D0153458

wwnorton.com/nawest

The StudySpace site that accompanies *The Norton Anthology of Western Literature* is FREE, but you will need the code below to register for a password that will allow you to access the copyrighted materials on the site.

WEST-WIND

THE NORTON ANTHOLOGY OF

WESTERN LITERATURE

NINTH EDITION

VOLUME 2

THE NORTON ANTHOLOGY OF

WESTERN LITERATURE

NINTH EDITION

MARTIN PUCHNER, *General Editor*
HARVARD UNIVERSITY

SUZANNE AKBARI
UNIVERSITY OF TORONTO

WIEBKE DENECKE
BOSTON UNIVERSITY

BARBARA FUCHS
UNIVERSITY OF CALIFORNIA, LOS ANGELES

CAROLINE LEVINE
UNIVERSITY OF WISCONSIN, MADISON

PERICLES LEWIS
YALE UNIVERSITY

EMILY WILSON
UNIVERSITY OF PENNSYLVANIA

VOLUME 2

W. W. NORTON & COMPANY | New York · London

W. W. Norton & Company has been independent since its founding in 1923, when William Warder Norton and Mary D. Herter Norton first published lectures delivered at the People's Institute, the adult education division of New York City's Cooper Union. The firm soon expanded its program beyond the Institute, publishing books by celebrated academics from America and abroad. By midcentury, the two major pillars of Norton's publishing program—trade books and college texts—were firmly established. In the 1950s, the Norton family transferred control of the company to its employees, and today—with a staff of four hundred and a comparable number of trade, college, and professional titles published each year—W. W. Norton & Company stands as the largest and oldest publishing house owned wholly by its employees.

Editor: Peter Simon
Associate Editor: Quynh Do
Managing Editor, College: Marian Johnson
Manuscript Editors: Alice Falk, Michael Fleming, Katharine Ings, Candace Levy
Project Editor: Rachel Mayer
Electronic Media Editor: Eileen Connell
Marketing Manager, Literature: Kim Bowers
Production Manager: Sean Mintus
Photo Editor: Patricia Marx
Permissions Manager: Megan Jackson
Permissions Clearing: Nancy Rodwan
Text Design: Jo Anne Metsch
Art Director: Debra Morton Hoyt
Composition: Jouve North America, Brattleboro, VT
Manufacturing: R. R. Donnelley & Sons—Crawfordsville, IN

The text of this book is composed in Fairfield Medium with the display set in Aperto.

Library of Congress Cataloging-in-Publication Data

The Norton Anthology of Western Literature / [edited by] Martin Puchner, Suzanne Akbari, Wiebke Denecke, Barbara Fuchs, Caroline Levine, Pericles Lewis, Emily Wilson.—Ninth edition.
    pages cm
  Includes bibliographical references and index.
  ISBN 978-0-393-93364-2 (pbk., vol 1 : alk. paper)—ISBN 978-0-393-93363-5 (pbk., vol 2 : alk. paper)
  1. Literature–Collections.   I. Puchner, Martin, 1969– editor of compilation.
II. Akbari, Suzanne Conklin, editor of compilation.   III. Denecke, Wiebke, editor of compilation.   IV. Fuchs, Barbara, 1970– editor of compilation.   V. Norton anthology of world masterpieces
 PN6014.N66 2014
 808.8–dc23

                                                                        2013045075

ISBN: 978-0-393-93363-5 (pbk.)

W. W. Norton & Company, Inc., 500 Fifth Avenue, New York, NY 10110-0017
wwnorton.com

W. W. Norton & Company Ltd., Castle House, 75/76 Wells Street, London W1T 3QT

1 2 3 4 5 6 7 8 9 0

Contents

I. THE ENLIGHTENMENT IN EUROPE AND THE AMERICAS   3

V. POSTWAR AND POSTCOLONIAL LITERATURE, 1945–1968

Preface

In this edition of *The Norton Anthology of Western Literature*, we seek to provide a generous collection of the Western literary tradition in a format that will suit the needs of instructors and students encountering that tradition for the first time. As editors of the Ninth Edition, we have looked back at what we have inherited, beginning with the first version of 1956, edited by Maynard Mack. At the same time, we recognize that the teaching of Western literature has undergone important changes. But before describing these changes in detail, let us pull back and ask just what we mean, in our age of globalization, by the Western tradition.

What Is Western Literature?

St. Lucia is a small island in the Caribbean with a tumultuous history. After European travelers came to the New World, it was dominated, in turns, by Britain and France, gaining independence only in the middle of the twentieth century. Western literary historians took little notice of this island, perhaps because the language spoken there was a language based on French called French Creole, sometimes combined with English, but also because other art forms such as carnival performances, music, and painting dominated. But all this changed when a young writer by the name of Derek Walcott embarked on a literary career that culminated in an epic poem, *Omeros*, which harked back to the Greek poet Homer. Suddenly, St. Lucia was connected to a tradition of literature that had begun thousands of years earlier on another group of islands in the Mediterranean Sea.

Classical Antiquity

We have come to know this tradition as Western literature. It begins with two epic poems: the *Iliad*, which tells the story of Greek armies laying siege to Ilium, or Troy, in Asia Minor; and the *Odyssey*, which follows one Greek hero involved in the siege back to his native island, Ithaca. Based on oral traditions of poetic performance that went back centuries, these two epic poems became foundational texts of Greek culture, with painters, sculptors, and musicians transforming Homer's characters and scenes into their own art forms. Students learned passages from these epics by heart, politicians quoted them, comedians riffed off of them, tragedians borrowed from them, lyric poets transformed them, and novelists and historians as well as later epic poets reworked them into their own narratives of wandering and conflict.

The *Iliad* and the *Odyssey* became important outside the Greek islands as well. When the Greek world was overtaken by Rome, the Roman poet Virgil imagined that his culture was founded by a character from the *Iliad*, the Trojan Aeneas, and proceeded to write a sequel to Homer's poems, the *Aeneid,* which became central to the identity of Romans and the Roman Empire. Centuries later, the Italian poet Dante wrote his own epic poem, *The Divine Comedy*, in which he cast Virgil as his guide and reworked classical epic for Christian Europe. The fortunes of both Greek and Roman literature changed when more and more scholars rediscovered the classical past in what came to be known as the Renaissance, or time of rebirth, thereby laying the ground for Homer's renewed influence on European culture. Yet Homer's influence was great not only in periods that looked back to the classical tradition, but also in those that attempted to break decisively with what had come before. The modernist Irish novelist James Joyce called his great novel *Ulysses* (after the Latin rendition of Odysseus's name), even though it was set in Dublin, Ireland, in 1904. And Joyce's example inspired Walcott to produce a reinvention of Homer set on his island in the Caribbean.

The recurrence of Homeric motifs across time and space provides a good illustration of how the traditions of Western literature have been formed: despite fractures, gaps, and discontinuities, great writers of literature repeatedly imagine themselves in conversation with each other across the centuries. As the Latin American writer Jorge Luis Borges wrote, "Every writer creates his own precursors; his work modifies our conception of the past, as it will modify the future." Reading Homer changes our reading of Joyce, and also the other way around. This is the real value of studying these texts together, examining the ways in which they interact with one another.

This view of Western literature works mostly in hindsight. Homer would have been astonished to learn that he was supposed to be writing something called Western literature. He was interested in the culture of the Greek islands and in defining that culture against those of their neighbors—for example, the cultures of Asia Minor. Our word "barbarians" is derived from the word the Greeks used to refer to these non-Greeks, the *barbaroi*, so-called because their languages sounded to Greek ears like "barbarbarbar." The Romans wouldn't have understood what we mean by Western literature either. They felt economically and militarily superior to the Greeks, but worried about their own lack of culture and therefore imitated Greek works while also reworking the originals, as Virgil did with the *Aeneid*. Even the early modern scholars who rediscovered classical Greece for Christian Europe (Islamic scholars had a much more continuous engagement with Greek thought) didn't use the term "Western literature." The sense of Europe as a coherent unit emerged only gradually and became more sharply drawn after European travelers encountered continents and cultures they had not even known existed.

A similar dynamic was at work in other genres crucial to Western literature. For instance, Athenian tragedians transformed the characters of Homer's epics for theatrical performances that showed heroic humans struggling in vain against forces larger than themselves. The genres of serious drama changed enormously in the course of the past two and a half thousand years, but the word "tragedy" has entered our language to help us describe scenes of suffering both in art and in life. Together with the epic poem, tragedy has had an astonishingly long history, even though dramatists also rebelled against its dominance over Western drama—for example, by combining tragedy with comedy as Samuel Beckett did in the twentieth century, following earlier attempts by Euripides and early modern dramatists. Indeed, Walcott tapped into the tradition of tragedy as well, writing tragedies modeled on ancient Greece but set on his native island.

Not all genres typical of Western literature originated in classical Greece. In the modern world, the most influential genre has been the novel, so-called because it seemed to have little precedent in antiquity and was therefore "novel." The modern novel is much less fixed in form or subject matter than epic or tragedy; indeed, it was dubbed a "loose, baggy monster" by Henry James. Its flexibility allowed writers to deal with a vast range of topics, including early modern trans-Atlantic slavery, as in Aphra Behn's *Oroonoko*, and domestic *ennui*, as in Gustave Flaubert's nineteenth-century masterpiece *Madame Bovary*.

The new genre of the novel was important not only for expanding the range of experiences that could be represented in literature, but also for expanding the range of authors who were enabled to write such literature in the first place. Female writers, for example, faced significant hurdles for entering the tradition of epic poetry and therefore tended to gravitate toward other genres. The Greek female poet Sappho, whose work now exists only in tantalizing fragments, became a powerful source for later female poets. But it was the new and therefore more open novel that allowed female writers, from Marie de la Fayette in the seventeenth century to Virginia Woolf in the twentieth, to flourish. At the same time, the emergence of mass literacy and mass education created new readers, many of them female, and thus a new audience for new types of literary texts, profoundly changing the shape of Western literature.

European colonists brought their literatures (and languages) to the four corners of the globe, and the novel in particular has become the prevalent form of world literature today. But colonized peoples were not merely passive recipients of these European exports. Instead, they transformed the languages and literatures coming from Europe, forging their own combination of local and European forms and idioms in response. This is how a boy born of a white mother and black father living in St. Lucia came to define his island in terms borrowed from Homer. Walcott had studied Western literature at school, but when he wrote *Omeros* he didn't simply follow a European model; rather, he made that model his own. Today, Western literature has become a resource available to anyone wishing to use it for his or her own purposes.

Christianity and the Religions of the Book

The idea that there existed something called the West that had its own, distinct literature had another source besides Greek and Roman antiquity: Christianity. The followers of Jesus slowly formed what was originally a splinter group opposed to the hierarchies of established Judaism into a religion in its own right. At first they were persecuted across the Roman Empire, but their religion slowly gained ground, tolerated at first and finally the official religion of the empire, spreading across Europe. It was as a Christian culture that Europe started to form a sense of identity.

These two sources of Western literature, classical Greece and Christianity, were not easily reconciled with each other. When Dante wrote *The Divine Comedy*, he didn't just write in the tradition of Homer and Virgil: he also put them in their places. They were models, but only pre-Christian ones, and for that reason, the Italian poet placed them, along with other writers of antiquity, in Limbo, to signal that Christian Europe had moved beyond pagan antiquity. The great English poet John Milton created a different mixture of continuity and hostility in his relationship to classical literature: his *Paradise Lost* tells the story of Adam and Eve in the form of a classical epic; but the character most closely associated with classical heroism is Satan.

Christianity separated Europe not only from its past, but also from its neighbors, especially from rising Islam. A foundational text in French literature, the *Song of Roland* has the Christian hero defend France from Muslim Saracens, just as Christian Europe began campaigns to spread Christianity, either by force or by persuasion, through crusades. And in the age of exploration and colonialism, Europeans sought to convert the rest of the world to their faith even as they were increasingly defining themselves against non-Christian cultures. In this way, Christian literature, beginning with the New Testament and through Dante's *Divine Comedy* and the *Song of Roland*, all the way to texts that record the encounter of Europeans with non-Europeans, forms a second tradition within Western literature.

Through this emphasis on the New Testament, however, Christian Europe also adopted the Hebrew Bible (called by Christians the Old Testament), as an antecedent and ultimate source of Christianity. In doing so, it came to share this text with Judaism and also with its younger rival, Islam, which likewise considered the Hebrew Bible as a source of its own religion. The three religions of the book emerged as fierce rivals, leading to bloody conflicts. Medieval and modern Europe prosecuted Jewish communities and fought repeated battles with Islam. At the same time, the three shared a scriptural legacy, the Hebrew Bible, that tied Western literature to Judaism and Islam.

The roots of Western literature were even more far-flung than Hebrew religious writing. When in the nineteenth century archeologists uncovered an ancient epic in Mesopotamia (today's Iraq) that contained the story of a great flood, it became clear that the Hebrew Bible itself derived from the older Babylonian tradition, and so the *Epic of Gilgamesh*, as this text was called, came to be considered as a new point of origin, making it clear that Western literature was intimately connected to traditions it had once considered its rivals.

As Christianity became a world religion, it did not remain the exclusive possession of Europe or the West. Missionaries brought the Bible but also secular literature to the rest of the world, where it often merged with local cultures. When Spanish missionaries encountered an epic poem in what is now southern Mexico, the Mayan *Popol Vuh*, they had it transcribed into the Latin alphabet; in the process, it also acquired material from the Bible, including the story of the flood. This way, the story of the flood traveled from the *Epic of Gilgamesh* to the Near East and through the dissemination of the Hebrew Bible influenced far-away Mayan culture.

Western Literature and World Literature

Western literature has always been engaged in a dynamic relation with other literatures, and today, it should be considered within the context of world literature. Europeans were fascinated by the region they referred to as "the Orient," helping to compile the work now known as *The Arabian Nights*, which became a Western best seller, and they incorporated elements of Middle Eastern and Asian literature into their own literature. Travelers chronicled encounters with foreign cultures, although often in fantastic (or derogatory) terms, which inspired other writers to invent fictional travel tales. The German writer and traveler Johann Wolfgang von Goethe, who coined the term "world literature" in 1827, was fascinated by Chinese novels, but also by Sanskrit drama and Arabic and Persian poetry. Once Western literature is placed within the context of world literature, it becomes clear just how porous the boundaries between Western and non-Western literatures really are.

To be sure, some continue to define Western literature against old and new rivals. In Europe, heated debates about Europe's Christian identity have erupted in the discussion of whether Turkey, a predominantly Muslim country, should be allowed to join the European Union. The rivalry between the United States and China is sometimes described as a new form of West versus East. In this context, the conception of a Western literature has not gone away, but it has considerably expanded. It now includes literature written in variants of European languages in other parts of the globe, including the Americas, Africa, and parts of Asia, but also literature that understands itself to be in dialogue with classics of Western literature, such as Walcott's *Omeros*.

The Norton Anthology of Western Literature

What does all of this mean for the book you are reading now—*The Norton Anthology of Western Literature*? It means that we have adopted an expansive and dynamic notion of Western literature. We have not only continued to represent but also have even strengthened the grand traditions of epic poetry from Homer to Walcott—for example, by adding selections from the great New World epic *Popol Vuh*. A new translation of the *Epic of Gilgamesh* reinforces the deep roots of Western literature in Mesopotamia, and we have given fuller representation to the three religions of the book by providing new selections from the Old Testament (Hebrew Bible), the New Testament, and the Qur'an.

Besides these religious and epic texts, we emphasize the emergence of other, crucial genres by providing separate clusters in which these genres are given particular attention. Lyric poetry in the Middle Ages, Petrarchan love lyric, and Romantic poetry are presented in this way, as is Athenian drama and, in the twentieth century, the new genre of the manifesto, with which artists sought to differentiate themselves from the past and from each other. We have also significantly enhanced the representation of contemporary literature, with exciting selections from Salman Rushdie, Jamaica Kincaid, and Roberto Bolaño, and we conclude with a text by the South African J. M. Coetzee, one of the most remarkable inheritors of the European tradition, in which his female alter ego finds herself on a cruise ship lecturing on literature; the piece is entitled "The Novel in Africa."

In order to chart paths through this enlarged territory, we have created clusters of texts that provide thematic centers of gravity. The anthology now opens with a group of texts called "Creation and the Cosmos," which includes creation myths that show us how writers captured the creation of the world in feats of religious and literary imagination. A cluster on travel writing in antiquity highlights the importance of cultural contact for the formation of Western literature; a cluster on Humanism explores the rediscovery of classical antiquity in the early modern world; and clusters on Enlightenment and Revolution capture these two crucial developments in Western civilization.

This edition of the *Norton Anthology of Western Literature* also introduces a new emphasis on geography. Both the ancient and the medieval world are represented in broad cultural spheres circling the Mediterranean, placing side by side texts from what later would come to be called Europe and its non-European neighbors. This is also the reason for including a text like *The Arabian Nights*, which was of particular interest to Western European readers and writers. Beginning with the age of European exploration and colonialism, we highlight the emerging sense of European identity through its relation to the New World and later to European empires all over the globe. European colonists not only occupied lands, but also brought their languages, with the effect that now literature written in English, French, Portuguese, Spanish, and other colonial languages is being produced all over the world. We have included many such texts, from the extraordinary nun Sor Juana Ines de la Cruz, writing in seventeenth-century New Spain (now Mexico) to the Chilean Isabel Allende's immensely popular writings in the twentieth century.

All of this is to say that Western literature is less a single tradition than a resource that has been used and adapted all over the world. No longer the exclusive possession of Europe and North America, Western literature belongs to all.

About the Ninth Edition

New Selections and Translations

This Ninth Edition represents a thoroughgoing, top-to-bottom revision of the anthology that altered nearly every section in important ways. Following is a list of the new sections and works, in order:

VOLUME 1

A new cluster, "Creation and the Cosmos" • Benjamin Foster's translation of *Gilgamesh* • Selections from chapters 12, 17, 28–29, 31–33, and 50 of Genesis, and from chapters 19 and 20 of Exodus • All selections from Genesis, Exodus, and Job are newly featured in Robert Alter's translation, and chapter 25 of Genesis (Jacob spurning his birthright) is presented as a graphic visualization by R. Crumb based on Alter's translation • Homer's *Iliad* and *Odyssey* are now featured in Stanley Lombardo's highly regarded translations • A selection of Aesop's *Fables* • A new selection and new translation of Sappho's lyrics • A new grouping, "Ancient Athenian Drama," brings together the three major Greek tragedians and Aristophanes • New translations of *Oedipus the King*, *Antigone* (both by Robert Bagg), *Medea* (by Diane Arnson Svarlien), and *Lysistrata* (by Sarah Ruden) • Plato's *Symposium* • A new cluster, "Travel and Conquest" • A new selection of Catullus's poems, in a new translation by Peter Green • The *Aeneid* is now featured in Robert Fagles's career-topping translation • New selections from book 1 of Ovid's *Metamorphoses* join the previous selection, now featured in Charles Martin's recent translation • Selections from the Christian Bible now featured in a new translation by Richmond Lattimore • A selection from book 3 of Apuleius's *The Golden Ass* • Selections from the Qur'an now featured in Abdel Haleem's translation • A new selection of Abolqasem Ferdowsi's *Shahnameh*, in a new translation by Dick Davis • Avicenna • Petrus Alfonsi • Additional material from Marie de France's *Lais*, in a translation by Robert Hanning and Joan Ferrante • Chretien de Troyes's *The Story of the Grail*, translated by Burton Raffel, newly included • Eirik the Red's *Thidrandi Whom the Goddesses Slew* and *Authun and the Bear*, both translated by Gwyn Jones, newly included • An expanded selection of poems fills out the "Medieval Lyrics" cluster • Dante's *Divine Comedy* now featured in Mark Musa's translation • An expanded selection from Boccaccio's *Decameron*, in a new translation by Wayne Rebhorn • A new translation by Sheila Fisher of Chaucer's *Canterbury Tales* • *Sir Gawain and the Green Knight* now featured in a new translation by Simon Armitage • Christine de Pizan's *Book of the City of Ladies*, translated by Rosalind Brown-Grant • Two new clusters, "Humanism and the Rediscovery of the Classical Past" and "Petrarch and the Love Lyric," open the new section "Europe and the New World" • Sir Thomas

More's *Utopia* in its entirety • Story 10 newly added to the selection of Marguerite de Navarre's *Heptameron* • *Lazarillo de Tormes* included in its entirety • A new cluster, "The Encounter of Europe and the New World" • Lope de Vega's *Fuente Ovejuna* now featured in G. J. Racz's recent translation • A new cluster, "God, Church, and Self."

VOLUME 2

A new cluster, "What Is Enlightenment?" • Molière's *Tartuffe* now featured in a new translation by Constance Congdon and Virginia Scott • A new translation of Jean Racine's *Phèdre* by Ted Hughes • Aphra Behn's *Oroonoko; or, The Royal Slave*, complete • New selections by Sor Juana Inés de la Cruz, in a new translation by Electa Arnela and Amanda Powell • A new cluster, "Revolutionary Contexts," features selections from the Declaration of Independence, the Declaration of the Rights of Man and of the Citizen, and the Declaration of Sentiments from the Seneca Falls convention, as well as pieces by Olympe de Gouges, Edmund Burke, Jean-Jacques Dessalines, William Wordsworth, and Simón Bólivar • New selection from book 2 of Rousseau's *Confessions* • Olaudah Equiano's *Interesting Narrative* • Selections from Domingo Sarmiento's *Facundo* • A new grouping, "Romantic Poets and Their Successors," features a generous sampling of lyric poetry from the period, including new poems by Anna Barbauld, William Wordsworth, Samuel Taylor Coleridge, Anna Bunina, Andrés Bello, John Keats, Heinrich Heine, Elizabeth Barrett Browning, Alfred Lord Tennyson, Robert Browning, Walt Whitman, Christina Rossetti, Rosalía de Castro, and José Martí, as well as an exciting new translation of Arthur Rimbaud's *Illuminations* by John Ashbery • New selections from Victor Hugo's *Les Misérables*, translated by Julie Rose • A new translation of Flaubert's *Madame Bovary* by Raymond Mackenzie, complete • A new translation of Tolstoy's *The Death of Ivan Ilyich* by Peter Carson • Ibsen's *Hedda Gabler*, now featured in a new translation by Rick Davis and Brian Johnston • Machado de Assis's *The Rod of Justice* • Chekhov's *The Cherry Orchard*, now featured in a new translation by Paul Schmidt • Rudyard Kipling's "The White Man's Burden" and selections from Mark Twain's "King Leopold's Soliloquy: A Defense of His Congo Rule," as part of the "Perspectives on European Empire" cluster • A new cluster, "Orature," with German, English, Irish, and Hawaiian folk tales; Anansi stories from Ghana, Jamaica, and the United States; and slave songs, stories, and spirituals, Malagasy wisdom poetry, and the Navajo Night Chant • Franz Kafka's *The Metamorphosis* now featured in Michael Hoffmann's translation • Chapter 1 of Woolf's *A Room of One's Own* newly added to the selections from chapters 2 and 3 • Octavio Paz • A new cluster, "Manifestos" • Leopold Sedar Senghor • Julio Cortázar • Tadeusz Borowski's *This Way for the Gas, Ladies and Gentlemen*, in a new translation by Barbara Vedder • Paul Celan • James Baldwin • Vladimir Nabokov • Clarice Lispector • Chinua Achebe's *Chike's School Days* • Carlos Fuentes • New poems by Derek Walcott • Seamus Heaney • V. S. Naipaul • Ngugi Wa Thiong'o • Wole Soyinka • Bessie Head • Salman Rushdie • Jamaica Kincaid • Toni Morrison • Isabel Allende • Junot Díaz • Roberto Bolaño • J. M. Coetzee

Supplements for Instructors and Students

Norton is pleased to provide instructors and students with several supplements to make the study and teaching of Western literature an even more interesting and rewarding experience.

Instructor Resource Disc

Designed to enhance large or small lecture environments, the Instructor's Resource Disc features approximately 200 images from the anthology and other sources, Lecture PowerPoints for each period introduction and for 30 widely taught works, and video tours of the Acropolis, the Parthenon, Ancient Rome, and the Sistine Chapel.

Instructor Course Guide

Teaching with The Norton Anthology of Western Literature: A Guide for Instructors, by Benedict Whalen, provides teaching plans, suggestions for in-class activities, discussion topics and writing projects, and extensive lists of scholarly and media resources.

Coursepacks

Available at no cost to professors or students, Norton coursepacks bring high-quality Norton digital media into a new or existing online course. Content includes all material from the StudySpace website, short-answer questions with suggested answers in the instructor area, and a new video series on writing about literature. Coursepacks are easy to download and install and are available in a variety of formats, including Blackboard, Desire2Learn, Angel, and Moodle.

StudySpace (wwnorton.com/nawest)

The free companion website helps students understand individual works and appreciate the places, sounds, and sights of literature. The site features a variety of review material, including more than 50 multiple-choice reading comprehension quizzes on widely taught individual works; bulleted summaries of the introductions; timelines; and illustrated, interactive maps. A new "Literary Places" feature uses Google Tours tools to offer students a practical way to (virtually) visit Western literature landmarks.

Writing about World Literature

Written by Karen Gocsik, Executive Director of the Writing Program at Dartmouth College, in collaboration with faculty in the world literature program at the University of Nevada, Las Vegas, *Writing about World Literature* provides course-specific guidance for writing papers and essay exams in the world literature course.

For more information about any of these supplements, instructors should contact their local Norton representative.

Acknowledgments

The editors would like to thank the following people, who have provided invaluable assistance by giving us sage advice, important encouragement, and help with the preparation of the manuscript: Sara Akbari, Alannah de Barra, Wendy Belcher, Jodi Bilinkoff, Freya Brackett, Psyche Brackett, Michaela Bronstein, Amanda Claybaugh, Rachel Carroll, Lewis Cook, David Damrosch, Dick Davis, Amanda Detry, Anthony Domestico, Merve Emre, Maria Fackler, Guillermina de Ferrari, Karina Galperín, Stanton B. Garner, Kimberly Dara Gordon, Elyse Graham, Stephen Greenblatt, Sara Guyer, Langdon Hammer, Iain Higgins, Mohja Kahf, Peter Kornicki, Paul Kroll, Lydia Liu, Bala Venkat Mani, Ann Matter, Barry McCrea, Alexandra McCullough-Garcia, Rachel McGuiness, Jon McKenzie, Mary Mullen, Djibril Tamsir Niane, Felicity Nussbaum, Andy Orchard, John Peters, Daniel Taro Poch, Daniel Potts, Megan Quigley, Imogen Roth, Catherine de Rose, Ellen Sapega, Jesse Schotter, Stephen Scully, Brian Stock, Tomi Suzuki, Joshua Taft, Sara Torres, Lisa Voigt, Kristen Wanner, and Emily Weissbourd.

All the editors would like to thank the wonderful people at Norton, principally our editor Pete Simon, the driving force behind this whole undertaking, as well as Marian Johnson (Managing Editor, College), Alice Falk, Michael Fleming, Katharine Ings, and Candace Levy (Copyeditors), Rachel Mayer (Project Editor), Quynh Do (Assistant Editor), Megan Jackson (College Permissions Manager), Nancy Rodwan (Permissions), Patricia Marx (Art Research Director), Debra Morton Hoyt (Art Director; cover design), Rubina Yeh (Design Director), Jo Anne Metsch (Designer; interior text design), Adrian Kitzinger (cartography), Agnieszka Gasparska (timeline design), Eileen Connell, (Media Editor), Sean Mintus (Production Manager), and Kim Bowers (Marketing Manager, Literature).

This anthology represents a collaboration not only among the editors and their close advisors, but also among the thousands of instructors who teach from the anthology and provide valuable and constructive guidance to the publisher and editors. *The Norton Anthology of Western Literature* is as much their book as it is ours, and we are grateful to everyone who has cared enough about this anthology to help make it better. We're especially grateful to the more than 500 professors of world literature who responded to an online survey in early 2008, whom we have listed below. Thank you all.

Michel Aaij (Auburn University Montgomery); Sandra Acres (Mississippi Gulf Coast Community College); Larry Adams (University of North Alabama); Mary Adams (Western Carolina University); Stephen Adams (Westfield State College); Roberta Adams (Roger Williams University); Kirk Adams (Tarrant County College); Kathleen Aguero (Pine Manor College); Richard Albright

(Harrisburg Area Community College); Deborah Albritton (Jefferson Davis Community College); Todd Aldridge (Auburn University); Judith Allen-Leventhal (College of Southern Maryland); Carolyn Amory (Binghamton University); Kenneth Anania (Massasoit Community College); Phillip Anderson (University of Central Arkansas); Walter Anderson (University of Arkansas at Little Rock); Vivienne Anderson (North Carolina Wesleyan College); Susan Andrade (University of Pittsburgh); Kit Andrews (Western Oregon University); Joe Antinarella (Tidewater Community College); Nancy Applegate (Georgia Highlands College); Sona Aronian (University of Rhode Island); Sona Aronian (University of Rhode Island); Eugene Arva (University of Miami); M. G. Aune (California University of Pennsylvania); Carolyn Ayers (Saint Mary's University of Minnesota); Diana Badur (Black Hawk College); Susan Bagby (Longwood University); Maryam Barrie (Washtenaw Community College); Maria Baskin (Alamance Community College); Samantha Batten (Auburn University); Charles Beach (Nyack College); Michael Beard (University of North Dakota); Bridget Beaver (Connors State College); James Bednarz (C. W. Post College); Khani Begum (Bowling Green State University); Albert Bekus (Austin Peay State University); Lynne Belcher (Southern Arkansas University); Karen Bell (Delta State University); Elisabeth Ly Bell (University of Rhode Island); Angela Belli (St. John's University); Leo Benardo (Baruch College); Paula Berggren (Baruch College, CUNY); Frank Bergmann (Utica College); Nancy Blomgren (Volunteer State Community College); Scott Boltwood (Emory & Henry College); Ashley Bonds (Copiah-Lincoln Community College); Thomas Bonner (Xavier University of Louisiana); Debbie Boyd (East Central Community College); Norman Boyer (Saint Xavier University); Nodya Boyko (Auburn University); Robert Brandon (Rockingham Community College); Alan Brasher (East Georgia College); Harry Brent (Baruch College); Charles Bressler (Indiana Wesleyan University); Katherine Brewer; Mary Ruth Brindley (Mississippi Delta Community College); Mamye Britt (Georgia Perimeter College); Gloria Brooks (Tyler Junior College); Monika Brown (University of North Carolina–Pembroke); Greg Bryant (Highland Community College); Austin Busch (SUNY Brockport); Barbara Cade (Texas College); Karen Caig (University of Arkansas Community College at Morrilton); Jonizo Cain-Calloway (Del Mar College); Mark Calkins (San Francisco State University); Catherine Calloway (Arkansas State University); Mechel Camp (Jackson State Community College); Robert Canary (University of Wisconsin–Parkside); Stephen Canham (University of Hawaii at Manoa); Marian Carcache (Auburn University); Alfred Carson (Kennesaw State University); Farrah Cato (University of Central Florida); Biling Chen (University of Central Arkansas); Larry Chilton (Blinn College); Eric Chock (University of Hawaii at West Oahu); Cheryl Clark (Miami Dade College–Wolfson Campus); Sarah Beth Clark (Holmes Community College); Jim Cody (Brookdale Community College); Carol Colatrella (Georgia Institute of Technology); Janelle Collins (Arkansas State University); Theresa Collins (St. John's University); Susan Comfort (Indiana University of Pennsylvania); Kenneth Cook (National Park Community College); Angie Cook (Cisco Junior College); Yvonne Cooper (Pierce College); Brenda Cornell (Central Texas College); Judith Cortelloni (Lincoln College); Robert Cosgrove (Saddleback College); Rosemary Cox (Georgia Perimeter College); Daniel Cozart (Georgia Perimeter College); Brenda Craven (Fort Hays

State University); Susan Crisafulli (Franklin College); Janice Crosby (Southern University); Randall Crump (Kennesaw State University); Catherine Cucinella (California State University San Marcos); T. Allen Culpepper (Manatee Community College–Venice); Rodger Cunningham (Alice Lloyd College); Lynne Dahmen (Purdue University); Patsy J. Daniels (Jackson State University); James Davis (Troy University); Evan Davis (Southwestern Oregon Community College); Margaret Dean (Eastern Kentucky University); JoEllen DeLucia (John Jay College, CUNY); Hivren Demir-Atay (Binghamton University); Rae Ann DeRosse (University of North Carolina–Greensboro); Anna Crowe Dewart (College of Coastal Georgia); Joan Digby (C. W. Post Campus Long Island University); Diana Dominguez (University of Texas at Brownsville); Dee Douglas-Jones (Winston-Salem State University); Jeremy Downes (Auburn University); Denell Downum (Suffolk University); Sharon Drake (Texarkana College); Damian Dressick (Robert Morris University); Clyburn Duder (Concordia University Texas); Dawn Duncan (Concordia College); Kendall Dunkelberg (Mississippi University for Women); Janet Eber (County College of Morris); Emmanuel Egar (University of Arkansas at Pine Bluff); David Eggebrecht (Concordia University of Wisconsin); Sarah Eichelman (Walters State Community College); Hank Eidson (Georgia Perimeter College); Monia Eisenbraun (Oglala Lakota College/Cheyenne-Eagle Butte High School); Dave Elias (Eastern Kentucky University); Chris Ellery (Angelo State University); Christina Elvidge (Marywood University); Ernest Enchelmayer (Arkansas Tech University); Niko Endres (Western Kentucky University); Kathrynn Engberg (Alabama A&M University); Chad Engbers (Calvin College); Edward Eriksson (Suffolk Community College); Donna Estill (Alabama Southern Community College); Andrew Ettin (Wake Forest University); Jim Everett (Mississippi College); Gene Fant (Union University); Nathan Faries (University of Dubuque); Martin Fashbaugh (Auburn University); Donald J. Fay (Kennesaw State University); Meribeth Fell (College of Coastal Georgia); David Fell (Carroll Community College); Jill Ferguson (San Francisco Conservatory of Music); Susan French Ferguson (Mountain View Comumunity College); Robyn Ferret (Cascadia Community College); Colin Fewer (Purdue Calumet); Hannah Fischthal (St. John's University); Jim Fisher (Peninsula College); Gene Fitzgerald (University of Utah); Monika Fleming (Edgecombe Community College); Phyllis Fleming (Patrick Henry Community College); Francis Fletcher (Folsom Lake College); Denise Folwell (Montgomery College); Ulanda Forbess (North Lake College); Robert Forman (St. John's University); Suzanne Forster (University of Alaska–Anchorage); Patricia Fountain (Coastal Carolina Community College); Kathleen Fowler (Surry Community College); Sheela Free (San Bernardino Valley College); Lea Fridman (Kingsborough Community College); David Galef (Montclair State University); Paul Gallipeo (Adirondack Community College); Jan Gane (University of North Carolina–Pembroke); Jennifer Garlen (University of Alabama–Huntsville); Anita Garner (University of North Alabama); Elizabeth Gassel (Darton College); Patricia Gaston (West Virginia University, Parkersburg); Marge Geiger (Cuyahoga Community College); Laura Getty (North Georgia College & State University); Amy Getty (Grand View College); Leah Ghiradella (Middlesex County College); Dick Gibson (Jacksonville University); Teresa Gibson (University of Texas–Brownsville); Wayne Gilbert (Community College of Aurora); Sandra Giles (Abraham

Baldwin Agricultural College); Pamela Gist (Cedar Valley College); Suzanne Gitonga (North Lake College); James Glickman (Community College of Rhode Island); R. James Goldstein (Auburn University); Jennifer Golz (Tennessee Tech University); Marian Goodin (North Central Missouri College); Susan Gorman (Massachusetts College of Pharmacy and Health Sciences); Anissa Graham (University of North Alabama); Eric Gray (St. Gregory's University); Geoffrey Green (San Francisco State University); Russell Greer (Texas Woman's University); Charles Grey (Albany State University); Frank Gruber (Bergen Community College); Alfonso Guerriero Jr. (Baruch College, CUNY); Letizia Guglielmo (Kennesaw State University); Nira Gupta-Casale (Kean University); Gary Gutchess (SUNY Tompkins Cortland Community College); William Hagen (Oklahoma Baptist University); John Hagge (Iowa State University); Julia Hall (Henderson State University); Margaret Hallissy (C. W. Post Campus Long Island University); Laura Hammons (Hinds Community College); Nancy Hancock (Austin Peay State University); Carol Harding (Western Oregon University); Cynthia Hardy (University of Alaska–Fairbanks); Steven Harthorn (Williams Baptist College); Stanley Hauer (University of Southern Mississippi); Leean Hawkins (National Park Community College); Kayla Haynie (Harding University); Maysa Hayward (Ocean County College); Karen Head (Georgia Institute of Technology); Sandra Kay Heck (Walters State Community College); Frances Helphinstine (Morehead State University); Karen Henck (Eastern Nazarene College); Betty Fleming Hendricks (University of Arkansas); Yndaleci Hinojosa (Northwest Vista College); Richard Hishmeh (Palomar College); Ruth Hoberman (Eastern Illinois University); Rebecca Hogan (University of Wisconsin–Whitewater); Mark Holland (East Tennessee State University); John Holmes (Virginia State University); Sandra Holstein (Southern Oregon University); Fran Holt (Georgia Perimeter College–Clarkston); William Hood (North Central Texas College); Glenn Hopp (Howard Payne University); George Horneker (Arkansas State University); Barbara Howard (Central Bible College); Pamela Howell (Midland College); Melissa Hull (Tennessee State University); Barbara Hunt (Columbus State University); Leeann Hunter (University of South Florida); Gill Hunter (Eastern Kentucky University); Helen Huntley (California Baptist University); Luis Iglesias (University of Southern Mississippi); Judith Irvine (Georgia State University); Miglena Ivanova (Coastal Carolina University); Kern Jackson (University of South Alabama); Kenneth Jackson (Yale University); M. W. Jackson (St. Bonaventure University); Robb Jackson (Texas A&M University–Corpus Christi); Karen Jacobsen (Valdosta State University); Maggie Jaffe (San Diego State University); Robert Jakubovic (Raymond Walters College); Stokes James (University of Wisconsin–Stevens Point); Beverly Jamison (South Carolina State University); Ymitri Jayasundera-Mathison (Prairie View A&M University); Katarzyna Jerzak (University of Georgia); Alice Jewell (Harding University); Elizabeth Jones (Auburn University); Jeff Jones (University of Idaho); Dan Jones (Walters State Community College); Mary Kaiser (Jefferson State Community College); James Keller (Middlesex County College); Jill Keller (Middlesex Community College); Tim Kelley (Northwest-Shoals Community College); Andrew Kelley (Jackson State Community College); Hans Kellner (North Carolina State); Brian Kennedy (Pasadena City College); Shirin Khanmohamadi (San Francisco State University); Jeremy Kiene (McDaniel College);

Mary Catherine Kiliany (Robert Morris University); Sue Kim (University of Alabama–Birmingham); Pam Kingsbury (University of North Alabama); Sharon Kinoshita (University of California, Santa Cruz); Lydia Kualapai (Schreiner University); Rita Kumar (University of Cincinnati); Roger Ladd (University of North Carolina–Pembroke); Daniel Lane (Norwich University); Erica Lara (Southwest Texas Junior College); Leah Larson (Our Lady of the Lake University); Dana Lauro (Ocean County College); Shanon Lawson (Pikes Peak Community College); Michael Leddy (Eastern Illinois University); Eric Leuschner (Fort Hays State University); Patricia Licklider (John Jay College, CUNY); Pamela Light (Rochester College); Alison Ligon (Morehouse College); Linda Linzey (Southeastern University); Thomas Lisk (North Carolina State University); Matthew Livesey (University of Wisconsin–Stout); Vickie Lloyd (University of Arkansas Community College at Hope); Judy Lloyd (Southside Virginia Community College); Mary Long (Ouachita Baptist University); Rick Lott (Arkansas State University); Scott Lucas (The Citadel); Katrine Lvovskaya (Rutgers University); Carolin Lynn (Mercyhurst College); Susan Lyons (University of Connecticut—Avery Point); William Thomas MacCary (Hofstra University); Richard Mace (Pace University); Peter Marbais (Mount Olive College); Lacy Marschalk (Auburn University); Seth Martin (Harrisburg Area Community College–Lancaster); Carter Mathes (Rutgers University); Rebecca Mathews (University of Connecticut); Marsha Mathews (Dalton State College); Darren Mathews (Grambling State University); Corine Mathis (Auburn University); Ken McAferty (Pensacola State College); Jeff McAlpine (Clackamas Community College); Kelli McBride (Seminole State College); Kay McClellan (South Plains College); Michael McClung (Northwest-Shoals Community College); Michael McClure (Virginia State University); Jennifer McCune (University of Central Arkansas); Kathleen McDonald (Norwich University); Charles McDonnell (Piedmont Technical College); Nancy McGee (Macomb Community College); Gregory McNamara (Clayton State University); Abby Mendelson (Point Park University); Ken Meyers (Wilson Community College); Barbara Mezeske (Hope College); Brett Millan (South Texas College); Sheila Miller (Hinds Community College); David Miller (Mississippi College); Matt Miller (University of South Carolina–Aiken); Yvonne Milspaw (Harrisburg Area Community College); Ruth Misheloff (Baruch College); Lamata Mitchell (Rock Valley College); D'Juana Montgomery (Southwestern Assemblies of God University); Lorne Mook (Taylor University); Renee Moore (Mississippi Delta Community College); Dan Morgan (Scott Community College); Samantha Morgan-Curtis (Tennessee State University); Beth Morley (Collin College); Vicki Moulson (College of the Albemarle); L. Carl Nadeau (University of Saint Francis); Wayne Narey (Arkansas State University); LeAnn Nash (Texas A&M University–Commerce); Leanne Nayden (University of Evansville); Jim Neilson (Wake Technical Community College); Jeff Nelson (University of Alabama–Huntsville); Mary Nelson (Dallas Baptist University); Deborah Nester (Northwest Florida State College); William Netherton (Amarillo College); William Newman (Perimeter College); Adele Newson-Horst (Missouri State University); George Nicholas (Benedictine College); Dana Nichols (Gainesville State College); Mark Nicoll-Johnson (Merced College); John Mark Nielsen (Dana College); Michael Nifong (Georgia College & State University); Laura Noell (North Virginia Community College); Bonnie

Noonan (Xavier University of Louisiana); Patricia Noone (College of Mount Saint Vincent); Paralee Norman (Northwestern State University–Leesville); Frank Novak (Pepperdine University); Kevin O'Brien (Chapman University); Sarah Odishoo (Columbia College Chicago); Samuel Olorounto (New River Community College); Jamili Omar (Lone Star College–CyFair); Michael Orlofsky (Troy University); Priscilla Orr (Sussex County Community College); Jim Owen (Columbus State University); Darlene Pagan (Pacific University); Yolanda Page (University of Arkansas–Pine Bluff); Lori Paige (Westfield State College); Linda Palumbo (Cerritos College); Joseph Parry (Brigham Young University); Carla Patterson (Georgia Highlands College); Andra Pavuls (Davenport University); Sunita Peacock (Slippery Rock University); Velvet Pearson (Long Beach City College); Joe Pellegrino (Georgia Southern University); Sonali Perera (Rutgers University); Clem Perez (St. Philip's College); Caesar Perkowski (Gordon College); Gerald Perkus (Collin College); John Peters (University of North Texas); Lesley Peterson (University of North Alabama); Judy Peterson (John Tyler Community College); Sandra Petree (Northwestern Oklahoma State University); Angela Pettit (Tarrant County College NE); Michell Phifer (University of Texas–Arlington); Ziva Piltch (Rockland Community College); Nancy Popkin (Harris-Stowe State University); Marlana Portolano (Towson University); Rhonda Powers (Auburn University); Lisa Propst (University of West Georgia); Melody Pugh (Wheaton College); Jonathan Purkiss (Pulaski Technical College); Patrick Quinn (College of Southern Nevada); Peter Rabinowitz (Hamilton College); Evan Radcliffe (Villanova University); Jody Ragsdale (Northeast Alabama Community College); Ken Raines (Eastern Arizona College); Gita Rajan (Fairfield University); Elizabeth Rambo (Campbell University); Richard Ramsey (Indiana University–Purdue University Fort Wayne); Jonathan Randle (Mississippi College); Amy Randolph (Waynesburg University); Rodney Rather (Tarrant County College Northwest); Helaine Razovsky (Northwestern State University); Rachel Reed (Auburn University); Karin Rhodes (Salem State College); Donald R. Riccomini (Santa Clara University); Christina Roberts (Otero Junior College); Paula Robison (Temple University); Jean Roelke (University of North Texas); Barrie Rosen (St. John's University); James Rosenberg (Point Park University); Sherry Rosenthal (College of Southern Nevada); Daniel Ross (Columbus State University); Maria Rouphail (North Carolina State University); Lance Rubin (Arapahoe Community College); Mary Ann Rygiel (Auburn University); Geoffrey Sadock (Bergen Community College); Allen Salerno (Auburn University); Mike Sanders (Kent State University); Deborah Scally (Richland College); Margaret Scanlan (Indiana University South Bend); Michael Schaefer (University of Central Arkansas); Tracy Schaelen (Southwestern College); Daniel Schenker (University of Alabama–Huntsville); Robyn Schiffman (Fairleigh Dickinson University); Roger Schmidt (Idaho State University); Robert Schmidt (Tarrant County College–Northwest Campus); Adrianne Schot (Weatherford College); Pamela Schuman (Brookhaven College); Sharon Seals (Ouachita Technical College); Su Senapati (Abraham Baldwin Agricultural College); Phyllis Senfleben (North Shore Community College); Theda Shapiro (University of California–Riverside); Mary Sheldon (Washburn University); Donald Shull (Freed-Hardeman University); Ellen Shull (Palo Alto College); Conrad Shumaker (University of Central Arkansas); Sara Shumaker (University of Central Arkansas); Dave Shuping (Spartanburg Methodist College); Horacio Sierra (University of Florida); Scott Simkins (Auburn University); Bruce Simon (SUNY Fredonia); LaRue Sloan (University of Louisiana–Monroe); Peter Smeraldo (Caldwell College); Renee Smith (Lamar University); Victoria Smith (Texas State University); Connie Smith (College of St. Joseph); Grant Smith (Eastern Washington University); Mary Karen Solomon (Coloardo NW Community College); Micheline Soong (Hawaii Pacific University); Leah Souffrant (Baruch College, CUNY); Cindy Spangler (Faulkner University); Charlotte Speer (Bevill State Community College); John Staines (John Jay College, CUNY); Tanja Stampfl (Louisiana State University); Scott Starbuck (San Diego Mesa College); Kathryn Stasio (Saint Leo University); Joyce Stavick (North Georgia College & State University); Judith Steele (Mid-America Christian University); Stephanie Stephens (Howard College); Rachel Sternberg (Case Western Reserve University); Holly Sterner (College of Coastal Georgia); Karen Stewart (Norwich University); Sioux Stoeckle (Palo Verde College); Ron Stormer (Culver-Stockton College); Frank Stringfellow (University of Miami); Ayse Stromsdorfer (Soldan I. S. H. S.); Ashley Strong-Green (Paine College); James Sullivan (Illinois Central College); Zohreh Sullivan (University of Illinois); Richard Sullivan (Worcester State College); Duke Sutherland (Mississippi Gulf Coast Community College/Jackson County Campus); Maureen Sutton (Kean University); Marianne Szlyk (Montgomery College); Rebecca Taksel (Point Park University); Robert Tally (Texas State University); Tim Tarkington (Georgia Perimeter College); Patricia Taylor (Western Kentucky University); Mary Ann Taylor (Mountain View College); Susan Tekulve (Converse College); Stephen Teller (Pittsburgh State University); Stephen Thomas (Community College of Denver); Freddy Thomas (Virginia State University); Andy Thomason (Lindenwood University); Diane Thompson (Northern Virginia Community College); C. H. Thornton (Northwest-Shoals Community College); Elizabeth Thornton (Georgia Perimeter); Burt Thorp (University of North Dakota); Willie Todd (Clark Atlanta University); Martin Trapp (Northwestern Michigan College); Brenda Tuberville (University of Texas–Tyler); William Tucker (Olney Central College); Martha Turner (Troy University); Joya Uraizee (Saint Louis University); Randal Urwiller (Texas College); Emily Uzendoski (Central Community College–Columbus Campus); Kenneth Van Dover (Lincoln University); Kay Walter (University of Arkansas–Monticello); Cassandra Ward-Shah (West Chester University); Gina Weaver (Southern Nazarene University); Cathy Webb (Meridian Community College); Eric Weil (Elizabeth City State University); Marian Wernicke (Pensacola Junior College); Robert West (Mississippi State University); Cindy Wheeler (Georgia Highlands College); Chuck Whitchurch (Golden West College); Julianne White (Arizona State University); Denise White (Kennesaw State University); Amy White (Lee University); Patricia White (Norwich University); Gwen Whitehead (Lamar State College–Orange); Terri Whitney (North Shore Community College); Tamora Whitney (Creighton University); Stewart Whittemore (Auburn University); Johannes Wich-Schwarz (Maryville University); Charles Wilkinson (Southwest Tennessee Community College); Donald Williams (Toccoa Falls College); Rick Williams (Rogue Community College); Lea Williams (Norwich University); Susan Willis (Auburn University–Montgomery); Sharon Wilson (University of Northern Colorado);

J. D. Wireman (Indiana State University); Rachel Wiren (Baptist Bible College); Bertha Wise (Oklahoma City Community College); Sallie Wolf (Arapahoe Community College); Rebecca Wong (James Madison University); Donna Woodford-Gormley (New Mexico Highlands University); Paul Woodruff (University of Texas–Austin); William Woods (Wichita State University); Marjorie Woods (University of Texas–Austin); Valorie Worthy (Ohio University); Wei Yan (Darton College); Teresa Young (Philander Smith College); Darcy Zabel (Friends University); Michelle Zenor (Lon Morris College); and Jacqueline Zubeck (College of Mount Saint Vincent).

THE NORTON ANTHOLOGY OF

WESTERN

LITERATURE

NINTH EDITION

VOLUME 2

I

The Enlightenment in Europe and the Americas

I s the latest thing always the best? On the whole, our society assumes that progress is likely and desirable. We move and communicate ever faster; we pursue the newest and shiniest things—our appetite for the modern knows no bounds. Yet we also indulge in moments of nostalgia, worrying that things are no longer what they used to be, that something has been lost in our tremendous rush. Before, we tell ourselves, there were standards; now all is confusion. Although the pace of change is now swifter, this ambivalence is nothing new.

The quarrel between "ancients" and "moderns"—those who believed, respectively, that old ideas or new ones were likely to prove superior to any alternatives—proved especially virulent in France and England during the late seventeenth and eighteenth centuries. Those who espoused the cause of the ancients feared—understandably—that the new commitment to individualism promoted by the moderns might lead to social alienation, unscrupulous self-seeking, and lack of moral responsibility. Believing in the universality of truth, they wished to uphold established values, not to invent new ones. On the other side, the moderns upheld the importance of individual autonomy, broad education for

A Philosopher Giving a Lecture in the Orrery, 1766, by Joseph Wright of Derby.

3

This engraving by J. Zucchi, a copy of a painting by Angelica Kauffmann, depicts Urania, the classical muse of astronomy.

women, and intellectual and geographical exploration. They stood for the new and are the recognizable forebears of what we even now call "modernity."

On both sides of the ancient/modern divide, thinkers believed in reason as a dependable guide. Both sides insisted that one should not take any assertion of truth on faith, blindly following the authority of others; instead, one should think skeptically about causes and effects, subjecting all truth-claims to logic and rational inquiry. **Dr. Johnson's** famous *Dictionary* defined reason as "the power by which man deduces one proposition from another, or proceeds from premises to consequences." By this definition, illumination occurs not by divine inspiration or by order of kings but by the reasoning powers of the ordinary human mind. Reason, some people argued, would lead human beings back to eternal truths. For others, reason provided a means for discovering fresh solutions to scientific, philosophical, and political questions.

In the realm of philosophy, thinkers turned their attention to defining what it meant to be human. "I think, therefore I am," **René Descartes** pronounced, declaring the mind the source of truth and meaning. But this idea proved less reassuring than it initially seemed. Subsequent philosophers, exploring the concept's implications, realized the possibility of the mind's isolation in its own constructions. Perhaps, Wilhelm Leibniz suggested, no real communication can take place between one consciousness and another. Possibly, according to **David Hume**, the idea of individual identity is a fiction constructed by our minds to make discontinuous experiences and memories seem continuous and whole. Philosophers pointed out the impossibility of knowing for sure even the reality of the external world: the only certainty is that we think it exists.

If contemplating the nature of human reason led philosophic skeptics to doubt our ability to know anything with certainty, other thinkers insisted on the existence, beyond ourselves, of an entirely rational physical and moral universe. Isaac Newton's demonstrations of the order of natural law greatly encouraged this line of thought, leading many to believe that the fullness and complexity of the perceived physical world testified to the sublime rationality of a divine plan. The Planner, however, did not necessarily supervise the day-to-day operations of His arrangements; He might rather, as a popular analogy had it, resemble the watchmaker who winds the watch and leaves it running.

God as a watchmaker was the central image for thinkers known as deists, who justified evil in the world by arguing that God never interfered with nature or with human action. Deism encouraged the separation of ethics from religion, as ethics was increasingly understood as a matter of reason.

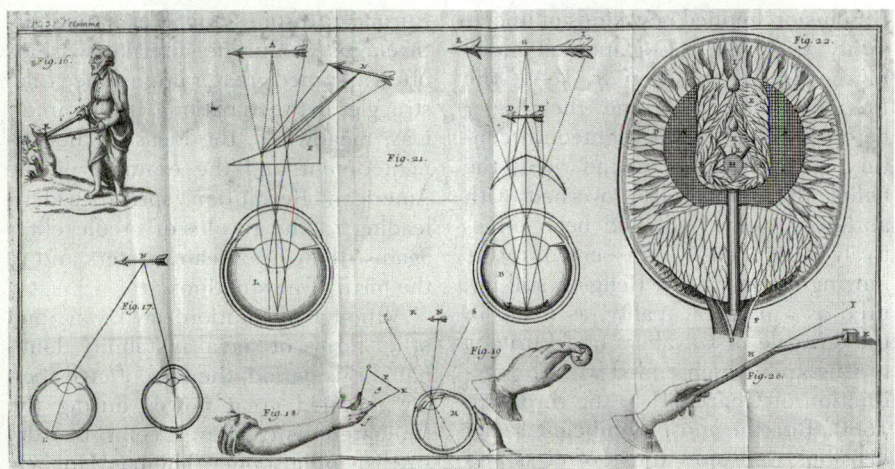

An illustration from an early eighteenth-century edition of the French philosopher René Descartes's unfinished book on the human body. Descartes saw the body as a machine whose operations could be understood mathematically.

Human beings, Enlightenment thinkers argued, could rely on their own authority—rather than looking to priests or princes—to decide how to act well in the world. Yet no one could fail to recognize that men and women embodied a capacity for passion as well as reason: "On life's vast ocean diversely we sail, / Reason the card, but Passion is the gale," **Alexander Pope's *Essay on Man*** (1733) pointed out. One could hope to steer with reason as guide, but one had to face the omnipresence of unreasonable passions. Life could be understood as a struggle between rationality and emotion, with feeling frequently exercising controlling force. Those who believed in the desirability of reason's governance often worried that it rarely prevailed over feelings of greed, lust, or the desire for power. For them as for us, the gap between the ideal and the actual caused frustration and often despair.

The questions raised by Enlightenment thinkers about human powers and limitations have left a legacy so lasting that it is hard to imagine our world without the Enlightenment. They are the ones who urged us to trust our own judgments and our own senses—while insisting on the need to think skeptically and critically—and they were the ones who shifted the dominant model of truth from divine revelation to human forms of knowledge: science, statistics, history, literature. They imagined conquering nature with ever-increasing knowledge—allowing humans to control their environment and harness nature's power for their own gain. And they ushered in a new sense of the equality of all human beings, launching the demand for universal human rights.

SOCIETY

The late seventeenth century, when the Enlightenment began, was a period of great turmoil, which persisted at intervals throughout the succeeding century. Reason had led many thinkers to the conclusion that kings and queens were ordinary mortals, and that conclusion implied new kinds of uncertainty. Civil war in England had ended in the king's execution in 1649; the French would guillotine their ruler before the end of the eighteenth century. The notion of divine right, the belief that monarchs governed with authority from God, had been effectively destroyed. God seemed to be moving further away. Religion still figured as a political reality, as it did in the struggle of Cavaliers and Puritans in England, which ended with the restoration of Charles II to the throne in 1660. But the most significant social divisions were now those of class and of political conviction—divisions no less powerful for lacking any claim of God-given authority. To England, the eighteenth century brought two unsuccessful but bitter rebellions on behalf of the deposed Stuart monarchs as well as the cataclysmic American Revolution. Throughout the eighteenth century, wars erupted over succession to European thrones and over nationalistic claims. In Europe, internal divisions often assumed greater importance than struggles between nations. In the Americas, meanwhile, the ideas of the Enlightenment and the example of the American Revolution spread widely, leading to the revolts of creole elites against their European masters and to the birth of new nations.

Although revolution, civil war, and other forms of social instability dominated this period, the idea of civil society retained great power during the Enlightenment. Seventeenth-century English philosopher Thomas Hobbes, who believed that human life before the formation of societies was inevitably "nasty, mean, brutish, and short," thought that men and women had originally banded together for the sake of preservation and progress. By the late seventeenth century in Europe as in the Americas, social organization had evolved into elaborate hierarchical

The Topsy-Turvy World, 1663, by the Dutch genre painter Jan Steen, presents a satirical picture of the disarray in the household of a newly wealthy middle-class family.

structures with the aristocracy at the top. Just below the aristocrats were the educated gentry—clergymen, lawyers, men of leisure with landed property. Below them were masses of workers of various kinds, many of them illiterate, and, in the Americas, the large populations of indigenous or *mestizo* (mixed-race) peoples, as well as slaves of African descent. Although literacy rates grew dramatically during the eighteenth century, those who wrote (and, for a long time, those who read) belonged almost entirely to the two upper classes. As new forms of commerce generated new wealth, and with it, newly wealthy people who felt entitled to their share of social power, the traditional social order faced increasing challenges. In the Americas, white creoles chafed at European entitlements while insisting on their own privilege over other races. By the eighteenth century, the abolitionist movement would begin to question whether slavery could be ethical, a challenge anticipated by **Aphra Behn's Oroonoko**, the story of an African prince tricked into slavery and spirited to the New World.

Among the privileged classes, men had many opportunities: for education, for service in government or diplomacy, for the exercise of political and economic power. Both men and women generally accepted as necessary the subordination of women, who, even in the upper classes, had few opportunities for education and occupation beyond the household. But the increasing value attached to individualism had implications for women as well as men. In the late seventeenth century, **Sor Juana Inés de la Cruz**, a Mexican nun, articulated her own passion for thought and reading, and became an eloquent advocate of the right of women to education and a life of the mind. During the next century, a number of women and an occasional man made the same case. It became increasingly common to argue that limiting women solely to childbearing and childrearing might not conform to the dictates of reason. If God had given all human beings reason, then women were just as entitled to develop and exercise their minds as their male counterparts. The emphasis on education in virtually all of the period's tracts about women provides proof that the concept of rational progress offered a device that could be used to gain at least some rights for women—if not civil rights, which were long in coming, at least the right to thought and knowledge.

Women of the upper classes occupied an important place in Enlightenment society, presiding over "salons," gatherings whose participants engaged in intellectual as well as frivolous conversation. In France as in England, by the late seventeenth century women also began writing novels, their books widely read by men and women alike. Although novels by women often focused attention on the domestic scene, they also ranged further, as in Behn's *Oroonoko*. Women published translations from the Greek as well as volumes of literary criticism, and were the most prolific writers in certain genres, such as Gothic fiction. Even if society as a whole did not acknowledge their full intellectual and moral capacities, individual women were beginning to claim for themselves more rights than those of motherhood.

Society in this period operated, as societies always do, by means of well-defined codes of behavior. Commentators at the time frequently showed themselves troubled by the possibility of sharp discrepancies between social appearance and the "truth" of human nature: **Molière's Tartuffe** provides a vivid example, with its exposé of religious sham. **Jonathan Swift**, lashing the English for institutionalized hypocrisy; Pope, calling attention to ambiguous sexual mores; **Voltaire** and Johnson, sending naive fictional protagonists to find that moralists don't always practice

Molière reading Tartuffe *at the home of Ninon de L'Enclos*, by Nicolas Andre Monsiau. This eighteenth-century painting of the seventeenth-century playwright is a tribute both to Molière and to L'Enclos, an author, courtesan, and patron of the arts who was host to some of the era's most celebrated literary salons.

what they preach—all of these writers call attention to the deceptiveness and the possible misuses of social norms as well as to their necessity. While the social codes may themselves not be at fault, people fail to live up to what they profess. The world would be a better place, these writers suggest, if people examined not only their standards of behavior but also their tendency to hide behind them.

In fiction, drama, poetry, and prose satire, writers of the Enlightenment in one way or another make society their subject. On occasion, they use domestic situations to provide microcosms of a wider social universe. Molière focuses on a private family to suggest how professed sentiment can obscure the operations of ambition; marriage comes to represent a society in miniature, not merely a structure for the fulfillment of personal desire. Marriage, an institution at once social and personal, provides a useful image for human re-

lationship as social and emotional fact. The developing eighteenth-century novel would assume marriage as the normal goal for men and women.

Other writers focus on a broader panorama. In **The Rape of the Lock**, Pope pokes fun at social structures by treating petty social squabbles in an epic form. Swift imagines idealized forms of social institutions ranging from marriage to Parliament, contrasting the ideals with their actual English counterparts. Johnson's and Voltaire's world travelers witness and participate in a vast range of sobering experiences. In general, women fill subordinate roles in the harsh social environments evoked by these satiric works: erotic love plays a less important part and the position of women becomes increasingly insignificant as the public life is privileged over the home. It is perhaps relevant to note that no literary work in this section (with the horrifying exception of Swift's **A Modest Proposal**) describes or evokes children, an omission that the generation of writers to follow—the Romantics—were eager to correct. But for the thinkers of the Enlightenment, it was only in adulthood that people assumed social responsibility; and so it was only then that they could provide interesting substance for social commentary.

HUMANITY AND NATURE

If the subject of human beings' relation to society occupied many writers, the problem of humankind's relation to the universe also perplexed them. Deism assumed the existence of a God who provided evidence of Himself only in His created works. Studying the natural world, therefore, might be seen as a religious act; the powers of reason would enable fruitful study. But how, exactly, should humanity's position in the created universe be understood? Alexander Pope, who in *An Essay on Man* investigates his subject in relation both to society and to the universe, understood creation as a great continuum, with man at the apex of the animal world. This view, sometimes described as belief in a Great Chain of Being, was widely shared. But if one turned the eye of reason on generic man himself, his dominance might seem questionable. Pope describes the inner life of human beings as a "Chaos of Thought and Passion, all confused," and sums up man as "the glory, jest, and riddle of the world." Glory? Perhaps. But when one adds jest and riddle, human preeminence seems less obvious.

Yet the natural order—however incomplete our grasp of it—remains a comfort. It suggests a *system*, a structure of relationships that makes sense at least in theory; rationality thus lies below all apparently irrational experience. It supplies a means of evaluating the natural world: every flower, every minnow, has meaning beyond itself as part of the great pattern. The passion with which the period's thinkers cling to belief in such a system suggests anxiety about what human reason could not do.

The notion of a permanent natural order corresponds to the notion of a permanent human nature, as conceived in the eighteenth century. It was generally believed that human nature remains in all times and places the same: all people hope and fear, are envious and lustful, and possess the capacity to reason. All suffer loss, all face death. Thinkers of the Enlightenment emphasized these common aspects of humanity far more than they considered cultural dissimilarities. Readers and writers alike could draw on this conviction about universality. It provided a test of excellence: if an author's imagining of character failed to conform to what eighteenth-century readers understood as human nature, a work might be securely judged inadequate. Conversely, the idea of a constant human nature held out the hope of longevity for writers who successfully evoked it. Moral philosophers could define human obligation and possibility, convinced that they, too, wrote for all time; ethical standards would never change. Like the vision of order in the physical universe, the notion of constancy in human nature provided bedrock.

CONVENTION AND AUTHORITY

Guides to manners proliferated in the eighteenth century, emphasizing the idea that commitment to decorum helped preserve society's standards. Literary conventions—agreed-on systems of verbal behavior—served comparable purposes in their own sphere, providing continuity between present and past. While these conventions may strike modern readers as antiquated and artificial, to contemporary readers they seemed both natural and proper, much as the plaintive lyrics of current country music or the extravagances of rap operate within restrictive conventions that appear "natural" only because they are familiar to us. Eighteenth-century writers had at their disposal an established set of conventions for every traditional literary genre. As the repetitive rhythms of the country ballad tell listeners what to expect, these literary conventions provided readers with clues about the kind of experience they could anticipate in a given poem or play.

Underlying all the conventions of this era was the classical assumption that literature existed to delight and instruct its readers. The various genres of this period embody such belief in literature's dual function. Stage comedy and tragedy, the early novel, satire in prose and verse, didactic poetry, the philosophical tale: each form developed its own set of devices for creating pleasure as well as for involving audiences and readers in situations requiring moral choice. The insistence in drama on unity of time and place (stage action occupying no more time than its representation, with no change of scene) exemplifies one such set of conventions, intended to produce in their audiences the maximum emotional and moral effect. The elevated diction of the *Essay on Man* ("Mark how it mounts, to Man's imperial race, / From the green myriads in the peopled grass"), like the mannered but less dignified language of *The Rape of the Lock* ("Here thou, great Anna! whom three realms obey, / Dost sometimes counsel take—and sometimes tea"), and the two-dimensional characters of Johnson's and Voltaire's tales all provide clues about whether the author intends us to read "straight" or to recognize a satirical intention.

One dominant convention of twenty-first-century poetry and prose is something we call "realism." In fiction, verse, and drama, writers often attempt to convey the literal feel of experience, the shape in which events actually occur in the world, the way people really talk. Behn, Pope, and Voltaire pursued no

Chiswick House in London, an early eighteenth-century villa modeled on the Renaissance architect Palladio's Villa Rotunda outside Vicenza. The Villa Rotunda itself was designed to hearken back to classical ideals.

such goal. Despite their concern with permanent patterns of thought and feeling, they employed deliberate and obvious forms of artifice as modes of emphasis and of indirection. The sonorous lines in which Behn's characters reflect on their passions ("Since I have sacrificed Imoinda to my revenge, shall I lose that Glory which I have purchased so dear, as at the Price of the fairest, dearest, softest Creature that ever Nature made?") embodies a characteristic form of stylization. Artistic transformation of life, the period's writers believed, involves the imposition of formal order on the endless flux of event and feeling. The formalities of this literature constitute part of its meaning: its statement that what experience shows as unstable, art makes stable.

By relying on convention, eighteenth-century writers attempted to control an unstable world. The classical past, for many, provided an emblem of that stability, a standard of permanence. But some felt that overvaluing the past was problematic, the problem epitomized by the quarrel of ancients versus moderns in England and France. At stake in this controversy was, among other things, the value of permanence as opposed to the value of change. Proponents of the ancients believed that the giants of Greece and Rome had not only established standards applicable to all future works but had provided models of achievement never to be excelled. Homer wrote the first great epics; subsequent epics could only imitate him. When innovation came, it came by making the old new, as Pope makes a woman's dressing for conquest new by comparing it to the arming of Achilles. Moderns who valued originality for its own sake, who claimed significance for worthless publications that time had not tested, thereby testified to their own inadequacies and their foolish pride.

Those proud to be moderns, on the other hand, held that men (possibly even women) standing on the shoulders of the ancients could see further than their predecessors. The new was conceivably more valuable than the old. One might discover flaws even in revered figures of the classic past, and not everything had yet been accomplished. This view, of course, corresponds to one widely current since the eighteenth century, but it did not triumph easily: many powerful thinkers of the late seventeenth and early eighteenth centuries adhered to the more conservative position.

Also at issue in this debate was the question of authority, which was to prove so perilous in the political sphere. What position should be assumed by one who hoped to write and be read? Did authority reside only in tradition? If so, must one write in classical forms, rely on classical allusions? Until late in the eighteenth century, virtually all important writers attempted to ally themselves with the authority of tradition, declaring themselves part of a community extending through time as well as space. The problems of authority became particularly important in connection with satire, a popular Enlightenment form. Satire involves criticism of vice and folly; Molière, Pope, Swift, Voltaire, and Johnson at least on occasion wrote in the satiric mode. The fact that satire flourished so richly in this period suggests another version of the central conflict between reason and passion: that of the forces of stability and of instability. In its heightened description of the world (people eating babies, young women initiating epic battles over the loss of a lock of hair), satire calls attention to the powerful presence of the irrational, opposing that presence with the clarity of the satirist's own claim to reason and tradition. As it chastises human beings for their eruptions of passion, urging resistance and control, satire reminds its readers of the universality of the irrational as well as of opposition to it.

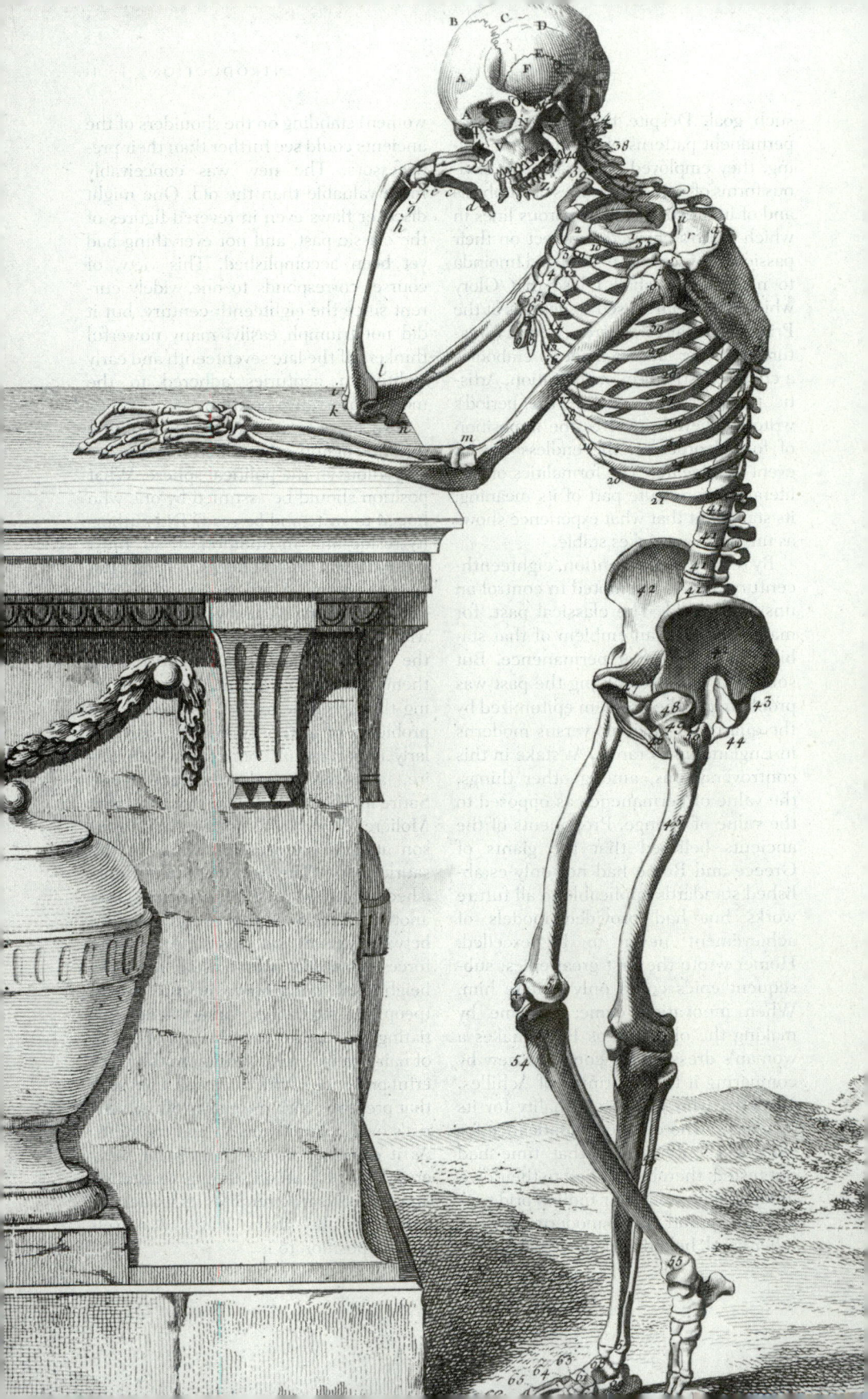

WHAT IS ENLIGHTENMENT?

One of the central goals of an education in our own time is the development of critical thinking. Rather than simply taking conventional wisdom on faith, we learn to stop and reflect on the arguments we hear, analyzing them for gaps and errors, exposing their unstated assumptions and evaluating their evidence. Instead of relying on external authorities, we put our own intelligence to work to distinguish between persuasive and misleading claims. Ideally, we learn to cultivate these habits in our everyday lives so that we become independent and skeptical adults, never carried away by mere prejudice or habit, and willing to examine all beliefs, including our own.

Critical thinking is a legacy of the Enlightenment. According to the great eighteenth-century French *Encyclopédie*, the enlightened person is one who "dares to think for himself . . . trampling on prejudice, tradition, conventional wisdom, authority, in a word, all that enslaves most minds." This was a bold new ideal, but one that had been in the works for a couple of centuries, as the principle of individualism had gained ground across Europe. By the seventeenth and eighteenth centuries, many educated people had begun to believe that they had a right to think and act for themselves, and to cast a critical eye on the pronouncements of priests and princes who had turned

An illustrated plate, *Anatomie*, from Diderot and D'Alembert's eighteenth-century *Encyclopédie*.

out, after all, to be merely human like themselves.

But what did it mean to be human? Enlightenment thinkers typically distinguished humans by the particular faculty of reason: unlike animals, they argued, humans had the capacity to think through relationships between objects or events. They could establish cause and effect, and follow logical arguments. **Mary Wollstonecraft**, the founder of modern feminism, made the case that women had as much right to freedom and authority as men because they too had been given the faculty of reason by God. While many, like Wollstonecraft, assumed that reason was a divine endowment, a commitment to thoroughgoing rationalism could also lead people to reject established religions. Determined to resist superstition and prejudice, some influential voices of the Enlightenment asked searching questions about Christianity: if God had given human beings the capacity to understand cause and effect, for example, then miracles seemed to make no sense. Why would God violate his own rules? The French writer **Voltaire** went further. Christianity for him was fundamentally corrupt and unreasonable and should therefore be altogether destroyed. "Écrasez l'infâme!" he is famous for saying, "Wipe out the infamous thing!" Although there was by no means a consensus about religion among Enlightenment thinkers, almost all of them urged people to look not to divine or priestly authority but to their own experience—human perception, human intelligence, and human reason—to guide them to truth and action in the world. In an intellectual revolution that has left a lasting mark on our world, humans started to see themselves, rather than gods or spirits, as the sole sources of experience, knowledge, and judgment.

While Enlightenment thinkers were upending what they saw as irrational and self-serving religions, scientific knowledge provided them with a new ideal. Guided by human reason, scientists claimed to take nothing on faith: they turned assertions into hypotheses, performing rigorous experiments that could be verified by others. And science also lent human beings an exciting and perilous new prospect of supremacy, the capacity to conquer nature and harness its forces for human ends: "the power of man over matter," as **Benjamin Franklin** called it, as he forecast endless new capabilities, enabled by scientific discovery, that would keep improving the lives of human beings for a thousand years and more. His own discovery of electricity in lightning certainly fit this image of science. Putting this natural form of energy to human use has transformed the world in countless ways since Franklin's breakthrough.

With its potential for endless technological advancement, science promised a bright future. Perhaps all human problems could be solved: sickness could be eradicated, natural disasters averted, human emotion fully understood. A vast optimistic prospect opened up. It was important to many Enlightenment thinkers to leave the past behind and to focus on a future made possible not only by scientific knowledge but by a thoroughgoing insistence on improving human conditions. The very metaphor of enlightenment rested on an idea of progress. People were moving from an immature darkness—superstition, ignorance, error—into the mature light of knowledge and reason. Advances would come from rationalizing life, making it more efficient and thereby increasing the store of human happiness. Enlightened governments were supposed to work not for a few privileged families but for the common good, committing themselves to maximizing the well-being of the people as a whole.

To be sure, there was a lot of debate about what the common good should be. The German philosopher **Immanuel Kant** argued that debate was itself crucial to the process of enlightenment. He claimed that societies would make progress only if they opened all questions to public deliberation, inviting a full discussion of alternatives. This insistence on rational public argument gained strength as literacy rates rose, and more and more people eagerly entered into debates about law, politics, and science. Newspapers and magazines reached a growing swathe of society, making it possible to envision a genuinely open public sphere. Two new kinds of reference book—the comprehensive dictionary and the grand encyclopedia—were also meant to foster progress by disseminating information widely: "to collect all the knowledge scattered over the face of the earth, to present its general outlines and structure to the men with whom we live, and to transmit this to those who will come after us, so that the work of past centuries may be useful to the following centuries, that our children, by becoming more educated, may at the same time become more virtuous and happier" (*Encyclopédie*).

The promise of future happiness began to shape the political landscape. Many thinkers, eager to hurry along the path of social progress, made the case for sweeping social reforms—such as new legal systems to protect natural and inalienable human rights. Others, disgusted at the corruption of traditional aristocracies and clerics, saw no possibility of genuine progress without revolution. And in fact Enlightenment thinking would help to inspire the dramatic political revolutions that broke out in the Americas and in France in the late eighteenth and early nineteenth centuries. Thomas Jefferson, for one, was very much a man of the Enlightenment. "We are not afraid to follow truth wherever it may lead," he wrote, "nor to tolerate any error so long as reason is left free to combat it."

Freedom was an Enlightenment watchword. Aside from the freedom to use one's own reason against traditional authorities, the new science of economics, whose most famous exponent was the Scottish thinker Adam Smith, argued that money worked according to rational laws just like physics, and that the marketplace, left free, would produce ever-increasing wealth. No government need interfere with its workings. The free market became an influential model for thinking about human liberty.

But the Enlightenment faith in freedom only went so far. Few writers at the time believed in a fully fledged democracy, where anyone—male or female, rich or poor, white or non-white—could participate equally, and as they set limits on political rights and liberties, they often concluded that enlightened monarchs were more trustworthy when it came to acting with reason than the mass of people, who were too likely to be swayed by prejudice and superstition. Though Kant favored open public discussion, for example, he actively argued against republicanism, praising King Frederick the Great of Prussia for imposing a rigid order and keeping a "well-disciplined army." It was only under such restrictive conditions, Kant argued, that enlightened discussion could occur. He, like many other thinkers of his time, rationalized arbitrary authority and so helped to legitimate distinctly undemocratic regimes.

There was a grim side to the Enlightenment embrace of progress as well. Europeans saw themselves as having emerged from a dark age—one they associated with immaturity and ignorance—and now, civilized and guided by reason, they were the only people who could understand and govern the world rationally. As Europeans set off from their native lands to find new markets for their products and new luxuries and natural resources to bring back, they increasingly encountered peoples whose lives were governed not by reason but by a great variety of traditions and faiths. All of these, according to numerous spokesmen for the Enlightenment, were primitive and unreasonable. What Europeans had begun as commercial interests overseas increasingly turned into imperial conquests, justified as the proper dominion of rational peoples over unreasonable and childlike ones. One had an obligation, it was argued, to bring the light of reason to those who lived in darkness.

What justified this worldview was a widespread faith in the universality of reason. Enlightenment was not only good for France or for Europe: it was what every nation needed. Enlightenment thinkers tended to be cosmopolitan in their outlook—imagining themselves as citizens of the world. Often they were travelers: Voltaire, for example, spent time in Britain, Switzerland, and Prussia; Wollstonecraft lived in Portugal and Ireland as well as her native Britain; and Benjamin Franklin was the American ambassador to France. And this international vantage point helped them to imagine that the light of reason would bring truth and understanding everywhere. Some even suggested that individual nations be abolished in favor of a single world state.

But others argued that reason could not be exported to everyone. It was during the Enlightenment that scientific theories of natural differences between the races emerged. Thus Thomas Jefferson argued that black slaves in the

United States were naturally inferior when it came to reason because they could not follow Euclidean geometry, and **David Hume**, the Scottish philosopher, could not think of any Africans who had shown "ingenuity." Others hotly disagreed. **James Beattie** criticized Hume's logic on the grounds of evidence gathered from around the world. "The Africans and Americans are known to have many ingenious manufactures and arts among them, which even Europeans would find it no easy matter to imitate," he wrote, pointing to the great civilizations of Mexico and Peru.

The question of racial difference was no matter of mere theoretical interest. The eighteenth century saw the height of the slave trade, as millions of Africans were forcibly taken to work land in the Americas, and Enlightenment thinkers had to defend their own theories of human rationality and progress in this charged context. As reports of cruelty and exploitation reached them, most of the leading figures of the Enlightenment—even Hume—found slavery abhorrent and argued fiercely against it. The French *Encyclopédie* put it simply: the slave trade is a "business that violates religion, morality, natural laws, and all the rights of human nature." When it comes to global justice, the Enlightenment left us a double legacy. While its thinkers were responsible for the harmful new science of race and helped to justify European imperial domination, Enlightenment ideas would also support struggles for universal human rights down to our own day.

SAMUEL JOHNSON

"Dr. Johnson," as he was known in his own time (1709–1784), was a British novelist, poet, essayist, biographer, and most famously, the sole author of the 40,000 definitions in his *Dictionary of the English Language*, first published in 1755. As the market for printed books and newspapers expanded dramatically in the early eighteenth century, demand grew for a standardization of spelling and word usage. Dr. Johnson's was not the first English dictionary, but it remained the standard until the *Oxford English Dictionary* appeared a century and a half later. It included many scientific and technical terms as a way of disseminating knowledge widely.

From A Dictionary of the English Language[1]

To ENLI'GHTEN. *v. a.* [from *light*.] 1. To illuminate; to supply with light. 2. To quicken in the faculty of vision. 3. To instruct; to furnish with encrease of knowledge. 4. To cheer; to exhilarate; to gladden. 5. To illuminate with divine knowledge.

1. From the 4th edition, 1777.

IMMANUEL KANT

One of the most influential thinkers in the Western tradition, Kant (1724–1804) made an impact that is still being felt among philosophers, who continue to debate the substance and implications of his thought. He spent his whole life in Königsberg, then in Prussia. In 1784, he responded to a monthly magazine that had posed the question: "What Is Enlightenment?" Kant's answer, which makes the case for a critical, skeptical, reflective approach to the world, has become a classic definition of what it means to be enlightened. He argues that people have slavishly followed the opinions of authorities, rather than having the courage to seek truth for themselves, and adopts the motto: "Dare to know!" Kant also dwells here on the ideal form of government for fostering enlightenment, and concludes that it is not democracy but enlightened monarchy.

What Is Enlightenment?[1]

Enlightenment is man's release from his self-incurred tutelage. Tutelage is man's inability to make use of his understanding without direction from another. This tutelage is self-incurred when its cause lies not in lack of reason but in lack of resolution and courage to use it without direction from another. *Sapere aude!*[2] "Have courage to use your own reason!"—that is the motto of enlightenment.

Laziness and cowardice are the reasons why so great a portion of mankind, after nature has long since discharged them from external direction (*naturaliter maiorennes*),[3] nevertheless remains under lifelong tutelage, and why it is so easy for others to set themselves up as their guardians. It is so easy not to be of age. If I have a book which understands for me, a pastor who has a conscience for me, a physician who decides my diet, and so forth, I need not trouble myself. I need not think, if I can only pay—others will readily undertake the irksome work for me.

That the step to competence is held to be very dangerous by the far greater portion of mankind (and by the entire fair sex)—quite apart from its being arduous—is seen to by those guardians who have so kindly assumed superintendence over them. After the guardians have first made their domestic cattle dumb and have made sure that these placid creatures will not dare take a single step without the harness of the cart to which they are confined, the guardians then show them the danger which threatens if they try to go alone. Actually, however, this danger is not so great, for by falling a few times they would finally learn to walk alone. But an example of this failure makes them timid and ordinarily frightens them away from all further trials.

1. Translated by Lewis White Beck.
2. Dare to know! (Latin; a quotation from the Roman poet Horace [65–8 B.C.E.]).
3. Those who come of age naturally (Latin).

For any single individual to work himself out of the life under tutelage which has become almost his nature is very difficult. He has come to be fond of this state, and he is for the present really incapable of making use of his reason, for no one has ever let him try it out. Statutes and formulas, those mechanical tools of the rational employment or rather misemployment of his natural gifts, are the fetters of an everlasting tutelage. Whoever throws them off makes only an uncertain leap over the narrowest ditch because he is not accustomed to that kind of free motion. Therefore, there are only few who have succeeded by their own exercise of mind both in freeing themselves from incompetence and in achieving a steady pace.

But that the public should enlighten itself is more possible; indeed, if only freedom is granted, enlightenment is almost sure to follow. For there will always be some independent thinkers, even among the established guardians of the great masses, who, after throwing off the yoke of tutelage from their own shoulders, will disseminate the spirit of the rational appreciation of both their own worth and every man's vocation for thinking for himself. But be it noted that the public, which has first been brought under this yoke by their guardians, forces the guardians themselves to remain bound when it is incited to do so by some of the guardians who are themselves incapable of some enlightenment— so harmful is it to implant prejudices, for they later take vengeance on their cultivators or on their descendants. Thus the public can only slowly attain enlightenment. Perhaps a fall of personal despotism or of avaricious or tyrannical oppression may be accomplished by revolution, but never a true reform in ways of thinking. Rather, new prejudices will serve as well as old ones to harness the great unthinking masses.

For this enlightenment, however, nothing is required but freedom, and indeed the most harmless among all the things to which this term can properly be applied. It is the freedom to make public use of one's reason at every point. But I hear on all sides, "Do not argue!" The officer says: "Do not argue but drill!" The tax-collector: "Do not argue but pay!" The cleric: "Do not argue but believe!" Only one prince in the world says, "Argue as much as you will, and about what you will, but obey!"[4] Everywhere there is restriction on freedom.

Which restriction is an obstacle to enlightenment, and which is not an obstacle but a promoter of it? I answer: The public use of one's reason must always be free, and it alone can bring about enlightenment among men. The private use of reason, on the other hand, may often be very narrowly restricted without particularly hindering the progress of enlightenment. By the public use of one's reason I understand the use which a person makes of it as a scholar before the reading public. Private use I call that which one may make of it in a particular civil post or office which is intrusted to him. Many affairs which are conducted in the interest of the community require a certain mechanism through which some members of the community must passively conduct themselves with an artificial unanimity, so that the government may direct

4. King Frederick II of Prussia (1712–1786), called "the Great," was an enlightened despot who expanded Prussia into a major European power; he was inspired by French philosophical ideas, including religious toleration.

them to public ends, or at least prevent them from destroying those ends. Here argument is certainly not allowed—one must obey. But so far as a part of the mechanism regards himself at the same time as a member of the whole community or of a society of world citizens, and thus in the role of a scholar who addresses the public (in the proper sense of the word) through his writings, he certainly can argue without hurting the affairs for which he is in part responsible as a passive member. Thus it would be ruinous for an officer in service to debate about the suitability or utility of a command given to him by his superior; he must obey. But the right to make remarks on errors in the military service and to lay them before the public for judgment cannot equitably be refused him as a scholar. The citizen cannot refuse to pay the taxes imposed on him; indeed, an impudent complaint at those levied on him can be punished as a scandal (as it could occasion general refractoriness). But the same person nevertheless does not act contrary to his duty as a citizen when, as a scholar, he publicly expresses his thoughts on the inappropriateness or even the injustice of these levies. Similarly a clergyman is obligated to make his sermon to his pupils in catechism and his congregation conform to the symbol of the church which he serves, for he has been accepted on this condition. But as a scholar he has complete freedom, even the calling, to communicate to the public all his carefully tested and well-meaning thoughts on that which is erroneous in the symbol and to make suggestions for the better organization of the religious body and church. In doing this, there is nothing that could be laid as a burden on his conscience. For what he teaches as a consequence of his office as a representative of the church, this he considers something about which he has no freedom to teach according to his own lights; it is something which he is appointed to propound at the dictation of and in the name of another. He will say, "Our church teaches this or that; those are the proofs which it adduces." He thus extracts all practical uses for his congregation from statutes to which he himself would not subscribe with full conviction but to the enunciation of which he can very well pledge himself because it is not impossible that truth lies hidden in them, and, in any case, there is at least nothing in them contradictory to inner religion. For if he believed he had found such in them, he could not conscientiously discharge the duties of his office; he would have to give it up. The use, therefore, which an appointed teacher makes of his reason before his congregation is merely private, because this congregation is only a domestic one (even if it be a large gathering); with respect to it, as a priest, he is not free, nor can he be free, because he carries out the orders of another. But as a scholar, whose writings speak to his public, the world, the clergyman in the public use of his reason enjoys an unlimited freedom to use his own reason and to speak in his own person. That the guardians of the people (in spiritual things) should themselves be incompetent is an absurdity which amounts to the eternalization of absurdities.

But would not a society of clergymen, perhaps a church conference or a venerable classis (as they call themselves among the Dutch), be justified in obligating itself by oath to a certain unchangeable symbol in order to enjoy an unceasing guardianship over each of its members and thereby over the people as a whole, and even to make it eternal? I answer that this is altogether impossible. Such a contract, made to shut off all further enlightenment from the human race, is absolutely null and void even if confirmed by the supreme power, by parliaments, and by the most ceremonious of peace treaties. An age cannot bind itself and ordain to put the succeeding one into such a condition that it cannot extend its (at best very occasional) knowledge, purify itself of errors, and progress in general enlightenment. That would be a crime against human nature, the proper destination of which lies precisely in this progress; and the descendants would be fully justified in rejecting those decrees as having been made in an unwarranted and malicious manner.

The touchstone of everything that can be concluded as a law for a people lies in the question whether the people could have imposed such a law on itself. Now such a religious compact might be possible for a short and definitely limited time, as it were, in expectation of a better. One might let every citizen, and especially the clergyman, in the role of scholar, make his comments freely and publicly, i.e., through writing, on the erroneous aspects of the present institution. The newly introduced order might last until insight into the nature of these things had become so general and widely approved that through uniting their voices (even if not unanimously) they could bring a proposal to the throne to take those congregations under protection which had united into a changed religious organization according to their better ideas, without, however, hindering others who wish to remain in the order. But to unite in a permanent religious institution which is not to be subject to doubt before the public even in the lifetime of one man, and thereby to make a period of time fruitless in the progress of mankind toward improvement, thus working to the disadvantage of posterity—that is absolutely forbidden. For himself (and only for a short time) a man can postpone enlightenment in what he ought to know, but to renounce it for himself and even more to renounce it for posterity is to injure and trample on the rights of mankind.

And what a people may not decree for itself can even less be decreed for them by a monarch, for his lawgiving authority rests on his uniting the general public will in his own. If he only sees to it that all true or alleged improvement stands together with civil order, he can leave it to his subjects to do what they find necessary for their spiritual welfare. This is not his concern, though it is incumbent on him to prevent one of them from violently hindering another in determining and promoting this welfare to the best of his ability. To meddle in these matters lowers his own majesty, since by the writings in which his subjects seek to present their views he may evaluate his own governance. He can do this when, with deepest understanding, he lays upon himself the reproach, *Caesar non est supra grammaticos.*[5] Far more does he injure his own majesty when he degrades his supreme power by supporting the ecclesiastical despotism of some tyrants in his state over his other subjects.

If we are asked, "Do we now live in an *enlightened age?*" the answer is, "No," but we do live in an *age of enlightenment.* As things now stand, much is lacking which prevents men from being, or easily becoming, capable of correctly using their own reason in religious matters with assurance and free from outside

---

5. Caesar is not above the grammarians (Latin); in other words, even an emperor has to abide by grammatical rules.

direction. But, on the other hand, we have clear indications that the field has now been opened wherein men may freely deal with these things and that the obstacles to general enlightenment or the release from self-imposed tutelage are gradually being reduced. In this respect, this is the age of enlightenment, or the century of Frederick.

A prince who does not find it unworthy of himself to say that he holds it to be his duty to prescribe nothing to men in religious matters but to give them complete freedom while renouncing the haughty name of *tolerance*, is himself enlightened and deserves to be esteemed by the grateful world and posterity as the first, at least from the side of government, who divested the human race of its tutelage and left each man free to make use of his reason in matters of conscience. Under him venerable ecclesiastics are allowed, in the role of scholars, and without infringing on their official duties, freely to submit for public testing their judgments and views which here and there diverge from the established symbol. And an even greater freedom is enjoyed by those who are restricted by no official duties. This spirit of freedom spreads beyond this land, even to those in which it must struggle with external obstacles erected by a government which misunderstands its own interest. For an example gives evidence to such a government that in freedom there is not the least cause for concern about public peace and the stability of the community. Men work themselves gradually out of barbarity if only intentional artifices are not made to hold them in it.

I have placed the main point of enlightenment—the escape of men from their self-incurred tutelage—chiefly in matters of religion because our rulers have no interest in playing the guardian with respect to the arts and sciences and also because religious incompetence is not only the most harmful but also the most degrading of all. But the manner of thinking of the head of a state who favors religious enlightenment goes further, and he sees that there is no danger to his lawgiving in allowing his subjects to make public use of their reason and to publish their thoughts on a better formulation of his legislation and even their open-minded criticisms of the laws already made. Of this we have a shining example wherein no monarch is superior to him whom we honor.

But only one who is himself enlightened, is not afraid of shadows, and has a numerous and well-disciplined army to assure public peace can say: "Argue as much as you will, and about what you will, only obey!" A republic could not dare say such a thing. Here is shown a strange and unexpected trend in human affairs in which almost everything, looked at in the large, is paradoxical. A greater degree of civil freedom appears advantageous to the freedom of mind of the people, and yet it places inescapable limitations upon it; a lower degree of civil freedom, on the contrary, provides the mind with room for each man to extend himself to his full capacity. As nature has uncovered from under this hard shell the seed for which she most tenderly cares—the propensity and vocation to free thinking—this gradually works back upon the character of the people, who thereby gradually become capable of managing freedom; finally, it affects the principles of government, which finds it to its advantage to treat men, who are now more than machines, in accordance with their dignity.

RENÉ DESCARTES

A mathematician, scientist, and philosopher, the French thinker René Descartes (1595–1650) wrote a book that transformed European thinking. *The Discourse on Method* (1637) asks how it is possible for human beings to know anything at all. It puts its emphasis not on what we know, but on the critical and rational methods by which we arrive at knowledge. The philosopher begins by resolving to strip away all claims to truth that cannot be grounded in certainty. Little remains apart from the fact that he is thinking. From this Descartes deduces that he himself exists: *Cogito ergo sum*, or "I think, therefore I am." With this conclusion he affirms that the mind is separate from the body, and more important than mere physical experience. Descartes believed that his own rational conclusions proved the existence of God, but others worried that his skeptical questioning might lead to atheism. Either way, Western thought has grappled ever since with the Cartesian "mind-body problem."

From The Discourse on Method[1]

Like a man who walks alone and in darkness, I resolved to go so slowly, and to use so much circumspection in everything, that if I did not advance speedily, at least I should keep from falling. I would not even have desired to begin by entirely rejecting any of the opinions which had formerly been able to slip into my belief without being introduced there by reason, had I not first spent much time in projecting the work which I was to undertake, and in seeking the true method of arriving at a knowledge of everything of which my understanding should be capable.

When I was younger, I had devoted a little study to logic, among philosophical matters, and to geometrical analysis and to algebra, among mathematical matters—three arts or sciences which, it seemed, ought to be able to contribute something to my design. But on examining them I noticed that the syllogisms of logic and the greater part of the rest of its teachings serve rather for explaining to other people the things we already know, or even, like the art of Lully,[2] for speaking without judgment of things we know not, than for instructing us of them. And although they indeed contain many very true and very good precepts, there are always so many others mingled therewith that it is almost as difficult to separate them as to extract a Diana or a Minerva[3] from a

---

1. Translated by Isaac Kramnick.
2. Ramón Llull (1232–1315), a medieval Catalán philosopher who tried to prove the existence of a Christian God by means of logic

machines; his reasoning was circular.
3. Roman goddesses often represented by sculptors in marble.

block of marble not yet rough hewn. Then, as to the analysis of the ancients and the algebra of the moderns, besides that they extend only to extremely abstract matters and appear to have no other use, the first is always so restricted to the consideration of figures that it cannot exercise the understanding without greatly fatiguing the imagination, and in the other one is so bound down to certain rules and ciphers that it has been made a confused and obscure art which embarrasses the mind, instead of a science which cultivates it. This made me think that some other method must be sought, which, while combining the advantages of these three, should be free from their defects. And as a multitude of laws often furnishes excuses for vice, so that a state is much better governed when it has but few, and those few strictly observed, so in place of the great number of precepts of which logic is composed, I believed that I should find the following four sufficient, provided that I made a firm and constant resolve not once to omit to observe them.

The first was, never to accept anything as true when I did not recognize it clearly to be so, that is to say, to carefully avoid precipitation and prejudice, and to include in my opinions nothing beyond that which should present itself so clearly and so distinctly to my mind that I might have no occasion to doubt it.

The second was, to divide each of the difficulties which I should examine into as many portions as were possible, and as should be required for its better solution.

The third was, to conduct my thoughts in order, by beginning with the simplest objects, and those most easy to know, so as to mount little by little, as if by steps, to the most complex knowledge, and even assuming an order among those which do not naturally precede one another.

And the last was, to make everywhere enumerations so complete, and surveys so wide, that I should be sure of omitting nothing.

The long chains of perfectly simple and easy reasons, which geometers are accustomed to employ in order to arrive at their most difficult demonstrations, had given me reason to believe that all things which can fall under the knowledge of man succeed each other in the same way, and that provided only we abstain from receiving as true any opinions which are not true, and always observe the necessary order in deducing one from the other, there can be none so remote that they may not be reached, or so hidden that they may not be discovered. And I was not put to much trouble to find out which it was necessary to begin with, for I knew already that it was with the simplest and most easily known; and considering that of all those who have heretofore thought truth in the sciences it is the mathematicians alone who have been able to find demonstrations, that is to say, clear and certain reasons, I did not doubt that I must start with the same things that they have considered, although I hoped for no other profit from them than that they would accustom my mind to feed on truths and not to content itself with false reasons. But I did not therefore design to try to learn all those particular sciences which bear the general name of mathematics: and seeing that although their objects were different they nevertheless all agree, in that they consider only the various relations or proportions found therein, I thought it would be better worth while if I merely examined these proportions in general, supposing them only in subjects which would serve to render the knowledge of them more easy to me, and even, also, without in any wise restricting them thereto, in order to be the better able to apply them subsequently to every other subject to which they should be suitable. Then, having remarked that in order to know them I should sometimes need to consider each separately, I had to suppose them in lines, because I found nothing more simple, or which I could more distinctly represent to my imagination and to my senses; but to retain them, or to comprehend many of them together, it was necessary that I should express them by certain ciphers as short as possible, and in this way I should borrow all the best in geometrical analysis, and in algebra, and correct all the faults of the one by means of the other.

I do not know whether I ought to discuss with you the earlier of my meditations, for they are so metaphysical and so out of the common that perhaps they would not be to everyone's taste; and yet, in order that it may be judged whether the bases I have taken are sufficiently firm, I am in some measure constrained to speak of them. I had remarked for long that, in conduct, it is sometimes necessary to follow opinions known to be very uncertain, just as if they were indubitable, as has been said above; but then, because I desired to devote myself only to the research of truth, I thought it necessary to do exactly the contrary, and reject as absolutely false all in which I could conceive the least doubt, in order to see if afterwards there did not remain in my belief something which was entirely indubitable. Thus, because our senses sometimes deceive us, I wanted to suppose that nothing is such as they make us imagine it; and because some men err in reasoning, even touching the simplest matters of geometry, and make paralogisms, and judging that I was as liable to fail as any other, I rejected as false all the reasons which I had formerly accepted as demonstrations; and finally, considering that all the thoughts which we have when awake can come to us also when we sleep, without any of them then being true, I resolved to feign that everything which had ever entered into my mind was no more true than the illusions of my dreams. But immediately afterwards I observed that while I thus desired everything to be false, I, who thought, must of necessity be something; and remarking that this truth, *I think, therefore I am*, was so firm and so assured that all the most extravagant suppositions of the skeptics were unable to shake it, I judged that I could unhesitatingly accept it as the first principle of the philosophy I was seeking.

Then, examining attentively what I was, and seeing that I could feign that I had no body, and that there was no world or any place where I was, but that nevertheless I could not feign that I did not exist, and that, on the contrary, from the fact that I thought to doubt of the truth of other things, it followed very evidently that I was; while if I had only ceased to think, although all else which I had previously imagined had been true I had no reason to believe that I might have been, therefore I knew that I was a substance whose essence or nature is only to think, and which, in order to be, has no need of any place, and depends on no material thing; so that this I, that is to say, the soul by which I am what I am, is entirely distinct from the body, and even easier to know than the body, and although the body were not, the soul would not cease to be all that it is.

After that I considered generally what is requisite to make a proposition true and certain; for since I had just found one which I knew to be so, I thought that I ought also to know in what this certainly consisted. And having remarked that there is nothing at all in this, *I think, therefore I am*, which assures me that I speak the truth, except that I see very clearly that in order to think it is necessary to exist, I judged that I might take it as a general rule that the things which we conceive very clearly and very distinctly are all true, and that there is difficulty only in seeing plainly which things they are that we conceive distinctly.

After this, and reflecting upon the fact that I doubted, and that in consequence my being was not quite perfect (for I saw clearly that to know was a greater perfection than to doubt), I bethought myself to find out from whence I had learned to think of something more perfect than I; and I knew for certain that it must be from some nature which was in reality more perfect. For as regards the thoughts I had of many other things outside myself, as of the sky, the earth, light, heat, and a thousand more, I was not so much at a loss to know whence they came, because, remarking nothing in them which seemed to make them superior to me, I could believe that if they were true they were dependencies of my nature, inasmuch as it had some perfection, and if they were not true that I derived them from nothing—that is to say, that they were in me because I had some defect. But it could not be the same with the idea of a Being more perfect than my own, for to derive it from nothing was manifestly impossible; and since it is no less repugnant to me that the more perfect should follow and depend on the less perfect than that out of nothing should proceed something, I could not derive it from myself; so that it remained that it had been put in me by a nature truly more perfect than I, which had in itself all perfections of which I could have any idea; that is, to explain myself in one word, God.

DENIS DIDEROT / JEAN LE ROND D'ALEMBERT

It may come as a surprise to learn that an encyclopedia could be considered one of the most dangerous books of its time. Edited by Denis Diderot (1713–1784) and Jean le Rond D'Alembert (1717–1783), two French thinkers, the thirty-volume illustrated *Encyclopédie* (1751–1777) broke with established knowledge and religious authority to affirm the kinds of knowledge that could be gained through human experience and human reason. A hundred and forty authors collaborated on the finished product, putting together more than 70,000 entries, starting with *asparagus* and ending with *zodiac*. Often considered the quintessential creation of the Enlightenment, it was written in French, rather than Latin, and intended to be accessible to a wide audience.

Diderot, who was especially interested in biology, and D'Alembert, who was an important mathematician, worked from an unshakable confidence in science, and deliberately inserted views unsettling to established religion in minor articles, which they cross-referenced with more orthodox articles on major topics. But it was not only unsettling, it was also useful: a collection of the latest scientific and technological advances that could be put to use for industrial development. The *Encyclopédie* proved enormously popular across Europe, reprinted in cheap editions to meet the demands of an ever-expanding readership. It helped to circulate the central values of the Enlightenment—universalism, reason, progress, and a thoroughgoing skepticism about authority—on an unprecedented new scale.

From The Encyclopédie

AFRICA,[1] one of the four principal parts of the Earth. It measures approximately 800 leagues from Tangiers to Suez; 1420 from Cape Verde to Cape Guardafui; and 1450 from the Cape of Good Hope to Bone. Long. 1-71. Lat. (southern) 1-35 and (northern) 1-37.30.

There is little trading on the *African* coasts; the interior of this part of the world is still insufficiently known, and Europeans began trading only around the middle of the XIVth century. There is little trade between the Kingdoms of Morocco and Fez and the area near Cape Verde. Trading posts can be found around Cape Verde and between the Senegal and the Sierra Leone rivers. The coast of Sierra Leone has been explored by the four Nations, but only the Portuguese and the English have established posts. Only the English have a trading post near Cape Miserado. We do some trading along the Melegueta and Greve Coasts: we trade even more along "little Dieppe" and the grand Sestre. The Ivory (or Tusk) Coast is frequented by all Europeans; they almost all have Settlements and Forts along the Gold Coast. The Cape of Corsica is the main settlement of the English; there is little trade at Asdres. Many Negroes are taken from Benin and Angola. There is no activity in Kafir country. The Portuguese are established in Sofala, in Mozambique, in Madagascar. They also handle all the Malindi trade. We will follow the branches of this trade in the different articles CAPE VERDE, SENEGAL, etc.

BEAST, ANIMAL, BRUTE.[2] People use *beast* in contradistinction to *man*; thus one says: "man has a soul, but some philosophers do not concede that beasts have any at all." *Brute* is a term of contempt applied to *beasts* and to man only in a bad sense. *He surrenders himself to all the fury of his inclinations like a brute. Animal* is a generic term suitable to all organic and living beings: *the animal lives, acts, and moves by itself, etc*. If we consider the animal as thinking, wanting, acting, reflecting, etc., then the sense of the word would be restricted to the human race. If we consider the animal to be limited in all the functions

---

1. Translated by Lauren Yoder.   2. Translated by Stephen J. Gendzier.

that indicate intelligence and will, but seem to have them in common with the human race, then it is restricted to the *beast*. If we consider the *beast* in its lowest depths of stupidity, released from the laws of reason and honesty according to which we must regulate our conduct, then we call it a *brute*. We do not know if *beasts* are governed by the general laws of motion or by a particular impulse. Both of these opinions present difficulties. If they act out of a particular impulse, if they think, if they have a soul, etc., then what is that soul? We cannot suppose that it is material in nature, but could it be spiritual? To declare that they do not have souls and do not think would reduce animals to the level of machines, which we hardly seem any more authorized to do than to maintain that a man whose speech we do not hear is an automaton. The argument based on the perfection of their works is strong, for it would seem, if we judge from their first steps, that they should go rather far. Nevertheless, they all stop at the same point, which is almost the character of machines. But the argument based on the uniformity of their productions does not appear quite as well-founded to me. The nests of swallows and the dwellings of beavers do not resemble each other any more than do the houses of men. If a swallow places its nest in an angle, the only circumference will be the arc covered between the sides of the angle. On the other hand, if the nest is set against a wall, it will measure half a circumference. If you dislodge beavers from their homes, and they go settle in another location, as it is not possible for them to find the same piece of ground, there will necessarily be variety in the techniques they use and the dwellings they construct.

However that may be, one cannot imagine that beasts have a much more intimate relationship with God than the other parts of the material world, otherwise, which one of us would dare to lay a hand on them and shed their blood without any qualms? Who would be able to kill a lamb with an easy conscience? The feelings they have, whatever their nature, are only useful in communicating with each other or with other creatures. With the incentive of pleasure they conserve their own being; and with the same incentive, they conserve their species. I have said *incentive of pleasure* for lack of a more precise expression, for if *beasts* were capable of the same feeling which we call *pleasure*, to cause them any harm would be an act of unprecedented cruelty. They have their own natural laws because they are united by common needs, interests, etc., but they do not have any positive ones because they are not united by any intellectual understanding. However, they do not seem to follow their natural laws in an invariable manner; and plants which we assume have neither understanding nor feeling are even more subject to these laws.

Beasts do not have the supreme advantage of human beings. However, they have some that we do not have: they do not have our hopes, but they do not have our fears. They suffer death as we do, but it is without knowing it. Most of them take better care of themselves and do not misuse their passions as much as we do. *See* the articles SOUL and ANIMAL.

EDUCATION[3] is the care one takes of feeding, bringing up and instructing children; thus education has as goals, 1) the health and good constitution of

---

3. Translated by Carolina Armenteros.

the body; 2) what regards the rectitude and the instruction of the mind; 3) manners, that is the conduct of life, and social qualities.

Of *education* in general. Children who come into the world, must form one day the society in which they will live. Their *education* is thus the most interesting subject, 1) for themselves, whom *education* must fashion such that they will be useful to that society, obtain its esteem, and find in it their well-being; 2) for their families, whom they must support and honor; 3) for the state itself, which must reap the fruits of the good *education* that the citizens that compose it receive.

All children who come into the world must be subjected to the care of *education*, for there is none who is born completely instructed and completely *educated*. So what advantage does not accrue everyday to a state whose head has had his mind cultivated early, who has learned in History that the most stable empires are exposed to revolutions; who has been as much instructed in what he owes his subjects, as in what his subjects owe to him; to whom the source, the motive, the extent and the limits of his authority have been made known; to whom it has been taught that the sole certain means of conserving it and making it be respected, is to make good use of it? *Erudimini qui judicatis terram* [be wise, you rulers of the earth] Psalm II, 10. What happiness that of a state in which magistrates have early learned their duties, and have manners; where each citizen is warned that in coming into the world he has received a talent to render valuable; that he is member of a political body, and that in this capacity he must contribute to the common good, search for everything that can procure true advantages to society, and avoid what can disrupt its harmony, and disturb tranquility and good order! It is evident that there is no order of citizens in a state, for whom some kind of *education* is not proper; *education* for the children of sovereigns; *education* for the children of the great, for those of magistrates, etc; *education* for the children of the countryside, where, in the same way that there are schools for learning the truths of religion, there should be also those in which the exercises, the practices, the duties and the virtues of their social state could be shown to them, so that they might act with greater knowledge.

If every kind of *education* were imparted with enlightenment and perseverance, the motherland would be well constituted, well governed, and protected from the insults of its neighbors.

Education is the greatest good that fathers can leave to their children. One finds only too frequently fathers who do not know their true interests, refuse to spend what is necessary for a good *education*, and who save nothing afterwards to provide an occupation for their children, or to lend to them an honorable office: yet what duty is more useful than a good *education*, which commonly does not cost so much, although it is the good whose product is the greatest, the most honorable and the most sensible? It pays back every day: other goods are often dissipated; but one cannot get rid of a good *education*, nor, unfortunately, of a bad one, which often is such because one has not wanted to defray the expenses of a good one:

* * *

You give your son to be *educated* by a slave, said one day an ancient philosopher to a rich father, very well, instead of one slave you shall have two.

There is much analogy between the cultivation of plants and the education of children; in one and in the other nature must furnish the base. The owner of a field cannot make it be usefully cultivated, unless the terrain is proper to what he wants to produce in it; likewise, an enlightened father, and a master who has discernment and experience, must observe their student; and after a certain period of observation, they must disentangle his penchants, his inclinations, his taste, his character, and know what he is good for, and what role, so to speak, he must play in the concert of society.

Do not force the inclinations of your children, but also do not allow them to choose lightly a station for which you foresee that they will realize in time they were not suitable. One must, as much as one can, spare them bad initiatives. Happy those children who have experienced parents capable of conducting them well in the choice of a station! A choice on which depends happiness or evil—without considering the rest of life.

* * *

With regard to the mind, the first years of childhood require much more care than is commonly given to them, so that it is often very difficult afterwards to erase the bad impressions that a young man has had through the discourses and the examples of people of little sense and little enlightenment, who were near him in those first years.

From the moment that a child lets it be known by his look and by his gestures that he understands what is said to him, he should be regarded as a subject proper to be submitted to the jurisdiction of *education*, whose goal is to form the mind, and set aside what can lead it astray. It would be desirable for him to be approached only by sensible people, and for him to see and hear nothing but good. The first instances of sensible acquiescence in our mind, or, to speak in common parlance, the first knowledge or the first ideas that form within us during the first years of our life, are as many models that it is difficult to refashion, and which later serve us as rules in the use that we make of our reason. Thus it is extremely important for a young man to acquiesce only to what is true, that is to what is, as soon as he has judgment. So keep him away from all fabulous stories, from all puerile tales of Fairies, of werewolves, of wandering Jews,[4] of goblins, of ghosts, of wizards, of spells, told by those makers of horoscopes, those fortune-tellers male and female, those interpreters of dreams, and so many other superstitious practices that serve only to lead astray children's reason, to frighten their imagination, and often even to make them regret having come into the world.

Persons who amuse themselves by frightening children are very reprehensible. It has often happened that the weak organs of children's brains have been deranged for the rest of their lives, besides their mind being filled with ridiculous prejudices, etc. The more these chimerical ideas are extraordinary, the more deeply ingrained they become in the brain.

One must not blame less those who amuse themselves by tricking children, leading them into error, deluding them into believing things, and who congratulate themselves instead of being ashamed. In such instances it is the

4. German legend of a Jew who insulted Jesus on his way to be crucified and was therefore doomed to wander the earth.

young man who has the good part; he does not yet know that there are persons whose soul is low enough to speak against their thought, and who affirm shameful falsehoods in the same tone in which honest people say the most certain truths; he has not yet learned to suspect; he puts himself in your hands, and you trick him: all those false ideas become as many exemplary ideas, which lead children's reason astray. I would have it that instead of thus taming the mind of young people with charm and lies, one never told them anything but the truth.

ENCYCLOPEDIA[5] (*Philosophy*). This word means the *interrelation of all knowledge*; it is made up of the Greek prefix *en*, in, and the nouns *kyklos*, circle, and *paideia*, instruction, science, knowledge. In truth, the aim of an *encyclopedia* is to collect all the knowledge scattered over the face of the earth, to present its general outlines and structure to the men with whom we live, and to transmit this to those who will come after us, so that the work of past centuries may be useful to the following centuries, that our children, by becoming more educated, may at the same time become more virtuous and happier, and that we may not die without having deserved well of the human race.

* * *

We have seen that our *Encyclopedia* could only have been the endeavor of a philosophical century; that this age has dawned, and that fame, while raising to immortality the names of those who will perfect man's knowledge in the future, will perhaps not disdain to remember our own names. We have been heartened by the ever so consoling and agreeable idea that people may speak to one another about us, too, when we shall no longer be alive; we have been encouraged by hearing from the mouths of a few of our contemporaries a certain voluptuous murmur that suggests what may be said of us by those happy and educated men in whose interests we have sacrificed ourselves, whom we esteem and whom we love, even though they have not yet been born. We have felt within ourselves the development of those seeds of emulation which have moved us to renounce the better part of ourselves to accomplish our task, and which have ravished away into the void the few moments of our existence of which we are genuinely proud. Indeed, man reveals himself to his contemporaries and is seen by them for what he is: a peculiar mixture of sublime attributes and shameful weaknesses. But our weaknesses follow our mortal remains into the tomb and disappear with them; the same earth covers them both, and there remains only the total result of our attributes immortalized in the monuments we raise to ourselves or in the memorials that we owe to public respect and gratitude—honors which a proper awareness of our own deserts enables us to enjoy in anticipation, an enjoyment that is as pure, as great, and as real as any other pleasure and in which there is nothing imaginary except, perhaps, the titles on which we base our pretensions. Our own claims are deposited in the pages of this work, and posterity will judge them.

5. Translated by Stephen J. Gendzier.

I have said that it could only belong to a philosophical age to attempt an *encyclopedia*; and I have said this because such a work constantly demands more intellectual daring than is commonly found in ages of pusillanimous taste. All things must be examined, debated, investigated without exception and without regard for anyone's feelings. . . . We must ride roughshod over all these ancient puerilities, overturn the barriers that reason never erected, give back to the arts and sciences the liberty that is so precious to them. . . . We have for quite some time needed a reasoning age when men would no longer seek the rules in classical authors but in nature, when men would be conscious of what is false and true about so many arbitrary treatises on aesthetics: and I take the term *treatise on aesthetics* in its most general meaning, that of a system of given rules to which it is claimed that one must conform in any genre whatsoever in order to succeed.

*   *   *

It would be desirable for the government to authorize people to go into the factories and shops, to see the craftsmen at their work, to question them, to draw the tools, the machines, and even the premises.

There are special circumstances when craftsmen are so secretive about their techniques that the shortest way of learning about them would be to apprentice oneself to a master or to have some trustworthy person do this. There would be few secrets that one would fail to bring to light by this method, and all these secrets would have to be divulged without any exception.

I know that this feeling is not shared by everyone. These are narrow minds, deformed souls, who are indifferent to the fate of the human race and who are so enclosed in their little group that they see nothing beyond its special interest. These men insist on being called good citizens, and I consent to this, provided that they permit me to call them *bad men*. To listen to them talk, one would say that a successful *encyclopedia*, that a general history of the mechanical arts, should only take the form of an enormous manuscript that would be carefully locked up in the king's library, inaccessible to all other eyes but his, an official document of the state, not meant to be consulted by the people. What is the good of divulging the knowledge a nation possesses, its private transactions, its inventions, its industrial processes, its resources, its trade secrets, its enlightenment, its arts, and all its wisdom? Are not these the things to which it owes a part of its superiority over the rival nations that surround it? This is what they say; and this is what they might add: would it not be desirable if, instead of enlightening the foreigner, we could spread darkness over him or even plunge all the rest of the world into barbarism so that we could dominate more securely over everyone? These people do not realize that they occupy only a single point on our globe and that they will endure only a moment in its existence. To this point and to this moment they would sacrifice the happiness of future ages and that of the entire human race.

They know as well as anyone that the average duration of empires is not more than two thousand years and that in less time, perhaps, the name *Frenchman*, a name that will endure forever in history, will be sought after in vain over the surface of the earth. These considerations do not broaden their point of view; for it seems that the word *humanity* is for them a word without meaning. All the same, they should be consistent! For they also fulminate against the impenetrability of the Egyptian sanctuaries;[6] they deplore the loss of the knowledge of the ancients; they accuse the writers of the past for having been silent or negligent in writing so badly on an infinite number of important subjects; and these illogical critics do not see that they demand of the writers of earlier ages something they call a crime when it is committed by a contemporary, that they are blaming others for having done what they think it honorable to do.

* * *

LYRIC POETRY.[7] * * * It is a type of *poetry* totally devoted to sentiment; that's its substance, its essential object. Whether it rises like a trembling flame; whether it seeps in, little by little, and excites us without noise; whether it is an eagle, a butterfly, a bee, it is always sentiment that guides it or carries it along.

In general, *lyric poetry* is destined to be set to music; it is for this that it is called *lyric*, and because, in times past, when it was sung, the lyre accompanied the voice. The word ode has the same origin; it means, song, hymn or canticle.

Thence, *lyric poetry* and music have an intimate connection between them, founded on things themselves, since they both have the same object to express; and if this is so, music being an expression of sentiments from the heart through inarticulate sound, musical or *lyric poetry* will be the expression of sentiments through articulate sound, that is to say, through words.

So, one can define *lyric poetry* as that which expresses sentiment in verse that is melodic; but as sentiments are hot, passionate and powerful, warmth must dominate in this genre of work. Thence are born all the rules of *lyric poetry*, as well as its privileges: that is what allows for the boldness of beginnings, the deviations, the energy of unconventional moments; it is from here that it derives this sublimity, which so specifically belongs to it, and this enthusiasm that brings it close to the divine.

Lyric poetry is as ancient as the world. When man had opened his eyes on to the universe, on the agreeable impressions that he received from all his senses, on the marvels that surrounded him, he raised his voice to pay the tribute of glory that he owed to the supreme benefactor. And that is the origin of hymns, odes, in a word, *lyric poetry*.

At the base of their holidays, the pagans had the same principle as the worshippers of the true God. It was joy and gratitude that made them institute solemn games to celebrate the gods to whom they believed they were indebted for their harvest. From there came the songs of joy that they devoted to the god of the harvest, and to that of love. If the beneficent gods were the natural material of lyric poetry, heroes, children of the gods naturally had to have their part in this sort of tribute, without counting that their virtue, their courage, or their favors either to a particular people or to the whole human race, made them resemble divinity. * * *

6. The holiest, innermost parts of ancient Egyptian temples.

7. Translated by Helen O'Connor.

We will only point out here that it is particularly to *lyric poets* that it is given to instruct with dignity and agreement. Dramatic and fable poetry rarely bring together these two advantages; the ode brings respect to a moral divinity by the sublimity of thoughts, the majesty of cadences, the boldness of figures, the force of expressions; at the same time it wards off distaste by brevity, by the variety of its turns, and by the choice of the embellishments that a skillful poet knows how to use at the right time.

POLITICAL AUTHORITY.[8] No man has received from nature the right to command others. Liberty is a gift from heaven, and each individual of the same species has the right to enjoy it as soon as he enjoys the use of reason. If nature has established any *authority*, it is paternal control; but paternal control has its limits, and in the state of nature it would terminate when the children could take care of themselves. Any other *authority* comes from another origin than nature. If one seriously considers this matter, one will always go back to one of these two sources: either the force and violence of an individual who has seized it, or the consent of those who have submitted to it by a contract made or assumed between them and the individual on whom they have bestowed *authority*.

Power that is acquired by violence is only usurpation and only lasts as long as the force of the individual who commands can prevail over the force of those who obey; in such a way that if the latter become in their turn the strongest party and then shake off the yoke, they do it with as much right and justice as the other who had imposed it upon them. The same law that made *authority* can then destroy it; for this is the law of might.

Sometimes *authority* that is established by violence changes its nature; this is when it continues and is maintained with the express consent of those who have been brought into subjection, but in this case it reverts to the second case about which I am going to speak; and the individual who had arrogated it then becomes a prince, ceasing to be a tyrant.

Power that comes from the consent of the people necessarily presupposes certain conditions that make its use legitimate, useful to society, advantageous to the republic, and set and restrict it between limits: for man must not nor cannot give himself entirely and without reserve to another man, because he has a master superior to everything, to whom he alone belongs in his entire being. It is God, whose power always has a direct bearing on each creature, a master as jealous as absolute, who never loses his rights and does not transfer them. He permits for the common good and for the maintenance of society that men establish among themselves an order of subordination, that they obey one of them, but he wishes that it be done with reason and proportion and not by blindness and without reservation, so that the creature does not arrogate the rights of the creator. Any other submission is the veritable crime of idolatry. To bend one's knee before a man or an image is merely an external ceremony about which the true God, who demands the heart and the mind, hardly cares and which he leaves to the institution of men to do with as they please

8. Translated by Stephen J. Gendzier.

the tokens of civil and political devotion or of religious worship. Thus it is not these ceremonies in themselves, but the spirit of their establishment that makes their observance innocent or criminal. An Englishman has no scruples about serving the king on one knee; the ceremonial only signifies what people wanted it to signify. But to deliver one's heart, spirit, and conduct without any reservation to the will and caprice of a mere creature, making him the unique and final reason for one's actions, is assuredly a crime of divine lese majesty[9] of the highest degree. Otherwise this power of God about which one speaks so much would only be empty noise that human politics would use out of pure fantasy and which the spirit of irreligion could play with in its turn; so that all ideas concerning power and subordination coming to the point of merging, the prince would trifle with God, and the subject with the prince.

* * *

The prince owes to his very subjects the *authority* that he has over them; and this *authority* is limited by the laws of nature and the state. The laws of nature and the state are the conditions under which they have submitted or are supposed to have submitted to its government. One of these conditions is that, not having any power or *authority* over them but by their choice and consent, he can never employ this *authority* to break the act or the contract by which it was transferred to him. From that time on he would work against himself, since his authority could only subsist by virtue of the right that established it. Whoever annuls one, destroys the other. The prince cannot therefore dispose of his power and his subjects without the consent of the nation and independently of the option indicated in the contract of allegiance. If he proceeded otherwise, everything would be nullified, and the laws would relieve him of the promises and the oaths that he would have been able to make, as a minor who would have acted without full knowledge of the facts, since he would have claimed to have at his disposal that which he only had in trust and with a clause of entail, in the same way as if he had had it in full ownership and without any condition.

Moreover the government, although hereditary in a family and placed in the hands of one person, is not private property, but public property that consequently can never be taken from the people, to whom it belongs exclusively, fundamentally, and as a freehold. Consequently it is always the people who make the lease or the agreement: they always intervene in the contract that adjudges its exercise. It is not the state that belongs to the prince, it is the prince who belongs to the state: but it does rest with the prince to govern in the state, because the state has chosen him for that purpose: he has bound himself to the people and the administration of affairs, and they in their turn are bound to obey him according to the laws. The person who wears the crown can certainly discharge himself of it completely if he wishes, but he cannot replace it on the head of another without the consent of the nation who has placed it on his. In a word, the crown, the government, and the public *authority* are possessions owned by the body of the nation, held as a usufruct by

---

9. An offense against God.

princes and as a trust by ministers. Although heads of state, they are nonetheless members of it; as a matter of fact the first, the most venerable, and the most powerful allowed everything in order to govern, allowed nothing legitimately to change the established government or to place another head in their place. The sceptre of Louis XV[1] necessarily passes to his eldest son, and there is no power who can oppose this; nor any nation because it is the condition of the contract; nor his father for the same reason.

The depository of *authority* is sometimes only for a limited time, as in the Roman republic. It is sometimes for the life of only one man, as in Poland; sometimes for all the time a family exists, as in England; sometimes for the time a family exists only through its male descendants, as in France.[2]

This depository is sometimes entrusted to a certain class in society, sometimes to several people chosen by all the classes, and sometimes to one man.

The conditions of this pact are different in different states. But everywhere the nation has a right to maintain against all forces the contract that they have made; no power can change it; and when it is no longer valid, the nation recovers its rights and full freedom to enter into a new one with whomever and however it pleases them. This is what would happen in France if by the greatest of misfortunes the entire reigning family happened to die out, including the most remote descendants; then the sceptre and the crown would return to the nation.

It seems that only slaves whose minds are as limited as their hearts are debased could think otherwise. Such men are born neither for the glory of the prince nor for the benefit of society; they have neither virtue nor greatness of soul. Fear and self-interest are the motives of their conduct. Nature only produces them to improve by contrast the worth of virtuous men; and Providence uses them to make tyrannical powers, with which it chastises as a rule the people and the sovereigns who offend God; the latter for usurping, the former for granting too much to man of supreme power, that the Creator reserved for Himself over the created being.

The observation of laws, the conservation of liberty, and the love of country are the prolific sources of all great things and of all beautiful actions. Here we can find the happiness of people, and the true luster of princes who govern them. Here obedience is glorious, and command august. On the contrary, flattery, self-interest, and the spirit of slavery are at the root of all the evils that overpower a state and of all the cowardice that dishonor it. There the subjects are miserable, and the princes hated; there the monarch has never heard himself proclaimed *the beloved*; submission is hateful there, and domination cruel. If I view France and Turkey[3] from the same perspective, I perceive on the one hand a society of men united by reason, activated by virtue, and governed by a head of state equally wise and glorious according to the laws of justice; on the other, a herd of animals assembled by habit, driven by the law of the rod, and led by an absolute master according to his caprice.

1. King of France (1710–1774).
2. The Roman Republic (ca. 509 B.C.E.– 49 B.C.E.) limited its dictators to six-month terms; Mieszko I (ca. 930–992) founded and ruled Poland before dividing the nation among his sons at his death; the unwritten Salic law in France excluded women from inheriting the throne.
3. Eighteenth-century Europeans frequently associated Turkey with despotism.

SAVAGES.[4] Barbarous peoples who live without law, without governance, without religion, and who have no fixed habitation.

This word comes from the Italian *salvagio*, derived from *salvaticus*, *selvaticus* and *silvaticus*, which signifies the same thing as *sylvestris—rustic*, or that which concerns woods and forests, because savages ordinarily dwell in forests.

A large part of America is peopled by *savages*, the majority of whom are still fierce and feed upon human flesh.

* * *

THE SLAVE TRADE[5] (*Commerce of Africa*) is the buying of unfortunate Negroes by Europeans on the coast of Africa to use as slaves in their colonies. This buying of Negroes, to reduce them to slavery, is one business that violates religion, morality, natural laws, and all the rights of human nature.

Negroes, says a modern Englishman full of enlightenment and humanity, have not become slaves by the right of war; neither do they deliver themselves voluntarily into bondage, and consequently their children are not born slaves. Nobody is unaware that they are bought from their own princes, who claim to have the right to dispose of their liberty, and that traders have them transported in the same way as their other goods, either in their colonies or in America, where they are displayed for sale.

If commerce of this kind can be justified by a moral principle, there is no crime, however atrocious it may be, that cannot be made legitimate. Kings, princes, and magistrates are not the proprietors of their subjects: they do not, therefore, have the right to dispose of their liberty and to sell them as slaves.

On the other hand, no man has the right to buy them or to make himself their master. Men and their liberty are not objects of commerce; they can be neither sold nor bought nor paid for at any price. We must conclude from this that a man whose slave has run away should only blame himself, since he had acquired for money illicit goods whose acquisition is prohibited by all the laws of humanity and equity.

There is not, therefore, a single one of these unfortunate people regarded only as slaves who does not have the right to be declared free, since he has never lost his freedom, which he could not lose and which his prince, his father, and any person whatsoever in the world had not the power to dispose of. Consequently the sale that has been completed is invalid in itself. This Negro does not divest himself and can never divest himself of his natural right; he carries it everywhere with him, and he can demand everywhere that he be allowed to enjoy it. It is, therefore, patent inhumanity on the part of judges in free countries where he is transported, not to emancipate him immediately by declaring him free, since he is their fellow man, having a soul like them.

There are authors who, posing as political jurists, come to tell us confidently that the questions relative to the state of persons must be decided by the laws of the countries in which they belong and that therefore a man who is declared a slave in America and who is transported from there to Europe must be regarded there as a slave. But this is to decide the rights of humanity by the

---

4. Translated by Richard Weyhing.   **5.** Translated by Stephen J. Gendzier.

civil laws of a gutter, as Cicero says.[6] Must the magistrates of a nation, out of consideration for another nation, have no regard for their own people? Must their deference to a law that binds them in no way make them trample underfoot the law of nature that binds all men at all times and in all places? Is there any law as obligatory as the eternal laws of equity? What problem is created if a judge is bound to observe them more than to respect the arbitrary and inhuman practices of the colonies?

One will say perhaps that these colonies will soon be ruined if the slavery of Negroes were abolished there. But if this were true, should we conclude from this that the human race must be horribly injured to enrich us and to provide us with luxuries? It is true that the pockets of highwaymen would be empty if robbery were to be entirely suppressed, but do men have the right to enrich themselves by cruel and criminal acts? What right has a bandit to rob travelers? Who is allowed to become opulent by making his fellow men unfortunate? Can it be legitimate to rob mankind of its most sacred rights solely to satisfy one's avarice, one's vanity, or one's particular passions? No . . . therefore let the European colonies be destroyed rather than make so many unfortunate people.

But I believe it is false that the suppression of slavery would entail its ruin. Commerce would suffer for some time, I agree; this is the effect of all new arrangements, because in this case new trade relations could not be readily found to follow another economic system; but out of this suppression other advantages would arise.

It is this *slave trade*, this practice of slavery, that has prevented America from being populated as promptly as it would have been. Let them free the Negroes, and in a few generations this vast and fertile country will have innumerable inhabitants. The arts and talent will flourish there, and instead of a land populated almost entirely by savages and wild beasts there will soon be a country of industrious men. It is freedom, it is industry that are the real sources of abundance. As long as a nation conserves this industry and this freedom, it has nothing to fear. Industry as well as necessity is ingenious and inventive: it finds a thousand different ways to procure riches for itself; and if one of the channels to opulence is blocked, a hundred others immediately open up.

Sensible and generous souls will without doubt applaud these reasons in favor of humanity; but avarice and greed which dominate the earth will never wish to hear them.

WIFE,[7] in Latin *uxor*, female of man, considered such when she is united to him by ties of marriage. See therefore Marriage [MARRIAGE (NATURAL LAW), MARRIAGE (JURISPRUDENCE), MARRIAGE (THEOLOGY)] and HUSBAND.

The Supreme Being having judged that it was not good for man to be alone, conceived a desire to unite him in close society with a companion, and this society is made through a voluntary accord between the parties. As this society has as its principal goal the procreation and protection of the children it produces, the father and mother of necessity devote all their energies to nourishing and

6. Marcus Tullius Cicero (106–43 B.C.E.), Roman philosopher, politician, and legal theorist who argued against despotism.
7. Translated by Naomi Andrews.

properly rearing the fruits of their love up until the time when they are able to care and judge for themselves.

But although the husband and the *wife* have fundamentally the same interests in their marriage, it is nevertheless essential that governing authority belong to one or the other: now the affirmative right of civilized nations, the laws and the customs of Europe give this authority unanimously to the male, being the one endowed with the greatest strength of mind and body, contributing more to the common good in matters of sacred and human things; such that the woman must necessarily be subordinated to her husband and obey his orders in all domestic affairs. This is the belief of the ancient and modern jurists and the formal decision of legislators.

In addition, the Frederician code,[8] which appeared first in 1750 and which seems to have attempted to introduce definitive and universal rights, declares that the husband is according to nature itself the master of the house, the chief of the family; and that it therefore follows that the *wife* resides there at his leave, she is in all regards under the power of the husband, from which fact devolve diverse prerogatives which pertain personally to him. Finally, holy scripture commands the wife to submit to him as to her master.[9]

However the reasons we've just listed for marital power are not without rejoinder, humanely speaking; and the character of this work allows us to boldly enunciate them.

It appears first of all that it would be difficult to demonstrate that the authority of the husband comes from nature; because this principle is contrary to the natural equality of men; and just because one is suited for commanding doesn't mean that it is actually one's right to do so: 2. man does not always have greater strength of body, wisdom, spirit or conduct than woman: 3. Scriptural precepts being established in punitive terms, indicates as well that there is only a positive right. One can therefore claim that there is no other type of subordination in marital relations than that of the civil law, and as a consequence, the only things preventing change in the civil law are particular conventions, and that natural law and religion do not determine anything to the contrary.

We do not deny that in a society composed of two people, it is necessary that the deliberative laws of one or the other carry the day; and since ordinarily men are more capable than women of ably governing particular matters, it is wise to establish as a general rule, that the voice of the man will carry more weight as long as the two have not made any agreement to the contrary, because general law results from human institutions, and not from natural right. In this way, a woman who knows the basis of civil law and who contracts her marriage purely and simply, has by law submitted, tacitly, to this civil law.

But if this woman, persuaded that she has more judgment and direction, or knowing that she has greater fortune or is of a higher station than that of the man who asks her to marry him, stipulates the contrary of that which the law implies, and with the consent of this husband, should she not have, by virtue

---

8. A body of laws drafted for King Frederick II of Prussia (1712–1786). The code combined ancient Roman traditions with Enlightenment theories of sociability.

9. Ephesians 5.22: "Wives, submit yourselves unto your own husbands, as unto the Lord."

of natural law, the same power her husband has by virtue of the law of the realm? The case of a queen, who, being sovereign in her own right, marries a prince below her rank, or if she likes, one of her subjects, is enough to show that the authority of a woman over her husband, even in matters concerning the governance of the family, is not incompatible with the nature of the marital contract.

In effect, we have seen among the most civilized nations, marriages which submit the husband to the domain of the *wife*; we have seen a princess, heir to the realm, reserve to herself, while marrying, the sovereign power of the state. Everyone knows the conventions of marriage which were made between Philip II and Mary Queen of England; those of Mary Queen of Scots and those of Ferdinand and Isabel, in order to govern the kingdom of Castile together.[1] * * *

The examples of England and of Muscovy[2] make evident that women can succeed equally, both in moderate and despotic government; and if it is not against reason and nature that they rule an empire, then it would seem that it is no more contradictory that they should be mistresses in a family.

When Lacedaemonian[3] marriages were ready to be consummated, the woman took the dress of a man; and it was a symbol of the equal power that she would share with her husband. On this subject we know what Gorgo, the wife of Leonidas, king of Sparta,[4] said to a foreign woman who was extremely surprised by this equality: Don't you know, responded the queen, that we bring men into the world? In other times, even in Egypt, marriage contracts between individuals, as much as those of the king and the queen, gave authority over the husband to the wife.

It makes no difference (because it is not a matter here of exploiting unique examples which prove too much); it makes no difference, I say, if the authority of a woman in marriage cannot exist within conventional bounds, between people of equal stature, at least let the legislature refrain from prohibiting exceptions to the law, made with the free consent of the parties.

Marriage is by its nature a contract; and as a result, in all things not expressly prohibited by natural law, the contractual engagements between the husband and the wife determine reciprocal rights.

Finally, why should the ancient maxim, *provisio hominis tollit provisionem legis*,[5] not be accepted in this case, such as one allows it in dowries, in the division of goods, and in several other things, where the law does not rule except when the parties have not stipulated provisions different from those prescribed by law?

---

1. Philip II of Spain (1527–1598) married Mary I of England (1516–1558), but she denied him the right to rule England and inherit the throne upon her death; Mary, Queen of Scots (1542–1587) refused monarchical power to her husband, Henry Stewart, Lord Darnley; Ferdinand II (1452–1516) and Isabella I (1451–1504) of Spain shared their powers of governance.

2. Catherine the Great (1729–1796) assumed control of Russia, called Muscovy, after her husband Peter III was dethroned.
3. From ancient Sparta.
4. Gorgo and Leonidas ruled Sparta in the early sixth and late fifth centuries B.C.E.
5. The provision made by an individual does not take away the provision made by the law (Latin).

BENJAMIN FRANKLIN

Few people have ever boasted the immense and various talents shown by Benjamin Franklin (1706–1790). This American started his adult life as a printer, moving to Philadelphia from his birthplace in Boston as a young man, and went on to become a successful businessman, inventor, scientist, writer, musician, diplomat, and signatory to the Declaration of Independence and the United States Constitution. He invented swimming fins and bifocal glasses and discovered new sources of electricity. Always looking for solutions to improve human life, he founded or improved libraries, hospitals, insurance companies, and volunteer fire departments. At first a slaveholder, Franklin eventually converted to the antislavery cause and freed the slaves he owned. In this letter to the Englishman Joseph Priestley (1733–1804), the discoverer of oxygen and one of the Enlightenment's most important scientists, Franklin articulates the belief that scientific knowledge will give rise to endless progress.

Letter to Joseph Priestley[1]

PASSY, Feb. 8, 1780.

DEAR SIR,

Your kind letter of September 27 came to hand but very lately, the bearer having stayed long in Holland. I always rejoice to hear of your being still employed in experimental researches into nature, and of the Success you meet with. The rapid Progress *true* Science now makes, occasions my regretting sometimes that I was born so soon. It is impossible to imagine the height to which may be carried, in a thousand years, the power of man over matter. We may perhaps learn to deprive large masses of their gravity, and give them absolute levity, for the sake of easy transport. Agriculture may diminish its labor and double its produce; all diseases may by sure means be prevented or cured, not excepting even that of old age, and our lives lengthened at pleasure even beyond the antediluvian standard. O that moral science were in as fair a way of improvement, that men would cease to be wolves to one another, and that human beings would at length learn what they now improperly call humanity!

I am glad my little paper on the *Aurora Borealis* pleased. If it should occasion further enquiry, and so produce a better hypothesis, it will not be wholly useless. I am ever, with the greatest and most sincere esteem, dear sir, yours very affectionately

B. FRANKLIN.

1. An English chemist (1733–1804) who experimented with electricity and discovered a range of gases; also a close friend of Franklin.

DAVID HUME

The Scottish-born philosopher David Hume (1711–1776) rejected the quest for abstract and theoretical truths. He favored an empirical approach, that is, the demand to "reject every system . . . however subtle or ingenious, which is not founded on fact and observation," and to "hearken to no arguments but those which are derived from experience." This insistence on trusting only the evidence of observable facts led readers to assume that he was an atheist, though in fact he refused to deny the existence of God, preferring rather to suspend judgment on what seemed to him an insoluble mystery.

While Hume stands for the quintessential Enlightenment values of skepticism and critical questioning, and was known to be a gentle and tolerant person, his work shows the more brutal side of the Enlightenment too: the belief that only Europeans were fully rational, human subjects. Always committed to empirical evidence, he makes a distinction between white and black races supposedly based on observed fact, though his own experience of African people was in fact exceptionally limited. While affirming a natural racial hierarchy, Hume also opposes slavery as disgusting and corrupting.

From Of National Characters

* * *

I am apt to suspect the negroes to be naturally inferior to the whites. There scarcely ever was a civilized nation of that complexion, nor even any individual eminent either in action or speculation. No ingenious manufactures amongst them, no arts, no sciences. On the other hand, the most rude and barbarous of the whites, such as the ancient GERMANS, the present TARTARS, have still something eminent about them, in their valour, form of government, or some other particular. Such a uniform and constant difference could not happen, in so many countries and ages, if nature had not made an original distinction between these breeds of men. Not to mention our colonies, there are NEGROE slaves dispersed all over EUROPE, of whom none ever discovered any symptoms of ingenuity; though low people, without education, will start up amongst us, and distinguish themselves in every profession. In JAMAICA, indeed, they talk of one negroe as a man of parts and learning; but it is likely he is admired for slender accomplishments, like a parrot, who speaks a few words plainly.

* * *

The chief difference between the *domestic* economy of the ancients and that of the moderns consists in the practice of slavery, which prevailed among the former, and which has been abolished for some centuries throughout the greater part of EUROPE. Some passionate admirers of the ancients, and zealous partisans of civil liberty, (for these sentiments, as they are, both of them, in the main, extremely just, are found to be almost inseparable) cannot forbear regretting the loss of this institution; and whilst they brand all submission to the government of a single person with the harsh denomination of slavery, they would gladly reduce the greater part of mankind to real slavery and subjection. But to one who considers coolly on the subject it will appear, that human nature, in general, really enjoys more liberty at present, in the most arbitrary government of EUROPE, than it ever did during the most flourishing period of ancient times. As much as submission to a petty prince, whose dominions extend not beyond a single city, is more grievous than obedience to a great monarch; so much is domestic slavery more cruel and oppressive than any civil subjection whatsoever. The more the master is removed from us in place and rank, the greater liberty we enjoy; the less are our actions inspected and controled; and the fainter that cruel comparison becomes between our own subjection, and the freedom, and even dominion of another. The remains which are found of domestic slavery, in the AMERICAN colonies, and among some EUROPEAN nations, would never surely create a desire of rendering it more universal. The little humanity, commonly observed in persons, accustomed, from their infancy, to exercise so great authority over their fellow-creatures, and to trample upon human nature, were sufficient alone to disgust us with that unbounded dominion. Nor can a more probable reason be assigned for the severe, I might say, barbarous manners of ancient times, than the practice of domestic slavery; by which every man of rank was rendered a petty tyrant, and educated amidst the flattery, submission, and low debasement of his slaves.

According to ancient practice, all checks were on the inferior, to restrain him to the duty of submission; none on the superior, to engage him to the reciprocal duties of gentleness and humanity. In modern times, a bad servant finds not easily a good master, nor a bad master a good servant; and the checks are mutual, suitably to the inviolable and eternal laws of reason and equity.

* * *

JAMES BEATTIE

James Beattie (1735–1803) read **David Hume**'s work and burned with anger. He was a Scottish philosopher, too, who made quite a reputation for himself by refuting Hume. In his *Essay on Truth* (1770), Beattie disputes claims about racial difference on Hume's own grounds— empirical evidence—and argues that such assertions of inferiority and superiority necessarily legitimate the practice of slavery. He thus exposes contradictions in Hume's own logic, using Enlightenment methods against one of the period's great philosophical heroes.

From An Essay on Truth

* * *

That I may not be thought a blind admirer of antiquity, I would here crave the reader's indulgence for one short digression more, in order to put him in mind of an important error in morals, inferred from partial and inaccurate experience, by no less a person than Aristotle himself.[1] He argues, "That men of little genius, and great bodily strength, are by Nature destined to serve, and those of better capacity to command; that the natives of Greece, and of some other countries, being superior in genius, have a natural right to empire; and that the rest of mankind, being naturally stupid, are destined to labour and slavery." This reasoning is now, alas! of little advantage to Aristotle's countrymen, who have for many ages been doomed to that slavery which, in his judgment, Nature had destined them to impose on others; and many nations whom he would have consigned to everlasting stupidity, have shown themselves equal in genius to the most exalted of human kind. It would have been more worthy of Aristotle, to have inferred man's natural and universal right to liberty, from that natural and universal passion with which men desire it, and from the salutary consequences to learning, to virtue, and to every human improvement, of which it never fails to be productive. He wanted, perhaps, to devise some excuse for servitude; a practice which to their eternal reproach, both Greeks and Romans tolerated even in the days of their glory.

Mr. Hume argues nearly in the same manner in regard to the superiority of white men over black. "I am apt to suspect," says he, "the negroes, and in general all the other species of men (for there are four or five different kinds), to be naturally inferior to the whites. There *never was* a civilized nation of any other complexion than white, *nor even any individual* eminent either in action or speculation. *No* ingenious manufactures among them, *no* arts, *no* sciences.— There are negro-slaves dispersed all over Europe, of which *none* ever discovered any symptoms of ingenuity." These assertions are strong; but I know not whether they have any thing else to recommend them.—For, first, though true, they would not prove the point in question, except it were also proved, that the Africans and Americans, even though arts and sciences were introduced among them, would still remain unsusceptible of cultivation. The inhabitants of Great Britain and France were as savage two thousand years ago, as those of Africa and America are at this day. To civilize a nation, is a work which requires long time to accomplish. And one may as well say of an infant, that he can never become a man, as of a nation now barbarous, that it never can be civilized.— Secondly, of the facts here asserted, no man could have sufficient evidence, except from a personal acquaintance with all the negroes that now are, or ever were, on the face of the earth. These people write no histories; and all the reports of all the travellers that ever visited them, will not amount to any thing like a proof of what is here affirmed.—But, thirdly, we know that these assertions are not true. The empires of Peru and Mexico could not have been governed, nor the metropolis of the latter built after so singular a manner, in the middle of a lake, without men eminent both for action and speculation. Every

---

1. Ancient Greek philosopher (384–322 B.C.E).

body has heard of the magnificence, good government, and ingenuity, of the ancient Peruvians. The Africans and Americans are known to have many ingenious manufactures and arts among them, which even Europeans would find it no easy matter to imitate. Sciences indeed they have none, because they have no letters; but in oratory, some of them, particularly the *Indians of the Five Nations*,[2] are said to be greatly our superiors. It will be readily allowed, that the condition of a slave is not favourable to genius of any kind; and yet the negro-slaves dispersed over Europe, have often discovered symptoms of ingenuity, notwithstanding their unhappy circumstances. They become excellent handicraftsmen, and practical musicians, and indeed learn every thing their masters are at pains to teach them, perfidy and debauchery not excepted. That a negro-slave, who can neither read nor write, nor speak any European language, who is not permitted to do any thing but what his master commands, and who has not a single friend on earth, but is universally considered and treated as if he were of a species inferior to the human;—that such a creature should so distinguish himself among Europeans, as to be talked of through the world as a man of genius, is surely no reasonable expectation. To suppose him of an inferior species, because he does not thus distinguish himself, is just as rational, as to suppose any private European of an inferior species, because he has not raised himself to the condition of royalty.

Had the Europeans been destitute of the arts of writing, and working in iron, they might have remained to this day as barbarous as the natives of Africa and America. Nor is the invention of these arts to be ascribed to our superior capacity. The genius of the inventor is not always to be estimated according to the importance of the invention. Gunpowder, and the mariner's compass, have produced wonderful revolutions in human affairs, and yet were accidental discoveries. Such, probably, were the first essays in writing, and working in iron. Suppose them the effect of contrivance, they were at least contrived by a few individuals; and if they required a superiority of understanding, or of species, in the inventors, those inventors, and their descendants, are the only persons who can lay claim to the honour of that superiority.

That every practice and sentiment is barbarous which is not according to the usages of modern Europe, seems to be a fundamental maxim with some of our philosophers. Their remarks often put us in mind of the fable of the man and the lion.[3] If negroes or Indians were disposed to recriminate; if a Lucian or a Voltaire,[4] from the coast of Guinea, or from *the Five Nations*, were to pay us a visit; what a picture of European manners might he present to his countrymen at his return! Nor would caricature, or exaggeration be necessary to render it hideous. A plain historical account of some of our most fashionable duellists, gamblers, and adulterers (to name no more), would exhibit specimens of brutish barbarity and sottish infatuation, such as might vie with any that ever appeared in Kamschatka, California, or the land of Hottentots.[5]

2. A confederacy of American Indian tribes: the Mohawk, Oneida, Onondaga, Cayuga, and Seneca peoples.
3. Story told by Aesop (620–564 B.C.E.) about a man and a lion, each of whom boasts of being superior to the other.

4. A French philosopher and satirist (1694–1778); Lucian (ca. 125–180), a Syrian satirist who wrote in Greek.
5. A southwest African people today better known as the Khoikhoi. "Kamschatka": a Russian peninsula that juts into the Pacific Ocean.

The natural inferiority of negroes is a favourite topic with some modern writers. They mean perhaps to invalidate the authority of that Book, which declares, that "Eve was the mother of all living," and that "God hath made of one blood all nations of men, for to dwell on all the face of the earth." And perhaps some of them may have it in view to vindicate a certain barbarous piece of policy, which, though it does no honour to the Christian world, and is not, I believe, attended with pecuniary advantage to the commercial, has notwithstanding many patrons even in this age of light and liberty.—But Britons are famous for generosity; a virtue in which it is easy for them to excel both the Romans and the Greeks. Let it never be said, that slavery is countenanced by the bravest and most generous people on earth; by a people who are animated with that heroic passion, the love of liberty, beyond all nations ancient or modern; and the fame of whose toilsome, but unwearied perseverance, in vindicating, at the expence of life and fortune, the sacred rights of mankind, will strike terror into the hearts of sycophants and tyrants, and excite the admiration and gratitude of all good men to the latest posterity.

MARY WOLLSTONECRAFT

Consorting with radicals in England who favored the French Revolution, with its overthrow of traditional authority and its embrace of universal principles of equality and reason, Mary Wollstonecraft (1759–1797) launched a powerful argument for inalienable human rights in her essay *A Vindication of the Rights of Men* (1791). Here she relied on rational principles to attack justifications for traditional privilege and power. She followed this essay in 1792 with the even more radical *A Vindication of the Rights of Woman*, where she argued that marriage was no better than prostitution, and that education and unequal laws for women at the time subjected them to a condition similar to slavery. For these political views, Wollstonecraft was widely mocked in her own lifetime. And when it emerged after her death that she had had a child out of wedlock, her reputation sank so low that few readers were willing to open her "immoral" books for more than a century. It was only in the 1960s that she became known as the great founder of feminism. Wollstonecraft also left a legacy of a different kind: her second daughter, Mary, the only legitimate child of Wollstonecraft and fellow radical writer William Godwin, grew up to write *Frankenstein*, one of the most influential works of nineteenth-century literature.

From A Vindication of the Rights of Woman

* * *

Men and women must be educated, in a great degree, by the opinions and manners of the society they live in. In every age there has been a stream of popular opinion that has carried all before it, and given a family character, as it were, to the century. It may then fairly be inferred, that, till society be differently constituted, much cannot be expected from education. It is, however, sufficient for my present purpose to assert, that, whatever effect circumstances have on the abilities, every being may become virtuous by the exercise of its own reason; for if but one being was created with vicious inclinations, that is positively bad, what can save us from atheism? or if we worship a God, is not that God a devil?

Consequently, the most perfect education, in my opinion, is such an exercise of the understanding as is best calculated to strengthen the body and form the heart. Or, in other words, to enable the individual to attain such habits of virtue as will render it independent. In fact, it is a farce to call any being virtuous whose virtues do not result from the exercise of its own reason. This was Rousseau's opinion[1] respecting men: I extend it to women, and confidently assert that they have been drawn out of their sphere by false refinement, and not by an endeavour to acquire masculine qualities. Still the regal homage which they receive is so intoxicating, that till the manners of the times are changed, and formed on more reasonable principles, it may be impossible to convince them that the illegitimate power, which they obtain, by degrading themselves, is a curse, and that they must return to nature and equality, if they wish to secure the placid satisfaction that unsophisticated affections impart. But for this epoch we must wait—wait, perhaps, till kings and nobles, enlightened by reason, and, preferring the real dignity of man to childish state, throw off their gaudy hereditary trappings: and if then women do not resign the arbitrary power of beauty—they will prove that they have *less* mind than man.

I may be accused of arrogance; still I must declare what I firmly believe, that all the writers who have written on the subject of female education and manners from Rousseau to Dr. Gregory,[2] have contributed to render women more artificial, weak characters, than they would otherwise have been; and, consequently, more useless members of society. I might have expressed this conviction in a lower key; but I am afraid it would have been the whine of affectation, and not the faithful expression of my feelings, of the clear result, which experience and reflection have led me to draw. When I come to that division of the subject, I shall advert to the passages that I more particularly disapprove of, in the works of the authors I have just alluded to; but it is first necessary to observe, that my objection extends to the whole purport of those books, which tend, in my opinion, to degrade one half of the human species, and render women pleasing at the expense of every solid virtue.

---

1. Jean-Jacques Rousseau (1712–1778), philosopher from Geneva whose ideas about human equality and freedom inspired many revolutionaries; he also wrote about education.

2. John Gregory (1724–1773), Scottish physician who wrote an influential book on educating girls called *A Father's Legacy to his Daughters* (1774).

Though, to reason on Rousseau's ground, if man did attain a degree of perfection of mind when his body arrived at maturity, it might be proper, in order to make a man and his wife *one*, that she should rely entirely on his understanding; and the graceful ivy, clasping the oak that supported it, would form a whole in which strength and beauty would be equally conspicuous. But, alas! husbands, as well as their helpmates, are often only overgrown children; nay, thanks to early debauchery, scarcely men in their outward form—and if the blind lead the blind, one need not come from heaven to tell us the consequence.

Many are the causes that, in the present corrupt state of society, contribute to enslave women by cramping their understandings and sharpening their senses. One, perhaps, that silently does more mischief than all the rest, is their disregard of order.

To do every thing in an orderly manner, is a most important precept, which women, who, generally speaking, receive only a disorderly kind of education, seldom attend to with that degree of exactness that men, who from their infancy are broken into method, observe. This negligent kind of guess-work, for what other epithet can be used to point out the random exertions of a sort of instinctive common sense, never brought to the test of reason? prevents their generalizing matters of fact—so they do to-day, what they did yesterday, merely because they did it yesterday.

This contempt of the understanding in early life has more baneful consequences than is commonly supposed; for the little knowledge which women of strong minds attain, is, from various circumstances, of a more desultory kind than the knowledge of men, and it is acquired more by sheer observations on real life, than from comparing what has been individually observed with the results of experience generalized by speculation. Led by their dependent situation and domestic employments more into society, what they learn is rather by snatches; and as learning is with them, in general, only a secondary thing, they do not pursue any one branch with that persevering ardour necessary to give vigor to the faculties, and clearness to the judgment. In the present state of society, a little learning is required to support the character of a gentleman; and boys are obliged to submit to a few years of discipline. But in the education of women, the cultivation of the understanding is always subordinate to the acquirement of some corporeal accomplishment; even while enervated by confinement and false notions of modesty, the body is prevented from attaining that grace and beauty which relaxed half-formed limbs never exhibit. Besides, in youth their faculties are not brought forward by emulation; and having no serious scientific study, if they have natural sagacity it is turned too soon on life and manners. They dwell on effects, and modifications, without tracing them back to causes; and complicated rules to adjust behaviour are a weak substitute for simple principles.

As a proof that education gives this appearance of weakness to females, we may instance the example of military men, who are, like them, sent into the world before their minds have been stored with knowledge or fortified by principles. The consequences are similar; soldiers acquire a little superficial knowledge, snatched from the muddy current of conversation, and, from continually mixing with society, they gain, what is termed a knowledge of the world; and this acquaintance with manners and customs has frequently been confounded with a knowledge of the human heart. But can the crude fruit of casual observation, never brought to the test of judgment, formed by comparing speculation and experience, deserve such a distinction? Soldiers, as well as women, practice the minor virtues with punctilious politeness. Where is then the sexual difference, when the education has been the same? All the difference that I can discern, arises from the superior advantage of liberty, which enables the former to see more of life.

It is wandering from my present subject, perhaps, to make a political remark; but, as it was produced naturally by the train of my reflections, I shall not pass it silently over.

Standing armies can never consist of resolute, robust men; they may be well disciplined machines, but they will seldom contain men under the influence of strong passions, or with very vigorous faculties. And as for any depth of understanding, I will venture to affirm, that it is as rarely to be found in the army as amongst women; and the cause, I maintain, is the same. It may be further observed, that officers are also particularly attentive to their persons, fond of dancing, crowded rooms, adventures, and ridicule.[3] Like the *fair* sex, the business of their lives is gallantry.—They were taught to please, and they only live to please. Yet they do not lose their rank in the distinction of sexes, for they are still reckoned superior to women, though in what their superiority consists, beyond what I have just mentioned, it is difficult to discover.

The great misfortune is this, that they both acquire manners before morals, and a knowledge of life before they have, from reflection, any acquaintance with the grand ideal outline of human nature. The consequence is natural; satisfied with common nature, they become a prey to prejudices, and taking all their opinions on credit, they blindly submit to authority. So that, if they have any sense, it is a kind of instinctive glance, that catches proportions, and decides with respect to manners; but fails when arguments are to be pursued below the surface, or opinions analyzed.

May not the same remark be applied to women? Nay, the argument may be carried still further, for they are both thrown out of a useful station by the unnatural distinctions established in civilized life. Riches and hereditary honours have made cyphers of women to give consequence to the numerical figure;[4] and idleness has produced a mixture of gallantry and despotism into society, which leads the very men who are the slaves of their mistresses to tyrannize over their sisters, wives, and daughters. This is only keeping them in rank and file, it is true. Strengthen the female mind by enlarging it, and there will be an end to blind obedience; but, as blind obedience is ever sought for by power, tyrants and sensualists are in the right when they endeavour to keep women in the dark, because the former only want slaves, and the latter a plaything. The sensualist, indeed, has been the most dangerous of tyrants, and women have been duped by their lovers, as princes by their ministers, whilst dreaming that they reigned over them.

3. Why should women be censured with petulant acrimony, because they seem to have a passion for a scarlet coat? Has not education placed them more on a level with soldiers than any other class of men? [Wollstonecraft's note].

4. Wealth and hereditary privilege have made women into "cyphers"—zeroes—which are nothing in themselves but valuable when added to the end of numbers.

MARQUIS DE SADE

The French aristocrat Donatien-Alphonse-François, the Marquis de Sade (1740–1814) is best known for his erotic writings, which are marked by an appetite for violence and cruelty (the word *sadism* is derived from his name). Not one of the standard figures of Enlightenment philosophy, he nonetheless represents a provocative extreme on the spectrum of Enlightenment thought. Like other influential thinkers of the period, he favored freedom—but in his case it was a freedom so complete that he saw no need for laws of any kind. Like others he asked how there could be a God when evil existed in the world, but rather than denying God's existence or justifying God's goodness in the face of evil, de Sade argued that God must be cruel and malicious himself. Humans therefore have the natural right to act as cruelly as they choose. In *Philosophy in the Bedroom* (1795), de Sade writes in a conventional philosophical form—the dialogue—and pursues a debate governed by the reasoned pursuit of truth. But his characters conclude that the only right way to act in the world involves rejecting modesty, compassion, and all moral and religious rules in favor of their own pleasure. In the selection included here, a libertine aristocrat asks whether murder is a crime in the eyes of nature and uses the eminently enlightened tools of logic and observed fact to reason through to his startling conclusions.

From Philosophy in the Bedroom[1]

* * *

Thus, my dear Eugénie, is the manner of these persons' arguing, and from my experience and studies I may add thereunto that cruelty, very far from being a vice, is the first sentiment Nature injects in us all. The infant breaks his toy, bites his nurse's breast, strangles his canary long before he is able to reason; cruelty is stamped in animals, in whom, as I think I have said, Nature's laws are more emphatically to be read than in ourselves; cruelty exists amongst savages, so much nearer to Nature than civilized men are; absurd then to maintain cruelty is a consequence of depravity. I repeat, the doctrine is false. Cruelty is natural. All of us are born furnished with a dose of cruelty education later modifies; but education does not belong to Nature, and is as deforming to Nature's sacred effects as arboriculture is to trees. In your orchards compare the tree abandoned to Nature's ministry with the other your art cares for, and you will see which is the more beautiful, you will discover from which you will pluck the superior fruit. Cruelty is simply the energy in a man civilization has not yet altogether corrupted: therefore it is a virtue, not a vice. Repeal your laws, do away with your constraints, your chastisements, your habits, and cruelty will have dangerous effects no more, since it will never manifest itself save

1. Translated by Richard Seaver and Austryn Wainhouse.

when it meets with resistance, and then the collision will always be between competing cruelties; it is in the civilized state cruelty is dangerous, because the assaulted person nearly always lacks the force or the means to repel injury; but in the state of uncivilization, if cruelty's target is strong, he will repulse cruelty; and if the person attacked is weak, why, the case here is merely that of assault upon one of those persons whom Nature's law prescribes to yield to the strong—'tis all one, and why seek trouble where there is none?

* * *

Have we not acquired the right to say anything? The time has come for the ventilation of great verities; men today will not be content with less. The time has come for error to disappear; that blindfold must fall beside the heads of kings. From Nature's point of view, is murder a crime? That is the first question posed.

It is probable that we are going to humiliate man's pride by lowering him again to the rank of all of Nature's other creatures, but the philosopher does not flatter small human vanities; ever in burning pursuit of truth, he discerns it behind stupid notions of pride, lays it bare, elaborates upon it, and intrepidly shows it to the astonished world.

What is man? and what difference is there between him and other plants, between him and all the other animals of the world? None, obviously. Fortuitously placed, like them, upon this globe, he is born like them; like them, he reproduces, rises, and falls; like them he arrives at old age and sinks like them into nothingness at the close of the life span Nature assigns each species of animal, in accordance with its organic construction. Since the parallels are so exact that the inquiring eye of philosophy is absolutely unable to perceive any grounds for discrimination, there is then just as much evil in killing animals as men, or just as little, and whatever be the distinctions we make, they will be found to stem from our pride's prejudices, than which, unhappily, nothing is more absurd. Let us all the same press on to the question. You cannot deny it is one and the same, to destroy a man or a beast; but is not the destruction of all living animals decidedly an evil, as the Pythagoreans believed, and as they who dwell on the banks of Ganges[2] yet believe? Before answering that, we remind the reader that we are examining the question only in terms of Nature and in relation to her; later on, we will envisage it with reference to men.

Now then, what value can Nature set upon individuals whose making costs her neither the least trouble nor the slightest concern? The worker values his work according to the labor it entails and the time spent creating it. Does man cost Nature anything? And, under the supposition that he does, does he cost her more than an ape or an elephant? I go further: what are the regenerative materials used by Nature? Of what are composed the beings which come into life? Do not the three elements of which they are formed result from the prior destruction of other bodies? If all individuals were possessed of eternal life,

---

2. River in India that is sacred to the Hindu religion, which encourages a vegetarian diet. "Pythagoreans": followers of the Greek philosopher Pythagoras (ca. 570–ca. 490 B.C.E.), who claimed that after death the soul migrated to a new human or animal body; Pythagoreans often espoused vegetarianism.

would it not become impossible for Nature to create any new ones? If Nature denies eternity to beings, it follows that their destruction is one of her laws. Now, once we observe that destruction is so useful to her that she absolutely cannot dispense with it, and that she cannot achieve her creations without drawing from the store of destruction which death prepares for her, from this moment onward the idea of annihilation which we attach to death ceases to be real; there is no more veritable annihilation; what we call the end of the living animal is no longer a true finis, but a simple transformation, a transmutation of matter, what every modern philosopher acknowledges as one of Nature's fundamental laws. According to these irrefutable principles, death is hence no more than a change of form, an imperceptible passage from one existence into another, and that is what Pythagoras called metempsychosis.

These truths once admitted, I ask whether it can ever be proposed that destruction is a crime? Will you dare tell me, with the design of preserving your absurd illusions, that transmutation is destruction? No, surely not; for, to prove that, it would be necessary to demonstrate matter inert for an instant, for a moment in repose. Well, you will never detect any such moment. Little animals are formed immediately a large animal expires, and these little animals' lives are simply one of the necessary effects determined by the large animal's temporary sleep. Given this, will you dare suggest that one pleases Nature more than another? To support that contention, you would have to prove what cannot be proven: that elongated or square are more useful, more agreeable to Nature than oval or triangular shapes; you would have to prove that, with what regards Nature's sublime scheme, a sluggard who fattens in idleness is more useful than the horse, whose service is of such importance, or than a steer, whose body is so precious that there is no part of it which is not useful; you would have to say that the venomous serpent is more necessary than the faithful dog.

Now, as not one of these systems can be upheld, one must hence consent unreservedly to acknowledge our inability to annihilate Nature's works; in light of the certainty that the only thing we do when we give ourselves over to destroying is merely to effect an alteration in forms which does not extinguish life, it becomes beyond human powers to prove that there may exist anything criminal in the alleged destruction of a creature, of whatever age, sex, or species you may suppose it. Led still further in our series of inferences proceeding one from the other, we affirm that the act you commit in juggling the forms of Nature's different productions is of advantage to her, since thereby you supply her the primary material for her reconstructions, tasks which would be compromised were you to desist from destroying.

Well, let *her* do the destroying, they tell you; one ought to let her do it, of course, but they are Nature's impulses man follows when he indulges in homicide; it is Nature who advises him, and the man who destroys his fellow is to Nature what are the plague and famine, like them sent by her hand which employs every possible means more speedily to obtain of destruction this primary matter, itself absolutely essential to her works.

Let us deign for a moment to illumine our spirit by philosophy's sacred flame; what other than Nature's voice suggests to us personal hatreds, revenges, wars, in a word, all those causes of perpetual murder? Now, if she incites us to murderous acts, she has need of them; that once grasped, how may we suppose ourselves guilty in her regard when we do nothing more than obey her intentions?

But that is more than what is needed to convince any enlightened reader, that for murder ever to be an outrage to Nature is impossible.

Is it a political crime? We must avow, on the contrary, that it is, unhappily, merely one of policy's and politics' greatest instruments. Is it not by dint of murders that France is free today? Needless to say, here we are referring to the murders occasioned by war, not to the atrocities committed by plotters and rebels; the latter, destined to the public's execration, have only to be recollected to arouse forever general horror and indignation. What study, what science, has greater need of murder's support than that which tends only to deceive, whose sole end is the expansion of one nation at another's expense? Are wars, the unique fruit of this political barbarism, anything but the means whereby a nation is nourished, whereby it is strengthened, whereby it is buttressed? And what is war if not the science of destruction? A strange blindness in man, who publicly teaches the art of killing, who rewards the most accomplished killer, and who punishes him who for some particular reason does away with his enemy! Is it not high time errors so savage be repaired?

Is murder then a crime against society? But how could that reasonably be imagined? What difference does it make to this murderous society, whether it have one member more, or less? Will its laws, its manners, its customs be vitiated? Has an individual's death ever had any influence upon the general mass? And after the loss of the greatest battle, what am I saying? after the obliteration of half the world—or, if one wishes, of the entire world—would the little number of survivors, should there be any, notice even the faintest difference in things? No, alas. Nor would Nature notice any either, and the stupid pride of man, who believes everything created for him, would be dashed indeed, after the total extinction of the human species, were it to be seen that nothing in Nature had changed, and that the stars' flight had not for that been retarded. Let us continue.

What must the attitude of a warlike and republican state be toward murder?

Dangerous it should certainly be, either to cast discredit upon the act, or to punish it. Republican mettle calls for a touch of ferocity: if he grows soft, if his energy slackens in him, the republican will be subjugated in a trice. A most unusual thought comes to mind at this point, but if it is audacious it is also true, and I will mention it. A nation that begins by governing itself as a republic will only be sustained by virtues because, in order to attain the most, one must always start with the least. But an already old and decayed nation which courageously casts off the yoke of its monarchical government in order to adopt a republican one, will only be maintained by many crimes; for it is criminal already, and if it were to wish to pass from crime to virtue, that is to say, from a violent to a pacific, benign condition, it should fall into an inertia whose result would soon be its certain ruin.

* * *

MOLIÈRE
(JEAN-BAPTISTE POQUELIN)
1622–1673

Jean-Baptiste Molière, one of the great comic dramatists in the Western tradition, wrote both broad farce and comedies of character in which he caricatured some form of vice or folly by embodying it in a single figure. His targets included the miser, the aspiring but vulgar middle class, female would-be intellectuals, the hypochondriac, and in *Tartuffe*, the religious hypocrite. Yet Molière's questioning goes far beyond witty farce: his works suggest not only the fallibility of specific types, but also the foolishness of trusting reason to arrange human affairs.

LIFE AND TIMES

Son of a prosperous Paris merchant, Molière (originally named Poquelin) devoted his entire adult life to the creation of stage illusion, as playwright and as actor. He was educated at a prestigious Jesuit school and seems to have studied law for some time, though without taking a degree. At about the age of twenty-five, he took his stage name and abandoned the comfortable life of a bourgeois to join the Illustre Théâtre, a company of traveling players established by the Béjart family. With them he toured the provinces for about twelve years, and, in 1662, he married Armande Béjart. Molière's lengthy experience as an actor doubtless honed his dramatic writing skills, although he first became known not for the tragedies that he preferred but for the short farces that he appended to them. Molière's particular talents, it would soon become clear, lay in satirizing an overly sophisticated society that was heavily invested in fashion, appearances, and proper behavior. Molière's skepticism about religious devotion, which he exposed as hypocrisy, would prove hugely controversial in a France that had recently been led by the powerful Cardinal Mazarin, chief minister while Louis XIV was a young boy, and where the Catholic Church still wielded considerable power.

Over the course of his long reign, Louis XIV, the "Sun King," consolidated royal power by upholding the divine right of kings, and became an important patron of the visual and literary arts. In Louis's France, the true measure of cultural worth was the approval of the court and the Paris stage. After years of courting noble patrons, in 1658 Molière's theatrical company was finally ordered to perform for the king in Paris; a year later, the playwright's first great success, *The High-Brow Ladies* (*Les Précieuses ridicules*), was produced. The company, now patronized by the king, became increasingly successful, developing finally (1680) into the Comédie Française. With success came opposition: the *parti des Devots* (party of the faithful) banded together to protest Molière's irreverence, as he took on more and more of his society's sacred cows. Yet the king continued to protect him, granting him a pension and allowing Molière to evade the censorship often demanded by the Church or the more conservative voices in society.

Molière became increasingly famous—and infamous—as his works met with increasing resistance, culminating in the furor over *Tartuffe*, discussed below. Over the course of his years in Paris, Molière wrote over thirty plays and produced many more on his stage. Ever the man of the theater, he died a few hours after performing in the lead role of his own play *The Imaginary Invalid*.

TARTUFFE

In *Tartuffe* (1664), as in his other plays, Molière employs classic comic devices of plot and character—here, a foolish, stubborn father blocking the course of young love; an impudent servant commenting on her superiors' actions; a happy ending involving a marriage facilitated by implausible means. He often uses such devices, however, to comment on his own immediate social scene, imagining how universal patterns play themselves out in a specific historical context. *Tartuffe* targeted the hypocrisy of piety so directly and transparently that the Catholic Church forced the king to ban it, although Molière managed to have it published and produced once more by 1669.

The play's emotional energy derives not from the simple discrepancy of man and mask in Tartuffe ("Is not a face quite different from a mask?" inquires Cléante, who has no trouble making such distinctions) but from the struggle for erotic, psychic, and economic power in which people employ their masks. Orgon, an aging man with grown children, seeks ways to preserve control and instead falls for the ploys of the hypocritical Tartuffe. A domestic tyrant, Orgon insists on submission from the women in the play, even when they prove far more perceptive than he about Tartuffe's deceptions. Tartuffe's lust, one of those passions forever eluding human mastery, disturbs Orgon's arrangements; in the end, the will of the offstage king orders everything, as though a benevolent god had intervened.

To make Tartuffe a specifically religious hypocrite is an act of inventive daring. Although one may easily accept Molière's defense of his intentions (not to mock faith but to attack its misuse), it is not hard to see why the play might trouble religious authorities. Molière suggests how readily religious faith lends itself to misuse, how high-sounding pieties allow men and women to evade self-examination and immediate responsibilities. Tartuffe deceives others by his grand gestures of mortification ("Hang up my hair shirt") and charity; he encourages his victims in their own grandiosities. Religion offers ready justification for a course as destructive as it is self-seeking.

Throughout the play, Orgon's brother-in-law Cléante speaks in the voice of wisdom, counseling moderation, common sense, and self-control, calling attention to folly. More important, he emphasizes how the issues Molière examines in this comedy relate to dominant late seventeenth-century themes:

> Ah, Brother, man's a strangely
> fashioned creature
> Who seldom is content to follow
> Nature,
> But recklessly pursues his inclination
> Beyond the narrow bounds of
> moderation,
> And often, by transgressing Reason's
> laws,
> Perverts a lofty aim or noble cause.

To follow Nature means to act appropriately to the human situation in the created universe, recognizing the limitations inherent in the human condition. As Cléante's observations suggest, "to follow Nature," given the rationality of the universe, implies adherence to "Reason's laws." All transgression involves failure to submit to reason's dictates, a point that Molière's stylized comic plot makes insistently.

Although the comedy suggests a social world in which women exist in utter subordination to fathers and husbands, in the plot two women bring about the unmasking of the villain. The virtuous wife, Elmire, object of Tartuffe's lust, and the clever servant girl, Dorine, confront the immediate situation with pragmatic inventiveness. Both women have a clear sense of right and wrong, although they express it in less resounding terms than does Cléante. Their concrete insistence on facing what is really going on, cutting through all obfuscation, rescues the men from entanglement in their own abstract formulations.

Molière achieves comic effects above all through style and language. Devoted to exposing the follies of his society, his plays use a number of devices that have become the gold standard of comic writing. His characters are often in the grip of a fixed idea, rigidly following a single principle of action, such as extreme religious devotion or sexual rejuvenation. These fixed ideas also manifest themselves in the characters' speech patterns, which are full of ticks and repetitions. Adhering to single abstractions, Molière's comic protagonists often seem like marionettes, whose rigid bearing, behavior and language is controlled by an outside force as if by a puppet master. Yet despite their singlemindedness, his characters are also recognizable portraits of human folly, closely observed and humorously rendered.

Comedies conventionally end in the restoration of order, declaring that good inevitably triumphs; rationality renews itself despite the temporary deviations of the foolish and the vicious. Although at the end of *Tartuffe* order is restored, the arbitrary intervention of the king leaves a disturbing emotional residue. The play has demonstrated that Tartuffe's corrupt will to power can ruthlessly aggrandize itself. Money speaks, in this society as in ours; possession of wealth implies total control over others. In the benign world of comedy, the play reminds its readers of the extreme precariousness with which reason finally triumphs. Tartuffe's monstrous lust—for women, money, power—genuinely endangers the social structure. The play forces us to recognize the constant threats to rationality, and how much we have at stake in trying to use reason as a principle of action.

Tartuffe[1]

CHARACTERS

MADAME PERNELLE, *mother of Orgon*
ORGON, *husband of Elmire*
ELMIRE, *wife of Orgon*
DAMIS, *son of Orgon*
MARIANE, *daughter of Orgon*
VALÈRE, *fiancé of Mariane*
CLÉANTE, *brother-in-law of Orgon*

TARTUFFE,[2] *a religious hypocrite*
DORINE, *lady's maid to Mariane*
MONSIEUR LOYAL, *a bailiff*
THE EXEMPT, *an officer of the king*
FLIPOTE, *lady's maid to Madame*
  Pernelle
LAURENT, *a servant of Tartuffe*

The scene is Paris, in ORGON's *house.*

1.1

[MADAME PERNELLE, FLIPOTE, ELMIRE,
  MARIANE, DORINE, DAMIS, CLÉANTE]

MADAME PERNELLE[3]   Flipote, come on! My visit here is through!
ELMIRE   You walk so fast I can't keep up with you!
MADAME PERNELLE   Then stop! That's your last step! Don't take another.
  After all, I'm just your husband's mother.
ELMIRE   And, as his wife, I have to see you out—   5
  Agreed? Now, what is this about?
MADAME PERNELLE   I cannot bear the way this house is run—
  As if I don't know how things should be done!
  No one even thinks about my pleasure,
  And, if I ask, I'm served at someone's leisure.   10
  It's obvious—the values here aren't good
  Or everyone would treat me as they should.
  The Lord of Misrule here has his dominion—
DORINE   But—
MADAME PERNELLE   See? A servant with an opinion.
  You're the former nanny, nothing more.   15
  Were I in charge here, you'd be out the door.
DAMIS   If—
MADAME PERNELLE   —You—be quiet. Now let Grandma spell
  Her special word for you: "F-O-O-L."
  Oh yes! Your dear grandmother tells you that,

---

1. Versification by Constance Congdon, from a translation by Virginia Scott.
2. The name Tartuffe is similar both to the Italian word *tartufo*, meaning "truffle," and to the French word for truffle, *truffe*, from which is derived the French verb *truffer*—one mean-

ing of which in Molière's day was "to deceive or cheat."
3. The role of Madame Pernelle was originally played by a male actor, a practice that was already a comic convention in Molière's time.

Just as I told my son, "Your son's a brat.   20
He won't become a drunkard or a thief,
And yet, he'll be a lifetime full of grief."
MARIANE   I think—
MADAME PERNELLE   —Oh, don't do that, my dear grandchild.
You'll hurt your brain. You think that we're beguiled
By your quietude, you fragile flower,   25
But as they say, still waters do run sour.
ELMIRE   But Mother—
MADAME PERNELLE   —Daughter-in-law, please take this well—
Behavior such as yours leads straight to hell.
You spend money like it grows on trees
Then wear it on your back in clothes like these.   30
Are you a princess? No? You're dressed like one!
One wonders whom you dress for—not my son.
Look to these children whom you have corrupted
When their mama's life was interrupted.
She spun in her grave when you were wed;   35
She's still a better mother, even dead.
CLÉANTE   Madame, I do insist—
MADAME PERNELLE   —You do? On what?
That we live life as you do, caring not
For morals? I hear each time you give that speech
Your sister memorizing what you teach.   40
I'd slam the door on you. Forgive my frankness.
That is how I am! And it is thankless.
DAMIS   Tartuffe would, from the bottom of his heart,
If he had one, thank you.
MADAME PERNELLE   Oh, now you start.
Grandson, it's "Monsieur Tartuffe" to you.   45
And he's a man who should be listened to.
If you provoke him with ungodly chat,
I will not tolerate it, and that's that.
DAMIS   Yet I should tolerate this trickster who
Has become the voice we answer to.   50
And I'm to be as quiet as a mouse
About this tyrant's power in our house?
All the fun things lately we have planned,
We couldn't do. And why? Because they're banned—
DORINE   By him! Anything we take pleasure in   55
Suddenly becomes a mortal sin.
MADAME PERNELLE   Then "he's here just in time" is what I say!
Don't you see? He's showing you the way
To heaven! Yes! So follow where he leads!
My son knows he is just what this house needs.   60
DAMIS   Now Grandmother, listen. Not Father, not you,
No one can make me follow this man who
Rules this house, yet came here as a peasant.
I'll put him in his place. It won't be pleasant.

DORINE   When he came here he wasn't wearing shoes.   65
    But he's no village saint—it's all a ruse.
    There was no vow of poverty—he's poor!
    And he was just some beggar at the door
    Whom we should have tossed. He's a disaster!
    To think this street bum now plays the master.   70
MADAME PERNELLE   May God have mercy on me. You're all blind.
    A nobler, kinder man you'll never find.
DORINE   So you think he's a saint. That's what he wants.
    But he's a hypocrite and merely flaunts
    This so-called godliness.   75
MADAME PERNELLE   Will you be quiet!?
DORINE   And that man of his—I just don't buy it—
    He's supposed to be his servant? No.
    They're in cahoots, I bet.
MADAME PERNELLE   How would you know?
    When, clearly, you don't understand, in fact,
    How a servant is supposed to act?   80
    This holy man you think of as uncouth,
    Tries to help by telling you the truth
    About yourself. But you can't hear it.
    He knows what heaven wants and that you fear it.
DORINE   So "heaven" hates these visits by our friends?   85
    I see! And that's why Tartuffe's gone to any ends
    To ruin our fun? But it is he who's zealous
    About "privacy"—and why? He's jealous.
    You can't miss it, whenever men come near—
    He's lusting for our own Madame Elmire.   90
MADAME PERNELLE   Since you, Dorine, have never understood
    Your place, or the concepts of "should"
    And "should not," one can't expect you to see
    Tartuffe's awareness of propriety.
    When these men visit, they bring noise and more—   95
    Valets and servants planted at the door,
    Carriages and horses, constant chatter.
    What must the neighbors think? These things matter.
    Is something going on? Well, I hope not.
    You know you're being talked about a lot.   100
CLÉANTE   Really, Madame, you think you can prevent
    Gossip? When most human beings are bent
    On rumormongering and defamation,
    And gathering or faking information
    To make us all look bad—what can we do?   105
    The fools who gossip don't care what is true.
    You would force the whole world to be quiet?
    Impossible! And each new lie—deny it?
    Who in the world would want to live that way?
    Let's live our lives. Let gossips have their say.   110

DORINE   It's our neighbor, Daphne. I just know it.
  They don't like us. It's obvious—they show it
  In the way they watch us—she and her mate.
  I've seen them squinting at us, through their gate.
  It's true—those whose private conduct is the worst   115
  Will mow each other down to be the first
  To weave some tale of lust, so hearts are broken
  Out of a simple kiss that's just a token
  Between friends—just friends and nothing more.
  See—those whose trysts are kept behind a door   120
  Yet everyone finds out? Well, then, they need
  New stories for the gossip mill to feed
  To all who'll listen. So they must repaint
  The deeds of others, hoping that a taint
  Will color others' lives in darker tone   125
  And, by this process, lighten up their own.
MADAME PERNELLE   Daphne and her mate are not the point.
  But when Orante says things are out of joint,
  There's a problem. She's a person who
  Prays every day and should be listened to.   130
  She condemns the mob that visits here.
DORINE   This good woman shouldn't live so near
  Those, like us, who run a bawdy house.
  I hear she lives as quiet as a mouse—
  Devout, though. Everyone applauds her zeal.   135
  She needed that when age stole her appeal.
  Her passion is policing—it's her duty.
  And compensation for her loss of beauty.
  She's a reluctant prude. And now, her art,
  Once used so well to win a lover's heart,   140
  Is gone. Her eyes, that used to flash with lust,
  Are steely from her piety. She must
  Have seen that it's too late to be a wife,
  And so she lives a plain and pious life.
  This is a strategy of old coquettes.   145
  It's how they manage once the world forgets
  Them. First, they wallow in a dark depression,
  Then see no recourse but in the profession
  Of a prude. They criticize the lives of everyone.
  They censure everything, and pardon none.   150
  It's envy. Pleasures that they are denied
  By time and age, now, they just can't abide.
MADAME PERNELLE   You do go on and on. [To ELMIRE] My dear Elmire,
  This is all your doing. It's so clear
  Because you let a servant give advice.   155
  Just be aware—I'm tired of being nice.
  It's obvious to anyone with eyes
  That what my son has done is more than wise

In welcoming this man who's so devout;
His very presence casts the devils out.   160
Or most of them—that's why I hope you hear him.
And I advise all of you to stay near him.
You need his protection and advice.
Your casual attention won't suffice.
It's heaven sent him here to fill a need,   165
To save you from yourselves—oh yes, indeed.
These visits from your friends you seem to want—
Listen to yourselves! So nonchalant!
As if no evil lurks in these events.
As if you're blind to what Satan invents.   170
And dances! What are those but food for slander!
It's to the worst desires these parties pander.
I ask you now, what purpose do they serve?
Where gossip's passed around like an hors-d'oeuvre.
A thousand cackling hens, busy with what?   175
It takes a lot of noise to cover smut.
It truly is the tower of Babylon,[4]
Where people babble on and on and on.
Ah! Case in point—there stands Monsieur Cléante,
Sniggering and eyeing me askant,   180
As if this has nothing to do with him,
And nothing that he does would God condemn.
And so, Elmire, my dear, I say farewell.
Till when? When it is a fine day in hell.
Farewell, all of you. When I pass through that door,   185
You won't have me to laugh at anymore.
Flipote! Wake up! Have you heard nothing I have said?
I'll march you home and beat you till you're dead.
March, slut, march.

1.2[5]

[DORINE, CLÉANTE]

CLÉANTE   I'm staying here. She's scary,
That old lady—
DORINE   I know why you're wary.
Shall I call her back to hear you say,
"That *old* lady"? That would make her day.

---

4. That is, the biblical Tower of Babel (the Hebrew equivalent of the Akkadian Bab-ilu, or Babylon—a name explained by the similar sounding but unrelated Hebrew verb *balal*, "confuse"), described in Genesis 11.1–9; to prevent it from being constructed and reaching heaven, God scattered all the people and confused their language, creating many tongues where there had been only one.

5. In classical French drama, a new scene begins whenever a character enters or leaves the stage, even if the action continues without interruption; this convention has become known as "French scenes." Characters remaining on-stage are listed; others from the previous scene can be assumed to have exited.

CLÉANTE   She's lost her mind, she's—now we have the proof—   5
    Head over heels in love with whom? Tartuffe.

DORINE   So here's what's worse and weird—so is her son.
    What's more—it's obvious to everyone.
    Before Tartuffe and he became entwined,
    Orgon once ruled this house in his right mind.   10
    In the troubled times,[6] he backed the prince,
    And that took courage. We haven't seen it since.
    He is intoxicated with Tartuffe—
    A potion that exceeds a hundred proof.
    It's put him in a trance, this devil's brew.   15
    And so he worships this imposter who
    He calls "brother" and loves more than one—
    This charlatan—more than daughter, wife, son.
    This charlatan hears all our master's dreams,
    And all his secrets. Every thought, it seems,   20
    Is poured out to Tartuffe, like he's his priest!
    You'd think they'd see the heresy, at least.
    Orgon caresses him, embraces him, and shows
    More love for him than any mistress knows.
    Come for a meal and who has the best seat?   25
    Whose preferences determine what we eat?
    Tartuffe consumes enough for six, is praised,
    And to his health is every goblet raised,
    While on his plate are piled the choicest bites.
    Then when he belches, our master delights   30
    In that and shouts, "God bless you!" to the beast,
    As if Tartuffe's the reason for the feast.
    Did I mention the quoting of each word,
    As if it's the most brilliant thing we've heard?
    And, oh, the miracles Tartuffe creates!   35
    The prophecies! We write while he dictates.
    All that's ridiculous. But what's evil
    Is seeing the deception and upheaval
    Of the master and everything he owns.
    He hands him money. They're not even loans—   40
    He's giving it away. It's gone too far.
    To watch Tartuffe play him like a guitar!
    And this Laurent, his man, found some lace.
    Shredded it and threw it in my face.
    He'd found it pressed inside *The Lives of Saints*,[7]   45
    I thought we'd have to put him in restraints.
    "To put the devil's finery beside

---

6. That is, during the Fronde (literally, "sling"; 1648–53), a civil war that took place while France was being ruled by a regent for Louis XIV—"the prince" whom Orgon supported—as various factions of the nobility sought to limit the growing authority of the monarchy.

7. A text (*Flos Sanctorum*, 1599–1601) by the Spanish Jesuit Pedro de Ribadeneyra, available in French translation by 1646.

The words and lives of saintly souls who died—
Is action of satanical transgression!"
And so, of course, I hurried to confession.   50

1.3

[ELMIRE, MARIANE, DAMIS, CLÉANTE, DORINE]

ELMIRE [to CLÉANTE]   Lucky you, you stayed. Yes, there was more,
   And more preaching from Grandma, at the door.
   My husband's coming! I didn't catch his eye.
   I'll wait for him upstairs. Cléante, good-bye.
CLÉANTE   I'll see you soon. I'll wait here below,   5
   Take just a second for a brief hello.
DAMIS   While you have him, say something for me?
   My sister needs for Father to agree
   To her marriage with Valère, as planned.
   Tartuffe opposes it and will demand   10
   That Father break his word, and that's not fair;
   Then I can't wed the sister of Valère.
   Listening only to Tartuffe's voice,
   He'd break four hearts at once—
DORINE   He's here.

1.4

[ORGON, CLÉANTE, DORINE]

ORGON   Rejoice!
   I'm back.
CLÉANTE   I'm glad to see you, but I'm on my way.
   Just stayed to say hello.
ORGON   No more to say?
   Dorine! Come back! And Cléante, why the hurry?
   Indulge me for a moment. You know I worry.
   I've been gone two days! There's news to tell.   5
   Now don't hold back. Has everyone been well?
DORINE   Not quite. There was that headache Madame had
   The day you left. Well, it got really bad.
   She had a fever—
ORGON   And Tartuffe?
DORINE   He's fine—
   Rosy-nosed and red-cheeked, drinking your wine.
ORGON   Poor man!
DORINE   And then, Madame became unable   10
   To eat a single morsel at the table.
ORGON   Ah, and Tartuffe?
DORINE   He sat within her sight,
   Not holding back, he ate with great delight,   15

A brace of partridge, and a leg of mutton.
In fact, he ate so much, he popped a button.

ORGON   Poor man!

DORINE   That night until the next sunrise,
Your poor wife couldn't even close her eyes.
What a fever! Oh, how she did suffer!   20
I don't see how that night could have been rougher.
We watched her all night long, worried and weepy.

ORGON   Ah, and Tartuffe?

DORINE   At dinner he grew sleepy.
After such a meal, it's not surprising.
He slept through the night, not once arising.   25

ORGON   Poor man!

DORINE   At last won over by our pleading,
Madame agreed to undergo a bleeding.[8]
And this, we think, has saved her from the grave.

ORGON   Ah, and Tartuffe?

DORINE   Oh, he was very brave.
To make up for the blood Madame had lost   30
Tartuffe slurped down red wine, all at your cost.

ORGON   Poor man!

DORINE   Since then, they've both been fine, although
Madame needs me. I'll go and let her know
How anxious you have been about her health,
And that you prize it more than all your wealth.   35

1.5

[ORGON, CLÉANTE]

CLÉANTE   You know that girl was laughing in your face.
I fear I'll make you angry, but in case
There is a chance you'll listen, I will try
To say that you are laughable and why.
I've never known of something so capricious   5
As letting this man do just as he wishes
In your home and to your family.
You brought him here, relieved his poverty,
And, in return—

ORGON   Now you listen to me!
You're just my brother-in-law, Cléante. Quite!   10
You don't know this man. And don't deny it!

CLÉANTE   I don't know him, yes, that may be so,
But men like him are not so rare, you know.

8. Bloodletting (whether by leeches or other means), for centuries a standard medical treatment
for a wide range of diseases.

ORGON   If you only could know him as I do,
    You would be his true disciple, too.   15
    The universe, your ecstasy would span.
    This is a man . . . who . . . ha! . . . well, such a man.
    Behold him. Let him teach you profound peace.
    When first we met, I felt my troubles cease.
    Yes, I was changed after I talked with him.   20
    I saw my wants and needs as just a whim!
    Everything that's written, all that's sung,
    The world, and you and me, well, it's all dung!
    Yes, it's crap! And isn't that a wonder!
    The real world—it's just some spell we're under!   25
    He's taught me to love nothing and no one!
    Mother, father, wife, daughter, son—
    They could die right now, I'd feel no pain.
CLÉANTE   What feelings you've developed, how humane.
ORGON   You just don't see him in the way I do,   30
    But if you did, you'd feel what I feel, too.
    Every day he came to church and knelt,
    And from his groans, I knew just what he felt.
    Those sounds he made from deep inside his soul,
    Were fed by piety he could not control.   35
    Of the congregation, who could ignore
    The way he humbly bowed and kissed the floor?
    And when they tried to turn away their eyes,
    His fervent prayers to heaven and deep sighs
    Made them witness his deep spiritual pain.   40
    Then something happened I can't quite explain.
    I rose to leave—he quickly went before
    To give me holy water at the door.
    He knew what I needed, so he blessed me.
    I found his acolyte, he'd so impressed me,   45
    To ask who he was and there I learned
    About his poverty and how he spurned
    The riches of this world. And when I tried
    To give him gifts, in modesty, he cried,
    "That is too much," he'd say, "A half would do."   50
    Then gave a portion back, with much ado.
    "I am not worthy. I do not deserve
    Your gifts or pity. I am here to serve
    The will of heaven, that and nothing more."
    Then takes the gift and shares it with the poor.   55
    So heaven spoke to me inside my head.
    "Just bring him home with you" is what it said
    And so I did. And ever since he came,
    My home's a happy one. I also claim
    A moral home, a house that's free of sin,   60
    Tartuffe's on watch—he won't let any in.
    His interest in my wife is reassuring,

She's innocent of course, but so alluring,
He tells me whom she sees and what she does.
He's more jealous than I ever was.   65
It's for my honor that he's so concerned.
His righteous anger's all for me, I've learned,
To the point that just the other day,
A flea annoyed him as he tried to pray,
Then he rebuked himself, as if he'd willed it—   70
His excessive anger when he killed it.

CLÉANTE   Orgon, listen. You're out of your mind.
Or you're mocking me. Or both combined.
How can you speak such nonsense without blinking?

ORGON   I smell an atheist! It's that freethinking!   75
Such nonsense is the bane of your existence.
And that explains your damnable resistance.
Ten times over, I've tried to save your soul
From your corrupted mind. That's still my goal.

CLÉANTE   You have been corrupted by your friends,   80
You know of whom I speak. Your thought depends
On people who are blind and want to spread it
Like some horrid flu, and, yes, I dread it.
I'm no atheist. I see things clearly.
And what I see is loud lip service, merely,   85
To make exhibitionists seem devout.
Forgive me, but a prayer is not a shout.
Yet those who don't adore these charlatans
Are seen as faithless heathens by your friends.
It's as if you think you'd never find   90
Reason and the sacred intertwined.
You think I'm afraid of retribution?
Heaven sees my heart and their pollution.
So we should be the slaves of sanctimony?
Monkey see, monkey do, monkey phony.   95
The true believers we should emulate
Are not the ones who groan and lay prostrate.
And yet you see no problem in the notion
Of hypocrisy as deep devotion.
You see as one the genuine and the spurious.   100
You'd extend this to your money? I'm just curious.
In your business dealings, I'd submit,
You'd not confuse the gold with counterfeit.
Men are strangely made, I'd have to say.
They're burdened with their reason, till one day,   105
They free themselves with such force that they spoil
The noblest of things for which they toil.
Because they must go to extremes. It's a flaw.
Just a word in passing, Brother-in-law.

ORGON   Oh, you are the wisest man alive, so   110
You know everything there is to know.

You are the one enlightened man, the sage.
You are Cato the Elder[9] of our age.
Next to you, all men are dumb as cows.

CLÉANTE   I'm not the wisest man, as you espouse,   115
Nor do I know—what—all there is to know?
But I do know, Orgon, that quid pro quo
Does not apply at all to "false" and "true,"
And I would never trust a person who
Cannot tell them apart. See, I revere   120
Everyone whose worship is sincere.
Nothing is more noble or more beautiful
Than fervor that is holy, not just dutiful.
So nothing is more odious to me
Than the display of specious piety   125
Which I see in every charlatan
Who tries to pass for a true holy man.
Religious passion worn as a facade
Abuses what's sacred and mocks God.
These men who take what's sacred and most holy   130
And use it as their trade, for money, solely,
With downcast looks and great affected cries,
Who suck in true believers with their lies,
Who ceaselessly will preach and then demand
"Give up the world!" and then, by sleight of hand,   135
End up sitting pretty at the court,
The best in lodging and new clothes to sport.
If you're their enemy, then heaven hates you.
That's their claim when one of them berates you.
They'll say you've sinned. You'll find yourself removed   140
And wondering if you'll be approved
For anything, at all, ever again.
Because so heinous was this fictional "sin."
When these men are angry, they're the worst,
There's no place to hide, you're really cursed.   145
They use what we call righteous as their sword,
To coldly murder in the name of the Lord.
But next to these imposters faking belief,
The devotion of the true is a relief.
Our century has put before our eyes   150
Glorious examples we can prize.
Look at Ariston, and look at Periandre,
Oronte, Alcidamas, Polydore, Clitandre:[1]
Not one points out his own morality,
Instead they speak of their mortality.   155

---

9. Roman statesman and author (234–149
B.C.E.), famous as a stern moralist devoted to
traditional Roman ideals of honor, courage,
and simplicity.
1. Made-up names.

They don't form cabals,[2] they don't have factions,
They don't censure other people's actions.
They see the flagrant pride in such correction
And know that humans can't achieve perfection.
They know this of themselves and yet their lives   160
Good faith, good works, all good, epitomize.
They don't exhibit zeal that's more intense
Than heaven shows us in its own defense.
They'd never claim a knowledge that's divine
And yet they live in virtue's own design.   165
They concentrate their hatred on the sin,
And when the sinner grieves, invite him in.
They leave to others the arrogance of speech.
Instead they practice what others only preach.
These are the men who show us how to live.   170
Their lives, the best example I can give.
These are my men, the ones whom I would follow.
Your man and his life, honestly, are hollow.
I believe you praise him quite sincerely,
I also think you'll pay for this quite dearly.   175
He's a fraud, this man whom you adore.

ORGON   Oh, you've stopped talking. Is there any more?

CLÉANTE   No.

ORGON   I am your servant, sir.

CLÉANTE   No! wait!
There's one more thing—no more debate—
I want to change the subject, if I might.   180
I heard that you said the other night,
To Valère, he'd be your son-in-law.

ORGON   I did.

CLÉANTE   And set the date?

ORGON   Yes.

CLÉANTE   Did you withdraw?

ORGON   I did.

CLÉANTE   You're putting off the wedding? Why?

ORGON   Don't know.   185

CLÉANTE   There's more?

ORGON   Perhaps.

CLÉANTE   Again I'll try:
You would break your word?

ORGON   I couldn't say.

CLÉANTE   Then, Orgon, why did you change the day?

ORGON   Who knows?

---

2. A possible allusion to the Compagnie de Saint-Sacrement, a tightly knit group of prominent French citizens known for public works as well as strict morality; they were pejoratively referred to as the *cabale*.

CLÉANTE   But we need to know, don't we now?
Is there a reason you would break your vow?
ORGON   That depends.   190
CLÉANTE   On what? Orgon, what is it?
Valère was the reason for my visit.
ORGON   Who knows? Who knows?
CLÉANTE   So there's some mystery there?
ORGON   Heaven knows.
CLÉANTE   It does? And now, Valère—
May he know, too?
ORGON   Can't say.
CLÉANTE   But, dear Orgon,
We have no information to go on.   195
We need to know—
ORGON   What heaven wants, I'll do.
CLÉANTE   Is that your final answer? Then I'm through.
But your pledge to Valère? You'll stand by it?
ORGON   Good-bye.

                                  [ORGON *exits*.]

CLÉANTE   More patience, yes, I should try it.
I let him get to me. Now I confess   200
I fear the worst for Valère's happiness.

                            2.1
                    [ORGON, MARIANE]

ORGON   Mariane.
MARIANE   Father.
ORGON   Come. Now. Talk with me.
MARIANE   Why are you looking everywhere?
ORGON   To see
If everyone is minding their own business.
So, Child, I've always loved your gentleness.
MARIANE   And for your love, I'm grateful, Father dear.   5
ORGON   Well said. And so to prove that you're sincere,
And worthy of my love, you have the task
Of doing for me anything I ask.
MARIANE   Then my obedience will be my proof.
ORGON   Good. What do you think of our guest, Tartuffe?   10
MARIANE   Who, me?
ORGON   Yes, you. Watch what you say right now.
MARIANE   Then, Father, I will say what you allow.
ORGON   Wise words, Daughter. So this is what you say:
"He is a perfect man in every way;
In body and soul, I find him divine."   15
And then you say, "Please Father, make him mine."
Huh?

MARIANE   Huh?
ORGON   Yes?
MARIANE   I heard . . .
ORGON   Yes.
MARIANE   What did you say?
   Who is this perfect man in every way,
   Whom in body and soul I find divine
   And ask of you, "Please, Father, make him mine?"   20
ORGON   Tartuffe.
MARIANE   All that I've said, I now amend
   Because you wouldn't want me to pretend.
ORGON   Absolutely not—that's so misguided.
   Have it be the truth, then. It's decided.
MARIANE   What?! Father, you want—   25
ORGON   Yes, my dear, I do—
   To join in marriage my Tartuffe and you.
   And since I have—

2.2

[DORINE, ORGON, MARIANE]

ORGON   Dorine, I know you're there!
   Any secrets in this house you don't share?
DORINE   "Marriage"—I think, yes, I heard a rumor,
   Someone's failed attempt at grotesque humor,
   So when I heard the story, I said, "No!   5
   Preposterous! Absurd! It can't be so."
ORGON   Oh, you find it preposterous? And why?
DORINE   It's so outrageous, it must be a lie.
ORGON   Yet it's the truth and you will believe it.
DORINE   Yet as a joke is how I must receive it.   10
ORGON   But it's a story that will soon come true.
DORINE   A fantasy!
ORGON   I'm getting tired of you.
   Mariane, it's not a joke—
DORINE   Says he,
   Laughing up his sleeve for all to see.
ORGON   I'm telling you—   15
DORINE   —more make-believe for fun.
   It's very good—you're fooling everyone.
ORGON   You have made me really angry now.
DORINE   I see the awful truth across your brow.
   How can a man who looks as wise as you
   Be such a fool to want—   20
ORGON   What can I do
   About a servant with a mouth like that?
   The liberties you take! Decorum you laugh at!
   I'm not happy with you—

DORINE   Oh sir, don't frown.
  A smile is just a frown turned upside down.
  Be happy, sir, because you've shared your scheme,   25
  Even though it's just a crazy dream.
  Because, dear sir, your daughter is not meant
  For this zealot—she's too innocent.
  She'd be alarmed by his robust desire
  And question heaven's sanction of this fire   30
  And then the gossip! Your friends will talk a lot,
  Because you're a man of wealth and he is not.
  Could it be your reasoning has a flaw—
  Choosing a beggar for a son-in-law?
ORGON   You, shut up! If he has nothing now   35
  Admire that, as if it were his vow,
  This poverty. His property was lost
  Because he would not pay the deadly cost
  Of daily duties nibbling life away,
  Leaving him with hardly time to pray.   40
  The grandeur in his life comes from devotion
  To the eternal, thus his great emotion.
  And at those moments, I can plainly see
  What my special task has come to be:
  To end the embarrassment he feels   45
  And the sorrow he so nobly conceals
  Of the loss of his ancestral domain.
  With my money, I can end his pain.
  I'll raise him up to be, because I can,
  With my help, again, a gentleman.   50
DORINE   So he's a gentleman. Does that seem vain?
  Then what about this piety and pain?
  Those with "domains" are those of noble birth.
  A holy man's domain is not on earth.
  It seems to me a holy man of merit   55
  Wouldn't brag of what he might inherit—
  Even gifts in heaven, he won't mention.
  To live a humble life is his intention.
  Yet he wants something back? That's just ambition
  To feed his pride. Is that a holy mission?   60
  You seem upset. Is it something I said?
  I'll shut up. We'll talk of her instead.
  Look at this girl, your daughter, your own blood.
  How will her honor fare covered with mud?
  Think of his age. So from the night they're wed,   65
  Bliss, if there is any, leaves the marriage bed,
  And she'll be tied unto this elderly person.
  Her dedication to fidelity will worsen
  And soon he will sprout horns,[3] your holy man,

---

3. The traditional sign of the cuckold.

And no one will be happy. If I can 70
Have another word, I'd like to say
Old men and young girls are married every day,
And the young girls stray, but who's to blame
For the loss of honor and good name?
The father, who proceeds to pick a mate, 75
Blindly, though it's someone she may hate,
Bears the sins the daughter may commit,
Imperiling his soul because of it.
If you do this, I vow you'll hear the bell,
As you die, summoning you to hell. 80

ORGON   You think that you can teach me how to live.

DORINE   If you'd just heed the lessons that I give.

ORGON   Can heaven tell me why I still endure
This woman's ramblings? Yet, of this I'm sure,
I know what's best for you—I'm your father. 85
I gave you to Valère, without a bother.
But I hear he gambles and what's more,
He thinks things that a Christian would abhor.
It's from free thinking that all evils stem.
No wonder, then, at church, I don't see him. 90

DORINE   Should he race there, if he only knew
Which Mass you might attend, and be on view?
He could wait at the door with holy water.

ORGON   Go away. I'm talking to my daughter.
Think, my child, he is heaven's favorite! 95
And age in marriage? It can flavor it,
A sweet comfit suffused with deep, deep pleasure.
You will be loving, faithful, and will treasure
Every single moment—two turtledoves—
Next to heaven, the only thing he loves. 100
And he will be the only one for you.
No arguments or quarrels. You'll be true,
Like two innocent children, you will thrive,
In heaven's light, thrilled to be alive.
And as a woman, surely you must know 105
Wives mold husbands, like making pies from dough.

DORINE   Four and twenty cuckolds baked in a pie.

ORGON   Ugh! What a thing to say!

DORINE   Oh, really, why?
He's destined to be cheated on, it's true.
You know he'd always question her virtue. 110

ORGON   Quiet! Just be quiet. I command it!

DORINE   I'll do just that, because you do demand it!
But your best interests—I will protect them.

ORGON   Too kind of you. Be quiet and neglect them.

DORINE   If I weren't fond of you— 115

ORGON   —Don't want you to

DORINE   I will be fond of you in spite of you.

ORGON   Don't!

DORINE   But your honor is so dear to me,
How can you expose yourself to mockery?

ORGON   Will you never be quiet!

DORINE   Oh, dear sir,
I can't let you do this thing to her,   120
It's against my conscience—

ORGON   You vicious asp!

DORINE   Sometimes the things you call me make me gasp.
And anger, sir, is not a pious trait.

ORGON   It's your fault, girl! You make me irate!
I am livid! Why won't you be quiet!   125

DORINE   I will. For you, I'm going to try it.
But I'll be thinking.

ORGON   Fine. Now, Mariane,
You have to trust—your father's a wise man.
I have thought a lot about this mating.
I've weighed the options—   130

DORINE   It's infuriating
Not to be able to speak.

ORGON   And so
I'll say this. Of up and coming men I know,
He's not one of them, no money in the bank,
Not handsome.

DORINE   That's the truth. Arf! Arf! Be frank.
He's a dog!   135

ORGON   He has manly traits.
And other gifts.

DORINE   And who will blame the fates
For failure of this marriage made in hell?
And whose fault will it be? Not hard to tell.
Since everyone you know will see the truth:
You gave away your daughter to Tartuffe.   140
If I were in her place, I'd guarantee
No man would live the night who dared force me
Into a marriage that I didn't want.
There would be war with no hope of détente.

ORGON   I asked for silence. This is what I get?   145

DORINE   You said not to talk to *you*. Did you forget?

ORGON   What do you call what you are doing now?

DORINE   Talking to myself.

ORGON   You insolent cow!
I'll wait for you to say just one more word.
I'm waiting . . .   150
      [ORGON *prepares to give* DORINE *a smack but each time he looks*
      over at her, she stands silent and still.]
                   Just ignore her. Look at me.
I've chosen you a husband who would be,
If rated, placed among the highest ranks.

[*To* DORINE]   Why don't you talk?

DORINE   Don't feel like it, thanks.

ORGON   I'm watching you.

DORINE   Do you think I'm a fool?

ORGON   I realize that you may think me cruel.   155
   But here's the thing, child, I will be obeyed,
   And this marriage, child, will not be delayed.

DORINE [*running from* ORGON, DORINE *throws a line to* MARIANE]
   You'll be a joke with Tartuffe as a spouse.
     [ORGON *tries to slap her but misses.*]

ORGON   What we have is a plague in our own house!
   It's her fault that I'm in the state I'm in,   160
   So furious, I might commit a sin.
   She'll drive me to murder. Or to curse.
   I need fresh air before my mood gets worse.   [ORGON *exits.*]

2.3

[DORINE, MARIANE]

DORINE   Tell me, have you lost the power of speech?
   I'm forced to play your role and it's a reach.
   How can you sit there with nothing to say
   Watching him tossing your whole life away?

MARIANE   Against my father, what am I to do?   5

DORINE   You want out of this marriage scheme, don't you?

MARIANE   Yes.

DORINE   Tell him no one can command a heart.
   That when you marry, you will have no part
   Of anyone unless he pleases you.
   And tell your father, with no more ado,   10
   That you will marry for yourself, not him,
   And that you won't obey his iron whim.
   Since he finds Tartuffe to be such a catch,
   He can marry him himself. There's a match.

MARIANE   You know that fathers have such sway   15
   Over our lives that I've nothing to say.
   I've never had the strength.

DORINE   Let's think. All right?
   Didn't Valère propose the other night?
   Do you or don't you love Valère?

MARIANE   You know the answer, Dorine—that's unfair.   20
   Just talking about it tears me apart.
   I've said a hundred times, he has my heart.
   I'm wild about him. I know. And I've told you.

DORINE   But how am I to know, for sure, that's true?

MARIANE   Because I told you. And yet you doubt it?   25
   See me blushing when I speak about it?

DORINE   So you do love him?

MARIANE   Yes, with all my might.
DORINE   He loves you just as much?
MARIANE   I think that's right.
DORINE   And it's to the altar you're both heading?
MARIANE   Yes.   30
DORINE   So what about this other wedding?
MARIANE   I'll kill myself. That's what I've decided.
DORINE   What a great solution you've provided!
    To get out of trouble, you plan to die!
    Immediately? Or sometime, by and by?
MARIANE   Oh, really, Dorine, you're not my friend,   35
    Unsympathetic—
DORINE   I'm at my wit's end,
    Talking to you whose answer is dying,
    Who, in a crisis, just gives up trying.
MARIANE   What do you want of me, then?
DORINE   Come alive!
    Love needs a resolute heart to survive.   40
MARIANE   In my love for Valère, I'm resolute.
    But the next step is his.
DORINE   And so, you're mute?
MARIANE   What can I say? It's the job of Valère,
    His duty, before I go anywhere,
    To deal with my father—   45
DORINE   —Then, you'll stay.
    "Orgon was born bizarre" is what some say.
    If there were doubts before, we have this proof—
    He is head over heels for his Tartuffe,
    And breaks off a marriage that he arranged.
    Valère's at fault if your father's deranged?   50
MARIANE   But my refusal will be seen as pride
    And, worse, contempt. And I have to hide
    My feelings for Valère, I must not show
    That I'm in love at all. If people know,
    Then all the modesty my sex is heir to   55
    Will be gone. There's more: how can I bear to
    Not be a proper daughter to my father?
DORINE   No, no, of course not. God forbid we bother
    The way the world sees you. What people see,
    What other people think of us, should be   60
    Our first concern. Besides, I see the truth:
    You really want to be Madame Tartuffe.
    What was I thinking, urging opposition
    To Monsieur Tartuffe! This proposition,
    To merge with him—he's such a catch!   65
    In fact, for you, he's just the perfect match.
    He's much respected, everywhere he goes,
    And his ruddy complexion nearly glows.
    And as his wife, imagine the delight

Of being near him, every day and night.   70
　　And vital? Oh, my dear, you won't want more.
MARIANE　　Oh, heaven help me!
DORINE　　　　　　　　　　　　　How your soul will soar,
　　Savoring this marriage down to the last drop,
　　With such a handsome—
MARIANE　　　　　　　　　　All right! You can stop!
　　Just help me. Please. And tell me there's a way   75
　　To save me. I'll do whatever you say.
DORINE　　Each daughter must choose always to say yes
　　To what her father wants, no more and no less.
　　If he wants to give her an ape to marry,
　　Then she must do it, without a query.   80
　　But it's a happy fate! What is this frown?
　　You'll go by wagon to his little town,
　　Eager cousins, uncles, aunts will greet you
　　And will call you "sister" when they meet you,
　　Because you're family now. Don't look so grim.   85
　　You will so adore chatting with them.
　　Welcomed by the local high society,
　　You'll be expected to maintain propriety
　　And sit straight, or try to, in the folding chair
　　They offer you, and never, ever stare   90
　　At the wardrobe of the bailiff's wife
　　Because you'll see her every day for life.[4]
　　Let's not forget the village carnival!
　　Where you'll be dancing at a lavish ball
　　To a bagpipe orchestra of locals,   95
　　An organ grinder's monkey doing vocals—
　　And your husband—
MARIANE　　　　　　　　　—Dorine, I beg you, please,
　　Help me. Should I get down here on my knees?
DORINE　　Can't help you.
MARIANE　　　　　　　　　Please, Dorine, I'm begging you!
DORINE　　And you deserve this man.   100
MARIANE　　　　　　　　　　That just not true!
DORINE　　Oh yes? What changed?
MARIANE　　　　　　　　　　　My darling Dorine . . .
DORINE　　No.
MARIANE　　You can't be this mean.
　　I love Valère. I told you and it's true.
DORINE　　Who's that? Oh. No, Tartuffe's the one for you.
MARIANE　　You've always been completely on my side.   105
DORINE　　No more. I sentence you to be Tartuffified!
MARIANE　　It seems my fate has not the power to move you,
　　So I'll seek my solace and remove to

---

4. Dorine's description reflects the stereotypes associated with rural pretensions to culture.

A private place for me in my despair.
To end the misery that brought me here.   110
    [MARIANE *starts to exit.*]
DORINE   Wait! Wait! Come back! Please don't go out that door.
I'll help you. I'm not angry anymore.
MARIANE   If I am forced into this martyrdom,
You see, I'll have to die, Dorine.
DORINE   Oh come,
Give up this torment. Look at me—I swear.   115
We'll find a way. Look, here's your love, Valère.
    [DORINE *moves to the side of the stage.*]

2.4

[VALÈRE, MARIANE, DORINE]

VALÈRE   So I've just heard some news that's news to me,
And very fine news it is, do you agree?
MARIANE   What?
VALÈRE   You have plans for marriage I didn't know.
You're going to marry Tartuffe. Is this so?
MARIANE   My father has that notion, it is true.   5
VALÈRE   Madame, your father promised—
MARIANE   —me to you?
He changed his mind, announced this change to me,
Just minutes ago . . .
VALÈRE   Quite seriously?
MARIANE   It's his wish that I should marry this man.
VALÈRE   And what do you think of your father's plan?   10
MARIANE   I don't know.
VALÈRE   Honest words—better than lies.
You don't know?
MARIANE   No.
VALÈRE   No?
MARIANE   What do you advise?
VALÈRE   I advise you to . . . marry Tartuffe. Tonight.
MARIANE   You advise me to . . .
VALÈRE   Yes.
MARIANE   Really?
VALÈRE   That's right.
Consider it. It's an obvious choice.   15
MARIANE   I'll follow your suggestion and rejoice.
VALÈRE   I'm sure that you can follow it with ease.
MARIANE   Just as you gave it. It will be a breeze.
VALÈRE   Just to please you was my sole intent.
MARIANE   To please you, I'll do it and be content.   20
DORINE   I can't wait to see what happens next.
VALÈRE   And this is love to you? I am perplexed.
Was it a sham when you—

MARIANE   That's in the past
  Because you said so honestly and fast
  That I should take the one bestowed on me.   25
  I'm nothing but obedient, you see,
  So, yes, I'll take him. That's my declaration,
  Since that's your advice and expectation.

VALÈRE   I see, you're using me as an excuse,
  Any pretext, so you can cut me loose.   30
  You didn't think I'd notice—I'd be blind
  To the fact that you'd made up your mind?

MARINE   How true. Well said.

VALÈRE   And so it's plain to see,
  Your heart never felt a true love for me.

MARIANE   If you want to, you may think that is true.   35
  It's clear this thought has great appeal for you.

VALÈRE   If I want? I will, but I'm offended
  To my very soul. But your turn's ended,
  And I can win this game we're playing at:
  I've someone else in mind.   40

MARIANE   I don't doubt that.
  Your good points—

VALÈRE   Oh, let's leave them out of this.
  I've very few—in fact, I am remiss.
  I must be. Right? You've made that clear to me.
  But I know someone, hearing that I'm free,
  To make up for my loss, will eagerly consent.   45

MARIANE   The loss is not that bad. You'll be content
  With your new choice, replacement, if you will.

VALÈRE   I will. And I'll remain contented still,
  In knowing you're as happy as I am.
  A woman tells a man her love's a sham.   50
  The man's been fooled and his honor blighted.
  He can't deny his love is unrequited,
  Then he forgets this woman totally,
  And if he can't, pretends, because, you see,
  It is ignoble conduct and weak, too,   55
  Loving someone who does not love you.

MARIANE   What a fine, noble sentiment to heed.

VALÈRE   And every man upholds it as his creed.
  What? You expect me to keep on forever
  Loving you after you blithely sever   60
  The bond between us, watching as you go
  Into another's arms and not bestow
  This heart you've cast away upon someone
  Who might welcome—

MARIANE   I wish it were done.
  That's exactly what I want, you see.   65

VALÈRE   That's what you want?

MARIANE   Yes.

VALÈRE   Then let it be.
   I'll grant your wish.
MARIANE   Please do.
VALÈRE   Just don't forget,
   Whose fault it was when you, filled with regret,
   Realize that you forced me out the door.
MARIANE   True.   70
VALÈRE   You've set the example and what's more,
   I'll match you with my own hardness of heart.
   You won't see me again, if I depart.
MARIANE   That's good!
      [VALÈRE *goes to exit, but when he gets to the door, he returns.*]
VALÈRE   What?
MARIANE   What?
VALÈRE   You said . . . ?
MARIANE   Nothing at all.
VALÈRE   Well, I'll be on my way, then.
         [*He goes, stops.*]
                              Did you call?
MARIANE   Me? You must be dreaming.   75
VALÈRE   I'll go away.
   Good-bye, then.
MARIANE   Good-bye.
DORINE   I am here to say,
   You both are idiots! What's this about?
   I left you two alone to fight it out,
   To see how far you'd go. You're quite a pair
   In matching tit for tat—Hold on, Valère!   80
   Where are you going?
VALÈRE   What, Dorine? You spoke?
DORINE   Come here.
VALÈRE   I'm upset and will not provoke
   This lady. Do not try to change my mind.
   I'm doing what she wants.
DORINE   You are so blind.
   Just stop.   85
VALÈRE   No. It's settled.
DORINE   Oh, is that so?
MARIANE   He can't stand to look at me, I know.
   He wants to go away, so please let him.
   No, I shall leave so I can forget him.
DORINE   Where are you going?
MARIANE   Leave me alone.
DORINE   Come back here at once.   90
MARIANE   No. Even that tone
   Won't bring me. I'm not a child, you see.
VALÈRE   She's tortured by the very sight of me.
   It's better that I free her from her pain.

DORINE   What more proof do you need? You are insane!
  Now stop this nonsense! Come here both of you.   95
VALÈRE   To what purpose?
MARIANE   What are you trying to do?
DORINE   Bring you two together! And end this fight.
  It's so stupid! Yes?
VALÈRE   No. It wasn't right
  The way she spoke to me. Didn't you hear?
DORINE   Your voices are still ringing in my ear.   100
MARIANE   The way he treated me—you didn't see?
DORINE   Saw and heard it all. Now listen to me.
  The only thing she wants, Valère, is you.
  I can attest to that right now. It's true.
  And Mariane, he wants you for his wife,   105
  And only you. On that I'll stake my life.
MARIANE   He told me to be someone else's bride!
VALÈRE   She asked for my advice and I replied!
DORINE   You're both impossible. What can I do?
  Give your hand—   110
VALÈRE   What for?
DORINE   Come on, you.
  Now yours, Mariane—don't make me shout.
  Come on!
MARIANE   All right. But what is this about?
DORINE   Here. Take each other's hand and make a link.
  You love each other better than you think.
VALÈRE   Mademoiselle, this is your hand I took,   115
  You think you could give me a friendly look?
      [MARIANE *peeks at* VALÈRE *and smiles.*]
DORINE   It's true. Lovers are not completely sane.
VALÈRE   Mariane, haven't I good reason to complain?
  Be honest. Wasn't it a wicked ploy?
  To say—   120
MARIANE   You think I told you that with joy?
  And you confronted me.
DORINE   Another time.
  This marriage to Tartuffe would be a crime,
  We have to stop it.
MARIANE   So, what can we do?
  Tell us.
DORINE   All sorts of things involving you.   125
  It's all nonsense and your father's joking.
  But if you play along, say, without choking,
  And give your consent, for the time being,
  He'll take the pressure off, thereby freeing
  All of us to find a workable plan   130
  To keep you from a marriage with this man.
  Then you can find a reason every day

To postpone the wedding, in this way;
One day you're sick and that can take a week.
Another day you're better but can't speak,   135
And we all know you have to say "I do,"
Or the marriage isn't legal. And that's true.
Now bad omens—would he have his daughter
Married when she's dreamt of stagnant water,
Or broken a mirror or seen the dead?   140
He may not care and say it's in your head,
But you will be distraught in your delusion,
And require bed rest and seclusion.
I do know this—if we want to succeed,
You can't be seen together. [*To* VALÈRE] With all speed,   145
Go, and gather all your friends right now,
Have them insist that Orgon keep his vow.
Social pressure helps. Then to her brother.
All of us will work on her stepmother.
Let's go.   150

VALÈRE   Whatever happens, can you see?
My greatest hope is in your love for me.

MARIANE   Though I don't know just what Father will do,
I do know I belong only to you.

VALÈRE   You put my heart at ease! I swear I will . . .

DORINE   It seems that lovers' tongues are never still.   155
Out, I tell you.

VALÈRE [*taking a step and returning*]   One last—

DORINE   No more chat!
You go out this way, yes, and you go that.

3.1

[DAMIS, DORINE]

DAMIS   May lightning strike me dead, right here and now,
Call me a villain, if I break this vow:
Forces of heaven or earth won't make me sway
From this my—

DORINE   Let's not get carried away.
Your father only said what he intends   5
To happen. The real event depends
On many things and something's bound to slip,
Between this horrid cup and his tight lip.

DAMIS   That this conceited fool Father brought here
Has plans? Well, they'll be ended—do not fear.   10

DORINE   Now stop that! Forget him. Leave him alone.
Leave him to your stepmother. He is prone,
This Tartuffe, to indulge her every whim.
So let her use her power over him.
It does seem pretty clear he's soft on her,   15
Pray God that's true. And if he will concur

That this wedding your father wants is bad,
That's good. But he might want it, too, the cad.
She's sent for him so she can sound him out
On this marriage you're furious about,   20
Discover what he feels and tell him clearly
If he persists that it will cost him dearly.
It seems he can't be seen while he's at prayers,
So I have my own vigil by the stairs
Where his valet says he will soon appear.   25
Do leave right now, and I'll wait for him here.

DAMIS   I'll stay to vouch for what was seen and heard.

DORINE   They must be alone.

DAMIS   I won't say a word.

DORINE   Oh, right. I know what you are like. Just go.
You'll spoil everything, believe me, I know.   30
Out!

DAMIS   I promise I won't get upset.
        [DORINE *pinches* DAMIS *as she used to do when he was a child.*]
                            Ow!

DORINE   Do as I say. Get out of here right *now!*

3.2

[TARTUFFE, LAURENT, DORINE]

TARTUFFE [*noticing* DORINE]   Laurent, lock up my scourge and
    hair shirt,[5] too.
And pray that our Lord's grace will shine on you.
If anyone wants me, I've gone to share
My alms at prison with the inmates there.

DORINE   What a fake! What an imposter! What a sleaze!   5

TARTUFFE   What do you want?

DORINE   To say—

TARTUFFE [*taking a handkerchief from his pocket*]   Good heavens, please,
    Do take this handkerchief before you speak.

DORINE   What for?

TARTUFFE   Cover your bust. The flesh is weak.
Souls are forever damaged by such sights,
When sinful thoughts begin their evil flights.   10

DORINE   It seems temptation makes a meal of you—
To turn you on, a glimpse of flesh will do.
Inside your heart, a furnace must be housed.
For me, I'm not so easily aroused.
I could see you naked, head to toe—   15
Never be tempted once, and this I know.

TARTUFFE   Please! Stop! And if you're planning to resume
This kind of talk, I'll leave the room.

---

5. Implements to mortify his flesh (penitential practices of religious ascetics).

DORINE   If someone is to go, let it be me.
   Yes, I can't wait to leave your company.   20
   Madame is coming down from her salon,
   And wants to talk to you, if you'll hang on.
TARTUFFE   Of course. Most willingly.
DORINE [aside]   Look at him melt.
   I'm right. I always knew that's how he felt.
TARTUFFE   Is she coming soon?   25
DORINE   You want me to leave?
   Yes, here she is in person, I believe.

3.3

[ELMIRE, TARTUFFE]

TARTUFFE   Ah, may heaven in all its goodness give
   Eternal health to you each day you live,
   Bless your soul and body, and may it grant
   The prayerful wishes of this supplicant.
ELMIRE   Yes, thank you for that godly wish, and please,   5
   Let's sit down so we can talk with ease.
TARTUFFE   Are you recovered from your illness now?
ELMIRE   My fever disappeared, I don't know how.
TARTUFFE   My small prayers, I'm sure, had not the power,
   Though I was on my knees many an hour.   10
   Each fervent prayer wrenched from my simple soul
   Was made with your recovery as its goal.
ELMIRE   I find your zeal a little disconcerting.
TARTUFFE   I can't enjoy my health if you are hurting,
   Your health's true worth, I can't begin to tell.   15
   I'd give mine up, in fact, to make you well.
ELMIRE   Though you stretch Christian charity too far,
   Your thoughts are kind, however strange they are.
TARTUFFE   You merit more, that's in my humble view.
ELMIRE   I need a private space to talk to you.   20
   I think that this will do—what do you say?
TARTUFFE   Excellent choice. And this is a sweet day,
   To find myself here tête-à-tête with you,
   That I've begged heaven for this, yes, is true,
   And now it's granted to my great relief.   25
ELMIRE   Although our conversation will be brief,
   Please open up your heart and tell me all.
   You must hide nothing now, however small.
TARTUFFE   I long to show you my entire soul,
   My need for truth I can barely control.   30
   I'll take this time, also, to clear the air—
   The criticisms I have brought to bear
   Around the visits that your charms attract,
   Were never aimed at you or how you act,

But rather were my own transports of zeal,   35
Which carried me away with how I feel,
Consumed by impulses, though always pure,
Nevertheless, intense in how—

ELMIRE   I'm sure
That my salvation is your only care.

TARTUFFE [*grasping her fingertips*]   Yes, you're right, and   40
    so my fervor there—

ELMIRE   Ouch! You're squeezing too hard.

TARTUFFE   —comes from this zeal . . .
    I didn't mean to squeeze. How does this feel?
        [*He puts his hand on* ELMIRE's *knee.*]

ELMIRE   Your hand—what is it doing . . . ?

TARTUFFE   So tender,
    The fabric of your dress, a sweet surrender
    Under my hand—   45

ELMIRE   I'm quite ticklish. Please, don't.
        [*She moves her chair back, and* TARTUFFE *moves his forward.*]

TARTUFFE   I want to touch this lace—don't fret, I won't,
    It's marvelous! I so admire the trade
    Of making lace. Don't tell me you're afraid.

ELMIRE   What? No. But getting back to business now,
    It seems my husband plans to break a vow   50
    And offer you his daughter. Is this true?

TARTUFFE   He mentioned it, but I must say to you,
    The wondrous gifts that catch my zealous eye,
    I see quite near in bounteous supply.

ELMIRE   Not earthly things for which you would atone.   55

TARTUFFE   My chest does not contain a heart of stone.

ELMIRE   Well, I believe your eyes follow your soul,
    And your desires have heaven as their goal.

TARTUFFE   The love that to eternal beauty binds us
    Doesn't stint when temporal beauty finds us.   60
    Our senses can as easily be charmed
    When by an earthly work we are disarmed.
    You are a rare beauty, without a flaw,
    And in your presence, I'm aroused with awe
    But for the Author of All Nature, so,   65
    My heart has ardent feelings, even though
    I feared them at first, questioning their source.
    Had I been ambushed by some evil force?
    I felt that I must hide from this temptation:
    You. My feelings threatened my salvation.   70
    Yes, I found this sinful and distressing,
    Until I saw your beauty as a blessing!
    So now my passion never can be wrong,
    And, thus, my virtue stays intact and strong.
    That is how I'm here in supplication,   75
    Offering my heart in celebration

Of the audacious truth that I love you,
That only you can make this wish come true,
That through your grace, my offering's received,
And accepted, and that I have achieved   80
Salvation of a sort, and by your grace,
I could be content in this low place.
It all depends on you, at your behest—
Am I to be tormented or be blest?
You are my welfare, solace, and my hope,   85
But, whatever your decision, I will cope.
Will I be happy? I'll rely on you.
If you want me to be wretched, that's fine, too.

ELMIRE   Well, what a declaration! How gallant!
But I'm surprised you want the things you want.   90
It seems your heart could use a talking to—
It's living in the chest of someone who
Proclaims to be pious—

TARTUFFE   —And so I am.
My piety's a true thing—not a sham,
But I'm no less a man, so when I find   95
Myself with you, I quickly lose my mind.
My heart is captured and, with it, my thought.
Yet since I know the cause, I'm not distraught.
Words like these from me must be alarming,
But it is your beauty that's so charming,   100
I cannot help myself, I am undone.
And I'm no angel, nor could I be one.
If my confession earns your condemnation,
Then blame your glance for the annihilation
Of my command of this: my inmost being.   105
A surrender of my soul is what you're seeing.
Your eyes blaze with more than human splendor,
And that first look had the effect to render
Powerless the bastions of my heart.
No fasting, tears or prayers, no pious art   110
Could shield my soul from your celestial gaze
Which I will worship till the End of Days.[6]
A thousand times my eyes, my sighs have told
The truth that's in my heart. Now I am bold,
Encouraged by your presence, so I say,   115
With my true voice, will this be the day
You condescend to my poor supplication,
Offered up with devout admiration,
And save my soul by granting this request:
Accept this love I've lovingly confessed?   120
Your honor has, of course, all my protection,
And you can trust my absolute discretion.

6. That is, the final days before human history ends and the Kingdom of God is established.

For those men that all the women die for,
Love's a game whose object is a high score.
Although they promise not to talk, they will.   125
They need to boast of their superior skill,
Receive no favors not as soon revealed,
Exposing what they vowed would be concealed.
And in the end, this love is overpriced,
When a woman's honor's sacrificed.   130
But men like me burn with a silent flame,
Our secrets safe, our loves we never name,
Because our reputations are our wealth,
When we transgress, it's with the utmost stealth.
Your honor's safe as my hand in a glove,   135
So I can offer, free from scandal, love,
And pleasure without fear of intervention.

ELMIRE   Your sophistry does not hide your intention.
In fact, you know, it makes it all too clear.
What if, through me, my husband were to hear   140
About this love for me you now confess
Which shatters the ideals you profess?
How would your friendship fare, then, I wonder?

TARTUFFE   It's your beauty cast this spell I suffer under.
I'm made of flesh, like you, like all mankind.   145
And since your soul is pure, you will be kind,
And not judge me harshly for my brashness
In speaking of my love in all its rashness.
I beg you to forgive me my offense,
I plead your perfect face as my defense.   150

ELMIRE   Some might take offense at your confession,
But I will show a definite discretion,
And keep my husband in the dark about
These sinful feelings for me that you spout.
But I want something from you in return: 155
There's a promised marriage, you will learn,
That supersedes my husband's recent plan—
The marriage of Valère and Mariane.
This marriage you will openly support,
Without a single quibble, and, in short,   160
Renounce the unjust power of a man
Who'd give his own daughter, Mariane,
To another when she's promised to Valère.
In return, my silence—

3.4

[ELMIRE, DAMIS, TARTUFFE]

DAMIS [*jumping out from where he had been hiding*]
            —Hold it right there!
No, no! You're done. All this will be revealed.
I heard each word. And as I was concealed,

Something besides your infamy came clear:
Heaven in its great wisdom brought me here,   5
To witness and then give my father proof
Of the hypocrisy of his Tartuffe,
This so-called saint anointed from above,
Speaking to my father's wife of love!

ELMIRE   Damis, there is a lesson to be learned,   10
And there is my forgiveness to be earned.
I promised him. Don't make me take it back.
It's not my nature to see as an attack
Such foolishness as this, or see the need
To tell my husband of the trivial deed.   15

DAMIS   So, you have your reasons, but I have mine.
To grant this fool forgiveness? I decline.
To want to spare him is a mockery,
Because he's more than foolish, can't you see?
This fanatic in his insolent pride,   20
Brought chaos to my house, and would divide
Me and my father—unforgivable!
What's more, he's made my life unlivable,
As he undermines two true love affairs,
Mine and Valère's sister, my sister and Valère's!   25
Father must hear the truth about this man.
Heaven helped me—I must do what I can
To use this chance. I'd deserve to lose it,
If I dropped it now and didn't use it.

ELMIRE   Damis—

DAMIS   No, please, I have to follow through.
I've never felt as happy as I do
Right now. And don't try to dissuade me—
I'll have my revenge. If you forbade me,
I'd still do it, so you don't have to bother.
I'll finish this for good. Here comes my father.   35

3.5

[ORGON, DAMIS, TARTUFFE, ELMIRE]

DAMIS   Father! You have arrived. Let's celebrate!
I have a tale that I'd like to relate.
It happened here and right before my eyes,
I offer it to you—as a surprise!
For all your love, you have been repaid   5
With duplicity. You have been betrayed
By your dear friend here, whom I just surprised
Making verbal love, I quickly surmised,
To your wife. Yes, this is how he shows you
How he honors you—he thinks he knows you.   10
But as your son, I know you much better—
You demand respect down to the letter.

Madame, unflappable and so discreet,
Would keep this secret, never to repeat.
But, as your son, my feelings are too strong,   15
And to be silent is to do you wrong.

ELMIRE   One learns to spurn without being unkind,
And how to spare a husband's peace of mind.
Although I understood just what he meant,
My honor wasn't touched by this event.   20
That's how I feel. And you would have, Damis,
Said nothing, if you had listened to me.

3.6

[ORGON, DAMIS, TARTUFFE]

ORGON   Good heavens! What he said? Can it be true?

TARTUFFE   Yes, my brother, I'm wicked through and through.
The most miserable of sinners, I.
Filled with iniquity, I should just die.
Each moment of my life's so dirty, soiled,   5
Whatever I come near is quickly spoiled.
I'm nothing but a heap of filth and crime.
I'd name my sins, but we don't have the time.
And I see that heaven, to punish me,
Has mortified my soul quite publicly.   10
What punishment I get, however great,
I well deserve so I'll accept my fate.
Defend myself? I'd face my own contempt,
If I thought that were something I'd attempt.
What you've heard here, surely, you abhor,   15
So chase me like a criminal from your door.
Don't hold back your rage, please, let it flame,
For I deserve to burn, in my great shame.

ORGON [to DAMIS]   Traitor! And how dare you even try
To tarnish this man's virtue with a lie?   20

DAMIS   What? This hypocrite pretends to be contrite
And you believe him over me?

ORGON   That's spite!
And shut your mouth!

TARTUFFE   No, let him have his say.
And don't accuse him. Don't send him away.
Believe his story—why be on my side?   25
You don't know what motives I may hide.
Why give me so much loyalty and love?
Do you know what I am capable of?
My brother, you have total trust in me,
And think I'm good because of what you see?   30
No, no, by my appearance you're deceived,
And what I say you think must be believed.
Well, believe this—I have no worth at all.

The world sees me as worthy, yet I fall
Far below. Sin is so insidious.   35
[*To* DAMIS] Dear son, do treat me as perfidious,
Infamous, lost, a murderer, a thief.
Speak on, because my sins, beyond belief,
Can bring this shameful sinner to his knees,
In humble, paltry effort to appease.   40
ORGON [*to* TARTUFFE]   Brother, there is no need . . .

         [*To* DAMIS] Will you
 relent?
DAMIS   He has seduced you!
ORGON   Can't you take a hint?
 Be quiet! [*To* TARTUFFE] Brother, please get up. [*To* DAMIS] Ingrate!
DAMIS   But father, this man
ORGON   —whom you denigrate.
DAMIS   But you should—   45
ORGON   Quiet!
DAMIS   But I saw and heard—
ORGON   I'll slap you if you say another word.
TARTUFFE   In the name of God, don't be that way.
 Brother, I'd rather suffer, come what may,
 Than have this boy receive what's meant for me.
ORGON [*to* DAMIS]   Heathen!   50
TARTUFFE   Please! I beg of you on bended knee.
ORGON [*to* DAMIS]   Wretch! See his goodness?!
DAMIS   But—
ORGON   No!
DAMIS   But—
ORGON   Be still!
 And not another word from you until
 You admit the truth. It's plain to see
 Although you thought that I would never be
 Aware and know your motives, yet I do.   55
 You all hate him. And I saw today, you,
 Wife, servants—everyone beneath my roof—
 Are trying everything to force Tartuffe
 Out of my house—this holy man, my friend.
 The more you try to banish him and end   60
 Our sacred brotherhood, the more secure
 His place is. I have never been more sure
 Of anyone. I give him as his bride
 My daughter. If that hurts the family pride,
 Then good. It needs humbling. You understand?   65
DAMIS   You're going to force her to accept his hand?
ORGON   Yes, traitor, and this evening. You know why?
 To infuriate you. Yes, I defy
 You all. I am master and you'll obey.
 And you, you ingrate, now I'll make you pay   70
 For your abuse of him—kneel on the floor,

And beg his pardon, or go out the door.

DAMIS   Me? Kneel and ask the pardon of this fraud?

ORGON   What? You refuse? Someone get me a rod!
A stick! Something! [*To* TARTUFFE] Don't hold me.   75
[*To* DAMIS] Here's your whack!
Out of my house and don't ever come back!

DAMIS   Yes, I'll leave, but—

ORGON   Get out of my sight!
I disinherit you, you traitor, you're a blight
On this house. And you'll get nothing now
From me, except my curse!   80

3.7

[ORGON, TARTUFFE]

ORGON   You have my vow,
He'll never more question your honesty.

TARTUFFE [*to heaven*]   Forgive him for the pain he's given me.
[*To* ORGON] How I suffer. If you could only see
What I go through when they disparage me.   5

ORGON   Oh no!

TARTUFFE   The ingratitude, even in thought,
Tortures my soul so much, it leaves me fraught
With inner pain. My heart's stopped. I'm near death,
I can barely speak now. Where is my breath?

ORGON [*running in tears to the door through which he chased* DAMIS]
You demon! I held back, you little snot   10
I should have struck you dead right on the spot!
[*To* TARTUFFE] Get up, Brother. Don't worry anymore.

TARTUFFE   Let us end these troubles, Brother, I implore.
For the discord I have caused, I deeply grieve,
So for the good of all, I'll take my leave.   15

ORGON   What? Are you joking? No!

TARTUFFE   They hate me here.
It pains me when I see them fill your ear
With suspicions.

ORGON   But that doesn't matter.
I don't listen.

TARTUFFE   That persistent chatter
You now ignore, one day you'll listen to.   20
Repetition of a lie can make it true.

ORGON   No, my brother. Never.

TARTUFFE   A man's wife
Can so mislead his soul and ruin his life.

ORGON   No, no.

TARTUFFE   Brother, let me, by leaving here,
Remove any cause for doubt or fear.   25

ORGON   No, no. You will stay. My soul is at stake.

TARTUFFE   Well, then, a hefty penance I must make.
   I'll mortify myself, unless . . .
ORGON   No need!
TARTUFFE   Then we will never speak of it, agreed?
   But the question of your honor still remains,   30
   And with that I'll take particular pains
   To prevent rumors. My absence, my defense—
   I'll never see your wife again, and hence—
ORGON   No. You spend every hour with her you want,
   And be seen with her. I want you to flaunt,   35
   In front of them, this friendship with my wife.
   And I know how to really turn the knife
   I'll make you my heir, my only one,
   Yes, you will be my son-in-law and son.[7]
   A good and faithful friend means more to me   40
   Than any member of my family.
   Will you accept this gift that I propose?
TARTUFFE   Whatever heaven wants I can't oppose.
ORGON   Poor man! A contract's what we need to write.
   And let all the envious burst with spite.   45

4.1

[CLÉANTE, TARTUFFE]

CLÉANTE   Yes, everyone is talking and each word
   Diminishes your glory, rest assured.
   Though your name's tainted with scandal and shame,
   I'm glad I ran across you, all the same,
   Because I need to share with you my view   5
   On this disaster clearly caused by you.
   Damis, let's say for now, was so misguided,
   He spoke before he thought. But you decided
   To just sit back and watch him be exiled
   From his own father's house. Were he a child,   10
   Then, really, would you dare to treat him so?
   Shouldn't you forgive him, not make him go?
   However, if there's vengeance in your heart,
   And you act on it, tell me what's the part
   That's Christian in that? And are you so base,   15
   You'd let a son fall from his father's grace?
   Give God your anger as an offering,
   Bring peace and forgive all for everything.
TARTUFFE   I'd do just that, if it were up to me.
   I blame him for nothing, don't you see?   20
   I've pardoned him already. That's my way.

7. In fact, French laws governing inheritance would have made such a change extremely difficult to accomplish.

And I'm not bitter, but have this to say:
Heaven's best interests will have been served,
When wrongdoers have got what they deserved.
In fact, if he returns here, I would leave,   25
Because God knows what people might believe.
Faking forgiveness to manipulate
My accuser, silencing the hate
He has for me could be seen as my goal,
When I would only wish to save his soul.   30
What he said to me, though unforgivable,
I give unto God to make life livable.

CLÉANTE   To this conclusion, sir, I have arrived:
Your excuses could not be more contrived.
Just how did you come by the opinion   35
Heaven's business is in your dominion,
Judging who is guilty and who is not?
Taking revenge is heaven's task, I thought.
And if you're under heaven's sovereignty,
What human verdict would you ever be   40
The least bit moved by. No, you wouldn't care—
Judging other's lives is so unfair.
Heaven seems to say "live and let live,"
And our task, I believe, is to forgive.

TARTUFFE   I said I've pardoned him. I take such pains   45
To do exactly what heaven ordains.
But after his attack on me, it's clear,
Heaven does not ordain that he live here.

CLÉANTE   Does it ordain, sir, that you nod and smile,
When taking what is not yours, all the while?   50
On this inheritance you have no claim
And yet you think it's yours. Have you no shame?

TARTUFFE   That this gift was, in any way, received
Out of self-interest, would not be believed
By anyone who knows me well. They'd say,   55
"The world's wealth, to him, holds no sway."
I am not dazzled by gold nor its glitter,
So lack of wealth has never made me bitter.
If I take this present from the father,
The source of all this folderol and bother,   60
I am saving, so everyone understands,
This wealth from falling into the wrong hands,
Waste of wealth and property's a crime,
And that is what would happen at this time.
But I would use it as part of my plan: 65
For glory of heaven, and the good of man.

CLÉANTE   Well, sir, I think these small fears that plague you,
In fact, may cause the rightful heir to sue.
Why trouble yourself, sir—couldn't you just
Let him own his property, if he must?   70

Let others say his property's misused
By him, rather than have yourself accused
Of taking it from its rightful owner.
Wouldn't a pious man be a donor
Of property? Unless there is a verse   75
Or proverb about how you fill your purse
With what's not yours, at all, in any part.
And if heaven has put into your heart
This obstacle to living with Damis,
The honorable thing, you must agree,   80
As well as, certainly, the most discreet,
Is pack your bags and, quickly, just retreat.
To have the son of the house chased away,
Because a guest objects, is a sad day.
Leaving now would show your decency,   85
Sir . . .

TARTUFFE   Yes. Well, it is half after three;
Pious duties consume this time of day,
You will excuse my hurrying away.

CLÉANTE   Ah!

4.2

[ELMIRE, MARIANE, DORINE, CLÉANTE]

DORINE   Please, come to the aid of Mariane.
She's suffering because her father's plan
To force this marriage, impossible to bear,
Has pushed her from distress into despair.
Her father's on his way here. Do your best,   5
Turn him around. Use subtlety, protest,
Whatever way will work to change his mind.

4.3

[ORGON, ELMIRE, MARIANE, CLÉANTE, DORINE]

ORGON   Ah! Here's everyone I wanted to find!
[To MARIANE] This document I have here in my hand
Will make you very happy, understand?

MARIANE   Father, in the name of heaven, I plead
To all that's good and kind in you, concede   5
Paternal power, just in this sense:
Free me from my vows of obedience.
Enforcing that inflexible law today
Will force me to confess each time I pray
My deep resentment of my obligation.   10
I know, father, that I am your creation,
That you're the one who's given life to me.
Why would you now fill it with misery?

If you destroy my hopes for the one man
I've dared to love by trying now to ban   15
Our union, then I'm kneeling to implore,
Don't give me to a man whom I abhor.
To you, Father, I make this supplication:
Don't drive me to some act of desperation,
By ruling me simply because you can.   20

ORGON [*feeling himself touched*]   Be strong! Human weakness
    shames a man!

MARIANE   Your affection for him doesn't bother me—
    Let it erupt, give him your property,
    And if that's not enough, then give him mine.
    Any claim on it, I do now decline.   25
    But in this gifting, don't give him my life.
    If I must wed, then I will be God's wife,
    In a convent, until my days are done.

ORGON   Ah! So you will be a holy, cloistered nun,
    Because your father thwarts your love affair.   30
    Get up! The more disgust you have to bear,
    The more of heaven's treasure you will earn,
    And the heaven will bless you in return.
    Through this marriage, you'll mortify your senses.
    Don't bother me with any more pretenses.   35

DORINE   But . . . !

ORGON   Quiet, you! I see you standing there.
    Don't speak a single word! don't even dare!

CLÉANTE   If you permit, I'd like to say a word . . .

ORGON   Brother, the best advice the world has heard
    Is yours—its reasoning, hard to ignore.   40
    But I refuse to hear it anymore.

ELMIRE [*to* ORGON]   And now, I wonder, have you lost your mind?
    Your love for this one man has made you blind.
    Can you stand there and say you don't believe
    A word we've said? That we're here to deceive?   45

ORGON   Excuse me—I believe in what I see.
    You, indulging my bad son, agree
    To back him up in this terrible prank,
    Accusing my dear friend of something rank.
    You should be livid if what you claim took place,   50
    And yet this look of calm is on your face.

ELMIRE   Because a man says he's in love with me,
    I'm to respond with heavy artillery?
    I laugh at these unwanted propositions.
    Mirth will quell most ardent ambitions.   55
    Why make a fuss over an indiscretion?
    My honor's safe and in my possession.
    You say I'm calm? Well, that's my constancy—
    It won't need a defense, or clemency.
    I know I'll never be a vicious prude   60

Who always seems to hear men being rude,
And then defends her honor tooth and claw,
Still snarling, even as the men withdraw.
From honor like that heaven preserve me,
If that's what you want, you don't deserve me,   65
Besides, you're the one who has been betrayed.

ORGON   I see through this trick that's being played.

ELMIRE   How can you be so dim? I am amazed
How you can hear these sins and stay unfazed.
But what if I could show you what he does?   70

ORGON   Show?

ELMIRE   Yes.

ORGON   A fiction!

ELMIRE   No, the truth because
I am quite certain I can find a way
To show you in the fullest light of day . . . .

ORGON   Fairy tales!

ELMIRE   Come on, at least answer me.
I've given up expecting you to be   75
My advocate. What have you got to lose,
By hiding somewhere, anyplace you choose,
And see for yourself. And then we can
Hear what you say about your holy man.

ORGON   Then I'll say nothing because it cannot be.   80

ELMIRE   Enough. I'm tired. You'll see what you see.
I'm not a liar, though I've been accused.
The time is now and I won't be refused.
You'll be a witness. And we can stop our rants.

ORGON   All right! I call your bluff, Miss Smarty Pants.   85

ELMIRE [to DORINE]   Tell Tartuffe to come.

DORINE   Watch out. He's clever.
Men like him are caught, well, almost never.

ELMIRE   Narcissism is a great deceiver,
And he has lots of that. He's a believer
In his charisma. [To CLÉANTE and MARIANE] Leave us for a bit.   90

4.4

[ELMIRE, ORGON]

ELMIRE   See this table? Good. Get under it.

ORGON   What!

ELMIRE   You are hiding. Get under there and stay.

ORGON   Under the table?

ELMIRE: Just do as I say.
I have a plan, but for it to succeed,
You must be hidden. So are we agreed?
You want to know? I'm ready to divulge it.   5

ORGON   This fantasy of yours—I'll indulge it.
But then I want to lay this thing to rest.

ELMIRE   Oh, that'll happen. Because he'll fail the test.
 You see, I'm going to have a conversation   10
 I'd never have—just as an illustration
 Of how this hypocrite behaved with me.
 So don't be scandalized. I must be free
 To flirt. Clearly, that's what it's going to take
 To prove to you your holy man's a fake.   15
 I'm going to lead him on, to lift his mask,
 Seem to agree to anything he'll ask,
 Pretend to respond to his advances.
 It's for you I'm taking all these chances.
 I'll stop as soon as you have seen enough;   20
 I hope that comes before he calls my bluff.
 His plans for me must be circumvented,
 His passion's strong enough to be demented,
 So the moment you're convinced, you let me know
 That I've revealed the fraud I said I'd show.   25
 Stop him so I won't have a minute more
 Exposure to your friend, this lecherous boor.
 You're in control. I'm sure I'll be all right.
 And . . . here he comes—so hush, stay out of sight.

4.5

[TARTUFFE, ELMIRE, ORGON (*under the table*)]

TARTUFFE   I'm told you want to have a word with me.
ELMIRE   Yes. I have a secret but I'm not free
 To speak. Close that door, have a look around,
 We certainly do not want to be found
 The way we were just as Damis appeared.   5
 I was terrified for you and as I feared,
 He was irate. You saw how hard I tried
 To calm him down and keep him pacified.
 I was so upset; I never had the thought
 "Deny it all," which might have helped a lot,   10
 But as it turns out, we've nothing to fear,
 My husband's not upset, it would appear.
 Things are good, to heaven I defer,
 Because they're even better than they were.
 I have to say I'm quite amazed, in fact,   15
 His good opinion of you is intact.
 To clear the air and quiet every tongue,
 And to kill any gossip that's begun—
 You could've pushed me over with a feather—
 He wants us to spend all our time together!   20
 That's why, with no fear of a critical stare,
 I can be here with you or anywhere.
 Most important, I am completely free

To show my ardor for you, finally.

TARTUFFE   Ardor? This is a sudden change of tone   25
From the last time we found ourselves alone.

ELMIRE   If thinking I was turning you away
Has made you angry, all that I can say
Is that you do not know a woman's heart!
Protecting our virtue keeps us apart,   30
And makes us seem aloof, and even cold.
But cooler outside, inside the more bold.
When love overcomes us, we are ashamed,
Because we fear that we might be defamed.
We must protect our honor—not allow   35
Our love to show. I fear that even now,
In this confession, you'll think ill of me.
But now I've spoken, and I hope you see
My ardor that is there. Why would I sit
And listen to you? Why would I permit   40
Your talk of love, unless I had a notion
Just like yours, and with the same emotion?
And when Damis found us, didn't I try
To quiet him? And did you wonder why,
In speaking of Mariane's marriage deal,   45
I not only asked you, I made an appeal
That you turn it down? What was I doing?
Making sure I'd be the one you'd be wooing.

TARTUFFE   It is extremely sweet, without a doubt,
To watch your lips as loving words spill out.   50
Abundant honey there for me to drink,
But I have doubts. I cannot help but think,
"Does she tell the truth, or does she lie,
To get me to break off this marriage tie?
Is all this ardor something she could fake,   55
And just an act for her stepdaughter's sake?"
So many questions, yet I want to trust,
But need to know the truth, in fact, I must.
Pleasing you, Elmire, is my main task,
And happiness, and so I have to ask   60
To sample this deep ardor felt for me
Right here and now, in blissful ecstasy.

ELMIRE [coughing to alert ORGON]
You want to spend this passion instantly?
I've been opening my heart consistently,
But for you, it's not enough, this sharing.   65
Yet for a woman, it is very daring.
So why can't you be happy with a taste,
Instead of the whole meal consumed in haste?

TARTUFFE   We dare not hope, all those of us who don't
Deserve a thing. And so it is I won't   70
Be satisfied with words. I'll always doubt,
Assume my fortune's taken the wrong route

On its way to me. And that is why
I don't believe in anything till I
Have touched, partaken until satisfied.   75

ELMIRE   So suddenly, your love can't be denied.
It wants complete dominion over me,
And what it wants, it wants violently.
I know I'm flustered, I know I'm out of breath—
Your power over me could be the death   80
Of my reason. Does this seem right to you?
To use my weakness against me, just to
Conquer? No one's gallant anymore.
I invite you in. You break down the door.

TARTUFFE   If your passion for me isn't a pretense,   85
Then why deny me its best evidence?

ELMIRE   But, heaven, sir, that place that you address
So often, would judge us both if we transgress.

TARTUFFE   That's all that's in the way of my desires?
These judgments heaven makes of what transpires?   90
All you fear is heaven's bad opinion.

ELMIRE   But I am made to fear its dominion.

TARTUFFE   And I know how to exorcise these fears.
To sin is not as bad as it appears
If, and stay with me on this, one can think   95
That in some cases, heaven gives a wink
        [It is a scoundrel speaking.]8
When it comes to certain needs of men
Who can remain upright but only when
There is a pure intention. So you see,
If you just let yourself be led by me,   100
You'll have no worries, and I can enjoy
You. And you, me. Because we will employ
This way of thinking—a real science
And a secret, thus, with your compliance,
Fulfilling my desires without fear,   105
Is easy now, so let it happen here.
        [ELMIRE coughs.]
That cough, Madame, is bad.

ELMIRE   I'm in such pain.

TARTUFFE   A piece of licorice might ease the strain.

ELMIRE [directed to ORGON]   This cold I have is very obstinate.
It stubbornly holds on. I can't shake it.   110

TARTUFFE   That's most annoying.

ELMIRE   More than I can say.

TARTUFFE   Let's get back to finding you a way,
Finally, to get around your scruples:
Secrecy—I'm one of its best pupils
And practitioners. Responsibility   115

---

8. This stage direction, inserted by Molière himself, supports the playwright's assertion that he took pains to demonstrate Tartuffe's true nature.

For any evil—you can put on me,
I will answer up to heaven if I must,
And give a good accounting you can trust.
There'll be no sins for which we must atone,
'Cause evil exists only when it's known.   120
Adam and Eve were public in their fall.
To sin in private is not to sin at all.

ELMIRE [*after coughing again*]   Obviously, I must give in to you,
    Because, it seems, you are a person who
    Refuses to believe anything I say.   125
    Live testimony only can convey
    The truth of passion here, no more, no less.
    That it should go that far, I must confess,
    Is such a pity. But I'll cross the line,
    And give myself to you. I won't decline   130
    Your offer, sir, to vanquish me right here.
    But let me make one point extremely clear:
    If there's a moral judgment to be made,
    If anyone here feels the least betrayed,
    Then none of that will be my fault. Instead,   135
    The sin weighs twice as heavy on your head.
    You forced me to this brash extremity.

TARTUFFE   Yes, yes, I will take all the sin on me.

ELMIRE   Open the door and check because I fear
    My husband—just look—might be somewhere near.   140

TARTUFFE   What does it matter if he comes or goes?
    The secret is, I lead him by the nose.
    He's urged me to spend all my time with you.
    So let him see—he won't believe it's true.

ELMIRE   Go out and look around. Indulge my whim.   145
    Look everywhere and carefully for him.

4.6

[ORGON, ELMIRE]

ORGON [*coming out from under the table*]
    I swear that is the most abominable man!
    How will I bear this? I don't think I can.
    I'm stupefied!

ELMIRE   What? Out so soon? No, no.
    You can't be serious. There's more to go.
    Get back under there. You can't be too sure.   5
    It's never good relying on conjecture.

ORGON   That kind of wickedness comes straight from hell.

ELMIRE   You've turned against this man you know so well?
    Good lord, be sure the evidence is strong
    Before you are convinced. You might be wrong.
        [*She steps in front of ORGON.*]

4.7

[TARTUFFE, ELMIRE, ORGON]

TARTUFFE   Yes, all is well; there's no one to be found,
  And I was thorough when I looked around.
  To my delight, my rapture, at last . . .
ORGON [*stopping him*]   Just stop a minute there! You move too fast!
  Delight and rapture? Fulfilling desire?   5
  Ah! Ah! You are a traitor and a liar!
  Some holy man you are, to wreck my life,
  Marry my daughter? Lust after my wife?
  I've had my doubts about you, but kept quiet,
  Waiting for you to slip and then deny it.   10
  Well, now it's happened and I'm so relieved,
  To stop pretending that I am deceived.
ELMIRE [*to* TARTUFFE]   I don't approve of what I've done today,
  But I needed to do it, anyway.
TARTUFFE   What? You can't think . . .   15
ORGON   No more words from you.
  Get out of here, you. . . . You and I are through.
TARTUFFE   But my intentions . . .
ORGON   You still think I'm a dunce?
  You shut your mouth and leave this house at once!
TARTUFFE   You're the one to leave, you, acting like the master.
  Now I'll make it known, the full disaster: 20
  This house belongs to me, yes, all of it,
  And I'll decide what's true, as I see fit.
  You can't entrap me with demeaning tricks,
  Yes, here's a situation you can't fix.
  Here nothing happens without my consent.   25
  You've offended heaven. You must repent.
  But I know how to really punish you.
  Those who harm me, they know not what they do.

4.8

[ELMIRE, ORGON]

ELMIRE   What was that about? I mean, the latter.
ORGON   I'm not sure, but it's no laughing matter.
ELMIRE   Why?
ORGON   I've made a mistake I now can see,
  The deed I gave him is what troubles me.
ELMIRE   The deed?   5
ORGON   And something else. I am undone.
  I think my troubles may have just begun.
ELMIRE   What else?
ORGON   You'll know it all. I have to race,
  To see if a strongbox is in its place.

5.1

[ORGON, CLÉANTE]

CLÉANTE   Where are you running to?
ORGON   Who knows.
CLÉANTE   Then wait.
   It seems to me we should deliberate,
   Meet, plan, and have some family talks.
ORGON   I can't stop thinking about the damned box
   More than anything, that's the loss I fear.   5
CLÉANTE   What about this box makes it so dear?
ORGON   I have a friend whom I felt sorry for,
   Because he chose the wrong side in the war;[9]
   Before he fled, he brought it to me,
   This locked box. He didn't leave a key.   10
   He told me it has papers, this doomed friend,
   On which his life and property depend.
CLÉANTE   Are you saying you gave the box away?
ORGON   Yes, that's true, that's what I'm trying to say.
   I was afraid that I would have to lie,   15
   If I were confronted. That is why
   I went to my betrayer and confessed
   And he, in turn, told me it would be best
   If I gave him the box, to keep, in case
   Someone were to ask me to my face   20
   About it all, and I might lie and then,
   In doing so, commit a venial sin.[1]
CLÉANTE   As far as I can see, this is a mess,
   And with a lot of damage to assess.
   This secret that you told, this deed you gave,   25
   Make the situation hard to save.
   He's holding all the cards, your holy man,
   Because you gave them to him. If you can,
   Restrain yourself a bit and stay away.
   That would be best. And do watch what you say.   30
ORGON   What? With his wicked heart and corrupt soul,
   Yet I'm to keep my rage under control?
   Yes, me who took him in, right off the street?
   Damn all holy men! They're filled with deceit!
   I now renounce them all, down to the man,   35
   And I'll treat them worse than Satan can.
CLÉANTE   Listen to yourself! You're over the top,
   Getting carried away again. Just stop.
   "Moderation." Is that a word you know?
   I think you've learned it, but then off you go.   40

---

9. That is, he opposed Louis in the Fronde (see 1.2.11 and note). Although Orgon supported the king, this act left him open to the charge of being a traitor to the throne—a capital offense.

1. A "pardonable" or relatively minor sin. Because Tartuffe had possession of the box, Orgon could deny that he had it without lying.

Always ignoring the strength in reason,
Flinging yourself from loyalty to treason.
Why can't you just admit that you were swayed
By the fake piety that man displayed?
But no. Rather than change your ways, you turned   45
Like that. [*Snaps fingers*] Attacking holy men who've earned
The right to stand among the true believers.
So now all holy men are base deceivers?
Instead of just admitting your delusion,
"They're all like that!" you say—brilliant conclusion.   50
Why trust reason, when you have emotion?
You've implied there is no true devotion.
Freethinkers are the ones who hold that view,
And yet, you don't agree with them, do you?
You judge a man as good without real proof.   55
Appearances can lie—witness: Tartuffe.
If your respect is something to be prized,
Don't toss it away to those disguised
In a cloak of piety and virtue.
Don't you see how deeply they can hurt you?   60
Look for simple goodness—it does exist.
And just watch for imposters in our midst,
With this in mind, try not to be unjust
To true believers, sin on the side of trust.

5.2

[DAMIS, ORGON, CLÉANTE]

DAMIS   Father, what? I can't believe it's true,
That scoundrel has the gall to threaten you?
And use the things you gave him in his case
'Gainst you? To throw you out? I'll break his face.
ORGON   My son, I'm in more pain than you can see.   5
DAMIS   I'll break both his legs. Leave it to me.
We must not bend under his insolence.
I'll finish this business, punish his offense,
I'll murder him and do it with such joy.
CLÉANTE   Damis, you're talking like a little boy.   10
Tantrums head the list of your main flaws.
We live in modern times, with things called "laws."
Murder is illegal. At least for us.

5.3

[MADAME PERNELLE, MARIANE, ELMIRE, DORINE,
DAMIS, ORGON, CLÉANTE]

MADAME PERNELLE   It's unbelievable! Preposterous!
ORGON   Believe it. I've seen it with my own eyes.
He returned kindness with deceit and lies.

I took in a man, miserable and poor,
Brought him home, gave him the key to my door,   5
I loaded him with favors every day,
To him, my daughter, I just gave away,
My house, my wealth, a locked box from a friend.
But to what depths this devil would descend.
This betrayer, this abomination,   10
Who had the gall to preach about temptation,
And know in his black heart he'd woo my wife.
Seduce her! Yes! And then to steal my life.
Using my property, which I transferred to him,
I know, I know—it was a stupid whim.   15
He wants to ruin me, chase me from my door,
He wants me as he was, abject and poor.

DORINE   Poor man!

MADAME PERNELLE   I don't believe a word, my son,
This isn't something that he could have done.

ORGON   What?   20

MADAME PERNELLE   Holy men always arouse envy.

ORGON   Mother, what are you trying to say to me?

MADAME PERNELLE   That you live rather strangely in this house;
He's hated here, especially by your spouse.

ORGON   What has this got to do with what I said?

MADAME PERNELLE   Heaven knows, I've beat into your head: 25
"In this world, virtue is mocked forever;
Envious men may die, but envy never."

ORGON   How does that apply to what's happened here?

MADAME PERNELLE   Someone made up some lies; it's all too clear.

ORGON   But I saw it myself, you understand.   30

MADAME PERNELLE   "Whoever spreads slander has a soiled hand."

ORGON   You'll make me, Mother, say something not nice.
I saw it for myself; I've told you twice.

MADAME PERNELLE   "No one can trust what gossips have to say,
Yet they'll be with us until Judgment Day."   35

ORGON   You're talking total nonsense, Mother!
I said I saw him, this man I called Brother!
I saw him with my wife, with these two eyes.
The word is "saw," past tense of "see." These "lies"
That you misnamed are just the truth.   40
I saw my wife almost beneath Tartuffe.

MADAME PERNELLE   Oh, is that all? Appearances deceive.
What we think we see, we then believe.

ORGON   I'm getting angry.

MADAME PERNELLE   False suspicions, see?
We are subject to them, occasionally,   45
Good deeds can be seen as something other.

ORGON   So I'm to see this as a good thing, Mother,
A man trying to kiss my wife?

MADAME PERNELLE   You must.
Because, to be quite certain you are just,

You should wait until you're very, very sure   50
  And not rely on faulty conjecture.
ORGON   Goddammit! You would have me wait until . . . ?
  And just be quiet while he has his fill,
  Right before my very eyes, Mother, he'd—
MADAME PERNELLE   I can't believe that he would do this "deed"   55
  Of which he's been accused. There is no way.
  His soul is pure.
ORGON   I don't know what to say!
  Mother!
DORINE   Just deserts, for what you put us through.
  You thought we lied, now she thinks that of you.
CLÉANTE   Why are we wasting time with all of this?   60
  We're standing on the edge of the abyss.
  This man is dangerous! He has a plan!
DAMIS   How could he hurt us? I don't think he can.
ELMIRE   He won't get far, complaining to the law—
  You'll tell the truth, and he'll have to withdraw.   65
CLÉANTE   Don't count on it; trust me, he'll find a way
  To use these weapons you gave him today.
  He has legal documents, and the deed.
  To kick us out, just what else does he need?
  And if he's doubted, there are many ways   70
  To trap you in a wicked legal maze.
  You give a snake his venom, nice and quick,
  And after that you poke him with a stick?
ORGON   I know. But what was I supposed to do?
  Emotions got the best of me, it's true.   75
CLÉANTE   If we could placate him, just for a while,
  And somehow get the deed back with a smile.
ELMIRE   Had I known we had all this to lose,
  I never would have gone through with my ruse.
  I would've—   80
        [A knock on the door.]
ORGON   What does that man want? You go find out.
  But I don't want to know what it's about.

5.4

[MONSIEUR LOYAL, MADAME PERNELLE, ORGON,
  DAMIS, MARIANE, DORINE, ELMIRE, CLÉANTE]

MONSIEUR LOYAL [to DORINE]   Dear sister, hello. Please, I beg of you,
  Your master is the one I must speak to.
DORINE   He's not receiving visitors today.
MONSIEUR LOYAL   I bring good news so don't send me away.
  My goal in coming is not to displease;   5
  I'm here to put your master's mind at ease.
DORINE   And you are . . . who?
MONSIEUR LOYAL   Just say that I have come

For his own good and with a message from
Monsieur Tartuffe.
DORINE [*to* ORGON] It's a soft-spoken man,
 Who says he's here to do just what he can   10
 To ease your mind. Tartuffe sent him.
CLÉANTE   Let's see
 What he might want.
ORGON   Oh, what's my strategy?
 He's come to reconcile us, I just know.
CLÉANTE Your strategy? Don't let your anger show,
 For heaven's sake. And listen for a truce.   15
MONSIEUR LOYAL My greetings, sir. I'm here to be of use.
ORGON Just what I thought. His language is benign.
 For the prospect of peace, a hopeful sign.
MONSIEUR LOYAL Your family's dear to me, I hope you know.
 I served your father many years ago.   20
ORGON I humbly beg your pardon, to my shame,
 I don't know you, nor do I know your name.
MONSIEUR LOYAL My name's Loyal. I'm Norman by descent.
 My job of bailiff is what pays my rent.
 Thanks be to heaven, it's been forty years   25
 I've done my duty free of doubts or fear.
 That you invited me in, I can report,
 When I serve you with this writ from the court.
ORGON What? You're here . . .
MONSIEUR LOYAL   No upsetting outbursts, please.
 It's just a warrant saying we can seize,   30
 Not me, of course, but this Monsieur Tartuffe—
 Your house and land as his. Here is the proof.
 I have the contract here. You must vacate
 These premises. Please, now, don't be irate.
 Just gather up your things now, and make way   35
 For this man, without hindrance or delay.
ORGON Me? Leave my house?
MONSIEUR LOYAL   That's right, sir, out the door.
 This house, at present, as I've said before,
 Belongs to good Monsieur Tartuffe, you see,
 He's lord and master of this property   40
 By virtue of this contract I hold right here.
 Is that not your signature? It's quite clear.
DAMIS He's so rude, I do almost admire him.
MONSIEUR LOYAL Excuse me. Is it possible to fire him?
 My business is with you, a man of reason,   45
 Who knows resisting would be seen as treason.
 You understand that I must be permitted
 To execute the orders as committed.
DAMIS I'll execute him, Father, to be sure.
 His long black nightgown won't make him secure.   50

MONSIEUR LOYAL   He's your son! I thought he was a servant.
   Control the boy. His attitude's too fervent,
   His anger is a bone of contention—
   Throw him out, or I will have to mention
   His name in this, my official report.   55
DORINE   "Loyal" is loyal only to the court.
MONSIEUR LOYAL   I have respect for all God-fearing men,
   So instantly I knew I'd come here when
   I heard your name attached to this assignment.
   I knew you'd want a bailiff with refinement.   60
   I'm here for you, just to accommodate,
   To make removal something you won't hate.
   Now, if I hadn't come, then you would find
   You got a bailiff who would be less kind.
ORGON   I'm sorry, I don't see the kindness in   65
   An eviction order.
MONSIEUR LOYAL   Let me begin:
   I'm giving you time. I won't carry out
   This order you are so upset about.
   I've come only to spend the night with you,
   With my men, who will be coming through.   70
   All ten of them, as quiet as a mouse,
   Oh, you must give me the keys to the house.
   We won't disturb you. You will have your rest—
   You need a full night's sleep—that's always best.
   There'll be no scandal, secrets won't be bared;   75
   Tomorrow morning you must be prepared,
   To pack your things, down to the smallest plate,
   And cup, and then these premises vacate.
   You'll have helpers; the men I chose are strong,
   And they'll have this house empty before long.   80
   I can't think of who would treat you better
   And still enforce the law down to the letter,
   Just later with the letter is my gift.
   So, no resistance. And there'll be no rift.
ORGON   From that which I still have, I'd give this hour,   85
   One hundred coins of gold to have the power
   To sock this bailiff with a punch as great
   As any man in this world could create.
CLÉANTE   That's enough. Let's not make it worse.
DAMIS   The nerve
   Of him. Let's see what my right fist can serve.   90
DORINE   Mister Loyal, you have a fine, broad back,
   And if I had a stick, you'd hear it crack.
MONSIEUR LOYAL   Words like that are punishable, my love—
   Be careful when a push becomes a shove.
CLÉANTE   Oh, come on, there's no reason to postpone.   95
   Just serve your writ and then leave us alone.

MONSIEUR LOYAL   May heaven keep you, till we meet again!
ORGON   And strangle you, and him who sent you in!

5.5

[ORGON, CLÉANTE, MARIANE, ELMIRE, MADAME
PERNELLE, DORINE, DAMIS]

ORGON   Well, Mother, look at this writ. Here is proof
   Of treachery supreme by your Tartuffe.
   Don't jump to judgment—that's what you admonished.
MADAME PERNELLE   I'm overwhelmed, I'm utterly astonished.
DORINE   I hear you blaming him and that's just wrong.   5
   You'll see his good intentions before long.
   "Just love thy neighbor" is here on this writ,
   Between the lines, you see him saying it.
   Because men are corrupted by their wealth,
   Out of concern for your spiritual health.   10
   He's taking, with a pure motivation,
   Everything that keeps you from salvation.
ORGON   Aren't you sick of hearing "Quiet!" from me?
CLÉANTE   Thoughts of what to do now? And quickly?
ELMIRE   Once we show the plans of that ingrate,   15
   His trickery can't get him this estate.
   As soon as they see his disloyalty,
   He'll be denied, I hope, this property.

5.6

[VALÈRE, ORGON, CLÉANTE, ELMIRE, MARIANE, *etc.*]

VALÈRE   I hate to ruin your day—I have bad news.
   Danger's coming. There's no time to lose.
   A good friend, quite good, as it turns out,
   Discovered something you must know about,
   Something at the court that's happening now.   5
   That swindler—sorry, if you will allow,
   That holy faker—has gone to the king,
   Accusing you of almost everything.
   But here's the worst: he says that you have failed
   Your duty as a subject, which entailed   10
   The keeping of a strongbox so well hidden,
   That you could deny knowledge, if bidden,
   Of a traitor's whereabouts. What's more,
   That holy fraud will come right through that door,
   Accusing you. You can't do anything.   15
   He had this box and gave it to the king.
   So there's an order out for your arrest!
   And evidently, it's the king's behest,
   That Tartuffe come, so justice can be done.

CLÉANTE   Well, there it is, at last, the smoking gun.   20
He can claim this house, at the very least.
ORGON   The man is nothing but a vicious beast.
VALÈRE   You must leave now, and I will help you hide.
Here's ten thousand in gold. My carriage is outside.
When a storm is bearing down on you   25
Running is the best thing one can do.
I have a place where both of us can stay.
ORGON   My boy, I owe you more than I can say.
I pray to heaven that, before too long,
I can pay you back and right the wrong   30
I've done to you. [*To* ELMIRE] Good-bye. Take care, my dear.
CLÉANTE   We'll plan. You go while the way is still clear.

5.7

[THE EXEMPT, TARTUFFE, VALÈRE, ORGON, ELMIRE,
MARIANE, DORINE, *etc.*[2]]

TARTUFFE   Easy, just a minute, you move too fast.
Your cowardice, dear sir, is unsurpassed.
What I have to say is uncontested.
Simply put, I'm having you arrested.
ORGON   You villain, you traitor, your lechery   5
Is second only to your treachery.
And you arrest me—that's the crowning blow.
TARTUFFE   Suffering for heaven is all I know,
So revile me. It's all for heaven's sake.
CLÉANTE   Why does he persist when we know it's fake?   10
DAMIS   He's mocking heaven. What a loathsome beast.
TARTUFFE   Get mad—I'm not bothered in the least.
It is my duty, what I'm doing here.
MARIANE   You really think that if you persevere
In this lie, you'll keep your reputation?   15
TARTUFFE   My honor is safeguarded by my station,
As I am on a mission from the king.
ORGON   You dog, have you forgotten everything?
Who picked you up from total poverty?
TARTUFFE   I know that there were things you did for me.   20
My duty to our monarch is what stifles
Memory, so your past gifts are trifles.
My obligations to him are so rife,
That I would give up family, friends, and life.
ELMIRE   Fraud!   25
DORINE   Now there's a lie that beats everything,
His pretended reverence for our king!

---

2. Molière himself added "etc." to the list of speaking characters. Thus Laurent and Flipote may return to the stage for this final scene.

CLÉANTE   This "duty to our monarch," as you say,
  Why didn't it come up before today?
  You had the box, you lived here for some time,
  To say the least, and yet this crime   30
  That you reported—why then did you wait?
  Orgon caught you about to desecrate
  The holy bonds of marriage with his wife.
  Suddenly, your obligations are so "rife"
  To our dear king, that you're here to turn in   35
  Your former friend and "brother" and begin
  To move into his house, a gift, but look,
  Why would you accept gifts from a crook?
TARTUFFE [to THE EXEMPT]   Save me from this whining! I have had my fill!
  Do execute your orders, if you will.   40
THE EXEMPT   I will. I've waited much too long for that.
  I had to let you have your little chat.
  It confirmed the facts our monarch knew,
  That's why, Tartuffe, I am arresting you.[3]
TARTUFFE   Who, me?   45
THE EXEMPT   Yes, you.
TARTUFFE   You're putting me in jail?
THE EXEMPT   Immediately. And there will be no bail.
  [To ORGON] You may compose yourself now, sir, because
  We're fortunate in leadership and laws.
  We have a king who sees into men's hearts,
  And cannot be deceived, so he imparts   50
  Great wisdom, and a talent for discernment,
  Thus frauds are guaranteed a quick internment.
  Our Prince of Reason sees things as they are,
  So hypocrites do not get very far.
  But saintly men and the truly devout,   55
  He cherishes and has no doubts about.
  This man could not begin to fool the king
  Who can defend himself against the sting
  Of much more subtle predators. And thus,
  When this craven pretender came to us,   60
  Demanding justice and accusing you,
  He betrayed himself. Our king could view
  The baseness lurking in his coward's heart.
  Evil like that can set a man apart,
  And so divine justice nodded her head,   65
  The king did not believe a word he said.
  It was soon confirmed, he has a crime
  For every sin, but why squander the time
  To list them or the aliases he used.
  For the king, it's enough that he abused   70

---

3. In his capacity as officer of the king, The Exempt becomes both Louis's representative and his surrogate.

Your friendship and your faith. And though we knew
Each accusation of his was untrue,
Our monarch himself, wanting to know
Just how far this imposter planned to go,
Had me wait to find this out, then pounce,   75
Arrest this criminal, quickly denounce
The man and all his lies. And now, the king
Orders delivered to you, everything
This scoundrel took, the deed, all documents,
This locked box of yours and all its contents,   80
And nullifies the contract giving away
Your property, effective today.
And finally, our monarch wants to end
Your worries about aiding your old friend
Before he went into exile because,   85
In that same way, and in spite of the laws,
You openly defended our king's right
To his throne. And you were prepared to fight.
From his heart, and because it makes good sense
That a good deed deserves a recompense,   90
He pardons you. And wanted me to add:
He remembers good longer than the bad.

DORINE   May heaven be praised!
MADAME PERNELLE   I am so relieved.
ELMIRE   A happy ending!
MARIANE   Can it be believed?
ORGON [to TARTUFFE]   Now then, you traitor . . .   95
CLÉANTE   Stop that, Brother, please.
You're sinking to his level. Don't appease
His expectations of mankind. His fate
Is misery. But it's never too late
To take another path, and feel remorse.
So let's wish, rather, he will change his course,   100
And turn his back upon his life of vice,
Embrace the good and know it will suffice.
We've all seen the wisdom of this great king,
Whom we should go and thank for everything.
ORGON   Yes, and well said. So come along with me,   105
To thank him for his generosity.
And then once that glorious task is done,
We'll come back here for yet another one—
I mean a wedding for which we'll prepare,
To give my daughter to the good Valère.   110

MARIE DE LA VERGNE DE LA FAYETTE

1634–1693

Despite its title, no one would confuse *The Princess of Clèves* with a fairy tale, for de La Fayette's princess lives in a recognizable world of political and historical turmoil. And unlike in a fairy tale, the princess's interiority— feelings, qualms, regrets—determines the plot. Yet this is a story about ethics as much as feeling: it explores the moral quandaries that evolving notions of the self and of marriage posed for the women, and also for the men, of de La Fayette's time, against a backdrop of high political intrigue.

LIFE AND TIMES

Marie de La Vergne was born to a family of the minor French nobility and raised in the lively, stylish metropolis that was seventeenth-century Paris. At sixteen, she became a maid-of-honor to the queen, Anne of Austria, and was tutored in Italian and Latin. At twenty-two, Marie married the Count of La Fayette, who took her to one of his estates in the remote rural Auvergne. She remained in the country for three years and gave birth to two sons, but when she was twenty-five she returned alone to Paris, where she handled some of her husband's business affairs and soon befriended key writers and critics, such as Madame de Sevigné, La Rochefoucauld, and Huet.

Madame de La Fayette was, like many noblewomen of her era, an active and celebrated contributor to the literary and intellectual culture of France under Louis XIV. His reign, marked as it was by centrist and absolutist policies, granted less power to the nobility than in earlier eras (including the era that de La Fayette describes in *The Princess of Clèves*), but the achievements of de La Fayette and her noble peers during this time buttressed France's reputation as Europe's cultural powerhouse. An important engine of all of this intellectual activity was the salon—a literary gathering hosted primarily by women, including de La Fayette. Noblewomen joined men as readers, writers, critics, and thinkers whose insights were noted and appreciated for their wit and elegance.

While the French court glittered with cosmopolitan wit and charm, Jansenism—a reform movement within the Catholic Church with distinctly Protestant overtones—offered a stern cultural counterpoint. Stressing a pessimistic view of human nature and the need to defend against temptation, Jansenism proved an intellectual and religious refuge for such central figures as Racine and Pascal, and there are subtle signs in de La Fayette's work (including *The Princess of Clèves*) that she too was sensitive to its admonitions.

At the heart of these conflicting currents, de La Fayette was widely recognized as a writer in her own time, despite the anonymous publication of her most famous work. She may have written as many as five novels, in close collaboration with members of her circle. She also wrote *Memoirs of the French Court for the Years 1688 and 1689*, a historical work on both public events, such as the English revolution that deposed James II, and the private affairs of figures connected with important happenings.

THE PRINCESS OF CLÈVES

First published anonymously in 1678, *The Princess of Clèves* won instantaneous popular success. The story's immediate interest, as well as its lasting appeal, lies in how it combines a historical setting with psychological depth. At a time when virtually all French fiction took the form of long, fanciful romances, it inaugurated a new novelistic tradition involving character development and narrative economy.

De La Fayette sets her story roughly one hundred years before her own time. Henri II of France (1519–1559), known as a patron of the arts and as a brave soldier, heads the court. The queen, Catherine de Médicis (1519–1589), has less social and political power than does the king's longtime mistress, Diane de Poitiers, Duchess of Valentinois (1499–1566). Also politically important is the woman usually referred to as "Madame," the king's sister, Marguerite (1525–1574). Both the Prince of Clèves, the heroine's husband in the novel, and the Duke of Nemours, whom she loves, actually existed. Conversely, the title character, the princess, and her mother, Madame de Chartres, are fictional, but they are said to belong to the family of another historical character, the powerful François de Vendôme, Vidame of Chartres (1522–1560).

The two dominant factions at court are headed by the Duke of Montmorency, constable of France (1492–1567), member of an enormously powerful family, and François de Lorraine, Chevalier of Guise (d. 1562). Various marital alliances link the families of these persons with the king's mistress, the Duchess of Valentinois, to whose patronage all aspire. The court intrigues reported in the novel mainly stem from the rivalries between the Duchess of Valentinois and the queen and between the Montmorency and Guise families.

Yet why does the reader need to understand all this in order to enjoy a love story? De La Fayette seems intent on showing how, in the confined social and political world that she depicts, shifting sexual alliances often determine movements of power. Hence the effort to understand people's sexual behavior involves, by extension, matters of public importance. When the king or his mistress play favorites, exiling certain figures and calling others back to the court, they affect the outcome of wars and negotiations. When the Duke of Nemours, newly enamored of the Princess, decides not to go to England to woo Queen Elizabeth, a possibly crucial alliance is voided. Most momentous, perhaps, when the king fatefully decides to continue jousting in a tournament held to celebrate his daughter's marriage to the king of Spain, he receives a fatal injury. Suddenly, the balance of power in the court is radically overthrown: under a new king, the elaborate circles of patronage around the former king's mistress become irrelevant. The personal is most definitely the political at this court. Not only is love rarely private, with everyone constantly watching everyone else, it also has powerful consequences in what we would call the public sphere.

For the princess herself, however, love remains an intensely personal matter, despite her full awareness that personal attachments can have wider implications. The princess thinks about her virtue, her commitments, her feelings, and about how to protect those feelings from the avid watchers and interpreters who compose her society. Through her characters' experience, de La Fayette explores changing notions of marriage in her time.

First promoted within sixteenth-century Protestantism, the revolutionary notion of companionate marriage, based on love rather than convenience or necessity, was far easier to adopt among the lower classes than among aristocrats, for whom huge fortunes and political alliances were at stake. The daughter of the king of France, for example, could not marry whom she chose: she was a pawn in the game of international politics, to be married off to the king of Spain. Thus aristocrats of de La Fayette's class would not have expected to find love in marriage, but simply a suitable alliance. Love was for outside marriage, in the long tradition of courtly love, and it also served as a political tool. This is why the Prince of Clèves is so unusual a figure: he is desperately in love with his wife, both before and after he marries her. She, despite her exposure to the cynicism of the court, sincerely wishes she could reciprocate his feelings. And although she never manages it, these aristocrats' longing for a love match is a striking reversal of the more usual pattern, in which the lower classes try to copy their social betters.

When the Duke of Nemours, the most desirable man at court, falls in love with the princess, she feels that passion she has never before experienced, and the stage is set for a standard conflict of love and duty. The novel renders this conflict in unconventional ways. The single event in *The Princess of Clèves* that most intrigued de La Fayette's contemporaries is the heroine's confession to her husband of her interest in another man. The princess acknowledges her attraction to the Duke of Nemours not to justify it but to ask for help in combating it; she yearns to retreat to the country to avoid constant anguishing temptation. Her husband finds this confession as astonishing as de La Fayette's readers did; her would-be lover, who overhears it, is equally amazed.

The remarkable action calls attention to the princess's overwhelming desire to keep her integrity as a person, which her desire would destroy. Her acceptance of female chastity as an ideal appears to us today to be a form of repression: she feels no erotic passion for her devoted husband, and the narrative provides no reason to expect her to develop such feeling. Yet *The Princess of Clèves* is not, as it may seem, only a story of female self-abnegation. The princess's lover, for his beloved's sake, gives up his chance to marry the queen of England, in a show of *male* abnegation, and an indication of the female protagonist's emotional power. The heroine suppresses her erotic impulse—or, at any rate, its expression—but she allows herself the virtuous satisfaction of her steady refusal.

These ambiguities are crucial for modern readers, who come to the text with different assumptions about gender roles and the psychology of desire. Is the princess honorable or needlessly cruel in confessing to her husband? Does she behave like a child or like a mature woman? Does she reject her lover out of virtue or (as she herself suggests) from fear of his eventual infidelity? Does she consolidate or yield her power by this rejection? Does she choose happiness or misery in celibate widowhood? Although *The Princess of Clèves,* like other works of its period, seems to endorse the control of passion by reason, it also reveals the costs of such control.

The Princess of Clèves has been read intensely in France and beyond since its original publication. De La Fayette's first readers debated the book so strenuously—was it plausible? was the princess acting as she should?—that an entire corpus of responses known as the "quarrel over de La Fayette" gathered around the novel. The work continues to cause controversy in our own day, if for very different reasons: in

2006, Nicolas Sarkozy, who would soon become the president of France, observed dismissively that people sitting for a civil service exam did not need to know *The Princess of Clèves*. Many intellectuals took this as an argument for a utilitarian or practical education over one that valued the French classics in all their complexity. Sarkozy's dismissal has led to a huge surge in the novel's popularity—always read, it is now all the more beloved as a symbol of dissent and of the French tradition and is celebrated in everything from public readings to film adaptations and popular songs.

The Princess of Clèves[1]

Part I

There never was in France so brilliant a display of magnificence and gallantry as during the last years of the reign of Henri II. This monarch was gallant, handsome, and susceptible; although his love for Diane de Poitiers, Duchess of Valentinois, had lasted twenty years, its ardor had not diminished, as his conduct testified.

He was remarkably skilful in physical exercises, and devoted much attention to them; every day was filled with hunting and tennis, dancing, running at the ring,[2] and sports of that kind. The favorite colors and the initials of Madame de Valentinois were to be seen everywhere, and she herself used to appear dressed as richly as Mademoiselle de la Marck, her granddaughter, who was then about to be married.

Madame de Valentinois's appearance at court was made acceptable by the presence there of the queen.[3] This princess, although she had passed her first youth, was still beautiful; she was fond of splendor, magnificence, and pleasure. The king had married her while still Duke of Orléans, in the lifetime of his elder brother, the dauphin, who afterward died at Tournon, mourned as a worthy heir to the position of Francis I, his father.

The queen's ambition made her like to reign. She seemed indifferent to the king's attachment to the Duchess of Valentinois, and never betrayed any jealousy; but she was so skilled a dissembler that it was hard to discover her real feelings, and she was compelled by policy to keep the duchess near her if she wanted to see anything of the king. As for him, he liked the society of women, even of those with whom he was not at all in love. He was with the queen every day at her audience,[4] when all the most attractive lords and ladies were sure to appear.

At no court had there ever been gathered together so many lovely women and brave men. It seemed as if Nature had made an effort to show her highest beauty in the greatest lords and ladies. Madame Elisabeth of France, afterwards queen of Spain, began to show her wonderful intelligence and that unrivalled beauty which was so fatal to her. Mary Stuart, the queen of Scotland,

1. Translated by Thomas Sergeant Perry.
2. A court game in which men, mounted on horseback, competed to carry away a suspended metal ring on the point of a lance.
3. We depart from the translation here.
4. A formal gathering.

who had just married the dauphin and was called the crown princess, or dauphiness, was faultless in mind and body. She had been brought up at the French court and had acquired all its polish; she was endowed by Nature with so strong a love for the softer graces that in spite of her youth she admired and understood them perfectly. Her mother-in-law, the queen, and Madame, the king's sister, were also fond of poetry, of comedy, and of music. The interest which King Francis I had felt in poetry and letters still prevailed in France and since the king, his son, was devoted to physical exercise, pleas- ures of all sorts were to be found at the court. But what rendered the court especially fine and majestic was the great number of princes and lords of exceptional merit; those I am about to name were, in their different ways, the ornament and the admiration of their age.

The King of Navarre inspired universal respect by his exalted rank and his royal bearing. He excelled in the art of war; but the Duke of Guise had shown himself so strong a rival that he had often laid aside his command to enter the duke's service as a private soldier in the most dangerous battles. This duke had manifested such admirable bravery with such remarkable success that he was an object of envy to every great commander. He had many conspicuous qualities besides his personal courage,—he possessed a vast and profound intelligence, a noble, lofty mind, and equal capacity for war and affairs. His brother, the Cardinal of Lorraine, was born with an unbridled ambition, and had acquired vast learning; this he turned to his profit by using it in defence of Catholicism, which had begun to be attacked. The Chevalier de Guise, afterwards known as the Grand Prior, was loved by all; he was handsome, witty, clever, and his courage was renowned throughout Europe. The short, ill-favored body of the Prince of Condé held a great and haughty soul, and an intelligence that endeared him to even the most beautiful women. The Duke of Nevers, famous for his military prowess and his important services to the state, though somewhat advanced in years was adored by all the court. He had three handsome sons,—the second, known as the Prince of Clèves, was worthy to bear that proud title; he was brave and grand, and was withal endowed with a prudence rare in the young. The Vidame[5] of Chartres, a scion of the old house of Vendôme, a name not despised by princes of the blood, had won equal triumphs in war and gallantry; he was handsome, attractive, brave, hardy, generous; all his good qualities were distinct and striking,—in short, he was the only man fit to be compared, if such comparison be possible, with the Duke of Nemours. This nobleman was a masterpiece of Nature; the least of his fascinations was his extreme beauty; he was the handsomest man in the world. What made him superior to every one else was his unrivalled courage and a charm manifested in his mind, his expression, and his actions, such as no other showed. He possessed a certain playfulness that was equally attractive to men and women; he was unusually skilful in physical exercises; and he dressed in a way that every one tried in vain to imitate; moreover, his bearing was such that all eyes followed him whenever he appeared. There was no lady in the court who would not have been flattered by his attentions; few of those to whom he had devoted himself could boast of having resisted him; and even many in whom he had

---

5. A title that designated the lay representative of a bishop and the commander of the bishop's troops.

shown no interest made very clear their affection for him. He was so gentle and courteous that he could not refuse some attentions to those who tried to please him,—hence he had many mistresses; but it was hard to say whom he really loved. He was often to be seen with the dauphiness; her beauty, her gentleness, her desire to please every one, and the especial regard she showed for this prince, made some imagine that he dared to raise his eyes to her. The Guises, whose niece she was, had acquired influence and position by her marriage; they aspired to an equality with the princes of the blood and to a share of the power exercised by the Constable[6] of Montmorency. It was to the constable that the king confided the greater part of the cares of state, while he treated the Duke of Guise and the Marshal of Saint-André as his favorites. But those attached to his person by favor or position could only keep their place by submitting to the Duchess of Valentinois, who, although no longer young or beautiful, ruled him so despotically that she may be said to have been the mistress of his person and of the state.

The king had always loved the constable, and at the beginning of his reign had summoned him from the exile into which he had been sent by Francis I. The court was divided between the Guises and the constable, who was the favorite of the princes of the blood. Both parties had always struggled for the favor of the Duchess of Valentinois. The Duke of Aumale, brother of the Duke of Guise, had married one of her daughters. The constable aspired to the same alliance, not satisfied with having married his eldest son to Madame Diane, a daughter of the king by a lady of Piedmont who entered a convent after the birth of her child. The promises which Monsieur de Montmorency had made to Mademoiselle de Piennes, one of the queen's maids-of-honor, had proved a serious obstacle to this match; and although the king had removed it with extreme patience and kindness, the constable still felt insecure until he had won over the Duchess of Valentinois and had separated her from the Guises, whose greatness had begun to alarm her. She had delayed in every way in her power the marriage between the dauphin and the Queen of Scotland; this young queen's beauty and intelligence, and the position given to the Guises by this marriage, were very odious to her. She especially detested the Cardinal of Lorraine, who had addressed her in bitter, even contemptuous terms. She saw that he was intriguing with the queen; hence the constable found her ready to join forces with him by bringing about the marriage of Mademoiselle de la Marck, her granddaughter, to Monsieur d'Anville, his second son, who succeeded to his post in the reign of Charles IX. The constable did not expect that Monsieur d'Anville would have any objections to this marriage, as had been the case with Monsieur de Montmorency; but though the reasons were more hidden, the difficulties were no less obstinate. Monsieur d'Anville was desperately in love with the crown princess; and although his passion was hopeless, he could not persuade himself to contract other ties. The Marshal of Saint-André was almost the only courtier who had taken sides with neither faction; he was one of the favorites, but this position he held simply by his own merits. Ever since he had been the dauphin, the king had been attached to this nobleman, and later had made him marshal of France, at an age when men are satisfied with lesser honors. His advance gave him a distinction which he maintained by

6. A title that designated the highest-ranking official of the court.

his personal worth and charm, by a costly table and rich surroundings, and by more splendor than any private individual had yet displayed. The king's generosity warranted this sumptuousness. There was no limit to this monarch's generosity to those he loved. He did not possess every great quality, but he had many, and among them the love of war and a good knowledge of it. This accounted for his many successes; and if we except the battle of St. Quentin, his reign was an unbroken series of victories. He had won the battle of Renty in person, Piedmont had been conquered, the English had been driven from France, and the Emperor Charles V had seen his good fortune desert him before the city of Metz,[7] which he had besieged in vain with all the forces of the Empire and of Spain. Nevertheless, since the defeat of St. Quentin had diminished our hope of conquest, and fortune seemed to favor one king as much as the other, they were gradually led to favor peace.

The Dowager Duchess of Lorraine had begun to lead the way to a cessation of hostilities at the time of the dauphin's marriage, and ever since then there had been secret negotiations. At last Cercamp, in the Province of Artois, was chosen as the place of meeting. The Cardinal of Lorraine, the constable, and the Marshal of Saint-André appeared in behalf of the King of France; the Duke of Alva and the Prince of Orange in behalf of Philip II. The Duke and Duchess of Lorraine were the mediators. The leading articles were the marriage of Madame Elisabeth of France to Don Carlos, Infanta of Spain, and that of Madame, the king's sister, with Monsieur de Savoie.

Meanwhile the king remained on the frontier, and there heard of the death of Mary, queen of England. He sent the Count of Randan to Elizabeth to congratulate her on ascending the throne. She was very glad to receive him, because her rights were so insecure that it was of great service to her to have them acknowledged by the king. The count found her well informed about the interests of France and the capabilities of those who composed the court, but especially familiar with the reputation of the Duke of Nemours. She spoke of this nobleman so often and with such warmth that when Monsieur de Randan returned and recounted his journey to the king, he told him that there was nothing to which Monsieur de Nemours could not aspire, and that she would be capable of marrying him. That very evening the king spoke to this nobleman, and made Monsieur de Randan repeat to him his conversation with Elizabeth, urging him to essay this great fortune. At first Monsieur de Nemours thought that the king was jesting; but when he saw his mistake he said,—

"At any rate, sire, if I undertake a fantastic enterprise under the advice and in behalf of your Majesty, I beg of you to keep it secret until success shall justify me before the public, and to guard me from appearing vain enough to suppose that a queen who has never seen me should wish to marry me from love."

The king promised to speak of the plan to no one but the constable, and agreed that secrecy was essential for its success. Monsieur de Randan advised Monsieur de Nemours to visit England as a simple traveller; but the latter

---

7. Henri II had continued the struggle of his father, Francis I, against Charles V, leader of the Holy Roman Empire, for supremacy in Europe and particularly for control in Italy. The battles mentioned here belong to that struggle. The French armies were defeated at St. Quentin in 1557. The French drove the English from Calais in 1558. The French captured Metz in 1552.

could not make up his mind to do this. He sent Lignerolles, an intelligent young man, one of his favorites, to ascertain the queen's feeling and to try to open the matter. Meanwhile he went to see the Duke of Savoy, who was then at Brussels with the King of Spain. The death of Mary of England[8] raised great obstacles to any treaty of peace; the commission broke up at the end of November, and the king returned to Paris.

At that moment there appeared at court a young lady to whom all eyes were turned, and we may well believe that she was possessed of faultless beauty, since she aroused admiration where all were well accustomed to the sight of handsome women. Of the same family as the Vidame of Chartres, she was one of the greatest heiresses in France. Her father had died young, leaving her under the charge of his wife, Madame de Chartres, whose kindness, virtue, and worth were beyond praise. After her husband's death she had withdrawn from court for many years; during this period she had devoted herself to the education of her daughter, not merely cultivating her mind and her beauty, but also seeking to inspire her with the love of virtue and to make her attractive. Most mothers imagine that it is enough never to speak of gallantry to their daughters to guard them from it forever. Madame de Chartres was of a very different opinion; she often drew pictures of love to her daughter, showing her its fascinations, in order to give her a better understanding of its perils. She told her how insincere men are, how false and deceitful; she described the domestic miseries which illicit love-affairs entail, and, on the other hand, pictured to her the peaceful happiness of a virtuous woman's life, as well as the distinction and elevation which virtue gives to a woman of rank and beauty. She taught her, too, how hard it was to preserve this virtue without extreme care, and without that one sure means of securing a wife's happiness, which is to love her husband and to be loved by him.

This heiress was, then, one of the greatest matches in France, and although she was very young, many propositions of marriage had been made to her. Madame de Chartres, who was extremely proud, found almost nothing worthy of her daughter, and the girl being in her sixteenth year, she was anxious to take her to court. The Vidame went to welcome her on her arrival, and was much struck by the marvellous beauty of Mademoiselle de Chartres,—and with good reason: her delicate complexion and her blond hair gave her a unique brilliancy; her features were regular, and her face and person were full of grace and charm.

The day after her arrival she went to match some precious stones at the house of an Italian who dealt in them. He had come from Florence with the queen, and had grown so rich by his business that his house seemed that of some great nobleman rather than of a merchant. The Prince of Clèves happened to come in while she was there; he was so struck by her beauty that he could not conceal his surprise, and Mademoiselle de Chartres could not keep from blushing when she saw his astonishment: she succeeded, however, in regaining her composure without paying any further attention to the prince than civility required for a man of his evident importance. Monsieur de Clèves gazed at her admiringly, wondering who this beauty was whom he did not

8. Mary Tudor (1516–1558), "Bloody Mary," wife of Philip II of Spain.

know. He perceived from her bearing and her suite[9] that she must be a lady of high rank. She was so young that he thought she must be unmarried; but since she had not her mother with her, and the Italian, who did not know her, addressed her as "madame," he was in great doubt, and stared at her with continual surprise. He saw that his glances embarrassed her, unlike most young women, who always take pleasure in seeing the effect of their beauty; it even seemed to him that his presence made her anxious to go away, and in fact she left very soon. Monsieur de Clèves consoled himself for her departure with the hope of finding out who she was, and was much disappointed to learn that no one knew. He was so struck by her beauty and evident modesty that from that moment he conceived for her the greatest love and esteem. That evening he called on Madame, the king's sister.

This princess was held in high esteem on account of her influence with the king, her brother; and this influence was so great that when the king made peace he consented to restore Piedmont to enable her to marry Monsieur de Savoie. Although she had always meant to marry, she had determined to give her hand to none but a sovereign, and had for that reason refused the King of Navarre when he was Duke of Vendôme, and had always felt an interest in Monsieur de Savoie after seeing him at Nice on the occasion of the interview between Francis I and Pope Paul III.[1] Since she possessed great intelligence and a fine taste, she drew pleasant persons about her, and at certain hours the whole court used to visit her.

Thither Monsieur de Clèves went, as was his habit. He was so full of the wit and beauty of Mademoiselle de Chartres that he could speak of nothing else; he talked freely of his adventure, and set no limit to his praise of the young woman he had seen but did not know. Madame said to him that there was no such person as he described, and that if there were, every one would have known about her. Madame de Dampierre, her lady-in-waiting and a friend of Madame de Chartres, when she heard the conversation moved near the princess and said to her in a low voice that doubtless it was Mademoiselle de Chartres whom Monsieur de Clèves had seen. Madame turned towards him and said that if he would return the next day, she would show him this beauty who had so impressed him. Mademoiselle de Chartres made her appearance the next day. The queen received her with every imaginable attention, and she was greeted with such admiration by every one that she heard around her nothing but praise. This she received with such noble modesty that she seemed not to hear it, or at least not to be affected by it. Then she visited the apartments of Madame, the king's sister. The princess, after praising her beauty, told her the surprise she had given to Monsieur de Clèves. A moment after, that person appeared.

"Come," she said to him, "see if I have not kept my word, and if, when I point out Mademoiselle de Chartres to you, I do not show you the beauty you sought; at any rate, thank me for telling her how much you already admire her."

Monsieur de Clèves was filled with joy to find that this young woman whom he had found so attractive was of a rank proportionate to her beauty. He went up to her and asked her to remember that he had been the first to admire her,

---

9. Group of attendants or servants.
1. The meeting took place in 1538. The pope helped arrange a ten-year truce between France and the empire.

and that without knowing her he had felt all the respect and esteem that were her due.

The Chevalier de Guise, his friend, and he left the house together. At first they praised Mademoiselle de Chartres without stint; then they found that they were praising her too much, and both stopped saying what they thought of her: but they were compelled to talk about her on the following days wherever they met. This new beauty was for a long time the general subject of conversation. The queen praised her warmly and showed an extraordinary regard for her; the dauphiness made her one of her favorites, and begged Madame de Chartres to bring her to see her very often; the daughters of the king invited her to all their entertainments,—in short, she was loved and admired by the whole court, except by Madame de Valentinois. It was not that this new beauty gave her any uneasiness,—her long experience had made her sure of the king,—but she so hated the Vidame of Chartres, whom she had desired to ally with herself by the marriage of one of her daughters, while he had joined the queen's party, that she could not look with favor on any one who bore his name and seemed to enjoy his friendship.

The Prince of Clèves fell passionately in love with Mademoiselle de Chartres, and was eager to marry her; but he feared lest the pride of Madame de Chartres should prevent her from giving her daughter to a man who was not the eldest of his family. Yet this family was so distinguished, and the Count of Eu, who was the head of the house, had just married a woman so near to royalty, that it was timidity rather than any true reason that inspired the fear of Monsieur de Clèves. He had many rivals; the Chevalier de Guise seemed to him the most formidable, on account of his birth, his ability, and the brilliant position of his family. This prince had fallen in love with Mademoiselle de Chartres the first day he saw her; he had noticed the passion of Monsieur de Clèves just as the latter had noticed his. Though the two men were friends, the separation which resulted from this rivalry gave them no chance to explain themselves, and their friendship cooled without their having courage to come to an understanding. The good fortune of Monsieur de Clèves in being the first to see Mademoiselle de Chartres seemed to him a happy omen, and to promise him some advantage over his rivals; but he foresaw serious obstacles on the part of the Duke of Nevers, his father. This duke was bound to the Duchess of Valentinois by many ties; she was an enemy of the Vidame, and this was reason enough to prevent the Duke of Nevers from consenting that his son should think of that nobleman's niece.

Madame de Chartres, who had already taken such pains to fill her daughter with a love of virtue, did not remit them in this place where they were still so necessary, and bad examples were so frequent. Ambition and gallantry were the sole occupation of the court, busying men and women alike. There were so many interests and so many different intrigues in which women took part that love was always mingled with politics, and politics with love. No one was calm or indifferent; every one sought to rise, to please, to serve, or to injure; no one was weary or idle, every one was taken up with pleasure or intrigue. The ladies had their special interest in the queen, in the crown princess, in the Queen of Navarre, in Madame the king's sister, or in the Duchess of Valentinois, according to their inclinations, their sense of right, or their humor. Those who had passed their first youth and assumed an austere virtue, were devoted to the queen; those who were younger and sought pleasure and gallantry, paid their court to the crown princess. The Queen of Navarre had her favorites; she was young, and had much influence over her husband the king,[2] who was allied with the constable, and hence highly esteemed. Madame the king's sister still preserved some of her beauty, and gathered several ladies about herself. The Duchess of Valentinois was sought by all those whom she deigned to regard; but the women she liked were few, and with the exception of those who enjoyed her intimacy and confidence, and whose disposition bore some likeness to her own, she received only on the days when she assumed to hold a court like the queen.

All these different cliques were separated by rivalry and envy. Then, too, the women who belonged to each one of them were also jealous of one another, either about their chances of advancement, or about their lovers; often their interests were complicated by other pettier, but no less important questions. Hence there was in this court a sort of well-ordered agitation, which rendered it very charming, but also very dangerous, for a young woman. Madame de Chartres saw this peril, and thought only of protecting her daughter from it. She besought her, not as a mother, but as a friend, to confide to her all the sweet speeches that might be made to her, and promised her aid in all those matters which so often embarrass the young.

The Chevalier de Guise made his feelings for Mademoiselle de Chartres and his intentions so manifest that every one could see them; yet he well knew the very grave difficulties that stood in his way. He was aware that he was not a desirable match, because his fortune was too small for his rank. He knew, too, that his brothers would disapprove of his marrying, through fear of the loss of position which sometimes befalls great families through the marriage of younger sons. The Cardinal of Lorraine soon proved to him that his fears were well grounded, for he denounced the chevalier's love for Mademoiselle de Chartres very warmly, though he concealed his true reasons. The cardinal nourished a hatred for the Vidame, which was hidden at the time, and only broke out later. He would have preferred to see his brother ally himself with any other family than that of the Vidame, and gave such public expression to his dislike that Madame de Chartres was plainly offended. She took great pains to show that the Cardinal of Lorraine had no cause for fear, and that she herself never contemplated the match. The Vidame adopted the same course, and with a better understanding of the cardinal's objection, because he knew the underlying reason.

The Prince of Clèves had concealed his passion quite as little as had the Chevalier de Guise. The Duke of Nevers was sorry to hear of this attachment, but thought that his son would forget it at a word from him; great was his surprise when he found him determined to marry Mademoiselle de Chartres. He opposed this determination with a warmth so ill concealed that the whole court soon had wind of it, and it came to the knowledge of her mother. She had never doubted that Monsieur de Nevers would regard this match as an advantageous one for his son, and was much surprised that both the house of Clèves and that of Guise dreaded the alliance instead of desiring it. She was so chagrined that she sought to marry her daughter to some one who could raise

---

2. Antoine de Bourbon (1518–1562), king of Navarre, father of Henri IV of France.

her above those who fancied themselves superior to her; and after carefully going over the ground, pitched on the prince dauphin, the son of the Duke of Montpensier. He was of the right age to marry, and held the highest position at court. Since Madame de Chartres was a very clever woman, and was aided by the Vidame, who at that time had great influence, while her daughter was in every way a good match, she played her cards so cleverly and successfully that Monsieur de Montpensier appeared to desire the marriage, and it seemed as if nothing could stand in its way.

The Vidame, though aware of Monsieur d'Anville's devotion to the crown princess, still thought that he might make use of the influence which she had over him to induce him to speak well of Mademoiselle de Chartres to the king and to the Prince of Montpensier, whose intimate friend he was. He mentioned this to the princess, who took up the matter eagerly, since it promised advancement to a young woman of whom she had become very fond. This she told the Vidame, assuring him that though she knew she should offend her uncle, the Cardinal of Lorraine, this would be no objection, because she had good grounds for disliking him, since he every day furthered the queen's interests in opposition to her own.

Persons in love are always glad of any excuse for talking about the object of their affection. As soon as the Vidame had gone, the crown princess ordered Châtelart, the favorite of Monsieur d'Anville and the confidant of his love for her, to tell him to be at the queen's reception that evening. Châtelart received this command with great delight. He belonged to a good family of Dauphiné, but his merit and intelligence had raised him to a higher place than his birth warranted. He was received and treated with kindness by all the great lords at the court, and the favor of the family of Montmorency had attached him especially to Monsieur d'Anville. He was handsome and skilled in all physical exercises; he sang agreeably, wrote verses, and had a gallant, ardent nature, which so attracted Monsieur d'Anville that he made him a confidant of his love for the crown princess. The confidence brought him into the society of that lady, and thus began that unhappy passion, which robbed him of his reason and finally cost him his life.

Monsieur d'Anville did not fail to make his appearance that evening in the queen's drawing-room; he was pleased that the dauphiness had chosen him to aid her, and he promised faithfully to obey her commands. But Madame de Valentinois had heard of the contemplated marriage and had laid her plans to thwart it; she had been so successful in arousing the king's opposition that when Monsieur d'Anville spoke of it, he showed his disapproval, and commanded him to apprise the Prince of Montpensier of it. It is easy to imagine the feelings of Madame de Chartres at the failure of a plan she had so much desired, especially when her ill-success gave so great an advantage to her enemies and did so much harm to her daughter.

The crown princess kindly expressed to Mademoiselle de Chartres her regrets at not being able to further her interests. "You see," she said, "I have but very little power; I am so detested by the queen and the Duchess of Valentinois that they or their attendants always oppose everything I desire. Still," she added, "I have always tried to please them, and they hate me only on account of my mother, who used to fill them with uneasiness and jealousy. The king had been in love with her before he loved Madame de Valentinois, and in his early married life, before he had any children, though he loved this duchess, he seemed bent on dissolving that marriage to marry the queen my mother. Madame de Valentinois dreaded the woman he had loved so well, lest her wit and beauty should diminish her own power, and entered into an alliance with the constable, who was also opposed to the king's marrying a sister of the Guises. They won over the late king; and though he hated the Duchess of Valentinois as much as he loved the queen, he joined with them in preventing the king from dissolving his marriage. In order to make this impossible, they arranged my mother's marriage with the King of Scotland, whose first wife had been Madame Magdeleine, the king's sister,—this they did because it was the first thing that offered; though they broke the promises that had been made to the King of England, who was deeply in love with her. In fact, this matter nearly caused a falling out between the two kings. Henry VIII could not be consoled for not marrying my mother; and whenever any other French princess was proposed to him, he used to say that she would never take the place of the one they had taken from him. It is true that my mother was a perfect beauty, and it is remarkable that when she was the widow of a duke of Longueville, three kings should have wanted to marry her. It was her misfortune to be married to the least important of them all, and to be sent to a kingdom where she has found nothing but unhappiness. I am told that I am like her; I dread the same sad fate, and whatever happiness seems to be awaiting me, I doubt if I ever enjoy it."

Mademoiselle de Chartres assured the crown princess that these gloomy presentiments were so fantastic that they could not long disturb her, and that she ought not to doubt that her good fortune would give the lie to her fears.

Henceforth no one dared to think of Mademoiselle de Chartres, through fear of displeasing the king or of not succeeding in winning a young woman who had aspired to a prince of the blood. None of these considerations moved Monsieur de Clèves. The death of his father, the Duke of Nevers, which happened at that time, left him free to follow his own inclinations, and as soon as the period of mourning had passed, he thought of nothing but marrying Mademoiselle de Chartres. He was glad to make his proposal at a time when circumstances had driven away all rivals and when he felt almost sure that she would not refuse him. What dimmed his joy was the fear of not being agreeable to her; and he would have preferred the happiness of pleasing her to the certainty of marrying her when she did not love him.

The Chevalier de Guise had somewhat aroused his jealousy; but since this was inspired more by his rival's merits than by the conduct of Mademoiselle de Chartres, he thought of nothing but ascertaining whether by good fortune she would approve of his designs. He met her only at the queen's rooms or in company, yet he managed to speak to her of his intentions and hopes in the most respectful way; he begged her to let him know how she felt towards him, and told her that his feelings for her were such that he should be forever unhappy if she obeyed her mother only from a sense of duty.

Mademoiselle de Chartres, having a very noble heart, was really grateful to the Prince of Clèves for what he did. This gratitude lent to her answer a certain gentleness, which was quite sufficient to feed the hope of a man as much in love as he was, and he counted on attaining at least a part of what he desired.

Mademoiselle repeated this conversation to her mother, who said that Monsieur de Clèves was of such high birth, possessed so many fine qualities, and seemed so discreet for a man of his age, that if she inclined to marry him she would herself gladly give her consent. Mademoiselle de Chartres replied that she had noticed the same fine qualities, and that she would rather marry him than any one else, but that she had no special love for him.

The next day the prince had his offer formally made to Madame de Chartres; she accepted it, being willing to give her daughter a husband she did not love. The marriage settlement was drawn up, the king was told of it, and the marriage became known to every one.

Monsieur de Clèves was very happy, although not perfectly satisfied; it gave him much pain to see that what Mademoiselle de Chartres felt for him was only esteem and gratitude, and he could not flatter himself that she nourished any warmer feeling; for had she done so, she would have readily shown it in their closer intimacy. Within a few days he complained to her of this.

"Is it possible," he said, "that I may not be happy in my marriage? Yet assuredly I am not happy. You have a sort of kindly feeling for me which cannot satisfy me; you are not impatient, uneasy, or grieved: you are as indifferent to my love as if this were given to your purse, and not to your charms."

"You do wrong to complain," she replied. "I do not know what more you can ask; it seems to me that you have no right to demand anything more."

"It is true," he said, "that you have a certain air with which I should be satisfied if there were anything behind it; but instead of your being restrained by a sense of propriety, it is a sense of propriety which inspires your actions. I do not touch your feelings or your heart; my presence causes you neither pleasure nor pain."

"You cannot doubt," she made answer, "that I am glad to see you, and I blush so often when I do see you that you may be sure that the sight of you affects me."

"I am not deceived by your blushes," he urged; "they come from modesty, and not from any thrill of your heart, and I do not exaggerate their importance."

Mademoiselle de Chartres did not know what to answer; these distinctions were outside of her experience. Monsieur de Clèves saw only too well how far removed she was from feeling for him as he should have liked, when he saw that she had no idea of what that feeling was.

The Chevalier de Guise returned from a journey a few days before the wedding. He had seen so many insurmountable obstacles in the way of his marrying Mademoiselle de Chartres that he knew he had no chance of success; yet he was evidently distressed at seeing her become the wife of another. This grief did not extinguish his passion, and he remained quite as much in love as before. Mademoiselle de Chartres had not been ignorant of his devotion. On his return he let her know that she was the cause of the deep gloom that marked his face; and he had so much merit and charm that it was almost impossible to make him unhappy without regretting it. Hence she was depressed; but this pity went no further, and she told her mother how much pain this prince's love caused her.

Madame de Chartres admired her daughter's frankness, and with good reason, for it could not be fuller or simpler; she regretted, however, that her heart was not touched, especially when she saw that the prince had not affected it any more than the others. Hence she took great pains to attach her to her future husband, and to impress upon her what she owed him for the interest he had taken in her before he knew who she was, and for the proof he had given of his love in choosing her at a time when no one else ventured to think of her.

The marriage ceremony took place at the Louvre,[3] and in the evening the king and queen, with all the court, supped at the house of Madame de Chartres, who received them with great splendor. The Chevalier de Guise did not venture to make himself conspicuous by staying away, but his dejection was evident.

Monsieur de Clèves did not find that Mademoiselle de Chartres had altered her feelings when she changed her name. His position as her husband gave him greater privileges, but no different place in her heart. Though he had married her, he did not cease to be her lover,[4] because there was always left something for him to desire; and though she lived on the best of terms with him, he was not yet perfectly happy. He preserved for her a violent and restless passion, which marred his joy. Jealousy had no part in it, for never had a husband been further from feeling it, or a wife from inspiring it. Yet she was exposed to all the temptations of the court, visiting the queen and the king's sister every day. All the young and fashionable men met her at her own house and at that of her brother-in-law, the Duke of Nevers, whose doors were always open; but she always had an air that inspired respect, and seemed so remote from gallantry that the Marshal of Saint-André, though bold and protected by the king's favor, was touched by her beauty without venturing to show it except by delicate attentions. There were many others who felt as did the marshal; and Madame de Chartres added to her daughter's natural modesty such a keen sense of propriety that she made her seem like a woman to be sighed for in vain.

The Duchess of Lorraine, while trying to bring about peace, had also tried to arrange the marriage of her son, the Duke of Lorraine, and had succeeded; he was to marry Madame Claude of France, the king's second daughter. The wedding had been settled for the month of February.

Meanwhile the Duke of Nemours had remained at Brussels, completely taken up with his plans for England. He was always sending and receiving messengers. His hopes grew from day to day, and at last Lignerolles told him that it was time for him to appear and finish in person what had been so well begun. He received this news with all the satisfaction that an ambitious man can feel at seeing himself raised to a throne simply through his reputation. He had gradually grown so accustomed to the contemplation of this great piece of good fortune that whereas at first he had regarded it as an impossibility, all difficulties had vanished, and he foresaw no obstacles.

He at once despatched to Paris orders for a magnificent outfit, that he might make his appearance in England with a splendor proportionate to his designs, and also hastened to court to be present at the wedding of the Duke of Lorraine. He arrived the day before the formal betrothal, and that same evening went to report to the king the condition of affairs and to receive his advice and commands about his future conduct. Thence he went to pay his respects to the queens. Madame de Clèves was not there, so that she did not see him, and was not even aware of his arrival. She had heard every one speak of this prince as the handsomest and most agreeable man at court, and Madame the Dauphi-

---

3. At this time, a royal residence.   **4.** I.e., he continued to love her.

ness had spoken of him so often and in such terms that she felt some curiosity to see him.

Madame de Clèves spent the day of the betrothal at home dressing herself for the ball in the evening at the Louvre. When she made her appearance, her beauty and the splendor of her dress aroused general admiration. The ball opened, and while she was dancing with Monsieur de Guise, there was a certain commotion at the door of the ballroom, as if some one were entering for whom way was being made. Madame de Clèves finished her dance, and while she was looking about for another partner, the king called out to her to take the gentleman who had just arrived. She turned, and saw a man, who she thought must be Monsieur de Nemours, stepping over some seats to reach the place where the dancing was going on. No one ever saw this prince for the first time without amazement; and this evening he was more striking than ever in the rich attire which set off his natural beauty to such great advantage; and it was also hard to see Madame de Clèves for the first time without astonishment.

Monsieur de Nemours was so amazed by her beauty that when he drew near her and bowed to her he could not conceal his wonder and delight. When they began their dance, a murmur of admiration ran through the ball-room. The king and the queens remembered that the pair had never met, and saw how strange it was that they should be dancing together without being acquainted. They summoned them when they had finished the set, and without giving them a chance to speak to any one, asked if each would not like to know who the other was, and whether either had any idea.

"As for me, Madame," said Monsieur de Nemours, "I have no doubts; but since Madame de Clèves has not the same reasons for guessing who I am that I have for recognizing her, I must beg your Majesty to be good enough to tell her my name."

"I fancy," said the dauphiness, "that she knows it as well as you know hers."

"I assure you, Madame," said Madame de Clèves, who seemed a little embarrassed, "that I cannot guess so well as you think."

"You can guess very well," replied the dauphiness, "and you are very kind to Monsieur de Nemours in your unwillingness to acknowledge that you recognize him without ever having seen him before."

The queen interrupted the conversation, that the ball might go on, and Monsieur de Nemours danced with the dauphiness. This lady was a perfect beauty, and had always appeared to be one in the eyes of Monsieur de Nemours before he went to Flanders; but all that evening he admired no one but Madame de Clèves.

The Chevalier de Guise, who never ceased worshipping her, was standing near, and this incident caused him evident pain. He regarded it as a sure sign that fate meant that Monsieur de Nemours should fall in love with Madame de Clèves; and whether it was that he saw something in her face, or that jealousy sharpened his fears, he believed that she had been moved by the sight of this prince, and he could not keep from telling her that Monsieur de Nemours was very fortunate in making her acquaintance in such a gallant and unusual way.

Madame de Clèves went home so full of what had happened at the ball that though it was very late, she went to her mother's room to tell her about it; and she praised Monsieur de Nemours with a certain air that made Madame de Chartres entertain the same suspicion as the Chevalier de Guise.

The next day the wedding took place; Madame de Clèves there saw the Duke of Nemours, and was even more struck by his admirable grace and dignity than before.

On succeeding days she met him at the drawing-room of the dauphiness, saw him playing tennis with the king and riding at the ring, and heard him talk; and she always found him so superior to every one else, and so much outshining all in conversation wherever he might be, by the grace of his person and the charm of his wit, that he soon made a deep impression on her heart.

Then, too, the desire to please made the Duke of Nemours, who was already deeply interested, more charming than ever; and since they met often, and found each other more attractive than any one else at court, they naturally experienced great delight in being together.

The Duchess of Valentinois took part in all the merry-making, and the king showed her all the interest and attention that he had done when first in love with her. Madame de Clèves, who was then of an age at which it is usual to believe that no woman can ever be loved after she is twenty-five years old, regarded with great amazement the king's attachment to this duchess, who was a grandmother and had just married[5] her granddaughter. She often spoke of it to Madame de Chartres. "Is it possible," she asked, "that the king has been in love so long? How could he get interested in a woman much older than himself, and who had been his father's mistress, as well as that of a great many other men, as I have heard?"

"It is true," was the answer, "that neither merit nor fidelity inspired the king's passion, or has kept it alive. And this is something which is scarcely to be excused; for had this woman had youth and beauty as well as rank, had she loved no one else, had she loved the king with untiring constancy, for himself alone, and not solely for his wealth and position, and had she used her power for worthy objects such as the king desired, it would have been easy to admire his great devotion to her. If," Madame de Chartres went on, "I were not afraid that you would say of me what is always said of women of my age, that we like to talk about old times, I would tell you the beginning of the king's love for this duchess; and many things that happened at the court of the late king bear much resemblance to what is now going on."

"So far from accusing you of repeating old stories," said Madame de Clèves, "I regret that you have told me so little about the present, and that you have not taught me the different interests and intrigues of the court. I am so ignorant of them that a few days ago I thought the constable was on the best of terms with the queen."

"You were very far from the truth," replied Madame de Chartres. "The queen hates the constable, and if she ever gets any power he will learn it very quickly. She knows that he has often told the king that of all his children it is only his bastards who look like him."

"I should never have imagined this hatred," interrupted Madame de Clèves, "after seeing the zeal with which the queen wrote to the constable when he was in prison, the joy she manifested at his return, and the familiarity of her address as regards him."

5. Married off.

"If you judge from appearances here," replied Madame de Chartres, "you will be often mistaken; what appears is seldom the truth.

"But to return to Madame de Valentinois: you know her name is Diane de Poitiers. She is of illustrious family, being descended from the old dukes of Aquitaine; her grandmother was a natural daughter of Louis XI,—in short, there is no common blood in her veins. Saint-Vallier, her father, was implicated in the affair of the Constable of Bourbon, of which you have heard, was condemned to be beheaded, and was led to the scaffold. His daughter, who was remarkably beautiful, and had already pleased the late king, managed, I don't know how, to save her father's life. His pardon was granted him when he was expecting the mortal stroke; but fear had so possessed him that he did not recover consciousness, but died a few days later. His daughter made her appearance at court as the king's mistress. His journey to Italy and his imprisonment interrupted this passion. When he returned from Spain and Madame de la Regente went to meet him at Bayonne, she had with her all her young women, among whom was Mademoiselle de Pisseleu, afterwards Duchess of Estampes. The king fell in love with her, though she was inferior in birth, beauty, and intelligence to Madame de Valentinois: the only advantage she had was that she was younger. I have often heard her say that she was born on the day that Diane de Poitiers was married; but that remark was more malicious than truthful, for I am much mistaken if the Duchess of Valentinois did not marry Monsieur de Brézé, grand seneschal of Normandy, at the same time that the king fell in love with Madame d'Estampes. Never was there fiercer hatred than existed between those two women. The Duchess of Valentinois could not forgive Madame d'Estampes for depriving her of the title of the king's mistress. Madame d'Estampes was madly jealous of Madame de Valentinois because the king maintained his relations with her. This king was never rigorously faithful to his mistresses; there was always one who had the title and the honors, but the ladies of what was called the little band shared his attentions. The death of his oldest son, it was supposed by poison, at Tournon, was a great blow to him. He had much less love for his second son, the present king, who was in every way far less to his taste, and whom he even regarded as lacking courage and spirit. He was lamenting this one day to Madame de Valentinois, whereupon she said she would like to make him fall in love with her, that he might become livelier and more agreeable. She succeeded, as you know. This love has lasted more than twenty years, without being dimmed by time or circumstances.

"At first the late king objected to it,—whether because he was still enough in love with Madame de Valentinois to feel jealous, or because he was influenced by Madame d'Estampes, who was in despair when the dauphin became attached to her enemy, is uncertain; however that may be, he viewed this passion with an anger and a disapproval that were apparent every day. His son feared neither his wrath nor his hate; and since nothing could induce him to abate or to conceal his attachment, the king was forced to endure it as best he could. His son's opposition to his wishes estranged him still more, and attached him more closely to the Duke of Orléans, his third son. This prince was handsome, energetic, ambitious, of a somewhat tempestuous nature, which needed to be controlled, but who in time would become a really fine man.

"The elder son's rank as dauphin and the father's preference for the Duke of Orléans inspired a rivalry between them which amounted to hatred. This rivalry had begun in their childhood, and lasted until the death of the latter. When the emperor entered French territory[6] he gave his whole preference to the Duke of Orléans. This so pained the dauphin that when the emperor was at Chantilly he tried to compel the constable to arrest him, without waiting for the king's orders; but the constable refused. Afterward the king blamed him for not following his son's advice; and this had a good deal to do with his leaving the court.

"The division between the two brothers induced the Duchess of Estampes to rely on the Duke of Orléans for protection against the influence which Madame de Valentinois had over the king. In this she succeeded; the duke, without falling in love with her, was as warm in defence of her interests as was the dauphin in defence of those of Madame de Valentinois. Hence there were two cabals in the court such as you can imagine; but the intrigues were not limited to two women's quarrels.

"The emperor, who had maintained his friendship for the Duke of Orléans, had frequently offered him the duchy of Milan. In the subsequent negotiations about peace, he raised hopes in the breast of the duke that he would give him the seventeen provinces[7] and his daughter's hand. The dauphin, however, desired neither peace nor this marriage. He made use of the constable, whom he had always loved, to convince the king how important it was not to give to his successor a brother so powerful as would be the Duke of Orléans in alliance with the emperor and governing the seventeen provinces. The constable agreed the more heartily with the dauphin's views because he also opposed those of Madame d'Estampes, who was his avowed enemy, and ardently desired that the power of the Duke of Orléans should be increased.

"At that time the dauphin was in command of the king's army in Champagne, and had reduced that of the emperor to such extremities that it would have utterly perished had not the Duchess of Estampes, fearing that too great success would prevent our granting peace and consenting to the marriage, secretly sent word to the enemy to surprise Epernay and Château-Thierry, which were full of supplies. This they did, and thereby saved their whole army.

"This duchess did not long profit by her treason. Soon afterward the Duke of Orléans died at Farmoutier of some contagious disease. He loved one of the most beautiful women of the court, and was beloved by her. I shall not tell you who it was, because her life since that time has been most decorous; and she has tried so hard to have her affection for the prince forgotten that she deserves to have her reputation left untarnished. It so happened that she heard of her husband's death on the same day that she heard of that of Monsieur d'Orléans; consequently she was able to conceal her real grief without an effort.

"The king did not long survive his son's decease,—he died two years later. He urged the dauphin to make use of the services of the Cardinal of Tournon and of the Amiral d'Annebauld, without saying a word about the constable, who at that time was banished to Chantilly. Nevertheless, the first thing the present king did after his father's death was to call the constable back and intrust him with the management of affairs.

---

6. Despite the enmity between France and the empire, Charles V was allowed to cross France in 1539 on his way to put down a revolt in the Netherlands.

7. The Spanish Netherlands, which included most of modern Belgium and Holland.

"Madame d'Estampes was sent away, and became the victim of all the ill-treatment she might have expected from an all-powerful enemy. The Duchess of Valentinois took full vengeance on this duchess and on all who had displeased her. Her power over the king seemed the greater because it had not appeared while he was dauphin. During the twelve years of his reign she has been in everything absolute mistress. She disposes of places and controls affairs of every sort; she secured the dismissal of the Cardinal of Tournon, of the Chancelier Olivier, and of Villeroy. Those who have endeavored to open the king's eyes to her conduct have been ruined for their pains. The Count of Taix, commander-in-chief of the artillery, who did not like her, could not keep from talking about her love affairs, and especially about one with the Count of Brissac, of whom the king was already very jealous. Yet she managed so well that the Count of Taix was disgraced and deprived of his position; and impossible as it may sound, he was succeeded by the Count of Brissac, whom she afterward made a marshal of France. Still, the king's jealousy became so violent that he could not endure having this marshal remain at court; but though usually jealousy is a hot and violent passion, it is modified and tempered in him by his extreme respect for his mistress, so that the only means he ventured to use to rid himself of his rival was by intrusting to him the government of Piedmont. There he has spent several years; last winter, however, he returned, under the pretext of asking for men and supplies for the army under his command. Possibly the desire of seeing Madame de Valentinois and dread of being forgotten had something to do with this journey. The king received him very coldly. The Guises, who do not like him, did not dare betray their feelings, on account of Madame de Valentinois, so they made use of the Vidame, his open enemy, to prevent his getting any of the things he wanted. It was not hard to injure him. The king hated him, and was made uneasy by his presence; consequently he was obliged to go back without getting any advantage from his journey,—unless, possibly, he had rekindled in the heart of Madame de Valentinois feelings which absence had nearly extinguished. The king has had many other grounds for jealousy, but either he has not known them, or he has not dared to complain.

"I am not sure, my dear," added Madame de Chartres, "that you may not think I have told you more than you cared to hear."

"Not at all," answered Madame de Clèves; "and if I were not afraid of tiring you, I should ask you many more questions."

Monsieur de Nemours' love for Madame de Clèves was at first so violent that he lost all interest in those he had formerly loved, and with whom he had kept up relations during his absence. He not merely did not seek any excuses for deserting them, he would not even listen to their complaints or reply to their reproaches. The dauphiness, for whom he had nourished very warm feelings, was soon forgotten by the side of Madame de Clèves. His impatience for his journey to England began to abate, and he ceased to hasten his preparations for departure. He often visited the crown princess, because Madame de Clèves was frequently in her apartments, and he was not unwilling to give some justification to the widespread suspicions about his feelings for the dauphiness. Madame de Clèves seemed to him so rare a prize that he decided to conceal all signs of his love rather than let it be generally known. He never spoke of it even to his intimate friend the Vidame de Chartres, to whom he usually confided everything. He was so cautious and discreet that no one suspected his love for Madame de Clèves except the Chevalier de Guise; and the lady herself would scarcely have perceived it had not her own interest in him made her watch him very closely, so that she became sure of it.

Madame de Clèves did not find herself so disposed to tell her mother what she thought of this prince's feelings as had been the case with her other lovers; and without definitely deciding on reserve, she yet never spoke of the subject. But Madame de Chartres soon perceived this, as well as her daughter's interest in him. This knowledge gave her distinct pain, for she well understood how dangerous it was for Madame de Clèves to be loved by a man like Monsieur de Nemours, especially when she was already disposed to admire him. An incident that happened a few days later confirmed her suspicions of this liking.

The Marshal of Saint-André, who was always on the look-out for opportunities to display his magnificence, made a pretext of desiring to show his house, which had just been finished, and invited the king to do him the honor of supping there with the queens. The marshal was also glad to be able to show to Madame de Clèves his lavish splendor.

A few days before the one of the supper, the dauphin, whose health was delicate, had been ailing and had seen no one. His wife, the crown princess, had spent the whole day with him, and toward evening, as he felt better, he received all the persons of quality who were in his ante-chamber. The crown princess went to her own apartment, where she found Madame de Clèves and a few other ladies with whom she was most intimate.

Since it was already late, and the crown princess was not dressed, she did not go to the queen, but sent word she could not come; she then had her jewels brought, to decide what she should wear at the Marshal of Saint-André's ball, and to give some, according to a promise she had made, to Madame de Clèves. While they were thus occupied, the Prince of Condé, whose rank gave him free admission everywhere, entered. The crown princess said to him that he doubtless came from her husband, and asked what was going on in his apartments.

"They are having a discussion, Madame, with Monsieur de Nemours," he answered. "He defends the side he has taken so eagerly that he must have a personal interest in it. I fancy he has a mistress who makes him uneasy when she goes to a ball, for he maintains that it makes a lover unhappy to see the woman he loves at such a place."

"What!" said the dauphiness, "Monsieur de Nemours does not want his mistress to go to a ball? I thought husbands might object, but I never supposed that lovers could have such a feeling."

"Monsieur de Nemours," replied the Prince of Condé, "declares that a ball is most distressing to lovers, whether they are loved or not. He says if their love is returned, they have the pain of being loved less for several days; that there is not a woman in the world who is not prevented from thinking of her lover by the demands of her toilet,[8] which entirely engrosses her attention; that women dress for every one as well as for those they love; that when they are at the ball they are anxious to please all who look at them; that when they are proud of their beauty, they feel a pleasure in which the lover plays but a small part. He says, too, that one who sighs in vain suffers even more when he sees his mis-

---

8. The process of dressing.

tress at an entertainment; that the more she is admired by the public, the more one suffers at not being loved, through fear lest her beauty should kindle some love happier than his own; finally, that there is no pain so keen as seeing one's mistress at a ball, except knowing that she is there while absent one's self."

Madame de Clèves, though pretending not to hear what the Prince of Condé was saying, listened attentively. She readily understood her share in the opinion expressed by Monsieur de Nemours, especially when he spoke of his grief at not being at the ball with his mistress, because he was not to be at that given by the Marshal of Saint-André, being ordered by the king to go to meet the Duke of Ferrara.

The crown princess laughed with the Prince of Condé, and expressed her disapproval of the views of Monsieur de Nemours. "There is only one condition, Madame," said the prince, "on which Monsieur de Nemours is willing that his mistress should go to a ball, and that is that he himself should give her permission. He said that last year when he gave a ball to your Majesty, he thought that his mistress did him a great favor in coming to it, though she seemed to be there only as one of your suite; that it is always a kindness to a lover to take part in any entertainment that he gives; and that it is also agreeable to a lover to have his mistress see him the host of the whole court and doing the honors fittingly."

"Monsieur de Nemours did well," said the dauphiness, with a smile, "to let his mistress go to that ball; for so many women claimed that position that if they had not come, there would have been scarcely any one there."

As soon as the Prince of Condé had begun to speak of what Monsieur de Nemours thought of the ball, Madame de Clèves was very anxious not to go to that of the Marshal of Saint-André. She readily agreed that it was not fitting for a woman to go to the house of a man who was in love with her, and she was glad to have so good a reason for doing a kindness to Monsieur de Nemours. Nevertheless, she took away the jewels which the crown princess had given her; that evening, however, when she showed them to her mother, she told her that she did not mean to wear them, that the Marshal of Saint-André had made his love for her so manifest that she felt sure he meant to have it thought that she was to have some part in the entertainment he was to give to the king, and that under the pretext of doing honor to the king he would pay her attentions which might perhaps prove embarrassing.

Madame de Chartres argued for some time against her daughter's decision, which she thought singular, but at last yielded, and told her she must pretend to be ill, in order to have a good excuse for not going, because her real reasons would not be approved and should not be suspected. Madame de Clèves gladly consented to stay at home for a few days, in order not to meet Monsieur de Nemours, who left without having the pleasure of knowing that she was not going to the ball.

The duke returned the day after the ball, and heard that she had not been there; but inasmuch as he did not know that his talk with the dauphin had been repeated to her, he was far from thinking that he was fortunate enough to be the cause of her absence.

The next day, when Monsieur de Nemours was calling on the queen and talking with the dauphiness, Madame de Chartres and Madame de Clèves happened to come in and approached this princess. Madame de Clèves was not in full dress, as if she were not very well, though her countenance belied her attire.

"You look so well," said the crown princess, "that I can scarcely believe that you have been ill. I fancy that the Prince of Condé, when he told you what Monsieur de Nemours thought about the ball, convinced you that you would do a kindness to the Marshal of Saint-André by going to his ball, and that that was the reason you stayed away."

Madame de Clèves blushed at the dauphiness's accurate guess which she thus expressed before Monsieur de Nemours.

Madame de Chartres saw at once why her daughter did not go to the ball, and in order to throw Monsieur de Nemours off the track, she at once addressed the dauphiness with an air of sincerity. "I assure you, Madame," she said, "that your Majesty pays an honor to my daughter which she does not deserve. She was really ill; but I am sure that if I had not forbidden it, she would have accompanied you, unfit as she was, to have the pleasure of seeing the wonderful entertainment last evening."

The dauphiness believed what Madame de Chartres said, and Monsieur de Nemours was vexed to see how probable her story was; nevertheless the confusion of Madame de Clèves made him suspect that the dauphiness's conjecture was not without some foundation in fact. At first Madame de Clèves had been annoyed because Monsieur de Nemours had reason to suppose that it was he who had kept her from going to the ball, and then she felt regret that her mother had entirely removed the grounds for this supposition.

Although the attempt to make peace at Cercamp had failed, negotiations still continued, and matters had assumed such a shape that toward the end of February a meeting was held at Cateau-Cambrésis.[9] The same commissioners had assembled there, and the departure of the Marshal of Saint-André freed Monsieur de Nemours from a rival who was more to be dreaded on account of his close observation of all those who approached Madame de Clèves than from any real success of his own.

Madame de Chartres did not wish to let her daughter see that she knew her feeling for this prince, lest she should make her suspicious of the advice she wanted to give her. One day she began to talk about him. She spoke of him in warm terms, but craftily praised his discretion in being unable to fall really in love and in seeking only pleasure, not a serious attachment, in his relations with women. "To be sure," she went on, "he has been suspected of a great passion for the dauphiness; I notice that he visits her very often, and I advise you to avoid talking with him as much as possible, especially in private, because you are on such terms with the crown princess that people would say that you were their confidant, and you know how disagreeable that would be. I think that if the report continues, you would do well to see less of the crown princess, that you may not be connected with love-affairs of that sort."

Madame de Clèves had never heard Monsieur de Nemours and the dauphiness talked about, and was much surprised by what her mother said. She was

---

9. Negotiations were beginning toward a peace treaty between France and the empire. The death of Queen Mary of England ended the preliminary meetings that had begun at Cercamp in 1558; they resumed the next year and ended with the Treaty of Cateau-Cambrésis.

so sure that she had misunderstood the prince's feelings for her that she changed color. Madame de Chartres noticed this, but company coming in at that moment, Madame de Clèves went home and locked herself up in her room.

It is impossible to express her grief when her mother's words opened her eyes to the interest she took in Monsieur de Nemours; she had never dared to acknowledge it to herself. Then she saw that her feelings for him were what Monsieur de Clèves had so often supplicated, and she felt the mortification of having them for another than a husband who so well deserved them. She felt hurt and embarrassed, fearing that Monsieur de Nemours might have used her as a pretext for seeing the dauphiness; and this thought decided her to tell Madame de Chartres what she had hitherto kept secret.

The next morning she went to her mother to carry out this decision; but Madame de Chartres was a little feverish, and did not care to talk with her. The illness seemed so slight, however, that Madame de Clèves called on the dauphiness after dinner, and found her in her room with two or three ladies with whom she was on intimate terms.

"We were talking about Monsieur de Nemours," said the queen when she saw her, "and were surprised to see how much he is changed since his return from Brussels; before he went, he had an infinite number of mistresses, and it was a positive disadvantage to him, because he used to be kind both to those who were worthy and to those who were not. Since his return, however, he will have nothing to do with any of them. There has never been such a change. His spirits, moreover, seem to be affected, as he is much less cheerful than usual."

Madame de Clèves made no answer; she thought with a sense of shame that she would have taken all that they said about the change in him for a proof of his passion if she had not been undeceived. She was somewhat vexed with the dauphiness for trying to explain and for expressing surprise at something of which she must know the real reason better than any one else. She could not keep from showing her annoyance, and when the other ladies withdrew, she went up to the crown princess and said in a low voice,—

"Is it for my benefit that you have just spoken, and do you want to hide from me that you are the cause of the altered conduct of Monsieur de Nemours?"

"You are unjust," said the crown princess; "you know that I never keep anything from you. It is true that before he went to Brussels, Monsieur de Nemours meant to have me understand that he did not hate me; but since his return he seems to have forgotten all about it, and I confess that I am a little curious about the reason of this change. I shall probably find it out," she went on, "as the Vidame de Chartres, his intimate friend, is in love with a young woman over whom I have some power, and I shall know from her what has made this change."

The dauphiness spoke with an air that carried conviction to Madame de Clèves, who found herself calmer and happier than she had been before. When she went back to her mother, she found her much worse than when she had left her. She was more feverish, and for some days it seemed as if she were going to be really ill. Madame de Clèves was in great distress, and did not leave her mother's room. Monsieur de Clèves spent nearly all his time there too, both to comfort his wife and to have the pleasure of seeing her: his love had not lessened.

Monsieur de Nemours, who had always been one of his friends, had not neglected him since his return from Brussels. During the illness of Madame de Chartres he found it possible to see Madame de Clèves very often, under pretence of calling on her husband or of stopping to take him to walk. He even sought him at hours when he knew he was not in; then he would say that he would wait for him, and used to stay in the ante-chamber of Madame de Chartres, where were assembled many persons of quality. Madame de Clèves would often look in, and although she was in great anxiety, she seemed no less beautiful to Monsieur de Nemours. He showed her how much he sympathized with her distress, and soon convinced her that it was not with the dauphiness that he was in love.

She could not keep from being embarrassed, and yet delighted to see him; but when he was out of her sight and she remembered that this pleasure was the beginning of an unhappy passion, she felt she almost hated him, so much did the idea of guilty love pain her.

Madame de Chartres rapidly grew worse, and soon her life was despaired of; she heard the doctors' opinion of her danger with a courage proportionate to her virtue and piety. After they had left her, she dismissed all who were present, and sent for Madame de Clèves.

"We have to part, my daughter," she said, holding out her hand; "and the peril in which you are and the need you have of me, double my pain in leaving you. You have an affection for Monsieur de Nemours; I do not ask you to confess it, as I am no longer able to make use of your sincerity in order to guide you. It is long since I perceived this affection, but I have been averse to speaking to you about it, lest you should become aware of it yourself. Now you know it only too well. You are on the edge of a precipice: a great effort, a violent struggle, alone can save you. Think of what you owe your husband, think of what you owe yourself, and remember that you are in danger of losing that reputation which you have acquired and which I have so ardently desired for you. Take strength and courage, my daughter: withdraw from the court; compel your husband to take you away. Do not be afraid of making a difficult decision. Terrible as it may appear at first, it will in the end be pleasanter than the consequences of a love-affair. If any other reasons than virtue and duty can persuade you to what I wish, let me say that if anything is capable of destroying the happiness I hope for in another world, it would be seeing you fall like so many women; but if this misfortune must come to you, I welcome death that I may not see it."

Madame de Clèves' tears fell on her mother's hand, which she held clasped in her own, and Madame de Chartres saw that she was moved. "Good-by, my daughter," she said; "let us put an end to a conversation which moves us both too deeply, and remember, if you can, all I have just said to you."

With these words she turned away and bade her daughter call her women, without hearing or saying more. Madame de Clèves left her mother's room in a state that may be imagined, and Madame de Chartres thought of nothing but preparing herself for death. She lingered two days more, but refused again to see her daughter,—the only person she loved.

Madame de Clèves was in sore distress; her husband never left her side, and as soon as Madame de Chartres had died, he took her into the country, to get her away from a place which continually renewed her grief, which was intense.

Although her love and gratitude to her mother counted for a great deal, the need she felt of her support against Monsieur de Nemours made the blow even more painful. She lamented being left to herself when she had her emotions so little under control, and when she so needed some one to pity her and give her strength. Her husband's kindness made her wish more than ever to be always true to him. She showed him more affection and kindliness than she had ever done before, and she wanted him always by her side; for it seemed to her that her attachment to him would prove a defence against Monsieur de Nemours.

This prince went to visit Monsieur de Clèves in the country, and did his best to see Madame de Clèves; but she declined to receive him, knowing that she could not fail to find him charming. Moreover, she resolutely determined to avoid every occasion of meeting him, so far as she was able.

Monsieur de Clèves repaired[1] to Paris to pay his respects at court, promising his wife to return the next day; but he did not return till the day after.

"I expected you all day yesterday," Madame de Clèves said to him when he arrived, "and I ought to find fault with you for not returning when you promised. You know that if I could feel a new sorrow in the state I am in, it would be at the death of Madame de Tournon, of which I heard this morning. I should have been distressed by it even if I had not known her. It is always painful when a young and beautiful woman like her dies after an illness of only two days, and much more so when it is one of the persons I liked best in the world, and who seemed as modest as she was worthy."

"I was sorry not to return yesterday," answered Monsieur de Clèves; "but it was so imperatively necessary that I should console an unhappy man that I could not possibly leave him. As for Madame de Tournon, I advise you not to be too profoundly distressed, if you mourn her as an upright woman who deserved your esteem."

"You surprise me," said Madame de Clèves, "as I have often heard you say that there was no woman at court whom you esteemed more highly."

"That is true," he answered; "but women are incomprehensible, and the more I see of them, the happier I feel that I have married you, and I cannot be sufficiently grateful for my good fortune."

"You think better of me than I deserve," exclaimed Madame de Clèves, with a sigh, "and it is much too soon to think me worthy of you. But tell me, please, what has undeceived you about Madame de Tournon."

"I have long been undeceived in regard to her," he replied, "and have long known that she loved the Count of Sancerre, to whom she held out hopes that she would marry him."

"I can scarcely believe," interrupted Madame de Clèves, "that Madame de Tournon, after the extraordinary reluctance to matrimony which she showed after she became a widow, and after her public assertions that she would never marry again, should have given Sancerre any hopes."

"If she had given them only to him," replied Monsieur de Clèves, "there would be little occasion for surprise; but what is astounding is that she also gave them to Estouteville at the same time, and I will tell you the whole story."

1. Went.

Part II

"You know," Monsieur de Clèves continued, "what good friends Sancerre and I are; yet when, about two years ago, he fell in love with Madame de Tournon, he took great pains to conceal it from me, as well as from every one else, and I was far from suspecting it. Madame de Tournon appeared still inconsolable for her husband's death, and was still living in the most absolute retirement. Sancerre's sister was almost the only person she saw, and it was at her house that the count fell in love with her.

"One evening when there was to be a play at the Louvre, and while they were waiting for the king and Madame de Valentinois in order to begin, word was brought that she was ill and that the king would not come. Every one guessed that the duchess's illness was some quarrel with the king. We knew how jealous he had been of the Marshal of Brissac during his stay at court; but the marshal had gone back to Piedmont a few days before, and we could not imagine the cause of this falling-out.

"While I was talking about it with Sancerre, Monsieur d'Anville came into the hall and whispered to me that the king was in a state of distress and anger most piteous to see; that when he and Madame de Valentinois were reconciled a few days before, after their quarrels about the Marshal of Brissac, the king had given her a ring and asked her to wear it. While she was dressing for the play, he had noticed its absence, and had asked her the reason. She seemed surprised to miss it, and asked her women for it; but they, unfortunately, perhaps because they had not been put on their guard, said that it was some four or five days since they had seen it.

" 'That exactly corresponded with the date of the Marshal of Brissac's departure,' Monsieur d'Anville went on; 'and the king is convinced that she gave him the ring when she bade him good-by. This thought has so aroused all his jealousy, which was by no means wholly extinguished, that, contrary to his usual custom, he flew into a rage and reproached her bitterly. He has gone back to his room in great distress, whether because he thinks that Madame de Valentinois has given away his ring, or because he fears that he has displeased her by his wrath, I do not know.'

"As soon as Monsieur d'Anville had finished, I went up to Sancerre to tell him the news, assuring him that it was a secret that had just been told me, and was to go no farther.

"The next morning I called rather early on my sister-in-law, and found Madame de Tournon there. She did not like Madame de Valentinois, and knew very well that my sister-in-law also had no reason for being fond of her. Sancerre had seen her when he left the play, and had told her about the king's quarrel with the duchess; this she had come to repeat to my sister-in-law, either not knowing or not remembering that it was I who had told her lover.

"When I came in, my sister-in-law said to Madame de Tournon that I could be trusted with what she had just told her, and without waiting for permission she repeated to me word for word everything I had told Sancerre the previous evening. You will understand my surprise. I looked at Madame de Tournon, who seemed embarrassed, and her embarrassment aroused my suspicions. I had mentioned the matter to no one but Sancerre, who had left me after the play, without saying where he was going; but I remembered hearing him praise

Madame de Tournon very warmly. All these things opened my eyes, and I soon decided that there was a love-affair between them, and that he had seen her after he left me.

"I was so annoyed to find that he kept the matter secret from me that I said a good many things that made it clear to Madame de Tournon that she had been imprudent; as I handed her to her carriage, I assured her that I envied the happiness of the person who had informed her of the falling-out of the king and Madame de Valentinois.

"At once I went to see Sancerre; I reproached him, and said that I knew of his passion for Madame de Tournon, but I did not say how I had found it out. He felt obliged to make a complete confession. I then told him how it was I had discovered his secret, and he told me all about the affair; he said that inasmuch as he was a younger son, and far from having any claims to such an honor, she was yet determined to marry him. No one could be more surprised than I was. I urged Sancerre to hasten his marriage, and told him that he would be justified in fearing anything from a woman who was so full of craft that she could play so false a part before the public. He said in reply that her grief had been sincere, but that it had yielded before her affection for him, and that she could not suddenly make this great change manifest. He brought up many other things in her defence, which showed me clearly how much in love he was; he assured me that he would persuade her to let me know all about the passion he had for her, since it was she who had let out the secret,—and in fact he compelled her to consent, though with much difficulty, and I was from that time fully admitted to their confidence.

"I have never seen a woman so honorable and agreeable toward her lover; yet I was always pained by her affectation of grief. Sancerre was so much in love, and so well satisfied with the way she treated him, that he was almost afraid to urge their marriage, lest she should think that he was moved thereto by interest rather than passion. Still, he often talked to her about it, and she seemed to have decided to marry him; she even began to leave her retirement and to reappear in the world,—she used to come to my sister-in-law's at the time when part of the court used to be there. Sancerre came very seldom; but those who were there every evening and met her often, found her very charming.

"Shortly after she began to come out again into society, Sancerre imagined that he detected some coolness in her love for him. He spoke to me about it several times without rousing any anxiety in me by his complaints; but when at length he told me that instead of hastening, she seemed to be postponing their marriage, I began to think that he had good grounds for uneasiness. I said that even if Madame de Tournon's passion should lessen after lasting for two years, he ought not to be surprised; that even if it did not lessen, and though it should not be strong enough to persuade her to marry him, he ought not to complain; since their marriage would injure her much in the eyes of the public, not only because he was not a very good match for her, but because it would affect her reputation: hence that all he could reasonably desire was that she should not deceive him and feed him with false hopes. I also said that if she had not the courage to marry him, or if she should confess that she loved some one else, he ought not to be angry or complain, but preserve his esteem and gratitude for her.

"'I give you the advice,' I said to him, 'which I should take myself; for I am so touched by sincerity that I believe that if my mistress, or my wife, were to confess that any one pleased her, I should be distressed without being angered, and should lay aside the character of lover or husband to advise and sympathize with her.'"

At these words Madame de Clèves blushed, finding a certain likeness to her own condition which surprised her and distressed her for some time.

"Sancerre spoke to Madame de Tournon," Monsieur de Clèves went on, "telling her everything I had advised; but she reassured him with such tact and seemed so pained by his suspicions that she entirely dispelled them. Nevertheless she postponed their marriage until after a long journey which he was about to make; but her conduct was so discreet up to the time of his departure, and she seemed so grieved at parting with him, that I, as well as he, believed that she truly loved him. He went away about three months ago. During his absence I saw Madame de Tournon very seldom; you have taken up all my time, and I only knew that Sancerre was to return soon.

"The day before yesterday, on my arrival in Paris, I heard that she was dead. I at once sent to his house to find out if they had heard from him, and was told that he had arrived the day before,—the very day of Madame de Tournon's death. I went at once to see him, knowing very well in what a state I should find him; but his agony far exceeded what I had imagined. Never have I seen such deep and tender grief. As soon as he saw me, he embraced me, bursting into tears. 'I shall never see her again,' he said, 'I shall never see her again; she is dead! I was not worthy of her; but I shall soon follow her.'

"After that he was silent; then from time to time he repeated: 'She is dead, and I shall never see her again!' Thereupon he would again burst into tears, and seemed out of his head. He told me he had received but few letters from her while away, but that this did not surprise him, because he well knew her aversion to running any risk in writing letters. He had no doubt that she would have married him on his return; and he looked upon her as the most amiable and faithful woman who had ever lived; he believed that she loved him tenderly, and that he had lost her at the moment when he made sure of winning her forever. These thoughts plunged him into the deepest distress, by which he was wholly overcome, and I confess that I was deeply moved.

"Nevertheless, I was obliged to leave him to go to the king, but I promised to return soon. This I did; but imagine my surprise when I found that he was in an entirely different mood. He was pacing up and down his room with a wild face, and he stopped as if he were beside himself and said: 'Come, come! see the most desperate man in the world; I am ten thousand times unhappier than I was before, and what I have just heard of Madame de Tournon is worse than her death.'

"I thought that his grief had crazed him, for I could imagine nothing more terrible than the death of a loved mistress who returns one's love. I told him that so long as his grief had been within bounds I had understood and sympathized with it; but that I should cease to pity him if he gave way to despair and lost his mind. 'I wish I could lose it, and my life too,' he exclaimed. 'Madame de Tournon was unfaithful to me; and I ascertained her infidelity and treachery the day after I heard of her death, at a time when my soul was filled with the deepest grief and the tenderest love that were ever felt,—at a time when my heart was filled with the thought of her as the most perfect creature that had ever lived, and the most generous to me. I find that I was mistaken in her, and that she does not deserve my tears; nevertheless, I have the same grief from her death as if she had been faithful to me, and I suffer from her infidelity as if she were not dead. Had I known of her changed feeling before she died, I should have been wild with wrath and jealousy, and should have been in some way hardened against the blow of her death; but now I can get no consolation from it or hate her.'

"You may judge of my surprise at what Sancerre told me; I asked him how he found this out. He told me that the moment I had left his room, Estouteville, an intimate friend of his, though he knew nothing of his love for Madame de Tournon, had come to see him; that as soon as he had sat down, he burst into tears and said he begged his pardon for not having told him before what he was about to say; that he had come to open his heart to him; and that he saw before him a man utterly crushed by the death of Madame de Tournon.

" 'That name,' said Sancerre, 'surprised me so that my first impulse was to tell him that I was much more distressed than he; but I was unable to speak a word. He went on and told me that he had been in love with her for six months; that he had always meant to tell me, but she had forbidden it so firmly that he had not dared to disobey her; that almost ever since he fell in love with her she had taken a tender interest in him; that he only visited her secretly; that he had had the pleasure of consoling her for the loss of her husband; and, finally, that he was on the point of marrying her at the time of her death, but that this marriage, which would have been one of love, would have appeared to be one of duty and obedience, because she had won over her father to command this marriage, in order that there should not be any great change in her conduct, which had indicated an unwillingness to contract a second marriage.

" 'While Estouteville was speaking,' Sancerre went on, 'I fully believed him, because what he said seemed likely, and the time he had mentioned as that when he fell in love with Madame de Tournon coincided with that of her altered treatment of me. But a moment after, I thought him a liar, or at least out of his senses, and I was ready to tell him so. I thought, however, I would first make sure; hence I began to question him and to show that I had my doubts. At last I was so persistent in the search of my unhappiness that he asked if I knew Madame de Tournon's handwriting, and placed on my bed four of her letters and her portrait. My brother happened to come in at that moment. Estouteville's face was so stained with tears that he had to go away in order not to be seen in that state; he told me that he would come back that evening to get the things he left. I sent my brother away, pretending that I was not feeling well, being impatient to read the letters, and still hoping to find something which would convince me that Estouteville was mistaken. But, alas, what did I not find! What tenderness, what protestations, what promises to marry him, what letters! She had never written me any like them. So,' he went on, 'I suffer at the same time grief for her death and for her faithlessness,—two misfortunes which have often been compared, but have never been felt at the same time by one person. I confess, to my shame, that I feel much more keenly her death than her change; I cannot find her guilty enough to deserve to die. If she were still alive, I should have the pleasure of reproaching her, of avenging myself by showing her how great was her injustice. But I shall never see her again.' He repeated, 'I shall never see her again,—that is the bitterest blow of all; I would gladly give up my life for hers. What a wish! If she were to return, she would live for Estouteville. How happy I was yesterday!' he exclaimed, 'how happy I was then! I was the most sorely distressed man in the world; but my distress was in the order of nature, and I drew some comfort from the thought that I could never be consoled. To-day all my feelings are false ones; I pay to the pretended love she felt for me the same tribute that I thought due to a real affection. I can neither hate nor love her memory; I am incapable of consolation or of grief. At least,' he said, turning suddenly toward me, 'let me, I beg of you, never see Estouteville again; his very name fills me with horror. I know very well that I have no reason to blame him; it is my own fault for concealing from him my love for Madame de Tournon: if he had known of it, he would perhaps have never cared for her, and she would not have been unfaithful to me. He came to see me to confide his grief; I really pity him. Yes, and with good reason,' he exclaimed; 'he loved Madame de Tournon and was loved by her. He will never see her again; yet I feel that I cannot keep from hating him. Once more, I beg of you never to let me see him again.'

"Thereupon Sancerre burst again into tears, mourning Madame de Tournon, saying to her the tenderest things imaginable; thence he changed to hatred, complaints, reproaches, and denunciations of her conduct. When I saw him in this desperate state I knew that I should need some aid in calming him, so I sent for his brother, whom I had just left with the king. I went out to speak to him in the hall before he came in, and I told him what a state Sancerre was in. We gave orders that he was not to see Estouteville, and spent a good part of the night trying to persuade him to listen to reason. This morning I found him in still deeper distress; his brother is staying with him, and I have returned to you."

"No one could be more surprised than I am," said Madame de Clèves, "for I thought Madame de Tournon incapable of both love and deception."

"Address and dissimulation,"[2] answered Monsieur de Clèves, "could not go further. Notice that when Sancerre thought she had changed toward him, she really had, and had begun to love Estouteville. She told her new lover that he consoled her for her husband's death, and that it was he who was the cause of her returning to society; while it seemed to Sancerre that it was because we had decided that she should no longer appear to be in such deep affliction. She was able to persuade Estouteville to conceal their relations, and to seem obliged to marry him by her father's orders, as if it were the result of her care for her reputation,—and this in order to abandon Sancerre without leaving him ground for complaint. I must go back," continued Monsieur de Clèves, "to see this unhappy man, and I think you had better return to Paris. It is time for you to see company and to begin to receive the number of visits that await you."

Madame de Clèves gave her consent, and they returned the next day. She found herself more tranquil about Monsieur de Nemours than she had been; Madame de Chartres' dying words and her deep grief had for a time dulled her feelings, and she thought they had entirely changed.

The evening of Madame de Clèves' arrival the dauphiness came to see her, and after expressing her sympathy with her affliction, said that in order to drive away her sad thoughts she would tell her everything that had taken place at court during her absence, and narrated many incidents. "But what I most want to tell you," she added, "is that it is certain that Monsieur de Nemours is pas-

---

2. Skill and tact.

sionately in love, and that his most intimate friends are not only not in his confidence, but they can't even guess whom it is whom he loves. Yet this love is strong enough to make him neglect, or rather give up, the hope of a crown."

The dauphiness then told Madame de Clèves the whole plan about England. "I heard what I have just told you," she went on, "from Monsieur d'Anville; and he said to me this morning that the king sent last evening for Monsieur de Nemours, after reading some letters from Lignerolles, who is anxious to return, and had written to the king that he was unable to explain to the Queen of England Monsieur de Nemours' delay; that she is beginning to be offended; and that although she has given no positive answer, she had said enough to warrant him in starting. The king read this letter to Monsieur de Nemours, who instead of talking seriously, as he had done in the beginning, only laughed and joked about Lignerolles' hopes. He said that the whole of Europe would blame his imprudence if he were to presume to go to England as a claimant for the queen's hand without being assured of success. 'It seems to me too,' he went on, 'that I should not choose the present time for my journey, when the King of Spain is doing his best to marry her.[3] In a love-affair he would not be a very formidable rival; but I think that in a question of marrying, your Majesty would not advise me to try my chances against him.' 'I do advise you so in the present circumstances,' answered the king. 'But you have no occasion to fear him. I know that he has other thoughts, and even if he had not, Queen Mary was too unhappy under the Spanish yoke for one to believe that her sister wishes to assume it, or would let herself be dazzled by the splendor of so many united crowns.' 'If she does not let herself be dazzled by them,' went on Monsieur de Nemours, 'probably she will wish to marry for love; she has loved Lord Courtenay for several years. Queen Mary also loved him, and she would have married him, with the consent of the whole of England, had she not known that the youth and beauty of her sister Elizabeth attracted him more than the desire of reigning. Your Majesty knows that her violent jealousy caused her to throw them both into prison, then to exile Lord Courtenay, and finally decided her to marry the King of Spain. I believe that Elizabeth, now that she is on the throne, will soon recall this lord and thus choose a man she has loved, who is very attractive, and who has suffered so much for her, rather than another whom she has never seen.' 'I should agree with you,' replied the king, 'if Courtenay were still living; but some days ago I heard that he had died at Padua, where he was living in banishment. I see very well,' he added, as he left Monsieur de Nemours, 'that it will be necessary to celebrate your marriage as we should celebrate the dauphin's, by sending ambassadors to marry the Queen of England by procuration.'

"Monsieur d'Anville and the Vidame, who were present while the king was talking with Monsieur de Nemours, are convinced that it is this great passion which has dissuaded him from this plan. The Vidame, who is more intimate than any one with him, said to Madame de Martigues that the prince is changed beyond recognition; and what amazes him still more is that he never finds him engaged or absent, so that he supposes he never meets the woman he loves; and what is so surprising, is to see Monsieur de Nemours in love with a woman who does not return his passion."

---

3. At the death of his wife, Mary Tudor, in 1558, Philip II of Spain (1527–1598) considered marrying her sister, Elizabeth of England.

All this story that the dauphiness told her was as poison to Madame de Clèves. It was impossible for her not to feel sure that she was the woman whose name was unknown; and she was overwhelmed with gratitude and tenderness when she learned from one who had the best means of knowing that this prince, who had already aroused her interest, hid his passion from every one, and for love of her gave up his chances of a crown. It is impossible to describe her agitation. If the dauphiness had observed her with any care, she would at once have seen that the story she had just repeated was by no means without interest to her; but having no suspicion of the truth, she went on without noticing her. "Monsieur d'Anville," she added, "who, as I said, told me all this, thinks that I know more about it than he does, and he has so high an opinion of my charms that he is convinced that I am the only person who can make such a great change in Monsieur de Nemours."

Madame de Clèves was agitated by this last remark of the crown princess, though not in the same way as a few moments before. "I should readily agree with Monsieur d'Anville," she replied, "and it is certainly probable, Madame, that no one but a princess like you could make him indifferent to the Queen of England."

"I should at once acknowledge it," said the dauphiness, "if I knew that was the case, and I should know if it were true. Love-affairs of that sort do not escape the notice of those who inspire them; they are the first to perceive them. Monsieur de Nemours has never paid me any but the most insignificant attentions; but there is nevertheless so great a difference between his way with me and his present conduct that I can assure you I am not the cause of the indifference he shows for the crown of England.

"I forget everything while I am with you," she went on, "and it had slipped my mind that I must go to see Madame Elisabeth.[4] You know that peace is nearly concluded, but what you don't know is that the King of Spain would not agree to a single article except on the condition that he, instead of the prince Don Carlos, his son, should marry this princess. The king had great difficulty in agreeing to this; at last he yielded, and has gone to tell Madame. I fancy she will be inconsolable; it certainly cannot be pleasant to marry a man of the age and temper of the King of Spain, especially for her, who, in all the pride of youth and beauty, expected to marry a young prince for whom she has a fancy, though she has never seen him. I don't know whether the king will find her as docile as he wishes, and he has asked me to go to see her; for he knows that she is fond of me, and imagines that I have some influence over her. I shall then make a very different visit, for I must go to congratulate Madame, the king's sister. Everything is arranged for her marriage with Monsieur de Savoie, and he will be here shortly. Never was a person of the age of that princess so glad to marry. The court will be finer and larger than it has ever been, and in spite of your afflictions you must come and help us show the foreigners that we have some famous beauties here."

Then the dauphiness left Madame de Clèves, and the next day Madame Elisabeth's marriage was known to every one. A few days later the king and the queens called on Madame de Clèves. Monsieur de Nemours, who had awaited

4. Elizabeth of France (1545–1568), daughter of Henri II. Philip indeed married her; although she was "inconsolable" about the idea, she was in fact happy with him.

her return with extreme impatience, and was very desirous of speaking to her alone, put off his call until every one should have left and it was unlikely that others would come in. His plan was successful, and he arrived just as the latest visitors were taking their departure.

The princess was still lying down;[5] it was warm, and the sight of Monsieur de Nemours gave her face an additional color, which did not lessen her beauty. He sat down opposite her with the timidity and shyness that real passion gives. It was some time before he spoke; Madame de Clèves was equally confused, so that they kept a long silence. At last Monsieur de Nemours took courage, and expressed his sympathy with her grief. Madame de Clèves, who was glad to keep the conversation on this safe topic, spoke for some time about the loss she had experienced; and finally she said that when time should have dimmed the intensity of her grief, it would still leave a deep and lasting impression, and that her whole nature had been changed by it.

"Great afflictions and violent passions," replied Monsieur de Nemours, "do greatly alter people; as for me, I am entirely changed since I returned from Flanders. Many persons have noticed this alteration, and even the dauphiness spoke of it last evening."

"It is true," said Madame de Clèves, "that she has noticed it, and I think I have heard her say something about it."

"I am not sorry, Madame," Monsieur de Nemours continued, "that she perceived it, but I should prefer that she should not be the only one to notice it. There are persons to whom one does not dare to give any other marks of the love one feels for them than those which do not affect them in any but an indirect way; and since one does not dare to show one's love, one would at least desire that they should see that one wishes not to be loved by any one else. One would like to have them know that there is no beauty, of whatever rank, whom one would not regard with indifference, and that there is no crown which one would wish to buy at the price of never seeing them. Women generally judge the love one has for them," he went on, "by the pains one takes to please them and to pursue them; but that is an easy matter, provided they are charming. What is difficult is not to yield to the pleasure of pursuing them—it is to avoid them, from fear of showing to the public or to them one's feelings; and the most distinctive mark of a true attachment is to become entirely different from what one was, to be indifferent to ambition or pleasure after having devoted one's whole life to one or the other."

Madame de Clèves readily understood the reference to her in these words. It seemed to her that she ought to answer them and express her disapproval; it also seemed to her that she ought not to listen to them or show that she took his remarks to herself: she believed that she ought to speak, and also that she ought to say nothing. The remarks of Monsieur de Nemours pleased and offended her equally; she saw in them a confirmation of what the crown princess had made her think,—she found them full of gallantry and respect, but also bold and only too clear. Her interest in the prince caused an agitation which she could not control. The vaguest words of a man one likes produce more emotion than the open declarations of a man one does not like. Hence she sat without saying a word, and Monsieur de Nemours noticed her silence,

---

5. It was common at this period for women to receive visitors in their bedroom.

which would have seemed to him a happy omen, if the arrival of Monsieur de Clèves had not put an end to the talk and to his visit.

The Prince de Clèves had come to tell his wife the latest news about Sancerre; but she had no great curiosity about the rest of that affair. She was so interested in what had just happened that she could hardly hide her inattention. When she was able to think it all over, she perceived that she had been mistaken when she fancied that she had become indifferent to Monsieur de Nemours. His words had made all the impression he could desire, and had thoroughly convinced her of his passion. His actions harmonized too well with his words for her to have any further doubts on the subject. She did not any longer indulge in the hope of not loving him; she merely determined to give him no further sign of it. This was a difficult undertaking,—how difficult she knew already. She was aware that her only chance of success lay in avoiding the prince, and her mourning enabled her to live in retirement; she made it a pretext for not going to places where she might meet him. She was in great dejection; her mother's death appeared to be the cause, and she sought no other.

Monsieur de Nemours was in despair at not seeing her oftener; and knowing that he should not meet her at any assembly or entertainment at which the whole court was present, he could not make up his mind to go to them; he pretended a great interest in hunting, and made up hunting-parties on the days of the queens' assemblies. For a long time a slight indisposition served as a pretext for staying at home, and thus escaping going to places where he knew that Madame de Clèves would not be.

Monsieur de Clèves was ailing at nearly the same time, and Madame de Clèves never left his room during his illness; but when he was better and began to see company, and among others Monsieur de Nemours, who, under the pretext of being still weak, used to spend a good part of every day with him, she determined not to stay there. Nevertheless, she could not make up her mind to leave during his first visits; it was so long since she had seen him that she was anxious to meet him again. He too managed to make her listen to him, by what seemed like general talk; though she understood, from its reference to what he had said in his previous visit to her, that he went hunting to get an opportunity for meditation, and that he stayed away from the assemblies because she was not there.

At last Madame de Clèves put into execution her decision to leave her husband's room when the duke should be there, though she found it a difficult task: Monsieur de Nemours observed that she avoided him, and was much pained.

Monsieur de Clèves did not at first notice his wife's conduct; but at last he saw that she was unwilling to stay in his room when company was present. He spoke to her about it, and she replied that she did not think it quite proper that she should meet every evening all the young men of the court. She begged him to let her lead a more retired life than she had done before, because the presence of her mother, who was renowned for her virtue, had authorized many things impossible for a woman of her age.

Monsieur de Clèves, who was generally kind and pleasant to his wife, was not so on this occasion; he told her he was averse to any change in her conduct. She was tempted to tell him that there was a report that Monsieur de Nemours was in love with her; but she did not feel able to mention his name.

She was also ashamed to assign a false reason, and to hide the truth from a man who had so good an opinion of her.

A few days later, the king happened to be with the queen when she was receiving, and the company was talking about horoscopes and predictions. Opinions were divided about the credence that ought to be given to them. The queen was inclined to believe in them; she maintained that after so many predictions had come true, it was impossible to doubt the exactness of this science. Others again held that the small number of lucky hits out of the numerous predictions that were made, proved that they were merely the result of chance.

"In former times," said the king, "I was very curious about the future; but I was told so much that was false or improbable that I became convinced that we can know nothing certain. A few years ago a famous astrologer came here. Every one went to see him, I as well as the rest, but without saying who I was; and I carried with me Monsieur de Guise and D'Escars, sending them into the room in front of me. Nevertheless the astrologer addressed me first, as if he thought I was their master; perhaps he knew me, although he said something to me which seemed to show that he did not know who I was. He prophesied that I should be killed in a duel; then he told Monsieur de Guise that he would be killed from behind, and D'Escars that he would have his skull broken by a kick from a horse. Monsieur de Guise was almost angry at hearing this,—as if he were accused of running away; D'Escars was no more pleased at learning that he was going to perish by such an unfortunate accident,—so that we all left the astrologer in extreme discontent. I have no idea what will happen to Monsieur de Guise or to D'Escars, but it is very unlikely that I shall be killed in a duel. The King of Spain and I have just made peace; and even if we had not, I doubt if we should resort to a personal combat, and it seems unlikely that I should challenge him, as my father challenged Charles V."

After the king had mentioned the unhappy end which had been foretold him, those who had supported astrology gave up and agreed that it was unworthy of belief. "For my part," said Monsieur de Nemours, "I am the last man in the world to place any confidence in it;" and turning to Madame de Clèves, near whom he was, he said in a low voice: "I was told that I should be made happy by the kindness of the woman for whom I should have the most violent and the most respectful passion. You may judge, Madame, whether I ought to believe in predictions."

The dauphiness, who fancied, from what Monsieur de Nemours had said aloud, that he was mentioning some absurd prophecy that had been made about him, asked him what he was saying to Madame de Clèves. He would have been embarrassed by this question if he had had less presence of mind; but he answered without hesitation: "I was saying, Madame, that it had been predicted about me that I should rise to a lofty position to which I should not even dare to aspire."

"If that is the only prediction that has been made about you," replied the dauphiness, smiling, and thinking of the English scheme, "I do not advise you to denounce astrology; you might find good reasons for supporting it."

Madame de Clèves understood what the crown princess referred to; but she also understood that the happiness of which Monsieur de Nemours spoke was not that of being king of England.

As it was some time since her mother's death, Madame de Clèves had to appear again in society and to resume her visits at court. She met Monsieur de Nemours at the dauphiness's and at her own house, whither he often came with young nobles of his own age, in order not to be talked about; but she never saw him without an agitation which he readily perceived.

In spite of the care she took to escape his glances and to talk less with him than with others, certain things inadvertently escaped her which convinced this prince that she was not indifferent to him. A less observant man than he would not, perhaps, have noticed them; but so many women had been in love with him that it was hard for him not to know when he was loved. He perceived that the Chevalier de Guise was his rival, and that prince knew that Monsieur de Nemours was his. He was the only man at court who would have discovered this truth; his interest had rendered him more clear-sighted than the others. The knowledge they had of each other's feelings so embittered their relations that although there was no open breach, they were opposed in everything. In running at the ring and in all the amusements in which the king took part they were always on different sides, and their rivalry was too intense to be hidden.

The English scheme often recurred to Madame de Clèves, and she felt that Monsieur de Nemours would not be able to withstand the king's advice and Lignerolles' urging. She noticed with pain that this last had not yet returned, and she awaited him with impatience. If she had followed his movements, she would have learned the condition of that matter; but the same feeling that inspired her curiosity compelled her to conceal it, and she contented herself with making inquiries about the beauty, intelligence, and character of Queen Elizabeth. A portrait of her was carried to the palace, and she found Elizabeth more beautiful than was pleasant to her, and she could not refrain from saying that it must flatter her.

"I don't think so," replied the dauphiness, who was present. "Elizabeth has a great reputation as a beauty and as the possessor of a mind far above the common, and I know that all my life she has been held up to me as an example. She ought to be attractive if she is like Anne Boleyn, her mother. Never was there a more amiable woman or one more charming both in appearance and disposition. I have been told that her face was exceptionally vivacious, and that she in no way resembled most English beauties."

"It seems to me," said Madame de Clèves, "that I have heard that she was born in France."

"Those who think so," replied the crown princess, "are in error, and I will tell you her history in a few words. She was born of a good English family. Henry VIII had been in love with her sister and her mother, and it had even been suspected that she was his daughter. She came here with the sister of Henry VII, who married Louis XII. This young and gallant princess found it very hard to leave the court of France after her husband's death; but Anne Boleyn, who shared her mistress's feelings, decided to stay. The late king was in love with her, and she remained as maid of honor to Queen Claude. This queen died, and Madame Marguerite, the king's sister, the Duchess of Alençon, since then Queen of Navarre, whose stories you have seen, added Anne to her suite; it was from her that this queen received her inclination toward the new religion. Then Anne returned to England, where she delighted every one. She had French manners, which please all nations; she sang well, and danced charmingly. She was made a lady in waiting to Queen Catherine of Aragon, and King Henry VIII fell desperately in love with her.

"Cardinal Wolsey, his favorite and prime minister, desired to be made pope; and being dissatisfied with the emperor for not supporting his claims, he resolved to avenge himself by allying the king his master with France. He suggested to Henry VIII that his marriage with the emperor's aunt was null and void, and proposed to him to marry the Duchess of Alençon, whose husband had just died. Anne Boleyn, being an ambitious woman, looked on this divorce as a possible step to the throne. She began to instill into the King of England the principles of Lutheranism, and persuaded the late king to urge at Rome Henry's divorce, in the hope of his marriage with Madame d'Alençon. Cardinal Wolsey contrived to be sent to France on other pretexts to arrange this affair; but his master would not consent to have the proposition made, and sent orders to Calais that this marriage was not to be mentioned.

"On his return from France, Cardinal Wolsey was received with honors equal to those paid to the king himself; never did a favorite display such haughtiness and vanity. He arranged an interview between the two kings, which took place at Boulogne. Francis I offered his hand to Henry VIII, who was unwilling to take it; they treated each other with great splendor, each giving the other clothes like those he himself wore. I remember having heard that those the late king sent to the King of England were of crimson satin trimmed with pearls and diamonds arranged in triangles, the cloak of white velvet embroidered with gold. After spending a few days at Boulogne, they went to Calais. Anne Boleyn was quartered in the house with Henry VIII in the queen's suite, and Francis I made her the same presents and paid her the same honors as if she had been a queen herself. At last, after being in love with her for nine years, Henry married her, without waiting for the annulment of his first marriage, which he had long been asking of Rome. The pope at once excommunicated him; this so enraged Henry that he declared himself the head of the Church, and carried all England into the unhappy change of religion in which you now see it.

"Anne Boleyn did not long enjoy her grandeur, for one day, when she thought her position assured by the death of Catherine of Aragon, she happened to be present with all the court when the Viscount Rochford, her brother, was running at the ring. The king was suddenly overwhelmed by such an access of jealousy that he instantly left the spot, hastened to London, and gave orders for the arrest of the queen, the Viscount Rochford, and many others whom he believed to be the queen's lovers or confidants. Although this jealousy seemed the work of a moment, it had for some time been instigated by the Viscountess Rochford, who could not endure her husband's intimacy with the queen, and represented it to the king as criminal intimacy; consequently he, being already in love with Jane Seymour, thought only of getting rid of Anne Boleyn. In less than three weeks he succeeded in having the queen and her brother brought to trial and beheaded, and he married Jane Seymour. He had afterward several wives, whom he either divorced or put to death, among others Catherine Howard, who had been the confidante of the Viscountess of Rochford, and was beheaded with her. Hence she was punished for the crimes with which she had blackened Anne Boleyn, and Henry VIII, having reached a monstrous size, died."

All the ladies present thanked the dauphiness for teaching them so much about the English court, and among others Madame de Clèves, who could not refrain from asking more questions about Queen Elizabeth.

The dauphiness had miniatures painted of all the beauties of the court to send to the queen her mother. The day when that of Madame de Clèves was receiving the last touches the crown princess came to spend the afternoon with her. Monsieur de Nemours was also there, for he neglected no opportunity of seeing Madame de Clèves, although he never seemed to court her society. She was so beautiful that day that he would surely have fallen in love with her then if he had not done so already; but he did not dare to sit with his eyes fixed on her, while she feared lest he should show too plainly the pleasure he found in looking at her.

The crown princess asked Monsieur de Clèves for a miniature he had of his wife, to compare it with the one that was painting. All who were there expressed their opinion of both, and Madame de Clèves asked the painter to make a little correction in the hair of the old one. The artist took the miniature out of its case, and after working on it, set it down on the table.

For a long time Monsieur de Nemours had been desiring to have a portrait of Madame de Clèves. When he saw this one, though it belonged to her husband, whom he tenderly loved, he could not resist the temptation to steal it; he thought that among the many persons present he should not be suspected.

The dauphiness was seated on the bed, speaking low to Madame de Clèves, who was standing in front of her. One of the curtains was only partly closed, and Madame de Clèves was able to see Monsieur de Nemours, whose back was against the table at the foot of the bed, without turning his head pick up something from this table. She at once guessed that it was her portrait, and she was so embarrassed that the crown princess noticed she was not listening to her, and asked her what she was looking at. At these words Monsieur de Nemours turned round and met Madame de Clèves' eyes fastened on him; he felt sure that she must have seen what he had just done.

Madame de Clèves was greatly embarrassed. Her reason bade her ask for her portrait; but if she asked for it openly, she would announce to every one the prince's feelings for her, and by asking for it privately, she would give him an opportunity to speak to her of his love, so that at last she judged it better to let him keep it,—and she was very glad to be able to grant him a favor without his knowing that she did it of her own choice. Monsieur de Nemours, who observed her embarrassment and guessed its cause, came up to her and said in a low voice: "If you saw what I ventured to do, be good enough, Madame, to let me suppose that you know nothing about it; I do not dare to ask anything more." Then he went away, without waiting for an answer.

The dauphiness, accompanied by all her ladies, went out for a walk. Monsieur de Nemours locked himself up in his own room, being unable to contain his joy at having in his possession a portrait of Madame de Clèves. He felt all the happiness that love can give. He loved the most charming woman of the court, and felt that in spite of herself she loved him; he saw in everything she did the agitation and embarrassment which love evokes in the innocence of early youth.

That evening every one looked carefully for the portrait; when they found the case, no one supposed that it had been stolen, but that it had been dropped somewhere. Monsieur de Clèves was distressed at its loss, and after hunting for it in vain, told his wife, but evidently in jest, that she doubtless had some mysterious lover to whom she had given the portrait, or who had stolen it, for no one but a lover would care for the portrait without the case.

Although these words were not said seriously, they made a deep impression on the mind of Madame de Clèves and filled her with remorse. She thought of the violence of her love for Monsieur de Nemours, and perceived that she could not control either her words or her face. She reflected that Lignerolles had returned, and that the English scheme had no terrors for her; that she had no longer grounds for suspecting the dauphiness; and finally, that, as she was without further defence, her only safety was in flight. Since, however, she knew she could not go away, she saw that she was in a most perilous condition, and ready to fall into what she judged to be the greatest possible misfortune,— namely, betraying to Monsieur de Nemours the interest she felt in him. She recalled everything her mother had said to her on her deathbed, and her advice to try everything rather than enter upon a love-affair. She remembered what her husband had said about her sincerity when he was speaking about Madame de Tournon, and it seemed to her that it was her duty to confess her passion for Monsieur de Nemours. She pondered over this for a long time; then she was astonished that the thought occurred to her: she deemed it madness, and fell back into the agony of indecision.

Part III

When peace was signed,[6] Madame Elisabeth, though with great repugnance, determined to obey her father the king. The Duke of Alva had been deputed to marry her in the name of the Catholic king, and he was expected to arrive shortly. The Duke of Savoy was also expected; he was to marry Madame the king's sister, and the two weddings were to take place at the same time. The king thought of nothing but making these events illustrious by entertainments at which he could display all the brilliancy and splendor of his court. It was suggested that plays and ballets should be sumptuously set upon the stage; but the king thought that too meagre a form of entertainment, and desired something more magnificent. He determined to have a tournament at which the foreigners might enter, and to admit the populace as spectators. All the princes and young noblemen gladly furthered the king's plan, and especially the Duke of Ferrara, Monsieur de Guise, and Monsieur de Nemours, who surpassed all others in exercises of this sort. The king chose them to be, with himself, the four champions of the tournament.

It was announced throughout the whole kingdom that a tournament would be opened in the city of Paris on the fifteenth day of June by His Very Christian Majesty and by the Prince Alphonso of Este Duke of Ferrara, Francis of Lorraine Duke of Guise, and James of Savoy Duke of Nemours, who were ready to meet all comers. The first combat was to be on horseback, with four antagonists, with four assaults with the lance, and one for the ladies; the second combat with swords, either singly or in couples, as should be determined; the third combat on foot, three assaults with the pike, and six with the sword. The

6. The peace treaty of Cateau-Cambrésis (April 1559).

champions were to supply the lances, swords, and pikes, from which the assailants might choose their weapons. Any one striking a horse in the attack was to
be put out of the ranks. There would be four masters of the camp who should
have command, and those of the assailants who should be most successful
would receive a prize, of a value to be determined by the judges. All the assailants, French or foreign, were to be obliged to come and touch one or more of
the shields hanging by the steps at the end of the lists; there they would find an
officer to receive and enroll them according to their rank and the shields they
had touched. The assailants were to have a gentleman bring their shields with
their arms, to be hung by the steps three days before the beginning of the tournament, otherwise they would not be received without the permission of the
champions.

A great field was made ready near the Bastile, extending from the caste of
Tournelles, across the Rue St. Antoine, to the royal mews. On each side scaf-
folding was raised, with rows of seats and covered boxes and galleries, fine to
look upon, and capable of holding a vast number of spectators. All the princes
and lords were thinking of nothing but their preparations to make a magnificent appearance, and were busily occupied in working some device into their
initials or mottoes that should flatter the woman they loved.

A few days before the Duke of Alva's arrival the king went to play tennis with
Monsieur de Nemours, the Chevalier de Guise, and the Vidame of Chartres.
The queens went with their suites, and Madame de Clèves among the others,
to watch the game. After it was over, and they were leaving the court, Châtelart
went up to the dauphiness and told her that he had just found a love-letter that
had fallen from Monsieur de Nemours' pocket. The crown princess, who was
always curious about everything that concerned that prince, told Châtelart to
give it to her; she took it, and followed the queen her mother-in-law, who was
going with the king to see the preparations for the tournament. After they had
been there some time the king sent for some horses which he had recently
bought. Though they had not been broken, he wanted to mount them, and he
also had them saddled for the gentlemen with him. The king and Monsieur de
Nemours got on the most fiery ones, and they tried to spring at one another.
Monsieur de Nemours, fearful of injuring the king, backed his horse suddenly
against a post with such violence that he was dismounted. The attendants ran
up to him and thought he was seriously injured; Madame de Clèves thought
him more hurt than did the others. Her interest in him inspired an agitation
which she did not think of concealing; she went up to him with the queens,
and her color was so changed that a man less interested than the Chevalier de
Guise would have noticed it. He remarked it at once, and gave much more
attention to the condition of Madame de Clèves than to that of Monsieur de
Nemours. This prince was so stunned by the fall that his head had to be supported by those about him. When he came to himself, the first person he saw
was Madame de Clèves; he read on her face all the pity she felt, and his expression showed that he was grateful. He then thanked the queens for their kindness, and apologized for appearing before them in such a state. The king
ordered him to go home and lie down.

After Madame had recovered from her fright she began to recall the way she
had betrayed it. The Chevalier de Guise did not leave her long to enjoy the
hope that no one had observed it. As he gave her his hand to lead her from the

field, he said: "I am more to be pitied, Madame, than Monsieur de Nemours. Pardon me if I abandon the profound reserve which I have always shown in regard to you, and if I betray the keen grief I feel at what I have just seen; it is the first time that I have been bold enough to speak to you, and it will be the last. Death, or at any rate an eternal separation, will remove me from a place where I cannot live, now that I have lost the sad consolation of believing that all those who dare to look upon you are as unhappy as I."

Madame de Clèves answered with a few disjointed words, as if she did not understand what the Chevalier de Guise meant. At any other time she would have been offended at his speaking of his feelings for her; but at that moment she thought only of her pain at perceiving that he had detected her own for Monsieur de Nemours. The Chevalier de Guise was so overwhelmed and pained by this discovery that he at once resolved never to think of winning Madame de Clèves' love; but the abandonment of a design which had seemed so difficult and glorious required one of equal moment to take its place, hence he thought of going to take Rhodes,[7]—a plan he had already meditated. When he died, in the flower of his youth, just when he had acquired a reputation as one of the greatest princes of his century, his only regret was that he had not been able to carry out that noble project, which seemed on the point of accomplishment.

Madame de Clèves at once went to the queen, with her mind intent on what had just happened. Monsieur de Nemours came there soon afterward, in magnificent attire, as if he had forgotten what had just happened. He appeared even gayer than usual, and his delight at what he thought he had seen added to his content. Every one was surprised to see him, and asked him how he felt, except Madame de Clèves, who remained by the fire-place, as if she did not see him. The king came out of his room, and observing him there, called him to ask about his mishap. As Monsieur de Nemours passed by Madame de Clèves, he said in a low voice: "I have received to-day, Madame, tokens of your pity, but not those I most deserve." Madame de Clèves had suspected that the prince had noticed her emotion at his accident, and his words showed her that she was not mistaken. She was deeply pained to see that she could not control her emotions, and had even made them manifest to the Chevalier de Guise. It distressed her, too, to perceive that Monsieur de Nemours had read them; but this distress was tempered by a certain pleasure.

The dauphiness, who was impatient to know what was in the letter that Châtelart had given her, went up to Madame de Clèves. "Read this letter," she said; "it is addressed to Monsieur de Nemours, and apparently is from that mistress for whom he has left all the others. If you cannot read it now, keep it; come to me this evening and give it back to me, and tell me whether you know the handwriting." With these words the crown princess turned away from Madame de Clèves, leaving her so astonished and agitated that she could scarcely move. Her emotion and impatience were so great that she could not stay longer with the queen, and she went home, though it was much earlier

7. The Turks had recaptured the island of Rhodes from the Christians in 1523. François de Lorraine, chevalier de Guise, in fact later led an expedition there. He was killed at the battle of Dreux in the religious wars against the Huguenots in 1563, at the age of twenty-nine.

than her usual hour of leaving. Her hands, in which she held the letter, trembled; her thoughts were all confused, and she felt an unendurable pain such as she had never known. As soon as she was safe in her room she opened the letter, and read as follows:—

"I love you too much to let you think that the change you see in me is the result of my fickleness; I want you to know that the real cause is your infidelity. You are surprised that I say your 'infidelity'; you have concealed it so craftily, and I have taken such pains to hide from you my knowledge of it, that you are naturally astonished that I should have detected it. I am myself surprised that I have been able to keep it from you. Never was there any grief like mine; I imagined that you felt for me a violent passion. I did not conceal what I felt for you, and at the time when I let you see it, I learned that you were deceiving me, that you loved another, and, according to all appearances, were sacrificing me to a new mistress. I knew it the day of the running at the ring, and that is why I was not there. I pretended to be ill, in order to conceal my emotion; but I really became so, for my body could not stand the intense agitation. When I began to get better, I pretended to be still suffering, in order to have an excuse for not seeing or writing to you; I wanted time to decide how I should act toward you. Twenty times at least I formed and changed my decision; but at last I judged you unworthy to see my grief, and I determined to hide it from you. I wished to wound your pride by letting you see my love for you fade away. I thought thus to diminish the price of the sacrifice you made of it; I did not wish you to have the pleasure of showing how much I loved you in order to appear more amiable. I resolved to write to you indifferent, dull letters, to suggest to the woman to whom you gave them that you were loved less. I did not wish her to have the pleasure of learning that I knew of her triumph over me, or to add to her triumph by my despair and reproaches. I thought I could not punish you sufficiently by breaking with you, and that I should inflict but a slight pain if I ceased to love you when you had ceased to love me. I thought you must love me, if you were to know the pang of not being loved, which tormented me so sorely. I thought that if anything could rekindle the feelings you had had for me, it was by showing that my own were changed, but to show this by pretending to hide it from you, as if I had not strength to tell you. I decided on this; but how hard it was to do so, and when I saw you, how almost impossible to carry it out! Hundreds of times I was ready to spoil all with my reproaches and tears. The state of my health helped me to conceal my emotion and distress. Afterward I was borne up by the pleasure of dissimulating to you as you dissimulated to me; nevertheless I did myself such violence to tell you and to write to you that I loved you, that you saw sooner than I had intended that I had not meant to let you see that my feelings were altered. You were wounded, and complained to me. I tried to reassure you, but in such an artificial way that you were more convinced than ever that I did not love you. At last I succeeded in what I had meant to do. The capriciousness of your heart made you turn again toward me when you saw me leaving you. I have tasted all the joy of vengeance; it has seemed to me that you loved me better than ever, and I have shown you that I did not love you. I have had reason to believe that you had entirely abandoned her for whom you had left me. I have also had grounds for supposing that you never spoke to her of me. But your return and your desertion have not been able to make good your fickleness; your heart has been divided between me and another; you have deceived me: that is enough to deprive me of the pleasure of being loved by you as I thought I deserved, and to fix me in the resolution that I had formed never to see you again, which so surprises you."

Madame de Clèves read and re-read this letter several times without understanding it; all that she made out was that Monsieur de Nemours did not love her as she had thought, and that he loved other women, whom he deceived as he did her. This was a grievous blow to a woman of her character, who was deeply in love, and had just shown this to a man whom she deemed unworthy, in sight of another whom she maltreated for love of his rival. Never was sorrow more bitter! It seemed to her that what had happened that day gave it a special sting, and that if Monsieur de Nemours had not had reason to suppose that she loved him, she would not care whether he had loved another woman. But she deceived herself; the pang she found so unendurable was that of jealousy, with all its hideous accompaniments. This letter showed her that Monsieur de Nemours had had a love affair for some time. She thought that it attested the writer's cleverness and worth, and she seemed a woman who deserved to be loved. She appeared to have more courage than herself, and she envied her the strength of character she showed in concealing her feelings from Monsieur de Nemours. The end of the letter showed that the woman thought herself still loved; she imagined that his constant discretion, which had so touched her, was perhaps only the effect of his love for the other, whom he feared to offend. In a word, all her thoughts only fed her grief and despair. How often she thought of herself; how often of her mother's counsels! How bitterly she regretted that she had not withdrawn from the world, in spite of Monsieur de Clèves, or that she had not followed her plan of confessing to him her feeling for Monsieur de Nemours! She judged that she would have done better to tell everything to a husband whose generosity she knew, and who would be interested in keeping her secret, than to betray it to a man unworthy of it, who was moved to love of her by no other feeling than pride or vanity. In a word, she deemed every evil that could befall her, every misery to which she might be reduced, insignificant by the side of letting Monsieur de Nemours see that she loved him, and knowing that he loved another woman. Her only consolation was that henceforth she need have no fear of herself, and that she was entirely cured of her love for him.

She gave no thought to the dauphiness's command to come to her that evening; she went to bed and pretended to be indisposed, so that when Monsieur de Clèves came back from seeing the king, he was told that she was asleep. But she was far from enjoying the calmness that induces sleep. She spent the night in self-reproach and in reading over the letter.

Madame de Clèves was not the only person whose rest was disturbed by this letter. The Vidame of Chartres, who had lost it, not Monsieur de Nemours, was very uneasy about it. He had spent the evening with Monsieur de Guise, who had given a grand supper to his brother-in-law, the Duke of Ferrara, and all the young men of the court. It so happened that during the supper the conversation turned to bright letters, and the Vidame said he had in his pocket the brightest letter that ever was written. He was asked to show it to them, but he refused. Monsieur de Nemours thereupon declared that he had never had it, and was only boasting. The Vidame replied that he tempted him to commit an indiscretion, but he would not show the letter, though he would read a few passages that would prove that few men ever received one like it. At the same time he felt for the letter, but could not find it; he sought everywhere in vain. They laughed at his discomfiture, but he seemed so uneasy that they soon stopped talking about it. He left before the others, hastening home to see if he had left the missing letter there. While he was still hunting for it, a first *valet de chambre*[8] of the queen came to tell him that the Vicomtesse d'Uzès thought it well to let him know that they were talking at the queen's apartment about a love-letter he had dropped from his pocket while he was playing tennis; that they had repeated a good deal that was in the letter; that the queen had expressed a strong desire to see it; that she had asked one of her gentlemen-in-waiting for it; but he had answered that he had given it to Châtelart.

The *valet de chambre* said many other things to the Vidame which only added to his distress. He went out at once to see a gentleman who was a great friend of Châtelart; he made him get out of bed, although it was very late, to go and ask for the letter, without telling him who wanted it or who had written it. Châtelart, who was confident that it had been written to Monsieur de Nemours, and that he was in love with the dauphiness, felt sure that he knew who had asked for it. He replied, with malicious joy, that he had handed the letter to the dauphiness. The gentleman brought this answer back to the Vidame of Chartres; it gave him only fresh uneasiness. After long hesitation about what he should do, he decided that Monsieur de Nemours was the only man who could aid him.

The Vidame thereupon went to the house of the duke, and entered his bedroom at about daybreak. The prince was sleeping calmly; what he had seen that day of Madame de Clèves gave him only agreeable thoughts. He was much surprised when he was awakened by the Vidame, and he asked him whether this had been done out of revenge for what he had said at the supper. The Vidame's countenance showed that he had come on some serious matter. "I have come," he said, "to confide to you the most important event of my life. I know very well that you have no cause to be grateful, because I do this at a moment when I need your aid; but I know that I should have sunk in your esteem if without being compelled by necessity I had told you what I am about to say. Some time yesterday I dropped the letter of which I was speaking last evening; it is of extreme importance that no one should know that it was written to me. It has been seen by a number of persons who were at the tennis-court when I dropped it. Now, you were there too, and I beg of you to say that it was you who lost it."

"You must suppose that I am not in love with any woman," answered Monsieur de Nemours, smiling, "to make such a proposition to me, and to imagine that there is no one with whom I might fall out if I let it be thought that I receive letters of that sort."

"I beg you," said the Vidame, "to listen to me seriously. If you have a mistress, as I do not doubt, though I have no idea who she is, it will be easy for you to explain yourself, and I will tell you how to do it. Even if you do not have an explanation with her, your falling-out will last but a few moments; whereas I by this mischance bring dishonor to a woman who has loved me passionately, and is one of the most estimable women in the world; and moreover, from another

---

8. A personal manservant.

quarter I bring upon myself an implacable hatred, which will certainly cost me my fortune, and may cost me something more."

"I do not understand what you tell me," replied Monsieur de Nemours; "but you imply that the current rumors about the interest a great princess takes in you are not entirely without foundation."

"They are not," exclaimed the Vidame; "but would to God they were! In that case I should not be in my present trouble. But I must tell you what has happened, to give you an idea of what I have to fear.

"Ever since I have been at court, the queen has always treated me with much distinction and amiability, and I have reason to believe that she has had a kindly feeling for me; yet there was nothing marked about it, and I had never dreamed of other feelings toward me than those of respect. I was even much in love with Madame de Themines; the sight of her is enough to prove that a man can have a great deal of love for her when she loves him,—and she loved me. Nearly two years ago, when the court was at Fontainebleau, I happened to talk with the queen two or three times when very few people were there. It seemed to me that I pleased her, and that she was interested in all that I said. One day especially we were talking about confidence. I said I did not confide wholly in any one; that one always repented absolute unreserve sooner or later; and that I knew a number of things of which I had never spoken to any one. The queen said that she thought better of me for that; that she had not found any one in France who had any reserve; and that this had troubled her greatly, because it had prevented her confiding in any one; that one must have somebody to talk to, especially persons of her rank. The following days she several times resumed the same conversation, and told me many tolerably secret things that were happening. At last it seemed to me that she wanted to test my reserve, and that she wished to intrust me with some of her own secrets. This thought attached me to her; I was flattered by the distinction, and I paid her my court with more assiduity than usual. One evening, when the king and all the ladies had gone out to ride in the forest, she remained at home, because she did not feel well, and I stayed with her. She went down to the edge of the pond and let go of the equerry's hand, to walk more freely. After she had made a few turns, she came near me and bade me follow her. 'I want to speak to you,' she said, 'and you will see from what I wish to say that I am a friend of yours.' Then she stopped and gazed at me intently. 'You are in love,' she went on, 'and because you do not confide in any one, you think that your love is not known; but it is known even to the persons interested. You are watched; it is known where you see your mistress: a plan has been made to surprise you. I do not know who she is, I do not ask you; I only wish to save you from the misfortunes into which you may fall.' Observe, please, the snare the queen set for me, and how difficult it was to escape it. She wanted to find out whether I was in love; and by not asking with whom, and by showing that her sole intention was to aid me, she prevented my thinking that she was speaking to me from curiosity or with premeditation.

"Nevertheless, in the face of all appearances I made out the truth. I was in love with Madame de Themines; but though she loved me, I was not fortunate enough to meet her in any private place where we could be surprised, hence I saw that it was not she whom the queen meant. I knew too that I had a love-affair with a woman less beautiful and less severe than Madame de Themines, and it was not impossible that the place where I used to meet her had been discovered; but since I took but little interest in her, it was easy for me to escape from perils of that sort by ceasing to see her. Hence I decided to confess nothing to the queen, but to assure her that I had long since given up the desire to win the love of such women as might smile on me, because I deemed them unworthy of an honorable man's devotion, and it would take women far above them to fascinate me. 'You are not frank,' replied the queen; 'I know the opposite of what you say. The way in which I speak to you binds you to conceal nothing from me. I want you to be one of my friends,' she went on; 'but when I give you that place, I must know all your ties. Consider whether you care to purchase it at the price of informing me; I give you two days to think it over. But be careful what you say to me at the expiration of that time, and remember that if I find out afterward that you have deceived me, I shall never pardon you so long as I live.' Thereupon the queen left me, without awaiting my reply.

"You may well imagine that I was much impressed by what she had just said. The two days she had given me for consideration did not seem to me too long. I perceived that she wished to know whether I was in love, and hoped that I was not. I saw the importance of the decision I was about to make. My vanity was not a little flattered by a love-affair with a queen, and a queen who was still so charming. To be sure, I love Madame de Themines, and although I was unfaithful to her in a way with that other woman I mentioned, I could not make up my mind to break with her. I also saw the danger to which I exposed myself in deceiving the queen, and how hard it would be to deceive her; yet I could not decide to refuse what fortune offered me, and I determined to risk the consequences of my evil conduct. I broke with that woman with whom my relations might be discovered, and I hoped to conceal those I had with Madame de Themines.

"At the expiration of the two days that the queen had granted me, as I was entering a room where all her ladies were assembled, she said to me aloud, with a seriousness that surprised me,—

" 'Have you thought over that matter of which I spoke to you, and do you know the truth about it?'

" 'Yes, Madame,' I replied, 'and it is as I told your Majesty.'

" 'Come this evening at the hour that I shall write to you, and I will give you the rest of my orders.'

"I made a deep bow, without answering, and did not fail to appear at the hour set. I found her in the gallery with her secretary and some of her ladies. As soon as she saw me, she came up to me and led me to the other end of the gallery.

" 'Well!' she said, 'is it after due reflection that you have nothing to say to me, and does not my treatment of you deserve that you should speak to me frankly?'

" 'It is because I am frank with you, Madame,' I replied, 'that I have nothing to tell you; and I swear to your Majesty, with all the respect I owe you, that I am not in love with any lady of the court.'

" 'I am willing to believe it,' resumed the queen, 'because I wish to; and I wish it because I desire that you should be unreservedly attached to me; and I could not possibly be satisfied with your friendship if you were in love. One may trust those who are, but it is impossible to have confidence in their secrecy. They are too inattentive and have too many distractions; their mistress is their main interest,—and that would not suit the way in which I want you to be attached to me. Remember, it is on account of your oath that you are free that I choose you for the recipient of my confidence. Remember that I wish yours without reserve, that I want you to have no friend, man or woman, except such as shall be agreeable to me, and that you will give up every aim except pleasing me. I shall not let harm come to your fortune,—I shall look after that more zealously than you do; and whatever I do for you, I shall consider myself more than paid if I find that you are to me what I hope. I choose you in order to confide in you all my anxieties, and to help me endure them. You will see that they are not light. To all appearance I suffer no pain from the king's attachment to Madame de Valentinois; but I can scarcely bear it. She controls the king; she is false to him; she despises me; all my people are devoted to her. My daughter-in-law, the crown princess, is vain of her beauty and of her uncle's power, and pays no respect to me. The Constable of Montmorency is master of the king and of the kingdom; he hates me, and has given me tokens of his hatred which I can never forget. The Marshal of Saint-André is an audacious young favorite, who treats me no better than do the others. The full list of my sufferings would arouse your compassion. Hitherto I have not dared to trust any one; I do put confidence in you: act in such a way that I shall not repent of it, and be my sole consolation.'

"The queen's eyes filled with tears as she said these last words, and I was on the point of throwing myself at her feet, so deeply was I moved by the kindness she showed me. Since that day she has had perfect confidence in me; she never takes a step without talking it over with me, and my alliance with her still lasts.

Part IV

"Still, though much taken up by my new intimacy with the queen, I was bound to Madame de Themines by a feeling which I could not overcome. It seemed to me that her love for me was waning; and although if I had been wise I should have taken advantage of this change I saw in her to try to forget her, as it was, my love for her redoubled, and I managed so ill that the queen in time learned something about this attachment. Persons of her nation[9] are always inclined to jealousy, and possibly her feelings toward me were warmer than she herself supposed. But at last the report that I was in love gave her such distress and grief that I very often felt sure that I had wholly lost her favor. I reassured her by my attentions, submissiveness, and by many false oaths; but I could not have long deceived her if Madame de Themines' altered demeanor had not at last set me free in spite of myself. She made me see that she loved me no longer, and I was so sure of this that I felt compelled to cease persecuting her with my attentions. Some time after, she wrote me the letter that I have lost. That told me that she knew about my relations with the other woman I mentioned, and that this was the reason of the change. Since, then, there was no one to divide my attentions, the queen was tolerably satisfied with me; but inasmuch as my feeling for her was not of a sort to render me incapable of another attachment, and it is impossible for a man to control his heart by force of will, I fell in love with Madame de Martigues, in whom I had been much interested before, when she was a

9. Italy.

Villemontais[1] and maid-of-honor to the dauphiness. I had reason for believing that she did not hate me, and that she was pleased with my discreet conduct, although she did not understand all its reasons. The queen has no suspicions about this affair, but there is another which torments her a great deal. Since Madame de Martigues is always with the crown princess, I go there oftener than usual. The queen has taken it into her head that it is with this princess that I am in love. The dauphiness's rank, which is equal to her own, and her advantages of youth and beauty, inspire a jealousy which amounts to madness, and she cannot conceal her hatred of her daughter-in-law. The Cardinal of Lorraine, who seems to me to have been for a long time an aspirant for the queen's good graces, and who sees me occupying a place that he would like to fill, under the pretence of bringing about a reconciliation between her and the crown princess is looking into the causes of their dissension. I do not doubt that he has found out the real cause of the queen's bitterness, and I fancy that he has done me many an evil turn, though without showing his hand. That is the state of affairs now. Judge then what will be the effect of the letter I lost when I was unfortunate enough to put it into my pocket to return it to Madame de Themines. If the queen sees this letter, she will know that I have deceived her, and that at almost the same time when I was false to her on account of Madame de Themines, I was false to Madame de Themines on account of another woman. Judge then what sort of an opinion she will have of me, and whether she will ever believe me again. If she does not see this letter, what shall I say to her? She knows that it has been in the dauphiness's hands; she will think that Châtelart recognized that princess's handwriting, and that the letter is from her; she will imagine that she is perhaps the woman whose jealousy is mentioned,—in a word, there is nothing which she may not think, and there is nothing I may not fear from her thoughts. Add to this that I am sincerely interested in Madame de Martigues, that the crown princess will certainly show her this letter, and that she will believe it was written very recently. So I shall be embroiled both with the woman I love best in the world and with the woman from whom I have most to fear. Consider now whether I am not justified in begging you to say that the letter is yours and in asking you as a favor to try to get it from the dauphiness."

"It is very plain," said Monsieur de Nemours, "that one could hardly be in more serious perplexity than you are; and you must confess that you got into it by your own fault. I have been accused of being a faithless lover and of carrying on several love-affairs at the same time; but I am nothing by the side of you, for I should never have dreamed of doing what you have done. Could you suppose it possible to keep on good terms with Madame de Themines when you formed your alliance with the queen; and did you hope to become intimate with the queen and yet succeed deceiving her? She is an Italian and a queen, and hence suspicious, jealous, and haughty. When your good luck rather than your good conduct got you out of one entanglement, you got into a new one, and imagined that here, amid the whole court, you could love Madame de Martigues without the queen's knowing anything about it. You could not have been too careful to rid her of the mortification of having taken the first steps. She has a violent passion for you. You are too discreet to say so, and I am too discreet to ask any questions; but she loves you, she distrusts you, and the facts justify her."

---

1. I.e., before her marriage. Villemontais was her maiden name.

"Is it for you to overwhelm me with reproaches?" interrupted the Vidame. "Ought not your experience to make you indulgent to my faults? Still, I am willing to confess that I did wrong; but consider, I beg of you, how to get me out of my present complications. It seems to me that you must see the crown princess as soon as she is up, and ask her for the letter as if it were yours."

"I have already told you," replied Monsieur de Nemours, "that this is a somewhat extraordinary request, and one that, the circumstances being what they are, I do not find very easy to grant. Then, too, if the letter was seen to fall from your pocket, how can I convince them that it fell from mine?"

"I thought I had said that they told the dauphiness that it was from yours that it fell."

"What!" said Monsieur de Nemours with some asperity, for he saw at once that this mistake might complicate matters with Madame de Clèves. "So the dauphiness has been told that I dropped this letter?"

"Yes," answered the Vidame; "that is what they told her,—and the mistake arose in this way: there were several of the queen's gentlemen in one of the rooms by the tennis-court where our clothes were hanging, and when we sent for them the letter dropped; these gentlemen took it up and read it aloud. Some thought it was written to you; others, that it was written to me. Chatelart, who took it, and from whom I have just tried to get it, said he had given it to the crown princess as a letter of yours; those who mentioned it to the queen unfortunately said it was mine,—so you can easily do what I wish, and get me out of this terrible complication."

Monsieur de Nemours had always been very fond of the Vidame of Chartres, and his relationship to Madame de Clèves rendered him still dearer. Nevertheless, he could not make up his mind to run the risk of her hearing of this letter as something in which he was concerned. He began to meditate profoundly, and the Vidame, guessing the nature of his thoughts, said: "I really believe you are afraid of falling out with your mistress; and I should be inclined to think that it is about the dauphiness that you are anxious, were it not that your freedom from any jealousy of Monsieur d'Anville forbids the thought. But however that may be, you must not sacrifice your peace of mind to mine, and I will make it possible for you to prove to the woman you love that this letter was written to me, and not to you. Here is a note from Madame d'Amboise; she is a friend of Madame de Themines, and to her she has confided all her feelings about me. In this note she asks me for her friend's letter,—the one I lost. My name is on the note, and its contents prove beyond the possibility of doubt that the letter she asks for is the one that has been picked up. I intrust this note to you, and I am willing that you should show it to your mistress in order to clear yourself. I beg of you not to lose a moment, but to go to the dauphiness this morning."

Monsieur de Nemours gave his promise to the Vidame of Chartres and took Madame d'Amboise's note. But his intention was not to see the crown princess; he thought he had something more urgent to do. He felt sure that she had already spoken about this letter to Madame de Clèves, and he could not endure that a woman he loved so much should have any reason for thinking that he was attached to any other.

He went to her house as soon as he thought she might be awake, and sent up word that he would not ask to have the honor at such an extraordinary hour if it were not on very important business. Madame de Clèves was not yet up; she was much embittered and agitated by the gloomy thoughts that had tormented her all night. She was extremely surprised when she heard that Monsieur de Nemours wanted to see her. Grieved as she was, she did not hesitate to send him word that she was ill, and unable to see him.

He was not pained by this refusal; an act of coolness at a time when she might be jealous was no unfavorable omen. He went to Monsieur de Clèves' apartments and told him that he had just called on his wife; that he was very sorry he could not see her, because he wished to speak to her of a matter of importance in which the Vidame of Chartres was interested. In a few words he told Monsieur de Clèves how serious the matter was, and Monsieur de Clèves took him at once to his wife's room. Nothing but the darkness enabled her to hide her agitation and surprise at seeing Monsieur de Nemours brought into her room by her husband. Monsieur de Clèves said that there was some question about a letter, and the Vidame's interests required her aid; he added that Monsieur de Nemours would tell her what was to be done, and that he should go to the king, who had just sent for him.

Monsieur de Nemours was left alone with Madame de Clèves,—which was exactly what he wanted. "I have come, Madame," he began, "to ask you if the dauphiness has not spoken to you about a letter which Châtelart gave her."

"She said something about it to me," answered Madame de Clèves; "but I don't understand how this letter concerns my uncle, and I am able to assure you that his name is not mentioned in it."

"True, Madame," Monsieur de Nemours went on, "his name is not mentioned; nevertheless, it was written to him, and it is of the utmost importance to him that you should get it out of her hands."

"I fail to understand," said Madame de Clèves, "how it concerns him that this letter should not be seen, and why it should be asked for in his name."

"If you will kindly listen to me," said Monsieur de Nemours, "I will speedily explain the matter to you, and you will soon see that the Vidame is so implicated that I should not have said anything about it even to the Prince of Clèves if I had not needed his assistance in order to have the honor of seeing you."

"I think that all that you might take the trouble to say to me would be useless," replied Madame de Clèves, somewhat tartly; "and it is much better that you should go to the crown princess and tell her frankly your interest in this letter, since it has been said that it belongs to you."

The vexation that Monsieur de Nemours saw in Madame de Clèves gave him the keenest pleasure he had yet known, and fully consoled him for his impatience to explain himself. "I do not know, Madame," he began, "what may have been said to the dauphiness; but this letter does not concern me personally, and it was written to the Vidame."

"That I believe," replied Madame de Clèves; "but the dauphiness has been told the contrary, and it will not seem to her likely that the Vidame's letters should fall out of your pockets. That is why, unless you have some good reason for concealing the truth from her, I advise you to confess it to her."

"I have nothing to confess to her," he went on; "the letter is none of mine, and if there is any one I wish to convince of this, it is not the crown princess. But, Madame, since the Vidame's fate is at stake, permit me to tell you some things which you will find quite worth listening to."

The silence of Madame de Clèves showed that she was willing to listen, and Monsieur de Nemours repeated in as few words as possible what the Vidame had told him. Although this might well have surprised, or at least interested, her, Madame de Clèves listened with such marked indifference that she seemed to doubt it or to find it unworthy of her attention. She maintained this indifference until Monsieur de Nemours mentioned Madame d'Amboise's note to the Vidame of Chartres, which was the proof of all he had just been saying. Since Madame de Clèves knew that she was a friend of Madame de Themines, it seemed to her possible that Monsieur de Nemours had been speaking the truth, and she began to think that possibly the letter in question had not been written to him. This thought suddenly dispelled her indifference. The prince read her the note, which exonerated him completely, and then handed it to her for examination, telling her that perhaps she knew the handwriting; she was compelled to take it and to read the address, and indeed every word, in order to make sure that the letter asked for was the one in her possession. Monsieur de Nemours said everything he could think of to convince her; and since a pleasant truth is readily believed, he succeeded in proving to Madame de Clèves that he had no part whatsoever in the letter.

Then she began to reflect on the Vidame's troubles and danger, to blame his evil conduct, and to desire means to aid him. She was surprised at the queen's behavior; she confessed to Monsieur de Nemours that the letter was in her possession,—in a word, so soon as she thought him innocent, she interested herself at once with the utmost cordiality in the very things that at first left her perfectly indifferent. They agreed that it was not necessary to return the letter to the crown princess, lest she should show it to Madame de Martigues, who knew Madame de Themines' handwriting, and would at once have guessed, from her interest in the Vidame, that the letter had been written to him. They also thought that it was better not to confide to the dauphiness the part concerning her mother-in-law, the queen. Madame de Clèves, under the pretext of her concern for her uncle's affairs, gladly promised to keep every secret that Monsieur de Nemours might intrust to her.

This prince would have talked with her about other things than the Vidame's affairs, and would have taken advantage of this opportunity to speak to her with greater freedom than he had ever done, were it not that word was brought to Madame de Clèves that the dauphiness had sent for her; Monsieur de Nemours consequently was obliged to withdraw. He went to see the Vidame, to tell him that after leaving him he had thought it better to see his niece, Madame de Clèves, than to go straight to the dauphiness. He brought forward many good arguments in support of what he had done and to make success seem probable.

Meanwhile Madame de Clèves dressed in all haste to go to the crown princess. She had scarcely entered the room when the dauphiness called her to her, and said in a low voice,—

"I have been waiting two hours for you, and never had more difficulty in concealing the truth than I have had this morning. The queen has heard about the letter I gave you yesterday, and thinks it was the Vidame of Chartres who dropped it; you know she takes a good deal of interest in him. She wanted to see the letter, and sent to ask Châtelart for it; he told her he had given it to me, and then they came to ask me for it, under the pretext that it was a very bright letter, which the queen was anxious to see. I did not dare say that you had it; I feared she would think that it had been placed in your hands because the Vidame is your uncle, and that there was some understanding between you and me. It has already occurred to me that she did not like his seeing me often; so I said the letter was in the pocket of the clothes I wore yesterday, and that those who had the key of the room in which they were locked had gone out. So give me the letter at once, that I may send it to her; and let me look at it before I send it, to see if I know the handwriting."

Madame de Clèves was even more embarrassed than she had expected. "I don't know, Madame," she answered, "what you will do; for Monsieur de Clèves, to whom I had given it, gave it back to Monsieur de Nemours, who came this morning to get him to ask you to return it to him. Monsieur de Clèves was imprudent enough to say that it was in his possession, and weak enough to yield to Monsieur de Nemours' entreaties and to give it to him."

"You have put me in the greatest possible embarrassment," said the dauphiness, "and you did very wrong to return the letter to Monsieur de Nemours; since I gave it you, you ought not to have returned it without my permission. What can I say to the queen, and what will she think? She will believe, and on good grounds, that this letter concerns me, and that there is something between the Vidame and me. She will never believe that the letter belongs to Monsieur de Nemours."

"I am extremely sorry," answered Madame de Clèves, "for the trouble I have caused,—I see just how great it is; but it is Monsieur de Clèves' fault, not mine."

"It is yours," retorted the dauphiness, "because you gave him the letter. There is not another woman in the world who would confide to her husband everything she knows."

"I acknowledge that I was wrong, Madame," said Madame de Clèves; "but think rather of repairing than of discussing my fault."

"Don't you remember pretty well what was in the letter?" asked the crown princess.

"Yes, Madame," was the reply; "I remember it, for I read it over more than once."

"In that case, you must go at once and write it in a disguised hand. This copy I will send to the queen. She will not show it to any one who has seen the original; and even if she should, I shall always maintain that it was the one that Châtelart gave me, and he will not dare to deny it."

Madame de Clèves agreed to this plan, and all the more readily because she thought she would send for Monsieur de Nemours to let her have the letter again, in order to copy it word for word, and so far as possible imitate the handwriting; in this way she thought the queen could not fail to be deceived. As soon as she got home she told her husband about the dauphiness's embarrassment, and begged him to send for Monsieur de Nemours; this was done, and he came at once. Madame de Clèves repeated to him what she had just told her husband, and asked him for the letter. Monsieur de Nemours replied that he had already given it back to the Vidame de Chartres, who was so glad to see it again and to be out of danger that he had at once sent it to Madame de Themines. Madame de Clèves was in new trouble; but at last, after discussing the matter together, they determined to write the letter from memory. They locked themselves up to work, left word at the door that no one was to be let in, and sent off Monsieur de Nemours' servants. This appearance of mystery and of confidence was far from unpleasant to this prince, and even to Madame de Clèves. The presence of her husband and the thought that she was furthering the Vidame's interests almost calmed her scruples. She felt only the pleasure of seeing Monsieur de Nemours; it was a fuller and purer joy than any she had ever felt, and it inspired her with a liveliness and ease that Monsieur de Nemours had never seen in her, and his love for her was only deepened. Since he had never before had such pleasant moments, his own spirits rose, and when Madame de Clèves wanted to recall the letter and to write, he, instead of aiding her seriously, did nothing but interrupt her with idle jests. Madame de Clèves was quite as merry; so that they had been long shut up together, and twice word had come from the dauphiness urging Madame de Clèves to make haste, before half the letter was written.

Monsieur de Nemours was only too happy to prolong so pleasant a visit, and forgot his friend's interests. Madame de Clèves was amusing herself, and forgot those of her uncle. At last, at four o'clock, the letter was hardly finished, and the handwriting was so unlike that of the original that it was impossible that the queen should not at once detect the truth; and she was not deceived by it. Although they did their best to convince her that the letter was written to Monsieur de Nemours, she remained convinced, not only that it was addressed to the Vidame de Chartres, but that the dauphiness had something to do with it, and that there was some understanding between him and her. This thought so intensified her hatred of this princess that she never forgave her, and persecuted her till she drove her from France.

As for the Vidame of Chartres, he was ruined so far as she was concerned; and whether it was that the Cardinal of Lorraine had already acquired an ascendency over her, or that the affair of this letter, in which she saw that she had been deceived, opened her eyes to the other deceptions of which the Vidame had been guilty, it is certain that he could never bring about a satisfactory reconciliation. Their intimacy was at an end, and she accomplished his ruin afterward at the time of the conspiracy of Amboise,[2] in which he was implicated.

After the letter had been sent to the crown princess, Monsieur de Clèves and Monsieur de Nemours went away. Madame de Clèves was left alone; and as soon as she was deprived of the presence of the man she loved, she seemed to awaken from a dream. She thought with surprise of the difference between her state of mind the previous evening and that she then felt; she pictured the coldness and harshness she had shown to Monsieur de Nemours so long as she had supposed that Madame de Themines' letter had been written to him, and the tranquillity and happiness that had succeeded them when he had proved to her that this letter in no way concerned him. When she recalled that the day before she had reproached herself, as if it were a crime, for having shown an interest that mere compassion had called forth, and that by her harshness she had betrayed a feeling of jealousy,—a certain proof of affection,—she scarcely

---

2. A 1560 conspiracy led by Louis de Bourbon, Prince of Condé, and the Huguenot Party in an effort to destroy the influence of the Guises over King Francis II. The plot failed.

recognized herself. When she thought further that Monsieur de Nemours saw that she was aware of his love; when he saw that, in spite of this, she treated him with perfect cordiality in her husband's presence,—indeed that she had treated him with more kindness than ever before, that she was the cause of her husband's sending for him, and that they had just passed an afternoon together privately,—she saw that there was an understanding between herself and Monsieur de Nemours; that she was deceiving a husband who deserved to be deceived less than any husband in the world; and she was ashamed to appear so unworthy of esteem even before the eyes of her lover. But what pained her more than all the rest was the memory of the state in which she had passed the night, and the acute grief she had suffered from the thought that Monsieur de Nemours loved another and that she had been deceived.

Up to that time she had not known the stings of mistrust and jealousy; her only thought had been to keep from loving Monsieur de Nemours, and she had not yet begun to fear that he loved another. Although the suspicions that this letter had aroused were wholly removed, they opened her eyes to the danger of being deceived, and gave her impressions of mistrust and jealousy such as she had never felt before. She was astounded that she had never yet thought how improbable it was that a man like Monsieur de Nemours, who had always treated women with such fickleness, should be capable of a sincere and lasting attachment. She thought it almost impossible that she could ever be satisfied with his love. "But if I could be," she asked herself, "what could I do with it? Do I wish it? Could I return it? Do I wish to begin a love-affair? Do I wish to fail in my duty to Monsieur de Clèves? Do I wish to expose myself to the cruel repentance and mortal anguish that are inseparable from love? I am over-whelmed by an affection which carries me away in spite of myself; all my reso-lutions are vain; I thought yesterday what I think to-day, and I act to-day in direct contradiction to my resolutions of yesterday. I must tear myself away from the society of Monsieur de Nemours; I must go to the country, strange as the trip may seem; and if Monsieur de Clèves persists in opposing it, or in demanding my reasons, perhaps I shall do him and myself the wrong of telling them to him." She held firm to this resolution, and spent the evening at home, instead of going to find out from the dauphiness what had become of the Vidame's pretended letter.

When Monsieur de Clèves came home she told him she wanted to go into the country; that she was not feeling well, and needed a change of air. Mon-sieur de Clèves, who felt sure from her appearance that there was nothing seri-ous ailed her, at first laughed at the proposed trip, and told her that she forgot the approaching marriages of the princesses and the tournament, and that she would not have time enough to make her preparations for appearing in due splendor alongside the other ladies. Her husband's arguments did not move her; she begged him, when he went to Compiègne with the king, to let her go to Coulommiers,[3]—a country-house they were building at a day's journey from Paris. Monsieur de Clèves gave his consent; so she went off with the intention of not returning at once, and the king left for a short stay at Compiègne.

Monsieur de Nemours felt very bad at not seeing Madame de Clèves again after the pleasant afternoon he had spent with her, which had so fired his

---

3. About twenty-five miles east of Paris.

hopes. His impatience to meet her once more left him no peace; so that when the king returned to Paris he determined to make a visit to his sister, the Duchess of Mercœur, who lived in the country not far from Coulommiers. He proposed to the Vidame to go with him; the latter gladly consented, to the delight of Monsieur de Nemours, who hoped to make sure of seeing Madame de Clèves by calling in company with the Vidame.

Madame de Mercœur was delighted to see them, and at once began to devise plans for their amusement. While they were deer-hunting, Monsieur de Nemours lost his way in the forest; and when he asked what road he should take, he was told that he was near Coulommiers. When he heard this word, "Coulommiers," he at once, without thinking, without forming any plan, dashed off in that direction. He got once more into the forest, and followed such paths as seemed to him to lead to the castle. These paths led to a summer-house, which consisted of a large room with two closets,[4] one opening on a flower-garden separated from the forest by a fence, and the other opening on one of the walks of the park. He entered the summer-house, and was about to stop and admire it, when he saw Monsieur and Madame de Clèves coming along the path, followed by a number of servants. Surprised at seeing Monsieur de Clèves, whom he had left with the king, his first impulse was to hide. He entered the closet near the flower-garden, with the intention of escaping by a door opening into the forest; but when he saw Madame de Clèves and her husband sitting in the summer-house, while their servants stayed in the park, whence they could not reach him without coming by Monsieur and Madame de Clèves, he could not resist the temptation to watch her, or overcome his curiosity to listen to her conversation with her husband, of whom he was more jealous than of any of his rivals.

He heard Monsieur de Clèves say to his wife: "But why don't you wish to return to Paris? What can keep you in the country? For some time you have had a taste for solitude which surprises me and pains me, because it keeps us apart. I find you in even lower spirits than usual, and I am afraid something distresses you."

"I have nothing on my mind," she answered, with some embarrassment; "but the bustle of a court is so great, and our house is always so thronged, that it is impossible for mind and body not to be tired and to need rest."

"Rest," he answered, "is not needed by persons of your age. Neither at home nor at court do you get tired, and I should be rather inclined to fear that you are glad to get away from me."

"If you thought that, you would do me great injustice," she replied, with ever-growing embarrassment; "but I beg of you to leave me here. If you could stay too I should be very glad, provided you would stay alone, and did not care for the throng of people who almost never leave you."

"Ah, Madame," exclaimed Monsieur de Clèves, "your air and your words show me that you have reasons for wishing to be alone which I don't know, and which I beg of you to tell me."

For a long time the prince besought her to tell him the reason, but in vain; and after she had refused in a way that only redoubled his curiosity, she stood for a time silent, with eyes cast down; then, raising her eyes to his, she said suddenly,—

---

4. Small private rooms for reading or meditation.

"Don't compel me to confess something which I have often meant to tell you, but had not the strength. Only remember that prudence does not require that a woman of my age, who is mistress of her actions, should remain exposed to the temptations of the court."

"What is it you suggest, Madame?" exclaimed Monsieur de Clèves. "I should not dare to say, for fear of offending you."

Madame de Clèves did not answer, and her silence confirming her husband's suspicions, he went on,—

"You are silent, and your silence tells me I am not mistaken."

"Well, sir," she answered, falling on her knees, "I am going to make you a confession such as no woman has ever made to her husband; the innocence of my actions and of my intentions gives me strength to do so. It is true that I have reasons for keeping aloof from the court, and I wish to avoid the perils that sometimes beset women of my age. I have never given the slightest sign of weakness, and I should never fear displaying any, if you would leave me free to withdraw from court, or if Madame de Chartres still lived to guide my actions. Whatever the dangers of the course I take, I pursue it with pleasure, in order to keep myself worthy of you. I beg your pardon a thousand times if my feelings offend you; at any rate I shall never offend you by my actions. Remember that to do what I am now doing requires more friendship and esteem for a husband than any one has ever had. Guide me, take pity on me, love me, if you can."

All the time she was speaking, Monsieur de Clèves sat with his head in his hands; he was really beside himself, and did not once think of lifting his wife up. But when she had finished, and he looked down and saw her, her face wet with tears, and yet so beautiful, he thought he should die of grief. He kissed her, and helped her to her feet.

"Do you, Madame, take pity on me," he said, "for I deserve it; and excuse me if in the first moments of a grief so poignant as mine I do not respond as I should to your appeal. You seem to me worthier of esteem and admiration than any woman that ever lived; but I also regard myself as the unhappiest of men. The first moment that I saw you, I was filled with love of you; neither your indifference to me nor the fact that you are my wife has cooled it: it still lives. I have never been able to make you love me, and I see that you fear you love another. And who, Madame, is the happy man that inspires this fear? Since when has he charmed you? What has he done to please you? What was the road he took to your heart? I found some consolation for not having touched it in the thought that it was beyond any one's reach; but another has succeeded where I have failed. I have all the jealousy of a husband and of a lover; but it is impossible to suffer as a husband after what you have told me. Your noble conduct makes me feel perfectly secure, and even consoles me as a lover. Your confidence and your sincerity are infinitely dear to me; you think well enough of me not to suppose that I shall take any unfair advantage of this confession. You are right, Madame,—I shall not; and I shall not love you less. You make me happy by the greatest proof of fidelity that a woman ever gave her husband; but, Madame, go on and tell me who it is you are trying to avoid."

"I entreat you, do not ask me," she replied; "I have determined not to tell you, and I think that the more prudent course."

"Have no fear, Madame," said Monsieur de Clèves; "I know the world too well to suppose that respect for a husband ever prevents men falling in love with his wife. He ought to hate those who do so, but without complaining; so once more, Madame, I beg of you to tell me what I want to know."

"You would urge me in vain," she answered; "I have strength enough to keep back what I think I ought not to say. My avowal is not the result of weakness, and it requires more courage to confess this truth than to undertake to hide it."

Monsieur de Nemours lost not a single word of this conversation, and Madame de Clèves' last remark made him quite as jealous as it made her husband. He was himself so desperately in love with her that he supposed every one else was just as much so. It was true in fact that he had many rivals, but he imagined even more than there were; and he began to wonder whom Madame de Clèves could mean. He had often believed that she did not dislike him, and he had formed this opinion from things which now seemed so slight that he could not imagine he had kindled a love so intense that it called for this desperate remedy. He was almost beside himself with excitement, and could not forgive Monsieur de Clèves for not insisting on knowing the name his wife was hiding.

Monsieur de Clèves, however, was doing his best to find it out, and after he had entreated her in vain, she said: "It seems to me that you ought to be satisfied with my sincerity; do not ask me anything more, and do not give me reason to repent what I have just done. Content yourself with the assurance I give you that no one of my actions has betrayed my feelings, and that not a word has ever been said to me at which I could take offence."

"Ah, Madame," Monsieur de Clèves suddenly exclaimed, "I cannot believe you! I remember your embarrassment the day your portrait was lost. You gave it away, Madame,—you gave away that portrait which was so dear to me, and belonged to me so legitimately. You could not hide your feelings; it is known that you are in love: your virtue has so far preserved you from the rest."

"Is it possible," the princess burst forth, "that you could suspect any misrepresentation in a confession like mine, which there was no ground for my making? Believe what I say: I purchase at a high price the confidence that I ask of you. I beg of you, believe that I did not give away the portrait; it is true that I saw it taken, but I did not wish to show that I saw it, lest I should be exposed to hearing things which no one had yet dared to say."

"How then did you see his love?" asked Monsieur de Clèves. "What marks of love were given to you?"

"Spare me the mortification," was her answer, "of repeating all the details which I am ashamed to have noticed, and have only convinced me of my weakness."

"You are right, Madame," he said, "I am unjust. Deny me when I shall ask such things, but do not be angry if I ask them."

At this moment some of the servants who were without, came to tell Monsieur de Clèves that a gentleman had come with a command from the king that he should be in Paris that evening. Monsieur de Clèves was obliged to leave at once, and he could say to his wife nothing except that he begged her to return the next day, and besought her to believe that though he was sorely distressed, he felt for her an affection and esteem which ought to satisfy her.

When he had gone, and Madame de Clèves was alone and began to think of what she had done, she was so amazed that she could scarcely believe it true.

She thought that she had wholly alienated her husband's love and esteem, and had thrown herself into an abyss from which escape was impossible. She asked herself why she had done this perilous thing, and saw that she had stumbled into it without intention. The strangeness of such a confession, for which she knew no precedent, showed her all her danger.

But when she began to think that this remedy, violent as it was, was the only one that could protect her against Monsieur de Nemours, she felt that she could not regret it, and that she had not gone too far. She spent the whole night in uncertainty, anxiety, and fear; but at last she grew calm. She felt a vague satisfaction in having given this proof of fidelity to a husband who so well deserved it, who had such affection and esteem for her, and who had just shown these by the way in which he had received her avowal.

Meanwhile Monsieur de Nemours had left the place where he had overheard a conversation which touched him keenly, and had hastened into the forest. What Madame de Clèves had said about the portrait gave him new life, by showing him that it was he whom she did not hate. He first gave himself up to this joy; but it was not of long duration, for he reflected that the same thing which showed him that he had touched the heart of Madame de Clèves, ought to convince him that he would never receive any token of it, and that it was impossible to gain any influence over a woman who resorted to so strange a remedy. He felt, nevertheless, great pleasure in having brought her to this extremity. He felt a certain pride in making himself loved by a woman so different from all others of her sex,—in a word, he felt a hundred times happier and unhappier. Night came upon him in the forest, and he had great difficulty in finding the way back to Madame de Mercœur's. He reached there at daybreak. He found it very hard to explain what had delayed him, but he made the best excuses he could, and returned to Paris that same day with the Vidame.

Monsieur de Nemours was so full of his passion and so surprised by what he had heard that he committed a very common imprudence,—that of speaking in general terms of his own feelings and of describing his own adventures under borrowed names. On his way back he turned the conversation to love: he spoke of the pleasure of being in love with a worthy woman; he mentioned the singular effects of this passion; and, finally, not being able to keep to himself his astonishment at what Madame de Clèves had done, he told the whole story to the Vidame, without naming her and without saying that he had any part in it. But he manifested such warmth and admiration that the Vidame at once suspected that the story concerned the prince himself. He urged him strongly to acknowledge this; he said that he had long known that he nourished a violent passion, and that it was wrong not to trust in a man who had confided to him the secret of his life. Monsieur de Nemours was too much in love to acknowledge his love; he had always hidden it from the Vidame, though he loved him better than any man at court. He answered that one of his friends had told him this adventure, and had made him promise not to speak of it, and he besought him to keep his secret. The Vidame promised not to speak of it; nevertheless, Monsieur de Nemours repented having told him.

Meanwhile, Monsieur de Clèves had gone to the king, his heart sick with a mortal wound. Never had a husband felt warmer love or higher respect for his wife. What he had heard had not lessened his respect, but this had assumed a new form. His most earnest desire was to know who had succeeded in pleasing her. Monsieur de Nemours was the first to occur to him, as the most fascinating man at court, and the Chevalier de Guise and the Marshal of Saint-André as two men who had tried to please her and had paid her much attention; so that he decided it must be one of these three. He reached the Louvre, and the king took him into his study to tell him that he had chosen him to carry Madame to Spain; that he had thought that the prince would discharge this duty better than any one; and that no one would do so much credit to France as Madame de Clèves. Monsieur de Clèves accepted this appointment with due respect, and even looked upon it as something that would remove his wife from court without attracting any attention; but the date of their departure was still too remote to relieve his present embarrassment. He wrote at once to Madame de Clèves to tell her what the king had said, and added that he was very anxious that she should come to Paris. She returned in obedience to his request, and when they met, each found the other in the deepest gloom.

Monsieur de Clèves addressed her in the most honorable terms, and seemed well worthy of the confidence she had placed in him.

"I have no uneasiness about your conduct," he said; "you have more strength and virtue than you think. It is not dread of the future that distresses me; I am only distressed at seeing that you have for another feelings that I have not been able to inspire in you."

"I do not know how to answer you," she said; "I am ready to die with shame when I speak to you. Spare me, I beg of you, these painful conversations. Regulate my conduct; let me see no one,—that is all I ask; but permit me never to speak of a thing which makes me seem so little worthy of you, and which I regard as so unworthy of me."

"You are right, Madame," he answered; "I abuse your gentleness and your confidence. But do you too take some pity on the state into which you have cast me, and remember that whatever you have told me, you conceal from me a name which excites an unendurable curiosity. Still, I do not ask you to gratify it; but I must say that I believe the man I must envy to be the Marshal of Saint-André, the Duke of Nemours, or the Chevalier de Guise."

"I shall not answer," she said, blushing, "and I shall give you no occasion for lessening or strengthening your suspicions; but if you try to find out by watching me, you will surely make me so embarrassed that every one will notice it. In Heaven's name," she went on, "invent some illness, that I may see no one!"

"No, Madame," he replied, "it would soon be found that it was not real; and moreover I want to place my confidence in you alone,—that is the course my heart recommends, and my reason too. In your present mood, by leaving you free, I protect you by a closer guard than I could persuade myself to set about you."

Monsieur de Clèves was right; the confidence he showed in his wife proved a stronger protection against Monsieur de Nemours and inspired her to make austerer resolutions than any form of constraint could have done. She went to the Louvre and visited the dauphiness as usual; but she avoided Monsieur de Nemours with so much care that she took away nearly all his happiness at thinking that she loved him. He saw nothing in her actions which did not prove the contrary. He was almost ready to believe that what he had heard was a dream, so unlikely did it appear. The only thing that assured him that he was not mistaken was the extreme sadness of Madame de Clèves, in spite of all her efforts to conceal it. Possibly kind words and glances would not have so fanned Monsieur de Nemours' love as did this austere conduct.

One evening, when Monsieur and Madame de Clèves were with the queen, some one said that it was reported that the king was going to name another nobleman of the court to accompany Madame to Spain. Monsieur de Clèves fixed his eyes on his wife when the speaker added that it would be either the Chevalier de Guise or the Marshal of Saint-André. He noticed that she showed no agitation at either of these names, or at the mention of their joining the party. This led him to think that it was neither of these that she dreaded to see; and wishing to determine the matter, he went to the room where the king was. After a short absence he returned to his wife and whispered to her that he had just learned that it would be Monsieur de Nemours who would go with them to Spain.

The name of Monsieur de Nemours and the thought of seeing him every day during a long journey, in her husband's presence, so agitated Madame de Clèves that she could not conceal it, and wishing to assign other reasons, she answered,—

"The choice of that gentleman will be very disagreeable for you; he will divide all the honors, and I think you ought to try to have some one else appointed."

"It is not love of glory, Madame," said Monsieur de Clèves, "that makes you dread that Monsieur de Nemours should come with me. Your regret springs from another cause. This regret tells me what another woman would have told by her delight. But do not be alarmed; what I have just told you is not true: I made it up to make sure of a thing which I had only too long inclined to believe." With these words he went away, not wishing by his presence to add to his wife's evident embarrassment.

At that moment Monsieur de Nemours entered, and at once noticed Madame de Clèves' condition. He went up to her, and said in a low voice that he respected her too much to ask what made her so thoughtful. His voice aroused her from her revery; and looking at him, without hearing what he said, full of her own thoughts and fearful that her husband would see him by her side, she said: "In Heaven's name, leave me alone!"

"Alas! Madame," he replied, "I leave you only too much alone. Of what can you complain? I do not dare to speak to you, or even to look at you; I never come near you without trembling. How have I brought such a remark on myself, and why do you make me seem to have something to do with the depression in which I find you?"

Madame de Clèves deeply regretted that she had given Monsieur de Nemours an opportunity to speak to her more frankly than he had ever done. She left him without giving him any answer, and went home in a state of agitation such as she had never known. Her husband soon noticed this; he perceived that she was afraid lest he should speak to her about what had just happened. He followed her into her room and said to her,—

"Do not try to avoid me, Madame; I shall say nothing that could displease you. I beg your pardon for surprising you as I did; I am sufficiently punished by what I learned. Monsieur de Nemours was the man whom I most feared. I see your danger: control yourself for your own sake, and, if possible, for mine. I do not ask this as your husband, but as a man, all of whose happiness you make, and who feels for you a tenderer and stronger love than he whom your heart prefers." Monsieur de Clèves nearly broke down at these last words, which he could hardly utter. His wife was much moved, and bursting into tears, she embraced him with a gentleness and a sorrow that almost brought him to the same condition. They remained for some time perfectly silent, and separated without having strength to utter a word.

The preparations for Madame Elisabeth's marriage were completed, and the Duke of Alva[5] arrived for the ceremony. He was received with all the pomp and formality that the occasion required. The king sent the Prince of Condé, the Cardinals of Lorraine and Guise, the Dukes of Lorraine, Ferrara, Aumale, Bouillon, Guise, and Nemours to meet him. They were accompanied by many gentlemen and a great number of pages wearing their liveries. The king himself received the Duke of Alva at the first door of the Louvre with two hundred gentlemen in waiting, with the constable at their head. As the duke drew near the king, he wished to embrace his knees;[6] but the king prevented him, and made him walk by his side to call on the queen and on Madame Elisabeth, to whom the Duke of Alva brought a magnificent present from his master. He then called on Madame Marguerite, the king's sister, to convey to her the compliments of Monsieur de Savoie, and to assure her that he would arrive in a few days. There were large receptions at the Louvre, to show the Duke of Alva and the Prince of Orange, who accompanied him, the beauties of the court.

Madame de Clèves did not dare to stay away, much as she desired it, through fear of displeasing her husband, who gave her special orders to go. What made him even more determined was the absence of Monsieur de Nemours. He had gone to meet Monsieur de Savoie, and after that prince's arrival he was obliged to be with him almost all the time, to help him in his preparations for the wedding ceremonies; hence Madame de Clèves did not meet him so often as usual, and she was able to enjoy a little peace.

The Vidame of Chartres had not forgotten the talk he had had with Monsieur de Nemours. He had made up his mind that the adventure this prince had told him was his own, and he watched him so closely that perhaps he would have made out the truth, had not the arrival of the Duke of Alva and of Monsieur de Savoie so changed and busied the court that he had no further opportunity. His desire for more information, or, rather, the natural tendency to tell all one knows to the woman one loves, made him mention to Madame de Martigues the extraordinary conduct of the woman who had confessed to her husband the love she felt for another man. He assured her that it was Monsieur de Nemours who had inspired this violent passion, and he besought her to aid him in observing this prince. Madame de Martigues was greatly interested in what the Vidame had told her, and her curiosity about the dauphiness's relations with Monsieur de Nemours made her more anxious than ever to get to the bottom of the affair.

A few days before the one set for the wedding the crown princess gave a supper to her father-in-law the king and the Duchess of Valentinois. Madame de Clèves, who was delayed in dressing, started for the Louvre a little later than usual, and on her way met a gentleman coming from the dauphiness to fetch her. When she entered the room the crown princess called out to her from the

5. He acted as a stand-in for Philip II at the marriage.
6. An act of homage.

bed on which she was lying that she had been waiting for her with the utmost impatience.

"I fancy, Madame," she replied, "that I have no cause to be grateful to you for this impatience; it is doubtless for some other reason that you were eager to see me."

"You are right," said the dauphiness; "but, nevertheless, you ought to be obliged to me, for I am going to tell you something that I am sure you will be very glad to hear."

Madame de Clèves knelt down by the side of the bed in such a way that, fortunately for her, her face was in the dark. "You know," said the crown princess, "how anxious we have been to find out the cause of the change in the Duke of Nemours; I think I have found out, and it is something that will surprise you. He is desperately in love with one of the most beautiful women of the court, and the lady returns his love."

These words, which Madame de Clèves could not take to herself, because she thought that no one knew of her love for this prince, gave her a pang that may be easily imagined.

"I see nothing in that," she replied, "which is surprising for a man of his age and appearance."

"But that," resumed the dauphiness, "is not the surprising part; what is amazing is the fact that this woman who loves Monsieur de Nemours has never given him any token of it, and that her fear that she may not always be able to control her passion has caused her to confess it to her husband to persuade him to take her away from court. And it is Monsieur de Nemours himself who is the authority for what I say."

If Madame de Clèves had been grieved at first by thinking that the affair in no way concerned her, these last words of the dauphiness filled her with despair, since they made it sure that it did concern her only too deeply. She could make no reply, but remained with her head resting on the bed while the dauphiness went on talking, too much taken up with what she was saying to notice her embarrassment. When Madame de Clèves had recovered some of her self-control, she answered,—

"This does not sound like a very probable story, and I wonder who told it to you."

"It was Madame de Martigues, who heard it from the Vidame. You know he is her lover; he told it to her as a secret, as he heard it from the Duke of Nemours. It is true that the Duke of Nemours did not mention the lady's name and did not even acknowledge that it was he who was loved; but the Vidame de Chartres has no doubt about that."

As the dauphiness pronounced these last words, some one drew near the bed. Madame de Clèves was turned away so that she could not see who it was; but she knew when the dauphiness exclaimed, with an air of surprise and amusement, "There he is himself, and I am going to ask how much truth there is in it."

Madame de Clèves knew that it must be the Duke of Nemours, and so it was. Without turning toward him, she leaned over to the crown princess and whispered to her to be careful not to say a word about this adventure, that he had told it to the Vidame in confidence, and that this would very possibly set them by the ears. The dauphiness answered laughingly that she was absurdly pru-

dent, and turned toward Monsieur de Nemours. He was arrayed for the evening entertainment, and addressed her with all his usual grace.

"I believe, Madame," he began, "that I can think, without impertinence, that
you were talking about me when I came in, that you wanted to ask me something, and that Madame de Clèves objected."

"You are right," replied the dauphiness; "but I shall not be as obliging to her
as I usually am. I want to know whether a story I have heard is true, and
whether you are the man who is in love with and is loved by a lady of the court
who carefully conceals her passion from you and has confessed it to her husband."

Madame de Clèves' agitation and embarrassment cannot be conceived, and
she would have welcomed death as an escape from her sufferings; but Monsieur de Nemours was even more embarrassed, if that is possible. This statement from the lips of the dauphiness, who, he had reason to believe, did not
hate him, in the presence of Madame de Clèves, whom he loved better than
any woman at court, and who also loved him, so overwhelmed him that he
could not control his face. The embarrassment into which his blunder had
plunged Madame de Clèves, and the thought of the good reason he gave her to
hate him, made it impossible for him to answer. The dauphiness, noticing his
intense confusion, said to Madame de Clèves: "Look at him, look at him, and
see whether this is not his own story!"

Meanwhile Monsieur de Nemours, recovering from his first agitation, and
recognizing the importance of escaping from this dangerous complication,
suddenly recovered his presence of mind and regained his composure.

"I must acknowledge, Madame," he said, "that no one could be more surprised and distressed than I am by the Vidame de Chartres' treachery in repeating the adventure of one of my friends which I told to him in confidence. I
might easily revenge myself," he went on, smiling in a way that almost dispelled the dauphiness's suspicions; "since he has confided to me matters of
considerable importance. But I fail to understand why you do me the honor of
implicating me in this affair. The Vidame cannot say that it concerns me,
because I told him the very opposite. It may do very well to represent me as a
man in love; but it will hardly do to represent me as a man who is loved,—
which, Madame, is what you do."

Monsieur de Nemours was very glad to say something to the dauphiness
which had some connection with his appearance in former times, in order to
divert her thoughts. She caught his meaning; but without referring to these
last words of his, she continued to harp on his evident confusion.

"I was embarrassed, Madame," he replied, "out of zeal for my friend and
from fear of the reproaches he would be justified in making to me for repeating
a thing dearer to him than life. Nevertheless, he only told me half, and did not
mention the name of the woman he loves. I simply know that he is more in love
and more to be pitied than any man in the world."

"Do you find him so worthy of pity," asked the crown princess, "because he
is loved?"

"Are you sure that he is?" he answered; "and do you think that a woman who
felt a real love would confide it to her husband? This woman, I am sure, knows
nothing about love, and has mistaken for it a faint feeling of gratitude for his
devotion to her. My friend cannot nourish any hope; but, wretched as he is, he

has at least the consolation of having made her fearful of loving him, and he would not change his fate for that of any man in the world."

"Your friend's love is easily satisfied," said the crown princess, "and I begin to think that you can't be talking about yourself; I am inclined to agree with Madame de Clèves, who maintains that there can be no truth in the whole story."

"I don't think there can be," said Madame de Clèves, who had not yet said a word; "and if it were true, how could it become known? It is extremely unlikely that a woman capable of such an extraordinary thing would have the weakness to tell of it. Evidently a husband would not think of doing such a thing, unless he were a husband very unworthy of the confidence that was placed in him."

Monsieur de Nemours, who saw that Madame de Clèves' suspicions had fallen on her husband, was very glad to strengthen them; he knew that he was his strongest rival.

"Jealousy," he replied, "and the desire to find out more than he had been told, may induce a husband to commit a great many indiscretions."

Madame de Clèves was at the end of her strength; and being unable to carry on the conversation further, she was about to say that she did not feel well, when, fortunately for her, the Duchess of Valentinois came in to tell the dauphiness that the king would arrive very soon. The crown princess accordingly went into her room to dress; whereupon Monsieur de Nemours came up to Madame de Clèves as she was about to follow her, and said,—

"Madame, I would give my life to speak to you a moment; but of all the important things I should have to say to you, nothing seems to me more important than to beg you to believe that if I have said anything which might seem to refer to the dauphiness, I have done so for reasons which do not concern her."

Madame de Clèves pretended not to hear him, but moved away without looking at him and joined the suite of the king, who had just come in. There being a great crowd present, her foot caught in her dress, and she made a misstep; she took advantage of this excuse to leave a place where she had no strength to stay longer, and went away pretending that she could not stand.

Monsieur de Clèves went to the Louvre, and being surprised not to see his wife, he was told of the accident that had just happened to her. He left at once, to find out how she was; he found her in bed, and she told him that she was but slightly hurt. When he had been with her for some time he saw that she was exceedingly sad; this surprised him, and he asked her, "What is the matter? You seem to suffer in some other way than that you have told me."

"I could not be in greater distress than I am," she answered. "What use did you make of the extraordinary, I might say foolish, confidence I had in you? Was I not worthy of secrecy on your part? And even if I was unworthy of it, did not your own interest urge it? Was it necessary that your curiosity to know a name which I ought not to tell you, could force you to confide in any one else in order to discover it? Nothing but curiosity could have led you to commit such an imprudence. The consequences have been most disastrous; the story is known, and has just been told to me, without any notion that I was the person most concerned."

"What do you say, Madame?" he replied. "You accuse me of having repeated what passed between us, and you tell me the story is known! I shall not defend myself from the charge of repeating it; you can't believe it, and you must have taken to yourself something said about some other woman."

"Oh, sir," she said, "in the whole world there is not another case like mine; there is not another woman capable of doing what I have done! Chance could not make any one invent it; no one has ever imagined it,—the very thought never entered any one's mind but mine. The dauphiness has just told me the whole story; she heard it from the Vidame of Chartres, and he had it from Monsieur de Nemours."

"Monsieur de Nemours!" exclaimed Monsieur de Clèves, with a gesture expressive of the wildest despair. "What, Monsieur de Nemours knows that you love him and that I know it!"

"You always want to fix on Monsieur de Nemours rather than any one else," she replied; "I told you that I should never say anything about your suspicions. I cannot say whether Monsieur de Nemours knows my share in this affair, or the part you assign to him; but he told it to the Vidame de Chartres, saying that he had it from one of his friends, who did not give the name of the woman. This friend of Monsieur de Nemours must be one of your friends, and you must have told the story to him in an effort to get some information."

"Is there a friend in the world," he exclaimed, "to whom any one would make a confidence of that sort? And would any one try to confirm his suspicions by telling another what one would wish to hide from one's self? Consider rather to whom you have spoken. It is more likely that the secret got out from you than from me. You could not endure your misery alone, and you sought solace in making a confidant of some friend who has played you false."

"Do not torment me further," she burst forth, "and do not be so cruel as to charge me with a fault which you have committed. Could you suspect me of that? And because I was capable of speaking to you, am I capable of speaking of it to any one else?"

His wife's confession had so convinced Monsieur de Clèves of her frankness, and she so warmly denied having mentioned the incident to any one, that Monsieur de Clèves did not know what to think. For his own part, he was sure that he had repeated nothing; it was something nobody could have guessed: it was known, and it must have become known through one of them. But what caused the liveliest grief was the knowledge that this secret was in somebody's hands, and apparently would be soon divulged.

Madame de Clèves' thoughts were nearly the same; she held it equally impossible that her husband should have spoken and should not have spoken. What Monsieur de Nemours had said, that curiosity might make a husband indiscreet, seemed to apply so well to just the state of mind in which Monsieur de Clèves was, that she could not think it was a mere strange coincidence; and this probability compelled her to believe that Monsieur de Clèves had abused her confidence in him. They were both so busy with their thoughts that they for a long time did not speak, and when they broke the silence, it was but to repeat what they had already said very often, and they felt farther apart than they had ever been.

It is easy to picture the way they passed the night. Monsieur de Clèves' constancy had been nearly worn out by his effort to endure the unhappiness of seeing his wife, whom he adored, touched with love for another man. His courage was wellnigh exhausted; he even doubted whether this was an opportunity to make use of it, in a matter in which his pride and honor were so sorely wounded. He no longer knew what to think of his wife; he could not decide what course of action he should urge her to take nor how he should himself act; on all sides he saw nothing but precipices and steep abysses. At last, after long distress and uncertainty, reflecting that he should soon have to go to Spain, he made up his mind to do nothing that should confirm any one's suspicions or knowledge of his unhappy condition. He went to Madame de Clèves and told her that it was not worth while to discuss which of them had betrayed their secret, but that it was very important to prove that the story that had been told was a mere invention in no way referring to her; that it depended on her to convince Monsieur de Nemours and the rest of this; that she had only to treat him with the severity and coldness which she ought to have for a man who made love to her, and that in this way she would soon dispel the notion that she had any interest in him. Hence, he argued, there was no need of her distressing herself about what he might have thought, because if henceforth she should betray no weakness, his opinion would necessarily change; and above all, he urged upon her the necessity of going to the palace and into the world as much as usual.

When he had finished, Monsieur de Clèves left his wife without awaiting her answer. She thought what he had said very reasonable, and her indignation against Monsieur de Nemours made her think it would be very easy to carry it out; but she found it very hard to appear at all the wedding festivities with a calm face and an easy mind. Nevertheless, since she had been selected to carry the train of the dauphiness's dress,—a special honor to her alone of all the princesses,—she could not decline it without exciting much attention and wonder. Hence she resolved to make a great effort to control herself; but the rest of the day she devoted to preparations and to indulging the feelings that harassed her. She shut herself up alone in her room. What most distressed her was to have grounds for complaint against Monsieur de Nemours, with no chance of excusing him. She felt sure that he had told the story to the Vidame,— this he had acknowledged; and she felt sure too, from the way in which he spoke of it, that he knew that she was implicated. What excuse could be found for so great a piece of imprudence, and what had become of the prince's discretion, that had once so touched her? "He was discreet," she said to herself, "so long as he thought himself unhappy; but the mere thought of happiness, vague as it was, put an end to his discretion. He could not imagine that he was loved without wishing it to be known. He has said everything he could say. I have not confessed that it was he whom I loved; he suspected it, and showed his suspicions. If he had been sure of it, he would have done the same thing. I did wrong to think that there ever was a man capable of concealing what flattered his vanity. Yet it is for this man, whom I thought so different from other men, that I find myself in the same plight as other women whom I so little resemble. I have lost the love and esteem of a husband who ought to make me happy; soon every one will look upon me as a woman possessed by a mad and violent passion. The man for whom I feel it is no longer ignorant of it, and it is to escape just these evils that I have imperilled all my peace of mind, and even my life." These sad reflections were followed by a torrent of tears; but whatever the grief by which she felt herself overwhelmed, she knew that she could have endured it if she had been satisfied with Monsieur de Nemours.

This prince's state of mind was no more tranquil. His imprudence in unbosoming himself to the Vidame of Chartres, and the cruel results of this imprudence, caused him great pain. He could not without intense mortification recall Madame de Clèves' agitation and embarrassment. He could not forgive himself for having spoken about that affair in terms which, though courteous in themselves, must have seemed coarse and impolite, since they had implied to Madame de Clèves that he knew that she was the woman who was deeply in love, and with him. All that he could wish was a conversation with her; but he thought this more to be dreaded than desired. "What should I have to say to her?" he exclaimed. "Should I once more undertake to tell her what I have already made too clear to her? Shall I let her see that I know she loves me,—I, who have never dared to tell her that I loved her? Shall I begin by speaking to her openly of my passion, in order to appear like a man emboldened by hope? Can I think merely of going near her, and should I dare to embarrass her by my presence? How could I justify myself? I have no excuse, I am unworthy to appear before Madame de Clèves, and I do not venture to hope that she will ever look at me again. By my own fault, I have given her a better protection against me than any she sought, and sought perhaps in vain. By my imprudence I have lost the happiness and pride of being loved by the most charming and estimable woman in the world. If I had lost this happiness without her suffering, without having inflicted on her a bitter blow, that would be some consolation; and at this moment I feel more keenly the harm I have done her than I did when I was in her presence."

Monsieur de Nemours long tortured himself with these thoughts. The desire to see Madame de Clèves perpetually haunted him, and he began to look about for means of communicating with her. He thought of writing to her; but he considered, after his blunder, and in view of her character, that the best thing he could do would be to show his profound respect, and by silence and evident distress to make it clear that he did not dare to meet her, and to wait until time, chance, or her own interest in him should work in his favor. He resolved also to forbear from reproaching the Vidame of Chartres for his treachery, lest he should confirm his suspicions.

The betrothal of Madame Elisabeth, which was to take place on the morrow, and the wedding, which was to be celebrated on the following day, so occupied the court that Madame de Clèves and Monsieur de Nemours had no difficulty in concealing their grief and annoyance from the public. The dauphiness referred only lightly to their talk with Monsieur de Nemours, and Monsieur de Clèves took pains not to say anything more to his wife about what had happened, so that soon she found herself more at ease than she had supposed possible.

The betrothal was celebrated at the Louvre; and after the banquet and the ball, the whole royal household went to the bishop's palace to pass the night, as was the custom. The next morning the Duke of Alva, who always dressed very simply, put on a coat of cloth of gold, mingled with red, yellow, and black, and all covered with precious stones; on his head he wore a crown. The Prince of Orange, arrayed in equal splendor, came with his servants, and all the Spaniards with theirs, to fetch the Duke of Alva from the Villeroy mansion, where he was staying; and they started, walking four abreast, for the bishop's palace. As soon as they arrived, they went in due order to the church. The king conducted Madame Elisabeth, who also wore a crown; her dress was held by Mesdemoiselles de Montpensier and De Longueville; then came the queen, but not wearing a crown; after her came the dauphiness, the king's sister, Madame de Lorraine, and the Queen of Navarre, with princesses holding their trains. The queens and princesses had all their maids-of-honor magnificently dressed in the same colors that they themselves wore, so that the maids-of-honor could be at once distinguished by the colors of their dresses. They ascended the platform set up in the church, and the wedding ceremony took place. Then they returned to dinner at the bishop's palace, and at about five left for the palace, to be present at the banquet to which the parliament, the sovereign courts,[7] and the city officials had been invited. The king, the queens, the princes, and princesses ate at the marble table in the great hall of the palace, the Duke of Alva being seated near the new Queen of Spain. Below the steps of the marble table, on the king's right hand, was a table for the ambassadors, the archbishops, and the knights of the order,[8] and on the other side a table for the members of parliament.

The Duke of Guise, dressed in a robe of cloth of gold, was the king's majordomo, the Prince of Condé his head butler, the Duke of Nemours his cupbearer.[9] After the tables were removed, the ball began; it was interrupted by the ballets and by extraordinary shows; then it was renewed, until, after midnight, the king and all the court returned to the Louvre. Though Madame de Clèves was very much depressed, she yet appeared in the eyes of every one, and especially in those of Monsieur de Nemours, incomparably beautiful. He did not dare to speak to her, although the confusion of the ceremony gave him many opportunities; but his demeanor was so dejected, and he showed such fear of approaching her, that she began to deem him less blameworthy, though he had not said a word in excuse of his conduct. His behavior was the same on the succeeding days, and continued to produce the same impression on Madame de Clèves.

At last the day of the tournament came. The queens betook themselves to the galleries and the raised seats set apart for them. The four champions appeared at the end of the lists, with a number of horses and servants, who formed the most magnificent spectacle ever seen in France.

The king's colors were plain black and white, which he always wore for the sake of Madame de Valentinois, who was a widow. The Duke of Ferrara and all his suite wore yellow and red. Monsieur de Guise appeared in pink and white: no one knew why he wore these colors; but it was remembered that they were those of a beautiful woman whom he had loved before she was married, and still loved, though he did not dare to show it. Monsieur de Nemours wore yellow and black,—why, no one knew. Madame de Clèves, however, had no difficulty in guessing: she remembered telling him one day that she liked yellow, and was sorry she was a blonde, because she could never wear that color. He believed that he could appear in it without indiscretion, because since Madame de Clèves never wore it, no one could suspect that it was hers.

---

7. Legal courts of appeal. The Parliament of Paris was essentially a judicial body.
8. The Order of the Knights of Malta, a military religious order that had led many battles against the Turks.
9. The positions of butler and cupbearer were honorific designations only for the duration of the ceremonies.

Never was there seen greater skill than the four champions displayed. Although the king was the best horseman in the kingdom, it was hard to know to whom to give the palm.[1] Monsieur de Nemours showed a grace in all he did that inclined in his favor women less interested than Madame de Clèves. As soon as she saw him at the end of the lists she felt an unusual emotion, and every time he ran she could scarcely conceal her joy when he escaped without harm.

Toward evening, when all was nearly over, and the company on the point of withdrawing, the evil fate of the country made the king wish to break another lance. He ordered the Count of Montgomery, who was very skilful, to enter the lists. The count begged the king to excuse him, and made every apology he could think of; but the king, with some annoyance, sent him word that he insisted upon it. The queen sent a message to the king beseeching him not to run again, saying that he had done so well he ought to be satisfied, and that she entreated him to come to her. He answered that it was for love of her that he was going to run again, and entered the field. She sent Monsieur de Savoie to beg him again to come; but all was in vain. He started, the lances broke, and a splinter from that of the Count of Montgomery struck him in the eye and remained in it. He fell at once to the ground. His equerries and Monsieur de Montgomery, one of the marshals of the field, ran up to him, and were alarmed to see him so severely wounded. The king was not alarmed; he said it was a slight matter, and that he forgave the count. It is easy to conceive the excitement and distress caused by this unhappy accident after a day devoted to merry-making. As soon as the king had been carried to his bed the surgeons examined his wound, which they found very serious. The constable at that moment recalled the prediction made to the king that he should be slain in single combat, and he had no doubt that the prophecy would come true.

As soon as the King of Spain, who was then in Brussels, heard of this accident, he sent his physician, a man of vast experience; but he thought the king's state desperate.

The court, thus distracted and torn by conflicting interests, was much excited on the eve of this great event; but all dissensions were quieted, and there seemed to be no other cause of anxiety than the king's health. The queens, the princes, and the princesses scarcely left his ante-chamber.

Madame de Clèves, knowing that she was compelled to be there and to meet Monsieur de Nemours, and that she could not hide from her husband the embarrassment that the sight of him would produce; knowing too that the mere presence of this prince would excuse him and overthrow all her plans,—decided to feign illness. The court was too busy to notice her conduct or to make out how much was true and how much feigned in her illness. Her husband alone could know the truth; but she was not sorry to have him know it, so she remained at home, thinking little of the great change that was impending, and perfectly free to indulge in her own reflections. Every one was with the king. Monsieur de Clèves came at certain hours to tell her the news. He treated her as he had always done, except that when they were alone his manner was a little colder and stiffer. He never spoke to her again about what had happened, and she lacked the strength and deemed it unwise to reopen the subject.

---

1. An ancient symbol of victory. Here, award the victory.

Monsieur de Nemours, who had expected to find a few moments to speak to Madame de Clèves, was much surprised and pained not to have even the pleasure of seeing her. The king grew so much worse that on the seventh day his physicians gave him up. He received the news of his approaching death with wonderful firmness, all the more admirable because he died by such an unfortunate accident, in the prime of life, full of happiness, adored by his subjects, and loved by a mistress whom he madly worshipped. The evening before his death he had Madame his sister married with Monsieur de Savoie, very quietly.

It is easy to conceive in what state was Madame de Valentinois. The queen did not permit her to see the king, and sent to her to ask for the king's seals and for the crown jewels, which were in her keeping. The duchess asked if the king was dead; and when they told her no, she said: "Then I have no master, and no one can compel me to return what he intrusted to my hands."

As soon as he had died, at the castle of Tournelles, the Duke of Ferrara, the Duke of Guise, and the Duke of Nemours conducted to the Louvre the queen-dowager, the king, and his wife the queen.[2] Monsieur de Nemours escorted the queen-dowager. Just as they were starting, she drew back a little and told her daughter-in-law she was to go first; but it was easy to see that there was more vexation than politeness in this compliment.

Part V

The Cardinal of Lorraine had acquired complete ascendency over the mind of the queen-dowager; the Vidame de Chartres had completely fallen from her good graces, but his love for Madame de Martigues and his enjoyment of his freedom had prevented him from suffering from this change as much as he might have done. During the ten days of the king's illness the cardinal had had abundant leisure to form his plans and to persuade the queen to take measures in conformity with his projects; hence as soon as the king was dead, the queen ordered the constable to remain at the castle of Tournelles to keep watch by the body of the late king and to take charge of the customary ceremonies. This order kept him aloof from everything, and prevented all action on his part. He sent a messenger to the king of Navarre to summon him in all diligence, in order that they might combine to oppose the promotion that evidently awaited the Guises. The command of the army was given to the Duke of Guise; that of the treasury to the Cardinal of Lorraine; the Duchess of Valentinois was driven from the court; the Cardinal of Tournon, the avowed enemy of the constable, was recalled, as well as the Chancelier Olivier, the open enemy of the Duchess of Valentinois, so that the aspect of the court was completely changed. The Duke of Guise was made equal to the princes of the blood, and allowed to carry the king's mantle at the funeral; he and his brothers were placed high in authority, not merely through the cardinal's influence over the queen, but also because she believed that she could overthrow them if they should offend her, while she would not be able to overthrow the constable, who was supported by the princes of the blood.

2. The new king, Francis II, married to Mary Stuart, who became Mary, queen of Scots, after her husband's death in 1560. "Queen-dowager": former king's widow, Catherine de Médicis.

After the funeral the constable went to the Louvre, but met with a cold reception from the king. He desired to speak with the king in private; but the king called the Guises and told him in their presence that he advised him to seek retirement, that the treasury and the command of the army were already disposed of, and that whenever he might need his counsels he should summon him. The queen-dowager received him even more coldly than the king; she went so far as to remind him of his insulting remark to the late king about his children not looking like him. The King of Navarre arrived, and was received no better. The Prince of Condé, who was less patient than his brother, complained bitterly, but all in vain; he was exiled from court under the pretext of sending him to Flanders to sign the ratification of the treaty of peace.[3] The King of Navarre was shown a forged letter of the King of Spain which accused him of making attempts on his territory, and he was made to fear for his own possessions, and induced to return to his kingdom. The queen made this easy for him by assigning to him the duty of escorting Madame Elisabeth; she even obliged him to start before her, so that there was no one left at court to oppose the power of the household of Guise.

Although it was most unfortunate for Monsieur de Clèves that he could not escort Madame Elisabeth, he still could not complain, in view of the lofty rank of the man who was preferred; but the deprivation of the dignity was not what pained him, but rather that his wife lost an opportunity of absenting herself from court without exciting comment.

A few days after the king's death it was decided that the court should go to Rheims for the coronation. Madame de Clèves, who had hitherto stayed at home under pretence of illness, begged her husband to excuse her from accompanying the court, and to let her go to Coulommiers to get strength from the change of air. He replied that he would not ask her whether it was care for her health that compelled her to give up the journey, but that he was willing she should not take it. He readily consented to a plan he had already decided on. High as was his opinion of his wife's virtue, he saw very clearly that it was not well for her to be exposed longer to meeting a man she loved.

Monsieur de Nemours soon learned that Madame de Clèves was not to accompany the court. He could not bear to think of leaving without seeing her; and the day before he was to start he called on her as late as he could, in order to find her alone. Fortune favored him, and as he entered the courtyard he met Madame de Nevers and Madame de Martigues coming out. They told him they had left her alone. He went upstairs in a state of agitation that can only be compared with that of Madame de Clèves when his name was announced. Her fear that he would mention his love; her apprehension lest she should give him a favorable answer; the anxiety that this visit would give her husband; the difficulty of repeating or concealing everything that happened,—all crowded on her mind at once, and so embarrassed her that she determined to avoid the thing she desired most in the world. She sent one of her maids to Monsieur de Nemours, who was in the hall, to tell him that she was not feeling well, and much regretted that she could not have the honor of receiving him. It was a grievous blow to him that he could not see Madame de Clèves because she was unwilling to receive him. He was to leave the next day, and there was no

---

3. Again, the Treaty of Cateau-Cambrésis, in which France gave up its claims in Italy.

chance of his meeting her. He had not spoken to her since their conversation at the crown princess's, and he had reason to believe that his mistake in speaking to the Vidame had shattered all his hopes; consequently, he went away in deep rejection.

As soon as Madame de Clèves had somewhat recovered from the agitation of the prince's threatened visit, all the arguments that had made her decline it vanished from her mind; she even thought she had made a mistake, and if she had dared, and there had still been time, she would have called him back.

Madame de Nevers and Madame de Martigues, after leaving her, went to the crown princess's and found Monsieur de Clèves there. The princess asked them where they had been. They said they had just come from Madame de Clèves', where they had spent the afternoon with a number of persons, and that they had left no one there except Monsieur de Nemours. These words, which they thought thoroughly insignificant, were quite the opposite for Monsieur de Clèves, although it must have been evident to him that Monsieur de Nemours could easily find opportunities to speak to his wife. Nevertheless, the thought that he was with her alone, and able to speak to her of his love, seemed to him at that moment such a new and unendurable thing that his jealousy flamed out with greater fury than ever. He was not able to stay longer with the dauphiness, but left, not knowing why he did so, or whether he meant to interrupt Monsieur de Nemours. As soon as he got home he looked to see if that gentleman was still there; and when he had the consolation of finding him gone, he rejoiced to think that he could not have stayed long. He fancied that perhaps it was not Monsieur de Nemours of whom he ought to be jealous; and although he did not really doubt it, he tried his best to do so: but so many things pointed in that direction that he could not long enjoy the happiness of uncertainty. He went straight to his wife's room, and after a little talk on indifferent matters, he could not refrain from asking her what she had done and whom she had seen. Observing that she did not mention Monsieur de Nemours, he asked her, trembling with excitement, if those were all she had seen, in order to give her an opportunity to mention him, and thus save him from the pain of thinking she was capable of deception. Since she had not seen him, she said nothing about him; whereupon Monsieur de Clèves, in a tone that betrayed his distress, asked:

"And Monsieur de Nemours, didn't you see him, or have you forgotten him?"

"I did not see him, in point of fact; I was not feeling well, and I sent my regrets by one of my maids."

"Then you were ill for him alone," he went on, "since you received everybody else? Why this difference for him? Why is he not the same to you as all the rest? Why should you dread meeting him? Why do you show him that you make use of the power his passion gives you over him? Would you dare to refuse to see him if you did not know that he is able to distinguish your severity from incivility? Why should you be severe to him? From a person in your position, Madame, everything is a favor except indifference."

"I never thought," answered Madame de Clèves, "that however suspicious you might be of Monsieur de Nemours, you would reproach me for not seeing him."

"I do, however," he went on, "and with good cause. Why do you decline to see him, if he has not said anything to you? But, Madame, he has spoken to you; had his silence been the only sign of his passion, it would have made no such deep impression. You have not been able to tell me the whole truth; you have even repented telling me the little you did, and you have not the strength to go on. I am more unhappy than I supposed,—I am the unhappiest of men. You are my wife, I love you devotedly, and I see you love another man! He is the most fascinating man at court, he sees you every day, he knows that you love him. And I," he exclaimed,—"I could bring myself to believe that you would overcome your passion for him! I must have lost my reason when I imagined such a thing possible."

"I don't know," replied Madame de Clèves, sadly, "whether you were wrong in judging such extraordinary conduct as mine so favorably; I don't feel sure that I was right in thinking that you would do me justice."

"Do not doubt it Madame," said Monsieur de Clèves. "You were mistaken; you expected of me things quite as impossible as what I expected of you. How could you expect me to retain my self-control? Have you forgotten that I loved you madly and that I was your husband? Either case is enough to drive a man wild: what must it be when the two combine? And see what they do! I am torn by wild and uncertain feelings that I cannot control; I find myself no longer worthy of you,—you seem no more worthy of me. I adore you, and I hate you; I offend you, and I beg your pardon; I admire you, and I am ashamed of my admiration,—in a word, I have lost all my calmness, all my reason. I do not know how I have been able to live since you spoke with me at Coulommiers, and since the day when you learned from the dauphiness that your adventure was known. I cannot conjecture how it came out, or what passed between Monsieur de Nemours and you on this subject. You will never tell me, and I don't ask you to tell me; I beg of you only to remember that you have made me the unhappiest man in the world."

With those words Monsieur de Clèves left his wife's room, and went away the next morning without seeing her, although he wrote her a letter full of grief, consideration, and gentleness. She wrote him a touching answer, containing such assurances about her past and future conduct that, since they sprang from the truth and were her real feelings, the letter carried great weight with Monsieur de Clèves and calmed him somewhat. Moreover, since Monsieur de Nemours was also on his way to join the king, her husband had the consolation of knowing that he was separated from Madame de Clèves. Whenever she spoke with her husband, the love he showed her, the uprightness of his treatment of her, her own affection for him, and her sense of duty, made an impression on her heart which effaced all thought of Monsieur de Nemours. But this was only for a time; the remembrance of him soon returned with greater force than ever.

The first days after that prince had left, she scarcely noticed his absence; then it began to appear painful,—for since she began to love him, hardly a day had passed in which she had not either feared or hoped to see him; and it was to her a melancholy thought that chance could no longer make her meet him.

She went to Coulommiers, taking with her copies she had had made of the large pictures with which Madame de Valentinois had adorned her fine house at Anet.[4] All the memorable events of the king's reign were represented in these pictures. Among others was one of the Siege of Metz, with excellent likenesses of the principal officers, among whom was Monsieur de Nemours; and that was perhaps why Madame de Clèves cared for the pictures.

Madame de Martigues, having been unable to accompany the court, promised to spend a few days with her at Coulommiers. The queen's favor, which they both enjoyed, did not make them jealous or hostile; they were good friends, although they did not confide to each other everything. Madame de Clèves knew that Madame de Martigues loved the Vidame, but Madame de Martigues did not know that Madame de Clèves loved Monsieur de Nemours and was loved by him. The fact that she was a niece of the Vidame endeared her to Madame de Martigues; and Madame de Clèves was drawn toward her as a woman who, like herself, was in love, and with her lover's most intimate friend.

Madame de Martigues kept her promise, and went to Coulommiers. She found Madame de Clèves leading a most retired life,—indeed, she had sought absolute solitude, spending her evenings in the gardens, unaccompanied by her servants. She used to go into the summer-house where Monsieur de Nemours had overheard her talking with her husband, and enter the closet which opened on the garden. Her women and the servants would stay in the summer-house or in the other closet, coming to her only when they were called. Madame de Martigues had never seen Coulommiers; she was delighted with all the loveliness she found there, and especially with the comfort of this summer-house, in which she and Madame de Clèves spent every evening. Their solitude after dark, in the most beautiful place in the world, made easy prolonged talks between these two young women, who were both in love; and although they did not confide in each other, they delighted in talking together. Madame de Martigues would have been very sorry to leave Coulommiers if she had not been going to meet the Vidame; she went to Chambord, where was the whole court.

The new king was crowned at Rheims by the Cardinal of Lorraine, and the rest of the summer was to be spent at the castle of Chambord, then newly built. The queen manifested great pleasure at seeing Madame de Martigues again; and after giving expression to her joy, she asked after Madame de Clèves and what she was doing in the country. Monsieur de Nemours and Monsieur de Clèves were then with the queen. Madame de Martigues, who had been delighted with Coulommiers, described its beauty, and spoke at great length of the summer-house in the wood and of the pleasant evenings she had passed there with Madame de Clèves. Monsieur de Nemours, who was sufficiently familiar with the place to know what Madame de Martigues was talking about, thought that it might be possible to see Madame de Clèves there without being seen by her. He questioned Madame de Martigues, in order to get further information; and Monsieur de Clèves, who had kept his eyes on him while Madame de Martigues was talking, fancied that he detected his design. The questions that Monsieur de Nemours asked only strengthened his suspicions, so that he felt sure the duke intended to go to see his wife. He was right; this plan so attracted Monsieur de Nemours that after spending the night in devis-

4. A château, about forty miles east of Paris, built for her by Henri II.

ing plans to carry it into execution, the next morning he asked leave of the king to go to Paris on some pretext he had invented.

Monsieur de Clèves had no doubt about his reasons for going away, but he determined to seek information on his wife's conduct, and no longer to remain in cruel uncertainty. He desired to leave at the same time with Monsieur de Nemours, and from some place of concealment to discover what success he might have; but he feared lest their simultaneous absence might attract attention, or that Monsieur de Nemours might get wind of it and adopt other measures; so he determined to rely on one of the gentlemen in his suite, in whose fidelity and intelligence he felt confidence. He told him in what trouble he was, and what Madame de Clèves' virtue had been hitherto, and ordered him to follow in Monsieur de Nemours' footsteps, to watch him closely, and to see if he did not go to Coulommiers and enter the garden by night.

This gentleman, who was well suited for the duty, discharged it with the utmost exactness. He followed Monsieur de Nemours to a village half a league from Coulommiers, where the prince stopped, and the gentleman easily guessed that this was to await the approach of night. He did not think it well to wait there too, but passed through the village and made his way into the forest, to a spot which he thought Monsieur de Nemours would have to pass. He was not mistaken; as soon as night had fallen, he heard footsteps, and though it was dark, he easily recognized Monsieur de Nemours. He saw him walk about the garden as if to find out if he could hear some one, and to choose the most convenient spot for entering it. The palings were very high, and there were some beyond to bar the way, so that it was not easy to get in; nevertheless, Monsieur de Nemours succeeded. As soon as he had made his way into the garden, he had no difficulty in making out where Madame de Clèves was, as he saw many lights in the closet. All the windows were open; and creeping along the palings, he approached it with an emotion that can easily be imagined. He hid behind one of the long windows by which one entered the closet, to see what Madame de Clèves was doing. He saw that she was alone; she was so beautiful that he could scarcely control his rapture at the spectacle. It was warm, and her head and shoulders had no other covering than her loosely fastened hair. She was on a couch behind a table, on which were many baskets of ribbons; she was picking some out, and Monsieur de Nemours observed that they were of the same colors that he had worn in the tournament. He saw that she was fastening bows on a very peculiar stick that he had carried for some time and had given to his sister, from whom Madame de Clèves had taken it, without seeming to recognize it as belonging to Monsieur de Nemours. When she had finished her work with a grace and gentleness that reflected on her face the feelings that filled her heart, she took a light and drew near to a large table opposite the picture of the Siege of Metz, in which was the portrait of Monsieur de Nemours; then she sat down and gazed at this portrait with a rapt attention such as love alone could give.

It would be impossible to describe everything that Monsieur de Nemours felt at this moment. To see, in the deep night, in the most beautiful spot in the world, the woman he adored; to see her without her seeing him, busied with things that bore reference to him and to the hidden love she felt for him,—all that is something no other lover ever enjoyed or imagined.

Monsieur de Nemours was so entranced that he stood motionless, contemplating Madame de Clèves, without remembering that every moment was precious.

When he had come to his senses again, he thought he ought to wait till she came into the garden before speaking to her; this he reflected would be safer, because then she would be farther from her maids. When, however, he saw that she remained in the closet, he decided to go in there. When he tried to do it, he was overwhelmed with agitation and with the fear of displeasing her. He could not bear the thought of seeing the face, just before so gentle, suddenly darken with anger and surprise.

He thought it madness, not his undertaking to see Madame de Clèves without being seen, but to think of showing himself; he saw everything that he had not before thought of. It seemed to him foolhardy to surprise at midnight a woman to whom he had never spoken of his love. He thought he had no right to assume that she would consent to listen to him, and he knew she would have good grounds for indignation at the danger to which he exposed her from the possible consequences of his acts. All his courage abandoned him, and more than once he was on the point of deciding that he would go back without seeing her. But he was so anxious to speak to her, and so encouraged by what he had seen, that he pushed on a few steps, though in such agitation that his scarf caught on the window and made a noise. Madame de Clèves turned her head; and whether it was that her mind was full of this prince, or that his face was actually in the light, she thought that she recognized him; and without hesitation or turning toward him, she rejoined her maids. She was so agitated that she had to trump up an excuse of not feeling well; and she said it also to attract their attention and thus give Monsieur de Nemours time to beat a retreat. After a little reflection she decided that she had been mistaken, and that the vision of Monsieur de Nemours was a mere illusion. She knew that he had been at Chambord, and she judged it extremely unlikely that he could have undertaken so perilous an enterprise; several times she was on the point of going back into the closet to see if there was any one in the garden. Perhaps she hoped as much as she feared to find Monsieur de Nemours there; but at last reason and prudence prevailed over every other feeling, and she decided that she should do better to stay where she was than to seek any further information. She was long in making up her mind to leave a place near which he might be, and it was almost morning when she returned to the castle.

Monsieur de Nemours stayed in the garden as long as he saw a light. He had not given up all hope of seeing Madame de Clèves again, although he was sure that she had recognized him and had only left in order to avoid him; but when he saw the servants locking the doors, he knew that he had no further chance. He retraced his steps, passing by the place where the friend of Monsieur de Clèves was in waiting. This gentleman followed him to the village, whence he had started in the evening. Monsieur de Nemours determined to spend the whole day there, in order to return to Coulommiers that night, to see if Madame de Clèves would be cruel enough to flee from him, or not to let him look at her. Although he was highly delighted to find that her mind was occupied with him, he was deeply pained to see her so instinctively taking flight.

Never was there a tenderer or intenser love than that which animated this prince. He strolled beneath the willows beside a little brook which ran behind the house in which he was concealed. He kept himself out of sight as much as possible, that no one might know of his presence. He gave himself up to the transports of love, and his heart was so full that he could not keep from shed-

Monsieur de Clèves' friend had watched him all the while. He also returned to Paris; and when he saw that Monsieur de Nemours had left for Chambord, he took the post in order to get there before him, and to make his report about his expedition. His master was awaiting his return to determine his life's unhappiness.

As soon as Monsieur de Clèves saw him, he read in his expression and his silence that he had brought only bad news. He remained for some time overwhelmed with grief, his head bowed, unable to speak; then he motioned to him to withdraw. "Go," he said; "I see what you have to tell me, but I am not strong enough to hear it."

"I have nothing to report," answered the gentleman, "from which it is possible to form an accurate judgment. It is true that Monsieur de Nemours entered the garden in the woods two nights running, and called at Coulommiers the next day with Madame de Mercœur."

"That is enough," replied Monsieur de Clèves, "that is enough;" and then, again motioning to him to leave, he added, "I have no need of further information."

The gentleman was forced to leave his master plunged in despair. Never, perhaps, has there been more poignant grief, and few men who possessed so much spirit and so affectionate a heart as Monsieur de Clèves have suffered the agony of discovering at the same time a wife's infidelity and the mortification of being deceived by a woman.

Monsieur de Clèves was overwhelmed by this grievous blow. That same night he was seized with a fever of such severity that at once his life was in peril. Word was sent to Madame de Clèves, and she went to him with all speed. He was worse when she reached him, and she noticed something cold and icy in his manner toward her that greatly surprised and pained her. He even seemed to be annoyed at the attention she paid him; but at last she thought this was perhaps a result of his illness.

As soon as Madame de Clèves had arrived at Blois, where the court was at that time, Monsieur de Nemours was filled with joy at knowing that she was in the same place as himself. He tried to see her, and called at the house every day, under pretext of inquiring after Monsieur de Clèves; but it was all in vain. She never left her husband's room, and was very anxious about him. Monsieur de Nemours regretted that she suffered so much; he readily saw how this grief would be likely to rekindle her love for Monsieur de Clèves, and how this affection would prove a dangerous foe to the love she bore in her heart. This feeling depressed him for some time; but the extreme seriousness of Monsieur de Clèves' illness soon gave him new hopes. He saw that Madame de Clèves would soon be free to follow her own wishes, and that in the future he might find lasting happiness. This thought filled him with almost painful rapture, and he banished it from his mind, lest he should be too miserable if his hopes were disappointed.

Meanwhile Monsieur de Clèves was almost given up. One of the last days of his illness, after he had passed a very bad night, he said, toward morning, that he would like to rest. Madame de Clèves alone stayed in his room. It seemed to her that, instead of resting, he was very uneasy; she went up to him and knelt down by his bed, with her face covered with tears. Monsieur de Clèves had made up his mind to say nothing about his grievance against her; but her attentions and her sorrow, which seemed genuine, and which he sometimes regarded as tokens of deceit and treachery, produced such conflicting and painful feelings that he could not repress them.

"You, Madame," he said, "are shedding a great many tears for a death of which you are the cause, and which cannot give you the sorrow which you display. I am no longer able to reproach you," he went on, in a voice weakened by illness and grief, "but I am dying of the cruel suffering you have inflicted on me. Was it necessary that so extraordinary an action as that of speaking to me as you did at Coulommiers should have so little result? Why confide to me your love for Monsieur de Nemours, if your virtue was not strong enough to resist it? I loved you so that I was glad to be deceived,—I confess it to my shame; I have since longed for the false tranquillity of which you robbed me. Why did you not leave me in the calm blindness in which so many husbands are happy? I should perhaps have never known that you loved Monsieur de Nemours. I am dying," he went on; "but bear it in mind that you make me welcome death, and that since you have robbed me of the love and esteem I felt for you, I dread living. What would life be to me, if I had to spend it with a woman I have loved so much and who has so cruelly deceived me, or if I had to live apart from her, after a scene of violence utterly repugnant to my disposition and to the love I bear you? My love for you, Madame, has been far deeper than you know; I have concealed the greater part of it, from fear of tormenting you or of lessening your esteem by a manner unbecoming to a husband; I really deserved your affection. I say it once more: I die without regret, since I could not win this, and now can no longer wish for it. Farewell, Madame. Some day you will mourn a man who had for you a true and lawful love. You will know the misery that overtakes women who fall into these entanglements, and you will learn the difference between being loved as I loved you, and being loved by men who, while protesting their love, seek only the honor of misleading you. But my death will leave you free, and you will be able to make Monsieur de Nemours happy without doing anything criminal. What do I care what may happen when I shall be no more? Must I be weak enough to look upon it?"

Madame de Clèves was so far from imagining that her husband could suspect her that she listened to him without understanding what he was saying, and supposing that he was blaming her interest in Monsieur de Nemours. At last, suddenly grasping his meaning, she exclaimed,—

"I a criminal! The very thought of it never entered my head. The severest virtue could command no different course of conduct than mine, and I have not done one thing of which I should not be glad to have you an eye-witness."

"Should you have been glad," asked Monsieur de Clèves, looking at her somewhat disdainfully, "to have had me for an eye-witness of the nights you spent with Monsieur de Nemours? Ah! Madame, am I speaking of you when I speak of a woman who has spent nights with a man?"

"No," she answered, "no; it is not of me that you are speaking,—I have never passed nights or moments with Monsieur de Nemours; he has never seen me in private; I have never had anything to do with him or listened to him, and I will swear—"

"Say no more," interrupted Monsieur de Clèves; "false oaths or a confession would give me equal pain."

Madame de Clèves could not answer; her tears and her grief choked her. At last, making a great effort, she said: "Look at me, at least; listen to me. If it concerned me alone, I should endure these reproaches; but it is your life that is at stake. Listen to me for your own sake; it is impossible that, with all the truth on my side, I should not convince you of my innocence."

"Would to God that you could convince me!" he exclaimed. "But what can you say to me? Was not Monsieur de Nemours at Coulommiers with his sister, and had he not passed the two previous nights with you in the garden in the forest?"

"If that is my crime," she replied, "I can clear myself easily. I don't ask you to believe me, but believe your servants: ask them if I was in the garden the evening Monsieur de Nemours came to Coulommiers, and if I didn't leave it the evening before, two hours earlier than usual."

She then told him how she had imagined she saw some one in the garden, and confessed that she had thought it was Monsieur de Nemours. She spoke with such earnestness, and the truth, even when improbable, carries such weight, that Monsieur de Clèves was almost convinced of her innocence.

"I do not know," he said, "whether I dare believe you; I am so near death that I do not want to see anything that might make me long to live. Your explanation comes too late; but it will always be a consolation to think that you are worthy of the esteem I have had for you. I beg of you to let me have the additional consolation of knowing that my memory will be dear to you, and that if it had depended on you, you would have had for me the feeling you have had for another."

He wanted to go on; but a sudden faintness made it impossible, and Madame de Clèves summoned the physicians. They found him almost lifeless. Nevertheless he lingered a few days longer, and at last died, having displayed admirable firmness.

Madame de Clèves was almost crazed by the intensity of her grief. The queen at once came to see her, and carried her to a convent, without her knowing whither she was going. Her sisters-in-law brought her to Paris before she was yet able to realize her afflictions. When she began to be strong enough to think about it, and saw what a husband she had lost, and reflected that she was the cause of his death by means of her love for another man, the horror she felt at herself and at Monsieur de Nemours cannot be described.

At first this prince did not venture to pay her any other attentions than such as etiquette required. He knew Madame de Clèves well enough to be sure that anything more marked would displease her; but what he learned later assured him that he would have to maintain this reserve for a long time. One of his equerries told him that Monsieur de Clèves' gentleman,[5] a friend of his, had told him, in his deep regret for the loss of his master, that Monsieur de Nemours' trip to Coulommiers was the cause of his death. Monsieur de Nemours was extremely surprised to hear this; but on thinking it over, he made out a part of the truth, and conjectured what would be the feelings of Madame de Clèves, and how she would detest him if she thought her husband's illness had been due to jealousy. He thought that the best thing would be not to have his name brought to her notice, and he regulated his conduct accordingly, painful as he found it.

5. Attendant. "Equerries": personal attendants.

The prince went to Paris, and could not refrain from calling on Madame de Clèves to ask how she was. He was informed that she saw no one, and had even given orders that she was not to be told who had inquired after her. Possibly these rigid orders were given solely on account of the prince, and to avoid hearing his name mentioned. But Monsieur de Nemours was too desperately in love to be able to live with absolutely no chance of seeing Madame de Clèves. He resolved to try every means, no matter how difficult, to escape from such an unendurable condition of affairs.

The princess's grief passed all bounds of reason. Her dying husband,—dying for her sake, and filled with such tender love for her,—was never sent from her mind; she continually recalled everything she owed him, and blamed herself for not having loved him,—as if that were a thing that depended on her will. Her sole consolation was the thought that she mourned him as he deserved, and that for the rest of her life she would only do what he would have approved if he had lived.

She had often wondered how he knew that Monsieur de Nemours had come to Coulommiers; she did not suspect that the prince had spoken of it, and it even seemed to her that it was immaterial whether he had said anything about it, so thoroughly rid of her passion did she feel. Nevertheless, she was deeply distressed to think that he was the cause of her husband's death, and she remembered with sorrow the fear that had tormented Monsieur de Clèves on his deathbed lest she should marry him; but all these various sources of grief were lost in that over her husband's death, and the others sank into insignificance.

After many months had passed, she recovered from her violent grief, becoming sad and languid. Madame de Martigues made a visit to Paris, and saw her repeatedly during her stay there. She talked with her about the court and of all that had happened; and although Madame de Clèves seemed to take no interest, Madame de Martigues went on talking in order to divert her. She told her all about the Vidame, Monsieur de Guise, and all the other men of note.

"As for Monsieur de Nemours," she said, "I do not know whether his occupations have taken the place of gallantry, but he is less cheerful than he used to be; he shuns the society of women; he continually runs up to Paris, and I believe is here now."

Monsieur de Nemours' name surprised Madame de Clèves and made her blush; she changed the subject, and Madame de Martigues did not notice her confusion.

The next day, the princess, being anxious to find some occupation suitable for her condition, went to see a man living close by who worked in silk in a peculiar way, with the intention of undertaking something of the sort herself. After looking at what he had to show, her eyes fell on the door of a room in which she thought there were some more, and asked to have it opened. The man replied that he did not have the key, and that it was occupied by a man who came there sometimes to draw the fine houses and gardens to be seen from the windows. "He is the handsomest man in the world," he went on, "and does not seem obliged to support himself by his work. Whenever he comes here, I see him always looking at the houses and gardens, but I have never seen him at work."

Madame de Clèves listened with great attention; what Madame de Martigues had said about Monsieur de Nemours coming some times to Paris, as well as her vision of this handsome man who had taken quarters near her house, made her think of that prince, and suggested that he was trying to see her. This thought produced in her an agitation which she could not understand. She went to the windows to see on what they looked, and saw that it was on her garden and her own apartment; and when she was in her room she saw the same window to which she had been told that the stranger used to come. The conjecture that it was Monsieur de Nemours entirely altered the current of her thoughts; she no longer felt the sad tranquillity which she had begun to enjoy,—she was uneasy and agitated. At last, unable to endure her loneliness, she went out to take the air in a garden in the faubourgs,[6] where she expected to find solitude. At first she supposed no one was there; the place seemed deserted, and she strolled about for some little time.

After passing through a little thicket, she saw at the end of the path, in the most retired part of the garden, a sort of summer-house open on all sides, and she turned in that direction. When she had got near it, she saw a man lying on the benches who seemed sunk in deep thought, and she recognized Monsieur de Nemours. At the sight of him she stopped short; but her servants, who were following her, made some noise that aroused him. Without looking at them, he arose, to avoid their company, and turned into another path, bowing deeply, so that he was unable to see whom he was saluting.

Had Monsieur de Nemours known from whom he was running away, he would have eagerly retraced his steps; but as it was, he followed the path and went out by a sidegate, at which his carriage was waiting. This incident made a deep impression on Madame de Clèves' heart; all her love was suddenly rekindled with its former fervor. She went on and sat down in the place which Monsieur de Nemours had just left, and there she remained, completely overwhelmed. Her mind was full of this prince, more fascinating than any man in the world; loving her long with respect and constancy; giving up everything for her; respecting even her grief; trying to see her, without himself being seen; abandoning the court, where he was a favorite, to look upon the walls behind which she was immured, to come and muse in places where he could not hope to meet her,—in short, a man worthy to be loved for his love alone, and for whom she felt a passion so violent that she would have loved him even if he had not loved her, and one moreover of a lofty nature perfectly in harmony with her own. Duty and virtue could not restrain her emotions; every obstacle vanished; and of all her past she remembered nothing but her love for Monsieur de Nemours and his for her.

All these thoughts were new to the princess; she had been so lost in grief for her husband's death that she had given them no attention. With the sight of Monsieur de Nemours they all recurred to her. But when they came fastest, and she remembered that this same man whom now she thought of as able to marry her was the one she had loved during her husband's lifetime and was the cause of his death; that on his deathbed he had manifested his fear lest she should marry him,—her rigid virtue was so pained by the thought that it seemed to her quite as grievous a crime to marry Monsieur de Nemours as it had been to love him while her husband was living. She gave herself up to these reflections, which were so hostile to her happiness, and confirmed them

6. Suburbs.

by many arguments concerning her peace of mind and the evils she foresaw in case she married him. At last, after spending two hours there, she returned home, convinced that she ought to avoid the sight of him as a real obstacle to her duty.

But this conviction, the product of reason and virtue, did not control her heart, which remained attached to Monsieur de Nemours with a violence that reduced her to a most restless and pitiable state. That night was one of the unhappiest she had ever known. In the morning her first thought was to go to see if there was any one at the window which commanded her house; she looked out and saw Monsieur de Nemours. This surprised her, and she drew back so quickly that he felt sure she must have recognized him. This he had long wished might happen, since he had devised this method of seeing her; and when it seemed hopeless, he used to go and meditate in the garden where she had seen him.

Worn out at last by grief and uncertainty, the duke made up his mind to find some way of determining his fate. "Why should I wait?" he asked. "I have long known she loved me; she is free, and duty no longer stands in her way. Why should she force me to see her without being seen by her and with no chance to speak to her? Can love have so absolutely destroyed my reason and my boldness that I am not what I was when in love before? I was bound to respect Madame de Clèves' grief; but I have respected it too long, and I am giving her time to forget the affection she feels for me."

Thereupon he began to devise some way of seeing her. He fancied that there was no good reason for concealing his love from the Vidame of Chartres, and he resolved to speak to him and to confide to him his plans about his niece. The Vidame was then in Paris, like all the rest of the court, who had come to town to make their preparations for accompanying the king, who was to escort the Queen of Spain. Accordingly, Monsieur de Nemours called on the Vidame and frankly told him everything he had kept hidden until then, except Madame de Clèves' feelings, which he did not wish to appear to know.

The Vidame heard him with great pleasure, and answered that, with no knowledge of his feelings, he had often, since Madame de Clèves had become a widow, thought that she was the only woman worthy of him. Monsieur de Nemours besought his aid in getting a chance to address her, in order to find out her intentions.

The Vidame proposed taking him to call on her; but Monsieur de Nemours feared that she would not like this, because she did not yet see any one. They decided that the Vidame should invite her to come and see him on some pretext or other, and that Monsieur de Nemours should enter by a hidden staircase, in order not to be seen. This was carried out according to their plans. Madame de Clèves came; the Vidame went to receive her, and led her into a small room at the end of his apartment. Shortly after, Monsieur de Nemours came in, as if by chance. Madame de Clèves was much surprised to see him; she blushed, and tried to hide her blushes. The Vidame began to talk about unimportant subjects, and then went away, under the pretext of having some orders to give. He asked Madame de Clèves to do the honors in his place, and said he should return in a moment.

It would be impossible to express the feelings of Monsieur de Nemours and Madame de Clèves when they for the first time found themselves alone and free to talk. They remained for a long time without a word; then at last Monsieur de Nemours broke the silence. "Will you, Madame, forgive the Vidame," he said, "for having given me an opportunity to see you and to speak with you, which you have always cruelly denied me?"

"I ought not to forgive him," she replied, "for having forgotten my position and to what he exposes my reputation." As she uttered these words she started to leave; but Monsieur de Nemours delayed her, saying:

"Do not be alarmed, Madame; no one knows that I am here, and there is no danger. Listen to me, Madame,—if not through kindness, at least through love of yourself, and in order to protect yourself against the extravagances to which I shall certainly be led by an uncontrollable passion."

For the first time Madame de Clèves yielded to her tenderness for Monsieur de Nemours, and looking at him with eyes full of gentleness and charm, she said: "But what do you hope from the kindness that you ask of me? You would certainly regret obtaining it, and I should regret granting it. You deserve a happier fate than you have yet had, and can have in the future, unless you seek it elsewhere."

"I, Madame, find such happiness elsewhere! Is there any other happiness than winning your love? Although I have never spoken with you, I cannot think that you are ignorant of my affection, or that you do not know that it is truer and warmer than ever. How much it has been tried by events unknown to you, and how much by your severity!"

"Since you wish me to speak, and I decide it best," answered Madame de Clèves, sitting down, "I will do so, with a frankness that you will not always find in women. I shall not tell you that I have not noticed your attachment to me,—perhaps you could not believe me if I were to say so; I confess, then, not only that I have noticed it, but also just as you wished it to appear."

"And, Madame, if you have seen it," he interrupted, "is it possible that you have not been touched by it; and may I venture to ask if it has made no impression on your heart?"

"You should have judged of that from my conduct," she replied; "but I should be glad to know what you have thought of it."

"I should have to be in a happier condition to dare to tell you," he answered, "and my fate has too little relation with what I should say. All that I can tell you, Madame, is that you would not have confessed to Monsieur de Clèves what you concealed from me, and that you would have concealed from him what you would have let me see."

"How were you able to find out," she asked, blushing, "that I confessed anything to Monsieur de Clèves?"

"I heard it from your own lips, Madame," he replied; "but as an excuse for my boldness in listening to you, consider whether I misused what I had heard, whether my hopes were strengthened by it, whether I became bold enough to speak to you."

He began to tell her how he had heard her conversation with Monsieur de Clèves: but she interrupted him in the middle.

"Say no more," she said; "I now see how you came to know too much: that you did, was very plain to me at the dauphiness's when she had heard the story from those to whom you had told it."

Monsieur de Nemours then explained to her how that had happened.

"Do not apologize," she resumed; "I forgave you a long time ago, before you told me how it occurred. But since you have yourself heard from me what I had meant to keep a secret from you all my life, I confess that you have inspired me with emotions unknown before I saw you, and so unfamiliar to me that they filled me with a surprise which greatly added to the agitation they produced. I confess this with the less shame because I may now do it innocently, and you have seen that my feelings did not guide my actions."

"Do you believe, Madame," exclaimed Monsieur de Nemours, falling on his knees, "that I am not ready to die at your feet with joy and rapture?"

"I only tell you," she answered, smiling, "what you already know only too well."

"Ah! Madame," he said, "what a difference between finding something out by accident, and hearing it from you, and seeing that you wish me to know it."

"It is true," said she, "that I wish you to know it, and that I take pleasure in telling you. I am not certain that I do not tell it more from love of myself than from love of you; for certainly this avowal will have no consequences, and I shall follow the rigid rules that my condition imposes."

"You will not think of such a thing, Madame," replied Monsieur de Nemours; "you are bound by no further duty; you are free; and if I dared, I should even tell you that it depends on you so to act that your duty shall some day oblige you to preserve the feelings that you have for me."

"My duty," she replied, "forbids my ever thinking of any one, and of you last of all, for reasons unknown to you."

"Perhaps they are not, Madame," he pleaded; "but those are no true reasons. I have reason to believe that Monsieur de Clèves thought me happier than I was, and imagined that you approved of mad freaks of mine which my passion suggested without your knowledge."

"Let us not speak of that affair," she said. "I cannot bear the thought of it; it fills me with shame, and its consequences were too painful. It is only too likely that you are the cause of Monsieur de Clèves' death; the suspicions you aroused, your inconsiderate conduct, cost him his life as truly as if you had taken it with your own hands. Think of what I should do if you had come to such extremities and the same unhappy result had followed. I know very well this is not the same thing in the eyes of the world; but in mine there is no difference, for I know it was from you he got his death, and on account of me."

"Oh! Madame," interposed Monsieur de Nemours, "what phantom of duty do you oppose to my happiness? What! Madame, a vain and baseless fancy can prevent your making happy a man you do not hate, when he has conceived the hope of passing his life with you, his fate leading him to love you as the best woman in the world, finding in you every charming trait, incurring not your hatred, and seeing in you everything that best becomes a woman,—for, Madame, there is no other woman who combines what you do. Men who marry their mistresses who love them, tremble from fear lest they should renew their misconduct with others; but nothing of the sort is to be feared in you: you are only to be admired. Can I have foreseen such felicity only to find you raising obstacles? Ah! Madame, you forget that you chose me from other men,—or rather, you did not; you made a mistake, and I have flattered myself."

"You did not flatter yourself," she replied; "the reasons for my acting as I do would not, perhaps, seem to me so strong, had I not chosen you as you suspect,—and that is what makes me foresee unhappiness if I should take an interest in you."

"I have no answer," he said, "when you show me that you fear unhappiness; but I confess that, after all you have been good enough to say to me, I did not expect to be opposed by such a cruel argument." "It is so far from uncomplimentary to you," she answered, "that I shall even find it hard to tell it to you."

"Alas! Madame, what can you fear will flatter me too much after what you have just said to me?"

"I wish still to speak to you as frankly as I began," she explained, "and I want to dispense with all the reserve and formalities that I should respect in a first conversation; but I beg of you to listen to me without interruption.

"I think it but a slight reward for your affection that I should hide from you none of my feelings, but should let you see them exactly as they are. This probably will be the only time in my life that I shall take the liberty of letting you see them; nevertheless, I cannot confess to you without deep shame that the certainty of not being loved by you as I am, seems to me a horrible misfortune; that if there were not already insurmountable claims of duty, I doubt if I could make up my mind to risk this unhappiness. I know that you are free, as I am, and that we are so situated that the world would probably blame neither of us if we should marry; but do men keep their love in these permanent unions? Ought I to expect a miracle in my case, and can I run the risk of seeing this passion, which would be my only happiness, fade away? Monsieur de Clèves was perhaps the only man in the world capable of keeping his love after marriage. My fate forbade my enjoying this blessing. Perhaps, too, his love only survived because he found none in me. But I should not have the same way of preserving yours; I believe that the obstacles you have met have made you constant; those were enough to make you yearn to conquer them, and my involuntary actions,—things you learned by chance,—gave you enough hope to keep you interested."

"Oh! Madame," replied Monsieur de Nemours, "I can no longer maintain the silence you impose on me; you do me too much injustice, and you let me see how far you are from being prejudiced in my favor."

"I confess," she said, "that I may be moved by my emotions, but they cannot blind me; nothing can prevent my seeing that you are born with every disposition for gallantry, and with all the qualities proper to secure speedy success. You have already been in love several times,—you would be again very often. I should not make you happy; I should see you interested in another as you have been in me: this would inflict on me a mortal blow, and I should never feel sure that I should not be jealous. I have said too much to try to hide from you that you have already made me feel this passion, and that I suffered cruel tortures that evening when the queen gave me that letter from Madame de Themines which was said to be directed to you, and that the impression left on me is that jealousy is the greatest unhappiness in the world.

"Vanity or taste makes all women try to secure you; there are few whom you do not please,—my own experience teaches me that there are few whom you might not please. I should always imagine that you were loved and in love, and I should not be often wrong. Yet in this condition I could only suffer,—I should not dare to complain. One may make reproaches to a lover, but can a woman reproach her husband for ceasing to love her? If I could become hardened to that misfortune, could I become hardened to imagining that I saw Monsieur de Clèves charging you with his death, reproaching me for loving you, and showing the difference between his affection and yours? It is impossible to resist such arguments; I must remain in my present position and in my immovable determination never to leave it."

"But do you think you can, Madame?" exclaimed Monsieur de Nemours. "Do you think that your resolutions can hold out against a man who worships you and is fortunate enough to please you? It is harder than you think, Madame, to resist what pleases us and one who loves us. You have done it by an austere virtue which is almost without a precedent; but this virtue no longer conflicts with your emotions, and these I hope you will follow, in spite of yourself."

"I know that there is nothing harder than what I undertake; I mistrust my own strength, supported by all my arguments. What I think due to the memory of Monsieur de Clèves would be ineffectual, if it were not reinforced by my anxiety for my own peace of mind; and these arguments need to be strengthened by those of duty. But though I mistrust myself, I think I shall never overcome my scruples, and I do not hope to overcome my interest in you. It will make me unhappy, and I shall deny myself the pleasure of seeing you, whatever pain this may cost me. I am in a position which makes that a crime which at any other time would be permissible, and mere etiquette forbids that we should meet."

Monsieur de Nemours flung himself at her feet and gave expression to all the emotion that filled him. He manifested, by his words and tears, the liveliest and tenderest passion that heart ever felt. Madame de Clèves was not unmoved; and looking at Monsieur de Nemours with eyes heavy with tears, she exclaimed,—

"Why must I charge you with the death of Monsieur de Clèves? Why did I not learn to know you when I was free; or why did I not know you before I was married? Why does fate divide us by such an insuperable obstacle?"

"There is no obstacle," pleaded Monsieur de Nemours; "you alone thwart my happiness, you alone impose a law which virtue and reason could not impose."

"It is true," she replied, "that I make a great sacrifice to a duty which exists only in my imagination. Wait to see what time will do. Monsieur de Clèves has but just died, and that fatal event is too recent for me to judge clearly. Meanwhile you have the pleasure of having won the love of a woman who would never have loved had she not seen you; be sure that my feelings for you will never change and will always survive, whatever I do.

"Good by," she said. "This conversation fills me with shame. Repeat it to the Vidame; I give my consent,—nay, I beg of you to do so."

With these words she left the room, Monsieur de Nemours being unable to prevent her. She found the Vidame in the next room. He saw her so agitated that he did not dare to speak to her, and he handed her to her carriage without a word. He went back to Monsieur de Nemours, who was in such a whirl of joy, sadness, surprise, and admiration,—in short, so possessed by all the emotions that spring from a passion full of hope and dread,—that he seemed beside himself. It was long before the Vidame got any clear notion of what they had said; finally, however, he succeeded; and Monsieur de Chartres, without being the least in love, had no less admiration for the virtue, intelligence, and worth of

Madame de Clèves than had Monsieur de Nemours himself. They tried to determine the prince's probable chances; and whatever the fears that love might arouse, the prince agreed with the Vidame that it was impossible that Madame de Clèves should persist in her resolutions. Nevertheless, they agreed to follow her orders, from fear lest, if the duke's love for her should become known, she should in some way bind herself, and would not change from fear of its being thought that she had loved him while her husband was living.

Monsieur de Nemours determined to join the king, as he could no longer stay away, and he made up his mind to start without even trying to see Madame de Clèves again. He begged the Vidame to speak to her. He told him a number of things to say to her, and suggested countless arguments with which to overcome her scruples. At last a good part of the night was gone before Monsieur de Nemours thought of leaving to seek repose.

Madame de Clèves was in no condition to find rest; it was for her such a new thing to lay aside the reserve which she had imposed upon herself, to permit a man to tell her that he loved her, to confess that she too was in love, that she did not recognize herself. She was amazed at what she had done, and repented it bitterly; she was also made happy by it,—she was completely upset by love and agitation. She went over once more the arguments in defence of her duty which stood in the way of her happiness; she lamented their strength, and regretted having stated them so strongly to Monsieur de Nemours. Although the thought of marrying him had occurred to her the moment she saw him again in the garden, it had not made so deep an impression on her as had her talk with him; and at moments she could scarcely believe that she would be unhappy if she should marry him. She would have liked to be able to say that she was wrong both in her scruples about the past and in her fears for the future. At other moments reason and duty convinced her of the opposite, and decided her not to marry again or ever to see Monsieur de Nemours; but this resolution was extremely repugnant to her when her heart was so much moved and had so recently seen the joys of love. At last, in order to allay her agitation, she thought it was not necessary for her to do herself the violence of forming a decision,—etiquette left her still much time for making up her mind; but she resolved to abide by her determination to have nothing to do with Monsieur de Nemours meanwhile.

The Vidame came to see her, and pleaded his friend's cause with all possible skill and earnestness; but he could not persuade her to modify her own conduct or that which she had imposed on Monsieur de Nemours. She told him that she did not mean to change her present condition, that she knew it would be hard for her to carry out this intention, but that she hoped she should be strong enough to do so. She showed him how firmly convinced she was that Monsieur de Nemours had caused her husband's death, and that she should do wrong in marrying him; so that the Vidame feared it would not be easy to convince her of the opposite. He did not confide to this prince what he thought, and when he reported his talk with her, he let him enjoy all the hope that reason can awaken in a man who is loved.

The next day they left to join the king. The Vidame, at the request of Monsieur de Nemours, wrote to Madame de Clèves, in order to speak of him; and in a second letter, which soon followed, Monsieur de Nemours added a few lines himself. But Madame de Clèves, who did not wish to infringe her rules, and who feared the perils of correspondence, told the Vidame that she should decline to receive his letters if he continued to write about Monsieur de Nemours; and this she said so earnestly that this prince himself begged his friend never to mention his name.

The court left to escort the Queen of Spain as far as Poitou. Madame de Clèves was left to herself during their absence, and the farther she was removed from Monsieur de Nemours and from anything that could remind her of him, the more she recalled the memory of Monsieur de Clèves, which she was bent on keeping ever present before her. Her reasons for not marrying Monsieur de Nemours seemed strong so far as her duty, and irrefutable so far as her tranquillity, was concerned. The fading of his love after marriage, and all the pangs of jealousy, which she regarded as certain, showed her the misery to which she would expose herself; but she saw too that she had assumed an impossible task in undertaking to resist the most fascinating of men, whom she loved and who loved her, in a matter which offended neither virtue nor propriety. She decided that only separation could give her strength; and this she felt that she needed, not merely to maintain her determination not to marry, but also to protect herself from the sight of Monsieur de Nemours. Hence she resolved to make a long journey during the time that etiquette forced her to spend in retirement. Some large estates that she owned in the Pyrénées seemed to her the best place she could choose. She started a few days before the court returned; and just before leaving, she wrote to the Vidame to beg that no one should inquire after her or write to her.

Monsieur de Nemours was as much afflicted by her absence as another man would have been by the death of the woman he loved. The thought of this long separation from Madame de Clèves was a constant source of suffering, especially after he had tasted the pleasure of meeting her and seeing that she loved him. He could do nothing but grieve, and his grief increased daily. Madame de Clèves, as a result of all her agitation, fell seriously ill after her arrival at her country place, and news of this reached the court. Monsieur de Nemours was inconsolable, and fell into the most unbounded despair. The Vidame had great difficulty in keeping him from letting his love be seen, as well as from following after her to find out how she was. The Vidame's relationship and intimacy served as a pretext for sending constant letters. At last word came that she had passed the turning point of her dangerous illness, but was still so weak that all were very anxious.

This long and near view of death enabled Madame de Clèves to judge mundane matters in a very different spirit from that of health. Her imminent peril taught her indifference to everything, and the length of her illness enforced this upon her. Yet when she had recovered, she found that she had not wholly forgotten Monsieur de Nemours; but she summoned to her aid every argument she could devise against marrying him. The conflict was a stern one; but at last she conquered what was left of this passion, which was already diminished by her reflections during her illness. The thought of death had revived her memory of Monsieur de Clèves; and this, harmonizing with her sense of duty, made a strong impression on her heart. The affections and ties of the world appeared to her as they appear to persons of enlarged views. Her health, which was still delicate, helped her to preserve those feelings; but knowing how circumstances affect the wisest resolutions, she was unwilling to run the risk of seeing her own altered, or of returning to the place where lived the man she had loved. Under the pretext of needing change of air, she withdrew to a religious house, without making known her determination to leave the court.

When Monsieur de Nemours heard of this, he at once saw what a decisive step it was, and feared that he had no more ground for hope. Yet the destruction of his hopes did not prevent his doing his utmost to bring about her return; he made the queen write to her, and even persuaded the Vidame to visit her: but it was all to no purpose. The Vidame saw her; she did not tell him that she had resolved upon this, but he decided that she would never return. At last Monsieur de Nemours went himself, under the pretext of going to the baths.[7] She was much moved and astonished when she heard that he had come. She sent him a message by one of her trusty companions that she begged him not to be surprised if she was unwilling to run the risk of seeing him again and of having the feelings she felt bound to maintain swept away by his presence; that she wanted him to know that having found her duty and her peace of mind unalterably opposed to her interest in him, everything else in the world seemed so indifferent that she had abandoned it entirely, had given all her thoughts to another life, and had no other feeling left but her desire to have him share the same sentiments.

Monsieur de Nemours thought he should die of grief in the presence of the woman who brought this message. He begged her twenty times to go back to Madame de Clèves, to entreat her to let him see her; but she told him that Madame de Clèves had forbidden her, not only to bring her any message from him, but even to repeat to her what he might say. At last he had to leave, as completely overwhelmed with grief as a man could be who had lost all hopes of ever seeing again a woman whom he loved with the most violent and the most natural passion possible. Yet he did not yield even then; he did everything he could to induce her to alter her decision. At last, when years had passed, time and separation allayed his grief and extinguished his passion. Madame de Clèves led such a life that it was evident she meant never to go into the world again; part of each year she spent in this religious house, and the other part at home, but in retirement, busied with severer tasks than those of the austerest convents. Her life, which was not long, furnished examples of the loftiest virtue.

---

7. At a resort or spa where bathing, usually in natural springs, is part of the medical treatment.

JEAN RACINE
1639–1699

Formally, Jean Racine was a classi-
cist: he took inspiration from
Europe's Greco-Roman heritage, and
he shaped his plays to conform to what
he imagined was a classical ideal. Yet
beneath their formal decorum and elevated tone, Racine's tragedies communicate intense passion and display
acute psychological insight, making
them as compelling today as they were
in his time.

LIFE AND TIMES

Born in the Valois district eighty miles
from Paris, Jean Racine came from a
bourgeois family that administered salt
granaries. After he was orphaned at age
four, his grandmother enrolled him in
the convent school at the Jansenist
center of Port-Royal des Champs,
where Racine received an education
unusual for his means. Jansenism was
a Catholic movement emphasizing
moral self-examination and severely
controlled conduct. Racine's strict
Jansenist upbringing would later create
tensions with his literary ambitions. In
1660 Racine came to Paris, then a
hotbed of literary salons, academies,
and patronage under the rule of the
absolutist Louis XIV. His first efforts
were encouraged by the poet and fabu-
list Jean de La Fontaine, a relative.
After an unsuccessful attempt to obtain
an ecclesiastical office in the provinces,
Racine returned to Paris in 1663, ready
to seek court patronage for his writing
despite the Jansenists' moral objection
to the theater. With Molière's support,
Racine rapidly developed a reputation
as a major playwright. Only one of
Racine's twelve plays, the early comedy

The Litigants, deviated from the tragic
mode. His first tragedies imitated the
work of his contemporary Pierre Corneille; later, he turned to biblical and
classical models. His success in the
theater and at court distanced Racine
from his Jansenist teachers, yet he
remained sensitive to attacks on his
morality and sought reconciliation
between the tragic arts and piety. In
1677, the same year *Phèdre* was first
performed, he married Catherine de
Romanet, with whom he had seven
children. The king also named Racine
one of his two royal historians. With a
royal post secured, and financially
independent from his theaterical
career, he left Paris and returned to
Port-Royal, an environment conducive
to his increasing interest in religion.
While living in the country, he wrote
and traveled with Louis XIV on his
campaigns; after *Phèdre* he never wrote
another classical tragedy. His last
known work is *Short History of Port-
Royal (1695–1699)*. He died in Port-
Royal in 1699.

PHÈDRE

Phèdre (1677) adapts Euripides's *Hippolytus* (428 B.C.E.), a tragedy about
Theseus, king of Athens; his unhappy
wife, Phèdre; and his illegitimate son,
Hippolytus. In Euripides' version of
the myth, Aphrodite, goddess of love,
punishes the stubbornly chaste Hippolytus by making his stepmother fall
in love with him. But Racine's *Phèdre*
introduces a key twist: it makes the
guilty woman rather than the relatively
passive man the protagonist and uses
the highly charged sexual situation

between the two to generate psychological tension. The play has all the formal hallmarks of classicism: the long declamatory speeches, the stylized exchanges in compressed half lines, the complicated relationships and histories artificially limited to the time span of a single day. Yet such devices (which would have seemed as artificial to seventeenth-century audiences as they do to us, although more familiar) intensify the impact of the central characters' anguish and their desperate attempts to deal with it. If the play's surface is formal, its depths seethe with passion.

Passion, of course, is the subject of *Phèdre*. The conflict between reason and passion that preoccupied many thinkers of the late seventeenth and early eighteenth centuries—that conflict resolved on the side of reason at such great cost to the Princess of Clèves—here plays itself out with stark urgency. Passion triumphs, in *Phèdre,* over all principles of control, bringing death to the two central characters and misery to their survivors. As in Greek tragedy, although by different means, the reader feels not only the self-destructiveness of the human psyche but the pathos and heroism of the characters' doomed efforts to transcend their condition. Like Molière, Racine uses the family as a microcosm of larger social orders, but the intense conflicts that throb beneath the surface in many real-life families here undergo no comic transformation. In their outsize dimension, the personal conflicts of rulers also impact the future of their kingdoms, and the fate of Athens is at stake.

The play opens not with Phèdre herself but with Hippolytus, meditating about his heroic father, Theseus. Blessed and burdened with this larger-than-life father, Hippolytus must choose whether to try to imitate him or to seek other ways of being a man. The-

seus has distinguished himself in two ways: by heroic action, the conquering and destruction of monsters human and inhuman, and by somewhat less heroic womanizing, leaving a trail of damaged women behind him wherever he goes. Now Hippolytus, becoming a man, acknowledges in himself the first incursions of love. His innocent desire to prove his manhood, to declare his separateness from and worthiness of his father, has been overwhelmed by his own passions in the absence and presumed death of Theseus. Far from loving Phèdre, the stepmother who caused his exile, Hippolytus falls for Aricia, the sole surviving member of the family who challenged his father's rule. Racine stresses the social and political backdrop to what seem the most personal and intimate of conflicts: is Hippolytus's love for Aricia not a betrayal of his father, in its own right? Yet how is future legitimacy to be ensured, if the claims of the past are not addressed? Would a union between Hippolytus and Aricia secure political stability for Athens?

Phèdre's impulses are similarly complex. She understands her own sin as an internal war between feeling and control; she speaks of desperately seeking her lost reason in the sacrifices she makes to Venus, trying to avert her fate. Never does she excuse herself, never does she believe herself justified in loving the son of the man who kidnapped her into marriage. When Theseus is thought dead, Phèdre declares herself unworthy to rule a nation because she cannot rule herself. Yet such moral awareness fails to help her: knowing her sin, she cannot overcome it. The play evokes the full torment of such experience.

As for powerful Theseus, conqueror of women, defier of the supernatural, ally of Neptune—this kingly figure returns from his presumed death to find himself powerless at home. The son and wife who by social convention exist in utter subordination to him appear to him as enemies he has no capacity to master. First his wife's nurse tells him that his son has attempted to seduce Phèdre. The rivalry of sons and fathers runs deep: if sons fear they can never equal their fathers, fathers fear that the young necessarily overcome the old. Theseus chooses to believe the nurse's bare assertion, unsupported by substantial evidence: he banishes his son and invokes Neptune's power to destroy him, in what is perhaps the rashest action in the play. Then Aricia's hints lead him to suspect his wife, who confesses her own emotional sin while already on the verge of self-inflicted death. Theseus remains alone, bereft, his tyrannical impulse now devoid of domestic object. His own passions, too quickly fired—jealous possessiveness of his wife, jealous rivalry with his son— have deprived him of two beings he loved.

The play provides no villains. Phèdre, in some versions of the story a monster of lust, here becomes a woman struggling against her nature, as profoundly committed to standards of control as to the violent feelings that overthrow them. Hippolytus, in the process of self-discovery, at a delicate balance point between youth and maturity, cannot protect himself against a woman whose passions, and whose self-awareness, far exceed his. Theseus, in the ignorance of success, fails to understand himself, his wife, or his son and cannot undo the destructiveness of the gods he has summoned. All three

exemplify the pathos and dignity of the struggle to be human.

Hippolytus dies in the beauty of his youth, deprived of age's suffering and fulfillment. Phèdre seeks self-purification in death, the only course now possible to her. Theseus lives to try once more to rule adequately, perhaps chastened by suffering into greater awareness, and recognizes Aricia's claims to legitimacy by adopting her. The names of the Greek gods survive in this drama: Aphrodite torments Phèdre; Neptune serves Theseus's impetuous will. But the gods now function as projections of human passion: Phèdre's sexual lust, Theseus's lust for power. Phèdre's torment suggests a Christian effort at purification, a Christian ideal of self-denial. The drama, in Racine's handling of the ancient story, magnifies the conflicts that all men and women undergo, the surge of feeling that wars with the ideal of self-restraint. By concentrating the play of passions, giving Theseus and Phèdre heroic dignity and stature, and linking this family with the fate of nations, Racine forces his readers to feel the significance of feelings and events that transcend the personal. He gives his characters timeless reality— speaking to his time and to ours.

Despite the difficulties involved in translating Racine's French alexandrine (twelve-syllable) lines into English, Racine's *Phèdre* has attracted the attention of many poet translators. Our version, by Ted Hughes, replaces rhyme with a taut and urgent free verse that moves the action along at a headlong pace.

Phèdre[1]

CHARACTERS

PHÈDRE, *Queen of Athens*
THESEUS, *King of Athens,* PHÈDRE'S *husband*
HIPPOLYTUS, *son of Theseus and Antiope, an Amazon*
ARICIA, *granddaughter of Erechtheus, once the King of Athens*
OENONE, *Phèdre's nurse and retainer*
THÉRAMÈNE, *Hippolytus's friend and counsellor*
ISMÈNE, *Aricia's attendant*
PANOPE, *citizen of Troezen*

Act I

[HIPPOLYTUS, THÉRAMÈNE.]

HIPPOLYTUS   I have made my decision.
It is six months now
And there hasn't been one word of my father.
Somebody somewhere knows what's happened to him.

Life here in Troezen is extremely pleasant   5
But I can't hang around doing nothing
With this uncertainty. My idleness makes me sweat.
I must find my father.
THÉRAMÈNE   But where, my lord, would you begin to look?
We have done all we can to find him.   10
Our ships have searched both seas, they have gone
As far as the Acheron[2]
Where it dives to the underworld, and nowhere
Can Theseus be found.
We have searched Elis, and on past Tenaros,[3]   15
As far as the ocean
That drowned Icarus[4] when he fell out of heaven.
We have searched every coast within reach
For news of the King and found nothing.
Do you think you'll fare better?   20

What unsearched patch of the earth do you think might hold him?
In any case, who knows—
He might have chosen to vanish.
He might be lying low for his own good reasons.
Perhaps while we rack ourselves   25
Imagining his death,
He is lolling at ease, tucked away
With some beauty—soon to be deserted.

1. Translated by Ted Hughes.
2. A river that flows into Hades; Charon ferried the dead across it.
3. A point of land in southern Greece, near Sparta. Elis is a district of Greece on the west coast of the Peloponnesus.
4. Son of Daedalus. Escaping from Crete by means of wings made by his father, Icarus flew so high that the sun melted the wax holding his wings together, and he fell to his death.

HIPPOLYTUS Théramène, Theseus is our King.
  He is also my father.   30
  His youthful follies are over.
  Phèdre need no longer fear a rival.
  Nothing of that kind can have detained him.
  But this is now my duty: to find him.
  I cannot stay here. Anyway, I dare not.   35
THÉRAMÈNE Dare not?
  Stay here—in your childhood sanctuary?
  As long as I have known you
  You have preferred this house,
  These gardens and woods and these hills,   40
  To the pompous tedium of the court
  And the din of Athens.
  What can have occurred in this household
  To make you fear it?
HIPPOLYTUS Everything has changed since the gods   45
  Decided to grace this palace
  With the daughter of Minos and Pasiphae.[5]
THÉRAMÈNE I understand. The world is not blind.
  Your problem is real. It is Phèdre.
  She persecutes you and she spoils your life.   50
  Your stepmother!
  Yes, a diabolical woman!
  She had hardly set eyes on you
  When she had you removed—right out of the country.
  But is her hatred still so virulent?   55
  Is it what it was?
  Besides—what could you fear from her?
  A dying woman, wanting only to die,
  Sick with some sickness of which she will say nothing,
  Tired of herself, tired of the very daylight!   60
  How could she plot anything against you?
HIPPOLYTUS Phèdre's futile hatred of me
  Is something I never feared. Théramène,
  What drives me away from this house
  Is a peril of another order.   65
  The girl Aricia![6] The surviving daughter
  Of that family sworn to eliminate ours.
  I have to get away from Aricia!
THÉRAMÈNE What?
  You can think that girl your enemy?   70
  What if she does belong
  To the venomous lineage of Pallas[7]—

5. Phèdre was the daughter of King Minos of
Crete and Pasiphae, sister to Circe. Enamored
of a white bull sent by Poseidon, Pasiphae
consequently gave birth to the Minotaur, the
Cretan monster later killed by Theseus. Phèdre
was thus half-sister to the Minotaur.
6. Pallas's daughter
7. Theseus killed all fifty sons of Pallas
because they threatened his kingdom of
Athens.

She never shared their guilt, not one spot of it.
She is utterly innocent. And such a beauty!
How can you hate her?   75
HIPPOLYTUS   If hate were what I felt, would I run from her?
THÉRAMÈNE   My lord—
How am I to understand you?
Is this the man I know?
Is this Hippolytus?   80
Our Prince of Scorn, who laughed at love and lovers?
Who mocked the yoke that time and again
Bent your father's neck and brought him down
On all fours, like any common man?
Maybe Venus   85
Has suffered your taunts
A day too long?
Maybe she now vindicates your father.
Has she forced you,
Even you,   90
To kneel at her altar
Bending your neck—
Hapless, her sacrificial victim?
Is she bringing the groans out of you?
Are you in love?   95
HIPPOLYTUS   My dear old friend,
From the first breath I drew you have known me.
You know my pride. It is inborn.
Do you think I could renounce it?
It is no small thing.   100
I drank this spirit in with my milk
From the breast of an Amazon.[8]
And when I grew up
I exulted to find it in me, like a strength.
You remember, in my boyhood,   105
When you told me stories about my father,
How I devoured your voice.
My whole body blazed when you described him
Filling the empty place of Hercules.
Monsters slaughtered, bandits rooted out,   110
Procrustes, Cercyon, Sciron, Sinis,
The giant's bones littered through Epidaurus,
Crete reeking with the blood of the Minotaur.
But when you came to his lighter conquests—remember
How little I liked it?   115
All those false vows given, and all swallowed!
Periboea's[9] tears at Salamis,

8. Hippolytus's mother was Antiope, sister of Hippolyta, queen of the Amazons.

9. One of the women Theseus seduced and abandoned.

Helen[1] stolen out of her bed in Sparta
So many, he has forgotten their names.
Ariadne[2] wailing under a cliff,
Phèdre kidnapped—though she became his wife.   120
Recall how I begged you to be brief?
I would have been happy
To see rased from the memory of mankind
That half of his record.   125
And now you think I could follow him
Into that kind of dishonour?
You think the gods
Could do that to me?
If I went that way   130
My sighs would be more than pathetic,
They would be contemptible.
Theseus
Has amassed huge wealth
In superhuman feats and trophies and triumphs   135
To excuse his occasional foible.
My story contains not one monster.
My only wealth is my pride,
Which leaves me no leeway for folly.
But even if I had to succumb   140
Would I have picked Aricia?
Do you think I am unaware
Of the gulf between that girl and me?
My father has condemned her never to marry.
He fears a shoot from that unruly stock.   145
He will bury their lineage with their sister,
Keeping it under guard until she dies.
Do you think I am mad enough
To take this girl's part against my father?
Defy such a man as my father?   150
Make my name
A synonym for—imbecility?
To launch my life with that doomed enterprise?
THÉRAMÈNE   My lord, once love has picked its man
The gods cancel all his protestations.   155
Theseus, trying to seal Aricia
From the eyes of every man,
Opened yours.
Theseus' hatred for Aricia
Surprised in you the opposite emotion.   160

1. Daughter of Zeus and Leda, later the wife
of Menelaus of Sparta (and the cause of the
Trojan War). In her girlhood she was abducted
by Theseus and Peirithoüs; her brothers rescued her and brought her back home.
2. Phèdre's sister, who was abandoned by
Theseus on the island of Naxos after she rescued him from the Minotaur.

Aricia
Has become irresistible—to you.
But why shy from this passion?
If you feel it—embrace it.
Why forever tangle yourself, my lord,   165
In these timid scruples?
Hercules never hesitated.
No heart ever begrudged the touch of Venus.
You reject love
But where would Hippolytus be   170
If Antiope,[3] your indomitable mother,
Had not nursed that flame for your father?
In any case,
This pride which has given you such a name,
What does it amount to?   175
Admit it, things have changed.
You are not seen much lately, my lord,
Unperturbed, untouched, untouchable,
Hurtling along the sands in your chariot.
Or imitating the god of the ocean   180
Breaking a wild horse to amuse yourself.
And why are you heard so rarely these days
Scouring the woods with your hounds?
In your eye there's a new kind of fire—
Secretive, heavy, like an ailment.   185
You try to hide it. But it is killing you.
There is no hiding it. You are in love.
Is this Aricia?

HIPPOLYTUS   I am going. The King must be found.

THÉRAMÈNE   Will you see Phèdre before you leave?   190

HIPPOLYTUS   Since it is my duty I cannot avoid it.
But here comes Oenone. Something has happened.

      [*Enter* OENONE.]

OENONE   My lord, I can't think how I can bear it.
The Queen is slipping away. She cannot last.
Day and night I watch her, but it's no use,   195
She is dying of some disease she hides from me.
Her soul is in turmoil. Her entire body
Is convulsed with anguish. She flings out of her bed
Desperate to see the day
At the same time she orders me   200
To shut the whole world from her sight.
Her suffering frightens me. She is coming.

HIPPOLYTUS   And I am going. At the very least
I will spare her the sight of a face she hates.

---

3. As an Amazon, Antiope was committed to chastity.

[*Exeunt* HIPPOLYTUS *and* THÉRAMÈNE. *Enter* PHÈDRE.]

PHÈDRE   No further, Oenone. I stop here.   205
   That last scrap of strength has left me suddenly.
   The sun's light is too painful.
   My wretched, trembling legs cannot support me.
OENONE   O you gods, look at her tears!
PHÈDRE   What a useless weight, all these jewels!   210
   And these veils! Whose interfering fingers
   Twisted up my hair in these knots?
   Everything conspires to torment me.
OENONE   No matter what you say, you contradict it.
   One minute ago you ordered us   215
   To braid and set those coils exactly so.
   And it was you, madam,
   Gathering all your strength, made the decision
   To face this splendid sun and the world.
   And now at your first glimpse of it you recoil.   220
   How can you fear the sun you longed to feel?
PHÈDRE   You brilliant founder of a benighted family,
   You whom my mother dared to call her father,[4]
   Maybe you blush to see me like this.
   You god of the sun—look at me for the last time.   225
OENONE   This longing for death is going to kill us both.
   I exhaust myself to keep you alive
   When all you are doing is trying to die.
PHÈDRE   I want to be hidden in a dark wood.
   I want to see the chariot go bounding past   230
   In a fearless cloud of dust.
OENONE   What do you mean?
PHÈDRE   Where am I? What am I saying?
   Where did those words come from? My mind is strange.
   Some god has taken my senses.   235
   My face feels to be coming apart
   With all the turmoil. Oenone!
   I can't hide it—everybody
   Stares into my shame and its secret.
   I can't control this weeping.   240
OENONE   If you have to weep—then weep
   For the way you are stifling what you suffer
   Which makes it all the more violent.
   You reject our care, our advice.
   Do you intend to die in this fashion?   245
   What kind of perversity
   Cuts off your days halfway? Is it witchcraft
   Shrivelling the springs of life? Is it poison?
   Three whole days and three whole nights
   You have not slept or broken your fast.   250

---

4. Helios, the sun god, was the father of Phèdre's mother, Pasiphae.

What right have you to throw away your life?
You insult the gods who gave it to you.
And you betray the oath you gave your husband.
Also remember your children.
What will your death mean for their future?   255
The day their mother dies—
The same day brings new hope
To the son of the foreign woman.
That born enemy of your blood.
That boy from the womb of an Amazon—   260
Hippolytus.

PHÈDRE   Aaagh!

OENONE   Now I have touched you.

PHÈDRE   The name! You spoke that name!

OENONE   Yes, let your rage blaze out. Curse that name!   265
I am glad to see you shudder at it.
Live. Renew yourself
With love, with duty. Live—
If only to prevent this sprig of a Scythian[5]
From crushing your sons and all the noble blood   270
Of Greece, and the gods, under his arrogant throne.

Hurry!
Every moment takes a little life.
You have damaged your strength. You can repair it.
Your flame has burned low, but it burns.   275
It will grow if you will nourish it.

PHÈDRE   I have lived too guilty for too long.

OENONE   Guilty of what? What is all this remorse?
What crime could be so awful?
You never stained your hands in innocent blood.   280

PHÈDRE   I thank heaven, my hands are clean enough.
I wish to God my heart resembled them.

OENONE   I think you have plotted something dreadful—
Something so evil you have frightened yourself.
What is it?   285

PHÈDRE   I have said too much. Let us leave it.
Let me die before I do something worse.

OENONE   Then die—and take your monstrous secret with you.
But find somebody else to close your eyes.
Your flame may have shrunk to next to nothing   290
But mine will be out before it.
Among the thousand roads to the land of the dead
Mine will be the shortest and the quickest.
Madam, when did I ever betray your trust?
When you dropped from the womb my arms caught you.   295
You know I gave up everything for you—

5. Scythia, home of the Amazons, was, to the Greeks, associated with barbarians.

Country, children, everything. And now
You repay my loyalty with this.

PHÈDRE   What do you hope to gain by such anger?
If I were to say what I could say   300
You would be struck dumb.

OENONE   What could be worse than standing here
Helpless—watching you kill yourself.

PHÈDRE   When you know my crime, when you know
The fate that has broken me,   305
My death will be no lighter. But my guilt
Will be by that much heavier.

OENONE   Madam,
By all the tears I have shed throughout your life,
For your sake, let me know. What is it?   310

PHÈDRE   Very well.

OENONE   Open your heart. Let me hear it.

PHÈDRE   What can I tell her? Where can I begin?

OENONE   These vague terrors mangle me. Be clear.

PHÈDRE   The curse of Venus is fatal.   315
What a crazed, pitiful thing
She made of my mother!

OENONE   Madam, forget that. Let the future too
Utterly forget it.

PHÈDRE   Remember Ariadne, my sister.   320
Her love was like some hideous injury
That killed her on the beach where she lay abandoned.[6]

OENONE   What is it? Why bring all this up?
Your family had bad luck in love.
Why mourn them again?   325

PHÈDRE   Because Venus demands it. And because
In our whole unfortunate succession
I die last and the most miserable.

OENONE   You are in love?

PHÈDRE   I am in love, yes, I am in love.   330

OENONE   Who is it?

PHÈDRE   I cannot think of the name steadily.
It fills me with fear to whisper it.
I love—the very name will kill me, I think.
I tremble at it, I shiver—   335

OENONE   Who?

PHÈDRE   You know him.
That son of the Amazon. That noble prince
I persecuted since the day we met.

OENONE   Hippolytus!   340

PHÈDRE   You named him.

OENONE   God in heaven!

6. Ariadne died on Naxos after Theseus's desertion of her.

Ah, my whole body's gone to ice.
What an inheritance!
Yes, your family is pitiable.   345
Why did we come to this accursèd country?

PHÈDRE   My sickness began much earlier.
That day I married Theseus in Athens,
The moment the ceremony was over,
That moment of the surest happiness   350
I had ever felt in my life—
Suddenly he was there
Standing in front of me,
He had simply appeared—
Staring at me,   355
The man created
To destroy me.
Before I could grasp what I'd seen
I felt my face flame crimson—then go numb.
My whole body scorched—then icy sweat.   360
My eyes went dark.
I could not speak. I could hardly stand.
I knew then the goddess had found me—
The latest in the lineage that she loathes.
I had fallen   365
Into her furnace—
And I was trapped.
I tried to appease her.
My prayers were incessant.
I built her a shrine.   370
I spent half my wealth to decorate it.
From dawn to dusk I sacrificed beasts,
Searching their bodies for my sanity.[7]
Futile placebo for a fatal illness!
And the incense I burned—equally futile!   375
All useless. Whenever I prayed
And bowed down to her image
I saw only his—
I adored only his.
Though I made the air shake with her titles   380
My whole heart and soul, my whole body
Worshipped only him—Hippolytus!
Then I began to avoid him.
But that was useless too.
I met him everywhere   385
In the face of his father—
Everywhere I saw him staring at me
Through his father's features.

7. Examining the entrails of an animal sacrifice was a means of prophecy.

So then I turned against him.
I turned against myself—to defend myself. 390
I forced myself
To make his life a misery. At last
I went the whole way—and drove him into exile.

Yes, I played the stepmother.
I pretended to hate him as my stepson. 395
As if his very presence poisoned me.
Night and day, Theseus had to hear that.
And finally he relented.
So—his own father forced him to go.
Then I could breathe again, Oenone. 400
Once he'd gone the days flowed past me calmly.

I could conceal my anguish. I could be faithful.
I could even bear children.
But then, of a sudden,
All my precautions came to nothing. 405
Fate is inescapable.
Theseus brought me to Troezen.
And here, in Troezen,
I had to confront the one I had banished.
The first sight of him ripped my wounds wide open. 410
No longer a fever in my veins,
Venus has fastened on me like a tiger.
I know my guilt, and it terrifies me.
My own craving fills me with horror.
I detest my life. 415
I would have preferred to die
With what ought to be hidden cleanly hidden,
And my name intact,
But now you know everything
I will not regret it. 420
If only you will let me die quietly
And stop lashing me with these pointless reproaches,
And stop making such efforts to keep me alive.

    [*Enter* PANOPE.]

PANOPE   Madam, against my will I bring bad news.
   And you will have to hear it. Forgive me. 425
   Death has taken your husband, Theseus.
   The whole world knows of it. Except you.
OENONE   What did you say?
PANOPE   The Queen must now accept that her prayers
   For the King's safe return are unavailing. 430
   His son, Prince Hippolytus, has learned
   From ships just docked in port: the King is dead.
PHÈDRE   Oh God!

PANOPE   Now the question is: who rules Athens?
The city is divided. Madam,   435
    One side gives its voice to your son.
    But the other, ignoring ancient law,[8]
    Gives its voice to the son of the foreign woman—
    To Hippolytus.
    And rumour has it that a turbulent faction   440
    Is determined to crown Aricia,
    Heiress to the blood of the Pallantes.
    I thought it right to warn you.
    Hippolytus is almost aboard.
    Once he sets foot among the Athenians   445
    In this broil, with everything so doubtful,
    That giddy population will be his.
    You would be right to fear it.
OENONE   You have said all that is needed, Panope.
    The Queen, you can be sure,   450
    Will not be blind to its significance.
         [Exit PANOPE.]

    Madam, I had given up all hope.
    I meant to go with you
    Into the grave. I had not a word left
    To restrain you one more hour.   455
    But this news demands a different spirit.
    Fortunes have changed and yours is smiling at you.
    The King is dead.
    Who takes his place?
    Your son is the heir.   460
    The King's death leaves you to enforce his claim.
    Die—and he's a slave.
    Live—and he is a king.
    If you die who will support him, or guide him,
    Or console him?   465
    You will have betrayed him.
    His bitterness
    Will be heard in heaven, the gods will hear it.
    He had forebears among them
    And they will not forgive you.   470
    Live—live! You have nothing to be ashamed of.
    Your love is as guiltless as love can be.
    Theseus' death has liberated it.
    It is no longer criminal and condemned.
    Hippolytus becomes accessible—   475
    No longer a man to be feared.
    You can meet him freely as you please.

8. Athenian law made the son of an Athenian and a non-Greek woman illegitimate. As noted, Hippolytus's mother was an Amazon. It is not clear why Phèdre's children are not similarly classified.

But you must move quickly.
Most likely,
Convinced as he is of your antipathy,
He will mount this coup—to seize Athens.   480
Madam, undeceive him.
Confuse his decision.
He knows too well that ancient law debars him
From the throne of Athens. Ancient law   485
Gives that throne to your son and to no other.
Hippolytus inherits
Only the crown of Troezen.
This is his lawful share of Theseus' realm.
Let him have this.   490
Then you can join with him, madam,
Against the common enemy: you and he
Combine your forces against Aricia.

PHÈDRE   Yes, yes, yes, your words are only too clear.
Now let me live—if that be possible.   495
Let my love for my son be strong enough
To revive what's left of my spirit.

Act II

[ARICIA, ISMÈNE.]

ARICIA   You say Hippolytus has asked to see me?
It can't be true. You must be mistaken.
You say he's looking for me?

ISMÈNE   To say farewell.
This is the first effect of the King's death.   5
Prepare yourself.
The hearts that Theseus diverted from you
Will now come flocking back. Aricia
Is queen of her own destiny—at last.
Soon the whole of Greece will be at your feet.   10

ARICIA   You are sure this isn't a rumour, Ismène?
Am I free? Is my jailer dead?

ISMÈNE   The gods are no longer against you.
The ghost of Theseus has joined your brothers.

ARICIA   How did he die?

ISMÈNE   Accounts conflict.   15
Mostly incredible. They say
This faithless husband drowned
In some escapade with a woman.
Others go further. They say   20
He went with his friend Pirithous
Down into the underworld.[9]

9. Theseus went to Hades with Pentithoüs, king of the Lapiths—with whom he had earlier abducted Helen—to help his friend steal Persephone. Hercules freed Theseus, whom the god Hades had imprisoned, but could not free Pentithoüs, who was later killed.

If it can be believed
He strolled along the banks of Hell's river
Letting the dead gaze at his living body.   25
Then found himself trapped in that black land
From which nothing emerges.
All Greece is buzzing with it.

ARICIA   Can you believe that a man before his death
Would visit the land of the dead? Why should he?   30
What could be the attraction?

ISMÈNE   The King is dead. Nobody doubts that.
Except you. Athens is in mourning.
Troezen confirms his death
By crowning Hippolytus.   35
Phèdre is frightened for her son.
She has summoned her anxious friends to advise her.

ARICIA   You think Hippolytus will treat me kindlier
Than his father did? A longer chain?
Will he pity me, do you think?   40

ISMÈNE   Madam, he will.

ARICIA   Haven't you heard? Hippolytus is bronze—
Dangerous and hard, without feeling.
To think he will pity me
And exempt me alone   45
From the revulsion he feels for all our sex
Ignores the reality. Have you not noticed
The lengths he goes to—simply to avoid me?
How carefully he limits all his movements
To my absence?   50

ISMÈNE   Of course I know what others say about him,
But I have also watched him in your presence.
That awesome, inflexible hauteur,
The very fame of it, as I observed him,
Doubled my curiosity. Madam,   55
What I had heard of him and what I saw
Were nothing like each other. Your first glance
Reduced him to total confusion.
I saw he could not take his eyes off you—
He tried to, but he could not. Those eyes, madam,   60
Were painful with longing—helpless longing.
The name of lover, perhaps, hurts his pride.
His words, maybe, protect his reputation.
But those eyes told everything.

ARICIA   Ismène,   65
What you say you might have imagined
But I am famished for it, I devour it.
You know my life—
You know how Fate has used me,
Like the toy of a cruel child.   70
Whatever feeling I had

Was what could survive on grief,
Nourished only by tears.
What can I know about love?
What can I know about the follies,   75
The luxury, the anguish?
How could I possibly know it?
Among all Erechtheus'[1] descendants
I am the last.
Of all my family, war spared only me.   80
The sword cut off our name.
It cut off all my brothers.
The earth could hardly stomach so much blood.
You know, too, when Theseus murdered them
He made a law   85
That no Greek should ever marry me.
Afraid my brothers' ashes might somehow
Blaze into life—out of their sister's womb.
But you know what contempt I felt
For this conqueror's petty vigilance.   90
Love had never interested me.
My whole life I despised it.
So I could almost thank him for his fears.
He merely officialised my chosen life.
But that—that was before I saw his son.   95

The whole world admires Hippolytus,
For grace, for beauty.
They are his natural gifts—the more dazzling
For seeming so unconscious.
I was dazzled.   100
I was even more dazzled
By something richer:
His father's strengths—without the weaknesses.
But what dazzled me most, and I admit it,
Was that pride—that flawless disdain   105
No woman has ever touched.
The dubious kisses of Theseus
May be the glory of Phèdre.
I set a higher value on myself.
I would be ashamed to cling to favours   110
Debased and distributed among hundreds.
To be locked up in a heart open to any.
No. But think—
To bring that obdurate spirit to its knees!
To render that unfeeling arrogant soul   115
Sick with desire.
To see him bound
In bonds he cannot break—

1. Their ancestor, son of Earth and reared by Athene.

Bonds he only prays to be tighter.
This thrills me. This is what I want. 120
Hercules was overpowered
Far too easily to bring much credit
To the various women who won him.
Perhaps I am prattling foolishly.
You may hear me regret these words. 125
More likely he will resist me, or ignore me,
And stay impenetrable.
This hard pride of his that fascinates me
Might yet break me. Hippolytus in love!
What freakish reversal of my fortunes 130
Could begin to sway—

ISMÈNE   Hear for yourself. He's coming.

[*Enter* HIPPOLYTUS.]

HIPPOLYTUS   Princess, before I leave I should inform you
What has been decided for you.
My father is dead. My fears were not misplaced. 135
Nothing but death could have imposed on Theseus
Such a protracted silence.
The gods have finally
Given to the fatal three sisters
Hercules' friend, and heir,[2] and sole equal. 140
You hated him, I know.
And yet I think you will grant him those honours,
And acknowledge his achievements.
I must mourn for my father.
But one thing lightens my grief: 145
You live a prisoner: I can free you.
I free you: from a law
That has always seemed to me barbarous.
Your life and your heart are now your own.
Do with them as you please. 150
Troezen has descended to me
Direct from my grandsire Pittheus.
By a unanimous voice, I am now King.
In this kingdom of mine
You are as free, madam, as I am myself. 155
Or rather, much freer.

ARICIA   Your generosity is too great—too sudden.
More than you can know,
Bestowing so much on my misfortune
You bind me 160
To the same austere law from which you have freed me.

HIPPOLYTUS   The Athenians cannot decide who shall rule them.
They have named the son of Phèdre. And me. And you.

ARICIA   Me?

---

2. In the sense of being, like Hercules, a destroyer of monsters.

HIPPOLYTUS   For myself I have no illusions.   165
  A Greek law discriminates against me
  Because my mother was a foreigner.
  Even so, if my only rival
  Were the son of Phèdre, my half-brother,
  My claim is strong enough. And I could assert it   170
  To push aside that scruple of the law.
  But, Princess,
  An even stronger claim reins me back
  From entering this race. I mean—your claim.
  I pass to you, or rather I restore it,   175
  The throne of Athens, which is yours by right—
  Descending directly to you
  From Erechtheus, the great son of Earth.
  Aegeus[3] came to it by adoption.
  Athens then confirmed the succession   180
  To Theseus, his son, for his tireless service
  Enlarging and defending the city.
  Your brothers' claim
  Was meanwhile passed over and forgotten.
  Now Athens wants you back.   185
  She is sick of this everlasting quarrel.
  Too much of your family's blood, for too long,
  Has gone smoking into the very soil
  That bore your progenitor.
  Troezen is mine. Crete and its territories   190
  Are kingdoms rich enough for Phèdre's child.
  And Greece is yours. What I shall do now
  Is reunite the votes scattered among us
  Behind your single name.
ARICIA   Everything you say is astonishing.   195
  It is too like a dream. Is it a dream?
  Am I awake? Who could believe this?
  Some god has possessed you to think such thoughts.
  I see now why the whole world honours you,
  And how far you surpass their admiration.   200
  To crown me you will depose yourself!
  It was enough simply not to hate me.
  Simply to have withheld yourself so long
  From that hostility—
HIPPOLYTUS   Me hate you?   205
  My pride, I know, is given hard names
  But do you think I came from the womb of a monster?
  There is no human temperament so brutal,
  No hatred so ossified with habit
  That could look at you and not soften,   210
  Not be enchanted, not be captivated.
  Could I be the exception?

---

3. Pandion's son by adoption, and Theseus's father.

ARICIA   My lord!

HIPPOLYTUS   No!

Now let me tell you. Now I have begun.   215
When passion boils, reason evaporates.
I mean—when the heart boils, when love moves.
My secret has become unbearable.
I cannot hold it in any longer.
Am I Hippolytus the arrogant?   220
Am I a prince? Or a king?
No, I am a beggar—to be pitied.
Not so much the exemplar of pride
As of the stupidity of pride.
I set this lofty pride against love.   225
I mocked her captives in their ridiculous chains,
I saw her clowns shipwrecked and I laughed
To watch their storms while I sat safe ashore.
But now you see me,
Flotsam in that tide of the common law.   230
A single surge has swept me far from myself.
A single wave, and it has overwhelmed me.
It happened in a moment.
Now this famous pride is crying for help.
Desperate, humiliated,   235
With the arrow in me,
Six months of mortification,
Fighting you, fighting myself.
I search your absence for you like a madman,
And yet I run from your presence.   240
Everywhere in the woods your image hunts me.
I try to escape you
But every shaft of sunlight,
Every night shadow
Sets you in front of me, surrounds me with you.   245
Everything competes to fling
The obstinate fool Hippolytus
Helpless at your feet.
All my studied care to preserve myself
Has brought me to this—I have lost myself,   250
I search—but I cannot find myself,
My bow, my spears, my chariot,
They beckon to me, I ignore them.
The breaking and taming of wild horses,
Everything the god of the sea taught me,   255
It is beyond me—I have forgotten it.
My own horses run wild—
They have forgotten my voice.
Nothing hears my voice but the forest—
The black echoing depth of the forest.   260
Yes, my love is a savage.
What raving words these are!

Maybe you blush to hear them.
All I had meant to do was declare my love.
Your delicate snare has caught a strange creature.   265
Princess, grant my words
Perhaps a little more than their face value.
You know this is a language alien to me.
My love speaks crudely, but do not reject it.
Without you, I never could have known it.   270

[*Enter* THÉRAMÈNE.]

THÉRAMÈNE   My lord, the Queen is coming.
She's looking for you.

HIPPOLYTUS   For me? Why?

THÉRAMÈNE   She instructed me
That she must speak with you before you go.   275
I know no more than that.

HIPPOLYTUS   Phèdre! What can I say?
What is she expecting me to say?

ARICIA   My lord, you cannot well refuse to hear her.
As your enemy, it is true,   280
She is implacable.
But in her state show her a little pity.

HIPPOLYTUS   You must go now. And I shall leave
Uncertain how far I have offended
This beauty I adore,   285
Or whether the heart I have given you—

ARICIA   Prince, do not delay!
Follow your noble plan and complete it.
Persuade Athens to acknowledge me.
Everything that you have given me—   290
I accept it. But the throne of Athens,
Glorious and great as it is,
To me is the least precious of your gifts.

[*Exeunt* ARICIA *and* ISMÈNE.]

HIPPOLYTUS   Old friend, are we all set? Here comes the Queen.
Go, make sure every man is ready   295
For immediate departure. That done,
Hurry back here and extract me
From a conversation I do not relish.

[*Exit* THÉRAMÈNE. *Enter* PHÈDRE *and* OENONE.]

PHÈDRE   He is there.
My heart labours. My legs tremble.   300
I had my words prepared but where are they?

OENONE   Only remember—
You are your son's sole hope.

PHÈDRE   My lord, we hear this sudden emergency
Is removing you from us. I had hoped   305

We might mourn a little together.
Also, dare I mention it,
I am anxious for my son. He is fatherless
And soon, very soon, he will be bowed
At the grave of his mother.　　　　　　　　　　310
The boy has few friends,
But, of a sudden, many enemies—
Already moving
To take advantage
Of this moment. My lord,　　　　　　　　　　315
You are the one man who can defend him.
But you know my fear:
It may be I have turned you against him.
I am afraid
A hatred created by his difficult mother　　　320
Will make him its object.

HIPPOLYTUS　Madam,
The very thought of that—I find repugnant.

PHÈDRE　I understand your distaste for me.
It is logical. Inevitable.　　　　　　　　　　325
You have seen me relentless to hurt you.
But you never looked any deeper.
Yes, I did all I could to provoke in you
A fury of revulsion for me.
I drove you away from wherever I came.　　　330
Public or private
In all I said
I was against you.
I set a whole ocean between us.
I made a law that even your name　　　　　　335
Should never be pronounced in my presence.
But if the measured penalty for all this
Were truly to match the motive, if your hatred
Answered my hatred and nothing but my hatred,
No woman ever earned more pity　　　　　　340
Or less enmity from you than I have.

HIPPOLYTUS　I know that a mother, jealous for her son,
Rarely tolerates the rivalry
Of a half-brother, the son of some other woman.
Seizures of resentment and suspicion　　　　345
Are expected of a stepmother.
No matter who my father had married
I would have faced the same, and perhaps worse.

PHÈDRE　My lord, God knows, I can swear
Heaven has exonerated me　　　　　　　　　350
From that common failing.
A far different passion
Oppresses me, devours me.

HIPPOLYTUS　Madam, our time to mourn has not yet come.

Your husband may be alive.   355
We weep, but the world might still produce him.
The god of the sea loves him. That great god
Will not have been deaf to his prayers.

PHÈDRE   Nobody goes twice to the underworld.
Once he strayed that far,   360
If you think some god can extricate him
You are deluded.
Hell never surrenders its prey.
But what am I saying? No—
You are right: he is not dead. I see him.   365
Theseus is alive. He lives in you.
I look at you and I see him.
My husband's face is this face.
And my love, my need, yes, in spite of myself,
My deprivation, my starvation, my fever—   370
I can't hide it. He has to know it.
It has to come out.

HIPPOLYTUS   Madam, the abnormal hunger of your love
Projects his image onto other faces.
Though he is dead, his love possesses you.   375

PHÈDRE   Prince, you are right. I am possessed.
I sicken for Theseus.
But not as the underworld saw him—
The laughing ravisher of a thousand women,
Ready to cuckold even the god of the dead.   380
Not like that, but loyal and proud,
Even a little diffident perhaps,
Young, and bewitching everybody
With an aura, a magic—
Just as they portray the gods.   385
Or just as I see you. Yes—
The Theseus I see
Has your bearing, exactly,
Your eyes, your lips,
The very pitch of your voice,   390
This noble modesty
Gives his cheeks just that flush of colour.
When he came over the sea, to my home in Crete,
The daughters of Minos[4] were besotted—
For a good reason.   395
Where were you then?
How could he have gathered the flower of Athens
To pay the tribute without Hippolytus?
You were too young! Even so
You could have come with him, on that voyage.   400
Why didn't you come with him?
To our shores, in that ship?

4. Phèdre and Ariadne.

In spite of all the labyrinth's knots and tangles
You would have slaughtered the Minotaur.
My sister Ariadne   405
Would have given the thread to you, not to Theseus,[5]
To lead you back to the light
Out of the heart of the monster's riddle.
No, she would not—no, no, she would not—
I would have been there before her   410
With the plan, and the spool of thread,
To unravel that snarl of dark tunnels
And bring you out of the maze.
Ah, what care and love I could have lavished
On this darling head! Phèdre   415
Would have come into the labyrinth with you.
She would have come the whole way beside you
To guide you back. Or be killed in there beside you.

HIPPOLYTUS   You gods, what am I hearing?
Have you forgotten that King Theseus   420
Is my father, and that you are his wife?

PHÈDRE   Can you believe I have lost my memory?
Could I be so reckless with my title?

HIPPOLYTUS   Forgive me, madam. I misinterpreted
Your words about my father.   425
They confused me. You see, I am blushing.
I am ashamed even to look at you:
I must go—

PHÈDRE   Now you torture me worse!
Prince, you have understood me perfectly.   430
I said enough to show you the truth.
Look at me—see a woman in frenzy.
I am in love.
But do not suppose for a second
I think myself guiltless   435
For loving you as I love you.
I have not
Indulged myself out of empty boredom.
I have not drunk this strychnine day after day
As an idle refreshment.   440
Wretched victim of a divine vengeance![6]
I detest myself
More than you can ever detest me.
You are right, the gods are watching me.
Yes, the same gods   445
Who have filled me with these horrible flames
That are killing me—as they have killed
All the women in my family.

5. The Minotaur inhabited the heart of a maze. Ariadne provided Theseus with a ball of thread, by which he left a trail behind him and so could retrace his steps after killing the monster.

6. Phèdre feels herself a victim of Venus, the goddess of love; she loves Hippolytus against her will.

Those sadistic gods
Who amuse themselves, and make their names,   450
Playing with human hearts.
You know too well how I have treated you.
I not only shunned you.
I acted like a tyrant, I had you banished.
I wanted you to hate me. I wanted you   455
To regard me as loathsome, inhuman—
Simply to help me to resist you.
All that agony—to no purpose!
Yes, you hated me more. And more and more—
But my love never lessened.   460
Your sufferings made your beauty more painful.
I writhed, I was consumed
In burnings and tears—
You only had to look at me to see it.
If you could force yourself to look at me.   465
What am I saying? Oh this is shameful.
Shameful confession! Shameful!
It's you—I have to speak.
You are crushing it out of me.
I came here with a simple small request: 470
Fearful for my son who depends on me,
I meant to beg you, Prince, not to hate him.
But see how I flung it aside!
My mania burst out, I cannot stop it!
O Prince, I cannot speak to you   475
Of anything but you. Avenge yourself.
I am depraved. Act. Punish me.
Prove yourself the son of your father—
Rid the world of a monster!
The widow of King Theseus has dared   480
To fall in love with his son, Hippolytus.
This disgusting pest should be killed.
Look—my heart. Here.
Bury your sword here.
This heart is utterly corrupt.   485
It cannot wait to expiate its evil.
I feel it lifting to meet your stroke. Strike!
Or am I beneath your contempt?
Maybe my death seems too light a sentence.
Or are you apprehensive   490
That my polluted blood might foul your hand?
If your hands are reluctant, give me your sword.
Give me that sword!

OENONE What are you doing, madam! Holy God!
Somebody's coming. Don't let them find you here.   495
Come, quickly, before they see too much.

    [*Exeunt* PHÈDRE *and* OENONE. *Enter* THÉRAMÈNE.]

THÉRAMÈNE   Was that the Queen? What has happened?
   Is there more bad news? My lord,
   You look half-crazed. Where is your sword?
HIPPOLYTUS   Théramène, we must leave and leave quickly.   500
   I cannot think of myself without horror.
   Phèdre—O you mighty gods in heaven,
   If there is a hole in your creation
   Drop this secret through it.
THÉRAMÈNE   The ship is rigged and ready. But I must tell you   505
   Athens has announced her decision.
   Her chieftains and their tribes have given the crown
   To your half-brother. Phèdre has triumphed.
HIPPOLYTUS   Phèdre!
THÉRAMÈNE   A delegation from Athens is here.   510
   Waiting to hand the reins of government
   Over to Phèdre. Her son will be King.
HIPPOLYTUS   You gods who know her—is this how you reward her?
THÉRAMÈNE   Meanwhile, my lord, there are murmurs
   That Theseus is alive. In Epirus—   515
   So it is said. But we have searched for him
   In that very place and we—
HIPPOLYTUS   No matter.
   Question everybody. Neglect nothing.
   Investigate this rumour. Follow it right back   520
   To its source in Epirus. If it is false
   Then it cannot hinder me. Come,
   Whatever the cost, I am going to set this crown
   On the head it belongs to.

Act III

[PHÈDRE, OENONE.]
PHÈDRE   Can't I be free of all this regalia?
   How can I parade myself now?
   Stop insisting.
   And stop trying to console me.
   You would be better to conceal me.   5
   I have said too much.
   This uncontainable obsession
   Has stooped to reveal itself.
   I have said what nobody alive
   Should ever have heard.   10
   Did you see him?
   How he stared as I spoke?
   Oh God—how he twisted about
   Pretending to misunderstand me.
   How he strained to be gone?   15
   And that blushing of his—
   The humiliation!

Why did you prevent me
When I had the solution there in my grasp?
That sword has a point like a needle.   20
When I rested it here, just touching my skin,
Here under my breast—
Did he go pale? For me?
Did he snatch the blade out of my hand?
It needed only a push, one little push—   25
But the mere fact that I'd touched it
Made his own sword horrifying to him.
He was afraid
That what I'd handled
Might profane   30
His sacred skin.
OENONE   Madam, enough of this. You must stop
Raking your miseries over.
You are feeding a fire that you should quench.
You are the daughter of Minos—   35
The grand-daughter of Zeus—
Far more fitting now to turn your mind
To practical matters.
And far wiser too, to forget this boy
Who has proved so unresponsive.   40
Take up your proper task, and rule your kingdom.
PHÈDRE   Me? Rule? Me take control
Of a state flying to pieces
When I cannot control myself?
When I have abdicated   45
The throne of my own being?
When I am occupied by an enemy
That hardly lets me breathe?
When I am all but dead?
OENONE   Get right away.   50
PHÈDRE   Ah!
I cannot remove myself from him.
OENONE   You dared to banish him. Dare to banish yourself.
PHÈDRE   Too late. He knows my whole madness.
Prudence and restraint are out of date.   55
Like weak prey torn open
I have bared my innermost, hidden pulse
To my killer. And I cannot help it—
In spite of myself, I still cling to a hope.
When my strength failed before   60
You brought me back to life.
When my soul was shivering at my lips
You restored it, you flattered its misery.
You gave it hope.
You made me think this love was possible.   65
OENONE   Whether I am guilty or innocent
I cannot tell. Could I have let you die?

But if my intervention vexes you
What about that spoiled brat's contempt?
Can you forget that face? That baleful blank.   70
That stone, hewn block. He hardly saw you
While you writhed at his feet.
His ferocious pride makes him repellent.
If only Phèdre had my eyes to see him.

PHÈDRE   Oenone, he might not be what we think.   75
The forests that bred him kept him wild.
Hunting has made him violent and harsh.
He never heard love speak until today.
He was silent because he was stunned.
It could be we have misunderstood him.   80

OENONE   Remember, an Amazon bore him.

PHÈDRE   Barbaric, maybe, but she must have loved.

OENONE   His hatred for all women is absolute.

PHÈDRE   In that case I need never fear a rival.
It is too late for this kind of discussion.   85
Serve my madness now, not my reason.
If his heart is walled up against me
We must find some other unguarded spot.
I noticed how the charms of kingship touched him.
Athens excited him. He could not hide it.   90
His ships were on the leash—ready to dash
Across the seas to pluck the Athenian crown.
Oenone, go now, work on him cleverly.
Dangle the crown until it dazzles him.
Let him understand—it can be his.   95
And tell him, Phèdre asks no other favour
Than to set that royal jewel on him.
I cede him all my power. I cannot defend it.
And he can teach my son how to command.
Perhaps be like a father to the boy.   100
I put both mother and son under his ward.
Go to any limit to persuade him.
Words from you will enter where mine cannot.
Be shameless, weep, groan, anything. Describe me
Close to death. Prostrate yourself. Implore him.   105
I grant you total licence. Oenone, quickly,
You are my only hope. I shall wait
Here till you return with my fate.
          [*Exit* OENONE.]

You great goddess Venus, are you watching?
Are you happy   110
To see just how far I have fallen?
It is impossible
To humiliate me any further.
Your victory is complete. Your every stroke
Has gone home.   115

Goddess of pure remorseless cruelty,
If you still seek for fame
Choose a harder target.
Hippolytus mocks you. He laughs at your furies.
He never uttered one prayer at your altar.   120
Your very name offends him.
He waves it aside like some polluted fly.
Why not choose him?
He pours the same derision
On you as on me. Avenge yourself.   125
Make him love.
     [*Enter* OENONE.]

Oenone, why are you back so quickly?
Wouldn't he listen? Is he still adamant?
OENONE   Madam,
  Now you need your former fortitude.   130
  Forget your great love: you can bury it.
PHÈDRE   What did he say?
OENONE   I could not find Hippolytus. Madam,
  All those rumours, that seemed so certain,
  That convinced everybody, have betrayed us.   135
  Do you hear the roar of the people?
  They are welcoming their King.
  Theseus is coming from the harbour.
PHÈDRE   Theseus is alive?
OENONE   Any moment   140
  He will be here.
PHÈDRE   Oenone, it's finished.
  I have confessed
  An appetite that is unspeakable.
  With a few greedy words   145
  I have stripped my husband of all honour.
  He is alive? Let me hear nothing else.
OENONE   Madam—
PHÈDRE   I foresaw all this.
  But you—you were blind.   150
  My guilt was unrelenting—
  I only wanted to die.
  Then your tears came like anaesthesia.
  Even this morning
  I could have died with honour.   155
  But then I drank your advice.
  However I die now, I die in shame.
OENONE   Die? Why must you always talk of dying?
PHÈDRE   What have I done, O God?
  My husband is coming. And his son   160
  Hippolytus—still dazed by my outburst.
  I shall have to face my enemy.

I shall have to feel his eyes on me—
Observing just what face I show his father.
Noting my loving words—which he spurned.   165
And my tears—which meant so little to him.
What do you think?
Is he so sensitive to his father's honour
That he will keep hidden at all costs
What I revealed?   170
How could he do that? How could he stay silent?
How could he rather connive
At the betrayal of his sire and monarch
Than spit out his loathing for me?
In any case   175
There's no point in him hiding it.
I am not one of those women
Who manage their infidelity
With a polished smile and a stone heart.
I have not forgotten my ravings.   180
Every gasp is still alive in me.
Even these walls remember them,
These ceilings are saturated with them,
Every room and passage in this palace
Is bursting to shout my secret   185
And accuse me. The air is quivering with it.
The moment he steps through the door
He will hear it.
Let me die. My one escape
From all this   190
Is annihilation.
Is it so dreadful to be nothing?
Despair can find death friendly.
But what a bequest for my children!
Descent from Jupiter is their confidence.   195
How will they lift their heads
Under my degradation?
Under my folly,
My self-immolation?
Ah!   200
How will their poor minds endure
The revelations about me, all too true?
The tales that every gossip will barb
And stick into them?
I dare not think   205
How they will live, buried in their mother's shame.
OENONE   They will not escape. I pity both.
No mother's fears were ever more prophetic.
But why create such a catastrophe?
Why mount this great case against yourself: 210
If you kill yourself, the whole world

Will be certain you did it because you were guilty,
And could not face the man you had deceived.
Who will be happier than Hippolytus
To have your suicide   215
Validate the story he will tell?
And what will my version of events
Amount to then? My voice will be wafted aside,
Like a feather. I shall have to listen
To his conceited triumphant sneer   220
While he regales the court with your behaviour.
Better a thunderbolt wipe me off the earth.
But, madam, has your feeling for him changed?
What do you feel? How do you see him now?

PHÈDRE   A monster! He terrifies me.   225

OENONE   Then why grant him so easy a victory?
You dread what he might say—that is your terror.
Madam—strike first.
Any moment now he can accuse you.
Accuse him first—of the same crime.   230
Who could contradict you? Everything
Is evidence against him. His own sword—
Which he left in your hand so luckily.
Your present agitation. Your past distress.
Your perpetual grievance—so emphatic   235
It turned even his own father against him.
The fact you went so far as to have him banished.

PHÈDRE   Me attack him? Perjure myself
To convict a man who is innocent?

OENONE   Say nothing.   240
All my plan requires is your silence.
I too have to smother a conscience.
I would rather confront death
A thousand times, than perform this.
But since without precarious surgery   245
Your death is inevitable, to my mind
The cost is meaningless.
Leave it to me to speak to Theseus.
He will go mad, for a while.
But in the end, like a wise horseman,   250
He'll halt the runaway furies.
He will punish his son, you can be sure,
With nothing more than exile, as before.
When a father judges his own son
He remains a daddy. For all that,   255
Innocent blood might still have to be spilt
If it threatens your name. They are coming,
I see Theseus.

PHÈDRE   Aye! And Hippolytus!
That arrogant gaze, plain as speech,   260
Tells me just how hopeless my case is.

Do what you want, Oenone.
I leave everything to your discretion.
I cannot make one move to help myself.

[*Enter* THESEUS, HIPPOLYTUS *and* THÉRAMÈNE.]
THESEUS   After my long ordeal, at last   265
Fate has let me through
To my Queen's arms—
PHÈDRE   Stop, Theseus.
Do not profane a greeting of such sweetness.
Phèdre is no longer fit to hear it.
The gods, you should know, are jealous of you.   270
In your long absence they have not spared your wife.
I cannot delight you. I am no longer worthy
Even to approach you.
Your honour, my lord, has been violated.   275
Nothing is left to me but to hide myself.
    [*Exeunt* PHÈDRE *and* OENONE.]

THESEUS   Hippolytus,
This is a strange welcome for your father.
HIPPOLYTUS   Nobody but Phèdre can explain it.
For my part, sir,   280
I want nothing more to do with her.
And I beg your permission to leave.
You see how this disturbs me. Let me go.
I cannot exist in her proximity.
Let me simply vanish.   285
THESEUS   You, my son, leave me?
HIPPOLYTUS   I never wanted her. I never sought her.
She was yours. You brought her into this country,
Into Troezen, with Aricia.
Before you left   290
You charged me, you remember, to protect them.
That duty is now redundant.
And I have squandered enough life in these forests,
Accumulating boars' tusks and antlers.
I cannot believe you would not prefer me   295
To be out of this nursery,
Facing something more formidable.
Before you were my age
You were the hero of your own epic,
You had emptied the known world   300
Of monsters and tyrants.
For every pirate of the two seas
You were Nemesis itself.
Wherever you turned, they simply ceased to exist.
To this day   305
Travellers are safe.
Hercules could rest on your laurels

And leave his work to you, confidently.
While I decayed here—
The unheard-of child of a prodigious father.   310
Unmentioned in the hymns of adulation
Sung to my heroic mother.[7]
Let me find employment for my strength.
Let me take up your work.
Or let me at least die the kind of death   315
That will be remembered
And prove to the world that I was your son.

THESEUS   What is happening?
What is it about me
Sends my family reeling from me?   320
Has that hellish pit done something to me?
Has it made me a pariah?
If it has
You gods that helped me out of it
Should have left me rotting inside it.   325
My friend Pirithous was responsible.
He let his idiot lust
Get the upper hand of his judgement.
He tried to ravish the consort
Of the tyrant of Epirus.[8]   330
Witless, rampant, suicidal folly!
And I—out of pure loyalty—
Was rash enough to aid and abet.
Fate was rightly angered—she made us stupid.
The tyrant surprised us—weaponless.   335
Then I was forced to watch as he flung
My lecherous companion Pirithous
To horrible reptiles, monsters of the swamp,
Which he kept as pets and fed on men.
For me he had a pit, a steep cavern,   340
Foetid with stench from the underworld.
I lay under the showering dung of bats.
It was a long time
Before the gods remembered me there.
But they did. They let me outwit my guards.   345
I paused only to pick up a sword
And butcher that King for his scavengers.
Then came hurrying home. And what meets me?
Just when I think I can be happy
With my family,   350
Just when I feel my soul
Is coming back to itself—
And only wants to feast and sate itself
In gazing at my family, my beloved,

7. Hippolytus's mother also performed brave deeds.
8. A district in western Greece on the Ionian Sea.

My children—   355
I see them staring at me horrified.
I see them shuddering as I approach them.
They squirm from my embraces, they back off,
They cannot get away from me fast enough.
I see such fear in their faces   360
It fills me with horror—at myself.
I would be happier back in that cavern.
What did my wife mean by what she said?
My honour violated? How? Who did it?
If it's true, why am I unavenged?   365
Greece looked to me to defend it—
Has it given asylum to the culprit?
You say nothing. Can't you say something?
Am I to assume my own son
Is in collusion with an enemy?   370
Where is Phèdre?
She swamps me with suspicions
Then disappears. Come.
No man on earth could endure this.
And only Phèdre can unravel it.   375
      [*Exit* THESEUS.]

HIPPOLYTUS   My father's words are more than ominous.
I have seen how far the Queen's derangement
Is beyond her control.
When he challenges her what will she do:
Denounce and destroy herself?   380
God in heaven, what will he make of it?
Love has unbalanced his entire family.
He thinks I am what I was.
But even I hide a passion
That subverts his law.   385
I am full of sickening premonitions.
Yet innocence has nothing to fear.
Maybe I can soften him a little,
Find the right words to bring him round,
Persuade him to forbearance   390
For a love he may not like, but cannot change.

Act IV

[THESEUS, OENONE.]
THESEUS   What? What? This is like vandalism.
Such malignity! So light-minded!
The whole thing so carefully designed
To desecrate his own father's honour.
To deface my name? Defile me?   5
Nothing could do me worse damage.
Shall I never get out of the labyrinth?

Where am I? Which way can I turn?
That he could think it, is inconceivable!
The brutalised audacity of it!   10
This is how he repays my paternal care.
And to drive the atrocity home
This thug did not reject the use of force.
I recognise that sword.
I gave it to him—for a different purpose.   15
The bonds of his own blood could not restrain him.
Phèdre has been at fault. Phèdre
Bears some blame. She deferred his exposure
For too long. Too loath to see him punished,
Phèdre's silence has protected him.   20

OENONE   Phèdre protected a pitiable father.
    She was so distraught to meet the lust
    Aroused in Hippolytus by her beauty,
    So shamed by his shamelessness, his importunate grossness—
    My lord, Phèdre was dying. I watched her own fingers   25
    Guide that point to a softness between her ribs.
    I saw her resolution. Had I not wrenched
    The sword out of her hands nothing could have saved her.
    It is my pity for her and for you
    Prompts me now to tell you what I know.   30

THESEUS   I saw it! He went white when I met him.
    And when I approached him—
    I recognise fear.
    To see his face so drawn—that made me wonder.
    And his embrace—   35
    It was so stiff and cold it froze mine.
    How long has he been possessed by this?
    Was it there earlier—in Athens?

OENONE   My lord, recall how Phèdre avoided him.
    His prurient attentions drove her mad.   40

THESEUS   He started it again—here in Troezen?

OENONE   My lord, I have described what I saw.
    You must excuse me. I have left the Queen
    Alone too long with her dangerous thoughts.
    Allow me to withdraw to be near her.   45
        [*Exit* OENONE. *Enter* HIPPOLYTUS.]

THESEUS   Ha! Here he comes. You gods in heaven,
    How nobly he carries himself!
    Who would not be deceived—
    As I have been?
    But isn't it natural—?   50
    The adulterer's gaze has to inveigle us
    With that seamless mask of probity.
    If only there were a window
    Fixed in the face of every blackguard

To show us the heart behind it! 55
HIPPOLYTUS   My lord, may I ask
What is weighing on you. I am aware
A dark cloud of some sort sits on you.
You know you can trust my discretion.
THESEUS   Trust you? How dare you 60
Show your impudent face in front of me?
The thunderbolt has spared you too long.
Last of the vermin to be exterminated!
After your ravenous lust
Has sated itself in your father's bed 65
You dare to confront him?
To bare that despicable face of yours
Within the reach of my weapon?
In this very palace you have despoiled?
You should be away. That would be wise. 70
You should be under some other heaven.
In some land ignorant of my name
Where nobody knows or could guess
How rabid you are.
Get out. Don't brave me with your lies. 75
Do not tempt me to the act
That I am reining back with difficulty.
I have enough—
The everlasting shame of such a son
Is enough 80
Without the last ignominy
Of having put an end to him myself.
That might soil the glory of all I have done.
Get out. Unless you want to die
Among the trash I have swept into ditches. 85
And make sure that the sun, the blessed sun,
Never again casts your accursèd shadow
On the threshold of this house
Or on the roads to it,
Or anywhere within my territories. 90
Get out. Now. Get out.

Neptune, O great God of the Oceans,
Remember how I scoured your shores clean
Of every ruffian.
Remember how you swore to reward me. 95
You promised me one wish. A single wish.
When I lay festering in that putrid dungeon
I didn't trouble you with it. I saved it.
I kept it for my moment of true need.
That moment has come. Grant me my wish. 100
Now! Avenge a heart-broken father.
Break your wrath on the head of this traitor.

Smash the bones of his effrontery.
Show how a great god can demolish a man.
Let me see the infinite of your favour   105
In how utterly you annihilate him.

HIPPOLYTUS   Am I to understand—the Queen has accused me?
I cannot speak for horror.
What you are saying is unthinkable.
The horror of it paralyses me.   110

THESEUS   You assumed that Phèdre, for shame,
Would hide her defilement,
So your assault on her fidelity
Would stay hidden with it.
You made a mistake. Have you forgotten?   115
You dropped your sword.
In her hand it convicts you.
You made another mistake. You omitted
To kill her—and cut off her voice.

HIPPOLYTUS   Sir, anger forces me to speak.   120
To stand accused by you, of such an outrage,
Should force me to give you the whole truth.
Yes, I know the truth. But I suppress it.
It touches you too close. My lord,
Consider a son's solicitude   125
For the father he loves.
That keeps my mouth sealed.
Unless you wish to open an abyss
Under the gulf that is already gaping.
Recall how I have lived, and what I am.   130
The first steps towards a great crime
Are trivial misdemeanours.
There is a stairway of degrees
To crime, just as to virtue.
Innocence is demure. A single day   135
Cannot transform a man of loyal conscience
To an incestuous lecher, a hardened killer.
My mother's chastity was her fame.
There's not a drop of dissolute blood in me.
She formed me. Then Pittheus[9] was my teacher.   140
The wisest, noblest, best man of his day.
I do not wish to boast but, my lord,
Above all other virtues, the one virtue
That I was born to, and have been bred up to,
Is hatred of this crime you charge me with.   145
My aversion to it is a legend.
Throughout Greece I am famed for just this.
Some say my rigour is so stubborn,
So severe, so blunt, they think it ugly,

---

9. The most learned man of his age, Theseus's guardian. After marrying Phèdre, Theseus sent Hippolytus to Pitteus (or Pitheus), who had adopted him as heir to the throne of Troezen.

Yet God knows the depth of my heart   150
Is pure as the blue sky! And still I hear you
Call me a hypocrite—
THESEUS   And I repeat it.
I see through your chastity—plain as day.
That frigid pride of yours is precisely   155
What betrays you.
Your lascivious eyes are locked on Phèdre.
Indifferent to every other woman
You have no trouble ignoring their attractions.
HIPPOLYTUS   Father, it is not so. You compel me   160
To tell you what I must withhold no longer.
I am in love.
This will anger you, but I must confess it.
I have done one thing you have forbidden.
Your son has submitted his whole being   165
To the daughter of the Pallantes—Aricia.
I worship Aricia.
Father, I adore her. My inmost soul
Belongs only to Aricia.
THESEUS   You love Aricia? Heaven sees what this is   170
As clearly as I do. A fairy tale for fools!
You concoct one crime to hide the other.
HIPPOLYTUS   Father, six months, against my will, I have loved her.
I came here to inform you. It is not easy.
What can I say to make you see the truth?   175
What heaven-shaking oaths do I have to swear
To make you understand you are mistaken?
I swear on the earth, the heavens, on all nature—
THESEUS   Blasphemy is child's play to a liar.
Stop! Spare me the babbling. You insult me.   180
Your posturing virtue is incredible.
HIPPOLYTUS   Only to you while you believe the lie.
Phèdre knows the truth. I am not guilty.
THESEUS   Ah! Your insolence is intolerable.
HIPPOLYTUS   If I am to be banished—where and when?   185
THESEUS   Beyond Atlas, far out in the Atlantic—
You would still be much too close to me.
HIPPOLYTUS   Once you have branded my name as a felon
Who in the world will befriend me? If Theseus
Casts me out, who dare take me in?   190
THESEUS   Find friends among men debauched enough
To approve adultery and relish incest.
Thankless, treacherous men, without laws or honour.
The kind who will welcome such as you.
HIPPOLYTUS   Adultery and incest! You are obsessed   195
With adultery and incest. Shall I say it?
Phèdre had a mother.
Remember Phèdre's mother.
Phèdre bears the blood of a lineage

Far more heavily charged with such crimes   200
    Than mine ever was and you know it.
THESEUS   What? You are mad!
    Get out. For the last time—get out.
    Must you wait till I'm speechless?
    Do you have to be flung out bodily?   205
            [Exit HIPPOLYTUS.]

    Yes, go, you filth. You will not escape.
    Destruction is hurrying towards you.
    The god of the oceans
    Swore on that river in Hell
    To give me satisfaction.   210
    A god of vengeance out of the seas pursues you.
    And yet in spite of your nature,
    So strangely diseased,
    I loved you. My bowels are twisting
    With a horrible foreboding.   215
    You forced me to curse you.
    How many fathers have known this?
    You gods, you see what I suffer.
    How did I sire this deformity?

            [Enter PHÈDRE.]
PHÈDRE   My lord, your voice rings through the palace.   220
    I could not help but hear it.
    I am terrified. O my lord,
    What if your prayers are answered?
    Is it too late to save him?
    He is your own blood—rescue him!   225
    Your own sacred blood—cherish it
    Before it is too late. I beg you
    Save me, Theseus,
    From having to hear his screams.
    Save me from a life   230
    Haunted by the screams of Hippolytus.
    Save me
    From the everlasting horror
    Of having prompted his own father's hand
    To destroy him.   235
THESEUS   No, Phèdre, I have refrained, not easily,
    From dipping my hand in my own blood.
    Nevertheless, this rapist is doomed.
    Immortal hands are already at it.
    Neptune's debt to me will avenge you.   240
PHÈDRE   Neptune's debt? What?
    You call on—
THESEUS   Would you prefer the god to ignore me
    Like some ordinary creditor?

My plea to him is holy—you should join me. 245
Recount my son's crime. In all its detail.
Let me hear the full enormity of it.
Shake up my sluggish spirits.
My blood is too torpid.
You do not know one half his perfidy. 250
He reviles you in particular—
Nothing but lies, he says, comes from your mouth.
He was almost incoherent.
Finally, as a last insult to me,
He dares to pretend 255
That he has fallen in love with Aricia.
He swears he has given his soul to Aricia.

PHÈDRE   Given his soul?

THESEUS   Another of his lies.
Everything he says is counterfeit. 260
He lies as he breathes—
To keep himself alive.
But Neptune, our great green god of the ocean,
His judgement will be swift.
And now I am going 265
To add my prayers to it.
          [*Exit* THESEUS.]

PHÈDRE   Can I believe this?
Am I sick? A smouldering
Here, under my ribs—
Trying to burst into hard flames. 270
This cannot be true.
I rushed here to save his son.
Oenone tried to stop me.
But her arms were powerless
To hold back the guilt that lashed me, 275
The remorse that dragged me—
I was out of my mind.
How far would I have let myself go?
Maybe, if what Theseus told me
Had not choked me 280
I would have gone on. I would have confessed.
The truth would have come vomiting out of my mouth.
But now—
Now I know Hippolytus can feel.
Only—he feels nothing for me. 285
He loves Aricia!
His heart, his soul, everything
Sworn to Aricia!
Oh God, when I howled at his feet—
When he stared at me 290
With that statue's face

I thought he was impenetrable, proof,
A bronze burnished visor, deflecting
The whole female sex—
Like his reputation. I was wrong.   295
It was all a front.
The right woman's touch undid his armour.
I thought his eyes were stone—she found tears in them.
Perhaps he is too susceptible to women.
I am the only one he cannot stand!   300
And I came rushing here to defend him!

    [*Enter* OENONE.]
  Oenone, I have learned something.
OENONE   Madam, when you ran out I almost fainted.
  You were in such a state.
  I feared it might be the end of you.   305
PHÈDRE   Would you believe it? I have a rival.
OENONE   What?
PHÈDRE   Hippolytus is in love.
  Beyond any doubt.
  This enemy of mine, so wild and shy,
  So alien to subjection,   310
  Who found my entreaty so appalling,
  My tears so irritating,
  This tiger
  That I could never approach without trembling—   315
  He has been tamed. He is humbled.
  And now he announces his love.
  Aricia has taken possession.
OENONE   Aricia!
PHÈDRE   What now, Oenone?   320
  What new constellations of torment,
  Reserved for this moment,
  Of a magnitude I never imagined,
  Rise for me now?
  All I have suffered before this—   325
  The terror, the delirium,
  The agonies of craving, the impossible pain
  Of that brutal rebuff, the horror of my guilt,
  The bottomless degradation,
  The loathing of myself, the despair—   330
  All that was no more than the overture
  For what is taking hold of me now.
  They love each other!
  What sort of witchcraft did they use
  To delude me?   335
  How long have they loved each other?
  Where have they been meeting? How often?
  You knew! You knew it! Oenone,
  Why did you let me be fooled?

Couldn't you breathe one whisper of their secret?   340
Wasn't it plain?
Weren't they forever
Running around looking for each other?
Heads together in corners, thinking themselves unnoticed
In plain view of everybody?   345
Or did they hide it all in the forest?
Ah! They were free!
Heaven was pleased with their innocent affection.
Wherever their love led, they went light-hearted.
For them the days dawned calm.   350
But for me, rejected by nature,
I dreaded every sunbeam.
I buried myself.
Daylight was a horror to me.
Death was the only god I prayed to.   355
I waited only for death.
Nothing but gall sustained me, and tears.
Surrounded by spies
I did not even dare
To unburden myself of my grief.   360
I concealed it.
I sank
Into the horrible secret luxury of it.
My sobbing was soundless.
My weeping was dry.   365
I trembled with calm.

OENONE   Their love is futureless. It has come to nothing.
           They will never meet again.

PHÈDRE   Yes, but their love exists.
           It exists. And it will last.   370
           I cannot bear to imagine it.
           Even this moment, as I speak,
           They have not a thought for me,
           They are heedless
           Of the fury of my love—   375
           It is meaningless to them.
           But I have to endure it—
           I have to burn in it.
           Banishment may separate them
           But it cannot injure their love,   380
           Only intensify their million vows
           To love each other for ever.
           No, it's their happiness—it's their hope
           That torments me.
           Oenone, I am going mad with jealousy.   385
           Aricia must die.
           Theseus must be made to kill her.
           No punishment is enough.
           She has outdone her criminal brothers.

I'll use every bit of rage in my body   390
To persuade him to kill her.
Oh God, what am I doing? What am I saying?
I think I'm losing my senses.
Me jealous? Me beg Theseus
To avenge my jealousy? Implore my husband   395
To remove my rival
From my monstrous passion for his son?
Everything I say makes my hair stand up.
My life is so bloated with my crimes
There's no room for another. I stink   400
Of incest and deceit. And worse—
My own hands are twitching
To squeeze the life out of that woman,
To empty that innocent blood out of her carcase
And smash her to nothing.   405
Yet I stand here facing the sun.
The light of heaven, my greatest ancestor,
Is the father and ruler of the gods.
The whole universe is full of my forebears.
Where can I hide?   410
I cannot hide even in Hell—
My father, Minos, is the judge of the dead.
There, the judgement favours nobody.
He will be stupefied
When I appear before him. His own daughter!   415
Forced to confess to such crimes,
So different and so many,
Some of them perhaps
Unknown even in Hell.
Father, how will you judge my life?   420
I see your hand fall from the dark urn
That contains the lots for the common dead.
I see you groping, aghast,
For the just sentence
That you must execute on your own daughter.   425
O Father, you have to forgive me.
The pitiless goddess
Would not loosen her grip on your family.
I am one more trophy of her vengeance.
My crimes were execrable.   430
Their shame walks with me like my shadow.
But they brought me no profit—
Not one flicker of gratification.
No, my every step
Carried me deeper into evil fortune.   435
My whole life has been wretched and ends in torment.

OENONE   Ah, madam, get rid of these thoughts.
You made mistakes, but view them in a new light.
You are in love: that's fate, it cannot be altered.

Destiny cast the spell that leads you spellbound. 440
Is that such a novelty?
Mankind is frail by nature.
Submit to being mortal. You are mortal.
The creation has laws.
Even the gods, the high Olympian gods, 445
Who come down so hard on our weakness,
They find passion uncontrollable.

PHÈDRE   What am I hearing?
How dare you go on mixing these drugs?
Will you try to poison me to the last? 450
Witch. This is how you have destroyed me.
When I tried to crawl out of my life
You won me to stay.
Your reasoning blinded me to my duty.
I shunned Hippolytus. You made me see him. 455
Can't you see what you've done?
Your evil incriminating mouth
Has ruined his name
And blasted his life.
It will have killed him 460
If the god fulfils the inhuman prayer
Of a father you have driven mad.
Get away from me.
Leave me to mourn what you have made of me.
And may the heavens 465
Pay you exactly
What you have earned.
And your punishment
Terrify
Everybody like you. 470
All those who do as you have done.
Bending their supple speeches to the failings
Of erratic monarchs.
Giving a little push to their inclinations,
Easing their descent into crime. 475
Vile whisperers!
Sycophants,
The most
Pernicious of the gifts an angered god
Can give to the wearer of the crown. 480

OENONE   Ah God, I have spent my life to save her.
Have I now been paid as I deserved?

Act V

[HIPPOLYTUS, ARICIA, ISMÈNE.]

ARICIA   You have to speak out.
The danger you are in numbs my mind.
Your father loves you.

You cannot let misapprehension craze him
Against you.   5
Speak, and save yourself from it. Save us.
You are forgetting us.
Are my tears meaningless? Can you accept
Our separation for ever
Without a word? Then go. Leave me hopeless.   10
But at least, if you must go, save your life.
Save your name, your fame
From this scandal and this preposterous lie.
Though the truth is vile, force him to face it.
Make him reverse the curse. There is still time.   15
What nicety of honour
Creeps off speechless leaving all the credit
With an unscrupulous liar? Tell your father,
Tell him everything.

HIPPOLYTUS   Ah God, what haven't I said?   20
You want me to disclose
The shame of his bedchamber
For the mere relief of feeling truthful?
Can I humiliate my own father
And make him laughable? Nobody   25
Has looked into this secret
Except you and the gods.
See now how I love you. I have shown you
What I tried to hide even from myself.
Aricia, forget you ever heard it.   30
I opened this to you in confidence.
Never mention it. It's too filthy a business.
It would contaminate your mouth.
But if the gods can be trusted,
If they want justice, they must favour me.   35
The situation can be left to them,
And I need fear nothing.
Sooner or later Phèdre and her great lie
Must meet their judgement, which is immovable.
Only for this I beg you to be patient.   40
But for everything else—I have done with patience.

Aricia, your prison
Need no longer hold you. Come with me.
Gather your courage. We can leave together.
Everything about this place is abhorrent.   45
The very air corrodes honesty.
Your disappearance now will pass unnoticed.
My sudden disgrace and banishment
Has turned the whole palace upside down.
We can use the confusion.   50
All that you require, I can give you.

Your guards are my men.
Across the sea our allies are powerful.
Argos calls us. Sparta welcomes us.
Our interests are theirs.   55
Phèdre shall never dethrone you or me.
She shall never build her empire
Out of our absence,
Or give what is ours to her son.
What now? You hold back?   60
This is the moment and we have to seize it.
Are you wavering?
Aricia! I am resolved.
If I seem to be moving too fast
It is for your sake.   65
Do you hesitate
To share your escape with a banished man?
ARICIA   I want no other freedom.
To share your fate is the only
Happiness I can imagine.   70
But if I come
There is one thing lacking between us
Not only to complete my happiness
But also preserve my honour.
If I can escape   75
From one who has dealt with me
As cruelly as your father has,
I break no code of honour.
Flight from a tyrant is acceptable.
And neither home nor kindred holds me here.   80
But, my lord, you love me, and my good name—
HIPPOLYTUS   Aricia, your good name is my first care.
Now hear my plan.
Desert your enemies and marry me.
Misfortune has freed us to do what the gods ordain.   85
We need no one's presence or permission,
No torches or procession.
Outside the gates of the city,
Among the tombs where my family are interred
There stands an ancient shrine.   90
That place is so holy
No perjurer dare come near it.
Whoever makes an oath in those precincts
And breaks it is instantly punished,
Their death follows quickly.   95
In that shrine, Aricia, if you will trust me,
We will consecrate together
An everlasting love. Our one witness
Will be the god of the place.
That god can perform   100

The role of priest and father to us both.
Then I will beseech Diana,
Goddess of chastity, brightest of all the gods,
To sanctify my vows, and to bless us.

ARICIA   Here's the King. Oh go. Oh God,   105
Go, go. I will stay here to cover you,
And allay his suspicions. Quickly, quickly.
But leave somebody who can guide me
To the place.
          [*Exit* HIPPOLYTUS. *Enter* THESEUS.]

THESEUS   You gods, permit me one ray of light.   110
Let me catch one glimmer of the truth I search for.
ARICIA   Ismène,
Have everything prepared. And be ready.
          [*Exit* ISMÈNE.]

THESEUS   Madam, you change colour. You seem startled.
What was Hippolytus doing here?   115
ARICIA   Giving me his last goodbye, my lord.
THESEUS   Those eyes of yours have humbled that arrogant stare.
His first sighs of passion—are all your work.
ARICIA   If that is true I shall not deny it.
One thing he has not inherited from you   120
Is your hatred for me.
He never saw me as a threat to the state.
THESEUS   Of course not. He was too busy
Swearing eternal love.
Do not depend, girl, on that facile mouth.   125
He has sworn the same to others.
ARICIA   He has?
THESEUS   You should have restrained him.
How can you entertain such a pretender?
ARICIA   And how can you let that rotten libel   130
Pollute his life—a current like sunlight!
Do you know your own son's heart so little?
Can't you distinguish between good and evil?
The whole world can see what he is.
Must you—his father—be the only one   135
Blundering about in the dark?
I can't leave him and his name
To the tongues and fangs of vipers.
Stop now: halt your homicidal curse
And beg the gods to forgive you for it.   140
Has it occurred to you
They may hate you enough to grant it?
Sometimes the gods accept our prayers
Just for the opportunity it gives them
To punish us in full, at our own request.   145
THESEUS   Enough. You have scolded enough.

You cannot change the nature of his crime.
Love has blinded you to his ugliness.
I have witnesses—impeccable.
I have seen tears that were incorruptible. 150
And I believe them.

ARICIA   Be careful, my lord. Your hands
May have eradicated many monsters
And never once failed. But let me say:
Not every monster has been accounted for. 155
There is one monster you have not recognised—
Your son, my lord, forbids me to say more.
He is concerned for you.
And his concern for you must also be mine.
If I told all I know—he too would be injured. 160
My lord, let me share his reticence.
And rather than be forced by you to break it
Allow me to withdraw.
        [*Exit* ARICIA.]

THESEUS   What's in her mind? What is this woman hiding?
She seems to be trying to tell me 165
Something she dare not tell me. Starting and stopping.
Going straight at it—then dodging past it.
Maybe the pair have put their heads together
To trick me, and lead me by the nose
Into some fresh maze of new clues— 170
And new darkness. At the same time,
In spite of my determination,
And in spite of my anger,
A voice—
Somewhere, beneath all this, a voice, 175
A pleading voice, inexplicable:
Pity—surprising and painful.
Oenone has to be questioned again—more thoroughly.
I need to know more about what happened.
Guards, bring Oenone. Here, alone. 180

        [*Enter* PANOPE.]
PANOPE   I dare not guess what is in Queen Phèdre's mind
But her agitation, my lord,
Puts her life in danger.
If despair can be fatal
And if we can recognise its signs, 185
I see it in her face. She is white as death.
As for Oenone—everything is too late.
She abandoned Phèdre and ran from the palace.
My lord, she leapt from the cliff-head—
And if that drop to the sea did not kill her 190
The sea did. Whatever her reasons
The waves that are now pounding her body on the rocks

Have washed them away, beyond recovery.

THESEUS   What?

PANOPE   This death has not quieted the Queen.   195
Only made her worse—if anything could.
She rushes to her children, like a mother
Seeking her own consolation,
Embracing them and sobbing over them,
But then she thrusts them away, with shrieks of horror,   200
As if maternal love were some contagion,
And staggers about the palace,
Falling on the stairs, colliding with walls
Like a blind madwoman.
She stares at everybody and sees nobody.   205
Three times she started a letter—
Each time changed her mind and tore it up.
You must see her, my lord. And perhaps help her.

THESEUS   Oh God—Oenone dead?
And Phèdre wanting to die?   210
Call my son back.
Let me hear my son defend himself.
Let him tell me all he has to tell me.
I will listen. Tell him I will listen.

         [*Exit* PANOPE.]

O Neptune,
If you heard my prayer, if you heard my curse,   215
Hear me. Withhold your favour to me.
Perhaps I believed the wrong story,
Perhaps I based my judgement on lies—
Too credulous and too precipitous.
Perhaps my berserk rage, that called on you   220
To destroy my son, was mistaken!
Oh God, God, if I am too late—

         [*Enter* THÉRAMÈNE.]

Where is Hippolytus? What have you done with him?
I gave him into your care, Théramène,
When he was only a child.   225
Where is my son?

THÉRAMÈNE   Ah—so much concern
Coming so late and so superfluously.
Such paternal love. And all so useless.
Hippolytus is dead.   230

THESEUS   Aaah!

THÉRAMÈNE   I have seen
The death of the most lovable of men.
And the most innocent, my lord.

THESEUS   My son dead? Ah! Only now   235
When I stretch my arms wide open to him
The gods rip him away.
What happened to him? How did they do it?

THÉRAMÈNE   We were hardly clear of the city gates
   And onto the beach road, towards Mycenae.   240
   Hippolytus was leading, in his chariot.
   His bodyguards close round him. A sombre troop.
   The prince was taciturn.
   His mood made the mood of every man.
   We all shared one dark thought and were silent.   245
   No sound but the click of hooves and jingle of harness.
   Those horses of his were strange.
   Usually so bursting with spirits—
   So headstrong, so eager to be off,
   They need the constant touch of his voice and the reins   250
   To hold them in—today they were listless.
   He left the pace to them,
   Letting the reins lie loose over their backs.
   They hung their heads, they seemed preoccupied,
   As if they were helping him, with their hanging heads,   255
   To think what he was thinking.
   I noticed it. It seemed very strange.
   As I was watching that,
   A sudden skull-splitting roar,
   An indescribable, terrible, tearing voice,   260
   Like lightning flash and thunderclap together,
   Made us all duck and cower.
   It came out of the sea, as if the whole sea
   Had bellowed.
   And then, like an echo to it,   265
   Another roaring groan, subterranean,
   As if something that groaned were trying to scream,
   Rolled through the earth under our feet.
   The ground was bulging, jumping beneath us.
   We were petrified and bewildered.   270
   The horses' manes and tails flared on end.
   And now I saw out at sea
   A mountain of water boiling up,
   Heaping higher,
   Irrupting from under the horizon   275
   And racing towards us.
   Till it towered above us, seeming to hang.
   And there, in slow motion,
   It collapsed, a solid fall of thunder.
   Quaking the bedrock. And out of it,   280
   The foam cascading from a colossal body,
   Came a beast—
   Up the sand, with the fury
   Of a supernatural existence.
   Its head was one huge monster all to itself,   285
   Like a bull's head, with bull's horns.
   But from the shoulders backwards
   The whole body was plated,

Humped and plated, the scales greeny yellow,
A nauseating colour, that sickened the eye.   290
And beyond the humped bulk of the body
Came scaled and lashing coils. Half bull, half dragon—
Mouth hanging open,
And bellowing, like a heavy surf
Exploding in a cavern.   295
The earth trembled, the air was thick with horror.
We breathed a mist of horror.
Weapons or courage were out of the question.
Everybody fled. We all took cover
In that small temple among the tombs.   300
Then I looked back and saw Hippolytus—
He was lashing his horses and making a run
Straight at the monster—at the last moment
I saw him swerve
Tight past its jaws and bury a javelin   305
All but for a span length of the shaft
Behind that thing's shoulder, right where the heart is
In creatures that have hearts.
I never saw anything so fearless.
But whether the javelin blade found a heart,   310
Or the beast was convulsed
With fury at his daring—the whole mass of it
Rose and collapsed on to Hippolytus,
Like another mountain of ocean,
Or like a giant octopus of water.   315
I saw horses and chariot
Tossing among foam and tentacles
That dragged back down towards the sea.
But then, a miracle.
The horses were clambering free,   320
Like a team scrambling across an avalanche.
And I saw Hippolytus braced in the chariot—
Fists bunched and legs wide,
I thought he was getting clear. But a god was watching.
In a surf of churning sand,   325
A last scything swipe of the monster's tail
Came round under their hooves,
Toppled the horses and smashed the wheels of the chariot.
Then the horses went mad—
I heard Hippolytus shouting among the screams   330
Of the horses, and the blasts of that beast.
The wonderful strength of Hippolytus was helpless.
Some of the others saw something
I can hardly credit, I did not see it.
They saw the glowing figure of a naked god   335
Astride the shoulders of the demented horses—
Goading and urging them
Among the rocks of the foreshore

With the chariot, stripped of its wheels,
Bounding like a bucket behind them.   340
Hippolytus had wound his arms in the reins.
He tore the horses' mouths but they felt nothing.
And the voice they had grown up with
Became a scream that added to their terror
As the chariot disintegrated beneath him.   345
Then it was two mad horses dragging a man.
Oh my lord, forgive me! The sight of it
Is like a great wound through my body,
It's never going to heal.
The horses galloped away with their weightless bundle   350
That had fed them, and that was your son.
We followed—all of us crying openly
Like forsaken children.
The trail was easy—he had signed every stone,
Left us a rag of flesh on every thorn.   355
The horses careered in a wide circle—
Till they were exhausted.
They came to a halt, as it happened,
Among the royal tombs. There we found them,
Streaming with lather and shuddering,   360
The eyes crazed in their heads. And there he lay.
It is part of the marvel of his strength
That he was still alive. When I clasped his hand
And called to him, his fingers squeezed my fingers.
His eyes opened—they stared past me awhile   365
At something he tried to recognise.
Then closed slowly. They did not open again.
He was trying to speak. I bent close.
'The gods have taken my life,' he whispered,
'Though it was innocent. Dear old friend,' he said,   370
'After my death protect Aricia.
And if my father ever frees himself
From his delusion, and feels any remorse
For that false charge which has destroyed his son,
Ask him to treat Aricia kindly.   375
Ask him to give back to her—' My lord,
With those words
His voice and his life failed together.
And I was left embracing the latest prize
Of the triumphant gods—an object   380
Hardly recognisable as a man.
I think his own father would not know him.
THESEUS   My son! I did it to myself—
Killed my only hope. Inexorable—
That is the word for the gods.   385
They kept their word too well.
Nothing is left to me now, but to mourn.
THÉRAMÈNE   There is a little more to tell you.

Aricia came running towards us.
My lord, she was running away from you,   390
And hurrying to meet Hippolytus
At that very temple, there, among the tombs,
Where they had planned a marriage solemnised
Only by the god. As she came near
She saw the horses steaming and shivering   395
In their broken traces. Then she saw
What we stood around and looked down at.
The drained rag of Hippolytus' body.
For a moment she could not recognise
That this was all that remained of her happiness.   400
Her eyes refused to understand it.
She stared at the corpse and asked for Hippolytus.
But then it sank in.
And she let it happen.
She cried out just once, then dropped, silent,   405
Like somebody jabbed through the heart.
Ismène was with her.
She managed to bring her round. Aricia
Returned to what was waiting for her—
Daylight, that mangled shape, her future.   410
And I have come, my lord,
Hating what I have to reveal
And to discharge the task allotted to me
By the dying breath of Hippolytus.
I pass his last wishes to you.   415
And here comes the cause of everything—

[*Enter* PHÈDRE.]

THESEUS   Now you can be happy. My son is dead.
I cannot help it, these vile fantasies
Overwhelm me—though I lack evidence.
I have only one fact—my son is dead.   420
Madam, he is your victim, rejoice.
Whether guilty or innocent
He can no longer aggrieve you. Accept it.
I am ready to look no deeper.
If you accuse him, let me live with that.   425
I will think him a criminal and a traitor.
His death alone is suffering enough
Without me searching for scraps and broken bits
Of information that could drive me mad
But never bring him back.   430
Let me get away from this land
That holds you
And the dismembered body of my boy.
Even if I found another universe
This memory would be with me.   435

Everything proclaims what I have done.
My very fame blazes with my shame.
If I were unknown I could hide.
The favour of the gods terrifies me—
I dare not ever again pray to them.   440
Their answers to my prayers have finished me.
However much they have helped me in the past
They have taken everything back, they have taken my son—
My son, my hope, my life.

PHÈDRE   No, Theseus. Now hear me speak.   445
Let me restore your son's lost innocence.
Hippolytus was not guilty.

THESEUS   My son was not guilty? So simple.
And it was on your word that I cursed him?
You are Hell itself.   450
You think this can be forgiven?

PHÈDRE   Listen to me carefully, Theseus.
Every moment now is precious to me.
Hippolytus was chaste. And loyal to you.
I was the monster in this riddle.   455
I was insane with an incestuous passion,
To amuse some malevolent deity.
That viper Oenone plotted the rest.
Once I had bared my affliction to your son
Oenone feared he might in time inform you   460
Of my shameless obsession, my shameless attempt
To force my lust on him. While I was helpless
That infernal woman slithered to you
And fixed the guilt on the prince
As if she had witnessed it. So you were poisoned.   465
She has been punished. She escaped my rage,
And found a gentler executioner
Where the sea breaks under the cliff.
The sword would have been my own choice, before this,
But that would have left the prince's innocence   470
To the play of suspicion and conjecture.
I have chosen a slower conveyance
To the land of the dead. This has allowed me
Time to show you, Theseus, my remorse.
Now I am drunk on an infallible poison   475
That my sister Medea[1] brought to Athens.
I feel my pulses pushing it icily
Into my feet, hands and the roots of my hair.
I see the sun's ball through a mist,
And you, whom my very presence sickens,   480
I see you in a mist, darkening.

1. A sorceress who helped Jason get the Golden Fleece; later, deserted by him, she killed her rival and her own children and burned her palace before fleeing to Athens. According to one legend, she tried to poison Theseus.

My eyes go dark. Now the light of the sun
Can resume its purity unspoiled.
PANOPE   My lord, she is dying.
THESEUS   If only   485
The results of her evil could die with her.
Come. Now my error of judgement
Is so monumental and plain
Let us go weep at my son's body.
Let us embrace the little of him that's left   490
And expiate the madness of my prayer.
We shall give him the honours he has earned.
And to appease his shade,
And in spite of the old crime of your brothers,
Aricia, from today you are my daughter.   495

JEAN DE LA FONTAINE
1621–1695

Although the stories that La Fon-taine tells in his fables are familiar from Aesop and other sources, his telling makes them new. He narrates the familiar fables so concisely that their impact is quick and sharp, making them seem thoroughly modern. In a few brilliant strokes, he renders our foibles and our fond hopes easily recognizable, even as they make us squirm.

Born into a bourgeois family at Château-Thierry, in northern France, La Fontaine eventually settled in Paris. His personal life was chaotic, more grasshopper than ant: he was constantly in debt and depended on his friends for financial support. While he lived in Paris, his wife and child remained in the provinces, so that he spent most of his time away from them. Yet La Fontaine succeeded in finding patrons who were happy to finance his literary pursuits, and did not disappoint them: he was widely admired and ultimately elected to the recently formed Académie Française.

La Fontaine's fables, 230 of them, were first published from 1668 to 1694. Mainly based on the tales of Aesop, the ancient Greek storyteller who used animals to comment on human foibles, they were immediately popular with children and adults alike. He also published a series of volumes called, in English, *Tales and Novels in Verse* (1664–74), in which he versified comic, sometimes bawdy, tales from **Boccaccio** and **Ariosto**, among others. He wrote poetry in several different genres, including opera librettos, but the collection of fables is still considered his masterpiece.

The wit of beast fables depends on an analogy between human beings and animals. To encounter a cicada talking like a man-about-town has an immediate comic effect. But the analogy also poses a serious question: if a cicada resembles a man, in what way is a man like a cicada? La Fontaine's playful vignettes are tinged with satire, as the animal traits reveal all-too-human failings—the cruelty of the powerful, the eagerness with which people take advantage of one another, the self-deceptions we use to feel good about ourselves. Yet La Fontaine also explores the more positive aspects of human nature—sometimes openly, as in "The Two Pigeons," a tale of love and loyalty as well as cruelty; sometimes subtly, as in "The Cicada and the Ant," where the wastrel cicada, a singer of songs, seems more attractive than the smug and contemptuous ant.

The traditional association between fables and teaching may mislead some readers into thinking that these tales are simple. After all, many of the fables state their morals openly, and those morals tend to be obvious. But La Fontaine goes beyond presenting a simple lesson. His subtle characterization and the economy and grace of his verse often undermine the proclaimed moral, as in "The Wolf and the Lamb," which may well show that "Might is right" but also illustrates precisely what is wrong with such a doctrine. The wolf, as he offers rationalizations for what he proposes to do with or without justification, seems more and more frightening, more and more recognizable. By the end, the reader understands not just how the powerful use self-justification but also the terror of powerlessness. Terrifyingly, from our own purview, this applies to individuals *and* to entire classes, for the wolf holds all sheep responsible in order to consume the single lamb.

The echoes and connections among the fables also complicate their meaning. "Might is right" may be one depressing conclusion of "The Wolf and the Lamb," but both "The Oak and the Reed" and "The Mouse and the Lion" offer more nuanced perspectives: those who appear mighty are not always the most resilient, and even the strongest need the help of the weak. Reading the fables together yields a more complete picture: the kaleidoscope of their various lessons offers a very different image than any single fable on its own, however self-sufficient they may at first appear. La Fontaine thereby adds a final, perhaps even more powerful lesson: all versions are partial, all received morals open to correction.

FABLES[1]

The Cicada and the Ant

The cicada,[2] having chirped her song
    All summer long,
Found herself bitterly deprived
When the north wind arrived—
Not a mouthful of worm or fly.   5
    Whereupon in her want
She rushed round to her neighbor the ant
    And begged her to supply
Some crumbs on loan to keep body and soul together
Till next spring. "On my word as an animal   10
    I swear," she said, "to repay

1. James Michie is the translator of all the fables appearing here except for "The Two Pigeons," which was translated by Francis Duke.
2. A grasshopperlike insect.

With interest before the harvest ends."
Of the ant's few faults the minimal
        Is that she never lends.
"What were you doing during the hot weather?"   15
She asked the importunate insect.
        "With all respect,
        I was singing night and day
For the pleasure of anyone whom chance
        Sent my way."   20
        "Singing, did you say?
I'm delighted to hear it. Now you can dance!"

The Crow and the Fox

Mr. Crow, perched in a tree, held in his beak
        A piece of cheese.
Mr. Fox, attracted by the smell,
        Began to speak
        In terms roughly like these: 5
        "Hullo!
I mean, good morning, honorable Crow,
        You look uncommonly well,
Indeed you look a veritable Romeo.
Honestly, if it were not for one thing   10
You would be the phoenix[1] of our woodland birds:
Your feathers are gorgeous—but how well can you sing?"
        At these words
The crow, beside himself with pleasure,
Opened his big mouth to show off, and dropped his treasure.   15
The fox snapped it up in a trice,
Remarking: "My dear sir, learn the hard way
        That all flatterers live
At the expense of those with a credulous ear to give—
A lesson cheap, surely, at the price   20
        Of your lost cheese-slice."
        Mortified and confused,
The crow vowed (rather late in the day)
Never again to be so abused.

The Wolf and the Lamb

Might is right: the verdict goes to the strong.
To prove the point won't take me very long.

---

1. A legendary bird of great beauty that is supposed to live five hundred years and then regenerate itself from the ashes of its funeral pyre.

A lamb was once drinking
From a clear stream when a foraging wolf came slinking
    Out of the woods, drawn to that quarter   5
    Of the countryside by hunger.
    "How dare you muddy my drinking water!"
    Said the beast of prey in anger.
"You shall be punished for your insolence."
    "Your Majesty," answered the lamb,   10
"I beg you not to be angry but to think
    Calmly about it. Here I am,
    Relieving my throat's dryness
At least twenty yards downstream from your Highness,
    And in consequence   15
    I cannot be in the least
    Guilty of sullying your royal drink."
    "But you are," said the pitiless beast.
"Besides, I know you spoke ill of me last year."
"How could I have done? I wasn't even here,"   20
The lamb replied. "I'm still at the teat of my mother."
"If it wasn't you, it must have been your brother."
"I haven't got one." "Well, then, one of you sheep;
For you and your shepherds and damned dogs keep
Making it harder and harder for me to eat.   25
But now revenge is mine—and revenge is sweet!"
    Whereupon he dragged the lamb deep
    Into the forest and had his meal.
    There was no right of appeal.

The Oak and the Reed

One day the oak said to the reed:
"You have good cause indeed
To accuse Nature of being unkind.
To you a wren must seem
An intolerable burden, and the least puff of wind   5
That chances to wrinkle the face of the stream
Forces your head low; whereas I,
Huge as a Caucasian peak, defy
Not only the sun's glare, but the worst the weather can do.
What seems a breeze to me is a gale for you.   10
Had you been born in the lee of my leaf-sheltered ground,
You would have suffered less, I should have kept you warm;
But you reeds are usually found
On the moist borders of the kingdom of the storm.
It strikes me that to you Nature has been unfair."   15
"Your pity," the plant replied, "springs from a kind heart.
But please don't be anxious on my part.
Your fear of the winds ought to be greater than mine.
I bend, but I never break. You, till now, have been able to bear
Their fearful buffets without flexing your spine.   20

But let us wait and see." Even as he spoke,
From the horizon's nethermost gloom
The worst storm the north had ever bred in its womb
    Furiously awoke.
The tree stood firm, the reed began to bend.   25
The wind redoubled its efforts to blow—
    So much so
    That in the end
It uprooted the one that had touched the sky with its head,
But whose feet reached to the region of the dead.   30

The Lion and the Rat

In this world we must do our best
    To oblige others; for we all
Occasionally have need to call
On the services of the weak and small.
    This truth two fables attest: 5
Indeed proofs of all such truths abound.

Rashly popping from a hole in the ground,
A rat came up between a lion's paws.
The king of beasts, sheathing his claws,
In this instance showed his royal nature   10
    And spared the little creature.
The kindness wasn't wasted. . . . But a rat
      Paying a lion back a debt—
      Could anyone credit that?
And yet it happened. On the fringe of the jungle   15
The same lion was later caught in a net
Which all his roars were powerless to untangle.
    Up ran Sir Rat and set
To work with his teeth, gnawing and fretting,
Till, mesh by mesh, he'd unpicked all the netting.   20

Patience and perseverance at length
Accomplish more than anger and brute strength.

The Fox and the Grapes

A starving fox—a Gascon, Normans[1] claim,
But Gascons say a Norman—saw a cluster
Of luscious-looking grapes of purplish luster
Dangling above him on a trellis-frame.
He would have dearly liked them for his lunch,   5

1. Normandy and Gascony, home of Normans and Gascons, respectively, are different regions of France that are sometimes in competition with one another.

But when he tried and failed to reach the bunch:
"Ah well, it's more than likely they're not sweet—
   Good only for green fools to eat!"

Wasn't he wise to say they were unripe
Rather than whine and gripe?   10

The Rooster and the Fox

   A shrewd, wily old rooster
   Was keeping look-out on a bough
When a fox, in the nicest voice he could muster,
   Addressed him: "Brother,
We are no longer at war with each other: 5
I've come to announce that it's peace now,
Total peace! Descend and accept my embrace.
   But for goodness' sake
Don't keep me waiting—today I'm in a hurry,
With twenty different calls to make.   10
From now on you and your race
Can go about your business free of worry—
We shall treat you as brothers. Let us light
   Jubilee bonfires tonight.
Meanwhile come and receive a fraternal kiss."   15
"My friend," the rooster replied, "I couldn't have heard
Better or more welcome news than this.
   Peace is a wonderful word,
   And to me it's a double delight
   To hear it from you. But wait!   20
I see two hounds—they must be envoys sent
Expressly to attend this great event.
They'll be here in a moment, to judge by their pace.
Then I'll get down and we can all four embrace."
"Goodbye," said the fox. "I've a long day ahead.   25
   We'll have to celebrate
   Tomorrow, or the day after. . . ."
   Whereupon, sick
   At the failure of his trick,
That gentleman hitched his trousers up and fled.   30
The old cock watched his panicky retreat
   With silent laughter;
   For the pleasure is twice as sweet
   When you cheat a cheat.

The Two Pigeons

Two Pigeons shared a tender love;
But one, being bored with life at home,
Made up his foolish mind to rove

Away, and through the world to roam.
"What shall you do?" exclaimed the other.   5
"Why must you desert your brother?
Absence is the worst of blows;
But, cruel, not to you! Would that a wanderer's woes,
   And risks, and cares, might serve for you
    A little to amend your view;   10
And later in the year you might fare better too!
Wait till the zephyrs[1] stir; who's goading you? A crow
Just now croaked warning that some bird would be brought low.
I'll dream of nothing but of travelers distressed
And hawks, and nets. I'll say: 'Dear, but the weather's wet;   15
   And are my brother's wants all met,
    Hot supper, warm bed, and the rest?' "
   This plea brought turmoil to the heart
   That on so mad a voyage would start;
But curiosity and restlessness at last   20
Prevailed, and he responded: "Wipe your tears away,
For I'll have had enough before three days have passed.
I'll soon be back, and in a circumstantial way
   I'll tell my brother my adventures
For his pleasure. Anyone who nothing ventures   25
Can't make conversation either. When you know
   My tale, you'll find it royal fare.
I'll say: 'That's where I was; this happened thus and so'—
   You'll think you actually are there."
Upon these words they wept, and said a fond good-bye.   30
The wanderer wings away. And now a cloud sails near,
And makes him seek some safer hiding-spot close by.
He finds a tree such that the tempest even here
Lashed at the Pigeon through the leaves. The air grows clear,
Until, with feathers sodden, he flies on ahead;   35
And as he flies, he does his best to dry the wet.
His eyes fall on a lonely field where wheat lies spread,
And where a pigeon pecks, his appetite to whet.
Alighting, he falls prisoner to a noose, await
   Beneath the wheat's delusive bait.   40
The noose was frayed, and so the bird, with beating wing,
And busy feet and bill, at last has broken loose
With only feathers lost. But fate allows no truce:
A certain sharp-clawed hawk, above him hovering,
Descries our luckless victim trailing bits of string   45
That as he flies he carries still about him draped,
   As might a convict just escaped.
The hawk being poised to strike, down out of clouds descended
Now an eagle with yet fiercer claws extended.
Profiting from this dispute of thief with thief,   50
The Pigeon flees, escapes, lands near a peasant's hut,

---

1. Gentle spring breezes.

And hopes that now perhaps his grief
    May end with this adventure. But
A vagrant boy (that age is heartless), with his sling
And pebblestones, came very near to murdering   55
    The hapless feathered flyer, who came,
    With curses on himself for an idle fling,
    And one foot dragging, and one wing,
    Half dead and more than halfway lame,
    Back to his home, which he contrived   60
    Somehow to reach, and so arrived
    Secure at last from ill luck's aim;
And so the two unite. I leave it to be guessed
With what extreme delight their sorrows they allay.

O lovers, happy lovers, must you fly the nest?   65
    Fly, then, but never far away.
Fly to a world of beauty fixed between you two,
    Forever different and new.
Be all things each to each, what though all else default.
There was a time when I too loved; and when I did,   70
    For all the Louvre[2] and all it hid,
And all the starry firmament and Heaven's vault,
    I'd not have given the woodland dell
Trod by the light step, and whereon the bright glance fell,
    Of that young shepherdess who'd won   75
    My heart—for whom, by Cythera's son[3]
Commanded, I served out my youth's first vows. But when,
Alas, shall moments such as those return again?
Must objects so beguiling and so charming, then,
Abandon me a victim to my spirit's thirst?   80
Ah, that love's flame still flared within my heart! Must I
Be warmed no more by charms that kept me young at first?
    Can love perhaps have passed me by?

2. The great royal palace in Paris, now its   3. Cupid.
most important museum.

APHRA BEHN
1640?–1689

Poised between Africa and the New World, *Oroonoko* follows the heroic prince of that name into captivity, slavery, and desperate violence. The novella tantalizes us with the fiction of a narrator who personally witnesses much of Oroonoko's story, and whose close friendship with the hero makes her both sympathetic to his plight and complicit in his fate. *Oroonoko* itself is similarly ambiguous: it makes a powerful case against slavery, long before the actual birth of abolitionism, yet it also presents the prince as an exceptional victim whose enslavement is tragic only because of his exalted, aristocratic nature.

As the first professional woman writer in England, Aphra Behn gave women "the right to speak their minds," as **Virginia Woolf** put it. She wrote popular plays, longer epistolary fiction, novellas such as *Oroonoko*, and occasional poetry. Early in her career, she probably served as a spy for the English in Holland, and in later years was associated with libertines and freethinkers. Both in her personal and in her professional life she showed a pronounced disregard for convention and for the limits imposed on women's behavior in her time.

Little is known about Behn's early life, though it seems likely that her father was a barber in Canterbury. In *Oroonoko* she creates a more exalted parentage for herself, claiming to be the daughter of the "lieutenant-general of six and thirty islands, besides the continent of Surinam." This purely fictional genealogy was repeated by her first biographer and has confused readers ever since. Behn did visit the English colony of Surinam, on the northern edge of South America, with her mother and siblings in 1663, and became involved in the political infighting there. On her return to London in 1664, she apparently married a German merchant, Johannes Behn, but the marriage did not last long, either because of his death or their separation.

In 1660, London playhouses reopened after an eighteen-year hiatus that coincided with Puritan control of England following the English Civil War. The restoration to the English throne of Charles II, an avid enthusiast of the theater, virtually guaranteed that the period later called "the Restoration" would witness a flowering of theatrical innovation and creativity. It also provided women with new opportunities to participate in the cultural life of London. For example, actresses, not actors, now routinely played female roles.

In this environment, Behn forged her writing career. It didn't hurt that her political sympathies would always lie with the king: in a time of continuing political turmoil, she supported first Charles and then James II. As political parties developed in England she consistently sided with the more conservative Tories, who supported a strong monarchy. Her ties to the monarchy were so strong that at one point, Behn was sent by the king to Holland as a spy. Her code name during this stint in espionage was "Astrea," the Greek goddess associated with purity and renewal, one of the many names given to another exceptional early modern Englishwoman, Elizabeth I. Behn would later adopt this name in her literary pursuits whenever she needed to conceal her identity. By 1670 she had become a playwright, writing for the Duke's Company in London. Uniquely for her time, she had at least nineteen plays staged, and probably contributed to many more. In keeping with the fashion of the times, Behn wrote tragicomedies on love and political restoration, as well as city comedies full of incorrigible rakes, duped husbands, and pert heroines. The most famous of these, *The Rover* (1677), is still produced regularly.

Behn was associated with the circle of the Earl of Rochester, the most famous libertine of a libertine time. She wrote a number of explicit poems on sexual matters, which led to many accusations of indecency, both from her contemporaries and especially during the Victorian era, when her work was dismissed for its "coarseness." Yet Behn was a famous and successful writer in her own time, whose work paved the way for playwrights and novelists, both male and female, in the eighteenth century. Today, her reputation rests primarily on *Oroonoko* and her city comedies, while her wider oeuvre is increasingly read and studied.

First published in 1688, *Oroonoko* describes the triangular trade in manufactured goods, slaves, and sugar among Europe, Africa, and the Caribbean. English slave traders picked up their human cargo on the west coast of Africa, transported them to the West Indies, where those who survived the cruel passage were sold to work on the sugar plantations, and then returned to England with a cargo of sugar to complete their profitable, if brutal, trajectory. Behn's novella is partly a frame narrative: it opens in the English sugar colony of Surinam, where the first-person narrator, who identifies herself as Behn, has traveled with her father, the new governor, and her sister. There the narrator befriends the imposing slave Oroonoko, who shares his story. His fantastic narrative takes us back to an exotic West Africa of harems and vulnerable virgins, a place overcivilized in its luxury, in contrast to the supposedly innocent New World. As the tale unfolds, we learn that Oroonoko, a prince in his own land, had managed to save his beloved Imoinda from his lecherous grandfather, only to be tricked into captivity by a greedy English slave trader.

In denouncing Oroonoko's fate, the narrator insists on Oroonoko's status as a virtual European and an aristocrat, as evinced by his elegant physique and European education. These claims underscore the text's ambivalence about slavery and race. The text leaves us wondering: Is Oroonoko meant to be a representative victim, or an exalted exception? How is he different from other Africans, who, in the world of the text, can be enslaved unproblematically? As Oroonoko and Imoinda's prolonged slavery becomes unbearable to the dignified hero, he leads his fellow slaves in a revolt, bringing down upon himself the fury of the slave-owning establishment and destroying the supposed harmony that the text relates. Are Oroonoko's violent acts justified? Does the text encourage us to see his resistance as necessary but unfortunate, or instead as evidence of his ultimate savagery?

Oroonoko's first-person narrator, closely identified with the author, raises for the reader basic questions of narrative authority and omniscience: what is this narrator privy to, and what are the limits of her power? What can she and can she not do for the enslaved prince, beyond narrating his story? Ultimately, how can we read her framed and partial account of him? In its short span, Behn's novella probes the dilemmas of personal versus political morality, of the legitimacy of government in a violent colonial space, and of the true nature of heroism.

Whatever its ambiguities, *Oroonoko* resonated profoundly with opponents of slavery and was repeatedly adapted both in prose and on the stage, from Thomas Southerne's 1695 tragicomedy through several tragic versions over the course of the eighteenth century, as the abolitionist movement in England found its voice.

Oroonoko; or, The Royal Slave

The Epistle Dedicatory

To The
Right Honourable
The
Lord MAITLAND.[1]

* * *

My Lord, the Obligations I have to some of the Great Men of your Nation, particularly to your Lordship, gives me an Ambition of making my Acknowledgments, by all the Opportunities I can; and such humble Fruits, as my Industry produces, I lay at your Lordship's Feet. This is a true Story, of a Man Gallant enough to merit your Protection; and, had he always been so Fortunate, he had not made so Inglorious an end: The Royal Slave I had the Honour to know in my Travels to the other World; and though I had none above me in that Country, yet I wanted power to preserve this Great Man. If there be any thing that seems Romantick, I beseech your Lordship to consider, these Countries do, in all things, so far differ from ours, that they produce unconceivable Wonders; at least, they appear so to us, because New and Strange. What I have mention'd I have taken care shou'd be Truth, let the Critical Reader judge as he pleases. 'Twill be no Commendation to the Book, to assure your Lordship I writ it in a few Hours, though it may serve to Excuse some of its Faults of Connexion; for I never rested my Pen a Moment for Thought: 'Tis purely the Merit of my Slave that must render it worthy of the Honour it begs; and the Author of that of Subscribing herself,

> My Lord,
> Your Lordship's most oblig'd
> and obedient Servant,
> A. BEHN.

The History of the Royal Slave

I do not pretend, in giving you the History of this *Royal Slave*, to entertain my Reader with the Adventures of a feign'd *Hero*, whose Life and Fortunes Fancy may manage at the Poet's Pleasure; nor in relating the Truth, design to adorn it with any Accidents, but such as arriv'd in earnest to him: And it shall come simply into the World, recommended by its own proper Merits, and natural Intrigues; there being enough of Reality to support it, and to render it diverting, without the Addition of Invention.

I was my self an Eye-Witness to a great part, of what you will find here set down; and what I cou'd not be Witness of, I receiv'd from the Mouth of the

---

1. Richard Maitland (1635–1695) held important posts in Scotland and was noted for his fine library.

chief Actor in this History, the *Hero* himself, who gave us the whole Transactions of his Youth; and though I shall omit, for Brevity's sake, a thousand little Accidents of his Life, which, however pleasant to us, where History was scarce, and Adventures very rare; yet might prove tedious and heavy to my Reader, in a World where he finds Diversions for every Minute, new and strange: But we who were perfectly charm'd with the Character of this great Man, were curious to gather every Circumstance of his Life.

The Scene of the last part of his Adventures lies in a Colony in *America*, called *Surinam*,[2] in the *West-Indies*.

But before I give you the Story of this *Gallant Slave*, 'tis fit I tell you the manner of bringing them to these new *Colonies*; for those they make use of there, are not *Natives* of the place; for those we live with in perfect Amity, without daring to command 'em; but on the contrary, caress 'em with all the brotherly and friendly Affection in the World; trading with 'em for their Fish, Venison, Buffilo's,[3] Skins, and little Rarities; as Marmosets, a sort of *Monkey* as big as a Rat or Weasel, but of a marvellous and delicate shape, and has Face and Hands like an Humane Creature: and *Cousheries*,[4] a little Beast in the form and fashion of a Lion, as big as a Kitten; but so exactly made in all parts like that noble Beast, that it is it in *Miniature*. Then for little *Parakeetoes*, great Parrots, *Muckaws*, and a thousand other Birds and Beasts of wonderful and surprizing Forms, Shapes, and Colours. For Skins of prodigious Snakes, of which there are some threescore Yards in length; as is the Skin of one that may be seen at His Majesty's *Antiquaries*: Where are also some rare Flies,[5] of amazing Forms and Colours, presented to 'em by my self; some as big as my Fist, some less; and all of various Excellencies, such as Art cannot imitate. Then we trade for Feathers, which they order into all Shapes, make themselves little short Habits of 'em, and glorious Wreaths for their Heads, Necks, Arms and Legs, whose Tinctures are unconceivable. I had a Set of these presented to me, and I gave 'em to the King's Theatre, and it was the Dress of the *Indian Queen*,[6] infinitely admir'd by Persons of Quality; and were unimitable. Besides these, a thousand little Knacks, and Rarities in Nature, and some of Art; as their Baskets, Weapons, Aprons, &c. We dealt with 'em with Beads of all Colours, Knives, Axes, Pins and Needles; which they us'd only as Tools to drill Holes with in their Ears, Noses and Lips, where they hang a great many little things; as long Beads, bits of Tin, Brass, or Silver, beat thin; and any shining Trincket. The Beads they weave into Aprons about a quarter of an Ell long, and of the same breadth;[7] working them very prettily in Flowers of several Colours of Beads; which Apron they wear just before 'em, as *Adam* and *Eve* did the Fig-leaves; the Men wearing a long Stripe of Linen, which they deal with us for. They thread these Beads also on long Cotton-threads, and make Girdles to tie their Aprons to, which come twenty times, or more, about the Waist; and then

---

2. An English colony in the region of Guiana, on the coast of South America east of Venezuela, now Suriname. It was settled by planters from Barbados seeking more land.
3. Buffalo or wild oxen.
4. A lion-headed marmoset.
5. Butterflies. "*Antiquaries*": the new Royal Society museum.
6. A play by Robert Howard and John Dryden, set in Mexico, first performed at the Theatre Royal in 1664.
7. About one foot square. "Ell": old English measure, about forty-five inches.

cross, like a Shoulder-belt, both ways, and round their Necks, Arms and Legs. This Adornment, with their long black Hair, and the Face painted in little Specks or Flowers here and there, makes 'em a wonderful Figure to behold. Some of the Beauties which indeed are finely shap'd, as almost all are, and who have pretty Features, are very charming and novel; for they have all that is called Beauty, except the Colour, which is a reddish Yellow; or after a new Oiling, which they often use to themselves, they are of the colour of a new Brick, but smooth, soft and sleek. They are extream modest and bashful, very shy, and nice[8] of being touch'd. And though they are all thus naked, if one lives for ever among 'em, there is not to be seen an indecent Action, or Glance; and being continually us'd to see one another so unadorn'd, so like our first Parents before the Fall, it seems as if they had no Wishes; there being nothing to heighten Curiosity, but all you can see, you see at once, and every Moment see; and where there is no Novelty, there can be no Curiosity. Not but I have seen a handsom young *Indian*, dying for Love of a very beautiful young *Indian* Maid; but all his Courtship was, to fold his Arms, pursue her with his Eyes, and Sighs were all his Language: While she, as if no such Lover were present; or rather, as if she desired none such, carefully guarded her Eyes from beholding him; and never approach'd him, but she look'd down with all the blushing Modesty I have seen in the most severe and cautious of our World. And these People represented to me an absolute *Idea* of the first State of Innocence, before Man knew how to sin: And 'tis most evident and plain, that simple Nature is the most harmless, inoffensive and vertuous Mistress. 'Tis she alone, if she were permitted, that better instructs the World, than all the Inventions of Man: Religion wou'd here but destroy that Tranquillity, they possess by Ignorance; and Laws wou'd but teach 'em to know Offence, of which now they have no Notion. They once made Mourning and Fasting for the Death of the *English* Governor, who had given his Hand to come on such a Day to 'em, and neither came, nor sent; believing, when once a Man's Word was past, nothing but Death cou'd or shou'd prevent his keeping it: And when they saw he was not dead, they ask'd him, what Name they had for a Man who promis'd a thing he did not do? The Governor told them, Such a man was a *Lyar*, which was a Word of Infamy to a Gentleman. Then one of 'em reply'd, *Governor, you are a Lyar, and guilty of that Infamy*. They have a Native Justice, which knows no Fraud; and they understand no Vice, or Cunning, but when they are taught by the *White Men*. They have Plurality of Wives, which, when they grow old, they serve those that succeed 'em, who are young; but with a Servitude easie and respected; and unless they take Slaves in War, they have no other Attendants.

Those on that *Continent* where I was, had no King; but the oldest War-Captain was obey'd with great Resignation.

A War-Captain is a Man who has led them on to Battel with Conduct,[9] and Success; of whom I shall have Occasion to speak more hereafter, and of some other of their Customs and Manners, as they fall in my way.

With these People, as I said, we live in perfect Tranquillity, and good Understanding, as it behooves us to do; they knowing all the places where to seek the best Food of the Country, and the Means of getting it; and for very small and

---

8. Fastidious, careful.

9. Good leadership.

unvaluable Trifles, supply us with what 'tis impossible for us to get; for they do not only in the Wood, and over the *Sevana's*,[1] in Hunting, supply the parts of Hounds, by swiftly scouring through those almost impassable places; and by the meer Activity of their Feet, run down the nimblest Deer, and other eatable Beasts: But in the water, one wou'd think they were Gods of the Rivers, or Fellow-Citizens of the Deep; so rare an Art they have in Swimming, Diving, and almost Living in Water; by which they command the less swift Inhabitants of the Floods. And then for Shooting; what they cannot take, or reach with their Hands, they do with Arrows; and have so admirable an Aim, that they will split almost an Hair; and at any distance that an Arrow can reach, they will shoot down Oranges, and other Fruit, and only touch the Stalk with the Dart's Point, that they may not hurt the Fruit. So that they being, on all Occasions, very useful to us, we find it absolutely necessary to caress 'em as Friends, and not to treat 'em as Slaves; nor dare we do other, their Numbers so far surpassing ours in that *Continent*.

Those then whom we make use of to work in our Plantations of Sugar, are *Negro's*, *Black*-Slaves altogether; which are transported thither in this manner.

Those who want Slaves, make a Bargain with a Master, or a Captain of a Ship, and contract to pay him so much a-piece, a matter of twenty Pound a Head for as many as he agrees for, and to pay for 'em when they shall be deliver'd on such a Plantation: So that when there arrives a Ship laden with Slaves, they who have so contracted, go a-board, and receive their Number by Lot;[2] and perhaps in one Lot that may be for ten, there may happen to be three or four Men; the rest, Women and Children: Or be there more or less of either Sex, you are oblig'd to be contented with your Lot.

Coramantien,[3] a Country of *Blacks* so called, was one of those places in which they found the most advantageous Trading for these Slaves; and thither most of our great Traders in that Merchandice traffick'd; for that Nation is very war-like and brave; and having a continual Campaign, being always in Hostility with one neighbouring Prince or other, they had the fortune to take a great many Captives; for all they took in Battel, were sold as Slaves; at least, those common Men who cou'd not ransom themselves. Of these Slaves so taken, the General only has all the profit; and of these Generals, our Captains and Masters of Ships buy all their Freights.

The King of *Coramantien* was himself a Man of a Hundred and odd Years old, and had no Son, though he had many beautiful *Black*-Wives; for most certainly, there are Beauties that can charm of that Colour. In his younger Years he had had many gallant Men to his Sons, thirteen of which died in Battel, conquering when they fell; and he had only left him for his Successor, one Grand-Child, Son to one of these dead Victors; who, as soon as he cou'd bear a Bow in his Hand, and a Quiver at his Back, was sent into the Field, to be trained up by one of the oldest Generals, to War; where, from his natural Inclination to Arms, and the Occasions given him, with the good Conduct of the

---

1. I.e., savannas, tropical and subtropical grasslands.
2. Groups.
3. An English fort and slave trading station in West Africa, in what is today Ghana. Slaves shipped out of this region were mainly Fante, Ashante, and other Akan-speaking peoples, whom the English referred to as Cormantines. They were known for their beauty and dignity, and their fierceness in war.

old General, he became, at the Age of Seventeen, one of the most expert Captains, and bravest Soldiers, that ever saw the Field of *Mars*:[4] So that he was ador'd as the Wonder of all that World, and the Darling of the Soldiers. Besides, he was adorn'd with a native Beauty so transcending all those of his gloomy Race, that he strook an Awe and Reverence, even in those that knew not his Quality; as he did in me, who beheld him with Surprize and Wonder, when afterwards he arriv'd in our World.

He had scarce arriv'd at his Seventeenth Year, when fighting by his Side, the General was kill'd with an Arrow in his Eye, which the Prince *Oroonoko* (for so was this gallant *Moor*[5] call'd) very narrowly avoided; nor had he, if the General, who saw the Arrow shot, and perceiving it aim'd at the Prince, had not bow'd his Head between, on purpose to receive it in his own Body rather than it shou'd touch that of the Prince, and so saved him.

'Twas then, afflicted as *Oroonoko* was, that he was proclaim'd General in the old Man's place; and then it was, at the finishing of that War, which had continu'd for two Years, that the Prince came to Court; where he had hardly been a Month together, from the time of his fifth Year, to that of Seventeen; and 'twas amazing to imagine where it was he learn'd so much Humanity; or, to give his Accomplishments a juster Name, where 'twas he got that real Greatness of Soul, those refin'd Notions of true Honour, that absolute Generosity, and that Softness that was capable of the highest Passions of Love and Gallantry, whose Objects were almost continually fighting Men, or those mangl'd, or dead; who heard no Sounds, but those of War and Groans: Some part of it we may attribute to the Care of a *French*-Man of Wit and Learning; who finding it turn to very good Account to be a sort of Royal Tutor to this young *Black*, & perceiving him very ready, apt, and quick of Apprehension, took a great pleasure to teach him Morals, Language and Science; and was for it extreamly belov'd and valu'd by him. Another Reason was, He lov'd, when he came from War, to see all the *English* Gentlemen that traded thither; and did not only learn their Language, but that of the *Spaniards* also, with whom he traded afterwards for Slaves.

I have often seen and convers'd with this great Man, and been a Witness to many of his mighty Actions; and do assure my Reader, the most Illustrious Courts cou'd not have produc'd a braver Man, both for Greatness of Courage and Mind, a Judgment more solid, a Wit more quick, and a Conversation more sweet and diverting. He knew almost as much as if he had read much: He had heard of, and admir'd the *Romans*; he had heard of the late Civil Wars in *England*, and the deplorable Death of our great Monarch;[6] and wou'd discourse of it with all the Sense, and Abhorrence of the Injustice imaginable. He had an extream good and graceful Mien, and all the Civility of a well-bred great Man. He had nothing of Barbarity in his Nature, but in all Points address'd himself, as if his Education had been in some *European* Court.

This great and just Character of *Oroonoko* gave me an extream Curiosity to see him, especially when I knew he spoke *French* and *English*, and that I cou'd talk with him. But though I had heard so much of him, I was as greatly surpriz'd

---

4. Battlefield, after the Roman god of war.
5. Variously used in the period for Muslims or for dark-skinned peoples.

6. Charles I, tried and executed in 1649 during the civil war between Royalists and Parliamentarians.

when I saw him, as if I had heard nothing of him; so beyond all Report I found him. He came into the Room, and address'd himself to me, and some other Women, with the best Grace in the World. He was pretty tall, but of a Shape the most exact that can be fancy'd: The most famous Statuary[7] cou'd not form the Figure of a Man more admirably turn'd from Head to Foot. His Face was not of that brown, rusty Black which most of that Nation are, but a perfect Ebony, or polish'd Jett. His Eyes were the most awful that cou'd be seen, and very piercing; the White of 'em being like Snow, as were his Teeth. His Nose was rising and *Roman*, instead of *African* and flat. His Mouth, the finest shap'd that cou'd be seen; far from those great turn'd Lips, which are so natural to the rest of the *Negroes*. The whole Proportion and Air of his Face was so noble, and exactly form'd, that bating[8] his Colour there cou'd be nothing in Nature more beautiful, agreeable and handsome. There was no one Grace wanting, that bears the Standard of true Beauty: His Hair came down to his Shoulders, by the Aids of Art; which was, by pulling it out with a Quill, and keeping it comb'd; of which he took particular Care. Nor did the Perfections of his Mind come short of those of his Person; for his Discourse was admirable upon almost any Subject; and who-ever had heard him speak, wou'd have been convinc'd of their Errors, that all fine Wit is confin'd to the *White* Men, especially to those of *Christendom*; and wou'd have confess'd that *Oroonoko* was as capable even, of reigning well, and of governing as wisely, had as great a Soul, as politick[9] Maxims, and was as sensible of Power as any Prince civiliz'd in the most refin'd Schools of Humanity and Learning, or the most Illustrious Courts.

This Prince, such as I have describ'd him, whose Soul and Body were so admirably adorn'd, was (while yet he was in the Court of his Grandfather) as I said, as capable of Love, as 'twas possible for a brave and gallant Man to be; and in saying that, I have nam'd the highest Degree of Love; for sure, great Souls are most capable of that Passion.

I have already said, the old General was kill'd by the shot of an Arrow, by the Side of this Prince, in Battel; and that *Oroonoko* was made General. This old dead *Hero* had one only Daughter left of his Race; a Beauty that, to describe her truly, one need say only, she was Female to the noble Male; the beautiful *Black Venus*,[1] to our young *Mars*; as charming in her Person as he, and of delicate Vertues. I have seen an hundred *White* Men sighing after her, and making a thousand Vows at her Feet, all vain, and unsuccessful: And she was, indeed, too great for any, but a Prince of her own Nation to adore.

Oroonoko coming from the Wars, (which were now ended) after he had made his Court to his Grand-father, he thought in Honour he ought to make a Visit to *Imoinda*, the Daughter of his Foster-father, the dead General; and to make some Excuses to her, because his Preservation was the Occasion of her Father's Death; and to present her with those Slaves that had been taken in this last Battel, as the Trophies of her Father's Victories. When he came, attended by all the young Soldiers of any Merit, he was infinitely surpriz'd at the Beauty of this fair Queen of Night, whose Face and Person was so exceeding all he had ever beheld, that lovely Modesty with which she receiv'd him, that Softness in her

---

7. Sculptor.
8. Except for.
9. Prudent, shrewd.

1. Roman goddess of love; lover of Mars, the god of war.

Look, and Sighs, upon the melancholy Occasion of this Honour that was done by so great a Man as *Oroonoko*, and a Prince of whom she had heard such admirable things; the Awfulness[2] wherewith she receiv'd him, and the Sweetness of her Words and Behaviour while he stay'd, gain'd a perfect Conquest over his fierce Heart, and made him feel, the Victor cou'd be subdu'd. So that having made his first Compliments, and presented her an hundred and fifty Slaves in Fetters, he told her with his Eyes, that he was not insensible of her Charms; while *Imoinda*, who wish'd for nothing more than so glorious a Conquest, was pleas'd to believe, she understood that silent Language of new-born Love; and from that Moment, put on all her Additions to Beauty.

The Prince return'd to Court with quite another Humour than before; and though he did not speak much of the fair *Imoinda*, he had the pleasure to hear all his Followers speak of nothing but the Charms of that Maid; insomuch that, even in the Presence of the old King, they were extolling her, and heightning, if possible, the Beauties they had found in her: So that nothing else was talk'd of, no other Sound was heard in every Corner where there were Whisperers, but *Imoinda! Imoinda!*

'Twill be imagin'd *Oroonoko* stay'd not long before he made his second Visit; nor, considering his Quality, not much longer before he told her, he ador'd her. I have often heard him say, that he admir'd by what strange Inspiration he came to talk things so soft, and so passionate, who never knew Love, nor was us'd to the Conversation of Women; but (to use his own Words) he said, Most happily, some new, and till then unknown Power instructed his Heart and Tongue in the Language of Love, and at the same time, in favour of him, inspir'd *Imoinda* with a Sense of his Passion. She was touch'd with what he said, and return'd it all in such Answers as went to his very Heart, with a Pleasure unknown before: Nor did he use those Obligations[3] ill, that Love had done him; but turn'd all his happy Moments to the best advantage; and as he knew no Vice, his Flame aim'd at nothing but Honour, if such a distinction may be made in Love; and especially in that Country, where Men take to themselves as many as they can maintain; and where the only Crime and Sin with Woman is, to turn her off, to abandon her to Want, Shame and Misery: Such ill Morals are only practis'd in *Christian*-Countries, where they prefer the bare Name of Religion; and, without Vertue or Morality, think that's sufficient. But *Oroonoko* was none of those Professors; but as he had right Notions of Honour, so he made her such Propositions as were not only and barely such; but, contrary to the Custom of his Country, he made her Vows, she shou'd be the only woman he wou'd possess while he liv'd; that no Age or Wrinkles shou'd incline him to change, for her Soul wou'd be always fine, and always young; and he shou'd have an eternal *Idea* in his Mind of the Charms she now bore, and shou'd look into his Heart for that *Idea*, when he cou'd find it no longer in her Face.

After a thousand Assurances of his lasting Flame, and her eternal Empire[4] over him, she condescended to receive him for her Husband; or rather, receiv'd him, as the greatest Honour the Gods cou'd do her.

---

2. Awe, reverence.   4. Rule, power.
3. Benefits.

There is a certain Ceremony in these Cases to be observ'd, which I forgot to ask him how perform'd; but 'twas concluded on both sides, that, in Obedience to him, the Grand-father was to be first made aequainted with the Design; for they pay a most absolute Resignation[5] to the Monarch, especially when he is a Parent also.

On the other side, the old King, who had many Wives, and many Concubines, wanted not Court-Flatterers to insinuate in his Heart a thousand tender Thoughts for this young Beauty; and who represented her to his Fancy, as the most charming he had ever possess'd in all the long Race of his numerous Years. At this Character his old Heart, like an extinguish'd Brand, most apt to take Fire, felt new Sparks of Love, and began to kindle; and now grown to his second Childhood, long'd with Impatience to behold this gay thing, with whom, alas! he cou'd but innocently play. But how he shou'd be confirm'd she was this *Wonder*, before he us'd his Power to call her to Court (where Maidens never came, unless for the King's private Use) he was next to consider; and while he was so doing, he had Intelligence brought him, that *Imoinda* was most certainly Mistress to the Prince *Oroonoko*. This gave him some *Shagrien*[6] however, it gave him also an Opportunity, one Day, when the Prince was a-hunting, to wait on a Man of Quality, as his Slave and Attendant, who shou'd go and make a Present to *Imoinda*, as from the Prince; he shou'd then, unknown, see this fair Maid, and have an Opportunity to hear what Message she wou'd return the Prince for his Present; and from thence gather the state of her Heart, and degree of her Inclination. This was put in Execution, and the old Monarch saw, and burnt: He found her all he had heard, and wou'd not delay his Happiness, but found he shou'd have some Obstacle to overcome her Heart; for she express'd her Sense of the Present the Prince had sent her, in terms so sweet, so soft and pretty, with an Air of Love and Joy that cou'd not be dissembl'd; insomuch that 'twas past doubt whether she lov'd *Oroonoko* entirely. This gave the old King some Affliction: but he salv'd[7] it with this, that the Obedience the People pay their King, was not at all inferior to what they pay'd their Gods: And what Love wou'd not oblige *Imoinda* to do, Duty wou'd compel her to.

He was therefore no sooner got to his Apartment, but he sent the Royal Veil to *Imoinda*; that is, the Ceremony of Invitation: he sends the Lady, he has a Mind to honour with his Bed, a Veil, with which she is cover'd, and secur'd for the King's Use; and 'tis Death to disobey; besides, held a most impious Disobedience.

'Tis not to be imagin'd the Surprize and Grief that seiz'd this lovely Maid at this News and Sight. However, as Delays in these Cases are dangerous, and Pleading worse than Treason; trembling, and almost fainting, she was oblig'd to suffer her self to be cover'd, and led away.

They brought her thus to Court; and the King, who had caus'd a very rich Bath to be prepar'd, was led into it, where he sate under a Canopy, in State, to receive this long'd for Virgin; whom he having commanded shou'd be brought to him, they (after dis-robing her) led her to the Bath, and making fast the Doors, left her to descend. The King, without more Courtship, bad her throw

5. Deference, submission.
6. I.e., chagrin.
7. Salved: soothed or remedied a wound.

off her Mantle, and come to his Arms. But *Imoinda*, all in Tears, threw her self on the Marble, on the Brink of the Bath, and besought him to hear her. She told him, as she was a Maid, how proud of the Divine Glory she should have been of having it in her power to oblige her King: but as by the Laws, he cou'd not; and from his Royal Goodness, wou'd not take from any Man his wedded Wife: So she believ'd she shou'd be the Occasion of making him commit a great Sin, if she did not reveal her State and Condition; and tell him, she was anothers, and cou'd not be so happy to be his.

The King, enrag'd at this Delay, hastily demanded the Name of the bold Man, that had marry'd a Woman of her Degree, without his Consent. *Imoinda*, seeing his Eyes fierce, and his Hands tremble; whether with Age, or Anger, I know not; but she fancy'd the last, almost repented she had said so much, for now she fear'd the Storm wou'd fall on the Prince; she therefore said a thousand things to appease the raging of his Flame, and to prepare him to hear who it was with Calmness; but before she spoke, he imagin'd who she meant, but wou'd not seem to do so, but commanded her to lay aside her Mantle, and suffer her self to receive his Caresses; or, by his Gods, he swore, that happy Man whom she was going to name shou'd die, though it were even *Oroonoko* himself. *Therefore* (said he) *deny this Marriage, and swear thy self a Maid. That* (reply'd *Imoinda*) *by all our Powers I do; for I am not yet known to my Husband.* 'Tis enough (said the King); *'tis enough to satisfie both my Conscience, and my Heart.* And rising from his Seat, he went, and led her into the Bath; it being in vain for her to resist.

In this time the Prince, who was return'd from Hunting, went to visit his *Imoinda*, but found her gone; and not only so, but heard she had receiv'd the Royal Veil. This rais'd him to a Storm; and in his Madness, they had much ado to save him from laying violent Hands on himself. Force first prevail'd, and then Reason: They urg'd all to him, that might oppose his Rage; but nothing weigh'd so greatly with him as the King's Old Age uncapable of injuring him with *Imoinda*.[8] He wou'd give way to that Hope, because it pleas'd him most, and flatter'd best his Heart. Yet this serv'd not altogether to make him cease his different Passions, which sometimes rag'd within him, and sometimes softned into Showers. 'Twas not enough to appease him, to tell him, his Grand-father was old, and cou'd not that way injure him, while he retain'd that awful[9] Duty which the young Men are us'd there to pay to their grave Relations. He cou'd not be convinc'd he had no Cause to sigh and mourn for the Loss of a Mistress, he cou'd not with all his Strength and Courage retrieve. And he wou'd often cry, *O my Friends! were she in wall'd Cities, or confin'd from me in Fortifications of the greatest Strength; did Inchantments or Monsters detain her from me, I wou'd venture through any Hazard to free her: But here, in the Arms of a feeble old Man, my Youth, my violent Love, my Trade in Arms, and all my vast Desire of Glory, avail me nothing: Imoinda is as irrecoverably lost to me, as if she were snatch'd by the cold Arms of Death: Oh! she is never to be retrive'd. If I wou'd wait tedious Years, till Fate shou'd bow the old King to his Grave; even that wou'd not leave me Imoinda free; but still that Custom that makes it so vile a Crime for a Son to marry his Father's Wives or Mistresses, wou'd hinder my Happiness;*

8. The king's great age suggests he is impotent. 9. Reverent.

unless I wou'd either ignobly set an ill President[1] to my Successors, or abandon my Country, and fly with her to some unknown World, who never heard our Story.

But it was objected to him, that his Case was not the same; for *Imoinda* being his lawful Wife, by solemn Contract, 'twas he was the injur'd Man, and might, if he so pleas'd, take *Imoinda* back, the Breach of the Law being on his Grand-father's side; and that if he cou'd circumvent him, and redeem her from the *Otan*,[2] which is the Palace of the King's Women, a sort of *Seraglio*, it was both just and lawful for him so to do.

This Reasoning had some force upon him, and he shou'd have been entirely comforted, but for the Thought that she was possess'd by his Grand-father. However, he lov'd so well, that he was resolv'd to believe what most favour'd his Hope; and to endeavour to learn from *Imoinda*'s own Mouth, what only she cou'd satisfie him in; whether she was robb'd of that Blessing, which was only due to his Faith and Love. But as it was very hard to get a Sight of the Women, for no Men ever enter'd into the *Otan*, but when the King went to entertain himself with some one of his Wives, or Mistresses; and 'twas Death at any other time, for any other to go in; so he knew not how to contrive to get a Sight of her.

While *Oroonoko* felt all the Agonies of Love, and suffer'd under a Torment the most painful in the World, the old King was not exempted from his share of Affliction. He was troubl'd for having been forc'd by an irresistable Passion, to rob his Son[3] of a Treasure, he knew, cou'd not but be extreamly dear to him, since she was the most beautiful that ever had been seen; and had besides, all the Sweetness and Innocence of Youth and Modesty, with a Charm of Wit surpassing all. He found that, however she was forc'd to expose her lovely Person to his wither'd Arms, she cou'd only sigh and weep there, and think of *Oroonoko*; and oftentimes cou'd not forbear speaking of him, though her Life were, by Custom, forfeited by owning her Passion. But she spoke not of a Lover only, but of a Prince dear to him, to whom she spoke; and of the Praises of a Man, who, till now, fill'd the old Man's Soul with Joy at every Recital of his Bravery, or even his Name. And 'twas this Dotage on our young *Hero*, that gave *Imoinda* a thousand Privileges to speak of him, without offending; and this Condescention in the old King, that made her take the Satisfaction of speaking of him so very often.

Besides, he many times enquir'd how the Prince bore himself; and those of whom he ask'd, being entirely Slaves to the Merits and Vertues of the Prince, still answer'd what they thought conduc'd best to his Service; which was, to make the old King fancy that the Prince had no more Interest in *Imoinda*, and had resign'd her willingly to the Pleasure of the King; that he diverted himself with his Mathematicians, his Fortifications, his Officers, and his Hunting.

This pleas'd the old Lover, who fail'd not to report these things again to *Imoinda*, that she might, by the Example of her young Lover, withdraw her Heart, and rest better contented in his Arms. But however she was forc'd to receive this unwelcome News, in all Appearance, with Unconcern, and Con-

---

1. Precedent, example.
2. *Odan* is the Fante word for house or apartment; *oda*, in Turkish, is a room in a harem or seraglio.
3. I.e., grandson.

tent, her Heart was bursting within, and she was only happy when she cou'd get alone, to vent her Griefs and Moans with Sighs and Tears.

What Reports of the Prince's Conduct were made to the King, he thought good to justifie as far as possibly he cou'd by his Actions; and when he appear'd in the Presence of the King, he shew'd a Face not at all betraying his Heart: So that in a little time the old Man, being entirely convinc'd that he was no longer a Lover of *Imoinda*, he carry'd him with him, in his Train, to the *Otan*, often to banquet with his Mistress. But as soon as he enter'd, one Day, into the Apartment of *Imoinda*, with the King, at the first Glance from her Eyes, notwithstanding all his determin'd Resolution, he was ready to sink in the place where he stood; and had certainly done so, but for the Support of *Aboan*, a young Man, who was next to him; which, with his Change of Countenance, had betray'd him, had the King chanc'd to look that way. And I have observ'd, 'tis a very great Error in those, who laugh when one says, A Negro *can change Colour*; for I have seen 'em as frequently blush, and look pale, and that as visibly as ever I saw in the most beautiful *White*. And 'tis certain that both these Changes were evident, this Day, in both these Lovers. And *Imoinda*, who saw with some Joy the Change in the Prince's Face, and found it in her own, strove to divert the King from beholding either, by a forc'd Caress, with which she met him; which was a new Wound in the Heart of the poor dying Prince. But as soon as the King was busy'd in looking on some fine thing of *Imoinda*'s making, she had time to tell the Prince with her angry, but Love-darting Eyes, that she resented his Coldness, and bemoan'd her own miserable Captivity. Nor were his Eyes silent, but answer'd hers again, as much as Eyes cou'd do, instructed by the most tender, and most passionate Heart that ever lov'd: And they spoke so well, and so effectually, as *Imoinda* no longer doubted, but she was the only Delight, and the Darling of that Soul she found pleading in 'em its Right of Love, which none was more willing to resign than she. And 'twas this powerful Language alone that in an Instant convey'd all the Thoughts of their Souls to each other; that they both found, there wanted[4] but Opportunity to make them both entirely happy. But when he saw another Door open'd by *Onahal*, a former old Wife of the King's, who now had Charge of *Imoinda*; and saw the Prospect of a Bed of State made ready, with Sweets and Flowers for the Dalliance of the King; who immediately led the trembling Victim from his Sight, into that prepar'd Repose; What Rage! what wild Frenzies seiz'd his Heart! which forcing to keep within Bounds, and to suffer without Noise, it became the more insupportable, and rent[5] his Soul with ten thousand Pains. He was forc'd to retire, to vent his Groans; where he fell down on a Carpet, and lay struggling a long time, and only breathing now and then,—O *Imoinda*! When *Onahal* had finish'd her necessary Affair within, shutting the Door, she came forth to wait, till the King call'd; and hearing some one sighing in the other Room, she pass'd on, and found the Prince in that deplorable Condition, which she thought needed her Aid: She gave him Cordials, but all in vain; till finding the nature of his Disease, by his Sighs, and naming *Imoinda*. She told him, he had not so much Cause as he imagin'd, to afflict himself; for if he knew the King so well as she did, he wou'd not lose a Moment in Jealousie, and that she was confident that *Imoinda* bore, at this Minute, part in his Affliction.

---

4. So that; wanted: lacked.   **5.** Tore apart.

Aboan was of the same Opinion; and both together, perswaded him to re-assume his Courage; and all sitting down on the Carpet, the Prince said so many obliging things to *Onahal*, that he half perswaded her to be of his Party. And she promis'd him, she wou'd thus far comply with his just Desires, that she wou'd let *Imoinda* know how faithful he was, what he suffer'd, and what he said.

This Discourse lasted till the King call'd, which gave *Oroonoko* a certain Satisfaction; and with the Hope *Onahal* had made him conceive, he assum'd a Look as gay as 'twas possible a Man in his Circumstances cou'd do; and presently after, he was call'd in with the rest who waited without. The King commanded Musick to be brought, and several of his young Wives and Mistresses came all together by his Command, to dance before him; where *Imoinda* perform'd her Part with an Air and Grace so passing all the rest, as her Beauty was above 'em; and receiv'd the Present, ordain'd as a Prize. The Prince was every Moment more charm'd with the new Beauties and Graces he beheld in this fair One: And while he gaz'd, and she danc'd, *Onahal* was retir'd to a Window with *Aboan*.

This *Onahal*, as I said, was one of the Cast-Mistresses of the old King; and 'twas these (now past their Beauty) that were made Guardians, or Governants[6] to the new, and the young Ones; and whose Business it was, to teach them all those wanton Arts of Love, with which they prevail'd and charm'd heretofore in their Turn; and who now treated the triumphing happy Ones with all the Severity, as to Liberty and Freedom, that was possible, in revenge of those Honours they rob them of; envying them those Satisfactions, those Gallantries and Presents, that were once made to themselves, while Youth and Beauty lasted, and which they now saw pass regardless by, and were pay'd only to the Bloomings.[7] And certainly, nothing is more afflicting to a decay'd Beauty, than to behold in it self declining Charms, that were once ador'd; and to find those Caresses paid to new Beauties, to which once she laid a Claim; to hear 'em whisper as she passes by, *That once was a delicate*[8] *Woman*. These abandon'd Ladies therefore endeavour to revenge all the Despights,[9] and Decays of Time, on these flourishing happy Ones. And 'twas this Severity, that gave *Oroonoko* a thousand Fears he shou'd never prevail with *Onahal*, to see *Imoinda*. But, as I said, she was now retir'd to a Window with *Aboan*.

This young Man was not only one of the best Quality, but a Man extreamly well made, and beautiful; and coming often to attend the King to the *Otan*, he had subdu'd the heart of the antiquated *Onahal*, which had not forgot how pleasant it was to be in Love: And though she had some decays in her Face, she had none in her Sense and Wit; she was there agreeable still, even to *Aboan*'s Youth, so that he took pleasure in entertaining her with Discourses of Love. He knew also, that to make his Court to these She-Favourites, was the way to be great; these being the Persons that do all Affairs and Business at Court. He had also observ'd that she had given him Glances more tender and inviting, than she had done to others of his Quality: And now, when he saw that her Favour cou'd so absolutely oblige the Prince, he fail'd not to sigh in her Ear,

---

6. Female caretakers or instructors. "Cast": cast-off, with a pun on chaste.
7. I.e., the younger women.
8. Delightful, lovely.
9. Insults.

and to look with Eyes all soft upon her, and give her Hope that she had made some Impressions on his Heart. He found her pleas'd at this, and making a thousand Advances to him; but the Ceremony ending, and the King departing, broke up the Company for that Day, and his Conversation.

Aboan fail'd not that Night to tell the Prince of his Success, and how advantageous the Service of *Onahal* might be to his Amour[1] with *Imoinda*. The Prince was overjoy'd with this good News, and besought him, if it were possible, to caress her so, as to engage her entirely; which he cou'd not fail to do, if he comply'd with her Desires: *For then* (said the Prince) *her Life lying at your Mercy, she must grant you the Request you make in my Behalf. Aboan* understood him; and assur'd him, he would make Love so effectually[2] that he wou'd defie the most expert Mistress of the Art, to find out whether he dissembl'd it, or had it really. And 'twas with Impatience they waited the next Opportunity of going to the *Otan*.

The Wars came on, the Time of taking the Field approach'd, and 'twas impossible for the Prince to delay his going at the Head of his Army, to encounter the Enemy: So that every Day seem'd a tedious Year, till he saw his *Imoinda*; for he believ'd he cou'd not live, if he were forc'd away without being so happy. 'Twas with Impatience therefore, that he expected the next Visit the King wou'd make; and, according to his Wish, it was not long.

The Parley of the Eyes of these two Lovers had not pass'd so secretly, but an old jealous Lover cou'd spy it; or rather, he wanted not Flatterers, who told him, they observ'd it: So that the Prince was hasten'd to the Camp, and this was the last Visit he found he shou'd make to the *Otan*; he therefore urg'd *Aboan* to make the best of this last Effort, and to explain himself so to *Onahal*, that she, deferring her Enjoyment of her young Lover no longer, might make way for the Prince to speak to *Imoinda*.

The whole Affair being agreed on between the Prince and *Aboan*, they attended the King, as the Custom was, to the *Otan*; where, while the whole Company was taken up in beholding the Dancing, and antick Postures the Women Royal made, to divert the King, *Onahal* singl'd out *Aboan*, whom she found most pliable to her Wish. When she had him where she believ'd she cou'd not be heard, she sigh'd to him, and softly cry'd, *Ah,* Aboan! *When will you be sensible of my Passion? I confess it with my Mouth, because I wou'd not give my Eyes the Lye; and you have but too much already perceiv'd they have confess'd my Flame: Nor wou'd I have you believe, that because I am the abandon'd Mistress of a King, I esteem my self altogether divested of Charms. No,* Aboan; *I have still a Rest of Beauty enough engaging, and have learn'd to please too well, not to be desirable. I can have Lovers still, but will have none but* Aboan. *Madam* (reply'd the half-feigning Youth) *you have already, by my Eyes, found, you can still conquer; and I believe 'tis in pity of me, you condescend to this kind Confession. But, Madam, Words are us'd to be so small a part of our Country-Courtship, that 'tis rare one can get so happy an Opportunity as to tell one's Heart; and those few Minutes we have are forc'd to be snatch'd for more certain Proofs of Love, than speaking and sighing; and such I languish for.*

He spoke this with such a Tone, that she hop'd it true, and cou'd not forbear believing it; and being wholly transported with Joy, for having subdu'd the finest

---

1. Love (French). 2. Diligently, thoroughly.

of all the King's Subjects to her Desires, she took from her Ears two large Pearls, and commanded him to wear 'em in his. He wou'd have refus'd 'em, *crying, Madam, these are not the Proofs of your Love that I expect; 'tis Opportunity, 'tis a Lone-hour only, that can make me happy.* But forcing the Pearls into his Hand, she whisper'd softly to him, *Oh! Do not fear a Woman's Invention, when Love sets her a-thinking.* And pressing his Hand, she cry'd, *This Night you shall be happy. Come to the Gate of the Orange-Groves, behind the* Otan; *and I will be ready, about Mid-night, to receive you.* 'Twas thus agreed, and she left him, that no notice might be taken of their speaking together.

The Ladies were still dancing, and the King, laid on a Carpet, with a great deal of pleasure, was beholding them, especially *Imoinda*; who that Day appear'd more lovely than ever, being enliven'd with the good Tidings *Onahal* had brought her of the constant Passion the Prince had for her. The Prince was laid on another Carpet, at the other end of the Room, with his Eyes fix'd on the Object of his Soul; and as she turn'd, or mov'd, so did they; and she alone gave his Eyes and Soul their Motions: Nor did *Imoinda* employ her Eyes to any other Use, than in beholding with infinite Pleasure the Joy she produc'd in those of the Prince. But while she was more regarding him, than the Steps she took, she chanc'd to fall; and so near him, as that leaping with extream force from the Carpet, he caught her in his Arms as she fell; and 'twas visible to the whole Presence, the Joy wherewith he receiv'd her: He clasp'd her close to his Bosom, and quite forgot that Reverence that was due to the Mistress of a King, and that Punishment that is the Reward of a Boldness of this nature; and had not the Presence of Mind of *Imoinda* (fonder of his Safety, than her own) befriended him, in making her spring from his Arms, and fall into her Dance again, he had, at that Instant, met his Death; for the old King, jealous to the last degree, rose up in Rage, broke all the Diversion, and led *Imoinda* to her Apartment, and sent out Word to the Prince, to go immediately to the Camp; and that if he were found another Night in Court, he shou'd suffer the Death ordain'd for disobedient Offenders.

You may imagine how welcome this News was to *Oroonoko*, whose unseasonable Transport and Caress of *Imoinda* was blam'd by all Men that lov'd him; and now he perceiv'd his Fault, yet cry'd, *That for such another Moment, he wou'd be content to die.*

All the *Otan* was in disorder about this Accident; and *Onahal* was particularly concern'd, because on the Prince's Stay depended her Happiness; for she cou'd no longer expect that of *Aboan*. So that, e'er the departed, they contriv'd it so, that the Prince and he shou'd come both that Night to the Grove of the *Otan*, which was all of Oranges and Citrons; and that there they shou'd wait her Orders.

They parted thus, with Grief enough, till Night; leaving the King in possession of the lovely Maid. But nothing cou'd appease the Jealousie of the old Lover: He wou'd not be impos'd on, but wou'd have it, that *Imoinda* made a false Step on purpose to fall into *Oroonoko's* Bosom and that all things look'd like a Design on both sides, and 'twas in vain she protested her Innocence: He was old and obstinate, and left her more than half assur'd that his Fear was true.

The King going to his Apartment, sent to know where the Prince was, and if he intended to obey his Command. The Messenger return'd, and told him, he found the Prince pensive, and altogether unpreparing for the Campaign; that he lay negligently on the Ground, and answer'd very little. This confirm'd the Jealousie of the King, and he commanded that they shou'd very narrowly and privately watch his Motions; and that he shou'd not stir from his Apartment, but one Spy or other shou'd be employ'd to watch him: So that the Hour approaching, wherein he was to go to the Citron-Grove; and taking only *Aboan* along with him, he leaves his Apartment, and was watch'd to the very Gate of the *Otan*; where he was seen to enter, and where they left him, to carry back the Tidings to the King.

Oroonoko and *Aboan* were no sooner enter'd, but *Onahal* led the Prince to the Apartment of *Imoinda*; who, not knowing any thing of her Happiness, was laid in Bed. But *Onahal* only left him in her Chamber, to make the best of his Opportunity, and took her dear *Aboan* to her own; where he shew'd the heighth of Complaisance for his Prince, when, to give him an Opportunity, he suffer'd himself to be caress'd in Bed by *Onahal*.

The Prince softly waken'd *Imoinda*, who was not a little surpriz'd with Joy to find him there; and yet she trembl'd with a thousand Fears. I believe, he omitted saying nothing to this young Maid, that might perswade her to suffer him to seize his own, and take the Rights of Love; and I believe she was not long resisting those Arms, where she so long'd to be; and having Opportunity, Night and Silence, Youth, Love and Desire, he soon prevail'd; and ravish'd in a Moment, what his old Grand-father had been endeavouring for so many Months.

'Tis not to be imagin'd the Satisfaction of these two young Lovers; nor the Vows she made him, that she remain'd a spotless Maid, till that Night; and that what she did with his Grand-father, had robb'd him of no part of her Virgin-Honour, the Gods, in Mercy and Justice, having reserv'd that for her plighted Lord, to whom of Right it belong'd. And 'tis impossible to express the Transports he suffer'd, while he listen'd to a Discourse so charming, from her lov'd Lips; and clasp'd that Body in his Arms, for whom he had so long languish'd; and nothing now afflicted him, but his suddain Departure from her; for he told her the Necessity, and his Commands; but shou'd depart satisfy'd in this, That since the old King had hitherto not been able to deprive him of those Enjoyments which only belong'd to him, he believ'd for the future he wou'd be less able to injure him; so that, abating the Scandal of the Veil, which was no otherwise so, than that she was Wife to another: He believ'd her safe, even in the Arms of the King, and innocent; yet wou'd he have ventur'd at the Conquest of the World, and have given it all, to have had her avoided that Honour of receiving the *Royal Veil*. 'Twas thus, between a thousand Caresses, that both bemoan'd the hard Fate of Youth and Beauty, so liable to that cruel Promotion: 'Twas a Glory that cou'd well have been spar'd here, though desir'd, and aim'd at by all the young Females of that Kingdom.

But while they were thus fondly employ'd, forgetting how Time ran on, and that the Dawn must conduct him far away from his only Happiness, they heard a great Noise in the *Otan*, and unusual Voices of Men; at which the Prince, starting from the Arms of the frighted *Imoinda*, ran to a little Battle-Ax he us'd to wear by his Side; and having not so much leisure, as to put on his Habit, he oppos'd himself against some who were already opening the Door; which they did with so much Violence, that *Oroonoko* was not able to defend it; but was forc'd to cry out with a commanding Voice, *Whoever ye are that have the Boldness to attempt to approach this Apartment thus rudely, know, that I, the Prince*

Oroonoko, *will revenge it with the certain Death of him that first enters: There-fore stand back, and know, this place is sacred to Love, and me this Night; to Morrow 'tis the King's.*

This he spoke with a Voice so resolv'd and assur'd, that they soon retir'd from the Door, but cry'd, *'Tis by the King's Command we are come; and being satisfy'd by thy Voice, O Prince, as much as if we had enter'd, we can report to the King the Truth of all his Fears, and leave thee to provide for thy own Safety, as thou art advis'd by thy Friends.*

At these Words they departed, and left the Prince to take a short and sad Leave of his *Imoinda*; who trusting in the strength of her Charms, believ'd she shou'd appease the Fury of a jealous King, by saying, She was surpriz'd, and that it was by force of Arms he got into her Apartment. All her Concern now was for his Life, and therefore she hasten'd him to the Camp; and with much a-do, prevail'd on him to go: Nor was it she alone that prevail'd, *Aboan* and *Onahal* both pleaded, and both assur'd him of a Lye that shou'd be well enough contriv'd to secure *Imoinda*. So that, at last, with a Heart sad as Death, dying Eyes, and sighing Soul, *Oroonoko* departed and took his way to the Camp.

It was not long after the King in Person came to the *Otan*; where beholding *Imoinda* with Rage in his Eyes, he upbraided her Wickedness and Perfidy, and threatning her Royal Lover, she fell on her Face at his Feet, bedewing the Floor with her Tears, and imploring his Pardon for a Fault which she had not with her Will committed; as *Onahal*, who was also prostrate with her, cou'd testifie: That, unknown to her, he had broke into her Apartment, and ravish'd her. She spoke this much against her Conscience; but to save her own Life, 'twas absolutely necessary she shou'd feign this Falsity. She knew it cou'd not injure the Prince, he being fled to an Army that wou'd stand by him, against any Injuries that shou'd assault him. However, this last Thought of *Imoinda*'s being ravish'd, chang'd the Measures of his Revenge; and whereas before he design'd to be himself her Executioner, he now resolv'd she shou'd not die. But as it is the greatest Crime in nature amongst 'em to touch a Woman, after hav-ing been possess'd by a Son, a Father, or a Brother; so now he look'd on *Imoinda* as a polluted thing, wholly unfit for his Embrace; nor wou'd he resign her to his Grand-son, because she had receiv'd the *Royal Veil*. He therefore removes her from the *Otan*, with *Onahal*; whom he put into safe Hands, with Order they should be both sold off, as Slaves, to another Country, either *Chris-tian*, or *Heathen*; 'twas no matter where.

This cruel Sentence, worse than Death, they implor'd, might be revers'd; but their Prayers were vain, and it was put in Execution accordingly, and that with so much Secrecy, that none, either without, or within the *Otan*, knew any thing of their Absence, or their Destiny.

The old King, nevertheless, executed this with a great deal of Reluctancy; but he believ'd he had made a very great Conquest over himself, when he had once resolv'd, and had perform'd what he resolv'd. He believ'd now, that his Love had been unjust; and that he cou'd not expect the Gods, or Captain of the Clouds (as they call the unknown Power) shou'd suffer a better Consequence from so ill a Cause. He now begins to hold *Oroonoko* excus'd; and to say, he had Reason for what he did: And now every Body cou'd assure the King, how passionately *Imoinda* was belov'd by the Prince; even those confess'd it now, who said the contrary before his Flame was abated. So that the King being old, and not able to defend himself in War, and having no Sons of all his Race[3] remaining alive, but only this, to maintain him on his Throne; and looking on this as a Man disoblig'd, first by the Rape of his Mistress, or rather, Wife; and now by depriving of him wholly of her, he fear'd, might make him desperate, and do some cruel thing, either to himself, or his old Grand-father, the Offender; he began to repent him extreamly of the Contempt he had, in his Rage, put on *Imoinda*. Besides, he consider'd he ought in Honour to have kill'd her, for this Offence, if it had been one: He ought to have had so much Value and Consideration for a Maid of her Quality, as to have nobly put her to death; and not to have sold her like a common Slave, the greatest Revenge, and the most disgraceful of any; and to which they a thousand times prefer Death, and implore it; as *Imoinda* did, but cou'd not obtain that Honour. Seeing therefore it was certain that *Oroonoko* wou'd highly resent this Affront, he thought good to make some Excuse for his Rashness to him; and to that End he sent a Messenger to the Camp, with Orders to treat with him about the Matter, to gain his Pardon, and to endeavour to mitigate his Grief; but that by no means he shou'd tell him, she was sold, but secretly put to death; for he knew he shou'd never obtain his Pardon for the other.

When the Messenger came, he found the Prince upon the point of Engaging with the Enemy; but as soon as he heard of the Arrival of the Messenger, he commanded him to his Tent, where he embrac'd him, and receiv'd him with Joy; which was soon abated, by the downcast Looks of the Messenger, who was instantly demanded the Cause by *Oroonoko*, who, impatient of Delay, ask'd a thousand Questions in a Breath; and all concerning *Imoinda*: But there needed little Return, for he cou'd almost answer himself of all he demanded, from his Sighs and Eyes. At last, the Messenger casting himself at the Prince's feet, and kissing them, with all the Submission of a Man that had something to implore which he dreaded to utter, he besought him to hear with Calmness what he had to deliver to him, and to call up all his noble and Heroick Courage, to encounter with his Words, and defend himself against the ungrateful[4] things he must relate. *Oroonoko* reply'd, with a deep Sigh, and a languishing voice,—*I am arm'd against their worst Efforts——; for I know they will tell me*, Imoinda *is no more——; and after that, you may spare the rest*. Then, commanding him to rise, he laid himself on a Carpet, under a rich Pavillion, and remain'd a good while silent, and was hardly heard to sigh. When he was come a little to himself, the Messenger ask'd him leave to deliver that part of his Embassy, which the Prince had not yet divin'd: And the Prince cry'd, *I permit thee*—. Then he told him the Affliction the old King was in, for the Rashness he had committed in his Cruelty to *Imoinda*; and how he deign'd to ask Pardon for his Offence, and to implore the Prince wou'd not suffer that Loss to touch his Heart too sensibly, which now all the Gods cou'd not restore him, but might recompence him in Glory, which he begg'd he wou'd pursue; and that Death, that common Revenger of all Injuries, wou'd soon even the Account between him, and a feeble old Man.

Oroonoko bad him return his Duty to his Lord and Master; and to assure him, there was no Account of Revenge to be adjusted between them; if there

3. Kin.   4. Offensive.

were, 'twas he was the Aggressor, and that Death wou'd be just, and, maugre[5] his Age, wou'd see him righted; and he was contented to leave his Share of Glory to Youths more fortunate, and worthy of that Favour from the Gods. That henceforth he wou'd never lift a Weapon, or draw a Bow; but abandon the small Remains of his Life to Sighs and Tears, and the continual Thoughts of what his Lord and Grand-father had thought good to send out of the World, with all that Youth, that Innocence, and Beauty.

After having spoken this, whatever his greatest Officers, and Men of the best Rank cou'd do, they cou'd not raise him from the Carpet, or perswade him to Action, and Resolutions of Life; but commanding all to retire, he shut himself into his Pavillion all that Day, while the Enemy was ready to engage; and wondring at the Delay, the whole Body of the chief of the Army then address'd themselves to him, and to whom they had much a-do to get Admittance. They fell on their Faces at the Foot of his Carpet; where they lay, and besought him with earnest Prayers and Tears, to lead 'em forth to Battel, and not let the Enemy take Advantages of them; and implor'd him to have regard to his Glory, and to the World, that depended on his Courage and Conduct. But he made no other Reply to all their Supplications but this. That he had now no more Business for Glory; and for the World, it was a Trifle not worth his Care. *Go,* (continu'd he, sighing) *and divide it amongst you; and reap with Joy what you so vainly prize, and leave me to my more welcome Destiny.*

They then demanded what they shou'd do, and whom he wou'd constitute in his Room[6] that the Confusion of ambitious Youth and Power might not ruin their Order, and make them a Prey to the Enemy. He reply'd, He wou'd not give himself the Trouble—; but wish'd 'em to chuse the bravest Man amongst 'em, let his Quality or Birth be what it wou'd: *For, O my Friends!* (said he) *it is not Titles make Men brave, or good; or Birth that bestows Courage and Generosity, or makes the Owner happy. Believe this, when you behold* Oroonoko, *the most wretched, and abandon'd by Fortune, of all the Creation of the Gods.* So turning himself about, he wou'd make no more Reply to all they cou'd urge or implore.

The Army beholding their Officers return unsuccessful, with sad Faces, and ominous Looks, that presag'd no good Luck, suffer'd a thousand Fears to take Possession of their Hearts, and the Enemy to come even upon 'em, before they wou'd provide for their Safety, by any Defence; and though they were assur'd by some, who had a mind to animate 'em, that they shou'd be immediately headed by the Prince, and that in the mean time *Aboan* had Orders to command as General; yet they were so dismay'd for want of that great Example of Bravery, that they cou'd make but a very feeble Resistance; and at last, downright, fled before the Enemy, who pursu'd 'em to the very Tents, killing 'em: Nor cou'd all *Aboan*'s Courage, which that Day gain'd him immortal Glory, shame 'em into a Manly Defence of themselves. The Guards that were left behind, about the Prince's Tent, seeing the Soldiers flee before the Enemy, and scatter themselves all over the Plain, in great Disorder, made such Outcries as rouz'd the Prince from his amorous Slumber, in which he had remain'd bury'd for two Days, without permitting any Sustenance to approach him: But, in spite of all his Resolutions, he had not the Constancy of Grief to that Degree, as to make him insensible of the Danger of his Army; and in that

---

5. Despite. Oroonoko hopes to die first.   **6.** I.e., in his place.

Instant he leap'd from his Couch, and cry'd,—*Come, if we must die, let us meet Death the noblest Way; and 'twill be more like* Oroonoko *to encounter him at an Army's Head, opposing the Torrent of a conquering Foe, than lazily, on a Couch, to wait his lingering Pleasure, and die every Moment by a thousand wrecking[7] Thoughts; or be tamely taken by an Enemy, and led a whining, Love-sick Slave, to adorn the Triumphs of* Jamoan, *that young Victor, who already is enter'd beyond the Limits I had prescrib'd him.*

While he was speaking, he suffer'd his People to dress him for the Field; and sallying out of his Pavillion, with more Life and Vigour in his Countenance than ever he shew'd, he appear'd like some Divine Power descended to save his Country from Destruction; and his People had purposely put on him all things that might make him shine with most Splendor, to strike a reverend Awe into the Beholders. He flew into the thickest of those that were pursuing his Men; and being animated with Despair, he fought as if he came on purpose to die, and did such things as will not be believ'd that Humane Strength cou'd perform; and such as soon inspir'd all the rest with new Courage, and new Order: And now it was, that they began to fight indeed; and so, as if they wou'd not be out-done, even by their ador'd *Hero*; who turning the Tide of the Victory, changing absolutely the Fate of the Day, gain'd an entire Conquest; and *Oroonoko* having the good Fortune to single out *Jamoan*, he took him Prisoner with his own Hand, having wounded him almost to death.

This *Jamoan* afterwards became very dear to him, being a Man very gallant, and of excellent Graces, and fine Parts; so that he never put him amongst the Rank of Captives, as they us'd to do, without distinction, for the common Sale, or Market; but kept him in his own Court, where he retain'd nothing of the Prisoner, but the Name, and return'd no more into his own Country, so great an Affection he took for *Oroonoko*; and by a thousand Tales and Adventures of Love and Gallantry, flatter'd[8] his Disease of Melancholy and Languishment; which I have often heard him say, had certainly kill'd him, but for the Conversation of this Prince and *Aboan*, and the *French* Governor[9] he had from his Childhood, of whom I have spoken before, and who was a Man of admirable Wit, great Ingenuity and Learning; all which he had infus'd into his young Pupil. This *French*-Man was banish'd out of his own Country, for some Heretical Notions he held; and though he was a Man of very little Religion, he had admirable Morals, and a brave Soul.

After the total Defeat of *Jamoan*'s Army, which all fled, or were left dead upon the Place, they spent some time in the Camp; *Oroonoko* chusing rather to remain a while there in his Tents, than enter into a Place, or live in a Court where he had so lately suffer'd so great a Loss. The Officers therefore, who saw and knew his Cause of Discontent, invented all sorts of Diversions and Sports, to entertain their Prince: So that what with those Amuzements abroad, and others at home, that is, within their Tents, with the Perswasions, Arguments and Care of his Friends and Servants that he more peculiarly priz'd, he wore off in time a great part of that *Shagrien*, and Torture of Despair, which the first Efforts of *Imoinda*'s Death had given him: Insomuch as having receiv'd a thousand kind Embassies from the King, and Invitations to return to Court, he

---

7. Racking.
8. Soothed.

9. Tutor.

obey'd, though with no little Reluctancy; and when he did so, there was a visible Change in him, and for a long time he was much more melancholy than before. But Time lessens all Extreams, and reduces 'em to *Mediums* and Unconcern; but no Motives or Beauties, though all endeavour'd it, cou'd engage him in any sort of Amour, though he had all the Invitations to it, both from his own Youth, and others Ambitions and Designs.

Oroonoko was no sooner return'd from this last Conquest, and receiv'd at Court with all the Joy and Magnificence that cou'd be express'd to a young Victor, who was not only return'd triumphant, but belov'd like a Deity, when there arriv'd in the Port an *English* Ship.

This Person[1] had often before been in these Countries, and was very well known to *Oroonoko*, with whom he had traffick'd for Slaves, and had us'd to do the same with his Predecessors.

This Commander was a Man of a finer sort of Address, and Conversation, better bred, and more engaging, than most of that sort of Men are; so that he seem'd rather never to have been bred out of a Court, than almost all his Life at Sea. This Captain therefore was always better receiv'd at Court, than most of the Traders to those Countries were; and especially by *Oroonoko*, who was more civiliz'd, according to the *European* Mode, than any other had been, and took more Delight in the *White* Nations; and, above all, Men of Parts and Wit. To this Captain he sold abundance of his Slaves; and for the Favour and Esteem he had for him, made him many Presents, and oblig'd him to stay at Court as long as possibly he cou'd. Which the Captain seem'd to take as a very great Honour done him, entertaining the Prince every Day with Globes and Maps, and Mathematical Discourses and Instruments; eating, drinking, hunting and living with him with so much Familiarity, that it was not to be doubted, but he had gain'd very greatly upon the Heart of this gallant young Man. And the Captain, in Return of all these mighty Favours, besought the Prince to honour his Vessel with his Presence, some Day or other, to Dinner, before he shou'd set Sail; which he condescended to accept, and appointed his Day. The Captain, on his part, fail'd not to have all things in a Readiness, in the most magnificent Order he cou'd possibly: And the Day being come, the Captain, in his Boat, richly adorn'd with Carpets and Velvet-Cushions, row'd to the shore to receive the Prince; with another Long-Boat, where was plac'd all his Musick and Trumpets, with which *Oroonoko* was extreamly delighted; who met him on the shore, attended by his *French* Governor, *Jamoan*, *Aboan*, and about an hundred of the noblest of the Youths of the Court: And after they had first carry'd the Prince on Board, the Boats fetch'd the rest off; where they found a very splendid Treat, with all sorts of fine Wines; and were as well entertain'd, as 'twas possible in such a place to be.

The Prince having drunk hard of Punch, and several Sorts of Wine, as did all the rest (for great Care was taken, they shou'd want nothing of that part of the Entertainment) was very merry, and in great Admiration of the Ship, for he had never been in one before; so that he was curious of beholding every place, where he decently might descend. The rest, no less curious, who were not quite overcome with Drinking, rambl'd at their pleasure *Fore* and *Aft*, as their Fancies guided 'em: So that the Captain, who had well laid his Design before,

---

1. The captain of the ship.

gave the Word, and seiz'd on all his Guests; they clapping great Irons suddenly on the Prince, when he was leap'd down in the Hold, to view that part of the Vessel; and locking him fast down, secur'd him. The same Treachery was us'd to all the rest; and all in one Instant, in several places of the Ship, were lash'd fast in Irons, and betray'd to Slavery. That great Design over, they set all Hands to work to hoise[2] Sail; and with as treacherous and fair a Wind, they made from the Shore with this innocent and glorious Prize, who thought of nothing less than such an Entertainment.

Some have commended this Act, as brave, in the Captain; but I will spare my sense of it, and leave it to my Reader, to judge as he pleases.

It may be easily guess'd, in what manner the Prince resented this Indignity, who may be best resembl'd to a Lion taken in a Toil[3] so he rag'd, so he struggl'd for Liberty, but all in vain; and they had so wisely manag'd his Fetters, that he cou'd not use a Hand in his Defence, to quit himself of a Life that wou'd by no Means endure Slavery; nor cou'd he move from the Place, where he was ty'd, to any solid part of the Ship, against which he might have beat his Head, and have finish'd his Disgrace that way: So that being depriv'd of all other means, he resolved to perish for want of Food: And pleased at last with that Thought, and toil'd and tired by Rage and Indignation, he laid himself down, and sullenly resolved upon dying, and refused all things that were brought him.

This did not a little vex the Captain, and the more so, because, he found almost all of 'em of the same Humour; so that the loss of so many brave Slaves, so tall and goodly to behold, wou'd have been very considerable: He therefore order'd one to go from him (for he wou'd not be seen himself) to *Oroonoko*, and to assure him he was afflicted for having rashly done so unhospitable a Deed, and which cou'd not be now remedied, since they were far from shore; but since he resented it in so high a nature, he assur'd him he wou'd revoke his Resolution, and set both him and his Friends a-shore on the next Land they shou'd touch at; and of this the Messenger gave him his Oath, provid'd he wou'd resolve to live: And *Oroonoko*, whose Honour was such as he never had violated a Word in his Life himself, much less a solemn Asseveration, believ'd in an instant what this Man said, but reply'd, He expected for a Confirmation of this, to have his shameful Fetters dismiss'd. This Demand was carried to the *Captain*, who return'd him answer, That the Offence had been so great which he had put upon the Prince, that he durst not trust him with Liberty while he remained in the Ship, for fear lest by a Valour natural to him, and a Revenge that would animate that Valour, he might commit some Outrage fatal to himself and the *King* his Master, to whom his Vessel did belong. To this *Oroonoko* replied, he would engage his Honour to behave himself in all friendly Order and Manner, and obey the Command of the *Captain*, as he was Lord of the *King*'s Vessel, and General of those Men under his Command.

This was deliver'd to the still doubting *Captain*, who could not resolve to trust a *Heathen*, he said, upon his Parole,[4] a Man that had no Sense or notion of the God that he Worshipp'd. *Oroonoko* then replied. He was very sorry to hear that the *Captain* pretended to the Knowledge and Worship of any *Gods*,

---

2. Hoist. Early accounts report the abduction of Africans who visited ships. Those of high rank were ransomed or returned to prevent the end of the slave trade.
3. Trap.
4. Word of honor.

who had taught him no better Principles, than not to Credit as he would be Credited: but they told him the Difference of their Faith occasion'd that Distrust: For the *Captain* had protested to him upon the Word of a *Christian*, and sworn in the Name of a Great *G O D*; which if he shou'd violate, he would expect eternal Torment in the World to come. *Is that all the Obligation he has to be Just to his Oath?* replied *Oroonoko. Let him know I Swear by my Honour, which to violate, wou'd not only render me contemptible and despised by all brave and honest Men, and so give my self perpetual pain, but it wou'd be eternally offending and diseasing all Mankind, harming, betraying, circumventing and outraging all Men; but Punishments hereafter are suffer'd by ones self; and the World takes no cognizances whether this God have revenged 'em, or not, 'tis done so secretly, and deferr'd so long: While the Man of no Honour, suffers every moment the scorn and contempt of the honester World, and dies every day ignominiously in his Fame, which is more valuable than Life: I speak not this to move Belief, but to shew you how you mistake, when you imagine, That he who will violate his Honour, will keep his Word with his Gods.* So turning from him with a disdainful smile, he refused to answer him, when he urg'd him to know what Answer he shou'd carry back to his *Captain*; so that he departed without saying any more.

The *Captain* pondering and consulting what to do, it was concluded that nothing but *Oroonoko*'s Liberty wou'd encourage any of the rest to eat, except the *French*-man, whom the *Captain* cou'd not pretend to keep Prisoner, but only told him he was secured because he might act something in favour of the Prince, but that he shou'd be freed as soon as they came to Land. So that they concluded it wholly necessary to free the Prince from his Irons, that he might show himself to the rest; that they might have an Eye upon him, and that they cou'd not fear a single Man.

This being resolv'd, to make the Obligation the greater, the Captain himself went to *Oroonoko*; where, after many Compliments, and Assurances of what he had already promis'd, he receiving from the Prince his *Parole*, and his Hand, for his good Behaviour, dismiss'd his Irons, and brought him to his own Cabin; where, after having treated and repos'd him a while, for he had neither eat nor slept in four Days before, he besought him to visit those obstinate People in Chains, who refus'd all manner of Sustenance, and intreated him to oblige 'em to eat, and assure 'em of their Liberty the first Opportunity.

Oroonoko, who was too generous, not to give Credit to his Words, shew'd himself to his People, who were transported with Excess of Joy at the sight of their Darling Prince; falling at his Feet, and kissing and embracing 'em; believing, as some Divine Oracle, all he assured 'em. But he besought 'em to bear their Chains with that Bravery that became those whom he had seen act so nobly in Arms; and that they cou'd not give him greater Proofs of their Love and Friendship, since 'twas all the Security the Captain (his Friend) cou'd have, against the Revenge, he said, they might possibly justly take, for the Injuries sustain'd by him. And they all, with one Accord, assur'd him, they cou'd not suffer enough, when it was for his Repose and Safety.

After this they no longer refus'd to eat, but took what was brought 'em, and were pleas'd with their Captivity, since by it they hop'd to redeem the Prince, who, all the rest of the Voyage, was treated with all the Respect due to his Birth, though nothing cou'd divert his Melancholy; and he wou'd often sigh for

Imoinda, and think this a Punishment due to his Misfortune, in having left that noble Maid behind him, that fatal Night, in the *Otan*, when he fled to the Camp.

Possess'd with a thousand Thoughts of past Joys with this fair young Person, and a thousand Griefs for her eternal Loss, he endur'd a tedious Voyage, and at last arriv'd at the Mouth of the River of *Surinam*, a Colony belonging to the King of *England*, and where they were to deliver some part of their Slaves. There the Merchants and Gentlemen of the Country going on Board, to demand those Lots of Slaves they had already agreed on; and, amongst those, the Over-seers of those Plantations where I then chanc'd to be, the Captain, who had given the Word, order'd his Men to bring up those noble Slaves in Fetters, whom I have spoken of; and having put 'em, some in one, and some in other Lots, with Women and Children (which they call *Pickaninies*), they sold 'em off, as Slaves, to several Merchants and Gentlemen; not putting any two in one Lot, because they wou'd separate 'em far from each other; not daring to trust 'em together, lest Rage and Courage shou'd put 'em upon contriving some great Action, to the Ruin of the Colony.

Oroonoko was first seiz'd on, and sold to our Over-seer, who had the first Lot, with seventeen more of all sorts and sizes, but not one of Quality with him. When he saw this, he found what they meant; for, as I said, he understood *English* pretty well; and being wholly unarm'd and defenceless, so as it was in vain to make any Resistance, he only beheld the Captain with a Look all fierce and disdainful, upbraiding him with Eyes, that forc'd Blushes on his guilty Cheeks, he only cry'd, in passing over the Side of the Ship, *Farewel, Sir: 'Tis worth my Suffering, to gain so true a Knowledge both of you, and of your Gods by whom you swear*. And desiring those that held him to forbear their pains, and telling 'em he wou'd make no Resistance, he cry'd, *Come, my Fellow-Slaves; let us descend, and see if we can meet with more Honour and Honesty in the next World we shall touch upon*. So he nimbly leap'd into the Boat, and shewing no more Concern, suffer'd himself to be row'd up the River, with his seventeen Companions.

The Gentleman that bought him was a young *Cornish* Gentleman, whose Name was *Trefry*; a Man of great Wit, and fine Learning, and was carry'd into those Parts by the Lord——— Governor,[5] to manage all his Affairs. He reflecting on the last Words of *Oroonoko* to the Captain, and beholding the Richness of his Vest,[6] no sooner came into the Boat, but he fix'd his Eyes on him; and finding something so extraordinary in his Face, his Shape and Mien, a Greatness of Look, and Haughtiness in his Air, and finding he spoke *English*, had a great mind to be enquiring into his Quality and Fortune; which, though *Oroonoko* endeavour'd to hide, by only confessing he was above the Rank of common Slaves, *Trefry* soon found he was yet something greater than he confess'd; and from that Moment began to conceive so vast an Esteem for him, that he ever after lov'd him as his dearest Brother, and shew'd him all the Civilities due to so great a Man.

Trefry was a very good Mathematician, and a Linguist; cou'd speak *French* and *Spanish*; and in the three Days they remain'd in the Boat (for so long were

---

5. Francis, Lord Willoughby of Parham, held a royal grant as coproprietor of Surinam. John   Trefry was his plantation overseer.
6. Robe.

they going from the Ship, to the Plantation) he entertain'd *Oroonoko* so agreeably with his Art and Discourse, that he was no less pleas'd with *Trefry*, than he was with the Prince; and he thought himself, at least, fortunate in this, that since he was a Slave, as long as he wou'd suffer himself to remain so, he had a Man of so excellent Wit and Parts for a Master: So that before they had finish'd their Voyage up the River, he made no scruple of declaring to *Trefry* all his Fortunes, and most part of what I have here related, and put himself wholly into the Hands of his new Friend, whom he found resenting all the Injuries were done him, and was charm'd with all the Greatness of his Actions; which were recited with that Modesty, and delicate Sense, as wholly vanquish'd him, and subdu'd him to his Interest. And he promis'd him on his Word and Honour, he wou'd find the Means to reconduct him to his own Country again: assuring him, he had a perfect Abhorrence of so dishonourable an Action; and that he wou'd sooner have dy'd, than have been the Author of such a Perfidy. He found the Prince was very much concern'd to know what became of his Friends, and how they took their Slavery; and *Trefry* promis'd to take care about the enquiring after their Condition, and that he shou'd have an Account of 'em.

Though, as *Oroonoko* afterwards said, he had little Reason to credit the Words of a *Backearary*,[7] yet he knew not why; but he saw a kind of Sincerity, and awful Truth in the Face of *Trefry*; he saw an Honesty in his Eyes, and he found him wise and witty enough to understand Honour; for it was one of his Maxims, *A Man of Wit cou'd not be a Knave or Villain.*

In their passage up the River, they put in at several Houses for Refreshment; and ever when they landed, numbers of People wou'd flock to behold this Man; not but their Eyes were daily entertain'd with the sight of Slaves, but the Fame of *Oroonoko* was gone before him, and all People were in Admiration of his Beauty. Besides, he had a rich Habit on, in which he was taken, so different from the rest, and which the Captain cou'd not strip him of, because he was forc'd to surprize his Person in the Minute he sold him. When he found his Habit made him liable, as he thought, to be gaz'd at the more, he begg'd *Trefry* to give him something more befitting a Slave; which he did, and took off his Robes. Nevertheless, he shone through all; and his *Osenbrigs* (a sort of brown *Holland*[8] Suit he had on) cou'd not conceal the Graces of his Looks and Mien; and he had no less Admirers, than when he had his dazzling Habit on: The Royal Youth appear'd in spite of the Slave, and People cou'd not help treating him after a different manner, without designing it: As soon as they approach'd him, they venerated and esteem'd him; his Eyes insensibly commanded Respect, and his Behaviour insinuated it into every Soul. So that there was nothing talk'd of but this young and gallant Slave, even by those who yet knew not that he was a Prince.

I ought to tell you, that the *Christians* never buy any Slaves but they give 'em some Name of their own, their native ones being likely very barbarous, and hard to pronounce; so that Mr. *Trefry* gave *Oroonoko* that of *Caesar*;[9] which

---

7. Master or white person, from *backra*, an Ibo or Efik word brought to Surinam by slaves.
8. A coarse linen or cotton cloth used to clothe slaves, also called *osnaburg* after a German town where it was made.
9. Slaves often received classical names. Julius Caesar was a famous Roman general and ruler.

Name will live in that Country as long as that (scarce more) glorious one of the great *Roman*; for 'tis most evident, he wanted no part of the Personal Courage of that *Caesar*, and acted things as memorable, had they been done in some part of the World replenish'd with People, and Historians, that might have given him his due. But his Misfortune was, to fall in an obscure World, that afforded only a Female Pen to celebrate his Fame; though I doubt not but it had liv'd from others Endeavours, if the *Dutch*, who, immediately after his Time, took that Country,[1] had not kill'd, banish'd and dispers'd all those that were capable of giving the World this great Man's Life, much better than I have done. And Mr. *Trefry*, who design'd it, dy'd before he began it; and bemoan'd himself for not having undertook it in time.

For the future therefore, I must call *Oroonoko, Caesar*, since by that Name only he was known in our Western World, and by that Name he was receiv'd on Shore at *Parham-House*, where he was destin'd a Slave. But if the King himself (God bless him) had come a-shore, there cou'd not have been greater Expectations by all the whole Plantation, and those neighbouring ones, than was on ours at that time; and he was receiv'd more like a Governor, than a Slave. Notwithstanding, as the Custom was, they assign'd him his Portion of Land, his House, and his Business, up in the Plantation. But as it was more for Form, than any Design, to put him to his Task, he endur'd no more of the Slave but the Name, and remain'd some Days in the House, receiving all Visits that were made him, without stirring towards that part of the Plantation where the *Negroes* were.

At last, he wou'd needs go view his Land, his House, and the Business assign'd him. But he no sooner came to the Houses of the Slaves, which are like a little Town by it self, the *Negroes* all having left Work, but they all came forth to behold him, and found he was that Prince who had, at several times, sold most of 'em to these Parts; and, from a Veneration they pay to great Men, especially if they know 'em, and from the Surprize and Awe they had at the sight of him, they all cast themselves at his Feet, crying out, in their Language, *Live, O King! Long Live, O King!* And kissing his Feet, paid him even Divine Homage.

Several *English* Gentlemen were with him; and what Mr. *Trefry* had told 'em, was here confirm'd; of which he himself before had no other Witness than *Caesar* himself: But he was infinitely glad to find his Grandure confirm'd by the Adoration of all the Slaves.

Caesar troubl'd with their Over-Joy, and Over-Ceremony, besought 'em to rise, and to receive him as their Fellow-Slave; assuring them, he was no better. At which they set up with one Accord a most terrible and hidious Mourning and condoling, which he and the *English* had much a-do to appease; but at last they prevail'd with 'em, and they prepar'd all their barbarous Musick, and every one kill'd and dress'd something of his own Stock (for every Family has their Land a-part, on which, at their leisure-times they breed all eatable things); and clubbing it together, made a most magnificent Supper, inviting their *Grandee*[2] *Captain*, their *Prince*, to honour it with his Presence; which he did, and several *English* with him; where they all waited on him, some playing, others dancing

1. The Dutch attacked and conquered Surinam in 1667, and the British exchanged it for
New York in the treaty of Breda.
2. Eminent or noble.

before him all the time, according to the Manners of their several Nations; and with unwearied Industry, endeavouring to please and delight him.

While they sat at Meat Mr. *Trefry* told *Caesar*, that most of these young *Slaves* were undone in Love, with a fine she-*Slave*, whom they had had about Six Months on their Land; the *Prince*, who never heard the Name of *Love* without a Sigh, nor any mention of it without the Curiosity of examining further into that tale, which of all Discourses was most agreeable to him, asked, how they came to be so Unhappy, as to be all undone for one fair *Slave*? *Trefry*, who was naturally Amorous, and lov'd to talk of Love as well as any body, proceeded to tell him, they had the most charming Black that ever was beheld on their *Plantation*, about Fifteen or Sixteen Years old, as he guess'd; that, for his part, he had done nothing but Sigh for her ever since she came; and that all the white Beautys he had seen, never charm'd him so absolutely as this fine Creature had done; and that no Man, of any Nation, ever beheld her, that did not fall in Love with her; and that she had all the *Slaves* perpetually at her Feet; and the whole Country resounded with the Fame of *Clemene*, for so, said he, we have Christ'ned her: But she denys us all with such a noble Disdain, that 'tis a Miracle to see, that she, who can give such eternal Desires, shou'd herself be all Ice, and all Unconcern. She is adorn'd with the most Graceful Modesty that ever beautifyed Youth; the softest Sigher—that, if she were capable of Love, one would swear she languish'd for some absent happy Man; and so retir'd, as if she fear'd a Rape even from the God of Day,[3] or that the Breezes would steal Kisses from her delicate Mouth. Her Task of Work some sighing Lover every day makes it his Petition to perform for her, which she accepts blushing, and with reluctancy, for fear he will ask her a Look for a Recompence, which he dares not presume to hope; so great an Awe she strikes into the Hearts of her Admirers. *I do not wonder*, replied the Prince, *that Clemene shou'd refuse Slaves, being as you say so Beautiful, but wonder how she escapes those who can entertain her as you can do; or why, being your Slave, you do not oblige her to yield. I confess*, said *Trefry*, *when I have, against her will, entertain'd her with Love so long, as to be transported with my Passion; even above Decency, I have been ready to make use of those advantages of Strength and Force Nature has given me. But oh! she disarms me, with that Modesty and Weeping so tender and so moving, that I retire, and thank my Stars she overcame me.* The Company laugh'd at his Civility to a *Slave*, and *Caesar* only applauded the nobleness of his Passion and Nature; since that Slave might be Noble, or, what was better, have true Notions of Honour and Vertue in her. Thus pass'd they this Night, after having received, from the *Slaves*, all imaginable Respect and Obedience.

The next Day *Trefry* ask'd *Caesar* to walk, when the heat was allay'd, and designedly carried him by the Cottage of the *fair Slave*; and told him, she whom he spoke of last Night liv'd there retir'd. *But*, says he, *I would not wish you to approach, for, I am sure, you will be in Love as soon as you behold her.* *Caesar* assur'd him, he was proof against all the Charms of that Sex; and that if he imagin'd his Heart cou'd be so perfidious to Love again, after *Imoinda*, he believ'd he shou'd tear it from his Bosom: They had no sooner spoke, but a little shock Dog, that *Clemene* had presented[4] her, which she took great Delight

3. The sun.
4. Clemene had presented to her a long-haired dog or poodle, associated with fashionable women.

in, ran out; and she, not knowing any body was there, ran to get it in again, and bolted out on those who were just Speaking of her: When seeing them, she wou'd have run in again; but *Trefry* caught her by the Hand, and cry'd, Clemene, *however you fly a Lover, you ought to pay some Respect to this Stranger* (pointing to *Caesar*). But she, as if she had resolv'd never to raise her Eyes to the Face of a Man again, bent 'em the more to the Earth, when he spoke, and gave the *Prince* the leisure to look the more at her. There needed no long Gazing, or Consideration, to examin who this fair Creature was; he soon saw *Imoinda* all over her; in a Minute he saw her Face, her Shape, her Air, her Modesty, and all that call'd forth his Soul with Joy at his Eyes, and left his Body destitute of almost Life; it stood without Motion, and, for a Minute, knew not that it had a Being; and, I believe, he had never come to himself, so opprest he was with over-Joy, if he had not met with this Allay,[5] that he perceiv'd *Imoinda* fall dead in the Hands of *Trefry*: this awaken'd him, and he ran to her aid, and caught her in his Arms, where, by degrees, she came to herself; and 'tis needless to tell with what transports, what extasies of Joy, they both a while beheld each other, without Speaking; then Snatcht each other to their Arms; then Gaze again, as if they still doubted whether they possess'd the Blessing: They Graspt; but when they recovered their Speech, 'tis not to be imagin'd, what tender things they exprest to each other; wondering what strange Fate had brought 'em again together. They soon inform'd each other of their Fortunes, and equally bewail'd their Fate; but, at the same time, they mutually protested, that even Fetters and Slavery were Soft and Easy; and wou'd be supported with Joy and Pleasure, while they cou'd be so happy to possess each other, and to be able to make good their Vows. *Caesar* swore he disdain'd the Empire of the World, while he cou'd behold his *Imoinda*; and she despis'd Grandure and Pomp, those Vanities of her Sex, when she cou'd Gaze on *Oroonoko*. He ador'd the very Cottage where she resided, and said, That little Inch of the World wou'd give him more Happiness than all the Universe cou'd do; and she vow'd, It was a Pallace, while adorn'd with the Presence of *Oroonoko*.

Trefry was infinitely pleas'd with this Novel,[6] and found this *Clemene* was the Fair Mistress of whom *Caesar* had before spoke; and was not a little satisfied, that Heaven was so kind to the *Prince*, as to sweeten his Misfortunes by so lucky an Accident; and leaving the Lovers to themselves, was impatient to come down to *Parham House*, (which was on the same *Plantation*) to give me an Account of what had hapned. I was as impatient to make these Lovers a Visit, having already made a Friendship with *Caesar*; and from his own Mouth learn'd what I have related, which was confirm'd by his *French*-man, who was set on Shore to seek his Fortunes; and of whom they cou'd not make a Slave, because a Christian; and he came daily to *Parham Hill* to see and pay his Respects to his Pupil *Prince*: So that concerning and intresting myself, in all that related to *Caesar,* whom I had assur'd of Liberty, as soon as the Governor arriv'd, I hasted presently to the Place where the Lovers were, and was infinitely glad to find this Beautiful young *Slave* (who had already gain'd all our Esteems, for her Modesty and be extraordinary Prettyness) to be the same I had heard *Caesar*

---

5. Intrusion.   6. New event.

speak so much of. One may imagine then, we paid her a treble Respect; and though from her being carv'd in fine Flowers and Birds all over her Body, we took her to be of Quality before, yet, when we knew *Clemene* was *Imoinda*, we cou'd not enough admire her.

I had forgot to tell you, that those who are Nobly born of that Country, are so delicately Cut and Rac'd all over the fore-part of the Trunk of their Bodies, that it looks as if it were Japan'd; the Works being raised like high Poynt[7] round the Edges of the Flowers: Some are only Carv'd with a little Flower, or Bird, at the Sides of the Temples, as was *Caesar* and those who are so Carv'd over the Body, resemble our Ancient *Picts*[8] that are figur'd in the Chronicles, but these Carvings are more delicate.

From that happy Day *Caesar* took *Clemene* for his Wife, to the general Joy of all People; and there was as much Magnificence as the Country wou'd afford at the Celebration of this Wedding: and in a very short time after she conceiv'd with Child; which made *Caesar* ever adore her, knowing he was the last of his Great Race. This new Accident made him more Impatient of Liberty, and he was every Day treating with *Trefry* for his and *Clemene*'s Liberty; and offer'd either Gold or a vast quantity of Slaves, which shou'd be paid before they let him go, provided he cou'd have any Security that he shou'd go when his Ransom was paid: They fed him from Day to Day with Promises, and delay'd him, till the Lord Governor shou'd come; so that he began to suspect them of falshood, and that they wou'd delay him till the time of his Wives delivery, and make a Slave of that too, for all the Breed is theirs to whom the Parents belong: This Thought made him very uneasy, and his Sullenness gave them some Jealousies[9] of him; so that I was oblig'd, by some Persons, who fear'd a Mutiny (which is very Fatal sometimes in those Colonies, that abound so with Slaves, that they exceed the Whites in vast Numbers) to discourse with *Caesar*, and to give him all the Satisfaction I possibly cou'd; they knew he and *Clemene* were scarce an Hour in a Day from my Lodgings; that they eat with me, and that I oblig'd 'em in all things I was capable of: I entertain'd him with the Lives of the Romans,[1] and great Men, which charm'd him to my Company; and her, with teaching her all the pretty Works that I was Mistress of; and telling her Stories of Nuns, and endeavouring to bring her to the knowledge of the true God. But of all Discourses *Caesar* lik'd that the worst, and wou'd never be reconcil'd to our Notions of the Trinity, of which he ever made a Jest; it was a Riddle, he said, wou'd turn his Brain to conceive, and one cou'd not make him understand what Faith was. However, these Conversations fail'd not altogether so well to divert him, that he lik'd the Company of us Women much above the Men; for he cou'd not Drink; and he is but an ill Companion in that Country that cannot: So that obliging him to love us very well, we had all the Liberty of Speech with him, especially my self, whom he call'd his *Great Mistress*; and indeed my Word wou'd go a great way with him. For these Reasons, I had Opportunity to take notice to him, that he was not well pleas'd of late, as he us'd to be; was more retir'd and thoughtful; and told him, I took it Ill he shou'd

---

7. An elaborate type of lace. "Rac'd": traced, incised. "Japan'd": like lacquerwork in the Japanese style.
8. Ancient British people, named *Picti*

(painted or tattooed) by the Romans.
9. Suspicions.
1. Plutarch's biographies of famous men, from the late first century.

Suspect we wou'd break our Words with him, and not permit both him and *Clemene* to return to his own Kingdom, which was not so long a way, but when he was once on his Voyage he wou'd quickly arrive there. He made me some Answers that shew'd a doubt in him, which made me ask him, what advantage it wou'd be to doubt? it would but give us a Fear of him, and possibly compel us to treat him so as I shou'd be very loath to behold: that is, it might occasion his Confinement. Perhaps this was not so Luckily spoke of me, for I perceiv'd he resented that Word, which I strove to Soften again in vain: However, he assur'd me, that whatsoever Resolutions he shou'd take, he wou'd Act nothing upon the White-People; and as for my self, and those upon that *Plantation* where he was, he wou'd sooner forfeit his eternal Liberty, and Life it self, than lift his Hand against his greatest Enemy on that Place: He besought me to suffer no Fears upon his Account, for he cou'd do nothing that Honour shou'd not dictate; but he accus'd himself for having suffer'd Slavery so long; yet he charg'd that weakness on Love alone, who was capable of making him neglect even Glory it self; and, for which, now he reproaches himself every moment of the Day. Much more to this effect he spoke, with an Air impatient enough to make me know he wou'd not be long in Bondage; and though he suffer'd only the Name of a Slave, and had nothing of the Toil and Labour of one, yet that was sufficient to render him Uneasy; and he had been too long Idle, who us'd to be always in Action, and in Arms: He had a Spirit all Rough and Fierce, and that cou'd not be tam'd to lazy Rest; and though all endeavors were us'd to exercise himself in such Actions and Sports as this World afforded, as Running, Wrastling, Pitching the Bar, Hunting and Fishing, Chasing and Killing *Tigers*[2] of a monstrous Size, which this Continent affords in abundance; and wonderful *Snakes*, such as *Alexander* is reported to have incounter'd at the River of *Amazons*,[3] and which *Caesar* took great Delight to overcome; yet these were not Actions great enough for his large Soul, which was still panting after more renown'd Action.

Before I parted that Day with him, I got, with much ado, a Promise from him to rest yet a little longer with Patience, and wait the coming of the Lord Governor, who was every Day expected on our Shore; he assur'd me he wou'd, and this Promise he desired me to know was given perfectly in Complaisance to me, in whom he had an intire Confidence.

After this, I neither thought it convenient to trust him much out of our View, nor did the Country who fear'd him; but with one accord it was advis'd to treat him Fairly, and oblige him to remain within such a compass, and that he shou'd be permitted, as seldom as cou'd be, to go up to the Plantations of the Negroes; or, if he did, to be accompany'd by some that shou'd be rather in appearance Attendants than Spys. This Care was for some time taken, and *Caesar* look'd upon it as a Mark of extraordinary Respect, and was glad his discontent had oblig'd 'em to be more observant to him; he received new assurance from the Overseer, which was confirmed to him by the Opinion of all the Gentlemen of the Country, who made their court to him. During this time that we had his Company more frequently than hitherto we had had, it may not be unpleasant to relate to you the Diversions we entertain'd him with, or rather he us.

---

2. Jaguars. "Pitching the bar": a game of distance throwing.

3. Alexander the Great supposedly encountered Amazons (and snakes) in India.

My stay was to be short in that Country, because my Father dy'd at Sea, and never arriv'd to possess the Honour was design'd him, (which was Lieutenant-General of Six and thirty Islands, besides the Continent of *Surinam*) nor the advantages he hop'd to reap by them;[4] so that though we were oblig'd to continue on our Voyage, we did not intend to stay upon the Place: Though, in a Word, I must say thus much of it, That certainly had his late Majesty, of sacred Memory, but seen and known what a vast and charming World he had been Master of in that Continent, he would never have parted so Easily with it to the *Dutch*. 'Tis a Continent whose vast Extent was never yet known, and may contain more Noble Earth than all the Universe besides; for, they say, it reaches from East to West; one Way as far as *China*, and another to *Peru*: It affords all things both for Beauty and Use; 'tis there Eternal Spring, always the very Months of *April*, *May* and *June*; the Shades are perpetual, the Trees, bearing at once all degrees of Leaves and Fruit, from blooming Buds to ripe Autumn; Groves of Oranges, Limons, Citrons, Figs, Nutmegs, and noble Aromaticks, continually bearing their Fragrancies. The Trees appearing all like Nosegays adorn'd with Flowers of different kinds; some are all White, some Purple, some Scarlet, some Blue, some Yellow; bearing, at the same time, Ripe Fruit and Blooming Young, or producing every Day new. The very Wood of all these Trees have an intrinsick Value above common Timber; for they are, when cut, of different Colours, glorious to behold; and bear a Price considerable, to inlay withal. Besides this, they yield rich Balm, and Gums; so that we make our Candles of such an Aromatick Substance, as does not only give a sufficient Light, but, as they Burn, they cast their Perfumes all about. Cedar is the common Firing, and all the Houses are built with it. The very Meat we eat, when set on the Table, if it be Native, I mean of the Country, perfumes the whole Room; especially a little Beast call'd an *Armadilly*, a thing which I can liken to nothing so well as a *Rhinoceros*; 'tis all in white Armor so joynted, that it moves as well in it, as if it had nothing on; this Beast is about the bigness of a Pig of Six Weeks old. But it were endless to give an Account of all the divers Wonderfull and Strange things that Country affords, and which we took a very great Delight to go in search of; though those adventures are oftentimes Fatal and at least Dangerous: But while we had *Caesar* in our Company on these Designs we fear'd no harm, nor suffer'd any.

As soon as I came into the Country, the best House in it was presented me, call'd *St. John's Hill*.[5] It stood on a vast Rock of white Marble, at the Foot of which the River ran a vast depth down, and not to be descended on that side; the little Waves still dashing and washing the foot of this Rock, made the softest Murmurs and Purlings in the World; and the Opposite Bank was adorn'd with such vast quantities of different Flowers eternally Blowing,[6] and every Day and Hour new, fenc'd behind 'em with lofty Trees of a Thousand rare Forms and Colours, that the Prospect was the most ravishing that fancy can create. On the Edge of this white Rock, towards the River, was a Walk or Grove of Orange and Limon Trees, about half the length of the *Mall*[7] here,

---

4. There is no record of Willoughby appointing anyone to the position of lieutenant-governor. "Continent": land joined to other lands.

5. A plantation near Willoughby's Parham Hill.

6. Blooming.

7. A fashionable park walk in London.

whose Flowery and Fruit-bearing Branches meet at the top, and hinder'd the Sun, whose Rays are very fierce there, from entering a Beam into the Grove; and the cool Air that came from the River made it not only fit to entertain People in, at all the hottest Hours of the Day, but refresh'd the sweet Blossoms, and made it always Sweet and Charming; and sure the whole Globe of the World cannot show so delightful a Place as this Grove was: Not all the Gardens of boasted *Italy* can produce a Shade to out-vie this, which Nature had joyn'd with Art to render so exceeding Fine; and 'tis a marvel to see how such vast Trees, as big as English Oaks, cou'd take footing on so solid a Rock, and in so little Earth, as cover'd that Rock; but all things by Nature there are Rare, Delightful and Wonderful. But to our Sports.

Sometimes we wou'd go surprizing,[8] and in search of young *Tigers* in their Dens, watching when the old Ones went forth to forage for Prey; and oftentimes we have been in great Danger, and have fled apace for our Lives, when surpriz'd by the Dams. But once, above all other times, we went on this Design, and *Caesar* was with us, who had no sooner stol'n a young *Tiger* from her Nest, but going off, we incounter'd the Dam, bearing a Buttock of a Cow, which he[9] had torn off with his mighty Paw, and going with it towards his *Den*; we had only found Women, *Caesar*, and an English Gentleman, Brother to *Harry Martin*,[1] the great *Oliverian*; we found there was no escaping this inrag'd and ravenous Beast. However, we Women fled as fast as we cou'd from it; but our Heels had not sav'd our Lives, if *Caesar* had not laid down his *Cub*, when he found the *Tiger* quit her Prey to make the more speed towards him; and taking Mr. *Martin*'s Sword desir'd him to stand aside, or follow the Ladies. He obey'd him, and *Caesar* met this monstrous Beast of might, size, and vast Limbs, who came with open Jaws upon him; and fixing his Awful stern Eyes full upon those of the Beast, and putting himself into a very steddy and good aiming posture of Defence, ran his Sword quite through his Breast down to his very Heart, home to the Hilt of the Sword; the dying Beast stretch'd forth her Paw, and going to grasp his Thigh, surpriz'd with Death in that very moment, did him no other harm than fixing her long Nails in his Flesh very deep, feebly wounded him, but cou'd not grasp the Flesh to tear off any. When he had done this, he hollow'd to us to return; which, after some assurance of his Victory, we did, and found him lugging out the Sword from the Bosom of the *Tiger*, who was laid in her Bloud on the Ground; he took up the *Cub*, and with an unconcern, that had nothing of the Joy or Gladness of a Victory, he came and laid the Whelp at my Feet: We all extreamly wonder'd at his Daring, and at the Bigness of the Beast, which was about the highth of an Heifer, but of mighty, great, and strong Limbs.

Another time, being in the Woods, he kill'd a *Tiger*, which had long infested that part, and born away abundance of Sheep and Oxen, and other things, that were for the support of those to whom they belong'd; abundance of People assail'd this Beast, some affirming they had shot her with several Bullets quite through the Body, at several times; and some swearing they shot her through the very Heart, and they believ'd she was a Devil rather than a Mortal thing.

---

8. Mounting sudden raids.
9. The tiger is alternatively she, he, and it.
1. Henry Martin had been one of judges who signed Charles I's death warrant. His younger brother George, a Barbados planter, moved to Surinam in 1658.

Caesar had often said, he had a mind to encounter this Monster, and spoke with several Gentlemen who had attempted her; one crying, I shot her with so many poyson'd Arrows, another with his Gun in this part of her, and another in that; so that he remarking all these Places where she was shot, fancy'd still he shou'd overcome her, by giving her another sort of a Wound than any had yet done; and one day said (at the Table) *What Trophies and Garlands, Ladies, will you make me, if I bring you home the Heart of this Ravenous Beast, that eats up all your Lambs and Pigs?* We all promis'd he shou'd be rewarded at all our Hands. So taking a Bow, which he chus'd out of a great many, he went up in the Wood, with two Gentlemen, where he imagin'd this Devourer to be; they had not past very far in it, but they heard her Voice, growling and grumbling, as if she were pleas'd with something she was doing. When they came in view, they found her muzzling in the Belly of a new ravish'd Sheep, which she had torn open; and seeing herself approach'd, she took fast hold of her Prey, with her fore Paws, and set a very fierce raging Look on *Caesar*, without offering to approach him; for fear, at the same time, of losing what she had in Possession. So that *Caesar* remain'd a good while, only taking aim, and getting an opportunity to shoot her where he design'd; 'twas some time before he cou'd accomplish it, and to wound her, and not kill her, wou'd but have enrag'd her more, and indanger'd him: He had a Quiver of Arrows at his side, so that if one fail'd he cou'd be supply'd; at last, retiring a little, he gave her opportunity to eat, for he found she was Ravenous, and fell to as soon as she saw him retire; being more eager of her Prey than of doing new Mischiefs. When he going softly to one side of her, and hiding his Person behind certain Herbage that grew high and thick, he took so good aim, that, as he intended, he shot her just into the Eye, and the Arrow was sent with so good a will, and so sure a hand, that it stuck in her Brain, and made her caper, and become mad for a moment or two; but being seconded by another Arrow, he fell dead upon the Prey: *Caesar* cut him Open with a Knife, to see where those Wounds were that had been reported to him, and why he did not Die of 'em. But I shall now relate a thing that possibly will find no Credit among Men, because 'tis a Notion commonly receiv'd with us, That nothing can receive a Wound in the Heart and Live; but when the Heart of this courageous Animal was taken out, there were Seven Bullets of Lead in it, and the Wounds seam'd up with great Scars, and she liv'd with the Bullets a great while, for it was long since they were shot: This Heart the Conqueror brought up to us, and 'twas a very great Curiosity, which all the Country came to see; and which gave *Caesar* occasion of many fine Discourses; of Accidents in War, and Strange Escapes.

At other times he wou'd go a Fishing; and discoursing on that Diversion, he found we had in that Country a very Strange Fish, call'd a *Numb Eel*,[2] (an *Eel* of which I have eaten) that while it is alive, it has a quality so Cold, that those who are Angling, though with a Line of never so great a length, with a Rod at the end of it, it shall, in the same minute the Bait is touched by this *Eel*, seize him or her that holds the Rod with benumb'dness, that shall deprive 'em of Sense, for a while; and some have fall'n into the Water, and others drop'd as dead on the Banks of the Rivers where they stood, as soon as this Fish touches the Bait. *Caesar* us'd to laugh at this, and believ'd it impossible a Man cou'd

2. Electric eel.

lose his Force at the touch of a Fish; and cou'd not understand that Philosophy,[3] that a cold Quality should be of that Nature: However, he had a great Curiosity to try whether it wou'd have the same effect on him it had on others, and often try'd, but in vain; at last, the sought for Fish came to the Bait, as he stood Angling on the Bank; and instead of throwing away the Rod, or giving it a sudden twitch out of the Water, whereby he might have caught both the *Eel*, and have dismiss'd the Rod, before it cou'd have too much Power over him; for Experiment sake, he grasp'd it but the harder, and fainting fell into the River; and being still possest of the Rod, the Tide carry'd him senseless as he was a great way, till an *Indian* Boat took him up; and perceiv'd, when they touch'd him, a Numbness seize them, and by that knew the Rod was in his Hand; which, with a Paddle (that is, a short Oar) they struck away, and snatch'd it into the Boat, *Eel* and all. If *Caesar* were almost Dead, with the effect of this Fish, he was more so with that of the Water, where he had remain'd the space of going a League; and they found they had much a-do to bring him back to Life: But, at last, they did, and brought him home, where he was in a few Hours well Recover'd and Refresh'd; and not a little Asham'd to find he shou'd be overcome by an *Eel*; and that all the People, who heard his Defiance, wou'd Laugh at him. But we cheared him up; and he, being convinc'd, we had the *Eel* at Supper; which was a quarter of an Ell about, and most delicate Meat; and was of the more Value, since it cost so Dear, as almost the Life of so gallant a Man.

About this time we were in many mortal Fears, about some Disputes the *English* had with the *Indians*; so that we cou'd scarce trust our selves, without great Numbers, to go to any *Indian* Towns, or Place, where they abode; for fear they shou'd fall upon us, as they did immediately after my coming away; and that it was in the possession of the *Dutch*, who us'd 'em not so civilly as the *English*; so that they cut in pieces all they cou'd take, getting into Houses, and hanging up the Mother, and all her Children about her; and cut a Footman, I left behind me, all in Joynts, and nail'd him to Trees.

This feud began while I was there; so that I lost half the satisfaction I propos'd, in not seeing and visiting the *Indian* Towns. But one Day, bemoaning of our Misfortunes upon this account, *Caesar* told us, we need not Fear; for if we had a mind to go, he wou'd undertake to be our Guard: Some wou'd, but most wou'd not venture; about Eighteen of us resolv'd, and took Barge; and, after Eight Days, arriv'd near an *Indian* Town: But approaching it, the Hearts of some of our Company fail'd, and they wou'd not venture on Shore; so we Poll'd who wou'd, and who wou'd not: For my part, I said, If *Caesar* wou'd, I wou'd go; he resolv'd, so did my Brother, and my Woman, a Maid of good Courage. Now none of us speaking the Language of the People, and imagining we shou'd have a half Diversion in Gazing only; and not knowing what they said, we took a Fisherman that liv'd at the Mouth of the River, who had been a long Inhabitant there, and oblig'd him to go with us: But because he was known to the *Indians*, as trading among 'em; and being, by long Living there, become a perfect *Indian* in Colour, we, who resolv'd to surprize 'em, by making 'em see something they never had seen, (that is, White People) resolv'd only my self, my Brother, and Woman shou'd go; so *Caesar*, the Fisherman, and the rest, hiding behind some thick Reeds and Flowers, that grew on the Banks, let

---

3. Principle or system.

us pass on towards the Town, which was on the Bank of the River all along. A little distant from the Houses, or Huts, we saw some Dancing, others busy'd in fetching and carrying of Water from the River: They had no sooner spy'd us, but they set up a loud Cry, that frighted us at first; we thought it had been for those that should Kill us, but it seems it was of Wonder and Amazement. They were all Naked, and we were Dress'd, so as is most comode,[4] for the hot Countries, very Glittering and Rich; so that we appear'd extreamly fine; my own Hair was cut short, and I had a Taffaty Cap, with Black Feathers, on my Head; my Brother was in a Stuff[5] Suit, with Silver Loops and Buttons, and abundance of Green Ribon; this was all infinitely surprising to them, and because we saw them stand still, till we approach'd 'em, we took Heart and advanc'd; came up to 'em, and offer'd 'em our Hands; which they took, and look'd on us round about, calling still for more Company; who came swarming out, all wondering, and crying out *Tepeeme*;[6] taking their Hair up in their Hands, and spreading it wide to those they call'd out to; as if they would say (as indeed it signify'd) *Numberless Wonders*, or not to be recounted, no more than to number the Hair of their Heads. By degrees they grew more bold, and from gazing upon us round, they touch'd us; laying their Hands upon all the Features of our Faces, feeling our Breasts and Arms, taking up one Petticoat, then wondering to see another; admiring our Shoes and Stockings, but more our Garters, which we gave 'em; and they ty'd about their Legs, being Lac'd with Silver Lace at the ends, for they much Esteem any shining things: In fine, we suffer'd 'em to survey us as they pleas'd, and we thought they wou'd never have done admiring us. When *Caesar*, and the rest, saw we were receiv'd with such wonder, they came up to us; and finding the *Indian* Trader whom they knew, (for 'tis by these Fishermen, call'd *Indian* Traders, we hold a Commerce with 'em; for they love not to go far from home, and we never go to them) when they saw him therefore they set up a new Joy; and cry'd, in their Language, *Oh! here's our* Tiguamy, *and we shall now know whether those things can speak*: So advancing to him, some of 'em gave him their Hands, and cry'd, *Amora Tiguamy*, which is as much as, *How do you*, or *Welcome Friend*; and all, with one din, began to gabble to him, and ask'd, If we had Sense, and Wit? if we cou'd talk of affairs of Life, and War, as they cou'd do? if we cou'd Hunt, Swim, and do a thousand things they use? He answer'd 'em, We cou'd. Then they invited us into their Houses, and dress'd Venison and Buffelo for us; and, going out, gathered a Leaf of a Tree, call'd a *Sarumbo* Leaf, of Six Yards long, and spread it on the Ground for a Table-Cloth; and cutting another in pieces instead of Plates, setting us on little bow *Indian* Stools, which they cut out of one intire piece of Wood, and Paint, in a sort of Japan Work: They serve every one their Mess[7] on these pieces of Leaves, and it was very good, but too high season'd with Pepper. When we had eat, my Brother, and I, took out our Flutes, and play'd to 'em, which gave 'em new Wonder; and I soon perceiv'd, by an admiration, that is natural to these People, and by the extream Ignorance and Simplicity of 'em, it were not difficult to establish any unknown or extravagant Religion among them; and to impose any Notions or Fictions upon 'em. For seeing a Kinsman

---

4. Appropriate.
5. Woven fabric. "Taffaty": taffeta.
6. *Tapouimé* (a modern transcription of the word Behn transcribed as *Tepeeme*) is the word for "many" in the indigenous Galibi language.
7. Serving.

of mine set some Paper a Fire, with a Burning-glass, a Trick they had never before seen, they were like to have Ador'd him for a God; and beg'd he wou'd give them the Characters or Figures of his Name, that they might oppose it against Winds and Storms; which he did, and they held it up in those Seasons, and fancy'd it had a Charm to conquer them; and kept it like a Holy Relique. They are very Superstitious, and call'd him the Great *Peeie*, that is, *Prophet*. They show'd us their *Indian Peeie*, a Youth of about Sixteen Years old, as handsom as Nature cou'd make a Man. They consecrate a beautiful Youth from his Infancy, and all Arts are us'd to compleat him in the finest manner, both in Beauty and Shape: He is bred to all the little Arts and cunning they are capable of; to all the Legerdemain Tricks, and Sleight of Hand, whereby he imposes upon the Rabble; and is both a Doctor in Physick and Divinity. And by these Tricks makes the Sick believe he sometimes eases their Pains; by drawing from the afflicted part little Serpents, or odd Flies, or Worms, or any Strange thing; and though they have besides undoubted good Remedies, for almost all their Diseases, they cure the Patient more by Fancy than by Medicines; and make themselves Fear'd, Lov'd, and Reverenc'd. This young *Peeie* had a very young Wife, who seeing my Brother kiss her, came running and kiss'd me; after this, they kiss'd one another, and made it a very great Jest, it being so Novel; and new Admiration and Laughing went round the Multitude, that they never will forget that Ceremony, never before us'd or known. *Caesar* had a mind to see and talk with their War *Captains*, and we were conducted to one of their Houses; where we beheld several of the great *Captains*, who had been at Councel: But so frightful a Vision it was to see 'em no Fancy can create; no such Dreams can represent so dreadful a Spectacle. For my part I took 'em for Hobgoblins, or Fiends, rather than Men; but however their Shapes appear'd, their Souls were very Humane and Noble; but some wanted their Noses, some their Lips, some both Noses and Lips, some their Ears, and others Cut through each Cheek, with long Slashes, through which their Teeth appear'd; they had other several formidable Wounds and Scars, or rather Dismemberings; they had *Comitias*, or little Aprons before 'em; and Girdles of Cotton, with their Knives naked, stuck in it; a Bow at their Backs, and a Quiver of Arrows on their Thighs; and most had Feathers on their Heads of divers Colours. They cry'd, *Amora Tigame* to us, at our entrance, and were pleas'd we said as much to 'em; they seated us, and gave us Drink of the best Sort; and wonder'd, as much as the others had done before, to see us. *Caesar* was marvelling as much at their Faces, wondering how they shou'd all be so Wounded in War; he was Impatient to know how they all came by those frightful Marks of Rage or Malice, rather than Wounds got in Noble Battel: They told us, by our Interpreter, That when any War was waging, two Men chosen out by some old *Captain*, whose Fighting was past, and who cou'd only teach the Theory of War, these two Men were to stand in Competition for the Generalship, or Great War Captain; and being brought before the old Judges, now past Labour, they are ask'd, What they dare do to shew they are worthy to lead an Army? When he, who is first ask'd, making no Reply, Cuts off his Nose, and throws it contemptably[8] on the Ground; and the other does something to himself that he thinks surpasses him, and perhaps deprives himself of Lips and an Eye; so they Slash on till one gives

---

8. With contempt.

out, and many have dy'd in this Debate. And 'tis by a passive Valour they shew and prove their Activity; a sort of Courage too Brutal to be applauded by our Black Hero; nevertheless he express'd his Esteem of 'em.

In this Voyage *Caesar* begot so good an understanding between the *Indians* and the *English*, that there were no more Fears, or Heart-burnings during our stay; but we had a perfect, open, and free Trade with 'em: Many things Remarkable, and worthy Reciting, we met with in this short Voyage; because *Caesar* made it his Business to search out and provide for our Entertainment, especially to please his dearly Ador'd *Imoinda*, who was a sharer in all our Adventures; we being resolv'd to make her Chains as easy as we cou'd, and to Compliment the Prince in that manner that most oblig'd him.

As we were coming up again, we met with some *Indians* of strange Aspects; that is, of a larger Size, and other sort of Features, than those of our Country: Our *Indian Slaves*, that Row'd us, ask'd 'em some Questions, but they cou'd not understand us; but shew'd us a long Cotton String, with several Knots on it;[9] and told us, they had been coming from the Mountains so many Moons as there were Knots; they were habited in Skins of a Strange Beast, and brought along with 'em Bags of Gold Dust; which, as well as they cou'd give us to understand, came streaming in little small Chanels down the high Mountains, when the Rains fell; and offer'd to be the Convoy to any Body, or Persons, that wou'd go to the Mountains. We carry'd these Men up to *Parham*, where they were kept till the Lord Governour came: And because all the Country was mad to be going on this Golden Adventure, the Governour, by his Letters, commanded (for they sent some of the Gold to him) that a Guard shou'd be set at the Mouth of the River of *Amazons*, (a River so call'd, almost as broad as the River of *Thames*) and prohibited all People from going up that River, it conducting to those Mountains of Gold.[1] But we going off for *England* before the Project was further prosecuted, and the Governour being drown'd in a Hurricane[2] either the Design dy'd, or the *Dutch* have the Advantage of it: And 'tis to be bemoan'd what his Majesty lost by losing that part of *America*.

Though this digression is a little from my Story, however since it contains some Proofs of the Curiosity and Daring of this great Man, I was content to omit nothing of his Character.

It was thus, for some time we diverted him; but now *Imoinda* began to shew she was with Child, and did nothing but Sigh and Weep for the Captivity of her Lord, her Self, and the Infant yet Unborn; and believ'd, if it were so hard to gain the Liberty of Two, 'twou'd be more difficult to get that for Three. Her Griefs were so many Darts in the great Heart of *Caesar*; and taking his Opportunity one *Sunday*, when all the Whites were overtaken in Drink, as there were abundance of several Trades, and *Slaves* for Four Years, that Inhabited among the *Negro* Houses; and *Sunday* was their Day of Debauch, (otherwise they were a sort of Spys upon Caesar); he went pretending out of Goodness to 'em, to Feast amongst 'em; and sent all his Musick, and order'd a great Treat for the whole Gang, about Three Hundred *Negros*; and about a Hundred and Fifty were able to bear Arms, such as they had, which were sufficient to do Execution

---

9. A *quipu*, used by the Incas of Peru for keeping records and accounts.
1. Spanish as well as English explorers had searched for the mythical golden city of El Dorado in Guiana.
2. Willoughby died in a storm in 1666.

with Spirits accordingly: For the *English* had none but rusty Swords, that no Strength cou'd draw from a Scabbard; except the People of particular Quality, who took care to Oyl 'em and keep 'em in good Order: The Guns also, unless here and there one, or those newly carry'd from *England*, wou'd do no good or harm; for 'tis the Nature of that Country to Rust and Eat up Iron, or any Metals, but Gold and Silver. And they are very Unexpert at the Bow, which the *Negros* and *Indians* are perfect Masters off.

Caesar, having singl'd out these Men from the Women and Children, made an Harangue to 'em of the Miseries, and Ignominies of Slavery; counting up all their Toyls and Sufferings, under such Loads, Burdens, and Drudgeries, as were fitter for Beasts than Men; Senseless Brutes, than Humane Souls. He told 'em it was not for Days, Months, or Years, but for Eternity; there was no end to be of their Misfortunes: They suffer'd not like Men who might find a Glory, and Fortitude in Oppression; but like Dogs that lov'd the Whip and Bell, and fawn'd the more they were beaten: That they had lost the Divine Quality of Men, and were become insensible Asses, fit only to bear; nay worse: and Ass, or Dog, or Horse having done his Duty, cou'd lye down in Retreat, and rise to Work again, and while he did his Duty indur'd no Stripes; but Men, Villanous, Senseless Men, such as they, Toyl'd on all the tedious Week till Black *Friday*; and then, whether they Work'd or not, whether they were Faulty or Meriting, they promiscuously, the Innocent with the Guilty, suffer'd the infamous Whip, the sordid Stripes, from their Fellow *Slaves* till their Blood trickled from all Parts of their Body; Blood, whose every drop ought to be Reveng'd with a Life of some of those Tyrants, that impose it; *And why*, said he, *my dear Friends and Fellow-sufferers, shou'd we be Slaves to an unknown People? Have they Vanquish'd us Nobly in Fight? Have they Won us in Honourable Battel? And are we, by the chance of War, become their Slaves? This wou'd not anger a Noble Heart, this wou'd not animate a Souldiers Soul; no, but we are Bought and Sold like Apes, or Monkeys, to be the Sport of Women, Fools and Cowards; and the Support of Rogues, Runagades,*[3] *that have abandon'd their own Countries, for Rapin, Murders, Thefts and Villanies: Do you not hear every Day how they upbraid each other with infamy of Life, below the Wildest Salvages; and shall we render Obedience to such a degenerate Race, who have no one Humane Vertue left, to distinguish 'em from the vilest Creatures? Will you, I say, suffer the Lash from such Hands?* They all Reply'd, with one accord, *No, no, no*; Caesar *has spoke like a Great Captain; like a Great King.*

After this he wou'd have proceeded, but was interrupted by a tall *Negro* of some more Quality than the rest, his Name was *Tuscan*; who Bowing at the Feet of *Caesar*, cry'd, *My Lord, we have listen'd with Joy and Attention to what you have said; and, were we only Men, wou'd follow so great a Leader through the World: But oh! consider, we are Husbands and Parents too, and have things more dear to us than Life; our Wives and Children unfit for Travel, in these unpassable Woods, Mountains and Bogs; we have not only difficult Lands to overcome, but Rivers to Wade, and Monsters to Incounter; Ravenous Beasts of Prey——.* To this, *Caesar* Reply'd, *That Honour was the First Principle in Nature, that was to be Obey'd; but as no Man wou'd pretend to that, without all the Acts of Vertue, Compassion, Charity, Love, Justice and Reason; he found it not*

---

3. Renegades.

inconsistent with that, to take an equal Care of their Wives and Children, as they wou'd of themselves; and that he did not Design, when he led them to Freedom, and Glorious Liberty, that they shou'd leave that better part of themselves to Perish by the Hand of the Tyrant's Whip: But if there were a Woman among them so degenerate from Love and Vertue to chuse Slavery before the pursuit of her Husband, and with the hazard of her Life, to share with him in his Fortunes; that such an one ought to be Abandon'd, and left as a Prey to the common Enemy.

To which they all Agreed,—and Bowed. After this, he spoke of the Impassable Woods and Rivers; and convinc'd 'em, the more Danger, the more Glory. He told them that he had heard of one *Hannibal* a great Captain, had Cut his Way through Mountains of solid Rocks; and shou'd a few Shrubs oppose them; which they cou'd Fire before 'em?[4] No, 'twas a trifling Excuse to Men resolv'd to die, or overcome. As for Bogs, they are with a little Labour fill'd and harden'd; and the Rivers cou'd be no Obstacle, since they Swam by Nature; at least by Custom, from their First Hour of their Birth: That when the Children were Weary they must carry them by turns, and the Woods and their own Industry wou'd afford them Food. To this they all assented with Joy.

Tuscan then demanded, What he wou'd do? He said, they wou'd Travel towards the Sea; Plant a New Colony, and Defend it by their Valour; and when they cou'd find a Ship, either driven by stress of Weather, or guided by Providence that way, they wou'd Seize it, and make it a Prize, till it had Transported them to their own Countries; at least, they shou'd be made Free in his Kingdom, and be Esteem'd as his Fellow-sufferers, and Men that had the Courage, and the Bravery to attempt, at least, for Liberty; and if they Dy'd in the attempt it wou'd be more brave, than to Live in perpetual Slavery.

They bow'd and kiss'd his Feet at this Resolution, and with one accord Vow'd to follow him to Death. And that Night was appointed to begin their March; they made it known to their Wives, and directed them to tie their Hamaca[5] about their Shoulder, and under their Arm like a Scarf; and to lead their Children that cou'd go, and carry those that cou'd not. The Wives, who pay an intire Obedience to their Husbands, obey'd, and stay'd for 'em, where they were appointed: The Men stay'd but to furnish themselves with what defensive Arms they cou'd get; and All met at the Rendezvous, where *Caesar* made a new incouraging Speech to 'em, and led 'em out.

But, as they cou'd not march far that Night, on Monday early, when the Overseers went to call 'em all together, to go to Work, they were extreamly surpris'd, to find not one upon the Place, but all fled with what Baggage they had. You may imagine this News was not only suddenly spread all over the *Plantation*, but soon reach'd the Neighbouring ones; and we had by Noon about Six hundred Men, they call the *Militia* of the Country, that came to assist us in the pursuit of the Fugitives: But never did one see so comical an Army march forth to War. The Men, of any fashion, wou'd not concern themselves, though it were almost the common Cause; for such Revoltings are very ill Examples, and have very fatal Consequences oftentimes in many Colonies: But they had a Respect for *Caesar*, and all hands were against the *Parhamites*, as they call'd those of *Parham Plantation*; because they did not, in the

---

4. Roman accounts relate how the Carthaginian general and his army hacked through the Alps on their way to attack Rome.
5. Hammock.

first place, love the Lord Governor; and secondly, they wou'd have it, that *Caesar* was Ill us'd, and Baffl'd with;[6] and 'tis not impossible but some of the best in the Country was of his Council in this Flight, and depriving us of all the *Slaves*; so that they of the better sort wou'd not meddle in the matter. The Deputy Governor,[7] of whom I have had no great occasion to speak, and who was the most Fawning fair-tongu'd Fellow in the World, and one that pretended the most Friendship to *Caesar*, was now the only violent Man against him; and though he had nothing, and so need fear nothing, yet talk'd and look'd bigger than any Man: He was a Fellow, whose Character is not fit to be mention'd with the worst of the *Slaves*. This Fellow wou'd lead his Army forth to meet *Caesar*, or rather to pursue him; most of their Arms were of those sort of cruel Whips they call *Cat with Nine Tayls*; some had rusty useless Guns for show; others old Basket-hilts,[8] whose Blades had never seen the Light in this Age; and others had long Staffs, and Clubs. Mr. *Trefry* went along, rather to be a Mediator than a Conqueror, in such a Battel; for he foresaw, and knew, if by fighting they put the Negroes into despair, they were a sort of sullen Fellows, that wou'd drown, or kill themselves, before they wou'd yield; and he advis'd that fair means was best: But *Byam* was one that abounded in his own Wit, and wou'd take his own Measures.

It was not hard to find these Fugitives; for as they fled they were forc'd to fire and cut the Woods before 'em, so that Night or Day they pursu'd 'em by the light they made, and by the path they had clear'd: But as soon as *Caesar* found he was pursu'd, he put himself in a Posture of Defence, placing all the Women and Children in the Rear; and himself, with *Tuscan* by his side, or next to him, all promising to Dye or Conquer. Incourag'd thus, they never stood to Parley, but fell on Pell-mell upon the *English*, and kill'd some, and wounded a good many; they having recourse to their Whips, as the best of their Weapons: And as they observ'd no Order, they perplex'd the Enemy so sorely, with Lashing 'em in the Eyes; and the Women and Children, seeing their Husbands so treated, being of fearful Cowardly Dispositions, and hearing the *English* cry out, *Yield and Live, Yield and be Pardon'd*; they all run in amongst their Husbands and Fathers, and hung about 'em, crying out, *Yield, yield; and leave* Caesar *to their Revenge*; that by degrees the Slaves abandon'd *Caesar*, and left him only *Tuscan* and his Heroick *Imoinda*; who, grown big as she was, did nevertheless press near her Lord, having a Bow, and a Quiver full of poyson'd Arrows, which she manag'd with such dexterity, that she wounded several, and shot the *Governor* into the Shoulder; of which Wound he had like to have Dy'd, but that an *Indian* Woman, his Mistress, suck'd the Wound, and cleans'd it from the Venom: But however, he stir'd not from the Place till he had Parly'd with *Caesar*, who he found was resolv'd to dye Fighting, and wou'd not be Taken; no more wou'd *Tuscan*, or *Imoinda*. But he, more thirsting after Revenge of another sort, than that of depriving him of Life, now made use of all his Art of talking, and dissembling; and besought *Caesar* to yield himself upon Terms, which he himself should propose, and should be Sacredly assented to and kept by him: He told him, It was not that he any longer fear'd him, or cou'd believe the force of Two Men, and a young Heroine, cou'd overcome all them, with all

6. Cheated.
7. William Byam, a Royalist exile from En- gland and Barbados.
8. Swords with hilt guards.

the Slaves now on their side also; but it was the vast Esteem he had for his Person; the desire he had to serve so Gallant a Man; and to hinder himself from the Reproach hereafter, of having been the occasion of the Death of a *Prince*, whose Valour and Magnanimity deserv'd the Empire of the World. He protested to him, he look'd upon this Action, as Gallant and Brave; however tending to the prejudice of his Lord and Master, who wou'd by it have lost so considerable a number of *Slaves*; that this Flight of his shou'd be look'd on as a heat of Youth, and rashness of a too forward Courage, and an unconsider'd impatience of Liberty, and no more; and that he labour'd in vain to accomplish that which they wou'd effectually perform, as soon as any Ship arriv'd that wou'd touch on his Coast. *So that if you will be pleas'd*, continued he, *to surrender your self, all imaginable Respect shall be paid you; and your Self, your Wife, and Child, if it be here born, shall depart free out of our Land*. But *Caesar* wou'd hear of no Composition,[9] though *Byam* urg'd, If he pursu'd, and went on in his Design, he wou'd inevitably Perish, either by great *Snakes*, wild Beasts, or Hunger; and he ought to have regard to his Wife, whose Condition required ease, and not the fatigues of tedious Travel; where she cou'd not be secur'd from being devoured. But *Caesar* told him, there was no Faith in the White Men, or the Gods they Ador'd; who instructed 'em in Principles so false, that honest Men cou'd not live amongst 'em; though no People profess'd so much, none perform'd so little; that he knew what he had to do, when he dealt with Men of Honour; but with them a Man ought to be eternally on his Guard, and never to Eat and Drink with *Christians* without his Weapon of Defence in his Hand; and, for his own Security, never to credit one Word they spoke. As for the rashness and inconsiderateness of his Action he wou'd confess the Governor is in the right; and that he was asham'd of what he had done, in endeavoring to make those Free, who were by Nature *Slaves*, poor wretched Rogues, fit to be us'd as *Christians* Tools; Dogs, treacherous and cowardly, fit for such Masters; and they wanted only but to be whipt into the knowledge of the *Christian Gods* to be the vilest of all creeping things; to learn to Worship such Deities as had not Power to make 'em Just, Brave, or Honest. In fine, after a thousand things of this Nature, not fit here to be recited, he told *Byam*, he had rather Dye than Live upon the same Earth with such Dogs. But *Trefry* and *Byam* pleaded and protested together so much, that *Trefry* believing the *Governor* to mean what he said; and speaking very cordially himself, generously put himself into *Caesar*'s Hands, and took him aside, and perswaded him, even with Tears, to Live, by Surrendring himself, and to name his Conditions. *Caesar* was overcome by his Wit and Reasons, and in consideration of *Imoinda*; and demanding what he desir'd, and that it shou'd be ratify'd by their Hands in Writing, because he had perceiv'd that was the common way of contract between Man and Man, amongst the Whites: All this was perform'd, and *Tuscan*'s Pardon was put in, and they Surrender to the Governor, who walked peaceably down into the *Plantation* with 'em, after giving order to bury their dead. *Caesar* was very much toyl'd with the bustle of the Day; for he had fought like a Fury, and what Mischief was done he and *Tuscan* perform'd alone; and gave their Enemies a fatal Proof that they durst do any thing, and fear'd no mortal Force.

9. Settlement.

But they were no sooner arriv'd at the Place, where all the Slaves receive their Punishments of Whipping, but they laid Hands on *Caesar* and *Tuscan*, faint with heat and toyl; and, surprising them, Bound them to two several Stakes, and Whipt them in a most deplorable and inhumane Manner, rending the very Flesh from their Bones; especially *Caesar*, who was not perceiv'd to make any Moan, or to alter his Face, only to roul his Eyes on the Faithless *Governor*, and those he believ'd Guilty, with Fierceness and Indignation; and, to compleat his Rage, he saw every one of those *Slaves*, who, but a few Days before, Ador'd him as something more than Mortal, now had a Whip to give him some Lashes, while he strove not to break his Fetters; though, if he had, it were impossible: But he pronounced a Woe and Revenge from his Eyes, that darted Fire, that 'twas at once both Awful and Terrible to behold.

When they thought they were sufficiently Reveng'd on him, they unty'd him, almost Fainting, with loss of Blood, from a thousand Wounds all over his Body; from which they had rent his Cloaths, and led him Bleeding and Naked as he was; and loaded him all over with Irons; and then rubbed his Wounds, to compleat their Cruelty, with *Indian Pepper*, which had like to have made him raving Mad; and, in this Condition, made him so fast to the Ground that he cou'd not stir, if his Pains and Wounds wou'd have given him leave. They spar'd *Imoinda*, and did not let her see this Barbarity committed towards her Lord, but carry'd her down to *Parham*, and shut her up; which was not in kindness to her, but for fear she shou'd Dye with the Sight, or Miscarry; and then they shou'd lose a young *Slave*, and perhaps the Mother.

You must know, that when the News was brought on Monday Morning, that *Caesar* had betaken himself to the Woods, and carry'd with him all the *Negroes*, we were possess'd with extream Fear, which no perswasions cou'd Dissipate, that he wou'd secure himself till Night; and then, that he wou'd come down and Cut all our Throats. This apprehension made all the Females of us fly down the River, to be secur'd; and while we were away, they acted this Cruelty: For I suppose I had Authority and Interest enough there, had I suspected any such thing, to have prevented it; but we had not gone many Leagues, but the News overtook us that *Caesar* was taken, and Whipt like a common *Slave*. We met on the River with Colonel *Martin*, a Man of great Gallantry, Wit, and Goodness, and whom I have celebrated in a Character of my New *Comedy*,[1] by his own Name, in memory of so brave a Man: He was Wise and Eloquent; and, from the fineness of his Parts, bore a great Sway over the Hearts of all the *Colony*: He was a Friend to *Caesar*, and resented this false Dealing with him very much. We carried him back to *Parham*, thinking to have made an Accommodation; when we came, the First News we heard was, that the *Governor* was Dead of a Wound *Imoinda* had given him; but it was not so well; But it seems he wou'd have the Pleasure of beholding the Revenge he took on *Caesar*; and before the cruel Ceremony was finish'd, he drop'd down; and then they perceiv'd the Wound he had on his Shoulder, was by a venom'd Arrow; which, as I said, his *Indian* Mistress heal'd, by Sucking the Wound.

We were no sooner Arriv'd, but we went up to the *Plantation* to see *Caesar*, whom we found in a very Miserable and Unexpressable Condition; and I have

---

1. Behn's *The Younger Brother, or The Amorous Jilt*, produced in 1696.

a Thousand times admired how he liv'd, in so much tormenting Pain. We said all things to him, that Trouble, Pitty, and Good Nature cou'd suggest; Protesting our Innocency of the Fact, and our Abhorance of such Cruelties; making a Thousand Professions of Services to him, and Begging as many Pardons for the Offenders, till we said so much, that he believ'd we had no Hand in his ill Treatment; but told us, he cou'd never Pardon *Byam*; as for *Trefry*, he confess'd he saw his Grief and Sorrow, for his Suffering, which he cou'd not hinder, but was like to have been beaten down by the very *Slaves*, for Speaking in his Defence: But for *Byam*, who was their Leader, their Head;——and shou'd, by his Justice, and Honor, have been an Example to 'em,——For him, he wish'd to Live, to take a dire Revenge of him, and said, *It had been well for him, if he had Sacrific'd me, instead of giving me the contemptable Whip*. He refus'd to Talk much, but Begging us to give him our Hands, he took 'em, and Protested never to lift up his, to do us any Harm. He had a great Respect for Colonel *Martin*, and always took his Counsel, like that of a Parent; and assur'd him, he wou'd obey him in any thing, but his Revenge on *Byam*. *Therefore*, said he, *for his own Safety, let him speedily dispatch me; for if I cou'd dispatch my self, I wou'd not, till that Justice were done to my injur'd Person, and the contempt of a Souldier: No, I wou'd not kill my self, even after a Whipping, but will be content to live with that Infamy, and be pointed at by every grinning Slave, till I have compleated my Revenge; and then you shall see that* Oroonoko *scoms to live with the Indignity that was put on* Caesar. All we cou'd do cou'd get no more Words from him; and we took care to have him put immediately into a healing Bath, to rid him of his Pepper; and order'd a Chirurgeon to anoint him with healing Balm, which he suffer'd, and in some time he began to be able to Walk and Eat; we fail'd not to visit him every Day, and, to that end, had him brought to an apartment at *Parham*.

The *Governor* was no sooner recover'd, and had heard of the menaces of *Caesar*, but he call'd his Council; who (not to disgrace them, or Burlesque the Government there) consisted of such notorious Villains as *Newgate*[2] never transported; and possibly originally were such, who understood neither the Laws of *God* or *Man*; and had no sort of Principles to make 'em worthy the Name of Men: But, at the very Council Table, wou'd Contradict and Fight with one another; and Swear so bloodily that 'twas terrible to hear, and see 'em. (Some of 'em were afterwards Hang'd, when the *Dutch* took possession of the place; others sent off in Chains.) But calling these special Rulers of the Nation together, and requiring their Counsel in this weighty Affair, they all concluded, that (Damn 'em) it might be their own Cases; and that *Caesar* ought to be made an Example to all the *Negroes*, to fright 'em from daring to threaten their Betters, their Lords and Masters; and, at this rate, no Man was safe from his own *Slaves*; and concluded, *nemine contradicente*,[3] that *Caesar* shou'd be Hang'd.

Trefry then thought it time to use his Authority; and told *Byam* his Command did not extend to his Lord's *Plantation*; and that *Parham* was as much exempt from the Law as *White-hall*,[4] and that they ought no more to touch the Servants of the Lord——— (who there represented the King's Person) than they cou'd

---

2. The main prison in London, from where criminals were transported to the colonies.
3. With no one disagreeing (Latin).

4. The king's palace in London. Trefry is Willoughby's deputy in Parham, Byam in the colony.

those about the King himself; and that *Parham* was a Sanctuary; and though his Lord were absent in Person, his Power was still in Being there; which he had intrusted with him, as far as the Dominions of his particular *Plantations* reach'd, and all that belong'd to it; the rest of the *Country*, as *Byam* was Lieutenant to his Lord, he might exercise his Tyrany upon. *Trefry* had others as powerful, or more, that int'rested themselves in *Caesar's* Life, and absolutely said, He shou'd be Defended. So turning the *Governor*, and his wise Council, out of Doors, (for they sate at *Parham-house*) they set a Guard upon our Landing Place, and wou'd admit none but those we call'd Friends to us and *Caesar*.

The *Governor* having remain'd wounded at *Parham*, till his recovery was compleated, *Caesar* did not know but he was still there; and indeed, for the most part, his time was spent there; for he was one that lov'd to Live at other Peoples Expence; and if he were a Day absent, he was Ten present there; and us'd to Play, and Walk, and Hunt, and Fish, with *Caesar*. So that *Caesar* did not at all doubt, if he once recover'd Strength, but he shou'd find an opportunity of being Reveng'd on him: Though, after such a Revenge, he cou'd not hope to Live; for if he escap'd the Fury of the English *Mobile*,[5] who perhaps wou'd have been glad of the occasion to have kill'd him, he was resolv'd not to survive his Whipping; yet he had, some tender Hours, a repenting Softness, which he called his fits of Coward; wherein he struggl'd with Love for the Victory of his Heart, which took part with his charming *Imoinda* there; but, for the most part, his time was past in melancholy Thought, and black Designs; he consider'd, if he shou'd do this Deed, and Dye, either in the Attempt, or after it, he left his lovely *Imoinda* a Prey, or at best a *Slave*, to the inrag'd Multitude; his great Heart cou'd not indure that Thought. *Perhaps*, said he, *she may be first Ravished by every Brute; exposed first to their nasty Lusts, and then a shameful Death*. No; he could not Live a Moment under that Apprehension, too insupportable to be born. These were his Thoughts, and his silent Arguments with his Heart, as he told us afterwards; so that now resolving not only to kill *Byam*, but all those he thought had inrag'd him; pleasing his great Heart with the fancy'd Slaughter he shou'd make over the whole Face of the *Plantation*; he first resolv'd on a Deed, that (however Horrid it at first appear'd to us all) when we had heard his Reasons, we thought it Brave and Just: Being able to Walk, and, as he believ'd, fit for the Execution of his great Design, he beg'd *Trefry* to trust him into the Air, believing a Walk wou'd do him good; which was granted him, and taking *Imoinda* with him, as he us'd to do in his more happy and calmer Days, he led her up into a Wood, where, after (with a thousand Sighs, and long Gazing silently on her Face, while Tears gusht, in spite of him, from his Eyes) he told her his Design first of Killing her, and then his Enemies, and next himself, and the impossibility of Escaping, and therefore he told her the necessity of Dying; he found the Heroick Wife faster pleading for Death than he was to propose it, when she found his fix'd Resolution; and, on her Knees, besought him, not to leave her a Prey to his Enemies. He (griev'd to Death) yet pleased at her noble Resolution, took her up, and imbracing her, with all the Passion and Languishment of a dying Lover, drew his Knife to kill this Treasure of his Soul, this Pleasure of his Eyes; while Tears trickl'd down his Cheeks, hers were Smiling with Joy she shou'd dye by so noble a Hand, and be

5. Mob.

sent in her own Country, (for that's their Notion of the next World) by him she so tenderly Lov'd, and so truly Ador'd in this; for Wives have a respect for their Husbands equal to what any other People pay a Deity; and when a Man finds any occasion to quit his Wife, if he love her, she dyes by his Hand; if not, he sells her, or suffers some other to kill her. It being thus, you may believe the Deed was soon resolv'd on; and 'tis not to be doubted, but the Parting, the eternal Leave taking of Two such Lovers, so greatly Born, so Sensible,[6] so Beautiful, so Young, and so Fond, must be very Moving, as the Relation of it was to me afterwards.

All that Love cou'd say in such cases, being ended; and all the intermitting Irresolutions being adjusted, the Lovely, Young, and Ador'd Victim lays her self down, before the Sacrificer; while he, with a Hand resolv'd, and a Heart breaking within, gave the Fatal Stroke; first, cutting her Throat, and then severing her yet Smiling Face from that Delicate Body, pregnant as it was with Fruits of tend'rest Love. As soon as he had done, he laid the Body decently on Leaves and Flowers; of which he made a Bed, and conceal'd it under the same cover-lid of Nature; only her Face he left yet bare to look on: But when he found she was Dead, and past all Retrieve, never more to bless him with her Eyes, and soft Language; his Grief swell'd up to Rage; he Tore, he Rav'd, he Roar'd, like some Monster of the Wood, calling on the lov'd Name of *Imoinda*; a thousand times he turn'd the Fatal Knife that did the Deed, toward his own Heart, with a Resolution to go immediately after her; but dire Revenge, which now was a thousand times more fierce in his Soul than before, prevents him; and he wou'd cry out, No; *since I have sacrificed* Imoinda *to my Revenge, shall I lose that Glory which I have purchas'd so dear, as at the Price of the fairest, dearest, softest Creature that ever Nature made? No, no!* Then, at her Name, Grief wou'd get the ascendant of Rage, and he wou'd lye down by her side, and water her Face with showers of Tears, which never were wont to fall from those Eyes: And however bent he was on his intended Slaughter, he had not power to stir from the Sight of this dear Object, now more Belov'd, and more Ador'd than ever.

He remain'd in this deploring Condition for two Days, and never rose from the Ground where he had made his sad Sacrifice; at last, rousing from her side, and accusing himself with living too long, now *Imoinda* was dead; and that the Deaths of those barbarous Enemies were deferr'd too long, he resolv'd now to finish the great Work; but offering to rise, he found his Strength so decay'd, that he reel'd to and fro, like Boughs assail'd by contrary Winds; so that he was forced to lye down again, and try to summons all his Courage to his Aid; he found his Brains turn round, and his Eyes were dizzy; and Objects appear'd not the same to him they were wont to do; his Breath was short; and all his Limbs surprised with a Faintness he had never felt before: He had not Eat in two Days, which was one occasion of this Feebleness, but excess of Grief was the greatest; yet still he hop'd he shou'd recover Vigour to act his Design; and lay expecting it yet six Days longer; still mourning over the dead Idol of his Heart, and striving every Day to rise, but cou'd not.

In all this time you may believe we were in no little affliction for *Caesar*, and his Wife; some were of Opinion he was escap'd never to return; others thought

6. Sensitive.

some Accident had hap'ned to him: But however, we fail'd not to send out an hundred People several ways to search for him; a Party, of about forty, went that way he took; among whom was *Tuscan*, who was perfectly reconcil'd to *Byam*; they had not go very far into the Wood, but they smelt an unusual Smell, as of a dead Body; for Stinks must be very noisom that can be distinguish'd among such a quantity of Natural Sweets, as every Inch of that Land produces. So that they concluded they shou'd find him dead, or some-body that was so; they past on towards it, as Loathsom as it was, and made such a rustling among the Leaves that lye thick on the Ground, by continual Falling, that *Caesar* heard he was approach'd; and though he had, during the space of these eight Days, endeavor'd to rise, but found he wanted Strength, yet looking up, and seeing his Pursuers, he rose, and reel'd to a Neighbouring Tree, against which he fix'd his Back; and being within a dozen Yards of those that advanc'd, and saw him, he call'd out to them, and bid them approach no nearer, if they wou'd be safe: So that they stood still, and hardly believing their Eyes, that wou'd perswade them that it was *Caesar* that spoke to 'em, so much was he alter'd, they ask'd him, What he had done with his Wife? for they smelt a Stink that almost struck them dead. He, pointing to the dead Body, sighing, cry'd, *Behold her there*; they put off the Flowers that cover'd her with their Sticks, and found she was kill'd; and cry'd out, *Oh monster! that hast murther'd thy Wife*: Then asking him, Why he did so cruel a Deed? He replied, he had no leasure to answer impertinent Questions; *You may go back*, continued he, *and tell the Faithless Governor, he may thank Fortune that I am breathing my last; and that my Arm is too feeble to obey my Heart, in what it had design'd him*: But his Tongue faultering, and trembling, he cou'd scarce end what he was saying. The *English* taking Advantage by his Weakness, cry'd, *Let us take him alive by all means*: He heard 'em; and, as if he had reviv'd from a Fainting, or a Dream, he cry'd out, *No, Gentlemen, you are deceiv'd; you will find no more Caesars to be Whipt; no more find a Faith in me: Feeble as you think me, I have Strength yet left to secure me from a second Indignity*. They swore all a-new, and he only shook his Head, and beheld them with Scorn; then they cry'd out, *Who will venture on this single Man? Will no body?* They stood all silent while *Caesar* replied, *Fatal will be the Attempt to the first Adventurer; let him assure himself*, and, at that Word, held up his Knife in a menacing Posture, *Look ye, ye faith-less Crew*, said he, *'tis not Life I seek, nor am I afraid of Dying*; and, at that Word, cut a piece of Flesh from his own Throat, and threw it at 'em, *yet still I wou'd Live if I cou'd, till I had perfected my Revenge. But oh! it cannot be; I feel Life gliding from my Eyes and Heart; and, if I make not haste, I shall yet fall a Victim to the shameful Whip*. At that, he rip'd up his own Belly; and took his Bowels and pull'd 'em out, with what Strength he cou'd; while some, on their Knees imploring, besought him to hold his Hand. But when they saw him tot-tering, they cry'd out, *Will none venture on him?* A bold *English* cry'd, *Yes, if he were the Devil*; (taking Courage when he saw him almost Dead) and swearing a horrid Oath for his farewell to the World, he rush'd on; *Caesar*, with his Arm'd Hand met him so fairly, as stuck him to the Heart, and he fell Dead at his Feet. *Tuscan* seeing that, cry'd out, *I love thee, oh* Caesar; *and therefore will not let thee Dye, if possible*: And, running to him, took him in his Arms; but, at the same time, warding a Blow that *Caesar* made at his Bosom, he receiv'd it quite through his Arm; and *Caesar* having not the Strength to pluck the Knife forth, though he attempted it, *Tuscan* neither pull'd it out himself, nor suffer'd it to be pull'd out; but came down with it sticking in his Arm; and the reason he gave for it was, because the Air shou'd not get into the Wound: They put their Hands a-cross, and carried *Caesar* between Six of 'em, fainted as he was; and they thought Dead, or just Dying; and they brought him to *Parham*, and laid him on a Couch, and had the Chirurgeon immediately to him, who drest his Wounds, and sew'd up his Belly, and us'd means to bring him to Life, which they effected. We ran all to see him; and, if before we thought him so beautiful a Sight, he was now so alter'd, that his Face was like a Death's Head black'd over; nothing but Teeth, and Eyeholes: For some Days we suffer'd no body to speak to him, but caused Cordials to be poured down his Throat, which sustained his Life; and in six or seven Days he recover'd his Senses: For, you must know, that Wounds are almost to a Miracle cur'd in the *Indies*; unless Wounds in the Legs, which rarely ever cure.

When he was well enough to speak, we talk'd to him; and ask'd him some Questions about his Wife, and the Reasons why he kill'd her; and he then told us what I have related of that Resolution, and of his Parting; and he besought us, we would let him Dye, and was extreamly Afflicted to think it was possible he might Live; he assur'd us, if we did not Dispatch him, he wou'd prove very Fatal to a great many. We said all we cou'd to make him Live, and gave him new Assurances; but he begg'd we wou'd not think so poorly of him, or of his love to *Imoinda*, to imagine we cou'd Flatter him to Life again; but the Chirurgeon assur'd him, he cou'd not Live, and therefore he need not Fear. We were all (but *Caesar*) afflicted at this News; and the Sight was gashly;[7] his Discourse was sad; and the earthly Smell about him so strong, that I was perswaded to leave the Place for some time (being my self but Sickly, and very apt to fall into Fits of dangerous Illness upon any extraordinary Melancholy); the Servants, and *Trefry*, and the Chirurgeons, promis'd all to take what possible care they cou'd of the Life of *Caesar*; and I, taking Boat, went with other Company to Colonel *Martin*'s, about three Days Journy down the River; but I was no sooner gon, but the *Governor* taking *Trefry*, about some pretended earnest Business, a Days Journy up the River; having communicated his Design to one *Banister*,[8] a wild *Irish* Man, and one of the Council; a Fellow of absolute Barbarity, and fit to execute any Villany, but was Rich. He came up to *Parham*, and forcibly took *Caesar*, and had him carried to the same Post where he was Whip'd; and causing him to be ty'd to it, and a great Fire made before him, he told him, he shou'd Dye like a Dog, as he was. *Caesar* replied, this was the first piece of Bravery that ever *Banister* did; and he never spoke Sense till he pronounc'd that Word; and, if he wou'd keep it, he wou'd declare, in the other World, that he was the only Man, of all the Whites, that ever he heard speak Truth. And turning to the Men that bound him, he said, *My Friends, am I to Dye, or to be Whip'd?* And they cry'd, *Whip'd! no; you shall not escape so well:* And then he replied, smiling, *A Blessing on thee*; and assur'd them, they need not tye him, for he wou'd stand fixt, like a Rock; and indure Death so as shou'd encourage them to Dye. *But if you Whip me,* said he, *be sure you tye me fast.*

7. Ghastly.
8. James Banister was the deputy governor in   1688, when Surinam was turned over to the Dutch.

He had learn'd to take Tobaco; and when he was assur'd he should Dye, he desir'd they would give him a Pipe in his Mouth, ready Lighted, which they did; and the Executioner came, and first cut off his Members[9] and threw them into the Fire; after that, with an ill-favoured Knife, they cut his Ears, and his Nose, and burn'd them; he still Smoak'd on, as if nothing had touch'd him; then they hack'd off one of his Arms, and still he bore up, and held his Pipe; but at the cutting off the other Arm, his Head sunk, and his Pipe drop'd; and he gave up the Ghost, without a Groan, or a Reproach. My Mother and Sister were by him all the while, but not suffer'd to save him; so rude and wild were the Rabble, and so inhumane were the Justices, who stood by to see the Execution, who after paid dearly enough for their Insolence. They cut *Caesar* in Quarters, and sent them to several of the chief *Plantations*: One Quarter was sent to Colonel *Martin*, who refus'd it; and swore, he had rather see the Quarters of *Banister*, and the *Governor* himself, than those of *Caesar*, on his *Plantations*; and that he cou'd govern his *Negroes* without Terrifying and Grieving them with frightful Spectacles of a mangl'd King.

Thus Dy'd this Great Man; worthy of a better Fate, and a more sublime Wit than mine to write his Praise; yet, I hope, the Reputation of my Pen is considerable enough to make his Glorious Name to survive to all Ages; with that of the Brave, the Beautiful, and the Constant *Imoinda*.

FINIS.

9. Genitals.

SOR JUANA INÉS DE LA CRUZ
1648–1695

Sor (Sister) Juana, a nun from New Spain (colonial Mexico), was one of the most famous writers of her time, celebrated as the "Tenth Muse" in Europe and the Americas. She is best known for her spirited defense of women's intellectual rights in *The Poet's Answer to the Most Illustrious Sor Filotea de la Cruz*. While ostensibly declaring her humility and her religious subordination in this text, Sor Juana also manages to advance claims for her sex that are more far-reaching and profound than any previously offered. At the same time, she paints a passionate yet nuanced picture of the life of the mind that combines rhetorical precision and intense emotion.

Born illegitimate to an upper-class creole woman and a Spanish captain, Sor Juana learned to read in her grandfather's library. Despite ongoing tensions among Spaniards, creoles, and the indigenous population, Sor Juana's Mexico was a huge metropole with a lively artistic and intellectual scene centered around the viceregal court. As a young girl, Juana served as lady-in-waiting at the court before entering the Convent of Saint Jerome when she was eighteen. Her *Answer* suggests that she became a nun in search of a safe environment in which to pursue her intellectual interests, and her religious vocation did not prevent her from writing in secular forms—lyric poetry and drama—for which she became known throughout the Spanish-speaking world. She wrote sixty-five sonnets, over sixty *romances* (ballads), and a profusion of poems in other metrical forms. She also wrote for the stage, producing everything from comedies and farces to *autos sacramentales*, religious plays that marked Catholic holidays.

Because her religious superiors rebuked her worldly interests, however, she struggled to continue writing secular literature without abandoning her faith. The natural disturbances and disasters that plagued Mexico City in the 1690s—a solar eclipse, storms, and famine—and the departure of some of her key supporters rekindled her religious passions and led her in 1694 to formally reaffirm her faith in a statement that she signed in her own blood with the words, "I, Sor Juana Inés de la Cruz, the worst of all." She died soon after, while nursing the convent sick during an epidemic.

The *Answer* stems directly from Sor Juana's venture into theological polemic. In 1690 she wrote a commentary on a sermon delivered forty years earlier, on the nature of Christ's love toward humanity. Her commentary, in the form of a letter, was published without her consent by the bishop of Puebla. The bishop provided the title, *Athenagoric Letter*, or "letter worthy of the wisdom of Athena," and also prefixed his own letter to Sor Juana, signed with the pseudonym "Filotea de la Cruz." In the letter, one "nun" advises the other to focus her attention and her talents on

religious matters. In her *Answer* (1691), Sor Juana nominally accepts the bishop's rebuke; the smooth surface of her elegant prose, however, conceals both rage and determination to assert her right—and that of other women—to a fully realized life of the mind.

The artistry of this piece of self-defense demonstrates Sor Juana's powers and thus constitutes part of her justification. While asserting her own unimportance, she illustrates the range of her knowledge and of her rhetorical skill. The sheer abundance of her biblical allusions and quotations from theological texts, for instance, proves that she has mastered a large body of religious material and that she has not sacrificed religious for secular study. Her elaborate protestations of deference, her vocabulary of insignificance, and her narrative of subservience all show the verbal dexterity that enables her to achieve her own rhetorical ends even as she denies her commitment to purely personal goals. No matter how often Sor Juana admits that her intellectual longings amount to a form of "vice," she embodies in her prose the energy and the vividness that they generate.

Her larger argument depends on her utter denial that intelligence or a thirst for knowledge should be attributed to only one gender. While she draws on history for evidence of female intellectual power, even more forceful is the testimony of her own experience: her account of how, deprived of books, she finds matter for intellectual inquiry everywhere—in the yolk of an egg, the spinning of a top, the reading of the Bible. If she arouses uneasiness when she implicitly equates herself, as object of persecution, with Christ, she also makes one feel directly the horror of women's official exclusion, in the past, from intellectual pursuits.

Sor Juana's sonnets offer a different perspective on this versatile writer. By turns playful and passionate, they often have a satiric edge that recalls the artful arguments of the *Answer*. In poem 145, she takes up the Spanish Baroque tradition of *desengaño* or disillusion, in which the poet finds behind the surface of things the emptiness and vanity of earthly existence. But instead of revealing the impermanence of a person or a building, as her models often do, Sor Juana writes about a portrait, so that her sonnet dismantles one piece of art as it makes another. Poem 164 is a passionate, intimate plea to end a lover's quarrel, reminding us of the remarkable poetic range available to this scholarly nun. In "Philosophical Satire," perhaps her most famous poem, Sor Juana methodically analyzes the contradictions in men's expectations of women, in a devastating anatomy of sexual hypocrisy that reverberates far beyond her own sophisticated milieu.

From The Poet's Answer to the Most Illustrious Sor Filotea de la Cruz[1]

Most illustrious Lady, my Lady:

It has not been my will, but my scant health and a rightful fear that have delayed my reply for so many days. Is it to be wondered that, at the very first step, I should meet with two obstacles that sent my dull pen stumbling? The first (and to me the most insuperable) is the question of how to respond to your immensely learned, prudent, devout, and loving letter. For when I consider how the Angelic Doctor, St. Thomas Aquinas, on being asked of his silence before his teacher Albertus Magnus,[2] responded that he kept quiet because he could say nothing worthy of Albertus, then how much more fitting it is that I should keep quiet—not like the Saint from modesty, but rather because, in truth, I am unable to say anything worthy of you. The second obstacle is the question of how to render my thanks for the favor, as excessive as it was unexpected, of giving my drafts and scratches to the press[3] a favor so far beyond all measure as to surpass the most ambitious hopes or the most fantastic desires, so that as a rational being I simply could not house it in my thoughts. In short, this was a favor of such magnitude that it cannot be bounded by the confines of speech and indeed exceeds all powers of gratitude, as much because it was so large as because it was so unexpected. In the words of Quintilian:[4] *"They produce less glory through hopes, more glory through benefits conferred."* And so much so, that the recipient is struck dumb.

---

1. Translated by Electa Arenal and Amanda Powell.
2. Thomas Aquinas (1225–1274), scholastic philosopher and theologian who held that faith and reason existed in harmony. The great thinker Albertus Magnus (ca. 1206?–1280) defended his student Thomas from criticisms.
3. "Sor Filotea" (from the Greek, lover of God) was the pseudonym used by Manuel Fernández de Santa Cruz, bishop of Puebla, who had published Sor Juana's commentary on a sermon without her consent.
4. Marcus Fabius Quintilianus (35–100), Roman orator and rhetorician from Hispania.

When the mother of [John] the Baptist—felicitously barren, so as to become miraculously fertile—saw under her roof so exceedingly great a guest as the Mother of the Word, her powers of mind were dulled and her speech was halted; and thus, instead of thanks, she burst out with doubts and questions: "*And whence is this to me . . . ?*" The same occurred with Saul when he was chosen and anointed[5] King of Israel: "*Am not I a son of Jemini of the least tribe of Israel, and my kindred the last among all the families of the tribe of Benjamin? Why then hast thou spoken this word to me?*"[6] Just so, I too must say: Whence, O venerable Lady, whence comes such a favor to me? By chance, am I something more than a poor nun, the slightest creature on earth and the least worthy of drawing your attention? Well, *why then hast thou spoken this word to me? And whence is this to me?*

I can answer nothing more to the first obstacle than that I am entirely unworthy of your gaze. To the second, I can offer nothing more than amazement, instead of thanks, declaring that I am unable to thank you for the slightest part of what I owe you. It is not false humility, my Lady, but the candid truth of my very soul, to say that when the printed letter reached my hands— that letter you were pleased to dub "Worthy of Athena"[7]—I burst into tears (a thing that does not come easily to me), tears of confusion. For it seemed to me that your great favor was nothing other than God's reproof aimed at my failure to return His favors, and while He corrects others with punishments, He wished to chide me through benefits. A special favor, this, for which I acknowledge myself His debtor, as I am indebted for infinitely many favors given by His immense goodness; but this is also a special way of shaming and confounding me. For it is the choicest form of punishment to cause me to serve, knowingly, as the judge who condemns and sentences my own ingratitude. And so when I consider this fully, here in solitude, it is my custom to say: Blessed are you, my Lord God, for not only did you forbear to give another creature the power to judge me, nor have you placed that power in my hands. Rather, you have kept that power for yourself and have freed me of myself and of the sentence I would pass on myself, which, forced by my own conscience, could be no less than condemnation. Instead you have reserved that sentence for your great mercy to declare, because you love me more than I can love myself.

My Lady, forgive the digression wrested from me by the power of truth; yet if I must make a full confession of it, this digression is at the same time a way of seeking evasions so as to flee the difficulty of making my answer. And therefore I had nearly resolved to leave the matter in silence; yet although silence explains much by the emphasis of leaving all unexplained, because it is a negative thing, one must name the silence, so that what it signifies may be understood. Failing that, silence will say nothing, for that is its proper function: to say nothing. The holy Chosen Vessel was carried off to the third Heaven and, having seen the arcane secrets of God, he says: "*That he was caught up into paradise, and heard secret words, which it is not granted to man to utter.*"[8] He

5. Luke 1.43.
6. I Samuel 9.21.
7. Fernández had entitled Sor Juana's commentary "Athenagoric Letter," letter worthy of Athena, after the Greek goddess of wisdom.

8. 2 Corinthians 12.4. "Chosen Vessel": in Acts 9.15, Christ describes St. Paul as his "chosen vessel" to carry his message to the Gentiles.

does not say what he saw, but he says that he cannot say it. In this way, of those things that cannot be spoken, it must be said that they cannot be spoken, so that it may be known that silence is kept not for lack of things to say, but because the many things there are to say cannot be contained in mere words. St. John says that if he were to write all of the wonders wrought by Our Redeemer, the whole world could not contain all the books.[9] Vieira says of this passage that in this one phrase the Evangelist says more than in all his other writings; and indeed how well the Lusitanian Phoenix[1] speaks (but when is he not well-spoken, even when he speaks ill?), for herein St. John says all that he failed to say and expresses all that he failed to express. And so I, my Lady, shall answer only that I know not how to answer; I shall thank you only by saying that I know not how to give thanks; and I shall say, by way of the brief label placed on what I leave to silence, that only with the confidence of one so favored and with the advantages granted one so honored, do I dare speak to your magnificence. If this be folly, please forgive it; for folly sparkles in good fortune's crown, and through it I shall supply further occasion for your good-will, and you shall better arrange the expression of my gratitude.

Moses, because he was a stutterer,[2] thought himself unworthy to speak to Pharaoh. Yet later, finding himself greatly favored by God, he was so imbued with courage that not only did he speak to God Himself, but he dared to ask of Him the impossible: "*Shew me thy face.*"[3] And so it is with me, my Lady, for in view of the favor you show me, the obstacles I described at the outset no longer seem entirely insuperable. For one who had the letter printed, unbeknownst to me, who titled it and underwrote its cost, and who thus honored it (unworthy as it was of all this, on its own account and on account of its author), what will such a one not do? What not forgive? Or what fail to do or fail to forgive? Thus, sheltered by the assumption that I speak with the safe-conduct granted by your favors and with the warrant bestowed by your goodwill, and by the fact that, like a second Ahasuerus,[4] you have allowed me to kiss the top of the golden scepter of your affection as a sign that you grant me kind license to speak and to plead my case in your venerable presence, I declare that I receive in my very soul your most holy admonition to apply my study to Holy Scripture; for although it arrives in the guise of counsel, it shall have for me the weight of law. And I take no small consolation from the fact that it seems my obedience, as if at your direction, anticipated your pastoral insinuation, as may be inferred from the subject matter and arguments of that very Letter. I recognize full well that your most prudent warning touches not on the letter, but on the many writings of mine on humane matters that you have seen.[5] And thus, all that

9. John 21.25.

1. Lusitania is the Roman name for Portugal; the phoenix was a mythical bird reborn from its own ashes, used as a term of praise for writers in the period. Sor Juana was herself called the Mexican Phoenix. Antonio Vieira (1608–1697), author of the sermon that Sor Juana had criticized in her commentary, was a Jesuit Portuguese priest, diplomat, and orator who served as a missionary in Brazil.

2. In Exodus 4.10, Moses complains to God that he lacks the eloquence to approach Pharaoh.

3. Exodus 33.13.

4. King Xerxes of Persia, 486–465 B.C.E. In Esther 5.2–3, Ahasuerus holds out his scepter to his queen, Esther, and promises to grant her whatever she wishes, an opportunity that the wise queen uses to save the Jews from destruction.

5. Sor Juana had published secular poetry and drama.

I have said can do no more than offer that letter to you in recompense for the failure to apply myself which you must have inferred (and reasonably so) from my other writings. And to speak more specifically, I confess, with all the candor due to you and with the truth and frankness that are always at once natural and customary for me, that my having written little on sacred matters has sprung from no dislike, nor from lack of application, but rather from a surfeit of awe and reverence toward those sacred letters, which I know myself to be so incapable of understanding and which I am so unworthy of handling. For there always resounds in my ears the Lord's warning and prohibition to sinners like me, bringing with it no small terror: *"Why does thou declare my justices, and take my convenant in thy mouth?"*[6] With this question comes the reflection that even learned men were forbidden to read the Song of Songs, and indeed Genesis[7] before they reached the age of thirty: the latter text because of its difficulty, and the former so that with the sweetness of those epithalamiums, imprudent youth might not be stirred to carnal feelings. My great father St. Jerome confirms this, ordering the Song of Songs to be the last text studied, for the same reason: *"Then at last she may safely read the Song of Songs: if she were to read it at the beginning, she might be harmed by not perceiving that it was the song of a spiritual bridal expressed in fleshly language."*[8] And Seneca[9] says, *"In early years, faith is not yet manifest."* Then how should I dare take these up in my unworthy hands, when sex, and age, and above all our customs oppose it? And thus I confess that often this very fear has snatched the pen from my hand and has made the subject matter retreat back toward that intellect from which it wished to flow; an impediment I did not stumble across with profane subjects, for a heresy against art is not punished by the Holy Office[1] but rather by wits with their laughter and critics with their censure. And this, *"just or unjust, is not to be feared,"* for one is still permitted to take Communion and hear Mass, so that it troubles me little if at all. For in such matters, according to the judgment of the very ones who slander me, I have no obligation to know how nor the skill to hit the mark, and thus if I miss it is neither sin nor discredit. No sin, because I had no obligation; no discredit, because I had no possibility of hitting the mark, and *"no one is obliged to do the impossible."* And truth to tell, I have never written save when pressed and forced and solely to give pleasure to others, not only without taking satisfaction but with downright aversion, because I have never judged myself to possess the rich trove of learning and wit that is perforce the obligation of one who writes. This, then, is my usual reply to those who urge me to write, and the more so in the case of a sacred subject: What understanding do I possess, what studies, what subject matter, or what instruction, save four profundities of a superficial scholar? They can leave such things to those who understand them; as for me,

---

6. Psalms 50.16.
7. First book of the Old Testament. "Song of Songs": Old Testament praise poem, uses erotic imagery.
8. St. Jerome (ca. 342–420), ascetic and scholar, learned Church Father, and founder of the Jeronymite order. He wrote this advice for the education of the Roman girl Paula, who would eventually collaborate with Jerome

and become a saint in her own right. Sor Juana's convent, St. Paula's of the Order of St. Jerome, was named after both figures.
9. Roman playwright, philosopher, and orator (ca. 3 B.C.E.–63 C.E.).
1. The Holy Office of the Inquisition, founded by the papacy in the 13th century to root out heresy and suppress challenges to religious orthodoxy.

I want no trouble with the Holy Office, for I am but ignorant and tremble lest I utter some ill-sounding proposition or twist the true meaning of some passage. I do not study in order to write, nor far less in order to teach (which would be boundless arrogance in me), but simply to see whether by studying I may become less ignorant. This is my answer, and these are my feelings.

My writing has never proceeded from any dictate of my own, but a force beyond me; I can in truth say, "*You have compelled me.*"[2] One thing, however, is true, so that I shall not deny it (first because it is already well known to all, and second because God has shown me His favor in giving me the greatest possible love of truth, even when it might count against me). For ever since the light of reason first dawned in me, my inclination to letters was marked by such passion and vehemence that neither the reprimands of others (for I have received many) nor reflections of my own (there have been more than a few) have sufficed to make me abandon my pursuit of this native impulse that God Himself bestowed on me. His Majesty knows why and to what end He did so, and He knows that I have prayed that He snuff out the light of my intellect, leaving only enough to keep His Law. For more than that is too much, some would say, in a woman; and there are even those who say that it is harmful. His Majesty knows too that, not achieving this, I have attempted to entomb my intellect together with my name and to sacrifice it to the One who gave it to me; and that no other motive brought me to the life of religion, despite the fact that the exercises and companionship of a community were quite opposed to the tranquillity and freedom from disturbance required by my studious bent. And once in the community, the Lord knows—and in this world only he who needs must know it, does[3]—what I did to try to conceal my name and renown from the public; he did not, however, allow me to do this, telling me it was temptation, and so it would have been. If I could repay any part of my debt to you, my Lady, I believe I might do so merely by informing you of this, for these words have never left my mouth save to that one to whom they must be said. But having thrown wide the doors of my heart and revealed to you what is there under seal of secrecy, I want you to know that this confidence does not gainsay the respect I owe to your venerable person and excessive favors.

To go on with the narration of this inclination of mine, of which I wish to give you a full account: I declare I was not yet three years old when my mother sent off one of my sisters, older than I, to learn to read in one of those girls' schools that they call *Amigas*.[4] Affection and mischief carried me after her; and when I saw that they were giving her lessons, I so caught fire with the desire to learn that, deceiving the teacher (or so I thought), I told her that my mother wanted her to teach me also. She did not believe this, for it was not to be believed; but to humor my whim she gave me lessons. I continued to go and she continued to teach me, though no longer in make-believe, for the experience undeceived her. I learned to read in such a short time that I already knew how by the time my mother heard of it. My teacher had kept it from my mother to give delight with a thing all done and to receive a prize for a thing done well. And I had kept still, thinking I would be whipped for having done this without

---

2. 1 Corinthians 12.11.
3. Presumably her confessor, Father Antonio Núñez.

4. Informal schools set up by cultured women in their homes to teach girls.

permission. The woman who taught me (may God keep her) is still living, and she can vouch for what I say.

I remember that in those days, though I was as greedy for treats as children usually are at that age, I would abstain from eating cheese, because I heard tell that it made people stupid, and the desire to learn was stronger for me than the desire to eat—powerful as this is in children. Later, when I was six or seven years old and already knew how to read and write, along with all the other skills like embroidery and sewing that women learn, I heard that in Mexico City there were a University and Schools where they studied the sciences. As soon as I heard this I began to slay my poor mother with insistent and annoying pleas, begging her to dress me in men's clothes and send me to the capital, to the home of some relatives she had there, so that I could enter the University and study. She refused, and was right in doing so; but I quenched my desire by reading a great variety of books that belonged to my grandfather, and neither punishments nor scoldings could prevent me. And so when I did go to Mexico City, people marveled not so much at my intelligence as at my memory and the facts I knew at an age when it seemed I had scarcely had time to learn to speak.

I began to study Latin, in which I believe I took fewer than twenty lessons. And my interest was so intense, that although in women (and especially in the very bloom of youth) the natural adornment of the hair is so esteemed, I would cut off four to six fingerlengths of my hair, measuring how long it had been before. And I made myself a rule that if by the time it had grown back to the same length I did not know such and such a thing that I intended to study, then I would cut my hair off again to punish my dull-wittedness. And so my hair grew, but I did not yet know what I had resolved to learn, for it grew quickly and I learned slowly. Then I cut my hair right off to punish my dull-wittedness, for I did not think it reasonable that hair should cover a head that was so bare of facts—the more desirable adornment. I took the veil because, although I knew I would find in religious life many things that would be quite opposed to my character (I speak of accessory rather than essential matters), it would, given my absolute unwillingness to enter into marriage, be the least unfitting and the most decent state I could choose, with regard to the assurance I desired of my salvation. For before this first concern (which is, at the last, the most important), all the impertinent little follies of my character gave way and bowed to the yoke. These were wanting to live alone and not wanting to have either obligations that would disturb my freedom to study or the noise of a community that would interrupt the tranquil silence of my books. These things made me waver somewhat in my decision until, being enlightened by learned people as to my temptation, I vanquished it with divine favor and took the state I so unworthily hold. I thought I was fleeing myself, but—woe is me!—I brought myself with me, and brought my greatest enemy in my inclination to study, which I know not whether to take as a Heaven-sent favor or as a punishment. For when snuffed out or hindered with every [spiritual] exercise known to Religion, it exploded like gunpowder; and in my case the saying "*privation gives rise to appetite*" was proven true.

I went back (no, I spoke incorrectly, for I never stopped)—I went on, I mean, with my studious task (which to me was peace and rest in every moment left over when my duties were done) of reading and still more reading, study and still more study, with no teacher besides my books themselves. What a hardship it is to learn from those lifeless letters, deprived of the sound of a teacher's voice and explanations; yet I suffered all these trials most gladly for the love of learning. Oh, if only this had been done for the love of God, as was rightful, think what I should have merited! Nevertheless I did my best to elevate these studies and direct them to His service, for the goal to which I aspired was the study of Theology. Being a Catholic, I thought it an abject failing not to know everything that can in this life be achieved, through earthly methods, concerning the divine mysteries. And being a nun and not a laywoman, I thought I should, because I was in religious life, profess the study of letters—the more so as the daughter of such as St. Jerome and St. Paula: for it would be a degeneracy for an idiot daughter to proceed from such learned parents. I argued in this way to myself, and I thought my own argument quite reasonable. However, the fact may have been (and this seems most likely) that I was merely flattering and encouraging my own inclination, by arguing that its own pleasure was an obligation.

I went on in this way, always directing each step of my studies, as I have said, toward the summit of Holy Theology; but it seemed to me necessary to ascend by the ladder of the humane arts and sciences in order to reach it; for who could fathom the style of the Queen of Sciences without knowing that of her handmaidens? Without Logic, how should I know the general and specific methods by which Holy Scripture is written? Without Rhetoric, how should I understand its figures, tropes, and locutions? Or how, without Physics or Natural Science, understand all the questions that naturally arise concerning the varied natures of those animals offered in sacrifice, in which a great many things already made manifest are symbolized, and many more besides? How should I know whether Saul's cure at the sound of David's harp was owing to a virtue and power that is natural in Music or owing, instead, to a supernatural power that God saw fit to bestow on David?[5] How without Arithmetic might one understand all those mysterious reckonings of years and days and months and hours and weeks that are found in Daniel[6] and elsewhere, which can be comprehended only by knowing the natures, concordances, and properties of numbers? Without Geometry, how could we take the measure of the Holy Ark of the Covenant or the Holy City of Jerusalem, each of whose mysterious measurements forms a perfect cube uniting their dimensions, and each displaying that most marvelous distribution of the proportions of every part?

Without the science of Architecture, how understand the mighty Temple of Solomon—where God Himself was the Draftsman who set forth His arrangement and plan, and the Wise King was but the overseer who carried it out; where there was no foundation without its mystery, nor column without its symbol, nor cornice without its allusion, nor architrave without its meaning, and likewise for every other part, so that even the very least fillet served not only for the support and enhancement of Art, but to symbolize greater things? How, without a thorough knowledge of the order and divisions by which History is composed, is one to understand the Historical Books[7]—as in those summaries, for example, which often postpone in the narration what happened

5. 1 Samuel 16.23.
6. The book of Daniel includes the numerical interpretation of complex visions (Daniel 9.21–27).
7. The sections of the Old Testament that recount history rather than law or prophecies.

first in fact? How, without command of the two branches of Law, should one understand the Books of Law?[8] Without considerable erudition, how should we understand the great many matters of profane history that are mentioned by Holy Scripture: all the diverse customs of the Gentiles, all their rituals, all their manners of speech? Without knowing many precepts and reading widely in the Fathers of the Church, how could one understand the obscure sayings of the Prophets? Well then, and without being expert in Music, how might one understand those musical intervals and their perfections that occur in a great many passages—especially in Abraham's petitions to God on behalf of the Cities,[9] beseeching God to spare them if there were found fifty righteous people within? And the number fifty Abraham reduced to forty-five, which is sesquinonal [10 to 9] or like the interval from mi to re; this in turn he reduced to forty, which is the sesquioctave [9 to 8] or like the interval from re to mi; thence he went down to thirty, which is sesquitertia, or the interval of the diatessaron [the perfect fourth]; thence to twenty, the sesquialtera or the diapente [the fifth]; thence to ten, the duple, which is the diapason [the interval and consonance of the octave]; and because there are no more harmonic intervals, Abraham went no further. How could all this be understood without knowledge of music?[1] Why, in the very Book of Job, God says to him: *Shalt thou be able to join together the shining stars the Pleiades, or canst thou stop the turning about of Arcturus? Canst thou bring forth the day star in its time, and make the evening star to rise upon the children of the earth?*[2] Without knowledge of Astronomy, these terms would be impossible to understand. Nor are these noble sciences alone represented; indeed, not one of the mechanical arts escapes mention. In sum, we see how this Book contains all books, and this Science[3] includes all sciences, all of which serve that She may be understood. And once each science is mastered (which we see is not easy, or even possible), She demands still another condition beyond all I have yet said, which is continual prayer and purity of life, to entreat God for that cleansing of the spirit and illumination of the mind required for an understanding of such high things. And if this be lacking, all the rest is useless.

The Church says these words of the Angelic Doctor, St. Thomas Aquinas: "*At the difficult passages of Holy Scripture, he added fasting to prayer. And he used to say to his companion Brother Reginald that he owed all his knowledge not so much to study or hard work, but rather he had received it from God.*" How then should I, so far from either virtue or learning, find the courage to write? And so, to acquire a few basic principles of knowledge, I studied constantly in a variety of subjects, having no inclination toward any one of them in particular but being drawn rather to all of them generally. Therefore, if I have studied some things more than others it has not been by my choice, but because by chance the books on certain subjects came more readily to hand, and this gave preference to those topics, without my passing judgment in the matter. I held

---

8. The sections of the Old Testament that give laws. "Two branches of law": canon and civil laws, or the codes for church and state.
9. Sodom and Gomorrah. Abraham beseeches God to save Sodom from destruction for the sake of its just inhabitants (Genesis 18.22–23).

1. Sor Juana refers here to the intervals of classical music theory.
2. Job 38.31–32. "Pleiades": a constellation. "Arcturus": a star in the Great Bear.
3. Theology, here feminized. "This Book": the Bible.

no particular interest to spur me, nor had I any limit to my time compelling me to reduce the continuous study of one subject, as is required in taking a degree. Thus almost at one sitting I would study diverse things or leave off some to take up others. Yet even in this I maintained a certain order, for some subjects I called my study and others my diversion, and with the latter I would take my rest from the former. Hence, I have studied many things but know nothing, for one subject has interfered with another. What I say is true regarding the practical element of those subjects that require practice, for clearly the compass must rest while the pen is moving, and while the harp is playing the organ is still, *and likewise with all things*. Much bodily repetition is needed to form a habit, and therefore a person whose time is divided among several exercises will never develop one perfectly. But in formal and speculative arts the opposite is true, and I wish I might persuade everyone with my own experience: to wit, that far from interfering, these subjects help one another, shedding light and opening a path from one to the next, by way of divergences and hidden links—for they were set in place so as to form this universal chain by the wisdom of their great Author.

* * *

I confess that I am far indeed from the terms of Knowledge and that I have wished to follow it, though *"afar off."* But all this has merely led me closer to the flames of persecution, the crucible of affliction; and to such extremes that some have even sought to prohibit me from study.

They achieved this once, with a very saintly and simple mother superior who believed that study was an affair for the Inquisition and ordered that I should not read. I obeyed her (for the three months or so that her authority over us lasted) in that I did not pick up a book. But with regard to avoiding study absolutely, as such a thing does not lie within my power, I could not do it. For although I did not study in books, I studied all the things that God created, taking them for my letters, and for my book all the intricate structures of this world. Nothing could I see without reflecting upon it, nothing could I hear without pondering it, even to the most minute, material things. For there is no creature, however lowly, in which one cannot recognize the great *"God made me"*; there is not one that does not stagger the mind if it receives due consideration. And so, I repeat, I looked and marveled at all things, so that from the very persons with whom I spoke and from what they said to me, a thousand speculations leapt to my mind: Whence could spring this diversity of character and intelligence among individuals all composing one single species? What temperaments, what hidden qualities could give rise to each? When I noticed a shape, I would set about combining the proportions of its lines and measuring it in my mind and converting it to other proportions. I sometimes walked back and forth along the forewall of one of our dormitories (which is a very large room), and I began to observe that although the lines of its two sides were parallel and the ceiling was flat, yet the eye falsely perceived these lines as though they approached each other and the ceiling as though it were lower in the distance than close by; from this I inferred that visual lines run straight, but not parallel, and that they form a pyramidal figure. And I conjectured whether this might be the reason the ancients were obliged to question whether the world is spherical or not. Because even though it seems so, this could be a delusion of the eye, displaying concavities where there were none.

This kind of observation has been continual in me and is so to this day, without my having control over it; rather, I tend to find it annoying, because it tires my head. Yet I believed this happened to everyone, as with thinking in verse, until experience taught me otherwise. This trait, whether a matter of nature or custom, is such that nothing do I see without a second thought. Two little girls were playing with a top in front of me, and no sooner had I seen the motion and shape than I began, with this madness of mine, to observe the easy movement of the spherical form and how the momentum lasted, now fixed and set free of its cause; for even far from its first cause, which was the hand of the girl, the little top went on dancing. Yet not content with this, I ordered flour to be brought and sifted on the floor, so that as the top danced over it, we could know whether its movement described perfect circles or no. I found they were not circular, but rather spiral lines that lost their circularity as the top lost its momentum. Other girls were playing at spillikins (the most frivolous of all childhood games). I drew near to observe the shapes they made, and when I saw three of the straws by chance fall in a triangle, I fell to intertwining one with another, recalling that this was said to be the very shape of Solomon's mysterious ring[4] where distantly there shone bright traces and representations of the Most Blessed Trinity, by virtue of which it worked great prodigies and marvels. And they say David's harp had the same shape, and thus was Saul cured by its sound; to this day, harps have almost the same form.

Well, and what then shall I tell you, my Lady, of the secrets of nature that I have learned while cooking? I observe that an egg becomes solid and cooks in butter or oil, and on the contrary that it dissolves in sugar syrup. Or again, to ensure that sugar flow freely one need only add the slightest bit of water that has held quince or some other sour fruit. The yolk and white of the very same egg are of such a contrary nature that when eggs are used with sugar, each part separately may be used perfectly well, yet they cannot be mixed together. I shall not weary you with such inanities, which I relate simply to give you a full account of my nature, and I believe this will make you laugh. But in truth, my Lady, what can we women know, save philosophies of the kitchen? It was well put by Lupercio Leonardo [sic][5] that one can philosophize quite well while preparing supper. I often say, when I make these little observations, "Had Aristotle[6] cooked, he would have written a great deal more." And so to go on with the mode of my cogitations: I declare that all this is so continual in me that I have no need of books. On one occasion, because of a severe stomach ailment, the doctors forbade me to study. I spent several days in that state, and then quickly proposed to them that it would be less harmful to allow me my books, for my cogitations were so strenuous and vehement that they consumed more vitality in a quarter of an hour than the reading of books could in four days. And so the doctors were compelled to let me read. What is more, my Lady, not even my sleep has been free of this ceaseless movement of my imagination. Rather, my mind operates in sleep still more freely and unobstructedly, ordering with greater clarity and ease the events it has preserved

---

4. It may, like Solomon's seal, have contained a Star of David, composed of triangles.
5. Sor Juana actually refers to his brother, Bernardo Leonardo de Argensola, Spanish poet and satirist (1562–1631).
6. Greek philosopher (384–322 B.C.E.) who studied with Plato and wrote on logic, politics, ethics, natural science, and poetics.

from the day, presenting arguments and composing verses. I could give you a very long catalogue of these, as I could of certain reasonings and subtle turns I have reached far better in my sleep than while awake; but I leave them out in order not to weary you. I have said enough for your judgment and your surpassing eminence to comprehend my nature with clarity and full understanding, together with the beginnings, the methods, and the present state of my studies.

If studies, my Lady, be merits (for indeed I see them extolled as such in men), in me they are no such thing: I study because I must. If they be a failing, I believe for the same reason that the fault is none of mine. Yet withal, I live always so wary of myself that neither in this nor in anything else do I trust my own judgment. And so I entrust the decision to your supreme skill and straightway submit to whatever sentence you may pass, posing no objection or reluctance, for this has been no more than a simple account of my inclination to letters.

I confess also that, while in truth this inclination has been such that, as I said before, I had no need of exemplars, nevertheless the many books that I have read have not failed to help me, both in sacred as well as secular letters. For there I see a Deborah[7] issuing laws, military as well as political, and governing the people among whom there were so many learned men. I see the exceedingly knowledgeable Queen of Sheba[8] so learned she dares to test the wisdom of the wisest of all wise men with riddles, without being rebuked for it; indeed, on this very account she is to become judge of the unbelievers. I see so many and such significant women: some adorned with the gift of prophecy, like an Abigail; others, of persuasion, like Esther; others, of piety, like Rahab; others, of perseverance, like Anna [Hannah] the mother of Samuel;[9] and others, infinitely more, with other kinds of qualities and virtues.

If I consider the Gentiles, the first I meet are the Sibyls,[1] chosen by God to prophesy the essential mysteries of our Faith in such learned and elegant verses that they stupefy the imagination. I see a woman such as Minerva,[2] daughter of great Jupiter and mistress of all the wisdom of Athens, adored as goddess of the sciences. I see one Polla Argentaria, who helped Lucan, her husband, to write the *Battle of Pharsalia*.[3] I see the daughter of the divine Tiresias,[4] more learned still than her father. I see, too, such a woman as Zenobia,[5] queen of the Palmyrians, as wise as she was courageous. Again, I see an Arete,[6] daughter of Aristippus, most learned. A Nicostrata,[7] inventor of Latin letters and most erudite in

7. Prophetess who judged the Israelites (Judges 4.4–14).
8. Sheba tested King Solomon with her questions (1 Kings 10.1–3).
9. Abigail saved her husband's life by prophesying for King David (1 Samuel 25.2–35). Esther persuaded King Ahasuerus to protect the Jews (Esther 5–9). The harlot Rahab protected two Israelites from the King of Jericho (Joshua 2.1–7). Anna persevered in her prayers until granted the birth of her son (1 Samuel 1.1–20).
1. Female prophets of the ancient world.

2. Roman name for Athena, goddess of wisdom.
3. Epic poem on the civil war between Caesar and Pompey.
4. A blind seer in ancient Thebes, whose daughter Manto was known for her skill in divination.
5. Matriarchal warrior queen of Palmyra (ruled 266–72 C.E.), much admired for her learning.
6. Founder of a Greek school of philosophy (4th century B.C.E.).
7. Mythical healer and teacher who adapted Greek characters into the Roman alphabet.

the Greek. An Aspasia Miletia,[8] who taught philosophy and rhetoric and was the teacher of the philosopher Pericles. An Hypatia, who taught astrology and lectured for many years in Alexandria. A Leontium, who won over the philosopher Theophrastus and proved him wrong. A Julia, a Corinna, a Cornelia;[9] and, in sum, the vast throng of women who merited titles and earned renown: now as Greeks, again as Muses, and yet again as Pythonesses.[1] For what were they all but learned women, who were considered, celebrated, and indeed venerated as such in Antiquity? Without mentioning still others, of whom the books are full; for I see the Egyptian Catherine,[2] lecturing and refuting all the learning of the most learned men of Egypt. I see a Gertrude[3] read, write, and teach. And seeking no more examples far from home, I see my own most holy mother Paula, learned in the Hebrew, Greek, and Latin tongues and most expert in the interpretation of the Scriptures. What wonder then can it be that, though her chronicler was no less than the unequaled Jerome, the Saint found himself scarcely worthy of the task, for with that lively gravity and energetic effectiveness with which only he can express himself, he says: "If all the parts of my body were tongues, they would not suffice to proclaim the learning and virtues of Paula." Blessilla, a widow, earned the same praises, as did the luminous virgin Eustochium, both of them daughters of the Saint herself [Paula][4] and indeed Eustochium was such that for her knowledge she was hailed as a World Prodigy. Fabiola,[5] also a Roman, was another most learned in Holy Scripture. Proba Falconia, a Roman woman, wrote an elegant book of centos[6] joining together verses from Virgil, on the mysteries of our holy Faith. Our Queen Isabella,[7] wife of Alfonso X, is known to have written on astrology—without mentioning others, whom I omit so as not merely to copy what others have said (which is a vice I have always detested): Well then, in our own day there thrive the great Christina Alexandra, Queen of Sweden,[8] as learned as she is brave and generous; and too those most excellent ladies, the Duchess of Aveyro and the Countess of Villaumbrosa.

* * *

My Lady, I have not wished to reply, though others have done so without my knowledge. It is enough that I have seen certain papers, among them one I send to you because it is learned, and because reading it will restore to you a portion of your time that I have wasted with what I am writing. If by your wisdom and sense, my Lady, you should be pleased for me to do other than what I propose, then as is only right, to the slightest motion of your pleasure I shall cede my own decision, which was as I have told you to keep still. For although

---

8. Reputed teacher of eloquence in ancient Athens.

9. Julia Domna (second century C.E.), wife of the Roman emperor Septimius Severus, known for her learning as Julia the Philosopher. Corinna (ca. 500? B.C.E.), a lyric poet of Tanagra who wrote for a female audience. Cornelia (2nd century B.C.E.), noted for her devotion to her children's education.

1. Seers.

2. St. Catherine of Alexandria (4th century?), allegedly so wise she could refute fifty philosophers at once.

3. St. Gertrude (d. 1302), Benedictine nun and mystic.

4. Blessilla and Eustochium, daughters of St. Paula, also taught by St. Jerome.

5. Another member of St. Jerome's circle.

6. Poems made up of verses from other authors.

7. Wife of Alfonso X of Spain (1221–1284), also known as Alfonso the Wise.

8. She attracted many scholars and writers to her court (1626–1689).

St. John Chrysostom[9] says, *"One's slanderers must be proven wrong, and one's questioners must be taught,"* I see too that St. Gregory[1] says, *"It is no less a victory to tolerate one's enemies than to defeat them,"* and that patience defeats by tolerance and triumphs by suffering. Indeed, it was the custom among the Roman Gentiles, for their captains at the very height of glory—when they entered triumphing over other nations, clothed in purple and crowned with laurel; with their carts drawn by the crowned brows of vanquished kings rather than by beasts of burden; accompanied by the spoils of the riches of all the world, before a conquering army decorated with the emblems of its feats; hearing the crowd's acclaim in such honorable titles and epithets as Fathers of the Fatherland, Pillars of the Empire, Ramparts of Rome, Refuge of the Republic, and other glorious names—it was the custom, at this supreme apex of pride and human felicity, that a common soldier should cry aloud to the conqueror, as if from his own feeling and at the order of the Senate: "Behold, how you are mortal; behold, for you have such and such a failing." Nor were the most shameful excused; as at the triumph of Caesar, when the most contemptible soldiers shouted in his ears, *"Beware, Romans, for we bring before you the bald adulterer."* All of this was done so that in the midst of great honor the conqueror might not puff up with pride, and that the ballast of these affronts might prove a counterweight to the sails of so much praise, so that the ship of sound judgment should not founder in the winds of acclaim. If, as I say, all this was done by mere Gentiles, guided only by the light of Natural Law, then for us as Catholics, who are commanded to *love* our enemies, is it any great matter for us to tolerate them? For my part, I can testify that these detractions have at times been a mortification to me, but they have never done me harm. For I think that man very foolish who, having the opportunity to earn due merit, undertakes the labor and then forfeits the reward. This is like people who do not want to resign themselves to death. In the end they die all the same, with their resistance serving not to exempt them from dying, but only to deprive them of the merit of conformity to God's will, and thus to give them an evil death when it could have been blessed. And so, my Lady, I think these detractions do more good than harm. I maintain that a greater risk to human frailty is worked by praise, which usually seizes what does not belong to it, so that one must proceed with great care and have inscribed in one's heart these words of the Apostle: *"Or what hast thou that thou hast not received? And if thou hast received, why dost thou glory, as if thou hadst not received it?"*[2] For these words should serve as a shield to deflect the prongs of praises, which are spears that, when not attributed to God to whom they belong, take our very lives and make us thieves of God's honor and usurpers of the talents that He bestowed on us, and of the gifts He lent us, for which we must one day render Him a most detailed account. And so, good Lady, I fear applause far more than slander. For the slander, with just one simple act of patience, is turned to a benefit, whereas praise requires many acts of reflection and humility and self-knowledge if it is not to cause harm. And so, for myself I know and own that this knowledge is a

---

9. Syrian prelate (ca. 347–407), known as a great orator.
1. Gregory the Great (ca. 540–604), pope

from 590.
2. Corinthians 11.4.

special favor from God, enabling me to conduct myself in the face of one as in the other, following that dictum of St. Augustine.[3] *One must believe neither the friend who speaks praises nor the enemy who reviles.*" Although I am such a one as most times must either let the opportunity go to waste, or mix it with such failings and flaws that I spoil what left to itself would have been good. And so, with the few things of mine that have been printed, the appearance of my name—and, indeed, permission for the printing itself—have not followed my own decision, but another's liberty that does not lie under my control, as was the case with the "Letter Worthy of Athena." So you see, only some little *Exercises for the Annunciation* and certain *Offerings for the Sorrows* were printed at my pleasure for the prayers of the public, but my name did not appear. I submit to you a few copies of the same, so that you may distribute them (if you think it seemly) among our sisters the nuns of your blessed community and others in this City. Only one copy remains of the *Sorrows*, because they have all been given away and I could find no more. I made them only for the prayers of my sisters, many years ago, and then they became more widely known. Their subjects are as disproportionate to my lukewarm ability as to my ignorance, and I was helped in writing them only by the fact that they dealt with matters of our great Queen; I know not why it is that in speaking of the Most Blessed Mary, the most icy heart is set aflame. It would please me greatly, my venerable Lady, to send you works worthy of your virtue and wisdom, but as the Poet[4] remarked:

> *Even when strength is lacking, still the intention must be praised.*
> *I surmise the gods would be content with that.*

If ever I write any more little trifles, they shall always seek haven at your feet and the safety of your correction, for I have no other jewel with which to repay you. And in the opinion of Seneca, he who has once commenced to confer benefits becomes obliged to continue them. Thus you must be repaid by your own generosity, for only in that way can I be honorably cleared of my debt to you, lest another statement, again Seneca's, be leveled against me: "*It is shameful to be outdone in acts of kindness.*" For it is magnanimous for the generous creditor to grant a poor debtor some means of satisfying the debt. Thus God behaved toward the world, which could not possibly repay Him: He gave His own Son, that He might offer Himself as a worthy amends.

If the style of this letter, my venerable Lady, has been less than your due, I beg your pardon for its household familiarity or the lack of seemly respect. For in addressing you, my sister, as a nun of the veil, I have forgotten the distance between myself and your most distinguished person, which should not occur were I to see you unveiled. But you, with your prudence and benevolence, will substitute or emend my terms; and if you think unsuitable the familiar terms of address I have employed—because it seems to me that given all the reverence I owe you, "Your Reverence" is very little reverence indeed—please alter it to whatever you think suitable. For I have not been so bold as to exceed

---

3. North African philosopher and theologian, one of the Latin Church Fathers (354–430). 4. Generally used to refer to Virgil, but this citation is from Ovid.

the limits set by the style of your letter to me, nor to cross the border of your modesty.

And hold me in your own good grace, so as to entreat divine grace on my behalf; of the same, may the Lord grant you great increase, and may He keep you, as I beg of Him and as I am needful. Written at the Convent of our Father St. Jerome in Mexico City, this first day of March of the year 1691. Receive the embrace of your most greatly favored,

Sor Juana Inés de la Cruz

Poem 145

[*She endeavors to expose the praises recorded in a portrait of the poetess by truth, which she calls passion.*]

> This object which you see—a painted snare
> exhibiting the subtleties of art
> with clever arguments of tone and hue—
> is but a cunning trap to snare your sense;
>   this object, in which flattery has tried   5
> to overlook the horrors of the years
> and, conquering the ravages of time,
> to overcome oblivion and age:
>   this is an empty artifice of care,
> a flower, fragile, set out in the wind,   10
> a letter of safe-conduct sent to Fate;
>   it is a foolish, erring diligence,
> a palsied will to please which, clearly seen,
> is a corpse, is dust, is shadow, and is gone.

Poem 164

[*In which she answers a suspicion with the eloquence of tears.*]

> This afternoon, my darling, when we spoke,
> and in your face and gestures I could see
> that I was not persuading you with words,
> I wished you might look straight into my heart;
>   and Love, who was assisting my designs,   5
> succeeded in what seemed impossible:
> for in the stream of tears which anguish loosed
> my heart itself, dissolved, dropped slowly down.
>   Enough unkindness now, my love, enough;
> don't let these tyrant jealousies torment you   10
> nor base suspicions shatter your repose
>   with foolish shadows, empty evidence:
> in liquid humor you have seen and touched
> my heart undone and passing through your hands.

Philosophical Satire

Poem 92

[The poet proves illogical both the whim and the censure of men who accuse, in women, that which they cause.]

You foolish and unreasoning men
who cast all blame on women,
not seeing you yourselves are cause
of the same faults you accuse:

if, with eagerness unequaled,   5
you plead against women's disdain,
why require them to do well
when you inspire them to fall?

You combat their firm resistance,
and then solemnly pronounce   10
that what you've won through diligence
is proof of women's flightiness.

What do we see, when we see you
madly determined to see us so,
but the child who makes a monster appear   15
and then goes trembling with fear?

With ridiculous conceit
you insist that woman be
a sultry Thais while you woo her;
a true Lucretia[1] once she's won.   20

Whose behavior could be odder
than that of a stubborn man
who himself breathes on the mirror,
and then laments it is not clear?

Women's good favor, women's scorn   25
you hold in equal disregard:
complaining, if they treat you badly;
mocking, if they love you well.

Not one can gain your good opinion,
for she who modestly withdraws   30
and fails to admit you is ungrateful;
yet if she admits you, too easily won.

---

1. A noble Roman woman (d. ca. 508 B.C.E.) who killed herself after being raped; a symbol of chastity. "Thais": a celebrated courtesan in ancient Greece.

So downright foolish are you all
that your injurious justice claims
to blame one woman's cruelty   35
and fault the other's laxity.

How then can she be moderate
to whom your suit aspires,
if, ingrate, she makes you displeased,
or, easy, prompts your ire?   40

Between such ire and such anguish
—the tales your fancy tells—
lucky is she who does not love you;
complain then, as you will!

Your doting anguish feathers the wings   45
of liberties that women take,
and once you've caused them to be bad,
you want to find them as good as saints.

But who has carried greater blame
in a passion gone astray: 50
she who falls to constant pleading,
or he who pleads with her to fall?

Or which more greatly must be faulted,
though either may commit a wrong:
she who sins for need of payment,   55
or he who pays for his enjoyment?

Why then are you so alarmed
by the fault that is your own?
Wish women to be what you make them,
or make them what you wish they were.   60

Leave off soliciting her fall
and then indeed, more justified,
that eagerness you might accuse
of the woman who besieges you.

Thus I prove with all my forces   65
the ways your arrogance does battle:
for in your offers and your demands
we have devil, flesh, and world: a man.

JONATHAN SWIFT

1667–1745

Jonathan Swift was such a thorough-going satirist that his definition of the genre was itself satirical. "Satire," he wrote, "is a sort of glass wherein beholders do generally discover everybody's face but their own; which is the chief reason for that kind reception it meets with in the world, and that so very few are offended with it." He was not wrong: his own brilliant, often bitter satirical writings were immensely popular in his own time, and have remained so for centuries, despite the fact that he pokes fun at all of us in some way or other, mocking political ambitions, religious convictions, scientific knowledge, war, power, lust, vanity, and greed. His derisive wit in fact takes in so much of the world that readers have had trouble figuring out whether he held any affirmative beliefs or values at all. But for Swift, that may not have been the point. What he said he most wanted was to "vex" his readers with an uncomfortable awareness of the follies of the world.

LIFE

Early in the seventeenth century, the English monarchy had seized great parcels of Irish land and sold them to loyal English families. These wealthy and powerful families were Protestants, and they struggled to prevent the Catholic majority from gaining power in Ireland: they officially barred Catholics from holding public office, joining the military, and teaching children. Jonathan Swift belonged to this small Protestant minority, born to English parents in 1667 in Dublin. His lawyer father died before he was born, and his mother moved to England when he was a small child. He was raised by a cold and unsympathetic uncle in Ireland, who had him educated at Trinity College in Dublin. A rebellious student, Swift was punished more than once for failing to attend religious services and carousing in the city. During a Catholic uprising in 1688, he left for England, and went to work for a powerful aristocrat and statesman named William Temple. There he made contact with influential writers and politicians, and he tutored a young girl named Esther Johnson, whom he nicknamed "Stella." He began as her teacher and mentor, but became her friend, and remained on close terms with her for the rest of his life.

In 1694, after earning his M.A. at Oxford, Swift was ordained a priest in the Protestant Church of England and was offered a position in Northern Ireland. Dissatisfied, he moved back and forth between England and Ireland, staying at the Temple household on and off for years. It was in this period that he began to develop a reputation as a witty writer, producing a comic picture of literary disputes called *The Battle of the Books* (1704) and in the same year, a clever satire of religious controversy called *The Tale of a Tub*. "What a genius I had when I composed that book!" he said later in life. He befriended **Alexander Pope** and other noted writers of the day, who together formed a club of satirists called the Scriblerians.

Swift hoped for church advancement in England, but in 1713 he was named dean of St. Patrick's Cathedral in Dublin and remained there for the rest of his life. "I reckon no man is thoroughly miserable unless he be condemned to live in Ireland," he wrote. And yet, he was to become an Irish national hero. For the rest of his life, he wrote passionately against the British government's treatment of Ireland, including his essay on economic policy called *Irish Manufacture*, later banned by the British government. "By the Laws of God, of Nature, of Nations, and of your Country," he urged Irish readers, "you are, and ought to be, as free a people as your brethren in England."

Swift's personal life in this period was both mysterious and complicated. Stella moved to Ireland, and spent a great deal of time with him. People have occasionally speculated that they were secretly married, but there is no evidence for this. Meanwhile, Swift made the acquaintance of one Esther Vanhomrigh, who fell passionately in love with him and moved to Ireland to pursue him, jealously demanding to know more about his relationship with Stella. She died shortly after Swift rejected her, some said of a broken heart.

In 1726, Swift published *Gulliver's Travels* anonymously. It sold out immediately. A friend in London wrote to tell him that the book was "the conversation of the whole town. . . . From the highest to the lowest it is universally read, from the Cabinet-council to the nursery." The next year Stella died, plunging him into misery. His last great work, the fiercely satirical *Modest Proposal*, appeared in 1729. In a touching and witty poem about his own demise called "The Death of Doctor Swift," Swift predicted madness and senility for his final years. Sadly, he guessed well. As he declined, guardians were appointed to take care of his finances and keep him from injuring himself. He died at the age of seventy-eight and was buried not far from Stella.

TIMES

Swift was a great coffee drinker, and this small fact points to a turning point in the history of English literature. In the late seventeenth century, English literary life began to shift away from its old status as a courtly culture, centered on the monarchy and its great palaces, to a more diffuse and democratic urban culture that revolved around coffeehouses. These establishments were not only places to eat and drink: one could see scientific experiments there, debate politics, attend lectures on religion, and gossip and share information. Altogether, there may have been as many as three thousand coffeehouses in London alone. Books and pamphlets were sold there, and as the reading public grew, so too did the printed matter available for reading. "Runners" appeared frequently to announce the latest news, making coffeehouses great places to catch up on what was current. In fact, they became the engine of an increasingly powerful new political force—public opinion. Thus coffeehouses helped move the weight of political authority from the old aristocracy into the hands of the urban middle class. Most coffeehouses charged a penny for those who wanted to enter, but beyond the entrance fee, there were few barriers. They therefore gathered a wide range of men (women were not expected to patronize them), including journalists, artisans, merchants, aspiring writers, and powerful politicians. Only the very poorest could not pass through the doors. And coffeehouses became the sites for new institutions. A coffeehouse in London called Jonathan's was a meeting ground for stockbrokers, which eventually became the London Stock Exchange; while Lloyd's coffeehouse was to become the most important British insurance company. Button's was the coffeehouse for the "Wits" during Swift's time, a hub where young writers struggled to make the right contacts and begin their careers.

As journalists, businesspeople, artisans, and aristocrats gathered in coffeehouses, they argued over the political affairs of their time. Governing England were two main political parties, the Whigs and the Tories. In 1688, the British Isles had deposed James II, a Catholic king, and put a new pair of Protestant rulers, William and Mary, in his place. The Whigs worried about monarchical tyranny and the return of the Catholic Church, and they favored a constitutional monarchy. The Tories believed in the divine right of kings, and feared the growing power of Parliament and the people. The two parties shared power until 1714, when the Protestant Queen Anne died. Her most immediate heir was a foreigner—he came from the German land of Hanover—and spoke no English. The Tories saw him as a break with the proper line of English kings who had been deposed in 1688, and many showed support for bringing back a Catholic king, the direct heir of James II, then in exile. The new King George suppressed this pro-Catholic uprising and expressed gratitude to his supporters by installing the Whigs in positions of power. Thus began a long period of Whig rule. Swift and his friend Alexander Pope, who were Tories, found that many of their supporters fled England or were imprisoned, and that they were on the losing side.

In this political context, satirical writing flourished. On the one hand, in an atmosphere of fierce political debate, persuasive writers were in great demand: Swift and Pope found they had great support from powerful politicians who wanted the best writers on their side. On the other hand, it could be dangerous to launch direct political challenges. After 1714, Tory writers often resorted to indirections such as innuendos and masks to avoid prosecution. And so satire seemed a perfect solution: veiled enough never to seem outright oppositional, it could still be pointed enough to hit political targets, including the king.

WORK

Gulliver's Travels and *A Modest Proposal* are two of the most famous satires in the English language. *Gulliver* is in part a parody of travel books, such as those of William Dampier (1651–1715), who published hugely popular descriptions of his three circumnavigations of the globe. Like Dampier, Gulliver seems intent on giving us precise facts: he offers exact dates and statistics and describes in copious detail the strange customs, flora, and fauna of the far-flung islands he happens to encounter. But the places where Gulliver alights carry uncanny echoes of his native England: in Lilliput, for example, he finds a people six inches tall whose pettiness and grandiose ambitions offer a recognizable commentary on political debates raging in England at the time. Opportunities for satire also emerge when Gulliver is asked to explain the customs of his own land to the inhabitants of the islands he visits. The covetousness, belligerence, and factionalism he describes at home in Britain horrify his audiences.

Gulliver typically fails to notice the ironies he generates. Swift deliberately opts for a naive narrator, allowing us to identify with him at times but also to distance ourselves from him to draw out the larger implications of his stories for ourselves. (Not all of Swift's readers got the point of this; one bishop reported "that the book was full of improbable lies, and for his part, he hardly believed a word of it.") One advantage of the gullible perspective is that it allows Swift to make his readers see themselves from an outsider's perspective: the writer thus makes ordinary life seem strange and prompts us to question what we might otherwise take for granted. More descriptive than contemplative, the language of the text is quite plain, and in fact *Gulliver's Travels* has long been read by children as well as by adults.

Gulliver makes three voyages before we reach the fourth and final book, included here. After his first journey to Lilliput, he goes to a land of giants, Brobdingnag, whose benevolent king, after hearing Gulliver's patriotic account of England, comments, "I cannot but conclude the bulk of your natives, to be the most pernicious race of odious little vermin that nature ever suffered to crawl upon the surface of the earth." In the third book, Gulliver aims at some intellectual targets: philosophers so deep in abstract thought they have to be attended by "flappers"—servants who flap them into an awareness of their immediate surroundings—and ghosts from the past who stress the lies of historians. The most terrifying group he meets are the Struldbrugs, who live forever but grow old and infirm like humans, surviving decrepit and senile into eternity.

On his fourth voyage, Gulliver finds himself on an island inhabited by Houyhnhnms—horses—and Yahoos, who are uncomfortably similar to human beings. But Swift turns the conventional distinction between humans and animals upside-down. On this island, the horses are the rational, clean, and articulate ones, and they keep the island under peaceful control, while the humans are greedy, filthy, violent, and irrational. As the Houyhnhnms ask Gulliver questions about his homeland, they are shocked by the depravity of the Yahoos of England. Gulliver offers a bitter indictment of British colonialism in this section and also comes to see his fellow Yahoos—including his own wife and children—with disgust.

Despite Gulliver's revulsion against British Yahoos, readers have long wondered whether the Houyhnhnms really are a model society, or whether there is something chilling in their cool, entirely rational resistance to close ties of affection and loyalty. In seventeenth-century England, Protestant philoso-phers had begun to put forward the notion that human beings, rather than being corrupt and fallen, were inherently rational and virtuous. This notion of a benevolent human nature gathered strength over the course of the eighteenth century. Swift, however, seems determined to keep alive the older belief in a naturally conceited, vain, greedy, lustful human nature. This sometimes made him seem misanthropic to his contemporaries. But understanding human beings as imperfect allowed him to make fun of all utopian projects and to cast his satirical eye on schemes for social improvement.

One such satire takes shape brilliantly in *A Modest Proposal*. Imitating the voice of rational social planners, who for the first time were depending on statistics and economic laws, Swift takes an extreme position and follows it to its logical conclusion. If the point of social reform is to produce solutions to social problems, maximizing profits along the way, then why not sell the infants of the poor as food for the rich? Surely this is a rational solution for the wealthy Protestant minority in England because they want to cut down on the number of Catholics in any case. Charges of cannibalism, so often used against non-European peoples, take on figurative force as Swift suggests that the English are in many ways feeding off Irish flesh.

In much of his work, Swift takes a particularly satirical look at the production of knowledge: while *Gulliver's Travels* satirizes travel narratives, with their detailed descriptions of exotic cultures, and mocks historians, clergymen, and philosophers along the way, *A Modest Proposal* explicitly relies on demographic facts and scientific rationality to come to its outrageous conclusions. These satires therefore ask us to reflect on the relationship between what we know and how we choose to act. Do facts and reason help us to make good decisions in the world? And if not, where should we turn instead? Swift leaves it up to us to develop solutions. For him, it is enough to make us confront the unsettling questions.

From Gulliver's Travels[1]

A Letter from Captain Gulliver to His Cousin Sympson

I hope you will be ready to own publicly, whenever you shall be called to it, that by your great and frequent urgency you prevailed on me to publish a very loose and uncorrect account of my travels; with direction to hire some young gentlemen of either University to put them in order, and correct the style, as my Cousin Dampier[2] did by my advice, in his book called *A Voyage round the World.* But I do not remember I gave you power to consent that anything should be omitted, and much less that anything should be inserted: therefore, as to the latter, I do here renounce everything of that kind; particularly a paragraph about her Majesty the late Queen Anne, of most pious and glorious memory; although I did reverence and esteem her more than any of human species. But you, or your interpolator, ought to have considered that as it was not my inclination, so was it not decent to praise any animal of our composition before my master Houyhnhnm; and besides, the fact was altogether false; for to my knowledge, being in England during some part of her Majesty's reign, she did govern by a chief Minister; nay, even by two successively; the first whereof was the Lord of Godolphin, and the second the Lord of Oxford; so that you have made me *say the thing that was not.* Likewise, in the account of the Academy of Projectors, and several passages of my discourse to my master Houyhnhnm, you have either omitted some material circumstances, or minced or changed them in such a manner, that I do hardly know mine own work. When I formerly hinted to you something of this in a letter, you were pleased to answer that you were afraid of giving offense; that people in power were very watchful over the press; and apt not only to interpret, but to punish everything which looked like an *inuendo* (as I think you called it). But pray, how could that which I spoke so many years ago, and at above five thousand leagues distance, in another reign, be applied to any of the Yahoos, who now are said to govern the herd; especially, at a time when I little thought on or feared the unhappiness of living under them. Have not I the most reason to complain, when I see these very Yahoos carried by Houyhnhnms in a vehicle, as if these were brutes, and those the rational creatures? And, indeed, to avoid so monstrous and detestable a sight was one principal motive of my retirement hither.[3]

---

1. Swift's full title for this work was *Travels into Several Remote Nations of the World. In Four Parts. By Lemuel Gulliver, First a Surgeon, and then a Captain of several Ships.* The text is based on the Dublin edition of Swift's work (1735). In this letter, first published in 1735, Swift complains, among other matters, of the alterations in his original text made by the publisher, Benjamin Motte, in the interest of what he considered political discretion.
2. William Dampier (1652–1715), the explorer, whose account of his circumnavigation of the globe Swift had read.
3. To Nottinghamshire in central England.

Thus much I thought proper to tell you in relation to yourself, and to the trust I reposed in you.

I do in the next place complain of my own great want of judgment, in being prevailed upon by the intreaties and false reasonings of you and some others, very much against mine own opinion, to suffer my travels to be published. Pray bring to your mind how often I desired you to consider, when you insisted on the motive of public good, that the Yahoos were a species of animals utterly incapable of amendment by precepts or examples; and so it hath proved; for instead of seeing a full stop put to all abuses and corruptions, at least in this little island, as I had reason to expect, behold, after above six months warning, I cannot learn that my book hath produced one single effect according to mine intentions; I desired you would let me know by a letter, when party and faction were extinguished; judges learned and upright; pleaders honest and modest, with some tincture of common sense; and Smithfield[4] blazing with pyramids of law books; the young nobility's education entirely changed; the physicians banished; the female Yahoos abounding in virtue, honor, truth, and good sense; courts and levees of great ministers thoroughly weeded and swept; wit, merit, and learning rewarded; all disgracers of the press in prose and verse, condemned to eat nothing but their own cotton,[5] and quench their thirst with their own ink. These, and a thousand other reformations, I firmly counted upon by your encouragement; as indeed they were plainly deducible from the precepts delivered in my book. And, it must be owned that seven months were a sufficient time to correct every vice and folly to which Yahoos are subject; if their natures had been capable of the least disposition to virtue or wisdom; yet so far have you been from answering mine expectation in any of your letters, that on the contrary, you are loading our carrier every week with libels, and keys, and reflections, and memoirs, and second parts; wherein I see myself accused of reflecting upon great statesfolk; of degrading human nature (for so they have still the confidence to style it) and of abusing the female sex. I find likewise, that the writers of those bundles are not agreed among themselves; for some of them will not allow me to be author of mine own travels; and others make me author of books to which I am wholly a stranger.

I find likewise that your printer hath been so careless as to confound the times, and mistake the dates of my several voyages and returns; neither assigning the true year, or the true month, or day of the month; and I hear the original manuscript is all destroyed, since the publication of my book. Neither have I any copy left; however, I have sent you some corrections, which you may insert, if ever there should be a second edition; and yet I cannot stand to them, but shall leave that matter to my judicious and candid readers, to adjust it as they please.

I hear some of our sea Yahoos find fault with my sea language, as not proper in many parts, nor now in use. I cannot help it. In my first voyages, while I was young, I was instructed by the oldest mariners, and learned to speak as they did. But I have since found that the sea Yahoos are apt, like the land ones, to become new fangled in their words; which the latter change every year; inso-

---

4. An area of London, used in the 16th century for burning heretics, that should now be used (Swift implies) to burn the incentives to litigation.

5. The fiber favored for paper making.

much, as I remember upon each return to mine own country, their old dialect was so altered, that I could hardly understand the new. And I observe, when any Yahoo comes from London out of curiosity to visit me at mine own house, we neither of us are able to deliver our conceptions in a manner intelligible to the other.

If the censure of Yahoos could any way affect me, I should have great reason to complain that some of them are so bold as to think my book of travels a mere fiction out of mine own brain; and have gone so far as to drop hints that the Houyhnhnms and Yahoos have no more existence than the inhabitants of Utopia.

Indeed I must confess that as to the people of Lilliput, Brobdingrag (for so the word should have been spelled, and not erroneously Brobdingnag) and Laputa, I have never yet heard of any Yahoo so presumptuous as to dispute their being, or the facts I have related concerning them; because the truth immediately strikes every reader with conviction. And, is there less probability in my account of the Houyhnhnms or Yahoos, when it is manifest as to the latter, there are so many thousands even in this city, who only differ from their brother brutes in Houyhnhnmland, because they use a sort of a jabber, and do not go naked. I wrote for their amendment, and not their approbation. The united praise of the whole race would be of less consequence to me, than the neighing of those two degenerate Houyhnhnms I keep in my stable; because, from these, degenerate as they are, I still improve in some virtues, without any mixture of vice.

Do these miserable animals presume to think that I am so far degenerated as to defend my veracity; Yahoo as I am, it is well known through all Houyhnhnmland, that by the instructions and example of my illustrious master, I was able in the compass of two years (although I confess with the utmost difficulty) to remove that infernal habit of lying, shuffling, deceiving, and equivocating, so deeply rooted in the very souls of all my species; especially the Europeans.

I have other complaints to make upon this vexatious occasion; but I forbear troubling myself or you any further. I must freely confess that since my last return, some corruptions of my Yahoo nature have revived in me by conversing with a few of your species, and particularly those of mine own family, by an unavoidable necessity; else I should never have attempted so absurd a project as that of reforming the Yahoo race in this kingdom; but I have now done with all such visionary schemes for ever.

The Publisher to the Reader

The author of these travels, Mr. Lemuel Gulliver, is my ancient and intimate friend; there is likewise some relation between us by the mother's side. About three years ago Mr. Gulliver, growing weary of the concourse of curious people coming to him at his house in Redriff,[6] made a small purchase of land, with a convenient house, near Newark, in Nottinghamshire, his native country; where he now lives retired, yet in good esteem among his neighbors.

Although Mr. Gulliver were born in Nottinghamshire, where his father dwelt, yet I have heard him say his family came from Oxfordshire; to confirm which, I have observed in the churchyard at Banbury, in that county, several tombs and monuments of the Gullivers.

---

6. Rotherhithe, a district in south London then frequented by sailors.

Before he quitted Redriff, he left the custody of the following papers in my hands, with the liberty to dispose of them as I should think fit. I have carefully perused them three times; the style is very plain and simple; and the only fault I find is that the author, after the manner of travelers, is a little too circumstantial. There is an air of truth apparent through the whole; and indeed the author was so distinguished for his veracity, that it became a sort of proverb among his neighbors at Redriff, when anyone affirmed a thing, to say, it was as true as if Mr. Gulliver had spoke it.

By the advice of several worthy persons, to whom, with the author's permission, I communicated these papers, I now venture to send them into the world; hoping they may be, at least for some time, a better entertainment to our young noblemen, than the common scribbles of politics and party.

This volume would have been at least twice as large, if I had not made bold to strike out innumerable passages relating to the winds and tides, as well as to the variations and bearings in the several voyages; together with the minute descriptions of the management of the ship in storms, in the style of sailors; likewise the account of the longitudes and latitudes, wherein I have reason to apprehend that Mr. Gulliver may be a little dissatisfied; but I was resolved to fit the work as much as possible to the general capacity of readers. However, if my own ignorance in sea affairs shall have led me to commit some mistakes, I alone am answerable for them; and if any traveler hath a curiosity to see the whole work at large, as it came from the hand of the author, I will be ready to gratify him.

As for any further particulars relating to the author, the reader will receive satisfaction from the first pages of the book.

RICHARD SYMPSON

Part IV

A Voyage to the Country of the Houyhnhnms[7]

CHAPTER I

The Author sets out as Captain of a ship. His men conspire against him, confine him a long time to his cabin, set him on shore in an unknown land. He travels up into the country. The Yahoos, a strange sort of animal, described. The Author meets two Houyhnhnms.

I continued at home with my wife and children about five months in a very happy condition, if I could have learned the lesson of knowing when I was well. I left my poor wife big with child, and accepted an advantageous offer made me to be Captain of the *Adventure*, a stout merchantman of 350 tons; for I understood navigation well, and being grown weary of a surgeon's employment at sea, which however I could exercise upon occasion, I took a skillful young man of that calling, one Robert Purefoy, into my ship. We set sail from Portsmouth upon the 7th day of September, 1710; on the 14th we met with Captain Pocock of Bristol, at Tenariff, who was going to the Bay of Campeachy[8] to cut

7. The word suggests the sound of a horse neighing.
8. Probably Campeche, in southeast Mexico, on the western side of the Yucatán Peninsula.

Tenariff (now Tenerife) is the largest of the Canary Islands, off northwest Africa in the Atlantic.

logwood. On the 16th he was parted from us by a storm; I heard since my return that his ship foundered and none escaped, but one cabin boy. He was an honest man and a good sailor, but a little too positive in his own opinions, which was the cause of his destruction, as it hath been of several others. For if he had followed my advice, he might at this time have been safe at home with his family as well as myself.

I had several men died in my ship of calentures, so that I was forced to get recruits out of Barbadoes and the Leeward Islands,[9] where I touched by the direction of the merchants who employed me; which I had soon too much cause to repent, for I found afterwards that most of them had been buccaneers. I had fifty hands on board; and my orders were that I should trade with the Indians in the South Sea, and make what discoveries I could. These rogues whom I had picked up debauched my other men, and they all formed a conspiracy to seize the ship and secure me; which they did one morning, rushing into my cabin, and binding me hand and foot, threatening to throw me overboard, if I offered to stir. I told them, I was their prisoner, and would submit. This they made me swear to do, and then unbound me, only fastening one of my legs with a chair near my bed, and placed a sentry at my door with his piece charged, who was commanded to shoot me dead if I attempted my liberty. They sent me down victuals and drink, and took the government of the ship to themselves. Their design was to turn pirates and plunder the Spaniards, which they could not do, till they got more men. But first they resolved to sell the goods in the ship, and then go to Madagascar for recruits, several among them having died since my confinement. They sailed many weeks, and traded with the Indians; but I knew not what course they took, being kept close prisoner in my cabin, and expecting nothing less than to be murdered, as they often threatened me.

Upon the 9th day of May, 1711, one James Welch came down to my cabin; and said he had orders from the Captain to set me ashore. I expostulated with him, but in vain; neither would he so much as tell me who their new Captain was. They forced me into the longboat, letting me put on my best suit of clothes, which were as good as new, and a small bundle of linen, but no arms except my hanger;[1] and they were so civil as not to search my pockets, into which I conveyed what money I had, with some other little necessaries. They rowed about a league, and then set me down on a strand. I desired them to tell me what country it was; they all swore, they knew no more than myself, but said that the Captain (as they called him) was resolved, after they had sold the lading, to get rid of me in the first place where they discovered land. They pushed off immediately, advising me to make haste, for fear of being overtaken by the tide, and bade me farewell.

In this desolate condition I advanced forward, and soon got upon firm ground, where I sat down on a bank to rest myself, and consider what I had best to do. When I was a little refreshed, I went up into the country, resolving to deliver myself to the first savages I should meet, and purchase my life from them by some bracelets, glass rings, and other toys, which sailors usually provide themselves with in those voyages, and whereof I had some about me. The

---

9. The northern group of the Lesser Antilles in the West Indies, extending southeast from Puerto Rico. Barbados is the easternmost of the West Indies. "Calentures": tropical fever.
1. A small sword.

land was divided by long rows of trees, not regularly planted, but naturally growing; there was great plenty of grass, and several fields of oats. I walked very circumspectly for fear of being surprised, or suddenly shot with an arrow from behind, or on either side. I fell into a beaten road, where I saw many tracks of human feet, and some of cows, but most of horses. At last I beheld several animals in a field, and one or two of the same kind sitting in trees. Their shape was very singular, and deformed, which a little discomposed me, so that I lay down behind a thicket to observe them better. Some of them coming forward near the place where I lay, gave me an opportunity of distinctly marking their form. Their heads and breasts were covered with a thick hair, some frizzled and others lank; they had beards like goats, and a long ridge of hair down their backs, and the fore parts of their legs and feet; but the rest of their bodies were bare, so that I might see their skins, which were of a brown buff color. They had no tails, nor any hair at all on their buttocks, except about the anus; which, I presume Nature had placed there to defend them as they sat on the ground; for this posture they used, as well as lying down, and often stood on their hind feet. They climbed high trees, as nimbly as a squirrel, for they had strong extended claws before and behind,[2] terminating in sharp points, and hooked. They would often spring, and bound, and leap with prodigious agility. The females were not so large as the males; they had long lank hair on their heads, and only a sort of down on the rest of their bodies, except about the anus, and pudenda. Their dugs hung between their forefeet, and often reached almost to the ground as they walked. The hair of both sexes was of several colors, brown, red, black, and yellow. Upon the whole, I never beheld in all my travels so disagreeable an animal; or one against which I naturally conceived so strong an antipathy. So that thinking I had seen enough, full of contempt and aversion, I got up and pursued the beaten road, hoping it might direct me to the cabin of some Indian: I had not gone far when I met one of these creatures full in my way, and coming up directly to me. The ugly monster, when he saw me, distorted several ways every feature of his visage, and stared as at an object he had never seen before; then approaching nearer, lifted up his forepaw, whether out of curiosity or mischief, I could not tell; but I drew my hanger, and gave him a good blow with the flat side of it; for I durst not strike him with the edge, fearing the inhabitants might be provoked against me, if they should come to know that I had killed or maimed any of their cattle. When the beast felt the smart, he drew back, and roared so loud, that a herd of at least forty came flocking about me from the next field, howling and making odious faces; but I ran to the body of a tree, and leaning my back against it, kept them off, by waving my hanger. Several of this cursed brood getting hold of the branches behind, leaped up into the tree, from whence they began to discharge their excrements on my head; however, I escaped pretty well, by sticking close to the stem of the tree, but was almost stifled with the filth, which fell about me on every side.

In the midst of this distress, I observed them all to run away on a sudden as fast as they could; at which I ventured to leave the tree, and pursue the road, wondering what it was that could put them into this fright. But looking on my left hand, I saw a horse walking softly in the field; which my persecutors having sooner discovered, was the cause of their flight. The horse started a little when

2. Concealed, or sheathed by flesh.

he came near me, but soon recovering himself, looked full in my face with manifest tokens of wonder; he viewed my hands and feet, walking round me several times. I would have pursued my journey, but he placed himself directly in the way, yet looking with a very mild aspect, never offering the least violence. We stood gazing at each other for some time; at last I took the boldness, to reach my hand towards his neck, with a design to stroke it; using the common style and whistle of jockies when they are going to handle a strange horse. But, this animal seeming to receive my civilities with disdain, shook his head, and bent his brows, softly raising up his left forefoot to remove my hand. Then he neighed three or four times, but in so different a cadence, that I almost began to think he was speaking to himself in some language of his own.

While he and I were thus employed, another horse came up; who applying himself to the first in a very formal manner, they gently struck each other's right hoof before, neighing several times by turns, and varying the sound, which seemed to be almost articulate. They went some paces off, as if it were to confer together, walking side by side, backward and forward, like persons deliberating upon some affair of weight; but often turning their eyes towards me, as it were to watch that I might not escape. I was amazed to see such actions and behavior in brute beasts; and concluded with myself that if the inhabitants of this country were endued with a proportionable degree of reason, they must needs be the wisest people upon earth. This thought gave me so much comfort, that I resolved to go forward until I could discover some house or village, or meet with any of the natives, leaving the two horses to discourse together as they pleased. But the first, who was a dapple grey, observing me to steal off, neighed after me in so expressive a tone that I fancied myself to understand what he meant; whereupon I turned back, and came near him, to expect his farther commands; but concealing my fear as much as I could; for I began to be in some pain, how this adventure might terminate; and the reader will easily believe I did not much like my present situation.

The two horses came up close to me, looking with great earnestness upon my face and hands. The grey steed rubbed my hat all round with his right fore hoof, and discomposed it so much that I was forced to adjust it better, by taking it off, and settling it again; whereat both he and his companion (who was a brown bay) appeared to be much surprised; the latter felt the lappet of my coat, and finding it to hang loose about me, they both looked with new signs of wonder. He stroked my right hand, seeming to admire the softness, and color; but he squeezed it so hard between his hoof and his pastern,[3] that I was forced to roar; after which they both touched me with all possible tenderness. They were under great perplexity about my shoes and stockings, which they felt very often, neighing to each other, and using various gestures, not unlike those of a philosopher, when he would attempt to solve some new and difficult phenomenon.

Upon the whole, the behavior of these animals was so orderly and rational, so acute and judicious, that I at last concluded, they must needs be magicians, who had thus metamorphosed themselves upon some design; and seeing a stranger in the way, were resolved to divert themselves with him; or perhaps were really amazed at the sight of a man so very different in habit, feature, and

---

3. The part of a horse's foot between the joint at the rear and the hoof.

complexion from those who might probably live in so remote a climate. Upon the strength of this reasoning, I ventured to address them in the following manner: "Gentlemen, if you be conjurers, as I have good cause to believe, you can understand any language; therefore I make bold to let your worships know that I am a poor distressed Englishman, driven by his misfortunes upon your coast; and I entreat one of you, to let me ride upon his back, as if he were a real horse, to some house or village, where I can be relieved. In return of which favor, I will make you a present of this knife and bracelet" (taking them out of my pocket). The two creatures stood silent while I spoke, seeming to listen with great attention; and when I had ended, they neighed frequently towards each other, as if they were engaged in serious conversation. I plainly observed, that their language expressed the passions very well, and the words might with little pains be resolved into an alphabet more easily than the Chinese.

I could frequently distinguish the word *Yahoo*, which was repeated by each of them several times; and although it was impossible for me to conjecture what it meant, yet while the two horses were busy in conversation, I endeavored to practice this word upon my tongue; and as soon as they were silent, I boldly pronounced "Yahoo" in a loud voice, imitating, at the same time, as near as I could, the neighing of a horse; at which they were both visibly surprised, and the grey repeated the same word twice, as if he meant to teach me the right accent, wherein I spoke after him as well as I could, and found myself perceivably to improve every time, although very far from any degree of perfection. Then the bay tried me with a second word, much harder to be pronounced; but reducing it to the English orthography, may be spelt thus, *Houyhnhnm*. I did not succeed in this so well as the former, but after two or three farther trials, I had better fortune; and they both appeared amazed at my capacity.

After some farther discourse, which I then conjectured might relate to me, the two friends took their leaves, with the same compliment of striking each other's hoof; and the grey made me signs that I should walk before him; wherein I thought it prudent to comply, till I could find a better director. When I offered to slacken my pace, he would cry, "Hhuun, Hhuun"; I guessed his meaning, and gave him to understand, as well as I could that I was weary, and not able to walk faster; upon which, he would stand a while to let me rest.

CHAPTER II

The Author conducted by a Houyhnhnm to his house. The house described. The Author's reception. The food of the Houyhnhnms. The Author in distress for want of meat is at last relieved. His manner of feeding in that country.

Having traveled about three miles, we came to a long kind of building, made of timber, stuck in the ground, and wattled across; the roof was low, and covered with straw. I now began to be a little comforted, and took out some toys, which travelers usually carry for presents to the savage Indians of America and other parts, in hopes the people of the house would be thereby encouraged to receive me kindly. The horse made me a sign to go in first; it was a large room with a smooth clay floor, and a rack and manger extending the whole length on one side. There were three nags, and two mares, not eating, but some of them sitting down upon their hams, which I very much wondered at; but wondered more to see the rest employed in domestic business; the last seemed but ordinary cattle; however this confirmed my first opinion, that a people who could so far civilize brute animals must needs excel in wisdom all the nations of the world. The grey came in just after, and thereby prevented any ill treatment, which the others might have given me. He neighed to them several times in a style of authority, and received answers.

Beyond this room there were three others, reaching the length of the house, to which you passed through three doors, opposite to each other, in the manner of a vista; we went through the second room towards the third; here the grey walked in first, beckoning me to attend; I waited in the second room, and got ready my presents, for the master and mistress of the house; they were two knives, three bracelets of false pearl, a small looking-glass and a bead necklace. The horse neighed three or four times, and I waited to hear some answers in a human voice, but I heard no other returns than in the same dialect, only one or two a little shriller than his. I began to think that this house must belong to some person of great note among them, because there appeared so much ceremony before I could gain admittance. But, that a man of quality should be served all by horses, was beyond my comprehension. I feared my brain was disturbed by my sufferings and misfortunes; I roused myself, and looked about me in the room where I was left alone; this was furnished as the first, only after a more elegant manner. I rubbed my eyes often, but the same objects still occurred. I pinched my arms and sides, to awake myself, hoping I might be in a dream. I then absolutely concluded that all these appearances could be nothing else but necromancy and magic. But I had no time to pursue these reflections; for the grey horse came to the door, and made me a sign to follow him into the third room; where I saw a very comely mare, together with a colt and foal, sitting on their haunches, upon mats of straw, not unartfully made, and perfectly neat and clean.

The mare soon after my entrance, rose from her mat, and coming up close, after having nicely observed my hands and face, gave me a most contemptuous look; then turning to the horse, I heard the word Yahoo often repeated betwixt them; the meaning of which word I could not then comprehend, although it were the first I had learned to pronounce; but I was soon better informed, to my everlasting mortification: for the horse beckoning to me with his head, and repeating the word, "Hhuun, Hhuun," as he did upon the road, which I understood was to attend him, led me out into a kind of court, where was another building at some distance from the house. Here we entered, and I saw three of those detestable creatures, which I first met after my landing, feeding upon roots, and the flesh of some animals, which I afterwards found to be that of asses and dogs, and now and then a cow dead by accident or disease. They were all tied by the neck with strong withes,[4] fastened to a beam; they held their food between the claws of their forefeet, and tore it with their teeth.

The master horse ordered a sorrel nag, one of his servants, to untie the largest of these animals, and take him into a yard. The beast and I were brought close together; and our countenances diligently compared, both by master and servant; who thereupon repeated several times the word "Yahoo." My horror and astonishment are not to be described, when I observed, in this abominable

4. Fibers braided into rope.

animal, a perfect human figure; the face of it indeed was flat and broad, the nose depressed, the lips large, and the mouth wide; but these differences are common to all savage nations, where the lineaments of the countenance are distorted by the natives suffering their infants to lie groveling on the earth, or by carrying them on their backs, nuzzling with their face against the mother's shoulders. The forefeet of the Yahoo differed from my hands in nothing else but the length of the nails, the coarseness and brownness of the palms, and the hairiness on the backs. There was the same resemblance between our feet, with the same differences, which I knew very well, although the horses did not, because of my shoes and stockings; the same in every part of our bodies, except as to hairiness and color, which I have already described.

The great difficulty that seemed to stick with the two horses, was to see the rest of my body so very different from that of a Yahoo, for which I was obliged to my clothes, whereof they had no conception; the sorrel nag offered me a root, which he held (after their manner, as we shall describe in its proper place) between his hoof and pastern; I took it in my hand, and having smelled it, returned it to him again as civilly as I could. He brought out of the Yahoo's kennel a piece of ass's flesh, but it smelled so offensively that I turned from it with loathing; he then threw it to the Yahoo, by whom it was greedily devoured. He afterwards showed me a wisp of hay, and a fetlock[5] full of oats; but I shook my head, to signify that neither of these were food for me. And indeed, I now apprehended that I must absolutely starve, if I did not get to some of my own species; for as to those filthy Yahoos, although there were few greater lovers of mankind, at that time, than myself, yet I confess I never saw any sensitive being so detestable on all accounts; and the more I came near them, the more hateful they grew, while I stayed in that country. This the master horse observed by my behavior, and therefore sent the Yahoo back to his kennel. He then put his forehoof to his mouth, at which I was much surprised, although he did it with ease, and with a motion that appeared perfectly natural; and made other signs to know what I would eat; but I could not return him such an answer as he was able to apprehend; and if he had understood me, I did not see how it was possible to contrive any way for finding myself nourishment. While we were thus engaged, I observed a cow passing by; whereupon I pointed to her, and expressed a desire to let me go and milk her. This had its effect; for he led me back into the house, and ordered a mare-servant to open a room, where a good store of milk lay in earthen and wooden vessels, after a very orderly and cleanly manner. She gave me a large bowl full, of which I drank very heartily, and found myself well refreshed.

About noon I saw coming towards the house a kind of vehicle, drawn like a sledge by four Yahoos. There was in it an old steed, who seemed to be of quality; he alighted with his hind feet forward, having by accident got a hurt in his left forefoot. He came to dine with our horse, who received him with great civility. They dined in the best room, and had oats boiled in milk for the second course, which the old horse eat warm, but the rest cold. Their mangers were placed circular in the middle of the room, and divided into several partitions, round which they sat on their haunches upon bosses of straw. In the middle

---

5. The joint at the back of a horse's foot, just above the hoof, in which the Houyhnhnm holds the oats.

was a large rack with angles answering to every partition of the manger. So that each horse and mare eat their own hay, and their own mash of oats and milk, with much decency and regularity. The behavior of the young colt and foal appeared very modest; and that of the master and mistress extremely cheerful and complaisant to their guest. The grey ordered me to stand by him; and much discourse passed between him and his friend concerning me, as I found by the stranger's often looking on me, and the frequent repetition of the word Yahoo.

I happened to wear my gloves; which the master grey observing, seemed perplexed; discovering signs of wonder what I had done to my forefeet; he put his hoof three or four times to them, as if he would signify, that I should reduce them to their former shape, which I presently did, pulling off both my gloves, and putting them into my pocket. This occasioned farther talk, and I saw the company was pleased with my behavior, whereof I soon found the good effects. I was ordered to speak the few words I understood; and while they were at dinner, the master taught me the names for oats, milk, fire, water, and some others which I could readily pronounce after him, having from my youth a great facility in learning languages.

When dinner was done, the master horse took me aside, and by signs and words made me understand the concern he was in that I had nothing to eat. Oats in their tongue are called *hlunnh*. This word I pronounced two or three times; for although I had refused them at first, yet upon second thoughts, I considered that I could contrive to make a kind of bread, which might be sufficient with milk to keep me alive, till I could make my escape to some other country, and to creatures of my own species. The horse immediately ordered a white mare-servant of his family to bring me a good quantity of oats in a sort of wooden tray. These I heated before the fire as well as I could, and rubbed them till the husks came off, which I made a shift to winnow from the grain; I ground and beat them between two stones, then took water, and made them into a paste or cake, which I toasted at the fire, and eat warm with milk. It was at first a very insipid diet, although common enough in many parts of Europe, but grew tolerable by time; and having been often reduced to hard fare in my life, this was not the first experiment I had made how easily nature is satisfied. And I cannot but observe that I never had one hour's sickness, while I staid in this island. It is true, I sometimes made a shift to catch a rabbit, or bird, by springes made of Yahoos' hairs; and I often gathered wholesome herbs, which I boiled, or ate as salads with my bread; and now and then, for a rarity, I made a little butter, and drank the whey. I was at first at a great loss for salt; but custom soon reconciled the want of it; and I am confident that the frequent use of salt among us is an effect of luxury, and was first introduced only as a provocative to drink; except where it is necessary for preserving of flesh in long voyages, or in places remote from great markets. For we observe no animal to be fond of it but man;[6] and as to myself, when I left this country, it was a great while before I could endure the taste of it in anything that I eat.

This is enough to say upon the subject of my diet, wherewith other travelers fill their books, as if the readers were personally concerned whether we fare well or ill. However, it was necessary to mention this matter, lest the world

---

6. Gulliver's error; many animals are very fond of salt.

should think it impossible that I could find sustenance for three years in such a country, and among such inhabitants.

When it grew towards evening, the master horse ordered a place for me to lodge in; it was but six yards from the house, and separated from the stable of the Yahoos. Here I got some straw, and covering myself with my own clothes, slept very sound. But I was in a short time better accommodated, as the reader shall know hereafter, when I come to treat more particularly about my way of living.

CHAPTER III

The Author studious to learn the language, the Houyhnhnm his master assists in teaching him. The language described. Several Houyhnhnms of quality come out of curiosity to see the Author. He gives his master a short account of his voyage.

My principal endeavor was to learn the language, which my master (for so I shall henceforth call him) and his children, and every servant of his house were desirous to teach me. For they looked upon it as a prodigy, that a brute animal should discover such marks of a rational creature. I pointed to everything, and enquired the name of it, which I wrote down in my journal book when I was alone, and corrected my bad accent, by desiring those of the family to pronounce it often. In this employment, a sorrel nag, one of the under servants, was very ready to assist me.

In speaking, they pronounce through the nose and throat, and their language approaches nearest to the High Dutch or German, of any I know in Europe; but is much more graceful and significant. The Emperor Charles V made almost the same observation, when he said, that if he were to speak to his horse, it should be in High Dutch.[7]

The curiosity and impatience of my master were so great, that he spent many hours of his leisure to instruct me. He was convinced (as he afterwards told me) that I must be a Yahoo, but my teachableness, civility, and cleanliness astonished him; which were qualities altogether so opposite to those animals. He was most perplexed about my clothes, reasoning sometimes with himself whether they were a part of my body; for I never pulled them off till the family were asleep, and got them on before they waked in the morning. My master was eager to learn from whence I came; how I acquired those appearances of reason, which I discovered in all my actions; and to know my story from my own mouth, which he hoped he should soon do by the great proficiency I made in learning and pronouncing their words and sentences. To help my memory, I formed all I learned into the English alphabet, and writ the words down with the translations. This last, after some time, I ventured to do in my master's presence. It cost me much trouble to explain to him what I was doing; for the inhabitants have not the least idea of books or literature.

In about ten weeks time I was able to understand most of his questions; and in three months could give him some tolerable answers. He was extremely curious to know from what part of the country I came, and how I was taught to

7. Charles was reputed to have said he would address God in Spanish, women in Italian, men in French, and his horse in German.

imitate a rational creature; because the Yahoos (whom he saw I exactly resembled in my head, hands, and face, that were only visible) with some appearance of cunning, and the strongest disposition to mischief, were observed to be the most unteachable of all brutes. I answered that I came over the sea, from a far place, with many others of my own kind, in a great hollow vessel made of the bodies of trees; that my companions forced me to land on this coast, and then left me to shift for myself. It was with some difficulty, and by the help of many signs, that I brought him to understand me. He replied that I must needs be mistaken, or that I *said the thing which was not.* (For they have no words in their language to express lying or falsehood.) He knew it was impossible that there could be a country beyond sea, or that a parcel of brutes could move a wooden vessel whither they pleased upon water. He was sure no Houyhnhnm alive could make such a vessel, or would trust Yahoos to manage it.

The word Houyhnhnm, in their tongue, signifies a Horse; and in its etymology, the Perfection of Nature. I told my master that I was at a loss for expression, but would improve as fast as I could; and hoped in a short time I should be able to tell him wonders; he was pleased to direct his own mare, his colt, and foal, and the servants of the family to take all opportunities of instructing me; and every day for two or three hours, he was at the same pains himself; several horses and mares of quality in the neighborhood came often to our house, upon the report spread of a wonderful Yahoo, that could speak like a Houyhnhnm, and seemed in his words and actions to discover some glimmerings of reason. These delighted to converse with me; they put many questions, and received such answers as I was able to return. By all which advantages, I made so great a progress, that in five months from my arrival, I understood whatever was spoke, and could express myself tolerably well.

The Houyhnhnms who came to visit my master, out of a design of seeing and talking with me, could hardly believe me to be a right Yahoo, because my body had a different covering from others of my kind. They were astonished to observe me without the usual hair or skin, except on my head, face, and hands; but I discovered that secret to my master, upon an accident, which happened about a fortnight before.

I have already told the reader, that every night when the family were gone to bed, it was my custom to strip and cover myself with my clothes; it happened one morning early, that my master sent for me, by the sorrel nag, who was his valet; when he came, I was fast asleep, my clothes fallen off on one side, and my shirt above my waist. I awaked at the noise he made, and observed him to deliver his message in some disorder; after which he went to my master, and in a great fright gave him a very confused account of what he had seen; this I presently discovered; for going as soon as I was dressed, to pay my attendance upon his honor, he asked me the meaning of what his servant had reported; that I was not the same thing when I slept as I appeared to be at other times; that his valet assured him, some part of me was white, some yellow, at least not so white, and some brown.

I had hitherto concealed the secret of my dress, in order to distinguish myself as much as possible, from that cursed race of Yahoos; but now I found it in vain to do so any longer. Besides, I considered that my clothes and shoes would soon wear out, which already were in a declining condition, and must be supplied by some contrivance from the hides of Yahoos, or other brutes; whereby the whole secret would be known. I therefore told my master, that in the country from whence I came, those of my kind always covered their bodies with the hairs of certain animals prepared by art, as well for decency, as to avoid inclemencies of air both hot and cold; of which, as to my own person I would give him immediate conviction, if he pleased to command me; only desiring this excuse, if I did not expose those parts that nature taught us to conceal. He said, my discourse was all very strange, but especially the last part; for he could not understand why Nature should teach us to conceal what Nature had given. That neither himself nor family were ashamed of any parts of their bodies; but however I might do as I pleased. Whereupon, I first unbuttoned my coat, and pulled it off. I did the same with my waistcoat; I drew off my shoes, stockings, and breeches. I let my shirt down to my waist, and drew up the bottom, fastening it like a girdle about my middle to hide my nakedness.

My master observed the whole performance with great signs of curiosity and admiration. He took up all my clothes in his pastern, one piece after another, and examined them diligently; he then stroked my body very gently, and looked round me several times; after which he said, it was plain I must be a perfect Yahoo; but that I differed very much from the rest of my species, in the whiteness and smoothness of my skin, my want of hair in several parts of my body, the shape and shortness of my claws behind and before, and my affectation of walking continually on my two hinder feet. He desired to see no more; and gave me leave to put on my clothes again, for I was shuddering with cold.

I expressed my uneasiness at his giving me so often the appellation of Yahoo, an odious animal, for which I had so utter an hatred and contempt. I begged he would forbear applying that word to me, and take the same order in his family, and among his friends whom he suffered to see me. I requested likewise, that the secret of my having a false covering to my body might be known to none but himself, at least as long as my present clothing should last; for as to what the sorrel nag his valet had observed, his honor might command him to conceal it.

All this my master very graciously consented to; and thus the secret was kept till my clothes began to wear out, which I was forced to supply by several contrivances, that shall hereafter be mentioned. In the meantime, he desired I would go on with my utmost diligence to learn their language, because he was more astonished at my capacity for speech and reason, than at the figure of my body, whether it were covered or no; adding that he waited with some impatience to hear the wonders which I promised to tell him.

From thenceforward he doubled the pains he had been at to instruct me; he brought me into all company, and made them treat me with civility, because, as he told them privately, this would put me into good humor, and make me more diverting.

Every day when I waited on him, beside the trouble he was at in teaching, he would ask me several questions concerning myself, which I answered as well as I could; and by those means he had already received some general ideas, although very imperfect. It would be tedious to relate the several steps, by which I advanced to a more regular conversation, but the first account I gave of myself in any order and length was to this purpose:

That, I came from a very far country, as I already had attempted to tell him, with about fifty more of my own species; that we traveled upon the seas, in a great hollow vessel made of wood, and larger than his honor's house. I described the ship to him in the best terms I could; and explained by the help of my handkerchief displayed, how it was driven forward by the wind. That, upon a quarrel among us, I was set on shore on this coast, where I walked forward without knowing whither, till he delivered me from the persecution of those execrable Yahoos. He asked me who made the ship, and how it was possible that the Houyhnhnms of my country would leave it to the management of brutes? My answer was that I durst proceed no farther in my relation, unless he would give me his word and honor that he would not be offended; and then I would tell him the wonders I had so often promised. He agreed; and I went on by assuring him, that the ship was made by creatures like myself, who in all the countries I had traveled, as well as in my own, were the only governing, rational animals; and that upon my arrival hither, I was as much astonished to see the Houyhnhnms act like rational beings, as he or his friends could be in finding some marks of reason in a creature he was pleased to call a Yahoo; to which I owned my resemblance in every part, but could not account for their degenerate and brutal nature. I said farther, that if good fortune ever restored me to my native country, to relate my travels hither, as I resolved to do; everybody would believe that I *said the thing which was not*; that I invented the story out of my own head; and with all possible respect to himself, his family, and friends, and under his promise of not being offended, our countrymen would hardly think it probable, that a Houyhnhnm should be the presiding creature of a nation, and a Yahoo the brute.

CHAPTER IV

The Houyhnhnms' notion of truth and falsehood. The author's discourse disapproved by his master. The author gives a more particular account of himself, and the accidents of his voyages.

My master heard me with great appearances of uneasiness in his countenance; because *doubting* or *not believing* are so little known in this country, that the inhabitants cannot tell how to behave themselves under such circumstances. And I remember in frequent discourses with my master concerning the nature of manhood, in other parts of the world, having occasion to talk of *lying* and *false representation*, it was with much difficulty that he comprehended what I meant; although he had otherwise a most acute judgment. For he argued thus: that the use of speech was to make us understand one another, and to receive information of facts; now if anyone *said the thing which was not*, these ends were defeated; because I cannot properly be said to understand him; and I am so far from receiving information, that he leaves me worse than in ignorance; for I am led to believe a thing *black* when it is *white*, and *short* when it is *long*. And these were all the notions he had concerning that faculty of *lying*, so perfectly well understood, and so universally practiced among human creatures.

To return from this digression; when I asserted that the Yahoos were the only governing animals in my country, which my master said was altogether past his conception, he desired to know, whether we had Houyhnhnms among us, and what was their employment; I told him we had great numbers; that in summer they grazed in the fields, and in winter were kept in houses, with hay and oats, where Yahoo servants were employed to rub their skins smooth, comb their manes, pick their feet, serve them with food, and make their beds. "I understand you well," said my master; "it is now very plain from all you have spoken, that whatever share of reason the Yahoos pretend to, the Houyhnhnms are your masters; I heartily wish our Yahoos would be so tractable." I begged his honor would please to excuse me from proceeding any farther, because I was very certain that the account he expected from me would be highly displeasing. But he insisted in commanding me to let him know the best and the worst; I told him he should be obeyed. I owned that the Houyhnhnms among us, whom we called Horses, were the most generous[8] and comely animal we had; that they excelled in strength and swiftness; and when they belonged to persons of quality, employed in traveling, racing, and drawing chariots, they were treated with much kindness and care, till they fell into diseases, or became foundered in the feet; but then they were sold, and used to all kind of drudgery till they died; after which their skins were stripped and sold for what they were worth, and their bodies left to be devoured by dogs and birds of prey. But the common race of horses had not so good fortune, being kept by farmers and carriers, and other mean people, who put them to greater labor, and fed them worse. I described as well as I could, our way of riding; the shape and use of a bridle, a saddle, a spur, and a whip; of harness and wheels. I added, that we fastened plates of a certain hard substance called iron at the bottom of their feet, to preserve their hoofs from being broken by the stony ways on which we often traveled.

My master, after some expressions of great indignation, wondered how we dared to venture upon a Houyhnhnm's back; for he was sure, that the weakest servant in his house would be able to shake off the strongest Yahoo; or by lying down, and rolling upon his back, squeeze the brute to death. I answered that our horses were trained up from three or four years old to the several uses we intended them for; that if any of them proved intolerably vicious, they were employed for carriages; that they were severely beaten while they were young for any mischievous tricks; that the males, designed for the common use of riding or draught, were generally castrated about two years after their birth, to take down their spirits, and make them more tame and gentle; that they were indeed sensible of rewards and punishments; but his honor would please to consider that they had not the least tincture of reason any more than the Yahoos in this country.

It put me to the pains of many circumlocutions to give my master a right idea of what I spoke; for their language doth not abound in variety of words, because their wants and passions are fewer than among us. But it is impossible to express his noble resentment at our savage treatment of the Houyhnhnm race; particularly after I had explained the manner and use of castrating horses among us, to hinder them from propagating their kind, and to render them more servile. He said, if it were possible there could be any country where Yahoos alone were endued with reason, they certainly must be the governing animal, because reason will in time always prevail against brutal strength. But, considering the frame of our bodies, and especially of mine, he thought no creature of equal bulk was so ill-contrived for employing that reason in the

8. Noble.

common offices of life; whereupon he desired to know whether those among whom I lived resembled me or the Yahoos of his country. I assured him that I was as well shaped as most of my age; but the younger and the females were much more soft and tender, and the skins of the latter generally as white as milk. He said I differed indeed from other Yahoos, being much more cleanly, and not altogether so deformed; but in point of real advantage, he thought I differed for the worse. That my nails were of no use either to my fore or hinder feet; as to my forefeet, he could not properly call them by that name, for he never observed me to walk upon them; that they were too soft to bear the ground; that I generally went with them uncovered, neither was the covering I sometimes wore on them of the same shape, or so strong as that on my feet behind. That I could not walk with any security; for if either of my hinder feet slipped, I must inevitably fall. He then began to find fault with other parts of my body; the flatness of my face, the prominence of my nose, my eyes placed directly in front, so that I could not look on either side without turning my head; that I was not able to feed myself without lifting one of my forefeet to my mouth; and therefore nature had placed those joints to answer that necessity. He knew not what could be the use of those several clefts and divisions in my feet behind; that these were too soft to bear the hardness and sharpness of stones without a covering made from the skin of some other brute; that my whole body wanted a fence against heat and cold, which I was forced to put on and off every day with tediousness and trouble. And lastly, that he observed every animal in his country naturally to abhor the Yahoos, whom the weaker avoided, and the stronger drove from them. So that supposing us to have the gift of reason, he could not see how it were possible to cure that natural antipathy which every creature discovered against us; nor consequently, how we could tame and render them serviceable. However, he would (as he said) debate the matter no farther, because he was more desirous to know my own story, the country where I was born, and the several actions and events of my life before I came hither.

I assured him how extremely desirous I was that he should be satisfied in every point; but I doubted much whether it would be possible for me to explain myself on several subjects whereof his honor could have no conception, because I saw nothing in his country to which I could resemble them. That however, I would do my best, and strive to express myself by similitudes, humbly desiring his assistance when I wanted proper words; which he was pleased to promise me.

I said, my birth was of honest parents, in an island called England, which was remote from this country, as many days journey as the strongest of his honor's servants could travel in the annual course of the sun. That I was bred a surgeon, whose trade it is to cure wounds and hurts in the body, got by accident or violence. That my country was governed by a female man, whom we called a queen.[9] That I left it to get riches, whereby I might maintain myself and family when I should return. That in my last voyage, I was Commander of the ship and had about fifty Yahoos under me, many of which died at sea, and I was forced to supply them by others picked out from several nations. That our ship was twice in danger of being sunk; the first time by a great storm, and the second, by striking against a rock. Here my master interposed, by asking me,

---

9. Queen Anne (1665–1714), the last Stuart ruler.

how I could persuade strangers out of different countries to venture with me, after the losses I had sustained, and the hazards I had run. I said, they were fellows of desperate fortunes, forced to fly from the places of their birth, on account of their poverty or their crimes. Some were undone by lawsuits; others spent all they had in drinking, whoring, and gambling; others fled for treason; many for murder, theft, poisoning, robbery, perjury, forgery, coining false money; for committing rapes or sodomy; for flying from their colors, or deserting to the enemy; and most of them had broken prison. None of these durst return to their native countries for fear of being hanged, or of starving in a jail; and therefore were under a necessity of seeking livelihood in other places.

During this discourse, my master was pleased often to interrupt me. I had made use of many circumlocutions in describing to him the nature of the several crimes, for which most of our crew had been forced to fly their country. This labor took up several days conversation before he was able to comprehend me. He was wholly at a loss to know what could be the use or necessity of practicing those vices. To clear up which I endeavored to give him some ideas of the desire of power and riches; of the terrible effects of lust, intemperance, malice, and envy. All this I was forced to define and describe by putting of cases, and making suppositions. After which, like one whose imagination was struck with something never seen or heard of before, he would lift up his eyes with amazement and indignation. Power, government, war, law, punishment, and a thousand other things had no terms, wherein that language could express them; which made the difficulty almost insuperable to give my master any conception of what I meant; but being of an excellent understanding, much improved by contemplation and converse, he at last arrived at a competent knowledge of what human nature in our parts of the world is capable to perform; and desired I would give him some particular account of that land, which we call Europe, especially, of my own country.

CHAPTER V

The Author, at his master's commands, informs him of the state of England. The causes of war among the princes of Europe. The Author begins to explain the English Constitution.

The reader may please to observe that the following extract of many conversations I had with my master contains a summary of the most material points, which were discoursed at several times for above two years; his honor often desiring fuller satisfaction as I farther improved in the Houyhnhnm tongue. I laid before him, as well as I could, the whole state of Europe; I discoursed of trade and manufactures, of arts and sciences; and the answers I gave to all the questions he made, as they arose upon several subjects, were a fund of conversation not to be exhausted. But I shall here only set down the substance of what passed between us concerning my own country, reducing it into order as well as I can, without any regard to time or other circumstances, while I strictly adhere to truth. My only concern is that I shall hardly be able to do justice to my master's arguments and expressions; which must needs suffer by my want of capacity, as well as by a translation into our barbarous English.

In obedience therefore to his honor's commands, I related to him the Revolution under the Prince of Orange; the long war with France entered into by the said Prince, and renewed by his successor the present queen; wherein the greatest powers of Christendom were engaged, and which still continued. I computed at his request, that about a million of Yahoos might have been killed in the whole progress of it; and perhaps a hundred or more cities taken, and five times as many ships burned or sunk.[1]

He asked me what were the usual causes or motives that made one country to go to war with another. I answered, they were innumerable; but I should only mention a few of the chief. Sometimes the ambition of princes, who never think they have land or people enough to govern; sometimes the corruption of ministers, who engage their master in a war in order to stifle or divert the clamor of the subjects against their evil administration. Difference in opinions hath cost many millions of lives; for instance, whether flesh be bread, or bread be flesh; whether the juice of a certain berry be blood or wine; whether whistling be a vice or a virtue; whether it be better to kiss a post, or throw it into the fire; what is the best color for a coat, whether black, white, red, or grey; and whether it should be long or short, narrow or wide, dirty or clean;[2] with many more. Neither are any wars so furious and bloody, or of so long continuance, as those occasioned by difference in opinion, especially if it be in things indifferent.

Sometimes the quarrel between two princes is to decide which of them shall dispossess a third of his dominions, where neither of them pretend to any right. Sometimes one prince quarreleth with another, for fear the other should quarrel with him. Sometimes a war is entered upon, because the enemy is too strong, and sometimes because he is too weak. Sometimes our neighbors want the things which we have, or have the things which we want; and we both fight, till they take ours or give us theirs. It is a very justifiable cause of war to invade a country after the people have been wasted by famine, destroyed by pestilence, or embroiled by factions amongst themselves. It is justifiable to enter into a war against our nearest ally, when one of his towns lies convenient for us, or a territory of land, that would render our dominions round and compact. If a prince send forces into a nation, where the people are poor and ignorant, he may lawfully put half of them to death, and make slaves of the rest, in order to civilize and reduce them from their barbarous way of living. It is a very kingly, honorable, and frequent practice, when one prince desires the assistance of another to secure him against an invasion, that the assistant, when he hath driven out the invader, should seize on the dominions himself, and kill, imprison, or banish the prince he came to relieve. Alliance by blood or marriage is a sufficient cause of war between princes; and the nearer the kindred is, the greater is their disposition to quarrel; poor nations are hungry, and rich nations are proud; and pride and hunger will ever be at variance. For these reasons, the trade of a soldier is held the most honorable of all others: because a soldier is a Yahoo hired to kill in cold blood as many of his own species, who have never offended him, as possibly he can.

There is likewise a kind of beggarly princes in Europe, not able to make war by themselves, who hire out their troops to richer nations for so much a day to

1. Gulliver relates recent English history: the Glorious Revolution of 1688 and the War of the Spanish Succession (1703–14). He greatly exaggerates the casualties in the war.
2. Gulliver refers to the religious controversies of the Reformation and Counter-Reformation: the doctrine of transubstantiation, the use of music in church services, the veneration of the crucifix, and the wearing of priestly vestments.

each man; of which they keep three fourths to themselves, and it is the best part of their maintenance; such are those in many northern parts of Europe.

"What you have told me," said my master, "upon the subject of war, doth indeed discover most admirably the effects of that reason you pretend to; however, it is happy that the shame is greater than the danger; and that Nature hath left you utterly uncapable of doing much mischief; for your mouths lying flat with your faces, you can hardly bite each other to any purpose, unless by consent. Then, as to the claws upon your feet before and behind, they are so short and tender, that one of our Yahoos would drive a dozen of yours before him. And therefore in recounting the numbers of those who have been killed in battle, I cannot but think that you have *said the thing which is not*."

I could not forebear shaking my head and smiling a little at his ignorance. And, being no stranger to the art of war, I gave him a description of cannons, culverins, muskets, carabines, pistols, bullets, powder, swords, bayonets, battles, sieges, retreats, attacks, undermines, countermines, bombardments, sea fights; ships sunk with a thousand men; twenty thousand killed on each side; dying groans, limbs flying in the air; smoke, noise, confusion, trampling to death under horses' feet; flight, pursuit, victory; fields strewed with carcasses left for food to dogs, and wolves, and birds of prey; plundering, stripping, ravishing, burning, and destroying. And, to set forth the valor of my own dear countrymen, I assured him that I had seen them blow up a hundred enemies at once in a siege, and as many in a ship; and beheld the dead bodies drop down in pieces from the clouds, to the great diversion of all the spectators.

I was going on to more particulars, when my master commanded me silence. He said, whoever understood the nature of Yahoos might easily believe it possible for so vile an animal, to be capable of every action I had named, if their strength and cunning equaled their malice. But, as my discourse had increased his abhorrence of the whole species, so he found it gave him a disturbance in his mind, to which he was wholly a stranger before. He thought his ears being used to such abominable words, might by degrees admit them with less detestation. That, although he hated the Yahoos of this country, yet he no more blamed them for their odious qualities, than he did a *gnnayh* (a bird of prey) for its cruelty, or a sharp stone for cutting his hoof. But, when a creature pretending to reason could be capable of such enormities, he dreaded lest the corruption of that faculty might be worse than brutality itself. He seemed therefore confident, that instead of reason, we were only possessed of some quality fitted to increase our natural vices; as the reflection from a troubled stream returns the image of an ill-shapen body, not only larger, but more distorted.

He added that he had heard too much upon the subject of war, both in this and some former discourses. There was another point which a little perplexed him at present. I had said that some of our crew left their country on account of being ruined by law: that I had already explained the meaning of the word; but he was at a loss how it should come to pass, that the law which was intended for every man's preservation, should be any man's ruin. Therefore he desired to be farther satisfied what I meant by law, and the dispensers thereof, according to the present practice in my own country; because he thought nature and reason were sufficient guides for a reasonable animal, as we pretended to be, in showing us what we ought to do, and what to avoid.

I assured his honor that law was a science wherein I had not much conversed, further than by employing advocates, in vain, upon some injustices that had been done me. However, I would give him all the satisfaction I was able.

I said there was a society of men among us, bred up from their youth in the art of proving by words multiplied for the purpose, that white is black, and black is white, according as they are paid. To this society all the rest of the people are slaves.

"For example. If my neighbor hath a mind to my cow, he hires a lawyer to prove that he ought to have my cow from me. I must then hire another to defend my right; it being against all rules of law that any man should be allowed to speak for himself. Now in this case, I who am the true owner lie under two great disadvantages. First, my lawyer being practiced almost from his cradle in defending falsehood is quite out of his element when he would be an advocate for justice, which as an office unnatural, he always attempts with great awkwardness, if not with ill-will. The second disadvantage is that my lawyer must proceed with great caution, or else he will be reprimanded by the judges, and abhorred by his breathren, as one who would lessen the practice of the law. And therefore I have but two methods to preserve my cow. The first is to gain over my adversary's lawyer with a double fee; who will then betray his client, by insinuating that he hath justice on his side. The second way is for my lawyer to make my cause appear as unjust as he can; by allowing the cow to belong to my adversary; and this if it be skillfully done, will certainly bespeak the favor of the bench.

"Now, your honor is to know that these judges are persons appointed to decide all controversies of property, as well as for the trial of criminals; and picked out from the most dextrous lawyers who are grown old or lazy; and having been biased all their lives against truth and equity, lie under such a fatal necessity of favoring fraud, perjury, and oppression, that I have known some of them to have refused a large bribe from the side where justice lay, rather than injure the faculty,[3] by doing anything unbecoming their nature or their office.

"It is a maxim among these lawyers, that whatever hath been done before may legally be done again; and therefore they take special care to record all the decisions formerly made against common justice and the general reason of mankind. These, under the name of *precedents*, they produce as authorities to justify the most iniquitous opinions; and the judges never fail of directing accordingly.

"In pleading, they studiously avoid entering into the merits of the cause; but are loud, violent, and tedious in dwelling upon all circumstances which are not to the purpose. For instance, in the case already mentioned, they never desire to know what claim or title my adversary hath to my cow; but whether the said cow were red or black; her horns long or short; whether the field I graze her in be round or square; whether she were milked at home or abroad; what diseases she is subject to, and the like. After which they consult precedents, adjourn the cause, from time to time, and in ten, twenty, or thirty years come to an issue.

"It is likewise to be observed, that this society hath a peculiar cant and jargon of their own, that no other mortal can understand, and wherein all their laws are written, which they take special care to multiply; whereby they have wholly

3. Profession.

confounded the very essence of truth and falsehood, of right and wrong; so that it will take thirty years to decide whether the field, left me by my ancestors for six generations, belong to me, or to a stranger three hundred miles off.

"In the trial of persons accused for crimes against the state, the method is much more short and commendable: the judge first sends to sound the disposition of those in power; after which he can easily hang or save the criminal, strictly preserving all the forms of law."

Here my master interposing said it was a pity that creatures endowed with such prodigious abilities of mind as these lawyers, by the description I gave of them must certainly be, were not rather encouraged to be instructors of others in wisdom and knowledge. In answer to which, I assured his honor that in all points out of their own trade, they were usually the most ignorant and stupid generation among us, the most despicable in common conversation, avowed enemies to all knowledge and learning; and equally disposed to pervert the general reason of mankind, in every other subject of discourse as in that of their own profession.

CHAPTER VI

A continuation of the state of England, under Queen Anne. The character of a first minister in the courts of Europe.

My master was yet wholly at a loss to understand what motives could incite this race of lawyers to perplex, disquiet, and weary themselves by engaging in a confederacy of injustice, merely for the sake of injuring their fellow animals; neither could he comprehend what I meant in saying they did it for hire. Whereupon I was at much pains to describe to him the use of money, the materials it was made of, and the value of the metals; that when a Yahoo had got a great store of this precious substance, he was able to purchase whatever he had a mind to; the finest clothing, the noblest houses, great tracts of land, the most costly meats and drinks; and have his choice of the most beautiful females. Therefore since money alone was able to perform all these feats, our Yahoos thought they could never have enough of it to spend or to save, as they found themselves inclined from their natural bent either to profusion or avarice. That the rich man enjoyed the fruit of the poor man's labor, and the latter were a thousand to one in proportion to the former. That the bulk of our people was forced to live miserably, by laboring every day for small wages to make a few live plentifully. I enlarged myself much on these and many other particulars to the same purpose, but his honor was still to seek, for he went upon a supposition that all animals had a title to their share in the productions of the earth; and especially those who presided over the rest. Therefore he desired I would let him know what these costly meats were, and how any of us happened to want[4] them. Whereupon I enumerated as many sorts as came into my head, with the various methods of dressing them, which could not be done without sending vessels by sea to every part of the world, as well for liquors to drink, as for sauces, and innumerable other conveniencies. I assured him, that this whole globe of earth must be at least three times gone round, before one

4. Lack.

of our better female Yahoos could get her breakfast, or a cup to put it in. He said, "That must needs be a miserable country which cannot furnish food for its own inhabitants." But what he chiefly wondered at, was how such vast tracts of ground as I described, should be wholly without fresh water, and the people put to the necessity of sending over the sea for drink. I replied that England (the dear place of my nativity) was computed to produce three times the quantity of food, more than its inhabitants are able to consume, as well as liquors extracted from grain, or pressed out of the fruit of certain trees, which made excellent drink; and the same proportion in every other convenience of life. But, in order to feed the luxury and intemperance of the males, and the vanity of the females, we sent away the greatest part of our necessary things to other countries, from whence in return we brought the materials of diseases, folly, and vice, to spend among ourselves. Hence it follows of necessity, that vast numbers of our people are compelled to seek their livelihood by begging, robbing, stealing, cheating, pimping, foreswearing, flattering, suborning, forging, gaming, lying, fawning, hectoring, voting, scribbling, star gazing, poisoning, whoring, canting, libeling, freethinking, and the like occupations; every one of which terms, I was at much pains to make him understand.

That, wine was not imported among us from foreign countries, to supply the want of water or other drinks, but because it was a sort of liquid which made us merry, by putting us out of our senses; diverted all melancholy thoughts, begat wild extravagant imaginations in the brain, raised our hopes, and banished our fears; suspended every office of reason for a time, and deprived us of the use of our limbs, until we fell into a profound sleep; although it must be confessed, that we always awaked sick and dispirited; and that the use of this liquor filled us with diseases, which made our lives uncomfortable and short.

But beside all this, the bulk of our people supported themselves by furnishing the necessities or conveniencies of life to the rich, and to each other. For instance, when I am at home and dressed as I ought to be, I carry on my body the workmanship of an hundred tradesmen; the building and furniture of my house employ as many more; and five times the number to adorn my wife.

I was going on to tell him of another sort of people, who get their livelihood by attending the sick; having upon some occasions informed his honor that many of my crew had died of diseases. But here it was with the utmost difficulty that I brought him to apprehend what I meant. He could easily conceive that a Houyhnhnm grew weak and heavy a few days before his death; or by some accident might hurt a limb. But that nature, who worketh all things to perfection, should suffer any pains to breed in our bodies, he thought impossible; and desired to know the reason of so unaccountable an evil. I told him, we fed on a thousand things which operated contrary to each other; that we eat when we were not hungry, and drank without the provocation of thirst; that we sat whole nights drinking strong liquors without eating a bit, which disposed us to sloth, enflamed our bodies, and precipitated or prevented digestion. That, prostitute female Yahoos acquired a certain malady, which bred rottenness in the bones of those who fell into their embraces; that this and many other diseases were propagated from father to son; so that great numbers come into the world with complicated maladies upon them; that it would be endless to give him a catalogue of all diseases incident to human bodies; for they could not be fewer than five or six hundred, spread over every limb, and joint; in short, every part, external and intestine, having diseases appropriated to each. To remedy which, there was a sort of people bred up among us, in the profession or pretense of curing the sick. And because I had some skill in the faculty, I would in gratitude to his honor let him know the whole mystery and method by which they proceed.

Their fundamental is that all diseases arise from repletion; from whence they conclude, that a great evacuation of the body is necessary, either through the natural passage, or upwards at the mouth. Their next business is, from herbs, minerals, gums, oils, shells, salts, juices, seaweed, excrements, barks of trees, serpents, toads, frogs, spiders, dead men's flesh and bones, birds, beasts and fishes, to form a composition for smell and taste the most abominable, nauseous, and detestable, that they can possibly contrive, which the stomach immediately rejects with loathing, and this they call a vomit. Or else from the same storehouse, with some other poisonous additions, they command us to take in at the orifice above or below (just as the physician then happens to be disposed) a medicine equally annoying and disgustful to the bowels; which relaxing the belly, drives down all before it; and this they call a purge, or a clyster. For nature (as the physicians allege) having intended the superior anterior orifice only for the intromission of solids and liquids, and the inferior posterior for ejection, these artists ingeniously considering that in all diseases nature is forced out of her seat; therefore to replace her in it, the body must be treated in a manner directly contrary, but interchanging the use of each orifice; forcing solids and liquids in at the anus, and making evacuations at the mouth.

But, besides real diseases, we are subject to many that are only imaginary, for which the physicians have invented imaginary cures; these have their several names, and so have the drugs that are proper for them; and with these our female Yahoos are always infested.

One great excellency in this tribe is their skill at prognostics, wherein they seldom fail; their predictions in real diseases, when they rise to any degree of malignity, generally portending death, which is always in their power, when recovery is not, and therefore, upon any unexpected signs of amendment, after they have pronounced their sentence, rather than be accused as false prophets, they know how to approve[5] their sagacity to the world by a seasonable dose.

They are likewise of special use to husbands and wives, who are grown weary of their mates; to eldest sons, to great ministers of state, and often to princes.

I had formerly upon occasion discoursed with my master upon the nature of government in general, and particularly of our own excellent constitution, deservedly the wonder and envy of the whole world. But having here accidentally mentioned a minister of state, he commanded me some time after to inform him what species of Yahoo I particularly meant by that appellation.

I told him that a first or chief minister of state, whom I intended to describe, was a creature wholly exempt from joy and grief, love and hatred, pity and anger; at least makes use of no other passions but a violent desire of wealth, power, and titles; that he applies his words to all uses, except to the indication of his mind; that he never tells a truth, but with an intent that you should take it for a lie; nor a lie, but with a design that you should take it for a truth; that

5. Prove.

those he speaks worst of behind their backs are in the surest way to preferment; and whenever he begins to praise you to others or to yourself, you are from that day forlorn. The worst mark you can receive is a promise, especially when it is confirmed with an oath; after which every wise man retires, and gives over all hopes.

There are three methods by which a man may rise to be chief minister: the first is by knowing how with prudence to dispose of a wife, a daughter, or a sister; the second, by betraying or undermining his predecessor; and the third is by a furious zeal in public assemblies against the corruptions of the court. But a wise prince would rather choose to employ those who practice the last of these methods; because such zealots prove always the most obsequious and subservient to the will and passions of their master. That, these ministers having all employments at their disposal, preserve themselves in power by bribing the majority of a senate or great council; and at last by an expedient called an Act of Indemnity (whereof I described the nature to him) they secure themselves from after-reckonings, and retire from the public, laden with the spoils of the nation.

The palace of a chief minister is a seminary to breed up others in his own trade; the pages, lackies, and porter, by imitating their master, become ministers of state in their several districts, and learn to excel in the three principal ingredients, of insolence, lying, and bribery. Accordingly, they have a subaltern court paid to them by persons of the best rank; and sometimes by the force of dexterity and impudence, arrive through several gradations to be successors to their lord.

He is usually governed by a decayed wench, or favorite footman, who are the tunnels through which all graces are conveyed, and may properly be called, in the last resort, the governors of the kingdom.

One day, my master, having heard me mention the nobility of my country, was pleased to make me a compliment which I could not pretend to deserve: that, he was sure, I must have been born of some noble family, because I far exceeded in shape, color, and cleanliness, all the Yahoos of his nation, although I seemed to fail in strength, and agility, which must be imputed to my different way of living from those other brutes; and besides, I was not only endowed with the faculty of speech, but likewise with some rudiments of reason, to a degree, that with all his acquaintance I passed for a prodigy.

He made me observe, that among the Houyhnhnms, the white, the sorrel, and the iron grey were not so exactly shaped as the bay, the dapple grey, and the black; nor born with equal talents of mind, or a capacity to improve them; and therefore continued always in the condition of servants, without ever aspiring to match out of their own race, which in that country would be reckoned monstrous and unnatural.

I made his honor my most humble acknowledgements for the good opinion he was pleased to conceive of me; but assured him at the same time, that my birth was of the lower sort, having been born of plain, honest parents, who were just able to give me a tolerable education; that, nobility among us was altogether a different thing from the idea he had of it; that, our young noblemen are bred from their childhood in idleness and luxury; that, as soon as years will permit, they consume their vigor, and contract odious diseases among lewd females; and when their fortunes are almost ruined, they marry some woman of mean birth, disagreeable person, and unsound constitution, merely for the sake of money, whom they hate and despise. That, the productions of such marriages are generally scrofulous, rickety or deformed children; by which means the family seldom continues above three generations, unless the wife take care to provide a healthy father among her neighbors, or domestics, in order to improve and continue the breed. That a weak diseased body, a meager countenance, and sallow complexion are the true marks of noble blood; and a healthy robust appearance is so disgraceful in a man of quality, that the world concludes his real father to have been a groom or a coachman. The imperfections of his mind run parallel with those of his body; being a composition of spleen, dullness, ignorance, caprice, sensuality, and pride.

Without the consent of this illustrious body, no law can be enacted, repealed, or altered, and these nobles have likewise the decision of all our possessions without appeal.

CHAPTER VII

The Author's great love of his native country. His master's observations upon the constitution and administration of England, as described by the Author, with parallel cases and comparisons. His master's observations upon human nature.

The reader may be disposed to wonder how I could prevail on myself to give so free a representation of my own species, among a race of mortals who were already too apt to conceive the vilest opinion of humankind, from that entire congruity betwixt me and their Yahoos. But I must freely confess that the many virtues of those excellent quadrupeds placed in opposite view to human corruptions had so far opened my eyes, and enlarged my understanding, that I began to view the actions and passions of man in a very different light; and to think the honor of my own kind not worth managing; which, besides, it was impossible for me to do before a person of so acute a judgment as my master, who daily convinced me of a thousand faults in myself, whereof I had not the least perception before, and which with us would never be numbered even among human infirmities. I had likewise learned from his example an utter detestation of all falsehood or disguise; and truth appeared so amiable to me, that I determined upon sacrificing everything to it.

Let me deal so candidly with the reader as to confess that there was yet a much stronger motive for the freedom I took in my representation of things. I had not been a year in this country, before I contracted such a love and veneration for the inhabitants, that I entered on a firm resolution never to return to humankind, but to pass the rest of my life among these admirable Houyhnhnms in the contemplation and practice of every virtue; where I could have no example or incitement to vice. But it was decreed by fortune, my perpetual enemy, that so great a felicity should not fall to my share. However, it is now some comfort to reflect that in what I said of my countrymen, I extenuated their faults as much as I durst before so strict an examiner; and upon every article, gave as favorable a turn as the matter would bear. For, indeed, who is there alive that will not be swayed by his bias and partiality to the place of his birth?

I have related the substance of several conversations I had with my master, during the greatest part of the time I had the honor to be in his service; but have indeed for brevity sake omitted much more than is here set down.

When I had answered all his questions, and his curiosity seemed to be fully satisfied; he sent for me one morning early, and commanding me to sit down at some distance (an honor which he had never before conferred upon me), he said he had been very seriously considering my whole story, as far as it related both to myself and my country: that, he looked upon us as a sort of animal to whose share, by what accident he could not conjecture, some small pittance of reason had fallen, whereof we made no other use than by its assistance to aggravate our natural corruptions, and to acquire new ones which nature had not given us. That we disarmed ourselves of the few abilities she had bestowed; had been very successful in multiplying our original wants, and seemed to spend our whole lives in vain endeavors to supply them by our own inventions. That, as to myself, it was manifest I had neither the strength or agility of a common Yahoo; that I walked infirmly on my hinder feet; had found out a contrivance to make my claws of no use or defense, and to remove the hair from my chin, which was intended as a shelter from the sun and the weather. Lastly, that I could neither run with speed, nor climb trees like my brethren (as he called them) the Yahoos in this country.

That our institutions of government and law were plainly owing to our gross defects in reason, and by consequence, in virtue; because reason alone is sufficient to govern a rational creature; which was therefore a character we had no pretense to challenge, even from the account I had given of my own people; although he manifestly perceived, that in order to favor them, I had concealed many particulars, and often *said the thing which was not*.

He was the more confirmed in this opinion, because he observed that I agreed in every feature of my body with other Yahoos, except where it was to my real disadvantage in point of strength, speed, and activity, the shortness of my claws, and some other particulars where nature had no part; so, from the representation I had given him of our lives, our manners, and our actions, he found as near a resemblance in the disposition of our minds. He said the Yahoos were known to hate one another more than they did any different species of animals; and the reason usually assigned was the odiousness of their own shapes, which all could see in the rest, but not in themselves. He had therefore begun to think it not unwise in us to cover our bodies, and by that invention, conceal many of our deformities from each other, which would else be hardly supportable. But he now found he had been mistaken; and that the dissentions of those brutes in his country were owing to the same cause with ours, as I had described them. For, if (said he) you throw among five Yahoos as much food as would be sufficient for fifty, they will, instead of eating peaceably, fall together by the ears, each single one impatient to have all to itself; and therefore a servant was usually employed to stand by while they were feeding abroad, and those kept at home were tied at a distance from each other. That, if a cow died of age or accident, before a Houyhnhnm could secure it for his own Yahoos, those in the neighborhood would come in herds to seize it, and then would ensue such a battle as I had described, with terrible wounds made by their claws on both sides, although they seldom were able to kill one another, for want of such convenient instruments of death as we had invented. At other times the like battles have been fought between the Yahoos of several neighborhoods without any visible cause; those of one district watching all opportunities to surprise the next before they are prepared. But if they find their project hath miscarried, they return home, and for want of enemies, engage in what I call a civil war among themselves.

That, in some fields of his country, there are certain shining stones of several colors, whereof the Yahoos are violently fond; and when part of these stones are fixed in the earth, as it sometimes happeneth, they will dig with their claws for whole days to get them out, and carry them away, and hide them by heaps in their kennels; but still looking round with great caution, for fear their comrades should find out their treasure. My master said he could never discover the reason of this unnatural appetite, or how these stones could be of any use to a Yahoo; but now he believed it might proceed from the same principle of avarice, which I had ascribed to mankind. That he had once, by way of experiment, privately removed a heap of these stones from the place where one of his Yahoos had buried it, whereupon, the sordid animal missing his treasure, by his loud lamenting brought the whole herd to the place, there miserably howled, then fell to biting and tearing the rest; began to pine away, would neither eat nor sleep, nor work, till he ordered a servant privately to convey the stones into the same hole, and hide them as before; which when his Yahoo had found, he presently recovered his spirits and good humor; but took care to remove them to a better hiding place; and hath ever since been a very serviceable brute.

My master farther assured me, which I also observed myself; that in the fields where these shining stones abound, the fiercest and most frequent battles are fought, occasioned by perpetual inroads of the neighboring Yahoos.

He said it was common when two Yahoos discovered such a stone in a field, and were contending which of them should be the proprietor, a third would take the advantage, and carry it away from them both; which my master would needs contend to have some resemblance with our suits at law; wherein I thought it for our credit not to undeceive him; since the decision he mentioned was much more equitable than many decrees among us; because the plaintiff and defendant there lost nothing beside the stone they contended for; whereas our courts of equity would never have dismissed the cause while either of them had anything left.

My master continuing his discourse said there was nothing that rendered the Yahoos more odious, than their undistinguished appetite to devour everything that came in their way, whether herbs, roots, berries, corrupted flesh of animals, or all mingled together; and it was peculiar in their temper, that they were fonder of what they could get by rapine or stealth at a greater distance, than much better food provided for them at home. If their prey held out, they would eat till they were ready to burst, after which nature had pointed out to them a certain root that gave them a general evacuation.

There was also another kind of root very juicy, but something rare and difficult to be found, which the Yahoos fought for with much eagerness, and would suck it with great delight; it produced the same effects that wine hath upon us. It would make them sometimes hug, and sometimes tear one another; they would howl and grin, and chatter, and reel, and tumble, and then fall asleep in the mud.

I did indeed observe that the Yahoos were the only animals in this country subject to any diseases; which however, were much fewer than horses have among us, and contracted not by any ill treatment they meet with, but by the nastiness and greediness of that sordid brute. Neither has their language any more than a general appellation for those maladies; which is borrowed from the name of the beast, and called *Hnea Yahoo*, or the Yahoo's Evil; and the cure prescribed is a mixture of their own dung and urine, forcibly put down the Yahoo's throat. This I have since often known to have been taken with success, and do here freely recommend it to my countrymen, for the public good, as an admirable specific against all diseases produced by repletion.

As to learning, government, arts, manufactures, and the like, my master confessed he could find little or no resemblance between the Yahoos of that country and those in ours. For he only meant to observe what parity there was in our natures. He had heard indeed some curious Houyhnhnms observe that in most herds there was a sort of ruling Yahoo (as among us there is generally some leading or principal stag in a park) who was always more deformed in body, and mischievous in disposition, than any of the rest. That this leader had usually a favorite as like himself as he could get, whose employment was to lick his master's feet and posteriors, and drive the female Yahoos to his kennel; for which he was now and then rewarded with a piece of ass's flesh. This favorite is hated by the whole herd; and therefore to protect himself, keeps always near the person of his leader. He usually continues in office till a worse can be found; but the very moment he is discarded, his successor, at the head of all the Yahoos in that district, young and old, male and female, come in a body, and discharge their excrements upon him from head to foot. But how far this might be applicable to our courts and favorites, and ministers of state, my master said I could best determine.

I durst make no return to this malicious insinuation, which debased human understanding below the sagacity of a common hound, who hath judgment enough to distinguish and follow the cry of the ablest dog in the pack, without being ever mistaken.

My master told me there were some qualities remarkable in the Yahoos, which he had not observed me to mention, or at least very slightly, in the accounts I had given him of humankind. He said, those animals, like other brutes, had their females in common; but in this differed, that the she-Yahoo would admit the male while she was pregnant; and that the hes would quarrel and fight with the females as fiercely as with each other. Both which practices were such degrees of infamous brutality, that no other sensitive creature ever arrived at.

Another thing he wondered at in the Yahoos was their strange disposition to nastiness and dirt; whereas there appears to be a natural love of cleanliness in all other animals. As to the two former accusations, I was glad to let them pass without any reply, because I had not a word to offer upon them in defense of my species, which otherwise I certainly had done from my own inclinations. But I could have easily vindicated humankind from the imputation of singularity upon the last article, if there had been any swine in that country (as unluckily for me there were not) which although it may be a sweeter quadruped than a Yahoo, cannot I humbly conceive in justice pretend to more cleanliness; and so his honor himself must have owned, if he had seen their filthy way of feeding, and their custom of wallowing and sleeping in the mud.

My master likewise mentioned another quality, which his servants had discovered in several Yahoos, and to him was wholly unaccountable. He said, a fancy would sometimes take a Yahoo, to retire into a corner, to lie down and howl, and groan, and spurn away all that came near him, although he were young and fat, and wanted neither food nor water; nor did the servants imagine what could possibly ail him. And the only remedy they found was to set him to hard work, after which he would infallibly come to himself. To this I was silent out of partiality to my own kind; yet here I could plainly discover the true seeds of spleen,[6] which only seizeth on the lazy, the luxurious, and the rich; who, if they were forced to undergo the same regimen, I would undertake for the cure.

His Honor had farther observed, that a female Yahoo would often stand behind a bank or a bush, to gaze on the young males passing by, and then appear, and hide, using many antic gestures and grimaces; at which time it was observed, that she had a most offensive smell; and when any of the males advanced, would slowly retire, looking back, and with a counterfeit show of fear, run off into some convenient place where she knew the male would follow her.

At other times, if a female stranger came among them, three or four of her own sex would get about her, and stare and chatter, and grin, and smell her all over; and then turn off with gestures that seemed to express contempt and disdain.

Perhaps my master might refine a little in these speculations, which he had drawn from what he observed himself, or had been told by others; however, I could not reflect without some amazement, and much sorrow, that the rudiments of lewdness, coquetry, censure, and scandal, should have place by instinct in womankind.

I expected every moment that my master would accuse the Yahoos of those unnatural appetites in both sexes, so common among us. But nature it seems hath not been so expert a school-mistress; and these politer pleasures are entirely the productions of art and reason, on our side of the globe.

CHAPTER VIII

The Author relateth several particulars of the Yahoos. The great virtues of the Houyhnhnms. The education and exercises of their youth. Their general assembly.

As I ought to have understood human nature much better than I supposed it possible for my master to do, so it was easy to apply the character he gave of the Yahoos to myself and my countrymen; and I believed I could yet make farther discoveries from my own observation. I therefore often begged his honor to let me go among the herds of Yahoos in the neighborhood; to which he always very graciously consented, being perfectly convinced that the hatred I bore those brutes would never suffer me to be corrupted by them; and his honor ordered one of his servants, a strong sorrel nag, very honest and good-natured, to be my guard; without whose protection I durst not undertake such adventures. For I have already told the reader how much I was pestered by those odious animals upon my first arrival. I afterwards failed very narrowly

6. Hypochondria.

three or four times of falling into their clutches, when I happened to stray at any distance without my hanger. And I have reason to believe, they had some imagination that I was of their own species, which I often assisted myself, by stripping up my sleeves, and shewing my naked arms and breast in their sight, when my protector was with me; at which times they would approach as near as they durst, and imitate my actions after the manner of monkeys, but ever with great signs of hatred; as a tame jackdaw with cap and stockings is always persecuted by the wild ones, when he happens to be got among them.

They are prodigiously nimble from their infancy; however, I once caught a young male of three years old, and endeavored by all marks of tenderness to make it quiet; but the little imp fell a squalling, scratching, and biting with such violence, that I was forced to let it go; and it was high time, for a whole troop of old ones came about us at the noise; but finding the cub was safe (for away it ran) and my sorrel nag being by, they durst not venture near us. I observed the young animal's flesh to smell very rank, and the stink was somewhat between a weasel and a fox, but much more disagreeable. I forgot another circumstance (and perhaps I might have the reader's pardon, if it were wholly omitted) that while I held the odious vermin in my hands, it voided its filthy excrements of a yellow liquid substance, all over my clothes; but by good fortune there was a small brook hard by, where I washed myself as clean as I could; although I durst not come into my master's presence until I were sufficiently aired.

By what I could discover, the Yahoos appear to be the most unteachable of all animals, their capacities never reaching higher than to draw or carry burdens. Yet I am of opinion, this defect ariseth chiefly from a perverse, restive disposition. For they are cunning, malicious, treacherous and revengeful. They are strong and hardy, but of a cowardly spirit, and by consequence insolent, abject, and cruel. It is observed that the red-haired of both sexes are more libidinous and mischievous than the rest, whom yet they much exceed in strength and activity.

The Houyhnhnms keep the Yahoos for present use in huts not far from the house; but the rest are sent abroad to certain fields, where they dig up roots, eat several kinds of herbs, and search about for carrion, or sometimes catch weasels and *luhimuhs* (a sort of wild rat) which they greedily devour. Nature hath taught them to dig deep holes with their nails on the side of a rising ground, wherein they lie by themselves; only the kennels of the females are larger, sufficient to hold two or three cubs.

They swim from their infancy like frogs, and are able to continue long under water, where they often take fish, which the females carry home to their young. And upon this occasion, I hope the reader will pardon my relating an odd adventure.

Being one day abroad with my protector the sorrel nag, and the weather exceeding hot, I entreated him to let me bathe in a river that was near. He consented, and I immediately stripped myself stark naked, and went down softly into the stream. It happened that a young female Yahoo standing behind a bank, saw the whole proceeding; and inflamed by desire, as the nag and I conjectured, came running with all speed, and leaped into the water within five yards of the place where I bathed. I was never in my life so terribly frighted; the nag was grazing at some distance, not suspecting any harm; she embraced me after a most fulsome manner; I roared as loud as I could, and the nag came galloping towards me, whereupon she quitted her grasp, with the utmost reluctancy, and leaped upon the opposite bank, where she stood gazing and howling all the time I was putting on my clothes.

This was matter of diversion to my master and his family, as well as of mortification to myself. For now I could no longer deny that I was a real Yahoo, in every limb and feature, since the females had a natural propensity to me as one of their own species; neither was the hair of this brute of a red color (which might have been some excuse for an appetite a little irregular) but black as a sole, and her countenance did not make an appearance altogether so hideous as the rest of the kind; for I think, she could not be above eleven years old.

Having already lived three years in this country, the reader I suppose will expect that I should, like other travelers, give him some account of the manners and customs of its inhabitants, which it was indeed my principal study to learn.

As these noble Houyhnhnms are endowed by Nature with a general disposition to all virtues, and have no conceptions or ideas of what is evil in a rational creature; so their grand maxim is to cultivate reason, and to be wholly governed by it. Neither is reason among them a point problematical as with us, where men can argue with plausibility on both sides of a question; but strikes you with immediate conviction; as it must needs do where it is not mingled, obscured, or discolored by passion and interest. I remember it was with extreme difficulty that I could bring my master to understand the meaning of the word "opinion," or how a point could be disputable; because reason taught us to affirm or deny only where we are certain; and beyond our knowledge we cannot do either. So that controversies, wranglings, disputes, and positiveness in false or dubious propositions are evils unknown among the Houyhnhnms. In the like manner when I used to explain to him our several systems of natural philosophy, he would laugh that a creature pretending to reason should value itself upon the knowledge of other people's conjectures, and in things, where that knowledge, if it were certain, could be of no use. Wherein he agreed entirely with the sentiments of Socrates, as Plato delivers them, which I mention as the highest honor I can do that prince of philosophers. I have often since reflected what destruction such a doctrine would make in the libraries of Europe; and how many paths to fame would be then shut up in the learned world.

Friendship and benevolence are the two principal virtues among the Houyhnhnms; and these not confined to particular objects, but universal to the whole race. For a stranger from the remotest part is equally treated with the nearest neighbor, and wherever he goes, looks upon himself as at home. They preserve decency and civility in the highest degrees, but are altogether ignorant of ceremony. They have no fondness for[7] their colts or foals; but the care they take in educating them proceedeth entirely from the dictates of reason. And I observed my master to show the same affection to his neighbor's issue that he had for his own. They will have it that nature teaches them to love the whole species, and it is reason only that maketh a distinction of persons, where there is a superior degree of virtue.

When the matron Houyhnhnms have produced one of each sex, they no longer accompany with their consorts, except they lose one of their issue by some

7. Attachment to.

casualty, which very seldom happens; but in such a case they meet again; or when the like accident befalls a person whose wife is past bearing, some other couple bestows on him one of their own colts, and then go together a second time, until the mother be pregnant. This caution is necessary to prevent the country from being overburdened with numbers. But the race of inferior Houyhnhnms bred up to be servants is not so strictly limited upon this article; these are allowed to produce three of each sex, to be domestics in the noble families.

In their marriages they are exactly careful to choose such colors as will not make any disagreeable mixture in the breed. Strength is chiefly valued in the male, and comeliness in the female; not upon the account of love, but to preserve the race from degenerating; for, where a female happens to excel in strength, a consort is chosen with regard to comeliness. Courtship, love, presents, jointures, settlements, have no place in their thoughts, or terms whereby to express them in their language. The young couple meet and are joined, merely because it is the determination of their parents and friends; it is what they see done every day; and they look upon it as one of the necessary actions in a reasonable being. But the violation of marriage, or any other unchastity, was never heard of; and the married pair pass their lives with the same friendship and mutual benevolence that they bear to all others of the same species who come in their way, without jealousy, fondness, quarreling, or discontent.

In educating the youth of both sexes, their method is admirable, and highly deserveth our imitation. These are not suffered to taste a grain of oats, except upon certain days, till eighteen years old; nor milk, but very rarely; and in summer they graze two hours in the morning, and as many in the evening, which their parents likewise observe; but the servants are not allowed above half that time; and a great part of the grass is brought home, which they eat at the most convenient hours, when they can be best spared from work.

Temperance, industry, exercise, and cleanliness are the lessons equally enjoined to the young ones of both sexes; and my master thought it monstrous in us to give the females a different kind of education from the males, except in some articles of domestic management; whereby, as he truly observed, one half of our natives were good for nothing but bringing children into the world; and to trust the care of their children to such useless animals, he said was yet a greater instance of brutality.

But the Houyhnhnms train up their youth to strength, speed, and hardiness, by exercising them in running races up and down steep hills, or over hard stony grounds; and when they are all in a sweat, they are ordered to leap over head and ears into a pond or a river. Four times a year the youth of certain districts meet to show their proficiency in running, and leaping, and other feats of strength or agility; where the victor is rewarded with a song made in his or her praise. On this festival the servants drive a herd of Yahoos into the field, laden with hay, and oats, and milk for a repast to the Houyhnhnms; after which these brutes are immediately driven back again, for fear of being noisome to the assembly.

Every fourth year, at the vernal equinox, there is a representative council of the whole nation, which meets in a plain about twenty miles from our house, and continueth about five or six days. Here they inquire into the state and condition of the several districts; whether they abound or be deficient in hay or oats, or cows or Yahoos? And wherever there is any want (which is but seldom) it is immediately supplied by unanimous consent and contribution. Here likewise the regulation of children is settled: as for instance, if a Houyhnhnm hath two males, he changeth one of them with another who hath two females, and when a child hath been lost by any casualty, where the mother is past breeding, it is determined what family in the district shall breed another to supply the loss.

CHAPTER IX

A grand debate at the general assembly of the Houyhnhnms, and how it was determined. The learning of the Houyhnhnms. Their buildings. Their manner of burials. The defectiveness of their language.

One of these grand assemblies was held in my time, about three months before my departure, whither my master went as the representative of our district. In this council was resumed their old debate, and indeed, the only debate that ever happened in their country; whereof my master after his return gave me a very particular account.

The question to be debated was whether the Yahoos should be exterminated from the face of the earth. One of the members for the affirmative offered several arguments of great strength and weight, alleging that, as the Yahoos were the most filthy, noisome, and deformed animal which nature ever produced, so they were the most restive and indocile, mischievous, and malicious; they would privately suck the teats of the Houyhnhnms' cows; kill and devour their cats, trample down their oats and grass, if they were not continually watched; and commit a thousand other extravagancies. He took notice of a general tradition, that Yahoos had not been always in their country, but that many ages ago, two of these brutes appeared together upon a mountain; whether produced by the heat of the sun upon corrupted mud and slime, or from the ooze and froth of the sea, was never known. That these Yahoos engendered, and their brood in a short time grew so numerous as to overrun and infest the whole nation. That the Houyhnhnms to get rid of this evil, made a general hunting, and at last enclosed the whole herd; and destroying the older, every Houyhnhnm kept two young ones in a kennel, and brought them to such a degree of tameness as an animal so savage by nature can be capable of acquiring, using them for draft and carriage. That there seemed to be much truth in this tradition, and that those creatures could not be *ylnhniamshy* (or aborigines of the land) because of the violent hatred the Houyhnhnms as well as all other animals bore them; which although their evil disposition sufficiently deserved, could never have arrived at so high a degree, if they had been aborigines, or else they would have long since been rooted out. That the inhabitants taking a fancy to use the service of the Yahoos, had very imprudently neglected to cultivate the breed of asses, which were a comely animal, easily kept, more tame and orderly, without any offensive smell, strong enough for labor, although they yield to the other in agility of body; and if their braying be no agreeable sound, it is far preferable to the horrible howlings of the Yahoos.

Several others declared their sentiments to the same purpose, when my master proposed an expedient to the assembly, whereof he had indeed borrowed the hint from me. He approved of the tradition, mentioned by the honorable member, who spoke before; and affirmed, that the two Yahoos said to be first seen among them, had been driven thither over the sea; that coming to land, and being forsaken by their companions, they retired to the mountains, and degenerating by degrees, became in process of time much more savage than those of their own species in the country from whence these two originals came. The reason of his assertion was that he had now in his possession a certain wonderful Yahoo (meaning myself) which most of them had heard of, and many of them had seen. He then related to them how he first found me; that my body was all covered with an artificial composure of the skins and hairs of other animals; that I spoke in a language of my own, and had thoroughly learned theirs; that I had related to him the accidents which brought me thither; that when he saw me without my covering, I was an exact Yahoo in every part, only of a whiter color, less hairy and with shorter claws. He added how I had endeavored to persuade him that in my own and other countries the Yahoos acted as the governing, rational animal, and held the Houyhnhnms in servitude; that he observed in me all the qualities of a Yahoo, only a little more civilized by some tincture of reason, which however was in a degree as far inferior to the Houyhnhnm race as the Yahoos of their country were to me; that among other things, I mentioned a custom we had of castrating Houyhnhnms when they were young, in order to render them tame; that the operation was easy and safe; that it was no shame to learn wisdom from brutes, as industry is taught by the ant, and building by the swallow (for so I translate the word *lyhannh*, although it be a much larger fowl). That this invention might be practiced upon the younger Yahoos here, which, besides rendering them tractable and fitter for use, would in an age put an end to the whole species without destroying life. That in the meantime the Houyhnhnms should be exhorted to cultivate the breed of asses, which, as they are in all respects more valuable brutes, so they have this advantage, to be fit for service at five years old, which the others are not till twelve.

This was all my master thought fit to tell me at that time, of what passed in the grand council. But he was pleased to conceal one particular, which related personally to myself, whereof I soon felt the unhappy effect, as the reader will know in its proper place, and from whence I date all the succeeding misfortunes of my life.

The Houyhnhnms have no letters, and consequently, their knowledge is all traditional. But there happening few events of any moment among a people so well united, naturally disposed to every virtue, wholly governed by reason, and cut off from all commerce with other nations, the historical part is easily preserved without burdening their memories. I have already observed that they are subject to no diseases, and therefore can have no need of physicians. However, they have excellent medicines composed of herbs, to cure accidental bruises and cuts in the pastern or frog of the foot by sharp stones, as well as other maims and hurts in the several parts of the body.

They calculate the year by the revolution of the sun and the moon, but use no subdivisions into weeks. They are well enough acquainted with the motions of those two luminaries, and understand the nature of eclipses; and this is the utmost progress of their astronomy.

In poetry they must be allowed to excel all other mortals; wherein the justness of their similes, and the minuteness, as well as exactness of their descriptions, are indeed inimitable. Their verses abound very much in both of these, and usually contain either some exalted notions of friendship and benevolence, or the praises of those who were victors in races and other bodily exercises. Their buildings, although very rude and simple, are not inconvenient, but well contrived to defend them from all injuries of cold and heat. They have a kind of tree, which at forty years old loosens in the root, and falls with the first storm; it grows very straight, and being pointed like stakes with a sharp stone (for the Houyhnhnms know not the use of iron), they stick them erect in the ground about ten inches asunder, and then weave in oat straw, or sometimes wattles, betwixt them. The roof is made after the same manner, and so are the doors.

The Houyhnhnms use the hollow part between the pastern and the hoof of their forefeet as we do our hands, and this with greater dexterity than I could at first imagine. I have seen a white mare of our family thread a needle (which I lent her on purpose) with that joint. They milk their cows, reap their oats, and do all the work which requires hands in the same manner. They have a kind of hard flints, which by grinding against other stones they form into instruments that serve instead of wedges, axes, and hammers. With tools made of these flints, they likewise cut their hay, and reap their oats, which there groweth naturally in several fields; the Yahoos draw home the sheaves in carriages, and the servants tread them in certain covered huts, to get out the grain, which is kept in stores. They make a rude kind of earthen and wooden vessels, and bake the former in the sun.

If they can avoid casualties, they die only of old age, and are buried in the obscurest places that can be found, their friends and relations expressing neither joy nor grief at their departure; nor does the dying person discover the least regret that he is leaving the world, any more than if he were upon returning home from a visit to one of his neighbors; I remember my master having once made an appointment with a friend and his family to come to his house upon some affair of importance; on the day fixed, the mistress and her two children came very late; she made two excuses, first for her husband, who, as she said, happened that very morning to *lhnuwnh*. The word is strongly expressive in their language, but not easily rendered into English; it signifies, *to retire to his first Mother*. Her excuse for not coming sooner was that her husband dying late in the morning, she was a good while consulting her servants about a convenient place where his body should be laid; and I observed she behaved herself at our house, as cheerfully as the rest; she died about three months after.

They live generally to seventy or seventy-five years, very seldom to four-score; some weeks before their death they feel a gradual decay, but without pain. During this time they are much visited by their friends, because they cannot go abroad with their usual ease and satisfaction. However, about ten days before their death, which they seldom fail in computing, they return the visits that have been made by those who are nearest in the neighborhood, being carried in a convenient sledge drawn by Yahoos; which vehicle they use, not only upon this occasion, but when they grow old, upon long journeys, or when they are lamed by any accident. And therefore when the dying Houyhnhnms return those visits, they take a solemn leave of their friends, as if they were going to some remote part of the country, where they designed to pass the rest of their lives.

I know not whether it may be worth observing, that the Houyhnhnms have no word in their language to express anything that is evil, except what they borrow from the deformities or ill qualities of the Yahoos. Thus they denote the folly of a servant, an omission of a child, a stone that cuts their feet, a continuance of foul or unseasonable weather, and the like, by adding to each the epithet of Yahoo. For instance, *hhnm Yahoo, whnaholm Yahoo, ynlhmndwihlma Yahoo*, and an ill-contrived house, *ynholmhnmrohlnw Yahoo*.

I could with great pleasure enlarge farther upon the manners and virtues of this excellent people; but intending in a short time to publish a volume by itself expressly upon that subject, I refer the reader thither. And in the meantime, proceed to relate my own sad catastrophe.

CHAPTER X

The Author's economy, and happy life among the Houyhnhnms. His great improvement in virtue, by conversing with them. Their conversations. The Author hath notice given him by his master that he must depart from the country. He falls into a swoon for grief, but submits. He contrives and finishes a canoe, by the help of a fellow servant, and puts to sea at a venture.

I had settled my little economy to my own heart's content. My master had ordered a room to be made for me after their manner, about six yards from the house; the sides and floors of which I plastered with clay, and covered with rush mats of my own contriving; I had beaten hemp, which there grows wild, and made of it a sort of ticking; this I filled with the feathers of several birds I had taken with springes made of Yahoos' hairs, and were excellent food. I had worked two chairs with my knife, the sorrel nag helping me in the grosser and more laborious part. When my clothes were worn to rags, I made myself others with the skins of rabbits, and of a certain beautiful animal about the same size, called *nnuhnoh*, the skin of which is covered with a fine down. Of these I likewise made very tolerable stockings. I soled my shoes with wood which I cut from a tree, and fitted to the upper leather, and when this was worn out, I supplied it with the skins of Yahoos, dried in the sun. I often got honey out of hollow trees, which I mingled with water, or eat it with my bread. No man could more verify the truth of these two maxims, that *Nature is very easily satisfied*; and, that *Necessity is the mother of invention*. I enjoyed perfect health of body, and tranquility of mind; I did not feel the treachery or inconstancy of a friend, nor the inquiries of a secret or open enemy. I had no occasion of bribing, flattering, or pimping to procure the favor of any great man, or of his minion. I wanted no fence against fraud or oppression; here was neither physician to destroy my body, nor lawyer to ruin my fortune; no informer to watch my words and actions, or forge accusations against me for hire; here were no gibers, censurers, backbiters, pickpockets, highwaymen, housebreakers, attorneys, bawds, buffoons, gamesters, politicians, wits, splenetics, tedious talkers, controvertists, ravishers, murderers, robbers, virtuosos; no leaders or followers of party and faction; no encouragers to vice, by seducement or examples; no dungeons, axes, gibbets, whipping posts, or pillories; no cheating shopkeepers or mechanics; no pride, vanity or affectation; no fops, bullies, drunkards, strolling whores, or poxes; no ranting, lewd, expensive wives; no stupid, proud pedants; no importunate, overbearing, quarrelsome, noisy, roaring, empty, conceited, swearing companions; no scoundrels raised from the dust upon the merit of their vices; or nobility thrown into it on account of their virtues; no lords, fiddlers, judges, or dancing masters.

I had the favor of being admitted to several Houyhnhnms, who came to visit or dine with my master; where his honor graciously suffered me to wait in the room, and listen to their discourse. Both he and his company would often descend to ask me questions, and receive my answers. I had also sometimes the honor of attending my master in his visits to others. I never presumed to speak, except in answer to a question; and then I did it with inward regret, because it was a loss of so much time for improving myself; but I was infinitely delighted with the station of an humble auditor in such conversations, where nothing passed but what was useful, expressed in the fewest and most significant words; where (as I have already said) the greatest decency was observed, without the least degree of ceremony; where no person spoke without being pleased himself, and pleasing his companions; where there was no interruption, tediousness, heat, or difference of sentiments. They have a notion, that when people are met together, a short silence doth much improve conversation; this I found to be true; for during those little intermissions of talk, new ideas would arise in their minds, which very much enlivened the discourse. Their subjects are generally on friendship and benevolence; on order and economy; sometimes upon the visible operations of nature, or ancient traditions; upon the bounds and limits of virtue; upon the unerring rules of reason; or upon some determinations, to be taken at the next great assembly; and often upon the various excellencies of poetry. I may add, without vanity, that my presence often gave them sufficient matter for discourse, because it afforded my master an occasion of letting his friends into the history of me and my country, upon which they were all pleased to discant in a manner not very advantageous to human kind; and for that reason I shall not repeat what they said; only I may be allowed to observe that his honor, to my great admiration, appeared to understand the nature of Yahoos much better than myself. He went through all our vices and follies, and discovered many which I had never mentioned to him; by only supposing what qualities a Yahoo of their country, with a small proportion of reason, might be capable of exerting; and concluded, with too much probability, how vile as well as miserable such a creature must be.

I freely confess, that all the little knowledge I have of any value was acquired by the lectures I received from my master, and from hearing the discourses of him and his friends; to which I should be prouder to listen, than to dictate to the greatest and wisest assembly in Europe. I admired the strength, comeliness, and speed of the inhabitants; and such a constellation of virtues in such amiable persons produced in me the highest veneration. At first, indeed, I did not feel that natural awe which the Yahoos and all other animals bear towards them; but it grew upon me by degrees, much sooner than I imagined, and was mingled with a respectful love and gratitude, that they would condescend to distinguish me from the rest of my species.

When I thought of my family, my friends, my countrymen, or human race in general, I considered them as they really were, Yahoos in shape and disposition, perhaps a little more civilized, and qualified with the gift of speech; but making no other use of reason than to improve and mutiply those vices, whereof their brethren in this country had only the share that nature allotted them. When I happened to behold the reflection of my own form in a lake or fountain, I turned away my face in horror and detestation of myself, and could better endure the sight of a common Yahoo than of my own person. By conversing with the Houyhnhnms, and looking upon them with delight, I fell to imitate their gait and gesture, which is now grown into a habit; and my friends often tell me in a blunt way, that I trot like a horse; which, however, I take for a great compliment; neither shall I disown, that in speaking I am apt to fall into the voice and manner of the Houyhnhnms, and hear myself ridiculed on that account without the least mortification.

In the midst of this happiness, when I looked upon myself to be fully settled for life, my master sent for me one morning a little earlier than his usual hour. I observed by his countenance that he was in some perplexity, and at a loss how to begin what he had to speak. After a short silence, he told me, he did not know how I would take what he was going to say; that, in the last general assembly, when the affair of the Yahoos was entered upon, the representatives had taken offense at his keeping a Yahoo (meaning myself) in his family more like a Houyhnhnm than a brute animal. That he was known frequently to converse with me, as if he could receive some advantage of pleasure in my company; that such a practice was not agreeable to reason or nature, or a thing ever heard of before among them. The assembly did therefore exhort him, either to employ me like the rest of my species, or command me to swim back to the place from whence I came. That the first of these expedients was utterly rejected by all the Houyhnhnms who had ever seen me at his house or their own; for, they alleged, that because I had some rudiments of reason, added to the natural pravity of those animals, it was to be feared, I might be able to seduce them into the woody and mountainous parts of the country, and bring them in troops by night to destroy the Houyhnhnms' cattle, as being naturally of the ravenous kind, and averse from labor.

My master added that he was daily pressed by the Houyhnhnms of the neighborhood to have the assembly's exhortation executed, which he could not put off much longer. He doubted[8] it would be impossible for me to swim to another country; and therefore wished I would contrive some sort of vehicle resembling those I had described to him, that might carry me on the sea; in which work I should have the assistance of his own servants, as well as those of his neighbors. He concluded that for his own part he could have been content to keep me in his service as long as I lived; because he found I had cured myself of some bad habits and dispositions, by endeavoring, as far as my inferior nature was capable, to imitate the Houyhnhnms.

I should here observe to the reader, that a decree of the general assembly in this country is expressed by the word *hnhloayn*, which signifies an exhortation, as near as I can render it; for they have no conception how a rational creature can be compelled, but only advised, or exhorted; because no person can disobey reason without giving up his claim to be a rational creature.

I was struck with the utmost grief and despair at my master's discourse; and being unable to support the agonies I was under, I fell into a swoon at his feet; when I came to myself, he told me that he concluded I had been dead (for these people are subject to no such imbecilities of nature). I answered, in a faint voice, that death would have been too great an happiness; that although I could not blame the assembly's exhortation, or the urgency of his friends; yet in my weak and corrupt judgment, I thought it might consist with reason to have been less rigorous. That I could not swim a league, and probably the nearest land to theirs might be distant above an hundred; that many materials, necessary for making a

8. Suspected.

small vessel to carry me off, were wholly wanting in this country, which, however, I would attempt in obedience and gratitude to his honor, although I concluded the thing to be impossible, and therefore looked on myself as already devoted[9] to destruction. That the certain prospect of an unnatural death was the least of my evils; for, supposing I should escape with life by some strange adventure, how could I think with temper[1] of passing my days among Yahoos, and relapsing into my old corruptions, for want of examples to lead and keep me within the paths of virtue. That I knew too well upon what solid reasons all the determinations of the wise Houyhnhnms were founded, not to be shaken by arguments of mine, a miserable Yahoo; and therefore after presenting him with my humble thanks for the offer of his servants' assistance in making a vessel, and desiring a reasonable time for so difficult a work, I told him I would endeavor to preserve a wretched being; and, if ever I returned to England, was not without hopes of being useful to my own species by celebrating the praises of the renowned Houyhnhnms, and proposing their virtues to the imitation of mankind.

My master in a few words made me a very gracious reply, allowed me the space of two months to finish my boat, and ordered the sorrel nag, my fellow servant (for so at this distance I may presume to call him), to follow my instructions, because I told my master that his help would be sufficient, and I knew he had a tenderness for me.

In his company my first business was to go to that part of the coast where my rebellious crew had ordered me to be set on shore. I got upon a height, and looking on every side into the sea, fancied I saw a small island towards the northeast; I took out my pocket glass, and could then clearly distinguish it about five leagues off, as I computed; but it appeared to the sorrel nag to be only a blue cloud; for, as he had no conception of any country besides his own, so he could not be as expert in distinguishing remote objects at sea, as we who so much converse in that element.

After I had discovered this island, I considered no farther; but resolved, it should, if possible, be the first place of my banishment, leaving the consequence to fortune.

I returned home, and consulting with the sorrel nag, we went into a copse at some distance, where I with my knife, and he with a sharp flint fastened very artificially,[2] after their manner, to a wooden handle, cut down several oak wattles about the thickness of a walking staff, and some larger pieces. But I shall not trouble the reader with a particular description of my own mechanics; let it suffice to say, that in six weeks time, with the help of the sorrel nag, who performed the parts that required most labor, I finished a sort of Indian canoe; but much larger, covering it with the skins of Yahoos, well stitched together, with hempen threads of my own making. My sail was likewise composed of the skins of the same animal; but I made use of the youngest I could get, the older being too tough and thick; and I likewise provided myself with four paddles. I laid in a stock of boiled flesh, of rabbits and fowls; and took with me two vessels, one filled with milk, and the other with water.

I tried my canoe in a large pond near my master's house, and then corrected in it what was amiss, stopping all the chinks with Yahoo's tallow, till I found it

9. Doomed.   2. Adroitly.
1. Equanimity.

staunch, and able to bear me and my freight. And when it was as complete as I could possibly make it, I had it drawn on a carriage very gently by Yahoos, to the seaside, under the conduct of the sorrel nag and another servant.

When all was ready, and the day came for my departure, I took leave of my master and lady, and the whole family, my eyes flowing with tears and my heart quite sunk with grief. But his honor, out of curiosity, and perhaps (if I may speak it without vanity) partly out of kindness, was determined to see me in my canoe; and got several of his neighboring friends to accompany him. I was forced to wait above an hour for the tide, and then observing the wind very fortunately bearing towards the island to which I intended to steer my course, I took a second leave of my master; but as I was going to prostrate myself to kiss his hoof, he did me the honor to raise it gently to my mouth. I am not ignorant how much I have been censured for mentioning this last particular. Detractors are pleased to think it improbable that so illustrious a person should descend to give so great a mark of distinction to a creature so inferior as I. Neither have I forgot how apt some travelers are to boast of extraordinary favors they have received. But, if these censurers were better acquainted with the noble and courteous disposition of the Houyhnhnms, they would soon change their opinion. I paid my respects to the rest of the Houyhnhnms in his honor's company; then getting into my canoe, I pushed off from shore.

CHAPTER XI

The Author's dangerous voyage. He arrives at New Holland, hoping to settle there. Is wounded with an arrow by one of the natives. Is seized and carried by force into a Portuguese ship. The great civilities of the Captain. The Author arrives at England.

I began this desperate voyage on February 15, 1714/5,[3] at 9 o'clock in the morning. The wind was very favorable; however, I made use at first only of my paddles; but considering I should soon be weary, and that the wind might probably chop about, I ventured to set up my little sail; and thus, with the help of the tide, I went at the rate of a league and a half an hour, as near as I could guess. My master and his friends continued on the shore, till I was almost out of sight; and I often heard the sorrel nag (who always loved me) crying out, *"Hnuy illa nyha maiah Yahoo"* ("Take care of thyself, gentle Yahoo").

My design was, if possible, to discover some small island uninhabited, yet sufficient by my labor to furnish me with necessaries of life, which I would have thought a greater happiness than to be first minister in the politest court of Europe, so horrible was the idea I conceived of returning to live in the society and under the government of Yahoos. For in such a solitude as I desired, I could at least enjoy my own thoughts, and reflect with delight on the virtues of those inimitable Houyhnhnms, without any opportunity of degenerating into the vices and corruptions of my own species.

The reader may remember what I related when my crew conspired against me, and confined me to my cabin, how I continued there several weeks, without knowing what course we took; and when I was put ashore in the longboat,

3. I.e., 1714. The year began on March 25.

how the sailors told me with oaths, whether true or false, that they knew not in what part of the world we were. However, I did then believe us to be about 10 degrees southward of the Cape of Good Hope, or about 45 degrees southern latitude, as I gathered from some general words I overheard among them, being I supposed to the southeast in their intended voyage to Madagascar. And although this were but little better than conjecture, yet I resolved to steer my course eastward, hoping to reach the southwest coast of New Holland, and perhaps some such island as I desired, lying westward of it. The wind was full west, and by six in the evening I computed I had gone eastward at least eighteen leagues; when I spied a very small island about half a league off, which I soon reached. It was nothing but a rock with one creek,[4] naturally arched by the force of tempests. Here I put in my canoe, and climbing a part of the rock, I could plainly discover land to the east, extending from south to north. I lay all night in my canoe; and repeating my voyage early in the morning, I arrived in seven hours to the southeast point of New Holland.[5] This confirmed me in the opinion I have long entertained, that the maps and charts place this country at least three degrees more to the east than it really is; which thought I communicated many years ago to my worthy friend Mr. Herman Moll,[6] and gave him my reasons for it, although he hath rather chosen to follow other authors.

I saw no inhabitants in the place where I landed; and being unarmed, I was afraid of venturing far into the country. I found some shellfish on the shore, and eat them raw, not daring to kindle a fire, for fear of being discovered by the natives. I continued three days feeding on oysters and limpets, to save my own provisions; and I fortunately found a brook of excellent water, which gave me great relief.

On the fourth day, venturing out early a little too far, I saw twenty or thirty natives upon a height, not above five hundred yards from me. They were stark naked, men, women, and children round a fire, as I could discover by the smoke. One of them spied me, and gave notice to the rest; five of them advanced towards me, leaving the women and children at the fire. I made what haste I could to the shore, and getting into my canoe, shoved off; the savages observing me retreat, ran after me; and before I could get far enough into the sea, discharged an arrow, which wounded me deeply on the inside of my left knee. (I shall carry the mark to my grave.) I apprehended the arrow might be poisoned; and paddling out of the reach of their darts (being a calm day) I made a shift to suck the wound, and dress it as well as I could.

I was at a loss what to do, for I durst not return to the same landing place, but stood to the north, and was forced to paddle; for the wind, although very gentle, was against me, blowing northwest. As I was looking about for a secure landing place, I saw a sail to the north northeast, which appearing every minute more visible, I was in some doubt whether I should wait for them or no; but at last my detestation of the Yahoo race prevailed; and turning my canoe, I sailed and paddled together to the south, and got into the same creek from whence I set out in the morning, choosing rather to trust myself among these barbarians than live with European Yahoos. I drew up my canoe as close as I could to the

---

4. A bay.
5. Present-day Republic of South Africa.

6. A famous contemporary mapmaker.

shore, and hid myself behind a stone by the little brook, which, as I have already said, was excellent water.

The ship came within half a league of this creek, and sent out her longboat with vessels to take in fresh water (for the place it seems was very well known), but I did not observe it until the boat was almost on shore; and it was too late to seek another hiding place. The seamen at their landing observed my canoe, and rummaging it all over, easily conjectured that the owner could not be far off. Four of them well armed searched every cranny and lurking hole, till at last they found me flat on my face behind the stone. They gazed a while in admiration at my strange uncouth dress; my coat made of skins, my wooden-soled shoes, and my furred stockings; from whence, however, they concluded I was not a native of the place, who all go naked. One of the seamen in Portuguese bid me rise, and asked who I was. I understood that language very well, and getting upon my feet, said I was a poor Yahoo, banished from the Houyh-nhnms, and desired they would please to let me depart. They admired to hear me answer them in their own tongue, and saw by my complexion I must be an European; but were at a loss to know what I meant by Yahoos and Houyh-nhnms, and at the same time fell a laughing at my strange tone in speaking, which resembled the neighing of a horse. I trembled all the while betwixt fear and hatred; I again desired leave to depart, and was gently moving to my canoe; but they laid hold on me, desiring to know what country I was of? whence I came? with many other questions. I told them I was born in England, from whence I came about five years ago, and then their country and ours was at peace. I therefore hoped they would not treat me as an enemy, since I meant them no harm, but was a poor Yahoo, seeking some desolate place where to pass the remainder of his unfortunate life.

When they began to talk, I thought I never heard or saw any thing so unnatural; for it appeared to me as monstrous as if a dog or a cow should speak in England, or a Yahoo in Houyhnhnmland. The honest Portuguese were equally amazed at my strange dress, and the odd manner of delivering my words, which however they understood very well. They spoke to me with great humanity, and said they were sure their Captain would carry me *gratis* to Lisbon, from whence I might return to my own country; that two of the seamen would go back to the ship, to inform the Captain of what they had seen, and receive his orders; in the meantime, unless I would give my solemn oath not to fly, they would secure me by force. I thought it best to comply with their proposal. They were very curious to know my story, but I gave them very little satisfaction; and they all conjectured, that my misfortunes had impaired my reason. In two hours the boat, which went laden with vessels of water, returned with the Captain's commands to fetch me on board. I fell on my knees to preserve my liberty; but all was in vain, and the men having tied me with cords, heaved me into the boat, from whence I was taken into the ship, and from thence into the Captain's cabin.

His name was Pedro de Mendez; he was a very courteous and generous person; he entreated me to give some account of myself, and desired to know what I would eat or drink; said I should be used as well as himself, and spoke so many obliging things, that I wondered to find such civilities from a Yahoo. However, I remained silent and sullen; I was ready to faint at the very smell of him and his men. At last I desired something to eat out of my own canoe; but he ordered me a chicken and some excellent wine, and then directed that

I should be put to bed in a very clean cabin. I would not undress myself, but lay on the bedclothes; and in half an hour stole out, when I thought the crew was at dinner; and getting to the side of the ship, was going to leap into the sea, and swim for my life, rather than continue among Yahoos. But one of the seamen prevented me, and having informed the Captain, I was chained to my cabin.

After dinner Don Pedro came to me, and desired to know my reason for so desperate an attempt; assured me he only meant to do me all the service he was able; and spoke so very movingly, that at last I descended to treat him like an animal which had some little portion of reason. I gave him a very short relation of my voyage; of the conspiracy against me by my own men; of the country where they set me on shore, and of my five years residence there. All which he looked upon as if it were a dream or a vision; whereat I took great offense; for I had quite forgot the faculty of lying, so peculiar to Yahoos in all countries where they preside, and consequently the disposition of suspecting truth in others of their own species. I asked him whether it were the custom of his country to *say the thing that was not*? I assured him I had almost forgot what he meant by falsehood; and if I had lived a thousand years in Houyhnhnmland, I should never have heard a lie from the meanest servant. That I was altogether indifferent whether he believed me or no; but however, in return for his favors, I would give so much allowance to the corruption of his nature, as to answer any objection he would please to make; and he might easily discover the truth.

The Captain, a wise man, after many endeavors to catch me tripping in some part of my story, at last began to have a better opinion of my veracity. But he added that since I professed so inviolable an attachment to truth, I must give him my word of honor to bear him company in this voyage without attempting anything against my life; or else he would continue me a prisoner till we arrived at Lisbon. I gave him the promise he required; but at the same time protested that I would suffer the greatest hardships rather than return to live among Yahoos.

Our voyage passed without any considerable accident. In gratitude to the Captain I sometimes sat with him at his earnest request, and strove to conceal my antipathy against humankind, although it often broke out; which he suffered to pass without observation. But the greatest part of the day, I confined myself to my cabin, to avoid seeing any of the crew. The Captain had often entreated me to strip myself of my savage dress, and offered to lend me the best suit of clothes he had. This I would not be prevailed on to accept, abhorring to cover myself with anything that had been on the back of a Yahoo. I only desired he would lend me two clean shirts, which having been washed since he wore them, I believed would not so much defile me. These I changed every second day, and washed them myself.

We arrived at Lisbon, Nov. 5, 1715. At our landing, the Captain forced me to cover myself with his cloak, to prevent the rabble from crowding about me. I was conveyed to his own house; and at my earnest request, he led me up to the highest room backwards.[7] I conjured him to conceal from all persons what I had told him of the Houyhnhnms; because the least hint of such a story would not only draw numbers of people to see me, but probably put me in danger of being imprisoned, or burned by the Inquisition. The Captain persuaded me to accept a suit of clothes newly made; but I would not suffer the tailor to

7. At the rear.

take my measure; however, Don Pedro being almost of my size, they fitted me well enough. He accoutred me with other necessaries, all new, which I aired for twenty-four hours before I would use them.

The Captain had no wife, nor above three servants, none of which were suffered to attend at meals; and his whole deportment was so obliging, added to very good human understanding, that I really began to tolerate his company. He gained so far upon me, that I ventured to look out of the back window. By degrees I was brought into another room, from whence I peeped into the street, but drew my head back in a fright. In a week's time he seduced me down to the door. I found my terror gradually lessened, but my hatred and contempt seemed to increase. I was at last bold enough to walk the street in his company, but kept my nose well stopped with rue, or sometimes with tobacco.

In ten days, Don Pedro, to whom I had given some account of my domestic affairs, put it upon me as a point of honor and conscience that I ought to return to my native country, and live at home with my wife and children. He told me there was an English ship in the port just ready to sail, and he would furnish me with all things necessary. It would be tedious to repeat his arguments, and my contradictions. He said it was altogether impossible to find such a solitary island as I had desired to live in; but I might command in my own house, and pass my time in a manner as recluse as I pleased.

I complied at last, finding I could not do better. I left Lisbon the 24th day of November, in an English merchantman, but who was the Master I never inquired. Don Pedro accompanied me to the ship, and lent me twenty pounds. He took kind leave of me, and embraced me at parting; which I bore as well as I could. During this last voyage I had no commerce with the Master, or any of his men; but pretending I was sick kept close in my cabin. On the fifth of December, 1715, we cast anchor in the Downs about nine in the morning, and at three in the afternoon I got safe to my house at Redriff.

My wife and family received me with great surprise and joy, because they concluded me certainly dead; but I must freely confess, the sight of them filled me only with hatred, disgust, and contempt; and the more, by reflecting on the near alliance I had to them. For, although since my unfortunate exile from the Houyhnhnm country, I had compelled myself to tolerate the sight of Yahoos, and to converse with Don Pedro de Mendez; yet my memory and imaginations were perpetually filled with the virtues and ideas of those exalted Houyhnhnms. And when I began to consider that by copulating with one of the Yahoo species, I had become a parent of more, it struck me with the utmost shame, confusion, and horror.

As soon as I entered the house, my wife took me in her arms, and kissed me; at which, having not been used to the touch of that odious animal for so many years, I fell in a swoon for almost an hour. At the time I am writing, it is five years since my last return to England; during the first year I could not endure my wife or children in my presence, the very smell of them was intolerable; much less could I suffer them to eat in the same room. To this hour they dare not presume to touch my bread, or drink out of the same cup; neither was I ever able to let one of them take me by the hand. The first money I laid out was to buy two young stone-horses,[8] which I keep in a good stable, and next to

8. Stallions.

them the groom is my greatest favorite; for I feel my spirits revived by the smell he contracts in the stable. My horses understand me tolerably well; I converse with them at least four hours every day. They are strangers to bridle or saddle; they live in great amity with me, and friendship to each other.

CHAPTER XII

The Author's veracity. His design in publishing this work. His censure of those travelers who swerve from the truth. The Author clears himself from any sinister ends in writing. An objection answered. The method of planting colonies. His native country commended. The right of the crown to those countries described by the Author is justified. The difficulty of conquering them. The Author takes his last leave of the reader; proposeth his manner of living for the future; gives good advice, and concludeth.

Thus, gentle reader, I have given thee a faithful history of my travels for sixteen years, and above seven months; wherein I have not been so studious of ornament as of truth. I could perhaps like others have astonished thee with strange improbable tales; but I rather chose to relate plain matter of fact in the simplest manner and style; because my principal design was to inform, and not to amuse thee.

It is easy for us who travel into remote countries, which are seldom visited by Englishmen or other Europeans, to form descriptions of wonderful animals both at sea and land. Whereas a traveler's chief aim should be to make men wiser and better, and to improve their minds by the bad as well as good example of what they deliver concerning foreign places.

I could heartily wish a law were enacted, that every traveler, before he were permitted to publish his voyages, should be obliged to make oath before the Lord High Chancellor that all he intended to print was absolutely true to the best of his knowledge; for then the world would no longer be deceived as it usually is, while some writers, to make their works pass the better upon the public, impose the grossest falsities on the unwary reader. I have perused several books of travels with great delight in my younger days; but, having since gone over most parts of the globe, and been able to contradict many fabulous accounts from my own observation, it hath given me a great disgust against this part of reading, and some indignation to see the credulity of mankind so impudently abused. Therefore, since my acquaintance were pleased to think my poor endeavors might not be unacceptable to my country; I imposed on myself as a maxim, never to be swerved from, that I would *strictly adhere to truth*; neither indeed can I be ever under the least temptation to vary from it, while I retain in my mind the lectures and example of my noble master, and the other illustrious Houyhnhnms, of whom I had so long the honor to be an humble hearer.

————*Nec si miserum Fortuna Sinonem*
Finxit, vanum etiam, mendacemque improba finget.[9]

———

9. Fortune has made a derelict of Sinon / but the bitch won't make an empty liar of him, too (Latin; Virgil's *Aeneid* 2).

I know very well how little reputation is to be got by writings which require neither genius nor learning, nor indeed any other talent, except a good memory, or an exact *Journal*. I know likewise, that writers of travels, like dictionary-makers, are sunk into oblivion by the weight and bulk of those who come last, and therefore lie uppermost. And it is highly probable that such travelers who shall hereafter visit the countries described in this work of mine, may be detecting my errors (if there be any) and adding many new discoveries of their own, jostle me out of vogue, and stand in my place, making the world forget that ever I was an author. This indeed would be too great a mortification if I wrote for fame; but, as my sole intention was the PUBLIC GOOD, I cannot be altogether disappointed. For, who can read the virtues I have mentioned in the glorious Houyhnhnms, without being ashamed of his own vices, when he considers himself as the reasoning, governing animal of his country? I shall say nothing of those remote nations where Yahoos preside; amongst which the least corrupted are the Brobdingnagians, whose wise maxims in morality and government it would be our happiness to observe. But I forbear descanting further, and rather leave the judicious reader to his own remarks and applications.

I am not a little pleased that this work of mine can possibly meet with no censurers; for what objections can be made against a writer who relates only plain facts that happened in such distant countries, where we have not the least interest with respect either to trade or negotiations? I have carefully avoided every fault with which common writers of travels are often too justly charged. Besides, I meddle not the least with any party, but write without passion, prejudice, or ill-will against any man or number of men whatsoever. I write for the noblest end, to inform and instruct mankind, over whom I may, without breach of modesty, pretend to some superiority, from the advantages I received by conversing so long among the most accomplished Houyhnhnms. I write without any view towards profit or praise. I never suffer a word to pass that may look like reflection, or possibly give the least offense even to those who are most ready to take it. So that, I hope, I may with justice pronounce myself an Author perfectly blameless; against whom the tribes of answerers, considerers, observers, reflectors, detecters, remarkers will never be able to find matter for exercising their talents.

I confess it was whispered to me that I was bound in duty as a subject of England, to have given in a memorial to a secretary of state, at my first coming over; because, whatever lands are discovered by a subject, belong to the Crown. But I doubt whether our conquests in the countries I treat of would be as easy as those of Ferdinando Cortez[1] over the naked Americans. The Lilliputians, I think, are hardly worth the charge of a fleet and army to reduce them; and I question whether it might be prudent or safe to attempt the Brobdingnagians; or, whether an English army would be much at their ease with the Flying Island over their heads. The Houyhnhnms, indeed, appear not to be so well prepared for war, a science to which they are perfect strangers, and especially against missive weapons. However, supposing myself to be a minister of state, I could never give my advice for invading them. Their prudence, unanimity, unacquaintedness with fear, and their love of their country would amply supply

1. Hernán Cortés (1485–1547), who destroyed the Aztec Empire.

all defects in the military art. Imagine twenty thousand of them breaking into the midst of an European army, confounding the ranks, overturning the carriages, battering the warriors' faces into mummy, by terrible yerks from their hinder hoofs: for they would well deserve the character given to Augustus, *Recalcitrat undique tutus*.[2] But instead of proposals for conquering that magnanimous nation, I rather wish they were in a capacity or disposition to send a sufficient number of their inhabitants for civilizing Europe; by teaching us the first principles of Honor, Justice, Truth, Temperance, Public Spirit, Fortitude, Chastity, Friendship, Benevolence, and Fidelity. The names of all which Virtues are still retained among us in most languages, and are to be met with in modern as well as ancient authors, which I am able to assert from my own small reading.

But I had another reason which made me less forward to enlarge his majesty's dominions by my discoveries: to say the truth, I had conceived a few scruples with relation to the distributive justice of princes upon those occasions. For instance, a crew of pirates are driven by a storm they know not whither; at length a boy discovers land from the topmast; they go on shore to rob and plunder; they see an harmless people, are entertained with kindness, they give the country a new name, they take formal possession of it for the king, they set up a rotten plank or a stone for a memorial, they murder two or three dozen of the natives, bring away a couple more by force for a sample, return home, and get their pardon. Here commences a new dominion acquired with a title by Divine Right. Ships are sent with the first opportunity; the natives driven out or destroyed, their princes tortured to discover their gold; a free license given to all acts of inhumanity and lust; the earth reeking with the blood of its inhabitants: and this execrable crew of butchers employed in so pious an expedition is a *modern colony* sent to convert and civilize an idolatrous and barbarous people.

But this description, I confess, doth by no means affect the British nation, who may be an example to the whole world for their wisdom, care, and justice in planting colonies; their liberal endowments for the advancement of religion and learning; their choice of devout and able pastors to propagate Christianity; their caution in stocking their provinces with people of sober lives and conversations from this the Mother Kingdom; their strict regard to the distribution of justice, in supplying the civil administration through all their colonies with officers of the greatest abilities, utter strangers to corruption: and to crown all, by sending the most vigilant and virtuous governors, who have no other views than the happiness of the people over whom they preside, and the honor of the king their master.

But, as those countries which I have described do not appear to have any desire of being conquered, and enslaved, murdered, or driven out by colonies, nor abound either in gold, silver, sugar, or tobacco, I did humbly conceive they were by no means proper objects of our zeal, our valor, or our interest. However, if those whom it may concern, think fit to be of another opinion, I am ready to depose, when I shall be lawfully called, that no European did ever visit these countries before me. I mean, if the inhabitants ought to be believed.

---

2. He kicks backward, at every point on his guard (Latin; Horace's *Satires* 2.20). "Mummy": pulp. "Yerks": kicks.

But, as to the formality of taking possession in my sovereign's name, it never came once into my thoughts; and if it had, yet as my affairs then stood, I should perhaps in point of prudence and self-preservation have put it off to a better opportunity.

Having thus answered the only objection that can be raised against me as a traveler, I here take a final leave of my courteous readers, and return to enjoy my own speculations in my little garden at Redriff; to apply those excellent lessons of virtue which I learned among the Houyhnhnms; to instruct the Yahoos of my own family as far as I shall find them docible animals; to behold my figure often in a glass, and thus if possible habituate myself by time to tolerate the sight of a human creature; to lament the brutality of Houyhnhnms in my own country, but always treat their persons with respect, for the sake of my noble master, his family, his friends, and the whole Houyhnhnm race, whom these of ours have the honor to resemble in all their lineaments, however their intellectuals came to degenerate.

I began last week to permit my wife to sit at dinner with me, at the farthest end of a long table; and to answer (but with the utmost brevity) the few questions I ask her. Yet the smell of a Yahoo continuing very offensive, I always keep my nose well stopped with rue, lavender, or tobacco leaves. And although it be hard for a man late in life to remove old habits, I am not altogether out of hopes in some time to suffer a neighbor Yahoo in my company, without the apprehensions I am yet under of his teeth or his claws.

My reconcilement to the Yahoo kind in general might not be so difficult, if they would be content with those vices and follies only which nature hath entitled them to. I am not in the least provoked at the sight of a lawyer, a pickpocket, a colonel, a fool, a lord, a gamester, politician, a whoremonger, a physician, an evidence, a suborner, an attorney, a traitor, or the like: this is all according to the due course of things. But when I behold a lump of deformity, and diseases both in body and mind, smitten with pride, it immediately breaks all the measures of my patience; neither shall I be ever able to comprehend how such an animal and such a vice could tally together. The wise and virtuous Houyhnhnms, who abound in all excellencies that can adorn a rational creature, have no name for this vice in their language, which hath no terms to express anything that is evil, except those whereby they describe the detestable qualities of their Yahoos, among which they were not able to distinguish this of pride, for want of thoroughly understanding human nature, as it showeth itself in other countries, where that animal presides. But I, who had more experience, could plainly observe some rudiments of it among the wild Yahoos.

But the Houyhnhnms, who live under the government of reason, are no more proud of the good qualities they possess, than I should be for not wanting a leg or an arm, which no man in his wits would boast of, although he must be miserable without them. I dwell the longer upon this subject from the desire I have to make the society of an English Yahoo by any means not insupportable; and therefore I here entreat those who have any tincture of this absurd vice, that they will not presume to appear in my sight.

A Modest Proposal

For Preventing the Children of Poor People in Ireland, from being a Burden to their Parents or Country; and for Making them Beneficial to the Public.

It is a melancholy object to those who walk through this great town,[1] or travel in the country, when they see the streets, the roads, and cabin-doors crowded with beggars of the female sex, followed by three, four, or six children, all in rags, and importuning every passenger for an alms. These mothers, instead of being able to work for their honest livelihood, are forced to employ all their time in strolling to beg sustenance for their helpless infants: who, as they grow up, either turn thieves for want of work, or leave their dear native country to fight for the Pretender in Spain, or sell themselves to the Barbadoes.[2]

I think it is agreed by all parties, that this prodigious number of children in the arms, or on the backs, or at the heels of their mothers, and frequently of their fathers, is, in the present deplorable state of the kingdom, a very great additional grievance; and, therefore, whoever could find out a fair, cheap, and easy method of making these children sound and useful members of the commonwealth, would deserve so well of the public, as to have his statue set up for a preserver of the nation.

But my intention is very far from being confined to provide only for the children of professed beggars; it is of a much greater extent, and shall take in the whole number of infants at a certain age, who are born of parents in effect as little able to support them as those who demand our charity in the streets.

As to my own part, having turned my thoughts for many years upon this important subject, and maturely weighed the several schemes of other projectors,[3] I have always found them grossly mistaken in their computation. It is true, a child, just dropped from its dam, may be supported by her milk for a solar year with little other nourishment; at most, not above the value of two shillings, which the mother may certainly get, or the value in scraps, by her lawful occupation of begging; and it is exactly at one year old that I propose to provide for them in such a manner, as, instead of being a charge upon their parents or the parish, or wanting food and raiment for the rest of their lives, they shall, on the contrary, contribute to the feeding, and partly to the clothing, of many thousands.

There is likewise another advantage in my scheme, that it will prevent those voluntary abortions, and that horrid practice of women murdering their bastard children, alas, too frequent among us, sacrificing the poor innocent babes, I doubt more to avoid the expense than the shame, which would move tears and pity in the most savage and inhuman breast.

The number of souls in this kingdom being usually reckoned one million and a half, of these I calculate there may be about two hundred thousand couple whose wives are breeders; from which number I subtract thirty thousand cou-

---

1. Dublin.
2. At this time a British possession, with a prosperous sugar industry. Workers were needed in the sugar plantations. The Pretender was James Edward (1688–1766), son of the Catholic king James II of England, called the "Old Pretender" (in distinction to his son Charles, nine years old at the time of this work, called the "Young Pretender"). Many thought him a legitimate claimant to the throne.
3. Planners.

ple, who are able to maintain their own children (although I apprehend there cannot be so many, under the present distresses of the kingdom); but this being granted, there will remain an hundred and seventy thousand breeders. I again subtract fifty thousand for those women who miscarry, or whose children die by accident or disease within the year. There only remain a hundred and twenty thousand children of poor parents annually born. The question therefore is how this number shall be reared and provided for? which, as I have already said, under the present situation of affairs, is utterly impossible by all the methods hitherto proposed. For we can neither employ them in handicraft or agriculture; we neither build houses (I mean in the country) nor cultivate land: they can very seldom pick up a livelihood by stealing until they arrive at six years old, except where they are of towardly parts;[4] although I confess they learn the rudiments much earlier; during which time they can, however, be properly looked upon only as probationers; as I have been informed by a principal gentleman in the county of Cavan, who protested to me, that he never knew above one or two instances under the age of six, even in a part of the kingdom so renowned for the quickest proficiency in that art.

I am assured by our merchants that a boy or a girl before twelve years old is no saleable commodity; and even when they come to this age they will not yield above three pounds or three pounds and half-a-crown at most, on the exchange; which cannot turn to account either to the parents or kingdom, the charge of nutriment and rags having been at least four times that value.

I shall now, therefore, humbly propose my own thoughts, which I hope will not be liable to the least objection.

I have been assured by a very knowing American of my acquaintance in London, that a young healthy child, well nursed, is, at a year old, a most delicious, nourishing, and wholesome food, whether stewed, roasted, baked, or boiled; and I make no doubt that it will equally serve in a fricassee or a ragout.

I do therefore humbly offer it to public consideration, that of the hundred and twenty thousand children already computed, twenty thousand may be reserved for breed, whereof only one-fourth part to be males; which is more than we allow to sheep, black cattle, or swine; and my reason is, that these children are seldom the fruits of marriage, a circumstance not much regarded by our savages, therefore one male will be sufficient to serve four females. That the remaining hundred thousand may, at a year old, be offered in sale to the persons of quality and fortune through the kingdom; always advising the mother to let them suck plentifully in the last month, so as to render them plump and fat for a good table. A child will make two dishes at an entertainment for friends; and when the family dines alone, the fore or hind quarter will make a reasonable dish, and, seasoned with a little pepper or salt, will be very good boiled on the fourth day, especially in winter.

I have reckoned, upon a medium,[5] that a child just born will weigh twelve pounds, and in a solar year, if tolerably nursed, increaseth to twenty-eight pounds.

I grant this food will be somewhat dear,[6] and therefore very proper for landlords, who, as they have already devoured most of the parents, seem to have the best title to the children.

---

4. Particularly talented, unusually gifted.
5. Average.
6. Expensive.

Infants' flesh will be in season throughout the year, but more plentifully in March, and a little before and after: for we are told by a grave author, an eminent French physician,[7] that fish being a prolific diet, there are more children born in Roman Catholic countries about nine months after Lent than at any other season; therefore, reckoning a year after Lent, the markets will be more glutted than usual, because the number of popish infants is at least three to one in this kingdom; and therefore it will have one other collateral advantage, by lessening the number of papists among us.

I have already computed the charge of nursing a beggar's child (in which list I reckon all cottagers, labourers, and four-fifths of the farmers) to be about two shillings per annum,[8] rags included; and I believe no gentleman would repine to give ten shillings for the carcass of a good fat child, which, as I have said, will make four dishes of excellent nutritive meat, when he has only some particular friend, or his own family, to dine with him. Thus the squire will learn to be a good landlord, and grow popular among his tenants; the mother will have eight shillings net profit, and be fit for work till she produces another child.

Those who are more thrifty (as I must confess the times require) may flay the carcass; the skin of which, artificially dressed, will make admirable gloves for ladies, and summer-boots for fine gentlemen.

As to our city of Dublin, shambles[9] may be appointed for this purpose in the most convenient parts of it, and butchers we may be assured will not be wanting; although I rather recommend buying the children alive, and dressing them hot from the knife, as we do roasting pigs.

A very worthy person, a true lover of his country, and whose virtues I highly esteem, was lately pleased, in discoursing on this matter, to offer a refinement upon my scheme. He said, that many gentlemen of this kingdom, having of late destroyed their deer, he conceived that the want of venison might be well supplied by the bodies of young lads and maidens, not exceeding fourteen years of age, nor under twelve; so great a number of both sexes in every country being now ready to starve for want of work and service; and these to be disposed of by their parents, if alive, or otherwise by their nearest relations. But, with due deference to so excellent a friend, and so deserving a patriot, I cannot be altogether in his sentiments; for as to the males, my American acquaintance assured me from frequent experience, that their flesh was generally tough and lean, like that of our schoolboys, by continual exercise, and their taste disagreeable; and to fatten them would not answer the charge. Then as to the females, it would, I think, with humble submission, be a loss to the public, because they soon would become breeders themselves: and besides, it is not improbable that some scrupulous people might be apt to censure such a practice (although indeed very unjustly) as a little bordering upon cruelty; which, I confess hath always been with me the strongest objection against any project, how well soever intended.

But in order to justify my friend, he confessed that this expedient was put into his head by the famous Psalmanazar,[1] a native of the island Formosa, who

---

7. François Rabelais (1494?–1553), French satirist and author of *Gargantua and Pantagruel* (1532–52).
8. Per year (Latin).
9. Slaughterhouses.
1. George Psalmanazar (1679?–1763), a liter-ary impostor born in southern France who claimed to be a native of Formosa and a recent Christian convert. He published a catechism in an invented language that he called Formosan as well as a description of Formosa with an introductory autobiography.

came from thence to London above twenty years ago; and in conversation told my friend, that in his country, when any young person happened to be put to death, the executioner sold the carcass to persons of quality as a prime dainty; and that in his time the body of a plump girl of fifteen, who was crucified for an attempt to poison the emperor, was sold to his Imperial Majesty's prime minister of state, and other great mandarins of the court, in joints from the gibbet,[2] at four hundred crowns. Neither indeed can I deny, that if the same use were made of several plump young girls in this town, who, without one single groat to their fortunes, cannot stir abroad without a chair,[3] and appear at playhouse and assemblies in foreign fineries which they never will pay for, the kingdom would not be the worse.

Some persons of a desponding spirit are in great concern about the vast number of poor people who are aged, diseased, or maimed; and I have been desired to employ my thoughts what course may be taken to ease the nation of so grievous an encumbrance. But I am not in the least pain upon that matter, because it is very well known, that they are every day dying, and rotting, by cold and famine, and filth and vermin, as fast as can be reasonably expected. And as to the younger labourers, they are now in almost as hopeful a condition: they cannot get work, and consequently pine away for want of nourishment, to a degree, that if at any time they are accidentally hired to common labour, they have not strength to perform it; and thus the country and themselves are happily delivered from the evils to come.

I have too long digressed, and therefore shall return to my subject. I think the advantages by the proposal which I have made are obvious and many, as well as of the highest importance.

For first, as I have already observed, it would greatly lessen the number of papists, with whom we are yearly overrun, being the principal breeders of the nation as well as our most dangerous enemies; and who stay at home on purpose with a design to deliver the kingdom to the Pretender, hoping to take their advantage by the absence of so many good Protestants, who have chosen rather to leave their country than stay at home and pay tithes against their conscience to an idolatrous Episcopal curate.

Secondly, the poorer tenants will have something valuable of their own, which by law may be made liable to distress,[4] and help to pay their landlord's rent; their corn and cattle being already seized, and money a thing unknown.

Thirdly, whereas the maintenance of an hundred thousand children, from two years old and upwards, cannot be computed at less than ten shillings a piece per annum, the nation's stock will be thereby increased fifty thousand pounds per annum; besides the profit of a new dish introduced to the tables of all gentlemen of fortune in the kingdom who have any refinement in taste. And the money will circulate among ourselves, the goods being entirely of our own growth and manufacture.

---

2. The post from which the bodies of criminals were hung in chains after execution. "Joints": portions of a carcass carved up by a butcher.

3. I.e., a sedan chair, an enclosed seat carried on poles by men.

4. The legal seizing of goods to satisfy a debt, particularly for unpaid rent.

Fourthly, the constant breeders, besides the gain of eight shillings sterling per annum by the sale of their children, will be rid of the charge of maintaining them after the first year.

Fifthly, this food would likewise bring great custom to taverns; where the vinters will certainly be so prudent as to procure the best receipts[5] for dressing it to perfection, and, consequently, have their houses frequented by all the fine gentlemen, who justly value themselves upon their knowledge in good eating: and a skilful cook, who understands how to oblige his guests, will contrive to make it as expensive as they please.

Sixthly, this would be a great inducement to marriage, which all wise nations have either encouraged by rewards, or enforced by laws and penalties. It would increase the care and tenderness of mothers towards their children, when they were sure of a settlement for life to the poor babes, provided in some sort by the public, to their annual profit instead of expense. We should soon see an honest emulation among the married women, which of them could bring the fattest child to the market. Men would become as fond of their wives during the time of their pregnancy, as they are now of their mares in foal, their cows in calf, or sows when they are ready to farrow; nor offer to beat or kick them (as is too frequent a practice) for fear of a miscarriage.

Many other advantages might be enumerated. For instance, the addition of some thousand carcasses in our exportation of barrelled beef; the propagation of swine's flesh, and improvement in the art of making good bacon, so much wanted among us by the great destruction of pigs, too frequent at our tables, which are no way comparable in taste or magnificence to a well-grown, fat yearling child, which, roasted whole, will make a considerable figure at a Lord Mayor's feast, or any other public entertainment. But this, and many others, I omit, being studious of brevity.

Supposing that one thousand families in this city would be constant customers for infants' flesh, besides others who might have it at merry meetings, particularly weddings and christenings. I compute that Dublin would take off annually about twenty thousand carcasses; and the rest of the kingdom (where probably they will be sold somewhat cheaper) the remaining eighty thousand.

I can think of no one objection that will possibly be raised against this proposal, unless it should be urged, that the number of people will be thereby much lessened in the kingdom. This I freely own, and it was indeed one principal design in offering it to the world. I desire the reader will observe, that I calculate my remedy for this one individual kingdom of Ireland, and for no other that ever was, is, or I think ever can be, upon earth. Therefore let no man talk to me of other expedients: of taxing our absentees at five shillings a pound: of using neither clothes nor household-furniture except what is of our own growth and manufacture: of utterly rejecting the materials and instruments that promote foreign luxury: of curing the expensiveness of pride, vanity, idleness, and gaming in our women; of introducing a vein of parsimony, prudence, and temperance: of learning to love our country, wherein we differ even from Laplanders, and the inhabitants of Topinamboo:[6] of quitting our animosities and factions, nor act any longer like the Jews, who were murdering one another at the very moment their city was taken: of being a little cautious not to sell our country and con-

---

5. Recipes.　　　　　　　　　　　　6. In Brazil.

sciences for nothing: of teaching landlords to have at least one degree of mercy towards their tenants: lastly, of putting a spirit of honesty, industry, and skill into our shopkeepers; who, if a resolution could now be taken to buy only our native goods, would immediately unite to cheat and exact upon us in the price, the measure, and the goodness, nor could ever yet be brought to make one fair proposal of just dealing, though often and earnestly invited to it.

Therefore I repeat, let no man talk to me of these and the like expedients, till he hath at least some glimpse of hope that there will ever be some hearty and sincere attempts to put them in practice.

But, as to myself, having been wearied out for many years with offering vain, idle, visionary thoughts, and at length utterly despairing of success, I fortunately fell upon this proposal; which, as it is wholly new, so it hath something solid and real, of no expense and little trouble, full in our own power, and whereby we can incur no danger in disobliging England. For this kind of commodity will not bear exportation, the flesh being of too tender a consistence to admit a long continuance in salt, although perhaps I could name a country[7] which would be glad to eat up our whole nation without it.

After all, I am not so violently bent upon my own opinion as to reject any offer proposed by wise men which shall be found equally innocent, cheap, easy, and effectual. But before something of that kind shall be advanced in contradiction to my scheme, and offering a better, I desire the author, or authors, will be pleased maturely to consider two points. First, as things now stand, how they will be able to find food and raiment for a hundred thousand useless mouths and backs? And, secondly, there being a round million of creatures in human figure throughout this kingdom, whose whole subsistence put into a common stock would leave them in debt two millions of pounds sterling, adding those who are beggars by profession, to the bulk of farmers, cottagers, and labourers, with the wives and children who are beggars in effect; I desire those politicians who dislike my overture, and may perhaps be so bold as to attempt an answer, that they will first ask the parents of these mortals, whether they would not at this day think it a great happiness to have been sold for food at a year old, in the manner I prescribe, and thereby have avoided such a perpetual scene of misfortunes as they have since gone through, by the oppression of landlords, the impossibility of paying rent without money or trade, the want of common sustenance, with neither house nor clothes to cover them from the inclemencies of weather, and the most inevitable prospect of entailing the like, or greater miseries, upon their breed for ever.

I profess, in the sincerity of my heart, that I have not the least personal interest in endeavouring to promote this necessary work, having no other motive than the public good of my country, by advancing our trade, providing for infants, relieving the poor, and giving some pleasure to the rich. I have no children by which I can propose to get a single penny; the youngest being nine years old, and my wife past child-bearing.

1729

7. England.

ALEXANDER POPE

1688–1744

Socially marginal and physically disabled, Alexander Pope might seem an unlikely candidate for celebrity, but he won great wealth and fame through his writing. Crowds parted when he entered a room, and people rushed to shake his hand. In 1741, the renowned actor David Garrick heard that Pope was in the audience: "I instantaneously felt a palpitation at my heart. . . . His look shot, and thrilled, like lightning through my frame; and I had some hesitation in proceeding, from anxiety, and from joy." What made Pope so celebrated in his own time? His writing did not strive to be innovative; he proudly turned backward to ancient Greek and Roman traditions of literature and morality—especially Homer, Virgil, and Horace—and borrowed from them to make critical and satirical commentaries on his own society. But his witty, graceful, often bitingly comic poetic lines, coupled with his deep sense of moral and philosophical authority, marked him as both the most respected and the most popular poet of his time.

LIFE

Born to Roman Catholic parents in a year when the last Catholic king of England, James II, was deposed in favor of the Protestant regime of William and Mary, Pope lived when repressive measures against Catholics restricted his freedom. He could not attend a university or hold public office. He was even forbidden to live within ten miles of London. Sickly and undersized in childhood, he never reached more than four feet six inches tall, and had a hunchback for his whole life. In his youth, he was educated sporadically at illegal Catholic schools and at home, learning Latin, Greek, French, and Italian. He began to write epic poetry at the age of twelve. He taught himself a great deal, and developed his understanding of the world through literary friendships that remained important to him throughout his career.

Pope first came to the attention of the literary world with his *Essay on Criticism*, an ambitious piece of writing for a twenty-three year old, since it offered advice to rising writers when he had not yet established himself. This work earned him as many attackers as defenders, and he entered into a lively, sometimes acrimonious, literary debate about whether the ancient writers could be surpassed by modern innovations. *The Rape of the Lock*, Pope's most popular work from his time to ours, appeared in 1714. It sold three thousand copies in the first week of its publication. Then, in the ten years that followed, he produced little new poetry of his own, instead translating Homer's *Iliad* and *Odyssey*, and editing the works of Shakespeare to make both newly accessible to English readers. A rival translation of Homer appeared around the same time, and debate about the two versions reached a fever pitch, with newspapers reporting on both sides. But Pope's translations soon won the field, establishing him as a literary representative of the whole nation. They also earned him substantial sums of money, making him perhaps the first English writer to make a fortune from his work.

Pope never married, but he had some notable friendships with women.

For some time he was on close terms with Lady Mary Wortley Montagu, a fellow writer, but they fell out, and she satirized him in print. His closest relationship was with a woman named Martha Blount, whom he had known since adolescence. He wrote her serious letters and for a period saw her every day, giving rise to some scandalous gossip about the pair. When he died he left her his estate.

In his later years, Pope was best known for two works: a philosophical poem that reflects on the role of human beings in the universe, called *The Essay on Man* (1733–34) and *The Dunciad* (completed in 1742), a satirical poem he wrote in response to criticisms of his edition of Shakespeare. Here he condemned almost all of his intellectual contemporaries, scientists, critics, and writers—with the notable exception of his friend **Jonathan Swift**—as hacks and dunces. This work earned him so many enemies that he refused to leave his house without a pair of loaded pistols. The money Pope made from his translations had allowed him to retire to Twickenham, where he built a small villa and a famous garden and grotto. He died there at the age of fifty-six.

TIMES

Although he was the richest poet of his era, Pope frequently condemned writers who wrote for monetary gain. This might make him seem hypocritical, but in fact his whole culture was feeling a new and profound ambivalence about money, which underwent a major transformation during his lifetime. In the eighteenth century European economies for the first time began to produce paper currencies rather than relying on exchanges of gold and silver, and people started to write checks. Lottery tickets went on sale as a new thrill. Among the most important new financial instruments of the period was the joint stock company—where an individual investor could advance a small sum that would be lumped in with money from others. It became popular to buy shares in these companies, and this wave of enthusiasm enabled large-scale economic projects that would never have been possible before.

The most famous—and ill-fated—of the new joint stock ventures was the South Sea Company. In the early eighteenth century, the British government found itself deep in debt, and in 1711, they sold a substantial portion of the debt to the South Sea Company, promising a return of 6 percent interest. The company publicized the fact that they had bought the rights to all new trading opportunities in South America, since Spain had just opened up access to British ships. Having heard about gold and silver mines in Mexico and Peru, people rushed to buy shares in the company, and the price of stocks rose precipitously. The South Sea Company abruptly failed in 1720. It turned out that many of the glowing rumors about it had been false. The directors wanted to sell and get out quickly. "And thus," wrote a historian looking back in 1803, "were seen, in the space of eight months, the rise, progress, and fall of that mighty fabric, which, being wound up by mysterious springs to a wonderful height, had fixed the eyes and expectations of all Europe, but whose foundation, being fraud, illusion, credulity, and infatuation, fell to the ground as soon as the artful management of its directors was discovered."

Intangible and sometimes illusory, the new paper economy often seemed simply immoral. Pope saw the crash as "God punishing the avaritious." But it was also hugely tempting, since it was clearly now possible to amass a great fortune from very little. As Pope himself put it, "'Tis ignominious (in this Age of Hope and Golden Mountains) not to Venture." The poet had in fact invested in the South Sea Company, but on the advice of a wise broker, he got much of his money out before the crash, losing only a part of his growing fortune. Torn between excitement at a fast-growing economy where ordinary people could accumulate riches, and alarm at the greed, deception, and catastrophic failure that the new financial world made possible, the whole of Europe was caught up in wonder and uncertainty at the new, strange fact of wealth on paper.

Pope was particularly shrewd about putting the changing marketplace to use for his own writing career. Since he was a Catholic outsider, he could not depend on powerful patrons in the Anglican Church or the court, and he suffered particular hardships when new anti-Catholic laws diminished his family's property in 1714. But like Jonathan Swift he figured out how to exploit a growing democratic and urban market for books and pamphlets. Pope retained his own copyright and acted as his own publisher. He also borrowed a trick out of the book of the new joint stock companies. That is, he sold subscriptions to his translation of Homer's *Iliad* before it appeared. Subscribers therefore "invested" in a promise rather than a concrete object, just as they bought stocks in new companies, and Pope could live on the cash that flowed in before the publication was complete. Unlike the South Sea Bubble, this turned out to be a good investment for his readers—and excellent for Pope's own finances. Where many contemporary writers might make a total £10 or £20 on a book they sold to a publisher, Pope made more than £800 on his *Iliad*, roughly equivalent to about $200,000 today. Thus he brought about his independence. As he put it proudly: "South-sea subscriptions take who please, / Leave me but Liberty and Ease!"

WORK

Alexander Pope wrote *The Rape of the Lock* in response to a real event. Arabella Fermor, the most famous beauty of her time, was deeply insulted one evening when a young aristocrat, Lord Petre, snipped off a lock of her hair without her permission. He bragged about the event, acting as if the young lady were the kind of person who invited such advances. Her family was outraged, and friends turned to the most celebrated poet of the time to intervene. Pope's poem pretends to belong to the genre of dignified epic poetry—traditionally poetry that commemorates heroic warriors—to describe this trifling social quarrel. His work is a "mock epic," one that relies on epic conventions while also poking fun at them. Thus Pope, like Homer and Virgil before him, stages the event as an elaborate military encounter, including the careful arming of the hero—which in this case involves the protagonist seated at her cosmetics table.

Part of the great wit of the poem lies in constant juxtaposition of two radically dissimilar worlds. Not only does Pope employ the conventions of epic for a high-society squabble, but he repeatedly joins the trivial and the serious in the fabric of the poem. Among the jumble of things on Belinda's dressing table, for example, are "Puffs, powders, patches, Bibles, billet-doux," and we are invited to wonder whether she "will stain her honor or her new brocade." In bringing the grave and the petty close together, Pope manages to move beyond mere comic lightness: he opens up questions about the relationship between femininity and masculinity, between private and public, and between sacred and secular. Criticism of social inequality appears on the margins ("wretches hang that jurymen may dine"), and the society Pope mocks revolves around tensions between the sexes. Most searchingly, he investigates the question of beauty, the target of much contemplation in the poem: is it a superficial quality, to be cast in with puffs and powders, or does it belong to the realms of timeless and even spiritual grandeur, like art itself? Reaching great heights and shallow depths, Pope also manages to take aim at the monarchy itself: the court is a place where Queen Anne, "whom three realms obey, / Dost sometimes counsel take—and sometimes tea." Thus the queen becomes at once powerful and domestic.

This idea of pairing suits the poetic form Pope was most famous for—pairs of lines called rhyming couplets. Although this form often seemed mechanical and forced in the hands of other poets, Pope used it with astonishing dexterity and variety: sometimes he follows a cheerful couplet with a solemn one; sometimes the two lines connect to one another thematically, while at other times he uses their closeness to accentuate opposition or difference; occasionally the line pairing makes a neat, self-enclosed whole, but Pope most often built his couplets into larger conceptual or thematic units. The pair of scissors used to cut Belinda's hair in *The Rape of the Lock* echoes the ways that the couplet form can both bring together and separate—"now joins it, to divide."

Pope used the couplet equally effectively for a very different kind of poem. His *Essay on Man* ambitiously sets out to consider humanity in relation to the universe, to itself, to society, and to happiness. He draws on a number of intellectual traditions—Catholic and Protestant theology, Platonic and Stoic philosophy, his own period's interest in a natural order—to reinforce the assumption of a timeless and universal human nature. Above all, the text is, like **Milton's** *Paradise Lost*, a theodicy—a genre that asks how, if God is good,

there can be evil in the world. The first section of the poem, included here, begins by insisting on the necessary limitations of human judgment: we see only parts, not the whole. And yet, our ignorance of future events and our hope for eternal life give us the possibility of happiness. He explores the nature of human pride and the place of humans in the Great Chain of Being that stretches from God down to the minutest living things, suggesting that this order extends farther than we can know and that any attempt to interfere with it will destroy the whole.

Pope draws us into the poem by addressing us directly, reminding us of our own tendencies to presumption. "In Pride, in reas'ning Pride, our error lies": we all share bewilderment at our situation, we all need to interpret it, we all face, every day, our necessary limitations. The poet rapidly shifts tone and perspective, sometimes berating his readers, sometimes reminding us (and himself) of his own participation in the universal dilemma, sometimes assuming a godlike perspective and suggesting his superior knowledge. And as he moves among voices and viewpoints, he comes to the conclusion that although we cannot see it, the universe works according to a design that is good, and thus demands "our absolute submission . . . to Providence."

Pope conceded that it was difficult to write a philosophical argument in poetic form, but he defended his choice. "This I might have done in prose," he wrote, "but I chose verse, and even rhyme, for two reasons. The one will appear obvious; that principles, maxims, or precepts, so written, both strike the reader more strongly at first, and are more easily retained by him afterwards: the other may seem odd, but it is true: I found I could express them more shortly this way than in prose itself; and nothing is more certain than that much of the force as well as grace of arguments or instructions depends on their conciseness." Forceful and concise, Pope's lines also offer concrete imagery—such as the Indian looking up at the clouds to find God or the eye of the fly, which sees more minutely than the human eye. And his perfectly turned couplets remind us of the complex dualities of humankind, at once godlike and animal, fallen and saved, capable of happy triviality and grim seriousness.

In the later eighteenth century, Pope's writing came under attack.

Romantic poets such as **William Wordsworth** saw Pope's elegant verse couplets as artificial, mechanical, lacking "soul." But he remained a well-loved poet for his moral wisdom and his remarkable technical skill. Most famous today for lines we may not even recognize as his—such as "A little learning is a dangerous thing" and "Hope springs eternal in the human breast"—Pope embodies a whole literary era in England, which has come to be known as the "age of Pope."

The Rape of the Lock[1]

An Heroi-Comical Poem

Nolueram, Belinda, tuos violare capillos;
sed juvat hoc precibus me tribuisse tuis.[2]
—MARTIAL

TO MRS. ARABELLA FERMOR

MADAM,

It will be in vain to deny that I have some regard for this piece, since I dedicate it to you. Yet you may bear me witness, it was intended only to divert a few young ladies, who have good sense and good humor enough to laugh not only at their sex's little unguarded follies, but at their own. But as it was communicated with the air of a secret, it soon found its way into the world. An imperfect copy having been offered to a bookseller, you had the good nature for my sake to consent to the publication of one more correct; this I was forced to, before I had executed half my design, for the machinery was entirely wanting to complete it.

The machinery, Madam, is a term invented by the critics, to signify that part which the deities, angels, or demons are made to act in a poem; for the ancient poets are in one respect like many modern ladies: let an action be never so trivial in itself, they always make it appear of the utmost importance. These machines I determined to raise on a very new and odd foundation, the Rosicrucian[3] doctrine of spirits.

1. Text and notes by Samuel Holt Monk.
2. "I was unwilling, Belinda, to ravish your locks; but I rejoice to have conceded this to your prayers" (Martial, *Epigrams* 12.84.1–2). Pope substituted his heroine for Martial's Polytimus. The epigraph is intended to suggest that

the poem was published at Miss Fermor's request.
3. A system of arcane philosophy introduced into England from Germany in the 17th century.

I know how disagreeable it is to make use of hard words before a lady; but 'tis so much the concern of a poet to have his works understood, and particularly by your sex, that you must give me leave to explain two or three difficult terms.

The Rosicrucians are a people I must bring you acquainted with. The best account I know of them is in a French book called *Le Comte de Gabalis*,[4] which both in its title and size is so like a novel, that many of the fair sex have read it for one by mistake. According to these gentlemen, the four elements are inhabited by spirits, which they call Sylphs, Gnomes, Nymphs, and Salamanders. The Gnomes or Demons of earth delight in mischief; but the Sylphs, whose habitation is in the air, are the best-conditioned creatures imaginable. For they say, any mortals may enjoy the most intimate familiarities with these gentle spirits, upon a condition very easy to all true adepts, an inviolate preservation of chastity.

As to the following cantos, all the passages of them are as fabulous as the vision at the beginning, or the transformation at the end; (except the loss of your hair, which I always mention with reverence). The human persons are as fictitious as the airy ones; and the character of Belinda, as it is now managed, resembles you in nothing but in beauty.

If this poem had as many graces as there are in your person, or in your mind, yet I could never hope it should pass through the world half so uncensured as you have done. But let its fortune be what it will, mine is happy enough, to have given me this occasion of assuring you that I am, with the truest esteem,

MADAM,
Your most obedient, humble servant,

A. POPE

CANTO I

What dire offense from amorous causes springs,
What mighty contests rise from trivial things,
I sing—This verse to Caryll,[5] Muse! is due:
This, even Belinda may vouchsafe to view:
Slight is the subject, but not so the praise,   5
If she inspire, and he approve my lays.
    Say what strange motive, Goddess! could compel
A well-bred lord t' assault a gentle belle?
Oh, say what stranger cause, yet unexplored,
Could make a gentle belle reject a lord?   10
In tasks so bold can little men engage,
And in soft bosoms dwells such mighty rage?
    Sol through white curtains shot a timorous ray,
And oped those eyes that must eclipse the day.
Now lapdogs give themselves the rousing shake,   15

4. By the Abbé de Montfaucon de Villars, published in 1670.
5. John Caryll (1666?–1736), a close friend of Pope's who suggested that he write this poem.

And sleepless lovers just at twelve awake:
Thrice rung the bell, the slipper knocked the ground,
And the pressed watch[6] returned a silver sound.
Belinda still her downy pillow pressed,
Her guardian Sylph prolonged the balmy rest: 20
'Twas he had summoned to her silent bed
The morning dream that hovered o'er her head.
A youth more glittering than a birthnight beau[7]
(That even in slumber caused her cheek to glow)
Seemed to her ear his winning lips to lay,   25
And thus in whispers said, or seemed to say:
    "Fairest of mortals, thou distinguished care
Of thousand bright inhabitants of air!
If e'er one vision touched thy infant thought,
Of all the nurse and all the priest have taught,   30
Of airy elves by moonlight shadows seen,
The silver token, and the circled green,[8]
Or virgins visited by angel powers,
With golden crowns and wreaths of heavenly flowers,
Hear and believe! thy own importance know,   35
Nor bound thy narrow views to things below.
Some secret truths, from learned pride concealed,
To maids alone and children are revealed:
What though no credit doubting wits may give?
The fair and innocent shall still believe.   40
Know, then, unnumbered spirits round thee fly,
The light militia of the lower sky:
These, though unseen, are ever on the wing,
Hang o'er the box,[9] and hover round the Ring.
Think what an equipage thou hast in air,   45
And view with scorn two pages and a chair.[1]
As now your own, our beings were of old,
And once enclosed in woman's beauteous mold
Thence, by a soft transition, we repair
From earthly vehicles to these of air.   50
Think not, when woman's transient breath is fled,
That all her vanities at once are dead:
Succeeding vanities she still regards,
And though she plays no more o'erlooks the cards.
Her joy in gilded chariots, when alive,   55
And love of ombre,[2] after death survive.

6. A watch that chimes the hour and the quarter hour when the stem is pressed down. "Thrice rung the bell": Belinda thus summons her maid.

7. Courtiers wore especially fine clothes on the sovereign's birthday.

8. According to popular belief, fairies skim off the cream from jugs of milk left standing overnight and leave a coin in payment. "The cir-

cled green": rings of bright green grass, which are common in England even in winter, were held to be due to the round dances of fairies.

9. "Box" in the theater and the fashionable circular drive ("Ring") in Hyde Park.

1. Sedan chair.

2. The popular card game. See III.27ff. and note.

For when the Fair in all their pride expire,
To their first elements[3] their souls retire:
The sprites of fiery termagants in flame
Mount up, and take a Salamander's name.[4]   60
Soft yielding minds to water glide away,
And sip, with Nymphs, their elemental tea.[5]
The graver prude sinks downward to a Gnome,
In search of mischief still on earth to roam.
The light coquettes in Sylphs aloft repair,   65
And sport and flutter in the fields of air.
   "Know further yet; whoever fair and chaste
Rejects mankind, is by some Sylph embraced:
For spirits, freed from mortal laws, with ease
Assume what sexes and what shapes they please.   70
What guards the purity of melting maids,
In courtly balls, and midnight masquerades,
Safe from the treacherous friend, the daring spark,
The glance by day, the whisper in the dark,
When kind occasion prompts their warm desires,   75
When music softens, and when dancing fires?
'Tis but their Sylph, the wise Celestials know,
Though Honor is the word with men below.
   "Some nymphs there are, too conscious of their face,
For life predestined to the Gnomes' embrace.   80
These swell their prospects and exalt their pride,
When offers are disdained, and love denied:
Then gay ideas[6] crowd the vacant brain,
While peers, and dukes, and all their sweeping train,
And garters, stars, and coronets appear,   85
And in soft sounds, 'your Grace' salutes their ear.
'Tis these that early taint the female soul,
Instruct the eyes of young coquettes to roll,
Teach infant cheeks a bidden blush to know,
And little hearts to flutter at a beau.   90
   "Oft, when the world imagine women stray,
The Sylphs through mystic mazes guide their way,
Through all the giddy circle they pursue,
And old impertinence expel by new.
What tender maid but must a victim fall   95
To one man's treat, but for another's ball?
When Florio speaks what virgin could withstand,
If gentle Damon did not squeeze her hand?
With varying vanities, from every part,

---

3. The four elements out of which all things were believed to have been made were fire, water, earth, and air. One or another of these elements was supposed to be predominant in both the physical and psychological makeup of each human being. In this context they are spoken of as "humors."

4. Pope borrowed his supernatural beings from Rosicrucian mythology. Each element was inhabited by a spirit, as the following lines explain. The salamander is a lizardlike animal, in antiquity believed to live in fire.
5. Pronounced *tay*.
6. Images.

They shift the moving toyshop[7] of their heart;   100
Where wigs with wigs, with sword-knots sword-knots strive,
Beaux banish beaux, and coaches coaches drive.
This erring mortals levity may call;
Oh, blind to truth! the Sylphs contrive it all.
   "Of these am I, who thy protection claim,   105
A watchful sprite, and Ariel is my name.
Late, as I ranged the crystal wilds of air,
In the clear mirror of thy ruling star
I saw, alas! some dread event impend,
Ere to the main this morning sun descend,   110
But Heaven reveals not what, or how, or where:
Warned by thy Sylph, O pious maid, beware!
This to disclose is all thy guardian can:
Beware of all, but most beware of Man!"
   He said; when Shock,[8] who thought she slept too long,   115
Leaped up, and waked his mistress with his tongue.
'Twas then, Belinda, if report say true,
Thy eyes first opened on a billet-doux;
Wounds, charms, and ardors were no sooner read,
But all the vision vanished from thy head.   120
   And now, unveiled, the toilet stands displayed,
Each silver vase in mystic order laid.
First, robed in white, the nymph intent adores,
With head uncovered, the cosmetic powers.
A heavenly image in the glass appears;   125
To that she bends, to that her eyes she rears.
The inferior priestess, at her altar's side,
Trembling begins the sacred rites of Pride.
Unnumbered treasures ope at once, and here
The various offerings of the world appear;   130
From each she nicely culls with curious toil,
And decks the goddess with the glittering spoil.
This casket India's glowing gems unlocks,
And all Arabia breathes from yonder box.
The tortoise here and elephant unite,   135
Transformed to combs, the speckled and the white.
Here files of pins extend their shining rows,
Puffs, powders, patches, Bibles, billet-doux.
Now awful Beauty puts on all its arms;
The fair each moment rises in her charms,   140
Repairs her smiles, awakens every grace,
And calls forth all the wonders of her face;
Sees by degrees a purer blush arise,
And keener lightnings quicken in her eyes.
The busy Sylphs surround their darling care,   145
These set the head, and those divide the hair,

7. A shop stocked with baubles and trifles.   8. Belinda's lapdog.

Some fold the sleeve, whilst others plait the gown;
And Betty's[9] praised for labors not her own.

CANTO II

Not with more glories, in the ethereal plain,
The sun first rises o'er the purpled main,
Than, issuing forth, the rival of his beams
Launched on the bosom of the silver Thames.
Fair nymphs and well-dressed youths around her shone,   5
But every eye was fixed on her alone.
On her white breast a sparkling cross she wore,
Which Jews might kiss, and infidels adore.
Her lively looks a sprightly mind disclose,
Quick as her eyes, and as unfixed as those: 10
Favors to none, to all she smiles extends;
Oft she rejects, but never once offends.
Bright as the sun, her eyes the gazers strike,
And, like the sun, they shine on all alike.
Yet graceful ease, and sweetness void of pride,   15
Might hide her faults, if belles had faults to hide:
If to her share some female errors fall,
Look on her face, and you'll forget 'em all.
   This nymph, to the destruction of mankind,
Nourished two locks which graceful hung behind   20
In equal curls, and well conspired to deck
With shining ringlets the smooth ivory neck.
Love in these labyrinths his slaves detains,
And mighty hearts are held in slender chains.
With hairy springes we the birds betray,   25
Slight lines of hair surprise the finny prey,
Fair tresses man's imperial race ensnare,
And beauty draws us with a single hair.
   The adventurous Baron the bright locks admired,
He saw, he wished, and to the prize aspired.   30
Resolved to win, he meditates the way,
By force to ravish, or by fraud betray;
For when success a lover's toil attends,
Few ask if fraud or force attained his ends.
   For this, ere Phoebus rose, he had implored   35
Propitious Heaven, and every power adored,
But chiefly Love—to Love an altar built,
Of twelve vast French romances, neatly gilt.
There lay three garters, half a pair of gloves,
And all the trophies of his former loves.   40
With tender billet-doux he lights the pyre,
And breathes three amorous sighs to raise the fire.

9. Belinda's maid, the "inferior priestess" mentioned in line I.127.

Then prostrate falls, and begs with ardent eyes
Soon to obtain, and long possess the prize:
The powers gave ear, and granted half his prayer,   45
The rest the winds dispersed in empty air.
    But now secure the painted vessel glides,
The sunbeams trembling on the floating tides,
While melting music steals upon the sky,
And softened sounds along the waters die.   50
Smooth flow the waves, the zephyrs gently play,
Belinda smiled, and all the world was gay.
All but the Sylph—with careful thoughts oppressed,
The impending woe sat heavy on his breast.
He summons straight his denizens of air;   55
The lucid squadrons round the sails repair:
Soft o'er the shrouds aërial whispers breathe
That seemed but zephyrs to the train beneath.
Some to the sun their insect-wings unfold,
Waft on the breeze, or sink in clouds of gold.   60
Transparent forms too fine for mortal sight,
Their fluid bodies half dissolved in light,
Loose to the wind their airy garments flew,
Thin glittering textures of the filmy dew,
Dipped in the richest tincture of the skies,   65
Where light disports in ever-mingling dyes,
While every beam new transient colors flings,
Colors that change whene'er they wave their wings.
Amid the circle, on the gilded mast,
Superior by the head was Ariel placed;   70
His purple[1] pinions opening to the sun,
He raised his azure wand, and thus begun:
    "Ye Sylphs and Sylphids, to your chief give ear!
Fays, Fairies, Genii, Elves, and Daemons, hear!
Ye know the spheres and various tasks assigned   75
By laws eternal to the aërial kind.
Some in the fields of purest ether play,
And bask and whiten in the blaze of day.
Some guide the course of wandering orbs on high,
Or roll the planets through the boundless sky.   80
Some less refined, beneath the moon's pale light
Pursue the stars that shoot athwart the night,
Or suck the mists in grosser air below,
Or dip their pinions in the painted bow,
Or brew fierce tempests on the wintry main,   85
Or o'er the glebe distill the kindly rain.
Others on earth o'er human race preside,
Watch all their ways, and all their actions guide:
Of these the chief the care of nations own,
And guard with arms divine the British Throne.   90

---

1. In 18th-century poetic diction, the word might mean "blood-red," "purple," or simply (as is likely here) "brightly colored." The word derives from Virgil, *Eclogue* 9.40, *pupureus*.

"Our humbler province is to tend the Fair,
Not a less pleasing, though less glorious care:
To save the powder from too rude a gale,
Nor let the imprisoned essences exhale;
To draw fresh colors from the vernal flowers   95
To steal from rainbows e'er they drop in showers
A brighter wash;[2] to curl their waving hairs,
Assist their blushes, and inspire their airs;
Nay oft, in dreams invention we bestow,
To change a flounce, or add a furbelow.   100
    "This day black omens threat the brightest fair,
That e'er deserved a watchful spirit's care;
Some dire disaster, or by force or slight,
But what, or where, the Fates have wrapped in night:
Whether the nymph shall break Diana's[3] law,   105
Or some frail china jar receive a flaw,
Or stain her honor or her new brocade,
Forget her prayers, or miss a masquerade,
Or lose her heart, or necklace, at a ball;
Or whether Heaven has doomed that Shock must fall.   110
Haste, then, ye spirits! to your charge repair:
The fluttering fan be Zephyretta's care;
The drops[4] to thee, Brillante, we consign;
And, Momentilla, let the watch be thine;
Do thou, Crispissa,[5] tend her favorite Lock;   115
Ariel himself shall be the guard of Shock.
    "To fifty chosen Sylphs, of special note,
We trust the important charge, the petticoat;
Oft have we known that sevenfold fence to fail,
Though stiff with hoops, and armed with ribs of whale.   120
Form a strong line about the silver bound,
And guard the wide circumference around.
    "Whatever spirit, careless of his charge,
His post neglects, or leaves the fair at large,
Shall feel sharp vengeance soon o'ertake his sins,   125
Be stopped in vials, or transfixed with pins,
Or plunged in lakes of bitter washes lie,
Or wedged whole ages in a bodkin's eye;[6]
Gums and pomatums shall his flight restrain,
While clogged he beats his silken wings in vain,   130
Or alum styptics with contracting power
Shrink his thin essence like a riveled[7] flower:
Or, as Ixion fixed,[8] the wretch shall feel
The giddy motion of the whirling mill,

2. Cosmetic lotion.
3. Diana was the goddess of chastity.
4. Diamond earrings.
5. From Latin *crispere*, to curl.
6. A blunt needle with a large eye, used for drawing ribbon through eyelets in the edging of women's garments.
7. To "rivel" is to "contract into wrinkles and corrugations" (Johnson's *Dictionary*).
8. In the Greek myth Ixion was punished in the underworld by being bound on an ever-turning wheel.

In fumes of burning chocolate shall glow,   135
And tremble at the sea that froths below!"
    He spoke; the spirits from the sails descend;
Some, orb in orb, around the nymph extend;
Some thread the mazy ringlets of her hair;
Some hang upon the pendants of her ear: 140
With beating hearts the dire event they wait,
Anxious, and trembling for the birth of Fate.

CANTO III

    Close by those meads, forever crowned with flowers,
Where Thames with pride surveys his rising towers,
There stands a structure of majestic frame,
Which from the neighboring Hampton[9] takes its name.
Here Britain's statesmen oft the fall foredoom   5
Of foreign tyrants and of nymphs at home;
Here thou, great Anna! whom three realms obey,
Dost sometimes counsel take—and sometimes tea.
    Hither the heroes and the nymphs resort,
To taste awhile the pleasures of a court;   10
In various talk the instructive hours they passed,
Who gave the ball, or paid the visit last;
One speaks the glory of the British Queen,
And one describes a charming Indian screen;
A third interprets motions, looks, and eyes;   15
At every word a reputation dies.
Snuff, or the fan, supply each pause of chat,
With singing, laughing, ogling, and all that.
    Meanwhile, declining from the noon of day,
The sun obliquely shoots his burning ray;   20
The hungry judges soon the sentence sign,
And wretches hang that jurymen may dine;
The merchant from the Exchange returns in peace,
And the long labors of the toilet cease.
Belinda now, whom thirst of fame invites,   25
Burns to encounter two adventurous knights,
At ombre[1] singly to decide their doom
And swells her breast with conquests yet to come.
Straight the three bands prepare in arms to join,
Each band the number of the sacred nine.   30
Soon as she spreads her hand, the aërial guard

---

9. Hampton Court, the royal palace, about fifteen miles up the Thames from London.
1. The game that Belinda plays against the baron and another young man is too complicated for complete explication here. Pope has carefully arranged the cards so that Belinda wins. The baron's hand is strong enough to be a threat, but the third player's is of little account.

The hand is played exactly according to the rules of ombre, and Pope's description of the cards is equally accurate. Each player holds nine cards (line 30). The "Matadores" (line 33), when spades are trumps, are "Spadillio" (line 49), the ace of spades; "Manillio" (line 51), the two of spades; "Basto" (line 53), the ace of clubs; Belinda holds all three of these.

Descend, and sit on each important card:
First Ariel perched upon a Matadore,
Then each according to the rank they bore;
For Sylphs, yet mindful of their ancient race,   35
Are, as when women, wondrous fond of place.
    Behold, four Kings in majesty revered,
With hoary whiskers and a forky beard;
And four fair Queens whose hands sustain a flower,
The expressive emblem of their softer power;   40
Four Knaves in garbs succinct,[2] a trusty band,
Caps on their heads, and halberts in their hand;
And parti-colored troops, a shining train,
Draw forth to combat on the velvet plain.
The skillful nymph reviews her force with care;   45
"Let Spades be trumps!" she said, and trumps they were.
    Now move to war her sable Matadores,
In show like leaders of the swarthy Moors.
Spadillio first, unconquerable lord!
Led off two captive trumps, and swept the board.   50
As many more Manillio forced to yield,
And marched a victor from the verdant field.
Him Basto followed, but his fate more hard
Gained but one trump and one plebeian card.
With his broad saber next, a chief in years,   55
The hoary Majesty of Spades appears,
Puts forth one manly leg, to sight revealed,
The rest his many-colored robe concealed.
The rebel Knave, who dares his prince engage,
Proves the just victim of his royal rage.   60
Even mighty Pam,[3] that kings and queens o'erthrew
And mowed down armies in the fights of loo,
Sad chance of war! now destitute of aid,
Falls undistinguished by the victor Spade.
    Thus far both armies to Belinda yield;   65
Now to the Baron fate inclines the field.
His warlike amazon her host invades,
The imperial consort of the crown of Spades.
The Club's black tyrant first her victim died,
Spite of his haughty mien and barbarous pride.   70
What boots the regal circle on his head,
His giant limbs, in state unwieldy spread?
That long behind he trails his pompous robe,
And of all monarchs only grasps the globe?
    The Baron now his Diamonds pours apace;   75
The embroidered King who shows but half his face,
And his refulgent Queen, with powers combined
Of broken troops an easy conquest find.

2. Girded up.
3. The knave of clubs, the highest trump in the game of loo.

Clubs, Diamonds, Hearts, in wild disorder seen,
With throngs promiscuous strew the level green. 80
Thus when dispersed a routed army runs,
Of Asia's troops, and Afric's sable sons,
With like confusion different nations fly,
Of various habit, and of various dye,
The pierced battalions disunited fall 85
In heaps on heaps; one fate o'erwhelms them all.
    The Knave of Diamonds tries his wily arts,
And wins (oh, shameful chance!) the Queen of Hearts.
At this, the blood the virgin's cheek forsook,
A livid paleness spreads o'er all her look; 90
She sees, and trembles at the approaching ill,
Just in the jaws of ruin, and Codille,[4]
And now (as oft in some distempered state)
On one nice trick depends the general fate.
An Ace of Hearts steps forth: the King unseen 95
Lurked in her hand, and mourned his captive Queen.
He springs to vengeance with an eager pace,
And falls like thunder on the prostrate Ace.
The nymph exulting fills with shouts the sky,
The walls, the woods, and long canals reply. 100
    O thoughtless mortals! ever blind to fate,
Too soon dejected, and too soon elate:
Sudden these honors shall be snatched away,
And cursed forever this victorious day.
    For lo! the board with cups and spoons is crowned, 105
The berries crackle, and the mill turns round;[5]
On shining altars of Japan[6] they raise
The silver lamp; the fiery spirits blaze:
From silver spouts the grateful liquors glide,
While China's earth receives the smoking tide. 110
At once they gratify their scent and taste,
And frequent cups prolong the rich repast.
Straight hover round the fair her airy band;
Some, as she sipped, the fuming liquor fanned,
Some o'er her lap their careful plumes displayed, 115
Trembling, and conscious of the rich brocade.
Coffee (which makes the politician wise,
And see through all things with his half-shut eyes)
Sent up in vapors to the Baron's brain
New stratagems, the radiant Lock to gain. 120
Ah, cease, rash youth! desist ere 'tis too late,
Fear the just Gods, and think of Scylla's fate![7]

---

4. The term applied to losing a hand at cards.
5. That is, coffee is roasted and ground.
6. That is, small, lacquered tables. The word "altars" suggests the ritualistic character of coffee drinking in Belinda's world.
7. Scylla, daughter of Nisus, was turned into a sea bird because, for the sake of her love for Minos of Crete, who was besieging her father's city of Megara, she cut from her father's head the purple lock on which his safety depended. She is not the Scylla of the "Scylla and Charybdis" episode in the *Odyssey*.

Changed to a bird, and sent to flit in air,
She dearly pays for Nisus' injured hair!
    But when to mischief mortals bend their will,   125
How soon they find fit instruments of ill!
Just then, Clarissa drew with tempting grace
A two-edged weapon from her shining case:
So ladies in romance assist their knight,
Present the spear, and arm him for the fight.   130
He takes the gift with reverence, and extends
The little engine on his fingers' ends;
This just behind Belinda's neck he spread,
As o'er the fragrant steams she bends her head.
Swift to the Lock a thousand sprites repair,   135
A thousand wings, by turns, blow back the hair,
And thrice they twitched the diamond in her ear,
Thrice she looked back, and thrice the foe drew near.
Just in that instant, anxious Ariel sought
The close recesses of the virgin's thought;   140
As on the nosegay in her breast reclined,
He watched the ideas rising in her mind,
Sudden he viewed, in spite of all her art,
An earthly lover lurking at her heart.
Amazed, confused, he found his power expired,   145
Resigned to fate, and with a sigh retired.
    The Peer now spreads the glittering forfex[8] wide,
T' enclose the Lock; now joins it, to divide.
Even then, before the fatal engine closed,
A wretched Sylph too fondly interposed;   150
Fate urged the shears, and cut the Sylph in twain
(But airy substance soon unites again):
The meeting points the sacred hair dissever
From the fair head, forever, and forever!
    Then flashed the living lightning from her eyes,   155
And screams of horror rend the affrighted skies.
Not louder shrieks to pitying heaven are cast,
When husbands, or when lapdogs breathe their last;
Or when rich china vessels fallen from high,
In glittering dust and painted fragments lie!   160
"Let wreaths of triumph now my temples twine,"
The victor cried, "the glorious prize is mine!
While fish in streams, or birds delight in air,
Or in a coach and six the British Fair,
As long as *Atalantis*[9] shall be read,   165
Or the small pillow grace a lady's bed,
While visits shall be paid on solemn days,
When numerous wax-lights in bright order blaze,
While nymphs take treats, or assignations give,

---

8. Scissors.
9. Mrs. Manley's *New Atalantis* (1709) was   notorious for its thinly concealed allusions to contemporary scandals.

So long my honor, name, and praise shall live!   170
What Time would spare, from Steel receives its date,
And monuments, like men, submit to fate!
Steel could the labor of the Gods destroy,
And strike to dust the imperial towers of Troy;
Steel could the works of mortal pride confound,   175
And hew triumphal arches to the ground.
What wonder then, fair nymph! thy hairs should feel,
The conquering force of unresisted Steel?"

CANTO IV

But anxious cares the pensive nymph oppressed,
And secret passions labored in her breast.
Not youthful kings in battle seized alive,
Not scornful virgins who their charms survive,
Not ardent lovers robbed of all their bliss,   5
Not ancient ladies when refused a kiss,
Not tyrants fierce that unrepenting die,
Not Cynthia when her manteau's[1] pinned awry,
E'er felt such rage, resentment, and despair,
As thou, sad virgin! for thy ravished hair.   10
    For, that sad moment, when the Sylphs withdrew
And Ariel weeping from Belinda flew,
Umbriel,[2] a dusky, melancholy sprite
As ever sullied the fair face of light,
Down to the central earth, his proper scene,   15
Repaired to search the gloomy Cave of Spleen.[3]
    Swift on his sooty pinions flits the Gnome,
And in a vapor[4] reached the dismal dome.
No cheerful breeze this sullen region knows,
The dreaded east is all the wind that blows.   20
Here in a grotto, sheltered close from air,
And screened in shades from day's detested glare,
She sighs forever on her pensive bed,
Pain at her side, and Megrim[5] at her head.
    Two handmaids wait the throne: alike in place,   25
But differing far in figure and in face.
Here stood Ill-Nature like an ancient maid,
Her wrinkled form in black and white arrayed;
With store of prayers for mornings, nights, and noons,
Her hand is filled; her bosom with lampoons.   30
    There Affectation, with a sickly mien,
Shows in her cheek the roses of eighteen,
Practiced to lisp, and hang the head aside,
Faints into airs, and languishes with pride,

1. Negligee, or loose robe.
2. The name suggests shade and darkness.
3. Ill humor.
4. Punning on *vapor* as (1) mist and (2) an

excessively emotional (even peevish) state of
mind, appropriate to the realm of "spleen."
5. Headache.

On the rich quilt sinks with becoming woe, 35
Wrapped in a gown, for sickness and for show.
The fair ones feel such maladies as these,
When each new nightdress gives a new disease.
 A constant vapor[6] o'er the palace flies,
Strange phantoms rising as the mists arise; 40
Dreadful as hermit's dreams in haunted shades,
Or bright as visions of expiring maids.
Now glaring fiends, and snakes on rolling spires,[7]
Pale specters, gaping tombs, and purple fires;
Now lakes of liquid gold, Elysian scenes, 45
And crystal domes, and angels in machines.[8]
 Unnumbered throngs on every side are seen
Of bodies changed to various forms by Spleen.
Here living teapots stand, one arm held out,
One bent; the handle this, and that the spout: 50
A pipkin[9] there, like Homer's tripod, walks;
Here sighs a jar, and there a goose pie talks;
Men prove with child, as powerful fancy works,
And maids, turned bottles, call aloud for corks.
 Safe passed the Gnome through this fantastic band, 55
A branch of healing spleenwort[1] in his hand.
Then thus addressed the Power: "Hail, wayward Queen!
Who rule the sex to fifty from fifteen:
Parent of vapors and of female wit,
Who give the hysteric or poetic fit, 60
On various tempers act by various ways,
Make some take physic, others scribble plays;
Who cause the proud their visits to delay,
And send the godly in a pet to pray.
A nymph there is that all your power disdains, 65
And thousands more in equal mirth maintains.
But oh! if e'er thy Gnome could spoil a grace,
Or raise a pimple on a beauteous face,
Like citron-waters[2] matrons' cheeks inflame,
Or change complexions at a losing game; 70
If e'er with airy horns[3] I planted heads,
Or rumpled petticoats, or tumbled beds,
Or caused suspicion when no soul was rude,
Or discomposed the headdress of a prude,

---

6. Emblematic of "the vapors"—hypochondria, melancholy, peevishness, often affected by fashionable women.
7. Coils.
8. Mechanical devices used in the theaters for spectacular effects. The fantasies of neurotic women here merge with the sensational stage effects popular with contemporary audiences.
9. An earthen pot. In *Iliad* 18.434–40, Vulcan furnishes the gods with self-propelling "tripods" (three-legged stools).

1. An herb, efficacious against the spleen. Pope alludes to the golden bough that Aeneas and the Cumaean sybil carry with them for protection into the underworld in *Aeneid* 6.
2. Brandy flavored with orange or lemon peel.
3. The symbol of the cuckold; here "airy," because they exist only in the jealous suspicions of the husband, the victim of the mischievous Umbriel.

Or e'er to costive lapdog gave disease, 75
Which not the tears of brightest eyes could ease,
Hear me, and touch Belinda with chagrin:[4]
That single act gives half the world the spleen."
  The Goddess with a discontented air
Seems to reject him though she grants his prayer. 80
A wondrous bag with both her hands she binds,
Like that where once Ulysses held the winds;[5]
There she collects the force of female lungs,
Sighs, sobs, and passions, and the war of tongues.
A vial next she fills with fainting fears, 85
Soft sorrows, melting griefs, and flowing tears.
The Gnome rejoicing bears her gifts away,
Spreads his black wings, and slowly mounts to day.
  Sunk in Thalestris'[6] arms the nymph he found,
Her eyes dejected and her hair unbound. 90
Full o'er their heads the swelling bag he rent,
And all the Furies issued at the vent.
Belinda burns with more than mortal ire,
And fierce Thalestris fans the rising fire.
"O wretched maid!" she spread her hands, and cried 95
(While Hampton's echoes, "Wretched maid!" replied),
"Was it for this you took such constant care
The bodkin, comb, and essence to prepare?
For this your locks in paper durance bound,
For this with torturing irons wreathed around? 100
For this with fillets strained your tender head,
And bravely bore the double loads of lead?[7]
Gods! shall the ravisher display your hair,
While the fops envy, and the ladies stare!
Honor forbid! at whose unrivaled shrine 105
Ease, pleasure, virtue, all, our sex resign.
Methinks already I your tears survey,
Already hear the horrid things they say,
Already see you a degraded toast,
And all your honor in a whisper lost! 110
How shall I, then, your helpless fame defend?
'Twill then be infamy to seem your friend!
And shall this prize, the inestimable prize,
Exposed through crystal to the gazing eyes,
And heightened by the diamond's circling rays, 115
On that rapacious hand forever blaze?
Sooner shall grass in Hyde Park Circus grow,

4. Ill humor.
5. Aeolus (later conceived of as god of the winds) gave Ulysses a bag containing all the winds adverse to his voyage home. When his ship was in sight of Ithaca, his companions opened the bag and the storms that ensued drove Ulysses far away (*Odyssey* 10.19ff.).

6. The name is borrowed from a queen of the Amazons, hence a fierce and warlike woman. Thalestris, according to legend, traveled thirty days in order to have a child by Alexander the Great. Plutarch denies the story.
7. The frame on which the elaborate coiffures of the day were arranged.

And wits take lodgings in the sound of Bow;[8]
Sooner let earth, air, sea, to chaos fall,
Men, monkeys, lapdogs, parrots, perish all!"   120
    She said; then raging to Sir Plume repairs,
And bids her beau demand the precious hairs
(Sir Plume of amber snuffbox justly vain,
And the nice conduct of a clouded cane).
With earnest eyes, and round unthinking face,   125
He first the snuffbox opened, then the case,
And thus broke out—"My Lord, why, what the devil!
Z—ds! damn the lock! 'fore Gad, you must be civil!
Plague on't! 'tis past a jest—nay prithee, pox!
Give her the hair"—he spoke, and rapped his box.   130
    "It grieves me much," replied the Peer again,
"Who speaks so well should ever speak in vain.
But by this Lock, this sacred Lock I swear
(Which never more shall join its parted hair;
Which never more its honors shall renew,   135
Clipped from the lovely head where late it grew),
That while my nostrils draw the vital air,
This hand, which won it, shall forever wear."
He spoke, and speaking, in proud triumph spread
The long-contended honors[9] of her head.   140
    But Umbriel, hateful Gnome, forbears not so;
He breaks the vial whence the sorrows flow.
Then see! the nymph in beauteous grief appears,
Her eyes half languishing, half drowned in tears;
On her heaved bosom hung her drooping head,   145
Which with a sigh she raised, and thus she said:
    "Forever cursed be this detested day,
Which snatched my best, my favorite curl away!
Happy! ah, ten times happy had I been,
If Hampton Court these eyes had never seen!   150
Yet am not I the first mistaken maid,
By love of courts to numerous ills betrayed.
Oh, had I rather unadmired remained
In some lone isle, or distant northern land;
Where the gilt chariot never marks the way,   155
Where none learn ombre, none e'er taste bohea![1]
There kept my charms concealed from mortal eye,
Like roses that in deserts bloom and die.
What moved my mind with youthful lords to roam?
Oh, had I stayed, and said my prayers at home!   160
'Twas this the morning omens seemed to tell,
Thrice from my trembling hand the patch box[2] fell;

8. A person born within sound of the bells of
St. Mary-le-Bow in Cheapside is said to be a
cockney. No fashionable wit would have so
vulgar an address.
9. Ornaments, hence locks; a Latinism.

1. A costly sort of tea.
2. A box to hold the ornamental patches of
court plaster worn on the face by both sexes.
Cf. *Spectator* 81.

The tottering china shook without a wind,
Nay, Poll sat mute, and Shock was most unkind!
A Sylph too warned me of the threats of fate,   165
In mystic visions, now believed too late!
See the poor remnants of these slighted hairs!
My hands shall rend what e'en thy rapine spares.
These in two sable ringlets taught to break,
Once gave new beauties to the snowy neck;   170
The sister lock now sits uncouth, alone,
And in its fellow's fate foresees its own;
Uncurled it hangs, the fatal shears demands,
And tempts once more thy sacrilegious hands.
Oh, hadst thou, cruel! been content to seize   175
Hairs less in sight, or any hairs but these!"

CANTO V

She said: the pitying audience melt in tears.
But Fate and Jove had stopped the Baron's ears.
In vain Thalestris with reproach assails,
For who can move when fair Belinda fails?
Not half so fixed the Trojan³ could remain,   5
While Anna begged and Dido raged in vain.
Then grave Clarissa graceful waved her fan;
Silence ensued, and thus the nymph began:
"Say why are beauties praised and honored most,
The wise man's passion, and the vain man's toast?   10
Why decked with all that land and sea afford,
Why angels called, and angel-like adored?
Why round our coaches crowd the white-gloved beaux,
Why bows the side box from its inmost rows?
How vain are all these glories, all our pains,   15
Unless good sense preserve what beauty gains;
That men may say when we the front box grace,
'Behold the first in virtue as in face!'
Oh! if to dance all night, and dress all day,
Charmed the smallpox, or chased old age away,   20
Who would not scorn what housewife's cares produce,
Or who would learn one earthly thing of use?
To patch, nay ogle, might become a saint,
Nor could it sure be such a sin to paint.
But since, alas! frail beauty must decay,   25
Curled or uncurled, since locks will turn to gray;
Since painted, or not painted, all shall fade,
And she who scorns a man must die a maid;
What then remains but well our power to use,
And keep good humor still whate'er we lose?   30

---

3. A reference to Aeneas, the epic hero of *The Aeneid*, by the Roman poet Virgil (70–19 B.C.E.). Aeneas abandons his lover Dido at the bidding of the gods, despite her reproaches; Virgil compares him to a steadfast oak that withstands a storm (*Aeneid* 4.427–43).

And trust me, dear, good humor can prevail
When airs, and flights, and screams, and scolding fail.
Beauties in vain their pretty eyes may roll;
Charms strike the sight, but merit wins the soul."
    So spoke the dame, but no applause ensued;   35
Belinda frowned, Thalestris called her prude.
"To arms, to arms!" the fierce virago cries,
And swift as lightning to the combat flies.
All side in parties, and begin the attack;
Fans clap, silks rustle, and tough whalebones crack;   40
Heroes' and heroines' shouts confusedly rise,
And bass and treble voices strike the skies.
No common weapons in their hands are found,
Like Gods they fight, nor dread a mortal wound.
    So when bold Homer makes the Gods engage,   45
And heavenly breasts with human passions rage;
'Gainst Pallas, Mars; Latona, Hermes arms;
And all Olympus rings with loud alarms:
Jove's thunder roars, heaven trembles all around,
Blue Neptune storms, the bellowing deeps resound: 50
Earth shakes her nodding towers, the ground gives way,
And the pale ghosts start at the flash of day!
    Triumphant Umbriel on a sconce's height
Clapped his glad wings, and sat to view the fight:
Propped on their bodkin spears, the sprites survey   55
The growing combat, or assist the fray.
    While through the press enraged Thalestris flies,
And scatters death around from both her eyes,
A beau and witling perished in the throng,
One died in metaphor, and one in song.   60
"O cruel nymph! a living death I bear,"
Cried Dapperwit, and sunk beside his chair.
A mournful glance Sir Fopling upwards cast,
"Those eyes are made so killing"—was his last.
Thus on Maeander's flowery margin lies   65
The expiring swan, and as he sings he dies.
    When bold Sir Plume had drawn Clarissa down,
Chloe stepped in, and killed him with a frown;
She smiled to see the doughty hero slain,
But, at her smile, the beau revived again.   70
Now Jove suspends his golden scales in air,
Weighs the men's wits against the lady's hair;
The doubtful beam long nods from side to side;
At length the wits mount up, the hairs subside.
    See, fierce Belinda on the Baron flies,   75
With more than usual lightning in her eyes;
Nor feared the chief the unequal fight to try,
Who sought no more than on his foe to die.
    But this bold lord with manly strength endued,
She with one finger and a thumb subdued: 80
Just where the breath of life his nostrils drew,
A charge of snuff the wily virgin threw;

The Gnomes direct, to every atom just,
The pungent grains of titillating dust.
Sudden, with starting tears each eye o'erflows,   85
And the high dome re-echoes to his nose.
    "Now meet thy fate," incensed Belinda cried,
And drew a deadly bodkin[4] from her side.
(The same, his ancient personage to deck,
Her great-great-grandsire wore about his neck,   90
In three seal rings; which after, melted down,
Formed a vast buckle for his widow's gown:
Her infant grandame's whistle next it grew,
The bells she jingled, and the whistle blew;
Then in a bodkin graced her mother's hairs,   95
Which long she wore, and now Belinda wears.)
    "Boast not my fall," he cried, "insulting foe!
Thou by some other shalt be laid as low.
Nor think to die dejects my lofty mind:
All that I dread is leaving you behind!   100
Rather than so, ah, let me still survive,
And burn in Cupid's flames—but burn alive."
    "Restore the Lock!" she cries; and all around
"Restore the Lock!" the vaulted roofs rebound.
Not fierce Othello in so loud a strain   105
Roared for the handkerchief that caused his pain.[5]
But see how oft ambitious aims are crossed,
And chiefs contend till all the prize is lost!
The lock, obtained with guilt, and kept with pain,
In every place is sought, but sought in vain: 110
With such a prize no mortal must be blessed,
So Heaven decrees! with Heaven who can contest?
    Some thought it mounted to the lunar sphere,
Since all things lost on earth are treasured there.
There heroes' wits are kept in ponderous vases,   115
And beaux' in snuffboxes and tweezer cases.
There broken vows and deathbed alms are found,
And lovers' hearts with ends of riband bound,
The courtier's promises, and sick man's prayers,
The smiles of harlots, and the tears of heirs,   120
Cages for gnats, and chains to yoke a flea,
Dried butterflies, and tomes of casuistry.
    But trust the Muse—she saw it upward rise,
Though marked by none but quick, poetic eyes
(So Rome's great founder[6] to the heavens withdrew,   125
To Proculus alone confessed in view);
A sudden star, it shot through liquid air,
And drew behind a radiant trail of hair.

---

4. An ornamental pin shaped like a dagger, to be worn in the hair.
5. A reference to Shakespeare's tragedy *Othello* (Act 3, Scene 4).

6. Romulus, the "founder" and first king of Rome, was snatched to heaven in a storm cloud while reviewing his army in the Campus Martius (Livy 1.16).

Not Berenice's[7] locks first rose so bright,
The heavens bespangling with disheveled light.   130
The Sylphs behold it kindling as it flies,
And pleased pursue its progress through the skies.
    This the beau monde shall from the Mall[8] survey,
And hail with music its propitious ray.
This the blest lover shall for Venus take,   135
And send up vows from Rosamonda's Lake.[9]
This Partridge soon shall view in cloudless skies,
When next he looks through Galileo's eyes;[1]
And hence the egregious wizard shall foredoom
The fate of Louis, and the fall of Rome.   140
    Then cease, bright nymph! to mourn thy ravished hair,
Which adds new glory to the shining sphere!
Not all the tresses that fair head can boast,
Shall draw such envy as the Lock you lost.
For, after all the murders of your eye,   145
When, after millions slain, yourself shall die:
When those fair suns shall set, as set they must,
And all those tresses shall be laid in dust,
This Lock the Muse shall consecrate to fame,
And 'midst the stars inscribe Belinda's name.   150

An Essay on Man

To Henry St. John, Lord Bolingbroke

EPISTLE I

ARGUMENT OF THE NATURE AND STATE OF MAN, WITH RESPECT TO THE UNIVERSE.
Of man in the abstract—I. That we can judge only with regard to our own system, being ignorant of the relations of systems and things, ver. 17, &c.—II.
That man is not to be deemed imperfect, but a being suited to his place and
rank in the creation, agreeable to the general order of things, and conformable
to ends and relations to him unknown, ver. 35, &c.—III. That it is partly upon
his ignorance of future events, and partly upon the hope of a future state, that
all his happiness in the present depends, ver. 77, &c.—IV. The pride of aiming
at more knowledge, and pretending to more perfection, the cause of man's
error and misery. The impiety of putting himself in the place of God, and judging of the fitness or unfitness, perfection or imperfection, justice or injustice of
his dispensations, ver. 113, &c.—V. The absurdity of conceiving himself the

7. Queen Berenice II of Egypt, wife of Ptolemy III
in the 3rd century B.C.E; she promised the goddess Aphrodite that she would sacrifice her
beautiful long hair if her husband returned
safely from war; Aphrodite was so pleased that
she turned the hair into a constellation of stars.
8. A walk laid out by Charles II in St. James's
Park, a resort for strollers of all sorts.
9. In St. James's Park; associated with unhappy
lovers.
1. A telescope. John Partridge was an astrologer whose annually published predictions had
been amusingly satirized by Swift and other
wits in 1708.

final cause of the creation, or expecting that perfection in the moral world which is not in the natural, ver. 131, &c.—VI. The unreasonableness of his complaints against Providence, while on the one hand he demands the perfections of the angels, and on the other the bodily qualifications of the brutes; though, to possess any of the sensitive faculties in a higher degree, would render him miserable, ver. 173, &c.—VII. That throughout the whole visible world, an universal order and gradation in the sensual and mental faculties is observed, which causes a subordination of creature to creature, and of all creatures to man. The gradations of sense, instinct, thought, reflection, reason: that reason alone countervails all the other faculties, ver. 207.—VIII. How much further this order and subordination of living creatures may extend, above and below us; were any part of which broken, not that part only, but the whole connected creation must be destroyed, ver. 233—IX. The extravagance, madness, and pride of such a desire, ver. 259.—X. The consequence of all, the absolute submission due to Providence, both as to our present and future state, ver. 281, &c., to the end.

> Awake, my St. John![1] leave all meaner things
> To low ambition, and the pride of Kings.
> Let us (since Life can little more supply
> Than just to look about us and to die)
> Expatiate free o'er all this scene of Man;   5
> A mighty maze! but not without a plan;
> A Wild, where weeds and flowers promiscuous shoot;
> Or Garden, tempting with forbidden fruit.
> Together let us beat this ample field,
> Try what the open, what the covert yield;   10
> The latent tracts, the giddy heights, explore
> Of all who blindly creep, or sightless soar;
> Eye Nature's walks, shoot Folly as it flies,
> And catch the Manners living as they rise;
> Laugh where we must, be candid where we can;   15
> But vindicate the ways of God to man.[2]
>
>   I. Say first, of God above, or Man below,
> What can we reason, but from what we know?
> Of Man, what see we but his station here,
> From which to reason, or to which refer?   20
> Through worlds unnumbered though the God be known,
> 'Tis ours to trace him only in our own.
> He, who through vast immensity can pierce,
> See worlds on worlds compose one universe,
> Observe how system into system runs,   25
> What other planets circle other suns,
> What varied Being peoples every star,

1. Henry St. John, Viscount Bolingbroke, Pope's friend, who had thus far neglected to keep his part of their friendly bargain: Pope was to write his philosophical speculations in verse; Bolingbroke was to write his in prose.

2. Cf. Milton's *Paradise Lost* 1.26. Pope's theme is essentially the same as Milton's, and even the opening image of the garden reminds one of the earlier poet's Paradise.

May tell why Heaven has made us as we are.
But of this frame the bearings, and the ties,
The strong connections, nice dependencies,   30
Gradations just, has thy pervading soul
Looked through? or can a part contain the whole?
    Is the great chain,[3] that draws all to agree,
And drawn supports, upheld by God, or thee?

    II. Presumptuous Man! the reason wouldst thou find,   35
Why formed so weak, so little, and so blind?
First, if thou canst, the harder reason guess,
Why formed no weaker, blinder, and no less?
Ask of thy mother earth, why oaks are made
Taller or stronger than the weeds they shade?   40
Or ask of yonder argent fields above,
Why Jove's satellites are less than JOVE?
    Of Systems possible, if 'tis confest
That Wisdom infinite must form the best,
Where all must full[4] or not coherent be,   45
And all that rises, rise in due degree;
Then, in the scale of reasoning life, 'tis plain,
There must be, somewhere, such a rank as Man:
And all the question (wrangle e'er so long)
Is only this, if God has placed him wrong?   50
    Respecting Man, whatever wrong we call,
May, must be right, as relative to all.
In human works, though laboured on with pain,
A thousand movements scarce one purpose gain;
In God's, one single can its end produce;   55
Yet serves to second too some other use.
So Man, who here seems principal alone,
Perhaps acts second to some sphere unknown,
Touches some wheel, or verges to some goal;
'Tis but a part we see, and not a whole.   60
    When the proud steed shall know why Man restrains
His fiery course, or drives him o'er the plains;
When the dull Ox, why now he breaks the clod,
Is now a victim, and now Egypt's God:
Then shall Man's pride and dullness comprehend   65
His actions', passions', being's use and end;
Why doing, suffering, checked, impelled; and why
This hour a slave, the next a deity.
    Then say not Man's imperfect, Heaven in fault;
Say rather, Man's as perfect as he ought: 70
His knowledge measured to his state and place;
His time a moment, and a point his space.
If to be perfect in a certain sphere,

3. A reference to the popular 18th-century notion of the Great Chain of Being, in which elements of the universe took their places in a hierarchy ranging from the lowest matter to God.

4. Theorists of the Great Chain of Being believed that there must be no gaps in the chain.

What matter, soon or late, or here or there?
The blest to-day is as completely so,   75
As who began a thousand years ago.

   III. Heaven from all creatures hides the book of Fate,
All but the page prescribed, their present state:
From brutes what men, from men what spirits know:
Or who could suffer Being here below?   80
The lamb thy riot dooms to bleed to-day,
Had he thy Reason, would he skip and play?
Pleased to the last, he crops the flowery food,
And licks the hand just raised to shed his blood.
Oh blindness to the future! kindly given,   85
That each may fill the circle marked by Heaven:
Who sees with equal eye, as God of all,
A hero perish, or a sparrow fall,
Atoms or systems into ruin hurled,
And now a bubble burst, and now a world.   90
   Hope humbly then; with trembling pinions soar;
Wait the great teacher Death; and God adore.
What future bliss, he gives not thee to know,
But gives that Hope to be thy blessing now.
Hope springs eternal in the human breast: 95
Man never Is, but always To be blest:
The soul, uneasy and confined from home,
Rests and expatiates in a life to come.
   Lo, the poor Indian! whose untutored mind
Sees God in clouds, or hears him in the wind;   100
His soul, proud Science never taught to stray
Far as the solar walk, or milky way;
Yet simple Nature to his hope has given,
Behind the cloud-topt hill, an humbler heaven;
Some safer world in depth of woods embraced,   105
Some happier island in the watery waste,
Where slaves once more their native land behold,
No fiends torment, no Christians thirst for gold.
To Be, contents his natural desire,
He asks no Angel's wing, no Seraph's fire;   110
But thinks, admitted to that equal sky,
His faithful dog shall bear him company.

   IV. Go, wiser thou! and, in thy scale of sense,
Weigh thy Opinion against Providence;
Call imperfection what thou fanciest such,   115
Say, here he gives too little, there too much:
Destroy all Creatures for thy sport or gust,
Yet cry, If Man's unhappy, God's unjust;
If Man alone engross not Heaven's high care,
Alone made perfect here, immortal there: 120
Snatch from his hand the balance and the rod,
Re-judge his justice, be the GOD of GOD.

In Pride, in reasoning Pride, our error lies;
All quit their sphere, and rush into the skies.
Pride still is aiming at the blest abodes,   125
Men would be Angels, Angels would be Gods.
Aspiring to be Gods, if Angels fell,
Aspiring to be Angels, Men rebel:
And who but wishes to invert the laws
Of ORDER, sins against the Eternal Cause.   130

    V. Ask for what end the heavenly bodies shine,
Earth for whose use? Pride answers, "'Tis for mine:
For me kind Nature wakes her genial Power,
Suckles each herb, and spreads out ev'ry flower;
Annual for me, the grape, the rose, renew,   135
The juice nectareous, and the balmy dew;
For me, the mine a thousand treasures brings;
For me, health gushes from a thousand springs;
Seas roll to waft me, suns to light me rise;
My footstool earth, my canopy the skies."   140
    But errs not Nature from this gracious end,
From burning suns when livid deaths descend,
When earthquakes swallow, or when tempests sweep
Towns to one grave, whole nations to the deep?
"No," 'tis replied, "the first Almighty Cause   145
Acts not by partial, but by general laws;
The exceptions few; some change since all began:
And what created perfect?"—Why then Man?
If the great end be human happiness,
Then Nature deviates; and can man do less?   150
As much that end a constant course requires
Of showers and sunshine, as of man's desires;
As much eternal springs and cloudless skies,
As Men forever temperate, calm, and wise.
If plagues or earthquakes break not Heaven's design,   155
Why then a Borgia, or a Catiline?[5]
Who knows but He whose hand the lightning forms,
Who heaves old Ocean, and who wings the storms;
Pours fierce Ambition in a Caesar's mind,
Or turns young Ammon[6] loose to scourge mankind?   160
From pride, from pride, our very reasoning springs;
Account for moral, as for natural things:
Why charge we Heaven in those, in these acquit?
In both, to reason right is to submit.
    Better for Us, perhaps, it might appear,   165
Were there all harmony, all virtue here;
That never air or ocean felt the wind;
That never passion discomposed the mind.

---

5. Roman who conspired against the state in 63 B.C.E. Cesare Borgia (1476–1507), an Italian prince notorious for his crimes.

6. Alexander the Great, who when he visited the oracle of Zeus Ammon in Egypt was hailed by the priest there as son of the god.

But ALL subsists by elemental strife;
And Passions are the elements of Life.   170
The general ORDER, since the whole began,
Is kept in Nature, and is kept in Man.

    VI. What would this Man? Now upward will he soar,
And little less than Angel, would be more;
Now looking downwards, just as grieved appears   175
To want the strength of bulls, the fur of bears.
Made for his use all creatures if he call,
Say what their use, had he the powers of all?
Nature to these, without profusion, kind,
The proper organs, proper powers assigned;   180
Each seeming want compénsated of course,
Here with degrees of swiftness, there of force;
All in exact proportion to the state;
Nothing to add, and nothing to abate.
Each beast, each insect, happy in its own: 185
Is Heaven unkind to Man, and Man alone?
Shall he alone, whom rational we call,
Be pleased with nothing, if not blessed with all?
    The bliss of Man (could Pride that blessing find)
Is not to act or think beyond mankind;   190
No powers of body or of soul to share,
But what his nature and his state can bear.
Why has not Man a microscopic eye?
For this plain reason, Man is not a Fly.
Say what the use, were finer optics[7] given,   195
T' inspect a mite, not comprehend the heaven?
Or touch, if tremblingly alive all o'er,
To smart and agonize at every pore?
Or quick effluvia[8] darting through the brain,
Die of a rose in aromatic pain?   200
If nature thundered in his opening ears,
And stunned him with the music of the spheres,[9]
How would he wish that Heaven had left him still
The whispering Zephyr, and the purling rill?
Who finds not Providence all good and wise,   205
Alike in what it gives, and what it denies?

    VII. Far as Creation's ample range extends,
The scale of sensual, mental powers ascends:
Mark how it mounts, to Man's imperial race,
From the green myriads in the peopled grass: 210
What modes of sight betwixt each wide extreme,
The mole's dim curtain, and the lynx's[1] beam:

---

7. Eyes.
8. Stream of minute particles.
9. The old notion that the movement of the planets created a "higher" music.

1. According to legend, one of the keenest sighted animals. "Dim curtain": the mole's poor vision.

Of smell, the headlong lioness between,
And hound sagacious[2] on the tainted green:
Of hearing, from the life that fills the Flood,   215
To that which warbles through the vernal wood:
The spider's touch, how exquisitely fine!
Feels at each thread, and lives along the line:
In the nice bee, what sense so subtly true
From poisonous herbs extracts the healing dew?   220
How Instinct varies in the grovelling swine,
Compared, half-reasoning elephant, with thine!
'Twixt that, and Reason, what a nice barriér,
For ever separate, yet for ever near!
Remembrance and Reflection how allied;   225
What thin partitions Sense from Thought divide:
And Middle natures,[3] how they long to join,
Yet never pass the insuperable line!
Without this just gradation, could they be
Subjected, these to those, or all to thee?   230
The powers of all subdued by thee alone,
Is not thy Reason all these powers in one?

    VIII. See, through this air, this ocean, and this earth,
All matter quick, and bursting into birth.
Above, how high, progressive life may go!   235
Around, how wide! how deep extend below!
Vast chain of Being! which from God began,
Natures ethereal, human, angel, man,
Beast, bird, fish, insect, what no eye can see,
No glass can reach; from Infinite to thee,   240
From thee to Nothing.—On superior powers
Were we to press, inferior might on ours:
Or in the full creation leave a void,
Where, one step broken, the great scale's destroyed:
From Nature's chain whatever link you strike,   245
Tenth or ten thousandth, breaks the chain alike.
    And, if each system in gradation roll
Alike essential to the amazing Whole,
The least confusion but in one, not all
That system only, but the Whole must fall.   250
Let Earth unbalanced from her orbit fly,
Planets and Suns run lawless through the sky;
Let ruling angels from their spheres be hurled,
Being on Being wrecked, and world on world;
Heaven's whole foundations to their center nod,   255
And Nature tremble to the throne of God.
All this dread ORDER break—for whom? for thee?
Vile worm!—oh Madness! Pride! Impiety!

2. Here, exceptionally quick of scent.
3. Animals that seem to share the characteris-   tics of several different classes, e.g., the duck-
billed platypus.

IX. What if the foot, ordained the dust to tread,
Or hand, to toil, aspired to be the head?   260
What if the head, the eye, or ear repined
To serve mere engines to the ruling Mind?
Just as absurd for any part to claim
To be another, in this general frame:
Just as absurd, to mourn the tasks or pains,   265
The great directing MIND of ALL ordains.
    All are but parts of one stupendous whole,
Whose body Nature is, and God the soul;
That, changed through all, and yet in all the same;
Great in the earth, as in the ethereal frame;   270
Warms in the sun, refreshes in the breeze,
Glows in the stars, and blossoms in the trees,
Lives through all life, extends through all extent,
Spreads undivided, operates unspent;
Breathes in our soul, informs our mortal part,   275
As full, as perfect, in a hair as heart;
As full, as perfect, in vile Man that mourns,
As the rapt Seraph that adores and burns:
To him no high, no low, no great, no small;
He fills, he bounds, connects, and equals all.   280

    X. Cease then, nor ORDER imperfection name:
Our proper bliss depends on what we blame.
Know thy own point: this kind, this due degree
Of blindness, weakness, Heaven bestows on thee.
Submit.—In this, or any other sphere,   285
Secure to be as blest as thou canst bear:
Safe in the hand of one disposing Power,
Or in the natal, or the mortal hour.
All Nature is but Art, unknown to thee;
All Chance, Direction, which thou canst not see;   290
All Discord, Harmony not understood;
All partial Evil, universal Good:
And, spite of Pride, in erring Reason's spite,
One truth is clear, WHATEVER IS, IS RIGHT.[4]

---

4. Epistle II deals with "the Nature and State of Man with respect to himself, as an Individual"; Epistle III examines "the Nature and State of Man with respect to Society"; and the last epistle concerns "the Nature and State of Man with Respect to Happiness."

VOLTAIRE
(FRANÇOIS-MARIE AROUET)
1694–1778

Imagine a writer so outspoken and so fearless that although his work landed him in prison and in exile—more than once—he never stopped writing defiantly. If he could not publish his work openly, he would have it printed secretly and smuggled across borders. If he could not circulate it by the post, he would have it hand-carried in suitcases and distributed by trusted friends. He seized freedom of speech even when it was not granted to him, and he used it to mock corrupt priests and self-regarding kings. The sheer gutsiness of Voltaire is breathtaking. In an atmosphere of stern censorship and absolute power, he managed to live to the ripe age of eighty-three, writing lively denunciations of dominant orthodoxies and powerful authorities almost every day. And his darkly comic imagination propelled him to enormous fame. He was so successful that he grew richer than many kings in Europe. His witty, light prose, and his clear and accessible style allowed him to popularize many of the revolutionary goals of the Enlightenment—human rights, the value of freedom and tolerance, the hope for progress through reasoned debate, and the urgent desire to end human suffering where we can. It is in no small part thanks to Voltaire that these ideals shape our own political landscape today.

LIFE AND TIMES

Bold, witty, and rebellious, François-Marie Arouet was a trouble to his parents as a child and became a trouble to the authorities for the rest of his life. He was born near Paris in 1694 to a middle-class family. At the age of ten he went to a boarding school run by Jesuits, where he developed an enthusiasm for literature and a passionate opposition to organized religion. His father wanted him to pursue a career in law, but he soon gave it up to write poetry and plays. So sparkling and brilliant was his conversation that he won powerful friends, but his propensity for satire also brought him enemies, and an attack on the acting head of state got him locked in the Bastille prison in Paris for almost a year. While there, he committed himself to writing, and his first play, *Oedipus*, turned into a huge success, bringing him considerable wealth and establishing his reputation.

The young writer, who was now known by his pen name, "Voltaire," spent three years in exile in England after a quarrel with a French nobleman. There he met the writers **Jonathan Swift** and **Alexander Pope**. He enjoyed the freedom from censorship and punishment allowed to writers in England, and returned to France with an even stronger sense of his right to dissent and oppose authority. His many subversive writings, called by the authorities "most dangerous to religion and civil order," earned him another spell of exile from Paris, which he spent with his longtime mistress and intellectual companion Madame du Châtelet. In 1750, Voltaire moved to Potsdam, in Prussia, where he joined the court of the young King Frederick, later to be known as Frederick the Great, who loved the arts and wanted philosophy and literature to flourish. Voltaire, like many other Enlightenment thinkers, did not see democracy as the best form of government. The masses seemed to him to impede reason, freedom, and progress (he said he would "rather obey one lion than 200 rats"). The regime he idealized was the enlightened despot—a sensitive, rational king who welcomed dissent and sought the counsel of philosophers like himself. Early on, Frederick promised to live up to that ideal, but Voltaire was soon to be disappointed. He and Frederick argued; Frederick waged violent warfare and asserted power high-handedly. Voltaire was invited to leave.

He took up residence for the rest of his life at Ferney, a town on the border between France and Switzerland, so that he could escape from France easily if necessary. It was here that he wrote the best-selling *Candide*—and a great deal more. Travelers and visitors brought suitcases filled with Voltaire's "scandal-sheets" back with them to Paris where the public eagerly gobbled them up. He repeatedly attacked religious extremism and stultifying tradition and argued for universal human rights. And he refused the traditional literary goal of immortality, casting his writing as a response to current debates and events.

Voltaire was no atheist (he once said that "if God did not exist it would be necessary to invent him"). His own religion is usually known as Deism; that is, faith in a God who created the world and then stands back, allowing nature to follow its own laws and never intervening. The Deists' signature metaphor was God as a watchmaker: the world he made was a mechanism, which then ticked away on its own. As far as human beings were concerned, God gave them reason, and then left them free to use it. Deists disagreed about whether God had instilled human beings with a love of virtue, and whether there was an

afterlife of rewards and punishments. Voltaire claimed that it was impossible for humans to know anything beyond their senses—so God's will must remain mysterious—and he believed that humans should use their senses and their reason to understand how the world works and, to the best of our ability, to make it better.

By the time of Voltaire's death, he had become a national hero. In all, he had produced enough work to fill 135 volumes, in a range of genres including tragedy, epic, philosophy, history, fiction, and journalism. In death as in life, he continued to generate scandal and division. Clergy in Paris refused to let him be buried in hallowed ground, so friends smuggled his body out of the city—propping it up on the journey like a sleeping passenger—and brought it to a monastery to be laid to rest. Later, leaders of the French Revolution, who had been inspired by Voltaire's attacks on authority and religion, had his body exhumed and reburied in Paris to huge national fanfare.

WORK

Voltaire wrote *Candide* in part as a response to a piece of news that shook him, and many of his contemporaries, badly. On November 1, 1755, a devastating earthquake hit Lisbon, in Portugal. Upwards of thirty thousand people died. Voltaire, writing almost obsessively about this tragedy in his letters, wondered how anyone could make a case for an optimistic philosophy in light of it. He worried over Alexander Pope's assertion in his **Essay on Man** that "Whatever is, is right." Could anyone really believe that this was God's will—that a just and rational God had created this world and that it was, in the words of the German philosopher Gottfried Wilhelm Leibniz, "the best of all possible worlds"? Voltaire's absurd philosopher Pangloss ("all-tongue") is a caricature of Leibniz.

Though philosophical, *Candide* is so brief and so easy to read that it was immediately popular with a wide range of readers. Voltaire deliberately opted for short, cheap, excitingly readable texts. Long works "will never make a revolution," he argued, and wrote that "if the New Testament had cost 4,200 sesterces, the Christian religion would never have taken root." Thus *Candide*'s brevity may be seen as part of its power.

It is also deliberately entertaining. Voltaire combines a lively appetite for humor with a horrifying sense of the real existence of evil. The exuberance and extravagance of the sufferings characters undergo may even prompt us to laugh: the plight of the old woman whose buttock has been cut off to make rump steak for her starving companions, the weeping of two girls whose monkey-lovers have been killed, the glum circumstances of six exiled, poverty-stricken kings. But Voltaire also manages to keep his readers off balance. Raped, cut to pieces, hanged, stabbed in the belly, the central characters of *Candide* keep coming back to life at opportune moments, as though no disaster could have permanent effects. Such reassuring fantasy at first suggests that it is all a joke, designed to ridicule an outmoded philosophical system. And yet, reality keeps intruding. An admiral really did face a firing squad and die for failing to engage an enemy ferociously enough. Those six hungry kings were actual historical figures who were dispossessed. The Lisbon earthquake was so real that it haunted Voltaire for years. And his satirical pen attacks genuine social problems as various as military discipline, class hierarchy, greed, religious extremism, slavery, and even the publishing industry. The extravagances of the story are therefore uncomfortably matched by the extravagances of real life, and despite the comic lightness of the telling, Voltaire demands that the reader confront these horrors.

The fantastic and exaggerated nature of the events stands out against the simplicity of the narrative style. Candide is a naive traveler, like Jonathan Swift's Gulliver, who does not grasp the ironies he witnesses. He travels widely, taking in Europe, South America, and the Ottoman Empire, where Catholics, Protestants, and Muslims all emerge as cruel and hypocritical. The only exception is the mythical Eldorado, which takes place almost exactly at the halfway point of the text, where corruption, crime, malice, and poverty do not exist. Candide nonetheless insists on leaving Eldorado to find his beloved Cunégonde. Readers have often wondered about the role of this paradise in an otherwise bleak picture of human experience: does Eldorado suggest that human beings are capable of virtue, and if so, then why does Voltaire compel his protagonist to leave? Is it too stagnant, too isolated, too dull? Is it like the Garden of Eden, a paradise no longer home to fallen humanity? The fact that Candide admires **Milton's *Paradise Lost*** and that the novella concludes with the protagonist cultivating a garden suggests that Voltaire may have been rethinking the story of Adam and Eve in his own imaginative way.

Candide encapsulated the many problems that stoked Voltaire's anger and fed his satire: absolutism and religious bigotry, unnecessary bloodshed, restrictions on freedom of speech and religion, and the intolerable reality of human suffering. This story has always been the most famous work of its author's incalculably influential career. Voltaire inspired leaders of the American Revolution—**Thomas Jefferson**, Thomas Paine, and **Benjamin Franklin**—and helped to shape the United States Constitution. The French Revolutionaries held Voltaire up as a hero, as did generations fighting against religious intolerance. He was hotly reviled by those who wanted to maintain the authority of established churches, and some went so far as to call him the Antichrist. But in the centuries that have followed, Voltaire's ideas have become part of the common fabric of our ideals.

Candide, or Optimism[1]

translated from the German of Doctor Ralph with the additions which were found in the Doctor's pocket when he died at Minden in the Year of Our Lord 1759

CHAPTER I

How Candide Was Brought up in a Fine Castle and How He Was Driven Therefrom

There lived in Westphalia,[2] in the castle of the Baron of Thunder-Ten-Tronckh, a young man on whom nature had bestowed the perfection of gentle manners. His features admirably expressed his soul; he combined an honest mind with great simplicity of heart; and I think it was for this reason that they called him Candide. The old servants of the house suspected that he was the son of the Baron's sister by a respectable, honest gentleman of the neighborhood, whom she had refused to marry because he could prove only seventy-one quarterings,[3] the rest of his family tree having been lost in the passage of time.

The Baron was one of the most mighty lords of Westphalia, for his castle had a door and windows. His great hall was even hung with a tapestry. The dogs of his courtyard made up a hunting pack on occasion, with the stable-boys as huntsmen; the village priest was his grand almoner. They all called him "My Lord," and laughed at his stories.

The Baroness, who weighed in the neighborhood of three hundred and fifty pounds, was greatly respected for that reason, and did the honors of the house with a dignity which rendered her even more imposing. Her daughter Cunégonde,[4] aged seventeen, was a ruddy-cheeked girl, fresh, plump, and desirable. The Baron's son seemed in every way worthy of his father. The tutor Pangloss was the oracle of the household, and little Candide listened to his lectures with all the good faith of his age and character.

---

1. Translated and with notes by Robert M. Adams.
2. A province of western Germany, near Holland and the lower Rhineland. Flat, boggy, and drab, it is noted chiefly for its excellent ham. In a letter to his niece, written during his German expedition of 1750, Voltaire described the "vast, sad, sterile, detestable countryside of Westphalia."

3. Genealogical divisions of one's family tree. Seventy-one of them is a grotesque number to have, representing something over 2,000 years of uninterrupted nobility.
4. Cunégonde gets her odd name from Kunigunda (wife to Emperor Henry II) who walked barefoot and blindfolded on red-hot irons to prove her chastity; Pangloss gets his name from Greek words meaning "all-tongue."

Pangloss gave instruction in metaphysico-theologico-cosmoloonigology.[5] He proved admirably that there cannot possibly be an effect without a cause and that in this best of all possible worlds the Baron's castle was the best of all castles and his wife the best of all possible Baronesses.

—It is clear, said he, that things cannot be otherwise than they are, for since everything is made to serve an end, everything necessarily serves the best end. Observe: noses were made to support spectacles, hence we have spectacles. Legs, as anyone can plainly see, were made to be breeched, and so we have breeches. Stones were made to be shaped and to build castles with; thus My Lord has a fine castle, for the greatest Baron in the province should have the finest house; and since pigs were made to be eaten, we eat pork all year round.[6] Consequently, those who say everything is well are uttering mere stupidities; they should say everything is for the best.

Candide listened attentively and believed implicitly; for he found Miss Cunégonde exceedingly pretty, though he never had the courage to tell her so. He decided that after the happiness of being born Baron of Thunder-Ten-Tronckh, the second order of happiness was to be Miss Cunégonde; the third was seeing her every day, and the fourth was listening to Master Pangloss, the greatest philosopher in the province and consequently in the entire world.

One day, while Cunégonde was walking near the castle in the little woods that they called a park, she saw Dr. Pangloss in the underbrush; he was giving a lesson in experimental physics to her mother's maid, a very attractive and obedient brunette. As Miss Cunégonde had a natural bent for the sciences, she watched breathlessly the repeated experiments which were going on; she saw clearly the doctor's sufficient reason, observed both cause and effect, and returned to the house in a distracted and pensive frame of mind, yearning for knowledge and dreaming that she might be the sufficient reason of young Candide—who might also be hers.

As she was returning to the castle, she met Candide, and blushed; Candide blushed too. She greeted him in a faltering tone of voice; and Candide talked to her without knowing what he was saying. Next day, as everyone was rising from the dinner table, Cunégonde and Candide found themselves behind a screen; Cunégonde dropped her handkerchief, Candide picked it up; she held his hand quite innocently, he kissed her hand quite innocently with remarkable vivacity and emotion; their lips met, their eyes lit up, their knees trembled, their hands wandered. The Baron of Thunder-Ten-Tronckh passed by the screen and, taking note of this cause and this effect, drove Candide out of the castle by kicking him vigorously on the backside. Cunégonde fainted; as soon as she recovered, the Baroness slapped her face; and everything was confusion in the most beautiful and agreeable of all possible castles.

5. The "looney" buried in this burlesque word corresponds to a buried *nigaud*—"booby" in the French. Christian Wolff, disciple of Leibniz, invented and popularized the word "cosmology." The catch phrases in the following sentence, echoed by popularizers of Leibniz, make reference to the determinism of his system, its linking of cause with effect, and its optimism.

6. The argument from design supposes that everything in this world exists for a specific reason; Voltaire objects not to the argument as a whole, but to the abuse of it.

CHAPTER 2
What Happened to Candide Among the Bulgars[7]

Candide, ejected from the earthly paradise, wandered for a long time without knowing where he was going, weeping, raising his eyes to heaven, and gazing back frequently on the most beautiful of castles which contained the most beautiful of Baron's daughters. He slept without eating, in a furrow of a plowed field, while the snow drifted over him; next morning, numb with cold, he dragged himself into the neighboring village, which was called Waldberghoff-trarbk-dikdorff; he was penniless, famished, and exhausted. At the door of a tavern he paused forlornly. Two men dressed in blue[8] took note of him:

—Look, chum, said one of them, there's a likely young fellow of just about the right size.

They approached Candide and invited him very politely to dine with them.

—Gentlemen, Candide replied with charming modesty, I'm honored by your invitation, but I really don't have enough money to pay my share.

—My dear sir, said one of the blues, people of your appearance and your merit don't have to pay; aren't you five feet five inches tall?

—Yes, gentlemen, that is indeed my stature, said he, making a bow.

—Then, sir, you must be seated at once; not only will we pay your bill this time, we will never allow a man like you to be short of money; for men were made only to render one another mutual aid.

—You are quite right, said Candide; it is just as Dr. Pangloss always told me, and I see clearly that everything is for the best.

They beg him to accept a couple of crowns, he takes them, and offers an I.O.U.; they won't hear of it, and all sit down at table together.

—Don't you love dearly . . . ?

—I do indeed, says he, I dearly love Miss Cunégonde.

—No, no, says one of the gentlemen, we are asking if you don't love dearly the King of the Bulgars.

—Not in the least, says he, I never laid eyes on him.

—What's that you say? He's the most charming of kings, and we must drink his health.

—Oh, gladly, gentlemen; and he drinks.

—That will do, they tell him; you are now the bulwark, the support, the defender, the hero of the Bulgars; your fortune is made and your future assured.

Promptly they slip irons on his legs and lead him to the regiment. There they cause him to right face, left face, present arms, order arms, aim, fire, doubletime, and they give him thirty strokes of the rod. Next day he does the drill a little less awkwardly and gets only twenty strokes; the third day, they give him only ten, and he is regarded by his comrades as a prodigy.

Candide, quite thunderstruck, did not yet understand very clearly how he was a hero. One fine spring morning he took it into his head to go for a walk, stepping straight out as if it were a privilege of the human race, as of animals in general, to

---

7. Voltaire chose this name to represent the Prussian troops of Frederick the Great because he wanted to make an insinuation of pederasty against both the soldiers and their master. Cf. French *bougre*, English "bugger."

8. The recruiting officers of Frederick the Great, much feared in 18th-century Europe, wore blue uniforms. Frederick had a passion for sorting out his soldiers by size; several of his regiments would accept only six-footers.

use his legs as he chose.[9] He had scarcely covered two leagues when four other heroes, each six feet tall, overtook him, bound him, and threw him into a dungeon. At the court-martial they asked which he preferred, to be flogged thirty-six times by the entire regiment or to receive summarily a dozen bullets in the brain. In vain did he argue that the human will is free and insist that he preferred neither alternative; he had to choose; by virtue of the divine gift called "liberty" he decided to run the gauntlet thirty-six times, and actually endured two floggings. The regiment was composed of two thousand men. That made four thousand strokes, which laid open every muscle and nerve from his nape to his butt. As they were preparing for the third beating, Candide, who could endure no more, begged as a special favor that they would have the goodness to smash his head. His plea was granted; they bandaged his eyes and made him kneel down. The King of the Bulgars, passing by at this moment, was told of the culprit's crime; and as this king had a rare genius, he understood, from everything they told him of Candide, that this was a young metaphysician, extremely ignorant of the ways of the world, so he granted his royal pardon, with a generosity which will be praised in every newspaper in every age. A worthy surgeon cured Candide in three weeks with the ointments described by Dioscorides.[1] He already had a bit of skin back and was able to walk when the King of the Bulgars went to war with the King of the Abares.[2]

CHAPTER 3

How Candide Escaped from the Bulgars, and What Became of Him

Nothing could have been so fine, so brisk, so brilliant, so well-drilled as the two armies. The trumpets, the fifes, the oboes, the drums, and the cannon produced such a harmony as was never heard in hell. First the cannons battered down about six thousand men on each side; then volleys of musket fire removed from the best of worlds about nine or ten thousand rascals who were cluttering up its surface. The bayonet was a sufficient reason for the demise of several thousand others. Total casualties might well amount to thirty thousand men or so. Candide, who was trembling like a philosopher, hid himself as best he could while this heroic butchery was going on.

Finally, while the two kings in their respective camps celebrated the victory by having *Te Deum*s sung, Candide undertook to do his reasoning of cause and effect somewhere else. Passing by mounds of the dead and dying, he came to a nearby village which had been burnt to the ground. It was an Abare village, which the Bulgars had burned, in strict accordance with the laws of war. Here old men, stunned from beatings, watched the last agonies of their butchered wives, who

---

9. This episode was suggested by the experience of a Frenchman named Courtilz, who had deserted from the Prussian army and been bastinadoed for it. Voltaire intervened with Frederick to gain his release. But it also reflects the story that Wolff, Leibniz's disciple, got into trouble with Frederick's father when someone reported that his doctrine denying free will had encouraged several soldiers to desert. "The argument of the grenadier," who was said to have pleaded preestablished harmony to justify his desertion, so infuriated the king that he

had Wolff expelled from the country.
1. Dioscorides' treatise on *materia medica*, dating from the 1st century C.E., was not the most up to date.
2. A tribe of semicivilized Scythians, who might be supposed at war with the Bulgars; allegorically, the Abares are the French, who opposed the Prussians in the Seven Years' War (1756–63). According to the title page of 1761, "Doctor Ralph," the dummy author of *Candide*, himself perished at the battle of Minden (Westphalia) in 1759.

still clutched their infants to their bleeding breasts; there, disemboweled girls, who had first satisfied the natural needs of various heroes, breathed their last; others, half-scorched in the flames, begged for their death stroke. Scattered brains and severed limbs littered the ground.

Candide fled as fast as he could to another village; this one belonged to the Bulgars, and the heroes of the Abare cause had given it the same treatment. Climbing over ruins and stumbling over corpses, Candide finally made his way out of the war area, carrying a little food in his knapsack and never ceasing to dream of Miss Cunégonde. His supplies gave out when he reached Holland; but having heard that everyone in that country was rich and a Christian, he felt confident of being treated as well as he had been in the castle of the Baron before he was kicked out for the love of Miss Cunégonde.

He asked alms of several grave personages, who all told him that if he continued to beg, he would be shut up in a house of correction and set to hard labor.

Finally he approached a man who had just been talking to a large crowd for an hour on end; the topic was charity. Looking doubtfully at him, the orator demanded:

—What are you doing here? Are you here to serve the good cause?

—There is no effect without a cause, said Candide modestly; all events are linked by the chain of necessity and arranged for the best. I had to be driven away from Miss Cunégonde, I had to run the gauntlet, I have to beg my bread until I can earn it; none of this could have happened otherwise.

—Look here, friend, said the orator, do you think the Pope is Antichrist?[3]

—I haven't considered the matter, said Candide; but whether he is or not, I'm in need of bread.

—You don't deserve any, said the other; away with you, you rascal, you rogue, never come near me as long as you live.

Meanwhile, the orator's wife had put her head out of the window, and, seeing a man who was not sure the Pope was Antichrist, emptied over his head a pot full of———Scandalous! The excesses into which women are led by religious zeal!

A man who had never been baptized, a good Anabaptist[4] named Jacques, saw this cruel and heartless treatment being inflicted on one of his fellow creatures, a featherless biped possessing a soul;[5] he took Candide home with him, washed him off, gave him bread and beer, presented him with two florins, and even undertook to give him a job in his Persian-rug factory—for these items are widely manufactured in Holland. Candide, in an ecstasy of gratitude, cried out:

—Master Pangloss was right indeed when he told me everything is for the best in this world; for I am touched by your kindness far more than by the harshness of that black-coated gentleman and his wife.

Next day, while taking a stroll about town, he met a beggar who was covered with pustules, his eyes were sunken, the end of his nose rotted off, his mouth twisted, his teeth black, he had a croaking voice and a hacking cough, and spat a tooth every time he tried to speak.

---

3. Voltaire is satirizing extreme Protestant sects that have sometimes seemed to make hatred of Rome the sum and substance of their creed.
4. Holland, as the home of religious liberty, had offered asylum to the Anabaptists, whose radical views on property and religious discipline had made them unpopular during the 16th century. Granted tolerance, they settled down into respectable burghers. Since this behavior confirmed some of Voltaire's major theses, he had a high opinion of contemporary Anabaptists.
5. Plato's famous minimal definition of man, which he corrected by the addition of a soul to distinguish man from a plucked chicken.

CHAPTER 4

How Candide Met His Old Philosophy Tutor, Doctor Pangloss, and What Came of It

Candide, more touched by compassion even than by horror, gave this ghastly beggar the two florins that he himself had received from his honest Anabaptist friend Jacques. The phantom stared at him, burst into tears, and fell on his neck. Candide drew back in terror.

—Alas, said one wretch to the other, don't you recognize your dear Pangloss any more?

—What are you saying? You, my dear master! you, in this horrible condition? What misfortune has befallen you? Why are you no longer in the most beautiful of castles? What has happened to Miss Cunégonde, that pearl among young ladies, that masterpiece of Nature?

—I am perishing, said Pangloss.

Candide promptly led him into the Anabaptist's stable, where he gave him a crust of bread, and when he had recovered:—Well, said he, Cunégonde?

—Dead, said the other.

Candide fainted. His friend brought him around with a bit of sour vinegar which happened to be in the stable. Candide opened his eyes.

—Cunégonde, dead! Ah, best of worlds, what's become of you now? But how did she die? It wasn't of grief at seeing me kicked out of her noble father's elegant castle?

—Not at all, said Pangloss; she was disemboweled by the Bulgar soldiers, after having been raped to the absolute limit of human endurance; they smashed the Baron's head when he tried to defend her, cut the Baroness to bits, and treated my poor pupil exactly like his sister. As for the castle, not one stone was left on another, not a shed, not a sheep, not a duck, not a tree; but we had the satisfaction of revenge, for the Abares did exactly the same thing to a nearby barony belonging to a Bulgar nobleman.

At this tale Candide fainted again; but having returned to his senses and said everything appropriate to the occasion, he asked about the cause and effect, the sufficient reason, which had reduced Pangloss to his present pitiful state.

—Alas, said he, it was love; love, the consolation of the human race, the preservative of the universe, the soul of all sensitive beings, love, gentle love.

—Unhappy man, said Candide, I too have had some experience of this love, the sovereign of hearts, the soul of our souls; and it never got me anything but a single kiss and twenty kicks in the rear. How could this lovely cause produce in you such a disgusting effect?

Pangloss replied as follows:—My dear Candide! you knew Paquette, that pretty maidservant to our august Baroness. In her arms I tasted the delights of paradise, which directly caused these torments of hell, from which I am now suffering. She was infected with the disease, and has perhaps died of it. Paquette received this present from an erudite Franciscan, who took the pains to trace it back to its source; for he had it from an elderly countess, who picked it up from a captain of cavalry, who acquired it from a marquise, who caught it from a page, who had received it from a Jesuit, who during his novitiate got it directly from one of the companions of Christopher Columbus. As for me, I shall not give it to anyone, for I am a dying man.

—Oh, Pangloss, cried Candide, that's a very strange genealogy. Isn't the devil at the root of the whole thing?

—Not at all, replied that great man; it's an indispensable part of the best of worlds, a necessary ingredient; if Columbus had not caught, on an American island, this sickness which attacks the source of generation and sometimes prevents generation entirely—which thus strikes at and defeats the greatest end of Nature herself—we should have neither chocolate nor cochineal. It must also be noted that until the present time this malady, like religious controversy, has been wholly confined to the continent of Europe. Turks, Indians, Persians, Chinese, Siamese, and Japanese know nothing of it as yet; but there is a sufficient reason for which they in turn will make its acquaintance in a couple of centuries. Meanwhile, it has made splendid progress among us, especially among those big armies of honest, well-trained mercenaries who decide the destinies of nations. You can be sure that when thirty thousand men fight a pitched battle against the same number of the enemy, there will be about twenty thousand with the pox on either side.

—Remarkable indeed, said Candide, but we must see about curing you.

—And how can I do that, said Pangloss, seeing I don't have a cent to my name? There's not a doctor in the whole world who will let your blood or give you an enema without demanding a fee. If you can't pay yourself, you must find someone to pay for you.

These last words decided Candide; he hastened to implore the help of his charitable Anabaptist, Jacques, and painted such a moving picture of his friend's wretched state that the good man did not hesitate to take in Pangloss and have him cured at his own expense. In the course of the cure, Pangloss lost only an eye and an ear. Since he wrote a fine hand and knew arithmetic, the Anabaptist made him his bookkeeper. At the end of two months, being obliged to go to Lisbon on business, he took his two philosophers on the boat with him. Pangloss still maintained that everything was for the best, but Jacques didn't agree with him.

—It must be, said he, that men have corrupted Nature, for they are not born wolves, yet that is what they become. God gave them neither twenty-four-pound cannon nor bayonets, yet they have manufactured both in order to destroy themselves. Bankruptcies have the same effect, and so does the justice which seizes the goods of bankrupts in order to prevent the creditors from getting them.[6]

—It was all indispensable, replied the one-eyed doctor, since private misfortunes make for public welfare, and therefore the more private misfortunes there are, the better everything is.

While he was reasoning, the air grew dark, the winds blew from all directions, and the vessel was attacked by a horrible tempest within sight of Lisbon harbor.

CHAPTER 5

Tempest, Shipwreck, Earthquake, and What Happened to Doctor Pangloss, Candide, and the Anabaptist, Jacques

Half of the passengers, weakened by the frightful anguish of seasickness and the distress of tossing about on stormy waters, were incapable of noticing their danger. The other half shrieked aloud and fell to their prayers, the sails were ripped to shreds, the masts snapped, the vessel opened at the seams. Everyone worked who could stir, nobody listened for orders or issued them. The Anabaptist was lending a hand in the after part of the ship when a frantic sailor struck him

---

6. Voltaire had suffered losses from various bankruptcy proceedings.

and knocked him to the deck; but just at that moment, the sailor lurched so violently that he fell head first over the side, where he hung, clutching a fragment of the broken mast. The good Jacques ran to his aid, and helped him to climb back on board, but in the process was himself thrown into the sea under the very eyes of the sailor, who allowed him to drown without even glancing at him. Candide rushed to the rail, and saw his benefactor rise for a moment to the surface, then sink forever. He wanted to dive to his rescue; but the philosopher Pangloss prevented him by proving that the bay of Lisbon had been formed expressly for this Anabaptist to drown in. While he was proving the point *a priori*, the vessel opened up and everyone perished except for Pangloss, Candide, and the brutal sailor who had caused the virtuous Anabaptist to drown; this rascal swam easily to shore, while Pangloss and Candide drifted there on a plank.

When they had recovered a bit of energy, they set out for Lisbon; they still had a little money with which they hoped to stave off hunger after escaping the storm.

Scarcely had they set foot in the town, still bewailing the loss of their benefactor, when they felt the earth quake underfoot; the sea was lashed to a froth, burst into the port, and smashed all the vessels lying at anchor there. Whirlwinds of fire and ash swirled through the streets and public squares; houses crumbled, roofs came crashing down on foundations, foundations split; thirty thousand inhabitants of every age and either sex were crushed in the ruins.[7] The sailor whistled through his teeth, and said with an oath:—There'll be something to pick up here.

—What can be the sufficient reason of this phenomenon? asked Pangloss.

—The Last Judgment is here, cried Candide.

But the sailor ran directly into the middle of the ruins, heedless of danger in his eagerness for gain; he found some money, laid violent hands on it, got drunk, and, having slept off his wine, bought the favors of the first streetwalker he could find amid the ruins of smashed houses, amid corpses and suffering victims on every hand. Pangloss however tugged at his sleeve.

—My friend, said he, this is not good form at all; your behavior falls short of that required by the universal reason; it's untimely, to say the least.

—Bloody hell, said the other, I'm a sailor, born in Batavia; I've been four times to Japan and stamped four times on the crucifix;[8] get out of here with your universal reason.

Some falling stonework had struck Candide; he lay prostrate in the street, covered with rubble, and calling to Pangloss:—For pity's sake bring me a little wine and oil; I'm dying.

—This earthquake is nothing novel, Pangloss replied; the city of Lima, in South America, underwent much the same sort of tremor, last year; same causes, same effects; there is surely a vein of sulphur under the earth's surface reaching from Lima to Lisbon.

—Nothing is more probable, said Candide; but, for God's sake, a little oil and wine.

7. The great Lisbon earthquake and fire occurred on November 1, 1755; between thirty and forty thousand deaths resulted.
8. The Japanese, originally receptive to foreign visitors, grew fearful that priests and proselytizers were merely advance agents of empire and expelled both the Portuguese and Spanish early in the 17th century. Only the Dutch were allowed to retain a small foothold, under humiliating conditions, of which the notion of stamping on the crucifix is symbolic. It was never what Voltaire suggests here, an actual requirement for entering the country.

—What do you mean, probable? replied the philosopher; I regard the case as proved.

Candide fainted and Pangloss brought him some water from a nearby fountain.

Next day, as they wandered amid the ruins, they found a little food which restored some of their strength. Then they fell to work like the others, bringing relief to those of the inhabitants who had escaped death. Some of the citizens whom they rescued gave them a dinner as good as was possible under the circumstances; it is true that the meal was a melancholy one, and the guests watered their bread with tears; but Pangloss consoled them by proving that things could not possibly be otherwise.

—For, said he, all this is for the best, since if there is a volcano at Lisbon, it cannot be somewhere else, since it is unthinkable that things should not be where they are, since everything is well.

A little man in black, an officer of the Inquisition,[9] who was sitting beside him, politely took up the question, and said:—It would seem that the gentleman does not believe in original sin, since if everything is for the best, man has not fallen and is not liable to eternal punishment.

—I most humbly beg pardon of your excellency, Pangloss answered, even more politely, but the fall of man and the curse of original sin entered necessarily into the best of all possible worlds.

—Then you do not believe in free will? said the officer.

—Your excellency must excuse me, said Pangloss; free will agrees very well with absolute necessity, for it was necessary that we should be free, since a will which is determined . . .

Pangloss was in the middle of his sentence, when the officer nodded significantly to the attendant who was pouring him a glass of port, or Oporto, wine.

CHAPTER 6

How They Made a Fine Auto-da-Fé to Prevent Earthquakes, and How Candide Was Whipped

After the earthquake had wiped out three quarters of Lisbon, the learned men of the land could find no more effective way of averting total destruction than to give the people a fine auto-da-fé;[1] the University of Coimbra had established that the spectacle of several persons being roasted over a slow fire with full ceremonial rites is an infallible specific against earthquakes.

In consequence, the authorities had rounded up a Biscayan convicted of marrying a woman who had stood godmother to his child, and two Portuguese who while eating a chicken had set aside a bit of bacon used for seasoning.[2] After dinner, men came with ropes to tie up Doctor Pangloss and his disciple Candide, one for talking and the other for listening with an air of approval; both were taken separately to a set of remarkably cool apartments, where the glare of the sun is

---

9. Specifically, a *familier* or *poursuivant*, an undercover agent with powers of arrest.
1. Literally, "act of faith," a public ceremony of repentance and humiliation. Such an auto-da-fé was actually held in Lisbon, June 20, 1756.

2. The Biscayan's fault lay in marrying someone within the forbidden bounds of relationship, an act of spiritual incest. The men who declined pork or bacon were understood to be crypto-Jews.

never bothersome; eight days later they were both dressed in *san-benitos* and crowned with paper mitres;[3] Candide's mitre and *san-benito* were decorated with inverted flames and with devils who had neither tails nor claws; but Pangloss's devils had both tails and claws, and his flames stood upright. Wearing these costumes, they marched in a procession, and listened to a very touching sermon, followed by a beautiful concert of plainsong. Candide was flogged in cadence to the music; the Biscayan and the two men who had avoided bacon were burned, and Pangloss was hanged, though hanging is not customary. On the same day there was another earthquake, causing frightful damage.[4]

Candide, stunned, stupefied, despairing, bleeding, trembling, said to himself:—If this is the best of all possible worlds, what are the others like? The flogging is not so bad, I was flogged by the Bulgars. But oh my dear Pangloss, greatest of philosophers, was it necessary for me to watch you being hanged, for no reason that I can see? Oh my dear Anabaptist, best of men, was it necessary that you should be drowned in the port? Oh Miss Cunégonde, pearl of young ladies, was it necessary that you should have your belly slit open?

He was being led away, barely able to stand, lectured, lashed, absolved, and blessed, when an old woman approached and said,—My son, be of good cheer and follow me.

CHAPTER 7

How an Old Woman Took Care of Candide, and How He Regained What He Loved

Candide was of very bad cheer, but he followed the old woman to a shanty; she gave him a jar of ointment to rub himself, left him food and drink; she showed him a tidy little bed; next to it was a suit of clothing.

—Eat, drink, sleep, she said; and may Our Lady of Atocha, Our Lord St. Anthony of Padua, and Our Lord St. James of Compostela watch over you. I will be back tomorrow.

Candide, still completely astonished by everything he had seen and suffered, and even more by the old woman's kindness, offered to kiss her hand.

—It's not *my* hand you should be kissing, said she. I'll be back tomorrow; rub yourself with the ointment, eat and sleep.

In spite of his many sufferings, Candide ate and slept. Next day the old woman returned bringing breakfast; she looked at his back and rubbed it herself with another ointment; she came back with lunch; and then she returned in the evening, bringing supper. Next day she repeated the same routine.

—Who are you? Candide asked continually. Who told you to be so kind to me? How can I ever repay you?

The good woman answered not a word; she returned in the evening, and without food.

—Come with me, says she, and don't speak a word.

Taking him by the hand, she walks out into the countryside with him for about a quarter of a mile; they reach an isolated house, quite surrounded by gardens

---

3. The cone-shaped paper cap (intended to resemble a bishop's mitre) and flowing yellow cape were customary garb for those pleading before the Inquisition.

4. In fact, the second quake occurred December 21, 1755.

and ditches. The old woman knocks at a little gate, it opens. She takes Candide up a secret stairway to a gilded room furnished with a fine brocaded sofa; there she leaves him, closes the door, disappears. Candide stood as if entranced; his life, which had seemed like a nightmare so far, was now starting to look like a delightful dream.

Soon the old woman returned; on her feeble shoulder leaned a trembling woman, of a splendid figure, glittering in diamonds, and veiled.

—Remove the veil, said the old woman to Candide.

The young man stepped timidly forward, and lifted the veil. What an event! What a surprise! Could it be Miss Cunégonde? Yes, it really was! She herself! His knees give way, speech fails him, he falls at her feet, Cunégonde collapses on the sofa. The old woman plies them with brandy, they return to their senses, they exchange words. At first they could utter only broken phrases, questions and answers at cross purposes, sighs, tears, exclamations. The old woman warned them not to make too much noise, and left them alone.

—Then it's really you, said Candide, you're alive, I've found you again in Portugal. Then you never were raped? You never had your belly ripped open, as the philosopher Pangloss assured me?

—Oh yes, said the lovely Cunégonde, but one doesn't always die of these two accidents.

—But your father and mother were murdered then?

—All too true, said Cunégonde, in tears.

—And your brother?

—Killed too.

—And why are you in Portugal? and how did you know I was here? and by what device did you have me brought to this house?

—I shall tell you everything, the lady replied; but first you must tell me what has happened to you since that first innocent kiss we exchanged and the kicking you got because of it.

Candide obeyed her with profound respect; and though he was overcome, though his voice was weak and hesitant, though he still had twinges of pain from his beating, he described as simply as possible everything that had happened to him since the time of their separation. Cunégonde lifted her eyes to heaven; she wept at the death of the good Anabaptist and at that of Pangloss; after which she told the following story to Candide, who listened to every word while he gazed on her with hungry eyes.

CHAPTER 8

Cunégonde's Story

—I was in my bed and fast asleep when heaven chose to send the Bulgars into our castle of Thunder-Ten-Tronckh. They butchered my father and brother, and hacked my mother to bits. An enormous Bulgar, six feet tall, seeing that I had swooned from horror at the scene, set about raping me; at that I recovered my senses, I screamed and scratched, bit and fought, I tried to tear the eyes out of that big Bulgar—not realizing that everything which had happened in my father's castle was a mere matter of routine. The brute then stabbed me with a knife on my left thigh, where I still bear the scar.

—What a pity! I should very much like to see it, said the simple Candide.

—You shall, said Cunégonde; but shall I go on?

—Please do, said Candide.

So she took up the thread of her tale:—A Bulgar captain appeared, he saw me covered with blood and the soldier too intent to get up. Shocked by the monster's failure to come to attention, the captain killed him on my body. He then had my wound dressed, and took me off to his quarters, as a prisoner of war. I laundered his few shirts and did his cooking; he found me attractive, I confess it, and I won't deny that he was a handsome fellow, with a smooth, white skin; apart from that, however, little wit, little philosophical training; it was evident that he had not been brought up by Doctor Pangloss. After three months, he had lost all his money and grown sick of me; so he sold me to a Jew named Don Issachar, who traded in Holland and Portugal, and who was mad after women. This Jew developed a mighty passion for my person, but he got nowhere with it; I held him off better than I had done with the Bulgar soldier; for though a person of honor may be raped once, her virtue is only strengthened by the experience. In order to keep me hidden, the Jew brought me to his country house, which you see here. Till then I had thought there was nothing on earth so beautiful as the castle of Thunder-Ten-Tronckh; I was now undeceived.

—One day the Grand Inquisitor took notice of me at mass; he ogled me a good deal, and made known that he must talk to me on a matter of secret business. I was taken to his palace; I told him of my rank; he pointed out that it was beneath my dignity to belong to an Israelite. A suggestion was then conveyed to Don Issachar that he should turn me over to My Lord the Inquisitor. Don Issachar, who is court banker and a man of standing, refused out of hand. The inquisitor threatened him with an auto-da-fé. Finally my Jew, fearing for his life, struck a bargain by which the house and I would belong to both of them as joint tenants; the Jew would get Mondays, Wednesdays, and the Sabbath, the inquisitor would get the other days of the week. That has been the arrangement for six months now. There have been quarrels; sometimes it has not been clear whether the night from Saturday to Sunday belonged to the old or the new dispensation. For my part, I have so far been able to hold both of them off; and that, I think, is why they are both still in love with me.

—Finally, in order to avert further divine punishment by earthquake, and to terrify Don Issachar, My Lord the Inquisitor chose to celebrate an auto-da-fé. He did me the honor of inviting me to attend. I had an excellent seat; the ladies were served with refreshments between the mass and the execution. To tell you the truth, I was horrified to see them burn alive those two Jews and that decent Biscayan who had married his child's godmother; but what was my surprise, my terror, my grief, when I saw, huddled in a *san-benito* and wearing a mitre, someone who looked like Pangloss! I rubbed my eyes, I watched his every move, I saw him hanged; and I fell back in a swoon. Scarcely had I come to my senses again, when I saw you stripped for the lash; that was the peak of my horror, consternation, grief, and despair. I may tell you, by the way, that your skin is even whiter and more delicate than that of my Bulgar captain. Seeing you, then, redoubled the torments which were already overwhelming me. I shrieked aloud, I wanted to call out, 'Let him go, you brutes!' but my voice died within me, and my cries would have been useless. When you had been thoroughly thrashed: 'How can it be,' I asked myself, 'that agreeable Candide and wise Pangloss have come to Lisbon, one to receive a hundred whiplashes, the other to be hanged by order of My Lord the Inquisitor, whose mistress I am? Pangloss must have deceived me cruelly when he told me that all is for the best in this world.'

—Frantic, exhausted, half out of my senses, and ready to die of weakness, I felt as if my mind were choked with the massacre of my father, my mother, my brother, with the arrogance of that ugly Bulgar soldier, with the knife slash he inflicted on me, my slavery, my cookery, my Bulgar captain, my nasty Don Issachar, my abominable inquisitor, with the hanging of Doctor Pangloss, with that great plainsong *miserere* which they sang while they flogged you—and above all, my mind was full of the kiss which I gave you behind the screen, on the day I saw you for the last time. I praised God, who had brought you back to me after so many trials. I asked my old woman to look out for you, and to bring you here as soon as she could. She did just as I asked; I have had the indescribable joy of seeing you again, hearing you and talking with you once more. But you must be frightfully hungry; I am, myself; let us begin with a dinner.

So then and there they sat down to table; and after dinner, they adjourned to that fine brocaded sofa, which has already been mentioned; and there they were when the eminent Don Issachar, one of the masters of the house, appeared. It was the day of the Sabbath; he was arriving to assert his rights and express his tender passion.

CHAPTER 9

What Happened to Cunégonde, Candide, the Grand Inquisitor, and a Jew

This Issachar was the most choleric Hebrew seen in Israel since the Babylonian captivity.

—What's this, says he, you bitch of a Christian, you're not satisfied with the Grand Inquisitor? Do I have to share you with this rascal, too?

So saying, he drew a long dagger, with which he always went armed, and, supposing his opponent defenceless, flung himself on Candide. But our good Westphalian had received from the old woman, along with his suit of clothes, a fine sword. Out it came, and though his manners were of the gentlest, in short order he laid the Israelite stiff and cold on the floor, at the feet of the lovely Cunégonde.

—Holy Virgin! she cried. What will become of me now? A man killed in my house! If the police find out, we're done for.

—If Pangloss had not been hanged, said Candide, he would give us good advice in this hour of need, for he was a great philosopher. Lacking him, let's ask the old woman.

She was a sensible body, and was just starting to give her opinion of the situation, when another little door opened. It was just one o'clock in the morning, Sunday morning. This day belonged to the inquisitor. In he came, and found the whipped Candide with a sword in his hand, a corpse at his feet, Cunégonde in terror, and an old woman giving them both good advice.

Here now is what passed through Candide's mind in this instant of time; this is how he reasoned:—If this holy man calls for help, he will certainly have me burned, and perhaps Cunégonde as well; he has already had me whipped without mercy; he is my rival; I have already killed once; why hesitate?

It was a quick, clear chain of reasoning; without giving the inquisitor time to recover from his surprise, he ran him through, and laid him beside the Jew.

—Here you've done it again, said Cunégonde; there's no hope for us now. We'll be excommunicated, our last hour has come. How is it that you, who were born so gentle, could kill in two minutes a Jew and a prelate?

—My dear girl, replied Candide, when a man is in love, jealous, and just whipped by the Inquisition, he is no longer himself.

The old woman now spoke up and said:—There are three Andalusian steeds in the stable, with their saddles and bridles; our brave Candide must get them ready: my lady has some gold coin and diamonds; let's take to horse at once, though I can only ride on one buttock; we will go to Cadiz. The weather is as fine as can be, and it is pleasant to travel in the cool of the evening.

Promptly, Candide saddled the three horses. Cunégonde, the old woman, and he covered thirty miles without a stop. While they were fleeing, the Holy Brotherhood[5] came to investigate the house; they buried the inquisitor in a fine church, and threw Issachar on the dunghill.

Candide, Cunégonde, and the old woman were already in the little town of Avacena, in the middle of the Sierra Morena; and there, as they sat in a country inn, they had this conversation.

CHAPTER 10

In Deep Distress, Candide, Cunégonde, and the Old Woman
Reach Cadiz; They Put to Sea

—Who then could have robbed me of my gold and diamonds? said Cunégonde, in tears. How shall we live? what shall we do? where shall I find other inquisitors and Jews to give me some more?

—Ah, said the old woman, I strongly suspect that reverend Franciscan friar who shared the inn with us yesterday at Badajoz. God save me from judging him unfairly! But he came into our room twice, and he left long before us.

—Alas, said Candide, the good Pangloss often proved to me that the fruits of the earth are a common heritage of all, to which each man has equal right. On these principles, the Franciscan should at least have left us enough to finish our journey. You have nothing at all, my dear Cunégonde?

—Not a maravedi, said she.

—What to do? said Candide.

—We'll sell one of the horses, said the old woman; I'll ride on the croup behind my mistress, though only on one buttock, and so we will get to Cadiz.

There was in the same inn a Benedictine prior; he bought the horse cheap. Candide, Cunégonde, and the old woman passed through Lucena, Chillas, and Lebrixa, and finally reached Cadiz. There a fleet was being fitted out and an army assembled, to reason with the Jesuit fathers in Paraguay, who were accused of fomenting among their flock a revolt against the kings of Spain and Portugal near the town of St. Sacrement.[6] Candide, having served in the Bulgar army, performed the Bulgar manual of arms before the general of the little army with such grace, swiftness, dexterity, fire, and agility, that they gave him a company of infantry to command. So here he is, a captain; and off he sails with Miss Cunégonde, the old woman, two valets, and the two Andalusian steeds which had belonged to My Lord the Grand Inquisitor of Portugal.

---

5. A semireligious order with police powers, very active in 18th-century Spain.
6. Actually, Colonia del Sacramento. Voltaire took great interest in the Jesuit role in Paraguay, which he has much oversimplified and largely misrepresented here in the interests of his satire. In 1750 they did, however, offer armed resistance to an agreement made between Spain and Portugal. They were subdued and expelled in 1769.

Throughout the crossing, they spent a great deal of time reasoning about the philosophy of poor Pangloss.

—We are destined, in the end, for another universe, said Candide; no doubt that is the one where everything is well. For in this one, it must be admitted, there is some reason to grieve over our physical and moral state.

—I love you with all my heart, said Cunégonde; but my soul is still harrowed by thoughts of what I have seen and suffered.

—All will be well, replied Candide; the sea of this new world is already better than those of Europe, calmer and with steadier winds. Surely it is the New World which is the best of all possible worlds.

—God grant it, said Cunégonde; but I have been so horribly unhappy in the world so far, that my heart is almost dead to hope.

—You pity yourselves, the old woman told them; but you have had no such misfortunes as mine.

Cunégonde nearly broke out laughing; she found the old woman comic in pretending to be more unhappy than she.

—Ah, you poor old thing, said she, unless you've been raped by two Bulgars, been stabbed twice in the belly, seen two of your castles destroyed, witnessed the murder of two of your mothers and two of your fathers, and watched two of your lovers being whipped in an auto-da-fé, I do not see how you can have had it worse than me. Besides, I was born a baroness, with seventy-two quarterings, and I have worked in a scullery.

—My lady, replied the old woman, you do not know my birth and rank; and if I showed you my rear end, you would not talk as you do, you might even speak with less assurance.

These words inspired great curiosity in Candide and Cunégonde, which the old woman satisfied with this story.

CHAPTER 11

The Old Woman's Story

—My eyes were not always bloodshot and red-rimmed, my nose did not always touch my chin, and I was not born a servant. I am in fact the daughter of Pope Urban the Tenth and the Princess of Palestrina.[7] Till the age of fourteen, I lived in a palace so splendid that all the castles of all your German barons would not have served it as a stable; a single one of my dresses was worth more than all the assembled magnificence of Westphalia. I grew in beauty, in charm, in talent, surrounded by pleasures, dignities, and glowing visions of the future. Already I was inspiring the young men to love; my breast was formed—and what a breast! white, firm, with the shape of the Venus de Medici;[8] and what eyes! what lashes, what black brows! What fire flashed from my glances and outshone the glitter of the stars, as the local poets used to tell me! The women who helped me dress and undress fell into ecstasies, whether they looked at me from in front or behind; and all the men wanted to be in their place.

---

7. Voltaire left behind a comment on this passage, a note first published in 1829: "Note the extreme discretion of the author; hitherto there has never been a pope named Urban X; he avoided attributing a bastard to a known pope. What circumspection! what an exquisite conscience!"

8. A famous Roman sculpture of Venus in marble from the 1st century B.C.E. that belonged to the Medici family in Italy; 18th-century Europeans considered it to be one of the best surviving works of art from ancient times.

—I was engaged to the ruling prince of Massa-Carrara; and what a prince he was! as handsome as I, softness and charm compounded, brilliantly witty, and madly in love with me. I loved him in return as one loves for the first time, with a devotion approaching idolatry. The wedding preparations had been made, with a splendor and magnificence never heard of before; nothing but celebrations, masks, and comic operas, uninterruptedly; and all Italy composed in my honor sonnets of which not one was even passable. I had almost attained the very peak of bliss, when an old marquise who had been the mistress of my prince invited him to her house for a cup of chocolate. He died in less than two hours, amid horrifying convulsions. But that was only a trifle. My mother, in complete despair (though less afflicted than I), wished to escape for a while the oppressive atmosphere of grief. She owned a handsome property near Gaeta.[9] We embarked on a papal galley gilded like the altar of St. Peter's in Rome. Suddenly a pirate ship from Salé swept down and boarded us. Our soldiers defended themselves as papal troops usually do; falling on their knees and throwing down their arms, they begged of the corsair absolution *in articulo mortis*.[1]

—They were promptly stripped as naked as monkeys, and so was my mother, and so were our maids of honor, and so was I too. It's a very remarkable thing, the energy these gentlemen put into stripping people. But what surprised me even more was that they stuck their fingers in a place where we women usually admit only a syringe. This ceremony seemed a bit odd to me, as foreign usages always do when one hasn't traveled. They only wanted to see if we didn't have some diamonds hidden there; and I soon learned that it's a custom of long standing among the genteel folk who swarm the seas. I learned that my lords the very religious knights of Malta never overlook this ceremony when they capture Turks, whether male or female; it's one of those international laws which have never been questioned.

—I won't try to explain how painful it is for a young princess to be carried off into slavery in Morocco with her mother. You can imagine everything we had to suffer on the pirate ship. My mother was still very beautiful; our maids of honor, our mere chambermaids, were more charming than anything one could find in all Africa. As for myself, I was ravishing, I was loveliness and grace supreme, and I was a virgin. I did not remain so for long; the flower which had been kept for the handsome prince of Massa-Carrara was plucked by the corsair captain; he was an abominable negro, who thought he was doing me a great favor. My Lady the Princess of Palestrina and I must have been strong indeed to bear what we did during our journey to Morocco. But on with my story; these are such common matters that they are not worth describing.

—Morocco was knee deep in blood when we arrived. Of the fifty sons of the emperor Muley-Ismael,[2] each had his faction, which produced in effect fifty civil wars, of blacks against blacks, of blacks against browns, halfbreeds against halfbreeds; throughout the length and breadth of the empire, nothing but one continual carnage.

—Scarcely had we stepped ashore, when some negroes of a faction hostile to my captor arrived to take charge of his plunder. After the diamonds and gold, we women were the most prized possessions. I was now witness of a struggle such as

---

9. About halfway between Rome and Naples.
1. Literally, when at the point of death. Absolution from a corsair in the act of murdering one is of very dubious validity.

2. Having reigned for more than fifty years, a potent and ruthless sultan of Morocco, he died in 1727 and left his kingdom in much the condition described.

you never see in the temperate climate of Europe. Northern people don't have hot blood; they don't feel the absolute fury for women which is common in Africa. Europeans seem to have milk in their veins; it is vitriol or liquid fire which pulses through these people around Mount Atlas. The fight for possession of us raged with the fury of the lions, tigers, and poisonous vipers of that land. A Moor snatched my mother by the right arm, the first mate held her by the left; a Moorish soldier grabbed one leg, one of our pirates the other. In a moment's time almost all our girls were being dragged four different ways. My captain held me behind him while with his scimitar he killed everyone who braved his fury. At last I saw all our Italian women, including my mother, torn to pieces, cut to bits, murdered by the monsters who were fighting over them. My captive companions, their captors, soldiers, sailors, blacks, browns, whites, mulattoes, and at last my captain, all were killed, and I remained half dead on a mountain of corpses. Similar scenes were occurring, as is well known, for more than three hundred leagues around, without anyone skimping on the five prayers a day decreed by Mohammed.

—With great pain, I untangled myself from this vast heap of bleeding bodies, and dragged myself under a great orange tree by a neighboring brook, where I collapsed, from terror, exhaustion, horror, despair, and hunger. Shortly, my weary mind surrendered to a sleep which was more of a swoon than a rest. I was in this state of weakness and languor, between life and death, when I felt myself touched by something which moved over my body. Opening my eyes, I saw a white man, rather attractive, who was groaning and saying under his breath: 'O che sciagura d'essere senza coglioni!'[3]

CHAPTER 12

The Old Woman's Story Continued

—Amazed and delighted to hear my native tongue, and no less surprised by what this man was saying, I told him that there were worse evils than those he was complaining of. In a few words, I described to him the horrors I had undergone, and then fainted again. He carried me to a nearby house, put me to bed, gave me something to eat, served me, flattered me, comforted me, told me he had never seen anyone so lovely, and added that he had never before regretted so much the loss of what nobody could give him back.

'I was born at Naples,' he told me, 'where they caponize two or three thousand children every year; some die of it, others acquire a voice more beautiful than any woman's, still others go on to become governors of kingdoms.[4] The operation was a great success with me, and I became court musician to the Princess of Palestrina . . .'

'Of my mother,' I exclaimed.

'Of your mother,' cried he, bursting into tears; 'then you must be the princess whom I raised till she was six, and who already gave promise of becoming as beautiful as you are now!'

'I am that very princess; my mother lies dead, not a hundred yards from here, buried under a pile of corpses.'

---

3. "Oh what a misfortune to have no testicles!"
4. The castrato Farinelli (1705–1782), originally a singer, came to exercise considerable political influence on the kings of Spain, Philip V and Ferdinand VI.

—I told him my adventures, he told me his: that he had been sent by a Christian power to the King of Morocco, to conclude a treaty granting him gunpowder, cannon, and ships with which to liquidate the traders of the other Christian powers.

'My mission is concluded,' said this honest eunuch; 'I shall take ship at Ceuta and bring you back to Italy. *Ma che sciagura d'essere senza coglioni!*'

—I thanked him with tears of gratitude, and instead of returning me to Italy, he took me to Algiers and sold me to the dey of that country. Hardly had the sale taken place, when that plague which has made the rounds of Africa, Asia, and Europe broke out in full fury at Algiers. You have seen earthquakes; but tell me, young lady, have you ever had the plague?

—Never, replied the baroness.

—If you had had it, said the old woman, you would agree that it is far worse than an earthquake. It is very frequent in Africa, and I had it. Imagine, if you will, the situation of a pope's daughter, fifteen years old, who in three months' time had experienced poverty, slavery, had been raped almost every day, had seen her mother quartered, had suffered from famine and war, and who now was dying of pestilence in Algiers. As a matter of fact, I did not die; but the eunuch and the dey and nearly the entire seraglio of Algiers perished.

—When the first horrors of this ghastly plague had passed, the slaves of the dey were sold. A merchant bought me and took me to Tunis; there he sold me to another merchant, who resold me at Tripoli; from Tripoli I was sold to Alexandria, from Alexandria resold to Smyrna, from Smyrna to Constantinople. I ended by belonging to an aga of janizaries, who was shortly ordered to defend Azov against the besieging Russians.[5]

—The aga, who was a gallant soldier, took his whole seraglio with him, and established us in a little fort amid the Maeotian marshes,[6] guarded by two black eunuchs and twenty soldiers. Our side killed a prodigious number of Russians, but they paid us back nicely. Azov was put to fire and sword without respect for age or sex; only our little fort continued to resist, and the enemy determined to starve us out. The twenty janizaries had sworn never to surrender. Reduced to the last extremities of hunger, they were forced to eat our two eunuchs, lest they violate their oaths. After several more days, they decided to eat the women too.

—We had an imam,[7] very pious and sympathetic, who delivered an excellent sermon, persuading them not to kill us altogether.

'Just cut off a single rumpsteak from each of these ladies,' he said, 'and you'll have a fine meal. Then if you should need another, you can come back in a few days and have as much again; heaven will bless your charitable action, and you will be saved.'

—His eloquence was splendid, and he persuaded them. We underwent this horrible operation. The imam treated us all with the ointment that they use on newly circumcised children. We were at the point of death.

—Scarcely had the janizaries finished the meal for which we furnished the materials, when the Russians appeared in flat-bottomed boats; not a janizary escaped. The Russians paid no attention to the state we were in; but there are French physicians everywhere, and one of them, who knew his trade, took care of

---

5. Azov, near the mouth of the Don, was besieged by the Russians under Peter the Great in 1695–96. "Janizaries": an elite corps of the Ottoman armies.

6. The Roman name of the so-called Sea of Azov, a shallow swampy lake near the town.

7. In effect, a chaplain.

us. He cured us, and I shall remember all my life that when my wounds were healed, he made me a proposition. For the rest, he counselled us simply to have patience, assuring us that the same thing had happened in several other sieges, and that it was according to the laws of war.

—As soon as my companions could walk, we were herded off to Moscow. In the division of booty, I fell to a boyar who made me work in his garden, and gave me twenty whiplashes a day; but when he was broken on the wheel after about two years, with thirty other boyars, over some little court intrigue,[8] I seized the occasion; I ran away; I crossed all Russia; I was for a long time a chambermaid in Riga, then at Rostock, Vismara, Leipzig, Cassel, Utrecht, Leyden, The Hague, Rotterdam; I grew old in misery and shame, having only half a backside and remembering always that I was the daughter of a Pope; a hundred times I wanted to kill myself, but always I loved life more. This ridiculous weakness is perhaps one of our worst instincts; is anything more stupid than choosing to carry a burden that really one wants to cast on the ground? to hold existence in horror, and yet to cling to it? to fondle the serpent which devours us till it has eaten out our heart?

—In the countries through which I have been forced to wander, in the taverns where I have had to work, I have seen a vast number of people who hated their existence; but I never saw more than a dozen who deliberately put an end to their own misery: three negroes, four Englishmen, four Genevans, and a German professor named Robeck.[9] My last post was as servant to the Jew Don Issachar; he attached me to your service, my lovely one; and I attached myself to your destiny, till I have become more concerned with your fate than with my own. I would not even have mentioned my own misfortunes, if you had not irked me a bit, and if it weren't the custom, on shipboard, to pass the time with stories. In a word, my lady, I have had some experience of the world, I know it; why not try this diversion? Ask every passenger on this ship to tell you his story, and if you find a single one who has not often cursed the day of his birth, who has not often told himself that he is the most miserable of men, then you may throw me overboard head first.

CHAPTER 13

How Candide Was Forced to Leave the Lovely Cunégonde and the Old Woman

Having heard out the old woman's story, the lovely Cunégonde paid her the respects which were appropriate to a person of her rank and merit. She took up the wager as well, and got all the passengers, one after another, to tell her their adventures. She and Candide had to agree that the old woman had been right.

—It's certainly too bad, said Candide, that the wise Pangloss was hanged, contrary to the custom of auto-da-fé; he would have admirable things to say of the physical evil and moral evil which cover land and sea, and I might feel within me the impulse to dare to raise several polite objections.

8. Voltaire had in mind an ineffectual conspiracy against Peter the Great known as the "revolt of the streltsy" or musketeers, which took place in 1698. Though easily put down, it provoked from the emperor a massive and atrocious program of reprisals.
9. Johann Robeck (1672–1739) published a treatise advocating suicide and showed his conviction by drowning himself at the age of sixty-seven.

As the passengers recited their stories, the boat made steady progress, and presently landed at Buenos Aires. Cunégonde, Captain Candide, and the old woman went to call on the governor, Don Fernando d'Ibaraa y Figueroa y Mascarenes y Lampourdos y Souza. This nobleman had the pride appropriate to a man with so many names. He addressed everyone with the most aristocratic disdain, pointing his nose so loftily, raising his voice so mercilessly, lording it so splendidly, and assuming so arrogant a pose, that everyone who met him wanted to kick him. He loved women to the point of fury; and Cunégonde seemed to him the most beautiful creature he had ever seen. The first thing he did was to ask directly if she were the captain's wife. His manner of asking this question disturbed Candide; he did not dare say she was his wife, because in fact she was not; he did not dare say she was his sister, because she wasn't that either; and though this polite lie was once common enough among the ancients,[1] and sometimes serves moderns very well, he was too pure of heart to tell a lie.

—Miss Cunégonde, said he, is betrothed to me, and we humbly beg your excellency to perform the ceremony for us.

Don Fernando d'Ibaraa y Figueroa y Mascarenes y Lampourdos y Souza twirled his moustache, smiled sardonically, and ordered Captain Candide to go drill his company. Candide obeyed. Left alone with My Lady Cunégonde, the governor declared his passion, and protested that he would marry her tomorrow, in church or in any other manner, as it pleased her charming self. Cunégonde asked for a quarter-hour to collect herself, consult the old woman, and make up her mind.

The old woman said to Cunégonde:—My lady, you have seventy-two quarterings and not one penny; if you wish, you may be the wife of the greatest lord in South America, who has a really handsome moustache; are you going to insist on your absolute fidelity? You have already been raped by the Bulgars; a Jew and an inquisitor have enjoyed your favors; miseries entitle one to privileges. I assure you that in your position I would make no scruple of marrying My Lord the Governor, and making the fortune of Captain Candide.

While the old woman was talking with all the prudence of age and experience, there came into the harbor a small ship bearing an alcalde and some alguazils.[2] This is what had happened.

As the old woman had very shrewdly guessed, it was a long-sleeved Franciscan who stole Cunégonde's gold and jewels in the town of Badajoz, when she and Candide were in flight. The monk tried to sell some of the gems to a jeweler, who recognized them as belonging to the Grand Inquisitor. Before he was hanged, the Franciscan confessed that he had stolen them, indicating who his victims were and where they were going. The flight of Cunégonde and Candide was already known. They were traced to Cadiz, and a vessel was hastily dispatched in pursuit of them. This vessel was now in the port of Buenos Aires. The rumor spread that an alcalde was aboard, in pursuit of the murderers of My Lord the Grand Inquisitor. The shrewd old woman saw at once what was to be done.

—You cannot escape, she told Cunégonde, and you have nothing to fear. You are not the one who killed my lord, and, besides, the governor, who is in love with you, won't let you be mistreated. Sit tight.

And then she ran straight to Candide:—Get out of town, she said, or you'll be burned within the hour.

---

1. Voltaire has in mind Abraham's adventures with Sarah (Genesis 12) and Isaac's with Rebecca (Genesis 26).

2. Police officers.

There was not a moment to lose; but how to leave Cunégonde, and where to go?

CHAPTER 14

How Candide and Cacambo Were Received by the Jesuits of Paraguay

Candide had brought from Cadiz a valet of the type one often finds in the provinces of Spain and in the colonies. He was one quarter Spanish, son of a half-breed in the Tucuman;[3] he had been choirboy, sacristan, sailor, monk, merchant, soldier, and lackey. His name was Cacambo, and he was very fond of his master because his master was a very good man. In hot haste he saddled the two Andalusian steeds.

—Hurry, master, do as the old woman says; let's get going and leave this town without a backward look.

Candide wept:—O my beloved Cunégonde! must I leave you now, just when the governor is about to marry us! Cunégonde, brought from so far, what will ever become of you?

—She'll become what she can, said Cacambo; women can always find something to do with themselves; God sees to it; let's get going.

—Where are you taking me? where are we going? what will we do without Cunégonde? said Candide.

—By Saint James of Compostela, said Cacambo, you were going to make war against the Jesuits, now we'll go make war for them. I know the roads pretty well, I'll bring you to their country, they will be delighted to have a captain who knows the Bulgar drill; you'll make a prodigious fortune. If you don't get your rights in one world, you will find them in another. And isn't it pleasant to see new things and do new things?

—Then you've already been in Paraguay? said Candide.

—Indeed I have, replied Cacambo; I was cook in the College of the Assumption, and I know the government of Los Padres[4] as I know the streets of Cadiz. It's an admirable thing, this government. The kingdom is more than three hundred leagues across; it is divided into thirty provinces. Los Padres own everything in it, and the people nothing; it's a masterpiece of reason and justice. I myself know nothing so wonderful as Los Padres, who in this hemisphere make war on the kings of Spain and Portugal, but in Europe hear their confessions; who kill Spaniards here, and in Madrid send them to heaven; that really tickles me; let's get moving, you're going to be the happiest of men. Won't Los Padres be delighted when they learn they have a captain who knows the Bulgar drill!

As soon as they reached the first barricade, Cacambo told the frontier guard that a captain wished to speak with My Lord the Commander. A Paraguayan officer ran to inform headquarters by laying the news at the feet of the commander. Candide and Cacambo were first disarmed and deprived of their Andalusian horses. They were then placed between two files of soldiers; the commander was at the end, his three-cornered hat on his head, his cassock drawn up, a sword at his side, and a pike in his hand. He nods, and twenty-four soldiers surround the newcomers. A sergeant then informs them that they must wait, that the commander

---

3. A province of Argentina, to the northwest of Buenos Aires.   4. The Jesuit fathers.

cannot talk to them, since the reverend father provincial has forbidden all Spaniards from speaking, except in his presence, and from remaining more than three hours in the country.

—And where is the reverend father provincial? says Cacambo.

—He is reviewing his troops after having said mass, the sergeant replies, and you'll only be able to kiss his spurs in three hours.

—But, says Cacambo, my master the captain, who, like me, is dying from hunger, is not Spanish at all, he is German; can't we have some breakfast while waiting for his reverence?

The sergeant promptly went off to report this speech to the commander.

—God be praised, said this worthy; since he is German, I can talk to him; bring him into my bower.

Candide was immediately led into a leafy nook surrounded by a handsome colonnade of green and gold marble and trellises amid which sported parrots, hummingbirds,[5] guinea fowl, and all the rarest species of birds. An excellent breakfast was prepared in golden vessels; and while the Paraguayans ate corn out of wooden bowls in the open fields under the glare of the sun, the reverend father commander entered into his bower.

He was a very handsome young man, with an open face, rather blonde in coloring, with ruddy complexion, arched eyebrows, liquid eyes, pink ears, bright red lips, and an air of pride, but a pride somehow different from that of a Spaniard or a Jesuit. Their confiscated weapons were restored to Candide and Cacambo, as well as their Andalusian horses; Cacambo fed them oats alongside the bower, always keeping an eye on them for fear of an ambush.

First Candide kissed the hem of the commander's cassock, then they sat down at the table.

—So you are German? said the Jesuit, speaking in that language.

—Yes, your reverence, said Candide.

As they spoke these words, both men looked at one another with great surprise, and another emotion which they could not control.

—From what part of Germany do you come? said the Jesuit.

—From the nasty province of Westphalia, said Candide; I was born in the castle of Thunder-Ten-Tronckh.

—Merciful heavens! cries the commander. Is it possible?

—What a miracle! exclaims Candide.

—Can it be you? asks the commander.

—It's impossible, says Candide.

They both fall back in their chairs, they embrace, they shed streams of tears.

—What, can it be you, reverend father! you, the brother of the lovely Cunégonde! you, who were killed by the Bulgars! you, the son of My Lord the Baron! you, a Jesuit in Paraguay! It's a mad world, indeed it is. Oh, Pangloss! Pangloss! how happy you would be, if you hadn't been hanged.

The commander dismissed his negro slaves and the Paraguayans who served his drink in crystal goblets. He thanked God and Saint Ignatius a thousand times, he clasped Candide in his arms, their faces were bathed in tears.

---

5. In this passage and several later ones, Voltaire uses in conjunction two words, both of which mean hummingbird. The French system of classifying hummingbirds, based on the work of the celebrated Buffon, distinguishes *oiseaux-mouches* with straight bills from *colibris* with curved bills. This distinction is wholly fallacious. Hummingbirds have all manner of shaped bills, and the division of species must be made on other grounds entirely.

—You would be even more astonished, even more delighted, even more beside yourself, said Candide, if I told you that My Lady Cunégonde, your sister, who you thought was disemboweled, is enjoying good health.

—Where?

—Not far from here, in the house of the governor of Buenos Aires; and to think that I came to make war on you!

Each word they spoke in this long conversation added another miracle. Their souls danced on their tongues, hung eagerly at their ears, glittered in their eyes. As they were Germans, they sat a long time at table, waiting for the reverend father provincial; and the commander spoke in these terms to his dear Candide.

CHAPTER 15

How Candide Killed the Brother of His Dear Cunégonde

—All my life long I shall remember the horrible day when I saw my father and mother murdered and my sister raped. When the Bulgars left, that adorable sister of mine was nowhere to be found; so they loaded a cart with my mother, my father, myself, two serving girls, and three little murdered boys, to carry us all off for burial in a Jesuit chapel some two leagues from our ancestral castle. A Jesuit sprinkled us with holy water; it was horribly salty, and a few drops got into my eyes; the father noticed that my lid made a little tremor; putting his hand on my heart, he felt it beat; I was rescued, and at the end of three weeks was as good as new. You know, my dear Candide, that I was a very pretty boy; I became even more so; the reverend father Croust,[6] superior of the abbey, conceived a most tender friendship for me; he accepted me as a novice, and shortly after, I was sent to Rome. The Father General had need of a resupply of young German Jesuits. The rulers of Paraguay accept as few Spanish Jesuits as they can; they prefer foreigners, whom they think they can control better. I was judged fit, by the Father General, to labor in this vineyard. So we set off, a Pole, a Tyrolean, and myself. Upon our arrival, I was honored with the posts of subdeacon and lieutenant; today I am a colonel and a priest. We are giving a vigorous reception to the King of Spain's men; I assure you they will be excommunicated as well as trounced on the battlefield. Providence has sent you to help us. But is it really true that my dear sister, Cunégonde, is in the neighborhood, with the governor of Buenos Aires?

Candide reassured him with a solemn oath that nothing could be more true. Their tears began to flow again.

The baron could not weary of embracing Candide; he called him his brother, his savior.

—Ah, my dear Candide, said he, maybe together we will be able to enter the town as conquerors, and be united with my sister Cunégonde.

—That is all I desire, said Candide; I was expecting to marry her, and I still hope to.

—You insolent dog, replied the baron, you would have the effrontery to marry my sister, who has seventy-two quarterings! It's a piece of presumption for you even to mention such a crazy project in my presence.

Candide, terrified by this speech, answered:—Most reverend father, all the quarterings in the world don't affect this case; I have rescued your sister out of

---

6. A Jesuit rector at Colmar with whom Voltaire had quarreled in 1754.

the arms of a Jew and an inquisitor; she has many obligations to me, she wants to marry me. Master Pangloss always taught me that men are equal; and I shall certainly marry her.

—We'll see about that, you scoundrel, said the Jesuit baron of Thunder-Ten-Tronckh; and so saying, he gave him a blow across the face with the flat of his sword. Candide immediately drew his own sword and thrust it up to the hilt in the baron's belly; but as he drew it forth all dripping, he began to weep.

—Alas, dear God! said he, I have killed my old master, my friend, my brother-in-law; I am the best man in the world, and here are three men I've killed already, and two of the three were priests.

Cacambo, who was standing guard at the entry of the bower, came running.

—We can do nothing but sell our lives dearly, said his master; someone will certainly come; we must die fighting.

Cacambo, who had been in similar scrapes before, did not lose his head; he took the Jesuit's cassock, which the commander had been wearing, and put it on Candide; he stuck the dead man's square hat on Candide's head, and forced him onto horseback. Everything was done in the wink of an eye.

—Let's ride, master; everyone will take you for a Jesuit on his way to deliver orders; and we will have passed the frontier before anyone can come after us.

Even as he was pronouncing these words, he charged off, crying in Spanish:—Way, make way for the reverend father colonel!

CHAPTER 16

What Happened to the Two Travelers with Two Girls, Two Monkeys, and the Savages Named Biglugs

Candide and his valet were over the frontier before anyone in the camp knew of the death of the German Jesuit. Foresighted Cacambo had taken care to fill his satchel with bread, chocolate, ham, fruit, and several bottles of wine. They pushed their Andalusian horses forward into unknown country, where there were no roads. Finally a broad prairie divided by several streams opened before them. Our two travelers turned their horses loose to graze; Cacambo suggested that they eat too, and promptly set the example. But Candide said:—How can you expect me to eat ham when I have killed the son of My Lord the Baron, and am now condemned never to see the lovely Cunégonde for the rest of my life? Why should I drag out my miserable days, since I must exist far from her in the depths of despair and remorse? And what will the *Journal de Trévoux*[7] say of all this?

Though he talked this way, he did not neglect the food. Night fell. The two wanderers heard a few weak cries which seemed to be voiced by women. They could not tell whether the cries expressed grief or joy; but they leaped at once to their feet, with that uneasy suspicion which one always feels in an unknown country. The outcry arose from two girls, completely naked, who were running swiftly along the edge of the meadow, pursued by two monkeys who snapped at their buttocks. Candide was moved to pity; he had learned marksmanship with the Bulgars, and could have knocked a nut off a bush without touching the leaves. He raised his Spanish rifle, fired twice, and killed the two monkeys.

---

7. A newspaper published by the Jesuit order, founded in 1701 and consistently hostile to Voltaire.

—God be praised, my dear Cacambo! I've saved these two poor creatures from great danger. Though I committed a sin in killing an inquisitor and a Jesuit, I've redeemed myself by saving the lives of two girls. Perhaps they are two ladies of rank, and this good deed may gain us special advantages in the country.

He had more to say, but his mouth shut suddenly when he saw the girls embracing the monkeys tenderly, weeping over their bodies, and filling the air with lamentations.

—I wasn't looking for quite so much generosity of spirit, said he to Cacambo; the latter replied:—You've really fixed things this time, master; you've killed the two lovers of these young ladies.

—Their lovers! Impossible! You must be joking, Cacambo; how can I believe you?

—My dear master, Cacambo replied, you're always astonished by everything. Why do you think it so strange that in some countries monkeys succeed in obtaining the good graces of women? They are one quarter human, just as I am one quarter Spanish.

—Alas, Candide replied, I do remember now hearing Master Pangloss say that such things used to happen, and that from these mixtures there arose pans, fauns, and satyrs, and that these creatures had appeared to various grand figures of antiquity; but I took all that for fables.

—You should be convinced now, said Cacambo; it's true, and you see how people make mistakes who haven't received a measure of education. But what I fear is that these girls may get us into real trouble.

These sensible reflections led Candide to leave the field and to hide in a wood. There he dined with Cacambo; and there both of them, having duly cursed the inquisitor of Portugal, the governor of Buenos Aires, and the baron, went to sleep on a bed of moss. When they woke up, they found themselves unable to move; the reason was that during the night the Biglugs,[8] natives of the country, to whom the girls had complained of them, had tied them down with cords of bark. They were surrounded by fifty naked Biglugs, armed with arrows, clubs, and stone axes. Some were boiling a caldron of water, others were preparing spits, and all cried out:—It's a Jesuit, a Jesuit! We'll be revenged and have a good meal; let's eat some Jesuit, eat some Jesuit!

—I told you, my dear master, said Cacambo sadly, I said those two girls would play us a dirty trick.

Candide, noting the caldron and spits, cried out:—We are surely going to be roasted or boiled. Ah, what would Master Pangloss say if he could see these men in a state of nature? All is for the best, I agree; but I must say it seems hard to have lost Miss Cunégonde and to be stuck on a spit by the Biglugs.

Cacambo did not lose his head.

—Don't give up hope, said he to the disconsolate Candide; I understand a little of the jargon these people speak, and I'm going to talk to them.

—Don't forget to remind them, said Candide, of the frightful inhumanity of eating their fellow men, and that Christian ethics forbid it.

—Gentlemen, said Cacambo, you have a mind to eat a Jesuit today? An excellent idea; nothing is more proper than to treat one's enemies so. Indeed, the law

---

8. Voltaire's name is "Oreillons" from Spanish "Orejones," a name mentioned in Garcilaso de Vega's *Historia General del Perú* (1609), on which Voltaire drew for many of the details in his picture of South America.

of nature teaches us to kill our neighbor, and that's how men behave the whole world over. Though we Europeans don't exercise our right to eat our neighbors, the reason is simply that we find it easy to get a good meal elsewhere; but you don't have our resources, and we certainly agree that it's better to eat your enemies than to let the crows and vultures have the fruit of your victory. But, gentlemen, you wouldn't want to eat your friends. You think you will be spitting a Jesuit, and it's your defender, the enemy of your enemies, whom you will be roasting. For my part, I was born in your country; the gentleman whom you see is my master, and far from being a Jesuit, he has just killed a Jesuit, the robe he is wearing was stripped from him; that's why you have taken a dislike to him. To prove that I am telling the truth, take his robe and bring it to the nearest frontier of the kingdom of Los Padres; find out for yourselves if my master didn't kill a Jesuit officer. It won't take long; if you find that I have lied, you can still eat us. But if I've told the truth, you know too well the principles of public justice, customs, and laws, not to spare our lives.

The Biglugs found this discourse perfectly reasonable; they appointed chiefs to go posthaste and find out the truth; the two messengers performed their task like men of sense, and quickly returned bringing good news. The Biglugs untied their two prisoners, treated them with great politeness, offered them girls, gave them refreshments, and led them back to the border of their state, crying joyously:—He isn't a Jesuit, he isn't a Jesuit!

Candide could not weary of exclaiming over his preservation.

—What a people! he said. What men! what customs! If I had not had the good luck to run a sword through the body of Miss Cunégonde's brother, I would have been eaten on the spot! But, after all, it seems that uncorrupted nature is good, since these folk, instead of eating me, showed me a thousand kindnesses as soon as they knew I was not a Jesuit.

CHAPTER 17

Arrival of Candide and His Servant at the Country of Eldorado, and What They Saw There

When they were out of the land of the Biglugs, Cacambo said to Candide:—You see that this hemisphere is no better than the other; take my advice, and let's get back to Europe as soon as possible.

—How to get back, asked Candide, and where to go? If I go to my own land, the Bulgars and Abares are murdering everyone in sight; if I go to Portugal, they'll burn me alive; if we stay here, we risk being skewered any day. But how can I ever leave that part of the world where Miss Cunégonde lives?

—Let's go toward Cayenne, said Cacambo, we shall find some Frenchmen there, for they go all over the world; they can help us; perhaps God will take pity on us.

To get to Cayenne was not easy; they knew more or less which way to go, but mountains, rivers, cliffs, robbers, and savages obstructed the way everywhere. Their horses died of weariness; their food was eaten; they subsisted for one whole month on wild fruits, and at last they found themselves by a little river fringed with coconut trees, which gave them both life and hope.

Cacambo, who was as full of good advice as the old woman, said to Candide:—We can go no further, we've walked ourselves out; I see an abandoned canoe on the bank, let's fill it with coconuts, get into the boat, and float with the current; a river always leads to some inhabited spot or other. If we don't find anything pleasant, at least we may find something new.

—Let's go, said Candide, and let Providence be our guide.

They floated some leagues between banks sometimes flowery, sometimes sandy, now steep, now level. The river widened steadily; finally it disappeared into a chasm of frightful rocks that rose high into the heavens. The two travelers had the audacity to float with the current into this chasm. The river, narrowly confined, drove them onward with horrible speed and a fearful roar. After twenty-four hours, they saw daylight once more; but their canoe was smashed on the snags. They had to drag themselves from rock to rock for an entire league; at last they emerged to an immense horizon, ringed with remote mountains. The countryside was tended for pleasure as well as profit; everywhere the useful was joined to the agreeable. The roads were covered, or rather decorated, with elegantly shaped carriages made of a glittering material, carrying men and women of singular beauty, and drawn by great red sheep which were faster than the finest horses of Andalusia, Tetuan, and Mequinez.

—Here now, said Candide, is a country that's better than Westphalia.

Along with Cacambo, he climbed out of the river at the first village he could see. Some children of the town, dressed in rags of gold brocade, were playing quoits at the village gate; our two men from the other world paused to watch them; their quoits were rather large, yellow, red, and green, and they glittered with a singular luster. On a whim, the travelers picked up several; they were of gold, emeralds, and rubies, and the least of them would have been the greatest ornament of the Great Mogul's throne.

—Surely, said Cacambo, these quoit players are the children of the king of the country.

The village schoolmaster appeared at that moment, to call them back to school.

—And there, said Candide, is the tutor of the royal household.

The little rascals quickly gave up their game, leaving on the ground their quoits and playthings. Candide picked them up, ran to the schoolmaster, and presented them to him humbly, giving him to understand by sign language that their royal highnesses had forgotten their gold and jewels. With a smile, the schoolmaster tossed them to the ground, glanced quickly but with great surprise at Candide's face, and went his way.

The travelers did not fail to pick up the gold, rubies, and emeralds.

—Where in the world are we? cried Candide. The children of this land must be well trained, since they are taught contempt for gold and jewels.

Cacambo was as much surprised as Candide. At last they came to the finest house of the village; it was built like a European palace. A crowd of people surrounded the door, and even more were in the entry; delightful music was heard, and a delicious aroma of cooking filled the air. Cacambo went up to the door, listened, and reported that they were talking Peruvian; that was his native language, for every reader must know that Cacambo was born in Tucuman, in a village where they talk that language exclusively.

—I'll act as interpreter, he told Candide; it's an hotel, let's go in.

Promptly two boys and two girls of the staff, dressed in cloth of gold, and wearing ribbons in their hair, invited them to sit at the host's table. The meal consisted of four soups, each one garnished with a brace of parakeets, a boiled condor which weighed two hundred pounds, two roast monkeys of an excellent flavor, three hundred birds of paradise in one dish and six hundred humming-birds in another, exquisite stews, delicious pastries, the whole thing served up in plates of what looked like rock crystal. The boys and girls of the staff poured them various beverages made from sugar cane.

The diners were for the most part merchants and travelers, all extremely polite, who questioned Cacambo with the most discreet circumspection, and answered his questions very directly.

When the meal was over, Cacambo as well as Candide supposed he could set-tle his bill handsomely by tossing onto the table two of those big pieces of gold which they had picked up; but the host and hostess burst out laughing, and for a long time nearly split their sides. Finally they subsided.

—Gentlemen, said the host, we see clearly that you're foreigners; we don't meet many of you here. Please excuse our laughing when you offered us in pay-ment a couple of pebbles from the roadside. No doubt you don't have any of our local currency, but you don't need it to eat here. All the hotels established for the promotion of commerce are maintained by the state. You have had meager enter-tainment here, for we are only a poor town; but everywhere else you will be given the sort of welcome you deserve.

Cacambo translated for Candide all the host's explanations, and Candide lis-tened to them with the same admiration and astonishment that his friend Cacambo showed in reporting them.

—What is this country, then, said they to one another, unknown to the rest of the world, and where nature itself is so different from our own? This probably is the country where everything is for the best; for it's absolutely necessary that such a country should exist somewhere. And whatever Master Pangloss said of the matter, I have often had occasion to notice that things went badly in Westphalia.

CHAPTER 18

What They Saw in the Land of Eldorado

Cacambo revealed his curiosity to the host, and the host told him:—I am an igno-rant man and content to remain so; but we have here an old man, retired from the court, who is the most knowing person in the kingdom, and the most talkative.

Thereupon he brought Cacambo to the old man's house. Candide now played second fiddle, and acted as servant to his own valet. They entered an austere little house, for the door was merely of silver and the paneling of the rooms was only gold, though so tastefully wrought that the finest paneling would not surpass it. If the truth must be told, the lobby was only decorated with rubies and emeralds; but the patterns in which they were arranged atoned for the extreme simplicity.

The old man received the two strangers on a sofa stuffed with bird-of-paradise feathers, and offered them several drinks in diamond carafes; then he satisfied their curiosity in these terms.

—I am a hundred and seventy-two years old, and I heard from my late father, who was liveryman to the king, about the astonishing revolutions in Peru which he had seen. Our land here was formerly part of the kingdom of the Incas, who rashly left it in order to conquer another part of the world, and who were ulti-mately destroyed by the Spaniards. The wisest princes of their house were those who had never left their native valley; they decreed, with the consent of the nation, that henceforth no inhabitant of our little kingdom should ever leave it; and this rule is what has preserved our innocence and our happiness. The

Spaniards heard vague rumors about this land, they called it Eldorado;[9] and an English knight named Raleigh even came somewhere close to it about a hundred years ago; but as we are surrounded by unscalable mountains and precipices, we have managed so far to remain hidden from the rapacity of the European nations, who have an inconceivable rage for the pebbles and mud of our land, and who, in order to get some, would butcher us all to the last man.

The conversation was a long one; it turned on the form of the government, the national customs, on women, public shows, the arts. At last Candide, whose taste always ran to metaphysics, told Cacambo to ask if the country had any religion.

The old man grew a bit red.

—How's that? he said. Can you have any doubt of it? Do you suppose we are altogether thankless scoundrels?

Cacambo asked meekly what was the religion of Eldorado. The old man flushed again.

—Can there be two religions? he asked. I suppose our religion is the same as everyone's, we worship God from morning to evening.

—Then you worship a single deity? said Cacambo, who acted throughout as interpreter of the questions of Candide.

—It's obvious, said the old man, that there aren't two or three or four of them. I must say the people of your world ask very remarkable questions.

Candide could not weary of putting questions to this good old man; he wanted to know how the people of Eldorado prayed to God.

—We don't pray to him at all, said the good and respectable sage; we have nothing to ask him for, since everything we need has already been granted; we thank God continually.

Candide was interested in seeing the priests; he had Cacambo ask where they were. The old gentleman smiled.

—My friends, said he, we are all priests; the king and all the heads of household sing formal psalms of thanksgiving every morning, and five or six thousand voices accompany them.

—What! you have no monks to teach, argue, govern, intrigue, and burn at the stake everyone who disagrees with them?

—We should have to be mad, said the old man; here we are all of the same mind, and we don't understand what you're up to with your monks.

Candide was overjoyed at all these speeches, and said to himself:—This is very different from Westphalia and the castle of My Lord the Baron; if our friend Pangloss had seen Eldorado, he wouldn't have called the castle of Thunder-Ten-Tronckh the finest thing on earth; to know the world one must travel.

After this long conversation, the old gentleman ordered a carriage with six sheep made ready, and gave the two travelers twelve of his servants for their journey to the court.

—Excuse me, said he, if old age deprives me of the honor of accompanying you. The king will receive you after a style which will not altogether displease you, and you will doubtless make allowance for the customs of the country if there are any you do not like.

9. The myth of this land of gold somewhere in Central or South America had been widespread since the 16th century. *The Discovery of Guiana*, published in 1595, described Sir Walter Ralegh's infatuation with the myth of Eldorado and served to spread the story still further.

Candide and Cacambo climbed into the coach; the six sheep flew like the wind, and in less than four hours they reached the king's palace at the edge of the capital. The entryway was two hundred and twenty feet high and a hundred wide; it is impossible to describe all the materials of which it was made. But you can imagine how much finer it was than those pebbles and sand which we call gold and jewels.

Twenty beautiful girls of the guard detail welcomed Candide and Cacambo as they stepped from the carriage, took them to the baths, and dressed them in robes woven of hummingbird feathers; then the high officials of the crown, both male and female, led them to the royal chamber between two long lines, each of a thousand musicians, as is customary. As they approached the throne room, Cacambo asked an officer what was the proper method of greeting his majesty: if one fell to one's knees or on one's belly; if one put one's hands on one's head or on one's rear; if one licked up the dust of the earth—in a word, what was the proper form?[1]

—The ceremony, said the officer, is to embrace the king and kiss him on both cheeks.

Candide and Cacambo fell on the neck of his majesty, who received them with all the dignity imaginable, and asked them politely to dine.

In the interim, they were taken about to see the city, the public buildings rising to the clouds, the public markets and arcades, the fountains of pure water and of rose water, those of sugar cane liquors which flowed perpetually in the great plazas paved with a sort of stone which gave off odors of gilly-flower and rose petals. Candide asked to see the supreme court and the hall of parliament; they told him there was no such thing, that lawsuits were unknown. He asked if there were prisons, and was told there were not. What surprised him more, and gave him most pleasure, was the palace of sciences, in which he saw a gallery two thousand paces long, entirely filled with mathematical and physical instruments.

Having passed the whole afternoon seeing only a thousandth part of the city, they returned to the king's palace. Candide sat down to dinner with his majesty, his own valet Cacambo, and several ladies. Never was better food served, and never did a host preside more jovially than his majesty. Cacambo explained the king's witty sayings to Candide, and even when translated they still seemed witty. Of all the things which astonished Candide, this was not, in his eyes, the least astonishing.

They passed a month in this refuge. Candide never tired of saying to Cacambo:— It's true, my friend, I'll say it again, the castle where I was born does not compare with the land where we now are; but Miss Cunégonde is not here, and you doubtless have a mistress somewhere in Europe. If we stay here, we shall be just like everybody else, whereas if we go back to our own world, taking with us just a dozen sheep loaded with Eldorado pebbles, we shall be richer than all the kings put together, we shall have no more inquisitors to fear, and we shall easily be able to retake Miss Cunégonde.

This harangue pleased Cacambo; wandering is such pleasure, it gives a man such prestige at home to be able to talk of what he has seen abroad, that the two happy men resolved to be so no longer, but to take their leave of his majesty.

---

1. Candide's questions are probably derived from those of Gulliver on a similar occasion, in the third part of Gulliver's Travels.

—You are making a foolish mistake, the king told them; I know very well that my kingdom is nothing much; but when you are pretty comfortable somewhere, you had better stay there. Of course I have no right to keep strangers against their will, that sort of tyranny is not in keeping with our laws or our customs; all men are free; depart when you will, but the way out is very difficult. You cannot possibly go up the river by which you miraculously came; it runs too swiftly through its underground caves. The mountains which surround my land are ten thousand feet high, and steep as walls; each one is more than ten leagues across; the only way down is over precipices. But since you really must go, I shall order my engineers to make a machine which can carry you conveniently. When we take you over the mountains, nobody will be able to go with you, for my subjects have sworn never to leave their refuge, and they are too sensible to break their vows. Other than that, ask of me what you please.

—We only request of your majesty, Cacambo said, a few sheep loaded with provisions, some pebbles, and some of the mud of your country.

The king laughed.

—I simply can't understand, said he, the passion you Europeans have for our yellow mud; but take all you want, and much good may it do you.

He promptly gave orders to his technicians to make a machine for lifting these two extraordinary men out of his kingdom. Three thousand good physicists worked at the problem; the machine was ready in two weeks' time, and cost no more than twenty million pounds sterling, in the money of the country. Cacambo and Candide were placed in the machine; there were two great sheep, saddled and bridled to serve them as steeds when they had cleared the mountains, twenty pack sheep with provisions, thirty which carried presents consisting of the rarities of the country, and fifty loaded with gold, jewels, and diamonds. The king bade tender farewell to the two vagabonds.

It made a fine spectacle, their departure, and the ingenious way in which they were hoisted with their sheep up to the top of the mountains. The technicians bade them good-bye after bringing them to safety, and Candide had now no other desire and no other object than to go and present his sheep to Miss Cunégonde.

—We have, said he, enough to pay off the governor of Buenos Aires—if, indeed, a price can be placed on Miss Cunégonde. Let us go to Cayenne, take ship there, and then see what kingdom we can find to buy up.

CHAPTER 19

What Happened to Them at Surinam, and How Candide Got to Know Martin

The first day was pleasant enough for our travelers. They were encouraged by the idea of possessing more treasures than Asia, Europe, and Africa could bring together. Candide, in transports, carved the name of Cunégonde on the trees. On the second day two of their sheep bogged down in a swamp and were lost with their loads; two other sheep died of fatigue a few days later; seven or eight others starved to death in a desert; still others fell, a little after, from precipices. Finally, after a hundred days' march, they had only two sheep left. Candide told Cacambo:— My friend, you see how the riches of this world are fleeting; the only solid things are virtue and the joy of seeing Miss Cunégonde again.

—I agree, said Cacambo, but we still have two sheep, laden with more treasure than the king of Spain will ever have; and I see in the distance a town which

I suspect is Surinam; it belongs to the Dutch. We are at the end of our trials and on the threshold of our happiness.

As they drew near the town, they discovered a negro stretched on the ground with only half his clothes left, that is, a pair of blue drawers; the poor fellow was also missing his left leg and his right hand.

—Good Lord, said Candide in Dutch, what are you doing in that horrible condition, my friend?

—I am waiting for my master, Mr. Vanderdendur,[2] the famous merchant, answered the negro.

—Is Mr. Vanderdendur, Candide asked, the man who treated you this way?

—Yes, sir, said the negro, that's how things are around here. Twice a year we get a pair of linen drawers to wear. If we catch a finger in the sugar mill where we work, they cut off our hand; if we try to run away, they cut off our leg: I have undergone both these experiences. This is the price of the sugar you eat in Europe. And yet, when my mother sold me for ten Patagonian crowns on the coast of Guinea, she said to me: 'My dear child, bless our witch doctors, reverence them always, they will make your life happy; you have the honor of being a slave to our white masters, and in this way you are making the fortune of your father and mother.' Alas! I don't know if I made their fortunes, but they certainly did not make mine. The dogs, monkeys, and parrots are a thousand times less unhappy than we are. The Dutch witch doctors who converted me tell me every Sunday that we are all sons of Adam, black and white alike. I am no genealogist; but if these preachers are right, we must all be remote cousins; and you must admit no one could treat his own flesh and blood in a more horrible fashion.

—Oh Pangloss! cried Candide, you had no notion of these abominations! I'm through, I must give up your optimism after all.

—What's optimism? said Cacambo.

—Alas, said Candide, it is a mania for saying things are well when one is in hell.

And he shed bitter tears as he looked at this negro, and he was still weeping as he entered Surinam.

The first thing they asked was if there was not some vessel in port which could be sent to Buenos Aires. The man they asked was a Spanish merchant who undertook to make an honest bargain with them. They arranged to meet in a café; Candide and the faithful Cacambo, with their two sheep, went there to meet with him.

Candide, who always said exactly what was in his heart, told the Spaniard of his adventures, and confessed that he wanted to recapture Miss Cunégonde.

—I shall take good care *not* to send you to Buenos Aires, said the merchant; I should be hanged, and so would you. The lovely Cunégonde is his lordship's favorite mistress.

This was a thunderstroke for Candide; he wept for a long time; finally he drew Cacambo aside.

—Here, my friend, said he, is what you must do. Each one of us has in his pockets five or six millions' worth of diamonds; you are cleverer than I; go get

2. A name perhaps intended to suggest Van-Duren, a Dutch bookseller with whom Voltaire had quarreled. In particular, the incident of gradually raising one's price recalls Van-Duren, to whom Voltaire had successively offered 1,000, 1,500, 2,000, and 3,000 florins for the return of the manuscript of Frederick the Great's *Anti-Machiavel*.

Miss Cunégonde in Buenos Aires. If the governor makes a fuss, give him a million; if that doesn't convince him, give him two millions; you never killed an inquisitor, nobody will suspect you. I'll fit out another boat and go wait for you in Venice. That is a free country, where one need have no fear either of Bulgars or Abares or Jews or inquisitors.

Cacambo approved of this wise decision. He was in despair at leaving a good master who had become a bosom friend; but the pleasure of serving him overcame the grief of leaving him. They embraced, and shed a few tears; Candide urged him not to forget the good old woman. Cacambo departed that very same day; he was a very good fellow, that Cacambo.

Candide remained for some time in Surinam, waiting for another merchant to take him to Italy, along with the two sheep which were left him. He hired servants and bought everything necessary for the long voyage; finally Mr. Vanderdendur, master of a big ship, came calling.

—How much will you charge, Candide asked this man, to take me to Venice—myself, my servants, my luggage, and those two sheep over there?

The merchant set a price of ten thousand piastres; Candide did not blink an eye.

—Oh, ho, said the prudent Vanderdendur to himself, this stranger pays out ten thousand piastres at once, he must be pretty well fixed.

Then, returning a moment later, he made known that he could not set sail under twenty thousand.

—All right, you shall have them, said Candide.

—Whew, said the merchant softly to himself, this man gives twenty thousand piastres as easily as ten.

He came back again to say he could not go to Venice for less than thirty thousand piastres.

—All right, thirty then, said Candide.

—Ah ha, said the Dutch merchant, again speaking to himself; so thirty thousand piastres mean nothing to this man; no doubt the two sheep are loaded with immense treasures; let's say no more; we'll pick up the thirty thousand piastres first, and then we'll see.

Candide sold two little diamonds, the least of which was worth more than all the money demanded by the merchant. He paid him in advance. The two sheep were taken aboard. Candide followed in a little boat, to board the vessel at its anchorage. The merchant bides his time, sets sail, and makes his escape with a favoring wind. Candide, aghast and stupefied, soon loses him from view.

—Alas, he cries, now there is a trick worthy of the old world!

He returns to shore sunk in misery; for he had lost riches enough to make the fortunes of twenty monarchs.

Now he rushes to the house of the Dutch magistrate, and, being a bit disturbed, he knocks loudly at the door; goes in, tells the story of what happened, and shouts a bit louder than is customary. The judge begins by fining him ten thousand piastres for making such a racket; then he listens patiently to the story, promises to look into the matter as soon as the merchant comes back, and charges another ten thousand piastres as the costs of the hearing.

This legal proceeding completed the despair of Candide. In fact he had experienced miseries a thousand times more painful, but the coldness of the judge, and that of the merchant who had robbed him, roused his bile and plunged him into a black melancholy. The malice of men rose up before his spirit in all its ugliness, and his mind dwelt only on gloomy thoughts. Finally, when a French vessel was ready to leave for Bordeaux, since he had no more diamond-laden sheep to transport, he took a cabin at a fair price, and made it known in the town that he would pay passage and keep, plus two thousand piastres, to any honest man who wanted to make the journey with him, on condition that this man must be the most disgusted with his own condition and the most unhappy man in the province.

This drew such a crowd of applicants as a fleet could not have held. Candide wanted to choose among the leading candidates, so he picked out about twenty who seemed companionable enough, and of whom each pretended to be more miserable than all the others. He brought them together at his inn and gave them a dinner, on condition that each would swear to tell truthfully his entire history. He would select as his companion the most truly miserable and rightly discontented man, and among the others he would distribute various gifts.

The meeting lasted till four in the morning. Candide, as he listened to all the stories, remembered what the old woman had told him on the trip to Buenos Aires, and of the wager she had made, that there was nobody on the boat who had not undergone great misfortunes. At every story that was told him, he thought of Pangloss.

—That Pangloss, he said, would be hard put to prove his system. I wish he was here. Certainly if everything goes well, it is in Eldorado and not in the rest of the world.

At last he decided in favor of a poor scholar who had worked ten years for the booksellers of Amsterdam. He decided that there was no trade in the world with which one should be more disgusted.

This scholar, who was in fact a good man, had been robbed by his wife, beaten by his son, and deserted by his daughter, who had got herself abducted by a Portuguese. He had just been fired from the little job on which he existed; and the preachers of Surinam were persecuting him because they took him for a Socinian.[3] The others, it is true, were at least as unhappy as he, but Candide hoped the scholar would prove more amusing on the voyage. All his rivals declared that Candide was doing them a great injustice, but he pacified them with a hundred piastres apiece.

CHAPTER 20
What Happened to Candide and Martin at Sea

The old scholar, whose name was Martin, now set sail with Candide for Bordeaux. Both men had seen and suffered much; and even if the vessel had been sailing from Surinam to Japan via the Cape of Good Hope, they would have been able to keep themselves amused with instances of moral evil and physical evil during the entire trip.

However, Candide had one great advantage over Martin, that he still hoped to see Miss Cunégonde again, and Martin had nothing to hope for; besides, he had gold and diamonds, and though he had lost a hundred big red sheep loaded with the greatest treasures of the earth, though he had always at his heart a memory of

3. A follower of Faustus and Laelius Socinus, 16th-century Polish theologians who proposed a form of "rational" Christianity that exalted the rational conscience and minimized such mysteries as the Trinity. The Socinians, by a special irony, were vigorous optimists.

the Dutch merchant's villainy, yet, when he thought of the wealth that remained in his hands, and when he talked of Cunégonde, especially just after a good dinner, he still inclined to the system of Pangloss.

—But what about you, Monsieur Martin, he asked the scholar, what do you think of all that? What is your idea of moral evil and physical evil?

—Sir, answered Martin, those priests accused me of being a Socinian, but the truth is that I am a Manichee.[4]

—You're joking, said Candide; there aren't any more Manichees in the world.

—There's me, said Martin; I don't know what to do about it, but I can't think otherwise.

—You must be possessed of the devil, said Candide.

—He's mixed up with so many things of this world, said Martin, that he may be in me as well as elsewhere; but I assure you, as I survey this globe, or globule, I think that God has abandoned it to some evil spirit—all of it except Eldorado. I have scarcely seen one town which did not wish to destroy its neighboring town, no family which did not wish to exterminate some other family. Everywhere the weak loathe the powerful, before whom they cringe, and the powerful treat them like brute cattle, to be sold for their meat and fleece. A million regimented assassins roam Europe from one end to the other, plying the trades of murder and robbery in an organized way for a living, because there is no more honest form of work for them; and in the cities which seem to enjoy peace and where the arts are flourishing, men are devoured by more envy, cares, and anxieties than a whole town experiences when it's under siege. Private griefs are worse even than public trials. In a word, I have seen so much and suffered so much, that I am a Manichee.

—Still there is some good, said Candide.

—That may be, said Martin, but I don't know it.

In the middle of this discussion, the rumble of cannon was heard. From minute to minute the noise grew louder. Everyone reached for his spyglass. At a distance of some three miles they saw two vessels fighting; the wind brought both of them so close to the French vessel that they had a pleasantly comfortable seat to watch the fight. Presently one of the vessels caught the other with a broadside so low and so square as to send it to the bottom. Candide and Martin saw clearly a hundred men on the deck of the sinking ship; they all raised their hands to heaven, uttering fearful shrieks; and in a moment everything was swallowed up.

—Well, said Martin, that is how men treat one another.

—It is true, said Candide, there's something devilish in this business.

As they chatted, he noticed something of a striking red color floating near the sunken vessel. They sent out a boat to investigate; it was one of his sheep. Candide was more joyful to recover this one sheep than he had been afflicted to lose a hundred of them, all loaded with big Eldorado diamonds.

The French captain soon learned that the captain of the victorious vessel was Spanish and that of the sunken vessel was a Dutch pirate. It was the same man who had robbed Candide. The enormous riches which this rascal had stolen were sunk beside him in the sea, and nothing was saved but a single sheep.

—You see, said Candide to Martin, crime is punished sometimes; this scoundrel of a Dutch merchant has met the fate he deserved.

4. Mani, a Persian sage and philosopher of the 3rd century, taught (probably under the influence of traditions stemming from Zoroaster and the worshipers of the sun god Mithra) that the earth is a field of dispute between two almost equal powers, one of light and one of darkness, both of which must be propitiated.

—Yes, said Martin; but did the passengers aboard his ship have to perish too? God punished the scoundrel, and the devil drowned the others.

Meanwhile the French and Spanish vessels continued on their journey, and Candide continued his talks with Martin. They disputed for fifteen days in a row, and at the end of that time were just as much in agreement as at the beginning. But at least they were talking, they exchanged their ideas, they consoled one another. Candide caressed his sheep.

—Since I have found you again, said he, I may well rediscover Miss Cunégonde.

CHAPTER 21

Candide and Martin Approach the Coast of France: They Reason Together

At last the coast of France came in view.

—Have you ever been in France, Monsieur Martin? asked Candide.

—Yes, said Martin, I have visited several provinces. There are some where half the inhabitants are crazy, others where they are too sly, still others where they are quite gentle and stupid, some where they venture on wit; in all of them the principal occupation is love-making, the second is slander, and the third stupid talk.

—But, Monsieur Martin, were you ever in Paris?

—Yes, I've been in Paris; it contains specimens of all these types; it is a chaos, a mob, in which everyone is seeking pleasure and where hardly anyone finds it, at least from what I have seen. I did not live there for long; as I arrived, I was robbed of everything I possessed by thieves at the fair of St. Germain; I myself was taken for a thief, and spent eight days in jail, after which I took a proofreader's job to earn enough money to return on foot to Holland. I knew the writing gang, the intriguing gang, the gang with fits and convulsions.[5] They say there are some very civilized people in that town; I'd like to think so.

—I myself have no desire to visit France, said Candide; you no doubt realize that when one has spent a month in Eldorado, there is nothing else on earth one wants to see, except Miss Cunégonde. I am going to wait for her at Venice; we will cross France simply to get to Italy; wouldn't you like to come with me?

—Gladly, said Martin; they say Venice is good only for the Venetian nobles, but that on the other hand they treat foreigners very well when they have plenty of money. I don't have any; you do, so I'll follow you anywhere.

—By the way, said Candide, do you believe the earth was originally all ocean, as they assure us in that big book belonging to the ship's captain?[6]

—I don't believe that stuff, said Martin, nor any of the dreams which people have been peddling for some time now.

—But why, then, was this world formed at all? asked Candide.

—To drive us mad, answered Martin.

—Aren't you astonished, Candide went on, at the love which those two girls showed for the monkeys in the land of the Biglugs that I told you about?

—Not at all, said Martin, I see nothing strange in these sentiments; I have seen so many extraordinary things that nothing seems extraordinary any more.

5. The Jansenists, a sect of strict Catholics, became notorious for spiritual ecstasies. Their public displays reached a height during the 1720s, and Voltaire described them in Le *Siècle de Louis XIV* (chap. 37), as well as in the article "Convulsions" in the *Philosophical Dictionary*.

6. The Bible: Genesis I.

—Do you believe, asked Candide, that men have always massacred one another as they do today? That they have always been liars, traitors, ingrates, thieves, weaklings, sneaks, cowards, backbiters, gluttons, drunkards, misers, climbers, killers, calumniators, sensualists, fanatics, hypocrites, and fools?

—Do you believe, said Martin, that hawks have always eaten pigeons when they could get them?

—Of course, said Candide.

—Well, said Martin, if hawks have always had the same character, why do you suppose that men have changed?

—Oh, said Candide, there's a great deal of difference, because freedom of the will . . .

As they were disputing in this manner, they reached Bordeaux.

CHAPTER 22

What Happened in France to Candide and Martin

Candide paused in Bordeaux only long enough to sell a couple of Eldorado pebbles and to fit himself out with a fine two-seater carriage, for he could no longer do without his philosopher Martin; only he was very unhappy to part with his sheep, which he left to the academy of science in Bordeaux. They proposed, as the theme of that year's prize contest, the discovery of why the wool of the sheep was red; and the prize was awarded to a northern scholar[7] who demonstrated by A plus B minus C divided by Z that the sheep ought to be red and die of sheep rot.

But all the travelers with whom Candide talked in the roadside inns told him:—We are going to Paris.

This general consensus finally inspired in him too a desire to see the capital; it was not much out of his road to Venice.

He entered through the Faubourg Saint-Marceau,[8] and thought he was in the meanest village of Westphalia.

Scarcely was Candide in his hotel, when he came down with a mild illness caused by exhaustion. As he was wearing an enormous diamond ring, and people had noticed among his luggage a tremendously heavy safe, he soon found at his bedside two doctors whom he had not called, several intimate friends who never left him alone, and two pious ladies who helped to warm his broth. Martin said:—I remember that I too was ill on my first trip to Paris; I was very poor; and as I had neither friends, pious ladies, nor doctors, I got well.

However, as a result of medicines and bleedings, Candide's illness became serious. A resident of the neighborhood came to ask him politely to fill out a ticket, to be delivered to the porter of the other world.[9] Candide wanted nothing to do with it. The pious ladies assured him it was a new fashion; Candide replied that he wasn't a man of fashion. Martin wanted to throw the resident out the window.

7. Maupertuis Le Lapon, philosopher and mathematician, whom Voltaire had accused of trying to adduce mathematical proofs of the existence of God.

8. A district on the left bank, notably grubby in the 18th century. "As I entered [Paris] through the Faubourg Saint-Marceau, I saw nothing but dirty stinking little streets, ugly black houses, a general air of squalor and pov-erty, beggars, carters, menders of clothes, sellers of herb-drinks and old hats." Jean-Jacques Rousseau, *Confessions*, Book IV.

9. In the middle of the 18th century in France, it became customary to require persons who were grievously ill to sign *billets de confession*, without which they could not be given absolution, admitted to the last sacraments, or buried in consecrated ground.

The cleric swore that without the ticket they wouldn't bury Candide. Martin swore that he would bury the cleric if he continued to be a nuisance. The quarrel grew heated; Martin took him by the shoulders and threw him bodily out the door; all of which caused a great scandal, from which developed a legal case.

Candide got better; and during his convalescence he had very good company in to dine. They played cards for money; and Candide was quite surprised that none of the aces were ever dealt to him, and Martin was not surprised at all.

Among those who did the honors of the town for Candide there was a little abbé from Perigord, one of those busy fellows, always bright, always useful, assured, obsequious, and obliging, who waylay passing strangers, tell them the scandal of the town, and offer them pleasures at any price they want to pay. This fellow first took Candide and Martin to the theatre. A new tragedy was being played. Candide found himself seated next to a group of wits. That did not keep him from shedding a few tears in the course of some perfectly played scenes. One of the commentators beside him remarked during the intermission:—You are quite mistaken to weep, this actress is very bad indeed; the actor who plays with her is even worse; and the play is even worse than the actors in it. The author knows not a word of Arabic, though the action takes place in Arabia; and besides, he is a man who doesn't believe in innate ideas. Tomorrow I will show you twenty pamphlets written against him.

—Tell me, sir, said Candide to the abbé, how many plays are there for performance in France?

—Five or six thousand, replied the other.

—That's a lot, said Candide; how many of them are any good?

—Fifteen or sixteen, was the answer.

—That's a lot, said Martin.

Candide was very pleased with an actress who took the part of Queen Elizabeth in a rather dull tragedy[1] that still gets played from time to time.

—I like this actress very much, he said to Martin, she bears a slight resemblance to Miss Cunégonde; I should like to meet her.

The abbé from Perigord offered to introduce him. Candide, raised in Germany, asked what was the protocol, how one behaved in France with queens of England.

—You must distinguish, said the abbé; in the provinces, you take them to an inn; at Paris they are respected while still attractive, and thrown on the dunghill when they are dead.[2]

—Queens on the dunghill! said Candide.

—Yes indeed, said Martin, the abbé is right; I was in Paris when Miss Monime herself[3] passed, as they say, from this life to the other; she was refused what these folk call 'the honors of burial,' that is, the right to rot with all the beggars of the district in a dirty cemetery; she was buried all alone by her troupe at the corner of the Rue de Bourgogne; this must have been very disagreeable to her, for she had a noble character.

—That was extremely rude, said Candide.

1. *Le Comte d'Essex* by Thomas Corneille.
2. Voltaire engaged in a long and vigorous campaign against the rule that actors and actresses could not be buried in consecrated ground. The superstition probably arose from a feeling that by assuming false identities they drained their own souls.

3. Adrienne Lecouvreur (1690–1730), so called because she made her debut as Monime in Racine's *Mithridate*. Voltaire had assisted at her secret midnight funeral and wrote an indignant poem about it.

—What do you expect? said Martin; that is how these folk are. Imagine all the contradictions, all the incompatibilities you can, and you will see them in the government, the courts, the churches, and the plays of this crazy nation.

—Is it true that they are always laughing in Paris? asked Candide.

—Yes, said the abbé, but with a kind of rage too; when people complain of things, they do so amid explosions of laughter; they even laugh as they perform the most detestable actions.

—Who was that fat swine, said Candide, who spoke so nastily about the play over which I was weeping, and the actors who gave me so much pleasure?

—He is a living illness, answered the abbé, who makes a business of slandering all the plays and books; he hates the successful ones, as eunuchs hate successful lovers; he's one of those literary snakes who live on filth and venom; he's a folliculator . . .

—What's this word *folliculator*? asked Candide.

—It's a folio filler, said the abbé, a Fréron.[4]

It was after this fashion that Candide, Martin, and the abbé from Perigord chatted on the stairway as they watched the crowd leaving the theatre.

—Although I'm in a great hurry to see Miss Cunégonde again, said Candide, I would very much like to dine with Miss Clairon,[5] for she seemed to me admirable.

The abbé was not the man to approach Miss Clairon, who saw only good company.

—She has an engagement tonight, he said; but I shall have the honor of introducing you to a lady of quality, and there you will get to know Paris as if you had lived here for years.

Candide, who was curious by nature, allowed himself to be brought to the lady's house, in the depths of the Faubourg St.-Honoré; they were playing faro;[6] twelve melancholy punters held in their hands a little sheaf of cards, blank summaries of their bad luck. Silence reigned supreme, the punters were pallid, the banker uneasy; and the lady of the house, seated beside the pitiless banker, watched with the eyes of a lynx for the various illegal redoublings and bets at long odds which the players tried to signal by folding the corners of their cards; she had them unfolded with a determination which was severe but polite, and concealed her anger lest she lose her customers. The lady caused herself to be known as the Marquise of Parolignac.[7] Her daughter, fifteen years old, sat among the punters and tipped off her mother with a wink to the sharp practices of these unhappy players when they tried to recoup their losses. The abbé from Perigord, Candide, and Martin came in; nobody arose or greeted them or looked at them; all were lost in the study of their cards.

—My Lady the Baroness of Thunder-Ten-Tronckh was more civil, thought Candide.

However, the abbé whispered in the ear of the marquise, who, half rising, honored Candide with a gracious smile and Martin with a truly noble nod; she gave a

---

4. A successful and popular journalist who had attacked several of Voltaire's plays, including *Tancrède*.

5. Actually Claire Leris (1723–1803). She had played the lead role in *Tancrède* and was for many years a leading figure on the Paris stage.

6. A game of cards, about which it is necessary to know only that a number of punters play against a banker or dealer. The pack is dealt out two cards at a time, and each player may bet on any card as much as he pleases. The sharp practices of the punters consist essentially of tricks for increasing their winnings without corresponding risks.

7. A *paroli* is an illegal redoubling of one's bet; her name therefore implies a title grounded in cardsharping.

seat and dealt a hand of cards to Candide, who lost fifty thousand francs in two turns; after which they had a very merry supper. Everyone was amazed that Candide was not upset over his losses; the lackeys, talking together in their usual lackey language, said:—He must be some English milord.

The supper was like most Parisian suppers: first silence, then an indistinguishable rush of words; then jokes, mostly insipid, false news, bad logic, a little politics, a great deal of malice. They even talked of new books.

—Have you seen the new novel by Dr. Gauchat, the theologian?[8] asked the abbé from Perigord.

—Oh yes, answered one of the guests; but I couldn't finish it. We have a horde of impudent scribblers nowadays, but all of them put together don't match the impudence of this Gauchat, this doctor of theology. I have been so struck by the enormous number of detestable books which are swamping us that I have taken up punting at faro.

—And the *Collected Essays* of Archdeacon T——[9] asked the abbé, what do you think of them?

—Ah, said Madame de Parolignac, what a frightful bore he is! He takes such pains to tell you what everyone knows; he discourses so learnedly on matters which aren't worth a casual remark! He plunders, and not even wittily, the wit of other people! He spoils what he plunders, he's disgusting! But he'll never disgust me again; a couple of pages of the archdeacon have been enough for me.

There was at table a man of learning and taste, who supported the marquise on this point. They talked next of tragedies; the lady asked why there were tragedies which played well enough but which were wholly unreadable. The man of taste explained very clearly how a play could have a certain interest and yet little merit otherwise; he showed succinctly that it was not enough to conduct a couple of intrigues, such as one can find in any novel, and which never fail to excite the spectator's interest; but that one must be new without being grotesque, frequently touch the sublime but never depart from the natural; that one must know the human heart and give it words; that one must be a great poet without allowing any character in the play to sound like a poet; and that one must know the language perfectly, speak it purely, and maintain a continual harmony without ever sacrificing sense to mere sound.

—Whoever, he added, does not observe all these rules may write one or two tragedies which succeed in the theatre, but he will never be ranked among the good writers; there are very few good tragedies; some are idylls in well-written, well-rhymed dialogue, others are political arguments which put the audience to sleep, or revolting pomposities; still others are the fantasies of enthusiasts, barbarous in style, incoherent in logic, full of long speeches to the gods because the author does not know how to address men, full of false maxims and emphatic commonplaces.

Candide listened attentively to this speech and conceived a high opinion of the speaker; and as the marquise had placed him by her side, he turned to ask her who was this man who spoke so well.

—He is a scholar, said the lady, who never plays cards and whom the abbé sometimes brings to my house for supper; he knows all about tragedies and

---

8. He had written against Voltaire, and Voltaire suspected him (wrongly) of having written the novel *L'Oracle des nouveaux philosophes*.
9. His name was Trublet, and he had said,

among other disagreeable things, that Voltaire's epic poem, the *Henriade*, made him yawn and that Voltaire's genius was "the perfection of mediocrity."

books, and has himself written a tragedy that was hissed from the stage and a book, the only copy of which ever seen outside his publisher's office was dedicated to me.

—What a great man, said Candide, he's Pangloss all over.

Then, turning to him, he said:—Sir, you doubtless think everything is for the best in the physical as well as the moral universe, and that nothing could be otherwise than as it is?

—Not at all, sir, replied the scholar, I believe nothing of the sort. I find that everything goes wrong in our world; that nobody knows his place in society or his duty, what he's doing or what he ought to be doing, and that outside of mealtimes, which are cheerful and congenial enough, all the rest of the day is spent in useless quarrels, as of Jansenists against Molinists,[1] parliament-men against churchmen, literary men against literary men, courtiers against courtiers, financiers against the plebs, wives against husbands, relatives against relatives—it's one unending warfare.

Candide answered:—I have seen worse; but a wise man, who has since had the misfortune to be hanged, taught me that everything was marvelously well arranged. Troubles are just the shadows in a beautiful picture.

—Your hanged philosopher was joking, said Martin; the shadows are horrible ugly blots.

—It is human beings who make the blots, said Candide, and they can't do otherwise.

—Then it isn't their fault, said Martin.

Most of the faro players, who understood this sort of talk not at all, kept on drinking; Martin disputed with the scholar, and Candide told part of his story to the lady of the house.

After supper, the marquise brought Candide into her room and sat him down on a divan.

—Well, she said to him, are you still madly in love with Miss Cunégonde of Thunder-Ten-Tronckh?

—Yes, ma'am, replied Candide. The marquise turned upon him a tender smile.

—You answer like a young man of Westphalia, said she; a Frenchman would have told me: 'It is true that I have been in love with Miss Cunégonde; but since seeing you, madame, I fear that I love her no longer.'

—Alas, ma'am, said Candide, I will answer any way you want.

—Your passion for her, said the marquise, began when you picked up her handkerchief; I prefer that you should pick up my garter.

—Gladly, said Candide, and picked it up.

—But I also want you to put it back on, said the lady; and Candide put it on again.

—Look you now, said the lady, you are a foreigner; my Paris lovers I sometimes cause to languish for two weeks or so, but to you I surrender the very first night, because we must render the honors of the country to a young man from Westphalia.

1. The Jansenists (from Corneille Jansen, 1585–1638) were a relatively strict party of religious reform; the Molinists (from Luis Molina) were the party of the Jesuits. Their central issue of controversy was the relative importance of divine grace and human will to the salvation of man.

The beauty, who had seen two enormous diamonds on the two hands of her young friend, praised them so sincerely that from the fingers of Candide they passed over to the fingers of the marquise.

As he returned home with his Perigord abbé, Candide felt some remorse at having been unfaithful to Miss Cunégonde; the abbé sympathized with his grief; he had only a small share in the fifty thousand francs which Candide lost at cards, and in the proceeds of the two diamonds which had been half-given, half-extorted. His scheme was to profit, as much as he could, from the advantage of knowing Candide. He spoke at length of Cunégonde, and Candide told him that he would beg forgiveness for his beloved for his infidelity when he met her at Venice.

The Perigordian overflowed with politeness and unction, taking a tender interest in everything Candide said, everything he did, and everything he wanted to do.

—Well, sir, said he, so you have an assignation at Venice?

—Yes indeed, sir, I do, said Candide; it is absolutely imperative that I go there to find Miss Cunégonde.

And then, carried away by the pleasure of talking about his love, he recounted, as he often did, a part of his adventures with that illustrious lady of Westphalia.

—I suppose, said the abbé, that Miss Cunégonde has a fine wit and writes charming letters.

—I never received a single letter from her, said Candide; for, as you can imagine, after being driven out of the castle for love of her, I couldn't write; shortly I learned that she was dead; then I rediscovered her; then I lost her again, and I have now sent, to a place more than twenty-five hundred leagues from here, a special agent whose return I am expecting.

The abbé listened carefully, and looked a bit dreamy. He soon took his leave of the two strangers, after embracing them tenderly. Next day Candide, when he woke up, received a letter, to the following effect:

—Dear sir, my very dear lover, I have been lying sick in this town for a week, I have just learned that you are here. I would fly to your arms if I could move. I heard that you had passed through Bordeaux; that was where I left the faithful Cacambo and the old woman, who are soon to follow me here. The governor of Buenos Aires took everything, but left me your heart. Come; your presence will either return me to life or cause me to die of joy.

This charming letter, coming so unexpectedly, filled Candide with inexpressible delight, while the illness of his dear Cunégonde covered him with grief. Torn between these two feelings, he took gold and diamonds, and had himself brought, with Martin, to the hotel where Miss Cunégonde was lodging. Trembling with emotion, he enters the room; his heart thumps, his voice breaks. He tries to open the curtains of the bed, he asks to have some lights.

—Absolutely forbidden, says the serving girl; light will be the death of her.

And abruptly she pulls shut the curtain.

—My dear Cunégonde, says Candide in tears, how are you feeling? If you can't see me, won't you at least speak to me?

—She can't talk, says the servant.

But then she draws forth from the bed a plump hand, over which Candide weeps a long time, and which he fills with diamonds, meanwhile leaving a bag of gold on the chair.

Amid his transports, there arrives a bailiff followed by the abbé from Perigord and a strong-arm squad.

—These here are the suspicious foreigners? says the officer; and he has them seized and orders his bullies to drag them off to jail.

—They don't treat visitors like this in Eldorado, says Candide.

—I am more a Manichee than ever, says Martin.

—But, please sir, where are you taking us? says Candide.

—To the lowest hole in the dungeons, says the bailiff.

Martin, having regained his self-possession, decided that the lady who pretended to be Cunégonde was a cheat, the abbé from Perigord was another cheat who had imposed on Candide's innocence, and the bailiff still another cheat, of whom it would be easy to get rid.

Rather than submit to the forms of justice, Candide, enlightened by Martin's advice and eager for his own part to see the real Cunégonde again, offered the bailiff three little diamonds worth about three thousand pistoles apiece.

—Ah, my dear sir! cried the man with the ivory staff, even if you have committed every crime imaginable, you are the most honest man in the world. Three diamonds! each one worth three thousand pistoles! My dear sir! I would gladly die for you, rather than take you to jail. All foreigners get arrested here; but let me manage it; I have a brother at Dieppe in Normandy; I'll take you to him; and if you have a bit of a diamond to give him, he'll take care of you, just like me.

—And why do they arrest all foreigners? asked Candide.

The abbé from Perigord spoke up and said:—It's because a beggar from Atrebatum[2] listened to some stupidities; that made him commit a parricide, not like the one of May, 1610, but like the one of December, 1594, much on the order of several other crimes committed in other years and other months by other beggars who had listened to stupidities.

The bailiff then explained what it was all about.[3]

—Foh! what beasts! cried Candide. What! monstrous behavior of this sort from a people who sing and dance? As soon as I can, let me get out of this country, where the monkeys provoke the tigers. In my own country I've lived with bears; only in Eldorado are there proper men. In the name of God, sir bailiff, get me to Venice where I can wait for Miss Cunégonde.

—I can only get you to Lower Normandy, said the guardsman.

He had the irons removed at once, said there had been a mistake, dismissed his gang, and took Candide and Martin to Dieppe, where he left them with his brother. There was a little Dutch ship at anchor. The Norman, changed by three more diamonds into the most helpful of men, put Candide and his people aboard the vessel, which was bound for Portsmouth in England. It wasn't on the way to Venice, but Candide felt like a man just let out of hell; and he hoped to get back on the road to Venice at the first possible occasion.

---

2. The Latin name for the district of Artois, from which came Robert-François Damiens, who tried to stab Louis XV in 1757. The assassination failed, like that of Châtel, who tried to kill Henri IV in 1594, but unlike that of Ravaillac, who succeeded in killing him in 1610.
3. The point, in fact, is not too clear since arresting foreigners is an indirect way at best to guard against homegrown fanatics, and the position of the abbé from Perigord in the whole transaction remains confused. Has he called in the officer just to get rid of Candide? If so, why is he sardonic about the very suspicions he is trying to foster? Candide's reaction is to the notion that Frenchmen should be capable of political assassination at all; it seems excessive.

CHAPTER 23

Candide and Martin Pass the Shores of England;
What They See There

—Ah, Pangloss! Pangloss! Ah, Martin! Martin! Ah, my darling Cunégonde! What is this world of ours? sighed Candide on the Dutch vessel.

—Something crazy, something abominable, Martin replied.

—You have been in England; are people as crazy there as in France?

—It's a different sort of crazy, said Martin. You know that these two nations have been at war over a few acres of snow near Canada, and that they are spending on this fine struggle more than Canada itself is worth.[4] As for telling you if there are more people in one country or the other who need a strait jacket, that is a judgment too fine for my understanding; I know only that the people we are going to visit are eaten up with melancholy.

As they chatted thus, the vessel touched at Portsmouth. A multitude of people covered the shore, watching closely a rather bulky man who was kneeling, his eyes blindfolded, on the deck of a man-of-war. Four soldiers, stationed directly in front of this man, fired three bullets apiece into his brain, as peaceably as you would want; and the whole assemblage went home, in great satisfaction.[5]

—What's all this about? asked Candide. What devil is everywhere at work?

He asked who was that big man who had just been killed with so much ceremony.

—It was an admiral, they told him.

—And why kill this admiral?

—The reason, they told him, is that he didn't kill enough people; he gave battle to a French admiral, and it was found that he didn't get close enough to him.

—But, said Candide, the French admiral was just as far from the English admiral as the English admiral was from the French admiral.

—That's perfectly true, came the answer; but in this country it is useful from time to time to kill one admiral in order to encourage the others.

Candide was so stunned and shocked at what he saw and heard, that he would not even set foot ashore; he arranged with the Dutch merchant (without even caring if he was robbed, as at Surinam) to be taken forthwith to Venice.

The merchant was ready in two days; they coasted along France, they passed within sight of Lisbon, and Candide quivered. They entered the straits, crossed the Mediterranean, and finally landed at Venice.

—God be praised, said Candide, embracing Martin; here I shall recover the lovely Cunégonde. I trust Cacambo as I would myself. All is well, all goes well, all goes as well as possible.

4. The wars of the French and English over Canada dragged intermittently through the 18th century till the peace of Paris sealed England's conquest (1763). Voltaire thought the French should concentrate on developing Louisiana, where the Jesuit influence was less marked.

5. Candide has witnessed the execution of Admiral John Byng, defeated off Minorca by the French fleet under Galisonnière and executed by firing squad on March 14, 1757. Voltaire had intervened to avert the execution.

CHAPTER 24

About Paquette and Brother Giroflée

As soon as he was in Venice, he had a search made for Cacambo in all the inns, all the cafés, all the stews—and found no trace of him. Every day he sent to investigate the vessels and coastal traders; no news of Cacambo.

—How's this? said he to Martin. I have had time to go from Surinam to Bordeaux, from Bordeaux to Paris, from Paris to Dieppe, from Dieppe to Portsmouth, to skirt Portugal and Spain, cross the Mediterranean, and spend several months at Venice—and the lovely Cunégonde has not come yet! In her place, I have met only that impersonator and that abbé from Perigord. Cunégonde is dead, without a doubt; and nothing remains for me too but death. Oh, it would have been better to stay in the earthly paradise of Eldorado than to return to this accursed Europe. How right you are, my dear Martin; all is but illusion and disaster.

He fell into a black melancholy, and refused to attend the fashionable operas or take part in the other diversions of the carnival season; not a single lady tempted him in the slightest. Martin told him:—You're a real simpleton if you think a half-breed valet with five or six millions in his pockets will go to the end of the world to get your mistress and bring her to Venice for you. If he finds her, he'll take her for himself; if he doesn't, he'll take another. I advise you to forget about your servant Cacambo and your mistress Cunégonde.

Martin was not very comforting. Candide's melancholy increased, and Martin never wearied of showing him that there is little virtue and little happiness on this earth, except perhaps in Eldorado, where nobody can go.

While they were discussing this important matter and still waiting for Cunégonde, Candide noticed in St. Mark's Square a young Theatine[6] monk who had given his arm to a girl. The Theatine seemed fresh, plump, and flourishing; his eyes were bright, his manner cocky, his glance brilliant, his step proud. The girl was very pretty, and singing aloud; she glanced lovingly at her Theatine, and from time to time pinched his plump cheeks.

—At least you must admit, said Candide to Martin, that these people are happy. Until now I have not found in the whole inhabited earth, except Eldorado, anything but miserable people. But this girl and this monk, I'd be willing to bet, are very happy creatures.

—I'll bet they aren't, said Martin.

—We have only to ask them to dinner, said Candide, and we'll find out if I'm wrong.

Promptly he approached them, made his compliments, and invited them to his inn for a meal of macaroni, Lombardy partridges, and caviar, washed down with wine from Montepulciano, Cyprus, and Samos, and some Lacrima Christi. The girl blushed but the Theatine accepted gladly, and the girl followed him, watching Candide with an expression of surprise and confusion, darkened by several tears. Scarcely had she entered the room when she said to Candide:—What, can it be that Master Candide no longer knows Paquette?

At these words Candide, who had not yet looked carefully at her because he was preoccupied with Cunégonde, said to her:—Ah, my poor child! so you are the one who put Doctor Pangloss in the fine fix where I last saw him.

6. A Catholic order founded in 1524 by Cardinal Cajetan and G. P. Caraffa, later Pope Paul IV.

—Alas, sir, I was the one, said Paquette; I see you know all about it. I heard of the horrible misfortunes which befell the whole household of My Lady the Baroness and the lovely Cunégonde. I swear to you that my own fate has been just as unhappy. I was perfectly innocent when you knew me. A Franciscan, who was my confessor, easily seduced me. The consequences were frightful; shortly after My Lord the Baron had driven you out with great kicks on the backside, I too was forced to leave the castle. If a famous doctor had not taken pity on me, I would have died. Out of gratitude, I became for some time the mistress of this doctor. His wife, who was jealous to the point of frenzy, beat me mercilessly every day; she was a gorgon. The doctor was the ugliest of men, and I the most miserable creature on earth, being continually beaten for a man I did not love. You will understand, sir, how dangerous it is for a nagging woman to be married to a doctor. This man, enraged by his wife's ways, one day gave her as a cold cure a medicine so potent that in two hours' time she died amid horrible convulsions. Her relatives brought suit against the bereaved husband; he fled the country, and I was put in prison. My innocence would never have saved me if I had not been rather pretty. The judge set me free on condition that he should become the doctor's successor. I was shortly replaced in this post by another girl, dismissed without any payment, and obliged to continue this abominable trade which you men find so pleasant and which for us is nothing but a bottomless pit of misery. I went to ply the trade in Venice. Ah, my dear sir, if you could imagine what it is like to have to caress indiscriminately an old merchant, a lawyer, a monk, a gondolier, an abbé; to be subjected to every sort of insult and outrage; to be reduced, time and again, to borrowing a skirt in order to go have it lifted by some disgusting man; to be robbed by this fellow of what one has gained from that; to be shaken down by the police, and to have before one only the prospect of a hideous old age, a hospital, and a dunghill, you will conclude that I am one of the most miserable creatures in the world.

Thus Paquette poured forth her heart to the good Candide in a hotel room, while Martin sat listening nearby. At last he said to Candide:—You see, I've already won half my bet.

Brother Giroflée[7] had remained in the dining room, and was having a drink before dinner.

—But how's this? said Candide to Paquette. You looked so happy, so joyous, when I met you; you were singing, you caressed the Theatine with such a natural air of delight; you seemed to me just as happy as you now say you are miserable.

—Ah, sir, replied Paquette, that's another one of the miseries of this business; yesterday I was robbed and beaten by an officer, and today I have to seem in good humor in order to please a monk.

Candide wanted no more; he conceded that Martin was right. They sat down to table with Paquette and the Theatine; the meal was amusing enough, and when it was over, the company spoke out among themselves with some frankness.

—Father, said Candide to the monk, you seem to me a man whom all the world might envy; the flower of health glows in your cheek, your features radiate pleasure; you have a pretty girl for your diversion, and you seem very happy with your life as a Theatine.

—Upon my word, sir, said Brother Giroflée, I wish that all the Theatines were at the bottom of the sea. A hundred times I have been tempted to set fire to my

7. His name means "carnation" and Paquette means "daisy."

convent, and go turn Turk. My parents forced me, when I was fifteen years old, to put on this detestable robe, so they could leave more money to a cursed older brother of mine, may God confound him! Jealousy, faction, and fury spring up, by natural law, within the walls of convents. It is true, I have preached a few bad sermons which earned me a little money, half of which the prior stole from me; the remainder serves to keep me in girls. But when I have to go back to the monastery at night, I'm ready to smash my head against the walls of my cell; and all my fellow monks are in the same fix.

Martin turned to Candide and said with his customary coolness:

—Well, haven't I won the whole bet?

Candide gave two thousand piastres to Paquette and a thousand to Brother Giroflée.

—I assure you, said he, that with that they will be happy.

—I don't believe so, said Martin; your piastres may make them even more unhappy than they were before.

—That may be, said Candide; but one thing comforts me, I note that people often turn up whom one never expected to see again; it may well be that, having rediscovered my red sheep and Paquette, I will also rediscover Cunégonde.

—I hope, said Martin, that she will some day make you happy; but I very much doubt it.

—You're a hard man, said Candide.

—I've lived, said Martin.

—But look at these gondoliers, said Candide; aren't they always singing?

—You don't see them at home, said Martin, with their wives and squalling children. The doge has his troubles, the gondoliers theirs. It's true that on the whole one is better off as a gondolier than as a doge; but the difference is so slight, I don't suppose it's worth the trouble of discussing.

—There's a lot of talk here, said Candide, of this Senator Pococurante,[8] who has a fine palace on the Brenta and is hospitable to foreigners. They say he is a man who has never known a moment's grief.

—I'd like to see such a rare specimen, said Martin.

Candide promptly sent to Lord Pococurante, asking permission to call on him tomorrow.

CHAPTER 25
Visit to Lord Pococurante, Venetian Nobleman

Candide and Martin took a gondola on the Brenta, and soon reached the palace of the noble Pococurante. The gardens were large and filled with beautiful marble statues; the palace was handsomely designed. The master of the house, sixty years old and very rich, received his two inquisitive visitors perfectly politely, but with very little warmth; Candide was disconcerted and Martin not at all displeased.

First two pretty and neatly dressed girls served chocolate, which they whipped to a froth. Candide could not forbear praising their beauty, their grace, their skill.

—They are pretty good creatures, said Pococurante; I sometimes have them into my bed, for I'm tired of the ladies of the town, with their stupid tricks, quarrels, jealousies, fits of ill humor and petty pride, and all the sonnets one has to make or order for them; but, after all, these two girls are starting to bore me too.

8. His name means "small care."

After lunch, Candide strolled through a long gallery, and was amazed at the beauty of the pictures. He asked who was the painter of the two finest.

—They are by Raphael, said the senator; I bought them for a lot of money, out of vanity, some years ago; people say they're the finest in Italy, but they don't please me at all; the colors have all turned brown, the figures aren't well modeled and don't stand out enough, the draperies bear no resemblance to real cloth. In a word, whatever people may say, I don't find in them a real imitation of nature. I like a picture only when I can see in it a touch of nature itself, and there are none of this sort. I have many paintings, but I no longer look at them.

As they waited for dinner, Pococurante ordered a concerto performed. Candide found the music delightful.

—That noise? said Pococurante. It may amuse you for half an hour, but if it goes on any longer, it tires everybody though no one dares to admit it. Music today is only the art of performing difficult pieces, and what is merely difficult cannot please for long. Perhaps I should prefer the opera, if they had not found ways to make it revolting and monstrous. Anyone who likes bad tragedies set to music is welcome to them; in these performances the scenes serve only to introduce, inappropriately, two or three ridiculous songs designed to show off the actress's sound box. Anyone who wants to, or who can, is welcome to swoon with pleasure at the sight of a castrate wriggling through the role of Caesar or Cato, and strutting awkwardly about the stage. For my part, I have long since given up these paltry trifles which are called the glory of modern Italy, and for which monarchs pay such ruinous prices.

Candide argued a bit, but timidly; Martin was entirely of a mind with the senator.

They sat down to dinner, and after an excellent meal adjourned to the library. Candide, seeing a copy of Homer in a splendid binding, complimented the noble lord on his good taste.

—That is an author, said he, who was the special delight of great Pangloss, the best philosopher in all Germany.

—He's no special delight of mine, said Pococurante coldly. I was once made to believe that I took pleasure in reading him; but that constant recital of fights which are all alike, those gods who are always interfering but never decisively, that Helen who is the cause of the war and then scarcely takes any part in the story, that Troy which is always under siege and never taken—all that bores me to tears. I have sometimes asked scholars if reading it bored them as much as it bores me; everyone who answered frankly told me the book dropped from his hands like lead, but that they had to have it in their libraries as a monument of antiquity, like those old rusty coins which can't be used in real trade.

Your Excellence doesn't hold the same opinion of Virgil? said Candide.

—I concede, said Pococurante, that the second, fourth, and sixth books of his *Aeneid* are fine; but as for his pious Aeneas, and strong Cloanthes, and faithful Achates, and little Ascanius, and that imbecile King Latinus, and middle-class Amata, and insipid Lavinia, I don't suppose there was ever anything so cold and unpleasant. I prefer Tasso and those sleepwalkers' stories of Ariosto.

—Dare I ask, sir, said Candide, if you don't get great enjoyment from reading Horace?

—There are some maxims there, said Pococurante, from which a man of the world can profit, and which, because they are formed into vigorous couplets, are more easily remembered; but I care very little for his trip to Brindisi, his description of a bad dinner, or his account of a quibblers' squabble between some fellow

Pupilus, whose words he says *were full of pus*, and another whose words *were full of vinegar*.[9] I feel nothing but extreme disgust at his verses against old women and witches; and I can't see what's so great in his telling his friend Maecenas that if he is raised by him to the ranks of lyric poets, he will strike the stars with his lofty forehead. Fools admire everything in a well-known author. I read only for my own pleasure; I like only what is in my style.

Candide, who had been trained never to judge for himself, was much astonished by what he heard; and Martin found Pococurante's way of thinking quite rational.

—Oh, here is a copy of Cicero, said Candide. Now this great man I suppose you're never tired of reading.

—I never read him at all, replied the Venetian. What do I care whether he pleaded for Rabirius or Cluentius? As a judge, I have my hands full of lawsuits. I might like his philosophical works better, but when I saw that he had doubts about everything, I concluded that I knew as much as he did, and that I needed no help to be ignorant.

—Ah, here are eighty volumes of collected papers from a scientific academy, cried Martin; maybe there is something good in them.

—There would be indeed, said Pococurante, if one of these silly authors had merely discovered a new way of making pins; but in all those volumes there is nothing but empty systems, not a single useful discovery.

—What a lot of stage plays I see over there, said Candide, some in Italian, some in Spanish and French.

—Yes, said the senator, three thousand of them, and not three dozen good ones. As for those collections of sermons, which all together are not worth a page of Seneca, and all these heavy volumes of theology, you may be sure I never open them, nor does anybody else.

Martin noticed some shelves full of English books.

—I suppose, said he, that a republican must delight in most of these books written in the land of liberty.

—Yes, replied Pococurante, it's a fine thing to write as you think; it is mankind's privilege. In all our Italy, people write only what they do not think; men who inhabit the land of the Caesars and Antonines dare not have an idea without the permission of a Dominican. I would rejoice in the freedom that breathes through English genius, if partisan passions did not corrupt all that is good in that precious freedom.

Candide, noting a Milton, asked if he did not consider this author a great man.

—Who? said Pococurante. That barbarian who made a long commentary on the first chapter of Genesis in ten books of crabbed verse?[1] That clumsy imitator of the Greeks, who disfigures creation itself, and while Moses represents the eternal being as creating the world with a word, has the messiah take a big compass out of a heavenly cupboard in order to design his work? You expect me to admire the man who spoiled Tasso's hell and devil? who disguises Lucifer now as a toad, now as a pigmy? who makes him rehash the same arguments a hundred times

---

9. *Satires* 1.7; Pococurante, with gentlemanly negligence, has corrupted Rupilius to Pupilus. Horace's poems against witches are *Epodes* 5.8, 12; the one about striking the stars with

his lofty forehead is *Odes* 1.1.
1. The first edition of *Paradise Lost* had ten books, which Milton later expanded to twelve.

over? who makes him argue theology? and who, taking seriously Ariosto's comic story of the invention of firearms, has the devils shooting off cannon in heaven? Neither I nor anyone else in Italy has been able to enjoy these gloomy extravagances. The marriage of Sin and Death, and the monster that Sin gives birth to, will nauseate any man whose taste is at all refined; and his long description of a hospital is good only for a gravedigger. This obscure, extravagant, and disgusting poem was despised at its birth; I treat it today as it was treated in its own country by its contemporaries. Anyhow, I say what I think, and care very little whether other people agree with me.

Candide was a little cast down by this speech; he respected Homer, and had a little affection for Milton.

—Alas, he said under his breath to Martin, I'm afraid this man will have a supreme contempt for our German poets.

—No harm in that, said Martin.

—Oh what a superior man, said Candide, still speaking softly, what a great genius this Pococurante must be! Nothing can please him.

Having thus looked over all the books, they went down into the garden. Candide praised its many beauties.

—I know nothing in such bad taste, said the master of the house; we have nothing but trifles here; tomorrow I am going to have one set out on a nobler design.

When the two visitors had taken leave of his excellency:—Well now, said Candide to Martin, you must agree that this was the happiest of all men, for he is superior to everything he possesses.

—Don't you see, said Martin, that he is disgusted with everything he possesses? Plato said, a long time ago, that the best stomachs are not those which refuse all food.

—But, said Candide, isn't there pleasure in criticizing everything, in seeing faults where other people think they see beauties?

—That is to say, Martin replied, that there's pleasure in having no pleasure?

—Oh well, said Candide, then I am the only happy man . . . or will be, when I see Miss Cunégonde again.

—It's always a good thing to have hope, said Martin.

But the days and the weeks slipped past; Cacambo did not come back, and Candide was so buried in his grief, that he did not even notice that Paquette and Brother Giroflée had neglected to come and thank him.

CHAPTER 26

About a Supper that Candide and Martin Had with Six Strangers, and Who They Were

One evening when Candide, accompanied by Martin, was about to sit down for dinner with the strangers staying in his hotel, a man with a soot-colored face came up behind him, took him by the arm, and said:—Be ready to leave with us, don't miss out.

He turned and saw Cacambo. Only the sight of Cunégonde could have astonished and pleased him more. He nearly went mad with joy. He embraced his dear friend.

—Cunégonde is here, no doubt? Where is she? Bring me to her, let me die of joy in her presence.

—Cunégonde is not here at all, said Cacambo, she is at Constantinople.

—Good Heavens, at Constantinople! but if she were in China, I must fly there, let's go.

—We will leave after supper, said Cacambo; I can tell you no more; I am a slave, my owner is looking for me, I must go wait on him at table; mum's the word; eat your supper and be prepared.

Candide, torn between joy and grief, delighted to have seen his faithful agent again, astonished to find him a slave, full of the idea of recovering his mistress, his heart in a turmoil, his mind in a whirl, sat down to eat with Martin, who was watching all these events coolly, and with six strangers who had come to pass the carnival season at Venice.

Cacambo, who was pouring wine for one of the strangers, leaned respectfully over his master at the end of the meal, and said to him:—Sire, Your Majesty may leave when he pleases, the vessel is ready.

Having said these words, he exited. The diners looked at one another in silent amazement, when another servant, approaching his master, said to him:—Sire, Your Majesty's litter is at Padua, and the bark awaits you.

The master nodded, and the servant vanished. All the diners looked at one another again, and the general amazement redoubled. A third servant, approaching a third stranger, said to him:—Sire, take my word for it, Your Majesty must stay here no longer; I shall get everything ready.

Then he too disappeared.

Candide and Martin had no doubt, now, that it was a carnival masquerade. A fourth servant spoke to a fourth master:—Your Majesty will leave when he pleases—and went out like the others. A fifth followed suit. But the sixth servant spoke differently to the sixth stranger, who sat next to Candide. He said:—My word, sire, they'll give no more credit to Your Majesty, nor to me either; we could very well spend the night in the lockup, you and I. I've got to look out for myself, so good-bye to you.

When all the servants had left, the six strangers, Candide, and Martin remained under a pall of silence. Finally Candide broke it.

—Gentlemen, said he, here's a funny kind of joke. Why are you all royalty? I assure you that Martin and I aren't.

Cacambo's master spoke up gravely then, and said in Italian:—This is no joke, my name is Achmet the Third.[2] I was grand sultan for several years; then, as I had dethroned my brother, my nephew dethroned me. My viziers had their throats cut; I was allowed to end my days in the old seraglio. My nephew, the Grand Sultan Mahmoud, sometimes lets me travel for my health; and I have come to spend the carnival season at Venice.

A young man who sat next to Achmet spoke after him, and said:—My name is Ivan; I was once emperor of all the Russias.[3] I was dethroned while still in my cradle; my father and mother were locked up, and I was raised in prison; I sometimes have permission to travel, though always under guard, and I have come to spend the carnival season at Venice.

The third said:—I am Charles Edward, king of England;[4] my father yielded me his rights to the kingdom, and I fought to uphold them; but they tore out the

2. Ottoman ruler (1673–1736); he was deposed in 1730.
3. Ivan VI reigned from his birth in 1740 until 1756, then was confined in the Schlusselberg, and executed in 1764.

4. This is the Young Pretender (1720–1788), known to his supporters as Bonnie Prince Charlie. The defeat so theatrically described took place at Culloden, April 16, 1746.

hearts of eight hundred of my partisans, and flung them in their faces. I have been in prison; now I am going to Rome, to visit the king, my father, dethroned like me and my grandfather; and I have come to pass the carnival season at Venice.

The fourth king then spoke up, and said:—I am a king of the Poles;[5] the luck of war has deprived me of my hereditary estates; my father suffered the same losses; I submit to Providence like Sultan Achmet, Emperor Ivan, and King Charles Edward, to whom I hope heaven grants long lives; and I have come to pass the carnival season at Venice.

The fifth said:—I too am a king of the Poles;[6] I lost my kingdom twice, but Providence gave me another state, in which I have been able to do more good than all the Sarmatian kings ever managed to do on the banks of the Vistula. I too have submitted to Providence, and I have come to pass the carnival season at Venice.

It remained for the sixth monarch to speak.

—Gentlemen, said he, I am no such great lord as you, but I have in fact been a king like any other. I am Theodore; I was elected king of Corsica.[7] People used to call me *Your Majesty*, and now they barely call me *Sir*; I used to coin currency, and now I don't have a cent; I used to have two secretaries of state, and now I scarcely have a valet; I have sat on a throne, and for a long time in London I was in jail, on the straw; and I may well be treated the same way here, though I have come, like your majesties, to pass the carnival season at Venice.

The five other kings listened to his story with noble compassion. Each one of them gave twenty sequins to King Theodore, so that he might buy a suit and some shirts; Candide gave him a diamond worth two thousand sequins.

—Who in the world, said the five kings, is this private citizen who is in a position to give a hundred times as much as any of us, and who actually gives it?[8]

Just as they were rising from dinner, there arrived at the same establishment four most serene highnesses, who had also lost their kingdoms through the luck of war, and who came to spend the rest of the carnival season at Venice. But Candide never bothered even to look at these newcomers because he was only concerned to go find his dear Cunégonde at Constantinople.

CHAPTER 27

Candide's Trip to Constantinople

Faithful Cacambo had already arranged with the Turkish captain who was returning Sultan Achmet to Constantinople to make room for Candide and Martin on board. Both men boarded ship after prostrating themselves before his miserable highness. On the way, Candide said to Martin:—Six dethroned kings that we had dinner with! and yet among those six there was one on whom I had to bestow charity! Perhaps there are other princes even more unfortunate. I myself

---

5. Augustus III (1696–1763), Elector of Saxony and King of Poland, dethroned by Frederick the Great in 1756.
6. Stanislas Leczinski (1677–1766), father-in-law of Louis XV, who abdicated the throne of Poland in 1736, was made Duke of Lorraine and in that capacity befriended Voltaire.
7. Theodore von Neuhof (1690–1756), an authentic Westphalian, an adventurer and a soldier of fortune, who in 1736 was (for about eight months) the elected king of Corsica. He spent time in an Amsterdam as well as a London debtor's prison.
8. Voltaire was very conscious of his situation as a man richer than many princes; in 1758 he had money on loan to no fewer than three highnesses, Charles Eugene, Duke of Wurtemburg; Charles Theodore, Elector Palatine; and the Duke of Saxe-Gotha.

have only lost a hundred sheep, and now I am flying to the arms of Cunégonde. My dear Martin, once again Pangloss is proved right, all is for the best.

—I hope so, said Martin.

—But, said Candide, that was a most unlikely experience we had at Venice. Nobody ever saw, or heard tell of, six dethroned kings eating together at an inn.

—It is no more extraordinary, said Martin, than most of the things that have happened to us. Kings are frequently dethroned; and as for the honor we had from dining with them, that's a trifle which doesn't deserve our notice.[9]

Scarcely was Candide on board than he fell on the neck of his former servant, his friend Cacambo.

—Well! said he, what is Cunégonde doing? Is she still a marvel of beauty? Does she still love me? How is her health? No doubt you have bought her a palace at Constantinople.

—My dear master, answered Cacambo, Cunégonde is washing dishes on the shores of the Propontis, in the house of a prince who has very few dishes to wash; she is a slave in the house of a onetime king named Ragotski,[1] to whom the Great Turk allows three crowns a day in his exile; but, what is worse than all this, she has lost all her beauty and become horribly ugly.

—Ah, beautiful or ugly, said Candide, I am an honest man, and my duty is to love her forever. But how can she be reduced to this wretched state with the five or six millions that you had?

—All right, said Cacambo, didn't I have to give two millions to Señor don Fernando d'Ibaraa y Figueroa y Mascarenes y Lampourdos y Souza, governor of Buenos Aires, for his permission to carry off Miss Cunégonde? And didn't a pirate cleverly strip us of the rest? And didn't this pirate carry us off to Cape Matapan, to Melos, Nicaria, Samos, Petra, to the Dardanelles, Marmora, Scutari? Cunégonde and the old woman are working for the prince I told you about, and I am the slave of the dethroned sultan.

—What a lot of fearful calamities linked one to the other, said Candide. But after all, I still have a few diamonds, I shall easily deliver Cunégonde. What a pity that she's become so ugly!

Then, turning toward Martin, he asked:—Who in your opinion is more to be pitied, the Emperor Achmet, the Emperor Ivan, King Charles Edward, or myself?

—I have no idea, said Martin; I would have to enter your hearts in order to tell.

—Ah, said Candide, if Pangloss were here, he would know and he would tell us.

—I can't imagine, said Martin, what scales your Pangloss would use to weigh out the miseries of men and value their griefs. All I will venture is that the earth holds millions of men who deserve our pity a hundred times more than King Charles Edward, Emperor Ivan, or Sultan Achmet.

—You may well be right, said Candide.

In a few days they arrived at the Black Sea canal. Candide began by repurchasing Cacambo at an exorbitant price; then, without losing an instant, he flung himself and his companions into a galley to go search out Cunégonde on the shores of Propontis, however ugly she might be.

There were in the chain gang two convicts who bent clumsily to the oar, and on whose bare shoulders the Levantine[2] captain delivered from time to time a few

9. Another late change adds the following question:—*What does it matter whom you dine with as long as you fare well at table?* I have omitted it, again on literary grounds.
1. Francis Leopold Rakoczy (1676–1735),

who was briefly king of Transylvania in the early 18th century. After 1720 he was interned in Turkey.
2. From the eastern Mediterranean.

lashes with a bullwhip. Candide naturally noticed them more than the other galley slaves, and out of pity came closer to them. Certain features of their disfigured faces seemed to him to bear a slight resemblance to Pangloss and to that wretched Jesuit, that baron, that brother of Miss Cunégonde. The notion stirred and saddened him. He looked at them more closely.

—To tell you the truth, he said to Cacambo, if I hadn't seen Master Pangloss hanged, and if I hadn't been so miserable as to murder the baron, I should think they were rowing in this very galley.

At the names of 'baron' and 'Pangloss' the two convicts gave a great cry, sat still on their bench, and dropped their oars. The Levantine captain came running, and the bullwhip lashes redoubled.

—Stop, stop, captain, cried Candide. I'll give you as much money as you want.

—What, can it be Candide? cried one of the convicts.

—What, can it be Candide? cried the other.

—Is this a dream? said Candide. Am I awake or asleep? Am I in this galley? Is that My Lord the Baron, whom I killed? Is that Master Pangloss, whom I saw hanged?

—It is indeed, they replied.

—What, is that the great philosopher? said Martin.

—Now, sir, Mr. Levantine Captain, said Candide, how much money do you want for the ransom of My Lord Thunder-Ten-Tronckh, one of the first barons of the empire, and Master Pangloss, the deepest metaphysician in all Germany?

—Dog of a Christian, replied the Levantine captain, since these two dogs of Christian convicts are barons and metaphysicians, which is no doubt a great honor in their country, you will give me fifty thousand sequins for them.

—You shall have them, sir, take me back to Constantinople and you shall be paid on the spot. Or no, take me to Miss Cunégonde.

The Levantine captain, at Candide's first word, had turned his bow toward the town, and he had them rowed there as swiftly as a bird cleaves the air.

A hundred times Candide embraced the baron and Pangloss.

—And how does it happen I didn't kill you, my dear baron? and my dear Pangloss, how can you be alive after being hanged? and why are you both rowing in the galleys of Turkey?

—Is it really true that my dear sister is in this country? asked the baron.

—Yes, answered Cacambo.

—And do I really see again my dear Candide? cried Pangloss.

Candide introduced Martin and Cacambo. They all embraced; they all talked at once. The galley flew, already they were back in port. A Jew was called, and Candide sold him for fifty thousand sequins a diamond worth a hundred thousand, while he protested by Abraham that he could not possibly give more for it. Candide immediately ransomed the baron and Pangloss. The latter threw himself at the feet of his liberator, and bathed them with tears; the former thanked him with a nod, and promised to repay this bit of money at the first opportunity.

—But is it really possible that my sister is in Turkey? said he.

—Nothing is more possible, replied Cacambo, since she is a dishwasher in the house of a prince of Transylvania.

At once two more Jews were called; Candide sold some more diamonds; and they all departed in another galley to the rescue of Cunégonde.

CHAPTER 28

What Happened to Candide, Cunégonde, Pangloss, Martin, &c.

—Let me beg your pardon once more, said Candide to the baron, pardon me, reverend father, for having run you through the body with my sword.

—Don't mention it, replied the baron. I was a little too hasty myself, I confess it; but since you want to know the misfortune which brought me to the galleys, I'll tell you. After being cured of my wound by the brother who was apothecary to the college, I was attacked and abducted by a Spanish raiding party; they jailed me in Buenos Aires at the time when my sister had just left. I asked to be sent to Rome, to the father general. Instead, I was named to serve as almoner in Constantinople, under the French ambassador. I had not been a week on this job when I chanced one evening on a very handsome young ichoglan.[3] The evening was hot; the young man wanted to take a swim; I seized the occasion, and went with him. I did not know that it is a capital offense for a Christian to be found naked with a young Moslem. A cadi sentenced me to receive a hundred blows with a cane on the soles of my feet, and then to be sent to the galleys. I don't suppose there was ever such a horrible miscarriage of justice. But I would like to know why my sister is in the kitchen of a Transylvanian king exiled among Turks.

—But how about you, my dear Pangloss, said Candide; how is it possible that we have met again?

—It is true, said Pangloss, that you saw me hanged; in the normal course of things, I should have been burned, but you recall that a cloudburst occurred just as they were about to roast me. So much rain fell that they despaired of lighting the fire; thus I was hanged, for lack of anything better to do with me. A surgeon bought my body, carried me off to his house, and dissected me. First he made a cross-shaped incision in me, from the navel to the clavicle. No one could have been worse hanged than I was. In fact, the executioner of the high ceremonials of the Holy Inquisition, who was a subdeacon, burned people marvelously well, but he was not in the way of hanging them. The rope was wet, and tightened badly; it caught on a knot; in short, I was still breathing. The cross-shaped incision made me scream so loudly that the surgeon fell over backwards; he thought he was dissecting the devil, fled in an agony of fear, and fell downstairs in his flight. His wife ran in, at the noise, from a nearby room; she found me stretched out on the table with my cross-shaped incision, was even more frightened than her husband, fled, and fell over him. When they had recovered a little, I heard her say to him: 'My dear, what were you thinking of, trying to dissect a heretic? Don't you know those people are always possessed of the devil? I'm going to get the priest and have him exorcised.' At these words, I shuddered, and collected my last remaining energies to cry: 'Have mercy on me!' At last the Portuguese barber[4] took courage; he sewed me up again; his wife even nursed me; in two weeks I was up and about. The barber found me a job and made me lackey to a Knight of Malta who was going to Venice; and when this master could no longer pay me, I took service under a Venetian merchant, whom I followed to Constantinople.

—One day it occurred to me to enter a mosque; no one was there but an old imam and a very attractive young worshipper who was saying her prayers. Her bosom was completely bare; and between her two breasts she had a lovely bouquet of tulips, roses, anemones, buttercups, hyacinths, and primroses. She

3. A page to the sultan.
4. The two callings of barber and surgeon, since they both involved sharp instruments, were interchangeable in the early days of medicine.

dropped her bouquet, I picked it up, and returned it to her with the most respectful attentions. I was so long getting it back in place that the imam grew angry, and, seeing that I was a Christian, he called the guard. They took me before the cadi, who sentenced me to receive a hundred blows with a cane on the soles of my feet, and then to be sent to the galleys. I was chained to the same galley and precisely the same bench as My Lord the Baron. There were in this galley four young fellows from Marseilles, five Neapolitan priests, and two Corfu monks, who assured us that these things happen every day. My Lord the Baron asserted that he had suffered a greater injustice than I; I, on the other hand, proposed that it was much more permissible to replace a bouquet in a bosom than to be found naked with an ichoglan. We were arguing the point continually, and getting twenty lashes a day with the bullwhip, when the chain of events within this universe brought you to our galley, and you ransomed us.

—Well, my dear Pangloss, Candide said to him, now that you have been hanged, dissected, beaten to a pulp, and sentenced to the galleys, do you still think everything is for the best in this world?

—I am still of my first opinion, replied Pangloss; for after all I am a philosopher, and it would not be right for me to recant since Leibniz could not possibly be wrong, and besides pre-established harmony is the finest notion in the world, like the plenum and subtle matter.[5]

CHAPTER 29

How Candide Found Cunégonde and the Old Woman Again

While Candide, the baron, Pangloss, Martin, and Cacambo were telling one another their stories, while they were disputing over the contingent or non-contingent events of this universe, while they were arguing over effects and causes, over moral evil and physical evil, over liberty and necessity, and over the consolations available to one in a Turkish galley, they arrived at the shores of Propontis and the house of the prince of Transylvania. The first sight to meet their eyes was Cunégonde and the old woman, who were hanging out towels on lines to dry.

The baron paled at what he saw. The tender lover Candide, seeing his lovely Cunégonde with her skin weathered, her eyes bloodshot, her breasts fallen, her cheeks seamed, her arms red and scaly, recoiled three steps in horror, and then advanced only out of politeness. She embraced Candide and her brother; everyone embraced the old woman; Candide ransomed them both.

There was a little farm in the neighborhood; the old woman suggested that Candide occupy it until some better fate should befall the group. Cunégonde did not know she was ugly, no one had told her; she reminded Candide of his promises in so firm a tone that the good Candide did not dare to refuse her. So he went to tell the baron that he was going to marry his sister.

—Never will I endure, said the baron, such baseness on her part, such insolence on yours; this shame at least I will not put up with; why, my sister's children would not be able to enter the Chapters in Germany.[6] No, my sister will never marry anyone but a baron of the empire.

5. Rigorous determinism requires that there be no empty spaces in the universe, so wherever it seems empty, one posits the existence of the "plenum." "Subtle matter" describes the soul, the mind, and all spiritual agencies— which can, therefore, be supposed subject to the influence and control of the great world machine, which is, of course, visibly material. Both are concepts needed to round out the system of optimistic determinism.
6. Knightly assemblies.

Cunégonde threw herself at his feet, and bathed them with her tears; he was inflexible.

—You absolute idiot, Candide told him, I rescued you from the galleys, I paid your ransom, I paid your sister's; she was washing dishes, she is ugly, I am good enough to make her my wife, and you still presume to oppose it! If I followed my impulses, I would kill you all over again.

—You may kill me again, said the baron, but you will not marry my sister while I am alive.

CHAPTER 30
Conclusion

At heart, Candide had no real wish to marry Cunégonde; but the baron's extreme impertinence decided him in favor of the marriage, and Cunégonde was so eager for it that he could not back out. He consulted Pangloss, Martin, and the faithful Cacambo. Pangloss drew up a fine treatise, in which he proved that the baron had no right over his sister and that she could, according to all the laws of the empire, marry Candide morganatically.[7] Martin said they should throw the baron into the sea. Cacambo thought they should send him back to the Levantine captain to finish his time in the galleys, and then send him to the father general in Rome by the first vessel. This seemed the best idea; the old woman approved, and nothing was said to his sister; the plan was executed, at modest expense, and they had the double pleasure of snaring a Jesuit and punishing the pride of a German baron.

It is quite natural to suppose that after so many misfortunes, Candide, married to his mistress, and living with the philosopher Pangloss, the philosopher Martin, the prudent Cacambo, and the old woman—having, besides, brought back so many diamonds from the land of the ancient Incas—must have led the most agreeable life in the world. But he was so cheated by the Jews[8] that nothing was left but his little farm; his wife, growing every day more ugly, became sour-tempered and insupportable; the old woman was ailing and even more ill-humored than Cunégonde. Cacambo, who worked in the garden and went into Constantinople to sell vegetables, was worn out with toil, and cursed his fate. Pangloss was in despair at being unable to shine in some German university. As for Martin, he was firmly persuaded that things are just as bad wherever you are; he endured in patience. Candide, Martin, and Pangloss sometimes argued over metaphysics and morals. Before the windows of the farmhouse they often watched the passage of boats bearing effendis, pashas, and cadis into exile on Lemnos, Mytilene, and Erzeroum; they saw other cadis, other pashas, other effendis coming, to take the place of the exiles and to be exiled in their turn. They saw various heads, neatly impaled, to be set up at the Sublime Porte.[9] These sights gave fresh impetus to their discussions; and when they were not arguing, the boredom was so fierce that one day the old woman ventured to say:—I should like to know which is worse, being raped a hundred times by negro pirates, having a buttock cut off, running the gauntlet in the Bulgar army, being flogged and hanged in an auto-da-fé, being

---

7. A morganatic marriage confers no rights on the partner of lower rank or on the offspring.
8. Voltaire's anti-Semitism, derived from various unhappy experiences with Jewish financiers, is not the most attractive aspect of his personality.

9. The gate of the sultan's palace is often used by extension to describe his government as a whole. But it was in fact a real gate where the heads of traitors and public enemies were gruesomely exposed.

dissected and rowing in the galleys—experiencing, in a word, all the miseries through which we have passed—or else just sitting here and doing nothing?

—It's a hard question, said Candide.

These words gave rise to new reflections, and Martin in particular concluded that man was bound to live either in convulsions of misery or in the lethargy of boredom. Candide did not agree, but expressed no positive opinion. Pangloss asserted that he had always suffered horribly; but having once declared that everything was marvelously well, he continued to repeat the opinion and didn't believe a word of it.

One thing served to confirm Martin in his detestable opinions, to make Candide hesitate more than ever, and to embarrass Pangloss. It was the arrival one day at their farm of Paquette and Brother Giroflée, who were in the last stages of misery. They had quickly run through their three thousand piastres, had split up, made up, quarreled, been jailed, escaped, and finally Brother Giroflée had turned Turk. Paquette continued to ply her trade everywhere, and no longer made any money at it.

—I told you, said Martin to Candide, that your gifts would soon be squandered and would only render them more unhappy. You have spent millions of piastres, you and Cacambo, and you are no more happy than Brother Giroflée and Paquette.

—Ah ha, said Pangloss to Paquette, so destiny has brought you back in our midst, my poor girl! Do you realize you cost me the end of my nose, one eye, and an ear? And look at you now! eh! what a world it is, after all!

This new adventure caused them to philosophize more than ever.

There was in the neighborhood a very famous dervish, who was said to be the best philosopher in Turkey; they went to ask his advice. Pangloss was spokesman, and he said:—Master, we have come to ask you to tell us why such a strange animal as man was created.

—What are you getting into? answered the dervish. Is it any of your business?

—But, reverend father, said Candide, there's a horrible lot of evil on the face of the earth.

—What does it matter, said the dervish, whether there's good or evil? When his highness sends a ship to Egypt, does he worry whether the mice on board are comfortable or not?

—What shall we do then? asked Pangloss.

—Hold your tongue, said the dervish.

—I had hoped, said Pangloss, to reason a while with you concerning effects and causes, the best of possible worlds, the origin of evil, the nature of the soul, and pre-established harmony.

At these words, the dervish slammed the door in their faces.

During this interview, word was spreading that at Constantinople they had just strangled two viziers of the divan,[1] as well as the mufti, and impaled several of their friends. This catastrophe made a great and general sensation for several hours. Pangloss, Candide, and Martin, as they returned to their little farm, passed a good old man who was enjoying the cool of the day at his doorstep under a grove of orange trees. Pangloss, who was as inquisitive as he was explanatory, asked the name of the mufti who had been strangled.

—I know nothing of it, said the good man, and I have never cared to know the name of a single mufti or vizier. I am completely ignorant of the episode you are

1. Intimate advisers of the sultan.

discussing. I presume that in general those who meddle in public business sometimes perish miserably, and that they deserve their fate; but I never listen to the
news from Constantinople; I am satisfied with sending the fruits of my garden to
be sold there.

Having spoken these words, he asked the strangers into his house; his two
daughters and two sons offered them various sherbets which they had made
themselves, Turkish cream flavored with candied citron, orange, lemon, lime,
pineapple, pistachio, and mocha coffee uncontaminated by the inferior coffee of
Batavia and the East Indies. After which the two daughters of this good Moslem
perfumed the beards of Candide, Pangloss, and Martin.

—You must possess, Candide said to the Turk, an enormous and splendid
property?

I have only twenty acres, replied the Turk; I cultivate them with my children,
and the work keeps us from three great evils, boredom, vice, and poverty.

Candide, as he walked back to his farm, meditated deeply over the words of the
Turk. He said to Pangloss and Martin:—This good old man seems to have found himself a fate preferable to that of the six kings with whom we had the honor of dining.

—Great place, said Pangloss, is very perilous in the judgment of all the philosophers; for, after all, Eglon, king of the Moabites, was murdered by Ehud; Absalom
was hung up by the hair and pierced with three darts; King Nadab, son of Jero-
boam, was killed by Baasha; King Elah by Zimri; Ahaziah by Jehu; Athaliah by
Jehoiada; and Kings Jehoiakim, Jeconiah, and Zedekiah were enslaved. You know
how death came to Croesus, Astyages, Darius, Dionysius of Syracuse, Pyrrhus,
Perseus, Hannibal, Jugurtha, Ariovistus, Caesar, Pompey, Nero, Otho, Vitellius,
Domitian, Richard II of England, Edward II, Henry VI, Richard III, Mary Stuart,
Charles I, the three Henrys of France, and the Emperor Henry IV? You know . . .

—I know also, said Candide, that we must cultivate our garden.

—You are perfectly right, said Pangloss; for when man was put into the garden
of Eden, he was put there *ut operaretur eum*, so that he should work it; this
proves that man was not born to take his ease.

—Let's work without speculation, said Martin; it's the only way of rendering
life bearable.

The whole little group entered into this laudable scheme; each one began to
exercise his talents. The little plot yielded fine crops. Cunégonde was, to tell the
truth, remarkably ugly; but she became an excellent pastry cook. Paquette took
up embroidery; the old woman did the laundry. Everyone, down even to Brother
Giroflée, did something useful; he became a very adequate carpenter, and even
an honest man; and Pangloss sometimes used to say to Candide:—All events are
linked together in the best of possible worlds for, after all, if you had not been
driven from a fine castle by being kicked in the backside for love of Miss Cunégonde, if you hadn't been sent before the Inquisition, if you hadn't traveled across
America on foot, if you hadn't given a good sword thrust to the baron, if you
hadn't lost all your sheep from the good land of Eldorado, you wouldn't be sitting
here eating candied citron and pistachios.

—That is very well put, said Candide, but we must cultivate our garden.

SAMUEL JOHNSON

1709–1784

Should you focus all of your energy on increasing your wealth? Should you dive into work or revel in idleness? Should you live in a stimulating city or the quiet countryside? Should you become a poet, a scientist, a trader? Should you marry young or wait until you are older—or not marry at all? Johnson's *Rasselas* follows a wealthy prince who has the freedom to adopt any kind of life and who sets out on his travels to determine which choice of life is best. What he discovers is cruelty, envy, delusion, and misery at every turn: "Human life is everywhere a state in which much is to be endured, and little to be enjoyed." And yet, *Rasselas* does not invite us to despair. Samuel Johnson was a famous conversationalist, and his characters' discussions are themselves pleasurable, engaging, and sometimes funny, allowing them to make meaningful connections to one another as they share their difficulties and insights. *Rasselas* never offers us a clear answer about how best to live, but it clearly values the act of throwing ourselves into the world and talking to others about what we can learn from experience.

LIFE

Samuel Johnson's father was a bookseller in Lichfield in the English Midlands. A few years after Samuel's birth in 1709, his father began to pile up huge debts, plunging the family into poverty. Samuel was a precocious child and a sickly one. Scarred by scrofula and smallpox and blind in one eye, he developed a muscular tic that lasted his whole life. He grew to be huge—tall and broad shouldered—and noticeably clumsy. One observer who took him to be an "idiot" at first glance was startled when he began to speak eloquently and wittily.

Johnson spent much of his life struggling to make ends meet. He started at Oxford University but was forced to withdraw after a year for lack of money. (Later Oxford would award him an honorary doctorate, which would allow him to become famous as "Dr. Johnson," but he never did finish his university degree.) He worked in his father's bookshop and tried teaching and some occasional writing, but his future looked dreary, and he sank into periods of depression. At the age of twenty-four, he surprised his friends and family by marrying a widow of forty-five. Johnson spent his wife's fortune establishing a school that quickly failed. Finally, in 1737, he set out for London, where he intended to make a career as a writer. Living apart from his wife, sometimes too poor to afford a bed for a night, Johnson would wander the city until dawn. He did write a great deal—poetry, essays, and a biography—and drew notice as a rising talent. Eventually he undertook a major project that allowed him to pay his bills: a new dictionary of the English language. Previous dictionaries had been poorly organized and focused only on difficult or arcane words. Dr. Johnson's dictionary, first published in 1755, strove to give reliable definitions of all English words in use. It succeeded, becoming the standard English dictionary for over 150 years. It was an astonishing achievement for a single person and a few helpers: Johnson read through the major writers of the previous two centuries, noting down the uses of more than forty thousand English words, comparing them, and bringing together the examples that would best reveal the range of each word's meanings. (For the word *dull,* Johnson's example is "To make dictionaries is dull work.")

While compiling this vast and laborious project, Johnson began to publish regular periodical essays on literature and morality that became immensely popular. *The Rambler* and *The Idler,* essays that appeared a couple of times a week over the course of several years, were sometimes attacked but more often praised, and they established Johnson as a celebrity, "the greatest Genius in the present age." Among his most impressive accomplishments was his skillful writing in a wide array of genres, including biography, poetry, philosophy, drama, and literary criticism. In a single week in 1759, Johnson composed *The History of Rasselas, Prince of Abissinia*, a philosophical story written to defray his mother's funeral expenses. "No man but a blockhead ever wrote, except for money," Johnson is famous for saying.

Politically, Johnson was a self-proclaimed Tory, which meant that he believed in upholding the traditional institutions of the monarchy and the Anglican Church. He objected to Britain's expanding empire and was firmly opposed to slavery. "How is it we hear the loudest yelps for liberty among the drivers of negroes?" he asked, referring to the North American colonies. *Rasselas* became a common name for freed slaves, and at his death Johnson left his estate to a former Jamaican slave, Francis Barber, who had been his servant for thirty years.

Johnson's wife had died in 1752, leaving him desolate. He developed a lively friendship with a literary woman named Hester Thrale, who, to Johnson's grave dismay, eventually chose to marry another man. He also struck up a friendship with a Scotsman named James Boswell, thirty-one years his junior, who took eighteen volumes of notes on Johnson's famously eloquent conversation and used these to craft one of the most famous literary biographies of all time, *The Life of Samuel Johnson* (1791). By the time of his death in 1784, Johnson was unquestionably the most famous literary figure in England.

WORK

In the same year, two literary giants in their own homelands—Voltaire in France and Samuel Johnson in England—wrote brief, popular stories about innocent young men who travel the world, accompanied by their teachers, in search of the best way to live. Voltaire's *Candide* is satirical, while Johnson's *Rasselas* is serious, but both ask us to confront the cruelty and suffering that trouble so much of human experience. The simultaneity of these works was not entirely a coincidence: at a moment when Europeans were encountering peoples around the world, interrogating their own values in relation to those of other cultures, and wondering whether there was anything universal in human nature, travel narratives—both real and fictional—offered an entertaining vehicle for thinking through the most urgent philosophical questions of the day.

Johnson starts his story in Abysinnia, a Christian kingdom in Africa that today is called Ethiopia. Like other "Oriental tales" popular across Europe at the time, the story takes place in an idealized and distant country to the east. As a young man, Johnson had translated an account of a Jesuit missionary in Abyssinia, and he remained fascinated by travel narratives throughout his life, though he himself never traveled farther than Scotland. What is remarkable about *Rasselas*, in this context, is its insistence on the universality of human nature, a depiction of African characters as remarkably similar to eighteenth-century Europeans. This might be seen as a sign of Johnson's ignorance of a world outside of Europe, but it is noteworthy that he does not assume that Europeans alone have reason and moral insight, as some of his contemporaries did. Johnson clearly imagines his African characters as fully human, virtuous, and sympathetic.

The travelers—Prince Rasselas; his sister, Nekayah; their wise teacher, Imlac; and Nekayah's servant, Pekuah—begin the story in "Happy Valley," a beautiful, enclosed place where all material needs are met, where one is constantly entertained and safe from danger. But this site "of pleasure and repose" is not enough for Rasselas, who is curious and imaginative and craves knowledge of a larger world. Johnson thus begins with what we might usually consider the quintessentially happy ending, a utopia of well-being and pleasure. This kind of happiness is clearly

not the aim of human life. But what would be a better purpose? As the characters travel to find the answer, they encounter frivolity, ill-feeling, and passion. They meet a tormented astronomer who has deluded himself into thinking that he controls the weather. Thus even the imagination, which has prompted Rasselas's journey in the first place, shows itself potentially false and dangerous.

The travelers come to realize that no course will satisfy human wishes. The prince shifts his own focus from "the choice of life" to "the choice of eternity," and some readers have taken this to be Johnson's answer. But it seems worth noting that Rasselas continues to struggle with his choice of life. Johnson pointedly titles the end the tale, "Conclusion, in Which Nothing Is Concluded." And yet, we cannot fail to notice one constant value throughout. The astronomer is cured when he is drawn back into social life and dialogue, and the characters continue to enjoy one another's company, answering and learning from one another. Thus Johnson suggests they will go on talking to one another, happily, long after the narrative has come to its end.

From The History of Rasselas, Prince of Abissinia[1]

CHAPTER 1

Description of a Palace in a Valley

Ye who listen with credulity to the whispers of fancy, and pursue with eagerness the phantoms of hope; who expect that age will perform the promises of youth, and that the deficiencies of the present day will be supplied by the morrow; attend to the history of Rasselas prince of Abissinia.

Rasselas was the fourth son of the mighty emperor, in whose dominions the Father of waters[2] begins his course; whose bounty pours down the streams of plenty, and scatters over half the world the harvests of Egypt.

---

1. The text is that of the sixth edition (London, 1783), the last version published in Johnson's lifetime.

2. The Nile.

According to the custom which has descended from age to age among the monarchs of the torrid zone, Rasselas was confined in a private palace, with the other sons and daughters of Abissinian royalty, till the order of succession should call him to the throne.

The place, which the wisdom or policy of antiquity had destined for the residence of the Abissinian princes, was a spacious valley in the kingdom of Amhara, surrounded on every side by mountains, of which the summits overhang the middle part. The only passage, by which it could be entered, was a cavern that passed under a rock, of which it has long been disputed whether it was the work of nature or of human industry. The outlet of the cavern was concealed by a thick wood, and the mouth which opened into the valley was closed with gates of iron, forged by the artificers of ancient days, so massy that no man could, without the help of engines,[3] open or shut them.

From the mountains on every side, rivulets descended that filled all the valley with verdure and fertility, and formed a lake in the middle inhabited by fish of every species, and frequented by every fowl whom nature has taught to dip the wing in water. This lake discharged its superfluities by a stream which entered a dark cleft of the mountain on the northern side, and fell with dreadful noise from precipice to precipice till it was heard no more.

The sides of the mountains were covered with trees, the banks of the brooks were diversified with flowers; every blast shook spices from the rocks, and every month dropped fruits upon the ground. All animals that bite the grass, or browse the shrub, whether wild or tame, wandered in this extensive circuit, secured from beasts of prey by the mountains which confined them. On one part were flocks and herds feeding in the pastures, on another all the beasts of chase frisking in the lawns; the spritely kid was bounding on the rocks, the subtle[4] monkey frolicking in the trees, and the solemn elephant reposing in the shade. All the diversities of the world were brought together, the blessings of nature were collected, and its evils extracted and excluded.

The valley, wide and fruitful, supplied its inhabitants with the necessaries of life, and all delights and superfluities were added at the annual visit which the emperor paid his children, when the iron gate was opened to the sound of music; and during eight days everyone that resided in the valley was required to propose whatever might contribute to make seclusion pleasant, to fill up the vacancies of attention, and lessen the tediousness of time. Every desire was immediately granted. All the artificers of pleasure were called to gladden the festivity; the musicians exerted the power of harmony, and the dancers showed their activity before the princes, in hope that they should pass their lives in this blissful captivity, to which these only were admitted whose performance was thought able to add novelty to luxury. Such was the appearance of security and delight which this retirement afforded, that they to whom it was new always desired that it might be perpetual; and as those, on whom the iron gate had once closed, were never suffered[5] to return, the effect of longer experience could not be known. Thus every year produced new schemes of delight, and new competitors for imprisonment.

---

3. Machines. "Massy": massive.
4. Cunning.

5. Permitted.

The palace stood on an eminence raised about thirty paces above the surface of the lake. It was divided into many squares or courts, built with greater or less magnificence according to the rank of those for whom they were designed. The roofs were turned into arches of massy stone joined with a cement that grew harder by time, and the building stood from century to century, deriding the solstitial rains and equinoctial hurricanes, without need of reparation.

This house, which was so large as to be fully known to none but some ancient officers who successively inherited the secrets of the place, was built as if suspicion herself had dictated the plan. To every room there was an open and secret passage, every square had a communication with the rest, either from the upper stories by private galleries, or by subterranean passages from the lower apartments. Many of the columns had unsuspected cavities, in which a long race of monarchs had reposited their treasures. They then closed up the opening with marble, which was never to be removed but in the utmost exigencies of the kingdom; and recorded their accumulations in a book which was itself concealed in a tower not entered but by the emperor, attended by the prince who stood next in succession.

CHAPTER II

The Discontent of Rasselas in the Happy Valley

Here the sons and daughters of Abissinia lived only to know the soft vicissitudes[6] of pleasure and repose, attended by all that were skillful to delight, and gratified with whatever the senses can enjoy. They wandered in gardens of fragrance, and slept in the fortresses of security. Every art was practiced to make them pleased with their own condition. The sages who instructed them, told them of nothing but the miseries of public life, and described all beyond the mountains as regions of calamity, where discord was always raging, and where man preyed upon man.

To heighten their opinion of their own felicity, they were daily entertained with songs, the subject of which was the *happy valley*. Their appetites were excited by frequent enumerations of different enjoyments, and revelry and merriment was the business of every hour from the dawn of morning to the close of even.

These methods were generally successful; few of the princes had ever wished to enlarge their bounds, but passed their lives in full conviction that they had all within their reach that art or nature could bestow, and pitied those whom fate had excluded from this seat of tranquillity, as the sport of chance, and the slaves of misery.

Thus they rose in the morning, and lay down at night, pleased with each other and with themselves, all but Rasselas, who, in the twenty-sixth year of his age, began to withdraw himself from their pastimes and assemblies, and to delight in solitary walks and silent meditation. He often sat before tables covered with luxury, and forgot to taste the dainties that were placed before him: he rose abruptly in the midst of the song, and hastily retired beyond the sound of music. His attendants observed the change and endeavored to renew his

6. Alternations.

love of pleasure: he neglected their officiousness,[7] repulsed their invitations, and spent day after day on the banks of rivulets sheltered with trees, where he sometimes listened to the birds in the branches, sometimes observed the fish playing in the stream, and anon cast his eyes upon the pastures and mountains filled with animals, of which some were biting the herbage, and some sleeping among the bushes.

This singularity of his humor made him much observed. One of the sages, in whose conversation he had formerly delighted, followed him secretly, in hope of discovering the cause of his disquiet. Rasselas, who knew not that any one was near him, having for some time fixed his eyes upon the goats that were browsing among the rocks, began to compare their condition with his own.

"What," said he, "makes the difference between man and all the rest of the animal creation? Every beast that strays beside me has the same corporal necessities with myself; he is hungry and crops the grass, he is thirsty and drinks the stream, his thirst and hunger are appeased, he is satisfied and sleeps; he rises again and is hungry, he is again fed and is at rest. I am hungry and thirsty like him, but when thirst and hunger cease I am not at rest; I am, like him, pained with want, but am not, like him, satisfied with fullness. The intermediate hours are tedious and gloomy; I long again to be hungry that I may again quicken my attention. The birds peck the berries or the corn, and fly away to the groves where they sit in seeming happiness on the branches, and waste their lives in tuning one unvaried series of sounds. I likewise can call the lutanist and the singer, but the sounds that pleased me yesterday weary me today, and will grow yet more wearisome tomorrow. I can discover within me no power of perception which is not glutted with its proper[8] pleasure, yet I do not feel myself delighted. Man has surely some latent sense for which this place affords no gratification, or he has some desires distinct from sense which must be satisfied before he can be happy."

After this he lifted up his head, and seeing the moon rising, walked towards the palace. As he passed through the fields, and saw the animals around him, "Ye," said he, "are happy, and need not envy me that walk thus among you, burthened with myself; nor do I, ye gentle beings, envy your felicity; for it is not the felicity of man. I have many distresses from which ye are free; I fear pain when I do not feel it; I sometimes shrink at evils recollected, and sometimes start at evils anticipated: surely the equity of providence has balanced peculiar[9] sufferings with peculiar enjoyments."

With observations like these the prince amused himself as he returned, uttering them with a plaintive voice, yet with a look that discovered him to feel some complacence in his own perspicacity, and to receive some solace of the miseries of life, from consciousness of the delicacy with which he felt, and the eloquence with which he bewailed them. He mingled cheerfully in the diversions of the evening, and all rejoiced to find that his heart was lightened.

* * *

[Rasselas remains dissatisfied in the happy valley and attempts to escape by means of wings; the wings, however, drop their inventor in the lake.]

7. Helpfulness.
8. Appropriate.

9. Distinctive.

CHAPTER VII

The Prince Finds a Man of Learning

The prince was not much afflicted by this disaster, having suffered himself to hope for a happier event, only because he had no other means of escape in view. He still persisted in his design to leave the happy valley by the first opportunity.

His imagination was now at a stand; he had no prospect of entering into the world; and, notwithstanding all his endeavors to support himself,[1] discontent by degrees preyed upon him, and he began to lose his thoughts in sadness, when the rainy season, which in these countries is periodical, made it inconvenient to wander in the woods.

The rain continued longer and with more violence than had been ever known: the clouds broke on the surrounding mountains, and the torrents streamed into the plain on every side, till the cavern was too narrow to discharge the water. The lake overflowed its banks, and all the level of the valley was covered with the inundation. The eminence, on which the palace was built, and some other spots of rising ground, were all that the eye could now discover. The herds and flocks left the pastures, and both the wild beasts and the tame retreated to the mountains.

This inundation confined all the princes to domestic amusements, and the attention of Rasselas was particularly seized by a poem, which Imlac rehearsed,[2] upon the various conditions of humanity. He commanded the poet to attend him in his apartment, and recite his verses a second time; then entering into familiar talk, he thought himself happy in having found a man who knew the world so well, and could so skillfully paint the scenes of life. He asked a thousand questions about things, to which, though common to all other mortals, his confinement from childhood had kept him a stranger. The poet pitied his ignorance, and loved his curiosity, and entertained him from day to day with novelty and instruction, so that the prince regretted the necessity of sleep, and longed till the morning should renew his pleasure.

As they were sitting together, the prince commanded Imlac to relate his history, and to tell by what accident he was forced, or by what motive induced, to close his life in the happy valley. As he was going to begin his narrative, Rasselas was called to a concert, and obliged to restrain his curiosity till the evening.

CHAPTER VIII

The History of Imlac

The close of the day is, in the regions of the torrid zone, the only season of diversion and entertainment, and it was therefore midnight before the music ceased, and the princesses retired. Rasselas then called for his companion and required him to begin the story of his life.

"Sir," said Imalac, "my history will not be long: the life that is devoted to knowledge passes silently away, and is very little diversified by events. To talk in public, to think in solitude, to read and to hear, to inquire, and answer

---

1. Keep up his spirits.   2. Recited.

inquiries, is the business of a scholar. He wanders about the world without pomp or terror, and is neither known nor valued but by men like himself.

"I was born in the kingdom of Goiama, at no great distance from the fountain[3] of the Nile. My father was a wealthy merchant, who traded between the inland countries of Afric and the ports of the Red Sea. He was honest, frugal and diligent, but of mean sentiments, and narrow comprehension: he desired only to be rich, and to conceal his riches, lest he should be spoiled[4] by the governors of the province."

"Surely," said the prince, "my father must be negligent of his charge, if any man in his dominions dares take that which belongs to another. Does he not know that kings are accountable for injustice permitted as well as done? If I were emperor, not the meanest[5] of my subjects should be oppressed with impunity. My blood boils when I am told that a merchant durst not enjoy his honest gains for fear of losing them by the rapacity of power. Name the governor who robbed the people, that I may declare his crimes to the emperor."

"Sir," said Imlac, "your ardor is the natural effect of virtue animated by youth: the time will come when you will acquit your father, and perhaps hear with less impatience of the governor. Oppression is, in the Abissinian dominions, neither frequent nor tolerated; but no form of government has been yet discovered, by which cruelty can be wholly prevented. Subordination supposes power on one part and subjection on the other; and if power be in the hands of men, it will sometimes be abused. The vigilance of the supreme magistrate may do much, but much will still remain undone. He can never know all the crimes that are committed, and can seldom punish all that he knows."

"This," said the prince, "I do not understand, but I had rather hear thee than dispute. Continue thy narration."

"My father," proceeded Imlac, "originally intended that I should have no other education, than such as might qualify me for commerce; and discovering in me great strength of memory, and quickness of apprehension, often declared his hope that I should be some time the richest man in Abissinia."

"Why," said the prince, "did thy father desire the increase of his wealth, when it was already greater than he durst discover or enjoy? I am unwilling to doubt thy veracity, yet inconsistencies cannot both be true."

"Inconsistencies," answered Imlac, "cannot both be right, but, imputed to man, they may both be true. Yet diversity is not inconsistency. My father might expect a time of greater security. However, some desire is necessary to keep life in motion, and he, whose real wants are supplied, must admit those of fancy."

"This," said the prince, "I can in some measure conceive. I repent that I interrupted thee."

"With this hope," proceeded Imlac, "he sent me to school; but when I had once found the delight of knowledge, and felt the pleasure of intelligence and the pride of invention, I began silently to despise riches, and determined to disappoint the purpose of my father, whose grossness of conception raised my pity. I was twenty years old before his tenderness would expose me to the

---

3. Source. Goiama, or Gojam, a province of ancient Abyssinia, indeed contains the source of the Blue Nile.

4. Plundered. "Mean": ignoble, small-minded.

5. Lowliest.

fatigue of travel, in which time I had been instructed, by successive masters, in all the literature of my native country. As every hour taught me something new, I lived in a continual course of gratifications; but, as I advanced towards manhood, I lost much of the reverence with which I had been used to look on my instructors; because, when the lesson was ended, I did not find them wiser or better than common men.

"At length my father resolved to initiate me in commerce, and, opening one of his subterranean treasuries, counted out ten thousand pieces of gold. 'This, young man,' said he, 'is the stock with which you must negotiate.'[6] I began with less than the fifth part, and you see how diligence and parsimony have increased it. This is your own to waste or to improve. If you squander it by negligence or caprice, you must wait for my death before you will be rich: if, in four years, you double your stock, we will thenceforward let subordination cease, and live together as friends and partners; for he shall always be equal with me, who is equally skilled in the art of growing rich.'

"We laid our money upon camels, concealed in bales of cheap goods, and traveled to the shore of the Red Sea. When I cast my eye on the expanse of waters my heart bounded like that of a prisoner escaped. I felt an unextinguishable curiosity kindle in my mind, and resolved to snatch this opportunity of seeing the manners of other nations, and of learning sciences[7] unknown in Abissinia.

"I remembered that my father had obliged me to the improvement of my stock, not by a promise which I ought not to violate, but by a penalty which I was at liberty to incur; and therefore determined to gratify my predominant desire, and by drinking at the fountains of knowledge, to quench the thirst of curiosity.

"As I was supposed to trade without connection with my father, it was easy for me to become acquainted with the master of a ship, and procure a passage to some other country. I had no motives of choice to regulate my voyage; it was sufficient for me that, wherever I wandered, I should see a country which I had not seen before. I therefore entered a ship bound for Surat,[8] having left a letter for my father declaring my intention."

CHAPTER IX

The History of Imlac Continued

"When I first entered upon the world of waters, and lost sight of land, I looked round about me with pleasing terror, and thinking my soul enlarged by the boundless prospect, imagined that I could gaze round for ever without satiety; but, in a short time, I grew weary of looking on barren uniformity, where I could only see again what I had already seen. I then descended into the ship, and doubted for a while whether all my future pleasures would not end like this in disgust and disappointment. Yet, surely, said I, the ocean and the land are very different; the only variety of water is rest and motion, but the earth has mountains and valleys, deserts and cities: it is inhabited by men of different

6. Do business.   8. An Indian port.
7. Forms of knowledge.

customs and contrary opinions; and I may hope to find variety in life, though I should miss it in nature.

"With this thought I quieted my mind; and amused myself during the voyage, sometimes by learning from the sailors the art of navigation, which I have never practiced, and sometimes by forming schemes for my conduct in different situations, in not one of which I have been ever placed.

"I was almost weary of my naval amusements when we landed safely at Surat. I secured my money, and purchasing some commodities for show, joined myself to a caravan that was passing into the inland country. My companions, for some reason or other, conjecturing that I was rich, and, by my inquiries and admiration,[9] finding that I was ignorant, considered me as a novice whom they had a right to cheat, and who was to learn at the usual expense the art of fraud. They exposed me to the theft of servants, and the exaction of officers, and saw me plundered upon false pretenses, without any advantage to themselves, but that of rejoicing in the superiority of their own knowledge."

"Stop a moment," said the prince. "Is there such depravity in man, as that he should injure another without benefit to himself? I can easily conceive that all are pleased with superiority; but your ignorance was merely accidental, which, being neither your crime nor your folly, could afford them no reason to applaud themselves; and the knowledge which they had, and which you wanted,[1] they might as effectively have shown by warning, as betraying you."

"Pride," said Imlac, "is seldom delicate, it will please itself with very mean advantages; and envy feels not its own happiness, but when it may be compared with the misery of others. They were my enemies because they grieved to think me rich, and my oppressors because they delighted to find me weak."

"Proceed," said the prince: "I doubt not of the facts which you relate, but imagine that you impute them to mistaken motives."

"In this company," said Imlac, "I arrived at Agra, the capital of Indostan, the city in which the great Mogul commonly resides. I applied myself to the language of the country, and in a few months was able to converse with the learned men; some of whom I found morose and reserved, and others easy and communicative; some were unwilling to teach another what they had with difficulty learned themselves; and some showed that the end of their studies was to gain the dignity of instructing.

"To the tutor of the young princes I recommended myself so much, that I was presented to the emperor as a man of uncommon knowledge. The emperor asked me many questions concerning my country and my travels; and though I cannot now recollect anything that he uttered above the power of a common man, he dismissed me astonished at his wisdom, and enamored of his goodness.

"My credit was now so high, that the merchants, with whom I had traveled, applied to me for recommendations to the ladies of the court. I was surprised at their confidence of solicitation, and gently reproached them with their practices on the road. They heard me with cold indifference, and showed no tokens of shame or sorrow.

"They then urged their request with the offer of a bribe; but what I would not do for kindness I would not do for money; and refused them, not because they

9. Astonishment.   1. Lacked.

had injured me, but because I would not enable them to injure others; for I knew they would have made use of my credit to cheat those who should buy their wares.

"Having resided at Agra till there was no more to be learned, I traveled into Persia, where I saw many remains of ancient magnificence, and observed many new accommodations[2] of life. The Persians are a nation eminently social, and their assemblies afforded me daily opportunities of remarking[3] characters and manners, and of tracing human nature through all its variations.

"From Persia I passed into Arabia, where I saw a nation at once pastoral and warlike; who live without any settled habitation; whose only wealth is their flocks and herds; and who have yet carried on, through all ages, an hereditary war with all mankind, though they neither covet nor envy their possessions."

CHAPTER X

Imlac's History Continued. A Dissertation upon Poetry

"Wherever I went, I found that poetry was considered as the highest learning, and regarded with a veneration somewhat approaching to that which man would pay to the angelic nature. And it yet fills me with wonder, that, in almost all countries, the most ancient poets are considered as the best: whether it be that every other kind of knowledge is an acquisition gradually attained, and poetry is a gift conferred at once; or that the first poetry of every nation surprised them as a novelty, and retained the credit by consent which it received by accident at first: or whether, as the province of poetry is to describe nature and passion, which are always the same, the first writers took possession of the most striking objects for description, and the most probable occurrences for fiction, and left nothing to those that followed them, but transcription of the same events, and new combinations of the same images. Whatever be the reason, it is commonly observed that the early writers are in possession of nature, and their followers of art: that the first excel in strength and invention, and the latter in elegance and refinement.

"I was desirous to add my name to this illustrious fraternity. I read all the poets of Persia and Arabia, and was able to repeat by memory the volumes that are suspended in the mosque of Mecca.[4] But I soon found that no man was ever great by imitation. My desire of excellence impelled me to transfer my attention to nature and to life. Nature was to be my subject, and men to be my auditors: I could never describe what I had not seen: I could not hope to move those with delight or terror, whose interests and opinions I did not understand.

"Being now resolved to be a poet, I saw everything with a new purpose; my sphere of attention was suddenly magnified: no kind of knowledge was to be overlooked. I ranged mountains and deserts for images and resemblances, and pictured upon my mind every tree of the forest and flower of the valley. I observed with equal care the crags of the rock and the pinnacles of the palace. Sometimes I wandered along the mazes of the rivulet, and sometimes watched the changes of the summer clouds. To a poet nothing can be useless. Whatever

---

2. Comforts, conveniences.
3. Noting.

4. Because they have won prizes.

is beautiful, and whatever is dreadful, must be familiar to his imagination: he must be conversant with all that is awfully[5] vast or elegantly little. The plants of the garden, the animals of the wood, the minerals of the earth, and meteors of the sky, must all concur to store his mind with inexhaustible variety: for every idea is useful for the enforcement or decoration of moral or religious truth; and he, who knows most, will have most power of diversifying his scenes, and of gratifying his reader with remote allusions and unexpected instruction.

"All the appearances of nature I was therefore careful to study, and every country which I have surveyed has contributed something to my poetical powers."

"In so wide a survey," said the prince, "you must surely have left much unobserved. I have lived, till now, within the circuit of these mountains, and yet cannot walk abroad without the sight of something which I had never beheld before, or never heeded."

"The business of a poet," said Imlac, "is to examine, not the individual, but the species; to remark general properties and large appearances: he does not number the streaks of the tulip, or describe the different shades in the verdure of the forest. He is to exhibit in his portraits of nature such prominent and striking features, as recall the original to every mind; and must neglect the minuter discriminations, which one may have remarked, and another have neglected, for those characteristics which are alike obvious to vigilance and carelessness.

"But the knowledge of nature is only half the task of a poet; he must be acquainted likewise with all the modes of life. His character requires that he estimate the happiness and misery of every condition; observe the power of all the passions in all their combinations, and trace the changes of the human mind as they are modified by various institutions and accidental influences of climate or custom, from the spriteliness of infancy to the despondence of decrepitude. He must divest himself of the prejudices of his age or country; he must consider right and wrong in their abstracted and invariable state; he must disregard present laws and opinions, and rise to general and transcendental truths, which will always be the same: he must therefore content himself with the slow progress of his name; contemn the applause of his own time, and commit his claims to the justice of posterity. He must write as the interpreter of nature, and the legislator of mankind, and consider himself as presiding over the thoughts and manners of future generations; as a being superior to time and place.

"His labor is not yet at an end: he must know many languages and many sciences; and, that his style may be worthy of his thoughts, must, by incessant practice, familiarize to himself every delicacy of speech and grace of harmony."

CHAPTER XI

Imlac's Narrative Continued. A Hint on Pilgrimage

Imlac now felt the enthusiastic fit,[6] and was proceeding to aggrandize his own profession, when the prince cried out, "Enough! Thou hast convinced me, that no human being can ever be a poet. Proceed with thy narration."

---

5. Impressively.　　　　　　　　　　　　6. A seizure of extravagant emotion.

"To be a poet," said Imlac, "is indeed very difficult." "So difficult," returned the prince, "that I will at present hear no more of his labors. Tell me whither you went when you had seen Persia."

"From Persia," said the poet, "I traveled through Syria, and for three years resided in Palestine, where I conversed with great numbers of the northern and western nations of Europe; the nations which are now in possession of all power and all knowledge; whose armies are irresistible, and whose fleets command the remotest parts of the globe. When I compared these men with the natives of our own kingdom, and those that surround us, they appeared almost another order of beings. In their countries it is difficult to wish for anything that may not be obtained: a thousand arts, of which we never heard, are continually laboring for their convenience and pleasure; and whatever their own climate has denied them is supplied by their commerce."

"By what means," said the prince, "are the Europeans thus powerful? or why, since they can so easily visit Asia and Africa for trade or conquest, cannot the Asiatics and Africans invade their coasts, plant colonies in their ports, and give laws to their natural princes? The same wind that carries them back would bring us thither."

"They are more powerful, Sir, than we," answered Imlac, "because they are wiser; knowledge will always predominate over ignorance, as man governs the other animals. But why their knowledge is more than ours, I know not what reason can be given, but the unsearchable will of the Supreme Being."

"When," said the prince with a sigh, "shall I be able to visit Palestine, and mingle with this mighty confluence of nations? Till that happy moment shall arrive, let me fill up the time with such representations as thou canst give me. I am not ignorant of the motive that assembles such numbers in that place, and cannot but consider it as the center of wisdom and piety, to which the best and wisest men of every land must be continually resorting."

"There are some nations," said Imlac, "that send few visitants to Palestine; for many numerous and learned sects in Europe, concur to censure pilgrimage as superstitious, or deride it as ridiculous."

"You know," said the prince, "how little my life has made me acquainted with diversity of opinions: it will be too long to hear the arguments on both sides; you, that have considered them, tell me the result."

"Pilgrimage," said Imlac, "like many other acts of piety, may be reasonable or superstitious, according to the principles upon which it is performed. Long journeys in search of truth are not commanded. Truth, such as is necessary to the regulation of life, is always found where it is honestly sought. Change of place is no natural cause of the increase of piety, for it inevitably produces dissipation of mind.[7] Yet, since men go every day to view the fields where great actions have been performed, and return with stronger impressions of the event, curiosity of the same kind may naturally dispose us to view that country whence our religion had its beginning; and I believe no man surveys those awful[8] scenes without some confirmation of holy resolutions. That the Supreme Being may be more easily propitiated in one place than in another, is the dream of idle superstition; but that some places may operate upon our own minds in an uncommon manner, is an opinion which hourly experience will

7. Scattering of attention.   8. Awe-inspiring.

justify. He who supposes that his vices may be more successfully combated in Palestine, will, perhaps, find himself mistaken, yet he may go thither without folly: he who thinks they will be more freely pardoned, dishonors at once his reason and religion."

"These," said the prince, "are European distinctions. I will consider them another time. What have you found to be the effect of knowledge? Are those nations happier than we?"

"There is so much infelicity," said the poet, "in the world, that scarce any man has leisure from his own distresses to estimate the comparative happiness of others. Knowledge is certainly one of the means of pleasure, as is confessed by the natural desire which every mind feels of increasing its ideas. Ignorance is mere privation, by which nothing can be produced: it is a vacuity in which the soul sits motionless and torpid for want of attraction; and, without knowing why, we always rejoice when we learn, and grieve when we forget. I am therefore inclined to conclude, that, if nothing counteracts the natural consequence of learning, we grow more happy as our minds take a wider range.

"In enumerating the particular comforts of life we shall find many advantages on the side of the Europeans. They cure wounds and diseases with which we languish and perish. We suffer inclemencies of weather which they can obviate. They have engines for the despatch of many laborious works, which we must perform by manual industry. There is such communication between distant places, that one friend can hardly be said to be absent from another. Their policy removes all public inconveniencies: they have roads cut through their mountains, and bridges laid upon their rivers. And, if we descend to the privacies of life, their habitations are more commodious, and their possessions are more secure."

"They are surely happy," said the prince, "who have all these conveniencies, of which I envy none so much as the facility with which separated friends interchange their thoughts."

"The Europeans," answered Imlac, "are less unhappy than we, but they are not happy. Human life is everywhere a state in which much is to be endured, and little to be enjoyed."

CHAPTER XII

The Story of Imlac Continued

"I am not yet willing," said the prince, "to suppose that happiness is so parsimoniously distributed to mortals; nor can believe but that, if I had the choice of life, I should be able to fill every day with pleasure. I would injure no man, and should provoke no resentment: I would relieve every distress, and should enjoy the benedictions of gratitude. I would choose my friends among the wise, and my wife among the virtuous; and therefore should be in no danger from treachery, or unkindness. My children should, by my care, be learned and pious, and would repay to my age what their childhood had received. What would dare to molest him who might call on every side to thousands enriched by his bounty, or assisted by his power? And why should not life glide quietly away in the soft reciprocation of protection and reverence? All this may be done without the help of European refinements, which appear by their effects to be rather specious than useful. Let us leave them and pursue our journey."

"From Palestine," said Imlac, "I passed through many regions of Asia; in the more civilized kingdoms as a trader, and among the Barbarians of the mountains as a pilgrim. At last I began to long for my native country, that I might repose after my travels, and fatigues, in the places where I had spent my earliest years, and gladden my old companions with the recital of my adventures. Often did I figure[9] to myself those, with whom I had sported away the gay hours of dawning life, sitting round me in its evening, wondering at my tales, and listening to my counsels.

"When this thought had taken possession of my mind, I considered every moment as wasted which did not bring me nearer to Abissinia. I hastened into Egypt, and, notwithstanding my impatience, was detained ten months in the contemplation of its ancient magnificence, and in inquiries after the remains of its ancient learning. I found in Cairo a mixture of all nations; some brought thither by the love of knowledge, some by the hope of gain, and many by the desire of living after their own manner without observation, and of lying hid in the obscurity of multitudes: for, in a city, populous as Cairo, it is possible to obtain at the same time the gratifications of society, and the secrecy of solitude.

"From Cairo I traveled to Suez, and embarked on the Red Sea, passing along the coast till I arrived at the port from which I had departed twenty years before. Here I joined myself to a caravan and re-entered my native country.

"I now expected the caresses of my kinsmen, and the congratulations of my friends, and was not without hope that my father, whatever value he had set upon riches, would own[1] with gladness and pride a son who was able to add to the felicity and honor of the nation. But I was soon convinced that my thoughts were vain. My father had been dead fourteen years, having divided his wealth among my brothers, who were removed to some other provinces. Of my companions the greater part was in the grave, of the rest some could with difficulty remember me, and some considered me as one corrupted by foreign manners.

"A man used to vicissitudes is not easily dejected. I forgot, after a time, my disappointment, and endeavoured to recommend myself to the nobles of the kingdom: they admitted me to their tables, heard my story, and dismissed me. I opened a school, and was prohibited to teach. I then resolved to sit down in the quiet of domestic life, and addressed[2] a lady that was fond of my conversation, but rejected my suit, because my father was a merchant.

"Wearied at last with solicitation and repulses, I resolved to hide myself forever from the world, and depend no longer on the opinion or caprice of others. I waited for the time when the gate of the *happy valley* should open, that I might bid farewell to hope and fear: the day came; my performance was distinguished with favor, and I resigned myself with joy to perpetual confinement."

"Hast thou here found happiness at last?" said Rasselas. "Tell me without reserve; art thou content with thy condition? or, dost thou wish to be again wandering and inquiring? All the inhabitants of this valley celebrate their lot, and, at the annual visit of the emperor, invite others to partake of their felicity."

"Great prince," said Imlac, "I shall speak the truth: I know not one of all your attendants who does not lament the hour when he entered this retreat. I am less unhappy than the rest, because I have a mind replete with images, which I

9. Imagine.   2. Courted.
1. Acknowledge.

can vary and combine at pleasure. I can amuse my solitude by the renovation of the knowledge which begins to fade from my memory, and by recollection of the accidents of my past life. Yet all this ends in the sorrowful consideration, that my acquirements are now useless, and that none of my pleasures can be again enjoyed. The rest, whose minds have no impression but of the present moment, are either corroded by malignant passions, or sit stupid in the gloom of perpetual vacancy."

"What passions can infest those," said the prince, "who have no rivals? We are in a place where impotence precludes malice, and where all envy is repressed by community of enjoyments."

"There may be community," said Imlac, "of material possessions, but there can never be community of love or of esteem. It must happen that one will please more than another; he that knows himself despised will always be envious; and still more envious and malevolent, if he is condemned to live in the presence of those who despise him. The invitations, by which they allure others to a state which they feel to be wretched, proceed from the natural malignity of hopeless misery. They are weary of themselves, and of each other, and expect to find relief in new companions. They envy the liberty which their folly has forfeited, and would gladly see all mankind imprisoned like themselves.

"From this crime, however, I am wholly free. No man can say that he is wretched by my persuasion. I look with pity on the crowds who are annually soliciting admission to captivity, and wish that it were lawful for me to warn them of their danger."

"My dear Imlac," said the prince, "I will open to thee my whole heart. I have long meditated an escape from the happy valley. I have examined the mountains on every side, but find myself insuperably barred: teach me the way to break my prison; thou shalt be the companion of my flight, the guide of my rambles, the partner of my fortune, and my sole director in the *choice of life*."

"Sir," answered the poet, "your escape will be difficult, and, perhaps, you may soon repent your curiosity. The world, which you figure to yourself smooth and quiet as the lake in the valley, you will find a sea foaming with tempests, and boiling with whirlpools: you will be sometimes overwhelmed by the waves of violence, and sometimes dashed against the rocks of treachery. Amidst wrongs and frauds, competitions and anxieties, you will wish a thousand times for these seats[3] of quiet, and willingly quit hope to be free from fear."

"Do not seek to deter me from my purpose," said the prince: "I am impatient to see what thou hast seen; and, since thou art thyself weary of the valley, it is evident, that thy former state was better than this. Whatever be the consequence of my experiment, I am resolved to judge with my own eyes of the various conditions of men, and then to make deliberately my *choice of life*."

"I am afraid," said Imlac, "you are hindered by stronger restraints than my persuasions; yet, if your determination is fixed, I do not counsel you to despair. Few things are impossible to diligence and skill."

* * *

[With the help of Imlac, Rasselas, joined by his sister, Nekayah, tunnels to freedom.]

3. Sites, locations.

CHAPTER XVI

They Enter Cairo, and Find Every Man Happy

As they approached the city, which filled the strangers with astonishment, "This," said Imlac to the prince, "is the place where travelers and merchants assemble from all the corners of the earth. You will here find men of every character, and every occupation. Commerce is here honorable: I will act as a merchant, and you shall live as strangers, who have no other end[4] of travel than curiosity; it will soon be observed that we are rich; our reputation will procure us access to all whom we shall desire to know; you will see all the conditions of humanity, and enable yourself at leisure to make your *choice of life*."

They now entered the town, stunned by the noise, and offended by the crowds. Instruction had not yet so prevailed over habit, but that they wondered to see themselves pass undistinguished along the street, and met by the lowest of the people without reverence or notice. The princess could not at first bear the thought of being leveled with the vulgar,[5] and, for some days, continued in her chamber, where she was served by her favorite Pekuah as in the palace of the valley.

Imlac, who understood traffic,[6] sold part of the jewels the next day, and hired a house, which he adorned with such magnificence, that he was immediately considered as a merchant of great wealth. His politeness attracted many acquaintance, and his generosity made him courted by many dependents. His table was crowded by men of every nation, who all admired his knowledge, and solicited his favor. His companions, not being able to mix in the conversation, could make no discovery[7] of their ignorance or surprise, and were gradually initiated in the world as they gained knowledge of the language.

The prince had, by frequent lectures, been taught the use and nature of money; but the ladies could not, for a long time, comprehend what the merchants did with small pieces of gold and silver, or why things of so little use should be received as equivalent to the necessaries of life.

They studied the language two years, while Imlac was preparing to set before them the various ranks and conditions of mankind. He grew acquainted with all who had anything uncommon in their fortune or conduct. He frequented the voluptuous and the frugal, the idle and the busy, the merchants and the men of learning.

The prince, being now able to converse with fluency, and having learned the caution necessary to be observed in his intercourse with strangers, began to accompany Imlac to places of resort, and to enter into all assemblies, that he might make his *choice of life*.

For some time he thought choice needless, because all appeared to him equally happy. Wherever he went he met gaiety and kindness, and heard the song of joy, or the laugh of carelessness. He began to believe that the world overflowed with universal plenty, and that nothing was withheld either from want or merit; that every hand showered liberality, and every heart melted with benevolence: "and who then," says he, "will be suffered to be wretched?"

4. Goal.
5. Common people.
6. Trade.
7. Revelation.

Imlac permitted the pleasing delusion, and was unwilling to crush the hope of inexperience; till one day, having sat awhile silent, "I know not," said the prince, "what can be the reason that I am more unhappy than any of our friends. I see them perpetually and unalterably cheerful, but feel my own mind restless and uneasy. I am unsatisfied with those pleasures which I seem most to court; I live in the crowds of jollity, not so much to enjoy company as to shun myself, and am only loud and merry to conceal my sadness."

"Every man," said Imlac, "may, by examining his own mind, guess what passes in the minds of others: when you feel that your own gaiety is counterfeit, it may justly lead you to suspect that of your companions not to be sincere. Envy is commonly reciprocal. We are long before we are convinced that happiness is never to be found, and each believes it possessed by others, to keep alive the hope of obtaining it for himself. In the assembly, where you passed the last night, there appeared such spriteliness of air, and volatility of fancy, as might have suited beings of an higher order, formed to inhabit serener regions inaccessible to care or sorrow: yet, believe me, prince, there was not one who did not dread the moment when solitude should deliver him to the tyranny of reflection."

"This," said the prince, "may be true of others, since it is true of me; yet, whatever be the general infelicity of man, one condition is more happy than another, and wisdom surely directs us to take the least evil in the *choice of life*."

"The causes of good and evil," answered Imlac, "are so various and uncertain, so often entangled with each other, so diversified by various relations, and so much subject to accidents which cannot be foreseen, that he who would fix his condition upon incontestable reasons of preference, must live and die inquiring and deliberating."

"But surely," said Rasselas, "the wise men, to whom we listen with reverence and wonder, chose that mode of life for themselves which they thought most likely to make them happy."

"Very few," said the poet, "live by choice. Every man is placed in his present condition by causes which acted without his foresight, and with which he did not always willingly cooperate; and therefore you will rarely meet one who does not think the lot of his neighbor better than his own."

"I am pleased to think," said the prince, "that my birth has given me at least one advantage over others, by enabling me to determine for myself. I have here the world before me; I will review it at leisure: surely happiness is somewhere to be found."

CHAPTER XVII

The Prince Associates with Young Men of Spirit and Gaiety

Rasselas rose next day, and resolved to begin his experiments upon life. "Youth," cried he, "is the time of gladness: I will join myself to the young men, whose only business is to gratify their desires, and whose time is all spent in a succession of enjoyments."

To such societies he was readily admitted, but a few days brought him back weary and disgusted. Their mirth was without images,[8] their laughter without motive; their pleasures were gross and sensual in which the mind had no part;

8. Ideas, conceptions.

their conduct was at once wild and mean; they laughed at order and at law, but the frown of power dejected, and the eye of wisdom abashed them.

The prince soon concluded, that he should never be happy in a course of life of which he was ashamed. He thought it unsuitable to a reasonable being to act without a plan, and to be sad or cheerful only by chance. "Happiness," said he, "must be something solid and permanent, without fear and without uncertainty."

But his young companions had gained so much of his regard by their frankness and courtesy, that he could not leave them without warning and remonstrance. "My friends," said he, "I have seriously considered our manners and our prospects, and find that we have mistaken our own interest. The first years of man must make provision for the last. He that never thinks never can be wise. Perpetual levity must end in ignorance; and intemperance, though it may fire the spirits for an hour, will make life short or miserable. Let us consider that youth is of no long duration, and that in maturer age, when the enchantments of fancy shall cease, and phantoms of delight dance no more about us, we shall have no comforts but the esteem of wise men, and the means of doing good. Let us, therefore, stop, while to stop is in our power: let us live as men who are sometime to grow old, and to whom it will be the most dreadful of all evils not to count their past years but by follies, and to be reminded of their former luxuriance of health only by the maladies which riot has produced."

They stared awhile in silence one upon another, and, at last, drove him away by a general chorus of continued laughter.

The consciousness that his sentiments were just, and his intentions kind, was scarcely sufficient to support him against the horror of derision. But he recovered his tranquillity, and pursued his search.

CHAPTER XVIII

The Prince Finds a Wise and Happy Man

As he [Rasselas] was one day walking in the street, he saw a spacious building which all were, by the open doors, invited to enter: he followed the stream of people, and found it a hall or school of declamation, in which professors read lectures to their auditory.[9] He fixed his eye upon a sage raised above the rest, who discoursed with great energy on the government of the passions. His look was venerable, his action graceful, his pronunciation clear, and his diction elegant. He showed, with great strength of sentiment, and variety of illustration, that human nature is degraded and debased, when the lower faculties predominate over the higher; that when fancy, the parent of passion, usurps the domination of the mind, nothing ensues but the natural effect of unlawful government, perturbation and confusion; that she betrays the fortresses of the intellect to rebels, and excites her children to sedition against reason their lawful sovereign. He compared reason to the sun, of which the light is constant, uniform, and lasting; and fancy to a meteor, of bright but transitory luster irregular in its motion, and delusive in its direction.

He then communicated the various precepts given from time to time for the conquest of passion, and displayed the happiness of those who had obtained the important victory, after which man is no longer the slave of fear, nor the

9. Audience.

fool of hope; is no more emaciated by envy, inflamed by anger, emasculated by tenderness, or depressed by grief; but walks on calmly through the tumults or the privacies of life, as the sun pursues alike his course through the calm or the stormy sky.

He enumerated many examples of heroes immovable by pain or pleasure, who looked with indifference on those modes or accidents to which the vulgar give the names of good and evil. He exhorted his hearers to lay aside their prejudices, and arm themselves against the shafts of malice or misfortune, by invulnerable patience; concluding that this state only was happiness, and that this happiness was in every one's power.

Rasselas listened to him with the veneration due to the instructions of a superior being, and, waiting for him at the door, humbly implored the liberty of visiting so great a master of true wisdom. The lecturer hesitated a moment, when Rasselas put a purse of gold into his hand, which he received with a mixture of joy and wonder.

"I have found," said the prince, at his return to Imlac, "a man who can teach all that is necessary to be known, who, from the unshaken throne of rational fortitude, looks down on the scenes of life changing beneath him. He speaks, and attention watches his lips. He reasons, and conviction closes his periods.[1] This man shall be my future guide: I will learn his doctrines, and imitate his life."

"Be not too hasty," said Imlac, "to trust, or to admire, the teachers of morality: they discourse like angels, but they live like men."

Rasselas, who could not conceive how any man could reason so forcibly without feeling the cogency of his own arguments, paid his visit in a few days, and was denied admission. He had now learned the power of money, and made his way by a piece of gold to the inner apartment, where he found the philosopher in a room half darkened, with his eyes misty, and his face pale. "Sir," said he, "you are come at a time when all human friendship is useless; what I suffer cannot be remedied, what I have lost cannot be supplied. My daughter, my only daughter, from whose tenderness I expected all the comforts of my age, died last night of a fever. My views, my purposes, my hopes are at an end: I am now a lonely being disunited from society."

"Sir," said the prince, "mortality is an event by which a wise man can never be surprised: we know that death is always near, and it should therefore always be expected." "Young man," answered the philosopher, "you speak like one that has never felt the pangs of separation." "Have you then forgot the precepts," said Rasselas, "which you so powerfully enforced? Has wisdom no strength to arm the heart against calamity? Consider, that external things are naturally variable, but truth and reason are always the same." "What comfort," said the mourner, "can truth and reason afford me? Of what effect are they now, but to tell me, that my daughter will not be restored?"

The prince, whose humanity would not suffer him to insult misery with reproof, went away convinced of the emptiness of rhetorical sound, and the inefficacy of polished periods and studied sentences.

1. Sentences.

CHAPTER XIX

A Glimpse of Pastoral Life

He was still eager upon the same inquiry; and, having heard of a hermit, that lived near the lowest cataract of the Nile, and filled the whole country with the fame of his sanctity, resolved to visit his retreat, and inquire whether that felicity, which public life could not afford, was to be found in solitude; and whether a man, whose age and virtue made him venerable, could teach any peculiar art of shunning evils, or enduring them.

Imlac and the princess agreed to accompany him, and, after the necessary preparations, they began their journey. Their way lay through fields, where shepherds tended their flocks, and the lambs were playing upon the pasture. "This," said the poet, "is the life which has been often celebrated for its innocence and quiet: let us pass the heat of the day among the shepherds' tents, and know whether all our searches are not to terminate in pastoral simplicity."

The proposal pleased them, and they induced the shepherds, by small presents and familiar questions, to tell their opinion of their own state: they were so rude[2] and ignorant, so little able to compare the good with the evil of the occupation, and so indistinct in their narratives and descriptions, that very little could be learned from them. But it was evident that their hearts were cankered with discontent; that they considered themselves as condemned to labor for the luxury of the rich, and looked up with stupid malevolence toward those that were placed above them.

The princess pronounced with vehemence, that she would never suffer these envious savages to be her companions, and that she should not soon be desirous of seeing any more specimens of rustic happiness; but could not believe that all the accounts of primeval pleasures were fabulous, and was yet in doubt whether life had anything that could be justly preferred to the placid gratifications of fields and woods. She hoped that the time would come, when, with a few virtuous and elegant companions, she should gather flowers planted by her own hand, fondle the lambs of her own ewe, and listen, without care, among brooks and breezes, to one of her maidens reading in the shade.

CHAPTER XX

The Danger of Prosperity

On the next day they continued their journey, till the heat compelled them to look round for shelter. At a small distance they saw a thick wood, which they no sooner entered than they perceived that they were approaching the habitations of men. The shrubs were diligently cut away to open walks where the shades were darkest; the boughs of opposite trees were artificially interwoven; seats of flowery turf were raised in vacant spaces, and a rivulet, that wantoned along the side of a winding path, had its banks sometimes opened into small basons,[3] and its stream sometimes obstructed by little mounds of stone heaped together to increase its murmurs.

---

2. Unpolished, boorish.   **3.** Ponds.

They passed slowly through the wood, delighted with such unexpected accommodations, and entertained each other with conjecturing what, or who, he could be, that, in those rude and unfrequented regions, had leisure and art for such harmless luxury.

As they advanced, they heard the sound of music, and saw youths and virgins dancing in the grove; and, going still further, beheld a stately palace built upon a hill surrounded with woods. The laws of eastern hospitality allowed them to enter, and the master welcomed them like a man liberal and wealthy.

He was skillful enough in appearances soon to discern that they were no common guests, and spread his table with magnificence. The eloquence of Imlac caught his attention, and the lofty courtesy of the princess excited his respect. When they offered to depart he entreated their stay, and was the next day still more unwilling to dismiss them than before. They were easily persuaded to stop, and civility grew up in time to freedom and confidence.

The prince now saw all the domestics cheerful, and all the face of nature smiling round the place, and could not forbear to hope that he should find here what he was seeking; but when he was congratulating the master upon his possessions, he answered with a sigh, "My condition has indeed the appearance of happiness, but appearances are delusive. My prosperity puts my life in danger; the Bassa[4] of Egypt is my enemy, incensed only by my wealth and popularity. I have been hitherto protected against him by the princes of the country; but, as the favor of the great is uncertain, I know not how soon my defenders may be persuaded to share the plunder with the Bassa. I have sent my treasures into a distant country, and, upon the first alarm, am prepared to follow them. Then will my enemies riot in my mansion, and enjoy the gardens which I have planted."

They all joined in lamenting his danger, and deprecating his exile; and the princess was so much disturbed with the tumult of grief and indignation, that she retired to her apartment. They continued with their kind inviter a few days longer, and then went forward to find the hermit.

CHAPTER XXI

The Happiness of Solitude. The Hermit's History

They came on the third day, by the direction of the peasants, to the hermit's cell: it was a cavern in the side of a mountain, overshadowed with palm trees; at such a distance from the cataract, that nothing more was heard than a gentle uniform murmur, such as composed the mind to pensive meditation, especially when it was assisted by the wind whistling among the branches. The first rude essay of nature had been so much improved by human labor, that the cave contained several apartments, appropriated to different uses, and often afforded lodging to travelers, whom darkness or tempests happened to overtake.

The hermit sat on a bench at the door, to enjoy the coolness of the evening. On one side lay a book with pens and papers, on the other mechanical instruments of various kinds. As they approached him unregarded, the princess observed that he had not the countenance of a man that had found, or could teach, the way to happiness.

---

4. A high official.

They saluted him with great respect, which he repaid like a man not unaccustomed to the forms of courts. "My children," said he, "if you have lost your way, you shall be willingly supplied with such conveniences for the night as this cavern will afford. I have all that nature requires, and you will not expect delicacies in a hermit's cell."

They thanked him, and, entering, were pleased with the neatness and regularity of the place. The hermit set flesh and wine before them, though he fed only upon fruits and water. His discourse was cheerful without levity, and pious without enthusiasm.[5] He soon gained the esteem of his guests, and the princess repented of her hasty censure.

At last Imlac began thus: "I do not now wonder that your reputation is so far extended; we have heard at Cairo of your wisdom, and came hither to implore your direction for this young man and maiden in the *choice of life*."

"To him that lives well," answered the hermit, "every form of life is good; nor can I give any other rule for choice, than to remove from all apparent evil."

"He will remove most certainly from evil," said the prince, "who shall devote himself to that solitude which you have recommended by your example."

"I have indeed lived fifteen years in solitude," said the hermit, "but have no desire that my example should gain any imitators. In my youth I professed arms, and was raised by degrees to the highest military rank. I have traversed wide countries at the head of my troops, and seen many battles and sieges. At last, being disgusted by the preferment of a younger officer, and feeling that my vigor was beginning to decay, I resolved to close my life in peace, having found the world full of snares, discord, and misery. I had once escaped from the pursuit of the enemy by the shelter of this cavern, and therefore chose it for my final residence. I employed artificers to form it into chambers, and stored it with all that I was likely to want.

"For some time after my retreat, I rejoiced like a tempest-beaten sailor at his entrance into the harbor, being delighted with the sudden change of the noise and hurry of war, to stillness and repose. When the pleasure of novelty went away, I employed my hours in examining the plants which grow in the valley, and the minerals which I collected from the rocks. But that inquiry is now grown tasteless and irksome. I have been for some time unsettled and distracted: my mind is disturbed with a thousand perplexities of doubt, and vanities of imagination, which hourly prevail upon me, because I have no opportunities of relaxation or diversion. I am sometimes ashamed to think that I could not secure myself from vice, but by retiring from the exercise of virtue, and begin to suspect that I was rather impelled by resentment, than led by devotion, into solitude. My fancy riots in scenes of folly, and I lament that I have lost so much, and have gained so little. In solitude, if I escape the example of bad men, I want likewise the counsel and conversation of the good. I have been long comparing the evils with the advantages of society, and resolve to return into the world tomorrow. The life of a solitary man will be certainly miserable, but not certainly devout."

They heard his resolution with surprise, but, after a short pause, offered to conduct him to Cairo. He dug up a considerable treasure which he had hid among the rocks, and accompanied them to the city, on which, as he approached it, he gazed with rapture.

5. Excessive ardor.

CHAPTER XXII

The Happiness of a Life Led According to Nature

Rasselas went often to an assembly of learned men, who met at stated times to unbend their minds, and compare their opinions. Their manners were somewhat coarse, but their conversation was instructive, and their disputations acute, though sometimes too violent, and often continued till neither controvertist remembered upon what question they began. Some faults were almost general among them: every one was desirous to dictate to the rest, and every one was pleased to hear the genius or knowledge of another depreciated.

In this assembly Rasselas was relating his interview with the hermit, and the wonder with which he heard him censure a course of life which he had so deliberately chosen, and so laudably followed. The sentiments of the hearers were various. Some were of opinion, that the folly of his choice had been justly punished by condemnation to perpetual perseverance.[6] One of the youngest among them, with great vehemence, pronounced him an hypocrite. Some talked of the right of society to the labor of individuals, and considered retirement as a desertion of duty. Others readily allowed, that there was a time when the claims of the public were satisfied, and when a man might properly sequester himself, to review his life, and purify his heart.

One, who appeared more affected with the narrative than the rest, thought it likely, that the hermit would, in a few years, go back to his retreat, and, perhaps, if shame did not restrain, or death intercept him, return once more from his retreat into the world: "For the hope of happiness," said he, "is so strongly impressed, that the longest experience is not able to efface it. Of the present state, whatever it be, we feel, and are forced to confess, the misery, yet, when the same state is again at a distance, imagination paints it as desirable. But the time will surely come, when desire will be no longer our torment, and no man shall be wretched but by his own fault."

"This," said a philosopher, who had heard him with tokens of great impatience, "is the present condition of a wise man. The time is already come, when none are wretched but by their own fault. Nothing is more idle, than to inquire after happiness, which nature has kindly placed within our reach. The way to be happy is to live according to nature, in obedience to that universal and unalterable law with which every heart is originally impressed; which is not written on it by precept, but engraven by destiny, not instilled by education, but infused at our nativity. He that lives according to nature will suffer nothing from the delusions of hope, or importunities of desire: he will receive and reject with equability of temper; and act or suffer as the reason of things shall alternately prescribe. Other men may amuse themselves with subtle definitions, or intricate raciocination. Let them learn to be wise by easier means: let them observe the hind of the forest, and the linnet of the grove: let them consider the life of animals, whose motions are regulated by instinct; they obey their guide and are happy. Let us therefore, at length, cease to dispute, and learn to live; throw away the incumbrance of precepts, which they who utter them with so much pride and pomp do not understand, and carry with us this simple and intelligible maxim, That deviation from nature is deviation from happiness."

6. Repetition; hence, monotony.

When he had spoken, he looked round him with a placid air, and enjoyed the consciousness of his own beneficence. "Sir," said the prince, with great modesty, "as I, like all the rest of mankind, am desirous of felicity, my closest attention has been fixed upon your discourse: I doubt not the truth of a position which a man so learned has so confidently advanced. Let me only know what it is to live according to nature."

"When I find young men so humble and so docile," said the philosopher, "I can deny them no information which my studies have enabled me to afford. To live according to nature, is to act always with due regard to the fitness arising from the relations and qualities of causes and effects; to concur with the great and unchangeable scheme of universal felicity; to cooperate with the general disposition and tendency of the present system of things."

The prince soon found that this was one of the sages whom he should understand less as he heard him longer. He therefore bowed and was silent, and the philosopher, supposing him satisfied, and the rest vanquished, rose up and departed with the air of a man that had cooperated with the present system.

CHAPTER XXIII

The Prince and His Sister Divide between Them the Work of Observation

Rasselas returned home full of reflections, doubtful how to direct his future steps. Of the way to happiness he found the learned and simple equally ignorant; but, as he was yet young, he flattered himself that he had time remaining for more experiments, and further inquiries. He communicated to Imlac his observations and his doubts, but was answered by him with new doubts, and remarks that gave him no comfort. He therefore discoursed more frequently and freely with his sister, who had yet the same hope with himself, and always assisted him to give some reason why, though he had been hitherto frustrated, he might succeed at last.

"We have hitherto," said she, "known but little of the world: we have never yet been either great or mean. In our own country, though we had royalty, we had no power, and in this we have not yet seen the private recesses of domestic peace. Imlac favors not our search, lest we should in time find him mistaken. We will divide the task between us: you shall try what is to be found in the splendor of courts, and I will range the shades of humbler life. Perhaps command and authority may be the supreme blessings, as they afford most opportunities of doing good: or, perhaps, what this world can give may be found in the modest habitations of middle fortune; too low for great designs, and too high for penury and distress."

CHAPTER XXIV

The Prince Examines the Happiness of High Stations

Rasselas applauded the design, and appeared next day with a splendid retinue at the court of the Bassa. He was soon distinguished for his magnificence, and admitted, as a prince whose curiosity had brought him from distant countries, to an intimacy with the great officers, and frequent conversation with the Bassa himself.

He was at first inclined to believe, that the man must be pleased with his own condition, whom all approached with reverence, and heard with obedience, and who had the power to extend his edicts to a whole kingdom. "There can be no pleasure," said he, "equal to that of feeling at once the joy of thousands all made happy by wise administration. Yet, since, by the law of subordination, this sublime delight can be in one nation but the lot of one, it is surely reasonable to think that there is some satisfaction more popular[7] and accessible, and that millions can hardly be subjected to the will of a single man, only to fill his particular breast with incommunicable content."

These thoughts were often in his mind, and he found no solution of the difficulty. But as presents and civilities gained him more familiarity, he found that almost every man who stood high in employment hated all the rest, and was hated by them, and that their lives were a continual succession of plots and detections, stratagems and escapes, faction and treachery. Many of those, who surrounded the Bassa, were sent only to watch and report his conduct; every tongue was muttering censure and every eye was searching for a fault.

At last the letters of revocation arrived, the Bassa was carried in chains to Constantinople, and his name was mentioned no more.

"What are we now to think of the prerogatives of power," said Rasselas to his sister; "is it without any efficacy to good? or, is the subordinate degree only dangerous, and the supreme safe and glorious? Is the Sultan the only happy man in his dominions? or, is the Sultan himself subject to the torments of suspicion, and the dread of enemies?"

In a short time the second Bassa was deposed. The Sultan, that had advanced him, was murdered by the Janisaries,[8] and his successor had other views and different favorites.

CHAPTER XXV

The Princess Pursues Her Inquiry with More Diligence Than Success

The princess, in the meantime, insinuated herself into many families; for there are few doors, through which liberality, joined with good humor, cannot find its way. The daughters of many houses were airy[9] and cheerful, but Nekayah had been too long accustomed to the conversation of Imlac and her brother to be much pleased with childish levity and prattle which had no meaning. She found their thoughts narrow, their wishes low, and their merriment often artificial. Their pleasures, poor as they were, could not be preserved pure, but were embittered by petty competitions and worthless emulation. They were always jealous of the beauty of each other; of a quality to which solicitude can add nothing, and from which detraction can take nothing away. Many were in love with triflers like themselves, and many fancied that they were in love when in truth they were only idle. Their affection was seldom fixed on sense or virtue, and therefore seldom ended but in vexation. Their grief, however, like their joy, was transient; everything floated in their mind unconnected with the past or future, so that one desire easily gave way to another, as a second stone cast into the water effaces and confounds the circles of the first.

---

7. Available to the people as a whole.   9. Lively.
8. Turkish guards.

With these girls she played as with inoffensive animals, and found them proud of her countenance,[1] and weary of her company.

But her purpose was to examine more deeply, and her affability easily persuaded the hearts that were swelling with sorrow to discharge their secrets in her ear: and those whom hope flattered, or prosperity delighted, often courted her to partake their pleasures.

The princess and her brother commonly met in the evening in a private summerhouse on the bank of the Nile, and related to each other the occurrences of the day. As they were sitting together, the princess cast her eyes upon the river that flowed before her. "Answer," said she, "great father of waters, thou that rollest thy floods through eighty nations, to the invocations of the daughter of thy native king. Tell me if thou waterest, through all thy course, a single habitation from which thou dost not hear the murmurs of complaint?"

"You are then," said Rasselas, "not more successful in private houses than I have been in courts." "I have, since the last partition of our provinces,"[2] said the princess, "enabled myself to enter familiarly into many families, where there was the fairest show of prosperity and peace, and know not one house that is not haunted by some fury that destroys its quiet.

"I did not seek ease among the poor, because I concluded that there it could not be found. But I saw many poor whom I had supposed to live in affluence. Poverty has, in large cities, very different appearances: it is often concealed in splendor, and often in extravagance. It is the care of a very great part of mankind to conceal their indigence from the rest: they support themselves by temporary expedients, and every day is lost in contriving for the morrow.

"This, however, was an evil, which, though frequent, I saw with less pain, because I could relieve it. Yet some have refused my bounties; more offended with my quickness to detect their wants, than pleased with my readiness to succor them: and others, whose exigencies compelled them to admit my kindness, have never been able to forgive their benefactress. Many, however, have been sincerely grateful without the ostentation of gratitude, or the hope of other favors."

CHAPTER XXVI

The Princess Continues Her Remarks upon Private Life

Nekayah perceiving her brother's attention fixed, proceeded in her narrative.

"In families, where there is or is not poverty, there is commonly discord: if a kingdom be, as Imlac tells us, a great family, a family likewise is a little kingdom, torn with factions and exposed to revolutions. An unpracticed observer expects the love of parents and children to be constant and equal; but this kindness seldom continues beyond the years of infancy: in a short time the children become rivals to their parents. Benefits are allayed by reproaches, and gratitude debased by envy.

"Parents and children seldom act in concert: each child endeavors to appropriate the esteem or fondness of the parents, and the parents, with yet less temptation, betray each other to their children; thus some place their confidence in the father, and some in the mother, and, by degrees, the house is filled with artifices and feuds.

1. Favor.   2. Division of assigned tasks.

"The opinions of children and parents, of the young and the old, are naturally opposite, by the contrary effects of hope and despondence, of expectation and experience, without crime or folly on either side. The colors of life in youth and age appear different, as the face of nature in spring and winter. And how can children credit the assertions of parents, which their own eyes show them to be false?

"Few parents act in such a manner as much to enforce their maxims by the credit of their lives. The old man trusts wholly to slow contrivance and gradual progression: the youth expects to force his way by genius, vigor, and precipitance. The old man pays regard to riches, and the youth reverences virtue. The old man deifies prudence: the youth commits himself to magnanimity and chance. The young man, who intends no ill, believes that none is intended, and therefore acts with openness and candor:[3] but his father, having suffered the injuries of fraud, is impelled to suspect, and too often allured to practice it. Age looks with anger on the temerity of youth, and youth with contempt on the scrupulosity of age. Thus parents and children, for the greatest part, live on to love less and less: and, if those whom nature has thus closely united are the torments of each other, where shall we look for tenderness and consolation?"

"Surely," said the prince, "you must have been unfortunate in your choice of acquaintance: I am unwilling to believe, that the most tender of all relations is thus impeded in its effects by natural necessity."

"Domestic discord," answered she, "is not inevitably and fatally necessary; but yet is not easily avoided. We seldom see that a whole family is virtuous: the good and evil cannot well agree; and the evil can yet less agree with one another: even the virtuous fall sometimes to variance, when their virtues are of different kinds, and tending to extremes. In general, those parents have most reverence who most deserve it: for he that lives well cannot be despised.

"Many other evils infest private life. Some are the slaves of servants whom they have trusted with their affairs. Some are kept in continual anxiety to the caprice of rich relations, whom they cannot please, and dare not offend. Some husbands are imperious, and some wives perverse: and, as it is always more easy to do evil than good, though the wisdom or virtue of one can very rarely make many happy, the folly or vice of one may often make many miserable."

"If such be the general effect of marriage," said the prince, "I shall, for the future, think it dangerous to connect my interest with that of another, lest I should be unhappy by my partner's fault."

"I have met," said the princess, "with many who live single for that reason; but I never found that their prudence ought to raise envy. They dream away their time without friendship, without fondness, and are driven to rid themselves of the day, for which they have no use, by childish amusements, or vicious delights. They act as beings under the constant sense of some known inferiority, that fills their minds with rancor, and their tongues with censure. They are peevish at home, and malevolent abroad; and, as the outlaws of human nature, make it their business and their pleasure to disturb that society which debars them from its privileges. To live without feeling or exciting sympathy, to be fortunate without adding to the felicity of others, or afflicted without tasting the balm of pity, is a state more gloomy than solitude: it is not

---

3. Generosity.

retreat but exclusion from mankind. Marriage has many pains, but celibacy has no pleasures."

"What then is to be done?" said Rasselas; "the more we inquire, the less we can resolve. Surely he is most likely to please himself that has no other inclination to regard."

CHAPTER XXVII

Disquisition upon Greatness

The conversation had a short pause. The prince, having considered his sister's observations, told her, that she had surveyed life with prejudice, and supposed misery where she did not find it. "Your narrative," says he, "throws yet a darker gloom upon the prospects of futurity: the predictions of Imlac were but faint sketches of the evils painted by Nekayah. I have been lately convinced that quiet is not the daughter of grandeur, or of power: that her presence is not to be bought by wealth, nor enforced by conquest. It is evident, that as any man acts in a wider compass, he must be more exposed to opposition from enmity or miscarriage from chance; whoever has many to please or to govern, must use the ministry of many agents, some of whom will be wicked, and some ignorant; by some he will be misled, and by others betrayed. If he gratifies one he will offend another: those that are not favored will think themselves injured; and, since favors can be conferred but upon few, the greater number will be always discontented."

"The discontent," said the princess, "which is thus unreasonable, I hope that I shall always have spirit to despise, and you, power to repress."

"Discontent," answered Rasselas, "will not always be without reason under the most just or vigilant administration of public affairs. None, however attentive, can always discover that merit which indigence or faction may happen to obscure; and none, however powerful, can always reward it. Yet, he that sees inferior desert[4] advanced above him, will naturally impute that preference to partiality or caprice; and, indeed, it can scarcely be hoped that any man, however magnanimous by nature, or exalted by condition, will be able to persist forever in fixed and inexorable justice of distribution: he will sometimes indulge his own affections, and sometimes those of his favorites; he will permit some to please him who can never serve him; he will discover in those whom he loves qualities which in reality they do not possess; and to those, from whom he receives pleasure, he will in his turn endeavor to give it. Thus will recommendations sometimes prevail which were purchased by money, or by the more destructive bribery of flattery and servility.

"He that has much to do will do something wrong, and of that wrong must suffer the consequences; and, if it were possible that he should always act rightly, yet when such numbers are to judge of his conduct, the bad will censure and obstruct him by malevolence, and the good sometimes by mistake.

"The highest stations cannot therefore hope to be the abodes of happiness, which I would willingly believe to have fled from thrones and palaces to seats[5] of humble privacy and placid obscurity. For what can hinder the satisfaction, or intercept the expectations, of him whose abilities are adequate to his employments, who sees with his own eyes the whole circuit of his influence, who

4. Merit, worth.   5. Residences.

chooses by his own knowledge all whom he trusts, and whom none are tempted to deceive by hope or fear? Surely he has nothing to do but to love and to be loved, to be virtuous and to be happy."

"Whether perfect happiness would be procured by perfect goodness," said Nekayah, "this world will never afford an opportunity of deciding. But this, at least, may be maintained, that we do not always find visible happiness in proportion to visible virtue. All natural and almost all political evils, are incident alike to the bad and good: they are confounded in the misery of a famine, and not much distinguished in the fury of a faction; they sink together in a tempest, and are driven together from their country by invaders. All that virtue can afford is quietness of conscience, a steady prospect of a happier state; this may enable us to endure calamity with patience; but remember that patience must suppose pain."

CHAPTER XXVIII

Rasselas and Nekayah Continue Their Conversation

"Dear princess," said Rasselas, "you fall into the common errors of exaggeratory declamation, by producing, in a familiar disquisition, examples of national calamities, and scenes of extensive misery, which are found in books rather than in the world, and which, as they are horrid, are ordained to be rare. Let us not imagine evils which we do not feel, nor injure life by misrepresentations. I cannot bear that querulous eloquence which threatens every city with a siege like that of Jerusalem,[6] that makes famine attend on every flight of locusts, and suspends pestilence on the wing of every blast that issues from the south.

"On necessary and inevitable evils, which overwhelm kingdoms at once, all disputation is vain: when they happen they must be endured. But it is evident, that these bursts of universal distress are more dreaded than felt: thousands and ten thousands flourish in youth, and wither in age, without the knowledge of any other than domestic evils, and share the same pleasures and vexations whether their kings are mild or cruel, whether the armies of their country pursue their enemies, or retreat before them. While courts are disturbed with intestine[7] competitions, and ambassadors are negotiating in foreign countries, the smith still plies his anvil, and the husbandman drives his plow forward; the necessaries of life are required and obtained, and the successive business of the seasons continues to make its wonted revolutions.

"Let us cease to consider what, perhaps, may never happen, and what, when it shall happen, will laugh at human speculation. We will not endeavor to modify the motions of the elements, or to fix the destiny of kingdoms. It is our business to consider what beings like us may perform; each laboring for his own happiness, by promoting within his circle, however narrow, the happiness of others.

"Marriage is evidently the dictate of nature; men and women were made to be companions of each other, and therefore I cannot be persuaded but that marriage is one of the means of happiness."

"I know not," said the princess, "whether marriage be more than one of the innumerable modes of human misery. When I see and reckon the various forms

6. The siege of 70 c.e., after which Titus cap-   7. Internal.
tured and destroyed the city.

of connubial infelicity, the unexpected causes of lasting discord, the diversities of temper, the oppositions of opinion, the rude collisions of contrary desire where both are urged by violent impulses, the obstinate contests of disagreeing virtues, where both are supported by consciousness of good intention, I am sometimes disposed to think with the severer casuists of most nations, that marriage is rather permitted than approved, and that none, but by the instigation of a passion too much indulged, entangle themselves with indissoluble compacts."

"You seem to forget," replied Rasselas, "that you have, even now, represented celibacy as less happy than marriage. Both conditions may be bad, but they cannot both be worst. Thus it happens when wrong opinions are entertained, that they mutually destroy each other, and leave the mind open to truth."

"I did not expect," answered the princess, "to hear that imputed to falsehood which is the consequence only of frailty. To the mind, as to the eye, it is difficult to compare with exactness objects vast in their extent, and various in their parts. Where we see or conceive the whole at once we readily note the discriminations and decide the preference: but of two systems, of which neither can be surveyed by any human being in its full compass of magnitude and multiplicity of complication, where is the wonder, that judging of the whole by parts, I am alternately affected by one and the other as either presses on my memory or fancy? We differ from ourselves just as we differ from each other, when we see only part of the question, as in the multifarious relations of politics and morality: but when we perceive the whole at once, as in numerical computations, all agree in one judgment, and none ever varies his opinion."

"Let us not add," said the prince, "to the other evils of life, the bitterness of controversy, nor endeavor to vie with each other in subtleties of argument. We are employed in a search, of which both are equally to enjoy the success, or suffer by the miscarriage. It is therefore fit that we assist each other. You surely conclude too hastily from the infelicity of marriage against its institution; will not the misery of life prove equally that life cannot be the gift of heaven? The world must be peopled by marriage, or peopled without it."

"How the world is to be peopled," returned Nekayah, "is not my care, and needs not be yours. I see no danger that the present generation should omit to leave successors behind them: we are not now inquiring for the world, but for ourselves."

CHAPTER XXIX

The Debate on Marriage Continued

"The good of the whole," says Rasselas, "is the same with the good of all its parts. If marriage be best for mankind it must be evidently best for individuals, or a permanent and necessary duty must be the cause of evil, and some must be inevitably sacrificed to the convenience of others. In the estimate which you have made of the two states, it appears that the incommodities of a single life are, in a great measure, necessary and certain, but those of the conjugal state accidental and avoidable.

"I cannot forbear to flatter myself that prudence and benevolence will make marriage happy. The general folly of mankind is the cause of general complaint. What can be expected but disappointment and repentance from a choice made in the immaturity of youth, in the ardor of desire, without judgment, without foresight, without inquiry after conformity of opinions, similarity of manners, rectitude of judgment, or purity of sentiment.

"Such is the common process of marriage. A youth and maiden meeting by chance, or brought together by artifice, exchange glances, reciprocate civilities, go home, and dream of one another. Having little to divert attention, or diversify thought, they find themselves uneasy when they are apart, and therefore conclude that they shall be happy together. They marry, and discover what nothing but voluntary blindness had before concealed; they wear out life in altercations, and charge nature with cruelty.

"From those early marriages proceeds likewise the rivalry of parents and children: the son is eager to enjoy the world before the father is willing to forsake it, and there is hardly room at once for two generations. The daughter begins to bloom before the mother can be content to fade, and neither can forbear to wish for the absence of the other.

"Surely all these evils may be avoided by that deliberation and delay which prudence prescribes to irrevocable choice. In the variety and jollity of youthful pleasures life may be well enough supported without the help of a partner. Longer time will increase experience, and wider views will allow better opportunities of inquiry and selection: one advantage, at least, will be certain; the parents will be visibly older than their children."

"What reason cannot collect," said Nekayah, "and what experiment has not yet taught, can be known only from the report of others. I have been told that late marriages are not eminently happy. This is a question too important to be neglected, and I have often proposed it to those, whose accuracy of remark, and comprehensiveness of knowledge, made their suffrages[8] worthy of regard. They have generally determined, that it is dangerous for a man and woman to suspend their fate upon each other, at a time when opinions are fixed, and habits are established; when friendships have been contracted on both sides, when life has been planned into method, and the mind has long enjoyed the contemplation of its own prospects.

"It is scarcely possible that two traveling through the world under the conduct of chance, should have been both directed to the same path, and it will not often happen that either will quit the track which custom has made pleasing. When the desultory levity of youth has settled into regularity, it is soon succeeded by pride ashamed to yield, or obstinacy delighting to contend. And even though mutual esteem produces mutual desire to please, time itself, as it modifies unchangeably the external mien, determines likewise the direction of the passions, and gives an inflexible rigidity to the manners. Long customs are not easily broken: he that attempts to change the course of his own life, very often labors in vain; and how shall we do that for others which we are seldom able to do for ourselves?"

"But surely," interposed the prince, "you suppose the chief motive of choice forgotten or neglected. Whenever I shall seek a wife, it shall be my first question, whether she be willing to be led by reason?"

"Thus it is," said Nekayah, "that philosophers are deceived. There are a thousand familiar disputes which reason never can decide; questions that elude

8. Opinions.

investigation, and make logic ridiculous; cases where something must be done, and where little can be said. Consider the state of mankind, and inquire how few can be supposed to act upon any occasions, whether small or great, with all the reasons of action present to their minds. Wretched would be the pair above all names of wretchedness, who should be doomed to adjust by reason every morning all the minute detail of a domestic day.

"Those who marry at an advanced age, will probably escape the encroachments of their children; but, in diminution of this advantage, they will be likely to leave them, ignorant and helpless, to a guardian's mercy: or, if that should not happen, they must at least go out of the world before they see those whom they love best either wise or great.

"From their children, if they have less to fear, they have less also to hope, and they lose, without equivalent, the joys of early love, and the convenience of uniting with manners pliant, and minds susceptible of new impressions, which might wear away their dissimilitudes by long cohabitation, as soft bodies, by continual attrition, conform their surfaces to each other.

"I believe it will be found that those who marry late are best pleased with their children, and those who marry early with their partners."

"The union of these two affections," said Rasselas, "would produce all that could be wished. Perhaps there is a time when marriage might unite them, a time neither too early for the father, nor too late for the husband."

"Every hour," answered the princess, "confirms my prejudice in favor of the position so often uttered by the mouth of Imlac, 'That nature sets her gifts on the right hand and on the left.' Those conditions, which flatter hope and attract desire, are so constituted, that, as we approach one, we recede from another. There are goods so opposed that we cannot seize both, but, by too much prudence, may pass between them at too great a distance to reach either. This is often the fate of long consideration; he does nothing who endeavors to do more than is allowed to humanity. Flatter not yourself with contrarieties of pleasure. Of the blessings set before you make your choice, and be content. No man can taste the fruits of autumn while he is delighting his scent with the flowers of the spring: no man can, at the same time, fill his cup from the source and from the mouth of the Nile."

* * *

[They decide to visit the pyramids, as monuments of the past. Nekayah's attendant, Pekuah, is frightened and remains behind.]

CHAPTER XXXII

They Enter the Pyramid

Pekuah descended to the tents, and the rest entered the pyramid: they passed through the galleries, surveyed the vaults of marble, and examined the chest in which the body of the founder is supposed to have been reposited. They then sat down in one of the most spacious chambers to rest awhile before they attempted to return.

"We have now," said Imlac, "gratified our minds with an exact view of the greatest work of man, except the wall of China."

"Of the wall it is very easy to assign the motives. It secured a wealthy and timorous nation from the incursions of Barbarians, whose unskillfulness in arts made it easier for them to supply their wants by rapine than by industry, and who from time to time poured in upon the habitations of peaceful commerce, as vultures descend upon domestic fowl. Their celerity and fierceness made the wall necessary, and their ignorance made it efficacious.

"But for the pyramids no reason has ever been given adequate to the cost and labor of the work. The narrowness of the chambers proves that it could afford no retreat from enemies, and treasures might have been reposited at far less expense with equal security. It seems to have been erected only in compliance with that hunger of imagination which preys incessantly upon life, and must be always appeased by some employment. Those who have already all that they can enjoy, must enlarge their desires. He that has built for use, till use is supplied, must begin to build for vanity, and extend his plan to the utmost power of human performance, that he may not be soon reduced to form another wish.

"I consider this mighty structure as a monument of the insufficiency of human enjoyments. A king, whose power is unlimited, and whose treasures surmount all real and imaginary wants, is compelled to solace, by the erection of a pyramid, the satiety of dominion and tastelessness of pleasures, and to amuse the tediousness of declining life, by seeing thousands laboring without end, and one stone, for no purpose, laid upon another. Whoever thou art, that, not content with a moderate condition, imaginest happiness in royal magnificence, and dreamest that command or riches can feed the appetite of novelty with perpetual gratifications, survey the pyramids, and confess thy folly!"

* * *

[Pekuah is kidnapped by an Arab, but eventually returns to her friends.]

CHAPTER XL

The History of a Man of Learning

They returned to Cairo, and were so well pleased at finding themselves together, that none of them went much abroad. The prince began to love learning, and one day declared to Imlac, that he intended to devote himself to science, and pass the rest of his days in literary solitude.

"Before you make your final choice," answered Imlac, "you ought to examine its hazards, and converse with some of those who are grown old in the company of themselves. I have just left the observatory of one of the most learned astronomers in the world, who has spent forty years in unwearied attention to the motions and appearances of the celestial bodies, and has drawn out his soul in endless calculations. He admits a few friends once a month to hear his deductions and enjoy his discoveries. I was introduced as a man of knowledge worthy of his notice. Men of various ideas and fluent conversation are commonly welcome to those whose thoughts have been long fixed upon a single point, and who find the images of other things stealing away. I delighted him with my remarks, he smiled at the narrative of my travels, and was glad to forget the constellations, and descend for a moment into the lower world.

"On the next day of vacation I renewed my visit, and was so fortunate as to please him again. He relaxed from that time the severity of his rule, and permitted me to enter at my own choice. I found him always busy, and always glad to be relieved. As each knew much which the other was desirous of learning, we exchanged our notions with great delight. I perceived that I had every day more of his confidence, and always found new cause of admiration in the profundity of his mind. His comprehension is vast, his memory capacious and retentive, his discourse is methodical, and his expression clear.

"His integrity and benevolence are equal to his learning. His deepest researches and most favorite studies are willingly interrupted for any opportunity of doing good by his counsel or his riches. To his closest retreat, at his most busy moments, all are admitted that want his assistance: 'For though I exclude idleness and pleasure, I will never,' says he, 'bar my doors against charity. To man is permitted the contemplation of the skies, but the practice of virtue is commanded.'"

"Surely," said the princess, "this man is happy."

"I visited him," said Imlac, "with more and more frequency, and was every time more enamored of his conversation: he was sublime[9] without haughtiness, courteous without formality, and communicative without ostentation. I was at first, great princess, of your opinion, thought him the happiest of mankind, and often congratulated him on the blessing that he enjoyed. He seemed to hear nothing with indifference but the praises of his condition, to which he always returned a general answer, and diverted the conversation to some other topic.

"Amidst this willingness to be pleased, and labor to please, I had quickly reason to imagine that some painful sentiment pressed upon his mind. He often looked up earnestly towards the sun, and let his voice fall in the midst of his discourse. He would sometimes, when we were alone, gaze upon me in silence with the air of a man who longed to speak what he was yet resolved to suppress. He would often send for me with vehement injunctions of haste, though, when I came to him, he had nothing extraordinary to say. And sometimes, when I was leaving him would call me back, pause a few moments and then dismiss me."

CHAPTER XLI

The Astronomer Discovers the Cause of His Uneasiness

"At last the time came when the secret burst his reserve. We were sitting together last night in the turret of his house, watching the emersion[1] of a satellite of Jupiter. A sudden tempest clouded the sky, and disappointed our observation. We sat awhile silent in the dark, and then he addressed himself to me in these words: 'Imlac, I have long considered thy friendship as the greatest blessing of my life. Integrity without knowledge is weak and useless, and knowledge without integrity is dangerous and dreadful. I have found in thee all the qualities requisite for trust, benevolence, experience, and fortitude. I have

---

9. Noble, exalted.
1. Reappearance (after having been obscured, for example, by clouds).

long discharged an office which I must soon quit at the call of nature, and shall rejoice in the hour of imbecility and pain to devolve it upon thee.'

"I thought myself honored by this testimony, and protested that whatever could conduce to his happiness would add likewise to mine.

" 'Hear, Imlac, what thou wilt not without difficulty credit. I have possessed for five years the regulation of weather, and the distribution of the seasons: the sun has listened to my dictates, and passed from tropic to tropic by my direction; the clouds, at my call, have poured their waters, and the Nile has overflowed at my command; I have restrained the rage of the Dog Star, and mitigated the fervors of the Crab.[2] The winds alone, of all the elemental powers, have hitherto refused my authority, and multitudes have perished by equinoctial tempests which I found myself unable to prohibit or restrain. I have administered this great office with exact justice, and made to the different nations of the earth an impartial dividend of rain and sunshine. What must have been the misery of half the globe, if I had limited the clouds to particular regions, or confined the sun to either side of the equator?' "

CHAPTER XLII

The Opinion of the Astronomer Is Explained and Justified

"I suppose he discovered in me, through the obscurity of the room, some tokens of amazement and doubt, for, after a short pause, he proceeded thus:

" 'Not to be easily credited will neither surprise nor offend me; for I am, probably, the first of human beings to whom this trust has been imparted. Nor do I know whether to deem this distinction a reward or punishment; since I have possessed it I have been far less happy than before, and nothing but the consciousness of good intention could have enabled me to support the weariness of unremitted vigilance.'

" 'How long, Sir,' said I, 'has this great office been in your hands?'

" 'About ten years ago,' said he, 'my daily observations of the changes of the sky led me to consider, whether, if I had the power of the seasons, I could confer greater plenty upon the inhabitants of the earth. This contemplation fastened on my mind, and I sat days and nights in imaginary dominion, pouring upon this country and that the showers of fertility, and seconding every fall of rain with a due proportion of sunshine. I had yet only the will to do good, and did not imagine that I should ever have the power.

" 'One day as I was looking on the fields withering with heat, I felt in my mind a sudden wish that I could send rain on the southern mountains, and raise the Nile to an inundation. In the hurry of my imagination I commanded rain to fall, and, by comparing the time of my command, with that of the inundation, I found that the clouds had listened to my lips.'

" 'Might not some other cause,' said I, 'produce this concurrence? The Nile does not always rise on the same day.'

" 'Do not believe,' said he with impatience, 'that such objections could escape me: I reasoned long against my own conviction, and labored against truth with

2. The constellation Cancer, associated with the summer solstice. "Dog Star": Sirius, which rises in late summer and was supposed to cause insanity.

the utmost obstinacy. I sometimes suspected myself of madness, and should not have dared to impart this secret but to a man like you, capable of distinguishing the wonderful from the impossible, and the incredible from the false.'

" 'Why, Sir,' said I, 'do you call that incredible, which you know, or think you know, to be true?'

" 'Because,' said he, 'I cannot prove it by any external evidence; and I know too well the laws of demonstration to think that my conviction ought to influence another, who cannot, like me, be conscious of its force. I, therefore, shall not attempt to gain credit by disputation. It is sufficient that I feel this power, that I have long possessed, and every day exerted it. But the life of man is short, the infirmities of age increase upon me, and the time will soon come when the regulator of the year must mingle with the dust. The care of appointing a successor has long disturbed me; the night and the day have been spent in comparisons of all the characters which have come to my knowledge, and I have yet found none so worthy as thyself.' "

CHAPTER XLIII

The Astronomer Leaves Imlac His Directions

" 'Hear therefore, what I shall impart, with attention, such as the welfare of a world requires. If the task of a king be considered as difficult, who has the care only of a few millions, to whom he cannot do much good or harm, what must be the anxiety of him, on whom depends the action of the elements, and the great gifts of light and heat!—Hear me therefore with attention.

" 'I have diligently considered the position of the earth and sun, and formed innumerable schemes in which I changed their situation. I have sometimes turned aside the axis of the earth, and sometimes varied the ecliptic of the sun: but I have found it impossible to make a disposition by which the world may be advantaged; what one region gains, another loses by any imaginable alteration, even without considering the distant parts of the solar system with which we are unacquainted. Do not, therefore, in thy administration of the year, indulge thy pride by innovation; do not please thyself with thinking that thou canst make thyself renowned of all future ages, by disordering the seasons. The memory of mischief is no desirable fame. Much less will it become thee to let kindness or interest[3] prevail. Never rob other countries of rain to pour it on thine own. For us the Nile is sufficient.'

"I promised that when I possessed the power, I would use it with inflexible integrity, and he dismissed me, pressing my hand. 'My heart,' said he, 'will be now at rest, and my benevolence will no more destroy my quiet: I have found a man of wisdom and virtue, to whom I can cheerfully bequeath the inheritance of the sun.' "

The prince heard this narration with very serious regard, but the princess smiled, and Pekuah convulsed herself with laughter. "Ladies," said Imlac, "to mock the heaviest of human afflictions is neither charitable nor wise. Few can attain this man's knowledge, and few practice his virtues; but all may suffer his calamity. Of the uncertainties of our present state, the most dreadful and alarming is the uncertain continuance of reason."

3. Self-interest.

The princess was recollected, and the favorite was abashed. Rasselas, more deeply affected, inquired of Imlac, whether he thought such maladies of the mind frequent, and how they were contracted.

CHAPTER XLIV
The Dangerous Prevalence of Imagination

"Disorders of intellect," answered Imlac, "happen much more often than superficial observers will easily believe. Perhaps, if we speak with rigorous exactness, no human mind is in its right state. There is no man whose imagination does not sometimes predominate over his reason, who can regulate his attention wholly by his will, and whose ideas will come and go at his command. No man will be found in whose mind airy notions do not sometimes tyrannize, and force him to hope or fear beyond the limits of sober probability. All power of fancy over reason is a degree of insanity; but while this power is such as we can control and repress, it is not visible to others, nor considered as any depravation of the mental faculties: it is not pronounced madness but when it comes ungovernable, and apparently[4] influences speech or action.

"To indulge the power of fiction, and send imagination out upon the wing, is often the sport of those who delight too much in silent speculation. When we are alone we are not always busy; the labor of excogitation is too violent to last long; the ardor of inquiry will sometimes give way to idleness or satiety. He who has nothing external that can divert him, must find pleasure in his own thoughts, and must conceive himself what he is not; for who is pleased with what he is? He then expatiates in boundless futurity, and culls from all imaginable conditions that which for the present moment he should most desire, amuses his desires with impossible enjoyments, and confers upon his pride unattainable dominion. The mind dances from scene to scene, unites all pleasures in all combinations, and riots in delights which nature and fortune, with all their bounty, cannot bestow.

"In time some particular train of ideas fixes the attention, all other intellectual gratifications are rejected, the mind, in weariness or leisure, recurs constantly to the favorite conception, and feasts on the luscious falsehood whenever she is offended with the bitterness of truth. By degrees the reign of fancy is confirmed; she grows first imperious, and in time despotic. Then fictions begin to operate as realities, false opinions fasten upon the mind, and life passes in dreams of rapture or of anguish.

"This, Sir, is one of the dangers of solitude, which the hermit has confessed not always to promote goodness, and the astronomer's misery has proved to be not always propitious to wisdom."

"I will no more," said the favorite, "imagine myself the queen of Abissinia. I have often spent the hours, which the princess gave to my own disposal, in adjusting ceremonies and regulating the court; I have repressed the pride of the powerful, and granted the petitions of the poor; I have built new palaces in more happy situations, planted groves upon the tops of mountains, and have exulted in the beneficence of royalty, till, when the princess entered, I had almost forgotten to bow down before her."

4. Obviously. "Comes": becomes.

"And I," said the princess, "will not allow myself any more to play the shepherdess in my waking dreams. I have often soothed my thoughts with the quiet and innocence of pastoral employments, till I have in my chamber heard the winds whistle, and the sheep bleat; sometimes freed the lamb entangled in the thicket, and sometimes with my crook encountered the wolf. I have a dress like that of the village maids, which I put on to help my imagination, and a pipe on which I play softly, and suppose myself followed by my flocks."

"I will confess," said the prince, "an indulgence of fantastic delight more dangerous than yours. I have frequently endeavored to image the possibility of a perfect government, by which all wrong should be restrained, all vice reformed, and all the subjects preserved in tranquility and innocence. This thought produced innumerable schemes of reformation, and dictated many useful regulations and salutary edicts. This has been the sport and sometimes the labor of my solitude; and I start, when I think with how little anguish I once supposed the death of my father and my brothers."

"Such," says Imlac, "are the effects of visionary schemes: when we first form them we know them to be absurd, but familiarize them by degrees, and in time lose sight of their folly."

CHAPTER XLV

They Discourse with an Old Man

The evening was now far past, and they rose to return home. As they walked along the bank of the Nile, delighted with the beams of the moon quivering on the water, they saw at a small distance an old man, whom the prince had often heard in the assembly of the sages. "Yonder," said he, "is one whose years have calmed his passions, but not clouded his reason: let us close the disquisitions of the night, by inquiring what are his sentiments of his own state, that we may know whether youth alone is to struggle with vexation, and whether any better hope remains for the latter part of life."

Here the sage approached and saluted them. They invited him to join their walk, and prattled[5] awhile as acquaintance that had unexpectedly met one another. The old man was cheerful and talkative, and the way seemed short in his company. He was pleased to find himself not disregarded, accompanied them to their house, and, at the prince's request, entered with them. They placed him in the seat of honor, and set wine and conserves before him.

"Sir," said the princess, "an evening walk must give to a man of learning, like you, pleasures which ignorance and youth can hardly conceive. You know the qualities and the causes of all that you behold, the laws by which the river flows, the periods in which the planets perform their revolutions. Everything must supply you with contemplation, and renew the consciousness of your own dignity."

"Lady," answered he, "let the gay and the vigorous expect pleasure in their excursions, it is enough that age can obtain ease. To me the world has lost its novelty: I look round, and see what I remember to have seen in happier days. I

5. Chatted.

rest against a tree, and consider, that in the same shade I once disputed upon the annual overflow of the Nile with a friend who is now silent in the grave. I cast my eyes upwards, fix them on the changing moon, and think with pain on the vicissitudes of life. I have ceased to take much delight in physical truth; for what have I to do with those things which I am soon to leave?"

"You may at least recreate yourself," said Imlac, "with the recollection of an honorable and useful life, and enjoy the praise which all agree to give you."

"Praise," said the sage, with a sigh, "is to an old man an empty sound. I have neither mother to be delighted with the reputation of her son, nor wife to partake the honors of her husband. I have outlived my friends and my rivals. Nothing is now of much importance; for I cannot extend my interest beyond myself. Youth is delighted with applause, because it is considered as the earnest of some future good, and because the prospect of life is far extended: but to me, who am now declining to decrepitude, there is little to be feared from the malevolence of men, and yet less to be hoped from their affection or esteem. Something they may yet take away, but they can give me nothing. Riches would now be useless, and high employment would be pain. My retrospect of life recalls to my view many opportunities of good neglected, much time squandered upon trifles, and more lost in idleness and vacancy.[6] I leave many great designs unattempted, and many great attempts unfinished. My mind is burthened with no heavy crime, and therefore I compose myself to tranquillity; endeavor to abstract my thoughts from hopes and cares, which, though reason knows them to be vain, still try to keep their old possession of the heart; expect; with serene humility, that hour which nature cannot long delay; and hope to possess in a better state that happiness which here I could not find, and that virtue which here I have not attained."

He rose and went away, leaving his audience not much elated with the hope of long life. The prince consoled himself with remarking, that it was not reasonable to be disappointed by this account; for age had never been considered as the season of felicity, and, if it was possible to be easy in decline and weakness, it was likely that the days of vigor and alacrity might be happy: that the noon of life might be bright, if the evening could be calm.

The princess suspected that age was querulous and malignant, and delighted to repress the expectations of those who had newly entered the world. She had seen the possessors of estates look with envy on their heirs, and known many who enjoy pleasure no longer than they can confine it to themselves.

Pekuah conjectured, that the man was older than he appeared, and was willing to impute his complaints to delirious dejection; or else supposed that he had been unfortunate, and was therefore discontented: "For nothing," said she, "is more common than to call our own condition, the condition of life."

Imlac, who had no desire to see them depressed, smiled at the comforts which they could so readily procure to themselves, and remembered, that at the same age, he was equally confident of unmingled prosperity, and equally fertile of consolatory expedients. He forbore to force upon them unwelcome knowl-

6. Inactivity.

edge, which time itself would too soon impress. The princess and her lady retired; the madness of the astronomer hung upon their minds, and they desired Imlac to enter upon his office, and delay next morning the rising of the sun.

CHAPTER XLVI

The Princess and Pekuah Visit the Astronomer

The princess and Pekuah having talked in private of Imlac's astronomer, thought his character at once so amiable and so strange, that they could not be satisfied without a nearer knowledge, and Imlac was requested to find the means of bringing them together.

This was somewhat difficult; the philosopher had never received any visits from women, though he lived in a city that had in it many Europeans who followed the manners of their own countries, and many from other parts of the world that lived there with European liberty. The ladies would not be refused, and several schemes were proposed for the accomplishment of their design. It was proposed to introduce them as strangers in distress, to whom the sage was always accessible; but, after some deliberation, it appeared, that by this artifice, no acquaintance could be formed, for their conversation would be short, and they could not decently importune him often. "This," said Rasselas, "is true; but I have yet a stronger objection against the misrepresentation of your state. I have always considered it as treason against the great republic of human nature, to make any man's virtues the means of deceiving him, whether on great or little occasions. All imposture weakens confidence and chills benevolence. When the sage finds that you are not what you seemed, he will feel the resentment natural to a man who, conscious of great abilities, discovers that he has been tricked by understandings meaner than his own, and, perhaps, the distrust, which he can never afterwards wholly lay aside, may stop the voice of counsel, and close the hand of charity; and where will you find the power of restoring his benefactions to mankind, or his peace to himself?"

To this no reply was attempted, and Imlac began to hope that their curiosity would subside; but, next day, Pekuah told him, she had now found an honest pretense for a visit to the astronomer, for she would solicit permission to continue under him the studies in which she had been initiated by the Arab, and the princess might go with her either as a fellow student, or because a woman could not decently come alone. "I am afraid," said Imlac, "that he will be soon weary of your company: men advanced far in knowledge do not love to repeat the elements of their art, and I am not certain that even of the elements, as he will deliver them connected with inferences, and mingled with reflections, you are a very capable auditress." "That," said Pekuah, "must be my care: I ask of you only to take me thither. My knowledge is, perhaps, more than you imagine it, and by concurring always with his opinions I shall make him think it greater than it is."

The astronomer, in pursuance of this resolution, was told, that a foreign lady, traveling in search of knowledge, had heard of his reputation, and was desirous to become his scholar. The uncommonness of the proposal raised at once his surprise and curiosity, and when, after a short deliberation, he consented to admit her, he could not stay without impatience till the next day.

The ladies dressed themselves magnificently, and were attended by Imlac to the astronomer, who was pleased to see himself approached with respect by persons of so splendid an appearance. In the exchange of the first civilities he was timorous and bashful; but when the talk became regular, he recollected his powers, and justified the character[7] which Imlac had given. Inquiring of Pekuah what could have turned her inclination towards astronomy, he received from her a history of her adventure at the pyramid, and of the time passed in the Arab's island. She told her tale with ease and elegance, and her conversation took possession of his heart. The discourse was then turned to astronomy: Pekuah displayed what she knew: he looked upon her as a prodigy of genius, and entreated her not to desist from a study which she had so happily begun.

They came again and again, and were every time more welcome than before. The sage endeavored to amuse them, that they might prolong their visits, for he found his thoughts grow brighter in their company; the clouds of solicitude vanished by degrees, as he forced himself to entertain them, and he grieved when he was left at their departure to his old employment of regulating the seasons.

The princess and her favorite had now watched his lips for several months, and could not catch a single word from which they could judge whether he continued, or not, in the opinion of his preternatural commission. They often contrived to bring him to an open declaration, but he easily eluded all their attacks, and on which side soever they pressed him escaped from them to some other topic.

As their familiarity increased they invited him often to the house of Imlac, where they distinguished him by extraordinary respect. He began gradually to delight in sublunary pleasures. He came early and departed late; labored to recommend himself by assiduity and compliance; excited their curiosity after new arts, that they might still want his assistance; and when they made any excursion of pleasure or inquiry, entreated to attend them.

By long experience of his integrity and wisdom, the prince and his sister were convinced that he might be trusted without danger; and lest he should draw any false hopes from the civilities which he received, discovered to him their condition, with the motives of their journey, and required his opinion on the choice of life.

"Of the various conditions which the world spreads before you, which you shall prefer," said the sage, "I am not able to instruct you. I can only tell that I have chosen wrong. I have passed my time in study without experience; in the attainment of sciences which can, for the most part, be but remotely useful to mankind. I have purchased knowledge at the expense of all the common comforts of life: I have missed the endearing elegance of female friendship, and the happy commerce[8] of domestic tenderness. If I have obtained any prerogatives above other students, they have been accompanied with fear, disquiet, and scrupulosity; but even of these prerogatives, whatever they were, I have, since

7. Characterization.   8. Exchange.

my thoughts have been diversified by more intercourse with the world, begun to question the reality. When I have been for a few days lost in pleasing dissipation,[9] I am always tempted to think that my inquiries have ended in error, and that I have suffered much, and suffered it in vain."

Imlac was delighted to find that the sage's understanding was breaking through its mists, and resolved to detain him from the planets till he should forget his task of ruling them, and reason should recover its original influence.

From this time the astronomer was received into familiar friendship, and partook of all their projects and pleasures: his respect kept him attentive, and the activity of Rasselas did not leave much time unengaged. Something was always to be done; the day was spent in making observations which furnished talk for the evening, and the evening was closed with a scheme for the morrow.

The sage confessed to Imlac, that since he had mingled in the gay tumults of life, and divided his hours by a succession of amusements, he found the conviction of his authority over the skies fade gradually from his mind, and began to trust less to an opinion which he never could prove to others, and which he now found subject to variation from causes in which reason had no part. "If I am accidentally left alone for a few hours," said he, "my inveterate persuasion rushes upon my soul, and my thoughts are chained down by some irresistible violence, but they are soon disentangled by the prince's conversation, and instantaneously released at the entrance of Pekuah. I am like a man habitually afraid of specters, who is set at ease by a lamp, and wonders at the dread which harassed him in the dark, yet, if his lamp be extinguished, feels again the terrors which he knows that when it is light he shall feel no more. But I am sometimes afraid lest I indulge my quiet by criminal negligence, and voluntarily forget the great charge with which I am entrusted. If I favor myself in a known error, or am determined by my own ease in a doubtful question of this importance, how dreadful is my crime!"

"No disease of the imagination," answered Imlac, "is so difficult of cure, as that which is complicated with the dread of guilt: fancy and conscience then act interchangeably upon us, and so often shift their places, that the illusions of one are not distinguished from the dictates of the other. If fancy presents images not moral or religious, the mind drives them away when they give it pain, but when melancholic notions take the form of duty, they lay hold on the faculties without opposition, because we are afraid to exclude or banish them. For this reason the superstitious are often melancholy, and the melancholy almost always superstitious.

"But do not let the suggestions of timidity overpower your better reason: the danger of neglect can be but as the probability of the obligation, which, when you consider it with freedom, you find very little, and that little growing every day less. Open your heart to the influence of the light, which, from time to time, breaks in upon you: when scruples importune you, which you in your lucid moments know to be vain, do not stand to parley, but fly to business or to Pekuah, and keep this thought always prevalent, that you are only one atom of the mass of humanity, and have neither such virtue nor vice, as that you should be singled out for supernatural favors or afflictions."

9. Frivolity.

CHAPTER XLVII

The Prince Enters, and Brings a New Topic

"All this," said the astronomer, "I have often thought, but my reason has been so long subjugated by an uncontrollable and overwhelming idea, that it durst not confide in its own decisions. I now see how fatally I betrayed my quiet, by suffering chimeras to prey upon me in secret; but melancholy shrinks from communication, and I never found a man before, to whom I could impart my troubles, though[1] I had been certain of relief. I rejoice to find my own sentiments confirmed by yours, who are not easily deceived, and can have no motive or purpose to deceive. I hope that time and variety will dissipate the gloom that has so long surrounded me, and the latter part of my days will be spent in peace."

"Your learning and virtue," said Imlac, "may justly give you hopes."

Rasselas then entered with the princess and Pekuah, and inquired whether they had contrived any new diversion for the next day. "Such," said Nekayah, "is the state of life, that none are happy but by the anticipation of change: the change itself is nothing; when we have made it, the next wish is to change again. The world is not yet exhausted; let me see something tomorrow which I never saw before."

* * *

[They visit the catacombs, "ancient repositories, in which the bodies of the earliest generations were lodged."]

CHAPTER XLVIII

Imlac Discourses on the Nature of the Soul

"What reason," said the prince, "can be given, why the Egyptians should thus expensively preserve those carcasses which some nations consume with fire, others lay to mingle with the earth, and all agree to remove from their sight, as soon as decent rites can be performed?"

"The original[2] of ancient customs," said Imlac, "is commonly unknown; for the practice often continues when the cause has ceased; and concerning superstitious ceremonies it is vain to conjecture; for what reason did not dictate reason cannot explain. I have long believed that the practice of embalming arose only from tenderness to the remains of relations or friends, and to this opinion I am more inclined, because it seems impossible that this care should have been general: had all the dead been embalmed, their repositories must in time have been more spacious than the dwellings of the living. I suppose only the rich or honorable were secured from corruption, and the rest left to the course of nature.

"But it is commonly supposed that the Egyptians believed the soul to live as long as the body continued undissolved, and therefore tried this method of eluding death."

"Could the wise Egyptians," said Nekayah, "think so grossly of the soul? If the soul could once survive its separation, what could it afterwards receive or suffer from the body?"

1. Even if.   2. Origin.

"The Egyptians would doubtless think erroneously," said the astronomer, "in the darkness of heathenism, and the first dawn of philosophy. The nature of the soul is still disputed amidst all our opportunities of clearer knowledge: some yet say, that it may be material, who, nevertheless, believe it to be immortal."

"Some," answered Imlac, "have indeed said that the soul is material, but I can scarcely believe that any man has thought it, who knew how to think; for all the conclusions of reason enforce the immateriality of mind, and all the notices of sense and investigations of science concur to prove the unconsciousness of matter.

"It was never supposed that cogitation is inherent in matter, or that every particle is a thinking being. Yet, if any part of matter be devoid of thought, what part can we suppose to think? Matter can differ from matter only in form, density, bulk, motion, and direction of motion: to which of these, however varied or combined, can consciousness be annexed? To be round or square, to be solid or fluid, to be great or little, to be moved slowly or swiftly one way or another, are modes of material existence, all equally alien from the nature of cogitation. If matter be once without thought, it can only be made to think by some new modification, but all the modifications which it can admit are equally unconnected with cogitative powers."

"But the materialists," said the astronomer, "urge that matter may have qualities with which we are unacquainted."

"He who will determine," returned Imlac, "against that which he knows, because there may be something which he knows not; he that can set hypothetical possibility against acknowledged certainty, is not to be admitted among reasonable beings. All that we know of matter is, that matter is inert, senseless and lifeless; and if this conviction cannot be opposed but by referring us to something that we know not, we have all the evidence that human intellect can admit. If that which is known may be overruled by that which is unknown, no being, not omniscient, can arrive at certainty."

"Yet let us not," said the astronomer, "too arrogantly limit the Creator's power."

"It is no limitation of omnipotence," replied the poet, "to suppose that one thing is not consistent with another, that the same proposition cannot be at once true and false, that the same number cannot be even and odd, that cogitation cannot be conferred on that which is created incapable of cogitation."

"I know not," said Nekayah, "any great use of this question. Does that immateriality, which, in my opinion, you have sufficiently proved, necessarily include eternal duration?"

"Of immateriality," said Imlac, "our ideas are negative, and therefore obscure. Immateriality seems to imply a natural power of perpetual duration as a consequence of exemption from all causes of decay: whatever perishes, is destroyed by the solution of its contexture, and separation of its parts; nor can we conceive how that which has no parts, and therefore admits no solution, can be naturally corrupted or impaired."

"I know not," said Rasselas, "how to conceive anything without extension: what is extended must have parts, and you allow, that whatever has parts may be destroyed."

"Consider your own conceptions," replied Imlac, "and the difficulty will be less. You will find substance without extension. An ideal form is no less real than material bulk: yet an ideal form has no extension. It is no less certain, when you think on a pyramid, that your mind possesses the idea of a pyramid, than that the pyramid itself is standing. What space does the idea of a pyramid occupy more than the idea of a grain of corn? or how can either idea suffer laceration? As is the effect such is the cause; as thought is, such is the power that thinks; a power impassive and indiscerptible."[3]

"But the Being," said Nekayah, "whom I fear to name, the Being which made the soul, can destroy it."

"He, surely, can destroy it," answered Imlac, "since, however unperishable, it receives from a superior nature its power of duration. That it will not perish by any inherent cause of decay, or principle of corruption, may be shown by philosophy; but philosophy can tell no more. That it will not be annihilated by him that made it, we must humbly learn from higher authority."

The whole assembly stood awhile silent and collected. "Let us return," said Rasselas, "from this scene of mortality. How gloomy would be these mansions of the dead to him who did not know that he shall never die; that what now acts shall continue its agency, and what now thinks shall think on forever. Those that lie here stretched before us, the wise and the powerful of ancient times, warn us to remember the shortness of our present state: they were, perhaps, snatched away while they were busy, like us, in the choice of life."

"To me," said the princess, "the choice of life is become less important; I hope hereafter to think only on the choice of eternity."

They then hastened out of the caverns, and, under the protection of their guard, returned to Cairo.

CHAPTER XLIX

The Conclusion, in Which Nothing Is Concluded

It was now the time of the inundation of the Nile: a few days after their visit to the catacombs, the river began to rise.

They were confined to their house. The whole region being underwater gave them no invitation to any excursions, and, being well supplied with materials for talk, they diverted themselves with comparisons of the different forms of life which they had observed, and with various schemes of happiness which each of them had formed.

Pekuah was never so much charmed with any place as the convent of St. Anthony, where the Arab restored her to the princess, and wished only to fill it with pious maidens, and to be made prioress of the order: she was weary of expectation and disgust, and would gladly be fixed in some unvariable state.

The princess thought, that of all sublunary things, knowledge was the best: she desired first to learn all sciences, and then purposed to found a college of learned women, in which she would preside, that, by conversing with the old, and educating the young, she might divide her time between the acquisition and communication of wisdom, and raise up for the next age models of prudence, and patterns of piety.

The prince desired a little kingdom, in which he might administer justice in his own person, and see all the parts of government with his own eyes; but he

3. Indivisible.

could never fix the limits of his dominion, and was always adding to the number of his subjects.

Imlac and the astronomer were contented to be driven along the stream of life without directing their course to any particular port.

Of these wishes that they had formed they well knew that none could be obtained. They deliberated awhile what was to be done, and resolved, when the inundation should cease, to return to Abissinia.

FINIS

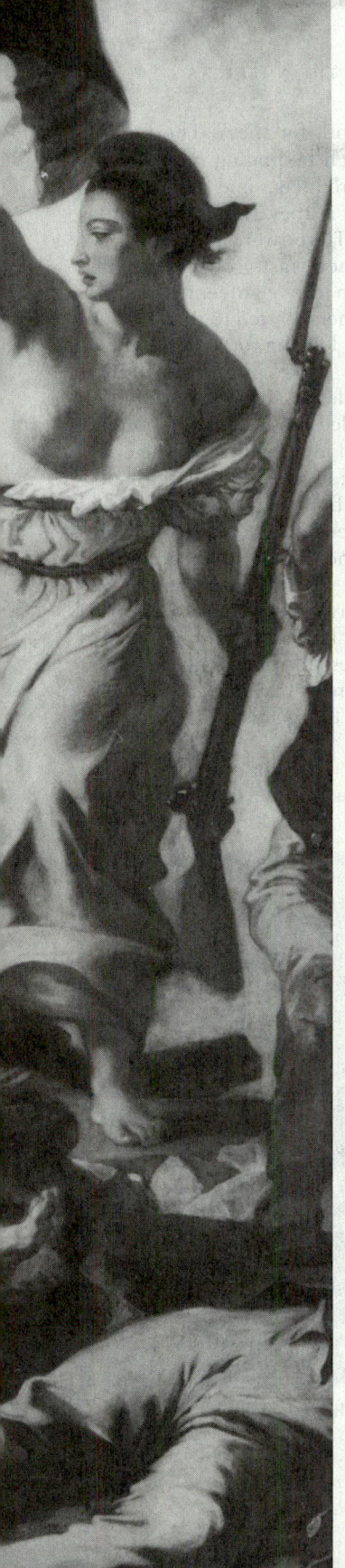

II

An Age of Revolutions in Europe and the Americas

If you were born in 1765, and you happened to live to a ripe old age, you would witness two dramatic revolutions. Together these revolutions would create a period of staggering upheaval unparalleled in prior human history. Whether you happened to find yourself in Texas or London or Buenos Aires, you would see daily life change for almost everyone—rich and poor, rural and urban—and the workings of governments and markets forever transformed. You would have to learn a whole new vocabulary to describe your social world: the terms "factory," "middle class," "capitalism," "industry," "journalism," "liberal," and "conservative" would come into use during your lifetime. You would learn of workers moving to cities in vast numbers. They would live in dismal conditions of filth, disease, and hunger, and at times would erupt in violent protest. You would listen to orators denouncing tyranny and demanding new rights and freedoms. You would hear about an ordinary soldier who rose to conquer most of Europe, and his name, Napoleon, would provoke either a chill of fear or a shiver of exhilaration. You would watch new constitutions take effect and new nations assert themselves. You would see the very map of the world redrawn.

Liberty Leading the People, 1830, Eugène Delacroix.

THE INDUSTRIAL REVOLUTION

The first of the two great upheavals was the industrial revolution, which began in England and then radiated outward, as other nations copied English innovations and as England's increasing commercial and military power conquered large portions of the globe. Before the 1780s economies everywhere changed only at a glacially slow pace. Most of Europe's inhabitants were peasants who worked the land which their forefathers had worked for generations before them, typically growing their own food and making their own clothes, and paying rent to their landowners in exchange for military protection. Many, including Russian serfs, were under the legal control of their landowners and thus forbidden to move from the places where they were born. But agriculture in England was different. There, large landowners rented tracts of land to tenant farmers, who then hired laborers to work for them. The farmers could get rich by finding new markets for their products, and the workers could move if they saw opportunities elsewhere. Here were the seeds of an entirely new, fast-growing capitalist economy. In the eighteenth century, English farmers started to turn into entrepreneurs, looking for faster and better ways to make profits from their lands. In order to attract investors, the nation needed to keep the economy growing, and in order to keep the economy growing, it needed to increase production and find new markets. Colonial expansion seemed like a perfect solution: England fought to acquire and control vast territories abroad, especially in North America, which would provide new land to till and new natural resources to use. Entrepreneurs also found new markets in the colonies to buy the goods which England produced.

The great spur for this new global economy was cotton. Grown and har-

An engraving depicting the interior of the Swainson & Birley Mill in Lancashire, England, ca. 1830.

vested by slaves in the colonies, the raw material was shipped to English entrepreneurs, whose textile factories spun and wove the slave-picked cotton into finished cloth. They eagerly developed new technologies to keep production growing, and that meant that iron and steel industries grew too, allowing for the ever faster production of machines for manufacture and transportation. Railways expanded swiftly. Historians often date the great acceleration of the economy to the 1780s, which was the moment when English exports surpassed imports for the first time. The growth was breathtaking and unprecedented. In 1785 England imported 11 million pounds of raw cotton; by 1850 the English were importing 588 million pounds. They established trade monopolies with India and Latin America, compelling overseas consumers to buy English goods, which meant that exports grew at an astonishing rate: English mill owners had sold more than two billion yards of cotton cloth by the middle of the nineteenth century. England had become the hub of a new world economy, and other nations rushed to imitate English techniques of production. Factories sprang up everywhere.

Not everyone benefited from this extraordinary growth. The workers who moved off ancestral lands to crowd into new industrial centers labored in unregulated factories, often inhaling dust or having their limbs broken in machines. Employers looked for the cheapest labor, typically hiring women and children, and forced them to work 14- and even 16-hour days. Barely paid a subsistence wage, the new urban working class made do with living conditions that were even more appalling than conditions in the factories where they worked. Cities grew at such a fast rate that urban populations quickly outpaced the availability of necessities such as adequate housing and the supply of clean water. The result was a sequence

Wentworth Street, Whitechapel, 1872, Gustave Doré. A late 19th-century depiction of the squalor in London's slums.

of major epidemics, including cholera and typhoid fever, which overwhelmed congested slums but hardly touched the middle and upper classes. To add to the general hardships for the poor, the economy had already begun the international cycles of boom and bust that would characterize the next two centuries. In periods of poor growth, unemployed workers literally starved. Feelings of angry discontent grew rapidly alongside the new economy.

Overseas, too, large populations began to suffer from industrialization. The huge acceleration in the English economy had absolutely depended on slavery. Six million slaves had been captured and sent from Africa to the Americas in the eighteenth century alone, many to serve the booming cotton trade. Meanwhile, India's economy plunged. Until the eighteenth century, India had had a thriving manufacturing sector that produced gorgeous textiles for export, but the new factory-made cloth from England came in at low prices and depressed the market. Many workers in India were forced back into agriculture, which deindustrialized India's economy, setting it on a slower track. Latin America, too, increasingly organized its economies of mining and agriculture around exports to England—including sugar, coffee, and silver—which made the new Latin American nations worryingly dependent on agriculture and on economic decisions made in England.

DEMOCRATIC REVOLUTIONS

As the industrial revolution was producing vast wealth, changing labor practices, molding a class of angry urban workers, rapidly expanding cities, and creating new and uneven global trade relations, a second revolution was also taking place. This revolution was political. Intent on throwing off old hierarchies that gave power to kings and compelled everyone else to act as obedient subjects, revolutionaries in North America and France argued that ordinary people should take political decision making into their own hands. This was a democratic revolution that, like the industrial revolution, had global effects, transforming expectations about basic rights and freedoms worldwide.

In North America, colonial subjects became increasingly resentful of the power of the English king, who made both political and economic decisions that favored England. In 1776 they declared independence not only from English rule but from the whole structure of the old regime, rejecting its hereditary monarchy in favor of a new elected president. They vested power in "the people," insisting that governments should derive their power only from the consent of the governed. This was a radical new foundation for politics, and it inspired many later constitutions.

In Europe, another, even more dramatic political revolution was brewing. The French monarchy had become ever more absolutist, and peasants were growing resentful of the traditional taxes and tithes they had to pay. Bad harvests in 1788 and 1789 doubled the cost of bread, but the king seemed entirely indifferent to the fate of a starving people. (When told that the peasants were calling for bread, Queen Marie Antoinette is famous for responding, "Let them eat cake.") On July 14, 1789, a loosely organized armed mob stormed the Bastille prison—a symbol of royal power—and called for the liberation of the French people. The news spread quickly. Within a month, uprisings all across France had wrecked the traditional feudal social hierarchy and ushered in a new era. **The Declaration of the Rights of Man and of the Citizen**, issued by the French National Assembly in August, asserted the equality and freedom of all men and abolished all privileges based on birth. The revolutionary government insisted on ruling by reason, not by tradition. They adopted the innovative new metric system, separated church and state, abolished slavery in the French colonies, and granted equal rights to everyone, including, for the first time, Jews. The French Revolution also helped to unleash a new force in world affairs: nationalism. France was no longer a land possessed by a powerful ruling family, but stood for a self-governing and autonomous "people." In a powerful symbolic gesture, the revolutionaries renamed 1789 as "Year Zero," suggesting that nothing that had happened before the revolution mattered. They then stunned Europe by sending the king to his death in 1793, executing him with a sleek new machine intended to make killing more humane: the guillotine.

The French Revolution sent shock waves around the world. Throughout Europe and the Americas, suddenly it seemed possible that people might rise

The siege of the Bastille, July 1789.

up against their oppressors, violently opposing traditional authority in the name of individual human rights. Huge divisions emerged between those who saw the revolutionaries as vicious and reckless, and those who heralded them as the opening of a whole new chapter in human history.

Other European powers, fearful that revolution might spread into their territories, went to war with France in 1792, and the whole country threatened to collapse in disarray. A small group of radicals, called the Jacobins, seized control and united the nation under a strong centralized dictatorship, mobilizing the nation for war and sending all traitors—and potential traitors—to the guillotine. Their short period of leadership in 1793–94 has come to be known as the "Reign of Terror." The blood they shed sickened many observers who had once sympathized with the aims of the revolution, and the "Reign of Terror" has, ever since, been seen as a symbol of revolutionary violence taken too far.

As the new French government faltered and changed leadership, a talented young soldier who had helped the French to defeat the British at Toulon in 1793 was rising up through the ranks. Born on the remote island of Corsica, Napoleon Bonaparte had few advantages of birth or connections, but his genius for military strategy, his extraordinary ambition, and his own huge popularity allowed him to take advantage of government weakness during a wave of foreign invasions and to position himself as the new leader of France. In 1799 he installed a new dictatorship and through a vast military campaign redrew the map of Europe, bringing large parts of Spain, Germany, Austria, Italy, and Poland under French control. He crowned himself emperor in 1804. Ravenous

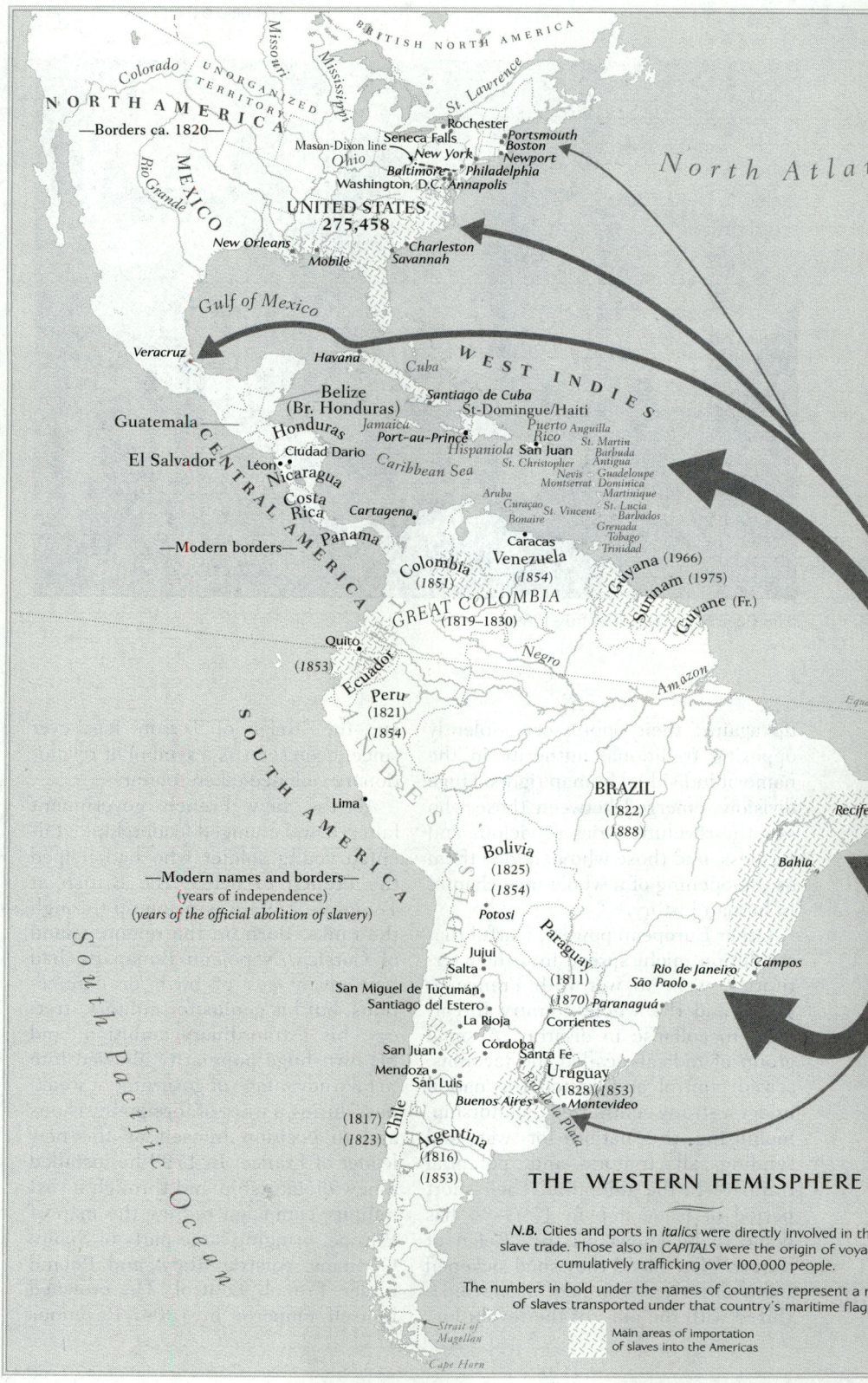

NORTH AMERICA
—Borders ca. 1820—

Colorado

UNORGANIZED TERRITORY

Missouri

Mississippi

BRITISH NORTH AMERICA

St. Lawrence

• Rochester
Portsmouth
Mason-Dixon line Seneca Falls *Boston*
Ohio *New York* *Newport*
Baltimore • *Philadelphia*
Washington, D.C. • *Annapolis*

UNITED STATES
275,458

New Orleans •

• Mobile • *Charleston*
Savannah

MEXICO

Rio Grande

Gulf of Mexico

Veracruz • • *Havana* *Cuba*

W E S T   I N D I E S

North Atlan

Belize
(Br. Honduras)

Guatemala —

Honduras

• *Santiago de Cuba*
St-Domingue/Haiti
Jamaica Puerto Anguilla
Port-au-Prince Rico St. Martin

Ciudad Dario

El Salvador León •

• Nicaragua
Costa
Rica

• Cartagena

Hispaniola *San Juan* Barbuda
St. Christopher • Antigua
Nevis • *Guadeloupe*
Montserrat *Dominica*
Martinique

Caribbean Sea

CENTRAL AMERICA

—Modern borders— Panama

Colombia
(1851)

Venezuela
(1854)

• Caracas

Aruba *St. Lucia*
Curaçao St. Vincent • *Barbados*
Bonaire Grenada
Tobago
Trinidad

Guyana (1966)

Surinam (1975)

GREAT COLOMBIA
(1819–1830)

Guyane (Fr.)

Quito •

(1853)

Ecuador

Negro

Amazon

Equat

Peru
(1821)
(1854)

SOUTH AMERICA

ANDES

BRAZIL
(1822)
(1888)

Recife

Lima •

—Modern names and borders—
(years of independence)
(years of the official abolition of slavery)

Bolivia
(1825)
(1854)

Potosi •

Bahia

Paraguay

Jujui •
Salta •

San Miguel de Tucumán •
Santiago del Estero •

• La Rioja

San Juan •
Mendoza • Córdoba •
San Luis • Santa Fe •

(1817)
(1823) Chile

Buenos Aires •

Argentina
(1816)
(1853)

Rio de Janeiro • • Campos
São Paolo •

(1811)

(1870) *Paranaguá*

Corrientes •

Uruguay
(1828)(1853)
Río de la Plata • *Montevideo*

South Pacific Ocean

*Strait of
Magellan*

Cape Horn

THE WESTERN HEMISPHERE

N.B. Cities and ports in *italics* were directly involved in the
slave trade. Those also in *CAPITALS* were the origin of voyac
cumulatively trafficking over 100,000 people.

The numbers in bold under the names of countries represent a m
of slaves transported under that country's maritime flag.

Main areas of importation
of slaves into the Americas

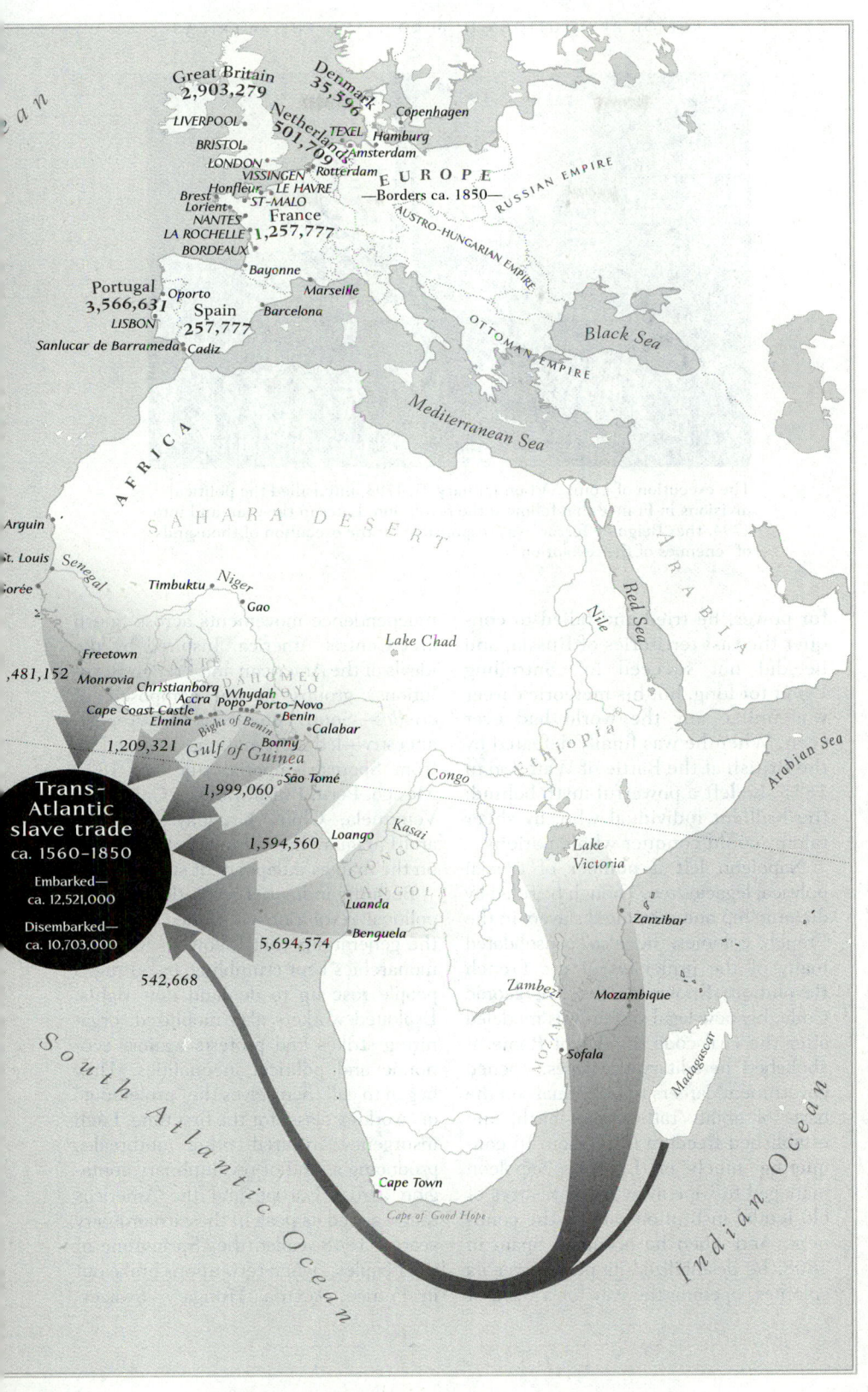

Great Britain
2,903,279

LIVERPOOL
BRISTOL
LONDON
VISSINGEN
Honfleur ST-MALO
Brest LE HAVRE
Lorient
NANTES
LA ROCHELLE France
BORDEAUX 1,257,777

Denmark
35,596

Copenhagen
Hamburg
Netherlands
501,709 Amsterdam
Rotterdam

EUROPE
—Borders ca. 1850—
AUSTRO-HUNGARIAN EMPIRE

RUSSIAN EMPIRE

Bayonne

Portugal
3,566,631
LISBON
Sanlucar de Barrameda Cadiz

Oporto
Marseille
Spain Barcelona
257,777

OTTOMAN EMPIRE

Black Sea

Mediterranean Sea

Arguin
St. Louis
Gorée

AFRICA

SAHARA DESERT

Senegal

Timbuktu Niger
Gao

Lake Chad

ARABIA

Red Sea

Nile

Arabian Sea

,481,152

Freetown
Monrovia Christianborg Whydah
Accra Popo Porto-Novo
Cape Coast Castle Benin
Elmina Bight of Benin Calabar
1,209,321 Gulf of Guinea Bonny

DAHOMEY

São Tomé

Congo

Ethiopia

1,999,060

**Trans-Atlantic
slave trade
ca. 1560–1850**

Embarked—
ca. 12,521,000

Disembarked—
ca. 10,703,000

1,594,560 Loango Kasai

Lake
Victoria

CONGO

ANGOLA

Luanda

Benguela

Zanzibar

5,694,574

542,668

Zambezi

Mozambique

South Atlantic Ocean

Sofala

Madagascar

Cape Town

Cape of Good Hope

Indian Ocean

The execution of Louis XVI on January 21, 1793, intensified the political divisions in France that followed the revolution. Later in the year, and into 1794, the "Reign of Terror" was responsible for the execution of thousands of "enemies of the revolution."

for power, he tried and failed to conquer the vast territories of Russia, and he did not succeed in controlling Egypt for long, but his meteoric career was unlike any the world had ever seen. When he was finally defeated by the British at the Battle of Waterloo in 1815, he left a powerful myth behind: the brilliant individual who, by sheer talent, could conquer whole nations.

Napoleon left a number of crucial political legacies too. Though he ruled by dictatorship and reinstated slavery in the French colonies, he also consolidated many of the principles of the French Revolution. Known as the Napoleonic Code, his new legal system was modeled after the civil code of ancient Rome: it abolished hereditary privileges, opened government careers to individuals on the basis of ability rather than birth, and established freedom of religion. In conquering much of Europe, Napoleon managed to wipe away many vestiges of old feudal institutions across the continent. And when he occupied Spain in 1808, he destabilized its power over its colonies, opening the way for a wave of

independence movements across South and Central America. Inspired by the ideals of the American and French Revolutions, groups mostly composed of *criollos*—South Americans of European ancestry—led new nations to freedom from Spanish imperial rule. By 1825 Mexico, Peru, Brazil, Bolivia, Colombia, Venezuela, Chile, Uruguay, Ecuador, and Paraguay had all taken their places on the map as independent states.

Both the industrial revolution and the political revolution continued to haunt the generations that followed. Absolute monarchies kept crumbling, as outraged people rose up to demand new rights. Exploited workers also mobilized, organizing strikes and protests against economic and political inequalities. They began to call themselves the "proletariat" or "working class" for the first time. Each insurgency inspired other outbreaks, producing a kind of revolutionary contagion across Europe and the Americas that reached its peak in the extraordinary year of 1848, called the "Springtime of the Peoples," when revolutions broke out in France, Austria, Hungary, Switzer-

Napoleon at the Battle of Waterloo, 1815, Charles Auguste Steuben. Most artists' portrayals of Napoleon, even in defeat (as here, where he is shown during the Battle of Waterloo), reinforced a romanticized, heroic ideal.

land, Spain, Germany, Italy, Denmark, and Romania. This was the year that Karl Marx and Friedrich Engels published the *Communist Manifesto*, which ended with the battle cry: "Workers of the world, unite!" It was in this year that the French abolished slavery for good. And it was in the same year that women's rights activists in the United States organized their first convention at Seneca Falls, New York, where, in a deliberate echo of the Declaration of Independence, they made the case "that all men and women are created equal."

LITERATURE IN THE AGE OF REVOLUTIONS

Utopian dreams have always driven political revolutionaries. In fact, there can be no revolution without acts of imagination. If the old world must be banished and a new world put in its place, what should that new world look like? The first wave of American and French revolutionaries were inspired by the work of eighteenth-century Enlightenment thinkers who envisioned a society governed by reason rather than by custom or superstition. In particular, the philosopher and novelist **Jean-Jacques Rousseau** powerfully stirred the French revolutionaries by imagining a universal emancipation from tyranny: "Man is born free," he wrote, "but everywhere is in chains." The industrial revolution, too, depended on the workings of the imagination: it was spurred by new schemes for increasing the speed of production, for the invention of huge new machines and the creation of fast modes of communication and transportation. It was fueled, too, by dreams of unprecedented wealth.

Since imagination seemed so crucial to the making of these modern revolutions, writers and artists began to see themselves as playing an important role in the tumult of the times. Art, it seemed, could have the power to transform the world. Many writers eagerly

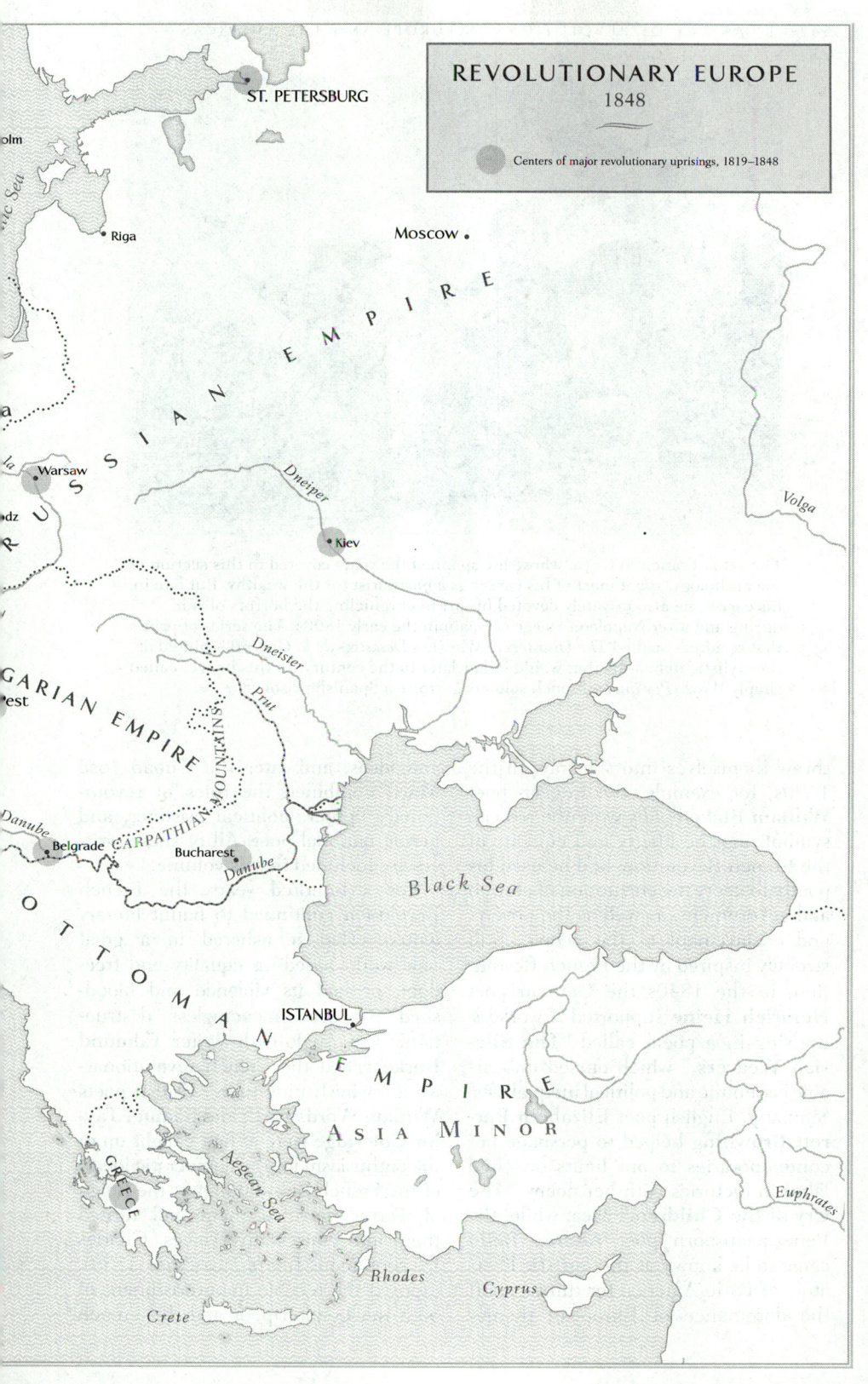

ST. PETERSBURG

Riga

Moscow

olm

ic Sea

RUSSIAN EMPIRE

Volga

Warsaw

dz

Dneiper

Kiev

GARIAN EMPIRE

est

Dneister

Prut

CARPATHIAN MOUNTAINS

Danube

Belgrade

Bucharest

Danube

Black Sea

OTTOMAN EMPIRE

ISTANBUL

ASIA MINOR

Aegean Sea

GREECE

Rhodes

Cyprus

Euphrates

Crete

The artist Francisco Goya, whose life spanned the years covered in this section of the anthology, spent most of his career as a portraitist for the wealthy. But late in his career, he also privately devoted his art to chronicling the horrors of war during and after Napoleon's siege of Spain in the early 1800s. The series of prints that resulted—called *The Disasters of War* (*Los Desastres de la Guerra*)—hinted at the stylistic upheavals that would follow later in the century. In this image, called simply *Why?* (*Por qué?*), French soldiers garrotte a Spanish prisoner.

threw themselves into the fray. In the 1790s, for example, the English poet **William Blake** boldly wore the red cap symbolizing the liberty and equality of the French Revolution, and he used his poetry to decry the corruption of church and government, as well as the poverty and enslavement of the people. Still strongly inspired by the French Revolution, in the 1840s the German poet **Heinrich Heine** supported a workers' uprising in a poem called **"The Silesian Weavers,"** which cursed unbearable economic and political inequalities. Similarly, English poet **Elizabeth Barrett Browning** helped to persuade her contemporaries to put limits on child labor in factories with her poem, **"The Cry of the Children."** Meanwhile, the Venezuelan-born poet **Andrés Bello** came to be known as the "artistic liberator" of Latin America for throwing off the dominance of European themes and ideas, and later the Cuban **José Martí** combined the roles of revolutionary fighter, political prisoner, and heroic national poet. All of these writers are included in this volume.

For a hundred years, the French Revolution continued to haunt literary writers. Had it ushered in a great new world based on equality and freedom, or had its violence and bloodshed produced meaningless destruction? The Anglo-Irish writer **Edmund Burke** called the French revolutionaries a "swinish multitude"; British poets **William Wordsworth** and **Samuel Taylor Coleridge** were at first caught up in the enthusiasm for the democratic ideals of the French Revolution, but the Reign of Terror horrified them and turned them into conservative voices. Charles Dickens, in his *Tale of Two Cities* (1859), exposed the terrible impoverishment of both the London poor and the French peasantry, and yet did not support the French Revolution: the sinister revolutionary Madame Defarge represents vengeful bloodshed. On the other hand, the revolutionaries continued to inspire passionate adherents. "Whatever else may be said of it," asserts a character in **Victor Hugo's novel** *Les Misérables* (1862), "the French Revolution was the greatest step forward by mankind since the coming of Christ." And whichever side one took, according to the English poet **Percy Shelley**, the French Revolution was simply "the master theme of the epoch in which we live."

Napoleon provided inspiration for novelists, who used his remarkable rise to shape both sensational adventures and political reflections. Alexandre Dumas, the grandson of a slave whose father had been dismissed from the French army by Napoleon because of the color of his skin, wrote an enormously popular novel called *The Count of Monte Cristo* (1844), where the protagonist is imprisoned for helping Napoleon. Russian writer **Leo Tolstoy** later set his magisterial *War and Peace* (1869) in Russia at the time of Napoleon's invasion, and **Herman Melville**, an American, looked back to the Napoleonic wars in *Billy Budd* (1891) to tell the story of a sailor on a British ship fighting against the French army.

The upheavals of this revolutionary moment did not only provide compelling subject matter for writers. This was a period that dramatically altered the very forms of art. Until the nineteenth century, artists in Europe had mostly worked for the old wealthy elites: powerful aristocrats or the Catholic Church. Now they began to create works of art for "the people." In this context, traditional modes of writing often seemed ill-suited to new democratic ideals. What was needed was a revolution in style and form. Thus when Wordsworth and Coleridge collaborated on a volume of poetry in 1798, they outright rejected "the gaudiness and inane phraseology" of earlier poetry in favor of "language really used by men." For generations to follow, writers would struggle to capture the revolutionary tumult of the times in startling and sometimes uncomfortable new forms, insisting on experimenting, on innovating, on seeing the world afresh—and never getting buried in old routines. This impulse to revolutionize the way people saw the world was to become part of the definition of art itself. The late nineteenth-century painter Paul Gauguin maintained that every artist was "either a plagiarist or a revolutionary." And if those were the only choices, then what self-respecting artist wouldn't choose revolution?

REVOLUTIONARY CONTEXTS

The word *revolution* comes from the Latin *revolvere*, "to turn." Once associated with astronomy to refer to the rotation of celestial bodies, in the eighteenth century the word came more and more frequently to signify a total overthrow of the existing political and social order. The American Revolution of 1776, the French Revolution of 1789, the Latin American independence movements, the outbreak of revolutions across Europe and the Americas in 1848, and the ongoing industrial revolution that spread worldwide throughout the nineteenth century all promised that kind of comprehensive transformation. Not every revolution delivered on that promise, however. While it might seem relatively straightforward to topple tyrants and resist established hierarchies, it turned out to be intensely difficult to put something radically different—and better—in their place. Thus revolutionary leaders often labored to create powerful declarations, proclamations, and constitutions that would lay down convincing foundations for a wholly new society. Many turned to traditions of philosophical thought, and in particular to the European philosophers of the Enlightenment, to answer the most difficult questions. What values and principles should guide relationships between governments and those they govern? Should ordinary life be transformed as well as political institu-

tions? What laws does a just society require? In this context, writing mattered. For the first time, societies around the world claimed to be governed by principles laid down in founding documents. The words that articulated the very grounds of new societies had to be forceful, widely persuasive, and durable.

Collected here are some of the most influential of those documents—the **U.S. Declaration of Independence**, the **Declaration of the Rights of Man and of the Citizen** issued by the revolutionary French government, two assertions of the rights of women (one from France and one from the United States), a proclamation from the Haitian Revolution, and **Simón Bolívar's** letter, in which an anticolonial leader announces the principles for revolution in Latin America. Each seeks to establish not only new laws and governments but also what it means to be human, what responsibilities we have to one another, and what justice and freedom entail. Included here with these documents are also the comments of two influential observers: **Edmund Burke**, a British politician who bitterly opposed the French Revolution and became one of the most influential voices for those ever since who favor conserving, rather than overthrowing, existing social arrangements; and **William Wordsworth**, a poet who had been inspired by the French Revolution, horrified by the Reign of Terror that followed it, and then sympathetic to the Haitian Revolution, though not hopeful. He captures in poetic form some of the ambivalence of living through the promise and the violence of revolutionary upheaval.

The Declaration of Independence, July 4, 1776, engraving based on a painting by John Trumbell.

U.S. DECLARATION OF INDEPENDENCE

Written by Thomas Jefferson (1743–1826), the Declaration of Independence draws on principles propounded by Enlightenment philosophers. Among these are the notion that human beings are given natural or "inalienable" rights by God, and that governments are not entitled to impose their will arbitrarily but instead derive their power from the people. Although these ideas were not new at the time of the American Revolution, no society before this moment had ever tried to found a state upon them. The Declaration passed the Continental Congress in Philadelphia on July 4, 1776.

This document is celebrated not only for its affirmation of radical principles for government but also for its compelling style. Rather than beginning with defenses or accusations, it "declares" a series of truths—foundational ideas about human nature and government—which it simply asserts as "self-evident." After affirming these general truths, it builds a dramatic picture of King George III's tyranny, presented as a sequence of incontrovertible facts which any impartial observer would decry. It builds to the rousing conclusion that the colonists are willing to stake their lives and their honor on the necessity of independence. Jefferson's brilliant writing—compact and logical, but also stirring and musical—has made this one of the most famous of all political documents.

The Declaration of Independence:

IN CONGRESS, JULY 4, 1776.

The unanimous Declaration of the thirteen united States of America,

When in the Course of human events, it becomes necessary for one people to dissolve the political bands which have connected them with another, and to assume among the powers of the earth, the separate and equal station to which the Laws of Nature and of Nature's God entitle them, a decent respect to the opinions of mankind requires that they should declare the causes which impel them to the separation.

We hold these truths to be self-evident, that all men are created equal, that they are endowed by their Creator with certain unalienable Rights, that among these are Life, Liberty and the pursuit of Happiness.—That to secure these rights, Governments are instituted among Men, deriving their just powers from the consent of the governed,—That whenever any Form of Government becomes destructive of these ends, it is the Right of the People to alter or to abolish it, and to institute new Government, laying its foundation on such principles and organizing its powers in such form, as to them shall seem most likely to effect their Safety and Happiness. Prudence, indeed, will dictate that Governments long established should not be changed for light and transient causes; and accordingly all experience hath shewn, that mankind are more disposed to suffer, while evils are sufferable, than to right themselves by abolishing the forms to which they are accustomed. But when a long train of abuses and usurpations, pursuing invariably the same Object evinces a design to reduce them under absolute Despotism, it is their right, it is their duty, to throw off such Government, and to provide new Guards for their future security.—Such has been the patient sufferance of these Colonies; and such is now the necessity which constrains them to alter their former Systems of Government. The history of the present King of Great Britain[1] is a history of repeated injuries and usurpations, all having in direct object the establishment of an absolute Tyranny over these States. To prove this, let Facts be submitted to a candid world.

He has refused his Assent to Laws, the most wholesome and necessary for the public good.

He has forbidden his Governors to pass Laws of immediate and pressing importance, unless suspended in their operation till his Assent should be obtained; and when so suspended, he has utterly neglected to attend to them.

He has refused to pass other Laws for the accommodation of large districts of people, unless those people would relinquish the right of Representation in the Legislature, a right inestimable to them and formidable to tyrants only.

He has called together legislative bodies at places unusual, uncomfortable, and distant from the depository of their public Records, for the sole purpose of fatiguing them into compliance with his measures.

He has dissolved Representative Houses repeatedly, for opposing with manly firmness his invasions on the rights of the people.

He has refused for a long time, after such dissolutions, to cause others to be elected; whereby the Legislative powers, incapable of Annihilation, have returned to the People at large for their exercise; the State remaining in the mean time exposed to all the dangers of invasion from without, and convulsions within.

He has endeavoured to prevent the population of these States; for that purpose obstructing the Laws for Naturalization of Foreigners; refusing to pass others to encourage their migrations hither, and raising the conditions of new Appropriations of Lands.

He has obstructed the Administration of Justice, by refusing his Assent to Laws for establishing Judiciary powers.

He has made Judges dependent on his Will alone, for the tenure of their offices, and the amount and payment of their salaries.

He has erected a multitude of New Offices, and sent hither swarms of Officers to harrass our people, and eat out their substance.

He has kept among us, in times of peace, Standing Armies without the Consent of our legislatures.

He has affected to render the Military independent of and superior to the Civil power.

He has combined with others to subject us to a jurisdiction foreign to our constitution, and unacknowledged by our laws; giving his Assent to their Acts of pretended Legislation:

---

1. George III (1738–1820).

For Quartering large bodies of armed troops among us:

For protecting them, by a mock Trial, from punishment for any Murders which they should commit on the Inhabitants of these States:

For cutting off our Trade with all parts of the world:

For imposing Taxes on us without our Consent:

For depriving us in many cases, of the benefits of Trial by Jury:

For transporting us beyond Seas to be tried for pretended offences:

For abolishing the free System of English Laws in a neighbouring Province, establishing therein an Arbitrary government, and enlarging its Boundaries so as to render it at once an example and it instrument for introducing the same absolute rule into these Colonies:

For taking away our Charters, abolishing our most valuable Laws, and altering fundamentally the Forms of our Governments:

For suspending our own Legislatures, and declaring themselves invested with power to legislate for us in all cases whatsoever.

He has abdicated Government here, by declaring us out of his Protection and waging War against us.

He has plundered our seas, ravaged our Coasts, burnt our towns, and destroyed the lives of our people.

He is at this time transporting large Armies of foreign Mercenaries to compleat the works of death, desolation and tyranny, already begun with circumstances of Cruelty & perfidy scarcely paralleled in the most barbarous ages, and totally unworthy the Head of a civilized nation.

He has constrained our fellow Citizens taken Captive on the high Seas to bear Arms against their Country, to become the executioners of their friends and Brethren, or to fall themselves by their Hands.

He has excited domestic insurrections amongst us, and has endeavoured to bring on the inhabitants of our frontiers, the merciless Indian Savages, whose known rule of warfare, is an undistinguished destruction of all ages, sexes and conditions.

In every stage of these Oppressions We have Petitioned for Redress in the most humble terms: Our repeated Petitions have been answered only by repeated injury. A Prince whose character is thus marked by every act which may define a Tyrant, is unfit to be the ruler of a free people.

Nor have We been wanting in attentions to our Brittish brethren. We have warned them from time to time of attempts by their legislature to extend an unwarrantable jurisdiction over us. We have reminded them of the circumstances of our emigration and settlement here. We have appealed to their native justice and magnanimity, and we have conjured them by the ties of our common kindred to disavow these usurpations, which, would inevitably interrupt our connections and correspondence. They too have been deaf to the voice of justice and of consanguinity. We must, therefore, acquiesce in the necessity, which denounces our Separation, and hold them, as we hold the rest of mankind, Enemies in War, in Peace Friends.

We, therefore, the Representatives of the united States of America, in General Congress, Assembled, appealing to the Supreme Judge of the world for the rectitude of our intentions, do, in the Name, and by Authority of the good

People of these Colonies, solemnly publish and declare, That these United Colonies are, and of Right ought to be Free and Independent States; that they are Absolved from all Allegiance to the British Crown, and that all political connection between them and the State of Great Britain, is and ought to be totally dissolved; and that as Free and Independent States, they have full Power to levy War, conclude Peace, contract Alliances, establish Commerce, and to do all other Acts and Things which Independent States may of right do. And for the support of this Declaration, with a firm reliance on the protection of divine Providence, we mutually pledge to each other our Lives, our Fortunes and our sacred Honor.

DECLARATION OF THE RIGHTS OF MAN AND OF THE CITIZEN

After the storming of the Bastille Prison in Paris on July 14, 1789, leaders of the French Revolution agreed on the need to draw up a declaration of rights. They debated whether to craft a short document that focused entirely on general rights, or to produce a detailed explanation of each principle. And should they include duties and obligations as well as rights? In the end, they opted for something easy to read and disseminate. Brief enough to take up one side of a sheet of paper, the Declaration of the Rights of Man and of the Citizen appeared all over France immediately after its passage on August 26, 1789. It was soon translated into every major European language and so conveyed the universalizing ideals of the French Revolution well beyond France.

Like the Continental Congress in the United States, the French National Assembly rested their founding document on the assertion of natural human rights. In fact, Thomas Jefferson, who was the U.S. envoy to France at the time, lent his help in drafting the language, though the rights asserted in France are interestingly different from those found in the U.S. Declaration of Independence.

Declaration of the Rights of Man and of the Citizen[1]

The representatives of the French people, organized in National Assembly,[2] considering that ignorance, forgetfulness or contempt of the rights of man are the sole causes of the public miseries and of the corruption of governments,

---

1. Translated by Frank Maloy Anderson.
2. The new French people's government, convened in 1789, responsible for the radical transformations that mark the beginning of the French Revolution.

have resolved to set forth in a solemn declaration the natural, inalienable, and sacred rights of man, in order that this declaration, being ever present to all the members of the social body, may unceasingly remind them of their rights and their duties; in order that the acts of the legislative power and those of the executive power may be each moment compared with the aim of every political institution and thereby may be more respected; and in order that the demands of the citizens, grounded henceforth upon simple and incontestable principles, may always take the direction of maintaining the constitution and the welfare of all.

In consequence, the National Assembly recognizes and declares, in the presence and under the auspices of the Supreme Being,[3] the following rights of man and citizen.

1. Men are born and remain free and equal in rights. Social distinctions can be based only upon public utility.

2. The aim of every political association is the preservation of the natural and imprescriptible rights of man. These rights are liberty, property, security, and resistance to oppression.

3. The source of all sovereignty is essentially in the nation; no body, no individual can exercise authority that does not proceed from it in plain terms.

4. Liberty consists in the power to do anything that does not injure others; accordingly, the exercise of the natural rights of each man has for its only limits those that secure to the other members of society the enjoyment of these same rights. These limits can be determined only by law.

5. The law has the right to forbid only such actions as are injurious to society. Nothing can be forbidden that is not interdicted by the law and no one can be constrained to do that which it does not order.

6. Law is the expression of the general will. All citizens have the right to take part personally or by their representatives in its formation. It must be the same for all, whether it protects or punishes. All citizens being equal in its eyes, are equally eligible to all public dignities, places, and employments, according to their capacities, and without other distinction than that of their virtues and their talents.

7. No man can be accused, arrested, or detained except in the cases determined by the law and according to the forms that it has prescribed. Those who procure, expedite, execute, or cause to be executed arbitrary orders ought to be punished; but every citizen summoned or seized in virtue of the law ought to render instant obedience; he makes himself guilty by resistance.

8. The law ought to establish only penalties that are strictly and obviously necessary and no one can be punished except in virtue of a law established and promulgated prior to the offence and legally applied.

9. Every man being presumed innocent until he has been pronounced guilty, if it is thought indispensable to arrest him, all severity that may not be necessary to secure his person ought to be strictly suppressed by law.

10. No one ought to be disturbed on account of his opinions, even religious, provided their manifestation does not derange the public order established by law.

---

3. Common term for divine power as understood by deists, who did not believe in a god who intervened in human affairs.

11. The free communication of ideas and opinions is one of the most precious of the rights of man; every citizen then can freely speak, write, and print, subject to responsibility for the abuse of this freedom in the cases determined by law.

12. The guarantee of the rights of man and citizen requires a public force; this force then is instituted for the advantage of all and not for the personal benefit of those to whom it is entrusted.

13. For the maintenance of the public force and for the expenses of administration a general tax is indispensable; it ought to be equally apportioned among all the citizens according to their means.

14. All the citizens have the right to ascertain, by themselves or by their representatives, the necessity of the public tax, to consent to it freely, to follow the employment of it, and to determine the quota, the assessment, the collection, and the duration of it.

15. Society has the right to call for an account from every public agent of its administration.

16. Any society in which the guarantee of the rights is not secured or the separation of powers not determined has no constitution at all.

17. Property being a sacred and inviolable right, no one can be deprived of it unless a legally established public necessity evidently demands it, under the condition of a just and prior indemnity.

OLYMPE DE GOUGES

One of the most radical voices for women's rights in the period was Olympe de Gouges (1748–1793). Born Marie Gouzes, the daughter of a rural butcher and a serving woman, Olympe de Gouges reinvented herself as a playwright and Parisian intellectual. She advanced highly progressive ideas, including the abolition of slavery and the rights of orphans and unwed mothers. Her political writings were so unsettling that they alienated many of her fashionable social and intellectual allies. The Rights of Woman (1791), which explicitly revises **the Declaration of the Rights of Man and of the Citizen**, insists that the logic of the French Revolution—its demands for freedom and equality and the overthrow of an old system of oppression—must be extended to women. Among her most famous assertions was article X: "Woman has the right to mount the scaffold; she must also have the right to take to the rostrum." That is, if women can be executed, then surely they should be permitted to make public speeches. She herself provided an ironic and tragic coda to this argument. Olympe de Gouges was guillotined during the Reign of Terror as a consequence of her inflammatory words. Too radical even for the revolutionaries, she died a "public enemy" in 1793.

The Rights of Woman[1]

Man, are you capable of being just? It is a WOMAN who asks you this question; you will not deprive her at least of this right. Tell me what gave you the supreme authority to oppress my sex? Your strength? Your talents? Observe the creator in his wisdom; Go through nature in all its grandeur, to which you seem to wish to be close. And if you dare, give me one example of this tyrannical empire. Go back to the animals, consult the elements, study plant life, and finally cast a glance, on all modifications in organized matter; and bow down before the evidence when I offer you the means to do so. Search, dig deeper and try to distinguish, if you can, sex in nature's administration. Everywhere you will find them indistinct; everywhere they cooperate in a harmonious whole in this immortal masterpiece.

Man alone is in principle tied down to this exception. Bizarre, blind, bloated with science and degenerated, in this century of enlightenment and wisdom, in the crassest of ignorance. He wishes to rule as a despot over a sex that is endowed with all intellectual faculties; he claims to enjoy the revolution and reclaim his rights to equality, in order to say nothing more.

The Rights of Woman

Declaration of the Rights of Woman and of the Woman-Citizen

To be decreed by the National Assembly in its last sessions or in those of the next legislature.

PREAMBLE

Mothers, daughters, sisters, representatives of the nation, demand to be constituted into a national assembly, considering that ignorance, forgetfulness or contempt of the rights of the WOMAN, are the sole causes of public miseries, and of the corruption of governments, have resolved to set forth in a solemn declaration, the natural inalienable and sacred rights of the WOMAN, in order that this declaration, being ever present to all members of the social body, may unceasingly remind them of their rights and duties, in order that the acts of the power of women, and those of the power of men may at each moment be compared with the aim of all political institutions and thereby be more respected, in order that the demands of women-citizens henceforth founded on simple and incontestable principles, may always turn to maintaining the constitution, good mores, and the happiness of all. In consequence, the sex superior in beauty as in courage, in maternal sufferings, recognizes and declares, in the presence and under the auspices of the Supreme Being, the following Rights of the Woman and of the Woman-Citizen.

1. Translated under the direction of Nirupama Rastogi.

I

Woman is born free and remains equal to man in rights. Social distinctions can be based only upon common utility.

II

The aim of every political association is the preservation of the natural and unwritten rights of woman and of man: these rights are liberty, prosperity, security and especially resistance to oppression.

III

The principle of all sovereignty resides essentially in the Nation, which is nothing but the coming together of woman and man: no body, no individual can exercise any authority that does not expressly emanate from it.

IV

Liberty and justice consist in restoring all that which belongs to others: accordingly the exercise of the natural rights of the woman has for its only limits the perpetual tyranny that man imposes on her; these limits must be reformed according to the laws of nature and of reason.

V

The laws of nature and of reason prohibit all actions injurious to society: all that is not forbidden by these wise and divine laws, cannot be prohibited, and no one can be constrained to do what they do not order.

VI

Law must be the expression of the general will; all women and male citizens must take part, personally, or through their representatives in its formation; it must be the same for all: all women and male citizens, being equal in its eyes, must be equally eligible to all dignities, places and public offices, according to their capacities, and without other distinctions than those of their virtues and talents.

VII

No woman is an exception; she is accused, arrested and detained according to cases determined by law. Women obey, just as men, this rigorous law.

VIII

The law must establish only penalties that are strictly and obviously necessary, and no one can be punished except by virtue of a law established and promulgated prior to the offence and legally applicable to women.

IX

Any woman being declared guilty, all severity is exercised by the law.

X

No one ought to be harmed on account of his opinions, even the fundamental ones. Woman has the right to mount the scaffold; she must also have the right to take to the rostrum;[2] provided her manifestations do not disturb the public order established by law.

XI

The free communication of thought and of opinion is one of the most precious rights of women, as this liberty assures the legitimacy of fathers in relation to children. Every woman-citizen can therefore say freely, I am the mother of the child that belongs to you without having to conceal the truth due to a barbarous prejudice only to respond to the abuse of this liberty in cases determined by law.

XII

The guarantee of the rights of women and the woman-citizen requires a major service, this guarantee must be instituted for the advantage of all, and not for the specific utility of the women to whom it is entrusted.

XIII

For the maintenance of the public force, and for administrative expenditure, the contribution of women and men is equal; she has a share in all chores, in all painful tasks; she should therefore have the same share in the distribution of posts, employment, responsibilities, dignities and industry.

XIV

Women and men-citizens have the right to ascertain, for themselves, or through their representatives, the necessity for a public fund. Women-citizens can become members only if they are eligible for an equal share, not only in fortune, but even in public administration, and to establish the quota, the taxable property, the collection and the duration of the tax.

XV

The mass of women along with men contributing to the public fund, have the right to ask for an account, from every public agent and its administration.

XVI

Every society, where guarantee of rights is not assured, nor the separation of powers determined, has no constitution: the constitution is nothing if the majority of the individuals who constitute the nation, has not cooperated in its drafting.

---

2. Women can be executed; they should also be allowed to make speeches.

XVII

Properties belong to all sexes united or separated; they are for everyone an inviolable and sacred right; no one can be deprived of it as a true heritage of nature, unless a public necessity, legally established, evidently demands it, and under the condition of a just and prior indemnity.

POSTAMBULE

Women, rouse yourself, the tolling of the bell of reason can be heard throughout the universe; recognize your rights. Nature's mighty empire is no longer encircled by prejudices, fanaticism, superstition and lies. Truth's flaming torch has dispelled all clouds of foolishness and usurpation. Man-slave has multiplied his strengths and he needs to resort to yours to break his shackles. Once free, he has become unjust towards his companion. O women! Women, when will you cease to be blind? What are the benefits that you have reaped from the revolution? A contempt all the more marked, a disdain all the more evident. During centuries of corruption you have only reigned over the weakness of men. Your empire is destroyed, what then are you left with? The conviction of man's injustices, the demand for your heritage, founded on wise decrees of nature; what would you have to fear for in such a beautiful enterprise? The wit of the legislator in the marriage of Cana?[3] Are you afraid that our French legislators, correctors of these morals, hanging for long to the branches of politics, but which are no longer in season, will repeat to you: WOMEN, what is common between you and us? Everything, you would have to answer. If they persisted stubbornly in their weaknesses, in putting this thoughtlessness in contradiction with their principles; oppose courageously with the force of reason the vain pretensions of superiority; assemble under the banner of philosophy; unfurl all the energy of your character, and you will soon see these arrogant ones become your servile worshippers, cringing at your feet, but proud to share with you the treasures of the Supreme Being. Whatever be the barriers against you, it is within your power to cross them; you only have to wish it. Let us move on now to the appalling picture of what you have been in society, and since there is talk, at this moment, of a national education, let us see if our wise legislators will think soundly about women's education.

Women have done more harm than good. Constraint and dissimulation have been their lot. What force took from them, has been returned to them by guile; they have resorted to all the resources of their charms, and the most irreproachable man could not resist them. Poison, chains, everything was subjugated to them; they controlled crime as well as virtue. The French government specially, for centuries, depended on the nocturnal administration of women,[4] the cabinet had no secrets to be indiscreet about. Be it the embassy, the armed forces, the ministry, the presidency, the pontificate or the cardinalship; in short all that characterizes the stupidity of men, secular or religious, all was submitted to the cupidity and to the ambition of this sex earlier disdainful and respected, and since the revolution, respectable and disdained.

---

3. At which Jesus performed his first miracle, turning water into wine.

4. The manipulations of women at night, presumably through "pillow talk."

In this sort of antithesis, how many remarks do I not have to offer! I only have a moment to make them, but this moment will arrest the attention of the most remote posterity. Under the Ancien Régime,[5] all was perverted, all guilty; but could we not notice an improvement of things in the very substance of vices? A woman only needed to be beautiful or pleasant; when she possessed these two qualities, she saw a hundred fortunes at her feet. If she did not take advantage of them, she had a bizarre personality, or a less common philosophy, which led her to scorn riches, thus she was only considered headstrong. The most indecent woman made herself respected with gold. Trade in women was a kind of industry accepted in the highest classes and which, henceforth, will have no credit. If it yet had any, the REVOLUTION would be lost, and under new relationships, we would still be corrupt. However, can reason conceal the fact that any other path to fortune is closed to the woman bought by man, like a slave on the African coast? The difference is considerable, we know it. The slave has command over the master, but if the master gives her freedom without reward, and at an age when the slave has lost all her charms, what becomes of this unfortunate woman? The toy of contempt; the very doors of charity are shut for her; she is poor and old, one says; why did she not know how to become rich? Other examples, even more touching, come to the mind. A young woman without any experience, seduced by the man she loves, will abandon her parents to follow him; the ungrateful man will leave her after a few years, and the more she has aged with him, the more inhuman his fickleness will be; if she has children he will abandon her all the same. If he is rich, he will think himself exempted from sharing his fortune with his noble victims. If some commitment binds him to his duties, he will violate its power, but hope for everything from the law. If he is married, all other commitments lose their force. What laws remain then to be formed in order to extirpate vice from its very roots? That of sharing wealth between men and women, and that of public administration. One can easily imagine that a woman born in a rich family earns a lot with equal sharing. But she who is born in a poor family, with merits and virtues, what is her lot? Poverty and opprobrium. If she does not excel precisely in music or in painting, she cannot be admitted to any public function even if she is fully capable. I will speak at length about them in the new edition of all my political writings, which I propose to give to the public in a few days' time, with notes.

I take up my text concerning mores.[6] Marriage is the tomb of confidence and love. The married woman can with impunity give bastards to her husband, and fortune which does not belong to them. The unmarried one, has but one weak right; the old and inhuman laws refused her and her children this right in the name and property of the father, and no new laws have been made on this subject. If an attempt to give an honorable and just place to my sex is, at this moment, considered as a paradox on my part and as attempting the impossible, I leave to future men the glory of treating this subject; but in the meanwhile, it can be prepared through national education by restoring customs and conjugal conventions.

---

5. The old monarchical, hierarchical system.   6. Morally binding customs.

EDMUND BURKE

Not everyone found the revolutionary tumult of the times inspiring or hopeful. The Anglo-Irish politician and writer Edmund Burke (1729–1797) was horrified when he read pamphlets enthusiastically supporting the French Revolution in England, and the response he wrote made him one of history's most famous champions of conservatism. His *Reflections on the Revolution in France* supports tradition for the sake of stability and freedom. It upholds monarchy, the inheritance of wealth and political power, and the value of conventional wisdom. To Burke, abstract rights and new constitutions seem monstrous and unnatural, and the angry mob violence of the French Revolution disrupts long-standing institutions and generates nothing better than terrifying chaos. The book was an immediate best seller when it appeared in 1790: thirteen thousand copies sold in the first month after publication, and it was reprinted eleven times in the next year. Part of its popularity had to do with Burke's sensational and gripping style. He is especially famous for his description of the march on Versailles in October of 1789, when a hungry mob composed mostly of women stormed the royal palace and captured the French king and queen.

From Reflections on the Revolution in France

* * * All circumstances taken together, the French revolution is the most astonishing that has hitherto happened in the world. The most wonderful things are brought about in many instances by means the most absurd and ridiculous; in the most ridiculous modes; and apparently, by the most contemptible instruments. Every thing seems out of nature in this strange chaos of levity and ferocity, and of all sorts of crimes jumbled together with all sorts of follies. In viewing this monstrous tragi-comic scene, the most opposite passions necessarily succeed, and sometimes mix with each other in the mind; alternate contempt and indignation; alternate laughter and tears; alternate scorn and horror.

* * * *

You will observe, that from Magna Charta to the Declaration of Right,[1] it has been the uniform policy of our constitution to claim and assert our liberties, as an *entailed inheritance*[2] derived to us from our forefathers, and to be transmitted to our posterity; as an estate specially belonging to the people of this kingdom without any reference whatever to any other more general or prior right.

---

1. Both the Magna Carta (1215) and the Declaration of Right (1689) are constitutional documents that limit the powers of the British monarchy and guarantee legal rights to subjects.

2. Property passed down through the family line that by law cannot be divided or sold by any future heirs.

By this means our constitution preserves an unity in so great a diversity of its parts. We have an inheritable crown; an inheritable peerage; and an house of commons and a people inheriting privileges, franchises, and liberties, from a long line of ancestors.

This policy appears to me to be the result of profound reflection; or rather the happy effect of following nature, which is wisdom without reflection, and above it. A spirit of innovation is generally the result of a selfish temper and confined views. People will not look forward to posterity, who never look backward to their ancestors. Besides, the people of England well know, that the idea of inheritance furnishes a sure principle of conservation, and a sure principle of transmission; without at all excluding a principle of improvement. It leaves acquisition free; but it secures what it acquires. Whatever advantages are obtained by a state proceeding on these maxims, are locked fast as in a sort of family settlement; grasped as in a kind of mortmain³ for ever. By a constitutional policy, working after the pattern of nature, we receive, we hold, we transmit our government and our privileges, in the same manner in which we enjoy and transmit our property and our lives. The institutions of policy, the goods of fortune, the gifts of Providence, are handed down, to us and from us, in the same course and order. Our political system is placed in a just correspondence and symmetry with the order of the world, and with the mode of existence decreed to a permanent body composed of transitory parts; wherein, by the disposition of a stupendous wisdom, moulding together the great mysterious incorporation of the human race, the whole, at one time, is never old, or middle-aged, or young, but in a condition of unchangeable constancy, moves on through the varied tenour of perpetual decay, fall, renovation, and progression. Thus, by preserving the method of nature in the conduct of the state, in what we improve we are never wholly new; in what we retain we are never wholly obsolete. By adhering in this manner and on those principles to our forefathers, we are guided not by the superstition of antiquarians, but by the spirit of philosophic analogy. In this choice of inheritance we have given to our frame of polity the image of a relation in blood; binding up the constitution of our country with our dearest domestic ties; adopting our fundamental laws into the bosom of our family affections; keeping inseparable, and cherishing with the warmth of all their combined and mutually reflected charities, our state, our hearths, our sepulchres, and our altars.

Through the same plan of a conformity to nature in our artificial institutions, and by calling in the aid of her unerring and powerful instincts, to fortify the fallible and feeble contrivances of our reason, we have derived several other, and those no small benefits, from considering our liberties in the light of an inheritance. Always acting as if in the presence of canonized forefathers, the spirit of freedom, leading in itself to misrule and excess, is tempered with an awful gravity. This idea of a liberal descent inspires us with a sense of habitual native dignity, which prevents that upstart insolence almost inevitably adhering to and disgracing those who are the first acquirers of any distinction. By this means our liberty becomes a noble freedom. It carries an imposing and majestic aspect. It has a pedigree and illustrating ancestors. It has its bearings and its ensigns armorial. It has its gallery of portraits; its monumental inscriptions; its records, evidences, and titles. We procure reverence to our civil institutions on the principle upon which nature teaches us to revere individual

---

3. Land held in perpetuity by an institution, such as a church.

men; on account of their age; and on account of those from whom they are descended. All your sophisters[4] cannot produce any thing better adapted to preserve a rational and manly freedom than the course that we have pursued, who have chosen our nature rather than our speculations, our breasts rather than our inventions, for the great conservatories and magazines of our rights and privileges.

* * *

Far am I from denying in theory; full as far is my heart from withholding in practice (if I were of power to give or to withhold) the *real* rights of men. In denying their false claims of right, I do not mean to injure those which are real, and are such as their pretended rights would totally destroy. If civil society be made for the advantage of man, all the advantages for which it is made become his right. It is an institution of beneficence; and law itself is only beneficence acting by a rule. Men have a right to live by that rule; they have a right to justice; as between their fellows, whether their fellows are in politic function or in ordinary occupation. They have a right to the fruits of their industry; and to the means of making their industry fruitful. They have a right to the acquisitions of their parents; to the nourishment and improvement of their offspring; to instruction in life, and to consolation in death. Whatever each man can separately do, without trespassing upon others, he has a right to do for himself; and he has a right to a fair portion of all which society, with all its combinations of skill and force, can do in his favor. In this partnership all men have equal rights; but not to equal things. He that has but five shillings in the partnership, has as good a right to it, as he that has five hundred pound has to his larger proportion. But he has not a right to an equal dividend in the product of the joint stock; and as to the share of power, authority, and direction which each individual ought to have in the management of the state, that I must deny to be amongst the direct original rights of man in civil society; for I have in my contemplation the civil social man, and no other. It is a thing to be settled by convention.

* * *

History, who keeps a durable record of all our acts, and exercises her awful censure over the proceedings of all sorts of sovereigns, will not forget, either those events, or the aera of this liberal refinement in the intercourse of mankind. History will record, that on the morning of the 6th of October 1789, the king and queen of France, after a day of confusion, alarm, dismay, and slaughter, lay down, under the pledged security of public faith, to indulge nature in a few hours of respite, and troubled melancholy repose. From this sleep the queen was first startled by the voice of the centinel at her door, who cried out to her, to save herself by flight—that this was the last proof of fidelity he could give—that they were upon him, and he was dead. Instantly he was cut down. A band of cruel ruffians and assassins, reeking with his blood, rushed into the chamber of the queen, and pierced with an hundred strokes of bayonets and poniards the bed, from whence this persecuted woman had but just time to fly almost naked, and through ways unknown to the murderers had escaped to seek refuge at the feet of a king and husband, not secure of his own life for a moment.

4. People who make devious or deceptive arguments.

This king, to say no more of him, and this queen, and their infant children (who once would have been the pride and hope of a great and generous people) were then forced to abandon the sanctuary of the most splendid palace in the world, which they left swimming in blood, polluted by massacre, and strewed with scattered limbs and mutilated carcases. Thence they were conducted into the capital of their kingdom. Two had been selected from the unprovoked, unresisted, promiscuous slaughter, which was made of the gentlemen of birth and family who composed the king's body guard. These two gentlemen, with all the parade of an execution of justice, were cruelly and publickly dragged to the block, and beheaded in the great court of the palace. Their heads were stuck upon spears, and led the procession; whilst the royal captives who followed in the train were slowly moved along, amidst the horrid yells, and shrilling screams, and frantic dances, and infamous contumelies, and all the unutterable abominations of the furies of hell, in the abused shape of the vilest of women. After they had been made to taste, drop by drop, more than the bitterness of death, in the slow torture of a journey of twelve miles, protracted to six hours, they were, under a guard, composed of those very soldiers who had thus conducted them through this famous triumph, lodged in one of the old palaces of Paris, now converted into a Bastile[5] for kings.

* * *

I hear that the august person, who was the principal object of our preacher's triumph, though he supported himself, felt much on that shameful occasion. As a man, it became him to feel for his wife and his children, and the faithful guards of his person, that were massacred in cold blood about him; as a prince, it became him to feel for the strange and frightful transformation of his civilized subjects, and to be more grieved for them, than solicitous for himself. It derogates little from his fortitude, while it adds infinitely to the honor of his humanity. I am very sorry to say it, very sorry indeed, that such personages are in a situation in which it is not unbecoming in us to praise the virtues of the great.

I hear, and I rejoice to hear, that the great lady, the other object of the triumph, has borne that day (one is interested that beings made for suffering should suffer well) and that she bears all the succeeding days, that she bears the imprisonment of her husband, and her own captivity, and the exile of her friends, and the insulting adulation of addresses, and the whole weight of her accumulated wrongs, with a serene patience, in a manner suited to her rank and race, and becoming the offspring of a sovereign distinguished for her piety and her courage;[6] that like her she has lofty sentiments; that she feels with the dignity of a Roman matron; that in the last extremity she will save herself from the last disgrace,[7] and that if she must fall, she will fall by no ignoble hand.

It is now sixteen or seventeen years since I saw the queen of France, then the dauphiness,[8] at Versailles; and surely never lighted on this orb, which she

5. Political prison in Paris that was attacked at the start of the French Revolution.
6. Marie Antoinette, the queen of France, was the daughter of the empress of Austria, Maria Theresa.
7. She is willing to commit suicide rather than submit to rape.
8. Wife of the heir to the French throne.

hardly seemed to touch, a more delightful vision. I saw her just above the horizon, decorating and cheering the elevated sphere she just began to move in,— glittering like the morning-star, full of life, and splendor, and joy. Oh! what a revolution! and what an heart must I have, to contemplate without emotion that elevation and that fall! Little did I dream when she added titles of veneration to those of enthusiastic, distant, respectful love, that she should ever be obliged to carry the sharp antidote against disgrace concealed in that bosom; little did I dream that I should have lived to see such disasters fallen upon her in a nation of gallant men, in a nation of men of honor and of cavaliers. I thought ten thousand swords must have leaped from their scabbards to avenge even a look that threatened her with insult.—But the age of chivalry is gone.— That of sophisters, oeconomists, and calculators, has succeeded; and the glory of Europe is extinguished for ever. Never, never more, shall we behold that generous loyalty to rank and sex, that proud submission, that dignified obedience, that subordination of the heart, which kept alive, even in servitude itself, the spirit of an exalted freedom. The unbought grace of life, the cheap defence of nations, the nurse of manly sentiment and heroic enterprize is gone! It is gone, that sensibility of principle, that chastity of honor, which felt a stain like a wound, which inspired courage whilst it mitigated ferocity, which ennobled whatever it touched, and under which vice itself lost half its evil, by losing all its grossness.

This mixed system of opinion and sentiment had its origin in the antient chivalry; and the principle, though varied in its appearance by the varying state of human affairs, subsisted and influenced through a long succession of generations, even to the time we live in. If it should ever be totally extinguished, the loss I fear will be great. It is this which has given its character to modern Europe. It is this which has distinguished it under all its forms of government, and distinguished it to its advantage, from the states of Asia, and possibly from those states which flourished in the most brilliant periods of the antique world. It was this, which, without confounding ranks, had produced a noble equality, and handed it down through all the gradations of social life. It was this opinion which mitigated kings into companions, and raised private men to be fellows with kings. Without force, or opposition, it subdued the fierceness of pride and power; it obliged sovereigns to submit to the soft collar of social esteem, compelled stern authority to submit to elegance, and gave a domination vanquisher of laws, to be subdued by manners.

But now all is to be changed. All the pleasing illusions, which made power gentle, and obedience liberal, which harmonized the different shades of life, and which, by a bland assimilation, incorporated into politics the sentiments which beautify and soften private society, are to be dissolved by this new conquering empire of light and reason. All the decent drapery of life is to be rudely torn off. All the superadded ideas, furnished from the wardrobe of a moral imagination, which the heart owns, and the understanding ratifies, as necessary to cover the defects of our naked shivering nature, and to raise it to dignity in our own estimation, are to be exploded as a ridiculous, absurd, and antiquated fashion.

On this scheme of things, a king is but a man; a queen is but a woman; a woman is but an animal; and an animal not of the highest order. All homage paid to the sex[9] in general as such, and without distinct views, is to be regarded as romance and folly. Regicide, and parricide, and sacrilege, are but fictions of superstition, corrupting jurisprudence by destroying its simplicity. The murder of a king, or a queen, or a bishop, or a father, are only common homicide; and if the people are by any chance, or in any way gainers by it, a sort of homicide much the most pardonable, and into which we ought not to make too severe a scrutiny.

On the scheme of this barbarous philosophy, which is the offspring of cold hearts and muddy understandings, and which is as void of solid wisdom, as it is destitute of all taste and elegance, laws are to be supported only by their own terrors, and by the concern, which each individual may find in them, from his own private speculations, or can spare to them from his own private interests. In the groves of *their* academy, at the end of every visto, you see nothing but the gallows. Nothing is left which engages the affections on the part of the commonwealth. On the principles of this mechanic philosophy, our institutions can never be embodied, if I may use the expression, in persons; so as to create in us love, veneration, admiration, or attachment. But that sort of reason which banishes the affections is incapable of filling their place. These public affections, combined with manners, are required sometimes as supplements, sometimes as correctives, always as aids to law. The precept given by a wise man, as well as a great critic, for the construction of poems, is equally true as to states. *Non satis est pulchra esse poemata, dulcia sunto.*[1] There ought to be a system of manners in every nation which a well-formed mind would be disposed to relish. To make us love our country, our country ought to be lovely.

But power, of some kind or other, will survive the shock in which manners and opinions perish; and it will find other and worse means for its support. The usurpation which, in order to subvert antient institutions, has destroyed antient principles, will hold power by arts similar to those by which it has acquired it. When the old feudal and chivalrous spirit of *Fealty,*[2] which, by freeing kings from fear, freed both kings and subjects from the precautions of tyranny, shall be extinct in the minds of men, plots and assassinations will be anticipated by preventive murder and preventive confiscation, and that long roll of grim and bloody maxims, which form the political code of all power, not standing on its own honor, and the honor of those who are to obey it. Kings will be tyrants from policy when subjects are rebels from principle.

When antient opinions and rules of life are taken away, the loss cannot possibly be estimated. From that moment we have no compass to govern us; nor can we know distinctly to what port we steer. Europe undoubtedly, taken in a mass, was in a flourishing condition the day on which your Revolution was compleated. How much of that prosperous state was owing to the spirit of our old manners and opinions is not easy to say; but as such causes cannot be indifferent in their operation, we must presume, that, on the whole, their operation was beneficial.

9. The female sex.
1. "It is not enough for poems to be beautiful; they must also be "sweet" (Latin, from the

Roman writer Horace [65–8 B.C.E.]).
2. A pledge of fidelity to a person of higher rank.

We are but too apt to consider things in the state in which we find them, without sufficiently adverting to the causes by which they have been produced, and possibly may be upheld. Nothing is more certain, than that our manners, our civilization, and all the good things which are connected with manners, and with civilization, have, in this European world of ours, depended for ages upon two principles; and were indeed the result of both combined; I mean the spirit of a gentleman, and the spirit of religion. The nobility and the clergy, the one by profession, the other by patronage, kept learning in existence, even in the midst of arms and confusions, and whilst governments were rather in their causes than formed. Learning paid back what it received to nobility and to priesthood; and paid it with usury,[3] by enlarging their ideas, and by furnishing their minds. Happy if they had all continued to know their indissoluble union, and their proper place! Happy if learning, not debauched by ambition, had been satisfied to continue the instructor, and not aspired to be the master! Along with its natural protectors and guardians, learning will be cast into the mire, and trodden down under the hoofs of a swinish multitude.

If, as I suspect, modern letters owe more than they are always willing to own to antient manners, so do other interests which we value full as much as they are worth. Even commerce, and trade, and manufacture, the gods of our oeconomical politicians, are themselves perhaps but creatures; are themselves but effects, which, as first causes, we choose to worship. They certainly grew under the same shade in which learning flourished. They too may decay with their natural protecting principles. With you, for the present at least, they all threaten to disappear together. Where trade and manufactures are wanting to a people, and the spirit of nobility and religion remains, sentiment supplies, and not always ill supplies their place; but if commerce and the arts should be lost in an experiment to try how well a state may stand without these old fundamental principles, what sort of a thing must be a nation of gross, stupid, ferocious, and at the same time, poor and sordid barbarians, destitute of religion, honor, or manly pride, possessing nothing at present, and hoping for nothing hereafter?

I wish you may not be going fast, and by the shortest cut, to that horrible and disgustful situation. Already there appears a poverty of conception, a coarseness and vulgarity in all the proceedings of the assembly and of all their instructors. Their liberty is not liberal. Their science is presumptuous ignorance. Their humanity is savage and brutal.

* * *

3. Interest.

JEAN-JACQUES DESSALINES

The French colony of Saint-Domingue—the western portion of the Caribbean island of Hispaniola—was the jewel of the French empire in the eighteenth century. A fertile source of sugar, coffee, tobacco and cotton, its 500,000 slaves produced extraordinary wealth for France. The slaves also chafed against their oppression, erupting frequently in rebellion. As the French Revolution abolished old hierarchies, the people of Saint-Domingue hotly debated new questions about natural rights, especially freedom and equality. The colony's free blacks, white plantation owners, and the poorer white population began to fight among themselves over property and privileges under the new French Declaration of the Rights of Man. In this unstable context in 1791, the slaves who made up the vast majority of the island rose up under the leadership of the brilliant strategist Toussaint L'Ouverture and launched a war that would last more than a decade. During this period, Britain and Spain struggled to take control of Saint-Domingue, and fearful of losing its richest colony, France officially liberated the slaves in the hope of retaining power there. The plan worked for a period: Toussaint L'Ouverture joined the French Republic and defeated the British and the Spanish. By 1801 he had succeeded in abolishing slavery on the island and had declared himself governor for life. Napoleon, however, nervous about this independent black leader, captured Toussaint and in 1802 forced him into exile in Europe, where he died less than a year later.

At this point, Toussaint's astute but also ruthless second-in-command, Jean-Jacques Dessalines (1758–1806), took charge of the revolution. He successfully defeated French troops in 1803 and proclaimed a new nation, which he called Haiti. He had himself crowned emperor. Dessalines' proclamation, "Liberty or Death," was published in June 1804, shortly after he had destroyed some of the French enclaves remaining in Haiti.

Rhetorically, the document is creative and skillful, especially for a former slave who had received no schooling: Dessalines recasts the French Revolutionary motif of the "Tree of Liberty" as "the ancient tree of slavery and prejudices," and portrays the slave trade as a cannibalistic consumption of fellow human beings. The proclamation is also explicitly critical of Toussaint, arguing for the need for absolutely ruthless determination. Dessalines was canny about targeting international audiences. His secretary sent letters accompanying this proclamation to American newspaper publishers, urging them to publish them. It appeared in about fifty different U.S. newspapers.

Assassinated in 1806, Dessalines left a complex legacy: on the one hand, horror at his autocratic rule and willingness to be brutal in battle, and on the other hand, admiration at his power to fight back against strong oppressors with both words and weapons. The Haitian national anthem is called the *Dessalinienne*.

LIBERTY or DEATH[1]

PROCLAMATION

Jean Jacques Dessalines, governor-general, to the inhabitants of Hayti.

CRIMES, the most atrocious, such as were until then unheard of, and would cause nature to shudder, have been perpetrated. The measure was over-heaped. At length the hour of vengeance has arrived, and the implacable enemies of the rights of man have suffered the punishment due to their crimes.

My arm, raised over their heads, has too long delayed to strike. At that signal which the justice of God has urged, your hands righteously armed, have brought the axe upon the ancient tree of slavery and prejudices. In vain had time, and more especially the infernal politics of Europeans, surrounded it with triple brass; you have stripped it of its armor: you have placed it upon your heart that you may become (like your natural enemies) cruel and merciless. Like an overflowing mighty torrent that tears down all opposition, your vengeful fury has carried away everything in its impetuous course. Thus perish all tyrants over innocence—all oppressors of mankind!

What then? bent for many ages under an iron yoke; the sport of the passions of men, of their injustice, and of the caprices of fortune; mutilated victims of the cupidity of white French men: after having fattened with our toils these insatiate bloodsuckers, with a patience and resignation unexampled, we should again have seen that sacrilegious horde make an attempt upon our destruction, without any distinction of sex or age; and we, men without energy, of no virtue, of no delicate sensibility, should not we have plunged in their breasts the dagger of desperation? Where is that vile Haytian, so unworthy of his regeneration, who thinks he has not accomplished the decrees of the eternal, by exterminating these blood-thirsty tigers? If there is one let him fly: indignant nature discards him our bosom; let him hide his shame far from hence; the air we breathe is not suited to his gross organs, it is the pure air of liberty, august and triumphant.

Yes, we have rendered to these true cannibals war for war, crime for crime, outrage for outrage; Yes, I have saved my country, I have avenged America. The avowal I make of it in the face of earth and heaven, constitutes my pride and my glory. Of what consequence to me is the opinion which contemporary and future generations will pronounce upon my conduct? I have performed my duty; I enjoy my own approbation; for me, that is sufficient. But what do I say? The preservation of my unfortunate brothers, the testimony of my own conscience, are not my only recompence: I have seen two classes of men,[2] born to cherish, assist and succour one another—mixed, in a word, and blended together—crying vengeance, and disputing the honor of the first blow.

Blacks and yellows,[3] whom the refined duplicity of Europeans has for a long time endeavoured to divide: you who are now consolidated and make but one family; without doubt it was necessary that our perfect reconciliation

---

1. Published in the *New York Commercial Advertiser*, June 4, 1804.
2. Black slaves and *gens de couleur* (free people of color); they united under Dessalines' leadership.
3. People of mixed-race ancestry.

should be sealed with the blood of our butchers. Similar calamities have hung over your proscribed heads: a similar ardour to strike your enemies has signalized you; the like fate is reserved for you: and the like interests must therefore render you forever one, indivisible and inseparable. Maintain that precious concord, that happy harmony amongst yourselves: it is the pledge of your happiness, your salvation, and your success: it is the secret of being invincible.

It is necessary, in order to strengthen these ties, to recall to your remembrance the catalogue of atrocities committed against our species; the massacre of the entire population of this island, meditated in the silence and sang froid of the cabinet:[4] the execution of that abominable project to me unblushingly proposed, and already begun by the French with the calmness and serenity of a countenance accustomed to similar crimes. Guadeloupe, pillaged and destroyed: its victims still reeking with the blood of the children, women and old men put to the sword. . . . Unfortunate people of Martinique,[5] could I but fly to your assistance, and break your fetters! Alas! an insurmountable barrier separates us. Perhaps a spark from the same fire which inflames us, will alight into your bosoms: perhaps at the sound of this commotion, suddenly awakening from your lethargy, with arms in your hands, you will reclaim your sacred and imprescriptable rights.

After the terrible example which I have just given, that sooner or later divine Justice will unchain on earth some mighty minds, above the weakness of the vulgar, for the destruction and terror of the wicked; tremble, tyrants, usurpers, scourges of the new world! our daggers are sharpened; your punishment is ready! sixty thousand men, equipped, inured to war, obedient to my orders, burn to offer a new sacrifice to the manes of their assassinated brothers. Let that nation come who may be mad and daring enough to attack me. Already at its approach, the irritated genius of Hayti, rising out of the bosom of the ocean, appears; his menacing aspect throws the waves into commotion, excites tempests, and with his mighty hand disperses ships, or dashes them in pieces; to his formidable voice the laws of nature pay obeisence: diseases, plague,[6] famine, conflagration, poison, are his constant attendants. But why calculate on the assistance of the climate and of the elements? Have I forgot that I command a people of no common cast, brought up in adversity, whose audacious daring frowns at obstacles, and increases by dangers? Let them come, then, these homicidal cohorts! I wait for them with firmness and with a steady eye. I abandon to them freely the sea shore, and the places where cities have existed; but woe to those who may approach us too near the mountains! It were better for them that the sea received them into its profound abyss, than to be devoured by the anger of the children of Hayti.

---

4. The French military leader Donatien-Marie-Joseph de Vimeur, Viscount of Rochambeau, had written to Napoleon to tell him that ruthless violence against slaves was the only way for France to reassert control over Saint-Domingue. **5.** French islands in the Caribbean that, unlike Saint-Domingue, did not achieve independence from France. **6.** Yellow fever helped to propel Dessalines to victory when it killed Napoleon's brother-in-law Le Clerc, the leader of French troops in Saint-Domingue, and thousands of his troops.

"War to death to tyrants!" this is my motto; "Liberty! Independence!" this is our rallying cry.

Generals, officers, soldiers, a little unlike him who has preceded me, the ex-general TOUSSAINT LOUVERTURE, I have been faithful to the promise which I made to you when I took up arms against tyranny, and whilst the last spark of life remains in me I shall keep my oath. *Never again shall a colonist or a European set his foot upon this territory with the title of master or proprietor.* This resolution shall henceforward form the fundamental basis of our constitution.

Should other chiefs, after me, by pursuing a conduct diametrically opposite to mine, dig their own grave and those of their species, you will have to accuse only the law of destiny which shall have taken me away from the happiness and welfare of my fellow citizens. May my successors follow the path I shall have traced out for them! It is the system best adapted for consolidating their power; it is the highest homage they can render to my memory.

As it is derogatory to my character and my dignity to punish the innocent for the crimes of the guilty, a handful of whites, commendable by the religion they have always professed, and who have besides taken the oath to live with us in the woods, have experienced my clemency. I order that the sword respect them, and that they be unmolested.

I recommend anew and order to all the generals of department, etc. to grant succours encouragement and protection, to all neutral and friendly nations who may wish to establish commercial relations in this island.

WILLIAM WORDSWORTH

The English poet William Words-worth (1770–1850) went through contradictory emotions as he watched the political revolutions of the period unfold. Living in France between 1790 and 1792, he caught the joyful spirit of freedom and possibility. He visited sites made famous by the revolutionar-ies and picked up rubble from the at-tack on the Bastille prison. At one point he saw a starving girl trudging through the streets. "'Tis against *that* / That we are fighting," a French friend explained, and Wordsworth committed himself to the cause of toppling mon-archy and eradicating poverty and in-equality.

Wordsworth's autobiographical poem, *The Prelude*, composed in 1799 and 1805 but not published (in a greatly revised version) until 1850, registers both the elation felt by the poet and his growing horror at the increasingly bloody revolution. The first passage selected here conveys his misery as he hears about the Terror; the second shows how the French Revolution raised exciting and profound political ques-tions: what kind of new society was now possible? Had the Revolution unleashed the promise of a world based on free-dom and reason?

In 1802 Wordsworth also published a poem to the Haitian revolutionary, Tous-saint l'Ouverture, who was at the time locked in a French prison, though the world did not know where he was or what his fate would be. Here the poet opts for the highly compact fourteen-line sonnet, a strict and traditional form usually associated with love. In this par-ticular sonnet the poet offers a troubling and ambivalent conclusion: Toussaint may die, but he should take comfort in the fact that nature—and human experience—will survive him.

The Prelude

From *Book X*

Domestic carnage now filled the whole year
With feast-days; old men from the chimney-nook,
The maiden from the bosom of her love,
The mother from the cradle of her babe,
The warrior from the field—all perished, all—   360
Friends, enemies, of all parties, ages, ranks,
Head after head, and never heads enough
For those that bade them fall. They found their joy,
They made it proudly, eager as a child,
(If like desires of innocent little ones   365
May with such heinous appetites be compared),
Pleased in some open field to exercise
A toy that mimics with revolving wings

The motion of a wind-mill; though the air
Do of itself blow fresh, and make the vanes   370
Spin in his eyesight, *that* contents him not,
But, with the plaything at arm's length, he sets
His front against the blast, and runs amain,
That it may whirl the faster.
                Amid the depth
Of those enormities, even thinking minds   375
Forgot, at seasons, whence they had their being;
Forgot that such a sound was ever heard,
As Liberty upon earth: yet all beneath
Her innocent authority was wrought,
Nor could have been, without her blessed name.   380
The illustrious wife of Roland,[1] in the hour
Of her composure, felt that agony,
And gave it vent in her last words. O Friend![2]
It was a lamentable time for man,
Whether a hope had e'er been his or not;   385
A woful time for them whose hopes survived
The shock; most woful for those few who still
Were flattered, and had trust in human kind:
They had the deepest feeling of the grief.
Meanwhile the Invaders[3] fared as they deserved: 390
The Herculean Commonwealth had put forth her arms,
And throttled with an infant godhead's might
The snakes about her cradle;[4] that was well,
And as it should be; yet no cure for them
Whose souls were sick with pain of what would be   395
Hereafter brought in charge against mankind.
Most melancholy at that time, O Friend!
Were my day-thoughts,—my nights were miserable;
Through months, through years, long after the last beat
Of those atrocities, the hour of sleep   400
To me came rarely charged with natural gifts,
Such ghastly visions had I of despair
And tyranny, and implements of death;
And innocent victims sinking under fear,
And momentary hope, and worn-out prayer,   405
Each in his separate cell, or penned in crowds
For sacrifice, and struggling with fond mirth
And levity in dungeons, where the dust
Was laid with tears. Then suddenly the scene
Changed, and the unbroken dream entangled me   410

1. Madame Roland (1754–1793), a prominent supporter of the moderate Girondist faction during the French Revolution, executed
by the Jacobins during the Reign of Terror.
Her last words were reportedly, "Oh Liberty,
how you have been played with!"
2. Samuel Taylor Coleridge (1772–1834),
Wordsworth's friend and collaborator.
3. Counterrevolutionary and foreign armies
attacking the new French Republic.
4. In Greek mythology, the infant Heracles
(Hercules to the Romans) strangled two snakes
sent by Hera to kill him.

In long orations, which I strove to plead
Before unjust tribunals,—with a voice
Laboring, a brain confounded, and a sense,
Death-like, of treacherous desertion, felt
In the last place of refuge—my own soul.   415

* * *

From *Book XI*

    O pleasant exercise of hope and joy!   105
For mighty were the auxiliars which then stood
Upon our side, us who were strong in love!
Bliss was it in that dawn to be alive,
But to be young was very Heaven! O times,
In which the meagre, stale, forbidding ways   110
Of custom, law, and statute, took at once
The attraction of a country in romance!
When Reason seemed the most to assert her rights
When most intent on making of herself
A prime enchantress—to assist the work,   115
Which then was going forward in her name!
Not favored spots alone, but the whole Earth,
The beauty wore of promise—that which sets
(As at some moments might not be unfelt
Among the bowers of Paradise itself)   120
The budding rose above the rose full blown.
What temper at the prospect did not wake
To happiness unthought of? The inert
Were roused, and lively natures rapt away!
They who had fed their childhood upon dreams,   125
The play-fellows of fancy, who had made
All powers of swiftness, subtilty, and strength
Their ministers,—who in lordly wise had stirred
Among the grandest objects of the sense,
And dealt with whatsoever they found there   130
As if they had within some lurking right
To wield it;—they, too, who of gentle mood
Had watched all gentle motions, and to these
Had fitted their own thoughts, schemers more mild,
And in the region of their peaceful selves;—   135
Nor was it that *both* found, the meek and lofty
Did both find helpers to their heart's desire,
And stuff at hand, plastic as they could wish,—
Were called upon to exercise their skill,
Not in Utopia,—subterranean fields,—   140
Or some secreted island, Heaven knows where!
But in the very world, which is the world
Of all of us,—the place where, in the end,
We find our happiness, or not at all!

Why should I not confess that Earth was then   145
To me, what an inheritance, new-fallen,
Seems, when the first time visited, to one
Who thither comes to find in it his home?
He walks about and looks upon the spot
With cordial transport, moulds it and remoulds,   150
And is half pleased with things that are amiss,
'Twill be such joy to see them disappear.

* * *

To Toussaint L'Ouverture[1]

Toussaint, the most unhappy Man of Men!
Whether the rural Milk-maid by her Cow
Sing in thy hearing, or thou liest now
Alone in some deep dungeon's earless den,
O miserable chieftain! where and when   5
Wilt thou find patience? Yet die not; do thou
Wear rather in thy bonds a chearful brow:
Though fallen Thyself, never to rise again,
Live, and take comfort. Thou hast left behind
Powers that will work for thee; air, earth, and skies;   10
There's not a breathing of the common wind
That will forget thee; thou hast great allies;
Thy friends are exultations, agonies,
And love, and Man's unconquerable mind.

---

1. L'Ouverture (1743–1803) was the slave-born leader of the Haitian Revolution, captured and imprisoned in France in 1802.

SIMÓN BOLÍVAR

Known as "El Libertador"—the Liberator—Simón Bolívar (1783–1830) led the movement for Latin American independence from Spain. Born in Venezuela, he took part in a battle that achieved a fragile independence there in 1811 before turning his attention to the rest of New Granada, a huge Spanish colony that comprised what are now Venezuela, Colombia, Ecuador, Guyana, Panama, Costa Rica, and Nicaragua, as well as the colony of Perú, comprising modern-day Peru, Chile, and Bolivia. In 1819 Bolívar's army beat back Spanish forces, liberating the Republic of Colombia, and he was elected president. Six years later he achieved victory in what was then known as Upper Perú, now named Bolivia in his honor.

Bolívar was a thinker as well as a fighter. He wrote Bolivia's constitution and a series of influential political manifestos. He had read works of French Enlightenment philosophers in his youth, including **Rousseau** and **Voltaire**, and was inspired by the French Revolution. After a defeat in 1815, Bolívar went into exile in Jamaica to reflect on the ideal course of action. His famous "Letter from Jamaica," ostensibly written to a single Englishman in Jamaica, was published with the intention of winning Britain over to the side of South American independence. Bolívar lists the crimes of Spain and its tenuous hold on the vast territories of Latin America, and he offers a theory of colonial power that is different, he argues, from other kinds of tyranny. He makes the case that Latin American independence will serve the interests of all of Europe. And he ends with a call to unity among all Latin American nations, foreseeing a great future for the continent.

Reply of a South American to a Gentleman of This Island[1] [Jamaica]

* * * With what a feeling of gratitude I read that passage in your letter in which you say to me: "I hope that the success which then followed Spanish arms may now turn in favor of their adversaries, the badly oppressed people of South America." I take this hope as a prediction, if it is justice that determines man's contests. Success will crown our efforts, because the destiny of America has been irrevocably decided; the tie that bound her to Spain has been severed. Only a concept maintained that tie and kept the parts of that immense monarchy together. That which formerly bound them now divides them. The hatred that the Peninsula has inspired in us is greater than the ocean between us. It would be easier to have the two continents meet than to reconcile the spirits of the two countries. The habit of obedience; a community of interest, of understanding, of religion; mutual goodwill; a tender regard for the birthplace and good name of our forefathers; in short, all that gave rise to our hopes, came to us from Spain. As a result there was born a principle of affinity that seemed

1. Translated by Lewis Bertrand.

eternal, notwithstanding the misbehavior of our rulers which weakened that sympathy, or, rather, that bond enforced by the domination of their rule. At present the contrary attitude persists: we are threatened with the fear of death, dishonor, and every harm; there is nothing we have not suffered at the hands of that unnatural step-mother—Spain. The veil has been torn asunder. We have already seen the light, and it is not our desire to be thrust back into darkness. The chains have been broken; we have been freed, and now our enemies seek to enslave us anew. For this reason America fights desperately, and seldom has desperation failed to achieve victory.

Because successes have been partial and spasmodic, we must not lose faith. In some regions the Independents triumph, while in others the tyrants have the advantage. What is the end result? Is not the entire New World in motion, armed for defense? We have but to look around us on this hemisphere to witness a simultaneous struggle at every point.

The war-like state of the La Plata River provinces has purged that territory and led their victorious armies to Upper Perú, arousing Arequipa and worrying the royalists in Lima.[2] Nearly one million inhabitants there now enjoy liberty.

The territory of Chile, populated by 800,000 souls, is fighting the enemy who is seeking her subjugation; but to no avail, because those who long ago put an end to the conquests of this enemy, the free and indomitable Araucanians,[3] are their neighbors and compatriots. Their sublime example is proof to those fighting in Chile that a people who love independence will eventually achieve it.

The viceroyalty of Perú, whose population approaches a million and a half inhabitants, without doubt suffers the greatest subjection and is obliged to make the most sacrifices for the royal cause; and, although the thought of coöperating with that part of America may be vain, the fact remains that it is not tranquil, nor is it capable of restraining the torrent that threatens most of its provinces.

New Granada,[4] which is, so to speak, the heart of America, obeys a general government, save for the territory of Quito which is held only with the greatest difficulty by its enemies, as it is strongly devoted to the country's cause; and the provinces of Panamá and Santa Marta endure, not without suffering, the tyranny of their masters. Two and a half million people inhabit New Granada and are actually defending that territory against the Spanish army under General Morillo,[5] who will probably suffer defeat at the impregnable fortress of Cartagena. But should he take that city, it will be at the price of heavy casualties, and he will then lack sufficient forces to subdue the unrestrained and brave inhabitants of the interior.

With respect to heroic and hapless Venezuela, events there have moved so rapidly and the devastation has been such that it is reduced to frightful desolation and almost absolute indigence, although it was once among the fairest

---

2. The Viceroyalty of Perú had been the center of Spanish power in Latin America for centuries; the city of Lima remained loyal to Spain, but the southern region of Arequipa housed many Peruvian nationalists.

3. Spanish name given to the Mapuche people, an indigenous group who live in Chile and Argentina.

4. Spanish colony fighting for independence in 1815; its territory has since been divided to become the nations of Panama, Colombia, Ecuador, and Venezuela.

5. Pablo Morillo y Morillo (1775–1837), commander of Spanish troops sent to quell revolts in the Latin American colonies.

regions that are the pride of America. Its tyrants govern a desert, and they oppress only those unfortunate survivors who, having escaped death, lead a precarious existence. A few women, children, and old men are all that remain. Most of the men have perished rather than be slaves; those who survive continue to fight furiously on the fields and in the inland towns, until they expire or hurl into the sea those who, insatiable in their thirst for blood and crimes, rival those first monsters who wiped out America's primitive race. Nearly a million persons formerly dwelt in Venezuela, and it is no exaggeration to say that one out of four has succumbed either to the land, sword, hunger, plague, flight, or privation, all consequences of the war, save the earthquake.

According to Baron von Humboldt, New Spain,[6] including Guatemala, had 7,800,000 inhabitants in 1808. Since that time, the insurrection, which has shaken virtually all of her provinces, has appreciably reduced that apparently correct figure, for over a million men have perished, as you can see in the report of Mr. Walton,[7] who describes faithfully the bloody crimes committed in that abundant kingdom. There the struggle continues by dint of human and every other type of sacrifice, for the Spaniards spare nothing that might enable them to subdue those who have had the misfortune of being born on this soil, which appears to be destined to flow with the blood of its offspring. In spite of everything, the Mexicans will be free. They have embraced the country's cause, resolved to avenge their forefathers or follow them to the grave. Already they say with Raynal:[8] The time has come at last to repay the Spaniards torture for torture and to drown that race of annihilators in its own blood or in the sea.

The islands of Puerto Rico and Cuba, with a combined population of perhaps 700,000 to 800,000 souls, are the most tranquil possessions of the Spaniards, because they are not within range of contact with the Independents. But are not the people of those islands Americans? Are they not maltreated? Do they not desire a better life?

This picture represents, on a military map, an area of 2,000 longitudinal and 900 latitudinal leagues at its greatest point, wherein 16,000,000 Americans either defend their rights or suffer repression at the hands of Spain, which, although once the world's greatest empire, is now too weak, with what little is left her, to rule the new hemisphere or even to maintain herself in the old. And shall Europe, the civilized, the merchant, the lover of liberty allow an aged serpent, bent only on satisfying its venomous rage, devour the fairest part of our globe? What! Is Europe deaf to the clamor of her own interests? Has she no eyes to see justice? Has she grown so hardened as to become insensible? The more I ponder these questions, the more I am confused. I am led to think that America's disappearance is desired; but this is impossible because all Europe is not Spain. What madness for our enemy to hope to reconquer America when she has no navy, no funds, and almost no soldiers! Those troops

6. Alexander von Humboldt (1769–1859), German explorer who published scientific accounts of Latin American geography. "New Spain": vast Spanish colony covering territory that today includes California, New Mexico, Texas, most of Central America, the Caribbean, and the Philippines.
7. William Walton (1784–1857), British resident of Santo Domingo, now capital of the Dominican Republic, who wrote *The Present State of the Spanish Colonies* (1810) and *An Exposé of the Dissensions of Spanish America* (1814).
8. Guillaume Thomas Raynal (1713–1796), French historian and philosopher who condemned European colonialism.

which she has are scarcely adequate to keep her own people in a state of forced obedience and to defend herself from her neighbors. On the other hand, can that nation carry on the exclusive commerce of one-half the world when it lacks manufactures, agricultural products, crafts and sciences, and even a policy? Assume that this mad venture were successful, and further assume that pacification ensued, would not the sons of the Americans of today, together with the sons of the European *reconquistadores*[9] twenty years hence, conceive the same patriotic designs that are now being fought for?

Europe could do Spain a service by dissuading her from her rash obstinacy, thereby at least sparing her the costs she is incurring and the blood she is expending. And if she will fix her attention on her own precincts she can build her prosperity and power upon more solid foundations than doubtful conquests, precarious commerce, and forceful exactions from remote and powerful peoples. Europe herself, as a matter of common sense policy, should have prepared and executed the project of American independence, not alone because the world balance of power so necessitated, but also because this is the legitimate and certain means through which Europe can acquire overseas commercial establishments. A Europe which is not moved by the violent passions of vengeance, ambition, and greed, as is Spain, would seem to be entitled, by all the rules of equity, to make clear to Spain where her best interests lie.

All of the writers who have treated this matter agree on this point. Consequently, we have had reason to hope that the civilized nations would hasten to our aid in order that we might achieve that which must prove to be advantageous to both hemispheres. How vain has been this hope! Not only the Europeans but even our brothers of the North have been apathetic bystanders in this struggle which, by its very essence, is the most just, and in its consequences the most noble and vital of any which have been raised in ancient or in modern times. Indeed, can the far-reaching effects of freedom for the hemisphere which Columbus discovered ever be calculated?

* * *

It is even more difficult to foresee the future fate of the New World, to set down its political principles, or to prophesy what manner of government it will adopt. Every conjecture relative to America's future is, I feel, pure speculation. When mankind was in its infancy, steeped in uncertainty, ignorance, and error, was it possible to foresee what system it would adopt for its preservation? Who could venture to say that a certain nation would be a republic or a monarchy; this nation great, that nation small? To my way of thinking, such is our own situation. We are a young people. We inhabit a world apart, separated by broad seas. We are young in the ways of almost all the arts and sciences, although, in a certain manner, we are old in the ways of civilized society. I look upon the present state of America as similar to that of Rome after its fall. Each part of Rome adopted a political system conforming to its interest and situation or was led by the individual ambitions of certain chiefs, dynasties, or associations. But this important difference exists: those dispersed parts later re-established their ancient nations, subject to the changes imposed by circumstances or events. But we scarcely retain a vestige of what once was; we are, moreover, neither

9. Reconquerors (Spanish).

Indian nor European, but a species midway between the legitimate proprietors of this country and the Spanish usurpers. In short, though Americans by birth we derive our rights from Europe, and we have to assert these rights against the rights of the natives, and at the same time we must defend ourselves against the invaders. This places us in a most extraordinary and involved situation. Notwithstanding that it is a type of divination to predict the result of the political course which America is pursuing, I shall venture some conjectures which, of course, are colored by my enthusiasm and dictated by rational desires rather than by reasoned calculations.

The rôle of the inhabitants of the American hemisphere has for centuries been purely passive. Politically they were non-existent. We are still in a position lower than slavery, and therefore it is more difficult for us to rise to the enjoyment of freedom. Permit me these transgressions in order to establish the issue. States are slaves because of either the nature or the misuse of their constitutions; a people is therefore enslaved when the government, by its nature or its vices, infringes on and usurps the rights of the citizen or subject. Applying these principles, we find that America was denied not only its freedom but even an active and effective tyranny. Let me explain. Under absolutism there are no recognized limits to the exercise of governmental powers. The will of the great sultan, khan, bey, and other despotic rulers is the supreme law, carried out more or less arbitrarily by the lesser pashas, khans, and satraps of Turkey and Persia, who have an organized system of oppression in which inferiors participate according to the authority vested in them. To them is entrusted the administration of civil, military, political, religious, and tax matters. But, after all is said and done, the rulers of Ispahan are Persians; the viziers of the Grand Turk are Turks; and the sultans of Tartary are Tartars. China does not bring its military leaders and scholars from the land of Genghis Khan,[1] her conqueror, notwithstanding that the Chinese of today are the lineal descendants of those who were reduced to subjection by the ancestors of the present-day Tartars.

How different is our situation! We have been harassed by a conduct which has not only deprived us of our rights but has kept us in a sort of permanent infancy with regard to public affairs. If we could at least have managed our domestic affairs and our internal administration, we could have acquainted ourselves with the processes and mechanics of public affairs. We should also have enjoyed a personal consideration, thereby commanding a certain unconscious respect from the people, which is so necessary to preserve amidst revolutions. That is why I say we have even been deprived of an active tyranny, since we have not been permitted to exercise its functions.

Americans today, and perhaps to a greater extent than ever before, who live within the Spanish system occupy a position in society no better than that of serfs destined for labor, or at best they have no more status than that of mere consumers. Yet even this status is surrounded with galling restrictions, such as being forbidden to grow European crops, or to store products which are royal monopolies, or to establish factories of a type the Peninsula[2] itself does not

---

1. Mongol chieftain (1165–1227), founder of the Mongol Empire in central Asia, who conquered huge swaths of territory, including present-day China, Korea, Russia, and Afghanistan.

2. The Iberian Peninsula, comprising Spain and Portugal.

possess. To this add the exclusive trading privileges, even in articles of prime necessity, and the barriers between American provinces, designed to prevent all exchange of trade, traffic, and understanding. In short, do you wish to know what our future held?—simply the cultivation of the fields of indigo, grain, coffee, sugar cane, cacao, and cotton; cattle raising on the broad plains; hunting wild game in the jungles: digging in the earth to mine its gold—but even these limitations could never satisfy the greed of Spain.

So negative was our existence that I can find nothing comparable in any other civilized society, examine as I may the entire history of time and the politics of all nations. Is it not an outrage and a violation of human rights to expect a land so splendidly endowed, so vast, rich, and populous, to remain merely passive?

* * *

Surely unity is what we need to complete our work of regeneration. The division among us, nevertheless, is nothing extraordinary, for it is characteristic of civil wars to form two parties, *conservatives* and *reformers*. The former are commonly the more numerous, because the weight of habit induces obedience to established powers; the latter are always fewer in number although more vocal and learned. Thus, the physical mass of the one is counterbalanced by the moral force of the other; the contest is prolonged, and the results are uncertain. Fortunately, in our case, the mass has followed the learned.

I shall tell you with what we must provide ourselves in order to expel the Spaniards and to found a free government. It is *union*, obviously; but such union will come about through sensible planning and well-directed actions rather than by divine magic. America stands together because it is abandoned by all other nations. It is isolated in the center of the world. It has no diplomatic relations, nor does it receive any military assistance; instead, America is attacked by Spain, which has more military supplies than any we can possibly acquire through furtive means.

When success is not assured, when the state is weak, and when results are distantly seen, all men hesitate; opinion is divided, passions rage, and the enemy fans these passions in order to win an easy victory because of them. As soon as we are strong and under the guidance of a liberal nation which will lend us her protection, we will achieve accord in cultivating the virtues and talents that lead to glory. Then will we march majestically toward that great prosperity for which South America is destined. Then will those sciences and arts which, born in the East, have enlightened Europe, wing their way to a free Colombia, which will cordially bid them welcome.

Such, Sir, are the thoughts and observations that I have the honor to submit to you, so that you may accept or reject them according to their merit. I beg you to understand that I have expounded them because I do not wish to appear discourteous and not because I consider myself competent to enlighten you concerning these matters.

DECLARATION OF SENTIMENTS

At the World Anti-Slavery Convention in London in 1840, two American delegates were denied the right to speak because they were women. Disturbed not least by the hypocrisy of the antislavery movement, supposedly dedicated to freedom and human rights, these two delegates—Lucretia Mott (1793–1880) and Elizabeth Cady Stanton (1815–1902)—convened a Women's Rights Convention in Seneca Falls, New York, in 1848. There more than 300 delegates hotly debated whether or not it was practical for the new women's movement to demand the right to vote. The great abolitionist leader **Frederick Douglass**, himself a former slave, spoke out powerfully in support of women's suffrage.

Stanton wrote the Declaration of Sentiments that was presented at Seneca Falls. Modeled explicitly on the Declaration of Independence, this document uses the language of the American Revolution to argue for freedom and equal rights for the half of the nation that had been excluded by the original Declaration. Ironically, the American men who had enumerated the wrongs perpetrated by a foreign tyrant were now the ones accused of tyranny. Many voices in the press, including religious leaders, treated the plea for women's rights with contempt or outright horror. It would be another seventy years before U.S. women won the right to vote.

Declaration of Sentiments

Put forth at Seneca Falls, N.Y., July 19th and 20th, 1848

WHEN, in the course of human events, it becomes necessary for one portion of the family of man to assume among the people of the earth a position different from that which they have hitherto occupied, but one to which the laws of nature, and of nature's God entitle them, a decent respect to the opinions of mankind requires that they should declare the causes that impel them to such a course.

We hold these truths to be self-evident; that all men and women are created equal; that they are endowed by their Creator with certain inalienable rights; that among these are life, liberty, and the pursuit of happiness; that to secure these rights governments are instituted, deriving their just powers from the consent of the governed. Whenever any form of Government becomes destructive of those ends, it is the right of those who suffer from it, to refuse allegiance to it, and to insist upon the institution of a new government, laying its foundation on such principles, and organizing its powers in such form as to them shall seem most likely to effect their safety and happiness. Prudence, indeed, will dictate that governments long established should not be changed for light and transient causes;

and accordingly, all experience hath shown that mankind are more disposed to suffer, while evils are sufferable, than to right themselves by abolishing the forms to which they are accustomed. But when a long train of abuses and usurpations, pursuing invariably the same object, evinces a design to reduce them under absolute despotism, it is their duty to throw off such government, and provide new guards for their future security. Such has been the patient sufferance of the women under this government, and such is now the necessity which constrains them to demand the equal station, to which they are entitled.

The history of mankind is a history of repeated injuries and usurpations on the part of man toward woman, having in direct object the establishment of an absolute tyranny over her. To prove this, let facts be submitted to a candid world.

He has never permitted her to exercise her inalienable right to the elective franchise.

He has compelled her to submit to laws, in the formation of which she had no voice.

He has withheld from her rights which are given to the most ignorant and degraded men—both natives and foreigners.

Having deprived her of this first right of a citizen, the elective franchise, thereby leaving her without representation in the halls of legislation, he has oppressed her on all sides.

He has made her, if married, in the eye of the law, civilly dead.[1]

He has taken from her all right in property, even to the wages she earns.

He has made her, morally, an irresponsible being, as she can commit many crimes with impunity, provided they be done in the presence of her husband. In the covenant of marriage, she is compelled to promise obedience to her husband, he becoming, to all intents and purposes, her master—the law giving him power to deprive her of her liberty, and to administer chastisement.

He has so framed the laws of divorce, as to what shall be the proper causes of divorce, in case of separation, to whom the guardianship of children shall be given; as to be wholly regardless of the happiness of women—the law, in all cases, going upon the false supposition of the supremacy of man, and giving all power into his hands.

After depriving her of all rights as a woman, if single and the owner of property, he has taxed her to support a government, which recognizes her only when her property can be made profitable to it.

He has monopolized nearly all the profitable employments; and from those she is permitted to follow, she receives but a scanty remuneration.

He closes against her all avenues to wealth and distinction, which he considers most honorable to himself. As a teacher of Theology, Medicine or Law, she is not known.

He has denied her the facilities for obtaining a thorough education—all colleges being closed against her.

He allows her in Church as well as State, but a subordinate position, claiming Apostolic authority for her exclusion from the ministry, and with some exceptions, from any public participation in the affairs of the Church.

---

1. "Civil death" is a legal term for those who have lost their civil rights, traditionally because they have committed a felony.

He has created a false public sentiment, by giving to the world a different code of morals for man and woman, by which moral delinquencies which exclude women from society, are not only tolerated but deemed of little account when committed by man.

He has usurped the prerogative of Jehovah himself, claiming it as his right to assign for her a sphere of action, when that belongs to her conscience and her God.

He has endeavored in every way that he could, to destroy her confidence in her own powers, to lessen her self-respect, and to make her willing to lead a dependent and abject life.

Now, in view of this entire disfranchisement of one half the people of this country, their social and religious degradation—in view of the unjust laws above mentioned and because women do feel themselves aggrieved, oppressed and fraudulently deprived of their most sacred rights, we insist that they have immediate admission to all the rights and privileges, which belong to them as citizens of these United States.

In entering upon the great work before us, we anticipate no small amount of misconception; misrepresentation and ridicule; but we shall use every instrumentality within our power to effect our object. We shall employ agents, circulate tracts, petition the State and National Legislatures, and endeavor to enlist the pulpit and the press in our behalf. We hope this Convention will be followed by a series of Conventions, embracing every part of the country.

Firmly relying upon the final triumph of the Right and the True, we do this day affix our signatures to this declaration.

JEAN-JACQUES ROUSSEAU

1712-1778

Jean-Jacques Rousseau played a significant role in three different revolutions: in politics, his work inspired and shaped revolutionary sentiment in the American colonies and France; in philosophy, he proposed radically unsettling ideas about human nature, justice, and progress that disrupted the dominant Enlightenment thinking of the moment and helped to spark the Romantic movement; and in literature, he invented a major new genre: the modern autobiography. The kind of life story he tells in the *Confessions* is now so familiar as to feel ordinary, recounting in detail the author's emotional life, including formative childhood experiences of desire, pain, and guilt. But in its moment this narrative broke with established conventions, erupting onto the literary scene as a shock so great that it was banned altogether. The text did not appear in full until more than a hundred years after it was written.

LIFE

As a young man, Rousseau did not seem bound for intellectual greatness. Born in the Protestant city of Geneva in 1712, the second son of a watchmaker, he spent very little time in school. Rousseau's mother died a few days after he was born, and his father, after having gotten himself involved in a violent quarrel, fled Geneva when Jean-Jacques was ten, sending his son to live with relatives. The boy did not seem adept enough to learn watchmaking, so at the age of thirteen he was apprenticed to an engraver, who turned out to be cruel and violent. Three years later, Rousseau ran away from Geneva and, craving the protection of a beautiful Catholic woman named Françoise-Louise de Warens, converted to Catholicism. Then began a period of aimless wandering, as Rousseau lived on and off with Madame de Warens, working for short periods as a domestic servant, a music teacher, a surveyor's clerk, and a tutor. Even in his thirties, he was given to idle drifting and was unable to hold down a job for long.

Despite his lack of formal schooling, the young Rousseau always read voraciously. In early childhood he developed a passionate enthusiasm for ancient Greek and Roman writers. A particular favorite was Plutarch, who wrote morally instructive biographies of ancient emperors and military leaders, including Julius Caesar and Alexander the Great. Rousseau was such an avid reader that while he was an apprentice he went so far as to sell his clothes in order to get his hands on books.

Madame de Warens helped the young man to pursue his intellectual interests and encouraged him to learn music. Their emotional relationship has become well known thanks to Rousseau's account of it in the *Confessions*. Rousseau called her "Mamma," while she called him "Little One." They became lovers in the period from 1733 to 1738, although, Rousseau writes, he felt considerable discomfort joining sexual longings with his love for this maternal figure. To make matters more complicated still, their household often included other men, with Rousseau at times the less favored figure in the *ménage à trois*. And yet, long after their relationship was over, he continued to speak of his lasting love for Madame de Warens and her pivotal importance in his life.

At the age of thirty, Rousseau went to Paris, where he became a personal assistant to a powerful and aristocratic family. In this period he met **Denis Diderot** and other important Enlightenment philosophers, and he contributed a few entries to the grand *Encyclopédie* they were compiling. At the same time that he was attracting patronage in the most refined Parisian circles, he started living with a barely literate chambermaid named Thérèse Levasseur, a relationship that lasted for three decades and finally resulted in marriage. He had five children with her—all of whom, shockingly, he insisted on leaving in a Paris orphanage.

Late in 1749 Rousseau was considering competing for an essay prize: the challenge was to write about whether advances in the arts and sciences had brought about a purification of human morals. As he was thinking about this question, he experienced a sudden flash of inspiration that would change his life. In one moment of "illumination," he said, he realized that intellectual advances had brought not moral purification but corruption, not improvement but decline. Human beings in a state of nature were compassionate and good; it was society itself that was to blame for creating inequality, greed, and aggression. He abruptly rejected the achievements that the Enlightenment philosophers were calling "progress." The essay won first prize, and it made

Rousseau famous. "I dared to strip man's nature naked," he wrote, "and showed that his supposed improvement was the true fount of all his miseries."

In the years that followed, Rousseau developed these innovative ideas. In 1754 he ascribed all of the evils of human experience to property and inequality: "You are undone if you once forget that the fruits of the earth belong to us all, and the earth itself to nobody." Deciding to live the simple life that he extolled in his works, he returned to Geneva, where he converted back to Protestantism. This second conversion prompted some detractors to accuse him of insincerity and opportunism. Soon after, he made a new enemy when he published a condemnation of the French philosopher **Voltaire**. Two years later he denounced the theater as a cause of moral corruption, and inserted a personal attack on his former friend Diderot. He soon found himself isolated and labeled a traitor. From this point onward, he constantly suspected that others were conspiring against him.

Julie, or the New Heloise, Rousseau's only novel, was published in 1761. The best-selling novel of the entire eighteenth century, *Julie* extolled passionate, authentic feeling, sincere faith, and rustic nature, and it struck audiences as dramatically different from most contemporary fiction, which prized artful wit and sophistication. Readers were enthralled, and Rousseau became one of the first literary celebrities. "Women were intoxicated by both the book and its author," he boasted, "and there were hardly any, even in the highest ranks, whose conquest I might not have made if I had undertaken it."

The year after *Julie* appeared, Rousseau developed his thinking in two major philosophical works. The first, *The Social Contract*, made the radical case that legitimate government rests on the will of the people. When rulers fail to protect the populace, Rousseau argued, they break the social contract, and the people are then free to choose new rulers. Thomas Jefferson would rely on this argument when he came to write the **Declaration of Independence**. The second major work, *Émile*, another major best seller, was a treatise on education which argued that children should be allowed to develop according to their senses and lived experience, and should be kept from books until the age of 12. This idea inspired numerous educational programs, including Montessori schools. In *Émile*, Rousseau also made a case for "natural religion," arguing that a knowledge of God comes not from orthodox doctrine or from revelation, but from one's own observations of nature. Parliaments in both Paris and Geneva saw the book as subversive and called for it to be banned and burned, while the French government ordered Rousseau's arrest. He escaped to a Prussian town, where he asked a priest if he could take communion. His detractors were shocked: was this the man who had just condemned all established religion? Then, in 1764, an anonymous pamphlet—which turned out to have been written by Voltaire—revealed that Rousseau had abandoned all five of his children. Since the moral purpose of *Émile* was to teach readers how to raise and educate children, this latest scandal seemed to many to expose Rousseau as a thoroughgoing hypocrite. In response, he began to write a defense of himself that would shield him from public blame—a story of his own life. This was to become the *Confessions*.

Looking for refuge from scandal and capture, Rousseau fled to England to stay with the philosopher **David Hume** in 1766. He had become so suspicious of those around him that after a few months he became convinced that Hume was part of a large conspiracy against him, and he wrote a public letter accusing his host of persecuting him. After wandering in exile, he finally settled down in Paris in 1770. A warrant was still out for his arrest, but no one seemed eager to enforce it, and he quietly took up copying music for a living. He also finished the *Confessions*. Since he knew that he would not be permitted to publish it, he confined himself to reading portions aloud to intimate aristocratic audiences. Even these readings alarmed many of his listeners, however, who feared that their own secrets would become public in Rousseau's narrative. Former friends convinced the police to ban these events. After an intense period of despair and hopelessness, Rousseau grew comparatively serene until his death in 1778.

CENSORSHIP AND SUBVERSION IN ROUSSEAU'S FRANCE

Rousseau was not the only writer of his time to endure censorship. At the beginning of the eighteenth century, France had been ruled for decades by an absolute monarch, Louis XIV, who consolidated power so effectively that he is remembered for his stark declaration, "I am the state." Under his rule, Catholic France became the most powerful nation in Europe. It was also highly repressive, silencing criticism of the state and persecuting Protestants who lived within French borders. The king's great-grandson, Louis XV, came to the throne in 1715, a less able and decisive ruler than his predecessor. After several serious military losses, sex scandals, and spending sprees, his popularity sank, and although the government controlled all publications and ordered the death penalty for any writer who attacked religious or state authority, a lively underground book and pamphlet trade flourished. The literate population of France almost doubled between 1680 and 1780, and it in-

cluded an ever greater variety of readers, including women and artisans. Printed works became cheaper and more available, and audiences began to change their habits, shifting from the conventional practice of reading a small number of works many times over to a new pattern of reading numerous works quickly, thereby gaining access to an unprecedented array of genres and points of view.

From the 1720s onward, a large network of underground printers published philosophical works outside of France in Protestant cities such as Geneva or Amsterdam and had them smuggled across the borders in oxcarts, or sewn into women's petticoats. A few publishers hid inflammatory pages inside respectable books such as Bibles. The king's advisors realized that they were losing the battle and in the 1750s became more permissive, but such an outpouring of radical publications followed that the state imposed new bans. Paradoxically, outlawing a work helped it to sell more copies, which meant that Louis XV's censorship helped to set off a vigorous public debate. For the first time, a democratic public sphere was emerging. Literary success began to depend on a wide reading public, rather than on specific patrons. And as those beyond the elite enjoyed a growing access to such innovative works, their willingness to tolerate the conventions of the old regime would start to falter.

Among the most influential critics of authority in Rousseau's time were the Enlightenment philosophers, such as Voltaire, who forcefully attacked the Catholic Church, and the Baron de Montesquieu, who denounced despotism and the slave trade. These thinkers called for individual reason to take the place of traditional authority, and they argued that human history was progressing toward perfection by casting off old habits and fetters. This was no marginal academic argument: it threatened to rock the very foundations of the state. Rousseau's friend Denis Diderot remained under police surveillance for years and was for a time imprisoned in a dungeon for writing subversively about religion. Later, his great Enlightenment project, the *Encyclopédie*, worried those in power by promising to diffuse knowledge widely, allowing ordinary people access to unsettling new ideas about natural rights, science, and religious tolerance. In the late 1750s Enlightenment thinkers felt intensely vulnerable, and it was in these same years that Rousseau— subversive and inflammatory in his own right—began to attack them from a new angle. Exalting feeling over reason, rejecting scientific advances, and imagining a return to uncorrupted nature as the key to human happiness, Rousseau became the lightning rod for critiques of Enlightenment reason and the personification of a whole new movement that would come to be known as Romanticism. Indeed, it was Rousseau's writing that first introduced a wide audience to the values that Romantic writers and artists would enthusiastically take up in the generations to follow: an admiration for simplicity and naturalness, a pleasure in the imagination, an assertion of the importance of unique, sincere, individual experience, and, in place of reason, a celebration of the whole range of emotions, from passionate love and intense horror to patriotic loyalty and harrowing grief.

WORK

Before Rousseau's *Confessions*, European readers had sometimes encountered life stories written by aristocrats and military heroes, which recounted their heroic exploits, and they had read confessional religious works, where authors had told stories about faith and conversion. But they had never seen anything quite like a modern autobiography. For the first time, an author's intimate emotional life became the subject of his work. The *Confessions* therefore helped to revolutionize notions of what a life was and what it meant. This was a text that took the uniqueness of individual feeling more seriously than any text had done before, prizing honest self-knowledge as a new moral value. In the process, it also offered a new kind of hero: the isolated but extraordinary individual, unhappy in his solitude but brave in his resistance to social mores. Rousseau departed from convention, too, in his insistence on the importance of childhood memories as essential to the formation of adult personality. Since previous writers had generally considered children's experience inconsequential, the *Confessions* challenged the most basic expectations about what was relevant to an understanding of the self. And then, even more strangely, the narrative focused specifically on sexual pleasures—including the pleasure of being spanked as a child— which struck many of Rousseau's first readers as embarrassingly petty. But these episodes would turn out to have a lasting impact. More than a century later, Sigmund Freud looked back on the *Confessions* as the forerunner of psychoanalysis, and into our own time, biographers, memoir writers, novelists, therapists, and talk-show hosts continue to understand childhood sexuality as a crucial shaping factor in an adult's life.

The book opens with Rousseau's own sense of his radical originality: "I am resolved on an undertaking that has no model and will have no imitator." Given this claim to being without precedent, Rousseau's title intriguingly suggests the opposite: by calling his autobiography the *Confessions*, he suggests that he is in fact modeling his own work on a famous fourth-century Christian story of spiritual conversion, St. Augustine's *Confessions*. And so he invites us to consider whether or not Augustine's autobiography acts as a "model" for his own work.

This is just one of many paradoxes and contradictions that readers have noticed in Rousseau. On the one hand, for example, he casts himself as a solitary outcast. On the other hand, the *Confessions* repeatedly mentions that its author is an international celebrity, hounded by adoring fans across Europe. In another seeming paradox, Rousseau borrows from the conventionally masculine genre of the public figure's memoir, while he draws equally from the much more feminine, private, domestic style of the novel to describe his childhood and love affairs. Rousseau himself said, "I would rather be a man of paradoxes than a man of prejudices," and it is possible to see these paradoxes forming the very backbone of the work. After all, while the *Confessions* presents the private, emotional life of a unique person, it also uses this personal experience to explore larger ideas about the relationship between the individual and society— the very ideas that are also at the heart of Rousseau's philosophical works. The *Confessions* can therefore be seen to interrogate and break down con-ventional distinctions between private and public, unique and representative, masculine and feminine.

Many readers have been troubled by yet another tension in the text. Rousseau insists throughout that he is telling the unvarnished truth about himself, however shameful, including acts of theft and masturbation. And yet, he also says that he intends the text to vindicate him to a wide public— to show that he is, by nature, essentially good. The struggle for truth and the attempt at self-justification can seem starkly at odds. In his own time, however, Rousseau's innovative style strengthened his claims to truth telling. Most contemporary writers reveled in elaborate wit and wordplay, but Rousseau spoke frankly and powerfully in the first person, giving his readers a startling new sense of direct contact with the author. Inventing a style of prose that felt unusually plain and honest, Rousseau helped to provoke a new appetite for authenticity in life-writing. Meanwhile, his insistence on direct democracy, natural rights, the value of authentic emotion, and the perils of property ownership would win numerous followers, political, philosophical, and literary. Napoleon himself is reputed to have said that Rousseau caused the French Revolution, and added, "without the Revolution, you would not have had me."

Confessions[1]

This is the only portrait of a man, painted exactly according to nature and in all its truth, that exists and will probably ever exist. Whoever you may be, whom destiny or my trust has made the arbiter of the fate of these notebooks, I entreat you, in the name of my misfortunes, of your compassion, and of all human kind, not to destroy a unique and useful work, which may serve as a first point of comparison in the study of man that certainly is yet to be begun, and not to

---

1. Translated by Angela Scholar.

take away from the honour of my memory the only sure monument to my character that has not been disfigured by my enemies. Finally, were you yourself to be one of those implacable enemies, cease to be so towards my ashes, and do not pursue your cruel injustice beyond the term both of my life and yours; so that you might do yourself the credit of having been, once at least, generous and good, when you might have been wicked and vindictive; if, that is, the evil directed at a man who has never himself done nor wanted to do any could properly bear the name of vengeance.

Part One

BOOK ONE

Intus, et in cute.[2]

I am resolved on an undertaking that has no model and will have no imitator. I want to show my fellow-men a man in all the truth of nature; and this man is to be myself.

Myself alone. I feel my heart and I know men. I am not made like any that I have seen; I venture to believe that I was not made like any that exist. If I am not more deserving, at least I am different. As to whether nature did well or ill to break the mould in which I was cast, that is something no one can judge until after they have read me.

Let the trumpet of judgement sound when it will, I will present myself with this book in my hand before the Supreme Judge. I will say boldly: 'Here is what I have done, what I have thought, what I was. I have told the good and the bad with equal frankness. I have concealed nothing that was ill, added nothing that was good, and if I have sometimes used some indifferent ornamentation, this has only ever been to fill a void occasioned by my lack of memory; I may have supposed to be true what I knew could have been so, never what I knew to be false. I have shown myself as I was, contemptible and vile when that is how I was, good, generous, sublime, when that is how I was; I have disclosed my innermost self as you alone know it to be. Assemble about me, Eternal Being, the numberless host of my fellow-men; let them hear my confessions, let them groan at my unworthiness, let them blush at my wretchedness. Let each of them, here on the steps of your throne, in turn reveal his heart with the same sincerity; and then let one of them say to you, if he dares: *I was better than that man.*'

I was born in 1712 in Geneva, the son of Isaac Rousseau and Suzanne Bernard, citizens.[3] Since an already modest family fortune to be divided between fifteen children had reduced to almost nothing my father's share of it, he was obliged to depend for his livelihood on his craft as a watchmaker, at which, indeed, he excelled. My mother, who was the daughter of M. Bernard, the minister, was wealthier; she was beautiful and she was good; and my father had not

---

2. "Inside and under the skin" (Latin), from Roman satirist Aulus Persius Flaccus (34–62 C.E.), referring to a man who looks back sadly on his loss of virtue.

3. Geneva, unlike its larger neighbors Savoy and France, was a republic with an elected legislature, though only a small number of adult men counted as citizens.

won her easily. They had loved one another almost from the day they were born; at the age of eight or nine years they were already taking walks together every evening along the Treille; by ten years they were inseparable. The sympathy, the harmony between their souls, reinforced the feelings that habit had formed. Tender and sensitive by nature, they were both of them waiting only for the moment when they would find another person of like disposition, or rather this moment was waiting for them, and each of them gave his heart to the first that opened to receive it. The destiny that had seemed to oppose their passion served only to kindle it. Unable to win his lady, the young man was consumed with grief; she counselled him to travel and to forget her. He travelled, to no avail, and returned more in love than ever. He found the woman he loved still tender and true. After such a test all that remained was for them to love one another till the end of their days; they swore to do so, and Heaven blessed the vow.

Gabriel Bernard, my mother's brother, fell in love with one of my father's sisters; but she consented to marry the brother only on condition that her brother marry the sister. Love prevailed, and the two weddings took place on the same day. And so my uncle was the husband of my aunt, and their children were my first cousins twice over. By the end of the first year a child had been born on each side; but there was to be a further separation.

My uncle Bernard was an engineer; he went away to serve in the Empire and in Hungary under Prince Eugène. He distinguished himself during the siege and the battle of Belgrade.[4] After the birth of my only brother, my father departed for Constantinople to take up a post as watchmaker to the seraglio. While he was away my mother's beauty, intelligence, and accomplishments[5] won her many admirers. M. de La Closure, the French resident in Geneva, was one of the most assiduous in his attentions. His passion must have been keenly felt; since thirty years later he still softened visibly when he spoke of her to me. My mother had more than her virtue with which to defend herself, she loved her husband tenderly; she pressed him to return; he abandoned everything and came. I was the sad fruit of this homecoming. Ten months later, I was born, weak and sickly; I cost my mother her life, and my birth was the first of my misfortunes.

I never knew how my father bore his loss; but I do know that he never got over it. He thought he could see my mother in me, without being able to forget that I had deprived him of her; he never caressed me without my sensing, from his sighs, from his urgent embraces, that a bitter regret was mingled with them, for which, however, they were the more tender. He had only to say to me: 'Let's talk about your mother, Jean-Jacques,' and I would reply: 'Very well, Father, and then we'll weep together,' and these words alone were enough to

---

4. François-Eugène, Prince of Savoy (1663–1736), led the Hungarian army to victory in the Battle of Belgrade, a famous and surprising triumph over the Turkish army in 1717.

5. These were too brilliant for her condition in life, for her father, the minister, adored her, and had taken great care over her education. She could draw and sing, she accompanied herself on the theorbo [a stringed instrument], she was well read and could write tolerable verse. Here is a little rhyme she wrote impromptu, while out walking with her sister-in-law and their children during the absence of her brother and her husband, in response to a remark that someone made to her about these latter:

These two young men, though far from here,
In many ways to us are dear;
They are our friends, our lovers;
Our husbands and our brothers,
And the fathers of these children here.
[Rousseau's note]

move him to tears. 'Ah!' he would sigh, 'bring her back to me, comfort me for losing her; fill the emptiness she has left in my soul. Would I love you as much if you were only my son?' Forty years after losing her he died in the arms of a second wife, but with the name of the first on his lips, and her image deep in his heart.

Such were the authors of my days. Of all the gifts bestowed on them by heaven, the only one they bequeathed to me was a tender heart; but to this they owed their happiness, just as I owe it all my misfortune.

I was born almost dying; they despaired of saving me. I already carried within me the germ of an indisposition which has worsened with the years, and which now allows me some occasional respite only in order that I might endure another, more cruel, form of suffering. One of my father's sisters, an amiable and virtuous young woman, took such good care of me that she saved me. She is still alive as I write this, and at eighty years old cares for a husband who is younger than she, but ravaged by drink. I forgive you, dear Aunt, for having preserved my life, and it grieves me that I cannot, at the end of your days, repay you for the tender care you lavished on me at the beginning of mine. My nurse Jacqueline, too, is still alive and in sound health. The hands that opened my eyes at my birth may yet close them at my death.

I had feelings before I had thoughts: that is the common lot of humanity. But I was more affected by it than others are. I have no idea what I did before the age of five or six: I do not know how I learned to read; all I remember is what I first read and its effect on me; this is the moment from which I date my first uninterrupted consciousness of myself. My mother had left some romances.[6] We began to read them after supper, my father and I. Our first intention was simply that I should practise my reading with the help of some entertaining books; but we soon became so engrossed in them that we spent whole nights taking it in turns to read to one another without interruption, unable to break off until we had finished the whole volume. Sometimes my father, hearing the swallows at dawn, would say shamefacedly: 'We'd better go to bed now; I'm more of a child than you are.'

By this dangerous method I acquired in a short time not only a marked facility for reading and comprehension, but also an understanding, unique in one of my years, of the passions. I had as yet no ideas about things, but already I knew every feeling. I had conceived nothing; I had felt everything. This rapid succession of confused emotions did not damage my reason, since as yet I had none; but it provided me with one of a different temper; and left me with some bizarre and romantic notions about human life, of which experience and reflection have never quite managed to cure me.

The romances lasted us until the summer of 1719. The following winter we found something else. Since my mother's books were exhausted, we resorted to what we had inherited of her father's library. Fortunately it contained some good books; and this could scarcely have been otherwise, since this library had been collected by a man who was not only an ordained minister and even, for such was the fashion of the day, a scholar, but also a man of taste and intelli-

---

6. Novels, often fanciful tales of adventure and heroism.

gence. Le Sueur's *History of Church and Empire*, Bossuet's discourses on universal history, Plutarch's on famous men, Nani's *History of Venice*, Ovid's *Metamorphoses*, La Bruyère, Fontenelle's *Plurality of Worlds* and his *Dialogues of the Dead*, and some volumes of Molière,[7] all these were moved into my father's studio, and there, every day, I read to him while he worked. I acquired a taste for these works that was rare, perhaps unique, in one of my age. Plutarch, in particular, became my favourite author. The pleasure I took in reading and rereading him cured me in part of my passion for romances, and I soon preferred Agesilaus, Brutus, and Aristides to Orondate, Artamène, and Juba.[8] These interesting books, and the conversations they occasioned between my father and me, shaped that free, republican spirit, that proud and indomitable character, that impatience with servitude and constraint, which it has been my torment to possess all my life in circumstances not at all favourable to its development. My mind was full of Athens and Rome; I lived, as it were, in the midst of their great men; I was, besides, by birth a citizen of a republic and the son of a father whose love for his country was his greatest passion, and I was fired by his example; I thought of myself as a Greek or a Roman; I became the person whose life I was reading: when I recounted acts of constancy and fortitude that had particularly struck me, my eyes would flash and my voice grow louder. One day at table, while I was relating the story of Scaevola,[9] my family were alarmed to see me stretch out my hand and, in imitation of his great deed, place it on a hot chafing-dish.

I had a brother seven years older than I, who was learning my father's trade. The extreme affection that was lavished upon me meant that he was a little neglected, which is not something of which I can approve. His upbringing suffered in consequence. He fell into dissolute ways even before the age at which one can, properly speaking, be considered dissolute. He was placed with a new master, from whom he ran away just as he had done at home. I hardly ever saw him; I can hardly claim to have known him; but I nevertheless loved him dearly, and he loved me too, in as far as such a rascal is capable of love. I remember once when my father, in a rage, was chastising him severely, throwing myself impetuously between the two of them and flinging my arms around him. I thus protected him by taking on my own body all the blows destined for him, and I kept this up so determinedly that my father was obliged in the end to spare him, either because he was moved by my cries and my tears, or because he was afraid of hurting me more than him. My brother went from bad to worse and in the end ran off and disappeared forever. A little while later we

7. The pseudonym of Jean Baptiste de Poquelin (1622–1673), French comic playwright. Jean Le Sueur (c. 1602–1681), French historian and Protestant minister. Jacques-Bénigne Bossuet (1627–1704), French bishop, writer, and orator. Plutarch (46–119), Roman historian and biographer. Giovanni Battista Nani (1616–1678), Venetian writer, historian, and ambassador. Ovid (43 B.C.E.–16 C.E.), Roman poet. Jean de la Bruyère (1645–1696), French satirist. Bernard le Bovier de Fontenelle (1657–1757), French writer, scientist, and philosopher.
8. Agesilaus, Brutus, and Aristides are historical figures; Orondate and Juba are characters from novels by Gauthier de Costes, called la Calprenède (1610–1663); Artamène is the hero of a long novel by Madeleine de Scudéry (1607–1701).
9. Gaius Mucius Scaevola, a mythical Roman hero who held his right hand in a fire without showing any signs of pain.

heard that he was in Germany. He never once wrote. No more was ever heard of him; and so it was that I became an only son.

If this poor boy's upbringing was neglected, the same could not be said of his brother, for royal princes could not have been cared for more zealously than I was during my early years, idolized by everyone around me, and, which is rarer, treated always as a much-loved child and never as a spoiled one. Never once while I remained in my father's house was I allowed to roam the streets alone with the other children; never was it necessary either to discourage in me or to indulge any of those fanciful whims which are generally attributed to nature, and which are entirely the product of upbringing. I had my childish faults: I prattled, I was greedy, I sometimes told lies. No doubt I stole fruit, sweets, things to eat; but I never, just for the fun of it, did any harm or damage, got others into trouble, or teased dumb animals. I remember on one occasion, however, peeing into the kettle belonging to one of our neighbours, Mme Clot, while she was at church. I must confess, too, that this memory still makes me laugh, for Mme Clot, although otherwise a thoroughly good person, was the grumpiest old woman I ever knew in my life. Such is the true but brief history of my childhood misdemeanours.

How could I have learnt bad ways, when I was offered nothing but examples of mildness and surrounded by the best people in the world? It was not that the people around me—my father, my aunt, my nurse, our relatives, our friends, our neighbours—obeyed me, but rather that they loved me; and I loved them in return. My whims were so little encouraged and so little opposed that it never occurred to me to have any. I am ready to swear that, until I was myself subjected to the rule of a master, I never even knew what a caprice was. When I was not reading or writing with my father, or going for walks with my nurse, I was always with my aunt, watching her at her embroidery, hearing her sing, sitting or standing at her side; and I was happy. Her good-humour, her gentleness, her agreeable features, all these have so imprinted themselves on my memory, that I can still see in my mind's eye her manner, her glance, her whole air; I still remember the affectionate little things she used to say; I could describe how she was dressed, and how she wore her hair, even to the two black curls which, after the fashion of the day, framed her temples.

I am convinced that it is to her that I owe the taste, or rather passion, for music that developed in me fully only much later. She knew a prodigious number of songs and airs, which she sang in a small, sweet voice. This excellent young woman possessed a serenity of soul that banished far from her and from everyone around her any reverie or sadness. I was so enchanted by her singing that, not only have many of her songs lingered in my memory, but, now that I have lost her, others too, totally forgotten since childhood, return to haunt me as I grow older, with a charm I cannot convey. Who would have thought that, old driveller that I am, worn out with worry and care, I should suddenly catch myself humming these little tunes in a voice already cracked and quavering, and weeping like a child? One air in particular has come back to me in full, although the words of the second verse have repeatedly resisted all my efforts to remember them, even though I dimly recall the rhymes. Here is the beginning followed by what I have been able to remember of the rest.

> Tircis,[1] I dare not stay
> Beneath the sturdy oak
> To hear your pipe's sweet play;
> Already I'm the talk
> Of all our village folk
>
> .   .   .   .
> .   .   .   a shepherd's vows
> .   .   .   his repose
> .   .   .   allows
> For always the thorn lies under the rose.

What is it about this song, I wonder, that so beguiles and moves my heart? It has a capricious charm I do not understand at all; nevertheless, I am quite incapable of singing it through to the end without dissolving into tears. I have often been on the point of writing to Paris to enquire about the rest of the words, in case there should be anyone there who still knows them. But I suspect that some of the pleasure I take in recalling this little tune would fade if I knew for certain that others apart from my poor aunt Suzanne had sung it.

Such were the affections that marked my entry into life; thus there began to take shape or to manifest themselves within me this heart, at once so proud and so tender, and this character, effeminate and yet indomitable, which, continually fluctuating between weakness and courage, between laxity and virtue, has to the end divided me against myself and ensured that abstinence and enjoyment, pleasure and wisdom have all eluded me equally.

This upbringing was interrupted by an accident whose consequences have affected my life ever since. My father had a quarrel with a M. Gautier, a French captain, who had relatives in the council.[2] This Gautier, an insolent and cowardly fellow, suffered a nose-bleed and, out of revenge, accused my father of having drawn his sword on him inside the city limits. My father, threatened with imprisonment, insisted that, in accordance with the law, his accuser be taken into custody with him. Unable to obtain this, he chose to leave Geneva and to exile himself for the rest of his life rather than give way on a point where it seemed to him that both his honour and his liberty were compromised.

I remained behind under the guardianship of my uncle Bernard, who at the time was employed on the fortifications of Geneva. His eldest daughter had died, but he had a son the same age as myself. We were sent off together to Bossey to board with the minister, M. Lambercier, so that, along with some Latin, we might acquire that hotchpotch of knowledge which usually accompanies it under the name of education.

Two years spent in this village softened, somewhat, my Roman harshness and restored my childhood to me. At Geneva, where nothing was imposed on me, I had loved reading and study; it was almost my only amusement. At Bossey I was made to work, and thus grew to love the games that served as relaxation. The countryside was so new to me that I never tired of enjoying it. I came to love it with a passion that has never faded. The memory of the happy days I spent there has filled me with regret for rural life and its pleasures at every stage of

---

1. A shepherd from pastoral poetry.   2. The legislature of Geneva.

my existence until the one that took me back there. M. Lambercier was a sensible man who, while not neglecting our education, did not overburden us with schoolwork. The proof that he went about this in the right way is that, in spite of my dislike of any form of compulsion, I have never remembered my hours of study with any distaste, and that, while I did not learn much from him, what I did learn, I learned without difficulty and have never forgotten.

This simple country life bestowed on me a gift beyond price in opening up my heart to friendship. Up until then I had only known feelings that, although exalted, were imaginary. Living peaceably day after day with my cousin Bernard, I became warmly attached to him, and soon felt a more tender affection for him than I had for my brother, and one that has not been erased by time. He was a tall boy, lanky and very thin, as mild-tempered as he was feeble-bodied, and who did not take unfair advantage of the preference that, as the son of my guardian, he was shown by the whole household. We shared the same tasks, the same amusements, the same tastes; we were on our own together; we were of the same age; each of us needed a friend; so that to be separated was for both of us, so to speak, to be annihilated. Although we rarely had occasion to demonstrate our mutual attachment, it was strong, and not only could we not bear to be separated for a moment, but we could not imagine ever being able to bear it. Since we both of us responded readily to affection and were good-humoured when not crossed, we always agreed about everything. If, as the favourite of our guardians, he took precedence over me when we were with them, when we were alone the advantage was mine, and this redressed the balance between us. When he was at a loss during lessons, I whispered the answer to him; when my exercise was finished, I helped him with his, and in games, where I was the more inventive, he always followed my lead. In other words, our characters were so compatible and the friendship that united us so real, that, during the more than five years that we were virtually inseparable, whether at Bossey or in Geneva, we often, it is true, fell out, but we never needed to be separated, none of our quarrels lasted for more than a quarter of an hour, and neither of us ever once informed against the other. These remarks may seem puerile, but they nevertheless draw attention to an example that is perhaps unique among children.

The kind of life I led at Bossey suited me so well that it would have fixed my character for ever, if only it had lasted longer. It was founded on feelings that were at once tender, affectionate, and tranquil. Never, I believe, has any individual of our species possessed less natural vanity than I do. I would soar to heights of sublime feeling, but as promptly fall back into my habitual indolence. To be loved by all who came near me was my most urgent wish. I was by nature gentle, so too was my cousin; so indeed were our guardians. During two whole years I neither witnessed nor was the victim of any kind of violence. Everything fostered the tendencies that nature herself had planted in my heart. I knew no greater happiness than to see everyone content with me and with the world in general. I will never forget how, when it was my turn in chapel to recite my catechism, nothing distressed me more, if I happened to hesitate in my replies, than to see on Mlle Lambercier's face signs of anxiety and distress. I was more upset by this than by the shame of failing in public, although that, too, affected me greatly: for, not much moved by praise, I was always susceptible to shame, and I can safely say that the expectation of a reprimand from Mlle Lambercier alarmed me less than did the fear of causing her pain.

And indeed, she was not afraid, any more than was her brother, to show severity when this was necessary; but since her severity was almost always justified and never excessive, it provoked in me feelings of distress rather than of rebellion. I was more concerned about occasioning displeasure than about being chastised, for marks of disapprobation seemed more cruel to me than physical punishment. I find it embarrassing to go into greater detail, but I must. How promptly we would change our methods of dealing with the young if only the long-term effects of the one that is presently employed, always indiscriminately and often indiscreetly, could be foreseen! The lesson that may be learned from just one example of this, as common as it is pernicious, is so important that I have decided to give it.

Just as Mlle Lambercier felt for us the affection of a mother, so too she had a mother's authority, which she sometimes exerted to the point of inflicting common childhood punishments on us, when we had deserved this. For a while she restricted herself to threats of punishment which were quite new to me and which I found very frightening; but after the threat had been carried out, I discovered that it was less terrible in the event than it had been in anticipation, and, what is even more bizarre, that this punishment made me even fonder of the woman who had administered it. Indeed, it took all the sincerity of my affection for her and all my natural meekness to prevent me from seeking to merit a repetition of the same treatment; for I had found in the pain inflicted, and even in the shame that accompanied it, an element of sensuality which left me with more desire than fear at the prospect of experiencing it again from the same hand. It is true that, since without doubt some precocious sexual instinct entered into all this, the same punishment received from her brother would not have seemed to me at all pleasant. But given his temperament, this arrangement was not something that needed to be feared, so that, if I resisted the temptation to earn punishment, this was solely because I was afraid of vexing Mlle de Lambercier; for so great is the power that human kindness exercises over me, even if it has its origin in the senses, that in my heart the former will always prevail over the latter.

This second offence, which I had avoided without fearing it, duly occurred, but without involving any misdeed or at least any conscious act of will on my part, so that it was with a clear conscience that I as it were profited from it. But this second was also the last: for Mlle de Lambercier, who no doubt inferred from some sign I gave that the punishment was not achieving its aim, declared that she could not continue with it, that it exhausted her too much. Up until then we had slept in her room and sometimes, in winter, even in her bed. Two days later we were moved to another room, and I had henceforward the honour, which I would gladly have foregone, of being treated by her as a big boy.

Who would have believed that this ordinary form of childhood punishment, meted out to a boy of eight years[3] by a young woman of thirty, should have

---

3. Rousseau was in fact eleven years old at the time, not eight.

decided my tastes, my desires, my passions, my whole self, for the rest of my life, and in a direction that was precisely the opposite of what might naturally have been expected? My senses were inflamed, but at the same time my desires, confused and indeed limited by what I had already experienced, never thought of looking for anything else. My blood had burned within my veins almost from the moment of my birth, but I kept myself pure of any taint until an age when even the coldest and slowest of temperaments begins to develop. Long tormented, but without knowing why, I devoured with ardent gaze all the beautiful women I encountered. My imagination returned to them again and again, but only to deploy them in its own way, and to make of each of them another Mlle de Lambercier.

This bizarre taste, which persisted beyond adolescence and indeed drove me to the verge of depravity and madness, nevertheless preserved in me those very standards of upright behaviour which it might have been expected to undermine. If ever an upbringing was proper and chaste, it was certainly the one that I had received. My three aunts were not only persons of exemplary respectability, they also practised a reticence that women have long since abandoned. My father, who liked his pleasures but was gallant in the old style, never uttered, even in the presence of the women he most admired, a single word that would make a virgin blush, and the consideration that is due to children has never been more scrupulously observed than it was in my family and in front of me. M. Lambercier's household was no less strict in this regard, and indeed a very good servant was dismissed for having said something a little too free and easy in front of us. Not only had I reached adolescence before I had any clear idea about sexual union, but such confused ideas as I did have always took some odious and disgusting form. I had a horror of common prostitutes that I have never lost; I could not look at a debauchee without disdain, without dread even, so extreme was the aversion that I had felt for debauchery ever since, going to Saconnex one day along a hollow lane, I saw holes in the earth along both sides of the path and was told that this was where these people did their coupling. What I had seen dogs doing always came into my mind too when I thought of how it might be for people, and the very memory was enough to sicken me.

These prejudices, which I owed to my upbringing and which were sufficient in themselves to delay the first eruptions of a combustible temperament, were further reinforced, as I have said, by the false direction in which I had been led by the first stirrings of sensuality. I imagined only what I had experienced; in spite of a troublesome agitation in the blood, I concentrated all my desires on the kind of pleasure I already knew, without ever getting as far as that which I had been made to think of as odious, and which so closely resembled the other, although I had not the least suspicion of this. When, in the midst of my foolish fantasies, of my wild erotic flights, and of the extravagant actions to which they sometimes drove me, I resorted in imagination to the assistance of the other sex, I never dreamt that it could be put to any other use than that which I burned to make of it.

In this way, then, in spite of an ardent, lascivious, and very precocious temperament, not only did I pass beyond the age of puberty without desiring, without knowing, any sensual pleasures beyond those to which Mlle de Lambercier had quite innocently introduced me; but also, when at last the passing years had made me a man, it was again the case that what should have ruined me preserved me. The taste I had acquired as a child, instead of disappearing, became so identified with that other pleasure that I was never able to dissociate it from the desires aroused through the senses; and this vagary, in conjunction with my natural timidity, has always inhibited me in my approaches to women, because I dare not tell them everything, but nor am I able to perform everything; since my kind of pleasure, of which the other sort is only the end point, cannot be extracted by the man who desires it, nor guessed at by the woman who alone can bestow it. And so I have spent my life coveting but never declaring myself to the women I loved most. Never daring to reveal my proclivities, I have at least kept them amused with relationships that allowed my mind to dwell on them. To lie at the feet of an imperious mistress, to obey her commands, to be obliged to beg for her forgiveness, these were sweet pleasures, and the more my inflamed imagination roused my blood, the more I played the bashful lover. This way of making love does not, needless to say, result in very rapid progress, nor does it pose much threat to the virtue of the women who are its object. I have thus possessed very few, but have nevertheless achieved much pleasure in my own way, that is, through my imagination. Thus it is that my senses, conspiring with my timid nature and my romantic spirit, have kept my heart pure and my behaviour honourable, thanks to those very inclinations which, if I had been a little bolder perhaps, would have plunged me into the most brutish pleasure-seeking.

I have taken the first step, and the most painful, into the dark and miry labyrinth of my confessions. It is not what is criminal that it is the hardest to reveal, but what is laughable or shameful. But from now on I can feel certain of myself: after what I have just dared to say, nothing can stop me.

* * *

BOOK TWO

My landlady who, as I have said, had taken a liking to me, told me that she might have found a situation for me, and that a lady of quality wanted to see me. This was enough to convince me that I was at last embarked upon adventures in high places, for this was the idea I always came back to. It turned out, however, not to be as brilliant as I had imagined. I was taken to see the lady by the servant who had told her about me. She questioned me, cross-examined me, and was, apparently, satisfied, for all of a sudden I found myself in her service, not exactly as a favourite, but as a footman. I was dressed in the same colour as the other servants, except that they had a shoulder-knot which I was not given; since there was no braid on her livery, it looked very little different from any ordinary suit of clothes. Such was the unexpected fulfilment of all my high hopes!

The Comtesse de Vercellis, whose household I had entered, was a widow with no children. Her husband had been from Piedmont; as for her, I have always assumed that she came from Savoy, since I could not imagine a Piedmontese speaking French so well and with such a pure accent. She was in her middle years, distinguished in appearance, cultivated in mind, with a great love and knowledge of French literature. She wrote a great deal and always in French. Her letters had the turn of phrase and the grace, almost, of Mme de Sévigné's:[4] some of them might even have been taken for hers. My main task, not at all an unpleasant one, was to take dictation of these letters, since she was prevented by a breast cancer, which caused her much suffering, from writing them herself.

Mme de Vercellis possessed not only great intelligence but a steadfast and noble soul. I watched her during her last illness, I saw her suffer and die without betraying a moment's weakness, without making the least apparent effort to contain herself, without abandoning her woman's dignity, and without suspecting that there was any philosophy in all of this; indeed, the word 'philosophy' was not yet in vogue, and she would not have known it in the sense in which it is used today. This strength of character was so marked as to be indistinguishable, sometimes, from coldness. She always seemed to me to be as indifferent to the feelings of others as she was to her own, so that, if she performed good works among the poor and needy, she did so because this was good in itself rather than out of any true compassion. I experienced something of this indifference during the three months I was with her. It would have been natural for her to conceive a liking for a young man of some promise, who was continually in her presence, and for it to occur to her, as she felt death approach, that afterwards he would still need help and support; however, either because she did not think me worthy of any special attention, or because the people who watched over her saw to it that she thought only of them, she did nothing for me.

I well remember, however, the curiosity she showed while getting to know me. She would sometimes ask me about myself; she liked me to show her the letters I was writing to Mme de Warens, and to describe my feelings to her. But she went about discovering them in quite the wrong way, since she never revealed hers to me. My heart was eager to pour itself out, provided it felt that another was open to receive it. Cold and curt interrogation, however, with no hint either of approbation or of blame at my replies, did not inspire me with confidence. Unable to judge whether my chatter was pleasing or displeasing, I became fearful and would try, not so much to say what I felt, as to avoid saying anything that might harm me. I have since observed that this habit of coldly interrogating people whom you are trying to get to know is fairly common among women who pride themselves on their intelligence. They imagine that, by revealing nothing of their own feelings, they will the better succeed in discovering yours; what they do not realize is that they thereby deprive you of the courage to reveal them. Anyone subjected to close questioning will, for that very reason, be put on his guard, and if he suspects that, far from inspiring any real interest, he is merely being made to talk, he will either lie, say nothing, or watch his tongue even more carefully than before, preferring to be thought a fool than to be the dupe of someone's mere curiosity. It is, in short, pointless to attempt to see into the heart of another while affecting to conceal one's own.

Mme de Vercellis never said a word to me that expressed affection, pity, or benevolence. She questioned me coldly, I replied with reserve. My replies were

4. French writer Marie de Rabutin-Chantal, marquise de Sévigné (1626–1696), famous for her letters.

so timid that she must have found them beneath her notice, and become bored. Towards the end she asked me no more questions and spoke to me only if she wanted me to do something for her. She judged me on the basis not so much of what I was but of what she had made me, and because she regarded me as nothing more than a footman, she prevented me from appearing to be anything else.

I think that this was my first experience of that malign play of hidden self-interest which has so often impeded me in life and which has left me with a very natural aversion towards the apparent order that produces it. Mme de Vercellis's heir, since she had no children, was a nephew, the Comte de la Roque, who was assiduous in his attentions towards her. In addition, her principal servants, seeing that her end was near, were determined not to be forgotten, and all in all she was surrounded by so many over-zealous people that it was unlikely that she would find time to think of me. The head of her household was a certain M. Lorenzini, an artful man, whose wife, even more artfully, had so insinuated herself into the good graces of her mistress that she was treated by her as a friend rather than a paid servant. She had persuaded her to take on as chambermaid a niece of hers, called Mlle Pontal, a crafty little creature who gave herself the airs of a lady's maid; together, she and her aunt were so successful in ingratiating themselves with their mistress that she saw only through their eyes and acted only through their agency. I had not the good fortune to find favour with these three people; I obeyed them, but I did not serve them; I did not see why, as well as attending our common mistress, I should be a servant to her servants. I presented, moreover, something of a threat to them. They could see very well that I was not in my rightful place; they feared that Madame would see it too, and that what she might do to rectify this would diminish their own inheritance; for people of that sort are too greedy to be fair, and look upon any legacy made to others as depriving them of what is properly theirs. And so they made a concerted effort to keep me out of her sight. She liked writing letters. It was a welcome distraction for someone in her condition; they discouraged it and persuaded her doctor to oppose it on the grounds that it was too tiring for her. On the pretext that I did not understand my duties, they hired in my place two great oafs to carry her about in her chair; and in short, they were so successful in all this that, when she came to make her will, I had not even entered her room during the whole of the previous week. It is true that thereafter I entered as before, and was more assiduous in my attentions than anyone else; for the poor woman's sufferings distressed me greatly, while the constancy with which she bore them inspired admiration and affection in me; indeed I shed genuine tears in that room, unnoticed by her or by anyone else.

At last we lost her. I saw her die. In life she had been a woman of wit and good sense; in death she was a sage. I can safely say that she endeared the Catholic religion to me by the serenity of spirit with which she fulfilled its duties, without omission and without affectation. She was by nature serious, but towards the end of her illness she assumed an air of gaiety, which was too constant to be simulated, and which was as though lent her by reason itself to compensate for the gravity of her situation. It was only during her last two days that she stayed in bed, and even then she kept up a tranquil conversation with the people round about her. At last, unable to speak and already in the throes of death, she gave a great fart. 'Good,' she said, as she turned over: 'A woman who farts cannot be dead.' These were the last words she uttered.

She had bequeathed a year's wages to each of her menial servants; but, since my name did not appear on her household list, I received nothing; in spite of this, the Comte de la Roque gave me thirty francs and let me keep the new suit of clothes which, although I was wearing it, M. Lorenzini had wanted to take away from me. He even promised to try to find me a new position and gave me permission to go and see him. I went two or three times, but without managing to speak to him. Easily deterred, I did not go again. As we will soon see, this was a mistake.

If only this were all that I have to relate about my time with Mme de Vercellis! But although my situation appeared unchanged, I was not the same on leaving her house as I had been when I entered it. I took away with me the enduring memory of a crime and the intolerable burden of a remorse, with which even now, after forty years, my conscience is still weighed down, and whose bitter knowledge, far from fading, becomes more painful with the years. Who would have thought that a child's misdeed could have such cruel consequences? But it is because of these all too probable consequences that my heart is denied any consolation. I may have caused to perish, in shameful and miserable circumstances, a young woman who, amiable, honest, and deserving, was, without a doubt, worth a great deal more than I.

It is almost inevitable that the dispersal of a household should generate a certain confusion and that items should go astray. And yet, such was the loyalty of the servants and the vigilance of M. and Mme Lorenzini that nothing was missing from the inventory. All that was lost was a little ribbon, silver and rose-coloured and already quite old, which belonged to Mlle Pontal. Many other, better things had been within my reach; but I was tempted only by this ribbon, I stole it, and since I made little attempt to conceal it, I was soon found with it. They asked me where I had got it. I hesitated, stammered, and finally said, blushing, that Marion had given it to me. Marion was a young girl from the Maurienne,[5] whom Mme de Vercellis had engaged as a cook when, because she no longer entertained and had more need of nourishing soups than of delicate ragouts, she decided to dismiss her own. Not only was Marion pretty, with a freshness of complexion that is found only in the mountains, and, above all, an air of modesty and sweetness that won the heart of everyone who saw her, she was also a good girl, virtuous and totally loyal. There was thus great surprise when I named her. I was regarded as scarcely less trustworthy, and so an enquiry was thought to be necessary to establish which of us was the thief. She was summoned; a large crowd of people was present, among them the Comte de la Roque. She arrived, was shown the ribbon, and, shamelessly, I made my accusation; taken aback, she said nothing, then threw me a glance which would have disarmed the devil himself, but which my barbarous heart resisted. At length she denied the charge, firmly but calmly, remonstrated with me, urged me to recollect myself and not to bring disgrace upon an innocent girl who had never done me any harm; I persisted in my infernal wickedness, however, repeated my accusation, and asserted to her face that it

5. A province in the kingdom of Savoy.

was she who had given me the ribbon. The poor girl began to cry, but said no more than, 'Ah Rousseau, and I always thought you had a good character! How wretched you are making me, and yet I would not for anything be in your place.' And that was all. She continued to defend herself with steadfast simplicity but without permitting herself any attack on me. The contrast between her moderation and my decided tone worked against her. It did not seem natural to suppose that there could be such diabolical effrontery on the one hand and such angelic sweetness on the other. No formal conclusion was reached, but the presumption was in my favour. Because of the general upheaval, the matter was left there, and the Comte de la Roque, dismissing us both, contented himself with saying that the conscience of the guilty party would be certain to avenge the innocent. This was no vain prophecy, but is every day fulfilled anew.

I do not know what became of the victim of my false witness; it seems unlikely that, after this, she would easily have found another good situation. She had suffered an imputation to her honour that was cruel in every way. The theft was trifling; nevertheless, it was a theft and, what was worse, had been used to seduce a young boy; finally, the lie and the obstinacy with which she clung to it left nothing to be hoped for from someone who combined so many vices. I fear, too, that wretchedness and destitution were not the worst of the dangers I exposed her to. Who knows to what extremes despair and injured innocence might not, at her age, have driven her? Ah, if my remorse at having made her unhappy is intolerable, only judge how it feels to have perhaps reduced her to being worse off than myself!

At times I am so troubled by this cruel memory, and so distressed, that I lie sleepless in my bed, imagining the poor girl advancing towards me to reproach me for my crime as though I had committed it only yesterday. While I still enjoyed some tranquillity in life it tormented me less, but in these tempestuous times it deprives me of the sweetest consolation known to persecuted innocence; it brings home to me the truth of an observation I think I have made in another work, that remorse is lulled during times of good fortune and aggravated in adversity. And yet I have never been able to bring myself to unburden my heart of this confession by entrusting it to a friend. I have never, in moments of the greatest intimacy, divulged it to anyone, even to Mme de Warens. The most that I have been able to do has been to confess my responsibility for an atrocious deed, without ever saying of what exactly it consisted. This burden, then, has lain unalleviated on my conscience until this very day; and I can safely say that the desire to be in some measure relieved of it has greatly contributed to the decision I have taken to write my confessions.

I have been outspoken in the confession I have just made, and surely no one could think that I have in any way sought to mitigate the infamy of my crime. But I would not be fulfilling the purpose of this book if I did not at the same time reveal my own innermost feelings, and if I were afraid to excuse myself, even where the truth of the matter calls for it. I have never been less motivated by malice than at this cruel moment, and when I accused this unfortunate girl, it is bizarre, but it is true, that it was my fondness for her that was the cause of it. She was on my mind, and I had simply used as an excuse the first object that presented itself to me. I accused her of having done what I wanted to do, and of having given me the ribbon, because my intention had been to give it to her. When she appeared shortly afterwards I was stricken with remorse, but the presence of so many people was stronger than my repentance. It was not that I was afraid of being punished but that I was afraid of being put to shame; and I feared shame more than death, more than crime, more than anything in the world. I would have wanted the earth to swallow me up and bury me in its depths. It was shame alone, unconquerable shame, that prevailed over everything and was the cause of all my impudence; and the more criminal I became, the more my terror at having to admit it made me bold. All I could think of was the horror of being found out and of being denounced, publicly and to my face, as a thief, a liar, a slanderer. The confusion that seized my whole being robbed me of any other feeling. If I had been given time to collect myself, I would unquestionably have admitted everything. If M. de la Roque had taken me aside and had said to me: 'Don't ruin this poor girl. If you are guilty, own up to it now,' I would have thrown myself at his feet forthwith; of that I am perfectly certain. But, when what I needed was encouragement, all I received was intimidation. My age, too, was a consideration that it is only fair to take into account. I was scarcely more than a child, or rather I still was one. Real wickedness is even more criminal in a young person than in an adult, but what is merely weakness is much less so, and my offence, when it comes down to it, was little more. Thus its memory distresses me less because of any evil in the act itself than because of that which it must have caused. It has even had the good effect of preserving me for the rest of my life from any inclination towards crime, because of the terrible impression that has remained with me of the only one I ever committed, and I suspect that my aversion towards lying comes in large part from remorse at having been capable of one that was so wicked. If, as I venture to believe, such a crime can be expiated, it must surely have been so by the many misfortunes that burden my old age; by forty years of rectitude and honour in difficult circumstances; indeed, poor Marion has found so many avengers in this world that, however grave my offence against her, I am not too afraid that I will carry the guilt for it into the next. That is all that I had to say on this subject. May I be spared from ever having to speak of it again.

OLAUDAH EQUIANO

ca. 1745–1797

To proslavery writers in Europe and the United States who insisted that Africans were not human beings, Olaudah Equiano offered an unsettling challenge. *The Interesting Narrative of the Life of Olaudah. Equiano, Or Gustavus Vassa, the African, Told by Himself* was the first autobiography to have been written by a freed slave. Barred from education, most slaves had to tell their stories to ghostwriters, but Equiano used his unusual access to literacy to present an intelligent, honest, and feeling self in his own compelling words. It was difficult to argue that Africans were not human when here was a person who evidently faced new experiences with puzzlement and curiosity; a person who encountered hardship with sensitivity; a person who felt love, pain, friendship, and deep religious faith. When the text first appeared in 1789, reviewers speculated that Equiano's story would shift the debate about slavery. "Written with much truth and simplicity," and showing "extraordinary intellectual powers,"

Equiano's story might be "sufficient to wipe off the stigma" attached to Africans. It was so popular that it went through 36 editions before 1857, and was translated into German, Dutch, and Russian. The debate about slavery might not have been the only source of the book's popularity: Equiano was one of the most widely traveled men of the eighteenth century, having been in Africa, the West Indies, the United States, Europe, Central America, Turkey, and even the Arctic Circle. His life made fascinating reading for European and American audiences who were showing a keen and growing appetite for stories of remote and exotic places.

LIFE

Equiano was born in about 1745 in the Niger River Delta area of present-day Nigeria. Kidnapped by local raiders around the age of eleven, he was carried to the coast and sold into slavery. There is no record of what price he commanded,

The frontispiece and title page of *The Interesting Narrative of the Life of Olaudah Equiano, or Gustavus Vassa, the African, Written by Himself* (1789).

but traders often exchanged several yards of fabric, a couple of barrels of rum, or a keg of gunpowder for a slave. After a harrowing journey across the Atlantic, Equiano was purchased by a Virginia slaveholder who put him to work in the fields. Soon after, a former British naval officer, Michael Henry Pascal, bought him as a present for friends in England. In a gesture of cruel irony, Pascal renamed his new slave "Gustavus Vassa," after a sixteenth-century Swedish hero who had liberated Sweden from Danish oppression.

On board Pascal's commercial ship, Equiano befriended a young American sailor named Dick Baker, who taught him the habits and values of his new environment. In England, Equiano received comparatively kind treatment; he learned to read and write, and was baptized. He also went to sea a number of times on Pascal's ship, serving under him in the Seven Years' War. In 1762 Equiano insisted to Pascal that he had a right to his freedom. Pascal promptly responded by selling him to a ship bound for the West Indies. There Equiano was lucky enough to be sold to a "charitable and humane" Quaker merchant from Philadelphia. He eventually earned the money he needed to purchase his freedom, and chose to live in London, where he worked as a hairdresser, valet, and doctor's assistant. In 1773 he joined an expedition to the Arctic, in search of a route from Europe, over the North Pole, to Asia; and two years later he went to Nicaragua as a missionary. He had by this point become a devout Methodist.

Equiano came to know the leading British abolitionists and with them, he took part in an effort to resettle former slaves in a colony in Sierra Leone. He was given the job of outfitting the ship with adequate food and equipment. As he worked, he discovered that other administrators were pocketing the money intended for the colony, and he drew public attention to their scheme. This attempt to redress injustice backfired,

and it was Equiano who was dismissed. History proved him right, however: Equiano had warned that the colony would fail without sufficient funds, and in fact it was so ill-equipped that fewer than one in five of the settlers survived the first few years.

The Interesting Narrative appeared in 1789. Equiano dedicated the book to the English Parliament; he then cannily persuaded prominent readers to pay for the book in advance, and published the list of all of his subscribers, beginning with the Prince of Wales and including eight dukes. Soon after the book's publication, he became the first modern author to go on a book tour. He lectured throughout Great Britain and Ireland, his presence helping to authenticate the claim that the text was "written by himself"—that is, that an African had been capable of writing this powerful story. A few years later, Equiano married an Englishwoman named Susannah Cullen, and had two daughters. He died in London at the age of fifty-two.

TIMES

Between the sixteenth century and the middle of the nineteenth, slave traders transported about 12 million Africans across the Atlantic Ocean to North America, South America, and the Caribbean. The journey across the Atlantic—called the Middle Passage—is infamous: chained and crowded together so closely that they could barely breathe, Africans had to be prevented from jumping overboard to their deaths to escape the sickness and pain that surrounded them. Often severed from family members and from anyone who shared their local language, faith, and customs, slaves endured a traumatic rupture from everything that had made life meaningful for them. And this was only the beginning. They then underwent the horrors of slavery itself: they were beaten, muzzled, raped, forced to work through sickness and hunger, separated from parents and children, and denied education and freedom of movement.

The slave trade reached its peak in the 1780s, when seventy thousand or more slaves traveled across the Atlantic to North and South America and the Caribbean each year. And the rewards for slave traders were considerable: if a voyage went smoothly, a trader might reap a profit of more than a hundred percent. Then, after selling the slaves that had survived the journey, traders used their profits to buy products of American slave labor, such as sugar, cotton, coffee, and tobacco, which they proceeded to sell in Europe.

As the traffic in slaves grew, so too did opposition to slavery. Quakers and Methodists were particularly active in the antislavery movement in Britain and the United States. They worked vigorously to publicize the horrors of the slave trade, organizing societies, publications, lectures, and petitions. Thanks to Olaudah Equiano's efforts, one incident in particular prompted public outcry. In 1781 the captain of the slave ship *Zong* ordered more than a hundred sick slaves to be thrown overboard. He reasoned that his insurance policy would pay for the loss of living slaves but would hold him responsible for those who had died of illness. Appalled by such brutality, the British Parliament eventually outlawed the transport of slaves to Britain or any of its colonies; the United States soon followed suit. The traffic in bodies did not stop, however; plenty of illicit ships continued to carry Africans across the Atlantic. In 1833 Britain outlawed slavery altogether, but it remained legal in the United States, Brazil, and Cuba well past midcentury.

WORK

Equiano begins the story of his life with a detailed description of the Ibo community of his childhood. Recent anthropologists have authenticated his account, praising Equiano for his meticulous depiction of a whole way of life. His own contemporaries were often fascinated by his images of contented African people, living in a bountiful nature, who existed without the luxuries and technologies of the Europeans but seemed happy and honorable. Some took *The Interesting Narrative* as confirmation of **Jean-Jacques Rousseau**'s claims that human beings are morally best when they are closest to nature.

To be sure, Equiano's writing goes far beyond mere anthropological interest: combining elements of the travelogue, spiritual autobiography, and antislavery argument, Equiano combined genres to create a new prototype which many later slave narratives would follow. The rootless Equiano also calls to mind the picaresque wanderers of popular eighteenth-century novels, such as **Gulliver** and Robinson Crusoe, who are thrown into unfamiliar situations and forced to survive among strangers. Like these heroes, too, the young slave comments on social conventions as he travels, using episodes in his story as opportunities for both wonder and critique.

Among the most famous of these episodes is Equiano's experience of "the talking book." Having seen Captain Pascal and his friend Dick reading, the slave puts a book to his ear to see if it will talk to him likewise, and is disappointed when it seems to say nothing. Here, he narrates the story from the perspective of the bewildered child, and so allows readers to see their own cultural habits and expectations through fresh, unfamiliar eyes. This scene also draws attention to the vast distance the hero himself will travel, moving from an illiterate slave to a successful author in his own right. Equiano tells us that the name Olaudah means "having a loud voice and well spoken," which suggests that his own book will speak more loudly than the silent ones he has tried to read as a child. *The Interesting Narrative* has certainly won a wide array of admiring readers over the centuries. And if recent audiences have been impressed by Equiano's complex and sophisticated narrative self-representation, his first readers were often most taken with his appealing, sensitive, and trustworthy persona. As one of his early reviewers put it, "anyone is to be pitied who does not feel affection for Vassa, after reading his memoirs."

From The Interesting Narrative of the Life of Olaudah Equiano, or Gustavus Vassa, the African, Written by Himself

Volume I

Behold, God is my salvation; I will trust and not be afraid, for the Lord Jehovah is my strength and my song; he also is become my salvation. And in that day shall ye say, Praise the Lord, call upon his name, declare his doings among the people.
—ISAIAH 12:2, 4

To the Lords Spiritual and Temporal, and the Commons of the Parliament of Great Britain.

My Lords and Gentlemen,

Permit me, with the greatest deference and respect, to lay at your feet the following genuine Narrative; the chief design of which is to excite in your august assemblies a sense of compassion for the miseries which the Slave-Trade has entailed on my unfortunate countrymen. By the horrors of that trade was I first torn away from all the tender connexions that were naturally dear to my heart; but these, through the mysterious ways of Providence, I ought to regard as infinitely more than compensated by the introduction I have thence obtained to the knowledge of the Christian religion, and of a nation which, by its liberal sentiments, its humanity, the glorious freedom of its government, and its proficiency in arts and sciences, has exalted the dignity of human nature.

I am sensible I ought to entreat your pardon for addressing to you a work so wholly devoid of literary merit; but, as the production of an unlettered African, who is actuated by the hope of becoming an instrument towards the relief of his suffering countrymen, I trust that *such a man*, pleading in *such a cause*, will be acquitted of boldness and presumption.

May the God of heaven inspire your hearts with peculiar benevolence on that important day when the question of Abolition is to be discussed, when thousands, in consequence of your Determination, are to look for Happiness or Misery!

I am,
MY LORDS AND GENTLEMEN,
Your most obedient,
And devoted humble Servant,
OLAUDAH EQUIANO,
OR
GUSTAVUS VASSA.

Union-Street, Mary-le-bone,
March 24, 1789.

CHAPTER I

I believe it is difficult for those who publish their own memoirs to escape the imputation of vanity; nor is this the only disadvantage under which they labour: it is also their misfortune, that what is uncommon is rarely, if ever, believed, and what is obvious we are apt to turn from with disgust, and to charge the writer with impertinence. People generally think those memoirs only worthy to be read or remembered which abound in great or striking events, those, in short, which in a high degree excite either admiration or pity: all others they consign to contempt and oblivion. It is therefore, I confess, not a little hazardous in a private and obscure individual, and a stranger too, thus to solicit the indulgent attention of the public; especially when I own I offer here the history of neither a saint, a hero, nor a tyrant. I believe there are few events in my life, which have not happened to many: it is true the incidents of it are numerous; and, did I consider myself an European, I might say my sufferings were great: but when I compare my lot with that of most of my countrymen, I regard myself as a *particular favourite of Heaven*, and acknowledge the mercies of Providence in every occurrence of my life. If then the following narrative does not appear sufficiently interesting to engage general attention, let my motive be some excuse for its publication. I am not so foolishly vain as to expect from it either immortality or literary reputation. If it affords any satisfaction to my numerous friends, at whose request it has been written, or in the smallest degree promotes the interests of humanity, the ends for which it was undertaken will be fully attained, and every wish of my heart gratified. Let it therefore be remembered, that, in wishing to avoid censure, I do not aspire to praise.

That part of Africa, known by the name of Guinea, to which the trade for slaves is carried on, extends along the coast above 3400 miles, from the Senegal to Angola, and includes a variety of kingdoms. Of these the most considerable is the kingdom of Benen,[1] both as to extent and wealth, the richness and cultivation of the soil, the power of its king, and the number and warlike disposition of the inhabitants. It is situated nearly under the line,[2] and extends along the coast about 170 miles, but runs back into the interior part of Africa to a distance hitherto I believe unexplored by any traveller; and seems only terminated at length by the empire of Abyssinia,[3] near 1500 miles from its beginning. This kingdom is divided into many provinces or districts: in one of the most remote and fertile of which, called Eboe,[4] I was born, in the year 1745, in a charming fruitful vale, named Essaka. The distance of this province from the capital of Benin and the sea coast must be very considerable; for I had never heard of white men or Europeans, nor of the sea: and our subjection to the king of Benin was little more than nominal; for every transaction of the government, as far as my slender observation extended, was conducted by the chiefs or elders of the place. The manners and government of a people who have little commerce with other countries are generally very simple; and the history of what passes in one family or village may serve as a specimen of a nation. My father was one of those elders or chiefs I have spoken of, and was styled

1. Benin, a country in West Africa.
2. South of the equator.
3. African empire that lasted for almost three millennia; it includes present-day Ethiopia and Eritrea, as well as parts of Egypt and Sudan.
4. The Ibo people of Nigeria.

Embrenche; a term, as I remember, importing the highest distinction, and signifying in our language a *mark* of grandeur. This mark is conferred on the person entitled to it, by cutting the skin across at the top of the forehead, and drawing it down to the eye-brows; and while it is in this situation applying a warm hand, and rubbing it until it shrinks up into a thick *weal* across the lower part of the forehead. Most of the judges and senators were thus marked; my father had long borne it: I had seen it conferred on one of my brothers, and I was also *destined* to receive it by my parents. Those Embrenche, or chief men, decided disputes and punished crimes; for which purpose they always assembled together. The proceedings were generally short; and in most cases the law of retaliation prevailed. I remember a man was brought before my father, and the other judges, for kidnapping a boy; and, although he was the son of a chief or senator, he was condemned to make recompense by a man or woman slave. Adultery, however, was sometimes punished with slavery or death; a punishment which I believe is inflicted on it throughout most of the nations of Africa:[5] so sacred among them is the honour of the marriage bed, and so jealous are they of the fidelity of their wives. Of this I recollect an instance:—a woman was convicted before the judges of adultery, and delivered over, as the custom was, to her husband to be punished. Accordingly he determined to put her to death: but it being found, just before her execution, that she had an infant at her breast; and no woman being prevailed on to perform the part of a nurse, she was spared on account of the child. The men, however, do not preserve the same constancy to their wives, which they expect from them; for they indulge in a plurality, though seldom in more than two. Their mode of marriage is thus:—both parties are usually betrothed when young by their parents, (though I have known the males to betroth themselves). On this occasion a feast is prepared, and the bride and bridegroom stand up in the midst of all their friends, who are assembled for the purpose, while he declares she is thenceforth to be looked upon as his wife, and that no other person is to pay any addresses to her. This is also immediately proclaimed in the vicinity, on which the bride retires from the assembly. Some time after she is brought home to her husband, and then another feast is made, to which the relations of both parties are invited: her parents then deliver her to the bridegroom, accompanied with a number of blessings, and at the same time they tie round her waist a cotton string of the thickness of a goose-quill, which none but married women are permitted to wear: she is now considered as completely his wife; and at this time the dowry is given to the new married pair, which generally consists of portions of land, slaves, and cattle, household goods, and implements of husbandry. These are offered by the friends of both parties; besides which the parents of the bridegroom present gifts to those of the bride, whose property she is looked upon before marriage; but after it she is esteemed the sole property of her husband. The ceremony being now ended the festival begins, which is celebrated with bonfires, and loud acclamations of joy, accompanied with music and dancing.

We are almost a nation of dancers, musicians, and poets. Thus every great event, such as a triumphant return from battle, or other cause of public rejoicing

---

5. See Benezet's 'Account of Guinea' throughout [Equiano's note]. Anthony Benezet (1713–1784) was an antislavery writer from the United States.

is celebrated in public dances, which are accompanied with songs and music suited to the occasion. The assembly is separated into four divisions, which dance either apart or in succession, and each with a character peculiar to itself. The first division contains the married men, who in their dances frequently exhibit feats of arms, and the representation of a battle. To these succeed the married women, who dance in the second division. The young men occupy the third; and the maidens the fourth. Each represents some interesting scene of real life, such as a great achievement, domestic employment, a pathetic story, or some rural sport; and as the subject is generally founded on some recent event, it is therefore ever new. This gives our dances a spirit and variety which I have scarcely seen elsewhere.[6] We have many musical instruments, particularly drums of different kinds, a piece of music which resembles a guitar, and another much like a stickado.[7] These last are chiefly used by betrothed virgins, who play on them on all grand festivals.

As our manners are simple, our luxuries are few. The dress of both sexes is nearly the same. It generally consists of a long piece of callico, or muslin, wrapped loosely round the body, somewhat in the form of a highland plaid. This is usually dyed blue, which is our favourite colour. It is extracted from a berry, and is brighter and richer than any I have seen in Europe. Besides this, our women of distinction wear golden ornaments; which they dispose with some profusion on their arms and legs. When our women are not employed with the men in tillage, their usual occupation is spinning and weaving cotton, which they afterwards dye, and make it into garments. They also manufacture earthen vessels, of which we have many kinds. Among the rest tobacco pipes, made after the same fashion, and used in the same manner, as those in Turkey.[8]

Our manner of living is entirely plain; for as yet the natives are unacquainted with those refinements in cookery which debauch the taste: bullocks, goats, and poultry, supply the greatest part of their food. These constitute likewise the principal wealth of the country, and the chief articles of its commerce. The flesh is usually stewed in a pan, to make it savoury we sometimes use also pepper, and other spices, and we have salt made of wood ashes. Our vegetables are mostly plantains, eadas, yams, beans, and Indian corn.[9] The head of the family usually eats alone; his wives and slaves have also their separate tables. Before we taste food we always wash our hands: indeed our cleanliness on all occasions is extreme; but on this it is an indispensable ceremony. After washing, libation is made, by pouring out a small portion of the food, in a certain place, for the spirits of departed relations, which the natives suppose to preside over their conduct, and guard them from evil. They are totally unacquainted with strong or spirituous liquors; and their principal beverage is palm wine. This is gotten from a tree of that name by tapping it at the top, and fastening a large gourd to it; and sometimes one tree will yield

6. When I was in Smyrna I have frequently seen the Greeks dance after this manner [Equiano's note]. Smyrna is a city that was once in Greece, now in Turkey.
7. The sticcado pastorale is an Italian instrument like a xylophone.
8. The bowl is earthen, curiously figured, to which a long reed is fixed as a tube. The tube is sometimes so long as to be borne by one, and frequently out of grandeur by two boys [Equiano's note].
9. Corn that comes from the New World. "Eadas": a species of yam.

three or four gallons in a night. When just drawn it is of a most delicious sweetness; but in a few days it acquires a tartish and more spirituous flavour: though I never saw any one intoxicated by it. The same tree also produces nuts and oil. Our principal luxury is in perfumes; one sort of these is an odoriferous wood of delicious fragrance: the other a kind of earth; a small portion of which thrown into the fire diffuses a most powerful odour.[1] We beat this wood into powder, and mix it with palm oil; with which both men and women perfume themselves.

In our buildings we study convenience rather than ornament. Each master of a family has a large square piece of ground, surrounded with a moat or fence, or enclosed with a wall made of red earth tempered; which, when dry, is as hard as brick. Within this are his houses to accommodate his family and slaves; which, if numerous, frequently present the appearance of a village. In the middle stands the principal building, appropriated to the sole use of the master, and consisting of two apartments; in one of which he sits in the day with his family, the other is left apart for the reception of his friends. He has besides these a distinct apartment in which he sleeps, together with his male children. On each side are the apartments of his wives, who have also their separate day and night houses. The habitations of the slaves and their families are distributed throughout the rest of the enclosure. These houses never exceed one story in height: they are always built of wood, or stakes driven into the ground, crossed with wattles,[2] and neatly plastered within, and without. The roof is thatched with reeds. Our day-houses are left open at the sides; but those in which we sleep are always covered, and plastered in the inside, with a composition mixed with cowdung, to keep off the different insects, which annoy us during the night. The walls and floors also of these are generally covered with mats. Our beds consist of a platform, raised three or four feet from the ground, on which are laid skins, and different parts of a spungy tree called plaintain. Our covering is calico or muslin, the same as our dress. The usual seats are a few logs of wood; but we have benches, which are generally perfumed, to accommodate strangers: these compose the greater part of our household furniture. Houses so constructed and furnished require but little skill to erect them. Every man is a sufficient architect for the purpose. The whole neighbourhood afford their unanimous assistance in building them and in return receive, and expect no other recompense than a feast.

As we live in a country where nature is prodigal of her favours, our wants are few and easily supplied; of course we have few manufactures. They consist for the most part of calicoes, earthern ware, ornaments, and instruments of war and husbandry. But these make no part of our commerce, the principal articles of which, as I have observed, are provisions. In such a state money is of little use; however we have some small pieces of coin, if I may call them such. They are made something like an anchor; but I do not remember either their value or denomination. We have also markets, at which I have been frequently with my mother. These are sometimes visited by stout mahogany-coloured men from

---

1. When I was in Smyrna, I saw the same kind of earth, and brought some of it with me to England; it resembles musk in strength but is more delicious in scent, and is not unlike the smell of a rose [Equiano's note].

2. Woven reeds or thin branches.

the south west of us: we call them Oye-Eboe, which term signifies red men living at a distance. They generally bring us fire-arms, gunpowder, hats, beads, and dried fish. The last we esteemed a great rarity, as our waters were only brooks and springs. These articles they barter with us for odoriferous woods and earth, and our salt of wood ashes. They always carry slaves through our land; but the strictest account is exacted of their manner of procuring them before they are suffered to pass. Sometimes indeed we sold slaves to them, but they were only prisoners of war, or such among us as had been convicted of kidnapping, or adultery, and some other crimes, which we esteemed heinous. This practice of kidnapping induces me to think, that, notwithstanding all our strictness, their principal business among us was to trepan[3] our people. I remember too they carried great sacks along with them, which not long after I had an opportunity of fatally seeing applied to that infamous purpose.

Our land is uncommonly rich and fruitful, and produces all kinds of vegetables in great abundance. We have plenty of Indian corn, and vast quantities of cotton and tobacco. Our pine apples grow without culture; they are about the size of the largest sugar-loaf,[4] and finely flavoured. We have also spices of different kinds, particularly pepper; and a variety of delicious fruits which I have never seen in Europe; together with gums of various kinds, and honey in abundance. All our industry is exerted to improve those blessings of nature. Agriculture is our chief employment; and every one, even the children and women, are engaged in it. Thus we are all habituated to labour from our earliest years. Every one contributes something to the common stock; and as we are unacquainted with idleness, we have no beggars. The benefits of such a mode of living are obvious. The West India planters prefer the slaves of Benin or Eboe to those of any other part of Guinea, for their hardiness, intelligence, integrity, and zeal. Those benefits are felt by us in the general healthiness of the people, and in their vigour and activity; I might have added too in their comeliness. Deformity is indeed unknown amongst us, I mean that of shape. Numbers of the natives of Eboe now in London might be brought in support of this assertion: for, in regard to complexion, ideas of beauty are wholly relative. I remember while in Africa to have seen three negro children, who were tawny, and another quite white, who were universally regarded by myself, and the natives in general, as far as related to their complexions, as deformed. Our women too were in my eyes at least uncommonly graceful, alert, and modest to a degree of bashfulness; nor do I remember to have ever heard of an instance of incontinence amongst them before marriage. They are also remarkably cheerful. Indeed cheerfulness and affability are two of the leading characteristics of our nation.

Our tillage is exercised in a large plain or common, some hours walk from our dwellings, and all the neighbours resort thither in a body. They use no beasts of husbandry; and their only instruments are hoes, axes, shovels, and beaks, or pointed iron to dig with. Sometimes we are visited by locusts, which come in large clouds, so as to darken the air, and destroy our harvest. This however happens rarely, but when it does, a famine is produced by it. I remember an instance or two wherein this happened. This common is often the theatre of war; and therefore when our people go out to till their land, they not only go in a body, but generally take their arms with them for fear of a surprise; and when they appre-

3. Deceive, betray.   4. Block of refined sugar for sale.

hend an invasion they guard the avenues to their dwellings, by driving sticks into the ground, which are so sharp at one end as to pierce the foot, and are generally dipped in poison. From what I can recollect of these battles, they appear to have been irruptions of one little state or district on the other, to obtain prisoners or booty. Perhaps they were incited to this by those traders who brought the European goods I mentioned amongst us. Such a mode of obtaining slaves in Africa is common; and I believe more are procured this way and by kidnapping, than any other.[5] When a trader wants slaves, he applies to a chief for them, and tempts him with his wares. It is not extraordinary, if on this occasion he yields to the temptation with as little firmness, and accepts the price of his fellow creatures liberty with as little reluctance as the enlightened merchant. Accordingly he falls on his neighbours, and a desperate battle ensues. If he prevails and takes prisoners, he gratifies his avarice by selling them; but, if his party be vanquished, and he falls into the hands of the enemy, he is put to death: for, as he has been known to foment their quarrels, it is thought dangerous to let him survive, and no ransom can save him, though all other prisoners may be redeemed. We have fire-arms, bows and arrows, broad two-edged swords and javelins: we have shields also which cover a man from head to foot. All are taught the use of these weapons; even our women are warriors, and march boldly out to fight along with the men. Our whole district is a kind of militia: on a certain signal given, such as the firing of a gun at night, they all rise in arms and rush upon their enemy. It is perhaps something remarkable, that when our people march to the field a red flag or banner is borne before them. I was once a witness to a battle in our common. We had been all at work in it one day as usual, when our people were suddenly attacked. I climbed a tree at some distance, from which I beheld the fight. There were many women as well as men on both sides; among others my mother was there, and armed with a broad sword. After fighting for a considerable time with great fury, and after many had been killed our people obtained the victory, and took their enemy's Chief prisoner. He was carried off in great triumph, and, though he offered a large ransom for his life, he was put to death. A virgin of note among our enemies had been slain in the battle, and her arm was exposed in our market-place, where our trophies were always exhibited. The spoils were divided according to the merit of the warriors. Those prisoners which were not sold or redeemed we kept as slaves: but how different was their condition from that of the slaves in the West Indies! With us they do no more work than other members of the community, even their masters; their food, clothing and lodging were nearly the same as theirs, (except that they were not permitted to eat with those who were free-born); and there was scarce any other difference between them, than a superior degree of importance which the head of a family possesses in our state, and that authority which, as such, he exercises over every part of his household. Some of these slaves have even slaves under them as their own property, and for their own use.

As to religion, the natives believe that there is one Creator of all things, and that he lives in the sun, and is girted round with a belt that he may never eat or drink; but, according to some, he smokes a pipe, which is our own favourite luxury. They believe he governs events, especially our deaths or captivity; but, as for the doctrine of eternity, I do not remember to have ever heard of it: some

5. See Benezet's 'Account of Guinea' throughout [Equiano's note].

however believe in the transmigration of souls[6] in a certain degree. Those spirits, which are not transmigrated, such as our dear friends or relations, they believe always attend them, and guard them from the bad spirits or their foes. For this reason they always before eating, as I have observed, put some small portion of the meat, and pour some of their drink, on the ground for them; and they often make oblations of the blood of beasts or fowls at their graves. I was very fond of my mother, and almost constantly with her. When she went to make these oblations at her mother's tomb, which was a kind of small solitary thatched house, I sometimes attended her. There she made her libations, and spent most of the night in cries and lamentations. I have been often extremely terrified on these occasions. The loneliness of the place, the darkness of the night, and the ceremony of libation, naturally awful and gloomy, were heightened by my mother's lamentations; and these, concuring with the cries of doleful birds, by which these places were frequented, gave an inexpressible terror to the scene.

We compute the year from the day on which the sun crosses the line, and on its setting that evening there is a general shout throughout the land; at least I can speak from my own knowledge throughout our vicinity. The people at the same time make a great noise with rattles, not unlike the basket rattles used by children here, though much larger, and hold up their hands to heaven for a blessing. It is then the greatest offerings are made; and those children whom our wise men foretell will be fortunate are then presented to different people. I remember many used to come to see me, and I was carried about to others for that purpose. They have many offerings, particularly at full moons; generally two at harvest before the fruits are taken out of the ground: and when any young animals are killed, sometimes they offer up part of them as a sacrifice. These offerings, when made by one of the heads of a family, serve for the whole. I remember we often had them at my father's and my uncle's, and their families have been present. Some of our offerings are eaten with bitter herbs. We had a saying among us to any one of a cross temper, "That if they were to be eaten, they should be eaten with bitter herbs."

We practised circumcision like the Jews, and made offerings and feasts on that occasion in the same manner as they did. Like them also, our children were named from some event, some circumstance, or fancied foreboding at the time of their birth. I was named *Olaudah*, which, in our language, signifies vicissitude or fortune also, one favoured, and having a loud voice and well spoken. I remember we never polluted the name of the object of our adoration; on the contrary, it was always mentioned with the greatest reverence; and we were totally unacquainted with swearing, and all those terms of abuse and reproach which find their way so readily and copiously into the languages of more civilized people. The only expressions of that kind I remember were "May you rot, or may you swell, or may a beast take you."

I have before remarked that the natives of this part of Africa are extremely cleanly. This necessary habit of decency was with us a part of religion, and therefore we had many purifications and washings; indeed almost as many, and used on the same occasions, if my recollection does not fail me, as the Jews. Those that touched the dead at any time were obliged to wash and purify themselves before they could enter a dwelling house. Every woman too, at certain

6. Reincarnation.

times, was forbidden to come into a dwelling house, or touch any person, or any thing we ate. I was so fond of my mother I could not keep from her, or avoid touching her at some of those periods, in consequence of which I was obliged to be kept out with her, in a little house made for that purpose, till offering was made, and then we were purified.

Though we had no places of public worship, we had priests and magicians, or wise men. I do not remember whether they had different offices, or whether they were united in the same persons, but they were held in great reverence by the people. They calculated our time, and foretold events, as their name imported, for we called them Ah-affoe-way-cah, which signifies calculators or yearly men, our year being called Ah-affoe. They wore their beards, and when they died they were succeeded by their sons. Most of their implements and things of value were interred along with them. Pipes and tobacco were also put into the grave with the corpse, which was always perfumed and ornamented, and animals were offered in sacrifice to them. None accompanied their funerals but those of the same profession or tribe. These buried them after sunset, and always returned from the grave by a different way from that which they went.

These magicians were also our doctors or physicians. They practised bleeding by cupping;[7] and were very successful in healing wounds and expelling poisons. They had likewise some extraordinary method of discovering jealousy, theft, and poisoning; the success of which no doubt they derived from their unbounded influence over the credulity and superstition of the people. I do not remember what those methods were, except that as to poisoning: I recollect an instance or two, which I hope it will not be deemed impertinent here to insert, as it may serve as a kind of specimen of the rest, and is still used by the negroes in the West Indies. A virgin had been poisoned, but it was not known by whom: the doctors ordered the corpse to be taken up by some persons, and carried to the grave. As soon as the bearers had raised it on their shoulders, they seemed seized with some[8] sudden impulse, and ran to and fro unable to stop themselves. At last, after having passed through a number of thorns and prickly bushes unhurt, the corpse fell from them close to a house, and defaced it in the fall; and, the owner being taken up, he immediately confessed the poisoning.[9]

The natives are extremely cautious about poison. When they buy any eatable the seller kisses it all round before the buyer, to shew him it is not poisoned;

---

7. The use of glass cups to create a heated air vacuum for drawing blood from the body.

8. See also Leut. Matthew's Voyage, p. 123 [Equiano's note]. He is referring to John Matthews, *A Voyage to the River Sierra Leone* (1788).

9. An instance of this kind happened at Montserrat in the West Indies in the year 1763. I then belonged to the Charming Sally, Capt. Doran.—The chief mate, Mr. Mansfield, and some of the crew being one day on shore, were present at the burying of a poisoned negro girl. Though they had often heard of the circumstance of the running in such cases, and had even seen it, they imagined it to be a trick of the corpse-bearers. The mate therefore desired two of the sailors to take up the coffin, and carry it to the grave. The sailors, who were all of the same opinion, readily obeyed; but they had scarcely raised it to their shoulders, before they began to run furiously about, quite unable to direct themselves, till, at last, without intention, they came to the hut of him who had poisoned the girl. The coffin then immediately fell from their shoulders against the hut, and damaged part of the wall. The owner of the hut was taken into custody on this, and confessed the poisoning.—I give this story as it was related by the mate and crew on their return to the ship. The credit which is due to it I leave with the reader [Equiano's note].

and the same is done when any meat or drink is presented, particularly to a stranger. We have serpents of different kinds, some of which are esteemed ominous when they appear in our houses, and these we never molest. I remember two of those ominous snakes, each of which was as thick as the calf of a man's leg, and in colour resembling a dolphin in the water, crept at different times into my mother's night-house, where I always lay with her, and coiled themselves into folds, and each time they crowed like a cock. I was desired by some of our wise men to touch these, that I might be interested in the good omens, which I did, for they were quite harmless, and would tamely suffer themselves to be handled; and then they were put into a large open earthen pan, and set on one side of the highway. Some of our snakes, however, were poisonous: one of them crossed the road one day when I was standing on it, and passed between my feet without offering to touch me, to the great surprise of many who saw it; and these incidents were accounted by the wise men, and therefore by my mother and the rest of the people, as remarkable omens in my favour.

Such is the imperfect sketch my memory has furnished me with of the manners and customs of a people among whom I first drew my breath. And here I cannot forbear suggesting what has long struck me very forcibly, namely, the strong analogy which even by this sketch, imperfect as it is, appears to prevail in the manners and customs of my countrymen and those of the Jews, before they reached the Land of Promise, and particularly the patriarchs[1] while they were yet in that pastoral state which is described in Genesis—an analogy, which alone would induce me to think that the one people had sprung from the other.

* * *

Like the Israelites in their primitive state, our government was conducted by our chiefs or judges, our wise men and elders; and the head of a family with us enjoyed a similar authority over his household with that which is ascribed to Abraham and the other patriarchs. The law of retaliation obtained almost universally with us as with them: and even their religion appeared to have shed upon us a ray of its glory, though broken and spent in its passage, or eclipsed by the cloud with which time, tradition, and ignorance might have enveloped it; for we had our circumcision (a rule I believe peculiar to that people:) we had also our sacrifices and burnt-offerings, our washings and purifications, on the same occasions as they had.

As to the difference of colour between the Eboan Africans and the modern Jews, I shall not presume to account for it. It is a subject which has engaged the pens of men of both genius and learning, and is far above my strength. The most able and Reverend Mr. T. Clarkson, however, in his much admired Essay on the Slavery and Commerce of the Human Species,[2] has ascertained the cause, in a manner that at once solves every objection on that account, and, on my mind at least, has produced the fullest conviction. I shall therefore refer to that

---

1. In the Bible, the patriarchs are the ancestors of the Israelites. "Land of Promise": land promised to the Israelites by God.

2. This was written in 1785 by antislavery writer Thomas Clarkson (1760–1846).

performance for the theory,[3] contenting myself with extracting a fact as related by Dr. Mitchel.[4] "The Spaniards, who have inhabited America, under the torrid zone, for any time, are become as dark coloured as our native Indians of Virginia; of which I *myself have been a witness*." There is also another instance[5] of a Portuguese settlement at Mitomba, a river in Sierra Leona;[6] where the inhabitants are bred from a mixture of the first Portuguese discoverers with the natives, and are now become in their complexion, and in the woolly quality of their hair, *perfect negroes*, retaining however a smattering of the Portuguese language.

These instances, and a great many more which might be adduced, while they shew how the complexions of the same persons vary in different climates, it is hoped may tend also to remove the prejudice that some conceive against the natives of Africa on account of their colour. Surely the minds of the Spaniards did not change with their complexions! Are there not causes enough to which the apparent inferiority of an African may be ascribed, without limiting the goodness of God, and supposing he forbore to stamp understanding on certainly his own image, because "carved in ebony." Might it not naturally be ascribed to their situation? When they come among Europeans, they are ignorant of their language, religion, manners, and customs. Are any pains taken to teach them these? Are they treated as men? Does not slavery itself depress the mind, and extinguish all its fire and every noble sentiment? But, above all, what advantages do not a refined people possess over those who are rude and uncultivated! Let the polished and haughty European recollect that his ancestors were once, like the Africans, uncivilized, and even barbarous. Did Nature make *them* inferior to their sons? and should *they too* have been made slaves? Every rational mind answers, No. Let such reflections as these melt the pride of their superiority into sympathy for the wants and miseries of their sable brethren, and compel them to acknowledge, that understanding is not confined to feature or colour. If, when they look round the world, they feel exultation, let it be tempered with benevolence to others, and gratitude to God, "who hath made of one blood all nations of men for to dwell on all the face of the earth;[7] and whose wisdom is not our wisdom, neither are our ways his ways."[8]

CHAPTER II

I hope the reader will not think I have trespassed on his patience in introducing myself to him with some account of the manners and customs of my country. They had been implanted in me with great care, and made an impression on my mind, which time could not erase, and which all the adversity and variety of fortune I have since experienced served only to rivet and record; for, whether the love of one's country be real or imaginary, or a lesson of reason, or

---

3. Page 178 to 216 [Equiano's note].
4. Philos. Trans. No. 476, Set. 4, cited by Mr. Clarkson, p. 205 [Equiano's note]. John Mitchell was the author of an "Essay on the Causes of the Different Colours of People in Different Climates," *Philosophical Transactions* (1744).

5. Same page [Equiano's note].
6. Portuguese port in West Africa for commerce in slaves and ivory; later used by the British government to resettle freed slaves.
7. Acts 17.26.
8. A paraphrase of Isaiah 5.58.

an instinct of nature, I still look back with pleasure on the first scenes of my life, though that pleasure has been for the most part mingled with sorrow.

I have already acquainted the reader with the time and place of my birth. My father, besides many slaves, had a numerous family, of which seven lived to grow up, including myself and a sister, who was the only daughter. As I was the youngest of the sons, I became, of course, the greatest favourite with my mother, and was always with her; and she used to take particular pains to form my mind. I was trained up from my earliest years in the art of war; my daily exercise was shooting and throwing javelins; and my mother adorned me with emblems, after the manner of our greatest warriors. In this way I grew up till I was turned the age of eleven, when an end was put to my happiness in the following manner:—Generally when the grown people in the neighbourhood were gone far in the fields to labour, the children assembled together in some of the neighbours' premises to play; and commonly some of us used to get up a tree to look out for any assailant, or kidnapper, that might come upon us; for they sometimes took those opportunities of our parents' absence to attack and carry off as many as they could seize. One day, as I was watching at the top of a tree in our yard, I saw one of those people come into the yard of our next neighbour but one, to kidnap, there being many stout young people in it. Immediately on this I gave the alarm of the rogue, and he was surrounded by the stoutest of them, who entangled him with cords, so that he could not escape till some of the grown people came and secured him. But alas! ere long it was my fate to be thus attacked, and to be carried off, when none of the grown people were nigh. One day, when all our people were gone out to their works as usual, and only I and my dear sister were left to mind the house, two men and a woman got over our walls, and in a moment seized us both, and, without giving us time to cry out, or make resistance, they stopped our mouths, and ran off with us into the nearest wood. Here they tied our hands, and continued to carry us as far as they could, till night came on, when we reached a small house, where the robbers halted for refreshment, and spent the night. We were then unbound, but were unable to take any food; and, being quite overpowered by fatigue and grief, our only relief was some sleep, which allayed our misfortune for a short time. The next morning we left the house, and continued travelling all the day. For a long time we had kept the woods, but at last we came into a road which I believed I knew. I had now some hopes of being delivered; for we had advanced but a little way before I discovered some people at a distance, on which I began to cry out for their assistance: but my cries had no other effect than to make them tie me faster and stop my mouth, and then they put me into a large sack. They also stopped my sister's mouth, and tied her hands; and in this manner we proceeded till we were out of the sight of these people. When we went to rest the following night they offered us some victuals; but we refused it; and the only comfort we had was in being in one another's arms all that night, and bathing each other with our tears. But alas! we were soon deprived of even the small comfort of weeping together. The next day proved a day of greater sorrow than I had yet experienced; for my sister and I were then separated, while we lay clasped in each other's arms. It was in vain that we besought them not to part us; she was torn from me, and immediately carried away, while I was left in a state of distraction not to be described. I cried and grieved continually; and for several days I did not eat any thing but what they forced into my mouth.

At length, after many days travelling, during which I had often changed masters, I got into the hands of a chieftain, in a very pleasant country. This man had two wives and some children, and they all used me extremely well, and did all they could to comfort me; particularly the first wife, who was something like my mother. Although I was a great many days journey from my father's house, yet these people spoke exactly the same language with us. This first master of mine, as I may call him, was a smith, and my principal employment was working his bellows, which were the same kind as I had seen in my vicinity. They were in some respects not unlike the stoves here in gentlemen's kitchens; and were covered over with leather, and in the middle of that leather a stick was fixed, and a person stood up, and worked it, in the same manner as is done to pump water out of a cask with a hand pump. I believe it was gold he worked, for it was of a lovely bright yellow colour, and was worn by the women on their wrists and ankles. I was there I suppose about a month, and they at last used to trust me some little distance from the house. This liberty I used in embracing every opportunity to inquire the way to my own home: and I also sometimes, for the same purpose, went with the maidens, in the cool of the evenings, to bring pitchers of water from the springs for the use of the house. I had also remarked where the sun rose in the morning, and set in the evening, as I had travelled along; and I had observed that my father's house was towards the rising of the sun. I therefore determined to seize the first opportunity of making my escape, and to shape my course for that quarter; for I was quite oppressed and weighed down by grief after my mother and friends; and my love of liberty, ever great, was strengthened by the mortifying circumstance of not daring to eat with the free-born children, although I was mostly their companion. While I was projecting my escape, one day an unlucky event happened, which quite disconcerted my plan, and put an end to my hopes. I used to be sometimes employed in assisting an elderly woman slave to cook and take care of the poultry; and one morning, while I was feeding some chickens, I happened to toss a small pebble at one of them, which hit it on the middle and directly killed it. The old slave, having soon after missed the chicken, inquired after it; and on my relating the accident (for I told her the truth, because my mother would never suffer me to tell a lie) she flew into a violent passion, threatened that I should suffer for it; and, my master being out, she immediately went and told her mistress what I had done. This alarmed me very much, and I expected an instant flogging, which to me was uncommonly dreadful; for I had seldom been beaten at home. I therefore resolved to fly; and accordingly I ran into a thicket that was hard by, and hid myself in the bushes. Soon afterwards my mistress and the slave returned, and, not seeing me, they searched all the house, but not finding me, and I not making answer when they called to me, they thought I had run away, and the whole neighbourhood was raised in the pursuit of me. In that part of the country (as in ours) the houses and villages were skirted with woods, or shrubberies, and the bushes were so thick that a man could readily conceal himself in them, so as to elude the strictest search. The neighbours continued the whole day looking for me, and several times many of them came within a few yards of the place where I lay hid. I then gave myself up for lost entirely, and expected every moment, when I heard a rustling among the trees, to be found out, and punished by my master: but they never discovered me, though they were often so near that I even heard their conjectures as they were looking about for me; and I now learned from them, that any attempt to return home would be hopeless. Most of them supposed I had fled towards home; but the distance was so great, and the way so intricate, that they thought I could never reach it, and that I should be lost in the woods. When I heard this I was seized with a violent panic, and abandoned myself to despair. Night too began to approach, and aggravated all my fears. I had before entertained hopes of getting home, and I had determined when it should be dark to make the attempt; but I was now convinced it was fruitless, and I began to consider that, if possibly I could escape all other animals, I could not those of the human kind; and that, not knowing the way, I must perish in the woods. Thus was I like the hunted deer:

—Ev'ry leaf and ev'ry whisp'ring breath
Convey'd a foe, and ev'ry foe a death.[9]

I heard frequent rustlings among the leaves; and being pretty sure they were snakes I expected every instant to be stung by them. This increased my anguish, and the horror of my situation became now quite insupportable. I at length quitted the thicket, very faint and hungry, for I had not eaten or drank any thing all the day; and crept to my master's kitchen, from whence I set out at first, and which was an open shed, and laid myself down in the ashes with an anxious wish for death to relieve me from all my pains. I was scarcely awake in the morning when the old woman slave, who was the first up, came to light the fire, and saw me in the fire place. She was very much surprised to see me, and could scarcely believe her own eyes. She now promised to intercede for me, and went for her master, who soon after came, and, having slightly repri-manded me, ordered me to be taken care of, and not to be ill-treated.

Soon after this my master's only daughter, and child by his first wife, sick-ened and died, which affected him so much that for some time he was almost frantic, and really would have killed himself, had he not been watched and prevented. However, in a small time afterwards he recovered, and I was again sold. I was now carried to the left of the sun's rising, through many different countries, and a number of large woods. The people I was sold to used to carry me very often, when I was tired, either on their shoulders or on their backs. I saw many convenient well-built sheds along the roads, at proper distances, to accommodate the merchants and travellers, who lay in those buildings along with their wives, who often accompany them; and they always go well armed.

From the time I left my own nation I always found somebody that understood me till I came to the sea coast. The languages of different nations did not totally differ, nor were they so copious as those of the Europeans, particularly the Eng-lish. They were therefore easily learned; and, while I was journeying thus through Africa, I acquired two or three different tongues. In this manner I had been travelling for a considerable time, when one evening, to my great surprise, whom should I see brought to the house where I was but my dear sister! As soon as she saw me she gave a loud shriek, and ran into my arms—I was quite over-powered: neither of us could speak; but, for a considerable time, clung to each

9. Lines from "Cooper's Hill," a 1642 work by British poet John Denham (1615–1669).

other in mutual embraces, unable to do any thing but weep. Our meeting affected all who saw us; and indeed I must acknowledge, in honour of those sable destroyers of human rights, that I never met with any ill treatment, or saw any offered to their slaves, except tying them, when necessary, to keep them from running away. When these people knew we were brother and sister they indulged us [to be] together; and the man, to whom I supposed we belonged, lay with us, he in the middle, while she and I held one another by the hands across his breast all night; and thus for a while we forgot our misfortunes in the joy of being together: but even this small comfort was soon to have an end; for scarcely had the fatal morning appeared, when she was again torn from me for ever! I was now more miserable, if possible, than before. The small relief which her presence gave me from pain was gone, and the wretchedness of my situation was redoubled by my anxiety after her fate, and my apprehensions lest her sufferings should be greater than mine, when I could not be with her to alleviate them.

Yes, thou dear partner of all my childish spats, thou sharer of my joys and sorrows; happy should I have ever esteemed myself to encounter every misery for you, and to procure your freedom by the sacrifice of my own! Though you were early forced from my arms, your image has been always rivetted in my heart, from which neither *time nor fortune* have been able to remove it; so that, while the thoughts of your sufferings have damped my prosperity, they have mingled with adversity and increased its bitterness. To that Heaven which protects the weak from the strong, I commit the care of your innocence and virtues, if they have not already received their full reward, and if your youth and delicacy have not long since fallen victims to the violence of the African trader, the pestilential stench of a Guinea ship, the seasoning[1] in the European colonies, or the lash and lust of a brutal and unrelenting overseer.

I did not long remain after my sister. I was again sold, and carried through a number of places, till, after travelling a considerable time, I came to a town called Tinmah, in the most beautiful country I had yet seen in Africa. It was extremely rich, and there were many rivulets which flowed through it, and supplied a large pond in the centre of the town, where the people washed. Here I first saw and tasted cocoa-nuts, which I thought superior to any nuts I had ever tasted before; and the trees, which were loaded, were also interspersed amongst the houses, which had commodious shades adjoining, and were in the same manner as ours, the insides being neatly plastered and whitewashed. Here I also saw and tasted for the first time sugar-cane. Their money consisted of little white shells, the size of the finger nail. I was sold here for one hundred and seventy-two of them by a merchant who lived and brought me there. I had been about two or three days at his house, when a wealthy widow, a neighbour of his, came there one evening, and brought with her an only son, a young gentleman about my own age and size. Here they saw me; and, having taken a fancy to me, I was bought of the merchant, and went home with them. Her house and premises were situated close to one of those rivulets I have mentioned, and were the finest I ever saw in Africa: they were very extensive, and she had a number of slaves to attend her. The next day I was washed and per-

---

1. One of the stages of the slave trade—first came capture; then the voyage across the ocean; then "seasoning," which was the preparation of slaves for hard labor; then enslavement.

fumed, and when meal-time came I was led into the presence of my mistress, and ate and drank before her with her son. This filled me with astonishment; and I could scarce help expressing my surprise that the young gentleman should suffer me, who was bound, to eat with him who was free; and not only so, but that he would not at any time either eat or drink till I had taken first, because I was the eldest, which was agreeable to our custom. Indeed every thing here, and all their treatment of me, made me forget that I was a slave. The language of these people resembled ours so nearly, that we understood each other perfectly. They had also the very same customs as we. There were likewise slaves daily to attend us, while my young master and I with other boys sported with our darts and bows and arrows, as I had been used to do at home. In this resemblance to my former happy state I passed about two months; and I now began to think I was to be adopted into the family, and was beginning to be reconciled to my situation, and to forget by degrees my misfortunes, when all at once the delusion vanished; for, without the least previous knowledge, one morning early, while my dear master and companion was still asleep, I was wakened out of my reverie to fresh sorrow, and hurried away even amongst the uncircumcised.

Thus, at the very moment I dreamed of the greatest happiness, I found myself most miserable; and it seemed as if fortune wished to give me this taste of joy, only to render the reverie more poignant. The change I now experienced was as painful as it was sudden and unexpected. It was a change indeed from a state of bliss to a scene which is inexpressible by me, as it discovered to me an element I had never before beheld, and till then had no idea of, and wherein such instances of hardship and cruelty continually occurred as I can never reflect on but with horror.

All the nations and people I had hitherto passed through resembled our own in their manners, customs, and language: but I came at length to a country, the inhabitants of which differed from us in all those particulars. I was very much struck with this difference, especially when I came among a people who did not circumcise, and are without washing their hands. They cooked also in iron pots, and had European cutlasses and cross bows, which were unknown to us, and fought with their fists amongst themselves. Their women were not so modest as ours, for they ate, and drank, and slept, with their men. But, above all, I was amazed to see no sacrifices or offerings among them. In some of those places the people ornamented themselves with scars, and likewise filed their teeth very sharp. They wanted sometimes to ornament me in the same manner, but I would not suffer them; hoping that I might some time be among a people who did not thus disfigure themselves, as I thought they did. At last I came to the banks of a large river, which was covered with canoes, in which the people appeared to live with their household utensils and provisions of all kinds. I was beyond measure astonished at this, as I had never before seen any water larger than a pond or a rivulet: and my surprise was mingled with no small fear when I was put into one of these canoes, and we began to paddle and move along the river. We continued going on thus till night; and when we came to land, and made fires on the banks, each family by themselves, some dragged their canoes on shore, others stayed and cooked in theirs, and laid in them all night. Those on the land had mats, of which they made tents, some in the shape of little houses: in these we slept; and after the morning meal we embarked again and proceeded as before. I was often very much astonished to see some of the women, as well as the men, jump into the water, dive to the bottom, come up again, and swim about. Thus I continued to travel, sometimes by land, sometimes by water, through different countries and various nations, till, at the end of six or seven months after I had been kidnapped, I arrived at the sea coast. It would be tedious and uninteresting to relate all the incidents which befell me during this journey, and which I have not yet forgotten; of the various hands I passed through, and the manners and customs of all the different people among whom I lived. I shall therefore only observe, that in all the places where I was the soil was exceedingly rich; the pomkins, eadas, plantains, yams, etc., etc. were in great abundance, and of incredible size. There were also vast quantities of different gums, though not used for any purpose; and every where a great deal of tobacco. The cotton even grew quite wild; and there was plenty of red-wood. I saw no mechanics whatever in all the way, except such as I have mentioned. The chief employment in all these countries was agriculture, and both the males and females, as with us, were brought up to it, and trained in the arts of war.

The first object which saluted my eyes when I arrived on the coast was the sea, and a slave ship, which was then riding at anchor, and waiting for its cargo. These filled me with astonishment, which was soon converted into terror when I was carried on board. I was immediately handled and tossed up to see if I were found by some of the crew; and I was now persuaded that I had gotten into a world of bad spirits, and that they were going to kill me. Their complexions too differing so much from ours, their long hair, and the language they spoke, (which was very different from any I had ever heard) united to confirm me in this belief. Indeed such were the horrors of my views and fears at the moment, that, if ten thousand worlds had been my own, I would have freely parted with them all to have exchanged my condition with that of the meanest slave in my own country. When I looked round the ship too and saw a large furnace or copper boiling, and a multitude of black people of every description chained together, every one of their countenances expressing dejection and sorrow, I no longer doubted of my fate; and, quite overpowered with horror and anguish, I fell motionless on the deck and fainted. When I recovered a little I found some black people about me, who I believed were some of those who brought me on board, and had been receiving their pay; they talked to me in order to cheer me, but all in vain. I asked them if we were not to be eaten by those white men with horrible looks, red faces, and loose hair. They told me I was not; and one of the crew brought me a small portion of spirituous liquor in a wine glass; but, being afraid of him, I would not take it out of his hand. One of the blacks therefore took it from him and gave it to me, and I took a little down my palate, which, instead of reviving me, as they thought it would, threw me into the greatest consternation at the strange feeling it produced, having never tasted any such liquor before. Soon after this the blacks who brought me on board went off, and left me abandoned to despair. I now saw myself deprived of all chance of returning to my native country, or even the least glimpse of hope of gaining the shore, which I now considered as friendly; and I even wished for my former slavery in preference to my present situation, which was filled with horrors of every kind, still heightened by my ignorance of what I was to undergo. I was not long suffered to indulge my grief; I was soon put down under the decks, and there I received such a salutation in my nostrils as I had never experienced in my life: so that, with the loathsomeness of the stench, and crying together, I became so sick and low that I was not able to eat, nor had I the least desire to taste any thing. I now wished for the last friend, death, to relieve me; but soon, to my grief, two of the white men offered me eatables; and, on my refusing to eat, one of them held me fast by the hands, and laid me across I think the windlass, and tied my feet, while the other flogged me severely. I had never experienced any thing of this kind before; and although, not being used to the water, I naturally feared that element the first time I saw it, yet nevertheless, could I have got over the nettings, I would have jumped over the side, but I could not; and, besides, the crew used to watch us very closely who were not chained down to the decks, lest we should leap into the water: and I have seen some of these poor African prisoners most severely cut for attempting to do so, and hourly whipped for not eating. This indeed was often the case with myself. In a little time after, amongst the poor chained men, I found some of my own nation, which in a small degree gave ease to my mind. I inquired to these what was to be done with us; they gave me to understand we were to be carried to these white people's country to work for them. I then was a little revived, and thought, if it were no worse than working, my situation was not so desperate: but still I feared I should be put to death, the white people looked and acted, as I thought, in so savage a manner; for I had never seen among any people such instances of brutal cruelty; and this not only shewn towards us blacks, but also to some of the whites themselves. One white man in particular I saw, when we were permitted to be on deck, flogged so unmercifully with a large rope near the foremast, that he died in consequence of it; and they tossed him over the side as they would have done a brute. This made me fear these people the more; and I expected nothing less than to be treated in the same manner. I could not help expressing my fears and apprehensions to some of my countrymen: I asked them if these people had no country, but lived in this hollow place (the ship): they told me they did not, but came from a distant one. "Then," said I, "how comes it in all our country we never heard of them?" They told me because they lived so very far off. I then asked where were their women? had they any like themselves? I was told they had: "and why," said I, "do we not see them?" They answered, because they were left behind. I asked how the vessel could go? they told me they could not tell; but that there were cloths put upon the masts by the help of the ropes I saw, and then the vessel went on; and the white men had some spell or magic they put in the water when they liked in order to stop the vessel. I was exceedingly amazed at this account, and really thought they were spirits. I therefore wished much to be from amongst them, for I expected they would sacrifice me: but my wishes were vain; for we were so quartered that it was impossible for any of us to make our escape. While we stayed on the coast I was mostly on deck; and one day, to my great astonishment, I saw one of these vessels coming in with the sails up. As soon as the whites saw it, they gave a great shout, at which we were amazed; and the more so as the vessel appeared larger by approaching nearer. At last she came to an anchor in my sight, and when the anchor was let go I and my countrymen who saw it were lost in astonishment to observe the vessel stop; and were now convinced it was done by magic. Soon after this the other ship got her boats out, and they came on board of us, and the people of both ships seemed very glad to see each other. Several of the strangers also shook hands with us black people, and made motions with their hands, signifying I suppose we were to go to their country; but we did not understand them. At last, when the ship we were in had got in all her cargo they made ready with many fearful noises and we were all put under deck, so that we could not see how they managed the vessel.

But this disappointment was the least of my sorrow. The stench of the hold while we were on the coast was so intolerably loathsome, that it was dangerous to remain there for any time, and some of us had been permitted to stay on the deck for the fresh air; but now that the whole ship's cargo were confined together, it became absolutely pestilential. The closeness of the place, and the heat of the climate, added to the number in the ship, which was so crowded that each had scarcely room to turn himself, almost suffocated us. This produced copious perspirations, so that the air soon became unfit for respiration, from a variety of loathsome smells, and brought on a sickness among the slaves, of which many died, thus falling victims to the improvident avarice, as I may call it, of their purchasers. This wretched situation was again aggravated by the galling of the chains, now become insupportable; and the filth of the necessary tubs, into which the children often fell, and were almost suffocated. The shrieks of the women, and the groans of the dying, rendered the whole a scene of horror almost inconceivable. Happily perhaps for myself I was soon reduced so low here that it was thought necessary to keep me almost always on deck; and from my extreme youth I was not put in fetters. In this situation I expected every hour to share the fate of my companions, some of whom were almost daily brought upon deck at the point of death, which I began to hope would soon put an end to my miseries. Often did I think many of the inhabitants of the deep much more happy than myself. I envied them the freedom they enjoyed, and as often wished I could change my condition for theirs. Every circumstance I met with served only to render my state more painful, and heighten my apprehensions, and my opinion of the cruelty of the whites. One day they had taken a number of fishes; and when they had killed and satisfied themselves with as many as they thought fit, to our astonishment who were on the deck, rather than give any of them to us to eat as we expected, they tossed the remaining fish into the sea again, although we begged and prayed for some as well as we could, but in vain; and some of my countrymen, being pressed by hunger, took an opportunity, when they thought no one saw them, of trying to get a little privately; but they were discovered, and the attempt procured them some very severe floggings. One day, when we had a smooth sea and moderate wind, two of my wearied countrymen who were chained together (I was near them at the time), preferring death to such a life of misery, somehow made through the nettings and jumped into the sea: immediately another quite dejected fellow, who, on account of his illness, was suffered to be out of irons, also followed their example; and I believe many more would very soon have done the same if they had not been prevented by the ship's crew, who were instantly alarmed. Those of us that were the most active were in a moment put down under the deck, and there was such a noise and confusion amongst the people of the ship as I never heard before, to stop her, and get the boat out to go after the slaves. However two of the wretches were drowned, but they got the other, and afterwards flogged him unmercifully for thus attempting to prefer death to slavery. In this manner we continued to undergo more hardships than I can now relate, hardships which are inseparable from this accursed trade. Many a time we were near suffocation from the want of fresh air, which we were often without for whole days together. This, and the stench of the necessary tubs, carried off many. During our passage I first saw flying fishes, which surprised me very much: they used frequently to fly across the ship, and many of them fell on the deck. I also now first saw the use of the quadrant;[2] I had often with astonishment seen the mariners make observations with it, and I could not think what it meant. They at last took notice of my surprise; and one of them, willing to increase it, as well as to gratify my curiosity, made me one day look through it. The clouds appeared to me to be land, which disappeared as they passed along. This heightened my wonder; and I was now more persuaded than ever that I was in another world, and that every thing about me was magic. At last we came in sight of the island of Barbadoes, at which the whites on board gave a great shout, and made many signs of joy to us. We did not know what to think of this; but as the vessel drew nearer we plainly saw the harbour, and other ships of different kinds and sizes; and we soon anchored amongst them off Bridge Town.[3] Many merchants and planters now came on board, though it was in the evening. They put us in separate parcels, and examined us attentively. They also made us jump, and pointed to the land, signifying we were to go there. We thought by this we should be eaten by these ugly men, as they appeared to us; and, when soon after we were all put down under the deck again, there was much dread and trembling among us, and nothing but bitter cries to be heard all the night from these apprehensions, insomuch that at last the white people got some old slaves from the land to pacify us. They told us we were not to be eaten, but to work, and were soon to go on land, where we should see many of our country people. This report eased us much; and sure enough, soon after we were landed, there came to us Africans of all languages. We were conducted immediately to the merchant's yard, where we were all pent up together like so many sheep in a fold, without regard to sex or age. As every object was new to me every thing I saw filled me with surprise. What struck me first was that the houses were built with stories, and in every other respect different from those in Africa: but I was still more astonished on seeing people on horseback. I did not know what this could mean; and indeed I thought these people were full of nothing but magical arts. While I was in this astonishment one of my fellow prisoners spoke to a countryman of his about the horses, who said they were the same kind they had in their country. I understood them, though they were from a distant part of Africa, and I thought it odd I had not seen any horses there; but afterwards, when I came to converse with different Africans, I found they had many horses amongst them, and much larger than those I then saw. We were not many days in the merchant's custody before we were sold after their usual manner, which is this:—On a signal given, (as the beat of a drum) the buyers rush at once into the yard where the slaves are confined, and make choice of that parcel they like best. The noise and clamour with which this is attended, and the eagerness visible in the countenances of the buyers, serve not a little to increase the apprehensions of the terrified Africans, who may well be supposed to consider them as the ministers of that destruction to which they think themselves devoted. In this manner, without

2. Measurement device used for the navigation of ships.

3. Capital of Barbados.

scruple, are relations and friends separated, most of them never to see each other again. I remember in the vessel in which I was brought over, in the men's apartment, there were several brothers, who, in the sale, were sold in different lots; and it was very moving on this occasion to see and hear their cries at parting. O, ye nominal Christians! might not an African ask you, learned you this from your God, who says unto you, Do unto all men as you would men should do unto you? Is it not enough that we are torn from our country and friends to toil for your luxury and lust of gain? Must every tender feeling be likewise sacrificed to your avarice? Are the dearest friends and relations, now rendered more dear by their separation from their kindred, still to be parted from each other, and thus prevented from cheering the gloom of slavery with the small comfort of being together and mingling their sufferings and sorrows? Why are parents to lose their children, brothers their sisters, or husbands their wives? Surely this is a new refinement in cruelty, which, while it has no advantage to atone for it, thus aggravates distress, and adds fresh horrors even to the wretchedness of slavery.

FROM CHAPTER III

I now totally lost the small remains of comfort I had enjoyed in conversing with my countrymen; the women too, who used to wash and take care of me, were all gone different ways, and I never saw one of them afterwards.

I stayed in this island for a few days; I believe it could not be above a fortnight; when I, and some few more slaves, that were not saleable amongst the rest, from very much fretting, were shipped off in a sloop for North America. On the passage we were better treated than when we were coming from Africa, and we had plenty of rice and fat pork. We were landed up a river a good way from the sea, about Virginia county, where we saw few or none of our native Africans, and not one soul who could talk to me. I was a few weeks weeding grass, and gathering stones in a plantation; and at last all my companions were distributed different ways, and only myself was left. I was now exceedingly miserable, and thought myself worse off than any of the rest of my companions, for they could talk to each other, but I had no person to speak to that I could understand. In this state, I was constantly grieving and pining, and wishing for death rather than anything else. While I was in this plantation the gentleman, to whom I suppose the estate belonged, being unwell, I was one day sent for to his dwelling-house to fan him; when I came into the room where he was I was very much affrighted at some things I saw, and the more so as I had seen a black woman slave as I came through the house, who was cooking the dinner, and the poor creature was cruelly loaded with various kinds of iron machines; she had one particularly on her head, which locked her mouth so fast that she could scarcely speak; and could not eat nor drink. I was much astonished and shocked at this contrivance, which I afterwards learned was called the iron muzzle. Soon after I had a fan put in my hand, to fan the gentleman while he slept; and so I did indeed with great fear. While he was fast asleep I indulged myself a great deal in looking about the room, which to me appeared very fine and curious. The first object that engaged my attention was a watch which hung on the chimney, and was going. I was quite surprised at the noise it made, and was afraid it would tell the gentleman anything I might do amiss; and when I immediately after observed a picture hanging in the room, which appeared constantly to look at me, I was still more affrighted, having never seen such things as these before. At one time I thought it was something relative to magic; and not seeing it move I thought it might be some way the whites had to keep their great men when they died, and offer them libations as we used to do to our friendly spirits. In this state of anxiety I remained till my master awoke, when I was dismissed out of the room, to my no small satisfaction and relief; for I thought that these people were all made up of wonders. In this place I was called Jacob; but on board the *African Snow*, I was called Michael. I had been some time in this miserable, forlorn, and much dejected state, without having anyone to talk to, which made my life a burden, when the kind and unknown hand of the Creator (who in very deed leads the blind in a way they know not) now began to appear, to my comfort; for one day the captain of a merchant ship, called the *Industrious Bee*, came on some business to my master's house. This gentleman, whose name was Michael Henry Pascal, was a lieutenant in the royal navy, but now commanded this trading ship, which was somewhere in the confines of the county many miles off. While he was at my master's house it happened that he saw me, and liked me so well that he made a purchase of me. I think I have often heard him say he gave thirty or forty pounds sterling for me; but I do not now remember which. However, he meant me for a present to some of his friends in England: and as I was sent accordingly from the house of my then master (one Mr. Campbell) to the place where the ship lay; I was conducted on horseback by an elderly black man (a mode of travelling which appeared very odd to me). When I arrived I was carried on board a fine large ship, loaded with tobacco, etc., and just ready to sail for England. I now thought my condition much mended; I had sails to lie on, and plenty of good victuals to eat; and everybody on board used me very kindly, quite contrary to what I had seen of any white people before; I therefore began to think that they were not all of the same disposition. A few days after I was on board we sailed for England. I was still at a loss to conjecture my destiny. By this time, however, I could smatter a little imperfect English; and I wanted to know as well as I could where we were going. Some of the people of the ship used to tell me they were going to carry me back to my own country, and this made me very happy. I was quite rejoiced at the sound of going back; and thought if I should get home what wonders I should have to tell. But I was reserved for another fate, and was soon undeceived when we came within sight of the English coast. While I was on board this ship, my captain and master named me *Gustavas Vassa*.[4] I at that time began to understand him a little, and refused to be called so, and told him as well as I could that I would be called Jacob; but he said I should not, and still called me Gustavus: and when I refused to answer to my new name, which at first I did, it gained me many a cuff; so at length I submitted, and was obliged to bear the present name, by which I have been known ever since.

* * *

It was about the beginning of the spring 1757, when I arrived in England and I was near twelve years of age at that time. I was very much struck with the buildings and

---

4. King Gustav of Sweden, called Gustav Vasa (1496–1560), who liberated the Swedes from the Danes but then ruled the nation as a brutal tyrant.

the pavement of the streets in Falmouth; and, indeed, every object I saw, filled me with new surprise. One morning, when I got upon deck, I saw it covered all over with the snow that fell over-night. As I had never seen anything of the kind before, I thought it was salt; so I immediately ran down to the mate and desired him, as well as I could, to come and see how somebody in the night had thrown salt all over the deck. He, knowing what it was, desired me to bring some of it down to him. Accordingly I took up a handful of it, which I found very cold indeed; and when I brought it to him he desired me to taste it. I did so, and I was surprised beyond measure. I then asked him what it was; he told me it was snow, but I could not in anywise understand him. He asked me if we had no such thing in my country; I told him, No. I then asked him the use of it, and who made it; he told me a great man in the heavens, called God. But here again I was to all intents and purposes at a loss to understand him; and the more so, when a little after I saw the air filled with it, in a heavy shower, which fell down on the same day. After this I went to church; and having never been at such a place before, I was again amazed at seeing and hearing the service. I asked all I could about it; and they gave me to understand it was worshipping God, who made us and all things. I was still at a great loss, and soon got into an endless field of inquiries, as well as I was able to speak and ask about things. However, my little friend Dick[5] used to be my best interpreter; for I could make free with him, and he always instructed me with pleasure. And from what I could understand by him of this God, and in seeing these white people did not sell one another as we did, I was much pleased; and in this I thought they were much happier than we Africans. I was astonished at the wisdom of the white people in all things I saw; but was amazed at their not sacrificing, or making any offerings, and eating with unwashed hands, and touching the dead. I likewise could not help remarking the particular slenderness of their women, which I did not at first like; and I thought they were not so modest and shame faced as the African women.

I had often seen my master and Dick employed in reading; and I had a great curiosity to talk to the books, as I thought they did; and so to learn how all things had a beginning: for that purpose I have often taken up a book, and have talked to it, and then put my ears to it, when alone, in hopes it would answer me; and I have been very much concerned when I found it remained silent.

* * *

---

5. Richard Baxter, an American boy who befriends Equiano on his first voyage to England.

JOHANN WOLFGANG VON GOETHE

1749–1832

Few writers have ever surpassed Goethe in global fame and influence. He was perhaps the last European to live up to the ideal of the Renaissance man: skilled in the arts, in science, and in politics. He made groundbreaking contributions not only in all the major literary genres, but also in art criticism and the study of classical culture. He did extensive work in the fields of botany, mineralogy, comparative anatomy, and optics. And he occupied many administrative and political positions at the court of Weimar, where he was responsible for finance, the military, and mining, as well as for the Weimar Court Theatre, which he turned from an amateur theater to a professional troupe that premiered many of his own plays. Distrusting both the French Revolution, whose effects he witnessed at close hand, and growing nationalist movements in Germany and elsewhere, Goethe did not consider himself a German, but a European, and he coined the visionary notion of "world literature," eager to open Europe to the intellectual and artistic production of the non-European world.

Goethe was born into a middle-class family in Frankfurt. Despite an early interest in the arts and the theater, he followed his father's wishes and studied law. But Goethe's artistic ambitions could not be held back for long and he soon started to publish literary works. His first significant play, *Götz of Ber-lechingen* (1773), was shaped by his discovery of Shakespeare, whom he especially admired for being willing to violate the strict rules of drama that prevailed at the time. Yet the most important work of Goethe's early period was a novel, *The Sorrows of Young Werther* (1774), which turned Goethe into the representative of a literary movement called *Sturm und Drang* ("storm and stress") that emphasized the expression of feelings over the strictures of literary form. Centered on subjective impressions, extreme emotions, and literary outbursts, the novel leads its tragic protagonist, who is caught in a love triangle, to his eventual suicide. *The Sorrows of Young Werther* prompted mass hysteria, also called "Werther fever," allegedly leading to several copycat suicides as well as to the marketing of Werther paraphernalia. Goethe became a European celebrity virtually overnight.

A year later, Duke Karl August of Weimar called the young writer to his elegant but provincial court, where Goethe first served as educator, but soon fulfilled more important functions and was ultimately elevated to the aristocracy. It was here, amid his extensive duties, that Goethe began his mature, more classical works: his influential novel, *Wilhelm Meister's Apprenticeship*, as well as the plays *Egmont, Iphigenia on Tauris, Torquato Tasso*, and *Faust*. He began all of these works shortly after he had arrived at Weimar, but they went through innumerable revisions, during which he slowly forged a new, less unruly and more measured style, leaving the earlier "storm and stress" behind.

Goethe was inspired by an extended voyage to Italy (1786–88), and he became the chief representative of a revival of classical forms and ideas in Germany and Europe more generally. This journey

Goethe in the Roman Campagna, 1786–1787, Johann Heinrich Wilhelm Tischbein.

led him to revise *Faust* and other works in accordance with the classical ideal. He collected classical sculpture (he contented himself with replicas) and adapted classical stories, poetry, and drama. But the theater stood at the center of the classical revival. He worried about the training of actors, developing guidelines later published as *Rules for Actors* (1803, 1832), and intervened in all other aspects of theater production. He also insisted on introducing international playwrights, including Shakespeare, Calderón, and Goldoni, to his provincial audience. Thus, although Goethe had started the Weimar Court Theatre as a vehicle for his revival of classical drama, he opened it to a variety of dramatic styles.

In the first decades of the nineteenth century, Goethe finally completed the long-awaited first part of *Faust* (1806). While he left his mark on numerous fields and genres, *Faust* stands out as his masterpiece. He began writing it in his early twenties and continued to work on it until his death. Even more than many of his other texts, it underwent significant changes, from the first drafts in the 1770s, through the publication of the first part in 1808, to the final version of the second part, completed just before his last birthday in 1832.

For *Faust* Goethe relied on an old folk legend, a quintessentially medieval morality tale, in which an arrogant scholar gives in to the temptations of the devil, makes a famous pact to trade his soul for the use of black magic, and finally suffers in hell for his sins. In the course of his many revisions, Goethe transformed this simple material into a text that captured the spirit and desires of modernity. Although he preserved important set pieces such as the pact with the devil, what mattered to Goethe was the relation between abstract learning and sensuous experience, as well as the nature of human striving. He used the character of Faust to explore the transformative energies unleashed by modern science, philosophy, and industry.

In revising the old legend, Goethe changed its moral structure. While earlier Fausts were always lost to the devil, Goethe has Faust escape Mephistopheles' clutches at the end of *Faust II*. This decision thoroughly alters the morality play, which had punished a blaspheming protagonist as a warning to Christian audiences. Goethe still depicts Faust as a sinner, as the earlier versions had done. But now Faust's sinning has to be balanced against his irreverent and limitless thirst for knowledge, which for Goethe has great esteem. Paradoxically, the very quality that drives Faust to his pact with the devil is the one that will lead him to salvation.

The "Prologue in Heaven" shows this shift. It is one of several scenes that frame the play before its proper action begins. Borrowed from the beginning of the biblical book of Job, the "Prologue" depicts a debate between God and Mephistopheles that ends in a wager. Mephistopheles has permission to lead Faust into temptation because God is certain that Faust's restless striving, his search for true knowledge, will eventually lead him back on the right path. Besides the "Prologue," Goethe also introduces the text with a "Dedication," in which he evokes the youthful world in which he began this work some thirty years ago. And he presents a kind of curtain riser, a "Prelude in the Theater," in which a Manager, a Poet, and a Clown debate their respective visions of a theater, poised between popular entertainment and high art, a debate undoubtedly grounded in Goethe's experience as a dramatist and theater director.

The main drama of *Faust I* can be divided into two parts. The first part introduces us to the medieval Doctor, who has mastered all the higher disciplines of the university—philosophy, law, medicine, and theology—but who still has not learned the inner essence of the world. Dissatisfied with this insufficient knowledge, he turns to the dangerous domains of magic and alchemy, and it is this daring that is, for Goethe, Faust's most modern attribute. Shunning inherited pieties and religious prejudices, Faust is ready to sacrifice everything to knowledge. He also longs to experience life to the fullest, and this makes him especially susceptible to the enticements of Mephistopheles, who offers him wide experience and the satisfaction of his sensual desires.

In the second part of *Faust I*, Mephistopheles tries to satisfy Faust's demands and yearnings. Although he often dismisses Mephistopheles' efforts at satisfaction as "mere spectacle," Faust nevertheless tries them all, culminating in the famous, orgiastic "Walpurgisnight" scene, a delirious meeting of all creatures of the night. None of these sensuous pleasures, however, can give Faust the kind of satisfaction he derives from the culminating event of the play: the seduction of Gretchen. It is with Gretchen that *Faust* earns its title to tragedy. Gretchen represents different pleasures from the other experiences provided by Mephistopheles. Faust genuinely falls in love with her, praising her innocence and simple religious faith. And yet he alternately neglects her and showers her with presents as he pursues, and finally achieves, his physical satisfaction, leading to a tragic end. Here the first part of *Faust* ends. These tragic events will be blissfully forgotten in the second part, which takes Faust and Mephistopheles on a wild tour through politics, science, and learning.

Not only did Goethe revise the Faust legend to rescue Faust from damnation at the end of part two, but in the first part, he shaped another, and possibly more radical, revision of the historical tale. For the real protagonist of this part is not Faust, who is alternatively pompous, idealistic, and fatuous, who does not know himself, and who manages to bring everything, including poor

Gretchen, to ruin. Instead, the real protagonist is the witty, realistic, and caustic Mephistopheles. It is Mephistopheles who criticizes the medieval world of Faust, and who deflates his grandiose speeches, including his self-serving declarations of love for Gretchen. Mephistopheles is the spirit of negation, as he says of himself, but it is a negation that serves to criticize authority. Mephistopheles thus embodies the principle of critique, of questioning all kinds of inherited religious belief and orthodoxies. Since this critical spirit is central to modernity, Mephistopheles becomes the truly modern character in the play. And Goethe clandestinely turns Mephistopheles into the main protagonist. He has all the best and wittiest lines. In the theater, he simply steals the show.

Outdoing a modernized Faust with an even more modern Mephistopheles, Goethe was also daring in his use of structure and form. The play rejects the narrow rules of Aristotelian drama, constraining time and space, and instead presents a play of epic length that is composed of loosely connected scenes. Faust contains passages in different meters and rhyme schemes as well as in prose. It includes interludes, an allegorical dream, a satire of the university, erotic songs, and scenes of outright bacchanalia. It seeks to encompass the entirety of the modern world, aspiring to a rare totality in its hybrid form. Thus Faust has been considered a total work of art, a modern epic, and a strikingly new type of drama.

Faust is so startling in its dramatic innovations that Goethe himself never sought to mount even the more manageable first part in his own Weimar Court Theatre, and in fact he did not even consider it fit for the stage. When it was performed at another theater a few years before his death, he did not show much interest in the production. The much more difficult, allegorical second part has been performed even less often. Given the length of both parts taken together, few theaters have ever tried to produce the entirety of Goethe's Faust. In the course of the twentieth century, however, the first part attracted the most renowned theater directors, composers, and actors. French composers Hector Berlioz and Charles Gounod based operas on it, and in the twentieth century, Gertrude Stein's Doctor Faustus Lights the Lights is among the most modernist responses to Goethe's text. Filmmakers have turned to it again and again for inspiration, including F. W. Murnau in 1926 and Czech director Jan Švankmajer in 1994. Goethe's Faust has thus remained an important touchstone for two centuries of art, a testament to Goethe's ability to turn a simple medieval morality tale into a complex investigation of modernity.

Faust[1]

Prologue in Heaven[2]

THE LORD. THE HEAVENLY HOST. Then MEPHISTOPHELES.[3] The three ARCHANGELS advance to front.

RAPHAEL   The sun sounds out his ancient measure
    In contest with each brother sphere,

---

1. Translated by Martin Greenberg.
2. The scene is patterned on Job 1.6–12 and 2.1–6.
3. The origin of the name remains debatable.

It may come from Hebrew, Persian, or Greek, with such meanings as "destroyer-liar," "no friend of Faust," and "no friend of light."

Marching round and around, with steps of thunder,
His appointed circle year after year.
To see him lends us angels strength,   5
But what he *is*, oh who can say?
The inconceivably great works are great
As on the first creating day.

GABRIEL   And swift, past all conception swift,
The jeweled globe spins on its axletree,   10
Celestial brightness alternating
With shuddering night's obscurity.
Against the rock-bound littoral
The sea is backwards seething hurled
And rock and sea together hurtle   15
With the eternally turning world.

MICHAEL   And tempests, vying, howling riot
From sea to land, from land to sea,
Linking in tremendous circuit
A chain of blazing energy.   20
The lightning bolt makes ready for
The thunderclap a ruinous way—
Yet Lord, your servants most prefer
The stiller motions of your day.

ALL THREE   From seeing this we draw our strength,   25
But what You *are*, oh who can say?
And all your great works are as great
As on the first creating day.

MEPHISTOPHELES   Lord, since you've stopped by here again,
    liking to know
How all of us are doing, for which we're grateful,   30
And since you've never made me feel *de trop*,
Well, here I am too with your other people.
Excuse, I hope, my lack of eloquence,
Though this whole host, I'm sure, will think I'm stupid.
Coming from me, high-sounding sentiments   35
Would only make you laugh—that is, provided
Laughing was a thing Your Worship still did.
About suns and worlds I don't know beans, I only see
How mortals find their lives pure misery.
Earth's little god's shaped out of the same old clay,   40
He's the same queer fish he was on the first day.
He'd be much better off, in my opinion, without
The bit of heavenly light you dealt him out.
He calls it Reason and the use he puts it to?
To act more beastly than beasts ever do.   45
To me he seems, if you'll pardon my saying so,
Like a long-legged grasshopper all of whose leaping
Only lands him back in the grass again chirping
The tune he's always chirped. And if only he'd
Stay put in the grass! But no! It's an absolute need   50
With him to creep and crawl and strain and sweat

And stick his nose in every pile of dirt.

THE LORD   Is that all you have got to say to me?
Is that all you can do, accuse eternally?
Is nothing ever right for you down there, sir?   55

MEPHISTOPHELES   No, nothing, Lord—all's just as bad as ever.
I really pity humanity's myriad miseries,
I swear I hate tormenting the poor ninnies.

THE LORD   Do you know Faust?

MEPHISTOPHELES   The Doctor?[4]

THE LORD   My good servant.

MEPHISTOPHELES   You[5] don't say! Well, he serves you, I think, very queerly,   60
Finds meat and drink, the fool, in nothing earthly,
Drives madly on, there's in him such a torment,
He himself is half aware he's crazy;
Heaven's brightest stars he imperiously requires,
And from the earth its most exciting pleasures,   65
And all that's near at hand or far and wide
Leaves your good servant quite unsatisfied.

THE LORD   If today his service shows confused, disordered,
With my help he'll see his way clearly forward.
When the sapling greens, the gardener can feel certain   70
Flower and fruit shall follow in due season.

MEPHISTOPHELES   Would you care to bet on that? You'll lose, I tell you,
If you'll give me leave to lead the fellow
Gently down my broad, my primrose path.

THE LORD   As long as Faustus walks the earth   75
I shan't, I promise, interfere.
While still man strives, still he must err.

MEPHISTOPHELES   Well thanks, Lord, for it's not the dead and gone
I like dealing with. By far what I prefer
Are round and rosy cheeks. When corpses come   80
A-knocking, sorry, Master's left the house;
My way of working's the cat's way with a mouse.

THE LORD   So it's agreed, you have my full consent.
Divert the soul of Faust from its true source
And if you're able, lead him along, Hell bent   85
With you, upon the downward course—
Then blush for shame when you find you must admit:
Impelled in this direction, then in that one,
A good man still knows which way is the right one.

MEPHISTOPHELES   Of course, of course! Yet I'll seduce him from it   90
Soon enough. I'm not afraid I'll lose my bet.
And after I have won it,
You won't, I trust, begrudge me
My whoops of triumph, shouts of victory.

---

4. Of philosophy.
5. In the German text, Mephistopheles shifts back and forth between the informal word for

"you" (*du*) and the more formal, respectful mode of address (*ihr*).

Dust he'll eat   95
And find that he enjoys it, exactly like
That old aunt of mine, the famous snake.
THE LORD   There too feel free, you have carte blanche.
I've never hated your likes much;
I find, of all the spirits of denial,   100
You jeerers not my severest trial.
Man's very quick to slacken in his effort,
What he likes best is Sunday peace and quiet;
So I'm glad to give him a devil—for his own good,
To prod and poke and incite him as a devil should.   105
[*To the* ANGELS] But you who are God's true and faithful progeny—
Delight in the world's wealth of living beauty!
May the force that makes all life-forms to evolve
Enfold you in the dear confines of love,
And the fitfulness, the flux of all appearance—   110
By enduring thoughts give enduring forms to its transience.
      [*The Heavens close, the* ARCHANGELS *withdraw.*]
MEPHISTOPHELES   I like to see the Old Man now and then,
And take good care I don't fall out with him.
How very decent of a Lord Celestial
To talk man to man with the Devil of all people.   115

Part I

NIGHT

In a narrow, high-vaulted Gothic room, FAUST, *seated restlessly in an armchair at his desk.*

FAUST   I've studied, alas, philosophy,
Law and medicine, recto and verso,
And how I regret it, theology also,
Oh God, how hard I've slaved away,
With what result? Poor foolish old man,   120
I'm no whit wiser than when I began!
I've got a Master of Arts degree,
On top of that a Ph.D.,
For ten long years, around and about,
Upstairs, downstairs, in and out,   125
I've led my students by the nose
With what result?—that nobody knows,
Or ever shall know, the tiniest crumb!
Which is why I feel completely undone.
    Of course I'm cleverer than these stuffed shirts,   130
These Doctors, M.A.s, Scribes and Priests,
I'm not bothered by a doubt or a scruple,
I'm not afraid of Hell or the Devil—
But the consequence is, my mirth's all gone.
No longer can I fool myself   135

I'm able to teach anyone
How to be better, love true worth;
I've got no money or property,
Worldly honors or celebrity—
A dog wouldn't put up with this life!   140
Which is why I've turned to magic,
Seeking to know, by ways occult,
From ghostly mouths, spells difficult;
So I no longer need to sweat
Painfully explaining what   145
I don't know anything about;
So I may penetrate the power
That holds the universe together,
Behold the source whence all proceeds
And no more torture words, words, words.   150

O full moon, melancholy-bright,
Friend I've watched for, many a night,
Till your quiet-shining circle
Appeared above my high-piled table,
If only you might never again   155
Look down from above on my pain,
If only I might stray at will
In your mild light, high on the hill,
Haunt with spirits upland hollows,
Fade with you in dim-lit meadows,   160
And soul no longer gasping in
The stink of learning's midnight oil,
Bathe in your dews till well again!

Oh misery! Oh am I still
Stuck here in this dismal prison?   165
A musty goddamned hole in the wall
Where even the golden light of heaven
Can only weakly make its way through
The painted panes of the gothic window;
Where all about me shelves of books   170
Rise up to the vault in stacks,
Books gray with dust, worm-eaten, rotten,
With soot-stained paper for a curtain;
Where instruments, retorts and glasses
Are crammed in everywhere a space is;   175
And squeezed in somehow with these things
My family's ancient furnishings
Make complete the sad confusion—
Call this a world, this world you live in?

Can you still wonder why your heart   180
Should clench in your breast so anxiously?

Why your every impulse is stopped short
By an inexplicable misery?
Instead of Nature's flourishing garden
God created and man to dwell there, 185
Rubbish, dirt are everywhere
Your gaze turns, old bones, a skeleton.

Off, off, to the open countryside!
And this mysterious book, inscribed
By Nostradamus'[6] own hand— 190
What better help to master the secrets
Of how the stars turn in their orbits,
From Nature learn to understand
The spirits' power to speak to spirits;
Sitting here and racking your brains 195
To puzzle out the sacred signs—
What a sterile, futile business!
Spirits, I feel your presence around me:
Announce yourselves if you hear me!
> [*He opens the book and his eye encounters the sign of
> the Macrocosm.*[7]]

The pure bliss flooding all my senses 200
Seeing this! Through every nerve and vein
I feel youth's fiery, fresh spirit race again.
Was it a god marked out these signs
By which my agitated bosom's stilled,
By which my bleak heart's filled with joy, 205
By whose mysterious agency
The powers of Nature all around me stand revealed?
Am *I* a god? All's bright as day!
By these pure tracings I can see,
At my soul's feet, great Nature unconcealed. 210
And the sage's words—I understand them, finally:
"The spirit world is not barred shut,
It's your closed mind, your dead heart!
Stand up unappalled, my scholar,
And bathe your breast in the rose of Aurora!" 215
> [*He contemplates the sign.*]

How all is woven one, uniting,
Each in the other living, working!
How Heavenly Powers rise, descend,
Passing gold vessels from hand to hand!
On wings that scatter sweet-smelling blessings 220
Everywhere they post in earth
And make a universal harmony sound forth!

6. The Latin name of the French astrologer and physician Michel de Notredame (1503–1566). His collection of rhymed prophecies, *The Centuries*, appeared in 1555.

7. The great world (literal trans.); the universe as a whole. It represents the ordered, harmonious universe in its totality.

Oh, what a show! But a show, nothing more!
How, infinite Nature, lay hold of you, where?
Where find your all-life-giving fountains?—breasts that sustain   225
The earth and the heavens, which my shrunken breast
Yearns for with a feverish thirst—
You flow, overflow, must I keep on thirsting in vain?
        [*Morosely, he turns the pages of the book and comes on the
        sign of the Spirit of Earth.*[8]]
What a different effect this sign has on me!
Spirit of Earth, how nearer you are to me!   230
Already fresh lifeblood pours through every vein,
Already I'm aglow as if with new wine—
Now I have the courage to dare
To venture into the world and bear
The ill and well of life, to battle   235
Storms, when the ship splits, not to tremble.

The air grows dark overhead—
The moon's put out her light,
The oil lamp looks like dying.
Vapors rise, red flashes dart   240
Around my head—fright,
Shuddering down from the vault,
Seizes me by the throat!
Spirit I have invoked, hovering near:
Reveal yourself!   245
Ha! How my heart beats! All of my being's
Fumbling and groping amid never felt feelings!
Spirit, I feel I am yours, body and breath!
Appear! Oh, you must! Though it costs me my life!
        [*He seizes the book and pronounces the* SPIRIT's *mystic spell.
        A red flame flashes, in the midst of which the* SPIRIT *appears.*]
SPIRIT   Who's calling?   250
FAUST [*Averting his face.*]   Overpowering! Dreadful!
SPIRIT   Potently you've drawn me here,
    A parched mouth sucking at my sphere.
    And now—?
FAUST   Oh, you're unbearable!
SPIRIT   You're breathless from your implorations   255
    To see my face, to hear me speak,
    I've yielded to your supplications
    And here I am.—Well, worried sick
    I find the superman! I come at your bidding
    And you're struck dumb! Is this the mind   260
    That builds a whole interior world, doting
    On its own creation, puffed to find

---

8. This figure seems to be a symbol for the energy of terrestrial nature—neither good nor bad, merely powerful.

Itself quite on a par, the equal,
Of us spirits? Wherever is that Faust
Who urged himself just now with boastful   265
Claims on me, made such a fuss?
You're Faust? The one who at my breath's
Least touch, shudders to his depths,
A thing that wriggles off scared, a worm!
FAUST   I shrink back from you, an airy flame?   270
I'm him, yes Faust, your equal, the same.
SPIRIT   In flood tides of life, in tempests of action,
I surge upwards, sink low,
Going here, going there,
Birth and the grave,   275
Unstopping exertion,
An eternal sea heaving,
A weaving, unweaving,
A life all aglow—
So seated before time's whirring loom   280
I weave divinity's living costume.
FAUST   We're equals, I know! I feel so close to you, near,
You busy spirit ranging everywhere!
SPIRIT   It's your idea of me you're equal to,
Not me! [Vanishes.]   285
FAUST [Deflated.]   Not you?
Then who?
Me, made in God's own image,
Not even equal to you?
      [A knocking.]
Death! My famulus⁹—I know that knock.   290
Finis my supremest moment—worse luck!
That visions richer than I could have guessed
Should be scattered by a shuffling dryasdust!
      [WAGNER in dressing gown and nightcap, carrying a lamp.
      FAUST turns around impatiently.]
WAGNER   Excuse me, sir, but wasn't that
Your voice I heard declaiming? A Greek tragedy,   295
I'm sure. Well, that's an art that comes in handy
Nowadays. I'd love to master it.
People say, how often I have heard it,
Actors could really give lessons to the clergy.
FAUST   Yes, so parsons can make a stage out of the pulpit—   300
Something I've seen done in more than one case.
WAGNER   Oh dear, to be so cooped up in one's study all day,
Seeing the world only now and then, on holiday,
Seeing people from far off, as if through a spyglass—
How persuade them to any effect in that way?   305
FAUST   Unless you really feel it, no, you cannot—

9. Assistant to a medieval scholar.

Unless the words your lips declare are heartfelt
And by their soul-born spontaneous power,
Seize with delight the soul of your hearer.
But no! Stick in your seats, you scholars!   310
Paste bits and pieces together, cook up
A beggar's stew from others' leftovers,
Over a flame you've sweated to coax up
From your own little heap of smoldering ashes,
Filling with wonder all the jackasses,   315
If that's the kind of stuff your taste favors—
But you'll never get heart to cleave to heart
Unless you spear from your own heart.

WAGNER   Still and all, a good delivery is what
Makes the orator. I'm far behind in that art.   320

FAUST   Advance yourself in an honest way!
Don't play the fool in cap and bells!
Good sense, good understanding, they
Are art enough, speak for themselves.
When you have something serious to say   325
What need is there for hunting up
Fancy words, high-sounding phrases?
Your brilliant speeches, smartened up
With bits and pieces collected out
Of a miscellany of commonplaces   330
From all the languages spoken by all the races,
Are about as bracing as the foggy autumnal breeze
Swaying the last leaves on the trees.

WAGNER   Dear God, but art is long
And our life—lots shorter.   335
Often in the middle of my labor
My confidence and courage falter.
How hard it is to master all the stuff
For dealing with each and every source,
And before you've traveled half the course,   340
Poor devil, you have gone and left this life.

FAUST   Parchment, tell me—that's the sacred fount
You drink out of, to slake your eternal thirst?
The only true refreshment that exists
You get from where? Yourself—where all things start.   345

WAGNER   But sir, it's such a pleasure, isn't it,
To enter into another age's spirit,
To see what the sages before us thought
And measure how far since we've got.

FAUST   As far as to the stars, no doubt!   350
Your history, why, it's a joke;
Bygone times are a seven-sealed book.[1]
What you call an age's spirit
Is nothing more than your own spirit

1. Revelation 5.1.

With the age reflected as you see it.   355
And it's pathetic, what's to be seen in your mirror!
One look and off I head for the exit:
A trash can, strewn attic, junk-filled cellar,
At best a blood-and-thunder thriller
Improved with the most high-minded sentiments   360
Exactly suited for mouthing by marionettes.

WAGNER   But this great world, the human mind and heart,
They are things everyone wants to know about.

FAUST   Yes, know as the world, knows knowing!
Who wants to know the real truth, tell me?   365
Those few with vision, feeling, understanding
Who failed to stand guard, most unwisely,
Over their tongues, speaking their minds and hearts
For the mob to hear—you know what's been their fate:
They were crucified, burnt, torn to bits.   370
But we must break off, friend, it's getting late.

WAGNER   I love such serious conversation, I do!
I'd stay up all night gladly talking to you.
But, sir, it's Easter Sunday in the morning
And perhaps I may ask you a question or two then, if you're willing?   375
I've studied hard, with unrelaxing zeal,
I know a lot, but I want, sir, to know all. [*Exit.*]

FAUST [*Alone.*]   Such fellows keep their hopes up by forever
Busying themselves with trivialities,
Dig greedily in the ground for treasure,   380
And when they turn a worm up—what ecstacies!
That banal, commonplace human accents
Should fill air just now filled with spirits' voices!
Still, this one time you've earned my thanks,
Oh sorriest, oh shallowest of wretches!   385
You snatched me from the grip of a dejection
So profound I was nearly driven off
My head. So gigantic was the apparition
It made me feel no bigger than a dwarf—

Me, the image of God, certain in my belief   390
Soon, soon I'd behold the mirror of eternal truth
Whose near presence I felt; already savoring
The celestial glory, stripped of all mortal clothing—
Me, higher placed than the angels, dreaming brashly
With the strength I possess I could flow freely,   395
Godlike creative, through Nature's live body—
Well, it had to be paid for: a single word
Thundered out knocked me flat, all vain conceit curbed.
No, I can't claim we are equals, presumptuously!
Though strong enough to draw you down to me,   400
Holding on to you was another matter entirely.
In that exalted-humbling moment of pure delight
I felt myself at once both small and great.

And then you thrust me remorselessly back
Into uncertainty, which is all of humanity's fate.   405
Who'll tell me what to do? Not to do?
Still seek out the spirits to learn what they know?
Oh what we do, as much as what's done to us,
Obstructs the way stretching clearly before us.

The noblest conceptions our minds ever attained   410
Are watered down more and more, corrupted, profaned;
When we've gained a bit of the good of the world as our prize,
Then the better's dismissed as delusion and lies;
Those radiant sentiments, once our breath of life,
Grow dim and expire in the madding crowd's strife.   415
Time was that hope and brave imagination
Boldly reached as far as to infinity,
But now misfortune piling on misfortune,
A little, confined space will satisfy.
It's then, heart-deep, Care builds her nest,   420
Dithering nervously, killing joy, ruining rest,
Masking herself as this, as that concern
For house and home, for wife and children,
Fearing fire and flood, daggers and poison;
You shrink back in terror from imagined blows   425
And cry over losing what you never in fact lose.

Oh no, I'm no god, only too well do I know it!
A worm's what I am, wriggling through the soot
And finding his nourishment in it,
Whom the passerby treads underfoot.   430

These high walls, every shelf crammed, every niche,
Dust is what shrinks them to a stifling cell,
This moth-eaten world with its oddments and trash,
It's the reason I feel shut up in jail.
And here I'll discover what it is that I lack?   435
Devour thousands of books so as to learn, shall I,
Mankind has always been stretched on the rack,
With now and then somebody, somewhere, who's been happy?
You, empty skull there, smirking so, I know why—
What does it tell me if not that your brain,   440
Whirling like mine, sought the bright sun of truth,
Only to wander, night-bewildered, in vain.
And all that apparatus, you mock me, you laugh
With your every wheel, cylinder, cog and ratchet;
I stood at the door, sure you provided the key,   445
Yet for all the bit's cunning design I couldn't unlatch it.
Mysterious even in broad daylight,
Nature lets no one part her veil,
And what she keeps hidden, out of sight,

All your levers and wrenches can't make her reveal.   450
You, ancient stuff I've left lying about,
You're here, and why?—my father[2] found you useful.
And you, old scrolls, have gathered soot
For as long as the lamp's smoked on this table.
Much better to have squandered the little I got   455
Than find myself sweating under the lot.
It's from our fathers, what we inherit,
To possess it really we have to earn it.
What you don't use is a dead weight,
What's worthwhile is what you spontaneously create.   460

But why do I find I must stare in that corner,
Is that bottle a magnet enchanting my sight?
Why is everything all at once brighter, clearer,
Like woods when the moon's up and floods them with light?

Vial, I salute you, exceptional, rare thing,   465
And reverently bring you down from the shelf,
Honoring in you man's craft and cunning;
Quintessence of easeful sleeping potions,
Pure distillation of subtle poisons,
Do your master the kindness that lies in your power!   470
One look at you and my agony lessens,
One touch and my feverish straining grows calmer
And my tight-stretched spirit bit by bit slackens.
The spirit's flood tide runs more and more out,
My way is clear, into death's immense sea;   475
The bright waters glitter before my feet,
A new day is dawning, new shores calling to me.

A fiery chariot, bird-winged, swoops down on me,
I am ready to follow new paths and higher,
Aloft into new spheres of purest activity.   480
An existence so exalted, so godlike a rapture,
Does the worm of a minute ago deserve it?
No matter. Never falter! Turn your back bravely
On the sunlight, sweet sunlight, of our earth forever!
Tear wide open those dark gates boldly   485
Which the whole world skulks past with averted heads.
The time has come to disprove by deeds,
Because the gods are great, man's a derision,
To cringe back no more from that black pit
Whose unspeakable tortures are your own invention,   490
To struggle toward that narrow gate
Around which all Hell flames in constant eruption,
To do it calmly, without regret,

2. Later we find that Faust's father was a doctor of medicine.

Even at the risk of utter extinction.
And now let me lift this long forgotten   495
Crystal wine cup out of its chest.
You used to shine bright at the family feast,
Making the solemn guests' faces lighten
When you went round with each lively toast.
The figures artfully cut in the crystal,   500
Which it was the duty of all at the table
In turn to make up rhymes about,
Then drain the cup at a single draught—
How they recall the nights of my youth!
But now there's no passing you on to my neighbor,   505
Or thinking up rhymes to parade my quick wit;[3]
Here is a juice that is quick too—to intoxicate,
A brownish liquid, see, filling the beaker,
Chosen by me, by me mixed together,
My last drink! Which now I lift up in festal greeting   510
To the bright new day I see dawning!

> [*He raises the cup to his lips. Bells peal, a choir bursts into song.*]

CHORUS OF ANGELS
    Christ is arisen!
    Joy to poor mortals
    By their own baleful,
    Inherited, subtle   515
    Failings imprisoned.

FAUST   What deep-sounding burden, what tremelo strain
Arrest the glass before I can drink?
Does that solemn ringing already proclaim
The glorious advent of Holy Week?   520
Already, choirs, are you intoning
What angels' lips sang once, a comforting chant,
Above the sepulcher's darkness sounding,
Certain assurance of a new covenant?

CHORUS OF WOMEN
    With spices and balm, we   525
    Prepared the body,
    Faithful ones all, we
    Laid him out in the tomb;
    Clean in linen we wound him
    And bound up his hair—   530
    Oh, what do we find now?
    Christ is not here.

CHORUS OF ANGELS
    Christ is arisen!
    Blest is the man of love,

---

3. Faust here alludes to the drinking of toasts. The maker of a toast often produced impromptu rhymes.

He who the anguishing, 535
Bitter, exacting test,
Salvation bringing, passed.

FAUST But why do you seek me out in the dust,
You music of Heaven, mild and magnificent?
Sound out where men and women are simple, 540
Your message is clear but it leaves me indifferent,
And where no belief is, no miracle's possible.
The spheres whence those glad tidings ring
Are not for me to try and enter—
Yet all's familiar from when I was young 545
And back to life I feel myself sent for.
Years ago loving Heaven's kiss
Flew down to me in the Sabbath stillness,
Oh, how the bells rang with such promise,
And fervently praying to Jesus, what bliss! 550
A yearning so sweet, not to be comprehended,
Drove me out into green wood and field,
In me an inner world expanded
As my cheeks ran wet from eyes tear-filled.
Your song gave the signal for the games we rejoiced in 555
When the springtime arrived with its gay festival,
Innocent childhood's remembered emotion
Holds me back from the last step of all—
O sound away, sound away, sweet songs of Heaven,
Earth claims me again, my tears well up, fall. 560

CHORUS OF DISCIPLES

Only just buried,
Ascended already,
Living sublimely,
Up rising in glory!
Joy of becoming, his, 565
Near to creating's bliss.
He on the earth's hard crust
Left us, his own, his best,
To languish and wait—
Oh! how we pity, 570
Master, your fate!

CHORUS OF ANGELS

Christ is arisen
From the bowels of decay,
Strike off your fetters
And shout for joy! 575
By good works praising him,
By loving raising him,
Feeding the least of all,
Preaching him east and west to all,
Promising bliss to all. 580
You have the Master near,
You have him here.

OUTSIDE THE CITY GATE

All sorts of people out walking.

SOME APPRENTICES   Where are you fellows off to?
OTHERS   To the hunters' lodge—over that way.
FIRST BUNCH   Well, we're on our way to the old mill.   585
ONE APPRENTICE   The river inn—that's what I say.
SECOND APPRENTICE   The way there's not pleasant, I feel.
SECOND BUNCH   And what about you?
THIRD APPRENTICE   I'll stick with the rest of us here.
FOURTH APPRENTICE   Let's go up to the village. There, I can promise you   590
     The best-looking girls, the best-tasting beer,
     And some very good roughhousing too.
FIFTH APPRENTICE   My, but aren't you greedy!
     A third bloody nose—don't you care?
     I'll never go there, it's too scary.   595
SERVANT GIRL   No, no, I'm turning back, no, I won't stay.
ANOTHER   We're sure to find him at those poplar trees.
FIRST GIRL   Is that supposed to make me jump for joy?
     It's you he wants to walk with, wants to please,
     And you're the one he'll dance with. Fine   600
     For you. And for me what? The spring sunshine!
THE OTHER   He's not alone, I know, today. He said
     He'd bring his friend—you know, that curlyhead.
A STUDENT   Those fast-stepping girls there, look at the heft of them!
     Into action, old fellow, we're taking out after them.   605
     Beer with body, tobacco with a good sharp taste
     And red-cheeked housemaids in their Sunday best
     Are just the things to make your Hermann happiest.
A BURGHER'S DAUGHTER   Oh look over there, such fine-looking boys!
     Really, I think they are simply outrageous,   610
     They have their pick of the nicest girls,
     Instead they run after overweight wenches.
SECOND STUDENT [*To the first*]   Hold up, go slow! I see two more,
     And the pair of them dressed so pretty, so proper.
     But I know that one! She lives next door,   615
     And she, I can tell you, I think I could go for.
     They loiter along, eyes lowered decorously,
     But after saying no twice, they'll jump at our company.
FIRST STUDENT   No, no—all that bowing and scraping, it makes me
          feel ill at ease,
     If we don't get a move on we'll lose our two birds in the bushes.   620
     The work-reddened hand that swings the broom Saturdays
     On Sundays knows how to give the softest caresses.
A BURGHER   No, you can have him, our new Mayor,
     Since he took office he's been a dictator,
     All he's done is make the town poorer,   625
     Every day I get madder and madder,

When he says a thing's so, not a peep, not a murmur,
Dare we express—and the taxes climb higher.
A BEGGAR [*Singing.*]

    Good sirs and all you lovely ladies,
    Healthy in body and handsome in dress,   630
    Turn, oh turn your eyes on me, please,
    And pity the beggarman's distress!
    Must I grind the organ fruitlessly,
    Only the charitable know true joy.
    This day when all the world dance merrily,   635
    Make it for me a harvest day.
ANOTHER BURGHER   On a Sunday or holiday nothing in all my experience
Beats talking about war and rumors of war,
When leagues away, in Turkey, for instance,
Armies are wading knee deep in gore.   640
You stand at the window, take long pulls at your schooner,
And watch the gaily colored boats glide past,
And then at sunset go home in the best of humor
And praise God for the peace by which we're blest.
THIRD BURGHER   Yes, neighbor, yes, exactly my opinion.   645
Let them go and beat each other's brains in,
Let them turn the whole world upside down,
As long as things are just as always in our town.
OLD CRONE [*To the* BURGHERS' DAUGHTERS.]

    Well, how smart we are! *And* so pretty and young.
    I'd like to see the man who could resist you.   650
    But not so proud, my dears! Just come along,
    Oh, I know how to get what you want for you.
BURGHER'S DAUGHTER   Agatha, come! The awful fright!
I'm afraid of being seen with that witchwoman.
It's true that last St. Andrew's Eve[4]   655
She showed me in a glass my very own one.
HER FRIEND   And mine she showed me in a crystal sphere
Looking a soldier, with swaggering friends around him,
And though I watch out everywhere,
I have no luck, I never seem to find him.   660
SOLDIERS

    Castles have ramparts,
    Great walls and towers,
    Girls turn their noses up
    At soldier-boy lovers—
    We'll make both ours!   665
    Boldly adventure
    And rake in the pay!

---

4. November 29, the traditional time for young girls to consult fortune-tellers about their future lovers or husbands.

Hear the shrill bugle
Summon to battle,
Forward to rapture   670
Or forward to ruin!
Oh what a struggle!
Our life—oh how stirring!
Haughty girls, high-walled castles,
We'll make them surrender!   675
Boldly adventure
And rake in the pay!
—And after, the soldiers
Go marching away.
[FAUST *and* WAGNER]

FAUST The streams put off their icy mantle   680
Under the springtime's quickening smile.
Hope's green banner flies in the valley;
White-bearded winter, old and frail,
Retreats back up into the mountains,
And still retreating, down he sends   685
Feeble volleys of sleet showers,
Whitening in patches new-green plains.
But the sun can bear with white no longer,
When life stirs, shaping all anew,
He wants a scene that has some color,   690
And since there's nowhere yet one flower,
Holiday crowds have got to do.
Now face about, and looking down
From the hilltop back to town,
See the brightly colored crowd   695
Pouring like a spring flood
Through the gaping, gloomy arch
To bask in the sun all love so much.
They celebrate the Savior's Rising,
For they themselves today are risen: 700
From airless rooms in huddled houses,
From drudgery at counters and benches,
From under cumbrous roofs and gables,
From crowded, suffocating alleys,
From the mouldering dimness of the churches,   705
They hurry to where all is brightness.
And look there, how the eager crowd
Scatters through the fields and gardens.
How over the river's length and breadth
Skiffs and sculls are busily darting,   710
And that last boat, packed near to sinking,
Already's pulled a good ways off.
Even from distant mountain slopes
Bright colored clothes wink back at us.

Now I can hear it, the village commotion,   715
Out here, you can tell, is the people's true heaven,
Young and old crying exultingly:
Here I am human, here I can be free.
WAGNER   To go for a walk with you, dear Doctor,
Is a treat for my mind as well as honoring me;   720
But by myself I'd never come near here,
For I can't abide the least vulgarity.
The fiddling, shrieking, clashing bowls
For me are all an unbearable uproar,
All scream and shout like possessed souls   725
And call it music, call it pleasure.
PEASANTS [*Singing and dancing under the linden tree.*]
The shepherd dressed up in his best,
Pantaloons and flowered vest,
   Oh my, how brave and handsome!
Within the broad-leaved linden's shade   730
Madly spun both man and maid,
      Tra-la! Tra-la!
      Tra-la-la-la! Tra-lay!
The fiddle bow flew, and then some.
He flung himself into their midst   735
And seized a young thing round the waist,
      While saying, "Care to dance, ma'am?"
The snippy miss she tossed her head,
"You boorish shepherd boy!" she said,
      Tra-la! Tra-la!   740
      Tra-la-la-la! Tra-lay!
"Observe, do, some decorum!"
But round the circle swiftly wheeled,
To right and left the dancers whirled,
      Till all the breath flew from them.   745
They got so red, they got so warm,
They rested, panting, arm in arm,
      Tra-la! Tra-la!
      Tra-la-la-la! Tra-lay!
And breast to breast—a twosome.   750

"I'll thank you not to make so free!
We girls know well how men betray,
   What snakes lurk in your bosom!"
But still he wheedled her away—
Far off they heard the fiddles play,   755
      Tra-la! Tra-la!
      Tra-la-la-la! Tra-lay!
   The shouting, uproar, bedlam.
OLD PEASANT   Professor, welcome! Oh how kind
To join us common folk today,   760

Though such a fine man, learned mind,
Not to scorn our holiday.
So please accept out best cup, sir,
Brimful with the freshest beer;
We hope that it will quench your thirst,   765
But more than that, we pray and hope
Your sum of days may be increased
By as many drops as fill the cup!
FAUST   Friends, thanks for this refreshment, I
In turn wish you all health and joy.   770
          [*The people make a circle around him.*]
OLD PEASANT   Indeed it's only right that you
Should be with us this happy day,
Who when our times were hard, a true
Friend he proved in every way.
Many a one stands in his boots here   775
Whom your good father, the last minute,
Snatched from the hot grip of the fever,
That time he quelled the epidemic.[5]
And you yourself, a youngster then,
Never shrank back; every house   780
The pest went in, you did too.
Out they carried many a corpse,
But never yours. Much you went through;
Us you saved, and God saved you.
ALL   Health to our tried and trusty friend,   785
And may his kindness have no end.
FAUST   Bow down to him who dwells above,
Whose love shows us how we should love.
          [*He continues on with* WAGNER.]
WAGNER   The gratification you must get from all of this,
From knowing the reverence these people hold you in!   790
The man whose gifts can gain him such advantages,
Oh, he's a lucky one in my opinion.
Who is it, each one asks as he runs to see,
Fathers point you out to their boys,
The fiddle stops, the dancers pause,   795
And as you pass between the rows
Of people, caps fly in the air, why,
Next you know they'll all be on their knees
As if the Host itself[6] were passing by.
FAUST   A few steps more to that rock where we'll rest   800
A bit, shall we, from our walk. How often
I would sit alone here thinking, sighing,
And torture myself with praying, fasting, crying.

5. Pestilence or plague.
6. The Eucharist, the consecrated bread of the Sacrament.

So much hope I had then, such great trust—
I'd wring my hands, I'd weep, fall on my knees,   805
Believing God, in this way forced
To look below, would cry halt to the disease.
But now these people's generous praise of me
I find a mockery. If only you could see
Into my heart, you'd realize   810
How little worthy father and son were really.
    My father was an upright man, a lonely,
Brooding soul who searched great Nature's processes
With a head crammed full of the most bizarre hypotheses.
Shutting himself with fellow masters up in   815
The vaulted confines of their vaporous Black Kitchen,
He mixed together opposites according
To innumerable recipes. A bold Red Lion,
Handsome suitor he, took for wedding
Partner a pure White Lily, the two uniting   820
In a tepid bath; then being tested by fire,
The pair precipitately fled
From one bridal chamber to another,
Till there appeared within the glass
The young Queen, dazzlingly dressed   825
In every color of the spectrum:
The Sovereign Remedy—a futile nostrum.
The patients died; none stopped to inquire
How many there were who'd got better.[7]
    So with our infernal electuary   830
We killed our way across the country.
I poisoned, myself, by prescription, thousands,
They sickened and faded; yet I must live to see
On every side the murderers' fame emblazoned.
WAGNER   But why be so distressed, there is no reason.   835
If an honest man with conscientious devotion
Practises the arts his forebears practised,
It's understandable, it's what's to be expected.
A youth who is respectful of his father
Listens and soaks up all he has to teach;   840
If the grown man lengthens science's reach,
His son in turn can reach goals even farther.
FAUST   Oh, he's a happy man who hopes
To keep from drowning in these seas of error!
What we know least, we need the most,   845
And what we do know is no use whatever.
    But such cheerlessness blasphemes
The quiet sweetness of this shining hour.
Look how the sunset's level beams
Gild those cottages in their green bower,   850

7. This confusing sequence evokes a kind of medicine closely allied to magic.

The brightness fades, the sun makes his adieu,
Hurrying off to kindle new life elsewhere—
If only I had wings to rise into
The air and follow ever after!
Then I would see the whole world at my feet,   855
Quietly shining in the eternal sunset,
The peaks ablaze, the valleys gone to sleep,
And babbling into golden stream the silver runlet.
The savage mountain with its plunging cliffs
Should never balk my godlike soaring,   860
And there's the ocean, see, already swelling
Before my wondering gaze, with its sun-warmed gulfs.
But finally the bright god looks like sinking,
Whereupon a renewed urgency
Drives me on to drink his eternal light,   865
The day always before, behind the night,
The heavens overhead, below the heaving sea . . .

    A lovely dream!—and meanwhile it grows dark.
Oh dear, oh dear, that our frames should lack
Wings with which to match the spirit's soaring.   870
Still our nature's such that all of us
Know feelings that strive upwards, always straining,
When high above, lost in the azure emptiness,
The skylark pours out his shrill rhapsody,
When over fir-clad mountain peaks   875
The eagle on his broad wings gyres silently,
And passing over prairies, over lakes,
The homeward-bound crane labors steadily.

WAGNER   Well, I've had more than one odd moment, I have,
But I have never felt those impulses you have.   880
Soon enough you get your fill of woods and things,
I don't really envy birds their wings.
How different are the pleasures of the intellect,
Sustaining one from page to page, from book to book,
And warming winter nights with dear employment   885
And with the consciousness your life's so lucky.
And goodness, when you spread out an old parchment,
Heaven's fetched straight down into your study.

FAUST   You know the one great driving force,
May you never know the other!   890
Two souls live in me, alas,
Irreconcilable with one another.
One, lusting for the world with all its might,
Grapples it close, greedy of all its pleasures,
The other rises up, up from the dirt,   895
Up to the blest fields where dwell our great forebears.

    O beings of the air, if you exist,
Holding sway between the heavens and earth,

Come down to me out of the golden mist
And translate me to a new, a vivid life! 900
Oh, if I only had a magic mantle
To bear me off to unknown lands,
I'd never trade it for the costliest gowns,
Or for a cloak however rich and royal.

WAGNER Never call them down, the dreadful swarm 905
That swoop and hover through the atmosphere,
Bringing mankind every kind of harm
From every corner of the terrestrial sphere.
From the North they bare their razor teeth
And prick you with their arrow-pointed tongues, 910
From the East, sighing with parched breath,
They eat away your dessicated lungs;
And when from Southern wastes they gust and sough,
Fire on fire on your sunk head heaping,
From the West they send for your relief 915
Cooling winds—then drown fields just prepared for reaping.
Their ears are cocked, on trickery intent,
Seem dutiful while scheming to defeat us,
Their pretense is that they are heaven-sent
And lisp like angels even as they cheat us. 920
    However, come, let's go, the world's turned gray
And chilly, evening mists are rising!
At nightfall it's indoors you want to be.
But why should you stand still, astonished, staring?
What can you see in the dusk to find upsetting? 925

FAUST Don't you see that black dog in the stubble,
Coursing back and forth?

WAGNER   I do. I noticed him.
A while back. What about him?

FAUST   Look again.
What kind of creature is it?

WAGNER   Kind? A poodle—
Worried where his master is, and always 930
Sniffing about to find his scent.

FAUST   Look, he's
Circling around us, coming near and nearer.
Unless I'm much mistaken, a wake of fire
Is streaming after him.

WAGNER   I see nothing
But a black-haired poodle. Your eyes are playing 940
Tricks on you, perhaps.

FAUST   I think I see
Him winding a magic snare, quietly,
Around our feet, a noose which he'll pull tight
In the future, when the time is right.

WAGNER He's circling us because he's timid and uncertain; 945
He's missed his master, come on men unknown to him.

FAUST The circle's getting tighter, he's much closer!

WAGNER   You see!—a dog, it's no ghost, sir.
  He growls suspiciously, he hesitates,
  He wags his tail, lies down and waits.   950
  Never fear, it's all just dog behavior.
FAUST   Come here, doggie, come here, do.
WAGNER   A silly poodle, a poor creature,
  When you stop, he stops too.
  Speak to him, he'll leap and bark,   955
  Throw something, he will fetch it back,
  Go after your stick right into the river.
FAUST   I guess you're right, it's just what he's been taught;
  I see no sign of anything occult.
WAGNER   A dog so good, so well-behaved by nature—   960
  Why, even a philosopher would stoop to pet him.
  Some students trained him, found him an apt scholar—
  Sir, he deserves you should adopt him.
      [*They enter at the City Gate.*]

FAUST'S STUDY [I]

FAUST [*Entering with the poodle.*]
  Behind me lie the fields and meadows
  Shrouded in the lowering dark,   965
  In dread of what waits in the shadows
  Our better soul now starts awake.
  Our worser one, unruly, reckless,
  Quietens and starts to nod;
  In me the love of my own fellows   970
  Begins to stir, and the love of God.

  Poodle, stop! How you race around! A dozen
  Dogs you seem. Why all that sniffing at the door?
  Here's my best cushion, it's yours to doze on,
  Behind the stove, there on the floor.   975
  Just now when we came down the hillside
  You gambolled like the friendliest beast.
  I'm glad to take you in, provide
  Your keep—provided you're a silent guest.

  When once again the lamp light brightens   980
  With its soft glow your narrow cell,
  Oh in your breast how then it lightens,
  And deeper in your heart as well.
  Again you hear the voice of reason,
  And hope revives, it breathes afresh,   985
  You long to drink the living waters,
  Mount upwards to our being's source.

  You're growling, poodle! Animal squealings
  Hardly suit the exalted feelings

Filling my soul to overflowing.   990
We're used to people ridiculing
What they hardly understand,
Grumbling at the good and beautiful—
It makes them so uncomfortable!
Do dogs now emulate mankind?   995
   Yet even with the best of will
I feel my new contentment fail.
Why must the waters cease so soon
And leave us thirsting once again?
Oh, this has happened much too often!   1000
But there's an answer to it all:
I mean the supernatural,
I mean our hope of revelation,
Which nowhere shines so radiant
As here in the New Testament.   1005
I'll look right now at the original[8]
And see if it is possible
For me to make a true translation
Into my beloved German.

       [He opens the volume and begins.]

"In the beginning was the Word"[9]—so goes   1010
The text. And right off I am given pause!
A little help, please, someone, I'm unable
To see the *word* as first, most fundamental.
If I am filled with the true spirit
I'll find a better way to say it.   1015
So: "In the beginning *mind* was"—right?
Give plenty of thought to what you write,
Lest your pen prove too impetuous:
Is it mind that makes and moves the universe?
Shouldn't it be: "In the beginning   1020
Power was, before it nothing"?
Yet even as I write this down on paper
Something tells me don't stop there, go further.
The Spirit's prompt in aid; now, now, indeed
I know for sure: "In the beginning was the *deed*!"   1025

If this cell's one that we'll be sharing,
Poodle, stop that barking, yelping!
You're giving me a splitting headache,
I can't put up with such a roommate.
I'm sorry to say that one of us   1030
Has got to quit the premises.
It goes against the grain with me
To renege on hospitality,
But there's the door, dog, leave, goodbye.

---

8. That is, the Greek.   9. John 1.1.

But what's that I'm seeing,   1035
A shadow or real thing?
It beggars belief—
My poodle swells up huger than life!
He heaves up his hulk—
No dog has such bulk!   1040
What a spook I have brought
Into my house without thought.
He looks, with his fierce eyes and jaws,
Just like a hippopotamus—
But I've got you, you're caught!   1045
For a half-hellhound like you are,
Solomon's Key[1] is what is called for.

SPIRITS [*Outside the door.*]

    Someone is locked in there!
    No one's allowed in there!
    Like a fox hunters snared,   1050
    Old Scratch shivers, he's scared.
    Be careful, watch out!
    Hover this way, now that,
    About and again about,
    You'll soon find he's got out.   1055
    If you can help him,
    Don't let him sit there,
    All of us owe him
    For many a favor.

FAUST   Against such a creature, my first defense: 1060
The Spell of the Four Elements.

    Salamander glow hot,
    Undine, wind about,
    Sylph, melt quick,
    Kobold,[2] to work.   1065

    Ignorance
    Of the elements,
    Their powers and properties,
    Denies you all mastery
    Over the demonry.   1070

    Vanish in flames,
    Salamander!
    Undine, make babbling streams
    All flow together!

---

1. The *Clavicula Salomonis*, a standard work used by magicians for conjuring. In many medieval legends, Solomon was noted as a great magician.

2. A spirit of the earth. "Salamander": spirit of fire. "Undine": spirit of water. "Sylph": spirit of air.

Glitter meteor-beauteous,   1075
Aërial Sylph!
Give household help to us,
Incubus! Incubus!
Come out, come out, enough's enough.

None of the four   1080
Is in the cur.
Calmly he lies there, grinning at me,
My spells glance off him harmlessly.
   Now hear me conjure
With something stronger.   1085

   Are you, grim fellow,
   Escaped here from Hell below?
   Then look at this symbol
   Before which the legions
   Of devils and demons   1090
   Fearfully bow.

How his hair bristles, how he swells up now!

   Creature cast into darkness,
   Can you make out its meaning?
   The never-begotten One.   1095
   Wholly ineffable One,
   Carelessly pierced in the side One,
   Whose blood in the heavens
   Is everywhere streaming?

Behind the stove by me sent,   1100
Bulging big as an elephant,
The entire cell filling,
Into mist himself willing—
—No, no, not through the ceiling!
At my feet fall, Master's bidding!   1105
My threats as you see are scarcely idle—
With fire I'll rout you out, yes, I will!
Wait if you wish,
For my triune[3] light's hot flash,
Wait till you force me   1110
To employ my most potent sorcery.
      [*The smoke clears, and* MEPHISTOPHELES, *dressed as an*
      itinerant student, emerges from behind the stove.]

3. Perhaps the Trinity or a triangle with divergent rays.

MEPHISTO   Why all the racket? What's your wish, sir?
FAUST   So it's you who was the poodle!
    I have to laugh—a wandering scholar!
MEPHISTO   My greetings to you, learned doctor,   1115
    You really had me sweating hard there.
FAUST   And what's your name?
MEPHISTO   Your question's trivial
    From one who finds words superficial,
    Who strives to pass beyond mere seeming
    And penetrate the heart of being.[4]   1120
FAUST   With gentry like yourself, it's common
    To find the name declares what you are
    Very plainly. I'll just mention
    Lord of the Flies,[5] Destroyer, Liar.
    So say who you are, if you would.   1125
MEPHISTO   A humble part of that great power
    Which always means evil, always does good.
FAUST   Those riddling words mean what, I'd like to know.
MEPHISTO   I am the spirit that says no,
    No always! And how right I am! For certainly   1130
    It's only fitting everything that comes to be
    Should cease to be. And so they do.
    Still better nothing ever was. Hence sin,
    And havoc and ruin—all you call evil, in sum—
    For me's the element that I swim in.   1135
FAUST   A part, you say? You look like the whole works to me.
MEPHISTO   I say what's so, it isn't modesty—
    Man in his world of self's a fool,
    He likes to think he's all in all.
    I'm part of the part which was all at first,   1140
    A part of the dark out of which light burst,
    Arrogant light which now usurps the air
    And seeks to thrust Night from her ancient chair,
    To no avail. Since light is one with all
    Things bodily, making them beautiful,   1145
    Streams from them, from them is reflected,
    Since light by matter's manifested—
    When by degrees all matter's burnt up and no more,
    Why, then light shall not matter any more.
FAUST   Oh, now I understand your office: 1150
    Since you can't wreck Creation wholesale,
    You're going at it bit by bit, retail.
MEPHISTO   And making, I fear, little progress.
    The opposite of nothing-at-all,
    The *something*, this great shambling world,   1155

---

4. Mephistopheles refers to Faust's substitu-   5. An almost literal translation of the name of
tion of *Deed* for *Word* in the passage from   the Philistine deity Beelzebub.
John (see line 1025).

In spite of how I exert myself against it,
Phlegmatically endures my every onset
By earthquake, fire, tidal wave and storm:
Next day the land and sea again are calm.
And all that *stuff*, those animal and human species— 1160
I can hardly make a dent in them.
The numbers I've already buried, armies!
Yet fresh troops keep on marching up again.
That's how it is, it's enough to drive you crazy!
From air, from water, from the earth 1165
Seeds innumerable sprout forth
In dry and wet and cold and warm!
If I hadn't kept back fire for myself,
What the devil could I call my own?

FAUST So against the good, the never-resting, 1170
Beneficent creative force
In impotent spite you ball your fist and
Try to arrest life's onward course?
Look around for work that's more rewarding,
You singular son of old Chaos! 1175

MEPHISTO Well, it's a subject for discussion—
At our next meeting. Now I wish
To go. That is, with your permission.

FAUST But why should *you* ask *me* for leave?
We've struck up an acquaintance, we two, 1180
Drop in on me whenever you please.
There's the door and there's the window,
And ever reliable, there's the chimney.

MEPHISTO Well . . . you see . . . an obstacle
Keeps me from dropping *out*—so sorry! 1185
That witch's foot chalked on your doorsill.

FAUST The pentagram's[6] the difficulty?
But if it's that that has you stopped,
How did you ever manage an entry?
And how should a devil like you get trapped? 1190

MEPHISTO Well, look close and you'll see that
A corner's open: the outward pointing
Angle's lines don't quite meet.

FAUST What a stroke of luck! I'm thinking
Now you are my prisoner. 1195
Pure chance has put you in my power!

MEPHISTO The poodle dashed right in, saw nothing;
But now the case is the reverse:
The Devil can't get out of the house!

FAUST There's the window, why don't you use it? 1200

MEPHISTO It's an iron law we devils can't flout,
The way we come in, we've got to go out,
We're free as to entrée, but not as to exit.

6. A magic five-pointed star designed to keep away evil spirits.

FAUST   So even in Hell there's law and order!
  I'm glad, for then a man might sign   1205
  A contract with you gentlemen.
MEPHISTO   Whatever we promise, you get, full measure,
  There's no cutting corners, no skulduggery—
  But it's not a thing to be done in a hurry;
  Let's save the subject for our next get-together.   1210
  And as for now, I beg you earnestly,
  Release me from the spell that binds me!
FAUST   Why rush off, stay a while, do.
  I'd love to hear some more from you.
MEPHISTO   Let me go now. I swear I'll come back,   1215
  Then you can ask me whatever you like.
FAUST   Trapping you was never my thought,
  You trapped yourself, it's your own fault.
  Who's nabbed the Devil must keep a tight grip,
  You don't grab him again once he gives you the slip.   1220
MEPHISTO   Oh, all right! To please you I
  Will stay and keep you company;
  Provided with my arts you let me
  Entertain you in my own way.
FAUST   Delighted, go ahead. But please   1225
  Make sure those arts of yours amuse!
MEPHISTO   You'll find, my friend, your senses, in one hour,
  More teased and roused than all the long dull year.
  The songs the fluttering spirits murmur in your ear,
  The visions they unfold of sweet desire,   1230
  Oh they are more than just tricks meant to fool.
  By Arabian scents you'll be delighted,
  Your palate tickled, never sated,
  The ravishing sensations you will feel!
  No preparation's needed, none.   1235
  Here we are. Let the show begin!
SPIRITS   Open, you gloomy
     Vaulted ceiling above him,
     Let the blue ether
     Look benignly in on him,   1240
     And dark cloudbanks scatter
     So that all is fair for him!
     Starlets are glittering,
     Milder suns glowing,
     Angelic troops shining   1245
     In celestial beauty
     Hover past smiling,
     Bending and bowing.
     Ardent desire
     Follows them yearning;   1250
     And their robes streaming ribbons
     Veil the fields, veil the meadows,

Veil the arbors where lovers
In pensive surrender
Give themselves to each other   1255
For ever and ever.
Arbor on arbor!
Vines clambering and twining!
Their heavy clusters,
Poured into presses,   1260
Pour out purple wines
Which descend in dark streams
Over beds of bright stones
Down the vineyards' steep slopes
To broaden to lakes   1265
At the foot of green hills.
Birds blissfully drink there,
With beating wings sunwards soar,
Soar towards the golden isles
Shimmering hazily   1270
On the horizon;
Where we hear voices
Chorusing jubilantly,
Where we see dancers
Whirling exuberantly   1275
Over the meadows,
Here, there and everywhere.
Some climb the heights,
Some swim in the lakes,
Others float in the air—   1280
Joying in life, all,
Beneath the paradisal
Stars glowing with love
Afar in the distance.

MEPHISTO   Asleep! Oh bravely done, my every airy youngling!   1285
Into a drowse you've sung him, never stumbling.
I am in your debt for this performance.
—As for you, sir, you were never born
To keep the Prince of Darkness down!
Let sweet dream-shapes crowd round him in confusion,   1290
Drown him in a deep sea of delusion.
But from this doorsill-magic to be freed
A rat's tooth is the thing I need.
No point to conjuring long-windedly—
There's one rustling nearby, he'll soon hear me.   1295

The lord of flies and rats and mice,
Of frogs and bedbugs, worms and lice,
Commands you forth from your dark hole
To gnaw, beast, for me that doorsill
Whereon I dab this drop of oil!   1300

—And there you are! Begin, begin!
The corner that is pointing in,
That's the one that shuts me in;
One last crunch to clear my way:
Now Faustus, till we meet next—dream away!   1305
FAUST [*Awakening*.]   Deceived again, am I, by tricks,
Those vanished spirits just a hoax,
A dream the Devil, nothing more,
The dog I took home just a cur?

FAUST'S STUDY [II]

FAUST, MEPHISTOPHELES.

FAUST   A knock, was that? Come in! Who is it this time?   1310
MEPHISTO   Me.
FAUST   Come in!
MEPHISTO   You have to say it still a third time.
FAUST   All right, all right—come in!
MEPHISTO   Good, very good!
We two will get along, I see, just as we should.
I've come here dressed up as a grandee,[7] Why?
To help you drive your blues away!   1315
In a scarlet suit, all over gold braid,
Across my shoulders a stiff silk cape,
A gay cock's feather in my cap,
At my side a gallant's long blade—
And bringing you advice that's short and sweet: 1320
Put fine clothes on like me, cut loose a bit,
Be free and easy, man, throw off your yoke
And find out what real life is like.
FAUST   In any clothes, I'd feel the misery
Of this cramped, suffocating life on earth.   1325
I'm too old for a life of gaiety,
Too young to live for nothing, wait for death.
The world—what has it got to say to me?
Renounce all that you long for, all—renounce!
That's the truth that all pronounce   1330
So sagely, so interminably,
The non-stop croak, the universal chant:
You can't have what you want, you can't!
I awake each morning, how? Horrified,
On the verge of tears, to confront a day   1335
Which at its close will not have satisfied
One smallest wish of mine, not one. Why,

---

7. In the popular plays based on the Faust legend, the Devil often appeared as a monk when the play catered to a Protestant audience and as a noble squire when the audience was mainly Catholic.

Even a hint of pleasure, some pleasantness,
Withers in the air of mean-spirited fault-finding;
My lively nature's quick inventiveness   1340
Is thwarted by cares that seem to have no ending.
And when the night draws on and all is hushed,
I go to bed not soothed at last but apprehensively,
Well knowing what awaits me is not rest,
But wild and whirling dreams that terrify me.   1345
The god who dwells inside my breast,
Able to stir me to my depths,
The master strength of all my strengths
Is impotent to effect a single thing outside me;
And so I find existence burdensome, wretched,   1350
Death eagerly desired, my life hated.
MEPHISTO   Yet the welcome men give death is never wholehearted.
FAUST   Oh that man's blest who, conquering gloriously,
Death winds the blood-stained laurel round his brows,
Who after dancing the night through furiously   1355
Death finds him in a girl's arms in a drowse.
If only, overwhelmed by the Spirit's power,
In raptures I had died right then and there!
MEPHISTO   And yet that very night, I seem to remember,
A fellow didn't down a drink I saw him prepare.   1360
FAUST   Spying around, I see, is what you like to do.
MEPHISTO   I don't know everything, but I know a thing or two.
FAUST   If a sweet, familiar harmony
When I was staggering, steadied me,
Beguiled what's left of childhood feeling   1365
From a time when all was smiling, gay,
Well, never again! I pronounce a curse on
All false and flattering persuasion,
All tales that cheat the soul, constrain
It to endure this vale of pain.   1370
First I curse man's mind for thinking
Much too well of itself; I curse
The show of things, so dazzling, glittering,
That assails us through our every sense;
Our dreams of fame, of our name's enduring,   1375
Oh what a sham, I curse them too;
I curse as hollow all our having,
Curse wife and child, peasant and plow;
I curse Mammon[8] when he incites us
With dreams of treasure to reckless deeds,   1380
Or plumps the cushions for our pleasure
As we lie lazily at ease;
Curse comfort sucked out of the grape,
Curse love on its pinnacle of bliss,

---

8. The Aramaic word for "riches," used in the New Testament of the Bible. Medieval writers interpreted the word as a proper noun, the name of the Devil, as representing greed.

Curse faith, so false, curse all vain hope, 1385
And patience most of all I curse!

SPIRIT CHORUS [*Invisible*.]

    Oh, what a pity,
    Now you've destroyed it!
    The world once so lovely,
    How you have wrecked it! 1390
    Down it goes, smashed
    By a demigod's fist!
    Out of existence
    We sweep its poor remnants,
    Sorrowing over 1395
    Beauty now lost forever.
    —Then build again, better,
    Potent son of the earth,
    Build a new world, a fairer,
    Inside your own self, 1400
    Within your own heart!
    With a mind clear and strong,
    On your lips a new song,
    Come, make a fresh start!

MEPHISTO   Lesser ones, these are, 1405
    Of my order.
    Active be, cheerful,
    Is their sage counsel.
    Out of your loneliness,
    Spiritless lustlessness, 1410
    Their voices draw you
    Into the wide world before you.

    Stop making love to your misery,
    It gnaws away at you like a vulture;
    Even in the meanest company 1415
    You'd feel yourself a man like any other.
    Not that I'm proposing to
    Thrust you down among the rabble.
    I'm not your grandest devil, no,
    But still, throw in with me—that way, united, 1420
    Together life's long road we'll travel,
    And my, how I would be delighted!
    I'll do your will as if my will,
    Every wish of yours fulfill,
    By your leave 1425
    Be your bond servant, be your slave.

FAUST   And in return what must I do?

MEPHISTO   There's plenty of time for that, forget it.

FAUST   No, no, the Devil must have his due,
    He doesn't do things for the hell of it, 1430
    Just to see another fellow through.

So let's hear the terms, what the fine print is;
Having you for a servant's a tricky business.
MEPHISTO   I promise I will serve your wishes—here,
    A slave who'll do your bidding faithfully;   1435
    But if we meet each other—there,
    Why, you must do the same for me.
FAUST   That "there" of yours—it doesn't scare me off;
    If you pull this world down about my ears,
    Let the other one come on, who cares?   1440
    My joys are part and parcel of this earth,
    It's under this sun that I suffer,
    And once it's goodbye, last leave taken,
    Then let whatever happens happen,
    And that is that. About the hereafter   1445
    We have had enough palaver,
    More than I want to hear, by far:
    If still we love and hate each other,
    If some stand high and some stand lower,
    Et cetera, et cetera.   1450
MEPHISTO   In that case an agreement's easy.
    Come, dare it! Come, your signature!
    Oh, how my tricks will tickle your fancy!
    I'll show you things no man has seen before.
FAUST   You poor devil, really, what have you got to offer?   1455
    The mind of man in its sublime endeavor,
    Tell me, have you ever understood it?
    Oh yes indeed, you've bread, and when I eat it
    I'm hungry still; you've yellow gold, it's flighty,
    Quicksilver-like it's gone, my purse is empty.   1460
    Games of chance no man can win at ever;
    Girls who wind me in their arms, their lover,
    While eyeing up a fresh one over my shoulder.
    There's fame, last failing of a noble nature,
    It shoots across the sky a second, then it's over—   1465
    Oh yes, do show me fruit that rots as you try
    To pick it, trees whose leaves bud daily, daily die!
MEPHISTO   Marvels like that? For a devil, not so daunting.
    I'm good for whatever you have in mind.
    —But friend, the day comes when you find   1470
    A share of your own in life's good things,
    And peace and quiet, are what you're wanting.
FAUST   If ever you see me loll at ease,
    Then it's all yours, you can have it, my life!
    If ever you fool me with flatteries   1475
    Into feeling satisfied with myself,
    Or tempt me with visions of luxuries,
    That's my last day on earth breathed,
    I'll bet you!
MEPHISTO   Done! A bet!

FAUST   A bet—agreed!
  If ever I plead with the passing moment,   1480
  "Linger awhile, you are so fair!"
  Then chain me up in close confinement,
  Then serving me's no more your care,
  Then let the death bell toll my finish,
  Then unreluctantly I'll perish,   1485
  The clock may stop, hands break, fall off,
  And time for me be over with.
MEPHISTO   Think twice. Forgetting's not a thing we do.
FAUST   Of course, quite right—a bet's a bet.
  This isn't anything I'm rushing into.   1490
  But if I fall into a rut,
  I'm a slave, no matter who to,
  To this or that one or to you.
MEPHISTO   My service starts now—no procrastinating!—
  At the dinner tonight for the just-made Ph.D.s.   1495
  But there's one thing: you know, for emergencies,
  I'd like to have our arrangement down in writing.
FAUST   In black and white you want it, pedant!
  You've never learnt a *man's* word's your best warrant?
  It's not enough for you that I'm committed   1500
  By what I promise till the end of days?
  —Yet the world's a flood sweeps all along before it,
  And why should I feel my word holds always?
  A strange idea, but that's the way we are,
  And who would want it otherwise?   1505
  That man's blessed who keeps his conscience clear,
  He'll regret no sacrifice.
  But parchment signed and stamped and sealed,
  Is a bogey all recoil from, scared.
  The pen does in the living word,   1510
  Only sealing wax and vellum count, honor must yield.
  Base spirit, say what you require!
  Brass or marble, parchment or paper?
  Shall I write with quill, with stylus, chisel,
  I leave it up to you, you devil!   1515
MEPHISTO   Why get so hot, make extravagant speeches?
  Ranting away does no good.
  A scrap of paper takes care of the business.
  And sign it with a drop of blood.
FAUST   Oh, all right. If that's what makes you happy,   1520
  I'll go along with the childish comedy.
MEPHISTO   Blood's a very special ink, you know.
FAUST   Are you afraid that I won't keep our bargain?
  With every sinew I'll strive, never slacken!
  So I've promised, that's what I will do.   1525
  I had ideas too big for me,
  Your level's mine, that's all I'm good for.

The Spirit laughed derisively,
Nature won't allow me near her.
Thinking is done with for me, I'm through,   1530
Learning I've loathed since long ago.
—Then fling ourselves into the dance
Of sensual extravagance!
Bring on your miracles, each one,
Veiled in impenetrable sorcery!   1535
We'll plunge into time's racing current,
The vortex of activity,
Where pleasure and distress,
Setbacks and success,
May come as they come, by turn-about, however;   1540
To be always up and doing is man's nature!

MEPHISTO   No limits restrain you, do just as you like.
A little taste here, a nibble, a lick,
You see something there, snatch it up on the run,
Let all that you do with gusto be done,   1545
Only don't be bashful, wade right in.

FAUST   I told you, I'm not out to enjoy myself, have fun,
I want frenzied excitements, gratifications that are painful,
Love and hatred violently mixed,
Anguish that enlivens, inspiriting trouble.   1550
Cured of my thirst to know at last,
I'll never again shun anything distressful;
From now on my wish is to undergo
What people everywhere undergo, their whole portion,
Make mine their heights and depths, their weal and woe,   1555
Everything human encompass in my one person,
And so enlarge my own self to embrace theirs, all,
And shipwreck with them when at last we shipwreck, all.

MEPHISTO   Believe me, I have chewed and chewed
At that tough meat, mankind, since long ago,   1560
From birth to death work at it, still that food
Is indigestible as sourdough.
Only a God can take in all of them,
The whole lot. For He dwells in eternal light,
While we poor devils are stuck down below   1565
In darkness and gloom, lacking even candlelight,
And all *you* qualify for is, half day, half night.

FAUST   Nevertheless I will!

MEPHISTO   Fine! Right!
Still, there's one thing worries me.
The time allotted you is very short,   1570
But art has always been around and shall be,
So listen, hear what is my thought:
Hire a poet, learn by his instruction.
Let the good gentleman search his mind
By careful, persevering reflection,   1575

And every noble attribute he can find
Heap on the head of his honored creation:
   The lion's fierceness,
   Mild hart's swiftness,
   Italian fieriness, 1580
   Northern steadiness.
Let him master for you the difficult feat
Of combining magnanimity with deceit,
How, driven by youthful impulsiveness, unrestrained,
To fall in love as beforehand planned. 1585
Such a creature—my, I'd love to know him!
I'd call him Mr. Microcosm.

FAUST   What am I, then, if it can never be:
The realization of all human possibility,
That crown my soul so avidly reaches for? 1590

MEPHISTO   In the end you are—just what you are.
Wear wigs high-piled with curls, oh millions,
Stick your legs in yard-high hessians,
You're still you, the one you always were.

FAUST   I feel it now, how pointless my long grind 1595
To make mine all the treasures of man's mind;
When I sit back and interrogate my soul,
No new powers answer to my call,
I'm not a hair's breadth more in height,
A step nearer to the infinite. 1600

MEPHISTO   The way you see things, my dear Faust,
Is superficial—I speak frankly.
If you go on repining weakly,
We'll lose our seat at life's rich feast.
Hell, man, you have hands and feet, 1605
A headpiece and a pair of balls,
And savors from fruit fresh and sweet,
That pleasure's yours, entirely yours.
If I've six studs, a sturdy span,
That horsepower's mine, my property, 1610
My coach bowls on, ain't I the man,
Two dozen legs I've got for me!
   Sir, come on, quit all that thinking,
Into the world, the pair of us!
The man who lives in his head only's 1615
Like a donkey in the rough
Led round and round by the bad fairies,
While green grass grows a stone's throw off.

FAUST   And how do we begin?

MEPHISTO   By clearing out—just leaving.
A torture chamber this place is, and that's the truth. 1620
You call it living, to be boring
Yourself and your young men to death?
Leave that to Dr. Bacon Fat next door!

Why toil and moil at threshing heaps of straw?
Anyhow, the deepest knowledge you possess   1625
You daren't let on to before your class.
—Oh now I hear one in the passageway!

FAUST   I can't see him—tell him to go away.

MEPHISTO   The poor boy's been so patient, don't be cross;
We mustn't let him leave here *désolé*.   1630
Let's have your cap and gown, Herr Doctor.
Won't I look the fine professor!
        [*Changes clothes.*]
Count on me to know just what to say,
Fifteen minutes's all I need for it—
Meanwhile get ready for our little junket!   1635

                    [*Exit* FAUST.]

MEPHISTO [*Wearing* FAUST's *gown.*]   Despise learning, heap contempt
        on reason,
The human race's best possession,
Only let the lying spirit draw you
Over into mumbo-jumbo,
Make-believe and pure illusion—   1640
And then you're mine, for sure I have you,
No matter what we just agreed to.
Fate's given him a spirit knows no measure,
On and on it strives relentlessly,
It soars away disdaining every pleasure,   1645
Yet I will lead him deep into debauchery
Where all is shallow, meaningless,
I'll have him writhing, ravening, berserk;
Before his lips' insatiable greediness
I'll dangle food and drink, he'll shriek   1650
In vain for relief from his torturing dryness.
And even if he weren't the Devil's already,
He'd still be sure to perish horribly.
        [*Enter a* STUDENT.]

STUDENT   Allow me, sir, but I am a beginner
And come in quest of an adviser,   1655
One whom all the people here
Greatly esteem, indeed revere.

MEPHISTO   I thank you for your courtesy.
But I'm a man, as you can see,
Like any other. Perhaps you should look further.   1660

STUDENT   It's you, sir, you, I want for adviser!
I came here full of youthful zeal,
Eager to learn everything worthwhile.
Mother cried to see me go;
I've got an allowance, not much, but it'll do.   1665

MEPHISTO   You've come to the right place, my son.

STUDENT   But I'm ready to turn right around and run!
It seems so sad inside these walls,

My heart misgives me; I find all's
Confined, shut in; there's nothing green,   1670
Not even a single tree to be seen.
I can't, on the bench in the lecture hall,
Hear or see or think at all!

MEPHISTO   It's a matter of getting used to things first.
An infant starts out fighting the breast,   1675
But soon it's feeding lustily.
Just so your appetite will sharpen day by day
The more you nurse at Wisdom's bosom.

STUDENT   I'll cling tight to her bosom, happily,
But where do I find her, by what way?   1680

MEPHISTO   First of all, then—have you chosen
A faculty?

STUDENT   Well, you see,
I'd like to be a learned man.
The earth below, the heavens on high—
All those things I long to understand,   1685
All the sciences; all nature.

MEPHISTO   You've got the right idea; however,
It demands close application.

STUDENT   Oh never fear, I'm in this heart and soul;
But still, a fellow gets so dull   1690
Without time off for recreation,
In the long and lovely days of summer.

MEPHISTO   Time slips away so fast you need to use it
Rationally, and not abuse it.
And for that reason I advise you: 1695
The Principles of Logic *primo*!
We will drill your mind by rote,
Strap it in the Spanish boot
So it never shall forget
The road that's been marked out for it   1700
And stray about incautiously,
A will-o'-the-wisp, this way, that way.
Day after day you'll be taught
All you once did just like that,
Like eating and drinking, thoughtlessly,   1705
Now needs a methodology—
Order and system: *A, B, C!*
    Our thinking instrument behaves
Like a loom: every thread
At a step on the treadle's set in motion,   1710
Back and forth the shuttle's sped,
The strands flow too fast for the eye,
A blow of the batten and there's cloth, woven!
Now enter your philosopher, he
Proves all is just as it should be: 1715
A being thus and *B* also,

Then *C* and *D* inevitably follow;
And if there were no *A* and *B*,
There'd never be a *C* and *D*.
They're struck all of a heap, his admiring hearers, 1720
But still, it doesn't make them weavers.
How do you study something living?
Drive out the spirit, deny it being,
So there're just parts with which to deal,
Gone is what binds it all, the soul. 1725
With lifeless pieces as the only things real,
The wonder's where's the life of the whole—
Encheiresis naturae,[9] the chemists then call it,
Make fools of themselves and never know it.
STUDENT I have trouble following what you say. 1730
MEPHISTO You'll get the hang of it by and by,
When you learn to distinguish and classify.
STUDENT How stupid all this makes me feel;
It spins around in my head like a wheel.
MEPHISTO Next metaphysics—a vital part 1735
Of scholarship, its very heart.
Exert your faculties to venture
Beyond the boundaries of our nature,
Gain intelligence the brain
Has difficulty taking in, 1740
And whether it goes in or not,
There's always a big word for it.
Be very sure, your first semester,
To do things right, attend each lecture.
Five of them you'll have daily; 1745
Be in your seat when the bell peals shrilly.
Come to class with your homework done,
The sections memorized, each one,
So you are sure nothing's mistook
And no word's said not in the book. 1750
Still, all you hear set down in your notes
As if it came from the Holy Ghost.
STUDENT No need to say that to me twice,
I realize notes help a lot;
What you've got down in black and white 1755
Goes home with you to a safe place.
MEPHISTO But your faculty—you've still not told me.
STUDENT Well, I don't think the law would hold me.
MEPHISTO I can't blame you, law is no delight.
What's jurisprudence?—a stupid rite 1760
That's handed down, a kind of contagion,
Passed from generation to generation,

9. The natural process by which substances are united into a living organism—a name for an
action no one understands.

From people to people, region to region;
What once made sense becomes nonsensical,
And benefaction a bothersome burden.   1765
O grandsons to come, how I do wince for you all!
As for the rights we have from Nature as her heir—
Never a word about *them* will you hear!
STUDENT   I hate the stuff now more than ever!
How lucky I am to have you for adviser.   1770
Perhaps I'll take theology.
MEPHISTO   I shouldn't want to lead you astray,
But it's a science, if you'll allow me to say it,
Where it's easy to lose your way.
There's so much poison hidden in it,   1775
It's very nearly impossible
To tell what's toxic from what's medicinal.
Here again it's safer to choose
One single master and echo his words dutifully—
As a general rule, put your trust in *words*,   1780
They'll guide you safely past doubt and dubiety
Into the Temple of Absolute Certainty.
STUDENT   But shouldn't words convey ideas, a meaning?
MEPHISTO   Of course they should! But why overdo it?
It's exactly when ideas are lacking   1785
Words come in so handy as a substitute.
With words we argue pro and con,
With words invent a whole system.
Believe in words! Have faith in them!
No jot or tittle shall pass from them.   1790
STUDENT   Forgive me, I've another query,
My last one and then I'll go.
Medicine, sir—what might you care to tell me
About that study I should know?
Three years, my God, are terribly short   1795
For so vast a field for the mind to survey;
A pointer or two would provide a start
And advance one quicker on one's way.
MEPHISTO [*Aside*]   Enough of all this academic chatter.
Back again to deviltry!   1800
[*Aloud*]   Medicine's an easy art to master.
Up and down you study the whole world
Only so as to discover
In the end it's all up to the Lord.
Plough your way through all the sciences you please,   1805
Each learns only what he can;
But the man who understands his opportunities,
Him I call a man.
You seem a pretty strapping fellow,
Not one to hang back bashfully.   1810
If you don't doubt yourself, I know,

Nobody else will doubt you, nobody.
Above all learn your way with women
If you mean to practise medicine;
The aches and pains that torture them   1815
From one place only, one, all stem.
Cure there, cure all. Act halfway decent
And you'll find the whole sex acquiescent.
With an M.D. you enjoy great credit,
Your art, they're sure, beats others' arts.   1820
The doctor, when he pays a visit,
For greeting reaches for those parts
It takes a layman years to get at;
You feel her pulse with extra emphasis,
And your arm slipping with an ardent glance   1825
Around her slender waist,
See if it's because she's so tight-laced.

STUDENT   Oh, that's much better—practical, down to earth!

MEPHISTO   All theory, my dear boy, is gray,
And green the golden tree of life.   1830

STUDENT   I swear it seems a dream to me!
Would you permit me, sir, to impose on
Your generous kindness another day
And drink still more draughts of your wisdom?

MEPHISTO   I'm glad to help you in any way.   1835

STUDENT   I mustn't leave without presenting
You my album. Do write something
In it for me, would you?

MEPHISTO   Happily.
[Writes and hands back the album.]

STUDENT [Reading.]   Eritis sicut Deus, scientes bonum et malum.[1]
[Closes the book reverently and exits.]

MEPHISTO   Faithfully follow that good old verse,   1840
That favorite line of my aunt's, the snake,
And for all your precious godlikeness,
You'll end up how? A nervous wreck.
[Enter FAUST.]

FAUST   And now where to?

MEPHISTO   Wherever you like.
First we'll mix with little people, then with great.   1845
The pleasure and the profit you will get
From our course—and never pay tuition for it!

FAUST   But me and my long beard—we're hardly suited
For the fast life. I feel myself defeated
Even before we start. I've never been   1850
A fellow to fit in. Among other men

---

1. A slight alteration of the serpent's words to Eve in Genesis: "Ye shall be as God, knowing good and evil" (Latin).

I feel so small, so mortified—I freeze.
Oh, in the world I'm always ill at ease!
MEPHISTO   My friend, that's all soon changed, it doesn't matter;
With confidence comes *savoir-vivre*.   1855
FAUST   But how do we get out of here?
Where are your horses, groom and carriage?
MEPHISTO   By air's how we make our departure,
On my cloak—you'll enjoy the voyage.
But take care, on so bold a venture,   1860
You're sparing in the matter of luggage.
I'll heat some gas, that way we'll lift up
Quickly off the face of earth;
If we're light enough we'll rise right up—
I offer my congratulations, sir, on your new life!   1865

AUERBACH'S CELLAR IN LEIPZIG

Drinkers carousing.

FROSCH   Faces glum and glasses empty?
I don't call this much of a party.
You fellows seem wet straw tonight,
Who always used to blaze so bright.
BRANDER   It's your fault—he just sits there, hardly speaks!   1870
Where's the horseplay, where's the dirty jokes?
FROSCH   [*Emptying a glass of wine on his head.*]
There! Both at once!
BRANDER   O horse and swine!
FROSCH   You asked for it, so don't complain.
SIEBEL   Out in the street if you want to punch noses!
—Now take a deep breath and roar out a chorus   1875
In praise of the grape and the jolly god Bacchus.
Come, all together with a rollicking round-o!
ALTMAYER   Stop, stop, man, I'm wounded, cotton, quick, someone
fetch some,
The terrible fellow has burst me an eardrum!
SIEBEL   Hear the sound rumble above in the vault?   1880
That tells you you're hearing the true bass note.
FROSCH   That's right! Out the door, whoever don't like it!
With a do-re-mi,
ALTMAYER   And a la-ti-do,
FROSCH   We will have us a concert!   1885
[*Sings.*]
Our dear Holy Roman Empire,
How does the damn thing hold together?
BRANDER   Oh, but that's dreadful, and dreadfully sung,
A dreary, disgusting *political* song!
Thank the Lord when you wake each morning   1890
You're not the one must keep the Empire running.
It's a blessing I'm grateful for

To be neither Kaiser nor Chancellor.
But we, too, need a chief for our group,
So let's elect ourselves a pope.   1895
To all of us here I'm sure it's well known
What a man must do to sit on that throne.

FROSCH [*Singing.*]
    Nightingale, fly away, o'er lawn, o'er bower,
    Tell her I love her ten thousand times over.

SIEBEL   Enough of that love stuff, it turns my stomach.   1900

FROSCH   Ten thousand times, though it drives you frantic!
    [*Sings.*]
    Unbar the door, the night is dark!
    Unbar the door, my love, awake!
    Bar up the door now it's daybreak.

SIEBEL   Go on, then, boast about her charms, her favor,   1905
But I will have the latest laugh of all.
She played me false—just wait, she'll play you falser.
A horned imp's what I wish her, straight from Hell,
To dawdle with her in the dust of crossroads,
And may an old goat stinking from the Brocken   1910
Bleat "Goodnight, dearie," to her, galloping homewards.
A fellow made of honest flesh and blood
For a slut like that is much too good.
What kind of love note would I send that scarecrow?—
A beribboned rock tossed through her kitchen window.   1915

BRANDER [*Banging on the table.*]
Good fellows, your attention! None here will deny
I know what should be done and shouldn't at all.
Now we have lovers in our company
Whom we must treat in manner suitable
To their condition, our jollity,   1920
With a song just lately written. So mind the air
And come in on the chorus loud and clear!
    [*He sings.*]
    A rat lived downstairs in the cellar,
    Dined every day on lard and butter,
    His paunch grew round as any burgher's,   1925
    As round as Dr. Martin Luther's.[2]
    The cook put poison down for it,
    Oh, how it groaned, the pangs it felt,
        As if by Cupid smitten.

CHORUS [*Loud and clear.*]
        As if by Cupid smitten!   1930

BRANDER
    It rushed upstairs, it raced outdoors
    And drank from every gutter,
    It gnawed the woodwork, scratched the floors,

2. Martin Luther (1483–1546), German leader of the Protestant Reformation, hence an object
of distaste for Catholics.

Its fever burned still hotter,
In agony it hopped and squealed   1935
Oh, piteously the the beast appealed,
  As if by Cupid smitten.

CHORUS
  As if by Cupid smitten!

BRANDER
Its torment drove it, in broad day,
Out into the kitchen,   1940
Collapsing on the hearth, it lay
Panting hard and twitching.
But that cruel Borgia smiled with pleasure,
That's it, that's that rat's final seizure,
  As if by Cupid smitten.   1945

CHORUS
  As if by Cupid smitten!

SIEBEL   You find it funny, you coarse louts,
  Oh, quite a stunt, so very cunning,
  To put down poison for poor rats!
BRANDER   You like rats, do you, find them charming?   1950
ALTMAYER   O big of gut and bald of pate!
  Losing out's subdued the oaf;
  What he sees in the bloated rat
  'S the spitting image of himself.
    [FAUST *and* MEPHISTOPHELES *enter*.]
MEPHISTO   What your case calls for, Doctor, first,   1955
  Is some diverting company,
  To teach you life affords some gaiety.
  For these men every night's a feast
  And every day a holiday;
  With little wit but lots of zest   1960
  All spin inside their little orbit
  Like young cats chasing their own tails.
  As long as the landlord grants them credit
  And they are spared a splitting headache,
  They find life good, unburdened by travails.   1965
BRANDER   They're travelers is what your Brander says,
  You can tell it by their foreign ways,
  They've not been here, I'll bet, an hour.
FROSCH   Right, right! My Leipzig's an attraction, how I love her,
  A little Paris spreading light and culture!   1970
SIEBEL   Who might they be? What's your guess?
FROSCH   Leave it to me. I'll fill their glass,
  Gently extract, as you do a baby's tooth,
  All there 's to know about them, the whole truth.
  I'd say we're dealing with nobility,   1975
  They look so proud, so dissatisfied, to me.
BRANDER   They're pitchmen at the Fair, is what I think.
ALTMAYER   Maybe so.

FROSCH   Now watch me go to work.

MEPHISTO [*To* FAUST.]

These dolts can't ever recognize Old Nick

Even when he's got them by the neck.   1980

FAUST   Gentlemen, good day.

SIEBEL   Thank you, the same.

       [*Aside, obliquely studying* MEPHISTOPHELES.]

What the hell, the fellow limps, he's lame![3]

MEPHISTO   We'd like to join you, sirs, if you'll allow it.

But our landlord's wine looks so-so, I am thinking,

So the company shall make up for it.   1985

ALTMAYER   Particular, you are, about your drinking?

FROSCH   Fresh from Dogpatch, right? From supper

On cabbage soup with Goodman Clodhopper?

MEPHISTO   We couldn't stop on this trip, more's the pity!

But last time he went on so tenderly   1990

About his Leipzig kith and kin,

And sent his very best to you, each one.

       [*Bowing to* FROSCH.]

ALTMAYER [*Aside to* FROSCH.]

Score one for him. He's got some wit.

SIEBEL   A sly one, he is.

FROSCH   Wait, I'll fix him yet!

MEPHISTO   Unless I err, weren't we just now hearing   1995

Some well-schooled voices joined in choral singing?

Voices, I am sure, must resonate

Inside this vault to very fine effect.

FROSCH   You know music professionally, I think.

MEPHISTO   Oh no—the spirit's eager, but the voice is weak.   2000

ALTMAYER   Give us a song!

MEPHISTO   Whatever you'd like to hear.

SIEBEL   The latest, nothing we've heard before.

MEPHISTO   Easily done. We've just come back from Spain,

Land where the air breathes song, the rivers run wine.

      [*Sings.*]

        Once upon a time a King   2005

          Had a flea, a big one—

FROSCH   Did you hear that? A flea, goddamn!

I'm all for fleas, myself, I am.

MEPHISTO [*Sings.*]

        Once upon a time a King

          Had a flea, a big one,   2010

        Doted fondly on the thing

          With fatherly affection.

        Calling his tailor in, he said,

          Fetch needles, thread and scissors,

---

3. By tradition, the Devil had a cloven foot, split like a sheep's hoof.

Measure the Baron up for shirts,   2015
   Measure him, too, for trousers.
BRANDER   And make it perfectly clear to the tailor
  He must measure exactly, sew perfect stitches,
  If he's fond of his head, not the least little error,
  Not a wrinkle, you hear, not one, in those breeches!   2020
MEPHISTO
   Glowing satins, gleaming silks
     Now were the flea's attire,
  Upon his chest red ribbons crossed
     And a great star shone like fire,
  In sign of his exalted post   2025
     As the King's First Minister.
  His sisters, cousins, uncles, aunts
     Enjoyed great influence too—
  The bitter torments that that Court's
     Nobility went through!   2030
  And the Queen as well, and her lady's maid,
     Though bitten till delirious,
  Forbore to squash the fleas, afraid
     To incur the royal animus.
  But we free souls, we squash all fleas   2035
     The instant they light on us!
CHORUS [*Loud and clear.*]
    But we free souls, we squash all fleas
     The instant they light on us!
FROSCH   Bravo, bravo! That was fine!
SIEBEL   May every flea's fate be the same!   2040
BRANDER   Between finger and nail, then crack! and they're done for.
ALTMAYER   Long live freedom, long live wine!
MEPHISTO   I'd gladly drink a glass in freedom's honor,
  If only your wine was a little better.[4]
SIEBEL   Again! You try, sir, our good humor!   2045
MEPHISTO   I'm sure our landlord wouldn't take it kindly,
  For otherwise I'd treat this company
  To wine that's wine—straight out of our own cellar.
SIEBEL   Go on, go on, let the landlord be my worry.
FROSCH   You're princes, you are, if you're able   2050
  To put good wine upon the table;
  But a drop or two, well, that's no trial at all,
  To judge right what I need's a real mouthful.
ALTMAYER [*In an undertone.*]   They're from the Rhineland,
  I would swear.
MEPHISTO   Let's have an auger, please.   2055
BRANDER   What for?
  Don't tell me you've barrels piled outside the door!
ALTMAYER   There's a basket of tools—look, over there.
MEPHISTO [*Picking out an auger, to* FROSCH.]

---

4. That is, not cursed.

Now gentlemen—name what you'll have, please?
FROSCH What do you mean? We have a choice?
MEPHISTO Whatever you wish, I'll produce. 2060
ALTMAYER [*To* FROSCH.] Licking his lips already, he is!
FROSCH Fine, fine! For me—a Rhine wine any day,
  The best stuff's from the Fatherland, I say.
MEPHISTO [*Boring a hole in the table edge at* FROSCH's *place.*]
  Some wax to stop the holes with, quick!
ALTMAYER Hell, it's just a sideshow trick. 2065
MEPHISTO [*To* BRANDER.]
  And you?
BRANDER The best champagne you have, friend, please,
  With lots of sparkle, lots of fizz.

  [MEPHISTOPHELES *goes round the table boring holes at all the places,
  which one of the drinkers stops with bungs made of wax.*]

You can't always avoid what's foreign;
About pleasure I'm nonpartisan. 2070
A man who's a true German can't stand Frenchmen,
But he can stand their wine, oh how he can!
SIEBEL [*As* MEPHISTOPHELES *reaches his place.*]
  I confess your dry wines don't
  Please my palate, I'll take sweet.
MEPHISTO Tokay[5] for you! Coming up shortly! 2075
ALTMAYER No, gentlemen! Look at me honestly,
  The whole thing's meant to make fools of us.
MEPHISTO Come on, my friend, I'm not so obtuse!
  Trying something like that on you would be risky.
  So what's your pleasure, I'm waiting—speak! 2080
ALTMAYER Whatever you like, just don't take all week.
MEPHISTO [*All the holes are now bored and stopped; gesturing grotesquely*]
  Grapes grow on the vine,
  Horns on the head of the goat,
  O vinestock of hard wood,
  O juice of the tender grape! 2085
  And a wooden table shall,
  When summoned, yield wine as well!
  O depths of Nature, mysterious, secret,
  Here is a miracle—if you believe it!
  Now pull the plugs, all, drink and be merry! 2090
ALL [*Drawing the bungs and the wine each drinker asked for gushing
  into his glass.*]
  Sweet fountain, flowing for us only!
MEPHISTO But take good care you don't spill any.
  [*They drink glass after glass.*]
ALL [*Singing.*]
  How lovely everything is, I'm dreaming!

5. A sweet Hungarian wine.

  Like cannibals having a feast,
  Like pigs in a pen full of slops!   2095
MEPHISTO The people feel free, what a time they're having!
FAUST I'd like to go now—nincompoops!
MEPHISTO Before we do, you must admire
 Their swinishness in its full splendor.
SIEBEL [*Spilling wine on the floor, where it bursts into flame.*]
 All Hell's afire, I burn, I burn!   2100
MEPHISTO [*Conjuring the flame.*]
 Peace, my own element, down, down!
  [*To the drinkers.*]
 Only a pinch, for the present, of the purgatorial fire.
SIEBEL What's going on here? For this you'll pay dear!
 You don't seem to know the kind of men you have here.
FROSCH Once is enough for that kind of business!   2105
ALTMAYER Throw him out on his ear, but quietly, no fuss!
SIEBEL You've got your nerve, trying out upon us
 Stuff like that—damned hocus-pocus!
MEPHISTO Quiet, you tub of guts!
SIEBEL   Bean pole, you!
 Now he insults us. I know what to do.   2110
BRANDER A taste of our fists is what: one-two, one-two.
ALTMAYER [*Drawing a bung and flames shooting out at him.*]
 I'm on fire, I'm on fire!
SIEBEL   It's witchcraft, no mistaking!
 Stick him, the rogue, he's free for the taking!
  [*They draw their knives and fall on* MEPHISTOPHELES.]
MEPHISTO [*Gesturing solemnly.*]
  False words, false shapes
  Addle wits, muddle senses!   2115
  Let here and otherwheres
  Exchange places!
  [*All stand astonished and gape at each other.*]
ALTMAYER Where am I? What a lovely country!
FROSCH Such vineyards! Do my eyes deceive me?
SIEBEL And grapes you only need to reach for!   2120
BRANDER Just look inside this green arbor!
 What vines, what grapes! Cluster on cluster!
  [*He seizes* SIEBEL *by the nose. The others do the same to each
  other and raise their knives.*]
MEPHISTO Unspell, illusion, eyes and ears!
 —Take note the Devil's a jester, my dears!
  [*He vanishes with* FAUST; *the drinkers recoil from each other.*]
SIEBEL What's happened?   2125
ALTMAYER   What?
FROSCH   Was that your nose?
BRANDER [*To* SIEBEL.] And I'm still holding on to yours!
ALTMAYER The shock I felt—in every limb!
 Get me a chair, I'm caving in.

FROSCH   But what the devil was it, tell me.

SIEBEL   Only let me catch that scoundrel,   2130
He won't go home alive, believe me!

ALTMAYER   I saw him, horsed upon a barrel,
Vault straight out through the cellar door—
My feet feel leaden, so unnatural.
        [*Turning toward the table.*]
Well—maybe some wine's still trickling here.   2135

SIEBEL   Lies, all, lies! Deluded! Dupes!

FROSCH   I was drinking wine, I'd swear.

BRANDER   But what was it with all those grapes?

ALTMAYER   Now try and tell me, you know-it-alls,
There's no such thing as miracles!   2140

WITCH'S KITCHEN

A low hearth, and on the fire a large cauldron. In the steam rising up from it, various figures can be glimpsed. A SHE-APE *is seated by the cauldron, skimming it to keep it from boiling over. The* MALE *with their young crouches close by, warming himself. Hanging on the walls and from the ceiling are all sorts of strange objects, the household gear of a witch.*

FAUST, MEPHISTOPHELES.

FAUST   Why, it's revolting, all this crazy witchery!
Are you telling me I'll be born a new man
Here amid this lunatic confusion?
Is an ancient hag the doctor who will cure me?
And the mess that that beast's boiling, that's the remedy   2145
To cancel thirty years, unbow my back?
If you can do no better, the outlook's black
For me, the hopes I nursed are dead already.
Hasn't man's venturesome mind, instructed by Nature,
Discovered some sort of potent elixir?   2150

MEPHISTO   Now you're speaking sensibly!
There *is* a natural way to recover your youth;
But that's another business entirely
And not your sort of thing, is my belief.

FAUST   No, no, come on, I want to hear it.   2155

MEPHISTO   All right. It's simple: you don't need to worry
About money, doctors, necromancy.
Go out into the fields right now, this minute,
Start digging and hoeing with never a stop or a respite.
Confine yourself and your thoughts to the narrowest sphere,   2160
Eat nothing but the plainest kind of fare,
Live with the cattle as cattle, don't think it too low
To spread your own dung on the fields that you plow.
So there you have it, the sane way, the healthy,
To keep yourself young till the age of eighty!   2165

FAUST   Yes, not my sort of thing, I'm afraid,

Humbling myself to work with a spade;
So straitened a life would never suit me.

MEPHISTO   So it's back to the witch, my friend, are we?

FAUST   That horrible hag—no one else will do?   2170
Why can't *you* concoct the brew?

MEPHISTO   A nice thing that, to waste the time of the Devil
When his every moment is claimed by the business of evil!
Please understand. Not only skill and science
Are called for here, but also patience: 2175
A mind must keep at it for years, very quietly,
Only time can supply the mixture its potency.
Such a deal of stuff goes into the process,
All very strange, all so secret.
The Devil, it's true, taught her how to do it,   2180
But it's no business of his to brew it.
        [*Seeing the* APES.]
See here, those creatures, aren't they pretty!
That one's the housemaid, that one's the flunkey.
        [*To the* APES.]
Madam is not at home, it seems?

APES   Flew up the chimney   2185
To dine out with friends.

MEPHISTO   And her feasting, how long does it usually take her?

APES   As long as we warm our paws by the fire.

MEPHISTO [*To* FAUST.]   What do you think of this elegant folk?

FAUST   Noisome enough to make me puke.   2190

MEPHISTO   Well, just this sort of causerie
Is what I find most pleases me.
        [*To the* APES.]
Tell me, you ugly things, oh do,
What's that you're stirring there, that brew?

APES   Beggars' soup, it's thin stuff, goes down easy.   2195

MEPHISTO   Your public's assured—they like what's wishy-washy.

HE-APE [*Sidling up to* MEPHISTOPHELES *fawningly*.]
            Oh roll the dice quick,
            How I long to be rich!
            I need some good luck,
            It's wrong, so few have so much.   2200
            With a purse full of thaler,
            An ape passes for clever.

MEPHISTO   How very happy that monkey would be
If he could buy chances in the lottery.
        [*Meanwhile the young* APES *have been rolling around a big ball
        to which they now give a push forward.*]

HE-APE   The world, sirs, behold it!   2205
            Down goes the upside,
            Up goes the downside,
            And never a respite.
            Touch it, it'll ring,

It's like glass, fractures easily. 2210
When all's said and done,
A hollow, void thing.
Here it shines brightly,
Here, even brighter.
—Oops, ain't I nimble! 2215
But you, son, be careful
And keep a safe distance,
Or it's your last day.
The thing's made of clay,
A knock, and it's fragments. 2220
MEPHISTO   What is that sieve for?
HE-APE [*Taking it down.*]
If you came here to thieve,
It would be my informer.
[*He scampers across to the* SHE-APE *and has her look through it.*]
Look through the sieve!
Now say, do you know him? 2225
Or you don't dare name him?
MEPHISTO [*Approaching the fire.*]   And this pot over here?
APES
Oh, you're a blockhead, sir—
Don't know what a pot's for!
Nor a kettle neither.
MEPHISTO   What a rude creature! 2230
HE-APE
Here, take this duster,
Sit down in the armchair.
[*Presses* MEPHISTOPHELES *down in the chair.*]
FAUST   [*Who meanwhile has been standing in front of a mirror,
going forward to peer into it from close up and then stepping back.*]
What do I see? What a marvellous vision
Shows itself in this magic glass!
Love, lend me your wings, your swiftest, to pass 2235
Through the air to the heaven she must dwell in!
Oh dear, unless I stay fixed to this spot,
If I dare to move nearer even a bit,
Mist blurs the vision and obscures her quite.
Woman unrivaled, beauty absolute! 2240
Can such things be, a creature so lovely?
The body so indolently stretched out there
Surely epitomizes all that is heavenly.
Can such a marvel inhabit down here?
MEPHISTO   Of course when a god's sweated six whole days, 2245
And himself cries bravo in his work's praise,
You can be certain the results are first class;
Look all you want now in the glass,
But I can find you just such a prize,
And lucky the man, his bliss is assured, 2250

Who can bring home such a beauty to his bed and board.
> [FAUST *continues to stare into the mirror, while*
> MEPHISTOPHELES, *leaning back comfortably in the armchair and toying*
> *with the feather duster, talks on.*]

Here I sit like a king on a throne,
Scepter in hand, all I'm lacking's my crown.

APES [*Who have been performing all sorts of queer, involved movements,*
with loud cries bring MEPHISTOPHELES *a crown.*]
> Here, your majesty,
> If you would,   2255
> Glue up the crown
> With sweat and blood!
> [*Their clumsy handling of the crown causes it to break in two,*
> *and they cavort around with the pieces.*]
> Oh, oh, now it's broken!
> We look and we listen,
> We chatter, scream curses,   2260
> And make up our verses—

FAUST [*Still gazing raptly into the mirror.*]
Good God, how my mind reels, it's going to snap!

MEPHISTO [*Nodding toward the* APES.]
My own head's starting to spin like a top.

APES
> And if by some fluke
> The words happen to suit   2265
> Then the rhyme makes a thought!

FAUST [*As above.*]   I feel like my insides are on fire!
Let's go, we've got to get out of here.

MEPHISTO [*Keeping his seat.*]   They tell the truth, these poets do,
You've got to give the creatures their due.   2270
> [*The cauldron, neglected by the* SHE-APE, *starts to boil over, causing*
> *a great tongue of flame to shoot up in the chimney.* THE WITCH *comes*
> *in riding down the flame, shrieking hideously.*]

THE WITCH   It hurts, it hurts!
Monkeys, apes, incompetent brutes!
Forgetting the pot and singeing your mistress—
The servants I have! Utterly useless!
> [*Catching sight of* FAUST *and* MEPHISTOPHELES.]
> What's this? What's this?   2275
> Who are you? Explain!
> What's your business?
> Got in by chicane!
> Hellfires parch and make
> Your bones crack, your bones break!   2280
> [*She plunges the spoon into the cauldron and scatters fire*
> *over* FAUST, MEPHISTOPHELES *and the* APES. *The apes whine.*]

MEPHISTO [*Turning the duster upside down and hitting out*
violently among the glasses and jars with the butt end.]
> In pieces, in pieces,
> Spilt soup and smashed dishes!

It's all in fun, really—
Beating time, you old carcass,
To your melody.   2285
    [THE WITCH *starts back in rage and fear.*]
Can't recognize me, rattlebones, old donkey, you?
Can't recognize your lord and master?
Why I don't chop up you and your monkey crew
Into the littlest bits and pieces is a wonder!
No respect at all for my red doublet?   2290
And my cock's feather means nothing to you, beldam?
Is my face masked, or can you plainly see it?
Must I tell *you* of all people who I am?
THE WITCH   Oh sir, forgive my discourteous salute!
But I look in vain for your cloven foot,   2295
And your two ravens, where are they?
MEPHISTO   All right, this time you're let off—I remember,
It's been so long since we've seen each other.
Also, the world's grown so cultured today,
Even the Devil's been swept up in it.   2300
The northern bogey has made his departure,
No horns now, no tail, to make people shiver,
And as for my hoof, though I can't do without it,
Socially it would raise too many eyebrows,
So like a lot of other young fellows   2305
I've padded my calves to try and conceal it.
THE WITCH [*Dancing with glee.*]
I'm out of my mind with delight, I swear!
My lord Satan's dropped out of the air.
MEPHISTO   Woman, that name—I forbid you to use it.
THE WITCH   Why not? Whyever now refuse it?   2310
MEPHISTO   Since God knows when, it belongs to mythology,
But that's hardly improved the morals of humanity.
The Evil One's no more, evil ones more than ever.
Address me as Baron, that will do,
A gentleman of rank like any other.   2315
And if you doubt my blood is blue,
See, here's my house's arms, the noblest ever!
    [*He makes an indecent gesture.*]
THE WITCH [*Laughing excessively.*]
Ha, ha! It's you, I see now, it's clear—
The same old rascal you always were!
MEPHISTO [*To* FAUST.]   Observe, friend, my diplomacy   2320
And learn the art of witch-mastery.
THE WITCH   Gentlemen, now what's your pleasure?
MEPHISTO   A generous glass of your famous liquor.
But please, let it be from your oldest supply;
It doubles in strength as the years multiply.   2325
THE WITCH   At once! Here I've got, as it happens, a bottle
From which I myself every now and then tipple,

And what is more, it's lost all its stink.
   I'll gladly pour you out a cup.
      [*Under her breath.*]
  But if the fellow's unprepared, the drink   2330
  Might kill him, you know, before an hour's up.
MEPHISTO   I know the man well, he'll thrive upon it.
  I wish him the best your kitchen affords.
  Now draw your circle, say the words,
  And pour him out a brimming goblet.   2335
      [*Making bizarre gestures,* THE WITCH *draws a circle and sets*
      down an assortment of strange objects inside it. All the glasses
      start to ring and the pots to resound, providing a kind of musical
      accompaniment. Last of all, she brings out a great tome and
      stands the APES *in the circle to serve as a lectern and to hold up*
      the torches. Then she signals FAUST *to approach.*]
FAUST [*To* MEPHISTOPHELES.]
  What's to be hoped for from this, would you tell me?
  That junk of hers, her waving her arms crazily,
  All the vulgar tricks she is performing,
  Well do I know them, don't find them amusing.
MEPHISTO   Jokes, just jokes! It's not all that serious;   2340
  Really, you're being much too difficult.
  Of course hocus-pocus, she's a sorceress—
  How else can her potion produce a result?
      [*He presses* FAUST *inside the circle.*]
THE WITCH [*Declaiming from the book, with great emphasis.*]
    Listen and learn!
    From one make ten,   2345
    And let two go,
    And add three in,
    And you are rich.
    Now cancel four!
    From five and six,   2350
    So says the witch,
    Make seven and eight—
    Thus all's complete.
    And nine is one,
    And ten is none,   2355
    And that's the witch's one-times-one.
FAUST   I think the old woman's throwing a fit.
MEPHISTO   We're nowhere near the end of it.
  I know the book, it's all like that.
  The time I've wasted over it!   2360
  For a thoroughgoing paradox is what
  Bemuses fools and wise men equally.
  The trick's old as the hills yet it's still going strong:
  With Three-in-One and One-in-Three[6]

---

6. The Christian doctrine of the Trinity.

Lies are sown broadcast, truth may go hang. 2365
Who questions professors about the claptrap they teach—
Who wants to debate and dispute with a fool?
People dutifully think, hearing floods of fine speech,
It can't be such big words mean nothing at all.

THE WITCH [*Continuing.*]
    The power of science 2370
    From the whole world kept hidden!
    Who don't have a thought,
    To them it is given
    Unbidden, unsought,
    It's theirs without sweat. 2375

FAUST   Did you hear that, my God, what nonsense,
It's giving me a headache, phew!
It makes me think I'm listening to
A hundred thousand fools in chorus.

MEPHISTO   Enough, enough, O excellent Sibyl! 2380
Bring on the potion, fill the stoup,
Your drink won't give my friend here trouble,
He's earned his Ph.D. in many a bout.
    [THE WITCH *very ceremoniously pours the potion into a bowl;*
    when FAUST *raises it to his lips, a low flame plays over it.*]
Drink, now drink, no need to diddle,
It'll put you into a fine glow. 2385
When you've got a sidekick in the Devil,
Why should some fire frighten you so?
    [THE WITCH *breaks the circle and* FAUST *steps out.*]
Now let's be off, you mustn't dally.

THE WITCH   I hope that little nip, sir, hits the spot!

MEPHISTO [*To* THE WITCH.]   Madam, thanks. If I can help *you* out, 2390
Don't fail, upon Walpurgis Night,[7] to ask me.

THE WITCH [*To* FAUST.]   Here is a song, sir, carol it now and then,
You'll find it assists the medicine.

MEPHISTO   Come away quick! You must do as I say.
To soak up the potion body and soul, 2395
A man's got to sweat a bucketful.
And after, I'll teach you the gentleman's way
Of wasting your time expensively.
Soon yours the delight outdelights all things—
Boy Cupid astir in you, stretching his wings. 2400

FAUST   One more look in the mirror, let me—
That woman was inexpressibly lovely!

MEPHISTO   No, no, soon enough, before you, vis-à-vis,
    Yours the fairest of fair women, I guarantee.
    [*Aside.*] With that stuff in him, old Jack will 2405
    Soon see a Helen in every Jill.

---

7. May Day Eve (April 30), when witches are supposed to assemble on the Brocken, the highest
peak in the Harz Mountains, which are in central Germany.

A STREET

FAUST. MARGARETE *passing by.*

FAUST   Pretty lady, here is my arm—
    Would you allow me to see you home?
MARGARETE   I'm neither pretty nor a lady,
    And I can find my way unaided.   2410
          [*She escapes his arm and passes by.*]
FAUST   By God, what a lovely girl,
    I've never seen her like, a pearl!
    A good girl, too, and quick-witted,
    Her behavior modest and yet spirited,
    Those red, ripe lips and cheeks abloom   2415
    Will haunt me till the crack of doom!
    The way she looked down, so demure,
    Had for me such allure!
    And bringing me up short, quite speechless—
    Oh that was charming, that was priceless!   2420
          [*Enter* MEPHISTOPHELES.]
FAUST   Get me that girl, do you hear, you must!
MEPHISTO   What girl?
FAUST   The one who just went past.
MEPHISTO   Oh, her. She's just been to confession
    To be absolved of all her sins.
    I sidled near the box to listen: 2425
    She could have spared herself her pains,
    She is the soul of innocence
    And has no reason, none at all,
    To visit the confessional.
    Her kind is too much for me.   2430
FAUST   She's over fourteen, isn't she?
MEPHISTO   Well, listen to him, an instant Don Juan,[8]
    Demands every favor, his shyness all gone,
    Conceitedly thinks it offends his honor
    To leave unplucked every pretty flower.   2435
    But it doesn't go so easy always.
FAUST   Dear Doctor of What's Right and Proper,
    Spare me your lectures, I can do without.
    Let me tell you it straight out:
    If I don't hold that darling creature   2440
    Tight in my arms this very night,
    We're through, we two, come twelve midnight.
MEPHISTO   Impossible! That's out of the question!
    I must have two weeks at least
    To spy out a propitious occasion.   2445

---

8. The German reads *Hans Liederlich*, meaning a profligate because *liederlich* means "careless" or "dissolute."

FAUST   With several hours or so, at the most,
   I could seduce her handily—
   Don't need the Devil to pimp for me.
MEPHISTO   You're talking like a Frenchman now.
   Calm down, there's no cause for vexation.   2450
   You'll find that instant gratification
   Disappoints; if you allow
   For compliments and billets doux,
   Whisperings and rendezvous,
   The pleasure's felt so much more keenly.   2455
   Italian novels teach you exactly.
FAUST   I've no use for your slow-paced courting;
   My appetite needs no supporting.
MEPHISTO   Please, I'm being serious.
   With such a pretty little miss   2460
   You mustn't be impetuous
   And assault the fortress frontally.
   What's called for here is strategy.
FAUST   Something of hers, do you hear, I require!
   Come, show me the way to the room she sleeps in,   2465
   Get me a scarf, a glove, a ribbon,
   A garter with which to feed my desire!
MEPHISTO   To prove to you my earnest intention
   By every means to further your passion,
   Not losing a minute, without delay,   2470
   I'll take you to her room today.
FAUST   I'll see her, yes? And have her?
MEPHISTO   No!
   She'll be at a neighbor's—you *must* go slow!
   Meanwhile alone there, in her room,
   You can breathe in her own person's perfume   2475
   And dream of the delights to come.
FAUST   Can we start now?
MEPHISTO   Too soon! Be patient!
FAUST   Then find me a pretty thing for a present.

                                 [*Exit.*]

MEPHISTO   Presents already? The man's proving a lover!
   Now for his gift. I know there's treasure   2480
   Buried in many an out-of-the-way corner.
   Off I go to reconnoiter!

EVENING

A small room, very neat and clean.

MARGARETE [*As she braids her hair and puts it up.*]
   I'd give a lot to know, I would.
   Who the gentleman was today.
   He seemed a fine man, decent, good,   2485

And from a noble house, I'm sure;
It shows on him as plain as day.
And so bold! Who else would dare?

        [Exit.]

    [MEPHISTOPHELES, FAUST.]

MEPHISTO   Come in now, in!—but take care, softly.

FAUST *[After a silent interval.]*   Leave, please leave, I'd like
   to be alone.   2490

MEPHISTO *[Sniffing around.]*   Not every girl keeps things so clean.

        [Exit.]

FAUST   Welcome, evening's twilight gloom,
  Stealing through this holy room.
  Possess my heart, O love's sweet anguish,
  That lives in hope, in hope must languish   2495
  Stillness reigns here, breathing quietly
  Peace, good order and contentment—
  What riches in this poverty,
  What bliss there is in this confinement!

      [He flings himself into a leather armchair by the bed.]

  Receive me as in generations past   2500
  You received the happy and distressed;
  How often, I know, children crowded around
  This chair where their grandfather sat enthroned.
  Perhaps my darling too, a round-cheeked child,
  Grateful for her Christmas present, held   2505
  Reverentially his shrunken hand.
  I feel, dear girl, where you are all is comfort,
  Where you are order, goodness all abound;
  Maternally instructed by your spirit,
  Daily you spread the clean cloth on the table,   2510
  Sprinkle the sand on the floor so evenly[9]—
  O lovely hand! Hand of a lovely angel
  That's made of this cottage something heavenly.
  And here—!

      [He lifts a bed curtain.]

             Why am I seized with awe-struck bliss?
  Here I could linger hour after hour.   2515
  Nature! Shaping here in dreaming peace
  The indwelling angel out of the budding creature.
  Here warm life in her tender bosom swelled,
  Here by a pure and holy weaving
  Of the strands, was revealed   2520
  The celestial being.

  But me? What is it brought me here?
  See how shaken I am, how nervous!
  What do I want? Why is my heart so anxious?
  Poor Faust, I hardly know you any more.   2525

---

9. Floors were sprinkled with sand after cleaning.

Has this room put a spell on me?
I came here burning up with lust,
And melt with love now, helplessly.
Are we blown about by every gust?

And if she came in now, this minute,   2530
How I would pay dear, I would, for it.
The big talker, Herr Professor,
Would dwindle to nothing, grovel before her.

MEPHISTO [*Entering.*]   Hurry! I saw her, she's coming up.

FAUST   Hurry indeed, I'll never come here again!   2535

MEPHISTO   Here's a jewel box I snatched up
When I—but who cares how or when.
Put it in the closet there,
She'll jump for joy when she comes on it.
It's got a number of choice things in it,   2540
Meant for another—but I declare,
Girls are girls, they're all the same,
The only thing that matters is the game.

FAUST   Should I, I wonder?

MEPHISTO   *Should* you, you say!   2545
Do you mean to keep it for yourself?
If what you're after's treasure, pelf,
Then I have wasted my whole day,
Been put to a lot of needless bother.
I hope you aren't some awful miser—
After all my head-scratching, scheming, labor!   2550
        [*He puts the box in the closet and shuts it.*]
Come on, let's go!
Our aim? Your darling's favor,
So you may do with her as you'd like to do.
And you do what?—only gape,
As if going into your lecture hall,   2555
There before you in human shape
Stood physics and metaphysics, old and stale.
                                                    [*Exit.*]

MARGARETE [*With a lamp.*]   How close, oppressive it's in here.
        [*She opens the window.*]
And yet outside it isn't warm.
I feel, I don't know why, so queer—   2560
I wish Mother would come home.
I shivering so in every limb.
What a foolish, frightened girl I am!
        [*She sings as she undresses.*]
There was a king in Thule,[1]

---

1. The fabled *ultima Thule* of Latin literature—those distant lands just beyond the reach of every explorer. Goethe wrote the ballad in 1774; it was published in 1782 and set to music by several composers.

No truer man drank up, 2565
To whom his mistress, dying,
Gave a golden cup.

Nothing he held dearer.
Amid the feasting's noise
Each time he drained the beaker 2570
Tears started in his eyes.

And when death knocked, he tallied
His towns and treasure up,
Yielded his heirs all gladly,
All except the cup. 2575

In the great hall of his fathers,
In the castle by the sea,
He and his knights sat down to
Their last revelry.

Up stood the old carouser, 2580
A last time knew wine's warmth,
Then pitched his beloved beaker
Down into the gulf.

He saw it fall and founder,
Deep in the sea it sank, 2585
His eyes grew dim and never
Another drop he drank.
[*She opens the closet to put her clothes away and sees the jewel box.*]
How did this pretty box get here?
I locked the closet, I'm quite sure.
Whatever's in the box? Maybe 2590
Mother took it in pledge today.
And there's the little key on a ribbon.
I think I'd like to open it.
—Look at all this, God in Heaven!
I've never seen the like of it! 2595
Jewels! And *such* jewels, that a fine lady
Might wear on a great holiday.
How would the necklace look on me?
Who is it owns these wonderful things?
[*She puts the jewelry on and stands in front of the mirror.*]
I wish they were mine, these lovely earrings! 2600
When you put them on, you're changed completely.
What good's your pretty face, your youth?
Nice to have but little worth.
Men praise you, do it half in pity,
The thing on their mind is money, money. 2605
Gold is their god, all,
Oh us poor people!

OUT WALKING

FAUST *strolling up and down, thinking. To him* MEPHISTOPHELES.

MEPHISTO   By true love cruelly scorned! By Hellfire fierce and fiery!
  If only I could think of worse to swear by!
FAUST   What's eating you, now what's the trouble?   2610
  Such a face I've not seen till today.
MEPHISTO   The Devil take me, that's what I would say,
  If it didn't so happen I'm the Devil.
FAUST   Are you in your right mind—behaving
  Like a madman, wildly raving?   2615
MEPHISTO   The jewels I got for Gretchen,[2] just imagine—
  Every piece a damned priest's stolen!
  The minute her mother saw them, she
  Began to tremble fearfully.
  The woman has a nose! It's stuck   2620
  Forever in her prayerbook;
  She knows right off, by the smell alone,
  If something's sacred or profane;
  One whiff of the jewelry was enough
  To tell her something's wrong with the stuff.   2625
  My child—she cried—and listen well to me,
  All property obtained unlawfully
  Does body and soul a mortal injury.
  These jewels we'll consecrate to the Blessed Virgin,
  And for reward have showers of manna from Heaven.   2630
  Our little Margaret pouted, loath—
  Why look a gift horse[3] in the mouth?
  And surely the one who gave her it
  So generously, was hardly wicked.
  Her mother sent for the priest, and he,   2635
  Seeing how the land lay,
  Was mightily pleased. You've done, he said,
  Just as you should, mother and maid.
  Who overcometh, is repaid.
  The Church's stomach's very capacious,   2640
  Gobbles up whole realms, everything precious,
  Nor once suffers qualms, not even belches.
  The Church alone, dear sister, God has named
  Receiver of goods unlawfully obtained.
FAUST   That's the way the whole world over,   2645
  From a king to a Jew, so all do, ever.
MEPHISTO   So then he pockets brooches, chains and rings
  As if they were quite ordinary things,

---

2. Diminutive of the German *Margarete*. She is given this name through much of the play.
3. Like the wooden horse in which Greek sol- diers entered Troy to capture it; an emblem of potential treachery.

And gives the women as much of a thank-you
As a body gets for a mouldy potato,   2650
In Heaven, he says, you'll be compensated—
And makes off leaving them feeling elevated.
FAUST   And Gretchen?
MEPHISTO   Sits there restlessly,
Her mind confused, her will uncertain,
Thinks about jewels night and day,   2655
Even more about her unknown patron.
FAUST   I can't bear that she should suffer.
Find her new ones immediately!
Poor stuff, those others, hardly suit her.
MEPHISTO   Oh yes indeed! With a snap of the fingers!   2660
FAUST   Do what I say, march, man—how he lingers!
Insinuate yourself with her neighbor!
Damn it, devil, you move so sluggishly!
Fetch Gretchen new and better jewelry!
MEPHISTO   Yes, yes, just as you wish, Your Majesty.   2665

[*Exit* FAUST.]

A lovesick fool! To amuse his girl he'd blow up
Sun, moon, stars, the whole damn shop.

THE NEIGHBOR'S HOUSE

MARTHE [*Alone.*]   May God forgive that man of mine,
He's done me wrong—disappeared
Into the night without a word   2670
And left me here to sleep alone.
I never gave him cause for grief
But loved him as a faithful wife.
    [*She weeps.*]
Suppose he's dead—oh I feel hopeless!
If only I had an official notice.   2675
    [*Enter* MARGARETE.]
MARGARETE   Frau Marthe!
MARTHE   Gretel, what's wrong, tell me!
MARGARETE   I feel so weak I'm near collapse!
Just now I found another box
Inside my closet. Ebony,
And such things in it, much more splendid   2680
Than the first ones, I'm dumbfounded!
MARTHE   Never a word to your mother about it,
Or the priest will have all the next minute.
MARGARETE   Just look at this, and this, and this here!
MARTHE [*Decking her out in the jewels.*]
Oh, what a lucky girl you are!   2685
MARGARETE   But I mustn't be seen in the streets with such jewelry,
And never in church. Oh, it's too cruel!
MARTHE   Come over to me whenever you're able,

Here you can wear them without worry,
March back and forth in front of the mirror— 2690
Won't we enjoy ourselves together!
And when it's a holiday, some such occasion,
You can start wearing them, with discretion.
First a necklace, then a pearl earring,
Your mother'll never notice a thing. 2695
And if she does we'll think of something.

MARGARETE Who put the jewelry in my closet?
There's something that's not right about it.
        [A knock.]
Dear God above, can that be Mother?

MARTHE [Peeping through the curtain.]
Please come in!—No, it's a stranger. 2700
        [Enter MEPHISTOPHELES.]

MEPHISTO With your permission, my good women!
I beg you to excuse the intrusion.
        [Steps back deferentially from MARGARETE.]
I'm looking for Frau Marthe Schwerdtlein.

MARTHE I'm her. And what have you to say, sir?

MEPHISTO [Under his breath to her.]
Now I know who you are, that's enough. 2705
You have a lady under your roof,
I'll go away and come back later.

MARTHE [Aloud.] Goodness, child, you won't believe me,
What the gentleman thinks is, you're a lady!

MARGARETE A poor girl's what I am, no more. 2710
The gentleman's kind—I thank you, sir.
These jewels don't belong to me.

MEPHISTO Ah, it's not just the jewelry,
It's the Fräulein herself, so clear-eyed, serene.
—So delighted I'm allowed to remain. 2715

MARTHE Why are you here, if you'll pardon the question?

MEPHISTO I wish my news were pleasanter.
Don't blame me, the messenger:
Your husband's dead. He sent his affection.

MARTHE The good man's dead, gone, departed? 2720
Then I'll die too. Oh, I'm broken-hearted!

MARGARETE Marthe dear, it's too violent, your sorrow!

MEPHISTO Hear the sad story I've come to tell you.

MARGARETE As long as I live I'll never love, no,
It would kill me with grief to lose my man so. 2725

MEPHISTO Joy's latter end is sorrow—and sorrow's joy.

MARTHE Tell me how the dear man died.

MEPHISTO He's buried in Padua, beside
The blessed saint, sweet Anthony,
In hallowed ground where he can lie 2730
In rest eternal, quietly.

MARTHE And nothing else, sir, that is all?

MEPHISTO   A last request. He enjoins you solemnly:
Let three hundred masses be sung for his soul!
As for anything else, my pocket's empty.   2735
MARTHE   What! No gold coin, jewel, souvenir,
Such as every journeyman keeps in his wallet,
And would sooner go hungry and beg than sell it?
MEPHISTO   Nothing, I'm sorry to say, Madam dear.
However—he never squandered his money,   2740
And he sincerely regretted his sins,
Regretted even more he was so unlucky.
MARGARETE   Why must so many be so unhappy!
I'll pray for him often, sing requiems.
MEPHISTO   What a lovable creature, there's none dearer!   2745
What you should have now, right away,
Is a good husband. It's true what I say.
MARGARETE   Oh no, it's not time yet, that must come later.
MEPHISTO   If not now a husband, meanwhile a lover.
What blessing from Heaven, which one of life's charms   2750
Rivals holding a dear thing like you in one's arms.
MARGARETE   With us people here it isn't the custom.
MEPHISTO   Custom or not, it's what's done and by more than some.
MARTHE   Go on with your story, sir, go on!
MEPHISTO   He lay on a bed of half-rotten straw,   2755
Better at least than a dunghill, and there
He died as a Christian, knowing well
Much remained outstanding on his bill.
"Oh how," he cried, "I hate myself!
To abandon my trade, desert my wife!   2760
It kills me even to think of it.
If only she would forgive and forget!"
MARTHE [Weeping.]   I did, long ago! He's forgiven, dear man.
MEPHISTO   "But she's more to blame, God knows, than I am."
MARTHE   Liar! How shameless! At death's very door!   2765
MEPHISTO   His mind wandered as the end drew near,
If I'm anything of a connoisseur here.
"No pleasure," he said, "no good times, nor anything nice;
First getting children, then getting them fed,
By fed meaning lots more things than bread.   2770
With never a moment for having my bite in peace."
MARTHE   How could he forget my love and loyalty,
My hard work day and night, the drudgery!
MEPHISTO   He didn't forget, he remembered all tenderly.
"When we set sail from Malta's port," he said,   2775
"For wife and children fervently I prayed.
And Heaven, hearing, smiled down kindly,
For we captured a Turkish vessel, stuffed
With the Sultan's treasure. How we rejoiced!
Our courage being recompensed,   2780
I left the ship with a fatter purse
Than ever I'd owned before in my life."

MARTHE   Treasure! Do you think he buried it?

MEPHISTO   Who knows what's become of it?

  In Naples, where he wandered about,   2785

  A pretty miss with a kind heart

  Showed the stranger such good will

  Till the day he died he felt it still.

MARTHE   The villain! Robbing his children, his wife!

  And for all his misery, dire need,   2790

  He would never give up his scandalous life.

MEPHISTO   Well, he's been paid, the man is dead.

  If I were in your shoes, my dear,

  I'd mourn him decently a year

  And meanwhile keep an eye out for another.   2795

MARTHE   Dear God, I'm sure it won't be easy

  To find, on this earth, his successor;

  So full of jokes he was, so jolly!

  But he was restless, always straying,

  Loved foreign women, foreign wine,   2800

  And how he loved, drat him, dice-playing!

MEPHISTO   Oh well, I'm sure things worked out fine

  If he was equally forgiving.

  With such an arrangement, why, I swear

  I'd marry you myself, my dear!   2805

MARTHE   Oh sir, you would? You're joking, I'm sure!

MEPHISTO [*Aside.*]   Time to leave! This one's an ogress,

  She'd sue the Devil for breach of promise!

      [*To* GRETCHEN.]

  And what's your love life like, my charmer?

MARGARETE   What do you mean?   2810

MEPHISTO [*Aside.*]   Oh you good girl,

  All innocence! [*Aloud.*] And now farewell.

MARGARETE   Farewell.

MARTHE   Quick, one last matter,

  If you would. I want to know

  If I might have some proof to show

  How and when my husband died   2815

  And where the poor man now is laid?

  I like to have things right and proper,

  With a notice published in the paper.

MEPHISTO   Madam, yes. To attest the truth,

  Two witnesses must swear an oath.   2820

  I know someone, a good man; we

  Will go before the notary.

  I'll introduce you to him.

MARTHE   Do.

MEPHISTO   And she'll be here, your young friend, too?—

  A very fine fellow who's been all over,   2825

  So polite to ladies, so urbane his behavior.

MARGARETE   I'd blush for shame before the gentleman.

MEPHISTO   No, not before a king or any man!

MARTHE   We'll wait for you tonight, the two of us,
    Inside my garden, just behind the house.   2830

A STREET

FAUST, MEPHISTOPHELES.

FAUST   Well? What's doing? When am I going to have her?
MEPHISTO   Bravo, bravo, I can see you're all on fire.
    Very shortly Gretchen will be all yours.
    This evening you will meet her at her neighbor's.
    The worthy Mistress Marthe, I confess,   2835
    Needs no instruction as a procuress.
FAUST   Good work.
MEPHISTO   There's something we must do for her, however.
FAUST   One good turn deserves another.
MEPHISTO   All it is is swear an oath
    Her husband's buried in the earth,   2840
    At Padua in consecrated ground.
FAUST   So we must make a trip there—very smart!
MEPHISTO   *Sancta simplicitas!*[4] Whoever said that?
    Just swear an oath. What's wrong? You frowned.
FAUST   If that's the best you're able, count me out.   2845
MEPHISTO   The saintly fellow! Turned devout!
    Declaring falsely—Heaven forbid!—
    Is something Faustus never did.
    Haven't you pontificated
    About God and the world, undisconcerted,   2850
    About man, man's mind and heart and being,
    As bold as brass, without blushing?
    Look at it closely and what's the truth?
    You know as much about those things
    As you know about Herr Schwerdtlein's death.   2855
FAUST   You always were a sophist and a liar.
MEPHISTO   Indeed, indeed. If we look ahead a little further,
    To tomorrow, what do we see?
    You swearing, oh so honorably,
    Your soul is Gretchen's—cajoling and deceiving her.   2860
FAUST   My soul, and all my heart as well.
MEPHISTO   Oh wonderful!
    You'll swear undying faith and love eternal,
    Go on about desire unique and irresistible,
    About longing, boundless, infinite:
    That, too, with all your heart—I'll bet!   2865
FAUST   With all my heart! And now enough.
    What I feel, an emotion of such depth,
    Such turbulence—when I try to find

---

4. Holy simplicity (Latin).

A name for it and nothing comes to mind,
And cast about, search heaven and earth   2870
For words to express its transcendent worth,
And call the fire in which I burn
Eternal, yes, eternal, yes, undying!
Do you really mean to tell me
That's just devil's doing, deception, lying?   2875

MEPHISTO   Say what you please, I'm right.

FAUST   One word more, one only,
And then I'll save my breath. A man who is unyielding,
Sure, absolutely, he's right, and has a tongue in his mouth—
Is right. So come, I'm sick of arguing.
You're right, and the reason's simple enough: 2880
I must do what I must, can't help myself.

A GARDEN

MARGARETE *with* FAUST, *her arm linked with his;* MARTHE *with*
MEPHISTOPHELES. *The two couples stroll up and down.*

MARGARETE   You are too kind, sir, I am sure it's meant
To spare a simple girl embarrassment.
A traveler finds whatever amusement he can,
You've been all over, you're a gentleman—   2885
How can anything I say
Interest you in any way?

FAUST   To me one word of yours, a loving look
'S worth all the wisdom in the great world's book.
        [*He kisses her hand.*]

MARGARETE   No, no, sir, please, you mustn't! How could you kiss   2890
A hand so ugly—red and coarse?
You can't imagine all the work I do;
My mother must have things just so.
        [*They walk on.*]

MARTHE   And you, sir, I believe, you constantly travel?

MEPHISTO   Business, business! It is so demanding!   2895
Leaving a place you like can be so painful,
Duty's duty, its voice strict, commanding.

MARTHE   How fine when young and full of ginger,
To travel the world, see all that's doing.
But with the years worse times arrive and worser,   2900
And find me, just do, someone somewhere choosing
To crawl to his grave a lonely bachelor.

MEPHISTO   When I look at what's ahead, I tremble.

MARTHE   Then, sir, bethink yourself while you're still able.
        [*They walk on.*]

MARGARETE   Yes, out of sight is out of mind.   2905
It's second nature with you, gallantry;
But you have heaps of friends of every kind

    Cleverer by far, oh much, than me.
FAUST   Dear girl, believe me, what's called cleverness
    Is mostly shallowness and vanity.   2910
MARGARETE   What do you mean?
FAUST   God, isn't it a pity
    That unspoiled innocence and simpleness
    Should never know itself and its own worth,
    That meekness, lowliness, those highest gifts
    Kindly Nature endows us with—   2915
MARGARETE   You'll think of me for a moment or two,
    I'll have hours enough to think of you.
FAUST   You're alone a good deal, are you?
MARGARETE   Our family's very small, it's true,
    But still it has to be looked to.   2920
    We have no maid, I sweep the floors, I cook and knit
    And sew, do all the errands, morning and night.
    Mother's very careful about money,
    All's accounted for to the last penny.
    Not that she really needs to pinch and save;   2925
    We could afford much more than others have.
    My father left us a good bit,
    With a small dwelling added to it,
    And a garden just outside the city.
    But lately I've lived quietly.   2930
    My brother is a soldier. My little sister died.
    The trouble that she cost me, the poor child!
    But I loved her very much, I'd gladly do
    It all again.
FAUST   An angel, if at all like you.
MARGARETE   All the care of her was mine,   2935
    And she was very fond of her sister.
    My father died before she was born,
    And Mother, well, we nearly lost her;
    It took so long, oh many months, till she got better.
    It was out of the question she should nurse   2940
    The poor little crying thing herself,
    So I nursed her, on milk and water,
    I felt she was my own daughter.
    In my arms, upon my lap,
    She smiled and kicked, grew round and plump.   2945
FAUST   The happiness it must have given you!
MARGARETE   But it was hard on me so often, too.
    Her crib stood at my bedside, near my head,
    A slightest movement, cradle's creak,
    And instantly I was awake;   2950
    I'd give her a bottle, or take her into my bed.
    If still she fretted, up I'd raise,
    Walk up and down with her, swaying and crooning,
    And be at the washtub early the next morning;

To market after that, and getting the hearth to blaze, 2955
And so it went, day after day, always.
Home's not always cheerful, be it said;
But still—how good your supper, good your bed.
　　　[*They walk on.*]

MARTHE　It's very hard on us poor women,
　　You bachelors don't listen, you're so stubborn! 2960
MEPHISTO　What's needed are more charmers like yourself
　　To bring us bachelors down from off the shelf.
MARTHE　There's never, sir, been anyone? Confess!
　　You've never lost your heart to one of us?
MEPHISTO　How does the proverb go? A loving wife, 2965
　　And one's own hearthside, are more worth
　　Than all the gold that's hidden in the earth.
MARTHE　I mean, you've had no wish, yourself?
MEPHISTO　Oh, everywhere I've been received politely.
MARTHE　No, what I mean is, hasn't there been somebody 2970
　　Who ever made your heart beat? Seriously?
MEPHISTO　It's never a joking matter with women, believe me.
MARTHE　Oh, you don't understand!
MEPHISTO　　　　　　　　　　So sorry! Still,
　　I can see that you are—amiable.
　　　[*They walk on.*]
FAUST　You recognized me, angel, instantly 2975
　　When I came through the gate into the garden?
MARGARETE　I dropped my eyes. Didn't you see?
FAUST　And you'll forgive the liberty, you'll pardon
　　My swaggering up in that insulting fashion
　　When you came out of the church door? 2980
MARGARETE　I was shocked. Never before
　　Had I been spoken to like that.
　　I'm a good girl. Who would dare
　　To be so free with me, so smart?
　　It seemed to me at once you thought 2985
　　There's a girl who can be bought
　　On the spot. Did I look a flirt?
　　Is that so, tell! Well, I'll admit
　　A voice spoke "Isn't he nice?" in my breast,
　　And oh how vexed with myself I felt 2990
　　That I wasn't vexed with you in the least.
FAUST　Dear girl!
MARGARETE　　　　　Just wait.
　　　[*Picking a daisy and plucking the petals one by one.*]
FAUST　　　　　　　　　What is it for, a bouquet?
MARGARETE　Only a little game of ours.
FAUST　　　　　　　　　　　A game, is it?
MARGARETE　Never mind. I'm afraid you'll laugh at me.
　　　[*Murmuring to herself as she plucks the petals.*]
FAUST　What are you saying? 2995

MARGARETE [*Under her breath.*]
                              Loves me—loves me not—
FAUST   Oh, what a creature, heavenly!
MARGARETE [*Continuing.*]   He loves me—not—he loves me—not—
    [*Plucking the last petal and crying out delightedly.*]
    He loves me!
FAUST   Dearest, yes! Yes, let the flower be
    The oracle by which the truth is said.
    He loves you! Do you understand?   3000
    He loves you! Let me take your hand.
        [*He takes her hands in his.*]
MARGARETE   I'm afraid!
FAUST   No, no, never! Read the look
    On my face, feel my hands gripping yours—
    They tell you what's impossible   3005
    Ever to put in words:
    Utter surrender, and such rapture
    As must never end, must last forever!
    Yes, forever! An end—it would betoken
    Utter despair, a heart forever broken!   3010
    No—no end! No end!
        [MARGARETE *squeezes his hands, frees herself and runs away.*
        He doesn't move for a moment, thinking, then follows her.]
MARTHE   It's getting dark.
MEPHISTO   That's right. We have to go.
MARTHE   Please forgive me if I don't invite
    You in. But ours is such a nasty-minded street,
    You'd think people had no more to do   3015
    Than watch their neighbors' every coming and going.
    The gossip that goes on here, about nothing!
    But where are they, our little couple?
MEPHISTO   Flew
    Up that path like butterflies.
MARTHE   He seems to like her.
MEPHISTO   And she him. Which is the way the world wags ever. 3020

                    A SUMMERHOUSE

GRETCHEN *runs in and hides behind the door, putting her fingertips*
to her lips and peeping through a crack.
MARGARETE   Here he comes!
FAUST   You're teasing me, are you?
    I've got you now. [*Kisses her.*]
MARGARETE [*Holding him around and returning the kiss.*]
                              I love you, yes, I do!
        [MEPHISTOPHELES *knocks.*]
FAUST [*Stamping his foot.*]
    Who's there?
MEPHISTO   A friend.

FAUST   A fiend!

MEPHISTO   We must be on our way.

MARTHE [*Coming up.*]   Yes, sir, it's late.   3025

FAUST   I'd like to walk you home.

MARGARETE   My mother, I'm afraid. . . . Goodbye!

FAUST   So we must say

Goodbye? Goodbye!

MARGARETE   I hope I'll see you soon.

[*Exit* FAUST *and* MEPHISTOPHELES.]

Good God, the thoughts that fill the head
Of such a man, oh it's astounding!
I stand there dumbly, my face red,   3030
And stammer yes to everything.
I don't understand. What in the world
Does he see in me, an ignorant child?

A CAVERN IN THE FOREST

FAUST [*Alone.*]   Sublime Spirit, all that I asked for, all,
You gave me. Not for nothing was it,   3035
The face you showed me, all ablaze with fire.
You gave me glorious Nature for my kingdom.
With the power to feel, to delight in her—nor as
A spectator only, coolly admiring her wonders,
But letting me see deep into her bosom   3040
As a man sees deep into a dear friend's heart.
Before me you make pass all living things,
From high to low, and teach me how to know
My brother creatures in the silent woods, the streams, the air.
And when the shrieking storm winds make the forest   3045
Groan, toppling the giant fir whose fall
Bears nearby branches down with it and crushes
Neighboring trees so that the hill returns
A hollow thunder—oh, then you lead me to
The shelter of this cave, lay bare my being to myself,   3050
And all the mysteries hidden in my depths
Unfold themselves and open to the day.
And when I see the moon ascend the sky,
Shedding a pure, assuaging light, out
Of the walls of rock, the dripping bushes, float   3055
The silver figures of antiquity
And temper meditation's austere joy.

That nothing perfect's ever ours, oh but
I know it now. Together with the rapture
That I owe you, by which I am exalted   3060
Nearer and still nearer to the gods, you gave me
A familiar, a creature whom already
I can't do without, though he's a cold

And shameless devil who drags me down
In my own eyes and with a whispered word   3065
Makes all you granted me to be as nothing.
The longing that I feel for that enchanting
Figure of a girl, he busily blows up
Into a leaping flame. And so desire
Whips me, stumbling on, to seize enjoyment,   3070
And once enjoyed, I languish for desire.

      [*Enter* MEPHISTOPHELES.]

MEPHISTO   Aren't you fed up with it by now,
  This mooning about? How can it still
  Amuse you? You do it for a while,
  All right; but enough's enough, on to the new!   3075
FAUST   Why, when I'm feeling a bit better,
  Do you badger me with your insidious chatter?
MEPHISTO   A breather you want? Very well, I grant it.
  But don't speak so, as if you really meant it—
  I wouldn't shed tears, losing a companion   3080
  Who is so mad, so rude, so sullen.
  I have my hands full every minute—
  Impossible to tell what pleases you or doesn't.
FAUST   Why, that's just perfect, isn't it?
  He bores me stiff and wants praise for it.   3085
MEPHISTO   You poor earthly creature, would
  You ever have managed at all without me?
  Whom do you have to thank for being cured
  Of your mad ideas, your feverish frenzy?
  If not for me you would have disappeared   3090
  From off the face of earth already.
  What kind of life do you call it, dully fretting
  Owl-like in caves, or toad-like feeding
  On oozing moss and dripping stone?
  That's a way to spend your time? Go on!   3095
  You're still living in your head—I have to say so;
  Only the old Dr. Faust would carry on so.
FAUST   Try to understand: my life's renewed
  When I wander, musing, in wild Nature.
  But even if you could, I know you would   3100
  Begrudge me, Devil that you are, my rapture.
MEPHISTO   Your superterrestrial joys! So spiritual!
  To sprawl on a hillside at night in the damp dewfall,
  Clasping heaven and earth blissfully to your bosom,
  Swelling up godlike in your enthusiasm,   3105
  Driven by vague intimations, delving
  Down to the bottommost depths of the earth;
  Feeling each day of Creation unfolding,
  All six at once, inside yourself,
  Arrogantly elated, by what I can't imagine.   3110
  And having ceased to be a mortal being,
  Ecstatically immerged with everything existing.

And your conclusion from such exalted insight?—
    [*Making a gesture.*]
I forbid myself to say, it's not polite.
FAUST   For shame! 3115
MEPHISTO   So that's not to your taste at all, sir?
You're right, "shame"'s right, the moral comment called for.
Never a word, when chaste ears are about,
Of what chaste hearts can't do without.
Oh well, go on, amuse yourself
By duping now and then yourself. 3120
Yet you can't keep on in this way much longer.
You look done in again, almost a goner.
And if you persist in this fashion,
You'll go mad with baffled passion.
Enough, I say! Your sweetheart sits down there 3125
And all's a dismal prison for her.
You haunt her mind continually,
She's mad about you, oh completely.
At first your passion, like a freshet,
Swollen with melted snow, overflowing 3130
Its peaceful banks, engulfed a soul unknowing.
But now the flood's thinned to a streamlet.
Instead of playing monarch of the wood,
My opinion is the Herr Professor
Should make the silly little creature 3135
Some return, in gratitude.
For her the hours creep along,
She stands at the window, watching the clouds
Pass slowly over the old town walls,
"Lend me, sweet bird, your wings," is the song 3140
She sings all day and half the night.
Sometimes she's cheerful, mostly she's downhearted,
Sometimes she cries as if brokenhearted,
Then she's calm again and seems all right,
And heart-sick always. 3145
FAUST   Serpent! Snake!
MEPHISTO [*Aside.*]   I'll have you yet!
FAUST   Away, you monster from some stinking fen!
Don't mention her, the soul itself of beauty,
Don't make my half-crazed senses crave again 3150
The sweetness of that lovely body!
MEPHISTO   Then what? She thinks you've taken flight,
And I must say, the girl's half right.
FAUST   Far off as I may wander, she's still near me,
She fills my thoughts both day and night, 3155
I even envy the Lord's body her warm kiss
Bestowed upon it at the Mass.[5]

5. When the bread of Communion miraculously turns to the body of Christ.

MEPHISTO   I understand. I've often envied *you*
    Her pair of roes that feed among the lilies.[6]
FAUST   Pimp, you! I won't hear your blasphemies!   3160
MEPHISTO   Fine! Insult me! And I laugh at you.
    The God that made you girls and boys
    Himself was first to recognize,
    And practice, what's the noblest calling,
    The furnishing of opportunities.   3165
    Away! A crying shame this, never linger!
    You act as if hard fate were dragging
    You to death, not to your true love's chamber.
FAUST   Heaven's out-heavened when she holds me tight,
    And though I'm warmed to life upon her breast,   3170
    Do I ever once forget her plight?
    A fugitive is what I am, a beast
    That's houseless, restless, purposeless,
    A furious, impatient cataract
    That plunges down from rock to rock to the abyss.   3175
    And she, her senses unawakened, a child still,
    Dwelt in her cottage on the Alpine meadow,
    Her life the same domestic ritual
    Within a little world where fell no shadow.
    And I, abhorred by God,   3180
    Was not content to batter
    Rocks to bits, I had
    To undermine her peace and overwhelm her!
    This sacrifice you claimed, Hell, as your due!
    Help me, Devil, please, to shorten   3185
    The anxious time I must go through!
    Let happen quick what has to happen!
    Let her fate fall on me, too, crushingly,
    And both together perish, her and me!
MEPHISTO   All worked up again, all in a sweat!   3190
    On your way, you fool, and comfort her.
    When blockheads think there's no way out,
    They give up instantly, they're done for.
    Long live the man who keeps on undeterred!
    I'd rate your progress as a devil pretty fair;   3195
    But tell me, what is there that's more absurd
    Than a moping devil, mewling in despair?

GRETCHEN'S ROOM

GRETCHEN [*Alone at her spinning wheel.*]
    My heart is heavy,
    My peace is gone,

---

6. Compare Song of Solomon 4.5: "Thy two breasts are like two young roes that are twins, which feed among the lilies."

I'll never know any   3200
Peace again.

For me it's death
Where he is not,
The whole green earth
All waste, all rot.   3205

My poor poor head
Is in a whirl,
I'm mad, for sure
A poor mad girl.

My heart is heavy,   3210
My peace is gone,
I'll never know any
Peace again.

I look out the window,
Walk out the door,   3215
Him, only him,
I look for.

His bold walk,
His princely person,
His look,
His eyes' persuasion,   3220

And his sweet speech—
Magicalness!
His fingers' touch,
And oh, his kiss!   3225

My heart is heavy,
My peace is gone,
I'll never know any
Peace again.

With aching breast   3230
I strain so toward him,
Oh if I just
Could catch and hold him,

And kiss and kiss him,
Never ceasing,   3235
Though I should die in
His arms kissing.

MARTHE'S GARDEN

MARGARETE, FAUST

MARGARETE   Heinrich,[7] the truth—I have to insist!
FAUST   As far as I'm able.
MARGARETE   Well, tell me, you must,
  About your religion—how do you feel?   3240
  You're such a good man, kind and intelligent,
  But I suspect you are indifferent.
FAUST   Enough of that, my child. You know quite well
  I cherish you so very dearly,
  For those I love I'd give my life up gladly,   3245
  And I never interfere with people's faith.
MARGARETE   That isn't right, you've got to have belief!
FAUST   You do?
MARGARETE   I know you think I am a dunce!
  You don't respect the sacraments.   3250
FAUST   I do respect them.
MARGARETE   Not enough to go to Mass.
  And tell me when you last went to confess?
  Do you believe in God?
FAUST   Who, my dear,
  Can say, I believe in God?
  Ask any priest or learned scholar   3255
  And what you get by way of answer
  Sounds like a joke, like words run wild.
MARGARETE   So you don't believe in him?
FAUST   Don't misunderstand me, lovely child.
  Who dares name him,   3260
  Dares affirm him,
  Declares I believe?
  And who, feeling doubt,
  Ventures to say right out,
  I don't believe?   3265
  The All-embracing,
  All-sustaining
  Sustains and embraces
  Himself and you and me.
  Overhead the great sky arches,   3270
  Firm lies the earth beneath our feet,
  And the friendly shining stars, don't they
  Mount aloft eternally?
  Don't my eyes, seeking your eyes, meet?
  And all that is, doesn't it weigh   3275
  On your mind and heart,
  In eternal secrecy working,
  Visibly, invisibly about you?

---

7. That is, Faust. In the legend, Faust's name was generally Johann (John). Goethe changed it to Heinrich (Henry).

Fill heart with it to overflowing
In an ecstasy of blissful feeling,   3280
Which then call what you would:
Happiness! Heart! Love! Call it God!—
I know no name for it, seek
For none. Feeling is all,
Names noise and smoke   3285
Dimming the heavenly fire.

MARGARETE   I guess what you say is all right,
The priest speaks so, or pretty near,
Except his language isn't yours, not quite.

FAUST   I speak as all speak here below,   3290
All souls beneath bright heaven's day,
They use the language that they know,
And I use mine. Why shouldn't I?

MARGARETE   It sounds fine when it's put your way,
But something's wrong, there's still a question: 3295
The truth is, you are not a Christian.

FAUST   Now darling!

MARGARETE   I have suffered so much, I can't sleep
To see the company you keep.

FAUST   Company?

MARGARETE   That man you always have with you,   3300
I loathe him, oh how much I do;
In all my life I can't remember
Anything that's made me shiver
More than his face has, so horrid, hateful!

FAUST   Silly thing, don't be so fearful.   3305

MARGARETE   His presence puts my blood into a turmoil.
I like people, most of them indeed;
But even as I long for you,
I think of him with secret dread—
And he's a scoundrel, he is too!   3310
If I'm unjust, forgive me, Lord.

FAUST   It takes all kinds to make a world.

MARGARETE   I wouldn't want to have his kind around me!
His lips curl so sarcastically,
Half angrily,   3315
When he pokes his head inside the door.
You can see there's nothing he cares for,
It's written on his face as plain as day
He loves no one, we're all his enemy.
I'm so happy with your arms around me,   3320
I'm yours, and feel so warm, so free, so easy,
But when he's here it knots up so inside me.

FAUST   You angel, you, atremble with foreboding!

MARGARETE   What I feel's so strong, so overwhelming,
That let him join us anywhere   3325
And right away I almost fear
I don't love you anymore.

And when he's near, my lips refuse to pray,
Which causes me such agony.
Don't you feel the same way too?   3330
FAUST   It's just that you dislike him so.
MARGARETE   I must go now.
FAUST   Shall we never
Pass a quiet time alone together,
Breast pressed to breast, our two souls one?
MARGARETE   Oh, if I only slept alone   3335
I'd draw the bolt for you tonight, yes, gladly.
But my mother sleeps so lightly,
And if we were surprised by her
I know I'd die right then and there.
FAUST   Angel, there's no need to worry.   3340
Here's a vial—three drops only
In her cup will subdue nature
And lull her into pleasant slumber.
MARGARETE   What is there that I'd say no to
When you ask?   3345
It won't harm her, though,
There is no risk?
FAUST   If there were,
Would I suggest you give it her?
MARGARETE   Let me only look at you   3350
And I don't know, I have to do
Your least wish.
I have gone so far already,
How much farther's left for me to go?
                                                        [*Exit.*]
        [*Enter* MEPHISTOPHELES.]
MEPHISTO   The girl's a goose! I hope she's gone.   3355
FAUST   Spying around, are you, again?
MEPHISTO   I heard it all, yes, every bit of it,
How she put the Doctor through his catechism,
From which he'll have, I trust, much benefit.
Does a fellow stick to the old, the true religion?—   3360
That's what all the girls are keen to know.
If he minds there, they think, he'll mind us too.
FAUST   Monster, lacking the least comprehension
How such a soul, so loving, pure,
Whose faith is all in all to her,   3365
The sole means to obtain salvation,
Should be tormented by the fear
The one she loves is damned forever!
MEPHISTO   You transcendental, hot and sensual Romeo,
See how a little skirt's got you in tow.   3370
FAUST   You misbegotten thing of filth and fire!
MEPHISTO   And she's an expert, too, in physiognomy.
When I come in, she feels—what, she's not sure;
This face I wear hides a dark mystery;

I am genius of some kind, a bad one,   3375
About that she is absolutely certain,
Even the Devil, very possibly.
Now about tonight—?

FAUST   What's it to you?

MEPHISTO   I get my fun out of it too.

AT THE WELL

GRETCHEN *and* LIESCHEN *carrying pitchers.*

LIESCHEN   You've heard about our Barbara, have you?   3380

GRETCHEN   No, not a word. I hardly see a soul.

LIESCHEN   Sybil told me; yes, the whole thing's true.
   She's gone and done it now, the little fool.
   You see what comes of being so stuck up!

GRETCHEN   What comes?   3385

LIESCHEN   Oh, it smells bad, I tell you, phew!—
   When she eats now, she's feeding two.

GRETCHEN   Oh dear!

LIESCHEN   Serves her right, if you ask me.
   How she kept after him, without a letup
   Gadding about, the pair, and gallivanting
   Off to the village for the music, dancing,   3390
   She had to be first always, everywhere,
   While he with wine and sweet cakes courted her.
   She thought her beauty echoed famously,
   Accepted his gifts shamelessly.
   They kissed and fondled by the hour,   3395
   Till it was goodbye to her little flower.

GRETCHEN   The poor thing!

LIESCHEN   Poor thing, you say!
   While we two sat home spinning the whole day
   And our mothers wouldn't let us out at night,
   She was where?—out hugging her sweetheart   3400
   On a bench or up a dark alley,
   And never found an hour passed too slowly.
   Well, now she's got to pay for it—
   Shiver in church, in her sinner's shift.

GRETCHEN   He'll marry her. How can he not?   3405

LIESCHEN   He won't—he can't.
   That one's too smart.
   He'll find a girlfriend elsewhere in a trice,
   In fact he's gone.

GRETCHEN   But that's not nice!   3410

LIESCHEN   And if he does, she'll rue the day,
   The boys will snatch her bridal wreath away
   And we'll throw dirty straw down in her doorway.[8]

[Exit.]

---

8. In Germany, this treatment was reserved for young women who had sexual relations before marriage.

GRETCHEN [*Turning to go home.*]

How full of blame I used to be, how scornful
Of any girl who got herself in trouble!　　　　　　　3415
I couldn't find words enough to express
My disgust for others' sinfulness.
Black as all their misdeeds seemed to be,
I blackened them still more, so cruelly,
And still they weren't black enough for me.　　　　3420
I blessed myself, was smug and proud
To think I was so very good,
And who's the sinner now? Me, me, oh God!
Yet everything that brought me to it,
God, was so good, oh, was so sweet!　　　　　　　3425

THE CITY WALL

In a niche in the wall, an image of the Mater Dolorosa[9] at the foot of the cross, with pots of flowers before it.

GRETCHEN [*Putting fresh flowers in the pots.*]

Look down, O
Thou sorrow-rich Lady,
On my need—in thy infinite mercy, aid me!

With the sword in your heart,
With your eternal hurt,　　　　　　　　　　　　3430
Upwards you look to your son's death.

To the Father you gaze up,
Send sighs upon sighs up
For His grief and your own sore grief.

Who's there knows　　　　　　　　　　　　　　3435
How it gnaws
Deep inside me, the pain?
The heart-anguish I suffer,
Fright, tremblings, desire?
You only know, you alone!　　　　　　　　　　　3440

I go no matter where,
The pain goes with me there,
Inside my bosom aching!
No sooner I'm alone
I moan, I moan, I moan—　　　　　　　　　　　3445
Mary, my heart is breaking!

---

9. "Sorrowful mother" (Latin; literal trans.); that is, the Virgin Mary in mourning.

From the box outside my window,
Dropping tears like dew,
Leaning into the dawning,
I picked these flowers for you.   3450

Into my bedroom early
The bright sun put his head,
Found me bolt upright sitting
Miserably on my bed.

Help! Save me from shame and death!   3455
Look down, O
Thou sorrow-rich Lady,
On my need—in thy infinite mercy, aid me!

NIGHT

The street outside GRETCHEN's *door.*

VALENTINE [*A soldier,* GRETCHEN's *brother.*]
    Whenever at a bout the boys
    Would fill the tavern with the noise   3460
    Of their loud bragging, swearing Mattie,
    Handsome Kate or blushing Mary
    The finest girl in all the country,
    Confirming what they said by drinking
    Many a bumper, I'd say nothing,   3465
    My elbows on the table propped
    Till all their boasting at last stopped.
    And then I'd stroke my beard and smiling,
    Say there was no point to quarreling
    About taste; but tell me where   3470
    There was one who could compare,
    A virgin who could hold a candle
    To my beloved sister, Gretel?
    Clink, clank, you heard the tankards rattle
    All around and voices shout   3475
    He's right, he is, she gets our vote,
    Among all her sex she has no equal!
    Which stopped those others cold. But now!—
    I could tear my hair out, all,
    Run right up the side of the wall!   3480
    All the drunks are free to crow
    Over me, to needle, sneer,
    And I'm condemned to sitting there
    Like a man with debts unpaid
    Who sweats in fear lest something's said.   3485
    I itch to smash them all, those beggars,
    But still that wouldn't make them liars.

Who's sneaking up here? Who is that?
There's two! And one I bet's that rat.
When I lay my hands on him   3490
He won't be going home again!
      [FAUST, MEPHISTOPHELES.]

FAUST   How through the window of the vestry, look,
The flickering altar lamp that's always lit,
Upward throws its light, while dim and weak,
By darkness choked, a gleam dies at our feet.   3495
Just so all's night and gloom within my soul.

MEPHISTO   And me, I'm itching like a tomcat on his prowls,
That slinks past fire ladders, hugs building walls.
An honest devil I am, after all;
It's nothing serious, the little thievery   3500
I have in mind, the little lechery—
It merely shows Walpurgis Night's already
Spooking up and down inside me.
Still another night of waiting, then
The glorious season's here again   3505
When a fellow finds out waking beats
Sleeping life away between the sheets.

FAUST   That flickering light I see, is that
Buried treasure rising, what?

MEPHISTO   Very soon you'll have the pleasure   3510
Of lifting out a pot of treasure.
The other day I stole a look—
Such lovely coins, oh you're in luck!

FAUST   No necklace, bracelet, some such thing
My darling can put on, a ring?   3515

MEPHISTO   I think I glimpsed a string of pearls—
Just the thing to please the girls.

FAUST   Good, good. It makes me feel unhappy
When I turn up with my hands empty.

MEPHISTO   Why should you mind it if you can   3520
Enjoy a free visit now and then?
Look up, how the heavens sparkle, starfull,
Time for a song, a cunning one, artful:
I'll sing her a ballad that's moral, proper,
So as to delude the baggage the better.   3525
     [Sings to the guitar.]
      What brings you out before[1]
      Your sweet William's door,
      O Katherine, my dear,
        In dawning's chill?
      You pretty child, beware,   3530
      The maid that enters there,

---

1. Lines 3526–41 are adapted by Goethe from Shakespeare's *Hamlet* 4.5.

Out she shall come ne'er
   A maiden still.

Girls, listen, trust no one,
Or when all's said and done,   3535
You'll find yourselves *undone*
   And, poor things, damned.
Of your good selves take care,
Yield nothing though he swear,
Until your finger wear   3540
   A silver band.

VALENTINE [*Advancing.*]
  Luring who here with that braying,
  Abominable ratcatcher!
  The devil take that thing you're playing,
  And then take you, you guitar scratcher!   3545

MEPHISTO   Smashed my guitar! Now it's no good at all.

VALENTINE   What I'll smash next's your skull!

MEPHISTO [*To* FAUST.]   Hold your ground, Professor! At the ready!
  Stick close to me, I'll show you how.
  Out with your pigsticker now!   3550
  You do the thrusting, I will parry.

VALENTINE   Parry that!

MEPHISTO   Why not?

VALENTINE   And this one too!

MEPHISTO   So delighted, I am, to oblige you.

VALENTINE   It's the Devil I think I'm fighting!
  What's this? My hand is feeling feeble.   3555

MEPHISTO [*To* FAUST.]   Stick him!

VALENTINE [*Falling.*]   Oh!

MEPHISTO   See how the lout's turned civil.
  What's called for now is legwork. Off and running!
  In no time they will raise a hue and cry.
  I can manage sheriffs without trouble,
  But not the High Judiciary.   3560

                        [*Exeunt.*]

MARTHE [*Leaning out of the window.*]
  Neighbors, help!

GRETCHEN   [*Leaning out of her window.*]
           A light, a light!

MARTHE   They curse and brawl, they scream and fight.

CROWD   Here's one on the ground. He's dead.

MARTHE [*Coming out.*]   Where are the murderers? All fled?

GRETCHEN [*Coming out.*]
  Who's lying here?   3565

CROWD   Your mother's son.

GRETCHEN   My God, the misery! On and on!

VALENTINE   I'm dying! Well, it's soon said, that,
  And sooner done. You women, don't

Stand there blubbering away.
Come here, I've something I must say.   3570
    [*All gather around him.*]
Gretchen, look here, you're young yet,
A green girl, not so smart about
Managing her business.
We know it, don't we, you and me,
You're a whore, quietly—   3575
Go public, don't be shy, miss.

GRETCHEN   My brother! God! What wretchedness!
VALENTINE   You can leave God out of this.
What's done can't ever be undone,
And as things went, so they'll go on.   3580
You let in one at the back door,
Soon there'll be others, more and more—
A whole dozen, hot for pleasure,
And then the whole town for good measure.

Shame is born in hugger-mugger,   3585
The lying-in veiled in black night,
And she is swaddled up so tight
In hopes the ugly thing will smother.
But as she thrives, grows bigger, bolder,
The hussy's eager to step out,   3590
Though she has grown no prettier.
The more she's hateful to the sight,
The more the creature seeks the light.

I look ahead and I see what?
The honest people of this place   3595
Standing back from you, you slut,
As from a plague-infected corpse.
When they look you in the face
You'll cringe with shame, pierced to the heart.
In church they'll drive you from the altar,   3600
No wearing gold chains any more,
No putting on a fine lace collar
For skipping round on the dance floor.
You'll hide in dark and dirty corners
With limping cripples, lousy beggars.   3605
God may pardon you at last,
But here on earth you stand accurst!

MARTHE   Look up to God and ask his mercy!
Don't add to all your other sins
Sacrilege and blasphemy.   3610
VALENTINE   If I could only lay my hands
On your scrawny, dried-up body,
Vile panderer, repulsive bawd,
Then I might hope to find forgiveness

Ten times over from the Lord!   3615

GRETCHEN My brother! Oh, what hellish anguish!

VALENTINE Stop your bawling, all your to-do.
  When you said goodbye to honor,
  That is what gave me the worst blow.
  And now I go down in the earth,   3620
  Passing through the sleep of death
  To God—who in his life was a brave soldier.

                                                    [*Dies.*]

THE CATHEDRAL

Requiem mass, organ music, singing. GRETCHEN *among a crowd of*
worshippers. Behind her an EVIL SPIRIT.

EVIL SPIRIT Oh, it was different,
  Wasn't it, Gretchen,
  When you then, an innocent,
  Used to come here   3625
  To the altar and kneeling,
  Prattle out prayers
  From the worn little prayer book,
  Half childish playing,
  Half God adoring,   3630
  Gretchen!
  In your heart's hidden
  What horrid sin?

  Do you pray for the soul of your mother,   3635
  Who by your contriving slept on,
  On into pain and more pain?
  That blood on your doorstep, whose is it?
  And under your heart, that faint stirring,
  A quickening in you, what is it?—   3640
  Affrighting both you and itself
  With its foreboding presence.

GRETCHEN Misery! Misery!
  To be rid of these thoughts
  That go round and around in me,   3645
  Accusing, accusing!

CHOIR *Dies irae, dies illa*
  Solvet saeclum in favilla.[2]
          [*Organ music.*]

EVIL SPIRIT The wrath of God grips you!
  The trumpet is sounding,   3650
  The sepulchers quaking,

---

2. "Day of wrath, that day that dissolves the world into ashes" (Latin). The choir sings a famous
mid-13th-century hymn by Thomas Celano (ca. 1200–ca. 1255).

And your heart,
　From its ashen peace waking,
　Trembles upwards in flames
　Of burning qualms!　　　　　　　　　　3655
GRETCHEN　To be out of here, gone!
　I feel as if drowning
　In the organ's sound,
　Dissolving into nothing
　In the singing's profound.　　　　　　　3660
CHOIR　*Judex ergo cum sedebit,*
　Quidquid latet apparebit,
　Nil inultum remanebit.[3]
GRETCHEN　I feel so oppressed here!
　The pillars imprison me!　　　　　　　3665
　The vaulting presses
　Down on me! Air!
EVIL SPIRIT　Hide yourself, try! Sin and shame
　Never stay hidden.
　Air! Light!　　　　　　　　　　　　　3670
　Poor thing that you are!
CHOIR　*Quid sum miser tunc dicturus?*
　Quem patronum rogaturus,
　Cum vix justus sit securus?[4]
EVIL SPIRIT　The blessed avert　　　　　3675
　Their faces from you.
　Pure souls snatch back
　Hands once offered you.
　Poor thing!
CHOIR　*Quid sum miser tunc dicturus?*　　3680
GRETCHEN　Neighbor, your smelling salts!
　　　[*She swoons.*]

WALPURGIS NIGHT

The Harz Mountains, near Schierke and Elend. FAUST, MEPHISTOPHELES.

MEPHISTO　What you would like now is a broomstick, right?
　Myself, give me a tough old billy goat.
　We've got a ways to go, still, on this route.
FAUST　While legs hold up and breath comes freely,　　3685
　This knotty blackthorn's all I want.
　Hastening our journey, what's the point?
　To loiter through each winding valley,
　Then clamber up this rocky slope
　Down which that stream there tumbles ceaselessly—　　3690

---

3. "When the judge shall be seated, what is hidden shall appear, nothing shall remain unavenged" (Latin).

4. "What shall I say in my wretchedness? To whom shall I appeal when scarcely the righteous man is safe?" (Latin.)

That's what gives the pleasure to our tramp.
The spring has laid her finger on the birch,
Even the fir tree feels her touch,
Then mustn't our limbs feel new energy?
MEPHISTO   Must they? I don't feel that way, not me.   3695
My season's strictly wintertime,
I'd much prefer we went through ice and snow.
The waning moon, making its tardy climb
Up the sky, gives off a reddish glow
So sad and dim, at every step you run   3700
Into a tree or stumble on a stone.
You won't mind my begging assistance
Of some will-o'-the-wisp?[5] And there's one no great distance,
Shining for all his worth, so merrily.
—Hello there, friend, we'd like your company!   3705
Why blaze away so uselessly, for nothing?
Do us a favor, light up this path we're climbing.
WILL-O'-THE-WISP   I hope the deep respect I hold you in, sir,
Will keep in check my all-too-skittish temper;
The way we go is zigzag, that's our nature.   3710
MEPHISTO   Trying to ape mankind, poor silly flame.
Now listen to me: fly straight, in the Devil's name,
Or out I'll blow your feeble, flickering light!
WILL-O'-THE-WISP   Yes, yes, you give the orders here, quite right;
I'll do what you require, eagerly.   3715
But don't forget, the mountain on this night
Is mad with magic, witchcraft, sorcery,
And if Jack-o'-Lantern is your guide,
Don't expect more than he can provide.
FAUST, MEPHISTOPHELES, WILL-O'-THE-WISP [*Singing in turn*]

    We have entered, as it seems,   3720
    Realm of magic, realm of dreams.
    Lead us well and win the honor
    His to have, bright-shining creature,
    By whose flicker we may hasten
    Forward through this wide, waste region!   3725

    See the trees, one then another,
    Spinning past us fast and faster,
    And the cliffs impending over,
    And the jutting crags, like noses
    Winds blow through with snoring noises!   3730

    Over stones and through the heather
    Rills and runnels downwards hasten.
    Is that water splashing, listen,

---

5. A wavering light formed by marsh gas. In German folklore, it was thought to lead travelers to their destruction.

Is it singing, that soft murmur,
Is it love's sweet voice, lamenting   3735
For the days when all was heaven?
How our hearts hoped, loving, yearning!
And like a tale, an old, familiar,
Echo once more tells it over.

Whoo-oo! owl's hoot's heard nearer,   3740
Cry of cuckoo and of plover—
Still not nested, still awake?
Are those lizards in the brake,
Straggle-legged, big of belly?
And roots, winding every which way   3745
In the rock and sand, send far out
Shoots to snare and make us cry out;
Tree warts, swollen, gross excrescents,
Send their tentacles like serpents
Out to catch us. And mice scamper   3750
In great packs of every color
Through the moss and through the heather.
And the glowworms swarm around us
In dense clouds and only lead us
Hither, thither, to confuse us.   3755

Tell me, are we standing still, or
Still advancing, climbing higher?
Everything spins round us wildly,
Rocks and trees grin at us madly,
And the errant lights, their number   3760
Ever greater, puffed up, swagger,

MEPHISTO   Seize hold of my coattails, quick,
   We're coming to a middling peak
   Where you'll marvel at the sight
   Of Mammon's mountain, burning bright.[6]   3765
FAUST   How strange that glow is, there, far down,
   Dim and reddish, like the dawn.
   Its faint luminescence reaches
   Deep into the yawning gorges.
   Mist rises here and streams away there,   3770
   Penetrated by pale fire.
   Here, like a thin thread, the glimmer
   Creeps along, then like a fountain
   Overflowing, spills down the mountain,
   And vein-like, spreading all about   3775
   Winds along the entire valley,
   And here, squeezed through a narrow gully,

---

6. Mammon is imagined as leading a group of fallen angels in digging out gold and gems from the ground of hell, presumably for Satan's palace, as described in Milton's *Paradise Lost* 1.678 ff.

Collects into a pool apart.
Sparks fly about as if a hand
Were scattering golden grains of sand. 3780
And look there, how from base to top
The whole cliffside is lit up.

MEPHISTO   Holiday time Lord Mammon's castle
Puts on a show that has no equal.
Don't you agree? You saw it, luckily. 3785
I hear our guests arriving—not so quietly!

FAUST   What a gale of wind is blowing,
Buffeting my back and shoulders!

MEPHISTO   Clutch with your fingers that outcropping
Or you'll fall to your death among the boulders. 3790
The mist is making it darker than ever.
Hear how the trees are pitching and tossing!
Frightened, the owls fly up in a flutter.
The evergreen palace's pillars are creaking
And cracking, boughs snapping and breaking, 3795
As down the trunks thunder
With a shriek of roots tearing,
Piling up on each other
In a fearful disorder!
And through the wreckage-strewn ravines 3800
The hurtling storm blast howls and keens.
And hear those voices in the air,
Some faroff and others near?
That's the witches' wizard singing,
Along the mountain shrilly ringing. 3805

CHORUS OF WITCHES
   The witches ride up to the Brocken,
   Stubble's yellow, new grain green.
   The great host meets upon the peak and
   There Urian[7] mounts his throne.
   So over stock and stone go stumping, 3810
   Witches farting, billy goats stinking!

VOICE   Here comes Mother Baubo[8] now,
   Riding on an old brood sow.

CHORUS
   Honor to whom honor is due!
   Old Baubo to the head of the queue! 3815
   A fat pig and a fat frau on her,
   And all the witches following after!

VOICE   How did you come?

VOICE   Ilsenstein way.
   I peeked in an owl's nest, passing by,
   Oh how it stared! 3820

---

7. A name for the devil.
8. In Greek mythology, the nurse of Demeter, noted for her obscenity and bestiality.

VOICE   Oh go to hell, all!
　Why such a rush, such a mad scramble?
VOICE   Too fast, too fast, my bottom's skinned sore!
　Oh my wounds! Look here and here!

CHORUS OF WITCHES
　　　Broad the way and long the road,
　　　What a bumbling, stumbling crowd!   3825
　　　Broomstraw scratches, pitchfork's pushed,
　　　Mother's ripped and baby's crushed.

HALF-CHORUS OF WARLOCKS
　　　We crawl like snails lugging their whorled shell,
　　　The women have got a good mile's lead.
　　　When where you're going's to the Devil,   3830
　　　It's woman knows how to get up speed.

OTHER HALF-CHORUS
　　　A mile or so, why should we care?
　　　Women may get the start of us,
　　　But for all of their forehandedness,
　　　One jump carries a man right there.   3835

VOICE [*Above.*]   Come along with us, you down at the lake.
VOICE [*From below.*]   Is there anything better we would like?
　We scrub ourselves clean as a whistle,
　But it's no use, still we're infertile.

BOTH CHORUSES
　　　The wind is still, the stars are fled,   3840
　　　The veiled moon's glad to hide her head.
　　　Rushing and roaring, the magic chorus
　　　Scatters sparks by the thousands around us.

VOICE [*From below.*]   Wait, please wait, only a minute!
VOICE [*Above.*]   A voice from that crevice, did you hear it?   3845
VOICE [*From below.*]   Take me along, don't forget me!
　For three hundred years I've tried to climb
　Up to the summit—all in vain.
　I long for creatures who are like me.

BOTH CHORUSES
　　　Straddle a broomstick, a pitchfork's fine too,   3850
　　　Get up on a goat, a plain stick will do.
　　　Who can't make it up today
　　　Forever is done for, and so bye-bye.

HALF-WITCH [*From below.*]   I trot breathlessly, and yet
　How far ahead the rest have got.   3855
　No peace at all at home, and here
　It's no better. Dear, oh dear!

CHORUS OF WITCHES
　　　The unction gives us hags a lift,
　　　A bit of rag will do for a sail,
　　　Any tub's a fine sky boat—   3860
　　　Don't fly now and you never will.

BOTH CHORUSES

And when we've gained the very top,
Light down, swooping, to a stop.
We'll darken the heath entirely
With all our swarming witchery.   3865
  [*They alight.*]

MEPHISTO What a crowding and shoving, rushing and clattering,
Hissing and shrieking, pushing and chattering,
Burning and sparking, stinking and kicking!
We're among witches, no mistaking!
Stick close to me or we'll lose each other.   3870
But where are you?

FAUST   Here, over here!

MEPHISTO Already swept away so far!
I must show this mob who's master.
Out of the way of Voland the Devil,
Out of the way, you charming rabble!   3875
Doctor, hang on, we'll make a quick dash
And get ourselves out of this terrible crush—
Even for me it's too much to endure.
Yonder's a light has a strange lure,
Those bushes, I don't know why, attract me,   3880
Quick now, dive in that shrubbery!

FAUST Spirit of Contradiction! However,
Lead the way!—He's clever, my devil:
Walpurgis Night up the Brocken we scramble
So as to do what? Hide ourselves in a corner!   3885

MEPHISTO Just look at that fire there, shining brightly,
Clubmen are meeting, how nice all looks, sprightly.
You don't feel alone when the company's fewer.

FAUST But I would feel much happier
To be on the summit. I can make out   3890
A red glow and black smoke swirling,
Satanwards a great crowd's toiling,
And there, I don't have any doubt,
Many a riddle's at last resolved.

MEPHISTO And many another riddle revealed.   3895
Let the great world rush on crazily,
We'll pass the time here cozily;
And doing what has been for a long time the thing done,
Inside that great world contrive us a little one.
Look there, young witches, all stark naked,   3900
And old ones wisely petticoated.
Don't sulk, be nice, if only to please me;
Much fun at small cost, really it's easy.
I hear music, a damned racket!
You must learn not to mind it.   3905
No backing out now, in with me!

You'll meet a distinguished company
And again be much obliged to me.
—Now what do you think of this place, my friend?
Our eyes can hardly see to its end.   3910
A hundred fires, all in a row,
People dance, people chatter, make love, drink and cook,
Did you ever in your life see such a show?
Find me the like, hard as ever you look!

FAUST   And when we enter into the revel,   3915
What part will you play, magician or devil?

MEPHISTO   I travel incognito normally,
But when it comes to celebrations
A man must show his decorations.
The Garter's never been awarded me,[9]   3920
But in these parts the split hoof's much respected.
That snail there, do you see it, creeping forwards,
Its face pushing this way, that way, towards us?
Already I've been smelt out, I'm detected.
Even if deception was my aim,   3925
Here there's no denying who I am.
Come on, we'll go along from fire to fire,
The go-between me, you the lover.

          [*Addressing several figures huddled around a fading fire.*]
Old sirs, you keep apart, you're hardly merry,
You'd please me better if you joined the party.   3930
You ought to be carousing with the youngsters,
At home we're all alone enough, we oldsters.

GENERAL   Put no trust in nations, for the people,
In spite of all you've done, are never grateful.
It's with them always as it is with women,   3935
The young come first, and we—ignored, forgotten.

MINISTER OF STATE   The world has got completely off the track.
Oh, they were men, the older generation!
When it was us held every high position,
That was the golden age, and no mistake.   3940

PARVENU   We were no simpletons ourselves, we weren't,
And often did the things we shouldn't.
But everything's turned topsy-turvy, now
That we are foursquare with the status quo.

AUTHOR   Who wants, today, to read a book   3945
With a modicum of sense or wit?
And as for our younger folk,
I've never seen such rude conceit.

MEPHISTO [*Suddenly transformed into an old man.*]
For Judgment Day all now are ripe and ready
Since I shan't ever again climb Brocken's top;   3950

---

9. That is, he has no decoration of nobility, such as the Order of the Garter.

And considering, too, my wine of life is running cloudy,
    The world also is coming to a stop.
JUNK-DEALER WITCH   Good sirs, don't pass me unawares,
    Don't miss this opportunity!
    Look here, will you, at my wares,   3955
    What richness, what variety!
    Yet there is not a single item
    Hasn't served to claim a victim,
    Nowhere on earth will you find such a stall!
    No dagger here but it has drunk hot blood,   3960
    No cup but from it deadly poison's flowed
    To waste a body once robust and hale,
    No gem but has seduced a loving girl,
    No sword but has betrayed an ally or a friend,
    Or struck an adversary from behind.   3965
MEPHISTO   Auntie, think about the times you live in—
    What's past is done! Done and gone!
    The new, the latest, that's what you should deal in;
    The nouveau only, turns us on.
FAUST   Oh let me not forget I'm me, me only!   3970
    This is a fair to beat all fairs, believe me!
MEPHISTO   The scrambling mob climbs upwards, jostling, rushed,
    You think you're pushing and you're being pushed.
FAUST   Who's that there?
MEPHISTO   Look at her close.
    Lilith.[1]   3975
FAUST   Lilith? What's she to us?
MEPHISTO   Adam's wife, his first. Beware of her.
    Her beauty's one boast is her dangerous hair.
    When Lilith winds it tight around young men
    She doesn't soon let go of them again.   3980
FAUST   Look, one old witch, one young one, there they sit—
    They've waltzed around a lot already, I will bet!
MEPHISTO   Tonight's no night for resting, but for fun,
    Let's join the dance, a new one's just begun.
FAUST [Dancing with the YOUNG WITCH.]
    A lovely dream I dreamt one day: 3985
    I saw a green-leaved apple tree,
    Two apples swayed upon a stem,
    So tempting! I climbed up for them.
THE PRETTY WITCH   Ever since the days of Eden
    Apples have been man's desire.   3990
    How overjoyed I am to think, sir,
    Apples grow, too, in my garden.

---

1. According to rabbinical legend, Adam's first wife; the *female* mentioned in Genesis 1.27: "So God created man in his own image, in the image of God created he him; male and female created he them." After Eve was created, Lilith became a ghost who seduced men and inflicted evil on children.

MEPHISTO [*Dancing with the* OLD WITCH.]
　　A naughty dream I dreamt one day:
　　I saw a tree split up the middle—
　　A huge cleft, phenomenal! 　　　　　　　　　　　3995
　　And yet it pleased me every way.
THE OLD WITCH　　Welcome, welcome, to you, sire,
　　Cloven-footed cavalier!
　　Stand to with a proper stopper,
　　Unless you fear to come a cropper. 　　　　　　　4000
PROCTOPHANTASMIST[2]　　Accurst tribe, so bold, presumptuous!
　　Hasn't it been proven past disputing
　　Spirits all are footless, they lack standing?
　　And here you're footing like the rest of us!
THE PRETTY WITCH [*Dancing.*]
　　What's he doing here, at our party? 　　　　　　4005
FAUST [*Dancing.*]
　　Him? You find him everywhere, that killjoy;
　　We others dance, he does the criticizing.
　　Every step one takes requires analyzing;
　　Until it's jawed about, it hasn't yet occurred.
　　He can't stand how we go forward undeterred; 　4010
　　If you keep going around in the same old circle,
　　As he plods year in, year out on his treadmill,
　　You might be favored with his good opinion,
　　Provided you most humbly beg it of him.
PROCTOPHANTASMIST　　Still here, are you? It's an outrage! 　4015
　　Vanish, ours is the Enlightened Age—
　　You devils, no respect for rule and regulation.
　　We've grown so wise, yet ghosts still walk in Tegel.[3]
　　How long I've toiled to banish superstition,
　　Yet it lives on. The whole thing is a scandal! 　4020
THE PRETTY WITCH　　Stop, stop, how boring, all your gabble!
PROCTOPHANTASMIST　　I tell you to your face you ghostly freaks,
　　I'll not endure this tyranny of spooks—
　　My spirit finds you spirits much too spiritual!
　　　　[*They go on dancing.*]
　　I see I'm getting nowhere with these devils, 　　4025
　　Still, it will add a chapter to my travels,
　　And I hope, before my sands of life run out,
　　To put foul fiends and poets all to rout.
MEPHISTO　　He'll go and plump himself down in a puddle—
　　It solaces him for all his ghostly trouble— 　　　4030

---

2. A German coinage meaning "one who exorcises evil spirits by sitting in a pond and applying leeches to his behind" (see lines 4029–32). The figure caricatures Friedrich Nicolai (1733–1811), who opposed modern movements in German thought and literature and had parodied Goethe's *The Sorrows of Young Werther* (1774).
3. A town near Berlin where ghosts had been reported.

And purge away his spirit and these other spirits
By having leeches feed on where the M'sieur sits.[4]
    [*To* FAUST, *who has broken off dancing and withdrawn.*]
What's this? You've left your partner in the lurch
As she was sweetly singing, pretty witch.

FAUST   Ugh! From her mouth a red mouse sprung   4035
In the middle of her song.

MEPHISTO   Is that anything to fuss about?
And anyway it wasn't gray, was it?
To take on so, to me, seems simply rudeness
When you are sporting with your Phyllis.   4040

FAUST   And then I saw—

MEPHISTO   Saw what?

FAUST   Look there, Mephisto,
At that lovely child, so pale with sorrow,
Standing by herself. How lifelessly
She makes her way along, with piteous pains,
As if her feet were bound in cruel chains.   4045
I must confess, it looks like Gretchen.

MEPHISTO   Let it be!
It's bad, that thing, a lifeless shape, a wraith
No man ever wants to meet up with.
Your blood freezes under her dead stare,
Almost turned to stone, you are.   4050
Medusa,[5] did you ever hear of her?

FAUST   Yes, yes, those are a corpse's eyes
No loving hand was by to close.
That's Gretchen's breast, which she so often
Gave to me to rest my head on,   4055
That shape her dear, her lovely body
She gave to me to enjoy freely.

MEPHISTO   It's all magic, idiot!
Each thinks her his sweetheart.

FAUST   What rapture! And what suffering!   4060
I stand here spellbound by her look.
How strange, that bit of scarlet string
That ornaments her lovely neck,
No thicker than a knife blade's back.

MEPHISTO   Right you are. I see it, too.   4065
She's also perfectly able to
Tuck her head beneath her arm
And stroll about. Perseus—remember him?—
He was the one who hacked it off her.
—Man, I'd think you'd have enough of   4070
The mad ideas your head is stuffed with!

---

4. Nicolai claimed that he had been bothered by ghosts but had repelled them by applying leeches to his rump.

5. The Gorgon with hair of serpents whose glance turned people to stone.

Come, we'll climb this little hill where
All's as lively as inside the Prater.[6]
And unless somebody has bewitched me,
The thing I see there is a theater.   4075
What's happening?

SERVIBILIS   A play, a new one, starting shortly,
   Last of seven. With us here it's customary
   To offer a full repertory.
   The playwright's a rank amateur,
   Amateurs, too, the whole company.   4080
   Well, I must hurry off now, please excuse me,
   I need to raise the curtain—amateurishly!

MEPHISTO   How right it is that I should find you here, sirs;
   The Blocksberg's just the place for amateurs.

WALPURGIS NIGHT'S DREAM;
OR
OBERON AND TITANIA'S GOLDEN WEDDING

INTERMEZZO[7]

STAGE MANAGER [*To crew.*]   Today we'll put by paint and canvas,   4085
   Mieding's[8] brave sons, all.
   Nature paints the scene for us:
   Gray steep and mist-filled vale.

HERALD   For the wedding to be golden,
   Years must pass, full fifty;   4090
   But if the quarrel is made up, then
   It is golden truly.

OBERON   Spirits hovering all around,
   Appear, dear imps, to me here!
   King and Queen are once more bound   4095
   Lovingly together.

PUCK[9]   Here's Puck, my lord, who spins and whirls
   And cuts a merry caper,
   A hundred follow at his heels,
   Skipping to the measure.   4100

ARIEL[1]   Ariel strikes up his song,
   The notes as pure as silver;
   Philistines all around him throng,
   But those, too, with true culture.

OBERON   Wives and husbands, learn from us   4105
   How two hearts unite:
   To find connubial happiness,
   Only separate.

---

6. A famous park in Vienna.
7. Brief interlude. Oberon and Titania are king and queen of the fairies.
8. Johann Martin Mieding (died 1782), a master carpenter and scene builder in the Weimar theater.
9. A mischievous spirit.
1. A helpful sprite.

TITANIA   If Master sulks and Mistress pouts,
    Here's the remedy: 4110
    Send her on a trip down south,
    Him the other way.

FULL ORCHESTRA [*Fortissimo.*]   Buzzing fly and humming gnat
    And all their consanguinity,
    Frog's hoarse croak, cicada's chat   4115
    Compose our symphony.

SOLO   Here I come, the bagpipes, who's
    Only a soap bubble.
    Hear me through my stumpy nose
    Tootle-doodle-doodle.   4120

A BUDDING IMAGINATION   A spider's foot, a green toad's gut,
    Two winglets—though a travesty
    Devoid of life and nature, yet
    It does as nonsense poetry.

A YOUNG COUPLE   Short steps, smart leaps, all done neatly   4125
    On the scented lawn—
    I grant you foot it very featly,
    Yet we remain un-airborne.

AN INQUIRING TRAVELER   Can it be a fairground fraud,
    The shape at which I'm looking?   4130
    Oberon the handsome god
    Still alive and kicking?

A PIOUS BELIEVER   I don't see claws, nor any tail,
    And yet it's indisputable:
    Like Greece's gods, his dishabille   4135
    Betrays the pagan devil.

AN ARTIST OF THE NORTH   Here everything I undertake
    Is weak, is thin, is sketchy;
    But I'm preparing soon to make
    My Italian journey.   4140

A STICKLER FOR DECORUM   I'm here, and most unhappily,
    Where all's impure, improper;
    Among this riotous witchery
    Only two wear powder.

A YOUNG WITCH   Powder, like a petticoat,   4145
    Is right for wives with gray hair;
    But I'll sit naked on my goat,
    Show off my strapping figure.

A MATRON   We are too well bred by far
    To bandy words about: 4150
    But may you, young thing that you are,
    Drop dead, and soon, cheap tart!

THE CONDUCTOR   Don't crowd so round the naked charmer,
    On with the concerto!
    Frog and blowfly, gnat, cicada—   4155
    Mind you keep the tempo.

A WEATHERCOCK [*Pointing one way.*]

No better company than maids
Like these, kind and complaisant,
And bachelors to match, old boys
Agog all, all impatient!   4160

WEATHERCOCK [*Pointing the other way.*]
And if the earth don't open up
And swallow this lewd rabble,
Off I'll race at a great clip,
Myself go to the Devil.

SATIRICAL EPIGRAMS [XENIEN[2]]   We are gadflies, plant our sting   4165
In hides highborn and bourgeois,
By so doing honoring
Satan, our dear dada.

HENNINGS[3]   Look there at the pack of them,
Like schoolboys jeering meanly.   4170
Next, I'm sure, they all will claim
It's all in fun, friends, really.

MUSAGET[4] ["LEADER OF THE MUSES"]
If I joined these witches here,
I'm sure I'd not repine;
I know I'd find it easier   4175
To lead them than the Nine.

[A JOURNAL] FORMERLY [ENTITLED] "THE SPIRIT OF THE AGE"[5]
What counts is knowing the right people,
With me, sir, you'll go places;
The Blocksberg's got a place for all,
Like Germany's Parnassus.[6]   4180

THE INQUIRING TRAVELER   Who's that fellow who's so stiff
And marches so majestical?
He sniffs away for all he's worth
"Pursuing things Jesuitical."

A CRANE   An earnest fisherman I am   4185
In clear and muddy waters,
And thus you see a pious man
Hobnobbing with devils.

A CHILD OF THIS WORLD   All occasions serve the godly
In their work. Atop   4190
The Blocksberg, even there, they
Set up religious shop.

A DANCER   What's that drumming, a new team
Of musicians coming?

---

2. Literally, polemical verses written by
Goethe and Friedrich von Schiller (1759–
1805). The characters here are versions of
Goethe himself.
3. August Adolf von Hennings (1746–1826),
publisher of a journal called *Genius of the Age*
that had attacked Schiller.
4. The title of a collection of Hennings's

poetry.
5. That is, former "Genius of the Age"; probably alludes to the journal's change of title in
1800 to *Genius of the Nineteenth Century*.
6. A mountain sacred to Apollo and the
Muses; hence, figuratively, the locale of poetic
excellence.

No, no, they're bitterns in the stream   4195
    All together booming.
THE DANCING MASTER   How cautiously each lifts a foot,
    Draws back in fear of tripping,
    The knock-kneed hop, they jump the stout,
    Heedless how they're looking.   4200
THE FIDDLER   This riffraff's so hate-filled, each lusts
    To slit the other's throat;
    Orpheus with his lute tamed beasts,[7]
    These march to the bagpipes' note.
A DOGMATIST   You can't rattle me by all   4205
    Your questionings and quibbles;
    The Devil is perfectly evil, hence real—
    For the perfect entails existence: so devils.
AN IDEALIST   The mind's creative faculty
    This time has gone too far.   4210
    If everything I see is me,
    I'm crazy, that's for sure.
A REALIST   It's pandemonium, it's mad,
    I'm floored, I am, dumbfounded.
    This is the first time I have stood   4215
    On ground on nothing founded.
A SUPERNATURALIST   The presence of these devils here
    For me's reassuring evidence;
    From the demonical I infer
    The angelical's existence.   4220
A SKEPTIC   They see a flickering light and gloat,
    There's treasure there, oh surely;
    Devil's a word that pairs with doubt,
    This is a place that suits me.
CONDUCTOR   Frogs in leaves, grasshoppers grass,   4225
    What damned amateurs!
    Cicadas chirr, mosquitos buzz—
    Call yourselves performers!
THE SMART ONES   Sans all souci[8] we are, shift
    About with lightning speed;   4230
    When walking on the feet is out,
    We walk on the head.
THE NOT-SO-SMART ONES   At court we sat down to free dinners,
    And now all doors are shut.
    We've worn out our dancing slippers   4235
    And must limp barefoot.
WILL-O'-THE-WISPS   We're from the muddy flats, marais,
    Such is our lowly origin.
    Today we shine as chevaliers
    And dance in the cotillion.   4240

---

7. In Greek mythology, Orpheus's music was said to have the power to quiet wild animals.   8. "Without any care or unhappiness" (French).

A SHOOTING STAR   I shot across the sky's expanse,
    A meteor, blazing bright.
    Now fallen, I sprawl in the grass—
    Who'll help me to my feet?
THE BRUISERS   Look out, look out, we're coming through,   4245
    Trampling your lawn.
    We're spirits too, but spirits who
    Have lots of beef and brawn.
PUCK   How you tramp, so heavily,
    Like infant elephants.   4250
    Elfin Puck's tread be today
    Heaviest of stamps.
ARIEL   Or gave you wings, our kindly Nature,
    Or gave you them the Spirit?
    As I fly, fly close after,   4255
    Up to the rose hill's summit.
ORCHESTRA [*Pianissimo.*]
    Shrouding mists and trailing clouds
    Lighten in the dawning,
    Breeze stirs leaves, wind rattles reeds,
    And all, all, gone in the morning.   4260

AN OVERCAST DAY. A FIELD

FAUST *and* MEPHISTOPHELES.

FAUST   In misery! In despair! Stumbling about pitifully over the earth for so long, and now a prisoner! A condemned criminal, shut up in a dungeon and suffering horrible torments, the poor unfortunate child! It's come to this, to this! And not a word about it breathed to me, you treacherous, odious spirit! Stand there rolling your Devil's eyes   4265 around in rage, oh do! Brazen it out with your intolerable presence! A prisoner! In misery, irremediable misery! Delivered up to evil spirits and the stony-hearted justice of mankind! And meanwhile you distract me with your insipid entertainments, keep her situation, more desperate every day, from me, and leave her to perish helplessly!   4270
MEPHISTO   She's not the first.
FAUST   You dog, you monster! Change him, O you infinite Spirit, change the worm back into a dog, give it back the shape it wore those evenings when it liked to trot ahead of me and roll under the feet of some innocent wayfarer, tripping him up and leaping on him as he   4275 fell. Give it back its favorite shape so it can crawl on its belly in the sand before me, and I can kick it as it deserves, the abomination!— Not the first!—Such misery, such misery! It's inconceivable, humanly inconceivable, that more than one creature should ever have plumbed such depths of misery, that the first who did, writhing in her last   4280 agony under the eyes of the Eternal Forgiveness, shouldn't have expiated the guilt of all the others who came after! I am cut to the quick, pierced to the marrow, by the suffering of this one being—you grin indifferently at the fate of thousands!

MEPHISTO   So once again we're at our wits' end, are we—reached the   4285
  point where you fellows start feeling your brain is about to explode?
  Why did you ever throw in with us if you can't see the thing through?
  You'd like to fly, but don't like heights. Did we force ourselves on you
  or you on us?

FAUST   Don't snarl at me that way with those wolfish fangs of yours, it   4290
  sickens me!—Great and glorious Spirit, Spirit who vouchsafed to
  appear to me, who knows me in my heart and soul, why did you tie
  me to this scoundrel who diets on destruction, delights to hurt?

MEPHISTO   Finished yet?

FAUST   Save her or you'll pay for it! With a curse on you, the dreadful-   4295
  est there is, for thousands of years to come!

MEPHISTO   I'm powerless to strike off the Great Avenger's chains or
  draw his bolts.—Save her indeed!—Who's the one who ruined her, I
  would like to know—you or me?

        [FAUST looks around wildly.]

  Looking for a thunderbolt, are you? A good thing you wretched mor-   4300
  tals weren't given them. That's the tyrant's way of getting out of
  difficulties—strike down any innocent person who makes an objection, gets in his way.

FAUST   Take me to where she is, you hear? She's got to be set free.

MEPHISTO   In spite of the risk you would run? There's blood guilt on   4305
  the town because of what you did. Where murder was, there the
  avenging spirits hover, waiting for the murderer to return.

FAUST   That from you, that too? Death and destruction, a world's
  worth, on your head, you monster! Take me there, I say, and set her
  free!   4310

MEPHISTO   All right, all right, I'll carry you there. But hear what I can
  do—do you think all the powers of heaven and earth are mine? I'll
  muddle the turnkey's senses, then you seize his keys and lead her out.
  Only a human hand can do it. I'll keep watch. The spirit horses are
  ready. Off I'll carry both of you. That's what I can do.   4315

FAUST   Away then!

NIGHT. OPEN COUNTRY

FAUST and MEPHISTOPHELES going by on black horses at a furious gallop.

FAUST   What's that they're doing at the ravenstone?

MEPHISTO   Cooking up, getting up, something, who cares?

FAUST   Soaring up, swooping down, bowing and stooping.

MEPHISTO   A pack of witches.   4320

FAUST   Strewing stuff, consecrating.

MEPHISTO   Keep going, keep going!

A PRISON

FAUST [With a bunch of keys and carrying a lamp, at a narrow iron door.]
  I shudder as I haven't for so long—
  She's shut up inside these dank walls, poor thing,
  And all her crime was love, the brave, the illusory.   4325

You're hanging back from going in!
You're afraid of meeting her eyes again!
In, in, your hesitation's her death, hurry!
  [*He puts the key in the lock.*]
SINGING [*From withins.*]
   My mother, the whore,
   She's the one slew me!   4330
   My father, the knave,
   He's the one ate me!
   My sister, wee thing,
   Heaped up my bones
   Under cool stones.   4335
   Then I became a pretty woodbird—
   Fly away, fly away!
FAUST [*Unlocking the door.*] She doesn't dream her lover's listening.
  Hears her chains rattle, the straw rustling.
    [*He enters.*]
MARGARETE [*Cowering on her paillasse.*]
  They're coming, they're coming! How bitter, death, bitter! 4340
FAUST [*Whispering.*] Hush, dear girl, hush! You'll soon be free.
MARGARETE [*Groveling before him.*]
  If your heart's human, think how I suffer.
FAUST You'll wake the guards. Speak quietly.
    [*Taking hold of the chains to unlock them.*]
MARGARETE [*On her knees.*] Headsman, so early, it isn't right.
  Have mercy on me! Too soon, too soon!   4345
  You come for me in the dead of night—
  Isn't it time enough at dawn?
    [*Stands up.*]
  I'm still so young, too young surely—
  Still I must die.
  How pretty I was, that's what undid me.   4350
  He held me so close, now he's far away,
  My wreath pulled apart, the flowers scattered.
  Don't grip me so hard. Please, won't you spare me?
  What did I ever do to you?
  Don't let me beg in vain for mercy.   4355
  I never before laid eyes on you.
FAUST It's unendurable, her misery.
MARGARETE What can I do, I'm in your power.
  Only let me nurse my baby first,
  All night long I hugged the dear creature;   4360
  How mean they were, snatched it from my breast,
  And now they say I murdered it.
  I'll never be happy, no, never again.
  They sing songs about me in the street;
  It's wicked of them.   4365
  There's an old fairy tale ends that way—
  What has it got to do with me?

FAUST [*Falling at her feet.*]   It's me here who loves you, me,
    at your feet,
  To rescue you from this miserable fate.
MARGARETE [*kneeling beside him.*]
  We'll kneel down, that's right, and pray to the saints.   4370
  Look, under those steps,
  Below the doorsill,
  All Hell's a-boil!
  The Evil One
  In his horrible rage   4375
  Makes such a noise.
FAUST [*Crying out.*]   Gretchen! Gretchen!
MARGARETE [*Listening.*]   That was my darling's own dear voice!
    [*She jumps up, the chains fall away.*]
  I heard him call. Where can he be?
  No one may stop me now, I'm free!   4380
  Into his arms I'll run so fast,
  Lie on his breast at last, at last.
  Gretchen, he called, from there on the sill.
  Through all the howlings and gnashings of Hell,
  Through the furious, devilish sneering and scorn,   4385
  I heard a dear voice, its sound so well known.
FAUST   It's me!
MARGARETE   It's you! Oh, say it again.
    [*Catching hold of him.*]
  It's him! Where is the torture now, it's him!
  Where's my fear of the prison, the chains they hung on me,
  It's you, it's you, you've come here to save me!   4390
  I'm saved!
  —I see it before me, so very plainly,
  The street I saw you the first time on,
  I see Marthe and me where we waited for you
  In the sunlit garden.   4395
FAUST [*Pulling her toward the door.*]
  Come along, come!
MARGARETE   Don't go, stay here!
  I love it so being wherever you are.
    [*Caressing him.*]
FAUST   Hurry!
  If you don't hurry,
  The price we will pay!   4400
MARGARETE   What? Don't know how to kiss anymore?
  Parted from me a short time only
  And quite forgotten what lips are for?
  Why am I frightened with your arms around me?
  Time was, at a word or a look from you,   4405
  Heaven herself threw her arms around me
  And you kissed me as if you'd devour me.
  Kiss me, kiss me!

Or I'll kiss you!
    [*She embraces him.*]
What cold lips you have,   4410
You don't speak, look dumbly.
What's become of your love?
Who took it from me?
    [*She turns away from him.*]
FAUST   Come, follow me! Darling, be brave!
Oh, the kisses I'll give you, my love—   4415
Only come now, we'll slip through that door.
MARGARETE [*Turning back to him.*]
Is it really you? Can I be sure?
FAUST   Yes, it's me—you must come!
MARGARETE   You strike off my chains,
Take me into your arms.
How is it you don't shrink away from me?   4420
Have you any idea who you're letting go free?
FAUST   Hurry, hurry! The night's almost over.
MARGARETE   I murdered my mother,
Drowned my infant,
Weren't both of us given it—you too its parent—   4425
Equally? It's you, I can hardly believe it.
Give me your hand. No, I haven't dreamt it.
Your dear hand.—But your hand is wet!
Wipe it off, there's blood on it!
My God, my God, what did you do?   4430
Put away your sword,
I beg you to!
FAUST   What's past is done, forget it all.
You're killing me.
MARGARETE   No, live on still.   4435
I'll tell you how the graves should be;
Tomorrow you must see to it.
Give my mother the best spot,
My brother put alongside her,
Me, put me some distance off,   4440
Yet not too far,
And at my right breast put my baby.
Nobody else shall lie beside me.
When I used to press up close to you,
How sweet it was, pure happiness,   4445
But now I can't, it's over, all such bliss—
I feel it as an effort I must make,
That I must force myself on you,
And you, I feel, resist me, push me back.
And yet it's you, with your good, kind look.   4450
FAUST   If it's me, then come, we can't delay.
MARGARETE   Out there?
FAUST   Out there, away!

MARGARETE   If the grave's out there, death waiting for me,
    Come, yes, come! The two of us together!
    But only to the last place, there, no other.   4455
    —You're going now?
    I'd go too if I could, Heinrich, believe me!
FAUST   You can! All you need is the will. Come on!
    The way is clear.
MARGARETE   No, I mayn't, for me all hope is gone.   4460
    It's useless, flight. They'd keep, I'm sure,
    A sharp watch out. I'd find it dreadful
    To have to beg my bread of people,
    Beg with a bad conscience, too;
    Dreadful to have to wander about   4465
    Where all is strange and new,
    Only to end up getting caught.
FAUST   But I'll stick to you!
MARGARETE   Quick, be quick!
    Save your poor child—   4470
    Run! Keep to the track
    That follows the brook;
    Over the bridge,
    Into the wood,
    Left where the plank is,   4475
    There, in the pool—
    Reach down, quick, catch it!
    It's fighting for breath!
    It's struggling still!
    Save it, save it!   4480
FAUST   Get hold of yourself!
    One step and you're free, dear girl!
MARGARETE   If only we were well past the hill!
    On the rock over there Mother sits, all atremble—
    Not a sign does she makes, doesn't speak.   4485
    On the rock over there Mother sits, head awobble,
    To look at her gives me a chill,
    She slept so long she will never wake.
    She slept so we might have our pleasure—
    The happy hours we passed together!   4490
FAUST   If all my persuading is no use,
    I'll have to carry you off by force.
MARGARETE   Let go, let go, how dare you compel me!
    You're gripping my arm so brutally!
    I always did what you wanted, once.   4495
FAUST   Soon day will be breaking! Darling, darling!
MARGARETE   Day? Yes, day, my last one, dawning,
    My wedding day it should have been.
    Not a word to a soul you've already been with your Gretchen.
    My poor wreath!   4500
    All's over and done.

We'll see one another again,
But not to go dancing.
The crowd presses in—not a sound, nothing,
Not the cry of a child.   4505
They are too many
For square and alley
To hold.
The bell calls, the staff's shattered,
I'm seized and I'm fettered   4510
And borne away, bound, to the block.
Every neck shivers with shock
As the axe-blade's brought down on my own.
Dumb lies the world as the grave.

FAUST   I wish I had never been born!   4515

MEPHISTOPHELES [*Appearing outside*]
Come, come, or all's up with you, friend—
Debating, vacillating, useless jabbering!
My horses are trembling.
A minute or two and it's day.

MARGARETE   Who's that rising up out of the ground?   4520
It's him, him, oh drive him away!
It's holy here, what is he after?
It's me he is after, it's me!

FAUST   Live, hear me, live!

MARGARETE   It's the judgment of God! I surrender!

MEPHISTO   Die both of you, I have to leave.   4525

MARGARETE   In your hands, our Father! Oh, save me!
You angelical hosts, stand about me,
Draw up in your ranks to protect me!
I'm afraid of you, Heinrich, afraid!

MEPHISTO   She's condemned!   4530

VOICE [*From above.*]
                                    She is saved!

MEPHISTO [*To* FAUST, *peremptorily.*]
Come with me!
        [*He disappears with* FAUST.]

VOICE [*From within, dying away.*]
Heinrich! Heinrich!

ALEXANDER SERGEYEVICH PUSHKIN

1799–1837

Before Pushkin's time, most Russian writers had translated or imitated French, English, and German literature. Pushkin forged a whole new path. Writing in a wide range of genres—lyric poems, short stories, dramas, a great novel in verse (*Eugene Onegin*), and versified folktales—he combined Russian styles and traditions with foreign influences to create an exciting new kind of literary voice that conveyed a lively new feeling for the variety and flexibility of the Russian language. Often called "the father of Russian literature," Pushkin inspired an extraordinary group of writers in the generations to follow, including **Leo Tolstoy**, **Fyodor Dostoyevsky**, and **Anton Chekhov**. His premature death was—and is—considered a catastrophe for Russian literature. During a memorial ceremony for Pushkin in Moscow long after he died in 1880, people in the audience felt such intense grief that many cried, screamed, and fainted away.

LIFE

Pushkin's life story sounds like a Romantic novel. His father, descended from an old aristocratic Russian family, married the granddaughter of a slave from the African empire of Abyssinia, who had risen to become a general in the Russian army. Pushkin's parents dedicated their lives to the pleasures of society—going to the theater and visiting literary salons—and neglected their five children. Their restless and irritable mother would sometimes refuse to speak to the young Pushkin for weeks on end. The boy read voraciously, including Homer, Plutarch, Molière, and Voltaire all before the age of twelve. He published his first poem at fifteen and at the same time started to become notorious for his many erotic involvements. At eighteen his poetry was already being received enthusiastically in literary circles. He graduated from a distinguished boarding school and accepted an appointment in the foreign service, where he spent much of his time drinking, gambling, and conducting turbulent love affairs with married women. In 1820, however, his revolutionary views brought him to the attention of the police: he was expelled from his job and confined to a family estate. In the years of exile that followed he wrote some of his most famous works, including his great lyrical drama, *Boris Godunov* (1825).

After the death of Czar Alexander I, Pushkin, by then a well-known poet, was befriended by the new czar, Nicholas. He moved to St. Petersburg and decided to settle down, saying that he intended to marry the most beautiful woman in Russia. At the age of thirty-one, he finished his great work, *Eugene Onegin*, and married the nineteen-year-old Natalya Nikolayevna Goncharova, who was widely admired and flirtatious. Six years later, Pushkin heard rumors that Natalya was having an affair. He challenged her alleged lover to a duel and died of gunshot wounds to the stomach.

WORK

In *The Queen of Spades,* Pushkin builds on the popularity of romantic tales of ghosts and lovers that circulated in his time, but he gives these a twist. He certainly offers us haunting characters: a beautiful young gambler who learns the secret of three infallible cards, a young foreigner who wants to make his way in the world, a servant girl longing for a "deliverer." A conventional symbol of death, the queen of spades itself fits the ghost story genre. But Pushkin continually undercuts both grand passions and supernatural thrills. Hermann, the observant German engineer who should be the romantic hero, turns out to be a greedy man who uses others as a means to an end. At one point, he goes so far as to imagine becoming the lover of an eighty-seven-year-old countess.

Pushkin uses ghosts and lovers to point us to a society corrupted by money. Gambling provides the chief activity in the story. The countess, whose days at the card table are past, uses her money to buy subservience; the servant girl, Lizaveta, is willing to risk her reputation, maybe even her chastity, for the possibility of escaping servitude; and Hermann literally frightens someone to death in an effort to make his fortune. Everyone seeks personal advantage.

The story moves among perspectives and narrators, and it continually points to the power of stories. Hermann becomes obsessed with a story of magical gambling, and he copies his love letter from someone else's novel. Lizaveta is too willing to live out other people's stories. The countess longs to read a novel that is not about strangling or drowning, and her grandson jokes that there are no other kinds of novels. What, Pushkin asks, is the right kind of story? The conclusion, told in a deadpan style, suggests an answer. It seems to belong to a totally different genre from the Romantic tale, as it calls up a mundane and fitting ending for each of the characters. Pushkin hints here that what really haunts us are not ghosts but our own desires and our own guilt. And perhaps the conclusion is more terrifying than any ghost story precisely because of its everyday reality—its revelation of a society entirely consumed by greed.

The Queen of Spades[1]

Chapter One

And on rainy days
They gathered
Often;
Their stakes—God help them!—
Wavered from fifty
To a hundred,
And they won
And marked up their winnings
With chalk.
Thus on rainy days
Were they
Busy.[2]

There was a card party one day in the rooms of Narumov, an officer of the Horse Guards. The long winter evening slipped by unnoticed; it was five o'clock in the morning before the assembly sat down to supper. Those who had won ate with a big appetite; the others sat distractedly before their empty plates. But champagne was brought in, the conversation became more lively, and everyone took a part in it.

'And how did you get on, Surin?' asked the host.

'As usual, I lost. I must confess, I have no luck: I never vary my stake, never get heated, never lose my head, and yet I always lose!'

'And weren't you tempted even once to back[3] on a series? Your strength of mind astonishes me.'

'What about Hermann then?' said one of the guests, pointing at the young Engineer.[4] 'He's never held a card in his hand, never doubled a single stake in his life, and yet he sits up until five in the morning watching us play.'

'The game fascinates me,' said Hermann, 'but I am not in the position to sacrifice the essentials of life in the hope of acquiring the luxuries.'

'Hermann's a German: he's cautious—that's all,' Tomsky observed. 'But if there's one person I can't understand, it's my grandmother, the Countess Anna Fedotovna.'

'How? Why?' the guests inquired noisily.

'I cannot understand why it is,' Tomsky continued, 'that my grandmother never gambles.'

'But what's so astonishing about an old lady of eighty not gambling?' asked Narumov.

'Then you don't know . . . ?'

'No, indeed; I know nothing.'

'Oh well, listen then:

'You must know that about sixty years ago my grandmother went to Paris, where she made something of a hit. People used to chase after her to catch a

---

1. Translated by Gillon R. Aitken.
2. Like most of the chapter epigraphs, this was presumably written by Pushkin himself.
3. Bet.
4. A member of the Corps of Engineers, concerned with fortifications.

glimpse of *la Vénus moscovite*; Richelieu[5] paid court to her, and my grand-mother vouches that he almost shot himself on account of her cruelty. At that time ladies used to play faro.[6] On one occasion at the Court, my grandmother lost a very great deal of money on credit to the Duke of Orleans. Returning home, she removed the patches[7] from her face, took off her hooped petticoat, announced her loss to my grandfather and ordered him to pay back the money. My late grandfather, as far as I can remember, was a sort of lackey to my grandmother. He feared her like fire; on hearing of such a disgraceful loss, however, he completely lost his temper. He produced his accounts, showed her that she had spent half a million francs in six months, pointed out that neither their Moscow nor their Saratov estates were in Paris, and refused point-blank to pay the debt. My grandmother gave him a box on the ear and went off to sleep on her own as an indication of her displeasure. In the hope that this domestic infliction would have had some effect upon him, she sent for her husband the next day; she found him unshakeable. For the first time in her life she approached him with argument and explanation, thinking that she could bring him to reason by pointing out that there are debts and debts, that there is a big difference between a Prince and a coach-maker. But my grandfather remained adamant, and flatly refused to discuss the subject any further. My grandmother did not know what to do. A little while before, she had become acquainted with a very remarkable man. You have heard of Count St-Germain,[8] about whom so many marvellous stories are related. You know that he held himself out to be the Wandering Jew, and the inventor of the elixir of life, the philosopher's stone and so forth. Some ridiculed him as a charlatan and in his memoirs Casanova declares that he was a spy. However, St-Germain, in spite of the mystery which surrounded him, was a person of venerable appearance and much in demand in society. My grandmother remains quite infatuated with him and becomes quite angry if anyone speaks of him with disrespect. My grandmother knew that he had large sums of money at his disposal. She decided to have recourse to him, and wrote asking him to visit her without delay. The eccentric old man at once called on her and found her in a state of terrible grief. She depicted her husband's barbarity in the blackest light, and ended by saying that she pinned all her hopes on his friendship and kindness.

'St-Germain reflected. "I could let you have this sum," he said, "but I know that you would not be at peace while in my debt, and I have no wish to bring fresh troubles upon your head. There is another solution—you can win back the money."

' "But, my dear Count," my grandmother replied, "I tell you—we have no money at all."

' "In this case money is not essential," St-Germain replied. "Be good enough to hear me out."

---

5. Louis-François-Armand de Vignerod du Plessis, duc de Richelieu (1696–1788), French aristocrat renowned throughout the 18th century for both his military and his sexual exploits. "*La vénus moscovite*": the Venus of Moscow (French). Venus was the Roman goddess of love.

6. A card game much used for gambling.
7. I.e., beauty patches, artificial "beauty marks" made of black silk or court plaster and worn on the face or neck.
8. A celebrated adventurer (ca. 1710–1784?) who frequented the French, German, and Russian courts.

'And at this point he revealed to her the secret for which any one of us here would give a very great deal ...'

The young gamblers listened with still greater attention. Tomsky lit his pipe, drew on it and continued:

'That same evening my grandmother went to Versailles, *au jeu de la Reine*.[9] The Duke of Orleans kept the bank. Inventing some small tale, my grandmother lightly excused herself for not having brought her debt, and began to play against him. She chose three cards and played them one after the other: all three won and my grandmother recouped herself completely.'

'Pure luck !' said one of the guests.

'A fairy-tale,' observed Hermann.

'Perhaps the cards were marked!' said a third.

'I don't think so,' Tomsky replied gravely.

'What!' cried Narumov. 'You have a grandmother who can guess three cards in succession, and you haven't yet contrived to learn her secret.'

'No, not much hope of that!' replied Tomsky. 'She had four sons, including my father; all four were desperate gamblers, and yet she did not reveal her secret to a single one of them, although it would have been a good thing if she had told them—told me, even. But this is what I heard from my uncle, Count Ivan Ilyitch, and he gave me his word for its truth. The late Chaplitsky—the same who died a pauper after squandering millions—in his youth once lost nearly 300,000 roubles—to Zoritch, if I remember rightly. He was in despair. My grandmother, who was most strict in her attitude towards the extravagances of young men, for some reason took pity on Chaplitsky. She told him the three cards on condition that he played them in order; and at the same time she exacted his solemn promise that he would never play again as long as he lived. Chaplitsky appeared before his victor; they sat down to play. On the first card Chaplitsky staked 50,000 roubles and won straight off; he doubled his stake, redoubled—and won back more than he had lost ...'

'But it's time to go to bed; it's already a quarter to six.'

Indeed, the day was already beginning to break. The young men drained their glasses and dispersed.

Chapter Two

—Il paraît que monsieur est décidément pour les suivantes.
—Que voulez-vous, madame? Elles sont plus fraîches.[1]

FASHIONABLE CONVERSATION

The old Countess ***[2] was seated before the looking-glass in her dressing-room. Three lady's maids stood by her. One held a jar of rouge, another a box of hairpins, and the third a tall bonnet with flame-coloured ribbons. The Countess no longer had the slightest pretensions to beauty, which had long

---

9. To the queen's game (French).
1. "It appears that the gentleman is decidedly in favor of servant girls." "What would you have me do, Madam? They are fresher [than upper-class women]" (French).
2. Asterisks in this selection are the author's and are intended to suggest that the proper name of an actual person has been omitted.

since faded from her face, but she still preserved all the habits of her youth, paid strict regard to the fashions of the 'seventies, and devoted to her dress the same time and attention as she had done sixty years before. At an embroidery frame by the window sat a young lady, her ward.

'Good morning, *grand'maman*!'[3] said a young officer as he entered the room. '*Bonjour, mademoiselle Lise. Grand'maman*, I have a request to make of you.'

'What is it, Paul?'

'I want you to let me introduce one of my friends to you, and to allow me to bring him to the ball on Friday.'

'Bring him straight to the ball and introduce him to me there. Were you at ***'s yesterday?'

'Of course. It was very merry; we danced until five in the morning. How charming Yeletskaya was!'

'But, my dear, what's charming about her? Isn't she like her grandmother, the Princess Darya Petrovna . . . ? By the way, I dare say she's grown very old now, the Princess Darya Petrovna?'

'What do you mean, "grown old"?' asked Tomsky thoughtlessly. 'She's been dead for seven years.'

The young lady raised her head and made a sign to the young man. He remembered then that the death of any of her contemporaries was kept secret from the old Countess, and he bit his lip. But the Countess heard the news, previously unknown to her, with the greatest indifference.

'Dead!' she said. 'And I didn't know it. We were maids of honour together, and when we were presented, the Empress . . .'

And for the hundredth time the Countess related the anecdote to her grandson.

'Come, Paul,' she said when she had finished her story, 'help me to stand up. Lisanka, where's my snuff-box?'

And with her three maids the Countess went behind a screen to complete her dress. Tomsky was left alone with the young lady.

'Whom do you wish to introduce?' Lisaveta Ivanovna asked softly.

'Narumov. Do you know him?'

'No. Is he a soldier or a civilian?'

'A soldier.'

'An Engineer?'

'No, he's in the Cavalry. What made you think he was an Engineer?'

The young lady smiled but made no reply.

'Paul!' cried the Countess from behind the screen. 'Bring along a new novel with you some time, will you, only please not one of those modern ones.'

'What do you mean, *grand'maman*?'

'I mean not the sort of novel in which the hero strangles either of his parents or in which someone is drowned.[4] I have a great horror of drowned people.'

'Such novels don't exist nowadays. Wouldn't you like a Russian one?'

'Are there such things? Send me one, my dear, please send me one.'

'Will you excuse me now, *grand'maman*, I'm in a hurry. Good-bye, Lisaveta Ivanovna. What made you think that Narumov was in the Engineers?'

---

3. Russian aristocrats often spoke French. Lisaveta is here called by the French name Lise, and Pavel, Paul.

4. Novels of the sort the countess does not wish to read were typical of the then current decadent movement in French literature.

And Tomsky left the dressing-room.

Lisaveta Ivanovna was left on her own. She put aside her work and began to look out of the window. Presently a young officer appeared from behind the corner house on the other side of the street. A flush spread over her cheeks. She took up her work again and lowered her head over the frame. At this moment, the Countess returned, fully dressed.

'Order the carriage, Lisanka,' she said, 'and we'll go for a drive.'

Lisanka got up from behind her frame and began to put her work away.

'What's the matter with you, my child? Are you deaf?' shouted the Countess. 'Order the carriage this minute.'

'I'll do so at once,' the young lady replied softly and hastened into the ante-room.

A servant entered the room and handed the Countess some books from the Prince Pavel Alexandrovitch.

'Good, thank him,' said the Countess. 'Lisanka, Lisanka, where are you running to?'

'To get dressed.'

'Plenty of time for that, my dear. Sit down. Open the first volume and read to me.'

The young lady took up the book and read a few lines.

'Louder!' said the Countess. 'What's the matter with you, my child? Have you lost your voice, or what . . . ? Wait . . . move that footstool up to me . . . nearer . . . that's right!'

Lisaveta Ivanovna read a further two pages. The Countess yawned.

'Put the book down,' she said. 'What rubbish! Have it returned to Prince Pavel with my thanks . . . But where is the carriage?'

'The carriage is ready,' said Lisaveta Ivanovna, looking out into the street.

'Then why aren't you dressed?' asked the Countess. 'I'm always having to wait for you—it's intolerable, my dear!'

Lisa ran up to her room. Not two minutes elapsed before the Countess began to ring with all her might. The three lady's maids came running in through one door and the valet through another.

'Why don't you come when you're called?' the Countess asked them. 'Tell Lisaveta Ivanovna that I'm waiting for her.'

Lisaveta Ivanovna entered the room wearing her hat and cloak.

'At last, my child!' said the Countess. 'But what clothes you're wearing . . . ! Whom are you hoping to catch? What's the weather like? It seems windy.'

'There's not a breath of wind, your Ladyship,' replied the valet.

'You never know what you're talking about! Open that small window. There, as I thought: windy and bitterly cold. Unharness the horses. Lisaveta, we're not going out—there was no need to dress up like that.'

'And this is my life,' thought Lisaveta Ivanovna.

And indeed Lisaveta Ivanovna was a most unfortunate creature. As Dante says: 'You shall learn the salt taste of another's bread, and the hard path up and down his stairs';[5] and who better to know the bitterness of dependence than the poor ward of a well-born old lady? The Countess *** was far from being

---

5. *Paradiso* 17.59.

wicked, but she had the capriciousness of a woman who has been spoiled by the world, and the miserliness and cold-hearted egotism of all old people who have done with loving and whose thoughts lie with the past. She took part in all the vanities of the *haut-monde*;[6] she dragged herself to balls, where she sat in a corner, rouged and dressed in old-fashioned style, like some misshapen but essential ornament of the ball-room. On arrival, the guests would approach her with low bows, as if in accordance with an established rite, but after that, they would pay no further attention to her. She received the whole town at her house, and although no longer able to recognise the faces of her guests, she observed the strictest etiquette. Her numerous servants, grown fat and grey in her hall and servants' room, did exactly as they pleased, vying with one another in stealing from the dying old lady. Lisaveta Ivanovna was the household martyr. She poured out the tea, and was reprimanded for putting in too much sugar; she read novels aloud, and was held guilty of all the faults of the authors; she accompanied the Countess on her walks, and was made responsible for the state of the weather and the pavement. There was a salary attached to her position, but it was never paid. Meanwhile, it was demanded of her to be dressed like everybody else—that is, like the very few who could afford to dress well. In society she played the most pitiable role. Everybody knew her, but nobody took any notice of her; at balls she danced only when there was a partner short, and ladies only took her arm when they needed to go to the dressing-room to make some adjustment to their dress. She was proud and felt her position keenly, and looked around her in impatient expectation of a deliverer; but the young men, calculating in their flightiness, did not honour her with their attention, despite the fact that Lisaveta Ivanovna was a hundred times prettier than the cold, arrogant but more eligible young ladies on whom they danced attendance. Many a time did she creep softly away from the bright but wearisome drawing-room to go and cry in her own poor room, where stood a papered screen, a chest of drawers, a small looking-glass and a painted bedstead, and where a tallow candle burned dimly in its copper candlestick.

One day—two days after the evening described at the beginning of this story, and about a week previous to the events just recorded—Lisaveta Ivanovna was sitting at her embroidery frame by the window when, happening to glance out into the street, she saw a young Engineer, standing motionless with his eyes fixed upon her window. She lowered her head and continued with her work; five minutes later she looked out again—the young officer was still standing in the same place. Not being in the habit of flirting with passing officers, she ceased to look out of the window, and sewed for about two hours without raising her head. Dinner was announced. She got up and began to put away her frame, and, glancing casually out into the street, she again saw the officer. She was considerably puzzled by this. After dinner, she approached the window with a feeling of some disquiet, but the officer was no longer outside, and she thought no more of him.

Two days later, while preparing to enter the carriage with the Countess, she saw him again. He was standing just by the front door, his face concealed by a beaver collar; his dark eyes shone from beneath his cap. Without knowing why,

6. High society (French).

Lisaveta Ivanovna felt afraid, and an unaccountable trembling came over her as she sat down in the carriage.

On her return home, she hastened to the window—the officer was standing in the same place as before, his eyes fixed upon her. She drew back, tormented by curiosity and agitated by a feeling that was quite new to her.

Since then, not a day had passed without the young man appearing at the customary hour beneath the windows of their house. A sort of mute acquaintance grew up between them. At work in her seat, she used to feel him approaching, and would raise her head to look at him—for longer and longer each day. The young man seemed to be grateful to her for this: she saw, with the sharp eye of youth, how a sudden flush would spread across his pale cheeks on each occasion that their glances met. After a week she smiled at him . . .

When Tomsky asked leave of the Countess to introduce one of his friends to her, the poor girl's heart beat fast. But on learning that Narumov was in the Horse Guards, and not in the Engineers, she was sorry that, by an indiscreet question, she had betrayed her secret to the light-hearted Tomsky.

Hermann was the son of a Russianised German from whom he had inherited a small amount of money. Being firmly convinced of the necessity of ensuring his independence, Hermann did not draw on the income that this yielded, but lived on his pay, forbidding himself the slightest extravagance. Moreover, he was secretive and ambitious, and his companions rarely had occasion to laugh at his excessive thrift. He had strong passions and a fiery imagination, but his tenacity of spirit saved him from the usual errors of youth. Thus, for example, although at heart a gambler, he never took a card in his hand, for he reckoned that his position did not allow him (as he put it) 'to sacrifice the essentials of life in the hope of acquiring the luxuries'—and, meanwhile, he would sit up at the card table for whole nights at a time, following the different turns of the game with feverish anxiety.

The story of the three cards had made a strong impression on his imagination, and he could think of nothing else all night.

'What if the old Countess should reveal her secret to me?' he thought the following evening as he wandered through the streets of Petersburg. 'What if she should tell me the names of those three winning cards? Why not try my luck . . . ? Become introduced to her, try to win her favour, perhaps become her lover . . . ? But all that demands time, and she's eighty-seven; she might die in a week, in two days . . . ! And the story itself . . . ? Can one really believe it . . . ? No! Economy, moderation and industry: these are my three winning cards, these will treble my capital, increase it sevenfold, and earn for me ease and independence!'

Reasoning thus, he found himself in one of the principal streets of Petersburg, before a house of old-fashioned architecture. The street was crowded with vehicles; one after another, carriages rolled up to the lighted entrance. From them there emerged, now the shapely little foot of some beautiful young woman, now a rattling jack-boot, now the striped stocking and elegant shoe of a diplomat. Furs and capes flitted past the majestic hall-porter. Hermann stopped.

'Whose house is this?' he asked the watchman at the corner.

'The Countess ***'s,' the watchman replied.

Hermann started. His imagination was again fired by the amazing story of the three cards. He began to walk around near the house, thinking of its owner and her mysterious faculty. It was late when he returned to his humble rooms. For a long time he could not sleep, and when at last he did drop off, cards, a green table,[7] heaps of banknotes and piles of golden coins appeared to him in his dreams. He played one card after the other, doubled his stake decisively, won unceasingly, and raked in the golden coins and stuffed his pockets with the banknotes. Waking up late, he sighed at the loss of his imaginary fortune, again went out to wander about the town and again found himself outside the house of the Countess ***. Some unknown power seemed to have attracted him to it. He stopped and began to look at the windows. At one he saw a head with long black hair, probably bent down over a book or a piece of work. The head was raised. Hermann saw a small, fresh face and a pair of dark eyes. That moment decided his fate.

Chapter Three

Vous m'écrivez, mon ange, des lettres de
quatre pages plus vite que je ne
puis les lire.[8]
CORRESPONDENCE

Scarcely had Lisaveta Ivanovna taken off her hat and cloak when the Countess sent for her and again ordered her to have the horses harnessed. They went out to take their seats in the carriage. At the same moment as the old lady was being helped through the carriage doors by two footmen, Lisaveta Ivanovna saw her Engineer standing close by the wheel. He seized her hand and, before she could recover from her fright the young man had disappeared—leaving a letter in her hand. She hid it in her glove and throughout the whole of the drive neither heard nor saw a thing. As was her custom when riding in her carriage, the Countess kept up a ceaseless flow of questions: 'Who was it who met us just now? What's this bridge called? What's written on that signboard?' This time Lisaveta Ivanovna's answers were so vague and inappropriate that the Countess became angry.

'What's the matter with you, my child? Are you in a trance or something? Don't you hear me or understand what I'm saying? Heaven be thanked that I'm still sane enough to speak clearly.'

Lisaveta Ivanovna did not listen to her. On returning home, she ran up to her room and drew the letter from her glove; it was unsealed. Lisaveta Ivanovna read it through. The letter contained a confession of love; it was tender, respectful and taken word for word from a German novel. But Lisaveta Ivanovna had no knowledge of German and was most pleased by it.

Nevertheless, the letter made her feel extremely uneasy. For the first time in her life she was entering into a secret and confidential relationship with a young man. His audacity shocked her. She reproached herself for her impru-

---

7. Tables on which gambling took place were typically covered with green baize.

8. My angel, you write me four-page-long letters faster than I can read them (French).

dent behaviour, and did not know what to do. Should she stop sitting at the window and by a show of indifference cool off the young man's desire for further acquaintance? Should she send the letter back to him? Or answer it with cold-hearted finality? There was nobody to whom she could turn for advice: she had no friend or preceptress. Lisaveta Ivanovna resolved to answer the letter.

She sat down at her small writing-table, took a pen and some paper, and lost herself in thought. Several times she began her letter—and then tore it up: her manner of expression seemed to her to be either too condescending or too heartless. At last she succeeded in writing a few lines that satisfied her:

> *'I am sure that your intentions are honourable, and that you did not wish to offend me by your rash behaviour, but our acquaintance must not begin in this way. I return your letter to you and hope that in the future I shall have no cause to complain of undeserved disrespect.'*

The next day, as soon as she saw Hermann approach, Lisaveta Ivanovna rose from behind her frame, went into the ante-room, opened a small window and threw her letter into the street, trusting to the agility of the young officer to pick it up. Hermann ran forward, took hold of the letter and went into a confectioner's shop. Breaking the seal of the envelope, he found his own letter and Lisaveta Ivanovna's answer. It was as he had expected, and he returned home, deeply preoccupied with his intrigue.

Three days afterwards, a bright-eyed young girl brought Lisaveta Ivanovna a letter from a milliner's shop. Lisaveta Ivanovna opened it uneasily, envisaging a demand for money, but she suddenly recognised Hermann's handwriting.

'You have made a mistake, my dear,' she said: 'this letter is not for me.'

'Oh, but it is!' the girl answered cheekily and without concealing a sly smile. 'Read it.'

Lisaveta Ivanovna ran her eyes over the note. Hermann demanded a meeting.

'It cannot be,' said Lisaveta Ivanovna, frightened at the haste of his demand and the way in which it was made: 'this is certainly not for me.'

And she tore the letter up into tiny pieces.

'If the letter wasn't for you, why did you tear it up?' asked the girl. 'I would have returned it to the person who sent it.'

'Please, my dear,' Lisaveta Ivanovna said, flushing at the remark, 'don't bring me any more letters in future. And tell the person who sent you that he should be ashamed of . . .'

But Hermann was not put off. By some means or other, he sent a letter to Lisaveta Ivanovna every day. The letters were no longer translated from the German. They were inspired by passion and written in a language, true to Hermann's character, which expressed his obsessive desires and the disorder of an unfettered imagination. Lisaveta Ivanovna no longer thought of returning them to him: she revelled in them, began to answer them, and with each day, her replies became longer and more tender. Finally, she threw out of the window the following letter:

> *'This evening there is a ball at the *** Embassy. The Countess will be there. We will stay until about two o'clock. Here is your chance to see me alone. As soon*

> *as the Countess has left the house, the servants will probably go to their quarters—with the exception of the hall-porter, who normally goes out to his closet anyway. Come at half-past eleven. Walk straight upstairs. If you meet anybody in the ante-room, ask whether the Countess is at home. You will be told "No"—and there will be nothing you can do but go away. But it is unlikely that you will meet anybody. The lady's maids sit by themselves, all in the one room. On leaving the hall, turn to the left and walk straight on until you come to the Countess' bedroom. In the bedroom, behind a screen, you will see two small doors: the one on the right leads into the study, which the Countess never goes into; the one on the left leads into a corridor and thence to a narrow winding staircase: this staircase leads to my bedroom.'*

Hermann quivered like a tiger as he awaited the appointed hour. He was already outside the Countess' house at ten o'clock. The weather was terrible; the wind howled, and a wet snow fell in large flakes upon the deserted streets, where the lamps shone dimly. Occasionally a passing cab-driver leaned forward over his scrawny nag, on the look-out for a late passenger. Feeling neither wind nor snow, Hermann waited, dressed only in his frock-coat. At last the Countess' carriage was brought round. Hermann saw two footmen carry out in their arms the bent old lady, wrapped in a sable fur, and immediately following her, the figure of Lisaveta Ivanovna, clad in a light cloak and with her head adorned with fresh flowers. The doors were slammed and the carriage rolled heavily away along the soft snow. The hall-porter closed the front door. The windows became dark. Hermann began to walk about near the deserted house. He went up to a lamp and looked at his watch; it was twenty minutes past eleven. He remained beneath the lamp, his eyes fixed upon the hands of his watch, waiting for the remaining minutes to pass. At exactly half-past eleven, Hermann ascended the steps of the Countess' house and reached the brightly-lit porch. The hall-porter was not there. Hermann ran up the stairs, opened the door into the ante-room and saw a servant asleep by the lamp in a soiled antique armchair. With a light, firm tread Hermann stepped past him. The drawing-room and reception-room were in darkness, but the lamp in the ante-room sent through a feeble light. Hermann passed through into the bedroom. Before an icon-case, filled with old-fashioned images,[9] glowed a gold sanctuary lamp. Faded brocade armchairs and dull gilt divans with soft cushions were ranged in sad symmetry around the room, the walls of which were hung with Chinese silk. Two portraits, painted in Paris by Madame Lebrun,[1] hung on one of the walls. One of these featured a plump, red-faced man of about forty, in a light-green uniform and with a star pinned to his breast; the other—a beautiful young woman with an aquiline nose and powdered hair, brushed back at the temples and adorned with a rose. In the corners of the room stood porcelain shepherdesses, table clocks from the workshop of the celebrated Leroy, little boxes, roulettes, fans and the various lady's playthings which had been popular at the end of the last century, when the Montgolfiers' balloon and Mesmer's

9. I.e., religious images.
1. Marie-Louise-Élisabeth Vigée-Lebrun (1755– 1842), French portrait painter, particularly of the aristocracy and royalty.

magnetism[2] were invented. Hermann went behind the screen, where stood a small iron bedstead. On the right was the door leading to the study; on the left the one which led to the corridor. Hermann opened the latter, and saw the narrow, winding staircase which led to the poor ward's room ... But he turned back and stepped into the dark study.

The time passed slowly. Everything was quiet. The clock in the drawing-room struck twelve; one by one the clocks in all the other rooms sounded the same hour, and then all was quiet again. Hermann stood leaning against the cold stove. He was calm; his heart beat evenly, like that of a man who has decided upon some dangerous but necessary action. One o'clock sounded; two o'clock; he heard the distant rattle of the carriage. He was seized by an involuntary agitation. The carriage drew near and stopped. He heard the sound of the carriage-steps being let down. The house suddenly came alive. Servants ran here and there, voices echoed through the house and the rooms were lit. Three old maid-servants hastened into the bedroom, followed by the Countess, who, tired to death, lowered herself into a Voltairean armchair.[3] Hermann peeped through a crack. Lisaveta Ivanovna went past him. Hermann heard her hurried steps as she went up the narrow staircase. In his heart there echoed something like the voice of conscience, but it grew silent, and his heart once more turned to stone.

The Countess began to undress before the looking-glass. Her rose-bedecked cap was unfastened; her powdered wig was removed from her grey, closely-cropped hair. Pins fell in showers around her. Her yellow dress, embroidered with silver, fell at her swollen feet. Hermann witnessed all the loathsome mysteries of her toilet. At last the Countess stood in her dressing-gown and night-cap; in this attire, more suitable to her age, she seemed less hideous and revolting.

Like most old people, the Countess suffered from insomnia. Having undressed, she sat down in the Voltairean armchair by the window and dismissed her maidservants. The candles were carried out; once again the room was lit by a single sanctuary lamp. Looking quite yellow, the Countess rocked from side to side in her chair, her flabby lips moving. Her dim eyes reflected a total absence of thought; looking at her, one would have thought that the awful old woman's rocking came not of her own volition, but by the action of some hidden galvanism.

Suddenly, an indescribable change came over her deathlike face. Her lips ceased to move, her eyes came to life: before the Countess stood an unknown man.

'Don't be alarmed, for God's sake, don't be alarmed,' he said in a clear, low voice. 'I have no intention of harming you; I have come to beseech a favour of you.'

The old woman looked at him in silence, as if she had not heard him. Hermann imagined that she was deaf, and bending right down over her ear, he repeated what he had said. The old woman kept silent as before.

'You can ensure the happiness of my life,' Hermann continued, 'and it will cost you nothing: I know that you can guess three cards in succession ... '

---

2. Franz Anton Mesmer (1734–1815) argued that a person can transmit personal force to others in the form of "animal magnetism." Julien Leroy (1686–1759), famous French clockmaker. "Roulettes": little balls, or possibly portable devices for playing the gambling game of roulette. Joseph-Michel (1740–1810) and Jacques-Étienne (1745–1799) Montgolfier, French brothers, helped develop the hot-air balloon and conducted the first untethered flights.

3. A large armchair with a high back.

Hermann stopped. The Countess appeared to understand what was demanded of her; she seemed to be seeking words for her reply.

'It was a joke,' she said at last. 'I swear to you, it was a joke.'

'There's no joking about it,' Hermann retorted angrily. 'Remember Chaplitsky whom you helped to win.'

The Countess was visibly disconcerted, and her features expressed strong emotion; but she quickly resumed her former impassivity.

'Can you name these three winning cards?' Hermann continued.

The Countess was silent. Hermann went on:

'For whom do you keep your secret? For your grandsons? They are rich and they can do without it; they don't know the value of money. Your three cards will not help a spend-thrift. He who cannot keep his paternal inheritance will die in want, even if he has the devil at his side. I am not a spend-thrift; I know the value of money. Your three cards will not be lost on me. Come . . . !'

He stopped and awaited her answer with trepidation. The Countess was silent. Hermann fell upon his knees.

'If your heart has ever known the feeling of love,' he said, 'if you remember its ecstasies, if you ever smiled at the wailing of your new-born son, if ever any human feeling has run through your breast, I entreat you by the feelings of a wife, a lover, a mother, by everything that is sacred in life, not to deny my request! Reveal your secret to me! What is it to you . . . ? Perhaps it is bound up with some dreadful sin, with the loss of eternal bliss, with some contract made with the devil . . . Consider: you are old; you have not long to live—I am prepared to take your sins on my own soul. Only reveal to me your secret. Realise that the happiness of a man is in your hands, that not only I, but my children, my grandchildren, my great-grandchildren will bless your memory and will revere it as something sacred . . .'

The old woman answered not a word.

Hermann stood up.

'You old witch!' he said, clenching his teeth. 'I'll force you to answer . . .'

With these words he drew a pistol from his pocket. At the sight of the pistol, the Countess, for the second time, exhibited signs of strong emotion. She shook her head and, raising her hand as though to shield herself from the shot, she rolled over on her back and remained motionless.

'Stop this childish behaviour now,' Hermann said, taking her hand. 'I ask you for the last time: will you name your three cards or won't you?'

The Countess made no reply. Hermann saw that she was dead.

Chapter Four

7 Mai 18**
Homme sans mœurs et sans religion![4]
CORRESPONDENCE

Still in her ball dress, Lisaveta Ivanovna sat in her room, lost in thought. On her arrival home, she had quickly dismissed the sleepy maid who had reluc-

---

4. A man without morals and without religion! (French).

tantly offered her services, had said that she would undress herself, and with a tremulous heart had gone up to her room, expecting to find Hermann there and yet hoping not to find him. Her first glance assured her of his absence and she thanked her fate for the obstacle that had prevented their meeting. She sat down, without undressing, and began to recall all the circumstances which had lured her so far in so short a time. It was not three weeks since she had first seen the young man from the window—and yet she was already in correspondence with him, and already he had managed to persuade her to grant him a nocturnal meeting! She knew his name only because some of his letters had been signed; she had never spoken to him, nor heard his voice, nor heard anything about him ... until that very evening. Strange thing! That very evening, Tomsky, vexed with the Princess Polina *** for not flirting with him as she usually did, had wished to revenge himself by a show of indifference: he had therefore summoned Lisaveta Ivanovna and together they had danced an endless mazurka. All the time they were dancing, he had teased her about her partiality to officers of the Engineers, had assured her that he knew far more than she would have supposed possible, and, indeed, some of his jests were so successfully aimed that on several occasions Lisaveta Ivanovna had thought that her secret was known to him.

'From whom have you discovered all this?' she asked, laughing.

'From a friend of a person you know well,' Tomsky answered. 'From a most remarkable man!'

'Who is this remarkable man?'

'He is called Hermann.'

Lisaveta made no reply, but her hands and feet turned quite numb.

'This Hermann,' Tomsky continued, 'is a truly romantic figure: he has the profile of a Napoleon, and the soul of a Mephistopheles. I should think he has at least three crimes on his conscience ... How pale you have turned ... !'

'I have a headache ... What did this Hermann—or whatever his name is—tell you?'

'Hermann is most displeased with his friend: he says that he would act quite differently in his place. I even think that Hermann himself has designs on you; at any rate he listens to the exclamations of his enamoured friend with anything but indifference.'

'But where has he seen me?'

'At church, perhaps; on a walk—God only knows! Perhaps in your room, whilst you were asleep: he's quite capable of it ... '

Three ladies approaching him with the question: '*Oublie ou regret?*'[5] interrupted the conversation which had become so agonisingly interesting to Lisaveta Ivanovna.

The lady chosen by Tomsky was the Princess Polina *** herself. She succeeded in clearing up the misunderstanding between them during the many turns and movements of the dance, after which he conducted her to her chair. Tomsky returned to his own place. He no longer had any thoughts for Hermann or Lisaveta Ivanovna, who desperately wanted to renew her interrupted

---

5. The ladies cut in, offering the man a choice: *oublie* (forgetting) or *regret*. He does not know which lady is which. He chooses correctly the one with whom he wants to dance.

conversation; but the mazurka came to an end and shortly afterwards the old Countess left.

Tomsky's words were nothing but ball-room chatter, but they made a deep impression upon the mind of the young dreamer. The portrait, sketched by Tomsky, resembled the image she herself had formed of Hermann, and thanks to the latest romantic novels, Hermann's quite commonplace face took on attributes that both frightened and captivated her imagination. Now she sat, her uncovered arms crossed, her head, still adorned with flowers, bent over her bare shoulders ... Suddenly the door opened, and Hermann entered. She shuddered.

'Where have you been?' she asked in a frightened whisper.

'In the old Countess' bedroom,' Hermann answered. 'I have just left it. The Countess is dead.'

'Good God! What are you saying?'

'And it seems,' Hermann continued, 'that I am the cause of her death.'

Lisaveta Ivanovna looked at him, and the words of Tomsky echoed in her mind: 'He has at least three crimes on his conscience!' Hermann sat down beside her on the window sill and told her everything.

Lisaveta Ivanovna listened to him with horror. So those passionate letters, those ardent demands, the whole impertinent and obstinate pursuit—all that was not love! Money—that was what his soul craved! It was not she who could satisfy his desire and make him happy! The poor ward had been nothing but the unknowing assistant of a brigand, of the murderer of her aged benefactress! She wept bitterly, in an agony of belated repentance. Hermann looked at her in silence. His heart was also tormented; but neither the tears of the poor girl nor the astounding charm of her grief disturbed his hardened soul. He felt no remorse at the thought of the dead old lady. He felt dismay for only one thing: the irretrievable loss of the secret upon which he had relied for enrichment.

'You are a monster!' Lisaveta Ivanovna said at last.

'I did not wish for her death,' Hermann answered. 'My pistol wasn't loaded.'

They were silent.

The day began to break. Lisaveta Ivanovna extinguished the flickering candle. A pale light lit up her room. She wiped her tear-stained eyes and raised them to Hermann. He sat by the window, his arms folded and with a grim frown on his face. In this position, he bore an astonishing resemblance to a portrait of Napoleon. Even Lisaveta Ivanovna was struck by the likeness.

'How am I going to get you out of the house?' Lisaveta Ivanovna said at last. 'I had thought of leading you down the secret staircase, but that would mean going past the Countess' bedroom, and I am afraid.'

'Tell me how to find this secret staircase. I'll go on my own.'

Lisaveta Ivanovna stood up, took a key from her chest of drawers, handed it to Hermann and gave him detailed instructions. Hermann pressed her cold, unresponsive hand, kissed her bowed head and left.

He descended the winding staircase and once more entered the Countess' bedroom. The dead old lady sat as if turned to stone; her face expressed a deep calm. Hermann stopped in front of her and gazed at her for a long time, as if wishing to assure himself of the dreadful truth. Finally, he went into the study, felt for the door behind the silk wall hangings and, agitated by strange feelings, began to descend the dark staircase.

'Along this very staircase,' he thought, 'perhaps at this same hour sixty years ago, in an embroidered coat, his hair dressed à l'oiseau royal,[6] his three-cornered hat pressed to his heart, there may have crept into this very bedroom a young and happy man now long since turned to dust in his grave—and to-day the aged heart of his mistress ceased to beat.'

At the bottom of the staircase Hermann found a door, which he opened with the key Lisaveta Ivanovna had given to him, and he found himself in a corridor which led to the street.

Chapter Five

That evening there appeared before me
*the figure of the late Baroness von V**.*
She was all in white and she said to me:
'How are you, Mr Councillor!'

SWEDENBORG[7]

Three days after the fateful night, at nine o'clock in the morning, Hermann set out for the *** monastery, where a funeral service for the dead Countess was going to be held. Although unrepentant, he could not altogether silence the voice of conscience, which kept repeating: 'You are the murderer of the old woman!' Having little true religious belief, he was extremely superstitious. He believed that the dead Countess could exercise a harmful influence on his life and he had therefore resolved to be present at her funeral, in order to ask for forgiveness.

The church was full. Hermann could scarcely make his way through the crowd of people. The coffin stood on a rich catafalque beneath a velvet canopy. Within it lay the dead woman, her arms folded upon her chest, dressed in a white satin robe and with a lace cap on her head. Around her stood the members of her household: servants in black coats, with armorial ribbons upon their shoulders and candles in their hands; the relatives—children, grandchildren, great-grandchildren—in deep mourning. Nobody cried; tears would have been *une affectation*. The Countess was so old that her death could have surprised nobody, and her relatives had long considered her as having outlived herself. A young bishop pronounced the funeral sermon. In simple, moving words, he described the peaceful end of the righteous woman, who for many years had been in quiet and touching preparation for a Christian end. 'The angel of death found her,' the speaker said, 'waiting for the midnight bridegroom, vigilant in godly meditation.' The service was completed with sad decorum. The relatives were the first to take leave of the body. Then the numerous guests went up to pay final homage to her who had so long participated in their frivolous amusements. They were followed by all the members of the Countess' household, the last of whom was an old housekeeper of the same age as the

---

6. In the style of the royal bird (French, literal trans.); an antiquated and elaborate hairstyle.
7. Emanuel Swedenborg (1688–1772), Swedish theologian, believed that he had several experiences of divine revelation, some involving appearances to him of the dead.

Countess. She was supported by two young girls who led her up to the coffin. She had not the strength to bow down to the ground—and merely shed a few tears as she kissed the cold hand of her mistress. After her, Hermann decided to approach the coffin. He knelt down and for several minutes lay on the cold floor, which was strewn with fir branches. At last he stood up, as pale as the dead woman herself, ascended the steps of the catafalque and bent his head over the body of the Countess . . . At that very moment, it seemed to him that the dead woman gave him a mocking glance, and winked at him. Hermann, hurriedly stepping back, missed his footing and crashed on to his back against the ground. He was helped to his feet. Simultaneously, Lisaveta Ivanovna was carried out in a faint to the porch of the church. These events disturbed the solemnity of the gloomy ceremony for a few moments. A subdued murmur arose among the congregation, and a tall, thin chamberlain, a near relative of the dead woman, whispered in the ear of an Englishman standing by him that the young officer was the Countess' illegitimate son, to which the Englishman replied coldly: 'Oh?'

For the whole of that day Hermann was exceedingly troubled. He went to a secluded inn for dinner and, contrary to his usual custom and in the hope of silencing his inward agitation, he drank heavily. But the wine fired his imagination still more. Returning home, he threw himself on to his bed without undressing and fell into a heavy sleep.

It was already night when he awoke: the moon lit up his room. He glanced at his watch; it was a quarter to three. He found he could not go back to sleep; he sat on his bed and thought about the funeral of the old Countess.

Just then, someone in the street glanced in at his window and immediately went away. Hermann paid no heed to the incident. A minute or so later, he heard the door into the front room being opened. Hermann imagined that it was his orderly, drunk as usual, returning from some nocturnal outing. But he heard unfamiliar footsteps and the soft shuffling of slippers. The door opened: a woman in a white dress entered. Hermann mistook her for his old wet-nurse and wondered what could have brought her out at this time of the night. But the woman in white glided across the room and suddenly appeared before him—and Hermann recognised the Countess!

'I have come to you against my will,' she said in a firm voice, 'but I have been ordered to fulfil your request. Three, seven, ace, played in that order, will win for you, but only on condition that you play not more than one card in twenty-four hours, and that you never play again for the rest of your life. I'll forgive you my death if you marry my ward, Lisaveta Ivanovna . . .'

With these words, she turned round quietly, walked towards the door and disappeared, her slippers shuffling. Herman heard the door in the hall bang, and again saw somebody look in at him through the window.

For a long time Hermann could not collect his senses. He went into the next room. His orderly was lying asleep on the floor. Hermann could scarcely awaken him. As ususal, the orderly was drunk, and it was impossible to get any sense out of him. The door into the hall was locked. Hermann returned to his room, lit a candle, and recorded the details of his vision.

Chapter Six

—*Attendez!*[8]
—*How dare you say to me: 'Attendez!'?*
—*Your Excellency, I said: 'Attendez, sir'!*

Two fixed ideas can no more exist in one mind than, in the physical sense, two bodies can occupy one and the same place. 'Three, seven, ace' soon eclipsed from Hermann's mind the form of the dead old lady. 'Three, seven, ace' never left his thoughts, were constantly on his lips. At the sight of a young girl, he would say: 'How shapely she is! Just like the three of hearts.' When asked the time, he would reply: 'About seven.' Every potbellied man he saw reminded him of an ace. 'Three, seven, ace,' assuming all possible shapes, persecuted him in his sleep: the three bloomed before him in the shape of some luxuriant flower, the seven took on the appearance of a Gothic gateway, the ace—of an enormous spider. To the exclusion of all others, one thought alone occupied his mind—making use of the secret which had cost him so much. He began to think of retirement and of travel. He wanted to try his luck in the public gaming-houses of Paris. Chance spared him the trouble.

There was in Moscow a society of rich gamblers, presided over by the celebrated Chekalinsky, a man whose whole life had been spent at the card-table, and who had amassed millions long ago, accepting his winnings in the form of promissory notes and paying his losses with ready money. His long experience had earned him the confidence of his companions, and his open house, his famous cook and his friendliness and gaiety had won him great public respect. He arrived in Petersburg. The younger generation flocked to his house, forgetting balls for cards, and preferring the enticements of faro to the fascinations of courtship. Narumov took Hermann to meet him.

They passed through a succession of magnificent rooms, full of polite and attentive waiters. Several generals and privy councillors were playing whist; young men, sprawled out on brocade divans, were eating ices and smoking their pipes. In the drawing-room, seated at the head of a long table, around which were crowded about twenty players, the host kept bank. He was a most respectable-looking man of about sixty; his head was covered with silvery grey hair, and his full, fresh face expressed good nature; his eyes, enlivened by a perpetual smile, shone brightly. Narumov introduced Hermann to him. Chekalinsky shook his hand warmly, requested him not to stand on ceremony and went on dealing.

The game lasted a long time. More than thirty cards lay on the table. Chekalinsky paused after each round, in order to give the players time to arrange their cards, and wrote down their losses. He listened politely to their demands, and more politely still allowed them to retract any stake accidentally left on the table. At last the game finished. Chekalinsky shuffled the cards and prepared to deal again.

'Allow me to place a stake,' Hermann said, stretching out his hand from behind a fat gentleman who was punting[9] there.

---

8. Wait! (French). Attendants at the gaming table called "Attendez" to indicate the end of the period to place bets.

9. Betting against the dealer.

Chekalinsky smiled and nodded silently, as a sign of his consent. Narumov laughingly congratulated Hermann on forswearing a longstanding principle and wished him a lucky beginning.

'I've staked,' Hermann said, as he chalked up the amount, which was very considerable, on the back of his card.

'How much is it?' asked the banker, screwing up his eyes. 'Forgive me, but I can't make it out.'

'47,000 roubles,' Hermann replied.

At these words every head in the room turned, and all eyes were fixed on Hermann.

'He's gone out of his mind!' Narumov thought.

'Allow me to observe to you,' Chekalinsky said with his invariable smile, 'that your stake is extremely high: nobody here has ever put more than 275 roubles on a single card.'

'What of it?' retorted Hermann. 'Do you take me or not?'

Chekalinsky, bowing, humbly accepted the stake.

'However, I would like to say,' he said, 'that, being judged worthy of the confidence of my friends, I can only bank against ready money. For my own part, of course, I am sure that your word is enough, but for the sake of the order of the game and of the accounts, I must ask you to place your money on the card.'

Hermann drew a banknote from his pocket and handed it to Chekalinsky who, giving it a cursory glance, put it on Hermann's card.

He began to deal. On the right a nine turned up, on the left a three.[1]

'The three wins,' said Hermann, showing his card.

A murmur arose among the players. Chekalinsky frowned, but instantly the smile returned to his face.

'Do you wish to take the money now?' he asked Hermann.

'If you would be so kind.'

Chekalinsky drew a number of banknotes from his pocket and settled up immediately. Hermann took up his money and left the table. Narumov was too astounded even to think. Hermann drank a glass of lemonade and went home.

The next evening he again appeared at Chekalinsky's. The host was dealing. Hermann walked up to the table; the players already there immediately gave way to him. Chekalinsky bowed graciously.

Hermann waited for the next deal, took a card and placed on it his 47,000 roubles together with the winnings of the previous evening.

Chekalinsky began to deal. A knave turned up on the right, a seven on the left.

Hermann showed his seven.

There was a general cry of surprise, and Chekalinsky was clearly disconcerted. He counted out 94,000 roubles and handed them to Hermann, who pocketed them coolly and immediately withdrew.

The following evening Hermann again appeared at the table. Everyone was expecting him. The generals and privy councillors abandoned their whist in

---

1. Bets in faro are made on the positions of cards. A player selects a card and places it facedown in front of him or her; if the card turns up on the dealer's left, the player wins; if on the right, the dealer wins.

order to watch such unusual play. The young officers jumped up from their divans; all the waiters gathered in the drawing-room. Hermann was surrounded by a crowd of people. The other players held back their cards, impatient to see how Hermann would get on. Hermann stood at the table and prepared to play alone against the pale but still smiling Chekalinsky. Each unsealed a pack of cards. Chekalinsky shuffled. Hermann drew and placed his card, covering it with a heap of banknotes. It was like a duel. A deep silence reigned all around.

His hands shaking, Chekalinsky began to deal. On the right lay a queen, on the left an ace.

'The ace wins,' said Hermann and showed his card.

'Your queen has lost,' Chekalinsky said kindly.

Hermann started: indeed, instead of an ace, before him lay the queen of spades. He could not believe his eyes, could not understand how he could have slipped up.

At that moment it seemed to him that the queen of spades winked at him and smiled. He was struck by an unusual likeness . . .

'The old woman!' he shouted in terror.

Chekalinsky gathered up his winnings. Hermann stood motionless. When he left the table, people began to converse noisily.

'Famously punted!' the players said.

Chekalinsky shuffled the cards afresh; play went on as usual.

Conclusion

Hermann went mad. Now installed in Room 17 at the Obukhov Hospital, he answers no questions, but merely mutters with unusual rapidity: 'Three, seven, ace! Three, seven, queen!'

Lisaveta Ivanovna married a very agreeable young man, the son of the old Countess's former steward and with a good position in the Service somewhere. Lisaveta Ivanovna is bringing up a poor relative.

Tomsky has been promoted to the rank of Captain and is to be married to Princess Polina.

NIKOLAI GOGOL

1809–1852

Is it possible for the same story to be both tragic and absurd, both realistic and fantastic? It is part of the genius of *The Overcoat* that it combines these opposing impulses. Many of Gogol's readers have praised the story as critical of the injustices of a stratified society. Others have argued that it is a comic tale with a mocking narrator. A few have read the story as a Christian allegory, with the lowly clerk protagonist as a saintly figure subjected to martyrdom. And in the past century, many readers have been taken most with Gogol's literary skill, his ornate language, his lively narration, and his bizarre distortions. Joining low comedy to high tragedy, realist details to ghostly hauntings, humorous digressions to sudden moral revelations, *The Overcoat* appeals to almost everyone—and puzzles everyone who tries to classify it.

LIFE

Nikolai Vasilievich Gogol-Yanovsky was born in 1809 in a village in rural Ukraine, then part of the Russian Empire, to a family of moderately prosperous landowners. His father was an amateur gardener, poet, and comic playwright who drew on local folklore and the Ukrainian puppet-theater tradition. His mother was a country woman of narrow views who married in her early teens. She pampered Nikolai, her firstborn son. Devout, superstitious, and steeped in local folklore, she also told him terrifying stories of malicious demons and the horrors of the Last Judgment, which sank into his anxious imagination. Gogol's fear of the devil lasted throughout his life.

When he was sent to boarding school at the age of nine, he joined the student literary club, read widely, and began to write. He was lonely and secretive, called the "Mysterious Dwarf" by his classmates. His greatest success in school came as an actor in plays, where his talent for mimicry was widely praised. In 1825, his father died. The family fortunes, already declining, dropped still further. But Gogol did not go home to take care of the family estate. He had high hopes of making a name for himself in some as yet undefined way: he wanted to avoid being merely an "exister," someone living in plantlike passivity who never made a mark on the world. In cosmopolitan St. Petersburg, the glittering capital of the Russian Empire, he hoped to find fame. He dropped the Polish-sounding Yanovsky from his name to emphasize his aristocratic Russian lineage, and set out for the city.

St. Petersburg was disappointing. Gogol could not find a job; he could not afford to live; he auditioned unsuccessfully for a part as an actor; and when he published a long romantic poem, the reviews were so bad that he bought and burned as many copies as he could find. Gogol eventually spent over a year as a clerk in the lowest level of the civil service, an experience that led him to hate and fear bureaucracy, and provided the material for the poor clerk characters that appear in his works. A series of jobs he did not much like—tutor, history teacher at a girls' school, adjunct professor of history at St. Petersburg University—allowed him to support himself, and he began to write articles and stories for literary magazines.

By the 1830s, Gogol had established himself as an innovative stylist and comic genius. Encouraged by the great writer **Alexander Pushkin**, Gogol at first wrote stories that developed themes and situations from Ukrainian folk culture. Experimenting with diverse narrative voices—melodramatic, comic, horror filled, and lyrical—he presented his first stories as regional tales collected by a garrulous beekeeper. These were a great popular success. Later, he began to establish a personal voice that changed mood within a single piece, being alternately comic, sympathetic, satiric, and lyrical.

Gogol never forgot his first love: the theater. In 1835, he wrote a play called *The Inspector General*. It is grotesquely realistic, a harsh, farcical exposure of human weakness and corruption. Public reaction was stormy: this was not a conventional light comedy of manners or romance, and the spectators were divided. Some were enraged; others thought it was a comic masterpiece; and still others praised the work as an example of social realism that had not yet been seen in Russia. Ironically, Nicholas I appreciated the play, though it lampooned his government and especially its inept bureaucracy. ("What a play!" he is reported to have said. "It gets at everyone and most of all at me!") The writer felt overwhelmed by the controversy. He fled for Rome and what would become a thirteen-year self-imposed exile.

Gogol's writing became more evangelical toward the end of his life. He planned to write a multivolume epic novel that would describe every facet of Russian society and bring about Russia's spiritual rebirth. Full of comic portraits and absurd situations, the first volume, *Dead Souls*, was published in 1842.

Devoting himself to prayer and ascetic living in an attempt to purify himself, Gogol never finished his grand epic work. He did write *Selected Passages from Correspondence with Friends*, a didactic book that enraged many of his friends with its religious preaching and politically reactionary views. After a trip to Jerusalem in 1848, Gogol returned to Russia, where he fell under the influence of a fanatical priest who advised extreme fasting and ordered him to give up literature. His health, precarious for several years, deteriorated further, and he began to have hallucinations. On February 11, 1852, after his priest threatened him with eternal damnation, he burned the recently completed second volume of his epic novel. He died ten days later. At his funeral, the streets were jammed for three days with mourners coming to pay their respect. But the authorities, who could not forgive Gogol's satire, canceled the publication of his collected works and arrested the novelist Ivan Turgenev for publishing a brief eulogy in the newspaper. It would not be long, however, before Gogol's works were back in print and critics began to speak of the "Gogolian period" in Russian literature.

WORK

It is one of Gogol's striking literary innovations to combine the oral speech of the lower classes with high literary style. To tell his extraordinary story, Gogol draws heavily on an old Russian oral genre called *skaz*, in which the storyteller is a lively, chatty presence, observing, commenting, and digressing, as in the tall tales of American literature. One of the most famous of these digressions is the absurd story of the hero's name, Akaky Akakievich. (Incorporating the sound *kaka*, the name might best be translated "Poop Poopson.") Mockery fades a moment later in a characteristic Gogolian shift when the clerk's pained protest penetrates the heart of a co-worker who is forever changed by it. The narrative voice also shifts registers, moving from humorous digression to lyrical interjection. Joining low comedy and tragic sadness, Gogol's style has often been called *grotesque*—that is, a mixture of incongruous or incompatible traits.

The premise of the story is itself absurd, as a low-level government clerk who delights in copying documents word for word discovers that he needs a new coat and is thereby transformed. The coat allows his existence to seem fuller, "as though he had married," with the coat as his wifely companion. Erotic images begin to crowd his mind: he stares at a suggestive picture in a shop window and nearly runs after a woman walking in the street. When the precious overcoat is stolen and the protagonist fails to move the bureaucracy to recover it for him, he is completely destroyed.

Why does a coat matter so much? Does it capture the pain of poverty, a Russia that cannot cover its people, where gaining access to the most basic of life's necessities is an almost insuperable struggle? Does the coat represent a misfit's chance to find a way into the social world? Or does putting on a new coat perhaps have religious overtones, covering Akaky Akakievich's nakedness as Adam and Eve are covered? Or perhaps the coat satisfies a material or erotic kind of desire, as the protagonist comes to love a mere object better than any person. Readers have never known for sure. What we do know is that in a life of mechanical copying, the making of the coat is Akaky Akakievich's sole creative act. He works with the tailor—his only real human connection in the story—to plan its thick padding and strong stitching. He is so caught up with ideas for the coat that he almost makes his first mistake as a copyist. A little like Gogol himself, perhaps, Akaky Akakievich has long had an inclination for imitation but now comes to create something new.

The Overcoat is one of a series of stories Gogol set in St. Petersburg. The city is itself almost a character in these works, appearing vast and impersonal, driven by an extensive bureaucracy and a grinding indifference to individual needs. Its dehumanized atmosphere precludes any feeling of collective identity, and its inhabitants are alienated from one another as they pursue their separate ambitions.

In the first years of the nineteenth century, Czar Alexander I had restructured the Russian government, instituting a series of ministries and launching a large-scale new bureaucracy organized according to a military-style hierarchy, or "table of ranks." As the capital city of the Russian Empire, St. Petersburg was home to many new government offices filled with civil servants. The city's architecture began to reflect new ideals of order, with grand classical buildings lining wide streets and majestic squares. Under Nicholas I, the czar who followed Alexander and ruled from 1825 to 1855, St. Petersburg became positively oppressive. Nicholas had been terrified by an uprising, leading him to develop an obsession with military order. He empowered censors and established a secret police force. The city began to look like a barracks. In *The Overcoat*, it feels nightmarish. Akaky Akakievich loses his way in the network of streets, coming at last to "an endless square, which looked like a fearful desert with its houses scarcely visible on the far side."

The end of the story is wonderfully rich in stylistic shifts: it offers tragedy and spiritual transformation, but it is also full of gossip, comic effects, and melodramatic touches that evoke old folktales. The conclusion is not purely sad, comic, critical, mystical, or surreal, but all of these.

Gogol's influence on world literature has been incalculable. A vast array of writers have been drawn to his work, from **Fyodor Dostoyevsky** and **Franz Kafka** to **Gabriel García Márquez** and Jhumpa Lahiri (who names a character "Gogol" in her 2003 novel, *The Namesake*). The filmmaker David Lynch, too, has embraced Gogol's mixing of humorous absurdity with wrenching tragedy. But few have been able to describe Gogol's strange power with any precision. Perhaps the great Russian writer **Vladimir Nabokov** comes closest. He characterized Gogol's style as a series of "jerks" and "glides" between rational and irrational planes: "Imagine a trapdoor that opens under your feet with absurd suddenness, and a lyrical gust that sweeps you up and then lets you fall with a bump." Perpetually in motion, Gogol's style never lets us come to rest, and his stories continue to haunt, amuse, and fascinate readers into our own time.

The Overcoat[1]

In the department of . . . but I had better not mention which department. There is nothing in the world more touchy than a department, a regiment, a government office, and, in fact, any sort of official body. Nowadays every private individual considers all society insulted in his person. I have been told that very lately a complaint was lodged by a police inspector of which town I don't remember, and that in this complaint he set forth clearly that the institutions of the State were in danger and that his sacred name was being taken in vain; and, in proof thereof, he appended to his complaint an enormously long volume of some romantic work in which a police inspector appeared on every tenth page, occasionally, indeed, in an intoxicated condition. And so, to avoid any unpleasantness, we had better call the department of which we are speaking "a certain department."

And so, in a *certain department* there was a *certain clerk*; a clerk of whom it cannot be said that he was very remarkable; he was short, somewhat pockmarked, with rather reddish hair and rather dim, bleary eyes, with a small bald patch on the top of his head, with wrinkles on both sides of his cheeks and the sort of complexion which is usually described as hemorrhoidal . . . nothing can be done about that, it is the Petersburg climate. As for his grade in the civil service (for among us a man's rank is what must be established first) he was what is called a perpetual titular councillor,[2] a class at which, as we all know, various writers who indulge in the praiseworthy habit of attacking those who cannot defend themselves jeer and jibe to their hearts' content. This clerk's surname was Bashmachkin. From the very name it is clear that it must have been derived from a shoe (*bashmak*); but when and under what circumstances it was derived from a shoe, it is impossible to say. Both his father and his grandfather and even his brother-in-law, and all the Bashmachkins without exception wore boots, which they simply resoled two or three times a year. His

---

1. Published in 1842. Translated by Constance Garnett; revised by Leonard J. Kent.
2. The ninth rank of the Russian imperial civil service. "Perpetual": ironic: he will not advance.

name was Akaky Akakievich.[3] Perhaps it may strike the reader as a rather strange and contrived name, but I can assure him that it was not contrived at all, that the circumstances were such that it was quite out of the question to give him any other name. Akaky Akakievich was born toward nightfall, if my memory does not deceive me, on the twenty-third of March. His mother, the wife of a government clerk, a very good woman, made arrangements in due course to christen the child. She was still lying in bed, facing the door, while on her right hand stood the godfather, an excellent man called Ivan Ivanovich Yeroshkin, one of the head clerks in the Senate, and the godmother, the wife of a police official and a woman of rare qualities, Arina Semeonovna Belobriush-kova. Three names were offered to the happy mother for selection—Mokky, Sossy, or the name of the martyr Khozdazat. "No," thought the poor lady, "they are all such names!" To satisfy her, they opened the calendar at another page, and the names which turned up were: Trifily, Dula, Varakhasy. "What an infliction!" said the mother. "What names they all are! I really never heard such names. Varadat or Varukh would be bad enough, but Trifily and Varakhasy!" They turned over another page and the names were: Pavsikakhy and Vakhisy. "Well, I see," said the mother, "it is clear that it is his fate. Since that is how it is, he had better be named after his father; his father is Akaky, let the son be Akaky, too." This was how he came to be Akaky Akakievich. The baby was christened and cried and made sour faces during the ceremony, as though he foresaw that he would be a titular councillor. So that was how it all came to pass. We have reported it here so that the reader may see for himself that it happened quite inevitably and that to give him any other name was out of the question.

No one has been able to remember when and how long ago he entered the department, nor who gave him the job. Regardless of how many directors and higher officials of all sorts came and went, he was always seen in the same place, in the same position, at the very same duty, precisely the same copying clerk, so that they used to declare that he must have been born a copying clerk, uniform, bald patch, and all. No respect at all was shown him in the department. The porters, far from getting up from their seats when he came in, took no more notice of him than if a simple fly had flown across the reception room. His superiors treated him with a sort of despotic aloofness. The head clerk's assistant used to throw papers under his nose without even saying "Copy this" or "Here is an interesting, nice little case" or some agreeable remark of the sort, as is usually done in well-bred offices. And he would take it, gazing only at the paper without looking to see who had put it there and whether he had the right to do so; he would take it and at once begin copying it. The young clerks jeered and made jokes at him to the best of their clerkly wit, and told before his face all sorts of stories of their own invention about him; they would say of his landlady, an old woman of seventy, that she beat him, would ask when the wedding was to take place, and would scatter bits of paper on his head, calling them snow. Akaky Akakievich never answered a word, however, but behaved as

---

3. "Akaky, son of Akaky." Gogol plays with comic-sounding names through this paragraph, and the repeated *kak* in "Akaky Akakievich" recalls *kaka,* a common word for "feces" in several European languages.

though there were no one there. It had no influence on his work; in the midst of all this teasing, he never made a single mistake in his copying. It was only when the jokes became too unbearable, when they jolted his arm, and prevented him from going on with his work, that he would say: "Leave me alone! Why do you insult me?" and there was something touching in the words and in the voice in which they were uttered. There was a note in it of something that aroused compassion, so that one young man, new to the office, who, following the example of the rest, had allowed himself to tease him, suddenly stopped as though cut to the heart, and from that time on, everything was, as it were, changed and appeared in a different light to him. Some unseen force seemed to repel him from the companions with whom he had become acquainted because he thought they were well-bred and decent men. And long afterward, during moments of the greatest gaiety, the figure of the humble little clerk with a bald patch on his head appeared before him with his heart-rending words: "Leave me alone! Why do you insult me?" and within those moving words he heard others: "I am your brother." And the poor young man hid his face in his hands, and many times afterward in his life he shuddered, seeing how much inhumanity there is in man, how much savage brutality lies hidden under refined, cultured politeness, and, my God! even in a man whom the world accepts as a gentleman and a man of honor. . . .

It would be hard to find a man who lived for his work as did Akaky Akaki-evich. To say that he was zealous in his work is not enough; no, he loved his work. In it, in that copying, he found an interesting and pleasant world of his own. There was a look of enjoyment on his face; certain letters were favorites with him, and when he came to them he was delighted; he chuckled to himself and winked and moved his lips, so that it seemed as though every letter his pen was forming could be read in his face. If rewards had been given according to the measure of zeal in the service, he might to his amazement have even found himself a civil councillor; but all he gained in the service, as the wits, his fellow clerks, expressed it, was a button in his buttonhole[4] and hemorrhoids where he sat. It cannot be said, however, that no notice had ever been taken of him. One director, being a good-natured man and anxious to reward him for his long service, sent him something a little more important than his ordinary copying; he was instructed to make some sort of report from a finished document for another office; the work consisted only of altering the headings and in places changing the first person into the third. This cost him so much effort that he was covered with perspiration: he mopped his brow and said at last, "No, I'd rather copy something."

From that time on they left him to his copying forever. It seemed as though nothing in the world existed for him except his copying. He gave no thought at all to his clothes; his uniform was—well, not green but some sort of rusty, muddy color. His collar was very low and narrow, so that, although his neck was not particularly long, yet, standing out of the collar, it looked as immensely long as those of the dozens of plaster kittens with nodding heads which foreigners carry about on their heads and peddle in Russia. And there were always

---

4. A button instead of a medal or decoration.

things sticking to his uniform, either bits of hay or threads; moreover, he had a special knack of passing under a window at the very moment when various garbage was being flung out into the street, and so was continually carrying off bits of melon rind and similar litter on his hat. He had never once in his life noticed what was being done and what was going on in the street, all those things at which, as we all know, his colleagues, the young clerks, always stare, utilizing their keen sight so well that they notice anyone on the other side of the street with a trouser strap hanging loose—an observation which always calls forth a sly grin. Whatever Akaky Akakievich looked at, he saw nothing but his clear, evenly written lines, and it was only perhaps when a horse suddenly appeared from nowhere and placed its head on his shoulder, and with its nostrils blew a real gale upon his cheek, that he would notice that he was not in the middle of his writing, but rather in the middle of the street.

On reaching home, he would sit down at once at the table, hurriedly eat his soup and a piece of beef with an onion; he did not notice the taste at all but ate it all with the flies and anything else that Providence happened to send him. When he felt that his stomach was beginning to be full, he would get up from the table, take out a bottle of ink and begin copying the papers he had brought home with him. When he had none to do, he would make a copy especially for his own pleasure, particularly if the document were remarkable not for the beauty of its style but because it was addressed to some new or distinguished person.

Even at those hours when the gray Petersburg sky is completely overcast and the whole population of clerks have dined and eaten their fill, each as best he can, according to the salary he receives and his personal tastes; when they are all resting after the scratching of pens and bustle of the office, their own necessary work and other people's, and all the tasks that an overzealous man voluntarily sets himself even beyond what is necessary; when the clerks are hastening to devote what is left of their time to pleasure; some more enterprising are flying to the theater, others to the street to spend their leisure staring at women's hats, some to spend the evening paying compliments to some attractive girl, the star of a little official circle, while some—and this is the most frequent of all—go simply to a fellow clerk's apartment on the third or fourth story, two little rooms with a hall or a kitchen, with some pretensions to style, with a lamp or some such article that has cost many sacrifices of dinners and excursions—at the time when all the clerks are scattered about the apartments of their friends, playing a stormy game of whist, sipping tea out of glasses, eating cheap biscuits, sucking in smoke from long pipes, telling, as the cards are dealt, some scandal that has floated down from higher circles, a pleasure which the Russian can never by any possibility deny himself, or, when there is nothing better to talk about, repeating the everlasting anecdote of the commanding officer who was told that the tail had been cut off the horse on the Falconet monument[5]—in short, even when everyone, was eagerly seeking entertainment, Akaky Akakievich did not indulge in any amusement. No one could say that they had ever seen him at an evening party. After working to his heart's content, he would go to bed, smiling at the thought of the next day and

---

5. A famous equestrian statue of Peter the Great created by French sculptor Étienne-Maurice Falconet (1716–1791). It was cast in bronze and known as *The Bronze Horseman*.

wondering what God would send him to copy. So flowed on the peaceful life of a man who knew how to be content with his fate on a salary of four hundred rubles and so perhaps it would have flowed on to extreme old age, had it not been for the various disasters strewn along the road of life, not only of titular, but even of privy, actual, court, and all other councillors,[6] even those who neither give counsel to others nor accept it themselves.

There is in Petersburg a mighty foe of all who receive a salary of about four hundred rubles. That foe is none other than our northern frost, although it is said to be very good for the health. Between eight and nine in the morning, precisely at the hour when the streets are filled with clerks going to their departments, the frost begins indiscriminately giving such sharp and stinging nips at all their noses that the poor fellows don't know what to do with them. At that time, when even those in the higher grade have a pain in their brows and tears in their eyes from the frost, the poor titular councillors are sometimes almost defenseless. Their only protection lies in running as fast as they can through five or six streets in a wretched, thin little overcoat and then warming their feet thoroughly in the porter's room, till all their faculties and talents for their various duties thaw out again after having been frozen on the way. Akaky Akakievich had for some time been feeling that his back and shoulders were particularly nipped by the cold, although he did try to run the regular distance as fast as he could. He wondered at last whether there were any defects in his overcoat. After examining it thoroughly in the privacy of his home, he discovered that in two or three places, on the back and the shoulders, it had become a regular sieve, the cloth was so worn that you could see through it and the lining was coming out. I must note that Akaky Akakievich's overcoat had also served as a butt for the jokes of the clerks. It had even been deprived of the honorable name of overcoat and had been referred to as the "dressing gown." It was indeed of rather a peculiar make. Its collar had been growing smaller year by year as it served to patch the other parts. The patches were not good specimens of the tailor's art, and they certainly looked clumsy and ugly. On seeing what was wrong, Akaky Akakievich decided that he would have to take the overcoat to Petrovich, a tailor who lived on the fourth floor up a back staircase, and, in spite of having only one eye and being pockmarked all over his face, was rather successful in repairing the trousers and coats of clerks and others—that is, when he was sober, be it understood, and had no other enterprise in his mind. Of this tailor I ought not, of course, say much, but since it is now the rule that the character of every person in a novel must be completely described, well, there's nothing I can do but describe Petrovich too. At first he was called simply Grigory, and was a serf belonging to some gentleman or other. He began to be called Petrovich[7] from the time that he got his freedom and began to drink rather heavily on every holiday, at first only on the main

---

6. There were fourteen levels in the civil service, each with its own title; distinctions were made between full (actual or active) positions and those that were inactive. Privy councillor was third level, actual (or active) privy councillor was second level, and court councillor was seventh level. "Rubles": basic units of Russian currency. In Gogol's time, four hundred rubles was a small salary.

7. "Son of Peter." A serf was addressed by his first name; free men could be addressed by their full name or just the patronymic (Petrovich).

holidays, but afterward, on all church holidays indiscriminately, wherever there was a cross in the calendar. In this he was true to the customs of his forefathers, and when he quarreled with his wife he used to call her a worldly woman and a German.[8] Since we have now mentioned the wife, it will be necessary to say a few words about her, too, but unfortunately not much is known about her, except indeed that Petrovich had a wife and that she wore a cap and not a kerchief, but apparently she could not boast of beauty; anyway, none but soldiers of the guard peered under her cap when they met her, and they twitched their mustaches and gave vent to a rather peculiar sound.

As he climbed the stairs leading to Petrovich's—which, to do them justice, were all soaked with water and slops and saturated through and through with that smell of ammonia which makes the eyes smart, and is, as we all know, inseparable from the backstairs of Petersburg houses—Akaky Akakievich was already wondering how much Petrovich would ask for the job, and inwardly resolving not to give more than two rubles. The door was open, because Petrovich's wife was frying some fish and had so filled the kitchen with smoke that you could not even see the cockroaches. Akaky Akakievich crossed the kitchen unnoticed by the good woman, and walked at last into a room where he saw Petrovich sitting on a big, wooden, unpainted table with his legs tucked under him like a Turkish pasha.[9] The feet, as is usual with tailors when they sit at work, were bare; and the first object that caught Akaky Akakievich's eye was the big toe, with which he was already familiar, with a misshapen nail as thick and strong as the shell of a tortoise. Around Petrovich's neck hung a skein of silk and another of thread and on his knees was a rag of some sort. He had for the last three minutes been trying to thread his needle, but could not get the thread into the eye and so was very angry with the darkness and indeed with the thread itself, muttering in an undertone: "She won't go in, the savage! You wear me out, you bitch." Akaky Akakievich was unhappy that he had come just at the minute when Petrovich was in a bad humor; he liked to give him an order when he was a little "elevated," or, as his wife expressed it, "had fortified himself with vodka, the one-eyed devil." In such circumstances Petrovich was as a rule very ready to give way and agree, and invariably bowed and thanked him. Afterward, it is true, his wife would come wailing that her husband had been drunk and so had asked too little, but adding a single ten-kopek piece would settle that. But on this occasion Petrovich was apparently sober and consequently curt, unwilling to bargain, and the devil knows what price he would be ready to demand. Akaky Akakievich realized this, and was, as the saying is, beating a retreat, but things had gone too far, for Petrovich was screwing up his solitary eye very attentively at him and Akaky Akakievich involuntarily said: "Good day, Petrovich!"

"I wish you a good day, sir," said Petrovich, and squinted at Akaky Akakievich's hands, trying to discover what sort of goods he had brought.

"Here I have come to you, Petrovich, do you see . . . !"

It must be noticed that Akaky Akakievich for the most part explained himself by apologies, vague phrases, and meaningless parts of speech which have abso-

---

8. A woman of suspect morals and a foreigner, both used as disparaging terms. Germans filled many privileged positions (such as doctor) that were not open to Russians, and anti-German bias was common among Russian nationalists.
9. A ruler or high official.

lutely no significance whatever. If the subject were a very difficult one, it was his habit indeed to leave his sentences quite unfinished, so that very often after a sentence had begun with the words, "It really is, don't you know . . ." nothing at all would follow and he himself would be quite oblivious to the fact that he had not finished his thought, supposing he had said all that was necessary.

"What is it?" said Petrovich, and at the same time with his solitary eye he scrutinized his whole uniform from the collar to the sleeves, the back, the skirts, the buttonholes—with all of which he was very familiar since they were all his own work. Such scrutiny is habitual with tailors; it is the first thing they do on meeting one.

"It's like this, Petrovich . . . the overcoat, the cloth . . . you see everywhere else it is quite strong; it's a little dusty and looks as though it were old, but it is new and it is only in one place just a little . . . on the back, and just a little worn on one shoulder and on this shoulder, too, a little . . . do you see? that's all, and it's not much work . . ."

Petrovich took the "dressing gown," first spread it out over the table, examined it for a long time, shook his head, and put his hand out to the window sill for a round snuffbox with a portrait on the lid of some general—which general I can't exactly say, for a finger had been thrust through the spot where a face should have been, and the hole had been pasted over with a square piece of paper. After taking a pinch of snuff, Petrovich held the "dressing gown" up in his hands and looked at it against the light, and again he shook his head; then he turned it with the lining upward and once more shook his head; again he took off the lid with the general pasted up with paper and stuffed a pinch into his nose, shut the box, put it away, and at last said: "No, it can't be repaired; a wretched garment!" Akaky Akakievich's heart sank at those words.

"Why can't it, Petrovich?" he said, almost in the imploring voice of a child. "Why, the only thing is, it is a bit worn on the shoulders; why, you have got some little pieces . . ."

"Yes, the pieces will be found all right," said Petrovich, "but it can't be patched, the stuff is rotten; if you put a needle in it, it would give way."

"Let it give way, but you just put a patch on it."

"There is nothing to put a patch on. There is nothing for it to hold on to; there is a great strain on it; it is not worth calling cloth; it would fly away at a breath of wind."

"Well, then, strengthen it with something—I'm sure, really, this is . . . !"

"No," said Petrovich resolutely, "there is nothing that can be done, the thing is no good at all. You had far better, when the cold winter weather comes, make yourself leg wrappings out of it, for there is no warmth in stockings; the Germans invented them just to make money." (Petrovich enjoyed a dig at the Germans occasionally.) "And as for the overcoat, it is obvious that you will have to have a new one."

At the word "new" there was a mist before Akaky Akakievich's eyes, and everything in the room seemed blurred. He could see nothing clearly but the general with the piece of paper over his face on the lid of Petrovich's snuffbox.

"A new one?" he said, still feeling as though he were in a dream; "why, I haven't the money for it."

"Yes, a new one," Petrovich repeated with barbarous composure.

"Well, and if I did have a new one, how much would it . . . ?"

"You mean what will it cost?"

"Yes."

"Well, at least one hundred and fifty rubles," said Petrovich, and he compressed his lips meaningfully. He was very fond of making an effect; he was fond of suddenly disconcerting a man completely and then squinting sideways to see what sort of a face he made.

"A hundred and fifty rubles for an overcoat!" screamed poor Akaky Akakievich—it was perhaps the first time he had screamed in his life, for he was always distinguished by the softness of his voice.

"Yes," said Petrovich, "and even then it depends on the coat. If I were to put marten on the collar, and add a hood with silk linings, it would come to two hundred."

"Petrovich, please," said Akaky Akakievich in an imploring voice, not hearing and not trying to hear what Petrovich said, and missing all his effects, "repair it somehow, so that it will serve a little longer."

"No, that would be wasting work and spending money for nothing," said Petrovich, and after that Akaky Akakievich went away completely crushed, and when he had gone Petrovich remained standing for a long time with his lips pursed up meaningfully before he began his work again, feeling pleased that he had not demeaned himself or lowered the dignity of the tailor's art.

When he got into the street, Akaky Akakievich felt as though he was in a dream. "So that is how it is," he said to himself. "I really did not think it would be this way . . ." and then after a pause he added, "So that's it! So that's how it is at last! and I really could never have supposed it would be this way. And there . . ." There followed another long silence, after which he said: "So that's it! well, it really is so utterly unexpected . . . who would have thought . . . what a circumstance . . ." Saying this, instead of going home he walked off in quite the opposite direction without suspecting what he was doing. On the way a clumsy chimney sweep brushed the whole of his sooty side against him and blackened his entire shoulder; a whole hatful of plaster scattered upon him from the top of a house that was being built. He noticed nothing of this, and only after he had jostled against a policeman who had set his halberd down beside him and was shaking some snuff out of his horn[1] into his rough fist, he came to himself a little and then only because the policeman said: "Why are you poking yourself right in one's face, haven't you enough room on the street?" This made him look around and turn homeward; only there he began to collect his thoughts, to see his position in a clear and true light, and began talking to himself no longer incoherently but reasonably and openly as with a sensible friend with whom one can discuss the most intimate and vital matters. "No," said Akaky Akakievich, "it is no use talking to Petrovich now; just now he really is . . . his wife must have been giving it to him. I had better go to him on Sunday morning; after Saturday night he will have a crossed eye and be sleepy, so he'll want a little drink and his wife won't give him a kopek.[2] I'll slip ten kopeks into his hand and then he will be more accommodating and maybe take the overcoat . . ."

---

1. A container made of horn. "Halberd": a weapon consisting of a long shaft with a blade at the end.

2. There are a hundred kopeks in a ruble.

So reasoning with himself, Akaky Akakievich cheered up and waited until the next Sunday; then, seeing from a distance Petrovich's wife leaving the house, he went straight in. Petrovich certainly had a crossed eye after Saturday. He could hardly hold his head up and was very drowsy; but, despite all that, as soon as he heard what Akaky Akakievich was speaking about, it seemed as though the devil had nudged him. "I can't," he said, "you must order a new one." Akaky Akakievich at once slipped a ten-kopek piece into his hand. "I thank you, sir, I will have just a drop to your health, but don't trouble yourself about the overcoat; it is no good for anything. I'll make you a fine new coat; you can have faith in me for that."

Akaky Akakievich would have said more about repairs, but Petrovich, without listening, said: "A new one I'll make you without fail; you can rely on that; I'll do my best. It could even be like the fashion that is popular, with the collar to fasten with silver-plated hooks under a flap."

Then Akaky Akakievich saw that there was no escape from a new overcoat and he was utterly depressed. How indeed, for what, with what money could he get it? Of course he could to some extent rely on the bonus for the coming holiday, but that money had long ago been appropriated and its use determined beforehand. It was needed for new trousers and to pay the cobbler an old debt for putting some new tops on some old boots, and he had to order three shirts from a seamstress as well as two items of undergarments which it is indecent to mention in print; in short, all that money absolutely must be spent, and even if the director were to be so gracious as to give him a holiday bonus of forty-five or even fifty, instead of forty rubles, there would be still left a mere trifle, which would be but a drop in the ocean compared to the fortune needed for an overcoat. Though, of course, he knew that Petrovich had a strange craze for suddenly demanding the devil knows what enormous price, so that at times his own wife could not help crying out: "Why, you are out of your wits, you idiot! Another time he'll undertake a job for nothing, and here the devil has bewitched him to ask more than he is worth himself." Though, of course, he knew that Petrovich would undertake to make it for eighty rubles, still where would he get those eighty rubles? He might manage half of that sum; half of it could be found, perhaps even a little more; but where could he get the other half? . . . But, first of all, the reader ought to know where that first half was to be found. Akaky Akakievich had the habit every time he spent a ruble of putting aside two kopeks in a little box which he kept locked, with a slit in the lid for dropping in the money. At the end of every six months he would inspect the pile of coppers there and change them for small silver. He had done this for a long time, and in the course of many years the sum had mounted up to forty rubles and so he had half the money in his hands, but where was he to get the other half; where was he to get another forty rubles? Akaky Akakievich thought and thought and decided at last that he would have to diminish his ordinary expenses, at least for a year; give up burning candles in the evening, and if he had to do any work he must go into the landlady's room and work by her candle; that as he walked along the streets he must walk as lightly and carefully as possible, almost on tiptoe, on the cobbles and flagstones, so that his soles might last a little longer than usual; that he must send his linen to the wash less frequently, and that, to preserve it from being worn, he must take it off every day when he came home and sit in a thin cotton dressing gown, a very ancient garment which Time itself had spared. To tell the truth, he found it at first rather difficult to get used to these privations, but after a while it became a habit and went smoothly enough—he even became quite accustomed to being hungry in the evening; on the other hand, he had spiritual nourishment, for he carried ever in his thoughts the idea of his future overcoat. His whole existence had in a sense become fuller, as though he had married, as though some other person were present with him, as though he were no longer alone but an agreeable companion had consented to walk the path of life hand in hand with him, and that companion was none other than the new overcoat with its thick padding and its strong, durable lining. He became, as it were, more alive, even more strong-willed, like a man who has set before himself a definite goal. Uncertainty, indecision, in fact all the hesitating and vague characteristics, vanished from his face and his manners. At times there was a gleam in his eyes; indeed, the most bold and audacious ideas flashed through his mind. Why not really have marten on the collar? Meditation on the subject always made him absent-minded. On one occasion when he was copying a document, he very nearly made a mistake, so that he almost cried out "ough" aloud and crossed himself. At least once every month he went to Petrovich to talk about the overcoat: where it would be best to buy the cloth, and what color it should be, and what price; and, though he returned home a little anxious, he was always pleased at the thought that at last the time was at hand when everything would be bought and the overcoat would be made. Things moved even faster than he had anticipated. Contrary to all expectations, the director bestowed on Akaky Akakievich a bonus of no less than sixty rubles. Whether it was that he had an inkling that Akaky Akakievich needed a coat, or whether it happened by luck, owing to this he found he had twenty rubles extra. This circumstance hastened the course of affairs. Another two or three months of partial starvation and Akaky Akakievich had actually saved up nearly eighty rubles. His heart, as a rule very tranquil, began to throb.

The very first day he set out with Petrovich for the shops. They bought some very good cloth, and no wonder, since they had been thinking of it for more than six months, and scarcely a month had passed without their going out to the shop to compare prices; now Petrovich himself declared that there was no better cloth to be had. For the lining they chose calico, but of such good quality, that in Petrovich's words it was even better than silk, and actually as strong and handsome to look at. Marten they did not buy, because it was too expensive, but instead they chose cat fur, the best to be found in the shop—cat which in the distance might almost be taken for marten. Petrovich was busy making the coat for two weeks, because there was a great deal of quilting; otherwise it would have been ready sooner. Petrovich charged twelve rubles for the work; less than that it hardly could have been; everything was sewn with silk, with fine double seams, and Petrovich went over every seam afterwards with his own teeth, imprinting various patterns with them. It was . . . it is hard to say precisely on what day, but probably on the most triumphant day in the life of Akaky Akakievich, that Petrovich at last brought the overcoat. He brought it in the morning, just before it was time to set off for the department. The overcoat could not have arrived at a more opportune time, because severe frosts were just beginning and seemed threatening to become even harsher. Petrovich brought the coat himself as a good tailor should. There was an expression of importance on his face, such as Akaky Akakievich had never seen there before. He seemed fully conscious of having completed a work of no little importance and of having shown by his own example the gulf that separates tailors who only put in linings and do repairs from those who make new coats. He took the coat out of the huge handkerchief in which he had brought it (the handkerchief had just come home from the wash); he then folded it up and put it in his pocket for future use. After taking out the overcoat, he looked at it with much pride and holding it in both hands, threw it very deftly over Akaky Akakievich shoulders, then pulled it down and smoothed it out behind with his hands; then draped it about Akaky Akakievich somewhat jauntily. Akaky Akakievich, a practical man, wanted to try it with his arms in the sleeves. Petrovich helped him to put it on, and it looked splendid with his arms in the sleeves, too. In fact, it turned out that the overcoat was completely and entirely successful. Petrovich did not let slip the occasion for observing that it was only because he lived in a small street and had no signboard, and because he had known Akaky Akakievich so long, that he had done it so cheaply, and that on Nevsky Prospekt[3] they would have asked him seventy-five rubles for the tailoring alone. Akaky Akakievich had no inclination to discuss this with Petrovich; besides he was frightened of the big sums that Petrovich was fond of flinging airily about in conversation. He paid him, thanked him, and went off, with his new overcoat on, to the department. Petrovich followed him out and stopped in the street, staring for a long time at the coat from a distance and then purposely turned off and, taking a short cut through a side street, came back into the street, and got another view of the coat from the other side, that is, from the front.

Meanwhile Akaky Akakievich walked along in a gay holiday mood. Every second he was conscious that he had a new overcoat on his shoulders, and several times he actually laughed from inward satisfaction. Indeed, it had two advantages: one that it was warm and the other that it was good. He did not notice how far he had walked at all and he suddenly found himself in the department; in the porter's room, he took off the overcoat, looked it over, and entrusted it to the porter's special care. I cannot tell how it happened, but all at once everyone in the department learned that Akaky Akakievich had a new overcoat and that the "dressing gown" no longer existed. They all ran out at once into the cloakroom to look at Akaky Akakievich's new overcoat; they began welcoming him and congratulating him so that at first he could do nothing but smile and then felt positively embarrassed. When, coming up to him, they all began saying that he must "sprinkle" the new overcoat and that he ought at least to buy them all a supper, Akaky Akakievich lost his head completely and did not know what to do, how to get out of it, nor what to answer. A few minutes later, flushing crimson, he even began assuring them with great simplicity that it was not a new overcoat at all, that it wasn't much, that it was an old overcoat. At last one of the clerks, indeed the assistant of the head clerk of the room, probably in order to show that he wasn't too proud to mingle with those beneath him, said: "So be it, I'll give a party instead of Akaky Akakievich and invite you all to tea with me this evening; as luck would have it, it is my

3. The main boulevard in St. Petersburg; a fashionable street and area.

birthday." The clerks naturally congratulated the assistant head clerk and eagerly accepted the invitation. Akaky Akakievich was beginning to make excuses, but they all declared that it was uncivil of him, that it would be simply a shame and a disgrace and that he could not possibly refuse. So, he finally relented, and later felt pleased about it when he remembered that through this he would have the opportunity of going out in the evening, too, in his new overcoat. That whole day was for Akaky Akakievich the most triumphant and festive day in his life. He returned home in the happiest frame of mind, took off the overcoat, and hung it carefully on the wall, admiring the cloth and lining once more, and then pulled out his old "dressing gown," now completely falling apart, and put it next to his new overcoat to compare the two. He glanced at it and laughed: the difference was enormous! And long afterwards he went on laughing at dinner, as the position in which the "dressing gown" was placed recurred to his mind. He dined in excellent spirits and after dinner wrote nothing, no papers at all, but just relaxed for a little while on his bed, till it got dark; then, without putting things off, he dressed, put on his overcoat, and went out into the street. Where precisely the clerk who had invited him lived we regret to say we cannot tell; our memory is beginning to fail sadly, and everything there in Petersburg, all the streets and houses, are so blurred and muddled in our head that it is a very difficult business to put anything in orderly fashion. Regardless of that, there is no doubt that the clerk lived in the better part of the town and consequently a very long distance from Akaky Akakievich. At first Akaky Akakievich had to walk through deserted streets, scantily lighted, but as he approached his destination the streets became more lively, more full of people, and more brightly lighted; passers-by began to be more frequent, ladies began to appear, here and there beautifully dressed, and beaver collars were to be seen on the men. Cabmen with wooden, railed sledges, studded with brass-topped nails, were less frequently seen; on the other hand, jaunty drivers in raspberry-colored velvet caps, with lacquered sledges and bearskin rugs, appeared and carriages with decorated boxes dashed along the streets, their wheels crunching through the snow.

Akaky Akakievich looked at all this as a novelty; for several years he had not gone out into the streets in the evening. He stopped with curiosity before a lighted shop window to look at a picture in which a beautiful woman was represented in the act of taking off her shoe and displaying as she did so the whole of a very shapely leg, while behind her back a gentleman with whiskers and a handsome imperial[4] on his chin was sticking his head in at the door. Akaky Akakievich shook his head and smiled and then went on his way. Why did he smile? Was it because he had come across something quite unfamiliar to him, though every man retains some instinctive feeling on the subject, or was it that he reflected, like many other clerks, as follows: "Well, those Frenchmen! It's beyond anything! If they go in for anything of the sort, it really is . . . !" Though possibly he did not even think that; there is no creeping into a man's soul and finding out all that he thinks. At last he reached the house in which the assistant head clerk lived in fine style; there was a lamp burning on the stairs, and the apartment was on the second floor. As he went into the hall Akaky Akaki-

---

4. A narrow pointed beard grown below the lower lip.

evich saw rows of galoshes. Among them in the middle of the room stood a hissing samovar[5] puffing clouds of steam. On the walls hung coats and cloaks among which some actually had beaver collars or velvet lapels. From the other side of the wall there came noise and talk, which suddenly became clear and loud when the door opened and the footman[6] came out with a tray full of empty glasses, a jug of cream, and a basket of biscuits. It was evident that the clerks had arrived long before and had already drunk their first glass of tea. Akaky Akakievich, after hanging up his coat with his own hands, went into the room, and at the same moment there flashed before his eyes a vision of candles, clerks, pipes and card tables, together with the confused sounds of conversation rising up on all sides and the noise of moving chairs. He stopped very awkwardly in the middle of the room, looking about and trying to think of what to do, but he was noticed and received with a shout and they all went at once into the hall and again took a look at his overcoat. Though Akaky Akakievich was somewhat embarrassed, yet, being a simple-hearted man, he could not help being pleased at seeing how they all admired his coat. Then of course they all abandoned him and his coat, and turned their attention as usual to the tables set for whist. All this—the noise, the talk, and the crowd of people—was strange and wonderful to Akaky Akakievich. He simply did not know how to behave, what to do with his arms and legs and his whole body; at last he sat down beside the players, looked at the cards, stared first at one and then at another of the faces, and in a little while, feeling bored, began to yawn—especially since it was long past the time at which he usually went to bed. He tried to say goodbye to his hosts, but they would not let him go, saying that he absolutely must have a glass of champagne in honor of the new coat. An hour later supper was served, consisting of salad, cold veal, pastry pies from the bakery, and champagne. They made Akaky Akakievich drink two glasses, after which he felt that things were much more cheerful, though he could not forget that it was twelve o'clock, and that he ought to have been home long ago. That his host might not take it into his head to detain him, he slipped out of the room, hunted in the hall for his coat, which he found, not without regret, lying on the floor, shook it, removed some fluff from it, put it on, and went down the stairs into the street. It was still light in the streets. Some little grocery shops, those perpetual clubs for servants and all sorts of people, were open; others which were closed showed, however, a long streak of light at every crack of the door, proving that they were not yet deserted, and probably maids and menservants were still finishing their conversation and discussion, driving their masters to utter perplexity as to their whereabouts. Akaky Akakievich walked along in a cheerful state of mind; he was even on the point of running, goodness knows why, after a lady of some sort who passed by like lightning with every part of her frame in violent motion. He checked himself at once, however, and again walked along very gently, feeling positively surprised at the inexplicable impulse that had seized him. Soon the deserted streets, which are not particularly cheerful by day and even less so in the evening, stretched before him. Now they were still more dead and deserted; the light of street lamps was

---

5. A Russian urn made of metal with a spigot at the bottom, that boils water for tea.

6. A servant, usually one who serves food or runs errands.

scantier, the oil evidently running low; then came wooden houses and fences; not a soul anywhere; only the snow gleamed on the streets and the low-pitched slumbering hovels looked black and gloomy with their closed shutters. He approached the spot where the street was intersected by an endless square, which looked like a fearful desert with its houses scarcely visible on the far side.

In the distance, goodness knows where, there was a gleam of light from some sentry box which seemed to be at the end of the world. Akaky Akakievich's lightheartedness faded. He stepped into the square, not without uneasiness, as though his heart had a premonition of evil. He looked behind him and to both sides—it was as though the sea were all around him. "No, better not look," he thought, and walked on, shutting his eyes, and when he opened them to see whether the end of the square was near, he suddenly saw standing before him, almost under his very nose, some men with mustaches; just what they were like he could not even distinguish. There was a mist before his eyes, and a throbbing in his chest. "Why, that overcoat is mine!" said one of them in a voice like a clap of thunder, seizing him by the collar. Akaky Akakievich was on the point of shouting "Help" when another put a fist the size of a clerk's head against his lips, saying: "You just shout now." Akaky Akakievich felt only that they took the overcoat off, and gave him a kick with their knees, and he fell on his face in the snow and was conscious of nothing more. A few minutes later he recovered consciousness and got up on his feet, but there was no one there. He felt that it was cold on the ground and that he had no overcoat, and began screaming, but it seemed as though his voice would not carry to the end of the square. Overwhelmed with despair and continuing to scream, he ran across the square straight to the sentry box beside which stood a policeman leaning on his halberd and, so it seemed, looking with curiosity to see who the devil the man was who was screaming and running toward him from the distance. As Akaky Akakievich reached him, he began breathlessly shouting that he was asleep and not looking after his duty not to see that a man was being robbed. The policeman answered that he had seen nothing, that he had only seen him stopped in the middle of the square by two men, and supposed that they were his friends, and that, instead of abusing him for nothing, he had better go the next day to the police inspector, who would certainly find out who had taken the overcoat. Akaky Akakievich ran home in a terrible state: his hair, which was still comparatively abundant on his temples and the back of his head, was completely disheveled; his sides and chest and his trousers were all covered with snow. When his old landlady heard a fearful knock at the door, she jumped hurriedly out of bed and, with only one slipper on, ran to open it, modestly holding her chemise over her bosom; but when she opened it she stepped back, seeing in what a state Akaky Akakievich was. When he told her what had happened, she clasped her hands in horror and said that he must go straight to the district commissioner,[7] because the local police inspector would deceive him, make promises and lead him a dance; that it would be best of all to go to the district commissioner, and that she knew him, because Anna, the Finnish girl who was once her cook, was now in service as a nurse at the commissioner's; and that she often saw him himself when he passed by their house, and that he

7. The local police commissioner.

used to be every Sunday at church too, saying his prayers and at the same time looking good-humouredly at everyone, and that therefore by every token he must be a kindhearted man. After listening to this advice, Akaky Akakievich made his way very gloomily to his room, and how he spent that night I leave to the imagination of those who are in the least able to picture the position of others.

Early in the morning he set off to the police commissioner's but was told that he was asleep. He came at ten o'clock, he was told again that he was asleep; he came at eleven and was told that the commissioner was not at home; he came at dinnertime, but the clerks in the anteroom would not let him in, and insisted on knowing what was the matter and what business had brought him and exactly what had happened; so that at last Akaky Akakievich for the first time in his life tried to show the strength of his character and said curtly that he must see the commissioner himself, that they dare not refuse to admit him, that he had come from the department on government business, and that if he made complaint of them they would see. The clerks dared say nothing to this, and one of them went to summon the commissioner. The latter received his story of being robbed of his overcoat in an extremely peculiar manner. Instead of attending to the main point, he began asking Akaky Akakievich questions: why had he been coming home so late? wasn't he going, or hadn't he been, to some bawdy house? so that Akaky Akakievich was overwhelmed with confusion, and went away without knowing whether or not the proper measures would be taken regarding his overcoat. He was absent from the office all that day (the only time that it had happened in his life). Next day he appeared with a pale face, wearing his old "dressing gown" which had become a still more pitiful sight. The news of the theft of the overcoat—though there were clerks who did not let even this chance slip of jeering at Akaky Akakievich—touched many of them. They decided on the spot to get up a collection for him, but collected only a very trifling sum, because the clerks had already spent a good deal contributing to the director's portrait and on the purchase of a book, at the suggestion of the head of their department, who was a friend of the author, and so the total realized was very insignificant. One of the clerks, moved by compassion, ventured at any rate to assist Akaky Akakievich with good advice, telling him not to go to the local police inspector, because, though it might happen that the latter might succeed in finding his overcoat because he wanted to impress his superiors, it would remain in the possession of the police unless he presented legal proofs that it belonged to him; he urged that by far the best thing would be to appeal to a Person of Consequence, that the Person of Consequence, by writing and getting into communication with the proper authorities, could push the matter through more successfully. There was nothing else to do. Akaky Akakievich made up his mind to go to the Person of Consequence. What precisely was the nature of the functions of the Person of Consequence has remained a matter of uncertainty. It must be noted that this Person of Consequence had only lately become a person of consequence, and until recently had been a person of no consequence. Though, indeed, his position even now was not reckoned of consequence in comparison with others of still greater consequence. But there is always to be found a circle of persons to whom a person of little consequence in the eyes of others is a person of consequence. It is true that he did his utmost to increase the consequence of his position in various ways, for instance by insisting that his subordinates should come out onto the stairs to meet him when he arrived at his office; that no one should venture to approach him directly but all proceedings should follow the strictest chain of command; that a collegiate registrar[8] should report the matter to the governmental secretary; and the governmental secretary to the titular councillor or whomsoever it might be, and that business should only reach him through this channel. Everyone in Holy Russia[9] has a craze for imitation; everyone apes and mimics his superiors. I have actually been told that a titular councillor who was put in charge of a small separate office, immediately partitioned off a special room for himself, calling it the head office, and posted lackeys[1] at the door with red collars and gold braid, who took hold of the handle of the door and opened it for everyone who went in, though the "head office" was so tiny that it was with difficulty that an ordinary writing desk could be put into it. The manners and habits of the Person of Consequence were dignified and majestic, but hardly subtle. The chief foundation of his system was strictness; "strictness, strictness, and—strictness!" he used to say, and at the last word he would look very significantly at the person he was addressing, though, indeed, he had no reason to do so, for the dozen clerks who made up the whole administrative mechanism of his office stood in appropriate awe of him; any clerk who saw him in the distance would leave his work and remain standing at attention till his superior had left the room. His conversation with his subordinates was usually marked by severity and almost confined to three phrases: "How dare you? Do you know to whom you are speaking? Do you understand who I am?" He was, however, at heart a good-natured man, pleasant and obliging with his colleagues, but his advancement to a high rank had completely turned his head. When he received it, he was perplexed, thrown off his balance, and quite at a loss as to how to behave. If he chanced to be with his equals, he was still quite a decent man, a very gentlemanly man, in fact, and in many ways even an intelligent man; but as soon as he was in company with men who were even one grade below him, there was simply no doing anything with him: he sat silent and his position excited compassion, the more so as he himself felt that he might have been spending his time to so much more advantage. At times there could be seen in his eyes an intense desire to join in some interesting conversation, but he was restrained by the doubt whether it would not be too much on his part, whether it would not be too great a familiarity and lowering of his dignity, and in consequence of these reflections he remained everlastingly in the same mute condition, only uttering from time to time monosyllabic sounds, and in this way he gained the reputation of being a terrible bore.

So this was the Person of Consequence to whom our friend Akaky Akakievich appealed, and he appealed to him at a most unpropitious moment, very unfortunate for himself, though fortunate, indeed, for the Person of Consequence. The latter happened to be in his study, talking in the very best of spirits with an old friend of his childhood who had only just arrived and whom he had not seen

---

8. The fourteenth, or lowest, level of the civil service.
9. A conventional epithet for Russia, originating in 11th-century epic poems and religious

verse that described the Christian state defending itself against invading pagans.
1. Uniformed servants.

for several years. It was at this moment that he was informed that a man called Bashmachkin was asking to see him. He asked abruptly, "What sort of man is he?" and received the answer. "A government clerk." "Ah! he can wait. I haven't time now," said the Person of Consequence. Here I must observe that this was a complete lie on the part of the Person of Consequence; he had time; his friend and he had long ago said all they had to say to each other and their conversation had begun to be broken by very long pauses during which they merely slapped each other on the knee saying, "So that's how things are, Ivan Abramovich!"—"So that's it, Stepan Varlamovich!" but, despite that, he told the clerk to wait in order to show his friend, who had left the civil service some years before and was living at home in the country, how long clerks had to wait for him. At last, after they had talked or rather been silent, to their heart's content and had smoked a cigar in very comfortable armchairs with sloping backs, he seemed suddenly to recollect, and said to the secretary, who was standing at the door with papers for his signature: "Oh, by the way, there is a clerk waiting, isn't there? tell him he can come in." When he saw Akaky Akakievich's meek appearance and old uniform, he turned to him at once and said: "What do you want?" in a firm and abrupt voice, which he had purposely rehearsed in his own room in solitude before the mirror for a week before receiving his present post and the grade of a general. Akaky Akakievich, who was overwhelmed with appropriate awe beforehand, was somewhat confused and, as far as his tongue would allow him, explained to the best of his powers, with even more frequent "ers" than usual, that he had had a perfectly new overcoat and now he had been robbed of it in the most inhuman way, and that now he had come to beg him by his intervention either to correspond with his honor, the head police commissioner, or anybody else, and find the overcoat. This mode of proceeding struck the general for some reason as too familiar. "What next, sir?" he went on abruptly. "Don't you know the way to proceed? To whom are you addressing yourself? Don't you know how things are done? You ought first to have handed in a petition to the office; it would have gone to the head clerk of the room, and to the head clerk of the section; then it would have been handed to the secretary and the secretary would have brought it to me . . ."

"But, your Excellency," said Akaky Akakievich, trying to gather the drop of courage he possessed and feeling at the same time that he was perspiring all over, "I ventured, your Excellency, to trouble you because secretaries . . . er . . . are people you can't depend on . . ."

"What? what? what?" said the Person of Consequence, "where did you get hold of that attitude? where did you pick up such ideas? What insubordination is spreading among young men against their superiors and their chiefs!" The Person of Consequence did not apparently observe that Akaky Akakievich was well over fifty, and therefore if he could have been called a young man it would only have been in comparison with a man of seventy. "Do you know to whom you are speaking? Do you understand who I am? Do you understand that, I ask you?" At this point he stamped, and raised his voice to such a powerful note that Akaky Akakievich was not the only one to be terrified. Akaky Akakievich was positively petrified; he staggered, trembling all over, and could not stand; if the porters had not run up to support him, he would have flopped on the floor; he was led out almost unconscious. The Person of Consequence, pleased that the effect had surpassed his expectations and enchanted at the idea that his words could even deprive a man of consciousness, stole a sideway glance at his friend to see how he was taking it, and perceived not without satisfaction that his friend was feeling very uncertain and even beginning to be a little terrified himself.

How he got downstairs, how he went out into the street—of all that Akaky Akakievich remembered nothing; he had no feeling in his arms or his legs. In all his life he had never been so severely reprimanded by a general, and this was by one of another department, too. He went out into the snowstorm that was whistling through the streets, with his mouth open, and as he went he stumbled off the pavement; the wind, as its way is in Petersburg, blew upon him from all points of the compass and from every side street. In an instant it had blown a quinsy into his throat, and when he got home he was not able to utter a word; he went to bed with a swollen face and throat. That's how violent the effects of an appropriate reprimand can be!

Next day he was in a high fever. Thanks to the gracious assistance of the Petersburg climate, the disease made more rapid progress than could have been expected, and when the doctor came, after feeling his pulse he could find nothing to do but prescribe a poultice, and that simply so that the patient might not be left without the benefit of medical assistance; however, two days later he informed him that his end was at hand, after which he turned to Akaky Akakievich's landlady and said: "And you had better lose no time, my good woman, but order him now a pine coffin, for an oak one will be too expensive for him." Whether Akaky Akakievich heard these fateful words or not, whether they produced a shattering effect upon him, and whether he regretted his pitiful life, no one can tell, for he was constantly in delirium and fever. Apparitions, each stranger than the one before, were continually haunting him: first he saw Petrovich and was ordering him to make an overcoat trimmed with some sort of traps for robbers, who were, he believed, continually under the bed, and he was calling his landlady every minute to pull out a thief who had even got under the quilt; then he kept asking why his old "dressing gown" was hanging before him when he had a new overcoat; then he thought he was standing before the general listening to the appropriate reprimand and saying, "I am sorry, your Excellency"; then finally he became abusive, uttering the most awful language, so that his old landlady positively crossed herself, having never heard anything of the kind from him before, and the more horrified because these dreadful words followed immediately upon the phrase "your Excellency." Later on, his talk was merely a medley of nonsense, so that it was quite unintelligible; all that was evident was that his incoherent words and thoughts were concerned with nothing but the overcoat. At last poor Akaky Akakievich gave up the ghost. No seal was put upon his room nor upon his things, because, in the first place, he had no heirs and, in the second, the property left was very small, to wit, a bundle of quills, a quire[2] of white government paper, three pairs of socks, two or three buttons that had come off his trousers, and the "dressing gown" with which the reader is already familiar. Who came into all this wealth God only knows; even I who tell the tale must admit that I

---

2. One-twentieth of a ream of paper, about twenty-five matching sheets. "Seal": usually placed on the room of a dead person in order to safeguard personal possessions for the estate.

have not bothered to inquire. And Petersburg carried on without Akaky Akakievich, as though, indeed, he had never been in the city. A creature had vanished and departed whose cause no one had championed, who was dear to no
one, of interest to no one, who never attracted the attention of a naturalist,
though the latter does not disdain to fix a common fly upon a pin and look at
him under the microscope—a creature who bore patiently the jeers of the
office and for no particular reason went to his grave, though even he at the very
end of his life was visited by an exalted guest in the form of an overcoat that for
one instant brought color into his poor, drab life—a creature on whom disease
fell as it falls upon the heads of the mighty ones of this world . . . !

Several days after his death, a messenger from the department was sent to
his lodgings with instructions that he should go at once to the office, for his
chief was asking for him; but the messenger was obliged to return without him,
explaining that he could not come, and to the inquiry "Why?" he added, "Well,
you see, the fact is he is dead; he was buried three days ago." This was how
they learned at the office of the death of Akaky Akakievich, and the next day
there was sitting in his seat a new clerk who was very much taller and who
wrote not in the same straight handwriting but made his letters more slanting
and crooked.

But who could have imagined that this was not all there was to tell about
Akaky Akakievich, that he was destined for a few days to make his presence felt
in the world after his death, as though to make up for his life having been
unnoticed by anyone? But so it happened, and our little story unexpectedly
finishes with a fantastic ending.

Rumors were suddenly floating about Petersburg that in the neighborhood of
the Kalinkin Bridge and for a little distance beyond, a corpse had begun
appearing at night in the form of a clerk looking for a stolen overcoat, and
stripping from the shoulders of all passersby, regardless of grade and calling,
overcoats of all descriptions—trimmed with cat fur or beaver or padded, lined
with raccoon, fox, and bear—made, in fact of all sorts of skin which men have
adapted for the covering of their own. One of the clerks of the department saw
the corpse with his own eyes and at once recognized it as Akaky Akakievich;
but it excited in him such terror that he ran away as fast as his legs could carry
him and so could not get a very clear view of him, and only saw him hold up his
finger threateningly in the distance.

From all sides complaints were continually coming that backs and shoulders,
not of mere titular councillors, but even of upper court councillors, had been
exposed to catching cold, as a result of being stripped of their overcoats.
Orders were given to the police to catch the corpse regardless of trouble or
expense, dead or alive, and to punish him severely, as an example to others,
and, indeed, they very nearly succeeded in doing so. The policeman of one
district in Kiryushkin Alley snatched a corpse by the collar on the spot of the
crime in the very act of attempting to snatch a frieze overcoat from a retired
musician, who used, in his day, to play the flute. Having caught him by the collar, he shouted until he had brought two other policemen whom he ordered to
hold the corpse while he felt just a minute in his boot to get out a snuffbox in
order to revive his nose which had six times in his life been frostbitten, but the
snuff was probably so strong that not even a dead man could stand it. The
policeman had hardly had time to put his finger over his right nostril and draw

up some snuff in the left when the corpse sneezed violently right into the eyes of all three. While they were putting their fists up to wipe their eyes, the corpse completely vanished, so that they were not even sure whether he had actually been in their hands. From that time forward, the policemen had such a horror of the dead that they were even afraid to seize the living and confined themselves to shouting from the distance: "Hey, you! Move on!" and the clerk's body began to appear even on the other side of the Kalinkin Bridge, terrorizing all timid people.

We have, however, quite neglected the Person of Consequence, who may in reality almost be said to be the cause of the fantastic ending of this perfectly true story. To begin with, my duty requires me to do justice to the Person of Consequence by recording that soon after poor Akaky Akakievich had gone away crushed to powder, he felt something not unlike regret. Sympathy was a feeling not unknown to him; his heart was open to many kindly impulses, although his exalted grade very often prevented them from being shown. As soon as his friend had gone out of his study, he even began brooding over poor Akaky Akakievich, and from that time forward, he was almost every day haunted by the image of the poor clerk who had been unable to survive the official reprimand. The thought of the man so worried him that a week later he actually decided to send a clerk to find out how he was and whether he really could help him in any way. And when they brought him word that Akaky Akakievich had died suddenly in delirium and fever, it made a great impression on him; his conscience reproached him and he was depressed all day. Anxious to distract his mind and to forget the unpleasant incident, he went to spend the evening with one of his friends, where he found respectable company, and what was best of all, almost everyone was of the same grade so that he was able to be quite uninhibited. This had a wonderful effect on his spirits. He let himself go, became affable and genial—in short, spent a very agreeable evening. At supper he drank a couple of glasses of champagne—a proceeding which we all know is not a bad recipe for cheerfulness. The champagne made him inclined to do something unusual, and he decided not to go home yet but to visit a lady of his acquaintance, a certain Karolina Ivanovna—a lady apparently of German extraction, for whom he entertained extremely friendly feelings. It must be noted that the Person of Consequence was a man no longer young. He was an excellent husband, and the respectable father of a family. He had two sons, one already serving in an office, and a nice-looking daughter of sixteen with a rather turned-up, pretty little nose, who used to come every morning to kiss his hand, saying: "*Bonjour,*[3] *Papa.*" His wife, who was still blooming and decidedly good-looking, indeed, used first to give him her hand to kiss and then turning his hand over would kiss it. But though the Person of Consequence was perfectly satisfied with the pleasant amenities of his domestic life, he thought it proper to have a lady friend in another quarter of the town. This lady friend was not a bit better looking nor younger than his wife, but these puzzling things exist in the world and it is not our business to criticize them. And so the Person of Consequence went downstairs, got into his sledge, and said to his coachman, "To Karolina Ivanovna." While luxuriously wrapped in his warm fur coat he remained in that agreeable frame of mind sweeter to a Russian than

3. Good morning (French). French, not Russian, was spoken in elegant society.

anything that could be invented, that is, when one thinks of nothing while thoughts come into the mind by themselves, one pleasanter than the other, without your having to bother following them or looking for them. Full of satisfaction, he recalled all the amusing moments of the evening he had spent, all the phrases that had started the intimate circle of friends laughing; many of them he repeated in an undertone and found them as amusing as before, and so, very naturally, laughed very heartily at them again. From time to time, however, he was disturbed by a gust of wind which, blowing suddenly, God knows why or where from, cut him in the face, pelting him with flakes of snow, puffing out his coat collar like a sail, or suddenly flinging it with unnatural force over his head and giving him endless trouble to extricate himself from it. All at once, the Person of Consequence felt that someone had clutched him very tightly by the collar. Turning around he saw a short man in a shabby old uniform, and not without horror recognized him as Akaky Akakievich. The clerk's face was white as snow and looked like that of a corpse, but the horror of the Person of Consequence was beyond all bounds when he saw the mouth of the corpse distorted into speech, and breathing upon him the chill of the grave, it uttered the following words: "Ah, so here you are at last! At last I've . . . er . . . caught you by the collar. It's your overcoat I want; you refused to help me and abused me into the bargain! So now give me yours!" The poor Person of Consequence very nearly dropped dead. Resolute and determined as he was in his office and before subordinates in general, and though anyone looking at his manly air and figure would have said: "Oh, what a man of character!" yet in this situation he felt, like very many persons of heroic appearance, such terror that not without reason he began to be afraid he would have some sort of fit. He actually flung his overcoat off his shoulders as far as he could and shouted to his coachman in an unnatural voice: "Drive home! Let's get out of here!" The coachman, hearing the tone which he had only heard in critical moments and then accompanied by something even more tangible, hunched his shoulders up to his ears in case of worse following, swung his whip, and flew on like an arrow. In a little over six minutes, the Person of Consequence was at the entrance of his own house. Pale, panic-stricken, and without his overcoat, he arrived home instead of at Karolina Ivanovna's, dragged himself to his own room, and spent the night in great distress, so that next morning his daughter said to him at breakfast, "You look very pale today, Papa"; but her papa remained mute and said not a word to anyone of what had happened to him, where he had been, and where he had been going. The incident made a great impression upon him. Indeed, it happened far more rarely that he said to his subordinates, "How dare you? Do you understand who I am?" and he never uttered those words at all until he had first heard all the facts of the case.

What was even more remarkable is that from that time on the apparition of the dead clerk ceased entirely; apparently the general's overcoat had fitted him perfectly; anyway nothing more was heard of overcoats being snatched from anyone. Many restless and anxious people refused, however, to be pacified, and still maintained that in remote parts of the town the dead clerk went on appearing. One policeman, in Kolomna,[4] for instance, saw with his own eyes

---

4. Bigger (or Greater) and Smaller Kolomna make up a large historic area of St. Petersburg. Gogol set many of his stories in the poor residential district of Smaller Kolomna.

an apparition appear from behind a house; but being by natural constitution somewhat frail—so much so that on one occasion an ordinary grown-up suckling pig, making a sudden dash out of some private building, knocked him off his feet to the great amusement of the cabmen standing around, whom he fined two kopeks each for snuff for such disrespect—he did not dare to stop it, and so followed it in the dark until the apparition suddenly looked around and, stopping, asked him: "What do you want?" displaying a huge fist such as you never see among the living. The policeman said: "Nothing," and turned back on the spot. This apparition, however, was considerably taller and adorned with immense mustaches, and directing its steps apparently toward Obukhov Bridge,[5] vanished into the darkness of the night.

5. One of the oldest bridges in St. Petersburg, spanning the Fontanka River. It was rebuilt in stone in 1785 by the contractor Obukhov.

DOMINGO FAUSTINO SARMIENTO

1811–1888

Part an attack on the rule of powerful dictators, part an exploration of the Latin American landscape and character, part a philosophical meditation on the problem of civilization, and part a racist polemic in favor of European-style modernization, Sarmiento's *Facundo* has shaped Latin American thinking so profoundly that one critic calls it "the most important book written by a Latin American in any discipline or genre." Sarmiento's controversial central claim is that "civilization" and "barbarism" form the fundamental tension in Latin American life: out of the opposition between these poles emerges the special character of culture and politics in Latin nations. But Sarmiento's impact also goes beyond this influential thesis. His commitment to modernizing Argentina catapulted him to the nation's presidency in 1868. And in terms of literary history, Sarmiento opened the way for later writers to explore Latin American identity and experience.

LIFE AND TIMES

Sarmiento was born in the Argentine province of San Juan in 1811, to a large family that had fallen on financial hard times. He had a haphazard education disrupted by political upheavals and an uneven educational system. He was an avid reader and found his chaotic schooling so frustrating that he would go on to make it his mission to revolutionize education in Argentina. Children still sing a "Hymn to Sarmiento" each year on Teacher's Day in Argentina.

During Sarmiento's early childhood, Argentina was waging a war against Spanish colonial rule. Revolutionary Argentine leaders declared independence in 1816 and went on to defeat Spain two years later. What followed was a civil war that pitted Argentine "Unitarists," who wanted to centralize the nation's power in the city of Buenos Aires, against the "Federalists," who sought to retain autonomy for the provinces. Out of this struggle emerged Juan Manuel de Rosas, the first dictator of the newly independent nation and a prototype for many Latin American dictators to come. Rosas had risen to power by commanding a regiment of notoriously ungovernable *gauchos*—Argentine hunters and cattle ranchers, who boasted the same kind of fierce independence as U.S. cowboys. Rosas, famous for his strongman style and ability to keep order, dressed like a *gaucho* himself and borrowed their tough and masculine style. He managed to impose a central national government on the provinces through a combination of populist rhetoric, a violent secret police force, and personal charisma. In 1835 he seized absolute power.

By this time, the young Sarmiento had already been jailed and exiled for his outspoken opposition to dictatorial rule. At the age of sixteen he had witnessed the invasion of his birthplace, the city of San Juan, by Facundo Quiroga, a charismatic *gaucho* military leader nicknamed "the Tiger of the Plains," whom Sarmiento loathed but also—ironically enough—would make world famous through his own writing. Warfare prevented Sarmiento from going to school, so he joined the military struggle against Facundo. He was arrested twice and escaped to Chile, where he taught in an elementary school, learned English, and became a prominent newspaper editor. As he moved back and forth between dissident activity in Argentina and exile in Chile, he formed part of a new cohort of urban intellectuals, opposed to the rural *gaucho* culture, called the "Generation of 1837." They committed themselves to freedom, modernization, and the defeat of the Rosas regime.

Sarmiento worked with enormous energy in Chile in the 1840s, publishing a memoir, a travelogue, and stream of attacks on the rule of dictators, including *Facundo,* his most famous work, composed in just a few weeks in 1845. He also founded a school and a newspaper, continued to work as a teacher, and traveled the world on behalf of the Peruvian government to investigate education systems in Brazil, Uruguay, Cuba, France, Spain, Italy, Algeria, Switzerland, England, and Canada. By this time he had earned the unfortunate nickname "Don Yo," or "Sir Self," for his egotistical personality. He also married Betina Martinez Pastoriza, a widow, and adopted her son.

In 1852 Sarmiento's nemesis Rosas was defeated and sent into exile by former supporters who had turned against him. His regime was followed by a period of political instability. Sarmiento participated in debates about a new constitution, and in 1855 he returned to Argentina, where he became editor of a major newspaper, *El Nacional*, and won a seat in the Senate. The following year, a writer and fellow activist from the "Generation of 1837," Bartolomé Mitre Martinez, was elected president of the unified republic of Argentina. The new government sent Sarmiento as Argentine ambassador to the United States. There, Sarmiento wrote an admiring life of Abraham Lincoln, comparing the U.S. Civil War to Argentina's conflicts. During this period, he argued for a policy of welcoming European immigrants to Argentina as a way to solve the nation's problems, and he openly subscribed to racist values that imagined white, Northern European bloodlines as superior to Southern European, African, and Native American ones.

Sarmiento arrived back in Buenos Aires in 1868 to begin a six-year term as the new president of Argentina. In his time in office, he oversaw progress in industry and technology, including a new system of telegraphs and railroads; he completed the country's first census; he set up schools to train new teachers and soldiers, and he enlarged the national library system. Under his leadership, Argentina built more schools and drew a higher enrollment of students than any other nation in Latin America. Sarmiento also opened Argentina to European immigrants, launching a policy that would bring more than two and a half million people there by 1914. Sarmiento's call for the "whitening" of Argentina led to genocidal attacks on Guarani and Mapuche Indians in 1879. Uruguayan author Eduardo Galeano writes of the paradox that "the most ferocious racism in Latin American history is to be found in the words of the most famed and celebrated intellectuals . . . and in the documents of liberal politicians who founded the modern state."

After Sarmiento stepped down from the presidency, he administered the national school system and made several unsuccessful bids for a return to political office. He died in Paraguay in 1888.

WORK

Sarmiento's best-known work is usually known by the single word *Facundo,* but the full title gives some sense of its actual reach and complexity: *Civilization and Barbarism: The Life of Juan Facundo Quiroga, and the Physical Aspect, Customs, and Practices of the Argentine*

Republic. Here, Sarmiento experiments with crafting a new form out of a mixture of existing genres: he borrows elements from biography, memoir, novel, natural history, epic, polemic, history, scientific treatise, and travelogue. His style, too, is hybrid, embracing passionate addresses, highly metaphorical passages, cool scientific facts, and poetic descriptions.

In spite of the text's heterogeneity, however, *Facundo*'s powerful influence can be traced, at least in part, to its stark and simple opposition between the two poles of civilization and barbarism. Europeans, Sarmiento argued, had advanced "civilization," meaning urbanization, technical and economic advances, civil freedoms, and reason. By contrast, the fertile terrain of Argentina, with its broad *pampas*, or plains, and immense woodlands populated by Native Americans, created what Sarmiento saw as the idle, backward, chaotic, rural, "barbaric" culture that gave rise to strongman dictators and violent *gauchos* like Facundo and Rosas.

Sarmiento divides the book into three parts. In the first section, he offers a detailed description of the geography of the Argentine landscape and describes the prominent "characters" who populate it, from the *gaucho* outlaw to the wandering minstrel. Although Sarmiento himself wanted to denounce these characters, readers have long felt that he produced a romantic image of life on the plains, and ironically these have remained the best-loved passages in the book. In the second part, he offers a vivid biography of Facundo Quiroga, whose violence, he claims, emerges out of the Argentine landscape. So vicious was Facundo, according to Sarmiento, that he tore off the ears of his mistress and split his son's head open with an axe. This focus on a single figure allows Sarmiento to explore the reasons for the rise of dictatorial rulers, and he uses Facundo as a representative of a whole way of life. In the final part, he explores the Rosas dictatorship and contemplates the future of Argentina. Sarmiento thus connects geography to biography and cultural life to politics to offer a comprehensive analysis of the new nation. In the process, Sarmiento gave Argentina a way to understand itself; *Facundo* produced a sense of national identity and prompted other Latin American writers to perform a similar task for their own nations.

Since its first appearance, *Facundo* has attracted as many critics as admirers. Sarmiento remains a hero for those resisting strongman dictators and a villain for those fighting against racism. For good and for ill, *Facundo* set the terms of debates that continue into our own time.

Civilization and Barbarism:
The Life of Juan Facundo Quiroga, and the Physical Aspect, Customs, and Practices of the Argentine Republic[1]

CHAPTER I

Physical Aspect of the Argentine Republic, and the Forms of Character, Habits, and Ideas Induced by It

> The extent of the Pampas is so prodigious that they are bounded on the north by groves of palm-trees and on the south by eternal snows.
>
> —HEAD[2]

The Continent of America ends at the south in a point, with the Strait of Magellan at its southern extremity. Upon the west the Chilian Andes run parallel to the coast at a short distance from the Pacific. Between that range of mountains and the Atlantic is a country whose boundary follows the River Plata up the course of the Uruguay into the interior, which was formerly known as the United Provinces of the River Plata, but where blood is still shed to determine whether its name shall be the Argentine Republic or the Argentine Confederation. On the north lie Paraguay, the Gran Chaco[3] and Bolivia, its assumed boundaries.

The vast tract which occupies its extremities is altogether uninhabited, and possesses navigable rivers as yet unfurrowed even by a frail canoe. Its own extent is the evil from which the Argentine Republic suffers; the desert encompasses it on every side and penetrates its very heart; wastes containing no human dwelling, are, generally speaking, the unmistakable boundaries between its several provinces. Immensity is the universal characteristic of the country: the plains, the woods, the rivers, are all immense; and the horizon is always undefined, always lost in haze and delicate vapors which forbid the eye to mark the point in the distant perspective, where the land ends and the sky begins. On the south and on the north are savages ever on the watch, who take advantage of the moonlight nights to fall like packs of hyenas upon the herds in their pastures, and upon the defenseless settlements. When the solitary caravan of wagons, as it sluggishly traverses the pampas, halts for a short period of rest, the men in charge of it, grouped around their scanty fire, turn their eyes mechanically toward the south upon the faintest whisper of the wind among the dry grass, and gaze into the deep darkness of the night, in search of the sinister visages of the savage horde, which, at any moment, approaching unperceived, may surprise them. If no sound reaches their ears, if their sight fails to pierce the gloomy veil which covers the silent wilderness, they direct their eyes, before entirely dismissing their apprehensions, to the ears of any horse standing within the firelight, to see if they are pricked up or turned carelessly backwards. Then they resume their interrupted conversation, or put into

---

1. Translated by Mary Mann.
2. Francis Bond Head (1793–1875), British soldier and colonial administrator, author of *Rough Notes Taken during some Rapid Jour-* *neys across the Pampas and among the Andes* (1826). "Pampas": a vast area of fertile grasslands in Argentina and Uruguay.
3. A lowland plain.

their mouths the half-scorched pieces of dried beef on which they subsist. When not fearful of the approach of the savage, the plainsman has equal cause to dread the keen eyes of the tiger, or the viper beneath his feet. This constant insecurity of life outside the towns, in my opinion, stamps upon the Argentine character a certain stoical resignation to death by violence, which is regarded as one of the inevitable probabilities of existence. Perhaps this is the reason why they inflict death or submit to it with so much indifference, and why such events make no deep or lasting impression upon the survivors.

The inhabited portion of this country—a country unusually favored by nature, and embracing all varieties of climates—may be divided into three sections possessing distinct characteristics, which cause differences of character among the inhabitants, growing out of the necessity of their adapting themselves to the physical conditions which surround them.

In the north, an extensive forest, reaching to the Chaco, covers with its impenetrable mass of boughs a space whose extent would seem incredible if there could be any marvel too great for the colossal types of Nature in America.

In the central zone, lying parallel to the former, the plain and the forest long contend with each other for the possession of the soil; the trees prevail for some distance, but gradually dwindle into stunted and thorny bushes, only reappearing in belts of forest along the banks of the streams, until finally in the south, the victory remains with the plain, which displays its smooth, velvet-like surface unbounded and unbroken. It is the image of the sea upon the land; the earth as it appears upon the map—the earth yet waiting for the command to bring forth every herb yielding seed after its kind. We may indicate, as a noteworthy feature in the configuration of this country, the aggregation of navigable rivers, which come together in the east, from all points of the horizon, to form the Plata by their union, and thus worthily to present their mighty tribute to the Ocean, which receives it, not without visible marks of disturbance and respect. But these immense canals, excavated by the careful hand of Nature, introduce no change into the national customs. The sons of the Spanish adventurers who colonized the country hate to travel by water, feeling themselves imprisoned when within the narrow limits of a boat or a pinnace. When their path is crossed by a great river, they strip themselves unconcernedly, prepare their horses for swimming, and plunging in, make for some island visible in the distance, where horse and horseman take breath, and by thus continuing their course from isle to isle, finally effect their crossing.

Thus is the greatest blessing which Providence bestows upon any people disdained by the Argentine gaucho,[4] who regards it rather as an obstacle opposed to his movements, than as the most powerful means of facilitating them thus the fountain of national growth, the origin of the early celebrity of Egypt, the cause of Holland's greatness, and of the rapid development of North America, the navigation of rivers, or the use of canals, remains a latent power, unappreciated by the inhabitants of the banks of the Bermejo, Pilcomayo, Paraná, and Paraguay.[5] A few small vessels, manned by Italians and adventurers, sail up stream from the Plata, but after ascending a few leagues, even this

---

4. A man who lived on the plains, hunting, herding cattle, and often leading a nomadic

life; similar to the North American cowboy.
5. Rivers of northern Argentina.

navigation entirely ceases. The instinct of the sailor, which the Saxon colonists of the north possess in so high a degree, was not bestowed upon the Spaniard. Another spirit is needed to stir these arteries in which a nation's life-blood now lies stagnant. Of all these rivers which should bear civilization, power, and wealth, to the most hidden recesses of the continent, and make of Santa Fé, Entre Rios, Corrientes, Cordova, Salta, Tucuman, and Jujui, rich and populous states, the Plata alone, which at last unites them all, bestows its benefits upon the inhabitants of its banks. At its mouth stand two cities, Montevideo and Buenos Ayres, which at present reap alternately the advantages of their enviable position. Buenos Ayres is destined to be some day the most gigantic city of either America. Under a benignant climate, mistress of the navigation of a hundred rivers flowing past her feet, covering a vast area, and surrounded by inland provinces which know no other outlet for their products, she would ere now have become the Babylon of America, if the spirit of the Pampa had not breathed upon her, and left undeveloped the rich offerings which the rivers and provinces should unceasingly bring. She is the only city in the vast Argentine territory which is in communication with European nations; she alone can avail herself of the advantages of foreign commerce; she alone has power and revenue. Vainly have the provinces asked to receive through her, civilization, industry, and European population; a senseless colonial policy made her deaf to these cries. But the provinces had their revenge when they sent to her in Rosas[6] the climax of their own barbarism.

Heavily enough have those who uttered it, paid for the saying, "The Argentine Republic ends at the Arroyo del Medio."[7] It now reaches from the Andes to the sea, while barbarism and violence have sunk Buenos Ayres below the level of the provinces. We ought not to complain of Buenos Ayres that she is great and will be greater, for this is her destiny. This would be to complain of Providence and call upon it to alter physical outlines. This being impossible, let us accept as well done what has been done by the Master's hand. Let us rather blame the ignorance of that brutal power which makes the gifts lavished by Nature upon an erring people of no avail for itself or for the provinces. Buenos Ayres, instead of sending to the interior, light, wealth, and prosperity, sends only chains, exterminating hordes, and petty subaltern tyrants. She, too, takes her revenge for the evil inflicted upon her by the provinces when they prepared for her a Rosas!

I have indicated the circumstance that the position of Buenos Ayres favors monopoly, in order to show that the configuration of the country so tends to centralization and consolidation, that even if Rosas had uttered his cry of "Confederation or Death!" in good faith, he would have ended with the consolidated system which is now established. Our desire, however, should be for union in civilization, and in liberty, while there has been given us only union in barbarism and in slavery. But a time will come when business will take its legitimate course. What it now concerns us to know is, that the progress of civilization must culminate only in Buenos Ayres; the pampa is a very bad medium of transmission and distribution through the provinces, and we are now about to see what is the result of this condition of things.

---

6. Juan Manuel de Rosas (1793–1877), military leader and first dictator of Argentina.

7. Small river that separates the provinces of Buenos Aires and Santa Fe.

But above all the peculiarities of special portions of the country, there predominates one general, uniform, and constant character. Whether the soil is covered with the luxuriant and colossal vegetation of the tropics, or stunted, thorny, and unsightly shrubs bear witness to the scanty moisture which sustains them; or whether finally the pampa displays its open and monotonous level, the surface of the country is generally flat and unbroken—the mountain groups of San Luis and Cordova in the centre, and some projecting spurs of the Andes toward the north, being scarcely an interruption to this boundless continuity.

We have, in this fact, a new element calculated to consolidate the nation which is hereafter to occupy these great solitudes, for it is well known that mountains and other natural obstacles interposed between different districts, keep up the isolation and the primitive peculiarities of their inhabitants. North America is destined to be a federation, not so much because its first settlements were independent of each other, as on account of the length of its Atlantic coast, and the various routes to the interior afforded by the St. Lawrence in the north, the Mississippi in the south, and the immense system of canals in the centre. The Argentine Republic is "one and indivisible."

Many philosophers have also thought that plains prepare the way for despotism, just as mountains furnish strongholds for the struggles of liberty. The boundless plain which permits the unobstructed passage of large and weighty wagons by routes upon which the hand of man has only been required to cut away a few trees and thickets, and which extend from Salta to Buenos Ayres, and thence to Mendoza, a distance of more than seven hundred leagues, constitutes one of the most noteworthy features of the internal conformation of the Republic. The exertions of the individual, aided by what rude nature has done already, suffice to provide ways and means of communication; if art shall offer its assistance, if the forces of society shall attempt to supply the strength lacking in the individual, the colossal dimensions of the work will repel the most enterprising, and insufficiency of labor will be an obstacle. Thus in the matter of roads, untamed nature will long have control, and the action of civilization will continue weak and inoperative.

Moreover, these outstretched plains impart to the life of the interior a certain Asiatic coloring, which we may even call very decided. I have often mechanically saluted the moon, as it rose calmly and brightly, with these words of Volney in his description of the Ruins: "La pleine lune à l'Orient s'élévait sur un fond bleuâtre aux plaines rives de l'Euphrate."[8] There is something in the wilds of the Argentine territory which brings to mind the wilds of Asia; the imagination discovers a likeness between the pampa and the plains lying between the Euphrates and the Tigris:[9] some affinity between the lonely line of wagons which crosses our wastes, arriving at Buenos Ayres after a journey lasting for months, and the caravan of camels which takes its way toward Bagdad or Smyrna. The wagons which make such journeys among us, constitute, so to speak, squadrons of little barks, the crews of which have a peculiar dress, dialect, and set of customs, which distinguish them from their fellow-countrymen,

8. The full moon in the East rose against a bluish background on the banks of the Euphrates (French). Constantin-François Volney (1757– 1820), French scholar.
9. Rivers that defined ancient Mesopotamia (present-day Iraq).

just as the sailor differs from the landsman. The head of each party is a military leader, like the chief of an Asiatic caravan; this position can be filled only by a man of iron will, and daring to the verge of rashness, that he may hold in check the audacity and turbulence of the land pirates who are to be directed and ruled by himself alone, for no help can be summoned in the desert. On the least symptom of insubordination, the captain raises his iron *chicote*,[1] and delivers upon the mutineer blows which make contusions and wounds; if the resistance is prolonged, before resorting to his pistols, the help of which he generally scorns, he leaps from his horse, grasps his formidable knife, and quickly reëstablishes his authority by his superior skill in handling it. If any one loses his life under such discipline, the leader is not answerable for the assassination, which is regarded as an exercise of legitimate authority.

From these characteristics arises in the life of the Argentine people the reign of brute force, the supremacy of the strongest, the absolute and irresponsible authority of rulers, the administration of justice without formalities or discussion. The caravan of wagons is provided, moreover, with one or two guns to each wagon, and sometimes the leading one has a small piece of artillery on a swivel. If the train is attacked by the savages, the wagons are tied together in a ring, and a successful resistance is almost always opposed to the blood-thirsty and rapacious plunder of the assailants. Defenseless droves of pack-mules often fall into the hands of these American Bedouins, and muleteers rarely escape with their lives. In these long journeys, the lower classes of the Argentine population acquire the habit of living far from society, of struggling single-handed with nature, of disregarding privation, and of depending for protection against the dangers ever imminent upon no other resources than personal strength and skill.

The people who inhabit these extensive districts, belong to two different races, the Spanish and the native; the combinations of which form a series of imperceptible gradations. The pure Spanish race predominates in the rural districts of Cordova and San Luis, where it is common to meet young shepherdesses fair and rosy, and as beautiful as the belles of a capital could wish to be. In Santiago del Estero, the bulk of the rural population still speaks the Quichua dialect, which plainly shows its Indian origin. The country people of Corrientes use a very pretty Spanish dialect. "Dame, general, una chiripá," said his soldiers to Lavalle.[2] The Andalusian soldier may still be recognized in the rural districts of Buenos Ayres; and in the city foreign surnames are the most numerous. The negro race, by this time nearly extinct (except in Buenos Ayres), has left, in its zambos[3] and mulattoes, a link which connects civilized man with the denizen of the woods. This race mostly inhabiting cities, has a tendency to become civilized, and possesses talent and the finest instincts of progress.

With these reservations, a homogeneous whole has resulted from the fusion of the three above-named families. It is characterized by love of idleness and incapacity for industry, except when education and the exigencies of a social

---

1. A type of whip.
2. "General, give me a *chiripá*." Spanish words are mixed here with a word from the indigenous *Guarani* language, *chiripá* meaning a kind of belt worn by *gauchos*. Juan Galo

Lavalle (1797–1841), Argentinian military and political leader.
3. People of mixed African and Native American ancestry.

position succeed in spurring it out of its customary pace. To a great extent, this unfortunate result is owing to the incorporation of the native tribes, effected by the process of colonization. The American aborigines live in idleness, and show themselves incapable, even under compulsion, of hard and protracted labor. This suggested the idea of introducing negroes into America, which has produced such fatal results. But the Spanish race has not shown itself more energetic than the aborigines, when it has been left to its own instincts in the wilds of America. Pity and shame are excited by the comparison of one of the German or Scotch colonies in the southern part of Buenos Ayres and some towns of the interior of the Argentine Republic; in the former the cottages are painted, the front-yards always neatly kept and adorned with flowers and pretty shrubs; the furniture simple but complete; copper or tin utensils always bright and clean; nicely curtained beds; and the occupants of the dwelling are always industriously at work. Some such families have retired to enjoy the conveniences of city life, with great fortunes gained by their previous labors in milking their cows, and making butter and cheese. The town inhabited by natives of the country, presents a picture entirely the reverse. There, dirty and ragged children live, with a menagerie of dogs; there, men lie about in utter idleness; neglect and poverty prevail everywhere; a table and some baskets are the only furniture of wretched huts remarkable for their general aspect of barbarism and carelessness.

This wretched manner of life of a people already on the decrease, and belonging to the pastoral districts, doubtless gave rise to the words which spite and the humiliation of the English arms drew from Sir Walter Scott: "The vast plains of Buenos Ayres," he says, "are inhabited only by Christian savages known as Guachos" (gauchos, he should have said), "whose furniture is chiefly composed of horses' skulls, whose food is raw beef and water, and whose favorite pastime is running horses to death. Unfortunately," adds the good foreigner, "they prefer their national independence to our cottons and muslins."[4]

It would be well to ask England to say at a venture how many yards of linen and pieces of muslin she would give to own these plains of Buenos Ayres!

Upon the boundless expanse above described stand scattered here and there fourteen cities, each the capital of a province. The obvious method of arranging their names would be to classify them according to their geographical position: Buenos Ayres, Santa Fé, Entre Rios, and Corrientes, on the banks of the Paraná; Mendoza, San Juan, Rioja, Catamarca, Tucuman, Salta, and Jujui, being on a line nearly parallel to the Chilian Andes; with Santiago, San Luis, and Cordova, in the centre. But this manner of enumerating the Argentine towns has no connection with any of the social results which I have in view. A classification adapted to my purpose must originate in the ways of life pursued by the country people, for it is this which determines their character and spirit. I have stated above that the proximity of the rivers makes no difference in this respect, because the extent to which they are navigated is so trifling as to be without influence upon the people.

All the Argentine provinces, except San Juan and Mendoza, depend on the products of pastoral life; Tucuman avails itself of agriculture also, and Buenos

4. From the *Life of Napoleon Bonaparte* (1827), by the Scottish writer Sir Walter Scott (1771–1832).

Ayres, besides raising millions of cattle and sheep, devotes itself to the numerous and diversified occupations of civilized life.

The Argentine cities, like almost all the cities of South America, have an appearance of regularity. Their streets are laid out at right angles, and their population scattered over a wide surface, except in Cordova, which occupies a narrow and confined position, and presents all the appearance of a European city, the resemblance being increased by the multitude of towers and domes attached to its numerous and magnificent churches. All civilization, whether native, Spanish, or European, centres in the cities, where are to be found the manufactories, the shops, the schools and colleges, and other characteristics of civilized nations. Elegance of style, articles of luxury, dress-coats, and frock-coats, with other European garments, occupy their appropriate place in these towns. I mention these small matters designedly. It is sometimes the case that the only city of a pastoral province is its capital, and occasionally the land is uncultivated up to its very streets. The encircling desert besets such cities at a greater or less distance, and bears heavily upon them, and they are thus small oases of civilization surrounded by an untilled plain, hundreds of square miles in extent, the surface of which is but rarely interrupted by any settlement of consequence.

The cities of Buenos Ayres and Cordova have succeeded better than the others in establishing about them subordinate towns to serve as new foci of civilization and municipal interests; a fact which deserves notice. The inhabitants of the city wear the European dress, live in a civilized manner, and possess laws, ideas of progress, means of instruction, some municipal organization, regular forms of government, etc. Beyond the precincts of the city everything assumes a new aspect; the country people wear a different dress, which I will call South American, as it is common to all districts; their habits of life are different, their wants peculiar and limited. The people composing these two distinct forms of society, do not seem to belong to the same nation. Moreover, the countryman, far from attempting to imitate the customs of the city, rejects with disdain its luxury and refinement; and it is unsafe for the costume of the city people, their coats, their cloaks, their saddles, or anything European, to show themselves in the country. Everything civilized which the city contains is blockaded there, proscribed beyond its limits; and any one who should dare to appear in the rural districts in a frock-coat, for example, or mounted on an English saddle, would bring ridicule and brutal assaults upon himself.

The whole remaining population inhabit the open country, which, whether wooded or destitute of the larger plants, is generally level, and almost everywhere occupied by pastures, in some places of such abundance and excellence, that the grass of an artificial meadow would not surpass them. Mendoza, and especially San Juan, are exceptions to this general absence of tilled fields, the people here depending chiefly on the products of agriculture. Everywhere else, pasturage being plenty, the means of subsistence of the inhabitants—for we cannot call it their occupation—is stock-raising. Pastoral life reminds us of the Asiatic plains, which imagination covers with Kalmuck, Cossack,[5] or Arab tents.

---

5. Members of independent military communities in southern Russia and Ukraine, known as adventurers. "Kalmuck": semi-nomadic, Mongolian-speaking people who migrated west to a region bordering the Caspian Sea.

The primitive life of nations—a life essentially barbarous and unprogressive—the life of Abraham, which is that of the Bedouin of to-day, prevails in the Argentine plains, although modified in a peculiar manner by civilization. The Arab tribe which wanders through the wilds of Asia, is united under the rule of one of its elders or of a warrior chief; society exists, although not fixed in any determined locality. Its religious opinions, immemorial traditions, unchanging customs, and its sentiment of respect for the aged, make altogether a code of laws and a form of government which preserves morality, as it is there understood, as well as order and the association of the tribe. But progress is impossible, because there can be no progress without permanent possession of the soil, or without cities, which are the means of developing the capacity of man for the processes of industry, and which enable him to extend his acquisitions.

Nomad tribes do not exist in the Argentine plains; the stock-raiser is a proprietor, living upon his own land; but this condition renders association impossible, and tends to scatter separate families over an immense extent of surface. Imagine an expanse of two thousand square leagues, inhabited throughout, but where the dwellings are usually four or even eight leagues apart, and two leagues, at least, separate the nearest neighbors. The production of movable property is not impossible, the enjoyments of luxury are not wholly incompatible with this isolation; wealth can raise a superb edifice in the desert. But the incentive is wanting; no example is near; the inducements for making a great display which exist in a city, are not known in that isolation and solitude. Inevitable privations justify natural indolence; a dearth of all the amenities of life induces all the externals of barbarism. Society has altogether disappeared. There is but the isolated self-concentrated feudal family. Since there is no collected society, no government is possible; there is neither municipal nor executive power, and civil justice has no means of reaching criminals. I doubt if the modern world presents any other form of association so monstrous as this. It is the exact opposite of the Roman municipality, where all the population were assembled within an inclosed space, and went from it to cultivate the surrounding fields. The consequence of this was a strong social organization, the good results of which have prepared the way for modern civilization. The Argentine system resembles the old Slavonic Sloboda,[6] with the difference that the latter was agricultural, and therefore more susceptible of government, while the dispersion of the population was not so great as in South America. It differs from the nomad tribes in admitting of no social reunion, and in a permanent occupation of the soil. Lastly, it has something in common with the feudal system of the Middle Ages, when the barons lived in their strongholds, and thence made war on the cities, and laid waste the country in the vicinity; but the baron and the feudal castle are wanting. If power starts up in the country, it lasts only for a moment, and is democratic; it is not inherited, nor can it maintain itself, for want of mountains and strong positions. It follows from this, that even the savage tribe of the pampas is better organized for moral development than are our country districts.

But the remarkable feature of this society, viewed in its social aspect, is its affinity to the life of the ancients—to the life of the Spartans or Romans; but again a radical dissimilarity appears when the subject is considered from another

6. An estate or a village that was technically free and did not have to pay taxes.

side. The free citizen of Sparta or of Rome threw upon his slaves the weight of material life, the care of providing for his subsistence, while he lived, free from such cares, in the forum or in the public place of assembly, exclusively occupied with the interests of the State—peace, war, and party contests. The stock-raiser has his share of the same advantages, and his herds fulfill the degrading office of the ancient Helot.[7] Their spontaneous multiplication constitutes and indefinitely augments his fortune; the help of man is superfluous; his labor, his intelligence, his time, are not needed to the preservation and increase of the means of life. But though he needs none of these forces for the supply of his physical wants, he is unable to make use of them, when thus saved, as the Roman did. He has no city, no municipality, no intimate associations, and thus the basis of all social development is wanting. As the land-owners are not brought together, they have no public wants to satisfy; in a word, there is no *res publica*.[8]

Moral progress, and the cultivation of the intellect, are here not only neglected, as in the Arab or Tartar tribe, but impossible. Where can a school be placed for the instruction of children living ten leagues apart in all directions? Thus, consequently, civilization can in no way be brought about. Barbarism is the normal condition,[9] and it is fortunate if domestic customs preserve a small germ of morality. Religion feels the consequences of this want of social organization. The offices of the pastor are nominal, the pulpit has no audience, the priest flees from the deserted chapel, or allows his character to deteriorate in inactivity and solitude. Vice, simony, and the prevalent barbarism penetrate his cell, and change his moral superiority into the means of gratifying his avarice or ambition, and he ends by becoming a party leader. I once witnessed a scene of rural life worthy of the primitive ages of the world, which preceded the institution of the priesthood. In 1838 I happened to be in the Sierra de San Luis, at the house of a proprietor whose two favorite occupations were saying prayers and gambling. He had built a chapel where he used to pray through the rosary on Sunday afternoons, to supply the want of a priest, and of the public divine service of which the place had been destitute for many years. It was a Homeric picture: the sun declining to the west; the sheep returning to the fold, and rending the air with their confused bleatings; the service conducted by the master of the house, a man of sixty, with a noble countenance, in which the pure European race was evident in the white skin, blue eyes, and wide and open forehead; while the responses were made by a dozen women and some young men, whose imperfectly broken horses were fastened near the door of the chapel. After finishing the rosary, he fervently offered up his own petitions. I never heard a voice fuller of pious feeling, nor a prayer of purer warmth, of firmer faith, of greater beauty, or better adapted to the circumstances, than that which he uttered. In this prayer he besought God to grant rain for the fields, fruitfulness for the herds and flocks, peace for the Republic, and safety for all wayfarers. I readily shed tears, and wept even with sobs, for the religious sentiment had been awakened in my soul to intensity, and like an unknown sensation, for I never witnessed a more religious scene. I seemed to be living in the times of Abraham, in his presence, in that of God, and of the nature which

7. A people who were treated much like slaves by the ancient Spartans.
8. Republic (Latin).
9. In 1826, during a year's residence at the Sierra San Luis, I taught the art of reading to six young people of good families, the youngest of whom was twenty-two years old [Sarmiento's note].

reveals Him. The voice of that sincere and pure-minded man made all my nerves vibrate, and penetrated to my inmost soul.

To this, that is, to natural religion, is all religion reduced in the pastoral districts. Christianity exists, like the Spanish idioms, as a tradition which is perpetuated, but corrupted; colored by gross superstitions and unaided by instruction, rites, or convictions. It is the case in almost all the districts which are remote from the cities, that when traders from San Juan or Mendoza arrive there, three or four children, some months or a year old, are presented to them for baptism, confidence being felt that their good education will enable them to administer the rite in a valid manner; and on the arrival of a priest, young men old enough to break a colt, present themselves to him to be anointed and have baptism *sub conditione*[1] administered to them.

In the absence of all the means of civilization and progress, which can only be developed among men collected into societies of many individuals, the education of the country people is as follows: The women look after the house, get the meals ready, shear the sheep, milk the cows, make the cheese, and weave the coarse cloth used for garments. All domestic occupations are performed by women; on them rests the burden of all the labor, and it is an exceptional favor when some of the men undertake the cultivation of a little maize, bread not being in use as an ordinary article of diet. The boys exercise their strength and amuse themselves by gaining skill in the use of the lasso and the bolas, with which they constantly harass and pursue the calves and goats. When they can ride, which is as soon as they have learned to walk, they perform some small services on horseback. When they become stronger, they race over the country, falling off their horses and getting up again, tumbling on purpose into rabbit burrows, scrambling over precipices, and practicing feats of horsemanship. On reaching puberty, they take to breaking wild colts, and death is the least penalty that awaits them if their strength or courage fails them for a moment. With early manhood comes complete independence and idleness.

Now begins the public life of the gaucho, as I may say, since his education is by this time at an end. These men, Spaniards only in their language and in the confused religious notions preserved among them, must be seen, before a right estimate can be made of the indomitable and haughty character which grows out of this struggle of isolated man with untamed nature, of the rational being with the brute. It is necessary to see their visages bristling with beards, their countenances as grave and serious as those of the Arabs of Asia, to appreciate the pitying scorn with which they look upon the sedentary denizen of the city, who may have read many books, but who cannot overthrow and slay a fierce bull, who could not provide himself with a horse from the pampas, who has never met a tiger[2] alone, and received him with a dagger in one hand and a poncho rolled up in the other, to be thrust into the animal's mouth, while he transfixes his heart with his dagger.

This habit of triumphing over resistance, of constantly showing a superiority to Nature, of defying and subduing her, prodigiously develops the consciousness of individual consequence and superior prowess. The Argentine people of every class, civilized and ignorant alike, have a high opinion of their national

1. Baptism performed when it is unknown whether the person has already been baptized.
2. The Spanish named South American jaguars "tigres" when they arrived there in the 16th century.

importance. All the other people of South America throw this vanity of theirs in their teeth, and take offense at their presumption and arrogance. I believe the charge not to be wholly unfounded, but I do not object to the trait. Alas, for the nation without faith in itself! Great things were not made for such a people. To what extent may not the independence of that part of America be due to the arrogance of these Argentine gauchos, who have never seen anything beneath the sun superior to themselves in wisdom or in power? The European is in their eyes the most contemptible of all men, for a horse gets the better of him in a couple of plunges.[3]

If the origin of this national vanity among the lower classes is despicable, it has none the less on that account some noble results; as the water of a river is no less pure for the mire and pollution of its sources. Implacable is the hatred which these people feel for men of refinement, whose garments, manners, and customs, they regard with invincible repugnance. Such is the material of the Argentine soldiery, and it may easily be imagined what valor and endurance in war are the consequences of the habits described above. We may add that these soldiers have been used to slaughtering cattle from their childhood, and that this act of necessary cruelty makes them familiar with bloodshed, and hardens their hearts against the groans of their victims.

Country life, then, has developed all the physical but none of the intellectual powers of the gaucho. His moral character is of the quality to be expected from his habit of triumphing over the obstacles and the forces of nature; it is strong, haughty, and energetic. Without instruction, and indeed without need of any, without means of support as without wants, he is happy in the midst of his poverty and privations, which are not such to one who never knew nor wished for greater pleasures than are his already. Thus if the disorganization of society among the gauchos deeply implants barbarism in their natures, through the impossibility and uselessness of moral and intellectual education, it has, too, its attractive side to him. The gaucho does not labor; he finds his food and raiment ready to his hand. If he is a proprietor, his own flocks yield him both; if he possesses nothing himself, he finds them in the house of a patron or a relation. The necessary care of the herds is reduced to excursions and pleasure parties; the branding, which is like the harvesting of farmers, is a festival, the arrival of which is received with transports of joy, being the occasion of the assembling of all the men for twenty leagues around, and the opportunity for displaying incredible skill with the lasso. The gaucho arrives at the spot on his best steed, riding at a slow and measured pace; he halts at a little distance and puts his leg over his horse's neck to enjoy the sight leisurely. If enthusiasm seizes him, he slowly dismounts, uncoils his lasso, and flings it at some bull, passing like a flash of lightning forty paces from him; he catches him by one hoof, as he intended, and quietly coils his leather cord again.

* * *

3. General Mansilla said, in a public meeting during the French blockade, "What have we to apprehend from those Europeans, who are not equal to one night's gallop?" and the vast plebeian audience drowned the speaker's voice with thunders of applause [Sarmiento's note].

CHAPTER V

Life of Juan Facundo Quiroga

Moreover these traits belong to the original character of the human race. The man of nature who has not yet learned to restrain or disguise his passions, displays them in all their energy, and gives himself up to their impetuosity.

—ALEX. *History of the Ottoman Empire*[4]

HIS INFANCY AND YOUTH

Between the cities of San Luis and San Juan, lies an extensive desert, called the Travesia, a word which signifies *want of water*. The aspect of that waste is mostly gloomy and unpromising, and the traveller coming from the east does not fail to provide his *chifles*[5] with a sufficient quantity of water at the last cistern which he passes as he approaches it. This Travesia once witnessed the following strange scene. The consequences of some of the encounters with knives so common among our gauchos had driven one of them in haste from the city of San Luis and forced him to escape to the Travesia on foot, and with his riding gear on his shoulder, in order to avoid the pursuit of the law. Two comrades were to join him as soon as they could steal horses for all three. Hunger and thirst were not the only dangers which at that time awaited him in the desert; a tiger that had already tasted human flesh had been following the track of those who crossed it for a year, and more than eight persons had already been the victims of this preference. In these regions, where man must contend with this animal for dominion over nature, the former sometimes falls a victim, upon which the tiger begins to acquire a preference for the taste of human flesh, and when it has once devoted itself to this novel form of chase, the pursuit of mankind, it gets the name of *man-eater*. The provincial justice nearest the scene of his depredations calls out the huntsmen of his district, who join, under his authority and guidance, in the pursuit of the beast, which seldom escapes the consequences of its outlawry.

When our fugitive had proceeded some six leagues, he thought he heard the distant roar of the animal, and a shudder ran through him. The roar of the tiger resembles the screech of the hog, but is prolonged, sharp, and piercing, and even when there is no occasion for fear, causes an involuntary tremor of the nerves as if the flesh shuddered consciously at the menace of death. The roaring was heard clearer and nearer. The tiger was already upon the trail of the man, who saw no refuge but a small carob-tree at a great distance. He had to quicken his pace, and finally to run, for the roars behind him began to follow each other more rapidly, and each was clearer and more ringing than the last. At length, flinging his riding gear to one side of the path, the gaucho turned to the tree which he had noticed, and in spite of the weakness of its trunk, happily quite a tall one, he succeeded in clambering to its top, and keeping himself half concealed among its boughs which oscillated violently. Thence he could see the swift approach of the tiger, sniffing the soil and roaring more frequently in proportion to its increasing perception of

---

4. Alexandre-Louis Félix (1795–1868), French civil servant and author of *The History of the Ottoman Empire* (1822–24).

5. Cattle horns carved for use as water carriers.

the nearness of its prey. Passing beyond the spot where our traveller had left the path, it lost the track, and becoming enraged, rapidly circled about until it discovered the riding gear, which it dashed to fragments by a single blow. Still more furious from this failure, it resumed its search for the trail, and at last found out the direction in which it led. It soon discerned its prey, under whose weight the slight tree was swaying like a reed upon the summit of which a bird has alighted. The tiger now sprang forward, and in the twinkling of an eye, its monstrous fore-paws were resting on the slender trunk two yards from the ground, and were imparting to the tree a convulsive trembling calculated to act upon the nerves of the gaucho, whose position was far from secure. The beast exerted its strength in an ineffectual leap; it circled around the tree, measuring the elevation with eyes reddened by the thirst for blood, and at length, roaring with rage, it crouched down, beating the ground frantically with its tail, its eyes fixed on its prey, its parched mouth half open. This horrible scene had lasted for nearly two mortal hours; the gaucho's constrained attitude, and the fearful fascination exercised over him by the fixed and bloodthirsty stare of the tiger, which irresistibly attracted and retained his own glances, had begun to diminish his strength, and he already perceived that the moment was at hand when his exhausted body would fall into the capacious mouth of his pursuer. But at this moment the distant sound of the feet of horses on a rapid gallop gave him hope of rescue. His friends had indeed seen the tiger's foot-prints, and were hastening on, though without hope of saving him. The scattered fragments of the saddle directed them to the scene of action, and it was the work of a moment for them to reach it, to uncoil their lassoes, and to fling them over the tiger, now blinded by rage. The beast, drawn in opposite directions by the two lassos, could not evade the swift stabs by which its destined victim took his revenge for his prolonged torments. "On that occasion I knew what it was to be afraid," was the expression of Don Juan Facundo Quiroga, as he related this incident to a group of officers.

He too was called "the tiger of the Llanos,"[6] a title which did not ill befit him. There are, in fact, as is proved by phrenology and comparative anatomy, relations between external forms and moral qualities, between the countenance of a man and that of some animal whose disposition resembles his own. Facundo, as he was long called in the interior,—or, General Don Facundo Quiroga, as he afterwards became, when society had received him into its bosom and victory had crowned him with laurels,—was a stoutly built man of low stature, whose short neck and broad shoulders supported a well-shaped head, covered with a profusion of black and closely curling hair. His somewhat oval face was half buried in this mass of hair and an equally thick black, curly beard, rising to his cheek-bones, which by their prominence evinced a firm and tenacious will. His black and fiery eyes, shadowed by thick eyebrows, occasioned an involuntary sense of terror in those on whom they chanced to fall, for Facundo's glance was never direct, whether from habit or intention.

* * *

6. Plains (Spanish).

Facundo Quiroga was the son of an inhabitant of San Juan, who had settled in the Llanos of La Rioja, and there had acquired a fortune in pastoral pursuits. In 1779, Facundo was sent to his father's native province to receive the limited education, consisting only of the arts of reading and writing, which he could acquire in its schools. After a man has come to employ the hundred trumpets of fame with the noise of his deeds, curiosity or the spirit of investigation is carried to such an extent as to scent out the insignificant history of the child, in order to connect it with the biography of the hero; and it is not seldom that the rudiments of the traits characteristic of the historical personage are met amid fables invented by flattery. The young Alcibiades[7] is said to have lain down at full length upon the pavement of the street where he was playing, in order to insist that the driver of an approaching vehicle should yield the way to avoid running over him. Napoleon is reported to have ruled over his fellow-students, and to have entrenched himself in his study to resist an apprehended insult. Many anecdotes are now in circulation relating to Facundo, many of which reveal his true nature. In the house where he lodged, he could never be induced to take his seat at the family table; in school he was haughty, reserved, and unsocial; he never joined the other boys except to head their rebellious proceedings or to beat them. The master, tired of contending with so untamable a disposition, on one occasion provided himself with a new and stiff strap, and said to the frightened boys, as he showed it to them, "This is to be made supple upon Facundo." Facundo, then eleven years old, heard this threat, and the next day he tested its value. Without having learned his lesson, he asked the head-master to hear it himself, because, as he said, the assistant was unfriendly to him. The master complied with the request. Facundo made one mistake, then two, three, and four; upon which the master used his strap upon him. Facundo, who had calculated everything, down to the weakness of the chair in which the master was seated, gave him a buffet, upset him on his back, and, taking to the street in the confusion created by this scene, hid himself among some wild vines where they could not get him out for three days. Was not such a boy the embryo chieftain who would afterwards defy society at large?

In early manhood his character took a more decided cast, constantly becoming more gloomy, imperious, and wild. From the age of fifteen years he was irresistibly controlled by the passion for gambling, as is often the case with such natures, which need strong excitement to awaken their dormant energies. This made him notorious in the city, and intolerable in the house which afforded him its hospitality; and finally under this influence, by a shot fired at one George Peña, he shed the first rill of blood which went to make up the wide torrent that marked his way through life.

On his becoming an adult, the thread of his life disappears in an intricate labyrinth of bouts and broils among the people of the surrounding region. Sometimes lying hid, always pursued, he passed his time in gambling, working as a common laborer, domineering over everybody around him, and distributing his stabs among them.

On the Godoy farm in San Juan are shown to this day mud-walls of Quiroga's treading; there are others in Fiambola, in La Rioja, made by him. He himself pointed out others in Mendoza, in the very place where one afternoon he had

7. Ancient Athenian military leader and strategist (ca. 450–404 B.C.E.).

twenty-six of the officers who surrendered at Chacon dragged from their houses and shot to avenge Villifañe.[8] He also showed some monuments of his wandering life of labor in the country districts of Buenos Ayres. What motives induced this man, brought up in a respectable family, son of a man of means and creditable life, to descend to a hireling's position, and moreover to select the dullest and most brutish kind of work, needing only bodily strength and endurance? Was it because the labor of building these mud-walls is recompensed with double wages, and that he was in haste to get together a little money?

The most connected account of this obscure and roaming part of his life that I can procure is as follows:

Towards 1806, he went to Chile with a consignment of grain on his parent's account. This he gambled away, as well as the animals, which had brought it, and the family slaves who had accompanied him.

He often took to San Juan and Mendoza droves of the stock on his father's estate, and these always shared the same fate; for with Facundo, gambling was a fierce and burning passion which aroused the deepest instincts of his nature. These successive gains and losses of his must have worn out his father's generosity, for at last he broke off all amicable relations with his family.

When he had become the terror of the Republic, he was once asked by one of his parasites, "What was the largest bet you ever made in your life, General?" "Seventy dollars," replied Quiroga, carelessly, and yet he had just won two hundred dollars at one stake. He afterwards explained that once when a young man, having only seventy dollars, he had lost them all at one throw. But this fact has its characteristic history. Facundo had been at work for a year as a laborer upon the farm of a lady, situated in the Plumerillo,[9] and had made himself conspicuous by his punctuality in going to work, and by the influence and authority which he exercised over the other laborers. When they wanted a holiday to get drunk in, they used to apply to Facundo, who informed the lady, and gave her his word, which was always fulfilled, to have all the men at work the next day. On this account the laborers called him *the father*. At the end of a year of steady work, Facundo asked for his wages, which amounted to seventy dollars, and mounted his horse without knowing where he was bound, but seeing a collection of people at a grocery store, he alighted, and reaching over the group around the card-dealer, bet his seventy dollars on one card. He lost them, and remounting, went on his way, careless in what direction, until after a little time a justice, Toledo by name, who happened to be passing, stopped him to ask for his passport. Facundo rode up as if about to give it to him, pretended to be feeling for something in his pocket, and stretched the justice on the ground with a stab. Was he taking his revenge upon the judge for his recent loss at play? or was it his purpose to satisfy the irritation against civil authority natural to a gaucho outlaw, and increase, by this new deed, the splendor of his rising fame? Both are true explanations. This mode of revenging himself for misfortunes upon whatever first offered itself, had many examples in his life. When he was addressed as General, and had colonels at his orders, he had two hundred lashes given one of them in his house at San Juan, for having, as he said, cheated at play. He ordered two hundred lashes to be given to a young

---

8. José Benito Villafañe (1790–1831), governor and ally of Facundo's assassinated by the Unitarists.

9. The region around the Argentine city of Mendoza.

man for having allowed himself a jest at a time when jests were not to his taste; and two hundred lashes was the penalty inflicted on a woman in Mendoza for having said to him as he passed, "Farewell, General," when he was going off in a rage at not having succeeded in intimidating a neighbor of his, who was as peaceable and judicious as Facundo was rash and gaucho-like.

Facundo reappears later in Buenos Ayres, where he was enrolled in 1810 as a recruit in the regiment of Arribeños, which was commanded by General Ocampo, a native of his own province, and afterwards president of Charcas. The glorious career of arms opened before him with the first rays of the sun of May; and doubtless, endowed with such capacity as his, and with his destructive and sanguinary instincts, Facundo, could he have been disciplined to submit to civil authority and ennobled in the sublimity of the object of the strife, might some day have returned from Peru, Chile, or Bolivia, as a General of the Argentine Republic, like so many other brave gauchos who began their careers in the humble position of a private soldier. But Quiroga's rebellious spirit could not endure the yoke of discipline, the order of the barrack, or the delay of promotion. He felt his destiny to be to rule, to rise at a single leap, to create for himself, without assistance, and in spite of a hostile and civilized society, a career of his own, combining bravery and crime, government and disorganization. He was subsequently recruited into the army of the Andes, and enrolled in the Mounted Grenadiers. A lieutenant named Garcia took him for an assistant, and very soon desertion left a vacant place in those glorious files. Quiroga, like Rosas, like all the vipers that have thriven under the shade of their country's laurels, made himself notorious in after-life by his hatred for the soldiers of Independence, among whom both the men above named made horrible slaughter.

Facundo, after deserting from Buenos Ayres, set out for the interior with three comrades. A squad of soldiery overtook him; he faced the pursuers and engaged in a real battle with them, which remained undecided for awhile, until, after having killed four or five men, he was at liberty to continue his journey, constantly cutting his way through detachments of troops which here and there opposed his progress, until he arrived at San Luis. He was, at a later day, to traverse the same route with a handful of men, to disperse armies instead of detachments, and proceed to the famous citadel of Tucuman to blot out the last remains of Republicanism and civil order.

Facundo now reappears in the Llanos, at his father's house. At this period occurred an event which is well attested. Yet one of the writers whose manuscripts I am using, replies to an inquiry about the matter, "that to the extent of his knowledge Quiroga never attempted forcibly to deprive his parents of money," and I could wish to adopt this statement, irreconcilable as it is with unvarying tradition and general consent. The contrary is shocking to relate. It is said that on his father's refusal to give him a sum of money which he had demanded, he watched for the time when both parents were taking an afternoon nap to fasten the door of the room they occupied, and to set fire to the straw roof, which was the usual covering of the buildings of the Llanos!

But what is certain in the matter is that his father once requested the governor of La Rioja to arrest him in order to check his excesses, and that Facundo, before taking flight from the Llanos, went to the city of La Rioja, where that official was to be found at the time, and coming upon him by surprise, gave him a blow, saying as he did so, "You have sent, sir, to have me arrested. There, have me arrested now!" On which he mounted his horse and set off for the open country at a gallop. At the end of a year he again showed himself at his father's house, threw himself at the feet of the old man whom he had used so ill, and succeeded amid the sobs of both, and the son's assurances of his reform in reply to the father's recriminations, in reëstablishing peace, although on a very uncertain basis.

But no change occurred in his character and disorderly habits; races, gambling parties, and expeditions into the country were the occasions of new acts of violence, stabbings, and assaults on his part, until he at length made himself intolerable to all, and rendered his own position very unsafe. Then a great thought which he announced without shame, got hold of his mind. The deserter from the Arribeños regiment, the mounted grenadier who refused to make himself immortal at Chacabuco or Maipù, determined to join the montonera of Ramirez, the offshoot from that led by Artigas,[1] whose renown for crime and hatred for the cities on which it was making war, had reached the Llanos, and held the provincial government in dread. Facundo set forth to join those buccaneers of the pampa. But perhaps the knowledge of his character, and of the importance of the aid which he would give to the destroyers, alarmed his fellow provincials, for they informed the authorities of San Luis, through which he was to pass, of his infernal design. Dupuis, then (1818) governor, arrested him, and for sometime he remained unnoticed among the criminals confined in the prison. This prison of San Luis, however, was to be the first step in his ascent to the elevation which he subsequently attained. San Martín had sent to San Luis a great number of Spanish officers of all ranks from among the prisoners taken in Chile. Irritated by their humiliations and sufferings, or thinking it possible that the Spanish forces might be assembled again, this party of prisoners rose one day and opened the doors of the cells of the common criminals, to obtain their aid in a general escape. Facundo was one of these criminals, and as soon as he found himself free from prison, he seized an iron bar of his fetters, split the skull of the very Spaniard who had released him, and passing through the group of insurgents, left a wide path strewn with the dead. Some say that the weapon he employed was a bayonet, and that only three men were killed by it. Quiroga, however, always talked of the iron bar of the fetters, and of fourteen dead men. This may be one of the fictions with which the poetic imagination of the people adorns the types of brute force they so much admire; perhaps the tale of the iron bar is an Argentine version of the jaw-bone of Samson, the Hebrew Hercules. But Facundo looked upon it as a crown of glory, in accordance with his idea of excellence, and whether by bar or bayonet, he succeeded, aided by other soldiers and prisoners whom his example encouraged, in suppressing the insurrection and reconciling society to himself by this act of bravery, and placing himself under his country's protection. Thus his name spread everywhere, ennobled and cleansed, though with blood, from the stains which had tarnished it.

Facundo returned to La Rioja covered with glory, his country's creditor; and with testimonials of his conduct, to show in the Llanos, among gauchos, the new titles which justified the terror his name began to inspire; for there is

1. José Gervasio Artigas Arnal (1764–1850), leader of Uruguayan independence. "Chacabuco or Maipù": sites of battles in the Chilean war of independence; both were important victories for rebel general José de San Martín. "Montonera of Ramirez": horseman who fought under Francisco Ramirez (1786–1821).

something imposing, something which subjugates and controls others in the man who is rewarded for the assassination of fourteen men at one time.

Something still remains to be noticed of the previous character and temper of this pillar of the Confederation. An illiterate man, one of Quiroga's companions in childhood and youth, who has supplied me with many of the above facts, sends me the following curious statements in a manuscript describing Quiroga's early years: "His public career was not preceded by the practice of theft; he never committed robbery even in his most pressing necessities. He was not only fond of fighting, but would pay for an opportunity, or for a chance to insult the most renowned champion in any company. He had a great aversion to respectable men. He never drank. He was very reserved from his youth, and desired to inspire others with awe as well as with fear, for which purpose he gave his confidants to understand that he had the gift of prophecy, in short was a soothsayer. He treated all connected with him as slaves. *He never went to confession, prayed, or heard mass*; I saw him once at mass after he became a general. He said of himself that he believed in nothing." The frankness with which these words are written, prove their truth.

And here ends the private life of Quiroga, in which I have omitted a long series of deeds which only show his evil nature, his bad education, and his fierce and bloody instincts. The facts stated appear to me to sum up the whole public life of Quiroga. I see in them the great man, the man of genius, in spite of himself and unknown to himself; a Caesar, Tamerlane, or Mohammed.[2] The fault is not his that thus he was born. In order to contend with, rule, and control the power of the city, and the judicial authority, he is willing to descend to anything. If he is offered a place in the army, he disdains it, because his impatience cannot wait for promotion. Such a position demands submission, and places fetters upon individual independence; the soldier's coat oppresses his body, and military tactics control his steps, all of which are insufferable! His equestrian life, a life of danger and of strong excitements, has steeled his spirit and hardened his heart. He feels an unconquerable and instinctive hatred for the laws which have pursued him, for the judges who have condemned him, and for the whole society and organism from which he has felt himself withdrawn from his childhood, and which regards him with suspicion and contempt. With these remarks is connected by imperceptible links the motto of this chapter, "He is the natural man, as yet unused either to repress or disguise his passions; he does not restrain their energy, but gives free rein to their impetuosity. This is the character of the human race." And thus it appears in the rural districts of the Argentine Republic. Facundo is a type of primitive barbarism. He recognized no form of subjection. His rage was that of a wild beast. The locks of his crisp black hair, which fell in meshes over his brow and eyes, resembled the snakes of Medusa's head.[3] Anger made his voice hoarse, and turned his glances into dragons. In a fit of passion he kicked out the brains of a man with whom he had quarreled at play. He tore off both the ears of a woman he had lived with, and had promised to marry, upon her asking him for

2. Famed world leaders. Julius Caesar (ca. 102–44 B.C.E.), Roman military leader and emperor; Tamerlane, or Timur (1336–1405), conqueror and founder of the Timurid Empire in Central Asia; Mohammed (570–632), prophet and founder of Islam.

3. Female monster from Greek myth, with snakes for hair, who turned those who looked at her to stone.

thirty dollars for the celebration of the wedding; and laid open his son John's head with an axe, because he could not make him hold his tongue. He violently beat a beautiful young lady at Tucuman, whom he had failed either to seduce or to subdue, and exhibited in all his actions a low and brutal yet not a stupid nature, or one wholly without lofty aims. Incapable of commanding noble admiration, he delighted in exciting fear; and this pleasure was exclusive and dominant with him to the arranging all his actions so as to produce terror in those around him, whether it was society in general, the victim on his way to execution, or his own wife and children. Wanting ability to manage the machinery of civil government, he substituted terror for patriotism and self-sacrifice. Destitute of learning, he surrounded himself with mysteries, and pretended to a foreknowledge of events which gave him prestige and reputation among the commonalty, supporting his claims by an air of impenetrability, by natural sagacity, an uncommon power of observation, and the advantage he derived from vulgar credulity.

The repertory of anecdotes relating to Quiroga, and with which the popular memory is replete, is inexhaustible; his sayings, his expedients, bear the stamp of an originality which gives them a certain Eastern aspect, a certain tint of Solomonic wisdom in the conception of the vulgar. Indeed, how does Solomon's advice for discovering the true mother of the disputed child differ from Facundo's method of detecting a thief in the following instances:—

An article had been stolen from a band, and all endeavors to discover the thief had proved fruitless. Quiroga drew up the troops and gave orders for the cutting of as many small wands of equal length as there were soldiers; then, having had these wands distributed one to each man, he said in a confident voice, "The man whose wand will be longer than the others to-morrow morning is the thief." Next day the troops was again paraded, and Quiroga proceeded to inspect the wands. There was one whose wand was, not *longer* but *shorter* than the others. "Wretch!" cried Facundo, in a voice which overpowered the man with dismay, "it is thou!" And so it was; the culprit's confusion was proof of the fact. The expedient was a simple one; the credulous gaucho, fearing that his wand would really grow, had cut off a piece of it. But to avail one's self of such means, a man must be superior in intellect to those about him, and must at least have some knowledge of human nature.

* * *

FREDERICK DOUGLASS

1818?–1895

There was no more important African American public figure in the nineteenth century than Frederick Douglass. Born into slavery, he could easily have remained illiterate his whole life. But with extraordinary ingenuity and perseverance, he taught himself to read, and soon turned himself into such an electrifying antislavery speaker and writer that some audiences simply could not believe that he had grown up a slave. Even skeptics found themselves won over by his charismatic personality, acerbic wit, and skillful arguments. Douglass's eloquence became a powerful weapon in the war against slavery, as he edited an influential abolitionist newspaper, stirred crowded lecture halls in the United States, Great Britain, and Ireland, and published his best-selling *Narrative of the Life of Frederick Douglass, an American Slave, Written by Himself* (1845).

LIFE

Frederick Augustus Washington Bailey was born in Talbot County in the slave state of Maryland sometime around 1818. He barely knew his mother, a slave, and never knew the identity of his father, probably a white man and perhaps his owner. At first he lived in his grandmother's cabin, and then at the age of six he went to live in the house of his owner, the chief overseer of a vast plantation belonging to one of the wealthiest men in Maryland. It was during this period, as Douglass recounts in horrifying detail in his autobiography, that he first witnessed the daily cruelty suffered by plantation slaves.

An important turning point came in 1826 when Frederick was sent to live with Hugh and Sophia Auld, relatives of his owner in Baltimore. One of the most famous episodes in the autobiography tells of the moment when Hugh Auld discovered that his wife was teaching the slave to read. He burst out angrily that literacy would make Frederick "discontented" and "unmanageable" and so "would forever unfit him to be a slave." This reprimand transformed the slave's life: "From that moment," Douglass writes, "I understood the pathway from slavery to freedom." In the seven years that he remained with the Aulds, Douglass used his best resources to learn how to read and write, discovering two texts that would significantly shape his later career: Caleb Bingham's *The Columbian Orator* (1807), and the speeches of Thomas Sheridan, an eighteenth-century Irish actor and educator. Both were guides to public speaking.

In 1833 Hugh Auld's brother, Thomas, who had become Frederick Bailey's official owner, called him back to work on his plantation. Thomas Auld was a cruel master, but he found the slave so unruly that he sent him to a harsh "slave breaker" for a year to tame him. Douglass was not tamed, however; he defied and bested this notoriously brutal master in a long physical struggle, which, he says, resolved him to break free from slavery altogether: "however long I might remain a slave in form, the day passed forever when I could be a slave in fact."

After a first abortive attempt at escape, Douglass returned to Hugh Auld in Baltimore, where he learned caulking skills in the shipyard and began to turn his weekly wages over to his master. During this period of relative independence he met and fell in love with a free black woman named Anna Murray. Then, in 1838, he managed a successful escape. In the *Narrative* he was reluctant to divulge his strategies in case publicizing them would endanger other slaves trying to escape, but much later, after slavery had ended, he told the full story. First he disguised himself as a sailor and borrowed the identification papers of a free black seaman; then he traveled by train and ferry to New York, and with the help of abolitionists, moved to New Bedford, Massachusetts. There he married Murray, changed his name, and worked odd jobs to make a living. He also began to read an abolitionist newspaper, *The Liberator*. In 1841 he met its celebrated and controversial editor, William Lloyd Garrison, who invited Douglass to work for him as a traveling lecturer, telling the story of his life and selling subscriptions to the newspaper.

This marked the beginning of Douglass's extraordinarily successful public career. From the outset, his lectures moved his audiences to laughter, tears, and rapt attention. "As a speaker, he has few equals," claimed a contemporary editor. "I would give twenty thousand dollars if I could deliver an address in that manner," said another. In a context where apologists for slavery argued that Southern slaves were contented— living comfortable lives with kindly owners—Douglass's story offered a compelling counternarrative. And yet, from the beginning, he was also accused of fabricating the facts. His oratorical elegance and skill were so striking that a few abolitionists pleaded with him to put a little more "plantation" into his speech, so that he would seem more authentic. Douglass refused.

The public lectures paved the way for the *Narrative of the Life of Frederick Douglass* in two ways. First, although Douglass's speeches regularly told of the cruelties of slaveholding, mocked hypocritical proslavery ministers, and asked Northern audiences to confront inequality and prejudice in the free states, the centerpiece of his lectures was his own life story. He had tested it out on audience after audience; he knew it had power, and he was eager to disseminate it widely. Second, given the many accusations of fraud against Douglass, he wanted to publish details about the people and places he had known as a slave, so that others could confirm the truthfulness of his account. But publishing the details also put Douglass in danger. There was always the threat that a fugitive slave would be recaptured and sent back to the South, and now his owners could recognize him from his narrative and come to claim him. Douglass left the United States for England in 1845, just a few months after the autobiography appeared.

For two years Douglass traveled through Great Britain and Ireland, lecturing to enthusiastic crowds. By 1848 the *Narrative* had gone through nine editions in England alone, and it was translated into French and German. Douglass was surprised at the relative lack of racial prejudice he encountered in Britain. Among the warmest receptions he had was from Daniel O'Connell, the leader of the struggle against British colonial rule in Ireland. In England two Quakers gave Douglass the money to buy his own freedom, and in December of 1846 he became officially a free man.

Back in the United States, Douglass broke from Garrison's organization. Garrison was a powerful voice in the antislavery cause, but he paid Douglass less than the white lecturers on his circuit and patronized him, urging him to focus only on telling the story of his own life because, Garrison suggested, a black man was not capable of analyzing slavery as a large-scale social problem. Garrison also refused to fight for the vote for African Americans. Setting up on his own, Douglass launched an antislavery newspaper called the *North Star* in Rochester, New York. This city was an important stop on the underground railroad—the secret route organized around safe houses which fugitive slaves followed to Canada. The Douglass household harbored so many runaway slaves that there were sometimes as many as eleven fugitives staying in the house at a time. But the city was less committed to full racial equality than the Douglasses had hoped: their oldest daughter, Rosetta, was not allowed to attend public school, and the private school she attended forbade her to learn with the white students. Douglass began a campaign to end segregation in the schools. In 1848 he attended the women's rights convention in Seneca Falls, and he emerged as a stalwart champion of women's suffrage. The motto of the *North Star* marked his commitment to gender as well as racial equality: "Right is of no sex," it read. "Truth is of no color."

When the Civil War broke out in 1861, Douglass led efforts to persuade Congress and President Lincoln to allow African American men to enlist in the Union Army. This struggle succeeded, and in 1863, Douglass actively recruited soldiers to fight, including his own two sons, Lewis and Charles. After the war was over, he led the campaign for black suffrage, and prevailed in 1870 with the passage of the Fifteenth Amendment to the U.S. Constitution, which states that citizens cannot be denied the vote "on account of race, color, or previous condition of servitude."

The following years saw Douglass working tirelessly to expose and denounce discrimination and violence. He moved to Washington, D.C., where he held several government offices. In 1889

he accepted the position of consul-general to Haiti and moved there, but later resigned when he was told that he was too sympathetic to Haitian interests. His wife died in 1882, and Douglass later married Helen Pitts, a white woman. After speaking at the National Council of Women, he died of a heart attack in 1895. On hearing the news of Douglass's death, the women's rights activist Elizabeth Cady Stanton remembered hearing him speak for the first time: "He stood there like an African prince, majestic in his wrath, as with wit, satire, and indignation he graphically described the bitterness of slavery. . . . Thus it was that I first saw Frederick Douglass, and wondered that any mortal man should have ever tried to subjugate a being with such talents, intensified with the love of liberty."

SLAVERY AND ABOLITION

In the southern United States in the nineteenth century, slaves worked in fields, in homes, and in mines; they built railroads and canals; they processed sugar and iron. But by far the most significant use of slave labor involved cotton production. Eli Whitney's 1793 invention of the cotton gin had accelerated the cleaning of cotton, and worldwide demand for cotton textiles—a source of cheap and lightweight clothing—had skyrocketed. But this was a crop that still needed to be handpicked in the fields. The booming cotton trade therefore demanded lots of arable land and a huge supply of labor—conditions met easily by the slave economy of the United States South. Nearly three quarters of all U.S. slaves labored on cotton plantations, and by 1840 the southern United States produced more than half of the world's cotton. Cotton helped to drive the whole nation's economy, contributing substantially to the growth of Northern industry, shipping, and banking. It powered the global economy too. African traders used the term *americani* to refer to inexpensive cottons from the United States. And even after Britain had officially abolished slavery in its own territories, British traders imported vast quantities of cotton picked by U.S. slaves, and British mills turned this raw material into textiles for sale around the world. About 10 percent of Britain's wealth came from the cotton trade. In 1858 U.S. Senator James Hammond of South Carolina declared, "You dare not make war upon cotton. No power on earth dare make war upon it. Cotton is king!"

Intent on reaping as much profit as possible from their crops, plantation holders increasingly turned to the "gang system" to organize slave labor. Groups of slaves, under the command of an overseer, were forced—typically with whips, clubs, and threats—to perform a single repetitive task from the break of dawn until night. To increase efficiency, slaveholders would often rotate corn and cotton—ready at different times of the year—and use the corn to feed both slaves and animals on the plantation.

The state of Maryland, where Douglass was a slave, differed from most of the South. Maryland farms mostly grew tobacco rather than cotton, and the demand for tobacco was on the decline. Also, by the time that Frederick Douglass was born, Maryland had the highest number of free black men and women in the United States, more than half of its African American population. (By contrast, more than 99 percent of black people in Alabama, Texas, and Mississippi were slaves.) Working in the bustling city of Baltimore, surrounded by free blacks, Douglass had significantly more opportunities for escape than the plantation would have afforded.

Maryland was reputed to have a less harsh and dehumanizing slaveholder population than the "deep" South. In this respect as in many others, Douglass's *Narrative* challenged his readers'

assumptions. In general the abolitionists felt that the best weapon against slavery was a campaign to reveal its horrors as fully and as accurately as possible. They went to significant trouble to demonstrate the evils of slavery and to confirm the truth of their claims. Some former slaves on the lecture circuit corroborated their accounts of violence by baring scars on their backs to horrified audiences.

Apart from organizing lecture tours and publishing books, abolitionists also sent volleys of pamphlets by mail to Southern states. But Southerners were not the only targets. As the abolitionist movement grew in the 1830s, activists increasingly focused their attention on the indifference of white Northerners, who mostly kept quiet on the subject of slavery. Neither major political party would mention it. And even in the North, angry mobs would descend on antislavery meetings and smash their printing presses. Douglass himself had his hand broken in Indiana. Dedicating themselves to exposing slavery to a wide public, abolitionists showed just how risky—and how powerful—words could be.

WORK

While the truthfulness of Douglass's story was a central question for his contemporaries, recent readers have been more inclined to admire the literary artfulness of the *Narrative*, its metaphorical richness, rhetorical complexity, and careful construction. Douglass casts his life as a long process of self-transformation—from an object, or an animal, to a free human being with a name. The contrast between the openings of the *Narrative* and of **Rousseau's *Confessions*** is instructive. Rousseau begins by proclaiming that he differs from everyone else in his unique personality and character. Douglass, on the other hand, starts by reporting what he does *not* know of himself. He must guess his own age, he doesn't know his birthday, he has only rumor to tell him of his father's identity. Although he knows his mother, he spends virtually no time with her; she comes to him and leaves him in the dark. Most children develop their sense of who they are by precisely the clues missing in Douglass's experience: age, parentage, and such ritual occasions as birthdays. Douglass has only a generic identity: slave. Everything in Douglass's early experience denies his individuality and declares his lack of particularized identity. By the end, however, he claims a right to affirm himself: "I subscribe myself, FREDERICK DOUGLASS." The name itself is a triumph, not his father's or his mother's but the freshly bestowed name of his freedom. Each step of the way to this point—learning to read, learning to write, acquiring a name—has involved a painful self-testing, but the *word* proves for Douglass quite literally a means to salvation.

If Douglass wins himself a name and an identity by the end of the *Narrative*, the triumphant individual is not the sole focus of the story. Along the way, Douglass uses his own experience to throw light on slavery in general. The first pages in fact tell us little about the uniqueness of the author, and Douglass is careful to explain how his own circumstances are common to many slaves. He also repeatedly argues that individuals emerge out of their circumstances. He goes to some trouble to show how masters systematically *create* the slaves' mindset, deliberately starving them of intellectual or spiritual nourishment. But he makes it clear that the masters, too, are created by their conditions. Sophia Auld begins as a compassionate and generous person, but the experience of owning another human being makes her suspicious and mean-spirited. Many readers have seen the *Narrative* as fundamentally a story

of self-transformation in which the illiterate and unthinking slave is prompted to recognize the injustice of his experience and to insist on his full personhood, but Douglass reminds us many times along the way that self-transformation always involves a set of opportunities, and that under slightly different conditions, this slave might never have sought out his freedom.

There is one way that Douglass's story has disappointed recent readers. He affirms his own manhood—rejecting the bestial and objectified status of the slave—but does so at the expense of women's experience. He entirely omits descriptions of important women in his life, such as his grandmother, who raised him, and his wife-to-be. He does give graphic depictions of women slaves enduring physical violence, and he refers to the rape of slaves by masters more than once. But since his central image for slavery is a physical struggle for dominance between men, and since he depicts women mostly as lacerated bodies, Douglass's *Narrative* cannot be said to speak for all slaves.

In recounting the internal and external shifts that take him from slave to free man, Douglass's story draws on a number of other genres. As in spiritual autobiographies, the *Narrative* calls attention to moments of revelation, when the central figure undergoes a kind of conversion experience, and sees himself and his world in a fresh light. As in rags-to-riches stories, Douglass tells us how he makes a dramatic rise in social status and wealth through virtues such as perseverance, bravery, self-reliance, and determination. He draws on the sentimental novel, too, in offering us images of innocent victims whose abuses tug at our heartstrings. And the *Narrative* draws on the language of politics, economics, and religious sermons, woven together throughout the text. But perhaps most important, this autobiography belongs in the tradition of the slave narrative, which, by Douglass's time, had become a well-established genre. There had been literally thousands of first-person accounts of slavery published since the late eighteenth century, and slave narratives had become a major American genre. They were so popular that most American readers might never have encountered an autobiography written by anyone other than a slave. Among these many narratives, Douglass's has been widely recognized as the richest, most subtle, and most beautifully conceived, remaining worthwhile reading not only for its searing indictment of slavery, but also for its complex literary artistry.

Narrative of the Life of Frederick Douglass, An American Slave[1]

CHAPTER I

I was born in Tuckahoe, near Hillsborough, and about twelve miles from Easton, in Talbot county, Maryland. I have no accurate knowledge of my age, never having seen any authentic record containing it. By far the larger part of the slaves know as little of their ages as horses know of theirs, and it is the wish of most masters within my knowledge to keep their slaves thus ignorant. I do not remember to have ever met a slave who could tell of his birthday. They seldom come nearer to it than planting-time, harvest-time, cherry-time, springtime, or fall-time. A want of information concerning my own was a source of unhappiness to me even during childhood. The white children could tell their ages. I could not tell why I ought to be deprived of the same privilege. I was not allowed to make any inquiries of my master concerning it. He deemed all such inquiries on the part of a slave improper and impertinent, and evidence of a restless spirit. The nearest estimate I can give makes me now between twenty-seven and twenty-eight years of age. I come to this, from hearing my master say, some time during 1835, I was about seventeen years old.

My mother was named Harriet Bailey. She was the daughter of Isaac and Betsey Bailey, both colored, and quite dark. My mother was of a darker complexion than either my grandmother or grandfather.

My father was a white man. He was admitted to be such by all I ever heard speak of my parentage. The opinion was also whispered that my master was my father; but of the correctness of this opinion, I know nothing; the means of knowing was withheld from me. My mother and I were separated when I was but an infant—before I knew her as my mother. It is a common custom, in the part of Maryland from which I ran away, to part children from their mothers at a very early age. Frequently, before the child has reached its twelfth month, its mother is taken from it, and hired out on some farm a considerable distance

1. The text, printed in its entirety, is that of the first American edition, published by the Massachusetts Anti-Slavery Society in Boston in 1845.

off, and the child is placed under the care of an old woman, too old for field labor. For what this separation is done, I do not know, unless it be to hinder the development of the child's affection toward its mother, and to blunt and destroy the natural affection of the mother for the child. This is the inevitable result.

I never saw my mother, to know her as such, more than four or five times in my life; and each of those times was very short in duration, and at night. She was hired by a Mr. Stewart, who lived about twelve miles from my home. She made her journeys to see me in the night, travelling the whole distance on foot, after the performance of her day's work. She was a field hand, and a whipping is the penalty of not being in the field at sunrise, unless a slave has special permission from his or her master to the contrary—a permission which they seldom get, and one that gives to him that gives it the proud name of being a kind master. I do not recollect of ever seeing my mother by the light of day. She was with me in the night. She would lie down with me, and get me to sleep, but long before I waked she was gone. Very little communication ever took place between us. Death soon ended what little we could have while she lived, and with it her hardships and suffering. She died when I was about seven years old, on one of my master's farms, near Lee's Mill. I was not allowed to be present during her illness, at her death, or burial. She was gone long before I knew anything about it. Never having enjoyed, to any considerable extent, her soothing presence, her tender and watchful care, I received the tidings of her death with much the same emotions I should have probably felt at the death of a stranger.

Called thus suddenly away, she left me without the slightest intimation of who my father was. The whisper that my master was my father, may or may not be true; and, true or false, it is of but little consequence to my purpose whilst the fact remains, in all its glaring odiousness, that slaveholders have ordained, and by law established, that the children of slave women shall in all cases follow the condition of their mothers; and this is done too obviously to administer to their own lusts, and make a gratification of their wicked desires profitable as well as pleasurable; for by this cunning arrangement, the slaveholder, in cases not a few, sustains to his slaves the double relation of master and father.

I know of such cases; and it is worthy of remark that such slaves invariably suffer greater hardships, and have more to contend with, than others. They are, in the first place, a constant offence to their mistress. She is ever disposed to find fault with them; they can seldom do any thing to please her; she is never better pleased than when she sees them under the lash, especially when she suspects her husband of showing to his mulatto children favors which he withholds from his black slaves. The master is frequently compelled to sell this class of his slaves, out of deference to the feelings of his white wife; and, cruel as the deed may strike any one to be, for a man to sell his own children to human flesh-mongers, it is often the dictate of humanity for him to do so; for, unless he does this, he must not only whip them himself, but must stand by and see one white son tie up his brother, of but few shades darker complexion than himself, and ply the gory lash to his naked back; and if he lisp one word of disapproval, it is set down to his parental partiality, and only makes a bad matter worse, both for himself and the slave whom he would protect and defend.

Every year brings with it multitudes of this class of slaves. It was doubtless in consequence of a knowledge of this fact, that one great statesman of the south predicted the downfall of slavery by the inevitable laws of population. Whether this prophecy is ever fulfilled or not, it is nevertheless plain that a very different-looking class of people are springing up at the south, and are now held in slavery, from those originally brought to this country from Africa; and if their increase will do no other good, it will do away the force of the argument, that God cursed Ham,[2] and therefore American slavery is right. If the lineal descendants of Ham are alone to be scripturally enslaved, it is certain that slavery at the south must soon become unscriptural; for thousands are ushered into the world, annually, who, like myself, owe their existence to white fathers, and those fathers most frequently their own masters.

I have had two masters. My first master's name was Anthony. I do not remember his first name. He was generally called Captain Anthony—a title which, I presume, he acquired by sailing a craft on the Chesapeake Bay. He was not considered a rich slaveholder. He owned two or three farms, and about thirty slaves. His farms and slaves were under the care of an overseer. The overseer's name was Plummer. Mr. Plummer was a miserable drunkard, a profane swearer, and a savage monster. He always went armed with a cowskin and a heavy cudgel. I have known him to cut and slash the women's heads so horribly, that even master would be enraged at his cruelty, and would threaten to whip him if he did not mind himself. Master, however, was not a humane slaveholder. It required extraordinary barbarity on the part of an overseer to affect him. He was a cruel man, hardened by a long life of slaveholding. He would at times seem to take great pleasure in whipping a slave. I have often been awakened at the dawn of day by the most heartrending shrieks of an own aunt of mine, whom he used to tie up to a joist, and whip upon her naked back till she was literally covered with blood. No words, no tears, no prayers, from his gory victim, seemed to move his iron heart from its bloody purpose. The louder she screamed, the harder he whipped; and where the blood ran fastest, there he whipped longest. He would whip her to make her scream, and whip her to make her hush; and not until overcome by fatigue, would he cease to swing the blood-clotted cowskin. I remember the first time I ever witnessed this horrible exhibition. I was quite a child, but I well remember it. I never shall forget it whilst I remember any thing. It was the first of a long series of such outrages, of which I was doomed to be a witness and a participant. It struck me with awful force. It was the blood-stained gate, the entrance to the hell of slavery, through which I was about to pass. It was a most terrible spectacle. I wish I could commit to paper the feelings with which I beheld it.

This occurrence took place very soon after I went to live with my old master, and under the following circumstances. Aunt Hester went out one night,—where or for what I do not know,—and happened to be absent when my master desired her presence. He had ordered her not to go out evenings, and warned

---

2. It was widely thought that Noah cursed his second son, Ham, for mocking him; that black skin resulted from the curse; and that all black people descended from Ham. In fact, according to Genesis 9.20–27 and 10.6–14, Noah cursed not Ham but Ham's son Canaan, while Ham's son Cush was black.

her that she must never let him catch her in company with a young man, who was paying attention to her, belonging to Colonel Lloyd. The young man's name was Ned Roberts, generally called Lloyd's Ned. Why master was so careful of her, may be safely left to conjecture. She was a woman of noble form, and of graceful proportions, having very few equals, and fewer superiors, in personal appearance, among the colored or white women of our neighborhood.

Aunt Hester had not only disobeyed his orders in going out, but had been found in company with Lloyd's Ned; which circumstance, I found, from what he said while whipping her, was the chief offence. Had he been a man of pure morals himself, he might have been thought interested in protecting the innocence of my aunt; but those who knew him will not suspect him of any such virtue. Before he commenced whipping Aunt Hester, he took her into the kitchen, and stripped her from neck to waist, leaving her neck, shoulders, and back, entirely naked. He then told her to cross her hands, calling her at the same time a d—d b—h. After crossing her hands, he tied them with a strong rope, and led her to a stool under a large hook in the joist, put in for the purpose. He made her get upon the stool, and tied her hands to the hook. She now stood fair for his infernal purpose. Her arms were stretched up at their full length, so that she stood upon the ends of her toes. He then said to her, "Now, you d—d b—h, I'll learn you how to disobey my orders!" and after rolling up his sleeves, he commenced to lay on the heavy cowskin, and soon the warm, red blood (amid heart-rending shrieks from her, and horrid oaths from him) came dripping to the floor. I was so terrified and horror-stricken at the sight, that I hid myself in a closet, and dared not venture out till long after the bloody transaction was over. I expected it would be my turn next. It was all new to me. I had never seen any thing like it before. I had always lived with my grandmother on the outskirts of the plantation, where she was put to raise the children of the younger women. I had therefore been, until now, out of the way of the bloody scenes that often occurred on the plantation.

CHAPTER II

My master's family consisted of two sons, Andrew and Richard; one daughter, Lucretia, and her husband, Captain Thomas Auld. They lived in one house, upon the home plantation of Colonel Edward Lloyd. My master was Colonel Lloyd's clerk and superintendent. He was what might be called the overseer of the overseers. I spent two years of childhood on this plantation in my old master's family. It was here that I witnessed the bloody transaction recorded in the first chapter; and as I received my first impressions of slavery on this plantation, I will give some description of it, and of slavery as it there existed. The plantation is about twelve miles north of Easton, in Talbot county, and is situated on the border of Miles River. The principal products raised upon it were tobacco, corn, and wheat. These were raised in great abundance; so that, with the products of this and the other farms belonging to him, he was able to keep in almost constant employment a large sloop, in carrying them to market at Baltimore. This sloop was named *Sally Lloyd*, in honor of one of the colonel's daughters. My master's son-in-law, Captain Auld, was master of the vessel; she was otherwise manned by the colonel's own slaves. Their names were Peter,

Isaac, Rich, and Jake. These were esteemed very highly by the other slaves, and looked upon as the privileged ones of the plantation; for it was no small affair, in the eyes of the slaves, to be allowed to see Baltimore.

Colonel Lloyd kept from three to four hundred slaves on his home plantation, and owned a large number more on the neighboring farms belonging to him. The names of the farms nearest to the home plantation were Wye Town and New Design. "Wye Town" was under the overseership of a man named Noah Willis. New Design was under the overseership of a Mr. Townsend. The overseers of these, and all the rest of the farms, numbering over twenty, received advice and direction from the managers of the home plantation. This was the great business place. It was the seat of government for the whole twenty farms. All disputes among the overseers were settled here. If a slave was convicted of any high misdemeanor, became unmanageable, or evinced a determination to run away, he was brought immediately here, severely whipped, put on board the sloop, carried to Baltimore, and sold to Austin Woolfolk, or some other slave-trader, as a warning to the slaves remaining.

Here, too, the slaves of all the other farms received their monthly allowance of food, and their yearly clothing. The men and women slaves received, as their monthly allowance of food, eight pounds of pork, or its equivalent in fish, and one bushel of corn meal. Their yearly clothing consisted of two coarse linen shirts, one pair of linen trousers, like the shirts, one jacket, one pair of trousers for winter, made of coarse negro cloth, one pair of stockings, and one pair of shoes; the whole of which could not have cost more than seven dollars. The allowance of the slave children was given to their mothers, or the old women having the care of them. The children unable to work in the field had neither shoes, stockings, jackets, nor trousers, given to them; their clothing consisted of two coarse linen shirts per year. When these failed them, they went naked until the next allowance-day. Children from seven to ten years old, of both sexes, almost naked, might be seen at all seasons of the year.

There were no beds given the slaves, unless one coarse blanket be considered such, and none but the men and women had these. This, however, is not considered a very great privation. They find less difficulty from the want of beds, than from the want of time to sleep; for when their day's work in the field is done, the most of them having their washing, mending, and cooking to do, and having few or none of the ordinary facilities for doing either of these, very many of their sleeping hours are consumed in preparing for the field the coming day; and when this is done, old and young, male and female, married and single, drop down side by side, on one common bed,—the cold, damp floor,—each covering himself or herself with their miserable blankets; and here they sleep till they are summoned to the field by the driver's horn. At the sound of this, all must rise, and be off to the field. There must be no halting; every one must be at his or her post; and woe betides them who hear not this morning summons to the field; for if they are not awakened by the sense of hearing, they are by the sense of feeling: no age nor sex finds any favor. Mr. Severe, the overseer, used to stand by the door of the quarter, armed with a large hickory stick and heavy cowskin, ready to whip any one who was so unfortunate as not to hear, or, from any other cause, was prevented from being ready to start for the field at the sound of the horn.

Mr. Severe was rightly named: he was a cruel man. I have seen him whip a woman, causing the blood to run half an hour at the time; and this, too, in the midst of her crying children, pleading for their mother's release. He seemed to take pleasure in manifesting his fiendish barbarity. Added to his cruelty, he was a profane swearer. It was enough to chill the blood and stiffen the hair of an ordinary man to hear him talk. Scarce a sentence escaped him but that was commenced or concluded by some horrid oath. The field was the place to witness his cruelty and profanity. His presence made it both the field of blood and of blasphemy. From the rising till the going down of the sun, he was cursing, raving, cutting, and slashing among the slaves of the field, in the most frightful manner. His career was short. He died very soon after I went to Colonel Lloyd's; and he died as he lived, uttering, with his dying groans, bitter curses and horrid oaths. His death was regarded by the slaves as the result of a merciful providence.

Mr. Severe's place was filled by a Mr. Hopkins. He was a very different man. He was less cruel, less profane, and made less noise, than Mr. Severe. His course was characterized by no extraordinary demonstrations of cruelty. He whipped, but seemed to take no pleasure in it. He was called by the slaves a good overseer.

The home plantation of Colonel Lloyd wore the appearance of a country village. All the mechanical operations for all the farms were performed here. The shoemaking and mending, the blacksmithing, cartwrighting, coopering, weaving, and grain-grinding, were all performed by the slaves on the home plantation. The whole place wore a business-like aspect very unlike the neighboring farms. The number of houses, too, conspired to give it advantage over the neighboring farms. It was called by the slaves the *Great House Farm*. Few privileges were esteemed higher, by the slaves of the out-farms, than that of being selected to do errands at the Great House Farm. It was associated in their minds with greatness. A representative could not be prouder of his election to a seat in the American Congress, than a slave on one of the out-farms would be of his election to do errands at the Great House Farm. They regarded it as evidence of great confidence reposed in them by their overseers; and it was on this account, as well as a constant desire to be out of the field from under the driver's lash, that they esteemed it a high privilege, one worth careful living for. He was called the smartest and most trusty fellow, who had this honor conferred upon him the most frequently. The competitors for this office sought as diligently to please their overseers, as the office-seekers in the political parties seek to please and deceive the people. The same traits of character might be seen in Colonel Lloyd's slaves, as are seen in the slaves of the political parties.

The slaves selected to go to the Great House Farm, for the monthly allowance for themselves and their fellow-slaves, were peculiarly enthusiastic. While on their way, they would make the dense old woods, for miles around, reverberate with their wild songs, revealing at once the highest joy and the deepest sadness. They would compose and sing as they went along, consulting neither time nor tune. The thought that came up, came out—if not in the word, in the sound;—and as frequently in the one as in the other. They would sometimes sing the most pathetic sentiment in the most rapturous tone, and the most rapturous sentiment in the most pathetic tone. Into all of their songs they would manage to weave something of the Great House Farm. Especially would they do this, when leaving home. They would then sing most exultingly the following words:—

> "I am going away to the Great House Farm!
> O, yea! O, yea! O!"

This they would sing, as a chorus, to words which to many would seem unmeaning jargon, but which, nevertheless, were full of meaning to themselves. I have sometimes thought that the mere hearing of those songs would do more to impress some minds with the horrible character of slavery, than the reading of whole volumes of philosophy on the subject could do.

I did not, when a slave, understand the deep meaning of those rude and apparently incoherent songs. I was myself within the circle; so that I neither saw nor heard as those without might see and hear. They told a tale of woe which was then altogether beyond my feeble comprehension; they were tones loud, long, and deep; they breathed the prayer and complaint of souls boiling over with the bitterest anguish. Every tone was a testimony against slavery, and a prayer to god for deliverance from chains. The hearing of those wild notes always depressed my spirit, and filled me with ineffable sadness. I have frequently found myself in tears while hearing them. The mere recurrence to those songs, even now, afflicts me; and while I am writing these lines, an expression of feeling has already found its way down my cheek. To those songs I trace my first glimmering conception of the dehumanizing character of slavery. I can never get rid of that conception. Those songs still follow me, to deepen my hatred of slavery, and quicken my sympathies for my brethren in bonds. If any one wishes to be impressed with the soul-killing effects of slavery, let him go to Colonel Lloyd's plantation, and, on allowance-day, place himself in the deep pine woods, and there let him, in silence, analyze the sounds that shall pass through the chambers of his soul,—and if he is not thus impressed, it will only be because "there is no flesh in his obdurate heart."

I have often been utterly astonished, since I came to the north, to find persons who could speak of the singing, among slaves, as evidence of their contentment and happiness. It is impossible to conceive of a greater mistake. Slaves sing most when they are most unhappy. The songs of the slave represent the sorrows of his heart; and he is relieved by them, only as an aching heart is relieved by its tears. At least, such is my experience. I have often sung to drown my sorrow, but seldom to express my happiness. Crying for joy, and singing for joy, were alike uncommon to me while in the jaws of slavery. The singing of a man cast away upon a desolate island might be as appropriately considered as evidence of contentment and happiness, as the singing of a slave; the songs of the one and of the other are prompted by the same emotion.

CHAPTER III

Colonel Lloyd kept a large and finely cultivated garden, which afforded almost constant employment for four men, besides the chief gardener (Mr. M'Durmond). This garden was probably the greatest attraction of the place. During the summer months, people came from far and near—from Baltimore, Easton, and

Annapolis—to see it. It abounded in fruits of almost every description, from the hardy apple of the north to the delicate orange of the south. This garden was not the least source of trouble on the plantation. Its excellent fruit was quite a temptation to the hungry swarms of boys, as well as the older slaves, belonging to the colonel, few of whom had the virtue or the vice to resist it. Scarcely a day passed, during the summer, but that some slave had to take the lash for stealing fruit. The colonel had to resort to all kinds of stratagems to keep his slaves out of the garden. The last and most successful one was that of tarring his fence all around; after which, if a slave was caught with tar upon his person, it was deemed sufficient proof that he had either been into the garden, or had tried to get in. In either case, he was severely whipped by the chief gardener. This plan worked well; the slaves became as fearful of tar as of the lash. They seemed to realize the impossibility of touching *tar* without being defiled.[3]

The colonel also kept a splendid riding equipage. His stable and carriage-house presented the appearance of some of our large city livery establishments. His horses were of the finest form and noblest blood. His carriage-house contained three splendid coaches, three or four gigs, besides dearborns and barouches[4] of the most fashionable style.

This establishment was under the care of two slaves—old Barney and young Barney—father and son. To attend to this establishment was their sole work. But it was by no means an easy employment; for in nothing was Colonel Lloyd more particular than in the management of his horses. The slightest inattention to these was unpardonable, and was visited upon those, under whose care they were placed, with the severest punishment; no excuse could shield them, if the colonel only suspected any want of attention to his horses—a supposition which he frequently indulged, and one which, of course, made the office of old and young Barney a very trying one. They never knew when they were safe from punishment. They were frequently whipped when least deserving, and escaped whipping when most deserving it. Every thing depended upon the looks of the horses, and the state of Colonel Lloyd's own mind when his horses were brought to him for use. If a horse did not move fast enough, or hold his head high enough, it was owing to some fault of his keepers. It was painful to stand near the stable-door, and hear the various complaints against the keepers when a horse was taken out for use. "This horse has not had proper attention. He has not been sufficiently rubbed and curried, or he has not been properly fed; his food was too wet or too dry; he got it too soon or too late; he was too hot or too cold; he had too much hay, and not enough of grain; or he had too much grain, and not enough of hay; instead of old Barney's attending to the horse, he had very improperly left it to his son." To all these complaints, no matter how unjust, the slave must answer never a word. Colonel Lloyd could not brook any contradiction from a slave. When he spoke, a slave must stand, listen, and tremble; and such was literally the case. I have seen Colonel Lloyd make old Barney, a man between fifty and sixty years of age, uncover his bald head, kneel down upon the cold, damp ground, and receive upon his

---

3. Cf. the proverb "He who touches pitch shall be defiled."

4. Light four-wheeled carriages (*dearborns*) and carriages with a front seat for the driver and two facing back seats for couples (*barouches*).

naked and toil-worn shoulders more than thirty lashes at the time. Colonel Lloyd had three sons—Edward, Murray, and Daniel,—and three sons-in-law, Mr. Winder, Mr. Nicholson, and Mr. Lowndes. All of these lived at the Great House Farm, and enjoyed the luxury of whipping the servants when they pleased, from old Barney down to William Wilkes, the coach-driver. I have seen Winder make one of the house-servants stand off from him a suitable distance to be touched with the end of his whip, and at every stroke raise great ridges upon his back.

To describe the wealth of Colonel Lloyd would be almost equal to describing the riches of Job.[5] He kept from ten to fifteen house-servants. He was said to own a thousand slaves, and I think this estimate quite within the truth. Colonel Lloyd owned so many that he did not know them when he saw them; nor did all the slaves of the out-farms know him. It is reported of him, that, while riding along the road one day, he met a colored man, and addressed him in the usual manner of speaking to colored people on the public highways of the south: "Well, boy, whom do you belong to?" "To Colonel Lloyd," replied the slave. "Well, does the colonel treat you well?" "No, sir," was the ready reply. "What, does he work you too hard?" "Yes, sir." "Well, don't he give you enough to eat?" "Yes, sir, he gives me enough, such as it is."

The colonel, after ascertaining where the slave belonged, rode on; the man also went on about his business, not dreaming that he had been conversing with his master. He thought, said, and heard nothing more of the matter, until two or three weeks afterwards. The poor man was then informed by his overseer that, for having found fault with his master, he was now to be sold to a Georgia trader. He was immediately chained and handcuffed; and thus, without a moment's warning, he was snatched away, and forever sundered, from his family and friends, by a hand more unrelenting than death. This is the penalty of telling the truth, of telling the simple truth, in answer to a series of plain questions.

It is partly in consequence of such facts, that slaves, when inquired of as to their condition and the character of their masters, almost universally say they are contented, and that their masters are kind. The slaveholders have been known to send in spies among their slaves, to ascertain their views and feelings in regard to their condition. The frequency of this has had the effect to establish among the slaves the maxim, that a still tongue makes a wise head. They suppress the truth rather than take the consequences of telling it, and in so doing prove themselves a part of the human family. If they have any thing to say of their masters, it is generally in their masters' favor, especially when speaking to an untried man. I have been frequently asked, when a slave, if I had a kind master, and do not remember ever to have given a negative answer; nor did I, in pursuing this course, consider myself as uttering what was absolutely false; for I always measured the kindness of my master by the standard of kindness set up among slaveholders around us. Moreover, slaves are like other people, and imbibe prejudices quite common to others. They think their own better than that of others. Many, under the influence of this prejudice, think

---

5. Job 1.3: "His substance also was seven thousand sheep, and three thousand camels, and five hundred yoke of oxen, and five hun- dred she asses, and a very great household; so that this man was the greatest of all the men of the East."

their own masters are better than the masters of other slaves; and this, too, in some cases, when the very reverse is true. Indeed, it is not uncommon for slaves even to fall out and quarrel among themselves about the relative goodness of their masters, each contending for the superior goodness of his own over that of the others. At the very same time, they mutually execrate their masters when viewed separately. It was so on our plantation. When Colonel Lloyd's slaves met the slaves of Jacob Jepson, they seldom parted without a quarrel about their masters; Colonel Lloyd's slaves contending that he was the richest, and Mr. Jepson's slaves that he was the smartest, and most of a man. Colonel Lloyd's slaves would boast his ability to buy and sell Jacob Jepson. Mr. Jepson's slaves would boast his ability to whip Colonel Lloyd. These quarrels would almost always end in a fight between the parties, and those that whipped were supposed to have gained the point at issue. They seemed to think that the greatness of their masters was transferable to themselves. It was considered as being bad enough to be a slave; but to be a poor man's slave was deemed a disgrace indeed!

CHAPTER IV

Mr. Hopkins remained but a short time in the office of overseer. Why his career was so short, I do not know, but suppose he lacked the necessary severity to suit Colonel Lloyd. Mr. Hopkins was succeeded by Mr. Austin Gore, a man possessing, in an eminent degree, all those traits of character indispensable to what is called a first-rate overseer. Mr. Gore had served Colonel Lloyd, in the capacity of overseer, upon one of the out-farms, and had shown himself worthy of the high station of overseer upon the home or Great House Farm.

Mr. Gore was proud, ambitious, and persevering. He was artful, cruel, and obdurate. He was just the man for such a place, and it was just the place for such a man. It afforded scope for the full exercise of all his powers, and he seemed to be perfectly at home in it. He was one of those who could torture the slightest look, word, or gesture, on the part of the slave, into impudence, and would treat it accordingly. There must be no answering back to him; no explanation was allowed a slave, showing himself to have been wrongfully accused. Mr. Gore acted fully up to the maxim laid down by slaveholders,—"It is better that a dozen slaves suffer under the lash, than that the overseer should be convicted, in the presence of the slaves, of having been at fault." No matter how innocent a slave might be—it availed him nothing, when accused by Mr. Gore of any misdemeanor. To be accused was to be convicted, and to be convicted was to be punished; the one always following the other with immutable certainty. To escape punishment was to escape accusation; and few slaves had the fortune to do either, under the overseership of Mr. Gore. He was just proud enough to demand the most debasing homage of the slave, and quite servile enough to crouch, himself, at the feet of the master. He was ambitious enough to be contented with nothing short of the highest rank of overseers, and persevering enough to reach the height of his ambition. He was cruel enough to inflict the severest punishment, artful enough to descend to the lowest trickery, and obdurate enough to be insensible to the voice of a reproving conscience. He was, of all the overseers, the most dreaded by the slaves. His presence was painful; his eye flashed confusion; and seldom was his sharp, shrill voice heard, without producing horror and trembling in their ranks.

Mr. Gore was a grave man, and, though a young man, he indulged in no jokes, said no funny words, seldom smiled. His words were in perfect keeping with his looks, and his looks were in perfect keeping with his words. Overseers will sometimes indulge in a witty word, even with the slaves; not so with Mr. Gore. He spoke but to command, and commanded but to be obeyed; he dealt sparingly with his words, and bountifully with his whip, never using the former where the latter would answer as well. When he whipped, he seemed to do so from a sense of duty, and feared no consequences. He did nothing reluctantly, no matter how disagreeable; always at his post, never inconsistent. He never promised but to fulfil. He was, in a word, a man of the most inflexible firmness and stone-like coolness.

His savage barbarity was equalled only by the consummate coolness with which he committed the grossest and most savage deeds upon the slaves under his charge. Mr. Gore once undertook to whip one of Colonel Lloyd's slaves, by the name of Demby. He had given Demby but few stripes, when, to get rid of the scourging, he ran and plunged himself into a creek, and stood there at the depth of his shoulders, refusing to come out. Mr. Gore told him that he would give him three calls, and that, if he did not come out at the third call, he would shoot him. The first call was given. Demby made no response, but stood his ground. The second and third calls were given with the same result. Mr. Gore then, without consultation or deliberation with any one, not even giving Demby an additional call, raised his musket to his face, taking deadly aim at his standing victim, and in an instant poor Demby was no more. His mangled body sank out of sight, and blood and brains marked the water where he had stood.

A thrill of horror flashed through every soul upon the plantation, excepting Mr. Gore. He alone seemed cool and collected. He was asked by Colonel Lloyd and my old master, why he resorted to this extraordinary expedient. His reply was, (as well as I can remember,) that Demby had become unmanageable. He was setting a dangerous example to the other slaves,—one which, if suffered to pass without some such demonstration on his part, would finally lead to the total subversion of all rule and order upon the plantation. He argued that if one slave refused to be corrected, and escaped with his life, the other slaves would soon copy the example; the result of which would be, the freedom of the slaves, and the enslavement of the whites. Mr. Gore's defence was satisfactory. He was continued in his station as overseer upon the home plantation. His fame as an overseer went abroad. His horrid crime was not even submitted to judicial investigation. It was committed in the presence of slaves, and they of course could neither institute a suit, nor testify against him; and thus the guilty perpetrator of one of the bloodiest and most foul murders goes unwhipped of justice, and uncensured by the community in which he lives. Mr. Gore lived in St. Michael's, Talbot county, Maryland, when I left there; and if he is still alive, he very probably lives there now; and if so, he is now, as he was then, as highly esteemed and as much respected as though his guilty soul had not been stained with his brother's blood.

I speak advisedly when I say this,—that killing a slave, or any colored person, in Talbot county, Maryland, is not treated as a crime, either by the courts or the community. Mr. Thomas Lanman, of St. Michael's, killed two slaves, one of whom he killed with a hatchet, by knocking his brains out. He used to boast of the commission of the awful and bloody deed. I have heard him do so laugh-

ingly, saying, among other things, that he was the only benefactor of his country in the company, and that when others would do as much as he had done,
we should be relieved of "the d——d niggers."

The wife of Mr. Giles Hicks, living but a short distance from where I used to
live, murdered my wife's cousin, a young girl between fifteen and sixteen years
of age, mangling her person in the most horrible manner, breaking her nose
and breastbone with a stick, so that the poor girl expired in a few hours afterward. She was immediately buried, but had not been in her untimely grave but
a few hours before she was taken up and examined by the coroner, who
decided that she had come to her death by severe beating. The offence for
which this girl was thus murdered was this:—She had been set that night to
mind Mrs. Hicks's baby, and during the night she fell asleep, and the baby
cried. She, having lost her rest for several nights previous, did not hear the crying. They were both in the room with Mrs. Hicks. Mrs. Hicks, finding the girl
slow to move, jumped from her bed, seized an oak stick of wood by the fireplace, and with it broke the girl's nose and breastbone, and thus ended her life.
I will not say that this most horrid murder produced no sensation in the community. It did produce sensation, but not enough to bring the murderess to
punishment. There was a warrant issued for her arrest, but it was never served.
Thus she escaped not only punishment, but even the pain of being arraigned
before a court for her horrid crime.

Whilst I am detailing bloody deeds which took place during my stay on Colonel Lloyd's plantation, I will briefly narrate another, which occurred about the
same time as the murder of Demby by Mr. Gore.

Colonel Lloyd's slaves were in the habit of spending a part of their nights and
Sundays in fishing for oysters, and in this way made up the deficiency of their
scanty allowance. An old man belonging to Colonel Lloyd, while thus engaged,
happened to get beyond the limits of Colonel Lloyd's, and on the premises of
Mr. Beal Bondly. At this trespass, Mr. Bondly took offence, and with his musket
came down to the shore, and blew its deadly contents into the poor old man.

Mr. Bondly came over to see Colonel Lloyd the next day, whether to pay him
for his property, or to justify himself in what he had done, I know not. At any
rate, this whole fiendish transaction was soon hushed up. There was very little
said about it at all, and nothing done. It was a common saying, even among
little white boys, that it was worth a half-cent to kill a "nigger," and a half-cent
to bury one.

CHAPTER V

As to my own treatment while I lived on Colonel Lloyd's plantation, it was very
similar to that of the other slave children. I was not old enough to work in the
field, and there being little else than field work to do, I had a great deal of leisure time. The most I had to do was to drive up the cows at evening, keep the
fowls out of the garden, keep the front yard clean, and run off errands for my
old master's daughter, Mrs. Lucretia Auld. The most of my leisure time I spent
in helping Master Daniel Lloyd in finding his birds, after he had shot them. My
connection with Master Daniel was of some advantage to me. He became quite
attached to me, and was a sort of protector of me. He would not allow the older
boys to impose upon me, and would divide his cakes with me.

I was seldom whipped by my old master, and suffered little from any thing else than hunger and cold. I suffered much from hunger, but much more from cold. In hottest summer and coldest winter, I was kept almost naked—no shoes, no stockings, no jacket, no trousers, nothing on but a coarse tow linen shirt, reaching only to my knees. I had no bed. I must have perished with cold, but that, the coldest nights, I used to steal a bag which was used for carrying corn to the mill. I would crawl into this bag, and there sleep on the cold, damp, clay floor, with my head in and feet out. My feet had been so cracked with the frost, that the pen with which I am writing might be laid in the gashes.

We were not regularly allowanced. Our food was coarse corn meal boiled. This was called *mush*. It was put into a large wooden tray or trough, and set down upon the ground. The children were then called, like so many pigs, and like so many pigs they would come and devour the mush; some with oyster-shells, others with pieces of shingle, some with naked hands, and none with spoons. He that ate fastest got most; he that was strongest secured the best place; and few left the trough satisfied.

I was probably between seven and eight years old when I left Colonel Lloyd's plantation. I left it with joy. I shall never forget the ecstasy with which I received the intelligence that my old master (Anthony) had determined to let me go to Baltimore, to live with Mr. Hugh Auld, brother to my old master's son-in-law, Captain Thomas Auld. I received this information about three days before my departure. They were three of the happiest days I ever enjoyed. I spent the most part of all these three days in the creek, washing off the plantation scurf, and preparing myself for my departure.

The pride of appearance which this would indicate was not my own. I spent the time in washing, not so much because I wished to, but because Mrs. Lucretia had told me I must get all the dead skin off my feet and knees before I could go to Baltimore; for the people in Baltimore were very cleanly, and would laugh at me if I looked dirty. Besides, she was going to give me a pair of trousers, which I should not put on unless I got all the dirt off me. The thought of owning a pair of trousers was great indeed! It was almost a sufficient motive, not only to make me take off what would be called by pig-drovers the mange, but the skin itself. I went at it in good earnest, working for the first time with the hope of reward.

The ties that ordinarily bind children to their homes were all suspended in my case. I found no severe trial in my departure. My home was charmless; it was not home to me; on parting from it, I could not feel that I was leaving any thing which I could have enjoyed by staying. My mother was dead, my grand-mother lived far off, so that I seldom saw her. I had two sisters and one brother, that lived in the same house with me; but the early separation of us from our mother had well nigh blotted the fact of our relationship from our memories. I looked for home elsewhere, and was confident of finding none which I should relish less than the one which I was leaving. If, however, I found in my new home hardship, hunger, whipping, and nakedness, I had the consolation that I should not have escaped any one of them by staying. Having already had more than a taste of them in the house of my old master, and having endured them there, I very naturally inferred my ability to endure them elsewhere, and especially at Baltimore; for I had something of the feeling about Baltimore that is expressed in the proverb, that "being hanged in England is preferable to dying a natural death in Ireland." I had the strongest desire to see Baltimore.

Cousin Tom, though not fluent in speech, had inspired me with that desire by his eloquent description of the place. I could never point out any thing at the Great House, no matter how beautiful or powerful, but that he had seen something at Baltimore far exceeding, both in beauty and strength, the object which I pointed out to him. Even the Great House itself, with all its pictures, was far inferior to many buildings in Baltimore. So strong was my desire, that I thought a gratification of it would fully compensate for whatever loss of comforts I should sustain by the exchange. I left without a regret, and with the highest hopes of future happiness.

We sailed out of Miles River for Baltimore on a Saturday morning. I remember only the day of the week, for at that time I had no knowledge of the days of the month, nor the months of the year. On setting sail, I walked aft, and gave to Colonel Lloyd's plantation what I hoped would be the last look. I then placed myself in the bows of the sloop, and there spent the remainder of the day in looking ahead, interesting myself in what was in the distance rather than in things near by or behind.

In the afternoon of that day, we reached Annapolis, the capital of the State. We stopped but a few moments, so that I had no time to go on shore. It was the first large town that I had ever seen, and though it would look small compared with some of our New England factory villages, I thought it a wonderful place for its size—more imposing even than the Great House Farm!

We arrived at Baltimore early on Sunday morning, landing at Smith's Wharf, not far from Bowley's Wharf. We had on board the sloop a large flock of sheep; and after aiding in driving them to the slaughterhouse of Mr. Curtis on Louden Slater's Hill, I was conducted by Rich, one of the hands belonging on board of the sloop, to my new home in Alliciana Street, near Mr. Gardner's ship-yard, on Fells Point.

Mr. and Mrs. Auld were both at home, and met me at the door with their little son Thomas, to take care of whom I had been given. And here I saw what I had never seen before; it was a white face beaming with the most kindly emotions; it was the face of my new mistress, Sophia Auld. I wish I could describe the rapture that flashed through my soul as I beheld it. It was a new and strange sight to me, brightening up my pathway with the light of happiness. Little Thomas was told, there was his Freddy,—and I was told to take care of little Thomas; and thus I entered upon the duties of my new home with the most cheering prospect ahead.

I look upon my departure from Colonel Lloyd's plantation as one of the most interesting events of my life. It is possible, and even quite probable, that but for the mere circumstance of being removed from that plantation to Baltimore, I should have to-day, instead of being here seated by my own table, in the enjoyment of freedom and the happiness of home, writing this Narrative, been confined in the galling chains of slavery. Going to live at Baltimore laid the foundation, and opened the gateway, to all my subsequent prosperity. I have ever regarded it as the first plain manifestation of that kind providence which has ever since attended me, and marked my life with so many favors. I regarded the selection of myself as being somewhat remarkable. There were a number of slave children that might have been sent from the plantation to Baltimore. There were those younger, those older, and those of the same age. I was chosen from among them all, and was the first, last, and only choice.

I may be deemed superstitious, and even egotistical, in regarding this event as a special interposition of divine Providence in my favor. But I should be false to the earliest sentiments of my soul, if I suppressed the opinion. I prefer to be true to myself, even at the hazard of incurring the ridicule of others, rather than to be false, and incur my own abhorrence. From my earliest recollection, I date the entertainment of a deep conviction that slavery would not always be able to hold me within its foul embrace; and in the darkest hours of my career in slavery, this living word of faith and spirit of hope departed not from me, but remained like ministering angels to cheer me through the gloom. This good spirit was from God, and to him I offer thanksgiving and praise.

CHAPTER VI

My new mistress proved to be all she appeared when I first met her at the door,—a woman of the kindest heart and finest feelings. She had never had a slave under her control previously to myself, and prior to her marriage she had been dependent upon her own industry for a living. She was by trade a weaver; and by constant application to her business, she had been in a good degree preserved from the blighting and dehumanizing effects of slavery. I was utterly astonished at her goodness. I scarcely knew how to behave towards her. She was entirely unlike any other white woman I had ever seen. I could not approach her as I was accustomed to approach other white ladies. My early instruction was all out of place. The crouching servility, usually so acceptable a quality in a slave, did not answer when manifested toward her. Her favor was not gained by it; she seemed to be disturbed by it. She did not deem it impudent or unmannerly for a slave to look her in the face. The meanest slave was put fully at ease in her presence, and none left without feeling better for having seen her. Her face was made of heavenly smiles, and her voice of tranquil music.

But, alas! this kind heart had but a short time to remain such. The fatal poison of irresponsible power was already in her hands, and soon commenced its infernal work. That cheerful eye, under the influence of slavery, soon became red with rage; that voice, made all of sweet accord, changed to one of harsh and horrid discord; and that angelic face gave place to that of a demon.

Very soon after I went to live with Mr. and Mrs. Auld, she very kindly commenced to teach me the A, B, C. After I had learned this, she assisted me in learning to spell words of three or four letters. Just at this point of my progress, Mr. Auld found out what was going on, and at once forbade Mrs. Auld to instruct me further, telling her, among other things, that it was unlawful, as well as unsafe, to teach a slave to read. To use his own words, further, he said, "If you give a nigger an inch, he will take an ell. A nigger should know nothing but to obey his master—to do as he is told to do. Learning would *spoil* the best nigger in the world. Now," said he, "if you teach that nigger (speaking of myself) how to read, there would be no keeping him. It would forever unfit him to be a slave. He would at once become unmanageable, and of no value to his master. As to himself, it could do him no good, but a great deal of harm. It would make him discontented and unhappy." These words sank deep into my heart, stirred up sentiments within that lay slumbering, and called into existence an entirely new train of thought. It was a new and special revelation, explaining dark and mysterious things, with which my youthful understanding had struggled, but struggled in vain. I now understood what had been to me a most perplexing difficulty—to wit, the white man's power to enslave the black man. It was a grand achievement, and I prized it highly. From that moment, I understood the pathway from slavery to freedom. It was just what I wanted, and I got it at a time when I the least expected it. Whilst I was saddened by the thought of losing the aid of my kind mistress, I was gladdened by the invaluable instruction which, by the merest accident, I had gained from my master. Though conscious of the difficulty of learning without a teacher, I set out with high hope, and a fixed purpose, at whatever cost of trouble, to learn how to read. The very decided manner with which he spoke, and strove to impress his wife with the evil consequences of giving me instruction, served to convince me that he was deeply sensible of the truths he was uttering. It gave me the best assurance that I might rely with the utmost confidence on the results which, he said, would flow from teaching me to read. What he most dreaded, that I most desired. What he most loved, that I most hated. That which to him was a great evil, to be carefully shunned, was to me a great good, to be diligently sought; and the argument which he so warmly urged, against my learning to read, only served to inspire me with a desire and determination to learn. In learning to read, I owe almost as much to the bitter opposition of my master, as to the kindly aid of my mistress. I acknowledge the benefit of both.

I had resided but a short time in Baltimore before I observed a marked difference, in the treatment of slaves, from that which I had witnessed in the country. A city slave is almost a freeman, compared with a slave on the plantation. He is much better fed and clothed, and enjoys privileges altogether unknown to the slave on the plantation. There is a vestige of decency, a sense of shame, that does much to curb and check those outbreaks of atrocious cruelty so commonly enacted upon the plantation. He is a desperate slaveholder, who will shock the humanity of his nonslaveholding neighbors with the cries of his lacerated slave. Few are willing to incur the odium attaching to the reputation of being a cruel master; and above all things, they would not be known as not giving a slave enough to eat. Every city slaveholder is anxious to have it known of him, that he feeds his slaves well; and it is due to them to say, that most of them do give their slaves enough to eat. There are, however, some painful exceptions to this rule. Directly opposite to us, on Philpot Street, lived Mr. Thomas Hamilton. He owned two slaves. Their names were Henrietta and Mary. Henrietta was about twenty-two years of age, Mary was about fourteen; and of all the mangled and emaciated creatures I ever looked upon, these two were the most so. His heart must be harder than stone, that could look upon these unmoved. The head, neck, and shoulders of Mary were literally cut to pieces. I have frequently felt her head, and found it nearly covered with festering sores, caused by the lash of her cruel mistress. I do not know that her master ever whipped her, but I have been an eye-witness to the cruelty of Mrs. Hamilton. I used to be in Mr. Hamilton's house nearly every day. Mrs. Hamilton used to sit in a large chair in the middle of the room, with a heavy cowskin always by her side, and scarce an hour passed during the day but was marked by the blood of one of these slaves. The girls seldom passed her without her saying. "Move faster, you *black gip!*"[6] at the same time giving

6. Cheat, swindler.

them a blow with the cowskin over the head or shoulders, often drawing the blood. She would then say, "Take that, you *black gip!*"—continuing, "If you don't move faster, I'll move you!" Added to the cruel lashings to which these slaves were subjected, they were kept nearly half-starved. They seldom knew what it was to eat a full meal. I have seen Mary contending with the pigs for the offal thrown into the street. So much was Mary kicked and cut to pieces, that she was oftener called "*pecked*" than by her name.

CHAPTER VII

I lived in Master Hugh's family about seven years. During this time, I suc-ceeded in learning to read and write. In accomplishing this, I was compelled to resort to various stratagems. I had no regular teacher. My mistress, who had kindly commenced to instruct me, had, in compliance with the advice and direction of her husband, not only ceased to instruct, but had set her face against my being instructed by any one else. It is due, however, to my mistress to say of her, that she did not adopt this course of treatment immediately. She at first lacked the depravity indispensable to shutting me up in mental dark-ness. It was at least necessary for her to have some training in the exercise of irresponsible power, to make her equal to the task of treating me as though I were a brute.

My mistress was, as I have said, a kind and tender-hearted woman; and in the simplicity of her soul she commenced, when I first went to live with her, to treat me as she supposed one human being ought to treat another. In entering upon the duties of a slaveholder, she did not seem to perceive that I sustained to her the relation of a mere chattel, and that for her to treat me as a human being was not only wrong, but dangerously so. Slavery proved as injurious to her as it did to me. When I went there, she was a pious, warm, and tender-hearted woman. There was no sorrow or suffering for which she had not a tear. She had bread for the hungry, clothes for the naked, and comfort for every mourner that came within her reach. Slavery soon proved its ability to divest her of these heavenly qualities. Under its influence, the tender heart became stone, and the lamblike disposition gave way to one of tiger-like fierceness. The first step in her down-ward course was in her ceasing to instruct me. She now commenced to practise her husband's precepts. She finally became even more violent in her opposition than her husband himself. She was not satisfied with simply doing as well as he had commanded; she seemed anxious to do better. Nothing seemed to make her more angry than to see me with a newspaper. She seemed to think that here lay the danger. I have had her rush at me with a face made all up of fury, and snatch from me a newspaper, in a manner that fully revealed her apprehension. She was an apt woman; and a little experience soon demonstrated, to her satis-faction, that education and slavery were incompatible with each other.

From this time I was most narrowly watched. If I was in a separate room any considerable length of time, I was sure to be suspected of having a book, and was at once called to give an account of myself. All this, however, was too late. The first step had been taken. Mistress, in teaching me the alphabet, had given me the *inch*, and no precaution could prevent me from taking the *ell*.

The plan which I adopted, and the one by which I was most successful, was that of making friends of all the little white boys whom I met in the street. As many of these as I could, I converted into teachers. With their kindly aid, obtained at different times and in different places, I finally succeeded in learning to read. When I was sent of errands, I always took my book with me, and by going one part of my errand quickly, I found time to get a lesson before my return. I used also to carry bread with me, enough of which was always in the house, and to which I was always welcome; for I was much better off in this regard than many of the poor white children in our neighborhood. This bread I used to bestow upon the hungry little urchins, who, in return, would give me that more valuable bread of knowledge. I am strongly tempted to give the names of two or three of those little boys, as a testimonial of the gratitude and affection I bear them; but prudence forbids;—not that it would injure me, but it might embarrass them; for it is almost an unpardonable offence to teach slaves to read in this Christian country. It is enough to say of the dear little fellows, that they lived on Philpot Street, very near Durgin and Bailey's ship-yard. I used to talk this matter of slavery over with them. I would sometimes say to them, I wished I could be as free as they would be when they got to be men. "You will be free as soon as you are twenty-one, *but I am a slave for life!* Have not I as good a right to be free as you have?" These words used to trouble them; they would express for me the liveliest sympathy, and console me with the hope that something would occur by which I might be free.

I was now about twelve years old, and the thought of being *a slave for life* began to bear heavily upon my heart. Just about this time, I got hold of a book entitled "The Columbian Orator."[7] Every opportunity I got, I used to read this book. Among much of other interesting matter, I found in it a dialogue between a master and his slave. The slave was represented as having run away from his master three times. The dialogue represented the conversation which took place between them, when the slave was retaken the third time. In this dialogue, the whole argument in behalf of slavery was brought forward by the master, all of which was disposed of by the slave. The slave was made to say some very smart as well as impressive things in reply to his master—things which had the desired though unexpected effect; for the conversation resulted in the voluntary emancipation of the slave on the part of the master.

In the same book, I met with one of Sheridan's[8] mighty speeches on and in behalf of Catholic emancipation. These were choice documents to me. I read them over and over again with unabated interest. They gave tongue to interesting thoughts of my own soul, which had frequently flashed through my mind, and died away for want of utterance. The moral which I gained from the dialogue was the power of truth over the conscience of even a slaveholder. What I got from Sheridan was a bold denunciation of slavery, and a powerful vindication of human rights. The reading of these documents enabled me to utter my thoughts, and to meet the arguments brought forward to sustain slavery; but while they relieved me of one difficulty, they brought on another even more painful than the one of which I was relieved. The more I read, the more I was led to abhor and detest my enslavers. I could regard them in no other light

---

7. Caleb Bingham, *The Columbian Orator: Containing a Variety of Original and Selected Pieces: Together with Rules, Calculated to Improve Youth and Others in the Ornamental* *and Useful Art of Eloquence* (1807).

8. Thomas Sheridan (1719–1788), Irish actor, lecturer, and writer on elocution.

than a band of successful robbers, who had left their homes, and gone to Africa, and stolen us from our homes, and in a strange land reduced us to slavery. I loathed them as being the meanest as well as the most wicked of men. As I read and contemplated the subject, behold! that very discontentment which Master Hugh had predicted would follow my learning to read had already come, to torment and sting my soul to unutterable anguish. As I writhed under it, I would at times feel that learning to read had been a curse rather than a blessing. It had given me a view of my wretched condition, without the remedy. It opened my eyes to the horrible pit, but to no ladder upon which to get out. In moments of agony, I envied my fellow-slaves for their stupidity. I have often wished myself a beast. I preferred the condition of the meanest reptile to my own. Any thing, no matter what, to get rid of thinking! It was this everlasting thinking of my condition that tormented me. There was no getting rid of it. It was pressed upon me by every object within sight or hearing, animate or inanimate. The silver trump of freedom had roused my soul to eternal wakefulness. Freedom now appeared, to disappear no more forever. It was heard in every sound, and seen in every thing. It was ever present to torment me with a sense of my wretched condition. I saw nothing without seeing it, I heard nothing without hearing it, and felt nothing without feeling it. It looked from every star, it smiled in every calm, breathed in every wind, and moved in every storm.

I often found myself regretting my own existence, and wishing myself dead; and but for the hope of being free, I have no doubt but that I should have killed myself, or done something for which I should have been killed. While in this state of mind, I was eager to hear any one speak of slavery. I was a ready listener. Every little while, I could hear something about the abolitionists. It was some time before I found what the word meant. It was always used in such connections as to make it an interesting word to me. If a slave ran away and succeeded in getting clear, or if a slave killed his master, set fire to a barn, or did any thing very wrong in the mind of a slaveholder, it was spoken of as the fruit of *abolition*. Hearing the word in this connection very often, I set about learning what it meant. The dictionary afforded me little or no help. I found it was "the act of abolishing"; but then I did not know what was to be abolished. Here I was perplexed. I did not dare to ask any one about its meaning, for I was satisfied that it was something they wanted me to know very little about. After a patient waiting, I got one of our city papers, containing an account of the number of petitions from the north, praying for the abolition of slavery in the District of Columbia, and of the slave trade between the States. From this time I understood the words *abolition* and *abolitionist*, and always drew near when that word was spoken, expecting to hear something of importance to myself and fellow-slaves. The light broke in upon me by degrees. I went one day down on the wharf of Mr. Waters; and seeing two Irishmen unloading a scow of stone, I went, unasked, and helped them. When we had finished, one of them came to me and asked me if I were a slave. I told him I was. He asked, "Are ye a slave for life?" I told him that I was. The good Irishman seemed to be deeply affected by the statement. He said to the other that it was a pity so fine a little fellow as myself should be a slave for life. He said it was a shame to hold me. They both advised me to run away to the north; that I should find friends there, and that I should be free. I pretended not to be interested in what they said, and treated them as if I did not understand them; for I feared they might be treacherous. White men have been known to encourage slaves to escape, and then, to get the reward, catch them and return them to their masters. I was afraid that these seemingly good men might use me so; but I nevertheless remembered their advice, and from that time I resolved to run away. I looked forward to a time at which it would be safe for me to escape. I was too young to think of doing so immediately; besides, I wished to learn how to write, as I might have occasion to write my own pass. I consoled myself with the hope that I should one day find a good chance. Meanwhile, I would learn to write.

The idea as to how I might learn to write was suggested to me by being in Durgin and Bailey's ship-yard, and frequently seeing the ship carpenters, after hewing, and getting a piece of timber ready for use, write on the timber the name of that part of the ship for which it was intended. When a piece of timber was intended for the larboard side, it would be marked thus—"L." When a piece was for the starboard side, it would be marked thus—"S." A piece for the larboard forward, would be marked thus—"L.F." When a piece was for starboard side forward, it would be marked thus—"S.F." For larboard aft, it would be marked thus—"L.A." For starboard aft, it would be marked thus—"S.A." I soon learned the names of these letters, and for what they were intended when placed upon a piece of timber in the ship-yard. I immediately commenced copying them, and in a short time was able to make the four letters named. After that, when I met with any boy who I knew could write, I would tell him I could write as well as he. The next word would be, "I don't believe you. Let me see you try it." I would then make the letters which I had been so fortunate as to learn, and ask him to beat that. In this way I got a good many lessons in writing, which it is quite possible I should never have gotten in any other way. During this time, my copy-book was the board fence, brick wall, and pavement; my pen and ink was a lump of chalk. With these, I learned mainly how to write. I then commenced and continued copying the Italics in Webster's Spelling Book, until I could make them all without looking on the book. By this time, my little Master Thomas had gone to school, and learned how to write, and had written over a number of copy-books. These had been brought home, and shown to some of our near neighbors, and then laid aside. My mistress used to go to class meeting at the Wilk Street meetinghouse every Monday afternoon, and leave me to take care of the house. When left thus, I used to spend the time in writing in the spaces left in Master Thomas's copy-book, copying what he had written. I continued to do this until I could write a hand very similar to that of Master Thomas. Thus, after a long, tedious effort for years, I finally succeeded in learning how to write.

CHAPTER VIII

In a very short time after I went to live at Baltimore, my old master's youngest son Richard died; and in about three years and six months after his death, my old master, Captain Anthony, died, leaving only his son, Andrew, and daughter, Lucretia, to share his estate. He died while on a visit to see his daughter at Hillsborough. Cut off thus unexpectedly, he left no will as to the disposal of his property. It was therefore necessary to have a valuation of the property, that it might be equally divided between Mrs. Lucretia and Master Andrew. I was immediately sent for, to be valued with the other property. Here again my feelings rose up in detestation of slavery. I had now a new conception of my degraded condition. Prior to this, I had become, if not insensible to my lot, at least partly so. I left Baltimore with a young heart overborne with sadness, and a soul full of apprehension. I took passage with Captain Rowe, in the schooner *Wild Cat*, and, after a sail of about twenty-four hours, I found myself near the place of my birth. I had now been absent from it almost, if not quite, five years. I, however, remembered the place very well. I was only about five years old when I left it, to go and live with my old master on Colonel Lloyd's plantation; so that I was now between ten and eleven years old.

We were all ranked together at the valuation. Men and women, old and young, married and single, were ranked with horses, sheep, and swine. There were horses and men, cattle and women, pigs and children, all holding the same rank in the scale of being, and all were subjected to the same narrow examination. Silvery-headed age and sprightly youth, maids and matrons, had to undergo the same indelicate inspection. At this moment, I saw more clearly than ever the brutalizing effects of slavery upon both slave and slaveholder.

After the valuation, then came the division. I have no language to express the high excitement and deep anxiety which were felt among us poor slaves during this time. Our fate for life was now to be decided. We had no more voice in that decision than the brutes among whom we were ranked. A single word from the white men was enough—against all our wishes, prayers, and entreaties—to sunder forever the dearest friends, dearest kindred, and strongest ties known to human beings. In addition to the pain of separation, there was the horrid dread of falling into the hands of Master Andrew. He was known to us all as being a most cruel wretch,—a common drunkard, who had, by his reckless mismanagement and profligate dissipation, already wasted a large portion of his father's property. We all felt that we might as well be sold at once to the Georgia traders, as to pass into his hands; for we knew that that would be our inevitable condition,—a condition held by us all in the utmost horror and dread.

I suffered more anxiety than most of my fellow-slaves. I had known what it was to be kindly treated; they had known nothing of the kind. They had seen little or nothing of the world. They were in very deed men and women of sorrow, and acquainted with grief.[9] Their backs had been made familiar with the bloody lash, so that they had become callous; mine was yet tender; for while at Baltimore I got few whippings, and few slaves could boast of a kinder master and mistress than myself; and the thought of passing out of their hands into those of Master Andrew—a man who, but a few days before, to give me a sample of his bloody disposition, took my little brother by the throat, threw him on the ground, and with the heel of his boot stamped upon his head till the blood gushed from his nose and ears—was well calculated to make me anxious as to my fate. After he had committed this savage outrage upon my brother, he turned to me, and said that was the way he meant to serve me one of these days,—meaning, I suppose, when I came into his possession.

Thanks to a kind Providence, I fell to the portion of Mrs. Lucretia, and was sent immediately back to Baltimore, to live again in the family of Master Hugh. Their joy at my return equalled their sorrow at my departure. It was a glad day

9. In Isaiah 53.3, the Lord's servant is described as "a man of sorrows, and acquainted with grief."

to me. I had escaped a [fate] worse than lion's jaws. I was absent from Baltimore, for the purpose of valuation and division, just about one month, and it seemed to have been six.

Very soon after my return to Baltimore, my mistress, Lucretia, died, leaving her husband and one child, Amanda; and in a very short time after her death, Master Andrew died. Now all the property of my old master, slaves included, was in the hands of strangers,—strangers who had had nothing to do with accumulating it. Not a slave was left free. All remained slaves, from the youngest to the oldest. If any one thing in my experience, more than another, served to deepen my conviction of the infernal character of slavery, and to fill me with unutterable loathing of slaveholders, it was their base ingratitude to my poor old grandmother. She had served my old master faithfully from youth to old age. She had been the source of all his wealth; she had peopled his plantation with slaves; she had become a great grandmother in his service. She had rocked him in infancy, attended him in childhood, served him through life, and at his death wiped from his icy brow the cold death-sweat, and closed his eyes forever. She was nevertheless left a slave—a slave for life—a slave in the hands of strangers; and in their hands she saw her children, her grandchildren, and her great-grandchildren, divided, like so many sheep, without being gratified with the small privilege of a single word, as to their or her own destiny. And, to cap the climax of their base ingratitude and fiendish barbarity, my grandmother, who was now very old, having outlived my old master and all his children, having seen the beginning and end of all of them, and her present owners finding she was of but little value, her frame already racked with the pains of old age, and complete helplessness fast stealing over her once active limbs, they took her to the woods, built her a little hut, put up a little mud-chimney, and then made her welcome to the privilege of supporting herself there in perfect loneliness; thus virtually turning her out to die! If my poor old grandmother now lives, she lives to suffer in utter loneliness; she lives to remember and mourn over the loss of children, the loss of grandchildren, and the loss of great-grandchildren. They are, in the language of the slave's poet, Whittier,—

"Gone, gone, sold and gone
To the rice swamp dank and lone,
Where the slave-whip ceaseless swings,
Where the noisome insect stings,
Where the fever-demon strews
Poison with the falling dews,
Where the sickly sunbeams glare
Through the hot and misty air:—
    Gone, gone, sold and gone
    To the rice swamp dank and lone,
    From Virginia hills and waters—
    Woe is me, my stolen daughters!"[1]

1. John Greenleaf Whittier, American poet (1807–1892), wrote a large group of antislavery poems. This one is *The Farewell of a Virginia Slave Mother to her Daughters Sold into Southern Bondage.*

The hearth is desolate. The children, the unconscious children, who once sang and danced in her presence, are gone. She gropes her way, in the darkness of age, for a drink of water. Instead of the voices of her children, she hears by day the moans of the dove, and by night the screams of the hideous owl. All is gloom. The grave is at the door. And now, when weighed down by the pains and aches of old age, when the head inclines to the feet, when the beginning and ending of human existence meet, and helpless infancy and painful old age combine together—at this time, this most needful time, the time for the exercise of that tenderness and affection which children only can exercise towards a declining parent—my poor old grandmother, the devoted mother of twelve children, is left all alone, in yonder little hut, before a few dim embers. She stands—she sits—she staggers—she falls—she groans—she dies—and there are none of her children or grandchildren present, to wipe from her wrinkled brow the cold sweat of death, or to place beneath the sod her fallen remains. Will not a righteous God visit[2] for these things?

In about two years after the death of Mrs. Lucretia, Master Thomas married his second wife. Her name was Rowena Hamilton. She was the eldest daughter of Mr. William Hamilton. Master now lived in St. Michael's. Not long after his marriage, a misunderstanding took place between himself and Master Hugh; and as a means of punishing his brother, he took me from him to live with himself at St. Michael's. Here I underwent another most painful separation. It, however, was not so severe as the one I dreaded at the division of property; for, during this interval, a great change had taken place in Master Hugh and his once kind and affectionate wife. The influence of brandy upon him, and of slavery upon her, had effected a disastrous change in the characters of both; so that, as far as they were concerned, I thought I had little to lose by the change. But it was not to them that I was attached. It was to those little Baltimore boys that I felt the strongest attachment. I had received many good lessons from them, and was still receiving them, and the thought of leaving them was painful indeed. I was leaving, too, without the hope of ever being allowed to return. Master Thomas had said he would never let me return again. The barrier betwixt himself and brother he considered impassable.

I then had to regret that I did not at least make the attempt to carry out my resolution to run away; for the chances of success are tenfold greater from the city than from the country.

I sailed from Baltimore for St. Michael's in the sloop *Amanda*, Captain Edward Dodson. On my passage, I paid particular attention to the direction which the steamboats took to go to Philadelphia. I found, instead of going down, on reaching North Point they went up the bay, in a north-easterly direction. I deemed this knowledge of the utmost importance. My determination to run away was again revived. I resolved to wait only so long as the offering of a favorable opportunity. When that came, I was determined to be off.

CHAPTER IX

I have now reached a period of my life when I can give dates. I left Baltimore, and went to live with Master Thomas Auld, at St. Michael's, in March, 1832.

---

2. I.e., visit vengeance. Cf. Exodus 32.34: "Nevertheless, in the day when I visit I will visit their sin upon them."

It was now more than seven years since I lived with him in the family of my old master, on Colonel Lloyd's plantation. We of course were now almost entire strangers to each other. He was to me a new master, and I to him a new slave. I was ignorant of his temper and disposition; he was equally so of mine. A very short time, however, brought us into full acquaintance with each other. I was made acquainted with his wife not less than with himself. They were well matched, being equally mean and cruel. I was now, for the first time during a space of more than seven years, made to feel the painful gnawings of hunger—a something which I had not experienced before since I left Colonel Lloyd's plantation. It went hard enough with me then, when I could look back to no period at which I had enjoyed a sufficiency. It was tenfold harder after living in Master Hugh's family, where I had always had enough to eat, and of that which was good. I have said Master Thomas was a mean man. He was so. Not to give a slave enough to eat, is regarded as the most aggravated development of meanness even among slaveholders. The rule is, no matter how coarse the food, only let there be enough of it. This is the theory; and in the part of Maryland from which I came, it is the general practice,—though there are many exceptions. Master Thomas gave us enough of neither coarse nor fine food. There were four of us slaves in the kitchen—my sister Eliza, my aunt Priscilla, Henny, and myself; and we were allowed less than a half of a bushel of corn-meal per week, and very little else, either in the shape of meat or vegetables. It was not enough for us to subsist upon. We were therefore reduced to the wretched necessity of living at the expense of our neighbors. This we did by begging and stealing, whichever came handy in the time of need, the one being considered as legitimate as the other. A great many times have we poor creatures been nearly perishing with hunger, when food in abundance lay mouldering in the safe and smoke-house, and our pious mistress was aware of the fact; and yet that mistress and her husband would kneel every morning, and pray that God would bless them in basket and store!

Bad as all slaveholders are, we seldom meet one destitute of every element of character commanding respect. My master was one of this rare sort. I do not know of one single noble act ever performed by him. The leading trait in his character was meanness; and if there were any other element in his nature, it was made subject to this. He was mean; and, like most other mean men, he lacked the ability to conceal his meanness. Captain Auld was not born a slaveholder. He had been a poor man, master only of a Bay craft. He came into possession of all his slaves by marriage; and of all men, adopted slaveholders are the worst. He was cruel, but cowardly. He commanded without firmness. In the enforcement of his rules, he was at times rigid, and at times lax. At times, he spoke to his slaves with the firmness of Napoleon and the fury of a demon; at other times, he might well be mistaken for an inquirer who had lost his way. He did nothing of himself. He might have passed for a lion, but for his ears.[3] In all things noble which he attempted, his own meanness shone most conspicuous. His airs, words, and actions, were the airs, words, and actions of born slaveholders, and, being assumed, were awkward enough. He was not even a good imitator. He possessed all the disposition to deceive, but wanted the

---

3. A variation on Aesop's fable of the ass in a lion's skin who frightened all of the animals. The fox says: "I would have been frightened too if I had not heard you bray."

power. Having no resources within himself, he was compelled to be the copyist of many, and being such, he was forever the victim of inconsistency; and of consequence he was an object of contempt, and was held as such even by his slaves. The luxury of having slaves of his own to wait upon him was something new and unprepared for. He was a slaveholder without the ability to hold slaves. He found himself incapable of managing his slaves either by force, fear, or fraud. We seldom called him "master"; we generally called him "Captain Auld," and were hardly disposed to title him at all. I doubt not that our conduct had much to do with making him appear awkward, and of consequence fretful. Our want of reverence for him must have perplexed him greatly. He wished to have us call him master, but lacked the firmness necessary to command us to do so. His wife used to insist upon our calling him so, but to no purpose. In August, 1832, my master attended a Methodist camp-meeting held in the Bay-side, Talbot county, and there experienced religion. I indulged a faint hope that his conversion would lead him to emancipate his slaves, and that, if he did not do this, it would, at any rate, make him more kind and humane. I was disappointed in both these respects. It neither made him to be humane to his slaves, nor to emancipate them. If it had any effect on his character, it made him more cruel and hateful in all his ways; for I believe him to have been a much worse man after his conversion than before. Prior to his conversion, he relied upon his own depravity to shield and sustain him in his savage barbarity; but after his conversion, he found religious sanction and support for his slaveholding cruelty. He made the greatest pretensions to piety. His house was the house of prayer. He prayed morning, noon, and night. He very soon distinguished himself among his brethren, and was soon made a class-leader and exhorter. His activity in revivals was great, and he proved himself an instrument in the hands of the church in converting many souls. His house was the preachers' home. They used to take great pleasure in coming there to put up; for while he starved us, he stuffed them. We have had three or four preachers there at a time. The names of those who used to come most frequently while I lived there, were Mr. Storks, Mr. Ewery, Mr. Humphry, and Mr. Hickey. I have also seen Mr. George Cookman at our house. We slaves loved Mr. Cookman. We believed him to be a good man. We thought him instrumental in getting Mr. Samuel Harrison, a very rich slaveholder, to emancipate his slaves; and by some means got the impression that he was laboring to effect the emancipation of all the slaves. When he was at our house, we were sure to be called in to prayers. When the others were there, we were sometimes called in and sometimes not. Mr. Cookman took more notice of us than either of the other ministers. He could not come among us without betraying his sympathy for us, and, stupid as we were, we had the sagacity to see it.

While I lived with my master in St. Michael's, there was a white young man, a Mr. Wilson, who proposed to keep a Sabbath school for the instruction of such slaves as might be disposed to learn to read the New Testament. We met but three times, when Mr. West and Mr. Fairbanks, both class-leaders, with many others, came upon us with sticks and other missiles, drove us off, and forbade us to meet again. Thus ended our little Sabbath school in the pious town of St. Michael's.

I have said my master found religious sanction for his cruelty. As an example, I will state one of many facts going to prove the charge. I have seen him tie up a lame young woman, and whip her with a heavy cowskin upon her naked shoulders, causing the warm red blood to drip; and, in justification of the bloody deed, he would quote this passage of Scripture—"He that knoweth his master's will, and doeth it not, shall be beaten with many stripes."[4]

Master would keep this lacerated young woman tied up in this horrid situation four or five hours at a time. I have known him to tie her up early in the morning, and whip her before breakfast; leave her, go to his store, return to dinner, and whip her again, cutting her in the places already made raw with his cruel lash. The secret of master's cruelty toward "Henny" is found in the fact of her being almost helpless. When quite a child, she fell into the fire, and burned herself horribly. Her hands were so burnt that she never got the use of them. She could do very little but bear heavy burdens. She was to master a bill of expense; and as he was a mean man, she was a constant offence to him. He seemed desirous of getting the poor girl out of existence. He gave her away once to his sister; but, being a poor gift, she was not disposed to keep her. Finally, my benevolent master, to use his own words, "set her adrift to take care of herself." Here was a recently-converted man, holding on upon the mother, and at the same time turning out her helpless child, to starve and die! Master Thomas was one of the many pious slaveholders who hold slaves for the very charitable purpose of taking care of them.

My master and myself had quite a number of differences. He found me unsuitable to his purpose. My city life, he said, had had a very pernicious effect upon me. It had almost ruined me for every good purpose, and fitted me for every thing which was bad. One of my greatest faults was that of letting his horse run away, and go down to his father-in-law's farm, which was about five miles from St. Michael's. I would then have to go after it. My reason for this kind of carelessness, or carefulness, was, that I could always get something to eat when I went there. Master William Hamilton, my master's father-in-law, always gave his slaves enough to eat. I never left there hungry, no matter how great the need of my speedy return. Master Thomas at length said he would stand it no longer. I had lived with him nine months, during which time he had given me a number of severe whippings, all to no good purpose. He resolved to put me out, as he said, to be broken; and, for this purpose, he let me for one year to a man named Edward Covey. Mr. Covey was a poor man, a farm-renter. He rented the place upon which he lived, as also the hands with which he tilled it. Mr. Covey had acquired a very high reputation for breaking young slaves, and this reputation was of immense value to him. It enabled him to get his farm tilled with much less expense to himself than he could have had it done without such a reputation. Some slaveholders thought it not much loss to allow Mr. Covey to have their slaves one year, for the sake of the training to which they were subjected, without any other compensation. He could hire young help with great ease, in consequence of this reputation. Added to the natural good qualities of Mr. Covey, he was a professor of religion—a pious soul—a member and a class-leader in the Methodist church. All of this added weight to his reputation as a "nigger-breaker." I was aware of all the facts, having been made acquainted with them by a young man who had lived there. I

4. Luke 12.47.

nevertheless made the change gladly; for I was sure of getting enough to eat, which is not the smallest consideration to a hungry man.

CHAPTER X

I left Master Thomas's house, and went to live with Mr. Covey, on the 1st of January, 1833. I was now, for the first time in my life, a field hand. In my new employment, I found myself even more awkward than a country boy appeared to be in a large city. I had been at my new home but one week before Mr. Covey gave me a very severe whipping, cutting my back, causing the blood to run, and raising ridges on my flesh as large as my little finger. The details of this affair are as follows: Mr. Covey sent me, very early in the morning of one of our coldest days in the month of January, to the woods, to get a load of wood. He gave me a team of unbroken oxen. He told me which was the in-hand ox, and which the off-hand ox. He then tied the end of a large rope around the horns of the in-hand ox, and gave me the other end of it, and told me, if the oxen started to run, that I must hold on upon the rope. I had never driven oxen before, and of course I was very awkward. I, however, succeeded in getting to the edge of the woods with little difficulty; but I had got a very few rods into the woods, when the oxen took fright, and started full tilt, carrying the cart against trees, and over stumps, in the most frightful manner. I expected every moment that my brains would be dashed out against the trees. After running thus for a considerable distance, they finally upset the cart, dashing it with great force against a tree, and threw themselves into a dense thicket. How I escaped death, I do not know. There I was, entirely alone, in a thick wood, in a place new to me. My cart was upset and shattered, my oxen were entangled among the young trees, and there was none to help me. After a long spell of effort, I succeeded in getting my cart righted, my oxen disentangled, and again yoked to the cart. I now proceeded with my team to the place where I had, the day before, been chopping wood, and loaded my cart pretty heavily, thinking in this way to tame my oxen. I then proceeded on my way home. I had now consumed one half of the day. I got out of the woods safely, and now felt out of danger. I stopped my oxen to open the woods gate; and just as I did so, before I could get hold of my ox-rope, the oxen again started, rushed through the gate, catching it between the wheel and the body of the cart, tearing it to pieces, and coming within a few inches of crushing me against the gate-post. Thus twice, in one short day, I escaped death by the merest chance. On my return, I told Mr. Covey what had happened, and how it happened. He ordered me to return to the woods again immediately. I did so, and he followed on after me. Just as I got into the woods, he came up and told me to stop my cart, and that he would teach me how to trifle away my time, and break gates. He then went to a large gum-tree, and with his axe cut three large switches, and, after trimming them up neatly with his pocket-knife, he ordered me to take off my clothes. I made him no answer, but stood with my clothes on. He repeated his order. I still made him no answer, nor did I move to strip myself. Upon this he rushed at me with the fierceness of a tiger, tore off my clothes, and lashed me till he had worn out his switches, cutting me so savagely as to leave the marks visible for a long time after. This whipping was the first of a number just like it, and for similar offences.

I lived with Mr. Covey one year. During the first six months, of that year, scarce a week passed without his whipping me. I was seldom free from a sore back. My awkwardness was almost always his excuse for whipping me. We were worked fully up to the point of endurance. Long before day we were up, our horses fed, and by the first approach of day we were off to the field with our hoes and ploughing teams. Mr. Covey gave us enough to eat, but scarce time to eat it. We were often less than five minutes taking our meals. We were often in the field from the first approach of day till its last lingering ray had left us; and at saving-fodder time, midnight often caught us in the field binding blades.[5]

Covey would be out with us. The way he used to stand it was this. He would spend the most of his afternoons in bed. He would then come out fresh in the evening, ready to urge us on with his words, example, and frequently with the whip. Mr. Covey was one of the few slaveholders who could and did work with his hands. He was a hard-working man. He knew by himself just what a man or a boy could do. There was no deceiving him. His work went on in his absence almost as well as in his presence; and he had the faculty of making us feel that he was ever present with us. This he did by surprising us. He seldom approached the spot where we were at work openly, if he could do it secretly. He always aimed at taking us by surprise. Such was his cunning, that we used to call him, among ourselves, "the snake." When we were at work in the cornfield, he would sometimes crawl on his hands and knees to avoid detection, and all at once he would rise nearly in our midst, and scream out, "Ha, ha! Come, come! Dash on, dash on!" This being his mode of attack, it was never safe to stop a single minute. His comings were like a thief in the night. He appeared to us as being ever at hand. He was under every tree, behind every stump, in every bush, and at every window, on the plantation. He would sometimes mount his horse, as if bound to St. Michael's, a distance of seven miles, and in half an hour afterwards you would see him coiled up in the corner of the wood-fence, watching every motion of the slaves. He would, for this purpose, leave his horse tied up in the woods. Again, he would sometimes walk up to us, and give us orders as though he was upon the point of starting on a long journey, turn his back upon us, and make as though he was going to the house to get ready; and, before he would get half way thither, he would turn short and crawl into a fence-corner, or behind some tree, and there watch us till the going down of the sun.

Mr. Covey's *forte* consisted in his power to deceive. His life was devoted to planning and perpetrating the grossest deceptions. Every thing he possessed in the shape of learning or religion, he made conform to his disposition to deceive. He seemed to think himself equal to deceiving the Almighty. He would make a short prayer in the morning, and a long prayer at night; and, strange as it may seem, few men would at times appear more devotional than he. The exercises of his family devotions were always commenced with singing; and, as he was a very poor singer himself, the duty of raising the hymn generally came upon me. He would read his hymn, and nod at me to commence. I would at times do so; at others, I would not. My noncompliance would almost always produce much

---

5. Gathering cut grain into bundles or sheaves.

confusion. To show himself independent of me, he would start and stagger through with his hymn in the most discordant manner. In this state of mind, he prayed with more than ordinary spirit. Poor man! such was his disposition, and success at deceiving, I do verily believe that he sometimes deceived himself into the solemn belief, that he was a sincere worshipper of the most high God; and this, too, at a time when he may be said to have been guilty of compelling his woman slave to commit the sin of adultery. The facts in the case are these: Mr. Covey was a poor man; he was just commencing in life; he was only able to buy one slave; and, shocking as is the fact, he bought her, as he said, for a *breeder*. This woman was named Caroline. Mr. Covey bought her from Mr. Thomas Lowe, about six miles from St. Michael's. She was a large, able-bodied woman, about twenty years old. She had already given birth to one child, which proved her to be just what he wanted. After buying her, he hired a married man of Mr. Samuel Harrison, to live with him one year; and him he used to fasten up with her every night! The result was, that, at the end of the year, the miserable woman gave birth to twins. At this result Mr. Covey seemed to be highly pleased, both with the man and the wretched woman. Such was his joy, and that of his wife, that nothing they could do for Caroline during her confinement was too good, or too hard, to be done. The children were regarded as being quite an addition to his wealth.

If at any one time of my life more than another, I was made to drink the bitterest dregs of slavery, that time was during the first six months of my stay with Mr. Covey. We were worked in all weathers. It was never too hot or too cold; it could never rain, blow, hail, or snow, too hard for us to work in the field. Work, work, work, was scarcely more the order of the day than of the night. The longest days were too short for him, and the shortest nights too long for him. I was somewhat unmanageable when I first went there, but a few months of this discipline tamed me. Mr. Covey succeeded in breaking me. I was broken in body, soul, and spirit. My natural elasticity was crushed, my intellect languished, the disposition to read departed, the cheerful spark that lingered about my eye died; the dark night of slavery closed in upon me; and behold a man transformed into a brute!

Sunday was my only leisure time. I spent this in a sort of beast-like stupor, between sleep and wake, under some large tree. At times I would rise up, a flash of energetic freedom would dart through my soul, accompanied with a faint beam of hope, that flickered for a moment, and then vanished. I sank down again, mourning over my wretched condition. I was sometimes prompted to take my life, and that of Covey, but was prevented by a combination of hope and fear. My sufferings on this plantation seem now like a dream rather than a stern reality.

Our house stood within a few rods of the Chesapeake Bay, whose broad bosom was ever white with sails from every quarter of the habitable globe. Those beautiful vessels, robed in purest white, so delightful to the eye of freemen, were to me so many shrouded ghosts, to terrify and torment me with thoughts of my wretched condition. I have often, in the deep stillness of a summer's Sabbath, stood all alone upon the lofty banks of that noble bay, and traced, with saddened heart and tearful eye, the countless number of sails moving off to the mighty ocean. The sight of these always affected me powerfully. My thoughts would compel utterance; and there, with no audience but the Almighty, I would pour out my soul's complaint, in my rude way, with an apostrophe[6] to the moving multitude of ships:—

"You are loosed from your moorings, and are free; I am fast in my chains, and am a slave! You move merrily before the gentle gale, and I sadly before the bloody whip! You are freedom's swift-winged angels, that fly round the world; I am confined in bands of iron! O that I were free! O, that I were on one of your gallant decks, and under your protecting wing! Alas! betwixt me and you, the turbid waters roll. Go on, go on. O that I could also go! Could I but swim! If I could fly! O, why was I born a man, of whom to make a brute! The glad ship is gone; she hides in the dim distance. I am left in the hottest hell of unending slavery. O God, save me! God, deliver me! Let me be free! Is there any God? Why am I a slave? I will run away. I will not stand it. Get caught, or get clear, I'll try it. I had as well die with ague as the fever. I have only one life to lose. I had as well be killed running as die standing. Only think of it; one hundred miles straight north, and I am free! Try it? Yes! God helping me, I will. It cannot be that I shall live and die a slave. I will take to the water. This very bay shall bear me into freedom. The steam boats steered in a north-east course from North Point. I will do the same; and when I get to the head of the bay, I will turn my canoe adrift, and walk straight through Delaware into Pennsylvania. When I get there, I shall not be required to have a pass; I can travel without being disturbed. Let but the first opportunity offer, and, come what will, I am off. Meanwhile, I will try to bear up under the yoke. I am not the only slave in the world. Why should I fret? I can bear as much as any of them. Besides, I am but a boy, and all boys are bound to some one. It may be that my misery in slavery will only increase my happiness when I get free. There is a better day coming."

Thus I used to think, and thus I used to speak to myself; goaded almost to madness at one moment, and at the next reconciling myself to my wretched lot.

I have already intimated that my condition was much worse, during the first six months of my stay at Mr. Covey's, than in the last six. The circumstances leading to the change in Mr. Covey's course toward me form an epoch in my humble history. You have seen how a man was made a slave; you shall see how a slave was made a man. On one of the hottest days of the month of August, 1833, Bill Smith, William Hughes, a slave named Eli, and myself, were engaged in fanning wheat.[7] Hughes was clearing the fanned wheat from before the fan, Eli was turning, Smith was feeding, and I was carrying wheat to the fan. The work was simple, requiring strength rather than intellect; yet, to one entirely unused to such work, it came very hard. About three o'clock of that day, I broke down; my strength failed me; I was seized with a violent aching of the head, attended with extreme dizziness; I trembled in every limb. Finding what was coming, I nerved myself up, feeling it would never do to stop work. I stood as long as I could stagger to the hopper with grain. When I could stand no longer, I fell, and felt as if held down by an immense weight. The fan of course stopped; every one had his own work to do; and no one could do the work of the other, and have his own go on at the same time.

6. An exclamatory form of address.   7. Separating the grain from the chaff.

Mr. Covey was at the house, about one hundred yards from the treading-yard where we were fanning. On hearing the fan stop, he left immediately, and came to the spot where we were. He hastily inquired what the matter was. Bill answered that I was sick, and there was no one to bring wheat to the fan. I had by this time crawled away under the side of the post and rail-fence by which the yard was enclosed, hoping to find relief by getting out of the sun. He then asked where I was. He was told by one of the hands. He came to the spot, and, after looking at me awhile, asked me what was the matter. I told him as well as I could, for I scarce had strength to speak. He then gave me a savage kick in the side, and told me to get up. I tried to do so, but fell back in the attempt. He gave me another kick, and again told me to rise. I again tried, and succeeded in gaining my feet; but, stooping to get the tub with which I was feeding the fan, I again staggered and fell. While down in this situation, Mr. Covey took up the hickory slat with which Hughes had been striking off the half-bushel measure, and with it gave me a heavy blow upon the head, making a large wound, and the blood ran freely; and with this again told me to get up. I made no effort to comply, having now made up my mind to let him do his worst. In a short time after receiving this blow, my head grew better. Mr. Covey had now left me to my fate. At this moment I resolved, for the first time, to go to my master, enter a complaint, and ask his protection. In order to [do] this, I must that afternoon walk seven miles; and this, under the circumstances, was truly a severe undertaking. I was exceedingly feeble; made so as much by the kicks and blows which I received, as by the severe fit of sickness to which I had been subjected. I, however, watched my chance, while Covey was looking in an opposite direction, and started for St. Michael's. I succeeded in getting a considerable distance on my way to the woods, when Covey discovered me, and called after me to come back, threatening what he would do if I did not come. I disregarded both his calls and his threats, and made my way to the woods as fast as my feeble state would allow; and thinking I might be overhauled by him if I kept the road, I walked through the woods, keeping far enough from the road to avoid detection, and near enough to prevent losing my way. I had not gone far before my little strength again failed me. I could go no farther. I fell down, and lay for a considerable time. The blood was yet oozing from the wound on my head. For a time I thought I should bleed to death; and think now that I should have done so, but that the blood so matted my hair as to stop the wound. After lying there about three quarters of an hour, I nerved myself up again, and started on my way, through bogs and briers, barefooted and bareheaded, tearing my feet sometimes at nearly every step; and after a journey of about seven miles, occupying some five hours to perform it, I arrived at master's store. I then presented an appearance enough to affect any but a heart of iron. From the crown of my head to my feet, I was covered with blood. My hair was all clotted with dust and blood; my shirt was stiff with blood. My legs and feet were torn in sundry places with briers and thorns, and were also covered with blood. I suppose I looked like a man who had escaped a den of wild beasts, and barely escaped them. In this state I appeared before my master, humbly entreating him to interpose his authority for my protection. I told him all the circumstances as well as I could, and it seemed, as I spoke, at times to affect him. He would then walk the floor, and seek to justify Covey by saying he expected I deserved it. He asked me what I wanted. I told him, to let me get a new home;

that as sure as I lived with Mr. Covey again, I should live with but to die with him; that Covey would surely kill me; he was in a fair way for it. Master Thomas ridiculed the idea that there was any danger of Mr. Covey's killing me, and said that he knew Mr. Covey; that he was a good man, and that he could not think of taking me from him; that, should he do so, he would lose the whole year's wages; that I belonged to Mr. Covey for one year, and that I must go back to him, come what might; and that I must not trouble him with any more stories, or that he would himself *get hold of me*. After threatening me thus, he gave me a very large dose of salts, telling me that I might remain in St. Michael's that night, (it being quite late) but that I must be off back to Mr. Covey's early in the morning; and that if I did not, he would *get hold of me*, which meant that he would whip me. I remained all night, and, according to his orders, I started off to Covey's in the morning, (Saturday morning), wearied in body and broken in spirit. I got no supper that night, or breakfast that morning. I reached Covey's about nine o'clock; and just as I was getting over the fence that divided Mrs. Kemp's fields from ours, out ran Covey with his cowskin, to give me another whipping. Before he could reach me, I succeeded in getting to the cornfield; and as the corn was very high, it afforded me the means of hiding. He seemed very angry, and searched for me a long time. My behavior was altogether unaccountable. He finally gave up the chase, thinking, I suppose, that I must come home for something to eat; he would give himself no further trouble in looking for me. I spent that day mostly in the woods, having the alternative before me,—to go home and be whipped to death, or stay in the woods and be starved to death. That night, I fell in with Sandy Jenkins, a slave with whom I was somewhat acquainted. Sandy had a free wife who lived about four miles from Mr. Covey's; and it being Saturday, he was on his way to see her. I told him my circumstances, and he very kindly invited me to go home with him. I went home with him, and talked this whole matter over, and got his advice as to what course it was best for me to pursue. I found Sandy an old adviser. He told me, with great solemnity, I must go back to Covey; but that before I went, I must go with him into another part of the woods, where there was a certain *root*, which, if I would take some of it with me, carrying it *always on my right side*, would render it impossible for Mr. Covey, or any other white man, to whip me. He said he had carried it for years; and since he had done so, he had never received a blow, and never expected to while he carried it. I at first rejected the idea, that the simple carrying of a root in my pocket would have any such effect as he had said, and was not disposed to take it; but Sandy impressed the necessity with much earnestness, telling me it could do no harm, if it did no good. To please him, I at length took the root, and, according to his direction, carried it upon my right side. This was Sunday morning. I immediately started for home; and upon entering the yard gate, out came Mr. Covey on his way to meeting. He spoke to me very kindly, bade me drive the pigs from a lot near by, and passed on towards the church. Now, this singular conduct of Mr. Covey really made me begin to think that there was something in the *root* which Sandy had given me; and had it been on any other day than Sunday, I could have attributed the conduct to no other cause than the influence of that root; and as it was, I was half inclined to think the *root* to be something more than I at first had taken it to be. All went well till Monday morning. On this morning, the virtue of the *root* was fully tested. Long before daylight, I was called to go and rub, curry, and feed, the horses. I obeyed, and was glad to obey. But whilst thus engaged, whilst in the act of throwing down some blades from the loft, Mr. Covey entered the stable with a long rope; and just as I was half out of the loft, he caught hold of my legs, and was about tying me. As soon as I found what he was up to, I gave a sudden spring, and as I did so, he holding to my legs, I was brought sprawling on the stable floor. Mr. Covey seemed now to think he had me, and could do what he pleased; but at this moment—from whence came the spirit I don't know—I resolved to fight; and, suiting my action to the resolution, I seized Covey hard by the throat; and as I did so, I rose. He held on to me, and I to him. My resistance was so entirely unexpected, that Covey seemed taken all aback. He trembled like a leaf. This gave me assurance, and I held him uneasy, causing the blood to run where I touched him with the ends of my fingers. Mr. Covey soon called out to Hughes for help. Hughes came, and, while Covey held me, attempted to tie my right hand. While he was in the act of doing so, I watched my chance, and gave him a heavy kick close under the ribs. This kick fairly sickened Hughes, so that he left me in the hands of Mr. Covey. This kick had the effect of not only weakening Hughes, but Covey also. When he saw Hughes bending over with pain, his courage quailed. He asked me if I meant to persist in my resistance. I told him I did, come what might; that he had used me like a brute for six months, and that I was determined to be used so no longer. With that, he strove to drag me to a stick that was lying just out of the stable door. He meant to knock me down. But just as he was leaning over to get the stick, I seized him with both hands by his collar, and brought him by a sudden snatch to the ground. By this time, Bill came. Covey called upon him for assistance. Bill wanted to know what he could do. Covey said, "Take hold of him, take hold of him!" Bill said his master hired him out to work, and not to help to whip me; so he left Covey and myself to fight our own battle out. We were at it for nearly two hours. Covey at length let me go, puffing and blowing at a great rate, saying that if I had not resisted, he would not have whipped me half so much. The truth was, that he had not whipped me at all. I considered him as getting entirely the worst end of the bargain; for he had drawn no blood from me, but I had from him. The whole six months afterwards, that I spent with Mr. Covey, he never laid the weight of his finger upon me in anger. He would occasionally say, he didn't want to get hold of me again. "No," thought I, "you need not; for you will come off worse than you did before."

This battle with Mr. Covey was the turning-point in my career as a slave. It rekindled the few expiring embers of freedom, and revived within me a sense of my own manhood. It recalled the departed self-confidence, and inspired me again with a determination to be free. The gratification afforded by the triumph was a full compensation for whatever else might follow, even death itself. He only can understand the deep satisfaction which I experienced, who has himself repelled by force the bloody arm of slavery. I felt as I never felt before. It was a glorious resurrection, from the tomb of slavery, to the heaven of freedom. My long-crushed spirit rose, cowardice departed, bold defiance took its place; and I now resolved that, however long I might remain a slave in form, the day had passed forever when I could be a slave in fact. I did not hesitate to let it be known of me, that the white man who expected to succeed in whipping, must also succeed in killing me.

From this time I was never again what might be called fairly whipped, though I remained a slave four years afterwards. I had several fights, but was never whipped.

It was for a long time a matter of surprise to me why Mr. Covey did not immediately have me taken by the constable to the whipping-post, and there regularly whipped for the crime of raising my hand against a white man in defence of myself. And the only explanation I can now think of does not entirely satisfy me; but such as it is, I will give it. Mr. Covey enjoyed the most unbounded reputation for being a first-rate overseer and negro-breaker. It was of considerable importance to him. That reputation was at stake; and had he sent me—a boy about sixteen years old—to the public whipping-post, his reputation would have been lost; so, to save his reputation, he suffered me to go unpunished.

My term of actual service to Mr. Edward Covey ended on Christmas day, 1833. The days between Christmas and New Year's day are allowed as holidays; and, accordingly, we were not required to perform any labor, more than to feed and take care of the stock. This time we regarded as our own, by the grace of our masters; and we therefore used or abused it nearly as we pleased. Those of us who had families at a distance, were generally allowed to spend the whole six days in their society. This time, however, was spent in various ways. The staid, sober, thinking and industrious ones of our number would employ themselves in making corn-brooms, mats, horse-collars, and baskets; and another class of us would spend the time in hunting opossums, hares, and coons. But by far the larger part engaged in such sports and merriments as playing ball, wrestling, running foot-races, fiddling, dancing, and drinking whisky; and this latter mode of spending the time was by far the most agreeable to the feelings of our masters. A slave who would work during the holidays was considered by our masters as scarcely deserving them. He was regarded as one who rejected the favor of his master. It was deemed a disgrace not to get drunk at Christmas; and he was regarded as lazy indeed, who had not provided himself with the necessary means, during the year, to get whisky enough to last him through Christmas.

From what I know of the effect of these holidays upon the slave, I believe them to be among the most effective means in the hands of the slaveholder in keeping down the spirit of insurrection. Were the slaveholders at once to abandon this practice, I have not the slightest doubt it would lead to an immediate insurrection among the slaves. These holidays serve as conductors, or safety-valves, to carry off the rebellious spirit of enslaved humanity. But for these, the slave would be forced up to the wildest desperation; and woe betide the slaveholder, the day he ventures to remove or hinder the operation of those conductors! I warn him that, in such an event, a spirit will go forth in their midst, more to be dreaded than the most appalling earthquake.

The holidays are part and parcel of the gross fraud, wrong, and inhumanity of slavery. They are professedly a custom established by the benevolence of the slaveholders; but I undertake to say, it is the result of selfishness, and one of the grossest frauds committed upon the down-trodden slave. They do not give the slaves this time because they would not like to have their work during its continuance, but because they know it would be unsafe to deprive them of it. This will be seen by the fact, that the slaveholders like to have their slaves spend those days just in such a manner as to make them as glad of their ending as of their beginning. Their object seems to be, to disgust their slaves with freedom, by plunging them into the lowest depths of dissipation. For instance, the slaveholders not only like to see the slave drink of his own accord, but will adopt various plans to make him drunk. One plan is, to make bets on their slaves, as to who can drink the most whisky without getting drunk; and in this way they succeed in getting whole multitudes to drink to excess. Thus, when the slave asks for virtuous freedom, the cunning slaveholder, knowing his ignorance, cheats him with a dose of vicious dissipation, artfully labelled with the name of liberty. The most of us used to drink it down, and the result was just what might be supposed: many of us were led to think that there was little to choose between liberty and slavery. We felt, and very properly too, that we had almost as well be slaves to man as to rum. So, when the holidays ended, we staggered up from the filth of our wallowing, took a long breath, and marched to the field,—feeling, upon the whole, rather glad to go, from what our master had deceived us into a belief was freedom, back to the arms of slavery.

I have said that this mode of treatment is a part of the whole system of fraud and inhumanity of slavery. It is so. The mode here adopted to disgust the slave with freedom, by allowing him to see only the abuse of it, is carried out in other things. For instance, a slave loves molasses; he steals some. His master, in many cases, goes off to town, and buys a large quantity; he returns, takes his whip, and commands the slave to eat the molasses, until the poor fellow is made sick at the very mention of it. The same mode is sometimes adopted to make the slaves refrain from asking for more food than their regular allowance. A slave runs through his allowance, and applies for more. His master is enraged at him; but, not willing to send him off without food, gives him more than is necessary, and compels him to eat it within a given time. Then, if he complains that he cannot eat it, he is said to be satisfied neither full nor fasting, and is whipped for being hard to please! I have an abundance of such illustrations of the same principle, drawn from my own observation, but think the cases I have cited sufficient. The practice is a very common one.

On the first of January, 1834, I left Mr. Covey, and went to live with Mr. William Freeland, who lived about three miles from St. Michael's. I soon found Mr. Freeland a very different man from Mr. Covey. Though not rich, he was what would be called an educated southern gentleman. Mr. Covey, as I have shown, was a well-trained negro-breaker and slave-driver. The former (slaveholder though he was) seemed to possess some regard for honor, some reverence for justice, and some respect for humanity. The latter seemed totally insensible to all such sentiments. Mr. Freeland had many of the faults peculiar to slaveholders, such as being very passionate and fretful; but I must do him the justice to say, that he was exceedingly free from those degrading vices to which Mr. Covey was constantly addicted. The one was open and frank, and we always knew where to find him. The other was a most artful deceiver, and could be understood only by such as were skilful enough to detect his cunningly-devised frauds. Another advantage I gained in my new master was, he made no pretensions to, or profession of, religion; and this, in my opinion, was truly a great advantage. I assert most unhesitatingly, that the religion of the south is a mere covering for the most horrid crimes,—a justifier of the most appalling barbarity,—a sanctifier of the most hateful frauds,—and a dark shelter under which the darkest, foulest, grossest, and most infernal deeds of slaveholders find the strongest protection. Were I to be again reduced to the chains of slavery, next to that enslavement, I should regard being the slave of a religious master the greatest calamity that could befall me. For of all slaveholders with whom I have ever met, religious slaveholders are the worst. I have ever found them the meanest and basest, the most cruel and cowardly, of all others. It was my unhappy lot not only to belong to a religious slaveholder, but to live in a community of such religionists. Very near Mr. Freeland lived the Rev. Daniel Weeden, and in the same neighborhood lived the Rev. Rigby Hopkins. These were members and ministers in the Reformed Methodist Church. Mr. Weeden owned, among others, a woman slave, whose name I have forgotten. This woman's back, for weeks, was kept literally raw, made so by the lash of this merciless, *religious* wretch. He used to hire hands. His maxim was, Behave well or behave ill, it is the duty of a master occasionally to whip a slave, to remind him of his master's authority. Such was his theory, and such his practice.

Mr. Hopkins was even worse than Mr. Weeden. His chief boast was his ability to manage slaves. The peculiar feature of his government was that of whipping slaves in advance of deserving it. He always managed to have one or more of his slaves to whip every Monday morning. He did this to alarm their fears, and strike terror into those who escaped. His plan was to whip for the smallest offences, to prevent the commission of large ones. Mr. Hopkins could always find some excuse for whipping a slave. It would astonish one, unaccustomed to a slaveholding life, to see with what wonderful ease a slaveholder can find things, of which to make occasion to whip a slave. A mere look, word, or motion,—a mistake, accident, or want of power,—are all matters for which a slave may be whipped at any time. Does a slave look dissatisfied? It is said, he has the devil in him, and it must be whipped out. Does he speak loudly when spoken to by his master? Then he is getting high-minded, and should be taken down a button-hole lower. Does he forget to pull off his hat at the approach of a white person? Then he is wanting in reverence, and should be whipped for it. Does he ever venture to vindicate his conduct, when censured for it? Then he is guilty of impudence,—one of the greatest crimes of which a slave can be guilty. Does he ever venture to suggest a different mode of doing things from that pointed out by his master? He is indeed presumptuous, and getting above himself; and nothing less than a flogging will do for him. Does he, while ploughing, break a plough,—or, while hoeing, break a hoe? It is owing to his carelessness, and for it a slave must always be whipped. Mr. Hopkins could always find something of this sort to justify the use of the lash, and he seldom failed to embrace such opportunities. There was not a man in the whole county, with whom the slaves who had the getting their own home, would not prefer to live, rather than with this Rev. Mr. Hopkins. And yet there was not a man any where round, who made higher professions of religion, or was more active in revivals,—more attentive to the class, love-feast, prayer and preaching meetings, or more devotional in his family,—that prayed earlier, later, louder, and longer,—than this same reverend slave-driver, Rigby Hopkins.

But to return to Mr. Freeland, and to my experience while in his employment. He, like Mr. Covey, gave us enough to eat; but, unlike Mr. Covey, he also gave us sufficient time to take our meals. He worked us hard, but always between sunrise and sunset. He required a good deal of work to be done, but gave us good tools with which to work. His farm was large, but he employed hands enough to work it, and with ease, compared with many of his neighbors. My treatment, while in his employment, was heavenly, compared with what I experienced at the hands of Mr. Edward Covey.

Mr. Freeland was himself the owner of but two slaves. Their names were Henry Harris and John Harris. The rest of his hands he hired. These consisted of myself, Sandy Jenkins,[8] and Handy Caldwell. Henry and John were quite intelligent, and in a very little while after I went there, I succeeded in creating in them a strong desire to learn how to read. This desire soon sprang up in the others also. They very soon mustered up some old spelling-books, and nothing would do but that I must keep a Sabbath school. I agreed to do so, and accordingly devoted my Sundays to teaching these my loved fellow-slaves how to read. Neither of them knew his letters when I went there. Some of the slaves of the neighboring farms found what was going on, and also availed themselves of this little opportunity to learn to read. It was understood, among all who came, that there must be as little display about it as possible. It was necessary to keep our religious masters at St. Michael's unacquainted with the fact, that, instead of spending the Sabbath in wrestling, boxing, and drinking whisky, we were trying to learn how to read the will of God; for they had much rather see us engaged in those degrading sports, than to see us behaving like intellectual, moral, and accountable beings. My blood boils as I think of the bloody manner in which Messrs. Wright Fairbanks and Garrison West, both class-leaders, in connection with many others, rushed in upon us with sticks and stones, and broke up our virtuous little Sabbath school, at St. Michael's—all calling themselves Christians! humble followers of the Lord Jesus Christ! But I am again digressing.

I held my Sabbath school at the house of a free colored man, whose name I deem it imprudent to mention; for should it be known, it might embarrass him greatly, though the crime of holding the school was committed ten years ago. I had at one time over forty scholars, and those of the right sort, ardently desiring to learn. They were of all ages, though mostly men and women. I look back to those Sundays with an amount of pleasure not to be expressed. They were great days to my soul. The work of instructing my dear fellow-slaves was the sweetest engagement with which I was ever blessed. We loved each other, and to leave them at the close of the Sabbath was a severe cross indeed. When I think that those precious souls are to-day shut up in the prison-house of slavery, my feelings overcome me, and I am almost ready to ask, "Does a righteous God govern the universe? and for what does he hold the thunders in his right hand, if not to smite the oppressor, and deliver the spoiled out of the hand of the spoiler?" These dear souls came not to Sabbath school because it was popular to do so, nor did I teach them because it was reputable to be thus engaged. Every moment they spent in that school, they were liable to be taken up, and given thirty-nine lashes. They came because they wished to learn. Their minds had been starved by their cruel masters. They had been shut up in

---

8. This is the same man who gave me the roots to prevent my being whipped by Mr. Covey. He was "a clever soul." We used frequently to talk about the fight with Covey, and as often as we did so, he would claim my success as the result of the roots which he gave me. This superstition is very common among the more ignorant slaves. A slave seldom dies but that his death is attributed to trickery [Douglass's note].

mental darkness. I taught them, because it was the delight of my soul to be doing something that looked like bettering the condition of my race. I kept up my school nearly the whole year I lived with Mr. Freeland; and, beside my Sabbath school, I devoted three evenings in the week, during the winter, to teaching the slaves at home. And I have the happiness to know, that several of those who came to Sabbath school learned how to read; and that one, at least, is now free through my agency.

The year passed off smoothly. It seemed only about half as long as the year which preceded it. I went through it without receiving a single blow. I will give Mr. Freeland the credit of being the best master I ever had, *till I became my own master*. For the ease with which I passed the year, I was, however, somewhat indebted to the society of my fellow-slaves. They were noble souls; they not only possessed loving hearts, but brave ones. We were linked and interlinked with each other. I loved them with a love stronger than any thing I have experienced since. It is sometimes said that we slaves do not love and confide in each other. In answer to this assertion, I can say, I never loved any or confided in any people more than my fellow-slaves, and especially those with whom I lived at Mr. Freeland's. I believe we would have died for each other. We never undertook to do any thing, of any importance, without a mutual consultation. We never moved separately. We were one; and as much so by our tempers and dispositions, as by the mutual hardships to which we were necessarily subjected by our condition as slaves.

At the close of the year 1834, Mr. Freeland again hired me of my master, for the year 1835. But, by this time, I began to want to live *upon free land* as well as *with Freeland*; and I was no longer content, therefore, to live with him or any other slaveholder. I began, with the commencement of the year, to prepare myself for a final struggle, which should decide my fate one way or the other. My tendency was upward. I was fast approaching manhood, and year after year had passed, and I was still a slave. These thoughts roused me—I must do something. I therefore resolved that 1835 should not pass without witnessing an attempt, on my part, to secure my liberty. But I was not willing to cherish this determination alone. My fellow-slaves were dear to me. I was anxious to have them participate with me in this, my life-giving determination. I therefore, though with great prudence, commenced early to ascertain their views and feelings in regard to their condition, and to imbue their minds with thoughts of freedom. I bent myself to devising ways and means for our escape, and meanwhile strove, on all fitting occasions, to impress them with the gross fraud and inhumanity of slavery. I went first to Henry, next to John, then to the others. I found, in them all, warm hearts and noble spirits. They were ready to hear, and ready to act when a feasible plan should be proposed. This was what I wanted. I talked to them of our want of manhood, if we submitted to our enslavement without at least one noble effort to be free. We met often, and consulted frequently, and told our hopes and fears, recounted the difficulties, real and imagined, which we should be called on to meet. At times we were almost disposed to give up, and try to content ourselves with our wretched lot; at others, we were firm and unbending in our determination to go. Whenever we suggested any plan, there was shrinking—the odds were fearful. Our path was beset with the greatest obstacles; and if we succeeded in gaining the end of it, our right to be free was yet questionable—we were yet liable to be returned to bondage. We could see no spot, this side of the ocean, where we could be free. We knew nothing about Canada. Our knowledge of the north did not extend farther than New York; and to go there, and be forever harassed with the frightful liability of being returned to slavery—with the certainty of being treated tenfold worse than before—the thought was truly a horrible one, and one which it was not easy to overcome. The case sometimes stood thus: At every gate through which we were to pass, we saw a watchman—at every ferry a guard—on every bridge a sentinel—and in every wood a patrol. We were hemmed in upon every side. Here were the difficulties, real or imagined—the good to be sought, and the evil to be shunned. On the one hand, there stood slavery, a stern reality, glaring frightfully upon us,—its robes already crimsoned with the blood of millions, and even now feasting itself greedily upon our own flesh. On the other hand, away back in the dim distance, under the flickering light of the north star, behind some craggy hill or snow-covered mountain, stood a doubtful freedom—half frozen—beckoning us to come and share its hospitality. This in itself was sometimes enough to stagger us; but when we permitted ourselves to survey the road, we were frequently appalled. Upon either side we saw grim death, assuming the most horrid shapes. Now it was starvation, causing us to eat our own flesh;—now we were contending with the waves, and were drowned;—now we were overtaken, and torn to pieces by the fangs of the terrible blood-hound. We were stung by scorpions, chased by wild beasts, bitten by snakes, and finally, after having nearly reached the desired spot,—after swimming rivers, encountering wild beasts, sleeping in the woods, suffering hunger and nakedness,—we were overtaken by our pursuers, and, in our resistance, we were shot dead upon the spot! I say, this picture sometimes appalled us, and made us

> "rather bear those ills we had,
> Than fly to others, that we knew not of."[9]

In coming to a fixed determination to run away, we did more than Patrick Henry,[1] when he resolved upon liberty or death. With us it was a doubtful liberty at most, and almost certain death if we failed. For my part, I should prefer death to hopeless bondage.

Sandy, one of our number, gave up the notion, but still encouraged us. Our company then consisted of Henry Harris, John Harris, Henry Bailey, Charles Roberts, and myself. Henry Bailey was my uncle, and belonged to my master. Charles married my aunt: he belonged to my master's father-in-law, Mr. William Hamilton.

The plan we finally concluded upon was, to get a large canoe belonging to Mr. Hamilton, and upon the Saturday night previous to Easter holidays, paddle directly up the Chesapeake Bay. On our arrival at the head of the bay, a distance of seventy or eighty miles from where we lived, it was our purpose to turn our canoe adrift, and follow the guidance of the north star till we got beyond the limits of Maryland. Our reason for taking the water route was, that we were

---

9. Shakespeare's *Hamlet* 3.1.81–82: "rather bear those ills we have, / Than fly to others, that we know not of."

1. American statesman and orator (1736–1799) whose most famous utterance was "Give me liberty or give me death."

less liable to be suspected as runaways; we hoped to be regarded as fishermen; whereas, if we should take the land route, we should be subjected to interruptions of almost every kind. Any one having a white face, and being so disposed, could stop us, and subject us to examination.

The week before our intended start, I wrote several protections, one for each of us. As well as I can remember, they were in the following words, to wit:—

> "This is to certify that I, the undersigned, have given the bearer, my servant, full liberty to go to Baltimore, and spend the Easter holidays. Written with mine own hand, &c., 1835.
>
> "WILLIAM HAMILTON,
> "Near St. Michael's, in Talbot county, Maryland."

We were not going to Baltimore; but, in going up the bay, we went toward Baltimore, and these protections were only intended to protect us while on the bay.

As the time drew near for our departure, our anxiety became more and more intense. It was truly a matter of life and death with us. The strength of our determination was about to be fully tested. At this time, I was very active in explaining every difficulty, removing every doubt, dispelling every fear, and inspiring all with the firmness indispensable to success in our undertaking; assuring them that half was gained the instant we made the move; we had talked long enough; we were now ready to move; if not now, we never should be; and if we did not intend to move now, we had as well fold our arms, sit down, and acknowledge ourselves fit only to be slaves. This, none of us were prepared to acknowledge. Every man stood firm; and at our last meeting, we pledged ourselves afresh, in the most solemn manner, that, at the time appointed, we would certainly start in pursuit of freedom. This was in the middle of the week, at the end of which we were to be off. We went, as usual, to our several fields of labor, but with bosoms highly agitated with thoughts of our truly hazardous undertaking. We tried to conceal our feelings as much as possible; and I think we succeeded very well.

After a painful waiting, the Saturday morning, whose night was to witness our departure, came. I hailed it with joy, bring what of sadness it might. Friday night was a sleepless one for me. I was, by common consent, at the head of the whole affair. The responsibility of success or failure lay heavily upon me. The glory of the one, and the confusion of the other, were alike mine. The first two hours of that morning were such as I never experienced before, and hope never to again. Early in the morning, we went, as usual, to the field. We were spreading manure; and all at once, while thus engaged, I was overwhelmed with an indescribable feeling, in the fulness of which I turned to Sandy, who was near by, and said, "We are betrayed!" "Well," said he, "that thought has this moment struck me." We said no more. I was never more certain of any thing.

The horn was blown as usual, and we went up from the field to the house for breakfast. I went for the form, more than for want of any thing to eat that morning. Just as I got to the house, in looking out at the lane gate, I saw four white men, with two colored men. The white men were on horseback, and the colored ones were walking behind, as if tied. I watched them a few moments till they got up to our lane gate. Here they halted, and tied the colored men to the gate-post. I was not yet certain as to what the matter was. In a few moments, in rode Mr. Hamilton, with a speed betokening great excitement. He came to the door, and inquired if Master William was in. He was told he was at the barn. Mr. Hamilton, without dismounting, rode up to the barn with extraordinary speed. In a few moments, he and Mr. Freeland returned to the house. By this time, the three constables rode up, and in great haste dismounted, tied their horses, and met Master William and Mr. Hamilton returning from the barn; and after talking awhile, they all walked up to the kitchen door. There was no one in the kitchen but myself and John. Henry and Sandy were up at the barn. Mr. Freeland put his head in at the door, and called me by name, saying, there were some gentlemen at the door who wished to see me. I stepped to the door, and inquired what they wanted. They at once seized me, and, without giving me any satisfaction, tied me—lashing my hands closely together. I insisted upon knowing what the matter was. They at length said, that they had learned I had been in a "scrape," and that I was to be examined before my master; and if their information proved false, I should not be hurt.

In a few moments, they succeeded in tying John. They then turned to Henry, who had by this time returned, and commanded him to cross his hands. "I won't!" said Henry, in a firm tone, indicating his readiness to meet the consequences of his refusal. "Won't you?" said Tom Graham, the constable. "No, I won't!" said Henry, in a still stronger tone. With this, two of the constables pulled out their shining pistols, and swore, by their Creator, that they would make him cross his hands or kill him. Each cocked his pistol, and, with fingers on the trigger, walked up to Henry, saying, at the same time, if he did not cross his hands, they would blow his damned heart out. "Shoot me, shoot me!" said Henry; "you can't kill me but once. Shoot, shoot,—and be damned! *I won't be tied!*" This he said in a tone of loud defiance; and at the same time, with a motion as quick as lightning, he with one single stroke dashed the pistols from the hand of each constable. As he did this, all hands fell upon him, and, after beating him some time, they finally overpowered him, and got him tied.

During the scuffle, I managed, I know not how, to get my pass out, and, without being discovered, put it into the fire. We were all now tied; and just as we were to leave for Easton jail, Betsy Freeland, mother of William Freeland, came to the door with her hands full of biscuits, and divided them between Henry and John. She then delivered herself of a speech, to the following effect:—addressing herself to me, she said, "*You devil! You yellow devil!* it was you that put it into the heads of Henry and John to run away. But for you, you long-legged mulatto devil! Henry nor John would never have thought of such a thing." I made no reply, and was immediately hurried off towards St. Michael's. Just a moment previous to the scuffle with Henry, Mr. Hamilton suggested the propriety of making a search for the protections which he had understood Frederick had written for himself and the rest. But, just at the moment he was about carrying his proposal into effect, his aid was needed in helping to tie Henry; and the excitement attending the scuffle caused them either to forget, or to deem it unsafe, under the circumstances, to search. So we were not yet convicted of the intention to run away.

When we got about half way to St. Michael's, while the constables having us in charge were looking ahead, Henry inquired of me what he should do with his pass. I told him to eat it with his biscuit, and own nothing; and we passed the word around, "*Own nothing*"; and "*Own nothing!*" said we all. Our confidence in each other was unshaken. We were resolved to succeed or fail together, after the calamity had befallen us as much as before. We were now prepared for any thing. We were to be dragged that morning fifteen miles behind horses, and then to be placed in the Easton jail. When we reached St. Michael's, we underwent a sort of examination. We all denied that we ever intended to run away. We did this more to bring out the evidence against us, than from any hope of getting clear of being sold; for, as I have said, we were ready for that. The fact was, we cared but little where we went, so we went together. Our greatest concern was about separation. We dreaded that more than any thing this side of death. We found the evidence against us to be the testimony of one person; our master would not tell who it was; but we came to a unanimous decision among ourselves as to who their informant was. We were sent off to the jail at Easton. When we got there, we were delivered up to the sheriff, Mr. Joseph Graham, and by him placed in jail. Henry, John, and myself, were placed in one room together—Charles, and Henry Bailey, in another. Their object in separating us was to hinder concert.

We had been in jail scarcely twenty minutes, when a swarm of slave traders, and agents for slave traders, flocked into jail to look at us, and to ascertain if we were for sale. Such a set of beings I never saw before! I felt myself surrounded by so many fiends from perdition. A band of pirates never looked more like their father, the devil. They laughed and grinned over us, saying, "Ah, my boys! we have got you, haven't we?" And after taunting us in various ways, they one by one went into an examination of us, with intent to ascertain our value. They would impudently ask us if we would not like to have them for our masters. We would make them no answer, and leave them to find out as best they could. Then they would curse and swear at us, telling us that they could take the devil out of us in a very little while, if we were only in their hands.

While in jail, we found ourselves in much more comfortable quarters than we expected when we went there. We did not get much to eat, nor that which was very good; but we had a good clean room, from the windows of which we could see what was going on in the street, which was very much better than though we had been placed in one of the dark, damp cells. Upon the whole, we got along very well, so far as the jail and its keeper were concerned. Immediately after the holidays were over, contrary to all our expectations, Mr. Hamilton and Mr. Freeland came up to Easton, and took Charles, the two Henrys, and John, out of jail, and carried them home, leaving me alone. I regarded this separation as a final one. It caused me more pain than any thing else in the whole transaction. I was ready for any thing rather than separation. I supposed that they had consulted together, and had decided that, as I was the whole cause of the intention of the others to run away, it was hard to make the innocent suffer with the guilty; and that they had, therefore, concluded to take the others home, and sell me, as a warning to the others that remained. It is due to the noble Henry to say, he seemed almost as reluctant at leaving the prison as at leaving home to come to the prison. But we knew we should, in all probability, be separated, if we were sold; and since he was in their hands, he concluded to go peaceably home.

I was now left to my fate. I was all alone, and within the walls of a stone prison. But a few days before, and I was full of hope. I expected to have been safe in a land of freedom; but now I was covered with gloom, sunk down to the utmost despair. I thought the possibility of freedom was gone. I was kept in this way about one week, at the end of which, Captain Auld, my master, to my surprise and utter astonishment, came up, and took me out, with the intention of sending me, with a gentleman of his acquaintance, into Alabama. But, from some cause or other, he did not send me to Alabama, but concluded to send me back to Baltimore, to live again with his brother Hugh, and to learn a trade.

Thus, after an absence of three years and one month, I was once more permitted to return to my old home at Baltimore. My master sent me away, because there existed against me a very great prejudice in the community, and he feared I might be killed.

In a few weeks after I went to Baltimore, Master Hugh hired me to Mr. William Gardner, an extensive ship-builder, on Fell's Point. I was put there to learn how to calk. It, however, proved a very unfavorable place for the accomplishment of this object. Mr. Gardner was engaged that spring in building two large man-of-war brigs, professedly for the Mexican government. The vessels were to be launched in the July of that year, and in failure thereof, Mr. Gardner was to lose a considerable sum; so that when I entered, all was hurry. There was no time to learn any thing. Every man had to do that which he knew how to do. In entering the shipyard, my orders from Mr. Gardner were, to do whatever the carpenters commanded me to do. This was placing me at the beck and call of about seventy-five men. I was to regard all these as masters. Their word was to be my law. My situation was a most trying one. At times I needed a dozen pair of hands. I was called a dozen ways in the space of a single minute. Three or four voices would strike my ear at the same moment. It was—"Fred., come help me to cant this timber here."—"Fred., come carry this timber yonder."—"Fred., bring that roller here."—"Fred., go get a fresh can of water."—"Fred., come help saw off the end of this timber."—"Fred., go quick, and get the crowbar."—"Fred., hold on the end of this fall."—"Fred., go to the blacksmith's shop, and get a new punch."—"Hurra,[2] Fred.! run and bring me a cold chisel."—"I say, Fred., bear a hand, and get up a fire as quick as lightning under that steam-box."—"Halloo, nigger! come, turn this grindstone."—"Come, come! move, move! and *bowse*[3] this timber forward."—"I say, darky, blast your eyes, why don't you heat up some pitch?"—"Halloo! halloo! halloo!" (Three voices at the same time.) "Come here!—Go there!—Hold on where you are! Damn you, if you move, I'll knock your brains out!"

This was my school for eight months, and I might have remained there longer, but for a most horrid fight I had with four of the white apprentices, in which my left eye was nearly knocked out, and I was horribly mangled in other respects. The facts in the case were these: Until a very little while after I went there, white and black ship-carpenters worked side by side, and no one seemed to see any impropriety in it. All hands seemed to be very well satisfied. Many of the black carpenters were freemen. Things seemed to be going on very well. All at once, the white carpenters knocked off, and said they would not work

2. Hurry.
3. Lift or haul (usually with the help of block and tackle).

with free colored workmen. Their reason for this, as alleged, was, that if free colored carpenters were encouraged, they would soon take the trade into their own hands, and poor white men would be thrown out of employment. They therefore felt called upon at once to put a stop to it. And, taking advantage of Mr. Gardner's necessities, they broke off, swearing they would work no longer, unless he would discharge his black carpenters. Now, though this did not extend to me in form, it did reach me in fact. My fellow-apprentices very soon began to feel it degrading to them to work with me. They began to put on airs, and talk about the "niggers" taking the country, saying we all ought to be killed; and, being encouraged by the journeymen, they commenced making my condition as hard as they could, by hectoring me around, and sometimes striking me. I, of course, kept the vow I made after the fight with Mr. Covey, and struck back again, regardless of consequences; and while I kept them from combining, I succeeded very well; for I could whip the whole of them, taking them separately. They, however, at length combined, and came upon me, armed with sticks, stones, and heavy handspikes. One came in front with a half brick. There was one at each side of me, and one behind me. While I was attending to those in front, and on either side, the one behind ran up with the handspike, and struck me a heavy blow upon the head. It stunned me. I fell, and with this they all ran upon me, and fell to beating me with their fists. I let them lay on for a while, gathering strength. In an instant, I gave a sudden surge, and rose to my hands and knees. Just as I did that, one of their number gave me, with his heavy boot, a powerful kick in the left eye. My eyeball seemed to have burst. When they saw my eye closed, and badly swollen, they left me. With this I seized the handspike, and for a time pursued them. But here the carpenters interfered, and I thought I might as well give it up. It was impossible to stand my hand against so many. All this took place in sight of not less than fifty white ship-carpenters, and not one interposed a friendly word; but some cried, "Kill the damned nigger! Kill him! kill him! He struck a white person." I found my only chance for life was in flight. I succeeded in getting away without an additional blow, and barely so; for to strike a white man is death by Lynch law,— and that was the law in Mr. Gardner's ship-yard; nor is there much of any other out of Mr. Gardner's ship-yard.

I went directly home, and told the story of my wrongs to Master Hugh; and I am happy to say of him, irreligious as he was, his conduct was heavenly, compared with that of his brother Thomas under similar circumstances. He listened attentively to my narration of the circumstances leading to the savage outrage, and gave many proofs of his strong indignation of it. The heart of my once overkind mistress was again melted into pity. My puffed-out eye and blood-covered face moved her to tears. She took a chair by me, washed the blood from my face, and, with a mother's tenderness, bound up my head, covering the wounded eye with a lean piece of fresh beef. It was almost compensation for my suffering to witness, once more, a manifestation of kindness from this, my once affectionate old mistress. Master Hugh was very much enraged. He gave expression to his feelings by pouring out curses upon the heads of those who did the deed. As soon as I got a little the better of my bruises, he took me with him to Esquire Watson's, on Bond Street, to see what could be done about the matter. Mr. Watson inquired who saw the assault committed. Master Hugh told him it was done in Mr. Gardner's ship-yard, at midday, where there were a large company of men at work. "As to that," he said, "the deed was done, and there was no question as to who did it." His answer was, he could do nothing in the case, unless some white man would come forward and testify. He could issue no warrant on my word. If I had been killed in the presence of a thousand colored people, their testimony combined would have been insufficient to have arrested one of the murderers. Master Hugh, for once, was compelled to say this state of things was too bad. Of course, it was impossible to get any white man to volunteer his testimony in my behalf, and against the white young men. Even those who may have sympathized with me were not prepared to do this. It required a degree of courage unknown to them to do so; for just at that time, the slightest manifestation of humanity toward a colored person was denounced as abolitionism, and that name subjected its bearer to frightful liabilities. The watchwords of the bloody-minded in that region, and in those days, were, "Damn the abolitionists!" and "Damn the niggers!" There was nothing done, and probably nothing would have been done if I had been killed. Such was, and such remains, the state of things in the Christian city of Baltimore.

Master Hugh, finding he could get no redress, refused to let me go back again to Mr. Gardner. He kept me himself, and his wife dressed my wound till I was again restored to health. He then took me into the ship-yard of which he was foreman, in the employment of Mr. Walter Price. There I was immediately set to calking, and very soon learned the art of using my mallet and irons. In the course of one year from the time I left Mr. Gardner's, I was able to command the highest wages given to the most experienced calkers. I was now of some importance to my master. I was bringing him from six to seven dollars per week. I sometimes brought him nine dollars per week: my wages were a dollar and a half a day. After learning how to calk, I sought my own employment, made my own contracts, and collected the money which I earned. My pathway became much more smooth than before; my condition was now much more comfortable. When I could get no calking to do, I did nothing. During these leisure times, those old notions about freedom would steal over me again. When in Mr. Gardner's employment, I was kept in such a perpetual whirl of excitement, I could think of nothing, scarcely, but my life; and in thinking of my life, I almost forgot my liberty. I have observed this in my experience of slavery,—that whenever my condition was improved, instead of its increasing my contentment, it only increased my desire to be free, and set me to thinking of plans to gain my freedom. I have found that, to make a contented slave, it is necessary to make a thoughtless one. It is necessary to darken his moral and mental vision, and, as far as possible, to annihilate the power of reason. He must be made to feel that slavery is right; and he can be brought to that only when he ceases to be a man.

I was now getting, as I have said, one dollar and fifty cents per day. I contracted for it; I earned it; it was paid to me; it was rightfully my own; yet, upon each returning Saturday night, I was compelled to deliver every cent of that money to Master Hugh. And why? Not because he earned it,—not because he had any hand in earning it,—not because I owed it to him,—nor because he possessed the slightest shadow of a right to it; but solely because he had the power to compel me to give it up. The right of the grim-visaged pirate upon the high seas is exactly the same.

CHAPTER XI

I now come to that part of my life during which I planned, and finally succeeded in making, my escape from slavery. But before narrating any of the peculiar circumstances, I deem it proper to make known my intention not to state all the facts connected with the transaction. My reasons for pursuing this course may be understood from the following: First, were I to give a minute statement of all the facts, it is not only possible, but quite probable, that others would thereby be involved in the most embarrassing difficulties. Secondly, such a statement would most undoubtedly induce greater vigilance on the part of slaveholders than has existed heretofore among them; which would, of course, be the means of guarding a door whereby some dear brother bondman might escape his galling chains. I deeply regret the necessity that impels me to suppress any thing of importance connected with my experience in slavery. It would afford me great pleasure indeed, as well as materially add to the interest of my narrative, were I at liberty to gratify a curiosity, which I know exists in the minds of many, by an accurate statement of all the facts pertaining to my most fortunate escape. But I must deprive myself of this pleasure, and the curious of the gratification which such a statement would afford. I would allow myself to suffer under the greatest imputations which evil-minded men might suggest, rather than exculpate myself, and thereby run the hazard of closing the slightest avenue by which a brother slave might clear himself of the chains and fetters of slavery.

I have never approved of the very public manner in which some of our western friends have conducted what they call the *underground railroad*,[4] but which, I think, by their open declarations, has been made most emphatically the *upperground railroad*. I honor those good men and women for their noble daring, and applaud them for willingly subjecting themselves to bloody persecution, by openly avowing their participation in the escape of slaves. I, however, can see very little good resulting from such a course, either to themselves or the slaves escaping; while, upon the other hand, I see and feel assured that those open declarations are a positive evil to the slaves remaining, who are seeking to escape. They do nothing towards enlightening the slave, whilst they do much towards enlightening the master. They stimulate him to greater watchfulness, and enhance his power to capture his slave. We owe something to the slaves south of the line[5] as well as to those north of it; and in aiding the latter on their way to freedom, we should be careful to do nothing which would be likely to hinder the former from escaping from slavery. I would keep the merciless slaveholder profoundly ignorant of the means of flight adopted by the slave. I would leave him to imagine himself surrounded by myriads of invisible tormentors, ever ready to snatch from his infernal grasp his trembling prey. Let him be left to feel his way in the dark; let darkness commensurate with his crime hover over him; and let him feel that at every step he takes, in pursuit of the flying bondman, he is running the frightful risk of having his hot brains dashed out by an invisible agency. Let us render the tyrant no aid; let us

---

4. A system set up by opponents of slavery to help fugitive slaves from the South escape to free states and to Canada.

5. The Mason-Dixon line, the boundary between Pennsylvania and Maryland and between slave and free states.

not hold the light by which he can trace the footprints of our flying brother. But enough of this. I will now proceed to the statement of those facts, connected with my escape, for which I am alone responsible, and for which no one can be made to suffer but myself.

In the early part of the year 1838, I became quite restless. I could see no reason why I should, at the end of each week, pour the reward of my toil into the purse of my master. When I carried to him my weekly wages, he would, after counting the money, look me in the face with a robber-like fierceness, and ask, "Is this all?" He was satisfied with nothing less than the last cent. He would, however, when I made him six dollars, sometimes give me six cents, to encourage me. It had the opposite effect. I regarded it as a sort of admission of my right to the whole. The fact that he gave me any part of my wages was proof, to my mind, that he believed me entitled to the whole of them. I always felt worse for having received any thing; for I feared that the giving me a few cents would ease his conscience, and make him feel himself to be a pretty honorable sort of robber. My discontent grew upon me. I was ever on the look-out for means of escape; and, finding no direct means, I determined to try to hire my time, with a view of getting money with which to make my escape. In the spring of 1838, when Master Thomas came to Baltimore to purchase his spring goods, I got an opportunity, and applied to him to allow me to hire my time. He unhesitatingly refused my request, and told me this was another stratagem by which to escape. He told me I could go nowhere but that he could get me; and that, in the event of my running away, he should spare no pains in his efforts to catch me. He exhorted me to content myself, and be obedient. He told me, if I would be happy, I must lay out no plans for the future. He said, if I behaved myself properly, he would take care of me. Indeed, he advised me to complete thoughtlessness of the future, and taught me to depend solely upon him for happiness. He seemed to see fully the pressing necessity of setting aside my intellectual nature, in order to [insure] contentment in slavery. But in spite of him, and even in spite of myself, I continued to think, and to think about the injustice of my enslavement, and the means of escape.

About two months after this, I applied to Master Hugh for the privilege of hiring my time. He was not acquainted with the fact that I had applied to Master Thomas, and had been refused. He too, at first, seemed disposed to refuse; but, after some reflection, he granted me the privilege, and proposed the following terms: I was to be allowed all my time, make all contracts with those for whom I worked, and find my own employment; and, in return for this liberty, I was to pay him three dollars at the end of each week; find myself in calking tools, and in board and clothing. My board was two dollars and a half per week. This, with the wear and tear of clothing and calking tools, made my regular expenses about six dollars per week. This amount I was compelled to make up, or relinquish the privilege of hiring my time. Rain or shine, work or no work, at the end of each week the money must be forthcoming, or I must give up my privilege. This arrangement, it will be perceived, was decidedly in my master's favor. It relieved him of all need of looking after me. His money was sure. He received all the benefits of slave-holding without its evils; while I endured all the evils of a slave, and suffered all the care and anxiety of a freeman. I found it a hard bargain. But, hard as it was, I thought it better than the old mode of getting along. It was a step towards freedom to be allowed to bear the responsibilities of a freeman, and

I was determined to hold on upon it. I bent myself to the work of making money. I was ready to work at night as well as day, and by the most untiring perseverance and industry, I made enough to meet my expenses, and lay up a little money every week. I went on thus from May till August. Master Hugh then refused to allow me to hire my time longer. The ground for his refusal was a failure on my part, one Saturday night, to pay him for my week's time. This failure was occasioned by my attending a camp meeting about ten miles from Baltimore. During the week, I had entered into an engagement with a number of young friends to start from Baltimore to the camp ground early Saturday evening; and being detained by my employer, I was unable to get down to Master Hugh's without disappointing the company. I knew that Master Hugh was in no special need of the money that night. I therefore decided to go to camp meeting, and upon my return pay him the three dollars. I staid at the camp meeting one day longer than I intended when I left. But as soon as I returned, I called upon him to pay him what he considered his due. I found him very angry; he could scarce restrain his wrath. He said he had a great mind to give me a severe whipping. He wished to know how I dared go out of the city without asking his permission. I told him I hired my time, and while I paid him the price which he asked for it, I did not know that I was bound to ask him when and where I should go. This reply troubled him, and, after reflecting a few moments, he turned to me, and said I should hire my time no longer; that the next thing he should know of, I would be running away. Upon the same plea, he told me to bring my tools and clothing home forthwith. I did so; but instead of seeking work, as I had been accustomed to do previously to hiring my time, I spent the whole week without the performance of a single stroke of work. I did this in retaliation. Saturday night, he called upon me as usual for my week's wages. I told him I had no wages; I had done no work that week. Here we were upon the point of coming to blows. He raved, and swore his determination to get hold of me. I did not allow myself a single word; but was resolved, if he laid the weight of his hand upon me, it should be blow for blow. He did not strike me, but told me that he would find me in constant employment in future. I thought the matter over during the next day, Sunday, and finally resolved upon the third day of September, as the day upon which I would make a second attempt to secure my freedom. I now had three weeks during which to prepare for my journey. Early on Monday morning, before Master Hugh had time to make any engagement for me, I went out and got employment of Mr. Butler, at his ship-yard near the draw-bridge, upon what is called the City Block, thus making it unnecessary for him to seek employment for me. At the end of the week, I brought him between eight and nine dollars. He seemed very well pleased, and asked me why I did not do the same the week before. He little knew what my plans were. My object in working steadily was to remove any suspicion he might entertain of my intent to run away; and in this I succeeded admirably. I suppose he thought I was never better satisfied with my condition than at the very time during which I was planning my escape. The second week passed, and again I carried him my full wages; and so well pleased was he, that he gave me twenty-five cents, (quite a large sum for a slaveholder to give a slave,) and bade me to make a good use of it. I told him I would.

Things went on without very smoothly indeed, but within there was trouble. It is impossible for me to describe my feelings as the time of my contemplated start drew near. I had a number of warm-hearted friends in Baltimore,—friends that I loved almost as I did my life,—and the thought of being separated from them forever was painful beyond expression. It is my opinion that thousands would escape from slavery, who now remain, but for the strong cords of affection that bind them to their friends. The thought of leaving my friends was decidedly the most painful thought with which I had to contend. The love of them was my tender point, and shook my decision more than all things else. Besides the pain of separation, the dread and apprehension of a failure exceeded what I had experienced at my first attempt. The appalling defeat I then sustained returned to torment me. I felt assured that, if I failed in this attempt, my case would be a hopeless one—it would seal my fate as a slave forever. I could not hope to get off with any thing less than the severest punishment, and being placed beyond the means of escape. It required no very vivid imagination to depict the most frightful scenes through which I should have to pass, in case I failed. The wretchedness of slavery, and the blessedness of freedom, were perpetually before me. It was life and death with me. But I remained firm, and, according to my resolution, on the third day of September, 1838, I left my chains, and succeeded in reaching New York without the slightest interruption of any kind. How I did so,— what means I adopted,— what direction I travelled, and by what mode of conveyance,—I must leave unexplained, for the reasons before mentioned.

I have been frequently asked how I felt when I found myself in a free State. I have never been able to answer the question with any satisfaction to myself. It was a moment of the highest excitement I ever experienced. I suppose I felt as one may imagine the unarmed mariner to feel when he is rescued by a friendly man-of-war from the pursuit of a pirate. In writing to a dear friend, immediately after my arrival at New York, I said I felt like one who had escaped a den of hungry lions. This state of mind, however, very soon subsided; and I was again seized with a feeling of great insecurity and loneliness. I was yet liable to be taken back, and subjected to all the tortures of slavery. This in itself was enough to damp the ardor of my enthusiasm. But the loneliness overcame me. There I was in the midst of thousands, and yet a perfect stranger; without home and without friends, in the midst of thousands of my own brethren—children of a common Father, and yet I dared not to unfold to any one of them my sad condition. I was afraid to speak to any one for fear of speaking to the wrong one, and thereby falling into the hands of money-loving kidnappers, whose business it was to lie in wait for the panting fugitive, as the ferocious beasts of the forest lie in wait for their prey. The motto which I adopted when I started from slavery was this—"Trust no man!" I saw in every white man an enemy, and in almost every colored man cause for distrust. It was a most painful situation; and, to understand it, one must needs experience it, or imagine himself in similar circumstances. Let him be a fugitive slave in a strange land—a land given up to be the hunting-ground for slaveholders—whose inhabitants are legalized kidnappers—where he is every moment subjected to the terrible liability of being seized upon by his fellow-men, as the hideous crocodile seizes upon his prey!—I say, let him place himself in my situation—without home or friends—without money or credit—wanting shelter, and no one to give it—wanting bread, and no money to buy it,—and at the same time let him feel that he is pursued by merciless men-hunters, and in total darkness as to what to do, where to go, or where to stay,—perfectly helpless both as to the means of defence and means of escape,—in the midst of plenty, yet suffering the terrible gnawings of hunger,—in the midst of houses, yet having no home,—among fellow-men, yet feeling as if in the midst of wild beasts, whose greediness to swallow up the trembling and half-famished fugitive is only equalled by that with which the monsters of the deep swallow up the helpless fish upon which they subsist,—I say, let him be placed in this most trying situation,—the situation in which I was placed,—then, and not till then, will he fully appreciate the hardships of, and know how to sympathize with, the toil-worn and whip-scarred fugitive slave.

Thank Heaven, I remained but a short time in this distressed situation. I was relieved from it by the humane hand of Mr. DAVID RUGGLES,[6] whose vigilance, kindness, and perseverance, I shall never forget. I am glad of an opportunity to express, as far as words can, the love and gratitude I bear him. Mr. Ruggles is now afflicted with blindness, and is himself in need of the same kind offices which he was once so forward in the performance of toward others. I had been in New York but a few days, when Mr. Ruggles sought me out, and very kindly took me to his boarding-house at the corner of Church and Lespenard Streets. Mr. Ruggles was then very deeply engaged in the memorable *Darg* case, as well as attending to a number of other fugitive slaves, devising ways and means for their successful escape; and, though watched and hemmed in on almost every side, he seemed to be more than a match for his enemies. Very soon after I went to Mr. Ruggles, he wished to know of me where I wanted to go; as he deemed it unsafe for me to remain in New York. I told him I was a calker, and should like to go where I could get work. I thought of going to Canada; but he decided against it, and in favor of my going to New Bedford, thinking I should be able to get work there at my trade. At this time, Anna,[7] my intended wife, came on; for I wrote to her immediately after my arrival at New York, (notwithstanding my homeless, houseless, and helpless condition,) informing her of my successful flight, and wishing her to come on forthwith. In a few days after her arrival, Mr. Ruggles called in the Rev. J. W. C. Pennington, who, in the presence of Mr. Ruggles, Mrs. Michaels, and two or three others, performed the marriage ceremony, and gave us a certificate, of which the following is an exact copy:—

"THIS may certify, that I joined together in holy matrimony Frederick Johnson[8] and Anna Murray, as man and wife, in the presence of Mr. David Ruggles and Mrs. Michaels.

"JAMES W. C. PENNINGTON.
"*New York, Sept.* 15, 1838."

Upon receiving this certificate, and a five-dollar bill from Mr. Ruggles, I shouldered one part of our baggage, and Anna took up the other, and we set out forthwith to take passage on board of the steamboat John W. Richmond for Newport, on our way to New Bedford. Mr. Ruggles gave me a letter to a Mr. Shaw in Newport, and told me, in case my money did not serve me to New

---

6. A black abolitionist (1810–1849), at this time living in New York, who helped many slaves to escape.

7. She was free [Douglass's note].

8. I had changed my name from Frederick *Bailey* to that of *Johnson* [Douglass's note].

Bedford, to stop in Newport and obtain further assistance; but upon our arrival at Newport, we were so anxious to get to a place of safety, that, notwithstanding we lacked the necessary money to pay our fare, we decided to take seats in the stage, and promise to pay when we got to New Bedford. We were encouraged to do this by two excellent gentlemen, residents of New Bedford, whose names I afterward ascertained to be Joseph Ricketson and William C. Taber. They seemed at once to understand our circumstances, and gave us such assurance of their friendliness as put us fully at ease in their presence. It was good indeed to meet with such friends, at such a time. Upon reaching New Bedford, we were directed to the house of Mr. Nathan Johnson, by whom we were kindly received, and hospitably provided for. Both Mr. and Mrs. Johnson took a deep and lively interest in our welfare. They proved themselves quite worthy of the name of abolitionists. When the stage-driver found us unable to pay our fare, he held on upon our baggage as security for the debt. I had but to mention the fact to Mr. Johnson, and he forthwith advanced the money.

We now began to feel a degree of safety, and to prepare ourselves for the duties and responsibilities of a life of freedom. On the morning after our arrival at New Bedford, while at the breakfast-table, the question arose as to what name I should be called by. The name given me by my mother was, "Frederick Augustus Washington Bailey." I, however, had dispensed with the two middle names long before I left Maryland so that I was generally known by the name of "Frederick Bailey." I started from Baltimore bearing the name of "Stanley." When I got to New York, I again changed my name to "Frederick Johnson," and thought that would be the last change. But when I got to New Bedford, I found it necessary again to change my name. The reason of this necessity was, that there were so many Johnsons in New Bedford, it was already quite difficult to distinguish between them. I gave Mr. Johnson the privilege of choosing me a name, but told him he must not take from me the name of "Frederick." I must hold on to that, to preserve a sense of my identity. Mr. Johnson had just been reading the "Lady of the Lake,"[9] and at once suggested that my name be "Douglass." From that time until now I have been called "Frederick Douglass"; and as I am more widely known by that name than by either of the others, I shall continue to use it as my own.

I was quite disappointed at the general appearance of things in New Bedford. The impression which I had received respecting the character and condition of the people of the north, I found to be singularly erroneous. I had very strangely supposed, while in slavery, that few of the comforts, and scarcely any of the luxuries, of life were enjoyed at the north, compared with what were enjoyed by the slaveholders of the south. I probably came to this conclusion from the fact that northern people owned no slaves. I supposed that they were about upon a level with the non-slaveholding population of the south. I knew *they* were exceedingly poor, and I had been accustomed to regard their poverty as the necessary consequence of their being non-slaveholders. I had somehow imbibed the opinion that, in the absence of slaves, there could be no wealth, and very little refinement. And upon coming to the north, I expected to meet with a rough, hard-handed, and uncultivated population, living in the most Spartan-like simplicity,

9. A narrative poem by Sir Walter Scott (1810) about the fortunes of the Douglas clan in Scotland.

knowing nothing of the ease, luxury, pomp, and grandeur of southern slavehold-ers. Such being my conjectures, any one acquainted with the appearance of New Bedford may very readily infer how palpably I must have seen my mistake.

In the afternoon of the day when I reached New Bedford, I visited the wharves, to take a view of the shipping. Here I found myself surrounded with the strongest proofs of wealth. Lying at the wharves, and riding in the stream, I saw many ships of the finest model, in the best order, and of the largest size. Upon the right and left, I was walled in by granite warehouses of the widest dimensions, stowed to their utmost capacity with the necessaries and comforts of life. Added to this, almost every body seemed to be at work, but noiselessly so, compared with what I had been accustomed to in Baltimore. There were no loud songs heard from those engaged in loading and unloading ships. I heard no deep oaths or horrid curses on the laborer. I saw no whipping of men; but all seemed to go smoothly on. Every man appeared to understand his work, and went at it with a sober, yet cheerful earnestness, which betokened the deep interest which he felt in what he was doing, as well as a sense of his own dig-nity as a man. To me this looked exceedingly strange. From the wharves I strolled around and over the town, gazing with wonder and admiration at the splendid churches, beautiful dwellings, and finely-cultivated gardens; evincing an amount of wealth, comfort, taste, and refinement, such as I had never seen in any part of slaveholding Maryland.

Every thing looked clean, new, and beautiful. I saw few or no dilapidated houses, with poverty-stricken inmates; no half-naked children and barefooted women, such as I had been accustomed to see in Hillsborough, Easton, St. Michael's, and Baltimore. The people looked more able, stronger, healthier, and happier, than those of Maryland. I was for once made glad by a view of extreme wealth, without being saddened by seeing extreme poverty. But the most astonishing as well as the most interesting thing to me was the condition of the colored people, a great many of whom, like myself, had escaped thither as a refuge from the hunters of men. I found many, who had not been seven years out of their chains, living in finer houses, and evidently enjoying more of the comforts of life, than the average of slave-holders in Maryland. I will venture to assert that my friend Mr. Nathan Johnson (of whom I can say with a grateful heart, "I was hungry, and he gave me meat; I was thirsty, and he gave me drink; I was a stranger, and he took me in")[1] lived in a neater house; dined at a better table; took, paid for, and read, more newspapers; better understood the moral, religious, and political character of the nation,—than nine tenths of the slave-holders in Talbot county Maryland. Yet Mr. Johnson was a working man. His hands were hardened by toil, and not his alone, but those also of Mrs. Johnson. I found the colored people much more spirited than I had supposed they would be. I found among them a determination to protect each other from the blood-thirsty kidnapper, at all hazards. Soon after my arrival, I was told of a circum-stance which illustrated their spirit. A colored man and a fugitive slave were on unfriendly terms. The former was heard to threaten the latter with informing his master of his whereabouts. Straightway a meeting was called among the colored

1. Matthew 25.35: "For I was an hungered, and ye gave me meat: I was thirsty, and ye gave me drink: I was a stranger, and ye took me in."

people, under the stereotyped notice, "Business of importance!" The betrayer was invited to attend. The people came at the appointed hour, and organized the meeting by appointing a very religious old gentleman as president, who, I believe, made a prayer, after which he addressed the meeting as follows: *"Friends, we have got him here, and I would recommend that you young men just take him outside the door, and kill him!"* With this, a number of them bolted at him; but they were intercepted by some more timid than themselves, and the betrayer escaped their vengeance, and has not been seen in New Bedford since. I believe there have been no more such threats, and should there be hereafter, I doubt not that death would be the consequence.

I found employment, the third day after my arrival, in stowing a sloop with a load of oil. It was new, dirty, and hard work for me; but I went at it with a glad heart and a willing hand. I was now my own master. It was a happy moment, the rapture of which can be understood only by those who have been slaves. It was the first work, the reward of which was to be entirely my own. There was no Master Hugh standing ready, the moment I earned the money, to rob me of it. I worked that day with a pleasure I had never before experienced. I was at work for myself and newly-married wife. It was to me the starting-point of a new existence. When I got through with that job, I went in pursuit of a job of calking; but such was the strength of prejudice against color, among the white calkers, that they refused to work with me, and of course I could get no employment.[2] Finding my trade of no immediate benefit, I threw off my calking habiliments, and prepared myself to do any kind of work I could get to do. Mr. Johnson kindly let me have his woodhorse and saw, and I very soon found myself a plenty of work. There was no work too hard—none too dirty. I was ready to saw wood, shovel coal, carry the hod, sweep the chimney, or roll oil casks,—all of which I did for nearly three years in New Bedford, before I became known to the anti-slavery world.

In about four months after I went to New Bedford there came a young man to me, and inquired if I did not wish to take the "Liberator."[3] I told him I did; but, just having made my escape from slavery, I remarked that I was unable to pay for it then. I, however, finally became a subscriber to it. The paper came, and I read it from week to week with such feelings as it would be quite idle for me to attempt to describe. The paper became my meat and my drink. My soul was set all on fire. Its sympathy for my brethren in bonds—its scathing denunciations of slaveholders—its faithful exposures of slavery—and its powerful attacks upon the upholders of the institution—sent a thrill of joy through my soul, such as I had never felt before!

I had not long been a reader of the "Liberator," before I got a pretty correct idea of the principles, measures and spirit of the anti-slavery reform. I took right hold of the cause. I could do but little; but what I could, I did with a joyful heart, and never felt happier than when in an anti-slavery meeting. I seldom had much to say at the meetings, because what I wanted to say was said so much better by others. But, while attending an anti-slavery convention at Nantucket, on the 11th of August, 1841, I felt strongly moved to speak, and was at

2. I am told that colored persons can now get employment at calking in New Bedford—a result of antislavery effort [Douglass's note].

3. William Lloyd Garrison's antislavery newspaper, which began publication in 1831.

the same time much urged to do so by Mr. William C. Coffin, a gentleman who had heard me speak in the colored people's meeting at New Bedford. It was a severe cross, and I took it up reluctantly. The truth was, I felt myself a slave, and the idea of speaking to white people weighed me down. I spoke but a few moments, when I felt a degree of freedom, and said what I desired with considerable ease. From that time until now, I have been engaged in pleading the cause of my brethren—with what success, and with what devotion, I leave those acquainted with my labors to decide.

APPENDIX

I find, since reading over the foregoing Narrative, that I have, in several instances, spoken in such a tone and manner, respecting religion, as may possibly lead those unacquainted with my religious views to suppose me an opponent of all religion. To remove the liability of such misapprehension, I deem it proper to append the following brief explanation. What I have said respecting and against religion, I mean strictly to apply to the *slaveholding religion* of this land, and with no possible reference to Christianity proper; for, between the Christianity of this land, and the Christianity of Christ, I recognize the widest possible difference—so wide, that to receive the one as good, pure, and holy, is of necessity to reject the other as bad, corrupt, and wicked. To be the friend of the one, is of necessity to be the enemy of the other. I love the pure, peaceable, and impartial Christianity of Christ: I therefore hate the corrupt, slaveholding, women-whipping, cradle-plundering, partial and hypocritical Christianity of this land. Indeed, I can see no reason, but the most deceitful one, for calling the religion of this land Christianity. I look upon it as the climax of all misnomers, the boldest of all frauds, and the grossest of all libels. Never was there a clearer case of "stealing the livery of the court of heaven to serve the devil in." I am filled with unutterable loathing when I contemplate the religious pomp and show, together with the horrible inconsistencies, which every where surround me. We have men-stealers for ministers, women-whippers for missionaries, and cradle-plunderers for church members. The man who wields the blood-clotted cowskin during the week fills the pulpit on Sunday, and claims to be a minister of the meek and lowly Jesus. The man who robs me of my earnings at the end of each week meets me as a class-leader on Sunday morning, to show me the way of life, and the path of salvation. He who sells my sister, for purposes of prostitution, stands forth as the pious advocate of purity. He who proclaims it a religious duty to read the Bible denies me the right of learning to read the name of the God who made me. He who is the religious advocate of marriage robs whole millions of its sacred influence, and leaves them to the ravages of wholesale pollution. The warm defender of the sacredness of the family relation is the same that scatters whole families,—sundering husbands and wives, parents and children, sisters and brothers,—leaving the hut vacant, and the hearth desolate. We see the thief preaching against theft, and the adulterer against adultery. We have men sold to build churches, women sold to support the gospel, and babes sold to purchase Bibles for the *poor heathen! all for the glory of God and the good of souls!* The slave auctioneer's bell and the church-going bell chime in with each other, and the bitter cries of the heart-broken slave are drowned in the religious shouts of his pious master. Revivals of religion and revivals in the slave-trade go hand in hand together. The slave prison and the church stand near each other. The clanking of fetters and the rattling of chains in the prison, and the pious psalm and solemn prayer in the church, may be heard at the same time. The dealers in the bodies and souls of men erect their stand in the presence of the pulpit, and they mutually help each other. The dealer gives his blood-stained gold to support the pulpit, and the pulpit, in return, covers his infernal business with the garb of Christianity. Here we have religion and robbery the allies of each other—devils dressed in angels' robes, and hell presenting the semblance of paradise.

> "Just God! and these are they,
> Who minister at thine altar, God of right!
> Men who their hands, with prayer and blessing, lay
> On Israel's ark of light.
>
> "What! preach, and kidnap men?
> Give thanks, and rob thy own afflicted poor?
> Talk of thy glorious liberty, and then
> Bolt hard the captive's door?
>
> "What! servants of thy own
> Merciful Son, who came to seek and save
> The homeless and the outcast, fettering down
> The tasked and plundered slave!
>
> "Pilate and Herod friends!
> Chief priests and rulers, as of old, combine!
> Just God and holy! is that church which lends
> Strength to the spoiler thine?"

The Christianity of America is a Christianity, of whose votaries it may be as truly said, as it was of the ancient scribes and Pharisees, "They bind heavy burdens, and grievous to be borne, and lay them on men's shoulders, but they themselves will not move them with one of their fingers. All their works they do for to be seen of men.—— They love the uppermost rooms at feasts, and the chief seats in the synagogues, ... and to be called of men, Rabbi, Rabbi.——But woe unto you, scribes and Pharisees, hypocrites! for ye neither go in yourselves, neither suffer ye them that are entering to go in. Ye devour widows' houses, and for a pretence make long prayers; therefore ye shall receive the greater damnation. Ye compass sea and land to make one proselyte, and when he is made, ye make him twofold more the child of hell than yourselves.——Woe unto you, scribes and Pharisees, hypocrites! for ye pay tithe of mint, and anise, and cumin, and have omitted the weightier matters of the law, judgment, mercy, and faith; these ought ye to have done, and not to leave the other undone. Ye blind guides! which strain at a gnat, and swallow a camel. Woe unto you, scribes and Pharisees, hypocrites! for ye make clean the outside of the cup and of the platter; but within, they are full of extortion and excess.——Woe unto you, scribes and Pharisees, hypocrites! for ye are like unto whited sepulchres, which indeed appear beautiful outward, but are within full of dead men's bones, and of all uncleanness. Even so ye also outwardly appear righteous unto men, but within ye are full of hypocrisy and iniquity."[4]

4. Matthew 23.

Dark and terrible as is this picture, I hold it to be strictly true of the over-whelming mass of professed Christians in America. They strain at a gnat, and swallow a camel. Could anything be more true of our churches? They would be shocked at the proposition of fellowshipping a *sheep*-stealer; and at the same time they hug to their communion a *man*-stealer, and brand me with being an infidel, if I find fault with them for it. They attend with Pharisaical strictness to the outward forms of religion, and at the same time neglect the weightier mat-ters of the law, judgment, mercy, and faith. They are always ready to sacrifice, but seldom to show mercy. They are they who are represented as professing to love God whom they have not seen, whilst they hate their brother whom they have seen. They love the heathen on the other side of the globe. They can pray for him, pay money to have the Bible put into his hand, and missionaries to instruct him; while they despise and totally neglect the heathen at their own doors.

Such is, very briefly, my view of the religion of this land; and to avoid any misunderstanding, growing out of the use of general terms, I mean, by the reli-gion of this land, that which is revealed in the words, deeds, and actions, of those bodies, north and south, calling themselves Christian churches, and yet in union with slaveholders. It is against religion, as presented by these bodies, that I have felt it my duty to testify.

I conclude these remarks by copying the following portrait of the religion of the south, (which is, by communion and fellowship, the religion of the north) which I soberly affirm is "true to the life," and without caricature or the slight-est exaggeration. It is said to have been drawn, several years before the present anti-slavery agitation began, by a northern Methodist preacher, who, while residing at the south, had an opportunity to see slaveholding morals, manners, and piety, with his own eyes. "Shall I not visit for these things? saith the Lord. Shall not my soul be avenged on such a nation as this?"[5]

"A Parody.

"Come, saints and sinners, hear me tell
How pious priests whip Jack and Nell,
And women buy and children sell,
And preach all sinners down to hell,
    And sing of heavenly union.

"They'll bleat and baa, dona[6] like goats,
Gorge down black sheep, and strain at motes,
Array their backs in fine black coats,
Then seize their negroes by their throats,
    And choke, for heavenly union.

"They'll church you if you sip a dram,
And damn you if you steal a lamb;
Yet rob old Tony, Doll, and Sam,
Of human rights, and bread and ham;
    Kidnapper's heavenly union.

---

5. Jeremiah 5.9.
6. Believed to be a printer's error in the original edition for "go on" or "go n-a-a-ah."

"They'll loudly talk of Christ's reward,
And bind his image with a cord,
And scold, and swing the lash abhorred,
And sell their brother in the Lord
    To handcuffed heavenly union.

"They'll read and sing a sacred song,
And make a prayer both loud and long,
And teach the right and do the wrong,
Hailing the brother, sister throng,
    With words of heavenly union.

"We wonder how such saints can sing,
Or praise the Lord upon the wing,
Who roar, and scold, and whip, and sting,
And to their slaves and mammon cling,
    In guilty conscience union.

"They'll raise tobacco, corn, and rye,
And drive, and thieve, and cheat, and lie,
And lay up treasures in the sky,
By making switch and cowskin fly,
    In hope of heavenly union.

"They'll crack old Tony on the skull,
And preach and roar like Bashan bull,
Or braying ass, of mischief full,
Then seize old Jacob by the wool,
    And pull for heavenly union.

"A roaring, ranting, sleek man-thief,
Who lived on mutton, veal, and beef,
Yet never would afford relief
To needy, sable sons of grief,
    Was big with heavenly union.

"'Love not the world,' the preacher said,
And winked his eye, and shook his head;
He seized on Tom, and Dick, and Ned,
Cut short their meat, and clothes, and bread,
    Yet still loved heavenly union.

"Another preacher whining spoke
Of One whose heart for sinners broke:
He tied old Nanny to an oak,
And drew the blood at every stroke,
    And prayed for heavenly union.

"Two others oped their iron jaws,
And waved their children-stealing paws;
There sat their children in gewgaws;
By stinting negroes' backs and maws,
    They kept up heavenly union.

"All good from Jack another takes,
And entertains their flirts and rakes,

Who dress as sleek as glossy snakes,
And cram their mouths with sweetened cakes;
And this goes down for union."

Sincerely and earnestly hoping that this little book may do something toward throwing light on the American slave system, and hastening the glad day of deliverance to the millions of my brethren in bonds—faithfully relying upon the power of truth, love, and justice, for success in my humble efforts—and solemnly pledging my self anew to the sacred cause,—I subscribe myself,

FREDERICK DOUGLASS.

Lynn, Mass., April 28, 1845.

HERMAN MELVILLE
1819–1891

"Bartleby, the Scrivener" takes place within a dark office on Wall Street, and its main character refuses to budge. This confined setting might seem unusual for a writer whose most famous works, including his most celebrated novel, *Moby-Dick*, are tales of adventure at sea. But "Bartleby" is typical of Melville's major work in that it revolves around questions of authority and rebellion, asking how and whether we may choose our own fates. Melville's memorable character Bartleby simply refuses to go along with the demands and expectations of others. "I would prefer not to," he repeats, politely but without compromise. And in his immovable way, he raises vexing social and philosophical questions: is it possible to opt out of the routines of modern life? Why should people continue to participate in the daily grind if it brings them neither satisfaction nor social mobility? And to what extent are we genuinely free to make our own choices?

LIFE

Two of the great literary giants of the United States in the nineteenth century—**Walt Whitman** and Herman Melville—were born in New York in 1819. Both believed in democracy and both opposed slavery. But Melville boasted an unusually patriotic pedigree: his paternal grandfather had participated in the Boston Tea Party, so attached to that revolutionary moment that he refused to change the style of his clothing even decades later, long after fashions had changed. His maternal grandfather, too, had been a hero in the American Revolutionary War. While Melville could claim a proud ancestry, however, his immediate family suffered shame and poverty after a series of poor business decisions. He and his father fled New York under cover of night when Herman was eleven years old to escape creditors, and they barely managed on loans from relatives until his father died in 1832. His own adulthood was hardly better financially: losing money even on his best-selling works, Melville would remain impoverished for most of his life.

In his teens, Melville worked unhappily as a copyist and errand boy in a bank, and then became a sailor, setting out for the South Pacific at the age of twenty. His first captain was harsh, and Melville jumped ship on an island reputed to be inhabited by cannibals. The local people treated Melville kindly, however, and he would remember them in his autobiographical novel *Typee* (1846) as sexually frank but also innocent, and morally good compared to the European missionaries then contributing to the disappearance of Polynesian cultural and spiritual traditions.

Back in the United States, Melville married Elizabeth Shaw, the daughter of a family friend, and they would go on to have four children. The marriage was not a happy one, and in the 1860s Elizabeth considered a legal separation, claiming that she was afraid of her husband. Their younger son Malcolm died in 1867 of a self-inflicted gunshot wound—almost certainly suicide—at the age of eighteen.

Melville's career as a writer went no more smoothly than his family life. *Typee* and its successor, *Omoo* (1847), both novels about the South Seas, proved popular with readers throughout the British Empire as well as the United States, but critics disliked the writer's defense of the "savages," his scenes of sexual pleasure, and his scathing portraits of Christian missionaries. Melville followed these early popular successes with a fantasy called *Mardi* (1849), which neither publishers nor readers liked much. And when he published *Moby-Dick* (1851)—which would later be seen by many readers as the best of all American novels—Melville lost the admiration of his contemporaries. A vast and bulky novel that folds into its story philosophy, science, and detailed myths and facts about whales and whal-

ing, it seemed to reviewers to be muddled, eccentric, and rambling. Most critics then agreed that Melville's next novel, *Pierre* (1852), was nothing more than the ravings of a "lunatic." This book lost him substantial money, and set him on the path to near total obscurity. He was dispirited. "What I feel most moved to write, that is banned,— it will not pay. Yet, altogether, write the *other* way I cannot. So the product is a final hash, and all my books are botches." It was in 1853, while still smarting from the hostile reviews of *Moby-Dick* and badly in need of money, that Melville published an anonymous short story in *Putnam's Magazine* called "Bartleby the Scrivener." It garnered little notice until a century later.

Though he continued to write for the rest of his life, Melville was forced to take up work as a customs inspector to pay his bills. He faded from the public eye almost entirely. One day in 1885 the English writer Robert Buchanan went to look for him: "I sought everywhere for this Triton, who is still living somewhere in New York. No one seemed to know anything of the one great writer fit to stand shoulder to shoulder with Whitman on that continent." At the very end of his life, Melville wrote *Billy Budd*, considered another of his greatest works, but it was not published until thirty-three years later. When the writer died in his sleep in 1891, some obituary writers declared themselves surprised to discover that he had been so recently alive.

It was not until the 1920s that Melville's star would begin to rise. Writers in the United States and Europe who were experimenting with new and unsettling techniques for writing fiction understood Melville's peculiarities as signs of brilliant originality and exciting innovation. Seen today as one of the greatest of all American writers, Herman Melville has ultimately earned a profound respect denied to him in his own time.

TIMES

The full title of Melville's story is "Bartleby, the Scrivener: A Story of Wall-Street." Already in the mid-nineteenth century, New York's Wall Street had become the major financial center of the United States. It was associated with the accumulation of tremendous wealth, often symbolized by one of the richest men in the nation, John Jacob Astor. But New York's financial district was also associated with large-scale economic meltdowns—such as the "Panic of 1837," which prompted a major economic depression and helped to put Melville's own father deep into debt. Mysterious and powerful, Wall Street already seemed like the hub of a vast web of economic transactions. Fluctuations in the stock market could put coal miners out of work in Pennsylvania, depress interest rates in Europe, bankrupt Southern slaveholders, and create a need for Chinese immigrants to help build railroads in California.

While some made fortunes on Wall Street and others lost all they had, many ordinary laborers were dissatisfied with their working conditions. Wages dropped in the northeastern United States in the 1830s and '40s, in part because large numbers of immigrants fleeing famine-wracked Ireland and political unrest in Germany brought new competition for scarce jobs. The quality of work was changing, too. Disappearing was the life of the self-sufficient artisan who grew materials and sold handmade products to buyers at local markets; now, more and more often, workers made only parts of objects in factories, to be assembled elsewhere and sold to far-flung consumers. Labor activists objected fiercely to the replacement of workers by machines, and to the transformation of workers *into* machines, performing repetitive, mind-numbing tasks. Some warned that a whole class of people was becoming violent as workers grew increasingly alienated from their labor. Meanwhile, entrepreneurs in New York and Philadelphia set out to defeat the growing trade unions, and more generally they preached the value of the free market as a cornerstone of American freedom. In the 1840s numerous labor struggles broke out in New York, including strikes by bookbinders, upholsterers, shoemakers, tailors, and railroad workers. Walt Whitman wrote admiringly of their resistance: "in all of them burns, almost with a fierceness, the divine fire which more or less, during all ages, has only waited a chance to leap forth and confound the calculations of tyrants, hunkers, and all their tribe. At this moment, New York is the most radical city in America."

A different version of resistance was emerging in the same moment. The writer Henry David Thoreau, outraged that the U.S. government was fighting to extend slavery into Mexico in the late 1840s, refused to pay his taxes and willingly went to prison to demonstrate his dissent. "I simply wish to refuse allegiance to the State, to withdraw and stand aloof from it effectually," wrote Thoreau in his essay "Civil Disobedience." The idea here was to resist unjust laws without violence, simply to refuse to cooperate and voluntarily to take the consequences as a form of peaceful protest. Thoreau would later have world-famous followers in Mohandas Gandhi and Martin Luther King Jr., but one of his first imitators may have been Melville's fictional Bartleby, who, by declining to make copies, ironically himself becomes a copy of Thoreau.

WORK

It could be said that Melville himself, like Bartleby, refused to make copies. That is, he would not write a predictable kind of literature that would sell but insisted on writing his own eccentric, highly original kind of work. Many readers have interpreted Bartleby, accordingly, as a figure for Melville the principled artist, punished for his unwillingness to go along with the crowd. But Bartleby can also be seen as an alienated member of the working class, a white-collar clerk only slightly higher on the social ladder than the angry factory workers agitating at the time, whose job of mechanically copying documents holds no possibility of fulfillment and whose comfortable employer lives off the proceeds of his labor. Or he can be read as the failure of freedom in modern society—the doomed struggle to assert a self in the face of economic and social pressures. Or even, as the narrator concludes, Bartleby cannot be interpreted at all: he is an unknowable cipher, one of the enigmas of a plural and puzzling "humanity."

And in fact, the narrator's response to Bartleby is as worthy of critical attention as Bartleby himself. In a story about a worker's refusal to obey, what can we make of the character who is both the boss and the storyteller? The prosperous lawyer who spins the narrative has a series of reactions to his employee's eccentric behavior, including first accommodating him, offering him friendship, then losing his temper, pleading, threatening, sympathizing, bribing, and eventually even fleeing altogether, as he feels compelled to abandon his own office to the unmoving Bartleby. Along the way, we hear far more about the narrator's thoughts than we do about Bartleby's: his unambitious life of ease, his anxiety about what other people think, his feelings about employees, and the prickings of his conscience. Most of all, we hear about his struggle to make some sense of Bartleby's resistance.

In his efforts to interpret the mysterious Bartleby, the narrator repeatedly runs into a wall, figuratively speaking, but the story is also filled with literal walls: the Wall Street of the title, the blank wall that can be seen from the office window, Bartleby's inclination to fall into "dead-wall reveries," and the high wall of the Tombs, New York's infamous prison. Filled with blockages and barriers, the story ends with the news that Bartleby has once worked for the Dead Letter Office—the resting place for undeliverable letters. Melville may have worried that his own writing was a kind of dead letter—doomed never to reach its destination, and thus to remain forever unread. Luckily for us, his work did not share the fate of its unfortunate character. And perhaps the story, in being read today, has finally reached the right address.

Bartleby, the Scrivener

A Story of Wall-Street

I am a rather elderly man. The nature of my avocations for the last thirty years has brought me into more than ordinary contact with what would seem an interesting and somewhat singular set of men, of whom as yet nothing that I know of has ever been written:—I mean the law-copyists or scriveners. I have known very many of them, professionally and privately, and if I pleased, could relate divers histories, at which good-natured gentlemen might smile, and sentimental souls might weep. But I waive the biographies of all other scriveners for a few passages in the life of Bartleby, who was a scrivener the strangest I ever saw or heard of. While of other law-copyists I might write the complete life, of Bartleby nothing of that sort can be done. I believe that no materials exist for a full and satisfactory biography of this man. It is an irreparable loss to literature. Bartleby was one of those beings of whom nothing is ascertainable, except from the original sources, and in his case those are very small. What my own astonished eyes saw of Bartleby, *that* is all I know of him, except, indeed, one vague report which will appear in the sequel.

Ere introducing the scrivener, as he first appeared to me, it is fit I make some mention of myself, my *employés*, my business, my chambers, and general surroundings; because some such description is indispensable to an adequate understanding of the chief character about to be presented.

Imprimis:[1] I am a man who, from his youth upwards, has been filled with a profound conviction that the easiest way of life is the best. Hence, though I belong to a profession proverbially energetic and nervous, even to turbulence, at times, yet nothing of that sort have I ever suffered to invade my peace. I am one of those unambitious lawyers who never addresses a jury, or in any way draws down public applause; but in the cool tranquillity of a snug retreat, do a snug business among rich men's bonds and mortgages and title-deeds. All who know me, consider me an eminently *safe* man. The late John Jacob Astor,[2] a personage little given to poetic enthusiasm, had no hesitation in pronouncing my first grand point to be prudence; my next, method. I do not speak it in vanity, but simply record the fact, that I was not unemployed in my profession by the late John Jacob Astor; a name which, I admit, I love to repeat, for it hath a rounded and orbicular sound to it, and rings like unto bullion. I will freely add, that I was not insensible to the late John Jacob Astor's good opinion.

Some time prior to the period at which this little history begins, my avocations had been largely increased. The good old office, now extinct in the State of New-York, of a Master in Chancery,[3] had been conferred upon me. It was not a very arduous office, but very pleasantly remunerative. I seldom lose my temper; much more seldom indulge in dangerous indignation at wrongs and outrages; but I must be permitted to be rash here and declare, that I consider the sudden and violent abrogation of the office of Master in Chancery, by the new Constitution, as a—premature act; inasmuch as I had counted upon a life-lease of the profits, whereas I only received those of a few short years. But this is by the way.

My chambers were up stairs at No. — Wall-street. At one end they looked upon the white wall of the interior of a spacious sky-light shaft, penetrating the building from top to bottom. This view might have been considered rather tame than otherwise, deficient in what landscape painters call "life." But if so, the view from the other end of my chambers offered, at least, a contrast, if nothing more. In that direction my windows commanded an unobstructed view of a lofty brick wall, black by age and everlasting shade; which wall required no spy-glass to bring out its lurking beauties, but for the benefit of all near-sighted spectators, was pushed up to within ten feet of my window panes. Owing to the great height of the surrounding buildings, and my chambers being on the

---

1. In the first place (Latin).
2. John Jacob Astor (1763–1848), successful businessman in the American fur trade and the country's first multimillionaire.

3. An anachronistic court position, associated with the British royalty, abolished in New York in 1848.

second floor, the interval between this wall and mine not a little resembled a huge square cistern.

At the period just preceding the advent of Bartleby, I had two persons as copyists in my employment, and a promising lad as an office-boy. First, Turkey; second, Nippers; third, Ginger Nut. These may seem names, the like of which are not usually found in the Directory.[4] In truth they were nicknames, mutu-ally conferred upon each other by my three clerks, and were deemed expressive of their respective persons or characters. Turkey was a short, pursy English-man of about my own age, that is, somewhere not far from sixty. In the morn-ing, one might say, his face was of a fine florid hue, but after twelve o'clock, meridian—his dinner hour—it blazed like a grate full of Christmas coals; and continued blazing—but, as it were, with a gradual wane—till 6 o'clock, P.M. or thereabouts, after which I saw no more of the proprietor of the face, which gaining its meridian with the sun, seemed to set with it, to rise, culminate, and decline the following day, with the like regularity and undiminished glory. There are many singular coincidences I have known in the course of my life, not the least among which was the fact, that exactly when Turkey displayed his fullest beams from his red and radiant countenance, just then, too, at that critical moment, began the daily period when I considered his business capaci-ties as seriously disturbed for the remainder of the twenty-four hours. Not that he was absolutely idle, or averse to business then; far from it. The difficulty was, he was apt to be altogether too energetic. There was a strange, inflamed, flurried, flighty recklessness of activity about him. He would be incautious in dipping his pen into his inkstand. All his blots upon my documents, were dropped there after twelve o'clock, meridian. Indeed, not only would he be reckless and sadly given to making blots in the afternoon, but some days he went further, and was rather noisy. At such times, too, his face flamed with augmented blazonry, as if cannel coal had been heaped on anthracite.[5] He made an unpleasant racket with his chair; spilled his sandbox;[6] in mending his pens, impatiently split them all to pieces, and threw them on the floor in a sud-den passion; stood up and leaned over his table, boxing his papers about in a most indecorous manner, very sad to behold in an elderly man like him. Never-theless, as he was in many ways a most valuable person to me, and all the time before twelve o'clock, meridian, was the quickest, steadiest creature too, accomplishing a great deal of work in a style not easy to be matched—for these reasons, I was willing to overlook his eccentricities, though indeed, occasion-ally, I remonstrated with him. I did this very gently, however, because, though the civilest, nay, the blandest and most reverential of men in the morning, yet in the afternoon he was disposed, upon provocation, to be slightly rash with his tongue, in fact, insolent. Now, valuing his morning services as I did, and resolved not to lose them; yet, at the same time made uncomfortable by his inflamed ways after twelve o'clock; and being a man of peace, unwilling by my admonitions to call forth unseemly retorts from him; I took upon me, one Sat-urday noon (he was always worse on Saturdays), to hint to him, very kindly, that perhaps now that he was growing old, it might be well to abridge his

4. List of the most established upper-class families in New York society.
5. Cannel coal burns quickly and brightly, whereas anthracite produces a dim, smokeless flame.
6. Sand was used to blot ink.

labors; in short, he need not come to my chambers after twelve o'clock, but, dinner over, had best go home to his lodgings and rest himself till tea-time. But no; he insisted upon his afternoon devotions. His countenance became intolerably fervid, as he oratorically assured me—gesticulating with a long ruler at the other end of the room—that if his services in the morning were useful, how indispensable, then, in the afternoon?

"With submission, sir," said Turkey on this occasion, "I consider myself your right-hand man. In the morning I but marshal and deploy my columns; but in the afternoon I put myself at their head, and gallantly charge the foe, thus!"— and he made a violent thrust with the ruler.

"But the blots, Turkey," intimated I.

"True,—but, with submission, sir, behold these hairs! I am getting old. Surely, sir, a blot or two of a warm afternoon is not to be severely urged against gray hairs. Old age—even if it blot the page—is honorable. With submission, sir, we *both* are getting old."

This appeal to my fellow-feeling was hardly to be resisted. At all events, I saw that go he would not. So I made up my mind to let him stay, resolving, nevertheless, to see to it, that during the afternoon he had to do with my less important papers.

Nippers, the second on my list, was a whiskered, sallow, and, upon the whole, rather piratical-looking young man of about five and twenty. I always deemed him the victim of two evil powers—ambition and indigestion. The ambition was evinced by a certain impatience of the duties of a mere copyist, an unwarrantable usurpation of strictly professional affairs, such as the original drawing up of legal documents. The indigestion seemed betokened in an occasional nervous testiness and grinning irritability, causing the teeth to audibly grind together over mistakes committed in copying; unnecessary maledictions, hissed, rather than spoken, in the heat of business; and especially by a continual discontent with the height of the table where he worked. Though of a very ingenious mechanical turn, Nippers could never get this table to suit him. He put chips under it, blocks of various sorts, bits of pasteboard, and at last went so far as to attempt an exquisite adjustment by final pieces of folded blotting-paper. But no invention would answer. If, for the sake of easing his back, he brought the table lid at a sharp angle well up towards his chin, and wrote there like a man using the steep roof of a Dutch house for his desk:— then he declared that it stopped the circulation in his arms. If now he lowered the table to his waistbands, and stooped over it in writing, then there was a sore aching in his back. In short, the truth of the matter was, Nippers knew not what he wanted. Or, if he wanted any thing, it was to be rid of a scrivener's table altogether. Among the manifestations of his diseased ambition was a fondness he had for receiving visits from certain ambiguous-looking fellows in seedy coats, whom he called his clients. Indeed I was aware that not only was he, at times, considerable of a ward-politician, but he occasionally did a little business at the Justices' courts, and was not unknown on the steps of the Tombs.[7] I have good reason to believe, however, that one individual who called upon him at my chambers, and who, with a grand air, he insisted was his client, was no other than a dun, and the alleged title-deed, a bill. But with all his

---

7. A New York prison and municipal court building complex.

failings, and the annoyances he caused me, Nippers, like his compatriot Turkey, was a very useful man to me; wrote a neat, swift hand; and, when he chose, was not deficient in a gentlemanly sort of deportment. Added to this, he always dressed in a gentlemanly sort of way; and so, incidentally, reflected credit upon my chambers. Whereas with respect to Turkey, I had much ado to keep him from being a reproach to me. His clothes were apt to look oily and smell of eating-houses. He wore his pantaloons very loose and baggy in summer. His coats were execrable; his hat not to be handled. But while the hat was a thing of indifference to me, inasmuch as his natural civility and deference, as a dependent Englishman, always led him to doff it the moment he entered the room, yet his coat was another matter. Concerning his coats, I reasoned with him; but with no effect. The truth was, I suppose, that a man with so small an income, could not afford to sport such a lustrous face and a lustrous coat at one and the same time. As Nippers once observed, Turkey's money went chiefly for red ink. One winter day I presented Turkey with a highly-respectable looking coat of my own, a padded gray coat, of a most comfortable warmth, and which buttoned straight up from the knee to the neck. I thought Turkey would appreciate the favor, and abate his rashness and obstreperousness of afternoons. But no. I verily believe that buttoning himself up in so downy and blanket-like a coat had a pernicious effect upon him; upon the same principle that too much oats are bad for horses. In fact, precisely as a rash, restive horse is said to feel his oats, so Turkey felt his coat. It made him insolent. He was a man whom prosperity harmed.

Though concerning the self-indulgent habits of Turkey I had my own private surmises, yet touching Nippers I was well persuaded that whatever might be his faults in other respects, he was, at least, a temperate young man. But indeed, nature herself seemed to have been his vintner, and at his birth charged him so thoroughly with an irritable, brandy-like disposition, that all subsequent potations were needless. When I consider how, amid the stillness of my chambers, Nippers would sometimes impatiently rise from his seat, and stooping over his table, spread his arms wide apart, seize the whole desk, and move it, and jerk it, with a grim, grinding motion on the floor, as if the table were a perverse voluntary agent, intent on thwarting and vexing him; I plainly perceive that for Nippers, brandy and water were altogether superfluous.

It was fortunate for me that, owing to its peculiar cause—indigestion—the irritability and consequent nervousness of Nippers, were mainly observable in the morning, while in the afternoon he was comparatively mild. So that Turkey's paroxysms only coming on about twelve o'clock, I never had to do with their eccentricities at one time. Their fits relieved each other like guards. When Nippers' was on, Turkey's was off; and *vice versa*. This was a good natural arrangement under the circumstances.

Ginger Nut, the third on my list, was a lad some twelve years old. His father was a carman,[8] ambitious of seeing his son on the bench instead of a cart, before he died. So he sent him to my office as student at law, errand boy, and cleaner and sweeper, at the rate of one dollar a week. He had a little desk to himself, but he did not use it much. Upon inspection, the drawer exhibited a great array of the shells of various sorts of nuts. Indeed, to this quick-witted

8. Railway car mechanic.

youth the whole noble science of the law was contained in a nut-shell. Not the least among the employments of Ginger Nut, as well as one which he discharged with the most alacrity, was his duty as cake and apple purveyor for Turkey and Nippers. Copying law papers being proverbially a dry, husky sort of business, my two scriveners were fain to moisten their mouths very often with Spitzenbergs[9] to be had at the numerous stalls nigh the Custom House and Post Office. Also, they sent Ginger Nut very frequently for that peculiar cake— small, flat, round, and very spicy—after which he had been named by them. Of a cold morning when business was but dull, Turkey would gobble up scores of these cakes, as if they were mere wafers—indeed they sell them at the rate of six or eight for a penny—the scrape of his pen blending with the crunching of the crisp particles in his mouth. Of all the fiery afternoon blunders and flurried rashnesses of Turkey, was his once moistening a ginger-cake between his lips, and clapping it on to a mortgage for a seal. I came within an ace of dismissing him then. But he mollified me by making an oriental bow, and saying— "With submission, sir, it was generous of me to find you in stationery on my own account."

Now my original business—that of a conveyancer and title hunter, and drawer-up of recondite documents of all sorts—was considerably increased by receiving the master's office. There was now great work for scriveners. Not only must I push the clerks already with me, but I must have additional help. In answer to my advertisement, a motionless young man one morning, stood upon my office threshold, the door being open, for it was summer. I can see that figure now—pallidly neat, pitiably respectable, incurably forlorn! It was Bartleby.

After a few words touching his qualifications, I engaged him, glad to have among my corps of copyists a man of so singularly sedate an aspect, which I thought might operate beneficially upon the flighty temper of Turkey, and the fiery one of Nippers.

I should have stated before that ground glass folding-doors divided my premises into two parts, one of which was occupied by my scriveners, the other by myself. According to my humor I threw open these doors, or closed them. I resolved to assign Bartleby a corner by the folding-doors, but on my side of them, so as to have this quiet man within easy call, in case any trifling thing was to be done. I placed his desk close up to a small side-window in that part of the room, a window which originally had afforded a lateral view of certain grimy back-yards and bricks, but which, owing to subsequent erections, commanded at present no view at all, though it gave some light. Within three feet of the panes was a wall, and the light came down from far above, between two lofty buildings, as from a very small opening in a dome. Still further to a satisfactory arrangement, I procured a high green folding screen, which might entirely isolate Bartleby from my sight, though not remove him from my voice. And thus, in a manner, privacy and society were conjoined.

At first Bartleby did an extraordinary quantity of writing. As if long famishing for something to copy, he seemed to gorge himself on my documents. There was no pause for digestion. He ran a day and night line, copying by sun-light and by candle-light. I should have been quite delighted with his application, had he been cheerfully industrious. But he wrote on silently, palely, mechanically.

9. Variety of apple.

It is, of course, an indispensable part of a scrivener's business to verify the accuracy of his copy, word by word. Where there are two or more scriveners in an office, they assist each other in this examination, one reading from the copy, the other holding the original. It is a very dull, wearisome, and lethargic affair. I can readily imagine that to some sanguine temperaments it would be altogether intolerable. For example, I cannot credit that the mettlesome poet Byron[1] would have contentedly sat down with Bartleby to examine a law document of, say five hundred pages, closely written in a crimpy hand.

Now and then, in the haste of business, it had been my habit to assist in comparing some brief document myself, calling Turkey or Nippers for this purpose. One object I had in placing Bartleby so handy to me behind the screen, was to avail myself of his services on such trivial occasions. It was on the third day, I think, of his being with me, and before any necessity had arisen for having his own writing examined, that, being much hurried to complete a small affair I had in hand, I abruptly called to Bartleby. In my haste and natural expectancy of instant compliance, I sat with my head bent over the original on my desk, and my right hand sideways, and somewhat nervously extended with the copy, so that immediately upon emerging from his retreat, Bartleby might snatch it and proceed to business without the least delay.

In this very attitude did I sit when I called to him, rapidly stating what it was I wanted him to do—namely, to examine a small paper with me. Imagine my surprise, nay, my consternation, when without moving from his privacy, Bartleby in a singularly mild, firm voice, replied, "I would prefer not to."

I sat awhile in perfect silence, rallying my stunned faculties. Immediately it occurred to me that my ears had deceived me, or Bartleby had entirely misunderstood my meaning. I repeated my request in the clearest tone I could assume. But in quite as clear a one came the previous reply, "I would prefer not to."

"Prefer not to," echoed I, rising in high excitement, and crossing the room with a stride. "What do you mean? Are you moon-struck? I want you to help me compare this sheet here—take it," and I thrust it towards him.

"I would prefer not to," said he.

I looked at him steadfastly. His face was leanly composed; his gray eye dimly calm. Not a wrinkle of agitation rippled him. Had there been the least uneasiness, anger, impatience or impertinence in his manner; in other words, had there been any thing ordinarily human about him, doubtless I should have violently dismissed him from the premises. But as it was, I should have as soon thought of turning my pale plaster-of-paris bust of Cicero[2] out of doors. I stood gazing at him awhile, as he went on with his own writing, and then reseated myself at my desk. This is very strange, thought I. What had one best do? But my business hurried me. I concluded to forget the matter for the present, reserving it for my future leisure. So calling Nippers from the other room, the paper was speedily examined.

A few days after this, Bartleby concluded four lengthy documents, being quadruplicates of a week's testimony taken before me in my High Court of

---

1. George Gordon, Lord Byron (1788–1824), aristocratic British poet noted for his rejection of social restrictions.

2. Marcus Tullius Cicero (106–43 B.C.E.), Roman philosopher, politician, and lawyer.

Chancery. It became necessary to examine them. It was an important suit, and great accuracy was imperative. Having all things arranged I called Turkey, Nippers and Ginger Nut from the next room, meaning to place the four copies in the hands of my four clerks, while I should read from the original. Accordingly Turkey, Nippers and Ginger Nut had taken their seats in a row, each with his document in hand, when I called to Bartleby to join this interesting group.

"Bartleby! quick, I am waiting."

I heard a slow scrape of his chair legs on the uncarpeted floor, and soon he appeared standing at the entrance of his hermitage.

"What is wanted?" said he mildly.

"The copies, the copies," said I hurriedly. "We are going to examine them. There"—and I held towards him the fourth quadruplicate.

"I would prefer not to," he said, and gently disappeared behind the screen.

For a few moments I was turned into a pillar of salt,[3] standing at the head of my seated column of clerks. Recovering myself, I advanced towards the screen, and demanded the reason for such extraordinary conduct.

"*Why* do you refuse?"

"I would prefer not to."

With any other man I should have flown outright into a dreadful passion, scorned all further words, and thrust him ignominiously from my presence. But there was something about Bartleby that not only strangely disarmed me, but in a wonderful manner touched and disconcerted me. I began to reason with him.

"These are your own copies we are about to examine. It is labor saving to you, because one examination will answer for your four papers. It is common usage. Every copyist is bound to help examine his copy. Is it not so? Will you not speak? Answer!"

"I prefer not to," he replied in a flute-like tone. It seemed to me that while I had been addressing him, he carefully revolved every statement that I made; fully comprehended the meaning; could not gainsay the irresistible conclusion; but, at the same time, some paramount consideration prevailed with him to reply as he did.

"You are decided, then, not to comply with my request—a request made according to common usage and common sense?"

He briefly gave me to understand that on that point my judgment was sound. Yes: his decision was irreversible.

It is not seldom the case that when a man is browbeaten in some unprecedented and violently unreasonable way, he begins to stagger in his own plainest faith. He begins, as it were, vaguely to surmise that, wonderful as it may be, all the justice and all the reason is on the other side. Accordingly, if any disinterested persons are present, he turns to them for some reinforcement for his own faltering mind.

"Turkey," said I, "what do you think of this? Am I not right?"

"With submission, sir," said Turkey, with his blandest tone, "I think that you are."

"Nippers," said I, "what do *you* think of it?"

---

3. In the Book of Genesis, Lot's wife disregards the angel's command not to look back while fleeing Sodom; as a punishment she is turned into a pillar of salt.

"I think I should kick him out of the office."

(The reader of nice perceptions will here perceive that, it being morning, Turkey's answer is couched in polite and tranquil terms, but Nippers replies in ill-tempered ones. Or, to repeat a previous sentence, Nippers's ugly mood was on duty, and Turkey's off.)

"Ginger Nut," said I, willing to enlist the smallest suffrage in my behalf, "what do *you* think of it?"

"I think, sir, he's a little *luny*," replied Ginger Nut, with a grin.

"You hear what they say," said I, turning towards the screen, "come forth and do your duty."

But he vouchsafed no reply. I pondered a moment in sore perplexity. But once more business hurried me. I determined again to postpone the consideration of this dilemma to my future leisure. With a little trouble we made out to examine the papers without Bartleby, though at every page or two, Turkey deferentially dropped his opinion that this proceeding was quite out of the common; while Nippers, twitching in his chair with a dyspeptic nervousness, ground out between his set teeth occasional hissing maledictions against the stubborn oaf behind the screen. And for his (Nippers's) part, this was the first and the last time he would do another man's business without pay.

Meanwhile Bartleby sat in his hermitage, oblivious to every thing but his own peculiar business there.

Some days passed, the scrivener being employed upon another lengthy work. His late remarkable conduct led me to regard his ways narrowly. I observed that he never went to dinner; indeed that he never went any where. As yet I had never of my personal knowledge known him to be outside of my office. He was a perpetual sentry in the corner. At about eleven o'clock though, in the morning, I noticed that Ginger Nut would advance toward the opening in Bartleby's screen, as if silently beckoned thither by a gesture invisible to me where I sat. The boy would then leave the office jingling a few pence, and reappear with a handful of ginger-nuts which he delivered in the hermitage, receiving two of the cakes for his trouble.

He lives, then, on ginger-nuts, thought I; never eats a dinner, properly speaking; he must be a vegetarian then; but no; he never eats even vegetables, he eats nothing but ginger-nuts. My mind then ran on in reveries concerning the probable effects upon the human constitution of living entirely on ginger-nuts. Ginger-nuts are so called because they contain ginger as one of their peculiar constituents, and the final flavoring one. Now what was ginger? A hot, spicy thing. Was Bartleby hot and spicy? Not at all. Ginger, then, had no effect upon Bartleby. Probably he preferred it should have none.

Nothing so aggravates an earnest person as a passive resistance. If the individual so resisted be of a not inhumane temper, and the resisting one perfectly harmless in his passivity; then, in the better moods of the former, he will endeavor charitably to construe to his imagination what proves impossible to be solved by his judgment. Even so, for the most part, I regarded Bartleby and his ways. Poor fellow! thought I, he means no mischief; it is plain he intends no insolence; his aspect sufficiently evinces that his eccentricities are involuntary. He is useful to me. I can get along with him. If I turn him away, the chances are he will fall in with some less indulgent employer, and then he will be rudely treated, and perhaps driven forth miserably to starve. Yes. Here I can cheaply purchase a delicious self-approval. To befriend Bartleby; to humor him in his strange wilfulness, will cost me little or nothing, while I lay up in my soul what will eventually prove a sweet morsel for my conscience. But this mood was not invariable with me. The passiveness of Bartleby sometimes irritated me. I felt strangely goaded on to encounter him in new opposition, to elicit some angry spark from him answerable to my own. But indeed I might as well have essayed to strike fire with my knuckles against a bit of Windsor soap. But one afternoon the evil impulse in me mastered me, and the following little scene ensued:

"Bartleby," said I, "when those papers are all copied, I will compare them with you."

"I would prefer not to."

"How? Surely you do not mean to persist in that mulish vagary?"

No answer.

I threw open the folding-doors near by, and turning upon Turkey and Nippers, exclaimed:

"Bartleby a second time says, he won't examine his papers. What do you think of it, Turkey?"

It was afternoon, be it remembered. Turkey sat glowing like a brass boiler, his bald head steaming, his hands reeling among his blotted papers.

"Think of it?" roared Turkey; "I think I'll just step behind his screen, and black his eyes for him!"

So saying, Turkey rose to his feet and threw his arms into a pugilistic position. He was hurrying away to make good his promise, when I detained him, alarmed at the effect of incautiously rousing Turkey's combativeness after dinner.

"Sit down, Turkey," said I, "and hear what Nippers has to say. What do you think of it, Nippers? Would I not be justified in immediately dismissing Bartleby?"

"Excuse me, that is for you to decide, sir. I think his conduct quite unusual, and indeed unjust, as regards Turkey and myself. But it may only be a passing whim."

"Ah," exclaimed I, "you have strangely changed your mind then—you speak very gently of him now."

"All beer," cried Turkey; "gentleness is effects of beer—Nippers and I dined together to-day. You see how gentle I am, sir. Shall I go and black his eyes?"

"You refer to Bartleby, I suppose. No, not to-day, Turkey," I replied; "pray, put up your fists."

I closed the doors, and again advanced towards Bartleby. I felt additional incentives tempting me to my fate. I burned to be rebelled against again. I remembered that Bartleby never left the office.

"Bartleby," said I, "Ginger Nut is away; just step round to the Post Office, won't you? (it was but a three minutes walk,) and see if there is any thing for me."

"I would prefer not to."

"You will not?"

"I prefer not."

I staggered to my desk, and sat there in a deep study. My blind inveteracy returned. Was there any other thing in which I could procure myself to be ignominiously repulsed by this lean, penniless wight?—my hired clerk? What added thing is there, perfectly reasonable, that he will be sure to refuse to do?

"Bartleby!"

No answer.

"Bartleby," in a louder tone.

No answer.

"Bartleby," I roared.

Like a very ghost, agreeably to the laws of magical invocation, at the third summons, he appeared at the entrance of his hermitage.

"Go to the next room, and tell Nippers to come to me."

"I prefer not to," he respectfully and slowly said, and mildly disappeared.

"Very good, Bartleby," said I, in a quiet sort of serenely severe self-possessed tone, intimating the unalterable purpose of some terrible retribution very close at hand. At the moment I half intended something of the kind. But upon the whole, as it was drawing towards my dinner-hour, I thought it best to put on my hat and walk home for the day, suffering much from perplexity and distress of mind.

Shall I acknowledge it? The conclusion of this whole business was, that it soon became a fixed fact of my chambers, that a pale young scrivener, by the name of Bartleby, had a desk there; that he copied for me at the usual rate of four cents a folio (one hundred words); but he was permanently exempt from examining the work done by him, that duty being transferred to Turkey and Nippers, out of compliment doubtless to their superior acuteness; moreover, said Bartleby was never on any account to be dispatched on the most trivial errand of any sort; and that even if entreated to take upon him such a matter, it was generally understood that he would prefer not to—in other words, that he would refuse point-blank.

As days passed on, I became considerably reconciled to Bartleby. His steadiness, his freedom from all dissipation, his incessant industry (except when he chose to throw himself into a standing revery behind his screen), his great stillness, his unalterableness of demeanor under all circumstances, made him a valuable acquisition. One prime thing was this,—*he was always there*;—first in the morning, continually through the day, and the last at night. I had a singular confidence in his honesty. I felt my most precious papers perfectly safe in his hands. Sometimes to be sure I could not, for the very soul of me, avoid falling into sudden spasmodic passions with him. For it was exceeding difficult to bear in mind all the time those strange peculiarities, privileges, and unheard of exemptions, forming the tacit stipulations on Bartleby's part under which he remained in my office. Now and then, in the eagerness of dispatching pressing business, I would inadvertently summon Bartleby, in a short, rapid tone, to put his finger, say, on the incipient tie of a bit of red tape with which I was about compressing some papers. Of course, from behind the screen the usual answer, "I prefer not to," was sure to come; and then, how could a human creature with the common infirmities of our nature, refrain from bitterly exclaiming upon such perverseness—such unreasonableness. However, every added repulse of this sort which I received only tended to lessen the probability of my repeating the inadvertence.

Here it must be said, that according to the custom of most legal gentlemen occupying chambers in densely-populated law buildings, there were several keys to my door. One was kept by a woman residing in the attic, which person weekly scrubbed and daily swept and dusted my apartments. Another was kept by Turkey for convenience sake. The third I sometimes carried in my own pocket. The fourth I knew not who had.

Now, one Sunday morning I happened to go to Trinity Church, to hear a celebrated preacher, and finding myself rather early on the ground, I thought I would walk round to my chambers for a while. Luckily I had my key with me; but upon applying it to the lock, I found it resisted by something inserted from the inside. Quite surprised, I called out; when to my consternation a key was turned from within; and thrusting his lean visage at me, and holding the door ajar, the apparition of Bartleby appeared, in his shirt sleeves, and otherwise in a strangely tattered dishabille, saying quietly that he was sorry, but he was deeply engaged just then, and—preferred not admitting me at present. In a brief word or two, he moreover added, that perhaps I had better walk round the block two or three times, and by that time he would probably have concluded his affairs.

Now, the utterly unsurmised appearance of Bartleby, tenanting my law-chambers of a Sunday morning, with his cadaverously gentlemanly *noncha-lance*, yet withal firm and self-possessed, had such a strange effect upon me, that incontinently I slunk away from my own door, and did as desired. But not without sundry twinges of impotent rebellion against the mild effrontery of this unaccountable scrivener. Indeed, it was his wonderful mildness chiefly, which not only disarmed me, but unmanned me, as it were. For I consider that one, for the time, is a sort of unmanned when he tranquilly permits his hired clerk to dictate to him, and order him away from his own premises. Further-more, I was full of uneasiness as to what Bartleby could possibly be doing in my office in his shirt sleeves, and in an otherwise dismantled condition of a Sunday morning. Was any thing amiss going on? Nay, that was out of the ques-tion. It was not to be thought of for a moment that Bartleby was an immoral person. But what could he be doing there?—copying? Nay again, whatever might be his eccentricities, Bartleby was an eminently decorous person. He would be the last man to sit down to his desk in any state approaching to nudity. Besides, it was Sunday; and there was something about Bartleby that forbade the supposition that he would by any secular occupation violate the proprieties of the day.

Nevertheless, my mind was not pacified; and full of a restless curiosity, at last I returned to the door. Without hindrance I inserted my key, opened it, and entered. Bartleby was not to be seen. I looked round anxiously, peeped behind his screen; but it was very plain that he was gone. Upon more closely examin-ing the place, I surmised that for an indefinite period Bartleby must have ate, dressed, and slept in my office, and that too without plate, mirror, or bed. The cushioned seat of a ricketty old sofa in one corner bore the faint impress of a lean, reclining form. Rolled away under his desk, I found a blanket; under the empty grate, a blacking box and brush; on a chair, a tin basin, with soap and a ragged towel; in a newspaper a few crumbs of ginger-nuts and a morsel of cheese. Yes, thought I, it is evident enough that Bartleby has been making his home here, keeping bachelor's hall all by himself. Immediately then the thought came sweeping across me, What miserable friendlessness and loneliness are here revealed! His poverty is great; but his solitude, how horrible! Think of it.

Of a Sunday, Wall-street is deserted as Petra;[4] and every night of every day it is an emptiness. This building too, which of week-days hums with industry and life, at nightfall echoes with sheer vacancy, and all through Sunday is forlorn. And here Bartleby makes his home, sole spectator of a solitude which he has seen all populous—a sort of innocent and transformed Marius brooding among the ruins of Carthage![5]

For the first time in my life a feeling of overpowering stinging melancholy seized me. Before, I had never experienced aught but a not-unpleasing sadness. The bond of a common humanity now drew me irresistibly to gloom. A fraternal melancholy! For both I and Bartleby were sons of Adam. I remembered the bright silks and sparkling faces I had seen that day, in gala trim, swan-like sailing down the Mississippi of Broadway; and I contrasted them with the pallid copyist, and thought to myself, Ah, happiness courts the light, so we deem the world is gay; but misery hides aloof, so we deem that misery there is none. These sad fancyings—chimeras, doubtless, of a sick and silly brain—led on to other and more special thoughts, concerning the eccentricities of Bartleby. Presentiments of strange discoveries hovered round me. The scrivener's pale form appeared to me laid out, among uncaring strangers, in its shivering winding sheet.

Suddenly I was attracted by Bartleby's closed desk, the key in open sight left in the lock.

I mean no mischief, seek the gratification of no heartless curiosity, thought I; besides, the desk is mine, and its contents too, so I will make bold to look within. Every thing was methodically arranged, the papers smoothly placed. The pigeon holes were deep, and removing the files of documents, I groped into their recesses. Presently I felt something there, and dragged it out. It was an old bandanna handkerchief, heavy and knotted. I opened it, and saw it was a savings' bank.

I now recalled all the quiet mysteries which I had noted in the man. I remembered that he never spoke but to answer; that though at intervals he had considerable time to himself, yet I had never seen him reading—no, not even a newspaper; that for long periods he would stand looking out, at his pale window behind the screen, upon the dead brick wall; I was quite sure he never visited any refectory or eating house; while his pale face clearly indicated that he never drank beer like Turkey, or tea and coffee even, like other men; that he never went any where in particular that I could learn; never went out for a walk, unless indeed that was the case at present; that he had declined telling who he was, or whence he came, or whether he had any relatives in the world; that though so thin and pale, he never complained of ill health. And more than all, I remembered a certain unconscious air of pallid—how shall I call it?—of pallid haughtiness, say, or rather an austere reserve about him, which had positively awed me into my tame compliance with his eccentricities, when I had feared to ask him to do the slightest incidental thing for me, even though I might know, from his long-continued motionlessness, that behind his screen he must be standing in one of those dead-wall reveries of his.

4. Ancient city in what is now Jordan, rediscovered in 1812 after centuries of neglect.
5. Gaius Marius (155–86 B.C.E.), a Roman
general who was exiled from Rome and denied
sanctuary in the African city of Carthage.

Revolving all these things, and coupling them with the recently discovered fact that he made my office his constant abiding place and home, and not forgetful of his morbid moodiness; revolving all these things, a prudential feeling began to steal over me. My first emotions had been those of pure melancholy and sincerest pity; but just in proportion as the forlornness of Bartleby grew and grew to my imagination, did that same melancholy merge into fear, that pity into repulsion. So true it is, and so terrible too, that up to a certain point the thought or sight of misery enlists our best affections; but, in certain special cases, beyond that point it does not. They err who would assert that invariably this is owing to the inherent selfishness of the human heart. It rather proceeds from a certain hopelessness of remedying excessive and organic ill. To a sensitive being, pity is not seldom pain. And when at last it is perceived that such pity cannot lead to effectual succor, common sense bids the soul be rid of it. What I saw that morning persuaded me that the scrivener was the victim of innate and incurable disorder. I might give alms to his body; but his body did not pain him; it was his soul that suffered, and his soul I could not reach.

I did not accomplish the purpose of going to Trinity Church that morning. Somehow, the things I had seen disqualified me for the time from church-going. I walked homeward, thinking what I would do with Bartleby. Finally, I resolved upon this;—I would put certain calm questions to him the next morning, touching his history, &c., and if he declined to answer them openly and unreservedly (and I supposed he would prefer not), then to give him a twenty dollar bill over and above whatever I might owe him, and tell him his services were no longer required; but that if in any other way I could assist him, I would be happy to do so, especially if he desired to return to his native place, wherever that might be; I would willingly help to defray the expenses. Moreover, if, after reaching home, he found himself at any time in want of aid, a letter from him would be sure of a reply.

The next morning came.

"Bartleby," said I, gently calling to him behind his screen.

No reply.

"Bartleby," said I, in a still gentler tone, "come here; I am not going to ask you to do any thing you would prefer not to do—I simply wish to speak to you."

Upon this he noiselessly slid into view.

"Will you tell me, Bartleby, where you were born?"

"I would prefer not to."

"Will you tell me *any thing* about yourself?"

"I would prefer not to."

"But what reasonable objection can you have to speak to me? I feel friendly towards you."

He did not look at me while I spoke, but kept his glance fixed upon my bust of Cicero, which as I then sat, was directly behind me, some six inches above my head.

"What is your answer, Bartleby?" said I, after waiting a considerable time for a reply, during which his countenance remained immovable, only there was the faintest conceivable tremor of the white attenuated mouth.

"At present I prefer to give no answer," he said, and retired into his hermitage.

It was rather weak in me I confess, but his manner on this occasion nettled me. Not only did there seem to lurk in it a certain calm disdain, but his perverseness seemed ungrateful, considering the undeniable good usage and indulgence he had received from me.

Again I sat ruminating what I should do. Mortified as I was at his behavior, and resolved as I had been to dismiss him when I entered my office, nevertheless I strangely felt something superstitious knocking at my heart, and forbidding me to carry out my purpose, and denouncing me for a villain if I dared to breathe one bitter word against this forlornest of mankind. At last, familiarly drawing my chair behind his screen, I sat down and said: "Bartleby, never mind then about revealing your history; but let me entreat you, as a friend, to comply as far as may be with the usages of this office. Say now you will help to examine papers to-morrow or next day: in short, say now that in a day or two you will begin to be a little reasonable:—say so, Bartleby."

"At present I would prefer not to be a little reasonable," was his mildly cadaverous reply.

Just then the folding-doors opened, and Nippers approached. He seemed suffering from an unusually bad night's rest, induced by severer indigestion than common. He overheard those final words of Bartleby.

"*Prefer not*, eh?" gritted Nippers—"I'd *prefer* him, if I were you, sir," addressing me—"I'd *prefer* him; I'd give him preferences, the stubborn mule! What is it, sir, pray, that he *prefers* not to do now?"

Bartleby moved not a limb.

"Mr. Nippers," said I, "I'd prefer that you would withdraw for the present."

Somehow, of late I had got into the way of involuntarily using this word "prefer" upon all sorts of not exactly suitable occasions. And I trembled to think that my contact with the scrivener had already and seriously affected me in a mental way. And what further and deeper aberration might it not yet produce? This apprehension had not been without efficacy in determining me to summary measures.

As Nippers, looking very sour and sulky, was departing, Turkey blandly and deferentially approached.

"With submission, sir," said he, "yesterday I was thinking about Bartleby here, and I think that if he would but prefer to take a quart of good ale every day, it would do much towards mending him, and enabling him to assist in examining his papers."

"So you have got the word too," said I, slightly excited.

"With submission, what word, sir," asked Turkey, respectfully crowding himself into the contracted space behind the screen, and by so doing, making me jostle the scrivener. "What word, sir?"

"I would prefer to be left alone here," said Bartleby, as if offended at being mobbed in his privacy.

"*That's* the word, Turkey," said I—"*that's* it."

"Oh, *prefer*? oh yes—queer word. I never use it myself. But, sir, as I was saying, if he would but prefer—"

"Turkey," interrupted I, "you will please withdraw."

"Oh certainly, sir, if you prefer that I should."

As he opened the folding-doors to retire, Nippers at his desk caught a glimpse of me, and asked whether I would prefer to have a certain paper copied on blue paper or white. He did not in the least roguishly accent the word prefer. It was plain that it involuntarily rolled from his tongue. I thought to myself, surely I must get rid of a demented man, who already has in some degree turned the tongues, if not the heads of myself and clerks. But I thought it prudent not to break the dismission at once.

The next day I noticed that Bartleby did nothing but stand at his window in his dead-wall revery. Upon asking him why he did not write, he said that he had decided upon doing no more writing.

"Why, how now? what next?" exclaimed I, "do no more writing?"

"No more."

"And what is the reason?"

"Do you not see the reason for yourself," he indifferently replied.

I looked steadfastly at him, and perceived that his eyes looked dull and glazed. Instantly it occurred to me, that his unexampled diligence in copying by his dim window for the first few weeks of his stay with me might have temporarily impaired his vision.

I was touched. I said something in condolence with him. I hinted that of course he did wisely in abstaining from writing for a while; and urged him to embrace that opportunity of taking wholesome exercise in the open air. This, however, he did not do. A few days after this, my other clerks being absent, and being in a great hurry to dispatch certain letters by the mail, I thought that, having nothing else earthly to do, Bartleby would surely be less inflexible than usual, and carry these letters to the post-office. But he blankly declined. So, much to my inconvenience, I went myself.

Still added days went by. Whether Bartleby's eyes improved or not, I could not say. To all appearance, I thought they did. But when I asked him if they did, he vouchsafed no answer. At all events, he would do no copying. At last, in reply to my urgings, he informed me that he had permanently given up copying.

"What!" exclaimed I; "suppose your eyes should get entirely well—better than ever before—would you not copy then?"

"I have given up copying," he answered, and slid aside.

He remained as ever, a fixture in my chamber. Nay—if that were possible—he became still more of a fixture than before. What was to be done? He would do nothing in the office: why should he stay there? In plain fact, he had now become a millstone to me, not only useless as a necklace, but afflictive to bear. Yet I was sorry for him. I speak less than truth when I say that, on his own account, he occasioned me uneasiness. If he would but have named a single relative or friend, I would instantly have written, and urged their taking the poor fellow away to some convenient retreat. But he seemed alone, absolutely alone in the universe. A bit of wreck in the mid Atlantic. At length, necessities connected with my business tyrannized over all other considerations. Decently as I could, I told Bartleby that in six days' time he must unconditionally leave the office. I warned him to take measures, in the interval, for procuring some other abode. I offered to assist him in this endeavor, if he himself would but take the first step towards a removal. "And when you finally quit me, Bartleby," added I, "I shall see that you go not away entirely unprovided. Six days from this hour, remember."

At the expiration of that period, I peeped behind the screen, and lo! Bartleby was there.

I buttoned up my coat, balanced myself; advanced slowly towards him, touched his shoulder, and said, "The time has come; you must quit this place; I am sorry for you; here is money; but you must go."

"I would prefer not," he replied, with his back still towards me.

"You *must*."

He remained silent.

Now I had an unbounded confidence in this man's common honesty. He had frequently restored to me sixpences and shillings carelessly dropped upon the floor, for I am apt to be very reckless in such shirt-button affairs. The proceeding then which followed will not be deemed extraordinary.

"Bartleby," said I, "I owe you twelve dollars on account; here are thirty-two; the odd twenty are yours.—Will you take it?" and I handed the bills towards him.

But he made no motion.

"I will leave them here then," putting them under a weight on the table. Then taking my hat and cane and going to the door I tranquilly turned and added—"After you have removed your things from these offices, Bartleby, you will of course lock the door—since every one is now gone for the day but you—and if you please, slip your key underneath the mat, so that I may have it in the morning. I shall not see you again; so good-bye to you. If hereafter in your new place of abode I can be of any service to you, do not fail to advise me by letter. Good-bye, Bartleby, and fare you well."

But he answered not a word; like the last column of some ruined temple, he remained standing mute and solitary in the middle of the otherwise deserted room.

As I walked home in a pensive mood, my vanity got the better of my pity. I could not but highly plume myself on my masterly management in getting rid of Bartleby. Masterly I call it, and such it must appear to any dispassionate thinker. The beauty of my procedure seemed to consist in its perfect quietness. There was no vulgar bullying, no bravado of any sort, no choleric hectoring, and striding to and fro across the apartment, jerking out vehement commands for Bartleby to bundle himself off with his beggarly traps. Nothing of the kind. Without loudly bidding Bartleby depart—as an inferior genius might have done—I *assumed* the ground that depart he must; and upon that assumption built all I had to say. The more I thought over my procedure, the more I was charmed with it. Nevertheless, next morning, upon awakening, I had my doubts,—I had somehow slept off the fumes of vanity. One of the coolest and wisest hours a man has, is just after he awakes in the morning. My procedure seemed as sagacious as ever,—but only in theory. How it would prove in practice—there was the rub. It was truly a beautiful thought to have assumed Bartleby's departure; but, after all, that assumption was simply my own, and none of Bartleby's. The great point was, not whether I had assumed that he would quit me, but whether he would prefer so to do. He was more a man of preferences than assumptions.

After breakfast, I walked down town, arguing the probabilities *pro* and *con*. One moment I thought it would prove a miserable failure, and Bartleby would be found all alive at my office as usual; the next moment it seemed certain that I should find his chair empty. And so I kept veering about. At the corner of Broadway and Canal-street, I saw quite an excited group of people standing in earnest conversation.

"I'll take odds he doesn't," said a voice as I passed.

"Doesn't go?—done!" said I, "put up your money."

I was instinctively putting my hand in my pocket to produce my own, when I remembered that this was an election day. The words I had overheard bore no reference to Bartleby, but to the success or non-success of some candidate for the mayoralty. In my intent frame of mind, I had, as it were, imagined that all Broadway shared in my excitement, and were debating the same question with me. I passed on, very thankful that the uproar of the street screened my momentary absent-mindedness.

As I had intended, I was earlier than usual at my office door. I stood listening for a moment. All was still. He must be gone. I tried the knob. The door was locked. Yes, my procedure had worked to a charm; he indeed must be vanished. Yet a certain melancholy mixed with this: I was almost sorry for my brilliant success. I was fumbling under the door mat for the key, which Bartleby was to have left there for me, when accidentally my knee knocked against a panel, producing a summoning sound, and in response a voice came to me from within—"Not yet; I am occupied."

It was Bartleby.

I was thunderstruck. For an instant I stood like the man who, pipe in mouth, was killed one cloudless afternoon long ago in Virginia, by summer lightning; at his own warm open window he was killed, and remained leaning out there upon the dreamy afternoon, till some one touched him, when he fell.

"Not gone!" I murmured at last. But again obeying that wondrous ascendancy which the inscrutable scrivener had over me, and from which ascendancy, for all my chafing, I could not completely escape, I slowly went down stairs and out into the street, and while walking round the block, considered what I should next do in this unheard-of perplexity. Turn the man out by an actual thrusting I could not; to drive him away by calling him hard names would not do; calling in the police was an unpleasant idea; and yet, permit him to enjoy his cadaverous triumph over me,—this too I could not think of. What was to be done? or, if nothing could be done, was there any thing further that I could *assume* in the matter? Yes, as before I had prospectively assumed that Bartleby would depart, so now I might retrospectively assume that departed he was. In the legitimate carrying out of this assumption, I might enter my office in a great hurry, and pretending not to see Bartleby at all, walk straight against him as if he were air. Such a proceeding would in a singular degree have the appearance of a home-thrust. It was hardly possible that Bartleby could withstand such an application of the doctrine of assumptions. But upon second thoughts the success of the plan seemed rather dubious. I resolved to argue the matter over with him again.

"Bartleby," said I, entering the office, with a quietly severe expression, "I am seriously displeased. I am pained, Bartleby. I had thought better of you. I had imagined you of such a gentlemanly organization, that in any delicate dilemma a slight hint would suffice—in short, an assumption. But it appears I am deceived. Why," I added, unaffectedly starting, "you have not even touched that money yet," pointing to it, just where I had left it the evening previous.

He answered nothing.

"Will you, or will you not, quit me?" I now demanded in a sudden passion, advancing close to him.

"I would prefer *not* to quit you," he replied, gently emphasizing the *not*.

"What earthly right have you to stay here? Do you pay any rent? Do you pay my taxes? Or is this property yours?"

He answered nothing.

"Are you ready to go on and write now? Are your eyes recovered? Could you copy a small paper for me this morning? or help examine a few lines? or step round to the post-office? In a word, will you do any thing at all, to give a coloring to your refusal to depart the premises?"

He silently retired into his hermitage.

I was now in such a state of nervous resentment that I thought it but prudent to check myself at present from further demonstrations. Bartleby and I were alone. I remembered the tragedy of the unfortunate Adams and the still more unfortunate Colt in the solitary office of the latter;[6] and how poor Colt, being dreadfully incensed by Adams, and imprudently permitting himself to get wildly excited, was at unawares hurried into his fatal act—an act which certainly no man could possibly deplore more than the actor himself. Often it had occurred to me in my ponderings upon the subject, that had that altercation taken place in the public street, or at a private residence, it would not have terminated as it did. It was the circumstance of being alone in a solitary office, up stairs, of a building entirely unhallowed by humanizing domestic associations—an uncarpeted office, doubtless, of a dusty, haggard sort of appearance;—this it must have been, which greatly helped to enhance the irritable desperation of the hapless Colt.

But when this old Adam of resentment rose in me and tempted me concerning Bartleby, I grappled him and threw him. How? Why, simply by recalling the divine injunction: "A new commandment give I unto you, that ye love one another."[7] Yes, this it was that saved me. Aside from higher considerations, charity often operates as a vastly wise and prudent principle—a great safeguard to its possessor. Men have committed murder for jealousy's sake, and anger's sake, and hatred's sake, and selfishness' sake, and spiritual pride's sake; but no man that ever I heard of, ever committed a diabolical murder for sweet charity's sake. Mere self-interest, then, if no better motive can be enlisted, should, especially with high-tempered men, prompt all beings to charity and philanthropy. At any rate, upon the occasion in question, I strove to drown my exasperated feelings towards the scrivener by benevolently construing his conduct. Poor fellow, poor fellow! thought I, he don't mean any thing; and besides, he has seen hard times, and ought to be indulged.

I endeavored also immediately to occupy myself, and at the same time to comfort my despondency. I tried to fancy that in the course of the morning, at such time as might prove agreeable to him, Bartleby, of his own free accord, would emerge from his hermitage, and take up some decided line of march in the direction of the door. But no. Half-past twelve o'clock came; Turkey began to glow in the face, overturn his inkstand, and become generally obstreperous;

6. In 1841 Samuel Adams, a New York printer, was murdered by John C. Colt, an accountant, after badgering Colt in his office about an outstanding loan; the distraught Colt committed suicide before he could be executed.
7. Jesus' command to his disciples before he is crucified (John 13.34).

Nippers abated down into quietude and courtesy; Ginger Nut munched his noon apple; and Bartleby remained standing at his window in one of his profoundest dead-wall reveries. Will it be credited? Ought I to acknowledge it? That afternoon I left the office without saying one further word to him.

Some days now passed, during which, at leisure intervals I looked a little into "Edwards on the Will," and "Priestley on Necessity."[8] Under the circumstances, those books induced a salutary feeling. Gradually I slid into the persuasion that these troubles of mine touching the scrivener, had been all predestinated from eternity, and Bartleby was billeted upon me for some mysterious purpose of an all-wise Providence, which it was not for a mere mortal like me to fathom. Yes, Bartleby, stay there behind your screen, thought I; I shall persecute you no more; you are harmless and noiseless as any of these old chairs; in short, I never feel so private as when I know you are here. At last I see it, I feel it; I penetrate to the predestinated purpose of my life. I am content. Others may have loftier parts to enact; but my mission in this world, Bartleby, is to furnish you with office-room for such period as you may see fit to remain.

I believe that this wise and blessed frame of mind would have continued with me, had it not been for the unsolicited and uncharitable remarks obtruded upon me by my professional friends who visited the rooms. But thus it often is, that the constant friction of illiberal minds wears out at last the best resolves of the more generous. Though to be sure, when I reflected upon it, it was not strange that people entering my office should be struck by the peculiar aspect of the unaccountable Bartleby, and so be tempted to throw out some sinister observations concerning him. Sometimes an attorney having business with me, and calling at my office, and finding no one but the scrivener there, would undertake to obtain some sort of precise information from him touching my whereabouts; but without heeding his idle talk, Bartleby would remain standing immovable in the middle of the room. So after contemplating him in that position for a time, the attorney would depart, no wiser than he came.

Also, when a Reference[9] was going on, and the room full of lawyers and witnesses and business was driving fast; some deeply occupied legal gentleman present, seeing Bartleby wholly unemployed, would request him to run round to his (the legal gentleman's) office and fetch some papers for him. Thereupon, Bartleby would tranquilly decline, and yet remain idle as before. Then the lawyer would give a great stare, and turn to me. And what could I say? At last I was made aware that all through the circle of my professional acquaintance, a whisper of wonder was running round, having reference to the strange creature I kept at my office. This worried me very much. And as the idea came upon me of his possibly turning out a long-lived man, and keep occupying my chambers, and denying my authority; and perplexing my visitors; and scandalizing my professional reputation; and casting a general gloom over the premises, keeping soul and body together to the last upon his savings (for doubtless he spent but half a dime a day), and in the end perhaps outlive me, and claim

8. Jonathan Edwards's *Freedom of the Will* (1754) claimed that God determines the kinds of choices that human beings will make; Joseph Priestley's *Doctrine of Philosophical Necessity Illustrated* (1777) argued that people cannot be blamed for wrongdoing because all human action ultimately fulfills the divine will.
9. Legal case referred to the Court of Chancery to be resolved.

possession of my office by right of his perpetual occupancy: as all these dark anticipations crowded upon me more and more, and my friends continually intruded their relentless remarks upon the apparition in my room; a great change was wrought in me. I resolved to gather all my faculties together, and for ever rid me of this intolerable incubus.

Ere revolving any complicated project, however, adapted to this end, I first simply suggested to Bartleby the propriety of his permanent departure. In a calm and serious tone, I commended the idea to his careful and mature consideration. But having taken three days to meditate upon it, he apprised me that his original determination remained the same; in short, that he still preferred to abide with me.

What shall I do? I now said to myself, buttoning up my coat to the last button. What shall I do? what ought I to do? what does conscience say I *should* do with this man, or rather ghost? Rid myself of him, I must; go, he shall. But how? You will not thrust him, the poor, pale, passive mortal,—you will not thrust such a helpless creature out of your door? you will not dishonor yourself by such cruelty? No, I will not, I cannot do that. Rather would I let him live and die here, and then mason up his remains in the wall. What then will you do? For all your coaxing, he will not budge. Bribes he leaves under your own paper-weight on your table; in short, it is quite plain that he prefers to cling to you.

Then something severe, something unusual must be done. What! surely you will not have him collared by a constable, and commit his innocent pallor to the common jail? And upon what ground could you procure such a thing to be done?—a vagrant, is he? What! he a vagrant, a wanderer, who refuses to budge? It is because he will *not* be a vagrant, then, that you seek to count him *as* a vagrant. That is too absurd. No visible means of support: there I have him. Wrong again: for indubitably he *does* support himself, and that is the only unanswerable proof that any man can show of his possessing the means so to do. No more then. Since he will not quit me, I must quit him. I will change my offices; I will move elsewhere; and give him fair notice, that if I find him on my new premises I will then proceed against him as a common trespasser.

Acting accordingly, next day I thus addressed him: "I find these chambers too far from the City Hall; the air is unwholesome. In a word, I propose to remove my offices next week, and shall no longer require your services. I tell you this now, in order that you may seek another place."

He made no reply, and nothing more was said.

On the appointed day I engaged carts and men, proceeded to my chambers, and having but little furniture, every thing was removed in a few hours. Throughout, the scrivener remained standing behind the screen, which I directed to be removed the last thing. It was withdrawn; and being folded up like a huge folio, left him the motionless occupant of a naked room. I stood in the entry watching him a moment, while something from within me upbraided me.

I re-entered, with my hand in my pocket—and—and my heart in my mouth.

"Good-bye, Bartleby; I am going—good-bye, and God some way bless you; and take that," slipping something in his hand. But it dropped upon the floor, and then,—strange to say—I tore myself from him whom I had so longed to be rid of.

Established in my new quarters, for a day or two I kept the door locked, and started at every footfall in the passage. When I returned to my rooms after any little absence, I would pause at the threshold for an instant, and attentively listen, ere applying my key. But these fears were needless. Bartleby never came nigh me.

I thought all was going well, when a perturbed looking stranger visited me, inquiring whether I was the person who had recently occupied rooms at No. — Wall-street.

Full of forebodings, I replied that I was.

"Then sir," said the stranger, who proved a lawyer, "you are responsible for the man you left there. He refuses to do any copying; he refuses to do any thing; he says he prefers not to; and he refuses to quit the premises."

"I am very sorry, sir," said I, with assumed tranquillity, but an inward tremor, "but, really, the man you allude to is nothing to me—he is no relation or apprentice of mine, that you should hold me responsible for him."

"In mercy's name, who is he?"

"I certainly cannot inform you. I know nothing about him. Formerly I employed him as a copyist; but he has done nothing for me now for some time past."

"I shall settle him then,—good morning, sir."

Several days passed, and I heard nothing more; and though I often felt a charitable prompting to call at the place and see poor Bartleby, yet a certain squeamishness of I know not what withheld me.

All is over with him, by this time, thought I at last, when through another week no further intelligence reached me. But coming to my room the day after, I found several persons waiting at my door in a high state of nervous excitement.

"That's the man—here he comes," cried the foremost one, whom I recognized as the lawyer who had previously called upon me alone.

"You must take him away, sir, at once," cried a portly person among them, advancing upon me, and whom I knew to be the landlord of No. — Wall-street. "These gentlemen, my tenants, cannot stand it any longer; Mr. B——" pointing to the lawyer, "has turned him out of his room, and he now persists in haunting the building generally, sitting upon the banisters of the stairs by day, and sleeping in the entry by night. Every body is concerned; clients are leaving the offices; some fears are entertained of a mob; something you must do, and that without delay."

Aghast at this torrent, I fell back before it, and would fain have locked myself in my new quarters. In vain I persisted that Bartleby was nothing to me—no more than to any one else. In vain:—I was the last person known to have any thing to do with him, and they held me to the terrible account. Fearful then of being exposed in the papers (as one person present obscurely threatened) I considered the matter, and at length said, that if the lawyer would give me a confidential interview with the scrivener, in his (the lawyer's) own room, I would that afternoon strive my best to rid them of the nuisance they complained of.

Going up stairs to my old haunt, there was Bartleby silently sitting upon the banister at the landing.

"What are you doing here, Bartleby?" said I.

"Sitting upon the banister," he mildly replied.

I motioned him into the lawyer's room, who then left us.

"Bartleby," said I, "are you aware that you are the cause of great tribulation to me, by persisting in occupying the entry after being dismissed from the office?"

No answer.

"Now one of two things must take place. Either you must do something, or something must be done to you. Now what sort of business would you like to engage in? Would you like to re-engage in copying for some one?"

"No; I would prefer not to make any change."

"Would you like a clerkship in a dry-goods store?"

"There is too much confinement about that. No, I would not like a clerkship; but I am not particular."

"Too much confinement," I cried, "why you keep yourself confined all the time!"

"I would prefer not to take a clerkship," he rejoined, as if to settle that little item at once.

"How would a bar-tender's business suit you? There is no trying of the eye-sight in that."

"I would not like it at all; though, as I said before, I am not particular."

His unwonted wordiness inspirited me. I returned to the charge.

"Well then, would you like to travel through the country collecting bills for the merchants? That would improve your health."

"No, I would prefer to be doing something else."

"How then would going as a companion to Europe, to entertain some young gentleman with your conversation,—how would that suit you?"

"Not at all. It does not strike me that there is any thing definite about that. I like to be stationary. But I am not particular."

"Stationary you shall be then," I cried, now losing all patience, and for the first time in all my exasperating connection with him fairly flying into a passion. "If you do not go away from these premises before night, I shall feel bound—indeed I *am* bound—to—to—to quit the premises myself!" I rather absurdly concluded, knowing not with what possible threat to try to frighten his immobility into compliance. Despairing of all further efforts, I was precipitately leaving him, when a final thought occurred to me—one which had not been wholly unindulged before.

"Bartleby," said I, in the kindest tone I could assume under such exciting circumstances, "will you go home with me now—not to my office, but my dwelling—and remain there till we can conclude upon some convenient arrangement for you at our leisure? Come, let us start now, right away."

"No: at present I would prefer not to make any change at all."

I answered nothing; but effectually dodging every one by the suddenness and rapidity of my flight, rushed from the building, ran up Wall-street towards Broadway, and jumping into the first omnibus was soon removed from pursuit. As soon as tranquillity returned I distinctly perceived that I had now done all that I possibly could, both in respect to the demands of the landlord and his tenants, and with regard to my own desire and sense of duty, to benefit Bartleby, and shield him from rude persecution. I now strove to be entirely care-free and quiescent; and my conscience justified me in the attempt; though indeed it was not so successful as I could have wished. So fearful was I of being again hunted out by the incensed landlord and his exasperated tenants, that, surrendering my business to Nippers, for a few days I drove about the upper part of the town and through the suburbs, in my rockaway;[1] crossed over to Jersey City and Hoboken, and paid fugitive visits to Manhattanville and Astoria. In fact I almost lived in my rockaway for the time.

When again I entered my office, lo, a note from the landlord lay upon the desk. I opened it with trembling hands. It informed me that the writer had sent to the police, and had Bartleby removed to the Tombs as a vagrant. Moreover, since I knew more about him than any one else, he wished me to appear at that place, and make a suitable statement of the facts. These tidings had a conflicting effect upon me. At first I was indignant; but at last almost approved. The landlord's energetic, summary disposition, had led him to adopt a procedure which I do not think I would have decided upon myself; and yet as a last resort, under such peculiar circumstances, it seemed the only plan.

As I afterwards learned, the poor scrivener, when told that he must be conducted to the Tombs, offered not the slightest obstacle, but in his pale unmoving way, silently acquiesced.

Some of the compassionate and curious bystanders joined the party; and headed by one of the constables arm in arm with Bartleby, the silent procession filed its way through all the noise, and heat, and joy of the roaring thoroughfares at noon.

The same day I received the note I went to the Tombs, or to speak more properly, the Halls of Justice. Seeking the right officer, I stated the purpose of my call, and was informed that the individual I described was indeed within. I then assured the functionary that Bartleby was a perfectly honest man, and greatly to be compassionated, however unaccountably eccentric. I narrated all I knew, and closed by suggesting the idea of letting him remain in as indulgent confinement as possible till something less harsh might be done—though indeed I hardly knew what. At all events, if nothing else could be decided upon, the alms-house must receive him. I then begged to have an interview.

Being under no disgraceful charge, and quite serene and harmless in all his ways, they had permitted him freely to wander about the prison, and especially in the inclosed grass-platted yards thereof. And so I found him there, standing all alone in the quietest of the yards, his face towards a high wall, while all around, from the narrow slits of the jail windows, I thought I saw peering out upon him the eyes of murderers and thieves.

"Bartleby!"

"I know you," he said, without looking round,—"and I want nothing to say to you."

"It was not I that brought you here, Bartleby," said I, keenly pained at his implied suspicion. "And to you, this should not be so vile a place. Nothing reproachful attaches to you by being here. And see, it is not so sad a place as one might think. Look, there is the sky, and here is the grass."

"I know where I am," he replied, but would say nothing more, and so I left him.

As I entered the corridor again, a broad meat-like man, in an apron, accosted me, and jerking his thumb over his shoulder said—"Is that your friend?"

"Yes."

1. A type of four-wheeled carriage.

"Does he want to starve? If he does, let him live on the prison fare, that's all."

"Who are you?" asked I, not knowing what to make of such an unofficially speaking person in such a place.

"I am the grub-man. Such gentlemen as have friends here, hire me to provide them with something good to eat."

"Is this so?" said I, turning to the turnkey.

He said it was.

"Well then," said I, slipping some silver into the grub-man's hands (for so they called him). "I want you to give particular attention to my friend there; let him have the best dinner you can get. And you must be as polite to him as possible."

"Introduce me, will you?" said the grub-man, looking at me with an expression which seemed to say he was all impatience for an opportunity to give a specimen of his breeding.

Thinking it would prove of benefit to the scrivener, I acquiesced; and asking the grub-man his name, went up with him to Bartleby.

"Bartleby, this is Mr. Cutlets; you will find him very useful to you."

"Your sarvant, sir, your sarvant," said the grub-man, making a low salutation behind his apron. "Hope you find it pleasant here, sir; nice grounds—cool apartments, sir—hope you'll stay with us some time—try to make it agreeable. May Mrs. Cutlets and I have the pleasure of your company to dinner, sir, in Mrs. Cutlets' private room?"

"I prefer not to dine to-day," said Bartleby, turning away. "It would disagree with me; I am unused to dinners." So saying he slowly moved to the other side of the inclosure, and took up a position fronting the dead-wall.

"How's this?" said the grub-man, addressing me with a stare of astonishment. "He's odd, aint he?"

"I think he is a little deranged," said I, sadly.

"Deranged? deranged is it? Well now, upon my word, I thought that friend of yourn was a gentleman forger; they are always pale and genteel-like, them forgers. I can't help pity 'em—can't help it, sir. Did you know Monroe Edwards?"[2] he added touchingly, and paused. Then, laying his hand pityingly on my shoulder, sighed, "he died of consumption at Sing-Sing.[3] So you weren't acquainted with Monroe?"

"No, I was never socially acquainted with any forgers. But I cannot stop longer. Look to my friend yonder. You will not lose by it. I will see you again."

Some few days after this, I again obtained admission to the Tombs, and went through the corridors in quest of Bartleby; but without finding him.

"I saw him coming from his cell not long ago," said a turnkey, "may be he's gone to loiter in the yards."

So I went in that direction.

"Are you looking for the silent man?" said another turnkey passing me. "Yonder he lies—sleeping in the yard there. 'Tis not twenty minutes since I saw him lie down."

---

2. Monroe Edwards (ca. 1808–1847), the "Great Forger" who posed as a wealthy southern plantation owner.

3. Prison on the Hudson River in New York State.

The yard was entirely quiet. It was not accessible to the common prison-ers. The surrounding walls, of amazing thickness, kept off all sounds behind them. The Egyptian character of the masonry weighed upon me with its gloom. But a soft imprisoned turf grew under foot. The heart of the eternal pyramids, it seemed, wherein, by some strange magic, through the clefts, grass-seed, dropped by birds, had sprung.

Strangely huddled at the base of the wall, his knees drawn up, and lying on his side, his head touching the cold stones, I saw the wasted Bartleby. But nothing stirred. I paused; then went close up to him; stooped over, and saw that his dim eyes were open; otherwise he seemed profoundly sleeping. Some-thing prompted me to touch him. I felt his hand, when a tingling shiver ran up my arm and down my spine to my feet.

The round face of the grub-man peered upon me now. "His dinner is ready. Won't he dine to-day, either? Or does he live without dining?"

"Lives without dining," said I, and closed the eyes.

"Eh!—He's asleep, aint he?"

"With kings and counsellors,"[4] murmured I.

• • • • • •

There would seem little need for proceeding further in this history. Imagina-tion will readily supply the meagre recital of poor Bartleby's interment. But ere parting with the reader, let me say, that if this little narrative has sufficiently interested him, to awaken curiosity as to who Bartleby was, and what manner of life he led prior to the present narrator's making his acquaintance, I can only reply, that in such curiosity I fully share, but am wholly unable to gratify it. Yet here I hardly know whether I should divulge one little item of rumor, which came to my ear a few months after the scrivener's decease. Upon what basis it rested, I could never ascertain; and hence, how true it is I cannot now tell. But inasmuch as this vague report has not been without a certain strange suggestive interest to me, however sad, it may prove the same with some oth-ers; and so I will briefly mention it. The report was this: that Bartleby had been a subordinate clerk in the Dead Letter Office[5] at Washington, from which he had been suddenly removed by a change in the administration. When I think over this rumor, hardly can I express the emotions which seize me. Dead let-ters! does it not sound like dead men? Conceive a man by nature and misfor-tune prone to a pallid hopelessness, can any business seem more fitted to heighten it than that of continually handling these dead letters, and assorting them for the flames? For by the cart-load they are annually burned. Sometimes from out the folded paper the pale clerk takes a ring:—the finger it was meant for, perhaps, moulders in the grave; a bank-note sent in swiftest charity:—he whom it would relieve, nor eats nor hungers any more; pardon for those who died despairing; hope for those who died unhoping; good tidings for those who died stifled by unrelieved calamities. On errands of life, these letters speed to death.

Ah Bartleby! Ah humanity!

---

4. After many misfortunes, the biblical Job longs for eternal rest "with kings and counsel-ors" (Job 3.14).

5. The U.S. Postal Service's depository for undeliverable mail.

ROMANTIC POETS AND THEIR SUCCESSORS

The twentieth century is often considered the era of radical experimentation in poetry, but in fact throughout the nineteenth century poets in Europe and the Americas were inventing startling new poetic forms and resisting traditional expectations. It all began with the period we now know as Romanticism, a movement across the arts—literature, visual art, and music—that lasted roughly from the 1780s to the 1830s in Europe and the Americas. *Romanticism* often feels like a frustratingly loose term, encompassing so many styles and practices that it ceases to mean anything at all. It is associated with nature, and especially wild and untamed natural settings. It is often defined as a rejection of neoclassical styles—the revival of Greek and Roman traditions that had grown dominant in the eighteenth century—as well as a rejection of reason as the organizing principle for art and society. Romanticism tended to valorize the ordinary individual, the solitary soul, the visionary, even the outcast. The term evokes imagination, excess, spontaneity, freedom, and revolution. Romantic art often dwells in wild, ghostly, and exotic settings, and embraces a turn inward to the emotions, dreams, and fantasies. Romanticism is also associated with nationalism and folk traditions. Its dominant literary form is the lyric poem, though there were Romantic novels, dramas, plays, and autobiographies.

One way to grasp Romanticism as a concept is to investigate the crucial role that nature plays in the period. Before the 1780s in Europe, there was very little art that depicted natural scenes apart from the highly artful tradition of pastoral—which tended to portray flute-playing, classical-style shepherds in distinctly sheepless environments. Romantic artists were really the first group in the West to take nature as an important subject matter in and of itself: turning away from the manners and artifices of social life, writers and artists celebrated the beauties of vast skies and towering mountains, a world free from court intrigues and urban poverty. But why did this new focus on nature emerge at this particular moment? Two different historical explanations help to make sense of the shift. First, as the industrial revolution forced huge masses of people out of agricultural life and into crowded cities, nature became exotic—and therefore interesting and valuable—in a whole new way. That is, when the majority of people lived in the countryside, it had seemed ordinary, mundane. But as more and more people began to lead urban lives, while railways cut ugly gashes through the fields and black smoke billowed into the sky, nature's beauty began to seem rare and precious—and increasingly under threat. From this perspective, the sudden upsurge in artistic treatments of nature makes sense as a way to capture and honor an increasingly vulnerable natural environment.

There is also a second explanation for the new embrace of nature. In the eighteenth century, both absolute monarchies and new kinds of human knowledge—including science and statistics—valued control over nature. The gardens built by King Louis XIV of France at his grand palace of Versailles followed a rigid geometrical design, marking the power to subdue and order the natural world in accordance with the demands of human reason. Resisting old regimes of power, some radical late-eighteenth-century thinkers rejected this entwining of order and authority, and saw a return to the wildness of nature as a new model of expressive freedom, liberated from the constraints of reason and authority. Nature could be not only a source of beauty and inspiration, but a very foundation for a new kind of society that would replace the rule of absolute monarchs and rigid regulations. This new society would be based on the fulfillment of what was natural within human beings. Thus thinkers started to explore and celebrate nature as a kind of foundation for human experience, putting forward "natural laws" as the basis for social organizations, and crafting new state constitutions based on them. Here we see the emergence of new ideas about human rights—the notion that certain freedoms are given by nature alone and cannot justly be taken away by any government. Also emergent was a notion of a human community based not on kings or laws but on natural ties that united a group—an organic set of folk traditions that bound a people together indissolubly. Called "romantic nationalists," these thinkers celebrated local folklore, language, and customs—and often ethnic and racial differences—as the basis for national identity.

This revolutionary set of political ideals went hand in hand with a thoroughgoing revolution in poetry. Throwing off classical models, poets now looked to children and to "primitive" peoples who seemed closer to nature as models for social experience. They sought out new poetic forms that would capture natural rhythms and patterns of human speech. They turned to traditional folk and fairy tales for inspiration, and wrote in local dialects that had seemed low and coarse in the era of neoclassicism. And they valued not rigid conventions but what seemed most natural in the self: impulsiveness, excess, imaginative freedom. **William Wordsworth** cast the best new poetry as "the spontaneous overflow of powerful feelings," and **John Keats** wrote that "if poetry comes not as naturally as the leaves to a tree it had better not come at all." Instead of insisting on reason, art, and order as their sources of inspiration, poets looked to the unconscious mind, to spiritual awakening, and to dreams. They also valued ruins and relics of past times and exotic settings—anything that would jolt readers out of their entrenched sense of order and habit. Some of these Romantic themes contradicted each other—exotic settings and local traditions, individualism and racial foundations for communities—but they coexisted as a constellation of reactions against the dominant eighteenth-century values of order, reason, and authority.

For many writers—especially in England—the ideal poetic form for these new principles seemed to be the lyric. A lyric poem expresses a process of perception, thought, or emotion, often in the first person. Traditionally a marginal European form compared to epic, elegy, pastoral, and the satires popular in the eighteenth century, lyric grew so powerfully central to the definition of poetry in the nineteenth century that today it seems to have little in the way of competition. And it is thanks to the Romantics, with their insistence on turning away from the imitation of classical forms and toward the truth of inner experience—toward the individual's sincere, spontaneous feeling—that lyric came to prominence. Lyric has few set rules—one can choose any meter, stanza length, or structuring arc—and so it embodies the freedom from set conventions that Romantic poets valued. And its focus on processes of thought and feeling allowed poets to celebrate the great range of human emotion that seemed to have been suddenly released from rigid authority—imagination and desire, memory and mourning, speculation and idealism, and above all, a passionate interest in the truth of nature as a guide to beauty, freedom, community, and humanity itself.

This volume collects Romantic poems from Britain, Germany, Russia, Italy, Spain, and Venezuela. In Britain, the Romantics are usually divided into two generations. The first, which included **Barbauld**, **Blake**, Wordsworth, and **Coleridge**, caught the initial excitement of the French Revolution and its promise of a wholly new kind of society based on equal rights and freedom. They had all reached adulthood, too, in time to be disillusioned by the murderous turn the revolution took, when its leader, Maximilien de Robespierre, presided over the mass executions of the thousands he deemed enemies of the revolutionary cause. Wordsworth and Coleridge both turned conservative, losing faith in the revolution. The second generation of Romantic poets—including Mary and **Percy Shelley** and John Keats—came of age in a significantly different world from their precursors. After the "Reign of Terror," British leaders tried to turn a divided France to their advantage by supporting the counterrevolutionaries, engaging in wars with France that would last, on and off, for twenty-two years. They imposed heavy taxes to pay for these expensive and protracted wars. The poor suffered especially from high taxes on grain and a severe economic depression. Concerned about rising unrest, Parliament imposed strict censorship, suspended the right to trial, suppressed politically subversive groups, and accused even moderate critics of treason. The second-generation Romantics experienced this oppressive regime as both children and adults. And while they were strongly influenced by the literary work that had gone before them, they also felt a need to renew Romanticism's initial emancipatory energies and to criticize the conservative turn of its leaders.

EXPERIMENTAL POETS AT MID-CENTURY

Romanticism has no clear end point, and in fact, writers can still be called "Romantic" today if their values seem to fit the mood and spirit of the period. But it is true that some poets in the middle of the nineteenth century began to turn a critical eye on some of the most crucial Romantic presumptions. These transitional figures, such as **Elizabeth Barrett Browning**, **Heinrich Heine**, and **Walt Whitman**, continued some of the impulses of Romantic poetry but experimented with transforming its voice and subject matter. Both Barrett Browning and Heine rejected the solitary first-person perspective of the individual poet in order to write in the collective voice of oppressed workers, attempting an unusual poetry in which whole groups would speak as one. Both also expressed bitterness at the betrayal of Romantic ideals by industrial exploitation and thus maintained the values of the Romantics even as they turned away from the natural landscapes that had so inspired their predecessors. Walt Whitman took Romanticism to a new extreme: he used the first-person voice of lyric in the interests of speaking for a nation emancipated from oppression, and yet his experimental voice pushed past the style and focus of his European forebears toward a wholly new poetic form that paved the way for the free verse that would become popular in the twentieth century. **Robert Browning**, **Christina Rossetti**, and **Emily Dickinson** can also be seen to be in dialogue—and sometimes in tension—with their Romantic precursors. All of these transitional poets pushed at the boundaries of convention, inventing new and sometimes profoundly unsettling poetic forms, but they formed no single school or movement.

EMERGENT MODERNISM

Just after the midpoint of the nineteenth century, a handful of French poets launched innovations that would have a profound influence on world literature. **Charles Baudelaire** is sometimes called "the first modern poet." His successors—**Stéphane Mallarmé**, **Paul Verlaine**, and **Arthur Rimbaud**—built on his resistance to poetic convention and together came to be known as the Symbolists. Preserving the Romantic notion of the poet as a seer or visionary, they brought together intensely evocative images that were not necessarily related by any external logic. In fact, they rejected the notion that poetic language should communicate or resolve itself into clear meanings. The goal was not to make sense; rather, they developed a deliberately allusive, sometimes brutally coarse poetry that played with multiple and shifting perspectives and frequently led to a blurring of boundaries between real and imaginary. They even abandoned the notion of the lyric speaker as a stable self, assuming that language precedes and makes up the self, rather than the other way around. For the Symbolists, poetry should be purified of everything but language itself.

The Symbolists were the first of a series of movements that would soon come to be known as *avant-garde*. Originally a military term, it means "advance guard" and evokes the image of artists doing battle. In this case, the war was being waged in the name of the future. Artists of the avant-garde saw themselves not as representing the world as it was but as bringing in a new world through startling breaks in perception. They shattered old views in favor of disconcerting new modes of seeing, which they hoped would then usher in radically new ways of living. Impressionism in painting, a famous avant-garde movement like Symbolism in poetry, literally broke color apart to lay bare its components of light and human perception.

In their struggle to make a radical break from the past, the Symbolists marked the beginnings of Modernism, an international movement that would flourish in the first half of the twentieth century. Already in the 1890s, the influence of the Symbolists could be felt far from Paris. Nicaraguan-born poet **Rubén Darío** was in fact the first person to use the term *modernismo* to describe what was happening in the arts. He drew on the inspiration of the French Symbolists but also brought indigenous American traditions into his work to create a new poetic movement in Latin America.

But perhaps the spirit of these avant-garde movements was not so new as it sometimes claimed to be. It was the Romantics of a century before, after all, who had insisted on freeing art from the past and experimenting with new forms and styles. The Modernists therefore drew upon a tradition of innovation launched by their Romantic precursors. And thus, while they inaugurated revolutionary new art forms for the new century, the Modernists remained in many ways Romanticism's rightful heirs.

ANNA LAETITIA BARBAULD

1743–1825

A fierce opponent of war and slavery and an early defender of animal rights, Anna Laetitia Barbauld was a sophisticated woman poet whose work was widely known and respected in England and the United States. Called "one of the great minds which belong to all time," she entered bravely into public debates that were traditionally the province of male writers, urging her readers to live up to the highest principles of morality and citizenship. But Barbauld was not only a fearless and tough-minded public poet: she also wrote playful and reflective poems on family life, exploring childhood, married love, and grief.

Born Anna Laetitia Aikin in rural England, she was the daughter of two Presbyterians. As a child, she persuaded her father to teach her Latin and Greek—typically forbidden to women in the period. Her first book of poems in 1772 met with excitement on the part of the literary world, and she soon came to prominence as a major poet in a culture that esteemed poetry as the highest of the arts. **Samuel Taylor Coleridge** walked forty miles just to meet her, and **William Wordsworth** regretted that he had not himself written some of her great lines. In 1774 she married Rochemont Barbauld, a convert to Presbyterianism, and together they administered a school for boys. "Mrs. Barbauld," as she became known, wrote poetry and popular textbooks for children in this period, including *Lessons for Children of Two to Three Years Old*. In 1808 her husband succumbed to mental illness, and they separated after he violently assaulted her. He soon committed suicide.

Taking women's domestic experience as seriously as she took national politics, Barbauld's poetry crossed back and forth between traditionally masculine and feminine domains. Her poem "To a little invisible Being, who is expected soon to become visible," written about 1795, considers the mysterious existence of the unborn child, a being, the poem speculates, that has senses but no objects to sense and a mind but no thoughts to fill it. Barbauld reflects on the baffling problem of individuality in pregnancy—still unresolved in our own time. Is the child the same as the mother, or different? In the poem, the mother eagerly awaits the arrival of a complex being—a "stranger guest," "Part of herself, yet to herself unknown."

Barbauld's political poetry is represented here by "Eighteen Hundred and Eleven," a satire of the "Juvenalian" variety, that is, a condemnation of social wrongs written in a deliberately scornful and indignant style. This poem was composed in response to a European war that had dragged on for almost two decades: by 1811 Napoleon Bonaparte had led France to victory over most of Europe and was doing his best to undermine Britain both militarily and economically, blockading ports, driving up prices, and provoking labor unrest. The British government refused to sue for peace, though the war seemed to have no end in sight. Barbauld's poem protested against the wasteful miseries of war, and predicted the demise of the

British Empire, to be surpassed in the future, she prophesied, by the Americas. This work prompted a volley of harsh reviews, labeling Barbauld unpatriotic. One writer went so far as to say that the poem was "only the more dangerous on account of its poetical excellence."

To a Little Invisible Being
Who Is Expected Soon to Become Visible

Germ of new life, whose powers expanding slow
For many a moon their full perfection wait,—
Haste, precious pledge of happy love, to go
Auspicious borne through life's mysterious gate.

What powers lie folded in thy curious frame,—   5
Senses from objects locked, and mind from thought!
How little canst thou guess thy lofty claim
To grasp at all the worlds the Almighty wrought!

And see, the genial season's warmth to share,
Fresh younglings shoot, and opening roses glow.   10
Swarms of new life exulting fill the air,—
Haste, infant bud of being, haste to blow!

For thee the nurse prepares her lulling songs,
The eager matrons count the lingering day;
But far the most thy anxious parent longs   15
On thy soft cheek a mother's kiss to lay.

She only asks to lay her burden down,
That her glad arms that burden may resume;
And nature's sharpest pangs her wishes crown,
That free thee living from thy living tomb.   20

She longs to fold to her maternal breast
Part of herself, yet to herself unknown;
To see and to salute the stranger guest,
Fed with her life through many a tedious moon.

Come, reap thy rich inheritance of love!   25
Bask in the fondness of a Mother's eye!
Nor wit nor eloquence her heart shall move
Like the first accents of thy feeble cry.

Haste, little captive, burst thy prison doors!
Launch on the living world, and spring to light!   30
Nature for thee displays her various stores,
Opens her thousand inlets of delight.

If charmed verse or muttered prayers had power,
With favouring spells to speed thee on thy way,

Anxious I'd bid my beads each passing hour,   35
Till thy wished smile thy mother's pangs o'erpay.

From Eighteen Hundred and Eleven, a Poem[1]

Still the loud death drum, thundering from afar,
O'er the vext nations pours the storm of war:
To the stern call still Britain bends her ear,
Feeds the fierce strife, the alternate hope and fear;
Bravely, though vainly, dares to strive with Fate,   5
And seeks by turns to prop each sinking state.
Colossal Power with overwhelming force
Bears down each fort of Freedom in its course;
Prostrate she lies beneath the Despot's sway,
While the hushed nations curse him—and obey.   10
      Bounteous in vain, with frantic man at strife,
Glad Nature pours the means—the joys of life;
In vain with orange blossoms scents the gale,
The hills with olives clothes, with corn the vale;
Man calls to Famine, nor invokes in vain,   15
Disease and Rapine follow in her train;
The tramp of marching hosts disturbs the plough,
The sword, not sickle, reaps the harvest now,
And where the Soldier gleans the scant supply,
The helpless Peasant but retires to die;   20
No laws his hut from licensed outrage shield,
And war's least horror is the ensanguined field.
      Fruitful in vain, the matron counts with pride
The blooming youths that grace her honoured side;
No son returns to press her widow'd hand,   25
Her fallen blossoms strew a foreign strand.
—Fruitful in vain, she boasts her virgin race,
Whom cultured arts adorn and gentlest grace;
Defrauded of its homage, Beauty mourns,
And the rose withers on its virgin thorns.   30
Frequent, some stream obscure, some uncouth name
By deeds of blood is lifted into fame;
Oft o'er the daily page some soft-one bends
To learn the fate of husband, brothers, friends,
Or the spread map with anxious eye explores,   35
Its dotted boundaries and penciled shores,
Asks *where* the spot that wrecked her bliss is found,
And learns its name but to detest the sound.
      And think'st thou, Britain, still to sit at ease,

1. A devastating year for Britain, which had been at war with France for almost 18 years and was suffering from widespread hunger, poverty, and unrest at home; King George III had descended into dementia, and war with the United States seemed imminent.

An island Queen amidst thy subject seas,   40
While the vext billows, in their distant roar,
But soothe thy slumbers, and but kiss thy shore?
To sport in wars, while danger keeps aloof,
Thy grassy turf unbruised by hostile hoof?
So sing thy flatterers; but, Britain, know,   45
Thou who hast shared the guilt must share the woe.
Nor distant is the hour; low murmurs spread,
And whispered fears, creating what they dread;
Ruin, as with an earthquake shock, is here,
There, the heart-witherings of unuttered fear,   50
And that sad death, whence most affection bleeds,
Which sickness, only of the soul, precedes.
Thy baseless wealth dissolves in air away,
Like mists that melt before the morning ray:
No more on crowded mart or busy street   55
Friends, meeting friends, with cheerful hurry greet;
Sad, on the ground thy princely merchants bend
Their altered looks, and evil days portend,
And fold their arms, and watch with anxious breast
The tempest blackening in the distant West.   60
    Yes, thou must droop; thy Midas[2] dream is o'er;
The golden tide of Commerce leaves thy shore,
Leaves thee to prove the alternate ills that haunt
Enfeebling Luxury and ghastly Want;
Leaves thee, perhaps, to visit distant lands,   65
And deal the gifts of Heaven with equal hands.

*   *   *

    London exults:—on London Art bestows   305
Her summer ices and her winter rose;
Gems of the East her mural crown adorn,
And Plenty at her feet pours forth her horn;
While even the exiles her just laws disclaim,
People a continent, and build a name: 310
August she sits, and with extended hands
Holds forth the book of life to distant lands.
    But fairest flowers expand but to decay;
The worm is in thy core, thy glories pass away;
Arts, arms and wealth destroy the fruits they bring;   315
Commerce, like beauty, knows no second spring.
Crime walks thy streets, Fraud earns her unblest bread,
O'er want and woe thy gorgeous robe is spread,
And angel charities in vain oppose:
With grandeur's growth the mass of misery grows.   320
For see,—to other climes the Genius soars,
He turns from Europe's desolated shores;
And lo, even now, midst mountains wrapt in storm,

2. Mythic king who turned everything he touched into gold.

On Andes' heights he shrouds his awful form;
On Chimborazo's summits treads sublime,[3]   325
Measuring in lofty thought the march of Time;
Sudden he calls:—"'Tis now the hour!" he cries,
Spreads his broad hand, and bids the nations rise.
La Plata[4] hears amidst her torrents' roar,
Porosi[5] hears it, as she digs the ore: 330
Ardent, the Genius fans the noble strife,
And pours through feeble souls a higher life,
Shouts to the mingled tribes from sea to sea,
And swears—Thy world, Columbus, shall be free.

---

3. The highest mountain in what was then New Granada, now Ecuador.
4. River running between Argentina and Uruguay.
5. City, famed for its silver deposits, in what is now Bolivia.

WILLIAM BLAKE
1757–1827

William Blake condemned authority of all kinds. He cast priests and kings as responsible for exploiting the poor, repressing sexuality, and stifling art, and he admired the devil himself for his disobedience. "I must Create a System or be enslaved by another Man's," claims one of his characters. But the rebellious Blake also harbored profound religious beliefs, developing his own unorthodox visions of divine love, justice, and creativity. When asked if he believed in the divinity of Jesus Christ, he is reported to have said, "*He is the only God,*" and then added: "And so am I and so are you." Some of his contemporaries hailed him as a saint: one legend has it that on his deathbed he burst out in songs of joy. To many others, he seemed a pitiable madman. Only a few admirers in his own time acclaimed him as the creative visionary he would appear to later generations.

LIFE

Born in 1757 in London, Blake was the third of six children. His father kept a hosiery shop, and both parents were lower-middle-class Londoners, radical in their politics and unorthodox in their religion. He grew up among small tradesmen and artisans, who typically took pride in their skilled labor and had a tradition of political radicalism that pitted them against the aristocratic elite. At the age of ten, Blake started drawing school, and at fourteen he was apprenticed to an engraver who taught him complex techniques of engraving and printmaking. He had no formal education beyond drawing school, but he read widely, including history, philosophy, classical literature, the Bible, Shakespeare, Milton, and other English poets, and he began writing poetry himself at around the age of thirteen.

From childhood onward he repeatedly saw visions. "I write when commanded by the spirits," he once said, "and the moment I have written I see the words fly about the room in all directions." After exhibiting engravings and watercolors at the prestigious Royal Academy of Arts in 1779, Blake went to work as an engraver for Joseph Johnson, a bookseller and publisher who associated with the most influential radical thinkers of the Enlightenment period.

At the age of 25 Blake married Catherine Boucher, an illiterate daughter of a small farmer, whom he taught to read and write. By all accounts, their married life was a happy one, if occasionally tempestuous, and Catherine actively helped William in his work. The couple had no children.

In the late 1780s Blake developed a revolutionary new technique which he called "illuminated printing." Conventional print shops at the time separated the printing of images and words, integrating them only in the final stage of book production. Blake's method, by contrast, involved combining visual and written materials. He drew and wrote directly on the same copper plate, which then formed the basis for print reproductions. This process allowed Blake to adopt a much more spontaneous multimedia artistic practice than was usual, and ensured that the end product was entirely his own: he was at once the writer, the illustrator, and the printer. In characteristically visionary fashion, Blake explained that the spirit of his dead brother Robert had come to teach him this new technique.

Excited by the radical energies unleashed by the French Revolution in 1789, Blake threw himself into his creative endeavors and produced many of his greatest works in the following few years. *Songs of Innocence* in 1789 marked the beginnings of Blake's innovations. Frustrated with the poetry of his contemporaries, he looked backward to ancient ballads and sixteenth- and seventeenth-century English poetry for models. But he also took his work into some startlingly new poetic directions, including experimental rhythms, prophecies, themes of madness and jealousy, and the beginnings of a grand cosmological history. He wrote directly about politics while also pursuing his growing interest in myths and symbols.

All of his books combined words and images, but Blake grew gradually more absorbed with freestanding visual images, and in 1795 he abandoned poetry altogether for a period and produced some of the greatest works in the history of British printmaking: twelve large color prints that showed a range of subjects, from the creation of Adam and Blake's own mythological figures to Isaac Newton. Blake experimented with adding glue to paint to produce a deeper color and a more complex texture than his earlier watercolor images.

Printing his own images and books involved such costly and painstaking labor that Blake struggled to make ends meet. Eventually he went to work for private patrons, but even then his path was not smooth: he repeatedly broke with benefactors, including the domineering William Hayley, who moved Blake from London to the seaside village of Felpham and employed him mostly as a drawing teacher and illustrator. Hayley tried to pull Blake away from his visionary art, and Blake, frustrated and angry, called him "the Enemy of my Spiritual Life."

A soldier came into the Blakes' garden in Felpham one day in 1803, uttering threats and curses; Blake physically pushed him out. The artist went on trial for sedition, then punishable by hanging. In the end, he was acquitted, but the experience drove him further into isolation than ever. He spent the rest of his life back in London, poor and obscure. In his final years, a group of young painters recognized Blake's innovations in visual art, hailing him as a genius and an inspiration. He began to feel less angry and isolated, and his last few years were probably his happiest. But although he had finally won admiration as a visual artist, it was only long after his death that Blake's extraordinary inventiveness as a poet would be understood and acclaimed.

TIMES

Blake was not alone in wanting to see tyrannical and corrupt authorities toppled, but he was often seen as eccentric even among revolutionaries. For example, the Enlightenment thinkers who frequented Joseph Johnson's shop —including Thomas Paine and **Mary Wollstonecraft**—wanted to see the monarchy overthrown and replaced with a new and more democratic society; Blake shared these ideals, but he rejected their insistence on cold rationality, mechanical science, and individual rights, envisioning a more spiritual, imaginative, and collective future. He wrote, "God is not a mathematical diagram." In a striking visual image, he depicted Isaac Newton— who was one of the heroes of the Enlightenment—as unable to appreciate the wonders of the natural world, obsessed only with tracing abstract geometrical patterns on the ground. Blake's famous poem "Mock on, mock on, **Voltaire**, **Rousseau**" expresses his sense of the dangers of Enlightenment philosophy.

Blake put a much greater emphasis on economic inequality than most English supporters of the French Revolution. While many of his Enlightenment contemporaries argued for legal rights and political representation, Blake fiercely condemned the vast economic gulf between rich and poor. This was a moment when working conditions were changing dramatically: factories were springing up in urban centers, drawing vast numbers of laborers from the rural countryside, and machines were beginning to replace traditional craftsmanship. Blake angrily denounced a society willing to thrust workers into "dark Satanic Mills." Britain was at this time becoming the first and wealthiest industrialized nation, but in the process it was also putting small children to work for long hours, allowing laborers to be injured and disfigured by machines, and offering little help to those who were too old or too ill to work. Chimney sweeps, notorious as emblems of child labor, endured particularly severe hardships. Typically, these boys started working around the age of five, and by the time they had grown too large to climb chimneys, at twelve or thirteen, their bodies had been deformed and broken, rendered incapable of further work. In "The Chimney Sweeper," Blake expressed horror at the life of the laboring child who worked in darkness, inhaled soot and smoke, and had to endure burns, bruises, and debilitating illnesses.

It was not an easy time to speak out against injustice. The 1790s saw a wave of repressive laws that clamped down on dissenting expression in Britain. Public speakers, inflamed by the French Revolution, were trying to whip up antimonarchical sentiment and crowds were actively protesting— even at one point attacking the king's carriage. The British government responded harshly, suspending habeas corpus (the right not to be detained indefinitely without trial), banning most meetings larger than fifty people, and prosecuting "wicked and seditious writing." In 1793 France declared war on England, and the two nations were at war almost continuously until 1815.

The wars intensified popular unrest, and revolutionary sympathizers were forced underground. Blake's former employer, Joseph Johnson, landed in jail for nine months for publishing an antiwar pamphlet. Blake himself published some of his work anonymously, and stopped work on his epic poem, *The French Revolution*, as fellow writers and publishers around him began to go to jail. Blake's explicit engagements with poverty, slavery, and revolution gave way to more cryptic, biblical, and mythological themes.

But it would also be a mistake to imagine too strict a separation between Blake's politics and his religion. British law had long denied civil liberties to those who did not belong to the Church of England, and many Protestants, such as Methodists, Baptists, and Presbyterians—called Dissenters—had a robust tradition of resistance to official power. They wove together their religious beliefs with their political opposition. Blake was no exception. His parents, like many other urban artisans and small shopkeepers, moved among Protestant denominations, and spent some time with the Moravian Church. Blake himself was drawn to the mystical, charitable Swedenborg Church of the New Jerusalem, though he later criticized and rejected its doctrines. The 1780s and '90s saw a rise in evangelical and millenarian enthusiasm, and many Dissenters took the French Revolution to be the sign of a coming apocalypse. Blake repeatedly treated politics in terms of biblical models, and he, like many of his dissenting contemporaries, understood political revolutions as a violent purifying process that would bring about prophecies foretold in the Bible. In Blake's *Jerusalem*, one character asks, "Are not Religion & Politics the same thing? Brotherhood is Religion." Although Blake can seem eccentric among his rationalist Enlightenment contemporaries, then, his fusion of radical political beliefs and unorthodox, mystical spirituality was not entirely unusual among Dissenters in London.

WORK

Blake called for an open, accessible, democratic poetry and claimed that children were often the best readers of his work. His poems typically reject regular rhythms and conventional images in favor of unorthodox forms and unusually plain, forceful language. But he also opted for complicated systems of allegorical images and symbols, and in his stories characters often meld into others, change names, and appear and disappear in new guises. Not surprisingly, then, Blake's meanings remain a subject of fierce debate after two centuries. Many readers protest that much of his work is impenetrable and obscure—precisely the opposite of what Blake himself seems to have intended. And yet this debate might not have surprised or bothered Blake, since deliberate oppositions are often at the very heart of his work. He moves back and forth between innocence and experience, mystical vision and wry irony, joyful optimism and bleak prophecy, visual art and poetry. In *The Marriage of Heaven and Hell*—a union of opposites—Blake invites us to see conflict as a vital force: "Without Contraries is no progression. Attraction and Repulsion, Reason and Energy, Love and Hate, are necessary to Human existence. From these contraries spring what the religious call Good & Evil. Good is the passive that obeys Reason. Evil is the active springing from Energy."

In *Songs of Innocence*, Blake explores in simple language what it would be like to perceive the world through the eyes of a child. This means rendering familiar ideas radically unfamiliar. For instance, if we are accustomed to living in a culture that associates darkness with evil, then what does it feel like to be a dark-skinned child? His later *Songs of Experience* (1794) offers a set of companion pieces that return to the same subject matter from a more knowing perspective. Blake juxtaposes the two sets of poems, inviting us to think about the different ways that an innocent child and an experienced adult might understand God, love, and justice. There are echoes and recurrences within as well as across these two groups of poems, and perhaps this is not surprising: after all, Blake's major occupation throughout his life involved

making copies—as an engraver, print-maker, and printer—and he seems to have been at least as interested in ideas of doubling and repetition as he was in uniqueness and originality. But he also complicates many of these echoes. In the famous "Tyger," for example, he rhymes "symmetry" and "eye"—a sight rhyme or pairing that might look like a rhyme but does not sound like one. He also unsettles conventional distinctions: the usual lines dividing human and divine states dissolve, for example, and the child leads the poet, rather than the other way around. These apparently simple but highly complex poems have remained Blake's most famous and beloved works.

Songs of Innocence and of Experience

SHEWING THE TWO CONTRARY STATES OF THE HUMAN SOUL

From Songs of Innocence[1]

Introduction

Piping down the valleys wild
Piping songs of pleasant glee
On a cloud I saw a child,
And he laughing said to me,

"Pipe a song about a Lamb"; 5
So I piped with merry chear;
"Piper pipe that song again"—
So I piped, he wept to hear.

"Drop thy pipe thy happy pipe
Sing thy songs of happy chear"; 10
So I sung the same again
While he wept with joy to hear.

---

1. The text for all of Blake's works is edited by David V. Erdman and Harold Bloom. *Songs of Innocence* (1789) was later combined with *Songs of Experience* (1794), and the poems were etched and accompanied by Blake's illustrations, the process accomplished by copper engravings stamped on paper, then colored by hand.

"Piper sit thee down and write
In a book that all may read"—
So he vanished from my sight.   15
And I plucked a hollow reed,

And I made a rural pen,
And I stained the water clear,
And I wrote my happy songs
Every child may joy to hear.   20

The Lamb

Little Lamb, who made thee?
    Dost thou know who made thee?
Gave thee life & bid thee feed,
By the stream & o'er the mead;
Gave thee clothing of delight,   5
Softest clothing wooly bright;
Gave thee such a tender voice,
Making all the vales rejoice!
    Little Lamb who made thee?
    Dost thou know who made thee?   10

    Little Lamb I'll tell thee,
    Little Lamb I'll tell thee!
He is callèd by thy name,
For he calls himself a Lamb:
He is meek & he is mild,   15
He became a little child:
I a child & thou a lamb,
We are callèd by his name.[1]
    Little Lamb God bless thee.
    Little Lamb God bless thee.   20

The Little Black Boy

My mother bore me in the southern wild,
And I am black, but O! my soul is white;
White as an angel is the English child:
But I am black as if bereaved of light.

My mother taught me underneath a tree,   5
And sitting down before the heat of day,

---

1. I.e., Christians use the name of Christ to designate themselves.

She took me on her lap and kissèd me,
And pointing to the east, began to say:

"Look on the rising sun: there God does live,
And gives his light, and gives his heat away;   10
And flowers and trees and beasts and men receive
Comfort in morning, joy in the noon day.

"And we are put on earth a little space,
That we may learn to bear the beams of love,
And these black bodies and this sun-burnt face   15
Is but a cloud, and like a shady grove.

"For when our souls have learned the heat to bear,
The cloud will vanish; we shall hear his voice,
Saying: 'Come out from the grove, my love & care,
And round my golden tent like lambs rejoice.'"   20

Thus did my mother say, and kissèd me;
And thus I say to little English boy:
When I from black and he from white cloud free,
And round the tent of God like lambs we joy,

I'll shade him from the heat till he can bear   25
To lean in joy upon our father's knee;
And then I'll stand and stroke his silver hair,
And be like him, and he will then love me.

Holy Thursday[1]

'Twas on a Holy Thursday, their innocent faces clean,
The children walking two & two, in red & blue & green,[2]
Grey headed beadles[3] walked before with wands as white as snow,
Till into the high dome of Paul's they like Thames' waters flow.

O what a multitude they seemed, these flowers of London town!   5
Seated in companies they sit with radiance all their own.
The hum of multitudes was there, but multitudes of lambs,
Thousands of little boys & girls raising their innocent hands.

Now like a mighty wind they raise to heaven the voice of song,
Or like harmonious thunderings the seats of heaven among.   10
Beneath them sit the agèd men, wise guardians[4] of the poor;
Then cherish pity, lest you drive an angel from your door.[5]

---

1. Ascension Day, forty days after Easter, when children from charity schools were marched to St. Paul's Cathedral.
2. Each school had its own distinctive uniform.
3. Ushers and minor functionaries, whose job was to maintain order.
4. The governors of the charity schools.
5. See Hebrews 13.2: "Be not forgetful to entertain strangers: for thereby some have entertained angels unawares."

The Chimney Sweeper

When my mother died I was very young,
And my father sold me[1] while yet my tongue
Could scarcely cry " 'weep![2] 'weep! 'weep! 'weep!"
So your chimneys I sweep & in soot I sleep.

There's little Tom Dacre, who cried when his head   5
That curled like a lamb's back, was shaved, so I said,
"Hush, Tom! never mind it, for when your head's bare,
You know that the soot cannot spoil your white hair."

And so he was quiet, & that very night,
As Tom was a-sleeping he had such a sight!   10
That thousands of sweepers, Dick, Joe, Ned, & Jack,
Were all of them locked up in coffins of black;

And by came an Angel who had a bright key,
And he opened the coffins & set them all free;
Then down a green plain, leaping, laughing they run,   15
And wash in a river and shine in the Sun;

Then naked[3] & white, all their bags left behind,
They rise upon clouds, and sport in the wind.
And the Angel told Tom, if he'd be a good boy,
He'd have God for his father & never want joy.   20

And so Tom awoke; and we rose in the dark
And got with our bags & our brushes to work.
Tho' the morning was cold, Tom was happy & warm;
So if all do their duty, they need not fear harm.

From Songs of Experience

Introduction

Hear the voice of the Bard!
Who Present, Past, & Future sees;
    Whose ears have heard
    The Holy Word
That walked among the ancient trees;[1]   5

1. It was common practice in Blake's day for fathers to sell, or indenture, their children to become chimney sweeps. The average age at which such children began working was six or seven; they were generally employed for seven years, until they were too big to ascend the chimneys.

2. The child's lisping effort to say "sweep," as he walks the streets looking for work.
3. They climbed up the chimneys naked.
1. Genesis 3.8: "And [Adam and Eve] heard the voice of the Lord God walking in the garden in the cool of the day."

Calling the lapsèd Soul
And weeping in the evening dew;[2]
That might control
The starry pole,
And fallen, fallen light renew!   10

"O Earth, O Earth, return!
Arise from out the dewy grass;
Night is worn,
And the morn
Rises from the slumberous mass.   15

"Turn away no more;
Why wilt thou turn away?
The starry floor
The watery shore
Is given thee till the break of day."   20

Earth's Answer

Earth raised up her head,
From the darkness dread & drear.
Her light fled:
Stony dread!
And her locks covered with grey despair.   5

"Prisoned on watery shore
Starry Jealousy does keep my den,
Cold and hoar
Weeping o'er
I hear the Father[1] of the ancient men.   10

"Selfish father of men,
Cruel, jealous, selfish fear!
Can delight
Chained in night
The virgins of youth and morning bear?   15

"Does spring hide its joy
When buds and blossoms grow?

---

2. Blake's ambiguous use of pronouns makes for interpretative difficulties. It would seem that *The Holy Word* (Jehovah, a name for God in the Old Testament of the Bible) calls *the lapsèd Soul*, and weeps—not the Bard.
1. In Blake's later prophetic works, one of the four Zoas, representing the four chief faculties of humankind, is Urizen. In general, he stands for the orthodox conception of the Divine Creator, sometimes Jehovah in the Old Testament, often the God conceived by Newton and Locke—in all instances a tyrant associated with excessive rationalism and sexual repression, and the opponent of the imagination and creativity. This may be "the Holy Word" in line 4 of "Introduction" (p. 911).

Does the sower
Sow by night,
Or the plowman in darkness plow?   20

"Break this heavy chain
That does freeze my bones around;
Selfish! vain!
Eternal bane!
That free Love with bondage bound."   25

The Tyger

Tyger! Tyger! burning bright
In the forests of the night,
What immortal hand or eye
Could frame thy fearful symmetry?

In what distant deeps or skies   5
Burnt the fire of thine eyes?
On what wings dare he aspire?
What the hand dare seize the fire?

And what shoulder, & what art,
Could twist the sinews of thy heart?
And when thy heart began to beat,   10
What dread hand? & what dread feet?

What the hammer? what the chain?
In what furnace was thy brain?
What the anvil? what dread grasp   15
Dare its deadly terrors clasp?

When the stars threw down their spears,
And watered heaven with their tears,
Did he smile his work to see?
Did he who made the Lamb make thee?   20

Tyger! Tyger! burning bright
In the forests of the night,
What immortal hand or eye
Dare frame thy fearful symmetry?

The Sick Rose

O Rose, thou art sick.
The invisible worm
That flies in the night
In the howling storm

Has found out thy bed   5
Of crimson joy,
And his dark secret love
Does thy life destroy.

London

I wander thro' each chartered[1] street,
Near where the chartered Thames does flow,
And mark in every face I meet
Marks of weakness, marks of woe.

In every cry of every Man,   5
In every Infant's cry of fear,
In every voice, in every ban,
The mind-forged manacles I hear:

How the Chimney-sweeper's cry
Every blackening Church appalls;[2]   10
And the hapless Soldier's sigh
Runs in blood down Palace walls.

But most thro' midnight streets I hear
How the youthful Harlot's curse
Blasts the new-born Infant's tear,[3]   15
And blights with plagues the Marriage hearse.

The Chimney Sweeper

A little black thing among the snow
Crying "'weep, 'weep," in notes of woe!
"Where are thy father & mother? say?"
"They are both gone up to the church to pray.

"Because I was happy upon the heath,   5
And smiled among the winter's snow;
They clothèd me in the clothes of death,
And taught me to sing the notes of woe.

"And because I am happy, & dance & sing,
They think they have done me no injury,   10

1. Hired (literally). Blake implies that the streets and the river are controlled by commercial interests.
2. Makes white (literally), punning also on *appall* (to dismay) and *pall* (the cloth covering a corpse or bier).
3. The harlot infects the parents with venereal disease, and thus the infant is inflicted with neonatal blindness.

And are gone to praise God & his Priest & King,
Who make up a heaven of our misery."

Mock On, Mock On, Voltaire, Rousseau

Mock on, Mock on, Voltaire, Rousseau;
Mock on, Mock on, 'tis all in vain.
You throw the sand against the wind,
And the wind blows it back again.

And every sand becomes a Gem   5
Reflected in the beams divine;
Blown back, they blind the mocking Eye,
But still in Israel's paths they shine.

The Atoms of Democritus[1]
And Newton's Particles of light[2]   10
Are sands upon the Red sea shore,
Where Israel's tents do shine so bright.

And Did Those Feet

And did those feet[1] in ancient time
Walk upon England's mountains green?
And was the holy Lamb of God
On England's pleasant pastures seen?

And did the Countenance Divine   5
Shine forth upon our clouded hills?
And was Jerusalem builded here,
Among those dark Satanic Mills?[2]

Bring me my Bow of burning gold:
Bring me my Arrows of desire: 10
Bring me my Spear: O clouds unfold!
Bring me my Chariot of fire!

I will not cease from Mental Fight,
Nor shall my Sword sleep in my hand,
Till we have built Jerusalem   15
In England's green & pleasant Land.

---

1. Greek philosopher (460?–362? B.C.E.), who advanced a theory that all things are merely patterns of atoms.
2. Sir Isaac Newton's (1642–1727) corpuscular theory of light. For Blake, both men were condemned as materialists.

1. A reference to an ancient legend that Jesus came to England with Joseph of Arimathea.
2. Possibly industrial England, but for Blake *mills* also meant 18th-century arid, mechanistic philosophy.

FRIEDRICH HÖLDERLIN

1770–1843

In his own moment, the poet Friedrich Hölderlin was little known, and after his death he was quickly forgotten, consigned to oblivion. But in the early twentieth century, his condensed, puzzling, unconventional poetry suddenly seemed up-to-date—quintessentially modern. By the mid-twentieth century Hölderlin would be considered one of the greatest figures in German poetry.

Born in the Swabian region of Germany, Hölderlin went to a Lutheran theological seminary, where he befriended two young men who would become world-famous philosophers: G. W. F. Hegel and F. W. J. Schelling. He too read deeply in ancient and modern philosophy, including Plato, **Kant**, and **Rousseau**, and became a fervent admirer of the French Revolution. Feeling unsuited to the ministry, he took work as a private tutor, whereupon he fell in love with Susette Gontard, the wife of his employer, and the two carried on a concealed relationship for several years. He translated two plays by the ancient Greek writer Sophocles, *Oedipus Rex* and *Antigone*, and wrote a highly philosophical novel called *Hyperion*. When Susette Gontard died, Hölderlin began to explode into episodes of violent rage and could be calmed only by having passages from Homer read aloud to him. His enthusiasm for the French Revolution got him arrested for sedition—a year after the English poet **William Blake** had been tried for the same offense—but he was not fit to stand trial. From this point onward, he descended into schizophrenia and was cared for by a carpenter's family for the rest of his life.

Hölderlin's poetry reveals an intense engagement with ancient Greece, a belief that Greek art and thought are not relics of a distant past but real and vibrant forces in the present. He combines a Christian God with his own unconventional sense of living Greek deities. The savage Dionysus, for example, is fully alive for Hölderlin, although his contemporaries preferred to imagine the Greeks as restrained and decorous, and barely acknowledged the untamed "holy drunkenness"—as Hölderlin called it—of Greek culture. And yet the poet is not simply joyous in his unorthodox faith: he feels the gods have withdrawn, leaving him bereft. However, their withdrawal also leaves him free. This dynamic movement is typical of the cycles of blending and dissolution that animate Hölderlin's poetry, as human beings struggle to bridge the gap between themselves and the gods, and between themselves and nature. These gaps govern the poetic forms Hölderlin uses, as he often juxtaposes images without explaining the connections between them—a style that can be bewildering but also mysterious and fascinating, provoking readers to make the links ourselves.

Starting in the late nineteenth century with Friedrich Nietzsche, philosophers began to take him seriously as a thinker who saw poetry as the best access to truth, and in the twentieth century Hölderlin found many enthusiasts. His work has been important for a number of major European philosophers, from Martin Heidegger to Jacques Derrida and Michel Foucault. Disturbingly, the Nazis also claimed

Hölderlin: his hymns to the "Father-land" were read to Hitler on his fiftieth birthday and distributed to German troops in 1943. But then, in the 1960s, the poet was taken up at the other end of the political spectrum by leftist readers who saw him as a radically sub-versive writer who applauded the dis-ruptions of the French Revolution and felt spurned by his countrymen. His greatest legacy, however, has been artistic. Acclaimed by poets, Hölderlin has also been beloved by composers, including Johannes Brahms, Richard Strauss, and Benjamin Britten, who have set his haunting works to music.

The Half of Life[1]

With yellow pears the country,
Brimming with wild roses,
Hangs into the lake,
You gracious swans,
And drunk with kisses   5
Your heads you dip
Into the holy lucid water.

Where, ah where shall I find,
When winter comes, the flowers,
And where the sunshine   10
And shadows of the earth?
Walls stand
Speechless and cold, in the wind
The weathervanes clatter.

Hyperion's[1] Song of Fate

You walk up there in the light
On floors like velvet, blissful spirits.
Shining winds divine
Touch you lightly
As a harper touches holy   5
Strings with her fingers.

Fateless as babes asleep
They breathe, the celestials.
Chastely kept
In a simple bud,   10
For them the spirit
Flowers eternal,

---

1. The following selection of Hölderlin's poems is translated by Christopher Middleton.

1. In Greek mythology, a Titan, father of Aurora, goddess of dawn.

And in bliss their eyes
Gaze in eternal
Calm clarity.   15

But to us it is given
To find no resting place,
We faint, we fall,
Suffering, human,
Blindly from one   20
To the next moment
Like water flung
From rock to rock down
Long years into uncertainty.

Brevity

Why make it so short? Have you lost your old liking
For song? Why, in days of hope, when young,
You sang and sang,
There scarce was an end of it.

My song is short as my luck was. Who'd go   5
Gaily swimming at sundown? It's gone, earth's cold,
And the annoying nightbird
Flits, close, blocking your vision.

To the Fates

Grant me a single summer, you lords of all,
A single autumn, for the fullgrown song,
So that, with such sweet playing sated,
Then my heart may die more willing.

The soul, in life robbed of its godly right,   5
Rests not, even in Orcus[1] down below;
Yet should I once achieve my heart's
First holy concern, the poem,

Welcome then, O stillness of the shadow world!
Even if down I go without my   10
Music, I shall be satisfied; once
Like gods I shall have lived, more I need not.

---

1. Hades, or the underworld in ancient Greek mythology.

WILLIAM WORDSWORTH
1770–1850

After Wordsworth, English poetry would never be the same again. The sense that poets should convey intensely personal, individual expression—which now feels like the ordinary stuff of poetry—can be traced to Wordsworth's deliberate rejection of his eighteenth-century precursors. He turned readers' attention away from classical models and Gothic supernatural stories to everyday emotion and imagination, championing the spontaneity of authentic feeling. Like **Jean-Jacques Rousseau**, he approached children's experience as crucial and determinative, in defiance of many of his contemporaries, who considered childhood trivial. And he chose to focus on common people—often poor and marginal figures such as elderly farmers and vagrant beggars. Just as important, Wordsworth also launched a new set of stylistic values for poetry, jettisoning "the gaudiness and inane phraseology" of contemporary poets in favor of a language that would feel direct, authentic, and plain. And finally, Wordsworth committed himself in surprising new ways to honoring the natural world as a benevolent nurturer and guide, and many have credited him with launching an ecological consciousness that continues to inspire environmentalists today.

LIFE

William Wordsworth was born in the small town of Cockermouth, in England's wild and rugged Lake District, in 1770. He was the second of four sons. His only sister, Dorothy, was a year younger. Separated for long periods as children, William and Dorothy were extremely close as adults. Their father worked as a lawyer and was often forced to travel, and their mother died when Wordsworth was eight years old. The boy was sent to a grammar school in the countryside, where he learned Greek and Latin and committed large portions of Shakespeare and Milton to memory. After his father's death in 1783, he began to feel restless and unsettled. While at Cambridge University, he failed to apply himself to his studies. "I am doomed to be an idler thro' my whole life," he wrote.

Wordsworth's perspective on the world took a turn in the summer of 1790, when he and a friend set off for a walking tour of France and the Alps. It was a critical moment in French history: the country was "mad with joy in consequence of the revolution," as Wordsworth put it. He also had a love affair with a Frenchwoman named Annette Vallon and had a child with her. He returned to England in 1793, meaning to make some money so that he could marry Vallon, but Britain went to war with France, and Wordsworth was not permitted to cross back for a decade.

The following few years were the most difficult of Wordsworth's life. He had no source of income, and his revolutionary sympathies made him an outsider in England. He moved to London and for a time became a disciple of the anarchist William Godwin, who favored the abolition of marriage and all forms of government. In 1795 Wordsworth began a formative friendship with another young radical poet, **Samuel Taylor Coleridge**. So close did Wordsworth and Coleridge become that they deliberately moved to within walking distance of one another in rural Somerset. There they entertained revolutionary thinkers and were suspected of being spies: "a mischievous gang of disaffected Englishmen," reported a government agent, "a Sett of violent Democrats." In fact, however, both Wordsworth and Coleridge were horrified by the bloody turn the revolution in France had taken, and they soon began to lose faith in radical politics. Loving the beauty of the countryside and each other's company, the two poets started to work together on a different kind of revolutionary ideal: the production of a new kind of poetry. Together, in 1798, they published a collection of poems called *Lyrical Ballads*. It contained works that would count among their best loved, including Wordsworth's "Tintern Abbey" and "We Are Seven," and Coleridge's "Rime of the Ancient Mariner." They published the first edition anonymously. ("Wordsworth's name is nothing," Coleridge explained, and "to a large number of persons mine *stinks*.")

This book succeeded in accomplishing a revolution in English poetry. Radically democratic, it focused on subject matter conventionally ignored by poets—the lives of lowly people, such as the very poor, the insane, children, shepherds, and tinkers. This new subject matter, Wordsworth wrote, demanded a simple and unaffected language, like the prose spoken by ordinary people. Thus *Lyrical Ballads* prized not only humble and simple subjects but also the poet's own internal state of mind, a focus that would become ever more important to Wordsworth's work. In 1801 he included a new preface, which has become as well known as his poetry. Here he put forward his revolutionary new ideas: "I have proposed to myself to imitate, and, as far as is possible, to adopt the very language of men," he wrote. Famously, he defined poetry as "the spontaneous overflow of powerful feelings," explaining that it comes from "emotion recollected in tranquility."

Critics were not prepared for this innovative volume, and Wordsworth's poetry garnered almost entirely hostile reviews. One critic wrote, "Than the volumes now before us we never saw any thing better calculated to excite disgust and anger in a lover of poetry. The drivelling nonsense of some of Mr. Wordsworth's poems is insufferable, and it is equally insufferable that such nonsense should have been written by a man capable, as he is, of writing well." Even Wordsworth's fellow poet, Lord Byron, wrote contemptuously of this "dull" poetry, which, he said, "shows / That prose is verse, and verse is merely prose."

In 1799 William and his sister Dorothy moved to Grasmere in the Lake District, near where they had grown up. Coleridge took a house nearby, and Wordsworth married a friend named Mary Hutchinson. At the time, Dorothy was reportedly so upset by the wedding that she could not attend the ceremony, but she and Mary settled into a happy domestic life in Grasmere. The Wordsworths went on to have five children.

Wordsworth was appalled by Napoleon's rise to power across Europe, and his political views turned increasingly conservative. Meanwhile, his life entered a period of stability, punctuated with several tragic events. He lost two young children to illness, and his friendship with Coleridge faltered. The Wordsworths had hosted Coleridge for lengthy periods, but he remained moody and depressed, and in 1810 the two poets quarreled. Although they patched up their friendship, they never regained their former closeness. In the following years, Wordsworth became very much part of the conservative establishment. He was appointed distributor of stamps, collecting taxes on government documents, a civil service job that seemed to many contemporary radicals to represent a betrayal of his earlier commitment to the artist's independence. In 1818 he campaigned for the Tories—the conservative party—in local elections.

It was in the last phase of Wordsworth's life that he became popular and widely respected, both in Britain and the United States, though the poetry he wrote in his final years is now usually considered much weaker than his earlier work. In 1843 Queen Victoria bestowed the title of Poet Laureate on him, and he received visiting fans from around the world, including the American writer Ralph Waldo Emerson. He died on April 23, traditionally thought to be Shakespeare's birth- and death-day, in 1850.

WORDSWORTH'S READERS

Expanding cities and industrialization brought with them a new kind of reading public. Before Wordsworth's time, writers had mostly published on a small scale for that tiny proportion of the public who were literate, many of whom would have known the writer personally. But around the turn of the nineteenth century, cheaper means of publication, rapidly increasing literacy, and growing leisure time for reading meant that printed matter suddenly started to reach a newly large and anonymous mass market. A few writers, including the poet Byron, became literary celebrities, selling every copy of a new work on its first day of publication and earning thousands of pounds from their writing. Other writers could not make ends meet unless they turned to private patrons. Wordsworth, for most of his life, knew that he was reaching the traditionally small literate audience but aspired to the new mass market,

often uncertain of his readers. He was trying out a new kind of democratic style and subject matter in his poetry, but was he actually reaching the working classes? Women? Radicals?

The uncertainty about audience gave way to a new sense of the literary marketplace over the next couple of decades, as the reading public in Britain increased markedly, reaching more widely into the reaches of the upper working classes—skilled artisans, shopkeepers, clerks, and servants. Churches played a major role in a dramatic expansion of literacy: Evangelicals insisted on reading as essential to spiritual development, and they set up charity schools and distributed Bibles and didactic tracts to the poor. Between 1804 and 1819 the British and Foreign Bible Society printed two and a half million Bibles for domestic use alone. Since print remained relatively costly, working people often banded together to buy newspapers, which they read aloud in pubs.

British opinion was split over the political consequences of this expanding readership. The government often feared the energetic radical press and worried that reading would incite revolutionary sentiment. They imposed a severe censorship, especially during the French Revolution and the Napoleonic wars. Others, however, held that education would quell agitation and increase worker productivity. "An instructed and intelligent people," wrote Scottish philosopher Adam Smith, "are always more decent and orderly than an ignorant and stupid one."

WORK

Since Wordsworth's style is often purposefully simple, his poetry can seem deceptively uncomplicated. For many readers, its pleasures lie in the philosophical questions it poses. "Tintern Abbey" asks what makes a self a self:

how do we become what we are? "We Are Seven" interrogates the abstraction of death and asks whether the dead may be considered part of the human community. And the "Ode on Intimations of Immortality" considers the immortality of the soul, using Plato's ideas as a touchstone.

But the poems also reward a close attention to their language. On first reading, Wordsworth's invocations of nature might seem simple acts of homage, but in fact the relationship between the poet and the natural world varies from poem to poem, and sometimes within the same poem. Even the most seemingly straightforward Wordsworthian lines often yield more questions than answers. Consider, for example, the title of the poem "Lines Composed a Few Miles above Tintern Abbey, on Revisiting the Banks of the Wye during a Tour, July 13, 1798." Why such a curiously long and descriptive title, going to such trouble to mark the place and date of composition? The poem itself, surprisingly, says nothing at all about the ruined abbey. Some readers have noted that Wordsworth is careful to use the title to note his position "above" the landscape; others have remarked on the date, which commemorates the anniversary of the day *before* the French Revolution started, hinting that Wordsworth's explorations of memory and selfhood in this poem are bound up with his ambivalence about the revolution. In another example, the central tension of "We Are Seven" turns on the definition of one of the simplest and most common words in the English language—"we." The poem explores the idea that two different uses of an ordinary pronoun reveal radically dissimilar ways of seeing the world. How is it, Wordsworth's poetry insistently asks, that complex conceptions of faith, nature, selfhood, community, and knowledge are revealed in the most commonplace language that we use?

Wordsworth is famous for his plain style and his philosophical explorations, but he is also notable for his ease in moving among poetic forms and genres. While "Tintern Abbey" is composed in the regular and highly traditional English form of iambic pentameter, "Ode on Intimations of Immortality" is strikingly irregular, with both lines and stanzas varying widely in length. Wordsworth borrows here from an English tradition of deliberately irregular odes in which the poet meditates on a problem or object in changing rhythms. Since both "Tintern Abbey" and the "Ode" are about time and memory, it is intriguing that Wordsworth should choose such different forms for the two poems.

The other genre represented here is the sonnet, a form that had languished for a couple of centuries but became popular again in the late eighteenth century. Wordsworth was among many Romantic poets—among them, numerous women—who brought the sonnet back to prominence. He wrote a poem called "Scorn not the Sonnet," which reminds the reader of the sonnet's illustrious history, begun by the Italian poet Petrarch and later taken up by Shakespeare and Milton. Wordsworth was clearly self-conscious about his place in this poetic tradition. The two examples included here, "Composed upon Westminster Bridge" and "The World Is Too Much with Us," steer clear of the sonnet's traditional focus on romantic love, meditating instead on the specific conditions of modern, industrial, and urban society, thus pointedly bringing this traditional poetic form into the present. In reimagining the sonnet, then, as in his innovative ideas about democracy, poetic style, nature, childhood, and the importance of individual experience, Wordsworth is a quintessentially modern poet.

We Are Seven

———A simple Child,
That lightly draws its breath,
And feels its life in every limb,
What should it know of death?

I met a little cottage Girl: 5
She was eight years old, she said;
Her hair was thick with many a curl
That clustered round her head.

She had a rustic, woodland air,
And she was wildly clad: 10
Her eyes were fair, and very fair;
———Her beauty made me glad.

"Sisters and brothers, little Maid,
How many may you be?"
"How many? Seven in all," she said,   15
And wondering looked at me.

"And where are they? I pray you tell."
She answered, "Seven are we;
And two of us at Conway[1] dwell,
And two are gone to sea.   20

"Two of us in the church-yard lie,
My sister and my brother;
And, in the church-yard cottage, I
Dwell near them with my mother."

"You say that two at Conway dwell,   25
And two are gone to sea,
Yet ye are seven! I pray you tell,
Sweet Maid, how this may be."

Then did the little Maid reply,
"Seven boys and girls are we;   30
Two of us in the church-yard lie,
Beneath the church-yard tree."

"You run about, my little Maid,
Your limbs they are alive;
If two are in the church-yard laid,   35
Then ye are only five."

1. Port town in Wales.

"Their graves are green, they may be seen,"
The little Maid replied,
"Twelve steps or more from my mother's door,
And they are side by side.   40

"My stockings there I often knit,
My kerchief there I hem;
And there upon the ground I sit,
And sing a song to them.

"And often after sun-set, Sir,   45
When it is light and fair,
I take my little porringer,[2]
And eat my supper there.

"The first that died was sister Jane;
In bed she moaning lay,   50
Till God released her of her pain;
And then she went away.

"So in the church-yard she was laid;
And, when the grass was dry,
Together round her grave we played,   55
My brother John and I.

"And when the ground was white with snow,
And I could run and slide,
My brother John was forced to go,
And he lies by her side."   60

"How many are you, then," said I,
"If they two are in heaven?"
Quick was the little Maid's reply,
"O Master! we are seven."

"But they are dead; those two are dead!   65
Their spirits are in heaven!"
'Twas throwing words away; for still
The little Maid would have her will,
And said, "Nay, we are seven!"

2. A bowl or dish.

Lines Composed a Few Miles above Tintern Abbey

On Revisiting the Banks of the Wye During a Tour, July 13, 1798

Five years have past; five summers, with the length
Of five long winters! and again I hear
These waters, rolling from their mountain-springs
With a soft inland murmur.—Once again
Do I behold these steep and lofty cliffs,   5
That on a wild secluded scene impress
Thoughts of more deep seclusion; and connect
The landscape with the quiet of the sky.
The day is come when I again repose
Here, under this dark sycamore, and view   10
These plots of cottage-ground, these orchard-tufts,
Which at this season, with their unripe fruits,
Are clad in one green hue, and lose themselves
'Mid groves and copses. Once again I see
These hedge-rows, hardly hedge-rows, little lines   15
Of sportive wood run wild: these pastoral farms,
Green to the very door; and wreaths of smoke
Sent up, in silence, from among the trees!
With some uncertain notice, as might seem
Of vagrant dwellers in the houseless woods,   20
Or of some Hermit's cave, where by his fire
The Hermit sits alone.

               These beauteous forms,
Through a long absence, have not been to me
As is a landscape to a blind man's eye:
But oft, in lonely rooms, and 'mid the din   25
Of towns and cities, I have owed to them,
In hours of weariness, sensations sweet,
Felt in the blood, and felt along the heart;
And passing even into my purer mind,
With tranquil restoration:—feelings too   30
Of unremembered pleasure: such, perhaps,
As have no slight or trivial influence
On that best portion of a good man's life,
His little, nameless, unremembered, acts
Of kindness and of love. Nor less, I trust,   35
To them I may have owed another gift,
Of aspect more sublime; that blessèd mood,
In which the burthen of the mystery,
In which the heavy and the weary weight
Of all this unintelligible world,   40
Is lightened:—that serene and blessèd mood,
In which the affections gently lead us on,—
Until, the breath of this corporeal frame
And even the motion of our human blood
Almost suspended, we are laid asleep   45

In body, and become a living soul:
While with an eye made quiet by the power
Of harmony, and the deep power of joy,
We see into the life of things.

                                    If this
Be but a vain belief, yet, oh! how oft—   50
In darkness and amid the many shapes
Of joyless daylight; when the fretful stir
Unprofitable, and the fever of the world,
Have hung upon the beatings of my heart—
How oft, in spirit, have I turned to thee,   55
O sylvan Wye! thou wanderer thro' the woods,
How often has my spirit turned to thee!

   And now, with gleams of half-extinguished thought,
With many recognitions dim and faint,
And somewhat of a sad perplexity,   60
The picture of the mind revives again:
While here I stand, not only with the sense
Of present pleasure, but with pleasing thoughts
That in this moment there is life and food
For future years. And so I dare to hope,   65
Though changed, no doubt, from what I was when first
I came among these hills; when like a roe
I bounded o'er the mountains, by the sides
Of the deep rivers, and the lonely streams,
Wherever nature led: more like a man   70
Flying from something that he dreads, than one
Who sought the thing he loved. For nature then
(The coarser pleasures of my boyish days,
And their glad animal movements all gone by)
To me was all in all.—I cannot paint   75
What then I was. The sounding cataract
Haunted me like a passion: the tall rock,
The mountain, and the deep and gloomy wood,
Their colours and their forms, were then to me
An appetite; a feeling and a love,   80
That had no need of a remoter charm,
By thought supplied, nor any interest
Unborrowed from the eye.—That time is past,
And all its aching joys are now no more,
And all its dizzy raptures. Not for this   85
Faint I, nor mourn nor murmur; other gifts
Have followed; for such loss, I would believe,
Abundant recompense. For I have learned
To look on nature, not as in the hour
Of thoughtless youth; but hearing oftentimes   90
The still, sad music of humanity,
Nor harsh nor grating, though of ample power
To chasten and subdue. And I have felt
A presence that disturbs me with the joy

Of elevated thoughts; a sense sublime   95
Of something far more deeply interfused,
Whose dwelling is the light of setting suns,
And the round ocean and the living air,
And the blue sky, and in the mind of man:
A motion and a spirit, that impels   100
All thinking things, all objects of all thought,
And rolls through all things. Therefore am I still
A lover of the meadows and the woods,
And mountains; and of all that we behold
From this green earth; of all the mighty world   105
Of eye, and ear,—both what they half create,
And what perceive; well pleased to recognise
In nature and the language of the sense,
The anchor of my purest thoughts, the nurse,
The guide, the guardian of my heart, and soul   110
Of all my moral being.

                    Nor perchance,
If I were not thus taught, should I the more
Suffer my genial[1] spirits to decay:
For thou art with me here upon the banks
Of this fair river; thou my dearest Friend,   115
My dear, dear Friend; and in thy voice I catch
The language of my former heart, and read
My former pleasures in the shooting lights
Of thy wild eyes. Oh! yet a little while
May I behold in thee what I was once,   120
My dear, dear Sister! and this prayer I make,
Knowing that Nature never did betray
The heart that loved her; 'tis her privilege,
Through all the years of this our life, to lead
From joy to joy: for she can so inform   125
The mind that is within us, so impress
With quietness and beauty, and so feed
With lofty thoughts, that neither evil tongues,
Rash judgments, nor the sneers of selfish men,
Nor greetings where no kindness is, nor all   130
The dreary intercourse of daily life,
Shall e'er prevail against us, or disturb
Our cheerful faith, that all which we behold
Is full of blessings. Therefore let the moon
Shine on thee in thy solitary walk;   135
And let the misty mountain-winds be free
To blow against thee: and, in after years,
When these wild ecstasies shall be matured
Into a sober pleasure; when thy mind
Shall be a mansion for all lovely forms,   140
Thy memory be as a dwelling-place
For all sweet sounds and harmonies; oh! then,

---

1. Generative, creative.

If solitude, or fear, or pain, or grief
Should be thy portion, with what healing thoughts
Of tender joy wilt thou remember me, 145
And these my exhortations! Nor, perchance—
If I should be where I no more can hear
Thy voice, nor catch from thy wild eyes these gleams
Of past existence—wilt thou then forget
That on the banks of this delightful stream 150
We stood together; and that I, so long
A worshipper of Nature, hither came
Unwearied in that service; rather say
With warmer love—oh! with far deeper zeal
Of holier love. Nor wilt thou then forget 155
That after many wanderings, many years
Of absence, these steep woods and lofty cliffs,
And this green pastoral landscape, were to me
More dear, both for themselves and for thy sake!

Ode on Intimations of Immortality

From Recollections of Early Childhood

The Child is father of the Man:
And I could wish my days to be
Bound each to each by natural piety.

I

There was a time when meadow, grove, and stream,
The earth, and every common sight,
    To me did seem
    Apparelled in celestial light,
The glory and the freshness of a dream. 5
It is not now as it hath been of yore;—
    Turn wheresoe'er I may,
        By night or day,
The things which I have seen I now can see no more.

II

The Rainbow comes and goes, 10
And lovely is the Rose;
    The Moon doth with delight
Look round her when the heavens are bare,
    Waters on a starry night
    Are beautiful and fair; 15
The sunshine is a glorious birth;
    But yet I know, where'er I go,
That there hath passed away a glory from the earth.

III

Now, while the birds thus sing a joyous song,
  And while the young lambs bound   20
    As to the tabor's sound,
To me alone there came a thought of grief:
A timely utterance gave that thought relief,
    And I again am strong:
The cataracts blow their trumpets from the steep;   25
No more shall grief of mine the season wrong;
I hear the Echoes through the mountains throng,
The Winds come to me from the fields of sleep,
    And all the earth is gay;
      Land and sea   30
  Give themselves up to jollity,
    And with the heart of May
  Doth every Beast keep holiday;—
    Thou Child of Joy,
Shout round me, let me hear thy shouts, thou happy   35
  Shepherd-boy!

IV

Ye blessèd Creatures, I have heard the call
  Ye to each other make; I see
The heavens laugh with you in your jubilee;
  My heart is at your festival,   40
    My head hath its coronal,
The fulness of your bliss, I feel—I feel it all.
    Oh evil day! if I were sullen
    While Earth herself is adorning,
      This sweet May-morning,   45
    And the Children are culling
      On every side,
    In a thousand valleys far and wide,
    Fresh flowers; while the sun shines warm,
And the Babe leaps up on his Mother's arm:—   50
    I hear, I hear, with joy I hear!
    —But there's a Tree, of many, one,
A single Field which I have looked upon,
Both of them speak of something that is gone:
    The Pansy at my feet   55
    Doth the same tale repeat:
Whither is fled the visionary gleam?
Where is it now, the glory and the dream?

V

Our birth is but a sleep and a forgetting:
The Soul that rises with us, our life's Star,   60
  Hath had elsewhere its setting,

And cometh from afar:
     Not in entire forgetfulness,
     And not in utter nakedness,
But trailing clouds of glory do we come   65
     From God, who is our home:
Heaven lies about us in our infancy!
Shades of the prison-house begin to close
     Upon the growing Boy,
But He beholds the light, and whence it flows,   70
     He sees it in his joy;
The Youth, who daily farther from the east
     Must travel, still is Nature's Priest,
     And by the vision splendid
     Is on his way attended;   75
At length the Man perceives it die away,
And fade into the light of common day.

                            VI

Earth fills her lap with pleasures of her own;
Yearnings she hath in her own natural kind,
And, even with something of a Mother's mind,   80
     And no unworthy aim,
     The homely Nurse doth all she can
To make her Foster-child, her Inmate, Man,
     Forget the glories he hath known,
And that imperial palace whence he came.   85

                           VII

Behold the Child among his new-born blisses,
A six years' Darling of a pigmy size!
See, where 'mid work of his own hand he lies,
Fretted by sallies of his mother's kisses,
With light upon him from his father's eyes!   90
See, at his feet, some little plan or chart,
Some fragment from his dream of human life,
Shaped by himself with newly-learnèd art;
     A wedding or a festival,
     A mourning or a funeral;   95
          And this hath now his heart,
          And unto this he frames his song:
          Then will he fit his tongue
To dialogues of business, love, or strife;
          But it will not be long   100
          Ere this be thrown aside,
          And with new joy and pride
The little Actor cons another part;
Filling from time to time his "humorous stage"
With all the Persons, down to palsied Age,   105
That Life brings with her in her equipage;
          As if his whole vocation
          Were endless imitation.

VIII

Thou, whose exterior semblance doth belie
      Thy Soul's immensity;   110
Thou best Philosopher, who yet dost keep
Thy heritage, thou Eye among the blind,
That, deaf and silent, read'st the eternal deep,
Haunted for ever by the eternal mind,—
      Mighty Prophet! Seer blest!   115
      On whom those truths do rest,
Which we are toiling all our lives to find,
In darkness lost, the darkness of the grave;
Thou, over whom thy Immortality
Broods like the Day, a Master o'er a Slave,   120
A Presence which is not to be put by;
      [To whom the grave
Is but a lonely bed without the sense or sight
      Of day or the warm light,
A place of thought where we in waiting lie;][1]   125
Thou little Child, yet glorious in the might
Of heaven-born freedom on thy being's height,
Why with such earnest pains dost thou provoke
The years to bring the inevitable yoke,
Thus blindly with thy blessedness at strife?   130
Full soon thy Soul shall have her earthly freight,
And custom lie upon thee with a weight,
Heavy as frost, and deep almost as life!

IX

      O joy! that in our embers
      Is something that doth live,   135
      That nature yet remembers
      What was so fugitive!
The thought of our past years in me doth breed
Perpetual benediction: not indeed
For that which is most worthy to be blest;   140
Delight and liberty, the simple creed
Of Childhood, whether busy or at rest,
With new-fledged hope still fluttering in his breast—
      Not for these I raise
      The song of thanks and praise;   145
      But for those obstinate questionings
      Of sense and outward things,
      Fallings from us, vanishings;
      Blank misgivings of a Creature
Moving about in worlds not realized,   150
High instincts before which our mortal Nature
Did tremble like a guilty Thing surprised:

1. The lines within brackets were included in the 1807 and 1815 editions of Wordsworth's poems but omitted in the 1820 and subsequent editions, as a result of Coleridge's severe censure of them.

But for those first affections,
　　Those shadowy recollections,
　　　Which, be they what they may,　　　　　　　　　　　155
Are yet the fountain-light of all our day,
Are yet a master-light of all our seeing;
　Uphold us, cherish, and have power to make
Our noisy years seem moments in the being
Of the eternal Silence: truths that wake,　　　　　　　　160
　　　To perish never;
Which neither listlessness, nor mad endeavour,
　　　Nor Man nor Boy,
Nor all that is at enmity with joy,
Can utterly abolish or destroy!　　　　　　　　　　　　165
　Hence in a season of calm weather
　　Though inland far we be,
Our Souls have sight of that immortal sea
　　Which brought us hither,
　　Can in a moment travel thither,　　　　　　　　　　170
And see the Children sport upon the shore,
And hear the mighty waters rolling evermore.

　　　　　　　　　　　X

Then sing, ye Birds, sing, sing a joyous song!
　　And let the young Lambs bound
　　As to the tabor's sound!　　　　　　　　　　　　　175
We in thought will join your throng,
　　Ye that pipe and ye that play,
　　Ye that through your hearts to-day
　　Feel the gladness of the May!
What though the radiance which was once so bright　　　180
Be now for ever taken from my sight,
　Though nothing can bring back the hour
Of splendour in the grass, of glory in the flower;
　　We will grieve not, rather find
　　Strength in what remains behind;　　　　　　　　185
　　In the primal sympathy
　　Which having been must ever be;
　　In the soothing thoughts that spring
　　Out of human suffering;
　　In the faith that looks through death,　　　　　　190
In years that bring the philosophic mind.

　　　　　　　　　　　XI

And O, ye Fountains, Meadows, Hills, and Groves,
Forebode not any severing of our loves!
Yet in my heart of hearts I feel your might;
I only have relinquished one delight　　　　　　　　　195
To live beneath your more habitual sway.
I love the Brooks which down their channels fret,
Even more than when I tripped lightly as they;
The innocent brightness of a new-born Day

Is lovely yet; 200
The Clouds that gather round the setting sun
Do take a sober colouring from an eye
That hath kept watch o'er man's mortality;
Another race hath been, and other palms are won.
Thanks to the human heart by which we live, 205
Thanks to its tenderness, its joys, and fears,
To me the meanest flower that blows can give
Thoughts that do often lie too deep for tears.

Composed upon Westminster Bridge, September 3, 1802

Earth has not anything to show more fair:
Dull would he be of soul who could pass by
A sight so touching in its majesty;
This City now doth, like a garment, wear
The beauty of the morning; silent, bare, 5
Ships, towers, domes, theatres, and temples lie
Open unto the fields, and to the sky;
All bright and glittering in the smokeless air.
Never did sun more beautifully steep
In his first splendour, valley, rock, or hill; 10
Ne'er saw I, never felt, a calm so deep!
The river glideth at his own sweet will:
Dear God! the very houses seem asleep;
And all that mighty heart is lying still!

The World Is Too Much with Us

The world is too much with us; late and soon,
Getting and spending, we lay waste our powers:
Little we see in Nature that is ours;
We have given our hearts away, a sordid boon![1]
This Sea that bares her bosom to the moon, 5
The winds that will be howling at all hours,
And are up-gathered now like sleeping flowers;
For this, for everything, we are out of tune;
It moves us not.—Great God! I'd rather be
A Pagan suckled in a creed outworn; 10
So might I, standing on this pleasant lea,
Have glimpses that would make me less forlorn;
Have sight of Proteus[2] rising from the sea;
Or hear old Triton[3] blow his wreathèd horn.

---

1. Gift. "Sordid": refers to the act of giving the heart away.
2. An old man of the sea who, in the *Odyssey*, could assume a variety of shapes.
3. A sea deity, usually represented as blowing on a conch shell.

SAMUEL TAYLOR COLERIDGE

1772–1834

Intellectually brilliant and highly learned, Coleridge led a chaotic life, addicted to opium, hopelessly in love with one woman while married to another, and typically unable to complete his literary and philosophical projects. But his groundbreaking poetic innovations, his wide and deep knowledge of religion, politics, and philosophy, and his compelling, improvised public lectures marked him as one of the most exceptional minds of his time. For many of his contemporaries, he was first and foremost a sparkling and impassioned conversationalist, so notable that admirers recorded and published his dinner table talk after his death. But long after his spirited conversation had gone, generations of readers would remember Coleridge for his most famous poem, "The Rime of the Ancient Mariner"—much quoted, imitated, and parodied—and for his dense philosophical meditations on literature and the mind.

LIFE

The youngest of ten children, Coleridge was a child prodigy who had read the Bible by the age of three. At school he was taught to read literature with exacting precision: "I learnt . . . that Poetry, even that of the loftiest, and, seemingly, that of the wildest odes, had a logic of its own, as severe as that of science." Always a voracious reader, Coleridge chose to immerse himself in philosophy and theology even as an adolescent. While studying at Cambridge University he won a medal for a poem he wrote on the slave trade, and found himself caught up in the enthusiasm for the French Revolution. But his commitment to "liberty" subjected him to intense anxieties. When the British declared war on France in 1793, antirevolutionary forces gathered strength, and Coleridge became vulnerable to accusations of treason. Plagued by uncertainty, he enlisted in the army under the unlikely alias of "Silas Tomkyn Comberbache." He was thoroughly unsuited to military life, and his brother, a military captain, obtained a release for him under the army's insanity clause.

Outside of the military context, Coleridge gained fame as a learned figure who spoke passionately in support of liberty. He published a radical journal and gave compelling lectures critical of the government and the slave trade. But he had no source of income, and when his wife gave birth to his first son, Hartley, in 1796, it was clear that he needed some stability. He set up house near his new friend, the poet **William Wordsworth**, and the two began a close relationship that would propel Coleridge into a period of intense poetic productivity that saw the composition of his most famous works, both his so-called conversation poems, which are written in response to his own feelings and experiences, and works on more mysterious, supernatural, even demonic themes. It was during 1797–98 that Coleridge wrote all three of the works collected here.

Around this time, Coleridge began to shift his political sympathies. He rejected the ideals of the French Revolution and adopted a patriotic, anti-Napoleonic position, which brought him under attack by radicals. Disillusioned with French thought, Coleridge grew increasingly fascinated by German philosophers, including G. W. F. Hegel, **Immanuel Kant**, and Friedrich Schelling, and he is often credited with having introduced these thinkers to British readers.

In the first years of the nineteenth century, Coleridge's life seemed bleak indeed. He found himself unable to write poetry, estranged from his wife, and in love with Sara Hutchinson, Wordsworth's future sister-in-law. She was highly intelligent, but thanks to Coleridge's marriage she remained permanently out of reach, and in his anguish the poet became increasingly dependent on both opium and alcohol. He left his family and worked as a journalist and lecturer. Addiction and both physical and mental illness brought Coleridge close to suicide in 1810, and he broke off his friendship with Wordsworth. He had a thoroughgoing breakdown a few years later, tormented by a sense of failure.

In 1814, however, his fortunes began to change. A new generation of poets, including **Percy Shelley, John Keats**, and most enthusiastically George Gordon Byron, professed themselves admirers of Coleridge's poetry, and he embarked on a new work, an exploration of poetic principles and practices, which grew into a complex intellectual autobiography—a combination of philosophy, theories of mind and language, literary history and criticism, and personal development—called the *Biographia Literaria*. There Coleridge elaborates theories of the imagination that would have great influence a century later. He also describes a rigorous discipline of reading poetry, a practice that would inspire literary critics in the twentieth century who wanted to foster skills of "close reading"—still a staple of literature classrooms today. Coleridge died a famous poet and thinker in 1834.

COLERIDGE'S WORKS IN A GLOBAL CONTEXT

The poems collected here give a sense of Coleridge's breadth as a poet. His conversation poem "Frost at Midnight," written soon after Hartley's birth, is sometimes considered the inspiration for Wordsworth's "Tintern Abbey," both of them meditations on childhood, memory, and nature written in a soothing blank verse. Intriguingly, Coleridge first published this in a pamphlet along with two highly political poems, "France: An Ode" and "Fears in Solitude," and some readers have interpreted this quiet work as a response to the atmosphere of censorship and oppressive government that prevailed during the wars with France.

Coleridge's supernatural poems, by contrast, are startling in their strangeness. "Kubla Khan" is haunting and fragmentary, and Coleridge prefaced it with a story about how the poem had come to him in an opium-induced dream that was unfortunately interrupted by a "person from Porlock." This account has become as famous as the poem itself. "The Ancient Mariner" also accumulated interpretive materials beyond the poem itself: it is written with archaic words and spellings, and over the years Coleridge made the language feel even more foreign by adding an explanatory gloss in the margins, also in an antiquated idiom, and a Latin epigraph. When it first appeared in the collection of poems by Wordsworth and Coleridge called *Lyrical Ballads*, critics were largely derisive, and the "Ancient Mariner" was called the worst in the volume. Wordsworth said later that "the old words and the strangeness of it have deterred readers from going on." (In the first version of *Lyrical Ballads*, Wordsworth had given it pride of place as the very first poem; just two years later he buried it second to last in the volume.)

Generations of readers have puzzled over Coleridge's theories of the human mind, and they have read "The Ancient Mariner" and "Kubla Khan" as meditations on the power and limits of the poetic imagination. But in recent years, readers have noticed that both poems depend on evocations of distant places. The Ancient Mariner travels as far as the South Pole, and "Kubla Khan" is quite specific in beginning with a Mongol emperor and ending with a girl from Abysinnia (now known as Ethiopia). Scholars have uncovered evidence of Coleridge's fascination with travel narratives, one of the most popular genres of his moment. And they have recommended reading these two poems in the context of Britain's global empire and the explosion of travel writing that accompanied it.

In Coleridge's time, books and newspapers brought constant news of imperial affairs: the loss of the American colonies, tensions with Spain and France over colonial territory, the first contact with Australia, the exploration of African territories unknown to Europeans, and the continuing administration of Ireland, India, Canada, and much of the Caribbean. Among the most popular books in late-eighteenth-century Britain were accounts of Captain James Cook's voyages around the globe. His crew brought back new maps of the world, accounts of cultures profoundly different from those of the Europeans, and also botanical and zoological specimens that surprised and fascinated English audiences. And yet the global explorations described in British travel writing of the time were not simply undertaken for the pursuit of knowledge: they formed an integral part of the British desire for the discovery and control of new raw materials, new trade goods, and new markets.

Travel writing thus formed one popular part of a wider colonizing culture preoccupied with economic gain and global conquest.

"The Rime of the Ancient Mariner" was partly inspired by Cook's second voyage, which attempted to discover the South Pole. "Kubla Khan" too might have evoked the British Empire for Coleridge's first readers, since the Khan was a legendary emperor: the grandson of Genghis Khan, he ruled over the Mongols of Northern China in the thirteenth century and controlled the largest empire that had existed up to that time, stretching as far as modern Korea, Iraq, Western Russia, and Hungary. It was the Mongols who first allowed trade between Europe and China, but they were also famous for their brutal violence—massacring and plundering wherever they encountered opposition.

At the time that Coleridge wrote "The Ancient Mariner" and "Kubla Khan," he was unsympathetic to British imperial expansion. He had begun his career in fierce opposition to slavery, and readers have noted resonances with contemporary slave ship voyages in the sorrowful tale of "The Ancient Mariner." Coleridge also wrote scathingly about imperialism in one of the poems he published alongside "Frost at Midnight": "From east to west," he wrote, the English have "borne to distant tribes slavery and pangs, / And, deadlier far, our vices, whose deep taint / With slow perdition murders the whole man."

As his poetry imaginatively ranges over the globe, Coleridge also explores the inner frontier, probing the powers and limits of the mind. And in all of his work, he offers a dense and thoughtful contemplation of human capacities: our knowledge, our inner vision, and our powers of creation and destruction.

The Rime of the Ancient Mariner

IN SEVEN PARTS

Facile credo, plures esse Naturas invisibiles quam visibiles in rerum universitate. Sed horum [sic] omnium familiam quis nobis enarrabit, et gradus et cognationes et discrimina et singulorum munera? Quid agunt? quae loca habitant? Harum rerum notitiam semper ambivit ingenium humanum, nunquam attigit. Juvat, interea, non diffiteor, quandoque in animo, tanquam in tabulâ, majoris et melioris mundi imaginem contemplari: ne mens assuefacta hodiernae vitae minutiis se contrahat nimis, et tota subsidat in pusillas cogitationes. Sed veritati interea invigilandum est, modusque servandus, ut certa ab incertis, diem a nocte, distinguamus.

T. BURNET, *Archaeol. Phil.* p. 68.[1]

Part 1

An ancient Mariner meeteth three gallants bidden to a wedding-feast, and detaineth one.

It is an ancient Mariner
And he stoppeth one of three.
"By thy long grey beard and glittering eye,
Now wherefore stopp'st thou me?

The Bridegroom's doors are opened wide,   5
And I am next of kin;
The guests are met, the feast is set:
May'st hear the merry din."

He holds him with his skinny hand,
"There was a ship," quoth he.   10
"Hold off! unhand me, grey-beard loon!"
Eftsoons[2] his hand dropt he.

The wedding guest is spellbound by the eye of the old sea-faring man, and constrained to hear his tale.

He holds him with his glittering eye—
The wedding-guest stood still,
And listens like a three years' child: 15
The Mariner hath his will.[3]

The wedding-guest sat on a stone:
He cannot choose but hear;

1. "I readily believe that there are more invisible Natures in the universe than visible ones. But who will explain the ways that these beings are related, their ranks and connections and features and functions? What do they do? Where do they dwell? The human mind has always searched for this knowledge but has never attained it. Meanwhile, I do not deny that from time to time it is useful to picture in the mind, as on a tablet, the image of a greater and better world, so that our minds, preoccu-pied with everyday trivial matters, do not narrow themselves too much and sink entirely into petty ideas. And yet we must watch for the truth and keep a sense of proportion, so that we may distinguish between the certain and uncertain, day and night" (Latin). Adapted by Coleridge from Thomas Burnet, *Archaeologiae philosophicae* (1692).
2. Immediately.
3. I.e., the mariner has mesmerized the wedding guest.

And thus spake on that ancient man,
The bright-eyed Mariner.   20

"The ship was cheered, the harbor cleared,
Merrily did we drop
Below the kirk,[4] below the hill,
Below the light house top.

*The Mariner tells
how the ship sailed
southward with a
good wind and fair
weather, till it
reached the line.*

The sun came up upon the left,   25
Out of the sea came he!
And he shone bright, and on the right
Went down into the sea.

Higher and higher every day,
Till over the mast at noon—"   30
The wedding-guest here beat his breast,
For he heard the loud bassoon.

*The Wedding Guest
heareth the bridal
music; but the mari-
ner continueth his
tale.*

The bride hath paced into the hall,
Red as a rose is she;
Nodding their heads before her goes   35
The merry minstrelsy.

The wedding-guest he beat his breast,
Yet he cannot choose but hear;
And thus spake on that ancient man,
The bright-eyed Mariner.   40

*The ship driven by a
storm toward the
south pole.*

"And now the storm-blast came, and he
Was tyrannous and strong:
He struck with his o'ertaking wings,
And chased us south along.

With sloping masts and dipping prow,   45
As who pursued with yell and blow
Still treads the shadow of his foe,
And forward bends his head,
The ship drove fast, loud roared the blast,
And southward aye we fled.   50

And now there came both mist and snow,
And it grew wondrous cold:
And ice, mast-high, came floating by,
As green as emerald.

*The land of ice, and
of fearful sounds
where no living thing
was to be seen.*

And through the drifts the snowy clifts   55
Did send a dismal sheen:
Nor shapes of men nor beasts we ken—
The ice was all between.

4. Church.

The ice was here, the ice was there,
The ice was all around:
It cracked and growled, and roared and howled,
Like noises in a swound![5]

At length did cross an Albatross,
Thorough the fog it came;
As if it had been a Christian soul,
We hailed it in God's name.

It ate the food it ne'er had eat,
And round and round it flew.
The ice did split with a thunder-fit;
The helmsman steered us through!

And a good south wind sprung up behind;
The Albatross did follow,
And every day, for food or play,
Came to the mariners' hollo!

In mist or cloud, on mast or shroud,
It perched for vespers nine;
Whiles all the night, through fog-smoke white,
Glimmered the white moon-shine."

"God save thee, ancient Mariner!
From the fiends, that plague thee thus!—
Why look'st thou so?"—With my cross-bow
I shot the Albatross.

Part 2

The Sun now rose upon the right:
Out of the sea came he,
Still hid in mist, and on the left
Went down into the sea.

And the good south wind still blew behind,
But no sweet bird did follow,
Nor any day for food or play
Came to the mariners' hollo!

And I had done a hellish thing,
And it would work 'em woe:
For all averred, I had killed the bird
That made the breeze to blow.
Ah wretch! said they, the bird to slay,
That made the breeze to blow!

60

65

70

75

80

85

90

95

5. Swoon.

*But when the fog
cleared off, they jus-
tify the same, and
thus make themselves
accomplices in the
crime.*

Nor dim nor red, like God's own head,
The glorious Sun uprist:
Then all averred, I had killed the bird
That brought the fog and mist.   100
'Twas right, said they, such birds to slay,
That bring the fog and mist.

*The fair breeze con-
tinues; the ship enters
the Pacific Ocean,
and sails northward,
even till it reaches the
Line.*

The fair breeze blew, the white foam flew,
The furrow followed free;
We were the first that ever burst   105
Into that silent sea.

*The ship hath been
suddenly becalmed.*

Down dropt the breeze, the sails dropt down,
'Twas sad as sad could be;
And we did speak only to break
The silence of the sea!   110

All in a hot and copper sky,
The bloody Sun, at noon,
Right up above the mast did stand,
No bigger than the Moon.

Day after day, day after day,   115
We stuck, nor breath nor motion;
As idle as a painted ship
Upon a painted ocean.

*And the Albatross
begins to be avenged.*

Water, water, every where,
And all the boards did shrink;   120
Water, water, every where,
Nor any drop to drink.

The very deep did rot: O Christ!
That ever this should be!
Yea, slimy things did crawl with legs   125
Upon the slimy sea.

About, about, in reel and rout
The death-fires danced at night;
The water, like a witch's oils,
Burnt green, and blue and white.   130

*A spirit had followed
them; one of the
invisible inhabitants
of this planet, neither
departed souls nor
angels; concerning*

And some in dreams assured were
Of the spirit that plagued us so;
Nine fathom deep he had followed us
From the land of mist and snow.

*whom the learned Jew, Josephus, and the Platonic Constantinopolitan, Michael Psellus, may be consulted.
They are very numerous, and there is no climate or element without one or more.*

And every tongue, through utter drought,   135
Was withered at the root;
We could not speak, no more than if
We had been choked with soot.

The shipmates, in their sore distress, would fain throw the whole guilt on the ancient Mariner: in sign whereof they hang the dead sea bird round his neck.

Ah! well-a-day! what evil looks
Had I from old and young!   140
Instead of the cross, the Albatross
About my neck was hung.

Part 3

There passed a weary time. Each throat
Was parched, and glazed each eye.
A weary time! a weary time!   145
How glazed each weary eye,
When looking westward, I beheld
A something in the sky.

The ancient Mariner beholdeth a sign in the element afar off.

At first it seemed a little speck,
And then it seemed a mist;
It moved and moved, and took at last   150
A certain shape, I wist.[6]

A speck, a mist, a shape, I wist!
And still it neared and neared:
As if it dodged a water-sprite,   155
It plunged and tacked and veered.

At its nearer approach, it seemeth him to be a ship; and at a dear ransom he freeth his speech from the bonds of thirst.

With throats unslaked, with black lips baked,
We could nor laugh nor wail;
Through utter drought all dumb we stood!
I bit my arm, I sucked the blood,   160
And cried, A sail! a sail!

A flash of joy;

With throats unslaked, with black lips baked,
Agape they heard me call:
Gramercy![7] they for joy did grin,
And all at once their breath drew in,   165
As they were drinking all.

And horror follows. For can it be a ship that comes onward without wind or tide?

See! see! (I cried) she tacks no more!
Hither to work us weal;[8]
Without a breeze, without a tide,
She steadies with upright keel!   170

6. Knew.
7. Great thanks!

8. Benefit.

The western wave was all a-flame.
The day was well nigh done!
Almost upon the western wave
Rested the broad bright Sun;
When that strange shape drove suddenly   175
Betwixt us and the Sun.

It seemeth him but the skeleton of a ship.

And straight the Sun was flecked with bars,
(Heaven's Mother send us grace!)
As if through a dungeon-grate he peered
With broad and burning face.   180

Alas! (thought I, and my heart beat loud)
How fast she nears and nears!
Are those her sails that glance in the Sun,
Like restless gossameres?

And its ribs are seen as bars on the face of the setting Sun. The specter-woman and her death-mate, and no other on board the skeleton-ship.

Are those her ribs through which the Sun   185
Did peer, as through a grate?
And is that Woman all her crew?
Is that a Death? and are there two?
Is Death that woman's mate?

Like vessel, like crew!

Her lips were red, her looks were free,   190
Her locks were yellow as gold:
Her skin was as white as leprosy,
The Night-mare Life-in-Death was she,
Who thicks man's blood with cold.

Death and Life-in-death have diced for the ship's crew, and she (the latter) winneth the ancient Mariner.

The naked hulk alongside came,   195
And the twain were casting dice;
"The game is done! I've won! I've won!"
Quoth she, and whistles thrice.

No twilight within the courts of the sun.

The Sun's rim dips; the stars rush out:
At one stride comes the dark;   200
With far-heard whisper, o'er the sea,
Off shot the spectre-bark.

At the rising of the Moon,

We listened and looked sideways up!
Fear at my heart, as at a cup,
My life-blood seemed to sip!   205
The stars were dim, and thick the night,
The steersman's face by his lamp gleamed white;

From the sails the dew did drip—
Till clomb above the eastern bar
The horned Moon, with one bright star   210
Within the nether tip.

One after one, by the star-dogged Moon,
Too quick for groan or sigh,
Each turned his face with a ghastly pang,
And cursed me with his eye.   215

Four times fifty living men,
(And I heard nor sigh nor groan)
With heavy thump, a lifeless lump,
They dropped down one by one.

The souls did from their bodies fly,—   220
They fled to bliss or woe!
And every soul, it passed me by,
Like the whizz of my cross-bow!

Part 4

"I fear thee, ancient Mariner!
I fear thy skinny hand!   225
And thou art long, and lank, and brown,
As is the ribbed sea-sand.

I fear thee and thy glittering eye,
And thy skinny hand, so brown."—
Fear not, fear not, thou wedding-guest!   230
This body dropt not down.

Alone, alone, all, all alone,
Alone on a wide wide sea!
And never a saint took pity on
My soul in agony.   235

The many men, so beautiful!
And they all dead did lie:
And a thousand thousand slimy things
Lived on; and so did I.

I looked upon the rotting sea,   240
And drew my eyes away;
I looked upon the rotting deck,
And there the dead men lay.

I looked to heaven, and tried to pray;
But or ever a prayer had gusht,   245
A wicked whisper came, and made
My heart as dry as dust.

I closed my lids, and kept them close,
And the balls like pulses beat;
For the sky and the sea, and the sea and the sky   250

Lay like a load on my weary eye,
And the dead were at my feet.

*But the curse liveth
for him in the eye of
the dead men.*

The cold sweat melted from their limbs,
Nor rot nor reek did they:
The look with which they looked on me   255
Had never passed away.

An orphan's curse would drag to hell
A spirit from on high;
But oh! more horrible than that
Is the curse in a dead man's eye!   260
Seven days, seven nights, I saw that curse,
And yet I could not die.

*In his loneliness and
fixedness he yearneth
towards the journey-
ing Moon, and the
stars that still sojourn,
yet still move onward;*

The moving Moon went up the sky,
And no where did abide:
Softly she was going up,   265
And a star or two beside—

*and everywhere the blue sky belongs to them, and is their appointed rest, and their native country and their own
natural homes, which they enter unannounced, as lords that are certainly expected and yet there is a silent joy at
their arrival.*

Her beams bemocked the sultry main,
Like April hoar-frost spread;
But where the ship's huge shadow lay,
The charmed water burnt alway   270
A still and awful red.

*By the light of the
Moon he beholdeth
God's creatures of the
great calm.*

Beyond the shadow of the ship,
I watched the water-snakes:
They moved in tracks of shining white,
And when they reared, the elfish light   275
Fell off in hoary flakes.

Within the shadow of the ship
I watched their rich attire:
Blue, glossy green, and velvet black,
They coiled and swam; and every track   280
Was a flash of golden fire.

*Their beauty and
their happiness.*

O happy living things! no tongue
Their beauty might declare:
A spring of love gushed from my heart,

*He blesseth them in
his heart.*

And I blessed them unaware: 285
Sure my kind saint took pity on me,
And I blessed them unaware.

*The spell begins to
break.*

The selfsame moment I could pray;
And from my neck so free
The Albatross fell off, and sank   290
Like lead into the sea.

Part 5

Oh sleep! it is a gentle thing,
Beloved from pole to pole!
To Mary Queen the praise be given!
She sent the gentle sleep from Heaven,   295
That slid into my soul.

By grace of the holy Mother, the ancient Mariner is refreshed with rain.

The silly⁹ buckets on the deck,
That had so long remained,
I dreamt that they were filled with dew;
And when I awoke, it rained.   300

My lips were wet, my throat was cold,
My garments all were dank;
Sure I had drunken in my dreams,
And still my body drank.

I moved, and could not feel my limbs: 305
I was so light—almost
I thought that I had died in sleep,
And was a blessed ghost.

He heareth sounds and seeth strange sights and commotions in the sky and the element.

And soon I heard a roaring wind:
It did not come anear;
But with its sound it shook the sails,   310
That were so thin and sere.

The upper air burst into life!
And a hundred fire-flags sheen,¹
To and fro they were hurried about!   315
And to and fro, and in and out,
The wan stars danced between.

And the coming wind did roar more loud,
And the sails did sigh like sedge;²
And the rain poured down from one black cloud;   320
The Moon was at its edge.

The thick black cloud was cleft, and still
The Moon was at its side:
Like waters shot from some high crag,
The lightning fell with never a jag,   325
A river steep and wide.

The bodies of the ship's crew are inspired, and the ship moves on;

The loud wind never reached the ship,
Yet now the ship moved on!
Beneath the lightning and the moon
The dead men gave a groan.   330

---

9. Simple.
1. Shone.

2. Flowering plant like a grass or rush.

They groaned, they stirred, they all uprose,
Nor spake, nor moved their eyes;
It had been strange, even in a dream,
To have seen those dead men rise.

The helmsman steered, the ship moved on;   335
Yet never a breeze up blew;
The mariners all 'gan work the ropes,
Where they were wont to do;
They raised their limbs like lifeless tools—
We were a ghastly crew.   340

The body of my brother's son
Stood by me, knee to knee:
The body and I pulled at one rope,
But he said nought to me.

But not by the souls of the men, nor by dæmons of earth or middle air, but by a blessed troop of angelic spirits, sent down by the invocation of the guardian saint.

"I fear thee, ancient Mariner!"   345
Be calm, thou Wedding-Guest!
'Twas not those souls that fled in pain,
Which to their corses[3] came again,
But a troop of spirits blest:

For when it dawned—they dropped their arms,   350
And clustered round the mast;
Sweet sounds rose slowly through their mouths,
And from their bodies passed.

Around, around, flew each sweet sound,
Then darted to the Sun;   355
Slowly the sounds came back again,
Now mixed, now one by one.

Sometimes a-dropping from the sky
I heard the sky-lark sing;
Sometimes all little birds that are,   360
How they seemed to fill the sea and air
With their sweet jargoning![4]

And now 'twas like all instruments,
Now like a lonely flute;
And now it is an angel's song,   365
That makes the heavens be mute.

It ceased; yet still the sails made on
A pleasant noise till noon,

3. Corpses.   4. Twittering.

A noise like of a hidden brook
In the leafy month of June,   370
That to the sleeping woods all night
Singeth a quiet tune.

Till noon we quietly sailed on,
Yet never a breeze did breathe:
Slowly and smoothly went the ship,   375
Moved onward from beneath.

The lonesome spirit
from the south-pole
carries on the ship as
far as the line, in obe-
dience to the angelic
troop, but still
requireth vengeance.

Under the keel nine fathom deep,
From the land of mist and snow,
The spirit slid: and it was he
That made the ship to go.   380
The sails at noon left off their tune,
And the ship stood still also.

The Sun, right up above the mast,
Had fixed her to the ocean:
But in a minute she 'gan stir,   385
With a short uneasy motion—
Backwards and forwards half her length
With a short uneasy motion.

Then like a pawing horse let go,
She made a sudden bound: 390
It flung the blood into my head,
And I fell down in a swound.

The Polar Spirit's fel-
low dæmons, the
invisible inhabitants
of the element, take
part in his wrong; and
two of them relate,
one to the other, that
penance long and
heavy for the ancient
Mariner hath been
accorded to the Polar
Spirit, who returneth
southward.

How long in that same fit I lay,
I have not to declare;
But ere my living life returned,   395
I heard and in my soul discerned
Two voices in the air.

"Is it he?" quoth one, "Is this the man?
By him who died on cross,
With his cruel bow he laid full low   400
The harmless Albatross.

The spirit who bideth by himself
In the land of mist and snow,
He loved the bird that loved the man
Who shot him with his bow."   405

The other was a softer voice,
As soft as honey-dew:
Quoth he, "The man hath penance done,
And penance more will do."

Part 6

FIRST VOICE

"But tell me, tell me! speak again,   410
Thy soft response renewing—
What makes that ship drive on so fast?
What is the ocean doing?"

SECOND VOICE

"Still as a slave before his lord,
The ocean hath no blast;   415
His great bright eye most silently
Up to the Moon is cast—

If he may know which way to go;
For she guides him smooth or grim.
See, brother, see! how graciously   420
She looketh down on him."

FIRST VOICE

"But why drives on that ship so fast,
Without or wave or wind?"

SECOND VOICE

"The air is cut away before,
And closes from behind.   425

Fly, brother, fly! more high, more high!
Or we shall be belated:
For slow and slow that ship will go,
When the Mariner's trance is abated."

I woke, and we were sailing on   430
As in a gentle weather:
'Twas night, calm night, the moon was high;
The dead men stood together.

All stood together on the deck,
For a charnel-dungeon fitter: 435
All fixed on me their stony eyes,
That in the Moon did glitter.

The pang, the curse, with which they died,
Had never passed away:
I could not draw my eyes from theirs,   440
Nor turn them up to pray.

*The Mariner hath
been cast into a
trance; for the angelic
power causeth the
vessel to drive north-
ward faster than
human life could
endure.*

*The supernatural
motion is retarded;
the Mariner awakes,
and his penance
begins anew.*

The curse is finally
expiated.

And now this spell was snapt: once more
I viewed the ocean green,
And looked far forth, yet little saw
Of what had else been seen—   445

Like one, that on a lonesome road
Doth walk in fear and dread,
And having once turned round walks on,
And turns no more his head;
Because he knows, a frightful fiend   450
Doth close behind him tread.

But soon there breathed a wind on me,
Nor sound nor motion made:
Its path was not upon the sea,
In ripple or in shade.   455

It raised my hair, it fanned my cheek
Like a meadow-gale of spring—
It mingled strangely with my fears,
Yet it felt like a welcoming.

Swiftly, swiftly flew the ship,   460
Yet she sailed softly too:
Sweetly, sweetly blew the breeze—
On me alone it blew.

And the ancient Mar-
iner beholdeth his
native country.

Oh! dream of joy! is this indeed
The light-house top I see?   465
Is this the hill? is this the kirk?
Is this mine own countree?

We drifted o'er the harbour-bar,
And I with sobs did pray—
O let me be awake, my God!   470
Or let me sleep alway.

The harbour-bay was clear as glass,
So smoothly it was strewn!
And on the bay the moonlight lay,
And the shadow of the moon.   475

The rock shone bright, the kirk no less,
That stands above the rock:
The moonlight steeped in silentness
The steady weathercock.

And the bay was white with silent light,   480
Till rising from the same,

The angelic spirits
leave the dead bodies,

Full many shapes, that shadows were,
In crimson colours came.

And appear in their
own forms of light.

A little distance from the prow
Those crimson shadows were: 485
I turned my eyes upon the deck—
Oh, Christ! what saw I there!

Each corse lay flat, lifeless and flat,
And, by the holy rood![5]
A man all light, a seraph-man,   490
On every corse there stood.

This seraph-band, each waved his hand:
It was a heavenly sight!
They stood as signals to the land,
Each one a lovely light;   495

This seraph-band, each waved his hand,
No voice did they impart—
No voice; but oh! the silence sank
Like music on my heart.

But soon I heard the dash of oars,   500
I heard the Pilot's cheer;
My head was turned perforce away,
And I saw a boat appear.

The Pilot and the Pilot's boy,
I heard them coming fast: 505
Dear Lord in Heaven! it was a joy
The dead men could not blast.

I saw a third—I heard his voice:
It is the Hermit good!
He singeth loud his godly hymns   510
That he makes in the wood.
He'll shrieve my soul, he'll wash away
The Albatross's blood.

Part 7

The Hermit of the
wood,

This Hermit good lives in that wood
Which slopes down to the sea.   515
How loudly his sweet voice he rears!
He loves to talk with marineres
That come from a far countree.

5. Cross.

He kneels at morn, and noon, and eve—
He hath a cushion plump:
It is the moss that wholly hides
The rotted old oak-stump.   520

The skiff-boat neared: I heard them talk,
"Why, this is strange, I trow!
Where are those lights so many and fair,   525
That signal made but now?"

Approacheth the ship   "Strange, by my faith!" the Hermit said—
with wonder.   "And they answered not our cheer!
The planks looked warped! and see those sails,
How thin they are and sere!   530
I never saw aught like to them,
Unless perchance it were

Brown skeletons of leaves that lag
My forest-brook along;
When the ivy-tod[6] is heavy with snow,   535
And the owlet whoops to the wolf below,
That eats the she-wolf's young."

"Dear Lord! it hath a fiendish look"—
(The Pilot made reply)
"I am a-feared"—"Push on, push on!"   540
Said the Hermit cheerily.

The boat came closer to the ship,
But I nor spake nor stirred;
The boat came close beneath the ship,
And straight a sound was heard.   545

The ship suddenly   Under the water it rumbled on,
sinketh.   Still louder and more dread:
It reached the ship, it split the bay;
The ship went down like lead.

The ancient Mariner   Stunned by that loud and dreadful sound,   550
is saved in the Pilot's   Which sky and ocean smote,
boat.   Like one that hath been seven days drowned
My body lay afloat;
But swift as dreams, myself I found
Within the Pilot's boat.   555

Upon the whirl, where sank the ship,
The boat spun round and round;
And all was still, save that the hill
Was telling of the sound.

6. Ivy bush.

I moved my lips—the Pilot shrieked   560
And fell down in a fit;
The holy Hermit raised his eyes,
And prayed where he did sit.

I took the oars: the Pilot's boy,
Who now doth crazy go,   565
Laughed loud and long, and all the while
His eyes went to and fro.
"Ha! ha!" quoth he, "full plain I see,
The Devil knows how to row."

And now, all in my own countree,   570
I stood on the firm land!
The Hermit stepped forth from the boat,
And scarcely he could stand.

The ancient Mariner
earnestly entreateth
the Hermit to shrieve
him; and the penance
of life falls on him.

"O shrieve me, shrieve me, holy man!"
The Hermit crossed his brow.   575
"Say quick," quoth he, "I bid thee say—
What manner of man art thou?"

Forthwith this frame of mine was wrenched
With a woful agony,
Which forced me to begin my tale;   580
And then it left me free.

And ever and anon
throughout his future
life an agony con-
straineth him to
travel from land to
land.

Since then, at an uncertain hour,
That agony returns:
And till my ghastly tale is told,
This heart within me burns.   585

I pass, like night, from land to land;
I have strange power of speech;
That moment that his face I see,
I know the man that must hear me:
To him my tale I teach.   590

What loud uproar bursts from that door!
The wedding-guests are there:
But in the garden-bower the bride
And bride-maids singing are:
And hark the little vesper bell,   595
Which biddeth me to prayer!

O Wedding-Guest! this soul hath been
Alone on a wide wide sea:
So lonely 'twas, that God himself
Scarce seemed there to be.   600

O sweeter than the marriage-feast,
'Tis sweeter far to me,

To walk together to the kirk
With a goodly company!—

To walk together to the kirk,   605
And all together pray,
While each to his great Father bends,
Old men, and babes, and loving friends,
And youths and maidens gay!

And to teach, by his own example, love and reverence to all things that God made and loveth.

Farewell, farewell! but this I tell   610
To thee, thou Wedding-Guest!
He prayeth well, who loveth well
Both man and bird and beast.

He prayeth best, who loveth best
All things both great and small;   615
For the dear God who loveth us,
He made and loveth all.

The Mariner, whose eye is bright,
Whose beard with age is hoar,
Is gone: and now the Wedding-Guest   620
Turned from the bridegroom's door.

He went like one that hath been stunned,
And is of sense forlorn:
A sadder and a wiser man,
He rose the morrow morn.   625

Kubla Khan

Or, a Vision in a Dream. A Fragment

The following fragment is here published at the request of a poet of great and deserved celebrity [Lord Byron], and, as far as the Author's own opinions are concerned, rather as a psychological curiosity, than on the ground of any supposed *poetic* merits.

In the summer of the year 1797, the Author, then in ill health, had retired to a lonely farm-house between Porlock and Linton, on the Exmoor confines of Somerset and Devonshire.[1] In consequence of a slight indisposition, an anodyne had been prescribed, from the effects of which he fell asleep in his chair at the moment that he was reading the following sentence, or words of the same substance, in "Purchas's Pilgrimage":[2] "Here the Khan Kubla commanded

1. A high moorland shared by the two southwestern counties in England.
2. Samuel Purchas (1575?–1626) published *Purchas, his Pilgrimage; or, Relations of the World and the Religions observed in all Ages* in 1613. The passage in Purchas is slightly different: "In Xamdu did Cublai Can build a stately Palace, encompassing sixteene miles of plaine ground with a wall, wherein are fertile meddowes, pleasant Springs, delightfull Streames, and all sorts of beasts of chase and game, and in the middest thereof a sumptuous house of pleasure, which may be removed from place to place" (IV.13).

a palace to be built, and a stately garden thereunto. And thus ten miles of fertile ground were inclosed with a wall." The Author continued for about three hours in a profound sleep, at least of the external senses, during which time he has the most vivid confidence, that he could not have composed less than from two to three hundred lines; if that indeed can be called composition in which all the images rose up before him as *things*, with a parallel production of the correspondent expressions, without any sensation or consciousness of effort.[3] On awaking he appeared to himself to have a distinct recollection of the whole, and taking his pen, ink, and paper, instantly and eagerly wrote down the lines that are here preserved. At this moment he was unfortunately called out by a person on business from Porlock, and detained by him above an hour, and on his return to his room, found, to his no small surprise and mortification, that though he still retained some vague and dim recollection of the general purport of the vision, yet, with the exception of some eight or ten scattered lines and images, all the rest had passed away like the images on the surface of a stream into which a stone has been cast, but, alas! without the after restoration of the latter!

> Then all the charm
> Is broken—all that phantom-world so fair
> Vanishes, and a thousand circlets spread,
> And each mis-shape[s] the other. Stay awhile,
> Poor youth! who scarcely dar'st lift up thine eyes—
> The stream will soon renew its smoothness, soon
> The visions will return! And lo, he stays,
> And soon the fragments dim of lovely forms
> Come trembling back, unite, and now once more
> The pool becomes a mirror.[4]

Yet from the still surviving recollections in his mind, the Author has frequently purposed to finish for himself what had been originally, as it were, given to him. Σαμερον αδιον ασω:[5] but the to-morrow is yet to come. . . .

> In Xanadu did Kubla Khan[6]
> A stately pleasure-dome decree:
> Where Alph,[7] the sacred river, ran
> Through caverns measureless to man
>   Down to a sunless sea.   5
> So twice five miles of fertile ground
> With walls and towers were girdled round:
> And there were gardens bright with sinuous rills,
> Where blossomed many an incense-bearing tree;

---

3. Coleridge's statement that he dreamed the poem and wrote down what he could later remember verbatim has been queried, most recently by medical opinion. The belief that opium produces special dreams or even any dreams at all lacks confirmation.
4. From Coleridge's poem *The Picture; or, The Lover's Resolution*, lines 91–100.

5. From Theocritus's *Idylls* 1.145: "I'll sing a sweeter song tomorrow" (Greek).
6. Mongol emperor (1215?–1294), visited by Marco Polo.
7. J. L. Lowes, in *The Road to Xanadu* (1927), thinks that Coleridge may have had in mind the river Alpheus—linked with the Nile—mentioned by Virgil.

And here were forests ancient as the hills,   10
Enfolding sunny spots of greenery.

But oh! that deep romantic chasm which slanted
Down the green hill athwart a cedarn cover!
A savage place! as holy and enchanted
As e'er beneath a waning moon was haunted   15
By woman wailing for her demon-lover!
And from this chasm, with ceaseless turmoil seething,
As if this earth in fast thick pants were breathing,
A mighty fountain momently was forced:
Amid whose swift half-intermitted burst   20
Huge fragments vaulted like rebounding hail,
Or chaffy grain beneath the thresher's flail:
And 'mid these dancing rocks at once and ever
It flung up momently the sacred river.
Five miles meandering with a mazy motion   25
Through wood and dale the sacred river ran,
Then reached the caverns measureless to man,
And sank in tumult to a lifeless ocean:
And 'mid this tumult Kubla heard from far
Ancestral voices prophesying war!   30

    The shadow of the dome of pleasure
    Floated midway on the waves;
    Where was heard the mingled measure
    From the fountain and the caves.
It was a miracle of rare device,   35
A sunny pleasure-dome with caves of ice!
    A damsel with a dulcimer
    In a vision once I saw:
    It was an Abyssinian maid,
    And on her dulcimer she played,   40
    Singing of Mount Abora.[8]
    Could I revive within me
    Her symphony and song,
    To such a deep delight 'twould win me,
That with music loud and long,   45
I would build that dome in air,
That sunny dome! those caves of ice!
And all who heard should see them there,
And all should cry, Beware! Beware!
His flashing eyes, his floating hair!   50
Weave a circle round him thrice,
And close your eyes with holy dread,
For he on honey-dew hath fed,
And drunk the milk of Paradise.

8. Lowes argues that this may have been "Mt. Amara," mentioned by Milton in *Paradise Lost*
(4.28), or Amhara in Samuel Johnson's *Rasselas*.

Frost at Midnight

The frost performs its secret ministry,
Unhelped by any wind. The owlet's cry
Came loud—and hark, again! loud as before.
The inmates of my cottage, all at rest,
Have left me to that solitude, which suits   5
Abstruser musings: save that at my side
My cradled infant slumbers peacefully.
'Tis calm indeed! so calm, that it disturbs
And vexes meditation with its strange
And extreme silentness. Sea, hill, and wood,   10
This populous village! Sea, and hill, and wood,
With all the numberless goings on of life,
Inaudible as dreams! the thin blue flame
Lies on my low burnt fire, and quivers not;
Only that film,¹ which fluttered on the grate,   15
Still flutters there, the sole unquiet thing.
Methinks, its motion in this hush of nature
Gives it dim sympathies with me who live,
Making it a companionable form,
Whose puny flaps and freaks the idling Spirit   20
By its own moods interprets, every where
Echo or mirror seeking of itself,
And makes a toy of Thought.

                            But O! how oft,
How oft, at school, with most believing mind,
Presageful, have I gazed upon the bars,   25
To watch that fluttering stranger! and as oft
With unclosed lids, already had I dreamt
Of my sweet birth-place, and the old church-tower,
Whose bells, the poor man's only music, rang
From morn to evening, all the hot Fair-day,   30
So sweetly, that they stirred and haunted me
With a wild pleasure, falling on mine ear
Most like articulate sounds of things to come!
So gazed I, till the soothing things I dreamt
Lulled me to sleep, and sleep prolonged my dreams!   35
And so I brooded all the following morn,
Awed by the stern preceptor's² face, mine eye
Fixed with mock study on my swimming book:
Save if the door half opened, and I snatched
A hasty glance, and still my heart leaped up,   40
For still I hoped to see the stranger's face,

---

1. In all parts of the kingdom these films are
called *strangers* and supposed to portend the
arrival of some absent friend [Coleridge's
note]. The term "film" here refers to a piece of
soot fluttering on the fire grate.
2. Teacher's.

Townsman, or aunt, or sister more beloved,
My play-mate when we both were clothed alike![3]

    Dear Babe, that sleepest cradled by my side,
Whose gentle breathings, heard in this deep calm,   45
Fill up the interspersed vacancies
And momentary pauses of the thought!
My babe so beautiful! it thrills my heart
With tender gladness, thus to look at thee,
And think that thou shalt learn far other lore   50
And in far other scenes! For I was reared
In the great city, pent 'mid cloisters dim,
And saw nought lovely but the sky and stars.
But thou, my babe! shalt wander like a breeze
By lakes and sandy shores, beneath the crags   55
Of ancient mountain, and beneath the clouds,
Which image in their bulk both lakes and shores
And mountain crags: so shalt thou see and hear
The lovely shapes and sounds intelligible
Of that eternal language, which thy God   60
Utters, who from eternity doth teach
Himself in all, and all things in himself.
Great universal Teacher! he shall mould
Thy spirit, and by giving make it ask.

    Therefore all seasons shall be sweet to thee,   65
Whether the summer clothe the general earth
With greenness, or the redbreast sit and sing
Betwixt the tufts of snow on the bare branch
Of mossy apple-tree, while the nigh thatch
Smokes in the sun-thaw; whether the eave-drops fall   70
Heard only in the trances of the blast,
Or if the secret ministry of frost
Shall hang them up in silent icicles,
Quietly shining to the quiet Moon.

3. Boys and girls were dressed in the same clothes when very young.

ANNA BUNINA

1774–1829

It was not easy to work as a woman writer in early nineteenth-century Russia, even for those who came from the highest ranks of the aristocracy. Women were largely dependent on husbands or fathers for their keep, and they received meager educations compared to their male counterparts. The small handful of women who did publish their writing typically won disparaging and sometimes hostile comments from critics and male writers, who insisted that women could act as readers and inspirations, but could not compose anything of value. It was in this context that the remarkable Anna Petrovna Bunina published a startling range of poems, in multiple styles and on themes that ranged from nationalistic military songs to conversational, intimate lyrics on love and mortality.

Born into an aristocratic family in 1774, Bunina struggled to maintain her independence. Her inheritance was so small that she soon exhausted it on attempts to improve her education, learning to read Latin and Greek and to speak a number of foreign languages. She started publishing her work in her late twenties, and soon attracted mentors and patrons. Remaining unmarried, she barely made ends meet as a poverty-stricken writer until her death in 1829 from breast cancer. And yet, although she was poor, her independence was an extraordinary accomplishment: she was the first Russian woman to earn her living as a writer. At the time it was rare for even male Russian writers to live by the pen. Only about 250 titles were published in Russia each year between 1800 and 1820, compared to 4,500 in France. As few as 6 percent of Russian men could read in 1800, and 4 percent of women. A financial turning point for Bunina came in 1808, when she published a manual for women poets called *The Rules of Poetry*. Here she explained principles of genre and meter in order to educate women who might not have taken up writing otherwise. The Administration of Schools adopted it as a textbook, and the ensuing profits allowed Bunina to become self-sufficient.

Some critics hailed Bunina as a "Russian Sappho," comparable to the great ancient Greek woman poet. Others, including the legendary writer Alexander Pushkin, scorned her as "the goddess of the lady-chatterboxes." Writers in the generation that followed hers saw her as painfully old-fashioned, and felt particular contempt for women poets who were only able to produce "a poetic knitting of stockings." Bunina's reputation never recovered, though readers have begun to show a renewed interest in recent years.

Bunina's poems frequently took gender as an explicit theme. Her "Conversation Between Me and the Women" sets up a dialogue between the poet and a chorus of modern, cosmopolitan women who reject Russian poetry and want the poetess to sing them flattering verses. She refuses, claiming that male readers will be the judges of her fame. But this seems like a puzzling conclusion. Is Bunina also writing for men in *this* poem, which is so clearly focused on women readers and writers? Is she trivializing women, or taking them seriously? And is she indicating her own preference for Russian styles and subjects, or is she undermining them by claiming that she writes about tsars and heroes merely for the approbation of a masculine readership? Bunina's ironic meditation on the role of the woman poet raises more questions than it answers.

Conversation Between Me and the Women[1]

Our sister dear, what joy for us!
You are a poetess! your palette's able,
Holding all shades, to paint an ode, a fable;
Your heart must brim with praise for us!
A man's tongue, though . . . Ah, God preserve us, dear!   5
Sharp as a knife is sharp!
In Paris, London—as in Russia here—
   They're all the same! On just one string they harp:
Naught but abuse—and ladies always suffer!
We wait for madrigals—it's epigrams they offer.   10
Don't expect brothers, husbands, fathers, sons
   To praise you even once.
How long we've lacked a songstress of our own!
So, do you sing? Pray answer, yes or no?

ME

Yes, yes, dear sisters! Thanks be to Providence   15
I have been singing now for five years since.

THE WOMEN

And in those years, what have you sung and how?
Though few of us, in truth, have Russian educations,
And Russian verses make such complications!
Besides, you know, they aren't in fashion now.   20

ME

I sing all Nature's beauteous hues,
Above the flood the hornèd sickle moon;
I count the little drops of dew,
I hymn the sun's ascension in the morn.
Flocks gambolling in the fields enjoy my care: 25
I give reed pipes unto the shepherdesses,
Flowers I entwine in their companions' tresses,
   That are so flaxen-fair;
I order them to take each other's hands,

1. Translated by Sibelan Forrester.

To caper to a dance,   30
And as their fleet feet pass,
To trample not a single blade of grass.
Up to the heavens rocky crags I raise,
  I plant out branchy trees
To rest an old man in their shady breeze   35
  On summer's sultry days;
I search the roses for bright insects' wings,
  And, having summoned feathered birds to sing,
  I languish pale
To the sweet warble of the nightingale.   40
Or, all at once, freeing the horse's manes.
  I order them to race the wind;
And with their hooves dust to the clouds they fling.
I draw a corn-field crowned with ears of grain,
  Which, from the sun's bright rays   45
    Takes on the look of seas
Of molten gold,
  Sways, ripples, dazzles, shines—
    Blinding the eye,
As humble ploughmen their reward behold.   50
In fortifying my own timid voice
Through Nature's loveliness,
  I'm braver in a flash!

THE WOMEN

Fie! what balderdash!
There's not one word in this for us!   55
Tell us what good such singing does?
What use are all your livestock, polled and horned
  To us, who weren't as herdsmen born?
So, with the beasts you feel at home?
Well! . . . if that's your topic, then,   60
    Hide in a den,
  Among the fields, pray, roam,
And never haunt the capitals in vain!

ME

O no, dear sisters, come!
People are also in my ken.   65

THE WOMEN

Commendable! but whom *have* you sung, then?

ME

At times I've hymned the deeds of mighty men,
  Who, when the bloody fight drew near,
Declared for faith and Tsar; they knew no fear.
Shaking with my lament the field of quarrels   70
  I bore them thence away with laurels,
    Dropping a tear.
At times I've left this grievous task,
And passed to those who keep the laws,
I've filled my soul with cheer,   75
And rested 'neath their aegis, free from cares.
  At times to poets I've inclined my ear
And bent the knee before their thunderous lyres.
    At times
    Moved by esteem,   80
I've made the chemist or astronomer my theme.

THE WOMEN

And here again we're missing from your rhymes!
  You do us quite a service!
So what good *are* you? Don't you make things worse?
  Why did you bother learning to sing verse?   85
You ought to take your themes from your own circle.
'Tis only men you honour with your lays,
As if their sex alone deserved your praise.
You traitress! Give our case some thought!
  For is this what you ought?   90
Are their own founts of flattery too few,
Or can they boast of more than our virtue?

ME

It's true, my dears, you are no less,
  But understand:
With men, not you, the courts of taste are manned   95
  Where authors all must stand,
And all an author's fame is in their hands,
And none can help loving himself the best.[2]

2. May I be forgiven for this jest in deference to the merry Muses, who love to mix business with idleness, lies with truth, and to enliven conversation with innocent playfulness [Bunina's note].

ANDRÉS BELLO
1781–1865

Sometimes known as "the artistic liberator" of Spanish America, Andrés Bello wrote at a moment when Latin American nations were throwing off the yoke of colonial rule. He insisted that it was time for poetry "to leave effete Europe . . . and fly to where Columbus's world / opens its great scene." And yet, while his work replaces the familiar natural landscape of European romantic poetry—mountains and daffodils—with a distinctively Latin American landscape, with cocoa beans and palm trees, yucca and sugar cane, Bello was not a thoroughgoing revolutionary. He began his life as a monarchist, an advocate of Spanish colonial rule, and only gradually became a supporter of democratic elections. Steadfastly, he favored long-term goals of stability and order, even in nature. In the "Ode to Tropical Agriculture," what he praises is not wilderness but human cultivation—plants in "proud rows and orderly design."

Born in Caracas, Venezuela, in 1781, Bello began working for the colonial government in 1802 and oversaw projects of national scope—including the first smallpox vaccination, which he made the subject of a poetic ode and a play. In response to the conquest of Spain by Napoleon in 1810, Venezuela claimed independence and established a series of military governments. One regime sent Bello on a diplomatic mission to London. He stayed there for nineteen years, working in temporary positions that left him too poor to return to Venezuela. It was in London, racked by homesickness, that he composed his most famous poetry, including the "Ode to Tropical Agriculture" in 1826. Three years later, the Chilean government invited him to work for their Foreign Ministry, and he went to live in Santiago, where he founded the University of Chile and became its rector until his death in 1865. Among the famous works he completed there were *Castilian Grammar Intended for Use by Americans* (1847), the first specifically Latin American grammar, and the Civil Code of Chile, which is still in force today. Over the course of his life, he exerted an astonishing breadth of influence—as a poet, essayist, editor, civil servant, diplomat, philosopher, grammarian, educator, and legal thinker.

Bello's poetry combines classical and romantic impulses. In "Ode to Tropical Agriculture" we find resonances of the Roman georgics of Virgil and Horace, who celebrate civic virtue, the simple life of farmers, and the beauties of nature. Bello also invokes the Roman republic as a model for the rising Latin American nations. But it would be a mistake to read Bello as simply nostalgic for an ancient past: he urges poets to draw inspiration from their native landscapes, suggesting that the unique characteristics of current politics, history, and geography will shape a dramatic and powerful art for the future.

Ode to Tropical Agriculture[1]

Hail, fertile zone, that circumscribes
the errant course of your enamored sun,
and, caressed by its light,

1. Translated by Frances M. Lopez-Morillas.

brings forth all living things
in each of your many climes! 5
You weave the summer's wreath of golden grain,
and offer grapes to the bubbling pail.
Your glorious groves lack no tone
of purple fruit, or red, or gold. In them the wind
imbibes a thousand odors, and innumerable flocks 10
crop your green meadow, from the plain
bordered by the horizon, to the mountain heights,
ever hoary with inaccessible snow.

      You give sweet sugarcane, whose pure sap
makes the world disdain the honeycomb. 15
In coral urns you prepare the beans
that overflow the foaming chocolate cup.
Living red teems on your cactus plants,
outdoing the purple of Tyre.[2]
And the splendid dye of your indigo 20
imitates the sapphire's glow.
Wine is yours, which the piercèd agave
pours out for Anahuac's happy brood.[3]
Yours too is the leaf that solaces
the tedium of idle hours, when its soft smoke 25
rises in wandering spirals.
You clothe with jasmine the bush of Sheba,[4]
and give it the perfume that cools
the wild fever of riotous excess.
For your children the lofty palm brings forth 30
its varied products, and the pineapple ripens
its ambrosia. The yucca grows its snowy bread,
and the potato yields its fair fruit,
and cotton opens to the gentle breeze
its golden roses and its milk-white fleece. 35
For you the passion plant displays
its fresh green branches, and sweet globes
and dangling flowers hang from climbing branches.
For you maize, proud chief of the tribe of grains
swells its ears; and for you the banana plant 40
sags under dulcet weight. Banana, first
of all the plants that Providence has offered
to happy tropic's folk with generous hand;
it asks no care by human arts, but freely yields
its fruit. It needs no pruning hook or plow. 45
No care does it require, only such heed
as a slave's hand can steal from daily toil.
It grows with swiftness, and when it is outworn
its full-grown children take its place.

2. Precious purple dye produced in the ancient Phoenician city of Tyre and used only for members of the emperor's family.
3. Anahuac is the Aztec region in the Valley of Mexico.
4. Ancient kingdom mentioned in the Hebrew Bible and the Qur'an.

But, fertile zone, though rich,   50
why did not Nature work with equal zeal
to make its indolent dwellers follow her?
Oh, would that they could recognize the joy
that beckons from the simple farmer's home,
and spurn vain luxury, false brilliance,   55
and the city's evil idleness!
What vain illusion has a grip on those
whom Fortune has made masters of this land,
so happy, rich and varied as it is,
to make them leave hereditary soil,   60
forsaking it to mercenary hands?
Shut in blind clamor of the wretched cities,
where sick ambition fans the flames
of civil strife, or indolence exhausts
the love of country. There it is   65
that luxury saps customs, and vices trap
unwary youth in ever stronger bonds.
There, youth does not tire from manly exercise,
but sickens in the arms of treacherous beauty
that sells its favors to the highest bidder;   70
whose pastime is to light the flame of outlaw love
in the chaste bosom of a youth.
Or dawn will find him drunk, perhaps,
at the base, sordid gaming table.

Meanwhile the wife lends an eager ear   75
to the ardent lover's seductive flattery.
The tender virgin grows in her mother's school
of dissipation and flirtation, and that example
spurs her to sin before she wishes to.
Is this the way to form the heroic spirits   80
that bravely found and undergird the state?
How will strong and modest youth emerge,
our country's hope and pride,
from the hubbub of foolish revels
or the choruses of lewd dances?   85
Can the man who even in the cradle
slept to the murmur of lascivious songs,
a man who curls his hair and scents himself,
and dresses with almost feminine care
and spends the day in idleness,   90
or worse, in criminal lust: can such a man
hold firmly to the reins of law,
or be serene in doubtful combat, or confront
the haughty spirit of a tyrannous leader?
Triumphant Rome did not thus view   95
the arts of peace and war; rather, she gave
the reins of state to the strong hand,
tanned by the sun and hardened by the plow,
who raised his sons under a smoky peasant roof,
and made the world submit to Latin valor.   100

Oh, you who are the fortunate possessors,
born in this beautiful land,
where bountiful Nature parades her gifts
as if to win you and attract you!
Break the harsh enchantment   105
that holds you prisoner within walls.
The common man, working at crafts,
the merchant who loves luxury and must have it,
those who pant after high place and noisy honour,
the troop of parasitic flatterers,   110
live happily in that filthy chaos.
The land is your heritage; enjoy it.
Do you love freedom? Go then to the country,
Not where the rich man lives
amid armed satellites, and where   115
Fashion, that universal dame,
drags reason tied to her triumphal car.
Go not where foolish common folk adore
Fortune, and nobles the adulation of the mob.
Or do you love virtue? then the best teacher   120
is the solitary calm where man's soul,
judge only of itself, displays its actions.
Do you seek lasting joys, and happiness,
as much as is given to man on earth?
Where laughter is close to tears, and always,   125
ah, always, among the flowers pricks the thorn?
Go and enjoy the farmer's life, his lovely peace,
untroubled by bitterness and envy.
His soft bed is prepared for him
by labor, purest air, and great content,   130
and the flavor of food easily won.
He is untouched by wasteful gluttony,
and in the safe haven of his loyal home
is host to health and happiness.
Go breathe the mountain air, that gives   135
lost vigor to the tired body, and retards
fretful old age, and tinges pink
the face of beauty. Is the flame of love,
tempered by modesty, less sweet, perchance?
Or is beauty less attractive   140
without false ornament and lying paint?
Does the heart hear unmoved
the innocent language that expresses love
openly, the intent equal to the promise?
No need to rehearse before the mirror   145
a laugh, a step, a gesture;
no lack there of an honest face
flushed with modesty and health, nor does
the sidelong glance cast by a timid lover
lose its way to the soul.   150
Could you expect a marriage bond to form,
arranged by an alien hand, tyrant of love,

swayed by base interests, for repute or fortune,
happier than one where taste and age agree,
and free choice reigns, and mutual ardor?   155

       There too are duties to perform: heal, oh heal
the bitter wounds of war; place the fertile soil,
now harsh and wild, under the unaccustomed yoke
of human skill, and conquer it.
Let pent-up pond and water mill   160
remember where their waters flowed,
let the axe break the matted trees
and fire burn the forest; in its barren splendor
let a long gash be cut.
Give shelter in the valleys   165
to thirsty sugarcane; in the cool mountains make
pear trees and apples forget their mother, Spain.
Make coffee trees adorn the slopes;
on river banks, let the maternal shade
of the *bucare* tree[5] guard the tender cacao plants.   170
Let gardens flourish, orchards laugh with joy.
Is this blind error, foolish fantasy?
Oh agriculture, wetnurse of mankind,
heeding your voice, now comes the servile crowd
with curving sickles armed.   175
It bursts into the dark wood's tangled growth.
I hear voices and distant sounds, the axe's noise.
Far off, echo repeats its blows; the ancient tree
for long the challenge of the laboring crowd,
groans, and trembles from a hundred axes,   180
topples at last, and its tall summit falls.
The wild beast flees; the doleful bird
leaves its sweet nest, its fledgling brood,
seeking a wood unknown to humankind.
What do I see? a tall and crackling flame   185
spills over the dry ruins of the conquered forest.
The roaring fire is heard afar,
black smoke eddies upward, piling cloud on cloud.
And only dead trunks, only ashes remain
of what before was lovely green and freshness,   190
the tomb of mortal joy, plaything of the wind.
But the wild growth of savage, tangled plants
gives way to fruitful plantings, that display
their proud rows and orderly design.
Branch touches branch, and steals   195
the light of day from sturdy shoots.
Now the first flower displays its buds,
lovely to see and breathing joyful hope.
Hope, that laughing mops the tired farmer's brow,
Hope, that from afar   200
paints the rich fruit, the harvest's bounty

---

5. Coral tree that provides the shade needed for growing cocoa beans.

that carries off the tribute of the fields
in heaping baskets and in billowing skirts,
and under the weight of plenty, the farmer's due,
makes vast storehouses creak and groan.   205

       Dear God! let not the Equator's farming folk
sweat vainly; be moved to pity and compassion.
Let them return now from their sad despair
with renewed spirit, and after such alarms,
anxiety and turmoil, and so many years   210
of fierce destruction and of military crimes,
may beg your mercy more than in the past.
May rustic piety, but no less sincere
find favor in your eyes. Let them not weep
for a vanished golden dream, a lying vision,   215
a future without tears, a smiling future
that lightens all the troubles of today.
Let not unseasonable rains
ruin the tender crops; let not the pitiless tooth
of gnawing insects devour them.   220
Let not the savage storm destroy,
or the tree's maternal sap
dry up in summer's long and heated thirst.
For you, supreme arbiter of fate,
were pleased at long last to remove the yoke   225
of foreign rule, and with your blessing
to raise American man toward heaven,
to make his freedom root and thrive.
Bury accursed war in deep abyss,
and, for fear of vengeful sword,   230
let the distrustful farmer not desist
from noble toil, that nourishes
families and whole countries too.
May anxious worry leave their souls,
and plows no longer sadly rust.   235
We have atoned enough for the savage conquest
of our unhappy fathers.
No matter where we look, do we not see
a stubbled wilderness where once were fields,
and cities too? Who can sum up the dreadful count   240
of deaths, proscriptions, tortures,
and orphans left abandoned?
The ghosts of Montezuma, Atahualpa,[6]
sleep now, glutted with Spanish blood.
Ah! from your lofty seat,   245
where choirs of winged angels veil their faces
in awe before the splendor of your face
(if luckless humankind deserves, perchance,
a single glance from you),

---

6. Montezuma II (ca. 1466–1529), Aztec emperor taken prisoner and killed during the Spanish conquest. "Atahualpa": last Inca emperor (1497–1533), captured and executed by the Spanish.

send down an angel, angel of peace, to make 250
the rude Spaniard forget his ancient tyranny,
and, reverent, hear the sacred vow,
the essential law you gave to men;
may he stretch out his unarmed hand,
(alas, too stained with blood!) 255
to his wronged brother.
And if innate gentleness should sleep
make it awake in the American breast.
The brave heart that scorns obscure content,
that beats more strongly in the bloody hap 260
of battle, and greedy for power or fame,
loves noble perils,
deems an insult, worthy of contempt,
and spurns the prize not given by his country.
May he find freedom sweeter far than power, 265
and olive branch more fair than laurel crown.
Let the soldier-citizen put off
the panoply of war; let the victory wreath
hang on his country's altar,
and glory be the only prize of merit. 270
Then may my country see the longed-for day
when peace will triumph:
peace, that fills the world
with joy, serenity, and happiness.
Man will return rejoicing to his task; 275
the ship lifts anchor, and entrusts herself
to friendly winds. Workshops swarm, farms teem,
the scythes do not suffice to cut the grain.

      Oh, youthful nations, with early laurels crowned,
who rise before the West's astonished gaze! 280
Honor the fields, honor the simple life,
and the farmer's frugal simplicity.
Thus freedom will dwell in you forever,
ambition be restrained, law have its temple.
Your people will set out bravely 285
on the hard, steep path of immortality,
always citing your example.
Those who come after you will imitate you eagerly,
adding new names to those whose fame
they now acclaim. For they will say, "Sons, sons 290
are these of men who won the Andes' heights;
those who in Boyacá, and on Maipo's sands,
and in Junín, and Apurima's glorious field,[7]
humbled in victory the lion of Spain."

---

7. Sites of military victories by revolutionary forces against Spanish colonial rule. "Andes": mountain range that runs along the west coast of South America. "Boyacá": a state in Colombia. "Maipo": river in Chile. "Junín": large lake in Peru. "Apurima": the Apurimac River in Peru, the source of the Amazon.

PERCY BYSSHE SHELLEY

1792–1822

A forthright advocate of vegetarianism, free love, anarchism, Irish nationalism, and atheism, the English poet Percy Shelley provoked so much alarm among his contemporaries that his critics accused him of spreading corruption, aligning himself with Satan, and undermining the nation. Shelley's work was inflammatory enough that only small portions of it found their way to publication in his lifetime, and he reported having escaped several attempts at assassination. Later generations would invoke an entirely different Shelley, one who looked beyond conventional pieties to a universal good, "a beautiful ineffectual angel, beating in the void his luminous wings in vain," as the poet and critic Matthew Arnold put it in 1888. Shelley remains an object of controversy into our own time: for some enthusiasts, he is the fiery radical who bravely flouted convention and inspired generations of revolutionary thinkers; for a still-sizable number of detractors he has emerged as a self-serving egoist who destroyed the lives of women he loved; and for some—admirers and critics alike—he appears as the abstract and philosophical poet-aristocrat who crafted beautiful and dreamy poetic reconciliations of humans with their world.

LIFE

Shelley came from a wealthy and aristocratic English family. His father was a member of Parliament who held to a strict standard of respectability. In 1811, after only five months at Oxford University, the young Shelley published a pamphlet titled *The Necessity of Atheism*, which he sent to all of the professors and heads of colleges at Oxford and Cambridge and all of the bishops of the Church of England. Oxford expelled him, and his father—deeply shocked—threw him on his own resources. Alone in London, he eloped with the daughter of a coffeehouse owner, Harriet Westbrook.

In these first years of his independence, Shelley moved in radical circles. Feeling disgust at the oppressiveness of British colonial rule, in 1812 he left for Ireland, where he spoke publicly in favor of Catholic rights and Irish nationalism. He claimed to have been the victim of an assassination attempt, though some have alleged that he was just trying to avoid mounting debts. Shelley's first major poem, *Queen Mab*, was distributed privately in 1813 because it was too revolutionary to be published. Advocating sexual freedom and a new era of egalitarianism as well as the overthrow of corrupt institutions, it continued to circulate underground among radicals throughout the nineteenth century.

Within just a few years, the Shelleys' marriage had begun to falter, and in 1814 Percy fell in love with Mary Wollstonecraft Godwin, the beautiful sixteen-year-old daughter of the two most famous radicals of the time, William Godwin and **Mary Wollstonecraft**. Godwin tried to separate the couple, and in desolation, Percy attempted suicide. When he recovered, the two lovers ran away together. Percy, in keeping with his unconventional beliefs about love and marriage, tried to persuade his wife Harriet to come and live with him and Mary—as a sister. She refused.

Ostracized, the young lovers wandered restlessly around Europe. They spent the summer of 1816 at Lake Geneva with the poet George Gordon Byron. Notorious for his many love affairs, Byron had a brief liaison with Mary's stepsister Claire. It was that summer, too, that Mary Shelley first had the idea for the novel that would soon make her famous—*Frankenstein*. During this period Shelley composed some of his best-known short works, including the "Hymn to Intellectual Beauty" and "Mont Blanc."

The next few years brought a sequence of terrible personal tragedies. In November of 1816, Harriet Shelley drowned herself, blaming Percy's abandonment of her in her suicide letter. The courts denied him custody of his two children, citing his immoral behavior and disturbing beliefs. Byron spurned Claire, Mary's stepsister, even before learning she was pregnant with his daughter. The Shelleys married with Godwin's consent, but their two living children died within nine months of each other in 1818 and 1819. (Only one son, Percy, born in 1819, would survive his parents.) Shattered by these losses, Mary descended into a bleak depression, and the relationship never regained its earlier harmony. Percy composed "Stanzas Written in Dejection" to mark his own anguish.

And yet, in the aftermath of these distressing events, Shelley also composed his finest poetry. He wrote his great odes—"To the West Wind" and "To a Skylark"—as well as his two verse dramas: *Prometheus Unbound*, which celebrates an ideal freedom that triumphs over oppression, drawing on Milton's Satan for its hero; and *The Cenci*, written in an accessible style and based on a true story of incest and murder. In these years Shelley also wrote powerful poems in response to political events, such as "England in 1819," and his "Essay on Christianity,"

which argued that Jesus' teachings had been corrupted and distorted. Like so many of Shelley's political and religious essays, it was too unsettling to be published during his lifetime.

Often ill and usually trying to escape creditors, Shelley continued to live a peripatetic life. He became friendly with poets and critics in London, including **John Keats**. In 1820 the Shelleys settled in the Italian town of Pisa, and it was there that he wrote his famous *Defense of Poetry*, where he made the case that creative artists were crucial to history, poets being "the unacknowledged legislators of the world." In 1822 Shelley went boating off the coast of Italy; a sudden storm wrecked the boat, and his body later washed ashore.

WORKS

Shelley is a deeply skeptical poet, always probing the foundations of his own thought and willing to subject his own and others' beliefs to interrogation. "Our words are dead," Shelley lamented; "our thoughts are cold and borrowed." Since we can only ever reuse words that have been used thousands of times before, Shelley argues, we are unable to have new thoughts—and so unable to revolutionize our approaches to experience. Only poetic images, in all of their strangeness and novelty, can reanimate "dead" words. And since oppressive power depends on static, deadened language, the poet's renewal of words becomes a means of upending social inequalities and tyrannical authorities. Poetic language can itself turn rigid through conventional use, however, and Shelley often experiments with endings that resist resolution and heapings of mismatched metaphors in order to keep his language surprising and unsettling.

If Shelley is famous for his resistance and rebellion, he is also a poet capable of remarkable formal control. "Stanzas Written in Dejection" modifies a poetic form borrowed from the Renaissance poet Edmund Spenser. It follows a strict pattern of eight regular lines, each composed of four feet (tetrameter), followed by a single longer line of six feet (hexameter). The rhyme, too, is tightly organized and regular. Since Shelley is writing to express an agonizing mood of desperation and failure, it is intriguing that he should choose a form that demands such artful and restrained craftsmanship.

"England in 1819" too follows a regular form. It stays very much within the tradition of the Shakespearian sonnet, with fourteen rhyming lines. And yet Shelley plays with the form in inventive ways. For example, he deliberately uses the sonnet, one of the smallest and most compact forms in English poetry, to convey vast wrongs that beset a whole nation. By 1819 the British government had imposed heavy taxes to pay for the nation's protracted wars with France, with the poor suffering especially from high taxes on grain. Concerned about rising unrest, Parliament imposed strict censorship, suspended the right to trial, suppressed politically subversive groups, and accused even moderate critics of treason. On August 16, 1819, a huge but orderly and unarmed crowd gathered at St. Peter's Field in the city of Manchester in support of democratic reforms. Between 60,000 and 80,000 men, women, and children arrived wearing their Sunday best. Ill-trained troops with sabers ignored the peaceful nature of the protest and charged through the crowd on horseback. Reporters counted eleven dead and estimated over 400 wounded. Contemporaries gave the event the nickname "Peterloo," an ironic echo of Waterloo, the great British victory against Napoleon in 1815. Parliament refused to conduct an inquiry into the violence, and powerful government ministers, Viscounts Castlereagh and Sidmouth, used the Peterloo massacre as an excuse to pass a new round of repressive laws. Shelley purposefully squeezes large-scale historical events into his first twelve lines, and imagines their redemption in an even briefer two.

"Ode to the West Wind" is the most complex of all the selections included here. It is written in an interlocking rhyme scheme called *terza rima*, invented by the thirteenth-century poet Dante for his *Divine Comedy*, and notoriously difficult to sustain in English (it follows the pattern aba bcb cdc ded, and so on). Shelley modifies Dante's model, however, by organizing his stanzas into five groups of fourteen lines—so that they become sonnets. While his formal choices are complex, his imagery is so fascinating that it has rewarded two centuries of attentive reading. Merging *terza rima* and sonnet, subject and object, death and life, nature and human history, poetry and prophecy, this magnificent ode has endured as one of Shelley's best-loved works.

Stanzas Written in Dejection—
December 1818, near Naples

The Sun is warm, the sky is clear,
The waves are dancing fast and bright,
Blue isles and snowy mountains wear
The purple noon's transparent might,
The breath of the moist earth is light   5
Around its unexpanded buds;
Like many a voice of one delight,
The winds, the birds, the Ocean-floods,
The City's voice, itself is soft like Solitude's.

    I see the Deep's untrampled floor   10
With green and purple seaweeds strown;
I see the waves upon the shore
Like light dissolved in star-showers, thrown;
I sit upon the sands alone;
The lightning of the noontide Ocean   15
Is flashing round me, and a tone
Arises from its measured motion,
How sweet! did any heart now share in my emotion.

    Alas, I have nor hope nor health
Nor peace within nor calm around,   20
Nor that content surpassing wealth
The sage in meditation found,
And walked with inward glory crowned;
Nor fame nor power nor love nor leisure—
Others I see whom these surround,   25
Smiling they live and call life pleasure:
To me that cup has been dealt in another measure.

    Yet now despair itself is mild,
Even as the winds and waters are;
I could lie down like a tired child   30
And weep away the life of care
Which I have borne and yet must bear
Till Death like Sleep might steal on me,
And I might feel in the warm air
My cheek grow cold, and hear the Sea   35
Breathe o'er my dying brain its last monotony.

    Some might lament that I were cold,
As I, when this sweet day is gone,
Which my lost heart, too soon grown old,
Insults with this untimely moan—   40
They might lament,—for I am one
Whom men love not, and yet regret;
Unlike this day, which, when the Sun
Shall on its stainless glory set,
Will linger though enjoyed, like joy in Memory yet.   45

England in 1819

An old, mad, blind, despised, and dying King;[1]
Princes,[2] the dregs of their dull race, who flow
Through public scorn,—mud from a muddy spring;
Rulers who neither see nor feel nor know,
But leechlike to their fainting country cling   5
Till they drop, blind in blood, without a blow.
A people starved and stabbed in th' untilled field;[3]
An army, whom liberticide and prey
Makes as a two-edged sword to all who wield;
Golden and sanguine[4] laws which tempt and slay;   10
Religion Christless, Godless—a book sealed;
A senate, Time's worst statute,[5] unrepealed—
Are graves from which a glorious Phantom may
Burst, to illumine our tempestuous day.

Ode to the West Wind

I

O wild West Wind, thou breath of Autumn's being,
Thou, from whose unseen presence the leaves dead
Are driven, like ghosts from an enchanter fleeing,

Yellow, and black, and pale, and hectic red,
Pestilence-stricken multitudes: O Thou,   5
Who chariotest to their dark wintry bed

The wingèd seeds, where they lie cold and low,
Each like a corpse within its grave, until
Thine azure sister of the Spring shall blow

Her clarion o'er the dreaming earth, and fill   10
(Driving sweet buds like flocks to feed in air)
With living hues and odours plain and hill:

Wild Spirit, which art moving everywhere;
Destroyer and Preserver; hear, O hear!

1. George III (1738–1820).
2. The king's sons, including the prince regent, whose dissolute behavior gave rise to public scandals.
3. A reference to the event called "Peterloo," the British military's massacre of unarmed protesters marching for political reform in St. Peter's Field, Manchester.
4. Bloody, causing bloodshed. "Golden": bought. The laws favor the rich and powerful.
5. The law by which the civil liberties of Roman Catholics and dissenters from the state religion (Anglicanism) were restricted.

II

Thou on whose stream, 'mid the steep sky's commotion,   15
Loose clouds like Earth's decaying leaves are shed,
Shook from the tangled boughs of Heaven and Ocean,

Angels of rain and lightning; there are spread
On the blue surface of thine aery surge,
Like the bright hair uplifted from the head   20

Of some fierce Mænad,[1] even from the dim verge
Of the horizon to the zenith's height,
The locks of the approaching storm. Thou Dirge

Of the dying year, to which this closing night
Will be the dome of a vast sepulchre,   25
Vaulted with all thy congregated might

Of vapors, from whose solid atmosphere
Black rain and fire and hail will burst: O hear!

III

Thou who didst waken from his summer dreams
The blue Mediterranean, where he lay,   30
Lulled by the coil of his crystalline streams,

Beside a pumice isle in Baiæ's bay,[2]
And saw in sleep old palaces and towers
Quivering within the wave's intenser day,

All overgrown with azure moss and flowers   35
So sweet, the sense faints picturing them! Thou
For whose path the Atlantic's level powers

Cleave themselves into chasms, while far below
The sea-blooms and the oozy woods which wear
The sapless foliage of the ocean, know   40

Thy voice, and suddenly grow grey with fear,
And tremble and despoil themselves: O hear!

IV

If I were a dead leaf thou mightest bear;
If I were a swift cloud to fly with thee;
A wave to pant beneath thy power, and share   45

1. Ecstatic female worshipper of Bacchus,   2. West of Naples; the Roman emperors built
Greek god of wine.   villas there.

The impulse of thy strength, only less free
Than thou, O Uncontrollable! If even
I were as in my boyhood, and could be

The comrade of thy wanderings over Heaven,
As then, when to outstrip thy skiey speed   50
Scarce seemed a vision; I would ne'er have striven

As thus with thee in prayer in my sore need.
Oh! lift me as a wave, a leaf, a cloud!
I fall upon the thorns of life! I bleed!

A heavy weight of hours has chained and bowed   55
One too like thee: tameless, and swift, and proud.

V

Make me thy lyre,[3] even as the forest is:
What if my leaves are falling like its own!
The tumult of thy mighty harmonies

Will take from both a deep, autumnal tone,   60
Sweet though in sadness. Be thou, Spirit fierce,
My spirit! Be thou me, impetuous one!

Drive my dead thoughts over the universe
Like withered leaves to quicken a new birth!
And, by the incantation of this verse,   65

Scatter, as from an unextinguished hearth
Ashes and sparks, my words among mankind!
Be through my lips to unawakened Earth

The trumpet of a prophecy! O Wind,
If Winter comes, can Spring be far behind?   70

A Defense of Poetry

[*Conclusion*]

* * * Poetry is the record of the best and happiest moments of the happiest
and best minds. We are aware of evanescent visitations of thought and feeling
sometimes associated with place or person, sometimes regarding our own mind
alone, and always arising unforeseen and departing unbidden, but elevating
and delightful beyond all expression: so that even in the desire and the regret
they leave, there cannot but be pleasure, participating as it does in the nature

---

3. Ancient harp. The allusion is also to the aeolian harp, an instrument played by the wind and
a frequent image for the poet played upon by inspiration.

of its object. It is as it were the interpenetration of a diviner nature through our own; but its footsteps are like those of a wind over a sea, which the coming calm erases, and whose traces remain only as on the wrinkled sand which paves it. These and corresponding conditions of being are experienced principally by those of the most delicate sensibility and the most enlarged imagination; and the state of mind produced by them is at war with every base desire. The enthusiasm of virtue, love, patriotism, and friendship is essentially linked with these emotions, and whilst they last, self appears as what it is, an atom to a Universe. Poets are not only subject to these experiences as spirits of the most refined organization, but they can colour all that they combine with the evanescent hues of this ethereal world; a word, or a trait in the representation of a scene or a passion, will touch the enchanted chord, and reanimate, in those who have ever experienced these emotions, the sleeping, the cold, the buried image of the past. Poetry thus makes immortal all that is best and most beautiful in the world; it arrests the vanishing apparitions which haunt the interlunations of life, and veiling them or[1] in language or in form sends them forth among mankind, bearing sweet news of kindred joy to those with whom their sisters abide—abide, because there is no portal of expression from the caverns of the spirit which they inhabit into the universe of things. Poetry redeems from decay the visitations of the divinity in man.

* * *

The first part of these remarks has related to Poetry in its elements and principles; and it has been shown, as well as the narrow limits assigned them would permit, that what is called poetry, in a restricted sense, has a common source with all other forms of order and of beauty according to which the materials of human life are susceptible of being arranged, and which is poetry in an universal sense.

The second part[2] will have for its object an application of these principles to the present state of the cultivation of Poetry, and a defense of the attempt to idealize the modern forms of manners and opinion, and compel them into a subordination to the imaginative and creative faculty. For the literature of England, an energetic development of which has ever preceded or accompanied a great and free development of the national will, has arisen as it were from a new birth. In spite of the low-thoughted envy which would undervalue contemporary merit, our own will be a memorable age in intellectual achievements, and we live among such philosophers and poets as surpass beyond comparison any who have appeared since the last national struggle for civil and religious liberty.[3] The most unfailing herald, companion, and follower of the awakening of a great people to work a beneficial change in opinion or institution, is Poetry. At such periods there is an accumulation of the power of communicating and receiving intense and impassioned conceptions respecting man and nature. The persons in whom this power resides, may often, as far as regards many portions of their nature, have little apparent correspondence with that spirit of good of which they are the ministers. But even whilst they

1. Either. "Interlunations": dark periods between the old and new moon.
2. The second part was never written.

3. The English Civil War. The great poet of that age was Milton.

deny and abjure, they are yet compelled to serve, the Power which is seated upon the throne of their own soul. It is impossible to read the compositions of the most celebrated writers of the present day without being startled with the electric life which burns within their words. They measure the circumference and sound the depths of human nature with a comprehensive and all-penetrating spirit, and they are themselves perhaps the most sincerely astonished at its manifestations, for it is less their spirit than the spirit of the age. Poets are the hierophants[4] of an unapprehended inspiration, the mirrors of the gigantic shadows which futurity casts upon the present, the words which express what they understand not; the trumpets which sing to battle, and feel not what they inspire: the influence which is moved not, but moves. Poets are the unacknowledged legislators of the World.

4. Interpreters, in the role of priests who interpret sacred mysteries.

JOHN KEATS

1795–1821

John Keats established himself as one of the greatest of all English poets in a career that lasted less than five years. His first published work appeared in 1816, and his life ended—"blighted in the bud," as the poet **Percy Shelley** put it—in 1821, just as he had reached the height of his powers. Readers have long speculated about what would have happened to his writing, and to the history of English poetry, if he had lived just a few years longer. Keats himself knew well that his life could be cut short; he had watched his mother and brother die of tuberculosis, and he diagnosed his own mortal illness. Written in the full awareness of a terrifying mortality, Keats's poetry exults in the intensity of bodily, sensual experience. And even in this briefest of writing careers, Keats produced a varied, original, and formally dazzling body of work. His linguistic richness, taut craftsmanship, and skill in harmonizing sounds and rhythms have influenced many poets to follow, while he grapples with themes that have moved generations of readers: aching desire, the dreadful coming of death, and the seductive power of beauty.

LIFE

John Keats began his life in comparatively lowly surroundings. He was the eldest son of an ostler, a laborer who looked after horses at a London inn, and the inn-owner's daughter. His father died when he was eight years old, and Keats's mother remarried within a few months. At the time Keats was a student at the progressive Enfield Academy, where the schoolmasters embraced political reform, skepticism, and religious dissent. The young Keats often started fights with other boys, earning a reputation for a hot temper. Called "little Keats" into adulthood, he never grew taller than five feet in height. After his father's death he began to work extraordinarily hard at his studies, hungrily reading poetry in particular, including the work of Edmund

Spenser—his favorite poet—as well as Virgil, Chaucer, Dante, Shakespeare, Milton, Wordsworth, and Byron.

Miserable in her second marriage, Keats's mother disappeared altogether for some time. Eventually she returned to her children, but only after she had begun to suffer from a deadly case of tuberculosis. John nursed her in her final illness, caring for her passionately and possessively. She died when he was fourteen years old. Soon afterward, Keats's guardian decided to apprentice him to a surgeon. These were the days before anesthesia, which meant patients writhed in pain under the surgeon's knife. Keats found this horrifying, and he stayed with his medical training only long enough to become an apothecary—the lowest rung on the medical ladder—before dedicating himself to writing poetry. His first volume garnered many harshly critical reviews, including one that called him "an uneducated and flimsy stripling."

At the end of 1818 Keats's younger brother Tom died of tuberculosis, and the poet threw himself into writing, producing all of his greatest work in just one remarkable year: "The Eve of Saint Agnes," "La Belle Dame sans Merci," "Lamia," the completion of his long poem *Hyperion*, all of his great odes, and a group of dazzling sonnets, including "Bright Star." This was the same year as the Peterloo Massacre, the government's violent killing of peaceful civilians. (Shelley's poem in this volume, "England in 1819," describes the corruption and severity of government censorship at this moment.) It was also the year that Keats fell in love with a London neighbor named Fanny Brawne. He was possessive, she flirtatious, and his letters reveal him as an impassioned and jealous lover.

Their love was doomed, however, by Keats's poverty and growing ill-health. A history of debts, unwise loans, and ongoing struggles to earn money prevented Keats from proposing marriage.

Then, early in 1820, he suffered a lung hemorrhage. His medical training led him to recognize this as his "death warrant." He was told that he would not survive another British winter, and so he set out for Italy. It was in this final stretch of his life that his work finally earned favorable reviews, and Keats felt hopeful that he would eventually be ranked with the great English poets. He died in Rome at the age of twenty-five.

KEATS AND THE "COCKNEY SCHOOL" OF POETRY

In 1817 the radical poet and editor Leigh Hunt published Keats's first poem and hailed him as one of the most exciting of a new generation of poets who were casting off the orderly, decorous, neoclassical poetic styles associated with the eighteenth century—in particular the work of Alexander Pope. Detractors lumped Keats and Hunt together as the "Cockney School" of poets. Cockneys are working-class Londoners from the heart of the city, and this name conveyed contempt for what critics saw as the poets' low social class, lack of education, and vulgarity. "Back to the shop, Mr John," urged one snobbish reviewer assessing Keats's work.

There was no question that the Cockney poets were up to something quite new. They flagrantly broke with poetic convention in a number of obvious ways: their work sparkled with clever, innovative turns of phrase—often making adverbs out of participles, such as "crushingly," or turning verbs into adjectives, as in "scattery light." They also refused Pope's favorite form of "closed couplets," which contained a completed sentence in two rhyming lines, in favor of "open couplets," where the thought spilled out beyond the end of the rhyme. Even more shockingly, they delighted in erotic imagery and sensuous language, which invited readers to linger on bodily pleasures: "delicious" was a particular favorite.

The Cockney poets also led a return to the roughness and sensuous vitality of the pagan ancient Greeks, which they saw as fundamentally different from the eighteenth-century English version of the Greeks as delicate "toys." Keats's poem "On First Looking into Chapman's Homer" would have seemed polemical at the time: the poet is pointedly celebrating Chapman's "loud and bold" seventeenth-century translation of the ancient Greek poet over the neatly rhymed, standard translation of his own time—that of Alexander Pope. (When one of Keats's readers expressed surprise that he evoked the Greeks so well, despite his meager education, Percy Shelley answered curtly, "He *was* a Greek.")

Contemporaries contrasted the Cockney School with the poets they called the "Lake School"—most prominently **William Wordsworth** and **Samuel Taylor Coleridge**. Keats mulled a great deal on Wordsworth, who provided both inspiration and irritation for the younger poet. In place of the "egotistical sublime"—Keats's term for Wordsworth's focus on the self—he embraced the model of the "chameleon poet" who has "no identity" but takes delight in things other than himself. Keats also criticized Coleridge, who lacked what he famously called "negative capability": "when a man is capable of being in uncertainties, Mysteries, doubts, without any irritable reaching after fact & reason."

WORKS

Keats's work richly rewards the reader in a broad range of ways. His luxurious language and sumptuous imagery invite us to take pleasure in the sensuous beauty of poetry; his meticulous crafting of poetic forms—the architecture of lines, stanzas, and figures—is flawless; his numerous allusions to other writers are thoughtful and suggestive; and his uses of poetic forms to dwell on death, love, pain, art, and nature are philosophically penetrating. For many readers, Keats is among the very few poets in English who have combined these elements with such skill.

Keats's poetry insistently dwells on antitheses and contradictions. "Bright Star" invokes the paradox of "sweet unrest," for example, while the "Ode to a Nightingale" opens with the oxymoronic claim that "numbness" can give "pain." These two poems also foreground a fundamental Keatsian opposition: the distance between the fully sensuous experience of human bodies, which are doomed to die, and that which lasts beyond the human lifespan but has no experience of its pleasures—the star or the transcendent song of the nightingale. But far from offering a simple contrast between these two states, Keats often pushes one of these so far that it turns into its opposite: in "Ode to a Nightingale," the poet longs for a lived experience of wine and sunshine so intense that he will "fade away" and become like the immortal nightingale, remote from lived experience. Leigh Hunt spoke of Keats's "poetical *concentrations*," and it is typical of his poetry to find conflicting experiences fused together. In "Ode to a Nightingale," for example, the poet speaks of "tasting . . . the country green," an example of synaesthesia—the mixing up of the senses—that violates conventional distinctions. And yet it would be misleading to see Keats as consumed only with oppositions and contradictions. His poems are thick with linguistic activity—meticulously wrought metaphors, puns, allusions, echoes within and across poems, and multiple kinds of poetic diction—all working together in a single text.

Keats's odes, perhaps his greatest works of all, participate in a tradition of English odes that are addressed to a serious and dignified object—such as an artwork, a mood, or a mythological figure. Keats, like other writers of odes, uses these objects to reflect on the nature and power of poetry. Each of his odes responds to and builds on the one before, and they echo and oppose one another in provocative ways. For example, "Ode to a Nightingale" and "Ode on a Grecian Urn" are like mirror images: the first compares poetry to music, suppressing visual experience in favor of aural; the second contrasts poetry to visual art while suppressing sound. Keats also builds his odes around repeated rhetorical forms: his insistent questions in "Ode on a Grecian Urn," for example, or the recurring form of the list in "To Autumn."

Collected here are four of Keats's greatest odes, as well as some shorter poems that give a sense of his variety as a writer: three sonnets and a ballad, "La Belle Dame sans Merci," a spare and haunting half-told story that draws on medieval style and subject matter. Two sonnets—"When I Have Fears That I May Cease to Be" and "Bright Star"—follow the Shakespearian sonnet form: three quatrains (groups of four alternately rhyming lines:

abab) followed by one rhyming couplet. Keats complained that the closing rhyme of Shakespearian sonnets was "seldom pleasing." He also disliked the "pouncing rhymes" of the traditional Petrarchan sonnet, though he used the form sometimes (as in "On First Looking into Chapman's Homer"). The ten-line stanza form of his odes can be seen as a joining of the two traditions: each starts with a Shakespearian quatrain and ends with a Petrarchan sestet (six lines that rhyme every third: cdecde). His discomfort with traditional forms and the desire for a more balanced and varied rhyme scheme attests to Keats's seriousness and originality as an architect of poetic structure: he cares deeply about the ways that stanzas, rhymes, rhythms, and line lengths punctuate, organize, and work together in complex composite wholes. But he is more than a mere craftsman: Keats's intricate structures are there to serve his exquisite meditations on poetry, love, and the looming fact of death.

On First Looking into Chapman's Homer[1]

Much have I traveled in the realms of gold,
   And many goodly states and kingdoms seen;
   Round many western islands have I been
Which bards in fealty to Apollo[2] hold.
Oft of one wide expanse had I been told   5
   That deep-browed Homer ruled as his demesne;[3]
   Yet did I never breathe its pure serene
Till I heard Chapman speak out loud and bold:
Then felt I like some watcher of the skies
   When a new planet swims into his ken;   10
Or like stout Cortez[4] when with eagle eyes
   He stared at the Pacific—and all his men
Looked at each other with a wild surmise—
   Silent, upon a peak in Darien.

1. Keats's friend and former teacher Charles Cowden Clarke had introduced Keats to George Chapman's (1559?–1634) translations of the *Iliad* (1611) and the *Odyssey* (1616) the night before this poem was written.
2. The Greek god of poetic inspiration.

3. Realm, kingdom.
4. In fact, Vasco Núñez de Balboa (ca. 1475–1519), Spanish conquistador, not Hernán Cortés (1485–1547), another Spaniard, was the European explorer who first saw the Pacific from Darién, Panama.

When I Have Fears That I May Cease to Be

When I have fears that I may cease to be
   Before my pen has glean'd my teeming brain,
Before high piled books, in charactry,[1]
   Hold like rich garners the full ripen'd grain;
When I behold, upon the night's starr'd face,   5
   Huge cloudy symbols of a high romance,
And think that I may never live to trace
   Their shadows, with the magic hand of chance;
And when I feel, fair creature of an hour,
   That I shall never look upon thee more,   10
Never have relish in the fairy power
   Of unreflecting love;—then on the shore
Of the wide world I stand alone, and think
Till love and fame to nothingness do sink.

Bright Star

Bright star, would I were steadfast as thou art—
   Not in lone splendor hung aloft the night,
And watching, with eternal lids apart,
   Like nature's patient, sleepless Eremite,[1]
The moving waters at their priestlike task   5
   Of pure ablution round earth's human shores,
Or gazing on the new soft fallen mask
   Of snow upon the mountains and the moors—
No—yet still steadfast, still unchangeable,
   Pillowed upon my fair love's ripening breast,   10
To feel forever its soft fall and swell,
   Awake forever in a sweet unrest,
Still, still to hear her tender-taken breath,
And so live ever—or else swoon to death.

1. Printed letters.   1. Hermit.

La Belle Dame sans Merci[1]

I

O what can ail thee, knight at arms,
   Alone and palely loitering?
The sedge has withered from the lake
   And no birds sing!

II

O what can ail thee, knight at arms,
   So haggard, and so woebegone?   5
The squirrel's granary is full
   And the harvest's done.

III

I see a lily on thy brow
   With anguish moist and fever dew,
And on thy cheeks a fading rose   10
   Fast withereth too.

IV

I met a lady in the meads,[2]
   Full beautiful, a faery's child,
Her hair was long, her foot was light   15
   And her eyes were wild.

V

I made a garland for her head,
   And bracelets too, and fragrant zone;[3]
She looked at me as she did love
   And made sweet moan.   20

VI

I set her on my pacing steed
   And nothing else saw all day long,
For sidelong would she bend and sing
   A faery's song.

1. "The beautiful lady without pity" (French); from a medieval poem by Alain Chartier.
2. Meadows. Here the knight answers the question asked in lines 5–6.
3. Girdle.

VII

She found me roots of relish sweet,   25
 And honey wild, and manna[4] dew,
And sure in language strange she said
 "I love thee true."

VIII

She took me to her elfin grot[5]
 And there she wept and sighed full sore,[6] 30
And there I shut her wild wild eyes
 With kisses four.

IX

And there she lullèd me asleep,
 And there I dreamed, ah woe betide!
The latest[7] dream I ever dreamt   35
 On the cold hill's side.

X

I saw pale kings, and princes too,
 Pale warriors, death-pale were they all;
They cried, "La belle dame sans merci
 Thee hath in thrall!"[8]   40

XI

I saw their starved lips in the gloam[9]
 With horrid warning gapèd wide,
And I awoke, and found me here
 On the cold hill's side.

XII

And this is why I sojourn here,   45
 Alone and palely loitering;
Though the sedge withered from the lake
 And no birds sing.

---

4. The supernatural substance with which God fed the children of Israel in the wilderness (Exodus 16 and Joshua 5.12).
5. Cavern.

6. With great grief.
7. Last.
8. Bondage.
9. Twilight.

Ode on a Grecian Urn

I

Thou still unravished bride of quietness,
　Thou foster-child of silence and slow time,
Sylvan historian, who canst thus express
　A flowery tale more sweetly than our rhyme:
What leaf-fringed legend haunts about thy shape　　　　　5
　Of deities or mortals, or of both,
　　In Tempe or the dales of Arcady?[1]
　　What men or gods are these? What maidens loth?
What mad pursuit? What struggle to escape?
　　What pipes and timbrels? What wild ecstasy?　　　　　10

II

Heard melodies are sweet, but those unheard
　Are sweeter; therefore, ye soft pipes, play on;
Not to the sensual ear, but, more endeared,
　Pipe to the spirit ditties of no tone:
Fair youth, beneath the trees, thou canst not leave　　　15
　Thy song, nor ever can those trees be bare;
　　Bold lover, never, never canst thou kiss,
Though winning near the goal—yet, do not grieve;
　　She cannot fade, though thou hast not thy bliss,
　For ever wilt thou love, and she be fair!　　　　　20

III

Ah, happy, happy boughs! that cannot shed
　Your leaves, nor ever bid the Spring adieu;
And, happy melodist, unwearièd,
　For ever piping songs for ever new;
More happy love! more happy, happy love!　　　　　25
　For ever warm and still to be enjoyed,
　　For ever panting, and for ever young;
All breathing human passion far above,
　　That leaves a heart high-sorrowful and cloyed,
　A burning forehead, and a parching tongue.　　　　　30

IV

Who are these coming to the sacrifice?
　To what green altar, O mysterious priest,
Lead'st thou that heifer lowing at the skies,
　And all her silken flanks with garlands drest?
What little town by river or sea shore,　　　　　35

---

1. A mountainous region in the Peloponnese, traditionally regarded as the place of ideal rustic, bucolic contentment. "Tempe": a valley in Thessaly between Mount Olympus and Mount Ossa.

Or mountain-built with peaceful citadel,
   Is emptied of this folk, this pious morn?
And, little town, thy streets for evermore
Will silent be; and not a soul to tell
   Why thou art desolate, can e'er return.   40

V

O Attic shape! Fair attitude! with brede[2]
   Of marble men and maidens overwrought,
With forest branches and the trodden weed;
   Thou, silent form, dost tease us out of thought
As doth eternity: Cold Pastoral!   45
   When old age shall this generation waste,
   Thou shalt remain, in midst of other woe
Than ours, a friend to man, to whom thou say'st,
   "Beauty is truth, truth beauty,"—that is all
   Ye know on earth, and all ye need to know.   50

Ode to a Nightingale

I

My heart aches, and a drowsy numbness pains
   My sense, as though of hemlock I had drunk,
Or emptied some dull opiate to the drains
   One minute past, and Lethe-wards[1] had sunk:
'Tis not through envy of thy happy lot,   5
   But being too happy in thy happiness,
      That thou, light-winged Dryad[2] of the trees,
         In some melodious plot
Of beechen green, and shadows numberless,
   Singest of summer in full-throated ease.   10

II

O for a draught of vintage! that hath been
   Cooled a long age in the deep-delvèd earth,
Tasting of Flora[3] and the country green,
   Dance, and Provençal[4] song, and sunburnt mirth!
O for a beaker full of the warm South!   15
   Full of the true, the blushful Hippocrene,[5]
      With beaded bubbles winking at the brim,
         And purple-stainèd mouth;

---

2. Pattern. "Attic": classical (literally, Athenian).
1. I.e., toward Lethe, the river of forgetfulness in Greek mythology.
2. Wood nymph.
3. The goddess of flowers and spring; here, flowers.
4. From Provence, the region in France associated with the troubadours.
5. The fountain on Mount Helicon, in Greece, sacred to the muse of poetry.

That I might drink, and leave the world unseen,
   And with thee fade away into the forest dim: 20

III

Fade far away, dissolve, and quite forget
   What thou among the leaves hast never known,
The weariness, the fever, and the fret
   Here, where men sit and hear each other groan;
Where palsy shakes a few, sad, last gray hairs,   25
   Where youth grows pale, and spectre-thin, and dies;
      Where but to think is to be full of sorrow
        And leaden-eyed despairs;
   Where beauty cannot keep her lustrous eyes,
      Or new love pine at them beyond tomorrow.   30

IV

Away! away! for I will fly to thee,
   Not charioted by Bacchus and his pards,[6]
But on the viewless wings of Poesy,
   Though the dull brain perplexes and retards:
Already with thee! tender is the night,   35
   And haply[7] the Queen-Moon is on her throne,
      Clustered around by all her starry Fays;[8]
        But here there is no light,
Save what from heaven is with the breezes blown
      Through verdurous glooms and winding mossy ways.   40

V

I cannot see what flowers are at my feet,
   Nor what soft incense hangs upon the boughs,
But, in embalmèd darkness, guess each sweet
   Wherewith the seasonable month endows
The grass, the thicket, and the fruit-tree wild;   45
   White hawthorn, and the pastoral eglantine;
      Fast-fading violets covered up in leaves;
        And mid-May's eldest child,
The coming musk-rose, full of dewy wine,
      The murmurous haunt of flies on summer eves.   50

VI

Darkling[9] I listen; and for many a time
I have been half in love with easeful Death,
Called him soft names in many a musèd rhyme,
   To take into the air my quiet breath;

6. Leopards. Bacchus (Dionysus) was traditionally supposed to be accompanied by leopards, lions, goats, and so on.

7. By chance.
8. Fairies.
9. In the dark.

Now more than ever seems it rich to die, 55
   To cease upon the midnight with no pain,
     While thou art pouring forth thy soul abroad
      In such an ecstasy!
Still wouldst thou sing, and I have ears in vain—
   To thy high requiem become a sod.[1] 60

VII

Thou wast not born for death, immortal Bird!
   No hungry generations tread thee down;
The voice I hear this passing night was heard
   In ancient days by emperor and clown:
Perhaps the self-same song that found a path 65
   Through the sad heart of Ruth, when, sick for home,
     She stood in tears amid the alien corn;[2]
      The same that ofttimes hath
Charmed magic casements, opening on the foam
   Of perilous seas, in faery lands forlorn. 70

VIII

Forlorn! the very word is like a bell
   To toll me back from thee to my sole self!
Adieu! the fancy cannot cheat so well
   As she is famed to do, deceiving elf.
Adieu! adieu! thy plaintive anthem fades 75
   Past the near meadows, over the still stream,
     Up the hill-side; and now 'tis buried deep
      In the next valley-glades:
Was it a vision, or a waking dream?
   Fled is that music:—do I wake or sleep? 80

Ode on Melancholy

I

No, no, go not to Lethe,[1] neither twist
   Wolfsbane, tight-rooted, for its poisonous wine;
Nor suffer thy pale forehead to be kissed
   By nightshade, ruby grape of Proserpine;[2]
Make not your rosary of yew-berries,[3] 5
   Nor let the beetle, nor the death-moth[4] be

1. I.e., like dirt, unable to hear.
2. See the Book of Ruth. After her Ephrathite husband died, she returned to his native land with her mother-in-law.
1. The river of forgetfulness in Hades.
2. Wife of Pluto, queen of the underworld.

3. Wolfsbane, nightshade, and yew berries are all poisonous.
4. The death's-head moth has markings that resemble a skull. The scarab beetle, often depicted in Egyptian tombs, was an emblem of death.

Your mournful Psyche,[5] nor the downy owl
A partner in your sorrow's mysteries;
  For shade to shade will come too drowsily,
    And drown the wakeful anguish of the soul.   10

II

But when the melancholy fit shall fall
  Sudden from heaven like a weeping cloud,
That fosters the droop-headed flowers all,
  And hides the green hill in an April shroud;
Then glut thy sorrow on a morning rose,   15
  Or on the rainbow of the salt sand-wave,
    Or on the wealth of globèd peonies;
Or if thy mistress some rich anger shows,
  Imprison her soft hand, and let her rave,
    And feed deep, deep upon her peerless eyes.   20

III

She[6] dwells with Beauty—Beauty that must die;
  And Joy, whose hand is ever at his lips
Bidding adieu; and aching Pleasure nigh,
  Turning to Poison while the bee-mouth sips:
Aye, in the very temple of Delight   25
  Veiled Melancholy has her sovereign shrine,
    Though seen of none save him whose strenuous tongue
Can burst Joy's grape against his palate fine;
His soul shall taste the sadness of her might,
  And be among her cloudy trophies hung.[7]   30

To Autumn

I

Season of mists and mellow fruitfulness,
  Close bosom-friend of the maturing sun;
Conspiring with him how to load and bless
  With fruit the vines that round the thatch-eaves run;
To bend with apples the mossed cottage-trees,   5
  And fill all fruit with ripeness to the core;
    To swell the gourd, and plump the hazel shells
With a sweet kernel; to set budding more,
  And still more, later flowers for the bees,
    Until they think warm days will never cease,   10
      For Summer has o'er-brimmed their clammy cells.

5. The soul, portrayed by the Greeks as a
butterfly.
6. Melancholy.

7. The Greeks placed war trophies in their
temples to commemorate victories.

II

Who hath not seen thee oft amid thy store?
    Sometimes whoever seeks abroad may find
Thee sitting careless on a granary floor,
    Thy hair soft-lifted by the winnowing wind;   15
Or on a half-reaped furrow sound asleep,
    Drowsed with the fume of poppies, while thy hook
        Spares the next swath and all its twinèd flowers:
And sometimes like a gleaner thou dost keep
    Steady thy laden head across a brook;   20
    Or by a cyder-press, with patient look,
        Thou watchest the last oozings hours by hours.

III

Where are the songs of Spring? Ay, where are they?
    Think not of them, thou hast thy music too,—
While barrèd clouds bloom the soft-dying day,   25
    And touch the stubble-plains with rosy hue;
Then in a wailful choir the small gnats mourn
    Among the river sallows,[8] borne aloft
        Or sinking as the light wind lives or dies;
And full-grown lambs loud bleat from hilly bourn;   30
    Hedge-crickets sing; and now with treble soft
    The red-breast whistles from a garden-croft;
        And gathering swallows twitter in the skies.

8. Willows.

HEINRICH HEINE

1797–1856

Born to Jewish parents in the German city of Düsseldorf, Heinrich Heine became one of the most famous of all German poets. He wrote at a historical moment dominated by Romantic literature, but experienced a growing disillusionment with the ideals of his contemporaries. "The Romantic School" was "where I spent the most agreeable days of my youth," he wrote, but he "ended up by beating the schoolmaster." He turned his sardonic pen on the very themes that had first animated him: instead of dreams, he focused on harsh awakenings; in place of beautiful love, he concentrated on falling out of love; and he treated nature itself with ironic detachment. He continued to rely on traditional rhyming forms, evocative of simple folk songs, but he deliberately modernized their content, and put them to complex, ironic, and often humorous ends.

Politically, Heine was a radical. He was a friend of Karl Marx, though he remained wary of communism. Early in his life he refused to use his poetic voice as a vehicle for political opinions, arguing that poetry belonged to a higher, more transcendent realm. (He once compared political poets to dancing bears.) But in the 1840s he would write a number of rousing poems on current political events: "The Silesian Weavers" commemorates a protest by Prussian laborers whose wages had fallen below starvation levels.

Throughout his life, the poet maintained an ambivalent relationship to both his Jewishness and his Germanness. Napoleon's conquest of Germany brought with it a guarantee of full civil rights to Jews, but after his defeat, many German cities and states reverted to repressive laws. In Frankfurt, for example, only twelve Jewish couples were permitted to marry in any given year. Heine was allowed to study law but not to practice, and he converted to Christianity in order to find work. He rejected Jewish communities and beliefs until late in life, but remained fiercely critical of Christian Germany. "Wherever they burn books," he wrote, "they will also, in the end, burn human beings."

[A pine is standing lonely][1]

A pine is standing lonely
In the North on a bare plateau.
He sleeps; a bright white blanket
Enshrouds him in ice and snow.

He's dreaming of a palm tree   5
Far away in the Eastern land
Lonely and silently mourning
On a sunburnt rocky strand.

To Tell the Truth[1]

When springtime comes, the sun and showers
Bring out a host of dancing flowers;
And when at night the moon peeps through,
The stars begin to twinkle too;
And when the bard sees two blue eyes,   5
Soulful songs materialise;—
But songs and stars and dancing flowers
And azure eyes and April showers,
However popular such stuff,
It's never *really* quite enough.   10

[A young man loves a maiden]

A young man loves a maiden
Who chooses another instead;

1. Translated by Hal Draper, as are the other Heine selections except "To tell the Truth."

1. Translated by T. J. Reed and David Cram.

This other loves still another
And these two haply[1] wed.

The maiden out of anger   5
Marries, with no regard,
The first good man she runs into—
The young lad takes it hard.

It is so old a story,
Yet somehow always new;   10
And he that has just lived it,
It breaks his heart in two.

The Silesian Weavers[1]

In somber eyes no tears of grieving;
Grinding their teeth, they sit at their weaving;
"O Germany, at your shroud we sit,
We're weaving a threefold curse in it—
    We're weaving, we're weaving!   5

"A curse on the god we prayed to, kneeling
With cold in our bones, with hunger reeling;
We waited and hoped, in vain persevered,
He scorned us and duped us, mocked and jeered—
    We're weaving, we're weaving!   10

"A curse on the king[2] of the rich man's nation
Who hardens his heart at our supplication,
Who wrings the last penny out of our hides
And lets us be shot like dogs besides—
    We're weaving, we're weaving!   15

"A curse on this false fatherland, teeming
With nothing but shame and dirty scheming,
Where every flower is crushed in a day,
Where worms are regaled on rot and decay—
    We're weaving, we're weaving!   20

"The shuttle[3] flies, the loom creaks loud,
Night and day we weave your shroud—
Old Germany, at your shroud we sit,
We're weaving a threefold curse in it,
    We're weaving, we're weaving!"   25

---

1. By chance.
1. Silesia was a province of the kingdom of Prussia in northeast Germany. This poem was occasioned by violent uprisings of weavers protesting intolerable working conditions during June 1844.

2. Friedrich Wilhelm IV (1795–1861). Heine's poem is prophetic: in 1848 the king, though not deposed, was forced by revolution to grant a constitution to Prussia.
3. Device used for weaving cloth on a loom.

GIACOMO LEOPARDI
1798–1837

Giacomo Leopardi is one of Italy's greatest lyric poets. Born into an aristocratic family in a dreary provincial town, he was extraordinarily precocious, learning faster than any tutor could teach him. As an adolescent, he read several hundred pages a day, translated and commented on ancient texts, and wrote volumes of his own plays, essays, and poems. Yet it was far from a happy childhood. In his well-known diary, Leopardi explained that his mother purposefully reproached her children in order to "make them well aware of their defects . . . and to convince them with a fierce, pitiless veracity of their inevitable misery." In late adolescence, Leopardi's health began to break down—he became almost blind, his spine curved over—and his family encouraged him to become a priest. But he had begun to lose faith in God, and what followed was thoroughgoing, even paralyzing skepticism, as he began to see human life as little more than agonizing suffering. Even as he grew to be a famous poet, he remained almost completely trapped in his parents' house, with no income of his own. He had three painful experiences of unrequited love, and died at the age of thirty-nine.

It is not surprising, then, that Leopardi is, above all, a poet of despair, one who casts life as doomed, sorrowful, and purposeless. And yet both natural and artistic beauty seem to provide a brief respite from this anguish. His own art has often felt to readers strangely uplifting, filled with pleasure and solace, despite the sadness of his themes. In his most famous lyric, "The Infinite" (1819), the poet has the sublime feeling—both pleasurable and frightening—of imagining infinity, which extends beyond his own restricted vision, and he willingly celebrates the feeling of drowning in this endlessness. Readers have long appreciated the musical beauty of "To Silvia" (1828). The despairing late poem "To Himself" (1833) was written after Leopardi had been rejected by a woman he loved. While most other Italian Romantic writers looked outward—toward national political struggles—Leopardi resolutely turned inward, to explore the painful intensity of an individual human life.

The Infinite[1]

This lonely hill has always been so dear
To me, and dear the hedge which hides away
The reaches of the sky. But sitting here
And wondering, I fashion in my mind
The endless spaces far beyond, the more   5
Than human silences, and deepest peace;
So that the heart is on the edge of fear.

---

1. All three poems are translated by Ottavio M. Casale.

And when I hear the wind come blowing through
The trees, I pit its voice against that boundless
Silence and summon up eternity,   10
And the dead seasons, and the present one,
Alive with all its sound. And thus it is
In this immensity my thought is drowned:
And sweet to me the foundering in this sea.

To Himself

   Now you may rest forever,
My tired heart. The last illusion is dead
That I believed eternal. Dead. I can
So clearly see—not only hope is gone
But the desire to be deceived as well.   5
Rest, rest forever.
You have beaten long enough. Nothing is worth
Your smallest motion, nor the earth your sighs.
This life is bitterness
And vacuum, nothing else. The world is mud.   10
From now on calm yourself.
Despair for the last time. The only gift
Fate gave our kind was death. Henceforth, heap scorn
Upon yourself, Nature, the ugly force
That, hidden, orders universal ruin,   15
And the boundless emptiness of everything.

To Sylvia

   Sylvia. Do you remember still
The moments of your mortal lifetime here,
When such a loveliness
Shone in the elusive laughter of your eyes,
And you, contemplative and gay, climbed toward   5
The summit of your youth?

   The tranquil chambers held,
The paths re-echoed, your perpetual song,
When at your woman's tasks
You sat, content to concentrate upon   10
The future beckoning within your mind.
It was the fragrant May,
And thus you passed your time.

   I often used to leave
The dear, belabored pages which consumed   15
So much of me and of my youth, and from

Ancestral balconies
Would lean to hear the music of your voice,
Your fingers humming through
The intricacies of the weaving work.   20
And I would gaze upon
The blue surrounding sky,
The paths and gardens golden in the sun,
And there the far-off sea, and here the mountain.
No human tongue can tell   25
What I felt then within my brimming heart.

What tendernesses then,
What hopes, what hearts were ours, O Sylvia mine!
How large a thing seemed life, and destiny!
When I recall those bright anticipations,   30
Bitterness invades,
And I turn once again to mourn my lot.
O Nature, Nature, why
Do you not keep the promises you gave?
Why trick the children so?   35

Before the winter struck the summer grass,
You died, my gentle girl,
Besieged by hidden illness and possessed.
You never saw the flowering of your years.
Your heart was never melted by the praise   40
Of your dark hair, your shy,
Enamoured eyes. Nor did you with your friends
Conspire on holidays to talk of love.

The expectation failed
As soon for me, and fate denied my youth.   45
Ah how gone by, gone by,
You dear companion of my dawning time,
The hope that I lament!
Is this the world we knew? And these the joys
The love, the labors, happenings we shared?   50
And this the destiny
Of human beings? My poor one, when
The truth rose up, you fell,
And from afar you pointed me the way
To coldest death and the stark sepulchre.   55

ELIZABETH BARRETT BROWNING
1806–1861

Elizabeth Barrett Browning was by far the most famous woman poet writing in English in the nineteenth century. She was adored to the point of hero-worship both in England and in the United States. In her view, poetry was capable of acting as a powerful vehicle for social protest, and in fact, when she wrote about slavery, women's rights, prostitution, and child labor, her audiences were often inspired to vocal debate and political action. Though widely acclaimed as both a poetic genius and a moral authority, after her death her fame was eclipsed by that of her husband, **Robert Browning**, and later writers dismissed her as a sentimental feminine soul rather than an accomplished poet in her own right. But this was a mistake. Few poets have been more technically skilled than Barrett Browning. She uses a vast range of existing poetic forms with staggering dexterity and subtlety, and when these forms are not enough, she boldly invents strange and innovative new rhythms, stanza structures, and rhyme schemes.

The eldest of twelve children, Elizabeth Barrett Moulton-Barrett was born to a prosperous English family that had made its money from slave plantations in Jamaica. Her education was highly unusual for an Englishwoman of her time: sitting in on her brother's private lessons, she learned Latin and Greek, and later taught herself Hebrew. She began writing poetry at the age of six and published her first volume at thirteen. Exceptionally learned, she translated the ancient Greek dramatist Aeschylus and experimented with writing epic poetry—something women were strongly discouraged from doing. As she came to understand the source of her family's wealth, she deliberately tried to distance herself from slavery, both renouncing money earned from plantation labor and writing antislavery poetry for abolitionist periodicals in the United States. A mysterious lung disease and a fall from a horse made her an invalid, and she spent much of her early adulthood confined to her bedroom, addicted to morphine. Her tyrannical father wanted none of his children to marry and leave his house, and he kept her secluded even as she became an increasingly prominent poet. This was to change, however, when the young poet Robert Browning launched a passionate correspondence with her. In 1846, when she was 39 and he 33, they eloped to Italy, where she recovered her strength and bore a son. The following years were exceptionally happy and productive. Elizabeth Barrett Browning died, in her husband's arms, unforgiven by her father, in 1861.

"The Cry of the Children" appeared in response to a government report about child laborers in mines and factories, who were expected to work as many as sixteen hours a day unprotected by any safety regulations. Rejecting the intensely personal voice of lyric poetry, Barrett Browning here makes confrontational direct addresses to her readers and adopts a collective first-person-plural "we" for the voice of the child workers. She also invents an uncomfortable, confrontational new rhythm rather than relying on existing poetic conventions. One reviewer wrote that "the cadence, lingering, broken, and full of wail, is one of the most perfect adaptations of sound to sense in literature." This poem was so powerful that Barrett Browning was credited with inspiring the British parliament to pass new laws regulating child labor.

Very different in tone and form are the *Sonnets from the Portuguese*—a series of love poems which Barrett Browning presented as if they were translations from a fictional Portuguese original. Typically, in these poems, she will use a single dominant image—the musician, the colorful gift, the sacrifice—and follow the logic of this image to a surprising conclusion. For example, in Sonnet III, she pictures her beloved as the chief musician at a royal court, while she is stuck outside, the wandering minstrel. But while casting herself as a marginal figure humbles her, it also masculinizes her in a context where women are closely associated with the home, deliberately shut in rather than out. Always noteworthy is the poet's use of the *volta*, or "turn" in the sonnet form—a break between the first two quatrains (sets of four lines) and the closing six lines. Barrett Browning will often turn here from question to answer, or from beloved to lover. But in the case of her most famous sonnet, "How Do I Love Thee? Let Me Count the Ways," it is intriguing to note that she makes no obvious turn at all.

In her own time, Barrett Browning's fierce frankness on politics, women's desire, and the power of poetry consistently drew attention to the ways that she defied conventional feminine constraints. One of her contemporaries wrote that she was the first woman writer to mix "masculine vigour, breadth, and culture" with "feminine subtlety of perception, feminine quickness of sensibility, and feminine tenderness."

The Cry of the Children

"Φεῦ, φεῦ, τι προσδέρκεσθέ μ' ὄμμασιν, τέκνα;"
—*Medea*[1]

Do ye hear the children weeping, O my brothers,
　　Ere the sorrow comes with years?
They are leaning their young heads against their mothers,
　　And *that* cannot stop their tears.
The young lambs are bleating in the meadows,　　　　　　　5
　　The young birds are chirping in the nest,
The young fawns are playing with the shadows,
　　The young flowers are blowing toward the west—
But the young, young children, O my brothers,
　　They are weeping bitterly!　　　　　　　　　　　　　10
They are weeping in the playtime of the others,
　　In the country of the free.

Do you question the young children in the sorrow
　　Why their tears are falling so?

---

1. Greek tragedy by Euripides (ca. 480–406 B.C.E.) about the mythological figure of Medea, a mother who kills her own children;　　Medea speaks the line in Greek: "Alas, my children, why do you look at me?"

The old man may weep for his to-morrow   15
     Which is lost in Long Ago;
The old tree is leafless in the forest,
   The old year is ending in the frost,
The old wound, if stricken, is the sorest,
   The old hope is hardest to be lost: 20
But the young, young children, O my brothers,
     Do you ask them why they stand
Weeping sore before the bosoms of their mothers,
     In our happy Fatherland?

They look up with their pale and sunken faces,   25
     And their looks are sad to see,
For the man's hoary anguish draws and presses
     Down the cheeks of infancy;
"Your old earth," they say, "is very dreary,"
     "Our young feet," they say, "are very weak;   30
Few paces have we taken, yet are weary—
   Our grave-rest is very far to seek:
Ask the aged why they weep, and not the children,
     For the outside earth is cold,
And we young ones stand without, in our bewildering,   35
     And the graves are for the old."

"True," say the children, "it may happen
     That we die before our time:
Little Alice died last year, her grave is shapen
     Like a snowball, in the rime.   40
We looked into the pit prepared to take her:
   Was no room for any work in the close clay!
From the sleep wherein she lieth none will wake her,
     Crying, 'Get up, little Alice! it is day.'
If you listen by that grave, in sun and shower,   45
     With your ear down, little Alice never cries;
Could we see her face, be sure we should not know her,
     For the smile has time for growing in her eyes:
And merry go her moments, lulled and stilled in
     The shroud by the kirk[2] chime.   50
It is good when it happens," say the children,
     "That we die before our time."

Alas, alas, the children! they are seeking
     Death in life, as best to have:
They are binding up their hearts away from breaking,   55
     With a ceremen[3] from the grave.
Go out, children, from the mine and from the city,
   Sing out, children, as the little thrushes do;
Pluck your handfuls of the meadow-cowslips pretty,
     Laugh aloud, to feel your fingers let them through!   60

2. Church.   3. Shroud.

But they answer, "Are your cowslips of the meadows
    Like our weeds anear the mine?
Leave us quiet in the dark of the coal-shadows,
    From your pleasures fair and fine!

"For oh," say the children, "we are weary,   65
    And we cannot run or leap;
If we cared for any meadows, it were merely
    To drop down in them and sleep.
Our knees tremble sorely in the stooping,
    We fall upon our faces, trying to go;   70
And, underneath our heavy eyelids drooping,
    The reddest flower would look as pale as snow.
For, all day, we drag our burden tiring
    Through the coal-dark, underground;
Or, all day, we drive the wheels of iron   75
    In the factories, round and round.

"For, all day, the wheels are droning, turning;
    Their wind comes in our faces,
Till our hearts turn, our heads with pulses burning,
    And the walls turn in their places: 80
Turns the sky in the high window blank and reeling,
    Turns the long light that drops adown the wall,
Turn the black flies that crawl along the ceiling,
    All are turning, all the day, and we with all.
And all day, the iron wheels are droning,   85
    And sometimes we could pray,
'O ye wheels,' (breaking out in a mad moaning)
    'Stop! be silent for to-day!'"

Ay, be silent! Let them hear each other breathing
    For a moment, mouth to mouth!   90
Let them touch each other's hands, in a fresh wreathing
    Of their tender human youth!
Let them feel that this cold metallic motion
    Is not all the life God fashions or reveals:
Let them prove their living souls against the notion   95
    That they live in you, or under you, O wheels!
Still, all day, the iron wheels go onward,
    Grinding life down from its mark;
And the children's souls, which God is calling sunward,
    Spin on blindly in the dark.   100

Now tell the poor young children; O my brothers,
    To look up to Him and pray;
So the blessed One who blesseth all the others,
    Will bless them another day.
They answer, "Who is God that He should hear us,   105
    While the rushing of the iron wheels is stirred?
When we sob aloud, the human creatures near us

Pass by, hearing not, or answer not a word.
And *we* hear not (for the wheels in their resounding)
  Strangers speaking at the door: 110
Is it likely God, with angels singing round Him,
  Hears our weeping any more?

Two words, indeed, of praying we remember,
  And at midnight's hour of harm,
'Our Father,' looking upward in the chamber,   115
  We say softly for a charm.
We know no other words except 'Our Father.'
 And we think that, in some pause of angels' song,
God may pluck them with the silence sweet to gather,
 And hold both within His right hand which is strong.   120
'Our Father!' If He heard us, He would surely
  (For they call Him good and mild)
Answer, smiling down the steep world very purely,
  'Come and rest with me, my child.'

"But, no!" say the children, weeping faster,   125
  "He is speechless as a stone:
And they tell us, of His image is the master
  Who commands us to work on.
Go to!" say the children,—"up in Heaven,
 Dark, wheel-like, turning clouds are all we find.   130
Do not mock us; grief has made us unbelieving:
We look up for God, but tears have made us blind."
Do you hear the children weeping and disproving,
  O my brothers, what ye preach?
For God's possible is taught by His world's loving,   135
  And the children doubt of each.

And well may the children weep before you!
  They are weary ere they run;
They have never seen the sunshine, nor the glory
  Which is brighter than the sun.   140
They know the grief of man, without its wisdom;
 They sink in man's despair, without its calm;
Are slaves, without the liberty in Christdom,
 Are martyrs, by the pang without the palm:
Are worn as if with age, yet unretrievingly   145
  The harvest of its memories cannot reap,—
Are orphans of the earthly love and heavenly.
  Let them weep! let them weep!

They look up with their pale and sunken faces,
  And their look is dread to see,   150
For they mind you of their angels in high places,
  With eyes turned on Deity.
"How long," they say, "how long, O cruel nation,
 Will you stand, to move the world, on a child's heart,—

Stifle down with a mailed[4] heel its palpitation,   155
    And tread onward to your throne amid the mart?
Our blood splashes upward, O gold-heaper,
    And your purple shows your path!
But the child's sob in the silence curses deeper
    Than the strong man in his wrath."   160

From Sonnets from the Portuguese

III

Unlike are we, unlike, O princely Heart!
Unlike our uses and our destinies.
Our ministering two angels look surprise
On one another, as they strike athwart
Their wings in passing. Thou, bethink thee, art   5
A guest for queens to social pageantries,
With gages from a hundred brighter eyes
Than tears even can make mine, to play thy part
Of chief musician. What hast *thou* to do
With looking from the lattice-lights at me,   10
A poor, tired, wandering singer, singing through
The dark, and leaning up a cypress tree?[1]
The chrism is on thine head,—on mine, the dew,—
And Death must dig the level where these agree.

VIII

What can I give thee back, O liberal
And princely giver, who hast brought the gold
And purple[2] of thine heart, unstained, untold,
And laid them on the outside of the wall
For such as I to take or leave withal,   5
In unexpected largesse? am I cold,
Ungrateful, that for these most manifold
High gifts, I render nothing back at all?
Not so; not cold,—but very poor instead.
Ask God who knows. For frequent tears have run   10
The colours from my life, and left so dead
And pale a stuff, it were not fitly done
To give the same as pillow to thy head.
Go farther! let it serve to trample on.

4. Armored, as with chainmail.   2. Traditionally, purple comes from a dye so
1. The cypress was connected to death in both   expensive that it was reserved for royalty.
Greek and Roman mythology.

XXXV

If I leave all for thee, wilt thou exchange
And be all to me? Shall I never miss
Home-talk and blessing and the common kiss
That comes to each in turn, nor count it strange,
When I look up, to drop on a new range   5
Of walls and floors, another home than this?
Nay, wilt thou fill that place by me which is
Filled by dead eyes too tender to know change?
That's hardest. If to conquer love, has tried,
To conquer grief, tries more, as all things prove;   10
For grief indeed is love and grief beside.
Alas, I have grieved so I am hard to love.
Yet love me—wilt thou? Open thine heart wide,
And fold within the wet wings of thy dove.

XLIII

How do I love thee? Let me count the ways.
I love thee to the depth and breadth and height
My soul can reach, when feeling out of sight
For the ends of Being and ideal Grace.
I love thee to the level of everyday's   5
Most quiet need, by sun and candlelight.
I love thee freely, as men strive for Right;
I love thee purely, as they turn from Praise.
I love thee with the passion put to use
In my old griefs, and with my childhood's faith.   10
I love thee with a love I seemed to lose
With my lost saints,—I love thee with the breath,
Smiles, tears, of all my life!—and, if God choose,
I shall but love thee better after death.

ALFRED, LORD TENNYSON
1809–1892

Alfred Tennyson exerted such a powerful influence on English poetry in the nineteenth century that the rebellious American poet **Walt** **Whitman** called him "the Boss." By the last decades of the century, British audiences looked to this post-Romantic poet as a voice of the whole nation, and readers of all classes could recite at least a few of his poems from memory. Many of his poems were set to music, and his works became a standard part of school curricula in Britain, the United States, Ireland, and India well into the twentieth century. The Modernist writers who followed found Tennyson's influence so stifling that they struggled to reject his legacy. (The Irish novelist **James Joyce** mockingly renamed him "Lawn Tennyson" to suggest that the poetry was tame and trivial.) And yet, Tennyson's appeal has long outlasted his fiercest critics. Using gorgeously melodious language to investigate the intensities of love, loss, longing, doubt, and despair, Tennyson remains one of the most moving of English poets.

Growing up in a family troubled by drunkenness, violence, and madness, Alfred Tennyson was the fourth of twelve children born in the space of fourteen years. The family was descended from the highest ranks of the aristocracy, but Tennyson's own father had been disinherited: he struggled to make ends meet while his younger brother enjoyed the immense riches of the ancestral estate. Given to paranoia and raging, abusive violence, Tennyson's father sunk into alcoholism in the 1820s. As soon as he could, Tennyson escaped the family home for Cambridge University. There he joined an undergraduate society called the Apostles, many of whom would become the leading intellectual lights of the nineteenth century in England. In particular he befriended a talented and brilliant young man named Arthur Henry Hallam, who encouraged Tennyson to write poetry, predicting that he would be recognized as the most important poetic genius of his time. Hallam died suddenly in 1833 at age twenty-two, plunging Tennyson into grief. He would later memorialize his friend in his great and wide-ranging elegy, *In Memoriam* (1850).

Tennyson's first two volumes of poetry, published in the 1830s, broke in surprising ways with Romantic themes and conventions. In luxuriantly musical cadences that evoked moods, personalities, and sensations, these poems seemed to their first audiences technically and thematically adventurous. Many of them explored an inexplicable melancholy and immobility. Reviewers at the time offered mostly harsh words, considering the work mystifying and pretentious. With his later volumes, Tennyson's fame and popularity grew; he became the favorite poet of Queen Victoria, who named him Poet Laureate in 1850. And yet, as Tennyson gained recognition, he lost some of his daringly experimental edge.

In his greatest early works, Tennyson explores feelings, thoughts, and experiences not through the poet's own voice, as the Romantics so often did, but instead through figures other than himself—Mariana, a minor character from Shakespeare's *Measure for Measure*, or Ulysses, the hero of Homer's *Odyssey*. Like his contemporary Robert Browning, he frequently turns to a genre called the dramatic monologue: a poem, such as *Ulysses*, in which the writer adopts a persona and speaks in the first person from that perspective.

Tennyson not only rejects himself as the source of poetic emotion, he also explores odd, neglected moments from the lives of the characters he chooses: Mariana when she feels most stuck, awaiting a lover who seems to have deserted her forever; Ulysses as an old man, when his celebrated days of heroic action are over. In the three poems collected here, we see how Tennyson draws on great literary forebears—Shakespeare, Homer, the Arthurian tradition—and yet concentrates on marginal experiences which his precursors ignored. Homer, after all, did not bother to think about what it might be like to be an epic hero past his prime; and

Shakespeare barely gives us a line— "Mariana in the moated grange"—to describe his character's experience of dejection. The Lady of Shalott is either a highly obscure character from Arthurian legend, or a completely fictional one created by Tennyson. These poems therefore rethink what literary tradition has left out. It is intriguing, in this context, that Tennyson so often focuses on women characters who are stalled, restrained, and confined.

Notably, too, Tennyson departs from many of the Romantic poets in his evocations of nature. Mariana's overgrown garden, for example, results from a mix of human cultivation and neglect, as the natural and social worlds merge together gloomily and inextricably, neither in harmony with the other. The Lady of Shalott is consumed with her mysterious isolation from human company, and Ulysses broods on that which lies beyond the natural and social environments that confine him. With Tennyson, that is, nature ceases to provide a model, an outlet, or a source of solace, while social relations remain broken and discouraging. His is a bleaker, less promising world than that of the Romantics—but it is also one that has resonated with readers from that day to this.

Mariana

"Mariana in the moated grange."

Measure for Measure[1]

With blackest moss the flower-plots
  Were thickly crusted, one and all;
The rusted nails fell from the knots
  That held the pear to the gable wall.
The broken sheds looked sad and strange: 5
  Unlifted was the clinking latch;
  Weeded and worn the ancient thatch
Upon the lonely moated grange.
    She only said, "My life is dreary,
      He cometh not," she said;   10
    She said, "I am aweary, aweary,
      I would that I were dead!"

Her tears fell with the dews at even;
  Her tears fell ere the dews were dried;
She could not look on the sweet heaven,   15
  Either at morn or eventide.
After the flitting of the bats,
  When thickest dark did trance[2] the sky,
  She drew her casement curtain by,
And glanced athwart the glooming flats.   20
    She only said, "The night is dreary,
      He cometh not," she said;
    She said, "I am aweary, aweary,
      I would that I were dead!"

1. Shakespeare's play *Measure for Measure* features a character named Mariana who is jilted by her lover; she waits for him in a moated grange, or farmhouse.
2. Pass across, transit.

Upon the middle of the night,
    Waking she heard the nightfowl crow;
The cock sung out an hour ere light;
    From the dark fen the oxen's low
Came to her; without hope of change,
    In sleep she seemed to walk forlorn,   30
Till cold winds woke the gray-eyed morn
About the lonely moated grange.
      She only said, "The day is dreary,
        He cometh not," she said;
      She said, "I am aweary, aweary,   35
        I would that I were dead!"

About a stonecast from the wall
    A sluice with blackened waters slept,
And o'er it many, round and small,
    The clustered marish-mosses[3] crept.   40
Hard by[4] a poplar shook alway,
    All silver-green with gnarlèd bark:
For leagues no other tree did mark
The level waste, the rounding gray.
      She only said, "My life is dreary,   45
        He cometh not," she said;
      She said, "I am aweary, aweary,
        I would that I were dead!"

And ever when the moon was low,
    And the shrill winds were up and away,   50
In the white curtain, to and fro,
    She saw the gusty shadow sway.
But when the moon was very low,
    And wild winds bound within their cell,
The shadow of the poplar fell   55
Upon her bed, across her brow.
      She only said, "The night is dreary,
        He cometh not," she said;
      She said, "I am aweary, aweary,
        I would that I were dead!"   60

All day within the dreamy house,
    The doors upon their hinges creaked;
The blue fly sung in the pane; the mouse
    Behind the moldering wainscot shrieked,
Or from the crevice peered about.   65
      Old faces glimmered through the doors,
      Old footsteps trod the upper floors,
    Old voices called her from without.

3. The little marsh-moss lumps that float on   4. Nearby.
the surface of water [Tennyson's note].

She only said, "My life is dreary,
    He cometh not," she said;
She said, "I am aweary, aweary,   70
    I would that I were dead!"

The sparrow's chirrup on the roof,
    The slow clock ticking, and the sound
Which to the wooing wind aloof   75
    The poplar made, did all confound
Her sense; but most she loathed the hour
    When the thick-moted sunbeam lay
Athwart the chambers, and the day
Was sloping toward his western bower.   80
    Then, said she, "I am very dreary,
        He will not come," she said;
    She wept, "I am aweary, aweary,
        Oh God, that I were dead!"

The Lady of Shalott[1]

Part 1

On either side the river lie
Long fields of barley and of rye,
That clothe the wold and meet the sky;
And through the field the road runs by
    To many-towered Camelot;[2]   5
And up and down the people go,
Gazing where the lilies blow
Round an island there below,
        The island of Shalott.

Willows whiten, aspens quiver,   10
Little breezes dusk and shiver
Through the wave that runs forever
By the island in the river
        Flowing down to Camelot.
Four gray walls, and four gray towers,   15
Overlook a space of flowers,
And the silent isle imbowers
        The Lady of Shalott.

By the margin, willow-veiled,
Slide the heavy barges trailed   20
By slow horses; and unhailed
The shallop[3] flitteth silken-sailed

---

1. An imaginary place; this story is loosely
based on medieval Arthurian legend, but Tennyson imagines most of the details.

2. King Arthur's legendary castle.
3. Small boat.

Skimming down to Camelot:
But who hath seen her wave her hand?
Or at the casement seen her stand? 25
Or is she known in all the land,
    The Lady of Shalott?

Only reapers, reaping early
In among the bearded barley,
Hear a song that echoes cheerly 30
From the river winding clearly,
    Down to towered Camelot;
And by the moon the reaper weary,
Piling sheaves in uplands airy,
Listening, whispers "'Tis the fairy 35
    Lady of Shalott."

Part 2

There she weaves by night and day
A magic web with colors gay.
She has heard a whisper say,
A curse is on her if she stay 40
    To look down to Camelot.
She knows not what the curse may be,
And so she weaveth steadily,
And little other care hath she,
    The Lady of Shalott. 45

And moving through a mirror clear
That hangs before her all the year,
Shadows of the world appear.
There she sees the highway near
    Winding down to Camelot. 50
There the river eddy whirls,
And there the surly village churls,
And the red cloaks of market girls,
    Pass onward from Shalott.

Sometimes a troop of damsels glad, 55
An abbot on an ambling pad,[4]
Sometimes a curly shepherd lad,
Or long-haired page in crimson clad,
    Goes by to towered Camelot;
And sometimes through the mirror blue 60
The knights come riding two and two:
She hath no loyal knight and true,
    The Lady of Shalott.

But in her web she still delights
To weave the mirror's magic sights, 65
For often through the silent nights

---

4. Walking horse.

A funeral, with plumes and lights
    And music, went to Camelot;
Or when the moon was overhead,
Came two young lovers lately wed: 70
"I am half sick of shadows," said
    The Lady of Shalott.

Part 3

A bowshot from her bower eaves,
He rode between the barley sheaves,
The sun came dazzling through the leaves,   75
And flamed upon the brazen greaves[5]
    Of bold Sir Lancelot.
A red-cross knight[6] forever kneeled
To a lady in his shield,
That sparkled on the yellow field,   80
    Beside remote Shalott.

The gemmy bridle glittered free,
Like to some branch of stars we see
Hung in the golden Galaxy.
The bridle bells rang merrily   85
    As he rode down to Camelot;
And from his blazoned baldric[7] slung
A mighty silver bugle hung,
And as he rode his armor rung,
    Beside remote Shalott.   90

All in the blue unclouded weather
Thick-jeweled shone the saddle leather,
The helmet and the helmet-feather
Burned like one burning flame together,
    As he rode down to Camelot;   95
As often through the purple night,
Below the starry clusters bright,
Some bearded meteor, trailing light,
    Moves over still Shalott.

His broad clear brow in sunlight glowed;   100
On burnished hooves his war horse trode;
From underneath his helmet flowed
His coal-black curls as on he rode,
    As he rode down to Camelot.
From the bank and from the river   105
He flashed into the crystal mirror,
"Tirra lirra," by the river
    Sang Sir Lancelot.

---

5. Leg armor.
6. Symbol of holiness and justice in *The Faerie Queene* by English poet Edmund

Spenser (ca. 1552–1599).
7. Shoulder belt used to support a weapon or drum.

She left the web, she left the loom,
She made three paces through the room,   110
She saw the water lily bloom,
She saw the helmet and the plume,
    She looked down to Camelot.
Out flew the web and floated wide;
The mirror cracked from side to side;   115
"The curse is come upon me," cried
    The Lady of Shalott.

Part 4

In the stormy east wind straining,
The pale yellow woods were waning,
The broad stream in his banks complaining,   120
Heavily the low sky raining
    Over towered Camelot;
Down she came and found a boat
Beneath a willow left afloat,
And round about the prow she wrote   125
    The Lady of Shalott.

And down the river's dim expanse
Like some bold seer in a trance,
Seeing all his own mischance—
With a glassy countenance   130
    Did she look to Camelot.
And at the closing of the day
She loosed the chain, and down she lay;
The broad stream bore her far away,
    The Lady of Shalott.   135

Lying, robed in snowy white
That loosely flew to left and right—
The leaves upon her falling light—
Through the noises of the night
    She floated down to Camelot;   140
And as the boat-head wound along
The willowy hills and fields among,
They heard her singing her last song,
    The Lady of Shalott.

Heard a carol, mournful, holy,   145
Chanted loudly, chanted lowly,
Till her blood was frozen slowly,
And her eyes were darkened wholly,
    Turned to towered Camelot.
For ere she reached upon the tide   150
The first house by the waterside,
Singing in her song she died,
    The Lady of Shalott.

Under tower and balcony,
By garden wall and gallery,   155
A gleaming shape she floated by,
Dead-pale between the houses high,
    Silent into Camelot.
Out upon the wharfs they came,
Knight and burgher, lord and dame,   160
And round the prow they read her name,
    The Lady of Shalott.

Who is this? and what is here?
And in the lighted palace near
Died the sound of royal cheer;   165
And they crossed themselves for fear,
    All the knights at Camelot:
But Lancelot mused a little space;
He said, "She has a lovely face;
God in his mercy lend her grace,   170
    The Lady of Shalott."

Ulysses[1]

    It little profits that an idle king,
By this still hearth, among these barren crags,
Matched with an aged wife, I mete and dole
Unequal laws unto a savage race,
That hoard, and sleep, and feed, and know not me.   5
    I cannot rest from travel; I will drink
Life to the lees.[2] All times I have enjoyed
Greatly, have suffered greatly, both with those
That loved me, and alone; on shore, and when
Through scudding drifts the rainy Hyades[3]   10
Vexed the dim sea. I am become a name;
For always roaming with a hungry heart
Much have I seen and known—cities of men
And manners, climates, councils, governments,
Myself not least, but honored of them all—   15
And drunk delight of battle with my peers,
Far on the ringing plains of windy Troy,
I am a part of all that I have met;
Yet all experience is an arch wherethrough
Gleams that untraveled world whose margin fades   20
Forever and forever when I move.
How dull it is to pause, to make an end,

---

1. In Dante's *Inferno*, Ulysses—the Roman name for the Greek hero Odysseus—persuades his crew to go on a new adventure rather than return home to his wife in Ithaca; Tennyson merges Dante's Ulysses with Homer's Odysseus, giving us a character who has spent time in Ithaca and then, in old age, sets out on a new journey.
2. That is, to the very end. (Lees are the dregs that settle at the bottom of a bottle of wine.)
3. Cluster of stars supposed to portend rain.

To rust unburnished, not to shine in use!
As though to breathe were life! Life piled on life
Were all too little, and of one to me   25
Little remains; but every hour is saved
From that eternal silence, something more,
A bringer of new things; and vile it were
For some three suns to store and hoard myself,
And this gray spirit yearning in desire   30
To follow knowledge like a sinking star,
Beyond the utmost bound of human thought.

    This is my son, mine own Telemachus,
To whom I leave the scepter and the isle—
Well-loved of me, discerning to fulfill   35
This labor, by slow prudence to make mild
A rugged people, and through soft degrees
Subdue them to the useful and the good.
Most blameless is he, centered in the sphere
Of common duties, decent not to fail   40
In offices of tenderness, and pay
Meet[4] adoration to my household gods,
When I am gone. He works his work, I mine.

    There lies the port; the vessel puffs her sail;
There gloom the dark, broad seas. My mariners,   45
Souls that have toiled, and wrought, and thought with me—
That ever with a frolic welcome took
The thunder and the sunshine, and opposed
Free hearts, free foreheads—you and I are old;
Old age hath yet his honor and his toil.   50
Death closes all; but something ere the end,
Some work of noble note, may yet be done,
Not unbecoming men that strove with Gods.
The lights begin to twinkle from the rocks;
The long day wanes; the slow moon climbs; the deep   55
Moans round with many voices. Come, my friends,
'Tis not too late to seek a newer world.
Push off, and sitting well in order smite
The sounding furrows; for my purpose holds
To sail beyond the sunset, and the baths   60
Of all the western stars, until I die.
It may be that the gulfs will wash us down;
It may be we shall touch the Happy Isles,[5]
And see the great Achilles, whom we knew.
Though much is taken, much abides; and though   65
We are not now that strength which in old days
Moved earth and heaven, that which we are, we are—
One equal temper of heroic hearts,
Made weak by time and fate, but strong in will
To strive, to seek, to find, and not to yield.   70

4. Proper, appropriate.
5. Summery paradise in the western ocean for heroes.

ROBERT BROWNING

1812–1889

Vengeful monks, murderous lovers, and megalomaniacal dukes: Robert Browning's characters are almost always outrageous in one way or another. Seeming quite unpoetic, they sputter, growl, and grunt. They also go to tremendous trouble to reason with us, elaborately explaining and justifying themselves. But the charms of Browning's poetry, while different from the delights of lyrical beauty we might usually associate with poetry, are great in their own way: vividly realized personalities—often extreme and eccentric—come to life in his pages, and as they talk to us, they hint at hidden truths which they do not mean to reveal. Reading Browning is therefore a little like reading a mystery novel: we have to figure out the real story from a character's self-justifying words.

The beloved son of an educated middle-class banker in London, Robert Browning read voraciously as a child and young man, learning Latin, Greek, French, and Italian. He was fascinated by the theater and tried to write verse drama, but eventually he found his vocation in the poetic genre of the dramatic monologue. Like monologues spoken on stage, these first-person poems are spoken by characters in a setting. Often the poet makes clear that there is a silent audience present. Many of Browning's first readers were thoroughly perplexed by these works: expecting lyric poetry to express the thoughts and feelings of the poet, they were shocked to find Browning's speakers confessing to murder, raging jealousy, and blasphemy. What could these poems mean? Condemned as obscure and incomprehensible, Browning's first works won him few admirers, but he adamantly refused to change his work to please the "hucksters," as he called his critics.

Stirred by admiration for **Elizabeth Barrett**, the most famous woman poet of his time, Browning wrote her a fan letter in 1845. He declared that he loved her books. He then added—without ever having met her—"and I love you too." She was an invalid, six years his senior, a world-renowned poet trapped in her home by a tyrannical father. He was self-confident and fashionable, a little-known young writer inclined to wear lemon-colored gloves. They eloped the following year to Italy, where he was often called "Mrs. Browning's husband." Her death in 1861 brought a happy marriage to an end. In the 1860s, he began to develop a reputation as a great writer in his own right, celebrated both as a Christian sage and as an exciting innovator who was paving the way for a newly skeptical, experimental, quintessentially modern kind of poetry.

Browning's dramatic monologues depart from the expressive lyrics so popular among the Romantic poets, which dwell on the thoughts and feelings of the individual self. Poems such as "Porphyria's Lover" and "My Last Duchess" imply that such an intense confidence in self-expression can lead to the silencing of others—even to murder. The dramatic monologue offers ideal opportunities for an ironic perspective on self-absorption: displaying a persona separate from the author, it can both draw us into another's viewpoint and distance us from it. "My Last

Duchess" is an especially brilliant example of this double experience, since we are likely to be initially seduced by the articulate and gracious Duke, only to realize, gradually, that he is so vain and jealous that he has had his wife killed on the strength of scant evidence.

Browning's characters are vibrant and brilliantly realized in ways that might remind us of the pleasures we associate with drama or fiction, and they can tempt us to overlook Browning's extraordinary technical skill as a poet. "My Last Duchess," for example, is a poem that both rhymes and resists rhyme: if we look at the last words of each line, they look as though they resonate with the adjacent line, but if we read the sentences of the poem as if we were reading prose, just trying to follow the meaning of sentences, then we do not hear the rhymes. Browning here makes canny use of enjambment—the break between poetic lines that interrupts the flow of the sentence, which

continues on without punctuation— to ensure that the rhymes fall into the background. Similarly intriguing is the wholly new form of "Love Among the Ruins." Here, Browning divides each stanza so that one half addresses the present and the other the past. He then introduces alternating short lines, which seem more like asides or interjections than meaning-laden phrases necessary to the poem's flow or sense. Browning's characters, like his poetic forms, seem consumed with interruption, constantly stopping themselves mid-sentence to exclaim or justify themselves.

Before his death, Browning societies grew up on both sides of the Atlantic Ocean, and he was hailed as a seer. Despite growing praise and fame, Browning never wrote for the critics. "As I began, so shall I end," he said, "taking my own course, pleasing myself, or aiming at doing so, and thereby, I hope, pleasing God."

Porphyria's Lover

The rain set early in tonight,
　　The sullen wind was soon awake,
It tore the elm-tops down for spite,
　　And did its worst to vex the lake:
　　I listened with heart fit to break. 5
When glided in Porphyria;[1] straight
　　She shut the cold out and the storm,
And kneeled and made the cheerless grate
　　Blaze up, and all the cottage warm;
　　Which done, she rose, and from her form 10
Withdrew the dripping cloak and shawl,
　　And laid her soiled gloves by, untied
Her hat and let the damp hair fall,
　　And, last, she sat down by my side
　　And called me. When no voice replied, 15
She put my arm about her waist,
　　And made her smooth white shoulder bare,

1. Her name comes from the Greek word for purple, the color of royalty.

And all her yellow hair displaced,
    And, stooping, made my cheek lie there,
    And spread, o'er all, her yellow hair,   20
Murmuring how she loved me—she
    Too weak, for all her heart's endeavor,
To set its struggling passion free
    From pride, and vainer ties dissever,
    And give herself to me forever.   25
But passion sometimes would prevail,
    Nor could tonight's gay feast restrain
A sudden thought of one so pale
    For love of her, and all in vain:
    So, she was come through wind and rain.   30
Be sure I looked up at her eyes
    Happy and proud; at last I knew
Porphyria worshiped me: surprise
    Made my heart swell, and still it grew
    While I debated what to do.   35
That moment she was mine, mine, fair,
    Perfectly pure and good: I found
A thing to do, and all her hair
    In one long yellow string I wound
    Three times her little throat around,   40
And strangled her. No pain felt she;
    I am quite sure she felt no pain.
As a shut bud that holds a bee,
    I warily oped her lids: again
    Laughed the blue eyes without a stain.   45
And I untightened next the tress
    About her neck; her cheek once more
Blushed bright beneath my burning kiss:
    I propped her head up as before,
    Only, this time my shoulder bore   50
Her head, which droops upon it still:
    The smiling rosy little head,
So glad it has its utmost will,
    That all it scorned at once is fled,
    And I, its love, am gained instead!   55
Porphyria's love: she guessed not how
    Her darling one wish would be heard.
And thus we sit together now,
    And all night long we have not stirred,
    And yet God has not said a word!   60

Soliloquy of the Spanish Cloister

1

Gr-r-r—there go, my heart's abhorrence!
    Water your damned flowerpots, do!
If hate killed men, Brother Lawrence,
    God's blood, would not mine kill you!
What? your myrtle bush wants trimming?   5
    Oh, that rose has prior claims—
Needs its leaden vase filled brimming?
    Hell dry you up with its flames!

2

At the meal we sit together:
    Salve tibi![1] I must hear   10
Wise talk of the kind of weather,
    Sort of season, time of year:
Not a plenteous cork crop: scarcely
    Dare we hope oak-galls,[2] *I doubt:*
What's the Latin name for "parsley"?   15
    What's the Greek name for Swine's Snout?[3]

3

Whew! We'll have our platter burnished,
    Laid with care on our own shelf!
With a fire-new spoon we're furnished,
    And a goblet for ourself,   20
Rinsed like something sacrificial
    Ere 'tis fit to touch our chaps
Marked with L. for our initial!
    (He-he! There his lily snaps!)

4

Saint, forsooth! While brown Dolores
    Squats outside the Convent bank   25
With Sanchicha, telling stories,
    Steeping tresses in the tank,
Blue-black, lustrous, thick like horsehairs,
    —Can't I see his dead eye glow,
Bright as 'twere a Barbary corsair's?[4]   30
    (That is, if he'd let it show!)

---

1. "Hail to thee!" (Latin). Brother Lawrence speaks the words in italics.
2. Growths on oak trees used in tanning leather.
3. A name for a dandelion.
4. North African Muslim pirates; they captured Christians and enslaved them.

5

When he finishes refection,
  Knife and fork he never lays
Cross-wise, to my recollection,   35
  As do I, in Jesu's praise.
I the Trinity illustrate,
  Drinking watered orange pulp—
In three sips the Arian[5] frustrate;
  While he drains his at one gulp.   40

6

Oh, those melons? If he's able
  We're to have a feast! so nice!
One goes to the Abbot's table,
  All of us get each a slice.
How go on your flowers? None double?   45
  Not one fruit-sort can you spy?
Strange!—And I, too, at such trouble,
  Keep them close-nipped on the sly!

7

There's a great text in Galatians,[6]
  Once you trip on it, entails   50
Twenty-nine distinct damnations,
  One sure, if another fails:
If I trip him just a-dying,
  Sure of heaven as sure can be,
Spin him round and send him flying   55
  Off to hell, a Manichee?[7]

8

Or, my scrofulous French novel
  On gray paper with blunt type!
Simply glance at it, you grovel
  Hand and foot in Belial's gripe:[8]   60
If I double down its pages
  At the woeful sixteenth print,
When he gathers his greengages,
  Ope a sieve and slip it in't?

---

5. Arius (250–336 C.E.) was a heretic; he and his followers denied the Trinity.
6. The speaker hopes to send Brother Lawrence to hell by tripping him up on rules he claims to find in the Bible's book of Galatians.
7. Follower of the Persian prophet Mani (ca. 216–276 C.E.), who saw the world as a great struggle between light and darkness; Manicheans were considered heretics by the Catholic Church.
8. The grip of Belial, a demon, one of the four princes of hell.

9

Or, there's Satan!—one might venture   65
    Pledge one's soul to him, yet leave
Such a flaw in the indenture
    As he'd miss till, past retrieve,
Blasted lay that rose-acacia[9]
    We're so proud of! *Hy, Zy, Hine*[1]   70
'St, there's Vespers! *Plena gratiâ*
    Ave, Virgo![2] Gr-r-r—you swine!

My Last Duchess[1]

Ferrara

That's my last Duchess painted on the wall,
Looking as if she were alive. I call
That piece a wonder, now: Frà Pandolf's[2] hands
Worked busily a day, and there she stands.
Will 't please you sit and look at her? I said   5
"Frà Pandolf" by design, for never read
Strangers like you that pictured countenance,
The depth and passion of its earnest glance,
But to myself they turned (since none puts by
The curtain I have drawn for you, but I)   10
And seemed as they would ask me, if they durst,
How such a glance came there; so, not the first
Are you to turn and ask thus. Sir, 'twas not
Her husband's presence only, called that spot
Of joy into the Duchess' cheek: perhaps   15
Frà Pandolf chanced to say "Her mantle laps
Over my lady's wrist too much," or "Paint
Must never hope to reproduce the faint
Half-flush that dies along her throat": such stuff
Was courtesy, she thought, and cause enough   20
For calling up that spot of joy. She had
A heart—how shall I say?—too soon made glad,
Too easily impressed; she liked whate'er
She looked on, and her looks went everywhere.
Sir, 'twas all one! My favor at her breast,   25
The dropping of the daylight in the West,

The bough of cherries some officious fool
Broke in the orchard for her, the white mule
She rode with round the terrace—all and each
Would draw from her alike the approving speech, 30
Or blush, at least. She thanked men—good! but thanked
Somehow—I know not how—as if she ranked
My gift of a nine-hundred-years-old name
With anybody's gift. Who'd stoop to blame
This sort of trifling? Even had you skill 35
In speech—(which I have not)—to make your will
Quite clear to such an one, and say, "Just this
Or that in you disgusts me; here you miss,
Or there exceed the mark"—and if she let
Herself be lessoned so, nor plainly set 40
Her wits to yours, forsooth, and made excuse
—E'en then would be some stooping; and I choose
Never to stoop. Oh sir, she smiled, no doubt,
Whene'er I passed her; but who passed without
Much the same smile? This grew; I gave commands; 45
Then all smiles stopped together. There she stands
As if alive. Will 't please you rise? We'll meet
The company below, then. I repeat,
The Count your master's known munificence
Is ample warrant that no just pretense 50
Of mine for dowry will be disallowed;
Though his fair daughter's self, as I avowed
At starting, is my object. Nay, we'll go
Together down, sir. Notice Neptune, though,
Taming a sea horse, thought a rarity, 55
Which Claus of Innsbruck³ cast in bronze for me!

Love among the Ruins

I

Where the quiet-colored end of evening smiles,
    Miles and miles
On the solitary pastures where our sheep
    Half-asleep
Tinkle homeward through the twilight, stray or stop 5
    As they crop—
Was the site once of a city great and gay
    (So they say),
Of our country's very capital, its prince
    Ages since 10
Held his court in, gathered councils, wielding far
    Peace or war.

---

3. An imaginary artist.

2

Now—the country does not even boast a tree,
　　As you see,
To distinguish slopes of verdure, certain rills　　　　　　15
　　From the hills
Intersect and give a name to (else they run
　　Into one),
Where the domed and daring palace shot its spires
　　Up like fires　　　　　　　　　　　　　　　　　20
O'er the hundred-gated circuit of a wall
　　Bounding all,
Made of marble, men might march on nor be pressed,
　　Twelve abreast.

3

And such plenty and perfection, see, of grass
　　Never was!　　　　　　　　　　　　　　　　　25
Such a carpet as, this summertime, o'erspreads
　　And embeds
Every vestige of the city, guessed alone,
　　Stock or stone—　　　　　　　　　　　　　　30
Where a multitude of men breathed joy and woe
　　Long ago;
Lust of glory pricked their hearts up, dread of shame
　　Struck them tame;
And that glory and that shame alike, the gold　　　　　35
　　Bought and sold.

4

Now—the single little turret that remains
　　On the plains,
By the caper overrooted, by the gourd
　　Overscored,　　　　　　　　　　　　　　　　40
While the patching houseleek's head of blossom winks
　　Through the chinks—
Marks the basement whence a tower in ancient time
　　Sprang sublime,
And a burning ring, all round, the chariots traced　　　45
　　As they raced,
And the monarch and his minions and his dames
　　Viewed the games.

5

And I know, while thus the quiet-colored eve
　　Smiles to leave
To their folding, all our many-tinkling fleece　　　　　50
　　In such peace,

And the slopes and rills in undistinguished gray
    Melt away—
That a girl with eager eyes and yellow hair   55
    Waits me there
In the turret whence the charioteers caught soul
    For the goal,
When the king looked, where she looks now, breathless, dumb
    Till I come.   60

6

But he looked upon the city, every side,
    Far and wide,
All the mountains topped with temples, all the glades
    Colonnades,
All the causeys,[1] bridges, aqueducts—and then,   65
    All the men!
When I do come, she will speak not, she will stand,
    Either hand
On my shoulder, give her eyes the first embrace
    Of my face,   70
Ere we rush, ere we extinguish sight and speech
    Each on each.

7

In one year they sent a million fighters forth
    South and north,
And they built their gods a brazen pillar high   75
    As the sky,
Yet reserved a thousand chariots in full force—
    Gold, of course.
Oh heart! oh blood that freezes, blood that burns!
    Earth's returns   80
For whole centuries of folly, noise, and sin!
    Shut them in,
With their triumphs and their glories and the rest!
    Love is best.

---

1. Causeways or raised roads.

WALT WHITMAN

1819–1892

Walt Whitman left an astonishing legacy. In rejecting conventional rhyme and meter he managed, almost single-handedly, to make free verse seem like the most appropriate form for a truly modern poetry. He insisted on a homegrown American art that would supplant European influence. He cast the poet as a fighter and a leader. He prized free and full sexual pleasure, celebrating "the body electric." And he gave voice to a vast range of ordinary people who had gone largely unnoticed by poets before him. "I am big—I contain multitudes," he wrote. Affirmative, inclusive, energetic, defiant, and radically experimental, Whitman ushered in a whole new era in American poetry.

LIFE

Born on Long Island, Whitman moved with his family to Brooklyn as a child. His father deeply admired American democracy, naming three of his sons George Washington, Thomas Jefferson, and Andrew Jackson. The young Whitman grew up among Deists and Quakers, creeds that favored an internal spirituality over formal religious doctrines. He left school at the age of eleven and worked odd jobs, first as a printer, later as a schoolteacher, builder, bookstore owner, journalist, and poet. He spent a few months in New Orleans and came to love the South, though he vehemently opposed slavery and petitioned to prevent its westward expansion. During the Civil War, Whitman felt a passionate admiration for Abraham Lincoln and was devoted to the Union cause. He was also deeply moved by the soldiers at the front, so much so that he went to Washington as a volunteer nurse, helping to care for the Civil War wounded and witnessing firsthand the devastating spectacle of corpses and amputated limbs. While in Washington he worked as a clerk in several government departments, including the Bureau of Indian Affairs. In 1865 Whitman met Peter Doyle, a young horsecar conductor who became his companion and almost certainly his lover. A few years later he settled in Camden, New Jersey, where he remained for the rest of his life.

WORK

Whitman began writing in his youth, producing a good deal of bad poetry and a novel about temperance, the movement advocating abstinence from alcohol. But something altogether different emerged in 1855 with his innovative collection of poems, *Leaves of Grass*. This volume departed from convention in startling ways. First of all, it did not look like the poetry of his contemporaries: there were no rhymes; the lines varied widely in length; and the words followed no particular rhythm. Second, the collection's themes were shocking: many readers were appalled by the unusually vivid sexual imagery and the intense evocations of bodily pleasure. Whitman also overturned convention by insisting on a vehemently democratic kind of verse, appealing to the common reader and celebrating the most overlooked people, from slaves and prostitutes to immigrants and prisoners. Finally, his poetic language was eccentrically various, moving between beauty and slang, between spirituality and obscenity. This was a poetry that aimed to include all of modern life. A poet fails, Whitman wrote, "if he does not flood himself with the immediate age as with vast oceanic tides . . . if he be not himself the age transfigured."

Whitman always loved the theater, and he deliberately adopted many voices and personae in his poetry. The *I* of his poems represents many selves. Perhaps most famously, the poet ventriloquizes a new urban type called the "b'hoy," a rebellious young working-class New Yorker known for his idle loafing and his willingness to fight, as well as his insolent, loud, slangy way of speaking. Whitman saw ordinary speech as the best source for poetry. "Language," he wrote, "is not an abstract construction of the learn'd, or of the dictionary-makers, but is something arising out of the work, needs, ties, joys, affections, tastes, of long generations of humanity, and has its bases broad and low, close to the ground. Its final decisions are made by the masses." Whitman's long lines also follow the patterns of ordinary language: rather than forming sentences broken up in accordance with conventions of rhyme or meter, each line is a statement complete in itself.

The innovations of *Leaves of Grass* did not sit well with the volume's first readers. "Walt Whitman," wrote one reviewer, "is as unacquainted with art as a hog is with mathematics." Another dismissed the book as "a mass of stupid filth." Even Henry David Thoreau said, "It is as if beasts spoke." Whitman was unperturbed by these attacks: he had intended to unsettle his readers, and he even publicized his most venomous reviews as a way of promoting his work.

But Whitman would soon come to be seen as one of the great poets of the United States, perhaps the greatest. In part this was because the nation was such a crucial focus for his work. He was deliberately writing a new, quin-tessentially American poetry, an art form that would leave European values and traditions behind to celebrate a modern, pluralistic democracy. At a moment when Europe was widely assumed to represent the standard for art and culture, Whitman wrote: "The Americans of all nations at any time upon the earth, have probably the fullest poetical nature. The United States themselves are essentially the greatest poem." And if the nation was a poem, the poet was its best leader. With the exception of Lincoln, Whitman despised politicians ("swarms of cringers, suckers, doughfaces, planners of the sly involutions for their own preferment to city offices or state legislatures or the judiciary or congress or the presidency"), and, as the United States fractured on the eve of Civil War, he imagined the poet alone as capable of healing and uniting the nation.

His way of healing, of course, involved confrontation and defiance. "I think agitation is the most important factor of all," he wrote. "To stir, to question, to suspect, to examine, to denounce!" What upset his contemporaries most was his willingness to defy conventions of silence around sex and sexuality. In 1882 he was threatened with an obscenity prosecution. Intriguingly, Whitman's contemporaries objected more to his eroticized representations of women than to the explicit expressions of male-male desire that appear often in his works. This was a cultural and historical context in which the "manly love" Whitman celebrated could be understood in idealized, nonsexual terms.

Whitman reworked *Leaves of Grass* many times, revising old poems and including new ones. Over time, he included explicitly patriotic work and toned down the most sexually offensive passages. By the end of his life he had come to seem not the rebellious purveyor of scandalous experiments, but simply "the good gray poet."

From Song of Myself[1]

1

I celebrate myself, and sing myself,
And what I assume you shall assume,
For every atom belonging to me as good belongs to you.

I loafe and invite my soul,
I lean and loafe at my ease observing a spear of summer grass.   5

My tongue, every atom of my blood, formed from this soil, this air,
Born here of parents born here from parents the same, and their parents
    the same,
I, now thirty-seven years old in perfect health begin,
Hoping to cease not till death.

Creeds and schools in abeyance,   10
Retiring back a while suffced at what they are, but never forgotten,
I harbor for good or bad, I permit to speak at every hazard,
Nature without check with original energy.

* * *

4

Trippers and askers surround me,
People I meet, the effect upon me of my early life or the ward and city
    I live in, or the nation,
The latest dates, discoveries, inventions, societies, authors old and new,
My dinner, dress, associates, looks, compliments, dues,
The real or fancied indifference of some man or woman I love,   5
The sickness of one of my folks or of myself, or ill-doing or loss or lack of
    money, or depressions or exaltations,
Battles, the horrors of fratricidal war, the fever of doubtful news, the fitful
    events;
These come to me days and nights and go from me again,
But they are not the Me myself.

Apart from the pulling and hauling stands what I am,   10
Stands amused, complacent, compassionating, idle, unitary,
Looks down, is erect, or bends an arm on an impalpable certain rest,
Looking with side-curved head curious what will come next,
Both in and out of the game and watching and wondering at it.

Backward I see in my own days where I sweated through fog with linguists
    and contenders,
I have no mockings or arguments, I witness and wait.   15

* * *

1. First published in 1855. This text is from the 1891–92 edition of *Leaves of Grass*, the so-
called Deathbed Edition.

7

Has any one supposed it lucky to be born?
I hasten to inform him or her it is just as lucky to die, and I know it.

I pass death with the dying and birth with the new-washed babe, and
    am not contained between my hat and boots,
And peruse manifold objects, no two alike and every one good,
The earth good and the stars good, and their adjuncts all good.   5

I am not an earth nor an adjunct of an earth,
I am the mate and companion of people, all just as immortal and fathomless
    as myself,
(They do not know how immortal, but I know.)

Every kind for itself and its own, for me mine male and female,
For me those that have been boys and that love women,   10
For me the man that is proud and feels how it stings to be slighted,
For me the sweet-heart and the old maid, for me mothers and the mothers
    of mothers,
For me lips that have smiled, eyes that have shed tears,
For me children and the begetters of children.

Undrape! you are not guilty to me, nor stale nor discarded,   15
I see through the broadcloth and gingham whether or no,
And am around, tenacious, acquisitive, tireless, and cannot be shaken away.

* * *

16

I am of old and young, of the foolish as much as the wise,
Regardless of others, ever regardful of others,
Maternal as well as paternal, a child as well as a man,
Stuffed with the stuff that is coarse and stuffed with the stuff that is fine,
One of the Nation of many nations, the smallest the same and the largest
    the same,   5
A Southerner soon as a Northerner, a planter nonchalant and hospitable
    down by the Oconee[2] I live,
A Yankee bound my own was ready for trade, my joints the limberest joints
    on earth and the sternest joints on earth,
A Kentuckian walking the vale of the Elkhorn in my deer-skin leggings, a
    Louisianian or Georgian,
A boatman over lakes or bays or along coasts, a Hoosier, Badger, Buckeye;
At home on Kanadian snow-shoes or up in the bush, or with fishermen off
    Newfoundland,   10
At home in the fleet of ice-boats, sailing with the rest and tacking,
At home on the hills of Vermont or in the woods of Maine, or the Texan
    ranch,

2. River in Georgia.

Comrade of Californians, comrade of free North-Westerners, (loving their
    big proportions,)
Comrade of raftsmen and coalmen, comrade of all who shake hands and
    welcome to drink and meat,
A learner with the simplest, a teacher of the thoughtfullest,   15
A novice beginning yet experient of myriads of seasons,
Of every hue and caste am I, of every rank and religion,
A farmer, mechanic, artist, gentleman, sailor, quaker,
Prisoner, fancy-man, rowdy, lawyer, physician, priest.

I resist any thing better than my own diversity,   20
Breathe the air but leave plenty after me,
And am not stuck up, and am in my place.

(The moth and the fish-eggs are in their place,
The bright suns I see and the dark suns I cannot see are in their place,
The palpable is in its place and the impalpable is in its place.)   25

* * *

21

I am the poet of the Body and I am the poet of the Soul,
The pleasures of heaven are with me and the pains of hell are with me,
The first I graft and increase upon myself, the latter I translate into a new
    tongue.

I am the poet of the woman the same as the man,
And I say it is as great to be a woman as to be a man,   5
And I say there is nothing greater than the mother of men.

I chant the chant of dilation or pride,
We have had ducking and deprecating about enough,
I show that size is only development.

Have you outstript the rest? are you the President?   10
It is a trifle, they will more than arrive there every one, and still pass on.

I am he that walks with the tender and growing night,
I call to the earth and sea half-held by the night.

Press close bare-bosomed night—press close magnetic nourishing night!
Night of south winds—night of the large few stars!   15
Still nodding night—mad naked summer night.

Smile O voluptuous cool-breathed earth!
Earth of the slumbering and liquid trees!
Earth of departed sunset—earth of the mountains misty-topt!
Earth of the vitreous pour of the full moon just tinged with blue!   20
Earth of shine and dark mottling the tide of the river!
Earth of the limpid gray of clouds brighter and clearer for my sake!

Far-swooping elbowed earth—rich apple-blossomed earth!
Smile, for your lover comes.

Prodigal, you have given me love—therefore I to you give love!   25
O unspeakable passionate love.

* * *

24

Walt Whitman, a kosmos, of Manhattan the son,
Turbulent, fleshy, sensual, eating, drinking and breeding,
No sentimentalist, no stander above men and women or apart from them,
No more modest than immodest.

Unscrew the locks from the doors!   5
Unscrew the doors themselves from their jambs!

Whoever degrades another degrades me,
And whatever is done or said returns at last to me.

Through me the afflatus surging and surging, through me the current and
      index.

I speak the pass-word primeval, I give the sign of democracy,   10
By God! I will accept nothing which all cannot have their counterpart of
      on the same terms.

* * *

32

I think I could turn and live with animals, they are so placid and self-
      contained,
I stand and look at them long and long.

They do not sweat and whine about their condition,
They do not lie awake in the dark and weep for their sins,
They do not make me sick discussing their duty to God,   5
Not one is dissatisfied, not one is demented with the mania of owning things,
Not one kneels to another, nor to his kind that lived thousands of years ago,
Not one is respectable or unhappy over the whole earth.

So they show their relations to me and I accept them,
They bring me tokens of myself, they evince them plainly in their
      possession.   10

I wonder where they get those tokens,
Did I pass that way huge times ago and negligently drop them?

Myself moving forward then and now and forever,
Gathering and showing more always and with velocity,

Infinite and omnigenous,[3] and the like of these among them,   15
Not too exclusive toward the reachers of my remembrancers,
Picking out here one that I love, and now go with him on brotherly terms.

A gigantic beauty of a stallion, fresh and responsive to my caresses,
Head high in the forehead, wide between the ears,
Limbs glossy and supple, tail dusting the ground,   20
Eyes full of sparkling wickedness, ears finely cut, flexibly moving.

His nostrils dilate as my heels embrace him,
His well-built limbs tremble with pleasure as we race around and return.

I but use you a minute, then I resign you, stallion,
Why do I need your paces when I myself out-gallop them?   25
Even as I stand or sit passing faster than you.

* * *

46

I know I have the best of time and space, and was never measured and
        never will be measured.

I tramp a perpetual journey, (come listen all!)
My signs are a rain-proof coat, good shoes, and a staff cut from the woods,
No friend of mine takes his ease in my chair,
I have no chair, no church, no philosophy,   5
I lead no man to a dinner-table, library, exchange,
But each man and each woman of you I lead upon a knoll,
My left hand hooking you round the waist,
My right hand pointing to landscapes of continents and the public road.
Not I, not any one else can travel that road for you,   10
You must travel it for yourself.

It is not far, it is within reach,
Perhaps you have been on it since you were born and did not know,
Perhaps it is everywhere on water and on land.

Shoulder your duds dear son, and I will mine, and let us hasten forth,   15
Wonderful cities and free nations we shall fetch as we go.

* * *

51

The past and present wilt—I have filled them, emptied them,
And proceed to fill my next fold of the future.

Listener up there! what have you to confide to me?
Look in my face while I snuff the sidle of evening[4]

---

3. Belonging to all races.

4. I.e., smell the fragrance of the slowly descending evening.

(Talk honestly, no one else hears you, and I stay only a minute longer.) 5
Do I contradict myself?
Very well then I contradict myself,
(I am large, I contain multitudes.)

I concentrate toward them that are nigh, I wait on the door-slab.

Who has done his day's work? who will soonest be through with his
    supper?
Who wishes to walk with me? 10

Will you speak before I am gone? will you prove already too late?

52

The spotted hawk swoops by and accuses me, he complains of my gab
    and my loitering.

I too am not a bit tamed, I too am untranslatable,
I sound my barbaric yawp over the roofs of the world.

The last scud of day holds back for me,
It flings my likeness after the rest and true as any on the shadowed wilds, 5
It coaxes me to the vapor and the dusk.

I depart as air, I shake my white locks at the runaway sun,
I effuse my flesh in eddies, and drift it in lacy jags.

I bequeath myself to the dirt to grow from the grass I love,
If you want me again look for me under your boot-soles. 10

You will hardly know who I am or what I mean,
But I shall be good health to you nevertheless,
And filter and fibre your blood.

Failing to fetch me at first keep encouraged,
Missing me one place search another, 15
I stop somewhere waiting for you.

Out of the Cradle Endlessly Rocking

Out of the cradle endlessly rocking,
Out of the mocking-bird's throat, the musical shuttle,
Out of the Ninth-month[1] midnight,
Over the sterile sands and the fields beyond, where the child leaving
    his bed wandered alone, bareheaded, barefoot,
Down from the showered halo, 5
Up from the mystic play of shadows twining and twisting as if they
    were alive,

---

1. September, in Quaker usage.

Out from the patches of briers and blackberries,
From the memories of the bird that chanted to me,
From your memories sad brother, from the fitful risings and fallings I
  heard.
From under that yellow half-moon late-risen and swollen as if with tears,   10
From those beginning notes of yearning and love there in the mist,
From the thousand responses of my heart never to cease,
From the myriad thence-aroused words,
From the word stronger and more delicious than any,
From such as now they start the scene revisiting,   15
As a flock, twittering, rising, or overhead passing,
Borne hither, ere all eludes me, hurriedly,
A man, yet by these tears a little boy again,
Throwing myself on the sand, confronting the waves,
I, chanter of pains and joys, uniter of here and hereafter,   20
Taking all hints to use them, but swiftly leaping beyond them,
A reminiscence sing.

Once Paumanok,[2]
When the lilac-scent was in the air and Fifth-month[3] grass was growing,
Up this seashore in some briers,   25
Two feathered guests from Alabama, two together,
And their nest, and four light-green eggs spotted with brown,
And every day the he-bird to and fro near at hand,
And every day the she-bird crouched on her nest, silent, with bright eyes,
And every day I, a curious boy, never too close, never disturbing them,   30
Cautiously peering, absorbing, translating.

Shine! shine! shine!
Pour down your warmth, great sun!
While we bask, we two together.

Two together!   35
Winds blow south, or winds blow north,
Day come white, or night come black,

Home, or rivers and mountains from home,
Singing all time, minding no time,
While we two keep together.   40

Till of a sudden,
Maybe killed, unknown to her mate,
One forenoon the she-bird crouched not on the nest,
Nor returned that afternoon, nor the next,
Nor ever appeared again.   45

And thenceforward all summer in the sound of the sea,
And at night under the full of the moon in calmer weather,
Over the hoarse surging of the sea,

2. Pronounced *paw-mah'-nok*. The Native
American name for Long Island, where Whit-

man grew up.
3. May.

Or flitting from brier to brier by day,
I saw, I heard at intervals the remaining one, the he-bird, 50
The solitary guest from Alabama.

Blow! blow! blow!
Blow up sea-winds along Paumanok's shore;
I wait and I wait till you blow my mate to me.

Yes, when the stars glistened, 55
All night long on the prong of a moss-scalloped stake,
Down almost amid the slapping waves,
Sat the lone singer wonderful causing tears.

He called on his mate,
He poured forth the meanings which I of all men know. 60

Yes my brother I know,
The rest might not, but I have treasured every note,
For more than once dimly down to the beach gliding,
Silent, avoiding the moonbeams, blending myself with the shadows,
Recalling now the obscure shapes, the echoes, the sounds and sights
    after their sorts, 65
The white arms out in the breakers tirelessly tossing,
I, with bare feet, a child, the wind wafting my hair,
Listened long and long.

Listened to keep, to sing, now translating the notes,
Following you my brother. 70

Soothe! soothe! soothe!
Close on its wave soothes the wave behind,
And again another behind embracing and lapping, every one close,
But my love soothes not me, not me.

Low hangs the moon, it rose late, 75
It is lagging—O I think it is heavy with love, with love.

O madly the sea pushes upon the land,
With love, with love.

O night! do I not see my love fluttering out among the breakers?
What is that little black thing I see there in the white? 80

Loud! loud! loud!
Loud I call to you, my love!
High and clear I shoot my voice over the waves,
Surely you must know who is here, is here,
You must know who I am, my love. 85

Low-hanging moon!
What is that dusky spot in your brown yellow?

O it is the shape, the shape of my mate!
O moon do not keep her from me any longer.

Land! land! O land!   90
Whichever way I turn, O I think you could give me my mate back again
    if you only would,
For I am almost sure I see her dimly whichever way I look.

O rising stars!
Perhaps the one I want so much will rise, will rise with some of you.

O throat! O trembling throat!   95
Sound clearer through the atmosphere!
Pierce the woods, the earth,
Somewhere listening to catch you must be the one I want.

Shake out carols!
Solitary here, the night's carols!   100
Carols of lonesome love! death's carols!
Carols under that lagging, yellow, waning moon!
O under that moon where she droops almost down into the sea!
O reckless despairing carols.

But soft! sink low!   105
Soft! let me just murmur,
And do you wait a moment you husky-noised sea,
For somewhere I believe I heard my mate responding to me,
So faint, I must be still, be still to listen,
But not altogether still, for then she might not come
    immediately to me.   110

Hither my love!
Here I am! here!
With this just-sustained note I announce myself to you,
This gentle call is for you my love, for you.

Do not be decoyed elsewhere,   115
That is the whistle of the wind, it is not my voice,
That is the fluttering, the fluttering of the spray,
Those are the shadows of leaves.

O darkness! O in vain!
O I am very sick and sorrowful.   120

O brown halo in the sky near the moon, drooping upon the sea!
O troubled reflection in the sea!
O throat! O throbbing heart!
And I singing uselessly, uselessly all the night.

O past! O happy life! O songs of joy!   125
In the air, in the woods, over fields,

Loved! loved! loved! loved! loved!
But my mate no more, no more with me!
We two together no more.

The aria sinking,　　　　　　　　　　　　　　　　　　　　　　130
All else continuing, the stars shining,
The winds blowing, the notes of the bird continuous echoing,
With angry moans the fierce old mother incessantly moaning,
On the sands of Paumanok's shore gray and rustling,
The yellow half-moon enlarged, sagging down, drooping, the face of
　　　the sea almost touching,　　　　　　　　　　　　　　135
The boy ecstatic, with his bare feet the waves, with his hair the
　　　atmosphere dallying,
The love in the heart long pent, now loose, now at last tumultuously bursting,
The aria's meaning, the ears, the soul, swiftly depositing,
The strange tears down the cheeks coursing,
The colloquy there, the trio, each uttering,　　　　　　　　　140
The undertone, the savage old mother incessantly crying,
To the boy's soul's questions sullenly timing, some drowned secret hissing,
To the outsetting bard.

Demon or bird! (said the boy's soul,)
Is it indeed toward your mate you sing? or is it really to me?　　145
For I, that was a child, my tongue's use sleeping, now I have heard you,
Now in a moment I know what I am for, I awake,
And already a thousand singers, a thousand songs, clearer, louder and
　　　more sorrowful than yours,
A thousand warbling echoes have started to life within me, never to die.

O you singer solitary, singing by yourself, projecting me,　　　150
O solitary me listening, never more shall I cease perpetuating you,
Never more shall I escape, never more the reverberations,
Never more the cries of unsatisfied love be absent from me,
Never again leave me to be the peaceful child I was before what there
　　　in the night,
By the sea under the yellow and sagging moon,　　　　　　155
The messenger there aroused, the fire, the sweet hell within,
The unknown want, the destiny of me.

O give me the clue! (it lurks in the night here somewhere,)
O if I am to have so much, let me have more!

A word then, (for I will conquer it,)　　　　　　　　　　　160
The word final, superior to all,
Subtle, sent up—what is it?—I listen;
Are you whispering it, and have been all the time, you sea-waves?
Is that it from your liquid rims and wet sands?

Whereto answering, the sea,　　　　　　　　　　　　　　165
Delaying not, hurrying not,
Whispered me through the night, and very plainly before daybreak,

Lisped to me the low and delicious word death,
And again death, death, death, death,
Hissing melodious, neither like the bird nor like my aroused child's heart,   170
But edging near as privately for me rustling at my feet,
Creeping thence steadily up to my ears and laving me softly all over.
Death, death, death, death, death.

Which I do not forget,
But fuse the song of my dusky demon and brother,   175
That he sang to me in the moonlight on Paumanok's gray beach,
With the thousand responsive songs at random,
My own songs awaked from that hour,
And with them the key, the word up from the waves,
The word of the sweetest song and all songs,   180
That strong and delicious word which, creeping to my feet,
(Or like some old crone rocking the cradle, swathed in sweet garments,
      bending aside,)
The sea whispered me.

When Lilacs Last in the Dooryard Bloom'd[1]

1

When lilacs last in the dooryard bloom'd,
And the great star early droop'd in the western sky in the night,
I mourn'd, and yet shall mourn with ever-returning spring.

Ever-returning spring, trinity sure to me you bring,
Lilac blooming perennial and drooping star in the west,   5
And thought of him I love.

2

O powerful western fallen star!
O shades of night—O moody, tearful night!
O great star disappear'd—O the black murk that hides the star!
O cruel hands that hold me powerless—O helpless soul of me!   10
O harsh surrounding cloud that will not free my soul.

3

In the dooryard fronting an old farm-house near the white-wash'd
      palings,
Stands the lilac-bush tall-growing with heart-shaped leaves of
      rich green,

1. Elegy written after the death of Abraham Lincoln; the poem follows Lincoln's coffin to its
burial place.

With many a pointed blossom rising delicate, with the perfume
    strong I love,
With every leaf a miracle—and from this bush in the dooryard,   15
With delicate-color'd blossoms and heart-shaped leaves of rich green,
A sprig with its flower I break.

4

In the swamp in secluded recesses,
A shy and hidden bird is warbling a song.
Solitary the thrush,   20
The hermit withdrawn to himself, avoiding the settlements,
Sings by himself a song.

Song of the bleeding throat,
Death's outlet song of life, (for well dear brother I know,
If though wast not granted to sing thou would'st surely die.)   25

5

Over the breast of the spring, the land, amid cities,
Amid lanes and through old woods, where lately the violets
    peep'd from the ground, spotting the gray debris,
Amid the grass in the fields each side of the lanes, passing
    the endless grass,
Passing the yellow-spear'd wheat, every grain from its shroud
    in the dark-brown fields uprisen,
Passing the apple-tree blows of white and pink in the orchards,   30
Carrying a corpse to where it shall rest in the grave,
Night and day journeys a coffin.

6

Coffin that passes through lanes and streets,
Through day and night with the great cloud darkening the land,
With the pomp of the inloop'd flags with the cities draped in   35
    black,
With the show of the States themselves as of crape-veil'd
    women standing,
With processions long and winding and the flambeaus of the night,
With the countless torches lit, with the silent sea of faces and
    the unbared heads,
With the waiting depot, the arriving coffin, and the sombre faces,
With dirges through the night, with the thousand voices rising
    strong and solemn,   40
With all the mournful voices of the dirges pour'd around the coffin,
The dim-lit churches and the shuddering organs—where amid
    these you journey,
With the tolling tolling bells' perpetual clang,
Here, coffin that slowly passes,
I give you my sprig of lilac.   45

7

(Nor for you, for one alone,
Blossoms and branches green to coffins all I bring,
For fresh as the morning, thus would I chant a song for you
    O sane and sacred death.

All over bouquets of roses,
O death, I cover you over with roses and early lilies,   50
But mostly and now the lilac that blooms the first,
Copious I break, I break the sprigs from the bushes,
With loaded arms I come, pouring for you,
For you and the coffins all of you O death.)

8

O western orb sailing the heaven,   55
Now I know what you must have meant as a month since I walk'd,
As I walk'd in silence the transparent shadowy night,
As I saw you had something to tell as you bent to me night after night,
As you droop'd from the sky low down as if to my side, (while
    the other stars all look'd on,)
As we wander'd together the solemn night, (for something I know
    not what kept me from sleep,)   60
As the night advanced, and I saw on the rim of the west how
    full you were of woe,
As I stood on the rising ground in the breeze in the cool
    transparent night,
As I watch'd where you pass'd and was lost in the netherward
    black of the night,
As my soul in its trouble dissatisfied sank, as where you sad orb,
Concluded, dropt in the night, and was gone.   65

9

Sing on there in the swamp,
O singer bashful and tender, I hear your notes, I hear your call,
I hear, I come presently, I understand you,
But a moment I linger, for the lustrous star has detain'd me,
The star my departing comrade holds and detains me.   70

10

O how shall I warble myself for the dead one there I loved?
And how shall I deck my song for the large sweet soul that has gone?
And what shall my perfume be for the grave of him I love?

Sea-winds blown from east and west,
Blown from the Eastern sea and blown from the Western sea,
    till there on the prairies meeting,   75
These and with these and the breath of my chant,
I'll perfume the grave of him I love.

11

O what shall I hang on the chamber walls?
And what shall the pictures be that I hang on the walls,
To adorn the burial-house of him I love?   80

Pictures of growing spring and farms and homes,
With the Fourth-month[2] eve at sundown, and the gray smoke
    lucid and bright,
With floods of the yellow gold of the gorgeous, indolent, sinking
    sun, burning, expanding the air,
With the fresh sweet herbage under foot, and the pale green leaves
    of the trees prolific,
In the distance the flowing glaze, the breast of the river, with a
    wind-dapple here and there,   85
With ranging hills on the banks, with many a line against the
    sky, and shadows,
And the city at hand with dwellings so dense, and stacks of
    chimneys,
And all the scenes of life and the workshops, and the workmen
    homeward returning.

12

Lo, body and soul—this land,
My own Manhattan with spires, and the sparkling and hurrying
    tides, and the ships,   90
The varied and ample land, the South and the North in the light,
    Ohio's shores and flashing Missouri,
And ever the far-spreading prairies cover'd with grass and corn.

Lo, the most excellent sun so calm and haughty,
The violet and purple morn with just-felt breezes,
The gentle soft-born measureless light,   95
The miracle spreading bathing all, the fulfill'd noon,
The coming eve delicious, the welcome night and the stars,
Over my cities shining all, enveloping man and land.

13

Sing on, sing on you gray-brown bird,
Sing from the swamps, the recesses, pour your chant from
    the bushes,
Limitless out of the dusk, out of the cedars and pines.   100

Sing on dearest brother, warble your reedy song,
Loud human song, with voice of uttermost woe.

O liquid and free and tender!
O wild and loose to my soul—O wondrous singer!   105

2. April.

You only I hear—yet the star holds me, (but will soon depart,)
Yet the lilac with mastering odor holds me.

14

Now while I sat in the day and look'd forth,
In the close of the day with its light and the fields of spring,
    and the farmers preparing their crops,
In the large unconscious scenery of my land with its lakes and
    forests,   110
In the heavenly aerial beauty, (after the perturb'd winds and the
    storms,)
Under the arching heavens of the afternoon swift passing, and
    the voices of children and women,
The many-moving sea-tides, and I saw the ships how they sail'd,
And the summer approaching with richness, and the fields all
    busy with labor,
And the infinite separate houses, how they all went on, each
    with its meals and minutia of daily usages,   115
And the streets how their throbbings throbb'd, and the cities
    pent—lo, then and there,
Falling upon them all and among them all, enveloping me with
    the rest,
Appear'd the cloud, appear'd the long black trail,
And I knew death, its thought, and the sacred knowledge of death.

Then with the knowledge of death as walking one side of me,   120
And the thought of death close-walking the other side of me,
And I in the middle as with companions, and as holding the hands
    of companions,
I fled forth to the hiding receiving night that talks not,
Down to the shores of the water, the path by the swamp in
    the dimness,
To the solemn shadowy cedars and ghostly pines so still.   125

And the singer so shy to the rest receiv'd me,
The gray-brown bird I know receiv'd us comrades three,
And he sang the carol of death, and a verse for him I love.

From deep secluded recesses,
From the fragrant cedars and the ghostly pines so still,   130
Came the carol of the bird.

And the charm of the carol rapt me,
As I held as if by their hands my comrades in the night,
And the voice of my spirit tallied the song of the bird.

Come lovely and soothing death,   135
Undulate round the world, serenely arriving, arriving,
In the day, in the night, to all, to each,
Sooner or later delicate death.

Prais'd be the fathomless universe,
For life and joy, and for objects and knowledge curious,   140
And for love, sweet love—but praise! praise! praise!
For the sure-enwinding arms of cool-enfolding death.

Dark mother always gliding near with soft feet,
Have none chanted for thee a chant of fullest welcome?
Then I chant it for thee, I glorify thee above all,   145
I bring thee a song that when thou must indeed come, come
*   unfalteringly.*

Approach strong deliveress,
When it is so, when thou hast taken them I joyously sing the dead,
Lost in the loving floating ocean of thee,
Laved in the flood of thy bliss O death.   150

From me to thee glad serenades,
Dances for thee I propose saluting thee, adornments and
*   feastings for thee,*
And the sights of the open landscape and the high-spread sky
*   are fitting,*
And life and the fields, and the huge and thoughtful night.
The night in silence under many a star,   155
The ocean shore and the husky whispering wave whose voice
*   I know,*
And the soul turning to thee O vast and well-veil'd death,
And the body gratefully nestling close to thee.

Over the tree-tops I float thee a song,
Over the rising and sinking waves, over the myriad fields and
*   the prairies wide,*
Over the dense-pack'd cities all and the teeming wharves and ways,   160
I float this carol with joy, with joy to thee O death.

15

To the tally of my soul,
Loud and strong kept up the gray-brown bird,
With pure deliberate notes spreading filling the night.   165

Loud in the pines and cedars dim,
Clear in the freshness moist and the swamp-perfume,
And I with my comrades there in the night.

While my sight that was bound in my eyes unclosed,
As to long panoramas of visions.   170

And I saw askant the armies,
I saw as in noiseless dreams hundreds of battle-flags,
Borne through the smoke of the battles and pierc'd with missiles
    I saw them,

And carried hither and yon through the smoke, and torn and
    bloody,
And at last but a few shreds left on the staffs, (and all in silence,)   175
And the staffs all splinter'd and broken.

I saw battle-corpses, myriads of them,
And the white skeletons of young men, I saw them,
I saw the debris and debris of all the slain soldiers of the war,
But I saw they were not as was thought,   180
They themselves were fully at rest, they suffer'd not,
The living remain'd and suffer'd, the mother suffer'd,
And the wife and the child and the musing comrade suffer'd,
And the armies that remain'd suffer'd.

16

Passing the visions, passing the night,   185
Passing, unloosing the hold of my comrades' hands,
Passing the song of the hermit bird and the tallying song of
    my soul,
Victorious song, death's outlet song, yet varying ever-altering song,
As low and wailing, yet clear the notes, rising and falling,
    flooding the night,
Sadly sinking and fainting, as warning and warning, and yet
    again bursting with joy,   190
Covering the earth and filling the spread of the heaven,
As that powerful psalm in the night I heard from recesses,
Passing, I leave thee lilac with heart-shaped leaves,
I leave thee there in the door-yard, blooming, returning with
    spring.

I cease from my song for thee,   195
From my gaze on thee in the west, fronting the west,
    communing with thee,
O comrade lustrous with silver face in the night.

Yet each to keep and all, retrievements out of the night,
The song, the wondrous chant of the gray-brown bird,
And the tallying chant, the echo arous'd in my soul,   200
With the lustrous and drooping star with the countenance full
    of woe,
With the holders holding my hand nearing the call of the bird,
Comrades mine and I in the midst, and their memory ever to
    keep, for the dead I loved so well,
For the sweetest, wisest soul of all my days and lands—and this
    for his dear sake,
Lilac and star and bird twined with the chant of my soul,   205
There in the fragrant pines and the cedars dusk and dim.

O Captain! My Captain![1]

O Captain! my Captain! our fearful trip is done,
The ship has weather'd every rack, the prize we sought is won,
The port is near, the bells I hear, the people all exulting,
While follow eyes the steady keel, the vessel grim and daring;
      But O heart! heart! heart!   5
        O the bleeding drops of red,
          Where on the deck my Captain lies,
            Fallen cold and dead.

O Captain! my Captain! rise up and hear the bells;
Rise up—for you the flag is flung—for you the bugle trills,   10
For you bouquets and ribbon'd wreaths—for you the shores
   a-crowding,
For you they call, the swaying mass, their eager faces turning;
        Here Captain! dear father!
         This arm beneath your head!
           It is some dream that on the deck,   15
            You've fallen cold and dead.

My Captain does not answer, his lips are pale and still,
My father does not feel my arm, he has no pulse nor will,
The ship is anchor'd safe and sound, its voyage closed and done,
From fearful trip the victor ship comes in with object won;   20
        Exult O shores, and ring O bells!
         But I with mournful tread,
          Walk the deck my Captain lies,
            Fallen cold and dead.

1. Elegy for Abraham Lincoln, who is imagined here as the captain of a ship.

CHARLES BAUDELAIRE

1821–1867

Crowds and prostitutes, boredom and hypocrisy, garbage and cheap perfume: from these ugly materials, Charles Baudelaire crafted such shocking, painful, and exquisite poetry that he became the most widely read French poet around the globe. Haunted by a vision of human nature as fallen and corrupt, he was drawn to explore his own weaknesses and transgressions, as well as the sins of society. Lust, hatred, laziness, a disabling self-awareness, a horror of death and decay, and above all an all-encompassing *ennui*—a kind of disgusted, existential boredom—consumed the poet. But it is not only this anguished worldview that makes Baudelaire so significant: for many thinkers who followed, he opened the way to understanding what it means to be modern, to live in the exciting, disorienting, technologically changing, often hideous world of the industrialized city. And for writers, what is so extraordinary about Baudelaire is that he examined the unsettling shocks of modernity through perfectly controlled and beautiful art forms.

LIFE

Born in Paris in 1821, Baudelaire quickly became a rebellious youth. His elderly father died when he was six, and his mother married a stern military man whom the young Baudelaire came to detest. In his late teens, he was expelled from boarding school and sent away on a boat to India to remove him from bad influences. He jumped ship on the African island of Mauritius, then slowly wended his way home without ever reaching India. Back in Paris, he began to consort with artists, bohemians, and prostitutes in the famous Latin Quarter. By his early twenties, he had contracted syphilis and had started to spend his father's inheritance with alarming speed, buying up gorgeous furniture, dandyish clothing, and costly paintings. In 1842 he fell passionately in love with a woman named Jeanne Duval, an actress of African descent, who lived with him on and off for most of his adult life. To his family, he seemed to be going nowhere. His mother was disturbed at his spending habits and obtained a court order to control his finances. Humiliated, Baudelaire remained for the rest of his life dependent on an allowance dispensed by the family lawyer.

In 1845 he published a work of art criticism that established his reputation as a writer, and he would go on to write important reviews of painting and photography, championing the most daring contemporary art. In the 1850s he reviewed and translated the works of American writer Edgar Allan Poe, who shared his dedication to beauty, his fascination with death, and his passion for perfectly crafted writing. Only in 1857, at the age of thirty-six, did his first slim volume of poetry appear. With its horrifyingly evocative images of lust, duplicity, and decay, *The Flowers of Evil* was fully intended to scandalize its readers. It succeeded. French authorities seized the book and fined the writer, making Baudelaire famous—but more reviled than admired. Ever more ill and in debt, Baudelaire spent his last years in distress. He added new poems to *The Flowers of Evil* and began to write some experimental works that would come to be known as *Paris Spleen*. He died in 1867, leaving behind few admirers. At the graveside, in the pouring rain, accompanied by a few stragglers, only one close friend predicted that Baudelaire would someday be recognized as a "poet of genius."

BAUDELAIRE'S PARIS

Most French poets of the first half of the nineteenth century were drawn to the beauties of the natural world: to mountains, lakes, and flowers. Baudelaire was different. "I find myself incapable of feeling moved by vegetation," he wrote. Instead, he observed the social life of the city.

At the time, Paris was an exciting and disorienting place. It grew rapidly over the first few decades of the nineteenth century, as new industries drew peasants from the impoverished countryside in search of work. Competing for badly paid jobs, the urban poor were visible everywhere, many of them sick from factory smoke, or reduced to beggary and prostitution. Also visible in the city, however, were the glossy carriages and flamboyant dresses of the rich. Commentators often remarked that on a single stroll through the city one might find ragpickers searching through street refuse for scraps to sell, as well as glittering new shopping arcades offering seductive, mass-produced commodities for wealthy consumers. Everything in this modern world, it seemed, could be bought and sold.

During the 1850s the streets of Paris underwent a huge transformation, as the government razed winding old alleyways and installed clean, wide boulevards in their place. These smooth streets radiated outward to allow easy access to the city center from many directions. The poor were evicted and moved in large numbers to the suburbs, while gleaming new apartment houses, street cafes, shops, and theaters rose up quickly. In this new urban milieu, one encountered vast numbers of strangers. Dramatically unlike village life, the city typically felt both crowded and lonely, both stimulating and alienating. Baudelaire used the term *flâneur*—meaning "saunterer"—to refer to those who wandered alone and detached through urban streets to experience the city's fleeting spectacles. Many of the first *flâneurs* were writers who found a new kind of inspiration in this fragmented experience. And so the bustling commercial city became an important literary theme, supplanting rural beauty for self-consciously "modern" writers in the decades to follow.

WORK

It is difficult to grasp just how shocking Baudelaire's work must have seemed to his contemporaries. French poets before him typically worked in what was called the "noble style," which was formal and elevated, deliberately remote from everyday speech. Poets were not supposed to refer to ordinary objects (even the word "nose" was forbidden as prosaic). We can only imagine, then, how outrageous Baudelaire's deliberately brutal wording— "pissing hogwash" or "lecherous whore"— must have seemed. And not only did he offer up explicit, often coarse, images of the body, but his contemporaries were horrified to find him willing to connect sexual desire to the horrors of sadism and putrefaction, as we see in his poem "A Carcass."

And yet it would be misleading to see Baudelaire as rejecting beauty: he luxuriated in gorgeous, lavish, and exotic images, and crafted passages of lyrical magnificence. Unlike some of his other rebellious-poet contemporaries—such as **Walt Whitman**, born just two years before him—Baudelaire loved strictly traditional metrical forms and rhyme schemes. And so it is worth exploring the ways that the poet associates the shockingly foul with the traditionally lovely. Even the very title of his volume, *The Flowers of Evil*, signals the juxtaposition of beauty with corruption.

Always attracted by dissonance and contrast, Baudelaire is famous for his irony—his willingness to undermine one perspective with another more-knowing, cynical point of view. Many of his works explore both lived experience and the desire to stand skeptically apart from that experience. In the process, Baudelaire's poetic speakers often emerge as self-divided, torn between beautiful ideals and what he called "spleen," a thoroughgoing disgust with life. (The ancient Greeks had believed that sadness originated with fluids of the spleen.)

Late in his life, Baudelaire experimented with "prose poems"—then highly innovative and, according to many of his contemporaries, confusingly paradoxical. Dissolving the distinction between poetry and prose, these brief pieces lack the line breaks associated with poetry, but they feel like lyric, capturing brief moments of experience in compressed and meditative passages. For Baudelaire, this kind of writing was momentous: he claimed to dream of "the miracle of a poetic prose, musical, without rhythm and without rhyme, supple enough and rugged enough to adapt itself to the lyrical impulses of the soul."

THE FLOWERS OF EVIL

To the Reader[1]

Infatuation, sadism, lust, avarice
possess our souls and drain the body's force;
we spoonfeed our adorable remorse,
like whores or beggars nourishing their lice.

Our sins are mulish, our confessions lies;   5
we play to the grandstand with our promises,
we pray for tears to wash our filthiness,
importantly pissing hogwash through our styes.

The devil, watching by our sickbeds, hissed
old smut and folk-songs to our soul, until   10
the soft and precious metal of our will
boiled off in vapor for this scientist.

Each day his flattery[2] makes us eat a toad,
and each step forward is a step to hell,
unmoved, though previous corpses and their smell   15
asphyxiate our progress on this road.

Like the poor lush who cannot satisfy,
we try to force our sex with counterfeits,
die drooling on the deliquescent tits,
mouthing the rotten orange we suck dry.   20

1. Translated by Robert Lowell. The translation pays primary attention to the insistent rhythm of the original poetic language and keeps the *abba* rhyme scheme.
2. The devil is literally described as a puppet master controlling our strings.

Gangs of demons are boozing in our brain—
ranked, swarming, like a million warrior-ants,[3]
they drown and choke the cistern of our wants;
each time we breathe, we tear our lungs with pain.

If poison, arson, sex, narcotics, knives   25
have not yet ruined us and stitched their quick,
loud patterns on the canvas of our lives,
it is because our souls are still too sick.[4]

Among the vermin, jackals, panthers, lice,
gorillas and tarantulas that suck   30
and snatch and scratch and defecate and fuck
in the disorderly circus of our vice,

there's one more ugly and abortive birth.
It makes no gestures, never beats its breast,
yet it would murder for a moment's rest,[5]   35
and willingly annihilate the earth.

It's BOREDOM. Tears have glued its eyes together.
You know it well, my Reader. This obscene
beast chain-smokes yawning for the guillotine—
you—hypocrite Reader—my double—my brother!   40

Correspondences[1]

Nature is a temple whose living colonnades
Breathe forth a mystic speech in fitful sighs;
Man wanders among symbols in those glades
Where all things watch him with familiar eyes.

Like dwindling echoes gathered far away   5
Into a deep and thronging unison
Huge as the night or as the light of day,
All scents and sounds and colors meet as one.

Perfumes there are as sweet as the oboe's sound,
Green as the prairies, fresh as a child's caress,[2]
—And there are others, rich, corrupt, profound[3]   10

And of an infinite pervasiveness,
Like myrrh, or musk, or amber,[4] that excite
The ecstasies of sense, the soul's delight.

---

3. Literally, intestinal worms.
4. Literally, not bold enough.
5. Literally, swallow the world in a yawn.
1. Translated by Richard Wilbur. The translation keeps the intricate melody of the sonnet's
original rhyme scheme.

2. Literally, flesh.
3. Literally, triumphant.
4. Or ambergris, a substance secreted by whales.
Ambergris and musk (a secretion of the male
musk deer) are used in making perfume.

Her Hair[1]

O fleece, that down the neck waves to the nape!
O curls! O perfume nonchalant and rare!
O ecstacy! To fill this alcove[2] shape
With memories that in these tresses sleep,
I would shake them like pennons in the air!   5

Languorous Asia, burning Africa,
And a far world, defunct almost, absent,
Within your aromatic forest stay!
As other souls on music drift away,
Mine, o my love! still floats upon your scent.   10

I shall go there where, full of sap, both tree
And man swoon in the heat of southern climes;
Strong tresses, be the swell that carries me!
I dream upon your sea of ebony
Of dazzling sails, of oarsmen, masts and flames: 15

A sun-drenched and reverberating port,
Where I imbibe color and sound and scent;
Where vessels, gliding through the gold and moire,
Open their vast arms as they leave the shore
To clasp the pure and shimmering firmament.   20

I'll plunge my head, enamored of its pleasure,
In this black ocean where the other hides;
My subtle spirit then will know a measure
Of fertile idleness and fragrant leisure,
Lulled by the infinite rhythm of its tides!   25

Pavilion, of blue-shadowed tresses spun,
You give me back the azure from afar;
And where the twisted locks are fringed with down
Lurk mingled odors I grow drunk upon
Of oil of coconut, of musk and tar.   30

A long time! always! my hand in your hair
Will sow the stars of sapphire, pearl, ruby,
That you be never deaf to my desire,
My oasis and gourd whence I aspire
To drink deep of the wine of memory![3]   35

1. Translated by Doreen Bell. The translation emulates the French original's challenging *abaab* rhyme pattern.
2. Bedroom.
3. The last two lines are a question: "Are you not . . . ?"

A Carcass[1]

Remember, my love, the item you saw
    That beautiful morning in June:
By a bend in the path a carcass reclined
    On a bed sown with pebbles and stones;

Her legs were spread out like a lecherous whore,   5
    Sweating out poisonous fumes,
Who opened in slick invitational style
    Her stinking and festering womb.

The sun on this rottenness focused its rays
    To cook the cadaver till done,   10
And render to Nature a hundredfold gift
    Of all she'd united in one.

And the sky cast an eye on this marvelous meat
    As over the flowers in bloom.
The stench was so wretched that there on the grass   15
    You nearly collapsed in a swoon.

The flies buzzed and droned on these bowels of filth
    Where an army of maggots arose,
Which flowed like a liquid and thickening stream
    On the animate rags of her clothes.[2]   20

And it rose and it fell, and pulsed like a wave,
    Rushing and bubbling with health.
One could say that this carcass, blown with vague breath,
    Lived in increasing itself.

And this whole teeming world made a musical sound   25
    Like babbling brooks and the breeze,
Or the grain that a man with a winnowing-fan
    Turns with a rhythmical ease.

The shapes wore away as if only a dream
    Like a sketch that is left on the page   30
Which the artist forgot and can only complete
    On the canvas, with memory's aid.

From back in the rocks, a pitiful bitch
    Eyed us with angry distaste,
Awaiting the moment to snatch from the bones   35
    The morsel she'd dropped in her haste.

1. Translated by James McGowan with special attention to imagery. The alternation of long and short lines in English emulates the French meter's rhythmic swing between twelve- and eight-syllable lines in an *abab* rhyme scheme.
2. By extension. The torn flesh is described as "living rags."

—And you, in your turn, will be rotten as this:
    Horrible, filthy, undone,
Oh sun of my nature and star of my eyes,
    My passion, my angel[3] in one!   40

Yes, such will you be, oh regent of grace,
    After the rites have been read,
Under the weeds, under blossoming grass
    As you molder with bones of the dead.

Ah then, oh my beauty, explain to the worms   45
    Who cherish your body so fine,
That I am the keeper for corpses of love
    Of the form, and the essence divine![4]

Invitation to the Voyage[1]

My child, my sister, dream
How sweet all things would seem
Were we in that kind land to live together,
    And there love slow and long,
    There love and die among   5
Those scenes that image you, that sumptuous weather.
    Drowned suns that glimmer there
    Through cloud-disheveled air
Move me with such a mystery as appears
    Within those other skies   10
    Of your treacherous eyes
When I behold them shining through their tears.

There, there is nothing else but grace and measure,
Richness, quietness, and pleasure.

    Furniture that wears   15
    The lustre of the years
Softly would glow within our glowing chamber,
    Flowers of rarest bloom
    Proffering their perfume
Mixed with the vague fragrances of amber;   20
    Gold ceilings would there be,
    Mirrors deep as the sea,
The walls all in an Eastern splendor hung—

3. Series of conventional Petrarchan images that idealize the beloved.
4. "Any form created by man is immortal. For form is independent of matter . . ." (from Baudelaire's journal *My Heart Laid Bare* 80).
1. Translated by Richard Wilbur. The translation maintains both the rhyme scheme and the rocking motion of the original meter, which follows an unusual pattern of two five-syllable lines followed by one seven-syllable line, and a seven-syllable couplet as refrain.

> Nothing but should address
> The soul's loneliness,   25
> Speaking her sweet and secret native tongue.
>
> There, there is nothing else but grace and measure,
> Richness, quietness, and pleasure.
>
> > See, sheltered from the swells
> > There in the still canals
> Those drowsy ships that dream of sailing forth;   30
> > It is to satisfy
> > Your least desire, they ply
> Hither through all the waters of the earth.
> > The sun at close of day   35
> > Clothes the fields of hay,
> Then the canals, at last the town entire
> > In hyacinth and gold:
> > Slowly the land is rolled
> Sleepward under a sea of gentle fire.   40
>
> There, there is nothing else but grace and measure,
> Richness, quietness, and pleasure.

Song of Autumn I[1]

Soon we shall plunge into the chilly fogs;
Farewell, swift light! our summers are too short!
I hear already the mournful fall of logs
Re-echoing from the pavement of the court.

All of winter will gather in my soul: 5
Hate, anger, horror, chills, the hard forced work;
And, like the sun in his hell by the north pole,
My heart will be only a red and frozen block.

I shudder, hearing every log that falls;
No scaffold could be built with hollower sounds.   10
My spirit is like a tower whose crumbling walls
The tireless battering-ram brings to the ground.

It seems to me, lulled by monotonous shocks,
As if they were hastily nailing a coffin today.
For whom?—Yesterday was summer. Now autumn knocks.   15
That mysterious sound is like someone's going away.

---

1. Translated by C. F. MacIntyre to follow the original rhyme pattern.

Spleen LXXVIII[1]

Old Pluvius,[2] month of rains, in peevish mood
Pours from his urn chill winter's sodden gloom
On corpses fading in the near graveyard,
On foggy suburbs pours life's tedium.

My cat seeks out a litter on the stones,   5
Her mangy body turning without rest.
An ancient poet's soul in monotones
Whines in the rain-spouts like a chilblained ghost.

A great bell mourns, a wet log wrapped in smoke
Sings in falsetto to the wheezing clock,   10
While from a rankly perfumed deck of cards
(A dropsical old crone's fatal bequest)
The Queen of Spades, the dapper Jack of Hearts
Speak darkly of dead loves, how they were lost.

Spleen LXXIX[1]

I have more memories than if I had lived a thousand years.

Even a bureau crammed with souvenirs,
Old bills, love letters, photographs, receipts,
Court depositions, locks of hair in plaits,
Hides fewer secrets than my brain could yield.   5
It's like a tomb, a corpse-filled Potter's Field,[2]
A pyramid where the dead lie down by scores.
I am a graveyard that the moon abhors:
Like guilty qualms, the worms burrow and nest
Thickly in bodies that I loved the best.   10
I'm a stale boudoir where old-fashioned clothes
Lie scattered among wilted fern and rose,
Where only the Boucher girls[3] in pale pastels
Can breathe the uncorked scents and faded smells.

---

1. Translated by Kenneth O. Hanson, with emphasis on the imagery. The French original uses identical *abab* rhymes in the two quatrains and shifts to *ccd, eed* in the tercets.
2. "The rainy time" (Latin, literal trans.); a period extending from January 20 to February 18 as the fifth month of the French Revolutionary calendar.
1. Translated by Anthony Hecht. The translation follows the original rhymed couplets,

except for one technical impossibility: Baudelaire's repetition (in a poem about monotony) of an identical rhyme for eight lines (lines 11–18, the sound of long *a*).
2. A general term describing the common cemetery for those buried at public expense.
3. François Boucher (1703–1770), court painter for Louis XV of France, drew many pictures of young women clothed and nude.

Nothing can equal those days for endlessness 15
When in the winter's blizzardy caress
Indifference expanding to Ennui[4]
Takes on the feel of Immortality.
O living matter, henceforth you're no more
Than a cold stone encompassed by vague fear 20
And by the desert, and the mist and sun;
An ancient Sphinx ignored by everyone,
Left off the map, whose bitter irony
Is to sing as the sun sets in that dry sea.[5]

Spleen LXXXI[1]

When the low heavy sky weighs like a lid
Upon the spirit aching for the light
And all the wide horizon's line is hid
By a black day sadder than any night;

When the changed earth is but a dungeon dank 5
Where batlike Hope goes blindly fluttering
And, striking wall and roof and mouldered plank,
Bruises his tender head and timid wing;

When like grim prison bars stretch down the thin,
Straight, rigid pillars of the endless rain, 10
And the dumb throngs of infamous spiders spin
Their meshes in the caverns of the brain,

Suddenly, bells leap forth into the air,
Hurling a hideous uproar to the sky
As 'twere a band of homeless spirits who fare 15
Through the strange heavens, wailing stubbornly.

And hearses, without drum or instrument,
File slowly through my soul; crushed, sorrowful,
Weeps Hope, and Grief, fierce and omnipotent,
Plants his black banner on my drooping skull. 20

---

4. Melancholy, paralyzing boredom.
5. Baudelaire combines two references to ancient Egypt, the Sphinx and the legendary statue of Memnon at Thebes, which was sup-

posed to sing at sunset.
1. Translated by Sir John Squire in accord with the original rhyme scheme.

The Voyage[1]

To Maxime du Camp[2]

I

The child, in love with prints and maps,
Holds the whole world in his vast appetite.
How large the earth is under the lamplight!
But in the eyes of memory, how the world is cramped!

We set out one morning, brain afire,   5
Hearts fat with rancor and bitter desires,
Moving along to the rhythm of wind and waves,
Lull the inner infinite on the finite of seas:

Some are glad, glad to leave a degraded home;
Others, happy to shake off the horror of their hearts,   10
Still others, astrologers drowned in the eyes of woman—
Oh the perfumes of Circe,[3] the power and the pig!—

To escape conversion to the Beast, get drunk
On space and light and the flames of skies;
The tongue of the sun and the ice that bites   15
Slowly erase the mark of the Kiss.

But the true voyagers are those who leave
Only to be going; hearts nimble as balloons,
They never diverge from luck's black sun,
And with or without reason, cry, Let's be gone!   20

Desire to them is nothing but clouds,
They dream, as a draftee dreams of the cannon,
Of vast sensualities, changing, unknown,
Whose name the spirit has never pronounced!

II

We imitate—horrible!—the top and ball   25
In their waltz and bounce; even in sleep
We're turned and tormented by Curiosity,
Who, like a mad Angel, lashes the stars.

---

1. Translated by Charles Henri Ford. The French poem is written in the traditional twelve-syllable (alexandrine) line with an *abab* rhyme scheme.
2. A wry dedication to the progress-oriented author of *Modern Songs* (1855), which began "I was born a traveler."
3. In Homer's *Odyssey*, an island sorceress who changed visitors into beasts. Odysseus's men were transformed into pigs.

Peculiar fortune that changes its goal,
And being nowhere, is anywhere at all!   30
And Man, who is never untwisted from hope,
Scrambling like a madman to get some rest!

The soul's a three-master seeking Icaria;[4]
A voice on deck calls: "Wake up there!"
A voice from the mast-head, vehement, wild: 35
"Love . . . fame . . . happiness!" We're on the rocks!

Every island that the lookout hails
Becomes the Eldorado[5] foretold by Fortune;
Then Imagination embarks on its orgy
But runs aground in the brightness of morning.   40

Poor little lover of visionary fields!
Should he be put in irons, dumped in the sea,
This drunken sailor, discoverer of Americas,
Mirage that makes the gulf more bitter?

So the old vagabond, shuffling in mud,   45
Dreams, nose hoisted, of a shining paradise,
His charmed eye lighting on Capua's[6] coast
At every candle aglow in a hovel.

III

Astounding voyagers! what noble stories
We read in your eyes, deeper than seas;   50
Show us those caskets, filled with rich memories,
Marvelous jewels, hewn from stars and aether.

Yes, we would travel, without sail or steam!
Gladden a little our jail's desolation,
Sail over our minds, stretched like a canvas,   55
All your memories, framed with gold horizons.

Tell us, what have you seen?

---

4. Greek island in the Aegean Sea named
after the mythological Icarus, who, escaping
from prison using wings made by his father,
Daedalus, plunged into nearby waters and
drowned when the wings gave way. His name
was associated with utopian flights, as in

Étienne Cabet's novel about a utopian community, Voyage to Icaria (1840). "Three-master":
a ship.
5. Fabled country of gold and abundance.
6. City on the Volturno River in southern
Italy, famous for its luxury and sensuality.

IV

"We have seen stars
And tides; we have seen sands, too,
And, despite shocks and unforeseen disasters,
We were often bored, just as we are here.   60

The glory of sun on a violet sea,
The glory of cities in the setting sun,
Kindled our hearts with torment and longing
To plunge into the sky's magnetic reflections.

Neither the rich cities nor sublime landscapes,   65
Ever possessed that mysterious attraction
Of Change and Chance having fun with the clouds.
And always Desire kept us anxious!

—Enjoyment adds force to Appetite!
Desire, old tree nurtured by pleasure,   70
Although your dear bark thicken and harden,
Your branches throb to hold the sun closer!

Great tree, will you outgrow the cypress?
Still we have gathered carefully
Some sketches for your hungry album,   75
Brothers, for whom all things from far away

Are precious! We've bowed down to idols;
To thrones encrusted with luminous rocks;
To figured palaces whose magic pomp
Would ruin your bankers with a ruinous dream;   80

To costumes that intoxicate the eye,
To women whose teeth and nails are dyed,
To clever jugglers, fondled by the snake."[7]

V

And then, and what more?

VI

"O childish minds!

Not to forget the principal thing,   85
We saw everywhere, without looking for it,
From top to toe of the deadly scale,
The tedious drama of undying sin:

7. Snake charmers. The images in this stanza evoke India.

Woman, low slave, vain and stupid,
Without laughter self-loving, and without disgust,   90
Man, greedy despot, lewd, hard and covetous,
Slave of the slave, rivulet in the sewer;

The hangman exulting, the martyr sobbing;
Festivals that season and perfume the blood;[8]
The poison of power unnerving the tyrant,   95
The masses in love with the brutalizing whip;

Many religions, very like our own,
All climbing to heaven; and Holiness,
Like a delicate wallower in a feather bed,
Seeking sensation from hair shirts and nails.   100

Jabbering humanity, drunk with its genius,
As crazy now as it was in the past,
Crying to God in its raging agony:
'O master, fellow creature, I curse thee forever!'

And then the least stupid, brave lovers of Lunacy,   105
Fleeing the gross herd that Destiny pens in,
Finding release in the vast dreams of opium!
—Such is the story, the whole world over."

VII

Bitter knowledge that traveling brings!
The globe, monotonous and small, today,   110
Yesterday, tomorrow, always, throws us our image:
An oasis of horror in a desert of boredom!

Should we go? Or stay? If you can stay, stay;
But go if you must. Some run, some hide
To outwit Time, the enemy so vigilant and   115
Baleful. And many, alas, must run forever

Like the wandering Jew[9] and the twelve apostles,
Who could not escape his relentless net[1]
By ship or by wheel; while others knew how
To destroy him without leaving home.   120

When finally he places his foot on our spine,
May we be able to hope and cry, Forward!
As in days gone by when we left for China,
Eyes fixed on the distance, hair in the wind,

8. Literally, "Festivals seasoned and perfumed by blood."
9. According to medieval legend, a Jew who mocked Christ on his way to the cross and was condemned to wander unceasingly until Judg-

ment Day.
1. These three stanzas describe Time (ultimately Death) as a Roman gladiator, the *retiarius*, who used a net to trap his opponent.

With heart as light as a young libertine's 125
We'll embark on the sea of deepening shadows.
Do you hear those mournful, enchanting voices[2]
That sing: "Come this way, if you would taste

The perfumed Lotus. Here you may pick
Miraculous fruits for which the heart hungers. 130
Come and drink deep of this strange,
Soft afternoon that never ends?"

Knowing his voice, we visualize the phantom—
It is our Pylades there, his arms outstretched.
While she whose knees we used to kiss cries out, 135
"For strength of heart, swim back to your Electra!"[3]

VIII

O Death, old captain, it is time! weigh anchor!
This country confounds us; hoist sail and away!
If the sky and sea are black as ink,
Our hearts, as you know them, burst with blinding rays. 140

Pour us your poison, that last consoling draft!
For we long, so the fire burns in the brain,
To sound the abyss, Hell or Heaven, what matter?
In the depths of the Unknown, we'll discover the New!

2. The voices of the dead, luring the sailor to the Lotus-land of ease and forgetfulness.
3. In Greek mythology, Orestes and Pylades were close friends ready to sacrifice their lives for each other. Electra was Orestes' faithful sister, who saved him from the Furies.

EMILY DICKINSON

1830–1886

In the 1880s, visitors to Amherst, Massachusetts, gossiped about the strange woman, dressed only in white gowns, who never left her father's house—except once, it was rumored, "to see a new church, when she crept out by night, and viewed it by moonlight." Neighbors and friends knew that this woman wrote, but she published only ten poems during her lifetime, and even those appeared anonymously. She begged those closest to her to burn her papers after her death. They refused, instead startling audiences by publishing Emily Dickinson's unusual lyrics, with their passionate intensity, broken meter, slant rhymes, and unconventional dashes and capitalizations. From the moment that they first appeared, these poems have been beloved by both readers and critics. Dickinson's works can seem, on the one hand, like child-like and accessible meditations on such universal themes as death, faith, and nature, and on the other hand, like highly artful, philosophically demanding, and radically innovative experiments in lyric form. It is with this unlikely combination of innocence and sophistication that the mysterious Dickinson has become one of the best-known of American poets.

LIFE

Born to a prominent Amherst family— her father was elected to Congress— Dickinson attended Amherst Academy and later, for a year, the Mount Holyoke Female Seminary. Conflicted and ambivalent about Christian orthodoxy even as a child, she resisted the Puritan attitudes that surrounded her, especially at school. "Christ is calling everyone here," she wrote, "and I am standing alone in rebellion." This sense of isolation would only deepen. From early in her twenties, she confined herself almost entirely to her family home, leading the life of a recluse with her tyrannical father and absent-minded mother. She did have close attachments to her brother and sister, and she developed a few close friendships, though she pursued these mainly through correspondence. Some of her works reflect on the pain of unrequited love and erotic desire, and biographers have speculated about Dickinson's passions, but no scholar has been able to determine indisputably the name of the one—or ones—she loved.

Dickinson began writing verse seriously in the 1850s, putting groups of her poems together in fascicles—booklets of pages bound together by hand. In these works she seldom remarked on the burning issues of the day, from slavery and women's rights to the violence of the Civil War. Concerned with domestic matters and the torments of the soul, she can seem excruciatingly inward-looking. But her literary life was expansive. She wrote more than a thousand letters, linking herself to the outside world more readily by mail than by face-to-face contact. Dickinson also read widely. Shakespeare was a major touchstone (she once asked: "why is any other book needed?"), and she named **John Keats**, **Elizabeth Barrett Browning**, **Robert Browning**, and Charlotte Brontë as among her foremost inspirations.

In 1862, after seeing an article with advice for aspiring writers by Thomas Wentworth Higginson, Dickinson wrote to solicit his opinion of her poems. He was both enthusiastic and shocked, warning her away from publishing such unconventional work. Their friendship continued to the end of Dickinson's life. After her death, Dickinson's sister Lavinia was surprised to discover almost two thousand poems stashed away in a box, and she began the difficult task of trying to figure out how to edit and organize these works for publication, a process that has puzzled and divided editors ever since. Higginson was one of the first to publish volumes of Dickinson's poetry, editing the work to make it seem as conventional as he could.

WORK

With singular conviction and independence, Dickinson produced poetry unlike anyone else of her time. Her works are noteworthy, first of all, for their brevity and compression, throwing readers immediately into the thick of the poem, eschewing any preparation. And while she draws on familiar poetic themes— nature, death, love, and faith—she pushes her explorations of feeling to their most extreme intensity, and her images persistently unsettle expectation. Nature can turn out to be revolting, as when a bird devours a worm; the grandest subjects can turn ordinary, as when death appears as an everyday conveyance; and the human body can be estranged from itself, turned into a corpse, a gun, or a tomb.

Dickinson's use of meter is as striking as her imagery. She relies most heavily on popular metrical patterns associated with Protestant hymns, such as common meter (quatrains that begin with one line of eight syllables followed by a line of six syllables, repeated to form an 8/6/8/6 pattern). But while she depends on the hymnal, she also breaks with it. Sometimes she speeds up or slows down its familiar rhythms; and sometimes she even interrupts them altogether. For example, she introduces dashes that cluster syllables together in a way that interrupts the feeling of a smooth rhythm (as in the first line of one of her most famous poems, "I heard a Fly buzz—when I died"); or she changes meter suddenly (as in "I like to see it lap the Miles," a poem that opens and closes with common-meter quatrains but swerves into a different pattern altogether in the third stanza). Dickinson's rhymes also play with traditional patterns. In "A Bird came down the Walk," for example, she offers us a couple of perfect rhymes (saw/raw, Grass/pass). But in the same poem she gives us two slant rhymes (Crumb/home, seam/swim), and in the middle, where one expects a rhyme, she presents sounds that share a rough resemblance but do not rhyme at all (around/Head).

Perhaps most strikingly experimental of all is Dickinson's use of punctuation. Her dramatic dashes are famous, and the manuscripts suggest that they are even more innovative than they look on the printed page. In her own handwriting, Dickinson's dashes are of varying lengths, and sometimes turn up or down (a few are completely vertical). These marks do not always work the same way: sometimes her dashes draw thoughts together; at other times they separate them. And finally, while Dickinson capitalizes many important proper nouns, such as Soul and Beauty, she also opts to capitalize some unexpected words: Onset, for example, or Buckets.

That Dickinson never published these outrageously unconventional and demanding poems might not surprise us. Higginson had led her to believe that the world would not appreciate them, and the few of her poems that did appear in print in her lifetime were heavily edited to conform to unadventurous tastes. "Publication—is the Auction / Of the Mind of Man," she wrote, disgusted by the idea of selling what she cared for most. And so she withdrew to what she called the "freedom" of her narrow room to create great poetry for herself alone.

216

Safe in their Alabaster Chambers—
Untouched by Morning
And untouched by Noon—
Sleep the meek members of the Resurrection—
Rafter of satin,
And Roof of stone.   5

Light laughs the breeze
In her Castle above them—
Babbles the Bee in a stolid Ear,
Pipe the Sweet Birds in ignorant cadence—
Ah, what sagacity perished here!   10

258

There's a certain Slant of light,
Winter Afternoons—
That oppresses, like the Heft
Of Cathedral Tunes—

Heavenly Hurt, it gives us—   5
We can find no scar,
But internal difference,
Where the Meanings, are—

None may teach it—Any—
'Tis the Seal Despair—   10
An imperial affliction
Sent us of the Air—

When it comes, the Landscape listens—
Shadows—hold their breath—
When it goes, 'tis like the Distance   15
On the look of Death—

303

The Soul selects her own Society—
Then—shuts the Door—
To her divine Majority—
Present no more—

Unmoved—she notes the Chariots—pausing   5
At her low Gate—
Unmoved—an Emperor be kneeling
Upon her Mat—

I've known her—from an ample nation—
Choose One—   10
Then—close the Valves of her attention—
Like Stone—

328

A Bird came down the Walk—
He did not know I saw—
He bit an Angleworm in halves
And ate the fellow, raw,

And then he drank a Dew   5
From a convenient Grass—

And then hopped sidewise to the Wall
To let a Beetle pass—

He glanced with rapid eyes
That hurried all around—   10
They looked like frightened Beads, I thought—
He stirred his Velvet Head

Like one in danger, Cautious,
I offered him a Crumb
And he unrolled his feathers   15
And rowed him softer home—

Than Oars divide the Ocean,
Too silver for a seam—
Or Butterflies, off Banks of Noon
Leap, plashless as they swim.   20

341

After great pain, a formal feeling comes—
The Nerves sit ceremonious, like Tombs—
The stiff Heart questions was it He, that bore,
And Yesterday, or Centuries before?

The Feet, mechanical, go round—   5
Of Ground, or Air, or Ought[1]—
A Wooden way
Regardless grown,
A Quartz contentment, like a stone—

This is the Hour of Lead—   10
Remembered, if outlived,
As Freezing persons, recollect the Snow—
First—Chill—then Stupor—then the letting go—

435

Much Madness is divinest Sense—
To a discerning Eye—
Much Sense—the starkest Madness—
'Tis the Majority
In this, as All, prevail—   5
Assent—and you are sane—
Demur—you're straightway dangerous—
And handled with a Chain—

1. Zero.

449

I died for Beauty—but was scarce
Adjusted in the Tomb
When One who died for Truth, was lain
In an adjoining Room—

He questioned softly "Why I failed"?   5
"For Beauty", I replied—
"And I—for Truth—Themself are One—
We Brethren, are", He said—

And so, as Kinsmen, met a Night—
We talked between the Rooms—   10
Until the Moss had reached our lips—
And covered up—our names—

465

I heard a Fly buzz—when I died—
The Stillness in the Room
Was like the Stillness in the Air—
Between the Heaves of Storm—

The Eyes around—had wrung them dry—   5
And Breaths were gathering firm
For that last Onset—when the King
Be witnessed—in the Room—

I willed my Keepsakes—Signed away
What portion of me be   10
Assignable—and then it was
There interposed a Fly—

With Blue—uncertain stumbling Buzz—
Between the light—and me—
And then the Windows failed—and then   15
I could not see to see—

519

'Twas warm—at first—like Us—
Until there crept upon
A Chill—like frost upon a Glass—
Till all the scene—be gone.

The Forehead copied Stone—   5
The Fingers grew too cold
To ache—and like a Skater's Brook—
The busy eyes—congealed—

It straightened—that was all—
It crowded Cold to Cold   10
It multiplied indifference—
As[1] Pride were all it could—

And even when with Cords—
'Twas lowered, like a Weight—
It made no Signal, nor demurred,   15
But dropped like Adamant.

585

I like to see it lap the Miles—
And lick the Valleys up—
And stop to feed itself at Tanks—
And then—prodigious step

Around a Pile of Mountains—   5
And supercilious peer
In Shanties—by the sides of Roads—
And then a Quarry pare

To fit its Ribs
And crawl between
Complaining all the while   10
In horrid—hooting stanza—
Then chase itself down Hill—

And neigh like Boanerges[1]—
Then—punctual as a Star
Stop—docile and omnipotent   15
At its own stable door—

632

The Brain—is wider than the Sky—
For—put them side by side—
The one the other will contain
With ease—and You—beside—

The Brain is deeper than the sea—   5
For—hold them—Blue to Blue—
The one the other will absorb—
As Sponges—Buckets—do—

1. As if.
1. "Sons of thunder," name given by Jesus to
the brothers and disciples James and John,
presumably because they were thunderous
preachers.

The Brain is just the weight of God—
For—Heft them—Pound for Pound—   10
And they will differ—if they do—
As Syllable from Sound—

657

I dwell in Possibility—
A fairer House than Prose—
More numerous of Windows—
Superior—for Doors—

Of Chambers as the Cedars—   5
Impregnable of Eye—
And for an Everlasting Roof
The Gambrels[1] of the Sky—

Of Visitors—the fairest—
For Occupation—This—   10
The spreading wide my narrow Hands
To gather Paradise—

712

Because I could not stop for Death—
He kindly stopped for me—
The Carriage held but just Ourselves—
And Immortality.

We slowly drove—He knew no haste   5
And I had put away
My labor and my leisure too,
For His Civility—

We passed the School, where Children strove
At Recess—in the Ring—   10
We passed the Fields of Gazing Grain—
We passed the Setting Sun—

Or rather—He passed Us—
The Dews drew quivering and chill—
For only Gossamer, my Gown—   15
My Tippet—only Tulle[1]—

We paused before a House that seemed
A Swelling of the Ground—

---

1. Slopes, as in the large, arched roofs often   1. Fine, silken netting. "Tippet": a scarf.
seen on barns.

The Roof was scarcely visible—
The Cornice—in the Ground—   20

Since then—'tis Centuries—and yet
Feels shorter than the Day
I first surmised the Horses' Heads
Were toward Eternity—

754

My Life had stood—a Loaded Gun—
In Corners—till a Day
The Owner passed—identified—
And carried Me away—

And now We roam in Sovereign Woods—   5
And now We hunt the Doe—
And every time I speak for Him—
The Mountains straight reply—

And do I smile, such cordial light
Upon the Valley glow—   10
It is as a Vesuvian face[1]
Had let its pleasure through—

And when at Night—Our good Day done—
I guard My Master's Head—
'Tis better than the Eider-Duck's   15
Deep Pillow—to have shared—

To foe of His—I'm deadly foe—
None stir the second time—
On whom I lay a Yellow Eye—
Or an emphatic Thumb—   20

Though I than He—may longer live
He longer must—than I—
For I have but the power to kill,
Without—the power to die—

1084

At Half past Three, a single Bird
Unto a silent Sky
Propounded but a single term
Of cautious melody.

---

1. A face glowing with light like that from an erupting volcano.

At Half past Four, Experiment   5
Had subjugated test
And lo, Her silver Principle
Supplanted all the rest.

At Half past Seven, Element
Nor Implement, be seen—   10
And Place was where the Presence was
Circumference between.

1129

Tell all the Truth but tell it slant—
Success in Circuit lies
Too bright for our infirm Delight
The Truth's superb surprise

As Lightning to the Children eased   5
With explanation kind
The Truth must dazzle gradually
Or every man be blind—

1207

He preached upon "Breadth" till it argued him narrow—
The Broad are too broad to define
And of "Truth" until it proclaimed him a Liar—
The Truth never flaunted a Sign—

Simplicity fled from his counterfeit presence   5
As Gold the Pyrites[1] would shun—
What confusion would cover the innocent Jesus
To meet so enabled[2] a Man!

1564

Pass to thy Rendezvous of Light,
Pangless except for us—
Who slowly ford the Mystery
Which thou hast leaped across!

1. Iron bisulfide, sometimes called fool's gold.   2. Competent.

1593

There came a Wind like a Bugle—
It quivered through the Grass
And a Green Chill upon the Heat
So ominous did pass
We barred the Windows and the Doors   5
As from an Emerald Ghost—
The Doom's electric Moccasin[1]
That very instant passed—
On a strange Mob of panting Trees
And Fences fled away   10
And Rivers where the Houses ran
Those looked that lived—that Day—
The Bell within the steeple wild
The flying tidings told—
How much can come   15
And much can go,
And yet abide the World!

1. I.e., water moccasin, a poisonous snake.

CHRISTINA ROSSETTI

1830–1894

Poems of thwarted desire and painful self-renunciation fill Christina Rossetti's body of work. But even as she explores the intensity of grief, longing, and death, her poems often express a whimsical playfulness and a wry humor. Like **Emily Dickinson**, born in the same year across the Atlantic, Rossetti refused a conventional life with marriage and children, and she broke poetic rules in ways that startled her first readers. Like Dickinson, too, she was secretive and largely withdrawn from social contact. "Beautiful, delightful, noble, memorable, as is the world," she wrote to her brother, "I yet am well content in my shady crevice."

Rossetti was born in London in 1830, the youngest of four talented children of an exiled Italian intellectual. Rossetti's two older brothers would go on to become famous artists, members of a group that called themselves the Pre-Raphaelite Brotherhood. Working in poetry and paint, they aimed to revitalize the arts in England by representing the details of the natural world and by returning to medieval themes and images. William Michael Rossetti was also a great admirer of the American poet **Walt Whitman** and introduced his work to English readers. Christina Rossetti's gender prevented her from being a central member of the Pre-Raphaelite

Brotherhood, but her first volume, *Goblin Market and Other Poems* (1862) was the first popular success associated with their movement, and it established her as a leading English poet.

Intensely religious and drawn to Christian models of austerity and self-renunciation, Rossetti rejected two suitors on the grounds that their faith was not firm enough for her, and gave up going to the theater and playing chess because these gave her too much pleasure. She wrote 450 devotional poems, and many of her other works also deal with questions of spirituality. Her mother led her to become an Anglo-Catholic, a member of the Protestant Church of England who wanted to revive traditional elements of the Catholic liturgy dating back centuries. This movement favored the doctrine of "reserve," which meant keeping sacred truths hidden from the profane and the uninitiated. Rossetti's secretiveness and her fascination with mysteries are sometimes associated with this doctrine. The Anglo-Catholic movement also encouraged women to work together, and Rossetti spent many years doing charitable service at a home for prostitutes. Her most famous poem, *Goblin Market*, ends with a moral about sisterhood which many readers have linked to Rossetti's membership in the Anglo-Catholic movement and her work with "fallen women."

But *Goblin Market* has also puzzled and captivated readers since it first appeared. "Is it a fable—or a mere fairy story—or an allegory against the pleasures of sinful love—or what is it?" asked the poet Caroline Norton. On the one hand, it is lavishly sensuous and wracked by aching temptation, a daring poem that refuses conventional patterns of rhyme and meter. On the other hand, it is moralizing and childlike, a didactic tale of temptation and redemption. On closer inspection, even its Christian warning against temptation starts to break down: the sinner is restored to her earlier happiness, and her savior is not Christ but her sister. Indeterminate, the poem has continued to tantalize readers with multiple meanings, and audiences have reached no consensus even about its central theme: the poem has been taken as a reflection on sin, on women's sexual desire, on addiction, and on imperial consumption (the fruit described in the poem comes from all over the world, like commodities to Britain from its colonies). The poem has also been celebrated as a feminist work that sets the violence of the male goblins against the solidarity of the sisters. In the end, like so much of Rossetti's life and work, it continues to entice us with its perpetually fascinating secrets.

After Death

The curtains were half drawn, the floor was swept
  And strewn with rushes, rosemary and may[1]
  Lay thick upon the bed on which I lay,
Where thro' the lattice ivy-shadows crept.
He leaned above me, thinking that I slept   5
  And could not hear him; but I heard him say:
  "Poor child, poor child": and as he turned away

---

1. Plants that symbolize death.

Came a deep silence, and I knew he wept.
He did not touch the shroud, or raise the fold
  That hid my face, or take my hand in his,   10
    Or ruffle the smooth pillows for my head:
  He did not love me living; but once dead
He pitied me; and very sweet it is
To know he still is warm tho' I am cold.

Winter: My Secret

I tell my secret? No indeed, not I:
Perhaps some day, who knows?
But not today; it froze, and blows, and snows,
And you're too curious: fie!
You want to hear it? well: 5
Only, my secret's mine, and I won't tell.

Or, after all, perhaps there's none:
Suppose there is no secret after all,
But only just my fun.
Today's a nipping day, a biting day;   10
In which one wants a shawl,
A veil, a cloak, and other wraps:
I cannot ope to every one who taps,
And let the draughts come whistling thro' my hall;
Come bounding and surrounding me,   15
Come buffeting, astounding me,
Nipping and clipping thro' my wraps and all.
I wear my mask for warmth: who ever shows
His nose to Russian snows
To be pecked at by every wind that blows?   20
You would not peck? I thank you for good will,
Believe, but leave that truth untested still.

Spring's an expansive time: yet I don't trust
March with its peck of dust,
Nor April with its rainbow-crowned brief showers,   25
Nor even May, whose flowers
One frost may wither thro' the sunless hours.

Perhaps some languid summer day,
When drowsy birds sing less and less,
And golden fruit is ripening to excess,   30
If there's not too much sun nor too much cloud,
And the warm wind is neither still nor loud,
Perhaps my secret I may say,
Or you may guess.

Goblin Market

Morning and evening
Maids heard the goblins cry:
"Come buy our orchard fruits,
Come buy, come buy:
Apples and quinces,   5
Lemons and oranges,
Plump unpecked cherries,
Melons and raspberries,
Bloom-down-cheeked peaches,
Swart-headed mulberries,   10
Wild free-born cranberries,
Crab-apples, dewberries,
Pine-apples, blackberries,
Apricots, strawberries;—
All ripe together   15
In summer weather,—
Morns that pass by,
Fair eves that fly;
Come buy, come buy:
Our grapes fresh from the vine,   20
Pomegranates full and fine,
Dates and sharp bullaces,
Rare pears and greengages,
Damsons[1] and bilberries,
Taste them and try: 25
Currants and gooseberries,
Bright-fire-like barberries,
Figs to fill your mouth,
Citrons from the South,
Sweet to tongue and sound to eye;   30
Come buy, come buy."

Evening by evening
Among the brookside rushes,
Laura bowed her head to hear,
Lizzie veiled her blushes: 35
Crouching close together
In the cooling weather,
With clasping arms and cautioning lips,
With tingling cheeks and finger tips.
"Lie close," Laura said,   40
Pricking up her golden head:
"We must not look at goblin men,
We must not buy their fruits:

1. Types of plum.

Who knows upon what soil they fed
Their hungry thirsty roots?"   45
"Come buy," call the goblins
Hobbling down the glen.
"Oh," cried Lizzie, "Laura, Laura,
You should not peep at goblin men."
Lizzie covered up her eyes,   50
Covered close lest they should look;
Laura reared her glossy head,
And whispered like the restless brook:
"Look, Lizzie, look, Lizzie,
Down the glen tramp little men.   55
One hauls a basket,
One bears a plate,
One lugs a golden dish
Of many pounds weight.
How fair the vine must grow   60
Whose grapes are so luscious;
How warm the wind must blow
Thro' those fruit bushes."
"No," said Lizzie: "No, no, no;
Their offers should not charm us,   65
Their evil gifts would harm us."
She thrust a dimpled finger
In each ear, shut eyes and ran:
Curious Laura chose to linger
Wondering at each merchant man.   70
One had a cat's face,
One whisked a tail,
One tramped at a rat's pace,
One crawled like a snail,
One like a wombat prowled obtuse and furry,   75
One like a ratel² tumbled hurry scurry.
She heard a voice like voice of doves
Cooing all together:
They sounded kind and full of loves
In the pleasant weather.   80

Laura stretched her gleaming neck
Like a rush-imbedded swan,
Like a lily from the beck,
Like a moonlit poplar branch,
Like a vessel at the launch   85
When its last restraint is gone.

Backwards up the mossy glen
Turned and trooped the goblin men,
With their shrill repeated cry,
"Come buy, come buy."   90

2. The honey badger, a mammal from Africa and south Asia.

When they reached where Laura was
They stood stock still upon the moss,
Leering at each other,
Brother with queer brother;
Signalling each other,   95
Brother with sly brother.
One set his basket down,
One reared his plate;
One began to weave a crown
Of tendrils, leaves and rough nuts brown   100
(Men sell not such in any town);
One heaved the golden weight
Of dish and fruit to offer her:
"Come buy, come buy," was still their cry.
Laura stared but did not stir,   105
Longed but had no money:
The whisk-tailed merchant bade her taste
In tones as smooth as honey,
The cat-faced purr'd,
The rat-paced spoke a word   110
Of welcome, and the snail-paced even was heard;
One parrot-voiced and jolly
Cried "Pretty Goblin" still for "Pretty Polly;"—
One whistled like a bird.

But sweet-tooth Laura spoke in haste: 115
"Good folk, I have no coin;
To take were to purloin:
I have no copper in my purse,
I have no silver either,
And all my gold is on the furze   120
That shakes in windy weather
Above the rusty heather."
"You have much gold upon your head,"
They answered all together:
"Buy from us with a golden curl."   125
She clipped a precious golden lock,
She dropped a tear more rare than pearl,
Then sucked their fruit globes fair or red:
Sweeter than honey from the rock.
Stronger than man-rejoicing wine,   130
Clearer than water flowed that juice;
She never tasted such before,
How should it cloy with length of use?
She sucked and sucked and sucked the more
Fruits which that unknown orchard bore;   135
She sucked until her lips were sore;
Then flung the emptied rinds away
But gathered up one kernel-stone,
And knew not was it night or day
As she turned home alone.   140

Lizzie met her at the gate
Full of wise upbraidings:
"Dear, you should not stay so late,
Twilight is not good for maidens;
Should not loiter in the glen   145
In the haunts of goblin men.
Do you not remember Jeanie,
How she met them in the moonlight,
Took their gifts both choice and many,
Ate their fruits and wore their flowers   150
Plucked from bowers
Where summer ripens at all hours?
But ever in the noonlight
She pined and pined away;
Sought them by night and day,   155
Found them no more but dwindled and grew grey;
Then fell with the first snow,
While to this day no grass will grow
Where she lies low:
I planted daisies there a year ago   160
That never blow.
You should not loiter so."
"Nay, hush," said Laura:
"Nay, hush, my sister:
I ate and ate my fill,   165
Yet my mouth waters still;
Tomorrow night I will
Buy more:" and kissed her:
"Have done with sorrow;
I'll bring you plums tomorrow   170
Fresh on their mother twigs,
Cherries worth getting;
You cannot think what figs
My teeth have met in,
What melons icy-cold   175
Piled on a dish of gold
Too huge for me to hold,
What peaches with a velvet nap,
Pellucid grapes without one seed:
Odorous indeed must be the mead   180
Whereon they grow, and pure the wave they drink
With lilies at the brink,
And sugar-sweet their sap."

Golden head by golden head,
Like two pigeons in one nest   185
Folded in each other's wings,
They lay down in their curtained bed:
Like two blossoms on one stem,
Like two flakes of new-fall'n snow,
Like two wands of ivory   190

Tipped with gold for awful[3] kings.
Moon and stars gazed in at them,
Wind sang to them lullaby,
Lumbering owls forbore to fly,
Not a bat flapped to and fro   195
Round their rest:
Cheek to cheek and breast to breast
Locked together in one nest.

Early in the morning
When the first cock crowed his warning,   200
Neat like bees, as sweet and busy,
Laura rose with Lizzie:
Fetched in honey, milked the cows,
Aired and set to rights the house,
Kneaded cakes of whitest wheat,   205
Cakes for dainty mouths to eat,
Next churned butter, whipped up cream,
Fed their poultry, sat and sewed;
Talked as modest maidens should:
Lizzie with an open heart,   210
Laura in an absent dream,
One content, one sick in part;
One warbling for the mere bright day's delight,
One longing for the night.

At length slow evening came: 215
They went with pitchers to the reedy brook;
Lizzie most placid in her look,
Laura most like a leaping flame.
They drew the gurgling water from its deep;
Lizzie plucked purple and rich golden flags,   220
Then turning homewards said: "The sunset flushes
Those furthest loftiest crags;
Come, Laura, not another maiden lags
No wilful squirrel wags,
The beasts and birds are fast asleep."   225
But Laura loitered still among the rushes
And said the bank was steep.

And said the hour was early still,
The dew not fall'n, the wind not chill:
Listening ever, but not catching   230
The customary cry,
"Come buy, come buy,"
With its iterated jingle
Of sugar-baited words:
Not for all her watching   235
Once discerning even one goblin

_____
3. Awe-inspiring.

Racing, whisking, tumbling, hobbling;
Let alone the herds
That used to tramp along the glen,
In groups or single,   240
Of brisk fruit-merchant men.
Till Lizzie urged, "O Laura, come:
I hear the fruit-call but I dare not look:
You should not loiter longer at this brook:
Come with me home.   245
The stars rise, the moon bends her arc,
Each glowworm winks her spark,
Let us get home before the night grows dark:
For clouds may gather
Tho' this is summer weather,   250
Put out the lights and drench us thro';
Then if we lost our way what should we do?"

Laura turned cold as stone
To find her sister heard that cry alone,
That goblin cry,   255
"Come buy our fruits, come buy."
Must she then buy no more such dainty fruit?
Must she no more such succous pasture find,
Gone deaf and blind?
Her tree of life drooped from the root: 260
She said not one word in her heart's sore ache;
But peering thro' the dimness, nought discerning,
Trudged home, her pitcher dripping all the way;
So crept to bed, and lay
Silent till Lizzie slept;   265
Then sat up in a passionate yearning,
And gnashed her teeth for baulked desire, and wept
As if her heart would break.

Day after day, night after night,
Laura kept watch in vain   270
In sullen silence of exceeding pain.
She never caught again the goblin cry:
"Come buy, come buy;"—
She never spied the goblin men
Hawking their fruits along the glen: 275
But when the noon waxed bright
Her hair grew thin and gray;
She dwindled, as the fair full moon doth turn
To swift decay and burn
Her fire away.   280

One day remembering her kernel-stone
She set it by a wall that faced the south;
Dewed it with tears, hoped for a root,
Watched for a waxing shoot,
But there came none;   285

It never saw the sun,
It never felt the trickling moisture run:
While with sunk eyes and faded mouth
She dreamed of melons, as a traveller sees
False waves in desert drouth   290
With shade of leaf-crowned trees,
And burns the thirstier in the sandful breeze.
She no more swept the house,
Tended the fowls or cows,
Fetched honey, kneaded cakes of wheat,   295
Brought water from the brook:
But sat down listless in the chimney-nook
And would not eat.

Tender Lizzie could not bear
To watch her sister's cankerous care   300
Yet not to share.
She night and morning
Caught the goblins' cry:
"Come buy our orchard fruits,
Come buy, come buy:"—   305
Beside the brook, along the glen,
She heard the tramp of goblin men,
The voice and stir
Poor Laura could not hear;
Longed to buy fruit to comfort her,   310
But feared to pay too dear.
She thought of Jeanie in her grave,
Who should have been a bride;
But who for joys brides hope to have
Fell sick and died   315
In her gay prime,
In earliest Winter time,
With the first glazing rime,
With the first snow-fall of crisp Winter time.

Till Laura dwindling   320
Seemed knocking at Death's door:
Then Lizzie weighed no more
Better and worse;
But put a silver penny in her purse,
Kissed Laura, crossed the heath with clumps of furze   325
At twilight, halted by the brook:
And for the first time in her life
Began to listen and look.

Laughed every goblin
When they spied her peeping: 330
Came towards her hobbling,
Flying, running, leaping,
Puffing and blowing,
Chuckling, clapping, crowing,

Clucking and gobbling,   335
Mopping and mowing,
Full of airs and graces,
Pulling wry faces,
Demure grimaces,
Cat-like and rat-like,   340
Ratel-and wombat-like,
Snail-paced in a hurry,
Parrot-voiced and whistler,
Helter skelter, hurry skurry,
Chattering like magpies,   345
Fluttering like pigeons,
Gliding like fishes,—
Hugged her and kissed her,
Squeezed and caressed her:
Stretched up their dishes,   350
Panniers, and plates:
"Look at our apples
Russet and dun,
Bob at our cherries,
Bite at our peaches,   355
Citrons and dates,
Grapes for the asking,
Pears red with basking
Out in the sun,
Plums on their twigs;   360
Pluck them and suck them,
Pomegranates, figs."—

"Good folk," said Lizzie,
Mindful of Jeanie:
"Give me much and many:"—   365
Held out her apron,
Tossed them her penny.
"Nay, take a seat with us,
Honour and eat with us,"
They answered grinning: 370
"Our feast is but beginning.
Night yet is early,
Warm and dew-pearly,
Wakeful and starry:
Such fruits as these   375
No man can carry;
Half their bloom would fly,
Half their dew would dry,
Half their flavour would pass by.
Sit down and feast with us,   380
Be welcome guest with us,
Cheer you and rest with us."—
"Thank you," said Lizzie: "But one waits
At home alone for me:

So without further parleying,   385
If you will not sell me any
Of your fruits tho' much and many,
Give me back my silver penny
I tossed you for a fee."—
They began to scratch their pates,   390
No longer wagging, purring,
But visibly demurring,
Grunting and snarling.
One called her proud,
Cross-grained, uncivil;   395
Their tones waxed loud,
Their looks were evil.
Lashing their tails
They trod and hustled her,
Elbowed and jostled her,   400
Clawed with their nails.
Barking, mewing, hissing, mocking,
Tore her gown and soiled her stocking,
Twitched her hair out by the roots,
Stamped upon her tender feet,   405
Held her hands and squeezed their fruits
Against her mouth to make her eat.

White and golden Lizzie stood,
Like a lily in a flood,—
Like a rock of blue-veined stone   410
Lashed by tides obstreperously,—
Like a beacon left alone
In a hoary roaring sea,
Sending up a golden fire,—
Like a fruit-crowned orange-tree   415
White with blossoms honey-sweet
Sore beset by wasp and bee,—
Like a royal virgin town
Topped with gilded dome and spire
Close beleaguerred by a fleet   420
Mad to tug her standard down.

One may lead a horse to water,
Twenty cannot make him drink.
Tho' the goblins cuffed and caught her,
Coaxed and fought her,   425
Bullied and besought her,
Scratched her, pinched her black as ink,
Kicked and knocked her,
Mauled and mocked her,
Lizzie uttered not a word;   430
Would not open lip from lip
Lest they should cram a mouthful in:
But laughed in heart to feel the drip

Of juice that syruped all her face,
And lodged in dimples of her chin,   435
And streaked her neck which quaked like curd.
At last the evil people
Worn out by her resistance
Flung back her penny, kicked their fruit
Along whichever road they took,   440
Not leaving root or stone or shoot;
Some writhed into the ground,
Some dived into the brook
With ring and ripple,
Some scudded on the gale without a sound,   445
Some vanished in the distance.

In a smart, ache, tingle,
Lizzie went her way;
Knew not was it night or day;
Sprang up the bank, tore thro' the furze,   450
Threaded copse and dingle,
And heard her penny jingle
Bouncing in her purse,
Its bounce was music to her ear.
She ran and ran   455
As if she feared some goblin man
Dogged her with gibe or curse
Or something worse:
But not one goblin skurried after,
Nor was she pricked by fear;   460
The kind heart made her windy-paced
That urged her home quite out of breath with haste
And inward laughter.

She cried "Laura," up the garden,
"Did you miss me?   465
Come and kiss me.
Never mind my bruises,
Hug me, kiss me, suck my juices
Squeezed from goblin fruits for you,
Goblin pulp and goblin dew.   470
Eat me, drink me, love me;
Laura, make much of me:
For your sake I have braved the glen
And had to do with goblin merchant men."

Laura started from her chair,   475
Flung her arms up in the air,
Clutched her hair:
"Lizzie, Lizzie, have you tasted
For my sake the fruit forbidden?
Must your light like mine be hidden,   480

Your young life like mine be wasted,
Undone in mine undoing
And ruined in my ruin,
Thirsty, cankered, goblin-ridden?"—
She clung about her sister,   485
Kissed and kissed and kissed her:
Tears once again
Refreshed her shrunken eyes,
Dripping like rain
After long sultry drouth;   490
Shaking with aguish fear, and pain,
She kissed and kissed her with a hungry mouth.

Her lips began to scorch,
That juice was wormwood to her tongue,
She loathed the feast: 495
Writhing as one possessed she leaped and sung,
Rent all her robe, and wrung
Her hands in lamentable haste,
And beat her breast.
Her locks streamed like the torch   500
Borne by a racer at full speed,
Or like the mane of horses in their flight,
Or like an eagle when she stems the light
Straight toward the sun,
Or like a caged thing freed,   505
Or like a flying flag when armies run.

Swift fire spread thro' her veins, knocked at her heart,
Met the fire smouldering there
And overbore its lesser flame;
She gorged on bitterness without a name: 510
Ah! fool, to choose such part
Of soul-consuming care!
Sense failed in the mortal strife:
Like the watch-tower of a town
Which an earthquake shatters down,   515
Like a lightning-stricken mast,
Like a wind-uprooted tree
Spun about,
Like a foam-topped waterspout
Cast down headlong in the sea,   520
She fell at last;
Pleasure past and anguish past,
Is it death or is it life?

Life out of death.
That night long Lizzie watched by her,   525
Counted her pulse's flagging stir,
Felt for her breath,

Held water to her lips, and cooled her face
With tears and fanning leaves:
But when the first birds chirped about their eaves,   530
And early reapers plodded to the place
Of golden sheaves,
And dew-wet grass
Bowed in the morning winds so brisk to pass,
And new buds with new day   535
Opened of cup-like lilies on the stream,
Laura awoke as from a dream,
Laughed in the innocent old way,
Hugged Lizzie but not twice or thrice;
Her gleaming locks showed not one thread of grey,   540
Her breath was sweet as May
And light danced in her eyes.

Days, weeks, months, years
Afterwards, when both were wives
With children of their own;   545
Their mother-hearts beset with fears,
Their lives bound up in tender lives;
Laura would call the little ones
And tell them of her early prime,
Those pleasant days long gone   550
Of not-returning time:
Would talk about the haunted glen,
The wicked, quaint fruit-merchant men,
Their fruits like honey to the throat
But poison in the blood;   555
(Men sell not such in any town:)
Would tell them how her sister stood
In deadly peril to do her good,
And win the fiery antidote:
Then joining hands to little hands   560
Would bid them cling together,
"For there is no friend like a sister
In calm or stormy weather;
To cheer one on the tedious way,
To fetch one if one goes astray,   565
To lift one if one totters down,
To strengthen whilst one stands."

ROSALÍA DE CASTRO
1837–1885

In northwestern Spain, just north of Portugal, lies the province called Galicia, where for centuries people have spoken a language, Galician, that is closer to Portuguese than to Castilian Spanish. Most writers considered this a low and vulgar dialect until the middle of the nineteenth century, when a poet and novelist named Rosalía de Castro began to celebrate this region, its customs, its folkways, and the language of its ordinary people. Her works helped to usher in what is called the "Galician Renaissance," and even now, every May 17, the anniversary of Rosalía de Castro's first Galician poetry collection, is celebrated as "Galician Literature Day."

Born in Santiago de Compostela, Rosalía de Castro was the child of an aristocratic mother and a Catholic priest who refused any contact with her. Doubly shamed as not only illegitimate but also "sacrilegious," she was raised by an aunt. Her first volume of poems, written in Castilian Spanish, brought her to the attention of an editor named Manuel Martinez Murguía, a champion of Galician culture. He published her work and encouraged her to write in Galician. Soon the two married and had seven children.

Over the course of her career, Rosalía de Castro wrote five novels and five volumes of poetry. Her fiction explores the subordinate position of women in Spanish society, and her poems turn again and again to quintessentially Romantic themes: the natural world, folk traditions, feelings of agonized, turbulent passion, and forebodings of death. Her intention, she said, was "to evoke all the splendor, and the sudden flashes of beauty, that emanate from every custom and thought of a people who have often been called stupid and sometimes judged insensitive or unfamiliar with refined poetry." She deliberately chose simple and accessible poetic forms, which would inspire such later Spanish writers as **Rubén Darío** and **Federico García Lorca**.

[As I composed this little book][1]

As I composed this little book, I thought:
Although my songs may never bring me fame,
    Simple they are and brief,
And may achieve, perhaps, my longed-for aim.
For they can be sure-fixed in memory   5
As are the prayers and rituals of belief,
Fervent though short, we learned in infancy.
Those we do not forget, in spite of grief
And time and distance and the destroying flame
Of passion. That is why my songs are brief   10
And simple,—though they may not bring me fame.

---

1. This and the following two poems were translated by S. Griswold Morley.

[A glowworm scatters flashes through the moss]

A glowworm scatters flashes through the moss;
A star gleams in its high remote domain.
Abyss above, and in the depths abyss:
What things come to an end and what remain?
   Man's thought—we call it science!—peers and pries   5
Into the soundless dark. But it is vain:
When all is done, we still are ignorant
Of what things reach an end, and what remain.

   Kneeling before an image rudely carved,
I sink my spirit in the Infinite,   10
And—is it impious?—I vacillate
And tremble, questioning Heaven and Hell of it.

   My Deity, shattered in a thousand bits,
Has fallen to chasms where I cannot see.
I rush to seek Him, and my groping meets   15
A solitary vast vacuity.

   When lo! from their lofty marble niches,
Angels gazed down in sorrow; and in my ears
Murmured a gentle voice: "Unhappy soul,
   Take hope; pour out thy tears   20
Before the feet of the Most High;
But well remember this: No insolent cry
   To Heaven makes its way
From one whose heart adores material things,
Who makes an idol out of Adam's clay."   25

[The ailing woman felt her forces ebb]

The ailing woman felt her forces ebb
With summer, and knew her time was imminent.
   "In autumn I shall die,"
She thought, half-melancholy, half-content,
"And I shall feel the leaves, that will be dead   5
Like me, drop on the grave in which I lie."

   Not even Death would do her so much pleasure.
   Cruel to her he too,
In winter spared her life, and when anew
The earth was being born in blossoming,   10
Slew her by inches to the joyous hymns
   Of fair and merry spring!

[I well know there is nothing]¹

I well know there is nothing
new under the sky,
that what I think of now
others have thought before.

Well, why do I write?   5
Well, because we are so,
clocks that repeat
forever the same.

[As the clouds]

As the clouds
borne by the wind,
now darken, now brighten
the immense spaces of the sky,
just so the mad   5
ideas I have,
the images of multiple forms,
of strange features, of vague colour,
now darken,
now brighten,   10
the abysmal depths of my mind.

[You will say about these verses, and it's true]

You will say about these verses, and it's true,
that they have a strange, unusual harmony,
that in them ideas wanly glow
as straying sparks
that explode at intervals   5
soon vanished;
that they resemble the unsteady leaf-fall
churning in the backyards,
and the pines monotonous sough
by the wild seashore.   10

And I will tell you, my songs
issue from my soul in confusion
as out of the deep oakwoods,
at the day's start,
an indefinable hum,   15
maybe the chafing of the breeze,
or the kissing of flowers,
or the rustic, mysterious harmonies
that in this sad world
are at a loss to find their way to Heaven.   20

1. This and the following three poems are translated by Michael Smith.

[Some say plants don't speak]

Some say plants don't speak, nor fountains, nor birds,
nor the wave with its swish, nor stars with their sparkle:
so say some, but it isn't true, since always as I pass by,
things whisper about me and exclaim:
                              —There goes the madwoman, dreaming   5
of the eternal spring of life and the fields,
though soon enough, all too soon, she will comb grey hair,
and shivering, numb, see the hoarfrost shroud the meadow.

—There's white hair on my head, hoarfrost in the meadows;
but I, poor soul, incurable sleepwalker, dream on and on   10
of expiring life's eternal spring
and the perennial freshness of fields and souls
even though these burn up and those wither.

Stars and fountains and flowers, don't murmur against my
                         dreams;
could I delight in you without them, without them, could I live?   15

[The feet of Spring are on the stair][1]

The feet of Spring are on the stair;
Her breath is sweet and warm and rare;
Beneath the soil in amorous heat
Seeds are astir with restless beat,
And atoms drifting in the air,   5
Afloat and silent, pair by pair,
     Kiss as they meet.

Youth's blood is eager, youth's heart is hot,
Its courage leaps, its bold mad thought
Believes that man—oh, dreams of youth!—   10
Is, like the gods, immortal. What
If dreams are lies? This much is truth:
Unblest are they who dreamless draw their breath,
And fortunate who in a dream find death.

How swift the passage of each thing   15
     In our sad world!
By a wild giant, quivering
     Our lives are whirled!
Yesterday bud, today a rose,
And then the sun-scorched blossom goes   20
     As Summer masters Spring.

1. Translated by S. Griswold Morley.

STÉPHANE MALLARMÉ
1842–1898

What would it be like to try to free poetry from the world of ordinary things? For Stéphane Mallarmé, it meant trying to figure out what makes poetry *poetry*—and not just another way of speaking about experience. It meant liberating poetic language from conventional everyday uses, such as the communication of facts and the reporting of events in newspapers. It meant refusing standard syntax, embracing incompleteness, moving fluidly among strange and disconnected images, and focusing on the sounds as much as the sense of words. The result was a kind of writing so deliberately strange and difficult that it has bewildered readers from its own time to ours. The writer **Marcel Proust** lamented, "How unfortunate that so gifted a man should become insane every time he takes up the pen." And the painter Edgar Degas ran out of a lecture by Mallarmé, shouting, "I do not understand!" But Mallarmé's poetry also sparked the intense enthusiasm of fellow writers, visual artists, and musicians—later called the "Symbolists"—who devoted themselves to creating an art of evocative moods and mysterious images and sensations.

LIFE

Mallarmé was born into a well-to-do middle-class family in Paris in 1842. His mother died when he was five, and his sister (his only sibling, whom Mallarmé adored) died when he was fifteen. Many critics have ascribed his existential anxiety and fascination with death to these painful early losses. As a young man, he married a German woman named Maria Gerhard, and together they had two children. Their son died at the age of eight.

Mallarmé had a long career as an English teacher, and even wrote an English textbook for French students. He was not a particularly good language teacher, had little aptitude for drills and discipline, and was often a figure of fun for his students. Frustrated that the French government repeatedly assigned him to teaching positions in the provinces, in 1871 he was relieved, finally, that he was able to move to Paris, capital of the arts. There he wrote reviews for newspapers and magazines, and he labored for months—sometimes even years—to perfect each of his innovative poems.

It was in Paris in 1880 that Mallarmé began holding exciting gatherings for artists, musicians, and writers, who flocked to hear him talk about the nature of art. These Tuesday-evening meetings became famous, and a whole generation of young artists found Mallarmé charismatic and inspiring. His influence spread widely: the painter Edouard Manet illustrated his verse, and the composer Claude Debussy famously set Mallarmé's "Afternoon of a Faun" to music. After he retired from teaching, he lectured on poetry and continued his radical experimentation with poetic form. He was elected "Prince of Poets" by his colleagues two years before his death in 1898.

WORK

"To tell, to teach, and even to describe have their place," wrote Mallarmé—but not in literature. Instead of "reporting," he insisted, literary writers should offer mysterious symbols and allusions.

Thus readers should not expect to enter a coherent and recognizable world, with descriptions and relationships explained. The poet urges us to take delight, instead, in images that remain elusive: "*To name* an object is to suppress three-quarters of the enjoyment of the poem, which derives from the pleasure of step-by-step discovery; to *suggest*, that is the dream . . . to evoke an object little by little, so as to bring to light a state of the soul or, inversely, to choose an object and bring out of it a state of the soul through a series of unravelings."

Mallarmé's best known and most influential work is the dramatic poem "The Afternoon of a Faun." The speaker is a woodland spirit from Roman mythology, part man and part goat, who is known both for his lustful appetites and for his skill in playing the flute. Mallarmé's faun tells us of his erotic pursuit of two beautiful water nymphs. Or was it a dream? The poem contemplates desire for beautiful objects that remain forever out of reach, and it interweaves erotic desire with questions about imagination and creativity. It has been especially celebrated for the extraordinary musicality of its verse, and the flute-playing faun may be a figure for the poet. In fact, Mallarmé often thought of music as a model for poetry, and in many of his works he focused intently on rhythm and sound. Sometimes he even began with a particular rhyme and worked backward to the text's images.

Mallarmé's poetry grew increasingly experimental with time. His last published work, "A Throw of the Dice Will Never Abolish Chance," took the form of a carefully designed visual object, printed in multiple typefaces with words arranged in unconventional ways, with huge gaps, across the page. This text is an important precursor to the concrete poetry of the twentieth century. Although Mallarmé's poems are immediately accessible on the level of visual imagery, they also offer the pleasure of a chess game for those who like to pursue intricate structures of thought. He works with sounds and letters, plays on words, and punning rhymes to produce rich patterns and echoes across each poem. Many of his early works also compel us to dwell on absences: hallmarks of his writing include hesitation and discontinuity, interruption and incompleteness. But his early poems, such as those included here, stay close to traditional verse forms. In French, "The Afternoon of a Faun" follows the alexandrine, or twelve-syllable line, in keeping with the most traditional French poetry, and "The Tomb of Edgar Poe," written for a memorial service for the American writer, is a sonnet.

So thought-provoking are his experiments in language that Mallarmé has been appreciated not only by poets and other artists but also by philosophers. This might not have surprised him. "Poetry," he insisted, is "the only possible human creation."

The Afternoon of a Faun[1]

Eclogue[2]

THE FAUN

These nymphs that I would perpetuate:

                              so clear
And light, their carnation,[3] that it floats in the air
Heavy with leafy slumbers.
My doubt, night's ancient hoard, pursues its theme
In branching labyrinths, which, being still   5
The veritable woods themselves, alas, reveal
My triumph as the ideal fault of roses.
Consider . . .

                    if the women of your glosses
Are phantoms of your fabulous[4] desires!
Faun, the illusion flees from the cold, blue eyes   10
Of the chaster nymph like a fountain gushing tears;
But the other, all in sighs, you say, compares
To a hot wind through the fleece that blows at noon?
No! through the motionless and weary swoon
Of stifling heat that suffocates the morning,   15
Save from my flute, no waters murmuring
In harmony flow out into the groves;
And the only wind on the horizon no ripple moves,
Exhaled from my twin pipes and swift to drain
The melody in arid drifts of rain,   20
Is the visible, serene and fictive air
Of inspiration rising as if in prayer.

RELATE, Sicilian shores,[5] whose tranquil fens
My vanity disturbs as do the suns,
Silent beneath the brilliant flowers of flame: 25
"That cutting hollow reeds my art would tame,
I saw far off, against the glaucous gold
Of foliage twined to where the springs run cold,
An animal whiteness languorously swaying;
To the slow prelude that the pipes were playing,   30
This flight of swans—no! naiads[6]*—rose in a shower*
Of spray . . ."

---

1. All poems translated by Henry Weinfield. In Greek mythology, a faun was a woodland satyr with goatlike hooves and horns.
2. A pastoral poem, usually in dialogue form, originating in Greek poetry. Here, italics indicate the divisions of the faun's internal dialogue.
3. A rosy flesh pink.
4. Fabled; i.e., both marvelous and narrated.
5. An invocation to the surrounding countryside, which recalls the openings of classical poems like the *Iliad* and the *Aeneid*.
6. Water nymphs.

Day burns inert in the tawny hour
And excess of hymen is escaped away—
Without a sign, from one who pined for the primal A:[7]
And so, beneath a flood of antique light,   35
As innocent as are the lilies white,
To my first ardors I awake alone.

Besides sweet nothings by their lips made known,
Kisses that only mark their perfidy,
My chest reveals an unsolved mystery . . .   40
The toothmarks of some strange, majestic creature:
Enough! Arcana such as these disclose their nature
Only through vast twin reeds played to the skies,
That, turning to music all that clouds the eyes,
Dream, in a long solo, that we amused   45
The beauty all around us by confused
Equations[8] with our credulous melody;
And dream that the song can make love soar so high
That, purged of all ordinary fantasies
Of back or breast—incessant shapes that rise   50
In blindness—it distills sonorities
From every empty and monotonous line.[9]

Then, instrument of flights; Syrinx[1] malign,
At lakes where you attend me, bloom once more!
Long shall my discourse from the echoing shore   55
Depict those goddesses: by masquerades,[2]
I'll strip the veils that sanctify their shades;
And when I've sucked the brightness out of grapes,
To quell the flood of sorrow that escapes,
I'll lift the empty cluster to the sky,   60
Avidly drunk till evening has drawn nigh,
And blow in laughter through the luminous skins.

Let us inflate our MEMORIES, O nymphs.
"Piercing the reeds, my darting eyes transfix,
Plunged in the cooling waves, immortal necks,   65
And cries of fury echo through the air;
Splendid cascades of tresses disappear
In shimmering jewels. Pursuing them, I find
There, at my feet, two sleepers intertwined,

---

7. The musical note A. In the French text it is
la (from the *do-re-mi* scale), which is also the
feminine article "the."
8. Playing his reed pipes, the faun creates a
musical line that is equated with the nymphs'
silhouette as he remembers it behind closed
eyes.

9. Lines 51 and 52 are one line in the French
text.
1. In Greek mythology, a nymph who fled
from the god Pan and was changed into a reed,
from which flutes, or panpipes, are made.
2. Literally, idolatrous pictures (of the
nymphs).

Bruised in the languor of duality,　　　　　　　　　70
Their arms about each other heedlessly.
I bear them, still entangled, to a height
Where frivolous shadow never mocks the light
And dying roses yield the sun their scent,
That with the day our passions might be spent."　　　75
I adore you, wrath of virgins—fierce delight
Of the sacred burden's writhing naked flight
From the fiery lightning of my lips that flash
With the secret terror of the thirsting flesh:
From the cruel one's feet to the heart of the shy,　　80
Whom innocence abandons suddenly,
Watered in frenzied or less woeful tears.
"Gay with the conquest of those traitorous fears,
I sinned when I divided the dishevelled
Tuft of kisses that the gods had ravelled.　　　　85
For hardly had I hidden an ardent moan
Deep in the joyous recesses of one
(Holding by a finger, that her swanlike pallor
From her sister's passion might be tinged with color,
The little one, unblushingly demure,　　　　　　90
When from my arms, loosened[3] *by death obscure,*
This prey, ungrateful to the end, breaks free,
Spurning the sobs that still transported me."

Others will lead me on to happiness,
Their tresses knotted round my horns, I guess.　　95
You know, my passion, that, crimson with ripe seeds,
Pomegranates burst in a murmur of bees,
And that our blood, seized by each passing form,
Flows toward desire's everlasting swarm.
In the time when the forest turns ashen and gold　100
And the summer's demise in the leaves is extolled,
Etna![4] when Venus visits her retreat,
Treading your lava with innocent feet,
Though a sad sleep thunders and the flame burns cold,
I hold the queen!
　　　　　　Sure punishment[5] . . .

　　　　　　　　　　　　No, but the soul,　　105
Weighed down by the body, wordless, struck dumb,
To noon's proud silence must at last succumb:
And so, let me sleep, oblivious of sin,
Stretched out on the thirsty sand, drinking in
The bountiful rays of the wine-growing star!　　110

Couple, farewell; I'll see the shade that now you are.

---

3. I.e., his arms were momentarily weakened.　　　in his heightened desire he fantasizes seizing
4. A volcano in Sicily.　　　　　　　　　　　　Venus, the goddess of love.
5. The faun imagines swift punishment when

The Tomb[1] of Edgar Poe

As to Himself at last eternity changes him
The Poet reawakens with a naked sword
His century appalled at never having heard
That in this voice triumphant death had sung its hymn.

They, like a writhing hydra, hearing seraphim[2]   5
Bestow a purer sense on the language of the horde,
Loudly proclaimed that the magic potion[3] had been poured
From the dregs of some dishonored mixture of foul slime.

From the war between earth and heaven, what grief!
If understanding cannot sculpt a bas-relief   10
To ornament the dazzling tomb of Poe:
Calm block here fallen from obscure disaster,[4]
Let this granite at least mark the boundaries evermore
To the dark flights of Blasphemy[5] hurled to the future.

Saint[1]

At the window frame concealing
The viol old and destitute
Whose gilded sandalwood, now peeling,
Once shone with mandolin or flute,

Is the Saint, pale, unfolding   5
The old, worn missal,[2] a divine
Magnificat[3] in rivers flowing
Once at vespers and compline:[4]

At the glass of this monstrance,[5] vessel
Touched by a harp that took its shape   10
From the evening flight of an Angel
For the delicate fingertip

1. A *tomb* is also a funeral poem. The poem
was written for a memorial ceremony honoring Edgar Allan Poe (1809–1849) in Baltimore, Maryland, and was first published in the
1877 memorial volume.
2. The Angel: the above said Poet [Mallarmé's
note]. Mallarmé explained this in English to
the memorial organizers. "Hydra": a mythical
many-headed serpent; here compared with
those who slandered Poe when he was alive.
3. In plain prose: Charged him with always
being drunk [Mallarmé's note]. Critics accused
Poe of finding inspiration in drunken fantasies.
4. The memorial marker ("Calm block") is seen
as a meteorite fallen from a dark or negative
star ("disaster"); a play on words: "aster" is Greek

for "star."
5. Blasphemy: against poets, such as the
charge of Poe being drunk [Mallarmé's note].
"Boundaries": literally, the milestone along
French roads, intended here to limit the batlike flights of slander.
1. The original title was "Saint Cecilia Playing on the Wing of an Angel."
2. Literally, an old book, probably containing
the music for the old instruments. Cecilia is
the patron saint of music.
3. A hymn of praise to God.
4. Evening church services. "Once": formerly.
5. An altar receptacle to hold the Host, with a
small glass window in front.

Which, without the old, worn missal
Or sandalwood, she balances
On the plumage instrumental,   15
Musician of silences.

[The virginal, vibrant, and beautiful dawn]

II

The virginal, vibrant, and beautiful dawn,
Will a beat of its drunken wing[1] not suffice
To rend this hard lake haunted beneath the ice
By the transparent glacier of flights never flown?

A swan of former times remembers it's the one   5
Magnificent but hopelessly struggling to resist
For never having sung of a land in which to exist
When the boredom of the sterile winter has shone.

Though its quivering neck will shake free of the agonies
Inflicted on the bird by the space it denies,   10
The horror of the earth will remain where it lies.
Phantom whose pure brightness assigns it this domain,
It stiffens in the cold dream of disdain
That clothes the useless exile of the Swan.[2]

---

1. A wild, impulsive gesture; also, an astonishing pun with "delivers" in French: *d'aile ivre/
délivre*.
2. The word *swan* rhymes with *sign* in French

(*cygne / signe*), and the capitalized Swan may
be read as a symbol of the writer's futile quest
for the absolute Sign.

PAUL VERLAINE
1844–1896

Most famous today for his decadent and bohemian life, Paul Verlaine spent time in prison for shooting his lover, and he passed his final years frequenting bars in Paris, hopelessly addicted to the notoriously dangerous green liquor, absinthe. But he was also, at the time, thought to be France's best poet. "You must have music first of all," he wrote, and indeed his poetry has often been praised above all for its rhythms and sounds. It is no accident, then, that he became a figurehead for the Symbolist movement—hailed, like **Mallarmé**, as a "Prince of Poets" by those artists who felt that writing should capture suggestive, atmospheric hints and feelings rather than reporting on the world. And if the abstract Mallarmé and the flamboyant **Rimbaud** are better known to modern readers, it is Verlaine whose asymmetrical lines and fleeting images most influenced twentieth-century poets in their rejection of traditional poetic forms and their exploration of free verse.

Born in Metz, Verlaine was the only son of indulgent parents. He began publishing poetry in his early twenties, and he would go on to write no fewer than twenty-four volumes, making him one of the most prolific poets of the nineteenth century. By his mid-twenties Verlaine was having problems with alcoholism and showing signs of sudden, violent rage, attacking his mother more than once. In an attempt to reform himself and settle down, he married Mathilde Mauté, a devout Catholic and sister of a friend. The next year, however, he met the seventeen-year old poet, Arthur Rimbaud, and they began a tempestuous relationship that ended his marriage. This new love affair, however, was also to be short-lived. In 1873 Verlaine shot Rimbaud in the arm and went to jail for two years. It was during this time that he published his most admired work, *Songs Without Words*, and critics have often remarked that Verlaine's best poetry was composed during the most tumultuous periods in his life. While in prison, Verlaine also turned to the religion of his childhood, Catholicism. When he was released from jail he took up with a new lover and together they tried farming, but this venture failed and Verlaine moved back in with his mother. Thrown into jail a second time for violence, he emerged to face a terrible end. His last years were spent in poverty and alcohol

addiction. During his last decade, however, his literary reputation was on the rise. The next generation of poets in France and England looked on him as a master, admiring both his poetry and his non-conformist ways.

In Verlaine's writing, his imagery is often elusive and fragmentary, even vague, and he evokes moods rather than describing detailed realities. He lavishes attention on sound, not only pursuing a variety of rhymes, but also exploring the many rich possibilities of assonance—the echoing of vowel sounds—and the repetition of consonants. He was especially fascinated by rhythms throughout his career, sometimes opting for long, slow lines, sometimes for broken and fragmentary ones. One of the most interesting examples of Verlaine's experiments in rhythm is the poem "Wooden Horses," which follows an insistent, harsh tempo to evoke a busy merry-go-round in an amusement park. The final poem included here, called "The Art of Poetry," outlines Verlaine's program for breaking from poetic tradition. No more even rhythms; no more fixed images with clear outlines and colors; no more witty epigrams or attempts at persuasion. These all belong to an outdated category Verlaine calls "literature"; they are not authentic poetry. Poetry, for Verlaine, must involve the joys of shade and nuance, and must pursue the *vers impair,* a poetic line with an odd number of syllables that often creates a floating effect. In French, "The Art of Poetry" follows a nine-syllable line, but otherwise it does not always practice what it preaches. For example, if all poetry should involve suggestion, dream, and nuance rather than definition, persuasion, and exactitude, then "The Art of Poetry," with its prescriptive formulas ("You must have music first of all," and "Never the Color, always the Shade"), does not meet its own requirements. Perhaps Verlaine decided to write one last work of ordinary "literature" in order to send conventional poetry to its grave. If so, he succeeded. This poem became Verlaine's most famous and was taken up as the unofficial manifesto of the Symbolist movement, which helped to revolutionize European poetry.

Autumn Song[1]

With long sobs
the violin-throbs
    of autumn wound
my heart with languorous
and monotonous   5
    sound.

Choking and pale
when I mind the tale
    the hours keep,
my memory strays   10
down other days
    and I weep;

and I let me go
where ill winds blow,
    now here, now there,   15
harried and sped,
even as a dead
    leaf, anywhere.

Wooden Horses[1]

By Saint-Gille
let's away,
my light-footed bay. —V. Hugo[2]

Turn, good wooden horses, round
a hundred turns, a thousand turns.
Forever turn till the axles burn,
turn, turn, to the oboes' sound.

The big soldier and the fattest maid   5
ride your backs as if in their chamber,

---

1. All poems translated by C. F. MacIntyre. The poem is one of the "Mournful Landscapes" in *Saturnian Poems* (1866).
1. From *Songs Without Words* (1874).

2. French poet (1802–1885). Saint-Gilles is a suburb of Brussels, Belgium, with a public fairground.

because their masters have also made
an outing today in the Bois de la Cambre.[3]

Turn, turn, horses of their hearts,
while all around your whirling there   10
are the clever sharpers[4] at their art;
turn to the cornet's bragging blare.

It's as much fun as getting dead
drunk, to ride in this silly ring!
Good for the belly, bad for the head,   15
a plenty good and a plenty bad thing.

Turn, turn, no need today
of any spurs to make you bound,
galloping around and round,
turn, turn, without hope of hay.   20

And hurry, horses of their love,
already night is falling here
and the pigeon flies to join the dove,
far from madame, far from the fair.

Turn! Turn! Slow evening comes,   25
in velvet, buttoned up with stars.
Away the lovers go, in pairs.
Turn to the beat of the joyous drums.

The Art of Poetry[1]

You must have music first of all,
and for that a rhythm uneven[2] is best,
vague in the air and soluble,
with nothing heavy and nothing at rest.

You must not scorn to do some wrong   5
in choosing the words to fill your lines:
nothing more dear than the tipsy song
where the Undefined and Exact combine.

It is the veiled and lovely eye,
the full noon quivering with light;   10
it is, in the cool of an autumn sky,
the blue confusion of stars at night!

---

3. An elegant park south of Brussels.
4. Literally, pickpockets.
1. From *Yesteryear and Yesterday* (1884), written in 1874.
2. The *vers impair* (line with an uneven number of syllables), which gives traditional
French readers a sense of "nothing at rest."
This poem uses a nine-syllable line and—as
here—often illustrates its points.

Never the Color, always the Shade,
always the nuance is supreme!
Only by shade is the trothal made   15
between flute and horn, of dream with dream!

Epigram's an assassin! Keep
away from him, fierce Wit, and vicious
laughter that makes the Azure[3] weep,
and from all that garlic of vulgar dishes!   20

Take Eloquence and wring his neck!
You would do well, by force and care,
wisely to hold Rhyme in check,
or she's off—if you don't watch—God knows where!

Oh, who will tell the wrongs of Rhyme?   25
What crazy negro or deaf child
made this trinket for a dime,
sounding hollow and false when filed?

Let there be music, again and forever!
Let your verse be a quick-wing'd thing and light—   30
such as one feels when a new love's fervor
to other skies wings the soul in flight.

Happy-go-lucky, let your lines
disheveled run where the dawn winds lure,
smelling of wild mint, smelling of thyme . . .   35
and all the rest is literature.

---

3. The sky's unbroken azure was, for many Symbolists, an image of absolute poetry as opposed to vulgarity.

JOSÉ MARTÍ
1853–1895

The Cuban writer José Martí always entwined his revolutionary political activities with his art. Arrested at the age of sixteen for writing subversive literature, he was killed twenty-six years later by a Spanish bullet in a war for Cuban independence. In the intervening years, he became known as an orator, a teacher, a diplomat, a widely respected journalist, a political and literary essayist, a groundbreaking poet, and a committed organizer of the struggle to free Cuba from Spanish colonial rule. His most important works, *Our America* (1891) and *Versos Sencillos* (*Simple Songs*, 1891), helped to formulate the concept of America for Latin Americans. Martí's dedication to freedom and human rights and his committed antiracism made him a political hero (today his face appears on Cuban coins, and the Havana airport is named after him), while his deliberately simplified poetic diction and his rejection of conventional Spanish verse forms paved the way for Latin American *modernismo*, the exciting experimental poetry that emerged at the end of the nineteenth century.

Martí's best-known poem, "I Am an Honest Man," with its values of sincerity, simplicity, and intense emotion,

astonished readers when it first appeared, dramatically overturning dominant traditions of Spanish poetry that had valued complex, artful structures and Romantic sentimentality. This poem has long been beloved by Cubans, but it became world famous when it was set to the tune of *Guantanamera* ("the woman from Guantánamo"), a popular Cuban melody. Julián Orbón, a musician and composer, wanted to dignify this popular song and did so by borrowing celebrated words for it from the martyred poet-hero Martí. It is now the unofficial anthem of both island and exiled Cubans, and musicians around the world have translated and recorded it. The U.S. folk singer Pete Seeger helped to propel the song to international fame in the 1960s.

I Am an Honest Man[1]

(Guantanamera)

I am an honest man
From where the palm grows
And before I die I wish
To fling my verses from my soul.
I come from everywhere   5
And I am going toward everywhere:
Among the arts, I am art
In the mountains, I am a mountain.
I know the strange names
Of the herbs and flowers   10
And of mortal deceits
And of sublime pains.
I have seen in the dark night
Rain over my head
The pure rays of lightning   15
Of divine beauty.
I saw wings born in men
Of beautiful women:
And coming out of rubbish
Butterflies flying.   20
I have seen a man live

1. Translated by Aviva Chomsky.

With his dagger at his side,
Without ever saying the name
Of she who had killed him.
Rapid, like a reflection,   25
I saw my soul, twice
When the poor old man died,
When she said good-bye to me.
I trembled once—at the fence,
At the entrance to the vineyard—   30
When a barbarous bee
Stung my daughter in the forehead.
I felt joy once, such that
Nobody ever felt joy: when
The mayor read the sentence   35
Of my death, crying.
I hear a sigh, across
The lands and the sea
And it is not a sigh, it is
That my son is going to wake up.   40
They say that from the jeweler
I took the best jewel,
I took a sincere friend
And left love aside.

ARTHUR RIMBAUD
1854–1891

In a brief, dazzling literary career, which lasted from the age of fifteen to the age of twenty, Arthur Rimbaud expanded the visionary and experimental possibilities of modern poetry. Taking literally the ancient notion of the poet as a prophet, he determined to push poetic vision beyond all familiar bounds, violently and dramatically, "by the systematic derangement *of all the senses.*" Rimbaud dedicated himself to a transformation of existence that exceeded even the written word: in ordinary life, he actively rebelled against rules of etiquette and conventional morality to produce a revolutionary reimagining of experience intended to explode entrenched patterns of thought and usher in a radically different future. Idealistic, defiant, deliberately rude, bitter, profoundly anti-conventional and astonishingly talented, Rimbaud, as one admirer explained, passed like a lightning bolt through French literature.

Jean-Nicholas-Arthur Rimbaud was born on October 20, 1854, in Charleville, a town in northeastern France. His military father abandoned the family when Arthur was seven, and his embittered mother raised her four children in a repressive, disciplinary atmosphere. Rimbaud was a highly gifted student who read widely, but he was also unruly, running away from home more than once to live as a vagrant. In 1871 the seventeen-year-old writer sent some of his work to an established Parisian poet, **Paul Verlaine**, who was so impressed that he invited Rimbaud to stay with him in Paris. Expecting to meet a man in his twenties, Verlaine was shocked to behold the "real head of a child, chubby and fresh, on a big, bony rather clumsy body of a still-growing adolescent." Far from innocent, however, Rimbaud sneered and swore, stole books and broke objects, and deliberately used literary magazines as toilet paper. He also wrote staggeringly innovative works of poetry. Verlaine was drawn to this gifted and uncompromising outsider, and the two began a tumultuous love affair, which ended two years later when Verlaine went to prison for shooting his young lover in a fight. At the age of nineteen Rimbaud decided to renounce poetry, and he traveled as a commercial trader to Cyprus, Java, and Aden, eventually becoming a gunrunner in Abyssinia (now Ethiopia). Falling ill with a cancerous tumor in one knee, he returned to France to die in 1891, one month after his thirty-seventh birthday.

Rimbaud's work resists Romantic traditions of lyric poetry that cherish the self as the site and source of meaningful experience. He suggests instead that multiple, disjointed, and borrowed experiences precede the self, making it what it is. One should not say "I think," he wrote, but rather "I am being thought," as if our thoughts come before us, rather than the other way around. In one of his most famous lines, he claimed "je est un autre" ("I is an other"), his deliberate grammatical error signaling a whole new way of regarding the self as if it were an external object.

We can see one radical revision of the lyric "I" in Rimbaud's most famous poem, "The Drunken Boat," which speaks from the perspective of the boat itself, one that leaves the rivers of Europe for the sea, where it experiences a thoroughgoing freedom and encounters a kind of total reality, both beautiful and terrifying, both creative and destructive, and ends in failure and the desire for self-annihilation, longing to be only a poor child's paper boat sailing in a black puddle. Rimbaud had at this point in his life never seen the sea, but the images he has borrowed from adventure novels, newspapers, and epic poetry allow him to bring together bits and pieces of imaginative intensity to see the world from the strange and unknowable vantage point of a boat.

The bitter prose poem, *A Season in Hell*, also unsettles the conventional first-person narrative. On the one hand it seems to be autobiographical, offering insight into the poet's life, but on the other hand it gives us as much hallucination as fact, and it turns into disjointed images in place of a coherent story: "I saw very plainly a mosque in place of a factory, a school of drummers composed of angels. . . . I became a fabulous opera." Similarly, the *Illuminations* offer a series of transformations that leave only traces of their points of departure, immersing the reader in free associations, cutting short all logical organization to develop an almost musical organization of themes and images. And "Barbarian," set outside recognizable parameters of time and space, gives us a vision—without logic or story—that operates according to a pattern of oppositions: red and white, heat and cold, subterranean volcanoes and starry sky. All of these works swing between an ideal world and the pain of repugnant and sordid realities, and all of them explode—often violently—dreams of a coherent and stable self.

The Drunken Boat[1]

As I descended black, impassive Rivers,
I sensed that haulers[2] were no longer guiding me:
Screaming Redskins took them for their targets,
Nailed nude to colored stakes: barbaric trees.

I was indifferent to all my crews;   5
I carried English cottons, Flemish wheat.
When the disturbing din of haulers ceased,
The Rivers let me ramble where I willed.

Through the furious ripping of the sea's mad tides,
Last winter, deafer than an infant's mind,   10
I ran! And drifting, green Peninsulas
Did not know roar more gleefully unkind.

A tempest blessed my vigils on the sea.
Lighter than a cork I danced on the waves,
Those endless rollers, as they say, of graves: 15
Ten nights beyond a lantern's[3] silly eye!

Sweeter than sourest apple-flesh to children,
Green water seeped into my pine-wood hull
And washed away blue wine[4] stains, vomitings,
Scattering rudder, anchor, man's lost rule.   20

And then I, trembling, plunged into the Poem
Of the Sea,[5] infused with stars, milk-white,
Devouring azure greens; where remnants, pale
And gnawed, of pensive corpses fell from light;

Where, staining suddenly the blueness, delirium.   25
The slow rhythms of the pulsing glow of day,
Stronger than alcohol and vaster than our lyres,
The bitter reds of love ferment the way!

I know skies splitting into light, whirled spouts
Of water, surfs, and currents: I know the night,   30
The dawn exalted like a flock of doves, pure wing,
And I have seen what men imagine they have seen.

I saw the low sun stained with mystic horrors,
Lighting long, curdled clouds of violet,
Like actors in a very ancient play,   35
Waves rolling distant thrills like lattice[6] light!

1. Translated by Stephen Stepanchev.
2. The image is of a commercial barge being towed along a canal.
3. Port beacons.
4. A cheap, ordinary, bitter wine.

5. A play on words, "Poem" suggests "creation" (Greek *poiein*, "making"); "Sea," the source or "mother" of life, sounds the same as "mother" in French (*mer / mère*).
6. Like the ripple of venetian blinds.

I dreamed of green night, stirred by dazzling snows,
Of kisses rising to the sea's eyes, slowly,
The sap-like coursing of surprising currents,
And singing phosphors,[7] flaring blue and gold!   40

I followed, for whole months, a surge like herds
Of insane cattle in assault on the reefs,
Unhopeful that three Marys,[8] come on luminous feet,
Could force a muzzle on the panting seas!

Yes, I struck incredible Floridas[9]   45
That mingled flowers and the eyes of panthers
In skins of men! And rainbows bridled green
Herds beneath the horizon of the seas.

I saw the ferment of enormous marshes, weirs
Where a whole Leviathan[1] lies rotting in the weeds!   50
Collapse of waters within calms at sea,
And distances in cataract toward chasms!

Glaciers, silver suns, pearl waves, and skies like coals,
Hideous wrecks at the bottom of brown gulfs
Where giant serpents eaten by red bugs   55
Drop from twisted trees and shed a black perfume!

I should have liked to show the young those dolphins
In blue waves, those golden fish, those fish that sing.
—Foam like flowers rocked my sleepy drifting,
And, now and then, fine winds supplied me wings.   60

When, feeling like a martyr, I tired of poles and zones,
The sea, whose sobbing made my tossing sweet,
Raised me its dark flowers, deep and yellow whirled,
And, like a woman, I fell on my knees . . .[2]

Peninsula, I tossed upon my shores   65
The quarrels and droppings of clamorous, blond-eyed birds.
I sailed until, across my rotting cords,
Drowned men, spinning backwards, fell asleep! . . .

Now I, a lost boat in the hair of coves,[3]
Hurled by tempest into a birdless air,   70
I, whose drunken carcass neither Monitors
Nor Hansa ships[4] would fish back for men's care;

---

7. *Noctiluca*, tiny marine animals.
8. A legend that the three biblical Marys crossed the sea during a storm to land in Camargue, a region in southern France famous for its horses and bulls.
9. A name (plural) given to any exotic country.
1. Vast biblical sea monster (Job 41.1–10).

2. The poet's ellipses; nothing has been omitted.
3. Seaweed.
4. Vessels belonging to the German Hanseatic League of commercial maritime cities. "Monitors": armored coast guard ships, after the iron-clad Union warship *Monitor* of the American Civil War.

Free, smoking, rigged with violet fogs,
I, who pierced the red sky like a wall
That carries exquisite mixtures for good poets,   75
Lichens of sun and azure mucus veils;

Who, spotted with electric crescents, ran
Like a mad plank, escorted by seashores,
When cudgel blows of hot Julys struck down
The sea-blue skies upon wild water spouts;   80

I, who trembled, feeling the moan at fifty leagues
Of rutting Behemoths[5] and thick Maelstroms, I,
Eternal weaver of blue immobilities,
I long for Europe with its ancient quays!

I saw sidereal archipelagoes! and isles   85
Whose delirious skies are open to the voyager:
—Is it in depthless nights you sleep your exile,
A million golden birds, O future Vigor?—

But, truly, I have wept too much! The dawns disturb.
All moons are painful, and all suns break bitterly: 90
Love has swollen me with drunken torpors.
Oh, that my keel might break and spend me in the sea!

Of European waters I desire
Only the black, cold puddle in a scented twilight
Where a child of sorrows squats and sets the sails   95
Of a boat as frail as a butterfly in May.

I can no longer, bathed in languors, O waves,
Cross the wake of cotton-bearers on long trips,
Nor ramble in a pride of flags and flares,
Nor swim beneath the horrible eyes of prison ships.[6]   100

From A Season in Hell[1]

Night of Hell

I have swallowed a first-rate draught of poison.—Thrice blessed be the counsel that came to me!—My entrails are on fire. The violence of the venom wrings my limbs, deforms me, fells me. I am dying of thirst, I am suffocating, I cannot cry out. This is hell, the everlasting punishment! Mark how the fire surges up again! I am burning properly. There you are, demon!

---

5. Biblical animal resembling a hippopotamus (Job 40.15–24).
6. Portholes of ships tied at anchor and used as prisons.
1. Translated by Enid Rhodes Peschel. *Night of Hell* is the second section (after the preface) of the autobiographical *A Season in Hell*.

The first section, *Bad Blood*, describes his solitary childhood and sense of being a member of an "inferior race." It also contrasts an authoritarian and hypocritical European society with African paganism, which is seen as a freer and more natural existence.

I had caught a glimpse of conversion to righteousness and happiness, salvation. May I describe the vision; the atmosphere of hell does not permit hymns! It consisted of millions of charming creatures, a sweet sacred concert, power and peace, noble ambitions, and goodness knows what else.

Noble ambitions![2]

And yet this is life!—What if damnation is eternal! A man who chooses to mutilate himself is rightly damned, isn't he? I believe that I am in hell, consequently I am there.[3] This is the effect of the catechism. I am the slave of my baptism.[4] Parents, you have caused my affliction and you have caused your own. Poor innocent!—Hell cannot assail pagans.—This is life, nevertheless! Later, the delights of damnation will be deeper. A crime, quickly, that I may sink to nothingness, in accordance with human law.

Be silent, do be silent! . . . There is shame, reproof, in this place: Satan who says that the fire is disgraceful, that my wrath is frightfully foolish.—Enough! . . . The errors that are whispered to me, enchantments, false perfumes, childish melodies.[5]—And to say that I possess truth, that I understand justice: I have a sound and steady judgment, I am prepared for perfection . . . Pride.—The skin of my head is drying up. Pity! Lord, I am terrified. I am thirsty, so thirsty! Ah! childhood, the grass, the rain, the lake upon the stones, *the moonlight when the bell tower was striking twelve*[6] . . . the devil is in the bell tower, at that hour. Mary! Blessed Virgin! . . . —The horror of my stupidity.

Over there, are they not honest-souls, who wish me well? . . . Come . . . I have a pillow over my mouth, they don't hear me, they are phantoms. Besides, no one ever thinks of others. Let no one approach. I reek of burning, that's certain.

The hallucinations are countless. It's exactly what I've always had: no more faith in history, neglect of principles. I shall be silent about this: poets and visionaries would be jealous. I am a thousand times the richest, let us be avaricious like the sea.

Now then! the clock of life has just stopped. I am no longer in the world.—Theology is serious, hell is certainly *below*—and heaven above.—Ecstasy, nightmare, sleep in a nest of flames.

What pranks during my vigilance in the country . . . Satan, Ferdinand,[7] races with wild seeds . . . Jesus walks on the purplish briers, without bending them . . . Jesus used to walk on the troubled waters.[8] The lantern revealed him to us, a figure standing, pale and with brown tresses, beside a wave of emerald. . . .

I am going to unveil all the mysteries: mysteries religious or natural, death, birth, futurity, antiquity, cosmogony, nothingness, I am a master of phantasmagories.

Listen! . . .

I have all the talents!—There is nobody here and there is somebody: I would not wish to scatter my treasure.—Do you wish for Negro chants, dances of

2. Mockery of his childhood idealism and attraction to traditional Catholicism.

3. A parody of French philosopher René Descartes's (1596–1650) phrase "I think, therefore I am," which had become a symbol of well-ordered thought.

4. Because baptism creates the possibility of both heaven and hell.

5. The poetic visions and harmonies that Rimbaud explored with Paul Verlaine.

6. A collection of romanticized childhood memories.

7. Peasant name for the devil.

8. Jesus' disciples saw him walking on the sea at night (John 6.16–21).

houris?[9] Do you wish me to vanish, to dive in search of the *ring*?[1] Do you? I shall produce gold, cures.

Rely, then, upon me: faith comforts, guides, heals. All of you, come,—even the little children,[2]—that I may console you, that one may pour out his heart for you,—the marvelous heart!—Poor men, laborers! I do not ask for prayers; with your confidence alone, I shall be happy.

—And let's think of me. This makes me miss the world very little. I have the good fortune not to suffer any longer. My life was nothing but sweet follies, regrettably.

Bah! let's make all the grimaces imaginable.

Decidedly, we are out of the world. No more sound. My sense of touch has disappeared. Ah! my castle, my Saxony,[3] my forest of willows. The evenings, the mornings, the nights, the days . . . Am I weary!

I ought to have my hell for wrath, my hell for pride,—and the hell of the caress; a concert of hells.

I am dying of weariness. This is the tomb, I am going to the worms, horror of horrors! Satan, jester, you wish to undo me, with your spells. I protest. I protest! one jab of the pitchfork, one lick of fire.

Ah! to rise again to life! To cast eyes upon our deformities. And that poison, that kiss a thousand times accursed! My weakness, the cruelty of the world! Dear God, your mercy, hide me, I regard myself too poorly!—I am hidden and I am not.

It is the fire that rises again with the soul condemned to it.

From THE ILLUMINATIONS[1]

The Bridges[2]

Crystal-gray skies. A bizarre pattern of bridges, some of them straight, others convex, still others descending or veering off at angles to the first ones, and these shapes multiplying in the other illuminated circuits of the canal,[3] but all of them so long and delicate that the riverbanks burdened with domes fall away and diminish. Some of these bridges are still lined with hovels.[4] Others support masts, signals, frail parapets. Minor chords meet and leave each other, ropes climb up from the banks. One can make out a red jacket, perhaps other costumes and musical instruments. Are these popular tunes, fragments of concerts offered by the aristocracy, snatches of public hymns? The water is gray and blue, wide as an arm of the sea.—A white ray, falling from the top of the sky, wipes out this bit of theatricality.

9. Beautiful virgins in the Koranic paradise.
1. At the end of Wagner's opera *Götterdämmerung*, Hagen plunges into the river Rhine to recapture the golden ring of world power.
2. Parody of Jesus' words "Suffer little children, and forbid them not, to come unto me" (Matthew 19.14).
3. Germanic duchy, part of Rimbaud's visionary memories.
1. This and the following selection are translated by John Ashbery.
2. An impressionistic memory of London.
3. The river Thames as it winds through the city.
4. Houses were once built on London Bridge.

Barbarian

Long after the days and the seasons, and the beings and the countries,

The pennant of bloody meat[1] against the silk of arctic seas and flowers; (they don't exist.)

Recovered from old fanfares of heroism—which still attack our hearts and heads—far from the ancient assassins—

Oh! The pennant of bloody meat against the silk of arctic seas and flowers; (they don't exist)

Sweetness!

Live coals raining down gusts of frost,—Sweetness!—those flashes in the rain of the wind of diamonds thrown down by the terrestrial heart eternally charred for us.—O world!—

(Far from the old refuges and the old fires that we can hear, can smell,)

The live coals and the foam. Music, wheeling of abysses and shock of ice floes against the stars.

O Sweetness, O world, O music! And there, shapes, sweat, tresses and eyes, floating. And the white, boiling tears.—O sweetness!—and the voice of woman reaching to the depths of the arctic volcanoes and caverns.

The pennant. . . .

1. Perhaps a reference to the Danish flag (a white cross on a red field), which Rimbaud would have seen on a visit to Iceland, then a Danish possession.

RUBÉN DARÍO

1867–1916

Rubén Darío was the first poet of *Modernismo*—a movement that revolutionized Spanish American poetry. He was inspired by the French Symbolists, and he fused their poetic innovations with a range of traditions, including his own indigenous ancestry, occult science, and ancient Greek mythology, to create a startling new sensibility. Darío's life, like his poetry, spanned continents and historical moments. He was born in Nicaragua, lived in Chile and Argentina, worked for the Colombian government, and spent many years in Europe as a reporter and diplomat, managing to serve as a bridge between countries and generations. When two later writers, **Pablo Neruda** and **García Lorca**, paid homage to Darío in 1933, they called him "that great Nicaraguan, Argentinian, Chilean, and Spanish poet" whose poetry, "crisscrossed with sounds and dreams . . . stands solidly outside of norms, forms, and schools."

LIFE

Rubén Darío was born Félix Rubén García y Sarmiento in a small village in Nicaragua now called Ciudad Darío (Darío City). His parents separated when he was only eight months old, and he was sent to live with an aunt and uncle in the old city of Léon. His autobiography describes the impression made on him by the antiquated house and the ghostly horror stories told after dinner, which gave him nightmares. Before he was eight, he had made a name for himself as a child-poet and soon became well known in the region. At fourteen he began submitting articles to newspapers, and in 1886 he moved to Chile, where he worked as a journalist and wrote poetry. It was here, two years later, that he published *Azul* (*Blue*), a collection of his writing that would come to be recognized as a turning point in Spanish American literary history.

In 1891 Nicaragua arranged to send a delegation to Spain for the fourth centennial of the European discovery of America, and Darío went as secretary to the delegation. Exhilarated by the warm reception he experienced as a representative of Spanish American letters, he moved to Argentina with new confidence in his role as a spokesperson for Latin American literature and culture.

Darío married twice and had two children who survived to adulthood. In the early years of the twentieth century, he lived in Madrid and then in Paris. Eventually, suffering from cirrhosis of the liver and barely making a living in Europe, he returned to Nicaragua, where he died in 1916. After his death, the government ordered national mourning and granted him the burial honors of a high-level minister, while the Church performed funeral services usually reserved for royalty.

BETWEEN TWO EMPIRES

To have grown up in Nicaragua in the late nineteenth century was to find oneself caught between two empires. Though the Spanish government had lost most of its colonies in the fierce battles for independence that had been waged in the early decades of the nineteenth century, Spain still exerted its powerful influence over Latin America through language and institutions—including the Catholic Church—as well as continued political control of Cuba and Puerto Rico. Meanwhile, the United States had become the major power in the region and was threatening to use its military strength against European states that might try to exert authority in the hemisphere. The 1823 Monroe Doctrine had proclaimed that the United States would interpret any European attempt to interfere with territory in the Americas as an act of aggression and would retaliate. Thus, when Cuba began to struggle for independence in 1868, tensions between Spain and the United States began to mount until 1898 when war erupted, and with Spain's defeat the United States took over almost all of Spain's remaining colonies, including the Philippines, Guam, and Puerto Rico. The Spanish-American War, as it came to be called, established the United States as an imperial power far more frightening to many in Latin America than Spain.

It was in this context that Darío turned toward Spain, and away from the United States. At the very end of the nineteenth century he traveled to Spain as a journalist to report on that country's defeat in the Spanish-American War. He quickly became a figure in Spanish intellectual and literary circles, and saw European culture as a rich resource for poets and intellectuals, while the United States seemed to him aggressive, greedy, and culturally barbaric. He started to envision a new literary geography that would include modern Spanish and Latin American writers, but would remain proudly separate from the looming influence of the United States. And yet his opposition to the U.S. was not absolute. At times Darío offered homage to the American poet **Walt Whitman**, and he remained fully conscious of Spain's long history of torturing and exploiting Indian peoples. Thus, like many of his contemporaries, he remained suspicious of both empires, and he longed for a Latin American cultural and political renewal that would entail a new kind of self-determination.

WORK

Although Darío is known for modernizing Latin American poetry, he was not one to discard traditional literary forms and conventions. His works deliberately recall forms with a long history—such as the *blasón* (blazon), a love poem that lists the beauties of the beloved. He also drew on age-old images, such as the swan, Darío's favorite symbol of artistic inspiration—ideally beautiful, and yet haunted by doubt, with its neck swerving into the shape of a question mark. All of this suggests a deep debt to tradition. But what felt strikingly new to his contemporaries was Darío's style. The poems, short stories, and sketches in the early collection *Blue* seemed far more similar to the evocative, jewel-like recent work of French Symbolist writers—such as **Verlaine**, one of Darío's great heroes—than to contemporary Spanish-language writers, who tended to favor long rhetorical passages. His sentences were surprisingly short, with rhythmic and stylistic variations; he preferred foreign, even exotic subjects, and rare and musical words. "Words should paint the color of a sound, the aroma of a star; they should capture the very soul of things," he wrote. Like many of the French Symbolists, then, he evoked ideal beauties in rich images rather than describing gritty realities, and he concentrated his attention on the musical qualities of his verse. He also purified his language of anything coarse or vulgar and produced a rigorously flawless technical brilliance that was entirely different from any poetry that had been written in Spanish before. At the same time, there was always a sense of melancholy, of longing and doubt, as if the pursuit of the ideal was always doomed to failure.

Darío's final collection, *Songs of Life and Hope*, continued the emphasis on musicality and technical perfection but also displayed a new poetic awakening to contemporary political and cultural concerns, as well as a somber interrogation of the poet's own mortality, as we see in the poem "Fatality." These final poems, including "Leda" and "To Roosevelt," invite a new sense of violence that breaks from the perfectly crafted, ideal gems that are the early work.

Darío's influence was already so overpowering by 1910 that a young Mexican poet named Enrique González Martínez urged his fellow poets to "wring the swan's neck." And yet poets have continued to return to Darío for inspiration. Indeed, his work has had such a profound impact that some literary historians have broken the story of Spanish-language poetry into two periods—before and after Darío.

Blazon[1]

For the Countess of Peralta

The snow-white Olympic[2] swan,
with beak of rose-red agate,
preens his eucharistic[3] wing,
which he opens to the sun like a fan.

His shining neck is curved   5
like the arm of a lyre,
like the handle of a Greek amphora,[4]
like the prow of a ship.

He is the swan of divine origin
whose kiss mounted through fields   10
of silk to the rosy peaks
of Leda's[5] sweet hills.

White king of Castalia's fount,
his triumph illumines the Danube;[6]
Da Vinci was his baron in Italy;   15
Lohengrin[7] is his blond prince.

His whiteness is akin to linen,
to the buds of white roses,
to the diamantine white
of the fleece of an Easter lamb.   20

He is the poet of perfect verses,
and his lyric cloak is of ermine;
he is the magic, the regal bird
who, dying, rhymes the soul in his song.

This wingèd aristocrat displays   25
white lilies on a blue field;
and Pompadour,[8] gracious and lovely,
has stroked his feathers.

---

1. This and the following poems are translated by Lysander Kemp. "Blazon": both a
heraldic coat of arms and a poem that enumerates various qualities of the beloved.
2. Associated with Mount Olympus, home of
the gods in Greek mythology.
3. Like the white wafer used in the Eucharist,
the Christian ritual of communion.
4. Large two-handled jar used in ancient
Greece for storing wine or oil.
5. In Greek mythology, a nymph raped by
Zeus, who had taken the form of a swan, she
gave birth to Helen of Troy.

6. A major river in central Europe. "Castalia's
fount": the spring of Castalia on Mount Parnassus, home of the Greek Muses.
7. The "Swan Knight" of Wagner's opera
Lohengrin (1850). "Da Vinci": Leonardo da
Vinci (1452–1519), the Renaissance artist
and inventor.
8. The Marquise de Pompadour (1721–1764)
was the mistress of King Louis XV of France.
"White lilies on a blue field": the fleur-de-lis.
The coat of arms of the French kings displayed
white lilies on a blue background.

He rows and rows on the lake
where dreams wait for the unhappy,   30
where a golden gondola waits
for the sweetheart of Louis of Bavaria.[9]

Countess, give the swans your love,
for they are gods of an alluring land
and are made of perfume and ermine,   35
of white light, of silk, and of dreams.

I Seek a Form . . .

I seek a form that my style cannot discover,
a bud of thought that wants to be a rose;
it is heralded by a kiss that is placed on my lips
in the impossible embrace of the Venus de Milo.[1]

The white peristyle[2] is decorated with green palms;   5
the stars have predicted that I will see the goddess;
and the light reposes within my soul like the bird
of the moon reposing on a tranquil lake.

And I only find the word that runs away,
the melodious introduction that flows from the flute,[3]   10
the ship of dreams that rows through all space,

and, under the window of my sleeping beauty,[4]
the endless sigh from the waters of the fountain,[5]
and the neck of the great white swan, that questions me.

To Roosevelt[1]

The voice that would reach you, Hunter, must speak
in Biblical tones, or in the poetry of Walt Whitman.[2]
You are primitive and modern, simple and complex;
you are one part George Washington and one part Nimrod.[3]
      You are the United States   5
future invader of our naive America[4]

---

9. The mad king of Bavaria (1864–86) who built a fairytale castle and retired from the world; he was Wagner's patron for many years.
1. Ancient Greek statue of Venus, goddess of love and beauty, found on the island of Melos; the statue's arms are missing.
2. A courtyard surrounded by columns.
3. Compare Mallarmé's *The Afternoon of a Faun*, lines 16–20.
4. Sleeping Beauty (capitalized in the original).

5. Compare Verlaine's *Moonlight*, lines 11–12.
1. President of the United States from 1901 to 1909, Theodore Roosevelt was well known as a hunter and as a political expansionist.
2. American poet (1819–1892) and author of *Leaves of Grass* (1855) whose poetry Darío liked and to whom he addressed a poem.
3. Mighty hunter and king of ancient Assyria (see Genesis 10.8–12).
4. I.e., Spanish-speaking South America.

with its Indian blood, an America
that still prays to Christ and still speaks Spanish.

You are a strong, proud model of your race;
you are cultured and able; you oppose Tolstoy.[5]   10
You are an Alexander-Nebuchadnezzar,[6]
breaking horses and murdering tigers.
(You are a Professor of Energy,
as the current lunatics say).

You think that life is a fire,   15
that progress is an irruption,
that the future is wherever
your bullet strikes.

No.

The United States is grand and powerful.
Whenever it trembles, a profound shudder   20
runs down the enormous backbone of the Andes.[7]
If it shouts, the sound is like the roar of a lion.
And Hugo said to Grant:[8] "The stars are yours."
(The dawning sun of the Argentine barely shines;
the star of Chile is rising . . .)[9] A wealthy country,   25
joining the cult of Mammon to the cult of Hercules;[1]
while Liberty, lighting the path
to easy conquest, raises her torch in New York.
But our own America, which has had poets
since the ancient times of Nezahualcóyotl;[2]   30
which preserved the footprints of great Bacchus,
and learned the Panic[3] alphabet once,
and consulted the stars; which also knew Atlantis[4]
(whose name comes ringing down to us in Plato)
and has lived, since the earliest moments of its life,   35

---

5. The Russian count and novelist Leo Tolstoy (1828–1910) in his later works preached piety, morality, and a simple peasant life.
6. A combination of the Macedonian conqueror Alexander the Great (356–323 B.C.E.) and Nebuchadnezzar (630–562 B.C.E.), king of Babylon, who destroyed Jerusalem and made its inhabitants slaves.
7. A mountain chain running the length of South America.
8. Ulysses S. Grant (1822–1885), Union general in the Civil War and president from 1869 to 1877. "Hugo": Darío admired the 19th-century French writer Victor Hugo (1802–1885).
9. The flags of Argentina and Chile display a sun and a star, respectively.
1. The Greek demigod known for his strength. "Mammon": in the New Testament, a false god who personified riches and greed.
2. An Aztec ruler and early poet.
3. Belonging to the woodland god Pan, a follower of Bacchus. "Bacchus": the Greek god of wine and fertility.
4. The lost civilization of Atlantis, described in Plato's dialogues *Timaeus* and *Critias*.

in light, in fire, in fragrance, and in love—
the America of Moctezuma and Atahualpa,[5]
the aromatic America of Columbus,
Catholic America, Spanish America,
the America where noble Cuauhtémoc said: 40
"I am not on a bed of roses"[6]—our America,
trembling with hurricanes, trembling with Love:
O men with Saxon[7] eyes and barbarous souls,
our America lives. And dreams: And loves.
And it is the daughter of the Sun. Be careful.   45
Long live Spanish America!
A thousand cubs of the Spanish lion are roaming free.
Roosevelt, you must become, by God's own will,
the deadly Rifleman and the dreadful Hunter
before you can clutch us in your iron claws.   50

And though you have everything, you are lacking one thing:
                                      God!

Leda

The swan in shadow seems to be of snow;
his beak is translucent amber in the daybreak;
gently that first and fleeting glow of crimson
tinges his gleaming wings with rosy light.

And then, on the azure waters of the lake,   5
when dawn has lost its colors, then the swan,
his wings outspread, his neck a noble arc,
is turned to burnished silver by the sun.

The bird from Olympus, wounded by love, swells out
his silken plumage, and clasping her in his wings   10
he ravages Leda there in the singing water,
his beak seeking the flower of her lips.

She struggles, naked and lovely, and is vanquished,
and while her cries turn sighs and die away,
the screen of teeming foliage parts and the wild   15
green eyes of Pan[1] stare out, wide with surprise.

---

5. Last Inca emperor (r. 1532–33), captured and held for ransom before being strangled by Pizarro's soldiers. "Moctezuma": Montezuma II (1466–1520), Aztec emperor in Mexico, slain for his wealth by Spanish invaders.
6. Words spoken to a fellow prisoner by the last Aztec emperor (d. 1525) while he was being tortured by Spanish invaders.
7. Of Germanic or British ancestry; here, North Americans.
1. The horned shepherd god of woods and field.

Fatality

The tree is happy because it is scarcely sentient;
the hard rock is happier still, it feels nothing:
there is no pain as great as being alive,
no burden heavier than that of conscious life.

To be, and to know nothing, and to lack a way,   5
and the dread of having been, and future terrors . . .
And the sure terror of being dead tomorrow,
and to suffer all through life and through the darkness,

and through what we do not know and hardly suspect . . .
And the flesh that tempts us with bunches of cool grapes,   10
and the tomb that awaits us with its funeral sprays,
and not to know where we go,
nor whence we came! . . .

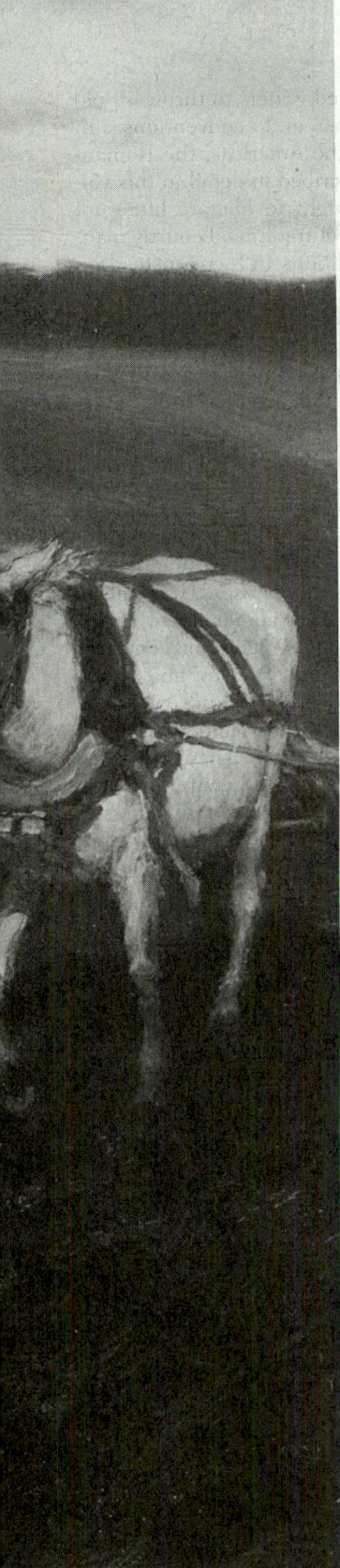

III

Realism

As the world grew closer together in the nineteenth century, thanks to rapidly expanding empires and new methods of transportation and communication, including the steamship and the telegraph, literary movements were able to spread fast, too. Writers could find inspiration in texts composed across the world; they could nurture new ideas at home that then spread quickly outward; and they could readily mix and fuse traditions that came from different continents. Symbolism, for example—the poetic movement launched by **Charles Baudelaire** in Paris—had an impact as far away as Nicaragua and Japan, and the *ghazal*, an Arabic poetic form used for many centuries in India and Persia, inspired imitators in nineteenth-century Europe, including **Johann Wolfgang von Goethe**, who made it a popular poetic form in Germany, and Thomas Hardy in Britain.

One of the most powerfully influential global artistic movements in the nineteenth century was realism. It began in Britain and France, hotbeds of industrial and political revolution, but it soon spread worldwide. And yet, it would be a mistake to see **Joaquim Maria Machado de Assis** in Brazil, Rabindranath Tagore in India, and Rebecca Harding Davis in the United States as mere imitators of

Leo Tolstoi Ploughing a Field, 1882, by Ilya Yefimovich Repin.

1111

the European model: they invented techniques, subjects, and plots, they altered conventions, and they experimented with styles to generate realisms all their own.

Despite its rich variety, realist writing around the world tended to share some crucial aims and characteristics. In the nineteenth century many artists felt a new urgency to tell the unvarnished truth about the world, to observe social life unsentimentally, and to convey it as objectively as possible. To be sure, the struggle to give a realistic representation of the world—sometimes called verisimilitude or mimesis—was nothing new. But while artists for many generations had been aiming at truth in their representations of the world, the nineteenth century ushered in a new realist philosophy, shocking new subject matter, and a specific new constellation of literary techniques.

The revolutionary overturning of old regimes and hierarchies, the rise of democracy and the middle class, and the industrial revolution—which created smoky, grimy cities teeming with an impoverished working class—had

already inspired writers to throw off old literary forms and conventions. In Europe and the Americas, the Romantic poets (described in detail in this volume) had sought to liberate literature from the grip of traditional courtly manners and traditions to focus instead on nature as a model of freedom and beauty. For them, the natural environment offered an antidote to the artifices and injustices of human societies. Realist writers, by and large, lost faith in this ideal: nature no longer seemed to provide a plausible alternative. Now all that was left of reality was what you could see with your naked eyes: gritty, ugly industries; the power of money; starving, broken workers; social hierarchies; dirt, decay, and disease. The realists thus shocked their audiences by representing characters who for centuries had been considered too low and coarse for art: ragged orphans and exhausted workers, washerwomen and prostitutes, drunks and thieves. They routinely chose the city over the countryside for their settings. And they were willing to lavish their descriptive attention on squalid surroundings—sickening slums,

The Stonebreakers, 1848, by Gustave Courbet. A realist masterpiece that was destroyed in the Allied bombing of Dresden during World War II, this painting now exists only in reproductions and photographs.

smoggy factories, dusty barrooms. Gone was the equation of art with beauty: visual art and literature could now be deliberately, powerfully hideous.

The realists were not only concerned with the unfortunate, however. In throwing off the ideals associated with earlier art forms, realist artists often threw their energies into representing the commonplace—the mundane experience of ordinary people. They wanted to capture the world as it was, and that meant describing plausible individuals in recognizable circumstances. Realism is as closely associated with middle-class characters, then, as it is with the poor, and many of the most famous realist writers of the nineteenth century—including Honoré de Balzac, Charles Dickens, and **Fyodor Dostoyevsky**—wrote fiction that deliberately cut across different classes, showing encounters between rich and poor in an attempt to give a realistic picture of a whole society.

While some realist writers tried to capture entire nations and social classes, others focused intensively on a few individuals. Some put their emphasis on internal, psychological reality, others on the shaping force of external circumstances. Usually those who stuck to the small scale implied larger social relationships, and they used individual characters to represent whole groups, but their fictions do feel more local and intimate than the vast and sprawling novels of the period—*Bleak House* or *War and Peace*—that contain many characters and strive to represent a whole nation. These differences were in part philosophical, revolving around the question of what it is possible to know. What *is* reality? Can we rely on our senses, or do we need to turn to facts and statistics, theories about hidden causes and social structures? Can we see reality from a single, individual perspective, or do we need to take a bird's-eye view?

The realists did not always agree about what constituted reality or how best to capture it in words or paint, but in general they resisted symbols and allegories, sentimentality and sensationalism, otherworldly ideals and timeless values in favor of the literal, the specific, and observable—the social world as it appeared in the here and the now. They tended to focus on the immediate, material causes of social

Place de la Concorde, 1875, by Edgar Degas. A portrait of a moment in the lives of the well-to-do.

Reading by Lamplight, 1858, by James Abbott McNeill Whistler.

misery and looked to scientists and social thinkers for solutions, rather than aspiring to transcendent or beautiful ideals. Though frequently the writers themselves were religious, realism was typically a secular project that put its emphasis on empirical experience— what we can know through our senses— rather than on providential explanations. Many realist writers were influenced by currents in science, and a later offshoot of realism, called naturalism, turned to the evolutionary science of Charles Darwin for a brutal explanatory model: human beings would only survive to the extent that they could adapt to their social environments; those who proved unfit would die.

Realist writers introduced a whole new range of formal techniques that transformed the literary landscape. Most wrote novels or short stories, though realist drama changed the history of theater in the late nineteenth century. The novel had the advantage of being relatively formless: it could be long or short; it could include many central characters or a single protagonist; it could be told in the first person

or the third person; it could focus on domestic settings or foreign travel; and it could entwine many stories or follow a single main path. Unlike more traditional and compact forms, such as the sonnet, it could swallow up other kinds of writing—letters, dialogue, description, history, biography, satire, even poetry—without being bound by the rules of any of those particular forms itself. In Europe, the novel was a new genre in the eighteenth century— hence its name "novel"—and its flexibility as a form allowed it to adapt to many different kinds of philosophies and social circumstances. Often written and read by more women than men, novels were a popular form that did not acquire a serious, highbrow status until the beginning of the twentieth century.

The novel and drama suited the aims of realism in some very specific ways. Prose is of course prosaic—suited to capturing ordinariness and even ugliness. Realist writers often opted for plain, unstylized diction and usually tried to convey the many ways of speaking that characterized the social groups they represented, including dialect speech. Prose and drama lend themselves much better to this linguistic variety than does poetry, with its strict forms and connotations of artful beauty. Fiction also lends itself well to movement between action and description: it can pause the plot to include highly detailed depictions of the characters and their environments. For writers wanting to capture the whole social world in a style that seemed objective, the omniscient third-person narrator provided the perfect, impersonal perspective. Other writers opted for first-person narrators, guided only by their own senses and experience as they try to make sense of the world. Fiction can accommodate both of these perspectives easily, and some realist novels even move back and forth between the narrator's bird's-eye view and the characters' more restricted knowledge.

The elements of both character and plot raised particular challenges and opportunities for realist writers. Some realists tried to present uniquely individual characters, conveying some of the complexity of real people in the world; others felt that the truth lay instead in types, and they used individual characters to represent whole social groups—the outraged worker, the subjugated wife, the social climber. As for plot, realist writers often tried to steer clear of sensational events and neat endings, which jeopardized the goal of unvarnished truth telling, but they also wanted to keep their readers absorbed. One solution was to put characters in believable social situations where they faced ethical dilemmas. The dramatic interest of the plot then lay in having the character make a difficult choice. Should the heroine choose respectable poverty or agree to a luxurious but disreputable life as a kept woman? Should the hero climb the social ladder at the expense of an innocent victim?

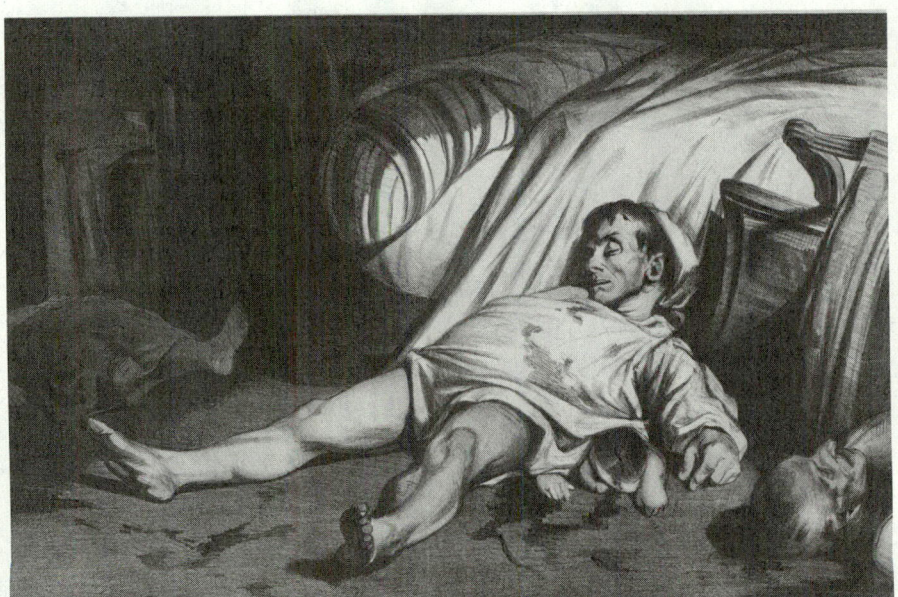

Rue Transnonain, 1834, by Honoré Daumier. This lithograph was Daumier's attempt to document the massacre of nineteen people, including women and children, by the French National Guard on April 14, 1834, in response to a strike of silk weavers in Lyon, France.

One of the advantages of dramatizing ethical predicaments is that these allowed fiction to engage the question of moral action in the new social environments of the nineteenth century. Can individuals have an impact on unjust social relationships? What responsibility does each of us have toward others in a city, a nation, or a densely interconnected world? For many realists, the purpose of describing the social world in great detail—with a particular emphasis on poverty and injustice—was to prompt readers to try to change that world.

With its emphasis on ordinary language, new social circumstances, and plausible human predicaments, realism transformed the literary landscape across the globe, inviting writers everywhere to try to capture the troubled, painful, struggling worlds of their own experience. And the mark these writers left remains palpable everywhere today, as realism continues to exert a powerful cultural force, still part of the daily fare of television, fiction, drama, and film around the world. Realism is nothing if not a capacious, roomy genre—able to move across borders and oceans, and as it moves, to take up new social relationships, new styles, new perspectives, and new resolutions.

VICTOR HUGO

1802–1885

Victor Hugo wrote the first novels to feature beggars as main characters. His massive, moving novel about the poor, *Les Misérables,* made him an international hero. When it hit the bookstores across Europe and beyond, it sold out in three days, Groups of French factory workers banded together to buy a single copy, while the Spanish government publicly burned the book. The pope put the book on his list of forbidden works. American soldiers on both sides of the U.S. Civil War read it, identifying with the downtrodden characters; influential writers around the world, including **Leo Tolstoy,** drew inspiration from it. Vast and sprawling, *Les Misérables* indicts a whole society for the pain in inflicts on the poorest and most vulnerable.

LIFE

Victor Hugo's father rose from humble origins as the son of a carpenter to become a general in the French army, an atheist who enthusiastically supported the French Revolution and Napoleon's rise. Hugo's mother was, by contrast, a Catholic supporter of the old monarchy who opposed the revolution. They separated when Victor, their youngest, was ten, and he lived with his mother in Paris until her death in 1821. Astonishingly precocious, Hugo wrote and published poetry that made him famous by the age of twenty. In his early life, he adopted his mother's conservative political and religious views, and when the Bourbon kings returned to the French throne after Napoleon's fall in 1815, Hugo professed himself a passionate royalist. His poetry, written in the strictest classical style, earned him a royal pension.

But Hugo's views of art and politics were about to change. In the late 1820s he started to join writers who were demanding freedom from classical literary styles and plots in favor of grotesque, strange, and wild experience. He soon became the leader of the Romantic movement, a group of mostly young writers and artists who were drawing inspiration from nature rather than from classical tradition and valuing freedom as their ultimate aim. "Down with theories and systems!" they cried. In 1830, Hugo's play *Hernani* deliberately broke the rules of classical theater. The author's anti-classical friends attended, dressed in deliberately absurd and archaic fashions, to argue with his classical enemies, who sneered at the play's poor plot and language. *Hernani* provoked fistfights every night of its hundred-night run.

In 1822, Hugo married a childhood friend named Adèle Foucher, and together they had four children. The marriage was not a happy one, and Hugo began a relationship with an actress that was to last more than fifty years. While on vacation with his mistress in 1843, Hugo learned from a newspaper story that his oldest daughter, Léopoldine, had drowned in the river Seine. The tragedy plunged him into a lifetime of mourning and prompted him to write numerous poems to Léopoldine's memory.

The revolution of 1848 marked a turning point in Hugo's political life.

As an elected member of the French Assembly, he had pushed for new civil rights and reforms, including the elimination of the death penalty, free public education, and prison reform, but when workers rose up against the government in June 1848, he worried about social chaos and took part in suppressing the revolts. He welcomed the rule of Napoleon's nephew, Louis-Napoleon, to impose civil order. His support for Louis-Napoleon soon soured, however, as the new ruler opposed parliamentary power and seized authority for himself, crowning himself the new emperor. Hugo denounced Louis-Napoleon as a traitor to France and fled the country, living in exile on the island of Guernsey for twenty years.

It was during his period of exile that Hugo took up work on a novel he had begun in 1845 about a convict who is unjustly persecuted. *Les Misérables* appeared in 1862 and took the literary world by storm, a huge popular success. When Hugo finally returned to Paris in 1870, he was a national icon. He continued to write and served again in the French Assembly. When he died in 1885, two million people—more than the entire population of Paris at the time—followed his funeral procession. He left his fortune to the poor and asked to be buried in a pauper's coffin.

WORK

Hugo was fascinated by how each of us comes to be the kind of person we are. What prompts any of us to be generous or spiteful, obedient or corrupt? In the short selection of *Les Misérables* here, Hugo's memorable character Jean Valjean undergoes two major transformations. The first is the change wrought by social conditions, including an unjust legal system that punishes a hard-working man who steals a loaf of bread to feed his hungry nieces and nephews. Imprisoned for nineteen years, shackled, forced into hard labor, denied his own name, and sent far from his home, Jean Valjean, when he finally leaves jail, has become an enemy of society: rebellious, ignorant, filled with hatred, and thoroughly alienated from others. But Hugo then puts his character in a context in which he will undergo another dramatic change. This time the transformation will take only an instant. One brief act of kindness, it would seem, can redeem a person as successfully as two decades of punishment can corrupt him.

Hugo liked extremes like these, and his writing style often adopts dramatic shifts of perspective. "Man overboard!" he writes, and then follows this immediately with, "Who cares! The ship does not stop." In brief chapters, often composed of short, choppy paragraphs, he moves back and forth between exciting narrative action and ruminations on philosophy, social analysis, architecture, religion, and history. Near the end of *Les Misérables,* Hugo interrupts a thrilling chase through the sewers of revolutionary Paris to dwell at length on ancient Roman sewers, reforms in sewer construction, and the very dependence of civilization on an underground of filth and waste. He moralizes while he offers up facts, generates symbolic images while analyzing pressing social problems, muses on sin and the possibilities of spiritual redemption, and squeezes a whole society into a fast-moving plot. We are a far cry here from the deliberately spare, detached, highly controlled realist style we will find in the next generation of writers, such as **Gustave Flaubert, Guy de Maupassant,** and **Giovanni Verga.** But Hugo nonetheless does crucial work for the realist novel by inviting us for the first time to imagine thieves, convicts, beggars, and prostitutes as the dignified and sympathetic heroes of serious art.

From Les Misérables

Book VI. Jean Valjean

In the middle of the night, Jean Valjean woke up.

Jean Valjean was from a poor peasant family from Brie.[1] As a child he had not learned to read. When he reached adulthood, he became a tree pruner in Faverolles. His mother's name was Jeanne Mathieu, his father's name was Jean Valjean or Vlajean, probably a nickname, a contraction of "voilà Jean."[2]

Jean Valjean was thoughtful without being glum, which is typical of affectionate natures. All in all, though, there was something rather sleepy and insignificant, in appearance at least, about Jean Valjean. He had lost his mother and his father when he was very young. His mother died after childbirth of a bout of milk fever that was not properly treated. His father, a pruner like him, died when he fell from a tree. All that remained to Jean Valjean was his sister, who was older than he was, a widow with seven children, girls and boys. This sister had brought Jean Valjean up and, while her husband was still alive, she had lodged and fed her younger brother. Then the husband died. The eldest of the seven children was eight years old, the youngest, one. Jean Valjean had just turned twenty-four. He took the father's place and in turn supported this sister who had brought him up. This was done automatically, as a duty, and even with a certain gruffness on Jean Valjean's part. His youth was thus spent in hard and badly paid labor. He had never been known to have a "sweetheart" in the region. He had never had the time to fall in love.

At night he came home tired out and ate his soup without a word. While he ate, his sister, mother Jeanne, would often take out the best bits of his meal from his bowl—the chunk of meat, the strip of bacon, the cabbage heart—to give to one of her children. He would go on eating, hunched over the table with his head practically in the soup, his long hair falling around the soup bowl, hiding his eyes. He behaved as though he didn't see a thing and did nothing to stop it. There was in Faverolles, not far from the Valjeans' cottage, on the other side of the lane, a farmer's wife named Marie-Claude. The Valjean children, who were always starving, sometimes went to "borrow" a pint of milk from Marie-Claude on their mother's behalf, which they then guzzled behind a hedge or in some corner of the alley, snatching the pot away from one another so greedily that the little girls would spill some on their smocks and down their gullets. If the mother had known about this pilfering, she would have chastised the delinquents severely. Jean Valjean, brusque and gruff as he was, paid for Marie-Claude's pint of milk behind their mother's back and the children went unpunished.

In the pruning season, he made twenty-four sous a day,[3] after that he would hire himself out as a harvester, as an unskilled worker, as a farmhand or cowherd, as any kind of casual laborer. He did what he could. His sister worked, too, but what can you do with seven children? They were a sad bunch, enveloped by a poverty that was slowly squeezing them dry. One winter was particularly rough.

---

1. A rural region of France, about a hundred miles south of Paris.
2. Behold John (French). An echo of "Behold the Man," the words of Pontius Pilate when he presents a suffering Jesus Christ to an angry crowd of people before the crucifixion.
3. A very small sum; two or three dollars.

Jean had no work. The family had no bread. No bread. Literally. Seven children!

One Sunday night, Maubert Isabeau, the baker on the church square in Faverolles, was getting ready to go to bed when he heard a loud crash and the sound of breaking glass at the barred window of his shop. He arrived just in time to see an arm shooting through the hole punched into the wire-meshed glass. The hand at the end of the arm grabbed a loaf of bread and the thief made off with it. Isabeau rushed out; the thief was running away as fast as his legs would carry him. Isabeau ran after him and stopped him. The thief had chucked the loaf of bread but his arm was still bleeding. It was Jean Valjean.

This happened in 1795. Jean Valjean was brought before the court of the day for "breaking and entering an inhabited house at night." He had a gun, which he could use better than any marksman in the world, and he was something of a poacher and that went against him. There is a legitimate prejudice against poachers. The poacher, like the smuggler, verges a little too closely on the out-and-out crook. And yet, we might just say in passing, there is still a gulf between this species of men and the murderous city-dwelling criminal. The poacher lives in the forest; the smuggler lives in the mountains or by the sea. Cities turn out ferocious men because they make men corrupt. The mountains, the sea, the forest, make men wild. They bring out the fierce side of human nature but often without destroying the human side.

Jean Valjean was found guilty. The terms of the code were categorical. There are some fearful moments in our civilization; these are the moments when a sentence delivers a verdict of shipwreck. What a mournful instant it is when society withdraws and consummates the irreparable abandonment of a sentient being! Jean Valjean was condemned to five years in the galleys.

On April 22, 1796, Paris resounded with the hue and cry over the victory of Montenotte, carried by the commander in chief of the Army of Italy, whom the message from the Directoire to the Five Hundred, dated Floréal 2, Year IV, called Buona-Parte; that same day a great human chain was shackled together at Bicêtre prison.[4] Jean Valjean was part of that chain. An old prison doorman, who is close to ninety years old today, still remembers perfectly the poor wretch who was put in irons at the end of the fourth row in the north corner of the courtyard. This man was sitting on the ground like the rest of them. He appeared not to comprehend anything about his situation, except that it was awful. Most likely he also made out, through all the hazy notions of a poor and completely ignorant man, something excessive in it. As they were riveting the bolt of his collar shackle with great whacks of the hammer at the back of his neck, he wept, he choked on tears that prevented him from speaking; the only thing he managed to get out from time to time was: "I was a pruner in Faverolles." Then, sobbing all the while, he raised his right hand and lowered it gradually seven times as though patting seven heads at different heights and through this gesture you could guess that whatever it was he had done, he had done it to feed and clothe seven small children.

4. In Paris, infamous for its dreadful conditions. Montenotte was an early victory for Napoleon, then twenty-seven years old and not yet famous. "Directoire of the Five Hundred": one of the two branches of the French government. "Floréal 2, Year IV": the leaders of the French Revolution of 1789 established a new calendar, which began with the end of Louis XVI's reign in 1792.

He left for Toulon. He arrived there after a journey of twenty-seven days, on a cart, with the chain at his neck. In Toulon he was dressed in a red smock known as a *paletot*. Everything about his life was erased, right down to his name; he was no longer even Jean Valjean, he was number 24601. What became of his sister? What became of the seven children? Who was going to worry about that? What becomes of the handful of leaves from the yellow tree sawn off at its base?

It's the same old story. These poor living beings, God's creatures, now without support, without a guide, without shelter, drifted off aimlessly, scattered on the wind, who knows? each on their own, perhaps, plunging further and further into the cold mist that swallows up solitary destinies, an opaque gloom into which so many luckless people disappear, one after the other, in the solemn march of the human race. They left their home county. The bell tower of what was once their village forgot them; the boundary of what was once their field forgot them; after a few years' sojourn in jail, Jean Valjean himself forgot them. In that heart where there once was a wound, was now a scar. That is all. During the whole time he was in Toulon he had only once heard talk of his sister. It was, I think, toward the end of his fourth year of captivity. I no longer remember through what channel the news reached him. Someone, who had known them back home, had seen his sister. She was in Paris. She lived in a mean street near Saint-Sulpice, the rue du Gindre. She had only one child with her by then, a little boy, the baby of the bunch. Where were the other six? She herself, perhaps, did not know. Every morning she went to a printer's in the rue du Sabot, no. 3, where she was a folder and stitcher. She had to be there at six in the morning, well before daybreak in winter. In the same building as the printing works there was a school and she took her little boy, who was seven, there. Only, as she started work at six o'clock, and the school did not open till seven, the child had to wait for an hour, in the courtyard, for the school to open; an hour in the dark in winter in the open air! They wouldn't let the boy come into the printer's because he got in the way, they said. As they passed by of a morning, the workers would see the poor little mite sitting on the cobblestones, nodding off to sleep and sometimes sound asleep in the dark, crouched and curled up over his basket. When it rained, an old lady, the concierge, would take pity on him; she would take him into her shabby squat, where there was nothing but a pallet, a spinning wheel, and two wooden chairs, and the little boy would sleep there in a corner, cuddling up to the cat for warmth. At seven o'clock, the school would open and in he would go. That is what someone told Jean Valjean. They spoke to him about it, one day, and just for a moment, there was a flash of lightning, like a window suddenly opening on the destiny of these creatures he had loved, then everything shut again; he never heard another word about them again, not ever. Nothing further about them ever reached him; he never saw them again, never ran into them, and for the rest of this painful story, we will not stumble across them again.

Toward the end of this fourth year, Jean Valjean's turn to escape arrived. His inmate pals helped him as they do in such sad places. He escaped. He wandered about for two days, free, in the fields; if you can call it being free to be hunted down, to whip your head round at every instant, to start at the slightest noise, to be frightened of anything and everything, of smoke coming from a roof, of a man passing by, of a dog, of a galloping horse, of the sound of the hour striking, of daylight because you can see, of night because you can't see, of the road, the path, the bushes, of sleep. The night of the second day he was nabbed again. He had not eaten or slept for thirty-six hours. The maritime court sentenced him for this felony to a further three years, which gave him eight years. The sixth year, it was his turn to escape again; he took it, but he was not able to consummate his flight. He had missed roll call. A cannon was fired and that night the men on patrol found him hiding under the keel of a boat that was being built. He resisted the guards who seized him. Escape and resisting arrest—this infraction was dealt with by the provisions of the special code; the punishment was an increase of five years, two of them in double chains. Thirteen years. The tenth year, his turn came again, he took advantage of it again. But he did not make a better go of it this time, either. Three years for this latest attempt. Sixteen years. Finally, it was, I think, during the thirteenth year that he tried one last time, succeeding only in being caught again after a mere four hours on the outside. Three years he copped for those four hours. Nineteen years. In October 1815 he was released; he had gone in in 1796 for having broken a windowpane and taken a loaf of bread.

This is the place for a short parenthesis. This is the second time, in his study of the penal issue and of damnation by the law, that the author of this book has come across the theft of a loaf of bread as the point of departure for the destruction of someone's life. Claude Gueux[5] stole a loaf of bread; Jean Valjean stole a loaf of bread. British statistics show that in London four out of five thefts have hunger as their immediate cause.

Jean Valjean had gone to jail sobbing and shaking; he came out impassive. He had gone in desperate; he came out grim.

What had gone on in his soul?

Book VII. Despair from the Inside

Let's try to put it into words.

Society must look these issues in the face since it is society that produces them.

The man was, as we have said, an ignoramus; but he was not an imbecile. That inborn light was on inside—and there was somebody home. Tragedy, which sheds its own light, intensified the thin light of day that was in his mind. Under the bludgeon, under the chains, in solitary confinement, in exhaustion, under the harsh sun of jail, on the plank bed of the convict, he withdrew into his conscience and reflected.

He turned himself into judge and jury.

He began by passing judgment on himself.

He acknowledged that he was not an innocent man unjustly punished. He admitted to himself that he had committed an extreme and blameworthy act; that he might not have been refused the loaf of bread if he had asked for it; that, in any case, he should have waited for it to come to him either through pity or through work; that it is not altogether an unchallengeable comeback to

5. A real French prisoner who was sentenced to death in the 1820s for stealing a loaf of bread to feed his mistress and child.

say: Who can wait when they're hungry?; that, to start with, it is extremely rare to literally die of hunger; second, that, happily or unhappily, man is so constituted that he can suffer for a long time and a great deal, morally and physically, without dying; that he should accordingly have had patience; that this would have been a lot better even for the seven poor children; that it was an act of madness, on his part, poor puny man, to grab society as a whole violently by the throat and to imagine that a person could get out of dire poverty by theft; that, in any case, it was the wrong door for getting out of dire poverty that admitted a man into infamy; in a word, that he had been in the wrong.

Then he asked himself:

If he were the only one who had been in the wrong in his fateful story? If it wasn't a serious matter to start with that he, who was a worker, lacked work; that he, who was industrious, lacked bread. If, subsequently, with the wrong committed and confessed, the punishment hadn't been ferocious and wildly excessive. If there hadn't been more abuse on the part of the law than on the part of the one guilty of the wrong. If there hadn't been too much weight in one of the pans of the scales, the one for expiation. If the excess weight of the penalty did not wipe out the crime and did not end in this result: reversing the situation, replacing the wrong of the delinquent with the wrong of the crackdown on him, turning the guilty party into the victim and the debtor into the creditor, and putting right squarely on the side of the very person who had violated it. If the sentence, complicated by the successive extensions of time for the escape attempts, did not wind up being a sort of assault by the strongest on the weakest, a crime committed by society against the individual, a crime that was committed afresh each day, a crime that went on for nineteen years.

He asked himself whether human society could have the right also to subject its members, on the one hand, to its crazy lack of foresight and, on the other, to its pitiless foresight, and to hold a poor man forever between a lack and an excess—lack of work and excess of punishment. If it were not outrageous that society dealt in this way precisely with those of its members who were the worst off in the parcelling out of goods, which is the work of chance, and so, the most worthy of being handled with care.

These questions being put and resolved, he passed judgment on society and he condemned it.

He condemned it to his hate.

He made it responsible for the fate he suffered and told himself that he would quite likely not hesistate to call it to account for this one day. He said to himself that there was no balance between the damage he had done and the damage done to him; he finally concluded that his punishment was not, in all honesty, an injustice, but that it was without the shadow of a doubt an iniquity.

Rage can be wild and unfounded; you can be wrongfully stirred up. But you only feel outraged when you are fundamentally right to do so somewhere along the line. Jean Valjean felt outraged.

And then, human society had only ever done him harm. Never had he seen anything of it but this wrathful face that it calls Justice and that it shows to those it strikes. People had only ever touched him to wound him. All contact with them had been, for him, a blow. Never, since his childhood, since his mother, since his sister, never had he met with a kind word or a kind look. He had lurched from one suffering to the next and had gradually arrived at the conviction that life was a war; and that in this war he was the vanquished. He had no other weapon but his hate, and he resolved to hone it in jail and to take it with him when he got out.

There was in Toulon a school for the convicts run by the Ignorantine friars,[6] where those of the wretched inmates who had the will to learn were taught the bare essentials. He was one of the ones who wanted to learn. At the age of forty, he started school and learned to read, write, and do sums. He felt that to strengthen his knowledge was to strengthen his hate. In certain cases, instruction and enlightenment can serve to shore up the harm done.

It is sad to have to say it, but after having judged the society that had brought him undone, he passed judgment on the Providence that had brought about that society.

He condemned it, too.

And so, during those nineteen years of torture and slavery, this poor soul both rose and fell at the same time. Light entered on one side and darkness on the other.

Jean Valjean was not, as we have seen, naturally bad. He was still good when he arrived in jail. Inside, he wrote society off and felt himself turn wicked; inside, he wrote Providence off and felt himself turn impious.

At this juncture it is hard not to ponder a little.

Can human nature turn itself inside out like that, so completely? Can man, created good by God, be made wicked by man? Can the soul be entirely remade by destiny and become bad if that destiny is bad? Can the heart become warped and catch incurable diseases and turn ugly under the pressure of some abnormally great woe, the way the vertebral column becomes warped under a too-low ceiling? Isn't there in every human soul, wasn't there in the soul of Jean Valjean, in particular, an initial spark, a divine element, incorruptible in this world, immortal in the next, that good can bring out, prime, ignite, set on fire and cause to blaze splendidly, and that evil can never entirely extinguish?

Grave and obscure questions, to the last of which any physiologist would probably have answered no, and without hestitating, if he had seen—in Toulon, in hours of rest, which were for Jean Valjean hours of reverie, as he sat, arms crossed, on the bar of some capstan, the end of his chain stuffed in his pocket to stop it from dragging—this forlorn galley slave, grave, silent, and pensive, a pariah of laws that look on man with anger, one of civilization's damned, who looked so harshly on the heavens.

Certainly, and we do not wish to pretend otherwise, the observant physiologist would have seen irremediable misery there, would perhaps have felt sorry for this man made sick by the law, but he would not even have attempted a cure; he would have averted his gaze from the bottomless pit he had glimpsed in that soul, and, like Dante at the gates of hell, he would have erased from that existence the word that the finger of God nonetheless writes on the forehead of every man: *Hope!*

Was the state of mind that we have been trying to analyze as perfectly clear for Jean Valjean as we have tried to make it for our readers? Did Jean Valjean distinctly see, once they were formed, and had he distinctly seen, as they were

---

6. Members of a Catholic religious fraternity dedicated to educating indigent children.

forming, all the ingredients that went into his moral destitution? Did this uncouth illiterate really grasp the succession of ideas by which he had, step by step, climbed and slid down until he reached that mournful outlook that had for so many years now been the inner horizon of his mind? Was he fully conscious of all that had happened within him and all that stirred there? We would not dare say such a thing; we do not even think it. There was too much ignorance in Jean Valjean for him not to remain fairly unclear, even after so much misery. At times, he did not really know for sure what he felt. Jean Valjean was in darkness; he suffered in darkness; he hated in darkness; you could say he hated whatever was in front of him. He lived constantly in such shadow, groping like a blind man or a dreamer. Only, at intervals, there would suddenly come to him, from within or from without, a gust of rage, an added burst of suffering, a pale and rapid flash of lightning that would illuminate his entire soul and would suddenly reveal all-around him, before and behind, in the glare of a ghastly light, the awful sheer drops and grim overhangs of his fate.

Once the lightning had passed, night would fall once more, and where was he? He could no longer tell.

The peculiar feature of sentences of this kind, in which what is pitiless, meaning brutalizing, dominates, is to gradually transform a man into a wild animal through a sort of stupid transfiguration. Sometimes into a ferocious animal, at that. Jean Valjean's repeated and dogged attempts to escape are enough to prove how strangely the law worked on the human soul. Jean Valjean would have tried to break out again and gone on trying, however utterly crazy and pointless such attempts might be, as many times as the occasion presented itself, without thinking for an instant about the consequences or about his previous experiences. He escaped impulsively, like a wolf that finds its cage open. Instinct told him: Run! Reason would have told him: Stay! But faced with such a violent temptation, reason vanished; only instinct remained. The animal alone acted. When he was nabbed again, the new severities inflicted on him only served to make him wilder.

There is one detail that we should not leave out and this is that not one of the galley inmates could hold a candle to him in physical strength. In hard labor, for twisting a cable or turning a windlass, Jean Valjean was equal to four men. He would sometimes lift and carry enormous weights on his back and would occasionally himself replace the tool known as a *cric*, or jack, which used to be called an *orgueil*, or pride, from which, by the way, the name of the rue Montorgueil near Les Halles in Paris derived. His inmate pals had nicknamed him Jean-le-Cric. Once, when the balcony of the Toulon *mairie* was being repaired, one of Puget's[7] wonderful caryatids, which support the balcony, came loose and was about to fall off. Jean Valjean, who happened to be there, propped the caryatid up by his shoulder, giving the workers time to get there.

His suppleness actually surpassed his strength. Certain convicts, who are always hatching escape plans, end up turning combined strength and skill into a veritable science—the science of muscles. A whole mysterious regimen of *statics* is practiced on a daily basis by prisoners, those eternal enviers of flies and birds. To scale a sheer vertical wall and find toeholds and handholds in

---

7. Pierre Puget (1620–1694), French artist whose sculptures can still be seen today on the Toulon *mairie*, or town hall.

places where you could barely see a bump was child's play for Jean Valjean. Give him a chunk of wall, and with the tension of his back and his knees, with his elbows and heels jammed into the rough edges of the stone, he would hoist himself up three stories, as though by magic. Sometimes he would climb up to the rooftop of the jail like this.

He said little. He never laughed. Some extreme emotion was required to wring out of him, once or twice a year, that lugubrious cackle of the convict, which is like the echo of a demon's laugh. To look at him, you would think he was busy staring endlessly at something terrible.

He was, in effect, absorbed.

Through the unhealthy perception of a stunted nature and an intelligence that had been laid to waste, he felt vaguely that something monstrous was sitting on his back. In the dim bleak haze in which he crawled, every time he craned his neck and tried to look up, he saw, with a mixture of terror and rage, piling up and looming in tiers that soared out of sight above him, with horrible sheer walls, a sort of horrifying heap of things, laws, prejudices, men, and deeds, whose contours escaped him, whose bulk terrified him, and which was nothing more than that prodigious pyramid we call civilization. Here and there he could make out, in this teeming, amorphous mass, now close up, now far away on inaccessibly high plains, some group, some detail sharply illuminated; here the guard with his truncheon, here the gendarme with his sword, over there the mitered bishop, and at the very top, in a sort of blaze of sunlight, the emperor, crowned and dazzling. It seemed to him that these remote splendors, far from dispelling his own darkness, made it all the more funereal and black. All that—laws, prejudices, deeds, men, things—was coming and going above him, according to the complex and mysterious movement God imparts to civilization, walking on top of him and crushing him with an unspeakably calm cruelty and remorseless indifference. Souls who have hit rock bottom as far as possible calamity goes, unhappy men lost in the depths of that limbo where no one looks anymore, the law's rejects feel the full weight on their heads of this human society, so forbidding if you are outside it, so terrifying if you are underneath it.

In this situation, Jean Valjean mused, and what do you think was the nature of his musings?

If the millet seed under the millstone had thoughts, it would doubtless think exactly what Jean Valjean thought.

All these things, realities full of phantoms, phantasmagoria full of realities, had ended up providing him with a sort of inner state you would be hard pressed to put into words.

At times, in the middle of his prison labors, he would stop . . . and think. His reason, at once more mature and more disturbed than before, would revolt. All that had happened to him seemed absurd; all that surrounded him did not seem possible. He told himself it was a dream. He looked at the guard standing a few feet away; the screw seemed like a phantom, yet suddenly the phantom would give him a whack with his truncheon.

The natural world scarcely existed for him. It would almost be true to say that for Jean Valjean, there was no sun, there were no lovely summer days, no radiant skies, no fresh April dawns. Only an awful thin light managed to reach him through the basement window of his soul.

By way of conclusion, to sum up what can be summed up and translated into concrete terms in all that we have just outlined, we will just say that, in nineteen years, Jean Valjean, the harmless tree pruner of Faverolles, the fearsome galley slave of Toulon, had become capable, thanks to the way the galleys had molded him, of two kinds of bad deed: first, some swift, unpremeditated act full of frenzy, performed entirely instinctively as a sort of reprisal for the wrong endured; second, some seriously criminal act, consciously debated and mulled over with the false notions such misery can give rise to. His premeditated ideas went through the three successive phases available only to natures of a certain cast: reasoning, will, determination. What moved him was habitual indignation, the bitterness in his soul, a profound sense of the iniquities he had been subject to, a reaction against even the good, the innocent, and the just, if such there be. The beginning and end of all his thoughts was the same: hatred of human law, the hatred that, if it is not nipped in the bud by some miraculous event, turns, within a certain time frame, into hatred of society, then hatred of the human race, then hatred of creation, and is translated into a vague and constant and brutal desire to do harm, to anyone at all, to any living being, whoever they may be.

So, as you can see, it was not for no reason that the passport described Jean Valjean as a very dangerous man.

Year by year, slowly but surely, his soul had dried up. Dry heart, dry eye. When he got out of jail, he had not shed a tear in nineteen years.

Book VIII. The Dark and the Deep

Man overboard!

Who cares! The ship does not stop. The wind is blowing and that particular doom-laden ship has a course to keep. On it sails.

The man disappears, then reappears, he dives down and comes back to the surface, he calls out, he waves his arms around; no one hears him. The ship shudders in the gale, fully focused on its maneuvering, and the sailors and the passengers can't even see the submerged man anymore; his miserable head is just a dot in the vastness of the waves.

He hurls desperate cries out into the depths. The sail looks so ghostly as it vanishes into the distance! He watches it, he watches it for all he's worth. It is moving away, it is becoming faint, it is getting smaller. He was on that ship just a moment ago, he was part of the crew, he came and went on deck with the rest of them, he had his share of air, of sunlight, he was alive. What the hell happened? He slipped, he fell, and now, the jig's up.

He is in the monstrous waters with only their roiling and heaving beneath him. The waves are torn and ripped to shreds by the wind and close in on him sickeningly; the rolling abyss sweeps him away, all the tattered water whips around his head, a mob of waves spits at him, vague tunnels of water half-devour him; every time he goes under, he glimpses sheer drops of unfathomable darkness; weird unfamiliar plants seize him, bind his feet, pull him under; he feels himself becoming one with the abyss, he is part of the foam, the waves toss him from one to the other, he gulps down bitterness, the spineless ocean is raring to drown him, the vastness toys with him, dragging out his last gasps. All that water feels like liquid hate.

Yet he struggles, he tries to defend himself, he tries to keep going, he makes an effort, he swims. His pitiful strength immediately exhausted, he struggles against the inexhaustible.

Where can the ship have got to? Over there. Barely visible in the pale blur of the horizon.

Gusts of wind come up; each head of foam batters him. He looks up and all he sees is the lividness of the clouds. In his death throes, he witnesses the immense madness of the sea. He is tortured to death by this insanity. He hears sounds unfamiliar to man that seem to come from beyond the earth—from some unimaginable and awful otherworld.

There are birds in the thick cloud cover, just as there are angels hovering over human hardships, but what can they do for him? They fly, sing, and soar while he, he moans in agony.

He feels buried at once by those two infinities, the ocean and the sky; the one a grave, the other a shroud.

Night comes bearing down and he has been swimming for hours, his strength is almost gone; the ship, that distant speck where once there were men, has faded from view; he is alone in the dreadful crepuscular gulf, he goes under, he is getting stiff, he thrashes around, he feels the monstrous waves of the invisible below him, he calls out.

There are no men anymore. Where is God?

He calls and calls. Anyone! Anyone! He goes on calling. Nothing on the horizon. Nothing in the sky.

He implores the expanse stretching away, the waves, the seaweed, the rocks; they are all deaf. He pleads with the storm; the imperturbable storm obeys only infinity.

Around him, darkness, mist, solitude, the oblivious thundering tumult, the endless chaotic puckering and churning of the wild waters. Inside him, horror and fatigue. Under him, the drop. Nothing to hang on to, no foothold. He thinks of the murky adventures of his corpse falling through the limitless gloom. The bottomless cold paralyzes him. His hands clench and curl up and grasp at nothingness. Winds, clouds, whirlpools, gusts, useless stars! What can he do? The despairing give up, the weary decide to die, they stop resisting, they go with the flow, let go, and off they go, the drowned, rolling away forever in the gloomy depths of engulfment.

O relentless march of human society! All the men and souls lost along the way, written off! Ocean into which all those that the law drops, fall! Vile withdrawal of all help! O moral death!

The sea is that inexorable social darkness into which the penal system casts those it has damned. The sea is measureless misery.

The soul, drifting with the current in the plumbless deep, can turn into a corpse. Who will resuscitate it?

Book IX. Fresh Grievances

When the time came for him to get out of jail, when Jean Valjean heard in his ear those strange words: *You are free!* the moment was unreal, unbelievable; a ray of blinding light, a ray of the real light of the living suddenly shot through him. But this light swiftly faded. Jean Valjean had been dazzled by the idea of freedom. He had believed in a new life. He very soon saw what kind of freedom a yellow passport[8] entails.

And this brought much more bitter disillusionment. He had calculated that what he had saved during his stay in jail amounted to one hundred and seventy-one francs. To be fair, we should add that he had forgotten to include in his calculations the fact that Sundays and public holidays were compulsory days off, which, over nineteen years, meant deducting around twenty-four francs. On top of that his savings had been reduced by various local charges to the sum of one hundred and nine francs and fifteen sous, which had been counted out and handed over to him as he was leaving.

He did not understand any of this and believed himself to have been short-changed—let's not mince words, robbed.

The day after he was released in Grasse,[9] he saw some men unloading bales of orange blossom outside a distillery. He offered his services. The job was urgent so they took him on. He set to work. He was smart, robust, and adroit; he did his best, and the foreman seemed happy. But while he was working, a gendarme came past, spotted him, and demanded to see his papers. He had to show his yellow passport. That done, Jean Valjean went back to work. A bit before this, he had quizzed one of the workers about the daily rate they earned for the job; they told him that it was thirty sous. That evening, since he was forced to head out the following morning, he turned up at the distillery foreman's and asked for his pay. The foreman didn't say a word, just handed him twenty-five sous. He demanded the rest. The foreman replied: "That's good enough for the likes of you." He stood his ground. The foreman looked him in the eyes and said: "Watch out you don't end up back inside!"

Once more, he considered himself robbed.

Society, the state, in diminishing his savings, had robbed him in a big way. Now it was the turn of the individual to rob him in a small way.

Release is not the same as liberation. You get out of jail, all right, but you never stop being condemned.

So that is what happened to him in Grasse. We have seen the welcome he was given in Digne.[1]

Book X. The Man Wakes Up

And so, as the cathedral clock struck two in the morning, Jean Valjean woke up.

What woke him up was that the bed was just too good. He had not gone to sleep in a bed for going on twenty years and although he had not taken his clothes off, the sensation was too novel not to disturb his sleep.

He had slept for over four hours. His weariness had passed. He was used to not giving many hours over to rest.

He opened his eyes and peered into the darkness around him for a while, then he closed them again to go back to sleep.

---

8. An identification card that distinguishes Jean Valjean as a convict.
9. Long famous as a center for perfume making.

1. All of the innkeepers in the town of Digne turned Jean Valjean away because of his yellow passport, but the kind bishop of Digne gave him a comfortable bed for the night.

When your day has been teeming with different sensations, when you have things on your mind, you can get to sleep to start with but you can't get back to sleep. Sleep comes a lot more easily than it comes back. This was the case with Jean Valjean. He could not get back to sleep and he began to think.

He was in one of those states where our ideas get blurred. There was a sort of cloudy swirling in his brain. His old memories and his most immediate memories floated around pell-mell and bumped into each other at random, losing their shapes, becoming crazily magnified, then evaporating suddenly, like mud stirred up in a pool of water. Many thoughts came to him, but there was one that would not go away and that sent all the others scurrying. This thought we will tell you without further ado: He had spotted the six silver knives and forks and the silver ladle that Madame Magloire[2] had laid on the table.

These six silver sets of cutlery obsessed him. They were just sitting there. A few feet away. The very moment he crossed the room next door to come into the room he was now in, the old servant had put them away in a cupboard at the head of the bed. He had, naturally, noted this cupboard. On the right, as you enter by the dining room. They were solid silver. And old silver, at that. For the ladle, you'd get at least two hundred francs. Double what he'd earned in nineteen years. True, he would have earned more if the "administration" hadn't "robbed him."

His mind wavered for a good hour, and his hesitation certainly involved some struggle. The clock struck three. He opened his eyes again, promptly sat up, shot out his arm, and groped for his haversack, which he had thrown into the corner of the alcove, then swung his legs over the side of the bed and placed his feet on the floor and found himself sitting up straight on the bed, not knowing how he'd got into that position.

He remained sitting there in that position, thinking, for some time, and anyone who'd seen him sitting there in the dark, the only person awake in the sleeping household, would have found him a sinister sight. Suddenly he bent down, took off his shoes, and put them gently on the mat beside the bed, then he resumed his position, sitting still and thinking.

In the middle of this vile rumination, the ideas we just mentioned kept stirring around in his brain, coming and going and coming back again, seemingly bearing down on him like a ton of bricks; and then, without knowing why, and with that automatic persistence of reverie, he thought at the same time about a convict named Brevet whom he had known in jail, and whose trousers used to be held up by a single brace of knitted cotton. The checked pattern of that brace kept coming back to him without letup.

He remained sitting there and would perhaps have stayed there like that until daybreak if the clock had not struck a single note—to mark the quarter hour or half hour. The clock seemed to say to him: Let's go!

He rose to his feet, hesitated a moment longer and listened; all was quiet in the house, so he headed straight for the window, which he could make out, taking small careful steps. The night was not very dark; there was a full moon with big clouds racing across it, chased by the wind. This produced bursts of light and dark outside, eclipses and lightning flashes, and inside, a sort of twi-

2. The bishop's servant.

light. This twilight, enough to guide his path, intermittent because of the clouds, was like the livid light that falls from a basement window when people are coming and going outside. When he reached the window, Jean Valjean looked closely at it. It had no bars, it opened on to the garden, and it was shut, in keeping with the custom of these parts, with only a tiny latch. He opened it, but as cold, sharp air rushed in, he closed it again instantly. He looked at the garden with that penetrating gaze that sizes up more than it sees. The garden was enclosed by a fairly low white wall, easily scaled. Behind it, on the other side, he could make out the tops of trees evenly spaced, which indicated that the wall divided the garden from an avenue or lane planted with trees.

Having given the scene the once-over, he acted like a man who knows what he's doing, walked over to his alcove, grabbed his haversack, opened it, fumbled around inside, took out something that he placed on the bed, stuck his shoes in one of his pockets, did the bag up again, hoisted it onto his shoulders, clapped his cap on his head, jamming the peak down over his eyes, felt for his stick, and went and put it in the corner of the window, then returned to the bed and resolutely seized the object he had laid on it. It was a short iron bar, sharpened at one end like a hunting spear.

In the dark it would have been hard to work out what this piece of iron was made for. Was it perhaps a lever? Was it perhaps a club?

In daylight, you would have recognized that it was just an ordinary miner's spike. In those days convicts were sometimes put to work quarrying stone from the high hills that surround Toulon, and it was not unusual for them to carry around miners' tools. Miner's spikes were made of solid iron, with a point at the bottom end for hoeing into the rock.

He took this spike in his right hand and, holding his breath and treading softly, he headed for the door of the room next door, the bishop's room, as you'll recall. When he reached the door, he found it ajar. The bishop had not closed it.

Book XI. What He Does Next

Jean Valjean listened. Not a sound.

He pushed the door.

He pushed it with one finger, lightly, with that furtive anxious restraint of a cat that wants to come inside.

The door yielded to the pressure, silently and imperceptibly opening the gap a little wider.

He waited a moment, then pushed the door again, more forcefully.

It continued to yield in silence. The gap was wide enough now for him to slip through. But near the door a small table was in the way, forming as it did a sort of awkward angle with the door.

Jean Valjean saw the problem. But he had to open the door wider no matter what.

He steeled his resolve and pushed the door a third time, more energetically. This time a badly oiled hinge suddenly sent out a prolonged and raucous screech into the darkness.

Jean Valjean jumped. The noise of the hinge rang in his ears, as resounding and terrible as the trumpet of the Last Judgment.

In the eerie amplification of that initial moment, he almost imagined that the hinge had come alive, suddenly taking on a terrible life of its own and barking a warning to the world like a dog rousing the sleeping from their slumber.

He stopped in his tracks, shivering, distraught, and tipped back from the balls of his feet onto his heels. He could hear his pulse thumping in his temples like a pair of sledgehammers, and it seemed to him that his breath came from his chest with the sound the wind makes rushing out of a cave. It seemed to him impossible that the horrible clamor of the outraged hinge had not shaken the whole house like the shock of an earthquake; the door, pushed by him, had taken fright and screamed; the old man would soon be up, the two old women would cry out, someone would come running to their aid; before a quarter of an hour was up, the town would be buzzing and the gendarmerie on the move. For a moment, he thought the jig was up.

He stayed where he was, petrified like the proverbial pillar of salt, not daring to make a move. Some minutes passed. The door was wide open now. He risked a peek at the room. Nothing had moved. He cocked an ear. Nothing in the house was stirring. The noise of the rusty hinge had woken no one.

This initial danger was over, but he still felt a dreadful turmoil inside. Yet he did not back down. Even when he had thought the jig was up, he had not backed down. His only thought now was to get it over with as quickly as possible. He stepped into the room. The room was perfectly still. Here and there various blurred shapes could vaguely be made out, which, by day, were papers scattered over the table, open folios, books piled on a stool, an armchair heaped with clothes, and a prie-dieu, but at this hour, they were no more than dark shadows and whitish spots. Jean Valjean crept forward carefully to avoid bumping into the furniture. At the back of the room he could hear the quiet, even breathing of the bishop, fast asleep.

Suddenly he stopped. He was on top of the bed before he knew it; it had taken no time at all.

Nature sometimes makes connections between our actions and its own special effects and star turns with a sort of somber and intelligent aptness, as though it wanted to make us sit up and think. For nearly half an hour, a huge cloud had covered the sky. The very moment Jean Valjean stopped, facing the bed, this cloud broke up as though it had done so on purpose and a ray of moonlight shot through the long window and suddenly lit up the bishop's pale face. He was sleeping peacefully, untroubled. Though in bed, he was almost fully dressed because of the bitterly cold nights of the Lower Alps, decked out in a brown woolen garment that covered his arms to the wrists. His head was thrown back against the pillow in the abandoned attitude of sleep; over the side of the bed his hand dangled, adorned with his pastoral ring—the hand that had performed so many good works and saintly deeds. His whole face was luminous with a vague expression of contentment, hope, and bliss. It was more than a smile; almost a radiance. On his forehead lay the ineffable reflection of a light invisible to the naked eye. The souls of the just in sleep contemplate a mysterious heaven.

A reflection of this heaven lay over the bishop.

It was at the same time a luminous transparency, for this heaven was inside him. This heaven was the internal light of his conscience.

At the moment that the moonlight superimposed itself, so to speak, on this inner limpidity, the sleeping bishop appeared bathed in glory. And yet that glory remained soft and veiled in an ineffable half-light. The moon in the sky, dozing nature, the garden so still, the house so calm, the hour, the moment, the silence, added something oddly solemn and moving to the venerable rest of this good man, and wrapped in a sort of majestic and serene aureole his white hair and those closed eyes, this face where all was hope and where all was trust, the head of an old man sleeping like a baby.

There was something almost divine about the man, so unself-consciously august was he.

Jean Valjean, on the other hand, was in the shadow, his iron spike in hand, standing erect, rigid, terrified at this luminous old man. He had never seen anything like it. Such trust horrified him. The moral world offers no greater sight than this: a troubled and overwrought conscience, brought to the brink of some evil deed, gazing upon the sleep of a just man.

Such sleep, in such isolation, with only the likes of him for company, had something sublime about it that he was dimly but powerfully aware of.

No one could have said what was happening inside him, not even himself. To try to grasp it, we need to imagine the most violent of men in the presence of the most gentle. Even on his face, you could not have made out anything distinct with any certainty. His expression was one of a sort of crazed amazement. He saw what he saw, and that was that. But what was he thinking? It would have been impossible to guess. What was obvious was that he was moved and deeply distressed. But what kind of emotion was that, exactly?

He couldn't take his eyes off the old man. The only thing that could clearly be discerned in his demeanor and on his countenance was a strange indecisiveness. You would have said he was hesitating on the brink of two yawning chasms, the one where you are lost and the one where you are saved—doom or salvation. He looked as though he was ready either to smash the old man's skull in or to kiss his hand.

After a few moments, Jean Valjean raised his left hand slowly to his forehead and took off his cap, then let his arm fall back just as slowly, and with that he retreated into his thoughts, his cap in his left hand, his club in his right, his hair standing up on end over his savage head.

The bishop went on sleeping in profound peace beneath this frightening stare.

A reflection of moonlight made the crucifix above the mantelpiece dimly visible, it seemed to be opening its arms to both of them, in benediction for the one and forgiveness for the other.

All of a sudden Jean Valjean clapped his cap back on his head, then strode to the head of the bed without giving the bishop another glance and straight to the cupboard, which he could make out next to the head of the bed; he raised the miner's spike as though he was about to force the lock. But the key was in it. So he turned it. The first thing he saw was the basket of silverware. He grabbed it, bounded across the room without worrying about the noise, whipped through the door, ran back to the oratory, shoved the window open, grabbed his stick, climbed over the windowsill, threw the silver into his knapsack, flung the basket away, raced across the garden, leaped over the wall like a tiger and fled.

Book XII. The Bishop at Work

The next day at sunrise, Monseigneur Bienvenu[3] was circling his garden. Madame Magloire ran to him, quite beside herself.

"Monseigneur, Monseigneur," she cried, "does Your Grace know where the silverware basket is?"

"Yes," said the bishop.

"God be praised!" she replied. "I didn't know what had happened to it."

The bishop had just picked the basket from out of a garden bed. He handed it to Madame Magloire.

"Here it is."

"But!" she said, flustered. "There's nothing in it! What about the silver?"

"Ah!" said the bishop. "So it's the silver you're worried about? I don't know where that is."

"Good God in heaven! It's been stolen! That man from last night! He's stolen it!"

In the blink of an eye, with all the sprightliness of a frisky old watchdog, Madame Magloire tore off to the oratory, into the alcove, and back again to the bishop. The bishop had just bent down, heaving a sigh, and was examining a cochlearia *des Guillons*[4] that the basket had broken when it landed in the garden bed. He straightened up again at Madame Magloire's shriek.

"Monseigneur, the man's gone! The silver's been stolen!"

While she was yelling the news, her eyes fell on a corner of the garden where you could see traces of a scramble. A brick in the wall had been ripped out.

"Look! That's where he got away. He jumped over into the ruelle Cochefiler! Ah! The swine! He stole our silver on us!"

The bishop remained silent for a moment, then he looked up with a grave expression on his face and spoke softly to Madame Magloire: "To start with, was the silver really ours?"

Madame Magloire was flabbergasted. There was another silence and then the bishop went on: "Madame Magloire, I was wrong to hang on to that silver—and for so long. It belonged to the poor. What was that man? He was poor, evidently."

"God help us!" Madame Magloire retorted. "It's not me or Mademoiselle I'm worried about. We couldn't care less. It's Monseigneur. What is Monseigneur going to eat with now?"

The bishop looked at her in amazement.

"Ah, is that all! Don't we have any pewter cutlery?"

Madame Magloire shrugged her shoulders.

"Pewter smells bad."

"Well, then, iron."

Madame Magloire pulled a face.

"Iron tastes bad."

"Well, then, wood."

A few moments later, he was eating at the same table that Jean Valjean had sat at the night before. While he ate, Monseigneur Bienvenu chirruped gaily to

---

3. Monsignor Welcome (French); the bishop's nickname. **4.** An herb that flowers.

his sister, who said nothing, and to Madame Magloire, who muttered under her breath that there really was no need for spoons or forks, even of wood, to dunk a bit of bread in a glass of milk.

"Did you ever hear such a thing!" Madame Magloire said to herself as she came and went. "Fancy letting a man like that come into your home! And to put him up, right next to your own bed! And what a stroke of luck that all he did was steal! Mary, Mother of God! It makes your hair stand on end just thinking about it!"

Just as the brother and sister were getting up from the table, there was a knock at the door.

"Come in," said the bishop.

The door opened. A weird and wild-looking bunch stood on the doorstep. Three men were holding a fourth by the scruff of the neck. The three men were gendarmes; the other man was Jean Valjean.

A sergeant of the gendarmerie, who seemed to be the leader of the group, stood nearest the door. He came in and strode over to the bishop, giving him a military salute.

"Monseigneur—" he began.

At that, Jean Valjean, who looked glum and broken, lifted his eyes, startled.

"Monseigneur," he murmured. "So this isn't the local curé?"[5]

"Quiet!" said one of the gendarmes. "This is Monseigneur, the bishop."

But Monseigneur Bienvenu had gone over to the men as fast as his old pins would carry him.

"Ah, there you are!" he cried, looking straight at Jean Valjean. "Am I glad to see you! But, heavens! I gave you the candlesticks, too, you know; they are made of silver like the rest and you can get two hundred francs for them, easily. Why didn't you take them with the cutlery?"

Jean Valjean's eyes nearly popped out of his head; he looked at the venerable bishop with an expression no human tongue could convey.

"Monseigneur," said the sergeant, "is what this man said true, then? We saw him hotfooting it out of town. He looked like he was on the run. So we arrested him to be on the safe side. He had all this silver—"

"And he told you," the bishop broke in with a smile, "that it had been given to him by some old codger of a priest whose place he'd spent the night in? I can see how it looks. So you've brought him back here? There has been a misunderstanding."

"If that's the case," the sergeant said, "can we let him go?"

"You must," said the bishop.

The gendarmes released Jean Valjean, who visibly shrank back.

"Are you really letting me go?" he said in a voice that was barely articulate, as muffled as if he were talking in his sleep.

"Yes, we're letting you go; something wrong with your ears!" said one of the gendarmes.

"My dear friend," said the bishop, "before you go, here are your candlesticks. Take them."

---

5. A parish priest, far below a bishop in the church hierarchy.

He went to the mantelpiece, swept up the two silver candlesticks, and handed them over to Jean Valjean. The two women watched the bishop without a word, without a movement, without a glance that might upset him.

Jean Valjean's whole body was shaking. He took the two candlesticks automatically and with a stricken look on his face.

"Now," said the bishop, "go in peace. Speaking of which, when you come back, my friend, there's no need to go through the garden. You can always come and go through the front door on the street. It is only ever on the latch, night and day."

He then turned to the policemen and said:

"Gentlemen, you may go."

The gendarmes headed off.

Jean Valjean looked as though he were about to pass out.

The bishop went over to him and said to him in a voice just above a whisper: "Don't forget, don't ever forget, that you promised me to use this silver to make an honest man of yourself."

Jean Valjean, who had no memory of ever having promised a thing, remained stunned. The bishop had emphasized every word as he spoke. He went on with a kind of solemnity: "Jean Valjean, my brother, you no longer belong to evil but to good. It is your soul that I am buying for you; I am taking it away from black thoughts and from the spirit of perdition, and I am giving it to God."

FYODOR DOSTOYEVSKY

1821–1881

At seven o'clock on a bitter winter morning in 1849, a young man, meagerly dressed and shivering, went to meet his death. He had been convicted of circulating subversive writings that attacked both the Russian Orthodox Church and the tsar. Led to a platform surrounded by a crowd, he looked out over a cart filled with coffins. He heard his name and faced a firing squad. A priest administered his last rites and pressed him to confess. His cap was pulled over his face. Then, just as the firing squad took aim, a carriage screeched to a halt, and a messenger leapt out, shouting, "Long live the tsar! The good tsar!" Fyodor Dostoyevsky had been allowed to live. Astonished and thankful, he pledged his lifelong loyalty to the tsar. Drawing on this and other experiences from his eventful life, he would go on to write some of the most gripping fiction of the nineteenth century, works characterized by dramatic extremes of authority and subjection. Intense and unforgettable, Dostoyevsky's characters are often, like their author, wracked by violence, guilt, obsession, and addiction.

LIFE

Fyodor Dostoyevsky was born in 1821, the son of a doctor in Moscow. He was the second of six children. The family lived next to a hospital for poor people, which also housed a morgue. Their father was stern and efficient, their mother compassionate, and both were devout members of the Russian Orthodox Church. The children were encouraged to read widely, and Fyodor became an admirer of such writers as William Shakespeare, Pierre Corneille, **Johann Wolfgang von Goethe**, and Charles Dickens.

In 1837 Dostoyevsky's beloved mother died, and his father sent him to be educated at the military Academy for Engineers in St. Petersburg. On the way there, he witnessed an act of violence that later became a famous scene in *Crime and Punishment*, one of his best-known novels. A government courier, after throwing back a few shots of vodka, jumped into a carriage and started beating the peasant driver mercilessly. The driver, in turn, began to thrash his horses. Dostoyevsky retained a lifelong fascination with what he considered the basic human desire to subdue those weaker than oneself. After his mother's death, his father withdrew and became violent, drinking excessively, talking aloud to his dead wife, and beating his servants. In 1839 he was mysteriously murdered on his own estate, probably by his serfs.

Once Dostoyevsky had finished his engineering courses, he worked at a government job, which he found as "tiresome as potatoes." He lived beyond his means, gambling and eating in expensive restaurants. Soon he quit his job to write *Poor Folk*, his first novel, which turned out to be a great success, especially with political radicals. In the revolutionary year 1848, he took up with a group of subversive St. Petersburg socialists and atheists. A spy who had infiltrated the group informed on them, leading to Dostoyevsky's arrest and death sentence.

After being pardoned at the last moment by the tsar, the writer was exiled to hard labor in remote Siberia.

For four years he marched with shackles on his legs, moving snow and firing bricks. "Every minute," he wrote later, "weighed upon my soul like a stone." The only book he was allowed was the New Testament, and he was not permitted to write letters or receive them. Dostoyevsky's thinking and writing would be transformed by the experience: in Siberia, he found renewed faith in the Orthodox Christianity of his childhood and artistic inspiration in the religious and folk traditions of the poorest Russian people.

Dostoyevsky served out the next four years of his sentence as a soldier in the small town of Semipalatinsk, where he fell in love for the first time with a married woman. In 1857, after her husband died, they were married. Then began a period of restlessness. The marriage was not a success. The couple traveled to Western Europe, where they were poor and unhappy. Ill with epilepsy and subject to increasingly serious episodes of the disease, Dostoyevsky gambled compulsively, squandering all of the money he had begged relatives to give him. As Dostoyevsky and his wife grew ever more estranged and her health declined from tuberculosis, he fell in love with another woman who disappointed him and then left him.

It was in 1864, during the lowest point of his bitter wandering, that he composed *Notes from Underground*. Soon after this his wife died, and he began work on the manuscript that would become *Crime and Punishment*, a novel about a young man named Raskolnikov who believes that he is superior to the ordinary run of humanity and therefore not subject to the usual moral laws. He kills two women with an axe and is consumed both with guilt and with the terror of being caught. Dostoyevsky burned the first draft of this novel and then rewrote it from scratch. All the while, he was miserably poor, forced to plead with

acquaintances for money and to sell everything he owned, including most of his clothes.

The next phase of the writer's life proved slightly more stable. He married a much younger woman with good business sense who managed his publications and their finances better than he had done on his own, though he remained in debt until the last year of his life. They had four children. The last, Alyosha, died from epilepsy at the age of three, and Dostoyevsky, heartbroken, blamed himself for having passed on the disease. His final novel, *The Brothers Karamazov*, features not only the murder of a father but also a saintly son named Alyosha. This novel proved extremely popular, hailed by fellow writer **Leo Tolstoy** as the best of the century. A life packed with dramatic incidents and great suffering came to an end soon after. At the time of his death in 1881, Dostoyevsky was acclaimed as one of the greatest Russian writers of all time. Thirty thousand people attended his funeral.

TIMES

By the middle of the nineteenth century, Russians had a long tradition of ambivalence toward Western Europe. On the one hand, Russia had been instituting Western-inspired reforms since the late seventeenth century, borrowing ideas about military organization, industry, law, and culture from France, Britain, and Germany. Most highborn Russians spoke French almost as a native language. On the other hand, the Russians had proudly fought off the invasion of Napoleon's French troops in 1812, and some saw European influences as weakening and corrupting Russian traditions. Tsar Nicholas I, who ruled the Russian empire from 1825 to 1855, instituted a policy he called Official Nationalism. He believed in exerting absolute power himself, and he imposed a regime of strict suppression, punishing dissenters, censoring subversive publications, and demanding allegiance to the Russian nation. He also insisted that everyone at court speak Russian. Nicholas I was followed by a very different kind of leader, Tsar Alexander II, who looked to the West for reformist ideas. His most sweeping reform was the abolition of serfdom—the possession of peasants by landowners, a system very much like slavery. He also introduced trial by jury and modest forms of representative government. His relatively liberal administration came to an end when he was assassinated in 1881.

Russian thinkers in this period tended to divide themselves into two broad camps. The first, called the Westernizers, favored European-style modernizations. Many of these were moderate liberals who defended gradual progress toward rights and freedoms, welcoming Alexander II's reforms, but others were more radical and utopian, imagining that only a thoroughgoing revolution would bring about the change Russia needed. Both liberals and radicals believed that the Western European Enlightenment, with its emphasis on reason and on universal rights, offered the best model for Russia's future.

Other Russians resisted this wholehearted embrace of Western Enlightenment values. Most of these, known as Slavophiles, envisioned all of the Slavic peoples uniting around a unique set of spiritual and cultural traditions, including a shared loyalty to the Orthodox Church. Dostoyevsky, after his brief flirtation with European radicalism, helped to bring into being a movement called "Native Soil" conservatism. He imagined all of Russia, rich and poor, joined in a new national union that would be spiritually superior to all of Western Europe. Somewhat ambivalent about the Orthodox Church, he was always drawn to the image of Christ

as a loving figure of universal reconciliation and self-sacrifice who could regenerate the nation. He saw the Russian peasantry as a repository of great spiritual wealth, and he felt that intellectuals must now return to their native soil to create a new bond with the vast mass of the people through *sobornost*, or spiritual oneness.

These "native soil" views sometimes come as a surprise to readers of Dostoyevsky's fiction, since he delves so compellingly into the minds of dogmatic atheists and violent killers that it seems he must in some way have shared their perspective. But part of what makes Dostoyevsky remarkable is his capacity to see from multiple, often conflicting viewpoints, and perhaps this is not surprising, given the extraordinary range of his experiences: his pious childhood, his fraternizing with socialists and atheists, his incarceration in a Siberian prison with murderous convicts and devout peasants, his humiliating poverty, his addiction to gambling, and his misery in love.

WORK

From the outset, *Notes from Underground* poses questions about what kind of human one should be. The narrator begins, "I am a sick man. . . . I am a spiteful man. I am a most unpleasant man." But if this character is sick, then what does it mean to be healthy? If he is spiteful and unpleasant, are others good and generous? Or, as the underground man suggests at times, are we all actually versions of him, and is humanity therefore sick, spiteful, and unpleasant? In the first few pages, the narrator compares himself to an insect, a mouse, a monkey, a slave, a peasant, and a civilized European. Later he mocks those who see humans as musical instruments—mechanical devices. But if we are not bugs, animals, machines, slaves, or civilized people, then what is the proper model for thinking about what it means to be human?

Dostoyevsky does not give us a character who can answer any of these questions to our satisfaction. Constantly contradicting himself, he calls himself a "paradoxicalist," taking pleasure in spitefulness and pride in pain. One of the most tortuous aspects of the narrator's experience is his acute self-awareness. He is horrified at being seen by others and then more troubled still by the idea that he may not be seen. And he cannot escape his obsessive self-consciousness even when alone, since he is always watching and judging himself and imagining himself through the eyes of others. Indeed, although he is painfully lonely, he is never truly free of the social world. We see him always in dialogue, constantly responding to another's views, anticipating someone else's response, even when that someone else is himself.

The "underground man" moves back and forth between casting his intense self-awareness as unique and seeing it as representative of all humanity. But Dostoyevsky also hints at a third possibility: that his antihero is a particular social type, a representative of a specifically *modern* condition. The "underground man" is a new kind of rootless urban intellectual, bombarded with fashionably progressive ideas about science, who cannot reason his way to any kind of satisfying conclusion. *Notes from Underground* is packed with references to contemporary ideas. For example, the socialist utopian novel *What Is to Be Done?*, published in 1863 (just a year prior to *Notes from Underground*), with its vision of an intrinsically good human nature governed by scientific laws, is one of the central targets of Dostoyevsky's biting critique, as is Charles Darwin's theory of evolution, first translated into Russian in 1864. The narrator also mocks an 1863 controversy over N. N. Ge's painting *The Last Supper*, which offered a star-

tling realism, showing Jesus recumbent and thoughtful instead of upright and authoritative, and presenting his disciples as scared and puzzled. This attention to up-to-date ideas was no accident: Dostoyevsky saw his own time as a "thunderous epoch permeated with so many colossal, astounding, and rapidly shifting actual events" that he could not imagine writing historical fiction, such as Leo Tolstoy's hugely popular *War and Peace*, which was set in 1812. *Notes from Underground*, then, may be less about the human condition in general than about the specific dilemma of being an educated man in modern, urban Russia.

Dostoyevsky captures this troubled mindset through a carefully crafted and complex work of literature. It is split into two quite distinct parts: in the first section we hear about the narrator from his own perspective in the present, and in the second we move backwards in time to see him through his encounters with others. The genre of *Notes from Underground* has long puzzled readers. It certainly draws on the tradition of the confession, as the narrator makes a declaration of guilt to an implied audience. And yet religious confessions require feelings of repentance, whereas Dostoyevsky's narrator defends himself and resists expressions of contrition. Is this novel, as some readers have believed, a parody of a confession? In many ways, the narrator is most like **Jean-Jacques Rousseau**, whose secular ***Confessions*** was the first text to explore the intimate psychological life of the author, including petty experiences of guilt and shame. And yet *Notes from Underground* is hardly a straightforward autobiography. The text's split structure does not follow a chronological arc. Instead, it gives us a picture of the narrator in two different pieces, first present and then past.

On first reading, this text may seem to meander with the narrator's tortured perceptions, but in fact it is tightly organized. After the long first section, in which he is entirely alone, we see him engaging with a sequence of other people, each of whom is lower on the social ladder than the one before. First, he becomes obsessed with a stranger—a military officer who is socially superior to him and snubs him by failing to recognize his existence. Next he meets with a group of his peers, schoolmates who refuse to take him seriously as an equal. In the final section we see him try to assert his superiority over two others: his dignified servant Apollon and the compassionate, self-sacrificing prostitute Liza.

However extreme and contradictory his characters, Dostoyevsky laid claim to a specific version of realism in his fiction. "They call me a psychologist," he said, but "it's not true. I'm merely a realist in a higher sense, that is to say I describe all the depths of the human soul." Reaching low, into the depths of the soul, as a way of achieving a "higher realism," his literature is nothing if not paradoxical. But Dostoyevsky's bril-liance lies precisely in its capacity to fold together extremes—it is in the poorest prostitute that one finds the greatest spiritual wealth, and in the cruelest spite that a man can experience pleasure. Not surprisingly, then, Dostoyevsky's realism did not involve attention to the humdrum, as did the work of other realists, but offered up extremes of emotion and violence. "What most people regard as fantastic and exceptional is sometimes for me the very essence of reality," he wrote. "Everyday trivialities and a conventional view of them, in my opinion, not only fall short of realism but are even contrary to it."

Dostoyevsky influenced an astonishing array of writers and thinkers. From **Franz Kafka** and **William Faulkner** to **Gabriel García Márquez** and Ralph Ellison, some of the most imaginative minds of the following century acknowledged him as an inspiration. Perhaps the most unexpected of these was Albert Einstein. "Dostoevsky," he wrote, "gives me more than any scientist."

Notes from Underground[1]

I

Underground[2]

I

I am a sick man. . . .[3] I am a spiteful man. I am a most unpleasant man. I think my liver is diseased. Then again, I don't know a thing about my illness; I'm not even sure what hurts. I'm not being treated and never have been, though I

---

1. Translated by Michael Katz.
2. Both the author of these notes and the *Notes* themselves are fictitious, of course. Nevertheless, people like the author of these notes not only may, but actually must exist in our society, considering the general circumstances under which our society was formed. I wanted to bring before the public with more prominence than usual one of the characters of the recent past. He's a representative of the cur-rent generation. In the excerpt entitled "Underground" this person introduces himself and his views, and, as it were, wants to explain the reasons why he appeared and why he had to appear in our midst. The following excerpt [*Apropos of Wet Snow*] contains the actual "notes" of this person about several events in his life [Dostoyevsky's note].
3. The ellipses are Dostoyevsky's and do not indicate omissions from the text.

respect both medicine and doctors. Besides, I'm extremely superstitious—well at least enough to respect medicine. (I'm sufficiently educated not to be superstitious; but I am, anyway.) No, gentlemen, it's out of spite that I don't wish to be treated. Now then, that's something you probably won't understand. Well, I do. Of course, I won't really be able to explain to you precisely who will be hurt by my spite in this case; I know perfectly well that I can't possibly "get even" with doctors by refusing their treatment; I know better than anyone that all this is going to hurt me alone, and no one else. Even so, if I refuse to be treated, it's out of spite. My liver hurts? Good, let it hurt even more!

I've been living this way for some time—about twenty years. I'm forty now. I used to be in the civil service. But no more. I was a nasty official. I was rude and took pleasure in it. After all, since I didn't accept bribes, at least I had to reward myself in some way. (That's a poor joke, but I won't cross it out. I wrote it thinking that it would be very witty; but now, having realized that I merely wanted to show off disgracefully, I'll make a point of not crossing it out!) When petitioners used to approach my desk for information, I'd gnash my teeth and feel unending pleasure if I succeeded in causing someone distress. I almost always succeeded. For the most part they were all timid people: naturally, since they were petitioners. But among the dandies there was a certain officer whom I particularly couldn't bear. He simply refused to be humble, and he clanged his saber in a loathsome manner. I waged war with him over that saber for about a year and a half. At last I prevailed. He stopped clanging. All this, however, happened a long time ago, during my youth. But do you know, gentlemen, what the main component of my spite really was? Why, the whole point, the most disgusting thing, was the fact that I was shamefully aware at every moment, even at the moment of my greatest bitterness, that not only was I not a spiteful man, I was not even an embittered one, and that I was merely scaring sparrows to no effect and consoling myself by doing so. I was foaming at the mouth—but just bring me some trinket to play with, just serve me a nice cup of tea with sugar, and I'd probably have calmed down. My heart might even have been touched, although I'd probably have gnashed my teeth out of shame and then suffered from insomnia for several months afterward. That's just my usual way.

I was lying about myself just now when I said that I was a nasty official. I lied out of spite. I was merely having some fun at the expense of both the petitioners and that officer, but I could never really become spiteful. At all times I was aware of a great many elements in me that were just the opposite of that. I felt how they swarmed inside me, these contradictory elements. I knew that they had been swarming inside me my whole life and were begging to be let out; but I wouldn't let them out, I wouldn't, I deliberately wouldn't let them out. They tormented me to the point of shame; they drove me to convulsions and—and finally I got fed up with them, oh how fed up! Perhaps it seems to you, gentlemen, that I'm repenting about something, that I'm asking your forgiveness for something? I'm sure that's how it seems to you. . . . But really, I can assure you, I don't care if that's how it seems. . . .

Not only couldn't I become spiteful, I couldn't become anything at all: neither spiteful nor good, neither a scoundrel nor an honest man, neither a hero nor an insect. Now I live out my days in my corner, taunting myself with the spiteful and entirely useless consolation that an intelligent man cannot seriously become anything and that only a fool can become something. Yes, sir, an intelligent man in the nineteenth century must be, is morally obliged to be, principally a characterless creature; a man possessing character, a man of action, is fundamentally a limited creature. That's my conviction at the age of forty. I'm forty now; and, after all, forty is an entire lifetime; why it's extreme old age. It's rude to live past forty, it's indecent, immoral! Who lives more than forty years? Answer sincerely, honestly. I'll tell you who: only fools and rascals. I'll tell those old men that right to their faces, all those venerable old men, all those silver-haired and sweet-smelling old men! I'll say it to the whole world right to its face! I have a right to say it because I myself will live to sixty. I'll make it to seventy! Even to eighty! . . . Wait! Let me catch my breath. . . .

You probably think, gentlemen, that I want to amuse you. You're wrong about that, too. I'm not at all the cheerful fellow I seem to be, or that I may seem to be; however, if you're irritated by all this talk (and I can already sense that you are irritated), and if you decide to ask me just who I really am, then I'll tell you: I'm a collegiate assessor. I worked in order to have something to eat (but only for that reason); and last year, when a distant relative of mine left me six thousand rubles in his will, I retired immediately and settled down in this corner. I used to live in this corner before, but now I've settled down in it. My room is nasty, squalid, on the outskirts of town. My servant is an old peasant woman, spiteful out of stupidity; besides, she has a foul smell. I'm told that the Petersburg climate is becoming bad for my health, and that it's very expensive to live in Petersburg with my meager resources. I know all that; I know it better than all those wise and experienced advisers and admonishers. But I shall remain in Petersburg; I shall not leave Petersburg! I shall not leave here because . . . Oh, what difference does it really make whether I leave Petersburg or not?

Now, then, what can a decent man talk about with the greatest pleasure?

Answer: about himself.

Well, then, I too will talk about myself.

II

Now I would like to tell you, gentlemen, whether or not you want to hear it, why it is that I couldn't even become an insect. I'll tell you solemnly that I wished to become an insect many times. But not even that wish was granted. I swear to you, gentlemen, that being overly conscious is a disease, a genuine, full-fledged disease. Ordinary human consciousness would be more than sufficient for everyday human needs—that is, even half or a quarter of the amount of consciousness that's available to a cultured man in our unfortunate nineteenth century, especially to one who has the particular misfortune of living in St. Petersburg, the most abstract and premeditated city in the whole world.[4] (Cities can be either premeditated or unpremeditated.) It would have been entirely sufficient, for example, to have the consciousness with which all so-called spontaneous people and men of action are endowed. I'll bet that you think I'm writing all this to show off, to make fun of these men of action, that I'm clanging my saber just like that officer did to show off in bad taste. But,

4. St. Petersburg was conceived of as an imposing city; plans called for regular streets, broad avenues, and spacious squares.

gentlemen, who could possibly be proud of his illnesses and want to show them off?

But what am I saying? Everyone does that; people do take pride in their illnesses, and I, perhaps, more than anyone else. Let's not argue; my objection is absurd. Nevertheless, I remain firmly convinced that not only is being overly conscious a disease, but so is being conscious at all. I insist on it. But let's leave that alone for a moment. Tell me this: why was it, as if on purpose, at the very moment, indeed, at the precise moment that I was most capable of becoming conscious of the subtleties of everything that was "beautiful and sublime,"[5] as we used to say at one time, that I didn't become conscious, and instead did such unseemly things, things that . . . well, in short, probably everyone does, but it seemed as if they occurred to me deliberately at the precise moment when I was most conscious that they shouldn't be done at all? The more conscious I was of what was good, of everything "beautiful and sublime," the more deeply I sank into the morass and the more capable I was of becoming entirely bogged down in it. But the main thing is that all this didn't seem to be occurring accidentally; rather, it was as if it all had to be so. It was as if this were my most normal condition, not an illness or an affliction at all, so that finally I even lost the desire to struggle against it. It ended when I almost came to believe (perhaps I really did believe) that this might really have been my normal condition. But at first, in the beginning, what agonies I suffered during that struggle! I didn't believe that others were experiencing the same thing; therefore, I kept it a secret about myself all my life. I was ashamed (perhaps I still am even now); I reached the point where I felt some secret, abnormal, despicable little pleasure in returning home to my little corner on some disgusting Petersburg night, acutely aware that once again I'd committed some revolting act that day, that what had been done could not be undone, and I used to gnaw and gnaw at myself inwardly, secretly, nagging away, consuming myself until finally the bitterness turned into some kind of shameful, accursed sweetness and at last into genuine, earnest pleasure! Yes, into pleasure, real pleasure! I absolutely mean that. . . . That's why I first began to speak out, because I want to know for certain whether other people share this same pleasure. Let me explain: the pleasure resulted precisely from the overly acute consciousness of one's own humiliation; from the feeling that one had reached the limit; that it was disgusting, but couldn't be otherwise; you had no other choice—you could never become a different person; and that even if there were still time and faith enough for you to change into something else, most likely you wouldn't even want to change, and if you did, you wouldn't have done anything, perhaps because there really was nothing for you to change into. But the main thing and the final point is that all of this was taking place according to normal and fundamental laws of overly acute consciousness and of the inertia which results directly from these laws; consequently, not only couldn't one change, one simply couldn't do anything at all. Hence it follows, for example, as a result of this overly acute consciousness, that one is absolutely right in being a

---

5. This phrase originated in Edmund Burke's *Philosophical Inquiry into the Origin of Our Ideas of the Sublime and Beautiful* (1756) and was repeated in Immanuel Kant's *Observations* *on the Feeling of the Beautiful and the Sublime* (1756). It became a cliché in the writings of Russian critics during the 1830s.

scoundrel, as if this were some consolation to the scoundrel. But enough of this. . . . Oh, my, I've gone on rather a long time, but have I really explained anything? How can I explain this pleasure? But I will explain it! I shall see it through to the end! That's why I've taken up my pen. . . .

For example, I'm terribly proud. I'm as mistrustful and as sensitive as a hunchback or a dwarf; but, in truth, I've experienced some moments when, if someone had slapped my face, I might even have been grateful for it. I'm being serious. I probably would have been able to derive a peculiar sort of pleasure from it—the pleasure of despair, naturally, but the most intense pleasures occur in despair, especially when you're very acutely aware of the hopelessness of your own predicament. As for a slap in the face—why, here the consciousness of being beaten to a pulp would overwhelm you. The main thing is, no matter how I try, it still turns out that I'm always the first to be blamed for everything and, what's even worse, I'm always the innocent victim, so to speak, according to the laws of nature. Therefore, in the first place, I'm guilty inasmuch as I'm smarter than everyone around me. (I've always considered myself smarter than everyone around me, and sometimes, believe me, I've been ashamed of it. At the least, all my life I've looked away and never could look people straight in the eye.) Finally, I'm to blame because even if there were any magnanimity in me, it would only have caused more suffering as a result of my being aware of its utter uselessness. After all, I probably wouldn't have been able to make use of that magnanimity: neither to forgive, as the offender, perhaps, had slapped me in accordance with the laws of nature, and there's no way to forgive the laws of nature; nor to forget, because even if there were any laws of nature, it's offensive nonetheless. Finally, even if I wanted to be entirely unmagnanimous, and had wanted to take revenge on the offender, I couldn't be revenged on anyone for anything because, most likely, I would never have decided to do anything, even if I could have. Why not? I'd like to say a few words about that separately.

III

Let's consider people who know how to take revenge and how to stand up for themselves in general. How, for example, do they do it? Let's suppose that they're seized by an impulse to take revenge—then for a while nothing else remains in their entire being except for that impulse. Such an individual simply rushes toward his goal like an enraged bull with lowered horns; only a wall can stop him. (By the way, when actually faced with a wall such individuals, that is, spontaneous people and men of action, genuinely give up. For them a wall doesn't constitute the evasion that it does for those of us who think and consequently do nothing; it's not an excuse to turn aside from the path, a pretext in which a person like me usually doesn't believe, but one for which he's always extremely grateful. No, they give up in all sincerity. For them the wall possesses some kind of soothing, morally decisive and definitive meaning, perhaps even something mystical . . . But more about the wall later.) Well, then, I consider such a spontaneous individual to be a genuine, normal person, just as tender mother nature wished to see him when she lovingly gave birth to him on earth. I'm green with envy at such a man. He's stupid, I won't argue with you about that; but perhaps a normal man is supposed to be stupid—how do we know? Perhaps it's even very beautiful. And I'm all the more convinced of the suspicion, so to speak, that if, for example, one were to take the antithesis of a normal man—that is, a man of overly acute consciousness, who emerged, of course, not from the bosom of nature, but from a laboratory test tube (this is almost mysticism, gentlemen, but I suspect that it's the case), then this test tube man sometimes gives up so completely in the face of his antithesis that he himself, with his overly acute consciousness, honestly considers himself not as a person, but a mouse. It may be an acutely conscious mouse, but a mouse nonetheless, while the other one is a person and consequently, . . . and so on and so forth. But the main thing is that he, he himself, considers himself to be a mouse; nobody asks him to do so, and that's the important point. Now let's take a look at this mouse in action. Let's assume, for instance, that it feels offended (it almost always feels offended), and that it also wishes to be revenged. It may even contain more accumulated malice than *l'homme de la nature et de la vérité*.[6] The mean, nasty, little desire to pay the offender back with evil may indeed rankle in it even more despicably than in *l'homme de la nature et de la vérité*, because *l'homme de la nature et de la vérité*, with his innate stupidity, considers his revenge nothing more than justice, pure and simple; but the mouse, as a result of its overly acute consciousness, rejects the idea of justice. Finally, we come to the act itself, to the very act of revenge. In addition to its original nastiness, the mouse has already managed to pile up all sorts of other nastiness around itself in the form of hesitations and doubts; so many unresolved questions have emerged from that one single question, that some kind of fatal blow is concocted unwillingly, some kind of stinking mess consisting of doubts, anxieties and, finally, spittle showered upon it by the spontaneous men of action who stand by solemnly as judges and arbiters, roaring with laughter until their sides split. Of course, the only thing left to do is dismiss it with a wave of its paw and a smile of assumed contempt which it doesn't even believe in, and creep ignominiously back into its mousehole. There, in its disgusting, stinking underground, our offended, crushed, and ridiculed mouse immediately plunges into cold, malicious, and, above all, everlasting spitefulness. For forty years on end it will recall its insult down to the last, most shameful detail; and each time it will add more shameful details of its own, spitefully teasing and irritating itself with its own fantasy. It will become ashamed of that fantasy, but it will still remember it, rehearse it again and again, fabricating all sorts of incredible stories about itself under the pretext that they too could have happened; it won't forgive a thing. Perhaps it will even begin to take revenge, but only in little bits and pieces, in trivial ways, from behind the stove, incognito, not believing in its right to be revenged, nor in the success of its own revenge, and knowing in advance that from all its attempts to take revenge, it will suffer a hundred times more than the object of its vengeance, who might not even feel a thing. On its deathbed it will recall everything all over again, with interest compounded over all those years and. . . . But it's precisely in that cold, abominable state of half-despair and

6. "The man of nature and truth" (French). The basic idea is borrowed from Jean-Jacques Rousseau's *Confessions* (1782–89), namely, that human beings in a state of nature are honest and direct and that they are corrupted only by civilization.

half-belief, in that conscious burial of itself alive in the underground for forty years because of its pain, in that powerfully created, yet partly dubious hopelessness of its own predicament, in all that venom of unfulfilled desire turned inward, in all that fever of vacillation, of resolutions adopted once and for all and followed a moment later by repentance—herein precisely lies the essence of that strange enjoyment I was talking about earlier. It's so subtle, sometimes so difficult to analyze, that even slightly limited people, or those who simply have strong nerves, won't understand anything about it. "Perhaps," you'll add with a smirk, "even those who've never received a slap in the face won't understand," and by so doing you'll be hinting to me ever so politely that perhaps during my life I too have received such a slap in the face and that therefore I'm speaking as an expert. I'll bet that's what you're thinking. Well, rest assured, gentlemen, I've never received such a slap, although it's really all the same to me what you think about it. Perhaps I may even regret the fact that I've given so few slaps during my lifetime. But that's enough, not another word about this subject which you find so extremely interesting.

I'll proceed calmly about people with strong nerves who don't understand certain refinements of pleasure. For example, although under particular circumstances these gentlemen may bellow like bulls as loudly as possible, and although, let's suppose, this behavior bestows on them the greatest honor, yet, as I've already said, when confronted with impossibility, they submit immediately. Impossibility—does that mean a stone wall? What kind of stone wall? Why, of course, the laws of nature, the conclusions of natural science and mathematics. As soon as they prove to you, for example, that it's from a monkey you're descended,[7] there's no reason to make faces; just accept it as it is. As soon as they prove to you that in truth one drop of your own fat is dearer to you than the lives of one hundred thousand of your fellow creatures and that this will finally put an end to all the so-called virtues, obligations, and other such similar ravings and prejudices, just accept that too; there's nothing more to do, since two times two is a fact of mathematics. Just you try to object.

"For goodness sake," they'll shout at you, "it's impossible to protest: it's two times two makes four! Nature doesn't ask for your opinion; it doesn't care about your desires or whether you like or dislike its laws. You're obliged to accept it as it is, and consequently, all its conclusions. A wall, you see, is a wall . . . etc. etc." Good Lord, what do I care about the laws of nature and arithmetic when for some reason I dislike all these laws and I dislike the fact that two times two makes four? Of course, I won't break through that wall with my head if I really don't have the strength to do so, nor will I reconcile myself to it just because I'm faced with such a stone wall and lack the strength.

As though such a stone wall actually offered some consolation and contained some real word of conciliation, for the sole reason that it means two times two makes four. Oh, absurdity of absurdities! How much better it is to understand it all, to be aware of everything, all the impossibilities and stone walls; not to be reconciled with any of those impossibilities or stone walls if it so disgusts you; to reach, by using the most inevitable logical combinations, the most revolting

7. A reference to the theory of evolution by natural selection developed by Charles Darwin (1809–1882). A book on the subject was translated into Russian in 1864.

conclusions on the eternal theme that you are somehow or other to blame even for that stone wall, even though it's absolutely clear once again that you're in no way to blame, and, as a result of all this, while silently and impotently gnashing your teeth, you sink voluptuously into inertia, musing on the fact that, as it turns out, there's no one to be angry with; that an object cannot be found, and perhaps never will be; that there's been a substitution, some sleight of hand, a bit of cheating, and that it's all a mess—you can't tell who's who or what's what; but in spite of all these uncertainties and sleights-of-hand, it hurts you just the same, and the more you don't know, the more it hurts!

IV

"Ha, ha, ha! Why, you'll be finding enjoyment in a toothache next!" you cry out with a laugh.

"Well, what of it? There is some enjoyment even in a toothache," I reply. I've had a toothache for a whole month; I know what's what. In this instance, of course, people don't rage in silence; they moan. But these moans are insincere; they're malicious, and malice is the whole point. These moans express the sufferer's enjoyment; if he didn't enjoy it, he would never have begun to moan. This is a good example, gentlemen, and I'll develop it. In the first place, these moans express all the aimlessness of the pain which consciousness finds so humiliating, the whole system of natural laws about which you really don't give a damn, but as a result of which you're suffering nonetheless, while nature isn't. They express the consciousness that while there's no real enemy to be identified, the pain exists nonetheless; the awareness that, in spite of all possible Wagenheims,[8] you're still a complete slave to your teeth; that if someone so wishes, your teeth will stop aching, but that if he doesn't so wish, they'll go on aching for three more months; and finally, that if you still disagree and protest, all there's left to do for consolation is flagellate yourself or beat your fist against the wall as hard as you can, and absolutely nothing else. Well, then, it's these bloody insults, these jeers coming from nowhere, that finally generate enjoyment that can sometimes reach the highest degree of voluptuousness. I beseech you, gentlemen, to listen to the moans of an educated man of the nineteenth century who's suffering from a toothache, especially on the second or third day of his distress, when he begins to moan in a very different way than he did on the first day, that is, not simply because his tooth aches; not the way some coarse peasant moans, but as a man affected by progress and European civilization, a man "who's renounced both the soil and the common people," as they say nowadays. His moans become somehow nasty, despicably spiteful, and they go on for days and nights. Yet he himself knows that his moans do him no good; he knows better than anyone else that he's merely irritating himself and others in vain; he knows that the audience for whom he's trying so hard, and his whole family, have now begun to listen to him with loathing; they don't believe him for a second, and they realize full well that he could moan in a different, much simpler way, without all the flourishes and affectation, and

---

8. The *General Address Book of St. Petersburg* listed eight dentists named Wagenheim; contemporary readers would have recognized the name from signs throughout the city.

that he's only indulging himself out of spite and malice. Well, it's precisely in this awareness and shame that the voluptuousness resides. "It seems I'm disturbing you, tearing at your heart, preventing anyone in the house from getting any sleep. Well, then, you won't sleep; you too must be aware at all times that I have a toothache. I'm no longer the hero I wanted to pass for earlier, but simply a nasty little man, a rogue. So be it! I'm delighted that you've seen through me. Does it make you feel bad to hear my wretched little moans? Well, then, feel bad. Now let me add an even nastier flourish. . . ." You still don't understand, gentlemen? No, it's clear that one has to develop further and become even more conscious in order to understand all the nuances of this voluptuousness! Are you laughing? I'm delighted. Of course my jokes are in bad taste, gentlemen; they're uneven, contradictory, and lacking in self-assurance. But that's because I have no respect for myself. Can a man possessing consciousness ever really respect himself?

V

Well, and is it possible, is it really possible for a man to respect himself if he even presumes to find enjoyment in the feeling of his own humiliation? I'm not saying this out of any feigned repentance. In general I could never bear to say: "I'm sorry, Daddy, and I won't do it again," not because I was incapable of saying it, but, on the contrary, perhaps precisely because I was all too capable, and how! As if on purpose it would happen that I'd get myself into some sort of mess for which I was not to blame in any way whatsoever. That was the most repulsive part of it. What's more, I'd feel touched deep in my soul; I'd repent and shed tears, deceiving even myself of course, though not feigning in the least. It seemed that my heart was somehow playing dirty tricks on me. . . . Here one couldn't even blame the laws of nature, although it was these very laws that continually hurt me during my entire life. It's disgusting to recall all this, and it was disgusting even then. Of course, a moment or so later I would realize in anger that it was all lies, lies, revolting, made-up lies, that is, all that repentance, all that tenderness, all those vows to mend my ways. But you'll ask why I mauled and tortured myself in that way? The answer is because it was so very boring to sit idly by with my arms folded; so I'd get into trouble. That's the way it was. Observe yourselves better, gentlemen; then you'll understand that it's true. I used to think up adventures for myself, inventing a life so that at least I could live. How many times did it happen, well, let's say, for example, that I took offense, deliberately, for no reason at all? All the while I knew there was no reason for it; I put on airs nonetheless, and would take it so far that finally I really did feel offended. I've been drawn into such silly tricks all my life, so that finally I lost control over myself. Another time, even twice, I tried hard to fall in love. I even suffered, gentlemen, I can assure you. In the depths of my soul I really didn't believe that I was suffering; there was a stir of mockery, but suffer I did, and in a genuine, normal way at that; I was jealous, I was beside myself with anger. . . . And all as a result of boredom, gentlemen, sheer boredom; I was overcome by inertia. You see, the direct, legitimate, immediate result of consciousness is inertia, that is, the conscious sitting idly by with one's arms folded. I've referred to this before. I repeat, I repeat emphatically: all spontaneous men and men of action are so active precisely because they're stupid and limited. How can one explain this? Here's how: as a result of their limitations they mistake immediate and secondary causes for primary ones, and thus they're convinced more quickly and easily than other people that they've located an indisputable basis for action, and this puts them at ease; that's the main point. For, in order to begin to act, one must first be absolutely at ease, with no lingering doubts whatsoever. Well, how can I, for example, ever feel at ease? Where are the primary causes I can rely upon, where's the foundation? Where shall I find it? I exercise myself in thinking, and consequently, with me every primary cause drags in another, an even more primary one, and so on to infinity. This is precisely the essence of all consciousness and thought. And here again, it must be the laws of nature. What's the final result? Why, the very same thing. Remember: I was talking about revenge before. (You probably didn't follow.) I said: a man takes revenge because he finds justice in it. That means, he's found a primary cause, a foundation: namely, justice. Therefore, he's completely at ease, and, as a result, he takes revenge peacefully and successfully, convinced that he's performing an honest and just deed. But I don't see any justice here at all, nor do I find any virtue in it whatever; consequently, if I begin to take revenge, it's only out of spite. Of course, spite could overcome everything, all my doubts, and therefore could successfully serve instead of a primary cause precisely because it's not a cause at all. But what do I do if I don't even feel spite (that's where I began before)? After all, as a result of those damned laws of consciousness, my spite is subject to chemical disintegration. You look—and the object vanishes, the arguments evaporate, a guilty party can't be identified, the offense ceases to be one and becomes a matter of fate, something like a toothache for which no one's to blame, and, as a consequence, there remains only the same recourse: that is, to bash the wall even harder. So you throw up your hands because you haven't found a primary cause. Just try to let yourself be carried away blindly by your feelings, without reflection, without a primary cause, suppressing consciousness even for a moment; hate or love, anything, just in order not to sit idly by with your arms folded. The day after tomorrow at the very latest, you'll begin to despise yourself for having deceived yourself knowingly. The result: a soap bubble and inertia. Oh, gentlemen, perhaps I consider myself to be an intelligent man simply because for my whole life I haven't been able to begin or finish anything. All right, suppose I am a babbler, a harmless, annoying babbler, like the rest of us. But then what is to be done[9] if the direct and single vocation of every intelligent man consists in babbling, that is, in deliberately talking in endless circles?

VI

Oh, if only I did nothing simply as a result of laziness. Lord, how I'd respect myself then. I'd respect myself precisely because at least I'd be capable of being lazy; at least I'd possess one more or less positive trait of which I could be cer-

9. Reference to a then-new novel by Nikolai Chernyshevsky (1828–1889) called *What Is to Be Done?* (1863). Dostoyevsky disliked the main idea of the novel, which was that Russians could be freed from the delusions of tradition and faith by scientific knowledge and could build a rational new nation; *Notes from Underground* is in part a response to Chernyshevsky.

tain. Question: who am I? Answer: a sluggard. Why, it would have been very pleasant to hear that said about oneself. It would mean that I'd been positively identified; it would mean that there was something to be said about me. "A sluggard!" Why, that's a calling and a vocation, a whole career! Don't joke, it's true. Then, by rights I'd be a member of the very best club and would occupy myself exclusively by being able to respect myself continually. I knew a gentleman who prided himself all his life on being a connoisseur of Lafite.[1] He considered it his positive virtue and never doubted himself. He died not merely with a clean conscience, but with a triumphant one, and he was absolutely correct. I should have chosen a career for myself too: I would have been a sluggard and a glutton, not an ordinary one, but one who, for example, sympathized with everything beautiful and sublime. How do you like that? I've dreamt about it for a long time. The "beautiful and sublime" have been a real pain in the neck during my forty years, but then it's been *my* forty years, whereas then—oh, then it would have been otherwise! I would've found myself a suitable activity at once—namely, drinking to everything beautiful and sublime. I would have seized upon every opportunity first to shed a tear into my glass and then drink to everything beautiful and sublime. Then I would have turned everything into the beautiful and sublime; I would have sought out the beautiful and sublime in the nastiest, most indisputable trash. I would have become as tearful as a wet sponge. An artist, for example, has painted a portrait of Ge.[2] At once I drink to the artist who painted that portrait of Ge because I love everything beautiful and sublime. An author has written the words, "Just as you please,"[3] at once I drink to "Just as you please," because I love everything "beautiful and sublime." I'd demand respect for myself in doing this, I'd persecute anyone who didn't pay me any respect. I'd live peacefully and die triumphantly—why, it's charming, perfectly charming! And what a belly I'd have grown by then, what a triple chin I'd have acquired, what a red nose I'd have developed—so that just looking at me any passerby would have said, "Now that's a real plus! That's something really positive!" Say what you like, gentlemen, it's extremely pleasant to hear such comments in our negative age.

VII

But these are all golden dreams. Oh, tell me who was first to announce, first to proclaim that man does nasty things simply because he doesn't know his own true interest; and that if he were to be enlightened, if his eyes were to be opened to his true, normal interests, he would stop doing nasty things at once and would immediately become good and noble, because, being so enlightened and understanding his real advantage, he would realize that his own advantage really did lie in the good; and that it's well known that there's not a single man capable of acting knowingly against his own interest; consequently, he would,

---

1. A variety of red wine from Médoc in France.
2. N. N. Ge (1831–1894), Russian artist who rebelled against official styles in favor of a new realism in art; just before *Notes from Underground* appeared, Ge's *Last Supper* (1863) provoked considerable controversy in St. Petersburg because the painter had refused the conventional imagery of Jesus seated at a long table and instead showed him reclined and meditative, with his disciples confused and frightened.
3. An attack on the writer M. E. Saltykov-Shchedrin, who published a sympathetic review of Ge's painting titled *Just As You Please*.

so to speak, begin to do good out of necessity. Oh, the child! Oh, the pure, innocent babe! Well, in the first place, when was it during all these millennia, that man has ever acted only in his own self interest? What does one do with the millions of facts bearing witness to the one fact that people knowingly, that is, possessing full knowledge of their own true interests, have relegated them to the background and have rushed down a different path, that of risk and chance, compelled by no one and nothing, but merely as if they didn't want to follow the beaten track, and so they stubbornly, willfully forged another way, a difficult and absurd one, searching for it almost in the darkness? Why, then, this means that stubbornness and willfulness were really more pleasing to them than any kind of advantage. . . . Advantage! What is advantage? Will you take it upon yourself to define with absolute precision what constitutes man's advantage? And what if it turns out that man's advantage sometimes not only may, but even must in certain circumstances, consist precisely in his desiring something harmful to himself instead of something advantageous? And if this is so, if this can ever occur, then the whole theory falls to pieces. What do you think, can such a thing happen? You're laughing; laugh, gentlemen, but answer me: have man's advantages ever been calculated with absolute certainty? Aren't there some which don't fit, can't be made to fit into any classification? Why, as far as I know, you gentlemen have derived your list of human advantages from averages of statistical data and from scientific-economic formulas. But your advantages are prosperity, wealth, freedom, peace, and so on and so forth; so that a man who, for example, expressly and knowingly acts in opposition to this whole list, would be, in your opinion, and in mine, too, of course, either an obscurantist or a complete madman, wouldn't he? But now here's what's astonishing: why is it that when all these statisticians, sages, and lovers of humanity enumerate man's advantages, they invariably leave one out? They don't even take it into consideration in the form in which it should be considered, although the entire calculation depends upon it. There would be no great harm in considering it, this advantage, and adding it to the list. But the whole point is that this particular advantage doesn't fit into any classification and can't be found on any list. I have a friend, for instance. . . . But gentlemen! Why, he's your friend, too! In fact, he's everyone's friend! When he's preparing to do something, this gentleman straight away explains to you eloquently and clearly just how he must act according to the laws of nature and truth. And that's not all: with excitement and passion he'll tell you all about genuine, normal human interests; with scorn he'll reproach the shortsighted fools who understand neither their own advantage nor the real meaning of virtue; and then—exactly a quarter of an hour later, without any sudden outside cause, but precisely because of something internal that's stronger than all his interests—he does a complete about-face; that is, he does something which clearly contradicts what he's been saying: it goes against the laws of reason and his own advantage, in a word, against everything. . . . I warn you that my friend is a collective personage; therefore it's rather difficult to blame only him. That's just it, gentlemen; in fact, isn't there something dearer to every man than his own best advantage, or (so as not to violate the rules of logic) isn't there one more advantageous advantage (exactly the one omitted, the one we mentioned before), which is more important and more advantageous than all others and, on behalf of

which, a man will, if necessary, go against all laws, that is, against reason, honor, peace, and prosperity—in a word, against all those splendid and useful things, merely in order to attain this fundamental, most advantageous advantage which is dearer to him than everything else?

"Well, it's advantage all the same," you say, interrupting me. Be so kind as to allow me to explain further; besides, the point is not my pun, but the fact that this advantage is remarkable precisely because it destroys all our classifications and constantly demolishes all systems devised by lovers of humanity for the happiness of mankind. In a word, it interferes with everything. But, before I name this advantage, I want to compromise myself personally; therefore I boldly declare that all these splendid systems, all these theories to explain to mankind its real, normal interests so that, by necessarily striving to achieve them, it would immediately become good and noble—are, for the time being, in my opinion, nothing more than logical exercises! Yes, sir, logical exercises! Why, even to maintain a theory of mankind's regeneration through a system of its own advantages, why, in my opinion, that's almost the same as . . . well, claiming, for instance, following Buckle,[4] that man has become kinder as a result of civilization; consequently, he's becoming less bloodthirsty and less inclined to war. Why, logically it all even seems to follow. But man is so partial to systems and abstract conclusions that he's ready to distort the truth intentionally, ready to deny everything that he himself has ever seen and heard, merely in order to justify his own logic. That's why I take this example, because it's such a glaring one. Just look around: rivers of blood are being spilt, and in the most cheerful way, as if it were champagne. Take this entire nineteenth century of ours during which even Buckle lived. Take Napoleon—both the great and the present one.[5] Take North America—that eternal union.[6] Take, finally, that ridiculous Schleswig-Holstein[7]. . . . What is it that civilization makes kinder in us? Civilization merely promotes a wider variety of sensations in man and . . . absolutely nothing else. And through the development of this variety man may even reach the point where he takes pleasure in spilling blood. Why, that's even happened to him already. Haven't you noticed that the most refined bloodshedders are almost always the most civilized gentlemen to whom all these Attila the Huns and Stenka Razins[8] are scarcely fit to hold a candle; and if they're not as conspicuous as Attila and Stenka Razin, it's precisely because they're too common and have become too familiar to us. At least if man hasn't become more bloodthirsty as a result of civilization, surely he's become bloodthirsty in a nastier, more repulsive way than before. Previously man saw justice in bloodshed and exterminated whomever he wished with a

---

4. In his *History of Civilization in England* (1857–61), Henry Thomas Buckle (1821–1862) argued that the development of civilization necessarily leads to the cessation of war. Russia had recently been involved in fierce fighting in the Crimea (1853–56).
5. The French emperors Napoleon I (1769–1821) and his nephew Napoleon III (1808–1873), both of whom engaged in numerous wars, though on vastly different scales.

6. The United States was in the middle of its Civil War (1861–65).
7. The German duchies of Schleswig and Holstein, held by Denmark since 1773, were reunited with Prussia after a brief war in 1864.
8. Cossack leader (d. 1671) who organized a peasant rebellion in Russia. Attila (406?–453 C.E.), king of the Huns, who conducted devastating wars against the Roman emperors.

clear conscience; whereas now, though we consider bloodshed to be abominable, we nevertheless engage in this abomination even more than before. Which is worse? Decide for yourselves. They say that Cleopatra (forgive an example from Roman history) loved to stick gold pins into the breasts of her slave girls and take pleasure in their screams and writhing. You'll say that this took place, relatively speaking, in barbaric times; that these are barbaric times too, because (also comparatively speaking), gold pins are used even now; that even now, although man has learned on occasion to see more clearly than in barbaric times, *he's still far from having learned* how to act in accordance with the dictates of reason and science. Nevertheless, you're still absolutely convinced that he will learn how to do so, as soon as he gets rid of some bad, old habits and as soon as common sense and science have completely re-educated human nature and have turned it in the proper direction. You're convinced that then man will voluntarily stop committing blunders, and that he will, so to speak, never willingly set his own will in opposition to his own normal interests. More than that: then, you say, science itself will teach man (though, in my opinion, that's already a luxury) that in fact he possesses neither a will nor any whim of his own, that he never did, and that he himself is nothing more than a kind of piano key or an organ stop;[9] that, moreover, there still exist laws of nature, so that everything he's done has been not in accordance with his own desire, but in and of itself, according to the laws of nature. Consequently, we need only discover these laws of nature, and man will no longer have to answer for his own actions and will find it extremely easy to live. All human actions, it goes without saying, will then be tabulated according to these laws, mathematically, like tables of logarithms up to 108,000, and will be entered on a schedule; or even better, certain edifying works will be published, like our contemporary encyclopedic dictionaries, in which everything will be accurately calculated and specified so that there'll be no more actions or adventures left on earth.

At that time, it's still you speaking, new economic relations will be established, all ready-made, also calculated with mathematical precision, so that all possible questions will disappear in a single instant, simply because all possible answers will have been provided. Then the crystal palace[1] will be built. And then . . . Well, in a word, those will be our halcyon days. Of course, there's no way to guarantee (now this is me talking) that it won't be, for instance, terribly boring then (because there won't be anything left to do, once everything has been calculated according to tables); on the other hand, everything will be extremely rational. Of course, what don't people think up out of boredom! Why, even gold pins get stuck into other people out of boredom, but that wouldn't matter. What's really bad (this is me talking again) is that for all I know, people might even be grateful for those gold pins. For man is stupid, phenomenally stupid. That is, although he's not really stupid at all, he's really so ungrateful that it's hard to find another being quite like him. Why, I, for

9. A reference to the last discourse of the French philosopher Denis Diderot (1713–1784) in the *Conversation of D'Alembert and Diderot* (1769).
1. An allusion to the crystal palace described in Vera Pavlovna's fourth dream in Cherny-

shevsky's *What Is to Be Done?* and to the actual building designed by Sir Joseph Paxton, erected for the Great Exhibition in London in 1851 and at that time admired as the newest wonder of architecture; Dostoevsky described it in *Winter Notes on Summer Impressions* (1863).

example, wouldn't be surprised in the least, if, suddenly, for no reason at all, in the midst of this future, universal rationalism, some gentleman with an offensive, rather, a retrograde and derisive expression on his face were to stand up, put his hands on his hips, and declare to us all: "How about it, gentlemen, what if we knock over all this rationalism with one swift kick for the sole purpose of sending all these logarithms to hell, so that once again we can live according to our own stupid will!" But that wouldn't matter either; what's so annoying is that he would undoubtedly find some followers; such is the way man is made. And all because of the most foolish reason, which, it seems, is hardly worth mentioning: namely, that man, always and everywhere, whoever he is, has preferred to act as he wished, and not at all as reason and advantage have dictated; one might even desire something opposed to one's own advantage, and sometimes (this is now my idea) one *positively must do so*. One's very own free, unfettered desire, one's own whim, no matter how wild, one's own fantasy, even though sometimes roused to the point of madness—all this constitutes precisely that previously omitted, most advantageous advantage which isn't included under any classification and because of which all systems and theories are constantly smashed to smithereens. Where did these sages ever get the idea that man needs any normal, virtuous desire? How did they ever imagine that man needs any kind of rational, advantageous desire? Man needs only one thing—his own *independent* desire, whatever that independence might cost and wherever it might lead. And as far as desire goes, the devil only knows. . . .

VIII

"Ha, ha, ha! But in reality even this desire, if I may say so, doesn't exist!" you interrupt me with a laugh. "Why science has already managed to dissect man so now we know that desire and so-called free choice are nothing more than . . ."

Wait, gentlemen, I myself wanted to begin like that. I must confess that even I got frightened. I was just about to declare that the devil only knows what desire depends on and perhaps we should be grateful for that, but then I remembered about science and I . . . stopped short. But now you've gone and brought it up. Well, after all, what if someday they really do discover the formula for all our desires and whims, that is, the thing that governs them, precise laws that produce them, how exactly they're applied, where they lead in each and every case, and so on and so forth, that is, the genuine mathematical formula—why, then all at once man might stop desiring, yes, indeed, he probably would. Who would want to desire according to some table? And that's not all: he would immediately be transformed from a person into an organ stop or something of that sort; because what is man without desire, without will, and without wishes if not a stop in an organ pipe? What do you think? Let's consider the probabilities—can this really happen or not?

"Hmmm . . . ," you decide, "our desires are mistaken for the most part because of an erroneous view of our own advantage. Consequently, we sometimes desire pure rubbish because, in our own stupidity, we consider it the easiest way to achieve some previously assumed advantage. Well, and when all this has been analyzed, calculated on paper (that's entirely possible, since it's repugnant and senseless to assume in advance that man will never come to understand the laws of nature) then, of course, all so-called desires will no longer exist. For if someday desires are completely reconciled with reason,

we'll follow reason instead of desire simply because it would be impossible, for example, while retaining one's reason, to *desire* rubbish, and thus knowingly oppose one's reason, and desire something harmful to oneself. . . . And, since all desires and reasons can really be tabulated, since someday the laws of our so-called free choice are sure to be discovered, then, all joking aside, it may be possible to establish something like a table, so that we could actually desire according to it. If, for example, someday they calculate and demonstrate to me that I made a rude gesture because I couldn't possibly refrain from it, that I had to make precisely that gesture, well, in that case, what sort of *free choice* would there be, especially if I'm a learned man and have completed a course of study somewhere? Why, then I'd be able to calculate in advance my entire life for the next thirty years; in a word, if such a table were to be drawn up, there'd be nothing left for us to do; we'd simply have to accept it. In general, we should be repeating endlessly to ourselves that at such a time and in such circum-stances nature certainly won't ask our opinion; that we must accept it as is, and not as we fantasize it, and that if we really aspire to prepare a table, a schedule, and, well . . . well, even a laboratory test tube, there's nothing to be done—one must even accept the test tube! If not, it'll be accepted even without you. . . ."

Yes, but that's just where I hit a snag! Gentlemen, you'll excuse me for all this philosophizing; it's a result of my forty years in the underground! Allow me to fantasize. Don't you see: reason is a fine thing, gentlemen, there's no doubt about it, but it's only reason, and it satisfies only man's rational faculty, whereas desire is a manifestation of all life, that is, of all human life, which includes both reason, as well as all of life's itches and scratches. And although in this manifestation life often turns out to be fairly worthless, it's life all the same, and not merely the extraction of square roots. Why, take me, for instance; I quite naturally want to live in order to satisfy all my faculties of life, not merely my rational faculty, that is, some one-twentieth of all my faculties. What does reason know? Reason knows only what it's managed to learn. (Some things it may never learn; while this offers no comfort, why not admit it openly?) But human nature acts as a whole, with all that it contains, consciously and uncon-sciously; and although it may tell lies, it's still alive. I suspect, gentlemen, that you're looking at me with compassion; you repeat that an enlightened and cul-tured man, in a word, man as he will be in the future, cannot knowingly desire something disadvantageous to himself, and that this is pure mathematics. I agree with you: it really is mathematics. But I repeat for the one-hundredth time, there is one case, only one, when a man may intentionally, consciously desire even something harmful to himself, something stupid, even very stupid, namely: in order *to have the right* to desire something even very stupid and not be bound by an obligation to desire only what's smart. After all, this very stupid thing, one's own whim, gentlemen, may in fact be the most advantageous thing on earth for people like me, especially in certain cases. In particular, it may be more advantageous than any other advantage, even in a case where it causes obvious harm and contradicts the most sensible conclusions of reason about advantage—because in any case it preserves for us what's most important and precious, that is, our personality and our individuality. There are some people who maintain that in fact this is more precious to man than anything else; of course, desire can, if it so chooses, coincide with reason, especially if it doesn't abuse this option, and chooses to coincide in moderation; this is useful and sometimes even commendable. But very often, even most of the time, desire

absolutely and stubbornly disagrees with reason and . . . and . . . and, do you know, sometimes this is also useful and even very commendable? Let's assume, gentlemen, that man isn't stupid. (And really, this can't possibly be said about him at all, if only because if he's stupid, then who on earth is smart?) But even if he's not stupid, he is, nevertheless, monstrously ungrateful. Phenomenally ungrateful. I even believe that the best definition of man is this: a creature who walks on two legs and is ungrateful. But that's still not all; that's still not his main defect. His main defect is his perpetual misbehavior, perpetual from the time of the Great Flood to the Schleswig-Holstein period of human destiny. Misbehavior, and consequently, imprudence; for it's long been known that imprudence results from nothing else but misbehavior. Just cast a glance at the history of mankind; well, what do you see? Is it majestic? Well, perhaps it's majestic; why, the Colossus of Rhodes,[2] for example—that alone is worth something! Not without reason did Mr Anaevsky[3] report that some people consider it to be the product of human hands, while others maintain that it was created by nature itself. Is it colorful? Well, perhaps it's also colorful; just consider the dress uniforms, both military and civilian, of all nations at all times—why, that alone is worth something, and if you include everyday uniforms, it'll make your eyes bulge; not one historian will be able to sort it all out. Is it monotonous? Well, perhaps it's monotonous, too: men fight and fight; now they're fighting; they fought first and they fought last—you'll agree that it's really much too monotonous. In short, anything can be said about world history, anything that might occur to the most disordered imagination. There's only one thing that can't possibly be said about it—that it's rational. You'll choke on the word. Yet here's just the sort of thing you'll encounter all the time: why, in life you're constantly running up against people who are so well-behaved and so rational, such wise men and lovers of humanity who set themselves the lifelong goal of behaving as morally and rationally as possible, so to speak, to be a beacon for their nearest and dearest, simply in order to prove that it's really possible to live one's life in a moral and rational way. And so what? It's a well-known fact that many of these lovers of humanity, sooner or later, by the end of their lives, have betrayed themselves: they've pulled off some caper, sometimes even quite an indecent one. Now I ask you: what can one expect from man as a creature endowed with such strange qualities? Why, shower him with all sorts of earthly blessings, submerge him in happiness over his head so that only little bubbles appear on the surface of this happiness, as if on water, give him such economic prosperity that he'll have absolutely nothing left to do except sleep, eat gingerbread, and worry about the continuation of world history—even then, out of pure ingratitude, sheer perversity, he'll commit some repulsive act. He'll even risk losing his gingerbread, and will intentionally desire the most wicked rubbish, the most uneconomical absurdity, simply in order to inject his own pernicious fantastic element into all this positive rationality. He wants to hold onto those most fantastic dreams, his own indecent stupidity solely for the purpose of assuring himself (as if it were necessary) that men are still men and not piano keys, and that even if the laws

2. A large bronze statue of the Greek sun god, Helios, built between 292 and 280 B.C.E. in the harbor of Rhodes (an island in the Aegean Sea) and considered one of the Seven Wonders of the Ancient World.

3. A. E. Anaevsky was a critic whose articles were frequently ridiculed in literary polemics of the period.

of nature play upon them with their own hands, they're still threatened by being overplayed until they won't possibly desire anything more than a schedule. But that's not all: even if man really turned out to be a piano key, even if this could be demonstrated to him by natural science and pure mathematics, even then he still won't become reasonable; he'll intentionally do something to the contrary, simply out of ingratitude, merely to have his own way. If he lacks the means, he'll cause destruction and chaos, he'll devise all kinds of suffering and have his own way! He'll leash a curse upon the world; and, since man alone can do so (it's his privilege and the thing that most distinguishes him from other animals), perhaps only through this curse will he achieve his goal, that is, become really convinced that he's a man and not a piano key! If you say that one can also calculate all this according to a table, this chaos and darkness, these curses, so that the mere possibility of calculating it all in advance would stop everything and that reason alone would prevail—in that case man would go insane deliberately in order not to have reason, but to have his own way! I believe this, I vouch for it, because, after all, the whole of man's work seems to consist only in proving to himself constantly that he's a man and not an organ stop! Even if he has to lose his own skin, he'll prove it; even if he has to become a troglodyte, he'll prove it. And after that, how can one not sin, how can one not praise the fact that all this hasn't yet come to pass and that desire still depends on the devil knows what . . . ?

You'll shout at me (if you still choose to favor me with your shouts) that no one's really depriving me of my will; that they're merely attempting to arrange things so that my will, by its own free choice, will coincide with my normal interests, with the laws of nature, and with arithmetic.

But gentlemen, what sort of free choice will there be when it comes down to tables and arithmetic, when all that's left is two times two makes four? Two times two makes four even without my will. Is that what you call free choice?

IX

Gentlemen, I'm joking of course, and I myself know that it's not a very good joke; but, after all, you can't take everything as a joke. Perhaps I'm gnashing my teeth while I joke. I'm tormented by questions, gentlemen; answer them for me. Now, for example, you want to cure man of his old habits and improve his will according to the demands of science and common sense. But how do you know not only whether it's possible, but even if it's *necessary* to remake him in this way? Why do you conclude that human desire *must* undoubtedly be improved? In short, how do you know that such improvement will really be to man's advantage? And, to be perfectly frank, why are you so *absolutely* convinced that not to oppose man's real, normal advantage guaranteed by the conclusions of reason and arithmetic is really always to man's advantage and constitutes a law for all humanity? After all, this is still only an assumption of yours. Let's suppose that it's a law of logic, but perhaps not a law of humanity. Perhaps, gentlemen, you're wondering if I'm insane? Allow me to explain. I agree that man is primarily a creative animal, destined to strive consciously toward a goal and to engage in the art of engineering, that, is, externally and incessantly building new roads for himself *wherever they lead*. But sometimes

he may want to swerve aside precisely because he's *compelled* to build these roads, and perhaps also because, no matter how stupid the spontaneous man of action may generally be, nevertheless it sometimes occurs to him that the road, as it turns out, almost always leads *somewhere or other*, and that the main thing isn't so much where it goes, but the fact that it does, and that the well-behaved child, disregarding the art of engineering, shouldn't yield to pernicious idleness which, as is well known, constitutes the mother of all vices. Man loves to create and build roads; that's indisputable. But why is he also so passionately fond of destruction and chaos? Now, then, tell me. But I myself want to say a few words about this separately. Perhaps the reason that he's so fond of destruction and chaos (after all, it's indisputable that he sometimes really loves it, and that's a fact) is that he himself has an instinctive fear of achieving his goal and completing the project under construction? How do you know if perhaps he loves his building only from afar, but not from close up; perhaps he only likes building it, but not living in it, leaving it afterward *aux animaux domestiques*,[4] such as ants or sheep, or so on and so forth. Now ants have altogether different tastes. They have one astonishing structure of a similar type, forever indestructible—the anthill.

The worthy ants began with the anthill, and most likely, they will end with the anthill, which does great credit to their perseverance and steadfastness. But man is a frivolous and unseemly creature and perhaps, like a chess player, he loves only the process of achieving his goal, and not the goal itself. And, who knows (one can't vouch for it), perhaps the only goal on earth toward which mankind is striving consists merely in this incessant process of achieving or to put it another way, in life itself, and not particularly in the goal which, of course, must always be none other than two times two makes four, that is, a formula; after all, two times two makes four is no longer life, gentlemen, but the beginning of death. At least man has always been somewhat afraid of this two times two makes four, and I'm afraid of it now, too. Let's suppose that the only thing man does is search for this two times two makes four; he sails across oceans, sacrifices his own life in the quest; but to seek it out and find it—really and truly, he's very frightened. After all, he feels that as soon as he finds it, there'll be nothing left to search for. Workers, after finishing work, at least receive their wages, go off to a tavern, and then wind up at a police station—now that's a full week's occupation. But where will man go? At any rate a certain awkwardness can be observed each time he approaches the achievement of similar goals. He loves the process, but he's not so fond of the achievement, and that, of course is terribly amusing. In short, man is made in a comical way; obviously there's some sort of catch in all this. But two times two makes four is an insufferable thing, nevertheless. Two times two makes four—why, in my opinion, it's mere insolence. Two times two makes four stands there brazenly with its hands on its hips, blocking your path and spitting at you. I agree that two times two makes four is a splendid thing; but if we're going to lavish praise, then two times two makes five is sometimes also a very charming little thing.

---

4. "To domestic animals" (French).

And why are you so firmly, so triumphantly convinced that only the normal and positive—in short, only well-being is advantageous to man? Doesn't reason ever make mistakes about advantage? After all, perhaps man likes something other than well-being? Perhaps he loves suffering just as much? Perhaps suffering is just as advantageous to him as well-being? Man sometimes loves suffering terribly, to the point of passion, and that's a fact. There's no reason to study world history on this point; if indeed you're a man and have lived at all, just ask yourself. As far as my own personal opinion is concerned, to love only well-being is somehow even indecent. Whether good or bad, it's sometimes also very pleasant to demolish something. After all, I'm not standing up for suffering here, nor for well-being, either. I'm standing up for . . . my own whim and for its being guaranteed to me whenever necessary. For instance, suffering is not permitted in vaudevilles,[5] that I know. It's also inconceivable in the crystal palace; suffering is doubt and negation. What sort of crystal palace would it be if any doubt were allowed? Yet, I'm convinced that man will never renounce real suffering, that is, destruction and chaos. After all, suffering is the sole cause of consciousness. Although I stated earlier that in my opinion consciousness is man's greatest misfortune, still I know that man loves it and would not exchange it for any other sort of satisfaction. Consciousness, for example, is infinitely higher than two times two. Of course, after two times two, there's nothing left, not merely nothing to do, but nothing to learn. Then the only thing possible will be to plug up your five senses and plunge into contemplation. Well, even if you reach the same result with consciousness, that is, having nothing left to do, at least you'll be able to flog yourself from time to time, and that will liven things up a bit. Although it may be reactionary, it's still better than nothing.

X[6]

You believe in the crystal palace, eternally indestructible, that is, one at which you can never stick out your tongue furtively nor make a rude gesture, even with your fist hidden away. Well, perhaps I'm so afraid of this building precisely because it's made of crystal and it's eternally indestructible, and because it won't be possible to stick one's tongue out even furtively.

Don't you see: if it were a chicken coop instead of a palace, and if it should rain, then perhaps I could crawl into it so as not to get drenched; but I would still not mistake a chicken coop for a palace out of gratitude, just because it sheltered me from the rain. You're laughing, you're even saying that in this case there's no difference between a chicken coop and a mansion. Yes, I reply, if the only reason for living is to keep from getting drenched.

But what if I've taken it into my head that this is not the only reason for living, and, that if one is to live at all, one might as well live in a mansion? Such is my wish, my desire. You'll expunge it from me only when you've changed my desires. Well, then, change them, tempt me with something else, give me some other ideal. In the meantime, I still won't mistake a chicken coop for a palace.

---

5. A dramatic genre, popular on the Russian stage, consisting of scenes from contemporary life acted with a satirical twist, often in racy dialogue.

6. This chapter was badly mutilated by the censor, as Dostoyevsky makes clear in the letter to his brother Mikhail, dated March 26, 1864.

But let's say that the crystal palace is a hoax, that according to the laws of nature it shouldn't exist, and that I've invented it only out of my own stupidity, as a result of certain antiquated, irrational habits of my generation. But what do I care if it doesn't exist? What difference does it make if it exists only in my own desires, or, to be more precise, if it exists as long as my desires exist? Perhaps you're laughing again? Laugh, if you wish; I'll resist all your laughter and I still won't say I'm satiated if I'm really hungry; I know all the same that I won't accept a compromise, an infinitely recurring zero, just because it exists according to the laws of nature and it *really* does exist. I won't accept as the crown of my desires a large building with tenements for poor tenants to be rented for a thousand years and, just in case, with the name of the dentist Wagenheim on the sign. Destroy my desires, eradicate my ideals, show me something better and I'll follow you. You may say, perhaps, that it's not worth getting involved; but, in that case, I'll say the same thing in reply. We're having a serious discussion; if you don't grant me your attention, I won't grovel for it. I still have my underground.

And, as long as I'm still alive and feel desire—may my arm wither away before it contributes even one little brick to that building! Never mind that I myself have just rejected the crystal palace for the sole reason that it won't be possible to tease it by sticking out one's tongue at it. I didn't say that because I'm so fond of sticking out my tongue. Perhaps the only reason I got angry is that among all your buildings there's still not a single one where you don't feel compelled to stick out your tongue. On the contrary, I'd let my tongue be cut off out of sheer gratitude, if only things could be so arranged that I'd no longer want to stick it out. What do I care if things can't be so arranged and if I must settle for some tenements? Why was I made with such desires? Can it be that I was made this way only in order to reach the conclusion that my entire way of being is merely a fraud? Can this be the whole purpose? I don't believe it.

By the way, do you know what? I'm convinced that we underground men should be kept in check. Although capable of sitting around quietly in the underground for some forty years, once he emerges into the light of day and bursts into speech, he talks on and on and on. . . .

XI

The final result, gentlemen, is that it's better to do nothing! Conscious inertia is better! And so, long live the underground! Even though I said that I envy the normal man to the point of exasperation, I still wouldn't want to be him under the circumstances in which I see him (although I still won't keep from envying him. No, no, in any case the underground is more advantageous!) At least there one can . . . Hey, but I'm lying once again! I'm lying because I know myself as surely as two times two, that it isn't really the underground that's better, but something different, altogether different, something that I long for, but I'll never be able to find! To hell with the underground! Why, here's what would be better: if I myself were to believe even a fraction of everything I've written. I swear to you, gentlemen, that I don't believe one word, not one little word of all that I've scribbled. That is, I do believe it, perhaps, but at the very same time, I don't know why, I feel and suspect that I'm lying like a trooper.

"Then why did you write all this?" you ask me.

"What if I'd shut you up in the underground for forty years with nothing to do and then came back forty years later to see what had become of you? Can a man really be left alone for forty years with nothing to do?"

"Isn't it disgraceful, isn't it humiliating!" you might say, shaking your head in contempt. "You long for life, but you try to solve life's problems by means of a logical tangle. How importunate, how insolent your outbursts, and how frightened you are at the same time! You talk rubbish, but you're constantly afraid of them and make apologies. You maintain that you fear nothing, but at the same time you try to ingratiate yourself with us. You assure us that you're gnashing your teeth, yet at the same time you try to be witty and amuse us. You know that your witticisms are not very clever, but apparently you're pleased by their literary merit. Perhaps you really have suffered, but you don't even respect your own suffering. There's some truth in you, too, but no chastity; out of the pettiest vanity you bring your truth out into the open, into the marketplace, and you shame it. . . . You really want to say something, but you conceal your final word out of fear because you lack the resolve to utter it; you have only cowardly impudence. You boast about your consciousness, but you merely vacillate, because even though your mind is working, your heart has been blackened by depravity, and without a pure heart, there can be no full, genuine consciousness. And how importunate you are; how you force yourself upon others; you behave in such an affected manner. Lies, lies, lies!"

Of course, it was I who just invented all these words for you. That, too, comes from the underground. For forty years in a row I've been listening to all your words through a crack. I've invented them myself, since that's all that's occurred to me. It's no wonder that I've learned it all by heart and that it's taken on such a literary form. . . .

But can you really be so gullible as to imagine that I'll print all this and give it to you to read? And here's another problem I have: why do I keep calling you "gentlemen"? Why do I address you as if you really were my readers? Confessions such as the one I plan to set forth here aren't published and given to other people to read. Anyway, I don't possess sufficient fortitude, nor do I consider it necessary to do so. But don't you see, a certain notion has come into my mind, and I wish to realize it at any cost. Here's the point.

Every man has within his own reminiscences certain things he doesn't reveal to anyone, except, perhaps, to his friends. There are also some that he won't reveal even to his friends, only to himself perhaps, and even then, in secret. Finally, there are some which a man is afraid to reveal even to himself; every decent man has accumulated a fair number of such things. In fact, it can even be said that the more decent the man, the more of these things he's accumulated. Anyway, only recently I myself decided to recall some of my earlier adventures; up to now I've always avoided them, even with a certain anxiety. But having decided not only to recall them, but even to write them down, now is when I wish to try an experiment: is it possible to be absolutely honest even with one's own self and not to fear the whole truth? Incidentally, I'll mention that Heine maintains that faithful autobiographies are almost impossible, and that a man is sure to lie about himself.[7] In Heine's opinion, Rousseau, for

---

7. A reference to the work *On Germany* (1853–54) by the German poet Heinrich Heine (1797–1856), in which on the very first page Heine speaks of Rousseau as lying and inventing disgraceful incidents about himself for his *Confessions*.

example, undoubtedly told untruths about himself in his confession and even lied intentionally, out of vanity. I'm convinced that Heine is correct; I understand perfectly well that sometimes it's possible out of vanity alone to impute all sorts of crimes to oneself, and I can even understand what sort of vanity that might be. But Heine was making judgments about a person who confessed to the public. I, however, am writing for myself alone and declare once and for all that if I write as if I were addressing readers, that's only for show, because it's easier for me to write that way. It's a form, simply a form; I shall never have any readers. I've already stated that. . . . I don't want to be restricted in any way by editing my notes. I won't attempt to introduce any order or system. I'll write down whatever comes to mind.

Well, now, for example, someone might seize upon my words and ask me, if you really aren't counting on any readers, why do you make such compacts with yourself, and on paper no less; that is, if you're not going to introduce any order or system, if you're going to write down whatever comes to mind, etc., etc.? Why do you go on explaining? Why do you keep apologizing?

"Well, imagine that," I reply.

This, by the way, contains an entire psychology. Perhaps it's just that I'm a coward. Or perhaps it's that I imagine an audience before me on purpose, so that I behave more decently when I'm writing things down. There may be a thousand reasons.

But here's something else: why is it that I want to write? If it's not for the public, then why can't I simply recall it all in my own mind and not commit it to paper?

Quite so; but somehow it appears more dignified on paper. There's something more impressive about it; I'll be a better judge of myself; the style will be improved. Besides, perhaps I'll actually experience some relief from the process of writing it all down. Today, for example, I'm particularly oppressed by one very old memory from my distant past. It came to me vividly several days ago and since then it's stayed with me, like an annoying musical motif that doesn't want to leave you alone. And yet you must get rid of it. I have hundreds of such memories; but at times a single one emerges from those hundreds and oppresses me. For some reason I believe that if I write it down I can get rid of it. Why not try?

Lastly, I'm bored, and I never do anything. Writing things down actually seems like work. They say that work makes a man become good and honest. Well, at least there's chance.

It's snowing today, an almost wet, yellow, dull snow. It was snowing yesterday too, a few days ago as well. I think it was apropos of the wet snow that I recalled this episode and now it doesn't want to leave me alone. And so, let it be a tale apropos of wet snow.

II

Apropos of Wet Snow

When from the darkness of delusion
I saved your fallen soul
With ardent words of conviction,
And, full of profound torment,
Wringing your hands, you cursed

> The vice that had ensnared you;
> When, punishing by recollection
> Your forgetful conscience,
> You told me the tale
> Of all that had happened before,
> And, suddenly, covering your face,
> Full of shame and horror,
> You tearfully resolved,
> Indignant, shaken . . .
> Etc., etc., etc.
> From the poetry of N. A. Nekrasov[8]

I

At that time I was only twenty-four years old. Even then my life was gloomy, disordered, and solitary to the point of savagery. I didn't associate with anyone; I even avoided talking, and I retreated further and further into my corner. At work in the office I even tried not to look at anyone; I was aware not only that my colleagues considered me eccentric, but that they always seemed to regard me with a kind of loathing. Sometimes I wondered why it was that no one else thinks that others regard him with loathing. One of our office-workers had a repulsive pock-marked face which even appeared somewhat villainous. It seemed to me that with such a disreputable face I'd never have dared look at anyone. Another man had a uniform so worn that there was a foul smell emanating from him. Yet, neither of these two gentlemen was embarrassed— neither because of his clothes, nor his face, nor in any moral way. Neither one imagined that other people regarded him with loathing; and if either had so imagined, it wouldn't have mattered at all, as long as their supervisor chose not to view him that way. It's perfectly clear to me now, because of my unlimited vanity and the great demands I accordingly made on myself, that I frequently regarded myself with a furious dissatisfaction verging on loathing; as a result, I intentionally ascribed my own view to everyone else. For example, I despised my own face; I considered it hideous, and I even suspected that there was something repulsive in its expression. Therefore, every time I arrived at work, I took pains to behave as independently as possible, so that I couldn't be suspected of any malice, and I tried to assume as noble an expression as possible. "It may not be a handsome face," I thought, "but let it be noble, expressive, and above all, extremely *intelligent*." But I was agonizingly certain that my face couldn't possibly express all these virtues. Worst of all, I considered it positively stupid. I'd have been reconciled if it had looked intelligent. In fact, I'd even have agreed to have it appear repulsive, on the condition that at the same time people would find my face terribly intelligent.

Of course, I hated all my fellow office-workers from the first to the last and despised every one of them; yet, at the same time it was as if I were afraid of them. Sometimes it happened that I would even regard them as superior to me. At this time these changes would suddenly occur: first I would despise them,

---

8. A Russian poet and editor of radical sympathies (1821–1878). The poem quoted dates from 1845 and is untitled. It ends with the lines "And enter my house bold and free / To become its full mistress!"

then I would regard them as superior to me. A cultured and decent man cannot be vain without making unlimited demands on himself and without hating himself, at times to the point of contempt. But, whether hating them or regarding them as superior, I almost always lowered my eyes when meeting anyone. I even conducted experiments: could I endure someone's gaze? I'd always be the first to lower my eyes. This infuriated me to the point of madness. I slavishly worshipped the conventional in everything external. I embraced the common practice and feared any eccentricity with all my soul. But how could I sustain it? I was morbidly refined, as befits any cultured man of our time. All others resembled one another as sheep in a flock. Perhaps I was the only one in the whole office who constantly thought of himself as a coward and a slave; and I thought so precisely because I was so cultured. But not only did I think so, it actually was so: I was a coward and a slave. I say this without any embarrassment. Every decent man of our time is and must be a coward and a slave. This is his normal condition. I'm deeply convinced of it. This is how he's made and what he's meant to be. And not only at the present time, as the result of some accidental circumstance, but in general at all times, a decent man must be a coward and a slave. This is a law of nature for all decent men on earth. If one of them should happen to be brave about something or other, we shouldn't be comforted or distracted: he'll still lose his nerve about something else. That's the single and eternal way out. Only asses and their mongrels are brave, and even then, only until they come up against a wall. It's not worthwhile paying them any attention because they really don't mean anything at all.

There was one more circumstance tormenting me at that time: no one was like me, and I wasn't like anyone else. "I'm alone," I mused, "and they are *everyone*"; and I sank deep into thought.

From all this it's clear that I was still just a boy.

The exact opposite would also occur. Sometimes I would find it repulsive to go to the office: it reached the point where I would often return home from work ill. Then suddenly, for no good reason at all, a flash of skepticism and indifference would set in (everything came to me in flashes); I would laugh at my own intolerance and fastidiousness, and reproach myself for my *romanticism*. Sometimes I didn't even want to talk to anyone; at other times it reached a point where I not only started talking, but I even thought about striking up a friendship with others. All my fastidiousness would suddenly disappear for no good reason at all. Who knows? Perhaps I never really had any, and it was all affected, borrowed from books. I still haven't answered this question, even up to now. And once I really did become friends with others; I began to visit their houses, play préférence,[9] drink vodka, talk about promotions. . . . But allow me to digress.

We Russians, generally speaking, have never had any of those stupid, transcendent German romantics, or even worse, French romantics, on whom nothing produces any effect whatever: the earth might tremble beneath them, all of France might perish on the barricades, but they remain the same, not even changing for decency's sake; they go on singing their transcendent songs, so to speak, to their dying day, because they're such fools. We here on Russian soil have no fools. It's a well-known fact; that's precisely what distinguishes us

9. A card game for three players.

from foreigners. Consequently, transcendent natures cannot be found among us in their pure form. That's the result of our "positive" publicists and critics of that period, who hunted for the Kostanzhouglo and the Uncle Pyotr Ivanoviches,[1] foolishly mistaking them for our ideal and slandering our own romantics, considering them to be the same kind of transcendents as one finds in Germany or France. On the contrary, the characteristics of our romantics are absolutely and directly opposed to the transcendent Europeans; not one of those European standards can apply here. (Allow me to use the word "romantic"—it's an old-fashioned little word, well-respected and deserving, familiar to everyone.) The characteristics of our romantics are to understand everything, *to see everything, often to see it much more clearly than our most positive minds*; not to be reconciled with anyone or anything, but, at the same time, not to balk at anything; to circumvent everything, to yield on every point, to treat everyone diplomatically; never to lose sight of some useful, practical goal (an apartment at government expense, a nice pension, a decoration)—to keep an eye on that goal through all his excesses and his volumes of lyrical verse, and, at the same time, to preserve intact the "beautiful and sublime" to the end of their lives; and, incidentally, to preserve themselves as well, wrapped up in cotton like precious jewelry, if only, for example, for the sake of that same "beautiful and sublime." Our romantic has a very broad nature and is the biggest rogue of all, I can assure you of that . . . even by my own experience. Of course, all this is true if the romantic is smart. But what am I saying? A romantic is always smart; I merely wanted to observe that although we've had some romantic fools, they really don't count at all, simply because while still in their prime they would degenerate completely into Germans, and, in order to preserve their precious jewels more comfortably, they'd settle over there, either in Weimar or in the Black Forest. For instance, I genuinely despised my official position and refrained from throwing it over merely out of necessity, because I myself sat there working and received good money for doing it. And, as a result, please note, I still refrained from throwing it over. Our romantic would sooner lose his mind (which, by the way, very rarely occurs) than give it up, if he didn't have another job in mind; nor is he ever kicked out, unless he's hauled off to the insane asylum as the "King of Spain,"[2] and only if he's gone completely mad. Then again, it's really only the weaklings and towheads who go mad in our country. An enormous number of romantics later rise to significant rank. What extraordinary versatility! And what a capacity for the most contradictory sensations! I used to be consoled by these thoughts back then, and still am even nowadays. That's why there are so many "broad natures" among us, people who never lose their ideals, no matter how low they fall; even though they never lift a finger for the sake of their ideals, even though they're outrageous villains and thieves, nevertheless they respect their original ideals to the point of tears and are extremely honest men at heart. Yes, only among us Russians

---

1. A character in Ivan Goncharov's novel *A Common Story* (1847); a high bureaucrat, a factory owner who teaches lessons of sobriety and good sense to the romantic hero, Alexander Aduyev. Konstanzhouglo is the ideal efficient landowner in the second part of Nikolai Gogol's novel *Dead Souls* (1852).

2. An allusion to the hero of Gogol's short story "Diary of a Madman" (1835). Poprishchin, a low-ranking civil servant, sees his aspirations crushed by the enormous bureaucracy. He ends by going insane and imagining himself to be king of Spain.

can the most outrageous scoundrel be absolutely, even sublimely honest at heart, while at the same time never ceasing to be a scoundrel. I repeat, nearly always do our romantics turn out to be very efficient rascals (I use the word "rascal" affectionately); they suddenly manifest such a sense of reality and positive knowledge that their astonished superiors and the general public can only click their tongues at them in amazement.

Their versatility is really astounding; God only knows what it will turn into, how it will develop under subsequent conditions, and what it holds for us in the future. The material is not all that bad! I'm not saying this out of some ridiculous patriotism or jingoism. However, I'm sure that once again you think I'm joking. But who knows? Perhaps it's quite the contrary, that is, you're convinced that this is what I really think. In any case, gentlemen, I'll consider that both of these opinions constitute an honor and a particular pleasure. And do forgive me for this digression.

Naturally, I didn't sustain any friendships with my colleagues, and soon I severed all relations after quarreling with them; and, because of my youthful inexperience at the same time, I even stopped greeting them, as if I'd cut them off entirely. That, however, happened to me only once. On the whole, I was always alone.

At home I spent most of my time reading. I tried to stifle all that was constantly seething within me with external sensations. And of all external sensations available, only reading was possible for me. Of course, reading helped a great deal—it agitated, delighted, and tormented me. But at times it was terribly boring. I still longed to be active; and suddenly I sank into dark, subterranean, loathsome depravity—more precisely, petty vice. My nasty little passions were sharp and painful as a result of my constant, morbid irritability. I experienced hysterical fits accompanied by tears and convulsions. Besides reading, I had nowhere else to go—that is, there was nothing to respect in my surroundings, nothing to attract me. In addition, I was overwhelmed by depression; I possessed a hysterical craving for contradictions and contrasts; and, as a result, I plunged into depravity. I haven't said all this to justify myself. . . . But, no, I'm lying. I did want to justify myself. It's for myself, gentlemen, that I include this little observation. I don't want to lie. I've given my word.

I indulged in depravity all alone, at night, furtively, timidly, sordidly, with a feeling of shame that never left me even in my most loathsome moments and drove me at such times to the point of profanity. Even then I was carrying around the underground in my soul. I was terribly afraid of being seen, met, recognized. I visited all sorts of dismal places.

Once, passing by some wretched little tavern late at night, I saw through a lighted window some gentlemen fighting with billiard cues; one of them was thrown out the window. At some other time I would have been disgusted; but just then I was overcome by such a mood that I envied the gentleman who'd been tossed out; I envied him so much that I even walked into the tavern and entered the billiard room. "Perhaps," I thought, "I'll get into a fight, and they'll throw me out the window, too."

I wasn't drunk, but what could I do—after all, depression can drive a man to this kind of hysteria. But nothing came of it. It turned out that I was incapable of being tossed out the window; I left without getting into a fight.

As soon as I set foot inside, some officer put me in my place.

I was standing next to the billiard table inadvertently blocking his way as he wanted to get by; he took hold of me by the shoulders and without a word of warning or explanation, moved me from where I was standing to another place, and he went past as if he hadn't even noticed me. I could have forgiven even a beating, but I could never forgive his moving me out of the way and entirely failing to notice me.

The devil knows what I would have given for a genuine, ordinary quarrel, a decent one, a more *literary* one, so to speak. But I'd been treated as if I were a fly. The officer was about six feet tall, while I'm small and scrawny. The quarrel, however, was in my hands; all I had to do was protest, and of course they would've thrown me out the window. But I reconsidered and preferred . . . to withdraw resentfully.

I left the tavern confused and upset and went straight home; the next night I continued my petty vice more timidly, more furtively, more gloomily than before, as if I had tears in my eyes—but I continued nonetheless. Don't conclude, however, that I retreated from that officer as a result of any cowardice; I've never been a coward at heart, although I've constantly acted like one in deed, but—wait before you laugh—I can explain this. I can explain anything, you may rest assured.

Oh, if only this officer had been the kind who'd have agreed to fight a duel! But no, he was precisely one of those types (alas, long gone) who preferred to act with their billiard cues or, like Gogol's Lieutenant Pirogov,[3] by appealing to the authorities. They didn't fight duels; in any case, they'd have considered fighting a duel with someone like me, a lowly civilian, to be indecent. In general, they considered duels to be somehow inconceivable, free-thinking, French, while they themselves, especially if they happened to be six feet tall, offended other people rather frequently.

In this case I retreated not out of any cowardice, but because of my unlimited vanity. I wasn't afraid of his height, nor did I think I'd receive a painful beating and get thrown out the window. In fact, I'd have had sufficient physical courage; it was moral fortitude I lacked. I was afraid that everyone present— from the insolent billiard marker to the foul-smelling, pimply little clerks with greasy collars who used to hang about—wouldn't understand and would laugh when I started to protest and speak to them in literary Russian. Because, to this very day, it's still impossible for us to speak about a point of honor, that is, not about honor itself, but a point of honor (*point d'honneur*), except in literary language. One can't even refer to a "point of honor" in everyday language. I was fully convinced (a sense of reality, in spite of all my romanticism!) that they would all simply split their sides laughing, and that the officer, instead of giving me a simple beating, that is, an inoffensive one, would certainly apply his knee to my back and drive me around the billiard table; only then perhaps would he have the mercy to throw me out the window. Naturally, this wretched story of mine couldn't possibly end with this alone. Afterward I used to meet this officer frequently on the street and I observed him very carefully. I don't know whether he ever recognized me. Probably not; I reached that conclusion

---

3. One of two main characters in Gogol's short story "Nevsky Prospect" (1835). A shallow and self-satisfied officer, he mistakes the wife of a German artisan for a woman of easy virtue and receives a sound thrashing. He decides to lodge an official complaint but, after consuming a cream-filled pastry, thinks better of it.

from various observations. As for me, I stared at him with malice and hatred, and continued to do so for several years! My malice increased and became stronger over time. At first I began to make discreet inquiries about him. This was difficult for me to do, since I had so few acquaintances. But once, as I was following him at a distance as though tied to him, someone called to him on the street: that's how I learned his name. Another time I followed him back to his own apartment and for a ten-kopeck piece learned from the doorman where and how he lived, on what floor, with whom, etc.—in a word, all that could be learned from a doorman. One morning, although I never engaged in literary activities, it suddenly occurred to me to draft a description of this officer as a kind of exposé, a caricature, in the form of a tale. I wrote it with great pleasure. I exposed him; I even slandered him. At first I altered his name only slightly, so that it could be easily recognized; but then, upon careful reflection, I changed it. Then I sent the tale off to *Notes of the Fatherland*.[4] But such exposés were no longer in fashion, and they didn't publish my tale. I was very annoyed by that. At times I simply choked on my spite. Finally, I resolved to challenge my opponent to a duel. I composed a beautiful, charming letter to him, imploring him to apologize to me; in case he refused, I hinted rather strongly at a duel. The letter was composed in such a way that if that officer had possessed even the smallest understanding of the "beautiful and sublime," he would have come running, thrown his arms around me, and offered his friendship. That would have been splendid! We would have led such a wonderful life! Such a life! He would have shielded me with his rank; I would have ennobled him with my culture, and, well, with my ideas. Who knows what might have come of it! Imagine it, two years had already passed since he'd insulted me; my challenge was the most ridiculous anachronism, in spite of all the cleverness of my letter in explaining and disguising that fact. But, thank God (to this day I thank the Almighty with tears in my eyes), I didn't send that letter. A shiver runs up and down my spine when I think what might have happened if I had. Then suddenly . . . suddenly, I got my revenge in the simplest manner, a stroke of genius! A brilliant idea suddenly occurred to me. Sometimes on holidays I used to stroll along Nevsky Prospect at about four o'clock in the afternoon, usually on the sunny side. That is, I didn't really stroll; rather, I experienced innumerable torments, humiliations, and bilious attacks. But that's undoubtedly just what I needed. I darted in and out like a fish among the strollers, constantly stepping aside before generals, cavalry officers, hussars, and young ladies. At those moments I used to experience painful spasms in my heart and a burning sensation in my back merely at the thought of my dismal apparel as well as the wretchedness and vulgarity of my darting little figure. This was sheer torture, uninterrupted and unbearable humiliation at the thought, which soon became an incessant and immediate sensation, that I was a fly in the eyes of society, a disgusting, obscene fly—smarter than the rest, more cultured, even nobler—all that goes without saying, but a fly, nonetheless, who incessantly steps aside, insulted and injured by everyone. For what reason did I inflict this torment on myself? Why did I stroll along Nevsky Prospect? I don't know. But something simply *drew* me there at every opportunity.

Then I began to experience surges of that pleasure about which I've already spoken in the first chapter. After the incident with the officer I was drawn

---

4. A radical literary and political journal published in St. Petersburg from 1839 to 1867.

there even more strongly; I used to encounter him along Nevsky most often, and it was there that I could admire him. He would also go there, mostly on holidays. He, too, would give way before generals and individuals of superior rank; he, too, would spin like a top among them. But he would simply trample people like me, or even those slightly superior; he would walk directly toward them, as if there were empty space ahead of him; and under no circumstance would he ever step aside. I revelled in my malice as I observed him, and . . . bitterly stepped aside before him every time. I was tortured by the fact that even on the street I found it impossible to stand on an equal footing with him. "Why is it you're always first to step aside?" I badgered myself in insane hysteria, at times waking up at three in the morning. "Why always you and not he? After all, there's no law about it; it isn't written down anywhere. Let it be equal, as it usually is when people of breeding meet: he steps aside halfway and you halfway, and you pass by showing each other mutual respect." But that was never the case, and I continued to step aside, while he didn't even notice that I was yielding to him. Then a most astounding idea suddenly dawned on me. "What if," I thought, "what if I were to meet him and . . . not step aside? Deliberately not step aside, even if it meant bumping into him: how would that be?" This bold idea gradually took such a hold that it afforded me no peace. I dreamt about it incessantly, horribly, and even went to Nevsky more frequently so that I could imagine more clearly how I would do it. I was in ecstasy. The scheme was becoming more and more possible and even probable to me. "Of course, I wouldn't really collide with him," I thought, already feeling more generous toward him in my joy, "but I simply won't turn aside. I'll bump into him, not very painfully, but just so, shoulder to shoulder, as much as decency allows. I'll bump into him the same amount as he bumps into me." At last I made up my mind completely. But the preparations took a very long time. First, in order to look as presentable as possible during the execution of my scheme, I had to worry about my clothes. "In any case, what if, for example, it should occasion a public scandal? (And the public there was *superflu*:[5] a countess, Princess D., and the entire literary world.) It was essential to be well-dressed; that inspires respect and in a certain sense will place us immediately on an equal footing in the eyes of high society." With that goal in mind I requested my salary in advance, and I purchased a pair of black gloves and a decent hat at Churkin's store. Black gloves seemed to me more dignified, more *bon ton*[6] than the lemon-colored ones I'd considered at first. "That would be too glaring, as if the person wanted to be noticed"; so I didn't buy the lemon-colored ones. I'd already procured a fine shirt with white bone cufflinks; but my overcoat constituted a major obstacle. In and of itself it was not too bad at all; it kept me warm; but it was quilted and had a raccoon collar, the epitome of bad taste. At all costs I had to replace the collar with a beaver one, just like on an officer's coat. For this purpose I began to frequent the Shopping Arcade; and, after several attempts, I turned up some cheap German beaver. Although these German beavers wear out very quickly and soon begin to look shabby, at first, when they're brand new, they look very fine indeed; after all, I only needed it for a single occasion. I asked the price: it was still expensive. After considerable reflection I resolved to sell my raccoon collar. I decided to request a loan for

---

5. "Excessively refined" (French).   6. "In good taste" (French).

the remaining amount—a rather significant sum for me—from Anton Antonych Setochkin, my office chief, a modest man, but a serious and solid one,
who never lent money to anyone, but to whom, upon entering the civil service,
I'd once been specially recommended by an important person who'd secured
the position for me. I suffered terribly. It seemed monstrous and shameful to
ask Anton Antonych for money. I didn't sleep for two or three nights in a row;
in general I wasn't getting much sleep those days, and I always had a fever. I
would have either a vague sinking feeling in my heart, or else my heart would
suddenly begin to thump, thump, thump! . . . At first Anton Antonych was surprised, then he frowned, thought it over, and finally gave me the loan, after
securing from me a note authorizing him to deduct the sum from my salary two
weeks later. In this way everything was finally ready; the splendid beaver
reigned in place of the mangy raccoon, and I gradually began to get down to
business. It was impossible to set about it all at once, in a foolhardy way; one
had to proceed in this matter very carefully, step by step. But I confess that
after many attempts I was ready to despair: we didn't bump into each other, no
matter what! No matter how I prepared, no matter how determined I was—it
seems that we're just about to bump, when I look up—and once again I've
stepped aside while he's gone by without even noticing me. I even used to pray
as I approached him that God would grant me determination. One time I'd
fully resolved to do it, but the result was that I merely stumbled and fell at his
feet because, at the very last moment, only a few inches away from him, I lost
my nerve. He stepped over me very calmly, and I bounced to one side like a
rubber ball. That night I lay ill with a fever once again and was delirious. Then,
everything suddenly ended in the best possible way. The night before I decided
once and for all not to go through with my pernicious scheme and to give it all
up without success; with that in mind I went to Nevsky Prospect for one last
time simply in order to see how I'd abandon the whole thing. Suddenly, three
paces away from my enemy, I made up my mind unexpectedly; I closed my eyes
and—we bumped into each other forcefully, shoulder to shoulder! I didn't
yield an inch and walked by him on a completely equal footing! He didn't even
turn around to look at me and pretended that he hadn't even noticed; but he
was merely pretending, I'm convinced of that. To this very day I'm convinced of
that! Naturally, I got the worst of it; he was stronger, but that wasn't the point.
The point was that I'd achieved my goal, I'd maintained my dignity, I hadn't
yielded one step, and I'd publicly placed myself on an equal social footing with
him. I returned home feeling completely avenged for everything. I was ecstatic.
I rejoiced and sang Italian arias. Of course, I won't describe what happened to
me three days later; if you've read the first part entitled "Underground," you
can guess for yourself. The officer was later transferred somewhere else; I
haven't seen him for some fourteen years. I wonder what he's doing nowadays,
that dear friend of mine! Whom is he trampling underfoot?

II

But when this phase of my nice, little dissipation ended I felt terribly nauseated. Remorse set in; I tried to drive it away because it was too disgusting.
Little by little, however, I got used to that, too. I got used to it all; that is, it
wasn't that I got used to it, rather, I somehow voluntarily consented to endure
it. But I had a way out that reconciled everything—to escape into "all that was

beautiful and sublime," in my dreams, of course. I was a terrible dreamer; I dreamt for three months in a row, tucked away in my little corner. And well you may believe that in those moments I was not at all like the gentleman who, in his faint-hearted anxiety, had sewn a German beaver onto the collar of his old overcoat. I suddenly became a hero. If my six-foot-tall lieutenant had come to see me then, I'd never have admitted him. I couldn't even conceive of him at that time. It's hard to describe now what my dreams consisted of then, and how I could've been so satisfied with them, but I was. Besides, even now I can take pride in them at certain times. My dreams were particularly sweet and vivid after my little debauchery; they were filled with remorse and tears, curses and ecstasy. There were moments of such positive intoxication, such happiness, that I felt not even the slightest trace of mockery within me, really and truly. It was all faith, hope and love. That's just it: at the time I believed blindly that by some kind of miracle, some external circumstance, everything would suddenly open up and expand; a vista of appropriate activity would suddenly appear—beneficent, beautiful, and most of all, *ready-made* (what precisely, I never knew, but, most of all, it had to be ready-made), and that I would suddenly step forth into God's world, almost riding on a white horse and wearing a laurel wreath. I couldn't conceive of a secondary role; and that's precisely why in reality I very quietly took on the lowest one. Either a hero or dirt—there was no middle ground. That was my ruin because in the dirt I consoled myself knowing that at other times I was a hero, and that the hero covered himself with dirt; that is to say, an ordinary man would be ashamed to wallow in filth, but a hero is too noble to become defiled; consequently, he can wallow. It's remarkable that these surges of everything "beautiful and sublime" occurred even during my petty depravity, and precisely when I'd sunk to the lowest depths. They occurred in separate spurts, as if to remind me of themselves; however, they failed to banish my depravity by their appearance. On the contrary, they seemed to add spice to it by means of contrast; they came in just the right amount to serve as a tasty sauce. This sauce consisted of contradictions, suffering, and agonizing internal analysis; all of these torments and trifles lent a certain piquancy, even some meaning to my depravity—in a word, they completely fulfilled the function of a tasty sauce. Nor was all this even lacking in a measure of profundity. Besides, I would never have consented to the simple, tasteless, spontaneous little debauchery of an ordinary clerk and have endured all that filth! How could it have attracted me then and lured me into the street late at night? No, sir, I had a noble loophole for everything. . . .

But how much love, oh Lord, how much love I experienced at times in those dreams of mine, in those "escapes into everything beautiful and sublime." Even though it was fantastic love, even though it was never directed at anything human, there was still so much love that afterward, in reality, I no longer felt any impulse to direct it: that would have been an unnecessary luxury. However, everything always ended in a most satisfactory way by a lazy and intoxicating transition into art, that is, into beautiful forms of being, ready-made, largely borrowed from poets and novelists, and adapted to serve every possible need. For instance, I would triumph over everyone; naturally, everyone else grovelled in the dust and was voluntarily impelled to acknowledge my superiority, while I would forgive them all for everything. Or else, being a famous poet and chamberlain, I would fall in love; I'd receive an enormous fortune and

would immediately sacrifice it all for the benefit of humanity, at the same time confessing before all peoples my own infamies, which, needless to say, were not simple infamies, but contained a great amount of "the beautiful and sublime," something in the style of Manfred.[7] Everyone would weep and kiss me (otherwise what idiots they would have been), while I went about barefoot and hungry preaching new ideas and defeating all the reactionaries of Austerlitz.[8] Then a march would be played, a general amnesty declared, and the Pope would agree to leave Rome and go to Brazil;[9] a ball would be hosted for all of Italy at the Villa Borghese on the shores of Lake Como,[1] since Lake Como would have been moved to Rome for this very occasion; then there would be a scene in the bushes, etc., etc.—as if you didn't know. You'll say that it's tasteless and repugnant to drag all this out into the open after all the raptures and tears to which I've confessed. But why is it so repugnant? Do you really think I'm ashamed of all this or that it's any more stupid than anything in your own lives, gentlemen? Besides, you can rest assured that some of it was not at all badly composed. . . . Not everything occurred on the shores of Lake Como. But you're right; in fact, it is tasteless and repugnant. And the most repugnant thing of all is that now I've begun to justify myself before you. And even more repugnant is that now I've made that observation. But enough, otherwise there'll be no end to it: each thing will be more repugnant than the last. . . .

I was never able to dream for more than three months in a row, and I began to feel an irresistible urge to plunge into society. To me plunging into society meant paying a visit to my office chief, Anton Antonych Setochkin. He's the only lasting acquaintance I've made during my lifetime; I too now marvel at this circumstance. But even then I would visit him only when my dreams had reached such a degree of happiness that it was absolutely essential for me to embrace people and all humanity at once; for that reason I needed to have at least one person on hand who actually existed. However, one could only call upon Anton Antonych on Tuesdays (his receiving day); consequently, I always had to adjust the urge to embrace all humanity so that it occurred on Tuesday. This Anton Antonych lived near Five Corners,[2] on the fourth floor, in four small, low-ceilinged rooms, each smaller than the last, all very frugal and yellowish in appearance. He lived with his two daughters and an aunt who used to serve tea. The daughters, one thirteen, the other fourteen, had little snub noses. I was very embarrassed by them because they used to whisper all the time and giggle to each other. The host usually sat in his study on a leather couch in front of a table together with some gray-haired guest, a civil servant either from our office or another one. I never saw more than two or three guests there, and they were always the same ones. They talked about excise

7. The romantic hero of Byron's poetic tragedy *Manfred* (1817), a lonely, defiant figure whose past conceals some mysterious crime.
8. The site of Napoleon's great victory in December 1805 over the combined armies of the Russian tsar Alexander I and the Austrian emperor Francis II.
9. Napoleon announced his annexation of the Papal States to France in 1809 and was promptly excommunicated by Pope Pius VII.

The pope was imprisoned and forced to sign a new concordat, but in 1814 he returned to Rome in triumph.
1. Located in the foothills of the Italian Alps in Lombardy. Villa Borghese was the elegant summer palace built by Scipione Cardinal Borghese outside the Porta del Popolo in Rome.
2. A well-known landmark in St. Petersburg.

taxes, debates in the Senate, salaries, promotions, His Excellency and how to please him, and so on and so forth. I had the patience to sit there like a fool next to these people for four hours or so; I listened without daring to say a word to them or even knowing what to talk about. I sat there in a stupor; several times I broke into a sweat; I felt numbed by paralysis; but it was good and useful. Upon returning home I would postpone for some time my desire to embrace all humanity.

I had one other sort of acquaintance, however, named Simonov, a former schoolmate of mine. In fact, I had a number of schoolmates in Petersburg, but I didn't associate with them, and I'd even stopped greeting them along the street. I might even have transferred into a different department at the office so as not to be with them and to cut myself off from my hated childhood once and for all. Curses on that school and those horrible years of penal servitude. In short, I broke with my schoolmates as soon as I was released. There remained only two or three people whom I would greet upon encountering them. One was Simonov, who hadn't distinguished himself in school in any way; he was even-tempered and quiet, but I detected in him a certain independence of character, even honesty. I don't even think that he was all that limited. At one time he and I experienced some rather bright moments, but they didn't last very long and somehow were suddenly clouded over. Evidently he was burdened by these recollections, and seemed in constant fear that I would lapse into that former mode. I suspect that he found me repulsive, but not being absolutely sure, I used to visit him nonetheless.

So once, on a Thursday, unable to endure my solitude, and knowing that on that day Anton Antonych's door was locked, I remembered Simonov. As I climbed the stairs to his apartment on the fourth floor, I was thinking how burdensome this man found my presence and that my going to see him was rather useless. But since it always turned out, as if on purpose, that such reflections would impel me to put myself even further into an ambiguous situation, I went right in. It had been almost a year since I'd last seen Simonov.

III

I found two more of my former schoolmates there with him. Apparently they were discussing some important matter. None of them paid any attention to me when I entered, which was strange since I hadn't seen them for several years. Evidently they considered me some sort of ordinary house fly. They hadn't even treated me like that when we were in school together, although they'd all hated me. Of course, I understood that they must despise me now for my failure in the service and for the fact that I'd sunk so low, was badly dressed, and so on, which, in their eyes, constituted proof of my ineptitude and insignificance. But I still hadn't expected such a degree of contempt. Simonov was even surprised by my visits. All this disconcerted me; I sat down in some distress and began to listen to what they were saying.

The discussion was serious, even heated, and concerned a farewell dinner which these gentlemen wanted to organize jointly as early as the following day for their friend Zverkov, an army officer who was heading for a distant province. Monsieur Zverkov had also been my schoolmate all along. I'd begun to hate him especially in the upper grades. In the lower grades he was merely an

attractive, lively lad whom everyone liked. However, I'd hated him in the lower grades, too, precisely because he was such an attractive, lively lad. He was perpetually a poor student and had gotten worse as time went on; he managed to graduate, however, because he had influential connections. During his last year at school he'd come into an inheritance of some two hundred serfs, and, since almost all the rest of us were poor, he'd even begun to brag. He was an extremely uncouth fellow, but a nice lad nonetheless, even when he was bragging. In spite of our superficial, fantastic, and high-flown notions of honor and pride, all of us, except for a very few, would fawn upon Zverkov, the more so the more he bragged. They didn't fawn for any advantage; they fawned simply because he was a man endowed by nature with gifts. Moreover, we'd somehow come to regard Zverkov as a cunning fellow and an expert on good manners. This latter point particularly infuriated me. I hated the shrill, self-confident tone of his voice, his adoration for his own witticisms, which were terribly stupid in spite of his bold tongue; I hated his handsome, stupid face (for which, however, I'd gladly have exchanged my own intelligent one), and the impudent bearing typical of officers during the 1840s. I hated the way he talked about his future successes with women. (He'd decided not to get involved with them yet, since he still hadn't received his officer's epaulettes; he awaited those epaulettes impatiently.) And he talked about all the duels he'd have to fight. I remember how once, although I was usually very taciturn, I suddenly clashed with Zverkov when, during our free time, he was discussing future exploits with his friends; getting a bit carried away with the game like a little puppy playing in the sun, he suddenly declared that not a single girl in his village would escape his attention—that it was his *droit de seigneur*,[3] and that if the peasants even dared protest, he'd have them all flogged, those bearded rascals; and he'd double their quit-rent.[4] Our louts applauded, but I attacked him—not out of any pity for the poor girls or their fathers, but simply because everyone else was applauding such a little insect. I got the better of him that time, but Zverkov, although stupid, was also cheerful and impudent. Therefore he laughed it off to such an extent that, in fact, I really didn't get the better of him. The laugh remained on his side. Later he got the better of me several times, but without malice, just so, in jest, in passing, in fun. I was filled with spite and hatred, but I didn't respond. After graduation he took a few steps toward me; I didn't object strongly because I found it flattering; but soon we came to a natural parting of the ways. Afterward I heard about his barrackroom successes as a lieutenant and about his *binges*. Then there were other rumors—about his *successes* in the service. He no longer bowed to me on the street; I suspected that he was afraid to compromise himself by acknowledging such an insignificant person as myself. I also saw him in the theater once, in the third tier, already sporting an officer's gold braids. He was fawning and grovelling before the daughters of some aged general. In those three years he'd let himself go, although he was still as handsome and agile as before; he sagged somehow and had begun to put on weight; it was clear that by the age of thirty

3. "Lord's privilege" (French); the feudal lord's right to spend the first night with the bride of a newly married serf.
4. The annual sum paid in cash or produce by serfs to landowners for the right to farm their land in feudal Russia, as opposed to the *corvée*, a certain amount of labor owed.

he'd be totally flabby. So it was for this Zverkov, who was finally ready to depart, that our schoolmates were organizing a farewell dinner. They'd kept up during these three years, although I'm sure that inwardly they didn't consider themselves on an equal footing with him.

One of Simonov's two guests was Ferfichkin, a Russified German, a short man with a face like a monkey, a fool who made fun of everybody, my bitterest enemy from the lower grades—a despicable, impudent show-off who affected the most ticklish sense of ambition, although, of course, he was a coward at heart. He was one of Zverkov's admirers and played up to him for his own reasons, frequently borrowing money from him. Simonov's other guest, Trudolyubov, was insignificant, a military man, tall, with a cold demeanor, rather honest, who worshipped success of any kind and was capable of talking only about promotions. He was a distant relative of Zverkov's, and that, silly to say, lent him some importance among us. He'd always regarded me as a nonentity; he treated me not altogether politely, but tolerably.

"Well, if each of us contributes seven rubles," said Trudolyubov, "with three of us that makes twenty-one altogether—we can have a good dinner. Of course, Zverkov won't have to pay."

"Naturally," Simonov agreed, "since we're inviting him."

"Do you really think," Ferfichkin broke in arrogantly and excitedly, just like an insolent lackey bragging about his master-the-general's medals, "do you really think Zverkov will let us pay for everything? He'll accept out of decency, but then he'll order *half a dozen bottles* on his own."

"What will the four of us do with half a dozen bottles?" asked Trudolyubov, only taking note of the number.

"So then, three of us plus Zverkov makes four, twenty-one rubles, in the Hôtel de Paris, tomorrow at five o'clock," concluded Simonov definitively, since he'd been chosen to make the arrangements.

"Why only twenty-one?" I asked in trepidation, even, apparently, somewhat offended. "If you count me in, you'll have twenty-eight rubles instead of twenty-one."

It seemed to me that to include myself so suddenly and unexpectedly would appear as quite a splendid gesture and that they'd all be smitten at once and regard me with respect.

"Do you really want to come, too?" Simonov inquired with displeasure, managing somehow to avoid looking at me. He knew me inside out.

It was infuriating that he knew me inside out.

"And why not? After all, I was his schoolmate, too, and I must admit that I even feel a bit offended that you've left me out," I continued, just about to boil over again.

"And how were we supposed to find you?" Ferfichkin interjected rudely.

"You never got along very well with Zverkov," added Trudolyubov frowning. But I'd already latched on and wouldn't let go.

"I think no one has a right to judge that," I objected in a trembling voice, as if God knows what had happened. "Perhaps that's precisely why I want to take part now, since we didn't get along so well before."

"Well, who can figure you out . . . such lofty sentiments . . . ," Trudolyubov said with an ironic smile.

"We'll put your name down," Simonov decided, turning to me. "Tomorrow at five o'clock at the Hôtel de Paris. Don't make any mistakes."

"What about the money?" Ferfichkin started to say in an undertone to Simonov while nodding at me, but he broke off because Simonov looked embarrassed.

"That'll do," Trudolyubov said getting up. "If he really wants to come so much, let him."

"But this is our own circle of friends," Ferfichkin grumbled, also picking up his hat. "It's not an official gathering. Perhaps we really don't want you at all. . . ."

They left. Ferfichkin didn't even say goodbye to me as he went out; Trudolyubov barely nodded without looking at me. Simonov, with whom I was left alone, was irritated and perplexed, and he regarded me in a strange way. He neither sat down nor invited me to.

"Hmmm . . . yes . . . , so, tomorrow. Will you contribute your share of the money now? I'm asking just to know for sure," he muttered in embarrassment.

I flared up; but in doing so, I remembered that I'd owed Simonov fifteen rubles for a very long time, which debt, moreover, I'd forgotten, but had also never repaid.

"You must agree, Simonov, that I couldn't have known when I came here . . . oh, what a nuisance, but I've forgotten. . . ."

He broke off and began to pace around the room in even greater irritation. As he paced, he began to walk on his heels and stomp more loudly.

"I'm not detaining you, am I?" I asked after a few moments of silence.

"Oh, no!" he replied with a start. "That is, in fact, yes. You see, I still have to stop by at . . . It's not very far from here . . . ," he added in an apologetic way with some embarrassment.

"Oh, good heavens! Why didn't you say so?" I exclaimed, seizing my cap; moreover I did so with a surprisingly familiar air, coming from God knows where.

"But it's really not far . . . only a few steps away . . . ," Simonov repeated, accompanying me into the hallway with a bustling air which didn't suit him well at all. "So, then, tomorrow at five o'clock sharp!" he shouted to me on the stairs. He was very pleased that I was leaving. However, I was furious.

"What possessed me, what on earth possessed me to interfere?" I gnashed my teeth as I walked along the street. "And for such a scoundrel, a pig like Zverkov! Naturally, I shouldn't go. Of course, to hell with them. Am I bound to go, or what? Tomorrow I'll inform Simonov by post. . . ."

But the real reason I was so furious was that I was sure I'd go. I'd go on purpose. The more tactless, the more indecent it was for me to go, the more certain I'd be to do it.

There was even a definite impediment to my going: I didn't have any money. All I had was nine rubles. But of those, I had to hand over seven the next day to my servant Apollon for his monthly wages; he lived in and received seven rubles for his meals.

Considering Apollon's character it was impossible not to pay him. But more about that rascal, that plague of mine, later.

In any case, I knew that I wouldn't pay him his wages and that I'd definitely go.

That night I had the most hideous dreams. No wonder: all evening I was burdened with recollections of my years of penal servitude at school and I

couldn't get rid of them. I'd been sent off to that school by distant relatives on whom I was dependent and about whom I've heard nothing since. They dispatched me, a lonely boy, crushed by their reproaches, already introspective, taciturn, and regarding everything around him savagely. My schoolmates received me with spiteful and pitiless jibes because I wasn't like any of them. But I couldn't tolerate their jibes; I couldn't possibly get along with them as easily as they got along with each other. I hated them all at once and took refuge from everyone in fearful, wounded and excessive pride. Their crudeness irritated me. Cynically they mocked my face and my awkward build; yet, what stupid faces they all had! Facial expressions at our school somehow degenerated and became particularly stupid. Many attractive lads had come to us, but in a few years they too were repulsive to look at. When I was only sixteen I wondered about them gloomily; even then I was astounded by the pettiness of their thoughts and the stupidity of their studies, games and conversations. They failed to understand essential things and took no interest in important, weighty subjects, so that I couldn't help considering them beneath me. It wasn't my wounded vanity that drove me to it; and, for God's sake, don't repeat any of those nauseating and hackneyed clichés, such as, "I was merely a dreamer, whereas they already understood life." They didn't understand a thing, not one thing about life, and I swear, that's what annoyed me most about them. On the contrary, they accepted the most obvious, glaring reality in a fantastically stupid way, and even then they'd begun to worship nothing but success. Everything that was just, but oppressed and humiliated, they ridiculed hard-heartedly and shamelessly. They mistook rank for intelligence; at the age of sixteen they were already talking about occupying comfortable little niches. Of course, much of this was due to their stupidity and the poor examples that had constantly surrounded them in their childhood and youth. They were monstrously depraved. Naturally, even this was more superficial, more affected cynicism; of course, their youth and a certain freshness shone through their depravity; but even this freshness was unattractive and manifested itself in a kind of rakishness. I hated them terribly, although, perhaps, I was even worse than they were. They returned the feeling and didn't conceal their loathing for me. But I no longer wanted their affection; on the contrary, I constantly longed for their humiliation. In order to avoid their jibes, I began to study as hard as I could on purpose and made my way to the top of the class. That impressed them. In addition, they all began to realize that I'd read certain books which they could never read and that I understood certain things (not included in our special course) about which they'd never even heard. They regarded this with savagery and sarcasm, but they submitted morally, all the more since even the teachers paid me some attention on this account. Their jibes ceased, but their hostility remained, and relations between us became cold and strained. In the end I myself couldn't stand it: as the years went by, my need for people, for friends, increased. I made several attempts to get closer to some of them; but these attempts always turned out to be unnatural and ended of their own accord. Once I even had a friend of sorts. But I was already a despot at heart; I wanted to exercise unlimited power over his soul; I wanted to instill in him contempt for his surroundings; and I demanded from him a disdainful and definitive break with those surroundings. I frightened him with my passionate friendship, and I reduced him to tears and convulsions. He was a naive and

giving soul, but as soon as he'd surrendered himself to me totally, I began to despise him and reject him immediately—as if I only needed to achieve a victory over him, merely to subjugate him. But I was unable to conquer them all; my one friend was not at all like them, but rather a rare exception. The first thing I did upon leaving school was abandon the special job in the civil service for which I'd been trained, in order to sever all ties, break with my past, cover it over with dust. . . . The devil only knows why, after all that, I'd dragged myself over to see this Simonov! . . .

Early the next morning I roused myself from bed, jumped up in anxiety, just as if everything was about to start happening all at once. But I believed that some radical change in my life was imminent and was sure to occur that very day. Perhaps because I wasn't used to it, but all my life, at any external event, albeit a trivial one, it always seemed that some sort of radical change would occur. I went off to work as usual, but returned home two hours earlier in order to prepare. The most important thing, I thought, was not to arrive there first, or else they'd all think I was too eager. But there were thousands of most important things, and they all reduced me to the point of impotence. I polished my boots once again with my own hands. Apollon wouldn't polish them twice in one day for anything in the world; he considered it indecent. So I polished them myself, after stealing the brushes from the hallway so that he wouldn't notice and then despise me for it afterward. Next I carefully examined my clothes and found that everything was old, shabby, and worn out. I'd become too slovenly. My uniform was in better shape, but I couldn't go to dinner in a uniform. Worst of all, there was an enormous yellow stain on the knee of my trousers. I had an inkling that the spot alone would rob me of nine-tenths of my dignity. I also knew that it was unseemly for me to think that. "But this isn't the time for thinking. Reality is now looming," I thought, and my heart sank. I also knew perfectly well at that time, that I was monstrously exaggerating all these facts. But what could be done? I was no longer able to control myself, and was shaking with fever. In despair I imagined how haughtily and coldly that "scoundrel" Zverkov would greet me; with what dull and totally relentless contempt that dullard Trudolyubov would regard me; how nastily and impudently that insect Ferfichkin would giggle at me in order to win Zverkov's approval; how well Simonov would understand all this and how he'd despise me for my wretched vanity and cowardice; and worst of all, how petty all this would be, not *literary*, but commonplace. Of course, it would have been better not to go at all. But that was no longer possible; once I began to feel drawn to something, I plunged right in, head first. I'd have reproached myself for the rest of my life: "So, you retreated, you retreated before reality, you retreated!" On the contrary, I desperately wanted to prove to all this "rabble" that I really wasn't the coward I imagined myself to be. But that's not all: in the strongest paroxysm of cowardly fever I dreamt of gaining the upper hand, of conquering them, of carrying them away, compelling them to love me—if only "for the nobility of my thought and my indisputable wit." They would abandon Zverkov; he'd sit by in silence and embarassment, and I'd crush him. Afterward, perhaps, I'd be reconciled with Zverkov and drink to our *friendship*, but what was most spiteful and insulting for me was that I knew even then, I knew completely and for sure, that I didn't need any of this at all; that in fact I really didn't want to crush them, conquer them, or attract them, and that if I could

have ever achieved all that, I'd be the first to say that it wasn't worth a damn. Oh, how I prayed to God that this day would pass quickly! With inexpressible anxiety I approached the window, opened the transom,[5] and peered out into the murky mist of the thickly falling wet snow. . . .

At last my worthless old wall clock sputtered out five o'clock. I grabbed my hat, and, trying not to look at Apollon—who'd been waiting since early morning to receive his wages, but didn't want to be the first one to mention it out of pride—I slipped out the door past him and intentionally hired a smart cab with my last half-ruble in order to arrive at the Hôtel de Paris in style.

IV

I knew since the day before that I'd be the first one to arrive. But it was no longer a question of who was first.

Not only was no one else there, but I even had difficulty finding our room. The table hadn't even been set. What did it all mean? After many inquiries I finally learned from the waiters that dinner had been ordered for closer to six o'clock, instead of five. This was also confirmed in the buffet. It was too embarrassing to ask any more questions. It was still only twenty-five minutes past five. If they'd changed the time, they should have let me know; that's what the city mail was for. They shouldn't have subjected me to such "shame" in my own eyes and . . . and, at least not in front of the waiters. I sat down. A waiter began to set the table. I felt even more ashamed in his presence. Toward six o'clock candles were brought into the room in addition to the lighted lamps already there, yet it hadn't occurred to the waiters to bring them in as soon as I'd arrived. In the next room two gloomy customers, angry-looking and silent, were dining at separate tables. In one of the distant rooms there was a great deal of noise, even shouting. One could hear the laughter of a whole crowd of people, including nasty little squeals in French—there were ladies present at that dinner. In short, it was disgusting. Rarely had I passed a more unpleasant hour, so that when they all arrived together precisely at six o'clock, I was initially overjoyed to see them, as if they were my liberators, and I almost forgot that I was supposed to appear offended.

Zverkov, obviously the leader, entered ahead of the rest. Both he and they were laughing; but, upon seeing me, Zverkov drew himself up, approached me unhurriedly, bowed slightly from the waist almost coquettishly, and extended his hand politely, but not too, with a kind of careful civility, almost as if he were a general both offering his hand, but also guarding against something. I'd imagined, on the contrary, that as soon as he entered he'd burst into his former, shrill laughter with occasional squeals, and that he'd immediately launch into his stale jokes and witticisms. I'd been preparing for them since the previous evening; but in no way did I expect such condescension, such courtesy characteristic of a general. Could it be that he now considered himself so immeasurably superior to me in all respects? If he'd merely wanted to offend me by this superior attitude, it wouldn't have been so bad, I thought; I'd manage to pay him back somehow. But what if, without any desire to offend, the notion had crept into his dumb sheep's brain that he really was immeasurably

---

5. A small hinged pane in the window of a Russian house, used for ventilation especially during the winter when the main part of the window is sealed.

superior to me and that he could only treat me in a patronizing way? From this possibility alone I began to gasp for air.

"Have you been waiting long?" Trudolyubov asked.

"I arrived at five o'clock sharp, just as I was told yesterday," I answered loudly and with irritation presaging an imminent explosion.

"Didn't you let him know that we changed the time?" Trudolyubov asked, turning to Simonov.

"No, I didn't. I forgot," he replied, but without any regret; then, not even apologizing to me, he went off to order the hors d'oeuvres.

"So you've been here for a whole hour, you poor fellow!" Zverkov cried sarcastically, because according to his notions, this must really have been terribly amusing. That scoundrel Ferfichkin chimed in after him with nasty, ringing laughter that sounded like a dog's yapping. My situation seemed very amusing and awkward to him, too.

"It's not the least bit funny!" I shouted at Ferfichkin, getting more and more irritated. "The others are to blame, not me. They neglected to inform me. It's, it's, it's . . . simply preposterous."

"It's not only preposterous, it's more than that," muttered Trudolyubov, naively interceding on my behalf. "You're being too kind. It's pure rudeness. Of course, it wasn't intentional. And how could Simonov have . . . hmm!"

"If a trick like that had been played on me," said Ferfichkin, "I'd . . ."

"Oh, you'd have ordered yourself something to eat," interrupted Zverkov, "or simply asked to have dinner served without waiting for the rest of us."

"You'll agree that I could've done that without asking anyone's permission," I snapped. "If I did wait, it was only because . . ."

"Let's be seated, gentlemen," cried Simonov upon entering. "Everything's ready. I can vouch for the champagne; it's excellently chilled. . . . Moreover, I didn't know where your apartment was, so how could I find you?" he said turning to me suddenly, but once again not looking directly at me. Obviously he was holding something against me. I suspect he got to thinking after what had happened yesterday.

Everyone sat down; I did, too. The table was round. Trudolyubov sat on my left, Simonov, on my right. Zverkov sat across; Ferfichkin, next to him, between Trudolyubov and him.

"Tell-l-l me now, are you . . . in a government department?" Zverkov continued to attend to me. Seeing that I was embarrassed, he imagined in earnest that he had to be nice to me, encouraging me to speak. "Does he want me to throw a bottle at his head, or what?" I thought in a rage. Unaccustomed as I was to all this, I was unnaturally quick to take offense.

"In such and such an office," I replied abruptly, looking at my plate.

"And . . . is it p-p-profitable? Tell-l-l me, what ma-a-de you decide to leave your previous position?"

"What ma-a-a-de me leave my previous position was simply that I wanted to," I dragged my words out three times longer than he did, hardly able to control myself. Ferfichkin snorted. Simonov looked at me ironically; Trudolyubov stopped eating and began to stare at me with curiosity.

Zverkov was jarred, but didn't want to show it.

"Well-l, and how is the support?"

"What support?"

"I mean, the s-salary?"

"Why are you cross-examining me?"

However, I told him right away what my salary was. I blushed terribly.

"That's not very much," Zverkov observed pompously.

"No, sir, it's not enough to dine in café-restaurants!" added Ferfichkin insolently.

"In my opinion, it's really very little," Trudolyubov observed in earnest.

"And how thin you've grown, how you've changed . . . since . . . ," Zverkov added, with a touch of venom now, and with a kind of impudent sympathy, examining me and my apparel.

"Stop embarrassing him," Ferfichkin cried with a giggle.

"My dear sir, I'll have you know that I'm not embarrassed," I broke in at last. "Listen! I'm dining in this 'café-restaurant' at my own expense, my own, not anyone else's; note that, Monsieur Ferfichkin."

"Wha-at? And who isn't dining at his own expense? You seem to be . . ." Ferfichkin seized hold of my words, turned as red as a lobster, and looked me straight in the eye with fury.

"Just so-o," I replied, feeling that I'd gone a bit too far, "and I suggest that it would be much better if we engaged in more intelligent conversation."

"It seems that you're determined to display your intelligence."

"Don't worry, that would be quite unnecessary here."

"What's all this cackling, my dear sir? Huh? Have you taken leave of your senses in that *duh*-partment of yours?"

"Enough, gentlemen, enough," cried Zverkov authoritatively.

"How stupid this is!" muttered Simonov.

"Really, it is stupid. We're gathered here in a congenial group to have a farewell dinner for our good friend, while you're still settling old scores," Trudolyubov said, rudely addressing only me. "You forced yourself upon us yesterday; don't disturb the general harmony now. . . ."

"Enough, enough," cried Zverkov. "Stop it, gentlemen, this'll never do. Let me tell you instead how I very nearly got married a few days ago . . ."

There followed some scandalous, libelous anecdote about how this gentleman very nearly got married a few days ago. There wasn't one word about marriage, however; instead, generals, colonels, and even gentlemen of the bed chamber figured prominently in the story, while Zverkov played the leading role among them all. Approving laughter followed; Ferfichkin even squealed.

Everyone had abandoned me by now, and I sat there completely crushed and humiliated.

"Good Lord, what kind of company is this for me?" I wondered. "And what a fool I've made of myself in front of them all! But I let Ferfichkin go too far. These numbskulls think they're doing me an honor by allowing me to sit with them at their table, when they don't understand that it's I who's done them the honor, and not the reverse. 'How thin I've grown! What clothes!' Oh, these damned trousers! Zverkov's already noticed the yellow spot on my knee. . . . What's the use? Right now, this very moment, I should stand up, take my hat, and simply leave without saying a single word. . . . Out of contempt! And tomorrow—I'll even be ready for a duel. Scoundrels! It's not the seven rubles I care about. But they may think that . . . To hell with it! I don't care about the seven rubles. I'm leaving at once! . . ."

Of course, I stayed.

In my misery I drank Lafite and sherry by the glassful. Being unaccustomed to it, I got drunk very quickly; the more intoxicated I became, the greater my annoyance. Suddenly I felt like offending them all in the most impudent manner—and then I'd leave. To seize the moment and show them all who I really was—let them say: even though he's ridiculous, he's clever . . . and . . . and . . . in short, to hell with them!

I surveyed them all arrogantly with my dazed eyes. But they seemed to have forgotten all about me. *They* were noisy, boisterous and merry. Zverkov kept on talking. I began to listen. He was talking about some magnificent lady whom he'd finally driven to make a declaration of love. (Of course, he was lying like a trooper.) He said that he'd been assisted in this matter particularly by a certain princeling, the hussar Kolya, who possessed some three thousand serfs.

"And yet, this same Kolya who has three thousand serfs hasn't even come to see you off," I said, breaking into the conversation suddenly. For a moment silence fell.

"You're drunk already," Trudolyubov said, finally deigning to notice me, and glancing contemptuously in my direction. Zverkov examined me in silence as if I were an insect. I lowered my eyes. Simonov quickly began to pour champagne.

Trudolyubov raised his glass, followed by everyone but me.

"To your health and to a good journey!" he cried to Zverkov. "To old times, gentlemen, and to our future, hurrah!"

Everyone drank up and pressed around to exchange kisses with Zverkov. I didn't budge; my full glass stood before me untouched.

"Aren't you going to drink?" Trudolyubov roared at me, having lost his patience and turning to me menacingly.

"I wish to make my own speech, all by myself . . . and then I'll drink, Mr. Trudolyubov."

"Nasty shrew!" Simonov muttered.

I sat up in my chair, feverishly seized hold of my glass, and prepared for something extraordinary, although I didn't know quite what I'd say.

"*Silence!*" cried Ferfichkin. "And now for some real intelligence!" Zverkov waited very gravely, aware of what was coming.

"Mr. Lieutenant Zverkov," I began, "you must know that I detest phrases, phrasemongers, and corsetted waists. . . . That's the first point; the second will follow."

Everyone stirred uncomfortably.

"The second point: I hate obscene stories and the men who tell them.[6] I especially hate the men who tell them!"

"The third point: I love truth, sincerity and honesty," I continued almost automatically, because I was beginning to become numb with horror, not knowing how I could be speaking this way. . . . "I love thought, Monsieur Zverkov. I love genuine comradery, on an equal footing, but not . . . hmmm . . . I

---

6. A phrase borrowed from the inveterate liar Nozdryov, one of the provincial landowners in the first volume of Gogol's *Dead Souls* (1842).

love . . . But, after all, why not? I too will drink to your health, Monsieur Zverkov. Seduce those Circassian[7] maidens, shoot the enemies of the fatherland, and . . . and . . . To your health, Monsieur Zverkov!"

Zverkov rose from his chair, bowed, and said: "I'm most grateful."

He was terribly offended and had even turned pale.

"To hell with him," Trudolyubov roared, banging his fist down on the table.

"No, sir, people should be whacked in the face for saying such things!" squealed Ferfichkin.

"We ought to throw him out!" muttered Simonov.

"Not a word, gentlemen, not a move!" Zverkov cried triumphantly, putting a stop to this universal indignation. "I'm grateful to you all, but I can show him myself how much I value his words."

"Mr. Ferfichkin, tomorrow you'll give me satisfaction for the words you've just uttered!" I said loudly, turning to Ferfichkin with dignity.

"Do you mean a duel? Very well," he replied, but I must have looked so ridiculous as I issued my challenge, it must have seemed so out of keeping with my entire appearance, that everyone, including Ferfichkin, collapsed into laughter.

"Yes, of course, throw him out! Why, he's quite drunk already," Trudolyubov declared in disgust.

"I shall never forgive myself for letting him join us," Simonov muttered again.

"Now's the time to throw a bottle at the lot of them," I thought. So I grabbed a bottle and . . . poured myself another full glass.

". . . No, it's better to sit it out to the very end!" I went on thinking. "You'd be glad, gentlemen, if I left. But nothing doing! I'll stay here deliberately and keep on drinking to the very end, as a sign that I accord you no importance whatsoever. I'll sit here and drink because this is a tavern, and I've paid good money to get in. I'll sit here and drink because I consider you to be so many pawns, nonexistent pawns. I'll sit here and drink . . . and sing too, if I want to, yes, sir, I'll sing because I have the right to . . . sing . . . hmm."

But I didn't sing. I just tried not to look at any of them; I assumed the most carefree poses and waited impatiently until they would be the first to speak to me. But, alas, they did not. How much, how very much I longed to be reconciled with them at that moment! The clock struck eight, then nine. They moved from the table to the sofa. Zverkov sprawled on the couch, placing one foot on the round table. They brought the wine over, too. He really had ordered three bottles at his own expense. Naturally, he didn't invite me to join them. Everyone surrounded him on the sofa. They listened to him almost with reverence. It was obvious they liked him. "What for? What for?" I wondered to myself. From time to time they were moved to drunken ecstasy and exchanged kisses. They talked about the Caucasus,[8] the nature of true passion, card games, profitable positions in the service; they talked about the income of a certain hussar Podkharzhevsky, whom none of them knew personally, and they

---

7. Women from the region between the Black Sea and the Caspian Sea, famous for their beauty and much in demand as concubines in the Ottoman Empire.

8. Region in which various peoples opposed Russian rule, and thus a constant source of trouble for the Russian Empire.

rejoiced that his income was so large; they talked about the unusual beauty and charm of Princess D., whom none of them had ever seen; finally, they arrived at the question of Shakespeare's immortality.

I smiled contemptuously and paced up and down the other side of the room, directly behind the sofa, along the wall from the table to the stove and back again. I wanted to show them with all my might that I could get along without them; meanwhile, I deliberately stomped my boots, thumping my heels. But all this was in vain. *They* paid me no attention. I had the forbearance to pace like that, right in front of them, from eight o'clock until eleven, in the very same place, from the table to the stove and from the stove back to the table. "I'm pacing just as I please, and no one can stop me." A waiter who came into the room paused several times to look at me; my head was spinning from all those turns; there were moments when it seemed that I was delirious. During those three hours I broke out in a sweat three times and then dried out. At times I was pierced to the heart with a most profound, venomous thought: ten years would pass, twenty, forty; and still, even after forty years, I'd remember with loathing and humiliation these filthiest, most absurd, and horrendous moments of my entire life. It was impossible to humiliate myself more shamelessly or more willingly, and I fully understood that, fully; nevertheless, I continued to pace from the table to the stove and back again. "Oh, if you only knew what thoughts and feelings I'm capable of, and how cultured I really am!" I thought at moments, mentally addressing the sofa where my enemies were seated. But my enemies behaved as if I weren't even in the room. Once, and only once, they turned to me, precisely when Zverkov started in about Shakespeare, and I suddenly burst into contemptuous laughter. I snorted so affectedly and repulsively that they broke off their conversation immediately and stared at me in silence for about two minutes, in earnest, without laughing, as I paced up and down, from the table to the stove, while *I paid not the slightest bit of attention to them*. But nothing came of it; they didn't speak to me. A few moments later they abandoned me again. The clock struck eleven.

"Gentlemen," exclaimed Zverkov, getting up from the sofa, "Now let's all go *to that place*."[9]

"Of course, of course!" the others replied.

I turned abruptly to Zverkov. I was so exhausted, so broken, that I'd have slit my own throat to be done with all this! I was feverish; my hair, which had been soaked through with sweat, had dried and now stuck to my forehead and temples.

"Zverkov, I ask your forgiveness," I said harshly and decisively. "Ferfichkin, yours too, and everyone's, everyone's. I've insulted you all!"

"Aha! So a duel isn't really your sort of thing!" hissed Ferfichkin venomously.

His remark was like a painful stab to my heart.

"No, I'm not afraid of a duel, Ferfichkin! I'm ready to fight with you tomorrow, even after we're reconciled. I even insist upon it, and you can't refuse me. I want to prove that I'm not afraid of a duel. You'll shoot first, and I'll fire into the air."

"He's amusing himself," Simonov observed.

"He's simply taken leave of his senses!" Trudolyubov added.

9. I.e., a brothel.

"Allow us to pass; why are you blocking our way? . . . Well, what is it you want?" Zverkov asked contemptuously. They were all flushed, their eyes glazed. They'd drunk a great deal.

"I ask for your friendship, Zverkov, I've insulted you, but . . ."

"Insulted me? You? In-sul-ted me? My dear sir, I want you to know that never, under any circumstances, could you possibly insult *me!*"

"And that's enough from you. Out of the way!" Trudolyubov added. "Let's go."

"Olympia is mine, gentlemen, that's agreed!" cried Zverkov.

"We won't argue, we won't," they replied, laughing.

I stood there as if spat on. The party left the room noisily, and Trudolyubov struck up a stupid song. Simonov remained behind for a brief moment to tip the waiters. All of a sudden I went up to him.

"Simonov! Give me six rubles," I said decisively and desperately.

He looked at me in extreme amazement with his dulled eyes. He was drunk, too.

"Are you really going *to that place* with us?"

"Yes!"

"I have no money!" he snapped; then he laughed contemptuously and headed out of the room.

I grabbed hold of his overcoat. It was a nightmare.

"Simonov! I know that you have some money. Why do you refuse me? Am I really such a scoundrel? Beware of refusing me: if you only knew, if you only knew why I'm asking. Everything depends on it, my entire future, all my plans. . . ."

Simonov took out the money and almost threw it at me.

"Take it, if you have no shame!" he said mercilessly, then ran out to catch up with the others.

I remained behind for a minute. The disorder, the leftovers, a broken glass on the floor, spilled wine, cigarette butts, drunkenness and delirium in my head, agonizing torment in my heart; and finally, a waiter who'd seen and heard everything and who was now looking at me with curiosity.

"*To that place!*" I cried. "Either they'll all fall on their knees, embracing me, begging for my friendship, or . . . or else, I'll give Zverkov a slap in the face."

V

"So here it is, here it is at last, a confrontation with reality," I muttered, rushing headlong down the stairs. "This is no longer the Pope leaving Rome and going to Brazil; this is no ball on the shores of Lake Como!"

"You're a scoundrel," the thought flashed through my mind, "if you laugh at that now."

"So what!" I cried in reply. "Everything is lost now, anyway!"

There was no sign of them, but it didn't matter. I knew where they were going.

At the entrance stood a solitary, late-night cabby in a coarse peasant coat powdered with wet, seemingly warm snow that was still falling. It was steamy and stuffy outside. The little shaggy piebald nag was also dusted with snow and was coughing; I remember that very well. I headed for the rough-hewn sledge; but as soon as I raised one foot to get in, the recollection of how Simonov had just given me six rubles hit me with such force that I tumbled into the sledge like a sack.

"No! There's a lot I have to do to make up for that!" I cried. "But make up for it I will or else I'll perish on the spot this very night. Let's go!" We set off. There was an entire whirlwind spinning around inside my head.

"They won't fall on their knees to beg for my friendship. That's a mirage, an indecent mirage, disgusting, romantic, and fantastic; it's just like the ball on the shores of Lake Como. Consequently, I *must* give Zverkov a slap in the face! I am obligated to do it. And so, it's all decided; I'm rushing there to give him a slap in the face."

"Hurry up!"

The cabby tugged at the reins.

"As soon as I go in, I'll slap him. Should I say a few words first before I slap him in the face? No! I'll simply go in and slap him. They'll all be sitting there in the drawing room; he'll be on the sofa with Olympia. That damned Olympia! She once ridiculed my face and refused me. I'll drag Olympia around by the hair and Zverkov by the ears. No, better grab one ear and lead him around the room like that. Perhaps they'll begin to beat me, and then they'll throw me out. That's even likely. So what? I'll still have slapped him first; the initiative will be mine. According to the laws of honor, that's all that matters. He'll be branded, and nothing can wipe away that slap except a duel.[1] He'll have to fight. So just let them beat me now! Let them, the ingrates! Trudolyubov will hit me hardest, he's so strong. Ferfichkin will sneak up alongside and will undoubtedly grab my hair, I'm sure he will. But let them, let them. That's why I've come. At last these blockheads will be forced to grasp the tragedy in all this! As they drag me to the door, I'll tell them that they really aren't even worth the tip of my little finger!"

"Hurry up, driver, hurry up!" I shouted to the cabby.

He was rather startled and cracked his whip. I'd shouted very savagely.

"We'll fight at daybreak, and that's settled. I'm through with the department. Ferfichkin recently said duh-partment, instead of department. But where will I get pistols? What nonsense! I'll take my salary in advance and buy them. And powder? Bullets? That's what the second will attend to. And how will I manage to do all this by daybreak? And where will I find a second? I have no acquaintances. . . ."

"Nonsense!" I shouted, whipping myself up into even more of a frenzy, "Nonsense!"

"The first person I meet on the street will have to act as my second, just as he would pull a drowning man from the water. The most extraordinary possibilities have to be allowed for. Even if tomorrow I were to ask the director himself to act as my second, he too would have to agree merely out of a sense of chivalry, and he would keep it a secret! Anton Antonych . . ."

The fact of the matter was that at that very moment I was more clearly and vividly aware than anyone else on earth of the disgusting absurdity of my intentions and the whole opposite side of the coin, but . . .

"Hurry up, driver, hurry, you rascal, hurry up!"

---

1. Duels as a means of resolving points of honor were officially discouraged but still fairly common.

"Hey, sir!" that son of the earth replied.

A sudden chill came over me.

"Wouldn't it be better . . . wouldn't it be better . . . to go straight home right now? Oh, my God! Why, why did I invite myself to that dinner yesterday? But no, it's impossible. And my pacing for three hours from the table to the stove? No, they, and no one else will have to pay me back for that pacing! They must wipe out that disgrace!"

"Hurry up!"

"What if they turn me over to the police? They wouldn't dare! They'd be afraid of a scandal. And what if Zverkov refuses the duel out of contempt? That's even likely; but I'll show them. . . . I'll rush to the posting station when he's supposed to leave tomorrow; I'll grab hold of his leg, tear off his overcoat just as he's about to climb into the carriage. I'll fasten my teeth on his arm and bite him. 'Look, everyone, see what a desperate man can be driven to!' Let him hit me on the head while others hit me from behind. I'll shout to the whole crowd, 'Behold, here's a young puppy who's going off to charm Circassian maidens with my spit on his face!'"

"Naturally, it'll all be over after that. The department will banish me from the face of the earth. They'll arrest me, try me, drive me out of the service, send me to prison; ship me off to Siberia for resettlement. Never mind! Fifteen years later when they let me out of jail, a beggar in rags, I'll drag myself off to see him. I'll find him in some provincial town. He'll be married and happy. He'll have a grown daughter. . . . I'll say, 'Look, you monster, look at my sunken cheeks and my rags. I've lost everything—career, happiness, art, science, a *beloved woman*—all because of you. Here are the pistols. I came here to load my pistol, and . . . and I forgive you.' Then I'll fire into the air, and he'll never hear another word from me again. . . ."

I was actually about to cry, even though I knew for a fact at that very moment that all this was straight out of Silvio and Lermontov's *Masquerade*.[2] Suddenly I felt terribly ashamed, so ashamed that I stopped the horse, climbed out of the sledge, and stood there amidst the snow in the middle of the street. The driver looked at me in amazement and sighed.

What was I to do? I couldn't go there—that was absurd; and I couldn't drop the whole thing, because then it would seem like . . . Oh, Lord! How could I drop it? After such insults!

"No!" I cried, throwing myself back into the sledge. "It's predestined; it's fate! Drive on, hurry up, *to that place!*"

In my impatience, I struck the driver on the neck with my fist.

"What's the matter with you? Why are you hitting me?" cried the poor little peasant, whipping his nag so that she began to kick up her hind legs.

Wet snow was falling in big flakes; I unbuttoned my coat, not caring about the snow. I forgot about everything else because now, having finally resolved on the slap, *I felt with horror that it was imminent* and that *nothing on earth could possibly stop it*. Lonely street lamps shone gloomily in the snowy mist like torches at a funeral. Snow got in under my overcoat, my jacket, and my necktie, and melted there. I didn't button up; after all, everything was lost, anyway.

2. A drama by Mikhail Lermontov (1835) about romantic conventions of love and honor. Silvio is the protagonist of Alexander Push- kin's short story "The Shot" (1830), about a man dedicated to revenge. Both works conclude with bizarre twists.

At last we arrived. I jumped out, almost beside myself, ran up the stairs, and began to pound at the door with my hands and feet. My legs, especially my knees, felt terribly weak. The door opened rather quickly; it was as if they knew I was coming. (In fact, Simonov had warned them that there might be someone else, since at this place one had to give notice and in general take precautions. It was one of those "fashionable shops" of the period that have now been eliminated by the police. During the day it really was a shop; but in the evening men with recommendations were able to visit as guests.) I walked rapidly through the darkened shop into a familiar drawing-room where there was only one small lit candle, and I stopped in dismay: there was no one there.

"Where are they?" I asked.

Naturally, by now they'd all dispersed. . . .

Before me stood a person with a stupid smile, the madam herself, who knew me slightly. In a moment a door opened, and another person came in.

Without paying much attention to anything, I walked around the room, and, apparently, was talking to myself. It was as if I'd been delivered from death, and I felt it joyously in my whole being. I'd have given him the slap, certainly, I'd certainly have given him the slap. But now they weren't here and . . . everything had vanished, everything had changed! . . . I looked around. I still couldn't take it all in. I glanced up mechanically at the girl who'd come in: before me there flashed a fresh, young, slightly pale face with straight dark brows and a serious, seemingly astonished look. I liked that immediately; I would have hated her if she'd been smiling. I began to look at her more carefully, as though with some effort: I'd still not managed to collect my thoughts. There was something simple and kind in her face, but somehow it was strangely serious. I was sure that she was at a disadvantage as a result, and that none of those fools had even noticed her. She couldn't be called a beauty, however, even though she was tall, strong, and well built. She was dressed very simply. Something despicable took hold of me; I went up to her. . . .

I happened to glance into a mirror. My overwrought face appeared extremely repulsive: it was pale, spiteful and mean; and my hair was dishevelled. "It doesn't matter. I'm glad," I thought. "In fact, I'm even delighted that I'll seem so repulsive to her; that pleases me. . . ."

VI

Somewhere behind a partition a clock was wheezing as if under some strong pressure, as though someone were strangling it. After this unnaturally prolonged wheezing there followed a thin, nasty, somehow unexpectedly hurried chime, as if someone had suddenly leapt forward. It struck two. I recovered, although I really hadn't been asleep, only lying there half-conscious.

It was almost totally dark in the narrow, cramped, low-ceilinged room, which was crammed with an enormous wardrobe and cluttered with cartons, rags, and all sorts of old clothes. The candle burning on the table at one end of the room flickered faintly from time to time, and almost went out completely. In a few moments total darkness would set in.

It didn't take long for me to come to my senses; all at once, without any effort, everything returned to me, as though it had been lying in ambush ready to pounce on me again. Even in my unconscious state some point had constantly remained in my memory, never to be forgotten, around which my sleepy visions had gloomily revolved. But it was a strange thing: everything that had happened to me that day now seemed, upon awakening, to have occurred in the distant past, as if I'd long since left it all behind.

My mind was in a daze. It was as though something were hanging over me, provoking, agitating, and disturbing me. Misery and bile were welling inside me, seeking an outlet. Suddenly I noticed beside me two wide-open eyes, examining me curiously and persistently. The gaze was coldly detached, sullen, as if belonging to a total stranger. I found it oppressive.

A dismal thought was conceived in my brain and spread throughout my whole body like a nasty sensation, such as one feels upon entering a damp, mouldy underground cellar. It was somehow unnatural that only now these two eyes had decided to examine me. I also recalled that during the course of the last two hours I hadn't said one word to this creature, and that I had considered it quite unnecessary; that had even given me pleasure for some reason. Now I'd suddenly realized starkly how absurd, how revolting as a spider, was the idea of debauchery, which, without love, crudely and shamelessly begins precisely at the point where genuine love is consummated. We looked at each other in this way for some time, but she didn't lower her gaze before mine, nor did she alter her stare, so that finally, for some reason, I felt very uneasy.

"What's your name?" I asked abruptly, to put an end to it quickly.

"Liza," she replied, almost in a whisper, but somehow in a very unfriendly way; and she turned her eyes away.

I remained silent.

"The weather today . . . snow . . . foul!" I observed, almost to myself, drearily placing one arm behind my head and staring at the ceiling.

She didn't answer. The whole thing was obscene.

"Are you from around here?" I asked her a moment later, almost angrily, turning my head slightly toward her.

"No."

"Where are you from?"

"Riga," she answered unwillingly.

"German?"

"No, Russian."

"Have you been here long?"

"Where?"

"In this house."

"Two weeks." She spoke more and more curtly. The candle had gone out completely; I could no longer see her face.

"Are your mother and father still living?"

"Yes . . . no . . . they are."

"Where are they?"

"There . . . in Riga."

"Who are they?"

"Just . . ."

"Just what? What do they do?"

"Tradespeople."

"Have you always lived with them?"

"Yes."

"How old are you?"

"Twenty."

"Why did you leave them?"

"Just because . . ."

That "just because" meant: leave me alone, it makes me sick. We fell silent.

Only God knows why, but I didn't leave. I too started to feel sick and more depressed. Images of the previous day began to come to mind all on their own, without my willing it, in a disordered way. I suddenly recalled a scene that I'd witnessed on the street that morning as I was anxiously hurrying to work. "Today some people were carrying a coffin and nearly dropped it," I suddenly said aloud, having no desire whatever to begin a conversation, but just so, almost accidentally.

"A coffin?"

"Yes, in the Haymarket; they were carrying it up from an underground cellar."

"From a cellar?"

"Not a cellar, but from a basement . . . well, you know . . . from down-stairs . . . from a house of ill repute . . . There was such filth all around. . . . Egg-shells, garbage . . . it smelled foul . . . it was disgusting."

Silence.

"A nasty day to be buried!" I began again to break the silence.

"Why nasty?"

"Snow, slush . . ." (I yawned.)

"It doesn't matter," she said suddenly after a brief silence.

"No, it's foul. . . ." (I yawned again.) "The grave diggers must have been curs-ing because they were getting wet out there in the snow. And there must have been water in the grave."

"Why water in the grave?" she asked with some curiosity, but she spoke even more rudely and curtly than before. Something suddenly began to goad me on.

"Naturally, water on the bottom, six inches or so. You can't ever dig a dry grave at Volkovo cemetery."

"Why not?"

"What do you mean, why not? The place is waterlogged. It's all swamp. So they bury them right in the water. I've seen it myself . . . many times. . . ."

(I'd never seen it, and I'd never been to Volkovo cemetery, but I'd heard about it from other people.)

"Doesn't it matter to you if you die?"

"Why should I die?" she replied, as though defending herself.

"Well, someday you'll die; you'll die just like that woman did this morning. She was a . . . she was also a young girl . . . she died of consumption."

"The wench should have died in the hospital. . . ." (She knows all about it, I thought, and she even said "wench" instead of "girl.")

"She owed money to her madam," I retorted, more and more goaded on by the argument. "She worked right up to the end, even though she had consump-tion. The cabbies standing around were chatting with the soldiers, telling them all about it. Her former acquaintances, most likely. They were all laughing. They were planning to drink to her memory at the tavern." (I invented a great deal of this.)

Silence, deep silence. She didn't even stir.

"Do you think it would be better to die in a hospital?"

"Isn't it just the same? . . . Besides, why should I die?" she added irritably.

"If not now, then later?"

"Well, then later . . ."

"That's what you think! Now you're young and pretty and fresh—that's your value. But after a year of this life, you won't be like that any more; you'll fade."

"In a year?"

"In any case, after a year your price will be lower," I continued, gloating. "You'll move out of here into a worse place, into some other house. And a year later, into a third, each worse and worse, and seven years from now you'll end up in a cellar on the Haymarket. Even that won't be so bad. The real trouble will come when you get some disease, let's say a weakness in the chest . . . or you catch cold or something. In this kind of life it's no laughing matter to get sick. It takes hold of you and may never let go. And so, you die."

"Well, then, I'll die," she answered now quite angrily and stirred quickly.

"That'll be a pity."

"For what?"

"A pity to lose a life."

Silence.

"Did you have a sweetheart? Huh?"

"What's it to you?"

"Oh, I'm not interrogating you. What do I care? Why are you angry? Of course, you may have had your own troubles. What's it to me? Just the same, I'm sorry."

"For whom?"

"I'm sorry for you."

"No need . . . ," she whispered barely audibly and stirred once again.

That provoked me at once. What! I was being so gentle with her, while she . . .

"Well, and what do you think? Are you on the right path then?"

"I don't think anything."

"That's just the trouble—you don't think. Wake up, while there's still time. And there is time. You're still young and pretty; you could fall in love, get married, be happy.[3] . . ."

"Not all married women are happy," she snapped in her former, rude manner.

"Not all, of course, but it's still better than this. A lot better. You can even live without happiness as long as there's love. Even in sorrow life can be good; it's good to be alive, no matter how you live. But what's there besides . . . stench? Phew!"

I turned away in disgust; I was no longer coldly philosophizing. I began to feel what I was saying and grew excited. I'd been longing to expound these cherished *little ideas* that I'd been nurturing in my corner. Something had suddenly caught fire in me, some kind of goal had "manifested itself" before me.

"Pay no attention to the fact that I'm here. I'm no model for you. I may be even worse than you are. Moreover, I was drunk when I came here." I hastened nonetheless to justify myself. "Besides, a man is no example to a woman. It's a different thing altogether; even though I degrade and defile myself, I'm still no one's slave; if I want to leave, I just get up and go. I shake it all off and I'm a

---

3. A popular theme treated by Gogol, Cherny-shevsky, and Nekrasov, among others. Typically, an innocent and idealistic young man attempts to rehabilitate a prostitute or "fallen" woman.

different man. But you must realize right from the start that you're a slave. Yes, a slave! You give away everything, all your freedom. Later, if you want to break this chain, you won't be able to; it'll bind you ever more tightly. That's the kind of evil chain it is. I know. I won't say anything else; you might not even understand me. But tell me this, aren't you already in debt to your madam? There, you see!" I added, even though she hadn't answered, but had merely remained silent; but she was listening with all her might. "There's your chain! You'll never buy yourself out. That's the way it's done. It's just like selling your soul to the devil. . . .

"And besides . . . I may be just as unfortunate, how do you know, and I may be wallowing in mud on purpose, also out of misery. After all, people drink out of misery. Well, I came here out of misery. Now, tell me, what's so good about this place? Here you and I were . . . intimate . . . just a little while ago, and all that time we didn't say one word to each other; afterward you began to examine me like a wild creature, and I did the same. Is that the way people love? Is that how one person is supposed to encounter another? It's a disgrace, that's what it is!"

"Yes!" she agreed with me sharply and hastily. The haste of her answer surprised even me. It meant that perhaps the very same idea was flitting through her head while she'd been examining me earlier. It meant that she too was capable of some thought. . . . "Devil take it; this is odd, this *kinship*," I thought, almost rubbing my hands together. "Surely I can handle such a young soul."

It was the sport that attracted me most of all.

She turned her face closer to mine, and in the darkness it seemed that she propped her head up on her arm. Perhaps she was examining me. I felt sorry that I couldn't see her eyes. I heard her breathing deeply.

"Why did you come here?" I began with some authority.

"Just so . . ."

"But think how nice it would be living in your father's house! There you'd be warm and free; you'd have a nest of your own."

"And what if it's worse than that?"

"I must establish the right tone," flashed through my mind. "I won't get far with sentimentality."

However, that merely flashed through my mind. I swear that she really did interest me. Besides, I was somewhat exhausted and provoked. After all, artifice goes along so easily with feeling.

"Who can say?" I hastened to reply. "All sorts of things can happen. Why, I was sure that someone had wronged you and was more to blame than you are. After all, I know nothing of your life story, but a girl like you doesn't wind up in this sort of place on her own accord. . . ."

"What kind of a girl am I?" she whispered hardly audibly; but I heard it.

"What the hell! Now I'm flattering her. That's disgusting! But, perhaps it's a good thing. . . ." She remained silent.

"You see, Liza, I'll tell you about myself. If I'd had a family when I was growing up, I wouldn't be the person I am now. I think about this often. After all, no matter how bad it is in your own family—it's still your own father and mother, and not enemies or strangers. Even if they show you their love only once a year, you still know that you're at home. I grew up without a family; that must be why I turned out the way I did—so unfeeling."

I waited again.

"She might not understand," I thought. "Besides, it's absurd—all this moralizing."

"If I were a father and had a daughter, I think that I'd have loved her more than my sons, really," I began indirectly, talking about something else in order to distract her. I confess that I was blushing.

"Why's that?"

Ah, so she's listening!

"Just because. I don't know why, Liza. You see, I knew a father who was a stern, strict man, but he would kneel before his daughter and kiss her hands and feet; he couldn't get enough of her, really. She'd go dancing at a party, and he'd stand in one spot for five hours, never taking his eyes off her. He was crazy about her; I can understand that. At night she'd be tired and fall asleep, but he'd wake up, go in to kiss her, and make the sign of the cross over her while she slept. He used to wear a dirty old jacket and was stingy with everyone else, but would spend his last kopeck on her, buying her expensive presents; it afforded him great joy if she liked his presents. A father always loves his daughters more than their mother does. Some girls have a very nice time living at home. I think that I wouldn't even have let my daughter get married."

"Why not?" she asked with a barely perceptible smile.

"I'd be jealous, so help me God. Why, how could she kiss someone else? How could she love a stranger more than her own father? It's even painful to think about it. Of course, it's all nonsense; naturally, everyone finally comes to his senses. But I think that before I'd let her marry, I'd have tortured myself with worry. I'd have found fault with all her suitors. Nevertheless, I'd have ended up by allowing her to marry whomever she loved. After all, the one she loves always seems the worst of all to the father. That's how it is. That causes a lot of trouble in many families."

"Some are glad to sell their daughters, rather than let them marry honorably," she said suddenly.

Aha, so that's it!

"That happens, Liza, in those wretched families where there's neither God nor love," I retorted heatedly. "And where there's no love, there's also no good sense. There are such families, it's true, but I'm not talking about them. Obviously, from the way you talk, you didn't see much kindness in your own family. You must be very unfortunate. Hmm . . . But all this results primarily from poverty."

"And is it any better among the gentry? Honest folk live decently even in poverty."

"Hmmm . . . Yes. Perhaps. There's something else, Liza. Man only likes to count his troubles; he doesn't calculate his happiness. If he figured as he should, he'd see that everyone gets his share. So, let's say that all goes well in a particular family; it enjoys God's blessing, the husband turns out to be a good man, he loves you, cherishes you, and never leaves you. Life is good in that family. Sometimes, even though there's a measure of sorrow, life's still good. Where isn't there sorrow? If you choose to get married, *you'll find out for yourself*. Consider even the first years of a marriage to the one you love: what happiness, what pure bliss there can be sometimes! Almost without exception. At first even quarrels with your husband turn out well. For some women, the more they love their husbands, the more they pick fights with them. It's true; I once knew a woman like that. 'That's how it is,' she'd say. 'I love you very much and I'm tormenting you out of love, so that you'll feel it.' Did you know that one can torment a person intentionally out of love? It's mostly women who do that. Then she thinks to herself, 'I'll love him so much afterward, I'll be so affectionate, it's no sin to torment him a little now.' At home everyone would rejoice over you, and it would be so pleasant, cheerful, serene, and honorable. . . . Some other women are very jealous. If her husband goes away, I knew one like that, she can't stand it; she jumps up at night and goes off on the sly to see. Is he there? Is he in that house? Is he with that one? Now that's bad. Even she herself knows that it's bad; her heart sinks and she suffers because she really loves him. It's all out of love. And how nice it is to make up after a quarrel, to admit one's guilt or forgive him! How nice it is for both of them, how good they both feel at once, just as if they'd met again, married again, and begun their love all over again. No one, no one at all has to know what goes on between a husband and wife, if they love each other. However their quarrel ends, they should never call in either one of their mothers to act as judge or to hear complaints about the other one. They must act as their own judges. Love is God's mystery and should be hidden from other people's eyes, no matter what happens. This makes it holier, much better. They respect each other more, and a great deal is based on this respect. And, if there's been love, if they got married out of love, why should love disappear? Can't it be sustained? It rarely happens that it can't be sustained. If the husband turns out to be a kind and honest man, how can the love disappear? The first phase of married love will pass, that's true, but it's followed by an even better kind of love. Souls are joined together and all their concerns are managed in common; there'll be no secrets from one another. When children arrive, each and every stage, even a very difficult one, will seem happy, as long as there's both love and courage. Even work is cheerful; even when you deny yourself bread for your children's sake, you're still happy. After all, they'll love you for it afterward; you're really saving for your own future. Your children will grow up, and you'll feel that you're a model for them, a support. Even after you die, they'll carry your thoughts and feelings all during their life. They'll take on your image and likeness, since they received it from you. Consequently, it's a great obligation. How can a mother and father keep from growing closer? They say it's difficult to raise children. Who says that? It's heavenly joy! Do you love little children, Liza? I love them dearly. You know—a rosy little boy, suckling at your breast; what husband's heart could turn against his wife seeing her sitting there holding his child? The chubby, rosy little baby sprawls and snuggles; his little hands and feet are plump; his little nails are clean and tiny, so tiny it's even funny to see them; his little eyes look as if he already understood everything. As he suckles, he tugs at your breast playfully with his little hand. When the father approaches, the child lets go of the breast, bends way back, looks at his father, and laughs—as if God only knows how funny it is—and then takes to suckling again. Afterward, when he starts cutting teeth, he'll sometimes bite his mother's breast; looking at her sideways his little eyes seem to say, 'See, I bit you!' Isn't this pure bliss—the three of them, husband, wife, and child, all together? You can forgive a great deal for such moments. No, Liza, I think you must first learn how to live by yourself, and only afterward blame others."

"It's by means of images," I thought to myself, "just such images that I can get to you," although I was speaking with considerable feeling, I swear it; and all at once I blushed. "And what if she suddenly bursts out laughing—where will I hide then?" That thought drove me into a rage. By the end of my speech I'd really become excited, and now my pride was suffering somehow. The silence lasted for a while. I even considered shaking her.

"Somehow you . . ." she began suddenly and then stopped.

But I understood everything already: something was trembling in her voice now, not shrill, rude or unyielding as before, but something soft and timid, so timid that I suddenly was rather ashamed to watch her and felt guilty.

"What?" I asked with tender curiosity.

"Well, you . . ."

"What?"

"You somehow . . . it sounds just like a book," she said, and once again something which was noticeably sarcastic was suddenly heard in her voice.

Her remark wounded me dreadfully. That's not what I'd expected.

Yet, I didn't understand that she was intentionally disguising her feelings with sarcasm; that was usually the last resort of people who are timid and chaste of heart, whose souls have been coarsely and impudently invaded; and who, until the last moment, refuse to yield out of pride and are afraid to express their own feelings to you. I should've guessed it from the timidity with which on several occasions she tried to be sarcastic, until she finally managed to express it. But I hadn't guessed, and a malicious impulse took hold of me.

"Just you wait," I thought.

VII

"That's enough, Liza. What do books have to do with it, when this disgusts me as an outsider? And not only as an outsider. All this has awakened in my heart . . . Can it be, can it really be that you don't find it repulsive here? No, clearly habit means a great deal. The devil only knows what habit can do to a person. But do you seriously think that you'll never grow old, that you'll always be pretty, and that they'll keep you on here forever and ever? I'm not even talking about the filth. . . . Besides, I want to say this about your present life: even though you're still young, good-looking, nice, with soul and feelings, do you know, that when I came to a little while ago, I was immediately disgusted to be here with you! Why, a man has to be drunk to wind up here. But if you were in a different place, living as nice people do, I might not only chase after you, I might actually fall in love with you. I'd rejoice at a look from you, let alone a word; I'd wait for you at the gate and kneel down before you; I'd think of you as my betrothed and even consider that an honor. I wouldn't dare have any impure thoughts about you. But here, I know that I need only whistle, and you, whether you want to or not, will come to me, and that I don't have to do your bidding, whereas you have to do mine. The lowliest peasant may hire himself out as a laborer, but he doesn't make a complete slave of himself; he knows that it's only for a limited term. But what's your term? Just think about it. What are you giving up here? What are you enslaving? Why, you're enslaving your soul, something you don't really own, together with your body! You're giving away your love to be defiled by any drunkard! Love! After all, that's all there is!

It's a precious jewel, a maiden's treasure, that's what it is! Why, to earn that love a man might be ready to offer up his own soul, to face death. But what's your love worth now? You've been bought, all of you; and why should anyone strive for your love, when you offer everything even without it? Why, there's no greater insult for a girl, don't you understand? Now, I've heard that they console you foolish girls, they allow you to see your own lovers here. But that's merely child's play, deception, making fun of you, while you believe it. And do you really think he loves you, that lover of yours? I don't believe it. How can he, if he knows that you can be called away from him at any moment? He'd have to be depraved after all that. Does he possess even one drop of respect for you? What do you have in common with him? He's laughing at you and stealing from you at the same time—so much for his love. It's not too bad, as long as he doesn't beat you. But perhaps he does. Go on, ask him, if you have such a lover, whether he'll ever marry you. Why, he'll burst out laughing right in your face, if he doesn't spit at you or smack you. He himself may be worth no more than a few lousy kopecks. And for what, do you think, did you ruin your whole life here? For the coffee they give you to drink, or for the plentiful supply of food? Why do you think they feed you so well? Another girl, an honest one, would choke on every bite, because she'd know why she was being fed so well. You're in debt here, you'll be in debt, and will remain so until the end, until such time comes as the customers begin to spurn you. And that time will come very soon; don't count on your youth. Why, here youth flies by like a stage-coach. They'll kick you out. And they'll not merely kick you out, but for a long time before that they'll pester you, reproach you, and abuse you—as if you hadn't ruined your health for the madam, hadn't given up your youth and your soul for her in vain, but rather, as if you'd ruined her, ravaged her, and robbed her. And don't expect any support. Your friends will also attack you to curry her favor, because they're all in bondage here and have long since lost both conscience and pity. They've become despicable, and there's nothing on earth more despicable, more repulsive, or more insulting than their abuse. You'll lose everything here, everything, without exception—your health, youth, beauty, and hope—and at the age of twenty-two you'll look as if you were thirty-five, and even that won't be too awful if you're not ill. Thank God for that. Why, you probably think that you're not even working, that it's all play! But there's no harder work or more onerous task than this one in the whole world and there never has been. I'd think that one's heart alone would be worn out by crying. Yet you dare not utter one word, not one syllable; when they drive you out, you leave as if you were the guilty one. You'll move to another place, then to a third, then somewhere else, and finally you'll wind up in the Haymarket. And there they'll start beating you for no good reason at all; it's a local custom; the clients there don't know how to be nice without beating you. You don't think it's so disgusting there? Maybe you should go and have a look sometime, and see it with your own eyes. Once, at New Year's, I saw a woman in a doorway. Her own kind had pushed her outside as a joke, to freeze her for a little while because she was wailing too much; they shut the door behind her. At nine o'clock in the morning she was already dead drunk, dishevelled, half-naked, and all beaten up. Her face was powdered, but her eyes were bruised; blood was streaming from her nose and mouth; a certain cabby had just fixed her up. She was sitting on a stone step, holding a piece of salted fish in her hand; she was howling, wailing something about her 'fate,' and slapping the fish against the stone step. Cabbies and drunken soldiers had gathered around the steps and were taunting her. Don't you think you'll wind up the same way? I wouldn't want to believe it myself, but how do you know, perhaps eight or ten years ago this same girl, the one with the salted fish, arrived here from somewhere or other, all fresh like a little cherub, innocent, and pure; she knew no evil and blushed at every word. Perhaps she was just like you—proud, easily offended, unlike all the rest; she looked like a queen and knew that total happiness awaited the man who would love her and whom she would also love. Do you see how it all ended? What if at the very moment she was slapping the fish against that filthy step, dead drunk and dishevelled, what if, even at that very moment she'd recalled her earlier, chaste years in her father's house when she was still going to school, and when her neighbor's son used to wait for her along the path and assure her that he'd love her all his life and devote himself entirely to her, and when they vowed to love one another forever and get married as soon as they grew up! No, Liza, you'd be lucky, very lucky, if you died quickly from consumption somewhere in a corner, in a cellar, like that other girl. In a hospital, you say? All right—they'll take you off, but what if the madam still requires your services? Consumption is quite a disease—it's not like dying from a fever. A person continues to hope right up until the last minute and declares that he's in good health. He consoles himself. Now that's useful for your madam. Don't worry, that's the way it is. You've sold your soul; besides, you owe her money—that means you don't dare say a thing. And while you're dying, they'll all abandon you, turn away from you—because there's nothing left to get from you. They'll even reproach you for taking up space for no good reason and for taking so long to die. You won't even be able to ask for something to drink, without their hurling abuse at you: 'When will you croak, you old bitch? You keep on moaning and don't let us get any sleep—and you drive our customers away.' That's for sure; I've overheard such words myself. And as you're breathing your last, they'll shove you into the filthiest corner of the cellar—into darkness and dampness; lying there alone, what will you think about then? After you die, some stranger will lay you out hurriedly, grumbling all the while, impatiently—no one will bless you, no one will sigh over you; they'll merely want to get rid of you as quickly as possible. They'll buy you a wooden trough and carry you out as they did that poor woman I saw today; then they'll go off to a tavern and drink to your memory. There'll be slush, filth, and wet snow in your grave—why bother for the likes of you? 'Let her down, Vanyukha; after all, it's her fate to go down with her legs up, that's the sort of girl she was. Pull up on that rope, you rascall!' 'It's okay like that.' 'How's it okay? See, it's lying on its side. Was she a human being or not? Oh, never mind, cover it up.' They won't want to spend much time arguing over you. They'll cover your coffin quickly with wet, blue clay and then go off to the tavern. . . . That'll be the end of your memory on earth; for other women, children will visit their graves, fathers, husbands—but for you—no tears, no sighs; no remembrances. No one, absolutely no one in the whole world, will ever come to visit you; your name will disappear from the face of the earth, just as if you'd never been born and had never existed. Mud and filth, no matter how you pound on the lid of your coffin at night when other corpses arise: 'Let me out, kind people, let me live on earth for a little while! I lived, but I didn't really see life; my life went down the drain; they drank it away in a tavern at the Haymarket; let me out, kind people, let me live in the world once again!'"

I was so carried away by my own pathos that I began to feel a lump forming in my throat, and . . . I suddenly stopped, rose up in fright, and, leaning over apprehensively, I began to listen carefully as my own heart pounded. There was cause for dismay.

For a while I felt that I'd turned her soul inside out and had broken her heart; the more I became convinced of this, the more I strived to reach my goal as quickly and forcefully as possible. It was the sport, the sport that attracted me; but it wasn't only the sport. . . .

I knew that I was speaking clumsily, artificially, even bookishly; in short, I didn't know how to speak except "like a book." But that didn't bother me, for I knew, I had a premonition, that I would be understood and that this bookishness itself might even help things along. But now, having achieved this effect, I suddenly lost all my nerve. No, never, never before had I witnessed such despair! She was lying there, her face pressed deep into a pillow she was clutching with her hands. Her heart was bursting. Her young body was shuddering as if she were having convulsions. Suppressed sobs shook her breast, tore her apart, and suddenly burst forth in cries and moans. Then she pressed her face even deeper into the pillow: she didn't want anyone, not one living soul, to hear her anguish and her tears. She bit the pillow; she bit her hand until it bled (I noticed that afterward); or else, thrusting her fingers into her dishevelled hair, she became rigid with the strain, holding her breath and clenching her teeth. I was about to say something, to ask her to calm down; but I felt that I didn't dare. Suddenly, all in a kind of chill, almost in a panic, I groped hurriedly to get out of there as quickly as possible. It was dark: no matter how I tried, I couldn't end it quickly. Suddenly I felt a box of matches and a candlestick with a whole unused candle. As soon as the room was lit up, Liza started suddenly, sat up, and looked at me almost senselessly, with a distorted face and a half-crazy smile. I sat down next to her and took her hands; she came to and threw herself at me, wanting to embrace me, yet not daring to. Then she quietly lowered her head before me.

"Liza, my friend, I shouldn't have . . . you must forgive me," I began, but she squeezed my hands so tightly in her fingers that I realized I was saying the wrong thing and stopped.

"Here's my address, Liza. Come to see me."

"I will," she whispered resolutely, still not lifting her head.

"I'm going now, good-bye . . . until we meet again."

I stood up; she did, too, and suddenly blushed all over, shuddered, seized a shawl lying on a chair, threw it over her shoulders, and wrapped herself up to her chin. After doing this, she smiled again somewhat painfully, blushed, and looked at me strangely. I felt awful. I hastened to leave, to get away.

"Wait," she said suddenly as we were standing in the hallway near the door, and she stopped me by putting her hand on my overcoat. She quickly put the candle down and ran off; obviously she'd remembered something or wanted to show me something. As she left she was blushing all over, her eyes were gleaming, and a smile had appeared on her lips—what on earth did it all mean? I waited against my own will; she returned a moment later with a glance that seemed to beg forgiveness for something. All in all it was no longer the same face or the same glance as before—sullen, distrustful, obstinate. Now her glance was imploring, soft, and, at the same time, trusting, affectionate, and timid. That's how children look at people whom they love very much, or when they're asking for something. Her eyes were light hazel, lovely, full of life, as capable of expressing love as brooding hatred.

Without any explanation, as if I were some kind of higher being who was supposed to know everything, she held a piece of paper out toward me. At that moment her whole face was shining with a most naive, almost childlike triumph. I unfolded the paper. It was a letter to her from some medical student containing a high-flown, flowery, but very respectful declaration of love. I don't remember the exact words now, but I can well recall the genuine emotion that can't be feigned shining through that high style. When I'd finished reading the letter, I met her ardent, curious, and childishly impatient gaze. She'd fixed her eyes on my face and was waiting eagerly to see what I'd say. In a few words, hurriedly, but with some joy and pride, she explained that she'd once been at a dance somewhere, in a private house, at the home of some "very, very good people, *family people*, where they *knew nothing*, nothing at all," because she'd arrived at this place only recently and was just . . . well, she hadn't quite decided whether she'd stay here and she'd certainly leave as soon as she'd paid off her debt. . . . Well, and this student was there; he danced with her all evening and talked to her. It turned out he was from Riga; he'd known her as a child, they'd played together, but that had been a long time ago; he was acquainted with her parents—but he knew nothing, absolutely nothing *about this place* and he didn't even suspect it! And so, the very next day, after the dance, (only some three days ago), he'd sent her this letter through the friend with whom she'd gone to the party . . . and . . . well, that's the whole story."

She lowered her sparkling eyes somewhat bashfully after she finished speaking.

The poor little thing, she'd saved this student's letter as a treasure and had run to fetch this one treasure of hers, not wanting me to leave without knowing that she too was the object of sincere, honest love, and that someone exists who had spoken to her respectfully. Probably that letter was fated to lie in her box without results. But that didn't matter; I'm sure that she'll guard it as a treasure her whole life, as her pride and vindication; and now, at a moment like this, she remembered it and brought it out to exult naively before me, to raise herself in my eyes, so that I could see it for myself and could also think well of her. I didn't say a thing; I shook her hand and left. I really wanted to get away. . . . I walked all the way home in spite of the fact that wet snow was still falling in large flakes. I was exhausted, oppressed, and perplexed. But the truth was already glimmering behind that perplexity. The ugly truth!

VIII

It was some time, however, before I agreed to acknowledge that truth. I awoke the next morning after a few hours of deep, leaden sleep. Instantly recalling the events of the previous day, even I was astonished at my *sentimentality* with Liza last night, at all of yesterday's "horror and pity." "Why, it's an attack of old woman's nervous hysteria, phew!" I decided. "And why on earth did I force my address on her? What if she comes? Then again, let her come, it doesn't make any difference. . . ." But *obviously* that was not the main, most important matter: I had to make haste and rescue at all costs my reputation in the eyes of Zverkov and Simonov. That was my main task. I even forgot all about Liza in the concerns of that morning.

First of all I had to repay last night's debt to Simonov immediately. I resolved on desperate means: I would borrow the sum of fifteen rubles from Anton Antonych. As luck would have it, he was in a splendid mood that morning and gave me the money at once, at my first request. I was so delighted that I signed a promissory note with a somewhat dashing air, and told him *casually* that on the previous evening "I'd been living it up with some friends at the Hôtel de Paris. We were holding a farewell dinner for a comrade, one might even say, a childhood friend, and, you know—he's a great carouser, very spoiled—well, naturally; he comes from a good family, has considerable wealth and a brilliant career; he's witty and charming, and has affairs with certain ladies, you understand. We drank up an extra 'half-dozen bottles' and . . ." There was nothing to it; I said all this very easily, casually, and complacently.

Upon arriving home I wrote to Simonov at once.

To this very day I recall with admiration the truly gentlemanly, good-natured, candid tone of my letter. Cleverly and nobly, and, above all, without unnecessary words, I blamed myself for everything. I justified myself, "if only I could be allowed to justify myself," by saying that, being so totally unaccustomed to wine, I'd gotten drunk with the first glass, which (supposedly) I'd consumed even before their arrival, as I waited for them in the Hôtel de Paris between the hours of five and six o'clock. In particular, I begged for Simonov's pardon; I asked him to convey my apology to all the others, especially to Zverkov, whom, "I recall, as if in a dream," it seems, I'd insulted. I added that I'd have called upon each of them, but was suffering from a bad headache, and, worst of all, I was ashamed. I was particularly satisfied by the "certain lightness," almost casualness (though, still very proper), unexpectedly reflected in my style; better than all possible arguments, it conveyed to them at once that I regarded "all of last night's unpleasantness" in a rather detached way, and that I was not at all, not in the least struck down on the spot as you, gentlemen, probably suspect. On the contrary, I regard this all serenely, as any self-respecting gentleman would. The true story, as they say, is no reproach to an honest young man.

"Why, there's even a hint of aristocratic playfulness in it," I thought admiringly as I reread my note. "And it's all because I'm such a cultured and educated man! Others in my place wouldn't know how to extricate themselves, but I've gotten out of it, and I'm having a good time once again, all because I'm an 'educated and cultured man of our time.' It may even be true that the whole thing occurred as a result of that wine yesterday. Hmmm . . . well, no, it wasn't really the wine. And I didn't have anything to drink between five and six o'clock when I was waiting for them. I lied to Simonov; it was a bold-faced lie—yet I'm not ashamed of it even now. . . ."

But, to hell with it, anyway! The main thing is, I got out of it.

I put six rubles in the letter, sealed it up, and asked Apollon to take it to Simonov. When he heard that there was money in it, Apollon became more respectful and agreed to deliver it. Toward evening I went out for a stroll. My head was still aching and spinning from the events of the day before. But as evening approached and twilight deepened, my impressions changed and became more confused, as did my thoughts. Something hadn't yet died within me, deep within my heart and conscience; it didn't want to die, and it expressed itself as burning anguish. I jostled my way along the more populous, commercial streets, along Meshchanskaya, Sadovaya, near the Yusupov Garden. I particularly liked to stroll along these streets at twilight, just as they became most crowded with all sorts of pedestrians, merchants, and tradesmen, with faces preoccupied to the point of hostility, on their way home from a hard day's work. It was precisely the cheap bustle that I liked, the crass prosaic quality. But this time all that street bustle irritated me even more. I couldn't get a hold of myself or puzzle out what was wrong. Something was rising, rising up in my soul continually, painfully, and didn't want to settle down. I returned home completely distraught. It was just as if some crime were weighing on my soul.

I was constantly tormented by the thought that Liza might come to see me. It was strange, but from all of yesterday's recollections, the one of her tormented me most, somehow separately from all the others. I'd managed to forget the rest by evening, to shrug everything off, and I still remained completely satisfied with my letter to Simonov. But in regard to Liza, I was not at all satisfied. It was as though I were tormented by her alone. "What if she comes?" I thought continually. "Well, so what? It doesn't matter. Let her come. Hmm. The only unpleasant thing is that she'll see, for instance, how I live. Yesterday I appeared before her such a . . . hero . . . but now, hmm! Besides, it's revolting that I've sunk so low. The squalor of my apartment. And I dared go to dinner last night wearing such clothes! And that oilcloth sofa of mine with its stuffing hanging out! And my dressing gown that doesn't quite cover me! What rags! . . . She'll see it all—and she'll see Apollon. That swine will surely insult her. He'll pick on her, just to be rude to me. Of course, I'll be frightened, as usual. I'll begin to fawn before her, wrap myself up in my dressing gown. I'll start to smile and tell lies. Ugh, the indecency! And that's not even the worst part! There's something even more important, nastier, meaner! Yes, meaner! Once again, I'll put on that dishonest, deceitful mask! . . ."

When I reached this thought, I simply flared up.

"Why deceitful? How deceitful? Yesterday I spoke sincerely. I recall that there was genuine feeling in me, too. I was trying no less than to arouse noble feelings in her . . . and if she wept, that's a good thing; it will have a beneficial effect. . . ."

But I still couldn't calm down.

All that evening, even after I returned home, even after nine o'clock, when by my calculations Liza could no longer have come, her image continued to haunt me, and, what's most important, she always appeared in one and the same form. Of all that had occurred yesterday, it was one moment in particular which stood out most vividly: that was when I lit up the room with a match and saw her pale, distorted face with its tormented gaze. What a pitiful, unnatural, distorted smile she'd had at that moment! But little did I know then that even fifteen years later I'd still picture Liza to myself with that same pitiful, distorted, and unnecessary smile which she'd had at that moment.

The next day I was once again prepared to dismiss all this business as nonsense, as the result of overstimulated nerves; but most of all, as exaggeration. I was well aware of this weakness of mine and sometimes was even afraid of it; "I exaggerate everything, that's my problem," I kept repeating to myself hour after hour. And yet, "yet, Liza may still come, all the same"; that was the refrain which concluded my reflections. I was so distressed that I sometimes became furious. "She'll come! She'll definitely come!" If not today, then tomorrow, she'll seek me out! That's just like the damned romanticism of all these *pure hearts*! Oh, the squalor, the stupidity, the narrowness of these "filthy, sentimental souls!' How could all this not be understood, how on earth could it not be understood? . . ." But at this point I would stop myself, even in the midst of great confusion.

"And how few, how very few words were needed," I thought in passing, "how little idyllic sentiment (what's more, the sentiment was artificial, bookish, composed) was necessary to turn a whole human soul according to my wishes at once. That's innocence for you! That's virgin soil!"

At times the thought occurred that I might go to her myself "to tell her everything," and to beg her not to come to me. But at this thought such venom arose in me that it seemed I'd have crushed that "damned" Liza if she'd suddenly turned up next to me. I'd have insulted her, spat at her, struck her, and chased her away!

One day passed, however, then a second, and a third; she still hadn't come, and I began to calm down. I felt particularly reassured and relaxed after nine o'clock in the evening, and even began to daydream sweetly at times. For instance, I'd save Liza, precisely because she'd come to me, and I'd talk to her. . . . I'd develop her mind, educate her. At last I'd notice that she loved me, loved me passionately. I'd pretend I didn't understand. (For that matter, I didn't know why I'd pretend; most likely just for the effect.) At last, all embarrassed, beautiful, trembling, and sobbing, she'd throw herself at my feet and declare that I was her saviour and she loved me more than anything in the world. I'd be surprised, but . . . "Liza," I'd say, "Do you really think that I haven't noticed your love? I've seen everything. I guessed, but dared not be first to make a claim on your heart because I had such influence over you, and because I was afraid you might deliberately force yourself to respond to my love out of gratitude, that you might forcibly evoke within yourself a feeling that didn't really exist. No, I didn't want that because it would be . . . despotism. . . . It would be indelicate (well, in short, here I launched on some European, George Sandian,[4] inexplicably lofty subtleties . . .). But now, now—you're mine, you're my creation, you're pure and lovely, you're my beautiful wife."

> And enter my house bold and free
> To become its full mistress![5]

---

4. George Sand was the pseudonym of the French woman novelist Aurore Dudevant (1804–1876), famous also as a promoter of feminism.

5. The last lines of the poem by Nekrasov used as the epigraph of Part II of this story (see pp. 1163–64).

"Then we'd begin to live happily together, travel abroad, etc., etc." In short, it began to seem crude even to me, and I ended it all by sticking my tongue out at myself.

"Besides, they won't let her out of there, the 'bitch,'" I thought. "After all, it seems unlikely that they'd release them for strolls, especially in the evening (for some reason I was convinced that she had to report there every evening, precisely at seven o'clock). Moreover, she said that she'd yet to become completely enslaved there, and that she still had certain rights; that means, hmm. Devil take it, she'll come, she's bound to come!"

It was a good thing I was distracted at the time by Apollon's rudeness. He made me lose all patience. He was the bane of my existence, a punishment inflicted on me by Providence. We'd been squabbling constantly for several years now and I hated him. My God, how I hated him! I think that I never hated anyone in my whole life as much as I hated him, especially at those times. He was an elderly, dignified man who worked part-time as a tailor. But for some unknown reason he despised me, even beyond all measure, and looked down upon me intolerably. However, he looked down on everyone. You need only glance at that flaxen, slicked-down hair, at that single lock brushed over his forehead and greased with vegetable oil, at his strong mouth, always drawn up in the shape of the letter V,[6] and you felt that you were standing before a creature who never doubted himself. He was a pedant of the highest order, the greatest one I'd ever met on earth; in addition he possessed a sense of self-esteem appropriate perhaps only to Alexander the Great, King of Macedonia. He was in love with every one of his buttons, every one of his fingernails—absolutely in love, and he looked it! He treated me quite despotically, spoke to me exceedingly little, and, if he happened to look at me, cast a steady, majestically self-assured, and constantly mocking glance that sometimes infuriated me. He carried out his tasks as if he were doing me the greatest of favors. Moreover, he did almost nothing at all for me; nor did he assume that he was obliged to do anything. There could be no doubt that he considered me the greatest fool on earth, and, that if he "kept me on," it was only because he could receive his wages from me every month. He agreed to "do nothing" for seven rubles a month. I'll be forgiven many of my sins because of him. Sometimes my hatred reached such a point that his gait alone would throw me into convulsions. But the most repulsive thing about him was his lisping. His tongue was a bit larger than normal or something of the sort; as a result, he constantly lisped and hissed. Apparently, he was terribly proud of it, imagining that it endowed him with enormous dignity. He spoke slowly, in measured tones, with his hands behind his back and his eyes fixed on the ground. It particularly infuriated me when he used to read the Psalter to himself behind his partition. I endured many battles on account of it. He was terribly fond of reading during the evening in a slow, even singsong voice, as if chanting over the dead. It's curious, but that's how he ended up: now he hires himself out to recite the Psalter over the dead; in addition, he exterminates rats and makes shoe polish. But at that time I couldn't get rid of him; it was as if he were chemically linked to my own existence. Besides, he'd never have agreed to leave for anything. It was impossible for me to live in a furnished room: my

6. The last letter of the old Russian alphabet, triangular in shape.

own apartment was my private residence, my shell, my case, where I hid from all humanity. Apollon, the devil only knows why, seemed to belong to this apartment, and for seven long years I couldn't get rid of him.

It was impossible, for example, to delay paying him his wages for even two or three days. He'd make such a fuss that I wouldn't know where to hide. But in those days I was so embittered by everyone that I decided, heaven knows why or for what reason, to *punish* Apollon by not paying him his wages for two whole weeks. I'd been planning to do this for some time now, about two years, simply in order to teach him that he had no right to put on such airs around me, and that if I chose to, I could always withhold his wages. I resolved to say nothing to him about it and even remain silent on purpose, to conquer his pride and force him to be the first one to mention it. Then I would pull all seven rubles out of a drawer and show him that I actually had the money and had intentionally set it aside, but that "I didn't want to, didn't want to, simply didn't want to pay him his wages, and that I didn't want to simply because *that's what I wanted*," because such was "my will as his master," because he was disrespectful and because he was rude. But, if he were to ask respectfully, then I might relent and pay him; if not, he might have to wait another two weeks, or three, or even a whole month. . . .

But, no matter how angry I was, he still won. I couldn't even hold out for four days. He began as he always did, because there had already been several such cases (and, let me add, I knew all this beforehand; I knew his vile tactics by heart), to wit: he would begin by fixing an extremely severe gaze on me. He would keep it up for several minutes in a row, especially when meeting me or accompanying me outside of the house. If, for example, I held out and pre- tended not to notice these stares, then he, maintaining his silence as before, would proceed to further tortures. Suddenly, for no reason at all, he'd enter my room quietly and slowly, while I was pacing or reading; he'd stop at the door, place one hand behind his back, thrust one foot forward, and fix his gaze on me, no longer merely severe, but now utterly contemptuous. If I were suddenly to ask him what he wanted, he wouldn't answer at all. He'd continue to stare at me reproachfully for several more seconds; then, compressing his lips in a par- ticular way and assuming a very meaningful air, he'd turn slowly on the spot and slowly withdraw to his own room. Two hours later he'd emerge again and suddenly appear before me in the same way. It's happened sometimes that in my fury I hadn't even asked what he wanted, but simply raised my head sharply and imperiously, and begun to stare reproachfully back at him. We would stare at each other thus for some two minutes or more; at last he'd turn slowly and self-importantly, and withdraw for another few hours.

If all this failed to bring me back to my senses and I continued to rebel, he'd suddenly begin to sigh while staring at me. He'd sigh heavily and deeply, as if trying to measure with each sigh the depth of my moral decline. Naturally, it would end with his complete victory: I'd rage and shout, but I was always forced to do just as he wished on the main point of dispute.

This time his usual maneuvers of "severe stares" had scarcely begun when I lost my temper at once and lashed out at him in a rage. I was irritated enough even without that.

"Wait!" I shouted in a frenzy, as he was slowly and silently turning with one hand behind his back, about to withdraw to his own room. "Wait! Come back, come back, I tell you!" I must have bellowed so unnaturally that he turned around and even began to scrutinize me with a certain amazement. He continued, however, not to utter one word, and that was what infuriated me most of all.

"How dare you come in here without asking permission and stare at me? Answer me!"

But after regarding me serenely for half a minute, he started to turn around again.

"Wait!" I roared, rushing up to him. "Don't move! There! Now answer me: why do you come in here to stare?"

"If you've got any orders for me now, it's my job to do 'em," he replied after another pause, lisping softly and deliberately, raising his eyebrows, and calmly shifting his head from one side to the other—what's more, he did all this with horrifying composure.

"That's not it! That's not what I'm asking you about, you executioner!" I shouted, shaking with rage. "I'll tell you myself, you executioner, why you came in here. You know that I haven't paid you your wages, but you're so proud that you don't want to bow down and ask me for them. That's why you came in here to punish me and torment me with your stupid stares, and you don't even sus-s-pect, you torturer, how stupid it all is, how stupid, stupid, stupid, stupid!"

He would have turned around silently once again, but I grabbed hold of him.

"Listen," I shouted to him. "Here's the money, you see! Here it is! (I pulled it out of a drawer.) All seven rubles. But you won't get it, you won't until you come to me respectfully, with your head bowed, to ask my forgiveness. Do you hear?"

"That can't be!" he replied with some kind of unnatural self-confidence.

"It will be!" I shrieked. "I give you my word of honor, it will be!"

"I have nothing to ask your forgiveness for," he said as if he hadn't even noticed my shrieks, "because it was you who called me an 'executioner,' and I can always go lodge a complaint against you at the police station."

"Go! Lodge a complaint!" I roared. "Go at once, this minute, this very second! You're still an executioner! Executioner! Executioner!" But he only looked at me, then turned and, no longer heeding my shouts, calmly withdrew to his own room without looking back.

"If it hadn't been for Liza, none of this would have happened!" I thought to myself. Then, after waiting a minute, pompously and solemnly, but with my heart pounding heavily and forcefully, I went in to see him behind the screen.

"Apollon!" I said softly and deliberately, though gasping for breath, "go at once, without delay to fetch the police supervisor!"

He'd already seated himself at his table, put on his eyeglasses, and picked up something to sew. But, upon hearing my order, he suddenly snorted with laughter.

"At once! Go this very moment! Go, go, or you can't imagine what will happen to you!"

"You're really not in your right mind," he replied, not even lifting his head, lisping just as slowly, and continuing to thread his needle. "Who's ever heard of a man being sent to fetch a policeman against himself? And as for trying to frighten me, you're only wasting your time, because nothing will happen to me."

"Go," I screeched, seizing him by the shoulder. I felt that I might strike him at any moment.

I never even heard the door from the hallway suddenly open at that very moment, quietly and slowly, and that someone walked in, stopped, and began to examine us in bewilderment. I glanced up, almost died from shame, and ran back into my own room. There, clutching my hair with both hands, I leaned my head against the wall and froze in that position.

Two minutes later I heard Apollon's deliberate footsteps.

"There's *some woman* asking for you," he said, staring at me with particular severity; then he stood aside and let her in—it was Liza. He didn't want to leave, and he scrutinized us mockingly.

"Get out, get out!" I commanded him all flustered. At that moment my clock strained, wheezed, and struck seven.

IX

And enter my house bold and free,
To become its full mistress!
From the same poem.[7]

I stood before her, crushed, humiliated, abominably ashamed; I think I was smiling as I tried with all my might to wrap myself up in my tattered, quilted dressing gown—exactly as I'd imagined this scene the other day during a fit of depression. Apollon, after standing over us for a few minutes, left, but that didn't make things any easier for me. Worst of all was that she suddenly became embarrassed too, more than I'd ever expected. At the sight of me, of course.

"Sit down," I said mechanically and moved a chair up to the table for her, while I sat on the sofa. She immediately and obediently sat down, staring at me wide-eyed, and, obviously, expecting something from me at once. This naive expectation infuriated me, but I restrained myself.

She should have tried not to notice anything, as if everything were just as it should be, but she . . . And I vaguely felt that she'd have to pay dearly *for everything*.

"You've found me in an awkward situation, Liza," I began, stammering and realizing that this was precisely the wrong way to begin.

"No, no, don't imagine anything!" I cried, seeing that she'd suddenly blushed. "I'm not ashamed of my poverty. . . . On the contrary, I regard it with pride. I'm poor, but noble. . . . One can be poor and noble," I muttered. "But . . . would you like some tea?"

"No . . . ," she started to say.

"Wait!"

I jumped up and ran to Apollon. I had to get away somehow.

"Apollon," I whispered in feverish haste, tossing down the seven rubles which *had been in my fist the whole time*, "here are your wages. There, you see, I've given them to you. But now you must rescue me: bring us some tea and a dozen rusks from the tavern at once. If you don't go, you'll make me a very miserable

7. I.e., from the poem quoted on pp. 1163–64 and 1203.

man. You have no idea who this woman is. . . . This means—everything! You may think she's . . . But you've no idea at all who this woman really is!"

Apollon, who'd already sat down to work and had put his glasses on again, at first glanced sideways in silence at the money without abandoning his needle; then, paying no attention to me and making no reply, he continued to fuss with the needle he was still trying to thread. I waited there for about three minutes standing before him with my arms folded *à la Napoleon*.[8] My temples were soaked in sweat. I was pale, I felt that myself. But, thank God, he must have taken pity just looking at me. After finishing with the thread, he stood up slowly from his place, slowly pushed back his chair, slowly took off his glasses, slowly counted the money and finally, after inquiring over his shoulder whether he should get a whole pot, slowly walked out of the room. As I was returning to Liza, it occurred to me: shouldn't I run away just as I was, in my shabby dressing gown, no matter where, and let come what may.

I sat down again. She looked at me uneasily. We sat in silence for several minutes.

"I'll kill him." I shouted suddenly, striking the table so hard with my fist that ink splashed out of the inkwell.

"Oh, what are you saying?" she exclaimed, startled.

"I'll kill him, I'll kill him!" I shrieked, striking the table in an absolute frenzy, but understanding full well at the same time how stupid it was to be in such a frenzy.

"You don't understand, Liza, what this executioner is doing to me. He's my executioner. . . . He's just gone out for some rusks; he . . . ."

And suddenly I burst into tears. It was a nervous attack. I felt so ashamed amidst my sobs, but I couldn't help it. She got frightened.

"What's the matter? What's wrong with you?" she cried, fussing around me.

"Water, give me some water, over there!" I muttered in a faint voice, realizing full well, however, that I could've done both without the water and without the faint voice. But I was *putting on an act*, as it's called, in order to maintain decorum, although my nervous attack was genuine.

She gave me some water while looking at me like a lost soul. At that very moment Apollon brought in the tea. It suddenly seemed that this ordinary and prosaic tea was horribly inappropriate and trivial after everything that had happened, and I blushed. Liza stared at Apollon with considerable alarm. He left without looking at us.

"Liza, do you despise me?" I asked, looking her straight in the eye, trembling with impatience to find out what she thought.

She was embarrassed and didn't know what to say.

"Have some tea," I said angrily. I was angry at myself, but she was the one who'd have to pay, naturally. A terrible anger against her suddenly welled up in my heart; I think I could've killed her. To take revenge I swore inwardly not to say one more word to her during the rest of her visit. "She's the cause of it all," I thought.

Our silence continued for about five minutes. The tea stood on the table; we didn't touch it. It reached the point of my not wanting to drink on purpose, to make it even more difficult for her; it would be awkward for her to begin alone.

8. In the style of Napoleon.

Several times she glanced at me in sad perplexity. I stubbornly remained silent. I was the main sufferer, of course, because I was fully aware of the despicable meanness of my own spiteful stupidity; yet, at the same time, I couldn't restrain myself.

"I want to . . . get away from . . . that place . . . once and for all," she began just to break the silence somehow; but, poor girl, that was just the thing she shouldn't have said at that moment, stupid enough as it was to such a person as me, stupid as I was. My own heart even ached with pity for her tactlessness and unnecessary straightforwardness. But something hideous immediately suppressed all my pity; it provoked me even further. Let the whole world go to hell. Another five minutes passed.

"Have I disturbed you?" she began timidly, barely audibly, and started to get up.

But as soon as I saw this first glimpse of injured dignity, I began to shake with rage and immediately exploded.

"Why did you come here? Tell me why, please," I began, gasping and neglecting the logical order of my words. I wanted to say it all at once, without pausing for breath; I didn't even worry about how to begin.

"Why did you come here? Answer me! Answer!" I cried, hardly aware of what I was saying. "I'll tell you, my dear woman, why you came here. You came here because I spoke some *words of pity* to you that time. Now you've softened, and want to hear more 'words of pity.' Well, you should know that I was laughing at you then. And I'm laughing at you now. Why are you trembling? Yes, I was laughing at you! I'd been insulted, just prior to that, at dinner, by those men who arrived just before me that evening. I came intending to thrash one of them, the officer; but I didn't succeed; I couldn't find him; I had to avenge my insult on someone, to get my own back; you turned up and I took my anger out at you, and I laughed at you. I'd been humiliated, and I wanted to humiliate someone else; I'd been treated like a rag, and I wanted to exert some power. . . . That's what it was; you thought that I'd come there on purpose to save you, right? Is that what you thought? Is that it?"

I knew that she might get confused and might not grasp all the details, but I also knew that she'd understand the essence of it very well. That's just what happened. She turned white as a sheet; she wanted to say something. Her lips were painfully twisted, but she collapsed onto a chair just as if she'd been struck down with an ax. Subsequently she listened to me with her mouth gaping, her eyes wide open, shaking with awful fear. It was the cynicism, the cynicism of my words that crushed her. . . .

"To save you!" I continued, jumping up from my chair and rushing up and down the room in front of her, "to save you from what? Why, I may be even worse than you are. When I recited that sermon to you, why didn't you throw it back in my face? You should have said to me, 'Why did you come here? To preach morality or what?' Power, it was the power I needed then, I craved the sport, I wanted to reduce you to tears, humiliation, hysteria—that's what I needed then! But I couldn't have endured it myself, because I'm such a wretch. I got scared. The devil only knows why I foolishly gave you my address. Afterward, even before I got home, I cursed you like nothing on earth on account of that address. I hated you already because I'd lied to you then, because it was all playing with words, dreaming in my own mind. But, do you know what I really want now? For you to get lost, that's what! I need some peace. Why, I'd sell the whole world for a kopeck if people would only stop bothering me. Should the world go to hell, or should I go without my tea? I say, let the world go to hell as long as I can always have my tea. Did you know that or not? And I know perfectly well that I'm a scoundrel, a bastard, an egotist, and a sluggard. I've been shaking from fear for the last three days wondering whether you'd ever come. Do you know what disturbed me most of all these last three days? The fact that I'd appeared to you then as such a hero, and that now you'd suddenly see me in this torn dressing gown, dilapidated and revolting. I said before that I wasn't ashamed of my poverty; well, you should know that I am ashamed, I'm ashamed of it more than anything, more afraid of it than anything, more than if I were a thief, because I'm so vain; it's as if the skin's been stripped away from my body so that even wafts of air cause pain. By now surely even you've guessed that I'll never forgive you for having come upon me in this dressing gown as I was attacking Apollon like a vicious dog. Your saviour, your former hero, behaving like a mangy, shaggy mongrel, attacking his own lackey, while that lackey stood there laughing at me! Nor will I ever forgive you for those tears which, like an embarrassed old woman, I couldn't hold back before you. And I'll never forgive *you* for all that I'm confessing now. Yes—you, you alone must pay for everything because you turned up like this, because I'm a scoundrel, because I'm the nastiest, most ridiculous, pettiest, stupidest, most envious worm of all those living on earth who're no better than me in any way, but who, the devil knows why, never get embarrassed, while all my life I have to endure insults from every louse—that's my fate. What do I care that you don't understand any of this? What do I care, what do I care about you and whether or not you perish there? Why, don't you realize how much I'll hate you now after having said all this with your being here listening to me? After all, a man can only talk like this once in his whole life, and then only in hysteria! . . . What more do you want? Why, after all this, are you still hanging around here tormenting me? Why don't you leave?"

But at this point a very strange thing suddenly occurred.

I'd become so accustomed to inventing and imagining everything according to books, and picturing everything on earth to myself just as I'd conceived of it in my dreams, that at first I couldn't even comprehend the meaning of this strange occurrence. But here's what happened: Liza, insulted and crushed by me, understood much more than I'd imagined. She understood out of all this what a woman always understands first of all, if she sincerely loves—namely, that I myself was unhappy.

The frightened and insulted expression on her face was replaced at first by grieved amazement. When I began to call myself a scoundrel and a bastard, and my tears had begun to flow (I'd pronounced this whole tirade in tears), her whole face was convulsed by a spasm. She wanted to get up and stop me; when I'd finished, she paid no attention to my shouting, "Why are you here? Why don't you leave?" She only noticed that it must have been very painful for me to utter all this. Besides, she was so defenseless, the poor girl. She considered herself immeasurably beneath me. How could she get angry or take offense? Suddenly she jumped up from the chair with a kind of uncontrollable impulse, and yearning toward me, but being too timid and not daring to stir from her place, she extended her arms in my direction. . . . At this moment my heart leapt inside me, too. Then suddenly she threw herself at me, put her arms around my neck, and burst into tears. I, too, couldn't restrain myself and sobbed as I'd never done before.

"They won't let me . . . I can't be . . . good!" I barely managed to say; then I went over to the sofa, fell upon it face down, and sobbed in genuine hysterics for a quarter of an hour. She knelt down, embraced me, and remained motionless in that position.

But the trouble was that my hysterics had to end sometime. And so (after all, I'm writing the whole loathsome truth), lying there on the sofa and pressing my face firmly into that nasty leather cushion of mine, I began to sense gradually, distantly, involuntarily, but irresistibly, that it would be awkward for me to raise my head and look Liza straight in the eye. What was I ashamed of? I don't know, but I was ashamed. It also occurred to my overwrought brain that now our roles were completely reversed; now she was the heroine, and I was the same sort of humiliated and oppressed creature she'd been in front of me that evening—only four days ago. . . . And all this came to me during those few minutes as I lay face down on the sofa!

My God! Was it possible that I envied her?

I don't know; to this very day I still can't decide. But then, of course, I was even less able to understand it. After all, I couldn't live without exercising power and tyrannizing over another person. . . . But . . . but, then, you really can't explain a thing by reason; consequently, it's useless to try.

However, I regained control of myself and raised my head; I had to sooner or later. . . . And so, I'm convinced to this day that it was precisely because I felt too ashamed to look at her, that another feeling was suddenly kindled and burst into flame in my heart—the feeling of domination and possession. My eyes gleamed with passion; I pressed her hands tightly. How I hated her and felt drawn to her simultaneously! One feeling intensified the other. It was almost like revenge! . . . At first there was a look of something resembling bewilderment, or even fear, on her face, but only for a brief moment. She embraced me warmly and rapturously.

X

A quarter of an hour later I was rushing back and forth across the room in furious impatience, constantly approaching the screen to peer at Liza through the crack. She was sitting on the floor, her head leaning against the bed, and she must have been crying. But she didn't leave, and that's what irritated me. By this time she knew absolutely everything. I'd insulted her once and for all, but . . . there's nothing more to be said. She guessed that my outburst of passion was merely revenge, a new humiliation for her, and that to my former, almost aimless, hatred there was added now a *personal, envious* hatred of her. . . . However, I don't think that she understood all this explicitly; on the other hand, she fully understood that I was a despicable man, and, most important, that I was incapable of loving her.

I know that I'll be told this is incredible—that it's impossible to be as spiteful and stupid as I am; you may even add that it was impossible not to return, or at least to appreciate, this love. But why is this so incredible? In the first place, I could no longer love because, I repeat, for me love meant tyrannizing and demonstrating my moral superiority. All my life I could never even conceive of any other kind of love, and I've now reached the point that I sometimes think that love consists precisely in a voluntary gift by the beloved person of the right to tyrannize over him. Even in my underground dreams I couldn't conceive of love in any way other than a struggle. It always began with hatred and ended with moral subjugation; afterward, I could never imagine what to do with the subjugated object. And what's so incredible about that, since I'd previously managed to corrupt myself morally; I'd already become unaccustomed to "real life," and only a short while ago had taken it into my head to reproach her and shame her for having come to hear "words of pity" from me. But I never could've guessed that she'd come not to hear words of pity at all, but to love me, because it's in that kind of love that a woman finds her resurrection, all her salvation from whatever kind of ruin, and her rebirth, as it can't appear in any other form. However, I didn't hate her so much as I rushed around the room and peered through the crack behind the screen. I merely found it unbearably painful that she was still there. I wanted her to disappear. I longed for "peace and quiet"; I wanted to remain alone in my underground. "Real life" oppressed me—so unfamiliar was it—that I even found it hard to breathe.

But several minutes passed, and she still didn't stir, as if she were oblivious. I was shameless enough to tap gently on the screen to remind her. . . . She started suddenly, jumped up, and hurried to find her shawl, hat, and coat, as if she wanted to escape from me. . . . Two minutes later she slowly emerged from behind the screen and looked at me sadly. I smiled spitefully; it was forced, however, for *appearance's sake only*; and I turned away from her look.

"Good-bye," she said, going toward the door.

Suddenly I ran up to her, grabbed her hand, opened it, put something in . . . and closed it again. Then I turned away at once and bolted to the other corner, so that at least I wouldn't be able to see. . . .

I was just about to lie—to write that I'd done all this accidentally, without knowing what I was doing, in complete confusion, out of foolishness. But I don't want to lie; therefore I'll say straight out, that I opened her hand and placed something in it . . . out of spite. It occurred to me to do this while I was rushing back and forth across the room and she was sitting there behind the screen. But here's what I can say for sure: although I did this cruel thing deliberately, it was not from my heart, but from my stupid head. This cruelty of mine was so artificial, cerebral, intentionally invented, *bookish*, that I couldn't stand it myself even for one minute—at first I bolted to the corner so as not to see, and then, out of shame and in despair, I rushed out after Liza. I opened the door into the hallway and listened. "Liza! Liza!" I called down the stairs, but timidly, in a soft voice.

There was no answer; I thought I could hear her footsteps at the bottom of the stairs.

"Liza!" I cried more loudly.

No answer. But at that moment I heard down below the sound of the tight outer glass door opening heavily with a creak and then closing again tightly. The sound rose up the stairs.

She'd gone. I returned to my room deep in thought. I felt horribly oppressed.

I stood by the table near the chair where she'd been sitting and stared senselessly into space. A minute or so passed, then I suddenly started: right before me on the chair I saw . . . in a word, I saw the crumpled blue five-ruble note, the very one I'd thrust into her hand a few moments before. It was the same one; it couldn't be any other; I had none other in my apartment. So she'd managed to toss it down on the table when I'd bolted to the other corner.

So what? I might have expected her to do that. Might have expected it? No. I was such an egotist, in fact, I so lacked respect for other people, that I couldn't even conceive that she'd ever do that. I couldn't stand it. A moment later, like a madman, I hurried to get dressed. I threw on whatever I happened to find, and rushed headlong after her. She couldn't have gone more than two hundred paces when I ran out on the street.

It was quiet; it was snowing heavily, and the snow was falling almost perpendicularly, blanketing the sidewalk and the deserted street. There were no passers-by; no sound could be heard. The street lights were flickering dismally and vainly. I ran about two hundred paces to the crossroads and stopped.

"Where did she go? And why am I running after her? Why? To fall down before her, sob with remorse, kiss her feet, and beg her forgiveness! That's just what I wanted. My heart was being torn apart; never, never will I recall that moment with indifference. But—why?" I wondered. "Won't I grow to hate her, perhaps as soon as tomorrow, precisely because I'm kissing her feet today? Will I ever be able to make her happy? Haven't I found out once again today, for the hundredth time, what I'm really worth? Won't I torment her?"

I stood in the snow, peering into the murky mist, and thought about all this.

"And wouldn't it be better, wouldn't it," I fantasized once I was home again, stifling the stabbing pain in my heart with such fantasies, "wouldn't it be better if she were to carry away the insult with her forever? Such an insult—after all, is purification; it's the most caustic and painful form of consciousness. Tomorrow I would have defiled her soul and wearied her heart. But now that insult will never die within her; no matter how abominable the filth that awaits her, that insult will elevate and purify her . . . by hatred . . . hmm . . . perhaps by forgiveness as well. But will that make it any easier for her?"

And now, in fact, I'll pose an idle question of my own. Which is better: cheap happiness or sublime suffering? Well, come on, which is better?

These were my thoughts as I sat home that evening, barely alive with the anguish in my soul. I'd never before endured so much suffering and remorse; but could there exist even the slightest doubt that when I went rushing out of my apartment, I'd turn back again after going only halfway? I never met Liza afterward, and I never heard anything more about her. I'll also add that for a long time I remained satisfied with my theory about the use of insults and hatred, in spite of the fact that I myself almost fell ill from anguish at the time.

Even now, after so many years, all this comes back to me as *very unpleasant*. A great deal that comes back to me now is very unpleasant, but . . . perhaps I should end these *Notes* here? I think that I made a mistake in beginning to write them. At least, I was ashamed all the time I was writing this *tale*: consequently, it's not really literature, but corrective punishment. After all, to tell you long stories about how, for example, I ruined my life through moral decay in my corner, by the lack of appropriate surroundings, by isolation from any living beings, and by futile malice in the underground—so help me God, that's not very interesting. A novel needs a hero, whereas here all the traits of an anti-hero have been assembled *deliberately*; but the most important thing is that all this produces an extremely unpleasant impression because we've all become estranged from life, we're all cripples, every one of us, more or less. We've become so estranged that at times we feel some kind of revulsion for genuine "real life," and therefore we can't bear to be reminded of it. Why, we've reached a point where we almost regard "real life" as hard work, as a job, and we've all agreed in private that it's really better in books. And why do we sometimes fuss, indulge in whims, and make demands? We don't know ourselves. It'd be even worse if all our whimsical desires were fulfilled. Go on, try it. Give us, for example, a little more independence; untie the hands of any one of us, broaden our sphere of activity, relax the controls, and . . . I can assure you, we'll immediately ask to have the controls reinstated. I know that you may get angry at me for saying this, you may shout and stamp your feet: "Speak for yourself," you'll say, "and for your own miseries in the underground, but don't you dare say *all of us.*'" If you'll allow me, gentlemen; after all, I'm not trying to justify myself by saying *all of us.* What concerns me in particular, is that in my life I've only taken to an extreme that which you haven't even dared to take halfway; what's more, you've mistaken your cowardice for good sense; and, in so deceiving yourself, you've consoled yourself. So, in fact, I may even be "more alive" than you are. Just take a closer look! Why, we don't even know where this "real life" lives nowadays, what it really is, and what it's called. Leave us alone without books and we'll get confused and lose our way at once—we won't know what to join, what to hold on to, what to love or what to hate, what to respect or what to despise. We're even oppressed by being men—men with real bodies and blood of *our very own.* We're ashamed of it; we consider it a disgrace and we strive to become some kind of impossible "general-human-beings." We're stillborn; for some time now we haven't been conceived by living fathers; we like it more and more. We're developing a taste for it. Soon we'll conceive of a way to be born from ideas. But enough; I don't want to write any more "from Underground. . . ."

However, the "notes" of this paradoxalist don't end here. He couldn't resist and kept on writing. But it also seems to us that we might as well stop here.

GUSTAVE FLAUBERT

1821–1880

Exquisitely crafted and powerfully imagined, *Madame Bovary* is one of the greatest of all novels. Gustave Flaubert said that he wanted to write "a book about nothing," one held together by the "internal force of its style" alone. The protagonist he developed for this was a doctor's wife in a stagnant provincial town who longs to lead a passionate life like the fictional heroines she encounters in books. Feeling trapped, she becomes increasingly reckless, refusing the moderation and reasonableness demanded by the provincial middle class in favor of sensual experience and extravagance. She becomes hungry for love, beauty, excitement, and freedom.

Flaubert identified closely with his heroine. Living mostly isolated in a small country town, he too condemned the stupidity and mediocrity of life in the provinces. "I am Madame Bovary," he insisted. But unlike his protagonist, he could throw himself into the making of art. He labored over every sentence he wrote, sometimes taking as much as a week to complete a paragraph, determined to perfect each phrase. Occasionally he traveled, spending months at a time in Paris and taking journeys to North Africa, Syria, Turkey, and Italy. He was even in Paris to witness the revolution of 1848, as workers rose up against the monarchy and demanded the vote. But Flaubert's greatest excitement lay in the act of writing: "I get drunk on ink as others do on wine," he wrote: "I love my work with a frenetic and perverted love, as the ascetic loves the hair shirt that scratches his belly."

LIFE

Gustave Flaubert was the son of a chief surgeon in the provincial French town of Rouen. He was precocious and began writing fiction in his teens. When he was fourteen, he developed an unrequited passion for an older married woman. A few years later he went to Paris to study law, which he hated. Anxious and unhappy, he failed his exams and suffered a sudden nervous breakdown, which sent him back to his family home in the small town of Croisset near Rouen, where he would stay for most of his life with his mother. It was there that he began to write seriously.

In 1846, on a visit to Paris, he made the acquaintance of the beautiful Louise Colet, a professional writer who lived and worked among bohemian artists. This was Flaubert's only serious love affair, though it would take place mostly by correspondence—for him the reality never lived up to the imagination—and he treated her coldly. Otherwise, he frequented prostitutes and had some fleeting sexual relationships with men. His mother declared that his "passion for sentences" had dried up his heart.

Flaubert's works did not make it easily into the world. In 1849, he asked his two closest friends to read a draft of his first novel, *The Temptation of Saint Anthony*. "We think you should throw it in the fire and never speak of it again," they advised. He put it aside and labored for five years on what would become his masterpiece, *Madame Bovary* (1857). When it appeared, sales were good, but critics denounced the book as disgusting, consumed with the ugly banality of everyday life with nothing uplifting or consoling to redeem it. The novel was so shocking in its distanced and ironic treatment of adultery that Flaubert was put on trial for "offending public morals and religion." Although he was acquitted, *Madame Bovary* maintained its reputation as an immoral book for decades to come. In 1869, Flaubert published *Sentimental Education*, a novel about the generation that lived through the revolutions of 1848. It flopped with the public, and reviewers sneered, but it has since come to be enormously influential and highly regarded.

Flaubert returned to *The Temptation of Saint Anthony* late in life, burying his manuscript in the ground temporarily when the Prussians invaded Normandy in 1870. In the next few years, his body succumbed to syphilis. Two weeks before he died in 1880, he said to his niece: "Sometimes I think I'm liquefying like an old Camembert cheese."

WORK

Before *Madame Bovary*, French fiction had never treated relatively humble and ordinary characters with such seriousness, restraint, verisimilitude, and clarity. The context is deliberately mundane, and the manner of telling the story is objective and detached. At the center of the novel is a dreamy young peasant woman brought up in a convent, who marries a dull doctor. Each of the other characters is a realistic and recognizable social type of the time: a pharmacist, a storekeeper, a notary and his clerk, a tax collector, a woman innkeeper, a priest, a landowner, a farmer, and the doctor himself (technically not quite a doctor, in fact, but a "health officer" with a lower

degree). Along the way, Flaubert's descriptions are painstakingly correct: a gruesome clubfoot operation and the effects of arsenic poisoning, for example, are all too meticulously rendered.

What particularly shocked readers when the novel was first published was their uncertainty about the author's attitude toward Emma. Readers were accustomed to being told clearly how to judge the morals of literary characters. **Victor Hugo** judges histrionically in *Les Miserables,* for example, hurling condemnations at the legal system and at characters who exploit others callously. In Flaubert's novel, by contrast, the author seemed to disappear altogether. He wrote that "the artist in his work should be like God in the universe, present everywhere and visible nowhere." For some, this made the narration feel impersonal, even heartless. One critic famously charged that Flaubert wielded his pen as a surgeon wields a scalpel. Another wrote: "In this novel there is no emotion, no feeling, no life, only the great force of an arithmetician." Seeming closer to science and mathematics than to conventional fiction, *Madame Bovary* broke new ground with its dispassionate narrative style.

The novel's moral ambiguity gave rise to a notorious trial. Flaubert was hauled into court, his novel described by the prosecutor as an incitement to adultery and atheism. In his rebuttal, the defense counsel argued that the novel was, rather, a highly moral work in which adultery is clearly punished. Flaubert was acquitted, but for him, the moral judgments were beside the point. *Madame Bovary* was first and foremost a literary experiment that ushered in an altogether new kind of novel: a precise, unsentimental, often ironic dissection of an actually existing society in which there can be no happy endings, no fulfilled fantasies. Flaubert had once loved such romantic extravagances, but now he sought carefully to eliminate every one of them from his writing. If we remember that it is fiction that shapes Emma Bovary in the first place—stories of passion and mystery, excitement and desire—then we can read *Madame Bovary* as a novel that deliberately sets itself against other novels. Conventional fictions create longings for endless luxuries and grand passions, but in the world these are always either short lived or dissatisfying. Flaubert's own fiction describes this painful cycle rather than participating in it.

And yet, it is not so much the world that he evokes as his stylistic innovations that mark Flaubert's greatest impact on the history of the novel. He always worked painstakingly to find what he saw as the one right word (*le mot juste*), and we can think of the most trivial cliché or the most obscure scientific term in this novel as the product of long thought and careful judgment. We know that it took him more than five years of grinding drudgery to write *Madame Bovary*: he recorded five days to write a single page, thirteen pages in seven weeks, a whole night spent in hunting for the right adjective. He also subjected his manuscript to ruthless pruning afterward, eliminating many images and descriptions of elusive mental states. He often made the text more rather than less morally ambiguous in the process.

The result is a novel that rewards the closest attention to images, patterns, and perspectives. What opens the novel is a laughably ugly cap, for example, worn by Charles Bovary, which marks him as a social outsider in the world of the school. The cap itself is an impossible composite, outlandish and remarkable and also perhaps more human than its owner; its "mute hideousness

suggests unplumbed depths, like an idiot's face." In a world where objects can matter a great deal—where gifts and luxuries plunge the Bovary household into overwhelming debt—it is an object that first makes a plea for our attention. Many of Flaubert's carefully described things, from the couple's absurd wedding cake to the heap of souvenirs from countless mistresses that blur together in Rodolphe's memory, hint at the empty relations between people.

Flaubert also offers startling, intriguing juxtapositions, like the famous scene at the country fair, where Emma is seduced by the virile Rodolphe against a backdrop of noisy farm animals and officials whose pompous rhetoric extols agricultural life. Is Flaubert satirizing passion, putting passionate words alongside mooing cows, or is he offering us an invitation to pity Emma, trapped as she is in a world that celebrates farming as its highest achievement? The author never explicitly comments. In another suggestive juxtaposition, Flaubert describes an argument between two characters—the insensitive village priest, who makes a case for the traditional, sacred world of the church, and the scientific pharmacist Homais, who argues for the rational values of the Enlightenment—but in the end he leaves them both snoring together beside a corpse.

When it comes to style, *Madame Bovary* is perhaps most deeply admired for its subtle handling of narrative perspective. The novel begins in the voice of a first-person narrator, one of Charles Bovary's classmates, and then begins telling the story from Charles's own perspective; eventually the narrative shifts to Emma's point of view, seeing much of the experience of the novel through her eyes. And yet, Flaubert retains the third-person narrator to render Emma's perspective. He is often praised for his skill in using a technique called *free indirect discourse*, which combines the third and first persons in ways that often produce an ironic effect. After Emma has begun her affair with Rodolphe, for instance, the narrator reports her experience this way: "At last she was going to know the joys of love, the fever of the happiness she had despaired of. She was entering a marvelous realm where all would be passion, ecstasy, rapture." Emma's exultant anticipations of the future are given to us not as direct thoughts ("At last I am going to know the joys of love") but in the third person and the past tense ("At last she was going to know the joys of love"), which has the effect of subtly distancing her perspective and making her hopes feel dubious. We are both inside her head and ever so slightly outside. It takes great skill to accomplish this delicate joining of perspectives, and the text's pervasive feeling of irony emerges not from any explicit authorial intrusion but from its skillful control of narrative perspective.

Emma is not, in fact, a particularly sympathetic heroine, despite the fact that we see the world through her eyes, and readers often find themselves both fascinated and repelled by her. Flaubert suggests sympathy here and there for those she rejects and abuses: the slow-witted, abused, but honest and loving Charles, who opens and closes the book; Justin, the pharmacist's apprentice who adores Emma from afar; the clubfoot stable boy exploited for a dream of medical reputation; poor neglected Berthe sent to the cotton mill; and the old peasant woman at the fair who for fifty-four years of service receives a medal worth twenty-five francs. We are invited to wonder whether Emma's society really is as mediocre and dimwitted—as undeserving of passionate emotion—as she herself believes.

But part of the power of the novel is that Madame Bovary is to be pitied, too. She has, at least, a spark of discontent, the yearning to escape the cage of her existence. She is the unfulfilled dreamer, the foiled romantic, a female Don Quixote, corrupted by sentimental reading, caught in a trap of circumstance. The novel reinforces her sense of despair, of alienation in an incomprehensible universe, and also her hatred for all the stupidity, mediocrity, and baseness of people there and everywhere. But even dreariness can be rendered beautifully, at least in Flaubert's gorgeously controlled prose. In a rare address to the reader in *Madame Bovary*, the narrator suggests that we are all doomed to produce ugly words, but as if to contradict his own point, his prose here is dazzling: "human speech is like a cracked kettle on which we tap crude rhythms for bears to dance to, while we long to make music that will melt the stars." This memorable passage helps us grasp the astonishing paradox at the heart of *Madame Bovary*: that it is precisely the dullest, most commonplace existence that can yield the most sublimely perfect work of art.

Madame Bovary[1]

Part One

CHAPTER I

We were at our studies when the headmaster came in, followed by a *new boy* still dressed in his street clothes, and a student assistant who was carrying a large desk. Those who were sleeping woke up, and everyone stood up as if interrupted in their work.

The headmaster signaled us to be seated; then, turning to the teacher:

"Monsieur Roger," he said quietly, "here is a pupil I'm putting in your charge; he'll start at the fifth level. If his work and his conduct are good, he'll move into the *upper grades*, where he belongs at his age."

Keeping back in the corner behind the door, so well concealed we could hardly see him, the *new one* was a country boy, about fifteen, taller than any of us. His hair was cut in a straight line across his forehead, like a village choirboy; he looked both sensible and completely embarrassed. Although his shoulders weren't especially broad, his green cloth jacket with its black buttons was clearly too tight under the arms, and it revealed, between the slits of the cuffs, a pair of red wrists accustomed to going bare. His legs, with blue socks, stuck out from a pair of yellowish trousers pulled up high by suspenders. He wore big, hobnail shoes, badly polished.

We began our recitation. He listened, all ears, as attentively as if it were a sermon, not daring even to cross his legs or lean on an elbow, and when the clock struck two, the teacher had to tell him to get in line with us.

We had a custom, when entering the classroom, of tossing our caps on the floor in order to have our hands free; what you had to do was stand in the doorway and pitch them under the bench hard enough to make them hit the wall and raise as much dust as possible; this was *how it was done*.

But, whether he hadn't observed this maneuver or he hadn't dared to try it himself, our prayer was over and the *new boy* still kept his cap held firmly on his two knees. This cap was one of those composite headpieces, in which could be detected elements of a fur cap, a lancer cap, a bowler hat, an otter-skin cap, and a cotton nightcap—in short, one of those poor things whose ugliness, even though voiceless, somehow suggests hidden depths of expression, like the face of an imbecile. Egg-shaped, swollen with whalebone, its base began with three circular sausages; and then, separated by a red band, came alternating diamond-shaped patches of velour and rabbit fur; finally, there was a kind of sack which ended in a cardboard-stiffened polygon covered with complicated braiding, from which hung, at the end of a long, flimsy cord, a clump of golden threads like a tassel. It was quite new; the visor gleamed.

"Stand up," said the teacher.

He got up; his cap fell to the floor. The whole class burst into laughter.

He bent down to pick it up. The boy next to him poked it with his elbow, making it fall again. He bent down again to pick it up.

"All right, get rid of that helmet!" said the teacher, who was a man of wit.

---

1. Translated by Raymond N. MacKenzie.

The students burst out in a roar of laughter, which flustered the poor boy, so that he didn't know if he should hold the cap in his hands, leave it on the floor, or put it on his head. He sat back down and put it on his knees.

"Stand up," the teacher went on, "and tell me your name."

The *new boy* mumbled an unintelligible name.

"Again!"

The same mumbled syllables came out, this time drowned out by the shouts of the class.

"Louder!" exclaimed the teacher. "Louder!"

The *new boy*, summoning every ounce of his courage, now opened wide his unusually large mouth, and at the top of his lungs as if he were calling out to someone, hurled out this word: *Charbovari*.

Now an uproar broke out, a rising *crescendo* of shrieking voices—they shouted, they howled, they stamped, they repeated: *Charbovari! Charbovari!*—which eventually diminished into isolated notes, subsiding only with difficulty, and then suddenly starting up all over again along a bench where a stifled burst of laughter shot up here and there, like fireworks that hadn't quite gone out.

But as threats of extra work rained down, order was bit by bit re-established in the class, and the teacher, having succeeded in grasping the name Charles Bovary by dint of having had it dictated, spelled out, and read over to him, swiftly ordered the poor devil to go sit in the dunce's seat at the foot of the lectern. He began to move there, but before starting off, hesitated.

"What are you looking for?" asked the teacher.

"My ha . . . " said the *new boy*, looking around anxiously.

"Five hundred lines for the whole class!" came the furious voice which, like Neptune's *"Quos ego"*[2] immediately calmed a new storm. "Keep quiet!" the indignant teacher continued, wiping his forehead with a handkerchief he had pulled out from under his cap. "As for you, the new boy, you'll write out for me the verb *ridiculus sum*[3] twenty times."

Then, in a gentler voice:

"Come, you'll find it, your hat; no one's stolen it!"

Everyone calmed down. Heads bent down over notebooks, and the *new boy* behaved in exemplary fashion for two hours, despite having his face peppered from time to time by a wad of paper launched from a penholder. But he would wipe them off with his hand and remain immobile, keeping his eyes lowered.

That evening during the study period he pulled the cuff guards from his desk, put all his little belongings in order, and carefully ruled his paper. We saw him working conscientiously, looking up all the words in the dictionary and taking the greatest pains. Thanks, no doubt, to all the good will and effort he showed, he wasn't made to move down to the lower class; for, though he knew the rules fairly well, he had no elegance at all in his style. He had started Latin with the village priest, his parents having kept him out of school as long as possible in order to save money.

His father, Monsieur Charles-Denis-Bartholome Bovary, the ex-assistant to a surgeon-major, implicated in a conscription scandal around 1812 and then

2. An unfinished threat (Latin: "you whom I . . . ") delivered by the sea god Neptune to winds that had caused ocean storms without his permission (*Aeneid* 1.135).

3. I am a fool (Latin).

forced to quit the service, had gone on to profit from his looks by getting his hands on a sixty-thousand-franc dowry that a haberdasher provided for his daughter, who had fallen in love with his elegance. A handsome and vain man, walking so as to make his spurs jangle, his sideburns trimmed to meet with his moustache, his fingers garnished with rings, wearing loud colors, he seemed to combine the looks of a warrior with the smooth talk of a traveling salesman. Once married, he lived for two or three years on his wife's money, dining well and rising late, smoking his porcelain pipes, coming home at night only after the theater, and frequenting the cafés. The father-in-law died, leaving very little; he was indignant about it, *took a shot at textile manufacturing*, losing money at it, and then returned to the countryside, where he wanted *to make it pay off*. But because he knew no more about agriculture than he had about calico, because he rode his horses rather than putting them to work, drank his bottled cider rather than selling it, ate the best poultry from his farmyard and used his pigs' lard to grease his hunting boots, he soon enough perceived that he might as well pack the whole thing in.

For two hundred francs'[4] rent a year, therefore, he found, in a village on the borders of Caux and Picardy, a sort of half-farm, half-country house; and there, bitter and resentful, blaming fate and envious of everyone else's lot, he shut himself up at the age of forty-five, disgusted with humankind, as he said, and determined to live in peace.

His wife had been crazy about him in the past; she had shown her love with a thousand servile attentions, which served only to detach him further from her. Playful, generous, and full of love at one time, as she aged she turned (like an uncorked wine that turns to vinegar) difficult, fretful, anxious. She had suffered a great deal without complaining, at first, when she saw him chasing every skirt in the village, and when he had been brought home to her at night from twenty different dives in a stupor, reeking of drunkenness! Then her own pride rose in revolt. But she silenced herself, swallowing her rage in mute stoicism and holding it in until her death. She kept herself constantly busy with errands and business matters. She went to see lawyers or local officials, always remembering when the bills came due, obtaining extensions; and at home she ironed, sewed, laundered, watched over the hired hands, and settled their accounts while Monsieur, entirely untroubled and continually sunk in a sullen lethargy from which he roused himself only to make nasty remarks, sat smoking by the fireside and spitting into the cinders.

When she had a child, he had to be put out to a wet nurse. When he returned home, the little brat was as spoiled as a prince. His mother fed him candies; his father let him run about without shoes and, playing the philosopher, even said he ought to go naked, like the offspring of the animals. To counter his wife's maternal tendencies, he got into his head a certain masculine ideal of childhood according to which he tried to form his son, wanting to see him grow up austerely, in the Spartan way, so he would develop a strong constitution. He

---

4. It is very difficult to transpose monetary values from 1840 into present-day figures, since relationships between the actual value of the franc, the cost of living, and the relative cost of specific items (e.g., rent and real estate) have undergone fundamental changes. A rough calculation of inflation and exchange rates between the franc and the dollar in 1840 and 2013 gives approximately $51.

sent him off to sleep without a fire, taught him to drink rum in big gulps and to hurl insults at religious processions. But the boy, naturally peace-loving, responded poorly to his efforts. His mother hauled him around with her at all times; she cut out little paper figures for him, told him stories, talked to him in endless monologues full of melancholy humor and baby talk. Isolated within her own life, she projected all her thin, broken fantasies and dreams onto this child. She dreamed of high positions, she pictured him already great, handsome, spiritual, established as a builder of bridges and roads or as a magistrate. She taught him to read and even, with the aid of an old piano she owned, to sing two or three little ballads. But all that, said Monsieur Bovary, who cared nothing for education, was *not worth the trouble*. Would they ever have the money to send him to government schools, buy him a position, or get him set up in a business? Anyway, *with enough nerve, a man will always get ahead in the world*. Madame Bovary bit her lips, and the child ran about the village freely.

He would follow the farmhands around, and would chase the surrounding crows away by throwing clumps of dirt at them. He ate the blackberries that grew along the ditches, herded the turkeys with a long stick, pitched the hay during harvest, ran around in the woods, played hopscotch under the church porch on rainy days, and on feast days begged the beadle to let him ring the bells so he could let himself hang from the heavy rope and feel himself swung along as the bells sounded.

And so he grew like an oak. His hands grew strong, his complexion ruddy.

When he was twelve, his mother arranged for him to begin his studies. The task of teaching him was given to the priest. But the lessons were so short and so badly done that they could hardly amount to anything. They took place at the odd free moment, in the sacristy, standing up, in haste, between a baptism and a burial; or the priest would send for his pupil after the Angelus, when he didn't have to go anywhere. They would go up to his room, make themselves comfortable; gnats and moths would circle about the candle. It was warm, and the boy would start to doze; and the good man, folding his hands over his stomach, would soon begin to snore, his mouth open. Other times, when the priest was returning from bringing the sacrament to some sick person in the neighborhood, he would see Charles wandering through the fields and would call to him, sermonize to him for a quarter of an hour, and take advantage of the moment by having him conjugate a verb at the foot of a tree. They would be interrupted by rain, or by some acquaintance passing by. In general he was very pleased with him, even saying that the *young man* had a fine memory.

But this could not be the end of it. His mother was emphatic about it. Ashamed or, rather, worn down, his father gave in without resistance, and they waited one more year until the little scamp had made his First Communion.

Six more months passed; and the following year, Charles was at last sent off to school in Rouen, brought there personally by his father toward the end of October, around the time of the Saint-Romain fair.

Today, it would be impossible for any of us to remember anything about him. He was an even-tempered boy who played during recess, worked at his studies, listened in class, slept well in the dormitory, and ate well in the dining hall. His local guardian was a wholesale hardware dealer on the Rue Ganterie, who came to take him out once a month on a Sunday, after his shop was closed, sent him out to walk by the port to look at the boats, then returned him to the school by seven, in time for supper. Each Thursday night he wrote his mother a long letter in red ink, sealing it with three wafers; then he went back over his history notebooks, or perhaps read an old volume of *Anacharsis*[5] that had been left in the classroom. When he went for walks, he would chat with the servant, who was from the country like him.

By dint of applying himself, he managed to stay about in the middle of the class; once he even won a prize in natural history. But at the end of his third year, his parents took him out of the school to study medicine, convinced that he could obtain his diploma by studying on his own.

His mother found a room for him, on the fourth floor, near the Eau-de-Robec,[6] in the house of a dyer she knew. She made the arrangements for his rent, found furniture for him, a table and two chairs, had an old cherry wood bed of hers sent to him, and also brought a small cast-iron stove with enough wood to keep her poor child warm. Then she left at the end of the week, after exhorting him a thousand times to behave himself now that he was going to be left on his own.

The list of courses affixed to the bulletin board made him dizzy when he read it: anatomy course, pathology course, physiology course, pharmacology course, chemistry course, and botany, clinical, and therapeutic courses, not to mention hygiene and medications, all names whose etymologies he did not know, and which seemed like so many doors leading in to sanctuaries teeming with noble shadows.

He understood none of it; listen as hard as he would, he couldn't grasp it. But he worked, he got bound notebooks. He attended every class, never missing a single day. He accomplished his little daily tasks like a blinkered horse at a mill, going round and round without any idea of the point of his work.

To save him money, his mother sent him baked veal by messenger each week; he lunched on it every day when he returned from the hospital, kicking his feet against the wall in the cold. Then he had to race off to his lessons in the lecture hall, then to the hospital, and then return home, crisscrossing the town. In the evening, after his landlord's meager dinner, he went back up to his room and went back to work, his wet clothes smoking on him as he sat before the hot stove.

On fine summer evenings, at the hour when the warm streets are empty and the maids play shuttlecock on doorsteps, he would open his window and lean out on his elbows. The river, which turns this part of Rouen into a sort of miserable little Venice, flowed below him, yellow, violet, or blue beneath its bridges and railings. Workingmen, squatting on the banks, washed their arms in the water. Hanks of cotton dried in the air, hanging from poles that projected from the lofts above. Opposite him, over the rooftops, the great, pure sky extended, the red sun setting. How good it would be to be back there! How fine the scents under the beeches! And he opened his nostrils wide, trying to inhale the good scent of the countryside, which did not reach him.

---

5. *Voyage du jeune Anacharsis en Grèce* (The voyage of young Anacharsis in Greece; 1788) was a popular account of ancient Greece as seen by a barbarian, by Jean-Jacques Barthélemy (1716–1795).

6. Small river, now covered up, that flows through the poorest neighborhood of Rouen, used as a sewer by the factories that border it, thus suggesting Flaubert's description as "*une ignoble petite Venise*" (squalid little Venice).

He thinned out, he grew taller, and his face took on a saddened expression that made him look almost interesting.

Inevitably, out of indifference, he came to forget all the resolutions he had made to himself. One day, he missed his hospital visit, the next day his lecture, and, savoring his idleness, he slowly stopped going back at all.

He took up the café habit, along with a passion for dominoes, Shutting himself up in a dirty public room and clicking little sheep bones with black dots on the marble tables seemed to him to be a significant act of freedom, something that heightened his sense of self-esteem. It was like an initiation into the world, an entry into forbidden pleasures; and when he entered, he would squeeze the doorknob with an almost sensual pleasure. Now, so many things that had been suppressed inside him began to expand; he learned by heart little songs that he would sing to women who came in, grew enthusiastic about Béranger,[7] learned how to make punch, and finally came to find out about lovemaking.

Thanks to this kind of preparatory study, he failed his examination for health officer[8] completely. They were waiting at home for him that very evening to celebrate his success!

He left on foot and stopped just outside the village, where he sent for his mother and told her everything. She made excuses for him, blaming his failure on the unfairness of the examiners, and, giving him a little encouragement, took it upon herself to arrange things. Monsieur Bovary only learned about it five years later; by then it was old news and he could accept it, incapable of believing that a son of his could be a fool.

So Charles went back to work and prepared nonstop for the examination, memorizing all the questions in advance. He passed with a respectable grade. What a great day for his mother! They gave him a fine dinner in celebration.

Where would he go to practice his art? To Tostes. There was only one old doctor there. Madame Bovary had been watching and waiting for news of his death for a long time, and the good old man had scarcely packed it in when Charles was installed across the street as his successor.

But it was not enough to have raised her son, to have had him learn medicine and to have discovered Tostes as the place he would practice: he needed a wife. She found him one: the widow of a Dieppe bailiff, who was forty-five, with an income of 1,200 livres.

Although she was ugly, as dried out as an old stick, and as pimpled as a budding springtime, Madame Dubuc nevertheless did not lack for suitors. To achieve her ends, Mother Bovary was obliged to oust them all, and she played her hand so well that she outmaneuvered a pork butcher who had had the support of the priests.

7. Pierre-Jean de Béranger (1780–1857), an extremely popular writer of songs that often exalt the glories of the empire of Napoleon I.
8. Health officer (French). Instituted during the French Revolution, a kind of second-class medical degree, well below the doctorate. The student was allowed to attend a medical school without having passed the equivalent of the *baccalauréat*, and could practice only in the administrative region in which the diploma had been conferred (Bovary is thus tied down to the vicinity of Rouen) and was not allowed to perform major operations, except in the presence of a full-fledged doctor. This diploma was suppressed in 1892.

Charles had expected that marriage would mean a better kind of life, imagining that he would be more free, that he would be in charge of both himself and his money. But his wife was the master: in company, he had to say this and not say that, to fast every Friday, to dress the way she wanted, to harass, on her orders, clients who had not paid up. She opened his letters, spied on his comings and goings, and listened through the partition when there were women in his consulting room.

She insisted on her chocolate every morning and made endless demands on him. She complained incessantly about her nerves, her chest, her moods. His footsteps annoyed her; he would go out; solitude became horrible for her; when he returned, she would complain that he had only come back to watch her die. In the evenings when Charles came home, she would extend her long skinny arms from beneath the covers, put them around his neck and, having made him sit down on the edge of the bed, would start to tell him about all her sufferings: he had forgotten her, he was in love with someone else! People had always predicted that she would end up unhappy, and they were right; and she concluded by asking him to give her some medicinal syrup for her health, and also a little more love.

CHAPTER 2

One night around eleven o'clock they were awakened by the sound of a horse stopping right outside their door. The maid opened her attic window and spoke for some time with the man down below, in the street. He had come to find the doctor; he had a letter. Nastasie came down the steps shivering, and went to draw all the bolts, one after the other. The man left his horse, and following the maid, came in right behind her. He pulled a letter, wrapped in a scrap of cloth, from his gray, tasseled wool cap; he handed it gingerly to Charles, who propped his elbow up on the pillow to read it. Nastasie, standing close to the bed, held the lamp. Madame, out of modesty, remained turned away, with her back toward them.

The letter, sealed with a little blue wax, entreated Monsieur Bovary to come at once to the farm of Les Bertaux to set a broken leg. Now, from Tostes to Les Bertaux is a good six leagues, past Longueville and Saint-Victor. The night was black. The wife was afraid of her husband having an accident. So it was decided that the stable boy would go on ahead. Charles would set out in three hours when the moon had come up. They would send a boy to meet him, show him the way to the farm, and open the fence gates for him.

About four in the morning, Charles, snugly wrapped up in his cloak, set out for Les Bertaux. Still drowsy with the warmth of sleep, he let himself be rocked by the peaceful gait of his horse. When the horse came to a stop on her own in front of the hollows, planted with thorns, that were dug at the ends of the furrows, Charles, abruptly starting awake, quickly remembered the broken leg, and he racked his memory trying to picture all the fractures he had learned. The rain had stopped falling; day began to break and, on the bare branches of apple trees, birds sat motionless, ruffling their little feathers in the cold wind of the morning.

The flat countryside spread out as far as the eye could see, and the clusters of trees around the farms formed, at distant intervals, little blurred patches of purplish black against the great gray surface that faded, at the horizon, into the bleak tone of the sky. Charles from time to time would open his eyes; then, his mind tiring and sleep returning upon him, he soon drifted into a kind of stupor in which recent events mixed with older memories, in which he seemed to be doubled, both student and husband, lying in his bed as he recently had been, passing through an operating room as he had in the past. The warm scent of poultices blended in his mind with the fresh scent of dew; he heard the tinkling of the curtain rings on the hospital beds and his wife sleeping . . . As he passed Vassonville, he saw a boy sitting on the grass beside a ditch.

"Are you the doctor?" the child asked.

And, upon Charles' reply, he took his wooden shoes in his hands and began to run ahead of him.

The health officer, as he rode on, gathered from his guide that Monsieur Rouault must be one of the more prosperous farmers. He had broken his leg the previous evening returning from a *faire les Rois* party at a neighbor's. His wife had been dead for two years. He had only his *young lady* living with him, helping him manage the house.

The ruts were becoming deeper. They were nearing Les Bertaux. The little boy, slipping through a hole in the hedges, disappeared, then reappeared at the edge of a courtyard to open the gate. The horse lost its footing and slipped on the wet grass; Charles had to bend down to pass below the branches. The guard dogs in their kennel howled and pulled at their chains. When they entered into Les Bertaux, his horse took fright and shied away powerfully.

It was a good-looking farm. He could see, through the open doors of the stables, huge workhorses eating leisurely from their new mangers. Alongside the buildings extended a large, steaming dunghill, where among the hens and the turkeys, five or six peacocks—considered luxuries in the Caux farmyards[9]— were pecking for food. The sheepfold was long, the barn high, with walls as smooth as a hand. Within the shed were two large carts and four plows with their whips, their collars, and their harnesses whose blue woolen fleeces were growing soiled from the fine dust that came down from the haylofts. The yard sloped upward, planted with symmetrically spaced trees, and the cheerful sounds of a flock of geese came up from the pond.

A young woman, in a blue wool dress adorned with three flounces, came to the doorway to welcome Monsieur Bovary and to show him into the kitchen, where a large fire was blazing. The farmhands' meal was simmering around it, in small pots of different sizes. Some damp clothes were drying inside the chimney. The scoop, the tongs, and the bellows' nozzle, all of huge proportions, gleamed like polished steel, while all along the walls hung an abundant supply of kitchen utensils, reflecting the fire's bright flames in different degrees, mingled with the first rays of the sun coming in through the curtains.

Charles went up to the second floor to see the injured man. He found him in his bed, sweating beneath the blankets and having thrown aside his cotton nightcap. He was a fat, small man of fifty with white skin and blue eyes, bald on the front part of his head, and wearing earrings. He had next to him, on a chain, a big bottle of brandy from which he would occasionally pour himself a glass to give himself courage; but the minute he saw the doctor, his feverish

---

9. From the Caux area, a large chalky plateau region in Normandy (northern France).

intoxication failed him, and instead of cursing—as he had been for the last twelve hours—he began to moan feebly.

The fracture was a simple one with no complications at all. Charles wouldn't have dared to wish for anything easier. Then, recalling the bedside manners of his teachers, he comforted the patient with all sorts of soothing words, those medical caresses that are like the oil used to grease scalpels. Then, for splints, a bundle of laths was fetched from the shed. Charles chose one, cut it into pieces, and smoothed it with a piece of broken window glass while the servant tore sheets to make a bandage and Mademoiselle Emma set herself to sewing some pads. When she took too long to find her sewing kit, her father became impatient; she said nothing; but, as she sewed, she would prick her fingers, and then put them in her mouth to suck them.

Charles was amazed at how white her fingernails were. They were gleaming, finely tapered, as polished as Dieppe ivory, and almond-shaped. Yet her hands were not beautiful, certainly not white enough, and a bit dry at the knuckles; and they were too long, with no softness in their contours. What was beautiful about her was her eyes; though they were brown, her eyelashes made them seem black, and she would gaze directly at you with a frank boldness.

The bandages in place, Monsieur Rouault himself invited the doctor to *have a bite* before leaving.

Charles came down to the dining room on the ground floor. Two place settings, with silver tumblers, had been laid at a small table, at the foot of a large bed whose canopy was decorated with figures representing Turks. The odor of iris and of damp sheets escaped from the high oak armoire that faced the window. On the floor, in the corner, stood upright sacks of wheat. This was the overflow from the granary attached to the house, to which one ascended by three stone steps. For decoration, the room featured a charcoal portrait of Minerva, hanging from a nail in the middle of the wall whose green paint was flaking off from the effects of saltpeter; the portrait, in a gilt frame, had written on it, in Gothic lettering, "To my dear Papa."

At first they talked about the patient, then the state of the weather, the cold spells, the wolves that ran in the fields at night. Mademoiselle Rouault didn't much like the country, especially now when she was essentially in sole charge of the farm. Because the room was cold, she shivered as she ate, making her full lips part a little; she had a habit of biting them in moments of silence.

Her neck rose above a white, turned-down collar. Her hair was parted into two black halves so smooth that they each seemed a single piece, the two segments separated by a slender part that followed the curve of her head; and, just barely revealing the tip of her ear, the two bands joined together in the back in a thick chignon, with little waves at the temples, which the country doctor now noticed for the first time in his life. Her cheeks were pink. She wore, as a man would, a pair of tortoise-shell glasses tucked between the buttons of her bodice.

When Charles, after having gone up to say good-bye to the father, came back to the dining room before leaving, he found her standing with her forehead against the window and gazing into the garden where the wind had blown down the bean-props. She turned to him.

"Are you looking for something?" she asked.

"My whip, please," he replied.

He began to rummage on the bed, behind the doors, under the chairs; it had fallen on the floor, between the wheat sacks and the wall. Mademoiselle Emma spotted it; she bent over the sacks. Out of gallantry, Charles rushed to help, and as he extended his own arm to reach for it, he felt his chest brush against the young woman's back, bent beneath him. She stood up blushing and looked at him over her shoulder as she passed him the riding crop.

Instead of returning to Les Bertaux three days later as he had promised, he came back the very next day, then regularly twice a week, not to mention the unexpected visits he made from time to time, as if by chance.

And everything was going well; the patient had healed according to the rules and when, after a month and a half, people saw the father out trying to walk around his farmyard unaided, they began to think of Monsieur Bovary as a man with great abilities. Rouault said he wouldn't have had any better treatment from the best doctors in Yvetot or even Rouen.

As for Charles, he never tried to ask himself why it was that he so enjoyed coming to Les Bertaux. If he had, he would no doubt have attributed his zeal to the seriousness of the case, or perhaps to the profit he hoped for from it. But was that the reason that his visits to the farm made such a delightful exception to the boring routines of his life? On those days he would rise early, set off at a gallop, urge his horse on, and then he would get down to wipe his boots on the grass and put on his black gloves before going in. He liked finding himself coming into the courtyard, feeling the gate opening against his shoulder, the rooster crowing on the wall, the farmhands coming to meet him. He liked the barn and the stables; he liked old man Rouault, who patted his hand and called him his savior; he liked the sound of Mademoiselle Emma's clogs on the scoured kitchen tiles; her heels made her a little taller, and when she walked ahead of him the wooden soles, lifting a bit, clacked with a dry sound against the leather of the ankle boot.

She would always accompany him to the first step of the porch. If his horse was not ready, she would wait there. They had already said good-bye, and now they spoke no more; the fresh air swept around her, lifting up little wisps of hair on the back of her neck, or shaking the apron strings from her hips so that they blew out like streamers. One time, during a thaw, when the bark on the trees was oozing and the snow on the buildings' roofs was melting, she stood on the threshold; then she went to fetch her umbrella, and she opened it. The umbrella was silk, the color of a pigeon's breast; when the sun passed through it, it lit up the white skin of her face with flickering glints of light. Beneath it, she smiled at the warm weather; you could hear drops of water, one by one, falling on the taut silk.

During those early times when Charles frequented Les Bertaux, Madame Bovary did not fail to inform herself about the patient and, in her double-columned account book, she had even set aside a fine white page for Monsieur Rouault. But when she learned that he had a daughter, she made inquiries; and she learned that Mademoiselle Rouault had been a student at the Ursuline convent and had received what is called *a fine education*, which meant that she had learned dancing, geography, drawing, embroidery, and how to play the piano. This was the limit!

So that's why, she said to herself, he lights up like that when he goes to see her, and why he wears his new waistcoat, even at the risk of getting it soaked in the rain? Oh, that woman! That woman! . . .

And she detested her instinctively. At first, she unburdened herself by making allusions. Charles didn't understand them; then she escalated to casual comments, which he ignored for fear of a storm; finally, she let loose with pointblank accusations, which he did not know how to answer. Why was it that he kept going back to Les Bertaux, since Monsieur Rouault was healed and since those people still hadn't paid up? Ah, it was because there was *a certain person* there, someone who knew how to make conversation, how to embroider, a clever person! So that was what he liked: he had to have city girls! And she went on:

"Old Rouault's daughter, a city girl! Come on now! Their grandfather was a shepherd, and they have a cousin who barely escaped being brought up on charges for some criminal act he committed during a quarrel. What's the point of making such a big display, or showing up on Sunday at church wearing a silk dress like a countess? And anyway, the man is so poor he couldn't have paid his bills without last year's rapeseed crop!"

Worn down, Charles ceased returning to Les Bertaux. Héloïse had made him swear, his hand on his Sunday missal, that he wouldn't go back, after countless sighs and tears that ended in a great explosion of love. So he obeyed; but the power of his desire fought against the servility of his behavior, and out of a sort of naïve hypocrisy, he reasoned that this prohibition against seeing her gave him the right to love her. And then, the widow was skinny; her teeth were long; she wore, no matter what the season, a little black shawl that trailed down between her shoulder blades; her bony body was sheathed in too-short dresses that fit her like a scabbard, revealing her ankles and the ribbons of her big shoes crisscrossing her gray stockings.

Charles' mother came to visit them from time to time, but after a few days the daughter-in-law seemed to whet and hone the mother's natural sharpness; and then, like a pair of knives, they would set to lacerate him with their comments and observations. He was wrong to eat so much! Why always offer a drink to anyone who stopped by? How pig-headed of him not to wear flannel!

Toward the beginning of spring, it happened that a notary in Ingouville, in charge of the widow Dubuc's funds, sailed off one fine day with all the money in his custody. True, Héloïse retained a share in a boat worth about six thousand francs, as well as her house on the Rue Saint François; but yet, out of all that fortune that had been boasted for so long, nothing had ever turned up in their household beyond a few pieces of furniture and some old clothes. It was time to get things clarified. The Dieppe house turned out to be worm-eaten with mortgages right down to the foundations; as to what she had deposited with her notary, God only knew, and the share in the boat was worth a thousand écus[1] at most. So, the upstanding lady had lied! Charles' father, in exasperation, broke a chair against the flagstones, accusing his wife of having brought about their son's ruin by getting him hitched up with an old nag whose harness wasn't worth its skin. They came to Tostes. Explanations were made. There were scenes. Héloïse, in tears, threw herself into her husband's arms, begging him to defend her against his parents. Charles tried to take her part. The parents got angry and left.

---

1. The *écu* was an obsolete coin, but the term continued to be used in the nineteenth century for five-franc pieces.

But *the die was cast*. One week later, as she was hanging out the laundry in the yard, she abruptly spat up blood, and the next day, while Charles had his back turned to pull the curtain across the window, she said, "Oh! My God!," let out a sigh, and fell unconscious. She was dead! What a surprise!

When everything at the cemetery was finished, Charles returned home. There was no one on the first floor; he went upstairs to the bedroom, saw her dress still hanging in the alcove; then, leaning against the desk, he remained all evening lost in a sorrowful reverie. She had loved him, after all.

CHAPTER 3

One morning, old Rouault came to bring Charles the payment for setting his leg: seventy-five francs in forty-sou pieces,[2] and a turkey. He had heard of Charles' misfortune, and he consoled him as best he could.

"I know what it's like!" he said, clapping him on the shoulder; "I've been in your shoes, me too! After I lost my poor wife, I would go out into the fields to be by myself; I would fall at the foot of a tree, I would weep, I would call on the good Lord, I would tell him foolish things. I wanted to be like the moles I saw up in the branches, with worms crawling around in their stomachs, I mean, dead. And when I would think how other men, at that very moment, were together with their fine little wives, holding them tightly up against themselves, I would beat my walking stick against the ground in fury; I was practically mad, I stopped eating; the idea of going to the café by myself was sickening, you wouldn't believe it. But then, quietly, one day passed and another began, a spring after a winter and an autumn after a summer, and all that flowed away, little by little, crumb by crumb; all that's gone, it's all disappeared, or I mean it's gone down inside, because something always remains deep inside you, so to speak . . . a weight, here, on the chest! But since we all have the same fate, a person shouldn't let himself waste away, and want to die just because others have died . . . You have to shake it off, Monsieur Bovary; it'll pass! Come see us; my daughter thinks about you now and then, you must know that, and she says that you're forgetting her. Look, spring is almost here; we'll get you out and have you shoot a rabbit in our field, to cheer you up a little."

Charles took his advice. He returned to Les Bertaux. He found everything was just as it had been yesterday, or that is, as it had been five months ago. The pear trees were already in flower, and good old Rouault, fully back on his feet now, was always on the go, making the farm seem even livelier.

Feeling it was his duty to lavish as much kindness on the doctor as possible, because of his sorrowful situation, he begged him not to remove his hat, spoke to him in a low voice as if he had been sick, and even made a show of being angry if the food prepared for him was not lighter than the rest, such as little pots of cream or stewed pears. He told stories. Charles was surprised to find himself laughing; but the memory of his wife, coming over him suddenly, sobered him again. Coffee was served; he thought no more about her.

He thought about her less as he grew used to living alone. The pleasure of independence very soon made solitude more endurable. He could change his meal times, come in or leave with no explanations and, when he was tired,

---

2. The *sou*, a coin created during the Revolution, was worth 5 centimes, 1/20th of a franc.

stretch out completely across his bed. And thus he pampered himself, indulged himself, and accepted the consolations people offered him. Moreover, the death of his wife had by no means hurt his practice, as people kept repeating for a month, "The poor young man! What a tragedy!" His reputation spread, and his clientele grew; and then he could go to Les Bertaux whenever he felt like it. He felt a hope without any particular object, a vague happiness; he thought his face looked more pleasing, as he brushed his side-burns before his mirror.

One day he arrived about three o'clock; everyone was out in the fields; he went in the kitchen, but at first failed to see Emma; the shutters were closed. Through the wooden slats, the sun's long thin rays stretched down to the tiles, broke across the corners of the furniture, and trembled on the ceiling. Some flies on the table crawled up the length of glasses that had been left out, buzzing as they drowned in the leftover cider at the bottom. The light coming in from the chimney turned the soot in the back of the fireplace velvety and gave a slightly blue tint to the cold ashes. Between the window and the hearth, Emma was sewing; she had no shawl on, and he could see tiny drops of sweat on her bare shoulders.

Following the country custom, she offered him something to drink. He refused, she insisted, and finally she suggested with a laugh that he take a glass of liqueur with her. Then she went to find a bottle of curaçao in the cupboard, reached for two small glasses, filled one to the brim, poured scarcely any in the other and, after clinking glasses with him, raised it to her mouth. Because it was nearly empty, she had to lean back in order to drink, and, with her head tilted back, her lips pouted, her neck extended, she laughed at getting nothing, while the tip of her tongue, passing between her small teeth, licked the bottom of the glass in short thrusts.

She sat back down and picked up her work again, which was a white cotton stocking she was darning: she worked with her head lowered; she didn't talk anymore. Nor did Charles. The breeze, passing below the door, blew a little dust along the tiles; he watched it blow along, and he heard only the pounding within his head and the distant cry of a hen laying an egg in the barnyard. From time to time Emma would cool her cheeks by pressing the palms of her hands against them, and she would cool the palms in turn against the iron knobs of the andirons.

She complained of feeling some dizziness with the onset of the new season; she asked if ocean bathing would be helpful; she began to chat about her convent, Charles about his school; words came easily. They went upstairs to her room. She showed him her her old music notebooks, the little books she had been given as prizes, and some oak-leaf wreaths that had been abandoned in the armoire. And she spoke about her mother, about the cemetery, and even showed him the flower bed in the garden from which she gathered flowers, the first Friday of every month, to take to her grave. But their gardener didn't understand anything; they had such poor servants. She would have liked very much to live in town, if only during the winter, although the long summer days might make the country even more boring then. Her voice changed according to her topic; it would be clear and sharp or, suddenly turning languorous, would trail off into modulations that were almost murmurs when she spoke about herself—sometimes she was joyous, with naïve, wide eyes, and then, with eyelids half closed, her gaze steeped in boredom, her thoughts would wander.

Returning home that night, Charles went over everything she had said, trying to remember, to interpret her meanings, to imagine the life she had lived before he knew her. But he never could visualize her any way other than the way she was when he first saw her, or as she was when he had just left her. Then he asked himself what she would be like if she were to get married, and to whom? Alas, old Rouault was very rich, and she was . . . so beautiful! But Emma's face rose continually before his eyes, and a monotonous sound like the humming of a top buzzed in his ears: "But what if you were to marry! If you were to marry!" That night, he couldn't sleep, his throat was tight, he was thirsty; he got up to drink from his water jug and he opened the window; the sky was covered with stars, a warm wind was blowing; far away, some dogs were barking. He turned his head toward Les Bertaux.

Thinking that, after all, he was risking nothing, Charles resolved to ask the question when the occasion presented itself; but every time it did, the fear of not finding the right words kept his lips shut tight.

Old Rouault would not have minded seeing someone take his daughter off his hands; she was of little use to him in the house. Inwardly, he excused her, feeling she was too intelligent for farming, that occupation cursed by heaven, because it never made anybody a millionaire. Far from having made his fortune in it, the old fellow actually lost money every year: for while he excelled at the market, where the wiliness that was needed suited him, the actual farming, on the other hand, along with the running of the household, agreed with him not at all. He kept his hands stuffed tightly in his pockets, but he spared no expense when it came to his own comforts, desiring to be well fed, to be warm enough, and to have a comfortable bed. He liked his cider strong, his mutton rare, and his *glorias*[3] carefully prepared. He liked his meals in the kitchen, alone, facing the fire, on a little table that was brought to him already set, as at a theater.

When he perceived that Charles was blushing around his daughter, which meant that one of these days he would ask for her in marriage, he carefully thought the whole thing out in advance. He found Charles a bit of a runt, and not the kind of man he would have wished for; but people said he conducted himself well, was thrifty, well educated, and there was no doubt he wouldn't dicker much over the dowry. Now, because Old Rouault was going to be forced to sell twenty-two acres of *his place*, because he owed a lot to the mason, and a lot to the saddler, because the winepress needed repair:

"If he asks me for her," he said to himself, "I'll give her to him."

At the feast of Saint Michael in September, Charles came to spend three days at Les Bertaux. The third day passed just like the preceding ones, with him putting the matter off from one quarter of an hour to the next. Old Rouault was seeing him off; they were walking down a rutted path, about to say good-bye; it was the moment. Charles gave himself until they reached the corner of the hedgerow, and finally, when they had passed it:

"Monsieur Rouault," he muttered, "I'd like to tell you something."

They stopped. Charles froze.

3. A *gloria* is a warm drink made from mixing coffee with sugar and either brandy or rum.

"But tell me what you have to say! As if I didn't already know it!" said old Rouault, with a gentle laugh.

"Father Rouault . . . father Rouault," Charles stammered.

"As for me, I couldn't ask for anything better," the farmer continued. "And the little one certainly feels the way I do, but still we have to ask her. You go on; I'll go back to the house. If it's yes, now follow me here, you won't have to come back, because people will see, and anyway she'll be too stirred up. But so you won't have to eat your heart out with worry, I'll push open the window shutter wide against the wall; you'll be able to see it from the back, if you lean over the hedge."

And he walked off.

Charles tied his horse to a tree. He ran to take up his place on the path; he waited. A half hour passed, and then he counted nineteen more minutes with his watch. Suddenly there was a noise against the wall; the shutter was opened; its hook was still rattling.

The next day at nine o'clock, he was at the farm. Emma blushed when he came in, but forced a little laughter to keep her composure. The father embraced his future son-in-law. They put off talking about the arrangements; in any case, they had plenty of time, since the wedding could not decently take place before the end of Charles' mourning period, that is, around the spring of the following year.

The winter passed in waiting. Mademoiselle Rouault busied herself with her trousseau. Part of it was ordered from Rouen, and she made chemises and nightcaps herself from fashion designs she borrowed. During Charles' visits to the farm, they would talk over the preparations for the wedding, consider what room would be best for the dinner, and think over the number of dishes needed and what entrees they would have.

Emma herself had other ideas: she wanted to get married at midnight with torchlight; but her father couldn't understand such a notion. And so there was a wedding, one to which forty-three people came, and at which they sat at the table for sixteen hours, the whole process beginning again the next day and to a lesser extent on the days following.

CHAPTER 4

The guests arrived early in their vehicles—one-horse carts, two-wheeled wagons, old open cabriolets,[4] vans with leather curtains—and the young people from the nearby villages came in wagons, standing upright in rows, hanging on to the railings to keep from falling off, moving along at a trot and thoroughly jolted about. People came from ten leagues off, from Goderville, from Normanville, and from Cany. Relatives of both families had been invited; they had reconciled with estranged friends; they had written to acquaintances long forgotten.

From time to time the crack of whips could be heard from behind the hedge; soon the gate opened; it was a cart coming in. Galloping up to the porch's first step, it stopped short and emptied its group, who got out from all sides, rubbing knees and stretching arms. The women, bonneted, wore dresses in city

4. A light, one-horse carriage that seats two people.

fashions, gold watch chains, capes with their ends tucked into their belts, or little colored scarves pinned behind, revealing the backs of their necks. The boys, dressed just like their papas, looked uncomfortable in their new suits (many of them were even breaking in, that very day, the first pair of boots in their lives), and near them could be seen some big girl of fourteen or sixteen, not breathing a word and wearing a white First-Communion dress lengthened for the occasion, a cousin or an older sister no doubt, ruddy, stunned-looking, hair greased with rose-pomade, greatly fearful of soiling her gloves. Since there weren't enough stable boys to unharness all the vehicles, the gentlemen rolled up their sleeves and took care of it themselves. In accordance with their varying social positions, they wore suits, frock coats, hunting jackets, or waistcoats— good suits, painstakingly cared for by a family, only allowed to leave the armoire for important occasions; frock coats with long tails afloat in the wind, with cylindrical collars and pockets big as sacks; jackets of coarse cloth, usually accompanied by caps with copper-rimmed visors; short waistcoats with two small buttons on the back close together like a pair of eyes, and tails that looked as if they had been cut from a single block by a carpenter's axe. And some others (but these, to be sure, would be seated at the lower end of the table) wore their better smocks, that is, with the collar turned down over the shoulder, the back gathered in little pleats, and the waistline very low and marked by a sewn-on belt.

And the shirts over the chests swelled like breastplates! Everyone's hair was freshly cut, ears sticking out of heads, everyone closely shaved; and some who had arisen before dawn, unable to see well enough for shaving, had diagonal gashes under their noses or, along the length of their jaws, scrapes the size of three-franc pieces, which had been inflamed by the fresh air on the way there, pink patches giving a marbled effect to all the fat, white, shining faces.

The mayor's office being about half a league from the farm, they went there on foot; and they returned the same way after the church service. The procession, united at first like a single, long, colored scarf undulating over the countryside, all along the narrow path winding between green wheat fields, soon stretched out and broke up into different groups, some of which stopped to chat. The village fiddler led the way, his violin decorated with ribbons on its shell; the newly-weds followed, then the relatives, the friends in no particular order, and the children stayed in the rear, amusing themselves by pulling out the ears of young oat shoots, or playing among themselves out of the adults' sight. Emma's dress, too long, dragged a little at the bottom; now and then she stopped to lift it, and then, delicately, with her gloved fingers she would pluck off the coarse grass and little burrs of thistle while Charles, his hands empty, would wait until she was done. Her father, a new silk hat on his head and the cuffs of his black suit covering his hands down to the fingernails, gave his arm to Charles' mother. As for Charles' father who, contemptuous of all these people, had come dressed simply in a frock coat of military cut with a single row of buttons, he was reeling off roadhouse gallantries to a young blond peasant. She curtsied and blushed, not knowing how to respond. The other wedding guests chatted about business or played practical jokes on each other, working themselves up in advance for the party; and, if they listened carefully, they could still hear the screeching of the village fiddler who continued to play through the countryside. When he realized they were all far behind him, he stopped to catch his breath, waxed his bow carefully with resin so the strings would produce a louder squeak, and then he set himself to walking on, raising and lowering the violin's neck to keep time for himself. The instrument's noise frightened off little birds from far away.

The table was set in the cart shed. On it were four sirloins, six chicken fricassees, stewed veal, three legs of lamb, and, in the middle, a fine roast suckling pig, flanked by four sorrel sausages. At the corners stood decanters of brandy. The bottles of sweet cider frothed around their corks, and all the glasses were already filled to the brim with wine. Big plates of yellow custard shuddered at the slightest bump of the table; they had the initials of the newlyweds traced on their smooth surfaces in arabesques of sugared almonds. They had had to go to Yvetot to find a baker for the pies and sweets. Because he was new to the area, he took extra care with things; and he personally delivered, for dessert, a layer cake that elicited cheers. At its base, first, it was a blue cardboard square that represented a temple, with porticoes, colonnades, and little stucco statuettes all around, with constellations of gilt paper stars in the niches; then, on the second stage, there was a dungeon made of Savoy cake entirely surrounded by tiny fortifications of angelica, almonds, raisins, and slices of oranges; and finally, on the topmost platform, which was a green meadow with rocks and lakes of jam and boats made of hazelnut shells, appeared a little Cupid balancing himself on a chocolate swing, whose two posts ended in two real rosebuds for knobs at their tops.

Until night fell, they ate. When they grew tired of sitting, they went for walks in the yard or played a game of *bouchon*[5] in the barn, and then returned to the table. Toward the end, some fell asleep and snored. But when the coffee was served, everything came back to life; then they began singing, did feats of strength, lifted heavy weights, played finger games, tried lifting carts on their shoulders, told bawdy jokes, kissed the women. At night when they left, the horses, stuffed to the nostrils with oats, could barely fit into the shafts; they kicked, they reared, their harnesses broke, their masters cursed or laughed; and all night long, by the light of the moon on the country roads, there were runaway carts hurtling along at a gallop, plunging into holes, leaping over the milestones, climbing up embankments, with women leaning out trying to catch hold of the reins.

Those who stayed at Les Bertaux spent the night drinking in the kitchen. The children had fallen asleep under the benches.

The bride had begged her father to be spared the customary wedding-night jokes. But among their cousins was a fishmonger (who had actually brought, as a wedding present, a pair of soles) who was about to spit water from his mouth through the keyhole when Monsieur Rouault came just in time to stop him, explaining that the distinguished position of his son-in-law would not admit of such improprieties. The cousin, all the same, did not readily give in to this reasoning. In his heart he accused the father of being stuck up, and he went off to join four of five other guests in a corner who, by chance, had been served the poorest cuts of meat several times, who also believed they had been ill-used, and who sat muttering about their host and hinting at their hopes for his ruin.

5. Game that involves knocking down a board on which pieces of money are balanced.

Madame Bovary senior had not opened her mouth all day. No one had consulted her either about her daughter-in-law's dress or about the arrangements for the feast; she went to bed early. Her husband, instead of following her, sent to Saint-Victor for cigars and stayed up smoking until daybreak, all the while drinking a punch made with kirsch, a mixture unknown to the others, which raised him even higher in their estimation.

Charles was decidedly not a joker, and he did not shine at the wedding. He responded rather weakly to the witty remarks, puns, double-entendres, compliments, and ribaldries that everyone felt obligated to hurl at him as early as the soup course.

The next day, on the other hand, he seemed to be a new man. He was the one who might have been taken for a virgin the night before, whereas the bride let nothing show from which anything could be inferred. Even the cleverest did not know what to think, and they watched her pass near them in utter perplexity. But Charles concealed nothing. He called her his wife, used the familiar *tu*[6] with her, asked everyone where she was, looked everywhere for her, and often pulled her out into the yard with him, where he could be seen from a distance among the trees, putting his arm around her and walking along half-bent over her, rumpling the front of her bodice with his head.

Two days after the wedding, the new couple left: Charles could not stay away any longer because of his patients. Emma's father sent them off in his cart and went with them as far as Vassonville. There, he kissed his daughter one last time, got down off the cart and started on his way back home. When he had gone about a hundred paces he stopped, and as he watched the cart moving away, its wheels turning up the dust, he heaved a great sigh. Then he remembered his own wedding, his own younger days, his wife's first pregnancy; he had been joyful then, he too, on the day he carried her off from her father's house, her behind him on the horse, trotting through the snow for it was near Christmas, and the countryside had been all white; she held onto him with one arm, and her basket with the other; the wind blew the long lace of her Cauchois bonnet, so that it drifted sometimes across his mouth, and when he turned his head he saw close to him, on his shoulder her little pink face silently smiling under her bonnet's gold ornament. To warm her fingers, she put them from time to time next to his chest. How long ago all that was! Their son, today, would be thirty.

Then he looked behind him and saw nothing on the road. He felt sad, like an emptied house; and these tender memories mixing with the dark thoughts in his brain, which was befogged by the vapors of the feast, he felt strongly inclined for a moment to take a detour toward the church. But because he feared that seeing it would make him even sadder, he went straight home.

Monsieur and Madame Charles arrived at Tostes about six o'clock. The neighbors stationed themselves at the windows to get a sight of their doctor's new wife.

The old servant introduced herself, made her greetings to Emma, apologized for not having dinner ready, and suggested that Madame, while she waited, get acquainted with her house.

---

6. The intimate form of "you" (French). *Ma femme:* my wife (French).

CHAPTER 5

The house's brick front was flush with the street, or rather the road. Behind the door hung a narrow-collared coat, a bridle, and a black leather cap, and, in a corner on the ground, a pair of leather leggings covered in dried mud. To the right was a combination dining and sitting room. Canary-yellow wallpaper, set off toward the top by a garland of pale flowers, shook loosely on its poorly hung canvas underlayer, white calico curtains with a red braided border hung open the length of the windows, and on the chimney's narrow mantle, a clock with a head of Hippocrates gleamed between two silver-plated candlesticks with oval shades. On the other side of the corridor was Charles' consulting room, a small room about six paces wide, with a table, three chairs, and a desk chair. The volumes of the *Dictionary of Medical Sciences*, their pages uncut but their bindings roughened from having suffered through a succession of sales, adorned almost alone the six shelves of a pinewood bookcase. During consultations, the smell of cooking butter penetrated through the wall, just as, in the kitchen, one heard the patients coughing in the consulting room and reciting their life stories. Next, opening directly onto the yard where the stable was, came a large dilapidated room with an oven, serving now as a wood shed, wine cellar, and storeroom, filled with old scrap metal, empty barrels, disused farm tools, and a heap of other dusty items whose purpose was impossible to guess.

The garden, longer than it was wide, ran between two clay walls covered by apricot trees and ended at a thorny hedge that separated it from the fields. In the middle there was a slate-grey sundial on a brick pedestal; four thin wild-rose bushes bounded the more useful vegetable patch. At the very back, beneath the spruce trees, a plaster curé was reading his breviary.

Emma went upstairs to the bedrooms. The first was entirely unfurnished; but the second, which was their nuptial chamber, had a mahogany bedstead set in an alcove with red curtains. A shell box adorned the chest of drawers; and on the writing desk near the window stood a bouquet of orange blossoms in a carafe, tied with white satin ribbons. It was a bridal bouquet, the bouquet of the other woman! She gazed at it. Charles saw this, and he picked it up and carried it to the attic while Emma, seating herself in an armchair (they were setting her things down around her), thought of her own wedding flowers, packed away in a box, and asked herself, in a kind of daydream, what would become of them if by chance she were to die.

She busied herself, those first days, in considering changes to be made to the house. She removed the shades from the candlesticks, had new wallpaper put up, had the staircase repainted, and had benches made for the garden, around the sundial; she even inquired how she could have a pond installed with fish and a fountain. Finally her husband, knowing she liked to go out for drives, found a secondhand cart that, once it was outfitted with new lamps and a mud-guard of padded leather, looked almost like a tilbury.[7]

He was happy then, and without a care in the world. A meal alone together, an evening walk along the highway, a gesture she would make in fixing her hair, the sight of her straw hat hung on the window latch, and many other things as well that Charles had never suspected could give him pleasure—

---

7. A *tilbury* was a fashionable two-wheeled carriage with no top [translator's note].

these now constituted his continuing happiness. In bed in the morning, side by side on the pillow, he watched the sunlight passing over the blond down on her cheeks, half covered by the scalloped edge of her nightcap. Seen from so close, her eyes looked enlarged to him, especially when she blinked them rapidly several times upon awaking; black in the shade and dark blue in the daylight, they seemed to have successive strata of colors, darker in their depths, becoming lighter closer to the eye's surface. And his own eyes lost themselves in those depths, and he saw himself there in miniature down to his shoulders, wearing his kerchief, the top of his shirt open. He would get up. She would place herself at the window to watch him leave; and she would stay leaning on the windowsill, between two geranium pots, dressed in the peignoir which hung loosely around her. Charles, in the street, would buckle his spurs, his foot on the mounting-block; and she would continue to talk to him from above while biting off a scrap of flower or leaf and blowing it toward him; fluttering, floating, it would make semicircles in the air like a bird until it caught in the poorly-groomed mane of the old white horse standing motionless before the door. Charles, on horse-back, would blow her a kiss; she would answer with a wave, close the window, and he would ride off. And then, along the highway stretching out its long ribbon of dust endlessly, along the empty roads beneath the bending tree branches, along the paths where the wheat rose up almost to his knees, with the sun on his shoulders and the morning air in his nostrils, his heart filled with the joys of the night before, his spirit at rest, his flesh contented, he would ride on, ruminating his happiness like those who, after dinner, continue to taste the truffles they are digesting.

Where had been the good in his life before now? Was it during his time in school, when he stayed shut up inside the high walls, alone amidst companions richer than him, or better than him at their schoolwork, who made fun of his clothes, who were amused by his accent, whose mothers came to the visitors' parlor with cakes in their muffs? Or was it later, when he was studying medicine, and never had a wallet fat enough to pay for a dance with some little working girl who might have become his mistress? And then he had lived fourteen months with the widow whose feet in bed were cold as icicles. But now, he possessed for life this pretty woman whom he adored. The universe, for him, was bounded by the silky flounces of her petticoat; he reproached himself for not loving her enough; he wanted to see her again; he would hurry back home, climb the staircase with his heart pounding. Emma, in her room, was dressing; he would come up behind her silently and kiss her back, and she would cry out.

He could not keep himself from constantly touching her comb, her rings, her shawl; sometimes, he would press big, full-mouthed, smacking kisses on her cheeks, or else trail a long row of little kisses along her bare arm, from her fingertips to her shoulders; and, half-smiling and half-irritated, she would push him away, the way one does with a clinging child.

Before she had married, she had believed herself to be in love; but since the happiness that should have resulted from this love had not arrived, she thought that she must have been mistaken. And Emma wanted to know exactly what people meant in life by words like *bliss*, like *passion* and *intoxication*, words that had seemed so beautiful to her in books.

CHAPTER 6

She had read *Paul et Virginie*,[8] and she had fantasized about the little bamboo cottage, the Negro Domingo, the dog Fidèle, but even more the sweet friend-ship of some good little brother who would go and gather ripe fruits for you from great trees taller than spires, or who would run barefoot in the sand, bringing you a bird's nest.

When she was thirteen, her father had taken her to town himself to place her in the convent school. They stopped at an inn in the Saint-Gervais quarter, where they ate from painted plates depicting the story of Mademoiselle de la Vallière.[9] The explanatory legends, cut into here and there by the scraping of knives, glorified religion, the delicacies of the heart, and the pomps of the court, all at the same time.

Far from being bored in the convent at first, she enjoyed the company of the good sisters who, to amuse her, took her to the chapel, which was linked to the refectory by a long corridor. She did not play much during recreation periods, learning her catechism well, and she was the one who could always answer the vicar's more difficult questions. Living thus, without ever leaving the warm, close atmosphere of classrooms and among those pale-faced women wearing rosaries with brass crucifixes, she drowsed softly in the mystic languor exhaled by the scents of the altar, the coolness of the holy water fonts, and the glow of the candles. Instead of following the Mass, she would gaze upon the pious little illustrations, with azure borders, in her missal, and she loved the sick lamb, the sacred heart pierced by sharp arrows, and poor Jesus, who stumbled as He car-ried His cross. She tried to mortify herself by going without food for a whole day. She tried to think of some vow she could fulfill.

When she went to confession, she would make up little sins in order to stay there as long as she could, on her knees in the darkness, hands joined together, her face close to the grill, below the priest's whispers. The analogies of fiancé, spouse, heavenly lover, and eternal marriage that recurred in the sermons aroused an unexpected sweetness in the depths of her soul.

In the evening before prayers, there was a religious reading in the study. During the week this would be some brief segment of sacred history or selec-tions from the Abbé Frayssinous' *Lectures* and on Sunday, passages from the *Génie du Christianisme*.[1] How she listened, those first times, to the sonorous lamentations of its romantic melancholy, echoing throughout the earth and all eternity! If she had spent her childhood in some back apartment in a business district, she might perhaps have been open to those lyrical invasions of Nature which normally reach us only through the interpretations of writers. But she

8. A 1784 story of the sentimental tragic love of two young people on the tropical island of Île de France (today, Mauritius). It was the most popular work of Bernardin de Saint-Pierre (1737–1814).

9. One of Louis XIV's mistresses, whose mythologized character is familiar to all readers of Alexandre Dumas's *Le Vicomte de Bragelonne* (a sequel to *The Three Musketeers*).

1. An enormously influential book (1802), by François-René de Chateaubriand, celebrating the truths and beauties of Roman Catholi-cism, just before Napoleon's concordat with Rome. Denis de Frayssinous (1765–1841) was a popular preacher who wrote *Défense du Christianisme* (1825). Under Louis XVIII (restored to the throne after the fall of Napo-leon I) he became a bishop and minister of ecclesiastical affairs.

knew the countryside all too well; she knew the lowing of herds, the milking, the plows. Accustomed to the calm side of things, she turned instead to the unpredictable. She loved the sea only for its tempests, and greenery only when it was scattered among ruins. She had to be able to take some personal profit out of things; and she rejected as useless anything that did not contribute to her heart's immediate gratification—being of a temperament more sentimental than artistic, seeking out emotions rather than landscapes.

There was an old maid at the convent who came for a week each month to mend the linen. She was protected by the Archbishop because she belonged to an old, noble family ruined in the Revolution, and she ate at the refectory with the nuns, chatting with them after dinner before returning to her work. The girls often slipped out of the study to go visit with her. She knew by heart the love songs of the previous century, and she sang them softly as she continued sewing. She would tell stories, bring news to you, do errands for you in town, and would secretly lend the older girls some novel, which she always carried in the pocket of her apron, long chapters of which she herself would consume during her breaks. It was always nothing but love, lovers, sweethearts, persecuted ladies fainting in deserted pavilions, postilions killed at every relay, horses ridden to death on every page, somber forests, troubled hearts, oaths, sighs, tears, and kisses, gondolas in the moonlight, nightingales in groves, gentlemen brave as lions, gentle as lambs, virtuous like nobody really is, always well dressed, pouring out tears like so many water jars. For six months, at the age of fifteen, Emma fouled her hands with this dust from old reading rooms. Later, with Walter Scott, she became smitten with historical subjects, fantasizing about old chests, guardrooms, and minstrels. She would have liked to live in some old manor, like those long-waisted chatelaines who, beneath trefoiled arches, spent their days leaning on stone balconies, chin in hand, watching a white-plumed knight on a black horse galloping toward them from the distant countryside. At that time she subscribed to the cult of Mary Stuart, and passionately venerated illustrious or doomed women. Joan of Arc, Héloise, Agnes Sorel, la belle Ferronière, and Clémence Isaure[2] stood out for her like comets from the shadowy immensity of history, from which also emerged here and there, more nearly lost in darkness and unrelated to each other, Saint Louis with his oak, the dying Bayard, some of Louis XI's savageries, a bit of Saint Bartholomew, the Béarnais' plume, and always the memory of those painted plates that praised Louis XIV.[3]

---

2. A half-fictional lady from Toulouse (14th century), popularized in a novel by Florian as an incarnation of the mystical poetry of the troubadours. Héloise, famous for her love affair with the philosopher Abelard (1101–1164). Agnès Sorel (1422–1450), a mistress of Charles VII, rumored to have been poisoned by the future Louis XI. La Belle Ferronière (d. 1540), one of François I's mistresses, wife of the lawyer Le Ferron, who is said to have contracted syphilis for the mere satisfaction of passing it on to the king.
3. Massacre of the Protestants ordered by Catherine de Medici in the night of August 23,

1572. St. Louis (1215–1270), king of France as Louis IX, led the seventh and eighth crusades and was canonized in 1297. According to tradition, he dispensed justice under an oak tree at Vincennes (near Paris). Bayard: Seigneur de Pierre du Terrail (1473–1542), one of the most famous French captains, distinguished himself by feats of bravery during the wars of François I. When dying, he chided the constable de Bourbon for his treason in a famous speech. Louis XI (b. 1421; ruled 1461–83), ruthlessly suppressed the rebellious noblemen.

In music class, the ballads she sang were full of little, golden-winged angels, Madonnas, lagoons, gondoliers, peaceful compositions that allowed her, despite the inanity of the style and the sloppiness of the music, a glimpse of the seductive phantasmagoria of sentimental realities. Some of her friends brought into the convent keepsake books that they had received as gifts. These had to be hidden, with a great deal of fuss; they would read them in the dormitory. Handling their beautiful satin bindings delicately, Emma fixed her dazzled gaze on the names of unknown authors who usually had signed their pieces as "count" or "viscount."

She would tremble, her breath lifting the tissue paper from the engraving, which rose up in a double fold and sank back softly upon the page. There, behind a balcony's balustrade, was a young man in a short cloak, holding tightly in his arms a young girl in a white dress with an alms purse hanging from her belt; or there were unnamed portraits of English ladies with blond curls who, beneath their round straw hats, gazed out at you with large clear eyes. Some could be seen relaxing in their carriages, gliding through parks, a greyhound leaping ahead in front of the horses being driven at a trot by two small postilions in white breeches. Others, dreaming on couches beside an opened letter, contemplated the moon through a partly opened window half draped by a black curtain. Naïve ones, with one tear on their cheeks, were kissing a dove through the bars of a gothic cage, or smiling, their heads leaned to one side, were plucking the petals of a daisy with their tapered fingers, which curved like pointed slippers. And you were there also, you sultans with your long pipes, swooning under arbors in the arms of dancing girls, giaours,[4] Turkish sabers, Greek caps, and above all you pallid landscapes of extravagant lands, which often present to us all at once palm trees and pines, tigers on the right with a lion on the left, Tartar minarets on the horizon, Roman ruins in the foreground, and then crouching camels; the whole framed by a well-tended virgin forest, with a great perpendicular sunbeam flickering on the water where, standing out in white scratches on a steel-gray background, swans are swimming.

And the oil-lamp's shade, hung from the wall over Emma's head, illuminated all these tableaus of the world, passing before her one after the other in the dormitory's silence, which was broken only by the distant sounds of some belated carriage still rolling across the boulevards.

When her mother died, she cried a great deal for the first few days. She had a funeral picture made of the deceased's hair, and she sent a long letter to Les Bertaux full of sad reflections on life, in which she asked to be buried herself, when the time came, in the same grave. Her father thought she must be sick and came to see her. Emma was inwardly pleased at having achieved on her first try that rare ideal of pallid existences that mediocre spirits never attain. She thus let herself glide into Lamartinian[5] meanderings, hearing harps on the lakes, all the songs of dying swans, all the falling leaves, the pure virgins ascending to heaven, and the voice of the eternal echoing in the valleys. She grew bored with it, refused to admit it, continued out of habit, then out of vanity, and was at last startled to realize she was healed, with no more sadness in her heart than wrinkles on her brow.

4. Romantic heroes of the outcast desperado type.
5. Alphonse de Lamartine (1790–1869), French Romantic poet whose *Méditations poétiques* (1820) resounds with amorous and religious melancholy.

The good sisters, who had been so certain of her vocation, began to see, to their astonishment, that Mademoiselle Rouault seemed to be slipping from their hands. They had in fact showered on her so many prayers, retreats, novenas, and sermons, so thoroughly preached the respect due to saints and martyrs, and given so much good counsel about bodily modesty and the soul's salvation, that she reacted the way a horse does when the bridle is too tight: she stopped short and the bit slipped from her teeth. Her nature, positive when amid its own enthusiasms, having loved the church for its flowers, music for its romantic lyrics, and literature for its emotional excitements, rebelled against the mysteries of faith precisely in proportion to her irritation with discipline, which had always been repugnant to her temperament. When her father came to take her from the school, no one was sorry to see her go. The mother superior even thought that she had recently started to become irreverent toward the community.

Emma, at home again, amused herself at first by taking charge of the servants, and then she began to detest the country and missed her convent. When Charles came to Les Bertaux for the first time, she thought of herself as entirely disillusioned, having nothing more to learn and nothing more to feel.

But the anxiety that came with her new status, or perhaps the irritation caused by the presence of this man, had been enough to make her believe that she at last knew that marvelous passion that, up to now, had seemed like a great pink-winged bird soaring in the splendor of poetic skies; and she could not believe, now, that this very calm in which she was living was the happiness of her dreams.

CHAPTER 7

She thought sometimes, however, that these were the most beautiful days of her life, the honeymoon, as they called it. To taste its real sweetness, it would no doubt have been necessary to travel to those countries with the sonorous names where the first days of a marriage are passed in exquisite idleness. In a post chaise, behind blue silk shades, one would slowly climb up steep, craggy roads, hearing the postilion's song echo through the mountains along with the goats' bells and the muffled sound of the waterfall. When the sun went down, one would inhale the scent of lemon trees on the gulf shores; then, in the evening, alone and holding hands on the villa's terrace, one would gaze at the stars while making future plans. It seemed to her that happiness must be a product of certain places on the earth, like a plant that needs a particular soil and dies out anywhere else. Why couldn't she lean on the balcony of a Swiss chalet or bury her sorrows in a Scottish cottage, with a husband wearing a black velvet suit with long coattails, wearing soft boots, a pointed hat, and long cuffs!

She would have perhaps liked someone to confide in about all these things. But how to express an elusive uneasiness that changes its shape as the clouds do, that swirls like the wind? She lacked the words for it, as well as an occasion, as well as the courage.

But if Charles had wanted, if he had even suspected, if his gaze had just once managed to align with her thoughts, she felt, it would have been as if a great weight had been lifted from her heart, the way fruit falls from a tree when it's shaken. But as the intimacy of their life together increased, an inner emotional detachment was growing within her, and distancing her from him.

Conversation from Charles was flat as a sidewalk, and every idea that walked over it was dressed in ordinary clothes, arousing neither emotion, nor laughter, nor reverie. He had never felt curious enough, he said, the whole time he lived in Rouen, to go see the visiting Parisian actors at the theater. He didn't know how to swim, nor how to fence, nor how to handle a pistol, and one day, he could not even explain an equestrian term she had run across in a novel.

But a man—shouldn't he know everything, excel in many, varied activities, initiate you into passion's energies, into the refinements of life, into all its mysteries? But this one—he taught nothing, knew nothing, desired nothing. He believed that she was happy; and she resented that placid calm, that dull serenity, the very happiness she gave to him.

Sometimes she would draw; and for Charles it was a great delight to stand upright near her and watch her as she bent over her drawing board, her eyes squinting to see her work better, or as she rolled little bread pellets between her fingers for erasers. And as for the piano playing, the faster her fingers flew, the more he marveled. She struck the keys with assurance, running up and down the keyboard from top to bottom without a break. Shaken thus by her, the old instrument with its frayed strings could be heard at the other end of the village if the window were open, and often the bailiff's clerk, passing bareheaded on the highway, wearing his moccasins, would stop to listen to her, his sheet of paper in his hand.

Emma, moreover, did know how to run the house. She sent patients the bills for their visits using such well-turned phrases that they didn't sound like bills. When, on a Sunday, they would have some neighbor over for dinner, she found a way to present some tasty dish, knew how to arrange pyramids of greengages on vine leaves, or preserves served turned up on a plate, and she even spoke of buying fingerbowls for dessert. All this resulted in greater public admiration for Bovary.

And Charles also ended up thinking more highly of himself for possessing such a wife. He proudly pointed out, in the sitting room, two of her small pencil sketches that he had had put in very large frames and hung against the wallpaper with long green cords. People coming back after Mass would see him in his doorway wearing fine needlepoint slippers.

He would get back home late, at ten o'clock or sometimes even midnight. At those times he would ask for supper, and since the maid was asleep, Emma would serve him. He would take off his coat so as to dine more comfortably. He would tell her, one after another, about every person he had run into, the villages he had been in and the prescriptions he had written, and, pleased with himself, he would finish off the stew, peel his cheese, munch on an apple, empty his carafe, and then take himself off to bed, lying on his back and snoring.

Since he had long been used to wearing a nightcap, his scarf would not stay in place around his ears; so his hair, in the morning, was flattened and askew all around his face and whitened from the feathers of the pillow, whose drawstrings had come undone during the night. He always wore heavy boots that had two thick creases over the instep running obliquely toward the ankles, whereas the rest of the boots' uppers ran in a straight line, as if stretched over a wooden leg. He said *they were good enough for the country*.

This economy won his mother's approval; for she came to visit him as before, whenever there had been some violent little blowup at her house; and yet,

Madame Bovary the elder seemed prejudiced against her daughter-in-law. She found her *living too high above her station in life;* firewood, sugar, and candles *flew away like the place was some great mansion,* and the amount of coal burned in the kitchen would have been enough for twenty-five meals! She arranged the linen in Emma's dresser and taught her to keep a close eye on the butcher when he delivered the meat. Emma tolerated these lessons; her mother-in-law lavished them on her; and the words *my daughter* and *my mother* were exchanged all day long, accompanied by a slight quivering about the lips, each one speaking gentle words in a voice trembling with rage.

Back in the era of Madame Dubuc, the old woman could still believe she was the favorite; but now Charles' love for Emma seemed to her to be a betrayal of her affection, an intrusion into what belonged to her; and she observed her son's happiness with a quiet sorrow, the way a bankrupt watches, through the windows, people dining in what was once his house. She would remind him, in the guise of reminiscences, of all her troubles and sacrifices, and, comparing these with Emma's carelessness, she would conclude that it was not at all rational for him to adore her so exclusively.

Charles didn't know how to respond; he respected his mother, and he loved his wife beyond all limits; he considered the judgment of the one to be infallible, but he also found the other to be beyond reproach. When his mother had left, he tried timidly to hazard, using his mother's terms, one or two of the more benign observations he had heard her make. Emma showed him how wrong he was in short order, and sent him right back to his patients.

But in keeping with what she believed to be the soundest theories, she wanted to give herself up to love. In the moonlight, in the garden, she would recite to him all the impassioned verses that she knew by heart, and would sing to him melancholy adagios with a sigh; but afterwards she found herself just as calm as before, and Charles appeared to be no more amorous and no more moved.

When she had thus beaten on the flint in her heart without eliciting any spark, and being, moreover, as incapable of understanding anything she did not feel as believing in anything that did not reveal itself in conventional forms, she easily persuaded herself that Charles' love no longer had anything intense about it. His effusions had become routine; he embraced her at certain hours. It was one habit among others, like a dessert one looked forward to after an insipid meal.

A gamekeeper, whose inflamed lungs Charles had healed, had given Madame a little Italian greyhound; she took it out for walks, for she went out sometimes in order to be alone for a few minutes and to get away from the eternal garden and the dusty road.

She would go as far as the beech wood at Banneville, near the abandoned summer house that stands at an angle to the wall, near the open fields. In the sunken ditch, among the grass, grew reeds with sharp-edged leaves.

She would begin by looking all around her to see if anything had changed since her last time there. She would find the foxgloves and the wild wall-flowers in the same places, the clumps of nettles surrounding the large stones, and the patches of lichen still stretched across the house's three windows, whose always-closed shutters were moldering on their rusty hinges. Her thoughts, aimless at first, roamed randomly like her greyhound, running in circles through the fields and yapping at yellow butterflies, chasing after little field mice or chewing on the poppies at the edge of the wheat field. Then her ideas bit by bit came into focus, and seated on the grass, into which she dug her parasol's tip with small, sharp thrusts, she would repeat to herself:

"Why, my God, did I get married?"

She would ask herself whether there might have been some way, some combination of circumstances that would have let her meet some other man; and she tried to imagine what those nonexistent events might have been, what that different life, that other husband might have been like. Certainly, none of them were at all like this one. He would have been handsome, a man of spirit, distinguished, attractive, like the ones who had undoubtedly married her old friends at the convent school. What were they doing now? In the city, with the sounds of the street, the buzzing of the theaters and the lights of the ballrooms, they led lives where the heart could expand and the senses could bloom. But she—her life was as cold as a garret facing north, and boredom, the silent spider, was spinning its web across all the dark corners of her heart. She remembered the prize days at school, when she would climb the platform to receive her little wreaths. With her hair in braids, her white dress, and her openwork twill shoes, she had a well-bred air, and when she returned to her seat the gentlemen would bend toward her and compliment her; the courtyard was full of carriages, people said good-bye to her through the windows, the music master bowed to her as he passed with his violin case. How far away it all was! How far away it was!

She called to Djali,[6] held her between her knees, passed her fingers over her long, delicate head, and spoke to her:

"Come, kiss your mistress; you don't have any sorrows."

Then, observing the graceful animal's melancholy face while it yawned slowly, she was moved, and comparing the dog to herself, she spoke aloud to her as if to an afflicted wretch who needed consolation.

Sometimes gusts of wind came up, breezes from the sea that with a single sweep would roll across the whole plateau of the Caux countryside, bringing a salt freshness all through the fields. The rushes whistled close to the ground and the beech leaves rustled in a swift shudder, while the treetops, swaying without stop, continued their deep murmur. Emma wrapped her shawl tight around her shoulders and got up.

In the avenue a green light filtering through the foliage lit up the low-growing moss that crunched softly beneath her feet. The sun was going down; the sky was reddening between the branches, and the uniform trunks of trees planted in a straight line were like brown columns standing out against a background of gold; feeling a sudden fear, she called Djali, and made her way quickly back to Tostes by the main road, slumped down into an armchair and did not speak a word all evening.

But toward the end of September, something extraordinary burst into her life: she was invited to La Vaubyessard, home of the Marquis d'Andervilliers.

Secretary of State under the Restoration, the Marquis, hoping now to get back into political life, was preparing well in advance his candidacy for the Chamber of Deputies. During the winter he presided over the distribution of a

---

6. The name of the little she-goat in Hugo's *Notre Dame de Paris*.

great deal of firewood, and in the General Council, he was always insisting on better roads for his district. He had had an abscess in his mouth during the warm weather, which Charles had cured, as if by a miracle, with a touch of his lancet. The steward he had sent to pay for the operation related, that evening, that he had seen some superb cherries in the doctor's little garden. Now, cherry trees did not grow well at La Vaubyessard, and the Marquis asked Bovary for a few cuttings, took it upon himself to thank him in person, got a look at Emma, found that she had a pretty shape and did not curtsey at all like a peasant—was pretty enough, in fact, that he felt it would not be going beyond the proper bounds of condescension, nor making a mistake, to invite the young couple to the chateau.

On a Wednesday at three o'clock, Monsieur and Madame Bovary, seated in their cart, set off for La Vaubyessard with a big trunk fastened to the rear and a hatbox fastened to the front. Charles had, also, a bandbox[7] balanced between his legs.

They arrived at nightfall, when the lamps in the park were being lit, to light the way for the carriages.

CHAPTER 8

The chateau was of modern construction, in the Italian style, with two projecting wings and three flights of steps; it spread itself out behind a vast lawn where a few cows grazed among clumps of large, evenly spaced trees, while groupings of shrubs, rhododendrons, syringa, and snowballs swelled out their unequal tufts of foliage along the winding lines of the sandy road. A river flowed under a bridge; through the mists one could make out buildings with thatched roofs scattered across the meadow, which was bordered by two gently sloping tree-covered hills, and beyond them, among the trees, in two parallel lines, were the coach-houses and stables, all that remained of the old, demolished chateau.

Charles' cart came to a stop before the middle flight of steps; servants appeared; the Marquis came forward and, offering his arm to the doctor's wife, conducted her into the foyer.

Its floor was marble tiles, it was high-ceilinged, and the sounds of footsteps and voices echoed as in a church. Straight ahead was a staircase, and to the left a gallery overlooked a garden and led to a billiard room, from which the clicking sounds of ivory balls could be heard when one approached the door. As she crossed it in order to get to the salon, Emma saw men with serious expressions around the billiard table, their chins bent over their high cravats, all wearing decorations, smiling silently as they shot with their cues. On the dark wood wall panels were big gilded frames inscribed on the lower borders with names in black letters. She read: "Jean-Antoine d'Andervilliers d'Yverbonville, Count of La Vaubyessard and Baron of La Fresnaye, killed in the battle of Coutras,[8] October 20, 1587." And on another: "Jean Antoine-Henry-Guy d'Andervilliers of La Vaubyessard, admiral of France and knight of

7. A *bandbox* was a light, thin, usually circular container used for carrying hats and other items of clothing [translator's note].

8. In the Gironde; the battle was won by Henri de Navarre against the duc de Joyeuse.

the Order of Saint Michael, wounded in the combat at La Hogue-Saint-Vaast on May 29, 1692, died at La Vaubyessard on January 23, 1693." The ones after that could barely be read because the lamplight, which was turned toward the green cloth of the billiard table, cast a shadow everywhere else in the room. Turning the hanging canvases brown, it highlighted only the cracks in the varnish; and from all those big, gilt-edged black squares, only the lighter parts of the paintings would emerge here and there: a pale forehead, two eyes that gazed out at you, wigs flowing down over powdered shoulders, red suits, or the buckle of a garter at the top of a plump calf.

The Marquis opened the door of the salon; one of the women arose (the Marquise herself), came to greet Emma, and seated her on a small love seat next to her, where she began to chat in a friendly way, as if she had known her for a long time. She was a woman of about forty, with handsome shoulders, a hooked nose, and a drawl, and tonight she was wearing a simple lace shawl over her brown hair, falling behind her head in a point. A young blond woman was sitting on her other side in a high-backed chair; and gentlemen, sporting little flowers in the boutonnieres of their suits, were chatting with ladies around the fireplace.

At seven o'clock, dinner was served. The men, more numerous than the ladies, were seated at the first table, in the foyer, while the ladies sat at the second, in the dining room, with the Marquis and Marquise.

Upon entering, Emma felt herself enveloped in a warm air, a mixture of scents of flowers, of fine linen, of the aroma of the meats and the truffles. The flames from the candelabras flickered on the silver; the faceted crystal pieces, thinly misted over with steam, reflected each other with pale gleams; flower bouquets were arranged in a line from one end of the table to the other; and on the wide-bordered dishes, napkins folded like bishop's miters held small, oval rolls between their gaping folds. The red claws of lobsters hung over the dishes; large pieces of fruit were piled high in open baskets; the quails still wore their feathers, steam rising from them; and, wearing silk stockings, knee breeches, white cravat, and a frilled shirt, as solemn as a magistrate, the steward, passing dishes of carved meat between shoulders, would make the piece you had chosen leap up with a flick of his spoon. And on the large porcelain stove, with inlaid copper, the statue of a woman draped to the chin gazed, immobile, on the room filled with people.

Madame Bovary noticed that many of the women had not placed their gloves in their wine glasses.[9]

But at the far end of the table, alone among all the women, bent over his full plate, his napkin tied around his neck like a child, an old man was eating, letting drops of gravy drip from his mouth. His eyes were bloodshot, and he wore a short ponytail tied with a black ribbon. This was the Marquis' father in-law, the old Duke de Laverdière, once the favorite of the Count d'Artois in the days of the Vaudreuil hunting parties hosted by the Marquis de Conflans, and rumored to have been the lover of Marie-Antoinette, between Messieurs de

9. The ladies in the provinces, unlike their Paris counterparts, did not drink wine at public dinner parties and signified their intention by putting their gloves in their wineglasses. The fact that they fail to do so suggests to Emma the high degree of sophistication of the company.

Coigny and de Lauzun. He had led a noisily debauched life full of duels, wagers, and abducted women; he had run through his fortune and terrorized his entire family. A servant stood behind his chair and spoke loudly into his ear, naming the dishes at which he pointed and stammered; and Emma's eyes were constantly drawn to this old man with drooping lips as if to something precious and hallowed. He had lived at Court and slept in the bed of queens!

Iced champagne was poured. Emma shivered all over when she felt the coldness in her mouth. She had never before seen pomegranates nor tasted pineapples. Even the powdered sugar seemed to her to be whiter and finer than it was elsewhere.

Afterwards, the ladies went up to their rooms to dress for the ball.

Emma dressed with the painstaking self-consciousness of an actress preparing for her debut. She arranged her hair according to the hairdresser's suggestions, and put on her muslin dress which had been laid out on the bed. Charles' trousers pinched him across the stomach.

"The shoe straps will get in the way for dancing," he said.

"Dancing?" Emma replied.

"Yes!"

"Are you out of your mind? Everyone will laugh at you; stay in your place. And besides, it's more seemly for a doctor," she added.

Charles said no more. He paced back and forth, waiting for Emma to finish dressing.

From behind, he watched her reflection in the mirror, between two candles. Her black eyes seemed even blacker. Her hair, puffed out gently around her ears, seemed to glow with a blue tint; a rose in her chignon trembled on its wavering stem, with artificial dewdrops on the tips of its leaves. She wore a gown of pale saffron, decorated with three small bouquets of pompon roses mixed with greenery.

Charles came and kissed her on the shoulder.

"Leave me alone!" she said. "You'll wrinkle my dress."

They heard the flourish of a violin and notes from a horn. She descended the stairs, barely able to keep herself from running.

The quadrilles[1] had begun. Everyone was arriving. There was pushing. She stationed herself on a seat near the door. After the quadrille, the floor stayed free for groups of men standing and talking, and for liveried servants carrying large platters. Down the line of seated women, painted fans were quivering, bouquets partly concealed smiling faces, and perfume bottles with gold stoppers were turning in half-opened hands whose thin white gloves revealed the shapes of fingernails and hugged the flesh tightly at the wrist. Lace ornaments, diamond brooches, and bracelets with lockets trembled on bodices, glimmered on breasts, rattled on bare arms. Hairdos, tight across foreheads and twisted at napes, wore as crowns clusters or bunches of forget-me-nots, jasmine, pomegranate flowers, wheat ears, or cornflowers. Sitting peacefully in their places, frowning mothers wore red turbans.

Emma's heart sped up when, her partner holding her by the fingertips, she took a place in the line and waited for the violinist's bow stroke to begin. But her emotion quickly passed; and swaying with the orchestra's rhythm, she glided

1. A square dance with four couples, fashionable in the 19th century.

forward, her neck moving lightly. A smile came to her lips at certain delicate touches from the violin, playing solo sometimes when the other instruments were mute; the distinctive sound of gold coins dropping on the card tables in the next room could be heard; and then suddenly everything began again, the cornet hurling out a sonorous figure. Feet fell back into rhythm, skirts swirled and billowed against each other, hands were joined, then separated; the same pair of eyes that had just fallen before you now rose back up to fix their gaze on yours.

Some men (about fifteen), ranging from twenty-five to forty were scattered among the dancers or chatting in the doorways; they were distinguished from the crowd by their family resemblance despite their differences in age, dress, and facial features.

Their clothes, better made, seemed of a suppler texture, and their hair, swept forward in curls at the temples, shone with a finer pomade. They had the coloring of wealth, that special white complexion that is accentuated by the pallor of porcelain, the sheen of satin, the varnish of fine furniture, and that is nurtured by a careful diet of exquisite foods. Their necks turned smoothly in low-folded cravats; their long sideburns fell over high collars; they wiped their lips with handkerchiefs embroidered with large monograms, from which an elegant scent emanated. Those who were beginning to age had a youthful air, while the young ones had a certain maturity about their faces. The indifference in their gazes revealed the calm of daily gratified passions; and through the veneer of their gentle manners pierced that particular brutality that bespeaks the casual domination of things in which force is exerted and vanity entertained: the handling of racehorses and the company of loose women.

A few feet away from Emma, a gentleman in a blue coat was chatting about Italy with a pale young woman wearing a pearl necklace. They were praising the size of the pillars in Saint Peter's, Tivoli, Vesuvius, Castellamare, and the Cascine,[2] the roses at Genoa, the Coliseum by moonlight. Emma listened, with her other ear, to a conversation full of words she didn't understand. People were gathered around a very young man who had outraced, the week before, *Miss Arabelle* and *Romulus*, and had won two thousand louis by jumping a ditch, in England. One man was complaining that his racehorses were getting fat; another, that a printer's error had misrepresented his horse's name.

The atmosphere in the ballroom grew heavy; the lights were growing dim. People streamed back into the billiard room. A servant got up on a chair and shattered two windowpanes; at the sound of the breaking glass, Emma turned her head, and she could make out the faces of peasants in the garden, pressed up against the window, looking in at them. And then the memory of Les Bertaux came back to her. She could see the farm again, the muddy pond, her father in his smock beneath the apple trees, and she could see herself again as she was then, skimming the cream off the milk pans in the dairy with her finger. But in the brilliance of this present moment, her past life, so clear and distinct until now, faded away completely, and she almost doubted that she had lived it. She was here now; and beyond the ball there was nothing but shadow darkening everything else. She was eating a maraschino ice, holding it in a silver gilt shell in her left hand, and she half-closed her eyes with the spoon between her teeth.

2. A park near Florence. Castellamare is a port south of Naples.

A woman near her let her fan drop. A man, dancing, passed by.

"Would you be so kind, Monsieur," the lady said, "as to pick up my fan from behind the sofa!"

The gentleman bowed, and as he bent forward to extend his arm, Emma saw the young lady's hand throw something white, folded into a triangle, into his hat. The gentleman retrieved the fan and offered it respectfully to the lady; she thanked him with a nod of her head and turned to sniff her bouquet.

After the supper, with a great many Spanish wines and Rhine wines, with bisque soups and cream of almond soups, Trafalgar puddings, and all sorts of cold meats surrounded by molded jellies trembling on their dishes, the carriages began to drive off, one after the other. By raising the corner of the muslin curtain, you could see their lanterns as they glimmered in the darkness. The seats began to empty; a few card players still remained; the musicians were cooling their fingertips on their tongues; Charles was half asleep, leaning up against a door.

At three in the morning, the cotillion began. Emma did not know how to waltz. Everyone was waltzing, even the young Mademoiselle d'Andervilliers and her mother the Marquise; the only people still there were the overnight guests at the chateau, about a dozen people.

But one of the waltzers, who was familiarly called the Viscount, wearing a low-cut waistcoat that seemed molded to his chest, came back a second time to invite Madame Bovary to dance, assuring her that he would lead her and that she would manage very well.

They began slowly, and then sped up. They whirled; everything was spinning around them, the lamps, the furniture, the wainscoting, and the floor, like a disc on a pivot. As they passed the doors, the hem of Emma's dress caught against his trousers; their legs intertwined; he lowered his eyes toward her, she raised her eyes to him; a sluggishness suddenly came over her, and she halted. They started up again; and with an even more rapid movement the Viscount, pulling her along, disappeared with her to the far end of the gallery where, out of breath, she almost fell and, for an instant, rested her head upon his chest. And then, still turning but more slowly now, he guided her back to her place; she leaned back against the wall and covered her eyes with her hand.

When she opened her eyes again, in the middle of the room was a lady seated on a stool with three waltzers kneeling before her. She chose the Viscount, and the violin started up again.

They all watched the pair. Back and forth they went, her body rigid, her chin lowered, and he always in the same pose, his back arched, his elbow rounded, his chin thrust forward. She knew how to waltz, that one! They continued for a long time, exhausting all the others.

People chatted for a few minutes more, and after saying good night, or rather good morning, the chateau's guests went off to bed.

Charles hauled himself upstairs by the banister; his legs *wouldn't hold him up another minute*. He had been standing up for five hours in a row around the tables watching people play whist without understanding a bit of it. And so he heaved a great, satisfied sigh when he had pulled off his boots.

Emma put a shawl around her shoulders, opened the window, and leaned out.

The night was black. A few drops of rain were falling. She breathed in the damp wind, and it refreshed her eyes. The music from the ball continued to hum in her ears, and she made an effort to stay awake, in order to prolong the illusion of this luxurious life that she would soon have to abandon.

Dawn began to break. She gazed, for a long while, across at the windows in the chateau's other wing, trying to guess which ones were the rooms of the people she had observed during the evening. She would have liked to know about their lives, to penetrate into them, to lose herself in them.

But she was shivering with cold. She undressed and nestled down between the sheets, against the sleeping Charles.

There were a lot of people at the breakfast. The meal lasted ten minutes; no liqueurs were served, which surprised the doctor. Then Mademoiselle d'Andervilliers collected some bits of rolls in a basket to take out to the swans on the little pond, and they all went for a walk in the hothouses, where strange plants bristling with hairs rose up in pyramids beneath hanging vases that, like over-full serpents' nests, let long, green, interlaced tendrils fall from their edges. The orangery, which they came to at the other end, led via a covered passage to the chateau's outbuildings. The Marquis, to amuse the young woman, took her to see the stables. Over the basket-shaped racks, porcelain slabs were inscribed in black with the horses' names. Each animal stirred in its stall when they came close to it and clicked their tongues. The flooring in the harness room shone as brightly as the polished floor of a drawing room. Carriage harnesses were set in the middle on two twisting columns, and the bits, the whips, the spurs, and the curbs were arranged in a line all along the wall.

In the meantime, Charles went to ask a servant to ready his cart. They brought it around to the front steps and, all the luggage having been crammed in, the Bovarys paid their respects to the Marquis and the Marquise, and set off for Tostes.

In silence, Emma watched the wheels turn. Charles, seated on the far edge of the bench, held the reins with his two arms spread wide apart, and the little horse trotted along between the shafts, which were too wide for him. The loose reins slapping against his cropper became wet with lather, and the box tied on to the back of the cart made loud, regular thumps against it.

They had reached the heights of Thibourville when suddenly, right in front of them, some men on horseback passed by, laughing, cigars in their mouths. Emma thought she recognized the Viscount; she turned, and saw nothing on the horizon except their heads rising and falling to the unequal cadences of a trot or a gallop.

A quarter of a league farther on, they had to stop to mend some broken traces with a rope.

But Charles, giving the harness one more look, saw something on the ground, between his horse's legs, and he picked up a cigar case bordered with green silk, emblazoned in the center with a coat of arms that resembled a carriage door.

"There are even two cigars in it," he said. "These will be for tonight after dinner."

"You smoke now?" she asked.

"Sometimes, when I get the chance."

He put his find in his pocket and whipped on the old horse.

When they got home, the dinner had not been prepared. Madame lost her temper. Nastasie talked back insolently.

"Get out!" said Emma. "Who do you think you are? I'm firing you!"

They had onion soup for dinner, and some veal cooked with sorrel. Charles, sitting across from Emma, rubbed his hands together happily and said:

"It's so good to be back home!"

They could hear Nastasie crying in the other room. He was rather fond of the poor girl. She had kept him company for many evenings during the rough times of his widowerhood. She had been his first patient, his oldest acquaintance in the region.

"Are you really going to send her away for good?" he finally asked.

"Yes. Who's going to stop me?" she replied.

Then they warmed themselves in the kitchen while their room was being readied. Charles began to smoke. He smoked by pushing out his lips, spitting constantly, recoiling with every puff.

"You're going to make yourself sick," she said disdainfully.

He threw away his cigar, and ran to the pump to swallow a glass of cold water. Emma picked up the cigar case and threw it quickly into the bottom of the cabinet.

It was a long day, that next day. She walked in her little garden, going up and down the same paths, stopping before the flowerbeds, before the trellis, before the plaster priest, considering with astonishment all these things that had once been so familiar to her. How far off the ball seemed already! Who was it that decreed so much distance between yesterday's morning and today's evening? Her trip to La Vaubyessard had created a kind of hole in her life, like one of those great crevasses that a storm can sometimes carve out in the mountains in a single night. But she resigned herself: she reverently packed away in her chest of drawers all her beautiful clothes, right down to the satin slippers, their soles yellow with the slick wax of the dance floor. Her heart was like them: by rubbing up against wealth, some layer had been added which would never come off.

It became, then, an occupation for Emma to remember the ball. Every time Wednesday came around, she would awaken and say to herself, "Ah! It was a week ago . . . . it was two weeks ago . . . three weeks ago, I was there!" And little by little, the faces grew confused in her memory; she forgot the tune of the quadrilles; she no longer saw clearly the liveries and the rooms; some of the details had gone, but the regret remained.

CHAPTER 9

Often, when Charles was out, she would go and take the green silk cigar case from the cabinet, from between the folds of linen where she had left it.

She would look at it, open it, and even sniff the scent of its lining, a mixture of verbena and tobacco. Who was its owner? . . . the Viscount. Perhaps it was a gift from his mistress. It had been embroidered on some rosewood frame, a pretty little thing that would have to be kept secret, that must have taken many hours, with the soft curls of the pensive worker bent over it. A sigh of love had passed through the canvas mesh; every prick of the needle had fixed there some hope or some memory, and all these interwoven silk threads were simply the continuation of the same silent passion. And then the Viscount, one morning, had taken it away with him. What would they have spoken about while it remained on the wide-mantled fireplace, between the vases of flowers and the Pompadour clocks? She was in Tostes. He, in Paris now; so far away! What was it like, that Paris? What a grand name! She would repeat it under her breath, for the pleasure of it; it sounded in her ears like a great cathedral bell; it flamed before her eyes across the labels of her cosmetics jars.

At night, when the fishmongers in their carts passed under her windows singing the "Marjolaine,"[3] she would awaken; and, listening to the sound of the iron-rimmed wheels dying away as they reached the country road, she would say to herself:

"They'll be there tomorrow!"

And she would follow them in her thoughts, as they ascended and descended the hills, passed through villages, made their way along the highway by the light of the stars. And at the end of some indeterminate distance, there would always be a confused, indistinct place where her dream expired.

She bought a map of Paris, and with her fingertip on the map, she would take walks in the capital. She would go up the boulevards, stopping at every corner, between the street lines, in front of the white squares that represented houses. When her eyes tired at last, she would close her eyelids and see in the shadows the gas jets fluttering in the wind, and see the carriages stop and lower their steps with a great clatter before the theater entrances.

She subscribed to the *Corbeille*, a lady's magazine, and to the *Sylphe des Salons*. She devoured all the reviews, without missing a single one, of opening nights, of races, of soirées, and she took an interest in a singer's debut, in the opening of a new shop. She knew the current fashions, the addresses of the best tailors, the right days for the Bois[4] or for the Opera. She studied the descriptions of furnishings in Eugène Sue;[5] she read Balzac and George Sand,[6] seeking in their books the vicarious satisfaction of her own desires. She took her book with her even to the table, and she would turn the pages while Charles ate and talked to her. The memory of the Viscount always returned as she read. She would invent relationships between him and the fictional characters. But the circle, at whose center he stood, bit by bit spread outward, and the halo that emanated from his face spread outward too, in order to illuminate other dreams.

Paris, vaster than the ocean, glimmered in Emma's eyes within a rose-tinted atmosphere. But the many lives bustling in that tumult were divided up into parts and classified into different types of pictures. Emma could only make out two or three, which hid all the others from her, but which, by themselves, represented all of humanity. In the world of the ambassadors one walked across gleaming parquet floors, through mirror-paneled salons, around oval tables covered with gold-fringed velvet cloths. There were dresses with bustles, great mysteries and private miseries hidden behind smiles. Then came the society of

3. The "Marjolaine" is an old, traditional Parisian workman's song, dating back to the twelfth century [translator's note].
4. Horse races at the Bois de Boulogne.
5. The novels of Eugène Sue (1804–57) were extremely popular in the period, especially his serialized novels about fashionable contemporary life. Flaubert detested his work, seeing it as the worst kind of commercial fiction [translator's note].
6. Pseudonym of Aurore Dudevant (1804–1876), prolific woman novelist. Sue (1804–1857), a popular novelist, was extremely successful at that period, both as a writer and as a fashionable dandy.

duchesses: everyone there was pale; everyone arose at four in the afternoon; the women—poor angels!—wore English lace on the hems of their petticoats, and the men, all unappreciated geniuses beneath their mild exteriors, rode horses to death at every country party, passed their summers at Baden,[7] and, at around forty, married heiresses. In the private rooms of those restaurants where one dines after midnight, the colorful crowd of writers and actresses laughed by candlelight. That group was as extravagant as kings, full of idealistic ambitions and fantastic dreams. Theirs was an existence higher than all the others, somewhere between heaven and earth, up in the storm clouds, something sublime. As for the rest of the world, it was lost, having no particular location, and being thus without substance. For the closer things were to her, the more her thoughts turned away from them. Everything that immediately surrounded her—the boring countryside, the middle-class imbeciles, the mediocrity of existence—all this seemed to her to be an exception in the world, some odd accident in which she was trapped, while beyond this place the immense country of happiness and of passions stretched out as far as the eye could see. In her desires, she confused the sensualities of luxury with the joys of the heart, the elegance of manners with the delicacy of sentiment. Didn't love require, like Indian plants, some special ground prepared for it, some particular climate? Sighs in the moonlight, long embraces, tears that flowed over yielding hands, all the fevers of the flesh and the languors of tenderness— these could not be separated from the balconies of grand, leisure-filled chateaux, from boudoirs with silk curtains and thick, plush carpets, from well-filled flowerboxes, from beds on raised platforms, nor from gleaming precious stones and lace-trimmed livery.

The postboy, who came every morning to groom the mare, passed through the corridor with his heavy wooden clogs; there were holes in his smock, and he wore no socks. And this was the groom in knee-breeches she had to be content with! When his work was done, he would not return for the rest of the day, because Charles, on his return, always put up his horse himself, unsaddling her and adjusting the halter, while the maid brought out a bucket of hay and, as best as she could, threw it into the manger.

To replace Nastasie (who had finally left Tostes in a stream of tears), Emma had hired a fourteen-year-old girl, an orphan with a sweet face. She forbade her to wear cotton bonnets, taught her that you need to address people in the third person, to carry a glass of water on a plate, to knock before entering, how to iron, to starch, and to dress herself; she wanted to make her into a lady's maid. The new maid obeyed without protest for fear of being fired; and since Madame usually left the key in the kitchen cabinet, Félicité would take a little supply of sugar away with her every night, which she would eat all alone in her bed after saying her prayers.

Sometimes in the afternoons, she would go off to chat with the postilions across the way. Madame stayed upstairs, in her rooms.

Emma would wear an open dressing gown, revealing, between the lapels of her bodice, a pleated chemisette with three gold buttons. For a belt, she wore a tasseled rope, and her little garnet-colored slippers had a tuft of wide ribbons that spilled over onto her instep. She had bought herself a blotter, a writing

7. A fashionable German spa with hot mineral-water springs.

case, a pen holder, and some envelopes, even though she had no one at all to write to; she would dust her shelves, look at herself in the mirror, pick up a book, and then, daydreaming between the lines, she would let it fall onto her knees. She felt urges to go traveling, or to return to her convent. She wanted at the same time to die and to live in Paris.

When it snowed or when it rained, Charles would ride his horse across the fields. He would eat omelets at farmhouse tables, poke his arms into damp beds, receive the warm jet of bloodlettings full in the face, listen to death rattles, investigate bedpans, and tuck in more than his share of dirty linen; but every night he returned to a roaring fire, a set table, comfortable furniture, and a well-dressed wife, charming and fresh-smelling, and he could not figure out the source of that scent, wondering whether it was in fact her skin that perfumed her chemise.

She charmed him by the sheer quantity of her refinements; now it was a new method of cutting paper sconces for the candles, now a flounce she had changed on her dress, now an extraordinary name for some simple dish that the maid had ruined, but whose every bite Charles gulped down with pleasure. In Rouen, she saw some women who wore charms on their watch chains; she bought charms. She wanted two large vases of blue glass for the fireplace, and a bit later, an ivory workbox with a silver-gilt thimble. The less Charles understood these refinements, the more he submitted to their seduction. They added something to his sensual pleasures and to the sweetness of his hearth. It was like some golden powder being spread all along the little path of his life.

His health was good, and he looked good; his reputation was firmly established. The country people cherished him because he was not proud. He would pat the children, never went to the café, and, in general, inspired trust by his good morals. He was especially successful with catarrhs and chest illnesses. Always greatly afraid of killing some patient, he rarely prescribed anything beyond sedatives, an occasional emetic, a foot bath, or leeches. It wasn't surgery that frightened him; he would bleed someone for you copiously, like a horse, and when it came to extracting teeth, he had *one hell of a grip*.

Eventually, *to keep himself up to date*, he took out a subscription to the *Ruche Médicale*, a new journal whose prospectus he had received. He would read a little of it after dinner, but the warmth of the room together with his digestion made him fall asleep within five minutes; and there he stayed, his chin propped on his hands and his hair falling like a mane down to the base of the reading lamp. Emma would look at him and shrug her shoulders. Why, at least, could she not have for a husband one of those taciturn but impassioned men who work all night at their books, those men who finally, at age sixty, when rheumatism sets in, wear a set of decorations on their ill-made black suits? She would have liked for this name Bovary, which was hers, to be illustrious, displayed in the bookshops, cited in the journals, known to all of France. But Charles had no ambition! A doctor from Yvetot, with whom he had lately been in consultation, had mildly humiliated him at the bedside of a patient, in front of the assembled relatives. When Charles told Emma about it later that night, Emma blew up at the colleague. Charles was touched. He kissed her forehead, a tear in his eye. But she was beside herself with shame, and she felt like striking him; to calm herself, she went into the corridor to open the window and breathe in the fresh air.

"What a man! What a man!" she repeated in a low voice, biting her lips.

She felt herself becoming in general more irritated with him. As he grew older, he took on some crude mannerisms: during dessert he would whittle the corks of the empty bottles; after eating, he would run his tongue over his teeth; with his soup, he made a gulping noise with every mouthful; and since he was starting to gain weight, his puffed-out cheeks seemed to push his already small eyes up toward his temples.

Emma would sometimes retuck the red border of his undershirt into his waistcoat, rearrange his cravat, and throw out the dirty gloves he was about to put on; and this was not, as he believed, for his sake; it was for herself, out of her own inflated ego, and out of nervous irritation. And sometimes she would tell him about things she had read, such as a passage in a novel, a new play, or some anecdote about *high society* that they were reporting in her magazines; because, after all, Charles was somebody, an always open ear, and always ready to approve of her. She did enough confiding to her greyhound! She would have done the same to the logs in the fireplaces or the pendulum of the clock.

But in the depths of her heart, she was waiting for something to happen. Like a shipwrecked sailor, she looked upon the solitude of her life with despairing eyes, searching far off for some white sail to appear in the mists of the horizon. She did not know what this chance event would be, what wind would blow it toward her, towards what shore it would drive her, whether it would be a rowboat or a three-deck ship, loaded down with anguish or stocked to the portholes with happiness. But every morning when she awoke, she hoped it would come that day; and she listened closely to every sound, leaped out of bed, and was shocked when it hadn't come; then at sunset, always sadder, she wished for the next day to come.

Springtime returned. She felt some shortness of breath during the first warm days, when the pear trees were in flower.

When July came, she counted on her fingers how many weeks there were until October, thinking that the Marquis d'Andervilliers might have another ball at La Vaubyessard. But September passed by with no letters and no visits.

After that bitter disappointment, her heart grew empty all over again, and then the series of identical days started over.

And that was how the days were going to be from now on, always the same, beyond numbering, and never bringing anything! Other lives, flat as they might be, at least had the chance of something happening. One little adventure sometimes brought with it an infinite series of twists, and the scene would change. But for her, nothing would happen; God had willed it that way! The future was a long black corridor with, at its end, a firmly locked door.

She gave up music. Why play? Who would listen? Since she would never wear a short-sleeved velvet gown and play in concert on an Érard piano,[8] swiftly touching the keys with her light fingers and sensing around her, like a breeze, a growing murmur of ecstasy, it wasn't worth the trouble to bore herself by practicing. She left her sketch pads and her tapestry in the cupboard. What was the point? What was the point? Needlework annoyed her.

8. The pianos designed by Sebastian Érard (1752–1831) were used by the finest musians of the era, including Beethoven, Chopin, and Liszt; it is difficult to imagine a health officer being able to afford one [translator's note].

"I've read everything," she said to herself.

And she would sit heating the tongs, or watching the rain come down.

On Sundays, how sad she was when they rang the bell for vespers! She would listen in a kind of attentive stupor to the cracked chimes of the bell, one by one. Some cat up on the rooftops, walking along slowly, would arch its back in the pale rays of the sun. The wind on the highway blew about great clouds of dust. Sometimes far away a dog would howl: and the church bell, its chimings evenly spaced, would continue its monotonous ringing, which faded and lost itself in the countryside.

But then the people would come out of the church. The women in waxed clogs, the peasants in new smocks, the little children who skipped along bareheaded in front of them—all of them were going back home. And then until night came, a group of five or six men, always the same ones, would stay on playing *bouchon* in front of the inn's large door.

The winter was cold. Every morning the windows were covered with frost, and the whitish light that came through them, as if through ground glass, sometimes did not change the whole day long. By four o'clock, the lamp had to be lit.

On days when the weather was good, she would go down into the garden. The dew had left a silver lace on the cabbages, with long, transparent threads stretching from one to the other. No birds could be heard; everything seemed to be asleep, the straw-covered espalier and the vine, like a huge, sick serpent strung under the wall coping where one could see, coming up close, the wood lice with their many feet crawling around. Among the spruce trees by the hedgerow, the priest in his three-cornered hat who was reading in his breviary had lost his right foot, and the plaster itself, peeling off in the frost, had made white scabs on his face.

Then she would go back in, close the door, stoke the coals, and, weakened by the heat from the hearth, would feel her boredom growing even heavier and weighing down upon her. She would have liked very much to go downstairs and chat with the maid, but a sense of propriety restrained her.

Every day at the same hour the schoolmaster in his black silk cap would open the shutters of his house, and the village policeman would pass by, his saber strapped over his smock. Evening and morning, the post-horses, three by three, would cross the street to drink from the pond. Sometimes the bell of the tavern door would tinkle, and when it was windy one could hear the creaking of the two little brass basins on their rod that served as a sign for the wigmaker's shop. The shop had for decoration an old engraving of women's fashions glued to one windowpane, as well as a wax bust of a woman with yellow hair. The wigmaker, he too, lamented his unfulfilled vocation, his lost future; and dreaming of owning a shop in a big town, Rouen for example, overlooking the quay, near the theater, he paced back and forth all day from the city hall to the church, somber, waiting for customers. When Madame Bovary looked up she always saw him there, like a sentry on duty, his cap pulled down over his ears, wearing his thick wool vest.

In the afternoons, sometimes a man's head would appear outside the window of her room—a tanned face, black sideburns, slowly smiling a wide, sweet smile, revealing white teeth. Then a waltz would begin; and on the organ was a little drawing room with dancers the size of a finger, women in pink turbans,

Tyroleans in jackets, monkeys in black suits, gentlemen in knee breeches, turning, turning around the armchairs, sofas, and tables, multiplying themselves in the little pieces of mirror held together at the corners by strips of gold paper. The man cranked the organ's handle, looking to the right, to the left, and toward the windows. From time to time, while he shot out a long jet of brown saliva toward the curb, he would use his knee to lift up his instrument, whose heavy strap was tiring his arm; and sometimes doleful and drawling, sometimes joyful and fast-paced, the music escaped from the box, droning through its pink taffeta curtain fastened by a copper arabesque grill. Those were the tunes that were being played elsewhere, in the theaters, sung in drawing rooms, danced to in the evenings under lighted chandeliers, echoes of the life that reached even to Emma. Sarabands without end whirled in her head, and like a dancer on a flowered carpet, her thoughts leaped with the notes, swaying from dream to dream, from sorrow to sorrow. When the man had received some money in his cap, he would pull down an old blue cloth cover, swing the organ onto his back, and go off with a heavy step. She would watch him depart.

But it was mealtimes above all that were hardest for her to bear, in that little room on the ground floor, with the smoking stove, the creaking door, the sweating walls, the damp flagstone floor; all the bitterness of life seemed to her to be served up on her plate, and with the steam from the boiled beef, there rose up from the depths of her soul other flavorless, sickening gusts. Charles was a slow eater; she would nibble on a few hazelnuts or, at times, would amuse herself by drawing lines on the oilcloth with the tip of her knife.

Now she neglected everything in the household, and when Charles' mother came to spend part of Lent at Tostes, she was amazed at the change. She who had formerly been so careful, so elegant, now went whole days without getting dressed, wearing gray cotton stockings, lighting the house with mere candles. She kept repeating that they had to economize since they weren't rich, and adding that she was quite contented, very happy, that she liked Tostes very much, and making up other little speeches that dumfounded her mother-in-law. But Emma seemed as little disposed as ever to follow her advice; one time, in fact, Charles' mother having thought it fit to maintain that masters ought to keep a close eye on their servants' religious habits, Emma responded with so angry a look and so cold a smile that the good woman never tried anything like that again.

Emma was becoming difficult, capricious. She would order dishes to be prepared for her, and then wouldn't eat a bite; one day she would drink only fresh milk, and the next day, cups of tea by the dozen. Often, she would obstinately refuse to go outside, and then she would feel suffocated and throw open the windows and put on light dresses. When she had harshly scolded her servant, she would then give her presents or send her out for a walk with the neighbors, just as she would sometimes toss all the coins in her purse to the poor, though she was by no means a tender-hearted person, or particularly sensitive to other people's feelings—like most country people who always retain something of their fathers' hard, calloused hands within their souls.

Toward the end of February, old Rouault commemorated his cure by bringing his son-in-law a superb turkey, and he stayed in Tostes for three days. Since Charles was with his patients, Emma kept him company. He smoked in the bedroom, spat on the andirons, talked farming, calves, cows, poultry, and the country council; so much so that she closed the door, when he departed, with a sense of satisfaction that surprised even herself. Anyway, she no longer hid her contempt for everything and everybody; and set herself to occasionally expressing eccentric opinions, condemning what others applauded and applauding perverse or immoral things, all of which often made her husband widen his eyes at her.

Would this suffering last forever? Would she never be able to get out of it? But she was just as good as all those people who lived happy lives! She had seen duchesses at La Vaubyessard with thicker waists and more vulgar ways, and she cursed God's injustice; she would lean her head against the walls and cry; she envied exciting lives, masked balls, and shameless pleasures with all the mad delights that she had never known and that other lives must include.

She grew pale and began to have heart palpitations. Charles gave her valerian and camphor baths. But all that only seemed to annoy her even more.

On certain days, she would begin to chatter with a feverish abandon; but these exaltations would be quickly followed by stupors into which she remained sunk without speaking, without moving. What would revive her then was splashing eau-de-cologne from a bottle over her arms.

Because she complained constantly about Tostes, Charles thought that the cause of her illness must be some local influence, and, fixing on this idea, he started to talk seriously about going elsewhere to set up his practice.

At that point, she began drinking vinegar to make herself thinner, contracted a dry little cough, and lost her appetite entirely.

Leaving Tostes was a serious matter for Charles, after living there for four years and at the very moment *when he was just beginning to get settled in*. But if it had to be done! He brought her to Rouen to consult with his old professor. It was a nervous malady: she had to have a change of air.

After looking around everywhere he could, Charles learned that there was a good-sized market town in the Neufchâtel district called Yonville-l'Abbaye, whose doctor, a Polish refugee, had cleared out just the week before. So he wrote to the local pharmacist to find out the size of the population, how far it was from the nearest doctor, how much his predecessor had made per year, et cetera; and, the replies having been satisfactory, he resolved to move there toward springtime, if Emma's health had not improved.

One day, in preparation for her move, she was arranging things in a drawer when something pricked her fingers. It was the metal wire from her wedding bouquet. The orange blossoms were yellowed with dust, and the satin ribbons with their silver border were shredded along the edges. She threw it in the fire. It flared up more quickly than dried straw. Then it looked like a little red bush against the cinders, slowly being consumed. She watched it burn. The little cardboard berries burst, the brass wires bent and twisted, the braiding melted down; and the paper flower petals, shriveling, swayed against the back of the stove like black butterflies and finally flew up the chimney.

When they left Tostes, in the month of March, Madame Bovary was pregnant.

Part Two

CHAPTER I

Yonville-l'Abbaye (so named for an old Capuchin abbey, even the ruins of which no longer exist) is a market town some twenty-four miles from Rouen, between the Abbeville and the Beauvais roads, lying in a valley watered by the Rieule, a small river that flows into the Andelle after having turned three watermills near its mouth, where there are a few trout; the boys amuse themselves by fishing for them on Sundays.

If you leave the highway at La Boissière and go straight on to the top of the Leux hills, you will see the valley below. The river running through it divides it into what seem to be two distinct physiognomies: everything on the left is pasture, and everything on the right is farmland. The meadow stretches along under a bulge of low hills, to join up behind in the pasture lands near Bray, while on the eastern side the gently rising plain broadens out, revealing its blond wheat fields as far as the eye can see. The water flowing by the edge of the grass creates a white line separating the color of the meadows from that of the cultivated farmland, and the countryside looks like a great cloak spread out, with a green velvet collar edged with a silver fringe.

On the horizon, when you arrive, you see straight ahead the oaks of the Argueil forest, with the slopes of the Saint-Jean hill scarred from top to bottom with long, irregular red lines; these are the tracks of the rains, and these bricktones, cut in fine streaks against the gray color of the mountain, are the effect of the iron-heavy waters that originate in springs in the surrounding regions.

This is the border region of Normandy, Picardy, and the Île-de-France, a bastard country where the language has no accent and the landscape no character. This is where they make the worst Neufchâtel cheeses in the whole district, and moreover, farming is an expensive proposition here, because it takes a lot of manure to enrich this crumbly soil, full as it is of sand and pebbles.

Up until 1835 there was no decent, passable road to get to Yonville; but around that time, a *connecting byroad* was established, linking up the road to Abbeville with that of the one to Amiens; the new road is sometimes used by Rouen wagoners on their way to Flanders. But for all that, Yonville-l'Abbaye has not changed a bit despite its *new outlets*. Instead of improving the soil, they stubbornly keep their land for pasture despite the depreciation in its value, and the lazy little town, turning its back on the plain, has continued its natural growth toward the river. You can see it from far off stretching along the water's edge, like a cowherd taking his siesta by the river.

At the foot of the hill, after the bridge, a roadway planted with young aspens leads you straight to the first homes in the area. They are enclosed by hedges, set in the midst of yards full of scattered outbuildings, wine presses, cart sheds, and distilleries under dense trees, from the lower branches of which are hung ladders, poles, and scythes. The thatched roofs, like fur caps pulled down over the eyes, hang down and cover the top third of the low windows—whose panes bulge out to a knot in the center, like the bottoms of bottles. Sometimes, a scraggly pear tree leans against a plaster wall crossed diagonally by black joists, and the ground floors have little swinging gates at their doors for protection from the chicks that come to the thresholds to peck at crumbs of brown bread dipped in cider. But the courtyards grow narrower, the houses come closer together, the hedges disappear; a bundle of ferns sways below a window, hanging from the end of a broomstick; there is a blacksmith's forge, then a wheelwright's shop with two or three new carts out in front, partly blocking the way. Then, across an open space, appears a white house in the middle of a lawn decorated by a Cupid, one finger pressed against his lips; two cast-iron urns stand at either side of the porch; a signboard gleams on the door: this is the notary's house, the finest one in the area.

The church is on the other side of the street, twenty paces further down, at the entrance to the square. The little cemetery surrounding it, enclosed by a wall chest high, is so full of graves that the old gravestones sunk in the ground form a continuous pavement of regular squares broken only by the grass growing between them. The church had been rebuilt during the last years of Charles X's[9] reign. The wooden roof is starting to rot from the top down, and here and there black holes appear in its blue paint. Over the doorway, where the organ would be, is a loft for the men, with a spiral staircase that echoes under their wooden shoes.

The daylight, coming in through the plain glass windows, obliquely lights up the pews ranged perpendicular to the wall, with here and there straw mats nailed to them, and just beneath them in big letters the words "Monsieur so-and-so's pew." Farther on, at the area where the nave narrows, the confessional is complemented by a statuette of the Virgin, dressed in a satin robe, a tulle veil sprinkled with silver stars on her head, her cheeks stained purple like some idol from the Sandwich Islands;[1] and finally, a copy of the *Holy Family, A Gift from the Minister of the Interior* dominates the high altar between four candlesticks, closing off the perspective. The choir stalls, of pinewood, remain unpainted.

The marketplace—that is, a tiled roof supported by twenty posts—itself occupies about half of Yonville's public square. The town hall, built *from the design of a Paris architect*, is a sort of Greek temple that forms the corner next to the pharmacist's shop. It has, on the ground floor, three Ionic columns and, on the second floor, a semicircular gallery terminating in a tympanum adorned with a Gallic cock who rests one foot upon the constitution[2] and holds in the other the scales of justice.

But what really attracts the eye, standing across from the *Golden Lion* inn, is the pharmacy of Monsieur Homais! Especially in the evening, when his lamp is lit, once the red and green apothecary jars that adorn his window cast their two bright colors across the sidewalk, then, looking through them, as if through Bengal lights,[3] one can see the shadow of the pharmacist leaning over his desk. His house from top to bottom is papered with inscriptions written in script, in round hand, in block letters: "Vichy, Seltzer, and Barège waters, purifying agents, Raspail medicine, Arabian racahout, Darcet lozenges, Regnault salve, bandages, baths, medicinal chocolate," et cetera. And the sign stretching across

9. The last Bourbon king (1757–1836), son of Louis XV. He was expelled by the July Revolution (1830).
1. Old name for Hawaii, after John Montagu, fourth earl of Sandwich (1718–1792), who served as first lord of the admiralty when the islands were discovered.

2. The *Charte constitutionelle de la France*, basis of the French constitution after the revolution, bestowed in 1814 by Louis XVIII and revised in 1830, after the downfall of Charles X.
3. Blue flares used in signaling.

the entire width of the shop reads, in golden letters, *Homais, Pharmacist*. Then, at the back of the shop, behind the big scales affixed to the counter, the word *Laboratory* appears above a glass door which, halfway up, repeats once more *Homais* in gold letters on a black background.

There is nothing more to see in Yonville. The street (the only one), about as long as a gunshot and lined with a few shops on either side, comes to a sudden end at the turn of the highway. Leaving it and heading off to the right, following the Saint-Jean hills, one soon comes to the cemetery.

In the time of cholera,[4] to enlarge it, they pulled down part of a wall and bought three adjoining acres; but this entire new section is largely empty, for the graves continue, as before, to crowd together near the gate. The grounds-keeper, who is also the gravedigger and the church's verger (thereby making a double profit out of the parish's corpses), has taken advantage of the empty ground to plant potatoes there. But from year to year his little field shrinks, and when there is an epidemic, he doesn't know whether to rejoice at the deaths or grieve at the burials.

"You feed yourself on the dead, Lestiboudois!" the priest said to him one day.

This somber remark made him think, and it made him stop for a while; but today he continues to cultivate his little tubers, and he even goes so far as to claim, with complete assurance, that they grow by themselves.

Since the time of the events we are about to narrate here, nothing has really changed in Yonville. The tin tricolor flag still turns at the top of the church steeple; the dry-goods merchant's shop still waves its two calico streamers in the wind; the pharmacist's fetuses, like little packets of white tinder, continue to rot away bit by bit in their muddy alcohol; and above the inn's big door, the old golden lion, faded by the rains, still shows off its poodle's mane to passersby.

On the evening when the Bovarys were due to arrive, the inn's landlady, the widow Madame Lefrançois, was so busy that the sweat poured off her in big drops as she shuffled her saucepans. The next day was the town's market day. She had to cut the meat in advance, clean the chickens, prepare the soup and the coffee. And she also had to make the meals for her boarders, and for the doctor, his wife, and their maid; the billiard room echoed with laughter; three millers in the little parlor were calling for brandy to be brought; the wood was blazing, the coals crackling, and, on the long kitchen table among the quarters of raw mutton, piles of plates rose up, rattling from the shaking of the cutting board where the spinach was being chopped. From the yard the squawking of chickens could be heard, as the servant chased them around to cut off their heads.

A pockmarked man wearing green leather slippers and a velvet cap with a gold tassel was warming his back at the fireplace. His face expressed nothing but self-satisfaction, and he seemed as content with life as the goldfinch suspended over his head in its wicker cage. This was the pharmacist.

"Artémise!" the landlady cried, "chop some wood, fill the pitchers, serve the brandy, hurry up! If only I knew what sort of dessert to serve the people you're expecting! Good heavens! Those moving men are starting up their racket again

---

4. The cholera epidemic in France was in 1832 [translator's note].

in the billiard room! And is their cart still up against the front door? The Hirondelle could crash into it when it gets here! Call 'Polyte to move it away! ... just think, Monsieur Homais, since this morning they've played fifteen games and drank eight jugs of cider! ... And they're going to rip the cloth for me," she continued, keeping an eye on them from a distance, her skimming ladle in her hand.

"That wouldn't be such a loss," Monsieur Homais replied. "you could buy another one."

"Another billiard cloth!" the widow exclaimed.

"Since that one's falling to pieces, Madame Lefrançois; I keep telling you, you're making a mistake! A big mistake! And anyway, the players nowadays want narrow pockets and heavy cues. People just don't play the way they used to; everything has changed! You have to keep up with the times! Look at Tellier ... "

The hostess reddened with irritation. The pharmacist added:

"His billiard table, say what you like, is nicer than yours; and suppose we had a patriotic pool tournament, for example, to benefit Poland, or the Lyons flood victims ... "[5]

"Good-for-nothings like him don't frighten me!" the hostess interrupted, shrugging her fat shoulders. "Come on, come on, Monsieur Homais! As long as the *Golden Lion* is here, people will be coming. We've feathered our nest just fine! One of these mornings you'll see the *Café Français* closed down, with a placard stuck on the shutters! ... Change my billiard table," she went on, talking to herself, "when this one is so handy for folding the laundry on, and when I've been able to fit six guests on it during hunting season! ... But that slowpoke Hivert still isn't here!"

"Are you waiting for him before you serve your gentlemen's dinner?" the pharmacist asked.

"Waiting for him? And what about Monsieur Binet? He'll walk in at six on the dot, because nobody on earth is more exact when it comes to being on time. He always has to have his place in the little parlor! You'd have to kill him to make him eat anywhere else! And he's so fussy! And so finicky about his cider! Not like Monsieur Léon—now him, he'll come in sometimes at seven, sometimes even at seven-thirty; and he doesn't pay any attention to what he's eating. What a nice young man! Never raises his voice!"

"That's the difference, you see, between someone who's had an education and an old soldier turned tax collector."

The clock struck six. Binet came in.

He was dressed in a blue frock coat that hung straight down on his thin body, and his leather cap, with its ear flaps tied up on top of his head, revealed below its turned-up visor a bald forehead, flattened out by the helmet he had worn for so long. He wore a black waistcoat, a horsehair collar, gray trousers, and, no matter what the season, well-polished boots that had two parallel bulges where his toes thrust upward. Not one hair was out of place in the careful line of blond whiskers that circled his jaws and framed, like a border in a

5. The allusion dates the action of the novel as taking place in 1840; during the winter of 1840, the Rhône overflowed with catastrophic results. At the same time, Louis Philippe was under steady attack for his failure to offer sufficient assistance to the victims of the repression that followed the insurrection of Warsaw (1831).

garden, his long, dull face with its little eyes and its hooked nose. Formidable at every kind of card game, a good hunter, a man of excellent penmanship, he had a lathe at his home with which he entertained himself by making napkin rings, cluttering his house with them, with the single-mindedness of an artist and the self-importance of a bourgeois.

He made straight for the little parlor: but first it was necessary to get the three millers out of it; and during the entire time it took to set his table, Binet remained silent in his place near the stove; then, he closed the door and removed his hat, in his customary way.

"He won't wear out *his* tongue with polite conversation!" said the pharmacist, when he was alone with the hostess.

"He never says much," she replied. "Last week, two traveling clothes salesmen were here, real funny guys who told so many jokes that evening I was crying from laughter: well! He just sat there like a fish and didn't say a word."

"Yes," said the pharmacist, "no imagination, no little bursts of wit, no social graces!"

"But they say he has his talents," she objected.

"Talents!" replied Monsieur Homais. "Him! Talents? In his own line of work, possibly," he added in a calmer tone.

And he went on: "Ah, if a businessman with important connections, a magistrate, a doctor, a pharmacist were to become so absorbed that they became eccentric or even gruff, I would understand that; history gives us examples! But at least it's because they're thinking about something. Take me for example: how many times have I looked all over my desk for a pen to write out a label, only to find that I'd put it behind my ear!"

But Madame Lefrançois went to the door to see if the *Hirondelle*[6] had come. She jumped: a man dressed in black suddenly strode into the kitchen. In the last gleams of the twilight one could see that his face was ruddy and his form athletic.

"What can I do for you, Monsieur le curé?" asked the landlady, while she reached up for one of the brass candlesticks that were arranged in a row with their candles. "Will you have a drink? A drop of cassis, a glass of wine?"

The priest very politely declined. He had come to look for his umbrella, which he had forgotten the other day at the Ernemont convent, and after having asked Madame Lefrançois to have it sent to him at the rectory that evening, he left to get back to the church, where the Angelus was ringing.

When the pharmacist could no longer hear the sound of his steps outside in the square, he said he found the priest's behavior just now quite unseemly. That refusal to accept some refreshment seemed to him the most loathsome hypocrisy; all priests guzzle liquor on the sly, and they were all trying to bring back the days of the tithe.

The hostess took up the priest's defense:

"Well, anyway, he could bend four men like you over his knee. Last year, he helped our folks bring in the hay; he could carry up to six bales at once, that's how strong he is!"

"Bravo!" said the pharmacist. "So send your daughters off to confess to strapping fellows like that! If I were the government, I'd like to have priests bled

---

6. The stagecoach is named for the swiftly flying swallow, the *hirondelle* [translator's note].

once a month. Yes, Madame Lefrançois, every month, a good strong bloodletting, for the sake of law and order!"

"Oh be quiet, Monsieur Homais! You're a blasphemer! You have no religion!"

The pharmacist replied, "Yes, I have a religion, my religion, and it's greater than all of theirs, with their mumbo-jumbo and their magic tricks! On the contrary, I worship God! I believe in a Supreme Being, in a Creator, whatever he is, it doesn't matter, who has placed us here below on Earth to fulfill our duties as citizens, and as fathers of families; but I don't have any need to go into a church to kiss silver plates and take money out of my pocket to fatten up a gang of frauds who eat better than we do! Because one can honor God just as well in the woods, in a field, or even in contemplating the ethereal vault above, the way the ancients did. My God, mine, is the God of Socrates, of Franklin, of Voltaire, and of Béranger! I'm for the *Profession of Faith of the Savoyard Vicar* and the immortal principles of 1789! Therefore I cannot accept some good old fellow of a God who walks in his garden with a cane in his hand, lodges his friends in the belly of whales, dies screeching, and revives himself three days later—things that are absurd in themselves, and what's more, completely opposed to all the laws of physics—which demonstrates, by the way, how the priests have always wallowed in base ignorance and want to drown the people in it right along with them!"

He stopped, and looked around for an audience, for in his excitement the pharmacist had for a moment imagined himself in the midst of a town council. But the inn's landlady didn't hear him; she was listening to the sound of distant wheels. They could hear the sounds of a carriage along with the clatter of loose horseshoes beating the ground, and at last the *Hirondelle* stopped in front of the door.

The coach was a yellow box mounted on two great wheels that reached all the way to the roof, preventing its passengers from being able to see the road, and muddying their shoulders. The little panes of the narrow windows rattled in their frames when the doors were closed, and they retained spots of mud here and there amid the old layers of dust that even the rainstorms never entirely washed off. It was drawn by three horses, the first one as the leader, and on the downhills, its bottom would bump the ground with a jolt.

Some Yonville townspeople came out into the square; they spoke all at once, asking for news, for information, for their food baskets: Hivert didn't know which one to answer first. He was the one who went to town and did errands and made purchases for the local people. He went to shops, brought back rolls of leather for the shoemaker, scrap iron for the blacksmith, a barrel of herring for the innkeeper, bonnets from the milliner, wigs from the hairdresser; and all along the road on his return trip, he distributed his packages, tossing them over fences and walls while standing upright on his seat, calling out at the top of his voice while his horses trotted along on their own.

He had been delayed by an accident: Madame Bovary's greyhound had run off across the fields. They had whistled for it for a quarter of an hour. Hivert had even turned and driven back a mile or so, thinking every moment that he would catch sight of it; but at last they had to move on. Emma had wept and was very angry; she blamed Charles for causing the disaster. Monsieur Lheureux, a dry-goods merchant who happened to be in the coach with her, tried to console her by telling numerous stories of lost dogs who years later recognized their masters. People talked about one, he said, who had found its way back from Constantinople to Paris. Another one had come a hundred and twenty miles in a straight line and had swum four rivers; and his own father had owned a poodle that, after being lost for twelve years, suddenly jumped up on his back one evening, as he was walking down the street on his way to dinner.

CHAPTER 2

Emma got out first, followed by Félicité, Monsieur Lheureux, and a nurse, and they had to wake Charles up; sitting in his corner, he had fallen sound asleep as soon as night fell.

Homais introduced himself; he offered Madame his compliments, and Monsieur his respects, said that he had been delighted to have been able to be of some service to them, and added cordially that he had been so bold as to invite himself to join their dinner, his wife being away.

Madame Bovary, when she had come in the kitchen, walked over to the fireplace. With the tips of two fingers, she grasped her dress at the knees and lifted it up to her ankles, holding out toward the fire, above the leg of lamb turning on a spit, her foot encased in a black boot. The flame fully illuminated her, its harsh light penetrating the cloth of her dress, the smooth pores of her white skin, even the eyelids that she blinked from time to time. A strong red glow moved over her, due to the wind coming through the half-open door.

On the other side of the fireplace, a young man with fair hair stood gazing at her silently.

Since he was enormously bored with Yonville, where he was a clerk to the notary Monsieur Guillaumin, Monsieur Léon Dupuis (for it was he, the second habitué of the *Golden Lion*) often put off his dinner hour in hopes that some traveler would turn up at the inn, someone with whom he could chat during the evening. On the days when he finished his work early, he had no choice but to arrive punctually, and then submit to the company of Binet from soup to cheese. And so it was with joy that he accepted the hostess' suggestion that he dine with the newcomers, and they all walked together into the large parlor where Madame Lefrançois, with great pomp, had set a table for four.

Homais begged permission to keep his skullcap on, for fear of catching a head cold.

Then, turning to his neighbor: "Madame is no doubt a bit tired? A person gets so terribly jolted around in our *Hirondelle*."

"That's true," Emma replied, "but all this trouble always amuses me; I love to have a change of scene."

"It's such a bore," the clerk said with a sigh, "to be always stuck in one place!"

"If you were like me," said Charles, "always obliged to be on horseback . . ."

"But," Léon continued, addressing himself to Madame Bovary, "there's nothing more pleasant, it seems to me—that is, when a person can—" he added.

"Anyway," said the pharmacist, "the practice of medicine is not so very difficult in our district; for the state of our roads allows the use of a cabriolet, and generally people pay well, the farmers being pretty well off. We have, speaking from the medical point of view, apart from the usual cases of enteritis, bronchitis, liver problems, and the like, from time to time a few intermittent fevers around harvest time, but, in general, very few serious illnesses, nothing worth mentioning, unless it be quite a lot of scrofula, which comes no doubt from the deplorable hygienic conditions of our peasant housing. Ah, you will find a great many prejudices to combat, Monsieur Bovary! Many stubborn habits, against which all the efforts of your science will have to do battle on a daily basis; for here people still turn to novenas, to relics, to the priest, rather than coming directly to the doctor or the pharmacist. The climate, however, is, to tell the truth, not all bad, and we even count some nonagenarians in the parish. The thermometer—I have made some observations—in winter goes down to about four degrees, and in the warmest season rises to twenty-five or thirty degrees centigrade at the most, which gives us twenty-four on the Réaumur scale at most, or in other words fifty-four degrees Fahrenheit (the English scale), no more than that! And in fact we are sheltered from the north winds by the forest of Argueil on the one side; from the west winds by the Saint-Jean hills on the other; and this heat, however, which, due to the water vapors given off from the river and the considerable presence of cattle in the fields, which exhale, as you know, a great deal of ammonia, or, that is, nitrogen, hydrogen, and oxygen—no, it's only nitrogen and hydrogen—and which, sucking up the earth's humus and blending together all these different emanations, reunites them into a single bundle, so to speak, and combining itself with the electricity in the atmosphere, when there is any, can, in the long run, as in tropical countries, give rise to insalubrious miasmas—this heat, I say, finds itself nicely tempered on the side it comes from, or rather on the side it would come from, that is to say the southern side, by the southeasterly winds that, being cooled themselves by passing over the Seine, come upon us abruptly sometimes, like breezes from Russia!"

"Are there at least some good walks around here?" Madame Bovary continued, speaking to the young man.

"Oh, hardly any," he replied. "There's a place they call the Pasture, on the top of a hill, on the edge of the forest. Sometimes on Sundays I go there with a book, to watch the sunset."

"I don't think there's anything as lovely as sunsets," she said, "but especially by the seaside."

"Oh, I love the sea!" said Monsieur Léon.

"And doesn't it seem to you," Madame Bovary replied, "that the spirit can roam more freely over that limitless expanse, the contemplation of which elevates the soul and suggests ideas of the infinite, of the ideal?"

"It's the same with mountain landscapes," said Léon. "I have a cousin who traveled to Switzerland last year, and he told me you simply can't imagine the poetry of the lakes, the delight of the waterfalls, the gigantic effect of the glaciers. You see pines of an unbelievable size across the torrents, little cottages practically hanging from precipices, and when the clouds part, a thousand feet below you, whole valleys. Sights like those just have to fill a person with enthusiasm, dispose him toward prayer, toward ecstasy! So it doesn't surprise me any more to think of that celebrated musician who, in order to stimulate his imagination more powerfully, used to play his piano in front of some imposing scene."

"Do you play music?" she asked.

"No, but I love it very much," he replied.

"Oh, don't believe him, Madame Bovary," Homais interrupted, bending over his plate, "it's pure modesty. Come on, my friend! Just the other day in your room you were singing the 'Guardian Angel'[7] delightfully! I was listening to you from my laboratory; you performed it like an actor."

Léon did room at the pharmacist's, where he had a little apartment on the third floor, overlooking the square. He blushed at his landlord's compliment, though Homais had already turned back toward the doctor and was enumerating for him, one after the other, the principal citizens of Yonville. He was telling anecdotes and supplying information; nobody knew what the notary's exact wealth amounted to, and *then there was the Tuvache concern*, which was facing some real problems.

Emma continued:

"And what music is your favorite?"

"Oh! German music, the kind that sets you dreaming."

"Are you familiar with the Italians?"

"Not yet; but I'll get to see them next year, when I go to live in Paris, to finish my law studies."

"I've just had the honor," the pharmacist said, "of explaining to your spouse all about that poor Yanoda who ran off; you'll find, thanks to his absurd extravagances, that you'll be enjoying one of Yonville's most comfortable houses. What makes it especially convenient for a doctor is its door onto the back lane, which lets people go in and leave without being seen. Moreover, it includes everything most pleasant in a household: laundry, kitchen with pantry, sitting room, fruit storeroom, et cetera. He was a lively fellow who didn't keep much of an eye on his expenses! He had an arbor built beside the river expressly for drinking his beer in the summer, and if Madame enjoys gardening, she will be able to . . ."

"My wife doesn't much care for it," said Charles; "and even though she has been advised to get some exercise, she'd rather stay in her room all day, reading."

"That's just like me," said Léon. "Really, what could be better than spending an evening by the fireside with a book, while the wind beats on the window-panes, while the lamp burns?"

"Isn't that true?" she said, fixing her great black eyes, wide open, upon him.

"At those times you think about nothing in particular," he went on, "and the hours pass by. Sitting still, you walk through lands that you feel you can see, and your thoughts merge with the fiction, hovering over the details or following along with the plot. You commune with the characters; it seems as if it's your heart beating beneath their clothes."

"So true! So true!" she said.

"Has it ever happened to you," Léon continued, "to come across, in a book, some vague idea that you once had, or some shadowy image that seems to return to you from a great distance, which seems to be the most complete expression possible of your most fleeting feelings?"

"I have felt that," she replied.

"That's why," he said, "I love the poets above all. I find verses to be more sensitive than prose, and they certainly bring me to tears more often."

---

7. A sentimental romance written by Mme. Pauline Duchambre, author of several such songs.

"Yet they're fatiguing in the long run," Emma replied. "And right now, on the contrary, I love those stories that you can read scarcely taking a breath, stories that frighten me. I detest common, everyday heroes and restrained emotions, like the ones in real life."

"And I really think," the clerk observed, "that those works that don't touch the heart are missing the true aim of Art. It's so sweet a thing, amidst all of life's disenchantments, to be able to come back and think about noble characters, pure feelings, and scenes of happiness. As for me, living here far away from the world, it's my only distraction; but Yonville has so few resources!"

"Just like Tostes, no doubt," replied Emma, "so I always subscribed to a lending library."

"If Madame would do me the honor of making use of it," said the pharmacist, who had just heard these last words, "I have at her disposal a library composed of the best authors: Voltaire, Rousseau, Delille,[8] Walter Scott, *The Literary Echo*, et cetera, and I subscribe, moreover, to various periodicals, among them the *Rouen Lantern*,[9] a daily, because I have the advantage of being their correspondent for the districts of Buchy, Forges, Neufchâtel, Yonville, and the vicinity."

They had been at the table for two and a half hours; for the servant Artémise, nonchalantly dragging her slippers over the tiles, brought the dishes in out of order, forgot everything, paid attention to nothing, and constantly left the billiard room door half open, so that its latch banged against the wall.

Without noticing it himself, as he talked Léon had placed his foot on one of the crossbars of Madame Bovary's chair. She was wearing a thin scarf of blue silk to keep her fluted cambric ruff in place; and, depending on the movement of her head, the lower part of her face would either sink into the fabric or gently rise up out of it. And sitting thus, close to each other, while Charles and the pharmacist talked, they entered into one of those vague conversations where chance phrases continually bring you back to the fixed center, to feelings held in common. Paris plays, the titles of novels, new quadrilles, and the world neither of them knew, Tostes, where she had lived, Yonville, where they were now—they discussed it all, up to the end of the dinner.

When coffee was served, Félicité went off to prepare the bedroom in the new house, and the group soon got up from the table. Madame Lefrançois was asleep beside the embers, while the stable boy with a lantern in his hand waited to lead Monsieur and Madame Bovary to their new home. His red hair had wisps of straw stuck in it, and he limped with his left leg. When he had picked up the priest's umbrella with his other hand, they all set off.

The town was asleep. The market pillars cast long shadows. The earth seemed entirely gray, as on a summer's night.

But since the doctor's house was only about fifty paces from the inn, they soon had to say their good-nights, and the group dispersed.

As soon as she entered the hall, Emma felt the coldness of the plaster walls seeming to fall over her shoulders like a damp cloth. The walls were newly done, and the wooden steps creaked. In the second-floor bedroom, a whitish light entered the uncurtained windows. Through them one could see treetops and, farther out, the meadow, half submerged in the fog that steamed up from

8. Jacques Delille (1738–1813) wrote idyllic nature poetry. 9. The *Rouen Beacon* (a fictitious newspaper).

the river in the moonlight. In the middle of the room was a jumble of dresser drawers, bottles, curtain rods, gilt poles, mattresses on the chairs, and basins on the floor: the two moving men had simply left everything there carelessly.

It was the fourth time she had gone to bed in an unknown environment. The first was on the day she had come to the convent, the second that of her arrival in Tostes, the third at La Vaubyessard, and the fourth was this time; and each one had been a kind of inauguration, a new phase in her life. She did not believe that things could be the same in different places, and since the part of her life she had already lived had been unpleasant, the part that remained would, no doubt, be better.

CHAPTER 3

The next day when she awoke she saw the clerk in the square. She was in her dressing gown. He looked up and bowed to her. She made a slight, rapid bow and reclosed the window.

Léon waited all day long for six o'clock to arrive; but when he came into the inn, he saw only Monsieur Binet, seated at his table.

The previous day's dinner had been a significant event for him; he had never before conversed for two hours straight with a *lady*. How was it that he had been able to express so many things to her, and in such language, so many things that he had never said so well before? He was normally shy, and kept up the sort of reserve that arose from a combination of modesty and dissimulation. In Yonville, people thought he had *the right sort* of manners. He listened to the opinions of his elders, and he was not all wrapped up in politics like so many young men. And then he had his talents: he painted in watercolors, could read music in the key of G, and was happy to discuss literature after dinner, when he wasn't playing cards. Monsieur Homais respected him for his education; Madame Homais was fond of him for his good nature, for he would often take the Homais children to the garden—brats whose faces were always dirty, very badly brought up, and tending to sluggishness like their mother. To look after them they had, besides the maid, Justin, the pharmacist's apprentice, a distant cousin of Homais whom they had taken in out of charity, and who thus was also useful as a servant.

The druggist showed himself to be the best of neighbors. He informed Madame Bovary about the local merchants, had his own cider merchant call on her, tasted the drink himself, and saw to it that the barrels were placed in the cellar properly; and he also showed her how to go about getting a good price on butter; and he made an arrangement with the sexton Lestiboudois who, apart from his churchly and mortuary functions, served as gardener to Yonville's principal homes, for hire by the hour or the year, according to the individual's wishes.

But it was not pure altruism that drove the pharmacist to such heights of obsequious cordiality; there was in fact another motive.

He had violated Article 1 of the law of the 19th of Ventose, year XI,[1] which forbids anyone without a diploma from practicing medicine; and the result was

1. The government of the French Republic established a new calendar. The new year began on September 22, 1792; thus the year is 1803. *Ventôse*: windy (French); the sixth month of the new calendar (from February 19 to March 20), making the date March 9.

that certain dark, anonymous accusations had landed Homais before the royal prosecutor in Rouen, in his own private office. The magistrate received him standing up, wearing his formal robes, ermine on his shoulders, and official cap on his head. This was in the morning, before the court session. He could hear the policemen's heavy boots in the corridor, and, in the distance, what sounded like huge locks being turned. The pharmacist's ears began to ring so much that he believed he would have a stroke; he vividly imagined the deepest reaches of a dungeon, his family in tears, the pharmacy put up for sale, all his jars dispersed; and he had to go into a café afterward to drink a glass of rum and seltzer water to calm his nerves.

But time slowly weakened the memory of his warning, and he continued, just as before, to give harmless consultations in the back room of his shop. But the mayor had his eye on him, some colleagues were jealous, and he had to be very careful; by binding Monsieur Bovary to him with his favors, he hoped to win his gratitude and prevent him from speaking out later if he happened to find out anything. And thus every morning he brought the newspaper to him, and many afternoons he would leave the pharmacy for a few moments to go over and chat with the health officer.

Charles was gloomy: patients were not coming. He would stay sitting in one place for long hours without speaking, would go nap in his office, or would sit and watch his wife sewing. For diversion, he busied himself at home playing handyman, and he even tried to brighten up the attic with some paint left behind by the painters. But money problems worried him. He had spent so much on repairs at Tostes, so much on Madame's wardrobe and on the move, that the entire dowry, over three thousand écus, had trickled away in two years. And then there had been so many things broken or lost in the move from Tostes to Yonville—not to mention the plaster priest, which had fallen off the cart after a severe jolt, shattering into a thousand pieces on the Quincampoix pavement.

But there was one more pleasant anxiety that helped to distract him, namely, his wife's pregnancy. The closer the due date came, the more he cherished her. It was another fleshly bond being established between them, and it seemed like a continuation and deepening of their union. When, standing off at a distance, he saw her heavy walk, and her uncorseted hips gently swaying—when they sat facing each other, and he could freely gaze at her while she wearily shifted positions in the armchair—then his happiness knew no limits. He would get up, kiss her, caress her face, call her "little mama," try to talk her into dancing, and, half laughing and half weeping, pour out every little endearment that came into his head. The idea of having fathered a child delighted him. There was nothing lacking in his life now. He knew the whole range of human existence now, and he sat down at the table before it, rested his elbows, and contemplated it with serenity.

Emma at first felt a great astonishment, and then she became anxious for the child to be born so she would learn what it was to be a mother. But not being able to spend as much as she wanted, to have a boat-shaped cradle with pink silk curtains and embroidered caps for the baby, she gave up caring about it all in a fit of bitterness, and she ordered everything from a village seamstress, without choosing or even discussing any of it. So she took no pleasure in those preparations that help to stimulate a mother's love, and her affection was perhaps weakened from the beginning.

But since Charles would speak about the baby at every meal, she soon began to think about it more seriously.

She wanted a boy; he would be strong, dark, and named Georges; and this idea of having a male child was like a hoped-for revenge upon all her former powerlessness. A man, whatever else he is, is free; he can explore passions and countries, overcome obstacles, taste the most exotic pleasure. But a woman is always held back. Inert and flexible at the same time, she is hampered both by the weakness of her flesh and by the legal restrictions imposed upon her. Her will, like the veil of her bonnet held by a string, flutters in every wind: there is always some desire luring her, some convention restraining her.

She gave birth on a Sunday about six in the morning, as the sun was rising.

"It's a girl!" said Charles.

She turned her head away and fainted.

Almost immediately Madame Homais ran over to embrace her, as did Madame Lefrançois of the *Golden Lion*. The pharmacist, a discreet man, only addressed a few provisional congratulations through the half-opened door. He wanted to see the infant and found it well formed.

During her convalescence, she busied herself a great deal in seeking out a name for her daughter. First she reviewed all the ones with Italian endings, like Clara, Louisa, Amanda, Atala; she liked Galsuinde well enough, and Yseult or Léocadie even more. Charles wanted to name the child after his mother; Emma opposed the idea. They ran through the saints' calendar from one end to the other, and they asked outsiders for advice.

"Monsieur Léon," said the pharmacist, "with whom I was conversing the other day, is quite surprised that you haven't chosen Madeleine, which is all the rage right now."

But Charles' mother protested strongly against that great sinner's name.[2] As for Monsieur Homais, he had a predilection for names that recalled great men, an illustrious deed, or a noble idea, and this was the system by which he had baptized his four children. Thus, Napoléon represented glory and Franklin liberty; Irma was, perhaps, a concession to Romanticism; but Athalie was an homage to the most immortal masterpiece of the French stage.[3] Because his philosophical convictions were no impediment to his aesthetic tastes, the thinker in him did not stifle the man of feeling; he knew how to make distinctions, to keep the roles of imagination and fanaticism quite separate. In the tragedy of *Athalie*, for example, he could condemn the ideas but admire the style; he could damn the conception, but applaud all the details; he could be infuriated by the characters but be carried away with enthusiasm over their speeches. When he read the great, famous passages, he was transported; but when he realized that the bigoted Catholics would draw some profit from them for their sales pitches, he despaired, and tangled up in these confused and contradictory feelings, he would have liked to put the laurel wreath on Racine with his own hands and at the same time sit down and argue with him for a good quarter of an hour.

---

2. *Madeleine* is French for Magdalene; Jesus' discipline, Mary Magdelene, was long thought to have been a prostitute.

3. *Athalie*: protagonist of a tragedy by Jean Racine (1639–1699), perhaps the greatest of all French playwrights.

Eventually, Emma recalled that at La Vaubyessard she had heard the Marquise call a young woman Berthe; from that moment it was settled. Since Monsieur Rouault was unable to come, they asked Homais to be the child's godfather. All the gifts he gave came right out of his shop, namely: six boxes of jujubes, a whole jar of racahout, three marshmallow cakes, and six sticks of sugar candy that he had found in a cupboard. There was a big dinner on the evening of the ceremony; the priest was there, and things began to heat up when the liqueurs were served: Homais recited from *The Good Man's God* by Béranger,[4] Monsieur Léon sang a barcarole, and Madame Bovary senior, who was godmother, sang a balled from the days of the Empire. Finally, Monsieur Bovary senior insisted that the infant be brought down, and he proceeded to baptize her with a glass of champagne, pouring it down from high over her head. This mockery of the first of the sacraments outraged the Abbé Bournisien; Bovary senior responded by quoting from *The War of the Gods*,[5] and the cleric got up to leave; the ladies pleaded with him; Homais intervened, and they succeeded in getting the priest to sit back down again, and he then went back to calmly sipping his half-finished coffee.

Monsieur Bovary senior stayed on for a month in Yonville, where he dazzled the locals with his superb silver-trimmed police hat; he wore it in the morning when he went out into the square to smoke. Having also the habit of consuming a great deal of brandy, he would often send the maid to the *Golden Lion* to fetch him a bottle, which he would charge to his son's account; and to scent his scarves, he used up the entirety of his daughter-in-law's eau de cologne.

She found his company by no means displeasing. He had gotten around in the world; he spoke about Berlin, Vienna, Strasbourg, his time as an officer, the mistresses he had had, the grand dinners he had attended; and then he was playful too, and from time to time, on the staircase or in the garden he would seize her around the waist and cry out:

"Charles, look out for yourself!"

Then Charles' mother began to fear for the happiness of her son, and fearing that her husband would in the long run have an immoral influence on the young woman's thinking, she hastened their departure. Perhaps she had even more serious concerns. Monsieur Bovary was a man who respected nothing.

One day, Emma was suddenly seized with an urge to visit her little girl, who had been put out to nurse with the carpenter's wife, and without looking at the almanac to be sure the six weeks of the Virgin[6] were over, she set out on the path to the Rollet house, located at the edge of town beneath the hills, between the highway and the fields.

It was noontime; the houses had their shutters closed, and the slate roofs gleaming under the harsh light of the bright blue sky seemed to be shooting sparks from the gable tops. A strong wind was blowing. Emma felt weak as she walked; the pebbles on the walkway hurt her feet; she was unsure whether she ought to turn back and go home or stop in somewhere and sit down.

---

4. A deistic song by Béranger.
5. A satirical poem by Évariste-Désiré Deforge (later vicomte de Parny; 1753–1814) published in 1799. It ridicules the Christian religion.

6. Originally the six weeks that separate Christmas from Purification (February 2); in those days, the normal period of confinement for a woman after childbirth.

At that moment Monsieur Léon came out of a neighboring doorway with a bundle of papers under his arm. He came over to greet her, and they stood in the shade in front of Lheureux's shop under the projecting gray awning.

Madame Bovary said she was going to see her child, but that she was beginning to feel tired.

"If . . . ," Léon replied, not daring to continue.

"Do you have business somewhere?" she asked.

And upon the clerk's reply, she asked him to accompany her. By that evening, everyone in Yonville knew all about it, and Madame Tuvache, the mayor's wife, declared to her maid that *Madame Bovary was compromising herself*.

To get to the wet nurse's house, they had to turn left off the street toward the cemetery and follow a narrow path, bordered with a privet hedge, that ran between cottages and yards. The hedge was in bloom, as were the blue veronicas, the wild briers, the nettles, and the thin brambles pushing out from the bushes. Through the gaps in the hedges they could see, in front of the huts, a pig on a manure pile, or tethered cows rubbing their horns against tree trunks. The two of them, side by side, walked along slowly, she leaning on him and he slowing his pace to match hers; in front of them, a swarm of flies was hovering, buzzing in the warm air.

They recognized the house by the old walnut tree shading it. Built low and covered with brown tiles, it had hanging in front, beneath the attic window, a string of onions. Sticks of firewood stood against a thorn fence enclosing a lettuce patch, a few lavender bushes, and some sweet peas that hung upon their trellises. There was dirty water running here and there over the grass, and miscellaneous rags were hung everywhere—some knitted stockings, a red calico nightdress—and a big, heavy linen sheet was spread along the length of the hedge. At the sound of the gate, the wet nurse appeared, holding a nursing child in one arm. With her other hand she was dragging along a poor scrawny little brat, his face covered with scrofula, the son of a Rouen hatmaker left in the country by his parents, who were too preoccupied with their business.

"Come in," she said. "Your little one is over there, the one that's sleeping."

The bedroom on the ground floor, the only one in the house, had a large uncurtained bed in the back, against the wall, while a kneading trough occupied the side with the window, one pane of which was patched with a blue, cut-out paper sun. In the corner, behind the door, shiny hobnail boots were set in a row under the drain board near a bottle of oil with a feather sticking out of it; a Mathieu Laensberg almanac[7] trailed along the dusty mantelpiece among gunflints, candle ends, and little bits of tinder. And the final luxury item in the room was a picture of *Fame Blowing Her Trumpet*, probably snipped out from some perfume advertisement, and nailed to the wall with six shoe nails.

Emma's child was asleep on the floor in a wicker cradle. She picked her up with the blanket she was wrapped in and began to sing softly while rocking her.

Léon walked around the room; it felt strange to him to observe this beautiful lady in her nankeen[8] dress right in the midst of all this poverty. Madame Bovary blushed; he turned away, thinking there might have been some imper-

---

7. A farmer's almanac, begun in 1635, frequently found in farms and country houses.

8. Nankeen is a kind of cotton, stiff and durable, usually yellow [translator's note].

tinence in the way he had been looking at her. Then she put the child back in its bed; it had just thrown up on her collar. The wet nurse hurried to wipe it off, protesting that it wouldn't show.

"She's done that to me plenty of times," she said, "and I'm forever washing her up! Would you be good enough to tell the grocer Camus to let me have a little soap when I need it? It would be more convenient for you, because then I wouldn't have to bother you for it."

"Yes, fine!" Emma said. "Good-bye, Madame Rollet."

And she went out, wiping her shoes on the doorstep.

The good woman followed her out through the yard, talking the whole way about how hard it was for her to get up during the nights.

"I'm so worn out sometimes that I fall asleep in my chair; also, you ought to at least give me a pound of ground coffee, because that would last me a month, and I could have it in the mornings with some milk."

Having put up with her thanks, Madame Bovary went on. She was only a little way down the path when the sound of wooden shoes made her turn around: it was the wet nurse!

"What is it?"

Then the peasant took her aside behind an elm tree and started talking about her husband who, what with his job and the six francs a year that the captain . . .

"Get to the point," said Emma.

"Well!" replied the wet nurse, heaving a sigh with every word, "I'm afraid that it'll make him angry to see me having coffee by myself: you know, these men . . ."

"But you'll have some," Emma repeated. "I'll get you some! You're beginning to annoy me!"

"Oh, my poor dear lady, it's just that, because of his wounds, he has terrible chest pains. He tells me even cider weakens him."

"But do hurry up, Madame Rollet!"

"So," she continued with a curtsy, "if it wouldn't be too much to ask of you . . ." She curtsied again: "whenever you could . . ." She said with pleading eyes: "just a jar of brandy," she said finally, "and I'll massage your little one's feet with it; they're just as soft as your tongue."

Finally rid of the wet nurse, Emma took Léon's arm again. She walked swiftly for a while; then she slowed down, and her gaze wandered to the young man's shoulder, whose frock coat had a black velvet collar. His light brown hair fell over it, straight and carefully combed. She noted his fingernails, longer than was usual for Yonville. Trimming them was one of the clerk's major occupations, and he kept, for that very purpose, a special knife in his desk.

They returned to Yonville by following the riverside. During the warm weather, the river's water level fell, revealing the garden walls down to their bases, with their few steps leading down to the water. The river flowed silently, rapid and cold-looking; long, thin grasses bent down within it, moving with the current, and like loosened hair, spread out green in the limpid water. Sometimes, at the tops of the reeds or on a leaf of the water lilies, a thin-legged insect was walking or alighting. A sunray pierced the little blue bubbles made by the breaking waves; the old, branchless willows reflected their gray bark in the water, and beyond, all around them, the meadows seemed empty. It was the dinner hour at the farms, and the young woman and her companion heard nothing as they walked along but the rhythm of their steps on the path, the words they said to each other, and the brushing sounds of Emma's dress as it rustled around her.

The garden walls, with pieces of bottles stuck in their copings, were as warm as windows in a greenhouse. Between the bricks, wallflowers had pushed their way out, and as Madame Bovary walked by, she used the tip of her opened parasol to make some of the withered flowers crumble into a yellow dust, and at times a branch of overhanging honeysuckle or clematis caught in its fringe and trailed along its silk.

They were talking about a troupe of Spanish dancers who were coming soon to the theater in Rouen.

"Are you going?" she asked.

"If I can," he replied.

Did they have nothing else to say to each other? But their eyes were filled with a more serious conversation, and while they were struggling to come up with banal phrases, they felt the same languor overcoming them both; it was like a murmuring of the soul, profound and continuous, more powerful than the sound of their voices. Surprised, wondering at this new sweetness, they never thought to speak about it or inquire into its cause. Future joys are like tropical shores: they project their native indolence, a perfumed breeze, over the vast spaces that precede them, and we let ourselves doze off within that intoxication, with no anxieties about the horizon that, in fact, we have not even seen.

The ground in one spot had been torn up by the hooves of cattle; they had to walk on the big green rocks spaced evenly across the mud. She frequently stopped to study her footing—and faltering on a wobbling stone, elbows in the air, bent forward, entirely uncertain, she laughed aloud, out of fear of falling into the puddles of water.

When they had reached her garden, Madame Bovary opened the little gate, ran up the steps, and disappeared.

Léon went back to his office. His employer was not there; he looked briefly at the files, then trimmed a pen, and then finally picked up his hat and left.

He went up to the Pasture at the top of the Argueil hills, where the forest began; he lay down beneath some pines and watched the sky through his fingers.

"How bored I am!" he said to himself. "How bored I am!"

He had grounds for complaint, he thought, having to live in this village, with Homais for a friend and Monsieur Guillaumin for a boss. The latter, entirely absorbed by his business, wearing his gold-rimmed spectacles, with his red whiskers hanging over his white cravat, understood nothing about intellectual refinement, even though he put on a stiff English style that had greatly impressed the clerk at first. As for the pharmacist's wife, she was the best wife in Normandy, gentle as a sheep, cherishing her children, her father, her mother, her cousins, weeping over the misfortune of others, letting household matters go, and detesting corsets—but so slow-moving, so boring to listen to, her looks so common and her conversation so limited that he had never even dreamed, though she was thirty and he twenty, though they slept next door to each other, and though they spoke every day, that she could be a wife to someone, or that she possessed anything of the female sex beyond her dress.

And then, what else was there? Binet, a few business people, two or three innkeepers, the priest, and finally Monsieur Tuvache, the mayor, with his two sons, rich, crude, obtuse, farming their own land and feasting with their own family, and pious on top of it all, and altogether insufferable companions.

But against the common background of all those human faces, the figure of Emma stood out, isolated from them, but even more distant; for he felt there was some vague abyss between him and her.

At the beginning, he came to visit her several times in the company of the pharmacist. Charles did not at all seem very interested in seeing him; and Léon didn't know what to do, torn between his fear of being indiscreet and his desire for an intimacy that seemed nearly impossible.

CHAPTER 4

During the first days of the cold weather, Emma moved from her bedroom to the parlor, a long, low-ceilinged room with a thick piece of coral branch spread out across the mirror on the mantel. Seated in her chair by the window, she could see the townspeople pass by on the sidewalk.

Léon, twice a day, left his office for the *Golden Lion*. Emma could hear him coming from far away; she bent forward, listening, and the young man slipped in through the inn's curtain, always dressed the same way, and without turning his head. But when, at dusk, her chin in her hand, she had abandoned her sewing and left it lying on her knees, she would often shudder at the apparition of the young man's shadow slipping past. She would stand up and give orders to set the table.

Monsieur Homais would come in during dinner. His skullcap in his hand, he would enter silently so as not to disturb anyone, and would always repeat the same phrase: "Good evening to the assembly!" Then, when he had settled himself in his place at the table, between husband and wife, he would ask the doctor for news about his patients, and the doctor would consult with him about the likelihood of getting paid. Then, they would discuss what there had been *in the paper*. By that hour, Homais knew it all pretty much by heart; and he would recount it all in its entirety, including the journalists' comments and the whole story of every single disaster that had occurred in France or anywhere else. But when the topics began to dry up, he did not hesitate to toss out little comments on the dishes he saw on the table before him. Sometimes he would even half rise and point out to Madame the tenderest slice or, turning himself toward the maid, would give her advice on the preparation of ragouts and the health effects of various seasonings; he would talk about aroma, osmazome, juices, and gelatin in a bewildering manner. His head, moreover, more stuffed with recipes than his pharmacy was with bottles, Homais excelled in making preserves, vinegars, and sweet liqueurs, and he also knew all about the newest fuel-saving stoves, along with the art of preserving cheeses and healing sick wines.

At eight, Justin would come looking for him to lock up the pharmacy. Then Monsieur Homais would give him a knowing look, especially if Félicité were there, having noticed that his apprentice had become unusually fond of the doctor's house.

"My fine lad," he would say, "is beginning to get ideas, and devil take me if he isn't in love with your maid!"

A more serious fault, for which Homais reproached him, was his constant eavesdropping on conversations. On Sundays, for instance, they couldn't get him out of the drawing room, when Madame Homais had called him to come and get the children who had fallen asleep in the armchairs, pulling off the oversized calico chair covers.

There was not much of a crowd at these gatherings at the pharmacist's, his malicious gossip and his political opinions having alienated, one by one, various respectable people. The clerk was always there. As soon as the doorbell sounded, he would run to Madame Bovary, take her shawl, and put away beneath the shop counter the thick felt slippers she wore over her shoes when there was snow.

First they played several games of *trente et un*; then Homais played *écarté*[9] with Emma; Léon, standing behind her, would give her advice. His hands on the back of her chair, he would gaze down at the teeth of her comb biting into her chignon. Every time she moved to throw down her cards, her dress would ride up on her right side. From her pinned up hair, a brown shadow was cast down her back until it was lost, little by little, in darkness. Her dress, then, fell in two billowing folds on either side of her chair, reaching to the floor. When Léon at times felt the sole of his boot touch it, he would jump back as if he had stepped on someone.

When the card playing was over, the pharmacist and the doctor would play dominoes, and Emma, changing her seat, would lean on the table to leaf through *L'Illustration*. She had brought along her fashion magazine. Léon would sit close to her; they would look at the engravings together, and each would wait for the other at the bottom of the pages. Often, she would ask him to recite poetry to her; Léon declaimed poems with a slow, languid voice that he would carefully allow to trail off at the love passages. But he was frustrated by the sound of the dominoes; Monsieur Homais was good at the game: he would beat Charles by a full double-six. And when they had reached three hundred, they would both stretch out in front of the fireplace and soon fall asleep. The fire died out in its embers; the teapot was empty; Léon would continue reading and Emma listening to him, mechanically turning the lampshade, the gauze of which was painted with Pierrots in carriages and tightrope dancers with their balancing poles. Léon would pause, pointing toward the sleeping audience; and then they would speak with lowered voices, their conversation seeming all the sweeter for not being overhead.

And so a kind of bond was established between them, a ongoing exchange of books and ballads; Monsieur Bovary, not a very jealous sort, was not concerned by it.

For his birthday, he received a fine phrenological head, marked with numbers down to the thorax and painted blue. This was a piece of thoughtfulness on the clerk's part. And there were many other instances of it, including running errands for him in Rouen; and when a novelist's book inspired a craze for cactus plants, Léon bought one for Madame, carrying it back on his knees in the *Hirondelle*, pricking his fingers on its spiky hairs.

9. A card game similar to euchre, in which players win tricks by playing a higher card in the suit. *Trente-et-un*: "Thirty-one" (French), also called "Red and Black": a French gambling game in which cards are dealt in two categories (red and black) until a total of thirty-one or more points is reached; players bet on the winning color.

She had a railed shelf fixed against her window for her flower pots. The clerk too had a hanging garden; they would see each other when tending their flowers at the window.

Among the windows in the village, there was one even more frequently occupied; for on Sundays from morning till night, and every afternoon if the sky was clear, one could see at his attic window the thin profile of Monsieur Binet bent over his lathe, whose monotonous hum could be heard as far away as the *Golden Lion*.

Coming home one evening, Léon found in his room a rug of velvet and wool, with a leaf design against a light background. He called Madame Homais, Monsieur Homais, Justin, the children, even the cook; he talked about it to his employer; everybody wanted to see this rug; but why was the doctor's wife giving the clerk *presents*? It seemed odd, and everyone decided that she must be his *girlfriend*.

He made it easy to believe, the way he would talk endlessly about her charms and her wit, so much so that Binet replied quite harshly to him:

"Why should I give a damn, since I'm not one of her crowd?"

He tortured himself trying to figure out how to *make his declaration* to her; and constantly hesitating between his fear of displeasing her and his shame at being such a coward, he wept out of discouragement and desire. Then he would make energetic decisions; he would write letters, then tear them up, put the matter off till a certain time, then put it off again. Often he would set off to see her, determined to risk everything; but his resolution deserted him in Emma's presence, and when Charles would turn up and invite him to climb into his cart and go see some patient in the neighborhood, he would accept right away, bow to Madame, and go off. Her husband—well, after all, wasn't he a part of her?

As for Emma, she never asked herself whether she was in love with him. Love, she believed, must come suddenly, with great thunderclaps and lightning—a hurricane from the skies crashing down upon your life, turning it upside down, ripping away the will like leaves from a tree, carrying off the whole of one's heart into the abyss. She did not know how the rain can fall softly on a house's terrace when the gutters are blocked up and slowly form lakes, and she would have remained securely unaware of this—until, one day, she suddenly discovered a crack in the wall.

CHAPTER 5

It was a Sunday in February, on a snowy afternoon.

They had all—Monsieur and Madame Bovary, Homais, and Monsieur Léon—gone to see, about a mile outside of Yonville, a flax mill that was being built in the valley. The pharmacist had brought along Napoléon and Athalie to give them some exercise, and Justin accompanied them, carrying umbrellas on his shoulder.

Nothing, however, could have been less curious than this curiosity. A large stretch of empty ground, upon which a number of already rusted gear wheels were scattered among heaps of sand and stones, surrounded a long rectangular building whose walls were pierced by a number of small windows. The building wasn't finished yet, and they could see the sky through the roof joists. Attached to the girder on the gable end was a bale of straw mixed with ears of wheat, tied with tricolor ribbons that fluttered in the wind.

Homais was talking. He was explaining to the *assembly* the future importance of the flax mill, calculating the strength of the flooring, the thickness of the walls, and greatly regretting not having a measuring rod with him, like the one Monsieur Binet had for his own personal use.

Emma, who had taken his arm, was leaning a little on his shoulder, and she was looking at the disc of the sun shining far off through the mist in a dazzling whiteness; then she turned her head: Charles was there. He had his cap pulled down over his eyebrows, and his two thick lips were shivering, which gave his face a look of stupidity; even his back, his calm, untroubled back, was irritating to look at, and she thought that his very coat displayed all the banality of his character.

While she was looking at him and taking a kind of perverse sensual pleasure in her irritation, Léon took a step forward. The cold made him pale, and it seemed to add a gentler, more languid air to his face: between his cravat and his slightly loosened shirt collar, his skin was visible; the tip of his ear showed under a lock of hair, and his large blue eyes, raised upward to the clouds, seemed to Emma more limpid and more beautiful than those mountain lakes that mirror the sky.

"You fool!" the pharmacist suddenly shouted.

And he ran to his son, who had just leaped into a pile of lime in order to whiten his boots. As reproaches were hurled at him, Napoléon began to wail, while Justin wiped off the shoes with a clump of straw. But a knife was needed; Charles offered his.

"Ah!" she said to herself: "He carries a knife in his pocket, just like a peasant!"

Frost was beginning to fall, and they turned back to Yonville.

That evening, Madame Bovary did not go to her neighbors', and when Charles had gone and she felt herself alone, the comparison arose again with an almost immediate clarity and with that greater perspective that memory gives to things. From her bed, looking at the bright-burning fire, she could see again, just as she had at the mill, Léon standing, leaning on his cane in one hand and holding Athalie with the other as she peacefully sucked on a piece of ice. She thought him charming; she could not tear her thoughts from him; she pictured his gestures and movements on other days, remembered things he had said, the sound of his voice, everything about him; and she repeated to herself, her lips advancing as if for a kiss:

"Yes, charming, charming! Could he be in love?" she asked herself. "But with whom? . . . It must be me!"

All the proofs arose at once before her, and her heart leaped. The flame in the fireplace made a joyous light shimmer on the ceiling; she turned onto her back, stretching out her arms.

And then began the eternal lamentation: "Oh, if heaven had only willed it! And why couldn't it be? Why did things have to be this way?"

When Charles came back at midnight, she acted as if she had just awakened, and, when he made some noise in getting undressed, she complained of a migraine; then she nonchalantly asked what had happened during the evening.

"Monsieur Léon," he said, "went up to his room early."

She couldn't keep from smiling, and she went to sleep, her soul filled with a new rapture.

The next day, just at nightfall, she received a visit from Monsieur Lheureux, who dealt in fashionable novelties. This shopkeeper was a clever man.

Born a Gascon but having become a Norman, he grafted the Cauchois cunning onto his southern talkativeness. His fat face, smooth and beardless, had a tint like watered-down licorice, and his white hair made his little black eyes seem even harder and brighter. Nobody knew what he had done before he came to Yonville: a traveling salesman, said some, a banker in Routot, said others. The one thing that was certain was that he could do in his head the kind of calculations that would frighten even Binet. Polite to the point of being obsequious, he always stood slightly bent forward, like someone greeting you, or making you a proposal.

After leaving his hat, banded with crêpe, at the door, he placed a green box on the table and began by complaining, in polite phrases, that Madame had not yet placed her confidence in him. A poor shop like his was not designed to attract an *elegant* lady; he stressed the word. But all she had to do was ask, and he would take it upon himself to provide her with whatever she wanted, whether cotton goods or lingerie, whether hats or novelties; for he went to the city regularly, four times a month. He had connections at the finest firms. She could ask about him at the *Trois Frères*, at the *Barbe d'Or*, or at the *Grand Sauvage*; all those gentlemen knew him as well as the insides of their pockets! Today, therefore, he had come by to show Madame just a few articles that he happened to have, thanks to the rarest of opportunities. And he pulled half a dozen embroidered collars out of the box.

Madame Bovary looked them over.

"I don't need anything," she said.

Then Monsieur Lheureux delicately laid out three Algerian scarves, several packets of English needles, a pair of straw slippers, and, finally, four eggcups made of coconut wood, carved in openwork by convicts. And then, both hands on the table, his neck stretched out, leaning forward, his mouth gaping open, he followed Emma's gaze as she paced, undecided, in front of his merchandise. From time to time, as if to remove a speck of dust, he would flick a finger over the silk of the scarves, spread out at their full length; and they would quiver in response with a light rustling sound, making the gold spangles of their tissue sparkle in the green light of the early evening.

"How much are they?"

"A pittance," he replied, "a pittance; but there's no hurry; you can pay whenever you're ready; we're not Jews!"

She considered for a few seconds, and ended by saying no thank you to Monsieur Lheureux, who replied calmly:

"Very well! We'll reach an understanding eventually; I've always managed to work things out with the ladies . . . all except my own!"

Emma smiled.

"I wanted to let you know," he went on good-naturedly after his little joke, "that I'm not concerned about the money. I could give you some, if you needed it."

She made a surprised gesture.

"Ah!" he said quickly, in a lowered voice, "I wouldn't have to go very far to find you some; you can count on that."

And he turned to ask her for news about Monsieur Tellier, the proprietor of the *Café Français*, who was just then a patient of Charles.

"What's the matter with Monsieur Tellier? . . . He coughs enough to shake the whole house, and I'm afraid that before long he'll need a wooden overcoat more than a flannel nightshirt! He had plenty of little adventures when he was young! People like that, Madame, have no sense of self-discipline! He's burned himself out with brandy! But it's too bad, all the same, to see an acquaintance on his way out."

And as he fastened up his box, he went on about the doctor's patients.

"It's the weather, I suppose," he said, looking out the window with a frown, "that causes all these illnesses? Me, I don't feel quite up to snuff myself; one of these days I'm going to have to come and see Monsieur myself, about this pain I have in my back. Well then, good-bye, Madame Bovary; I'm at your service; your very humble servant!"

And he closed the door quietly.

Emma had her dinner served in her bedroom, on a tray by the fireside; she took her time eating; everything tasted good to her.

"How wise I was!" she said to herself, thinking about the scarves.

She heard steps on the stairs: it was Léon. She stood up and snatched up the top dust cloth from a pile on the dresser waiting to be mended. She seemed very busy when he came in.

Their conversation languished, Madame Bovary letting it drop every few minutes, while he himself seemed embarrassed. Seated on a low chair near the fire, he turned her ivory needle case in his fingers; she kept on with her needle-work or, now and then, straightened out the folds in the cloth with her finger-nail. She didn't speak; he became quiet too, as enthralled by her silence as he had been by her words.

"Poor boy!" she thought.

"How have I displeased her?" he asked himself.

But Léon eventually spoke, saying that one of these days he would have to go to Rouen on some office business.

"Your music subscription has run out—should I renew it?"

"No," she replied.

"Why not?"

"Because . . ."

And pursing her lips, she slowly drew out a long stitch of gray thread.

Her working irritated Léon. The tips of Emma's fingers seemed to be roughening from it; a gallant phrase came into his head, but he didn't risk it.

"So you're giving it up?" he continued.

"What?" she asked quickly. "Music? Oh, my God, yes! Don't I have a house to keep up, a husband to take care of, a thousand things really, so many duties that have to come first?"

She looked at the clock. Charles was late. So she acted as if she were anxious. She repeated two or three times:

"He's so good!"

The clerk was fond of Monsieur Bovary. But all these expressions of tenderness surprised and annoyed him; nonetheless he went on singing his praises, as did everyone else, he said, and above all, the pharmacist.

"Ah, he's a fine man," Emma replied.

"Certainly," said the clerk.

And he began to talk about Madame Homais, whose unkempt appearance usually made them both laugh.

Emma interrupted: "But what difference does that make? A good housewife and mother shouldn't be all that concerned about her looks."

Then she relapsed into silence.

It was the same on the following days: her talk, her manners, everything had changed. She was seen taking her household work more seriously, going regularly to church, and being stricter with her maid.

She took Berthe back from the wet nurse. Félicité brought her in when there were visitors, and Madame Bovary undressed her to show her legs. She declared that she adored children; they were her consolation, her joy, her obsession, and she accompanied her caresses with lyrical outbursts that, to anyone but Yonvillians, would have called up memories of Sachette in *Notre-Dame de Paris*.[1]

When Charles came home, he would find his slippers warming by the fire. His waistcoats no longer lacked lining, nor his shirts buttons, and he even had the pleasure of seeing his cotton nightcaps arranged in neat piles in the armoire. She no longer grumbled, as she had before, at taking walks in the garden; she consented to whatever he proposed, although she did not understand what it was that was making her submit without a murmur—and when Léon saw him by the fireside after dinner, his two hands folded over his stomach, his two feet propped on the andirons, his cheeks flushed from digestion, and his eyes moist with happiness, with the baby crawling on the carpet and that woman with the slim waist standing behind his easy chair and bending over to kiss his forehead:

"What insanity!" he said to himself. "How could I ever get close to her?"

And so she seemed to him so virtuous, so inaccessible, that every hope, even the vaguest, abandoned him.

But through this renunciation, he was granting her an extraordinary status. She now stood apart from those carnal qualities that he could never hope to experience; and in his heart she continued to rise up, mounting high above him, detaching herself from him, taking wing like a goddess. It was one of those pure sentiments, which don't interfere with real life, which one cultivates because they are rare, and the loss of which would cause more pain than possessing it gives pleasure.

Emma became thinner, her cheeks paler, her face longer. With her black hair parted in two, her large eyes, her straight nose, her birdlike walk, and her new habit of silence: didn't she seem to be passing through life scarcely touching it, bearing on her forehead the mysterious imprint of some sublime destiny? She was so sad and so calm, at the same time so gentle and so reserved, that to be near her was to feel a glacial charm, like the shudder one feels in churches when the scent of the flowers mingles with the chill of the marble. Even the others felt that seductive power. The pharmacist said:

"She's a woman of great abilities; she wouldn't be out of place in a subprefecture."

---

1. A historical novel (1831) by Victor Hugo, in which the mother of Agnes, a girl abducted by gypsies who takes the name Esmeralda, worships a shoe of her stolen child.

The townswomen admired her thrift, the patients her politeness, the poor her charity.

But inside, she seethed with lusts, with rage, with hatred. That dress with its neat folds concealed a heart in turmoil, and those so-chaste lips uttered no hints about the torment she felt. She was in love with Léon, and she sought out solitude in order to be able to delight undisturbed in the mental image of him. Actually seeing him troubled the sensual pleasure of that meditation. Emma's heart raced at the sound of his footsteps: then, in his presence, the emotion subsided, and all that remained of it was an enormous astonishment that always ended in sorrow.

Léon did not know that when he left her house in his own despair, she would get up after him so as to be able to watch him go down the street. She worried over his comings and goings; she secretly watched his face; she would invent a whole complex story as a pretext for visiting his room. She thought the pharmacist's wife was lucky to sleep under the same roof as he did; and her thoughts continually swooped down upon that house, like the pigeons from the *Golden Lion* who came to dip their pink feet and their white wings in its gutters. But the more aware Emma was of her love, the more she repressed it so as to hide it, and allow it to diminish. She would have liked Léon to suspect; and she imagined chance events or catastrophes that would have made it clear to him. But what held her back, no doubt, was laziness or fear as much as modesty. She thought that she had pushed him away too firmly, that the moment had passed, that everything was lost. Then pride, the joy of saying to herself, "I am virtuous," gazing at herself in the mirror making poses of resignation, consoled her a little for the sacrifice she believed she was making.

Then, the appetites of the flesh, the lust for money, and the melancholy of her passion all combined into one agony—and instead of turning her thoughts away from it, she attached herself to it all the more, stimulating herself with suffering and seeking it out on all occasions. She would get angry over a poorly served dish or a door left open, would groan for the velvet she didn't own, the happiness she didn't have, her dreams too lofty and her house too small.

What exasperated her was that Charles didn't appear to suspect her torment. His belief that he was making her happy seemed to her to be an imbecilic insult, and his certainty about it seemed ingratitude. For whom, then, was she being so sensible? Wasn't it him, that obstacle to all her happiness, that cause of all her misery, who was like the sharp clasp of a complicated strap that was binding her in on all sides?

Thus, she transferred onto him the host of hatreds that resulted from her boredom, and every effort to lessen it only intensified it; for that wasted effort only added to her other reasons for despair, and to her alienation from him. She was naturally kind to herself, and this led her to more rebellions. Domestic mediocrity drove her to fantasies of luxury, and maternal tenderness to adulterous desires. She would have liked Charles to beat her so as to be able to detest him with more justification, to avenge herself on him. She was shocked sometimes by the horrific possibilities that crossed her mind; and did she have to go on smiling, repeating that she was happy, act as if she were, let it always seem that way?

But she felt disgust at all this hypocrisy. The temptation to run away with Léon seized her, to run somewhere far away, to try for a different fate; but immediately a dark abyss opened up within her soul, shadowy and obscure.

"Besides, he doesn't love me anymore," she thought. "What will become of me? What help can I expect, what consolation, what relief?"

She was left broken, breathless, inert, sobbing in a low voice, her tears flowing down.

"Why not tell Monsieur about it?" the maid would ask, when she came in during one of these crises.

"It's only nerves," Emma replied. "Don't tell him about it; you'll only worry him."

"Oh, yes!" Félicité went on. "You're just like Mademoiselle Guérin, the daughter of old Guérin, the fisherman at Pollet[2] that I knew at Dieppe before coming to you. She was so sad, so sad that seeing her standing in her doorway made you think of a burial shroud hanging in front of the door. Her sickness, they said, was like a kind of fog that she had in her head, and the doctors couldn't do anything, the priest either. When it came on too strong, she'd go off all alone to the seashore, so bad off that the customs officer on duty often found her lying flat on her stomach, crying into the pebbles. But then it went away after her marriage, they say."

"But for me," Emma replied, "it was after the marriage that it started."

CHAPTER 6

One evening when the window was open, and she was watching the sexton Lestiboudois trim the hedges, she suddenly heard the church bell ringing the Angelus.

It was the beginning of April, when the primroses are blooming; a warm wind blows over the flowerbeds, and the gardens seem like women dressing themselves up for the summer holidays. Through the arbor's lattice and everywhere far beyond, one could see the river tracing its sinuous and vagabond course through the grassy meadows. The evening mist was passing through the leafless poplars, giving a violet tint to their outlines, more pale, more transparent than a delicate gauze draped across their branches. In the distance, cattle were walking along; but neither their steps nor their lowings could be heard; and the church bell, still ringing, continued to sound its peaceful lamentation through the air.

In that repeated chiming, the young woman's thoughts strayed back to memories of her youth and of the convent school. She remembered the candelabra standing taller than the altar, with its flower-filled vases, and the tabernacle's thin columns. She wished she could lose herself once more in that long line of white veils, here and there accented by the black, stiff veils worn by the good sisters, bent over their *prie-Dieux;* on Sundays at Mass, when she raised her head she would behold the Virgin's sweet face through the billowing blue incense smoke rising upward. Then she would be gripped by a tender lassitude: she would feel herself weak and abandoned, like a bird's feather turning in a stormy wind; and so it was that, almost without being aware of it, she was walking toward the church, bent on any devotion at all so long as it would absorb her soul, and so long as her entire existence could become lost in it.

In the square she ran into Lestiboudois, who was returning from the church; for, in order not to clip his working day too short, he preferred to interrupt one

---

2. Suburb of Dieppe, where the fishermen live.

task and then come back to it, and so he ended up ringing the Angelus whenever it suited him. Besides, ringing it earlier alerted the children to the hour of their catechism class.

Already a few of them had arrived early and were playing at marbles on the cemetery stones. Others, sitting astride the wall, were swinging their legs, using their wooden shoes to crush down the big nettles growing between the smaller wall and the most recent graves. This was the only green space; everything else was stone, and it was always covered with a fine powdery dust, despite the sacristan's sweeping.

The children in felt shoes ran around as if the church were a playground built for them, and their shouts could be heard over the booming of the bell. The sound diminished with the oscillation of the thick rope that hung from the top of the bell and dragged its end along the ground. Some swallows flew by, emitting little cries, cutting through the air, returning swiftly to their yellow nests beneath the eaves. At the far end of the church's interior, a lamp was burning, or rather a wick in a nightlight, in a hanging glass. From a distance, its light was a white spot, trembling upon its oil. A long ray of sun was crossing the nave, making the side aisles and the corners even darker.

"Where is the priest?" Madame Bovary asked a young boy, who was amusing himself by shaking the gate's latch in its worn hole.

"He's coming," he answered.

And in fact the presbytery door creaked open, revealing Abbé Bournisien; the children flew wildly into the church.

"Those rascals!" the cleric muttered. "Always the same!"

And picking up a tattered catechism that he had almost tripped over: "No respect for anything!"

But when he noticed Madame Bovary: "Excuse me," he said. "I didn't see you there."

He stuck the catechism in his pocket and stood there, swinging the heavy sacristy key between his fingers.

The light from the setting sun, falling directly upon his face, turned his woolen cassock gray; its elbows were shiny, and it was frayed at the hem. Grease and tobacco stains ran in a line, following the buttons, up over his large chest, and they grew more numerous the closer they came to his neck band, upon which the abundant folds of his red flesh reposed; his face was sprinkled with yellow pimples that disappeared under the coarse hair of his graying beard. He had just had his dinner, and he was breathing noisily.

"And how are you?" he added.

"Not well," she answered; "I'm suffering."

"Ah, well, me too!" the cleric replied. "These first warm days, you know, they weaken a person surprisingly. But what can you do! We are born to suffer, as Saint Paul says. But Monsieur Bovary, what does he think?"

"Oh, him!" she said with a disdainful gesture.

"What?" said the priest, surprised. "Hasn't he prescribed something for you?"

"Oh," said Emma, "it isn't earthly remedies that I need."

But the priest was looking back from time to time into the church, where all the kneeling boys were shoving each other and falling over like packs of cards.

"I'd like to know . . . ," she continued.

"Just wait, Riboudet," the cleric called out in an angry voice, "I'll warm your ears for you, you little brat!"

Then, turning back to Emma:

"He's the son of Boudet the carpenter; his parents are well off, and they let him do whatever he likes. He'd be a quick learner, if he only wanted to, because he's a clever boy. So I sometimes, just for a joke, I call him Riboudet—after the hill, you know, on the way to Maromme—and sometimes I'll even say 'Mon Riboudet.' Ha ha! You see, Mont Riboudet! The other day I told it to the Monsignor, and he laughed at it—yes, he deigned to laugh! . . . And Monsieur Bovary, how is he doing?"

She seemed not to hear. He continued:

"Always busy, I suppose? Because he and I are the two busiest people in the parish. But he, he's the doctor of the body," he added with a thick laugh, "and me, I'm in charge of the souls!"

She fixed her pleading eyes on the priest.

"Yes . . . ," she said; "you ease every pain."

"Oh, don't even talk about it, Madame Bovary! Just this morning, I had to go into Bas-Diauville to see about a cow that was all swollen up; they thought it was some witchcraft. All their cows, I don't know how . . . Excuse me. Longuemarre and Boudet! Nitwits! Will you stop it!"

And with a bound, he leaped into the church.

Now the boys were crowding around the pulpit, climbing up on the cantor's stool, opening up the missal; others were tiptoeing their way to the confessional. But the priest came upon them suddenly and distributed a hailstorm of slaps among all of them. Grasping them by the shirt collars, he picked them up off the ground and set them down kneeling on the choir's stone floor, firmly, as if he meant to plant them there.

"So," he said when he returned to Emma, unfolding his big calico handkerchief, "the farmers have plenty to complain about!"

"And others too," she replied.

"Definitely! The town workers, for instance."

"They're not the ones . . . "

"Excuse me! I've known poor mothers, virtuous women I assure you, veritable saints, who didn't even have enough bread."

"But the ones," Emma said, the corners of her mouth twitching as she spoke, "the ones, Father, those who do have bread but who don't have . . . "

"Fire in the winter," said the priest.

"What? What does that matter?"

"What does it matter? It seems to me, I think, that if a person is warm, well fed, . . . because, after all . . . "

"My God! My God!" she sighed.

"You don't feel well?" he said, approaching her with a concerned air. "It's your digestion, I assume? You need to go back home, Madame Bovary, and drink a little tea; that will strengthen you, or maybe a glass of cold water with some brown sugar."

"Why?"

She looked like someone who had just awakened from a dream.

"It's just that you put your hand to your forehead. I thought you were having a dizzy spell."

Then, suddenly remembering: "But you wanted to ask me something? What was it? I don't remember any more."

"Me? Nothing . . . nothing," Emma repeated.

And her gaze, which she had been casting around her, slowly came to rest on the old man in the cassock. They considered each other, face to face, without speaking.

"Well, Madame Bovary," he said at last, "my excuses, but duty comes first, you know; I have to see to my little brats. First Communion is coming up. We won't be ready, I fear! So after Ascension, I'm going to keep them an extra hour every Wednesday. These poor children! You can't set them too soon on the path of the Lord because, after all, He recommended it Himself through the mouth of his divine Son . . . Good health to you, Madame; and give my respects to Monsieur, your husband."

And he went into the church, making a genuflection at the door.

Emma watched him disappear between the double line of pews, walking with heavy steps, his head bent slightly to his shoulder, and his two hands together behind him, half open.

Then she turned on her heels, in a single movement, like a statue on a pivot, and set off toward her house. But she continued to hear the priest's loud voice, and the clear voices of the children, from behind her as she walked:

"Are you a Christian?"

"Yes, I am a Christian."

"What is a Christian?"

"A Christian is one who, being baptized . . . baptized . . . baptized . . ."

She walked up her stairs clinging to the banister and, when she reached her bedroom, let herself fall into an armchair.

The whitish light coming in through the windows fell in gentle waves. The furniture in the room seemed to have become more immobile, and it was fading into the shadows as into a dark ocean. The fire had gone out, the clock ticked continually, and Emma felt vaguely astounded at the calm of these things, while there was so much turmoil inside her. But between the window and worktable was little Berthe, tottering unsteadily in her knitted booties, and trying to come toward her mother in order to catch hold of her apron strings.

"Leave me alone!" she said, pushing the child away with her hand.

The little girl soon came closer, up against her knees, and leaning on them with her arms, she raised her big blue eyes up toward her, while a string of pure saliva dribbled from her lips onto the silk of the apron.

"Leave me alone!" the young woman repeated, angrily.

The expression on her face frightened the child, and she began to cry.

"Oh! Leave me alone, will you!" she said, pushing her with her elbow.

Berthe fell onto the base of the chest of drawers, against the brass hook; she cut her cheek, and the blood flowed. Madame Bovary rushed to pick her up, broke the bell-rope, called for the maid as loud as she could, and she was about to begin cursing herself when Charles appeared. It was his dinner hour, and he was returning home.

"Look, dear," she said in a calm voice: "Look, the little one was playing, and she fell down and hurt herself."

Charles reassured her that it was not at all serious, and he went off to find some adhesive plaster for the cut.

Madame Bovary did not go down to the parlor; she wanted to stay alone and care for the child. Then as she watched her sleeping, what remained of her anxiety dissipated by degrees, and she felt she was both foolish and good-hearted to have been so worried about so small a thing. Berthe was no longer sobbing. Her breathing now was lifting the cotton coverlet very slightly. Big teardrops hung in the corners of her almost closed eyelids, which showed her pale, deep-set pupils behind the eyelashes; the adhesive plaster stuck on her cheek was pulling the skin away at an angle.

"It's a strange thing," Emma thought, "how ugly this child is!"

At eleven o'clock, when Charles returned from the pharmacy (where he had gone to return what was left of the adhesive plaster), he found his wife standing up beside the cradle.

"But I promise you, it's nothing!" he said, kissing her forehead. "Don't torture yourself, my poor darling; you'll make yourself ill!"

He had stayed on a long time at the pharmacist's. Even though he had not seemed terribly upset, Monsieur Homais nonetheless was determined to steady him, to *keep up his morale*. They went on to talk about the various dangers that menace children, and how scatterbrained servants were. Madame Homais knew something about that subject, still carrying the scars on her chest from a bowlful of hot food that a cook, long ago, had dropped down her smock. As a result, these good parents took plenty of precautions. Knives were never sharpened, nor floors waxed. The windows had iron grates, and the fireplace strong bars. The little Homais children, despite their independence, couldn't take a step without someone watching them from behind; at the slightest sign of a cold, their father stuffed them with cough syrup, and until they were four they were pitilessly swaddled with thick quilts. This was, to tell the truth, one of Madame Homais' obsessions; her husband was inwardly worried that such compression could have negative effects on the intellectual organs, and once he forgot himself so much as to say:

"Are you trying to make Caribs or Botocudos[3] out of them?"

Charles, however, had been trying to interrupt the conversation a number of times.

"I'd like to talk to you," he whispered quietly into the clerk's ear, and so Léon led him upstairs.

"Does he suspect something?" he asked himself. His heart was hammering, and one possibility after another was passing through his mind.

At last Charles, having closed the door, asked him if he would go to Rouen and find out the price of a good daguerreotype; it was a sentimental surprise he had in mind for his wife, a special gift, a portrait of himself dressed in black. But he had to know *how much it was going to take;* this sort of errand shouldn't cause Léon much trouble, since he went to the city almost every week.

But for what purpose? Homais suspected there was some *young man's affair* at the bottom of it, some intrigue. But he was wrong; Léon was not involved in any infatuation. He had been more unhappy than usual, as Madame Lefrançois could see perfectly well from the amount of food he left on his plate. To find out more about it, she questioned the tax collector; Binet replied haughtily that he was *certainly not in the pay of the police.*

3. Two South American peoples.

His dinner companion, nonetheless, did seem quite eccentric to him; for Léon would often throw himself back in his chair, stretch out his arms, and complain vaguely about life.

"It's because you don't give yourself enough distractions," said the tax collector.

"Like what?"

"If I were in your shoes, I'd get myself a lathe!"

"But I don't know how to operate one."

"Well, yes, that's true!" said the other, stroking his jaw with a mixture of disdain and self-satisfaction.

Léon was tired of loving without any results; he was beginning to feel that depression caused by a repetitive, unvaried life, when no particular interest drives you and no hope sustains you. He was so bored with Yonville and Yonvillians that the mere sight of certain people or certain houses irritated him beyond endurance; and the pharmacist, good fellow that he was, had become absolutely unbearable to him. On the other hand, the prospect of a real change in life frightened him as much as it tempted him.

That apprehension soon evolved into impatience, and then Paris beckoned to him, from far off in the distance, with its sounds of masked balls and laughing grisettes. Since he was supposed to finish his law studies there, why not go? What was holding him back? And mentally he began making preparations; he arranged his daily schedule in advance. In his head, he furnished an apartment. He would lead an artist's life! He would take guitar lessons! He would have a dressing gown, a Basque beret, slippers of blue velvet! And he even delighted in picturing two crossed fencing foils hung over his mantel, with a skull and the guitar above them.

The hard part was getting his mother to consent; but nothing could appear more reasonable. His employer had even been urging him to look into another office where he could develop his talents more fully. Taking a middle course, then, Léon looked for a second clerk's position in Rouen, found nothing, and finally wrote a long, detailed letter to his mother where he set out his reasons for going to live in Paris immediately. She consented to it.

He did not hurry about it, though. Every day for a month, Hivert carried boxes, suitcases, packages for him from Yonville to Rouen, from Rouen to Yonville; and when Léon had packed up his wardrobe, had his three armchairs restuffed, purchased a supply of neckties—when, in short, he had made more preparations than he would have needed for a trip around the world—he put it off from week to week, until he received a second letter from his mother urging him to leave soon, if he wanted to pass his second examination before the vacations.

When the moment for farewell embraces had come, Madame Homais cried; Justin sobbed; Homais, as a rational man, hid his emotion; he wanted to carry his friend's coat for him as far as the gate of the notary, who would take Léon to Rouen in his own carriage. He just had time to say his good-byes to Monsieur Bovary.

When he reached the top of the stairs he stopped, feeling out of breath. As he entered, Madame Bovary got up quickly.

"It's me again!" Léon said.

"I was sure of it!"

She bit her lips, and the blood surging beneath reddened her skin from the roots of her hair to the edge of her collar. She remained standing, leaning her shoulder against the wood paneling.

"Monsieur isn't here?" he continued.

"He's gone."

She repeated: "He's gone."

Then there was a silence. They looked at each other; and their thoughts merged together in the same anguish, embracing each other tightly like two throbbing hearts.

"I'd like to kiss Berthe," Léon said.

Emma went down a few steps and called Félicité.

He threw one long look around the room, taking in the walls, the shelves, the fireplace, as if to penetrate it all, to carry it all along with him.

But she came back in, and the servant brought Berthe, who was dangling a toy windmill, roof side down, on the end of a string.

Léon gave her several kisses on the neck.

"Good-bye, poor child! Good-bye, dear little one, good-bye!"

And he handed her back to her mother.

"Take her away," she said.

They remained standing there, alone.

Madame Bovary, her back turned, had her face pressed up against a window-pane; Léon was holding his cap in his hand, tapping it softly against his thigh.

"It's going to rain," said Emma.

"I have an overcoat," he replied.

"Ah!"

She turned around, her chin lowered, her forehead bent down. The light slipped over it as it would over marble, down to the curve of her eyebrows, but it was impossible to guess what it was Emma was watching in the distance, nor what it was she was thinking deep inside.

"Well, good-bye!" he sighed.

She raised her head abruptly:

"Yes, good-bye . . . Go then!"

They both took a step toward each other: he held out his hand, and she hesitated.

"Well, English style then," she said, surrendering her hand to his, and forcing herself to laugh.

Léon felt her hand with his fingers, and the very essence of his entire being felt as if it were flowing into that warm palm.

Then he opened his hand; their eyes met again, and he left.

When he was outside in the marketplace, he stopped and hid himself behind a pillar in order to contemplate one last time that white house with its four green blinds. He thought he could see a shadow behind the window, within the bedroom; but the curtain, slipping off its peg as if on its own, slowly straightened its long slanting folds, and in a single movement spread itself out, hanging straight and motionless as a plaster wall. Léon turned and began to run.

He could see from afar his employer's carriage in the road, and beside it a man in a thick apron holding the horse. Homais and Monsieur Guillaumin were chatting together. They were waiting for him.

"Embrace me," said the pharmacist, tears in his eyes. "Here's your coat, my good friend; be careful about the cold. Take care of yourself! Be good to yourself!"

"Come on, Léon, get in!" said the notary.

Homais bent over the mudguard and, in a voice broken by sobs, only got two sad words out:

"Safe journey!"

"Good evening," said Monsieur Guillaumin. "Off we go!"

They left, and Homais went back home.

Madame Bovary had opened her window onto the garden, and she was watching the clouds. They were piling up in the sunset, toward Rouen, their black, scrolling shapes moving swiftly, and behind them were the great rays of the sun, like golden arrows stuck in a hanging trophy, while the rest of the sky was empty and white as porcelain. But a gust of wind came up, bending the poplars, and suddenly rain began to fall; it pattered on the green leaves. Then quickly the sun came back out, the hens cackled, sparrows were beating their wings in the warm foliage, and pools of water on the gravel crept outward, carrying off the pink flowers of an acacia.

"Oh, how far away he must be by now!" she thought.

Monsieur Homais, as usual, came by at six-thirty during their dinner.

"Well!" he said as he seated himself. "So we've got our young man sent off on his way!"

"So it seems," the doctor replied.

Then, turning in his chair:

"And what's new with you?"

"Not much. But my wife was a little sentimental this afternoon. You know, women—the littlest things upset them! And mine more than others! And it would be wrong to try to change them, since their nervous system is so much more volatile than ours."

"That poor Léon!" said Charles. "How will he live in Paris? Will he be able to get used to it?"

Madame Bovary sighed.

"Oh, come on now," said the pharmacist, clucking his tongue. "The dinner parties at restaurants! The masked balls! The champagne! He'll get along just fine, I promise you."

"I don't think he'll turn bad," Bovary objected.

"Nor do I!" Monsieur Homais quickly replied. "Though he'll have to do like the others do, or risk looking like a Jesuit. And you don't know the kind of life those jokers lead in the Latin Quarter, with the actresses! And besides, people think well of students in Paris. As long as they have a little charm, they're received into the best society, and there have even been cases of ladies from the Faubourg Saint Germain[4] falling in love with them, which gives them the chance to make very good marriages."

"But," said the doctor, "I fear for him that . . . living there . . . ."

4. The aristocratic quarter of Paris.

"You're right," the pharmacist interrupted, "and that's the other side of the coin! A person has to keep his hand on his wallet at all times. So, let's suppose you're in a public park; an individual comes up to you, well dressed, even decorated, someone you'd take for a diplomat; he approaches you: you converse; he ingratiates himself, offers you a pinch of snuff, or maybe picks up your hat for you. Now he's made friends with you; he takes you to a café, invites you to visit his house in the country, introduces you, over a couple of drinks, to all sorts of acquaintances, and three-quarters of the time, all this is only to swindle you out of your purse and get you involved in wicked doings."

"That's true," Charles replied; "but I was thinking more of the diseases, like typhoid fever for example, that attack students from the provinces."

Emma shuddered.

"Because of the change of diet," the pharmacist continued, "and of the disturbance it causes in the system as a whole. And then, the water in Paris, I tell you! And the dishes they serve in restaurants, all those spicy foods end up heating the blood, and if you ask me they can't compare with a good stew. As for me, I've always preferred home cooking: it's more healthful! And when I was studying pharmacy in Rouen, I made sure to live in a boarding house; I ate with the professors."

And he continued in this vein, laying out his general opinions and his personal feelings, right up to the moment when Justin came to find him to mix an eggnog that needed preparing.

"Not one second of rest!" he exclaimed. "My nose always to the grindstone! I can't go out for a minute! Like a workhorse, always having to sweat blood! What a yoke I have to wear!"

Then, when he was at the door:

"By the way, have you heard the news?"

"What's that?"

"That it's very probable," Homais replied, raising his eyebrows and putting on one of his most serious expressions, "that the agricultural fair of the Seine-Inférieure will be held this year in Yonville-l'Abbaye. That's the word, anyway, that's going around. The paper said something about it this morning. This would be of the greatest importance for our district! But we'll talk about it later. I can see my way very well, thank you; Justin has the lantern."

CHAPTER 7

The next day for Emma was a depressing one. Everything seemed to be enveloped in a kind of blackness that hovered confusedly over the surface of things, and the grief sinking into her soul howled softly like a winter wind in an abandoned chateau. Her state of mind was that kind of reverie we slip into over something that is gone forever, the fatigue that sets in when we have done everything we could have done—the pain, in short, that you feel when everything you are accustomed to doing is interrupted, when a prolonged vibration comes to an abrupt end.

As with her return from La Vaubyessard, when the quadrilles were whirling in her head, she felt a dreary melancholy, a numbing despair. Léon reappeared, taller, more handsome, sweeter, more vague; although he was separated from her, he had not left, he was there, and the walls of the house still seemed to retain his shadow. She could not take her eyes off the carpet on which he had walked, the empty furniture where he had sat. The river continued to flow, slowly pushing its little waves along the slippery banks. They had walked there many times, with the same murmuring of the waves over the moss-covered pebbles. What fine sunny days they had had! What fine afternoons, alone in the shade at the foot of the garden! He would read aloud, bareheaded, seated on a footstool made of dried sticks; the cool breeze from the meadows would make the pages of his book tremble, and the nasturtiums in the arbor . . . Oh! He was gone, the only delight in her life, her only possible hope for happiness! Why didn't she seize that happiness when it presented itself! Why didn't she hold onto it with both hands, go down on her knees when it wanted to flee from her? And she cursed herself for not having loved Léon; she thirsted for his lips. She felt an urge to run to him, to rejoin him, to throw herself into his arms, to say to him, "Here I am, and I am yours!" But Emma was weighed down in advance by the impracticalities of the idea, and her desires, augmented by regret, only intensified.

From then on, the memory of Léon occupied the center point of her unhappiness; it gleamed there, more vividly than a fire abandoned by travelers on a snow-covered Russian steppe. She would hurry toward it, huddle herself next to it, carefully stir the almost-dying embers, look all around for anything that would help revive it; and the most distant memories as well as the most recent events, things she had experienced as well as things she had imagined, her voluptuous desires that were now scattering away, her plans for happiness that now creaked in the wind like dead branches, her sterile virtue, her lost hopes, the dead debris of her domestic life—she gathered it all, took it all up, and used it to rekindle the fire of her sorrow.

But the flame did die down, whether because she exhausted the fuel or because she had built the fire too high. Absence snuffed out her love bit by bit, and her regret was stifled by daily routine; and the burning gleam that had made her pale sky purple was increasingly covered over by shadow, and it faded out by degrees. In the numbness of her consciousness, she even took her repugnance toward her husband as a yearning for her lover, the fires of hatred for the warmth of tenderness; but as the tempest outside went on raging, and as passion was burned down to cinders, and no help came, no sun appeared, darkness fell on all sides, and she remained lost within a terrible cold that pierced her through and through.

And then the bad days of Tostes started up again. She considered her present situation even more miserable, because now she had the experience of grief along with the certitude that it would never end.

A woman who had had to endure such great sacrifice deserved a few self-indulgences. She bought an old Gothic *prie-Dieu*, and she spent fourteen francs in one month on lemons for polishing her nails; she ordered a blue cashmere dress from Rouen; from Lheureux, she bought one of his most beautiful scarves; she tied it around her waist, over her dressing gown, and with the blinds closed and a book in her hand, she lounged, stretched out on a couch, dressed in her new purchases.

She changed her hairstyle frequently: she did her hair in Chinese fashion, or in long, flowing curls, or plaited in braids; she parted it on one side and rolled it under, like a man.

She wanted to learn Italian: she bought dictionaries, a grammar, and a supply of white paper. She tried to do some serious reading, in history and philosophy. Sometimes at night Charles would awaken with a start, thinking he was being called to tend to a patient:

"I'm on my way," he would stammer.

But it had been the sound of Emma striking a match to relight her lamp. But her reading turned out just like her embroidery projects—half-finished, piled away in the cupboard; she would start something, drop it, and move on to something else.

She had wild moods, in which she could easily have been persuaded to commit any extreme act. She insisted one day, to her husband's disbelief, that she could easily drink an entire large glass of brandy, and when Charles was foolish enough to dare her, she swallowed every last drop.

Despite her "giddy" airs (the Yonville housewives' term for it), Emma nonetheless never seemed happy, and the corners of her mouth were fixed in that pursed look that puckers the faces of old maids and of people whose hopes have been dashed. She was pale all over, as white as linen; the skin on her nose was drawn taut at the nostrils, and her eyes would gaze at you vaguely. When she discovered three gray hairs on her temples, she started referring to her old age.

She often had fainting fits. One day she coughed up some blood, and when Charles fussed over her, revealing how worried he really was: "Oh," she said, "what does it matter?"

Charles sought refuge in his office; and he wept, his elbows on the table, sitting in his office chair below the phrenological head.

Then he wrote to his mother to beg her to come, and together they had long discussions on the subject of Emma.

What should they decide to do? What could they do, considering that she refused every suggestion they made?

"Do you know what your wife needs?" said Charles' mother. "She needs to be forced into some kind of work, some manual labor! If she had to earn her bread, like so many other women do, she wouldn't have these foolish whims; they come from those ideas she has in her head, and from not doing anything all day."

"But she keeps busy," Charles said.

"Oh? Busy? With what? Reading novels, wicked books, books against religion, where they make fun of priests in speeches taken from Voltaire. But all that has its consequences, my poor boy, and a person who doesn't have religion will always turn out bad."

Thus, they resolved to prevent Emma from reading novels. But the plan didn't look so easy to carry out. The good mother took on the task herself: when she was in Rouen, she would go personally to the lending library and tell them Emma was canceling her subscription. And wouldn't they have the right to call in the police then, if the book lender insisted on poisoning her?

The good-byes between mother-in-law and daughter-in-law were dry. In the three weeks they had been together, they hadn't exchanged half a dozen words about anything other than household matters, and polite phrases when they were at the table or going to bed.

The elder Madame Bovary left on a Wednesday, which was market day in Yonville.

Since morning the square had been blocked by a row of carts, their back ends tilted up and their shafts in the air, stretching out in front of the houses from the church to the inn. Along the other side were canvas booth selling cotton goods, blankets, and wool stockings, together with halters for horses and packets of blue ribbons, their ends fluttering in the air. There was heavy hardware spread out on the ground amid pyramids of eggs, and hampers filled with cheeses with wisps of sticky straw jutting out from them; near the wheat machinery, clucking hens were poking their heads out through the bars of their cages. People crowded together into the same spot, unwilling to budge, putting the pharmacist's shop window in some danger. On Wednesdays his place was never empty, and people crowded in less to buy medicine than to ask for advice—so famous was Monsieur Homais in the surrounding villages. His robust self-certainty had fascinated the country people. They saw him as a greater physician than any of the real doctors.

Emma was leaning out the window (where she often was: in the provinces, the window substitutes for the theater and the public promenades), and she was amusing herself watching the swarm of country louts, when she noticed a gentleman dressed in a green velvet coat. He wore fine yellow gloves, though he also wore sturdy gaiters on his legs; and he was heading toward the doctor's house, followed by a peasant who walked with his head bent down and a very determined air about him.

"May I see Monsieur?" he asked Justin, who was chatting with Félicité in the doorway. And, taking him for the house's servant:

"Tell him that Monsieur Rodolphe Boulanger, of La Huchette, is here."

It was not territorial vanity that made him add the name of his estate, but simply the desire to identify himself better. La Huchette was in fact an estate near Yonville, where he had recently purchased the chateau, along with its two farms, which he was running himself—without, however, putting out any great effort in doing so. He lived as a bachelor, and was said to have *at least fifteen thousand in rents!*

Charles came in the room. Monsieur Boulanger introduced his man, who was asking to be bled because he was feeling *pins and needles all over.*

"That'll cure it," he insisted, against all arguments.

So Bovary began by bringing out a bandage and a basin, and he asked Justin to hold it. Then, addressing the peasant, who had already gone pale:

"Don't be afraid, my friend."

"No, no," said the other, "go ahead!"

And with an air of bravado, he held out his thick arm. With the first prick of the lancet, the blood shot out and spattered against the mirror.

"Hold the basin closer!" Charles exclaimed.

"Gawd!" said the peasant. "You'd swear it was a fountain, the way it runs. Look how red my blood is! That must be a good sign, don't you think?"

The health officer said, "Now sometimes, they don't feel anything at first, but then comes a fainting fit, especially with strong people like this one."

At these words, the peasant dropped the little box he had been turning in his fingers. A great shudder in his shoulders made the back of his chair creak. His hat fell to the floor.

"I was afraid of this," Bovary said, pressing his finger against the vein.

The basin began to shake in Justin's hands; his knees shook, and he turned pale.

sign of an eccentric life, the discords that arise from profound feeling, from the tyranny of art, and from a certain contempt for social conventions—all of which may strike them as either seductive or exasperating. Thus, the wind would puff his cotton shirt with frilled cuffs out from the opening of his gray jacket, and his broad-striped trousers revealed at the ankle his nankeen boots with patent leather uppers. They were so highly polished that the grass was reflected in them. He stamped over horse dung in them, one hand in his jacket pocket, his straw hat tilted to one side.

"And besides," he continued, "when one lives in the country . . ."

"It's all wasted effort," said Emma.

"Exactly!" Rodolphe replied. "To think that not one of these fine people is capable of appreciating the cut of a suit!"

They went on to talk about provincial mediocrity, the lives it stifled, the ideals it crushed.

"And so," Rodolphe said, "I retreat into my own sadness . . ."

"You!" she cried, astonished. "But you seem so carefree!"

"Oh yes, in appearance, because I know how to put on a mocking mask for other people; but for all that, there are times when the sight of a cemetery in the moonlight makes me wonder if I wouldn't be better off to go and join the ones who are at peace there . . ."

"Oh! But what about your friends?" she said. "You must think of them."

"My friends? Which ones? Do I have any? Who really cares about me?"

He accompanied these last words with a sort of hissing sound.

But now they had to separate from each other because of a great pile of chairs that a man behind them was carrying. He was so overloaded that the only visible parts of him were the points of his shoes and the ends of his two extended arms. It was Lestiboudois, the gravedigger, who was carrying chairs from the church out to the multitude. Always inventive when it came to his own interests, he had discovered this means of making a profit from the agricultural show, and his idea was so successful that he hardly knew which way to turn. In fact the townspeople, who had grown hot and tired, were quarreling over these chairs, their straw smelling of incense, and they leaned themselves against their thick backs, stained with candle wax, with a certain veneration.

Madame Bovary again took Rodolphe's arm; he continued, as if talking to himself:

"Yes, so many things have been denied to me! Always alone! Oh, if I had only had some goal in my life, if I had only met with some affection, if I had found someone . . . Oh, how I would have expended all the energy I'm capable of, how I would have overcome everything, conquered everything!"

"But it seems to me," Emma said, "that you hardly have much to complain about."

"You think so?" he exclaimed.

"Because after all . . . ," she replied, "you are free."

She hesitated.

"And rich."

"Don't make fun of me," he replied.

And she swore she was not mocking him, when a blast from the cannon sounded; suddenly, everyone began to surge wildly toward the village.

It was a false alarm. The prefect had not arrived; and the jury members were greatly embarrassed, uncertain whether they ought to begin the proceedings or continue to wait.

Finally, at the back of the square, a big rented landau coach appeared, drawn by two skinny horses being whipped on forcefully by a coachman in a white hat. Binet scarcely had time to cry, "To your arms!" and the colonel to follow suit. The men rushed toward their stacked rifles. They hurled themselves at them. A few even forgot to attach their collars. But the prefectorial carriage seemed to anticipate this shortcoming, and the two yoked nags, waddling along in their harness, came up in a little trot to the front of the town hall's peristyle at exactly the moment when the National Guard and the firemen were deployed, beating their drums and marching in place.

"Present!" Binet shouted.

"Halt!" cried the colonel. "Left face!"

And after presenting arms, the clattering of which sounded like a brass kettle tumbling down a flight of stairs, all the guns were lowered.

Then could be seen, stepping down from the carriage, a gentleman wearing a short jacket with silver braiding, bald in the front with a tuft of hair in the back, with a pallid complexion and the most benign appearance. His eyes, very large and heavy-lidded, half closed to contemplate the crowd, while he raised his pointed nose and made his sunken mouth form a smile. He could tell the mayor by his sash, and he explained to him that the prefect had not been able to come. He was himself one of the Counselors of the prefecture; to this he added some excuses. Tuvache responded with his compliments, and the other admitted that he didn't know how to proceed; and there they stood, face to face, their foreheads almost touching, with the jury members all around them, the dignitaries, the National Guard, and the crowd. The Counselor, pressing his little black tri-cornered hat against his chest, repeated his greetings while Tuvache bent into an arc, smiled back at him, stammered, sought for some appropriate phrases, and avowed his devotion to the monarchy and his appreciation of the honor being done to Yonville.

Hippolyte, the groom from the inn, came up to take the coach horses' bridle, and limping on his clubfoot, conducted them to the door of the *Golden Lion*, where a crowd of peasants had gathered to look at the coach. The drum beat, the howitzer boomed, and the gentlemen mounted the stage in a line, seating themselves in the armchairs of red Utrecht velvet that Madame Tuvache had provided.

Everyone on the platform looked alike. Their soft blond faces, a little tanned by the sun, had the color of sweet cider, and their bushy side whiskers emerged from high, stiff collars, held up by white cravats with wide bows. All the waistcoats were velvet; all the watches had oval carnelian seals at the end of long ribbons; every man rested his two hands on his two thighs, carefully tending the drape of his trousers, whose starched cloth shone more brightly than the leather of his heavy boots.

The ladies of the group were behind them, below the porch and between the pillars, while the common crowd faced them, some standing and some sitting on chairs. In fact, Lestiboudois had carried over all the ones he could bring from the meadow, and he was constantly running back to find more in the church, causing such a commotion with his business that it was very difficult to make one's way to the little stair steps leading up to the platform.

"I happen to think," Monsieur Lheureux said to the pharmacist (who was passing by to get to his seat), "that they should have put two Venetian poles up there: with something both rich and a little severe for ornamentation, it would have been quite striking."

"Certainly," Homais replied. "But what can you do! The mayor took charge of everything himself. He's not a man of much taste, poor Tuvache; he is entirely devoid of what they call the artistic sense."

Meanwhile, Rodolphe with Madame Bovary had gone up to the second floor of the town hall, to the *council chamber*, and seeing it was empty, he had declared that they could enjoy the show more comfortably from there. He picked up three stools from the oval table beneath the king's bust, and when he had brought them over to one of the windows, they sat down next to each other.

There was some commotion going on below on the platform, with lengthy whisperings and discussions. Finally, the Counselor arose. By now it was known that his name was Lieuvain, and people were repeating the name to each other throughout the crowd. When he had put a series of pages in order, and brought them up close enough to his eyes to read them, he began:

"Gentlemen,

"May I be permitted to begin—before discussing with you the object of today's gathering, and this feeling, I feel quite sure, will by shared by all of you—may I be permitted, I say, to pay my respects to the national administration, to the government, to the monarch, gentlemen, to our sovereign, to that well-beloved king to whom no branch of either public or private prosperity is a thing indifferent, and who directs, with a hand at once firm and wise, the ship of state amidst the unceasing perils of a stormy sea, and who knows, moreover, how to make peace as respected as war, industry, commerce, agriculture, and the fine arts."

"I should move back a bit," said Rodolphe.

"Why?" asked Emma.

But just then the Counselor's voice rose to an extraordinary pitch. He was declaiming:

"The days have passed, gentlemen, when civil discord bloodied our public squares, when the landlord, the businessman, the workingman himself, falling asleep in the evening, a peaceful sleep, had to tremble at the thought of being suddenly awakened by the sound of inflammatory tocsins, when the most subversive ideas were audaciously undermining the bases . . ."

"It's just that I might be seen from down there," Rodolphe replied; "and then I'd have to be making excuses for weeks, and with my bad reputation . . ."

"Oh, you're exaggerating," said Emma.

"No, no, it's terrible, I assure you."

"But, gentlemen," the Counselor continued, "if I remove those dark images from my sight, and I turn my eyes to the current situation of our beautiful nation, what do I see there? Everywhere, commerce and the arts are flourishing; everywhere new paths of communication, like so many arteries in the body of the State, are establishing new connections; our great manufacturing centers have resumed their activity; religion, stronger than ever, smiles on every one of us; our ports are full, trust is reborn, and France, at last, can breathe!"

"Besides," Rodolphe went on, "from the world's point of view, perhaps they're right."

"How do you mean?" she asked.

"Well," he said, "you know, don't you, that there are some souls in constant torment? They have to alternate, back and forth, between dream and action, the purest of passions, the wildest of joys, and they thus thrust themselves into all sorts of fantasies, all sorts of madness."

At this, she looked at him the way one looks at a person who has visited strange, unknown countries, and she replied:

"We don't even have that distraction, we poor women!"

"A sad distraction, because it doesn't lead to happiness."

"But does a person ever find happiness?"

"Yes—one day, it will be found," he answered.

"And this is precisely what you have understood," the Counselor was saying. "You, farmers and farm workers; you, the peaceful pioneers in the great work of civilization! You, men of progress, men of morality! You have understood, I say, that political storm clouds are far more frightening than any disturbances in the atmosphere . . . ."

"It will be found one day," Rodolphe repeated, "all at once, and just when one has despaired of it. Then the clouds will part, the skies open, and it will be like a voice crying out, 'Here it is!' You sense a need to tell that woman everything, to sacrifice everything for her! It's not a matter of explaining yourself; she will intuit everything. You've both already met, in your dreams." He looked at her. "And finally, there it is, that treasure you've searched for so long, there, right in front of you; it gleams, it sparkles But there is still doubt; one dares not believe in it; one stands still, bedazzled as if coming out of shadows and into daylight."

And as he finished speaking these words, Rodolphe added a sort of panto-mime. He passed his hand across his eyes, like a person who felt dizzy all of a sudden; then he let his hand fall back down, on top of Emma's. She pulled hers back. But the Counselor continued to read his speech:

"And who would be surprised at this, gentlemen? Only a man who is so blind, so entirely immersed—I do not hesitate to use the word—so entirely immersed in the prejudices of another age as to misunderstand still the spirit of our agricultural population. Where can we find, truly, more patriotism than in the country, more devotion to the public good, in short, more intelligence? And I do not mean, gentlemen, that superficial intelligence, that vain orna-ment of idlers, but rather that profound and moderate intelligence that applies itself above all else to pursuing useful ends, and thus contributing to the good of all, to common improvement, to upholding the State, the fruit of respect for the law and the practice of one's duties . . . "

"Oh, there it is again," said Rodolphe. "Always duties—words like that bore me to death. They're all a heap of old fools in flannel waistcoats, and bigoted old women with their footwarmers and their rosaries, constantly droning into our ears that word 'Duty! Duty!' My God, what is duty but to feel what is great, to cherish what's beautiful, and not to accept all the social conventions, along with the humiliations they impose on us."

"But still . . . but still . . . ," Madame Bovary objected.

"No! Why preach against the passions? Are they not the only beautiful thing there is on earth, the source of heroism, of enthusiasm, of poetry and music, of the arts, of everything?"

"But one has to have some concern for the world's opinion, and obey its moral code," Emma said.

"Oh, but there are two moralities," he replied. "The little one, the conventional one, the morality of men, the one that varies constantly and that makes so much noise and fuss here on earth, like this assembly of imbeciles you see down there. But the other morality, the eternal one, that one is all around and above us, like the landscape surrounding us, and the blue sky that gives us light."

Monsieur Lieuvain had just paused to wipe his lips with his pocket handkerchief. He continued:

"But why should I point out to you here, gentlemen, the usefulness of agriculture? Who is it that fulfills our needs? Who is it who provides our subsistence? Is it not the farmer? The farmer, gentlemen, who, sowing the fecund furrows of the countryside with hard-working hands, causes the wheat to spring forth, which, being ground and turned to powder by ingenious technical means and exiting the process under the name of flour, is thence transported to the cities, and is soon brought to the baker, who makes of it nutrition for both poor and rich. And is it not the farmer who fattens his abundant flocks in the meadows to clothe us? For how would we clothe ourselves, how nourish ourselves, without the farmer? And gentlemen, do we need to go even that far afield for examples? Who among us has not frequently reflected on the important things we receive from that humble animal, the ornament of our farmyards, who furnishes us with soft pillows for our beds, succulent meat for our tables, and eggs? But I would never come to an end if I had to enumerate, one after another, all the different products that the earth, well-cultivated, like a generous mother, provides for her children. Here, the vine; elsewhere, apples for cider; there, rapeseed oil; farther away, cheeses; and flax: gentlemen, let us not forget flax! Which has grown considerably in importance over these last several years, and to which I would particularly draw your attention."

He didn't have to draw very hard, because every mouth in the crowd was gaping open, as if to drink in his words. Tuvache, right next to him, listened with his eyes wide open; Monsieur Derozerays would softly close his eyelids from time to time; and farther away, the pharmacist, with his son Napoléon between his knees, cupped his hand behind his ear so as not to miss a single syllable. The other jury members nodded their chins slowly into their waistcoats to single their approval. The firemen, below the platform, leaned on their bayonets; and Binet, motionless, stood with one elbow out, the point of his saber in the air. He may have been listening, but he could not see anything, because his helmet's visor had slipped down onto his nose. His lieutenant, the youngest son of Tuvache, had tilted his own visor at an even more extreme angle, for he was wearing an enormous helmet that wobbled on his head, revealing the border of his cotton kerchief. He smiled underneath it with a childlike sweetness, and his small, pale face, running with sweat, wore an expression that combined pleasure, despondency, and sleepiness.

The square was packed with people up to the house fronts. They were leaning out of every window, others standing in every doorway, and Justin, in front of the pharmacy, seemed transfixed by what he was seeing. Despite the hushed silence, Monsieur Lieuvain's voice was lost as it came through the air. You would catch bits of phrases, interrupted here and there by the creaking of chairs in the crowd; and then you would suddenly hear from behind you the long bellow of a bull or the bleating of lambs replying to each other on the street corners. In fact, the cowherds and the shepherds had driven their beasts right up to the edge of the square, and they lowed from time to time, while they ripped off some bit of foliage that hung within reach of their mouths.

Rodolphe had moved closer to Emma, and he was saying in a low voice, speaking quickly:

"Doesn't this conspiracy of society disgust you? Is there one single feeling that it doesn't condemn? The noblest instincts, the purest sympathies are persecuted, slandered, and, if it does so happen that two poor souls find each other, everything is organized to keep them apart. But they will try, they will beat their wings, they will call to each other. Oh! But it doesn't matter, because sooner or later, in six months, in ten years, they will come together, they will love each other, because fate demands it, and because they were born for each other."

He had his arms folded across his knees, and in that pose lifting his face up toward Emma, close to her, he gazed at her fixedly. She could see small gold flecks in his eyes, radiating outward from his black pupils, and she could even smell the scent of the pomade gleaming in his hair. And then she felt a weakness overcoming her, and she recalled the Viscount who had made her waltz at La Vaubyessard, whose beard had given off the same vanilla and citron scent as this man's hair; and mechanically, she half closed her eyes to breathe it in the better. But in making that movement and arching in her chair, she saw off in the distance the old *Hirondelle* coach coming slowly down the Leux hillside, a long plume of dust trailing behind it. It was in that yellow coach that Léon so often had returned to her; and it was by that very route that he had gone away forever! She thought she could see his face in the window, and then everything became confused: some clouds were passing by; she felt as if she were turning again in the waltz under the chandeliers' lights, in the Viscount's arms, and that Léon was not far off, that he was on his way . . . and still she sensed Rodolphe's head very close to her. The sweetness of this sensation thus seeped into her old desires and, like grains of sand in a gust of wind, they whirled within the subtle rush of the scent that was spreading itself throughout her soul. She dilated her nostrils several times to breathe in deeply the freshness of the ivy wound around the columns. She removed her gloves, she wiped her hands; then, with her handkerchief, she fanned her face, while over the beating of her temples she could hear the murmur of the crowd and the voice of the Counselor as he intoned his sentences.

He was saying:

"Continue! Persevere! Listen neither to the suggestions of routine nor the too hasty counsels of a reckless empiricism! Above all, apply yourself to the enrichment of the soil, to good manures, to the development of the equine, bovine, ovine, and porcine races! May this agricultural fair be for you like a peaceful arena from which the victor, as he departs, extends his hand to the vanquished and fraternizes with him, in the hope of an even better success! And you, venerable servants! Humble domestics, whose painful labor no government until now has taken into account, come forward and receive the recompense for your silent virtues, and rest assured that the State henceforth has its eyes fixed upon you, that it encourages you, that it protects you, that it will do right by all your justifiable complaints and will lighten, insofar as it is able, the burdens of your painful sacrifices!"

Monsieur Lieuvain then sat down; Monsieur Derozerays got up, and began another speech. His was, perhaps, considerably less flowery than the Counselor's, but he made up for this with a more positive style, that is, by more specialized knowledge and more exalted considerations. Thus, praise of the government took up less space in it; religion and agriculture took up more. He demonstrated the relations between the two, and how they had always contributed to civilization. Rodolphe, with Madame Bovary, was talking dreams, premonitions, magnetism. The orator went back to the cradle of society, painting for us those savage days when men ate acorns and lived deep in the woods. But then they moved beyond animal skins, put on clothes, plowed the fields, planted vines. Was this a good thing, or did these discoveries result in more inconveniences than advantages? Monsieur Derozerays homed in on this problem. From magnetism, Rodolphe had bit by bit approached the topic of affinities, and while the Président was citing Cincinnatus at the plow, Diocletian planting his cabbages,[5] and the Chinese emperors launching the new year by sowing seed, the young man was explaining to the young woman that such irresistible attractions had their origins in a previous existence.

"And so, consider ourselves," he was saying. "Why is it that we met? What chance brought it about? It can only be because our particular inclinations were pushing us toward each other across the distance, like two rivers that eventually flow into each other."

And he took her hand; she did not withdraw it.

"For good farming practices in general!" cried the Président.

"So, for example, when I came to your house today . . . "

"To Monsieur Bizet, of Quincampoix!"

"Did I know I would be accompanying you?"

"Seventy francs!"

"A hundred times I wanted to leave, and yet I followed you, I stayed."

"Manures."

"Just as I will remain this evening, tomorrow, the next days, all my life!"

5. Diocletian (245–313 C.E.), Roman emperor from 284 to 305. He resigned in 305 and retired to Salonae (now Split), in Dalmatia, to cultivate his garden. Cincinnatus was a Roman consul (460 B.C.E.) who was supposedly called to his office while found plowing.

"To Monsieur Caron of Argeuil, a gold medal!"

"Because I have never found so complete a charm in the company of any other woman."

"To Monsieur Bain, of Givry-Saint-Martin!"

"And so I will carry with me the memory of you."

"For a merino ram."

"But you will forget about me, I will have passed away like a shadow."

"To Monsieur Belot, of Notre-Dame . . . ."

"Oh no! I will remain, won't I, somewhere in your thoughts, in your life?"

"Porcine race, a shared prize: sixty francs to Messieurs Lehérissé and Cullembourg!"

Rodolphe pressed her hand, and he felt it all warm and trembling, like a captive dove anxious to resume its flight; but, whether because she was trying to withdraw her hand or because she was responding to the pressure of his, she moved her fingers slightly, and he exclaimed:

"Oh, thank you! You do not reject me! You are good! You understand that I'm yours! Let me just look at you, let me contemplate you!"

A gust of wind blew in through the window and ruffled the cloth on the table, and in the square below, it lifted all the great bonnets of the peasant women, like the wings of so many white butterflies all beating at once.

"The use of oil cakes," the Président continued.

And now he began to speed up.

"Flemish manure—flax cultivation—drainage, long leases—domestic service."

Rodolphe spoke no more. They were looking at each other. A supreme desire caused their dry lips to quiver; and gently, effortlessly, their fingers joined.

"Catherine-Nicaise-Elisabeth Leroux, of Sassetot-la-Guerrière, for fifty-four years of service on the same farm, a silver medal—value, twenty-five francs!"

"Where is she, Catherine Leroux?" the Counselor repeated.

She did not come forward, and voices could be heard whispering:

"Go on."

"No."

"To the left!"

"Don't be afraid!"

"Oh, how stupid the woman is!"

"Is that her finally?" Tuvache asked.

"Yes—there she is!"

"Make her come up then!"

Then up to the platform came a little old woman, fearful looking, seeming to shrink inward under her poor clothes. She wore big wooden clogs on her feet, and a large blue apron hung from her waist. Her scrawny face, framed by a borderless cap, was more wrinkled than a withered old russet apple, and from the sleeves of her red jacket extended two long hands, with gnarled joints. Barn dust, soapsuds, and the grease from sheep's wool had so thoroughly encrusted, scratched, hardened them that they seemed dirty, even though they had been rinsed in clear water; and they remained half open as a result of having worked for so long, as if presenting themselves as humble witnesses of all the suffering she had endured. A kind of monastic rigidity gave a dignity to her expression. There was nothing sorrowful and nothing sentimental in her pale gaze. Through a long life with animals, she had taken on their muteness and their placidity. This was the first time she had found herself in so numerous a company; and inwardly terrified by the flags, the drums, by the men in black suits and the Counselor's Cross of Honor, she remained absolutely motionless, not knowing whether to go forward or to turn and run away, nor why the crowd was pushing her and the jurymen smiling at her. And there she stood, before all the beaming townspeople, this half a century of servitude.

"Come forward, venerable Catherine-Nicaise-Elisabeth Leroux!" said the Counselor, who had taken the list of winners out of the Président's hands.

And looking back and forth between the piece of paper and the old woman, he repeated in a paternal tone:

"Come forward, come forward!"

"Are you deaf?" said Tuvache, twitching in his chair.

And he began to shout in her ear:

"Fifty-four years of service! A silver medal! Twenty-five francs! It's for you."

Then, when she had her medal, she looked at it thoughtfully. And a beatific smile spread over her face, and they could hear her murmuring as she walked away:

"I'll give it to the priest back home, so he'll say Masses for me."

"What a fanatic!" the pharmacist exclaimed, bending toward the notary.

The program was over; the crowd dispersed; and now that the speeches had been read out, everyone returned to his station, and everything went back to normal: the masters bullied the servants, and the latter beat the animals, the indolent winners who now returned to their stables, a green wreath between their horns.

In the meantime, the National Guardsmen had gone up to the second floor of the town hall, with buns skewered on their bayonets, the battalion's drummer hauling up a basket of bottles. Madame Bovary took Rodolphe's arm; he escorted her to her house; they separated in front of her door; then he went for a walk alone in the meadow, waiting for the banquet hour.

The feast was lengthy, raucous, and poorly served; people were so crowded together they could barely move their elbows, and the narrow planks being used for benches almost broke under the guests' weight. They ate copiously. Each one was determined to eat his share. Sweat was running down every forehead; and a whitish vapor, like a river mist on an autumn day, floated over the tables between the hanging lamps. Rodolphe, leaning his back against the canvas tent, was thinking so intently about Emma that he heard nothing around him. Behind him, outside the tent, on the grass, servants were piling up the dirty plates; his neighbors were speaking, and he didn't reply; they refilled his glass, and a silence took root in his thought, despite the growing noise around him. He was thinking of what she had said, and the shape of her lips; her face, as in a magic mirror, gleamed at him from the polished visors of the military caps; the folds of her dress hung all down the walls, and days of love unfurled before him, stretching out infinitely into the future.

He saw her again that evening during the fireworks; but she was with her husband, Madame Homais, and the pharmacist, who was terribly worried about the danger of stray rockets; and he constantly left the group to go give advice to Binet.

The fireworks sent to Monsieur Tuvache's house had been locked up in the basement, out of an excess of precaution; and so the damp powder would scarcely light, and the major piece, which was supposed to be a dragon biting its tail, fizzled out altogether. From time to time, there was a pathetic Roman candle, and then the gaping crowd would set up a clamor that mingled with the squeals of women whose waists were being squeezed in the darkness. Emma, silent, nestled gently against Charles' shoulder; then, her chin raised up, she would follow the luminous jet of the fireworks in the black sky. Rodolphe contemplated her in the light of the burning lanterns.

They were extinguished one by one. The stars came out. A few drops of rain began to fall. She tied her scarf over her head.

At that moment, the Counselor's carriage came out from the inn. His coachman, who was drunk, abruptly nodded off, and from a distance they could see, above the coach's hood, between the two lanterns, the large mass of his body being swayed to the right and to the left, depending on which way the coach rocked.

"Really," said the pharmacist, "they ought to clamp down on drunkenness! I'd like to see the names of all those who were intoxicated during the week inscribed on a tablet *ad hoc* and hung on the town hall door! And besides, from a statistical point of view, you'd then have a public record to use in case of . . . But excuse me."

And off he ran again to the captain.

The latter was going back to his house. He was going to get back to his lathe.

"Perhaps it might not be a bad idea," Homais said to him, "to send one of your men, or to go yourself . . ."

"Leave me alone," the tax collector replied. "There's nothing to worry about!"

"Rest easy," said the pharmacist when he returned to his friends. "Monsieur Binet has assured me that measures have been taken. No sparks will fall. The pumps are full. Let's go home to bed."

"Heavens! I'm ready for it," said Madame Homais, who was yawning considerably. "But that's all right; we've had a beautiful day for our celebration."

Rodolphe echoed her quietly, with a tender look: "Oh yes! Very beautiful."

And having said good night to each other, they separated.

Two days later, in the *Rouen Lantern*, there was a long article about the agricultural fair. Homais had written it—with gusto—the day after:

"Why these festoons, these flowers, these garlands? Where is the crowd hurrying, like the waves of a furious sea, under a pitiless tropical sun spreading its torrential heat over our fallow lands?"

Then he went on to speak about the condition of the peasants. Certainly, the government was doing a great deal, but it was not enough! "Have courage!" he exclaimed. "A thousand reforms are essential; let us accomplish them!" Then, touching upon the Counselor's entry, he did not fail to note "the martial air of our militia," nor "our most vivacious village girls," nor the old bald men "like patriarchs who were there, some of whom are the remains of our immortal legions, whose hearts still throb at the manly sound of the drums." He noted himself among the most prominent of the jury, and he even pointed out, in a footnote, that Monsieur Homais, pharmacist, had written a memorandum on cider for the Agriculture Society. When he came to the distribution of the prizes, he depicted the joy of the winners in dithyrambic strains. "Father embraced his son, brother his brother, husband his wife. More than one proudly displayed his humble medal to the crowd, and, no doubt, when he returns home to his good housewife, he will have hung it up, weeping, on the modest walls of his cottage.

"Around six o'clock, a banquet, set up in Monsieur Liegeard's meadow, brought all the celebration's principal figures together. The greatest cordiality never ceased to reign. Various toasts were proposed: Monsieur Lieuvain, to the monarch! Monsieur Tuvache, to the Prefect! Monsieur Derozerays, to agriculture! Monsieur Homais, to industry and the fine arts, those two sisters! Monsieur Leplichey, to progress! In the evening, a brilliant fireworks display suddenly illuminated the skies. One might say it was a veritable kaleidoscope, a true scene from the opera, and for a moment, our little town could imagine itself transported into a dream from the *Thousand and One Nights*.

"Let us note that not a single untoward event arose to disturb this family gathering."

And he added:

"However, the absence of the clergy was noted. No doubt the priests have a different definition of progress. As you wish, men of Loyola!"[6]

CHAPTER 9

Six weeks passed by. Rodolphe did not return. One evening, at last, he appeared.

"Better not come around too soon," he had said to himself the day after the agricultural fair. "That would be a mistake."

So, at the end of that week, he had left to go hunting.

When the hunt was over, he worried that perhaps he was proceeding too slowly, but then he reasoned to himself:

"But if she loved me from that very first day, she'll have to love me even more out of her impatience to see me again. So let's carry on!"

And he knew that he had calculated correctly when, coming into the room now, he saw Emma go pale.

She was alone. Daylight was fading. The thin muslin curtains across the windows thickened in the dusk, and the gilt front of the barometer, struck by a ray of the sun, reflected like fire in the coral-edged mirror.

Rodolphe remained standing; and Emma scarcely made any replies to his opening polite sentences.

"As for me," he said, "I've been busy. I've been sick."

"Seriously sick?" she cried.

"Well!" Rodolphe said, sitting down on a stool next to her. "No! . . . It's more that I didn't want to come back."

"Why?"

"You can't guess?"

He looked directly at her now, and so intensely that she lowered her head and reddened. He continued:

6. Ignatius of Loyola (1491–1556), a Spaniard, founded the order of the Jesuits in 1534. The Jesuits were expelled from France in 1762.

"Emma . . . "

"Sir!" she said, and moved slightly away from him.

"Ah, you see," he continued in a melancholic tone, "that I was right not to want to come back; because this name, this name that fills my heart and just now slipped out, you deny it to me! Madame Bovary! . . . Yes, everybody calls you that! . . . But it's not your name, after all; it's another man's name!"

And he repeated: "Another man's!"

And he hid his face in his hands.

"Yes, I think about you continually! . . . The memory of you tears at me! . . . Oh, forgive me! . . . I'll leave you alone . . . Farewell! I'll go far away . . . so far that you'll never hear anyone speak of me again! But still . . . today . . . I can't say what force it was that drove me toward you! Because you can't fight against heaven, you can't resist the smiles of the angels! You simply have to let yourself be pulled along by the beautiful, the charming, the adorable!"

This was the first time Emma had had such things said to her; and her pride, like someone relaxing in a steam bath, languorously stretched out its whole length in the warmth of this language.

"But," he went on, "if I had not come, if I hadn't been able to see you, ah, at least I know your surroundings so very well. At night, every night, I got up, I came by here, I gazed at your house, the roof shining in the moonlight, the trees in the garden swaying against your window, and the small lamp, that glow, shining through the curtains, in the darkness. Ah, you couldn't know that there was, so close and yet so far from you, a poor, miserable . . . "

She turned toward him with a sob.

"Oh, you are so good!" she said.

"No, I love you, that's all! You don't doubt it! Say it to me, one word, one single word!"

And Rodolphe had, imperceptibly, let himself slide down off the stool, and he knelt on the floor beside her; but they heard the sound of boots in the kitchen, and the door, he suddenly realized, had not been closed.

"How good it would be of you," he said as he quickly stood up, "to satisfy that whim of mine!"

That is, to visit her house; he had wanted to see it, and Madame Bovary had seen nothing at all inappropriate in the request, and now they both were standing when Charles entered the room.

"Hello, Doctor," Rodolphe said to him.

The health officer, flattered by this unexpected title, began to gush obsequiously, which gave the other the opportunity to pull himself together.

Then he said, "Madame has been telling me about her health . . . "

Charles interrupted: he had a thousand anxieties, in fact; his wife's respiratory problems were starting up again. At that, Rodolphe asked whether some exercise on horseback wouldn't do her good.

"Certainly! Excellent, perfect! . . . Now there's an idea! You should follow up on that," he said to her.

And when she objected that she had no horse, Monsieur Rodolphe offered her one of his; she refused the offer; he did not insist; and then, to give his visit a better motive, he invented a story about his farmhand, the one Charles had bled, saying he was still experiencing dizzy spells.

"I'll come by," said Bovary.

"No, no, I'll bring him to you; we'll come here, to make it more convenient for you."

"Ah, fine. Thank you."

And then, when they were alone:

"Why didn't you accept Monsieur Boulanger's offer, which was so gracious?"

She put on a sulky air, tried out a thousand excuses, and at last declared *that it might seem strange*.

"Oh, I couldn't care less!" Charles said, pirouetting around. "Health above all else! You're making a mistake!"

"Well then! How am I supposed to ride, when I don't have a riding outfit?"

"We'll have to get you one!" he replied.

The outfit decided her.

When the riding habit was ready, Charles wrote to Monsieur Boulanger that his wife was now available for him, and that they appreciated his kindness.

The next day, at noon, Rodolphe came up to Charles' door with two horses. One of them wore little pink pompons on its ears, and a woman' saddle made of buckskin.

Rodolphe had put on his high, soft boots, saying to himself that she would undoubtedly never have seen the like; and in fact Emma was charmed by the figure he cut when he appeared in front of the house in his velvet coat and his white knit riding breeches. She was ready, she was waiting for him.

Justin slipped out of the pharmacy to look at her, and the apothecary likewise troubled himself to emerge for the occasion. He gave Monsieur Boulanger some advice.

"Bad luck happens so quickly! Be careful! Your horses might be too spirited!"

She heard sounds from over her head: it was Félicité beating out a rhythm on the windowpanes to amuse little Berthe. The child threw a kiss; her mother signaled back with the pommel of her riding crop.

"Have a good ride!" cried Monsieur Homais. "Prudence above all! Prudence!"

And he waved his newspaper at them as he watched them ride off.

As soon as he felt the softer earth beneath him, Emma's horse broke into a gallop. Rodolphe galloped alongside her. Now and then they exchanged a word or two. Bent slightly forward, keeping her hand up and her right arm extended, she gave herself up to the rhythmic movement that rocked her in the saddle.

At the foot of the hill, Rodolphe loosened the reins: they raced off together as one; then, at the top, abruptly, the horses stopped, and Emma's long blue veil settled back into place.

These were the first days of October. A low fog lay on the landscape. Mists spread out on the horizon, settling in the hollows of the hillsides; some wisps detached themselves, rose up, and were lost. At times when the clouds parted and a ray of sun shone through, they could see the distant rooftops of Yonville with its gardens alongside the river, its barnyards, its walls, and the church steeple. Emma squinted to make out her house, and never had this poor village in which she lived seemed so very small. From the high ground where they were, the whole valley seemed an immense pale lake evaporating into the air. Here and there, great clumps of trees sprung up like black rocks; and the tall lines of poplars, overtopping the fog, looked like shorelines stirred by the wind.

To one side, among the firs, a brown light was moving over the grass in the warm air. The earth, reddish brown like powdered tobacco, deadened the sounds of the horses' steps; as they walked along, their iron-shod hooves nudged fallen pine cones before them.

Rodolphe and Emma followed the edge of the forest. She turned away frequently to avoid his gaze, and then she only saw the long rows of fir trunks, the endless succession of which made her a little dizzy. The horses panted. The leather saddles creaked.

At the moment they turned to enter the forest, the sun came out.

"God is protecting us!" said Rodolphe.

"Do you think so?" she said.

"Let's go on! Let's go on!" he replied.

He clicked his tongue. The two beasts began to trot more quickly.

Some long ferns on the edge of the path got tangled in Emma's stirrup. Rodolphe, without dismounting, bent over and pulled them off as they rode. Other times, to pull back the branches, he passed closer to her, and Emma felt his knee rub against her leg. The sky had become blue. The leaves were still. There were great open spaces of heather in bloom; and patches of violets alternated with the jumbled undergrowth, gray, fawn-colored, or golden, colors as diverse as the various trees. Often they heard a soft beating of wings in the bushes, or the harsh but muffled cries of the crows as they flew up off the oaks.

They dismounted. Rodolphe tethered the horses. She walked ahead, on the moss between the wagon ruts.

But her too-long dress got in the way, even though she held it up behind her by the train, and Rodolphe, walking behind, contemplated the delicate white of her stocking between the black hem and the black boot, and he felt he was glimpsing her nudity.

She stopped.

"I'm so tired," she said.

"Come, let's push on!" he replied. "You can do it!"

Then, after another hundred steps, she stopped again; and, through the long veil falling from her masculine hat all the way to her hips, he could see her face; the veil gave it a bluish cast, as if she had swum up from an azure wave.

"Where are we going?"

He made no reply. She was almost panting. Rodolphe looked around, and he silently chewed at his moustache.

They came to a wider clearing where the young trees had been cut down. They sat down on a fallen tree trunk, and Rodolphe began to speak to her of his love.

She was not at all frightened by his compliments at first. He was calm, serious, melancholic.

Emma listened with her head lowered, poking at some wood shavings on the ground with the toe of her boot.

"Isn't it true that our destinies are linked now?"

"No!" she replied. "You know very well. It's impossible."

She got up to leave. He seized her by the wrist. She stopped. Then, having looked at him for a few moments with a moist, loving gaze, she spoke sharply:

"Oh, come, let's not talk about it any more . . . Where are the horses? Let's go back."

He made an angry, bored gesture. She repeated:

"Where are the horses? Where are the horses?"

Then, smiling strangely, with his eyes fixed and his teeth clenched, he came forward, his arms outstretched. She recoiled, trembling. She stammered:

"Oh, you're frightening me! You're hurting me! Let's go back."

"If we must," he replied, immediately changing the look on his face.

And he instantly became respectful again, reassuring and mild-mannered. She gave him her arm. They turned back. He said:

"What's wrong? Why? I don't understand. You must have misunderstood me? You stand in my soul like a Madonna on a pedestal, in a high, immaculate place. But I need you in order to live! I need your eyes, your voice, your thoughts. Be my friend, my sister, my angel!"

And he stretched out his arm, encircling her waist. She tried gently to disengage him. He held on as they continued to walk.

But they heard the two horses ahead, grazing on the leaves.

"Oh, once more," said Rodolphe, "let's not leave! Stay!"

He drew her further away, near to a small pond where floating weeds spread their green color over the water. Withered water lilies were held immobile by the reeds. At the sound of their footsteps on the grass, frogs leaped away to hide.

"It's wrong, it's wrong," she was saying. "I'm mad to listen to you."

"Why? . . . . Emma! Emma!"

"Oh, Rodolphe! . . . ." said the young woman slowly, turning to lean her head on his shoulder.

The cloth of her dress caught on the velvet of his coat, she tilted back her white throat, which was swelling with a sigh, and overcome, in tears, with a long shudder, hiding her face, she gave herself up to him.

The shadows of the evening descended; the sun, on the horizon, passed between the branches and blinded her. Here and there, all around her, little luminous patches trembled, as if hummingbirds in flight had scattered their feathers on the ground. Silence was everywhere; the trees seemed to emanate a sort of sweetness; she felt her heart begin to beat again, and felt the blood circulating in her flesh like a stream of milk. Then she heard far away, beyond the forest, coming from the hills on the other side of the valley, a vague, prolonged cry, a voice that faded away, and she listened silently, the voice blending like music with the last vibrations of her pulsating nerves. Rodolphe, a cigar between his teeth, was using his pocket knife to repair one of the broken bridles.

They came back to Yonville by the same path. They saw the tracks of their own horses in the mud, side by side, the same bushes, the same stones in the grass. Nothing around them had changed; yet, for her, something greater had happened than if the mountains themselves had moved. Rodolphe from time to time bent and took her hand to kiss it.

She was charming on horseback! Sitting erect with her narrow waist, her knee bent against the horse's mane, a little flushed in the fresh air, in the red glow of the evening.

Entering Yonville, she made her horse prance a little on the paving stones. Everyone watched her from their windows.

At dinner, her husband said that she looked healthier; but she seemed not to hear him when he asked her about her day's outing; and she remained still, leaning her elbow next to her plate, between the two lit candles.

"Emma!" he said.

"What?"

"Well, I spent this afternoon with Monsieur Alexandre; he has an old mare that's still in good shape, just a little bad in the knees, which we could buy, I'm sure of it, for a hundred écus . . . ."

He added:

"And, thinking that it would please you, I took it . . . I bought it . . . Did I do the right thing? Tell me."

She nodded her head in assent; then, fifteen minutes later:

"Are you going out this evening?" she asked.

"Yes. Why?"

"Oh, nothing, nothing, dear."

And once she was rid of Charles, she went up to her room and locked the door.

At first it was all a whirl; she saw the trees, the pathways, the ditches, Rodolphe, and she still felt the pressure of his arms while the leaves trembled and the reeds sighed in the wind.

But seeing herself in the mirror, she was startled by her face. Never had her eyes been so large, so black, never of such depths. Some subtle thing had spread through her and transfigured her.

She repeated: "I have a lover! A lover!" delighting in the concept as if it were another puberty that she was passing through. She was at last going to feel those joys of love, that fever of happiness that she had despaired of. She was entering into something marvelous where everything would be passion, ecstasy, delirium; a bluish immensity surrounded her, the heights of passion sparkling within her exalted thoughts, ordinary existence appearing only at a distance, far below, in the darkness, down in the valleys between these high peaks.

Then she remembered the heroines in the books she had read, and the lyrical legion of adulterous women sang in her memory with the voices of sisters casting their spell on her. She was herself becoming a real part of these imaginations, realizing the long dream of her youth, seeing herself now as one of those lovers she had so long envied. And more: Emma now experienced a satisfaction that felt like revenge. Hadn't she suffered enough! But now she triumphed, and love, stifled for so long, burst forth, effervescing in joy. She savored it without remorse, without disquiet, without anxiety.

The following day went by in a new kind of sweetness. They made promises to each other. She told him about her sorrows. Rodolphe interrupted her with kisses; and gazing on him with half-closed eyes, she asked him again to say her name and to tell her that he loved her. This was in the forest, like the day before, but now in a shoemaker's hut. The walls were of straw, and the roof hung so low that they had to remain bent over. They sat side by side, on a bed of dry leaves.

From that day on, they wrote each other regularly every evening. Emma carried her letter to the end of the garden by the river, to a fissure in the terrace wall. Rodolphe would come to get it and put another one there, which she always complained was too short.

One morning, when Charles had left before dawn, she was seized by a whim to see Rodolphe right then. She could get to La Huchette quickly, stay there an hour, and be back in Yonville while everyone else was still asleep. The idea made her pant with desire; she quickly found herself in the middle of the meadow, walking rapidly, without looking back.

Day began to dawn. From afar, Emma recognized her lover's home, with its two dove-tailed weathervanes forming a black silhouette against the pale dawn sky.

After the barnyard, she found a building that had to be the chateau. She went in, as if the walls had opened of themselves at her approach. A large, straight staircase led up to a corridor. Emma turned the handle of a door and there, suddenly, at the back of the room, she saw a sleeping man. It was Rodolphe. She cried out to him.

"You here! You here!" he repeated. "How did you manage to get here? Oh, your dress is wet!"

"I love you!" she replied, putting her arms around him.

This first audacity having been a success, now every time Charles left early, Emma would quickly dress herself and hurry stealthily down the steps that led to the riverside.

But when the crossing plank for the cows had been removed, she had to follow the garden walls running along the river; the bank was slippery; to keep from falling, she had to grip the overhanging tufts of wilted wildflowers. Then she had to cross the ploughed fields where she sank in the mud, stumbled, and got her thin boots stuck. Her scarf, tied around her head, fluttered in the wind that blew across the meadows; she was afraid of the cattle; she began to run; she arrived out of breath, her cheeks pink, her whole person exhaling the fresh scent of sap, of greenery, and of the open air. At that hour, Rodolphe would still be asleep. It was as if a spring morning had entered his room.

The yellow curtains, hanging down the whole length of the window allowed in a heavy, blond kind of light. Emma groped her way, blinking her eyes, while drops of dew hung suspended from her hair, creating a kind of topaz halo all around her face. Rodolphe, laughing, would pull her to him and press her to his heart.

Later, she began examining his quarters, opening drawers, combing her hair with his comb and looking at herself in his shaving mirror. Often, she would even put between her teeth the stem of a huge pipe that lay on the night table, among lemons and lumps of sugar, next to a water carafe.

It would take them a good quarter of an hour to say their good-bye. Then Emma would cry; she would have liked never to leave Rodolph. Something stronger than her was pushing her toward him, so much so that one day, seeing her turn up unexpectedly, he frowned, as if he was displeased.

"What's the matter with you?" she said. "Are you ill? Speak to me!"

At last he declared, in his most serious tone, that her visits were becoming indiscreet and that she was compromising herself.

CHAPTER 10

Rodolphe's fears slowly took possession of her. Love had at first intoxicated her, and she had thought of nothing beyond that. But now that it had become indispensable to her life, she was afraid of losing any part of it or even of disturbing it in any way. When she came back from his house, she would cast anxious glances all around her, carefully scanning every shape passing on the horizon, and every village window from which she might be seen. She would listen for footsteps, for shouts, for the sound of plows; and she would come to a halt, more pale and trembling than the leaves of the poplars that swayed over her head.

One morning when she was returning, she suddenly thought she could make out the long barrel of a rifle that seemed to be aimed directly at her. It was sticking out sideways from the rim of a small barrel, half buried in the grass, on the edge of a ditch. Emma, ready to faint from fright, came forward nonetheless, and a man emerged from the barrel like a jack-in-the-box. He had leggings buckled up to his knees, a cap pulled down to his eyes, shivering lips, and a red nose. It was captain Binet, out hunting wild ducks.

"You should have called out before you got so close!" he cried. "When you see a gun, you should always give a warning."

In this way, the tax collector tried to hide the scare he had just had; for a decree from the prefecture had outlawed duck hunting except in boats. Monsieur Binet, despite his respect for the laws, was acting quite illegally. So he was expecting to encounter a game warden any minute. But this anxiety only added a thrill to his hunting pleasure, and all alone in his barrel, he congratulated himself on his good fortune and on his cleverness.

At the sight of Emma, he felt a great weight lifted off him, and he quickly struck up a conversation:

"It's definitely not warm; *it's nippy!*"

Emma didn't reply. He went on:

"And here you are, out and about so early?"

"Yes," she stammered. "I'm just coming back from the wet nurse's, where my daughter is."

"Ah, good! Good! As for me, just as you can see, I've been here since dawn; but the weather's so nasty that unless you have the bird right in front of you . . ."

"Good day, Monsieur Binet," she interrupted, turning on her heel.

"Your servant, Madame," he replied in a dry tone.

And he got back into his barrel.

Emma regretted having left the tax collector in such a brusque way. He would undoubtedly start to from unpleasant suspicions. The story about the nurse was the worst excuse possible, everybody in Yonville knowing perfectly well that the child had been home for a year. Besides, nobody lived near the place; the path she had been on led only to La Huchette; Binet, therefore, had guessed where she had been, and he wouldn't keep quiet about it, he would gossip, it was certain! She spent the entire day tormenting herself, thinking up every lie she possibly could, and having always before her eyes that imbecile with his game bag.

After dinner, Charles, seeing her fretful, wanted to distract her by taking her to the pharmacist's; and who was the first person she saw upon entering the pharmacy but the tax collector! He was standing in front of the counter, in the glow of a red jar, and he was saying:

"Give me, please, half an ounce of vitriol."

"Justin!" cried the pharmacist. "Bring us the sulfuric acid."

Then, turning to Emma who was about to go up to Madame Homais' room:

"No, wait, it's not worth your trouble, she's coming down. You can warm yourself up at the stove while you're waiting ... Pardon me ... Hello, Doctor," (because the pharmacist loved to pronounce that word *doctor*, as if, in addressing somebody else with the term, something of its splendor reflected back on himself). " . . . But look out, Justin, don't knock the mortars over! Go up instead to the little room and find some chairs; and you know very well we don't move the armchairs from the drawing room."

Homais was hurrying out from behind the counter to put his armchair back where it belonged when Binet asked for half an ounce of sugar acid.

"Sugar acid?" said the pharmacist disdainfully. "I don't know what it is, never heard of it! Do you perhaps mean oxalic acid? It's oxalic, isn't it?"

Binet explained that he wanted a corrosive to make a copper solution for cleaning his various hunting gear. Emma shuddered. The pharmacist began to say:

"Actually, the weather isn't right for it now, because of the humidity."

"All the same," the tax collector replied in a cunning tone of voice, "there are some people who like it just fine."

She couldn't breathe.

"And also give me . . . "

"He'll never leave!" she thought.

"A half ounce of resin and of turpentine, four ounces of yellow wax, and three half ounces of animal black, please, to polish the patent leather on my gear."

The pharmacist was starting to cut the wax when Madame Homais appeared with Irma in her arms, Napoléon at her side, and Athalie behind. She went to sit down on the velvet-covered bench by the window, and the little boy squatted down on a stool while his older sister prowled around the jujube box near her papa. He was filling funnels and corking flasks, sticking on labels, making up packages. All were quiet around him, and the only sounds were the occasional clinking of the scale's weights, along with a few softly spoken words from the pharmacist to his pupil.

"How is your little daughter doing?" Madame Homais suddenly asked.

"Silence!" exclaimed her husband, who was writing down some figures in his account book.

"Why didn't you bring her along?" she continued in a low voice.

"Hush, hush!" said Emma, pointing to the pharmacist.

But Binet, entirely absorbed in going over his bill, had probably not heard anything. At last he left the shop. Then Emma, relieved, let out a great sigh.

"How hard you're breathing!" said Madame Homais.

"Oh, it's because it's so warm," she replied.

The next day they discussed how to arrange their meetings; Emma wanted to bribe her servant with a present; but it would be much better to find some discreet house in Yonville. Rodolphe promised to look for one.

All that winter, three or four times a week, he would come to her garden in the dark of night. Emma had purposely taken the key out of the gate, and Charles thought it had been lost.

To let her know he was there, Rodolphe would throw a handful of sand up against her shutters. She would leap up at once; but sometimes he would have to wait, for Charles had the absurd habit of chatting by the fireside, and he would go on and on.

She burned with impatience; if looks could have done it, she would have hurled him out of the window. Finally, she would begin to get ready for bed, then pick up a book and continue to read peacefully, acting as if the book fascinated her. Charles, in bed, would call for her to come.

"Come along to bed, Emma," he would say. "It's time."

"Yes, I'm coming!" she would reply.

Then, since the candles bothered his eyes, he would turn toward the wall and go to sleep. Then she would escape, holding her breath, smiling, her heart throbbing, in her nightdress.

Rodolphe had a large cloak; he would wrap her entirely in it, and putting his arm around her waist, he would lead her without saying a word to the bottom of the garden.

It was under the same arbor, on the same bench made of dry sticks where, in the past, Léon used to gaze at her so amorously during those summer nights. Now she hardly ever thought about him.

The stars were shining through the bare branches of the jasmine tree. They could hear the river flowing behind them, and from time to time the rustling of the dead reeds on the banks. Great masses of shadows would loom up here and there against the darkness and sometimes, rising up together in a single shuddering movement, would hang over them like immense black waves coming to engulf them. The cold of the night would make them hold each other even more tightly; the sighs from their lips seemed stronger; their eyes, which they could scarcely see, seemed larger to them, and in the midst of the silence, there were soft words spoken that fell upon their souls, crystalline, sonorous, reverberating in multiplying echoes.

When the night was rainy, they would take shelter in the consulting room, between the cart shed and the stable. She would light one of the kitchen candles, which she had hidden behind the books. Rodolphe would settle in as if he were at home. The sight of the bookshelves, the desk, the whole room, made him merrier; and he couldn't keep himself from making a series of jokes about Charles, which embarrassed Emma. She wanted to see him be more serious, and even more dramatic for the occasion, as she did the time she thought she heard footsteps approaching in the lane outside.

"Someone's coming!" she said.

He snuffed out the candle.

"Do you have your pistols?"

"What for?"

"Well—to defend yourself with," Emma replied.

"From your husband? Oh, the poor boy!"

And Rodolphe said this with a gesture signifying, "I'd crush him with a flick of my finger."

She was stunned by his courage, while at the same time she felt there was something vulgar and indelicate in it that shocked her.

Rodolphe thought quite a lot about this incident with the pistols. If she had been speaking seriously, it was totally ridiculous, he thought, and even odious, because he had no reason at all to hate that poor old Charles, not being the sort one would call devoured by jealousy—and on that subject, Emma had made a solemn vow to him that he didn't find in the best of taste.

Besides, she was becoming sentimental. They had had to exchange miniatures, they had had to cut off locks of hair, and now she was asking for a ring, a regular marriage ring, a symbol of their eternal union. She would often talk to him about the chimes of the evening or the *voices of nature;* and then she would talk about her mother, and about his. Rodolphe had lost his mother twenty years ago. Emma nevertheless would console him with simpering phrases, the sort you would use with a lost child, and more than once she had even said, while looking up at the moon:

"I am certain that up there, together, they both approve of our love."

But she was so very pretty! He had had so few women who were that candid! This love affair without anything libertine about it was something new for him, something that, by getting him out of his normal, easy habits, flattered both his pride and his sensuality. Emma's exaltation, which his good bourgeois sense disdained, seemed charming to him, deep down in his heart, since it was directed at him. Then, sure of being loved, he no longer took any trouble about it, and his ways began to change imperceptibly.

He no longer used any of those sweet words that used to make her weep, nor those impassioned caresses that used to drive her mad; and so their great love, into which she had plunged herself entirely, now seemed to be shrinking beneath her, like the water of a stream being absorbed into its bed, and now she could see the sludge on the bottom. She did not want to believe it; she redoubled her tendernesses; and Rodolphe concealed his indifference less and less.

She didn't know whether she regretted having yielded to him or whether, on the contrary, she wanted only to love him more. The humiliation of sensing her own weakness turned into a resentment that was only tempered by voluptuous pleasures. This was not an attachment; it was more like a continuous seduction. It subjugated her. She was almost afraid of it.

On the surface, though, things seemed calmer than ever, Rodolphe having succeeded in conducting the adultery to suit his wishes; and after six months, when spring came, they found themselves facing each other like a married couple tending their domestic flame peacefully.

This was the time of year when Monsieur Rouault would send his turkey in remembrance of his healed leg. The gift always arrived with a letter. Emma cut the string that attached it to the basket, and read these lines:

My Dear Children,

I hope this turkey finds you in good health, and that it's as good as the others; because it seems a little more tender, if I do say so, and heavier. But the next time, for a change, I'll give you a turkey cock, unless you prefer the gobblers, and send me back the basket, if you don't mind, along with the two other ones. I had a problem with my cart shed, its roof flew off into the trees, one night when it was blowing hard. The harvest is not very good either. Finally, I don't know when I'll see you. It's hard for me to leave the house now, since I'm all alone, my poor Emma!

There was a space after these lines, as if the old man had let his pen drop to daydream for a while.

> As for me, I'm doing well, except for a cold I caught the other day at the Yvetot fair, where I went to hire a shepherd, having fired mine because he was too particular about his food. Those bandits give us plenty to complain about! And he wasn't honest, either.
>
> I heard from a peddler who was passing through your parts this winter, who had to have a tooth pulled, that Bovary is still working hard. That didn't surprise me, and he showed me his tooth; we had a coffee together. I asked him if he'd seen you, and he said no, but he saw two animals in the stable, which seems to imply business is good. That's good, my dear children, and may the good God send you every imaginable happiness.
>
> It grieves me that I haven't got to know my much-loved granddaughter Berthe Bovary. I planted a plum tree with those little hard black plums for her in the garden, under your window, and I won't let anybody touch it except to make jam for her in the future, which I'll keep in the cupboard and save for her, when she comes to visit.
>
> Farewell, my dear children. I kiss you, my daughter, you too, my son-in-law, and the little one, on both cheeks.
>
> I am, with compliments,
> Your loving father,
> THÉODORE ROUAULT.

She stayed holding the coarse piece of paper in her hand for a few minutes. There were spelling errors all through it, and Emma followed the sweet thoughts that cackled through them like a hen half hidden in a thorn hedge. He had blotted the ink dry with ashes from the fireplace, and a little gray dust slipped from the letter onto her dress, and she felt as if she could almost see her father bending toward the hearth to pick up the tongs. What a long time it had been since she sat with him on the stool next to the fireplace, when she would hold a stick into the blazing flame of rushes until it caught fire! She remembered evenings in summer, filled with sun. The colts would whinny when anyone passed them, and gallop, gallop . . . Beneath her window there was a honey-bee hive, and sometimes the bees would whirl in the light, beating against the window like little bouncing balls of gold. What happiness she had had then! What freedom! What hope! What an abundance of illusions! None of them remained anymore! She had slowly dispersed them all in the course of her soul's life, through all her successive situations, in her virginity, her marriage, and in her love—losing them continually all along the path of her life, like a traveler who leaves behind some part of his wealth at every inn along the way.

But what was it that was making her so unhappy? Where was it, the great catastrophe that had overwhelmed her? And she raised up her head, looking around her, as if searching for what it was that caused her suffering.

An April sunray was shimmering over the porcelain on the shelves; the fire was burning; she felt, beneath her slippers, the softness of the carpet; the day was clear, the air was warm, and she heard her child outside shouting with laughter.

In fact, the little girl was rolling on the lawn, while the grass was being cut. She lay flat on her stomach atop a pile of cut grass. Her maid was holding her by the skirt. Lestiboudois was raking next to her, and every time he came close, she leaned forward, beating her arms in the air.

"Bring her to me!" said her mother, rushing out to embrace her. "How much I love you, my poor child! How much I love you!"

Then, noticing that her ears were a bit dirty, she quickly rang for warm water and bathed her, changed her underwear, stockings, and shoes, asked a thousand questions about her health, as if she had just returned from a long voyage, and finally, kissing her again and weeping a little, she gave the child back to the servant, who stood there stunned by this excess of maternal affection.

That evening Rodolphe found her more serious than usual.

"It'll pass," he concluded; "it's a whim."

And he skipped three meetings in a row. When he returned, she was cold and almost disdainful.

"Ah! You're wasting your time, my little one . . . "

And he pretended not to notice her melancholy sighs, nor the handkerchief she held on to.

That was when Emma repented!

She asked herself why she so loathed Charles, and whether it would not have been better to be able to love him. But he had no particular reaction to this new feeling of hers, so that she was stymied in her vague desire to sacrifice something, until the pharmacist arrived just in time to provide her an opportunity.

CHAPTER 11

He had recently read an article praising a new treatment for clubfoot; and since he was on the side of progress, he conceived the patriotic idea that Yonville, *to be in the forefront of things*, ought to have some operations for strephopodia.[7]

"For after all," he said to Emma, "what's the risk? Let's think it through." He counted off on his fingers the advantages of trying it. "Success virtually certain, relief and improvement for the patient, and immediate celebrity for the surgeon. Why shouldn't your husband, for example, cure that poor Hippolyte from the *Golden Lion*? Note that he would certainly tell all the travelers who come to the inn all about his cure, and then," (Homais lowered his voice, and looked carefully all around) "what would prevent me from sending a little note about it to the newspaper? Well, good lord, an article circulates—people talk about it—and the whole thing ends up snowballing! And who knows? Who knows?"

In fact, Bovary might succeed; Emma had no reason to doubt his ability, and what satisfaction there would be in having engaged him in an endeavor that would enhance his reputation and his fortune! She was looking for something more solid than love to lean on.

Charles, urged on by both the pharmacist and her, let himself be convinced. He had Doctor Duval's book sent from Rouen, and every evening, his head in his hands, he buried himself in reading it.

While he was studying equin, varus, and valgus—that is to say, strephocatopodia, strephendopodia, and strephexopodia—or, to speak more

7. Strephopodia is a technical term for club-foot. Technical terms abound in this chapter; Flaubert generally clarifies them by means of context, but at times they are meant to be somewhat bewildering [translator's note].

plainly, the different ways the foot turns, whether downward, inward, or outward—along with strephypodia and strephanopodia (in other words, torsion either downward or upward)—Monsieur Homais was using every argument he could think of to convince the boy from the inn to let himself be operated upon.

"You'll hardly feel anything, maybe, or just a little pain; it's a simple prick like you'd feel with a bloodletting, less than the extraction of certain corns."

Hippolyte, thinking it over, rolled his eyes stupidly.

"Anyway," the pharmacist continued, "it has nothing to do with me! It's for you! Out of a pure feeling of humanity! I want to see you, my friend, rid of this hideous limping and that swinging movement in your lumbar region which, whatever you say, must be a considerable hindrance to you in the exercise of your calling."

Then Homais described for him how much more cheerful and capable he would feel, and even implied how much more attractive he would be to women, which made the stable boy break into a leering grin. Then he approached him by way of his vanity:

"You're a man, aren't you, damn it? What would happen if you were called to serve in the military, and you had to go fight to defend our flag? Ah, Hippolyte!"

And Homais walked away, declaring that he simply could not understand this stubbornness, this blindness, this rejection of the benefits of Science.

The unfortunate boy gave in, because it was like a conspiracy against him. Binet, who never meddled in other people's affairs, Madame Lefrançois, Artémise, the neighbors, and even the mayor, Monsieur Tuvache—everyone was urging him, lecturing him, making him feel ashamed; but the thing that finally made him decide, was that *it wouldn't cost him a thing*. Bovary would even pay for the machine that was necessary for the operation. Emma was the one who came up with the idea for that generosity; and Charles agreed to it, telling himself that his wife was an angel.

Working with the pharmacist's advice, and starting over three different times, he had the carpenter, with the locksmith's help, build a kind of box weighing about eight pounds; neither iron, wood, sheet metal, leather, screws, or nuts were spared.

Meanwhile, in order to know which of Hippolyte's tendons to clip, it was first necessary to know what sort of clubfoot he had.

He had a foot that formed almost a straight line with the leg, which did not keep it from being turned inward, so that it appeared to be an equin mixed with a bit of varus, or perhaps a light varus with a strong tendency toward equin. But with that equin—which was in fact as wide as a horse's hoof, with rough skin, delicate tendons, and huge toes whose black nails looked like they were made of iron—the clubfooted stable boy bounded around the village from morning till night like a deer. He could always be seen on the square, leaping around the carts, thrusting his bad foot forward. The bad leg, in fact, seemed to be more vigorous than the other. Through long service, it had acquired what seemed like the moral qualities of patience and energy, and when he was given heavy work to do, he put his weight on it rather than the good foot.

Now, since it was an equin, the Achilles tendon would have to be cut, after which the anterior tibial muscle could be looked to for eliminating the varus;

for the doctor dared not risk both operations at once, and in fact he was already trembling for fear of damaging some important region he knew nothing about.

Neither Ambrose Paré, when he applied a ligature to an artery for the first time since Celsus, the first time in fifteen hundred years; nor Dupuytren, about to cut open an abscess through a thick layer of brain; nor Gensoul, when he made the first removal of a superior maxillary—none had a heart so throbbing, a hand so shaky, a mind so strained as Monsieur Bovary when he approached Hippolyte, his tenotomy scalpel in his hand. And just as in a hospital, on a table next to him lay a heap of gauze, waxed threads, and many bandages, a whole pyramid of bandages, all the bandages there were in the pharmacist's shop. It was Monsieur Homais who had organized all the preparations since the morning, as much to dazzle the multitudes as to flatter his sense of self-importance. Charles pricked the skin; a dry crack was heard. The tendon was cut, the operation over. Hippolyte was so surprised that he couldn't get over it; he bent over Bovary's hands to cover them with kisses.

"Come now, calm yourself," the pharmacist said. "You'll have plenty of time to show your gratitude toward your benefactor!"

And he went out to narrate the results to five or six curious types who were standing in the courtyard, and who imagined that Hippolyte would come out walking normally. Then Charles, having buckled his patient in the machine, went back home, where Emma was anxiously awaiting him in the doorway. She leaped up to embrace him; they sat down at the table; he ate a great deal, and he even asked, at dessert, for a cup of coffee, an extravagance he only allowed himself on Sundays when there was company.

The evening was delightful, full of conversation and sharing of dreams. They talked about their future fortune, of improvements they would make in the household; he pictured how people would think more highly of him, how his comforts would increase, how his wife would always continue to love him; and she felt herself happy, and renewed, by a new, healthier, purer feeling, even feeling some tenderness for this poor boy who cherished her so. The idea of Rodolphe passed through her mind for a moment; but her gaze returned to Charles: she even noticed, with surprise, that his teeth were not horrible.

They were in bed when Monsieur Homais, rushing past the servant, suddenly entered their bedroom holding a sheet of paper with fresh writing on it. It was the publicity piece he was sending to the *Rouen Lantern*. He brought it for them to read.

"Read it to us yourself," said Bovary.

He read:

"Despite the prejudices which are still spread over part of the face of Europe like a web, enlightenment has begun to dawn in our countryside. Thus it was that on Tuesday, our little town of Yonville was the theater of a surgical experiment that was at the same time an act of the highest philanthropy. Monsieur Bovary, one of our most distinguished practitioners . . . ."

"Oh, no! It's too much! Too much!" said Charles, overcome with emotion.

"No, no, not at all! How is it too much! . . . 'Operated on a clubfoot . . . ' I didn't want to use the technical term because, you know, it's a newspaper . . . not everyone would understand it; with the masses, one has to . . . "

"That's true," said Bovary. "Go on."

"I'll start over," said the pharmacist. "Monsieur Bovary, one of our most distinguished practitioners, operated on a clubfoot named Hippolyte Tautain, a stable boy for twenty-five years at the *Golden Lion* hotel, managed by Madame Lefrançois, on the Place d'Armes. The novelty of the attempt and the interest attaching to the subject had attracted such a crowd from the local population that the doorway to the establishment was packed. The operation, moreover, was carried out as if by magic, with only a very few drops of blood coming up onto the skin, as if to signify that the rebel tendon had finally ceded to the efforts of Science. The patient, strange as it may seem (and we can affirm this as having witnessed it with our own eyes), appeared to feel no pain at all. His state at present leaves nothing to be desired. Everything leads us to believe that his convalescence will be brief, and who knows whether, at the next village festival, we won't see our Hippolyte among the Bacchic dancers, in the midst of other jolly fellows, and thus prove to every observer, by his verve and by his gambols, his complete cure? All honor to the generous savants! All honor to those untiring spirits who consecrate themselves to the improvement or at least the relief of their species! Honor! Three times honor! Is it not true that the blind will see, the deaf hear, and the lame walk? But what fanaticism used to promise to its elect in the old times, Science now will accomplish for all mankind! We will keep our readers up to date as to the subsequent phases of this remarkable cure."

But none of this in any way prevented Madame Lefrançois, five days later, from coming to them in a state of terror and crying out:

"Help! He's dying! . . . I'm going out of my mind!"

Charles hurried over to the *Golden Lion*, and the pharmacist, seeing him rushing past on the square without his hat on, left the pharmacy. He arrived out of breath himself, red in the face, worried, and asking everyone on the stairway:

"What's the trouble with our interesting strephopode?"

He was twisting, the strephopode, in horrific convulsions, so violent that the machine enclosing his leg was smashing against the wall hard enough to break it down.

Taking many precautions so as not to disturb the position of the limb, they took the box off, and they saw a hideous spectacle. The shape of the foot had disappeared into such a swelling that the skin seemed about to burst entirely, and it was covered with bruises caused by the famous machine. Hippolyte had already complained that he was in pain; no one took heed of it; now they had to admit that he was not entirely wrong, and they left the limb free for a few hours. But the swelling had hardly subsided when the two savants judged it best to put the limb back inside the apparatus, and to even tighten it further, so as to hurry things along. Finally, three days later, Hippolyte could endure it no longer, and they again removed the machine, utterly shocked at what they saw. A bluish gray swelling extended all along the leg, with blisters here and there that oozed a black liquid. Things had taken a serious turn. Hippolyte was beginning to worry, and Madame Lefrançois installed him in the little room near the kitchen so that he would at least have some distraction.

But the tax collector, who dined there every day, complained bitterly about having such a neighbor. So they took Hippolyte into the billiard room.

There he was, groaning beneath his thick blankets, pale, his beard untrimmed, his eyes hollow, turning his sweaty head from time to time on the dirty pillow where flies would alight. Madame Bovary came to see him. She brought him some linens for his poultices, and consoled and encouraged him. And he certainly didn't lack for company, especially on market days when the peasants pushed their billiard cues all around him, or fenced with them, smoking, drinking, singing, shouting.

"How are you doing?" they would say, slapping him on the shoulder. "Ah, you don't look all that good, do you! But it's your own fault. You should do this, you should do that."

And they would tell him stories about people who had been cured entirely by other means; and then, as a sort of consolation, they would add:

"You give up too easily! Get up! You're coddling yourself like a king! Oh, don't you worry, old boy! Say, you don't smell so good!"

In fact, the gangrene was mounting higher and higher. It was making even Bovary sick. He came every hour, every moment. Hippolyte would look at him with terror-filled eyes, stammering and sobbing:

"When will I be better? . . . . Oh, save me! . . . . I'm so miserable! I'm so miserable!"

And the doctor would leave, always suggesting he take care with his diet.

"Don't listen to that, my boy," Madame Lefrançois would say; "they've already made a martyr out of you! That will just make you weaker. Here, swallow this."

And she would bring some good bouillon to him, a slice of lamb, a bit of bacon, and sometimes some little glasses of brandy, which he lacked the strength to raise to his lips.

The Abbé Bournisien, learning that he was worsening, asked to see him. He began by expressing pity for his suffering, but at the same time declaring that he really ought to rejoice, for this was the will of the Lord, and he should profit from the occasion by reconciling himself with heaven.

"Because," the cleric said in a fatherly tone, "you have been neglecting your obligations somewhat; we rarely see you at Mass; and how many years has it been since you approached the Holy Communion table? I understand that your work, and the whirlwind of the world have been able to turn you away from your salvation. But now, this is the time to think about it. Don't fall into despair, however; I have known some great sinners who, when they were about to appear before God (and you're not close to that yet, of course), had begged for His mercy, and who certainly died in the best possible states of mind. Let us hope that, just like them, you'll provide us all with a good example! And so, out of precaution, what's there to stop you from saying a 'Hail Mary, full of grace' in the morning and the evening, and an 'Our Father, who art in heaven'? Yes, do that! Do it for me, as a favor. What's it going to cost you? . . . Will you promise me?"

The poor devil promised. The priest returned on the following days. He chatted with the innkeeper and even told some humorous stories with puns that Hippolyte didn't understand. Then, as soon as circumstances permitted, he returned to religious matters, his face resuming an appropriate expression.

His zeal looked as if it might succeed; for soon the strephopode declared his wish to make a pilgrimage to Bon-Secours, if he recovered: to which Monsieur Bournisien replied that he saw nothing inappropriate in that; two precautions were better than one. *What's the risk?*

The pharmacist was indignant at what he called *the priest's maneuverings;* they would do harm, he argued, to Hippolyte's convalescence, and he repeated to Madame Lefrançois:

"Leave him alone! Leave him alone! You're going to damage his morale with your mysticism!"

But the good woman didn't want to hear it. He was *the cause of it all*. In the spirit of contradiction, she even hung a holy water font, a full one, at his bedside, along with a little sprig of boxwood.

Meanwhile, neither religion nor surgery seemed to be helping him, and the unstoppable rot continued to mount up his extremities toward his stomach. In vain did they vary the medicines and change the poultices; the muscles weakened more every day, and at last Charles responded with an affirmative nod when Madame Lefrançois asked him whether, out of desperation, she couldn't send for Monsieur Canivet from Neufchâtel, who was quite famous.

A medical doctor aged fifty, enjoying a solid reputation and very sure of himself, the distinguished colleague did not hesitate to burst out in a disdainful laugh when he uncovered the leg, gangrenous to the knee. Then, having declared that they would have to amputate, he went over to the pharmacist's to rant against the asses who could have reduced an unlucky man to such a state. Shaking Homais by the button of his coat, he shouted angrily in the pharmacy.

"These are the great Parisian inventions! Here we can see the ideas of the gentlemen from the Capital! It's just like strabismus, chloroform, or lithotrity, a heap of monstrosities that the government ought to outlaw! But they want to be clever, and they'll stuff you full of their remedies without worrying about the consequences. But out here in the country, we're not as good as they are; we aren't sages, braggarts, fops! No, we're practitioners, healers, and we wouldn't dream of operating on someone who's getting along just fine! Straighten a clubfoot! Can anybody straighten a clubfoot? It's as absurd as if you were to, say, try to straighten out a hunchback!"

Homais suffered as he listened to all this, but he hid his discomfort behind a sycophantic smile, for he had to get along with Monsieur Canivet, whose prescriptions often found their way to Yonville; nor did he speak up in defense of Bovary, nor did he make any other comment at all, and abandoning his principles, he sacrificed his dignity in favor of the more serious demands of his business.

This was a major event in the village, this amputation at the thigh by Doctor Canivet! All the inhabitants were up early on that day, and the main road, despite being filled with people, had something lugubrious about it, as if there were going to be an execution. They were talking about Hippolyte's illness at the grocer's; the shops didn't sell a thing, and Madame Tuvache, the mayor's wife, didn't budge from her window, so impatient was she to see the arrival of the surgeon.

He arrived in his gig, which he drove himself. But over the years, the spring on the right side had weakened under his corpulence, and as a result the gig tilted a bit to the one side as he drove, revealing on the cushion next to him a huge box covered in red leather, its three copper clasps shining magnificently.

When, like a whirlwind, he entered the *Golden Lion's* courtyard, the doctor cried out loudly, ordering his horse to be unhitched; then he went to the stable to be sure the horse would have plenty of oats; for whenever he visited a patient, his first concern was for his mare and his gig. People even remarked on it, saying, "Oh, that Monsieur Canivet, what a character!" And they actually thought more highly of him because of his unshakable calm. The universe could have crushed the last man living before he would change the least of his habits.

Homais appeared.

"I'm counting on you," said the doctor. "Everything ready? Let's go!"

But the pharmacist, blushing, admitted that he was too sensitive to assist at such an operation.

"When one is simply a spectator," he said, "the imagination, you understand, gets the better of one! And then I have such a nervous system that . . . ."

"Bah!" Canivet interrupted. "You seem to me, on the contrary, to be the apoplectic type. But anyway, it doesn't surprise me, because you fellows, you pharmacists, you're always burrowed into your kitchens working, and that will inevitably have an effect on your constitution. Look at me, on the other hand: every day, I get up at four, I shave with cold water (I never feel the cold), I don't wear flannel, I never catch colds, the old body's in fine shape! I live sometimes this way, sometimes that, like a philosopher, take whatever kind of meal comes along! And that's why I'm not delicate like you, and why to me it's all the same to cut up a Christian or the first chicken that comes along. I suppose you'll say, it's all habit, just habit . . . ."

Then, without any regard for Hippolyte, who was sweating with anguish beneath his covers, the two gentlemen got into a conversation in which the pharmacist compared the self-control of a surgeon to that of a general; and the comparison was agreeable to Canivet, who talked at length about the demands of his profession. He considered it like a priesthood, although those health officers did it dishonor. At last, coming back to the patient, he examined the bandages Homais had brought, the same ones he had brought before, and asked for someone to hold the limb for him. They sent for Lestiboudois, and Monsieur Canivet, having rolled up his sleeves, walked into the billiard room while the pharmacist stayed with Artémise and the innkeeper, the two of them paler than their aprons, their ears glued to the door.

Bovary, during all this, didn't dare to budge from his house. He stayed downstairs in the parlor, sitting beside the unlit fireplace, his chin on his chest, his hands gripped together, staring straight ahead. "What a disaster!" he thought. "What a disappointment!" But he had taken every imaginable precaution. Fate must be mixed up in it. But what difference did that make—for if Hippolyte did die, it would be he who had murdered him. And then, what would he say when he made his visits, when people questioned him about it? Perhaps, though, he had made some mistake? He sought for it, but didn't find it. But the very best surgeons made mistakes. But they would never believe that! On the contrary, they would laugh at him, jeer! They'd be talking about it all the way to Forges! In Neufchâtel! In Rouen! Everywhere! Who knows if some of his colleagues might write against him? There would be a scandal, he'd have to respond in the newspapers. Hippolyte could even bring him to trial. He saw himself dishonored, ruined, lost! And his imagination, assailed by a multitude of hypotheses, rolled among them like an empty barrel taken by the sea, and tossing on the waves.

Emma, sitting across from him, watched him; she didn't share in his humiliation, but she was feeling a different one: it was to have imagined that such a man could be worth anything, as if she had not sufficiently perceived his mediocrity twenty times over.

Charles paced to and fro in the room. His boots creaked on the floor.

"Sit down, will you," she said, "you're getting on my nerves!"

He sat back down.

How could she—she who was so intelligent!—have been so wrong yet again? And besides, what lamentable madness could have led her to ruin her life in these continual sacrifices? She recalled all her natural instincts for luxury, all the deprivations of her soul, all the basenesses of her marriage, her household, her dreams fallen into the mud like wounded swallows, all that she had desired, all that she had given up, all that she could have had! And why, why?

In the midst of the silence that filled the village, a wrenching shriek cut through the air. Bovary paled almost to fainting. Her brows contracted, she made a nervous gesture, and she continued thinking. It was for him, though, for that creature, for that man who understood nothing! And there he was, completely calm, without even any concern that the ridicule attached to his name henceforth would also sully hers as well! She had tried to love him, and she had repented in tears for having given herself to another.

"But maybe it was a valgus?"[8] suddenly exclaimed Bovary, who had been deep in his own thoughts.

At the unexpected shock of this statement, falling into the midst of her thoughts like a lead bullet on a silver platter, Emma shuddered and raised her head to divine what it was he was saying; and they looked at each other silently, almost dumbfounded to see each other, so far away had their separate thoughts taken them. Charles looked at her with the disturbed gaze of a drunken man, while continuing to listen, motionless, to the final cries of the amputee, which followed each other in drawn-out modulations, accented by sharp screams, like the far off howls of an animal being slaughtered. Emma bit her pale lips, and rolling a piece of coral she had broken between her fingers, she fixed an intense gaze on Charles, her eyes like two fiery arrows about to be released. Everything about him irritated her now, his face, his clothing, what he failed to say, his entire person, his very existence. She repented of her past virtue as if it had been a crime, and what was left of it crumbled now under the hammer blows of her pride. She felt delight in all the ugly ironies of triumphant adultery. The memory of her lover returned to her with dizzying seductiveness; she threw her soul into it, carried forward toward his image with a new enthusiasm; and Charles himself seemed detached from her life, absent forever, as impossible and annihilated as if he were in the process of dying before her eyes.

They heard footsteps on the sidewalk. Charles looked, and through the lowered blind he saw, at the corner of the market, in bright daylight, Doctor Canivet wiping his brow with his scarf. Homais, behind him, carried the big red box, and they were both heading toward the pharmacy.

Then, out of a sudden burst of tenderness and discouragement, Charles turned toward his wife, saying to her:

"Kiss me, my dear one!"

"Leave me alone!" she said, red with rage.

"What's wrong? What's wrong?" he repeated, stupefied. "Calm yourself, get hold of yourself! You know how much I love you! . . . Come to me!"

"Enough!" she cried in a terrible voice.

8. A twisting of the first toe above or below the other toes.

And making her escape from the room, Emma slammed the door so hard that the barometer bounced off the wall and broke on the floor.

Charles sank back into his armchair, overwhelmed, wondering what could be wrong with her, imagining some nervous illness, weeping, and vaguely sensing something fatal and incomprehensible circling around him.

When Rodolphe came to the garden that evening, he found his mistress waiting for him on the stairs, standing on the first step. They embraced, and all their bitterness melted away like snow in the heat of that kiss.

CHAPTER 12

They started to love each other all over again. Often, even in the middle of the day, Emma would suddenly write to him; then, through the window, she would make a sign to Justin who would quickly take off his apron and take the note over to La Huchette: Rodolphe would come; she wanted him to come to tell him that she was bored, that her husband was odious, and that her life was hideous!

"What can I do about it?" he cried one day, impatient with her.

"Oh, if you wanted to . . . ."

She was seated on the ground between his knees, her hair undone, a lost look in her eyes.

"What then?" Rodolphe asked.

She sighed:

"We could go live somewhere else . . . someplace . . ."

"You're mad, you really are!" he said, smiling. "How could we do it?"

She repeated the idea; he pretended not to understand her, and changed the subject.

What he really couldn't understand was making so much trouble out of something as simple as a love affair. But she had a motive, a reason, something that served as a kind of driving force behind her affection for him.

Her affection for him, in fact, grew greater every day right along with the revulsion she felt for her husband. The more she devoted herself to the one, the more she detested the other; Charles never seemed so unpleasant to her, his fingers so coarse, his mind so flat, his manners so common, as when she had to return to him after one of her meetings with Rodolphe. And then, while she was playing the role of the virtuous wife, she would become inwardly enflamed with the idea of that head, its black hair curled over the tanned forehead, that body at once so robust and so elegant, that man, in short, who was so experienced intellectually, so passionate in his desire! It was for him that she trimmed her nails with the precision of a sculptor, for him that she could never have enough cold cream on her skin, nor enough patchouli in her handkerchiefs. She loaded herself with bracelets, rings, necklaces. When he was going to visit her, she filled the two big blue-glass vases with roses, arranging her room and her person like a courtesan expecting a prince. The maid was forever tasked with washing her underthings; and all day long, Félicité couldn't budge from the kitchen, where little Justin, who often kept her company, would watch her working.

His elbow resting on the long ironing board where she worked, he eagerly gazed upon all these feminine things spread out around him: the petticoats of fine stitched cotton, the shawls, the collars, the pantaloons with drawstrings, so wide at the hips and narrowing below.

"And what's this for?" the boy asked, passing his hand over the crinoline or the hook-and-eye.

"You've never seen one of those?" Félicité laughed. "As if your employer, Madame Homais, didn't have the same kind of things!"

"Oh, of course—Madame Homais!"

And then he added, meditatively:

"She's not a lady, like Madame."

But Félicité was getting impatient with him always hovering around her. She was six years older, and Théodore, Monsieur Guillaumin's servant, was beginning to court her.

"Let me be!" she said, picking up her starching pot. "Go on and grind some almonds instead; you're always nosing around women; wait a bit before you get all mixed up in that, you naughty little boy, at least until you have a beard on your chin."

"Come on, don't get angry; I'm going to *do her boots* for you."

And he went right over to get Emma's shoes from the doorsill; they were crusted with mud—the mud from her meetings with Rodolphe—which fell off in a powder beneath his fingers, and which he observed as it rose up gently in a sunbeam.

"How afraid you are of spoiling them!" the kitchen maid said, for she never took such care when she cleaned them herself, because Madame would discard them as soon as the fabric was no longer new.

Emma had a great many of them in her armoire, and she would squander them freely, without Charles allowing himself to make any comment.

That is how she was able to spend three hundred francs for a wooden leg, which she felt was a suitable gift for Hippolyte. It had cork at the top, along with spring joints and a complex mechanism, and was covered by a black trouser leg ending in a patent-leather boot. But Hippolyte, not daring to make use of such a superb leg every day, begged Madame Bovary to find him another, more ordinary one. The doctor, needless to say, again paid the bill for this purchase.

And so the stable boy bit by bit took up his old profession again. He could be seen as before crisscrossing the village, and when Charles heard him from a distance making that sharp sound with his cane on the pavement, he quickly turned and took another route.

It was the shopkeeper, Monsieur Lheureux, who had taken the order, which gave him the opportunity to visit Emma frequently. He chatted with her about all the latest things from Paris, about a thousand feminine trifles, always making himself agreeable and never asking for money. Emma surrendered to that ability of his to satisfy her every whim. Thus, she wanted to get a beautiful riding whip for Rodolphe, one that could only be found in the Rouen umbrella-maker's shop. The very next week, Monsieur Lheureux placed it on her table.

But the next day he presented her with a bill of two hundred and seventy francs, not counting the centimes. Emma was very much embarrassed: all the drawers in the writing desk were empty; they owed two weeks' wages to Lestiboudois, two trimesters' worth to the servant, along with a number of other debts, and Bovary was anxiously waiting for Monsieur Derozerays' payment, which usually came in around Saint Peter's day, at the end of June.

She succeeded initially in putting Lheureux off; finally he lost patience: his creditors were dogging him, his capital was tied up, and unless he could get some money in he would be forced to take back all the things she had purchased.

"Oh, take it back then!" Emma said.

"Oh no! I was only joking" he replied. "The only problem is the riding whip. I will really have to ask Monsieur to give it back."

"No, no!" she exclaimed.

"Ah—I've got you now!" Lheureux thought.

And assured by this discovery, he left, repeating softly, with the whistling sound he always made:

"Very well! We'll see! We'll see!"

She was wondering how to get out of this, when the kitchen maid entered, placing a small roll of money on the mantel, wrapped in blue paper and inscribed *for Monsieur Derozeray's account*. Emma jumped up and opened it. There were fifteen napoléons[9] in it. It was the whole amount. She heard Charles on the staircase; she threw the money in the back of her drawer and turned the key.

Three days later, Lheureux came back.

"I have an arrangement to propose to you," he said. "If, in lieu of the amount you owe, you would be willing to take . . . "

"Here it is!" she said, putting fourteen napoléons in his hand.

The shopkeeper was astounded. Then, to hide his disappointment, he expansively made excuses and offers for other services, all of which Emma refused; when he was gone, she stood fingering in her apron pocket the two hundred-sou pieces he had given her in change. She promised herself she would economize, so she would be able to repay Charles' money later . . .

"Bah!" she thought. "He won't even notice it."

Apart from the riding whip with its silver-gilt pommel, Rodolphe had been given a seal with this motto: *Amor nel cor;*[1] a scarf to be used as a muffler; and a cigarette case exactly like the Viscount's, which Charles had long ago found on the road and which Emma still kept. But he found these gifts humiliating. He refused several of them; she insisted, and Rodolphe ended by accepting them, but thinking her tyrannical and too demanding.

And then she had some strange ideas:

"On the stroke of midnight," she would say, "you must think about me."

And if he admitted that he hadn't thought about her, there would be a flood of reproaches, always ending in the same, eternal phrases:

"Do you love me?"

"Yes, of course I love you!" he would reply.

"Very much!"

"Certainly!"

"You've never loved anyone as much, have you?"

"Did you think I was a virgin before you?" he would exclaim with a laugh.

9. A *napoléon* was a gold coin worth 20 francs [translator's note].

1. Love in the heart (Italian).

Emma would cry, and he would force himself to console her, embellishing his protestations with little jokes.

"Oh, it's just that I love you so!" she would continue. "I love you so much that I couldn't live without you, don't you know that? There are times when I want to see you again so badly that I feel like love is tearing me apart. I ask myself: 'Where is he? Maybe he's with other women? They're smiling at him, he goes to them . . . ' Oh, it isn't true is it, you aren't attracted to anyone else? Some are more beautiful; but I, I know how to love better! I'm your slave, your concubine! You're my king, my idol! You are good! You're handsome! You're strong!"

He had heard things like this so many times, there was nothing fresh about them for him. Emma was like all the other mistresses; and the charm of novelty, slipping away inch by inch like a dress, left nakedly visible the eternal monotony of passion, which always takes on the same forms and the same language. He did not distinguish—this man of so much experience—the difference of feeling beneath the sameness of expression. Because libertine or mercenary lips had murmured similar phrases to him, he believed very little in the sincerity of Emma's; it seemed to him that one had to discount such exaggerated discourse that masked mediocre feelings: as if the fullness of the soul did not sometimes overflow into the emptiest metaphors, since no one can ever state the exact measure of his needs, nor his ideas nor his sorrows, and since human language is like a cracked kettle on which we beat out rhythms for bears to dance to, when what we want is to bring the stars themselves to tears.

But with that superior critical judgment belonging to someone who always holds back and never fully commits to anything, Rodolphe saw other sorts of pleasures to exploit in this love affair. He felt all modesty was an inconvenience. He treated her entirely without ceremony. He turned her into something supple and corrupt. It was a mindless sort of attachment, composed of admiration on his side and sensuality on hers, a beatitude that benumbed her; and her soul sank down into that intoxication and drowned and shriveled there, like the Duke of Clarence in his butt of malmsey.[2]

As a result of her amorous habits, Madame Bovary began to change. Her gaze became bolder, her language freer; she even had the impudence to walk out with Monsieur Rodolphe with a cigarette between her lips, *as if to defy the whole world*; and finally, those who still doubted had their doubts removed when they saw her, one day, get down from the *Hirondelle*, dressed in a tight-fitting waistcoat like a man; and Madame Bovary senior, who had come to her son's for refuge after an appalling scene with her husband, was by no means the least scandalized woman in town. There were plenty of other things to displease her: to begin with, Charles had not followed through on the interdiction against novels; then, *the state of the house* displeased her; she permitted herself to make some comments, which led to quarrels, one in particular concerning Félicité.

On the preceding night, Madame Bovary senior in passing down the corridor had surprised her in the company of a man, a man with dark whiskers, about

2. The duke of Clarence was the younger brother of King Edward IV of England and the elder brother of Richard, duke of Gloucester. He was condemned to death for treason and, according to rumor, drowned in a butt of malmsey (a sweet aromatic wine) in February 1478. See Shakespeare's *Richard III* 1.4.155.

forty years of age; at the sound of her footsteps, he had quickly escaped through the kitchen. This made Emma laugh; but the good mother was outraged, and declared that unless morals were a laughing matter, one ought to look after those of one's servants.

"What world do you come from?" asked the daughter-in-law, with so impertinent a look on her face that the elder asked if she was in fact defending her own behavior.

"Get out!" said the young woman, leaping up.

"Emma! . . . Mama!" Charles cried, trying to reconcile them.

But they both rushed out separately in frustration. Emma stamped her feet, repeating:

"Oh! What manners! What a peasant!"

He ran after his mother; she was in a fit of rage, and she stammered:

"She's insolent! Irresponsible! And maybe worse!"

And she wanted to leave immediately, if the other would not apologize. Charles returned to his wife and begged her to give in: he went down on his knees, and finally she said:

"All right! I'll do it."

In fact, she offered her hand to her mother-in-law with the dignity of a marquise, saying to her:

"Pardon me, Madame."

Then, back upstairs in her room, she threw herself flat on her bed and cried like a child, her face buried in the pillow.

She and Rodolphe had agreed that in the case of some extraordinary event she would fasten a small piece of white paper to the window blind so that if he happened to be in Yonville, he would hurry to the lane behind the house. Emma made the signal; she had waited three-quarters of an hour when she suddenly saw Rodolphe at the corner of the market. She was tempted to open the window and call out to him, but he had already disappeared. She sank back, in despair.

But soon she thought she heard someone on the sidewalk. It was him, undoubtedly; she ran down the stairs and crossed the yard. He was there, outside. She threw herself into his arms.

"Be careful," he said.

"Oh, if you only knew!" she replied.

And she began to recount everything, in haste, disconnectedly, exaggerating the facts, inventing many more, and lavishing so many parenthetical remarks so abundantly that he couldn't understand any of it.

"Come, my poor angel, be brave, be comforted, be patient!"

"But I've been patient for four years, and I'm suffering! . . . A love like ours should avow itself openly in the face of heaven! They're torturing me. I can't take it any more! Save me!"

She held Rodolphe tightly. Her eyes, brimming with tears, sparkled like flames under a wave; her throat was throbbing as she gasped for air; never had he loved her so much; so much in fact that he lost his head, and said to her:

"What should we do? What do you want?"

"Take me away!" she cried. "Carry me off! . . . Oh, I'm begging you!"

And she threw herself upon his mouth, as if to draw from his kiss the consent she did not expect.

"But . . . ," Rodolphe said.

"What? What is it?"

"Your daughter?"

She thought for a few minutes, and then replied:

"We'll take her with us; it can't be helped!"

"What a woman!" he said to himself, as he watched her leaving.

For she had just run off into the garden: someone was calling for her.

Madame Bovary senior, on the following days, was very surprised at the metamorphosis her daughter-in-law had undergone. Emma was in fact more docile, and was even deferential to the point of asking her for a recipe for pickling gherkins.

Was it all in order to fool the two of them? Or was it that she wanted, through a sort of voluptuous stoicism, to feel more deeply the bitterness of the things she was about to abandon? But on the contrary, she paid them no attention: she was living as if she were lost in relishing the anticipation of her coming happiness. With Rodolphe, it was the eternal subject of every conversation. She leaned on his shoulder, murmuring:

"Imagine, when we're in the mail coach! . . . Can you believe it? Is it possible? It seems to me that the moment we feel the carriage start off, it'll be as if we're going up in a balloon, as if we were heading up to the clouds. Did you know I'm counting the days? Are you?"

Never was Madame Bovary as beautiful as she was at that period; she had that indefinable beauty that results from joy, from enthusiasm, from success, and which is nothing more than one's temperament being in harmony with one's circumstances. Her longings, her regrets, the experience of pleasure, and her ever-youthful illusions had all nurtured her gradually, the way fertilizer, rain, wind, and sun do a flower, and she was finally blossoming in the fullness of her nature. Her eyelids seemed to have been purposely formed for those long amorous looks in which the pupils disappeared, while her heavy breathing flared her thin nostrils outward and raised up the full corners of her lips, which in the light were slightly shaded with a black down. One would have said that some artist skilled in corruption had arranged the tangles of her hair on her neck; they wound negligently in a heavy mass, altering with her chance adulterous encounters, which loosened them every day. Her voice now took on a softer inflection, as did her body; something subtle and penetrating emanated from the very folds of her dress and the curve of her foot. Charles, as in the first days of his marriage, found her delicious and completely irresistible.

When he came home in the middle of the night, he dared not wake her. The porcelain nightlight cast a soft, trembling light on the ceiling, and the little cradle's drawn curtains were like a billowing white tent in the shadow beside the bed. Charles gazed at them. He thought he could hear his daughter's light breathing. She was going to start growing now; every season would show quick changes, and he could already picture her returning from school at the day's end, laughing, her blouse stained with ink, her basket on her arm; then she would have to be sent to boarding school, which cost a lot; how would he afford it? He pondered. He thought he could rent a little farm in the neighborhood, which he would oversee himself in the mornings before he went to visit his patients. He would carefully save the income, and put it in the bank; then he would buy some stocks, somewhere, no matter where; and besides, his clientele would grow; he counted on it, because he wanted Berthe to be well brought up, to develop talents, to learn to play the piano. Oh, how pretty she would be later on, at fifteen, when she would resemble her mother and wear, just like her, big straw hats in the summer! From a distance, people would take them for sisters. He pictured her working in the evenings next to them, in the lamplight; she would be mending his slippers for him; she would busy herself taking care of the house; she would fill the place with her sweetness and her gaiety. And then he imagined her marrying: they would find her some good young man with a solid occupation; he would make her happy; it would last forever.

Emma was not asleep, but only pretending to be; and while he gradually dozed off beside her, she was dreaming other dreams.

Drawn by four galloping horses, for the last week she had been carried off to a new land, from which the two of them would never return. They were racing ahead, their arms intertwined, without speaking. Often, from a mountain's top, they would suddenly catch sight of some splendid city with domes, bridges, ships, forests of lemon trees, white marble cathedrals with storks nesting in their spires. They would walk slowly because of the large flagstones, and there would be bouquets of flowers on the ground, offered to you by women dressed in red bodices. They heard the bells ringing, the mules whinnying, along with the murmur of guitars and the sound of fountains, whose spray floated up and cooled the fruit piled in the shape of pyramids at the foot of pale statues smiling under the jets of water. And then one evening, they would arrive at a fishing village, where brown nets were drying in the wind, along the cliffs and near the cabins. It was there that they would stop and live: they would inhabit a low house with a flat roof, shaded by a palm tree, at the edge of a gulf, close to the sea. They would float in gondolas, sway in hammocks; and their life would be as easy and loose as their silk garments, as warm and star-spangled as the sweet nights they would contemplate. But in the vastness of this future that she was creating, no specifics emerged: the days, all of them magnificent, resembled each other as closely as waves of the sea; and the waves swayed on the infinite horizon, harmonious, pale blue, and bathed in sun. But the child began to cough in her cradle, or perhaps Bovary snored more loudly, and Emma would not sleep until morning, when the dawn whitened the windows, and when young Justin was already opening the pharmacy's shutters.

She told Lheureux to come, and she said to him:

"I need a cloak, a large one, lined, with a big collar."

"You're going on a trip?" he asked.

"No! But . . . it doesn't matter; I can count on you, can't I? And soon!"

He bowed.

"And I also need," she continued, "a trunk—not too heavy—but large."

"Yes, yes, I see, about three feet by a foot and a half, the way they're making them nowadays."

"Along with an overnight bag."

"There's definitely," Lheureux thought, "something going on here."

"And wait," said Madame Bovary, taking her watch from her belt; "take this; you can pay for my things with it."

But the merchant insisted she had it all wrong; they knew each other; didn't he trust her? What childishness! But she insisted he at least take the chain, and Lheureux had already put it in his pocket and started to leave when she called him back.

"Leave everything at your shop. As for the cloak," and she paused to think, "don't bring that either; just give me the tailor's address, and tell him to hold it for me."

The next month was the date set for their flight. She would leave Yonville as if she were going to do errands in Rouen. Rodolphe would have got their tickets, arranged their passports, and would even have written to Paris so they would have the mail coach to themselves all the way to Marseilles, where they would buy a carriage, and continue from there without stopping, following the Genoa route. She would have taken care to send her baggage to Lheureux, who would have it put on the *Hirondelle*, in such a way that no one would have any suspicions; and in all this planning, not one word was said about the child. Rodolphe avoided the subject; and perhaps she did not think about it.

He wanted to have two more weeks to finish up some business affairs; then, after a week, he asked for two more, and then he said he was ill; then he went off on a trip; the month of August passed, and after all these delays, they decided that the date was definitely to be September 4, a Monday.

At last the Saturday before arrived.

Rodolphe came that evening, earlier than usual.

"Is everything ready?" she asked him.

"Yes."

Then they walked around the flowerbed and went to sit near the terrace, on the edge of the wall.

"You seem sad," Emma said.

"No—why?"

And he looked at her in an unusual way, but with tenderness.

"Is it because you're leaving?" she continued. "Leaving all your ties here, your life? Oh, I understand . . . But me, I have nothing at all in the world! You are everything to me. And just so, I'll be everything to you, I'll be your family, your country: I'll care for you, I'll love you."

"How delightful you are!" he said, seizing her in his arms.

"Really?" she asked with a sensual laugh. "Do you love me? Swear that you do!"

"Yes I love you! Yes I love you! I adore you, my love."

The moon, full and crimson colored, was rising from the level of the earth, from the far reaches of the meadow. It rose quickly between the poplar branches, which hid it in places, like a black curtain with holes in it. And then it appeared, elegant and white, illuminating the empty sky; and then, slowing its progress, it dropped a large patch of light onto the river, which splintered it into an infinity of stars, and that silver gleam seemed to slither all down the river, like a headless serpent covered with luminous scales. It also resembled some monstrous candelabra with diamonds running all along it. The sweet night spread out all around them; patches of shadow hung among the leaves. Emma, her eyes half closed, breathed in the cool wind deeply. They spoke no more, lost as they were in the onrush of their reverie. The tenderness of their early days returned to their hearts, abundant and silent as the flowing river, soft as the syringa's perfume, and it projected into their memories shadows more immense, more melancholy than those that the motionless willows cast on the grass. At times, some night animal, a hedgehog or a weasel, would begin its hunting, rustling the leaves, or they would hear at times a ripe peach falling, solitary, from the trellis.

"Ah, such a beautiful night!" Rodolphe said.

"We'll have many others!" Emma replied.

And then, as if speaking to herself:

"Yes, it will be good to travel . . . But why do I feel sad? Is it fear of the unknown . . . leaving my routines . . . or is it . . . No, it's an overflow of happiness! I'm so weak, aren't I? Forgive me!"

"There's still time!" he cried. "Think it over; you may perhaps regret it."

"Never!" she said impetuously.

And drawing closer to him:

"What harm could happen to me? There's no desert, no precipice, no ocean that I wouldn't cross with you. The longer we live together, the more life will be like an embrace, one that grows ever tighter, more complete! We'll have nothing to trouble us, no worries, no obstacles! We'll be alone together, eternally . . . Say something—answer me."

He responded "Yes . . . Yes . . . ," at regular intervals.

She ran her hands through his hair, and she repeated in a childlike voice, with big tears falling from her eyes:

"Rodolphe! Rodolphe! Oh, Rodolphe, dear little Rodolphe!"

The clock struck midnight.

"Midnight!" she said. "Now it's just one day! Now it will be tomorrow!"

He got up to leave; and as if that movement had been the signal for them to begin their flight, Emma suddenly became lively and cheerful:

"You have the passports?"

"Yes."

"You're not forgetting anything?"

"No."

"You're sure?"

"Definitely."

"You'll wait for me at the Hotel *de Provence*, right? At noon?"

He nodded.

"Until tomorrow, then!" Emma said, with a last caress.

And she watched him walking away.

He didn't turn around. She ran after him, and leaning over the water's edge among the reeds:

"Until tomorrow!" she exclaimed.

He was already on the other side of the river and walking swiftly through the meadow.

After a few minutes, Rodolphe stopped; and when he saw her, with her white dress, slowly vanish into the darkness like a phantom, his heart began to beat so fast that he had to lean against a tree to keep from falling down.

"What an idiot I am!" he said, swearing furiously. "But what's the difference; she was a pretty mistress!"

And then Emma's beauty, with all the pleasures her love had given him, rose up before him. At first he was saddened, but then he revolted against her.

"Because after all, I can't leave the country—and with a child on my hands!"

He said these things to himself in order to strengthen his resolve.

"And besides, all the trouble, all the expense ... Oh, no, no, a thousand times no! It really would be just too stupid!"

CHAPTER 13

As soon as he arrived home, Rodolphe quickly sat down at his desk, below the stag's head trophy on his wall. But when he had his pen in his hand, he could not find the right words to say, and so, leaning on his elbows, he began to think. Emma already seemed to have receded into a distant past, as if the resolution he had made had already put an immense gulf between them.

In order to retrieve something of her, he went to the cupboard by his bed to get an old box of Rheims biscuits, in which he always stored women's letters to him; from it escaped an odor of damp dust and of decayed roses. First he found a pocket handkerchief, covered with little faint spots. It was her handkerchief; once when they were out walking, she had had a nosebleed; he no longer recalled anything else about it. Next to it was the miniature Emma had given him, with all its corners chipped; her clothes seemed pretentious to him, and the intimate expression on her face was in the worst possible taste; then, by reflecting on that picture and trying to evoke the memory of the model, he found Emma's traits becoming confused in his memory, as if the living woman and the painted one, rubbing up one against the other, were reciprocally effacing each other. Finally, he read over some of her letters; they were full of details regarding their journey, short, specific, and urgent as business letters. He wanted to find the long ones from the early days; in order to get to them at the bottom of the box, he had to sift through all the others, and he began mechanically rummaging through the heap of papers and objects, coming up with a jumble of bouquets, a garter, a black mask, hairpins, and locks of hair—so much hair!—brunette, blond; some of it, catching on the box's hinges, broke when it was opened.

Amusing himself thus with his souvenirs, he looked closely at the handwriting and the varied styles of the letters. They were tender or jovial, facetious, melancholic; some of them demanded his love, and some his money. A given word would remind him of faces, of certain gestures, of a tone of voice; and sometimes, he remembered nothing at all.

These women, rushing all at once through his thoughts, actually crowded each other so that they began to shrink down to one single level of love where they were all equalized. So, picking up a random handful of the jumbled letters, he let them fall in cascades from his right hand to his left. Finally, bored and sleepy, Rodolphe put the box back in the cupboard, saying:

"What a pile of nonsense!"

And that summed up his view of the matter; for pleasures, like schoolboys in a schoolyard, had so trampled over his heart that nothing green could grow there, and what did pass through it was even more thoughtless than schoolboys, for it did not even leave its name scratched on the wall.

"All right," he said to himself, "let's get started!"

He wrote:

"Be brave, Emma! Be brave! I don't want to be a curse upon your life."

"After all, that's true," Rodolphe thought; "I'm acting in her interest; I'm being honest."

"Have you carefully thought your decision through? Do you know the abyss into which I was leading you, my poor angel? You really don't, do you? You were going forward, trusting and rash, with faith in happiness, in the future . . . Oh, how miserable we are! How senseless!"

Here Rodolphe paused, to find some good excuse.

"What if I told her that I'd lost all my money? No—and anyway that wouldn't stop her. It would all start up again later. Is there any way to talk sense to women like this?"

He pondered, and then added:

"I will not forget you, believe me, and I will always feel a profound devotion to you; but one day, sooner or later, this ardor—like the destiny of all human things—will diminish, without a doubt! Weariness would come upon us, and who can say if I might not have had the terrible sorrow of having to witness your remorse, and of sharing in it myself, because I was its cause. The very idea of your regret is a torture to me, Emma! Forget me! Oh, why did I ever come to know you? Why were you so beautiful? Is it my fault? Oh, my God! No, no—only fate is to blame."

"Now that's a word that's always effective," he said to himself.

"Oh, if you had only been one of those women with a frivolous heart, the kind that's common enough, then I might indeed have tried the experiment, for it would have held no danger for you. But that delicious exaltation, which is at once your charm and your torment, has kept you from seeing, adorable woman that you are, the falsity of our future position. And I too did not at first think it through, and I rested in the shade of that ideal happiness as if in the shade of a poisonous tropical tree, without foreseeing the consequences."

"Maybe she'll think I'm rejecting her out of stinginess . . . Well, it doesn't matter; it's too bad, but I have to finish it!"

"The world is cruel, Emma. Wherever we might have gone, it would have pursued us. It would have subjected you to indiscreet questions, to calumny, to disdain, perhaps even to insults. Insults to you! Oh! . . . And I, who would have placed you upon a throne! I, who carry the thought of you with me like a talisman! For I will punish myself with exile for all the evil I've done you. I am leaving. Where? I don't have any idea—I am mad! Farewell! Be good always! And keep a memory of the unhappy one who has lost you. Teach my name to your child, so that she may repeat it in her prayers."

The wicks of his two candles flickered. Rodolphe got up to close the window, and, when he had reseated himself:

"I think that's about all. Oh! One more thing, so she won't come *charging after me*:"

"I will be far away by the time you read these sad lines; for I wanted to flee quickly to avoid the temptation of seeing you again. No more weakness! I will return; and perhaps, later on, we will talk dispassionately together about our old love. Farewell!"

And he wrote another farewell, separated into two words—*Fare well!*—which he thought in excellent taste.

"Now how am I going to sign it?" he said to himself. "Your devoted . . . No. Your friend? . . . Yes, that's it."

"Your friend."

He reread the letter. He thought it was good.

"Poor little woman!" he thought, with a feeling of tenderness. "She's going to think I'm as unfeeling as a rock. There ought to be a few teardrops on it; but I've never been able to cry; it's not my fault." Then, having poured some water into a glass, Rodolphe dipped his finger in it and let a big drop fall on the paper, which blotched the ink slightly. Then, as he looked around for a seal, the *Amor nel cor* seal turned up.

"This doesn't much fit the occasion. But bah! What's the difference!"

After which he smoked three pipes, and then went to bed.

The next day, when he got up (he had slept late, and it was about two), he had a basket of apricots picked. He hid the letter at the bottom, under some grape leaves, and ordered his ploughman, Girard, to deliver it discreetly to Madame Bovary. He used this method to communicate with her, sending her fruits or game, according to the season.

"If she asks for news about me," he said, "tell her that I've gone on a trip. Be sure to give the basket only to her—put it in her hands. Go, and be careful!"

Girard put on his new smock, knotted his handkerchief around the apricots, and walking with heavy steps in his big hobnailed clogs, set off placidly down the path to Yonville.

Madame Bovary, when he arrived at her house, was with Félicité, folding linen on the kitchen table.

"Here," said the servant, "master sends you this."

She was seized with apprehension, and while she searched in her pocket for some money, she looked at the peasant with such a dire expression that he looked back at her in amazement, not understanding how such a gift could so upset someone. Finally he left. Félicité stayed. She couldn't wait; she ran into the drawing room as if she were taking the apricots there, turned the basket upside down, tore through the leaves, found the letter, opened it; and, in horror, she began to run upstairs to her room as if she were pursued by a terrible fire.

Charles was there, she saw him; he spoke to her, she heard nothing, and she continued to climb the stairs quickly, breathless, lost, drunk, and always holding on to that terrible sheet of paper, crackling in her hand like a piece of tin. On the third floor, she stopped in front of the attic door, which was closed.

Then she wanted to calm herself; she remembered the letter; she had to read it through, she didn't dare. Besides, where? How? They would see her.

"Ah! No, here I'll be safe," she thought.

Emma pushed open the door and went in.

The roof slates emitted a heavy heat that pressed down on her temples and stifled her; she dragged herself to the closed attic window; she pulled back its bolt, and a blinding light burst instantly into the room.

Opposite her, over the rooftops, the open countryside extended as far as the eye could see. Below her, the village square was empty; the stones of the sidewalk glittered, the weathervanes on the houses were utterly still; on the corner, coming from a lower storey, there was a sort of humming sound, strident and harsh. It was Binet, working at his lathe.

Leaning against the window frame, she reread the letter with angry sneers. But the more she focused on it, the more confused her thoughts became. She saw him again, she heard his voice, she held him in her arms; and her throbbing heart, beating in her chest like great blows from a hammer, began to accelerate and to become irregular. She cast her eyes around her, hoping the world would crumble. Why not end it? What was holding her back? She was free. And she stepped forward, looking down at the paving stones, saying to herself:

"Let's go! Let's go!"

The luminous beam of sunlight reflecting up from below was pulling the weight of her body forward to the abyss. It seemed to her that the ground of the swaying square was creeping upward along the walls, and that the floor she stood on was tilted like a tossing boat. She stood at the edge, almost suspended in air, surrounded by an immense space. The blue of the sky swept over her, the air rushing through her hollowed brain, all she had to do was to let go, let herself fall; and the lathe's buzzing never stopped, sounding like a furious voice calling to her.

"Emma! Emma!" Charles cried.

She stopped.

"Where are you? Come down!"

The idea that she had just escaped from death made her almost faint with terror; she closed her eyes; then she shuddered when she felt a hand on her sleeve: it was Félicité.

"Monsieur is waiting for you, Madame; the soup is on the table."

And she had to go downstairs! She had to go sit at the table!

She tried to eat. The bites she took choked her. Then she unfolded her napkin as if to examine its mending, and she wanted very much to apply herself to this task, to count the threads in the linen. Suddenly, the memory of the letter came back to her. Had she lost it? Where could it be? But she felt such an inner weariness that she was unable to invent a pretext for leaving the table. And she had become cowardly too; she was afraid of Charles; he knew everything, it was certain! And in fact he pronounced these words, strangely:

"We won't be seeing Monsieur Rodolphe anytime soon, it appears."

"Who told you that?" she asked, trembling.

"Who told me?" he replied, a bit surprised by her brusque tone. "It was Girard, who I met just now at the doorway of the *Café Français*. He's gone on a trip, or he's about to go."

A sob escaped her.

"What's so surprising about that? He goes off now and then for his own distraction, and, by God, I approve of it. When a person has money, and is a young bachelor! . . . Besides, he has himself some good times, our friend! He's quite a playboy! Monsieur Langlois told me . . . "

He stopped speaking, for decorum's sake, because the maid had entered.

She put the apricots spilled on the shelf back in the basket; Charles, without noticing his wife's reddening, picked one out and bit into it.

"Oh! Perfect!" he said. "Here, try one."

He held the basket out to her, and she gently pushed it away.

"Smell them, then: what an aroma!" he said, passing it back and forth under her nose.

"I'm choking!" she cried, leaping up suddenly.

But by an effort of will, the spasm disappeared; then she said:

"It's nothing! It's nothing! It's just nerves! Sit back down, eat!"

For she feared he would question her if he tried to care for her, and that he would never leave her alone.

Charles, to obey her, sat back down, and he spit the apricot pits into his hand, and then deposited them on his plate.

Suddenly a blue tilbury coach passed rapidly through the square. Emma uttered a loud cry and fell down, rigid, onto the floor.

In fact Rodolphe, after thinking it all over, had decided to leave for Rouen. Now, since there was no other road from La Huchette to Buchy except through Yonville, he had to go through the village, and Emma had recognized him in the glow of the lanterns, which flashed through the dusk like lightning.

The pharmacist, hearing the uproar, ran to the Bovarys' at once. The table and all the dishes had been knocked over; sauce, meat, cutlery, salt, and oil were scattered all over the room; Charles was shouting for help; Berthe, frightened, was crying; and Félicité, her hands shaking, was unlacing her mistress, whose whole body was shuddering in convulsions.

"I'll run to my laboratory to find some aromatic vinegar," said the pharmacist.

Then, when she smelled the bottle and opened her eyes:

"I was sure it would do the trick," he said; "that would wake the dead."

"Talk to us!" said Charles. "Talk to us! Pull yourself together! It's me, your Charles, the one who loves you! Do you recognize me? Look, here's your little girl: kiss her!"

The child stretched her arms out to her mother to hug her. But Emma, turning her head away, said in a clipped voice:

"No, no . . . No one!"

She fainted again. They carried her to her bed.

She lay there stretched out, her mouth open, her eyelids closed, hands open, motionless and white as a wax statue. Two streams of tears ran from her eyes, and slowly dropped onto the pillow.

Charles stood in the back of the alcove, and the pharmacist, next to him, kept that meditative silence that is befitting during life's serious occasions.

"Don't worry," he said, nudging his elbow, "I think the crisis is past."

"Yes, she's resting a little now!" replied Charles, as he watched her sleep. "Poor woman! Poor woman! . . . She's fallen asleep now!"

Then Homais asked how the accident had happened. Charles replied that she had been seized suddenly while she was eating apricots.

"Extraordinary!" said the pharmacist. "But it might be that the apricots precipitated a syncope! There are some systems just that impressionable when they encounter certain odors! And this could be quite a good question to examine, as much from a pathological angle as from a physiological one. The priests know how important this is, which is why they have always mixed scents in with their rituals. It's in order to stupefy your senses and provoke ecstasies, which is, moreover, very easy to bring about with persons of the weaker sex, who are more delicate than the others. Cases have been cited of people fainting at the scent of burnt hartshorn, of fresh bread . . ."

"Be careful not to wake her up!" said Bovary in a low voice.

"And it's not only humans," the pharmacist continued, "who are subject to these anomalies, but animals as well. Thus, you are certainly aware of the singularly aphrodisiac effect that *nepeta cataria*, vulgarly known as catnip, has on the feline race; and moreover, to cite an example I can personally warrant as genuine, Bridoux (one of my old comrades, currently living on the Rue Malpalu) owns a dog who falls into convulsions the minute anyone shows him a snuffbox. He has often demonstrated this for his friends, at his summerhouse in the Bois Guillaume. Can you believe that a simple sternutation could effect such ravages on the organism of a quadruped? It's exceptionally curious, wouldn't you agree?"

"Yes," said Charles, who wasn't listening.

"It proves," said the other, smiling with a self-important air, "that irregularities are beyond number with regard to the nervous system. In the case of Madame, she has always seemed to me, I must say, a very sensitive type. And therefore I would by no means recommend to you, my old friend, any of those so-called remedies that, on the pretext of attacking the symptoms, in fact attack the constitution! No, none of those pointless medications! Just diet, that's all! Sedatives, emollients, dulcifiers. Also, don't you think that it might be necessary to arouse her imagination?"

"In what way? How?" said Bovary.

"Ah, that's the question! That's definitely the question: 'That is the question!'[3]—as I recently read in a newspaper."

But Emma, awaking, cried out, "And the letter? And the letter?"

They thought she was delirious; and by midnight, she was; a cerebral fever was diagnosed.

For forty-three days, Charles did not leave her side. He abandoned all his patients; he no longer went to bed, but was continually taking her pulse, applying mustard plasters, cold-water compresses. He sent Justin to Neufchâtel to find some ice; on the way back, the ice melted; he sent him again. He called in Monsieur Canivet for a consultation; he sent for his old master from Rouen, Doctor Larivière; he was desperate. What frightened him the most was Emma's complete prostration; for she didn't speak, didn't hear, and didn't even seem to be suffering—as if her body and soul were now both resting together after their struggles.

Toward the middle of October, she was able to sit up in bed, propped up with pillows. Charles wept when he saw her eat her first bread and jam. Her strength returned; she would get up for a few hours in the afternoon, and, on one day when she felt herself to be better, he tried to get her to take a turn in the garden, leaning on his arm. The gravel on the path had disappeared beneath the dead leaves; she walked along step by step, dragging her slippers, and leaning on Charles' shoulder, she continued to smile.

They walked in this way to the bottom of the garden, near the terrace. She slowly straightened herself up, using her hand to shade her eyes and look around her. She looked far off, as far away as she could, but there was nothing on the horizon but great grass fires, smoking on the hillsides.

---

3. In English in the original. Homais is unaware that he's quoting from Shakespeare's *Hamlet* [translator's note].

"You're going to get overtired, my dear one," said Bovary.

And pushing her gently to get her to enter the arbor:

"Sit on this bench: you'll be more comfortable."

"Oh no! Not there, not there!" she exclaimed, her voice faltering.

She had a dizzy spell, and from that evening on, her illness returned, in a less clearly defined way, true, and with more complicated symptoms. Sometimes she felt pain in her heart, and sometimes in her chest, then the head, then the limbs; there were fits of vomiting, in which Charles thought he could see the first signs of cancer.

And as if that weren't enough, the poor man had money worries!

CHAPTER 14

In the first place, he didn't know how he could pay Homais for all the medications he brought to him; and even though as a doctor he was not required to pay for them, still he blushed at the obligation. Then the household expenses, now that the kitchen maid had taken charge, had become horrific; bills rained upon the house; the tradesmen grumbled; Monsieur Lheureux in particular harassed him. In fact, when Emma's illness was at its worst, the latter took advantage of the circumstances to increase his bill, hurriedly delivering the cloak, the overnight bag, two trunks instead of one, and a great many other things as well. In vain Charles said he didn't need them, for the merchant responded arrogantly that all these things had been ordered, and he could not return them; besides, this would only upset Madame during her convalescence; Monsieur ought to think it over; in short, he was determined to pursue his case in court rather than give up his rights and take back the merchandise. Afterward, Charles gave orders that it should all be returned to his shop; Félicité forgot to do it; Charles had other worries; he thought no more about it; Monsieur Lheureux went back on the attack and, alternating between menacing and whining, managed to get Bovary to sign a promissory note, due in full in six months. But he had scarcely signed the note when an audacious idea occurred to him: to borrow a thousand francs from Monsieur Lheureux. So he asked, with an embarrassed air, whether it would be possible, adding that the loan would be for a year, at whatever rate of interest he wanted. Lheureux ran back to his shop, bringing back the money and dictating another note, by which Bovary agreed to pay, on September 1 of the following year, the sum of one thousand and seventy francs, which, along with the one hundred and eighty already stipulated, came to exactly twelve hundred and fifty. Thus the loan, at six percent, and his twenty-five percent commission, and the goods bringing in another third at minimum—all of this ought to give him, twelve months hence, a hundred and thirty francs in profit; and he hoped the business would not stop there, that they would be unable to pay the debt, that it would have to be renewed, and that his poor, thin money, after being nourished and fed at the doctor's as at a rest home, would one day return to him much plumper, and fat enough to burst the money bag.

Besides, everything he did was successful. He had the contract to supply cider to the Neufchâtel hospital; Monsieur Guillaumin had promised him some shares in the peat bogs at Grumesnil, and he was thinking about establishing a new coach line between Argueil and Rouen, which would certainly

thoughts, to impure temptations. Such at any rate is the opinion of all the Fathers. And finally," he added in a mystical tone of voice, while rolling a pinch of snuff between his fingers, "if the Church has condemned plays, she must have been right; we must submit to her decrees."

"Why," the pharmacist asked, "does she excommunicate actors? Because in other eras they openly took part in the religious ceremonies. Yes, they acted right in the middle of the choir a species of farce called mysteries, which often offended against the laws of decency."

The cleric contented himself with uttering a groan, and the pharmacist pursued the point:

"It's just like in the Bible; there is . . . you know . . . more than one detail . . . spicy sorts of things, really . . . lively ones!"

And when Monsieur Bournisien made an irritated gesture:

"Ah! You agree then that it isn't a book that should be put into the hands of a young person, and I would be very sorry if Athalie . . . "

"But it's the Protestants, not us, who recommend the Bible!" cried the other, impatiently.

"It doesn't matter!" said Homais. "I'm surprised that in our days, in this enlightened century, anyone stubbornly continues to proscribe an intellectual relaxation that is inoffensive, moralizing, and even sometimes therapeutic; wouldn't you agree, Doctor?"

"No doubt," replied the doctor casually, either because he shared the same ideas and didn't want to offend anyone, or because in fact he had no ideas at all.

The conversation seemed to be concluded, when the pharmacist judged it opportune to take one more shot.

"I've known of priests who dress like townsfolk in order to go watch dancing girls jiggling."

"Come now!" said the priest.

"Ah yes, I've known some!"

And separating the syllables of his phrase, Homais repeated:

"I-have-known-some!"

"Well then, they were in the wrong," said Bournisien, resigned to having to listen to anything.

"By heaven, they get up to more tricks than that too!" exclaimed the pharmacist.

"Monsieur!" said the cleric with so fierce a look in his eyes that the pharmacist was intimidated.

"I only mean to say," he went on in a softer tone, "that tolerance is the surest way of attracting souls to religion."

"That's true! That's true!" the good priest conceded, sitting back down in his chair.

But he only stayed a couple of minutes. Then, once he was gone, Monsieur Homais said to the doctor:

"Now that's what I call a real dustup! I showed him up, you saw it! . . . Anyway, believe me, take Madame to the theater, if only to irritate one of these crows for once in your life, damn it! If anyone could replace me, I'd come along with you myself. Hurry! Lagardy is only giving one performance; he's engaged to go to England for quite a high fee. People say he's quite the playboy! He's rolling in money! He travels with three mistresses and a cook! All these great artists burn the candle at both ends; they have to live a debauched life to keep their imaginations stimulated. But they die in the poorhouse because they haven't got the sense, while they're young, to save their money. Well, have a pleasant dinner; see you tomorrow!"

This idea of the theater quickly germinated in Bovary's head; he mentioned it to his wife soon after, but she rejected it at first, pleading fatigue, the trouble, and the expense; but, most unusually for him, Charles did not give in, so strongly did he believe that this recreation would be good for her. He saw nothing to prevent them; his mother had unexpectedly sent them three hundred francs, the current debts were not unmanageable, and the payments due to Monsieur Lheureux were so far off that he didn't have to think much about them. And besides, believing that she was refusing out of consideration for him, Charles insisted all the more; so much so that she finally gave in to his ceaseless arguments. And the next day, at eight o'clock, they set off in the *Hirondelle*.

There was nothing at all keeping the pharmacist in Yonville, but believing that he dare not leave, he sighed at seeing them depart.

"Well then, have a good journey!" he said to them. "Fortunate mortals that you are!"

Then, speaking to Emma, who was wearing a blue silk dress with four flounces:

"You're as pretty as a goddess of love! You'll *positively thrive* in Rouen!"

The coach stopped at the *Red Cross* inn, on the Place Beauvoisine. It was the sort of inn found in every provincial town, with large stables and little bedrooms, where one can see chickens in the courtyard pecking at oats under the muddy gigs of traveling salesmen—a good old inn with a worm-eaten wooden balcony that creaks in the wind on winter nights, always full of people, noise, and food, with black tables sticky from *glorias*, thick windows yellowed by flies, damp napkins stained with cheap wine; a place that, smelling always of the village, like a country boy dressed in city clothes, has a café on the street, and, on the country side, a vegetable garden. Charles got right to business. He confused the stage boxes with the gallery, the pit with the boxes, asked for explanations, failed to understand them, was sent from the box office to the manager, returned to the inn, then returned to the theater, and ended by covering the whole length of the town from the theater to the boulevard several times.

Madame bought herself a hat, gloves, a bouquet. Monsieur was terribly afraid of missing the beginning; and without even giving themselves the time to consume a bowl of soup, they presented themselves in front of the theater doors, which were still closed.

CHAPTER 15

The crowd was waiting against the wall, divided symmetrically between railings. At the corner of the nearby streets, gigantic posters repeated in flamboyant script, "*Lucia di Lammermoor*[8] . . . Lagardy . . . Opera" et cetera. The

8. Fictional tenor who plays Edgar in the opera. *Lucie de Lammermoor*: an opera by Gaetano Donizetti (1797–1848), first performed in Naples in 1835 (in Paris in 1837), based on Walter Scott's novel *The Bride of Lammermoor* (1819). There are substantial differences between the French version, which Flaubert followed, and the original Italian libretto. Here, Edgar of Ravenswood has sworn vengeance on Lord Henry Ashton, his father's killer; Edgar and Ashton's sister Lucie are in love, but Ashton forces her to marry a rich suitor, Lord Arthur; Gilbert is a treacherous servant.

weather was fine; people were hot; sweat was running under hairdos; handkerchiefs were dabbing at reddened foreheads; from time to time a warm wind blowing up from the river would gently flutter the awnings hanging from the doorways of the bars. A little further down, however, people were cooled by a glacial current of air that smelled of tallow, leather, and oil. This was the exhalation from the Rue des Charrettes, full of big dark warehouses where casks are stored.

For fear of seeming ridiculous, Emma wanted to take a walk along the harbor before going in, and Bovary, out of prudence, kept the tickets in his hand, in his trouser pocket, pressing them tightly against his stomach.

Her heart began beating faster as soon as they reached the vestibule. She smiled involuntarily out of vanity at seeing the crowd rushing to the right down the other corridor while she walked up the staircase toward the reserved seats. She felt a childlike pleasure in pushing open the wide, tapestried doors with her finger; she breathed in deeply the dusty odor of the corridor, and when she was seated in her box, she leaned forward as casually as a duchess.

The theater was beginning to fill; opera glasses were taken out of their cases, and the subscribers, catching sight of each other, were bowing. They had come to the arts to relax from the anxieties of their commerce; but by no means did they forget about *business*, and they continued talking about cotton, alcohol, or indigo. The heads of older people could be seen, impassive and peaceful, their white hair and complexions making them resemble silver medals tarnished by lead fumes. Good-looking young men were strutting in the pit, revealing, in their open waistcoats, cravats of pink or apple-green; and Madame Bovary admired them from above, as they draped the open palms of their yellow gloves over the golden knobs of their canes.

Meanwhile, the orchestra's candles were lit; the chandelier with its glittering crystals descended from the ceiling, casting a sudden gaiety over the theater; then the musicians entered, one after the other, and there was at first an extended din of snoring basses, squeaking violins, blaring cornets, and cheeping flutes and flageolets. But then three taps were heard on the stage; a drum roll began, the brass instruments played some chords, and the curtain rose up, revealing a landscape.

There was a crossroads in a forest, with a fountain on the left, shaded by an oak tree. Peasants and lords with plaids over their shoulders were singing a hunting song together; then a captain suddenly came on, invoking the angel of evil, lifting both arms up to heaven; another appeared; they exited, and the hunters started up again.

She found herself taken back to her childhood reading, to the world of Walter Scott. She felt she could hear, coming through the mist, the sound of Scottish bagpipes echoing across the heather. Her memory of the novel made it easier to follow the libretto, and she could follow the story phrase by phrase, while vague thoughts came and went in her mind, dispersed by gusts of music. She gave herself up to the rocking, lulling movement of the melodies, feeling her entire being vibrating as if the violin bows were being drawn over her nerves. She stared avidly at the costumes, the sets, the characters, the painted trees that shook when the actors walked past them, the velvet caps, the cloaks, the swords, all those imaginary things fluttering past within the harmony as if in the air of another world. But one young woman stepped forward, throwing a purse to a squire in green. She remained there alone, and then the flute began to play like the murmur of a fountain or like the warbling of a bird. Lucia solemnly started into her cavatina[9] in G major; she lamented for love, she wished to have wings. Emma too would have liked to flee from life, carried off in an embrace. Suddenly, Edgar Lagardy appeared.

He had that splendid pallor that gives a marble-like appearance to the passionate races of the South. His robust body was tightly clad in a brown doublet; a little carved dagger hung against his left thigh, and he cast languishing glances around him, revealing his white teeth. People said that a Polish princess, hearing him sing one night on the beach at Biarritz[1] where he then mended boats, had fallen in love with him. She ruined herself over him. He had left her there for other women, and those romantic stories only served to enhance his artistic reputation. The clever ham always took care to have some poetic phrase dropped into his publicity material, something regarding the fascination of his person and the sensitivity of his soul. A fine vocal organ, an imperturbable cool, more temperament than intelligence, more overstatement than real lyricism—all these came together to make up the charm of this marvelous charlatan, in whom there was something of both the hairdresser and the toreador.

From the very first scene, the audience was enraptured. He pressed Lucia in his arms, he left her, he returned, he seemed desperate; he had outbursts of rage, and then elegiac gurgles of infinite sweetness, the notes escaping from his bared throat, full of sighs and kisses. Emma leaned forward to watch him, digging her fingernails into the velvet railing of the box. Her heart swelled with those melodious lamentations accompanied by the double basses, like the cries of the shipwrecked in a furious tempest. In them she recognized all the intoxications, all the anguish from which she had almost died. The soprano's voice seemed only an echo of her own consciousness, and this illusion charming her seemed something from her own life. But no one on earth had ever loved her with a love like this. He had not wept the way Edgar did, that last night in the moonlight when they were saying to each other, "until tomorrow! Until tomorrow . . . " The room resounded with bravos; they repeated the passage all over again; the lovers spoke of the flowers on their tomb, of vows, of exile, of fate, of hopes, and when they finally sent forth their final adieu, Emma burst out with a sharp cry that blended with the vibrations of the final chords.

"But why," asked Bovary, "is that lord persecuting her?"

"No, no," Emma replied; "he's her lover."

"But he swears to take vengeance on her family, while the other one, the one who was on before, said, 'I love Lucia and I believe she loves me!' And besides, he went off with her father, arm in arm. Because it is her father, isn't it, the short ugly one wearing the cock's feather in his hat?"

Despite Emma's explanations, as soon as the recitative duet began in which Gilbert reveals his heinous plots to his master Ashton, Charles, seeing the false engagement ring meant to deceive Lucia, thought that it was a love token sent by Edgar. He admitted, moreover, that he couldn't understand the story because of the music, which very much got in the way of the words.

9. A short, simple song.
1. A fashionable French resort on the Bay of Biscay.

"What's the difference?" said Emma. "Be quiet!"

"It's because I like to know what's going on," he said, leaning against her shoulder. "You know that."

"Be quiet! Be quiet!" she repeated impatiently.

Lucia came forward, partly supported by her ladies, a wreath of orange blossoms in her hair, and paler than the white satin of her dress. Emma thought of her wedding day; and she saw herself there again, among the wheat fields, on the little path, when they were walking to the church. Why hadn't she, like this woman, resisted, pleaded? But on the contrary, she had been joyful, without seeing the abyss into which she was hurling herself . . . Oh! If only, in the springtime of her beauty, before the defilement of marriage and the disillusionment of adultery, she had been able to base her life upon some great, solid heart, then virtue, tenderness, sensuality, and duty would have been harmoniously blended, and she would never have fallen from so high a state of happiness. But that happiness, no doubt, was a lie dreamed up to cause the despair of every desire. She now knew the pettiness of the passions that art exaggerated. Forcing herself to turn away from such thoughts, Emma now wanted to see in this reproduction of her sorrows nothing more than a plastic fantasy to amuse the eyes, and she even smiled to herself with a scornful pity when, at the back of the stage, a man dressed in a black cloak appeared.

He swept off his large Spanish hat with a single gesture; and at once the instruments and singers began the sextet. Edgar, flashing with fury, dominated all the others with his stronger voice; Ashton hurled murderous provocations at him in profound tones; Lucia sent up her shrill lamentation; Arthur, to the side, modulated his tones in the middle register, and the minister's bass boomed like an organ while the ladies' voices repeated his words and took them up in a delightful chorus. All were lined up in a row gesticulating; and anger, vengeance, jealousy, terror, mercy, and astonishment were all breathed out at the same time from their open mouths. The offended lover brandished his bare sword: his lace ruffle jerked up and down according to the movements of his chest, and he stalked from right to left, making the stage boards rattle with the silver-gilt spurs on his soft boots, which flared out at the ankles. He must, she thought, possess an inexhaustible love, to be able to pour it out over the crowd in such streams. All her attempts to be critical faded away under the force of the poetic role that was absorbing her; and, drawn to the man by the illusion of the character he was playing, she tried to imagine his life, that captivating, extraordinary, splendid life of his, one that could have been hers if fate had willed it so. They would have known each other, they would have loved each other! With him, through all the capitals of Europe, she would have traveled, sharing his fatigue, his pride, gathering up the flowers people threw to him, sewing his costumes herself; and then, every evening, standing in the back of the box behind a golden trellis, she would have eagerly breathed in the outpourings of his soul, which would always be sung only for her; even as he was acting on the stage, he would be looking at her! But now a mad idea seized hold of her: he was looking directly at her, she was sure of it! She felt like running into his arms to take refuge in his strength as in the incarnation of love itself, and to say to him, to cry out to him, "Take me away! Carry me off with you! Let us go now! Yours, yours—all my passion, all my dreams!"

The curtain came down.

The odor of gas mixed with that of the crowd's breath; the waving of the ladies' fans only made the air more stifling. Emma wanted to go outside; the crowd blocked the corridors, and she fell back into her chair with palpitations that were suffocating. Charles, fearing she might faint, ran off to the bar to get her a glass of barley water.

He had a great deal of difficulty getting back to his seat with the glass of water in his hands, because people kept bumping his elbows at every step, and he spilled three-fourths of it on the shoulders of a Rouen lady in short sleeves; feeling the cold liquid trickling down her back, she shrieked like a peacock, as if she were being assassinated. Her husband, a mill owner, shouted angrily at the clumsy fool; and while she used her handkerchief to sponge up the stains from her lovely cherry-colored taffeta gown, he was gruffly muttering words about indemnity, costs, reimbursement. At last Charles got back to Emma, and, out of breath, said to her:

"I thought, good lord, that I'd never make it back! There is such a crowd! Such a crowd!"

He added:

"But guess who I met up there? Monsieur Léon!"

"Léon?"

"Himself! He's going to come to pay you his respects."

And just as he finished saying those words, the one-time clerk of Yonville stepped into their box.

He held out his hand with a gentleman's ease: and Madame Bovary mechanically extended her own, evidently obeying the attraction of a will stronger than her own. She had not touched that hand since that spring evening when rain was falling on the green leaves, when they said good-bye to each other, standing in front of the window. But quickly remembering the requisite courtesies of the present situation, she made an effort to shake off that torpor of her memories, and began to stammer out rapid phrases.

"Ah, hello! . . . Imagine! You here?"

"Silence!" cried a voice from the pit, for the third act was about to begin.

"So you're in Rouen?"

"Yes."

"And since when?"

"Throw them out! Throw them out!"

Other people had turned to stare at them; they were silent.

But from that moment on, she didn't listen to the music anymore; and the chorus of the guests, the scene between Ashton and his servant, the great duet in D major: for her, all of it took place in the distance, as if the instruments had become less sonorous, the characters more remote; she remembered the card parties at the pharmacist's, and the walk to the wet nurse's, the readings in the arbor, the intimate moments by the fireside, the whole impoverished love so calm and so long, so discreet, so tender, which she had nonetheless forgotten until now. Why had he come back? What combination of events had placed him back in her life? He stood behind her, leaning his shoulder against the wall of the box; and she now and then felt herself trembling beneath the warmth of his breath upon her hair.

"Are you enjoying this?" he asked, bending down so close to her that the tip of his moustache brushed her cheek.

She replied carelessly:

"Oh, my God, no! Not very much."

Then he proposed that they leave the theater, to go and have an ice somewhere.

"Ah, but not yet! Let's stay!" said Bovary. "Her hair has come undone: this is going to be tragic."

But the mad scene did not interest Emma at all, and the singer's acting seemed exaggerated to her.

"She's shouting too loud," she said to Charles, who was listening.

"Yes, perhaps . . . a little," he replied, undecided between the genuineness of his pleasure and his respect for the opinions of his wife.

Then Léon said with a sigh:

"The heat today is . . ."

"Unendurable! That's right."

"Are you uncomfortable?" asked Bovary.

"Yes, I'm stifling: let's go."

Monsieur Léon carefully placed her long, lace shawl over her shoulders, and the three of them went to sit down by the harbor in the fresh air, outside the windows of a café.

They began to talk about her illness, but Emma interrupted Charles from time to time, afraid, she said, of boring Monsieur Léon; and the latter told them that he had come to Rouen to spend two years in a big firm in order to get some experience with business in Normandy, which was different from that in Paris. Then he asked about Berthe, the Homais family, Madame Lefrançois; and since they had nothing else to say to each other, in the presence of the husband, the conversation soon came to a halt.

Some people coming back from the theater were passing on the sidewalk, humming or shouting at the tops of their voices, "O bel ange, ma Lucia!" Then Léon, adopting the role of the dilettante, began to talk about music. He had seen Tamburini, Rubini, Persiani, Grisi;[2] and compared to them, Lagardy, despite his great reputation, wasn't worth much.

"Still," interrupted Charles, who had been eating his rum sherbet little spoonfuls at a time, "they say that he's really wonderful in the last act; I'm sorry we left before the end, because I was beginning to enjoy it."

"Well," said the clerk, "he'll be giving another performance soon."

But Charles replied that they had to leave the next day.

"Unless," he added, turning to his wife, "you'd like to stay on alone, my little kitten?"

And changing his strategy in the face of this unexpected and hopeful development, the young man began singing Lagardy's praises, especially his performance in the last act. It was something superb, something sublime! Then Charles insisted:

"You can come back on Sunday. Come on, decide! If you feel this would do you even the slightest good, you really ought to stay."

<hr>

2. Antonio Tamburini (1800–1876); Gian-Battista Rubini (1794–1854); Fanny Tacchinardi Persiani, who was the first Lucia (1812–1867); and Giulia Grisi (1811–1869) were all famous bel-canto singers who appeared in Paris in the operas of Rossini and Donizetti.

Meanwhile the tables around them were emptying; a waiter came and stood discreetly near them; Charles, who understood, reached for his purse; but the clerk reached out and held back his arm, and he did not forget to leave two extra silver coins for the waiter, which he made resound on the marble table.

"I feel bad, really," Bovary murmured, "about the money that you're . . ."

The other made a cordially dismissive gesture, and, picking up his hat:

"So it's settled? Tomorrow at six o'clock?"

Charles objected again that he could not stay away that long, but there was nothing to prevent Emma . . .

"It's just that . . . ," she stammered with an unusual smile, "I'm not too . . ."

"Well! You'll think it over, and we'll see. The night brings counsel . . ."

Then to Léon, who was walking along with them:

"Now that you're back in our part of the world, I trust you'll come by, sometime or other, and have dinner with us?"

The clerk assured him that he wouldn't fail to do so, for in any case he had to go to Yonville to take care of some business for his firm. And they separated in front of the Saint-Herbland Passage, at the very moment when the cathedral clock was sounding eleven-thirty.

Part Three

CHAPTER I

During his law studies in Paris, Monsieur Léon was a frequent presence at the *Chaumière*,[3] where he actually had pretty good success with the grisettes, who thought he had a *distinguished air*. He was the most decorous of students: he wore his hair neither too short nor too long, nor did he burn through all his money on the first day of the trimester, and he kept on good terms with the professors. As for any excesses, he avoided them as much out of timidity as moral scrupulousness.

Often, when he stayed in his rooms reading, or when he sat for an evening under the linden trees in the Luxembourg Gardens, he would let his law book fall from his hands, and the memory of Emma would come back to him. But the feeling weakened bit by bit, and other desires grew, took over, and covered it up, even though it persisted beneath them; for Léon did not lose all hope, and a kind of uncertain promise swayed ahead of him in the future, like some golden fruit suspended from a fantastic tree.

And then, when he saw her again after three years of absence, his passion came to life again. He simply must, he thought to himself, make up his mind to possess her. Moreover, his old shyness had been worn away by contact with more frolicsome company, and when he returned to the provinces he felt scorn for anyone who had not trodden the boulevards of Paris with polished boots. If he had to face an elegant Parisian woman in lace, or in the salon of some illustrious doctor, a man with decorations and a carriage, the poor clerk would no doubt tremble like a child; but here, in Rouen, on the harbor, before the wife of this little doctor, he was comfortable, certain in advance that he would dazzle

3. *La Chaumière* was a long–established (1788–1855) nightclub/cabaret with a bohemian, even scandalous reputation; it was situ- ated on the corner of the Boulevard d'Enfer and the Boulevard Montparnasse. A *chaumière* is a thatched cottage [translator's note].

her. Such confidence depends on our surroundings: we don't speak in the drawing room in the same way we would in a garret; and the wealthy woman can feel that all the bank notes surrounding her are guarding her virtue invisibly, like armor in the lining of her corset.

When Monsieur and Madame Bovary left him the night before, Léon followed them at a distance; and having seen them stopping at the *Red Cross*, he turned on his heels and spent the rest of the night devising a plan.

So the next day at about five o'clock he entered the inn's kitchen, his throat constricted, his cheeks pale, with the coward's determination to let nothing stop him this time.

"Monsieur is not here," a servant replied.

He took that as a good omen. He went upstairs.

Emma was not disturbed by his coming; on the contrary, she apologized for not having told him where they were staying.

"Oh! I guessed," Léon replied.

"How?"

He claimed he had been guided to her by chance, by instinct. She began to smile, and Léon quickly moved to cover his foolishness by saying that he spent the morning looking for her at all the hotels in town.

"So you have decided to stay on?" he added.

"Yes," she said, "and it was a mistake. I can't let myself get used to impractical pleasures, when there are a thousand responsibilities . . . ."

"Oh, yes, I can imagine . . ."

"No, you can't, because you're not a woman."

But men also have their own difficulties, and the conversation turned toward some philosophical reflections. Emma expounded at length on the poverty of earthly affections, and the eternal isolation in which the human soul is buried.

Whether out of a need to make himself seem impressive, or out of a naïve imitation of Emma's melancholy, the young man declared that he had been immensely bored throughout his law studies. Legal procedure irritated him, other vocations were attractive to him, and his mother never ceased to torment him with every letter she sent. As they talked and became increasingly specific about the causes of their unhappiness, each of them became more enthusiastic in their progressive confidences. But sometimes they would stop just short of a complete explanation, searching for some phrase that would translate it in the right way for the situation. She by no means confessed her passion for another man; he did not say that he had forgotten her.

It may be that he no longer remembered his late suppers after balls with costumed girls; and she no longer recalled, perhaps, those mornings when she would run through the grass toward her lover's chateau. The sounds of the city barely reached them; and the room seemed small, as if to bring them even closer together in their solitude. Emma, wearing a dimity dressing gown, was leaning her head against the back of the old armchair; the yellow wallpaper was like a background of gold for her; and her bare head was repeated in the mirror, with its firm white part in the middle, and with the tips of her ears showing beneath her hair.

"But do excuse me," she said, "I'm so wrong to bore you with my eternal complaints!"

"No, never! Never!"

"If you only knew," she replied, raising her beautiful eyes up toward the ceiling, a tear forming in each of them, "all the things I've dreamed of!"

"And me too! Oh, I've suffered so much! Often I'd go out, to get away, and drag myself along the docks, drowning myself in the noise of the crowd, but without being able to escape the obsession that always pursued me. On the boulevard there is an engraver's shop, with an Italian print that represents a Muse. She's clothed in a tunic and she's looking at the moon, with forget-me-nots in her uncovered hair. Something always pushed me toward that place; I would stay there for whole hours."

And then, in a trembling voice:

"She looked a little like you."

Madame Bovary turned her face away, so that he would not see the irrepressible smile she felt forming on her lips.

"Many times," he went on, "I would write letters to you, and then I would tear them up."

She did not reply. He continued:

"I would often fantasize that some chance event would bring you to me. I thought I saw you on street corners; and I would run after all the carriages from which a shawl or a veil like yours was fluttering from the window . . ."

She seemed determined to let him speak without interrupting him. Crossing her arms and lowering her head, she looked at the rosette on her slippers, and she occasionally made little movements with her toes inside their satin.

Then at last she sighed:

"The saddest thing, don't you think, is dragging out a pointless existence like mine? If our sorrows at least did someone some good, we could console ourselves with the thought of making a sacrifice!"

He began to praise virtue, duty, and acts of silent self-denial, feeling in himself an incredible need for self-sacrifice that he could not satisfy.

"I would very much like," she said, "to be a nun working in a hospital."

"Alas!" he replied, "we men have no such holy missions, and I can't see any career . . . unless maybe that of a doctor . . ."

With a light shrug of her shoulders, Emma interrupted to say she regretted that she hadn't died of her illness; what a pity! She wouldn't be suffering even more now. Léon quickly spoke of envying the *peace of the tomb*, and he had even written out his will one evening, asking that he be buried in that beautiful coverlet with velvet bands that she had given him; for that is how they both wanted to have been, each of them creating an ideal to which they now were adjusting their past lives. And besides, speech is a rolling pin, stretching and drawing the feelings outward.

But with regard to this story about the coverlet:

"But why?" she asked.

"Why?"

He hesitated.

"Because I have loved you so much!"

And applauding himself for having crossed this difficult threshold, Léon watched her face out of the corner of his eye.

It was like the sky, when a sudden wind chases the clouds away. The heap of sad thoughts that had darkened them seemed to drift away from her blue eyes; her whole face shone.

He waited. Finally she replied:

"I always suspected it ... "

Then they went on to tell each other about little events from their far-away life, whose pleasures and sorrows had just been summed up in that single word. He reminisced about the clematis arbor, the dresses she had worn, the furniture in her room, everything in her house.

"And our poor cacti, what happened to them?"

"The cold killed them off last winter."

"Ah, do you know how much I've thought about them? I would often picture them just as they were when, in the summer mornings, the sun struck them through the blinds ... and I would picture your two bare arms working around the flowers."

"My poor friend!" she said, holding her hand out to him.

Léon with alacrity raised it to his lips. Then, after he had taken a deep breath:

"You were, in those days, some incomprehensible force that had taken over my life. One time, for example, I came to your house; but—you probably won't remember it."

"I do," she said. "Go on."

"You were downstairs in the hall, ready to go out, on the bottom stair—I even remember you had a hat with little blue flowers; and without any invitation on your part, and despite myself, I went out with you. But with every passing minute I was more and more aware of my foolishness, and I continued walking along by you, not daring to commit myself to actually following you, and not wanting to leave you. When you went into a shop, I stayed out in the street, and I watched you through the window taking off your gloves and counting the change on the counter. Then you went on to call on Madame Tuvache, they let you in, and I stayed standing, like an idiot, outside that big heavy door that closed behind you."

Madame Bovary, as she listened to him, was surprised at feeling so old; all these things reappearing before her seemed to be widening her existence; it created a vastness of sentiment to which she now was returning; and she said from time to time, her voice low and her eyelids half closed:

"Yes, that's right! ... That's right! ... That's right!"

They heard eight o'clock sounding from the various clocks in the Beauvoisine Quarter, which is full of schools, churches, and large, abandoned houses. They no longer spoke; but they felt, as they looked at each other, a kind of reverberation in their heads, as if some sonorous thing had escaped from each one's fixed stare. They had just joined their hands; and the past, the future, reminiscences, and dreams all were blended together in the sweetness of that ecstasy. Night was darkening the walls, on which still shone, half lost in the shadow, the crude colors of four prints representing four scenes from the *Tour de Nesle*,[4] each with a caption below, in both Spanish and French. Through the sashed window, they could see a corner of the black sky, between the pointed roofs.

She got up to light two candles on the chest of drawers, and then sat down again.

4. The Nesle Tower (French); a melodrama by Alexandre Dumas the elder (1803–1870) and Gaillardet (1832) in which Marie de Bourgogne, famous for her crimes, is the main heroine.

"Well? . . . " said Léon.

"Well? . . . " she replied.

And he was trying to find a way to restart their interrupted conversation, when she said to him:

"Why is it that no one, up until this moment, has ever spoken to me like this before?"

The clerk exclaimed that ideal natures were difficult for others to understand. As for him, from the moment he first saw her, he had loved her; and he despaired when he thought about the happiness they would have had if, by the grace of fate, they had met earlier; they would have been bound to each other indissolubly.

"I've sometimes dreamed about it," she replied.

"What a dream!" Léon murmured.

And gently fingering the blue border of her long white sash, he added:

"What is there to prevent us from starting over?"

"No, my friend," she replied. "I am too old . . . you are too young . . . forget me! Others will love you . . . you will love them."

"Not like you!" he cried.

"What a child you are! Come, let's be wiser. I want us to be."

She explained to him how impossible their love would be, and that they would have to remain, as in the past, on the simple terms of a fraternal friendship.

Was she saying this seriously? No doubt Emma herself didn't know, entirely occupied as she was with the charm of this seduction and the necessity of defending herself from it; and contemplating the young man with a tender look, she gently fended off the timid caresses his trembling hands were attempting.

"Ah, pardon me," he said, drawing them back.

And Emma was seized with a vague fright in the face of this timidity, more dangerous for her than Rodolphe's boldness had been when he stepped toward her with his arms open. No other man had ever seemed so beautiful to her as this one. His countenance breathed an exquisite candor. He lowered his long, fine, curled eyelashes. His soft-skinned cheek was reddened—she thought— with desire for her body, and Emma felt an overpowering urge to press her lips to it. And then, bending toward the clock as if to see what time it was:

"It's so late—my God!" she said. "How we've chattered!"

He understood the inference, and looked around for his hat.

"I've even forgotten the theater! That poor Bovary left me here specifically for that! Monsieur Lormaux, from the Rue Grand-Pont, was supposed to take me, along with his wife."

And the opportunity was lost, because she was to leave the next day.

"Really?" said Léon.

"Yes."

"But I have to see you again," he said, "I have something to tell you . . . "

"What?"

"A thing . . . very grave, very serious. Oh, no, no! You won't leave me, it's impossible! If you only knew . . . Listen to me . . . Haven't you understood me? Haven't you guessed? . . . "

"You speak plainly enough," said Emma.

"Oh, jokes! Enough, enough! Arrange it, for pity's sake, that I can see you again . . . just once . . . one time."

"All right . . . "

She stopped herself, as if changing her mind:

"Oh! But not here!"

"Wherever you like."

"Would you like . . . "

She seemed to be thinking, and then she said abruptly:

"Tomorrow, at eleven o'clock, in the cathedral."

"I'll be there!" he cried, taking hold of her hands, which she pulled away.

And because they found themselves standing up, him behind her and Emma lowering her head, he bent toward her neck and kissed her, a lingering kiss, on the nape.

"You're mad! Ah, you're mad!" she said with little, throaty laughs, as his kisses multiplied.

Then, advancing his head over her shoulders, he seemed to be seeking permission from her eyes. They fell upon him, full of an icy majesty.

Léon took three steps back, to leave. He stood on the threshold. Then he whispered, his voice trembling:

"Until tomorrow."

She replied with a nod of her head, and disappeared like a bird into the next room.

That evening, Emma wrote an interminable letter to the clerk, in which she broke off the meeting; everything was over, and for their own happiness they should not meet. But when the letter was finished, since she didn't know Léon's address, she was vexed.

"I'll give it to him myself," she said to herself; "he will come."

The next day, Léon, his window open, humming to himself on the balcony, polished his shoes himself, applying several layers. He put on white trousers, thin socks, a green jacket, applied every scent he had to his handkerchief and then, having curled his hair, uncurled it so as to give himself a more natural elegance.

"It's still too early!" he thought, looking over at the wigmaker's cuckoo clock, which sounded nine o'clock.

He read an old fashion magazine, went out, smoked a cigar, walked up three different streets, thought that it must be time and slowly headed toward the Notre-Dame square.

It was a beautiful summer morning. Silver plate shone in the jewelers' windows, and the light slanting down on the cathedral glittered in the cracks between the gray paving stones; a flock of birds was whirling up in the blue sky, around the trefoils of the steeples; the square, echoing with shouts, smelled of the flowers lining its pavement, roses, jasmine, carnations, narcissus, and tuberoses, spaced irregularly between the damp greenery, the catnip, and the chickweed for the birds; the fountain gurgled in the middle, and bareheaded merchant women under large umbrellas, among melons piled in pyramids, were wrapping bouquets of violets in paper.

The young man took one. It was the first time that he had bought flowers for a woman; and his chest, as he breathed in their scent, swelled with pride, as if this homage he planned for another somehow reflected back on himself.

But he was afraid of being seen; he went resolutely into the church.

The verger was standing on the doorstep, in the middle of the left doorway, beneath the *Marianne Dancing* with a plumed hat, a rapier at his side, and a cane in his hand, more majestic than a cardinal and gleaming like a ciborium.

He advanced toward Léon, and with that oily, benevolent smile that clerics adopt when they catechize children:

"Monsieur is perhaps not from around here? Monsieur would like to see the curiosities of the church?"

"No," said the other.

At first he walked down the side aisles. Then he went back to look out on the square. Emma had not arrived. He went back up into the choir.

The nave was reflected in the full holy-water fonts, as were the beginnings of the arches and parts of the stained-glass windows. But the reflection of the painted windows, breaking off at the border of the marble, continued further on, on the stone floors, like a multicolored carpet. The full daylight outside stretched into the church in three enormous rays, through the three open doorways. Now and then at the upper end, a sacristan passed, performing that sideways genuflection before the altar made by the devout when they're in a hurry. The crystal chandeliers hung motionless. In the choir, a silver lamp was burning; and, from the side chapels, the darker parts of the church, sometimes arose a sound like sighs, along with the sound of a grate being closed, its echo reverberating under the high vaults.

Léon was walking near the walls at a measured pace. Never had life seemed so good to him. She was going to come soon, charming and nervous, glancing over her shoulder to see who was looking at her—and with her flounced dress, her gold lorgnette, her thin boots, with all those elegances that he had not yet tasted, and with the indescribable allure of virtue seduced. The church, like a gigantic boudoir, spread out around her; the arches bent forward to receive in the shadows the confession of her love: the windows shone resplendent to illuminate her face, and the censers were going to burn so that she would appear like an angel in the perfumed smoke.

However, she did not come. He sat down on a chair, and his eyes encountered a blue window depicting boatmen carrying baskets. He gazed at it at length, attentively, counting the scales on the fish and the buttonholes in the doublets, while his thoughts wandered off in search of Emma.

The verger, off to the side, was inwardly indignant about this individual who gave himself permission to admire the cathedral on his own. It seemed to him a monstrous thing to do, a kind of theft, and almost a sacrilege.

But then a rustling of silk over the stones, the border of a hat, a black cape . . . It was she! Léon got up and rushed to meet her.

Emma was pale. She was walking rapidly.

"Read this!" she said, handing him some paper. "Oh! No."

And she abruptly pulled back her hand, in order to go into the chapel of the Virgin where, kneeling down against a chair, she began to pray.

The young man was annoyed by this fantastical piety; but then he felt there was a certain charm in the way she looked, lost in prayer like an Andalusian marquise right in the middle of their rendezvous; but then he quickly grew bored with it, because she didn't stop.

Emma was praying, or rather trying hard to pray, hoping that some sudden sense of resolution would come down to her from the sky; and, trying to attract some divine intervention, she filled her eyes with the tabernacle's splendors, breathing in the perfume of the white flowers blooming in the large vases, and taking in the church's silence, which, however, only made the tumult in her heart grow all the more.

She got back up, and they started to leave, when the verger rapidly approached them, saying:

"Madame is perhaps not from around here? Madame would like to see the curiosities of the church?"

"No!" exclaimed the clerk.

"But why not?" she asked.

For in her tottering virtue, she was trying to hang on to the Virgin, the sculptures, the tombs—to anything.

Then, so as to proceed in the proper order, the verger took them back to the entrance near the square where he pointed with his cane at a large circle of black stones with neither inscription nor carving:

"That," he said majestically, "is the circumference of the beautiful Amboise bell. It weighed forty thousand pounds. It had no equal in all of Europe. The workman who forged it died of joy . . . "

"Let's leave," said Léon.

The old man started off again; then, coming back to the Virgin's chapel, he extended his arms in an all-embracing gesture, and with more pride than a country squire showing off his fruit trees to you:

"This simple stone covers Pierre de Brézé, lord of Varenne and of Brissac, grand marshal of Poitou and governor of Normandy, who died in the battle of Montlhery, July 16, 1465."

Léon, biting his lips, was fuming.

"And to the right, this gentleman encased in iron, on a prancing horse, is his grandson Louis de Brézé, lord of Breval and of Montchauvet, Count de Maulevrier, Baron de Mauny, chamberlain to the king, Knight of the Order, and likewise governor of Normandy, who died July 23, 1531, on a Sunday as the inscription reports; and below, this figure about to descend into his tomb represents the same. It would be impossible, would it not, to find a more perfect representation of our mortality?"

Madame Bovary took out her lorgnette. Léon, motionless, watched her, no longer even trying to say a single word, or make a single gesture, so discouraged was he under this double assault of chatter and indifference.

The eternal guide continued:

"Near to him, this woman on her knees weeping is his wife, Diane de Poitiers, Countess of Brézé, Duchess of Valentinois, born in 1499 and dead in 1566; and to the left, the one holding an infant, is the holy Virgin. And now, turn to this side: here are the tombs of the Amboise family. Two of them were cardinals and archbishops of Rouen. That one was a minister under Louis XII. He did a great deal of good for the cathedral. In his will, he left thirty thousand gold écus for the poor."

And without stopping, talking the whole time, he pushed them into a chapel full of railings and moved a few of them aside, revealing a sort of block that might once have been an ill-made statue.

"This once decorated," he said with a lengthy groan, "the tomb of Richard the Lion-Hearted,[5] King of England and Duke of Normandy. It was the Calvinists, Monsieur, who reduced it to this state. Out of spite, they buried it in the ground under the episcopal seat of Monsignor. See, here is the door that Monsignor uses to return to his home. Let us go on now to see the Gargoyle windows."

5. Richard the Lion-Hearted (b.1157), who was king of England from 1189 to 1199, when he died at the siege of the castle of Châlus.

But Léon suddenly drew a silver piece from his pocket and seized Emma by the arm. The verger stood there stupefied, unable to understand this untimely generosity, while there were so many things left to see. So he called them back:

"Monsieur! The steeple! The steeple!"[6]

"Thank you anyway," Léon said.

"Monsieur is making a mistake! It is four hundred and forty feet high, just nine less than the great pyramid of Egypt. It is entirely cast iron, and it . . . ."

Léon fled; for he felt that his love, which for two hours now had been as immobilized as the stones in the church, was going to evaporate like smoke and go up that sort of truncated funnel, that oblong cage, that open chimney that rises up so grotesquely from the cathedral like the outlandish fantasy of some overly imaginative metal worker.

"Where are we going, then?" she asked.

Without replying, he continued to walk rapidly, and Madame Bovary had already moistened her finger in the holy water font when they heard a great puffing coming up behind them, punctuated by the tapping of a cane. Léon turned around.

"Monsieur!"

"What?"

And he recognized the verger, holding about twenty heavy, bound volumes in his arms, balancing them against his chest. These were books *that discussed the cathedral*.

"Imbecile!" Léon muttered, hurrying out of the church.

There was a little urchin playing outside on the square:

"Go and find me a cab!"

The child shot off like a bullet down the Rue Quatre-Vents; then they stood face to face for a few minutes, a little uncomfortable.

"Oh, Léon! . . . Really . . . I don't know . . . if I should . . . !"

She whimpered. Then, in a more serious tone:

"It's very improper, don't you know that?"

"How so?" the clerk replied. "They do it in Paris!"

And that word, like an irresistible argument, convinced her.

However, the cab did not come. Léon was afraid she might go back into the church. At last the cab appeared.

"At least go out through the north door!" the verger shouted to them, still standing in the doorway, "so as to see the *Resurrection*, the *Last Judgment*, the *Paradise*, the *King David*, and the *Condemned* in the flames of hell."

"Where to, Monsieur?" asked the driver.

"Wherever you like!" said Léon, pushing Emma into the cab.

And the slow-moving vehicle set off.

It went down the Rue Grand-Pont, crossed the Place des Arts, the Quai Napoléon, the Pont Neuf, and stopped short in front of the statue of Pierre Corneille.

"Go on!" came a voice from the inside. The cab started off again, and when it reached the Carrefour LaFayette, it sped up on the descent, and entered the train station at a full gallop.

---

6. Added to the cathedral of Rouen, which was built in the Gothic style in stages from the 13th to the 16th century, it is a high cast-iron spire (485 feet), generally considered a tasteless disfigurement. Construction was begun in 1824 but not finished until 1876.

"No, keep going!" the same voice cried.

The cab drove through the city gate and soon, arriving at the Cours, trotted quietly beneath the tall elm trees. The cab driver wiped his forehead, put his leather cap between his legs, and drove the cab beyond the side alley by the meadow, along the riverside.

It drove along the river, on the towing path paved with cobblestones, and then proceeded for a long time toward the Oyssel side, beyond the islands.

But then suddenly it turned and crossed Quatremares, Sotteville, Grande-Chaussée, Rue d'Elbeuf, and then made its third stop in front of the botanical gardens.

"Keep going!" said the voice inside, even more furiously.

And so, taking up its course again, it passed by Saint-Sever, by the Quaides Curandiers, the Quai aux Meules, once more past the bridge, by the Place du Champ-de-Mars and behind the hospital gardens, where old men in black coats stroll in the sun, all along the terrace green with ivy. It went back up the Boulevard Bouvreuil, crossed the Boulevard Cauchoise, and then crossed the whole of Mont-Riboudet as far as the Deville hills.

It returned; and then, with no plan and no direction, it wandered. People saw it in Saint-Pol, at Lescure, at Mont Gargan, at Rouge-Mare and the Place du Gaillardbois; on the Rue Maladrerie, Rue Dinanderie, in front of Saint-Romain, Saint-Vivien, Saint-Maclou, Saint-Nicaise—in front of the Customs—at Basse-Vieille-Tour, at the Trois-Pipes, and at the Cimetière Monumental. From time to time the cab driver, from his seat, would cast desperate glances at the passing cafés. He could not understand what rage for locomotion possessed these individuals who would not consider stopping. He did try sometimes, and as soon as he did he heard angry exclamations from behind him. Then he lashed his sweating nags anew, but without caring anymore when they bumped up against things here and there; he was entirely demoralized, and almost weeping with thirst, with fatigue, and depression.

And on the harbor, among the wagons and barrels, and in the streets and on the corners, the townspeople stared in amazement at this sight, so unusual in the provinces, of a cab that kept reappeaing, its blinds drawn, shut up more tightly than a tomb, and tossing about like a ship.

Once, in the middle of the day, in the open countryside, at the time when the sun beat most fiercely against the old silver-plated lanterns, a naked hand emerged from beneath the little yellow-canvas blinds, and it tossed out some torn-up scraps of paper, which dispersed in the wind and alit further on, like white butterflies, on a field of red clover all in bloom.

And then, about six o'clock, the cab stopped in a back street in the Beauvoisine Quarter, and a woman got down from it, walking with her veil down and without looking back.

CHAPTER 2

When she reached the inn, Madame Bovary was surprised not to see the *Hirondelle*. Hivert, who had waited fifty-three minutes for her, had given up and gone without her.

There was nothing forcing her to leave; but she had promised that she would come back that night. And Charles was waiting for her; and she already felt in her heart that cowardly docility that is, for a great many women, both the punishment accepted and the payment made for adultery.

She quickly packed her bags, paid the bill, got a cab in the courtyard, and urging the driver to hurry, asking him every minute about the time and the miles they had covered, finally caught up with the *Hirondelle* on the outskirts of Quincampoix.

As soon as she had settled in her seat, she closed her eyes and didn't open them until they reached the foot of the hill, where she saw Félicité in the distance, standing in front of the blacksmith's shop, keeping watch for her. Hivert stopped the horses, and the kitchen maid, standing on tiptoe to reach the coach window, said mysteriously:

"Madame, you must go right away to Monsieur Homais' house. It's for something urgent."

The village was as quiet as it always was. There were little pink, steaming mounds at the street corners, because it was jam-making time, and everybody in Yonville was preparing the year's supply at the same time. But most impressive was the much larger mound in front of the pharmacist's shop, surpassing all the others with the superiority that a laboratory must have over ordinary ovens, a general demand over individual needs.

She went in. The big armchair was turned over, and the *Rouen Lantern* was spread out on the floor between the two pestles. She pushed open the hall door; and in the middle of the kitchen, among the brown jars full of currants, powdered and lump sugar, the scales on the table, the pans on the fire, she saw the entire Homais family, both big and small, wearing aprons reaching up to their chins and holding forks in their hands. Justin was standing there, his head lowered, and the pharmacist was shouting:

"Who told you to go get it from the capharnaüm?"

"What is it? What's the matter?"

"What's the matter?" the pharmacist responded. "We're making preserves: they're cooking; but things were about to boil over because there's too much heat, and I asked for another pan. And then he, out of feeble-mindedness, out of laziness, went to the laboratory and took the key, hanging on its hook, to the capharnaüm!"

That is what the pharmacist called a little room under the roof full of the tools and materials of his trade. He often spent long hours alone there, labeling, decanting, and repacking; and he thought of it not as a simple storeroom but as a veritable sanctuary from which would emerge afterwards, from his own hands, all the sorts of pills, boluses, tisanes, lotions, and potions that would make their way into the world and enhance his renown. No one else ever set foot in there; and he had such veneration for the place that he even swept it himself. Finally, if the pharmacy, open to anyone, was the place where he displayed his pride, the capharnaüm was the refuge where, egotistically secluding himself, Homais delighted in indulging his personal obsessions; and thus Justin's thoughtlessness seemed to him to be a monstrous irreverence; and redder than the currants, he repeated:

"Yes, the capharnaüm! The key that locks away the acids and the caustic alkalis! In order to find a spare pan! A pan with a lid! One I may never use! Everything is crucial in the delicate operations of our art! But, what the devil! You have to make distinctions and not employ something destined for pharmaceutical use for a domestic one! It's as if you were to carve a fowl with a scalpel, as if a magistrate . . . "

"Calm down!" Madame Homais said.

And Athalie, tugging at his coat:

"Papa! Papa!"

"No, leave me alone!" said the pharmacist. "Leave me alone! Goodness! Might as well be a grocer, I swear! Go on, go on! Respect nothing! Break! Smash! Let the leeches out! Burn the all-heal! Pickle the cucumbers in the window display jars, rip up the bandages!"

"But you had . . . ," Emma said.

"In a minute! Do you know what you exposed yourself to? Didn't you see anything, in the corner, to the left, on the third shelf? Speak, respond, say something!"

"I d-don't know," the boy stammered.

"Ah! You don't know! Well, I know! You saw a bottle of blue glass, sealed with yellow wax, containing a white powder, on which I had written: *Dangerous!* And do you know what was inside? Arsenic! And you went and touched it! And you took a pan that was right next to it!"

"Right next to it!" cried Madame Homais, wringing her hands. "Arsenic? You could have poisoned us all!"

And the children all began to cry, as if they already felt hideous pains in their entrails.

"Or perhaps poisoned a patient!" the pharmacist continued. "Do you want to see me hauled to court and put in the criminal's dock? See me dragged up to the gallows? Don't you see the care I take in handling my materials, even though I'm thoroughly used to all this? Sometimes I even frighten myself when I think about my responsibility! Because the government persecutes us, and the absurd legislation that rules us is a veritable Damoclean sword over our heads!"

Emma was no longer thinking of what she had come for, and the pharmacist raged on breathlessly:

"This is how you repay all the good that has been done for you! This is my recompense for all the paternal cares I've lavished on you! Because without me, where would you be? What would you do? Who gives you your food, education, clothing, and all the means you need to someday become an honorable figure in the ranks of society? But for that you have to pull hard on the oars, and you have to acquire, as they say, calluses on your hands. *Fabricando fit faber, age quod agis.*"[7]

He was so exasperated that he was speaking in Latin. He would have broken into Chinese and Greenlandish if he had known those languages; for he found himself in one of those crises where the entire soul opens up and reveals vaguely what is hidden within it—like the ocean in a tempest, when it opens itself up to reveal everything, from the seaweed on its shores to the sands at the bottom of its abysses.

And he went on:

"I'm beginning to seriously regret taking you into my charge! I would have certainly done better to have left you to rot in the poverty and filth you were

7. The artisan becomes proficient through practice; practice what you are supposed to do (Latin).

born in! You'll never be good for anything except herding cattle! You have absolutely no scientific aptitude! You barely know how to affix a label! And there you are living in my house, like a mooching cleric, in clover, pampering yourself!

But Emma, turning to Madame Homais:

"They said I should come here . . . "

"Oh! My God," the pharmacist's wife interrupted with a sad expression, "how can I tell you? . . . It's a terrible thing!"

She couldn't finish. The pharmacist was thundering:

"Empty it! Clean it! Take it back! And hurry up!" And gripping Justin by the collar of his smock, he caused a book to tumble out of his pocket.

The boy bent down. But Homais was faster and, having picked up the book, he stared at it, wide eyed, mouth agape.

"*Conjugal . . . Love!*" he said, slowly drawing out the two words. "Ah! Very good! Very good! Very nice! And with pictures! . . . Oh, this is too much!"

Madame Homais stepped forward.

"No—don't touch it!"

The children wanted to look at the pictures.

"Get out!" he said imperiously.

And they went out.

At first he walked up and down the room, taking big steps, keeping the volume open between his fingers, rolling his eyes, choking, huffing and puffing, apoplectic. Then he walked straight up to his pupil and, planting himself right in front of him, his arms crossed:

"So you have all the vices, do you, you little wretch? Take care, you're on a steep path! You haven't thought what it could do, this vile book, if it fell into the hands of my children, kindled a spark in their minds, tarnished Athalie's purity, corrupted Napoléon! He's already built like a man. Can you be sure, at least, that they have not read it? Can you guarantee me . . . "

"But please, Monsieur," Emma said, "you had something to tell me?"

"Yes, that's correct, Madame. Your father-in-law is dead!"

In fact Charles' father had died suddenly two nights before, from an attack of apoplexy, right after getting up from the table; and out of an excess of concern for Emma's sensibilities, Charles had asked Monsieur Homais to break the horrible news to her gently.

He had carefully thought out his phrasing, rounding it and polishing it and making it rhythmical; it was a masterpiece of prudence and smooth transitions, of subtle and delicate wording; but anger had driven out rhetoric.

Emma, abandoning hope of getting any details, left the pharmacy; for Monsieur Homais had resumed his vituperations. He was calming himself, though, and now he was growling in more paternal tones, while fanning himself with his cap.

"It's not that I entirely disapprove of such a book! The author was a doctor. There are certain scientific aspects of the subject that are not so bad for a man to know about, even, I would dare to say, that a man should know about. But later, later! At least wait until you're a man yourself, and your character has been formed."

At Emma's knock on the door, Charles, who had been waiting for her, came forward with his arms open, saying to her with tears in his voice:

"Oh, my dearest one . . . "

And he bent forward gently to kiss her. But when his lips touched her, the memory of the other one seized hold of her, and she passed her hand over her face with a shudder.

Still, she did manage to say:

"Yes, I know . . . I know . . . "

He showed her the letter in which his mother narrated the events without any sentimental hypocrisy. She only regretted that her husband had not received the aid of religion, having died in Doudeville, in the street, outside the door of a café, after a patriotic celebration with some of his old officer friends.

Emma gave the letter back to him; then, at dinner, for the sake of appearances, she pretended to have no appetite. But when he insisted, she resolutely forced herself to eat while Charles, across the table, sat motionless and dejected.

From time to time, lifting up his head, he would give her a long look full of distress. Once he sighed:

"I would have liked to see him again!"

She said nothing. Finally, seeing that she had to make some reply:

"How old was he, your father?"

"Fifty-eight!"

"Ah!"

And that was all.

Fifteen minutes later he added:

"And my poor mother? What will become of her now?"

She made a gesture signifying she didn't know.

Seeing her so taciturn, Charles assumed she was emotionally overcome, which touched him, and he forced himself to say nothing more, for fear of making her grieving worse. And then, shaking off his own sadness:

"Did you have a good time yesterday?" he asked.

"Yes."

When the tablecloth was removed, Bovary remained sitting, as did Emma; and the longer she looked at him, the monotony of the spectacle banished bit by bit all the pity from her heart. She thought he seemed puny, weak, a nobody—in short, an impoverished man in every respect. How could she get rid of him? What an interminable evening! Something as stupefying as opium fumes came over her.

They heard the sharp sound of a stick on the floor in the entry. It was Hippolyte, bringing Madame's bags in. In order to set them down, he painfully executed a ninety-degree turn with his stump.

"He doesn't even think about it anymore!" she said to herself as she watched the poor devil, whose thick red hair was wet with sweat.

Bovary was trying to find a coin in the bottom of his purse; and without appearing to comprehend what humiliation there was for him simply in the presence of the man standing there, like the personification of his incurable ineptitude:

"Say, that's a pretty bouquet you have!" he said, noticing on the mantel the violets Léon had given her.

"Yes," she said indifferently; "it's a bouquet I bought earlier . . . from a beggar."

Charles picked up the violets, refreshing his red, tearful eyes against them, and inhaled their scent delicately. She quickly pulled them out of his hand and went off to put them in a glass of water.

The next day, Madame Bovary senior arrived. She and her son wept a great deal. Emma, on the pretext of having chores to do, disappeared.

The next day, they had to discuss the mourning details. Taking their work-boxes, they went to sit in the arbor near the riverside.

Charles was thinking about his father, and he was surprised to be feeling so much affection for the man who, up until now, he would have said meant little to him. Madame Bovary senior was thinking about her husband. The worst days of the past now seemed enviable to her. Everything was erased under the instinctive regret of such a long habit of life; and from time to time, while she was working with her needle, a big tear would descend along her nose and hang there suspended for a moment. Emma was thinking that scarcely forty-eight hours before, they were together, far from this world, totally intoxicated with each other, unable to get enough of each other. She tried to recall the smallest details of that vanished day. But the presence of the mother-in-law and the husband got in the way. She would have liked to hear nothing and see nothing in order to preserve the memory of her love, which was fading, no matter how hard she tried, beneath external sensations.

She was taking out the lining of a dress, the pieces of which were strewn around her; Charles' mother was working with her scissors without looking up, and Charles, with his cloth slippers and the old brown jacket that served him as a dressing gown, stood there with his hands in his pockets, saying nothing; near them, Berthe, in a little white apron, was scraping at the sand in the path with a little spade.

Suddenly they saw Monsieur Lheureux, the dry-goods merchant, coming in through the gate.

He came to offer his services, *with regard to these tragic circumstances.* Emma replied that she thought they wouldn't need anything from him. The merchant did not accept this as a defeat.

"I do apologize," he said, "but I wanted to talk about something privately with you."

Then, in a lowered voice:

"It's about that business . . . you understand?"

Charles reddened to the tips of his ears.

"Oh—yes! Of course."

And in some confusion, turning to his wife:

"Do you think you could . . . my dear?"

She seemed to understand, for she got up, and Charles said to his mother:

"It's nothing! Probably just some little household matter."

He by no means wanted her to know about the promissory note, fearing what she would say about it.

When he and Emma were alone, Monsieur Lheureux began by openly congratulating her on her inheritance, and then went on to talk about inconsequential things, the fruit trees, the harvest, his own state of health, which, he said, was *always just up and down, sometimes good, sometimes not.* But to tell her the truth, he was working like five hundred devils, and even so, no matter what people thought about him, he could barely afford to butter his bread.

Emma let him talk on. She had been so massively bored these last two days!

"And everything is better with you?" he continued. "Good lord, I saw your husband in quite a state! He's a good sort, even though he and I had some difficulties."

She asked him which ones, because Charles had concealed from her their dispute over her purchases.

"You know perfectly well, don't you?" said Lheureux. "It was about your little whims, all that traveling gear."

He had shaded his eyes with his hat, and now, his hands behind his back, smiling and making a whistling sound, he looked her right in the face in an insolent manner. Did he suspect something? She stood there, paralyzed by all sorts of anxieties. But finally he went on:

"We've made up, and I came to propose another arrangement to him."

This was to renew the promissory note Bovary had signed. Naturally, the doctor would do what seemed best to him; but he needn't torture himself over it, especially now when he was going to have all sorts of other problems.

"And it might be even better for him to give it all over to someone else—you for example; with a power of attorney, it would be easy enough, and then you and I could take care of our own little dealings together . . ."

She didn't understand. He said no more. And then, returning to his business, Lheureux declared that Madame simply couldn't do without buying something from him. He would send her some black barège, about twelve meters, enough to make a dress.

"The one you have there is fine for the house. But you need another one for paying visits. I noticed it the minute I came in. I've got the American eye!"[8]

He didn't send the material; he brought it himself. Then he came back to take the measurements; he came back on other pretexts, always trying to make himself amiable, helpful, being her vassal, as Homais would have said, and always slipping in a few words to Emma about the power of attorney. He didn't say a word about the promissory note. She never thought about it; at the beginning of her convalescence, Charles had told her something about it, but there was so much confusion in her head then that she didn't remember it anymore. Besides, she was very careful not to bring up any topics related to money; this was a surprise to Charles' mother, who attributed the change in her personality to the religious sentiments she had developed when she was sick.

But as soon as she was gone, Emma wasted no time in making Bovary marvel at her good practical sense. It would be necessary for them to acquire information, verify mortgages, see if there should be an auction or a liquidation. She threw technical terms around almost randomly, pronouncing grand-sounding terms like 'order,' 'the future,' and 'foresight,' and she always exaggerated the complexity of the inheritance: so much so that one day she showed him the template for a general authorization "to manage and administer his business concerns, oversee all loans, sign and endorse all bills, pay all sums due," et cetera. She had profited from Lheureux's lessons.

---

8. To have "the American eye" (l'oeil américain) is to have a sharp eye, not to miss a thing. The idiom came from the popularity, in France, of James Fenimore Cooper's novels and their depiction of the Native American's hunting and tracking prowess [translator's note].

Charles naively asked where the form had come from.

"From Monsieur Guillaumin."

And with all the coolness in the world, she added:

"I personally don't trust him all that much. Notaries have such a bad reputation! Maybe we should consult . . . But we only know . . . well, nobody!"

"Except for Léon . . . ," Charles replied thoughtfully.

But it would be difficult to make it all clear through letters. Then she offered to make the trip herself. He thanked her but refused to let her go to all that trouble. She insisted. It was a virtual battle of politenesses. At last, she exclaimed in a tone of playful rebellion:

"No, please, I will go!"

"You're so good!" he said, kissing her on the forehead.

The very next day, she was in the *Hirondelle* on her way to Rouen to consult with Monsieur Léon; and she stayed there three days.

CHAPTER 3

They were three full, exquisite, splendid days, a real honeymoon.

They stayed at the *Hotel de Boulogne*, on the harbor. And they stayed in, curtains shut, doors closed, with flowers on the floor and iced syrups, which they had delivered in the mornings.

Toward evening, they took a covered boat and went to have their dinner on one of the islands.

It was the time of evening when the shipyards echo with the sound of caulking mallets striking against ships' hulls. Smoke from the tar escaped upward through the trees, and there were large, fat drops of tar on the river, undulating on the water in the purple of sunset, looking like floating plaques of Florentine bronze.

Their boat moved down among the moored vessels, whose long slanting cables grazed the bottom of theirs.

The sound of the city gradually faded away—the wheels of the carts, the uproar of shouting voices, the yapping dogs on the decks of the ships. She untied her bonnet, and they landed on their island.

They sat down in the low-ceilinged room of a tavern, which had black fishnets hanging at the door. They ate fried smelts, and cream and cherries. They lay down on the grass; they kissed in the shade, under the poplars; and they would have liked, like two Robinson Crusoes, to live forever on this little island, which seemed to them, in their bliss, to be the most beautiful place on earth. It was not the first time that they had seen trees, a blue sky, meadows, that they heard water flowing and the wind rustling the leaves—but they had certainly never before admired all these things in this way, as if nature had not existed before, or as if it had only begun to be beautiful since the fulfillment of their desires.

At night, they returned. Their boat hugged the islands' shorelines. They remained in the back, both of them hidden in shadow, without speaking. The squared oars resounded in the iron oarlocks; and in the stillness, the sound seemed to mark time like a beating metronome, while the rudder trailing behind never ceased its gentle splashing in the water.

Once, the moon appeared; it didn't take long before they were making fine phrases, finding the orb melancholy and filled with poetry; Emma even began to sing:

"One night, do you recall, when we were sailing," et cetera.[9]

Her harmonious but weak voice was lost among the waves; and the wind carried off the trills that Léon heard passing by him, like the beating of wings.

She sat facing him, leaning on the partition, the moonlight coming in through one of the open shutters. Her black dress, spread out fan-like around her, made her thinner, made her taller. Her head was raised, her hands joined, her eyes fixed on the sky. Sometimes the shadow of the willow trees would hide her completely, and then she would reappear suddenly, like a vision, in the light of the moon.

Léon, sitting on the floor next to her, found a scarlet silk ribbon under his hand.

The boatman looked at it and concluded:

"Ah! Maybe it's from the party I was rowing the other day. A whole group of jokers, gentlemen and ladies, with cakes, champagne, instruments, and everything you could imagine. There was one of them especially, a tall, good-looking man with a small moustache, who was really funny! And they all were saying: 'Come on, tell us another one ..., Adolphe ..., Dodolphe,' I think it was."

She shuddered.

"Is something wrong?" Léon said, drawing closer to her.

"Oh, it's nothing! Probably just the cool night air."

"And he sure didn't lack for lady friends either," the old boatman added quietly, thinking he was paying the stranger a compliment.

Then, spitting in his hands, he took up the oars again.

Still they had to part! Their good-byes were sorrowful. He should send his letters to her care of Madame Rolet; and she gave him such precise instructions about the double envelope that he greatly admired her shrewdness as a lover.

"So, you can promise me that everything's all right?" she said during their final kiss.

"Yes, of course it is!"

"But why," he thought afterwards, as he was walking back through the streets alone, "is she so anxious to get that power of attorney?"

CHAPTER 4

Léon soon began to adopt a superior attitude around his friends, avoiding their company, and he began to neglect his work completely.

He waited for her letters; he reread them. He wrote to her. He called her image up in his mind with all the strength of his desire and of his memories. His desire to see her again, rather than diminishing in her absence, grew so much that on Saturday morning he escaped from the office.

When, from the summit of the hill, he saw the church spire in the valley below with its tin flag turning in the wind, he felt that delight combining triumphant vanity and egotistical sentimentality that millionaires must feel when they return to visit their old village.

9. The beginning of Alphonse de Lamartine's *The Lake*.

He went to prowl around her house. A light was shining in the kitchen. He looked for her shadow behind the curtains. No one was there.

Madame Lefrançois, when she saw him, let out a series of loud exclamations, and she thought he was "taller and thinner," while Artémise, on the contrary, found him "stouter and darker."

He ate in the little room just as he used to, but alone, without the tax collector; for Binet, *sick and tired* of waiting for the *Hirondelle's* arrival, had definitively moved his dinner time up by an hour, and now, though he dined precisely at five o'clock, he still often complained that *the miserable old clock was slow.*

Léon, however, eventually made up his mind; he went to knock on the doctor's door. Madame was in her room, and didn't come down for a quarter of an hour. Monsieur seemed thrilled to see him; but he didn't leave the house all evening, nor the next day either.

He saw her alone, that next evening, very late, behind the garden, in the lane—in the lane, where she met the other one! It was storming, and they talked beneath an umbrella, in the flashing of the lightning.

Their separation was becoming intolerable.

"I'd rather die!" Emma said.

She was writhing in his arms, weeping.

"Farewell! . . . Farwell! . . . When will I see you again?"

They turned back and embraced each other again; and that was when she promised him she would somehow find a permanent way of seeing him freely, at least once a week, she was certain of it. Emma was full of hope: some money was going to be coming to her.

And so she bought a pair of yellow curtains with wide stripes for her bedroom, which Monsieur Lheureux had declared were a bargain; she thought about a new carpet, and Lheureux, affirming that "it was the easiest thing in the world," politely took it upon himself to get her one. She couldn't bring herself to say no to his offers anymore. She sent for him twenty times a day, and he dropped whatever he was doing without so much as a murmur. No one could understand at all why Madame Rolet had breakfast with her every day and even came to visit her privately.

This was the period—that is, around the beginning of winter—when she was taken with a grand passion for music.

One evening when Charles was listening to her play, she restarted the same piece four times in a row, becoming more annoyed each time, while he, unable to tell the difference, cried:

"Bravo! . . . Very good! . . . There's nothing wrong with that! Go on!"

"Oh! No, it's terrible! My fingers are rusty."

The next day, he begged her *to play him something again.*

"Very well, to please you!"

And Charles admitted that she had regressed a bit. She hit wrong notes, smeared notes together; then, stopping short:

"Oh, that's enough! I really ought to take lessons; but . . . "

She bit her lips, and added:

"At twenty francs a time, that's too much!"

"Yes, actually . . . a bit . . . ," Charles said with a stupid giggle. "But it seems to me that a person might be able to do it for less; because there are some teachers who aren't famous as artists but who are often better than the celebrities."

"Find them," said Emma.

The next day when he came back home, he gave her a cunning look, and couldn't keep himself from saying to her:

"You can be so stubborn sometimes! I was at Barfeuchères today. Well! Madame Liégeard assured me that her three daughters, at Miséricorde, are taking lessons for fifty sous a time, and from a well-known teacher to boot!"

She shrugged her shoulders, and did not open her piano any more.

But whenever she passed by it (if Bovary were nearby), she would sigh:

"Ah, my poor piano!"

And when visitors came to see her, she never failed to inform them that she had given up music and couldn't take it up again now for important reasons. Then they would pity her. What a shame it was! She had such a fine talent! They even spoke about it to Bovary. They shamed him, especially the pharmacist:

"You're making a mistake! Natural talents should never be allowed to lie fallow! And besides, think, my friend, that by engaging your wife in study, you'll be saving money later on your child's musical education! I've always believed mothers ought to instruct their children themselves. It's an idea of Rousseau's, perhaps a little too modern still, but it will be triumphant in the end, I'm sure of it, like maternal breastfeeding, and vaccination."

So Charles once again raised the question of the piano. Emma responded bitterly, saying it would be better to sell it. That old piano, which had so pleased her vanity and given her so much satisfaction in the past—for Bovary, seeing it go was like seeing some part of her commit suicide.

"If you wanted . . . ," he said, "to take a lesson from time to time, it might not be all that ruinous after all."

"But lessons," she replied, "are only worthwhile if you follow through with them."

And that is how she came to obtain permission from her husband to go to the city once a week to meet her lover. At the end of a month, everyone noticed that she had made considerable progress.

CHAPTER 5

It was Thursday. She got up, and she dressed herself silently to avoid waking Charles, who would have made some objections that she was getting ready too early. Then she paced up and down; she placed herself at the window and kept an eye on the square. The early dawn was creeping in among the pillars of the marketplace, and she could begin to read the large block letters of the sign on the pharmacist's house, its shutters still closed.

When the clock read seven-fifteen, she went to the *Golden Lion*, where Artémise, yawning, came to open the door for her. She also swept out the ashes from the fire for Madame. Emma stayed in the kitchen alone. From time to time, she would walk out. Hivert, without hurrying, was harnessing his horses while listening to Madame Lefrançois who, poking her night-capped head out through the grill, was giving him a list of errands and instructions that would have befuddled any other man. Emma tapped the soles of her boots against the courtyard's paving stones.

At last, after he had eaten his soup, put on his driving cloak, lit his pipe, and taken hold of his whip, he would calmly get up into his seat.

The *Hirondelle* started off at a slow pace and, for the first mile or so, stopped repeatedly to pick up the travelers who were standing behind their gates by the roadside, watching for it. Those who had reserved a place the night before kept it waiting; some were even still in bed inside their houses; Hivert would call them, shout, curse, and then get down from his seat and go knock loudly on their doors. The wind whistled through the cracked windows.

But when the four benches were filled, the coach rolled off, the rows of apple trees passed by, and the road, between its two long ditches filled with yellow water, climbed up continually and stretched out to the horizon.

Emma knew it from one end to the other; she knew that after the meadow there was a signpost, then an elm tree, a barn, the hut for the road repairman; sometimes she would close her eyes for a time to try to surprise herself. But she never lost her clear sense of exactly how much distance remained.

At last the brick houses grew closer together, the earth sounded different beneath the wheels, the *Hirondelle* slipped between gardens where, through openings, she could see statues, a periwinkle, some clipped yew trees and a swing. Then, all of a sudden, the city appeared.

Sloping downward like an amphitheater and drowned in the fog, it stretched out confusedly beyond the bridges. Then, open countryside ascended from it in a monotonous stretch until, in the far distance, it touched the vague line of the pale sky. Seen from above like this, the landscape was motionless as a painting; the ships at anchor were massed in one corner; the river made a round curve around the foot of the green hills, and the islands, oblong shaped, seemed like great black fish fixed motionless on the water. The factory chimneys pushed immense brown plumes up and out, plumes that dissolved in the wind at their tops. The rumbling noise of the foundries mixed with the sharp chimes ringing from the churches rising up through the mist. The leafless trees on the boulevards formed patches of violet undergrowth amid the houses, and the roofs, all gleaming with rain, gave off unequal reflections, depending on the height of the buildings in that section of town. Sometimes a gust of wind would carry the clouds off toward Saint-Catherine's Hill, like aerial waves silently breaking against a cliff.

There was something dizzying for her in the thought of those lives massed below, and her heart swelled greatly, as if the hundred and twenty thousand hearts beating down there had sent forth all at once the hot breath of the passions she attributed to them. Her love grew larger in the face of this vastness, and it expanded itself to encompass the tumult of that vague humming sound rising up toward her. She poured it out on the squares, the public walks, the streets; and the old Norman city enlarged before her eyes into a boundless capital, like a Babylon she was about to enter. She leaned out the coach window, holding on with both hands, and breathed in the breeze; the three horses broke into a gallop. The stones made grating sounds in the mud, the coach swayed, and Hivert from afar hailed the carts on the road, while the townsfolk who had spent the night in the Bois Guillaume were descending the hill sedately in their small family carriages.

They came to a stop at the city gate; Emma took off her overshoes, put on a different pair of gloves, adjusted her shawl, and twenty paces farther on, she got down from the *Hirondelle*.

The city was just then awakening. Clerks in caps were cleaning the shop windows, and women with baskets on their hips were rhythmically hawking their wares on street corners. She walked along, eyes to the ground, staying close to the walls and smiling with pleasure under her lowered black veil.

For fear of being seen, she did not ordinarily take the shortest route. She plunged into dark alleys, and she emerged, sweating, at the bottom of the Rue Nationale, near the fountain there. This is the theater quarter, the district for taverns and whores. Often a wagon would pass near her, carrying some shaky piece of scenery. Waiters in aprons were scattering sand over the flagstones, between green shrubs. The area smelled of absinthe, cigars, and oysters.

She turned a corner; she recognized him by the curled hair escaping from beneath his hat.

Léon, on the sidewalk, would continue walking. She would follow him to the hotel; he would go up the steps, he would open the door, he would go in . . . and then, what an embrace!

And then words, after the kisses, would pour out. They would narrate all the irritations of their week, their fears, their anxieties over the letters; but now, all that was forgotten, and they would look at each other face to face, with sensuous laughter and tender names.

The bed was large, mahogany, boat-shaped. The heavy red silk curtains hung from the ceiling were bunched low by the headboard—and there was nothing in the world so beautiful as her dark hair and white skin set off against that deep red when, in a modest gesture, she would cross her naked arms and hide her face behind her hands.

The warm room with its discreet, muffling carpet, its playful ornaments, and its tranquil light seemed perfectly suited to passionate intimacy. The curtain rods ending in little arrows, their brass pegs, and the oversized balls on the andirons would flash and gleam when the sun came in. On the chimney, between the candelabra, there were two of those big pink shells in which you can hear the sea, when you hold them to your ear.

How they loved that good room full of joy, despite its somewhat faded splendor! They always found the furniture in its rightful place, and sometimes they found the hairpins that she had forgotten the previous Thursday, beneath the clock's pedestal. They would eat by the fireside, on a little table inlaid with rosewood. Emma would carve, serve him bits on his plate with every kind of flirtatious gesture; and she would give a loud, libertine laugh when the champagne foam overflowed the glass onto the rings on her fingers. They were so completely lost in the possession of each other that they thought of the place as their own home, the place in which they would live on until they died, like two spouses eternally young. They would say "our room," "our carpet," "our armchairs," and she even said "my slippers," referring to a gift from Léon in response to a whim of hers. The slippers were pink satin, with swan's-down borders. When she sat on his knees, her leg was too short to reach the floor, and it would dangle in the air; and the dainty little backless slipper would be held on only by the toes of her bare foot.

He was savoring for the first time in his life the inexpressible delicacies of feminine elegance. He had never encountered this refined language, this understated elegance of clothing, these poses like a sleeping dove. He marveled at the exaltation of her soul and the lace on her petticoat. And besides, was this not a *woman of the world*, and a married woman? In short, a real mistress?

Through her changing moods—by turns mystical or joyous, talkative, taciturn, exultant, nonchalant—she awakened in him a thousand desires, calling up instincts or memories. She was the woman in love from a thousand novels, the heroine of every drama, the vague *she* of all the volumes of poetry. On her shoulders, he found the amber coloring of the *odalisque bathing*; she had the long waist of medieval chatelaines; she also resembled the *pale woman of Barcelona*,[1] but above all these, she was an Angel!

Often, as he gazed at her, it seemed to him that his soul was escaping toward her, spreading, wavelike, around the contours of her face, and then descending, being pulled down into the whiteness of her breast.

He would sit on the floor in front of her; and with both his elbows on her knees, his face upturned, he would smile at her.

She would bend down toward him and murmur, as if suffocating in her passion:

"Oh, don't move! Don't speak! Look at me! There's something so sweet in your eyes, and it does me so much good!"

She would call him child:

"Child, do you love me?"

And she would scarcely hear his answer in the rush of his lips upward to her mouth.

On the clock there was a small bronze Cupid with a simpering smile, his arm crooked beneath a gilded garland. They had laughed at it many times; but when it was time for them to part, everything became serious.

Standing motionless, facing each other, they would repeat:

"Until Thursday! . . . Until Thursday!"

Suddenly she would take his head in her hands, kiss him quickly on the forehead while exclaiming "Farewell!" and then hurry to the stairs.

She would go to a hairdresser in the Rue de la Comédie to have her hair put in order. Night would be falling, and they would be lighting the gas lamps in the shop.

She could hear the theater bell calling the actors for the performance; and she could see, across the street, men with white faces and women in faded gowns going in the stage door.

It was hot in that little, cramped room, where the stove hummed amid the wigs and the pomades. The smell of the curling irons, along with the greasy hands handling her head, soon made her tired, and she would doze a little in her robe. Often, the man doing her hair would offer her tickets to the masked ball.

And then she would be on her way! She walked back up the streets; she arrived at the *Red Cross* inn; she would put her overshoes back on (which she had hidden under a bench that morning), and she would sink into her place among the impatient travelers. Some of them got out at the foot of the hill. She would remain alone in the coach.

At every bend, she could see the city lights more and more completely, as they formed a luminous vapor around the obscured houses. She would kneel on the cushions, and she would let her gaze wander over that dazzling light.

1. Pale woman of Barcelona (French). Alfred de Musset (1810–1857) frequently incarnates, for Flaubert, the type of stilted romantic sensibility he despises.

She would sob, call Léon's name, and send tender phrases out to him, along with kisses that were lost in the wind.

There was, on the hillside, a poor devil who wandered around with his cane, coming right up to the coaches. A pile of rags covered his shoulders, and a beat-up old beaver hat, round like a bowl, hid his face; but when he pulled it off, he revealed two blank, bloody orbits where there should have been eyelids. The flesh on his face peeled in red strips; and it oozed liquid matter that hardened into green scales as far down as his nose, whose black nostrils sniffed convulsively. To speak to you, he would throw his head back with an idiot's grin—and then the bluish pupils of his eyes, constantly rolling, would beat up against his temples, at the edge of an open wound.

He would sing a little song while he followed the coaches:

> Often the warmth of a beautiful day
> Makes a young girl dream of love.

And all the rest was birds, sunshine, and foliage.

Sometimes, he would appear suddenly right behind Emma, his head bared. She would recoil with a cry. Hivert would joke with him. He would suggest he open a booth at the Saint-Romain fair, or he would ask him with a laugh how his girlfriend was doing.

Often, they were moving along when his hat would fly into the coach through the window while he clung with his other arm to the footboard between the wheels spattering mud. His voice, feeble and quavering at first, would become shrill. It would echo through the night, like an indistinct lamentation over some vague distress; and coming to her across the ringing of bells, the murmur of the trees, and the rumblings of the empty vehicle, it had a far-off sound that overwhelmed Emma. It drove down into the depths of her soul like a whirlwind into an abyss and carried her along with it into a borderless, melancholy region. But Hivert, sensing a weight behind him, would lash the blind man off with sharp blows from his whip. The thong would slash into his wounds, and he would fall off into the mud with a howl.

Then the *Hirondelle* passengers would settle into sleep, some with their mouths open, some with their chins lowered, leaning against their neighbors' shoulders, or with their arm passed through the strap, swaying regularly with the jolting of the coach; and the reflection of the lantern, swinging outside, above the rumps of the horses, would penetrate the interior through the chocolate-colored calico curtains, casting blood-red shadows over all the motionless people. Emma, overwhelmed with sorrow, shivered beneath her clothing and felt her feet grow colder and colder, with death in her soul.

At home, Charles would be waiting; the *Hirondelle* was always late on Thursdays. At last, Madame arrived! She scarcely kissed the child. Dinner was not ready—but it didn't matter! She made excuses for the servant. Everything, it seemed, was now permitted to the girl.

Often her husband, noticing how pale she was, would ask if she didn't feel ill.

"No," Emma would say.

"But," he would continue, "you seem strange this evening."

"Oh, it's nothing! It's nothing!"

There were even some days when she would go directly up to her room immediately after arriving; and Justin, who happened to be there, walked around on tiptoes, more ingenious in serving her than the most excellent of maids. He would set out the matches, the candle, a book, lay out her night-dress, turn down the covers.

"Enough!" she would say. "That's fine; run along."

For he would remain standing there, his hands hanging and his eyes wide open, as if he were enmeshed in the complex web of some sudden reverie.

The next day was horrible, and the following ones even more intolerable as Emma's impatience to recapture her happiness grew—a bitter lust, inflamed by remembered images that would, on the seventh day, erupt under Léon's caresses. As for his ardors, they were concealed beneath outbursts of wonder and gratitude. Emma savored this love in a discreet but intense way, nourishing it with all the artifices of tenderness she knew, and trembling a little at the thought of losing it eventually.

She would often say to him, in a sweet, melancholic voice:

"Ah, you'll leave me, you will! . . . You'll get married! . . . You'll be like all the others."

"What others?"

"I mean men in general," she said.

Then she added, pushing him away with a languid gesture:

"You're all vile!"

One day when they were talking philosophically about earthly disillusionments, she said—perhaps to explore how jealous he would be, or perhaps out of too great a need to open her heart—that in the past, before him, she had loved someone. "But not like you!" she quickly added, swearing on her daughter's head *that nothing had happened*.

The young man believed it, but nonetheless questioned her to find out who it had been.

"He was a ship's captain, my dear."

Was this not a means of preventing further inquiry, and at the same time a way of elevating herself, through this imaginary fascination that she had exercised over a man who must have been both aggressive and accustomed to dominating women?

The clerk then sensed the weakness of his position; he envied epaulettes, crosses of honor, titles. All that would surely please her; her expensive habits proved it.

Even so, Emma concealed a great many of her expensive fantasies, such as the desire to have a blue tilbury coach to take her to Rouen, drawn by an English horse, and driven by a groom with top-boots. It was Justin who had inspired this particular whim, by begging her to hire him on as her valet; and if having no tilbury in no way lessened the pleasure of her arrival at each rendezvous, it certainly did augment the bitterness of her return.

Often, when they were speaking together about Paris, she would end by murmuring:

"Ah! How happy we would be living there!"

"But aren't we happy now?" the young man gently asked, passing his hand over her hair.

"Oh, yes, that's true," she would say. "I'm being foolish. Kiss me!"

For her husband, she was more charming than ever, making him pistachio creams and playing him waltzes after dinner. So he thought of himself as the happiest of mortals, and so Emma lived without any anxieties—until suddenly, one night:

"It's Mademoiselle Lempereur, isn't it, who gives you your lessons?"

"Yes."

"Well! I saw her today," Charles replied, "at Madame Liégeard's. I talked about you to her: she doesn't know you."

This was like a lightning bolt. But she replied in a natural tone:

"Oh, she's probably forgotten my name!"

"But couldn't there be," the doctor said, "several Mademoiselle Lempereurs in Rouen, all of them piano teachers?"

"It's possible!"

Then, quickly:

"I've got her receipts here. Take a look at them!"

And she went over to the desk, rummaged through the drawers, confused all the papers and at last lost her head so completely that Charles begged her not to take so much trouble over those miserable receipts.

"Oh, I'll find them!" she said.

In fact, on the following Friday, when Charles was putting on his boots in the dark room where his clothes were kept, he felt a piece of paper between his sock and the shoe leather; he took it out and read:

"Received, for three months of lessons and miscellaneous supplies, the sum of sixty-five francs. FÉLICIE LEMPEREUR, music teacher."

"How the devil did this get into my boot?"

"It must have fallen out of the old box of bills, up on the edge of the shelf."

From that moment on, her existence was nothing more than a long tissue of lies, in which she enveloped her love as if under a veil, to keep it hidden.

It was a need, a mania, a pleasure, to the point where, if she said she walked down the right side of the street yesterday, you would have to believe that she had gone down the left.

One morning when she had just left lightly dressed as she usually did, snow suddenly began to fall; and as Charles watched it out the window, he saw Monsieur Bournisien sitting in the chaise of Monsieur Tuvache, who was taking him to Rouen. So he went down and gave the cleric a thick shawl to give to Emma as soon as he arrived at the _Red Cross_. As soon as he got to the inn, Bournisien asked where the doctor's wife from Yonville was. The landlady replied that she rarely came in to her establishment. That evening, when he met Madame Bovary in the _Hirondelle_, he told her about his problem, without seeming to attach any importance to it; for he began to praise a preacher who was doing great things at the cathedral, and who all the ladies were rushing to hear.

But no matter—if he had not asked for any explanations, others later on might be less discreet. So she thought it would be useful to get out each morning at the _Red Cross_, so that the good people from her village, seeing her on the staircase, would suspect nothing.

One day, however, Monsieur Lheureux met her leaving the _Hotel de Boulogne_ on Léon's arm; and she felt fear, imagining that he would gossip about it. He was not that stupid.

But three days later, he came into her room, closed the door, and said:

"I'm going to need some money."

She said she couldn't give him any. Lheureux burst into groans and reminded her of all the kindnesses he had done for her.

In fact, of the two notes signed by Charles, Emma so far had paid only one. As for the second, the merchant, at her entreaty, had agreed to replace it with two others, which had been renewed for a long period again. Then he took out of his pocket a list of goods she hadn't paid for, to wit: the curtains, the carpet, the material for the armchairs, a number of dresses, and various clothing items, the value of which amounted to the sum of about two thousand francs.

She lowered her head; he went on:

"But if you don't have the cash, you do have *property*."

And he mentioned a miserable hovel located in Barneville, near Aumale, that brought in very little income. It had formerly been part of a little farm sold by Charles' father—for Lheureux knew everything, from the number of acres to the names of the neighbors.

"If I were in your situation," he said, "I'd get rid of it, and I'd have money left over."

She objected that it would be difficult to find a buyer; he suggested he might be able to find one; but she asked him how she would be able to sell it.

"Don't you have the power of attorney?" he replied.

The word struck her like a gust of fresh air.

"Leave me your bill," Emma said.

"Oh! It's not worth the trouble!" Lheureux said.

He came back the following week, boasting of having found, after a lot of trouble, a man named Langlois, who had had an eye on the property for a long time, though he hadn't specified a price.

"The price doesn't matter!" she cried.

On the contrary, they should wait and feel the fellow out. The thing was worth a trip there, and since she couldn't go, he offered to go over himself to discuss it with Langlois. When he returned, he announced that the buyer proposed a price of four thousand francs.

Emma lit up at the news.

"Frankly," he added, "it's a good price."

She drew out half the sum right away, and when she offered to pay off her debt, the merchant said to her:

"It pains me, word of honor, to see you deprive yourself all at once of a sum as *consequential* as that."

Then she gazed at the bank notes; and, dreaming of the number of lovers' meetings that those two thousand francs represented:

"What! What!" she stammered.

"Oh," he replied, laughing in a good-natured tone, "you can put any numbers you like on the sales receipts! Don't you think I know all about household management?"

And he looked at her fixedly, while he held in his hand two long sheets of paper, sliding his nails over them. At last, opening his pocketbook, he spread out on the table four promissory notes, of a thousand francs each.

"Sign these for me," he said, "and you can keep it all."

She cried out, shocked.

"But if I give you the surplus," Monsieur Lheureux replied shamelessly, "isn't that doing you a service?"

And taking a pen, he wrote at the bottom of the account: "Received from Madame Bovary, four thousand francs."

"What is there to worry about, since you'll get the remaining payment on your cottage in six months, and I'll set up your due date for after that?"

Emma was growing a little confused by these calculations, and her ears were ringing as if the gold pieces had burst out of their sacks and were jingling all around her on the floor. Then Lheureux explained that he had a friend, Vinçart, a banker in Rouen, who would discount the four notes, and then he would remit to Madame the surplus of the real debt.

But, instead of two thousand francs, he brought her only eighteen hundred, because friend Vinçart had taken two hundred for his commission and expenses (as was *only fair*).

Then he nonchalantly asked for a receipt.

"You understand . . . in business . . . sometimes. And with the date, please, the date."

A horizon then opened up before Emma, of fantasies she could now make come true. She had enough prudence to set aside three thousand francs, with which the first three notes were paid, when they matured; but the fourth, by chance, came to the house on a Thursday, and Charles, stunned, waited patiently for his wife to return and give him some explanation.

The only reason she had not told him about this bill was to spare him from domestic worries; she sat on his knees, caressed him, cooed, and gave him a long list of all the essential things that had been purchased on credit.

"When it's all said and done, you have to admit that, considering the quantity of things, it really wasn't too expensive."

Charles, at his wits' end, soon had recourse to the inevitable Lheureux, who assured him he could smooth everything out if Monsieur would sign two notes, one of which was for seven hundred francs, payable in three months. In order to be able to meet this, he wrote a pathetic letter to his mother. Instead of mailing a reply, she came in person; and when Emma asked him if he had managed to get anything out of her:

"Yes," he replied. "But she wants to see the account."

The next day at dawn, Emma ran to Lheureux's to beg him to make out another note, of no more than a thousand francs; because, in order to show the one for four thousand, she would have to say she had paid two thirds of it, and that would entail her having to tell them that she had sold the property, a business deal carried out so quietly by the merchant that it didn't come to light until later.

Despite the low prices paid for each individual article purchased, Madame Bovary senior did not fail to point out the extravagance of it all.

"Couldn't she do without a carpet? Why did the armchairs have to be recovered? In my day, a house had one armchair, for elderly people—at least that's the way it was at my mother's, and she was an honest woman, I can assure you.—Everybody can't be rich! No fortune can survive wastefulness! I would blush if I pampered myself the way you do! And look at me, I'm an old woman, I need attention . . . And here! Here, alterations, frills! What! Silk for linings for two francs!—when you can get cotton for ten sous, or even eight sous, and it will do perfectly well!"

Emma, lying on the couch, replied in as tranquil a tone as possible:

"Oh, Madame! Enough! Enough!"

The other continued to lecture her, predicting that they would all end up in the poorhouse. Besides, it was all Bovary's fault. Fortunately, though, he had promised to destroy that power of attorney . . .

"What?"

"Ah! He promised me," the good woman replied.

Emma opened the window, called Charles in, and the poor man was obliged to admit that his mother had forced him to promise.

Emma disappeared, then quickly came back in, majestically holding out a thick sheet of paper to her.

"Thank you," said the old woman.

And she threw the power of attorney into the fire.

Emma began to laugh a shrill, piercing, prolonged laugh: she was having a nervous attack.

"Oh, my God!" Charles cried. "It's your fault too! You come here just to make scenes!"

His mother, shrugging her shoulders, insisted that *all this was just playacting*.

But Charles, rebelling for the first time, took up his wife's defense, so strongly that Madame Bovary senior wanted to leave. She left the next morning, and when, on the threshold, he tried to make her stay, she replied:

"No, no! You love her more than me, and that's the way it should be; it's natural. As for everything else, so much the worse! You'll see! Good day to you—because I'm not going to stay, as you put it, just to make scenes."

This did not make Charles any the less sheepish around Emma, who by no means hid the resentment she felt toward him for lacking trust in her; and it took him a great deal of begging before she would consent to signing another power of attorney, and he even accompanied her to Monsieur Guillaumin's to have a second one drawn up, just like the first.

"I can understand this," said the notary. "A man of science can't let himself be bothered with the practical details of life."

And Charles was soothed by this unctuous observation, which lent to his weakness the flattering appearance of a preoccupation with higher things.

What an outburst, the next Thursday, at the hotel, in their room, with Léon! She laughed, wept, sang, danced, had sherbets sent up, wanted to smoke cigarettes—and she seemed excessive to him, but adorable, superb.

He did not know what reaction was at work within her that made her throw her whole being into the pleasures of life. She was becoming irritable, gluttonous, and voluptuous; and she would walk out with him in the streets, head held high, unafraid, she would declare, of compromising herself. Sometimes, however, she would shudder at the sudden thought of encountering Rodolphe; for it seemed to her, though they had separated forever, that she was not entirely free of her attachment to him.

One evening, she did not return at all to Yonville. Charles lost his head, and little Berthe, not wanting to go to bed without her mama, sobbed as if her heart were breaking. Justin had gone out to wander aimlessly along the road. Monsieur Homais even left his pharmacy.

Finally, at eleven o'clock, Charles harnessed up his chaise, leaped in, whipped his horse, and arrived at about two in the morning at the *Red Cross* inn. No one. He thought that perhaps the clerk had seen her; but where did he live? Luckily, Charles remembered the address of his employer. He raced there.

Day was beginning to break. He made out the sign over a door; he knocked. Someone, without opening the door, shouted out the information he asked for, while adding to it a number of curses on the kind of people who bothered others during the night.

The house where the clerk lived had neither a bell, nor a knocker, nor a porter. Charles banged loudly on the shutters with his fists. A policeman passed by; then he was afraid, and he left.

"I'm insane," he said to himself. "They must have kept her after dinner at Monsieur Lormeaux's house."

The Lormeaux family no longer lived in Rouen.

"She must have stayed to care for Madame Dubreuil. Oh! Madame Dubreuil has been dead for ten months! Where is she?"

An idea struck him. He asked in a café for the *Annuaire* directory, and quickly found the name of Mademoiselle Lempereur, who lived at 74 Rue de la Renelle-des-Maroquiniers.

Just as he turned into that street, Emma herself appeared at the other end; he did not so much embrace her as throw himself upon her, crying:

"What kept you yesterday?"

"I was sick."

"Sick? What was it? Where?"

She passed her hand over her forehead and answered:

"At Mademoiselle Lempereur's."

"I knew it! I was just going there."

"Oh, it's not worth the trouble," said Emma. "She has just gone out; but in the future, calm yourself down. How can I be free, don't you understand, if being the slightest bit late throws you into such a state?"

This was a way of giving herself permission not to trouble herself about her escapades. And she made full and free use of it. Whenever she felt a desire to see Léon, she left under any pretext at all, and if it was on a day he wasn't expecting her, she would go seek him out at his office.

This was a great pleasure, the first few times; but soon he no longer hid the truth from her: that his employer complained vigorously about these interruptions.

"Bah! Come along," she would say.

And he would slip away.

She wanted him to dress all in black and to grow a pointed beard, so as to look like the portraits of Louis XIII.[2] She wanted to see his lodgings, and found them mediocre; he blushed, she took no notice of it, and then she advised him to buy some curtains like her own, and when he objected to the expense:

"Ah, ah! You're holding on tight to your little francs!" she said, laughing.

Every time, Léon had to tell her everything he had done since their last meeting. She asked for a poem, a poem for her, *a love poem* in her honor; he could never find a rhyme for the second line, and ultimately he copied out a sonnet from a keepsake book.

---

2. French king (1601–1643), who ruled 1610–43; the father of Louis XIV.

This was less out of vanity than for the sole aim of pleasing her. He did not question her ideas; he accepted all her tastes; he became her mistress more than she was his. She had tender words and kisses that swept his soul away. But where had she learned this corruption, so profound and so deeply disguised that it seemed almost spiritual?

CHAPTER 6

On the trips he made to see her, Léon often dined at the pharmacist's, and he felt obliged, out of politeness, to invite him in return.

"Gladly!" Monsieur Homais had replied. "Anyway, I really ought to dip my toe into the outside world a bit, because I'm getting into a rut here. We'll go to the theater, to a restaurant, we'll get a little wild!"

"Oh, my dear," Madame Homais murmured tenderly, feeling fearful of the vague perils he was proposing to risk.

"Well, what? Don't you think I'm endangering my health by living every day with the emanations in this pharmacy? There you have it, the character of women: they're jealous of Science, but at the same time they're opposed to the most legitimate distractions. But never mind: you can count on me; one of these days I'll roll into Rouen, and we'll go out and throw some money around!"

The pharmacist would normally have taken care never to use such an expression: but now he wanted to sound frolicsome and Parisian, which he thought to be in the best of taste; and like Madame Bovary, his neighbor, he questioned the clerk curiously about the customs in the capital, and he even talked enough slang to dazzle—at least, to dazzle the bourgeois of Yonville, saying *turne, bazar, chicard, chicandard, Breda-Street*,[3] and "I'm cutting out," to mean I'm leaving.

So one Thursday, Emma was surprised to encounter Monsieur Homais in the *Golden Lion's* kitchen, wearing traveler's clothes, that is to say, covered in an old cloak no one had seen before, carrying a valise in one hand and the pharmacy's foot warmer in the other. He had told no one about his planned trip, out of concern that the public might be uneasy if they knew he was out of town.

The idea of revisiting the places where he had spent his youth was no doubt a thrill for him, because he didn't stop talking for the entire journey; and then, as soon as they arrived, he leaped out of the coach to go in search of Léon; the clerk's protests were in vain, as Monsieur Homais dragged him to the big *Normandie* café, which he entered with a stately air, without removing his hat, thinking it too provincial to be seen bareheaded in a public place.

Emma waited for Léon for three-quarters of an hour. Finally she ran to his office; and then, confusedly proposing every sort of explanation to herself, accusing him inwardly of indifference to her, reproaching herself for her weakness, she passed the afternoon with her head pressed against the windowpanes.

---

3. *Turne*: sweet. *Bazar*: fabulous. *Chicard*: "in." *Chicanard*: con artist. (All these terms are French.)

At two o'clock, the two men were still sitting across from each other at the table. The large dining room was emptying out; the stove pipe, designed to look like a palm tree, spread its gilt leaves over the white ceiling; near them, through the café window, in the bright sunshine, a little fountain of water gurgled in a marble basin where, among the watercress and the asparagus, three somnolent lobsters were stretching their claws toward the quail, piled in a heap on both sides of them.

Homais was enjoying himself. Although he was more drunk from the luxury than from the rich fare, the Pomard wine nonetheless had overstimulated his brain a bit, and by the time the omelet *au rhum* arrived, he was propounding immoral theories about women. The one thing above all others that always seduced him was *chic*. He adored an elegantly dressed woman in the setting of a beautifully furnished apartment, and as to the physical aspects, he wouldn't say no to a nice *piece*.

Léon watched the clock in despair. The pharmacist continued to drink, eat, talk.

"You must feel pretty deprived," he suddenly said, "here in Rouen. But after all, your lover doesn't live that far away."

And, when the other blushed:

"Come on, tell the truth! Would you deny that in Yonville . . . "

The young man began to stammer.

"At Madame Bovary's, you weren't courting . . . ?"

"Who was I courting?"

"The maid!"

He wasn't joking; but his vanity overcoming his prudence, Léon, despite himself, protested. And anyway, he only liked brunettes.

"I approve," the pharmacist said. "They're more passionate."

And bending toward his friend's ear, he listed the symptoms by which one could recognize a passionate woman. He even launched into an ethnographic digression: German women were nervous, French ones libertine, Italians hot-tempered.

"And Negresses?" asked the clerk.

"Artists like them," said Homais. "Waiter! Two demitasses!"

"Shall we leave?" Léon impatiently said at last.

"Yes," Homais said in English.

But before leaving, he wanted to see the manager of the establishment and offer him a few compliments.

Then the young man, in order to be left alone, claimed that he had some business to attend to.

"Ah! I'll go along with you!" Homais said.

And as he walked along the streets with him, he talked about his wife, his children, their future, and his pharmacy, describing the decayed state it used to be in and the point of perfection to which he had now raised it.

Arriving in front of the *Hotel de Boulogne*, Léon brusquely left him, raced up the stairs, and found his mistress in a highly emotional state.

At the pharmacist's name, she flew into a rage. However, he listed a series of good reasons; it wasn't his fault, didn't she know Monsieur Homais? Could she possibly believe he preferred his company? But she turned away from him; he drew her back; and sinking down on his knees, he put both arms around her waist in a languorous pose that combined sensuality and supplication.

She was standing up; her great flashing eyes glared at him intensely, almost frighteningly. Then tears clouded them, her reddened eyelids lowered, she held her hands out to him, and Léon was bringing them up to his mouth when a servant appeared, saying that Monsieur was being asked for.

"You're going to come back?" she said.

"Yes."

"But when?"

"Right away."

"It's a *trick*," the pharmacist said when he saw Léon. "I wanted to interrupt this visit, because I could tell it annoyed you. Let's go to Bridoux's and have a glass of *garus*[4] to settle our stomachs."

Léon swore that he had to get back to his office. Then the pharmacist made jokes about paper-pushers and the law.

"Leave Cujas and Barthole[5] for a while, what the devil! What's to stop you? Have some backbone! Let's go to Bridoux's; you'll get to see his dog. It's extremely curious!"

And when the clerk continued to insist:

"All right, I'll come along with you. I'll read a paper while I wait for you, or maybe I'll leaf through a law book."

Léon, stunned by Emma's anger, the chatter of Monsieur Homais, and perhaps the heavy lunch, remained undecided, almost as if he were under a spell cast by the pharmacist, who kept repeating:

"Let's go to Bridoux's! It's just a few steps from here, on the Rue Malpalu."

Then, whether out of cowardice, or out of stupidity, or out of that inexplicable feeling that leads us into doing the things we least want to do, he let himself be taken to Bridoux's; and they found him in his small courtyard, overseeing three workmen who were panting as they turned the big wheel of a machine for making seltzer water. Homais gave them some advice; he embraced Bridoux; they had their drinks. Twenty times, Léon wanted to leave; but the other would seize him by the arm, saying:

"In a minute! I'm leaving. We'll go to the *Rouen Lantern* to see the gentlemen there. I'll introduce you to Thomassin."

But he managed to get rid of him and ran immediately to the hotel. Emma was no longer there.

She had just left, infuriated. She hated him now. This failure to keep his word about their rendezvous seemed an insult to her, and she was trying to think of other reasons to break it off with him: he was incapable of heroism, weak, banal, more spineless than a woman, a tightwad besides, and cowardly.

Then, when she calmed down, she decided that she had in fact slandered him unjustly. But when we disparage those we love, we begin to detach ourselves from them a little. Idols must never be touched: the gilt will come off on our hands.

They gradually began to talk more often of things other than their love; and in the letters Emma sent him, it was always a matter of flowers, verses, the

4. Garus elixir is an alcohol–based tonic [translator's note].
5. Or Bartole (1313–1357), an Italian jurist

in Bologna. Jacques Cujas (1552–1590), a famous jurist who interpreted Roman law in contemporary terms.

moon and the stars, all the naïve resources that a weakening passion employs in trying to revive itself through external props. She always promised herself that her next trip would bring her a profound happiness; but then she would have to admit that she had felt nothing extraordinary. The disillusionment would be erased by a new hope, and Emma would return to him more impassioned, more ardent. She would undress brutally, tearing off the thin laces of her corset, which would hiss like a snake as it slipped over her hips. She would tiptoe, barefoot, to check once more that the door was locked, and then, with a single gesture, she would throw all her clothes off—and pale, unspeaking, unsmiling, she would throw herself against his chest with a long shudder.

But upon that forehead with its droplets of cold sweat, on those quivering lips, within those wild eyes, in the embrace of those arms, there was something extreme, something indefinite and mournful that Léon felt subtly slipping between them, as if to separate them.

He dared not question her; but perceiving how experienced she was, he said to himself that she must have known every excess of pain and pleasure. What had at first charmed him now frightened him a little. Moreover, he was rebelling against the way her personality, more and more every day, was absorbing his own. He resented Emma's permanent dominance. He forced himself to care less about her; then, at the creaking of her boots, he felt his cowardice return, the way drunkards do at the sight of hard liquor.

But it is true too that she never failed to lavish every kind of attention on him, from the fine foods she chose, to the flirtatious clothes she wore, to the languorous looks she cast at him. She brought roses from Yonville, holding them next to her breast, and she would toss them at his face; she showed great concern over his health, gave him advice on how to conduct himself, and in order to keep her hold over him—perhaps in the hope that heaven would step in—she put a medal of the Virgin around his neck. Like a virtuous mother, she asked about his friends. She said to him:

"Don't see them, don't go out, think only of us, love me!"

She wanted to be able to keep a close watch on his life, and she considered the idea of having him followed in the streets. There was always a kind of tramp near the hotel who accosted the travelers, and he would probably agree to it . . . But her pride revolted at this finally.

"Well, so what then! Let him cheat on me, what's the difference! Why should I care?"

One day when they had parted early, and she was walking back alone on the boulevard, she saw the outer walls of her old convent school; she sat down on a bench, in the shade of the elm trees. How peaceful those days were! How she missed those ineffable feelings about love that she had tried to imagine from books!

The first months of her marriage, horseback rides through the forest, the Viscount who waltzed with her, and Lagardy singing, all of it passed before her eyes . . . And Léon suddenly appeared to her, but just as far away as the others.

"But I do love him!" she said to herself.

What does it matter! She was not happy, had never been. Where did it come from, this insufficiency in life, this immediate corruption of everything she tried to lean on? But if there really existed somewhere a strong, beautiful being, brave and capable of both exaltation and refinement, with the heart of a poet in the form of an angel, a lyre whose ethereal strings sang out elegiac nuptial songs to the heavens—why, why could she not find him? Oh, how impossible it all was! Nothing was worth all the struggle of such a search; everything was a lie! Every smile hid beneath it a yawn of boredom, every joy a curse, every pleasure its disgust, and the finest kisses only left on your lips the impossible desire for an even greater sensuality.

A metallic groan sounded through the air, and the convent clock rang out four strokes. Four o'clock! And she felt that she had been there, on that bench, for an eternity. But we can feel an infinity of passions in a moment, like a crowd in a little space.

Emma lived wholly preoccupied with her own passions, and she bothered no more about money than an archduchess.

One time, however, a scrawny looking man, ruddy and bald, came into her home, saying he had been sent by Monsieur Vinçart from Rouen. He removed the pins that held together the side pocket of his long green coat, stuck them in his cuff, and politely handed her a paper.

It was a bill for seven hundred francs, signed by her, which Lheureux had passed on to Vinçart despite all her objections.

She sent a servant to fetch him. He could not come.

Then the stranger, who had remained standing and looking around curiously to the right and the left, though his glances were partly hidden by his thick blonde eyebrows, asked innocently:

"What reply should I take to Monsieur Vinçart?"

"All right!" Emma answered. "Tell him . . . that I don't have it . . . It will be next week . . . Ask him to wait . . . yes, next week."

And the man went off without saying a word.

But the next day at noon, she received a formal protest of nonpayment; and the sight of the stamped paper, on which was written several times in large letters, "Maître Hareng, bailiff of Buchy," so frightened her that she ran as fast as she could to the dry-goods merchant.

She found him in his shop, in the process of trying up a parcel.

"Your servant!" he said. "I'm all yours."

But Lheureux nevertheless did not stop what he was doing, assisted by a girl of around thirteen years of age, slightly hunchbacked, who worked as both his clerk and his cook.

Then, making his clogs clomp loudly across the shop floor, he led Madame up to the second floor, and brought her into a narrow office where a pine desk held several ledgers, protected by a crosswise padlocked iron bar. Against the wall, beneath some calico samples, was a safe so unusually large that it had to contain something other than bills and money. Monsieur Lheureux was in fact also something of a pawnbroker, and it was there that he kept Madame Bovary's gold chain, along with the earrings of poor old Tellier, who, having finally been forced to sell out, had bought a tiny grocery store in Quincampoix, where he was currently dying of his catarrh among candles less yellow than his own face.

Lheureux seated himself on his large cane armchair, saying:

"What's the news?"

"Look."

And she handed him the paper.

"Well! What can I do about it?"

At that, she flew into a rage, reminding him of his promise not to sell her promissory notes; he admitted it.

"But I was forced to do it; the knife was at my throat."

"And what's going to happen now?" she asked.

"Oh, it's very simple: a legal judgment, then a seizure of goods, and then— *nothing more to it!*"

Emma had to restrain herself from striking him. She quietly asked if there wasn't some way to calm Vinçart down.

"Oh, sure! Calm Vinçart down; you don't know him; he's fiercer than an Arab."

Still, Monsieur Lheureux simply had to help her out.

"Look, it seems to me that, up to now, I've been good enough to you!"

And, opening up his ledger:

"Look at this!"

Then, running his finger up the page:

"Let's see . . . Let's see . . . August 3rd, two hundred francs . . . June 17th, a hundred and fifty . . . March 23rd, forty-six . . . In April . . . "

He stopped, as if afraid of being at all imprecise.

"And I'm not even mentioning the notes signed by Monsieur, one for seven hundred francs, another for three hundred! As for your little payments, with interest, there's no end to them, they'd completely confuse a person. I'll have nothing more to do with it!"

She wept, she even called him "my good Monsieur Lheureux." But he kept referring to "that bulldog Vinçart." In any case, he himself didn't have a centime; nobody was paying him; they were stealing the clothes off his back; a poor shopkeeper like him couldn't be advancing money to people.

Emma said nothing; and Monsieur Lheureux, who was chewing on the feathers of his quill, evidently grew uneasy with her silence, for he continued:

"At least, if one of these days I had some cash coming in . . . I could . . . "

"Besides, once the rest of the Barneville payments . . . "

"What?"

And when he learned that Langlois had not yet paid in full, he seemed very surprised. Then, in a honeyed voice:

"And we can agree, you say . . . "

"Oh! Anything you want!"

Then he closed his eyes to think, wrote down a few figures, and declaring that all this was very bad for him, that the whole thing was very complicated and that people were *bleeding* him, he wrote out four notes of two hundred and fifty francs apiece, their due dates spaced out at one per month.

"Provided that Vinçart will be willing to listen to me! But otherwise, it's all settled. I don't play games. I'm as straight as an arrow."

He then went on nonchalantly to show a few new items he had for sale, none of which, in his opinion, was worthy of Madame.

"When I think that this is supposedly dress quality at seven sous a meter, and guaranteed to be colorfast! And they'll believe it! Of course, I don't tell them what it really is, you understand"—intending, by this confession of his dishonesty to others, to convince her of his honesty toward her.

Then he called her back, to show her three yards of lace that he had recently come across "at a *sale*."

"Beautiful, isn't it?" Lheureux said. "People use this nowadays to protect armchairs; it's quite in style."

And as swiftly as a juggler, he wrapped the lace up in blue paper and put it into Emma's hands.

"But at least tell me . . . "

"Oh! Some other time," he said, turning away.

That evening, she pressed Bovary to write to his mother so that she would send them the rest of the inheritance quickly. The mother-in-law replied that there was nothing more: the liquidation was finished, and all that remained, apart from Barneville, was six hundred francs in rents, which she would send to them punctually.

Madame then sent bills to three or four of Charles' patients, and soon was using this method frequently, as it had some success. She was always careful to add as a postscript: "Don't mention this to my husband, for you know how proud he is . . . Please pardon me . . . Your servant . . . " There were a few complaints; she intercepted them.

To raise money, she began to sell her old gloves, her old hats, old household items; and she bargained ruthlessly—her peasant blood coming to her aid. Then, in her trips to the city, she would pick up trinkets that Monsieur Lheureux, if no one else, would surely buy from her. She bought some ostrich feathers, some Chinese porcelain, some chests; she borrowed from Félicité, from Madame Lefrançois, from the innkeeper at the *Red Cross*, from everybody, no matter where. With the money that she finally got for Barneville, she paid off two of the notes; the other fifteen hundred francs flew away. She renewed the notes, and so it went on!

Sometimes, it's true, she tried to do some calculations, but the sums she came up with were so exorbitant that she couldn't believe they were correct. Then she would try again, quickly become confused, stop trying, and think no more about it.

The house was sad enough, nowadays! Tradesmen were seen leaving it with angry looks on their faces. There were handkerchiefs left lying on the stoves, and little Berthe, to the great scandal of Madame Homais, was wearing stockings with holes in them. If Charles timidly ventured some remark about it, she would respond brutally that it wasn't her fault!

Why these fits of anger? He attributed it all to her old nervous illness; and reproaching himself for having taken her infirmities for faults, he accused himself of egoism, and felt like running over to embrace her.

"Oh, no," he would say to himself, "I'd only annoy her."

And he stayed where he was.

After dinner, he would walk alone in the garden; he would put little Berthe on his knees and, using his medical journal, try to teach her to read. The child, who never had any schooling, lost no time in opening her big sad eyes wide and beginning to cry. Then he would comfort her; he would go fill her watering can so she could make rivers in the sand, or break off branches from the privet hedge to plant little trees in the flower beds—none of which did the garden any harm, overgrown with weeds as it had become; they owed too much back pay to Lestiboudois! Then the child would feel cold and ask for her mother.

"Call your nanny," Charles would say. "You know, little one, that Mama doesn't like to be disturbed."

Autumn began, and already the leaves were falling—it's been two years since her illness! When will all this end! And he would continue to pace, his hands behind his back.

Madame was in her room. No one went up there. She stayed there all day long, drowsing, half-dressed, and from time to time burning incense that she had bought in Rouen, in an Algerian's shop. To rid herself of that man who slept stretched out next to her every night, she complained long enough that she got him to move up to the third floor; and she would stay up all night reading extravagant books depicting orgies and bloody events. Sometimes a sudden terror would seize her, and she would cry out. Charles would come running.

"Oh, go away!" she would say.

Or, at other times, burning more intensely from that inner, intimate flame that adultery had awakened in her, breathless and impassioned and filled with desire, she would open her window, breathe in the cool air, shake her too-heavy hair loose in the wind, and looking up at the stars, wish for the love of a prince. She thought of him, of Léon. At such a moment she would have given everything for just one of those meetings that sated her.

Those were her gala days. She wanted them to be splendid! And when he wasn't able to pay for everything, she made up the difference liberally, which happened just about every time. He tried to make her understand that they would do just as well elsewhere, in some more modest hotel; but she always found objections.

One day she took six small silver spoons out of her bag (they were a wedding present from her father, Rouault), and begged him to take them right away, for her, to a pawnshop; and Léon obeyed, even though he disliked the task. He feared compromising himself.

Later, upon reflection, he considered that his mistress' behavior was becoming too strange, and that perhaps the people who wanted him to leave her were not so wrong.

In fact, someone had sent his mother a long anonymous letter, letting her know that her son was *ruining himself with a married woman;* and the good woman, immediately seeing before her that eternal specter of respectable families, that is to say that vague, pernicious creature the siren, the fantastic monster that lurks in the depths of love, wrote off to Maître Dubocage, his employer, who played his role perfectly. He lectured him for three-quarters of an hour, trying to open his eyes, to warn him away from the abyss. Such an intrigue eventually would do damage to his future. He begged him to break with her, and if he wouldn't make this sacrifice for his own self-interest, would he please do it for him, for Dubocage!

Léon finally swore not to see Emma again; and he reproached himself for not keeping his word, considering all the difficulties and the sermons that seeing this woman could draw down upon him, not to mention the jokes his friends made as they sat around the stove every morning. Besides, he was about to be made chief clerk: this was the time to get serious. And so he gave up his flute, his exalted feelings, his poetic imaginings—for every bourgeois, in the heat of his youth, has believed himself capable of immense passions and high enterprises, even if only for a day or a minute. The cheapest libertine has dreamed of sultanas; every notary carries within himself the debris of a poet.

He was bored now when Emma suddenly began to sob against his chest; and his heart—like those people who can only endure a certain amount of music— slept, indifferent now to the frantic sounds made by a love whose subtle delights he no longer noticed.

They knew each other too well by now for any of those sensual surprises that multiply the joy of possession. She was as disgusted with him as he was tired of her. Emma was discovering in adultery all the dreary monotonies of marriage.

But how to get rid of him? For even though she felt humiliated by the baseness of such happiness, she still hung on to it, whether out of habit or out of corruption; and every day she clung to it even more, withering up every joy by wishing it were a greater joy. She blamed Léon for her disappointed hopes, as if he had betrayed her; and she even wished for some catastrophe that would bring about their separation, since she lacked the courage to act on it herself.

Nevertheless she continued to write him love letters, on the principle that a woman must always write to her lover.

But in writing to him, she pictured another man, a phantom made up of her most ardent memories, her most beautiful books, her most powerful desires; and he became in the end so real, so accessible that she trembled with wonder, though she was unable to picture him clearly, so lost was he, like a god, under the abundance of his attributes. He inhabited that bluish country where silk ladders sway from balconies, in the soft breath of the flowers, in the bright moonlight. She felt him close to her; he was going to come and sweep her away entirely in a kiss. Then she fell back to the flat earth, broken; for these vague ecstasies of love fatigued her more than actual debauchery.

She now was feeling a constant ache all over her. Often, she received summonses on stamped, official paper, and she would scarcely glance at them. She wanted to be done with living, or to sleep endlessly.

On the day of Mid-Lent, she did not return to Yonville; she went that evening to a masked ball. She went wearing velvet trousers and red stockings, with a pony-tailed wig and a cocked hat tilted over one ear. She danced all night to the raging sound of the trombones; people formed a circle around her; and in the morning she found herself in front of the theater's entrance among five or six partiers in masks, women dressed like longshoremen or sailors, some of Léon's friends, who were talking about going to find something to eat.

The nearby cafés were full. They found one of the most mediocre restaurants on the harbor, where the proprietor opened up a little room for them on the fifth floor.

The men were whispering in a corner, no doubt consulting about money. There was a clerk, two medical students, and a shop worker: what company for her! As for the women, Emma quickly perceived that they were almost all of the lowest order of society. She felt fear then, pushed herself back in her chair, and cast down her eyes.

The others began to eat. She did not eat; her forehead was on fire, her eyelids were stinging, and her skin felt as cold as ice. She felt, within her head, the floorboards at the dance, rebounding under the rhythmic pulses of a thousand dancing feet. And soon the smell of the punch together with the cigar smoke made her dizzy. She fainted: they carried her over to the window.

Day was breaking, and a large smear of purple was widening in the white sky over Saint-Catherine's Hill. The pale river shimmered in the wind; there was no one on the bridges; the streetlights were going out.

Meanwhile, she revived, and began to think of Berthe, who was sleeping far away, in the maid's room. But a cart carrying long strips of iron passed by, making a deafening metallic vibration against the walls.

She abruptly slipped out, getting rid of her costume, saying to Léon that she had to go back, and finally was alone at the *Hotel de Boulogne*. Everything, including herself, was unendurable. She wished she could escape like a bird, go somewhere and recover her youth, somewhere far away in the immaculate regions.

She went out, crossed the boulevard, the Place Cauchoise and the outskirts of the city, as far as an open street that overlooked some gardens. She walked swiftly, the fresh air calming her: and little by little the faces in the crowd, the masks, the quadrilles, the lights, the supper, those women, all disappeared like a fog carried off by the wind. Then, returning to the *Red Cross*, she threw herself in her bed, in the little room on the third floor with the pictures of the *Tour de Nesle*. At four o'clock, Hivert awakened her.

When she got back home, Félicité showed her a gray paper document hidden behind the clock:

"By virtue of the seizure, following the legal judgment . . ."

What judgment? The previous day, in fact, they had delivered another document that she hadn't seen; and she was stupefied by these words:

"By the order of the king, the law, and justice, to Madame Bovary . . ."

Then, skipping down several lines, she read:

"Within twenty-four hours without delay." But what? "To pay the total sum of eight thousand francs." And then, farther down: "She shall be constrained thereunto by the power of the law, and specifically by the seizure of her furniture and effects."

What to do? It said within twenty-four hours: tomorrow! Lheureux, she thought, was trying to frighten her again; for she could see right through all his maneuvers, see the real goal of all his kind indulgences. The one thing that reassured her was the exaggerated sum.

However, as a result of all her buying and not paying, her borrowing, her signing promissory notes and then renewals of them that grew larger every time, she had ended up building up a nice capital sum for Lheureux, who was patiently awaiting the payout on his speculations.

She arrived at his shop with a casual air.

"Do you know what's happened to me? It must be some kind of joke!"

"No."

"What do you mean?"

He turned away from her slowly, and folding his arms, said to her:

"Did you think, my little lady, that I was going to be your provider and banker till the end of time, and all for the love of God? I have to get back what I've laid out, let's be fair!"

She protested the amount of the debt.

"Oh, that's too bad! The court has recognized it! There's a judgment against you! You've been notified! And anyway, it isn't me, it's Vinçart."

"But can't you . . . "

"Oh no—nothing at all."

"But surely . . . let's discuss it."

And she began to flail about; she hadn't known . . . it was a surprise . . .

"Whose fault is that?" said Lheureux, bowing to her ironically. "Look at me: all the time I'm slaving away like a Black while you're out having fine times."

"Oh, don't lecture me!"

"It wouldn't hurt," he replied.

She turned cowardly, she begged him; and she even laid her pretty white hand on the merchant's knees.

"Leave me alone! A person would think you wanted to seduce me."

"You're terrible!" she cried.

"Oh, my, how you do carry on!" he answered with a laugh.

"I'll tell people what you are. I'll tell my husband . . . "

"Fine! As for me, I have something to show your husband!"

And Lheureux pulled out of his safe a receipt for eighteen hundred francs, which she had given him when Vinçart discounted the note.

"Do you really think," he added, "that he won't understand this little theft of yours, the poor dear man?"

She sank back, more stunned than if he had struck her with a club. He was walking back and forth between the window and the desk, repeating to himself:

"Oh yes, I'll show it all to him . . . I'll show it all to him . . . "

Then he came over to her and said, in a more gentle voice:

"I know, it isn't pleasant; but after all, nobody's died, and since this is the only way you have to get me my money . . . "

"But where am I going to find it?" said Emma, wringing her hands.

"Bah! When a person has friends like you do!"

And he gave her such a knowing and such a terrible look that she shuddered to the depths of her being.

"I promise you," she said, "that I'll sign . . . "

"I've had enough of your signatures!"

"I'll sell . . . "

"Come on!" he said, shrugging his shoulders. "You don't have anything left to sell."

And he called through the peephole that looked down into the shop:

"Annette! Don't forget those three samples of number 14."

The servant appeared; Emma understood, and asked, "how much money it would take to stop all these proceedings."

"It's too late!"

"But if I were to bring you several thousand francs, a quarter of the sum, a third, almost all of it?"

"No, no, it's a waste of time."

He pushed her gently toward the staircase.

"I beg you, Monsieur Lheureux, just a few more days!"

She was sobbing.

"Oh of course, tears now!"

"You're making me desperate!"

"I couldn't care less!" he said, closing the door on her.

CHAPTER 7

She was stoical the next day when Maître Hareng, the bailiff, along with his two witnesses, arrived at her house to draw up the inventory for the seizure.

They began with Bovary's consulting room, but didn't note down the phrenological head, which was considered an instrument of his profession; but they did go into the kitchen and count the plates, the saucepans, the chairs, the candlesticks, and all the trinkets on the shelves in the bedroom. They examined her dresses, the linen, the dressing room; and her whole existence, right down to its most intimate details, was spread out before these three men like a corpse for an autopsy.

Maître Hareng, buttoned up in his thin black coat, with a white cravat and very tight bootstraps, repeated from time to time:

"With your permission, Madame? With your permission?"

Often, he made little exclamations:

"Charming! . . . How pretty!"

Then he would return to writing, dipping his pen into the inkwell he carried in his left hand.

When they had finished with the rooms, they went up to the attic.

She kept a desk up there, in which she had hidden Rodolphe's letters. It had to be opened.

"Ah! A correspondence," Maître Hareng said with a discreet smile. "But, permit me! Because I must be sure the box contains nothing else."

And he tilted the letters, lightly, as if to make gold coins fall out of them. At that point she was seized with indignation, watching that fat hand with its red fingers, as soft as slugs, touching the pages that had made her heart throb.

At last they left! Félicité came back in. Emma had sent her out to keep an eye out for Bovary; and they quickly installed the bailiff's watchman in the attic, where he promised to remain.

Emma thought that Charles seemed worried that evening. She watched him with an anguished look, thinking she could see accusations in the lines of his face. Then, when her eyes fell upon the mantel piece with the ornamental Chinese screens, upon the thick curtains, upon the armchairs, upon all those things that had sweetened the bitterness of her life, she was overcome with remorse, or rather with an immense regret that, rather than suppressing her passion, only stoked it. Charles poked the fire placidly, resting his feet on the andirons.

There was a moment when the bailiff's watchman, probably bored in his hiding place, made a little noise.

"Is somebody walking up there?" said Charles.

"No!" she answered. "It's an open window, rattling in the wind."

She left for Rouen on the next day, Sunday, to try all the bankers whose names she knew. They were all in the countryside or off on trips. But she was not discouraged, and with the ones that she did see, she asked them for money, insisting that she needed it, and that she would pay it back. Some laughed in her face; all of them refused.

At two o'clock, she ran to Léon's and knocked on his door. No one opened. Finally, he appeared.

"What brings you here?"

"I'm bothering you!"

"No ... But ... "

And he admitted that his landlord didn't like for the tenants to receive "women" in their rooms.

"I have to speak with you," she went on.

He reached for his key. She stopped him.

"Oh, no! Down there, at our place."

And they went to their room in the *Hotel de Boulogne*.

As soon as they went in she drank a large glass of water. She was very pale. She said to him:

"Léon, you have to do me a favor."

And shaking him by his two hands, which she was gripping tightly, she added:

"Listen, I need eight thousand francs!"

"You must be mad!"

"Not yet!"

And soon, narrating the story of the seizure, she explained her desperation to him; because Charles knew nothing of it: her mother-in-law detested her, her father Rouault could do nothing for her; but he, Léon, he could exert himself to find this crucial sum ...

"What do you think I ... ?"

"What a coward you are!" she exclaimed.

Then he said, stupidly:

"You're exaggerating how bad it is. Maybe a few thousand would calm your man down."

All the more reason to try everything they could; it simply wasn't possible that they could fail to come up with three thousand francs. Besides, Léon could sign the notes instead of her.

"Go! Try! It's essential! Run! ... Oh, try, try! I'll love you so!"

He went out, and returned after an hour, saying with a solemn expression:

"I've tried three people ... It's no use."

They remained seated and facing each other, at the two corners of the fireplace, motionless, not speaking. Then Emma shrugged her shoulders and stamped her feet. He could hear her muttering:

"If I were in your place, I'd know where to find it!"

"Where?"

"At your office!"

And she stared at him.

An infernal boldness was emanating from her burning eyes, and the eyelids narrowed in what was both a lascivious and encouraging manner—so much so that the young man felt himself weakening under the mute will of this woman who was counseling him into crime. And then he was afraid, and to avoid entering into any understanding with her, he slapped his forehead and exclaimed:

"Morel is coming back tonight! He won't refuse me, I hope"—this was one of his friends, the son of a very rich businessman—"and I'll bring it to you tomorrow," he added.

Emma didn't seem to receive this hope of his with as much joy as he had expected. Did she suspect he was lying? He continued, his face reddening:

"But, if you don't see me by three o'clock, don't wait for me, dearest. I have to go now, pardon me. Farewell!"

He squeezed her hand, but he felt it was entirely inert. Emma no longer had enough energy for any kind of feeling.

Four o'clock struck; and she got up to return to Yonville, as obedient to the force of habit as an automaton.

It was a beautiful day; it was one of those clear, crisp March days when the sun glistens in a completely white sky. Some citizens of Rouen in their Sunday clothes were out walking, seeming happy. She came to the Place du Parvis. People were coming out of vespers; the crowd was streaming out of the three doors, like a river through the three arches of a bridge, and in the midst of them, more motionless than a rock, stood the verger.

Then she remembered that day when, all anxious and filled with hope, she had entered into that great nave that extended out before her so deeply, but not as deeply as her love; and she continued walking, weeping behind her veil, dizzy, staggering, close to fainting.

"Careful!" cried a voice coming out of a courtyard gate that was opening.

She stopped to let a black horse pass, pawing the ground between the traces of a tilbury, carrying a gentleman dressed in sable fur. Who was that? She knew him ... The vehicle shot forward and disappeared.

It was him, the Viscount! She turned around; the street was deserted. And she was so overcome, so sorrowful, that she had to lean against a wall to keep from falling down.

But then she thought she was mistaken. Besides, she wasn't sure of anything anymore. Everything, both within her and outside of her, was abandoning her. She felt herself lost and falling beyond control into indefinable abysses; and it was almost with joy that she caught sight of the good Homais when she reached the *Red Cross* inn; he was overseeing a large box of pharmaceutical supplies being loaded onto the *Hirondelle*; in his hand he held six *cheminots* for his wife, wrapped up in a handkerchief.

Madame Homais was very fond of these small, heavy turban-shaped loaves of bread that people ate with salted butter during Lent—a last vestige of medieval food, dating back to the century of the Crusades, on which the robust Normans of old gorged themselves, imagining that they saw on the table, in the light of yellow torches, between their tankards of mead and their enormous cuts of meat, the heads of Saracens waiting to be devoured. The pharmacist's wife chewed them as they did, heroically, despite the foul state of her teeth; and so, every time Homais made a trip to the city, he never failed to bring some back to her, always purchasing them at the big bakery on the Rue Massacre.

"Delighted to see you!" he said, offering Emma his hand to help her into the *Hirondelle*.

He then hung up his *cheminots* on the baggage rack's strap, and he remained bareheaded, his arms crossed, in a pensive, Napoleonic pose.

But when the blind man appeared, as usual, at the foot of the hill, he exclaimed:

"I cannot understand why the authorities continue to tolerate such begging! They ought to lock up these miserable people and force them to do some work.

My word, Progress moves at a turtle's pace! We are floundering into downright barbarism!"

The blind man held out his hat, which flopped on the edge of the window, as if it were a loose piece of upholstery.

"Now there," said the pharmacist, "is a scrofulous infection!"

And although he was completely familiar with the poor devil, he pretended to be seeing him for the first time, muttering words like *cornea, opaque cornea, sclerotic, facies;* and then he asked in a paternal tone:

"Have you suffered a long time, my friend, from this frightful infirmity? Instead of getting drunk in bars, you'd do much better to follow a prescribed diet."

He urged him to take only good wine, good beer, and good meats. The blind man continued singing; he appeared, in fact, to be almost an idiot. Finally, Monsieur Homais opened his purse.

"Look, here's a sou; give me half of it back in change: and don't forget to follow my advice; you'll be the better for it."

Hivert permitted himself to express some doubts about the efficacy of Homais' advice. But the pharmacist insisted that he could cure him himself, with an antiphlogistic[6] salve of his own making, and he gave his address:

"Monsieur Homais, near the marketplace, I'm well known."

"And now," said Hivert, "to reward us for all this trouble, you should *show us your act.*"

The blind man sank down on his haunches, and his head thrown back, rolling his greenish eyes and sticking out his tongue, he rubbed his stomach with both hands while he emitted a sort of low howl like a starving dog. Emma, filled with disgust, tossed him a five-franc piece over her shoulder. It was the entirety of her fortune. It seemed a fine thing to her, throwing it away like that.

The coach had started off again when, suddenly, Monsieur Homais leaned out of the window and shouted back:

"No farinaceous foods, and no dairy products! Wear wool next to your skin, and expose the diseased parts to the smoke of juniper berries!"

Bit by bit, the sight of familiar objects drifting past her eyes distracted Emma from her present troubles. An overwhelming fatigue came over her, and she arrived at home dazed, discouraged, almost asleep.

"What will be will be!" she said to herself.

And after all, who knows? Why couldn't something extraordinary happen at any moment? Lheureux himself could even die.

At nine the next morning, she was awakened by the sound of voices in the square. A crowd had gathered in the market to read a large poster affixed to one of the poles, and she saw Justin climb up onto a stone in order to tear it down. But just at that moment, the village policeman grabbed him by the collar. Monsieur Homais came out of the pharmacy, and Madame Lefrançois, in the midst of the crowd, seemed to be making a speech.

"Madame! Madame!" cried Félicité as she ran in: "It's horrible!"

And the poor girl, very upset, handed her a sheet of yellow paper she had just torn off the door. Emma read, in a single glance, that all her furniture was up for sale.

6. Anti-inflammatory.

Then they looked at each other in silence. They had, servant and mistress, no secrets from each other. At last Félicité sighed:

"If I were you, Madame, I'd go see Monsieur Guillaumin."

"You think so?"

The question meant:

"You know their house through their servant: does the master ever speak about me?"

"Yes, go; you'll do well."

She dressed herself, putting on her black dress and her hood with jet beads; and, so that no one would see her (the crowd was still in the square), she took the river path, circling around the village.

When she reached the notary's gate, she was out of breath; the sky was dark, and a little snow was falling.

At the sound of the bell, Théodore, wearing a red vest, appeared on the steps; he came and opened the door almost familiarly, as he would for an acquaintance, and showed her into the dining room.

A large porcelain stove was humming below a cactus that occupied a niche in the wall, and in black frames, hanging against the oak-grained wallpaper, were Steuben's *Esmeralda* and Schopin's *Potiphar*.[7] The table was set, and the two silver warming dishes, the crystal doorknobs, the floor, the furniture—everything gleamed with a meticulous, English tidiness; the windows were ornamented with stained glass in their corners.

"This is the kind of dining room," Emma thought, "that I ought to have."

The notary came in, pressing his dressing gown patterned with palm trees tightly against his chest with one hand; with the other, he rapidly raised and then replaced his cap of brown velvet, tilted pretentiously to the right side, from which hung three blond strands of hair, drawn forward from the back and contoured around his bald head.

After offering her a seat, he sat down to eat, while making many excuses for his impoliteness.

"Monsieur," she said, "I would like to ask you . . . ."

"What, Madame? I'm listening."

She began to explain her situation to him.

Maître Guillaumin knew it all already, being secretly in league with the dry-goods merchant, from whom he could always get the capital he needed for the mortgages he was asked to arrange.

Thus, he knew (and better than she did) the long history of those promissory notes, minimal at first, endorsed by various people, with their due dates broadly spaced out and endlessly renewed, right up to the day when the merchant, gathering all his bills together, had his friend Vinçart begin the proceedings in his name, not wanting to appear quite such a predator in the eyes of his fellow citizens.

She mixed recriminations against Lheureux into her story, recriminations to which the notary responded from time to time with a noncommittal word.

7. The official in the court of Egypt who was Joseph's master; the wife of Potiphar tried to seduce him. The painting represents the seduction scene. Karl Steuben (1788–1856), a German history painter. Esmeralda is the gypsy girl in Hugo's *Notre Dame de Paris*. A painting titled *Esmeralda et Quasimodo* was exhibited in 1839. Schopin was the brother of the composer Chopin.

Eating his cutlet and drinking his tea, he lowered his chin into his sky-blue cravat, which was fastened with two diamond pins linked with a golden chain, and he smiled an odd smile, in an overly sweet, ambiguous manner. But seeing that her feet were damp:

"Come closer to the stove ... put them higher up ... against the porcelain."

She was afraid of getting it dirty. The notary replied gallantly:

"Beautiful things never do any harm."

She then tried to get him emotionally involved in her plight, and becoming emotional herself, she started telling him about how tight things were in her home, her worries, her needs. He understood all that: a woman of elegance! And without interrupting his dinner, he turned himself completely around toward her, so that his knee brushed against her boot, its sole curling and steaming slightly from the stove.

But when she asked him for three thousand francs, he pursed his lips, and then declared himself to be most sorry that he had not been in charge of managing her fortune, because there were a hundred very easy ways, even for a lady, to have made her money work for her. In the Grumesnil peat bogs, for instance, or in the building developments in Le Havre, she could have invested very safely and profitably; and he let her seethe in rage at the thought of the fantastic sums she would have certainly earned.

"Why was it," he continued, "that you didn't come to me?"

"I just don't know," she said.

"But why? Did I frighten you? I'm the one, really, who ought to be complaining! We know each other so little! And yet I'm so devoted to you: you don't doubt that any more, do you?"

He reached out his hand and took hers, covered it with a voracious kiss, and then held it on his knee; and he played delicately with her fingers, while he uttered a stream of compliments.

His insipid voice rustled like a running brook; a gleam in his eyes shone though his glasses, and his hands advanced into Emma's sleeve, so as to finger her arm. She felt the panting of his breath against her cheek. This man was making her horribly uncomfortable.

She sprang up abruptly and said to him:

"Monsieur, I'm waiting!"

"For what?" said the notary, who had suddenly gone extremely pale.

"That money."

"But ...."

Then, giving way to the eruption of a desire too strong to check:

"All right, yes!"

He dragged himself toward her on his knees, with no concern for his dressing gown.

"Please, stay! I love you!"

He seized her around the waist.

A purple flush raced up Madame Bovary's face. She recoiled with a terrible expression, crying out:

"You're trying to profit from my distress, Monsieur! I'm to be pitied, not to be sold!"

And she left.

The notary remained there astounded, his eyes fixed on his beautifully embroidered slippers. They were a lover's gift. The sight of them consoled him. And besides, he reflected that such an affair would have gotten him more involved than he wanted.

"What a monster! What a boor! . . . How contemptible!" she said to herself, rushing along nervously beneath the aspens lining the road. The disappointment over her failure reinforced the indignation she felt over her outraged honor; it seemed to her as if Providence was deliberately hunting her down; her pride swelled up again, and she had never had so much esteem for herself nor so much contempt for others. Something warrior-like was transporting her. She would have liked to strike men, spit in their faces, crush them all; and she continued walking swiftly straight ahead, pale, trembling, enraged, casting her tear-filled gaze all around the empty horizon, almost delighting in the hatred that was suffocating her.

When she caught sight of her house, a numbness came over her. She couldn't go any farther; but she had to; and anyway, where could she run to?

Félicité was waiting for her at the door.

"Well?"

"No!" said Emma.

And for a quarter of an hour, the two of them discussed the different people in Yonville who might be disposed to help her. But every time Félicité mentioned someone, Emma would reply:

"It's impossible! They wouldn't!"

"And Monsieur will be coming home!"

"I know, I know . . . Leave me alone."

She had tried everything. There was nothing more to do now; and when Charles appeared, she was, therefore, going to have to say to him:

"Go back. The carpet you're standing on is no longer ours. You don't own a single piece of furniture in your house, not a pin, not a straw, and I'm the one who has ruined you, you poor man!"

This would lead to a great sob, then he would cry abundantly, and finally, once the surprise of it had passed, he would forgive her.

"Yes," she muttered through clenched teeth, "he will forgive me, he who couldn't purchase my forgiveness for having known me if he had a million . . . Never! Never!"

The idea of Bovary being superior to her infuriated her. And then, whether she confessed or not, soon, very soon, tomorrow, he would know the whole catastrophe anyway; so she had to await that terrible scene and bow down under the weight of his magnanimity. She felt an urge to return to Lheureux's: what for? Then, to write to her father: it was too late; and it may be that now she repented for not having given in to that man who— when she heard the sound of a horse in the lane. It was him, he was opening the gate, he was whiter than the plaster on the wall. Rushing down the stairs, she escaped swiftly into the square; and the mayor's wife, who was chatting in front of the church with Lestiboudois, saw her go into the tax collector's.

She ran to tell Madame Caron. The two women went up into the attic; and, hidden behind some linen hanging on clothes racks, they posted themselves comfortably so as to be able to see directly into Binet's house.

He was alone, in his attic room, in the process of imitating, with his wood carving, one of those indescribable ivory shapes composed of crescents, of spheres dug one inside the other, the whole forming a sort of obelisk and having no function whatsoever; and he was entering upon the final phase—he was finally approaching his goal! In the dim light of his studio, the yellowish dust was flying from his tool, like a shower of sparks under the iron shoes of a galloping horse; the two wheels were turning, rumbling; Binet was smiling, his chin lowered, his nostrils flaring, seeming to be lost in one of those moments of utter happiness that occur, no doubt, only in the lower professions, where the intelligence is amused by easy difficulties, and is entirely satisfied, blissfully unaware of any larger sphere beyond it.

"Ah! There she is!" said Madame Tuvache.

But it was hardly possible, with the sound of the lathe, to hear what it was that she was saying.

At last, though, the two ladies thought they could make out the word *francs*, and Madame Tuvache whispered quietly:

"She's pleading with him, for more time to pay her taxes."

"So it seems!" replied the other.

They saw her walk up and down the room, examining the walls with all the napkin rings, the candle holders, the newel posts, while Binet caressed his beard with evident satisfaction.

"Is she going to order something from him?" said Madame Tuvache.

"But he doesn't sell any of his things!" her neighbor objected.

The tax collector seemed to be listening, his eyes widening as if he didn't understand. She continued in what seemed to be a gentle, suppliant manner. She drew close to him; her breast heaved; they spoke no more.

"Is she making advances to him?" said Madame Tuvache.

Binet blushed to the tips of his ears. She took his hands in hers.

"Oh, this is too much!"

And no doubt she was proposing some abomination; because the tax collector—but he was a brave man, he had fought at Bautzen and Lutzen, served in the French campaign,[8] and had even been recommended *for the cross of the Legion of Honor*—suddenly, as if he had seen a snake, jumped back and cried out:

"Madame! What are you thinking?"

"They ought to whip women like that!" said Madame Tuvache.

"Where did she go?" replied Madame Caron.

For she had disappeared as those words were being spoken; then, catching sight of her going down the main road and turning right as if headed for the cemetery, they lost themselves in conjectures.

"Madame Rolet," she said on reaching the wet nurse's house, "I'm choking! Unlace me."

8. The battles in France before the Allies captured Paris and forced the abdication of Napoleon and his banishment to Elba in 1814. Bautzen, in Saxony, was the scene of an 1813 battle in which Napoleon defeated the Prussians and Russians. Lützen, in Saxony, was the scene of another victory by Napoleon.

She threw herself on the bed; she sobbed. Madame Rolet covered her with a petticoat and remained standing beside her. When Emma didn't respond to her, the nurse walked away, sat down at her wheel, and began spinning flax.

"Oh! Stop it!" she muttered, thinking she heard Binet's lathe.

"What's bothering her?" the nurse asked herself. "What's she doing here?"

She had run there, impelled by some terror that that had driven her out of her house.

Lying on her back, immobile, her eyes fixed, she could perceive her surroundings only vaguely, though she tried—with an idiotic persistence—to make things out. She stared at the scales of peeling plaster on the wall, at two smoking sticks in the fire, burning end to end, and at a large spider walking up above her head, in a crack in the rafter. Finally, she began to collect her thoughts. She remembered ... One day, with Léon ... Oh, how long ago that was! ... The sun was glinting on the river, and clematis scent filled the air ... And then, carried away by her memories as if on a raging torrent, she soon arrived at the day before.

"What time is it?" she asked.

Madame Rolet went outside, lifted the fingers of her right hand toward the spot where the sky was brightest, and ambled slowly back inside, saying:

"Just about three o'clock."

"Ah! Thank you, thank you!"

Because he was going to come: she was sure of it! He would have found the money. But maybe he would go down there, not suspecting that she was here; and she ordered the nurse to run to her house and bring him.

"Hurry!"

"My dear lady, I'm going! I'm going!"

Now she was surprised that she hadn't thought of him right away; yesterday, he had given her his word, and he wouldn't fail; and she could already picture herself at Lheureux's, spreading out the three bank notes on his desk. Then she would have to invent some story to explain everything to Bovary. What should she say?

Meanwhile, the nurse was taking a long time in returning. But since there was no clock in the cottage, Emma feared she might be exaggerating the length of time. She went out and walked around the garden slowly, step by step; she went down the path all along the hedge, and then hurried back in hopes that the woman would have returned by another route. Finally, tired of waiting and assailed by suspicions that she tried to keep at bay, no longer sure whether she had been there for a century or a moment, she sat down in a corner and closed her eyes, covering her ears with her hands. Then the gate squeaked: she jumped up; before she could speak, Madame Rolet said to her:

"There's nobody at your house!"

"What?"

"No, nobody! And Monsieur is crying. He's calling for you. Everyone's looking for you."

Emma didn't respond. Her breath turned heavy, and her eyes rolled, while the peasant instinctively drew back, frightened by what she saw in her face, thinking she had gone mad. Suddenly she slapped her forehead and cried out, for the memory of Rodolphe had just penetrated her soul, like a great flash of lightning across a dark night sky. He was so good, so delicate, so generous! And besides, even if he did hesitate to do her this kindness, she knew very well that she could force him to, in the blink of an eye, by reminding him of their lost love. So she left for La Huchette, without perceiving that she was now hurrying to offer the very thing that had so horrified her earlier that same day, nor did she suspect in the least that she was prostituting herself.

CHAPTER 8

As she walked, she asked herself: "What am I going to say? Where will I start?" And the farther along she walked, the more she recognized the bushes, the trees, the rushes growing on the hillside, the chateau below. She found herself reliving the sensations of her first tender affections, and her poor shrunken heart felt itself expanding with the memory of love. A warm wind was blowing against her face; the snow, melting, was falling drop by drop from the buds onto the grass.

She went in, just as she used to do, through the little park gate, then came to the courtyard, bordered by a double row of densely planted lime trees. They swayed, rustling their long branches. The dogs in the kennels were all barking, and the sounds of their voices echoed, though no one came out.

She ascended the large, straight staircase with wooden balustrades, which led to the hallway paved with dusty stone; a row of rooms opened onto it, as in monasteries or inns. His was all the way at the end, on the left. When she came to put her fingers on the lock, all her strength suddenly abandoned her. She was afraid he wasn't there, almost wished for it, even though this was her only hope, her last chance for salvation. She collected herself for a moment, and reviving her courage in the feeling of how urgent her present need was, she entered.

He was in front of the low fire, both feet up on the chimneypiece, in the process of smoking a pipe.

"What! It's you!" he said, jumping up quickly.

"Yes, it's me! . . . I wanted, Rodolphe, to ask you for some advice."

But despite all her efforts, it was impossible for her to open her mouth.

"You haven't changed, you're as charming as ever!"

"Oh," she replied bitterly, "they must be pitiful charms, my friend, since you were able to reject them."

Then he began to explain his behavior, excusing himself in vague terms, unable to come up with any better ones.

She let his words work on her, and then his voice even more, and then, even more, the sight of him; so much so that she pretended to believe, or perhaps did believe, in his pretext for their rupture; this was, evidently, a secret on which a third person's honor and even life depended.

"It doesn't matter!" she said, looking at him sadly. "I've suffered enough!"

He replied in a philosophical tone:

"Such is life!"

"Has it at least," Emma replied, "been good for you since our separation?"

"Oh—neither good . . . nor bad."

"It might have been better if we hadn't parted."

"Yes—maybe so!"

"Do you think so?" she said, drawing closer to him.

And she sighed:

"Oh, Rodolphe! If you only knew! . . . I've loved you so much!"

At this point she took his hand, and they stayed a while with their fingers interlaced—as on the very first day, at the Agricultural Fair! Out of a sense of pride, he struggled against the feeling of tenderness. But, sinking down against his breast, she said to him:

"How did you think I could live without you? A person can't just drop the habit of being happy! I was desperate! I thought I would die! I'll tell you all about it, you'll see! And you, you ran away from me! . . . "

For in fact, during those three years he had very carefully avoided her, out of that natural cowardice that characterizes the stronger sex; and Emma continued, gently nodding her head, as affectionate as an amorous kitten:

"You've been in love with others, admit it. Oh, I understand that, of course! I forgive them; you will have seduced them the way you seduced me. You're a man, after all! You have everything it takes to make yourself loved. But we'll begin again, won't we? We'll love each other! Look, I'm laughing, I'm happy! . . . Say something!"

And she was ravishing to look at, with those eyes in which a tear still trembled, like the water from a storm cupped in a blue flower.

He pulled her onto his knees, and with the back of his hand he caressed the smooth bands of her hair, where, in the light of the dusk, a last ray of the sun flashed like a golden arrow. She bent her forehead down; he kissed her on the eyelids, very gently, with the tips of his lips.

"But you've been crying!" he said. "Why?"

She burst into sobs. Rodolphe believed it was the outpouring of her love; as she said nothing, he took her silence for one last gesture of modesty, and then he exclaimed:

"Oh, forgive me! You're the only one I really care for! I was an imbecile, and mean! I love you, I'll always love you! What's wrong? Tell me!"

He was kneeling down beside her.

"All right! . . . I'm ruined, Rodolphe. You have to give me three thousand francs!"

"But . . . But . . . ," he said, slowly getting back up, while his face took on a more serious expression.

"You know," she went on quickly, "that my husband has entrusted his entire fortune to a notary; he's run away. We've had to borrow; the patients don't pay us. But the liquidation of the estate isn't finished; we'll have money later on. But today, if we don't get three thousand francs, they're going to seize our property; it's going on right now, this very minute; and I've come here, counting on your friendship."

"Ah!" Rodolphe thought, becoming very pale very quickly. "So that's why she's come!"

At last he said, in a very calm tone:

"I don't have it, my dear Madame."

He was not at all lying. If he had had it, he probably would have given it to her, even though he generally found such noble gestures disagreeable: out of all the winds that blow against love, a request for money is the coldest, the one most likely to uproot it.

She stood still a few minutes, looking at him.

She repeated several times:

"You don't have it! . . . I should have spared myself this last humiliation. You never loved me! You're no better than all the others!"

She was betraying herself, losing control.

Rodolphe interrupted her, insisting that he himself was "hard up" at the moment.

"Oh, I feel sorry for you!" Emma said. "Yes, very much."

And, her eyes pausing on a damascened carbine that glinted in the gun rack:

"But when a person is that poor, he doesn't have silver on the butt of his rifle! He doesn't buy a clock inlaid with tortoiseshell!" she went on, pointing out a Boulle clock; "nor silver-gilt whistles for his whips"—she touched them!—"nor charms for his watch chain. Oh, he lacks for nothing! Right down to a liquor stand in his bedroom; because you love yourself, you live very well, with your chateau, your farms, your forests; you hunt with hounds, you travel to Paris . . . Oh! And even these," she cried, picking up a pair of cufflinks from the mantel, "the least of these little stupid things! You could turn any of this into money! . . . Oh, but I don't want it! Keep it!"

And she threw the cufflinks as hard as she could across the room, so their gold chain broke as they hit the wall.

"But me, I would have given you everything! I would have sold everything, I would have worked with my hands, I would have begged on the roadsides, for a smile, for a look, to hear you say 'thank you.' And you sit there calmly in your armchair, as if you haven't already made me suffer enough! If it hadn't been for you, and you know it perfectly well, I could have had a happy life! What drove you to do it? Was it a bet? But you loved me, you said so . . . And again just now . . . Oh, you would have done better to chase me away! My hands are still warm with your kisses, and look, there's the place on the carpet where you swore, at my knees, an eternity of love. You made me believe it: for two years, you led me along through the most magnificent, the sweetest dream! . . . Well? And our plans for our trip, you remember? Oh! Your letter, that letter! It tore my heart out! And then, when I come back to him, to him, and he's rich, happy, free!—to beg for some help, the kind of help that a total stranger would offer, a supplicant, bringing to him all my tenderness, he repulses me, because it would cost him three thousand francs!"

"I haven't got it!" Rodolphe replied, with that perfect calm that acts like a shield covering angry resignation.

She left. The walls were trembling, the ceiling crushing down upon her; and she went back down the long lane, slipping on the heaps of dead leaves the wind was scattering around. At last she reached the ditch in front of the gate; she was so anxious to open it that she broke her fingernails against the lock. Then, a hundred paces on, out of breath, ready to collapse, she stopped. And turning back, she looked one more time at the impassive chateau, with its park, its gardens, its three courtyards, and all the windows on its façade.

She remained, lost in a stupor, her only awareness of herself being the pulsing in her arteries, which seemed to have escaped from her and to have become a muffled, rhythmic music that filled the entire countryside. The ground under her feet was as soft as a wave, and the furrows in the fields looked to her like immense brown billows breaking around her. Everything that she had held in her mind—memories, thoughts—slipped out all at once, like a thousand fireworks going off. She saw her father, Lheureux's office, their hotel room down there, another landscape. Madness seized her, she was afraid, and she succeeded in getting hold of herself, but in fact only in a confused way; for she could not at all remember the cause of her terrifying state—that is, the money issue. Her only suffering was from her love, and she could feel her soul slipping away from her in that memory, like the mortally injured who feel their lives leaving them through their bleeding wound.

Night was falling, crows were flying.

It seemed to her suddenly that globes the color of fire were bursting in the air like bullets being fired and turning, turning, to melt at last into the snow, between the branches of the trees. In the middle of one of them, Rodolphe's face appeared. They multiplied, and they closed in upon her, penetrated her; everything disappeared. She recognized again the lights of the houses, shining far off through the fog.

Then her situation presented itself to her, like an abyss. She panted hard enough to burst her chest. Then, in a heroic exaltation that made her almost joyful, she ran down the hillside, crossed the cow bridge, the path, the lane, the marketplace, and arrived in front of the pharmacist's shop.

No one was there. She was going to enter; but the sound of the bell might make someone come out; and slipping in by the gate, holding her breath, feeling her way along the walls, she came almost to the door of the kitchen, where a candle was burning on the stove. Justin, in his shirtsleeves, was carrying out a dish.

"Ah! They're having their dinner. Wait."

He came back in. She rapped on the window. He came out to her.

"The key! The one for upstairs, where the . . . "

"What?"

And he looked at her, startled by how pale her face was, a white slash against the black background of the night. She seemed extraordinarily beautiful to him, and as majestic as a phantom; without understanding what she wanted, he had a presentiment of something terrible.

But she repeated quickly, her voice low, her voice sweet, melting:

"I want it! Give it to me."

Because the partition was so thin, they could hear the forks scraping against plates in the dining room.

She claimed she needed to kill some rats who were disturbing her sleep.

"I have to tell Monsieur."

"No! Wait!"

Then, in an indifferent tone:

"Oh, it's not worth the bother, I'll tell him myself later. Let's go, light the way for me!"

She entered the hallway that led to the laboratory. Against one wall hung a key labeled *capharnaüm*.

"Justin!" the pharmacist called, impatiently.

"Let's go!"

And he followed her.

The key turned in the lock, and she went directly to the third shelf, so well did her memory guide her, picked up the blue jar, pulled out its cork, plunged her hand in, and pulling it out filled with a white powder, she began to eat.

"Stop!" he cried, throwing himself at her.

"Be quiet! Someone will come . . ."

He stood in despair, wanting to call out.

"Don't say anything about this, or the blame will fall on your master!"

Then she turned around, suddenly feeling relieved, almost serene with the feeling of having completed a duty.

When Charles, shocked by the news of the household seizure, had come back home, Emma had just left. He cried out, wept, fainted, but she didn't return. Where could she be? He sent Félicité to Homais', to Monsieur Tuvache's, to Lheureux's, to the *Golden Lion*, everywhere; and in the intervals of his anxiety, he could see his reputation destroyed, their fortune lost, Berthe's future ruined! For what reason? Not a word! He waited until six o'clock. Finally, unable to stand it any longer, and imagining that she had gone to Rouen, he went out on the highway, walked down it a mile, encountered no one, waited longer, and then returned home.

She had come back.

"What happened? . . . Why? . . . Explain it to me? . . ."

She sat at her desk and wrote a letter that she then slowly sealed, adding the date and the time. Then she said in a solemn voice:

"You'll read this tomorrow; from now until then, I beg you, do not ask me a single question! . . . No, not one!"

"But . . ."

"Oh! Leave me alone!"

And she lay down full length on her bed.

A bitter taste in her mouth awakened her. She saw Charles, and she closed her eyes again.

She watched herself with curiosity, to discern whether she felt any pain. No! Nothing yet. She heard the ticking of the clock, the sound of the fire, and the breathing of Charles, standing close to her bed.

"Ah! Death isn't such a difficult thing!" she thought to herself. "I'm going to go to sleep, and it will all be over!"

She drank a mouthful of water and turned toward the wall.

That awful taste, like ink, continued.

"I'm thirsty! . . . Oh, I'm so thirsty!" she sighed.

"What's the matter?" said Charles, handing her a glass.

"It's nothing! Open the window . . . I'm stifling!"

And she was seized by an attack of nausea, so sudden that she barely had the time to get her handkerchief from under the pillow.

"Take it away!" she said quickly. "Throw it out!"

He asked her questions; she didn't respond. She was holding herself absolutely still, in the fear that the slightest movement would make her vomit. At the same time, she felt an icy cold rising from her feet up toward her heart.

"Ah! So now it's starting," she murmured.

"What did you say?"

She rolled her head from side to side, gently, but filled with anguish, and she kept opening her jaws, as if she felt something very heavy weighing on her tongue. At eight o'clock, the vomiting started again.

Charles, examining the basin, saw that there was a sort of white gritty substance sticking to the bottom of the porcelain.

"That's strange! That's extraordinary!" he repeated.

But she said loudly:

"No, you're mistaken!"

Then, as delicately as a caress, he passed his hand over her stomach. She let out a piercing cry. He recoiled, very frightened.

Then she began to moan, weakly at first. A great shuddering started in her shoulders, and she became paler than the sheet her clenched fingers were digging themselves into. Her pulse was irregular, and almost imperceptible now.

Drops of sweat were oozing from her bluish face, which was stiffening now as if some metallic vapor were exhaling itself from inside her. Her teeth were chattering, her wide-open eyes were gazing vaguely all around her, and to every question her only reply was to nod her head; she even smiled two or three times. Bit by bit, her moans grew stronger. A low howl burst from her; she claimed that she was feeling better and that she would be getting up soon. But she was seized by convulsions; she cried out:

"Oh, it's horrible, my God!"

He threw himself down on his knees against the bed.

"Speak! What did you eat? Answer me, in the name of God!"

And he looked at her with a tenderness in his eyes like nothing she had ever seen.

"All right, there . . . there!" she said in a faltering voice.

He ran to the desk, broke open the seal and read the letter out loud: *No one should be blamed* . . . He stopped, passed his hand over his eyes, and read it again.

"What? Help! Help me!"

And he could only repeat the word: "Poisoned! Poisoned!" Félicité ran to Homais', who shouted it out as he crossed the square; Madame Lefrançois heard it in the *Golden Lion;* some got up to tell their neighbors, and all night the entire village was awake.

Desperate, stammering, ready to collapse, Charles paced back and forth in the bedroom. He bumped into the furniture, pulled at his hair, and the pharmacist had never thought he would see such a frightful spectacle.

He went back home to write to Monsieur Canivet and to Doctor Larivière. He lost his head; he ruined more than fifteen drafts. Hippolyte set out for Neufchâtel, and Justin spurred Bovary's horse on so hard that he was forced to leave it by the Bois-Guillaume Hill, exhausted and three-quarters dead.

Charles wanted to flip through his medical dictionary; he couldn't see, the lines danced in front of his eyes.

"Stay calm!" said the pharmacist. "It's just a matter of administering some powerful antidote. What was the poison?"

Charles showed him the letter. It was arsenic.

"All right!" Homais replied. "We'll have to do an analysis."

Because he knew that for every case of poisoning, one must do an analysis; and the other, who didn't understand, replied:

"Ah—do it! Do it! Save her . . . "

Then, coming back near her, he sank down upon the carpet, and he lay his head against the edge of her bed, sobbing.

"Don't cry!" she said to him. "I won't be tormenting you much longer!"

"But why? What made you do it?"

She replied:

"It had to be done, my friend."

"But weren't you happy? Was it my fault? But I did everything I could!"

"Yes, that's true . . . You are good, you are!"

And she ran her hand through his hair, slowly. The sweetness of that sensation redoubled his grief; he felt his entire being crumbling in despair at the thought that he was going to have to lose her, just when she had avowed more love for him than she ever had before; and he couldn't think of anything to do; he didn't know, he didn't dare, the urgent need for an immediate decision had overwhelmed him completely.

She was finished now, she thought, with all the betrayals, all the basenesses and the innumerable lusts that had tortured her. She hated no one right now; a confusion like the dusk was settling over her thoughts, and out of all the sounds on the earth, Emma heard only the intermittent lamentation of that poor heart, sweet and indistinct, like the last fading echo of a symphony.

"Bring me the little one," she said, rising up on one elbow.

"You aren't feeling any worse, are you?" asked Charles.

"No! No!"

The child, serious and still half asleep, entered in the arms of the servant, in her long nightdress, from which her naked feet were poking out. She looked with astonishment at the disordered room and blinked her eyes, blinded by the candles burning on all the tables. They must have reminded her of the mornings of New Year's Day or of Mid-Lent when, awakened early like this and amid similar candles, she would come to her mother's bed to receive her present, because she began to say:

"Where is it, Mama?"

And when no one said anything:

"I don't see my little slipper."

Félicité bent her down over the bed, while she continued to look over toward the mantelpiece.

"Has Nurse taken it?" she asked.

And at that name, which brought back the memory of her adulteries and her calamities, Madame Bovary turned her head away, as if from a more disgusting poison than the one she had put in her mouth. But Berthe remained on the bed.

"Oh! Your eyes are so big, Mama! And you're so pale! Look how you're sweating!"

Her mother looked at her.

"I'm afraid!" said the little one, starting away from her.

Emma took her hand to kiss it, but she tried to pull it away.

"That's enough! Take her away!" exclaimed Charles, who stood sobbing in the alcove.

At that point the symptoms stopped for a time; she appeared less agitated; and at every insignificant word, at every slightly calmer breath she took, he began to regain hope. Finally, when Canivet came in, he threw himself upon him, weeping.

"Oh, it's you! Thank you! You're so good! But everything is getting better. Here, have a look at her . . ."

His colleague was not at all of that opinion, and, preferring *not to take half-measures*, as he put it, he prescribed an emetic, in order to empty the stomach completely.

Very soon she was vomiting blood. Her lips were clenching more tightly. Her limbs were stiffening, her body covered with brown spots, and her pulse slid away underneath his fingers like a stretched thread, like a harp's string about to break.

Then she began screaming, horribly. She cursed the poison, hurled abuse at it, implored it to hurry, and with her rigid arms she pushed away everything that Charles, in even more agony than she, was trying to make her drink. He was standing, his handkerchief to his lips, moaning, weeping, suffocating from the sobs that shook him all the way down to his heels; Félicité was running back and forth in the room; Homais, motionless, was letting out great sighs, and Monsieur Canivet, keeping his calm as always, was nonetheless beginning to feel troubled.

"The devil! . . . Still, she's been purged, and as soon as the cause ceases . . ."

"The effect must cease," said Homais; "it's obvious."

"But save her!" Bovary exclaimed.

So, without listening to the pharmacist, who was hazarding the hypothesis that "It may be a salutary paroxysm," Canivet was beginning to administer an antidote, when they all heard the cracking of a whip; all the windows rattled, and a post-chaise drawn by three horses abreast, up to their ears in mud, galloped around the corner of the marketplace. It was Doctor Larivière.

The apparition of a god could not have caused more excitement. Bovary raised his hands to heaven, Canivet stopped short what he was doing, and Homais removed his cap as soon as the doctor entered.

He belonged to that great surgical school begotten of Bichat,[9] to that generation, now disappeared, of philosophical practitioners who, cherishing their art with a fanatical love, exercised it with passion and with wisdom! In his hospital, everyone trembled when he got angry, and his students venerated him so much that the moment they were established, they set about imitating him as closely as possible; so that one would see them, in the towns all over the region, wearing the same long, comfortable merino coat and black frock jacket that he wore, whose unbuttoned sleeves came down slightly over his brawny hands, which never wore gloves, as if to be more ready to plunge themselves into human suffering. Scorning medals, titles, and academies—hospitable, generous, fatherly with the poor and practicing virtue without believing in it—he might have passed for a saint if the strength of his intellect didn't make him feared like a demon. His gaze, more incisive than his scalpels, would penetrate right into your soul, right through every pretension and every reticence, and excise every lie hiding beneath. And so he went on through life, filled with that relaxed majesty that comes with the awareness of a great talent, of a solid fortune, and of forty years of hard-working, irreproachable life.

He frowned as soon as he entered the doorway, seeing Emma's cadaverous face as she lay stretched out on her back, her mouth open. Then, while appearing to listen to Canivet, he rubbed his index finger under his nose, repeating:

"That's fine, that's fine."

9. Marie-Françoise-Xavier Bichat (1771–1802), author of an *Anatomie générale* (1801).

But he made a slight shrug with his shoulders. Bovary observed it; they looked at each other; and this man, so habituated to the sight of misery, could not restrain a tear from dropping and falling on his shirtfront.

He brought Canivet into the neighboring room. Charles followed.

"She's very sick, isn't she? What if we applied some mustard plasters? I don't know what to do! Find something, you've saved so many!"

Charles put both arms around him, and he looked at him in a bewildered, supplicating way, half fainting against his breast.

"Come on, poor man, be brave! There's nothing more to be done."

And Doctor Larivière turned away.

"You're leaving?"

"I'll come back."

He went out, as if to give orders to the postilion, along with Monsieur Canivet, who likewise had no desire to see Emma die under his hands.

The pharmacist joined them on the square. He was temperamentally incapable of separating himself from celebrated men. Thus, he begged Monsieur Larivière to do him the great honor of dining with him.

He immediately sent to the *Golden Lion* for some pigeons, to the butcher for every cutlet he had, to Tuvache for cream, to Lestiboudois for eggs; and the pharmacist himself helped in the preparations, while Madame Homais said, pulling the strings of her jacket:

"You must pardon us, Monsieur; for, in our poor village, unless one has a day's warning . . ."

"Wine glasses!" hissed Homais.

"If we were in town, at least, we could have served you stuffed pig's feet."

"Be quiet! . . . Come to the table, Doctor!"

He thought it would be a good idea, after they had begun to eat, to furnish a few details about the catastrophe.

"We first observed a siccative pharynx, followed by intolerable epigastric pains, then superpurgation, then coma."

"How did she poison herself?"

"I don't know, Doctor, and I can hardly imagine where she could have procured that arsenious acid."

Justin, who was carrying a pile of dishes, was suddenly seized with a fit of trembling.

"What's the matter with you?" asked the pharmacist.

At that question, the young man let everything fall to the ground, with a great crash.

"Imbecile!" Homais exclaimed. "Clumsy oaf! Stupid donkey!"

But abruptly mastering himself:

"I wanted, Doctor, to try an analysis, and *primo*, I delicately introduced into a tube . . ."

"It would have been much better," said the surgeon, "to have introduced your fingers into her throat."

His colleague said nothing, having just a moment before received a strong reprimand regarding his own emetic—so that the good Canivet, so arrogant and long-winded with the incident of the clubfoot, was very modest today; he never stopped smiling, with a look of approval on his face.

Homais was basking in the pride of playing host, and the thought of Bovary's affliction contributed subtly to his own pleasure through an egoistic contrast with his own situation. And then the presence of the doctor positively transported him. He displayed his erudition, alluding almost at random to cantharides, upas, manchineel, adder . . .

"And I have even read that various people have become poisoned, Doctor, and virtually struck down by black puddings that have been over-smoked! At least, so it was reported in a fine paper composed by one of our leading pharmaceutical experts, the celebrated Cadet de Gassicourt!"[1]

Madame Homais reappeared, carrying one of those shaky machines that have to be heated with a spirit lamp; for Homais insisted on making his coffee at the table, having roasted, ground, and blended it himself as well.

"*Saccharum*, Doctor," he said, offering the sugar.

Then he had all his children come down, curious to have the surgeon's opinion on their constitutions.

Finally, Monsieur Larivière was leaving when Madame Homais asked for some advice concerning her husband. He was thickening his blood by going to sleep every evening after dinner.

"Oh! I don't think *thick blood's* his problem."

And, smiling a little at this joke that went over his listener's head, the doctor opened the door. But the pharmacy was stuffed with people, and he had a great deal of trouble getting rid of, first, Monsieur Tuvache, who was afraid his wife would get her lungs inflamed from her habit of spitting into the fire; then of Binet, who suffered from sudden attacks of hunger; then of Madame Caron, who had tinglings; then of Lheureux, who had vertigo; then of Lestiboudois, who had rheumatism; then of Madame Lefrançois, who had heartburn. At last the three horses went off, and the general feeling was that he had not been at all helpful.

Their attention was distracted by the appearance of Monsieur Bournisien, who was walking through the marketplace with the holy oils.

Homais—out of duty to his principles—compared priests to crows attracted by the smell of the dead; the sight of a cleric was personally disagreeable to him, because cassocks reminded him of shrouds, and he cursed the one out of fear of the other.

Nevertheless, not slacking before what he termed his *mission*, he returned to Bovary's in the company of Canivet—who had been strongly urged to stay on by Monsieur Larivière before he left. If it had not been for his wife's objections, Homais would have brought his two sons along, in order to accustom them to difficult circumstances, as a lesson, an example, a solemn tableau that would remain in their heads afterward.

When they went in, the room was filled with mournful solemnity. On the worktable, covered over with a white napkin, there were five or six small cotton balls on a silver plate, near a large crucifix, between two burning candles. Emma lay with her chin sunk down upon her chest and her eyes unnaturally wide open: and her poor hands were dragging themselves over the covers, with that hideous, gentle gesture of the dying, who seem to be already drawing the

1. The pharmacist of Emperor Napoleon I who had considerable trouble under the Restoration because of his liberal ideas.

shroud over them. Pale as a statue, his eyes red as coals, Charles, not crying now, was facing her from the foot of the bed while the priest, kneeling on one knee, was murmuring some words in a low voice.

She turned her face slowly and appeared to be seized with sudden joy at seeing the violet stole, no doubt rediscovering, in this moment of extraordinary calm, the lost pleasures of her first mystical flights, along with visions of the eternal beatitude that was now beginning.

The priest rose to pick up the crucifix; and she stretched out her neck like someone thirsting, and pressing her lips to the body of the Man-God with all her dying powers, she placed there the most loving kiss she had ever given. He went on to recite the *Misereatur* and the *Indulgentiam*, dipped his right thumb in the oil, and began the unctions: first upon the eyes, which had so lusted after earthly luxuries; then upon the nostrils, so fond of warm breezes and amorous scents; then upon the mouth, which had opened to lie, which had moaned with pride and cried out in sensuality; then upon the hands, which had delighted in lustful contact; and finally upon the soles of the feet, so swift in the past when she had run to satisfy her desires, and which now would never walk again.

The priest wiped his fingers, threw the bits of cotton soaked in oil into the fire, and returned to sit beside the dying woman to tell her that she should now join her sufferings with those of Jesus Christ and surrender herself to divine mercy.

As he completed his exhortations, he tried to place a blessed candle in her hands, a symbol of the celestial glories that would soon surround her. Emma, too weak, could not close her fingers, and the candle, but for Monsieur Bournisien, would have fallen to the ground.

But she was no longer quite so pale, and on her face was an expression of serenity, as if the sacrament had cured her.

The priest did not fail to point this out; he even explained to Bovary that the Lord, sometimes, lengthened the lives of individuals when He thought it right for their salvation; and Charles remembered the day when, close to death then also, she had received Communion.

"Maybe there's still room for hope," he thought.

And in fact she looked all around her, slowly, like someone awakening from a dream, and then, in a clear voice, she asked for her mirror, and she remained bent over it for some time; until the moment when big tears began to fall from her eyes. Then she turned her head away with a sigh, and fell back on the pillow.

Her chest soon began to heave rapidly; her entire tongue protruded from her mouth; her eyes were rolling as they grew dimmer, like two lamp globes about to die out, so that one might have thought she was already dead, except for the frightening heaving of her sides, shaking with violent breaths, as if the soul were leaping inside, trying to get itself free. Félicité knelt before the crucifix, and even the pharmacist flexed his knees a little, while Monsieur Canivet looked abstractedly outside at the square. Bournisien began to pray again, his face bowed against the edge of the bed, his long black cassock trailing behind him into the room. Charles was on the other side, on his knees, his arms stretched out toward Emma. He had taken her hands and was holding them tightly, shuddering with every beat of her heart, as if at the aftershocks of a collapsing building. As the death-rattle grew stronger, the priest sped up his prayers; they mixed with the stifled sobs of

Bovary, and sometimes every sound seemed to be lost, absorbed into the murmur of the Latin syllables, which tolled like a death-bell.

Abruptly, they could hear the sound of loud clogs outside on the sidewalk, and the rapping of a stick; and a voice rose up, a hoarse voice, that sang:

> Often the warmth of a beautiful day
> Makes a young girl dream of love.

Emma sprang up like a galvanized corpse, her hair undone, her eyes fixed, gaping.

> To glean with care the ears of corn
> The scythe has all cut down,
> My Nanette herself bends down
> Toward the giving earth.

"The blind man!" she cried.

And Emma began to laugh, a horrible laugh, frenetic and despairing, believing she could see the hideous face of the beggar, standing out against the eternal shadows like a sudden terror.

> The wind was plenty strong that day,
> And up her short skirt blew!

A convulsion seized her and threw her back upon the mattress. They all drew closer to her. She was no longer living.

CHAPTER 9

There is always a period of shock that sets in after someone's death, so difficult it is to comprehend that visitation from nothingness, and to resign ourselves to believe in it. But even so, when Charles saw her completely motionless, he threw himself upon her, crying out:

"Farewell! Farewell!"

Homais and Canivet pulled him out of the bedroom.

"Control yourself!"

"Yes," he said, struggling free of them, "I'll be reasonable, I won't do anything foolish. But leave me alone! I want to see her! She's my wife!"

And he wept.

"Cry," said the pharmacist. "Give nature a free rein; it will console you!"

As weak now as a child, Charles let himself be guided downstairs to the drawing room, and soon Monsieur Homais returned home.

Outside, on the square, he was accosted by the blind man who, having dragged himself to Yonville in hopes of getting the antiphlogistic salve, was asking every passerby where the pharmacist lived.

"Oh, fine! As if I didn't have more important fish to fry right now! No, come back later."

And he hurried into the pharmacy.

He had to write two letters, to make up a sedative potion for Bovary, to find some lie to cover up the poisoning, and to write up an article about it for the *Lantern*, not to mention all the people waiting for him in order to hear the news; and when the Yonvillians had all heard his story about the arsenic she had mistaken for sugar while making a vanilla cream, Homais, once again, returned to Bovary's.

He found him alone (Monsieur Canivet having just left), sitting in the armchair near the window, staring at the floor with the expression of an idiot.

"You have to decide on the time for the ceremony," said the pharmacist.

"Why? What ceremony?"

Then, stammering and afraid:

"Oh! No—not really? No, I want to keep her with me."

Homais, to maintain his composure, picked up a carafe from the shelf to water the geraniums.

"Oh, thank you!" said Charles. "You're so good!"

But he broke down again, suffocating under the abundance of memories that this gesture of the pharmacist's brought back to him.

So, to distract him, Homais thought it would be wise to talk a bit of horticulture; plants needed humidity. Charles bowed his head in a sign of agreement.

"Besides, the good weather will be coming back soon."

"Ah!" said Bovary.

The pharmacist, running out of ideas, began to draw back the small window curtains.

"Look, it's Monsieur Tuvache going by."

Charles repeated, like a machine:

"Monsieur Tuvache going by."

Homais didn't dare bring up the subject of the funeral preparations again; the cleric was the one who finally got him to resolve the issue.

He shut himself up in his consulting room, took a pen, and after having sobbed for a while, he wrote:

"I want her to be buried in her wedding dress, with white shoes and a wreath. Let them spread her hair out over her shoulders; three coffins, one of oak, one of mahogany, one of lead. Let no one speak about it to me at all, I'll be strong enough. Let a large sheet of green velvet be placed over everything. This is my will. Let it be done."

The gentlemen were shocked by such romantic ideas coming from Bovary, and soon the pharmacist came to say to him:

"The velvet seems to me to be excessive. Besides, the expense . . . "

"Is it any of your business?" cried Charles. "Leave me alone! You didn't love her! Go away!"

The cleric took him by the arm to make him take a walk in the garden. He discoursed upon the vanity of all earthly things. God was truly great, truly good; one had to submit to His decrees, and even to be thankful for them.

Charles burst out in blasphemy:

"I detest that God of yours!"

"The spirit of rebellion is still within you," sighed the cleric.

Charles was already far away. He walked with great strides, along the wall, by the fruit trees, and he ground his teeth, and he looked upward, cursing the heavens; but not one single leaf stirred.

A light rain was falling. Charles, his shirt open, began to shiver; he went back inside and sat down in the kitchen.

At six o'clock, the sound of clanking iron could be heard in the square: it was the *Hirondelle* arriving; and he leaned his head against the window, watching the travelers descend one after the other. Félicité spread out a mattress for him in the drawing room; he threw himself upon it and went to sleep.

Despite being a philosopher, Monsieur Homais respected the dead. Thus, without holding any grudge against poor Charles, he came back in the evening to sit up with the corpse, bringing three books along with him and a pocketbook for taking notes.

Monsieur Bournisien was already there, and two large candles were burning at the head of the bed, which had been taken out from the alcove.

Silence always weighed on the pharmacist, so he was not long in formulating some laments for the "unfortunate young woman"; and the priest answered that there was nothing to be done now except to pray for her.

"However," Homais replied, "it has to be one of two possibilities: either she has died in a state of grace (as the Church terms it), in which case she has no need of our prayers; or she has died impenitent (which is, I believe, the ecclesiastical expression), and in that case . . . "

Bournisien interrupted, replying peevishly that prayer was necessary in any case.

"But," the pharmacist objected, "since God knows all our needs, what's the point of praying?"

"What!" exclaimed the cleric. "The point of prayer! So you aren't a Christian?"

"Excuse me!" Homais said. "I admire Christianity. It has, to begin with, freed the slaves and introduced into the world a morality . . . "

"That's not the point of it! All the texts . . . "

"Oh, oh! As for the texts, open up your history books; it's well known that the texts have been falsified by the Jesuits."

Charles came in and, moving toward the bed, slowly opened the curtains.

Emma's head was bent toward her right shoulder. The corner of her mouth, which was open, looked like a black hole in the lower half of her face, and her two thumbs remained curled against the palms of her hands; a sort of white dust seemed to be sprinkled on her eyelashes, and her eyes were beginning to disappear behind a thick pallor that resembled a fine web, as if spiders had been spinning over them. The sheet sank down from her breasts to her knees, and then rose up again at the tips of her toes; and it seemed to Charles that some infinite mass, some enormous weight was pressing down upon her.

The church clock struck two o'clock. They could hear the river's loud murmur, running past out there in the shadows, at the foot of the terrace. Monsieur Bournisien now and then would blow his nose loudly, and Homais' pen would scratch on the paper.

"Come along, my friend," he said, "get to bed; this sight is tearing you apart!"

Once Charles had gone, the pharmacist and the priest resumed their discussion.

"Read Voltaire!" said the one. "Read D'Holbach, read the *Encyclopédie*!"[2]

2. Paul-Henri Dietrich, baron d'Holbach (1723–1789), friend and disciple of Diderot and one of the most outspoken opponents of religion in the French Enlightenment. The *Encyclopedia*, a dictionary of the sciences, arts, and letters, edited by Diderot and d'Alembert (1751–72), is the intellectual monument of the French Enlightenment, a fountainhead of later secular and agnostic thought.

"Read the *Letters of Some Portuguese Jews!*"[1] said the other. "Read the *Reason of Christianity*[3] by Nicolas, a retired judge!"

They grew heated; they grew red in the face; they talked over each other, without listening; Bournisien was shocked at the other's audacity; Homais marveled at such stupidity; and the two of them were not far from exchanging open insults when Charles suddenly reappeared. A kind of fascination drew him back. He continually came back up the staircase.

He stood facing her, in order to see her better, and he lost himself in a contemplation of her so profound that he no longer felt his sorrow.

He remembered stories about catalepsy, about the miracles of magnetism; and he told himself that if he could will it intensely enough, he might be able to bring her back to life. Once he even bent toward her and called in a low voice, "Emma! Emma!" His breathing was so strong that it made the candle flames tremble against the wall.

At dawn, Madame Bovary senior arrived; when Charles embraced her, he burst into a new fit of weeping. She tried, as the pharmacist had, to make a few comments about the expenses of the burial. He flew into such a rage that she said no more, and he even ordered her to go into town at once to buy what was needed.

Charles remained alone all afternoon; Berthe had been taken to Madame Homais; Félicité stayed upstairs, in the bedroom, along with Madame Lefrançois.

In the evening, he received some visitors. He would get up, shake hands without being able to speak; then the guest would find a seat among the others, forming a big semicircle around the fireplace. Their faces lowered, their legs crossed, they would swing their legs and now and then give a sigh; and every one of them was bored beyond measure; but no one would leave.

Homais, when he returned at nine o'clock (he had been constantly running back and forth on the square for two days), was carrying a stock of camphor, benzene, and aromatic herbs. He also carried a vase full of chlorine to keep miasmas away. At just that moment, the maid, Madame Lefrançois, and Madame Bovary senior were working with Emma, finishing dressing her; and they drew down a long, stiff veil that covered her all the way down to her satin slippers.

Félicité was sobbing:

"Oh! My poor mistress! My poor mistress!"

"Look at her," said the innkeeper with a sigh, "how pretty she still is! You'd swear she would be getting up any minute."

Then they bent down to arrange the wreath on her head.

They had to lift the head a little, and at that a stream of black liquids came out of her mouth, as if she were vomiting.

"Oh! My God! Look out for the dress!" cried Madame Lefrançois. "Help us!" she said to the pharmacist. "You aren't afraid, are you?"

"Me? Afraid?" he replied, with a shrug of his shoulders. "Hardly! I saw plenty of them at the Hôtel-Dieu, when I was studying pharmacy! We would make punch in the dissecting amphitheater! Nothingness holds no terrors for the

3. One of the many books defending Roman Catholicism by Jean-Jacques-Auguste Nicolas (1807–1888). *Letters of Some Portuguese Jews* (1769) refers to a book by Abbé Antoine Guéné directed against Voltaire.

philosopher; and I might add that I even plan to bequeath my body to the hospitals, in order to serve the cause of Science."

When the priest arrived, he asked how Monsieur was holding up; and, when the pharmacist told him, he replied:

"The blow, you understand, is still too recent!"

Then Homais congratulated him on not having to worry, as everyone else did, about the eventual loss of a beloved; and from there the discussion turned to the celibacy of priests.

"Because," the pharmacist said, "it just isn't natural for a man to do without women! There have been crimes . . ."

"Oh, for pity's sake!" exclaimed the cleric. "How would you expect a married person to keep the secrets of the confessional, for example?"

Homais attacked confession. Bournisien defended it; he expounded on the acts of restitution that it brought about. He cited anecdotes about thieves who turned honest all of a sudden. Military men, when they approached the tribunal of penitence, had felt the scales falling from their eyes. And there was a minister in Fribourg . . .

His companion was asleep. Then, finding the air stuffy in the room, he opened the window, which awakened the pharmacist.

"Here, have a pinch of snuff!" he said to him. "Take it; it'll clear your head."

A continual barking could be heard somewhere off in the distance.

"Do you hear a dog howling?" asked the pharmacist.

"They say that they can sense death," replied the cleric. "It's like bees; they come flying out of their hives when a person passes away." But Homais made no comment on these superstitions, because he had fallen asleep again.

Monsieur Bournisien, more robust, continued to move his lips quietly for a while; then, insensibly, his chin began to lower, his great black book fell, and he began to snore.

They were facing each other, stomachs protruding, faces puffy, seeming to frown: after all their discord, they were united at last in the same human weakness; and they moved no more than the corpse next to them, which seemed to be sleeping as well.

When Charles came in, he did not wake them. It was the final time. He had come to say his good-byes.

The aromatic herbs were still smoking, and little clouds of bluish vapor mingled, near the open window, with the morning fog that was entering. There were still a few stars out, and the night was gentle.

The wax from the candles dropped in big tears on the bed sheets. Charles watched the candles burn, wearying his eyes with the shine of their yellow flame.

The moiré texture on Emma's satin dress shimmered, white as moonlight. Emma was disappearing beneath it; and it seemed to him that, spreading out beyond the boundaries of her self, she was confusedly lost and blended in the surrounding things, in the silence, in the night, in the passing wind, in the damp odors rising.

Then suddenly he saw her in the garden at Tostes, on the bench, against the thorn hedge, or again at Rouen, in the streets, in the doorway of their house, in the yard at Les Bertaux. He could hear again the boys laughing happily as they danced under the apple trees; the room was filled with the perfume of her hair, and her dress rustled in his arms with a crackling sound. It was the same one, this dress!

He stayed a long time remembering all the lost happy moments, her attitudes, her gestures, the sound of her voice. After one wave of despair, another came, and then another, unstoppable, like the waves of an overflowing sea.

He felt a terrible curiosity: slowly, with the tips of his fingers, trembling, he raised up her veil. But he cried out with horror, awakening the two others. They pulled him back downstairs to the parlor.

Then Félicité came to say that he was asking for a lock of her hair.

"Cut one!" replied the pharmacist.

And since she did not dare, he came over himself, the scissors in his hand. He was shaking so badly that he pricked the skin of her temples in several places. Finally, stiffening himself against his fears, Homais chopped two or three places at random, leaving white patches in that beautiful head of black hair.

The pharmacist and the priest plunged back into their preoccupations, not without dozing off from time to time, for which they mutually reproached each other upon awakening. Then Monsieur Bournisien sprinkled the room with holy water and Homais spread some chlorine on the floor.

Félicité had taken care to provide a bottle of brandy, some cheese, and a large roll for them, on the chest of drawers. Around four o'clock in the morning, the pharmacist could hold out no longer, sighing:

"Good lord, I could eat something!"

The cleric needed no persuading; he went out to say Mass and then returned; the two of them ate, clinking their glasses together, chuckling a little without knowing why, stimulated by that vague gaiety that comes over us after a sorrowful vigil; and, with the last glass, the priest said to the pharmacist, clapping him on the shoulder:

"You and I will end up being friends yet!"

Downstairs in the entryway they met the workmen as they arrived. Then for two hours Charles had to endure the sound of the hammer resounding on the wood planks. Next, they lowered her into her oak coffin, which was then put inside the other two; but since the outer one was too large, they had to fill up the gaps with wool from a mattress. Finally, when the three lids had been planed, nailed in place, and soldered, they set it outside the door; the house doors were opened wide, and the Yonville people began to gather around.

Old Rouault arrived. When he saw the black cloth, he fainted on the square.

CHAPTER 10

He had not received the pharmacist's letter until thirty-six hours after the event; and out of consideration for his feelings, Monsieur Homais had written it in such a way that it was impossible to tell what it was about.

First, the old man had collapsed as if struck by apoplexy. Then he reread, and decided she was not dead. But on the other hand, she might be . . . At last, he put on his smock, took his hat, put on his spurs, and rode off as quickly as he could go; and all along the route, old Rouault, panting, was tormented by anxiety. Once, he had to get down from the horse. He couldn't see anymore, he was hearing voices around him, he thought he was going mad.

Day broke, and he saw three black hens sleeping in a tree; he shuddered, taking it as an omen. He promised the Holy Virgin he would buy three new chasubles for the church, and that he would walk barefoot from the cemetery at Les Bertaux to the Vassonville chapel.

He got to Maromme, calling out for innkeepers, pushed open the door with his shoulder, headed straight for the oat sack, poured a bottle of sweet cider into the feedbag, and leaped back onto his nag, whose hoofs struck sparks as it flew off.

He told himself that they would undoubtedly be able to save her; the doctors would surely come up with some remedy. He remembered all the miraculous cures he had heard people tell about.

But then he seemed to see her dead. There she was, in front of him, lying stretched out on her back, in the middle of the road. He pulled back on the reins, and the hallucination disappeared.

At Quincampoix, to give himself courage, he drank three cups of coffee, one after the other.

He imagined that they had got the name wrong. He searched for the letter in his pocket, found it, but didn't dare open it.

He came to wonder if the whole thing hadn't perhaps been a joke, someone's revenge, the fantasy of someone who'd been drinking; and besides, if she had been dead, wouldn't he have known it? But no! There was nothing unusual about the countryside: the sky was blue, the trees were swaying in the wind; a flock of sheep was passing by. He caught sight of the village; people saw him riding fast, bent forward on his horse, beating it with great blows, its flanks bleeding.

When he had regained consciousness, he fell weeping into Bovary's arms:

"My daughter! Emma! My child! Tell me what happened . . . ?"

And the other replied, sobbing:

"I don't know, I don't know! It's a curse!"

The pharmacist separated them.

"These terrible details aren't important. I'll tell Monsieur all about it. Here, everyone's coming. Have some dignity, for goodness' sake! Be philosophical!"

The poor boy wanted to seem strong, and he repeated several times:

"Yes . . . Be brave!"

"All right!" cried the old man. "I will, by God's name! I'll stay right with her up to the end."

The bell tolled. Everything was ready. It was time to start.

And seated together in a choir stall, the one next to the other, they watched the three choristers pass back and forth in front of them continually, chanting. The musician playing the serpent[4] made it blast as loudly as he could. Monsieur Bournisien, in his grandest vestments, was singing in a shrill voice; he bowed before the tabernacle, lifted up his hands, extended his arms. Lestiboudois circulated through the church with his whalebone staff; near the lectern, the coffin reposed, surrounded by four rows of candles. Charles felt an urge to get up and extinguish them.

But he tried to stimulate his sense of devotion, to throw himself into the hope of a future life in which he would see her again. He imagined that she had gone on a journey, far away, for a long time. But when he recalled that she was lying

---

4. A woodwind instrument no longer in use.

there, and that everything was over, that they would be taking her to lie in the ground, he felt a ferocious, black, desperate rage. At times, he thought he couldn't feel anything; and he savored those intervals in his grief, while at the same time reproaching himself for doing so.

They could hear a sharp sound on the church floor, a metal-tipped cane rapping at regular intervals. It was coming from the back and stopped abruptly in the lower aisles of the church. A man in a coarse brown jacket knelt down awkwardly. It was Hippolyte, the stable boy from the *Golden Lion*. He had put on his new leg.

One of the choristers was going around the nave to take up the collection, and heavy sou pieces, one after another, were clattering on the silver collection plate.

"Hurry up, will you! I can't take any more of this!" Bovary cried, while angrily throwing him a five-franc piece.

The churchman thanked him with a long bow.

They sang, they knelt, they stood up again—this would never end! He remembered once, in their early days, they had both come to Mass, and they sat on the other side, on the right, against the wall. The bell began tolling again. There was a great movement of chairs. The pallbearers slipped their three poles under the coffin, and the crowd left the church.

Justin appeared, all alone, in the pharmacy doorway. He went right back in, pale and staggering.

People leaned out their windows to watch the funeral procession pass. Charles came first, his head erect. He was putting on a brave front, nodding to those who came out from the side streets or from their doorways, and stood among the crowd.

The six men, three on each side, walked slowly, panting a little. The priests, the choristers, and the two choir boys recited the *De Profundis*; and their voices carried out over the countryside, rising and falling in waves. Sometimes they disappeared at the turning of the path; but the big silver cross could always be seen among the trees.

The women followed, covered in black mantles with turned-down hoods; they each carried a thick, burning candle, and Charles thought he would collapse under this continued repetition of prayers and candles, under the sickly odors of wax and cassock. A cool breeze was blowing, the rye and the colza were turning green, little droplets of dew shimmered on the thorn hedges bordering the pathway. Every sort of joyful sound was filling the air: the clattering of a distant cart rolling along the rutted path, the repeated crowing of a cock, the galloping sound of a foal, running away under the apple trees. The pure sky was dotted with pink clouds; a bluish haze spread over the iris-covered cottages; Charles, as he passed, recognized the yards. He was remembering mornings like this one when, after having visited some patient, he would come back outside and go home to her.

The black cloth, strewn with white, teardrop-shaped beads, lifted up from time to time, revealing the coffin. The fatigued pallbearers were slowing down; the coffin jerked forward continually, like a rowboat pitching with every wave.

They arrived.

The men continued onward, to a place in the grass where the hole had been dug.

They stood around it; and while the priest was speaking, the red soil thrown up on the edges rolled back in, quietly, continually.

Then, when the four ropes were arranged, they put the coffin atop them. He watched it being lowered. It went on forever.

At last they heard a thudding sound; the ropes, with a creak, were pulled back up. Then Bournisien took the spade that Lestiboudois handed him; sprinkling holy water with his right hand, with his left he vigorously pushed in a large spadeful of earth; and the coffin wood, struck by the pebbles, made that tremendous sound that seems to us to be the echo of eternity.

The cleric passed the holy water bottle to his neighbor. It was Monsieur Homais. He shook it solemnly, and then passed it to Charles, who collapsed on his knees onto the earth, and he threw in handfuls, crying out, "Farewell!" He threw her kisses; he dragged himself toward the open grave to be swallowed up along with her.

They pulled him away; and it wasn't long before he grew calmer, perhaps feeling that same vague satisfaction they all felt at having it over.

Old Rouault, on the way back, began calmly smoking his pipe, which Homais inwardly judged to be inappropriate. He likewise observed that Monsieur Binet had not bothered to attend, that Tuvache had "run out" after the Mass, and that Théodore, the notary's servant, had worn a blue suit, "as if a person couldn't find a black one, which happens to be the custom—what the devil!" And to communicate his observations, he went from one group to another. Everyone deplored Emma's death, and especially Lheureux, who had not failed to attend the burial.

"That poor little lady! What a tragedy for her husband!"

The pharmacist took up the subject:

"If it hadn't been for me, believe me, who knows what harm he would have done to himself!"

"Such a good person she was! And to think it was just this last Saturday when she was in my shop!"

"I didn't have the leisure," Homais said, "to prepare a little speech that I might have delivered at the grave."

When he got home, Charles changed his clothes, and old Rouault put his blue smock on again. It was new, and as he had often wiped his eyes with its sleeves on his way to Yonville, it had left dye stains on his face; and the traces of tears made little lines in the dust on the smock.

Madame Bovary senior was with them. All three of them were silent. Finally the old man sighed:

"Do you remember, my friend, that I came to Tostes once, when you had just lost your first deceased. I consoled you back then! I knew what to say; but now . . ."

Then, after a lengthy groan that lifted his entire chest:

"Ah, it's the end for me, you know! I've seen my wife go . . . later on, my son . . . and now today, my daughter!"

He wanted to return to Les Bertaux right away, saying that he couldn't sleep in that house. He even refused to see his granddaughter.

"No! No! It will be too sad. But you kiss her for me! Farewell! . . . . You're a good fellow! And you know, I'll never forget," he said, slapping his thigh. "Don't worry: you'll always get your turkey!"

But when he reached the summit of the hill, he turned around, just as he had turned around once long ago on the road to Saint-Victor, when she was leaving him. The windows of the village houses were all alit with the slanting rays of the sun, setting now over the meadows. He put his hand over his eyes, and he saw on the horizon a walled enclosure, with little black bunches of trees here and there like bouquets against the white stone; and then he continued on his way, but slowly, for his old horse was limping.

Charles and his mother, despite their fatigue, stayed up a long time that evening talking together. They talked about the past, and about the future. She would come to live in Yonville, she would manage the household for him, she would never leave him again. She was ingenious and comforting, and she rejoiced inwardly at having regained an affection that had escaped her for so many years. Midnight struck. The village was silent, as usual, and Charles, sleepless, thought constantly about her.

Rodolphe, who, to distract himself, had been hunting in the woods all day, was sleeping peacefully in his chateau; and Léon, farther away, was also asleep.

But there was one other who, at that particular hour, was not sleeping.

On the grave, among the pines, a boy was kneeling and crying, and his heart, broken with sobbing, throbbed in the darkness under the pressure of an immense regret, sweeter than the moon and deeper than the night. Suddenly the gate creaked. It was Lestiboudois; he had come to look for the spade he had forgotten earlier. He recognized Justin scaling the wall, and then he knew at last who the culprit was who had been stealing his potatoes.

CHAPTER 11

The next day, Charles had his little girl brought back home. She asked for her mother. They told her that she was gone, that she would be bringing toys back for her. Berthe spoke about her several more times; then, as time went by, she stopped thinking about her. The child's cheerfulness saddened Bovary, and he also had to put up with the pharmacist's intolerable consolations.

Soon, the money problems started up again, Monsieur Lheureux inciting his friend Vinçart all over again, and Charles signed notes for exorbitant sums; because he would never consent to selling the least of the household goods that belonged to *her*. This exasperated his mother. He waxed more indignant than she. He had changed entirely. She left the house.

Then everyone started trying to *profit*. Mademoiselle Lempereur billed him for six months of lessons, even though Emma had never taken a single one (despite that receipt she had shown Bovary): the two women had had an agreement; the bookseller billed for three years' subscription; Madame Rolet billed for the postage for twenty letters, and when Charles asked for an explanation, she had the delicacy to reply:

"Ah, I don't know anything about it! It was for her business matters."

With every debt he paid, Charles thought he had come to an end of it. But there were always others, without end.

He billed his patients for past visits. They showed him the letters that his wife had sent them. Then he had to apologize.

Félicité was now wearing Madame's dresses; not all of them, as he had kept back some of them, and he went to look at them in her dressing room, shutting himself in with them; Félicité was just about the same build, and sometimes Charles would catch sight of her from behind, and seized by the illusion, he would cry out:

"Oh! Stay! Stay!"

But at Pentecost, she ran away from Yonville, carried off by Théodore, and stealing everything that was left in the wardrobe.

It was about that time when the widow, old Madame Dupuis, had the honor to inform him of the "marriage of Monsieur Léon Dupuis, notary of Yvetot, to Mademoiselle Léocadie Lebœuf, of Bondeville." Charles wrote him congratulations, including this sentence:

"How happy this news would have made my poor wife!"

One day when he was wandering aimlessly through the house, he went up into the attic, and he felt a piece of thin paper under his slipper. He opened it and he read: "Be brave, Emma! Be brave! I don't want to be a curse upon your life." It was Rodolphe's letter, which had remained on the floor after falling between the boxes, and which the wind from the open window had blown over toward the door. And Charles stood motionless and agape in that place where once Emma, desperate and even paler than he was, had wanted to die. At length he discovered a small R at the bottom of the second page. Who was it? He remembered Rodolphe's kindnesses, his abrupt disappearance and the constrained tone he adopted when they had met again, two or three times. But the letter's respectful tone allowed him to delude himself:

"Perhaps they were platonic friends," he said to himself.

In any case, Charles was not one of those who like to get to the bottom of things; he recoiled before the proofs, and his vague jealousy was lost in the immensity of his sorrow.

People must have adored her, he thought. Every man, you could be sure of it, desired her. It made her even more beautiful to him; and he conceived a permanent, limitless desire for her that only inflamed his despair, because it was now forever unachievable.

To please her—as if she were still alive—he adopted her tastes, her ideas; he bought patent leather boots, he began wearing white cravats. He put cosmetics on his mustache, and like her, he signed promissory notes. She was corrupting him from beyond the grave.

He was forced to sell off the silver, piece by piece, and then all the drawing-room furniture. All the rooms were emptied; but the bedroom, her own bedroom, was maintained just as it always had been. After his dinner, Charles would go up there. He would push the round table up close to the fire and bring *her* armchair up. He would sit down facing it. A candle would burn in one of the gilded candlesticks. Berthe, next to him, would color pictures.

He suffered, the poor man, at seeing her so badly dressed, her boots missing their laces, the armholes of her smock torn down to her hips, for the housekeeper paid no attention to her. But she was so sweet, so pretty, and her little head bent forward so gracefully, letting her blond hair tumble forward onto her pink cheeks, that an infinite delight penetrated him, a pleasure mixed with a bitterness, like those poorly-made wines that taste of resin. He would repair her toys, make puppets out of cardboard for her, or sew up the ripped stomach of her dolls. Then, if he happened to see a ribbon trailing out of the workbox, or even a pin lying in a crack in the table, he would begin to dream, and he looked so sad that she became just as sad as he was.

No one ever came to see them; for Justin had run off to Rouen, where he became a grocer's assistant, and the pharmacist's children saw the little girl less and less, Monsieur Homais not wishing them to continue the friendship, in view of their different social standings.

The blind man, whom he was never able to cure with his pomade, returned to the Bois-Guillaume hillside, where he narrated the pharmacist's failure to so many travelers that Homais, when he went to the city, hid himself behind the *Hirondelle*'s curtains, to avoid being recognized. He hated him; and in the interests of his own reputation, wanting to rid himself of the problem at all costs, he waged a secret campaign against him—which revealed both the depth of his intelligence and the violence of his vanity. For six months running, one could read editorial items like this one in the *Rouen Lantern*:

> "Anyone who travels to the fertile plains of Picardy will undoubtedly have noticed, on the Bois-Guillaume hillside, a beggar marked with a horrible facial wound. He bothers you, persecutes you, and levies a veritable tax on every traveler. Are we still living in the monstrous Middle Ages, when it was permissible for tramps to display, in our public places, the leprosy and scrofula they brought back from the Crusades?"

Or:

> "Despite the laws against vagrancy, the approaches to our big cities continue to be infested with bands of poor beggars. Some of them can be seen wandering around alone, though this is perhaps no less dangerous. What are our local officials thinking about?"

Then, Homais went on to invent anecdotes:

> "Yesterday, on the Bois-Guillaume hillside, a skittish horse . . . "

And this introduced a story about an accident caused by the blind man's presence.

He worked all this so well that they jailed the beggar. But then he was released. He started up again, and Homais started up again too. It was a battle. Victory was his; for his enemy was condemned to life in an asylum.

This success emboldened him; and since then the district didn't see a dog run over, a wife beaten, or a barn burned without his informing the public about it, always guided by his love of progress and his hatred of priests. He drew up comparisons between the public schools and those run by the *frères ignorantins*,[5] much to the detriment of the latter; when there was a question of a hundred-franc grant to the church, he brought up the Saint Bartholomew's Day Massacre; he denounced abuses, and tossed off witticisms. That was his term for it. Homais was laying mines; he was becoming dangerous.

Meanwhile, the narrow limits of journalism were beginning to feel stifling to him, and soon he felt he had to produce a real work, a book! So he composed his *General Statistics of the Canton of Yonville, Followed by Climatological Observa-*

5. The *Freres Ignorantins* were organized in the 1680s with the purpose of providing free education to poor children; they adopted the adjective "ignorant" because they specifically excluded theologians from joining their ranks. Anticlerical people, like Homais, easily mocked the name, as here, by omitting the capital letters.

tions, and from statistics he was propelled toward philosophy. He busied himself with the big questions: social problems, improving the morality of the lower classes, fish farming, rubber manufacturing, railroads, et cetera. He came to blush at being a bourgeois. He affected the *artistic style*; he took up smoking! He bought two *chic* Pompadour statuettes to adorn his drawing room.

He by no means abandoned his pharmacy; on the contrary! He kept up with all the latest discoveries. He carefully followed the chocolate fad. He was the first to introduce both *cho-ca* and *revalentia*[6] to the district. He was an enthusiast for the Pulvermacher hydro-electric chain;[7] he wore one himself; and when he took off his flannel vest at night, Madame Homais was dazzled by the golden spiral wound around him, and she felt her passion redoubled for this man more swathed up than a Scythian and as splendid as a Mage.

He had some fine ideas for Emma's tomb. He first suggested a broken column with some drapery, then a pyramid, then a Vestal temple, a kind of rotunda . . . or perhaps "a pile of ruins." But with all his plans, he refused to give up the weeping willow, which he considered the obligatory symbol of sorrow.

He and Charles took a trip to Rouen together to look at tombstones at a gravestone dealer's—accompanied by an artist named Vaufrylard, a friend of Bridoux's, who made puns constantly. Finally, after having examined a hundred designs, having ordered an estimate, and having made a second trip to Rouen, Charles decided upon a mausoleum with "a spirit holding an extinguished torch" on both sides.

As for the inscription, Homais could find nothing more beautiful than *Sta viator*, and he got stuck there; he wracked his brains for the next line; he repeated constantly, *Sta viator . . .* " At last, he came up with: *amabilem conjugem calcas!*—which was adopted.[8]

It was a strange thing that Bovary, in thinking continually about Emma, was forgetting her; and he felt desperate when he sensed her image slipping away from his memory despite all his efforts to retain it. But every night, he dreamed about her; it was always the same dream: he would come up close to her; but when he tried to embrace her, she turned into mere dust in his arms.

For about a week, he was seen going to church every evening. Monsieur Bournisien even came to visit him two or three times, then gave him up. Anyway, the fellow was becoming intolerant and fanatical, Homais said; he preached against the spirit of the age, and every other week in his sermon he always brought up the deathbed agony of Voltaire, who died eating his own excrement, as everyone knows.

Even though Bovary lived very sparingly, he was far from being able to clear his old debts. Lheureux refused to renew any of his notes. A seizure was imminent. He then turned to his mother, who consented to let him take out a mortgage on her property, but not without expressing strong recriminations

---

6. *Cho-ca* was a kind of cocoa powder, and *relaventia* was a newly fashionable cure-all composed of diverse vegetables including lentils and beans.
7. The Pulvermacher chain was a hugely successful pseudoscientific device during the early 1850s; it was worn against the skin and was promised to cure or prevent many diseases.

8. You are treading on a beloved spouse (Latin). Based on the Latin inscription placed over the spot where the valorous Bavarian field marshal Baron Franz von Mercy died in the Second Battle of Nördlingen (1645): *Sta viator, heroem calcas* (Halt, traveler, you are treading on a hero).

against Emma; and in recompense for her sacrifice, she asked for a shawl that had escaped the ravages of Félicité. Charles refused. They quarreled.

She made the first overtures toward a reconciliation, by suggesting to him that the child come and live with her, where she could help around the house. Charles agreed to it. But at the moment of departure, his courage failed him. And that was the definitive, complete rupture.

As his other relationships vanished, he clung even more tightly to the love of his child. She caused him anxiety, though, because she coughed sometimes, and there were red spots on her cheeks.

Directly across from him was the pharmacist's family, flourishing and merry, and everything in the world seemed to contribute to their well-being. Napoléon helped out in the laboratory, Athalie embroidered a skullcap for her father, Irma cut out rounds of paper for labeling the preserves, and Franklin could recite the multiplication tables in a single breath. He was the happiest of fathers, the most fortunate of men.

But not quite! One secret ambition devoured him: Homais desired the Cross of the Legion of Honor. He was not lacking in qualifications for it:

"(1) In the time of cholera, was distinguished by boundless devotion; (2) have published, and at my own expense, various works for the public good, such as [here he listed his memorandum titled *On Cider, Its Manufacture and Its Effects*; and his observations on the wool-bearing aphid, which were sent to the Academy; his volume on statistics; and even his thesis from pharmacy school]; not to mention that I am a member of several learned societies [he was a member of exactly one]."

"For that matter," he cried as he pirouetted in excitement, "they could grant it to me for my service as a volunteer fireman alone!"

Then Homais turned himself toward the seats of Power. He secretly did great services for Monsieur the Prefect during the elections. In short, he sold himself; he prostituted himself. He even sent a petition to the Sovereign, in which he begged him to *do justice to him*; he addressed him as *our good king*, and compared him to Henri IV.

And every morning, the pharmacist pounced on the newspaper to see if his nomination would be in it: it was never there. Finally, able to endure it no longer, he had a little grass plot in his garden cut in the shape of the Cross of Honor, with two little grass strips running off it to suggest the ribbon. He would walk around it with his arms crossed, meditating on the ineptitude of the government and the ingratitude of men.

Out of respect, or out of a sort of laziness that made him proceed slowly in his investigations, Charles had not yet opened the secret drawer in the rosewood desk that Emma had always used. Finally, one day he sat down in front of it, turned the key, and pushed the spring. All Léon's letters were there. No more doubts this time! He read every single one of them, rummaged in all the corners, in all the furniture, all the drawers, behind the walls, sobbing, moaning, frantic, wild. He discovered a box and broke it open with a kick. Rodolphe's portrait flew out, directly into his face, from among the overturned love letters.

People were surprised at his despondency. He never went out anymore, never had visitors, and even refused to go see his patients. Then people claimed that he had *locked himself in to drink*.

Sometimes, though, some curious person would pull himself up over the garden hedge and look with amazement at the man with the long beard, dressed in shabby clothes, savage-looking, who wept out loud as he paced.

In the evenings during the summer, he would take his little girl and walk with her to the cemetery. They would come back at nightfall, when the only light on in the square was from Binet's attic.

However, he was unable to revel fully in his misery, because he had no one with whom he could share it; and he made visits to Madame Lefrançois in order to be able to speak about her. But the innkeeper only listened with one ear, having her own troubles, for Monsieur Lheureux had finally established his own coach service called Business Express, and Hivert, who enjoyed a solid reputation as a runner of errands, was asking for a raise and threatening to go over "to the competition."

One day, when he had gone to the Argueil market to sell his horse—his last remaining asset—he ran into Rodolphe.

They both paled when they saw each other. Rodolphe, who had only sent his card, stammered some excuses, then grew bolder and even confident enough (it was very hot, this being the month of August) to invite him for a bottle of beer at the tavern.

Leaning on the table and facing him, he chewed his cigar as he talked, and Charles became lost in reverie, looking at this face that she had loved. It seemed to him that there was something of her in it. It was a marvel. He would have liked to be this man.

The other went on talking agriculture, animals, fertilizer, deftly employing banal phrases to plug up quickly any gap where there might have been an awkward allusion. Charles wasn't listening; Rodolphe perceived this, and he was able to follow the passage of Charles' memories by the movements of his face. It grew redder, moment by moment, the nostrils flared, the lips trembled; there was even an instant when Charles, filled with a somber rage, fixed his eyes upon Rodolphe, who, feeling a kind of fright, interrupted his talking. But soon the same look of mournful weariness reappeared on his face.

"I don't blame you," he said.

Rodolphe remained silent. And Charles, his head in his two hands, repeated lifelessly, with the resigned tone of infinite sorrow:

"No, I don't blame you any more!"

He added one fine phrase, the only one he ever uttered:

"Fate is to blame!"

Rodolphe, who had been in charge of that particular fate, found him awfully easygoing for a man in his situation, comical even, and a bit cowardly.

The next day, Charles went to sit on the bench in the arbor. Rays of sunlight streamed through the trellis; the vine leaves threw their shadows on the sand path, the jasmine scented the air, the sky was blue, flies were buzzing around the lilies in bloom, and Charles was suffocating like an adolescent under the vague waves of love that were swelling his despondent heart.

At seven o'clock, little Berthe, who had not seen him all afternoon, went to find him for dinner.

His head was leaning back against the wall, his eyes closed, his mouth open, and his hands holding a long lock of black hair.

"Papa, come in!" she said.

And thinking he wanted to play, she pushed him gently. He fell to the ground. He was dead.

Thirty-six hours later, at the request of the pharmacist, Monsieur Canivet hurried over. He performed an autopsy and found nothing.

When everything was sold, there were twelve francs, seventy-five centimes left over to pay for Mademoiselle Bovary's trip to her grandmother's. The good old woman died that same year; old Rouault was paralyzed, and it was an aunt who took her in. She is poor, and she sends the girl to a cotton mill to earn a living.

Since Bovary's death, three different doctors have followed him in Yonville without being able to succeed, so soundly does Homais defeat them. He has a hell of a practice; the authorities watch over him, and public opinion protects him.

He has just been awarded the Cross of the Legion of Honor.

LEO TOLSTOY

1828–1910

A gambler, womanizer, and aristocrat of the highest rank, Count Leo Tolstoy was also a vegetarian, pacifist, and anarchist and a passionate advocate for the Russian peasantry. He was world famous for his wisdom on the subject of marriage but suffered through a remarkably stormy marriage himself. He became widely known as a moral and religious sage but was excommunicated from the Russian Orthodox Church. He produced some of the century's best fiction but came to believe that novels were immoral. And yet this heap of contradictions should not be seen as the mark of a hypocrite. Tolstoy was always fully conscious of the disparity between his ideals and his life. "Blame *me*," he wrote, "and not the path I tread." This painful self-division reflects his intense, lifelong struggle to find the best way to live in the world—how to respond to the pressures of guilt and pleasure, authority and money, sex and war. And it suggests the source of one of his great talents as a writer: the capacity to represent a vast, various, and conflicting array of desires and ideals.

LIFE

Born in 1828, Tolstoy was the fourth of five children. Both of his parents belonged to the highest class of Russian society—aristocrats who had access to the tsar and the tsar's court. And yet Tolstoy never took advantage of his high birth to pursue a grand career as a diplomat or courtier. Having lost his mother at the age of two and his father at nine, he spent a relatively isolated youth. Much of his long life was passed on the family estate, Yasnaya Polyana, about 130 miles from Moscow, in the company of his close family members and his serfs—Russian peasants who were the property of aristocratic landowners, much like slaves.

Despite the fact that he was an orphan and moved from one guardian to another, Tolstoy looked back on his childhood as idyllic. He was close to his

siblings, and together they imagined a perfect society based on the ideal of universal love. At the age of fourteen Tolstoy started to visit brothels, which prompted terrible bouts of remorse and self-revulsion. After his first experience, he claimed to have stood next to the bed and wept. A few years later he started to write in a diary, which he then kept compulsively for the rest of his life. This daily writing often furnished material for his fiction as well as developing his skills and habits as a writer. There he would explore questions about how to act and what to believe, wondering about the purpose and meaning of life. He would also repeatedly make vows to give up his dalliances with women and, just as often, break his promises. Thus began a chronicle of sex and shame, played out in countless affairs with women, almost all of them members of the peasant class.

Intending to take up a diplomatic career, Tolstoy went to the provincial university at Kazan to study Arabic, Turko-Tartar, French, and German. He later switched to law, a course of study open only to the highest-ranking aristocrats. But this too he dropped in 1847 when he inherited the family estate, a large sum of money, and the ownership of over three hundred serfs. This sudden inheritance allowed him to drift aimlessly for a while, moving in aristocratic circles in the cities of St. Petersburg and Moscow, where he spent night after night at gambling tables.

Tolstoy's life changed radically in 1851 when he followed his older brother Nikolay, a soldier, to the mountains of the Caucasus, where the Russian army was protecting the hotly contested boundary between Russia and the Ottoman and Persian Empires. It was there, observing military life and conflict, that Tolstoy began publishing his work. He decided to join the army and to serve in the war between Russia and Britain in Crimea. There he witnessed appalling devastation, incompetence, and confusion. He also gambled away his fortune, observed the heat of battle and the pettiness of military life, and became a literary sensation with his detailed descriptions of the war in *Sebastopol Sketches* (1854). He began to be known in literary circles as an emerging genius and in government circles as a potentially dangerous critic.

Although he had been an indifferent student, Tolstoy was a great reader, and from adolescence he passionately admired the French Romantic **Jean-Jacques Rousseau**, who argued against the artificiality of social manners and institutions in favor of the simplicity of life in and through nature. Tolstoy read widely in European and American literature, from **Johann Wolfgang von Goethe** to Harriet Beecher Stowe. One of his greatest influences was the English novelist Charles Dickens, who was highly popular in Russia. Tolstoy would often read a Dickens novel when he needed a catalyst to begin writing himself.

At the age of thirty-four, Tolstoy, now a famous writer, married Sofya Andreyevna Bers, an eighteen-year-old, upper-class St. Petersburg girl. A day after he proposed, he offered his fiancée the chance to read his diaries, which recorded, among other things, twenty years of sexual activity with prostitutes, gypsies, and serfs. "I forgive you," she said to him after reading it, "but it's dreadful." From the beginning, both Tolstoys wrote constantly about one another in their diaries, and read each other's accounts, leading to many jealous battles—and perhaps the most documented marriage in history. Over their long and tumultuous life together, Sofya bore thirteen children, made four handwritten copies of the fifteen-hundred-page *War and Peace*, and did her best to protect her husband's literary property.

By his mid-thirties, Tolstoy had run afoul of the Russian government. As a local justice of the peace, he had made eccentric and radical decisions, taking the side of serfs against his fellow landowners, and he had founded an experimental school for peasant children at Yasnaya Polyana based on new theories of education emerging out of France, Belgium, Germany, and England. Instead of cramming children with information, Tolstoy argued, it made sense for education to draw on their own experience. This seemed dangerously foreign, and his writing seemed unsettling, too. The tsar, concerned about threats to his life and his regime, had a team of censors who excised paragraphs from a number of Tolstoy's early short stories. In 1862 the police made a raid on his house. They found little evidence of subversive writings or activity, but the search infuriated Tolstoy, whose antigovernment sentiment increased as he grew older. Arguing that governments always relied on violence, he became a vocal anarchist and pacifist, advocating civil disobedience rather than submission to the state.

Tolstoy's two greatest works, *War and Peace* (1865–69) and *Anna Karenina* (1875–77), were hugely popular and established him as the greatest novelist of the Russian experience. *War and Peace* was an epic that recounted Napoleon's invasion of Russia in 1812, a huge swarming story of a nation's resistance to a foreign power. Tolstoy unsettles the myth of Napoleon as one of the world's greatest heroes, interpreting history instead as a struggle of anonymous collective forces; events are the consequences of waves of irrational communal feeling. *Anna Karenina* is a moving story of marriage and adultery that juxtaposes characters who are searching for meaning and fulfillment. Its hero, Levin, ends a painful struggle with the promise of salvation,

adopting the ideal of a simple life in which we should "remember God." So bound up with national pride were these two works that they survived successive waves of censorship. In fact, the repressive Russian government was so fearful of making a martyr out of the much-beloved novelist that they left Tolstoy almost entirely alone, even while they imprisoned and executed a vast number of his fellow writers for subversive antitsarist sentiment. As Tolstoy became an increasingly outspoken critic of the state, his own fiction protected him.

After he published *Anna Karenina* Tolstoy underwent an acute personal and spiritual crisis, thrown into such despair by the pointlessness of existence that he considered suicide (a despair shared by some of the characters in the novel). Then he had a conversion experience that set him on a new path. After exploring and rejecting the Russian Orthodox Church, he began to pursue his own search for God. It was the peasants who seemed to Tolstoy to know how to live best, and in the late 1870s he started to try to live a peasant life, dressing like them, eating peasant food, and even making his own shoes. Rereading the Gospels closely, he founded his own religion. This involved rejecting any idea of an afterlife and following the model of Jesus's life as closely as possible, giving away wealth and rejecting all forms of violence. Tolstoy's first work of fiction after his conversion was *The Death of Ivan Ilyich* in 1886.

The last decades of his life saw Tolstoy writing mostly religious and philosophical treatises. By the 1880s the writer was arguing in favor of complete sexual abstinence. He condemned literature and singled out **Shakespeare** as particularly bad. He became an outspoken vegetarian. At one point, an elderly relative visiting Yasnaya Polyana asked that meat be served to her; when

she came to the table, she discovered a meat cleaver at her place and a live chicken tied to her chair. In his later years, many followers saw Tolstoy as a wise prophet and made long journeys to Yasnaya Polyana from distant places to meet the great man. They often reported that he seemed larger than life—saintly and heroic.

At Tolstoy's death in 1910 students rioted, anarchists were rounded up by the police, and thousands of people followed his coffin. Seven years later, when Russia erupted in political turmoil, some saw the first tide of communism as a "Tolstoyan revolution." But Tolstoy left another kind of political legacy as well. So influential was his notion of nonviolent resistance for a young Indian man named Mohandas Gandhi that he called his first political base "Tolstoy farm."

TIMES

In the century leading up to Tolstoy's birth, Russian society was divided into three major groups: the aristocracy, which was small in number but exerted all of the nation's political power; town merchants, who had fixed duties and privileges; and serfs, who made up the vast majority of the population but had no power at all. The aristocrats were the only Russians who could attend universities, hold civil service positions, and remain exempt from taxation. Meanwhile, serfs had neither freedom nor authority: one tsar after another reduced serfs' rights, and by the middle of the eighteenth century, serfs were forbidden to travel and had the legal status of personal property, exactly like slaves. When Tolstoy was young, twenty-three million Russians were privately owned serfs.

This drastically lopsided political and social system was clearly unstable, and anxious tsars struggled to stave off outright revolution. Alexander II emancipated the serfs in 1861 for purely pragmatic reasons: "It is better to abolish serfdom from above," he explained, "than to wait for the time when it will begin to abolish itself from below." The emancipation did not put an end to social unrest, however. By 1880 there had been six attempts to kill the tsar by anarchists and nihilists. Alexander increased his secret police force, imposed severe censorship, and promised political reforms. In 1881 an assassin succeeded in killing him, and he was succeeded by his son, Alexander III, who rejected his father's reform efforts in favor of harsh and repressive measures, including even tighter censorship and persecution of non-Orthodox minorities, especially Jews. Most writers were persecuted—thrown in jail or kept under house arrest. In this context, it is astonishing that Tolstoy managed to remain free, especially given his sharp and vocal criticism of both church and state.

In Russian intellectual circles, one urgent question constantly reemerged in the nineteenth century: should Russia follow the lead of a modernizing Western Europe in terms of culture, politics, and industry or should the nation instead reach for models drawn from its own religious and national history, developing its own distinctive heritage? On the one side, the so-called Westernizers, based largely in St. Petersburg, argued for liberal democracy, religious freedom, and the emancipation of the serfs. They spoke French, and often felt ashamed of Russian backwardness. On the other side, the Moscow-based Slavophiles resisted rationalism and technological innovation, embraced the Russian Orthodox Church, and typically favored bringing together all Slavic peoples under the Russian tsar. Tolstoy belonged to neither camp—or to both. While he favored European models of education and rejected the Orthodox Church, he also

prized the Russian peasantry as a source of national renewal and meaning.

WORK

Tolstoy's great novels, *War and Peace* and *Anna Karenina*, told vast and sweeping realist stories of nineteenth-century Russian life, filled with vivid depictions of aristocratic pursuits, military battles, and the complexities of love and marriage. Later he turned to a different kind of writing, producing impassioned and often didactic stories and nonfiction essays in favor of spiritual principles. *The Death of Ivan Ilyich*, the story included here, falls midway between these two phases of his career. As the first piece of fiction written after the writer's conversion, it has seemed to many readers to combine Tolstoy's earlier, richly realistic representations of contemporary life with his later turn to religious ideals.

There may be a biographical source for this novella. In 1856—thirty years before he began writing it—Tolstoy's brother Dmitry had died of tuberculosis in the arms of a prostitute. Revolted by his brother's emaciated body and the smell of illness, Tolstoy felt remarkably little concern for Dmitry and selfishly rushed back to St. Petersburg to enjoy his growing literary fame. This experience—Dmitry's death, his own indifference, and his resulting guilt—seems to have provided the writer with the contrasting perspectives he explores in *The Death of Ivan Ilyich*.

This is the story of an average man of the prosperous middle class who faces the unbearable fact that he is soon going to die. Tolstoy is famous for peppering his prose with startlingly opinionated, intrusive judgments, and among the most famous of these is the narrator's assessment of his protagonist's life at the opening of Chapter II: "Ivan Ilyich's life had been the most simple and most ordinary and therefore most terrible."

The relationship between terror and ordinariness here appears straightforward and categorical, but the story then asks us to think about how we respond to such blunt claims of truth. Ivan Ilyich himself knows that everyone must die—"Caius is a man, men are mortal, therefore Caius is mortal"—but he rebels against applying this to himself: "he was not Caius, not an abstract man, but a creature quite, quite separate from all others." What, Tolstoy asks us, is the relationship between abstract, universal truths and our intensely felt personal experience?

Ordinary social life, it seems, allows us to avoid this question, as characters immerse themselves in card games, interior decorating, career advancement, financial dealings, and the desire to "live pleasantly." Ivan Ilyich, whose first symptoms of illness appear when he tries to hang his curtains properly, comes to see his family, friends, and doctors as false and deceitful. Gerasim, the peasant, represents the only appealing alternative described in the narrative.

Tolstoy experiments with perspective, choosing to begin the story at its chronological endpoint, as the news of Ivan Ilyich's death comes to his acquaintances. For them it appears as an interruption of ordinary life, and we see the event through their uncomfortable eyes. It is only after this introduction that the narrator switches to Ivan Ilyich's perspective. In the first draft, two characters, Peter Ivanovich and Ivan Ilyich, told the story in the first person. Later Tolstoy shifted to a third-person omniscient narrator, who filters our experience through these two characters.

Tolstoy not only multiplies perspectives, he also multiplies metaphors: dying is like being "thrust into a narrow, deep black sack"; it is also like a "stone falling downwards," like flying, and "like the sensation one sometimes experiences in a railway carriage when one thinks one is going backwards while one

is really going forwards." Death emerges variously as nothingness, a black hole, a judge (like the character himself), and perhaps most memorably, as "It." In Russian this pronoun is feminine and thus closer to the English "She." As death slowly comes to the protagonist, language itself begins to break down. In the final chapter, he starts screaming, "I won't," but this becomes simply "Oh! Oh! Oh!"—a sound that lasts for three solid days. In his final moments of illumination, the protagonist tries to ask his son to "forgive" him but says only "forgo." As Ivan Ilyich's viewpoint develops and changes, the story narrows in time and space; the focus tightens, his range of movements contracts, the chapters get shorter, and the time of the events shrinks.

Guy de Maupassant, a French writer whom Tolstoy admired, read *The Death of Ivan Ilyich* late in his own life, and said, sadly: "I realize that everything I have done now was to no purpose, and that my ten volumes are worthless."

The Death of Ivan Ilyich[1]

I

During a break in the hearing of the Melvinsky case, the members of the court and the prosecutor met in Ivan Yegorovich Shebek's room in the big law courts building, and began talking about the famous Krasovsky case. Fyodor Vasilyevich became heated, contending that it didn't come under their jurisdiction, Ivan Yegorovich held his ground, while Pyotr Ivanovich, not having joined in the argument at the beginning, took no part in it and was looking through the *Gazette* which had just been delivered.

'Gentlemen!' he said. 'Ivan Ilyich has died.'

'He hasn't!'

"Look, read this,' he said to Fyodor Vasilyevich, handing him a fresh copy which still smelled of ink.

Within a black border was printed: "Praskovya Fyodorovna Golovina with deep sorrow informs family and friends of the passing of her beloved spouse Ivan Ilyich Golovin, Member of the Court of Justice, which took place on the 4th of February of this year 1882. The funeral will be on Friday at 1 p.m.'

Ivan Ilyich was a colleague of the gentlemen meeting there and they all liked him. He had been ill for several weeks; people were saying his illness was incurable. His position had been kept for him, but there had been conjectures that, in the event of his death, Alekseyev might be appointed to his position, and either Vinnikov or Shtabel to Alekseyev's. So on hearing of Ivan Ilyich's death the first thought of each of the gentlemen meeting in the room was of the significance the death might have for the transfer or promotion of the members themselves or their friends.

'Now I will probably get Shtabel's or Vinnikov's position,' thought Fyodor Vasilyevich. 'It was promised to me long ago and this promotion means a raise of eight hundred roubles, plus a private office.'

1. Translated by Peter Carson.

'Now I must ask about the transfer of my brother-in-law from Kaluga,' thought Pyotr Ivanovich. 'My wife will be very pleased. Now she won't be able to say that I've never done anything for her family.'

'I thought he wouldn't leave his bed,' Pyotr Ivanovich said aloud. 'Such a pity.'

'What was actually wrong with him?'

'The doctors couldn't make a diagnosis. That is they did, but different ones. When I saw him the last time, I thought he would recover.'

'And I didn't go and see him after the holidays. I kept meaning to.'

'Did he have any money?'

'I think his wife had a very small income. But next to nothing.'

'Yes, we'll have to go and see her. They lived a terribly long way off.'

'That is, a long way from you. Everything's a long way from you.'

'He just can't forgive me for living on the other side of the river,' said Pyotr Ivanovich, smiling at Shebek. And they started talking about distances in the city, and went back into the court.

Apart from the thoughts the death brought each of them about the moves and possible changes at work that might follow, the actual fact of the death of a close acquaintance evoked, as always, in all who learned of it a complacent feeling that it was 'he who had died, not I'.

'So—he's dead; but here I am still,' each thought or felt. At this point his closer acquaintances, the so-called friends of Ivan Ilyich, involuntarily thought that they now needed to carry out the very tedious requirements of etiquette and go to the requiem service and pay a visit of condolence to the widow.

Closest of all were Fyodor Vasilyevich and Pyotr Ivanovich.

Pyotr Ivanovich was a friend from Law School and considered himself under an obligation to Ivan Ilyich.

Having given his wife at dinner the news of Ivan Ilyich's death and his thoughts about the possibility of his brother-in-law's transfer to their district, Pyotr Ivanovich didn't lie down to have a rest but put on a formal tail coat and drove to Ivan Ilyich's.

At the entrance to Ivan Ilyich's apartment stood a carriage and two cabs. Downstairs in the hall by the coat-stand, leaning against the wall, was the brocade-covered lid of the coffin with tassels and a gold braid that had been cleaned with powder. Two ladies in black were taking off their fur coats. One of them, Ivan Ilyich's sister, he knew, the other was an unknown lady. Pyotr Ivanovich's colleague Schwarz was coming downstairs and seeing from the top step who had come in he winked at him as if to say, 'Ivan Ilyich has made a silly mess of things; you and I have done things differently.'

Schwarz's face with his English side-whiskers and his whole thin figure in a tail coat as usual had an elegant solemnity, and this solemnity, which was always at odds with Schwarz's playful character, was especially piquant here. So Pyotr Ivanovich thought.

Pyotr Ivanovich let the ladies go in front of him and slowly followed them up the stairs. Schwarz didn't come down but stayed at the top. Pyotr Ivanovich understood why: he obviously wanted to arrange where they should play vint[2] today. The ladies went up the stairs to the widow but Schwarz, with a serious set

---

2. A Russian card game, similar to whist and bridge.

to his strong lips and a playful look, indicated by a twitch of his eyebrows that Pyotr Ivanovich should go to the right, into the room where the corpse lay.

Pyotr Ivanovich went in, feeling as is always the case at a loss, as to what he should do there. One thing he did know was that in these circumstances it never does any harm to cross oneself. He wasn't altogether sure whether one should also bow and so he chose a middle course: entering the room, he started to cross himself and made a kind of slight bow. In so far as the movements of his head and hands would allow, he looked round the room at the same time. Two young men, probably nephews, one of them a Gymnasium pupil, were crossing themselves as they were leaving the room. An old woman stood motionless, and a lady with oddly arched eyebrows was saying something to her in a whisper. A church lector[3] in a frock coat, with a vigorous and decisive way to him, was reading out something loudly with an expression that permitted no contradiction; the peasant manservant Gerasim, stepping lightly in front of Pyotr Ivanovich, scattered something on the ground. Seeing that, Pyotr Ivanovich at once sensed the faint smell of a decomposing body. He had seen on his last visit to Ivan Ilyich this peasant in the study; he carried out the duties of a sick-nurse and Ivan Ilyich was especially fond of him. Pyotr Ivanovich kept on crossing himself and bowing slightly in an intermediate direction between the coffin, the lector and the icons on a table in the corner. Then, when he thought the movement of crossing himself with his hand had gone on for too long, he stopped and started to examine the dead man.

The dead man lay, as dead men always do, especially heavily, his stiffened limbs sunk in the padded lining of the coffin with his head bent back forever on the pillow, and, as always with dead men, his yellow waxen forehead sticking out, showing bald patches on his hollow temples, his nose protruding as if it pressed on his upper lip. He had greatly changed, had become even thinner since Pyotr Ivanovich had seen him, but like all dead men, his face was handsomer, above all more imposing than when he was alive. On his face was an expression that said what had to be done had been done, and done properly. This expression also held a reproach or reminder to the living. Pyotr Ivanovich found this reminder inappropriate or at the least one not applying to himself. This gave Pyotr Ivanovich an unpleasant feeling and so he hurriedly crossed himself once more and turned, too hurriedly he thought, and not in accordance with the proprieties, and went to the door. Schwarz was waiting for him in the next room, his legs wide apart and both hands playing behind his back with his top hat. One look at Schwarz's playful, neat and elegant figure refreshed Pyotr Ivanovich. Pyotr Ivanovich felt that Schwarz stood above all this and didn't allow himself to give in to depressing thoughts. The very way he looked stated the following: the fact of Ivan Ilyich's requiem cannot serve as a sufficient reason to consider the order of the courts disrupted; in other words nothing can stop us unsealing and shuffling a pack of cards this evening while the manservant puts out four fresh candles; in general there are no grounds for assuming that this fact can prevent us from spending a pleasant evening, even today. He said this in a whisper to Pyotr Ivanovich as he came in, proposing

---

3. High position in the minor orders of the Eastern Orthodox Church, responsible for reading from scripture during services.

they meet for a game at Fyodor Vasilyevich's. But apparently Pyotr Ivanovich was not fated to play vint this evening. Praskovya Fyodorovna, a short, plump woman who broadened from the shoulders down in spite of all her efforts to achieve the opposite, was dressed all in black with her head covered in lace and with oddly arched eyebrows like the lady standing by the coffin. She came out of her rooms with the other ladies, and taking them to the door where the dead man lay, said:

'Now there'll be the requiem; do go in.'

Schwarz stopped, making a vague bow—clearly neither accepting nor rejecting this proposal. Praskovya Fyodorovna, recognising Pyotr Ivanovich, sighed, went right up to him, took him by the hand and said:

'I know that you were a true friend of Ivan Ilyich . . .' and looked at him, waiting for an action on his part that corresponded to these words.

Pyotr Ivanovich knew that just as in that room one had had to cross oneself, so here one must press the hand, sigh and say, 'Believe me!' And that's what he did. And having done it he felt that the desired result had been obtained: he was moved and she was moved.

'Come while they haven't started in there; I need to talk to you,' said the widow. 'Give me your hand.'

Pyotr Ivanovich gave his hand and they went off into the inner rooms, past Schwarz who sadly gave a wink at Pyotr Ivanovich. 'There's your vint gone! Don't take it out on us, we'll find another partner. Maybe you can cut in once you've gotten free,' said his playful look.

Pyotr Ivanovich sighed even more deeply and sadly and Praskovya Fyodorovna gratefully pressed his hand. They went into her dimly lit drawing room, hung with pink cretonne, and sat down by a table, she on a sofa and Pyotr Ivanovich on a low pouffe built on springs which awkwardly gave way as he sat down. Praskovya Fyodorovna was going to warn him to sit on another chair but found such a warning inappropriate for her situation and changed her mind. As he sat down on the pouffe, Pyotr Ivanovich remembered how Ivan Ilyich had arranged this drawing room and consulted him about this very pink cretonne[4] with green leaves. On her way to sit down on the sofa, as she passed the table (the whole drawing room was full of furniture and knick-knacks), the widow caught the black lace of her black mantilla on the carving of the table. Pyotr Ivanovich got up to unhook her, and the sprung pouffe now released below him began to sway and push at him. The widow started to unhook the lace herself and Pyotr Ivanovich sat down again, quelling the rebellious pouffe underneath him. But the widow hadn't unhooked it all and Pyotr Ivanovich again got up and the pouffe again rebelled and even made a noise. When all this was over she took out a clean cambric handkerchief and began to cry. Pyotr Ivanovich felt chilled by the episode of the lace and the battle with the pouffe and sat frowning. This awkward situation was interrupted by Sokolov, Ivan Ilyich's butler, reporting that the place in the cemetery Praskovya Fyodorovna had selected would cost two hundred roubles. She stopped crying and, looking at Pyotr Ivanovich with the air of a victim, said in French[5] that she was suffering greatly. Pyotr Ivanovich made a silent sign expressing a firm conviction that it couldn't be otherwise.

---

4. Heavy upholstery fabric, often printed with a fancy or gaudy pattern.
5. It was common for members of the upper classes in Russia in the 19th century to speak French to one another.

'Do smoke, please,' she said in a gracious and, at the same time, broken voice and talked to Sokolov about the matter of the price of the place in the cemetery. Pyotr Ivanovich smoked and heard her asking very detailed questions about the different prices of plots and deciding on the one that should be bought. When that was done, she went on to give instructions about the singers. Sokolov went out.

'I do everything myself,' she said to Pyotr Ivanovich, moving some albums lying on the table to one side; and noticing that his ash was posing a threat to the table, she speedily pushed an ashtray towards Pyotr Ivanovich and said, 'I find it a pretence to state that because of grief I can't deal with practical matters. On the contrary, if there is something that can . . . not console . . . but distract me, then it's bothering about him.' She again took out her handkerchief as if she were going to cry, and suddenly, as if pulling herself together, she shook herself and began to speak quietly:

'However, I have to talk to you about something.'

Pyotr Ivanovich bowed, not letting the pouffe release its springs which had at once started to move underneath him.

'He suffered terribly in the last days.'

'Did he suffer very much?' Pyotr Ivanovich asked.

'Oh. Terribly! At the end he never stopped screaming, not for minutes, for hours. For three whole days he screamed without drawing breath. It was unbearable. I can't understand how I bore it; one could hear it from three doors away. Oh, what I've been through!'

'And was he really conscious?' Pyotr Ivanovich asked.

'Yes,' she whispered, 'till the final moment. He said goodbye to us a quarter of an hour before he died and asked as well for Volodya to be taken out.'

The thought of the sufferings of a man he had known so well, first as a cheerful lad, a schoolboy, then as an adult colleague, suddenly horrified Pyotr Ivanovich in spite of his unpleasant consciousness of his own and this woman's pretence. He saw again that forehead, the nose pressing on the lip, and he became fearful for himself.

'Three days of terrible suffering and death. That can happen to me too, now, any minute,' he thought and for a moment he became frightened. But right away, he himself didn't know how, there came to his aid the ordinary thought that this had happened to Ivan Ilyich and not to him, and this ought not and could not happen to him; that in thinking like this he was giving in to gloomy thoughts, which one shouldn't, as had been clear from Schwarz's face. And having reached this conclusion, Pyotr Ivanovich was reassured and started to ask with interest about the details of Ivan Ilyich's end, as if death were an adventure peculiar to Ivan Ilyich but absolutely not to himself.

After some talk about the details of the truly terrible physical sufferings which Ivan Ilyich had undergone (details that Pyotr Ivanovich learned only by way of the effect that Ivan Ilyich's torment had on Praskovya Fyodorovna's nerves), the widow apparently found it necessary to move on to business.

'Ah, Pyotr Ivanovich, it's so hard, so terribly hard, so terribly hard,' and she again started to cry.

Pyotr Ivanovich sighed and waited for to her to blow her nose. When she had blown her nose, he said:

'Believe me . . .' and again she talked away and unburdened herself of what was clearly her main business with him—how on her husband's death she could

get money from the treasury. She gave the appearance of asking Pyotr Ivanovich for advice about the pension; but he saw that she already knew down to the smallest details even what he didn't know—everything that one could extract from the public purse on this death—but that she wanted to learn if one couldn't somehow extract a bit more money. Pyotr Ivanovich tried to think of a way, but, having thought a little and out of politeness abusing the government for its meanness, he said that he thought one couldn't get more. Then she sighed and clearly began to think of a way to get rid of her visitor. He understood this, put out his cigarette, got up, shook her hand and went into the hall.

In the dining room, with the clock that Ivan Ilyich had been so pleased to buy in a junkshop, Pyotr Ivanovich met the priest and also a few acquaintances who had come to the requiem, and he saw a beautiful young lady he knew, Ivan Ilyich's daughter. She was all in black. That made her very slender waist seem even more so. She had a sombre, decisive, almost angry expression. She bowed to Pyotr Ivanovich as if he had done something wrong. Behind the daughter, with a similarly offended expression, stood a rich young man whom Pyotr Ivanovich knew, an examining magistrate, who he'd heard was her fiancé. He glumly bowed to them and was about to go on into the room where the dead man lay when from under the stairs there appeared the figure of the son, a Gymnasium student, who looked terribly like Ivan Ilyich. He was a little Ivan Ilyich just as Pyotr Ivanovich remembered him at Law School. His eyes were tear-stained and had the look that the eyes of boys with impure thoughts have at the age of thirteen or fourteen. When he recognized Pyotr Ivanovich the boy began to scowl sullenly and shame-facedly. Pyotr Ivanovich nodded to him and went into the dead man's room. The requiem began—candles, groans, incense, tears, sobs. Pyotr Ivanovich stood frowning, looking at the feet in front of him. He didn't look once at the dead man and right until the end didn't give in to any depressing influences. He was one of the first to leave. There was no one in the hall. Gerasim, the peasant manservant, darted out of the dead man's study, rummaged with his strong hands among all the fur coats to find Pyotr Ivanovich's, and gave it to him.

'So, Gerasim my friend?' said Pyotr Ivanovich in order to say something. 'It's sad, isn't it?'

'It's God's will. We'll all be there,' said Gerasim, showing his white, regular, peasant's teeth, and like a man in the full swing of intensive work, briskly opened the door, called the coachman, helped Pyotr Ivanovich in and jumped back to the steps as if trying to think what else he might do.

It was particularly pleasant for Pyotr Ivanovich to breathe the fresh air after the smell of incense, the dead body and the carbolic acid.

'Where to, sir?' asked the coachman.

'It's not late. So I'll still drop in at Fyodor Vasilyevich's.'

And off Pyotr Ivanovich went. And indeed he found his friends finishing the first rubber;[6] so it was easy for him to cut in as a fifth.

II

Ivan Ilyich's past life had been very simple and ordinary and very awful.

Ivan Ilyich had died at the age of forty-five, a member of the Court of Justice. He was the son of a St Petersburg civil servant who had had in various minis-

6. A round of a card game.

tries and departments the kind of career which brings people to a position in which, although it is quite clear that they are incapable of performing any meaningful job, they still by reason of their long past service and their seniority cannot be dismissed; so they receive invented, fictitious positions and thousands of roubles, from six to ten thousand, which are not fictitious, with which they live on to a ripe old age.

Such was Privy Councillor Ilya Yefimovich Golovin, the superfluous member of various superfluous institutions.

He had three sons. Ivan Ilyich being the second. The eldest had had the same kind of career as his father, only in a different ministry, and he was already nearly approaching the age at which salary starts increasing automatically. The third son was a failure. Wherever he had been in various positions he had made a mess of things and was now working in the railways: both his father and his brothers, and especially their wives, not only didn't like to see him but didn't even mention his existence unless absolutely compelled to do so. Their sister was married to Baron Gref, the same kind of Petersburg civil servant as his father-in-law. Ivan Ilyich was *le phénix de la famille*,[7] as they said. He wasn't as cold and precise as the eldest or as hopeless as the youngest. He was somewhere between them—a clever, lively, pleasant and decent man. He had been educated with his younger brother in the Law School. The younger one didn't finish and was expelled from the fifth class. Ivan Ilyich completed the course with good marks. In Law School he was already what he would be later during his entire life: a capable, cheerful, good-natured and sociable man, but one who strictly did what he considered his duty; and he considered his duty to be everything that it was considered to be by his superiors. Neither as a boy nor afterwards as a grown man did he seek to ingratiate himself, but there was in him from a young age the characteristic of being drawn to people of high station, like a fly towards the light; he adopted their habits and their views on life and established friendly relations with them. All the passions of childhood and youth went by without leaving much of a trace in him; he gave in both to sensuality and to vanity, and—towards the end, in the senior classes—to liberalism, but always within the defined limits which his sense accurately indicated to him as correct.

At Law School he had done things which previously had seemed to him quite vile and had filled him with self-disgust while he did them; but later, seeing these things were done by people in high positions and not thought by them to be bad, he didn't quite think of them as good but he completely forgot them and wasn't at all troubled by memories of them.

Having left Law School in the tenth class and having received money from his father for fitting himself out, Ivan Ilyich ordered clothes at Sharmer's,[8] hung on his watch-chain a medallion with the inscription 'respice finem',[9] took his leave of the princely patron of the school and his tutor, dined with his schoolmates at Donon's[1] and, equipped with a new and fashionable trunk, linen, clothes, shaving and toilet things and travelling rug, ordered and bought

---

7. "The phoenix of the family" (French). The word *phoenix* is used here to mean "rare bird," "prodigy."

8. A fashionable St. Petersburg tailor.
9. "Regard the end" (a Latin motto).
1. One of St. Petersburg's better restaurants.

from the very best shops, he went off to a provincial city to the post of assistant to the governor for special projects, which his father had procured for him.

In the provincial city Ivan Ilyich at once established for himself the kind of easy and pleasant position he had had at Law School. He worked, he made his career and at the same time he amused himself in a pleasant and seemly way; from time to time he went around the district towns on a mission from his chief, he behaved to both superiors and inferiors with dignity and he carried out the responsibilities he had been given, mainly for the affairs of religious dissenters,[2] with an exactness and incorruptible honesty of which he could not but be proud.

In his work, despite his youth and liking for frivolous amusement, he was exceptionally reserved, formal and even severe; but in society he was often playful and witty and always good-humoured, well-behaved and *bon enfant*,[3] as his chief and his chief's wife used to say of him, with whom he was one of the family.

There was also in the provincial city an affair with one of the ladies who attached herself to the smart lawyer; there was a little dressmaker; there were drinking sessions with visiting aides-de-camp and trips to a remote street after supper; there was also some fawning deference to his chief and even to his chief's wife but all this wore such a high tone of probity that it couldn't be described in bad words; all this could only go under the rubric of the French expression: *il faut que jeunesse se passe*.[4] Everything took place with clean hands, in clean shirts, with French words and, most importantly, in the highest society, consequently with the approval of people in high position.

Ivan Ilyich worked in this way for five years, and then there came changes in his official life. New legal bodies were founded; new men were needed.

And Ivan Ilyich was this new man.

Ivan Ilyich was offered the position of examining magistrate and he accepted it, despite the fact that this position was in another province and he had to abandon the relationships he had established and establish new ones. His friends saw Ivan Ilyich off, they took a group photograph, they presented him with a silver cigarette-case and off he went to his new position.

As an examining magistrate Ivan Ilyich was just as *comme il faut*,[5] well-behaved, capable of separating his official duties from his private life and of inspiring general respect as he had been as a special projects officer. The actual work of a magistrate had much more interest and attraction for him than his previous work. In his previous position it had been pleasant to walk with a light step in his Sharmer uniform past trembling petitioners and envious officials waiting to be seen, straight into his chief's room and to sit down with him over a cup of tea with a cigarette. But there were few people who depended directly on his say-so—only district police officers and religious schismatics when he was sent on missions—and he liked to treat such people dependent on him politely, almost as comrades; he liked to let them feel that here he was, someone who could crush them, treating them in a simple and friendly way.

---

2. The Old Believers, a large group of Russians (about 25 million in 1900), members of a sect that originated in a break with the Orthodox Church in the 17th century; they were subject to many legal restrictions.

3. A nice boy (French).
4. "Youth must have its fling" [translators' note].
5. Literally, "as one must" (French): proper.

There were only a few such people then. Now, as an examining magistrate, Ivan Ilyich felt that all of them, all without exception, even the most important, self-satisfied people, were all in his hands, and that he only had to write certain words on headed paper and this or that important, self-satisfied man would be brought to him as a defendant or a witness, and if he wouldn't let him sit down, would have to stand before him and answer his questions. Ivan Ilyich never abused this power of his; on the contrary he tried to use it lightly; but the consciousness of this power and the possibility of using it lightly constituted for him the chief interest and attraction of his new job. In the work itself, in the actual investigations, Ivan Ilyich very quickly mastered a way of setting aside all circumstances which didn't relate to the investigation, and expressing the most complicated case in a terminology in which the case only appeared on paper in its externals and in which his personal view was completely excluded, and most important all the requisite formality was observed. This work was something new. And he was one of the first people who worked out the practical application of the statutes of 1864.[6]

Moving to a new city to the post of examining magistrate, Ivan Ilyich made new acquaintances and connections, positioned himself afresh and adopted a slightly different tone. He positioned himself at a certain respectable distance from the governing authorities, but chose the best circle of the lawyers and nobles who lived in the city, and adopted a tone of slight dissatisfaction with government, moderate liberalism and enlightened civic-mindedness. Moreover, without changing the elegance of his dress, in his new job Ivan Ilyich stopped shaving his chin and let his beard grow freely.

Ivan Ilyich's life turned out very pleasantly in the new city as well: the society that took a critical tone of the governor was good and friendly; his salary was larger and a not inconsiderable pleasure was then added to his life by whist, which Ivan Ilyich started to play, having an ability to play cards cheerfully, quick-wittedly and very shrewdly so that generally he won.

After two years working in the new city Ivan Ilyich met his future wife. Praskovya Fyodorovna Mikhel was the most attractive, cleverest, most brilliant girl of the group in which Ivan Ilyich moved. Among the other amusements and relaxations from the labours of a magistrate Ivan Ilyich developed a playful, easy relationship with Praskovya Fyodorovna.

While he had been a special assignments official Ivan Ilyich used to dance as a matter of course; as an examining magistrate he now danced only on exceptional occasions. He danced now in the sense that although he was a part of the new institutions and in the fifth grade[7]—if it comes to dancing, then I can show that in this field I can do things better than others. So from time to time at the end of an evening he used to dance with Praskovya Fyodorovna and it was during these dances in particular that he conquered her. She fell in love with him. Ivan Ilyich didn't have a clear, defined intention of marrying, but when the girl fell in love with him, he asked himself a question. 'Actually, why not get married?' he said to himself.

6. The emancipation of the serfs in 1861 was followed by a thorough all-round reform of judicial proceedings [translators' note].

7. That is, government service sector of the Table of Ranks.

Miss Praskovya Fyodorovna was from a good noble family, was not bad looking and had a bit of money. Ivan Ilyich could aspire to a more brilliant match, but this too was a good match. Ivan Ilyich had his salary; she, he hoped, would have as much again. The family connection was good; she was a sweet, pretty and absolutely decent woman. To say that Ivan Ilyich married because he fell in love with his bride and found in her sympathy for his views on life would have been as unjust as to say that he married because people in his social circle approved of the match. Ivan Ilyich married because of both considerations: he was doing something pleasant for himself in acquiring such a wife and at the same time he was doing something his superiors thought a right thing to do.

And so Ivan Ilyich married.

The actual process of marriage and the first period of married life, with its conjugal caresses, new furniture, new china, new linen, went very well till his wife's pregnancy, so that Ivan Ilyich was beginning to think that marriage not only would not destroy the character of an easy, pleasant, cheerful life, one wholly decorous and approved of by society, which Ivan Ilyich thought the true quality of life, but would enhance it further. But then from the first months of his wife's pregnancy something new appeared, something unexpected, unpleasant, oppressive and indecorous which one couldn't expect and from which one couldn't escape.

His wife for no reasons, so Ivan Ilyich thought, as he said to himself, began *de gaîté de coeur*[8] to destroy the pleasant tenor and decorum of life: she was jealous of him without any cause, demanded attentions to herself from him, found fault with everything and made crude and unpleasant scenes.

At first Ivan Ilyich had hoped to be freed from the unpleasantness of this situation by the same easy and decorous attitude to life which had rescued him before—he tried to ignore his wife's state of mind and continued to live pleasantly and decorously as before: he invited friends home for a game of cards, he tried to go out to his club or to see his friends. But on one occasion his wife started to abuse him rudely with such energy and continued to abuse him so persistently every time he didn't fulfil her demands, clearly having made a firm decision not to stop until he would submit, that is, sit at home and be miserable like her, that Ivan Ilyich was horrified. He understood that married life—at any rate with his wife—does not always make for the pleasures and decorum of life but on the contrary often destroys them and therefore it was essential to protect himself from this destruction. And Ivan Ilyich began to seek the means for this. His official work was one thing that impressed Praskovya Fyodorovna and Ivan Ilyich through his official work and the duties which arose out of it began to fight his wife, securing his own independent world.

A child was born. There were attempts at feeding and various failures in this, along with the real and imaginary illnesses of child and mother. Sympathy for all this was demanded from Ivan Ilyich but of which he could understand nothing. So the requirement of Ivan Ilyich to fence in a world for himself outside of the family became all the more pressing.

As his wife became more irritable and demanding, so Ivan Ilyich moved the center of gravity of his life more and more into his official work. He came to like his work more and became more ambitious than he had been before.

8. Literally, "from gaiety of heart" (French); from sheer impulsiveness.

Very soon, not more than a year after their marriage, Ivan Ilyich understood that married life, which offers certain conveniences in life, in reality is a very complicated and difficult business with which in order to do one's duty, that is to lead a decorous life that is approved of by society, one has to develop a defined relationship as one does with one's work.

And Ivan Ilyich did develop for himself such a relationship with married life. He required of family life only those conveniences which it could give him, of dinner at home, a mistress of the house, a bed, and most important, that decorum of external appearances which were defined by public opinion. For the rest he looked for cheerfulness and pleasure and if he found them was very grateful; if he met rejection and querulousness, he at once went off into the separate world of official work that he had fenced in for himself and found pleasure there.

Ivan Ilyich was valued as a good official and in three years he was made assistant prosecutor. His new responsibilities, their importance, the ability to bring anyone to trial and send him to prison, the public nature of his speeches, the success Ivan Ilyich had in this work—all of this tied him even more closely to his official work.

More children came. His wife became more and more querulous and angry, but the relationship Ivan Ilyich had developed with domestic life had made him almost impervious to her querulousness.

After seven years of working in one city Ivan Ilyich was promoted to the position of prosecutor in a different province. They moved, they now had little money and his wife didn't like the place to which they had moved. Though his salary was more than it had been, life cost more; also two children died and so family life became even more unpleasant for Ivan Ilyich.

Praskovya Fyodorovna blamed her husband for all the misfortunes that befell them in their new home. Most subjects of conversation between husband and wife, particularly the education of the children, led to questions that recalled past disputes, and quarrels were ready to break out every minute. There remained only those rare periods of tenderness which came to the married couple but did not last long. These were islands on which they landed for a while but then again sailed off into the sea of hidden animosity which expressed itself in their alienation from each other. This alienation might have distressed Ivan Ilyich if he had thought that it should not be like this, but he now recognized this situation not just as normal but as the actual goal of his family life. His object was to free himself more and more from these unpleasant things and to give them a character of innocuous decorum; and he achieved it by spending less and less time with his family and when he was forced to do it, he tried to protect his situation by the presence of outsiders. The important thing was that Ivan Ilyich had his official work. For him all the interest of life was concentrated in that official world. And this interest absorbed him. The consciousness of his power, of his ability to bring down anyone he chose to, his importance, even in externals when he entered the court and at meetings with subordinates, his mastery of conducting the work—all this made him feel glad and together with talking to his friends, with dinners and whist it filled up his life. So that overall Ivan Ilyich's life continued to go on as he thought that it should: pleasantly and with decorum.

So he lived for another seven years. His elder daughter was now sixteen, another child had died, and there only remained a boy at the Gymnasium, a

subject of dissension. Ivan Ilyich had wanted to send him to Law School but to spite him Praskovya Fyodorovna had sent the boy to the Gymnasium. The daughter was taught at home and had grown into a good-looking girl, the boy too wasn't bad at his studies.

III

That was Ivan Ilyich's life for seventeen years after his marriage. He was now a senior prosecutor, having refused various promotions in the expectation of a more desirable position, when something very unpleasant happened which completely destroyed the tranquillity of his life. Ivan Ilyich was expecting the position of president of the tribunal in a university town but somehow Hoppe overtook him and got the place. Ivan Ilyich was angry, started to make accusations and quarrelled with him and his closest superiors; they cooled towards him and passed him over for the next appointment.

That was in 1880. That year was the hardest in Ivan Ilyich's life. In that year his salary wasn't sufficient for living; everyone forgot him and what appeared to him to be the greatest, the cruellest injustice towards him was found by others to be something completely ordinary. Even his father didn't see it as his duty to help him. He felt everyone had abandoned him, considering his situation on a 3,500 rouble salary quite normal and even fortunate. He alone knew that with his consciousness of the injustices done to him and with his wife's constant nagging, and with the debts he was beginning to run, living above his means—he alone knew that his situation was far from normal.

In the summer of that year to ease his finances he took some leave and went with his wife to spend the summer at Praskovya Fyodorovna's brother's home.

In the country, without his work, Ivan Ilyich for the first time felt not just boredom but unbearable depression, felt that he could not live like that and that he absolutely had to take some decisive action.

Having spent a sleepless night the whole of which he spent pacing the terrace, Ivan Ilyich decided to go to Petersburg to make a petition and in order to punish *them*, those who could not appreciate him, to transfer to another ministry.

The next day, in spite of all the attempts of his wife and brother-in-law to dissuade him, he travelled to Petersburg.

He went for one thing: to obtain a 5,000 rouble salary. He was no longer holding out for any particular ministry or direction or type of work. He just needed a position, a position on 5,000 roubles, in government, in banking, in the railways, in the Empress Maria's Foundations,[9] even in the customs, but he absolutely had to have 5,000 roubles and he absolutely had to leave the ministry where they couldn't appreciate him.

And now this trip of Ivan Ilyich's was crowned with amazing, unexpected success. In Kursk he was joined in a first class carriage by F. S. Ilyin, someone he knew, who told him about a telegram the governor of Kursk had just received, which announced a reorganization to take place in the ministry: Pyotr Ivanovich's position was going to be taken by Ivan Semyonovich.

9. Reference to the charitable organization founded by the Empress Maria, wife of Paul I, late in the 18th century.

The planned upheaval, apart from its significance for Russia, had a particular significance for Ivan Ilyich: by promoting a new face, Pyotr Petrovich, and of course Zakhar Ivanovich, his classmate and friend, it was highly propitious for him.

In Moscow the news was confirmed. And when he reached Petersburg, Ivan Ilyich found Zakhar Ivanovich and got the promise of a sure place in his old ministry of justice.

After a week he telegraphed his wife: *'Zakhar has Miller's place stop I receive position at next report.'*

Thanks to this change of personnel Ivan Ilyich got this position in his old ministry which placed him two ranks above his old colleagues; also a salary of 5,000 rubles and 3,500 removal expenses. All his anger against his former enemies and the entire ministry was forgotten, and Ivan Ilyich was altogether happy.

Ivan Ilyich returned to the country more cheerful and content than he had ever been. Praskovya Fyodorovna cheered up too and a truce was established between them. Ivan Ilyich told her how in Petersburg everyone had feted him, how all his old enemies had been shamed and were now crawling before him, how he was envied for his position, and especially how highly he was regarded by everyone in Petersburg.

Praskovya Fyodorovna listened to all this and appeared to believe it and didn't contradict him in anything but just made plans for arranging their new life in the city to which they were moving. And Ivan Ilyich joyfully saw that these plans were his plans, that the plans were tallying, and that his life which had faltered was again taking on its true and natural character of cheerful pleasantness and decorum.

Ivan Ilyich had come just for a short time. On 10 September he had to take up the new job and furthermore he needed time to settle in the new home, to move everything from the provincial city, and to buy and order many more things; in a word, to settle as had been decided in his own mind and almost exactly as had been decided in that of Praskovya Fyodorovna.

And now, when everything had worked out so well and he and his wife were agreed about their goals and furthermore weren't living much together, they got on harmoniously as they hadn't done since the first years of married life. Ivan Ilyich thought of taking his family away with him immediately but the insistence of his brother-in-law and his wife, who had suddenly become particularly friendly and familial towards Ivan Ilyich and his family, resulted in Ivan Ilyich going away alone.

Ivan Ilyich left and the cheerful state of mind brought about by his success and the harmony with his wife, one reinforcing the other, stayed with him the whole time. A delightful apartment was found, the very one husband and wife had been dreaming of. High, spacious, old-fashioned reception rooms, a comfortable, imposing study, rooms for his wife and daughter, a schoolroom for his son—everything as if devised purposely for them. Ivan Ilyich set about arranging it himself, he chose wallpaper, he bought more furniture, antiques in particular whose style he found particularly *comme il faut*, he had things upholstered, and it all grew and grew and approached the ideal he had composed for himself. Even when he had half arranged things, his arrangements exceeded his expectation. He understood the *comme il faut* look, elegant

without vulgarity, which everything would take on once it was ready. As he went to sleep he imagined to himself how the salon would be. Looking at the drawing-room, which wasn't yet finished, he could already see the fireplace, the screen, the whatnot and the little chairs disposed about the room, the plates and saucers on the walls and the bronzes all standing in their places. He was pleased by the thought that he would surprise Pasha and Lizanka, his wife and daughter, who also had a taste for this. They were certainly not expecting this. He was particularly successful in finding old things and buying them cheaply: they gave everything a particularly aristocratic air. In his letters he deliberately described everything in less attractive terms than the reality, to surprise them. All this absorbed him so much that even his new job absorbed him less than he had expected—though he loved his work. During sittings of the court he had moments of absent-mindedness: he started thinking about whether the curtain pelmets should be straight or curved. He was so absorbed by this that he often did things himself; he even moved the furniture about and re-hung the curtains himself. Once he got up on a ladder to show a slow-witted decorator how he wanted the drapes hung; he missed his footing and fell but being a strong and agile man he held his balance, and only knocked his side on the handle of the window-frame. The bruise was painful but soon disappeared. During all this time Ivan Ilyich felt particularly well and cheerful. He wrote, 'I feel I'm fifteen years younger.' He thought the work would be finished in September but it dragged on till mid October. But the apartment was delightful—it wasn't just he who said this but everyone who saw it said so to him.

In actual fact it was the same as in the houses of all people who are not so rich but want to be like the rich and so are only like one another: brocade, ebony, flowers, carpets and bronzes, everything dark and shiny—everything that all people of a certain type do to be like all people of a certain type. And what he had was so like that that one couldn't even notice it, but to him it all looked somehow special. When he met his family at the railway station and took them to his apartment, all finished and lit up, and a manservant in a white tie opened the door into the flower-decked hall, and then they went into the drawing-room and study—he was very happy, he took them everywhere, drank in their praise and beamed with pleasure. That evening, when over tea Praskovya Fyodorovna asked him among other things how he had fallen, he laughed and in front of them showed how he had gone flying and frightened the decorator.

'It's lucky I am a gymnast. Someone else might have been killed but I only knocked myself a bit here; when you touch it—it hurts, but it'll pass; it's just a bruise.'

And they started to live in the new home which as always, once they had settled in properly, turned out to have one room too few, and with the new income which as always turned out to be too little—only not by very much— 500 roubles. And life was very good. Especially good at first when all was not yet done and more still had to be done: things to be bought, to be ordered, moved, adjusted. Although there were some disagreements between husband and wife, they were both so pleased and there was so much to do that everything was finished without serious quarrels. When there was nothing left to do, it became a bit more boring and something seemed lacking, but now friendships were made and habits established and life filled up.

After spending the morning in court, Ivan Ilyich returned for dinner, and at first his mood was good although it suffered a little, specifically because of their home. (Every stain on a tablecloth or brocade, or a broken curtain cord irritated him; he had put in so much work into the arrangement that every disruption of it was painful to him.) But in general Ivan Ilyich's life went on just as in his view life should flow: easily, pleasantly and decorously. He rose at nine, drank his coffee, read the newspapers, then put on his uniform and drove to the court. There the harness in which he worked was already moulded for him and he slipped into it right away: petitioners, chancery inquiries, the chancery itself, public and executive sittings of the court. In all of these one had to know how to exclude anything raw and vital which always destroys the even flow of official work: one couldn't admit any human relationships, except official ones; the occasion for a relationship had to be solely official and so had the relationship itself. For example, a man would come in and want to find out something. Outside his official role Ivan Ilyich could not have any relationship with him; but if this man had a relationship with him as a member of the court, one that could be expressed on headed paper—then within the bounds of this relationship Ivan Ilyich would do everything, absolutely everything he could, and in doing this would observe the semblance of friendly relations, i.e. courtesy. As soon as the official relationship was ended, so was any other. This ability to separate out the official side without combining it with his real life Ivan Ilyich possessed in the highest degree and by his talents and long practice he had developed it to such a point that he even sometimes like a virtuoso would allow himself as if in jest to combine personal and official relationships. He would allow himself this because he always felt in himself the power to split off the official again when necessary, and to reject the personal. Ivan Ilyich handled this work of his not just easily, agreeably and decorously but even with the mastery of a virtuoso. Between cases he would smoke, drink tea, chat a bit about politics, a bit about generalities, a bit about cards and most of all about official appointments. And he would return home tired but with the feeling of a virtuoso who had given a lucid performance of his part, one of the first violins in the orchestra. At home mother and daughter would go out somewhere or someone came to see them; his son was at the Gymnasium, preparing his lessons with tutors and diligently studying the things they teach in a Gymnasium. Everything was good. After dinner, if there were no guests, Ivan Ilyich would sometimes read a book about which people were talking a lot and in the evening he would sit down to his work, that is read his papers, consult the law, examine testimony and check it against the law. All this he found neither boring nor amusing. It was boring if he could be playing *vint*; but if there was no *vint*—then all the same this was better than sitting by himself or with his wife. Ivan Ilyich's pleasures were little dinners to which he would invite ladies and gentlemen who were important in terms of worldly position, and spending his time with them: that was just like the usual way such people spend their time, just as his drawing room was like all drawing rooms.

Once they even had an evening party, with dancing. And Ivan Ilyich felt cheerful and everything was good, except he had a big quarrel with his wife over the cakes and sweets: Praskovya Fyodorovna had her own plan but Ivan Ilyich insisted on getting everything from an expensive confectioner and the quarrel was because there were cakes left over and the confectioner's bill came

to forty-five rubles. The quarrel was a big and unpleasant one to such a point that Praskovya Fyodorovna called him 'an idiot and a misery,' and he took his head in his hands and in a fit of temper said something about divorce. But the actual party was enjoyable. The very best society was there and Ivan Ilyich danced with Princess Trufonova, sister of the famous founder of the 'Goodbye Sorrow' Society. His official pleasures were pleasures of pride; his social pleasures were pleasures of vanity; but Ivan Ilyich's real pleasures were the pleasures of playing *vint*. He admitted that after all the various unhappy events in his life the pleasure which burnt like a candle above all others was to sit down at *vint* with good players and partners who didn't shout, definitely in a four (when you're five it's really annoying to have to stand out, although you pretend you very much like it), and to have an intelligent, serious game (when the cards are right), and then to have supper and drink a glass of wine. After *vint*, especially after a little win (a big win was unpleasant) Ivan Ilyich went to bed in an especially good mood.

That's how they lived. They formed around them a group of the best society, important people went to them and young people too.

Husband, wife and daughter were agreed in their views of their circle of acquaintances and without any formal understanding they dropped and were rid of all sorts of shabby little friends and relatives, who used to drop in to see them, spouting endearments into the drawing room with Japanese plates hanging on the wall. Soon these shabby little friends stopped dropping in and the Golovins were left with just the very best society. Young men paid court to Lizanka and Petrishchev, an examining magistrate, the son of Dmitry Ivanovich Petrishchev and sole heir to his property, began to pay so much attention to her that Ivan Ilyich even talked about it to Praskovya Fyodorovna: shouldn't they bring them together in a troika ride or organize some theatricals? That's how they lived. And everything went on like that, without any change, and everything was very good.

IV

They were all in good health. One couldn't call poor health the fact that Ivan Ilyich sometimes said he had an odd taste in his mouth and something felt uncomfortable on the left side of his stomach.

But it happened that this discomfort started to grow and to become not quite pain but the consciousness of a constant heaviness in his side accompanied by a bad mood. This bad mood, which got worse and worse, began to spoil the pleasant course of the easy and decorous life which had been established in the Golovin house. Husband and wife began to quarrel more and more often, and soon the ease and pleasantness disappeared and only decorum was preserved, with difficulty. Again scenes became more frequent. Again there remained just some islands of calm, and only a few of those, on which husband and wife could meet without an outburst.

And Praskovya Fyodorovna now said, not without cause, that her husband had a difficult character. With her natural habit of exaggeration she said he had always had this dreadful character, and that one needed her good nature to stand it for twenty years. It was true that the quarrels now started with him. His fault-finding always began just before dinner and often when he was start-

ing to eat, over the soup. He would remark that one of the dishes was damaged, or the food wasn't right, or his son had his elbow on the table, or it was his daughter's hair style. And he blamed Praskovya Fyodorovna for everything. At first Praskovya Fyodorovna answered back and was rude to him but a couple of times at the beginning of dinner he flew into such a rage that she understood that this was a morbid condition brought on in him by the intake of food, so she controlled herself and didn't answer back but ate her dinner quickly. Praskovya Fyodorovna regarded her self-control as greatly to her own credit. Having decided that her husband had a dreadful character and that he had created the unhappiness of her life, she started to feel sorry for herself. And the more she felt sorry for herself, the more she hated her husband. She began to wish that he would die, but she couldn't wish for that because then there would be no salary. And that irritated her against him even more. She considered herself terribly unhappy precisely because even his death could not rescue her and she became irritated; she concealed it and her concealed irritation increased his own irritation.

After one scene, in which Ivan Ilyich was particularly unfair, and after which in explaining himself he said he was indeed prone to irritability but that it came from his illness, she said to him that if he was ill, then he must get treatment and demanded from him that he see a famous doctor.

He went. Everything was as he had expected; everything happened as it always does. The waiting and the doctor's assumed pompousness, something familiar to him, which he knew from himself in court, and the tapping and the auscultation and the questions requiring predetermined and clearly unnecessary answers, and the meaningful air suggesting that you just submit to us, we'll fix everything—we know, we have no doubts about how to fix everything, in the very same way for any man you choose. Everything was precisely as in court. Just as he in court put on an air towards the accused, so in precisely the same way the famous doctor put on an air towards him.

The doctor said: such and such shows that you have such and such inside; but if that isn't confirmed by examining such and such, then one must assume you have such and such. If one does assume such and such, then . . . and so forth. Only one question was important to Ivan Ilyich: was his condition dangerous or not? But the doctor ignored this inappropriate question. From the doctor's point of view the question was pointless and wasn't the one under discussion; it was only a question of assessing various possibilities—a floating kidney, chronic catarrh or an infection of the appendix. It wasn't a question of Ivan Ilyich's life but an argument between a floating kidney and the appendix. And before Ivan Ilyich's eyes the doctor resolved the argument brilliantly in favour of the floating kidney, with the reservation that an examination of his urine could provide new evidence and then the case would be looked at again. All this was very precisely what Ivan Ilyich himself had done a thousand times with defendants and as brilliantly. The doctor did his summing up just as brilliantly, triumphantly, even cheerfully, looking at the defendant over his glasses. From the doctor's summing up Ivan Ilyich drew the conclusion that things were bad; that it didn't matter much to the doctor or probably to anyone else, but that for him things were bad. And Ivan Ilyich was painfully struck by this conclusion which aroused in him a feeling of great self pity and of great anger towards this doctor who was indifferent to such an important question.

But he didn't say anything and got up, put the money on the desk and said with a sigh:

'Probably we patients often put inappropriate questions to you,' he said. 'In general terms, is this a dangerous illness or not? . . .'

The doctor gave him one stern look through his glasses as if to say: accused, if you will not stay within the boundaries of the questions that are put to you, then I will be compelled to give instructions for your removal from the courtroom.

'I have already told you what I consider necessary and proper,' said the doctor. 'An examination will show the rest.' And the doctor bowed.

Ivan Ilyich slowly went out, despondently got into the sleigh and went home. For the whole journey he ceaselessly went over everything the doctor had said, trying to turn those confused, unclear, scientific words into simple language and to read in them an answer to the question: am I in a bad way, or a very bad way, or aren't things yet so bad? And he thought that the sense of everything the doctor had said was that he was in a very bad way. Everything in the streets looked sad to Ivan Ilyich. The cab drivers were sad, the houses were sad, the passers by, the shops. This pain, this dull nagging pain which didn't stop for a single second combined with the doctor's unclear pronouncements acquired another more serious meaning. Ivan Ilyich listened to his pain with a new heavy feeling.

He arrived home and started to tell his wife. His wife listened but in the middle of his account his daughter came in wearing a hat: she and her mother were going out. She sat down for a moment to listen to this boring stuff but she couldn't stand it for long, and her mother didn't listen to the end.

'Now I'm very pleased,' his wife said, 'so mind you take your medicine properly. Give me the prescription, I'll send Gerasim to the chemist's.' And she went to dress.

While she was in the room he was barely able to breathe and he sighed heavily when she went out.

'Well then,' he said. 'Perhaps it's not so bad.'

He began to take the medicines and to follow the doctor's directions, which changed after the urine examination. But it was the case now that there had been some kind of confusion in the examination and in what followed from it. It was impossible to get through to the doctor himself but it turned out that what was happening was not what the doctor had told him. Either he had forgotten or he had lied or he had concealed something from him.

But Ivan Ilyich still started to follow the directions precisely and in doing so at first found some comfort.

From the time he visited the doctor Ivan Ilyich's chief occupation became the precise following of the doctor's directions about hygiene and the monitoring of his pain and all the functions of his organism. Ivan Ilyich's chief interests became human illness and human health. When they talked in front of him about people who were ill or had died or got better and in particular about any illness that resembled his own, he would listen, trying to conceal his agitation, and ask questions and apply what was said to his own illness.

The pain got no less but Ivan Ilyich made an effort to force himself to think he was better. And he could deceive himself as long as nothing disturbed him. But as soon as there was some unpleasantness with his wife or something went wrong at work or he had bad cards at *vint*, he at once felt the full force of

his illness; in the past he had endured things going wrong in the expectation that 'I'll soon put things right, I'll overcome, I'll be successful, I'll get a grand slam.' Now anything that went wrong brought him down and cast him into despair. He would say to himself, 'I was just starting to get better and the medicine was already beginning to work, and along comes this cursed accident or unpleasantness . . .' And he was angry with the accident or with the people who were causing him unpleasantnesses and killing him, and he felt that this anger was killing him but he couldn't restrain himself. One might have thought it would have been clear to him that this anger against circumstances and people made his illness worse and that therefore he shouldn't pay any attention to unpleasant incidents; but his reasoning was quite the reverse: he said he needed calm, he watched out for anything that might breach that calm and at the smallest breach he got angry. His condition was made worse by the fact that he consulted medical books and doctors. His deterioration progressed so evenly that comparing one day with another he could deceive himself—there was little difference. But when he consulted doctors, he thought he was getting worse and that very quickly. And in spite of that he constantly consulted doctors.

That month he went see another celebrity; this other celebrity said almost the same as the first but put the questions differently. And consulting this celebrity only deepened Ivan Ilyich's doubt and terror. A friend of a friend—a very good doctor—diagnosed his illness quite differently and in spite of promising recovery, with his questions and assumptions he confused Ivan Ilyich even more and increased his doubts. A homeopath diagnosed his illness again quite differently and gave him some medicine, and Ivan Ilyich took it in secret from everyone for about a week. But after a week, feeling no relief and having lost confidence both in the previous treatments and in this one, he fell into greater despair. On one occasion a lady he knew was talking about the healing powers of icons. Ivan Ilyich found himself listening carefully and believing the reality of this. This incident frightened him. 'Have I really become so feeble-minded?' he said to himself. 'What rubbish! It's all nonsense, I mustn't give in to hypochondria, but having chosen one doctor I must firmly stick to his treatment. That's what I'll do. Now it's settled. I'm not going to think and I'm strictly going to follow the treatment till the summer. Then there'll be something to show. Let's now have an end to all this wavering! . . .' It was easy to say that but impossible to put it into action. The pain in his side wore him down, it seemed to keep getting worse, it became constant, the taste in his mouth became stronger, he thought a disgusting smell was coming from his mouth, and his appetite and strength were going. He couldn't deceive himself: something terrible, new and important was happening in him, something more important than anything that had happened to Ivan Ilyich in his life. And only he knew about this, all those around him either didn't understand or didn't want to understand and thought that everything in the world was going on as before. That was what tormented Ivan Ilyich most of all. He could see that his household— chiefly his wife and daughter who were in the full swing of visits and parties— understood nothing, and they were vexed that he was so gloomy and demanding, as if he were guilty in that. Although they tried to conceal it, he saw that he was a burden to them but that his wife had evolved a particular attitude to his illness and adhered to that irrespective of what he said and did. Her attitude was like this:

'You know,' she would say to friends, 'Ivan Ilyich can't strictly follow a prescribed treatment, as most good people can. Today he'll take his drops and eat

what he's been told to, and go to bed in good time; but tomorrow if I don't look properly, he'll suddenly forget to take them and eat oysters (which are forbidden him) and sit down to *vint* till one in the morning.'

'When did I do that?' Ivan Ilyich would say crossly. 'Once at Pyotr Ivanovich's.'

'Yesterday with Shebek.'

'I just couldn't sleep from the pain . . .'

'Well, whatever it was from, like that you won't get better and you make us miserable.'

Praskovya Fyodorovna's public attitude to her husband's illness, which she expressed to others and to him, was that this illness was Ivan Ilyich's own fault and that the whole illness was a new unpleasantness he was bringing down on his wife. Ivan Ilyich felt that this came out in her involuntarily, but that didn't make it any easier for him.

In court Ivan Ilyich noticed or thought he noticed the same strange attitude to him: now he would think that people were scrutinising him like a man whose position was soon going to be vacant; now all of a sudden his friends would start to joke in an amicable way about his hypochondria, as if this thing, this awful, terrible, unheard of thing that had grown in him and was ceaselessly gnawing at him and irrepressibly dragging him somewhere, were the most pleasant subject for a joke. He was especially irritated by Schwarz with his playfulness and energy and *comme il faut* ways, all of which reminded Ivan Ilyich of himself ten years back.

Friends came to make up a game, they sat down. They dealt, bending the new cards, he put diamonds next to diamonds, seven of them. His partner bid no trumps—and held two diamonds. What could be better? Things were cheerful and bright—they had a grand slam. And suddenly Ivan Ilyich felt that gnawing pain, that taste in the mouth and there seemed to him to be something absurd in the fact that he could rejoice in a grand slam.

He looked at Mikhail Mikhaylovich, his partner, rapping his powerful hand on the table and politely and condescendingly refraining from scooping up the tricks but pushing the cards toward Ivan Ilyich to give him the pleasure of picking them up without straining himself and stretching out his arm. 'Does he think I'm so weak I can't stretch out my arm?' Ivan Ilyich thought. He forgot about trumps and trumped his partner, losing the grand slam by three tricks— and what was really dreadful was that he saw how Mikhail Mikhaylovich was suffering, but he didn't care. And it was dreadful to think just why he didn't care.

They all saw he was feeling bad and said to him, 'We can stop if you are tired. You must rest.' Rest? No, he wasn't tired at all, and they finished the rubber. They were all gloomy and silent. Ivan Ilyich felt he had brought down this gloom upon them and he couldn't dispel it. They had supper and went their ways, and Ivan Ilyich was left alone with the knowledge that his life had been poisoned for him and that it was poisoning the life of others and this poison wasn't losing its power but was penetrating his whole being more and more.

And with this knowledge and with the physical pain too and the terror, he had to get into bed and often be unable to sleep from the pain the greater part of the night. And the next morning he had to get up again, dress, go to court, talk, write, or if he didn't go to court he had stay at home with those twenty-

four hours of the day, each one of which was a torment. And he had to live like that on the brink of the abyss, all alone, without a single person who could understand and take pity on him.

V

A month went by like that and then another. Before the New Year his brother-in-law came to the city and stayed with them. Ivan Ilyich was in court. Praskovya Fyodorovna had gone out shopping. When Ivan Ilyich went into his study he found his brother-in-law, a healthy, full-blooded fellow, unpacking his suitcase himself. He raised his head when he heard Ivan Ilyich's footsteps and looked at him for a second in silence. That look revealed everything to Ivan Ilyich. His brother-in-law opened his mouth to say 'oh' and stopped himself. That movement confirmed everything.

'So, I've changed, haven't I?'

'Yes . . . there is a change.'

And however much afterwards Ivan Ilyich turned the conversation with his brother-in-law to his appearance, the brother-in-law said nothing. Praskovya Fyodorovna arrived, the brother-in-law went out to her. Ivan Ilyich locked his door and started to examine himself in the mirror—full face, then from the side. He took up a photograph of himself with his wife and compared the image with the one he saw in the mirror. The change was huge. Then he bared his arms to the elbow, looked, let back his sleeves and sat on an ottoman, and his mood became darker than night.

'You mustn't, you mustn't,' he said to himself; he jumped up, went to the desk, opened a case file and began to read it, but he couldn't. He unlocked the door and went into the salon. The drawing-room door was shut. He tiptoed to it and began to listen.

'No, you're exaggerating,' said Praskovya Fyodorovna.

'Exaggerating? You don't see—he's a dead man, look at his eyes. There's no light in them. What's the matter with him?'

'Nobody knows. Nikolayev [that was the second doctor] said something but I don't know what. Leshchetitsky [that was the celebrated doctor] said the opposite . . .'

Ivan Ilyich moved away, went to his room, lay down and started to think: 'A kidney, a floating kidney.' He remembered everything the doctor had told him—how it had become detached and was floating. And with an effort of the imagination he tried to understand his kidney and to halt it and strengthen it; so little was needed for that, he thought. 'No, I'll go again to Pyotr Ivanovich.' (That was the friend who had a friend who was a doctor.) He rang, gave orders for the horse to be harnessed and got ready to leave.

'Where are you off to, *Jean*?'[1] his wife said with a particularly sad and unusually kind expression.

This unusual kindness angered him. He looked at her morosely.

'I have to go to Pyotr Ivanovich.'

He went to his friend who had a friend who was a doctor. He found him at home and had a long conversation with him.

1. French for Ivan (in English, John).

When he considered both the anatomical and physiological details of what in the doctor's opinion had been happening inside him, he understood everything.

There was some thing, a little something in the appendix. All that might be put right. Stimulate the activity of one organ, weaken the activity of another, the something would be absorbed and everything would be put right. He got back a little late for dinner, talked cheerfully for a bit, but for a long time he couldn't go to his room to work. Finally he went into his study and at once sat down to work. He read his cases and worked, but the consciousness that he had set something aside, an important and intimate matter which he would take up once his work was over—did not leave him. When he had finished his cases, he remembered that this intimate matter was his thinking about his appendix. But he didn't indulge it, he went to the drawing-room for tea. There were guests, including the examining magistrate, his daughter's intended; they talked and played the piano and sang. Ivan Ilyich spent the evening, as Praskovya Fyodorovna noticed, more cheerfully than he had spent others but he didn't forget for one minute that he had set aside some important thinking about his appendix. At eleven o'clock he said goodnight and went to his room. Since he had become ill he slept in a little room next to his study. He went in, undressed and picked up a novel of Zola's[2] which he didn't read. He began thinking instead. The desired cure of the appendix took place in his imagination. Matter was absorbed, matter was expelled and normal activity was restored. 'Yes, that's how it all is,' he said to himself. 'Only nature needs a little help.' He remembered his medicine, sat up, took it, watching for the beneficial effects of the medicine and the removal of the pain. 'Just take it regularly and avoid unhealthy influences; I already feel a bit better, much better.' He started to feel his side—it wasn't painful to the touch. 'Yes, I can't feel it, I'm really much better now.' He put out the candle and lay on his side . . . The appendix is getting better, things are being absorbed. Suddenly he felt the familiar old dull nagging pain, the persistent, quiet, serious pain. The familiar nastiness in his mouth. His heart began to pump, his head turned. 'My God, my God!' he said. 'It's here again, it's here again and it's never going to stop.' And suddenly his case presented itself to him from a different perspective. 'Appendix! Kidney!' he said to himself. 'It's not a case of the appendix or of the kidney, but of life . . . and death. Yes, I had life and now it's passing, passing, and I can't hold it back. That's it. Why deceive oneself? Isn't it obvious to everyone but myself that I am dying, and it's only a question of the number of weeks, days—maybe now. There was light and now there's darkness. I was here but now I'm going there! Where?' A chill came over him, his breathing stopped. He could only hear the beating of his heart.

'I won't exist, so what will exist? Nothing will exist. So where will I be when I don't exist? Is this really death? No, I don't want it.' He got up quickly, tried to light a candle, groped with shaking hands, dropped the candle and candlestick on the floor and slumped back again onto the pillow. 'Why? Nothing matters,' he said to himself, looking into the darkness with open eyes. 'Death. Yes, death. And none of them knows and they don't want to know and they have no pity for

---

2. Émile Zola (1840–1902), French novelist, author of the *Rougon-Macquart* novels (*Nana, Germinal*, etc.). Tolstoy condemned Zola for his naturalistic theories and considered his novels crude.

me. They're enjoying themselves. [Outside the door he could hear the distant noise of music and singing.] They don't care but they too will die. Fools. It'll come to me first; to them later; they too will have the same. But they're having fun, the beasts!' Anger choked him. And he felt painful, unbearable misery. It cannot be that we're all doomed to this terrible fear. He raised himself.

'Something's not right; I must calm down, I must think over everything from the outset.' And he began to think. 'Yes, the start of my illness. I knocked my side, and I stayed just the same that day and the next; it ached a bit, then more, then the doctors, then depression, despair, the doctors again; and I kept getting nearer and nearer to the abyss. Less strength. Nearer and nearer. And now I've wasted away, there's no light in my eyes. And death, and I think about my appendix. I think of how to mend my appendix, but this is death. Is it really death?' Again horror came over him, he bent down, tried to find the matches, and banged his elbow on the night-table. It got in his way and hurt him, he got angry with it, in his irritation he banged his elbow harder and knocked the night-table over. And in his despair he fell back, gasping for breath, expecting death to come now.

Now the guests were leaving. Praskovya Fyodorovna was seeing them out. She heard something fall and came in.

'What's the matter with you?'

'Nothing. I knocked it over by mistake.'

She went out and brought back a candle. He lay breathing heavily and very fast, like a man who has run a mile, looking at her with motionless eyes.

'What's the matter with you, *Jean*?'

'No . . . thing. I . . . knocked . . . it . . . over.' ('What should I say? She won't understand,' he thought.)

Indeed she didn't. She picked the table up, lit a candle for him and quickly went out; she had to see a guest out.

When she returned, he was lying in the same position, on his back, looking up.

'How are you feeling? Is it worse?'

'Yes, it is.'

She shook her head and sat down.

'You know, *Jean*. I am wondering whether we shouldn't ask Leshchetitsky to the house.'

That meant asking the celebrated doctor regardless of cost. He smiled venomously and said, 'No.' She sat for a while, then went over to him and kissed him on the forehead.

When she kissed him he hated her with all his might and made an effort not to push her away.

'Good night. With God's help you'll go to sleep.'

'Yes.'

VI

Ivan Ilyich saw that he was dying and was in constant despair.

Ivan Ilyich knew that he was dying in the very depths of his soul but not only could he not get accustomed to this, he simply didn't understand it, he just couldn't understand it.

All his life the example of a syllogism which he had studied in Kiesewetter's[3] logic—'Caius is a man, men are mortal, therefore Caius is mortal'—had seemed to him to be true only in relation to Caius but in no way to himself. There was Caius-the-man, man in general, and it was quite justified, but he wasn't Caius and wasn't man in general, and he had always been something quite, quite special apart from all other beings; he was Vanya, with Mama, with Papa, with Mitya and Volodya, with his toys and the coachman, with Nyanya, then with Katenka, with all the joys, sorrows, passions of childhood, boyhood, youth. Did Caius know the smell of the striped leather ball Vanya loved so much? Did Caius kiss his mother's hand like that and did the silken folds of Caius's mother's dress rustle like that for him? Was Caius in love like that? Could Caius chair a session like that?

And Caius is indeed mortal and it's right that he should die, but for me, Vanya, Ivan Ilyich, with all my feelings and thoughts—for me it's quite different. And it cannot be that I should die. It would be too horrible.

That's what he felt.

'If I had to die like Caius, then I would know it, an inner voice would be telling me, but nothing like that happened in me; and I and all my friends—we understood that things weren't at all like with Caius. But now there's this!' he said to himself. 'It can't be. It can't be, but it is. How has this happened? How can one understand it?'

And he couldn't understand it and tried to banish this thought as false, inaccurate, morbid, and to replace it by other true and healthy thoughts. But this thought, and not just the thought but as it were reality came and stopped in front of him.

And in the place of this thought he called up others in turn, in the hope of finding support in them. He tried to return to his previous ways of thought, which had previously concealed the thought of death from him. But—strangely—everything which previously had concealed and covered up and obliterated the awareness of death now could no longer produce this result. Ivan Ilyich now spent most of his time attempting to restore his previous ways of feeling which had concealed death. Now he would say to himself, 'I'll take up some work, that's what I live by.' And he went to court, banishing all his doubts; he talked to friends and sat down, absentmindedly looking over the crowd of people with a pensive look as he used to and supporting both wasted hands on the arms of his oak chair; leaning over towards a friend as usual, moving the papers of a case, whispering together, and then suddenly raising his eyes and sitting up straight, he would pronounce the particular words and open the case. But suddenly in the middle of it the pain in his side ignoring the stages of the case's development, began its own gnawing work. Ivan Ilyich listened, and tried not to think about it, but it kept on. It came and stood right in front of him and looked at him, and he became petrified, the fire in his eyes died down, and he again began to ask himself, 'Is It alone the truth?' And his friends and staff saw with surprise and dismay that he, such a brilliant, subtle judge, was getting confused and making mistakes. He would give himself a shake, make an effort

---

3. Karl Kiesewetter (1766–1819) was a German popularizer of Kant's philosophy. His *Outline of Logic According to Kantian Princi-* *ples* (1796) was widely used in Russian adaptations as a schoolbook.

to recover himself and somehow or other bring the session to an end, and he would return home with the depressing awareness that his work as a judge couldn't hide from him as it used to what he wanted it to hide; that with his work as a judge he couldn't be rid of It. And what was worst of all was that It was distracting him not for him to do anything but only for him to look at It, right in the eye, look at it and without doing anything endure inexpressible sufferings.

And to rescue himself from this condition, Ivan Ilyich looked for relief—for new screens—and new screens appeared and for a short time seemed to offer him salvation but very soon they again not so much collapsed as let the light through, as if It penetrated everything and nothing could hide it.

Latterly he would go into the drawing room he had arranged—the drawing room where he had fallen, for which—how venomously comic it was to think of it—for the arrangement of which he had sacrificed his life, for he knew that his illness had started with that injury; he would go in and see that something had made a scratch on a polished table. He would look for the cause and find it in the bronze ornament of an album which had become bent at the edge. He would pick up the album, an expensive one he had lovingly compiled, and be cross at the carelessness of his daughter and her friends—things were torn and the photographs bent. He would carefully set things to rights and bend the decoration back again.

He then would have the thought of moving this whole *établissement*[4] of albums over into another corner by the flowers. He would call the manservant: either his daughter or his wife would come to his help; they would disagree, contradict him, he would argue, get angry; but everything would be all right because he didn't remember It, couldn't see It.

And then his wife would say when he himself was moving something: 'Let the servants do it, you'll hurt yourself again', and suddenly It would flash through the screens, he would see It; flash just for a moment, and he still would hope It would disappear, but without wanting to he would pay attention to his side—the same thing would still be sitting there, still aching, and he couldn't forget it, and It would be looking at him quite openly from behind the flowers. Why?

'It's true, it was here, on these curtains that I lost my life as if in an assault. Did I really? How terrible and how stupid! It can't be so! It can't be, but it is.'

He would go into his study, lie down and be left alone with It. Face to face with It, but nothing to be done with It. Just look at It and turn cold.

VII

How it happened in the third month of Ivan Ilyich's illness is impossible to say because it happened step by step, imperceptibly, but it did happen that his wife and his daughter and his son and the servants and his friends and the doctors and, above all, he himself knew that all interest that others had in him lay solely in whether he would soon, at last, vacate his place, free the living from the constraint brought about by his presence, and himself be liberated from his sufferings.

4. Arrangement (French).

He slept less and less; they gave him opium and started to inject morphine. But that gave him no relief. The dull pangs he felt in his half somnolent state at first gave him relief as being something new, but then they became as agonising as outright pain or even more so.

They prepared special food to the doctors' prescriptions, but this food he found more and more tasteless, more and more disgusting.

Special contrivances had to be made for excretion and every time this was a torment for him. A torment because of the uncleanliness, the loss of decorum and the odor, from the consciousness that another person had to take part in this.

But some comfort for Ivan Ilyich did come out of this unpleasant business. Gerasim, the serving man, always came to take things out for him.

Gerasim was a clean, fresh young peasant who had filled out on city food. He was always cheerful and sunny. At first Ivan Ilyich was embarrassed by seeing this man, always dressed in his clean traditional clothes, having to do this repulsive job.

Once getting up from the pan and lacking the strength to pull up his trousers, he collapsed into an easy chair and looked with horror at his feeble bared thighs with their sharply defined muscles.

Gerasim came in with firm, light steps in his heavy boots, giving off round him a pleasant smell of tar from the boots and of fresh winter air; he had on a clean hessian apron and a clean cotton shirt, the sleeves rolled up over his strong young bare arms; without looking at Ivan Ilyich, he went to the vessel, obviously masking the joy in living shining out from his face so as not to hurt the sick man.

'Gerasim,' Ivan Ilyich said weakly.

Gerasim started, obviously scared he had made some mistake, and with a quick movement turned towards the sick man his fresh, kind, simple, young face which was just beginning to grow a beard.

'Do you need something, sir?'

'I think this must be unpleasant for you. You must forgive me. I can't manage.'

'No, sir.' And Gerasim's eyes were shining and he showed his young white teeth. 'What's a little trouble? You've got an illness.'

And with strong, dexterous hands he did his usual job and went out, treading lightly. And in five minutes, treading just as lightly, he came back.

Ivan Ilyich was still sitting there like that in the armchair.

'Gerasim,' he said when he had put down the clean, rinsed vessel, 'please, come here and help me.' Gerasim came. 'Lift me up. It's difficult by myself and I've sent Dmitry away.'

Gerasim came over to him; he put his strong arms around him, and gently and deftly, in the same way as he walked, lifted and supported him; he pulled up his trousers with one hand and was going to sit him down. But Ivan Ilyich asked him to take him to the sofa. Effortlessly and with next to no pressure, Gerasim led him, almost carrying him, to the sofa and sat him down.

'Thank you. How easily, how well . . . you do everything.'

Gerasim again smiled and was about to go out. But Ivan Ilyich felt so good with him around that he didn't want to let him go.

'Now. Please move this chair over to me. No, that one, underneath my legs. I feel better when my legs are higher.'

Gerasim brought the chair, placed it without making any noise, lowered it in one movement to the floor and lifted Ivan Ilyich's legs onto the chair; Ivan Ilyich thought he felt better the moment Gerasim raised up his legs.

'I feel better when my legs are higher,' Ivan Ilyich said. 'Put that cushion under me.'

Gerasim did that. Again he lifted his legs up and put the cushion into position. Again Ivan Ilyich felt better when Gerasim held his legs up. When he lowered them, he thought he felt worse.

'Gerasim,' he said to him, 'are you busy now?'

'No sir, not at all,' said Gerasim who had learned from the townsfolk how to talk to the gentry.

'What do you still have to do?'

'What is there to do? I've done everything, I've just got to chop the wood for tomorrow.'

'So hold my legs up a bit higher, can you do that?'

'Of course I can.' Gerasim lifted up his legs and Ivan Ilyich thought that in this position he felt absolutely no pain.

'But what about the wood?'

'Don't worry, sir. We'll manage.'

Ivan Ilyich told Gerasim to sit down and hold up his legs and he talked to him. And—strange to say—he thought he felt better while Gerasim held up his legs.

From that day Ivan Ilyich started sometimes to call Gerasim in to him and made him hold up his legs on his shoulders and he liked to talk to him. Gerasim did this easily, willingly, simply and with a goodness of heart which touched Ivan Ilyich. In all other people Ivan Ilyich was offended by health, strength, high spirits; only Gerasim's strength and high spirits didn't depress but calmed Ivan Ilyich.

Ivan Ilyich's chief torment was the lie—that lie, for some reason recognized by everyone, that he was only ill but not dying and that he only needed rest and treatment and that then there would be some very good outcome. But he knew that whatever they did, there would be no outcome except even more painful suffering and death. And he was tormented by this lie, he was tormented by their unwillingness to acknowledge what everyone knew and he knew; by their wanting to lie to him about his terrible situation, by their wanting him and making him to take part in that lie himself. The lie, this lie being perpetrated above him on the eve of his death, the lie which could only bring down this terrible solemn act of his death to the level of all their visits and curtains and sturgeon for dinner . . . was horribly painful for Ivan Ilyich. And, strangely, many times when they were performing their tricks above him, he was within a hairs breadth of crying out to them, 'Stop lying; you know and I know that I am dying; so at least stop lying.' But he never had the strength to do it. The terrible, horrific act of his dying, he saw, had been brought down by all those surrounding him to the level of a casual unpleasantness, in part of some breach of decorum (as one treats a man who entering a drawing room emits a bad smell); brought down by that very 'decorum' he had served his whole life; he saw that no one had pity for him because no one wanted even to understand his situation. Only Gerasim understood this situation and felt pity for him. And so Ivan Ilyich only felt comfortable with Gerasim. He felt comfortable when Gerasim

held up his legs, sometimes for whole nights without a break, and wouldn't go off to bed, saying, 'Please, sir, don't worry, Ivan Ilyich, I'll still get plenty of sleep'; or when he would suddenly add, going over to the familiar 'thou', 'You're sick, so why shouldn't I do something for you?' Gerasim was the only one not to lie, everything showed he was the only one who understood what the matter was and didn't think it necessary to hide it, and simply felt pity for his wasted, feeble master. He even once said directly when Ivan Ilyich was dismissing him:

'We'll all die. So why not take a little trouble?' He said this conveying by it that he wasn't bothered by the work precisely because he was doing it for a dying man and hoped that in his time someone would do this work for him.

Apart from this lie, or as a consequence of it, what was most painful for Ivan Ilyich was that no one had pity on him as he wanted them to have pity: at some moments after prolonged sufferings Ivan Ilyich wanted most of all, however much he felt ashamed to admit it, wanted someone to have pity on him like a sick child. He wanted them to caress him, to kiss him, to cry over him as one caresses and comforts children. He knew he was an important legal official, that he had a greying beard and that therefore this was impossible; but he still wanted it. And in his relations with Gerasim there was something close to that, and therefore his relations with Gerasim comforted him. Ivan Ilyich would want to cry, would want them to caress him and cry over him; then in would come his friend, the lawyer Shebek, and instead of crying and caresses Ivan Ilyich would assume a serious, stern, pensive expression and out of inertia would give his opinion on the meaning of a verdict of the Court of Appeal and stubbornly insist on it. This lie all around him and inside him more than anything poisoned the last days of Ivan Ilyich's life.

VIII

It was morning. It was morning only because Gerasim had gone out and Pyotr the manservant came in, put out the candles, opened one curtain and started quietly to tidy up. Whether it was morning or evening, Friday or Sunday, was immaterial, it was all one and the same: the gnawing, agonizing pain that didn't abate for a moment; the consciousness of life departing without hope but still not yet departed; the same terrible, hateful death advancing, which was the only reality, and always the same lie. What did days, weeks and the times of day matter here?

'Would you like some tea?'

'He has to have order, masters should drink tea in the mornings,' he thought and only said:

'No.'

'Would you like to move to the sofa?'

'He has to tidy the chamber, and I'm in the way, I am dirt, disorder,' he thought and only said:

'No, leave me be.'

The manservant did some more things. Ivan Ilyich stretched out his hand. Pyotr came up, to serve.

'What do you want?'

'My watch.'

Pyotr got the watch which was lying right there and handed it to him.

'Half past eight. Have they got up?'

'No, sir. Vasily Ivanovich [that was his son] has gone to the Gymnasium, but Praskovya Fyodorovna gave orders to wake her if you asked for her. Shall I?'

'No, don't.' 'Shall I try some tea?' he thought. 'Yes, tea . . . bring it.'

Pyotr went to the door. Ivan Ilyich felt terrified of being left alone. 'How can I detain him? Yes, my medicine.' 'Pyotr, give me my medicine.' 'Why not, maybe the medicine will still help.' He took the spoon and drank. 'No, it won't help. It's all nonsense and a sham,' he decided as soon as he sensed the familiar sickly, hopeless taste. 'No, I can't believe in it any more. But the pain, why the pain, if it would just go down even for a minute.' And he groaned. Pyotr turned round again. 'No, go away. Bring me some tea.'

Pyotr went out. Left alone, Ivan Ilyich groaned not so much from the pain, however frightful it was, as from anguish. 'Always the same, always these endless days and nights. If only it could be soon. What could be soon? Death, darkness. No, no. Anything is better than death!'

When Pyotr came in with the tea on a tray, Ivan Ilyich looked at him for a long time distractedly, not taking in who and what he was. Pyotr was embarrassed by this stare. And when Pyotr was embarrassed, Ivan Ilyich came to himself.

'Yes,' he aid, 'tea . . . good, put it down. Only help me wash and give me a clean shirt.'

And Ivan Ilyich began to wash. Stopping to rest, he washed his hands, his face, cleaned his teeth, began to brush his hair and looked in the mirror. He felt frightened; especially frightened by the way his hair stuck flat to his forehead.

When his shirt was being changed, he knew that he would be even more frightened if he looked at his body, and so he didn't look at himself. But now it was all done. He put on a dressing gown, covered himself with a blanket and sat in an armchair to have his tea. For one minute he felt refreshed, but as soon as he began to drink the tea, again the same taste, the same pain. With an effort he finished the tea and lay down, stretching out his legs. He lay down and sent Pyotr away.

Always the same. There'd be a small flash of hope, then a sea of despair would surge, and always pain, always pain, always despair and always the same. It was horribly depressing being alone, he wanted to ask for someone but he knew in advance that with others there it would be even worse. 'If only I could have morphine again—and lose consciousness. I'll tell him, the doctor, to think of something else. Like this it's impossible, impossible.'

An hour, a couple of hours would go by like that. But now there's a bell in the hall. Maybe it's the doctor. It is, it's the doctor, fresh, bright, plump, cheerful, his expression saying, 'You've got frightened of something there but now we'll fix all that for you.' The doctor knows that this expression isn't appropriate here but he has assumed it once and for all and he can't take it off, like a man who has put on a tailcoat in the morning and is paying visits.

The doctor rubs his hands briskly and reassuringly.

'I'm cold. There's a cracking frost. Let me warm myself up,' he says, his expression being as if one just had to wait a little for him to warm himself, and when he had, then he would set everything to rights.

'So, how are we?'

Ivan Ilyich feels the doctor wants to say, 'How are tricks?' but feels one can't talk like that, and he says, 'How did you spend the night?'

Ivan Ilyich looks at the doctor, his expression asking, 'Will you really never be ashamed of telling lies?' But the doctor doesn't want to understand the question.

And Ivan Ilyich says:

'Just as dreadfully. The pain isn't going, it isn't going away. If I could just have something!'

'Yes, you patients are always like that. Well, sir, now I've warmed up, even our very particular Praskovya Fyodorovna wouldn't have anything to say against my temperature. So, sir, good morning.' And the doctor shakes his hand.

And, dropping all his earlier playfulness, the doctor begins to examine the patient with a serious expression, takes pulse and temperature and then begins the tappings and auscultations.

Ivan Ilyich knows firmly and without any doubt that all this is nonsense, an empty fraud, but when the doctor on his knees stretches over him, applying his ear first higher, then lower, and performs over him various gymnastic exercises, Ivan Ilyich succumbs to all this as he used to succumb to lawyers' speeches when he knew very well that they were lying and why they were lying.

The doctor, kneeling on the sofa, was still tapping something when there was a rustling at the door of Praskovya Fyodorovna's silk dress and they could hear her scolding Pyotr for not informing her of the doctor's arrival.

She comes in, kisses her husband and at once starts to make it clear that she has got up long ago and that it's because of a misunderstanding that she wasn't there when the doctor came.

Ivan Ilyich looks at her, examines her closely and holds against her the whiteness and plumpness and cleanliness of her arms and neck, the gloss of her hair and the shine of her eyes that are so full of life. He hates her with his whole soul. And her touch makes him suffer from a surge of hatred towards her.

Her attitude to him and to his illness is always the same. Just as the doctor has developed for himself an attitude towards his patients which he hasn't been able to put aside, so she has developed a simple attitude towards him—he isn't doing something of what he should be doing, and it's his fault, and she lovingly scolds him for this—and she hasn't yet managed to put this attitude towards him aside.

'He just doesn't listen. He doesn't take it when he should. And above all—he lies in a position which has to be bad for him—with his legs up.'

She described how he makes Gerasim hold his legs.

The doctor smiled a smile of amiable scorn, as if saying, 'What can one do, sometimes these patients dream up such silly things; but one can forgive them.'

When the examination was over, the doctor looked at his watch, and then Praskovya Fyodorovna announced to Ivan Ilyich that whatever he might want, today she had asked in a famous doctor and he and Mikhail Danilovich (that was the usual doctor's name) would examine him together and discuss the case.

'So please don't go against this. I'm doing this for myself,' she said ironically, letting him understand that she does everything for him and just by her saying this he is given no right to refuse her. He said nothing and frowned. He felt

that the lies surrounding him had become so tangled that it was difficult now to see anything clearly.

Everything she did for him, she did only for herself and she told him so, as if that was something so unlikely that he had to understand it in the opposite sense.

Indeed the famous doctor did arrive at half-past eleven. Again there started the auscultations and serious conversations both in front of him and in another room about his kidney and appendix, and questions and answers delivered with such a serious air that again, instead of the real question about life and death which now was the only one which confronted him, there came a question about his kidney and appendix, which were doing something not quite as they should be and which Mikhail Danilovich and the celebrity would get to grips with right away and make them correct themselves.

The famous doctor said his goodbyes with a serious expression but one which hadn't given up hope. And to the timid question which Ivan Ilyich put to him, raising eyes that were shining with fear and hope—is there any possibility of recovery—he answered that though one can't guarantee it, there is a possibility. The look of hope with which Ivan Ilyich said goodbye to the doctor was so pitiful that when she saw it Praskovya Fyodorovna burst into tears as she went through the study doors to give the famous doctor his fee.

The rise in his spirits brought about by the doctor's encouragement didn't last long. Again it was the same room, the same pictures, curtains, wallpaper, medicine bottles, and his same hurting, suffering body. And Ivan Ilyich started to groan; they gave him an injection and he lost consciousness.

When he came to, it was beginning to get dark; they brought in his dinner. With some effort he took some broth; and again all those same things and again night was coming on.

After dinner at seven o'clock Praskovya Fyodorovna came into his room, dressed for an evening out, her breasts large and lifted and with traces of powder on her face. That morning she had reminded him that they were going to the theatre. Sarah Bernhardt[5] was visiting and they had a box which he had insisted they take. Now he had forgotten that and her clothes outraged him. But he concealed his outrage when he remembered that he himself had insisted they get a box and go because it was a cultural treat for their children.

Praskovya Fyodorovna came in pleased with herself but also with a kind of guilty feeling. She sat down, asked about his health, as he could see just for the sake of asking rather than to learn, knowing that there was nothing to learn, and began to say what she needed to: that she wouldn't have gone out for anything but the box was taken and Hélène was going and their daughter and Petrishchev (the examining magistrate, the daughter's fiancé) and it was impossible to let them go alone. But it would be so much more agreeable for her to sit with him. He must just do what the doctor had ordered without her.

'Yes, and Fyodor Petrovich [the fiancé] wanted to come in. Can he? Liza too.'

'Let them come in.'

5. Stage name of French actress Rosine Bernard (1844–1923), famed for romantic and tragic roles.

His daughter came in, with her young body bared, that body which made him suffer so. But she was displaying it. Strong, healthy, clearly in love and angry at the illness, suffering and death which stood in the way of her happiness.

Fyodor Petrovich came too, in a tail coat, his hair curled à la Capoul, his long sinewy neck encased in a white collar, with a huge white shirtfront and powerful thighs squeezed into narrow black trousers, with one white glove pulled onto his hand and an opera hat.

After him the schoolboy crept in inconspicuously, in a new school uniform, poor fellow, wearing white gloves and with terrible dark patches under his eyes, the meaning of which Ivan Ilyich knew.

His son always made him feel sorry for him. And the look he gave him was terrible, full of sympathy and fear. Apart from Gerasim, only Vasya understood him and felt pity for him, so Ivan Ilyich thought.

They all sat down, asked again about his health. A silence fell. Liza asked her mother about the opera glasses. There ensued an argument between mother and daughter about who had put them where. It felt unpleasant.

Fyodor Petrovich asked Ivan Ilyich if he had seen Sarah Bernhardt. At first Ivan Ilyich didn't understand what he was being asked and then said:

'No, but have you?'

'Yes, in *Adrienne Lecouvreur*.'[6]

Praskovya Fyodorovna said that she was particularly good in something or other. Their daughter disagreed. There began a conversation about the elegance and realism of her acting—that conversation which is always exactly the same.

In the middle of the conversation Fyodor Petrovich looked at Ivan Ilyich and fell silent. The others looked and fell silent. Ivan Ilyich looked straight ahead with shining eyes, clearly becoming angry with them. This had to be put right but it was quite impossible to put right. Somehow this silence had to be broken. No one had the resolve and they all became frightened that somehow the decorous lie would collapse and the true state of things would become obvious to all. Liza was the first to take the resolve. She broke the silence. She wanted to hide what they were all feeling but she said it wrong.

'So, *if we are going to go*, it's time,' she said looking at her watch, a present from her father, and she gave a barely perceptible smile to the young man, which had a meaning about something known to them alone, and got up, her dress rustling.

They all got up, said goodbye and went off.

When they had gone out, Ivan Ilyich thought he felt better: the lie wasn't there—it had gone out with them, but the pain remained. The same constant pain, the same constant fear made nothing more difficult, nothing easier. Everything was worse.

Again minute followed minute, hour followed hour, it was always the same and there was still no end and the inevitable end became more terrifying.

'Yes, send me Gerasim,' he said in reply to a question Pyotr asked.

6. A play (1849) by the French dramatist Eugène Scribe (1791–1861), in which the heroine was a famous actress of the 18th century. Tolstoy considered Scribe, who wrote over four hundred plays, a shoddy, commercial playwright.

IX

His wife came back late at night. She walked on tiptoe but he heard her: he opened his eyes and quickly shut them again. She wanted to send Gerasim away and sit with him herself. He opened his eyes and said:

'No. Go away.'

'Are you in a lot of pain?'

'It doesn't matter.'

'Take some opium.'

He agreed and drank. She went out.

Till three o'clock he was in a tormented stupor. He thought that in some way they were pushing him and his pain into a narrow, deep black sack; they kept pushing further but they couldn't push them right in. And this terrible business for him was being crowned by his suffering. And he was both struggling and wanting to drop right down, both fighting against it and assisting. And suddenly he was free and fell and came to. The same Gerasim is still sitting on the bed at his feet, dozing quietly, patiently. And Ivan Ilyich is lying there having lifted his emaciated legs in their socks onto Gerasim's shoulders; there's the same candle with its shade and the same unceasing pain.

'Go, Gerasim,' he whispered.

'It doesn't matter, sir, I'll sit a bit longer.'

'No, go.'

He removed his legs and lay on his side on top of his arm, and he began to feel sorry for himself. He just waited for Gerasim to go out into the next room and he couldn't control himself any more and burst into tears like a child. He wept for his helplessness, for his horrible loneliness, for people's cruelty, for God's cruelty, for God's absence.

'Why have you done all this? Why have you brought me here? Why, why do you torment me so horribly? . . .'

He didn't expect an answer but he also wept because there wasn't and couldn't be an answer. The pain increased again but he didn't move or call anyone. He said to himself, 'More, go on, beat me! But why? What have I done to you, why?'

Then he calmed down, he not only stopped weeping, he stopped breathing and became all attention: as if he was listening not to a voice speaking in sounds but to the voice of his soul, to the train of thoughts rising within him.

'What do you want?' was the first clear idea capable of being expressed in words that he heard. 'What do you want? What do you want?' he repeated to himself. 'What? Not to suffer. To live,' he answered.

And again he became absorbed with such intense attention that even the pain did not distract him.

'To live? To live how?' asked the voice of his soul.

'Yes, to live, as I lived before: well and pleasantly.'

'As you lived before, lived well, pleasantly?' asked the voice. And he began to go over in his imagination the best moments of his pleasant life. But—strange to relate—all these best moments of a pleasant life now seemed quite different from what they had seemed then. All of them—except for his first memories of childhood. There, in childhood was something so truly pleasant, with which he could live, if it returned. But the person who had experienced those pleasant things no longer existed: it was like a memory of something else.

As soon as the process began which had resulted in Ivan Ilyich, the man of today, all the things which had seemed joys melted away before his eyes and were changed into something worthless and often vile.

And the further from childhood, the nearer to the present, the more worthless and dubious were the joys. That began with Law School. There was still something there truly good: there was gaiety, there was friendship, there were hopes. But in the senior classes these good moments were already less frequent. After that, at the time of his first period of service with the governor, again good moments appeared: there were memories of love for a woman. After that all this became confused and there was even less of what was good. Further on there was still less good, and the further he went the less there was.

Marriage . . . so casually entered, and disillusionment, and the smell that came from his wife's mouth, and sensuality, hypocrisy! And that deadly work of his and those worries about money, and on for a year, and two, and ten, and twenty—and always the same. And the further he went, the more deadly it became. 'As if I was walking downhill at a regular pace, imagining I am walking uphill. That's how it was. In the eyes of the world I was walking uphill, and to just that extent life was slipping away from under me . . . And now it's time, to die!

'So what is this? Why? It can't be. It can't be that life was so meaningless and vile. But if was indeed so meaningless and vile, then why die and die suffering? Something is wrong.

'Maybe I have lived not as I should have'—the thought suddenly came into his head. 'But how so when I did everything in the proper way?' he said to himself and immediately rejected this sole solution of the whole riddle of life as something wholly impossible.

'What do you want now? To live? To live how? To live as you lived in court when the court officer pronounces, "The court is opening! . . ."' 'The court is opening, opening, the court,' he repeated to himself. 'Here's the court! But I'm not guilty!' he shouted angrily. 'For what?' And he stopped weeping and turning his face to the wall, he began to think of just the one thing: why all this horror, for what?

But however much he thought, he found no answer. And when there came to him the thought, as it did often, that all this was happening because he had lived wrongly, he at once remembered all the correctness of his life and rejected this strange thought.

X

Two weeks more went by. Ivan Ilyich didn't get up from the sofa any more. He didn't want to lie in bed and instead lay on the sofa. And, lying almost all the time with his face to the wall, he suffered in his loneliness all those same insoluble sufferings and in his loneliness thought the same insoluble thought. What is this? Is it really true that this is death? And a voice within answered: yes, it's true. Why these torments? And the voice answered: that's the way it is, there is no why. Apart from that there was nothing more.

From the very start of his illness, when Ivan Ilyich went to the doctor for the first time, his life was divided into two diametrically opposed moods, which alternated with each other: on the one hand despair and the expectation of an

incomprehensible and horrible death, on the other hope and the absorbed observation of the activity of his body. Now he had before his eyes just a kidney or appendix which for a time had deviated from the performance of its duties; now there was just incomprehensible, horrible death from which it was impossible to escape in any way.

From the very beginning of his illness these two moods alternated with each other; but the more the illness progressed, the more fantastic and questionable became thoughts about his kidney and the more real the consciousness of approaching death.

He only had to remember what he had been three months previously and what he was now—to remember how he had been walking downhill at a regular pace—for all possibility of hope to crumble.

In the recent loneliness in which he found himself, lying with his face to the back of the sofa, loneliness in the midst of a crowded city and his numerous acquaintances and family—loneliness which could not be more absolute anywhere, either at the bottom of the sea or underneath the earth, in his recent terrible loneliness Ivan Ilyich lived only by his imagination in the past. One after another pictures of his past presented themselves to him. It always began with the closest in time and went back to the most remote, to his childhood, and rested there. If Ivan Ilyich thought of the stewed prunes he was offered to eat now, he remembered the moist, wrinkled French prunes of his childhood, their particular taste and the flow of saliva when he got to the stone, and alongside this memory of taste there arose a whole row of memories of that time; his *nyanya*, his brother, his toys. 'You mustn't think of that . . . it's too painful,' Ivan Ilyich said to himself and was again transported into the present. A button on the back of the sofa and the creases in its morocco leather. 'Morocco is expensive and wears badly; there was a quarrel because of it. But it was different leather and a different row when we ripped our father's briefcase and were punished, but Mama brought us some pies.' And again he stopped in his childhood and again it was painful for Ivan Ilyich and he tried to push it away and think of something else.

And here again, together with this train of memories, another train of memories went through his mind—of how his illness had intensified and grown. It was the same, the further back he went, the more life there was. There was more good in life and more of life itself. And the two merged together. 'As my torments kept getting worse and worse, so the whole of life became worse and worse,' he thought. One bright spot, there, at the start of his life, and after that everything blacker and blacker, and everything quicker and quicker. 'In inverse ratio to the square of the distance from death,' thought Ivan Ilyich. And an image of a stone flying downwards with increasing speed became fixed in his mind. Life, a sequence of increasing sufferings, flies quicker and quicker to the end, to the most terrible suffering of all. 'I am flying . . .' He shivered, moved, tried to resist; but he now knew that resistance was impossible, and again, with eyes that were tired of looking but which couldn't help looking at what was in front of him, he gazed at the back of the sofa and waited—waited for that terrible fall, the crash and annihilation. 'I can't resist,' he said to himself. 'But if I could just understand why. That too I can't. I might be able to explain it if I said I had lived not as I should have. But it's impossible to admit that,' he said to himself, remembering all the lawfulness, the correctness and the decorum of his life. It's impossible to admit that now, he said to himself, grimacing with

his lips, as if anyone could see this smile of his and be deceived by it. 'There's no explanation! Torment, death . . . Why?'

XI

Two weeks went by like that. In those weeks an event took place that had been desired by Ivan Ilyich and his wife: Petrishchev made a formal proposal. It happened in the evening. The next day Praskovya Fyodorovna went in to her husband, wondering how to announce Fyodor Petrovich's proposal to him, but that very night Ivan Ilyich had had a turn for the worse. Praskovya Fyodorovna found him on the same sofa, but in a new position. He was lying on his back, groaning and looking ahead with a fixed gaze.

She started talking about medicines. He turned his eyes to her. She didn't finish what she had begun to say: there was so much anger expressed in those eyes, aimed directly at her. 'For Christ's sake, let me die in peace,' he said.

She was about to go but at that moment his daughter came in and went up to say good morning. He looked at his daughter as he had at his wife and to her questions about his health he drily said to her that he would soon liberate them all from himself. They both said nothing, sat briefly and went out.

'What can we be blamed for?' Liza said to her mother. 'As if we'd done this! I'm sorry for Papa, but why must he torment us?'

The doctor came at the usual time. Ivan Ilyich answered him 'yes, no', not taking his angry eyes from him, and finally said:

'You know that you won't be of any help, so leave me.'

'We can relieve the suffering,' the doctor said.

'You can't do that either; leave me.'

The doctor went out into the drawing-room and informed Praskovya Fyodorovna that things were very bad and that there was only one resource—opium, to relieve the sufferings, which must be terrible.

The doctor said that his physical sufferings were terrible, and that was true; but even more terrible than his physical sufferings were his mental sufferings, and there was his chief torment.

His mental sufferings lay in the fact that that night, as he looked at Gerasim's sleepy, good-natured face, with its high cheekbones, there had suddenly entered his head the thought: 'But what if in actual fact all my life, my conscious life, has been "wrong"?'

It occurred to him that the notion that had previously seemed to him a complete impossibility, that he had lived his life not as he should have done, could be the truth. It occurred to him that his barely noticeable attempts at struggling against what was considered good by those in high positions above him, those barely noticeable attempts which he had immediately rejected—could be genuine and everything else wrong. His work and the structure of his life and his family and his social and professional interests—all that could be wrong. He tried to defend all that to himself. And suddenly he felt the fragility of what he was defending. And there was nothing to defend.

'But if this is so,' he said to himself, 'and I am leaving life with the realization that I have lost everything I was given and that it's impossible to put right, then what?' He lay on his back and started to go over his whole life afresh. When in the morning he saw the manservant, then his wife, then his daughter, then the

doctor—every one of their movements, every one of their words confirmed for him the terrible truth that had been disclosed to him in the night. He saw in them himself, everything by which he had lived, and saw clearly that all this was wrong, all this was a terrible, huge fraud, concealing both life and death. This realization increased, increased tenfold his physical sufferings. He groaned and tossed about and pulled at the clothes on him. He felt suffocated and crushed. And he hated them for that.

They gave him a big dose of opium, he lost consciousness; but at dinner time the same began again. He drove them all away from him and tossed about from side to side.

His wife came to him and said:

'Jean, my dear, do this for me (for me?). It can't do any harm, but it often helps. So, it's nothing. And people in good health often . . .'

He opened his eyes wide.

'What? Take communion? Why? There's no need to! But then . . .'

She started crying.

'Yes, my dear? I'll call for our man, he's so sweet.'

'Fine, very well,' he said.

When the priest came and took his confession, he was calmed, he felt a kind of relief from his doubts and as a consequence of that from his sufferings, and a moment of hope came to him. He again began to think of his appendix and the possibility of curing it. He received communion with tears in his eyes.

When after communion he was put to bed, for a moment he felt comfortable and hope for life appeared again. He began to think of the operation being suggested to him. 'To live, I want to live,' he said to himself. His wife came to congratulate him on taking communion; she said the usual words and added:

'You feel better, don't you?'

Without looking at her he said, 'Yes.'

Her clothes, her body, the expression of her face, the sound of her voice—everything said to him one thing: 'Wrong. Everything by which you have lived and are living is a lie, a fraud, concealing life and death from you.' And as soon as he thought that, hatred rose up in him and together with hatred agonizing physical sufferings and with those sufferings an awareness of the end, near by and unavoidable. Something new happened: his breath started to strain and come in spurts and be squeezed out.

His expression when he said 'yes' was terrible. Having said that 'yes', he looked at her straight in the eyes and with unusual strength for his weakness turned himself face down and cried:

'Go away, go away, leave me!'

XII

From that minute began those three days of unceasing screams which were so horrible that one couldn't hear them from two doors away without feeling horror. The minute he answered his wife, he understood that he was lost, that there was no return, that the end had come, the very end, but the doubt still wasn't resolved, it still remained doubt.

'Oh! Oh! Oh!' he cried out in various tones. He began to cry out, 'I don't want to, no!' and went on like that crying out the letter O.

For the whole three days, during which time for him did not exist, he tossed about in the black sack into which he was being pushed by an invisible, insurmountable force. He struggled as a man condemned to death struggles in the arms of the executioner, knowing he cannot save himself; and with every minute he felt that for all his efforts at struggling he was coming nearer and nearer to what filled him with horror. He felt that his agony lay both in being pushed into that black hole and even more in being unable to get into it. He was prevented from climbing in by his declaration that his life had been good. This justification of his life caught on something and stopped him going forward and that distressed him most of all.

Suddenly some kind of force struck him in the chest and on the side, his breath was constricted even more, he collapsed into the hole and there at the bottom of the hole some light was showing. There happened to him what he used to experience in a railway carriage when you think you are going forward but are going backward and suddenly realize your true direction.

'Yes, everything was wrong,' he said to himself, 'but it doesn't matter. I can, I can do what is right. But what is right?' he asked himself and at once fell silent.

It was at the end of the third day, an hour before his death. At that very time the Gymnasium schoolboy quietly slipped into his father's room and approached his bed. The dying man was still crying out despairingly and waving his arms about. One of his hands hit the schoolboy's head. The schoolboy took it, pressed it to his lips and wept.

At that very time Ivan Ilyich fell through and saw a light, and it was revealed to him that his life had been wrong but that it was still possible to mend things. He asked himself, 'What is right?' and fell silent, listening. Now he felt someone was kissing his hand. He opened his eyes and looked at his son. He felt sorry for him. His wife came to him. He looked at her. She looked at him, mouth open and tears on her nose and cheek that she hadn't wiped away. He felt sorry for her.

'Yes, I make them unhappy,' he thought. 'They are sorry for me but it'll be better for them when I die.' He wanted to say that but didn't have the strength to utter it. 'However, why say things, one must act,' he thought. With a look to his wife he pointed to his son and said:

'Take him away . . . sorry for him . . . and for you . . .' He wanted to add 'forgive' but said 'give' and not having the strength to correct himself, waved his hand, knowing that He who needed to understand would understand.

And suddenly it became clear to him that what had been oppressing him and not coming to an end—now everything was coming to an end at once, on two sides, on ten sides, on every side. He was sorry for them, he must make it so they had no pain. Free them and free himself from these sufferings. 'So good and so simple,' he thought. 'And the pain?' he asked himself. 'Where's it gone? Well, where are you, pain?'

He began to listen.

'There it is. So—let the pain be.'

'And death? Where is it?'

He searched for his old habitual fear of death and didn't find it. Where is death? What death? There was no fear, because there was no death.

Instead of death there was light.

'So that's it!' he suddenly said aloud. 'Such joy!'

For him all this took place in a moment and the significance of this moment didn't change. For those there his death agony lasted two hours more. Something bubbled in his chest; his emaciated body shivered. Then the gurgling and wheezing became less and less frequent.

'It is finished!' someone said above him.

He heard these words and repeated them in his heart. 'Death is finished,' he said to himself. 'It is no more.'

He breathed in, stopped halfway, stretched himself and died.

HENRIK IBSEN

1828–1906

Writing in an era when drama had become a second-rate occupation, with most gifted writers turning instead to novels or poetry, Henrik Ibsen restored prestige and relevance to the theater. Over the course of the nineteenth century, the invention of new theatrical machinery and techniques had turned theater into spectacle. Theater producers spent their time and money on special effects, dazzling audiences with lighting, horses, or even nautical battles in addition to, of course, trying to sign the latest acting stars. One might compare nineteenth-century theater with present-day Hollywood and its focus on blockbuster action movies packed with special effects and star actors. Ibsen showed Europe that theater could be more than just spectacle, that it could be an art form addressing the most serious moral and social questions of the time. The theatergoing public was first shocked, and later thrilled, to have controversial themes presented on the stage, and to have them presented not through special effects but through carefully drawn characters and well-constructed dramatic situations. Honing his dramatic technique over half a century, Ibsen almost single-handedly brought a new seriousness to the theater, and he has been regarded as the originator of modern drama ever since.

Ibsen achieved his unparalleled success against all odds. He was born in Skien, a small town in Norway, far removed from the cultural centers of Europe, and he spoke Norwegian, a marginal language unlikely to launch a European career in literature. When Ibsen left his provincial home at the age of fifteen, he was apprenticed to a chemist. Only at the age of twenty-two was he able to free himself from his apprenticeship—and from a liaison with a maid that had resulted in an illegitimate child—and move to the capital, Christiania (now Oslo), to study for the university entrance exam. During this time his first play was performed. After a few years spent learning the craft, he assumed positions of greater responsibility—as artistic director and dramaturge—at theaters in Bergen and Christiania.

Ibsen at first learned from the standard dramatic form of the time, the so-called well-made play. Popularized by the French playwrights Victorien Sardou and Augustine-Eugène Scribe, the well-made play revolved around

complicated plots and well-timed confrontations. Immensely popular with audiences, well-made plays excelled at fast-moving action, intrigues, alliances, and sudden revelations.

But Ibsen would soon turn against these sensational formulas. In two plays, *Brand* (1866) and *Peer Gynt* (1867), Ibsen startlingly rejected not only the well-made play, but the theater as such. He wrote these works as "dramatic poems," plays that were not supposed to be performed but were written exclusively to be read. All the rules that governed conventional stage action could thus be circumvented entirely. Drawing on literary models such as **Goethe's** *Faust* and Byron's *Don Juan*, *Peer Gynt* freely mixes fantasy and reality, conjuring mountain trolls, mad German philosophers, and the devil himself. The play established Ibsen as a writer of European significance.

And so Europe, rather than Norway, became Ibsen's home: he would spend the next twenty-seven years on the continent, mostly in Italy and Germany, before moving back to Norway at the age of sixty-three. After *Brand* and *Peer Gynt* had secured his Europe-wide reputation, he changed course and started writing for the stage once more, but in an entirely different style. He gave up on Norway's past and chose to write, once and for all, about the world he knew best: the contemporary Norwegian middle class. His singular purpose was to lay bare the ugly reality behind the façade of middle-class respectability, to expose the lies of bourgeois characters and indeed of bourgeois society as a whole. The five plays of this period, *The Pillars of Society* (1877), *A Doll's House* (1879), *Ghosts* (1881), *Enemy of the People* (1882), and *The Wild Duck* (1884), made Ibsen notorious throughout Europe and established him as an author of shock, confrontation, and revolt.

The main reason why these plays caused such consternation and excitement is that they introduced realism to the theater. Realism had already been established in the novel, but not in drama. In these realist plays, Ibsen wrote in ordinary language and devoted his drama to undoing deceit and pretense, to unveiling hidden motives and past misdeeds so that the truth would shine forth on the stage. Realism, for Ibsen, meant creating a theater of emotional and moral truth, where audiences could understand both the subjective experience and the objective conditions of modern life.

After becoming notorious with his realist plays, Ibsen changed course once more. He had been trying to write modern versions of Greek tragedy for a long while, but it was only in the last phase of his career that he managed to give definite shape to the tragedy of modern middle-class life. Of these plays, *Hedda Gabler* (1890) is the most compelling and famous. It is set in the same bourgeois milieu as his realist plays, but is no longer directed towards social deceptions and pretense. Instead it is interested in the bourgeois characters themselves, presenting them in all their complexity, with the hidden yearnings and fantasies that take them outside of the constricted worlds in which they live.

Hedda Gabler is a play about the daughter of a general who marries Tesman, an aspiring scholar waiting for his university post. As the play begins, we see almost immediately that the marriage is unequal and unsettled. Tesman is eager to start his new life and he is clearly proud of his trophy wife. Hedda, by contrast, is dismissive of his affectionate tone and also his values. She snubs him, is impatient, abruptly changes the topic of conversation, and sulks. There is a clear class difference between them. As the daughter of a general, Hedda is used to an upper-middle-class life. Tesman, by contrast, is lower middle class,

with all the difference in habit and taste that entails. The collision between Hedda's and Tesman's respective classes, expectations, and attitudes centers on the bourgeois home. Gradually we learn that Hedda only married Tesman and convinced him to get the house out of boredom, feeling that no other options were available to her. But now she finds herself trapped: trapped in her marriage and trapped in the house.

Far from merely a setting for the characters, the house and its furnishings emerge as the main object of Hedda's scorn. The play revolves around furniture and what it represents: class and taste. Hedda despises those objects associated with Tesman and his class, and she admires the remnants of her former life. Tesman's scholarly study is also a set of objects: the handicrafts of the Middle Ages. For Ibsen tangible things become pawns in larger struggles between classes and wills.

Hedda Gabler, bored and without a function except to bear children—a thought she rejects with horror—manipulates every single character in the play, from Tesman and his aunt to Løvborg and his companion, her old school friend, Mrs. Elvsted. She gets them to do her bidding through force, lies, flattery, and utter ruthlessness. As the play progresses, we find her destroying careers and lives without blinking an eye. Hedda sees plotting as an end in itself and for this reason she is often seen as a modern version of Medea or Lady Macbeth.

The main victim of Hedda's plotting is Tesman's rival, Løvborg, who has written nothing less than a book about the future (after completing one about the history of civilization). Ibsen again here focuses on an object, Løvberg's sole manuscript, which becomes a central plot device, a stage prop that drives the action forward. Ibsen had learned from the well-made play how to weave objects and characters into suspenseful plots. But these props are rich in meaning too, throwing light on characters and themes, multifaceted devices that develop a life of their own.

Hedda Gabler may be a manipulator, but she is a manipulator with a vision. She is driven by her hunger for a more fulfilling, ideal, and beautiful life. She fantasizes about acts of heroism and beauty, and she tries to bring about such acts by directing the people around her the way a director assigns roles to actors. She shares her desire for a better life with many tragic characters of Ibsen's later plays, characters who cannot get rid of the chains that bind them to their houses, their objects, their habits, their class, and their past. Ibsen's attitude towards his characters' desire for beauty tends to be ambivalent. On the one hand, he sympathizes with them, even with the cold-hearted Hedda Gabler. On the other hand, his plays show that the single-minded desire to achieve an ideal life leads to destruction. Hedda Gabler's vision is an escape fantasy, the stuff of historical and idealist plays of the kind Ibsen had written in his youth. Ibsen saw both: the intense longing to live a life of ideals as well as the destructive effects of that idealism.

Since his own time, Ibsen's work has inspired important actors and directors worldwide. In England, George Bernard Shaw and the writer William Archer led what some have called the Ibsen campaign, turning the Norwegian playwright into the central figure in modern British drama, and the influential Russian director Konstantin Stanislavski, whose Moscow Art Theater promoted an acting style based on authentic emotional responses, drew on Ibsen's drama. His later plays, including *Hedda Gabler*, have attracted a different set of directors, less interested in naturalism and truth telling than in symbolism and poetry. Film directors drawn to surrealism and suggestive stage

craft, such as Ingmar Bergman, continue to be attracted first and foremost to Ibsen's late plays.

Ibsen's influential career is full of enigmas and contradictions. He began with historical dramas, looking to the past, and yet he would become the herald of modern drama. He rejected the dramatic techniques of standard nineteenth-century drama, but he also managed to transform them into something that seemed new, shocking, and modern to his audience. He received the most attention for his realist plays but later turned realism itself in a more poetic and symbolist direction. In the end, he created a dramatic oeuvre of unparalleled variety and complexity, and this versatility has allowed him to become one of the most popular dramatists of all time. Today, he ranks second only to Shakespeare as the world's most-performed playwright. Shocking and novel when it was first presented to audiences, Ibsen's work has also stood the test of time.

Hedda Gabler[1]

CHARACTERS

GEORGE TESMAN, *research fellow in cultural history*
HEDDA TESMAN, *his wife*
MISS JULIANE TESMAN, *his aunt*

MRS. ELEVSTED
JUDGE BRACK
EILERT LØVBORG
BERTA, *the maid to the Tesmans*

The action takes place in the fashionable west side of Christiania, Norway's capital.

Act 1

A large, pleasantly and tastefully furnished drawing room, decorated in somber tones. In the rear wall is a wide doorway with the curtains pulled back. This doorway leads into a smaller room decorated in the same style. In the right wall of the drawing room is a folding door leading into the hall. In the opposite wall, a glass door, also with its curtains pulled back. Outside, through the windows, part of a covered veranda can be seen, along with trees in their autumn colors. In the foreground, an oval table surrounded by chairs. Downstage, near the right wall, is a broad, dark porcelain stove, a high-backed armchair, a footstool with cushions and two stools. Up in the right-hand corner, a corner-sofa and a small round table. Downstage, on the left side, a little distance from the wall, a sofa. Beyond the glass door, a piano. On both sides of the upstage doorway stand shelves displaying terra cotta and majolica objects. By the back wall of the inner room, a sofa, a table and a couple of chairs can be seen. Above the sofa hangs the portrait of a handsome elderly man in a general's uniform. Above the table, a hanging lamp with an opalescent glass shade. There are many flowers arranged in vases and glasses all around the drawing room. More flowers lie on the tables. The floors of both rooms are covered with thick rugs.

1. Translated by Rick Davis and Brian Johnston.

Morning light. The sun shines in through the glass door.

[MISS JULIE TESMAN, *with hat and parasol, comes in from the hall, followed by* BERTA, *who carries a bouquet wrapped in paper.* MISS TESMAN *is a kindly, seemingly good-natured lady of about sixty-five, neatly but simply dressed in a grey visiting outfit.* BERTA *is a housemaid, getting on in years, with a homely and somewhat rustic appearance.*]

MISS TESMAN [*Stops just inside the doorway, listens, and speaks softly.*] Well—
I believe they're just now getting up!

BERTA [*Also softly.*] That's what I said, Miss. Just think—the steamer got in so late last night, and then—Lord, the young mistress wanted so much unpacked before she could settle down.

MISS TESMAN Well, well. Let them have a good night's sleep at least. But— they'll have some fresh morning air when they come down. [*She crosses to the glass door and throws it wide open.*]

BERTA [*By the table, perplexed, holding the bouquet.*] Hmm. Bless me if I can find a spot for these. I think I'd better put them down here, Miss. [*Puts the bouquet down on the front of the piano.*]

MISS TESMAN So, Berta dear, now you have a new mistress. As God's my witness, giving you up was a heavy blow.

BERTA And me, Miss—what can I say? I've been in yours and Miss Rina's service for so many blessed years—

MISS TESMAN We must bear it patiently, Berta. Truly, there's no other way. You know George has to have you in the house with him—he simply has to. You've looked after him since he was a little boy.

BERTA Yes, but Miss—I keep worrying about her, lying there at home—so completely helpless, poor thing. And that new girl! She'll never learn how to take care of sick people.

MISS TESMAN Oh, I'll teach her how soon enough. And I'll be doing most of the work myself, you know. Don't you worry about my sister, Berta dear.

BERTA Yes, but there's something else, Miss. I'm so afraid I won't satisfy the new mistress—

MISS TESMAN Ffft—Good Lord—there might be a thing or two at first—

BERTA Because she's so particular about things—

MISS TESMAN Well, what do you expect? General Gabler's daughter—the way she lived in the general's day! Do you remember how she would go out riding with her father? In that long black outfit, with the feather in her hat?

BERTA Oh, yes—I remember that all right. But I never thought she'd make a match with our Mr. Tesman.

MISS TESMAN Neither did I. But—while I'm thinking about it, don't call George "Mister Tesman" any more. Now it's "Doctor Tesman."

BERTA Yes—that's what the young mistress said as soon as they came in last night. So it's true?

MISS TESMAN Yes, it's really true. Think of it, Berta—they've made him a doctor. While he was away, you understand. I didn't know a thing about it, until he told me himself, down at the pier.

BERTA   Well, he's so smart he could be anything he wanted to be. But I never thought he'd take up curing people too!

MISS TESMAN   No, no, no. He's not that kind of doctor. [*Nods significantly.*] As far as that goes, you might have to start calling him something even grander soon.

BERTA   Oh no! What could that be?

MISS TESMAN [*Smiling.*]   Hmm—wouldn't you like to know? [*Emotionally.*] Oh, dear God . . . if our sainted Joseph could look up from his grave and see what's become of his little boy. [*She looks around.*] But, Berta—what's this now? Why have you taken all the slipcovers off the furniture?

BERTA   The mistress told me to. She said she can't stand covers on chairs.

MISS TESMAN   But are they going to use this for their everyday living room?

BERTA   Yes, they will. At least she will. He—the doctor—he didn't say anything.

[GEORGE TESMAN *enters, humming, from the right of the inner room, carrying an open, empty suitcase. He is a youthful-looking man of thirty-three, of medium height, with an open, round, and cheerful face, blond hair and beard. He wears glasses and is dressed in comfortable, somewhat disheveled clothes.*]

MISS TESMAN   Good morning, good morning, George!

TESMAN   Aunt Julie! Dear Aunt Julie! [*Goes over and shakes her hand.*] All the way here—so early in the day! Hm!

MISS TESMAN   Yes, you know me—I just had to peek in on you a little.

TESMAN   And after a short night's sleep at that!

MISS TESMAN   Oh, that's nothing at all to me.

TESMAN   So—you got home all right from the pier, hm?

MISS TESMAN   Yes, as it turned out, thanks be to God. The Judge was kind enough to see me right to the door.

TESMAN   We felt so bad that we couldn't take you in the carriage—but you saw how many trunks and boxes Hedda had to bring.

MISS TESMAN   Yes, it was amazing.

BERTA [*To* TESMAN.]   Perhaps I should go in and ask the mistress if there's anything I can help her with.

TESMAN   No, thank you, Berta. You don't have to do that. If she needs you, she'll ring—that's what she said.

BERTA [*Going out to right.*]   Very well.

TESMAN   Ah—but—Berta—take this suitcase with you.

BERTA [*Takes the case.*]   I'll put it in the attic.

TESMAN   Just imagine, Auntie. I'd stuffed that whole suitcase with notes—just notes! The things I managed to collect in those archives—really incredible! Ancient, remarkable things that no one had any inkling of.

MISS TESMAN   Ah yes—you certainly haven't wasted any time on your honeymoon.

TESMAN   Yes—I can really say that's true. But, Auntie, take off your hat—Here, let's see. Let me undo that ribbon, hm?

MISS TESMAN [*While he does so.*]   Ah, dear God—this is just what it was like when you were home with us.

TESMAN [*Examining the hat as he holds it.*]   My, my—isn't this a fine, elegant hat you've got for yourself.

MISS TESMAN   I bought it for Hedda's sake.

TESMAN   For Hedda's—hm?

MISS TESMAN   Yes, so Hedda won't feel ashamed of me if we go out for a walk together.

TESMAN   [*Patting her cheek.*]   You think of everything, Auntie Julie, don't you? [*Putting her hat on a chair by the table.*] And now—let's just settle down here on the sofa until Hedda comes. [*They sit. She puts her parasol down near the sofa.*]

MISS TESMAN   [*Takes both his hands and gazes at him.*]   What a blessing to have you here, bright as day, right before my eyes again, George. Sainted Joseph's own boy!

TESMAN   For me too. To see you again, Aunt Julie—who've been both father and mother to me.

MISS TESMAN   Yes, I know you'll always have a soft spot for your old aunts.

TESMAN   But no improvement at all with Rina, hm?

MISS TESMAN   Oh dear no—and none to be expected poor thing. She lies there just as she has all these years. But I pray that Our Lord lets me keep her just a little longer. Otherwise I don't know what I'd do with my life, George. Especially now, you know—when I don't have you to take care of any more.

TESMAN   [*Patting her on the back.*]   There. There. There.

MISS TESMAN   Oh—just to think that you've become a married man, George. And that you're the one who carried off Hedda Gabler! Beautiful Hedda Gabler. Imagine—with all her suitors.

TESMAN   [*Hums a little and smiles complacently.*]   Yes, I believe I have quite a few friends in town who envy me, hm?

MISS TESMAN   And then—you got to take such a long honeymoon—more than five—almost six months . . .

TESMAN   Yes, but it was also part of my research, you know. All those archives I had to wade through—and all the books I had to read!

MISS TESMAN   I suppose you're right. [*Confidentially and more quietly.*] But listen, George—isn't there something—something extra you want to tell me?

TESMAN   About the trip?

MISS TESMAN   Yes.

TESMAN   No—I can't think of anything I didn't mention in my letters. I was given my doctorate—but I told you that yesterday.

MISS TESMAN   So you did. But I mean—whether you might have any—any kind of—prospects—?

TESMAN   Prospects?

MISS TESMAN   Good Lord, George—I'm your old aunt.

TESMAN   Well of course I have prospects.

MISS TESMAN   Aha!

TESMAN   I have excellent prospects of becoming a professor one of these days. But Aunt Julie dear, you already know that.

MISS TESMAN   [*With a little laugh.*]   You're right, I do. [*Changing the subject.*] But about your trip. It must have cost a lot.

TESMAN   Well, thank God, that huge fellowship paid for a good part of it.

MISS TESMAN   But how did you make it last for the both of you?

TESMAN   That's the tricky part, isn't it?

MISS TESMAN   And on top of that, when you're travelling with a lady! That's always going to cost you more, or so I've heard.

TESMAN   You're right—it was a bit more costly. But Hedda just had to have that trip, Auntie. She really had to. There was no choice.

MISS TESMAN   Well, I suppose not. These days a honeymoon trip is essential, it seems. But now tell me—have you had a good look around the house?

TESMAN   Absolutely! I've been up since dawn.

MISS TESMAN   And what do you think about all of it?

TESMAN   It's splendid! Only I can't think of what we'll do with those two empty rooms between the back parlor and Hedda's bedroom.

MISS TESMAN [*Lightly laughing.*]   My dear George—when the time comes, you'll think of what to do with them.

TESMAN   Oh, of course—as I add to my library, hm?

MISS TESMAN   That's right, my boy—of course I was thinking about your library.

TESMAN   Most of all I'm just so happy for Hedda. Before we got engaged she'd always say how she couldn't imagine living anywhere but here—in Prime Minister Falk's house.

MISS TESMAN   Yes—imagine. And then it came up for sale just after you left for your trip.

TESMAN   Aunt Julie, we really had luck on our side, hm?

MISS TESMAN   But the expense, George. This will all be costly for you.

TESMAN [*Looks at her disconcertedly.*]   Yes. It might be. It might be, Auntie.

MISS TESMAN   Ah, God only knows.

TESMAN   How much, do you think? Approximately. Hm?

MISS TESMAN   I can't possibly tell before all the bills are in.

TESMAN   Luckily Judge Brack lined up favorable terms for me—he wrote as much to Hedda.

MISS TESMAN   That's right—don't you ever worry about that, my boy. All this furniture, and the carpets? I put up the security for it.

TESMAN   Security? You? Dear Auntie Julie, what kind of security could you give?

MISS TESMAN   I took out a mortgage on our annuity.

TESMAN   What? On your—and Aunt Rina's annuity!

MISS TESMAN   I couldn't think of any other way.

TESMAN [*Standing in front of her.*]   Have you gone completely out of your mind, Auntie? That annuity is all you and Aunt Rina have to live on.

MISS TESMAN   Now, now, take it easy. It's just a formality, you understand. Judge Brack said so. He was good enough to arrange it all for me. Just a formality, he said.

TESMAN   That could very well be, but all the same . . .

MISS TESMAN   You'll be earning your own living now, after all. And, good Lord, so what if we do have to open the purse a little, spend a little bit at first? That would only make us happy.

TESMAN   Auntie . . . you never get tired of sacrificing yourself for me.

MISS TESMAN [*Rises and lays her hands on his shoulders.*]   What joy do I have in the world, my dearest boy, other than smoothing out the path

for you? You, without a father or mother to take care of you . . . but we've reached our destination, my dear. Maybe things looked black from time to time. But, praise God, George, you've come out on top!

TESMAN Yes, it's really amazing how everything has gone according to plan.

MISS TESMAN And those who were against you—those who would have blocked your way—they're at the bottom of the pit. They've fallen, George. And the most dangerous one, he fell the farthest. Now he just lies there where he fell, the poor sinner.

TESMAN Have you heard anything about Eilert—since I went away, I mean?

MISS TESMAN Nothing, except they say he published a new book.

TESMAN What? Eilert Løvborg? Just recently, hm?

MISS TESMAN That's what they say. God only knows how there could be anything to it. But when *your* book comes out—now that will be something else again, won't it, George? What's it going to be about?

TESMAN It will deal with the Domestic Craftsmanship Practices of Medieval Brabant.[2]

MISS TESMAN Just think—you can write about that kind of thing too.

TESMAN However, it might be quite a while before that book is ready. I've got all these incredible collections that have to be put in order first.

MISS TESMAN Ordering and collecting—you're certainly good at that. You're not the son of sainted Joseph for nothing.

TESMAN And I'm so eager to get going. Especially now that I've got my own snug house and home to work in.

MISS TESMAN And most of all, now that you've got her—your heart's desire, dear, dear George!

TESMAN [*Embracing her.*] Yes, Auntie Julie! Hedda . . . that's the most beautiful thing of all! [*Looking toward the doorway.*] I think that's her, hm?

[HEDDA *comes in from the left side of the inner room. She is a lady of twenty-nine. Her face and figure are aristocratic and elegant. Her complexion is pale. Her eyes are steel-grey, cold and clear. Her hair is an attractive medium brown but not particularly full. She is wearing a tasteful, somewhat loose-fitting morning gown.*]

MISS TESMAN [*Going to meet* HEDDA.] Good morning, Hedda, my dear. Good morning.

HEDDA [*Extending her hand.*] Good morning, Miss Tesman, my dear. You're here so early. How nice of you.

MISS TESMAN [*Looking somewhat embarrassed.*] Well now, how did the young mistress sleep in her new home?

HEDDA Fine thanks. Well enough.

TESMAN [*Laughing.*] Well enough! That's a good one, Hedda. You were sleeping like a log when I got up.

HEDDA Yes, lucky for me. But of course you have to get used to anything new, Miss Tesman. A little at a time. [*Looks toward the window.*] Uch! Look at that. The maid opened the door. I'm drowning in all this sunlight.

MISS TESMAN [*Going to the door.*] Well then, let's close it.

---

2. In the Middle Ages, Brabant was a duchy located in parts of what are now Belgium and the Netherlands.

HEDDA No, no, don't do that. Tesman my dear, just close the curtains. That gives a gentler light.

TESMAN [*By the door.*] All right, all right. Now then, Hedda. You've got both fresh air and sunlight.

HEDDA Yes, fresh air. That's what I need with all these flowers all over the place. But Miss Tesman, won't you sit down?

MISS TESMAN No, but thank you. Now that I know everything's all right here, I've got to see about getting home again. Home to that poor dear who's lying there in pain.

TESMAN Be sure to give her my respects, won't you? And tell her I'll stop by and look in on her later today.

MISS TESMAN Yes, yes I'll certainly do that. But would you believe it, George? [*She rustles around in the pocket of her skirt.*] I almost forgot. Here, I brought something for you.

TESMAN And what might that be, Auntie, hm?

MISS TESMAN [*Brings out a flat package wrapped in newspaper and hands it to him.*] Here you are, my dear boy.

TESMAN [*Opening it.*] Oh my Lord. You kept them for me, Aunt Julie. Hedda, isn't this touching, hm?

HEDDA Well, what is it?

TESMAN My old house slippers. My slippers.

HEDDA Oh yes, I remember how often you talked about them on our trip.

TESMAN Yes, well, I really missed them. [*Goes over to her.*] Now you can see them for yourself, Hedda.

HEDDA [*Moves over to the stove.*] Oh, no thanks. I don't really care to.

TESMAN [*Following after her.*] Just think, Aunt Rina lying there embroidering for me, sick as she was. Oh, you couldn't possibly believe how many memories are tangled up in these slippers.

HEDDA [*By the table.*] Not for me.

MISS TESMAN Hedda's quite right about that, George.

TESMAN Yes, but now that she's in the family I thought—

HEDDA That maid won't last, Tesman.

MISS TESMAN Berta—?

TESMAN What makes you say that, hm?

HEDDA [*Pointing.*] Look, she's left her old hat lying there on that chair.

TESMAN [*Terrified, dropping the slippers on the floor.*] Hedda—!

HEDDA What if someone came in and saw that.

TESMAN But Hedda—that's Aunt Julie's hat.

HEDDA Really?

MISS TESMAN [*Taking the hat.*] Yes, it really is. And for that matter it's not so old either, my dear little Hedda.

HEDDA Oh, I really didn't get a good look at it, Miss Tesman.

MISS TESMAN [*Tying the hat on her head.*] Actually I've never worn it before today—and the good Lord knows that's true.

TESMAN And an elegant hat it is too. Really magnificent.

MISS TESMAN [*She looks around.*] Oh that's as may be, George. My parasol? Ah, here it is. [*She takes it.*] That's mine too. [*She mutters.*] Not Berta's.

TESMAN A new hat and a new parasol. Just think, Hedda.

HEDDA   Very charming, very attractive.

TESMAN   That's true, hm? But Auntie, take a good look at Hedda before you go. Look at how charming and attractive she is.

MISS TESMAN   Oh my dear, that's nothing new. Hedda's been lovely all her life. [*She nods and goes across to the right.*]

TESMAN   [*Following her.*]   Yes, but have you noticed how she's blossomed, how well she's filled out on our trip?

HEDDA   Oh, leave it alone!

MISS TESMAN   [*Stops and turns.*]   Filled out?

TESMAN   Yes, Aunt Julie. You can't see it so well right now in that gown— but I, who have a little better opportunity to—

HEDDA   [*By the glass door impatiently.*]   Oh you don't have the opportunity for anything.

TESMAN   It was that mountain air down in the Tyrol.

HEDDA   [*Curtly interrupting.*]   I'm the same as when I left.

TESMAN   You keep saying that. But it's true, isn't it Auntie?

MISS TESMAN   [*Folding her hands and gazing at* HEDDA.]   Lovely . . . lovely . . . lovely. That's Hedda. [*She goes over to her and with both her hands takes her head, bends it down, kisses her hair.*]   God bless and keep Hedda Tesman for George's sake.

HEDDA   [*Gently freeing herself.*]   Ah—! Let me out!

MISS TESMAN   [*With quiet emotion.*]   I'll come look in on you two every single day.

TESMAN   Yes, Auntie, do that, won't you, hm?

MISS TESMAN   Good-bye, good-bye.

> [*She goes out through the hall door.* TESMAN *follows her out. The door remains half open.* TESMAN *is heard repeating his greetings to Aunt Rina and his thanks for the slippers. While this is happening,* HEDDA *walks around the room raising her arms and clenching her fists as if in a rage. Then she draws the curtains back from the door, stands there and looks out. After a short time,* TESMAN *comes in and closes the door behind him.*]

TESMAN   [*Picking up the slippers from the floor.*]   What are you looking at, Hedda?

HEDDA   [*Calm and controlled again.*]   Just the leaves. So yellow and so withered.

TESMAN   [*Wrapping up the slippers and placing them on the table.*]   Yes, well—we're into September now.

HEDDA   [*Once more uneasy.*]   Yes—It's already—already September.

TESMAN   Didn't you think Aunt Julie was acting strange just now, almost formal? What do you suppose got into her?

HEDDA   I really don't know her. Isn't that the way she usually is?

TESMAN   No, not like today.

HEDDA   [*Leaving the glass door.*]   Do you think she was upset by the hat business?

TESMAN   Not really. Maybe a little, for just a moment—

HEDDA   But where did she get her manners, flinging her hat around any way she likes here in the drawing room. People just don't act that way.

TESMAN   Well, I'm sure she won't do it again.

HEDDA   Anyway, I'll smooth everything over with her soon enough.

TESMAN   Yes, Hedda, if you would do that.

HEDDA   When you visit them later today, invite her here for the evening.

TESMAN   Yes, that's just what I'll do. And there's one more thing you can do that would really make her happy.

HEDDA   Well?

TESMAN   If you just bring yourself to call her Aunt Julie, for my sake, Hedda, hm?

HEDDA   Tesman, for God's sake, don't ask me to do that. I've told you that before. I'll try to call her Aunt once in a while and that's enough.

TESMAN   Oh well, I just thought that now that you're part of the family . . .

HEDDA   Hmm. I don't know—[She crosses upstage to the doorway.]

TESMAN   [After a pause.]   Is something the matter, Hedda?

HEDDA   I was just looking at my old piano. It really doesn't go with these other things.

TESMAN   As soon as my salary starts coming in, we'll see about trading it in for a new one.

HEDDA   Oh, no, don't trade it in. I could never let it go. We'll leave it in the back room instead. And then we'll get a new one to put in here. I mean, as soon as we get the chance.

TESMAN   [A little dejectedly.]   Yes, I suppose we could do that.

HEDDA   [Taking the bouquet from the piano.]   These flowers weren't here when we got in last night.

TESMAN   I suppose Aunt Julie brought them.

HEDDA   [Looks into the bouquet.]   Here's a card. [Takes it out and reads.] "Will call again later today." Guess who it's from.

TESMAN   Who is it, hm?

HEDDA   It says Mrs. Elvsted.

TESMAN   Really. Mrs. Elvsted. She used to be Miss Rysing.

HEDDA   Yes, that's the one. She had all that irritating hair she'd always be fussing with. An old flame of yours, I've heard.

TESMAN   [Laughs.]   Oh, not for long and before I knew you, Hedda. And she's here in town. How about that.

HEDDA   Strange that she should come visiting us. I hardly know her except from school.

TESMAN   Yes, and of course I haven't seen her since—well God knows how long. How could she stand it holed up out there so far from everything, hm?

HEDDA   [Reflects a moment and then suddenly speaks.]   Just a minute, Tesman. Doesn't he live out that way, Eilert Løvborg, I mean?

TESMAN   Yes, right up in that area.

[BERTA comes in from the hallway.]

BERTA   Ma'am, she's back again. The lady who came by with the flowers an hour ago. [Pointing.] Those you've got in your hand, Ma'am.

HEDDA   Is she then? Please ask her to come in.

[BERTA opens the door for MRS. ELVSTED and then leaves. MRS. ELVSTED is slender with soft, pretty features. Her eyes are light blue, large, round and slightly protruding. Her expression is one of alarm and question. Her hair is remarkably light, almost a white gold and exceptionally rich and full. She

is a couple of years younger than Hedda. Her costume is a dark visiting dress, tasteful but not of the latest fashion.]

HEDDA [*Goes to meet her in a friendly manner.*]   Hello my dear Mrs. Elvsted. So delightful to see you again.

MRS. ELVSTED [*Nervous, trying to control herself.*]   Yes, it's been so long since we've seen each other.

TESMAN [*Shakes her hand.*]   And we could say the same, hm?

HEDDA   Thank you for the lovely flowers.

MRS. ELVSTED   I would have come yesterday right away but I heard you were on a trip—

TESMAN   So you've just come into town, hm?

MRS. ELVSTED   Yesterday around noon. I was absolutely desperate when I heard you weren't home.

HEDDA   Desperate, why?

TESMAN   My dear Miss Rysing—I mean Mrs. Elvsted.

HEDDA   There isn't some sort of trouble—?

MRS. ELVSTED   Yes there is—and I don't know another living soul to turn to here in town.

HEDDA [*Sets the flowers down on the table.*]   All right then, let's sit down here on the sofa.

MRS. ELVSTED   Oh no, I'm too upset to sit down.

HEDDA   No you're not. Come over here. [*She draws* MRS. ELVSTED *to the sofa and sits beside her.*]

TESMAN   Well, and now Mrs.—

HEDDA   Did something happen up at your place?

MRS. ELVSTED   Yes—That's it—well, not exactly—Oh, I don't want you to misunderstand me—

HEDDA   Well then the best thing is just to tell it straight out, Mrs. Elvsted—why?

TESMAN   That's why you came here, hm?

MRS. ELVSTED   Yes, of course. So I'd better tell you, if you don't already know, that Eilert Løvborg is in town.

HEDDA   Løvborg?

TESMAN   Eilert Løvborg's back again? Just think, Hedda.

HEDDA   Good Lord, Tesman, I can hear.

MRS. ELVSTED   He's been back now for about a week. The whole week alone here where he can fall in with all kinds of bad company. This town's a dangerous place for him.

HEDDA   But my dear Mrs. Elvsted, how does this involve you?

MRS. ELVSTED [*With a scared expression, speaking quickly.*]   He was the children's tutor.

HEDDA   Your children?

MRS. ELVSTED   My husband's. I don't have any.

HEDDA   The stepchildren then?

MRS. ELVSTED   Yes.

TESMAN [*Somewhat awkwardly.*]   But was he sufficiently—I don't know how to say this—sufficiently regular in his habits to be trusted with that kind of job, hm?

MRS. ELVSTED   For the past two years no one could say anything against him.

TESMAN   Really, nothing. Just think, Hedda.

HEDDA   I hear.

MRS. ELVSTED   Nothing at all, I assure you. Not in any way. But even so, now that I know he's here in the city alone and with money in his pocket I'm deathly afraid for him.

TESMAN   But why isn't he up there with you and your husband, hm?

MRS. ELVSTED   When the book came out he was too excited to stay up there with us.

TESMAN   Yes, that's right. Aunt Julie said he'd come out with a new book.

MRS. ELVSTED   Yes, a major new book on the progress of civilization—in its entirety I mean. That was two weeks ago. And it's been selling wonderfully. Everyone's reading it. It's created a huge sensation—why?

TESMAN   All that really? Must be something he had lying around from his better days.

MRS. ELVSTED   From before, you mean?

TESMAN   Yes.

MRS. ELVSTED   No, he wrote the whole thing while he was up there living with us. Just in the last year.

TESMAN   That's wonderful to hear, Hedda. Just think!

MRS. ELVSTED   Yes, if only it continues.

HEDDA   Have you met him here in town?

MRS. ELVSTED   No, not yet. I had a terrible time hunting down his address but this morning I finally found it.

HEDDA [Looks searchingly.]   I can't help thinking this is a little odd on your husband's part.

MRS. ELVSTED [Starts nervously.]   My husband—What?

HEDDA   That he'd send you to town on this errand. That he didn't come himself to look for his friend.

MRS. ELVSTED   Oh no, no, no. My husband doesn't have time for that. And anyway I had to do some shopping too.

HEDDA [Smiling slightly.]   Oh well, that's different then.

MRS. ELVSTED [Gets up quickly, ill at ease.]   And now I beg you, Mr. Tesman, please be kind to Eilert Løvborg if he comes here—and I'm sure he will. You were such good friends in the old days. You have interests in common. The same area of research, as far as I can tell.

TESMAN   Yes, that used to be the case anyway.

MRS. ELVSTED   Yes, that's why I'm asking you—from the bottom of my heart to be sure to—that you'll—that you'll keep a watchful eye on him. Oh, Mr. Tesman, will you do that—will you promise me that?

TESMAN   Yes, with all my heart, Mrs. Rysing.

HEDDA   Elvsted.

TESMAN   I'll do anything in my power for Eilert. You can be sure of it.

MRS. ELVSTED   Oh, that is so kind of you. [She presses his hands.] Many, many thanks. [Frightened.] Because my husband thinks so highly of him.

HEDDA [Rising.]   You should write to him, Tesman. He might not come to you on his own.

TESMAN   Yes, that's the way to do it, Hedda, hm?

HEDDA   And the sooner the better. Right now, I think.

MRS. ELVSTED [*Beseechingly.*]   Yes, if you only could.

TESMAN   I'll write to him this moment. Do you have his address, Mrs. Elvsted?

MRS. ELVSTED   Yes. [*She takes a small slip of paper from her pocket and hands it to him.*] Here it is.

TESMAN   Good, good. I'll go write him—[*Looks around just a minute.*]— Where are my slippers? Ah, here they are. [*Takes the packet and is about to leave.*]

HEDDA   Make sure your note is very friendly—nice and long too.

TESMAN   Yes, you can count on me.

MRS. ELVSTED   But please don't say a word about my asking you to do it.

TESMAN   Oh, that goes without saying.

[TESMAN *leaves to the right through the rear room.*]

HEDDA [*Goes over to* MRS. ELVSTED, *smiles and speaks softly.*]   There, now we've killed two birds with one stone.

MRS. ELVSTED   What do you mean?

HEDDA   Didn't you see that I wanted him out of the way?

MRS. ELVSTED   Yes, to write the letter—

HEDDA   So I could talk to you alone.

MRS. ELVSTED [*Confused.*]   About this thing?

HEDDA   Yes, exactly, about this thing.

MRS. ELVSTED [*Apprehensively.*]   But there's nothing more to it, Mrs. Tesman, really there isn't.

HEDDA   Ah, but there is indeed. There's a great deal more. I can see that much. Come here, let's sit down together. Have a real heart-to-heart talk.

[*She forces* MRS. ELVSTED *into the armchair by the stove and sits down herself on one of the small stools.*]

MRS. ELVSTED [*Nervously looking at her watch.*]   Mrs. Tesman, I was just thinking of leaving.

HEDDA   Now you can't be in such a hurry, can you? Talk to me a little bit about how things are at home.

MRS. ELVSTED   Oh, that's the last thing I want to talk about.

HEDDA   But to me? Good Lord, we went to the same school.

MRS. ELVSTED   Yes, but you were one class ahead of me. Oh, I was so afraid of you then.

HEDDA   Afraid of me?

MRS. ELVSTED   Horribly afraid. Whenever we'd meet on the stairs you always used to pull my hair.

HEDDA   No, did I do that?

MRS. ELVSTED   Yes, you did—and once you said you'd burn it off.

HEDDA   Oh, just silly talk, you know.

MRS. ELVSTED   Yes, but I was so stupid in those days and anyway since then we've gotten to be so distant from each other. Our circles have just been totally different.

HEDDA   Well let's see if we can get closer again. Listen now, I know we were good friends in school. We used to call each other by our first names.

MRS. ELVSTED   No, no, I think you're mistaken.

HEDDA I certainly am not. I remember it perfectly and so we have to be perfectly open with each other just like in the old days. [*Moves the stool closer.*] There now. [*Kisses her cheek.*] Now you must call me Hedda.

MRS. ELVSTED [*Pressing and patting her hands.*] Oh, you're being so friendly to me. I'm just not used to that.

HEDDA There, there, there. I'll stop being so formal with you and I'll call you my dear Thora.

MRS. ELVSTED My name is Thea.

HEDDA That's right, of course, I meant Thea. [*Looks at her compassionately.*] So you're not used to friendship, Thea, in your own home?

MRS. ELVSTED If I only had a home, but I don't. I've never had one.

HEDDA [*Glances at her.*] I suspected it might be something like that.

MRS. ELVSTED [*Staring helplessly before her.*] Yes, yes, yes.

HEDDA I can't exactly remember now, but didn't you go up to Sheriff Elvsted's as a housekeeper?

MRS. ELVSTED Actually I was supposed to be a governess but his wife—at that time—she was an invalid, mostly bedridden, so I had to take care of the house too.

HEDDA So in the end you became mistress of your own house.

MRS. ELVSTED [*Heavily.*] Yes, that's what I became.

HEDDA Let me see. How long has that been?

MRS. ELVSTED Since I was married?

HEDDA Yes.

MRS. ELVSTED Five years now.

HEDDA That's right, it must be about that.

MRS. ELVSTED Oh these five years—! Or the last two or three anyway—! Ah, Mrs. Tesman, if you could just imagine.

HEDDA [*Slaps her lightly on the hand.*] Mrs. Tesman; really, Thea.

MRS. ELVSTED No, no, of course, I'll try to remember. Anyway, Hedda, if you could only imagine.

HEDDA [*Casually.*] It seems to me that Eilert Løvborg's been living up there for about three years, hasn't he?

MRS. ELVSTED [*Looks uncertainly at her.*] Eilert Løvborg? Yes, that's about right.

HEDDA Did you know him from before—from here in town?

MRS. ELVSTED Hardly at all. I mean his name of course.

HEDDA But up there he'd come to visit you at the house?

MRS. ELVSTED Yes, every day. He'd read to the children. I couldn't manage everything myself, you see.

HEDDA No, of course not. And what about your husband? His work must take him out of the house quite a bit.

MRS. ELVSTED Yes, as you might imagine. He's the sheriff so he has to go traveling around the whole district.

HEDDA [*Leaning against the arm of the chair.*] Thea, my poor sweet Thea— You've got to tell me everything just the way it is.

MRS. ELVSTED All right, but you've got to ask the questions.

HEDDA So, Thea, what's your husband really like? I mean, you know, to be with? Is he good to you?

MRS. ELVSTED [*Evasively.*] He thinks he does everything for the best.

HEDDA I just think he's a little too old for you. He's twenty years older, isn't he?

MRS. ELVSTED [*Irritatedly.*] There's that too. There's a lot of things. I just can't stand being with him. We don't have a single thought in common, not a single thing in the world, he and I.

HEDDA But doesn't he care for you at all in his own way?

MRS. ELVSTED I can't tell what he feels. I think I'm just useful to him, and it doesn't cost very much to keep me. I'm very inexpensive.

HEDDA That's a mistake.

MRS. ELVSTED [*Shaking her head.*] Can't be any other way, not with him. He only cares about himself and maybe about the children a little.

HEDDA And also for Eilert Løvborg, Thea.

MRS. ELVSTED [*Stares at her.*] For Eilert Løvborg? Why do you think that?

HEDDA Well, my dear, he sent you all the way into town to look for him. [*Smiling almost imperceptibly.*] And besides, you said so yourself, to Tesman.

MRS. ELVSTED [*With a nervous shudder.*] Oh yes, I suppose I did. No, I'd better just tell you the whole thing. It's bound to come to light sooner or later anyway.

HEDDA But my dear Thea.

MRS. ELVSTED All right, short and sweet. My husband doesn't know that I'm gone.

HEDDA What, your husband doesn't know?

MRS. ELVSTED Of course not. Anyway he's not at home. He was out traveling. I just couldn't stand it any longer, Hedda, it was impossible. I would have been so completely alone up there.

HEDDA Well, then what?

MRS. ELVSTED Then I packed some of my things, just the necessities, all in secret, and I left the house.

HEDDA Just like that?

MRS. ELVSTED Yes, and I took the train to town.

HEDDA Oh, my good, dear Thea. You dared to do that!

MRS. ELVSTED [*Gets up and walks across the floor.*] Well, what else could I do?

HEDDA What do you think your husband will say when you go home again?

MRS. ELVSTED [*By the table looking at her.*] Up there to him?

HEDDA Of course, of course.

MRS. ELVSTED I'm never going back up there.

HEDDA [*Gets up and goes closer to her.*] So you've really done it? You've really run away from everything?

MRS. ELVSTED Yes, I couldn't think of anything else to do.

HEDDA But you did it—so openly.

MRS. ELVSTED Oh, you can't keep something like that a secret anyway.

HEDDA Well, what do you think people will say about you, Thea?

MRS. ELVSTED They'll say whatever they want, God knows. [*She sits tired and depressed on the sofa.*] But I only did what I had to do.

HEDDA [*After a brief pause.*] So what will you do with yourself now?

MRS. ELVSTED I don't know yet. All I know is that I've got to live here where Eilert Løvborg lives if I'm going to live at all.

HEDDA [*Moves a chair closer from the table, sits beside her and strokes her hands.*] Thea, my dear, how did it come about, this—bond between you and Eilert Løvborg?

MRS. ELVSTED Oh, it just happened, little by little. I started to have a kind of power over him.

HEDDA Really?

MRS. ELVSTED He gave up his old ways—and not because I begged him to. I never dared do that. But he started to notice that those kinds of things upset me, so he gave them up.

HEDDA [*Concealing an involuntary, derisive smile.*] So you rehabilitated him, as they say. You, little Thea.

MRS. ELVSTED That's what he said, anyway. And for his part he's made a real human being out of me. Taught me to think, to understand all sorts of things.

HEDDA So he read to you too, did he?

MRS. ELVSTED No, not exactly, but he talked to me. Talked without stopping about all sorts of great things. And then there was that wonderful time when I shared in his work, when I helped him.

HEDDA You got to do that?

MRS. ELVSTED Yes. Whenever he wrote anything, we had to agree on it first.

HEDDA Like two good comrades.

MRS. ELVSTED [*Eagerly.*] Yes, comrades. Imagine, Hedda, that's what he called it too. I should feel so happy, but I can't yet because I don't know how long it will last.

HEDDA Are you that unsure of him?

MRS. ELVSTED [*Dejectedly.*] There's the shadow of a woman between Eilert Løvborg and me.

HEDDA [*Stares intently at her.*] Who could that be?

MRS. ELVSTED I don't know. Someone from his past. Someone he's never really been able to forget.

HEDDA What has he told you about all this?

MRS. ELVSTED He's only talked about it once and very vaguely.

HEDDA Yes, what did he say?

MRS. ELVSTED He said that when they broke up she was going to shoot him with a pistol.

HEDDA [*Calm and controlled.*] That's nonsense, people just don't act that way here.

MRS. ELVSTED No they don't—so I think it's got to be that red-haired singer that he once—

HEDDA Yes, that could well be.

MRS. ELVSTED Because I remember they used to say about her that she went around with loaded pistols.

HEDDA Well, then it's her, of course.

MRS. ELVSTED [*Wringing her hands.*] Yes, but Hedda, just think, I hear this singer is in town again. Oh, I'm so afraid.

HEDDA [*Glancing toward the back room.*] Shh, here comes Tesman. [*She gets up and whispers.*] Now, Thea, all of this is strictly between you and me.

MRS. ELVSTED [*Jumping up.*]   Oh yes, yes, for God's sake!

[GEORGE TESMAN, *a letter in his hand, comes in from the right side of the inner room.*]

TESMAN   There now, the epistle is prepared.

HEDDA   Well done—but Mrs. Elvsted's got to leave now, I think. Just a minute, I'll follow you as far as the garden gate.

TESMAN   Hedda dear, do you think Berta could see to this?

HEDDA [*Takes the letter.*]   I'll instruct her.

[BERTA *comes in from the hall.*]

BERTA   Judge Brack is here. Says he'd like to pay his respects.

HEDDA   Yes, ask the Judge to be so good as to come in, and then—listen here now—Put this letter in the mailbox.

BERTA [*Takes the letter.*]   Yes, ma'am.

[*She opens the door for* JUDGE BRACK *and then goes out.* JUDGE BRACK *is forty-five years old, short, well built and moves easily. He has a round face and an aristocratic profile. His short hair is still almost black. His eyes are lively and ironic. He has thick eyebrows and a thick moustache, trimmed square at the ends. He is wearing outdoor clothing, elegant, but a little too young in style. He has a monocle in one eye. Now and then he lets it drop.*]

BRACK [*Bows with his hat in his hand.*]   Does one dare to call so early?

HEDDA   One does dare.

TESMAN [*Shakes his hand.*]   You're welcome any time. Judge Brack, Mrs. Rysing. [HEDDA *sighs.*]

BRACK [*Bows.*]   Aha, delighted.

HEDDA [*Looks at him laughing.*]   Nice to see you by daylight for a change, Judge.

BRACK   Do I look different?

HEDDA   Yes, younger.

BRACK   You're too kind.

TESMAN   Well, how about Hedda, hm? Doesn't she look fine? Hasn't she filled out?

HEDDA   Stop it now. You should be thanking Judge Brack for all of his hard work—

BRACK   Nonsense. It was my pleasure.

HEDDA   There's a loyal soul. But here's my friend burning to get away. Excuse me, Judge, I'll be right back.

[*Mutual good-byes.* MRS. ELVSTED *and* HEDDA *leave by the hall door.*]

BRACK   Well, now, your wife's satisfied, more or less?

TESMAN   Oh yes, we can't thank you enough. I gather there might be a little more rearrangement here and there and one or two things still missing. A couple of small things yet to be procured.

BRACK   Is that so?

TESMAN   But nothing for you to worry about. Hedda said that she'd look for everything herself. Let's sit down.

BRACK   Thanks. Just for a minute. [*Sits by the table.*] Now, my dear Tesman, there's something we need to talk about.

TESMAN   Oh yes, ah, I understand. [*Sits down.*] Time for a new topic. Time for the serious part of the celebration, hm?

BRACK Oh, I wouldn't worry too much about the finances just yet—although I must tell you that it would have been better if we'd managed things a little more frugally.

TESMAN But there was no way to do that. You know Hedda, Judge, you know her well. I couldn't possibly ask her to live in a middle-class house.

BRACK No, that's precisely the problem.

TESMAN And luckily it can't be too long before I get my appointment.[3]

BRACK Well, you know, these things often drag on and on.

TESMAN Have you heard anything further, hm?

BRACK Nothing certain. [*Changing the subject.*] But there is one thing. I've got a piece of news for you.

TESMAN Well?

BRACK Your old friend Eilert Løvborg's back in town.

TESMAN I already know.

BRACK Oh, how did you find out?

TESMAN She told me, that lady who just left with Hedda.

BRACK Oh, I see. I didn't quite get her name.

TESMAN Mrs. Elvsted.

BRACK Ah yes, the sheriff's wife. Yes, he's been staying up there with them.

TESMAN And I'm so glad to hear that he's become a responsible person again.

BRACK Yes, one is given to understand that.

TESMAN And he's come out with a new book, hm?

BRACK He has indeed.

TESMAN And it's caused quite a sensation.

BRACK It's caused an extraordinary sensation.

TESMAN Just think, isn't that wonderful to hear. With all his remarkable talents, I was absolutely certain he was down for good.

BRACK That was certainly the general opinion.

TESMAN But I can't imagine what he'll do with himself now. What will he live on, hm?

[*During these last words,* HEDDA *has entered from the hallway.*]

HEDDA [*To* BRACK, *laughing a little scornfully.*] Tesman is constantly going around worrying about what to live on.

TESMAN My Lord, we're talking about Eilert Løvborg, dear.

HEDDA [*Looking quickly at him.*] Oh yes? [*Sits down in the armchair by the stove and asks casually.*] What's the matter with him?

TESMAN Well, he must have spent his inheritance a long time ago, and he can't really write a new book every year, hm? So I was just asking what was going to become of him.

BRACK Perhaps I can enlighten you on that score.

TESMAN Oh?

BRACK You might remember that he has some relatives with more than a little influence.

TESMAN Unfortunately they've pretty much washed their hands of him.

---

3. Tesman expects to be appointed to a professorship. These positions were much less numerous and more socially prominent than their contemporary American counterparts.

BRACK In the old days they thought of him as the family's great shining hope.

TESMAN Yes, in the old days, possibly, but he took care of that himself.

HEDDA Who knows? [*Smiles slightly.*] Up at the Elvsteds' he's been the target of a reclamation project.

BRACK And there's this new book.

TESMAN Well, God willing, they'll help him out some way or another. I've just written to him, Hedda, asking him to come over this evening.

BRACK But my dear Tesman, you're coming to my stag party[4] this evening. You promised me on the pier last night.

HEDDA Had you forgotten, Tesman?

TESMAN Yes, to be perfectly honest, I had.

BRACK For that matter, you can be sure he won't come.

TESMAN Why do you say that, hm?

BRACK [*Somewhat hesitantly getting up and leaning his hands on the back of his chair.*] My dear Tesman, you too, Mrs. Tesman, in good conscience I can't let you go on living in ignorance of something like this.

TESMAN Something about Eilert, hm?

BRACK About both of you.

TESMAN My dear Judge, tell me what it is.

BRACK You ought to prepare yourself for the fact that your appointment might not come through as quickly as you expect.

TESMAN [*Jumps up in alarm.*] Has something held it up?

BRACK The appointment might just possibly be subject to a competition.

TESMAN A competition! Just think of that, Hedda!

HEDDA [*Leans further back in her chair.*] Ah yes—yes.

TESMAN But who on earth would it—surely not with—?

BRACK Yes, precisely, with Eilert Løvborg.

TESMAN [*Clasping his hands together.*] No, no, this is absolutely unthinkable, absolutely unthinkable, hm?

BRACK Hmm—well, we might just have to learn to get used to it.

TESMAN No, but Judge Brack, that would be incredibly inconsiderate. [*Waving his arms.*] Because—well—just look, I'm a married man. We went and got married on this very prospect, Hedda and I. Went and got ourselves heavily into debt. Borrowed money from Aunt Julie too. I mean, good Lord, I was as much as promised the position, hm?

BRACK Now, now, you'll almost certainly get it but first there'll have to be a contest.

HEDDA [*Motionless in the armchair.*] Just think, Tesman, it will be a sort of match.

TESMAN But Hedda, my dear, how can you be so calm about this?

HEDDA Oh I'm not, not at all. I can't wait for the final score.

BRACK In any case, Mrs. Tesman, it's a good thing that you know how matters stand. I mean, before you embark on any more of these little purchases I hear you're threatening to make.

HEDDA What's that got to do with this?

---

4. A party for men only, whether single or married.

BRACK   Well, well, that's another matter. Good-bye. [*To* TESMAN.] I'll come by for you when I take my afternoon walk.

TESMAN   Oh yes, yes, forgive me—I don't know if I'm coming or going.

HEDDA [*Reclining, stretching out her hand.*]   Good-bye, Judge, and do come again.

BRACK   Many thanks. Good-bye, good-bye.

TESMAN [*Following him to the door.*]   Good-bye, Judge. You'll have to excuse me.

[JUDGE BRACK *goes out through the hallway door.*]

TESMAN [*Pacing about the floor.*]   We should never let ourselves get lost in a wonderland, Hedda, hm?

HEDDA [*Looking at him and smiling.*]   Do you do that?

TESMAN   Yes, well, it can't be denied. It was like living in wonderland to go and get married and set up housekeeping on nothing more than prospects.

HEDDA   You may be right about that.

TESMAN   Well, at least we have our home, Hedda, our wonderful home. The home both of us dreamt about, that both of us craved, I could almost say, hm?

HEDDA [*Rises slowly and wearily.*]   The agreement was that we would live in society, that we would entertain.

TESMAN   Yes, good Lord, I was so looking forward to that. Just think, to see you as a hostess in our own circle. Hm. Well, well, well, for the time being at least we'll just have to make do with each other, Hedda. We'll have Aunt Julie here now and then. Oh you, you should have such a completely different—

HEDDA   To begin with, I suppose I can't have the liveried footmen.[5]

TESMAN   Ah no, unfortunately not. No footmen. We can't even think about that right now.

HEDDA   And the horse!

TESMAN [*Horrified.*]   The horse.

HEDDA   I suppose I mustn't think about that any more.

TESMAN   No, God help us, you can see that for yourself.

HEDDA [*Walking across the floor.*]   Well, at least I've got one thing to amuse myself with.

TESMAN [*Beaming with pleasure.*]   Ah, thank God for that, and what is that, Hedda?

HEDDA [*In the center doorway looking at him with veiled scorn.*]   My pistols, George.

TESMAN [*Alarmed.*]   Pistols?

HEDDA [*With cold eyes.*]   General Gabler's pistols.

[*She goes through the inner room and out to the left.*]

TESMAN [*Running to the center doorway and shouting after her.*]   No, for the love of God, Hedda, dearest, don't touch those dangerous things. For my sake, Hedda, hm?

5. Uniformed servants.

Act 2

The TESMANS' *rooms as in the first act except that the piano has been moved out and an elegant little writing table with a bookshelf has been put in its place. Next to the sofa a smaller table has been placed. Most of the bouquets have been removed.* MRS. ELVSTED'S *bouquet stands on the larger table in the foreground. It is afternoon.*

[HEDDA, *dressed to receive visitors, is alone in the room. She stands by the open glass door loading a pistol. The matching pistol lies in an open pistol case on the writing table.*]

HEDDA [*Looking down into the garden and calling.*]   Hello again, Judge.

BRACK [*Is heard some distance below.*]   Likewise, Mrs. Tesman.

HEDDA [*Raises the pistol and aims.*]   Now, Judge Brack, I am going to shoot you.

BRACK [*Shouting from below.*]   No, no, no. Don't stand there aiming at me like that.

HEDDA   That's what you get for coming up the back way. [*She shoots.*]

BRACK   Are you out of your mind?

HEDDA   Oh, good Lord, did I hit you?

BRACK [*Still outside.*]   Stop this nonsense.

HEDDA   Then come on in, Judge.

[JUDGE BRACK, *dressed for a bachelor party, comes in through the glass doors. He carries a light overcoat over his arm.*]

BRACK   In the devil's name, are you still playing this game? What were you shooting at?

HEDDA   Oh, I just stand here and shoot at the sky.

BRACK [*Gently taking the pistol out of her hands.*]   With your permission, ma'am? [*Looks at it.*] Ah, this one. I know it well. [*Looks around.*] And where do we keep the case? I see, here it is. [*Puts the pistol inside and shuts the case.*] All right, we're through with these little games for today.

HEDDA   Then what in God's name am I to do with myself?

BRACK   No visitors?

HEDDA [*Closes the glass door.*]   Not a single one. Our circle is still in the country.

BRACK   Tesman's not home either, I suppose.

HEDDA [*At the writing table, locks the pistol case in the drawer.*]   No, as soon as he finished eating he was off to the aunts. He wasn't expecting you so early.

BRACK   Hmm, I never thought of that. Stupid of me.

HEDDA [*Turns her head, looks at him.*]   Why stupid?

BRACK   Then I would have come a little earlier.

HEDDA [*Going across the floor.*]   Then you wouldn't have found anyone here at all. I've been in my dressing room since lunch.

BRACK   Isn't there even one little crack in the door wide enough for a negotiation?

HEDDA   Now that's something you forgot to provide for.

BRACK   That was also stupid of me.

HEDDA   So we'll just have to flop down here and wait. Tesman won't be home any time soon.

BRACK   Well, well, Lord knows I can be patient.

[HEDDA *sits in the corner of the sofa.* BRACK *lays his overcoat over the back of the nearest chair and sits down, keeps his hat in his hand. Short silence. They look at each other.*]

HEDDA   So?

BRACK [*In the same tone.*]   So?

HEDDA   I asked first.

BRACK [*Leaning a little forward.*]   Yes, why don't we allow ourselves a cozy little chat, Mrs. Hedda.

HEDDA [*Leaning further back in the sofa.*]   Doesn't it feel like an eternity since we last talked together? A few words last night and this morning, but I don't count them.

BRACK   Like this, between ourselves, just the two of us?

HEDDA   Well, yes, more or less.

BRACK   I wished you were back home every single day.

HEDDA   The whole time I was wishing the same thing.

BRACK   You, really, Mrs. Hedda? Here I thought you were having a wonderful time on your trip.

HEDDA   Oh yes, you can just imagine.

BRACK   But that's what Tesman always wrote.

HEDDA   Yes, him! He thinks it's the greatest thing in the world to go scratching around in libraries. He loves sitting and copying out old parchments or whatever they are.

BRACK [*Somewhat maliciously.*]   Well, that's his calling in the world, at least in part.

HEDDA   Yes, so it is, and no doubt it's—but for me, oh dear Judge, I've been so desperately bored.

BRACK [*Sympathetically.*]   Do you really mean that? You're serious?

HEDDA   Yes, you can imagine it for yourself. Six whole months never meeting with a soul who knew the slightest thing about our circle. No one we could talk with about our kinds of things.

BRACK   Ah no, I'd agree with you there. That would be a loss.

HEDDA   Then what was most unbearable of all.

BRACK   Yes?

HEDDA   To be together forever and always—with one and the same person.

BRACK [*Nodding agreement.*]   Early and late, yes, night and day, every waking and sleeping hour.

HEDDA   That's it, forever and always.

BRACK   Yes, all right, but with our excellent Tesman I would have imagined that you might—

HEDDA   Tesman is—a specialist, dear Judge.

BRACK   Undeniably.

HEDDA   And specialists aren't so much fun to travel with. Not for the long run anyway.

BRACK   Not even the specialist that one loves?

HEDDA   Uch, don't use that syrupy word.

BRACK [*Startled.*]   Mrs. Hedda.

HEDDA [*Half laughing, half bitterly.*] Well, give it a try for yourself. Hearing about the history of civilization every hour of the day.

BRACK Forever and always.

HEDDA Yes, yes, yes. And then his particular interest, domestic crafts in the Middle Ages. Uch, the most revolting thing of all.

BRACK [*Looks at her curiously.*] But, tell me now, I don't quite understand how—hmmm.

HEDDA That we're together? George Tesman and I, you mean?

BRACK Well, yes. That's a good way of putting it.

HEDDA Good Lord, do you think it's so remarkable?

BRACK I think—yes and no, Mrs. Hedda.

HEDDA I'd danced myself out, dear Judge. My time was up. [*Shudders slightly.*] Uch, no, I'm not going to say that or even think it.

BRACK You certainly have no reason to think it.

HEDDA Ah, reasons—[*Looks watchfully at him.*] And George Tesman? Well, he'd certainly be called a most acceptable man in every way.

BRACK Acceptable and solid, God knows.

HEDDA And I can't find anything about him that's actually ridiculous, can you?

BRACK Ridiculous? No—I wouldn't quite say that.

HEDDA Hmm. Well, he's a very diligent archivist anyway. Some day he might do something interesting with all of it. Who knows.

BRACK [*Looking at her uncertainly.*] I thought you believed, like everyone else, that he'd turn out to be a great man.

HEDDA [*With a weary expression.*] Yes, I did. And then when he went around constantly begging with all his strength, begging for permission to let him take care of me, well, I didn't see why I shouldn't take him up on it.

BRACK Ah well, from that point of view . . .

HEDDA It was a great deal more than any of my other admirers were offering.

BRACK [*Laughing.*] Well, of course I can't answer for all the others, but as far as I'm concerned you know very well that I've always maintained a certain respect for the marriage bond, that is, in an abstract kind of way, Mrs. Hedda.

HEDDA [*Playfully.*] Oh, I never had any hopes for you.

BRACK All I ask is an intimate circle of good friends, friends I can be of service to in any way necessary. Places where I am allowed to come and go as a trusted friend.

HEDDA Of the man of the house, you mean.

BRACK [*Bowing.*] No, to be honest, of the lady. Of the man as well, you understand, because you know that kind of—how should I put this— that kind of triangular arrangement is really a magnificent convenience for everyone concerned.

HEDDA Yes, you can't imagine how many times I longed for a third person on that trip. Ach, huddled together alone in a railway compartment.

BRACK Fortunately, the wedding trip is over now.

HEDDA [*Shaking her head.*] Oh no, it's a very long trip. It's nowhere near over. I've only come to a little stopover on the line.

BRACK Then you should jump out, stretch your legs a little, Mrs. Hedda.

HEDDA I'd never jump out.

BRACK Really?

HEDDA No, because there's always someone at the stop who—

BRACK [*Laughing.*] Who's looking at your legs, you mean?

HEDDA Yes, exactly.

BRACK Yes, but for heaven's sake.

HEDDA [*With a disdainful gesture.*] I don't hold with that sort of thing. I'd rather remain sitting, just like I am now, a couple alone. On a train.

BRACK But what if a third man climbed into the compartment with the couple?

HEDDA Ah yes. Now that's quite different.

BRACK An understanding friend, a proven friend—

HEDDA Who can be entertaining on all kinds of topics—

BRACK And not a specialist in any way!

HEDDA [*With an audible sigh.*] Yes, that would be a relief.

BRACK [*Hears the front door open and glances toward it.*] The triangle is complete.

HEDDA [*Half audibly.*] And there goes the train.

> [GEORGE TESMAN *in a gray walking suit and with a soft felt hat comes in from the hallway. He is carrying a large stack of unbound books under his arm and in his pockets.*]

TESMAN [*Goes to the table by the corner, sofa.*] Phew—hot work lugging all these here. [*Puts the books down.*] Would you believe I'm actually sweating, Hedda? And you're already here, Judge, hm. Berta didn't mention anything about that.

BRACK [*Getting up.*] I came up through the garden.

HEDDA What are all those books you've got there?

TESMAN [*Stands leafing through them.*] All the new works by my fellow specialists. I've absolutely got to have them.

HEDDA By your fellow specialists.

BRACK Ah, the specialists, Mrs. Tesman. [BRACK *and* HEDDA *exchange a knowing smile.*]

HEDDA You need even more of these specialized works?

TESMAN Oh, yes, my dear Hedda, you can never have too many of these. You have to keep up with what's being written and published.

HEDDA Yes, you certainly must do that.

TESMAN [*Searches among the books.*] And look here, I've got Eilert Løvborg's new book too. (*Holds it out.*) Maybe you'd like to look at it, Hedda, hm?

HEDDA No thanks—or maybe later.

TESMAN I skimmed it a little on the way.

HEDDA And what's your opinion as a specialist?

TESMAN I think the argument's remarkably thorough. He never wrote like this before. [*Collects the books together.*] Now I've got to get all these inside. Oh, it's going to be such fun to cut the pages.[6] Then I'll go and change. [*To* BRACK.] We don't have to leave right away, hm?

---

6. Books used to be sold with the pages folded but uncut; one had to cut the pages to read the book.

BRACK   No, not at all. No hurry at all.

TESMAN   Good, I'll take my time then. [*Leaves with the books but stands in the doorway and turns.*] Oh, Hedda, by the way, Aunt Julie won't be coming over this evening.

HEDDA   Really? Because of that hat business?

TESMAN   Not at all. How could you think that of Aunt Julie? No, it's just that Aunt Rina is very ill.

HEDDA   She always is.

TESMAN   Yes, but today she's gotten quite a bit worse.

HEDDA   Well, then it's only right that the other one should stay at home with her. I'll just have to make the best of it.

TESMAN   My dear, you just can't believe how glad Aunt Julie was, in spite of everything, at how healthy and rounded out you looked after the trip.

HEDDA   [*Half audibly getting up.*]   Oh, these eternal aunts.

TESMAN   Hm?

HEDDA   [*Goes over to the glass door.*]   Nothing.

TESMAN   Oh, all right. [*He goes out through the rear room and to the right.*]

BRACK   What were you saying about a hat?

HEDDA   Oh, just a little run-in with Miss Tesman this morning. She'd put her hat down there on that chair [*Looks at him smiling.*] and I pretended I thought it was the maid's.

BRACK   [*Shaking his head.*]   My dear Mrs. Hedda, how could you do such a thing to that harmless old lady.

HEDDA   [*Nervously walking across the floor.*]   Oh, you know—these things just come over me like that and I can't resist them. [*Flings herself into the armchair by the stove.*] I can't explain it, even to myself.

BRACK   [*Behind the armchair.*]   You're not really happy—that's the heart of it.

HEDDA   [*Staring in front of her.*]   And why should I be happy? Maybe you can tell me.

BRACK   Yes. Among other things, be happy you've got the home that you've always longed for.

HEDDA   [*Looks up at him and laughs.*]   You also believe that myth?

BRACK   There's nothing to it?

HEDDA   Yes, heavens, there's something to it.

BRACK   So?

HEDDA   And here's what it is. I used George Tesman to walk me home from parties last summer.

BRACK   Yes, regrettably I had to go another way.

HEDDA   Oh yes, you certainly were going a different way last summer.

BRACK   [*Laughs.*]   Shame on you, Mrs. Hedda. So you and Tesman . . .

HEDDA   So we walked past here one evening and Tesman, the poor thing, was twisting and turning in his agony because he didn't have the slightest idea what to talk about and I felt sorry that such a learned man—

BRACK   [*Smiling skeptically.*]   You did . . .

HEDDA   Yes, if you will, I did, and so just to help him out of his torment I said, without really thinking about it, that this was the house I would love to live in.

BRACK   That was all?

HEDDA   For that evening.

BRACK   But afterward?

HEDDA   Yes, dear Judge, my thoughtlessness has had its consequences.

BRACK   Unfortunately, our thoughtlessness often does, Mrs. Hedda.

HEDDA   Thanks, I'm sure. But it so happens that George Tesman and I found our common ground in this passion for Prime Minister Falk's villa. And after that it all followed. The engagement, the marriage, the honeymoon and everything else. Yes, yes, Judge, I almost said: you make your bed, you have to lie in it.

BRACK   That's priceless. Essentially what you're telling me is you didn't care about any of this here.

HEDDA   God knows I didn't.

BRACK   What about now, now that we've made it into a lovely home for you?

HEDDA   Ach, I feel an air of lavender and dried roses in every room—or maybe Aunt Julie brought that in with her.

BRACK   [Laughing.]   No, I think that's probably a relic of the eminent prime minister's late wife.

HEDDA   Yes, that's it, there's something deathly about it. It reminds me of a corsage the day after the ball. [Folds her hands at the back of her neck, leans back in her chair and gazes at him.] Oh, my dear Judge, you can't imagine how I'm going to bore myself out here.

BRACK   What if life suddenly should offer you some purpose or other, something to live for? What about that, Mrs. Hedda?

HEDDA   A purpose? Something really tempting for me?

BRACK   Preferably something like that, of course.

HEDDA   God knows what sort of purpose that would be. I often wonder if— [Breaks off.] No, that wouldn't work out either.

BRACK   Who knows. Let me hear.

HEDDA   If I could get Tesman to go into politics, I mean.

BRACK   [Laughing.]   Tesman? No, you have to see that politics, anything like that, is not for him. Not in his line at all.

HEDDA   No, I can see that. But what if I could get him to try just the same?

BRACK   Yes, but why should he do that if he's not up to it? Why would you want him to?

HEDDA   Because I'm bored, do you hear me? [After a pause.] So you don't think there's any way that Tesman could become a cabinet minister?

BRACK   Hmm, you see my dear Mrs. Hedda, that requires a certain amount of wealth in the first place.

HEDDA   [Rises impatiently.]   Yes, that's it, this shabby little world I've ended up in. [Crosses the floor.] That's what makes life so contemptible, so completely ridiculous. That's just what it is.

BRACK   I think the problem's somewhere else.

HEDDA   Where's that?

BRACK   You've never had to live through anything that really shakes you up.

HEDDA   Anything serious, you mean.

BRACK   Yes, you could call it that. Perhaps now, though, it's on its way.

HEDDA   [Tosses her head.]   You mean that competition for that stupid professorship? That's Tesman's business. I'm not going to waste a single thought on it.

BRACK   No, forget about that. But when you find yourself facing what one calls in elegant language a profound and solemn calling—[Smiling.] a new calling, my dear little Mrs. Hedda.

HEDDA [*Angry.*]   Quiet. You'll never see anything like that.

BRACK [*Gently.*]   We'll talk about it again in a year's time, at the very latest.

HEDDA [*Curtly.*]   I don't have any talent for that, Judge. I don't want anything to do with that kind of calling.

BRACK   Why shouldn't you, like most other women, have an innate talent for a vocation that—

HEDDA [*Over by the glass door.*]   Oh, please be quiet. I often think I only have one talent, one talent in the world.

BRACK [*Approaching.*]   And what is that may I ask?

HEDDA [*Standing, staring out.*]   Boring the life right out of me. Now you know. [*Turns, glances toward the inner room and laughs.*] Perfect timing; here comes the professor.

BRACK [*Warning softly.*]   Now, now, now, Mrs. Hedda.

[GEORGE TESMAN, *in evening dress, carrying his gloves and hat, comes in from the right of the rear room.*]

TESMAN   Hedda, no message from Eilert Løvborg?

HEDDA   No.

BRACK   Do you really think he'll come?

TESMAN   Yes, I'm almost certain he will. What you told us this morning was just idle gossip.

BRACK   Oh?

TESMAN   Yes, at least Aunt Julie said she couldn't possibly believe that he would stand in my way anymore. Just think.

BRACK   So, then everything's all right.

TESMAN [*Puts his hat with his gloves inside on a chair to the right.*]   Yes, but I'd like to wait for him as long as I can.

BRACK   We have plenty of time. No one's coming to my place until seven or even half past.

TESMAN   Meanwhile, we can keep Hedda company and see what happens, hm?

HEDDA [*Sets* BRACK's *overcoat and hat on the corner sofa.*]   At the very worst, Mr. Løvborg can stay here with me.

BRACK [*Offering to take his things.*]   At the worst, Mrs. Tesman, what do you mean?

HEDDA   If he won't go out with you and Tesman.

TESMAN [*Looking at her uncertainly.*]   But, Hedda dear, do you think that would be quite right, him staying here with you? Remember, Aunt Julie can't come.

HEDDA   No, but Mrs. Elvsted will be coming and the three of us can have a cup of tea together.

TESMAN   Yes, that's all right then.

BRACK [*Smiling.*]   And I might add, that would be the best plan for him.

HEDDA   Why so?

BRACK   Good Lord, Mrs. Tesman, you've had enough to say about my little bachelor parties in the past. Don't you agree they should be open only to men of the highest principle?

HEDDA   That's just what Mr. Løvborg is now, a reclaimed sinner.

[BERTA *comes in from the hall doorway.*]

BERTA   Madam, there's a gentleman who wishes to—

HEDDA   Yes, please, show him in.

TESMAN [*Softly.*] It's got to be him. Just think.

[EILERT LØVBORG *enters from the hallway. He is slim and lean, the same age as* TESMAN, *but he looks older and somewhat haggard. His hair and beard are dark brown. His face is longish, pale, with patches of red over the cheekbones. He is dressed in an elegant suit, black, quite new dark gloves and top hat. He stops just inside the doorway and bows hastily. He seems somewhat embarrassed.*]

TESMAN [*Goes to him and shakes his hands.*] Oh my dear Eilert, we meet again at long last.

LØVBORG [*Speaks in a low voice.*] Thanks for the letter, George. [*Approaches* HEDDA.] May I shake your hand also, Mrs. Tesman?

HEDDA [*Takes his hand.*] Welcome, Mr. Løvborg. [*With a gesture.*] I don't know if you two gentlemen—

LØVBORG [*Bowing.*] Judge Brack, I believe.

BRACK [*Similarly.*] Indeed. It's been quite a few years—

TESMAN [*To* LØVBORG, *his hands on his shoulders.*] And now Eilert, make yourself completely at home. Right, Hedda? I hear you're going to settle down here in town, hm?

LØVBORG Yes, I will.

TESMAN Well, that's only sensible. Listen, I got your new book. I haven't really had time to read it yet.

LØVBORG You can save yourself the trouble.

TESMAN What do you mean?

LØVBORG There's not much to it.

TESMAN How can you say that?

BRACK But everyone's been praising it so highly.

LØVBORG Exactly as I intended—so I wrote the sort of book that everyone can agree with.

BRACK Very clever.

TESMAN Yes, but my dear Eilert.

LØVBORG Because I want to reestablish my position, begin again.

TESMAN [*A little downcast.*] Yes, I suppose you'd want to, hm.

LØVBORG [*Smiling, putting down his hat and pulling a package wrapped in paper from his coat pocket.*] But when this comes out, George Tesman— this is what you should read. It's the real thing. I've put my whole self into it.

TESMAN Oh yes? What's it about?

LØVBORG It's the sequel.

TESMAN Sequel to what?

LØVBORG To my book.

TESMAN The new one?

LØVBORG Of course.

TESMAN But my dear Eilert, that one takes us right to the present day.

LØVBORG So it does—and this one takes us into the future.

TESMAN The future. Good Lord! We don't know anything about that.

LØVBORG No, we don't—but there are still one or two things to say about it, just the same. [*Opens the packages.*] Here, you'll see.

TESMAN That's not your handwriting, is it?

LØVBORG   I dictated it. [*Turns the pages.*] It's written in two sections. The first is about the cultural forces which will shape the future, and this other section [*Turning the pages.*] is about the future course of civilization.

TESMAN   Extraordinary. It would never occur to me to write about something like that.

HEDDA [*By the glass door, drumming on the pane.*]   Hmm, no, no.

LØVBORG [*Puts the papers back in the packet and sets it on the table.*]   I brought it along because I thought I might read some of it to you tonight.

TESMAN   Ah, that was very kind of you, Eilert, but this evening [*Looks at* BRACK.] I'm not sure it can be arranged—

LØVBORG   Some other time then, there's no hurry.

BRACK   I should tell you, Mr. Løvborg, we're having a little party at my place this evening, mostly for Tesman, you understand—

LØVBORG [*Looking for his hat.*]   Aha, well then I'll—

BRACK   No, listen, why don't you join us?

LØVBORG [*Briefly but firmly.*]   No, that I can't do, but many thanks just the same.

BRACK   Oh come now, you certainly can do that. We'll be a small, select circle and I guarantee we'll be "lively," as Mrs. Hed—Mrs. Tesman would say.

LØVBORG   No doubt, but even so—

BRACK   And then you could bring your manuscript along and read it to Tesman at my place. I've got plenty of rooms.

TESMAN   Think about that, Eilert. You could do that, hm?

HEDDA [*Intervening.*]   Now, my dear, Mr. Løvborg simply doesn't want to. I'm quite sure Mr. Løvborg would rather settle down here and have supper with me.

LØVBORG [*Staring at her.*]   With you, Mrs. Tesman?

HEDDA   And with Mrs. Elvsted.

LØVBORG   Ah—[*Casually.*] I saw her this morning very briefly.

HEDDA   Oh did you? Well, she's coming here; so you might almost say it's essential that you stay here, Mr. Løvborg. Otherwise she'll have no one to see her home.

LØVBORG   That's true. Yes, Mrs. Tesman, many thanks. I'll stay.

HEDDA   I'll go and have a word with the maid.

     [*She goes over to the hall door and rings.* BERTA *enters.* HEDDA *speaks quietly to her and points toward the rear room.* BERTA *nods and goes out again.*]

TESMAN [*At the same time to* LØVBORG.]   Listen, Eilert, your lecture—Is it about this new subject? About the future?

LØVBORG   Yes.

TESMAN   Because I heard down at the bookstore that you'd be giving a lecture series here this fall.

LØVBORG   I plan to. Please don't hold it against me.

TESMAN   No, God forbid, but—?

LØVBORG   I can easily see how this might make things awkward.

TESMAN [*Dejectedly.*]   Oh, for my part, I can't expect you to—

LØVBORG   But I'll wait until you get your appointment.

TESMAN   You will? Yes but—yes but—you won't be competing then?

LØVBORG   No. I only want to conquer you in the marketplace of ideas.

TESMAN   But, good Lord, Aunt Julie was right after all. Oh yes, yes, I was quite sure of it. Hedda, imagine, my dear—Eilert Løvborg won't stand in our way.

HEDDA [*Curtly.*]   Our way? Leave me out of it.

    [*She goes up toward the rear room where* BERTA *is placing a tray with decanters and glasses on the table.* HEDDA *nods approvingly, comes forward again.* BERTA *goes out.*]

TESMAN [*Meanwhile.*]   So, Judge Brack, what do you say about all this?

BRACK   Well now, I say that honor and victory, hmm—they have a powerful appeal—

TESMAN   Yes, yes, I suppose they do but all the same—

HEDDA [*Looking at* TESMAN *with a cold smile.*]   You look like you've been struck by lightning.

TESMAN   Yes, that's about it—or something like that, I think—

BRACK   That was quite a thunderstorm that passed over us, Mrs. Tesman.

HEDDA [*Pointing toward the rear room.*]   Won't you gentlemen go in there and have a glass of punch?

BRACK [*Looking at his watch.*]   For the road? Yes, not a bad idea.

TESMAN   Wonderful, Hedda, wonderful! And I'm in such a fantastic mood now.

HEDDA   You too, Mr. Løvborg, if you please.

LØVBORG [*Dismissively.*]   No, thank you, not for me.

BRACK   Good Lord, cold punch isn't exactly poison, you know.

LØVBORG   Maybe not for everybody.

HEDDA   Then I'll keep Mr. Løvborg company in the meantime.

TESMAN   Yes, yes, Hedda dear, you do that.

    [TESMAN *and* BRACK *go into the rear room, sit down and drink punch, smoking cigarettes and talking animatedly during the following.* EILERT LØVBORG *remains standing by the stove and* HEDDA *goes to the writing table.*]

HEDDA [*In a slightly raised voice.*]   Now, if you like, I'll show you some photographs. Tesman and I—we took a trip to the Tyrol on the way home.

    [*She comes over with an album and lays it on the table by the sofa, seating herself in the farthest corner.* EILERT LØVBORG *comes closer, stooping and looking at her. Then he takes a chair and sits on her left side with his back to the rear room.*]

HEDDA [*Opening the album.*]   Do you see these mountains, Mr. Løvborg? That's the Ortler group. Tesman's written a little caption. Here. "The Ortler group near Meran."[7]

LØVBORG [*Who has not taken his eyes off her from the beginning, says softly and slowly.*]   Hedda Gabler.

HEDDA [*Glances quickly at him.*]   Shh, now.

LØVBORG [*Repeating softly.*]   Hedda Gabler.

HEDDA [*Staring at the album.*]   Yes, so I was once, when we knew each other.

---

7. I.e., Merano, a city in the Austrian Tyrol, since 1918 in Italy. The scenic features mentioned here and later are tourist attractions. The Ortler group and the Dolomites are Alpine mountain ranges. The Ampezzo Valley lies beyond the Dolomites to the east. The Brenner Pass is a major route through the Alps to Austria.

LØVBORG And from now—for the rest of my life—do I have to teach myself never to say Hedda Gabler?

HEDDA [*Turning the pages.*] Yes, you have to. And I think you'd better start practicing now. The sooner the better, I'd say.

LØVBORG [*In a resentful voice.*] Hedda Gabler married—and then—with George Tesman.

HEDDA That's how it goes.

LØVBORG Ah, Hedda, Hedda—how could you have thrown yourself away like that?

HEDDA [*Looks sharply at him.*] What? Now stop that.

LØVBORG Stop what, what do you mean?

HEDDA Calling me Hedda and[8]—

[TESMAN *comes in and goes toward the sofa.*]

HEDDA [*Hears him approaching and says casually.*] And this one here, Mr. Løvborg, this was taken from the Ampezzo Valley. Would you just look at these mountain peaks. [*Looks warmly up at* TESMAN.] George, dear, what were these extraordinary mountains called?

TESMAN Let me see. Ah, yes, those are the Dolomites.

HEDDA Of course. Those, Mr. Løvborg, are the Dolomites.

TESMAN Hedda, dear, I just wanted to ask you if we should bring some punch in here, for you at least.

HEDDA Yes, thank you my dear. And a few pastries perhaps.

TESMAN Any cigarettes?

HEDDA No.

TESMAN Good.

[*He goes into the rear room and off to the right.* BRACK *remains sitting, from time to time keeping his eye on* HEDDA *and* LØVBORG.]

LØVBORG [*Quietly, as before.*] Then answer me, Hedda—how could you go and do such a thing?

HEDDA [*Apparently absorbed in the album.*] If you keep talking to me that way, I just won't speak to you.

LØVBORG Not even when we're alone together?

HEDDA No. You can think whatever you want but you can't talk about it.

LØVBORG Ah, I see. It offends your love for George Tesman.

HEDDA [*Glances at him and smiles.*] Love? Don't be absurd.

LØVBORG Not love then either?

HEDDA But even so—nothing unfaithful. I will not allow it.

LØVBORG Answer me just one thing—

HEDDA Shh.

[TESMAN, *with a tray, enters from the rear room.*]

TESMAN Here we are, here come the treats. [*He places the tray on the table.*]

HEDDA Why are you serving us yourself?

TESMAN [*Filling the glasses.*] I have such a good time waiting on you, Hedda.

---

8. This line is interpolated in an attempt to suggest the difference between the informal *du* (thee or thou) and the formal *de* (you) in the Norwegian text. Løvborg has just addressed Hedda in the informal manner and she is warning him not to [translators' note].

HEDDA   But now you've gone and poured two drinks and Mr. Løvborg definitely does not want—

TESMAN   No, but Mrs. Elvsted's coming soon.

HEDDA   Yes, that's right, Mrs. Elvsted.

TESMAN   Did you forget about her?

HEDDA   We were just sitting here so completely wrapped up in these. [*Shows him a picture.*] Do you remember this little village?

TESMAN   Yes, that's the one below the Brenner Pass. We spent the night there—

HEDDA   —and ran into all those lively summer visitors.

TESMAN   Ah yes, that was it. Imagine—if you could have been with us, Eilert, just think. [*He goes in again and sits with* BRACK.]

LØVBORG   Just answer me one thing—

HEDDA   Yes?

LØVBORG   In our relationship—wasn't there any love there either? No trace? Not a glimmer of love in any of it?

HEDDA   I wonder if there really was. For me it was like we were two good comrades, two really good, faithful friends. [*Smiling.*] I remember you were particularly frank and open.

LØVBORG   That's how you wanted it.

HEDDA   When I look back on it, there was something really beautiful—something fascinating, something brave about this secret comradeship, this secret intimacy that no living soul had any idea about.

LØVBORG   Yes, Hedda, that's true isn't it? That was it. When I'd come to your father's in the afternoon—and the General would sit in the window reading his newspaper with his back toward the room—

HEDDA   And us on the corner sofa.

LØVBORG   Always with the same illustrated magazine in front of us.

HEDDA   Instead of an album, yes.

LØVBORG   Yes, Hedda—and when I made all those confessions to you—telling you things about myself that no one else knew in those days. Sat there and told you how I'd lost whole days and nights in drunken frenzy, frenzy that would last for days on end. Ah, Hedda—what kind of power was in you that drew these confessions out of me?

HEDDA   You think it was a power in me?

LØVBORG   Yes. I can't account for it in any other way. And you'd ask me all those ambiguous leading questions—

HEDDA   Which you understood implicitly—

LØVBORG   How did you sit there and question me so fearlessly?

HEDDA   Ambiguously?

LØVBORG   Yes, but fearlessly all the same. Questioning me about—About things like that.

HEDDA   And how could you answer them, Mr. Løvborg?

LØVBORG   Yes, yes. That's just what I don't understand anymore. But now tell me, Hedda, wasn't it love underneath it all? Wasn't that part of it? You wanted to purify me, to cleanse me—when I'd seek you out to make my confessions. Wasn't that it?

HEDDA   No, no, not exactly.

LØVBORG   Then what drove you?

HEDDA   Do you find it so hard to explain that a young girl—when it becomes possible—in secret—

LØVBORG   Yes?

HEDDA   That she wants a glimpse of a world that—

LØVBORG   That—

HEDDA   That is not permitted to her.

LØVBORG   So that was it.

HEDDA   That too, that too—I almost believe it.

LØVBORG   Comrades in a quest for life. So why couldn't it go on?

HEDDA   That was your own fault.

LØVBORG   You broke it off.

HEDDA   Yes, when it looked like reality threatened to spoil the situation. Shame on you, Eilert Løvborg, how could you do violence to your comrade in arms?

LØVBORG   [Clenching his hands together.]   Well, why didn't you do it for real? Why didn't you shoot me dead right then and there like you threatened to?

HEDDA   Oh, I'm much too afraid of scandal.

LØVBORG   Yes, Hedda, underneath it all, you're a coward.

HEDDA   A terrible coward. [Changes her tone.] Lucky for you. And now you've got plenty of consolation up there at the Elvsteds'.

LØVBORG   I know what Thea's confided to you.

HEDDA   And no doubt you've confided to her about us.

LØVBORG   Not one word. She's too stupid to understand things like this.

HEDDA   Stupid?

LØVBORG   In things like this she's stupid.

HEDDA   And I'm a coward. [Leans closer to him without looking him in the eyes and says softly.] Now I'll confide something to you.

LØVBORG   [In suspense.]   What?

HEDDA   My not daring to shoot you—

LØVBORG   Yes?!

HEDDA   —that wasn't my worst cowardice that evening.

LØVBORG   [Stares at her a moment, understands and whispers passionately.] Ah, Hedda Gabler, now I see the hidden reason why we're such comrades. This craving for life in you—

HEDDA   [Quietly, with a sharp glance at him.]   Watch out, don't believe anything of the sort.

[It starts to get dark. The hall door is opened by BERTA.]

HEDDA   [Clapping the album shut and crying out with a smile.]   Ah, finally. Thea, darling, do come in.

[MRS. ELVSTED enters from the hall. She is in evening dress. The door is closed after her.]

HEDDA   [On the sofa, stretching out her arms.]   Thea, my sweet, you can't imagine how I've been expecting you.

[MRS. ELVSTED, in passing, exchanges a greeting with the gentlemen in the inner room, crosses to the table, shakes HEDDA's hand. EILERT LØVBORG has risen. He and MRS. ELVSTED greet each other with a single nod.]

MRS. ELVSTED   Perhaps I should go in and have a word with your husband.

HEDDA   Not at all. Let them sit there. They'll be on their way soon.

MRS. ELVSTED They're leaving?

HEDDA Yes, they're going out on a little binge.

MRS. ELVSTED [*Quickly to* LØVBORG.] You're not?

LØVBORG No.

HEDDA Mr. Løvborg . . . he'll stay here with us.

MRS. ELVSTED [*Takes a chair and sits down beside him.*] It's so nice to be here.

HEDDA No, you don't, little Thea, not there. Come right over here next to me. I want to be in the middle between you.

MRS. ELVSTED All right, whatever you like. [*She goes around the table and sits on the sofa to the right of* HEDDA. LØVBORG *takes his chair again.*]

LØVBORG [*After a brief pause, to* HEDDA.] Isn't she lovely to look at?

HEDDA [*Gently stroking her hair.*] Only to look at?

LØVBORG Yes. We're true comrades, the two of us. We trust each other completely and that's why we can sit here and talk so openly and boldly together.

HEDDA With no ambiguity, Mr. Løvborg.

LØVBORG Well—

MRS. ELVSTED [*Softly, clinging to* HEDDA.] Oh, Hedda, I'm so lucky. Just think, he says I've inspired him too.

HEDDA [*Regards her with a smile.*] No, dear, does he say that?

LØVBORG And she has the courage to take action, Mrs. Tesman.

MRS. ELVSTED Oh God, me, courage?

LØVBORG Tremendous courage when it comes to comradeship.

HEDDA Yes, courage—yes! That's the crucial thing.

LØVBORG Why is that, do you suppose?

HEDDA Because then—maybe—life has a chance to be lived. [*Suddenly changing her tone.*] But now, my dearest Thea. Why don't you treat yourself to a nice cold glass of punch?

MRS. ELVSTED No thank you, I never drink anything like that.

HEDDA Then for you, Mr. Løvborg.

LØVBORG No thank you, not for me either.

MRS. ELVSTED No, not for him either.

HEDDA [*Looking steadily at him.*] But if I insisted.

LØVBORG Doesn't matter.

HEDDA [*Laughing.*] Then I have absolutely no power over you? Ah, poor me.

LØVBORG Not in that area.

HEDDA But seriously now, I really think you should, for your own sake.

MRS. ELVSTED No, Hedda—

LØVBORG Why is that?

HEDDA Or to be more precise, for others' sakes.

LØVBORG Oh?

HEDDA Because otherwise people might get the idea that you don't, deep down inside, feel really bold, really sure of yourself.

LØVBORG Oh, from now on people can think whatever they like.

MRS. ELVSTED Yes, that's right, isn't it.

HEDDA I saw it so clearly with Judge Brack a few minutes ago.

LØVBORG What did you see?

HEDDA That condescending little smile when you didn't dare join them at the table.

LØVBORG   Didn't dare? I'd just rather stay here and talk with you, of course.

MRS. ELVSTED   That's only reasonable, Hedda.

HEDDA   How was the Judge supposed to know that? I saw how he smiled and shot a glance at Tesman when you didn't dare join them in their silly little party.

LØVBORG   Didn't dare. You're saying I don't dare.

HEDDA   Oh, I'm not. But that's how Judge Brack sees it.

LØVBORG   Well let him.

HEDDA   So you won't join them?

LØVBORG   I'm staying here with you and Thea.

MRS. ELVSTED   Yes, Hedda, you can be sure he is.

HEDDA [Smiling and nodding approvingly to LØVBORG.]   What a strong foundation you've got. Principles to last a lifetime. That's what a man ought to have. [Turns to MRS. ELVSTED.] See now, wasn't that what I told you when you came here this morning in such a panic—

LØVBORG [Startled.]   Panic?

MRS. ELVSTED [Terrified.]   Hedda, Hedda, no.

HEDDA   Just see for yourself. No reason at all to come running here in mortal terror. [Changing her tone.] There, now all three of us can be quite jolly.

LØVBORG [Shocked.]   What does this mean, Mrs. Tesman?

MRS. ELVSTED   Oh God, oh God, Hedda. What are you doing? What are you saying?

HEDDA   Keep calm now. That disgusting Judge is sitting there watching you.

LØVBORG   In mortal terror on my account?

MRS. ELVSTED [Quietly wailing.]   Oh, Hedda—

LØVBORG [Looks at her steadily for a moment; his face is drawn.]   So that, then, was how my brave, bold comrade trusted me.

MRS. ELVSTED [Pleading.]   Oh, my dearest friend, listen to me—

LØVBORG [Takes one of the glasses of punch, raises it and says in a low, hoarse voice.]   Your health, Thea. [Empties the glass, takes another.]

MRS. ELVSTED [Softly.]   Oh Hedda, Hedda—how could you want this to happen?

HEDDA   Want it? I want this? Are you mad?

LØVBORG   And your health too, Mrs. Tesman. Thanks for the truth. Long may it live. [He drinks and goes to refill the glass.]

HEDDA [Placing her hand on his arm.]   That's enough for now. Remember, you're going to the party.

MRS. ELVSTED   No, no, no.

HEDDA   Shh. They're watching us.

LØVBORG [Putting down the glass.]   Thea, be honest with me now.

MRS. ELVSTED   Yes.

LØVBORG   Was your husband told that you came here to look for me?

MRS. ELVSTED [Wringing her hands.]   Oh, Hedda, listen to what he's asking me!

LØVBORG   Did he arrange for you to come to town to spy on me? Maybe he put you up to it himself. Aha, that's it. He needed me back in the office again. Or did he just miss me at the card table?

MRS. ELVSTED [Softly moaning.]   Oh, Løvborg, Løvborg—

LØVBORG [*Grabs a glass intending to fill it.*] Skøal to the old Sheriff too.

HEDDA [*Preventing him.*] No more now. Remember, you're going out to read to Tesman.

LØVBORG [*Calmly putting down his glass.*] Thea, that was stupid of me. What I did just now. Taking it like that I mean. Don't be angry with me, my dear, dear comrade. You'll see. Both of you and everyone else will see that even though I once was fallen—now I've raised myself up again, with your help, Thea.

MRS. ELVSTED [*Radiant with joy.*] Oh God be praised.

[*Meanwhile* BRACK *has been looking at his watch. He and* TESMAN *get up and come into the drawing room.*]

BRACK [*Taking his hat and overcoat.*] Well, Mrs. Tesman, our time is up.

HEDDA Yes, it must be.

LØVBORG [*Rising.*] Mine too.

MRS. ELVSTED [*Quietly pleading.*] Løvborg, don't do it.

HEDDA [*Pinching her arm.*] They can hear you.

MRS. ELVSTED [*Crying out faintly.*] Ow.

LØVBORG [*To* BRACK.] You were kind enough to ask me along.

BRACK So you're coming after all.

LØVBORG Yes, thanks.

BRACK I'm delighted.

LØVBORG [*Putting the manuscript packet in his pocket and saying to* TESMAN.] I'd really like you to look at one or two things before I send it off.

TESMAN Just think, that will be splendid. But, Hedda dear, how will you get Mrs. Elvsted home?

HEDDA Oh, there's always a way out.

LØVBORG [*Looking at the ladies.*] Mrs. Elvsted? Well, of course, I'll come back for her. [*Coming closer.*] Around ten o'clock, Mrs. Tesman, will that do?

HEDDA Yes, that will be fine.

TESMAN Well, everything's all right then; but don't expect me that early, Hedda.

HEDDA No dear, you stay just as long—as long as you like.

MRS. ELVSTED [*With suppressed anxiety.*] Mr. Løvborg—I'll stay here until you come.

LØVBORG [*His hat in his hand.*] That's understood.

BRACK All aboard then, the party train's pulling out. Gentlemen, I trust it will be a lively trip, as a certain lovely lady suggested.

HEDDA Ah yes, if only that lovely lady could be there—invisible, of course.

BRACK Why invisible?

HEDDA To hear a little of your liveliness, Judge, uncensored.

BRACK [*Laughing.*] Not recommended for the lovely lady.

TESMAN [*Also laughing.*] You really are the limit, Hedda. Think of it.

BRACK Well, well, my ladies. Good night. Good night.

LØVBORG [*Bowing as he leaves.*] Until ten o'clock, then.

[BRACK, LØVBORG *and* TESMAN *leave through the hall door. At the same time* BERTA *comes in from the rear room with a lighted lamp which she places on the drawing room table, going out the way she came in.*]

MRS. ELVSTED [*Has gotten up and wanders uneasily about the room.*] Oh, Hedda, where is all this going?

HEDDA Ten o'clock—then he'll appear. I see him before me with vine leaves in his hair,[9] burning bright and bold.

MRS. ELVSTED Yes, if only it could be like that.

HEDDA And then you'll see—then he'll have power over himself again. Then he'll be a free man for the rest of his days.

MRS. ELVSTED Oh God yes—if only he'd come back just the way you see him.

HEDDA He'll come back just that way and no other. [Gets up and comes closer.] You can doubt him as much as you like. I believe in him. And so we'll see—

MRS. ELVSTED There's something behind this, something else you're trying to do.

HEDDA Yes, there is. Just once in my life I want to help shape someone's destiny.

MRS. ELVSTED Don't you do that already?

HEDDA I don't and I never have.

MRS. ELVSTED Not even your husband?

HEDDA Oh yes, that was a real bargain. Oh, if you could only understand how destitute I am while you get to be so rich. [She passionately throws her arms around her.] I think I'll burn your hair off after all.

MRS. ELVSTED Let me go, let me go. I'm afraid of you.

BERTA [In the doorway.] Tea is ready in the dining room, Madam.

HEDDA Good. We're on our way.

MRS. ELVSTED No, no, no! I'd rather go home alone! Right now!

HEDDA Nonsense! First you're going to have some tea, you little bubble-head, and then—at ten o'clock—Eilert Løvborg—with vine leaves in his hair! [She pulls MRS. ELVSTED toward the doorway almost by force.]

Act 3

The room at the TESMANS'. The curtains are drawn across the center door-way and also across the glass door. The lamp covered with a shade burns low on the table. In the stove, with its door standing open, there has been a fire that is almost burned out.

[MRS. ELVSTED, wrapped in a large shawl and with her feet on a footstool, sits sunk back in an armchair. HEDDA, fully dressed, lies sleeping on the sofa with a rug over her.]

MRS. ELVSTED [After a pause suddenly straightens herself in the chair and listens intently. Then she sinks back wearily and moans softly.] Still not back . . . Oh God, oh God . . . Still not back.

[BERTA enters tiptoeing carefully through the hall doorway; she has a letter in her hand.]

MRS. ELVSTED Ah—did someone come?

BERTA Yes, a girl came by just now with this letter.

---

9. Like Bacchus, the Greek god of wine, and his followers.

MRS. ELVSTED [*Quickly stretching out her hand.*] A letter? Let me have it.

BERTA No ma'am, it's for the doctor.

MRS. ELVSTED Oh.

BERTA It was Miss Tesman's maid who brought it. I'll put it on the table here.

MRS. ELVSTED Yes, do that.

BERTA [*Puts down the letter.*] I'd better put out the lamp; it's starting to smoke.

MRS. ELVSTED Yes, put it out. It'll be light soon anyway.

BERTA [*Putting out the light.*] Oh, ma'am, it's already light.

MRS. ELVSTED So, morning and still not back—!

BERTA Oh, dear Lord—I knew all along it would go like this.

MRS. ELVSTED You knew?

BERTA Yes, when I saw a certain person was back in town. And then when he went off with them—oh we'd heard plenty about that gentleman.

MRS. ELVSTED Don't speak so loud, you'll wake your mistress.

BERTA [*Looks over to the sofa and sighs.*] No, dear Lord—let her sleep, poor thing. Shouldn't I build the stove up a little more?

MRS. ELVSTED Not for me, thanks.

BERTA Well, well then. [*She goes out quietly through the hall doorway.*]

HEDDA [*Awakened by the closing door, looks up.*] What's that?

MRS. ELVSTED Only the maid.

HEDDA [*Looking around.*] In here—! Oh, now I remember. [*Straightens up, stretches sitting on the sofa and rubs her eyes.*] What time is it, Thea?

MRS. ELVSTED [*Looks at her watch.*] It's after seven.

HEDDA What time did Tesman get in?

MRS. ELVSTED He hasn't.

HEDDA Still?

MRS. ELVSTED [*Getting up.*] No one's come back.

HEDDA And we sat here waiting and watching until almost four.

MRS. ELVSTED [*Wringing her hands.*] Waiting for him!

HEDDA [*Yawning and speaking with her hand over her mouth.*] Oh yes— we could have saved ourselves the trouble.

MRS. ELVSTED Did you finally manage to sleep?

HEDDA Yes, I think I slept quite well. Did you?

MRS. ELVSTED Not a wink. I couldn't, Hedda. It was just impossible for me.

HEDDA [*Gets up and goes over to her.*] Now, now, now. There's nothing to worry about. I know perfectly well how it all turned out.

MRS. ELVSTED Yes, what do you think? Can you tell me?

HEDDA Well, of course they dragged it out dreadfully up at Judge Brack's.

MRS. ELVSTED Oh God yes—that must be true. But all the same—

HEDDA And then you see, Tesman didn't want to come home and create a fuss by ringing the bell in the middle of the night. [*Laughing.*] He probably didn't want to show himself either right after a wild party like that.

MRS. ELVSTED For goodness sake—where would he have gone?

HEDDA Well, naturally, he went over to his aunt's and laid himself down to sleep there. They still have his old room standing ready for him.

MRS. ELVSTED   No, he's not with them. A letter just came for him from Miss Tesman. It's over there.

HEDDA   Oh? [*Looks at the inscription.*] Yes, that's Aunt Julie's hand all right. So then, he's still over at Judge Brack's and Eilert Løvborg—he's sitting—reading aloud with vine leaves in his hair.

MRS. ELVSTED   Oh, Hedda, you don't even believe what you're saying.

HEDDA   You are such a little noodlehead, Thea.

MRS. ELVSTED   Yes, unfortunately I probably am.

HEDDA   And you look like you're dead on your feet.

MRS. ELVSTED   Yes, I am. Dead on my feet.

HEDDA   And so now you're going to do what I tell you. You'll go into my room and lie down on my bed.

MRS. ELVSTED   Oh no, no—I couldn't get to sleep anyway.

HEDDA   Yes, you certainly will.

MRS. ELVSTED   But your husband's bound to be home any time now and I've got to find out right away—

HEDDA   I'll tell you as soon as he comes.

MRS. ELVSTED   Promise me that, Hedda?

HEDDA   Yes, that you can count on. Now just go in and sleep for a while.

MRS. ELVSTED   Thanks. At least I'll give it a try. [*She goes in through the back room.*]

[HEDDA *goes over to the glass door and draws back the curtains. Full daylight floods the room. She then takes a small hand mirror from the writing table, looks in it and arranges her hair. Then she goes to the hall door and presses the bell. Soon after* BERTA *enters the doorway.*]

BERTA   Did Madam want something?

HEDDA   Yes, build up the stove a little bit. I'm freezing in here.

BERTA   Lord, in no time at all it'll be warm in here. [*She rakes the embers and puts a log inside. She stands and listens.*] There's the front doorbell, Madam.

HEDDA   So, go answer it. I'll take care of the stove myself.

BERTA   It'll be burning soon enough. [*She goes out through the hall door.*]

[HEDDA *kneels on the footstool and puts more logs into the stove. After a brief moment,* GEORGE TESMAN *comes in from the hall. He looks weary and rather serious. He creeps on tiptoes toward the doorway and is about to slip through the curtains.*]

HEDDA   [*By the stove, without looking up.*]   Good morning.

TESMAN   [*Turning around.*]   Hedda. [*Comes nearer.*] What in the world— Up so early, hm?

HEDDA   Yes, up quite early today.

TESMAN   And here I was so sure you'd still be in bed. Just think, Hedda.

HEDDA   Not so loud. Mrs. Elvsted's lying down in my room.

TESMAN   Has Mrs. Elvsted been here all night?

HEDDA   Yes. No one came to pick her up.

TESMAN   No, no, they couldn't have.

HEDDA   [*Shuts the door of the stove and gets up.*]   So, did you have a jolly time at the Judge's?

TESMAN   Were you worried about me?

HEDDA   No, that would never occur to me. I asked if you had a good time.

TESMAN Yes, I really did, for once, in a manner of speaking—Mostly in the beginning, I'd say. We'd arrived an hour early. How about that? And Brack had so much to get ready. But then Eilert read to me.

HEDDA [*Sits at the right of the table.*] So, tell me.

TESMAN Hedda, you can't imagine what this new work will be like. It's one of the most brilliant things ever written, no doubt about it. Think of that.

HEDDA Yes, yes, but that's not what I'm interested in.

TESMAN But I have to confess something, Hedda. After he read—something horrible came over me.

HEDDA Something horrible?

TESMAN I sat there envying Eilert for being able to write like that. Think of it, Hedda.

HEDDA Yes, yes, I'm thinking.

TESMAN And then, that whole time, knowing that he—even with all the incredible powers at his command—is still beyond redemption.

HEDDA You mean he's got more of life's courage in him than the others?

TESMAN No, for heaven sakes—he just has no control over his pleasures.

HEDDA And what happened then—at the end?

TESMAN Well, Hedda, I guess you'd have to say it was a bacchanal.

HEDDA Did he have vine leaves in his hair?

TESMAN Vine leaves? No, I didn't see anything like that. But he did make a long wild speech for the woman who had inspired him in his work. Yes—that's how he put it.

HEDDA Did he name her?

TESMAN No, he didn't, but I can only guess that it must be Mrs. Elvsted. Wouldn't you say?

HEDDA Hmm—where did you leave him?

TESMAN On the way back. Most of our group broke up at the same time and Brack came along with us to get a little fresh air. And you see, we agreed to follow Eilert home because—well—he was so far gone.

HEDDA He must have been.

TESMAN But here's the strangest part, Hedda! Or maybe I should say the saddest. I'm almost ashamed for Eilert's sake—to tell you—

HEDDA So?

TESMAN There we were walking along, you see, and I happened to drop back a bit, just for a couple of minutes, you understand.

HEDDA Yes, yes, good Lord but—

TESMAN And then when I was hurrying to catch up—can you guess what I found in the gutter, hm?

HEDDA How can I possibly guess?

TESMAN Don't ever tell a soul, Hedda. Do you hear? Promise me that for Eilert's sake. [*Pulls a package out of his coat pocket.*] Just think—this is what I found.

HEDDA That's the package he had with him here yesterday, isn't it?

TESMAN That's it. His precious, irreplaceable manuscript—all of it. And he's lost it—without even noticing it. Oh just think, Hedda—the pity of it—

HEDDA Well, why didn't you give it back to him right away?

TESMAN   Oh, I didn't dare do that—The condition he was in—

HEDDA   You didn't tell any of the others that you found it either?

TESMAN   Absolutely not. I couldn't, you see, for Eilert's sake.

HEDDA   So nobody knows you have Eilert's manuscript? Nobody at all?

TESMAN   No. And they mustn't find out either.

HEDDA   What did you talk to him about later?

TESMAN   I didn't get a chance to talk to him any more. We got to the city limits, and he and a couple of the others went a different direction. Just think—

HEDDA   Aha, they must have followed him home then.

TESMAN   Yes, I suppose so. Brack also went his way.

HEDDA   And, in the meantime, what became of the bacchanal?

TESMAN   Well, I and some of the others followed one of the revelers up to his place and had morning coffee with him—or maybe we should call it morning-after coffee, hm? Now, I'll rest a bit—and as soon as I think Eilert has managed to sleep it off, poor man, then I've got to go over to him with this.

HEDDA   [*Reaching out for the envelope.*]   No, don't give it back. Not yet, I mean. Let me read it first.

TESMAN   Oh no.

HEDDA   Oh, for God's sake.

TESMAN   I don't dare do that.

HEDDA   You don't dare?

TESMAN   No, you can imagine how completely desperate he'll be when he wakes up and realizes he can't find the manuscript. He's got no copy of it. He said so himself.

HEDDA   [*Looks searchingly at him.*]   Couldn't it be written again?

TESMAN   No, I don't believe that could ever be done because the inspiration— you see—

HEDDA   Yes, yes—That's the thing, isn't it? [*Casually.*] But, oh yes—there's a letter here for you.

TESMAN   No, think of that.

HEDDA   [*Hands it to him.*]   It came early this morning.

TESMAN   From Aunt Julie, Hedda. What can it be? [*Puts the manuscript on the other stool, opens the letter and jumps up.*] Oh Hedda—poor Aunt Rina's almost breathing her last.

HEDDA   It's only what's expected.

TESMAN   And if I want to see her one more time, I've got to hurry. I'll charge over there right away.

HEDDA   [*Suppressing a smile.*]   You'll charge?

TESMAN   Oh, Hedda dearest—if you could just bring yourself to follow me. Just think.

HEDDA   [*Rises and says wearily and dismissively.*]   No, no. Don't ask me to do anything like that. I won't look at sickness and death. Let me stay free from everything ugly.

TESMAN   Oh, good Lord, then—[*Darting around.*] My hat—? My overcoat—? Ah, in the hall—Oh, I hope I'm not too late, Hedda, hm?

HEDDA   Then charge right over—

[BERTA *appears in the hallway.*]

BERTA   Judge Brack is outside.

HEDDA   Ask him to come in.

TESMAN   At a time like this! No, I can't possibly deal with him now.

HEDDA   But I can. [*To* BERTA.] Ask the Judge in.

[BERTA *goes out.*]

HEDDA [*In a whisper.*]   The package, Tesman. [*She snatches it off the stool.*]

TESMAN   Yes, give it to me.

HEDDA   No, I'll hide it until you get back.

[*She goes over to the writing table and sticks the package in the bookcase.* TESMAN *stands flustered, and can't get his gloves on.* BRACK *enters through the hall doorway.*]

HEDDA [*Nodding to him.*]   Well, you're an early bird.

BRACK   Yes, wouldn't you say. [*To* TESMAN.] You're going out?

TESMAN   Yes, I've got to go over to my aunt's. Just think, the poor dear is dying.

BRACK   Good Lord, is she really? Then don't let me hold you up for even a moment, at a time like this—

TESMAN   Yes, I really must run—Good-bye. Good-bye. [*He hurries through the hall doorway.*]

HEDDA [*Approaches.*]   So, things were livelier than usual at your place last night, Judge.

BRACK   Oh yes, so much so that I haven't even been able to change clothes, Mrs. Hedda.

HEDDA   You too.

BRACK   As you see. But, what has Tesman been telling you about last night's adventures?

HEDDA   Oh, just some boring things. He went someplace to drink coffee.

BRACK   I've already looked into the coffee party. Eilert Løvborg wasn't part of that group, I presume.

HEDDA   No, they followed him home before that.

BRACK   Tesman too?

HEDDA   No, but a couple of others, he said.

BRACK [*Smiles.*]   George Tesman is a very naïve soul, Mrs. Hedda.

HEDDA   God knows, he is. But is there something more behind this?

BRACK   I'd have to say so.

HEDDA   Well then, Judge, let's be seated. Then you can speak freely. [*She sits to the left side of the table,* BRACK *at the long side near her.*] Well, then—

BRACK   I had certain reasons for keeping track of my guests—or, more precisely, some of my guests' movements last night.

HEDDA   For example, Eilert Løvborg?

BRACK   Yes, indeed.

HEDDA   Now I'm hungry for more.

BRACK   Do you know where he and a couple of the others spent the rest of the night, Mrs. Hedda?

HEDDA   Why don't you tell me, if it can be told.

BRACK   Oh, it's certainly worth the telling. It appears that they found their way into a particularly animated soirée.[1]

---

1. "Evening party" (French).

HEDDA   A lively one?

BRACK   The liveliest.

HEDDA   Tell me more, Judge.

BRACK   Løvborg had received an invitation earlier—I knew all about that. But he declined because, as you know, he's made himself into a new man.

HEDDA   Up at the Elvsteds', yes. But he went just the same?

BRACK   Well, you see, Mrs. Hedda—unfortunately, the spirit really seized him at my place last evening.

HEDDA   Yes, I hear he was quite inspired.

BRACK   Inspired to a rather powerful degree. And so, he started to reconsider, I assume, because we men, alas, are not always so true to our principles as we ought to be.

HEDDA   Present company excepted, Judge Brack. So, Løvborg—?

BRACK   Short and sweet—He ended up at the salon of a certain Miss Diana.

HEDDA   Miss Diana?

BRACK   Yes, it was Miss Diana's soirée for a select circle of ladies and their admirers.

HEDDA   Is she a redhead?

BRACK   Exactly.

HEDDA   A sort of a—singer?

BRACK   Oh, yes—She's also that. And a mighty huntress—of men, Mrs. Hedda. You must have heard of her. Eilert Løvborg was one of her most strenuous admirers—in his better days.

HEDDA   And how did all this end?

BRACK   Apparently less amicably than it began. Miss Diana, after giving him the warmest of welcomes, soon turned to assault and battery.

HEDDA   Against Løvborg?

BRACK   Oh, yes. He accused her, or one of her ladies, of robbing him. He insisted that his pocketbook was missing, along with some other things. In short, he seems to have created a dreadful spectacle.

HEDDA   And what did that lead to?

BRACK   A regular brawl between both the men and the women. Luckily the police finally got there.

HEDDA   The police too?

BRACK   Yes. It's going to be quite a costly little romp for Eilert Løvborg. What a madman.

HEDDA   Well!

BRACK   Apparently, he resisted arrest. It seems he struck one of the officers on the ear, and ripped his uniform to shreds, so he had to go to the police station.

HEDDA   How do you know all this?

BRACK   From the police themselves.

HEDDA   [Gazing before her.]   So, that's how it ended? He had no vine leaves in his hair.

BRACK   Vine leaves, Mrs. Hedda?

HEDDA   [Changing her tone.]   Tell me now, Judge, why do you go around snooping and spying on Eilert Løvborg?

BRACK   For starters, I'm not a completely disinterested party—especially if the hearing uncovers the fact that he came straight from my place.

HEDDA   There's going to be a hearing?

BRACK   You can count on it. Be that as it may, however—My real concern was my duty as a friend of the house to inform you and Tesman of Løvborg's nocturnal adventures.

HEDDA   Why, Judge Brack?

BRACK   Well, I have an active suspicion that he'll try to use you as a kind of screen.

HEDDA   Oh! What makes you think that?

BRACK   Good God—we're not that blind, Mrs. Hedda. Wait and see. This Mrs. Elvsted—she won't be in such a hurry to leave town again.

HEDDA   If there's anything going on between those two, there's plenty of places they can meet.

BRACK   Not one single home. Every respectable house will be closed to Eilert Løvborg from now on.

HEDDA   And mine should be too—Is that what you're saying?

BRACK   Yes. I have to admit it would be more than painful for me if this man secured a foothold here. If this—utterly superfluous—and intrusive individual—were to force himself into—

HEDDA   Into the triangle?

BRACK   Precisely! It would leave me without a home.

HEDDA   [Looks smilingly at him.]   I see—The one cock of the walk—That's your goal.

BRACK   [Slowly nodding and dropping his voice.]   Yes, that's my goal. And it's a goal that I'll fight for—with every means at my disposal.

HEDDA   [Her smile fading.]   You're really a dangerous man, aren't you—when push comes to shove.

BRACK   You think so?

HEDDA   Yes, I'm starting to. And that's all right—just as long as you don't have any kind of hold on me.

BRACK   [Laughing ambiguously.]   Yes, Mrs. Hedda—you might be right about that. Of course, then, who knows whether I might not find some way or other—

HEDDA   Now listen, Judge Brack! That sounds like you're threatening me.

BRACK   [Gets up.]   Oh, far from it. A triangle, you see—is best fortified by free defenders.

HEDDA   I think so too.

BRACK   Well, I've had my say so I should be getting back. Good-bye, Mrs. Hedda. [He goes toward the glass doors.]

HEDDA   Out through the garden?

BRACK   Yes, it's shorter for me.

HEDDA   And then, it's also the back way.

BRACK   That's true. I have nothing against back ways. Sometimes they can be very piquant.

HEDDA   When there's sharpshooting.

BRACK   [In the doorway, laughing at her.]   Oh, no—you never shoot your tame cocks.

HEDDA   [Also laughing.]   Oh, no, especially when there's only one—

[Laughing and nodding they take their farewells. He leaves. She closes the door after him. HEDDA stands for a while, serious, looking out. Then she goes and peers through the curtains in the back wall. She goes to the writ-

ing table, takes Løvborg's package from the bookcase, and is about to leaf through it. BERTA's voice, raised in indignation, is heard out in the hall. HEDDA turns and listens. She quickly locks the package in the drawer and sets the key on the writing table. EILERT LØVBORG, wearing his overcoat and carrying his hat, bursts through the hall doorway. He looks somewhat confused and excited.]

LØVBORG [*Turned toward the hallway.*]   And I'm telling you, I've got to go in! And that's that! [*He closes the door, sees HEDDA, controls himself immediately, and bows.*]

HEDDA [*By the writing table.*]   Well, Mr. Løvborg, it's pretty late to be calling for Thea.

LØVBORG   Or a little early to be calling on you. I apologize.

HEDDA   How do you know that she's still here?

LØVBORG   I went to where she was staying. They told me she'd been out all night.

HEDDA [*Goes to the table.*]   Did you notice anything special when they told you that?

LØVBORG [*Looks inquiringly at her.*]   Notice anything?

HEDDA   I mean—did they seem to have any thought on the subject—one way or the other?

LØVBORG [*Suddenly understanding.*]   Oh, of course, it's true. I'm dragging her down with me. Still, I didn't notice anything. Tesman isn't up yet, I suppose?

HEDDA   No, I don't think so.

LØVBORG   When did he get home?

HEDDA   Very late.

LØVBORG   Did he tell you anything?

HEDDA   Yes. I heard Judge Brack's was very lively.

LØVBORG   Nothing else?

HEDDA   No, I don't think so. I was terribly tired, though—
[MRS. ELVSTED *comes in through the curtains at the back.*]

MRS. ELVSTED [*Runs toward him.*]   Oh, Løvborg—at last!

LØVBORG   Yes, at last, and too late.

MRS. ELVSTED [*Looking anxiously at him.*]   What's too late?

LØVBORG   Everything's too late. I'm finished.

MRS. ELVSTED   Oh no, no—Don't say that!

LØVBORG   You'll say it too, when you've heard—

MRS. ELVSTED   I won't listen—

HEDDA   Shall I leave you two alone?

LØVBORG   No, stay—You too, I beg you.

MRS. ELVSTED   But I won't listen to anything you tell me.

LØVBORG   I don't want to talk about last night.

MRS. ELVSTED   What is it, then?

LØVBORG   We've got to go our separate ways.

MRS. ELVSTED   Separate!

HEDDA [*Involuntarily.*]   I knew it!

LØVBORG   Because I have no more use for you, Thea.

MRS. ELVSTED   You can stand there and say that! No more use for me! Can't I help you now, like I did before? Won't we go on working together?

LØVBORG   I don't plan to work any more.

MRS. ELVSTED [*Desperately.*]   Then what do I have to live for?

LØVBORG   Just try to live your life as if you'd never known me.

MRS. ELVSTED   I can't do that.

LØVBORG   Try, Thea. Try, if you can. Go back home.

MRS. ELVSTED [*Defiantly.*]   Where you are, that's where I want to be. I won't let myself be just driven off like this. I want to stay at your side—be with you when the book comes out.

HEDDA [*Half aloud, tensely.*]   Ah, the book—Yes.

LØVBORG [*Looking at her.*]   Mine and Thea's, because that's what it is.

MRS. ELVSTED   Yes, that's what I feel it is. That's why I have a right to be with you when it comes out. I want to see you covered in honor and glory again, and the joy. I want to share that with you too.

LØVBORG   Thea—our book's never coming out.

HEDDA   Ah!

MRS. ELVSTED   Never coming out?

LØVBORG   It can't ever come out.

MRS. ELVSTED [*In anxious foreboding.*]   Løvborg, what have you done with the manuscript?

HEDDA [*Looking intently at him.*]   Yes, the manuscript—?

MRS. ELVSTED   What have you—?

LØVBORG   Oh, Thea, don't ask me that.

MRS. ELVSTED   Yes, yes, I've got to know. I have the right to know.

LØVBORG   The manuscript—all right then, the manuscript—I've ripped it up into a thousand pieces.

MRS. ELVSTED [*Screams.*]   Oh no, no!

HEDDA [*Involuntarily.*]   But that's just not—!

LØVBORG [*Looking at her.*]   Not true, you think?

HEDDA [*Controls herself.*]   All right then. Of course it is, if you say so. It sounds so ridiculous.

LØVBORG   But it's true, just the same.

MRS. ELVSTED [*Wringing her hands.*]   Oh God—oh God, Hedda. Torn his own work to pieces.

LØVBORG   I've torn my own life to pieces. I might as well tear up my life's work too—

MRS. ELVSTED   And you did that last night!

LØVBORG   Yes. Do you hear me? A thousand pieces. Scattered them all over the fjord.[2] Way out where there's pure salt water. Let them drift in it. Drift with the current in the wind. Then, after a while, they'll sink. Deeper and deeper. Like me, Thea.

MRS. ELVSTED   You know, Løvborg, all this with the book—? For the rest of my life, it will be just like you'd killed a little child.

LØVBORG   You're right. Like murdering a child.

MRS. ELVSTED   But then, how could you—! That child was partly mine, too.

HEDDA [*Almost inaudibly.*]   Ah, the child—

MRS. ELVSTED [*Sighs heavily.*]   So it's finished? All right, Hedda, now I'm going.

2. "Inlet of the sea" (Norwegian).

HEDDA You're not going back?

MRS. ELVSTED Oh, I don't know what I'm going to do. I can't see anything out in front of me. [*She goes out through the hall doorway.*]

HEDDA [*Standing a while, waiting.*] Don't you want to see her home, Mr. Løvborg?

LØVBORG Through the streets? So that people can get a good look at us together?

HEDDA I don't know what else happened to you last night but if it's so completely beyond redemption—

LØVBORG It won't stop there. I know that much. And I can't bring myself to live that kind of life again either. Not again. Once I had the courage to live life to the fullest, to break every rule. But she's taken that out of me.

HEDDA [*Staring straight ahead.*] That sweet little fool has gotten hold of a human destiny. [*Looks at him.*] And you're so heartless to her.

LØVBORG Don't call it heartless.

HEDDA To go and destroy the thing that has filled her soul for this whole long, long time. You don't call that heartless?

LØVBORG I can tell you the truth, Hedda.

HEDDA The truth?

LØVBORG First, promise me—Give me your word that Thea will never find out what I'm about to confide to you.

HEDDA You have my word.

LØVBORG Good. Then I'll tell you—What I stood here and described—It wasn't true.

HEDDA About the manuscript?

LØVBORG Yes. I haven't ripped it up. I didn't throw it in the fjord, either.

HEDDA No, well—so—Where is it?

LØVBORG I've destroyed it just the same. Utterly and completely, Hedda!

HEDDA I don't understand any of this.

LØVBORG Thea said that what I'd done seemed to her like murdering a child.

HEDDA Yes, she did.

LØVBORG But killing his child—that's not the worst thing a father can do to it.

HEDDA Not the worst?

LØVBORG No. And the worst—that is what I wanted to spare Thea from hearing.

HEDDA And what is the worst?

LØVBORG Imagine, Hedda, a man—in the very early hours of the morning—after a wild night of debauchery, came home to the mother of his child and said, "Listen—I've been here and there to this place and that place, and I had our child with me in this place and that place. And the child got away from me. Just got away. The devil knows whose hands it's fallen into, who's got a hold of it."

HEDDA Well—when you get right down to it—it's only a book—

LØVBORG All of Thea's soul was in that book.

HEDDA Yes, I can see that.

LØVBORG And so, you must also see that there's no future for her and me.

HEDDA So, what will your road be now?

LØVBORG   None. Only to see to it that I put an end to it all. The sooner the better.

HEDDA [*Comes a step closer.*]   Eilert Løvborg—Listen to me now—Can you see to it that—that when you do it, you bathe it in beauty?

LØVBORG   In beauty? [*Smiles.*] With vine leaves in my hair, as you used to imagine?

HEDDA   Ah, no. No vine leaves—I don't believe in them any longer. But in beauty, yes! For once! Good-bye. You've got to go now. And don't come here any more.

LØVBORG   Good-bye, Mrs. Tesman. And give my regards to George Tesman. [*He is about to leave.*]

HEDDA   No, wait! Take a souvenir to remember me by.

    [*She goes over to the writing table, opens the drawer and the pistol case. She returns to* LØVBORG *with one of the pistols.*]

LØVBORG [*Looks at her.*]   That's the souvenir?

HEDDA [*Nodding slowly.*]   Do you recognize it? It was aimed at you once.

LØVBORG   You should have used it then.

HEDDA   Here, you use it now.

LØVBORG [*Puts the pistol in his breast pocket.*]   Thanks.

HEDDA   In beauty, Eilert Løvborg. Promise me that.

LØVBORG   Good-bye, Hedda Gabler. [*He goes out the hall doorway.*]

    [HEDDA *listens a moment at the door. Afterward, she goes to the writing table and takes out the package with the manuscript, looks inside the wrapper, pulls some of the pages half out and looks at them. She then takes it all over to the armchair by the stove and sits down. She has the package in her lap. Soon after she opens the stove door and then opens the package.*]

HEDDA [*Throws one of the sheets into the fire and whispers to herself.*]   Now, I'm burning your child, Thea—You with your curly hair. [*Throws a few more sheets into the fire.*] Your child and Eilert Løvborg's. [*Throws in the rest.*] Now I'm burning—burning the child.

Act 4

The same room at the TESMANS'. *It is evening. The drawing room is in darkness. The rear room is lit with a hanging lamp over the table. The curtains are drawn across the glass door.*

    [HEDDA, *dressed in black, wanders up and down in the darkened room. Then she goes into the rear room, and over to the left side. Some chords are heard from the piano. Then she emerges again, and goes into the drawing room.* BERTA *comes in from the right of the rear room, with a lighted lamp, which she places on the table in front of the sofa, in the salon. Her eyes show signs of crying, and she has black ribbons on her cap. She goes quietly and carefully to the right.* HEDDA *goes over to the glass door, draws the curtains aside a little, and stares out into the darkness. Soon after,* MISS TESMAN *enters from the hallway dressed in black with a hat and a veil.* HEDDA *goes over to her and shakes her hand.*]

MISS TESMAN   Yes, here I am, Hedda—in mourning black. My poor sister's struggle is over at last.

HEDDA   As you can see, I've already heard. Tesman sent me a note.

MISS TESMAN   Yes, he promised he would but I thought I should bring the news myself. This news of death into this house of life.

HEDDA   That was very kind of you.

MISS TESMAN   Ah, Rina shouldn't have left us right now. Hedda's house is no place for sorrow at a time like this.

HEDDA [*Changing the subject.*]   She died peacefully, Miss Tesman?

MISS TESMAN   Yes, so gently—Such a peaceful release. And she was happy beyond words that she got to see George once more and could say a proper good-bye to him. Is it possible he's not home yet?

HEDDA   No. He wrote saying I shouldn't expect him too early. But, please sit down.

MISS TESMAN   No, thank you, my dear—blessed Hedda. I'd like to, but I have so little time. She'll be dressed and arranged the best that I can. She'll look really splendid when she goes to her grave.

HEDDA   Can I help you with anything?

MISS TESMAN   Oh, don't even think about it. These kinds of things aren't for Hedda Tesman's hands or her thoughts either. Not at this time. No, no.

HEDDA   Ah—thoughts—Now they're not so easy to master—

MISS TESMAN [*Continuing.*]   Yes, dear God, that's how this world goes. Over at my house we'll be sewing a linen shroud for Aunt Rina, and here there will be sewing too, but of a whole different kind, praise God.

[GEORGE TESMAN *enters through a hall door.*]

HEDDA   Well, it's good you're finally here.

TESMAN   You here, Aunt Julie, with Hedda. Just think.

MISS TESMAN   I was just about to go, my dear boy. Well. Did you manage to finish everything you promised to?

TESMAN   No, I'm afraid I've forgotten half of it. I have to run over there tomorrow again. Today my brain is just so confused. I can't keep hold of two thoughts in a row.

MISS TESMAN   George, my dear, you mustn't take it like that.

TESMAN   Oh? How should I take it, do you think?

MISS TESMAN   You must be joyful in your sorrow. You must be glad for what has happened, just as I am.

TESMAN   Ah, yes. You're thinking of Aunt Rina.

HEDDA   You'll be lonely now, Miss Tesman.

MISS TESMAN   For the first few days, yes. But that won't last long, I hope. Our sainted Rina's little room won't stand empty. That much I know.

TESMAN   Really? Who'll be moving in there, hm?

MISS TESMAN   Oh, there's always some poor invalid or other who needs care and attention, unfortunately.

HEDDA   You'd really take on a cross like that again?

MISS TESMAN   Cross? God forgive you child. It's not a cross for me.

HEDDA   But a complete stranger—

MISS TESMAN   It's easy to make friends with sick people. And I so badly need someone to live for. Well, God be praised and thanked—there'll be a thing or two to keep an old aunt busy here in this house soon enough.

HEDDA   Oh, please don't think about us.

TESMAN   Yes. The three of us could be quite cozy here if only—

HEDDA   If only—?

TESMAN [*Uneasily.*] Oh, it's nothing. Everything'll be fine. Let's hope, hm?

MISS TESMAN Well, well, you two have plenty to talk about, I'm sure. [*Smiling.*] And Hedda may have something to tell you, George. Now it's home to Rina. [*Turning in the doorway.*] Dear Lord, isn't it strange to think about. Now Rina's both with me and our sainted Joseph.

TESMAN Yes, just think, Aunt Julie, hm?

[MISS TESMAN *leaves through the hall door.*]

HEDDA [*Follows* TESMAN *with cold, searching eyes.*] I think all this has hit you harder than your aunt.

TESMAN Oh, it's not just this death. It's Eilert I'm worried about.

HEDDA [*Quickly.*] Any news?

TESMAN I wanted to run to him this afternoon and tell him that his manuscript was safe—in good hands.

HEDDA Oh? Did you find him?

TESMAN No, he wasn't home. But later I met Mrs. Elvsted, and she told me he'd been here early this morning.

HEDDA Yes, just after you left.

TESMAN And apparently he said that he'd ripped the manuscript up into a thousand pieces, hm?

HEDDA That's what he said.

TESMAN But, good God, he must have been absolutely crazy. So you didn't dare give it back to him, Hedda?

HEDDA No, he didn't get it back.

TESMAN But, you told him we had it?

HEDDA No. [*Quickly.*] Did you tell Mrs. Elvsted?

TESMAN No, I didn't want to. But you should have told him. What would happen if in his desperation he went and did something to himself? Let me have the manuscript, Hedda. I'll run it over to him right away. Where did you put it?

HEDDA [*Cold and impassively leaning on the armchair.*] I don't have it any more.

TESMAN Don't have it! What in the world do you mean?

HEDDA I burned it up—every page.

TESMAN [*Leaps up in terror.*] Burned? Burned? Eilert's manuscript!

HEDDA Don't shout like that. The maid will hear you.

TESMAN Burned! But good God—! No, no, no—That's absolutely impossible.

HEDDA Yes, but all the same it's true.

TESMAN Do you have any idea what you've done, Hedda? That's—that's criminal appropriation of lost property. Think about that. Yes, just ask Judge Brack, then you'll see.

HEDDA Then it's probably wise for you not to talk about it, isn't it? To the Judge or anyone else.

TESMAN How could you have gone and done something so appalling? What came over you? Answer me that, Hedda, hm?

HEDDA [*Suppressing an almost imperceptible smile.*] I did it for your sake, George.

TESMAN My sake?

HEDDA Remember you came home this morning and talked about how he had read to you?

TESMAN Yes, yes.

HEDDA You confessed that you envied him.

TESMAN Good God, I didn't mean it literally.

HEDDA Nevertheless, I couldn't stand the idea that someone would over-shadow you.

TESMAN [*Exclaiming between doubt and joy.*] Hedda—Oh, is this true?—What you're saying?—Yes, but. Yes, but. I never noticed that you loved me this way before. Think of that!

HEDDA Well, you need to know—that at a time like this—[*Violently breaking off.*] No, no—go and ask your Aunt Julie. She'll provide all the details.

TESMAN Oh, I almost think I understand you, Hedda. [*Clasps his hands together.*] No, good God—Can it be, hm?

HEDDA Don't shout like that. The maid can hear you.

TESMAN [*Laughing in extraordinary joy.*] The maid! Oh, Hedda, you are priceless. The maid—why it's—why it's Berta. I'll go tell Berta myself.

HEDDA [*Clenching her hands as if frantic.*] Oh, I'm dying—Dying of all this.

TESMAN All what, Hedda, what?

HEDDA [*Coldly controlled again.*] All this—absurdity—George.

TESMAN Absurdity? I'm so incredibly happy. Even so, maybe I shouldn't say anything to Berta.

HEDDA Oh yes, go ahead. Why not?

TESMAN No, no. Not right now. But Aunt Julie, yes, absolutely. And then, you're calling me George. Just think. Oh, Aunt Julie will be so happy—so happy.

HEDDA When she hears I've burned Eilert Løvborg's manuscript for your sake?

TESMAN No, no, you're right. All this with the manuscript. No. Of course, nobody can find out about that. But, Hedda—you're burning for me—Aunt Julie really must share in that. But I wonder—all this—I wonder if it's typical with young wives, hm?

HEDDA You'd better ask Aunt Julie about that too.

TESMAN Oh yes, I certainly will when I get the chance. [*Looking uneasy and thoughtful again.*] No, but, oh no, the manuscript. Good Lord, it's awful to think about poor Eilert, just the same.

[MRS. ELVSTED, *dressed as for her first visit with hat and coat, enters through the hall door.*]

MRS. ELVSTED [*Greets them hurriedly and speaks in agitation.*] Oh, Hedda, don't be offended that I've come back again.

HEDDA What happened to you, Thea?

TESMAN Something about Eilert Løvborg?

MRS. ELVSTED Oh yes, I'm terrified that he's had an accident.

HEDDA [*Grips her arm.*] Ah, do you think so?

TESMAN Good Lord, where did you get that idea, Mrs. Elvsted?

MRS. ELVSTED I heard them talking at the boarding house—just as I came in. There are the most incredible rumors about him going around town today.

TESMAN Oh yes, imagine, I heard them too. And still I can swear he went straight home to sleep. Just think.

HEDDA So—What were they saying at the boarding house?

MRS. ELVSTED   Oh, I couldn't get any details, either because they didn't know or—or they saw me and stopped talking. And I didn't dare ask.

TESMAN [*Uneasily pacing the floor.*]   Let's just hope—you misunderstood.

MRS. ELVSTED   No, I'm sure they were talking about him. Then I heard them say something about the hospital—

TESMAN   Hospital?

HEDDA   No—That's impossible.

MRS. ELVSTED   I'm deathly afraid for him, so I went up to his lodgings and asked about him there.

HEDDA   You dared to do that?

MRS. ELVSTED   What else should I have done? I couldn't stand the uncertainty any longer.

TESMAN   You didn't find him there either, hm?

MRS. ELVSTED   No. And the people there didn't know anything at all. They said he hadn't been home since yesterday afternoon.

TESMAN   Yesterday? How could they say that?

MRS. ELVSTED   It could only mean one thing—Something terrible's happened to him.

TESMAN   You know, Hedda—What if I were to go into town and ask around at different places—?

HEDDA   No! You stay out of this.

[JUDGE BRACK, *carrying his hat, enters through the hall door, which* BERTA *opens and closes after him. He looks serious and bows in silence.*]

TESMAN   Oh, here you are, Judge, hm?

BRACK   Yes, it was essential for me to see you this evening.

TESMAN   I see you got the message from Aunt Julie.

BRACK   Yes, that too.

TESMAN   Isn't it sad, hm?

BRACK   Well, my dear Tesman, that depends on how you look at it.

TESMAN [*Looks at him uneasily.*]   Has anything else happened?

BRACK   Yes, it has.

HEDDA [*Tensely.*]   Something sad, Judge Brack?

BRACK   Once again, it depends on how you look at it, Mrs. Tesman.

MRS. ELVSTED [*In an uncontrollable outburst.*]   It's Eilert Løvborg.

BRACK [*Looks briefly at her.*]   How did you guess, Mrs. Elvsted? Do you already know something—?

MRS. ELVSTED [*Confused.*]   No, no, I don't know anything but—

TESMAN   Well, for God's sake, tell us what it is.

BRACK [*Shrugging his shoulders.*]   Well then—I'm sorry to tell you—that Eilert Løvborg has been taken to the hospital. He is dying.

MRS. ELVSTED [*Crying out.*]   Oh God, oh God.

TESMAN   Dying?

HEDDA [*Involuntarily.*]   So quickly—?

MRS. ELVSTED [*Wailing.*]   And we were quarrelling when we parted, Hedda.

HEDDA [*Whispers.*]   Now, Thea—Thea.

MRS. ELVSTED [*Not noticing her.*]   I'm going to him. I've got to see him alive.

BRACK   It would do you no good, Mrs. Elvsted. No visitors are allowed.

MRS. ELVSTED   At least tell me what happened. What—?

TESMAN   Yes, because he certainly wouldn't have tried to—hm?

HEDDA   Yes, I'm sure that's what he did.

TESMAN   Hedda. How can you—

BRACK [*Who is watching her all the time.*]   Unfortunately, Mrs. Tesman, you've guessed right.

MRS. ELVSTED   Oh, how awful.

TESMAN   To himself, too. Think of it.

HEDDA   Shot himself!

BRACK   Right again, Mrs. Tesman.

MRS. ELVSTED [*Tries to compose herself.*]   When did this happen, Mr. Brack?

BRACK   Just this afternoon, between three and four.

TESMAN   Oh, my God—Where did he do it, hm?

BRACK [*Slightly uncertain.*]   Where? Oh, I suppose at his lodgings.

MRS. ELVSTED   No, that can't be. I was there between six and seven.

BRACK   Well then, some other place. I don't know precisely. All I know is that he was found—he'd shot himself—in the chest.

MRS. ELVSTED   Oh, how awful to think that he should die like that.

HEDDA [*To* BRACK.]   In the chest?

BRACK   Yes, like I said.

HEDDA   Not through the temple?

BRACK   The chest, Mrs. Tesman.

HEDDA   Well, well. The chest is also good.

BRACK   What was that, Mrs. Tesman?

HEDDA [*Evasively.*]   Oh, nothing—nothing.

TESMAN   And the wound is fatal, hm?

BRACK   The wound is absolutely fatal. In fact, it's probably already over.

MRS. ELVSTED   Yes, yes, I can feel it. It's over. It's all over. Oh, Hedda—!

TESMAN   Tell me, how did you find out about all this?

BRACK [*Curtly.*]   From a police officer. One I spoke with.

HEDDA [*Raising her voice.*]   Finally—an action.

TESMAN   God help us, Hedda, what are you saying?

HEDDA   I'm saying that here, in this—there is beauty.

BRACK   Uhm, Mrs. Tesman.

TESMAN   Beauty! No, don't even think it.

MRS. ELVSTED   Oh, Hedda. How can you talk about beauty?

HEDDA   Eilert Løvborg has come to terms with himself. He's had the courage to do what had to be done.

MRS. ELVSTED   No, don't ever believe it was anything like that. What he did, he did in a moment of madness.

TESMAN   It was desperation.

MRS. ELVSTED   Yes, madness. Just like when he tore his book in pieces.

BRACK [*Startled.*]   The book. You mean his manuscript? Did he tear it up?

MRS. ELVSTED   Yes, last night.

TESMAN [*Whispering softly.*]   Oh, Hedda, we'll never get out from under all this.

BRACK   Hmm, that's very odd.

TESMAN [*Pacing the floor.*]   To think that Eilert Løvborg should leave the world this way. And then not to leave behind the work that would have made his name immortal.

MRS. ELVSTED   Oh, what if it could be put together again.

TESMAN   Yes—just think—what if it could? I don't know what I wouldn't give—

MRS. ELVSTED   Maybe it can, Mr. Tesman.

TESMAN   What do you mean?

MRS. ELVSTED [*Searching in the pocket of her skirt.*]   See this? I saved all the notes he dictated from.

HEDDA [*A step closer.*]   Ah.

TESMAN   You saved them, Mrs. Elvsted, hm?

MRS. ELVSTED   Yes, they're all here. I brought them with me when I came to town, and here they've been. Tucked away in my pocket—

TESMAN   Oh, let me see them.

MRS. ELVSTED [*Gives him a bundle of small papers.*]   But they're all mixed up, completely out of order.

TESMAN   Just think. What if we could sort them out. Perhaps if the two of us helped each other.

MRS. ELVSTED   Oh yes. Let's at least give it a try—

TESMAN   It will happen. It must happen. I'll give my whole life to this.

HEDDA   You, George, your life?

TESMAN   Yes, or, anyway, all the time I have. Every spare minute. My own research will just have to be put aside. Hedda—you understand, don't you, hm? I owe this to Eilert's memory.

HEDDA   Maybe so.

TESMAN   Now, my dear Mrs. Elvsted, let's pull ourselves together. God knows there's no point brooding about what's happened. We've got to try to find some peace of mind so that—

MRS. ELVSTED   Yes, yes, Mr. Tesman. I'll do my best.

TESMAN   Well. So, come along then. We've got to get started on these notes right away. Where should we sit? Here? No. In the back room. Excuse us, Judge. Come with me, Mrs. Elvsted.

MRS. ELVSTED   Oh God—if only it can be done.

[TESMAN *and* MRS. ELVSTED *go into the rear room. She takes her hat and coat off. Both sit at the table under the hanging lamp and immerse themselves in eager examination of the papers. Hedda goes across to the stove and sits in the armchair. Soon after,* BRACK *goes over to her.*]

HEDDA [*Softly.*]   Ah, Judge—This act of Eilert Løvborg's—there's a sense of liberation in it.

BRACK   Liberation, Mrs. Hedda? Yes, I guess it's a liberation for him, all right.

HEDDA   I mean, for me. It's a liberation for me to know that in this world an act of such courage, done in full, free will, is possible. Something bathed in a bright shaft of sudden beauty.

BRACK [*Smiles.*]   Hmm—Dear Mrs. Hedda—

HEDDA   Oh, I know what you're going to say, because you're a kind of specialist too, after all, just like—Ah well.

BRACK [*Looking steadily at her.*]   Eilert Løvborg meant more to you than you might admit—even to yourself. Or am I wrong?

HEDDA   I don't answer questions like that. All I know is that Eilert Løvborg had the courage to live life his own way, and now—his last great act—

bathed in beauty. He—had the will to break away from the banquet of life—so soon.

BRACK   It pains me, Mrs. Hedda—but I'm forced to shatter this pretty illusion of yours.

HEDDA   Illusion?

BRACK   Which would have been taken away from you soon enough.

HEDDA   And what's that?

BRACK   He didn't shoot himself—so freely.

HEDDA   Not freely?

BRACK   No. This whole Eilert Løvborg business didn't come off exactly the way I described it.

HEDDA   [*In suspense.*]   Are you hiding something? What is it?

BRACK   I employed a few euphemisms for poor Mrs. Elvsted's sake.

HEDDA   Such as—?

BRACK   First, of course, he's already dead.

HEDDA   At the hospital?

BRACK   Yes. And without regaining consciousness.

HEDDA   What else?

BRACK   The incident took place somewhere other than his room.

HEDDA   That's insignificant.

BRACK   Not completely. I have to tell you—Eilert Løvborg was found shot in—Miss Diana's boudoir.

HEDDA   [*About to jump up but sinks back again.*]   That's impossible, Judge. He can't have gone there again today.

BRACK   He was there this afternoon. He came to demand the return of something that he said they'd taken from him. He talked crazily about a lost child.

HEDDA   Ah, so that's why—

BRACK   I thought maybe he was referring to his manuscript but I hear he'd already destroyed that himself so I guess it was his pocketbook.

HEDDA   Possibly. So—that's where he was found.

BRACK   Right there, with a discharged pistol in his coat pocket, and a fatal bullet wound.

HEDDA   In the chest, yes?

BRACK   No—lower down.

HEDDA   [*Looks up at him with an expression of revulsion.*]   That too! Oh absurdity—! It hangs like a curse over everything I so much as touch.

BRACK   There's still one more thing, Mrs. Hedda. Also in the ugly category.

HEDDA   And what is that?

BRACK   The pistol he had with him—

HEDDA   [*Breathless.*]   Well, what about it?

BRACK   He must have stolen it.

HEDDA   [*Jumping up.*]   Stolen? That's not true. He didn't.

BRACK   There's no other explanation possible. He must have stolen it—Shh.
   [TESMAN *and* MRS. ELVSTED *have gotten up from the table in the rear room and come into the living room.*]

TESMAN   [*With papers in both hands.*]   Hedda, my dear—I can hardly see anything in there under that lamp. Just think—

HEDDA   I'm thinking.

TESMAN Do you think you might let us sit a while at your desk, hm?

HEDDA Oh, gladly. [*Quickly.*] No, wait. Let me just clean it up a bit first.

TESMAN Oh, not necessary, Hedda. There's plenty of room.

HEDDA No, no, I'll just straighten it up, I'm telling you. I'll just move these things here under the piano for a while.

> [*She has pulled an object covered with sheet music out of the bookcase. She adds a few more sheets and carries the whole pile out to the left of the rear room.* TESMAN *puts the papers on the desk and brings over the lamp from the corner table. He and* MRS. ELVSTED *sit and continue their work.*]

HEDDA Well, Thea, my sweet. Are things moving along with the memorial?

MRS. ELVSTED [*Looks up at her dejectedly.*] Oh, God—It's going to be so difficult to find the order in all of this.

TESMAN But it must be done. There's simply no other choice. And finding the order in other people's papers—that's precisely what I'm meant for.

> [HEDDA *goes over to the stove and sits on one of the stools.* BRACK *stands over her, leaning over the armchair.*]

HEDDA [*Whispers.*] What were you saying about the pistol?

BRACK [*Softly.*] That he must have stolen it.

HEDDA Why stolen exactly?

BRACK Because there shouldn't be any other way to explain it, Mrs. Hedda.

HEDDA I see.

BRACK [*Looks briefly at her.*] Eilert Løvborg was here this morning, am I correct?

HEDDA Yes.

BRACK Were you alone with him?

HEDDA Yes, for a while.

BRACK You didn't leave the room at all while he was here?

HEDDA No.

BRACK Think again. Weren't you out of the room, even for one moment?

HEDDA Yes. Perhaps. Just for a moment—out in the hallway.

BRACK And where was your pistol case at that time?

HEDDA I put it under the—

BRACK Well, Mrs. Hedda—

HEDDA It was over there on the writing table.

BRACK Have you looked since then to see if both pistols are there?

HEDDA No.

BRACK It's not necessary. I saw the pistol Løvborg had, and I recognized it immediately from yesterday, and from before as well.

HEDDA Have you got it?

BRACK No, the police have it.

HEDDA What will the police do with that pistol?

BRACK Try to track down its owner.

HEDDA Do you think they can do that?

BRACK [*Bends over her and whispers.*] No, Hedda Gabler, not as long as I keep quiet.

HEDDA [*Looking fearfully at him.*] And what if you don't keep quiet—then what?

BRACK Then the way out is to claim that the pistol was stolen.

HEDDA I'd rather die.

BRACK [*Smiling.*] People make those threats but they don't act on them.

HEDDA [*Without answering.*] So—let's say the pistol is not stolen and the owner is found out? What happens then?

BRACK Well, Hedda—then there'll be a scandal.

HEDDA A scandal?

BRACK Oh, yes, a scandal. Just what you're so desperately afraid of. You'd have to appear in court, naturally. You and Miss Diana. She'd have to detail how it all occurred. Whether it was an accident or a homicide. Was he trying to draw the pistol to threaten her? Is that when the gun went off? Did she snatch it out of his hands to shoot him, and then put the pistol back in his pocket? That would be thoroughly in character for her. She's a feisty little thing, that Miss Diana.

HEDDA But all this ugliness has got nothing to do with me.

BRACK No. But you would have to answer one question. Why did you give the pistol to Eilert Løvborg? And what conclusions would people draw from the fact that you gave it to him?

HEDDA [*Lowers her head.*] That's true. I didn't think of that.

BRACK Well. Fortunately you have nothing to worry about as long as I keep quiet.

HEDDA [*Looking up at him.*] So I'm in your power now, Judge. You have a hold over me from now on.

BRACK [*Whispering more softly.*] Dearest Hedda—Believe me—I won't abuse my position.

HEDDA But in your power. Totally subject to your demands—And your will. Not free. Not free at all. [*She gets up silently.*] No, that's one thought I just can't stand. Never!

BRACK [*Looks mockingly at her.*] One can usually learn to live with the inevitable.

HEDDA [*Returning his look.*] Maybe so. [*She goes over to the writing table, suppressing an involuntary smile and imitating* TESMAN's *intonation.*] Well, George, this is going to work out, hm?

TESMAN Oh, Lord knows, dear. Anyway, at this rate, it's going to be months of work.

HEDDA [*As before.*] No, just think. [*Runs her fingers lightly through* MRS. ELVSTED's *hair.*] Doesn't it seem strange, Thea. Here you are, sitting together with Tesman—just like you used to sit with Eilert Løvborg.

MRS. ELVSTED Oh, God, if only I could inspire your husband too.

HEDDA Oh, that will come—in time.

TESMAN Yes, you know what, Hedda—I really think I'm beginning to feel something like that. But why don't you go over and sit with Judge Brack some more.

HEDDA Can't you two find any use for me here?

TESMAN No, nothing in the world. [*Turning his head.*] From now on, my dear Judge, you'll have to be kind enough to keep Hedda company.

BRACK [*With a glance at* HEDDA.] That will be an infinite pleasure for me.

HEDDA Thanks, but I'm tired tonight. I'll go in there and lie down on the sofa for a while.

TESMAN Yes, do that, Hedda, hm?

[HEDDA *goes into the rear room and draws the curtains after her. Short pause. Suddenly she is heard to play a wild dance melody on the piano.*]

MRS. ELVSTED [*Jumping up from her chair.*] Oh—what's that?

TESMAN [*Running to the doorway.*] Oh, Hedda, my dear—Don't play dance music tonight. Just think of poor Aunt Rina and of Eilert Løvborg too.

HEDDA [*Putting her head out from between the curtains.*] And Aunt Julie and all the rest of them too. From now on I shall be quiet. [*She closes the curtains again.*]

TESMAN [*At the writing table.*] This can't be making her very happy—Seeing us at this melancholy work. You know what, Mrs. Elvsted—You're going to move in with Aunt Julie. Then I can come over in the evening, and we can sit and work there, hm?

MRS. ELVSTED Yes, maybe that would be the best—

HEDDA [*From the rear room.*] I can hear you perfectly well, Tesman. So, how am I supposed to get through the evenings out here?

TESMAN [*Leafing through the papers.*] Oh, I'm sure Judge Brack will be good enough to call on you.

BRACK [*In the armchair, shouts merrily.*] I'd be delighted, Mrs. Tesman. Every evening. Oh, we're going to have some good times together, the two of us.

HEDDA [*Loudly and clearly.*] Yes, that's what you're hoping for, isn't it, Judge? You, the one and only cock of the walk—

[*A shot is heard within.* TESMAN, MRS. ELVSTED *and* BRACK *all jump to their feet.*]

TESMAN Oh, she's playing around with those pistols again.

[*He pulls the curtains aside and runs in.* MRS. ELVSTED *follows.* HEDDA *is stretched out lifeless on the sofa. Confusion and cries.* BERTA *comes running in from the right.*]

[*Shrieking to* BRACK.] Shot herself! Shot herself in the temple! Just think!

BRACK [*Half prostrate in the armchair.*] But God have mercy—People just don't act that way!

END OF PLAY

GIOVANNI VERGA

1840–1922

Giovanni Verga startled his readers with harsh, even brutal, stories of peasant life in Sicily. He developed an impersonal narrative voice, seeking to create a kind of literature that would efface all signs of the author, allowing the work of art, as he said, to "seem *to have made itself.*" Conveying a stark world in stripped-down, plain language, his fiction describes the excruciating struggles of people locked in a stagnant and unjust social order. The foremost exponent of *verismo*, an Italian version of realism, Verga is considered one of the greatest of all Italian novelists.

LIFE AND TIMES

Giovanni Carmelo Verga was born in 1840 in the city of Catania, on the island of Sicily, one of the poorest regions in Europe. His father was a prosperous and politically liberal gentleman-landowner, and his mother an educated woman who was interested in current literature and ideas. Verga attended one of the few secular schools in the area, where he read classic Italian authors as well as local writers. Catania was a dangerous place. It was frequently ravaged by cholera and subject to famines, and it had for many years been torn by political strife. In 1820 and 1848, Sicilian nationalists had struggled for independence from the rule of the royal Bourbon family, who held the thrones of Spain and southern Italy. Repeated antigovernment revolts all failed in bloody violence. More bloodshed was to follow, as the military leader Giuseppe Garibaldi seized Sicily from the Bourbons and made it part of the newly united

kingdom of Italy. The poor continued to revolt against local landowners, and in the 1860s Sicily was placed under martial law. Thousands of peasants were killed, deported, and imprisoned.

In 1865, the young Verga moved to Florence, then Italy's capital, which was also its main cultural center and a magnet for aspiring writers who wished to cast off provincial ideas. For the next three decades, he would divide his time between summers in the Sicilian countryside and winters in the north. Verga's novels during this period are chiefly tales of doomed passion. When he moved to Milan in 1872, he became part of a lively bohemian society of artists, writers, and composers. The novels of the Milan years continued to investigate the psychology of unhappy love. The composer Pietro Mascagni turned one of these stories into a popular opera, *Cavalliera Rusticana*, which played in Milan in 1890 and then traveled to New York, Chicago, and Philadelphia in 1891, performed to great acclaim. It remains a favorite of opera companies today.

In the 1880s Verga's style began to change. Experimenting with clinically accurate description, and influenced by the stylistic innovations of French writers **Gustave Flaubert, Guy de Maupassant**, and **Emile Zola**, he told stories of Sicilian life in a newly spare, objective manner, recording facts but not openly interpreting them. Economic themes began to dominate Verga's work, as he became more and more convinced of the role played by poverty and wealth in human affairs and by Darwinian concepts of the struggle for existence. He produced his greatest

fiction during this Sicilian period. The selection included here is taken from his finest collection of stories, the *Novelle rusticane* (Rustic Tales, 1883).

Verga's new style disturbed his readers. Audiences attacked and dismissed this bleak work. Disappointed, the author busied himself with small projects and in 1894 retired to Catania, where he also cared for his dead brother's family. Verga had a number of love affairs with women in his life but had never married. In his last years, he lived relatively secluded, traveling occasionally to collect background material for his fiction, and adapting previous works for stage and film.

When he died in 1922, Verga's reputation was on the rise. Readers began to see his stories and novels as masterworks of modern prose, and his work influenced a range of twentieth-century writers and artists, including the British novelist D. H. Lawrence, the Italian playwright **Luigi Pirandello**, and the filmmaker Luchino Visconti.

WORK

Verga's version of realism, *verismo*, rejects romantic musings on human emotions and develops a deliberately dispassionate style of narration. It is brusque, wastes no words, emphasizes dialogue, and does not dwell in psychological analysis. Verga said he wanted to the truth of his characters' lives to be conveyed in their own simple language. This was a challenging task because the peasants' local dialect could not be understood outside of Sicily. Verga therefore invented a new literary language, an Italian that captured his Sicilian characters' thought patterns and the syntactic patterns of their speech.

Most writers before Verga had imagined the countryside as an idyllic, innocent place. Writers and artists in the pastoral tradition, which reaches as far

back as ancient Greece, cultivated a deliberately idealized vision of rural life, imagining peaceful shepherds and farmers in a lost golden age, when people and nature existed harmoniously together in settings of wild beauty. Verga bluntly rejects this tradition. In place of an innocent peasant world of the past, he offers grating accounts of the gulf between rich and poor in a modern agricultural society whose economic, political, and religious institutions offer only the bleakest prospects for the peasants. Turning his clear-eyed observation on the rural experience of his own time, Verga saw not pastoral, but its opposite: political corruption, ugliness, ignorance, and outright bloodshed.

The story printed here, *Freedom,* recreates a gruesome peasant uprising that had taken place when Verga was twenty years old in the town of Bronte, not far from his home. At the time, the revolutionaries who unseated the Bourbon monarchy had promised to redistribute the land owned by the upper classes to the peasants. For the poor, *freedom* meant the right to own a piece of land. But they were to get little or nothing. The crown lands were sold off to the wealthy. Finding themselves denied even traditional grazing privileges, the lowest rung of society rebelled, massacring anyone who had wealth or privilege. Decades later Verga would use all the techniques of *verismo* to recount the event.

The story begins in the midst of a violent mob scene. Verga offers little background information, hinting at the political situation quickly through dialogue or significant images. The tricolor streamer in the first sentence situates the event after Garibaldi's invasion of Sicily in 1860, which promised the peasants an end to the old regime of inequality. Their shouts catalog a range of complaints as the peasants strike down the authority figures

who have humiliated and exploited them: baron, priest, rich man, police officer, and gamekeeper. Verga's narrator does not comment on events, but he does isolate richly resonant individual details. Don Paolo is wearing "an old cap that his daughter had embroidered for him" when he is killed in front of his family, for example, and we learn that as a baroness flees from room to room ahead of the avenging crowd, "there were plenty of rooms for her to run through."

Verga ends the tale in the words of one of the bewildered workers, who does not understand why he is being imprisoned and why he has been denied even a scrap of land. We are left to wonder how one could explain or justify his society to him. What does the *freedom* of the title mean? Who can be free, and why? Whatever answer Verga's powerful story suggests, it is neither a comforting nor a hopeful one.

Freedom[1]

They unfurled a tricolor streamer above the campanile,[2] rang the bells like merry hell, and began shouting "Hooray for freedom!" in the square.

Like the sea in a storm, the crowd foamed and heaved in front of the bigwigs' club, outside the town hall, on the steps leading up to the church: a solid mass of white headscarves, axes and sickles flashing in the sun. Then they burst into a narrow street.

"You, baron, for a start! That's for getting your farm-watchmen to beat up the people!" At the head of the mob, a harridan with ancient hair sticking straight up, armed only with her fingernails.

"You next, priest of the devil, for sucking away our souls!"

"That's for you, rich pig, who grew so fat on the flesh of the poor that you can't even run away!"

"That's for you, constable, for prosecuting no one except the penniless!"

"And that's for you, woodkeepers, for selling the body and soul of yourselves and your neighbors for a couple of *tarì*[3] a day!"

The smell of blood made them drunk. Sickles, hands, rags, stones were all dripping with it. "Get the bigwigs! Get the felt hats![4] Kill 'em! Kill 'em. Get the felt hats!"

Don Antonio was slipping off home through the back streets. The first blow floored him, face bleeding, on to the pavement. "Why? Why d'you want to kill me?"

"You as well! The devil take you!" A crippled street urchin grabbed his filth-covered hat and spat into it. "Down with the felt hats! Hooray for freedom!"

"Take that! You too!" This to The Reverend who preached that anyone stealing bread would go to Hell.

---

1. Translated by G. H. McWilliam. The story is based on a peasant uprising in the town of Bronte, on Mount Etna, in 1860.
2. A bell tower. "Tricolor": the flag of Garibaldi's army of liberation was red, green, and white; it would become the national flag of Italy.

3. A tarò is a small coin worth about 0.85 lira.
4. The upper classes wore felt hats; peasants wore caps or berets.

He was on his way back from saying Mass, with the consecrated Host in his belly. "Please don't kill me! I'm in mortal sin!" Gnà[5] Lucia was the mortal sin he meant. Her father had sold her to The Reverend when she was fourteen, the winter of the famine, and she'd been filling the Cloister Wheel[6] and the streets with starving brats ever since. If all that dog's meat were worth anything to them that day, they could have stuffed themselves with it as they went about carving it up with their sickles in the doorways and the cobbled streets. The same thing happens when a starving wolf turns up in a flock of sheep: it doesn't think of filling its belly, but just slaughters everything in sight from pure rage. First, the Grand Lady's son, who had rushed out to see what was happening; then the chemist[7] as he was shutting up shop in a tearing hurry; and then Don Paolo, who was riding back from the vineyard on his donkey with a couple of saddlebags that looked half-empty. And he was even wearing an old cap that his daughter had embroidered for him ages ago, before the disease struck the vineyard. She saw him fall at the front door, as she was waiting with her five children for the few vegetables he had in his saddlebags to make the minestra.[8] "Paolo! Paolo!"

One of them struck him in the back with a blow from an axe. Another fell upon him with a sickle, and ripped him open as his bloody arm was reaching for the door-knocker.

But the worst moment of all was when the notary's son, an eleven-year-old with a head of golden blond hair, managed somehow to fall in the midst of the crowd. His father had raised his head two or three times and called out, 'Neddu! Neddu!' before dragging himself to die in the gutter.

Neddu was running away in absolute terror, eyes and mouth wide open, unable to utter a sound. He took a tumble, and raised himself on one knee, like his father. The torrent poured over him. One of them put the boot in and smashed his cheek, and the boy still pleading for mercy with clasped hands. No, he didn't want to die in the way he'd seen his father killed! It was heartbreaking! The woodcutter, out of pity, landed him a massive blow with his axe using both hands as if he were felling a fifty-year-old oak, as he lay there shaking like a leaf.

Another one cried out, "What the hell! He would only have grown up a lawyer!"

What did it matter? Now they had their hands covered in so much blood, they had to spill all the rest. Get them all! All the felt hats! It was no longer the hunger, the bullying, the beatings, that were fueling their anger. It was innocent blood. The women were even more ferocious, waving their skinny arms, shrieking with anger in high-pitched voices, their tender flesh showing beneath the rags they were wearing. "So much for you, that came praying to the good Lord in your silk dress! And you, that loathed having to kneel alongside the poor! Take that! Take that!" Into the houses, up the stairs, into the bedrooms, tearing up the silk and the fine curtains. No end of ear-rings decorating those bleeding faces! And what a collection of gold rings on the hands trying to ward off the blows from the axes!

The baroness had ordered a barricade of wooden beams, country carts, and casks full of wine to be placed behind the main entrance. Her watchmen were firing away from the windows to sell their lives dearly. The crowd kept their heads

---

5. Signora, Mrs.—i.e., a grown woman.
6. A revolving horizontal wheel fixed into an opening in the wall of an orphanage (usually a convent). Unwanted babies were left anonymously on the wheel outside, a bell was rung, and someone inside came to collect the child,

who was raised by the orphanage until he or she grew old enough to work and could be turned over to an employer.
7. Pharmacist.
8. Vegetable soup.

down against the shotgun pellets, having no weapons of their own to fire back. Before all this, anyone carrying firearms faced the death penalty. "Hooray for freedom!" Once they broke down the door, they charged into the courtyard and up the steps, trampling over the wounded. They left the watchmen alone. "We'll get the watchmen later!" First of all they were after the flesh of the baroness, flesh fattened on partridges and precious wines. She was running from one room to the next with a suckling[9] at her breast, hair disheveled, and there were plenty of rooms for her to run through. You could hear the crowd yelling along the corridors, closing in on her like a river in spate.

Her eldest son, a boy of sixteen with a body still as pale as his mother's, propped up the door with his trembling hands, shouting, "Mother! Mother!" At the first push, they crashed the door down on top of him. He clung on to legs stamping over it, but soon stopped shouting. His mother had taken refuge on the balcony, clinging frantically to the baby with a hand over its mouth to stop it bawling. Staring wildly around him, her other son was trying to shield her with his body, grabbing all those axes by the blades as though he had a hundred hands to do it with. They were separated in a flash. One of them took her by the hair, another by the waist, another by her dress, and they lifted her in the air above the balcony rail. The charcoal-burner seized the suckling baby from her arms. The other brother could see nothing of all this, only black and red everywhere. They were stamping on him and breaking every bone in his body with their hob-nailed boots; he had sunk his teeth into a hand that had him by the throat and refused to let it go. The throng was so tightly packed that they were unable to strike with their axes, that were glistening in the air.

And in that raging carnival of the month of July, amid the drunken shouting of the ravenous mob, the church bell went on tolling furiously away until evening, without either noon or Angelus as if in the land of the Turks.[1] Eventually they began to split up, weary of the slaughter and crept slowly away, each avoiding his companion. By nightfall all the doors were closed out of fear, and in every house a lamp kept vigil. In the narrow streets all you could hear were the dogs, rummaging in the corners, gnawing hungrily away at the bones by the light of the moon, which washed over everything and cast its glow over the wide-open doorways and windows of the empty houses.

Daylight came. It was Sunday, with nobody in the square, and no bell ringing for Mass. The sexton[2] had made himself scarce, there was not a priest to be found anywhere. The first group of people to form in front of the church looked suspiciously at one another, each wondering what his neighbor had on his conscience. Then, once a tidy number had turned up, they started to grumble, saying, "People can't go without their Sunday Mass, like a pack of dogs!" The bigwigs club was boarded up, and no one knew where to go to take the masters' orders for the week to follow. From the campanile the tricolor streamer still dangled flabbily in the stifling midsummer heat.

As the shaded area in front of the church grew gradually smaller, they all crowded together in a corner. Between a pair of shabby-looking houses, at the foot of a narrow lane that sloped down steeply from the square, you could see the

---

9. A nursing baby.
1. The Angelus, a Roman Catholic devotion, was announced by a church bell that rang in the morning, at noon, and in the evening. It would not be rung in a Muslim country like Turkey.
2. A church employee, one of whose tasks was to ring the bells.

parched fields of the plain, and the dark woods on the slopes of Mount Etna.[3] Now it was time for them to share out those woods and those fields. Everyone was adding up on his fingers how big his own portion ought to be, and casting hostile glances at his neighbor.

"Freedom meant there was going to be enough for everyone!" they were saying. "That swine of a Nino, and that Ramurazzo, would like to take over from the felt hats, and carry on the bullying where they left off! With no surveyor left to measure out the land, and no notary to put it down in writing, it's everyone for himself, and the devil take the hindmost!"

"And what if you guzzle up your own share in the tavern? Do we have to divide everything up all over again?"

"You call me a thief, and I'll call you a thief. Now there's freedom, anyone can go for a double helping and live it up like the bigwigs!" The woodcutter waved his arm in the air as if he were still wielding his axe.

Next day they heard the general[4] was coming, the one who frightened the life out of people, to deal out justice. You could see the red shirts of his soldiers making their way slowly up the ravine towards the village. All that was needed was to roll boulders down on them and wipe out the lot. But nobody moved. The women were screaming and tearing out their hair. The men, black as coal and with long beards, waited on the hillside, dangling their hands between their thighs, and watched the young soldiers arriving, bending exhausted beneath their rusty old rifles, with that tiny general on his big black horse riding alone ahead of them.

The general had straw brought into the church, and put his boys to bed like a father. In the morning, before dawn, if they failed to get up at the sound of the trumpet, he would ride into the church on horseback, swearing like a Turk. That was the sort of man he was. The first thing he did was to order five or six to be shot: Pippo, the cripple, Pizzanello, whoever happened to come within reach. The woodcutter, while they were making him kneel against the wall of the cemetery, was crying like a child because of something his mother had said to him, and because of the scream she had let out when they tore him away from her arms. From a distance, in the remotest lanes of the village, behind closed doors, that series of rifle shots sounded like rockets going off at festival time.

Afterwards the real judges arrived, bespectacled gents perched on mules, travel weary, who were still complaining about being overworked as they were questioning the accused in the convent refectory.[5] They were seated side by side on the bench, and letting out a groan every time they changed position. The trial went on and on for ages. The ones they found responsible were led away to the city on foot, chained together in pairs, between two lines of soldiers with muskets at the ready. Their womenfolk ran after them beside the country lanes, across plowland, through cactus groves, vineyards and golden cornfields, staggering along out of breath, calling out to them by name every time the road turned a corner, and they could see the prisoners' faces. On reaching the city they were locked up in the great, tall prison, huge as a monastery, dotted all over with tiny barred windows. If the women wanted to see their menfolk, it was Mondays only, in the presence of warders, behind the iron gate. The poor wretches inside became more and more pallid-looking in that eternal half-light, never catching a glimpse of the sun. Monday after Monday they became more reticent, hardly giving an

3. A high volcano on the east coast of Sicily.
4. I.e., General Nino Bixio, a lieutenant under Garibaldi, whose army of "red shirts" had entered Catania earlier that year.
5. Dining hall.

answer, complaining less and less. On the other days of the week, if the women were to buzz around the square by the prison, the sentries would threaten them with their rifles. They had no idea what to do for the best, where to find work in the city, or how to get themselves something to eat. The bed in the stable cost two *soldi*,[6] the white bread was no more than a single mouthful and never filled their stomachs. If they huddled down to spend the night in the doorway of a church, the police arrested them. Gradually they returned to the village, first the wives, then the mothers. One fine-looking young woman disappeared in the city and was never heard of again. All the rest of the villagers had returned to what they were doing before. The bigwigs couldn't work their lands by themselves, and the poor couldn't live without the bigwigs. They declared peace.

The orphan of the chemist stole Neli Pirru's wife from him, and thought it a good way of avenging himself against the man who had killed his father. Now and again, when the woman had qualms because she feared her husband would slash her face when he came out of prison, he would say, "Don't worry, he'll never come out." Nobody gave them a second thought any more, except for a few mothers and a few older men whenever they cast their eyes towards the plain, where the city lay, or else on Sundays, when they saw the others calmly discussing their affairs with the bigwigs in front of the club, cap in hand, which only went to show that the poor always came off worse in the end.

The trial lasted three years! Imagine! Three whole years locked up without a glimpse of the sun. The accused looked like so many corpses dug up from the graveyard, every time they were led handcuffed into the courtroom. Everyone who could manage it dashed in from the village as though to a festival: witnesses, relatives, rubbernecks,[7] so as to take a look at their fellow-villagers cooped up in the dock like so many fattening fowl, which was all they became after such a long time in jail. And there was Neli Pirru, standing face to face with the chemist's son, who had played him such a trick to become his in-law!

They were made to stand up one after the other. "What is your name?" And each of them heard himself spouting it out, name, surname and what he had done. The lawyers fought it out in their broad-sleeved gowns amid the hubbub, getting over-excited and foaming at the mouth, then drying themselves off with their white handkerchiefs and taking a pinch of snuff. The judges were dropping off to sleep so often behind their spectacle lenses that your heart absolutely froze. In the jury-box opposite sat twelve good men and true,[8] so tired and bored by the proceedings that they were yawning, scratching their beards, or twittering among themselves. Of course people said it was lucky for them that the good men and true were not from that village up in the hills, when they had struck a blow for freedom. The poor devils in the dock tried to read their faces. Then they went away to have a chat among themselves, and the prisoners waited, pale in the face, their eyes fixed on that closed door. When they came back, the foreman, looking almost as white-faced as the accused, speaking with his hand on his belly, said, "On my honor and on my conscience. . . . !"

As they were putting on his handcuffs again, the charcoal-burner muttered, "Where are you taking me? To prison? What for? I never even got a square meter of land out of it! They told me it was all in the cause of freedom . . . !"

---

6. Twenty *soldi* made up 1 lira, the basic unit of Italian currency at the time.
7. Gawking onlookers, stretching their necks so as not to miss anything.

8. The traditional English expression for members of the jury. The Italian term is *galantuomini*, "gentlemen," translated as "bigwigs" elsewhere in the story.

GUY DE MAUPASSANT

1850–1893

An enormously popular writer in his own time and ever since, Guy de Maupassant had a gift for the special economy required by short fiction. Although he also wrote poetry, plays, and novels, it is the short stories that made their mark on later generations. Ernest Hemingway put Maupassant's work on his list of compulsory reading for any hopeful writer, admiring his unobtrusive narrators and his talent for crispness and brevity. Self-contained, Maupassant's short stories are perfectly shaped, like little gems.

LIFE

Henri-René-Albert-Guy de Maupassant was born on August 5, 1850, in Normandy, in the agricultural north of France. Both parents were well-to-do; the Maupassant family had recently been granted recognition as members of the minor nobility. A brother, Hervé, was born six years later, and the family lived in comfort until 1859, when financial setbacks forced the boys' father to take a job in a Paris bank. Guy was close to his mother, who was a great lover of literature—her favorite writer was Shakespeare. The boy took his mother's side in his parents' quarrels, condemning his father's many infidelities. The strong-willed Madame de Maupassant was able to obtain a formal separation from her husband in 1863, a rare step for a woman at the time.

On being enrolled in a Catholic boarding school, the young Maupassant developed a hatred of religion and deliberately got himself expelled for writing lewd poems. When he was not in school, he roamed the outdoors, learning how to handle a boat, a lifelong passion and the setting for many of his fictions. (He also reported that as a teenager he happened to be on hand to save the famous British poet Algernon Swinburne from drowning.) In these years, Maupassant began to write poetry, and his mother arranged for him to meet the novelist **Gustave Flaubert**, who was a family friend and who would later become his literary mentor. It was in his teens, too, that Maupassant began to have many sexual affairs and contracted syphilis.

In 1869, the young man moved to Paris to study law. When the Franco-Prussian War broke out a year later, he enlisted in the army. After the armistice, he returned to Paris, where he resumed his law studies and found a job in the Naval Ministry and later in the Ministry of Public Education. He performed his duties well and was promoted several times, but neither the jobs nor the law interested him. He abandoned law school in 1875 and spent his free time in parties on a boat, carousing at a floating cabaret, and learning martial arts, including shooting and fencing. At twenty-three, he heard that newspapers were paying well for short stories to entertain their readers, and he began to write prose.

Paris was a global literary center at the time, and Maupassant met many well-known writers, including Ivan Turgenev, **Stephane Mallarmé**, and Emile Zola. Flaubert considered Maupassant his talented disciple. The older writer read Maupassant's drafts and offered critiques over lunch every Sunday in 1875 and 1876, all the time lecturing him on artistic dedication and

the principles of realism. Maupassant later described this training as an education in precision. In 1880, Maupassant's *Ball of Fat,* the tale of a patriotic prostitute's sacrifice during the Franco-Prussian War, was hailed as a masterpiece. The young writer became suddenly famous, and his income soared. He left the Ministry of Public Education in 1882. During these years he began to show the first symptoms of syphilis, then incurable.

Between 1880 and 1890, Maupassant published three hundred stories in a variety of styles. He wrote quickly and vividly, attracting a large audience. There were stories of the Norman countryside and of outings on city rivers, sketches of crafty peasants, tales set in wartime, stories of love affairs and fears of infidelity, sympathetic descriptions of the plight of women, and tales of the supernatural that were also tales of horror and madness.

The last years of Maupassant's life were shadowed by the progress of his illness and by the terrifying example of his brother Hervé's insanity and death in 1889. He found it difficult to write: his eyes would not focus; he had frequent migraine headaches; he took drugs for severe stomach pains, and he suffered from hallucinations. Despite these, he kept writing to support his aging mother and his brother's family. He consulted at least twelve doctors without improvement and, after attempting suicide in January 1892, was confined to a mental hospital outside Paris, where his condition deteriorated rapidly. His death from syphilis came on July 6, 1892, a month before his forty-third birthday.

WORK

In his own lifetime, Maupassant gained an international reputation for superbly constructed stories that were told in an objective and economical form. Unfor-

tunately for Maupassant, some of his stories—especially those with a twist at the end—also provided a commercially successful model for other writers, and he was widely imitated and adapted. At one point, another writer even stole his identity. These imitations did considerable damage to Maupassant's reputation, allowing him to be cast as a writer of clever but mechanical fiction. But this account does not do justice to Maupassant's richly textured language, subtly telling details, and profound psychological insight. In fact, he was deeply interested in the new fields of psychiatry and psychoanalysis, and his stories often show the signs of this fascination.

Hautot and His Son, first published in 1889, limits itself to four main characters. Hautot senior, a forceful and dominating landowner, has tried to raise his son in his own image, but Hautot junior, César, has turned out to be loving and submissive. Hautot's secret mistress of some years has a little son, Emile. The three male figures echo one another. Invited to step into his father's shoes, César also sees a resemblance between himself and Emile. ("Poor boy, he is an orphan now," says the mother. "And so am I," says César.) Strangely, then, Hautot junior manages to take on all of the masculine roles in the family at once: father, husband, son, and brother. Caroline, the mistress, has herself been a replacement for his mother, like a second wife to Hautot senior; and now, Hautot junior becomes the ghost of his own father, repeating his actions as if they formed part of his inheritance. Through these acts of substitution, the three characters who remain create a new family out of the pattern of the old. It is as if Maupassant understands people not primarily as unique individuals but as roles that endlessly fill and refill places in the structure of the family.

Like other influential realist writers, including his mentor Flaubert and his successor **Giovanni Verga**, Maupassant deliberately eliminates authorial commentary and avoids overt moralizing. The narrator conveys contemporary social contexts especially well through dialogues that let the characters themselves communicate their relationships and the social expectations that shape them. We learn from Hautot senior, for example, that mistresses are a common enough fact: "These things happen, everyone knows that, but no one talks about them unless they are obliged." It is typical of Maupassant to write about sexual relationships which most people would not mention in polite conversation at the time: he was famous for having the courage and the will to expose aspects of society that were hidden from view.

But the story is atypical in other respects. In contrast to Maupassant's harsher stories, this tale is permeated with sympathy for its characters and with a gently ironic humor. This story is unusual, too, in that Maupassant very rarely describes a loving and meaningful relationship between a father and a son. And yet, the pleasures that always draw readers to his stories are fully in evidence: intriguing characters, entangled in surprising ways through a powerful and tightly constructed plot.

Hautot and His Son[1]

I

In front of the building, half farm-house, half manor-house—one of those semi-feudal country dwellings of mixed character now occupied by wealthy farmers—the dogs chained to the apple-trees in the court-yard were barking and howling at the sight of the bags carried by the gamekeepers, and at the mischievous boys. In the large dining-room-kitchen, Hautot and his son, M. Bermont the tax-collector, and M. Mondaru the notary, were having a bite and a mouthful of wine before they went out shooting, for it was the first day of the season.

The elder Hautot, proud of his possessions, was boasting of the game that his guests would find in his shoot. He was a big Norman, one of those powerful, ruddy, big-boned men who can lift a cart-load of apples on to their shoulders. Half peasant, half gentleman, rich, respected, influential, autocratic, he had first insisted that his son César should work up to the third form[2] so that he might be well informed, and then he had stopped his education for fear of his becoming a fine gentleman without any interest in the farm.

Nearly as tall as his father, but thinner, César Hautot was a good son, docile, contented, full of admiration and respect and regard for the wishes and opinions of the elder Hautot.

M. Bermont, the tax-collector, a short stout man whose red cheeks showed a thin network of violet veins like the tributaries and winding streams of a river on a map, asked:

"And hares—are there any hares?"

1. Written in 1883; published in 1889. Translated by Margaret Storm Jameson.

2. A basic education; third-form pupils were fourteen years old.

The elder Hautot replied:

"As many as you please, especially in the hollows of Puysatier."

"Where shall we begin?" asked the good-natured notary; he was pale and fat, his flesh bulging out in his tight-fitting, brand-new shooting-kit recently bought at Rouen.[3]

"In that direction, through the bottoms. We will drive the partridges into the open and fall upon them."

Hautot got up. The others followed his example, took their guns from the corner, examined the locks, stamped their feet to ease them in their boots, not yet softened by the warmth within. Then they went out, and the dogs straining at the leash barked and beat the air with their paws.

They set out towards the hollows, which were in a little glen, or rather in a long undulating stretch of poor land unfit for cultivation, furrowed with ditches and covered with ferns—an excellent preserve for game.

The sportsmen took their places, Hautot senior to the right, Hautot junior to the left, with the two guests in the center. The keepers and game-bag carriers followed. The solemn moment had come when sportsmen are waiting for the first shot, their hearts beating more rapidly, and their nervous fingers unable to leave the trigger alone.

Suddenly there was a shot. Hautot had fired. They all stopped and saw a partridge, one of a covy flying as swiftly as possible, drop into a ditch covered with thick shrubs. The excited sportsman started to run, taking big strides, dragging aside the briers in his path, and disappeared into the thicket to look for the bird.

Almost immediately a second shot was heard.

"Ha! Ha! the rascal," exclaimed M. Bermont, "he must have started a hare from the undergrowth."

They all waited with eyes fixed on the mass of dense underwood. The notary, making a trumpet of his hands, shouted: "Have you got them?"

As there was no reply from the elder Hautot, César, turning towards the game-keeper, said: "Go and help him, Joseph. We must keep in line. We'll wait."

And Joseph, a man with an old, lean body and swollen joints, set off at an easy pace down to the ditch, searching for a suitable opening with the caution of a fox. Then, suddenly, he shouted: "Oh, hurry up! Hurry up! There has been an accident!"

They all hurried along and plunged through the briers. Hautot had fallen on his side in a faint with both hands pressed on his abdomen, from which long trickles of blood flowed on to the grass through his linen jacket torn by a bullet. In letting go of his gun to pick up the dead partridge that lay within reach, he had dropped it and the second discharge going off in the fall had torn open his bowels. They drew him out of the ditch, undressed him and saw a frightful wound through which the intestines protruded. Then after binding him up as well as they could they carried him home and waited for the doctor who had been sent for, as well as the priest.

When the doctor arrived, he shook his head gravely, and turning towards young Hautot, who was sobbing on a chair, he said:

"My poor boy, this looks bad."

3. A major city in Normandy.

But when the wound was dressed, the patient moved his fingers, first opened his mouth, then his eyes, cast around him a troubled, haggard glance, then appeared to be trying to recall, to understand, and he murmured:

"Good God, I am done for."

The doctor held his hand.

"No, no; a question of a few days' rest, it will be all right."

Hautot resumed:

"I am done for! I am torn to bits! I know!"

Then, suddenly:

"I want to talk to my son, if there is time."

In spite of himself, César was weeping, and repeated like a little boy:

"Papa, papa, poor papa!"

But the father said in a more determined tone:

"Come, stop crying, this is no time for tears. I have something to say to you. Sit down there, close to me, it will soon be over, and I shall be easier in my mind. You others, please leave us alone for a minute."

As soon as they were alone:

"Listen, my boy. You are twenty-four, one can talk to you. After all there is not such a mystery about these matters as we attach to them. You know that your mother has been dead seven years and that I am only forty-five, seeing that I married when I was nineteen. Is that not true?"

The son stammered:

"Yes, quite true."

"So then your mother has been dead for seven years, and I am still a widower. Well! a man like me cannot remain a widower at thirty-seven, you agree?"

The son replied:

"That's quite true."

Gasping for breath, very pale and his face drawn with pain, the father continued:

"God! how I suffer! Well, you understand. Man is not made to live alone, but I did not want to give your mother a successor, since I had promised I would not do so. Well . . . you understand?"

"Yes, father."

"Well, I kept a girl at Rouen, number 18 Rue de l'Éperlan, the second door on the third floor—I am telling you all this, don't forget—this young girl has been as nice as nice to me, loving, devoted, a real wife. You understand, my lad?"

"Yes, father."

"Well, if I am taken, I owe her something, something substantial that will place her out of the reach of want. You understand?"

"Yes, father."

"I tell you she is good, really good, and but for you and the memory of your mother and also because we three lived here together in this house, I would have brought her here, and then married her, sure enough . . . listen . . . listen . . . my lad, I might have made a will . . . I have not done so! I did not want to . . . you must never write things down . . . not things of that sort . . . it is bad for the rightful heirs . . . then it muddles up everything . . . it ruins everyone. . . . Look you, never go in for legal documents, never have anything to do

with them. If I am rich it is because I have avoided them all my life. You understand, my boy!"

"Yes, father."

"Now listen. . . . Listen attentively. . . . So I have made no will. . . . I did not want to. . . . Besides, I know you, you are kind-hearted, you are not greedy, not stingy. I said to myself that when I saw the end within sight, I would tell you all about it and would beg you not to forget my darling: Caroline Donet, 18 Rue de l'Éperlan, the second door on the right, don't forget. Further, go there directly I am gone—and make such arrangements that she will have no reason to complain. You have plenty. . . . You can spare it.—I am leaving you well provided for. Listen! You won't find her at home on week-days. She works at Madame Moreau's in the Rue Beauvoisine.⁴ Go on a Thursday. She always expects me on Thursdays. It has been my day for six years. Poor thing, how she will cry! I tell you all this, my boy, because I know you so well. You cannot tell these things to everybody, either to the notary or to the priest. These things happen, everyone knows that, but no one talks about them except when they are obliged. Then again there must be no outsider in the secret, nobody except the family, because a family is the same as an individual! You understand?"

"Yes, father."

"You promise?"

"Yes, father."

"You swear to this?"

"Yes, father."

"I beg, I pray, do not forget, my boy. It means so much to me."

"No, father."

"You will go yourself. I want you to make sure of everything."

"Yes, father."

"And then, you will see . . . you will see what she says. I can't tell you more about it. You swear?"

"Yes, father."

"That's right, my boy. Embrace me. Adieu, I am done for, I know it. Tell the others they may come in."

The son embraced his father, sobbing as he did so, then, obedient as usual, he opened the door and the priest appeared in a white surplice carrying the holy oils.

But the dying man had closed his eyes and refused to open them again, he would not make any response nor would he make any sign to show that he understood.

The man had talked enough, he could not continue. Besides, he now felt quiet in his mind and wanted to die in peace. He felt no need to confess to the priest when he had just made his confession to his son who at all events belonged to the family.

Surrounded by his friends and servants on their bended knees, he received the last rites, was purified, and was given absolution, no change of expression on his face showing that he still lived.

4. An actual street in Rouen.

He died towards midnight after four hours of convulsive movements indicating terrible suffering.

II

He was buried on Tuesday, the shooting season having opened on Sunday. On returning home from the cemetery César Hautot spent the rest of the day weeping. He scarcely slept that night and felt so sad when he awoke that he wondered how he could manage to go on living.

However, until evening he kept on thinking that in accordance with his father's dying wish he must go to Rouen the following day, and see this girl, Caroline Donet, who lived at 18 Rue de l'Éperlan, the second door on the third story. He went on repeating the blindly obeyed the will of his dead father. But now name and address under his breath—just as a prayer is repeated—so as not to forget, and he ended by stammering them unceasingly, without thinking about anything, to such a point had his mind become obsessed by the set phrase.

Accordingly, about eight o'clock next day he ordered Graindorge to be harnessed to the tilbury and set out at the long, swinging pace of the heavy Norman horse along the high road from Ainville to Rouen. He was wearing a black frock-coat, a silk hat, and trousers strapped under his shoes. Owing to the circumstances he had not put on his flowing blue blouse, so easily taken off at the journey's end, over his black clothes to protect them from dust and dirt.

He got to Rouen just as it was striking ten, put up as usual at the Hôtel des Bons Enfants,[5] in the Rue des Trois-Mares, submitted to being embraced by the landlord, his wife and their five sons, for they had heard the sad news; later on he had to tell them all about the accident, which made him shed tears, repel their offers of service thrust upon him on account of his wealth, and even refuse luncheon, which hurt their feelings.

Having wiped the dust off his hat, brushed his coat and cleaned his boots, he started off to seek the Rue de l'Eperlan without daring to make any inquiries, for fear of being recognized and of arousing suspicion.

At last, unable to find the place, he caught sight of a priest, and trusting to the professional discretion of the priesthood, he asked for help.

It was only about one hundred steps farther on—the second street to the right.

Then he hesitated. Up to the present he had felt agitated, confused, humiliated at the idea of finding himself—he, the son—in the presence of the woman who had been his father's mistress.

All our better feelings developed by centuries of family training, all that he had been taught since early childhood about women of loose character, the instinctive distrust that all men feel of these women even when they marry them, all his narrow-minded peasant virtue; all combined to disturb him, to make him hesitate, and fill him with shame.

But he said to himself: "I promised my father. I must not fail." So he pushed the partly-opened door of number 18, discovered a dark staircase, went up three flights, saw first one door, then a second, then found a bell rope, which he pulled.

5. Good Children's Hotel (literal trans.).

The ding-dong that sounded in the next room sent a shiver through his body. The door opened and he found himself face to face with a well-dressed young lady, a brunette with rosy cheeks, who gazed at him with eyes full of astonishment.

He did not know what to say, and she, who suspected nothing and was expecting the father, did not invite him in. They looked at each other about thirty seconds until, at last, she said:

"What do you want, sir?"

He muttered:

"I am the young Hautot."

She started, turned pale, and stammered as if she had known him for a long time:

"Monsieur César?"

"Yes."

"Well?"

"I have a message for you from my father."

She exclaimed: "My God!" and moved away so that he might enter. He closed the door and followed her.

Then he caught sight of a little boy of four or five years playing with a cat, seated on the ground in front of a stove from which rose the odor of food being kept hot.

"Sit down," she said.

He sat down. She said: "Well?"

He dare not say anything, he fixed his eyes on the table standing in the middle of the room that was laid for two grown-ups and a child. He looked at the chair with its back to the fire, the plate, the table napkin and glasses, the bottle of red wine already opened, and the bottle of white wine still uncorked. That was his father's chair, with its back to the fire. They were expecting him. That was his bread near the fork, he knew that because the crust had been removed on account of Hautot's bad teeth. Then, raising his eyes, he noticed his father's portrait hanging on the wall, the large photograph taken at Paris the year of the Exhibition,[6] the same one that hung above the bed in the room at Ainville.

The young woman asked again:

"Well, Monsieur César?"

She stared at him. Her face was deathly white with anxiety, and she waited, her hands trembling with fear.

Then he picked up courage:

"Well, Miss, papa died on Sunday, the first day of the season."

She was too overcome to make any movement. After a silence of a few seconds, she faltered almost inaudibly:

"Oh, it's not possible?"

Then the tears came to her eyes, and covering her face with her hands, she burst out sobbing.

Seeing his mother cry, the little boy turned round and began to roar at the top of his voice. Then, understanding that the sudden grief was caused by the unknown visitor, he threw himself upon César, caught hold of his trousers

6. Probably a reference to the upcoming Exposition Universelle (World's Fair) of 1889 in Paris, at which the Eiffel Tower was introduced.

with one hand and hit his shins as hard as he could with the other. César felt bewildered, deeply affected, thus placed between the woman mourning for his father, and the child who was defending his mother. Their emotion communicated itself to him and his eyes filled with tears, so, to regain his self-control, he began to talk.

"Yes," he said, "the accident occurred on Sunday morning, at eight o'clock." And he told the story in detail, as if she were listening to him, mentioning the most trivial matters with the characteristic thoroughness of the peasant. The child, who had kept on beating César, was now kicking his ankles.

When he reached the point of Hautot's anxiety for her, she heard her name mentioned and, taking her hands from face, asked:

"Excuse me! I was not following you. I would like to know—would it be a bother to you to begin all over again?"

He began the story in the same words: "The accident occurred Sunday morning at eight o'clock."

He repeated everything, at great length, with pauses and occasional reflections of his own. She listened eagerly, feeling with a woman's keen sensitiveness the events as they were unfolded, and, trembling with horror, exclaimed at intervals: "My God!" The boy, thinking that she was all right again, took hold of his mother's hand instead of beating César, and listened attentively as if he understood what was happening.

When the story was finished, young Hautot continued:

"Now, we'll settle matters together according to his wishes. Listen! I am well off, he has left me plenty. I don't want you to have anything to complain about."

She interrupted quickly:

"Oh! Mr. César, not to-day. My heart is . . . Another time . . . another day. . . . No, not to-day. . . . If I accept, listen . . . it is not for myself . . . no, no, no, I swear. It is for the child. Besides, what you give will be placed to his account."

Whereupon César, feeling troubled, guessed the truth and stammered:

"So then . . . it is his . . . the little one?"

"Why, yes," she said.

The young Hautot looked at his brother with confused feelings both intense and painful.

After a long silence, for she was crying again, César, very embarrassed, went on:

"Well, Mam'zelle[7] Donet, I am going. When would you like to talk this over?"

She exclaimed:

"Oh! no, don't go! don't go! Don't leave me all alone with Emile. I would die of grief. I have nobody in the world, nobody but my little one. Oh! what misery, what misery, Mr. César. Do sit down. Tell me some more. Tell me how he spent his time at home."

César, accustomed to obey, sat down again.

She drew another chair near to his, in front of the stove on which the food prepared for lunch was bubbling, took Emile on her lap and asked César hundreds of questions about his father—such simple questions about his ordinary

7. I.e., Mademoiselle or Miss.

everyday life that without reasoning on the subject he felt that she had loved Hautot with all the strength of her aching heart.

And by the natural association of his scanty thoughts he returned to the accident and began to tell her all about it again giving the same details as before.

When he said: "He had a hole in the stomach into which you could put your two fists," she uttered a faint cry and her eyes again filled with tears. Infected by her grief, César began to weep too, and as tears always soften the heart, he bent over Emile, whose forehead was close to his own mouth, and kissed him.

Recovering her breath, the mother murmured:

"Poor boy, he is an orphan now."

"And so am I," said César.

They said no more.

But suddenly the housewife's practical instinct, accustomed to think of everything, reawakened.

"I expect you have had nothing to eat this morning, Mr. César?"

"No, mam'zelle."

"Oh! You must be hungry. You will have a bite?"

"Thank you," he said, "I am not hungry; I have been too worried."

She replied:

"In spite of grief one must go on living, you are surely not going to refuse. Then that will keep you here a little longer. When you are gone, I don't know what I shall do."

He yielded after a little hesitation, and sitting down with his back to the fire, facing her, he ate some of the tripe that was crackling in the oven and drank a glass of red wine. But he would not allow her to uncork the white wine. Several times he wiped the small boy's mouth who had smeared his chin all over with gravy.

As he got up to go, he asked:

"When would you like me to come back to talk the matter over, Mam'zelle Donet?"

"If it is all the same to you, next Thursday, Mr. César. I shall not waste any time that way, as I am always free on Thursdays."

"That will suit me—next Thursday."

"You will come to lunch, won't you?"

"Oh! as for that, I can't promise."

"Well, you know, it is easier to talk when eating. Besides, there is more time."

"Well, all right. At twelve o'clock then."

And off he went after having kissed little Emile and shaken hands with Mademoiselle Donet.

III

The week seemed long to César Hautot. He had never felt so lonely, and the solitude seemed unbearable. Hitherto he had lived with his father, just like his shadow, following him to the fields and superintending the execution of his orders; and when he did leave him for a short time it was only to meet again at dinner. They spent their evenings sitting opposite each other, smoking their pipes and talking about horses, cows or sheep; and the handshake they exchanged every morning was the symbol of deep family affection.

Now César was alone. He strolled about looking on while the harvesters worked, expecting at any moment to see his father's tall gesticulating form at the far end of a field. To kill time he visited his neighbors, telling all about the accident to those who had not already heard it and telling it over again to those who had. Then having reached the end of all that interested him, he would sit down at the side of the road and wonder whether this kind of life would last very long.

He often thought of Mademoiselle Donet. He remembered her with pleasure. He had found her ladylike, gentle and good, exactly as father had described her. Undoubtedly, so far as goodness was concerned, she was good. He was determined to do the thing handsomely and give her two thousand francs a year, settling the capital on the child. He even felt a certain pleasure at the prospect of seeing her again on the following Thursday, and making all the arrangements for her future. Then, although the idea of the brother, the little chap of five—his father's son—did worry and annoy him, it also filled him with a friendly feeling. This illegitimate youngster, though he would never bear the name of Hautot, was, in a sense, a member of the family life, whom he might adopt or abandon as he pleased but who would always remind him of his father.

So that when, on Thursday morning, he was trotting along the road to Rouen on Graindorge's back, he felt lighter-hearted, more at peace than he had done since his bereavement.

On entering Mademoiselle Donet's apartment, he saw the table laid as on the previous Thursday, the only difference being that the crust had been left on the bread.

He shook hands with the young woman, kissed Emile on both cheeks and sat down feeling more or less at home in spite of his heart being heavy. Mademoiselle Donet seemed to him to have grown thinner and paler. She must have wept bitterly. She appeared rather awkward in his presence, as if she now understood what she had not felt the previous week when under the first impression of her loss. She treated him with exaggerated respect, showing stricken humility, and waiting upon him with solicitude as if to repay by her attentions and devotion the kindness he had shown her. The lunch dragged on as they discussed the business that had brought him to the house. She did not want so much money. It was too much, far too much. She earned enough to keep herself and she only wanted Emile to find a small sum awaiting him when he was grown up. César was firm, and even added a present of one thousand francs for her mourning.

When he had finished his coffee, she asked:

"Do you smoke?"

"Yes . . . I have my pipe."

He felt his pocket. Good heavens! he had forgotten it. He was quite miserable until she brought out his father's pipe, which had been put away in a cupboard. He accepted her offer of the pipe, took hold of it, recognized it and smelled it, said what a good one it was, in a voice choked with feeling, filled it with tobacco and lighted it. Then he set Emile astride on his knee and let him play at horses while the mother removed the table-cloth and put the dirty dishes aside in the bottom of the cupboard, intending to wash up as soon as he had gone.

About three o'clock he got up reluctantly, very depressed at the idea of leaving.

"Well, Mademoiselle Donet," he said, "I wish you good afternoon. It has been a pleasure to make your further acquaintance."

She stood before him, blushing, deeply moved, and gazed at him while she thought of the father.

"Shall we never see each other again?" she said.

He replied simply:

"Why, yes, Mademoiselle, if it give you any pleasure."

"Indeed it will, Mr. César. So till next Thursday, if that suits you?"

"Yes, Mademoiselle Donet."

"You will come to lunch, without fail?"

"Well—as you are so kind, I won't refuse."

"It's settled then, next Thursday, at twelve, the same as to-day."

"Thursday at twelve, Mademoiselle Donet!"

JOAQUIM MARIA MACHADO DE ASSIS
1839–1908

No one could have predicted that Joaquim Maria Machado de Assis would became Brazil's greatest writer. Born the grandson of freed slaves in a dilapidated corner of Rio de Janeiro, subject to fits of epilepsy, afflicted with a pronounced stutter, and having no more than an elementary school education, this man of color became the first president of Brazil's Academy of Letters and one of the most innovative, playful, and technically adventurous writers of the whole nineteenth century. Particularly skilled at revealing gaps between high-flown rhetoric and bleak reality, Machado—as he is called—used his fiction to expose hypocrisy and pretension at the heart of Brazilian society.

Machado's father was a housepainter of mixed race, his mother a white Portuguese woman who died when he was a small child. He taught himself largely by listening in on lessons at a girls' school where his stepmother worked in the kitchen. In his early teens he took a job as an apprentice printer and began to write for publication. By the age of twenty-five he was a literary star, having established himself as an editor, translator, poet, and writer of criticism and drama. Elegant, reserved, and courteous, he was happily married to the sister of a close poet friend. Despite his literary success, he took bureaucratic posts in the Brazilian government to ensure a steady income.

Machado eventually became best known for his novels and short stories, which in the 1880s broke with all established schools and styles. Drawing on a huge range of influences that included Shakespeare and Jonathan Swift, Machado often anticipated twentieth-century Modernist fiction by experimenting with unreliable narrators and mischievous addresses to the reader. But he also expanded the possibilities of realism, exploring the complex

psychology and social structures of modern urban life.

The city of Rio de Janeiro was an especially strange and frustrating place to live in the late nineteenth century. Brazil abolished slavery only in 1888, when Machado was forty-nine years old—the last country in the Americas to do so. Over the previous three centuries Brazil had brought in four and a half million Africans, more slaves than any other nation in the New World. Even very poor people—some of them free blacks—often owned a slave or two. The social life of Rio de Janeiro looked quite peculiar to nineteenth-century observers: its elite class turned to Europe for fashion and ideas, imitating especially the upper classes in France and Britain; its "middle class" was typically quite poor, composed of white immigrants from Europe and free black workers; and the whole city was propped up by slave labor.

Machado, more than any of his contemporaries, set out to expose the attitudes and the lies that sustained this lopsided society. Slavery often remains on the margins of Machado's work, but he had a longstanding fascination with questions of authority and control. How do people wield power? Why do others submit? "The Rod of Justice" (1891), our selection below, follows a subtle chain of influence, as a young seminary student tries to figure out how to escape a career in the priesthood. He locates his best chance of help in his godfather's mistress, who herself is eager to show her power over both her lover and her slaves. As the main character is torn between ideals of justice and compassion on the one hand and a desire to realize his own freedom on the other, Machado reveals the subtle and conflicting sources of power organizing Brazilian society.

The Rod of Justice[1]

Damião ran away from the seminary at eleven o'clock in the morning, on a Friday in August. I am not sure of the year, but it was before 1850.[2] After a few minutes he stopped in embarrassment. He had not counted on the effect his appearance would have on other people—a seminarist in his cassock, hurrying along with a dazed, fearful look. He did not recognize the streets, he kept missing his way and retracing his steps. Finally he stopped altogether. Where would he go? Home? No, that was where his father was, and his father would send him back to the seminary, after a good trouncing. He had not settled upon a place of refuge, because his departure had been planned for a later date: an unforeseen circumstance hastened it. Where would he go? He thought of his godfather, João Carneiro, a soft muttonhead with no will of his own. He'd be of no help. It was he who took him to the seminary in the first place and presented him to the rector.

"I bring you the great-man-to-be," he had said to the rector.

"Let him enter, let the great man enter, provided he be also meek and good. True greatness is humble. Young man . . ."

Such was his introduction. Not long after, he ran away. And now we see him in the street, dazed, uncertain, with no idea of where to take refuge, or even

1. Translated by Helen Caldwell.
2. The end of the international slave trade in Brazil.

ask for advice. He mentally ran over the houses of relatives and friends without regarding any one of them with much favor. Suddenly he cried out, "I'll go beg Sinhá[3] Rita to protect me! She will send for my godfather, tell him that she wants me to leave the seminary . . . Maybe . . ."

Sinhá Rita was a widow, the sweetheart of João Carneiro. Damião had certain vague ideas about this situation and decided to turn it to his advantage. Where did she live? He was so confused that it was several minutes before he could remember where her house was. It was in the Largo do Capim.[4]

"Holy name of Jesus! What's this?" screamed Sinhá Rita sitting upright on the settee where she had been reclining. Damião entered terror-stricken. At the very moment of reaching the house, he had seen a priest walking along, had given the door a shove, and by great good luck it was neither locked nor bolted. Once inside, he peeked through the lattice to watch the padre. The latter had not noticed him, and kept on his way.

"But what's this, Senhor Damião?" the mistress of the house again screamed, for it was only now that she recognized him. "What are you doing here?"

Damião, trembling, scarcely able to speak, told her not to be afraid, it was nothing, he would explain everything.

"There, there, go ahead and explain."

"First of all, I have not perpetrated any crime, that I swear! Wait."

Sinhá Rita looked at him with a startled air, and all the little slave girls—those of the household and those from outside—who were seated around the room before their work cushions, all stopped moving their bobbins and their hands. Sinhá Rita made her living, for the most part, by teaching lacemaking, drawn work, and embroidery. While the boy caught his breath, she ordered the little girls back to work, and waited. At last Damião poured out everything: the misery the seminary caused him, he was sure he could never be a good padre. He spoke with passion and begged her to save him.

"How? I can't do anything."

"Yes, you can, if you really want to."

"No," she answered, shaking her head, "I'm not butting into your family's affairs. I scarcely know them. And your father—they say he has a terrible temper!"

Damião saw his hopes fading. He knelt at her feet, kissed her hands in desperation.

"You can do a great deal, Sinhá Rita. I beg you for the love of God—by whatever you hold most sacred, by the soul of your late husband—save me from death, because I'll kill myself if I have to go back to that place."

Sinhá Rita, flattered by the young man's entreaties, tried to recall him to a more cheerful frame of mind. A priest's life was holy and fine, she told him, time would teach him it was better to overcome one's dislikes, and one day . . .

"No, nohow, never!" he retorted shaking his head and kissing her hands, and he kept repeating that it would be his death.

Even then, Sinhá Rita hesitated, for a long time. Finally she asked him why he did not go talk to his godfather.

---

3. Variant of *senhora*, or "mistress"; used by slaves as a form of address.

4. Street in Rio de Janeiro where there was a hangman's scaffold and a slave cemetery.

"My godfather? He's even worse than papa, he doesn't pay any attention to what I say, I don't believe he'd pay attention to anyone . . ."

"No?" interrupted Sinhá Rita, her pride pricked. "Well, I'll show him whether he'll pay attention or not . . ."

She called a slave and ordered him in a loud voice to go to João Carneiro's house and tell him to come at once, and if he was not at home to ask where he could be found, and to run and tell him that she had to speak to him immediately.

"Get along, darky!"

Damião sighed heavily.

To cover up the authority with which she had given these orders, she explained to the youth that Senhor João Carneiro had been a friend of her dead husband and had got her some of these slaves as pupils. Then, as Damião continued to lean gloomily against the door jamb, she smiled and tweaked his nose, "Come, come, your reverence! Don't worry, everything will be all right."

Sinhá Rita was forty years old by her baptismal certificate, but her eyes were seven and twenty. She was a fine figure of a woman, lively, merry, and fond of a joke, but, if need be, fierce as the devil. She set out to cheer the boy up, and it was not hard for her. In a little while they were both laughing: she told him funny stories and asked him to tell her some, which he did with singular wit and charm. One of them, thanks to his crazy capering and grimacing, was so absurd that it made one of Sinhá Rita's pupils laugh: she had forgotten her work to stare at the young man and listen to him. Sinhá Rita grabbed a birch rod that was lying beside the settee and called out in a threatening voice, "Lucretia, mind the rod!"

The little girl lowered her head to parry the blow, but the blow did not fall. It was a warning. If her task was not finished at nightfall, Lucretia would receive the usual punishment. Damião looked at the child: she was a little Negress, a frail wisp of a thing with a scar on her forehead and a burn on her left hand. She was eleven years old. Damião noticed that she kept coughing, but inwardly, and muffled, so as not to interrupt the conversation. He was sorry for the little black girl, and resolved to protect her if she did not finish her task. Sinhá Rita would not refuse to forgive her . . . Besides, she had laughed because she found him amusing; the fault was his, if it is a fault to be witty.

At this point, João Carneiro arrived. He turned pale when he saw his godson there, and looked at Sinhá Rita, who wasted no time in preliminaries. She told him it was necessary to remove the boy from the seminary, that he had no talent for an ecclesiastical life, and better one priest the less than a bad priest. One could love and serve Our Lord out in the world just as well.

João Carneiro was thunderstruck. For several minutes he could find nothing to say. Finally he opened his mouth and began to reprimand his godson for coming and bothering "strangers," and then he asserted he would punish him.

"Punish, nothing!" interrupted Sinhá Rita. "Punish for what? Go on, go talk to the boy's father."

"I don't guarantee anything. I don't believe it will be possible to . . ."

"And I guarantee it will be possible, it has to be. If you have a will to do it, senhor," she continued in an insinuating tone, "everything is bound to be arranged. Keep after him; he'll give in. Get along, João Carneiro, your godson is not going back to the seminary. I tell you, he is not going back . . ."

"But, my dear senhora . . ."

"Go, go on."

João Carneiro was in no hurry to leave, and he could not remain. He was caught between two opposing forces. It really made no difference to him whether his godson ended up a priest, a doctor, a lawyer, or what—even if he turned out to be a good-for-nothing bum and loafer. But, the worst of it was, he was being pushed into a terrible struggle against the most intimate feelings of his friend the boy's father, with no certainty as to the result. If the result proved negative, he would have another fight on his hands with Sinhá Rita, whose final words were, "I tell you he is not going back." There was bound to be a row. João Carneiro's gaze became unsteady, his eyelids twitched, his chest heaved, and the eyes he turned upon Sinhá Rita were full of supplication, mixed with a mild gleam of censure. Why couldn't she ask something else of him? Why couldn't she command him to walk up Tijuca in a pouring rain, or up Jacarèpaguá?[5] But to persuade his godson's father, like that, to change his son's whole career . . . He knew the man, he was quite capable of breaking a water pitcher over his head. Oh, if his godson would only drop dead, then and there, of a fit of apoplexy! It would be a solution, cruel, it is true, but conclusive.

"Well?" insisted Sinhá Rita.

He held up his hand for her to wait. He scratched his beard, hunting for an expedient. God in heaven! a decree of the pope dissolving the Church, or at the least abolishing seminaries, would fix up everything. João Carneiro would go back home and play *três-setes*.[6] Imagine Napoleon's barber entrusted with the command of the battle of Austerlitz[7] . . . But the Church lived on, seminaries lived on, his godson lived on, shrunk against the wall, his eyes downcast, hoping, and giving no promise of an apoplectic solution.

"Be off, be off," said Sinhá Rita, handing him his hat and cane.

There was no help for it. The barber put the razor in its case, girded on his sword, and sallied forth to battle. Damião began to breathe again. Outwardly, however, he was the same, eyes fixed on the ground, dispirited. This time, Sinhá Rita chucked him under the chin. "Come on to dinner, and stop brooding."

"Do you really think, senhora, that he'll do anything?"

"He'll do everything," she asserted with a self-confident air. "Come along or the soup'll get cold."

In spite of Sinhá Rita's boisterous good humor and his own lighthearted nature, Damião was less cheerful at dinner than he had been earlier in the day. He distrusted his godfather's flabby character. Still, he ate a good dinner, and toward the end returned to his jesting mood of that morning. During dessert he heard the sound of voices in the sitting room and asked if they had come to arrest him.

"It must be the girls."

They got up from the table and went into the other room. The "girls" were five young women of the neighborhood who came every afternoon to take coffee with Sinhá Rita, and stayed until nightfall.

---

5. Neighborhoods in Rio de Janeiro.
6. Card game.
7. Defining victory in Napoleon's military career, often considered the height of his tactical genius; Austerlitz is the present-day Slavkov, a town in the Czech Republic.

The pupils finished their dinner and returned to their work cushions. Sinhá Rita was mistress of all this womenfolk—slaves of her own household and from outside. The whisper of the bobbins and the chattering of the "girls" were such worldly echoes, so far from theology and Latin, that the young man gave himself up to them and forgot those other things.

During the first few minutes there was a certain constraint on the part of the neighbor women, but it soon wore off. One of them sang a popular song, to a guitar accompaniment played by Sinhá Rita. And so the afternoon passed quickly. Sinhá Rita asked Damião to tell a certain funny story that had particularly delighted her. It was the one that had made Lucretia laugh.

"Come on, Senhor Damião, don't be coy, the girls have to leave. You'll be crazy about it."

There was nothing for Damião to do but obey. Although the announcement and the expectation served to lessen the drollery and the effect, the story ended amid the loud laughter of the girls. Damião, pleased with himself, did not forget Lucretia, and glanced in her direction to see if she had laughed too. He saw her with her head bent over the work cushion, trying to complete her task. She was not laughing, or she may have been laughing inwardly, just as she coughed.

The neighbor women left, and the day was gone in earnest. Damião's soul grew dark before the night. What was happening? Every other second he went and peered through the lattice and returned each time more downhearted. Not a sign of his godfather. It was certain his father had made him shut up, called a couple of slaves, gone to the police station for an officer, and was on his way thither to seize him by force and drag him back to the seminary. He asked Sinhá Rita if the house happened to have a back door, he ran into the yard and figured he could jump over the wall. He tried to find out if there was a way of escape down the Rua da Valla, or if it was better to speak to one of the neighbors, and see if they would take him in. The worst thing was the cassock: if Sinhá Rita could only get him a man's jacket, an old coat . . . Sinhá Rita just happened to have a man's jacket in the house, a remembrance—or a forgetfulness—of João Carneiro.

"I do have a jacket . . . that belonged to my late husband," she said with a laugh, "but why are you so scared? Everything will be all right. Don't worry."

Finally, at nightfall, there appeared one of his godfather's slaves with a letter for Sinhá Rita. The business was not yet settled; the father was furious and wanted to smash things. He had shouted "no sir," the young dandy would go to the seminary, or he would have him locked up in the Aljube[8] or on a prison ship. João Carneiro fought hard to get him not to make a decision right away, to sleep on it, and think over carefully whether it was *right* to offer the Church such an unruly and vicious character. He explained in the letter that he had spoken in this manner the better to win his case. He did not consider it yet won, but he would go to see him the next day and have another try. He concluded by saying that the young man should go to his house.

Damião finished reading the letter and glanced toward Sinhá Rita. She is my only hope, he thought. Sinhá Rita sent for her inkstand of carved horn, and on

8. Archbishop's prison, famous for its abominable conditions.

the same sheet of paper, below the letter itself, she wrote this reply: "Joãozinho,[9] either you rescue the boy, or we never see each other again." She folded the paper and sealed it with wax, handed it to the slave, and told him to take it back with all speed. She returned to the job of cheering up the seminarist, for he was once more very low and shrouded in despair. She told him to rest easy and leave the matter to her.

"They'll find out what I'm made of! No, I won't stand for any foolishness!"

It was now time to gather up the pieces of needle-work. Sinhá Rita inspected them. All the others had finished their tasks. Only Lucretia still sat before her cushion, moving the bobbins in and out, for some time now without seeing. Sinhá Rita came to where she sat, saw that the allotted task was not finished, became furious, and grabbed her by the ear.

"Ah! low-down good-for-nothing!"

"Nhanhã, Nhanhã,[1] for the love of God! by Our Lady that is in heaven!"

"Trashy good-for-nothing! Our Lady does not protect lazy-bones."

With a tremendous effort, Lucretia wrenched herself free from the hands of her mistress, and ran out of the room. The mistress went after her and grabbed her.

"Come back here!"

"Mistress, forgive me!" coughed the little black girl.

"No, I won't forgive you! Where is the rod?"

They both came back into the sitting room: one held by the ear, struggling, crying, begging; the other saying "no," that she was going to punish her.

"Where is the rod?"

The rod lay on the floor by the settee, on the other side of the room. Sinhá Rita was unwilling to loose her hold on the little girl and yelled to the seminarist, "Senhor Damião, give me that rod, if you please!"

Damião froze . . . Cruel moment! A cloud passed before his eyes. Yes, he had sworn to protect the little girl; it was because of him that she was behind with her work . . .

"Give me the rod, Senhor Damião!"

Damião finally started to walk toward the settee. The little Negress begged him then by all he held most sacred, in the name of his mother, his father, of Our Lord . . .

"Help me, sweet young master!"

Sinhá Rita, her face on fire, her eyes starting from her head, kept calling for the rod, without letting go of the little black girl, who was now held in a fit of coughing.

Damião was pricked by an uneasy sense of guilt, but he wanted so much to get out of the seminary! He reached the settee, picked up the rod, and handed it to Sinhá Rita.

---

9. Diminutive nickname for João, a term of endearment.

1. Variant of *senhora*, mistress.

ANTON CHEKHOV

1860–1904

Anton Chekhov visited the literary giant **Leo Tolstoy** late in the great novelist's life. Tolstoy embraced him warmly, and said: "I can't stand your plays. Shakespeare's are terrible, but yours are worse!" Tolstoy particularly objected that the dramas lacked purpose. "Where does one get to with your heroes?" he asked the young dramatist. "From the sofa to the privy and from the privy back to the sofa?" The ever-modest Chekhov was apparently amused, finding it hard to take offense at a judgment that likened him to Shakespeare. And perhaps he was pleased, too, that Tolstoy's perplexity got at the very heart of Chekhov's innovative writing, which both puzzled and startled his early audiences by refusing grand actions and melodramatic plots: no deaths, no great love affairs, no shocking revelations. Tolstoy was looking for heroes, and Chekhov refuses to give us any, typically offering a constellation of characters, each of whom—even the most minor—can lay claim to a separate life and perspective. Aged servants and bumbling tutors have as much to say as aristocrats and beauties. His plays are like life, Chekhov said, "just as complex and just as simple."

LIFE

Anton Chekhov was born in the thriving Russian seaport town of Taganrog in 1860. His grandfather had been a serf who eventually saved enough money to purchase his freedom. Chekhov himself never forgot how narrowly he had escaped being born into serfdom, and he struggled his whole life against feelings of subservience and inferiority.

Chekhov's father owned a grimy and decrepit grocery store and forced his children to work there. A tyrannical man, he had outbursts of temper, beat his children, insulted his wife, and held fervent religious beliefs. When Chekhov was sixteen, his father went bankrupt and slunk off to Moscow to escape his debtors, where his family soon joined him. They left only Anton to fend for himself in Taganrog. Survival was difficult. His parents insisted that he send them money, so he sold the family furniture and lived with relatives, begging them for small sums.

In 1879, Chekhov won a scholarship to study medicine at Moscow University. In Moscow he found his family poverty-stricken and gloomy, his two older brothers spending what money they earned on drinking and women. Anton took financial responsibility for all of them, writing humorous stories for magazines to make money while studying medicine. He was so prolific that by the age of twenty-six, he had published more than four hundred short pieces in popular magazines as well as two books of stories.

During this period, Chekhov developed two techniques as a writer that would serve him for the rest of his life. First, his medical training taught him a close attention to details, and readers have long praised his skill as an objective observer of subtle signs and gestures. Second, his work as a humor writer demanded brevity: he wrote frequently for a magazine called *Splinters*, which had a strict limit of one hundred words, forcing the young writer to

express his ideas within tight constraints. A friend once found him condensing a story by Tolstoy; he frequently did this kind of exercise, he explained, to practice conciseness.

In his third year of medical school, Chekhov began writing for more serious literary magazines. He was launched on two careers, managing to work as both a physician and a writer until he died. "Medicine is my lawful wife," he once said. "Writing is my mistress." His medical practice was draining because he often treated poor patients for nothing and was called out to visit the sick in the middle of the night. Alarmingly, he started showing symptoms of tuberculosis in 1884.

Chekhov's first full-length play, *Ivanov*, went on stage in 1887. The production was a disaster: none of the actors had learned his or her lines, and one was clearly drunk on stage. Chekhov later dismissed his early plays as conventional and frivolous. It would be another decade before his drama would be treated as seriously as his short fiction, which was making him famous. He won the prestigious Pushkin Prize for his short stories in 1888.

Surprising everyone who knew him, Chekhov decided to write a report about Sakhalin, a penal colony off the coast of Siberia that was notorious for its appalling conditions. What he found was worse even than he had imagined: a "perfect hell." Chained to wheelbarrows, flogged, starved, and sometimes raped and murdered, the prisoners endured a life of daily horror. The women survived mostly by prostitution. Because the Russian government had never collected much information about the prisoners and their families, Chekhov decided to perform a full census of the island himself. This was a massive task, and the writer took notes on the brutal conditions as he moved, offering his medical services to sick prisoners. When he returned, he lobbied for

reform of Sakhalin, especially for the island's children, and published a long and detailed book on the colony in 1894, filled with statistics and shocking truths. The press praised the book; the public was scandalized by the conditions in Sakhalin, and the government began to undertake reforms.

In the 1890s Chekhov finally turned his hand to writing drama again, and this time the plays he wrote were radically experimental, casting off the conventions of sensational melodrama that had dominated Russian theater and ushering in a new style that stressed ensembles rather than heroes and moods rather than actions. The first of these dramas, *The Seagull*, had such a disastrous opening that Chekhov vowed never to write another play. But this failure marked the beginning of a new era in Russian drama. In 1897, a theater opened in Moscow that insisted on naturalistic, modern styles, and its great director, Konstantin Stanislavsky, saw *The Seagull* as the ideal play to mark this innovation. His new production astonished its first audiences. When the curtain fell on the first act, there was total silence. The hush went on for so long that one actress tried to keep from sobbing aloud. But then the audience burst into wild applause. The actors were too stunned to take their bow. What followed were rave reviews and packed houses. Stanislavsky's production of *The Seagull* was hailed as "one of the greatest events in the history of Russian theatre and one of the greatest new developments in the history of world drama." The Moscow Art Theatre took the seagull as its emblem, and it staged all of Chekhov's late dramatic works, including his very last, *The Cherry Orchard*.

The Moscow Art Theatre launched a new phase in Chekhov's personal life as well. He fell in love with one of the actresses in *The Seagull*, Olga Knipper, and married her in 1901, at the age of

forty-one. They moved to Yalta, where they hoped that his health would improve. It did not. Chekhov died of tuberculosis in 1904.

TIMES

Huge social inequalities, fast-paced economic change, and rising political instability produced the pervasive anxiety that characterized Russia at the end of the nineteenth century. The country had begun a phase of rapid industrialization—about a century later than most of western Europe—and saw a dramatic rise in the production of coal, steel, iron, oil, textiles, and beet sugar after 1850. Its population exploded from fifty million in 1860 to about a hundred million in 1900. Russian cities grew quickly, and the railroad expanded dramatically. Tsar Alexander II officially abolished serfdom in 1860, diminishing the traditional influence of landowners, while business and bureaucratic sectors grew and employed ever larger numbers. Newly rich merchants and professionals began to buy property from the old aristocracy.

This profound shift in wealth and power brought a sense of impending crisis. Social groups that had new access to wealth and education frequently expressed anger at the autocratic tsarist regime, and voices across the class spectrum criticized the government for allowing the poor to suffer miserable hardships. Numerous high-ranking officials were assassinated by anarchists and other revolutionary groups, including Tsar Alexander II himself in 1881. The government tried to crack down on social turmoil with widespread arrests. Writers and intellectuals lived in constant fear that they would be thrown into prison, and their work was subject to frequent censorship. Chekhov was among the writers who signed a petition for freedom of the press, which brought him under the surveillance of the tsar's secret police. The end of the century witnessed massive demonstrations against tsarist authority, with students often acting as the leading agitators. In 1901, the Russian minister of education tried to draft two hundred student leaders into the army. In *The Cherry Orchard*, the perpetual student Trofimov would have evoked these dissidents for contemporary audiences, and in fact the censors forced Chekhov to revise his character's most inflammatory speeches.

In the final years of Chekhov's life, Russian society was turning ever more volatile. Tsar Nicholas II was a weak-willed leader, inclined to bow to the dictates of reactionary ministers. Russian liberals clamored for constitutional reforms, while increasingly visible socialists responded to widespread crop failures, cholera epidemics, and grinding rural poverty by demanding outright revolution. In 1904, mounting tensions between Japan and Russia exploded into war. The very day that Chekhov died, July 15, 1904, a homemade bomb thrown by a socialist revolutionary killed the minister of the interior in his carriage. A year later, the Imperial Guard killed a thousand peaceful demonstrators, who had been singing patriotic songs and hymns. Bloody Sunday, as this event came to be called, inflamed antimonarchical sentiment, launched the Russian Revolution of 1905, and heralded the ultimate end of tsarism. In 1917 the Bolshevik-led revolution would bring about a wholly new kind of social organization—the communist state.

Writers and artists working in this atmosphere of violence and instability hotly debated the proper role of the arts. Should art act as provocative political opposition, offering criticism of the status quo and images of a better future? Should it instead glorify the nation, prompting patriotism and loyalty? Or should art retain a fierce inde-

pendence from politics, dedicated to purely aesthetic aims and aspirations? Chekhov had friends who propounded all of these positions, but he managed to elude all of them. Throughout his career, for example, Chekhov stood up for oppressed and marginalized groups, but his stories and plays often steered clear of strong political and moral messages. From the 1930s onward, Chekhov became a favorite among Soviet leaders, who saw him as a proponent of communist ideals and insisted that his plays be produced across the USSR. Meanwhile, his work was taken to stand for individualism—and against Soviet collectivism—in the West. Throughout the twentieth century, Chekhov remained widely popular around the world, and exceptionally difficult to categorize.

WORK

Chekhov made a lasting mark on two major genres: short fiction and drama. When twenty-five famous short story writers in our own time were asked to name the authors who had had the greatest influence on their art, ten of them—including Eudora Welty, Nadine Gordimer, and Raymond Carver—named Chekhov, more than any other writer. (Tied for second place, with five votes each, were Henry James and **James Joyce**.) Chekhov's special aptitude, and what makes him seem especially modern, is his reliance on small, delicate details in place of sensational actions or sudden plot twists. The driving force of his narratives is often not external events at all but mental processes that are subtle and unsettling: unexpected emotions, ambivalent desires, and dawning recognitions.

Vladimir Nabokov called "The Lady with the Dog" (printed here) "one of the greatest stories ever written." Contradictory impulses propel the two

main characters from the beginning: the jaded philanderer Gurov scorns women and yet craves their company, whereas the bored young woman he casually seduces at a seaside resort deceives a husband she condemns as a "flunky" but is then rocked by waves of remorse. Gurov thinks of the affair as a passing thrill, but later, in the woman's absence, he is surprised to discover that he has actually fallen in love with her. Chekhov invites us to recognize this as a major crisis in Gurov's life— his old life becomes unbearable—but it does not interrupt the narrative as a sudden turning point. Instead, the crisis unfolds as a series of fleeting, quiet moments of painful perception. Chekhov does not judge his characters' adultery, as most of his contemporaries would have done, but hints at the value of their transformation, as both are slowly estranged from their earlier selves. And in characteristically Chekhovian fashion, he does not end with a clear or comforting resolution but with a fragile, fleeting, inconclusive moment of genuine intimacy.

Chekhov's drama, like his short fiction, is so subtle and subdued that audiences have often had trouble fitting his work into conventional categories. From the very beginning, for example, there has been a dispute over whether *The Cherry Orchard* (the second selection printed here) is a comedy or a tragedy. The original director Stanislavsky saw the play as a tear-jerker. He wept when he read the text for the first time, and many directors since have foregrounded the pain and loss at the center of the play. Chekhov himself, however, insisted that it was a comic farce, to be played at an almost breakneck speed. (He imagined the fourth act taking a quick twelve minutes, while Stanislavsky stretched it to last forty.) Conventional comedies end in marriage, tragedies in death, and this play does end with the death of the

ancient servant Firs, whom the family has forgotten to send to a nursing home. On the other hand, slapstick moments occur throughout the play, as when Varya smacks her beloved Lopakhin over the head by mistake. Carlotta's magic tricks and Yepikhidov's comically grandiose language compete for attention with passages of poetic beauty. Chekhov wrote that directors like Stanislavsky were misreading him: "First they turn me into a weeper and then into a boring writer." In the century since, directors and actors have had to wrestle with the question of the proper mood and pace for *The Cherry Orchard*, which can change significantly from production to production.

Productions of *The Cherry Orchard* also have to grapple with the political implications of the play. Since the Russian Revolution of 1917, it has been difficult to avoid reading the play as a warning of the coming upheaval. The single event in the drama—the sale of a beautiful but unprofitable aristocratic estate—suggests the passing of the old regime and the coming of a new order. Like the vast expanse of Russia, the orchard is huge, bigger than any real orchard, and like Russian land it is owned by the few rather than the many. Toward the end of Act II Trofimov says explicitly, "This whole country is our orchard." But Chekhov does not agitate for revolution here: instead he captures a feeling of stagnation, the quiet before the storm.

Soviet directors tended to cast the workers as heroic characters—serious and grand—while the aristocrats appeared decadent and foolish. But it is equally plausible to represent the socialist student as a naive idealist with his head so much in the clouds that he cannot even make it down a flight of stairs. Many Western productions have played *The Cherry Orchard* in this way. A third perspective, probably closest to Chekhov's own, is to see the cast as an ensemble, with no characters claiming the heroic center. In such productions, Chekhov offers us representatives from many social groups, all comically misguided but all sympathetic as well.

At the same time as Chekhov gives us a surprisingly wide cross section of Russian society, he diminishes the usual scale of the dramatic action. As the only major event in the play, the sale of the orchard, takes place offstage, what happens onstage is largely banter, offhand remarks, distracted conversation, foundering intentions, and other markers of sheer ordinariness. Notably, Chekhov paid considerable attention to writing meticulous stage directions, which some readers have found poetic in themselves and which suggest that he cared a great deal about the smallest details of clothing, setting, and character arrangement.

Chekhov is perhaps at his most innovative when it comes to the play's extraordinarily complex structure. His drama is more like a musical composition than a traditional dramatic plot: certain words, themes, and images appear, then reappear later, somewhat changed, like leitmotifs. The play organizes itself around multiple, overlapping patterns: it follows the cycle of the cherry trees, from their first blossoming in an unseasonably cold early spring to the ax that chops them down at the end, but it also follows the fates of three young women, Anya, Varya, and Dunyasha, all of whom consider the possibility of marriage, just as it tracks the intensity of loss, from the mother's loss of her child to the aristocrats' loss of land. Echoes and resonances among the characters reverberate in visible groupings onstage: clusters of characters converge and then disperse, and their collective moods shift, like a network of emotions that has its own life. Chekhov's play also follows the model of music in quite a literal way: it orga-

nizes itself around specific, nonverbal *sounds*: the mysterious, sad noise that sounds like a harp string breaking or an echo in a mine shaft, the noise of the axes chopping down the cherry trees, and more comically, Yepikhidov's squeaking boots (which resonate with Pishchik's name, meaning "squeaker"). Throughout, too, music plays a prominent role: among Chekhov's many specific stage directions are details about the music played by the Jewish orchestra, Yepikhidov's guitar, and Ranevskaya's humming. As one director wrote to Chekhov: "Your play is abstract, like a Tchaikovsky symphony."

Although Chekhov's admirers have disagreed about the nature of *The Cherry Orchard*, from those who compared it to a musical abstraction to those who praised it as a politically charged historical chronicle, there has been no disputing its radical originality and its contribution to the history of drama. As Chekhov himself said, in characteristically self-effacing fashion: "I think that, however boring it may be, there's something new about my play."

The Lady with the Dog[1]

I

People were telling one another that a newcomer had been seen on the promenade—a lady with a dog. Dmitri Dmitrich Gurov had been a fortnight in Yalta,[2] and was accustomed to its ways, and he, too, had begun to take an interest in fresh arrivals. From his seat in Vernet's outdoor café, he caught sight of a young woman in a toque, passing along the promenade; she was fair and not very tall; after her trotted a white Pomeranian.

Later he encountered her in the municipal park and in the square several times a day. She was always alone, wearing the same toque, and the Pomeranian always trotted at her side. Nobody knew who she was, and people referred to her simply as "the lady with the dog."

"If she's here without her husband, and without any friends," thought Gurov, "it wouldn't be a bad idea to make her acquaintance."

He was not yet forty but had a twelve-year-old daughter and two sons in high school. He had been talked into marrying in his second year at college, and his wife now looked nearly twice as old as he did. She was a tall woman with dark eyebrows, erect, dignified, imposing, and, as she said of herself, a "thinker." She was a great reader, omitted the "hard sign"[3] at the end of words in her letters, and called her husband "Dimitry" instead of Dmitry; and though he secretly considered her shallow, narrow-minded, and dowdy, he stood in awe of her, and disliked being at home. He had first begun deceiving her long ago and he was now constantly unfaithful to her, and this was no doubt why he spoke slightingly of women, to whom he referred as *the lower race*.

---

1. Translated by Ivy Litvinov.
2. A fashionable seaside resort in the Crimea.
3. Certain progressive intellectuals, anticipating the reform of the Russian alphabet, omitted the hard sign after consonants in writing; here, however, it is an affectation.

He considered that the ample lessons he had received from bitter experience entitled him to call them whatever he liked, but without this "lower race" he could not have existed a single day. He was bored and ill-at-ease in the company of men, with whom he was always cold and reserved, but felt quite at home among women, and knew exactly what to say to them, and how to behave; he could even be silent in their company without feeling the slightest awkwardness. There was an elusive charm in his appearance and disposition which attracted women and caught their sympathies. He knew this and was himself attracted to them by some invisible force.

Repeated and bitter experience had taught him that every fresh intimacy, while at first introducing such pleasant variety into everyday life, and offering itself as a charming, light adventure, inevitably developed, among decent people (especially in Moscow, where they are so irresolute and slow to move), into a problem of excessive complication leading to an intolerably irksome situation. But every time he encountered an attractive woman he forgot all about this experience, the desire for life surged up in him, and everything suddenly seemed simple and amusing.

One evening, then, while he was dining at the restaurant in the park, the lady in the toque came strolling up and took a seat at a neighboring table. Her expression, gait, dress, coiffure, all told him that she was from the upper classes, that she was married, that she was in Yalta for the first time, alone and bored. . . . The accounts of the laxity of morals among visitors to Yalta are greatly exaggerated, and he paid no heed to them, knowing that for the most part they were invented by people who would gladly have transgressed themselves, had they known how to set about it. But when the lady sat down at a neighboring table a few yards away from him, these stories of easy conquests, of excursions to the mountains, came back to him, and the seductive idea of a brisk transitory liaison, an affair with a woman whose very name he did not know, suddenly took possession of his mind.

He snapped his fingers at the Pomeranian and, when it trotted up to him, shook his forefinger at it. The Pomeranian growled. Gurov shook his finger again.

The lady glanced at him and instantly lowered her eyes.

"He doesn't bite," she said, and blushed.

"May I give him a bone?" he asked, and on her nod of consent added in friendly tones: "Have you been long in Yalta?"

"About five days."

"And I am dragging out my second week here."

Neither spoke for a few minutes.

"The days pass quickly, and yet one is so bored here," she said, not looking at him.

"It's the thing to say it's boring here. People never complain of boredom in godforsaken holes like Belyev or Zhizdra, but when they get here it's: 'Oh, the dullness! Oh, the dust!' You'd think they'd come from Granada[4] to say the least."

---

4. A famous medieval city in Spain, once capital of the Moorish kingdom of Granada and now a tourist center known for its art and architecture. Belyev and Zhizdra are small provincial towns.

She laughed. Then they both went on eating in silence, like complete strangers. But after dinner they left the restaurant together, and embarked upon the light, jesting talk of people free and contented, for whom it is all the same where they go, or what they talk about. They strolled along, remarking on the strange light over the sea. The water was a warm, tender purple, the moonlight lay on its surface in a golden strip. They said how close it was, after the hot day. Gurov told her he was from Moscow, that he was really a philologist, but worked in a bank; that he had at one time trained himself to sing in a private opera company, but had given up the idea; that he owned two houses in Moscow. . . . And from her he learned that she had grown up in Petersburg,[5] but had gotten married in the town of S., where she had been living two years, that she would stay another month in Yalta, and that perhaps her husband, who also needed a rest, would join her. She was quite unable to explain whether her husband was a member of the province council, or on the board of the *zemstvo*,[6] and was greatly amused at herself for this. Further, Gurov learned that her name was Anna Sergeyevna.

Back in his own room he thought about her, and felt sure he would meet her the next day. It was inevitable. As he went to bed he reminded himself that only a very short time ago she had been a schoolgirl, like his own daughter, learning her lessons, he remembered how much there was of shyness and constraint in her laughter, in her way of conversing with a stranger—it was probably the first time in her life that she found herself alone, and in a situation in which men could follow her and watch her, and speak to her, all the time with a secret aim she could not fail to divine. He recalled her slender, delicate neck, her fine gray eyes.

"And yet there's something pathetic about her," he thought to himself as he fell asleep.

II

A week had passed since the beginning of their acquaintance. It was a holiday. Indoors it was stuffy, but the dust rose in clouds out of doors, and people's hats blew off. It was a parching day and Gurov kept going to the outdoor café for fruit drinks and ices to offer Anna Sergeyevna. The heat was overpowering.

In the evening, when the wind had dropped, they walked to the pier to see the steamer come in. There were a great many people strolling about the landing-place; some, bunches of flowers in their hands, were meeting friends. Two peculiarities of the smart Yalta crowd stood out distinctly—the elderly ladies all tried to dress very youthfully, and there seemed to be an inordinate number of generals about.

Owing to the roughness of the sea the steamer arrived late, after the sun had gone down, and it had to maneuver for some time before it could get alongside the pier. Anna Sergeyevna scanned the steamer and passengers through her lorgnette,[7] as if looking for someone she knew, and when she turned to Gurov her eyes were glistening. She talked a great deal, firing off abrupt questions and forgetting immediately what it was she had wanted to know. Then she lost her lorgnette in the crush.

---

5. St. Petersburg, the former capital of Russia: an important port and cultural center.

6. District administration.

7. Small eyeglasses on a short handle.

The smart crowd began dispersing, features could no longer be made out, the wind had quite dropped, and Gurov and Anna Sergeyevna stood there as if waiting for someone else to come off the steamer. Anna Sergeyevna had fallen silent, every now and then smelling her flowers, but not looking at Gurov.

"It's turned out a fine evening," he said. "What shall we do? We might go for a drive."

She made no reply.

He looked steadily at her and suddenly took her in his arms and kissed her lips, and the fragrance and dampness of the flowers closed round him, but the next moment he looked behind him in alarm—had anyone seen them?

"Let's go to your room," he murmured.

And they walked off together, very quickly.

Her room was stuffy and smelt of some scent she had bought in the Japanese shop.[8] Gurov looked at her, thinking to himself: "How full of strange encounters life is!" He could remember carefree, good-natured women who were exhilarated by love-making and grateful to him for the happiness he gave them, however short-lived; and there had been others—his wife among them—whose caresses were insincere, affected, hysterical, mixed up with a great deal of quite unnecessary talk, and whose expression seemed to say that all this was not just lovemaking or passion, but something much more significant; then there had been two or three beautiful, cold women, over whose features flitted a predatory expression, betraying a determination to wring from life more than it could give, women no longer in their first youth, capricious, irrational, despotic, brainless, and when Gurov had cooled to these, their beauty aroused in him nothing but repulsion, and the lace trimming on their underclothes reminded him of fish-scales.

But here the timidity and awkwardness of youth and inexperience were still apparent; and there was a feeling of embarrassment in the atmosphere, as if someone had just knocked at the door. Anna Sergeyevna, "the lady with the dog," seemed to regard the affair as something very special, very serious, as if she had become a fallen woman, an attitude he found odd and disconcerting. Her features lengthened and drooped, and her long hair hung mournfully on either side of her face. She assumed a pose of dismal meditation, like a repentant sinner in some classical painting.[9]

"It isn't right," she said. "You will never respect me anymore."

On the table was a watermelon. Gurov cut himself a slice from it and began slowly eating it. At least half an hour passed in silence.

Anna Sergeyevna was very touching, revealing the purity of a decent, naïve woman who had seen very little of life. The solitary candle burning on the table scarcely lit up her face, but it was obvious that her heart was heavy.

"Why should I stop respecting you?" asked Gurov. "You don't know what you're saying."

"May God forgive me!" she exclaimed, and her eyes filled with tears. "It's terrible."

8. Probably a tourist shop with imported goods.
9. A famous painting of Mary Magdalen (see Luke 7.36–50) by the French classical artist Georges de la Tour (1593–1652) shows her seated at a table meditating, her face and long hair illuminated by a candle.

"No need to seek to justify yourself."

"How can I justify myself? I'm a wicked, fallen woman, I despise myself and have not the least thought of self-justification. It isn't my husband I have deceived, it's myself. And not only now, I have been deceiving myself for ever so long. My husband is no doubt an honest, worthy man, but he's a flunky. I don't know what it is he does at his office, but I know he's a flunky. I was only twenty when I married him, and I was devoured by curiosity, I wanted something higher. I told myself that there must be a different kind of life I wanted to live, to live. . . . I was burning with curiosity . . . you'll never understand that, but I swear to God I could no longer control myself, nothing could hold me back, I told my husband I was ill, and I came here. . . . And I started going about like one possessed, like a madwoman . . . and now I have become an ordinary, worthless woman, and everyone has the right to despise me."

Gurov listened to her, bored to death. The naïve accents, the remorse, all was so unexpected, so out of place. But for the tears in her eyes, she might have been jesting or play-acting.

"I don't understand," he said gently. "What is it you want?"

She hid her face against his breast and pressed closer to him.

"Do believe me, I implore you to believe me," she said. "I love all that is honest and pure in life, vice is revolting to me, I don't know what I'm doing. The common people say they are snared by the Devil. And now I can say that I have been snared by the Devil, too."

"Come, come," he murmured.

He gazed into her fixed, terrified eyes, kissed her, and soothed her with gentle affectionate words, and gradually she calmed down and regained her cheefulness. Soon they were laughing together again.

When, a little later, they went out, there was not a soul on the promenade, the town and its cypresses looked dead, but the sea was still roaring as it dashed against the beach. A solitary fishing-boat tossed on the waves, its lamp blinking sleepily.

They found a carriage and drove to Oreanda.[1]

"I discovered your name in the hall, just now," said Gurov, "written up on the board. Von Diederitz. Is your husband a German?"

"No. His grandfather was, I think, but he belongs to the Orthodox Church himself."

When they got out of the carriage at Oreanda they sat down on a bench not far from the church, and looked down at the sea, without talking. Yalta could be dimly discerned through the morning mist, and white clouds rested motionless on the summits of the mountains. Not a leaf stirred, the grasshoppers chirruped, and the monotonous hollow roar of the sea came up to them, speaking of peace, of the eternal sleep lying in wait for us all. The sea had roared like this long before there was any Yalta or Oreanda, it was roaring now, and it would go on roaring, just as indifferently and hollowly, when we had passed away. And it may be that in this continuity, this utter indifference of life and death, lies the secret of our ultimate salvation, of the stream of life on our planet, and of its never-ceasing movement towards perfection.

1. A hotel and beach compound near Yalta; the whole area is known as the Ukrainian Riviera.

Side by side with a young woman, who looked so exquisite in the early light, soothed and enchanted by the sight of all this magical beauty—sea, mountains, clouds and the vast expanse of the sky—Gurov told himself that, when you came to think of it, everything in the world is beautiful really, everything but our own thoughts and actions, when we lose sight of the higher aims of life, and of our dignity as human beings.

Someone approached them—a watchman, probably—looked at them and went away. And there was something mysterious and beautiful even in this. The steamer from Feodosia[2] could be seen coming towards the pier, lit up by the dawn, its lamps out.

"There's dew on the grass," said Anna Sergeyevna, breaking the silence.

"Yes. Time to go home."

They went back to the town.

After this they met every day at noon on the promenade, lunching and dining together, going for walks, and admiring the sea. She complained of sleeplessness, of palpitations, asked the same questions over and over again, alternately surrendering to jealousy and the fear that he did not really respect her. And often, when there was nobody in sight in the square or the park, he would draw her to him and kiss her passionately. The utter idleness, these kisses in broad daylight, accompanied by furtive glances and the fear of discovery, the heat, the smell of the sea, and the idle, smart, well-fed people continually crossing their field of vision, seemed to have given him a new lease of life. He told Anna Sergeyevna she was beautiful and seductive, made love to her with impetuous passion, and never left her side, while she was always pensive, always trying to force from him the admission that he did not respect her, that he did not love her a bit, and considered her just an ordinary woman. Almost every night they drove out of town, to Oreanda, the waterfall, or some other beauty-spot. And these excursions were invariably a success, each contributing fresh impressions of majestic beauty.

All this time they kept expecting her husband to arrive. But a letter came in which he told his wife that he was having trouble with his eyes, and implored her to come home as soon as possible. Anna Sergeyevna made hasty preparations for leaving.

"It's a good thing I'm going," she said to Gurov. "It's the intervention of fate."

She left Yalta in a carriage, and he went with her as far as the railway station. The drive took nearly a whole day. When she got into the express train, after the second bell had been rung, she said:

"Let me have one more look at you. . . . One last look. That's right."

She did not weep, but was mournful, and seemed ill, the muscles of her cheeks twitching.

"I shall think of you . . . I shall think of you all the time," she said. "God bless you! Think kindly of me. We are parting forever, it must be so, because we ought never to have met. Good-bye—God bless you."

The train steamed rapidly out of the station, its lights soon disappearing, and a minute later even the sound it made was silenced, as if everything were conspiring to bring this sweet oblivion, this madness, to an end as quickly as possi-

2. A coastal town seventy miles northeast of Yalta.

ble. And Gurov, standing alone on the platform and gazing into the dark distance, listened to the shrilling of the grasshoppers and the humming of the telegraph wires, with a feeling that he had only just awakened. And he told himself that this had been just one more of the many adventures in his life, and that it, too, was over, leaving nothing but a memory. . . . He was moved and sad, and felt a slight remorse. After all, this young woman whom he would never again see had not been really happy with him. He had been friendly and affectionate with her, but in his whole behaviour, in the tones of his voice, in his very caresses, there had been a shade of irony, the insulting indulgence of the fortunate male, who was, moreover, almost twice her age. She had insisted in calling him good, remarkable, high-minded. Evidently he had appeared to her different from his real self, in a word he had involuntarily deceived her. . . .

There was an autumnal feeling in the air, and the evening was chilly.

"It's time for me to be going north, too," thought Gurov, as he walked away from the platform. "High time!"

III

When he got back to Moscow it was beginning to look like winter; the stoves were heated every day, and it was still dark when the children got up to go to school and drank their tea, so that the nurse had to light the lamp for a short time. Frost had set in. When the first snow falls, and one goes for one's first sleigh-ride, it is pleasant to see the white ground, the white roofs; one breathes freely and lightly, and remembers the days of one's youth. The ancient lime-trees and birches, white with hoarfrost, have a good-natured look, they are closer to the heart than cypresses and palms, and beneath their branches one is no longer haunted by the memory of mountains and the sea.

Gurov had always lived in Moscow, and he returned to Moscow on a fine frosty day, and when he put on his fur-lined overcoat and thick gloves, and sauntered down Petrovka Street, and when, on Saturday evening, he heard the church bells ringing, his recent journey and the places he had visited lost their charm for him. He became gradually immersed in Moscow life, reading with avidity three newspapers a day, while declaring he never read Moscow newspapers on principle. Once more he was caught up in a whirl of restaurants, clubs, banquets, and celebrations, once more he glowed with the flattering consciousness that well-known lawyers and actors came to his house, that he played cards in the Medical Club opposite a professor. He could once again eat a whole serving of Moscow Fish Stew served in a pan.

He had believed that in a month's time Anna Sergeyevna would be nothing but a vague memory, and that hereafter, with her wistful smile, she would only occasionally appear to him in dreams, like others before her. But the month was now well over and winter was in full swing, and all was as clear in his memory as if he had parted with Anna Sergeyevna only the day before. And his recollections grew ever more insistent. When the voices of his children at their lessons reached him in his study through the evening stillness, when he heard a song, or the sounds of a music-box in a restaurant, when the wind howled in the chimney, it all came back to him: early morning on the pier, the misty mountains, the steamer from Feodosia, the kisses. He would pace up and down his room for a long time, smiling at his memories, and then memory

turned into dreaming, and what had happened mingled in his imagination with what was going to happen. Anna Sergeyevna did not come to him in his dreams, she accompanied him everywhere, like his shadow, following him everywhere he went. When he closed his eyes, she seemed to stand before him in the flesh, still lovelier, younger, tenderer than she had really been, and looking back, he saw himself, too, as better than he had been in Yalta. In the evenings she looked out at him from the bookshelves, the fireplace, the corner, he could hear her breathing, the sweet rustle of her skirts. In the streets he followed women with his eyes, to see if there were any like her. . . .

He began to feel an overwhelming desire to share his memories with someone. But he could not speak of his love at home, and outside his home who was there for him to confide in? Not the tenants living in his house, and certainly not his colleagues at the bank. And what was there to tell? Was it love that he had felt? Had there been anything exquisite, poetic, anything instructive or even amusing about his relations with Anna Sergeyevna? He had to content himself with uttering vague generalizations about love and women, and nobody guessed what he meant, though his wife's dark eyebrows twitched as she said:

"The role of a coxcomb doesn't suit you a bit, Dimitry."

One evening, leaving the Medical Club with one of his card-partners, a government official, he could not refrain from remarking:

"If you only knew what a charming woman I met in Yalta!"

The official got into his sleigh, and just before driving off, turned and called out:

"Dmitry Dmitrich!"

"Yes?"

"You were quite right, you know—the sturgeon was just a *leetle* off."

These words, in themselves so commonplace, for some reason infuriated Gurov, seemed to him humiliating, gross. What savage manners, what people! What wasted evenings, what tedious, empty days! Frantic card-playing, gluttony, drunkenness, perpetual talk always about the same thing. The greater part of one's time and energy went on business that was no use to anyone, and on discussing the same thing over and over again, and there was nothing to show for it all but a stunted, earth-bound existence and a round of trivialities, and there was nowhere to escape to, you might as well be in a madhouse or a convict settlement.

Gurov lay awake all night, raging, and went about the whole of the next day with a headache. He slept badly on the succeeding nights, too, sitting up in bed, thinking, or pacing the floor of his room. He was sick of his children, sick of the bank, felt not the slightest desire to go anywhere or talk about anything.

When the Christmas holidays came, he packed his things, telling his wife he had to go to Petersburg in the interests of a certain young man, and set off for the town of S. To what end? He hardly knew himself. He only knew that he must see Anna Sergeyevna, must speak to her, arrange a meeting, if possible.

He arrived at S. in the morning and engaged the best suite in the hotel, which had a carpet of gray military frieze, and a dusty ink-pot on the table, surmounted by a headless rider, holding his hat in his raised hand. The hall porter told him what he wanted to know: von Diederitz had a house of his own in Staro-Goncharnaya Street. It wasn't far from the hotel, he lived on a grand scale, luxuriously, kept carriage-horses, the whole town knew him. The hall porter pronounced the name "Drideritz."

Gurov strolled over to Staro-Goncharnaya Street and discovered the house. In front of it was a long gray fence with inverted nails hammered into the tops of the palings.

"A fence like that is enough to make anyone want to run away," thought Gurov, looking at the windows of the house and the fence.

He reasoned that since it was a holiday, Anna's husband would probably be at home. In any case it would be tactless to embarrass her by calling at the house. And a note might fall into the hands of the husband, and bring about catastrophe. The best thing would be to wait about on the chance of seeing her. And he walked up and down the street, hovering in the vicinity of the fence, watching for his chance. A beggar entered the gate, only to be attacked by dogs, then, an hour later, the faint, vague sounds of a piano reached his ears. That would be Anna Sergeyevna playing. Suddenly the front door opened and an old woman came out, followed by a familiar white Pomeranian. Gurov tried to call to it, but his heart beat violently, and in his agitation he could not remember its name.

He walked on, hating the gray fence more and more, and now ready to tell himself irately that Anna Sergeyevna had forgotten him, had already, perhaps, found distraction in another—what could be more natural in a young woman who had to look at this accursed fence from morning to night? He went back to his hotel and sat on the sofa in his suite for some time, not knowing what to do, then he ordered dinner, and after dinner, had a long sleep.

"What a foolish, restless business," he thought, waking up and looking towards the dark windowpanes. It was evening by now. "Well, I've had my sleep out. And what am I to do in the night?"

He sat up in bed, covered by the cheap gray quilt, which reminded him of a hospital blanket, and in his vexation he fell to taunting himself.

"You and your lady with a dog . . . there's adventure for you! See what you get for your pains."

On his arrival at the station that morning he had noticed a poster announcing in enormous letters the first performance at the local theatre of *The Geisha*.[3] Remembering this; he got up and made for the theatre.

"It's highly probable that she goes to first nights," he told himself.

The theatre was full. It was a typical provincial theatre, with a mist collecting over the chandeliers, and the crowd in the gallery fidgeting noisily. In the first row of the stalls the local dandies stood waiting for the curtain to go up, their hands clasped behind them. There, in the front seat of the governor's box, sat the governor's daughter, wearing a boa, the governor himself hiding modestly behind the drapes, so that only his hands were visible. The curtain stirred, the orchestra took a long time tuning up their instruments. Gurov's eyes roamed eagerly over the audience as they filed in and occupied their seats.

Anna Sergeyevna came in, too. She seated herself in the third row of the stalls, and when Gurov's glance fell on her, his heart seemed to stop, and he knew in a flash that the whole world contained no one nearer or dearer to him, no one more important to his happiness. This little woman, lost in the provincial crowd, in no way remarkable, holding a silly lorgnette in her hand, now filled his whole life, was his grief, his joy, all that he desired. Lulled by the sounds coming from the wretched orchestra, with its feeble, amateurish violinists, he thought how beautiful she was . . . thought and dreamed. . . .

---

3. An operetta (1896) by the English composer Sidney Jones.

Anna Sergeyevna was accompanied by a tall, round-shouldered young man with small whiskers, who nodded at every step before taking the seat beside her and seemed to be continually bowing to someone. This must be her husband, whom, in a fit of bitterness, at Yalta, she had called a "flunky." And there really was something of a lackey's servility in his lanky figure, his side-whiskers, and the little bald spot on the top of his head. And he smiled sweetly, and the badge of some scientific society gleaming in his buttonhole was like the number on a footman's livery.

The husband went out to smoke in the first interval, and she was left alone in her seat. Gurov, who had taken a seat in the stalls, went up to her and said in a trembling voice, with a forced smile: "How d'you do?"

She glanced up at him and turned pale, then looked at him again in alarm, unable to believe her eyes, squeezing her fan and lorgnette in one hand, evidently struggling to overcome a feeling of faintness. Neither of them said a word. She sat there, and he stood beside her, disconcerted by her embarrassment, and not daring to sit down. The violins and flutes sang out as they were tuned, and there was a tense sensation in the atmosphere, as if they were being watched from all the boxes. At last she got up and moved rapidly towards one of the exits. He followed her and they wandered aimlessly along corridors, up and down stairs; figures flashed by in the uniforms of legal officials, high-school teachers and civil servants, all wearing badges; ladies, coats hanging from pegs flashed by; there was a sharp draft, bringing with it an odor of cigarette butts. And Gurov, whose heart was beating violently, thought:

"What on earth are all these people, this orchestra for? . . ."

The next minute he suddenly remembered how, after seeing Anna Sergeyevna off that evening at the station, he had told himself that all was over, and they would never meet again. And how far away the end seemed to be now!

She stopped on a dark narrow staircase over which was a notice bearing the inscription "To the upper circle."[4]

"How you frightened me!" she said, breathing heavily, still pale and half-stunned. "Oh, how you frightened me! I'm almost dead! Why did you come? Oh, why?"

"But, Anna," he said, in low, hasty tones. "But, Anna. . . . Try to understand . . . do try. . . ."

She cast him a glance of fear, entreaty, love, and then gazed at him steadily, as if to fix his features firmly in her memory.

"I've been so unhappy," she continued, taking no notice of his words. "I could think of nothing but you the whole time, I lived on the thoughts of you. I tried to forget—why, oh, why did you come?"

On the landing above them were two schoolboys, smoking and looking down, but Gurov did not care, and, drawing Anna Sergeyevna towards him, began kissing her face, her lips, her hands.

"What are you doing, oh, what are you doing?" she said in horror, drawing back. "We have both gone mad. Go away this very night, this moment. . . . By all that is sacred, I implore you. . . . Somebody is coming."

Someone was ascending the stairs.

"You must go away," went on Anna Sergeyevna in a whisper. "D'you hear me, Dmitry Dmitrich? I'll come to you in Moscow. I have never been happy, I am

4. The stalls or back rows; a medium-priced area behind the orchestra seats on the main floor.

unhappy now, and I shall never be happy—never! Do not make me suffer still more! I will come to you in Moscow, I swear it! And now we must part! My dear one, my kind one, my darling, we must part."

She pressed his hand and hurried down the stairs, looking back at him continually, and her eyes showed that she was in truth unhappy. Gurov stood where he was for a short time, listening, and when all was quiet, went to look for his coat, and left the theatre.

IV

And Anna Sergeyevna began going to Moscow to see him. Every two or three months she left the town of S., telling her husband that she was going to consult a specialist on female diseases, and her husband believed her and did not believe her. In Moscow she always stayed at the Slavyanski Bazaar,[5] sending a man in a red cap to Gurov the moment she arrived. Gurov went to her, and no one in Moscow knew anything about it.

One winter morning he went to see her as usual (the messenger had been to him the evening before, but had not found him at home). His daughter was with him, for her school was on the way and he thought he might as well see her to it.

"It is forty degrees," said Gurov to his daughter, "and yet it is snowing. You see it is only above freezing close to the ground, the temperature in the upper layers of the atmosphere is quite different."

"Why doesn't it ever thunder in winter, Papa?"

He explained this, too. As he was speaking, he kept reminding himself that he was going to a rendezvous and that not a living soul knew about it, or, probably, ever would. He led a double life—one in public, in the sight of all whom it concerned, full of conventional truth and conventional deception, exactly like the lives of his friends and acquaintances, and another which flowed in secret. And, owing to some strange, possibly quite accidental chain of circumstances, everything that was important, interesting, essential, everything about which he was sincere and never deceived himself, everything that composed the kernel of his life, went on in secret, while everything that was false in him, everything that composed the husk in which he hid himself and the truth which was in him—his work at the bank, discussions at the club, his "lower race," his attendance at anniversary celebrations with his wife—was on the surface. He began to judge others by himself, no longer believing what he saw, and always assuming that the real, the only interesting life of every individual goes on as under cover of night, secretly. Every individual existence revolves around mystery, and perhaps that is the chief reason that all cultivated individuals insisted so strongly on the respect due to personal secrets.

After leaving his daughter at the door of her school Gurov set off for the Slavyanski Bazaar. Taking off his overcoat in the lobby, he went upstairs and knocked softly on the door. Anna Sergeyevna, wearing the gray dress he liked most, exhausted by her journey and by suspense, had been expecting him since the evening before. She was pale and looked at him without smiling, but was in his arms almost before he was fairly in the room. Their kiss was lingering, prolonged, as if they had not met for years.

5. A luxurious hotel in Moscow.

"Well, how are you?" he asked. "Anything new?"

"Wait, I'll tell you in a minute. . . . I can't. . . ."

She could not speak, because she was crying. Turning away, she held her handkerchief to her eyes.

"I'll wait till she's had her cry out," he thought, and sank into a chair.

He rang for tea, and a little later, while he was drinking it, she was still standing there, her face to the window. She wept from emotion, from her bitter consciousness of the sadness of their life; they could only see one another in secret, hiding from people, as if they were thieves. Was not their life a broken one?

"Don't cry," he said.

It was quite obvious to him that this love of theirs would not soon come to an end, and that no one could say when this end would be. Anna Sergeyevna loved him ever more fondly, worshipped him, and there would have been no point in telling her that one day it must end. Indeed, she would not have believed him.

He moved over and took her by the shoulders, intending to fondle her with light words, but suddenly he caught sight of himself in the looking-glass.

His hair was already beginning to turn gray. It struck him as strange that he should have aged so much in the last few years. The shoulders on which his hands lay were warm and quivering. He felt a pity for this life, still so warm and exquisite, but probably soon to fade and droop like his own. Why did she love him so? Women had always believed him different from what he really was, had loved in him not himself but the man their imagination pictured him, a man they had sought for eagerly all their lives. And afterwards when they discovered their mistake, they went on loving him just the same. And not one of them had ever been happy with him. Time had passed, he had met one woman after another, become intimate with each, parted with each, but had never loved. There had been all sorts of things between them, but never love.

And only now, when he was gray-haired, had he fallen in love properly, thoroughly, for the first time in his life.

He and Anna Sergeyevna loved one another as people who are very close and intimate, as husband and wife, as dear friends love one another. It seemed to them that fate had intended them for one another, and they could not understand why she should have a husband, and he a wife. They were like two migrating birds, the male and the female, who had been caught and put into separate cages. They forgave one another all that they were ashamed of in the past and in the present, and felt that this love of theirs had changed them both.

Formerly, in moments of melancholy, he had consoled himself by the first argument that came into his head, but now arguments were nothing to him, he felt profound pity, desired to be sincere, tender.

"Stop crying, my dearest," he said. "You've had your cry, now stop. . . . Now let us have a talk, let us try and think what we are to do."

Then they discussed their situation for a long time, trying to think how they could get rid of the necessity for hiding, deception, living in different towns, being so long without meeting. How were they to shake off these intolerable fetters?

"How? How?" he repeated, clutching his head. "How?"

And it seemed to them that they were within an inch of arriving at a decision, and that then a new, beautiful life would begin. And they both realized that the end was still far, far away, and that the hardest, the most complicated part was only just beginning.

The Cherry Orchard

A Comedy in Four Acts[1]

CHARACTERS

LIUBÓV RANYÉVSKAYA [Lyúba, Liúba
   Andréyevna], *who owns the estate*
ÁNYA, *her daughter, seventeen years old*
VÁRYA, *her adopted daughter,*
   twenty-four years old
LEONÍD GÁYEV [Lonya, Lyónya
   Andréyich], *Liubóv's brother*
YERMOLÁI LOPÁKHIN [Yermolái
   Alexéyich], *a businessman*
PÉTYA TROFÍMOV, *a graduate student*
BORÍS SEMYÓNOV-PÍSHCHIK, *who owns*
   land in the neighborhood

CARLOTTA, *the governess*
SEMYÓN YEPIKHÓDOV, *an accountant*
DUNYÁSHA [Avdótya Fyódorovna,
   Dunyáhsa Kozoyédov],
   the maid
FIRS, *the butler, eighty-seven*
   years old
YÁSHA, *the valet*
A HOMELESS MAN
THE STATIONMASTER
THE POSTMASTER
GUESTS, SERVANTS

The action takes place on RANYÉVSKAYA'S *estate.*

Act 1

[*A room they still call the nursery. A side door leads to* ÁNYA'S *room. Almost dawn; the sun is about to rise. It's May; the cherry orchard is already in bloom, but there's a chill in the air. The windows are shut. Enter* DUNYÁSHA *with a lamp, and* LOPÁKHIN *with a book in his hand.*]

LOPÁKHIN   The train's finally in, thank God. What time is it?

DUNYÁSHA   Almost two. [*She blows out the lamp.*] It's getting light.

LOPÁKHIN   How late is the train this time? Must be at least two hours. [*He yawns and stretches.*] That was dumb. I came over on purpose just to meet them at the station, and then I fell asleep. Sat right here and fell asleep. Too bad. You should have woke me up.

DUNYÁSHA   I thought you already left. [*She listens.*] Listen, that must be them.

LOPÁKHIN [*he listens*]   No, they still have the luggage to get, and all that. [*Pause*] She's been away five years now; no telling how she's changed. She was always a good person. Very gentle, never caused a fuss. I remember one time when I was a kid, fifteen or so, they had my old man working in the store down by the village, and he hit me, hard, right in the face; my nose started to bleed. And we had to come up here to make a delivery or something; he was still drunk. And Liubóv Andréyevna—she wasn't much older than I was, kind of thin—she brought me inside the house, right into the nursery here, and washed the blood off my face for me. "Don't cry," she told me. "Don't cry, poor boy; you'll live long enough to get married." [*Pause*] Poor boy . . . Well, my father was poor, but take a look at me now, all dressed up, brand-new suit and tan shoes. Silk purse out of a sow's ear, I guess . . . I'm rich now, got lots of money, but when you think about it, I

---

1. Translated by Paul Schmidt.

guess I'm still a poor boy from the country. [*He flips the pages of the book.*] I tried reading this book, couldn't figure out a word it said. Put me to sleep.

[*Pause.*]

DUNYÁSHA   The dogs were barking all night long; they know their mistress is coming home.

LOPÁKHIN   Don't be silly.

DUNYÁSHA   I'm so excited I'm shaking. I may faint.

LOPÁKHIN   You're getting too full of yourself, Dunyásha. Look at you, all dressed up like that, and that hairdo. You watch out for that. You got to remember who you are.

[*Enter* YEPIKHÓDOV *with a bunch of flowers; he wears a jacket and tie and brightly polished boots, which squeak loudly. As he comes in, he drops the flowers.*]

YEPIKHÓDOV [*picking up the flowers*]   Here. The gardener sent these over; he said put them on the dining room table. [*He gives the flowers to* DUNYÁSHA.]

LOPÁKHIN   And bring me a beer.

DUNYÁSHA   Right away.

[*She goes out.*]

YEPIKHÓDOV   It's freezing this morning—it must be in the thirties—and the cherry blossoms are already out. I cannot abide the climate here. [*He sighs.*] I never have abided it, ever. [*Beat*]² Yermolái Alexéyich, would you examinate something for me, please? Day before yesterday I bought myself a new pair of boots, and listen to them squeak, will you? I just cannot endear it. Do you know anything I can put on them?

LOPÁKHIN   Will you shut up? You drive me crazy.

YEPIKHÓDOV   Every day something awful happens to me. It's like a habit. But I don't complain. I just try to keep smiling.

[*Enter* DUNYÁSHA; *she brings* LOPÁKHIN *a beer.*]

YEPIKHÓDOV   I'm going. [*He bumps into a chair, which falls over.*] You see? [*He seems proud of it.*] You see what I was referring about? Excuse my expressivity, but what a concurrence. It's almost uncanny, isn't it?

[*He leaves.*]

DUNYÁSHA   You know what? That Yepikhódov proposed to me!

LOPÁKHIN   Oh?

DUNYÁSHA   I just don't know what to think. He's kind of nice. . . . He's a real quiet boy, but then he opens his mouth, and you can't ever understand what he's talking about. I mean, it sounds nice, but it just doesn't make any sense. I do like him, though. Kind of. And he's crazy about me. It's funny, you know, every day something awful happens to him. People around here call him Double Trouble.

LOPÁKHIN [*he listens*]   That must be them.

DUNYÁSHA   It's them! Oh, I don't know what's the matter with me! I feel so funny; I'm cold all over.

LOPÁKHIN   It really is them this time. Let's go; we should be there at the door. You think she'll recognize me? It's been five years.

2. Pause.

DUNYÁSHA [*excited*]   Oh, my God! I'm going to faint! I think I'm going to faint!

> [*The sound of two carriages outside the house.* LOPÁKHIN *and* DUNYÁSHA *hurry out. The stage is empty. The sound outside gets louder.* FIRS, *leaning heavily on his cane, crosses the room, heading for the door; he wears an old-fashioned butler's livery and a top hat; he says something to himself, but you can't make out the words. The offstage noise and bustle increases. A voice: "Here we are . . . this way." Enter* LIUBÓV ANDRÉYEVNA, ÁNYA, *and* CAR-LOTTA, *dressed in traveling clothes.* VÁRYA *wears an overcoat, and a kerchief on her head.* GÁYEV, SEMYÓNOV-PÍSHCHIK, LOPÁKHIN, DUNYÁSHA *with a bundle and an umbrella, Servants with the luggage—all pass across the stage.*]

ÁNYA   Here we are. Oh, Mama, do you remember this room?

LIUBÓV ANDRÉYEVNA   The nursery!

VÁRYA   It's freezing; my hands are like ice. We kept your room exactly as you left it, Mama. The white and lavender one.

LIUBÓV ANDRÉYEVNA   The nursery! Oh, this house, this beautiful house! I slept in this room when I was a child. . . . [*She weeps.*] And I feel like a child again! [*She hugs* GÁYEV, VÁRYA, *then* GÁYEV *again.*] And Várya hasn't changed at all—still looks like a nun! And Dunyásha dear! Of course I remember you! [*She hugs* DUNYÁSHA.]

GÁYEV   The train was two hours late. What kind of efficiency is that? Eh?

CARLOTTA   And my dog loves nuts.

SEMYÓNOV-PÍSHCHIK   Really! I don't believe it!

> [*Everyone leaves, except* ÁNYA *and* DUNYÁSHA.]

DUNYÁSHA   We've been up all night, waiting. . . . [*She takes* ÁNYA's *coat and hat.*]

ÁNYA   I've been up for four nights now. . . . I didn't sleep the whole trip. And now I'm freezing.

DUNYÁSHA   When you went away it was still winter, it was snowing, and now look! Oh, sweetie, you're back! [*She laughs and hugs Ánya.*] I've been up all night, waiting to see you. Sweetheart, I just can't wait—I've got to tell you what happened. I can't wait another minute!

ÁNYA [*wearily*]   Now what?

DUNYÁSHA   Yepikhódov proposed the day after Easter! He wants to marry me!

ÁNYA   That's all you ever think about. . . . [*She fixes her hair.*] I lost all my hairpins. . . .

DUNYÁSHA   I just don't know what to do about him. He really, really loves me!

ÁNYA [*looking through the door to her room*]   My own room, just as if I'd never left. I'm back home! Tomorrow I'll get up and go for a walk in the orchard. I just wish I could get some sleep. I didn't sleep the whole trip, I was so worried.

DUNYÁSHA   Pétya's here. He got here day before yesterday.

ÁNYA [*joyfully*]   Pétya!

DUNYÁSHA   He's staying out in the barn. Said he didn't want to bother anybody. [*She looks at her watch.*] He told me to get him up, but Várya said not to. You let him sleep, she said.

> [*Enter* VÁRYA. *She has a big bunch of keys attached to her belt.*]

VÁRYA   Dunyásha, go get the coffee. Mama wants her coffee.

DUNYÁSHA   Oh, I forgot!

    [*She goes out.*]

VÁRYA   You're back. Thank God! You're home again! [*She embraces Ánya.*] My angel is home again! My beautiful darling!

ÁNYA   You won't believe what I've been through!

VÁRYA   I can imagine.

ÁNYA   I left just before Easter; it was cold. Carlotta never shut up the whole trip; she kept doing those silly tricks of hers. I don't know why you had to stick me with her.

VÁRYA   Darling, you couldn't go all that way by yourself! You're only seventeen!

ÁNYA   We got to Paris, it was cold and snowy, and my French is just awful! Mama was living in this fifth-floor apartment, we had to walk up, we get there and there's all these French people, some old priest reading some book, and it was crowded, and everybody was smoking these awful cigarettes—and I felt so sorry for Mama, I just threw my arms around her and couldn't let go. And she was so glad to see me, she cried—

VÁRYA   [*almost crying*]   I know, I know . . .

ÁNYA   And she sold the villa in Mentón,[3] and the money was already gone, all of it! And I spent everything you gave me for the trip; I haven't got a thing left. And Mama still doesn't understand! We have dinner at the train station, and she orders the most expensive things on the menu, and then she tips the waiters a ruble[4] each! And Carlotta does the same! And Yásha expects the same treatment—he's just awful. You know, Yásha, that flunky of Mama's—he came back with us.

VÁRYA   I saw him, the lazy good-for-nothing.

ÁNYA   So what happened? Did you get the interest paid?

VÁRYA   With what?

ÁNYA   Oh, my God, my God . . .

VÁRYA   The place goes up for sale in August.

ÁNYA   Oh, my God.

    [LOPÁKHIN *sticks his head in the doorway and makes a mooing sound, then goes away.*]

VÁRYA   Oh, that man! I'd like to— [*She shakes her fist.*]

ÁNYA [*she hugs her*]   Várya, did he propose yet? [VÁRYA *shakes her head no.*] But you know he loves you! Why don't the two of you just sit down and be honest with each other? What are you waiting for?

VÁRYA   I don't think anything will ever come of it. He's always so busy, he never has time for me. He just isn't interested! It's hard for me when I see him, but I don't care anymore. Everybody talks about us getting married, people even congratulate me, but there's nothing. . . . I mean, it's all just a dream. [*A change of tone*] Oh, you've got a new pin, a little bee. . . .

ÁNYA [*with a sigh*]   I know. Mama bought it for me. [*She goes into her room and starts to giggle, like a little girl.*] You know what? In Paris I went for a ride in a balloon!

VÁRYA   Oh, darling, you're back! My angel is home again!

---

3. Resort town on the French Riviera.

4. Basic unit of Russian currency, worth about $20; one ruble is equal to one hundred kopecks.

[DUNYÁSHA *comes in, carrying a tray with coffee things, and begins setting them out on the table.* VÁRYA *stands at the doorway and talks to* ÁNYA *in the other room.*]

You know, dear, I spend the livelong day trying to keep this house going, and all I do is dream. I want to see you married off to somebody rich, then I can rest easy. And I think then I'll go away by myself, maybe live in a convent, or just go traveling: Kiev, Moscow . . . spend all my time making visits to churches. I'd start walking and just go and go and go. That would be heaven!

ÁNYA   Listen to the birds in the orchard! What time is it?

VÁRYA   It must be almost three. You should get some sleep, darling. [*She goes into* ÁNYA's *room.*] Yes, that would be heaven!

[*Enter* YÁSHA *with a suitcase and a lap robe. He walks with an affected manner.*]

YÁSHA   I beg pardon! May I intrude?

DUNYÁSHA   I didn't even recognize you, Yásha. You got so different there in France.

YÁSHA   *I'm* sorry—who are you exactly?

DUNYÁSHA   When you left, I wasn't any higher than this. [*She holds her hand a distance from the floor.*] I'm Dunyásha. You know, Dunyásha Kozoyédov. Don't you remember me?

YÁSHA   Well! You sure turned out cute, didn't you? [*He looks around carefully, then grabs and kisses her; she screams and drops a saucer;* YÁSHA *leaves in a hurry.*]

VÁRYA   [*at the door, annoyed*]   Now what happened?

DUNYÁSHA   [*almost in tears*]   I broke a saucer.

VÁRYA   [*ironically*]   Well, isn't that lucky!

ÁNYA   [*entering*]   Somebody should let Mama know Pétya's here.

VÁRYA   I told them to let him sleep.

ÁNYA   [*lost in thought*]   Father died six years ago, and a month later our little brother, Grísha, drowned. Sweet boy, he was only seven. And Mama couldn't face it, that's why she went away, just went away and never looked back. [*Shivers.*] And I understand exactly how she felt. I wish she knew that.

[*Pause.*]

And Pétya Trofímov was Grísha's tutor. He might remind her . . .

[*Enter* FIRS *in his old-fashioned butler's livery. He crosses to the table and begins looking over the coffee things.*]

FIRS   The missus will have her breakfast here. [*He puts on a pair of white gloves.*] Is the coffee ready? [*To* DUNYÁSHA, *crossly*] Where's the cream? Go get the cream!

DUNYÁSHA   Oh, my God, I'm sorry. . . .

[*Hurries off.*]

FIRS   [*he starts fussing with the coffee things*]   Young flibbertigibbet . . . [*He mumbles to himself.*] They're all back from Paris. . . . In the old days they went to Paris too . . . had to go the whole way in a horse and buggy. [*He laughs.*]

VÁRYA   Firs, what are you talking about?

FIRS   Beg pardon? [*Joyfully*] The missus is home! Going to see her at last! Now I can die happy. . . . [*He starts to cry with joy.*]

[*Enter* LIUBÓV, GÁYEV, LOPÁKHIN, *and* SEMYÓNOV-PÍSHCHIK, *who wears a crumpled linen suit. As* GÁYEV *enters, he gestures as if he were making a billiard shot.*]

LIUBÓV ANDRÉYEVNA   How did it go? I'm trying to remember. . . . Yellow ball
in the side pocket! Bank shot off the corner!

GÁYEV   And right down the middle! Oh, sister, sister, just think . . . when you
and I were little we used to sleep in this room, and now I'm almost fifty-one!
Strange, isn't it?

LOPÁKHIN   Time sure passes. . . .

GÁYEV [*beat*]   Say again?

LOPÁKHIN   I said, time sure passes.

GÁYEV [*looking at* LOPÁKHIN]   Who's wearing that cheap cologne?

ÁNYA   I'm going to bed. Good night, Mama. [*She kisses her mother.*]

LIUBÓV ANDRÉYEVNA   Oh, my darling little girl, my baby! Are you glad you're
home? I still can't quite believe I'm here.

ÁNYA   Good night, Uncle.

GÁYEV [*he kisses her*]   God bless you, dear. You're getting to look so much like
your mother! Liúba, she looks just like you when you were her age. She
really does.

[ÁNYA *says good night to* LOPÁKHIN *and* PÍSHCHIK, *goes into her room, and
closes the door behind her.*]

LIUBÓV ANDRÉYEVNA   She's tired to death.

PÍSHCHIK   Well, that's such a long trip!

VÁRYA   Gentlemen, please. It's almost three; time you were going.

LIUBÓV ANDRÉYEVNA [*laughs*]   You're the same as ever, Várya. [*Hugs and kisses
her.*] Just let me have my coffee, then we'll all be going.

[FIRS *puts a pillow beneath her feet.*]

Thank you, dear. I've really gotten addicted to coffee; I drink it day and
night. You old darling, you! Thank you.

VÁRYA   I'll just go make sure they've got everything unloaded.

[*Goes out.*]

LIUBÓV ANDRÉYEVNA   I can't believe I'm really here! [*Laughs.*] I feel like jumping up and waving my arms in the air! [*Covers her face with her hands.*] It's
still like a dream. I love this country, really I do, I adore it. I started to cry
every time I looked out the train windows. [*Almost in tears*] But I do need my
coffee! Thank you, Firs, thank you, darling. I'm so glad you're still alive.

FIRS   Day before yesterday.

GÁYEV   He doesn't hear too well anymore.

LOPÁKHIN   Time for me to go. I have to leave for Hárkow[5] at five. I'm really
disappointed; I was looking forward to seeing you, have a chance to talk. . . .
You look wonderful, just the way you always did.

PÍSHCHIK [*breathes hard*]   Better than she always did. That Paris outfit. . . .
She makes me feel young again!

LOPÁKHIN   Your brother here thinks I'm crude, calls me a money grubber. That
doesn't bother me; he can call me whatever he wants. I just hope you'll trust
me the way you used to, look at me the way you used to. . . . My God, my
father slaved for your father and grandfather, my whole family worked for
yours; but you, you treated me different. You did so much for me I forgot
about all that. Fact is, I . . . I love you like you were family . . . more, even.

---

5. Kharkov, city in present-day Ukraine.

LIUBÓV ANDRÉYEVNA   I can't sit still; I'm just not in the mood! [*Gets up excit-edly, moves about the room.*] I'm so happy I could die! I know I sound stupid—go ahead, laugh. . . . Dear old bookcase. . . . [*Kisses the bookcase.*] My little desk . . .

GÁYEV   Did I tell you Nanny died while you were away?

LIUBÓV ANDRÉYEVNA [*sits back down and drinks her coffee*]   Yes, you wrote me. God rest her.

GÁYEV   Stásy died too. And Petrúsha Kosói quit and moved into town; he works at the police station. [*Takes out a little box of hard candies and puts one in his mouth.*]

PÍSHCHIK   Dáshenka—you remember Dáshenka? My daughter? Anyway, she sends her regards. . . .

LOPÁKHIN   Well, I'd like to give you some very good news. [*Looks at his watch.*] Afraid there's no time to talk now, though; I've got to go. Well, just to make it short, you know you haven't kept up the mortgage payments on your place here. So now they foreclosed and your estate is up for sale. At auction. They set a date already, August twenty-second, but don't you worry, you can rest easy. We can take care of this—I've got a great idea. Now listen, here's how it works: your place here is fifteen miles from town, and it's only a short drive from the train station. All you've got to do is clear out the old cherry orchard, plus that land down by the river, and subdivide! You lease the plots, build vacation homes, and I swear that'll bring you in twenty-five thousand[6] a year, maybe more.

GÁYEV   What an outrageous thing to say!

LIUBÓV ANDRÉYEVNA   Excuse me . . . Excuse me, I don't think I quite understand. . . .

LOPÁKHIN   You'll get at least twenty-five hundred an acre! And if you start advertising right away, I swear to God come this fall you won't have a single plot left. You see what I'm saying? Your troubles are over! Congratulations! The location is terrific; the river's a real selling point. Only thing is, you've got to start clearing right away. Get rid of all the old buildings. This house, for instance, will have to go. You can't get people to live in a barn like this anymore. And you'll have to cut down that old cherry orchard.

LIUBÓV ANDRÉYEVNA   Cut down the cherry orchard? My dear man, you don't understand! Our cherry orchard is a landmark! It's famous for miles around!

LOPÁKHIN   The only thing famous about it is how big it is. You only get cherries every two years, and even then you can't get rid of them. Nobody buys them. It's just not a commercial crop.

GÁYEV   Our cherry orchard is mentioned in the encyclopedia![7]

LOPÁKHIN [*looks at his watch*]   We have to think of something to do and then do it. Otherwise the cherry orchard will be sold at auction on August twenty-second, this house and all the land with it. Make up your minds! Believe me, I've thought this through; there isn't any other way to do it. There just isn't.

FIRS   Back in the old days, forty, fifty years ago, they used to make dried cherries, pickled cherries, preserved cherries, cherry jam, and sometimes—

6. Roughly equivalent to $500,000 today (all references to money are in rubles).
7. Probably a reference to the *Great Russian Encyclopedic Dictionary* (1890–1906), an authoritative 86-volume reference work published by F. A. Brockhaus and I. A. Efron.

GÁYEV   Oh, Firs, just shut up.

FIRS   —sometimes they sent them off to Moscow by the wagonload. People paid a lot for them! Back then the dried cherries were soft and juicy and sweet, and they smelled just lovely; back then they knew how to fix them. . . .

LIUBÓV ANDRÉYEVNA   Does anybody know how to fix them nowadays?

FIRS   Nope. They all forgot.

PÍSHCHIK   Tell us about Paris. What was it like? Did you eat frogs?

LIUBÓV ANDRÉYEVNA   I ate crocodiles.

PÍSHCHIK   Crocodiles? Really! I don't believe it!

LOPÁKHIN   You see, it used to be out here in the country there were only landlords and poor farmers, but now all of a sudden there are summer people moving in; they want vacation homes. Every town you can name is surrounded by them—it's the coming thing. In twenty years they'll expand and multiply! Right now maybe they're only places to relax on the weekend, but I bet you eventually people will put down roots out here, they'll create neighborhoods, and then your cherry orchard will blossom and bear fruit once again—and even bring in a profit!

GÁYEV [indignantly]   That's outrageous!

   [Enter VÁRYA and YÁSHA.]

VÁRYA   Mama, a couple of telegrams came for you. [Takes a key and opens the old bookcase; the lock creaks.] Here they are.

LIUBÓV ANDRÉYEVNA   They're from Paris. [She tears them up without opening them.] I'm through with Paris.

GÁYEV   Liúba, have you any idea how old this bookcase is? Last week I pulled out the bottom drawer, and there was the date on the back, burned right into the wood. A hundred years! This bookcase is exactly a hundred years old! What do you say to that, eh? We should have a birthday celebration. Of course, it's an inanimate object, any way you look at it, but still, it's a . . . well, it's a . . . a bookcase.

PÍSHCHIK   A hundred years old! Really! I don't believe it!

GÁYEV   Yes, yes, it is. [He caresses the bookcase.] Dear old bookcase! Wonderful old bookcase! I rejoice in your existence. For a hundred years now you have borne the shining ideals of goodness and justice, a hundred years have not dimmed your silent summons to useful labor. To generations of our family [Almost in tears] you have offered courage, a belief in a better future, you have instructed us in ideals of goodness and social awareness. . . .

   [Pause.]

LOPÁKHIN   Right. Well . . .

LIUBÓV ANDRÉYEVNA   Oh, Lonya, you're still the same as ever!

GÁYEV [somewhat embarrassed]   Yellow ball in the side pocket! Bank shot off the center!

LOPÁKHIN   Well, I've got to be off.

YÁSHA [gives LIUBÓV a pillbox]   Isn't it perhaps time for your pills?

PÍSHCHIK   No, no, no, dear lady! Never take medicine! Won't do any good! Won't do any harm either, though. Watch! [Takes the pillbox, dumps the contents into his hand, puts them in his mouth, and swallows them with a swig of beer.] There! All gone!

LIUBÓV ANDRÉYEVNA [alarmed]   Are you out of your mind?

PÍSHCHIK   I have just taken all your pills for you.

LOPÁKHIN   What a glutton.

    [*Everybody laughs.*]

FIRS   He was here over the holidays, ate half a crock of pickles. . . .
  [*Mumbles.*]

LIUBÓV ANDRÉYEVNA   What's he mumbling about?

VÁRYA   He's been going on like that for the last three years. We're used to it
by now.

YÁSHA   He's getting senile.

    [*Enter* CARLOTTA, *in a white dress with a lorgnette on a chain. She starts to
cross the room.*]

LOPÁKHIN   Oh, excuse me, Carlotta, I didn't get a chance to say hello yet.
[*Tries to kiss her hand.*]

CARLOTTA [*takes her hand away*]   I let you kiss my hand, first thing I know,
you'll want to kiss my elbow, then my shoulder . . .

LOPÁKHIN   This isn't my lucky day.

    [*Everybody laughs.*]

  Carlotta, show us a trick!

LIUBÓV ANDRÉYEVNA   Yes, do, Carlotta—show us a trick!

CARLOTTA   Not now. I'm off to bed.

    [*Leaves.*]

LOPÁKHIN   Well, I'll see you in three weeks. [*Kisses* LIUBÓV's *hand.*] Goodbye
now. I've got to be off. [*To* GÁYEV] Goodbye. [*Hugs* PÍSHCHIK.] So long.
[*Shakes hands with* VÁRYA, *then with* FIRS *and* YÁSHA.] I sort of hate to leave.
[*To* LIUBÓV] Think over what I said about subdividing the place. You decide
to do it, let me know, and I'll take care of everything. I'll get you a loan of
fifty thousand. Think it over now, seriously.

VÁRYA [*angry*]   Will you please just go?

LOPÁKHIN   I'm going, I'm going.

    [*Leaves.*]

GÁYEV   What a bore. Oh, excuse me, *pardon*,[8] I forgot—that's Várya's boy-
friend. He's going to marry our Várya.

VÁRYA   Uncle, will you please not talk nonsense?

LIUBÓV ANDRÉYEVNA   Oh, but Várya, that's wonderful! He's a fine man!

PÍSHCHIK   One of the finest, in fact . . . the very, very finest . . . My Dáshenka
always says . . . she says . . . she says a lot of things. [*Snores, but immediately
wakes up.*] Dear lady, yes, always respected you, hmm. . . . You think you
could lend me, say, two hundred and forty rubles? Mortgage payment, you
know, due tomorrow . . .

VÁRYA [*terrified*]   We can't; we don't have any!

LIUBÓV ANDRÉYEVNA   I'm afraid that's the truth. We haven't any money.

PÍSHCHIK   I'll get it somewhere. [*Laughs.*] I never give up hope. There was
that time I thought I was finished, it was all over, and all of a sudden—
boom! The railroad cut across some of my land and paid me for it. You'll see,
something will turn up tomorrow or the next day. Dáshenka will win two
hundred thousand in the lottery; she just bought a ticket.

LIUBÓV ANDRÉYEVNA   Well, the coffee's gone. We might as well go to bed.

---

8. Gáyev uses the French word *pardon* (excuse me); it was typical for upper-class Russians in
the 19th century to speak French to one another.

FIRS [*takes out a clothes brush and brushes* GÁYEV's *clothes; scolds him*]   You've got on the wrong trousers again. What am I supposed to do with you?

VÁRYA [*softly*]   Ánya's asleep. [*Quietly opens the window.*] The sun's coming up; it's not as cold as it was. Look, Mama, what wonderful trees! Smell the perfume! Oh, Lord! And the orioles are singing!

GÁYEV [*opens another window*]   The whole orchard is white. You remember, Liúba? That long path, stretched out like a ribbon, on and on, the way it used to shine in the moonlight? You remember? You haven't forgotten?

LIUBÓV ANDRÉYEVNA   Oh, my childhood! My innocence! I slept in this room, I could look out over the orchard, when I woke up in the morning I was happy, and it all looked exactly the same as this! Nothing has changed! [*Laughs delightedly.*] White, white, all white! My whole orchard is white! Autumn was dark and drizzly, and winter was cold, but now you're young again, flowering with happiness—the angels of heaven have never abandoned you. If only I could shake off this weight I've been carrying so long. If only I could forget my past!

GÁYEV   Yes, and now they're selling the orchard to pay our debts. Strange, isn't it?

LIUBÓV ANDRÉYEVNA   Look! There . . . in the orchard . . . it's Mother! In her white dress! [*Laughs delightedly.*] It's Mother!

GÁYEV   Where?

VÁRYA   Oh, Mama, for God's sake . . .

LIUBÓV ANDRÉYEVNA   It's all right; I was just imagining things. There to the right, by the path to the summerhouse, that little white tree all bent over . . . it looked just like a woman.

[*Enter* TROFÍMOV. *He is dressed like a student and wears wire-rimmed glasses.*] What a glorious orchard! All those white blossoms, and the blue sky—

TROFÍMOV   Liubóv Andréyevna!

[*She turns to look at him.*]

I don't mean to disturb you; I just wanted to say hello. [*Shakes her hand warmly.*] They told me to wait until later, but I couldn't. . . .

[LIUBÓV *stares at him, bewildered.*]

VÁRYA   It's Pétya Trofímov. . . .

TROFÍMOV   Pétya Trofímov—I was your little boy Grísha's tutor. . . . Have I really changed all that much?

[LIUBÓV *embraces him and begins to weep softly.*]

GÁYEV [*embarrassed*]   Liúba, that'll do, that'll do. . . .

VÁRYA [*weeps*]   Oh, Pétya, I told you to wait till tomorrow.

LIUBÓV ANDRÉYEVNA   Grísha . . . my little boy. Grísha . . . my son . . .

VÁRYA   Oh, Mama, don't; it was God's will.

TROFÍMOV [*gently, almost in tears*]   There, there . . .

LIUBÓV ANDRÉYEVNA [*weeps softly*]   My little boy drowned, lost forever . . . Why? What for? My dear boy, why? [*Quiets down.*] Ánya's asleep, and here I am carrying on like this. . . . Pétya, what's happened to you? You used to be such a nice-looking boy. What happened? You look dreadful. You've gotten so old!

TROFÍMOV   Some lady on the train called me a high-class tramp.

LIUBÓV ANDRÉYEVNA   You were only a boy then, just out of high school, you were adorable, and now you've got glasses and you're losing your hair. And haven't you graduated yet? [*Goes to the door.*]

TROFÍMOV   I suppose I'm what you'd call a permanent graduate student.

LIUBÓV ANDRÉYEVNA [kisses GÁYEV, then VÁRYA]   Time for bed. You've gotten old too, Leoníd.

PÍSHCHIK [follows LIUBÓV]   Time for bed, time to go . . . Ooh, my gout! I'd better stay the night. Now, dear, look, look . . . Liubóv Andréyevna, tomorrow morning I need . . . two hundred and forty rubles. . . .

GÁYEV   He never gives up, does he?

PÍSHCHIK   Two hundred and forty rubles; my mortgage payment due. . . .

LIUBÓV ANDRÉYEVNA   Darling, I simply have no money.

PÍSHCHIK   But, dear, I'll give it right back. . . . It's such a *trivial* amount. . . .

LIUBÓV ANDRÉYEVNA   Oh, all right. Leoníd will get it for you. Leoníd, you give him the money.

GÁYEV   I should give him money? That'll be the day.

LIUBÓV ANDRÉYEVNA   We have to give it to him; he needs it. He'll give it back.

[Exit LIUBÓV, TROFÍMOV, PÍSHCHIK, and FIRS. GÁYEV, VÁRYA, and YÁSHA remain.]

GÁYEV   She still thinks money grows on trees. [To YÁSHA] My good man, will you leave us, please? Go back to the barn, where you belong.

YÁSHA [smiles]   Leoníd Andréyich, you're the same as you always were.

GÁYEV   What say? [To VÁRYA] What did he just say?

VÁRYA [to YÁSHA]   Your mother came in from the country to see you. She's been sitting in the kitchen for two days now, waiting.

YÁSHA   Oh, for God's sake, can't she leave me alone?

VÁRYA   You are really disgraceful!

YÁSHA   That's all I need right now. Why couldn't she wait till tomorrow? [Goes out.]

VÁRYA   Mama hasn't changed; she's the same as she always was. If it were up to her, she'd give away everything.

GÁYEV   Yes. . . . [Pause] Someone gets sick, you know, and the doctor tries one thing after another, that means there's no cure. I've been thinking and thinking, racking my brains, I come up with one thing, then another, but the truth is, none of them will work. It would be wonderful if somebody left us a lot of money, it would be wonderful if we could marry off Ánya to somebody with a lot of money, it would be wonderful if we could go see Ánya's godmother in Yároslavl,[9] try to borrow the money from her. She's very, very rich.

VÁRYA [weeps]   If only God would help us!

GÁYEV   Oh, stop crying. She's very, very rich, but she doesn't like us. Because in the first place, my sister married a mere lawyer instead of a man with a title. . . .

[ÁNYA appears in the doorway.]

She married a lawyer, and then her behavior has not been—how shall I put it?—particularly exemplary. She's a lovely woman, goodhearted, charming, and of course she's my sister and I love her very much, and there are extenuating circumstances and such, but the fact is, she's what you'd have to call a . . . a loose woman. And she doesn't care who knows it; you can feel it in every move she makes.

9. Russian city northeast of Moscow.

VÁRYA [*whispers*] Ánya's here.

GÁYEV What say? [*Pause*] Funny, I must have gotten something in my eye: I can't see too well. . . . Did I tell you what happened Thursday, when I was at the county courthouse?

> [ÁNYA *comes into the room.*]

VÁRYA Why aren't you asleep?

ÁNYA I tried. I couldn't sleep.

GÁYEV Kitten . . . [*Kisses* ÁNYA's *cheek, then her hands.*] My dear child . . . [*Almost in tears*] You're more than just my niece, you're my angel, you know that? You're my whole world, believe me, believe me. . . .

ÁNYA I believe you, Uncle. And I love you; we all love you. . . . But, Uncle dear, you should learn not to talk so much. The things you were saying just now about Mama, about your own sister . . . What were you saying all that for?

GÁYEV I know, I know. . . . [*Covers his face with her hand.*] It's awful, I know. My God, a few minutes ago I made a speech to a piece of furniture. . . . It was so stupid! The thing is, I never realize how stupid I sound until I'm done.

VÁRYA She's right, Uncle. You just have to learn to keep still, that's all.

ÁNYA If you do, you'll feel much better about yourself, you know you will. . . .

GÁYEV I will, I will, I promise. [*Kisses* ÁNYA's *and* VÁRYA's *hands.*] I'll keep still. Only right now I have to talk a little more. Business! On Thursday I was at the county courthouse; there was a group of us talking—just this and that—and it turns out I might be able to arrange a promissory note for enough money to pay off the mortgage.

VÁRYA If only God would help us!

GÁYEV I'm going in on Tuesday, I'll talk to them again. [*To* VÁRYA] Don't whine! [*To* ÁNYA] Your mother will talk to Lopákhin; he can't refuse to help her. And you, as soon as you're rested, you go to Yároslavl, go talk to your godmother. There. We'll be operating on three fronts at once; we're sure to succeed. We *will* pay off this mortgage, I know we will. . . . [*He pops a hard candy into his mouth.*] I swear by my honor, I swear by anything you want, the estate will not be sold! [*Excitedly*] I swear by my own happiness! Here, you have my hand on it. You may call me . . . dishonorable, call me anything you will, if I ever let this estate go on the auction block! I swear by my entire existence!

ÁNYA [*her calm mood has returned; she is happy*] You're so smart, Uncle! You're such a wonderful man! [*Hugs* GÁYEV.] Now I feel better! So much better! I'm happy again!

> [*Enter* FIRS.]

FIRS [*reproachfully*] Leoníd Andréyich, why aren't you in bed, like decent God-fearing people?

GÁYEV I'm coming, I'm coming. You go to bed, Firs. I can get undressed by myself. All right, children, nighty-night. We can talk about the details tomorrow, now it's time for bed. [*Kisses* ÁNYA *and* VÁRYA.] I am a man of the eighties, you know. People don't think much of that era now, but I can tell you frankly that I have had the courage of my convictions and often had to pay the price.[1]

---

1. When Alexander III (1845–1894) became tsar in 1881, he initiated repressive measures to combat liberal and revolutionary elements in Russian society.

But these local peasants all love me. You have to get to know them, that's all. You have to get to know them, and—

ÁNYA   Uncle. You're at it again.

VÁRYA   Just be quiet, Uncle.

FIRS [*angrily*]   Leoníd Andréyich!

GÁYEV   I'm coming, I'm coming. . . . Go to bed now. Yellow ball in the side pocket! Clean shot!

[*Goes out;* FIRS *follows him, limping.*]

ÁNYA   I feel much better. I don't much want to go to Yároslavl, I don't like my godmother, but I feel better now. Thanks to Uncle. [*Sits down.*]

VÁRYA   We've got to get some sleep. I'm going to bed. Oh, there's something came up since you left. You know we've got all those old retired servants living out back—Paulina, old Karp, and the rest of them. And what happened, they started inviting people in to spend the night. Well, it's annoying, but I never said a thing. Then what happened was, they started telling everybody all they were getting to eat was beans. Because I was so cheap, you see. It was that old Karp was doing it. So I said to myself, All right, that's the way you want it, all right, just wait, and I sent for him [*Yawns*], and in he comes, so I say, Karp, you're such an idiot—[*Looks at* ÁNYA.] Ánya!

[*Pause.*]

She's asleep. [*Lifts* ÁNYA *by the arms.*] Come on, time for bed. . . . Come on, let's go. . . . [*Leads her off.*] My angel fell asleep! Come on. . . . [*They start out.*]

[*In the distance, beyond the orchard, a shepherd plays a pipe.* TROFÍMOV *enters, sees* ÁNYA *and* VÁRYA, *stops.*]

VÁRYA   Shh! She's asleep. . . . Come on, darling, let's go. . . .

ÁNYA [*softly, half asleep*]   I was so tired. . . . All those bells . . . Uncle dear . . . and Mama. Uncle and Mama.

VÁRYA   Come on, darling, come on. . . .

[*They go off into* ÁNYA's *room.*]

TROFÍMOV [*deeply moved*]   My sunshine! My springtime!

Curtain.

Act 2

[*An open space. The overgrown rain of an abandoned chapel. There is a well beside it and some large stones that must once have been grave markers. An old bench. Beyond, the road to the Gáyev estate. On one side a shadowy row of poplar trees; they mark the limits of the cherry orchard. A row of telegraph poles, and on the far distant horizon, on a clear day, you can just make out the city. It's late afternoon, almost sunset.* CARLOTTA, YÁSHA, *and* DUNYÁSHA *are sitting on the bench;* YEPIKHÓDOV *stands nearby, strumming his guitar; each seems lost in his own thoughts.* CARLOTTA *wears an old military cap and is adjusting the strap on a hunting rifle.*]

CARLOTTA [*meditatively*]   I haven't got a birth certificate, so I don't know how old I really am. I just think of myself as young. When I was a little girl, Mama and my father used to travel around to fairs and put on shows, good ones. I did back flips, things like that. And after they died this German woman brought me up, taught me a few things. And that was it. Then I grew up and

had to go to work. As a governess. Where I'm from . . . who I am . . . no idea. Who my parents were—maybe they weren't even married—no idea. [*Takes a large cucumber pickle out of her pocket and takes a bite*.] No idea at all.

[*Pause.*]

And I feel like talking all the time, but there's no one to talk to. No one.

YEPIKHÓDOV [*plays the guitar and sings*]

"What do I care for the rest of the world,
or care what it cares for me . . ."[2]

Very agreeable, playing a mandolin.

DUNYÁSHA   That's not a mandolin, it's a guitar. [*Takes out a compact with a mirror and powders herself*.]

YEPIKHÓDOV   When a man is madly in love, a guitar is a mandolin. [*Sings.*]

"As long as my heart is on fire with love,
and the one I love loves me."

[YÁSHA *sings harmony*.]

CARLOTTA   Oof! You people sound like hyenas.

DUNYÁSHA   But it must have been just lovely, being in Europe.

YÁSHA   Oh, it was. Quite, quite lovely. I have to agree with you there. [*Yawns, then lights a cigar*.]

YEPIKHÓDOV   That's understandable. In Europe, things have already come to a complex.

YÁSHA [*beat*]   I suppose you could say that.

YEPIKHÓDOV   I'm a true product of the educational system; I read all the time. All the right books too, but I have no chosen directive in life. For me, strictly speaking, it's live or shoot myself. That's why I always carry a loaded pistol. See? [*Takes out a revolver*.]

CARLOTTA   All done. Time to go. [*Slings the rifle over her shoulder*.] You're a very smart man, Yepikhódov, and a very scary one. Ooh! The women must adore you. [*Starts off*.] They're all so dumb, these smart boys. Never anyone to talk to . . . Always alone, all by myself, no one to talk to . . . and I still don't know who I am. Or why. No idea.

[*Walks slowly off*.]

YEPIKHÓDOV   I should explain, by the way, for the sake of expressivity, that fate has been, ah, *rigorous* to me. I am, strictly speaking, tempest-tossed. Always have been. Now, you may say to me, Oh, you're imagining things, but then why, when I wake up this morning—here's an example—and I look down, why is there this spider on my stomach? Detrimentally large too. [*Makes a circle with his two hands*.] Big as that. Or take a beer, let's say. I go to drink it, what do I see floating around in it? Something highly unappreciative, like a cockroach.

[*Pause.*]

Have you ever read Henry Thomas Buckle?[3]

[*Pause.*]

May I design to disturb you, Avdótya Fyódorovna, with something I have to say?

---

2. Words from a popular turn-of-the-century ballad.
3. English historian (1821–1862) who wrote

A History of Civilization in England (1857–61), considered daringly freethinking and materialistic.

DUNYÁSHA So say it.

YEPIKHÓDOV Preferentially alone. [*Sighs.*]

DUNYÁSHA [*embarrassed*] All right. . . . Only first get me my wrap; it's by the kitchen door. It's getting kind of damp.

YEPIKHÓDOV Ah, I see. Yes, get the wrap, of course. Now I know what to do with my gun.

[*Takes his guitar and goes off, strumming.*]

YÁSHA Double Trouble. He's an idiot, if you ask me. [*Yawns.*]

DUNYÁSHA I hope to God he doesn't shoot himself.

[*Pause.*]

I get upset over every little thing anymore. Ever since I started working for them here, I've gotten used to their *lifestyle*. Just look at my hands. Look at how white they are, just like I was rich. I'm different now from like I was. I'm more delicate, I'm more sensitive; everything upsets me. . . . It's just awful how things upset me. So if you cheat on me, Yásha, I may just have a nervous breakdown.

YÁSHA [*kisses her*] Oh, you little cutie! Just remember, though: a girl has to watch her step. What I'm after is a *nice* girl.

DUNYÁSHA I really love you, Yásha, I really do. You're so smart, you know so many things. . . .

[*Pause.*]

YÁSHA [*yawns*] Yeah. . . . But my theory is, a girl says she loves you, she's not a nice girl.

[*Pause.*]

Nothing like smoking a cigar out here in the fresh air. . . . [*Listens.*] Somebody's coming. . . . It's them. . . .

[DUNYÁSHA *hugs him impulsively.*]

YÁSHA Go on back to the house. Go back the other way, make believe you've been swimming down by the river, so they don't think we've been . . . we've been getting together out here like this. I don't want them to think that.

DUNYÁSHA [*a little cough*] That cigar smoke is giving me a headache. . . .

[*Goes out.*]

[YÁSHA *sits beside the chapel wall. Enter* LIUBÓV, GÁYEV, *and* LOPÁKHIN.]

LOPÁKHIN You have to make up your mind one way or the other; time's running out. There's no argument left. You want to subdivide or don't you? Just give me an answer, one word, yes or no.

LIUBÓV ANDRÉYEVNA Who's been smoking those cheap cigars? [*Sits down.*]

GÁYEV Everything's so convenient, now that there's the railroad. We went into town just to have lunch. Yellow ball in the side pocket! What do you say—why don't we go back to the house, eh? Have ourselves a little game . . .

LIUBÓV ANDRÉYEVNA Let's wait till later.

LOPÁKHIN Just one word! [*Imploringly*] Why don't you give me an answer?

GÁYEV [*yawns*] To what?

LIUBÓV ANDRÉYEVNA [*rummages in her purse*] Yesterday I had a lot of money, today it's all gone. My poor Várya feeds us all on soup to economize, the poor old people get nothing but beans, and I just spend and spend. . . . [*Drops her purse; gold coins spill out.*] Oh, I've spilled everything. . . .

YÁSHA Here, allow me. [*Picks up the money.*]

LIUBÓV ANDRÉYEVNA Oh, please do, Yásha: thank you. And why I had to go into that town for lunch—that stupid restaurant of yours, those stupid musi-

cians, those stupid tablecloths; they smelled of soap. . . . Why do we drink so much, Lyónya? And eat so much? Why do we talk so much? The whole time we were in the restaurant, you kept talking, and none of it made any sense. Talking about the seventies, about Symbolism.[4] And to who? The waiters! Talking about Symbolism to waiters!

LOPÁKHIN Yes.

GÁYEV [*makes a deprecating gesture*] I'm incorrigible, I suppose. . . . [*To* YÁSHA, *irritably*] What are *you* doing here? Why are you always underfoot every time I turn around?

YÁSHA [*laughs*] Because every time I hear your voice it makes me laugh.

GÁYEV Either he goes or I do!

LIUBÓV ANDRÉYEVNA Yásha, please . . . just go 'way, will you?

YÁSHA [*gives* LIUBÓV *her purse*] I'm going. Right now. [*Barely containing his laughter*] Right this very minute . . .
 [*Goes out.*]

LOPÁKHIN You know who Derigánov is? You know how much money he has? You know he's planning to buy your property? They say he's coming to the auction himself.

LIUBÓV ANDRÉYEVNA Who told you that?

LOPÁKHIN Everybody in town knows about it.

GÁYEV The old lady in Yároslavl promised to send money. . . . But when, and how much, she didn't say.

LOPÁKHIN How much will she send? A hundred thousand? Two hundred?

LIUBÓV ANDRÉYEVNA Ten or fifteen thousand. And we're lucky to get that much.

LOPÁKHIN Excuse me, but you people . . . I have never met anyone so unbusinesslike, so impractical, so . . . so *crazy* as the pair of you! Somebody tells you flat out your land is about to be sold, you don't even seem to understand!

LIUBÓV ANDRÉYEVNA But what should we do? Just tell us what we should do!

LOPÁKHIN I tell you every day what you should do! Every day I come out here and say the same thing. The cherry orchard and the rest of the land has to be subdivided and developed for leisure homes, and it has to be done right away. The auction date is getting closer! Can't you understand? All you have to do is make up your mind to subdivide, you'll have more money than even you can spend! Your troubles will be over!

LIUBÓV ANDRÉYEVNA Subdivide, leisure homes . . . excuse me, but it's all so hopelessly vulgar.

GÁYEV I couldn't agree more.

LOPÁKHIN You people drive me crazy! Another minute, I'll be shouting my head off! Oh, I give up, I give up! Why do I even bother? [*To* GÁYEV] You're worse than an old lady!

GÁYEV What say?

LOPÁKHIN I said you're an old lady! [*Starts to leave.*]

---

4. Symbolism was an unsettling artistic movement, launched by French poets Stéphane Mallarmé and Paul Verlaine in the late 19th century; they emphasized evocative images and sounds rather than logic or facts. "The seventies": a time of peasant unrest in Russia.

LIUBÓV ANDRÉYEVNA [*fearfully*]   No, no, no, please, my dear, don't go. Please.
I'm sure we'll think of something.

LOPÁKHIN   What's there to think of?

LIUBÓV ANDRÉYEVNA   Please. Don't go. Things are easier when you're
around. . . .
　　[*Pause.*]
I keep waiting for something to happen. It's as if the house were about to
fall down around our ears or something. . . .

GÁYEV [*meditatively*]   Yellow ball in the side pocket . . . Clean shot down the
middle . . .

LIUBÓV ANDRÉYEVNA   We're guilty of so many sins, I know—

LOPÁKHIN   Sins? What are you talking about?

GÁYEV [*pops a hard candy into his mouth*]   People say I've eaten up my entire
inheritance in candy. [*Laughs.*]

LIUBÓV ANDRÉYEVNA   All my sins . . . I've always wasted money, just thrown it
away like a madwoman, and I married a man who never paid a bill in his life.
He was an alcoholic; he drank himself to death—on champagne. And I was
so unhappy I fell in love with another man, *unfortunately*, and had an affair
with him, and that was when—that was the first thing, my first punishment,
right down there, in the river, my little boy drowned, and I left, I went to
France, I left and never wanted to come back, I never wanted to see that
river again, I just closed my eyes and *ran*, forgot about everything, and that
man followed me. He just wouldn't let up. And he was so mean to me, so
cruel! I bought a villa in Mentón because he got sick while we were there,
and for the next three years I never had a moment's peace, day or night. He
tormented me from his sickbed. I could feel my soul dry up. And last year I
couldn't afford the villa anymore, so I sold it and we moved to Paris, and
once we were in Paris he took everything I had left and ran off with another
woman, and I tried to kill myself. It was so stupid, and so shameful! Finally
all I wanted was to come back home, to where I was born, to my daughter.
[*Wipes away her tears.*] Oh, dear God, dear God, forgive me! Forgive me my
sins! Don't punish me again! [*Takes a telegram from her purse.*] This came
today, from Paris. . . . He says he's sorry, he wants me back. . . . [*Tears up
the telegram.*] Where's [*Listens.*] . . . where's that music coming from?

GÁYEV   That's our famous local orchestra. Those Jewish musicians, you
remember? Four fiddles, a clarinet, and a double bass.

LIUBÓV ANDRÉYEVNA   Are they still around? We should have them over some
evening and throw a party.

LOPÁKHIN [*listens*]   I don't hear anything. [*Sings to himself.*]

　　"Ooh-la-la . . .
　　Just a little bit of money
　　makes a lady very French . . ."[5]

[*Laughs.*] I went to the theater last night, saw this musical. Very funny.

---

5. Satirical reference to Russian efforts to imitate Parisian culture since the time of Tsar Peter
the Great (1672–1725).

LIUBÓV ANDRÉYEVNA   I doubt there was anything funny about it. You ought to stop going to see playacting and take a good look at your own reality. What a boring life you lead! And what uninteresting things you talk about.

LOPÁKHIN   Well . . . yeah, there's some truth to that. It is a pretty dumb life we lead. . . .

[*Pause.*]

My father was a . . . he was a dirt farmer, an idiot, never understood me, never taught me anything, just got drunk and beat me up. With a stick. Fact is, I'm not much better myself. Never did well in school, my writing's terrible, I'm ashamed if anybody sees it. I write like a pig.

LIUBÓV ANDRÉYEVNA   My dear man, you should get married.

LOPÁKHIN   Yes. . . . Yes, I should.

LIUBÓV ANDRÉYEVNA   And you should marry our Várya. She's a wonderful girl.

LOPÁKHIN   She is.

LIUBÓV ANDRÉYEVNA   Her people were quite ordinary, but she works like a dog, and the main thing is, she loves you. And you like her, I know you do. You always have.

LOPÁKHIN   Look, I've got nothing against it. I . . . She's wonderful girl.

[*Pause.*]

GÁYEV   They offered me a position at the bank. Six thousand a year. Did I tell you?

LIUBÓV ANDRÉYEVNA   Don't be silly! You stay right here where you belong.

[*Enter* FIRS, *carrying an overcoat.*]

FIRS   Sir, sir, please put this on. It's getting damp.

GÁYEV [*puts it on*]   Firs, you're getting to be a bore.

FIRS   That so? Went out this morning, didn't even tell me. [*Tries to adjust* GÁYEV's *clothes.*]

LIUBÓV ANDRÉYEVNA   Poor Firs! You've gotten so old!

FIRS   Beg pardon?

LOPÁKHIN   She said you got very old!

FIRS   I've lived a long time. They were trying to marry me off way back before your daddy was born. [*Laughs.*] By the time we got our freedom back,[6] I was already head butler. I had all the freedom I needed, so I stayed right here with the masters.

[*Pause.*]

I remember everybody got all excited about it, but they never even knew what they were getting excited about.

LOPÁKHIN   Oh, sure, things were wonderful back in the good old days! They had the right to beat you if they wanted, remember?

FIRS [*doesn't hear*]   That's right. Masters stood by the servants, servants stood by the masters. Nowadays it's all mixed up; you can't tell who's who.

GÁYEV   Shut up, Firs. . . . I have to go into town tomorrow. A friend promised to introduce me to someone who might be able to arrange a loan. Some general.

LOPÁKHIN   That's never going to work. Trust me, you won't get enough even for the interest payments.

6. Tsar Alexander II emancipated the serfs in 1861.

LIUBÓV ANDRÉYEVNA   He's imagining things. There's no general.

[Enter ÁNYA, VÁRYA, and TROFÍMOV.]

GÁYEV   Here come our young people.

ÁNYA   Mama's resting.

LIUBÓV ANDRÉYEVNA [tenderly]   Here we are, dears, over here. [Kisses ÁNYA and VÁRYA.] If you only knew how much I love you both. Come sit here by me . . . that's right.

[They all sit down.]

LOPÁKHIN   Our permanent graduate student seems to spend all his time studying the ladies.

TROFÍMOV   Mind your own business.

LOPÁKHIN   Almost in his fifties, he's still in school.

TROFÍMOV   Just stop the silly jokes, will you?

LOPÁKHIN   Oh, the scholar is losing his temper!

TROFÍMOV   Will you please just leave me alone?

LOPÁKHIN [laughs]   Let me ask you a question: You look at me, what do you see?

TROFÍMOV   When I look at you, Yermolái Alexéyich, what I see is a rich man. One who will soon be a millionaire. You are as necessary a part of the evolution of the species as the wild animal that eats up anything in its path.

[Everybody laughs.]

VÁRYA   Forget biology, Pétya. You should stick to counting stars.

LIUBÓV ANDRÉYEVNA   I want to hear more about what we were talking about last night.

TROFÍMOV   What were we talking about?

GÁYEV   About human dignity.

TROFÍMOV   We talked about a lot last night, but we never got anywhere. You people talk about human dignity as if it were something mystical. I suppose it is, in a way, for you anyway, but when you really get down to it, what have humans got to be proud of? Biologically we're pretty minor specimens—besides which, the great majority of human beings are vulgar and unhappy and totally undignified. We should stop patting ourselves on the back and get to work.

GÁYEV   You still have to die.

TROFÍMOV   Who says? Anyway, what does that mean, to die? Maybe we have a hundred senses, and all we lose when we die are the five we're familiar with, and the other ninety-five go on living.

LIUBÓV ANDRÉYEVNA   Oh, Pétya, you're so smart!

LOPÍKHIN [with irony]   Oh, yes, very.

TROFÍMOV   Remember, human beings are constantly progressing, and their power keeps growing. Things that seem impossible to us nowadays, the day will come when they're not a problem at all, only we have to work toward that day. We have to seek out the truth. We don't do that, you know. Most of the people in this country aren't working toward anything. People I come in contact with—at the university, for instance—they're supposed to be educated, but they're not interested in the truth. They're not interested in much of anything, actually. They certainly don't do much. They call themselves intellectuals and think that gives them the right to look down on the rest of the world. They never read anything worthwhile, they're completely ignorant

where science is concerned, they talk about art and they don't even know what it is they're talking about. They take themselves so seriously, they're full of theories and ideas, but just go look at the cities they live in. Miles and miles of slums, where people go hungry and where they live packed into unheated tenements full of cockroaches and garbage, and their lives are full of violence and immorality. So what are all the theories for? To keep people like us from seeing all that. Where are the day-care centers they talk so much about, and the literacy programs? It's all just talk. You go out to the parts of town where the poor people live, you can't find them. All you find is dirt and ignorance and crime. That's why I don't like all this talk, all these theories. Bothers me, makes me afraid. If that's all our talk is good for, we'd better just shut up.

LOPÁKHIN   I get up at five and work from morning to night, and you know, my business involves a lot of money, my own and other people's, so I see lots of people, see what they're like. And you just try to get anything accomplished: you'll see how few decent, honest people there really are. Sometimes at night I can't sleep, and I think: Dear God, you gave us this beautiful earth to live on, these great forests, these wide fields, the broad horizons . . . by rights we should be giants.

LIUBÓV ANDRÉYEVNA   What do you want giants for? The only good giants are in fairy tales. Real ones would scare you to death.

[Upstage, YEPIKHÓDOV strolls by, playing his guitar.]

[Dreamily] There goes Yepikhódov. . . .

ÁNYA [dreamily]   There goes Yepikhódov. . . .

GÁYEV   The sun, ladies and gentlemen, has just set.

TROFÍMOV   Yes.

GÁYEV [as if reciting a poem, but not too loud]   O wondrous nature, cast upon us your eternal rays, forever beautiful, forever indifferent. . . . Mother, we call you; life and death reside within you; you bring forth and lay waste—

VÁRYA [pleading]   Uncle, please!

ÁNYA   Uncle, you're doing it again.

TROFÍMOV   We'd rather have the yellow ball in the side pocket.

GÁYEV   Sorry, sorry. I'll keep still.

[They all sit in silence. The only sound we hear is old FIRS mumbling. Suddenly a distant sound seems to fall from the sky, a sad sound, like a harp string breaking. It dies away.]

LIUBÓV ANDRÉYEVNA   What was that?

LOPÁKHIN   Can't tell. Sounds like it could be an echo from a mine shaft. But it must be far away.

GÁYEV   Or some kind of bird . . . like a heron.

TROFÍMOV   Or an owl.

LIUBÓV ANDRÉYEVNA [shivers]   Makes me nervous.

[Pause.]

FIRS   It's like just before the trouble started. They heard an owl screech, and the kettle wouldn't stop whistling. . . .

GÁYEV   Before what trouble?

FIRS   The day we got our freedom back.

[Pause.]

LIUBÓV ANDRÉYEVNA   My dears, it's getting dark; we should be going in. [To ÁNYA] You've got tears in your eyes, darling. What's the matter? [Hugs ÁNYA.]

ÁNYA   Nothing, Mama. It's all right.

TROFÍMOV   Someone's coming.

[*Enter a* HOMELESS MAN *in a white cap and an overcoat; he's slightly drunk.*]

HOMELESS MAN   Can anyone please tell me, can I get to the train station this way?

GÁYEV   Of course you can. Just follow this road.

HOMELESS MAN   Much obliged. [*Bows.*] Wonderful weather we're having . . . [*Recites.*] "Behold one of the poor in spirit, just trying to inherit a little of the earth. . . ."[7] [*To* VÁRYA] Listen, you think you could spare some money for a hungry man?

[VÁRYA *is terrified; she screams.*]

LOPÁKHIN [*angrily*]   Now hold on just a minute!

LIUBÓV ANDRÉYEVNA [*panicked*]   Here . . . here . . . take this. [*Fumbles in her purse.*] Oh, I don't seem to have anything smaller. Here, take this. [*Gives him a gold piece.*]

HOMELESS MAN   Very much obliged!

[*Goes out.*]

[*Everybody laughs.*]

VÁRYA   Get me out of here! Oh, please get me out! Mama, how could you! We can't even feed the servants, and you go and give him a gold piece!

LIUBÓV ANDRÉYEVNA   I know, darling, I'm just stupid about money. When we get home I'll give you whatever I've got left; you can take care of it. Yermolái Alexéyich, can you lend me some money?

LOPÁKHIN   Of course.

LIUBÓV ANDRÉYEVNA   My darlings, it really is time to go in. Várya dear, we've just gotten you engaged. Congratulations.

VÁRYA [*almost in tears*]   Mama, that's nothing to joke about!

LOPÁKHIN   Amelia, get thee to a nunnery![8]

GÁYEV   Look how my hands shake. I don't know if I could play billiards anymore. . . .

LOPÁKHIN   Nymph, in thy horizons be all my sins remembered![9]

LIUBÓV ANDRÉYEVNA   Please, let's go. It's almost suppertime.

VÁRYA   He scared me half to death. I can feel my heart pounding.

LOPÁKHIN   But keep in mind, the cherry orchard is going to be sold. On August twenty-second! You hear what I'm saying? You've got to think about this! You've got to!

[*They all go off except* ÁNYA *and* TROFÍMOV.]

ÁNYA [*laughs*]   I'm so glad that tramp scared Várya off. Now we can be alone.

TROFÍMOV   Várya's afraid we're going to fall in love; that's why she never leaves us alone. She's so narrow-minded; she simply can't understand that we are above love. Our goal is to get rid of the silly illusions that keep us from being free and happy. We are moving forward, toward the future! Toward one bright star that burns ahead of us! Forward, friends! Come join us in our journey!

---

7. Reference to Jesus' Sermon on the Mount: "Blessed are the poor in spirit, for theirs is the kingdom of heaven. . . . Blessed are the meek, for they shall inherit the earth" (Matthew 5.3, 5).

8. Hamlet, in Shakespeare's play, suspects Ophelia of spying for her father and sends her off with "Get thee to a nunnery!" (3.1.22).

9. Lopákhin transforms a line from *Hamlet*: "Nymph, in thy orisons, / Be all my sins remembered" (3.1.91–92).

ÁNYA [*claps her hands*]   Oh, you talk so beautifully!
   [*Pause.*]
   It's just heavenly out here today!
TROFÍMOV   Yes, the weather's been really good lately.
ÁNYA   I don't know what it is you've done to me, Pétya, but I don't love the cherry orchard anymore, not the way I used to. I used to think there was no place on earth like our orchard.
TROFÍMOV   This whole country is our orchard. It's a big country and a beautiful one; it has lots of wonderful places in it.
   [*Pause.*]
   Just think, Ánya: your grandfather, and his father, and his father's fathers, they *owned* the people who slaved away for them all over this estate, and now the voices and faces of human beings hide behind every cherry in the orchard, every leaf, every tree trunk. Can't you see them? And hear them? And owning human beings has left its mark on all of you. Look at your mother and your uncle! They live off the labor of others, they always have, and they've never even noticed! They owe their entire lives to those other people, people they wouldn't even let walk through the front gate of their beloved cherry orchard! This whole country has fallen behind; it'll take us at least two hundred years to catch up. The thing is, we don't have any real sense of our own history; all we do is sit around and talk, talk, talk, then we feel depressed, so we go out and get drunk. If there's one thing that's clear to me, it's this: if we want to have any real life in the present, we have to do something to make up for our past, we have to get over it, and the only way to do that is to make sacrifices, get down to work, and work harder than we've ever worked before. Do you understand what I mean, Ánya?
ÁNYA   The house we live in isn't our house anymore. It hasn't ever been, really. And I'll leave it all behind, I promise you I will.
TROFÍMOV   Yes, you will! Throw away your house keys and go as far away as you can! You'll be free as the wind.
ÁNYA [*radiant*]   I love the way you say things!
TROFÍMOV   You have to understand me, Ánya. I'm not thirty yet, I'm still young; I may still be in school, but I've learned a lot. Winter comes, sometimes I get cold and hungry, or sick and upset, I don't have a cent to my name; things work out or they don't. . . . But no matter what, my heart and soul are always full of feelings, all kinds . . . I can't even explain them. And I feel happiness coming, Ánya, I can feel it. I can almost see it—
ÁNYA [*dreamily*]   Look, the moon's rising.
   [*The sound of* YEPIKHÓDOV's *guitar, still playing the same mournful song. The moon rises. Somewhere beyond the poplar trees,* VÁRYA *can be heard calling.*]
VÁRYA [*off*]   Ánya! Ánya, where are you?
TROFÍMOV   Yes, the moon is rising.
   [*Pause.*]
   It's happiness, that's what it is: it's rising, it's coming closer and closer, I can hear it. And even if we miss it, if we never find it, that's all right! Someone will!
VÁRYA [*off*]   Ánya! Ánya, where are you?
TROFÍMOV [*angrily*]   That Várya! Why won't she let us alone!
ÁNYA   Don't let her bother you. Let's take a walk by the river. It's so nice there.

TROFÍMOV   All right, let's go.

[*They leave. The stage is empty.*]

VÁRYA [*off*]   Ánya! Ánya!

Curtain.

Act 3

[*A sitting room, separated from the ballroom in back by an archway. The chandeliers are lit. From the entrance hall comes the sounds of an orchestra, the Jewish musicians GÁYEV mentioned in Act 2. Evening. In the ballroom, everyone is dancing a grande ronde. SEMYÓNOV-PÍSHCHIK's voice is heard calling the figures of the dance: "Promenade à une paire!"*[1] *The dancers dance through the sitting room in pairs in the following order: PÍSHCHIK and CARLOTTA, TROFÍMOV and LIUBÓV ANDREYÉVNA, ÁNYA and the POSTMASTER, VÁRYA and the STATIONMASTER, etc. VÁRYA is in tears, which she tries to wipe away as she dances. The final pair includes DUNYÁSHA. As the dancers return to the ballroom, PÍSHCHIK calls out: "Grande roude, balancez!" and "Les cavaliers à genoux et remercier vos dames."*[2] *FIRS in his butler's uniform crosses the stage, carrying a seltzer bottle on a tray. PÍSHCHIK and TROFÍMOV come into the sitting room.*]

PÍSHCHIK   I'm prone to strokes, already had two of 'em, I really shouldn't be dancing, but you know what they say: When in Rome. Besides, I'm really strong as a horse. Speaking of Romans, my father—what a joker he was—he used to claim our family was descended from the emperor Caligula's horse—you know, the one he made a senator?[3] [*Sits down.*] The only problem is we have no money. [*His head nods, he snores, then immediately wakes up.*] So the only thing I ever think about is money.

TROFÍMOV   Your father was right. You do look a little like a horse.

PÍSHCHIK   Nothing wrong with horses. Wonderful animals. If I had one, I could sell it. . . .

[*From the adjacent billiard room come the sounds of a game. VÁRYA appears in the archway.*]

TROFÍMOV [*teases her*]   Mrs. Lopákhin! Mrs. Lopákhin!

VÁRYA [*angrily*]   High-class tramp!

TROFÍMOV   Yes, I'm a high-class tramp, and I'm proud of it!

VÁRYA [*bitterly*]   We've hired an orchestra! And what are we supposed to pay them with?

[*Goes out.*]

TROFÍMOV [*to PÍSHCHIK*]   All the energy you've used trying to find money to pay your mortgage, if you'd spent that energy on something else, you could have moved the world.

PÍSHCHIK   Nietzsche,[4] you know, the philosopher—a great thinker, Nietzsche, a man of genius, one of the great minds of the century—now Nietzsche, you

---

1. "Promenade with your partner!" (French).
2. "Make a large circle, swing with your arms! Gentlemen, kneel and thank your ladies!" (French).
3. The mad emperor Caligula (12–41 C.E.)

brought his favorite horse into the Roman senate to make it a senator.
4. Friedrich Nietzsche (1844–1900), influential German philosopher.

know, says, in his memoirs, that counterfeit money's just as good as real. . . .

TROFÍMOV I didn't know you'd read Nietzsche.

PÍSHCHIK Well . . . actually, Dáshenka told me. And I'm desperate enough. I'm ready to start counterfeiting. I need three hundred and ten rubles, day after tomorrow. All I've got so far is a hundred and thirty. . . . [*He feels in his pockets anxiously.*] It's gone! My money's gone! [*Almost in tears*] I've lost my money! [*Joyfully*] Oh, here it is! It slipped down into the lining of my coat! God, I'm all in a sweat!

[*Enter* LIUBÓV *and* CARLOTTA.]

LIUBÓV ANDREYÉVNA [*she hums a dance tune*] Why is it taking so long? What's Leoníd doing all this time in town? He should be back by now. [*Calls to* DUNYÁSHA *in the ballroom.*] Dunyásha, tell the musicians they can take a break.

TROFÍMOV They probably postponed the auction.

LIUBÓV ANDREYÉVNA I suppose it was a mistake to hire an orchestra. Or to have a party in the first place. Oh, well . . . what difference does it make? [*Sits down and hums quietly.*]

CARLOTTA [*hands* PÍSHCHIK *a deck of cards*] Here's the deck. Pick a card, any card. . . . No, no, just think of one.

PÍSHCHIK All right, I'm thinking of one.

CARLOTTA Good. Now shuffle the deck. Very good. Now give it to me. Observe, my dear Píshchik! *Eins, zwei, drei!*[5] Now look in your jacket pocket, and you will find your card.

PÍSHCHIK [*takes a card from his jacket pocket*] That's it, the eight of spades! [*Amazed*] Really! I don't believe it!

CARLOTTA [*holds out the deck to* TROFÍMOV] Quick, what's the top card?

TROFÍMOV The top card? Oh . . . uh . . . the queen of spades.

CARLOTTA Correct! [*To* PÍSHCHIK] Now which card's on top?

PÍSHCHIK Ace of hearts!

CARLOTTA Correct! [*Claps her hands, and the deck disappears.*] Well, isn't this a lovely day we're having?

[*A mysterious woman's voice answers; it seems to come from the floorboards: "A lovely day indeed. I couldn't agree more."*]

Whoever you are, I adore you!

[*The voice: "I adore you too!"*]

MASTER [*applauds*] Bravo! A lady ventriloquist!

PÍSHCHIK [*amazed*] Really! I don't believe it! Carlotta, you are amazing! I'm completely in love with you!

CARLOTTA In love? [*Shrugs her shoulders.*] What do you know about love? *Guter Mensch aber schlechter Musikant.*[6]

TROFÍMOV [*slaps* PÍSHCHIK *on the shoulder*] You're just an old horse!

CARLOTTA All right, everybody, watch closely! One more trick! [*Takes a lap robe from a chair.*] See, what a lovely blanket! I'm thinking of selling it. [*Shakes out the lap robe and holds it up.*] Who wants to buy?

PÍSHCHIK [*amazed*] Really! I don't believe it!

---

5. "One, two, three!" (German).
6. "A good man but a bad musician" (German); that is, an incompetent (from the poet
Heinrich Heine).

CARLOTTA   *Eins, zwei, drei!* [*Quickly raises the lap robe.*]
     [ÁNYA *appears behind the lap robe; she curtsies, runs to her mother and kisses her, then runs back into the ballroom. General applause and cries of delight.*]

LIUBÓV ANDREYÉVNA [*applauding*]   Bravo! Bravo!

CARLOTTA   Now one more! *Eins, zwei, drei!*
     [*She raises the lap robe;* VÁRYA *appears; she takes a bow.*]

PÍSHCHIK   Really! I don't believe it!

CARLOTTA   That's all. The show is over.
     [*Throws the lap robe to* PÍSHCHIK, *takes a bow, goes through the ballroom and out.*]

PÍSHCHIK [*goes after her*]   Enchanting! What a woman! What a woman!
     [*Goes out.*]

LIUBÓV ANDRÉYEVNA   Leoníd still isn't back from town yet. I don't understand what could be taking him so long! It's got to be all over by now: either the estate has been sold or they've postponed the auction. Why does he have to keep us in suspense like this?

VÁRYA [*tries to comfort her*]   Uncle bought the estate, I'm sure he has.

TROFÍMOV [*ironically*]   Oh, I'm sure.

VÁRYA   Ánya's godmother sent him a power of attorney to buy the estate in her name; she agreed to take over the mortgage. She did it for Ánya. So God *has* helped us. Uncle has saved the estate.

LIUBÓV ANDREYÉVNA   The old lady in Yároslavl sent us fifteen thousand to buy the place in her name—she doesn't trust us—but that's not even enough to pay the interest. [*Covers her face with her hands.*] My fate . . . my entire life . . . It's all being decided today.

TROFÍMOV [*teases* VÁRYA]   Mrs. Lopákhin! Mrs. Lopákhin!

VÁRYA [*angrily*]   And you're a permanent graduate student! Who's been suspended twice!

LIUBÓV ANDRÉYEVNA   Don't get so angry, Várya; he's only teasing you. What's wrong with that? And what's wrong with Lopákhin? If you want to marry him, do; he's a nice man. Interesting, even. If you don't want to marry him, don't; nobody's forcing you.

VÁRYA   It's not a joking matter, Mama, believe me. I'm serious about him. He is a nice man, and I like him.

LIUBÓV ANDRÉYEVNA   Then go ahead and marry him! I don't understand what you're waiting for!

VÁRYA   Mama, I can't propose to him myself! For two years now everybody's been telling me to marry him, everybody, but he never mentions it. Or he jokes about it! Look, I understand, he's busy getting rich, he doesn't have time for me. Oh, if I had just a little money—I don't care how much, even a couple of hundred—I'd get out of here and go someplace far away. I'd go join a convent.

TROFÍMOV   Now, there's an exalted idea!

VÁRYA [*to* TROFÍMOV]   I thought students were supposed to be smart! [*Her tone softens; almost crying.*] Oh, Pétya, you used to be so nice-looking, and now you're getting old! [*To* LIUBÓV, *in a normal tone*] It's just that I need something to do all the time, Mama; it's the way I am. I can't sit around and do nothing.
     [*Enter* YÁSHA.]

YÁSHA [*barely controlling his laughter*]   Yepikhódov broke a billiard cue!
   [*Goes out.*]
VÁRYA   What is Yepikhódov doing here? Who asked him to come? And what's
   he doing playing billiards? I just don't understand these people. . . .
   [*Goes out.*]
LIUBÓV ANDRÉYEVNA   Pétya, don't tease her like that; you can see she's upset
   already.
TROFÍMOV   Oh, she's such a busybody, always poking her nose into other
   people's business. She hasn't left Ánya and me alone the whole summer;
   she's afraid we're having a . . . an *affair*. What business is it of hers? Besides,
   it's not true. I'd never do anything so sordid. We're above love!
LIUBÓV ANDRÉYEVNA   And I, I suppose, am beneath love. [*Upset*] Why isn't
   Leoníd back yet? I just want to know: has the estate been sold or not? The whole
   disaster seems so impossible to me, I don't know what to think, or do. . . . Oh,
   God, I'm losing my mind! I want to scream, or do something completely stupid . . . Help me, Pétya! Save me! Say something, say something!
TROFÍMOV   Whether they sell it or not, does it make any difference really? You
   can't go back to the past. Everything here came to an end a long time ago.
   Try to calm down. You can't go on deceiving yourself; at least once in your
   life you have to look the truth straight in the eye.
LIUBÓV ANDRÉYEVNA   What truth? You seem so sure what's truth and what
   isn't, but I'm not. I've lost any sense of it. I've lost sight of the truth. You're
   so sure of yourself, aren't you, so sure you have all the answers to everything,
   but darling, have you ever really had to live with one of your answers? You're
   too young. Of course *you* look into the future and see a brave new world,
   you don't expect any difficulties, but that's because you know nothing about
   life! Yes, you have more courage than my generation has, and better morals,
   and you're better educated, but for God's sake have a little sense of what it's
   like for me, and be easier on me. Pétya, I was born here! My parents lived
   here all their lives; so did my grandfather. I love this house! Without the
   cherry orchard my life makes no sense, and if you have to sell it, you might
   as well sell me with it. [*She embraces* TROFÍMOV *and kisses his forehead.*] And
   it was here my son drowned, you know that. . . . [*Weeps.*] Have some feeling
   for me, Pétya, you're such a good, sweet boy.
TROFÍMOV   I pity you. [*Beat*] I do, from the bottom of my heart.
LIUBÓV ANDRÉYEVNA   You should have said that differently, just a little differently. . . . [*Takes out her handkerchief; a telegram falls to the floor.*] You can't
   imagine how miserable I am today. All this noise, and every new sound
   makes me shake. I can't get away from it, but then when I'm alone in my
   room I can't stand the silence. Don't judge me, Pétya! I love you like one of
   my own family; I'd be very happy to see you and Ánya married, you know I
   would, only, darling, you must finish school first! You have *got* to graduate!
   You don't do anything except drift around from place to place—what kind
   of life is that? It's true, isn't it? Isn't that the truth? And we have to do something about that beard of yours; it's so scraggly. . . . [*Laughs.*] You've gotten
   so funny-looking!
TROFÍMOV [*picks up the telegram*]   I have no desire to be good-looking.
LIUBÓV ANDRÉYEVNA   The telegram's from Paris. I get a new one every day.
   One yesterday, now again today. That madman is sick again and in trou-

everybody, you got forty-six minutes till train time! And it's twenty minutes from here to the station, so you better get a move on.

[*Enter* TROFÍMOV *from outside; he's wearing an overcoat.*]

TROFÍMOV It must be time to go. The carts are here. Where the hell are my galoshes? I've lost them somewhere. [*At the door*] Ánya, where are my galoshes? I can't find them anyplace!

LOPÁKHIN I'm off to Hárkov. I'll be taking the same train as you. Off to Hárkov, spend the winter there. I've been hanging around here too long, doing nothing; I can't stand that. I got to keep working, otherwise I don't know what to do with my hands; if they're not doing something, they feel like they don't belong to me.

TROFÍMOV So. We're leaving, and you're going back to your useful labors in the real world.

LOPÁKHIN Have a glass of champagne.

TROFÍMOV No, thanks.

LOPÁKHIN So you're off to Moscow?

TROFÍMOV Yes. I'll go into town with them today, and then leave tomorrow for Moscow.

LOPÁKHIN Sure. I'll bet all those professors are waiting for you to show up, wouldn't want to start their lectures without you!

TROFÍMOV Mind your own business.

LOPÁKHIN How long you say you've been at that university?

TROFÍMOV Come on! Think up something new, will you? You're getting boring. [*Pokes around, looking for his galoshes.*] You know, we probably won't ever see each other again, so you mind my giving you a little advice? As a farewell present? Don't wave your arms around so much. Bad habit. And this development you're putting in out here—you think that's going to improve the world? You think your leisure home buyers are going to turn into yeoman farmers? That's a lot of arm waving too. Well, what the hell. I like you anyway. You've got nice hands. Gentle and sensitive. You could have been an artist. And you're like that inside too—gentle and sensitive.

LOPÁKHIN [*hugs him*] Goodbye, boy. Thanks for everything. Here, let me give you a little money. You may need it for the trip.

TROFÍMOV What for? I don't need money!

LOPÁKHIN What *for*? You don't have any!

TROFÍMOV I do too. Thanks all the same. I got paid for a translation I did. I have money right here in my pocket. [*Worried*] I just wish I could find my galoshes!

VÁRYA [*from the next room*] Here they are! The smelly things . . . [*Throws a pair of galoshes into the room.*]

TROFÍMOV What are you always getting mad for? Hmm . . . These aren't my galoshes.

LOPÁKHIN This past spring I planted a big crop of poppies. Three hundred acres. Sold the poppy seed, made forty thousand clear. And when those poppies were all in flower, what a picture that was! So look, I just made forty thousand, I can afford to loan you some money. Why turn up your nose at it? Because you think I'm just a dirt farmer?

TROFÍMOV So your father was a dirt farmer. Mine worked in a drugstore. What does that prove?

[LOPÁKHIN *takes out his wallet.*]

Forget it, forget it. Look, you could give me a couple of hundred thousand, I still wouldn't take it. I'm a free man. And you people, everything you think is so valuable, it doesn't mean a thing to me. I don't care whether you're rich or poor; you've got no power over me. I can do without you, I can go right on past you, because I am proud and I am strong. Humanity is moving onward, toward a higher truth and a higher happiness, higher than anyone can imagine. And I'm ahead of the rest!

LOPÁKHIN   You think you'll ever get there?

TROFÍMOV   I'll get there.

[*Pause.*]

I'll get there. Or I'll make sure the rest of them get there.

[*From the orchard comes the sound of axes; they've started chopping down the cherry trees.*]

LOPÁKHIN   Well, boy, goodbye. Time to go. You and I don't see eye to eye, but life goes on anyway. Whenever I work real hard, round the clock practically, that clears my mind somehow, and for a minute I think maybe I know what we're all here for. But God, boy, think of the thousands of people in this country who don't know what they're doing or why they're doing it. But . . . I guess that doesn't have much to do with the price of eggs. They told me Leoníd Andréyich got a job at the bank, six thousand a year. He won't last; he's too lazy.

ÁNYA [*at the door*]   Mama asks you to please wait until she's gone before you start cutting down the orchard.

TROFÍMOV   I agree. That isn't very tactful, you know.

[*Goes out into the front hall.*]

LOPÁKHIN   All right, all right, I'll take care of it. God, these people . . .

[*Goes out after him.*]

ÁNYA   Have they taken Firs to the nursing home?

YÁSHA   I told them about it this morning. So I imagine they have.

ÁNYA [*to* YEPIKHÓDOV, *who crosses the room*]   Yepikhódov, could you please go and make sure they've taken Firs to the nursing home?

YÁSHA [*offended*]   I already told them this morning! Why keep asking?

YEPIKHÓDOV   The aged Firs, in my ultimate opinion, is beyond nursing. They ought to take him to the cemetery. And I can only envy him. [*Sets a suitcase down on a cardboard hatbox and crushes it.*] There. Finally. Wouldn't you know.

[*Goes out.*]

YÁSHA [*snickers*]   Old Double Trouble.

VÁRYA [*from the next room*]   Have they taken Firs to the nursing home?

ÁNYA   They took him this morning.

VÁRYA   Then why didn't they take the letter for the doctor?

ÁNYA   They must have forgotten. We'll have to send someone after them with it.

VÁRYA   Where's Yásha? Tell him his mother is here; she wants to say goodbye.

YÁSHA [*with a dismissive gesture*]   What a bore! Why can't she just leave me alone?

[DUNYÁSHA *has been drifting in and out, fussing with the baggage; now that she sees* YÁSHA *alone, she goes to him.*]

DUNYÁSHA   Oh ... oh, Yásha, why won't you even look at me? You're going away ... you're leaving me behind. ... [*Starts to cry and throws her arms around his neck.*]

YÁSHA   What are you crying about? [*Drinks some champagne.*] Six days from now, I'll be back in Paris. Tomorrow we get on the express train, and we're off! And that's the last you'll ever see of me! I can't hardly believe it myself. *Vive la France!*[1] I can't live around here anymore; it's just not my kind of place. They're all so ignorant, and I can't stand that. [*Drinks more champagne.*] What are you crying about? If you'd been a nice girl, you wouldn't have anything to cry about.

DUNYÁSHA [*powders her nose in a mirror*]   Don't forget to send me a letter from Paris. Because I loved you, Yásha, I really did. I'm a very sensitive person, Yásha, I really am—

YÁSHA   Watch it, someone's coming. [*He starts fussing with the luggage, whistling quietly.*]

[*Enter* LIUBÓV, GÁYEV, ÁNYA, *and* CARLOTTA.]

GÁYEV   We should be going. We're already a little late. [*Looks at* YÁSHA.] Who smells like herring?

LIUBÓV ANDRÉYEVNA   We've only got ten minutes; then we absolutely must start out. [*Glances around the room.*] Goodbye, house! Wonderful old house! Winter's almost here, and come spring you'll be gone. They'll tear you down. Think of everything these walls have seen! [*Kisses* ÁNYA *with great feeling.*] My treasure, look at you! You're radiant today! Your eyes are shining like diamonds! Are you happy? Really happy?

ÁNYA   Oh, yes, Mama, really! We're starting a new life!

GÁYEV   She's right—everything worked out extremely well. Before the cherry orchard was sold we were at our wit's end—remember how painful it was?— and now everything's finally settled, once and for all, no turning back, and see? We've all calmed down. We're even rather happy. I'm going to work at the bank, I'm about to become a financier! Yellow ball in the side pocket ... And you look better than you have in a long time, Lyúba; you do, you know.

LIUBÓV ANDRÉYEVNA   I know. My nerves have quieted down. You're quite right.

[*Someone holds out her hat and coat.*]

And I sleep much better now. Take my things, Yásha, will you? It's time to go. [*To* ÁNYA] Darling, we'll see each other soon enough. I'm off to Paris—I kept the money your godmother in Yároslavl sent to buy the estate. [*A hard laugh*] Thank God for the old lady! That ought to get me through the winter at least. ...

ÁNYA   And you'll come back soon, won't you? You promise? I'll study hard and get my diploma, and then I'll get a job and help you out. We can read together the way we used to, can't we? [*Kisses her mother's hands.*] We'll spend long autumn evenings together; we'll read lots of books and learn all about the wonderful new world of the future. ... [*Dreamily*] Don't forget, Mama, you promised. ...

LIUBÓV ANDRÉYEVNA   I will, my angel, I promise. [*Embraces her.*]

1. "Long live France!" (French).

[*Enter* LOPÁKHIN. CARLOTTA *hums a tune under her breath.*]

GÁYEV   Carlotta must be happy; she's singing!

CARLOTTA   [*picks up a bundle that looks like a baby in swaddling clothes*]
Here's my little baby. Bye, bye, baby . . .

[*We hear a baby's voice: "Wah! Wah!"*]

Shh, baby, shh, shh . . . good little children don't cry. . . .

[*Again: "Wah! Wah!"*]

I feel so sorry for the poor thing. [*Hurls the bundle to the floor.*] You will find
me a job, won't you? I can't go on like this anymore.

LOPÁKHIN   Don't worry, Carlotta; we'll take care of you.

GÁYEV   Everybody's just thrown us away. Várya's leaving. . . . All of a sudden
we're useless.

CARLOTTA   How can I live in that town of yours? There must be someplace I
can go. . . . [*Hums.*] What difference does it make . . . ?

[*Enter* PÍSHCHIK.]

LOPÁKHIN   Here comes the wonder boy.

PÍSHCHIK [*panting*]   Ooh, give me a minute . . . I'm all worn out. Good morning, good morning, good morning. Could I get a drink of water?

GÁYEV [*sarcastic*]   You're sure it isn't money you want? You'll all have to excuse
me if I remove myself from the approaching negotiations.

[*Goes out.*]

PÍSHCHIK   I'm so glad to see you all. . . . Dear lady . . . I've been a stranger, I
know. [*To* LOPÁKHIN] And you're here too. Delighted, delighted, a man I
admire, always have. . . . Here. Here. This is for you. [*Gives* LOPÁKHIN
money.] Four hundred. And I still owe you eight hundred and forty.

LOPÁKHIN [*a bewildered shrug*]   I must be dreaming. Where did you get
money?

PÍSHCHIK   Wait a minute; let me cool off. Well, it was an absolutely extraordinary thing. These Englishmen showed up, they poked around on my land,
found some kind of white clay. . . . [*To* LIUBÓV] Here . . . Here's the four
hundred. You've been so kind . . . so sweet . . . [*Gives her money.*] And you'll
have the rest before you know it. [*Takes a drink of water.*] You know, there
was a young man on the train just now, he was saying . . . there was this
philosopher, he said, who wanted us all to jump off the roof. "Jump!" he
said. "Jump!" That was his whole philosophy. [*Amazed*] Really! I don't
believe it! Give me some more water. . . .

LOPÁKHIN   What Englishmen are you talking about?

PÍSHCHIK   I gave them a lease on the land, the place where the clay is, a
twenty-four-year lease. And now excuse me, but I'm off. Lots of people to
see, pay back what I owe. I owe money all over the place. [*Takes a drink of
water.*] Well, I just wanted to say hello. I'll come by again on Thursday.

LIUBÓV ANDRÉYEVNA   But we're leaving for town today. And tomorrow I'm
going back to Paris.

PÍSHCHIK   What? [*Astonished*] Leaving for town? Oh, my . . . Oh, of course; the
furniture's gone. And all these trunks. I didn't realize. [*Almost in tears*] I didn't
realize. Great thinkers, these English . . . God bless you all. And be happy. I
didn't realize. Well, all things must come to an end. [*Kisses* LIUBÓV's *hand.*] I'll
come to an end myself one of these days. And when I do, I want you all to say:
"Semyónov-Píshchik . . . he was a good old horse. God bless him." Wonderful

weather we're having. Yes. . . . [*Starts out, overcome with emotion, stops in the doorway and turns.*] Oh, by the way, Dáshenka says hello.

    [*Goes out.*]

LIUBÓV ANDRÉYEVNA Now we can go. There are just two things still on my mind. The first is old Firs. [*Looks at her watch.*] We've still got five minutes. . . .

ÁNYA Mama, they took Firs to the nursing home this morning. Yásha took care of it.

LIUBÓV ANDRÉYEVNA . . . And then there's our Várya. She's used to getting up early and working around here all day long, and now she's . . . out of a job. Like a fish out of water. Poor thing—she's so nervous, she cries, she's losing weight . . .

    [*Pause.*]

You know, Yermolái Alexéyich—well, of course you know—I'd always dreamed . . . always dreamed she'd marry you; you know we all think it's a wonderful idea. . . . [*Whispers to* ÁNYA, *who nods to* CARLOTTA; *they both leave.*] She loves you, you like her. . . . I don't know why, I just don't know why the two of you keep avoiding the issue. Really!

LOPÁKHIN I don't know why either. It's all a little funny. Well, I don't mind. If there's still time, I'll do it. . . . All right, *basta*,[2] let's just get it over with. But I don't know, I don't think I can propose without you—

LIUBÓV ANDRÉYEVNA Of course you can. All it takes is a minute. I'll send her right in. . . .

LOPÁKHIN We've even got some champagne all ready. [*Looks at the tray of empty glasses.*] Or at least we did. Somebody must have drunk it all up.

    [YÁSHA *coughs.*]

Guzzled it down, I should say.

LIUBÓV ANDRÉYEVNA Wonderful! We'll leave you alone. Yásha, *allez!*[3] I'll go call her. [*At the door*] Várya, leave that alone; come here a minute, will you? Come on, dear!

    [*Goes out with* YÁSHA.]

LOPÁKHIN [*looks at his watch*] Well . . .

    [*Pause. A few stifled laughs and whispers behind the door. Finally* VÁRYA *enters.*]

VÁRYA [*examines the luggage; takes her time*] That's funny, I can't find them. . . .

LOPÁKHIN What are you looking for?

VÁRYA I packed them myself, and now I don't remember where.

    [*Pause.*]

LOPÁKHIN What . . . ah . . . where are you off to, Várya?

VÁRYA Me? I'm going to work for the Ragúlins. I talked to them about it already; they need a housekeeper. And look after things, you know. . . .

LOPÁKHIN All the way over there? That's fifty miles away.

    [*Pause.*]

Well, looks like this is the end of things around here. . . .

VÁRYA [*still examining the luggage*] Where are they . . . ? Or maybe I put them in the trunk. You're right: this is the end of things here. The end of one life—

---

2. "That's enough" (Italian).   3. "Go on!" (French).

LOPÁKHIN   I'm going too. To Hárkov. Taking the same train, actually. I've got a million things waiting for me. I'm leaving Yepikhódov, though. Hired him to take charge here.

VÁRYA   You hired *who*?

LOPÁKHIN   Last year this time it was snowing already, remember? Today it's still sunny. Nice day. A little chilly, though . . . It was freezing this morning; must have been in the thirties.

VÁRYA   I didn't notice.

[*Pause.*]

Anyway, the thermometer's broken.

[*Pause. A voice from outside calls: "Lopákhin!"*]

LOPÁKHIN [*as if he'd been waiting for the call*]   I'm coming!

[*Goes out.*]

[VÁRYA *sits down on the floor, leans her head on a bundle of dresses, and cries. The door opens;* LIUBÓV *enters carefully.*]

LIUBÓV ANDRÉYEVNA   Well?

[*Pause.*]

We have to go.

VÁRYA [*already stopped crying, wipes her eyes*]   Right, Mama, we have to go. I can get to the Ragúlins' today, if I don't miss the train.

LIUBÓV ANDRÉYEVNA   Ánya, get your coat on.

[*Enter* ÁNYA, GÁYEV, CARLOTTA. GÁYEV *wears a winter overcoat. Servants and drivers come in to pick up the luggage.* YEPIKHÓDOV *directs the operation.*]

Well, we're ready to start.

ÁNYA [*joyfully*]   Ready to start!

GÁYEV   My dear friends, my very dear friends! On this occasion, this farewell to our beloved house, I cannot keep still. I feel I must say a few words to express the emotion that overwhelms me, overwhelms us all—

ÁNYA [*pleads*]   Uncle, please!

VÁRYA   That's enough, Uncle.

GÁYEV [*crushed*]   All right . . . Yellow ball in the side pocket . . . I'll keep still.

[*Enter* TROFÍMOV, *then* LOPÁKHIN.]

TROFÍMOV   Ladies and gentlemen, time to go! You'll be late!

LOPÁKHIN   Yepikhódov, get my coat.

LIUBÓV ANDRÉYEVNA   Let me stay a little minute longer. I never really noticed these walls before, or the ceilings. I want a last look, one last long look. . . .

GÁYEV   I remember when I was six, I was watching out that window, right over there. It was a holy day, Trinity Sunday,[4] I think, and I saw Father on his way to church. . . .

LIUBÓV ANDRÉYEVNA   Have we got everything?

LOPÁKHIN   I guess so. [*To* YEPIKHÓDOV, *who helps him on with his coat*] You keep an eye on things, Yepikhódov.

YEPIKHÓDOV [*loud, businesslike tone*]   You can count on me, Yermolái Alexéyich!

LOPÁKHIN   Why are you talking like that all of a sudden?

YEPIKHÓDOV   I just had a drink—water. . . . It went down the wrong way.

YÁSHA [*with contempt*]   Dumb hick!

---

4. Also known as Pentecost, a Christian holy day occurring on the seventh Sunday after Easter.

LIUBÓV ANDRÉYEVNA   We're all going away. There won't be a soul left on the place. . . .

LOPÁKHIN   But wait till you see what happens here come spring!

[VÁRYA *grabs an umbrella from the luggage, as if she were going to hit him.* LOPÁKHIN *pretends to be terrified.*]

VÁRYA   Don't get excited. It was just a joke.

TROFÍMOV   You've all got to get moving! It's time to go! You'll miss your train!

VÁRYA   Here's your galoshes, Pétya, behind this suitcase. [*With tears in her eyes*] Smelly old things . . .

TROFÍMOV [*puts them on*]   It's time to go!

GÁYEV [*deeply moved, afraid he'll start crying*]   Yes, the train . . . mustn't miss the train . . . Yellow ball in the side pocket, white in the corner . . .

LIUBÓV ANDRÉYEVNA   Let's go!

LOPÁKHIN   Everybody here? Nobody left? [*Closes and locks the door, left.*] Got to lock up; I've got a few things stored here. All right, let's go!

ÁNYA   Goodbye, house! Goodbye, old life!

TROFÍMOV   No, hello, new life!

[*Goes out with* ÁNYA.]

[VÁRYA *looks around the room again; she's not eager to go.* YÁSHA *goes out with* CARLOTTA *and her little dog.*]

LOPÁKHIN   So. Until next spring. Come on, let's go, everybody. Goodbye!

[LIUBÓV *and* GÁYEV *are left alone. It's as if they'd been waiting for this moment. They throw their arms around each other and burst out crying, but try to keep the others outside from hearing.*]

GÁYEV [*in despair*]   Oh, sister, sister . . .

LIUBÓV ANDRÉYEVNA   Oh, my orchard, my beautiful orchard! My life, my youth, my happiness, goodbye! Goodbye! Goodbye!

[ÁNYA's *voice, joyful:* "Mama!" TROFÍMOV's *voice, joyful, excited:* "Yoo-hoo!"]

These walls, these windows, for the last time . . . And Mama loved this room . . .

GÁYEV   Oh, sister, sister . . .

[ÁNYA: "Mama!" TROFÍMOV: "Yoo-hoo!"]

LIUBÓV ANDRÉYEVNA   We're coming!

[*They leave.*]

[*The stage is empty. We hear the sound of the door being locked, then the carriages as they drive away. It grows very quiet. In the silence, we hear the occasional sound of an ax chopping down the cherry trees, a mournful, lonely sound. Then we hear steps. Enter* FIRS *from the door, right. He wears his usual butler's livery, but with bedroom slippers. He's very ill.*]

FIRS [*goes to the door, tries the handle*]   Locked. They're gone. [*Sits on the sofa.*] They forgot about me. That's all right; I'll just sit here for a bit. . . . And Leoníd Andréyich probably forgot his winter coat. [*A worried sigh*] I should have looked. . . . He's still all wet, that one. . . . [*Mumbles something we can't make out.*] Well, it's all over now, and I never even had a life to live. . . . [*Lies back.*] I'll just lie here for a bit. . . . No strength left, nothing left, not a thing . . . Oh, you. You young flibbertigibbet. [*Lies there, no longer moving.*]

[*In the distance we hear a sound that seems to come from the sky, a sad sound, like a string snapping. It dies away. Everything grows quiet. We can hear the occasional sound of an ax on a tree.*]

Curtain.

Perspectives
on
European Empire

A great deal of our experience of the world today is a consequence of the dominance of European empires in the nineteenth century. Both our feelings of global interconnectedness and the deep economic inequalities that divide the developed world from developing nations are effects of Europe's imperial reach. Britain and France became the world's major superpowers then, centers of vast empires that stretched across the globe. These empires had emerged out of fierce economic competition among European nations going back several centuries. Hoping to profit from new natural resources and new markets, England, France, Spain, Holland, and Portugal had sent ships both eastward and westward, trying to establish monopolies on trade relations with Turkey, Russia, India, and China, and establishing colonies in North and South America. European consumers developed a growing appetite for products from these distant places, including tea, coffee, sugar, furs, cotton, silver, tobacco, rubber, silk, spices, and opium. The profits of European companies soared. The slave trade played a crucial role in this new economy: traders would buy slaves in Africa and sell them to plantation owners in the United States, Brazil, and the Caribbean. Slave traders

The Rhodes Colossus, a caricature of Cecil John Rhodes published in *Punch* magazine in 1892.

would then use these profits to buy products of slave labor, such as tobacco and sugar, which they would transport to Europe to sell to eager customers there.

Because all of Europe coveted the same valuable markets, tensions rose among European nations, frequently erupting into outright war. In the eighteenth century, France lost a series of wars with Britain, which frustrated its dreams of controlling North America, the Caribbean, and India. France then looked elsewhere. Long interested in opening up trade with Vietnam, France invaded in the 1850s and took control. They industrialized the Vietnamese economy, investing in railroads and factories and making huge profits from Vietnamese rubber, coal, and sugar. But few Vietnamese people benefited: under French rule, poverty, disease, and starvation became commonplace.

Conflicts among European empires redrew the maps of whole continents. When Napoleon invaded Spain and put his brother on the throne there, he destabilized monarchical authority so profoundly that leaders in Latin America led wars of independence from Spanish rule. Many of these were helped by Britain, which was eager to limit Spanish economic and political power. In the 1880s, European powers, which had held various territories on the African coast, began to compete for power inland, dividing up Africa into spheres of control. The diverse territories of South Africa prompted the Boer Wars, battles between the British army and Dutch settlers. In west central Africa, Great Britain, Germany, France, and Portugal vied for territory. By the turn of the century, 90 percent of the African continent was under European control. Around this time, the United States and Japan also began to build

empires, entering into the competition with European states. In 1898, the United States intervened in Cuba and the Philippines, starting the Spanish-American War and beginning its new role as another powerful imperial player on the world stage.

Among these many global powers, Britain held an exceptionally powerful position. There is a famous phrase—The sun never sets on the British Empire—that points to the extraordinary reach of British commercial, financial, and naval power. In an empire that stretched from Hong Kong, Singapore, and New Zealand to Nigeria, South Africa, and Kenya, to Ireland, Jamaica, and Canada, the British imposed their language, education system, and culture, including their literature, on millions of people. The spread of British power around the world is the reason so much of the world knows at least a little bit of English today.

Until the nineteenth century, European nations had been unashamed to admit their imperial missions were above all about profits. But if the Europeans traveled to distant lands for economic reasons, they often stayed for political ones. For a long time, the British had tended to leave local leaders in place, for example in India, rather than get involved in direct governmental administration. But in the nineteenth century, a new generation of British career men, feeling superior to the Indians, began a campaign to impose their own moral, linguistic, and cultural traditions on India, whipping up enthusiasm back in England for the task of advancing the "backward" peoples of India.

Over the course of the nineteenth century, the rhetoric of racial difference deepened, as Europeans saw themselves less and less as economic actors and more and more as libera-

tors and civilizers of less "advanced" races. Advocates of colonialism often argued that empires existed not for the benefit of the conquerors but for the sake of the conquered, "primitive" peoples, who were incapable of self-government but who could, with European guidance, eventually become civilized. Global empires had filled European coffers, but this the Europeans often conveniently forgot, speaking of themselves instead as responsible world leaders, reluctantly taking up what Rudyard Kipling famously called "the white man's burden."

But while Europeans often claimed to be motivated by a high-minded responsibility to spread reason and progress, reports of their atrocities made it clear that the zeal to civilize was often a mask for brutal exploitation. King Leopold II of Belgium sent explorers to Congo Free State, for example, under the guise of a scientific and charitable association but really intending to subdue the Congolese through economic and military force. Eager to profit from the rubber trade, he enslaved workers in Congo and brutally tortured and mutilated them, often leaving them to starve. As much as half the population—ten million people—died under Leopold's regime.

The violence and exploitation of European empires fostered resentment and out-and-out insurrection. A major blow to British imperialism came in 1857, for example, when Indian soldiers rebelled against the British army. The British violently suppressed the rebellion, a brutality that left lasting scars. Indian subjects began to feel a profound mistrust of the British, which would foster increasingly insistent movements for independence. A number of other countries, including Australia and Canada, successfully broke away and formed separate states. These rebellions became more frequent and more successful after World War I. But poverty remained a feature of many of the regions exploited by European empires. Many new nations successfully fought for political sovereignty but remain, into our own time, enmeshed in asymmetrical economic relations, providing natural and human resources largely for the benefit of wealthier Western nations.

This cluster offers a variety of perspectives on imperialism. Several writers are enthusiastic champions. Macaulay's *Minute on Indian Education* is a confident and influential assertion of the supremacy of Western civilization and of the English language as a treasure house of civilized learning. The businessman-conqueror Cecil Rhodes and the poet Rudyard Kipling welcome England's imperial destiny and what they see as the duty of white races to advance world civilization. English South African writer Olive Schreiner criticizes the Europeans who come to Africa to make fortunes, but she defends the rights of white colonial settlers and ignores indigenous Africans almost completely. Other writers here argue forcefully against European empires. The first of these voices comes from within Europe. Giuseppe Garibaldi, an Italian revolutionary who tired of imperialist wars of aggression, proposes to restructure the imperial nation-states into a European confederation, whose energy could then turn to the development of global trade. Also included here is a letter of protest by an East African leader, Chief Machemba, to a German officer, defiantly refusing to capitulate to imperial aggression. Finally, U.S. writer Mark Twain offers a bitter satire of imperial rule by imagining what goes

on inside the head of the rapacious Belgian King Leopold II.

Inventing fast new modes of communication and transportation to conduct business and government affairs, European empires linked distant peoples for the first time, laying the groundwork for globalization today. But their insistence on the superiority of Western culture, Christianity, and racial whiteness also laid down deep tracks of prejudice and inequality. Not until the next century would the claims of European "civilization" be systematically called into question, and even now we can see the legacy of nineteenth-century European empires powerfully at work every day in economic, political, and cultural experience around the globe.

THOMAS BABINGTON MACAULAY

No voice argued more effectively for the superiority of Western culture in the nineteenth century than T. B. Macaulay (1800–1859), a famous essayist, orator, and member of the British Parliament. In the early 1830s, the British government was engaged in a fierce debate about education in colonial India: some assumed that Indian students should study the classical languages of South Asia (Arabic and Sanskrit); others felt strongly that they should learn English from the beginning, so that they might absorb European knowledge and values effectively. Although Macaulay admits that he does not know either Arabic or Sanskrit himself, he forcefully asserts the preeminence of English. He gives a variety of reasons here, from the advances of English science and superiority of their morals to practical opportunities for employment and political influence. Along the way, he assumes a vast chasm between advanced European civilization and Asian backwardness: "a single shelf of a good European library," he claims, is "worth the whole native literature of India and Arabia."

It is worth noting that in Macaulay's argument, education emerges as crucial to the work of maintaining an empire. He imagines that a new class of English-educated Indians, "English in taste, in opinions, in morals, and in intellect," will help Britain to govern the vast and diverse territories of India. This proved persuasive, and Macaulay's proposal had far-reaching consequences: English became the official language of Indian education, government, and the national press, and although it was replaced by Hindi in 1963, it remains a widely used language in Indian media and education today.

[*From* Minute on Indian Education, February 2, 1835][1]

* * * A sum is set apart "for the revival and promotion of literature and the encouragement of the learned natives of India, and for the introduction and promotion of a knowledge of the sciences among the inhabitants of the British territories."[2] It is argued, or rather taken for granted, that by literature, the Parliament can have meant only Arabic and Sanscrit literature, that they never would have given the honorable appellation of "a learned native" to a native who was familiar with the poetry of Milton, the metaphysics of Locke, and the physics of Newton; but that they meant to designate by that name only such persons as might have studied in the sacred books of the Hindoos all the uses of cusa-grass,[3] and all the mysteries of absorption into the Deity. This does not appear to be a very satisfactory interpretation. To take a parallel case; suppose

1. A memorandum written by Macaulay, in his capacity as president of the Committee of Public Instruction, to Lord Bentinck, governor-general of India.

2. Macaulay cites an 1813 act of Parliament that established a fund for Indian education.
3. Also called *darbha*, a sacred grass required in various Hindu rituals.

that the Pacha of Egypt, a country once superior in knowledge to the nations of Europe, but now sunk far below them, were to appropriate a sum for the purpose of "reviving and promoting literature, and encouraging learned natives of Egypt," would anybody infer that he meant the youth of his pachalic to give years to the study of hieroglyphics, to search into all the doctrines disguised under the fable of Osiris,[4] and to ascertain with all possible accuracy the ritual with which cats and onions were anciently adored? Would he be justly charged with inconsistency, if, instead of employing his young subjects in deciphering obelisks, he were to order them to be instructed in the English and French languages, and in all the sciences to which those languages are the chief keys?

* * *

We now come to the gist of the matter. We have a fund to be employed as government shall direct for the intellectual improvement of the people of this country. The simple question is, what is the most useful way of employing it?

All parties seem to be agreed on one point, that the dialects commonly spoken among the natives of this part of India, contain neither literary nor scientific information, and are, moreover, so poor and rude that, until they are enriched from some other quarter, it will not be easy to translate any valuable work into them. It seems to be admitted on all sides, that the intellectual improvement of those classes of the people who have the means of pursuing higher studies can at present be effected only by means of some language not vernacular amongst them.

What then shall that language be? One-half of the committee maintain that it should be the English. The other half strongly recommend the Arabic and Sanscrit. The whole question seems to me to be, which language is the best worth knowing?

I have no knowledge of either Sanscrit or Arabic.—But I have done what I could to form a correct estimate of their value. I have read translations of the most celebrated Arabic and Sanscrit works. I have conversed both here and at home with men distinguished by their proficiency in the Eastern tongues. I am quite ready to take the oriental learning at the valuation of the orientalists themselves. I have never found one among them who could deny that a single shelf of a good European library was worth the whole native literature of India and Arabia. The intrinsic superiority of the Western literature is, indeed, fully admitted by those members of the committee who support the oriental plan of education.

It will hardly be disputed, I suppose, that the department of literature in which the Eastern writers stand highest is poetry. And I certainly never met with any orientalist who ventured to maintain that the Arabic and Sanscrit poetry could be compared to that of the great European nations. But when we pass from works of imagination to works in which facts are recorded, and general principles investigated, the superiority of the Europeans becomes absolutely immeasurable. It is, I believe, no exaggeration to say, that all the

4. In ancient Egypt, the god of the underworld. "Pachalic": the district over which the pacha, or pasha, rules.

historical information which has been collected from all the books written in the Sanscrit language is less valuable than what may be found in the most paltry abridgments used at preparatory schools in England. In every branch of physical or moral philosophy, the relative position of the two nations is nearly the same.

How, then, stands the case? We have to educate a people who cannot at present be educated by means of their mother-tongue. We must teach them some foreign language. The claims of our own language it is hardly necessary to recapitulate. It stands pre-eminent even among the languages of the west. It abounds with works of imagination not inferior to the noblest which Greece has bequeathed to us; with models of every species of eloquence; with historical compositions, which, considered merely as narratives, have seldom been surpassed, and which, considered as vehicles of ethical and political instruction, have never been equaled; with just and lively representations of human life and human nature; with the most profound speculations on metaphysics, morals, government, jurisprudence, and trade; with full and correct information respecting every experimental science which tends to preserve the health, to increase the comfort, or to expand the intellect of man. Whoever knows that language has ready access to all the vast intellectual wealth, which all the wisest nations of the earth have created and hoarded in the course of ninety generations. It may safely be said, that the literature now extant in that language is of far greater value than all the literature which three hundred years ago was extant in all the languages of the world together. Nor is this all. In India, English is the language spoken by the ruling class. It is spoken by the higher class of natives at the seats of government. It is likely to become the language of commerce throughout the seas of the East. It is the language of two great European communities which are rising, the one in the south of Africa, the other in Australasia; communities which are every year becoming more important, and more closely connected with our Indian empire. Whether we look at the intrinsic value of our literature, or at the particular situation of this country, we shall see the strongest reason to think that, of all foreign tongues, the English tongue is that which would be the most useful to our native subjects.

The question now before us is simply whether, when it is in our power to teach this language, we shall teach languages in which, by universal confession, there are no books on any subject which deserve to be compared to our own; whether, when we can teach European science, we shall teach systems which, by universal confession, whenever they differ from those of Europe, differ for the worse; and whether, when we can patronize sound philosophy and true history, we shall countenance, at the public expense, medical doctrines, which would disgrace an English farrier[5]—astronomy, which would move laughter in girls at an English boarding school,—history, abounding with kings thirty feet high, and reigns thirty thousand years long,—and geography, made up of seas of treacle and seas of butter.

We are not without experience to guide us. History furnishes several analogous cases, and they all teach the same lesson. There are in modern times, to go no further, two memorable instances of a great impulse given to the mind of a whole society,—of prejudices overthrown,—of knowledge diffused,—of taste

---

5. A person who shoes horses or, by extension, cares for them.

purified,—of arts and sciences planted in countries which had recently been ignorant and barbarous.

The first instance to which I refer, is the great revival of letters among the Western nations at the close of the fifteenth and the beginning of the sixteenth century. At that time almost every thing that was worth reading was contained in the writings of the ancient Greeks and Romans. Had our ancestors acted as the Committee of Public Instruction has hitherto acted; had they neglected the language of Cicero and Tacitus;[6] had they confined their attention to the old dialects of our own island; had they printed nothing and taught nothing at the universities but chronicles in Anglo-Saxon, and romances in Norman-French, would England have been what she now is? What the Greek and Latin were to the contemporaries of More and Ascham,[7] our tongue is to the people of India. The literature of England is now more valuable than that of classical antiquity. I doubt whether the Sanscrit literature be as valuable as that of our Saxon and Norman progenitors. In some departments,—in history, for example, I am certain that it is much less so.

Another instance may be said to be still before our eyes. Within the last hundred and twenty years, a nation which has previously been in a state as barbarous as that in which our ancestors were before the crusades, has gradually emerged from the ignorance in which it was sunk, and has taken its place among civilized communities.—I speak of Russia. There is now in that country a large educated class, abounding with persons fit to serve the state in the highest functions, and in no wise inferior to the most accomplished men who adorn the best circles of Paris and London. There is reason to hope that this vast empire, which in the time of our grandfathers was probably behind the Punjab,[8] may, in the time of our grandchildren, be pressing close on France and Britain in the career of improvement. And how was this change effected? Not by flattering national prejudices: not by feeding the mind of the young Muscovite with the old women's stories which his rude fathers had believed: not by filling his head with lying legends about St. Nicholas: not by encouraging him to study the great question, whether the world was or was not created on the 13th of September;[9] not by calling him "a learned native," when he has mastered all these points of knowledge: but by teaching him those foreign languages in which the greatest mass of information had been laid up, and thus putting all that information within his reach. The languages of Western Europe civilized Russia. I cannot doubt that they will do for the Hindoo what they have done for the Tartar.

---

6. Gaius Cornelius Tacitus (ca. 56–120 C.E.), Roman historian and eminent prose stylist. Marcus Tullius Cicero (106–43 B.C.E.), Roman statesman, orator, and author whose Ciceronian style became a model for later writers.
7. Roger Ascham (1515–1568), humanist scholar and author of *The Scholemaster* (1570). Sir Thomas More (1477–1535), humanist and chancellor of England (1529–32).
8. A large region of the Indian subcontinent, currently divided between India and Pakistan.

9. According to the Byzantine calendar, which the Russians accepted together with Christianity, the world was created on September 1, 5508 B.C.E. Peter the Great moved Russia to the Julian calendar (to be superseded by the current Gregorian calendar) in an attempt to reconcile discrepancies that had crept in over the centuries: By the 19th century, there was a difference of twelve days between the Byzantine and Julian calendars, so the Byzantine date of creation would appear as September 13 in the new reckoning.

* * *

To sum up what I have said, I think it clear that we are not fettered by the Act of Parliament of 1813; that we are not fettered by any pledge expressed or implied; that we are free to employ our funds as we choose; that we ought to employ them in teaching what is best worth knowing; that English is better worth knowing than Sanscrit or Arabic; that the natives are desirous to be taught English, and are not desirous to be taught Sanscrit or Arabic;[1] that neither as the languages of law, nor as the languages of religion, have the Sanscrit and Arabic any peculiar claim to our engagement; that it is possible to make natives of this country thoroughly good English scholars, and that to this end our efforts ought to be directed.

In one point I fully agree with the gentlemen to whose general views I am opposed. I feel with them, that it is impossible for us, with our limited means, to attempt to educate the body of the people. We must at present do our best to form a class who may be interpreters between us and the millions whom we govern; a class of persons, Indian in blood and color, but English in taste, in opinions, in morals, and in intellect. To that class we may leave it to refine the vernacular dialects of the country, to enrich those dialects with terms of science borrowed from the Western nomenclature, and to render them by degrees fit vehicles for conveying knowledge to the great mass of the population.

* * *

1. Graduates of the Sanscrit (i.e., Sanskrit) and Arabic curriculum had complained that they could not find jobs.

GIUSEPPE GARIBALDI

Because European nations were locked in a battle for global power over the course of the nineteenth century, it is unusual to come across a vision of international cooperation. But Giuseppe Garibaldi (1807–1882) was no ordinary voice. Born in southern France to Italian parents, he became a "hero of two worlds," fighting wars of liberation in South America and Italy. Although he helped form the Italian nation, Garibaldi's main allegiance was to common people regardless of nation.

A brilliant guerrilla leader and strategist, he was distrusted as an unpredictable revolutionary by most heads of state. In Sicily, however, he was welcomed by the peasants as a liberator, when he landed there with his forces in 1860 and proceeded to defeat the much larger army of the king of Naples.

The conquest of Sicily turned sour, however, and Garibaldi was unable to forget the atrocities he witnessed there after the peasants took revenge on their oppressors. (Giovanni Verga's *Freedom*,

printed in this volume, describes this violence.) Tired of war and taking advantage of his international fame, Garibaldi sent a public letter, dated October 15, 1860, to all the heads of Europe, suggesting a plan to stop wars between nations and allow resources to be used for peaceful ends. It is a surprising memorandum, one that was ignored at the time but anticipates international political organizations to come, including the United Nations and the European Union. Unlike contemporary imperialists, Garibaldi does not seek local solutions in foreign conquests but imagines instead a reconfigured Europe and a nonviolent construction of empire.

Memorandum[1]

[Monte Tifata, Campania,
15 October 1860]

It is well known to all intelligent people that Europe is far from finding itself in a normal state and justifiable to its populations.

France, which undisputably occupies the first position among the European powers, maintains under arms six hundred thousand soldiers, one of the first fleets in the world, and an immense quantity of employees for its internal security.

Great Britain does not have the same number of soldiers, but a superior fleet, and perhaps a superior number of employees, for the security of its possessions abroad.

Russia and Prussia, in order to maintain themselves in equilibrium, also need to employ immense armies.

The secondary States, if for no other reason than their spirit of imitation and to show their presence, are obliged to maintain themselves proportionately at the same level.

I will not speak of Austria and the Ottoman Empire[2] both of which are damned to destruction for the good of the unfortunate peoples they oppress.

In sum, one may ask himself: why this agitated and violent state of Europe? Everyone speaks of civilization and progress . . . But to me it seems, excepting our elegance, that instead we do not differ much from primitive times, when men tore each other apart in order to possess themselves of another's prey. We pass our lives threatening each other continuously and reciprocally, while in Europe the large majority of the people, not only the intelligent, but also those of good sense, understand perfectly that we can also pass our poor lives without this perpetual state of threats and hostilities of some against the others, and without this necessity, which seems to be fatally imposed upon peoples by some secret and invisible enemy of mankind, by killing ourselves with so much science and finesse.

1. This document, translated here by Anthony P. Campanella, was sent by Garibaldi to the heads of all European governments.
2. During the 19th century, both the Ottoman Turkish Empire and the Austrian Habsburg Empire suppressed, or tried to suppress, a series of nationalist revolts among their subject peoples. In addition, Austrian soldiers had put down numerous rebellions in Italy, and Austria declared war on Piedmont in 1859.

For example, let us suppose one thing:

Let us suppose that Europe should form a single State.

Who ever would think of disturbing it in its own domain? Who would ever consider, I ask you, disturbing the tranquility of this sovereign of the world?

And in such a supposition there would be no more armies, no more fleets, and the immense capital sums wrested almost always from the needs and misery of peoples in order to be squandered in the service of extermination, would be converted instead to the advantage of the people in one colossal development of industry, by improving roads, in the construction of bridges, in the excavation of canals, in founding public buildings, and in the erection of schools which would divert from misery and ignorance so many poor creatures in all countries of the world, regardless of their grade of civilization, now condemned by egoism, connivance and bad administration of privileged classes bent upon the bestialization and prostitution of mankind and its surroundings.

However, the realization of the social reforms to which I allude, rarely depends upon a sole initiative, regardless of its strength and exuberance. But when has Europe ever presented greater probabilities for success in achieving these humanitarian benefits than now?

Let us examine the situation. Alexander II in Russia proclaims the emancipation of slaves.[3]

Victor Emmanuel in Italy throws his scepter onto the battlefield and shows himself to be in favor of regenerating a noble race and great nation.[4]

In Great Britain there is a virtuous queen[5] and a generous and wise nation, which associates itself enthusiastically for the cause of oppressed nationalities.

Finally France, because of the mass of its concentrated population, because of the valor of its soldiers, and because of its recent prestige from the most brilliant period of its military history, is called upon to be the arbiter of Europe.[6]

But who shall initiate this great undertaking?

The nation which marches in the vanguard of the revolution! The idea of a European confederation, which would be placed ahead of the French Emperor and which would spread security and happiness in the world, would that not be better than all the political combinations which torment and make uneasy each day of this poor people?

Concerning the thought of atrocious destruction which a single battle among the great fleets of western powers could bring, he who would dare give such an order would be frightened with terror, and probably there will never be a man so vilely daring as to assume such a frightful responsibility.

---

3. Alexander II, czar of Russia, had announced a plan to abolish serfdom in 1856; the law was enacted in 1861 after extensive negotiations with the serfs' former owners.

4. The king of Piedmont, Victor Emmanuel II (1820–1878), personally commanded his troops against Austrian forces in the battles of Magenta and Solferino (June 1859). He was proclaimed king of the new kingdom of Italy on March 17, 1861.

5. Queen Victoria (1819–1901).

6. Napoleon III of France had earned the reputation of arbiter of Europe during the negotiations leading to the Treaty of Paris (1856), which concluded the Crimean War. "Military history": a joint force of Piedmontese and French troops, commanded by Napoleon III, defeated the Austrians at the Battle of Solferino.

The rivalry which has persisted between France and Great Britain from the fourteenth century to today exists still; but today we will show it to be for the glory of human progress, which is infinitely less intensive so that a compromise between the two greatest nations of Europe, that is a compromise which would have as its aim the welfare of humanity, could no longer figure among the dreams and utopias of serious men.

Therefore the foundation of a European Confederation is naturally based upon France and Great Britain. Then France and Great Britain should frankly and faithfully shake hands, while Italy, Spain, Portugal, Hungary, Belgium, Switzerland, Greece and Rumania will come along too, in fact they will instinctively group themselves around them.

In this manner all divided and oppressed nationalities, that is the Slavic, Celtic, Germanic, Scandinavian races, gigantic Russia included, will not want to remain outside of this political regeneration to which they are drawn by the genius of the century.

I realize that an objection arises naturally in opposition to the preceding project:

What is to be done with the innumerable mass of men now employed in the military armies and navies?

The answer is simple:

During the same time that these masses are discharged, we would also be getting rid of the cumbersome and damaging institutions; and the spirit of the sovereigns, no longer preoccupied with the ambition of conquest, war and destruction, would be turned instead towards the creation of useful institutions and would descend from the study of generalities to that of the families and also of individuals.

Furthermore with the growth of industry, with commerce protected, the merchant marine will reclaim from the military marine all the financial support from the latter at once, and the incalculable quantity of enterprises created by the peace, from our association and security, would swallow up all this armed population, perhaps even twice that which it is today.

War becoming practically impossible again, armies would become useless. But that which would not become useless is maintaining the soldierly and generous customs of the people by means of national militias, so that they would be ready to suppress disorders and any ambitions which might attempt to destroy the European pact.

I strongly desire that my words become known to those to whom God confided the holy mission of doing well, and they will do it, certainly preferring instead of a false and ephemeral greatness, true greatness, that which has its foundation in love and in the gratitude of the people.

G. Garibaldi

MACHEMBA

"I find no reason why I should obey you. I would rather die," writes East African chief Machemba (late 1800s) defiantly to Major Hermann von Wissmann, the officer in command of subduing Tanganyika for the German Empire. Von Wissmann had recently completed a bloody suppression of coastal resistance and was now turning his attention to the interior and requiring the submission of all local chiefs, demanding that they pay new taxes and give up their lands.

Machemba was chief of the numerous Yao tribes who lived near the southern end of Lake Malawi. He was a wealthy trader, with a vast commercial network inside and outside Tanganyika. When the Germans first tried to lure him with promises of friendship, he turned them away. But for all his wealth and power and the advantage of guerrilla warfare on his own terrain, Machemba knew he would be vulnerable in the long term to the kind of scorch-and-burn attack that had already reduced the coast. The Germans had cannons and a large military force that included hundreds of Sudanese mercenaries.

Von Wissmann's letter requires Machemba to come to the German station at Lindi and submit. Using reason, appeals to fairness, and biblical morality, Machemba insists that he and his family present no danger for the Germans, and he leaves the door open for friendship. He also emphatically refuses to submit.

Friendship was not what the Germans had in mind, and they tried to subdue Machemba three times. Each time he disappeared and harassed them with guerrilla tactics until they finally returned to the coast to report failure. In 1891, after his people's villages had been destroyed, Machemba did go to Lindi to accept the Germans' conditions. The peace did not last, however; he refused to collect their taxes and in 1899 was forced to flee to neighboring Mozambique, where he conducted a similar resistance against the Portuguese.

Machemba's letter is a dramatic statement of resistance to colonial subjugation. The only copy of the document is a German translation preserved in the German Colonial Archives along with other records, which means that the lost Swahili original comes to us filtered through the conqueror's language.

Letter to Major von Wissmann[1]

[undated—ca. Fall 1890]

Addressed to my friend and brother, the Commander-in-Chief:

I am informing you that your letter has arrived, and that I have read it and know everything it contains. Moreover, I have heard what you have to say;[2] but I find no reason that I should obey you. I would rather die. I have no relationship

---

1. This letter was written by Chief Machemba of the Yao people to Major Hermann von Wissmann, commander of the German forces in Tanganyika and head of the station at Lindi.

Translated from the German by Robert Sullivan and Sarah Lawall.
2. The spoken message accompanying the letter.

to you, and I cannot recall that you ever gave me a paisa[3] or a quarter paisa or a needle or a thread. I look for a reason why I should obey you, and I find not the slightest. If it is only a matter of friendship, then I am not opposed, now or in the future. But to be your subject—that I cannot do. If it is only a matter of friendship, then we are agreed.

If you want to fight, I am ready. But to be your subject—never.

What you are hearing here is said without ambush. I will not fall at your feet, for you are a creature of God,[4] and I, too, am created. I am no God to be able to help you, and if you hear anything in my message, it is that we have no relationship.

I am sultan in my land. You are sultans in your land. Behold,[5] I am by no means saying to you that you should obey me. Not at all: indeed, I know that you are a free man. Not since I was born have I ever set foot on the coast; should I set foot on it now because you summon me? I will not come, and, if you are strong enough, then come get me. I would rather lose your respect [by being captured] than submit to you.

Besides, my child is called "Weakling,"[6] and, ever since he was born, has not known what war is. God willing, if you want to get me, then come: I will not come in person. Greetings.

This letter comes from your friend Machemba, son of M'chakama of the family of Masaninga, written in his own hand.

---

3. Or pice, a small coin, one-sixty-fourth of the Indian rupee in the East India Company's currency system. Machemba lists a descending order of possible gifts. The colonial trading companies initially gave gifts to local rulers whom they wished to persuade. "Relationship": i.e., personal, commercial, or diplomatic ties.
4. In the German text, would be recognized as a phrase from the Lutheran Bible.

5. Echoes biblical language in German and is more than simply "look" or "see." "Sultans": kings or rulers. The sultan of Zanzibar, now displaced by the Germans, was the traditional ruler of the mainland peoples of Tanganyika.
6. Literal translation from German. The lost Swahili term may have had special cultural significance, such as describing a youth who has not yet seen combat.

CECIL RHODES

On a journey to South Africa, the U.S. writer Mark Twain was startled by the power of a single man: Cecil Rhodes (1853–1902). "He is the only colonial in the British dominions whose goings and comings are chronicled and discussed under all the globe's meridians, and whose speeches, unclipped, are cabled from the ends of the earth; and he is the only unroyal outsider whose arrival in London can compete for attention with an eclipse." South Africa seems "to stand in a kind of shuddering awe of him, friend and enemy alike."

Rhodes was a British businessman and imperialist whose wealth, energy, and manipulation of public opinion made him a force capable of overthrowing native rulers and bending colonial governments to his will. He was born in England and moved to South Africa in 1870; within ten years he had become wealthy as a diamond speculator, founding the De Beers diamond-mining company. In 1889, he created and controlled the British South Africa Company, whose royal charter gave it unlimited power to acquire lands and rule them in the name of the British

Empire. Rhodes stopped at nothing to expand his holdings in the name of British imperialism, deceiving the Ndebele ruler Lobengula into signing away all rights to Matabeleland and Mashonaland (now Zimbabwe). As prime minister of Cape Colony from 1890 to 1896, Rhodes maintained his power base with the Afrikaners by laws that restricted the rights of black Africans to vote, to own land, and to live where they wished. This was the beginning of what became the apartheid system.

Rhodes dreamed of colonizing the world with Anglo-Saxon settlers. He even imagined bringing the United States back into the British Empire. The prestigious Rhodes Scholarships, which he established, are a philanthropic version of this dream. A charismatic speaker, his 1899 speech in Cape Town offers a picture of ever-expanding imperial horizons and limitless prosperity for "every civilized man" in a "union of races"—by which he means only whites. In fact, there is no mention of the African population in Rhodes's speech. He simply states that the country has been "given to us" for profitable exploitation.

From Speech at Drill Hall, Cape Town, South Africa[1]

* * *

"And, sir, my people have changed. I speak of the English people, with their marvelous common sense, coupled with their powers of imagination—all thoughts of a Little England are over. They are tumbling over each other, Liberals and Conservatives, to show which side are the greatest and most enthusiastic Imperialists. The people have changed, and so do all the parties, just like the Punch and Judy show at a country fair.[2] The people have found out that

1. Published in 1900. The speech was delivered on July 18, 1899.
2. A traditional puppet play that showed con-

stant battles between a brutal husband and his nagging wife. "Parties": i.e., political parties.

England is small, and her trade is large, and they have also found out that other people are taking their share of the world, and enforcing hostile tariffs. The people of England are finding out that "trade follows the flag," and they have all become Imperialists. They are not going to part with any territory. And the bygone ideas of nebulous republics are over. The English people intend to retain every inch of land they have got, and perhaps, sir, they intend to secure a few more inches. And so the thought of my country has changed. When I began this business of annexation, both sides were most timid. They would ask one to stop at Kimberley, then they asked one to stop at Khama's country. I remember Lord Salisbury's Chief Secretary imploring me to stop at the Zambesi.[3] Mr. Mayor, excuse me for using the word "I," but unfortunately I have been alone in these efforts. Now, sir, they won't stop anywhere; they have found out that the world is not quite big enough for British trade and the British flag; and that the operation of even conquering the planets is only something which has yet to be known. I have little doubt about the Colonial people, and in saying so, I cover in the Colonial people the Dutch as well as the English. Notwithstanding my past little temporary difficulty, if we were all to accept equal rights,[4] I feel convinced that we should all be united on the proposition that Africa is not, after all, big enough for us.

"And, gentlemen, with that comes the development of our own country. * * * You have the sheep, the wine, the gold, the diamonds, and the health, and a marvelous climate. There is no place in the world to touch this; there is no place to touch it for the beauty of its climate, and the variety of its products, and yet we stupid human mortals are quarreling over the equality of rights, instead of thinking of the great country that has been given to us. * * * That is what we are working for, not only union of the country but union of the races, and, if I may put it, that will come right once the principle of equal rights is accepted—equal rights for every civilized man south of the Zambesi.

* * *

---

3. A large river flowing through south-central Africa. Kimberley is a city in the northern Cape of Africa, known for its diamond mines. Rhodes's company (De Beers Consolidated Mines) took control of the mines in 1888. Khama III was ruler of Bechuanaland (now Botswana), which was a British protectorate. He made a journey to England in 1895 to confirm British protection for his country. "Chief Secretary": the representative of Lord Salisbury, who was prime minister of Britain.

4. Specifically for settlers of Dutch ancestry (the Boers) and the English. "Temporary difficulty": in January 1896, Rhodes was forced to resign as prime minister of the Cape after being implicated in the Jameson Raid, an unsuccessful attempt to overthrow the government of the Transvaal (a neighboring Boer state). The following year, a committee of the British House of Commons condemned him for grave breaches of official duty.

OLIVE SCHREINER

Olive Schreiner (1853–1920), an English South African, hated the "small knot" of European speculators, including Cecil Rhodes, who were ruthlessly exploiting her birthplace. Schreiner was born in the Cape Colony in 1855, the child of missionary parents who had moved to South Africa in 1838. As a young woman, Schreiner went to London in search of a more cosmopolitan environment. Her controversial first novel, *The Story of an African Farm* (1883), published in England under a pseudonym, was an immediate success for its vivid writing and its intellectually bold attacks on the social, educational, and religious narrowness of colonial society. She was not happy in London, however, and returned to South Africa in 1889 where she became actively engaged in politics.

In 1899, Schreiner wrote a public letter to the British people. It was a moment when war between the British and Dutch settlers in South Africa was looming. She suggests in her letter that the most urgent problem is European greed. She makes a passionate statement in defense of the Boer settlers and, by extension, all settlers in South Africa who dream of a new African nation built by their own hands. Notably, Schreiner almost never mentions the plight of the indigenous Africans, whose soil the settlers occupy. Instead, this letter focuses on the risk of war between two colonial states whose image of a developed and "civilized" Africa is, she believes, more shared than not.

From An English–South African's View of the Situation[1]

* * *

Amid all this chorus of opinion, there is one voice which, though heard, has not yet been heard with that distinctness and fullness which its authority demands—it is the voice of the African-born Englishman who loves England, the man who, born in South Africa, and loving it as all men, who are men, love their birth-land, is yet an Englishman, bound to England not only by ties of blood, but that much more intense passion which springs from personal contact alone. Our position is unique, and it would seem that we are marked out, at the present juncture of South African affairs, for an especial function, which imposes on us at whatever cost to ourselves the duty of making our voices heard and taking our share in the life of our two nations at their

Most Critical Juncture.[2]

For let us consider what exactly our position is.

Born in South Africa, our eyes first opened on these African hills and plains; around us, of other parentage, but born with us in the land, our birth-fellows,

1. Published in 1899.
2. Typographical emphasis found in the original text.

were men of another white race, and we grew up side by side with them. Is it strange that, like all men living who have the hearts of men, we learnt to love this land in which we first saw light? * * * Is it strange that when, after long years of absence, years it may be of success and the joy which springs from human fellowship and youth, our ship has cast its anchor in sight of Table Bay, and the great front of Table Mountain[3] has reared up before us, a cry of passionate joy has welled up within us; and when we saw the black men with their shining skins unloading in the docks, and the rugged faces of South Africans browned with our African sun, we put our foot on the dear old earth again, and our hearts have cried: "We are South Africans! We have come back again to our land and to our people"? * * * Side by side with us in South Africa are other South Africans whose position is not and cannot be exactly what ours is. Shading away from us by imperceptible degrees, stand on one side of us those English South Africans who, racially English, yet know nothing or little personally of her; the grandparents, and not the parents of such men, have left England; they are proud of being Englishmen; proud of England's great record and great names, as a man is proud of his grandmother's family; they are before all things essentially South African. He desires to see England increase and progress, and to remain in harmony and union with her while she does not interfere with internal affairs of South Africa, but he does not and cannot feel to her as those of us do whose love is personal and whose intellectual sympathies center largely in England.

Yet further from us on the same side stand our oldest white fellow South Africans; who were, many, not of English blood originally, though among that body of early white settlers, men who preceded us in South Africa by three centuries, were a few with English names, and though by intermarriage Dutch and English South Africans are daily and hourly blending, the bulk of these folk were Dutchmen from Holland and Friesland, with a few Swedes, Germans, and Danes, and later was intermingled with them a strong strain of Huguenot[4] blood from France. These men were mainly of that folk which, in the sixteenth century, held Philip and the Spanish Empire at bay,[5] and struck the first death-blow into the heart of that mighty Imperial system whose death-gasp we have witnessed to-day. A brave, free, fearless folk with the

Blood of the Old Sea Kings[6]

in their veins; a branch of that old Teutonic race which came with the Angles and Saxons into England and subdued the Britons, and who in the persons of the Franks entered Gaul,[7] and spread its blood across Europe. They are a

---

3. Cape Town is situated on the harbor of Table Bay, on the western coast of South Africa and at the foot of a flattop mountain called Table Mountain.
4. In the 16th and 17th centuries, French Protestants. Many Huguenots were driven out of France by religious persecution. Friesland is a region of northern Europe settled by Germanic peoples. Part of the original area is now a province of the northern Netherlands.
5. In 1588, Philip II of Spain sent a fleet of large ships (the Armada) to invade England. It was destroyed in a memorable sea battle by a fleet of smaller but more maneuverable English ships.
6. I.e., Vikings, Norse sailors, and explorers.
7. Ancient name for the part of western Europe that is now France and Belgium. The Franks were Germanic tribes who invaded Gaul in the 5th century C.E., when it was part of the Roman Empire.

people most nearly akin to the English of all European folk; in language, form, and feature resembling them, and in a certain dogged persistence, and an inalienable, indestructible air of personal freedom.

* * *

We South Africans, Dutch and English alike, are a curious folk, strong, brave, with a terrible intensity and perseverance, but we are not a sharp people well versed in the movements of the speculative world. In a few years the entire wealth of South Africa, its mines of gold and diamonds, its coalfields, and even its most intractable lands from the lovely Hex River Valley to Magaliesberg, had largely passed into the hands of a very small knot of speculators.[8] In hardly any instances are they South Africans. That they were not South Africans born would in itself matter less than nothing, had they thrown in their lot with us, if in sympathies, hopes, and fears they were one with us. They are not. It is not merely that the wealth which should have made us one of the richest peoples in the world has left us one of the poorest, and is exported to other countries, that it builds palaces in Park Lane, buys yachts in the Mediterranean, fills the bags of the croupiers at Monte Carlo,[9] decks foreign women with jewels, while our citizens toil in poverty; this is a small matter. But those men are not of us! That South Africa we love whose great future is dearer to us than our own interests, in the thought of whose great and noble destiny lies the source of our patriotism and highest inspiration, for whose good in a far-distant future we, Dutch and English alike, would sacrifice all in the present—this future is no more to them than the future of the Galapago Islands.[1] We are a hunting ground to them, a field for extracting wealth, for

Building up Fame and Fortune;

nothing more. This matter does not touch the Transvaal alone; from the lovely Hex River Valley, east, west, north, and south, our lands are being taken from us, and passing into the hands of men who not only care nothing for South Africa, but apply the vast wealth they have drawn from South Africa soil in an attempt to corrupt our public life, and put their own nominees into our parliaments, to grasp the reins of power, that their wealth may yet more increase. Is it strange that from the hearts of South Africans, English and Dutch alike, there is arising an exceedingly great and bitter cry, "We have sold our birthright for a mess of pottage![2] The lands, the mineral wealth which should have been ours to build up the great Africa of the future, has gone into strange hands! And they

---

8. Chief among them Schreiner's archenemy, the diamond and gold magnate Cecil Rhodes and his British South Africa Company. The Hex River Valley is a picturesque grape-growing region. The Magaliesberg is an ancient mountain range with rare geological formations, fauna, and flora.
9. A resort in Monaco on the French Riviera, known for its casino. Park Lane is a fashionable shopping district in central London.

1. Volcanic islands in the Pacific Ocean, west of Ecuador, that are home to a variety of rare and endangered species.
2. In Genesis 25.29–34 Esau comes in hungry from the fields, and his younger twin brother, Jacob, offers him vegetable stew (pottage) in exchange for his birthright. Esau accepts but regrets it later (Genesis 27.36).

use the gold they gain out of us to enslave us; they strike at our hearts with a sword gilded with South African gold! While the gold and stones remained undiscovered in the bosom of our earth, it was saved up for us and for our grand-children to build up the great future; it is going from us never to return; and when they have rifled our earth and picked the African bones bare, as the vultures clear the carcase of their prey, they will leave us with a broken skeleton!"

* * *

RUDYARD KIPLING

Born to English parents in Bombay (now Mumbai), Rudyard Kipling (1865–1936) won the Nobel Prize for literature in 1907. He is most famous for his popular stories for children set in India, *The Jungle Book* and the *Just So Stories*, and his poetry about empire, including a series of poems that take the common soldier's perspective, adopting the dialect of the London working class. His most famous poem, however, is a sober work that casts imperialism as a painful duty to the world's less advanced peoples. *The White Man's Burden* was first published in 1899, as Spain and the United States went to war over the Philippines. Kipling justi-fied the expanding U.S. empire, con-tending that white people have a responsibility to govern "new-caught, sullen peoples" because they are too backward to govern themselves. Empire, here, does not profit the conqueror, but answers to a higher and more serious purpose—the development of people who will resist and resent imperial con-quest but, the poet urges, will benefit from conquest in the long run. Some readers have claimed that Kipling is being satirical in this poem, but his other writings, taken together, suggest that he is being quite serious.

The White Man's Burden[1]

Take up the White Man's burden—
   Send forth the best ye breed—
Go bind your sons to exile
   To serve your captives' need;
To wait in heavy harness,   5
   On fluttered folk and wild—
Your new-caught, sullen peoples,
   Half-devil and half-child.

1. Written during the Spanish-American War, as the United States took control of the Philippines.

Take up the White Man's burden—
    In patience to abide,   10
To veil the threat of terror
    And check the show of pride;
By open speech and simple,
    An hundred times made plain,
To seek another's profit,   15
    And work another's gain.

Take up the White Man's burden—
    The savage wars of peace—
Fill full the mouth of Famine
    And bid the sickness cease.   20
And when your goal is nearest
    The end for others sought,
Watch Sloth and heathen Folly
    Bring all your hope to naught.

Take up the White Man's burden—   25
    No tawdry rule of kings,
But toil of serf and sweeper—
    The tale of common things.
The ports ye shall not enter,
    The roads ye shall not tread,   30
Go make them with your living,
    And mark them with your dead.

Take up the White Man's burden—
    And reap his old reward:
The blame of those ye better,   35
    The hate of those ye guard—
The cry of hosts ye humour
    (Ah, slowly!) toward the light:—
"Why brought ye us from bondage,
    Our loved Egyptian night?"[2]   40

Take up the White Man's burden—
    Ye dare not stoop to less—
Nor call too loud on Freedom
    To cloak your weariness;
By all ye cry or whisper,   45
    By all ye leave or do,
The silent, sullen peoples
    Shall weigh your Gods and you.

Take up the White Man's burden—
    Have done with childish days—   50

2. In Exodus 16:2–3, the hungry Israelites complain that Moses and Aaron have taken them from the comforts of Egypt.

The lightly proffered laurel,[3]
　The easy, ungrudged praise.
Comes now, to search your manhood
　Through all the thankless years,
Cold, edged with dear-bought wisdom,　　　　55
　The judgment of your peers!

3. Ancient Greek and Roman symbol of victory.

MARK TWAIN (SAMUEL CLEMENS)

Best known around the world for *The Adventures of Tom Sawyer* (1876) and *The Adventures of Huckleberry Finn* (1885), the Missouri-born humorist Mark Twain (1835–1910) was also a fierce opponent of imperialism. When the United States went to war with Spain over the Philippines, Twain at first cheered his own nation on, believing that U.S. power would bring freedom to Filipinos: "We can make them as free as ourselves, give them a government and country of their own, put a miniature of the American Constitution afloat in the Pacific, start a brand new republic to take its place among the free nations of the world." But Twain's views changed when he realized that the U.S. government was subjugating, rather than liberating, Filipinos. He began to work for the American Anti-Imperialist League and wrote scathing critiques of other empires as well. He condemned Cecil Rhodes, the British imperialist in South Africa, in *Following the Equator* (1898) and a few years later turned his attention to Leopold II of Belgium, whose atrocities in the Congo Free State were being reported here and there but not prompting the kind of revulsion Twain thought they should. The United States and Britain recognized Leopold's regime and looked the other way, for the most part, when they heard of his willingness to torture and mutilate Congolese workers. Twain's *King Leopold's Soliloquy* (1905), excerpted here, is an inventive kind of satire. It adopts Leopold's persona and imagines him attempting to justify himself in response to reports of his cruelties. This technique allows Twain to quote at length from horrifying eyewitness accounts of Leopold's regime while also revealing the king as a mad and ruthless monster of a ruler.

From King Leopold's Soliloquy[1]

[*Contemplating, with an unfriendly eye, a stately pile of pamphlets*] Blister the meddlesome missionaries! They write tons of these things. They seem to be always around, always spying, always eye-witnessing the happenings; and everything they see they commit to paper. They are always prowling from place to place; the natives consider them their only friends; they go to them with their sorrows; they show them their scars and their wounds, inflicted by my soldier police; they hold up the stumps of their arms and lament because their hands have been chopped off, as punishment for not bringing in enough rubber, and as proof to be laid before my officers that the required punishment was well and truly carried out. One of these missionaries saw eighty-one of these hands drying over a fire for transmission to my officials—and of course he must go and set it down and print it. They travel and travel, they spy and spy! And nothing is too trivial for them to print. [*Takes up a pamphlet. Reads a passage from Report of a "Journey made in July, August and September, 1903, by Rev. A. E. Scrivener, a British missionary"*]

"... Soon we began talking, and without any encouragement on my part the natives began the tales I had become so accustomed to. They were living in peace and quietness when the white men came in from the lake with all sorts of requests to do this and that, and they thought it meant slavery. So they attempted to keep the white men out of their country but without avail. The rifles were too much for them. So they submitted and made up their minds to do the best they could under the altered circumstances. First came the command to build houses for the soldiers, and this was done without a murmur. Then they had to feed the soldiers and all the men and women—hangers on—who accompanied them. Then they were told to bring in rubber. This was quite a new thing for them to do. There was rubber in the forest several days away from their home, but that it was worth anything was news to them. A small reward was offered and a rush was made for the rubber. 'What strange white men, to give us cloth and beads for the sap of a wild vine.' They rejoiced in what they thought their good fortune. But soon the reward was reduced until at last they were told to bring in the rubber for nothing. To this they tried to demur; but to their great surprise several were shot by the soldiers, and the rest were told, with many curses and blows, to go at once or more would be killed. Terrified, they began to prepare their food for the fortnight's absence from the village which the collection of rubber entailed. The soldiers discovered them sitting about. 'What, not gone yet?' Bang! bang! bang! and down fell one and another, dead, in the midst of wives and companions. There is a terrible wail and an attempt made to prepare the dead for burial, but this is not allowed. All must go at once to the forest. Without food? Yes, without food. And off the poor wretches had to go without even their tinder boxes to make fires. Many died in the forests of hunger and exposure, and still more from the rifles of the ferocious soldiers in charge of the post. In spite of all their efforts

1. This selection is spoken in the voice of King Leopold II of Belgium (1835–1909), who was one of the most vicious of all imperial rulers, conquering the people of Congo in the 1880s and remaining their ruler until he was forced to cede in 1908. In 1905, at the time this piece was written, reports by missionaries and other witnesses had begun to stir up international outcry over Leopold's actions.

the amount fell off and more and more were killed. I was shown around the place, and the sites of former big chiefs' settlements were pointed out. A careful estimate made the population of, say, seven years ago, to be 2,000 people in and about the post, within a radius of, say, a quarter of a mile. All told, they would not muster 200 now, and there is so much sadness and gloom about them that they are fast decreasing."

"We stayed there all day on Monday and had many talks with the people. On the Sunday some of the boys had told me of some bones which they had seen, so on the Monday I asked to be shown these bones. Lying about on the grass, within a few yards of the house I was occupying, were numbers of human skulls, bones, in some cases complete skeletons. I counted thirty-six skulls, and saw many sets of bones from which the skulls were missing. I called one of the men and asked the meaning of it. 'When the rubber palaver began,' said he, 'the soldiers shot so many we grew tired of burying, and very often we were not allowed to bury; and so just dragged the bodies out into the grass and left them. There are hundreds all around if you would like to see them.' But I had seen more than enough, and was sickened by the stories that came from men and women alike of the awful time they had passed through. The Bulgarian atrocities[2] might be considered as mildness itself when compared with what was done here. How the people submitted I don't know, and even now I wonder as I think of their patience. That some of them managed to run away is some cause for thankfulness. I stayed there two days and the one thing that impressed itself upon me was the collection of rubber. I saw long files of men come in, as at Bongo, with their little baskets under their arms; saw them paid their milk tin full of salt, and the two yards of calico flung to the headmen; saw their trembling timidity, and in fact a great deal that all went to prove the state of terrorism that exists and the virtual slavery in which the people are held."

That is their way; they spy and spy, and run into print with every foolish trifle. And that British consul, Mr. Casement, is just like them. He gets hold of a *diary which had been kept by one of my government officers*, and, although it is a private diary and intended for no eye but its owner's, Mr. Casement is so lacking in delicacy and refinement as to print passages from it. [*Reads a passage from the diary*]

"Each time the corporal goes out to get rubber, cartridges are given him. He must bring back all not used, and for every one used he must bring back a right hand. M. P. told me that sometimes they shot a cartridge at an animal in hunting; they then cut off a hand from a living man. As to the extent to which this is carried on, he informed me that in six months the State on the Mambogo River had used 6,000 cartridges, which means that 6,000 people are killed or mutilated. It means more than 6,000, for the people have told me repeatedly that the soldiers kill the children with the butt of their guns."

When the subtle consul thinks silence will be more effective than words, he employs it. Here he leaves it to be recognized that a thousand killings and mutilations a month is a large output for so small a region as the Mambogo River concession, silently indicating the dimensions of it by accompanying his report with a map of the prodigious Congo State, in which there is not room

2. In the 1870s the Ottoman Empire violently suppressed an uprising of Christians in Bulgaria who were resisting Ottoman rule.

for so small an object as that river. That silence is intended to say, "If it is a thousand a month in this little corner, imagine the output of the whole vast State!" A gentleman would not descend to these furtivenesses.

Now as to the mutilations. You can't head off a Congo critic and make him stay headed-off; he dodges, and straightway comes back at you from another direction. They are full of slippery arts. When the mutilations (severing hands, unsexing men, etc.) began to stir Europe, we hit upon the idea of excusing them with a retort which we judged would knock them dizzy on that subject for good and all, and leave them nothing more to say; to wit, we boldly laid the custom on the natives, and said we did not invent it, but only followed it. Did it knock them dizzy? did it shut their mouths? Not for an hour. They dodged, and came straight back at us with the remark that "if a Christian king can perceive a saving moral difference between inventing bloody barbarities, and *imitating them from savages,* for charity's sake let him get what comfort he can out of his confession!"

It is most amazing, the way that that consul acts—that spy, that busy-body. *[Takes up pamphlet "Treatment of Women and Children in the Congo State; what Mr. Casement Saw in 1903"] Hardly two years ago! Intruding* that date upon the public was a piece of cold malice. It was intended to weaken the force of my press syndicate's assurances to the public that my severities in the Congo *ceased,* and ceased utterly, *years and years ago.* This man is fond of trifles— revels in them, gloats over them, pets them, fondles them, sets them all down. One doesn't need to drowse through his monotonous report to see that; the mere subheadings of its chapters prove it. *[Reads]*

> "Two hundred and forty persons, *men, women and children,* compelled to supply government with *one ton* of carefully prepared foodstuffs *per week,* receiving in remuneration, all told, the princely sum of 15s. 10d!"[3]

Very well, it was liberal. It was not much short of a penny a week for each nigger. It suits this consul to belittle it, yet he knows very well that I could have had both the food and the labor for nothing. I can prove it by a thousand instances. *[Reads]*

> "Expedition against a village behindhand in its (compulsory) supplies; result, slaughter of sixteen persons; among them three women and a boy of five years. Ten carried off, to be prisoners till ransomed; among them a child, who died during the march."

But he is careful not to explain that we are *obliged* to resort to ransom to collect debts, where the people have nothing to pay with. Families that escape to the woods sell some of their members into slavery and thus provide the ransom. He knows that I would stop this if I could find a less objectionable way to collect their debts. . . . Mm—here is some more of the consul's delicacy! He reports a conversation he had with some natives:

> Q. "How do you know it was the *white* men themselves who ordered these cruel things to be done to you? These things must have been done without the white man's knowledge by the black soldiers."

3. Fifteen shillings and ten pence in British money, worth between seventy-five and a hundred dollars today.

A. "The white men told their soldiers: 'You only kill *women*; you cannot kill men. You must prove that you kill men.' So then the soldiers when they killed us" (here he stopped and hesitated and then pointing to . . . he said:) "then they . . . and took them to the white men, who said: 'It is true, you have killed *men*.'"

Q. "You say this is true? Were many of you so treated after being shot?"

All [*shouting out*]: "Nkote! Nkoto!" ("Very many! Very many!")

There was no doubt that these people were not inventing. Their vehemence, their flashing eyes, their excitement, were not simulated."

Of course the critic had to divulge that; he has no self-respect. All his kind reproach me, although they know quite well that I took no pleasure in punishing the men in that particular way, but only did it as a warning to other delinquents. Ordinary punishments are no good with ignorant savages; they make no impression. [*Reads more sub-heads*]

"Devastated region; population reduced from 40,000 to 8,000."

He does not take the trouble to say how it happened. He is fertile in concealments. He hopes his readers and his Congo reformers, of the Lord-Aberdeen-Norbury-John-Morley-Sir Gilbert-Parker stripe,[4] will think they were all killed. They were not. The great majority of them escaped. They fled to the bush with their families because of the rubber raids, and it was there they died of hunger. Could we help that?

One of my sorrowing critics observes: "Other Christian rulers tax their people, but furnish schools, courts of law, roads, light, water and protection to life and limb in return; King Leopold taxes his stolen nation, but provides *nothing in return but hunger, terror, grief, shame, captivity, mutilation and massacre*." That is their style! I furnish "nothing"! I send the gospel to the survivors; these censure-mongers know it, but they would rather have their tongues cut out than mention it. I have several times required my raiders to give the dying an opportunity to kiss the sacred emblem; and if they obeyed me I have without doubt been the humble means of saving many souls. None of my traducers have had the fairness to mention this; but let it pass; there is One who has not overlooked it, and that is my solace, that is my consolation.

[*Puts down the Report, takes up a pamphlet, glances along the middle of it*]

This is where the "death-trap" comes in. Meddlesome missionary spying around—Rev. W. H. Sheppard. Talks with a black raider of mine after a raid; cozens him into giving away some particulars. The raider remarks:

"I demanded 30 slaves from this side of the stream and 30 from the other side; 2 points of ivory, 2,500 balls of rubber, 13 goats, 10 fowls and 6 dogs, some corn chumy, etc.

'How did the fight come up?' I asked.

'I sent for all their chiefs, sub-chiefs, men and women, to come on a certain day, saying that I was going to finish all the palaver. When they entered these small gates (the walls being made of fences brought from other villages, the high native ones) I demanded all my pay or I would kill them; so they refused to pay me, and I ordered the fence to be closed so they couldn't run away; then we killed them here inside the fence. The panels of the fence fell down and some escaped.'

'How many did you kill?' I asked.

---

4. British leaders who opposed Leopold's atrocities.

'We killed plenty, will you see some of them?'

That was just what I wanted.

He said: 'I think we have killed between eighty and ninety, and those in the other villages I don't know, I did not go out but sent my people.'

He and I walked out on the plain just near the camp. There were three dead bodies with the flesh carved off from the waist down.

'Why are they carved so, only leaving the bones?' I asked.

'My people ate them,' he answered promptly. He then explained, 'The men who have young children do not eat people, but all the rest ate them.' On the left was a big man, shot in the back and without a head. (All these corpses were nude.)

'Where is the man's head?' I asked.

'Oh, they made a bowl of the forehead to rub up tobacco and diamba in.'

We continued to walk and examine until late in the afternoon, and counted forty-one bodies. The rest had been eaten up by the people.

On returning to the camp, we crossed a young woman, shot in the back of the head, one hand was cut away. I asked why, and Mulunba N'Cusa explained that they always cut off the right hand to give to the State on their return.

'Can you not show me some of the hands?' I asked.

So he conducted us to a framework of sticks, under which was burning a slow fire, and there they were, the right hands—I counted them, eighty-one in all.

There were not less than sixty women (Bena Pianga)[5] prisoners. I saw them.

We all say that we have as fully as possible investigated the whole outrage, and find it was a plan previously made to get all the stuff possible and to catch and kill the poor people in the 'death-trap.'"

Another detail, as we see!—cannibalism. They report cases of it with a most offensive frequency. My traducers do not forget to remark that, inasmuch as I am absolute and with a word can prevent in the Congo anything I choose to prevent, then whatsoever is done there by my permission is my act, my *personal* act; that *I* do it; that the hand of my agent is as truly *my* hand as if it were attached to my own arm; and so they picture me in my robes of state, with my crown on my head, munching human flesh, saying grace, mumbling thanks to Him from whom all good things come. Dear, dear, when the soft-hearts get hold of a thing like that missionary's contribution they quite lose their tranquility over it They speak out profanely and reproach Heaven for allowing such a fiend to live. Meaning me. They think it irregular. They go shuddering around, brooding over the reduction of that Congo population from 25,000,000 to 15,000,000 in the twenty years of my administration; then they burst out and call me "the King with Ten Million Murders on his Soul." They call me a "record." The most of them do not stop with charging merely the 10,000,000 against me. No, they reflect that but for me the population, by natural increase, would now be 30,000,000, so they charge another 5,000,000 against me and make my total death-harvest 15,000,000. They remark that the man who killed the goose that laid the golden egg was responsible for the eggs she would subsequently have laid if she had been let alone. Oh, yes, they call me a "record." They remark that twice in a generation, in India, the Great Famine destroys 2,000,000 out of a population of 320,000,000, and the whole world holds up its hands in pity and horror; then they fall to wondering where the world would find room for its emotions if I had a chance to trade places with the Great Famine for twenty years! The idea fires their fancy, and they go on and imagine

5. A Congolese group.

the Famine coming in state at the end of the twenty years and prostrating itself before me, saying: "Teach me, Lord, I perceive that I am but an apprentice." And next they imagine Death coming, with his scythe and hour-glass, and begging me to marry his daughter and reorganize his plant and run the business. For the whole world, you see! By this time their diseased minds are under full steam, and they get down their books and expand their labors, with me for text. They hunt through all biography for my match, working Attila, Torquemada, Ghengis Khan, Ivan the Terrible,[6] and the rest of that crowd for all they are worth, and evilly exulting when they cannot find it. Then they examine the historical earthquakes and cyclones and blizzards and cataclysms and volcanic eruptions: verdict, none of them "in it" with me. At last they do really hit it (as they think), and they close their labors with conceding—reluctantly—that I have *one* match in history, but only one—the *Flood*. This is intemperate.

But they are always that, when they think of me. They can no more keep quiet when my name is mentioned than can a glass of water control its feelings with a seidlitz powder[7] in its bowels. The bizarre things they can imagine, with me for an inspiration! One Englishman offers to give me the odds of three to one and bet me anything I like, up to 20,000 guineas,[8] that for 2,000,000 years I am going to be the most conspicuous foreigner in hell. The man is so beside himself with anger that he does not perceive that the idea is foolish. Foolish and unbusiness-like: you see, there could be no winner; both of us would be losers, on account of the loss of interest on the stakes; at four or five per cent. compounded, this would amount to—I do not know how much, exactly, but, by the time the term was up and the bet payable, a person could buy hell itself with the accumulation.

Another madman wants to construct a memorial for the perpetuation of my name, out of my 15,000,000 skulls and skeletons, and is full of vindictive enthusiasm over his strange project. He has it all ciphered out and drawn to scale. Out of the skulls he will build a combined monument and mausoleum to me which shall exactly duplicate the Great Pyramid of Cheops,[9] whose base covers thirteen acres, and whose apex is 451 feet above ground. He desires to stuff me and stand me up in the sky on that apex, robed and crowned, with my "pirate flag" in one hand and a butcher-knife and pendant handcuffs in the other. He will build the pyramid in the centre of a depopulated tract, a brooding solitude covered with weeds and the mouldering ruins of burned villages, where the spirits of the starved and murdered dead will voice their laments forever in the whispers of the wandering winds. Radiating from the pyramid, like the spokes of a wheel, there are to be forty grand avenues of approach, each thirty-five miles long, and each fenced on both sides by skulless skeletons standing a yard and a half apart and festooned together in line by short chains stretching from wrist to wrist and attached to tried and true old handcuffs stamped with my private trade-mark, a crucifix and butcher-knife crossed, with motto, "By this sign we prosper;" each osseous fence to consist of 200,000 skeletons on a side, which is 400,000 to each avenue. It is remarked with satisfaction that it aggregates three or four thousand

6. All rulers infamous for their cruelty. Attila, ruler of the Huns in the fifth century (?–453). Tomás de Torquemada (1420–1498), fanatical priest who led the Spanish Inquisition. Tsar Ivan IV of Russia (1530–1584), called "the Terrible."
7. A common medication used to aid digestion.

8. A large sum, worth several million U.S. dollars today.
9. This ancient Egyptian pyramid is almost five hundred feet high, and considered one of the Seven Wonders of the World. It was built about 2500 B.C.E.

miles (single-ranked) of skeletons,—15,000,000 all told—and would stretch across America from New York to San Francisco. It is remarked further, in the hopeful tone of a railroad company forecasting showy extensions of its mileage, that my output is 500,000 corpses a year when my plant is running full time, and that therefore if I am spared ten years longer there will be fresh skulls enough to add 175 feet to the pyramid, making it by a long way the loftiest architectural construction on the earth, and fresh skeletons enough to continue the transcontinental file (on piles) a thousand miles into the Pacific. The cost of gathering the materials from my "widely scattered and innumerable private graveyards," and transporting them, and building the monument and the radiating grand avenues, is duly ciphered out, running into an aggregate of millions of guineas, and then— why then, (————— —————!! ————— —————!!) this idiot asks me to *furnish the money! [Sudden and effusive application of the crucifix]* He reminds me that my yearly income from the Congo is millions of guineas, and that *"only"* 5,000,000 would be required for his enterprise. Every day wild attempts are made upon my purse; they do not affect me, they cost me not a thought. But *this one*—this one troubles me, makes me nervous; for there is no telling what an unhinged creature like this may think of next. . . . *If he should think of Carnegie*[1]—but I must banish that thought out of my mind! it worries my days; it troubles my sleep. That way lies madness. *[After a pause]* There is no other way—I have got to buy Carnegie.

[*Harrassed and muttering, walks the floor a while, then takes to the Consul's chapter-headings again. Reads*]

"Government starved a woman's children to death and killed her sons."

"Butchery of women and children."

"The native has been converted into a being without ambition because without hope."

"Women chained by the neck by rubber sentries."

"Women refuse to bear children because, with a baby to carry, they cannot well run away and hide from the soldiers."

"Statement of a child. 'I, my mother, my grandmother and my sister, we ran away into the bush. A great number of our people were killed by the soldiers. . . . After that they saw a little bit of my mother's head, and the soldiers ran quickly to where we were and caught my grandmother, my mother, my sister and another little one younger than us. Each wanted my mother for a wife, and argued about it, so they finally decided to kill her. They shot her through the stomach with a gun and she fell, and when I saw that I cried very much, because they killed my grandmother and mother and I was left alone. I saw it all done!'"

It has a sort of pitiful sound, although they are only blacks. It carries me back and back into the past, to when my children were little, and would fly—to the bush, so to speak—when they saw me coming. . . . [*Resumes the reading of chapter-headings of the Consul's report*]

"They put a knife through a child's stomach."

"They cut off the hands and brought them to C. D. (white officer) and spread them out in a row for him to see. They left them lying there, because the white man had seen them, so they did not need to take them to P."

"Captured children left in the bush to die, by the soldiers."

1. Andrew Carnegie (1835–1919) was one of the richest men in the world. Scottish born, he made his fortune in the United States in steel.

"Friends came to ransom a captured girl; but sentry refused, saying the white man wanted her because she was young."

"Extract from a native girl's testimony. 'On our way the soldiers saw a little child, and when they went to kill it the child laughed, so the soldier took the butt of his gun and struck the child with it and then cut off its head. One day they killed my half-sister and cut off her head, hands and feet, because she had bangles on. Then they caught another sister, and sold her to the W. W. people, and now she is a slave there.'"

The little child laughed! [*A long pause. Musing*] That innocent creature. Somehow—I wish it had not laughed. [*Reads*]

"Mutilated children."

"Government encouragement of inter-tribal slave-traffic. The monstrous fines levied upon villages tardy in their supplies of foodstuffs compel the natives to sell their fellows—and children—to other tribes in order to meet the fine."

"A father and mother forced to sell their little boy."

"Widow forced to sell her little girl."

[*Irritated*] Hang the monotonous grumbler, what would he have me do! Let a widow off merely because she is a widow? He knows quite well that there is nothing much left, now, *but* widows. I have nothing against widows, as a class, but business is business, and I've got to live, haven't I, even if it does cause inconvenience to somebody here and there? [*Reads*]

"Men intimidated by the torture of their wives and daughters. (To make the men furnish rubber and supplies and so get their captured women released from chains and detention.) The sentry explained to me that he caught the women and brought them in (chained together neck to neck) by direction of his employer."

"An agent explained that he was forced to catch women in preference to men, as then the men brought in supplies quicker; but he did not explain how the children deprived of their parents obtained their own food supplies."

"A file of 15 (captured) women."

"Allowing women and children to die of starvation in prison."

[*Musing*] Death from *hunger*. A lingering, long misery that must be. Days and days, and still days and days, the forces of the body failing, dribbling away, little by little—yes, it must be the hardest death of all. And to see food carried by, every day, and you can have none of it! Of course the little children cry for it, and that wrings the mother's heart. . . . [*A sigh*] Ah, well, it cannot be helped; circumstances make this discipline necessary. * * *

[*Studies some photographs of mutilated negroes—throws them down. Sighs*] The kodak[2] has been a sore calamity to us. The most powerful enemy that has confronted us, indeed. In the early years we had no trouble in getting the press to "expose" the tales of the mutilations as slanders, lies, inventions of busy-body American missionaries and exasperated foreigners who had found the "open door" of the Berlin-Congo charter[3] closed against them when they innocently

---

2. The first camera that was easy to use and carry, it was extremely popular from its introduction in 1888.
3. In 1884–85, European powers met to decide on a policy to govern imperial activity in Africa, agreeing that any European nation could take control of African land. "Open Door": a policy allowing free trade and travel along the Congo and Niger Rivers.

went out there to trade; and by the press's help we got the Christian nations everywhere to turn an irritated and unbelieving ear to those tales and say hard things about the tellers of them. Yes, all things went harmoniously and pleasantly in those good days, and I was looked up to as the benefactor of a downtrodden and friendless people. Then all of a sudden came the crash! That is to say, the incorruptible *kodak*—and all the harmony went to hell! The only witness I have encountered in my long experience that I couldn't bribe. Every Yankee missionary and every interrupted trader sent home and got one; and now—oh, well, the pictures get sneaked around everywhere, in spite of all we can do to ferret them out and suppress them. Ten thousand pulpits and ten thousand presses are saying the good word for me all the time and placidly and convincingly denying the mutilations. Then that trivial little kodak, that a child can carry in its pocket, gets up, uttering never a word, and knocks them dumb!

. . . What is this fragment? [*Reads*]

"But enough of trying to tally off his crimes! His list is interminable, we should never get to the end of it. His awful shadow lies across his Congo Free State, and under it an unoffending nation of 15,000,000 is withering away and swiftly succumbing to their miseries. It is a land of graves; it is *The* Land of Graves; it is the Congo Free Graveyard. It is a majestic thought: that is, this ghastliest episode in all human history is the work of *one man alone*; one solitary man; just a single individual—Leopold, King of the Belgians. He is personally and solely responsible for all the myriad crimes that have blackened the history of the Congo State. He is *sole* master there; he is absolute. He could have prevented the crimes by his mere command; he could stop them today with a word. He withholds the word. For his pocket's sake.

It seems strange to see a king destroying a nation and laying waste a country for mere sordid money's sake, and solely and only for that. Lust of conquest is royal; kings have always exercised that stately vice; we are used to it, by old habit we condone it, perceiving a certain dignity in it; but *lust of money—lust of shillings—lust of nickels—lust of dirty coin*, not for the nation's enrichment but for *the king's alone*—this is new. It distinctly revolts us, we cannot seem to reconcile ourselves to it, we resent it, we despise it, we say it is shabby, unkingly, out of character. Being democrats we ought to jeer and jest, we ought to rejoice to see the purple dragged in the dirt, but—well, account for it as we may, we don't. We see this awful king, this pitiless and blood-drenched king, this money-crazy king towering toward the sky in a world-solitude of sordid crime, unfellowed and apart from the human race, sole butcher for personal gain findable in all his caste, ancient or modern, pagan or Christian, proper and legitimate target for the scorn of the lowest and the highest, and the execrations of all who hold in cold esteem the oppressor and the coward; and—well, it is a mystery, but *we do not wish to look*; for he is a king, and it hurts us, it troubles us, by ancient and inherited instinct it shames us to see a king degraded to this aspect, and we shrink from hearing the particulars of how it happened. *We shudder* and *turn away* when we come upon them in print."

Why, certainly—*that* is my protection. And you will continue to do it. I know the human race.

ORATURE

The written word reached only a tiny sliver of the world's population before the twentieth century. The United Nations estimates that around 10 percent of the world was literate in 1850. By the 1920s the number was up to 28 percent. But low levels of literacy worldwide did not mean that people lacked stories and poetry, philosophy and religious wisdom. For most of human history, people used the spoken word to pass on laws, skills, common values, founding legends, and thrilling tales. In fact, world literature as we know it today would not exist without the nourishment of oral traditions. Homer's great ancient Greek epics, the *Iliad* and the *Odyssey*, began as oral tales, becoming "literature" only after generations had passed them down from memory. From Walt Disney's *Snow White* to **Toni Morrison**'s Nobel Prize–winning fiction, from experimental poetry to African jazz, long and complex histories of oral performance continue to circulate as a living part of world culture, whether we recognize them or not.

The Ugandan linguist Pio Zirimu coined the term *orature* to convey the serious artistic value of oral expression. In most predominantly oral cultures, performance is a highly refined skill. Those who recite stories and poems aloud adopt individual performance styles and alter details for dramatic effect. A talented few come to be renowned as great artists. Unlike the fixed written word, an oral tradition is not a single,

Zouave storyteller (North Africa, 1857). Photograph by Gustave le Gray.

knowable object: live performances involve vocal modulations and cadences, dramatic silences and bodily movements that change with each telling; and performers often introduce creative transformations, adapting old stories to suit new circumstances. Live audiences respond to the teller in ways that can shape the telling, and they sometimes participate in the performance.

The relationship between oral literature and the written word took on a new importance in the nineteenth century. When it comes to reading and writing, this was a time of great unevenness and rapid change. In traditional agrarian societies such as Russia, where most people worked the land, only 5 percent of the population could read. But in the United States and Protestant Europe, where churches formed schools to teach people how to read the Bible, and industrialization and urbanization demanded new skills and new mobility, literacy rates reached almost universal levels. Around mid-century, about 60 percent of French and British people could read, 30 percent of Japanese people, and 5 percent across the Ottoman Empire. In some regions literacy rates varied by gender: in Brazil 12 percent of women were literate compared to 20 percent of men, and India's female literacy was at 8 percent across the country, while in the Kerala region almost a third of adult women could read. In the United States, the most important differentiating factor was race: while the United States boasted an 80 percent overall literacy rate in 1870, four-fifths of African Americans were illiterate because under slavery they had been denied education.

Literacy rates rose dramatically in many places over the course of the century: in Argentina, adult literacy stood at less than one-third in 1869, but thanks to education reforms launched by **Domingo Faustino Sarmiento**, it rose to two-thirds by 1914. Toward the end of the nineteenth century, British colonial administrators in South Africa actually worried that too many black people were literate and so were beginning to rebel against the expectation that they would perform only the most menial kinds of work. Literacy, as the American slave **Frederick Douglass** had discovered, could be a powerful tool of resistance and political freedom. But so too could orature, which often eluded official scrutiny and could bring a sense of cohesion and solidarity to social groups under threat.

Interest in oral traditions rose sharply in the nineteenth century, as many nations made the shift to widespread literacy. When people learn how to read, they usually stop developing the skills and methods of memorization, and this means that oral traditions fade as literacy rates rise. Thanks to the huge upsurge in literacy, the nineteenth century saw the end of many vibrant oral traditions around the world. This threat of disappearing cultural riches prompted some, like **Jacob and Wilhelm Grimm**, to try to preserve spoken stories in print before they vanished. The Grimms' fairy tales, first published in 1812, included "Snow White" and "Hansel and Gretel," stories that had been passed down orally for generations. For the Grimms, fairy tales were important because they were thought to reveal a deep, longstanding cultural life that bound the German people together. And the Grimms were not the only ones to turn to folktales and fairy tales to build nationalist sentiment: around the world, traditional oral stories were often thought to be the authentic expressions of a unified people.

The nineteenth century was also a time when European powers were conquering peoples around the world, and some Europeans became fascinated by similarities between their own oral traditions and those they found thriving elsewhere. Did folktales provide a key to understanding a universal human nature? Did all cultures tell the same basic stories? The examples collected below suggest intriguing similarities between African stories and those told by slaves in the Americas and peasants in Europe: all of these groups return again and again to tales of oppressive labor. Many Europeans assumed that cultures in Africa and Asia represented "immature" stages in a single story of human development, and that one could see Europe as it had once been by studying Iroquois or Zulu culture in the present. In the 1870s, for example, a Dutch scholar by the name of Willem Bleek took advantage of the imprisonment of a number of nomadic Kung people by the British in southern Africa. These prisoners were the perfect subjects to teach him about oral traditions, he realized, since they could not wander off, as nomadic people were inclined to do. Acknowledging that the Kung were in danger of extinction because their traditional hunting and gathering lands had been seized by European settlers, Bleek said that he had made an urgent journey to collect their stories so that Europeans could come to know a disappearing race "that had made little, if any, advance since the far-distant days when members of it shot their flint-headed arrows at reindeer in France." Bleek assumed that oral stories from Africa needed to be transcribed as a way for Europeans to understand their own past—the prehistory of civilization—before they themselves eradicated that prehistory through colonization.

Although orature might have seemed fragile in the context of rapid industrialization and modernization, sometimes it survived, forceful and vigorous. The twelve million African slaves who crossed

the ocean between the seventeenth and the nineteenth centuries carried stories, styles, and cadences to the United States, Latin America, and the Caribbean, which pervaded their new home cultures. The roots of jazz and hip-hop rhythms, for example, can be traced to African musical traditions. Collected below are three stories of **Anansi** the spider-trickster, a character who originates with the Ashanti people in West Africa and then travels on the slave ships, appearing in lots of different retellings in the Americas.

As vibrant oral cultures continued to coexist with rising literacy in the nineteenth century, many people tried their hands at translating oral stories and poems into written form. Among these were colonial administrators, missionaries, curious travelers, and scholars of language, folklore, and anthropology, as well as representatives of cultures under threat. The British in West Africa, for example, wanted to study local lore so that they could control the Ashanti people, while the German Grimms feared that their own traditions were disappearing. Whether intending to oppress or to conserve, all of these writers had to make difficult choices in the translation from oral to written forms: should they try to express the particular style of one performer, or should they listen to multiple versions of the same story to try to distill the common features of a tradition? Should the written version convey the idiosyncratic features of spoken language—

conversational interjections, cadences, repetitions, and colloquialisms—or should it follow a tidier, more conventionally literary style? The selections here vary: the transcriber of "**A Donegal Fairy**," an Irish tale, tries to keep the texture of the particular oral performance intact, down to the details of local pronunciation and conversational interruptions, while **Julius Lester**, a contemporary American writer, retells slave stories from the past in his own fluent and dramatic style.

However they were preserved and transcribed, a vast range of oral traditions have survived into our time, nourishing the richness of modern world cultures, sometimes unseen or overlooked but nonetheless still vital. Many of the most prominent twentieth- and twenty-first-century writers around the world have drawn inspiration from orature. **William Butler Yeats**, the Irish poet, collected and published traditional tales from his own country and drew from them for his groundbreaking Modernist poetry, while the Nigerian novelist **Chinua Achebe** has made complex use of Igbo orature. American Indian writers, such as **Leslie Marmon Silko**, frequently ground their fiction in folktales passed down orally through the generations, while Indian-born **Salman Rushdie** deliberately stylizes traditional oral storytelling in his novels. Surprisingly, perhaps, even the most modern, technologically driven cultures have been built on oral foundations.

GERMAN FOLKTALE: THE THREE SPINNERS

The folktales and fairy tales collected by the brothers Grimm—Jacob (1785–1863) and Wilhelm (1786–1859)—have become some of the most famous stories in the world: "Little Red Riding Hood," "Rapunzel," "Hansel and Gretel," "Rumpelstiltskin," "Snow White," "Cinderella," and "Sleeping Beauty." The Grimm versions can be surprising or even shocking today. They include scenes of sexual and physical violence that seem like strange material for children. But in fact these stories were originally entertainment for a whole village.

The Grimms were the editors of these stories rather than their authors. They were serious German scholars who came of age just as Napoleon's French armies invaded and imposed new laws and customs, threatening to wipe out generations of traditional German lore. Eager to preserve a national heritage, the brothers set about collecting the stories told by peasants. Ironically, however, they did not hear actual peasants tell the tales. Instead, most of their sources were educated women who had absorbed traditional stories from household servants and nursemaids in their childhoods. The Grimms then heavily edited the stories. They were keen to preserve a rustic feel, sometimes inserting old proverbs for effect. But they also added new material that explored the psychological motives of the characters. In this way, they joined traditional folk elements with rounded characters who appealed to a growing middle-class audience. This combination would prove enormously popular, influencing many other collectors of folktales around the world and making these tales classics well beyond Germany within a generation.

"The Three Spinners" is not one of the most famous Grimm fairy tales, but it reveals the ways that traditional folktales could appeal to poor peasants. It is primarily about the burden of physical work, which is so oppressive that it deforms the very body of the worker. The story shows how the different social classes have strikingly different relationships to work, and it is interesting to speculate what its happy ending would have meant to those facing a life of hard and unrelenting labor.

The Three Spinners[1]

There was once a girl who was idle and would not spin, and her mother, say what she would, could not bring her to it. At last the mother lost her temper and beat her, at which the girl began to weep loudly. Now at this very moment the Queen drove by, and when she heard the weeping she stopped her carriage, went into the house, and asked the mother why she was beating her daughter so that the cries could be heard out in the road?

The woman was ashamed to tell how lazy her daughter was, and said,—

"I cannot get her to leave off spinning. She insists on spinning for ever and ever, and I am poor, and cannot get the flax for her." Then the Queen answered,—

---

1. Translated by Jack Zipes.

"There is nothing I like better to hear than spinning, and I am never happier than when the wheels are humming. Let me have your daughter with me in the palace; I have flax enough, and there she shall spin as much as she likes."

The mother was well pleased with this, and the Queen took the girl with her. When they had arrived at the palace, the Queen led the girl up into three rooms which were filled from the bottom to the top with the finest flax.

"Now spin me this flax," said she, "and when you have done it, you shall have my eldest son for a husband, even if you are poor. I care not for that; you are a hard-working girl, and that is enough."

The girl was scared out of her wits, for she could not have spun the flax, no, not if she had lived till she was three hundred years old, and had sat at it every day from morning till night. So when she was alone, she began to weep, and sat thus for three days without moving a finger. On the third day the Queen came, and wondered when she saw nothing had been spun yet; but the girl said she had not been able to begin because she felt so badly at leaving her mother's house. The Queen was sorry for her, but said when she was going away,—

"To-morrow you must begin to work."

When the girl was alone again, she did not know what to do, and in her distress went to the window. There she saw three women coming toward her; the first had a broad flat foot, the second had such a great under lip that it hung down over her chin, and the third had a broad thumb. They stood before the window, and looked up, and asked the girl what was the matter with her? She told her trouble, and they said they would help her, but added,—

"If you will invite us to the wedding, not be ashamed of us, and will call us your aunts; and if you will place us at your table, we will spin the flax for you, and that in a very short time."

"With all my heart," she replied; "do but come in and begin the work at once." Then she let in the three strange women, and cleared a place in the first room, where they sat down and began their spinning. One drew the thread and trod the wheel, the second wetted the thread, the third twisted it, and struck the table with her finger; and as often as she struck it, a skein of thread, that was spun in the finest manner possible, fell to the ground. The girl hid the three spinners from the Queen, and showed her, whenever she came, the great heap of spun thread, until the Queen could not praise her enough. When the first room was empty she went to the second, and at last to the third, and that too was quickly cleared. Then the three women took leave, and said to the girl,—

"Do not forget what you have promised us,—it will make your fortune."

When the maiden showed the Queen the empty rooms, and the great heap of yarn, she gave orders for the wedding. Her son was glad that he was to have such a clever and hard-working wife, and praised her well.

"I have three aunts," said the girl, "and as they have been very kind to me, I should not like to forget them in my good fortune; let me ask them to the wedding, and let them sit with us at table." The Queen and the bridegroom said,—

"Why not?" So when the feast began, the three women entered in strange dress, and the bride said,—

"Welcome, dear aunts."

"Ah," said the bridegroom, "how do you come by these odious friends?" He went to the one with the broad flat foot, and said,—

"How do you come by such a broad foot?"

"By treading," she answered, "by treading." Then the bridegroom went to the second and said,—

"How do you come by your falling lip?"

"By licking," she answered, "by licking." Then he asked the third,—

"How do you come by your broad thumb?"

"By twisting the thread," she answered, "by twisting the thread." On this the King's son took fright and said,—

"Neither now nor ever shall my beautiful bride touch a spinning-wheel." And thus she got rid of the hateful flax-spinning.

ENGLISH FOLKTALE: TOM TIT TOT

An Australian-born Jew who settled in the United States, Joseph Jacobs (1854–1916) might seem a surprising person to have collected folklore for the sake of preserving a traditional English culture. He complained that the Grimms had had too much of an effect on England, wiping out local traditions, and he set about gathering authentically English stories and editing them for children so that they could grow up absorbing their national heritage, hearing each story "as a good old nurse" would have told it. He worried that the middle and upper classes had lost access to the lore that continued to thrive among working people, and argued, like the Grimms, for folktales as a key to national unity: it is "no unpatriotic task," he wrote, "to help to bridge over this gulf, by giving a common fund of nursery literature to all classes of the English people."

Jacobs took most of the stories from published sources. He then actively created his own versions of these tales, reducing the frequency of dialect speech but adding local words here and there for effect. Jacobs felt that "Tom Tit Tot," the first story in his volume, was "one of the best folktales that have ever been collected," better than any French or German version of the same story, including "Rumpelstiltskin" and "The Three Spinners." He praised it particularly for its humor and claimed that the tale reveals the staying power of the ancient superstition that to know someone's name gives you power over that person.

Tom Tit Tot

Once upon a time there was a woman, and she baked five pies. And when they came out of the oven, they were that overbaked the crusts were too hard to eat. So she says to her daughter:

"Darter," says she, "put you them there pies on the shelf, and leave 'em there a little, and they'll come again."—She meant, you know, the crust would get soft.

But the girl, she says to herself: "Well, if they'll come again, I'll eat 'em now." And she set to work and ate 'em all, first and last.

Well, come supper-time the woman said: "Go you, and get one o' them there pies. I dare say they've come again now."

The girl went and she looked, and there was nothing but the dishes. So back she came and says she: "Noo, they ain't come again."

"Not one of 'em?" says the mother.

"Not one of 'em," says she.

"Well, come again, or not come again," said the woman, "I'll have one for supper."

"But you can't, if they ain't come," said the girl.

"But I can," says she. "Go you, and bring the best of 'em."

"Best or worst," says the girl, "I've ate 'em all, and you can't have one till that's come again."

Well, the woman she was done, and she took her spinning to the door to spin, and as she span she sang:

> "My darter ha' ate five, five pies to-day.
> My darter ha' ate five, five pies to-day."

The king was coming down the street, and he heard her sing, but what she sang he couldn't hear, so he stopped and said:

"What was that you were singing, my good woman?"

The woman was ashamed to let him hear what her daughter had been doing, so she sang, instead of that:

> "My darter ha' spun five, five skeins to-day.
> My darter ha' spun five, five skeins to-day."

"Stars o' mine!" said the king, "I never heard tell of any one that could do that."

Then he said: "Look you here, I want a wife, and I'll marry your daughter. But look you here," says he, "eleven months out of the year she shall have all she likes to eat, and all the gowns she likes to get, and all the company she likes to keep; but the last month of the year she'll have to spin five skeins every day, and if she don't I shall kill her."

"All right," says the woman; for she thought what a grand marriage that was. And as for the five skeins, when the time came, there'd be plenty of ways of getting out of it, and likeliest, he'd have forgotten all about it.

Well, so they were married. And for eleven months the girl had all she liked to eat, and all the gowns she liked to get, and all the company she liked to keep.

But when the time was getting over, she began to think about the skeins and to wonder if he had 'em in mind. But not one word did he say about 'em, and she thought he'd wholly forgotten 'em.

However, the last day of the last month he takes her to a room she'd never set eyes on before. There was nothing in it but a spinning-wheel and a stool. And says he: "Now, my dear, here you'll be shut in to-morrow with some victuals and some flax, and if you haven't spun five skeins by the night, your head 'll go off."

And away he went about his business.

Well, she was that frightened, she'd always been such a gatless[1] girl, that she didn't so much as know how to spin, and what was she to do to-morrow with no

1. Careless.

one to come nigh her to help her? She sat down on a stool in the kitchen, and law! how she did cry!

However, all of a sudden she heard a sort of a knocking low down on the door. She upped and oped it, and what should she see but a small little black thing with a long tail. That looked up at her right curious, and that said:

"What are you a-crying for?"

"What's that to you?" says she.

"Never you mind," that said, "but tell me what you're a-crying for."

"That won't do me no good if I do," says she.

"You don't know that," that said, and twirled that's tail round.

"Well," says she, "that won't do no harm, if that don't do no good," and she upped and told about the pies, and the skeins, and everything.

"This is what I'll do," says the little black thing, "I'll come to your window every morning and take the flax and bring it spun at night."

"What's your pay?" says she.

That looked out of the corner of that's eyes, and that said: "I'll give you three guesses every night to guess my name, and if you haven't guessed it before the month's up you shall be mine."

Well, she thought she'd be sure to guess that's name before the month was up. "All right," says she, "I agree."

"All right," that says, and law! how that twirled that's tail.

Well, the next day, her husband took her into the room, and there was the flax and the day's food.

"Now there's the flax," says he, "and if that ain't spun up this night, off goes your head." And then he went out and locked the door.

He'd hardly gone, when there was a knocking against the window.

She upped and she oped it, and there sure enough was the little old thing sitting on the ledge.

"Where's the flax?" says he.

"Here it be," says she. And she gave it to him.

Well, come the evening a knocking came again to the window. She upped and she oped it, and there was the little old thing with five skeins of flax on his arm.

"Here it be," says he, and he gave it to her.

"Now, what's my name?" says he.

"What, is that Bill?" says she.

"Noo, that ain't," says he, and he twirled his tail.

"Is that Ned?" says she.

"Noo, that ain't," says he, and he twirled his tail.

"Well, is that Mark?" says she.

"Noo, that ain't," says he, and he twirled his tail harder, and away he flew.

Well, when her husband came in, there were the five skeins ready for him. "I see I shan't have to kill you to-night, my dear," says he; "you'll have your food and your flax in the morning," says he, and away he goes.

Well, every day the flax and the food were brought, and every day that there little black impet used to come mornings and evenings. And all the day the girl sate trying to think of names to say to it when it came at night. But she never hit on the right one. And as it got towards the end of the month, the impet began to look so maliceful, and that twirled that's tail faster and faster each time she gave a guess.

At last it came to the last day but one. The impet came at night along with the five skeins, and that said:

"What, ain't you got my name yet?"

"Is that Nicodemus?" says she.

"Noo, t'ain't," that says.

"Is that Sammle?" says she.

"Noo, t'ain't," that says.

"A-well, is that Methusalem?" says she.

"Noo, t'ain't that neither," that says.

Then that looks at her with that's eyes like a coal o' fire, and that says: "Woman, there's only to-morrow night, and then you'll be mine!" And away it flew.

Well, she felt that horrid. However, she heard the king coming along the passage. In he came, and when he sees the five skeins, he says, says he:

"Well, my dear," says he. "I don't see but what you'll have your skeins ready to-morrow night as well, and as I reckon I shan't have to kill you, I'll have supper in here to-night." So they brought supper, and another stool for him, and down the two sate.

Well, he hadn't eaten but a mouthful or so, when he stops and begins to laugh.

"What is it?" says she

"A-why," says he, "I was out a-hunting to-day, and I got away to a place in the wood I'd never seen before. And there was an old chalk pit. And I heard a kind of a sort of a humming. So I got off my hobby,[2] and I went right quiet to the pit, and I looked down. Well, what should there be but the funniest little black thing you ever set eyes on. And what was that doing, but that had a little spinning-wheel, and that was spinning wonderful fast, and twirling that's tail. And as that span that sang:

> "Nimmy nimmy not
> My name's Tom Tit Tot."

Well, when the girl heard this, she felt as if she could have jumped out of her skin for joy, but she didn't say a word.

Next day that there little thing looked so maliceful when he came for the flax. And when night came, she heard that knocking against the window panes. She oped the window, and that come right in on the ledge. That was grinning from ear to ear, and Oo! that's tail was twirling round so fast.

"What's my name?" that says, as that gave her the skeins.

"Is that Solomon?" she says, pretending to be afeard.

"Noo, t'ain't," that says, and that came further into the room.

"Well, is that Zebedee?" says she again.

"Noo, 'tain't," says the impet. And then that laughed and twirled that's tail till you couldn't hardly see it.

"Take time, woman," that says; "next guess, and you're mine." And that stretched out that's black hands at her.

2. Small horse.

Well, she backed a step or two, and she looked at it, and then she laughed out, and says she, pointing her finger at it:

> "Nimmy nimmy not
> Your name's Tom Tit Tot."

Well, when that heard her, that gave an awful shriek and away that flew into the dark, and she never saw it anymore.

IRISH FOLKTALES: A DONEGAL FAIRY *AND* THE BREWERY OF EGG-SHELLS

"Poetry in Ireland," wrote the great poet **William Butler Yeats**, "has always been mysteriously connected with magic." Frustrated by the schooling of Irish children by the British government, who saw fairy tales and local superstitions as primitive and backward, Yeats collected and published *Fairy and Folk Tales of Ireland* in 1889, aiming to celebrate the poetic value of Irish orature as the most inspiring source of art in a rapidly modernizing age: for Yeats it had a "simplicity sought for so much in these days by all the poets, and not to be had at any price." Yeats drew his stories from previous collections. "The Brewery of Egg-Shells" came from a compilation put together by Thomas Crofton Croker (1798–1854), who had traveled around Ireland transcribing local stories and describing customs. His book *The Fairy Legends and Traditions of the South of Ireland* (1825) was popular throughout the nineteenth century. Letitia Maclintock, who transcribed "A Donegal Fairy," was a novelist in her own right. Little is known about her, but Yeats praised her for capturing the distinctive dialect speech of Northern Ireland. Her story appears without a narrator to frame it, as though being told directly by "old Matt Craig," the man she claimed was her source.

A Donegal Fairy

Ay, it's a bad thing to displeasure the gentry,[1] sure enough—they can be unfriendly if they're angered, an' they can be the very best o' gude neighbours if they're treated kindly.

My mother's sister was her lone in the house one day, wi' a big pot o' water boiling on the fire, and ane o' the wee folk fell down the chimney, and slipped wi' his leg in the hot water.

---

1. Respectful term for fairies in order not to offend them.

He let a terrible squeal out o' him, an' in a minute the house was full o' wee crathurs[2] pulling him out o' the pot, an' carrying him across the floor.

"Did she scald you?" my aunt heard them saying to him.

"Na, na, it was mysel' scalded my ainsel',"[3] quoth the wee fellow.

"A weel, a weel," says they. "If it was your ainsel scalded yoursel', we'll say nothing, but if she had scalded you, we'd ha' made her pay."

The Brewery of Egg-Shells

Mrs. Sullivan fancied that her youngest child had been exchanged by "fairies theft,"[4] and certainly appearances warranted such a conclusion; for in one night her healthy, blue-eyed boy had become shrivelled up into almost nothing, and never ceased squalling and crying. This naturally made poor Mrs. Sullivan very unhappy; and all the neighbours, by way of comforting her, said that her own child was, beyond any kind of doubt, with the good people,[5] and that one of themselves was put in his place.

Mrs. Sullivan of course could not disbelieve what every one told her, but she did not wish to hurt the thing; for although its face was so withered, and its body wasted away to a mere skeleton, it had still a strong resemblance to her own boy. She, therefore, could not find it in her heart to roast it alive on the griddle, or to burn its nose off with the red-hot tongs, or to throw it out in the snow on the road-side, notwithstanding these, and several like proceedings, were strongly recommended to her for the recovery of her child.

One day who should Mrs. Sullivan meet but a cunning woman, well known about the country by the name of Ellen Leah (or Grey Ellen). She had the gift, however she got it, of telling where the dead were, and what was good for the rest of their souls; and could charm away warts and wens, and do a great many wonderful things of the same nature.

"You're in grief this morning, Mrs. Sullivan," were the first words of Ellen Leah to her.

"You may say that, Ellen," said Mrs. Sullivan, "and good cause I have to be in grief, for there was my own fine child whipped off from me out of his cradle, without as much as 'by your leave' or 'ask your pardon,' and an ugly dony[6] bit of a shrivelled-up fairy put in his place; no wonder, then, that you see me in grief, Ellen."

"Small blame to you, Mrs. Sullivan," said Ellen Leah, "but are you sure 'tis a fairy?"

"Sure!" echoed Mrs. Sullivan, "sure enough I am to my sorrow, and can I doubt my own two eyes? Every mother's soul must feel for me!"

"Will you take an old woman's advice?" said Ellen Leah, fixing her wild and mysterious gaze upon the unhappy mother; and, after a pause, she added, "but maybe you'll call it foolish?"

2. Creatures.
3. My own self.
4. Fairies were said to steal human infants

and replace them with supernatural creatures.
5. Fairies.
6. A fairy trick intended to fool humans.

"Can you get me back my child, my own child, Ellen?" said Mrs. Sullivan with great energy.

"If you do as I bid you," returned Ellen Leah, "you'll know." Mrs. Sullivan was silent in expectation, and Ellen continued, "Put down the big pot, full of water, on the fire, and make it boil like mad; then get a dozen new-laid eggs, break them, and keep the shells, but throw away the rest; when that is done, put the shells in the pot of boiling water, and you will soon know whether it is your own boy or a fairy. If you find that it is a fairy in the cradle, take the red-hot poker and cram it down his ugly throat, and you will not have much trouble with him after that I promise you."

Home went Mrs. Sullivan, and did as Ellen Leah desired. She put the pot on the fire, and plenty of turf[7] under it, and set the water boiling at such a rate, that if ever water was red-hot, it surely was.

The child was lying, for a wonder, quite easy and quiet in the cradle, every now and then cocking his eye, that would twinkle as keen as a star in a frosty night, over at the great fire, and the big pot upon it; and he looked on with great attention at Mrs. Sullivan breaking the eggs and putting down the egg-shells to boil. At last he asked, with the voice of a very old man, "What are you doing, mammy?"

Mrs. Sullivan's heart, as she said herself, was up in her mouth ready to choke her, at hearing the child speak. But she contrived to put the poker in the fire, and to answer, without making any wonder at the words, "I'm brewing, *a vick*" (my son).

"And what are you brewing, mammy?" said the little imp, whose supernatural gift of speech now proved beyond question that he was a fairy substitute.

"I wish the poker was red," thought Mrs. Sullivan; but it was a large one, and took a long time heating; so she determined to keep him in talk until the poker was in a proper state to thrust down his throat, and therefore repeated the question.

"Is it what I'm brewing, *a vick*," said she, "you want to know?"

"Yes, mammy: what are you brewing?" returned the fairy.

"Egg-shells, *a vick*," said Mrs. Sullivan.

"Oh!" shrieked the imp, starting up in the cradle, and clapping his hands together, "I'm fifteen hundred years in the world, and I never saw a brewery of egg-shells before!" The poker was by this time quite red, and Mrs. Sullivan, seizing it, ran furiously towards the cradle; but somehow or other her foot slipped, and she fell flat on the floor, and the poker flew out of her hand to the other end of the house. However, she got up without much loss of time and went to the cradle, intending to pitch the wicked thing that was in it into the pot of boiling water, when there she saw her own child in a sweet sleep, one of his soft round arms rested upon the pillow—his features were as placid as if their repose had never been disturbed, save the rosy mouth, which moved with a gentle and regular breathing.

7. Peat, a low-burning fuel cut from bogs in Ireland.

THREE ANANSI STORIES:
GHANA, JAMAICA, UNITED STATES

Tricky, mischievous, mostly clever but sometimes very foolish, the spider Anansi manages to outsmart most other animals and sometimes even the gods. He is a trickster—a character who compensates for his physical weakness by using his cunning to play tricks on powerful characters. He can be a shape-shifter, and sometimes takes the form of a human, or a human-spider hybrid. Spiders spin webs that connect spaces: they are therefore border-crossers, and belong to no one place. They also hide in corners, and disappear easily. Anansi usually breaks taboos and upsets expectations. And he is almost always selfish, aiming to survive in hard conditions, stealing food and money or bamboozling other creatures into working to get food for him. Anansi's maneuvers do not always succeed: sometimes they backfire and he is temporarily set back, but he is nothing if not resilient, and he simply returns to his old tricks again in the next story.

For the Ashanti people of West Africa, where he originates, Anansi is almost always the underdog, though he sometimes takes on qualities of the gods. Ashanti village elders typically tell Anansi stories after dark, with an audience sitting in a circle to listen. Sometimes in the middle of a telling, an actor will enter the circle and start impersonating one of the characters, to the great amusement of those watching. The stories typically reinforce a shared sense of moral norms and appropriate behavior precisely by having Anansi break taboos in a humorous way. One characteristic of the African versions of the Anansi stories is that they often explain how the world has come to be the way it is.

In Ghana, stories of all kinds are called *Anansesem*, and the first tale included here explains why all stories belong to Anansi.

The first English-language transcriber of the Anansi stories was R. S. Rattray, an anthropologist for the British government, which had established a colony called the Gold Coast (now Ghana). The more the British knew, they thought, the more successfully they would be able to assert and maintain power over the Ashanti. The collection of oral traditions was thus considered "of incalculable importance from an administrative point of view." The version included here comes out of a later collaboration between American anthropologist Harold Courlander and a student from Ghana, Albert Kofi Prempeh.

Trickster figures are found in many cultures, but what is most remarkable about the Anansi stories is their global reach. They can be found not only in West Africa but also in the Bahamas, Jamaica, Haiti, Trinidad, Barbados, Curaçao, Grenada, Costa Rica, Belize, Colombia, Nicaragua, Suriname, and the United States. The stories vary, and the character's name changes from place to place—Ananse, Annancy, Nansi, Aunt Nancy, Bre Nancy, Anansi Tori, and Ti Malice—but this oral tradition has remained remarkably resilient despite its transmission through centuries and across oceans.

The geographical scope of the Anansi tradition has everything to do with the slave trade. Enforced illiteracy meant that slaves who were taken from West Africa to the New World had severely restricted educations, but it also meant that they kept alive oral traditions that

might have faded under different conditions. Oppressed by a system that was based on a hypocritical morality, and surrounded by an abundance that was denied to them, slaves might well find Anansi appealing: his egocentrism, his willingness to use cunning to survive, his undermining of authority, and his resistance to moral constraints all suggested ways of coping with cruel and hypocritical slaveholders.

As Anansi traveled to the Caribbean, Latin America, and the United States, he tended to lose the divine qualities which he sometimes had in West Africa. In the American versions, he also faces harsher realities; moreover, he is more inclined to trick characters who are weaker than he is, and more frequently his tricks go wrong and he loses. Sometimes his arrogance or his greed brings about a downfall. He also adapts to new social conditions, sometimes getting involved in gambling and bootlegging. The stories are frequently entangled with tales and characters from other traditions, including European and American Indian orature.

Walter Jekyll, a British folklorist, collected the Jamaican version of the Anansi story included here, published in 1906. The "men and boys" who told the stories he collected were his own paid workers. (The British government had abolished slavery in Jamaica in 1834.) Around the same time that he was transcribing these stories, Jekyll met and encouraged a young Jamaican poet, Claude McKay, urging him to write in his native dialect. With money and advice, Jekyll helped McKay to move to the United States, where he became a leading writer in New York's Harlem Renaissance.

Some slaves in the United States transformed Anansi into a mischievous female. The story included here features Brer Rabbit, a famous trickster figure of Cherokee origin, who meets a frightening spider named "Aunt Nancy." This melding of American Indian and African traditions was not uncommon. Before 1776 many Indians had been enslaved and made to work alongside African slaves, with English as their common language. With Julius Lester's retelling of "Brer Rabbit and Aunt Nancy," we see how far-flung oral traditions can cross the world, meet, enrich, and transform one another, all without the need of writing.

All Stories Are Anansi's[1]

In the beginning, all tales and stories belonged to Nyame, the Sky God. But Kwaku Anansi, the spider, yearned to be the owner of all the stories known in the world, and he went to Nyame and offered to buy them.

The Sky God said: "I am willing to sell the stories, but the price is high. Many people have come to me offering to buy, but the price was too high for them. Rich and powerful families have not been able to pay. Do you think you can do it?"

Anansi replied to the Sky God: "I can do it. What is the price?"

"My price is three things," the Sky God said. "I must first have Mmoboro, the hornets. I must then have Onini, the great python. I must then have Osebo, the leopard. For these things I will sell you the right to tell all stories."

Anansi said: "I will bring them."

He went home and made his plans. He first cut a gourd from a vine and made a small hole in it. He took a large calabash and filled it with water. He

1. As told by Harold Courlander and Albert Kofi Prempeh.

went to the tree where the hornets lived. He poured some of the water over himself, so that he was dripping. He threw some water over the hornets, so that they too were dripping. Then he put the calabash on his head, as though to protect himself from a storm, and called out to the hornets: "Are you foolish people? Why do you stay in the rain that is falling?"

The hornets answered: "Where shall we go?"

"Go here, in this dry gourd," Anansi told them.

The hornets thanked him and flew into the gourd through the small hole. When the last of them had entered, Anansi plugged the hole with a ball of grass, saying: "Oh, yes, but you are really foolish people!"

He took his gourd full of hornets to Nyame, the Sky God. The Sky God accepted them. He said: "There are two more things."

Anansi returned to the forest and cut a long bamboo pole and some strong vines. Then he walked toward the house of Onini, the python, talking to himself. He said: "My wife is stupid. I say he is longer and stronger. My wife says he is shorter and weaker. I give him more respect. She gives him less respect. Is she right or am I right? I am right, he is longer. I am right, he is stronger."

When Onini, the python, heard Anansi talking to himself, he said: "Why are you arguing this way with yourself?"

The spider replied: "Ah, I have had a dispute with my wife. She says you are shorter and weaker than this bamboo pole. I say you are longer and stronger."

Onini said: "It's useless and silly to argue when you can find out the truth. Bring the pole and we will measure."

So Anansi laid the pole on the ground, and the python came and stretched himself out beside it.

"You seem a little short," Anansi said.

The python stretched further.

"A little more," Anansi said.

"I can stretch no more," Onini said.

"When you stretch at one end, you get shorter at the other end," Anansi said. "Let me tie you at the front so you don't slip."

He tied Onini's head to the pole. Then he went to the other end and tied the tail to the pole. He wrapped the vine all around Onini, until the python couldn't move.

"Onini," Anansi said, "it turns out that my wife was right and I was wrong. You are shorter than the pole and weaker. My opinion wasn't as good as my wife's. But you were even more foolish than I, and you are now my prisoner."

Anansi carried the python to Nyame, the Sky God, who said: "There is one thing more."

Osebo, the leopard, was next. Anansi went into the forest and dug a deep pit where the leopard was accustomed to walk. He covered it with small branches and leaves and put dust on it, so that it was impossible to tell where the pit was. Anansi went away and hid. When Osebo came prowling in the black of night, he stepped into the trap Anansi had prepared and fell to the bottom. Anansi heard the sound of the leopard falling, and he said: "Ah, Osebo, you are half-foolish!"

When morning came, Anansi went to the pit and saw the leopard there.

"Osebo," he asked, "what are you doing in this hole?"

"I have fallen into a trap," Osebo said. "Help me out."

"I would gladly help you," Anansi said. "But I'm sure that if I bring you out, I will have no thanks for it. You will get hungry, and later on you will be wanting to eat me and my children."

"I swear it won't happen!" Osebo said.

"Very well. Since you swear it, I will take you out," Anansi said.

He bent a tall green tree toward the ground, so that its top was over the pit, and he tied it that way. Then he tied a rope to the top of the tree and dropped the other end of it into the pit.

"Tie this to your tail," he said.

Osebo tied the rope to his tail.

"Is it well tied?" Anansi asked.

"Yes, it is well tied," the leopard said.

"In that case," Anansi said, "you are not merely half-foolish, you are all-foolish."

And he took his knife and cut the other rope, the one that held the tree bowed to the ground. The tree straightened up with a snap, pulling Osebo out of the hole. He hung in the air head downward, twisting and turning. And while he hung this way, Anansi killed him with his weapons.

Then he took the body of the leopard and carried it to Nyame, the Sky God, saying: "Here is the third thing. Now I have paid the price."

Nyame said to him: "Kwaku Anansi, great warriors and chiefs have tried, but they have been unable to do it. You have done it. Therefore, I will give you the stories. From this day onward, all stories belong to you. Whenever a man tells a story, he must acknowledge that it is Anansi's tale."

In this way Anansi, the spider, became the owner of all stories that are told. To Anansi all these tales belong.

Annancy, Monkey and Tiger

One day Annancy an' Tiger get in a rum-shop, drink an' drink, an' then Monkey commence to boast. Monkey was a great boaster.

Annancy say:—"You boast well; I wonder if you have sense as how you boast."

Monkey say:—"Get 'way you foolish fellah you, can come an' ask me if me have sense. You go t'rough de whole world you never see a man again have the sense I have."

Annancy say:—"Bro'er Monkey, how many sense you have, tell me?"

Monkey say:—"I have dem so till I can't count dem to you, for dem dé[1] all over me body."

Annancy say:—"Me no have much, only two, one fe[2] me an' one fe me friend."

One day Monkey was travelling an' was going to pass where Tiger live. Annancy was working on that same road.

1. There.   2. For.

As Monkey passing, Tiger was into a stone-hole an' jump out on the fellah an' catch him. All his sense was gone, no sense to let him get 'way. Tiger was so glad, have him before him well ready to kill.

Here come the clever man Mr. Annancy.

When he saw his friend Monkey in the hand of such a wicked man he was frighten, but he is going to use his sense.

He said:—"Marnin', Bro'er Tiger, I see you catch dat fellah; I was so glad to see you hold him so close in hand. You must eat him now. But before you eat him take you two hand an' cover you face an' kneel down with you face up to Massa God an' say, 'T'ank God fe what I goin' to receive.'"

An' so Tiger do.

An' by the time Tiger open his eyes Monkey an' Annancy was gone.

When they get to a distant Annancy said to Monkey:—"T'ink you say you have sense all over you 'kin, why you no been get 'way when Bro'er Tiger catch you?"

Monkey don't have nothing to say.

Annancy say:—"Me no tell you say me have two sense, one fe me an' one fe me friend? Well! a him me use to-day."

From that day Tiger hate Annancy up to now.

Jack Mantora me no choose any.[3]

Brer Rabbit and Aunt Nancy

Once a year all the creatures—winged and claw, big and little, long-tail, bobtail, and no-tail—had to go see Aunt Nancy. Aunt Nancy was the great-grandmother of the Witch-Rabbit, Mammy-Bammy-Big-Money. She ruled all the animals, even King Lion. When she wanted them to know that she was watching their every move, all she had to do was suck in her breath and the creatures would get a chill.

One year it came time for the creatures to go pay their respects.

"I ain't going!" Brer Rabbit announced.

"You got to go," the other animals argued with him.

"Says who? I don't feel like going way up in the country and into that thick swamp just to see Aunt Nancy."

"You better go," they told him.

"I done already been and seen. But, when you get where you going, ask Aunt Nancy to shake hands with you. Then you'll see what I saw."

The creatures went off. After a while they came to Aunt Nancy's house. If you had seen her house, you would've said it looked like a big chunk of fog.

Brer Bear hollered, "Hallooooo!"

Aunt Nancy came out wearing a big black cloak and sat down on a pine stump. Her eyeballs sparkled red like they were on fire.

"Let me call the roll to be sure everybody is here," she said in a voice like chalk on a blackboard.

"Brer Wolf!"

---

3. Jamaican storytellers typically end Annancy stories with these words, indicating that the moral is not intended for any particular listener.

"Here!"

"Brer Possum!"

"Here!"

Finally she got to the last one. "Brer Rabbit!"

Silence.

Brer Rabbit!

More silence.

"BRER RABBIT!!!!!"

Silence and more silence.

"Did Brer Rabbit send an excuse as to why he ain't here?" Aunt Nancy asked the creatures.

Brer Wolf said, "No, he didn't."

Brer Bear added, "He said to tell you howdy and he told us to tell you to shake hands with us and remember him in your dreams."

Aunt Nancy rolled her eyes and chomped her lips together. "Is that what he told you? Well, you tell him that if he'll come, I'll shake hands with him. Tell him that if he don't come, then I'll come and shake hands with him where he lives."

Brer Bear persisted. "Why won't you shake hands with us? You're hurting my feelings."

Aunt Nancy rolled her eyes again. She got up. But her cloak got caught on the tree stump and slipped off. The creatures looked. She was half woman and half spider, with seven arms and no hands. That's why her house looked like fog. It was a web.

The creatures got away from there as fast as their legs could take them.

When they got back and told Brer Rabbit what they had seen, he chuckled but didn't say a word.

That was the last time the animals went to see Aunt Nancy.

UNITED STATES SLAVE STORY: ALL GOD'S CHILLEN HAD WINGS

Geographically and culturally isolated from the mainland, the islands off the coast of Georgia and South Carolina are home to a group of African Americans called "Gullah," who retained African stories, rituals, intonations, common words, and even grammatical constructions well into the twentieth century. Many of their linguistic practices can be traced to Bantu, a family of languages found across central and southern Africa. In the early part of the twentieth century, Caesar Grant, a Gullah worker on John's Island off the coast of South Carolina, told a story of slaves making plans in a language not understood by their masters and escaping from a cruel slave driver by intoning an African word that allows them to fly away. Like **"The Three Spinners"** and **"Tom Tit Tot,"** it offered the fantasy of an escape from a life of painful labor. A

white novelist named John Bennett wrote Grant's story down, though he felt free to translate many of the teller's Gullah phrases into standard English. Bennett published the story in 1943, concerned that the grim and ghostly Gullah stories common in Charleston would vanish with the older generations who had lived under slavery.

Across the American South there were many versions of this legend of slaves who could fly. The great African American poet Langston Hughes (1902–1967) claimed that this story was important because it showed that there was more to slave folklore than humorous trickster tales. Later, the U.S. novelist **Toni Morrison** (b. 1931) shaped her novel *Song of Solomon* around this oral tradition. The image of flying slaves, she has said, "is everywhere—people used to talk about it, it's in the spirituals and gospels. Perhaps it was wishful thinking: escape, death, and all that. But suppose it wasn't. What might that mean?"

All God's Chillen Had Wings

Once all Africans could fly like birds; but owing to their many transgressions, their wings were taken away. There remained, here and there, in the sea islands and out-of-the-way places in the low country, some who had been overlooked, and had retained the power of flight, though they looked like other men.

There was a cruel master on one of the sea islands who worked his people till they died. When they died he bought others to take their places. These also he killed with overwork in the burning summer sun, through the middle hours of the day, although this was against the law.

One day, when all the worn-out Negroes were dead of overwork, he bought, of a broker in the town, a company of native Africans just brought into the country, and put them at once to work in the cottonfield.

He drove them hard. They went to work at sunrise and did not stop until dark. They were driven with unsparing harshness all day long, men, women and children. There was no pause for rest during the unendurable heat of the midsummer noon, though trees were plenty and near. But through the hardest hours, when fair plantations gave their Negroes rest, this man's driver pushed the work along without a moment's stop for breath, until all grew weak with heat and thirst.

There was among them one young woman who had lately borne a child. It was her first; she had not fully recovered from bearing, and should not have been sent to the field until her strength had come back. She had her child with her, as the other women had, astraddle on her hip, or piggyback.

The baby cried. She spoke to quiet it. The driver could not understand her words. She took her breast with her hand and threw it over her shoulder that the child might suck and be content. Then she went back to chopping knot-grass; but being very weak, and sick with the great heat, she stumbled, slipped and fell.

The driver struck her with his lash until she rose and staggered on.

She spoke to an old man near her, the oldest man of them all, tall and strong, with a forked beard. He replied; but the driver could not understand what they said; their talk was strange to him.

She returned to work; but in a little while she fell again. Again the driver lashed her until she got to her feet. Again she spoke to the old man. But he said: "Not yet, daughter; not yet." So she went on working, though she was very ill.

Soon she stumbled and fell again. But when the driver came running with his lash to drive her on with her work, she turned to the old man and asked: "Is it time yet, daddy?" He answered: "Yes, daughter; the time has come. Go; and peace be with you!". . . and stretched out his arms toward her . . . so.

With that she leaped straight up into the air and was gone like a bird, flying over field and wood.

The driver and overseer ran after her as far as the edge of the field; but she was gone, high over their heads, over the fence, and over the top of the woods, gone, with her baby astraddle of her hip, sucking at her breast.

Then the driver hurried the rest to make up for her loss; and the sun was very hot indeed. So hot that soon a man fell down. The overseer himself lashed him to his feet. As he got up from where he had fallen the old man called to him in an unknown tongue. My grandfather told me the words that he said; but it was a long time ago, and I have forgotten them. But when he had spoken, the man turned and laughed at the overseer, and leaped up into the air, and was gone, like a gull, flying over field and wood.

Soon another man fell. The driver lashed him. He turned to the old man. The old man cried out to him, and stretched out his arms as he had done for the other two; and he, like them, leaped up, and was gone through the air, flying like a bird over field and wood.

Then the overseer cried to the driver, and the master cried to them both: "Beat the old devil! He is the doer!"

The overseer and the driver ran at the old man with lashes ready; and the master ran too, with a picket pulled from the fence, to beat the life out of the old man who had made those Negroes fly.

But the old man laughed in their faces, and said something loudly to all the Negroes in the field, the new Negroes and the old Negroes.

And as he spoke to them they all remembered what they had forgotten, and recalled the power which once had been theirs. Then all the Negroes, old and new, stood up together; the old man raised his hands; and they all leaped up into the air with a great shout; and in a moment were gone, flying, like a flock of crows, over the field, over the fence, and over the top of the wood; and behind them flew the old man.

The men went clapping their hands; and the women went singing; and those who had children gave them their breasts; and the children laughed and sucked as their mothers flew, and were not afraid.

The master, the overseer, and the driver looked after them as they flew, beyond the wood, beyond the river, miles on miles, until they passed beyond the last rim of the world and disappeared in the sky like a handful of leaves. They were never seen again.

Where they went I do not know; I never was told. Nor what it was that the old man said . . . that I have forgotten. But as he went over the last fence he made a sign in the master's face, and cried "Kuli-ba! Kuli-ba!" I don't know what that means.

But if I could only find the old wood sawyer, he could tell you more; for he was there at the time, and saw the Africans fly away with their women and children. He is an old, old man, over ninety years of age, and remembers a great many strange things.

UNITED STATES SLAVE SPIRITUALS AND SECULAR SONGS

In 1801 a Methodist preacher named Richard Allen (1760–1831), who had been born into slavery, published the first hymnal intended specifically for African American congregations. He collected and wrote songs of religious faith in the face of persecution which would come to be known as *spirituals*. Sung not only in churches but also during times of work and leisure, African American spirituals played many roles: often they were outlets for fervent belief and strong emotion, but they might also help to synchronize work rhythms, and they could even be used to pass on coded information about secret meetings or plans to escape. Typically these songs have a double meaning: on the one hand, they express a desire to flee an oppressive earthly world into the arms of a loving Christian God who understands suffering; on the other hand, they suggest dreams of escape from slavery in this world, using the underground railroad system of safe houses, for example, to reach Canada. Some incorporated specific instructions, such as constellations of stars that would lead the way for slaves on the run. "Steal Away to Jesus" is famous for having functioned as a signal for escaped slaves.

Combining European Protestant church music with African musical rhythms and patterns of call-and-response, slave songs created a new hybrid tradition. This music laid the groundwork for jazz and the blues, and has influenced rock, reggae, and hip-hop artists. In the twentieth century, musicians in apartheid South Africa adopted some of the styles and patterns of American jazz, completing a global circuit in which oral traditions that had moved west with the slave trade returned to Africa in a new form. Certainly music around the world as we know it today would not have been the same without the songs of American slaves.

No More Auction Block

No more auction block for me,
No more, no more,
No more auction block for me,
Many thousand gone.

No more peck of corn for me,   5
No more, no more,
No more peck of corn for me,
Many thousand gone.

No more pint of salt for me,
No more, no more,   10
No more pint of salt for me,
Many thousand gone.

No more driver's lash for me,
No more, no more,
No more driver's lash for me,   15
Many thousand gone.

Swing Low, Sweet Chariot

Swing low, sweet chariot,
Coming for to carry me home,
Swing low, sweet chariot,
Coming for to carry me home.

I looked over Jordan[1] and what did I see   5
Coming for to carry me home,
A band of angels, coming after me,
Coming for to carry me home.

If you get there before I do,
Coming for to carry me home,   10
Tell all my friends I'm coming too,
Coming for to carry me home.

Swing low, sweet chariot,
Coming for to carry me home,
Swing low, sweet chariot,   15
Coming for to carry me home.

Steal Away to Jesus

Steal away, steal away, steal away to Jesus,
Steal away, steal away home,
I ain't got long to stay here.

My Lord, He calls me,
He calls me by the thunder,
The trumpet sounds within-a my soul,   5
I ain't got long to stay here.

Steal away, steal away, steal away to Jesus,
Steal away, steal away home,
I ain't got long to stay here.   10

Green trees a-bending,
Po' sinner stands a-trembling,
The trumpet sounds within-a my soul,
I ain't got long to stay here.

1. A river that appears in the Bible; for slaves, crossing Jordan symbolized going to heaven and escaping from slavery.

Steal away, steal away, steal away to Jesus,   15
Steal away, steal away home,
I ain't got long to stay here.

Promises of Freedom

My ole Mistiss promise me,
W'en she died, she'd set me free.
She lived so long dat 'er head got bal',
An' she give out'n de notion a dyin' at all.

My ole Mistiss say to me: 5
"Sambo, I'se gwine ter set you free."
But w'en dat head git slick an' bal',
De Lawd couldn' a' killed 'er wid a big green maul.

My ole Mistiss never die,
Wid 'er nose all hooked an' skin all dry.   10
But my ole Miss, she's somehow gone,
An' she lef' "Uncle Sambo" a-hillin' up co'n.

Ole Mosser lakwise promise me,
W'en he died, he'd set me free.
But ole Mosser go an' make his Will   15
Fer to leave me a-plowin' ole Beck still.

Yes, my ole Mosser promise me;
But "his papers" didn't leave me free.
A dose of pizen he'ped 'im along.
May de Devil preach 'is funer'l song.   20

NAVAJO CEREMONY: THE NIGHT CHANT

Navajo ceremonialism ranks among the glories of native American achievement. Directed primarily toward restoring a harmony between individuals and the environment, the ceremonies called Nightway, Mountainway, Beautyway, Enemyway, and Blessingway—to name only a few of the best known—create a spiritual universe of song, prayer, drama, and graphic art. These are healing ceremonies that have proven their therapeutic power and earned the respect of Western medicine. In fact, they cross the boundaries of art, religion, and science. Their shared quest for *beauty*—a broad term that includes perfection, normality, success, and well-being—reflects a central value of Navajo culture, located mostly in the southwestern United States, in Arizona and New Mexico.

With its induction of new initiates, its unique all-night sing, and its lofty portrayal of deities, the famous Nightway chant occupies a place of honor among these "ways." Its nineteenth-century translator, Washington Matthews, a U.S. army surgeon posted to New Mexico, called it by the name "Night Chant." Although a large audience of relatives, friends, and visitors usually attend the Nightway ceremony, a single person is its focus. Each of the Navajo ceremonials is said to be effective against a particular group of illnesses, and the Night Chant heals strokes and other disorders of the brain. It remains in huge demand every year. But the value of the ceremony also goes beyond the task of healing one person: the host who sponsors it gains prestige, and it provides opportunities for broader cultural reaffirmation, socializing, and spiritual renewal.

Performed in only fall or winter, the Night Chant falls into two four-day parts, followed by a climactic ninth-night reprise, the night of nights, in which the ceremonial leader, or chanter, summons the long-awaited spirit of thunder. At this point the ceremony breaks free in a torrent of song that continues unabated until dawn. In the first part the emphasis is on rites that exorcise evil influences and invoke the distant gods. The second part is distinguished by spacious and intricate sand paintings made of dry pigments sprinkled on the earth. The paintings depict the gods and allow the sick to take on some divine invulnerability. Through it all, the ceremonial leader directs the song recitals and intones the prescribed prayers. The two selections included here are the prayer to thunder that begins the final night and the last of the Finishing Songs that bring it to a close.

From The Night Chant[1]

Prayer to Thunder[2]

* * *

In Tsegíhi,[3]
In the house made of the dawn,

---

1. Translated by Washington Matthews.
2. In performance each line is first recited by the chanter, then repeated by the patient.

3. Pronounced *tsay-gee'-hee*, a distant canyon and site of the *house made of the dawn* (line 2), a prehistoric ruin, regarded as the home of deities.

In the house made of the evening twilight,
In the house made of the dark cloud,
In the house made of the he-rain,   5
In the house made of the dark mist,
In the house made of the she-rain,[4]
In the house made of pollen,[5]
In the house made of grasshoppers,
Where the dark mist curtains the doorway,   10
The path to which is on the rainbow,
Where the zigzag lightning stands high on top,
Where the he-rain stands high on top,
Oh, male divinity![6]
With your moccasins of dark cloud, come to us.   15
With your leggings of dark cloud, come to us.
With your shirt of dark cloud, come to us.
With your headdress of dark cloud, come to us.
With your mind enveloped in dark cloud, come to us.
With the dark thunder above you, come to us soaring.   20
With the shapen cloud at your feet, come to us soaring.
With the far darkness made of the dark cloud
    over your head, come to us soaring.
With the far darkness made of the he-rain
    over your head, come to us soaring.
With the far darkness made of the dark mist
    over your head, come to us soaring.
With the far darkness made of the she-rain
    over your head, come to us soaring.   25
With the zigzag lightning flung out on high
    over your head, come to us soaring.
With the rainbow hanging high over your head,
    come to us soaring.
With the far darkness made of the dark cloud on
    the ends of your wings, come to us soaring.
With the far darkness made of the he-rain on
    the ends of your wings, come to us soaring.
With the far darkness made of the dark mist
    on the ends of your wings, come to us soaring.   30
With the far darkness made of the she-rain
    on the ends of your wings, come to us soaring.
With the zigzag lightning flung out on high
    on the ends of your wings, come to us soaring.
With the rainbow hanging high on the ends of
    your wings, come to us soaring.
With the near darkness made of the dark cloud, of
    the he-rain, of the dark mist, and of the
    she-rain, come to us.
With the darkness on the earth, come to us.   35

4. Rain without thunder. "He-rain": rain with thunder.
5. Emblem of peace, of happiness, of prosper-

ity [translator's note].
6. Thunder, regarded as a bird.

With these I wish the foam floating on the flowing
   water over the roots of the great corn.
I have made your sacrifice.
I have prepared a smoke[7] for you.
My feet restore for me.
My limbs restore for me.   40
My body restore for me.
My mind restore for me.
My voice restore for me.
Today, take out your spell for me.
Today, take away your spell for me.   45
Away from me you have taken it.
Far off from me it is taken.
Far off you have done it.
Happily I recover.
Happily my interior becomes cool.   50
Happily my eyes regain their power.
Happily my head becomes cool.
Happily my limbs regain their power.
Happily I hear again.
Happily for me *the spell*[8] is taken off.   55
Happily may I walk.
Impervious to pain, may I walk.
Feeling light within, may I walk.
With lively feelings, may I walk.
Happily abundant dark clouds I desire.   60
Happily abundant dark mists I desire.
Happily abundant passing showers I desire.
Happily an abundance of vegetation I desire.
Happily an abundance of pollen I desire.
Happily abundant dew I desire.   65
Happily may fair white corn, to the ends of the
   earth, come with you.
Happily may fair yellow corn, to the ends of the
   earth, come with you.
Happily may fair blue corn, to the ends of the
   earth, come with you.
Happily may fair corn of all kinds, to the ends
   of the earth, come with you.
Happily may fair plants of all kinds, to the ends
   of the earth, come with you.   70
Happily may fair goods of all kinds, to the ends
   of the earth, come with you.
Happily may fair jewels of all kinds, to the ends
   of the earth, come with you.
With these before you, happily may they come with you.
With these behind you, happily may they come with you.
With these below you, happily may they come with you.   75

---

7. Painted reed filled with native tobacco, offered as a sacrifice.   8. Words added by the translator.

With these above you, happily may they come with you.
With these all around you, happily may they come with you.
Thus happily you accomplish your tasks.
Happily the old men will regard you.
Happily the old women will regard you.   80
Happily the young men will regard you.
Happily the young women will regard you.
Happily the boys will regard you.
Happily the girls will regard you.
Happily the children will regard you.   85
Happily the chiefs will regard you.
Happily, as they scatter in different directions,
    they will regard you.
Happily, as they approach their homes, they will
    regard you.
Happily may their roads home be on the trail of pollen.
Happily may they all get back.   90
In beauty I walk.
With beauty before me, I walk.
With beauty behind me, I walk.
With beauty below me, I walk.
With beauty above me, I walk.   95
With beauty all around me, I walk.
It is finished in beauty,
It is finished in beauty,
It is finished in beauty,
It is finished in beauty.   100

Finishing Song

From the pond in the white valley—
The young man doubts it—
He takes up his sacrifice,
With that he now heals.
With that your kindred thank you now.   5

From the pools in the green meadow[9]—
The young woman doubts it—
He takes up his sacrifice,[1]
With that he now heals.
With that your kindred thank you now.   10

9. A contrast of landscapes, of the beginning and end of a stream. It rises in a green valley in the mountains and flows down to the lower plains, where it spreads into a single sheet of water. As the dry season approaches, it shrinks, leaving a white saline efflorescence called alkali. The male is associated with the sterile, unattractive alkali flat in the first stanza, while the female is named with the pleasant mountain meadow in the second stanza [adapted from translator's note].

1. The deity accepts the sacrificial offering (see p. 946, n. 7) and effects the healing that benefits the patient and his kindred—though young men and young women, with the irreverence of youth, may doubt the truth of the ceremony.

IV

Modernity and Modernism, 1900–1945

At the beginning of the twentieth century, the world was interconnected as never before. New means of transportation, such as the steamship, the railroad, the automobile, and the airplane, allowed people in the industrialized West to cover vast distances quickly. Other technologies, such as the telegraph and the telephone, allowed them to communicate instantaneously. In the decades to come, such inventions, powered either by electricity or by the internal combustion engine, along with improvements in agriculture, nutrition, public health, and medical care, would foster remarkable growth in human health and material prosperity. Infant mortality declined and world population more than tripled, from under two billion to around six billion. In unprecedented numbers, people were living in large cities; correspondingly, the experience of urban life is one of the major themes of twentieth-century literature. Together, these vast transformations in human experience can be characterized as *modernization*.

Yet the technological advances that undeniably improved human life led, as well, to the production of weapons that were increasingly effective, and therefore increasingly destructive. As distant parts of the

"Books!" (1925), a promotional poster by the Russian artist Alexander Rodchenko (1891–1956). Rodchenko, Alexander (1891–1956) © VAGA, NY Advertisement: "Books!" 1925. Scala/Art Resource, NY. Art © Estate of Alexander Rodchenko/RAO.

globe grew closer through trade, immigration, and communications, they often came into deadly conflict. Indeed, the twentieth century was the bloodiest in human history: as many as 200 million died in wars, revolutions, genocides, and related famines. In response to the century's horrors, the old dream of a unified, peaceful world became ever more appealing; and to many, in the splendid light of new technologies and optimistic ideas of progress, it even seemed achievable as never before. Frequently, those who sought to end war looked to supranational bodies, such as the League of Nations, the United Nations, the European Community (later the European Union), the Organization of American States, and the Organization for African Unity, as the future guarantors of "peaceful coexistence," a term that gained currency during the Cold War to refer to the arms race between the United States and the Soviet Union.

MODERNITY AND CONFLICT IN WORLD HISTORY, 1900–1945

As Europe and North America became industrialized over the course of the nineteenth century, they extended their political power to cover most of the globe. By 1900, after centuries of European expansion, there were no longer, in the words of **Joseph Conrad's *Heart of Darkness***, any "blank spaces" on the map. Within a few years, explorers would even reach the North and South Poles. At the 1884 Berlin Conference, the European powers had carved up Africa among themselves; they also controlled most of southern Asia. The remaining independent nations in the Americas and the antipodes maintained close ties with their former colonial masters—Britain, Spain, France, Portugal, and the Netherlands. The small kingdom of Belgium and the recently unified nations of Germany and Italy sought to acquire overseas empires of their own. The British Empire was still at its zenith, and since Britain retained colonial possessions in all parts of the world, it was known as "the empire on which the sun never sets."

Yet as the twentieth century advanced, the sun did set on the British Empire—and on every other European empire as well. During the first half of the century, the world system that the European powers dominated experienced massive crises in the forms of two world wars, the Russian Revolution, the Great Depression, and the Holocaust. These upheavals became central concerns for the literature of the period and contributed to a rethinking of traditional literary forms and techniques.

The First World War (1914–18) took place mainly in Europe; it was the most mechanized war to date and killed some 15 million people. Much of the war on the Western Front (in Belgium and France) was characterized by stalemate, as each side ferociously defended entrenched positions with machine guns, resulting in massive battles over tiny slices of territory, as at Ypres, Vimy Ridge, and Verdun. It was only after the United States joined the war, in 1917, that the Allies (France, Britain and its colonies, Italy, and the United States) gained the initiative and were able to repel Germany.

In the East, Germany and Austria-Hungary drove deep into Russian territory. Russia's near-defeat contributed to the revolution of 1917, in which the Bolsheviks under V. I. Lenin sought to establish a Communist "dictatorship of the proletariat," with a tiny vanguard of party members taking power in the name of the working classes. During the succeeding decades, forced collectivization of agriculture and enterprise (which led to widespread famine), as well as purges of people considered enemies of the Communist Party (especially under Lenin's successor, Joseph Stalin), caused tens of millions of deaths, both in Russia

Emmeline Pankhurst, a leading British suffragette, is shown here speaking in the early 1920s, several years after passage of the 1918 Representation of the People Act, which acknowledged the right of women over thirty to vote. In the 1920s, Pankhurst devoted herself to speaking out against Bolshevism and in favor of British imperialism.

and in other former territories of the Russian Empire, such as the Ukraine. (They were united under the Communist regime of the Soviet Union.) The Communist movement, initially supportive of some literary experiments, increasingly restricted the scope of acceptable artistic expression in the countries where it gained control. In response, a dissident literature developed, published abroad or in informal, private editions that could circulate without being censored. Writers such as **Anna Akhmatova** and **Alexander Solzhenitsyn** had to work within these constraints.

The Treaty of Versailles (1919) formalized the end of the war, and of four great empires—the German, Austro-Hungarian, Russian, and Ottoman—dividing most of Central and Eastern Europe into a multitude of smaller nations (some of which would later be reabsorbed by the resurgent Soviet Union and Nazi Germany). The treaty also founded the first of the great international organizations, the League of Nations—which, despite its idealistic beginnings, proved incapable of enforcing the demilitarization of Germany.

Making matters worse, the Allies' demand for huge reparations contributed to the economic chaos in Germany that, in turn, furthered the cause of the National Socialists (Nazis). The party came to power under Adolf Hitler in 1933 with a program of national rearmament and authoritarian politics held together by the glue of anti-Semitism. The Nazis were unremittingly hostile to modern literature, and writers such as **Thomas Mann** and **Bertolt Brecht** went into exile.

Beginning on October 24, 1929, the liberal capitalist world also experienced financial disaster, with the stock market crash that heralded the Great Depression. Within a few years, a third of American workers were unemployed; hunger and joblessness spread throughout the industrialized world. Despite fears that radical parties like the Communists or the Nazis would emerge from the economic devastation in the United States, Franklin D. Roosevelt (president from 1933 to 1945) was able to reverse the worst effects of the Depression with the New Deal, which included public works spending and

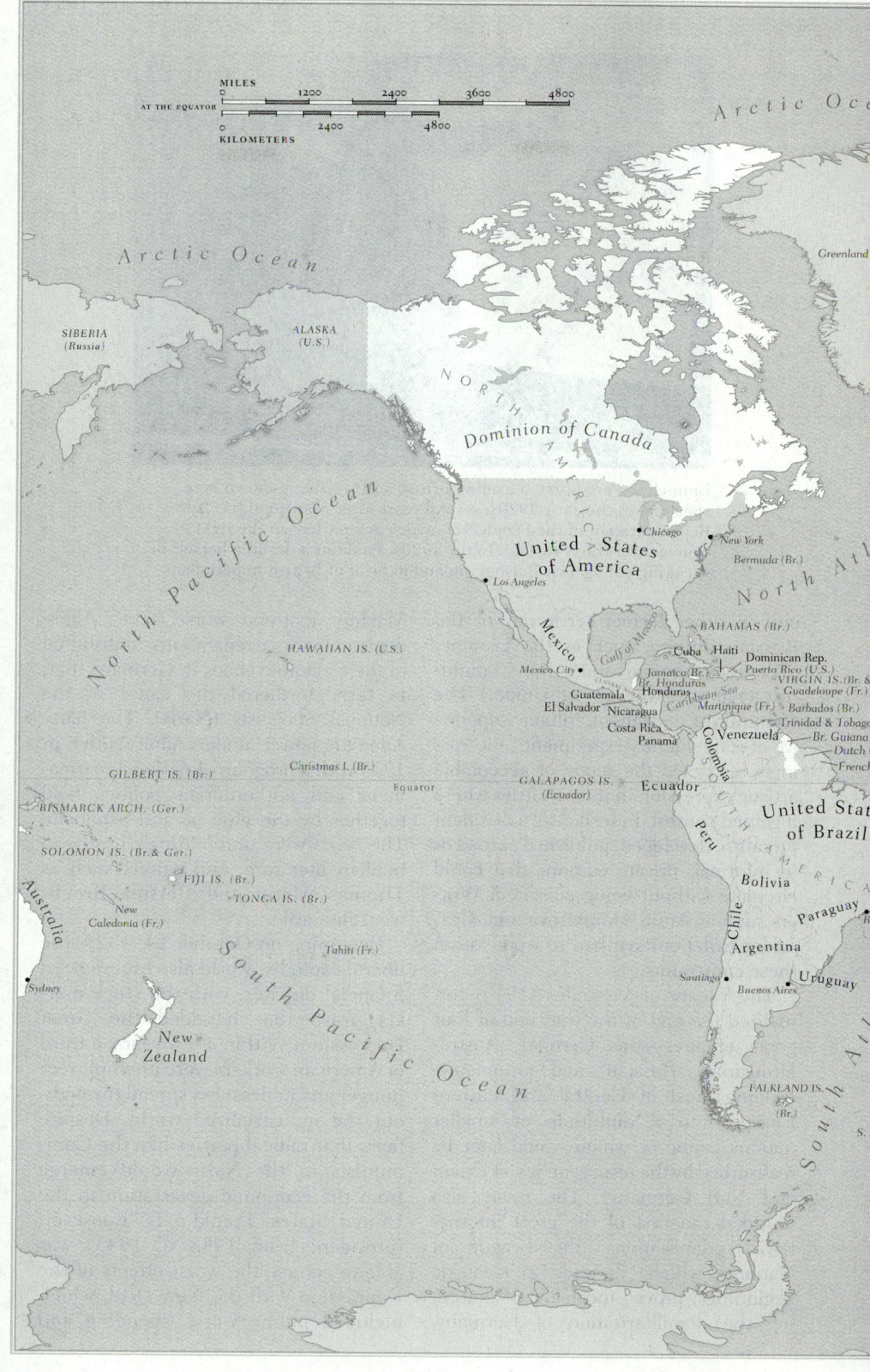

MILES

| 0 | 1200 | 2400 | 3600 | 4800 |

AT THE EQUATOR

KILOMETERS

| 0 | 2400 | 4800 |

Arctic Oce

Arctic Ocean

SIBERIA
(Russia)

ALASKA
(U.S.)

Greenland

N O R T H

A M E R I C A

Dominion of Canada

United States
of America

Chicago

New York

Bermuda (Br.)

North Atl

North Pacific Ocean

HAWAIIAN IS. (U.S.)

Los Angeles

Mexico

Gulf of Mexico

BAHAMAS (Br.)

Mexico City

Cuba

Haiti

Dominican Rep.

Jamaica (Br.)

Puerto Rico (U.S.)

Br. Honduras

VIRGIN IS. (Br. &

Guatemala

Honduras

Guadeloupe (Fr.)

El Salvador

Nicaragua

Caribbean Sea

Martinique (Fr.)

Barbados (Br.)

Costa Rica

Trinidad & Tobago

Panama

Venezuela

Br. Guiana

Colombia

Dutch &

French

GILBERT IS. (Br.)

Christmas I. (Br.)

GALAPAGOS IS.
(Ecuador)

Ecuador

Equator

BISMARCK ARCH. (Ger.)

United Stat
of Brazil

SOLOMON IS. (Br.& Ger.)

Peru

S O U T H

A M E R I C A

FIJI IS. (Br.)

Bolivia

Australia

New
Caledonia (Fr.)

TONGA IS. (Br.)

Paraguay

South Pacific Ocean

Tahiti (Fr.)

Chile

Argentina

Sydney

Santiago

Uruguay

Buenos Aires

New
Zealand

South Pacific Ocean

FALKLAND IS.
(Br.)

South Atl

S.

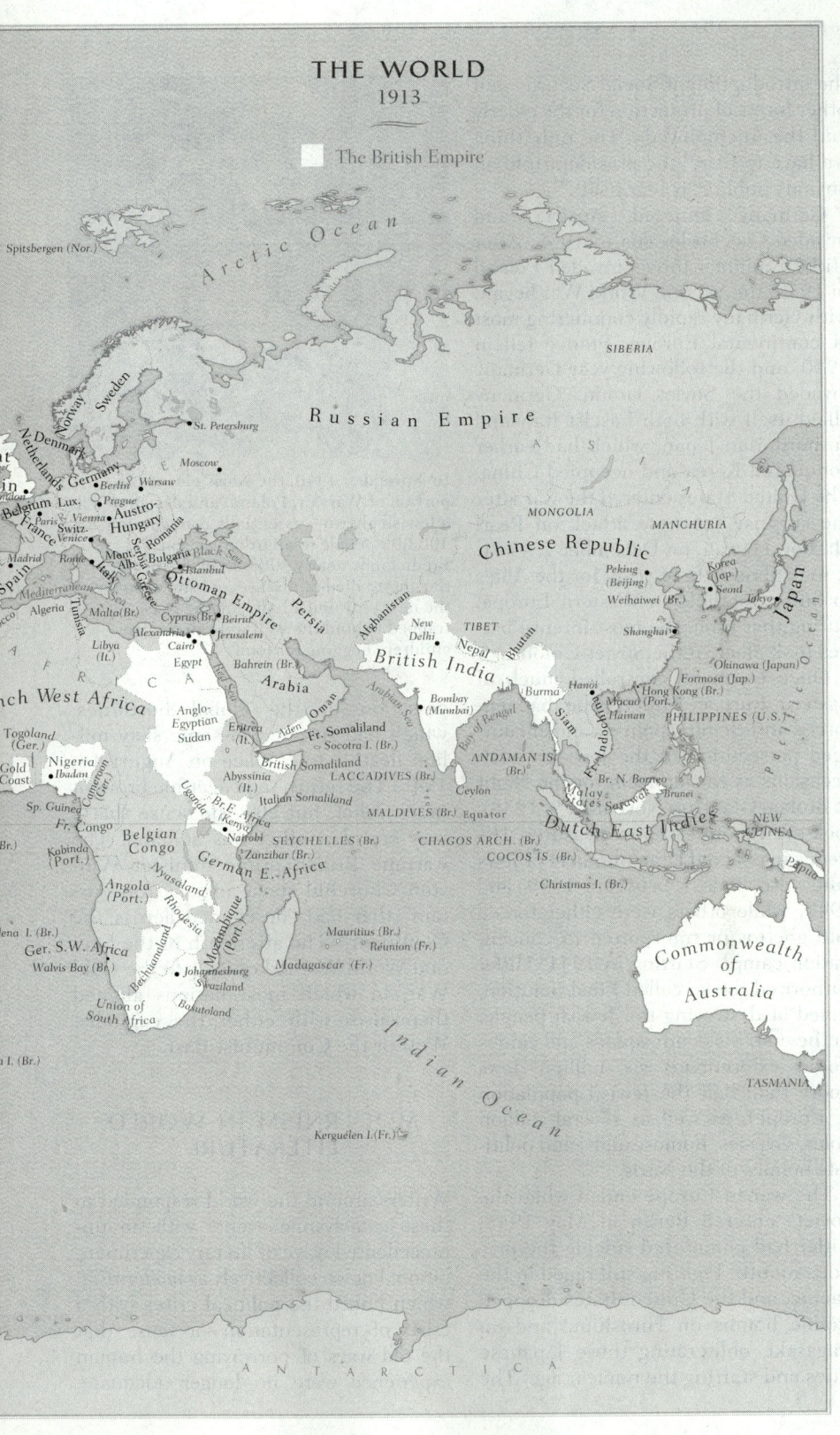

THE WORLD
1913

◻ The British Empire

Spitsbergen (Nor.)

Arctic Ocean

SIBERIA

Russian Empire

St. Petersburg

Moscow

Sweden

Norway

Denmark

Netherlands

Germany

Belgium Lux.

Berlin

Warsaw

Prague

Paris

Vienna

Austro-Hungary

France

Switz.

Venice

Romania

Madrid

Rome

Italy

Alb.

Bulgaria

Mont.

Greece

Istanbul

Black Sea

Spain

Mediterranean Sea

Madrid

Algeria

Tunisia

Malta (Br.)

Cyprus (Br.)

Beirut

Jerusalem

Ottoman Empire

Persia

Afghanistan

MONGOLIA

MANCHURIA

Chinese Republic

Peking (Beijing)

Weihaiwei (Br.)

Shanghai

Korea (Jap.)

Seoul

Tokyo

Japan

New Delhi

TIBET

Nepal

Bhutan

British India

Mal.

Burma

Hanoi

Okinawa (Japan)

Formosa (Jap.)

Macao (Port.)

Hong Kong (Br.)

Hainan

PHILIPPINES (U.S.)

Libya (It.)

Egypt

Cairo

Arabia

Bahrein (Br.)

Oman

Aden

Arabian Sea

Bombay (Mumbai)

Bay of Bengal

Siam

French Indo-China

Pacific Ocean

French West Africa

Togoland (Ger.)

Gold Coast

Nigeria

Ibadan

Cameroon (Ger.)

Sp. Guinea

Fr. Congo

Kabinda (Port.)

Belgian Congo

Angola (Port.)

Ger. S.W. Africa

Walvis Bay (Br.)

Anglo-Egyptian Sudan

Uganda

Br. E. Africa (Kenya)

Nairobi

Zanzibar (Br.)

German E. Africa

Nyasaland

Rhodesia

Mozambique (Port.)

Bechuanaland

Johannesburg

Swaziland

Basutoland

Union of South Africa

Eritrea (It.)

Fr. Somaliland

British Somaliland

Abyssinia

Italian Somaliland

Socotra I. (Br.)

LACCADIVES (Br.)

Ceylon

MALDIVES (Br.)

Equator

ANDAMAN IS. (Br.)

Malay States

Br. N. Borneo

Sarawak

Brunei

Dutch East Indies

NEW GUINEA

Papua

SEYCHELLES (Br.)

CHAGOS ARCH. (Br.)

COCOS IS. (Br.)

Christmas I. (Br.)

Mauritius (Br.)

Réunion (Fr.)

Madagascar (Fr.)

Indian Ocean

Commonwealth of Australia

TASMANIA

ena I. (Br.)

a I. (Br.)

Kerguélen I. (Fr.)

ANTARCTICA

the introduction of Social Security and other forms of protection for the elderly and the unemployed. "The only thing we have to fear," the president told an anxious public, "is fear itself."

Germany annexed Austria and invaded Czechoslovakia in 1938. After Hitler's military forces invaded Poland in 1939, the Second World War began, with Germany rapidly conquering most of continental Europe. France fell in 1940, and the following year Germany invaded the Soviet Union. Germany allied itself with both Fascist Italy and authoritarian Japan, which had earlier conquered Korea and occupied China. The United States entered the war after the surprise Japanese attack on Pearl Harbor, Hawaii, on December 7, 1941. It took almost three years for the Allies to find a foothold in Western Europe; during that time, the most intense battles took place in the Soviet Union.

In November 1940, the Nazis closed off a portion of Warsaw, Poland, and designated it a Jewish ghetto—essentially condemning 400,000 people to an urban prison. Predictably, nearly 100,000 of the people in the ghetto died of disease and starvation over the next year and a half. Among those trapped behind the wall were these two children, begging for food.

Once Germany controlled much of Eastern Europe, Hitler, who had enforced anti-Semitic policies and encouraged persecution of the Jews on such occasions as *Kristallnacht,* or the Night of Broken Glass (on November 9, 1938), took even more extreme measures. His troops massacred large numbers of Jews (and also Poles) between 1939 and 1941, while others were either forced into ghettos or transported to concentration camps. Starting in 1941, Hitler authorized the so-called Final Solution, aimed at destroying the Jewish people. In the end, his death squads and camps would exterminate six million Jews (more than half the Jewish population of Europe), as well as several million Poles, Gypsies, homosexuals, and political enemies of the Nazis.

The war in Europe ended when the Soviets entered Berlin in May 1945; Hitler had committed suicide the previous month. Fighting still raged in the Pacific, and the United States dropped atomic bombs on Hiroshima and on Nagasaki, obliterating those Japanese cities and starting the nuclear age. The cessation of the global hostilities, which had resulted in some sixty million deaths, took place on August 14, 1945. The return to peacetime brought much relief, but also the sense that a new era of conflict was at hand. The wartime British prime minister Winston Churchill spoke of an "iron curtain" that had "descended across the Continent." The aftermath of the Second World War led quickly to the Cold War, in which most nations aligned themselves with either the capitalist West or the Communist East.

MODERNISM IN WORLD LITERATURE

Writers around the world responded to these cataclysmic events with an unprecedented wave of literary experimentation, known collectively as *modernism,* which linked the political crises with a crisis of representation—a sense that the old ways of portraying the human experience were no longer adequate.

The modernists therefore broke away from such conventions as standard plots, verse forms, narrative techniques, and the boundaries of genre. They often grouped themselves in avant-garde movements with names like futurism, Dadaism, and surrealism, seeing their literary experiments in the context of a broader search for a type of society to replace the broken prewar consensus.

The modernist crisis of representation also reflected a broader "crisis of reason" that had begun in Europe in the late nineteenth century, as radical thinkers challenged the ability of human reason to understand the world. In the wake of Charles Darwin's discovery of the process of natural selection, human beings could no longer be so easily distinguished from the other animals; the animal nature of human existence was a crucial concept to three thinkers from the nineteenth century who wielded significant influence in the twentieth. Karl Marx saw the struggle between social classes for control of the means of economic production as the motor force of history; his thought inspired the Communist revolutions in Russia and China during the twentieth century and also the more moderate Socialist and Communist Parties of Western Europe. Friedrich Nietzsche attacked both a belief in God and the conviction that humans are fundamentally rational. His emphasis on the variety of perspectives from which we shape our notions of truth would have a substantial affect on both modernists and post-modernists. Sigmund Freud published the first major work of psychoanalysis, *The Interpretation of Dreams*, in 1900. His exploration of the unconscious, the power of sexual and destructive instincts, the shaping force of early childhood, and the Oedipal conflict between fathers and sons led many writers to reimagine the wellsprings of family interactions. More specifically, Freud's stress on the hidden, or "latent," meanings contained in dreams, jokes, and slips of the tongue lent itself to creative wordplay.

While philosophers and psychologists were examining the dynamics of the human mind, scientists found that the natural world does not necessarily function in the way it appears to. The most famous of the scientific discoveries of the early twentieth century was Albert Einstein's theory of relativity (Special Theory, 1905; General Theory, 1915). Other discoveries around the turn of the century, such as radioactivity, X-rays, and quantum theory, presented counterintuitive understandings of the physical universe that conflicted with classical Newtonian physics and even with common sense.

Modernism began in Europe and can be traced both to these new currents of thought and to the experimental literature of the late nineteenth century, including the symbolist poets and the realist novelists. Like such symbolists as **Charles Baudelaire** and **Stéphane Mallarmé**, the modernist poets held a high conception of the power and significance of poetry. In their works, they often drew on symbolist techniques, such as ambiguous and esoteric meanings. **T. S. Eliot's *The Waste Land*** (1922) responded to the prevalent sense of devastation after the First World War and was seen at the

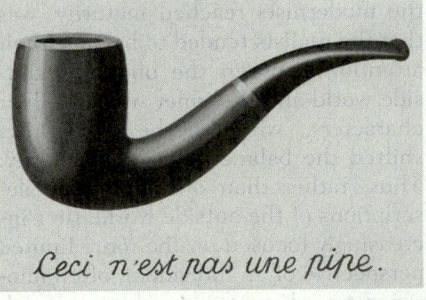

Ceci n'est pas une pipe.

The title of this work by the Belgian painter René Magritte (1898–1967), *La Trahison des Images* (1929), translates as *The Treason of Images*. "Ceci n'est pas une pipe" means "This is not a pipe."

Although Pablo Picasso's *Guernica* (1937) memorializes a historical event—the bombing of Guernica, in the Basque region of Spain, in April 1937, during the Spanish Civil War—the painting stresses the psychological horror, rather than the physical appearance, of the event.

time as the high-water mark of modernism in the English language.

Modernist fiction followed the realists, especially **Gustave Flaubert**, in attempting to portray life "as it is" by using precise language. Modernists found, however, that in depicting characters, settings, and events with directness and without sentiment, they discovered mysteries that lay beyond language. The great modern novelists, including Conrad, **Marcel Proust**, Thomas Mann, **James Joyce**, and **Virginia Woolf**, all started out by writing realistic works in the manner of Flaubert or **Leo Tolstoy**. The great difference, which became more apparent as the modernists reached maturity, was that the realists tended to balance their attention between the objective, outside world and the inner world of their characters, whereas the modernists shifted the balance toward interiority. Thus, rather than offer objective descriptions of the outside world, they increasingly focused on the more limited perspective of an individual, often idiosyncratic, character. In this approach they were following the lead of another great nineteenth-century precursor, **Fyodor Dostoyevsky**.

It would be too simple to say that the modernists did away with the omniscient narrator. They might retain a narrator who seemed to be observing the characters and events with an objective, all-knowing eye, but the authors counterbalanced such narrators with storytellers like Conrad's Marlow or Proust's Marcel, who were themselves characters in the stories they related and whose reliability might therefore be in doubt. Joyce's story "**The Dead**," with its narrator who sees into the mind of the protagonist Gabriel Conroy, could easily belong to the nineteenth century, but Joyce later pioneered the move toward a deeper interiority in two novels, *A Portrait of the Artist as a Young Man* (1916) and *Ulysses* (1922)—the latter is, in fact, the most famous and influential of all modernist novels. The new method, called "the stream of consciousness," was well described by another of its great practitioners, Woolf, when she wrote: "Let us record the atoms as they fall upon the mind in the order in which they fall, let us trace the pattern, however disconnected and incoherent in appearance, which each sight or incident scores upon the consciousness."

Bertolt Brecht and Kurt Weill's *The Threepenny Opera*, staged at the Kammer (Chamber) Theater, Moscow, in 1930.

A similar, possibly even farther-reaching transformation took place in the theater. Just as novelists questioned the role of an omniscient narrator, dramatists challenged the separation of the audience from the action of the play—specifically, the tradition of the "fourth wall." According to this concept, developed in realist and naturalist theater of the nineteenth century, the actors on stage went about their business as if they did not know that an audience was watching them. In different ways, the major modernist playwrights, represented in this section by **Luigi Pirandello** and Bertolt Brecht, broke down the fourth wall. Pirandello introduced a playful "metatheater," calling attention to the fictionality of his works by having his characters debate the nature of drama. In Brecht's Epic Theater, audience members were encouraged not to identify with the characters and be carried away by the drama but to think critically about the actions they were witnessing. The German writer's notion of an "estrangement effect" that would shock audiences out of their complacency was linked closely to broader modernist theories in which the task of art was to break through our habitual assumptions to make the world appear strange and new.

Many of these modernist experiments took place on the level of form; but modernism also entailed a change in the content of literature, specifically in the inclusion of previously taboo subject matter (especially sexuality), as well as greater attention to shifting social roles (often relating to the impact of feminism). Woolf was famous both as a novelist and as an essayist on feminist issues. Her work *A Room of One's Own* makes the case for women's writing and, more broadly, for women's admission into traditionally male professions and institutions of learning, which were gradually becoming more open to women during the first decades of the century. Feminism had won a major victory with the achievement of women's suffrage in 1918 in Britain; the United States would guarantee all women the vote in 1920. Conrad's novel *Heart of Darkness* criticizes the actions of European imperialists in Africa, although he seems to make

an exception for the British Empire. Joyce addresses the political situation of Ireland in the midst of its quest for independence from Britain. **Franz Kafka's** work has been seen as a commentary on the status of the Jews in a hostile world. Mann addresses homosexuality, which was becoming socially acceptable even though it remained illegal in many countries. **William Faulkner** documents the decline of an aristocratic South and the persistence of racial tensions. Even the seemingly most intimate of works, Proust's *Swann's Way*, documents the social changes that France was undergoing in the late nineteenth century. (In subsequent volumes of his masterpiece, *Remembrance of Things Past*, Proust also treats both anti-Semitism and homosexuality at length.) In their later works, Mann and Proust were conscious of reconstructing the bygone Europe of the years before the First World War.

Modernist experimentation persisted in various forms throughout the century. Somewhat younger than the European novelists represented here, **Jorge Luis Borges** wrote short pieces that present alternative universes; in "**The Garden of the Forking Paths**," the fictional universe he creates starts out as a commentary on a work of history. Whereas Pirandello's play with theatricality came to be known as "metatheater," Borges's games with the border between fact and fiction have been called "metafiction" or even "metahistory." Borges is also representative of the mobility of writers in the twentieth century: educated mostly in Europe, he returned home to Argentina and formed a bridge between European modernism and the significant expansion of Latin American fiction in the second half of the century.

In other parts of the world, nationalist movements against colonization were gathering force and would result in a wave of independence after the Second World War. The African American writer and activist W. E. B. Du Bois had said early in the century that "the problem of the Twentieth Century is the problem of the color line." Literature played a major role both in the articulation of this challenge and in the attempts to solve it. During the 1920s, when, in the words of Langston Hughes, "Harlem was in vogue," a group of African American intellectuals and writers enjoyed unprecedented success in what came to be known as the Harlem Renaissance. During the 1930s, a group of African and Caribbean intellectuals, led by **Léopold Sédar Senghor** and **Aimé Césaire**, met in Paris, where they had come to pursue higher education, and formed the Négritude movement. It would celebrate the culture of Africa and the African diaspora and provide intellectual support and political leadership for decolonization movements after the war.

These developments pointed the way to a postwar and postcolonial literature that often rejected the formal experiments of the modernist generation and sought a more direct engagement with the pressing political issues of the day, such as decolonization, civil rights, and economic empowerment. The Holocaust also presented a distinct challenge to writers who sought to record the unspeakable: some took a straightforward, documentary style, while others turned to a minimalist, almost mystical language. While Europe, after 1945, set about rebuilding the cities destroyed in the war, much of the rest of the world entered a period of decolonization, establishing nation-states on the basis of the principles (democracy, equality) that the Allies had defended during the war and that they now had to acknowledge as the basis for their colonies' self-determination. The postwar world would inspire both avant-garde literary movements and a return to more traditional forms, but the literature of the twentieth century had been decisively marked by the experiments of the modernists, who created a diverse, remarkable range of masterpieces during a period of continual social crisis.

JOSEPH CONRAD

1857–1924

Born in Polish Ukraine, learning English at twenty-one, and then serving as a sailor for sixteen years, Joseph Conrad nonetheless became a prolific, innovative writer of English fiction. Works like *Heart of Darkness* and *Lord Jim* have influenced novelists throughout the twentieth century, because of Conrad's ability to evoke the feel and color of distant places as well as the complexity of human responses to moral crisis. Conrad's sense of separation and exile, his yearning for the kinship and solidarity of humanity, permeates these works, along with the despairing vision of a universe in which even the most ardent idealist finds no ultimate meaning or moral value.

He was born Jozef Teodor Konrad Korzeniowski on December 3, 1857, the only child of Polish patriots who were involved in resistance to Russian rule. (He changed his name to the more English-sounding Conrad for the publication of his first novel, in 1895.) Their country had been partitioned through most of the nineteenth century among Russia, Prussia, and Austria. The town where Conrad was born, now part of Ukraine, had traditionally been ruled by the Polish aristocracy, and Conrad's family bore a coat of arms. When his father was condemned for conspiracy in 1862, the family went into exile in northern Russia, where Conrad's mother died three years later from tuberculosis. Conrad's father, a poet and a translator, supported the small family by translating Shakespeare and Victor Hugo; Conrad himself read English novels by William Makepeace Thackeray, Walter Scott, and Charles Dickens in Polish and in French translation. When his father,

too, succumbed to tuberculosis in 1869, the eleven-year-old orphan went to live with his maternal uncle, Tadeusz Bobrowski, who sent him to school in Cracow (in Austrian-ruled Poland) and Switzerland. Bobrowski supported his orphaned nephew both financially and emotionally, and, when Conrad asked to fulfill a long-standing dream of going to sea, he gave him an annual allowance (which Conrad consistently overspent) and helped him find a berth in the merchant marine. The decision to go to sea reflected the gallant and romantic aspirations of a child who had often been frail and sickly; it also marked a permanent departure from the nation that his parents had fought and, as Conrad saw it, died for.

During the next few years, he worked on French ships, traveling to the West Indies and participating in various activities—some of which, such as smuggling, were probably illegal—that would play a role in his novels of the sea. He also lost money at the casino in Monte Carlo, may have had an unhappy romance, and attempted suicide. Many events of these years are known only through the fictionalized versions Conrad used in short stories written years later. After signing onto a British ship in 1878 to avoid conscription by the French or the Russians (he had just turned twenty-one), Conrad visited England for the first time, speaking the language only haltingly. He served for sixteen years on British merchant ships, earning his Master's Certificate in 1886 (the same year that he became a British subject) and learning English fast and well. During this period, he made trips to the Far East and India that would provide

material for his fiction throughout his writing career, including major works like *The Nigger of the "Narcissus"* (1897) and *Typhoon* (1903). When he married in 1896, he turned his back on the sea as a profession and, buoyed by the publication of his first novel, *Almayer's Folly* (1895), chose writing as his new career. His early novels, including *An Outcast of the Islands* (1896), established his initial literary reputation as an exotic storyteller and novelist of adventure at sea.

Among the many voyages that furnished material for his fiction, one stands out as the most emotional and intense: the trip up the Congo River that Conrad made in 1890, straight into the heart of King Leopold II's privately owned Congo Free State. Like many nineteenth-century explorers, Conrad was fascinated by the mystery of this "dark" (because uncharted by Europeans) continent, and he persuaded a relative to find him a job as pilot on a Belgian merchant steamer. The steamer that Conrad was supposed to pilot had been damaged, and while he waited for a replacement, his supervisors shifted him to another where he could help out and learn about the river. The boat traveled upstream to collect a seriously ill trader, Georges Antoine Klein (who died on the return trip), and Conrad, after speaking with Klein and observing the inhuman conditions imposed by slave labor and the ruthless search for ivory, returned seriously ill and traumatized by his journey. The experience marked Conrad both physically and mentally. After a few years, he began to write about it with a moral rage that emerged openly at first and subsequently in more complex, ironic form. *An Outpost of Progress*, a harshly satirical story of two murderous incompetents in a jungle trading post, was published in 1897, and Conrad wrote *Heart of Darkness* two years later; it appeared in *Blackwood's Magazine* in 1899 and in the volume *"Youth" and Other Stories* in 1902.

Along with *Lord Jim* (1900) and *Nostromo* (1904), this volume established him as one of the leading novelists of the day. He became friendly with other writers such as Henry James, Stephen Crane, H. G. Wells, John Galsworthy, and Ford Madox Ford. Yet he preferred a quiet life in the country to the attractions of literary London. From 1898 he lived on Pent Farm in Kent, near James, Wells, and Crane. He found writing difficult, often suffering from insomnia and physical ailments while trying to complete a novel (one biographer remarks that each of his later novels "cost him a tooth"). His novels from this period, *The Secret Agent* (1907) and *Under Western Eyes* (1911), revolve around political conflicts, but Conrad usually refrained from taking sides in politics—his interest lay in the effect that espionage and intrigue have on individual character. He hated autocratic rule but opposed revolution and was skeptical of social reform movements. His two abiding political commitments were to his adoptive homeland, England, and to the cause of Polish independence; he traveled to Poland on the eve of the First World War, returning with difficulty to England once war broke out. Although he had struggled financially throughout his writing life, Conrad had his first popular success with *Chance* (1913), which is now less highly regarded than his other works. His later works returned, typically with a more optimistic tone, to the Eastern settings with which he began. They have not received much appreciation from critics, although *The Shadow Line* (1917) recaptures some of the earlier works' appreciation of the moment of crisis in a youthful life.

HEART OF DARKNESS

Although the subject matter of *Heart of Darkness* is clearly one of the reasons for its continued influence, equally

important is Conrad's introduction of many literary techniques that would be central to modern fiction. In the preface to *The Nigger of the "Narcissus,"* Conrad describes the task of the writer as "before all, to make you *see*," and his works stress the visual perception of reality. His technique of registering the way that a scene appears to an individual before explaining the scene's contents has been described as "delayed decoding"; it is an element of his literary impressionism, his emphasis on how the mind processes the information that the senses provide. In *Heart of Darkness*, Conrad records first the impressions that an event makes on Marlow and only later Marlow's arrival at an explanation of the event. The reader must continually decide when to accept Marlow's account as accurate and when to treat it as ironic and unreliable. Marlow describes his experiences in Africa from a position of experience, having contemplated the episode for many years, but the reader, like the narrator, may question some aspects of Marlow's story as self-justification. Conrad also uses symbolism in a distinctly modern way. As he later wrote, "a work of art is very seldom limited to one exclusive meaning and not necessarily tending to a definite conclusion. And this for the reason that the nearer it approaches art, the more it acquires a symbolic character." Frequently, Marlow's story seems to carry symbolic overtones that are not easily extracted from the story as a simple kernel of wisdom. This symbolic character has its exemplar in the primary narrator's comment that "the yarns of seamen have a direct simplicity, the whole meaning of which lies within the shell of a cracked nut. . . . [But to Marlow,] the meaning of an episode was not inside like a kernel but outside, enveloping the tale which brought it out only as a glow brings out a haze." *Heart of Darkness* does not reveal its meaning in digestible morsels, like the kernel of a

nut. Rather, its meanings evade the interpreter; they are larger than the story itself. The story's hazy atmosphere, rich symbolic suggestiveness, and complex narrative structure have all appealed to later readers and writers. Although it was published at the end of the nineteenth century, *Heart of Darkness* became one of the most influential works of the twentieth century. It greatly influenced Nobel Prize winners **T. S. Eliot, William Faulkner, Gabriel García Márquez,** and **J. M. Coetzee.** In the second half of the century, the novella was seen as so relevant to the aftermath of imperialism that the filmmaker Francis Ford Coppola used it as the basis of his film about the Vietnam War, *Apocalypse Now*.

The "darkness" of the title exemplifies this symbolism. Although it is both a conventional metaphor for obscurity and evil and a cliché referring to Africa and the "unenlightened" state of its indigenous population, the story leaves it unclear where the heart of darkness is located: in the "uncivilized" jungle or in the hearts of the European imperialists. Leopold II of Belgium, who owned the trading company that effectively was the Congo Free State, gained a free hand in the area after calling an international conference in 1876 "to open to civilization the only part of our globe where Christianity has not penetrated and to pierce the darkness which envelops the entire population." Leopold had pledged to end the slave trade in central Africa, but his rule continued slavery under another guise, extracting forced labor for infrastructure projects, such as road building, that were poorly managed. Throughout the novella, Conrad plays on images of darkness and savagery and complicates any simple opposition by associating moral darkness—the evil that lurks within humans and underlies their predatory idealism—with a white exterior, beginning with the town (Brussels) that

serves as the Belgian firm's headquarters and that Marlow describes as a "whited sepulchre."

Still, it is not surprising that later critics and writers, most notably the Nigerian novelist and essayist **Chinua Achebe**, would criticize *Heart of Darkness* for its racist portrayal of Africans. Marlow's words and behavior—indeed, the selectivity of his narrative—can be as distant and cruelly patronizing as those of any European colonialist. Yet he also recognizes his "kinship" with the Africans and often sees them as morally superior to the Europeans; Marlow's quiet critique of imperialism has inspired many postcolonial writers. For the most part, however, the Africans in his story constitute the background for the strange figure of Kurtz, the charismatic, once idealistic, now totally corrupt trader who becomes the destination of Marlow's journey. Marlow's strange bond with this maddened soul stems initially from a desire to see a man whom others have described to him as a universal genius—an "emissary of pity, and science, and progress" and part of the "gang of virtue." In time, though, it becomes a horrified fascination with someone who has explored moral extremes to their furthest end. Kurtz's famous judgment on what he has lived and seen—"The horror! The horror!"—speaks at once to personal despair, to the political realities of imperialism, and to a broader sense of the human condition.

Heart of Darkness

1

The *Nellie*, a cruising yawl,[1] swung to her anchor without a flutter of the sails, and was at rest. The flood had made, the wind was nearly calm, and being bound down the river, the only thing for it was to come to[2] and wait for the turn of the tide.

The sea-reach of the Thames stretched before us like the beginning of an interminable waterway. In the offing[3] the sea and the sky were welded together without a joint, and in the luminous space the tanned sails of the barges drifting up with the tide seemed to stand still in red clusters of canvas sharply peaked, with gleams of varnished sprits. A haze rested on the low shores that ran out to sea in vanishing flatness. The air was dark above Gravesend,[4] and farther back still seemed condensed into a mournful gloom, brooding motionless over the biggest, and the greatest, town on earth.

The Director of Companies was our captain and our host. We four affectionately watched his back as he stood in the bows looking to seaward. On the whole river there was nothing that looked half so nautical. He resembled a pilot, which to a seaman is trustworthiness personified. It was difficult to realise his work was not out there in the luminous estuary, but behind him, within the brooding gloom.

1. A two-masted boat.
2. To come to a standstill in a fixed position.
3. The part of the sea distant but visible from the shore.
4. A port on the Thames River, and the last major town in the estuary.

Between us there was, as I have already said somewhere, the bond of the sea.[5] Besides holding our hearts together through long periods of separation, it had the effect of making us tolerant of each other's yarns—and even convictions. The Lawyer—the best of old fellows—had, because of his many years and many virtues, the only cushion on deck, and was lying on the only rug. The Accountant had brought out already a box of dominoes, and was toying architecturally with the bones. Marlow sat cross-legged right aft, leaning against the mizzenmast.[6] He had sunken cheeks, a yellow complexion, a straight back, an ascetic aspect, and, with his arms dropped, the palms of hands outwards, resembled an idol. The Director, satisfied the anchor had good hold, made his way aft and sat down amongst us. We exchanged a few words lazily. Afterwards there was silence on board the yacht. For some reason or other we did not begin that game of dominoes. We felt meditative, and fit for nothing but placid staring. The day was ending in a serenity of still and exquisite brilliance. The water shone pacifically; the sky, without a speck, was a benign immensity of unstained light; the very mist on the Essex marshes was like a gauzy and radiant fabric, hung from the wooded rises inland, and draping the low shores in diaphanous folds. Only the gloom to the west, brooding over the upper reaches, became more sombre every minute, as if angered by the approach of the sun.

And at last, in its curved and imperceptible fall, the sun sank low, and from glowing white changed to a dull red without rays and without heat, as if about to go out suddenly, stricken to death by the touch of that gloom brooding over a crowd of men.

Forthwith a change came over the waters, and the serenity became less brilliant but more profound. The old river in its broad reach rested unruffled at the decline of day, after ages of good service done to the race that peopled its banks, spread out in the tranquil dignity of a waterway leading to the uttermost ends of the earth. We looked at the venerable stream not in the vivid flush of a short day that comes and departs for ever, but in the august light of abiding memories. And indeed nothing is easier for a man who has, as the phrase goes, "followed the sea" with reverence and affection, than to evoke the great spirit of the past upon the lower reaches of the Thames. The tidal current runs to and fro in its unceasing service, crowded with memories of men and ships it has borne to the rest of home or to the battles of the sea. It had known and served all the men of whom the nation is proud, from Sir Francis Drake to Sir John Franklin, knights all, titled and untitled—the great knights-errant of the sea. It had borne all the ships whose names are like jewels flashing in the night of time, from the *Golden Hind* returning with her round flanks full of treasure, to be visited by the Queen's Highness and thus pass out of the gigantic tale, to the *Erebus* and *Terror*,[7] bound on other conquests—and that never returned. It had known the ships and the men. They had sailed from Deptford, from

---

5. "The bond of the sea" appears in "Youth," Conrad's first story to feature Marlow. "Youth" and *Heart of Darkness* were first published in book form as part of the same volume, with "Youth" immediately preceding *Heart of Darkness*.
6. The mast aft (to the rear) of the mainmast on any ship with two or more masts.

7. The *Erebus* and the *Terror* were ships commanded by Arctic explorer Sir John Franklin (1786–1847) and lost in an attempt to find a passage from the Atlantic Ocean to the Pacific. *Golden Hind*: the ship in which Elizabethan explorer Sir Francis Drake (1540–1596) sailed around the world.

Greenwich, from Erith—the adventurers and the settlers; kings' ships and the ships of men on 'Change; captains, admirals, the dark "interlopers"[8] of the Eastern trade, and the commissioned "generals" of East India fleets. Hunters for gold or pursuers of fame, they all had gone out on that stream, bearing the sword, and often the torch, messengers of the might within the land, bearers of a spark from the sacred fire.[9] What greatness had not floated on the ebb of that river into the mystery of an unknown earth! . . . The dreams of men, the seed of commonwealths, the germs of empires.

The sun set; the dusk fell on the stream, and lights began to appear along the shore. The Chapman lighthouse, a three-legged thing erect on a mudflat, shone strongly. Lights of ships moved in the fairway[1]—a great stir of lights going up and going down. And farther west on the upper reaches the place of the monstrous town[2] was still marked ominously on the sky, a brooding gloom in sunshine, a lurid glare under the stars.

"And this also," said Marlow suddenly, "has been one of the dark places of the earth."

He was the only man of us who still "followed the sea." The worst that could be said of him was that he did not represent his class. He was a seaman, but he was a wanderer too, while most seamen lead, if one may so express it, a sedentary life. Their minds are of the stay-at-home order, and their home is always with them—the ship; and so is their country—the sea. One ship is very much like another, and the sea is always the same. In the immutability of their surroundings the foreign shores, the foreign faces, the changing immensity of life, glide past, veiled not by a sense of mystery but by a slightly disdainful ignorance; for there is nothing mysterious to a seaman unless it be the sea itself, which is the mistress of his existence and as inscrutable as Destiny. For the rest, after his hours of work, a casual stroll or a casual spree on shore suffices to unfold for him the secret of a whole continent, and generally he finds the secret not worth knowing. The yarns of seamen have a direct simplicity, the whole meaning of which lies within the shell of a cracked nut. But Marlow was not typical (if his propensity to spin yarns be excepted), and to him the meaning of an episode was not inside like a kernel but outside, enveloping the tale which brought it out only as a glow brings out a haze, in the likeness of one of these misty halos that sometimes are made visible by the spectral illumination of moonshine.

His remark did not seem at all surprising. It was just like Marlow. It was accepted in silence. No one took the trouble to grunt even; and presently he said, very slow:

"I was thinking of very old times, when the Romans first came here, nineteen hundred years ago[3]—the other day. . . . Light came out of this river since—you

---

8. Private ships intruding on the East India Company's legal trade monopoly. "Deptford, Greenwich, Erith": ports on the Thames between London and Gravesend. "'Change": the stock exchange.
9. An allusion to the myth of Prometheus, who stole fire from the gods to give to humankind; by extension, refers to civilization, human ingenuity, and adventurousness.

1. A navigable passage in a river between rocks or sandbanks; the usual route into or out of a port.
2. I.e., London.
3. Romans first invaded England under Julius Caesar, in 55 and 54 B.C.E. These attempts were unsuccessful; in 43 C.E. a lengthy and effective conquest began.

say Knights? Yes; but it is like a running blaze on a plain, like a flash of lightning in the clouds. We live in the flicker—may it last as long as the old earth
keeps rolling! But darkness was here yesterday. Imagine the feelings of a commander of a fine—what d'ye call 'em?—trireme[4] in the Mediterranean, ordered
suddenly to the north; run overland across the Gauls[5] in a hurry; put in charge
of one of these craft the legionaries[6]—a wonderful lot of handy men they must
have been too—used to build, apparently by the hundred, in a month or two, if
we may believe what we read. Imagine him here—the very end of the world, a
sea the colour of lead, a sky the colour of smoke, a kind of ship about as rigid
as a concertina[7]—and going up this river with stores, or orders, or what you
like. Sandbanks, marshes, forests, savages—precious little to eat fit for a civi-
lised man, nothing but Thames water to drink. No Falernian wine[8] here, no
going ashore. Here and there a military camp lost in a wilderness, like a needle
in a bundle of hay—cold, fog, tempests, disease, exile, and death—death skulk-
ing in the air, in the water, in the bush. They must have been dying like flies
here. Oh yes—he did it. Did it very well, too, no doubt, and without thinking
much about it either, except afterwards to brag of what he had gone through in
his time, perhaps. They were men enough to face the darkness. And perhaps
he was cheered by keeping his eye on a chance of promotion to the fleet at
Ravenna[9] by and by, if he had good friends in Rome and survived the awful
climate. Or think of a decent young citizen in a toga—perhaps too much dice,
you know—coming out here in the train of some prefect, or tax-gatherer, or
trader, even, to mend his fortunes. Land in a swamp, march through the
woods, and in some inland post feel the savagery, the utter savagery, had
closed round him—all that mysterious life of the wilderness that stirs in the
forest, in the jungles, in the hearts of wild men. There's no initiation either
into such mysteries. He has to live in the midst of the incomprehensible, which
is also detestable. And it has a fascination, too, that goes to work upon him.
The fascination of the abomination—you know. Imagine the growing regrets,
the longing to escape, the powerless disgust, the surrender, the hate."

He paused.

"Mind," he began again, lifting one arm from the elbow, the palm of the
hand outwards, so that, with his legs folded before him, he had the pose of a
Buddha preaching in European clothes and without a lotus-flower[1]—"Mind,
none of us would feel exactly like this. What saves us is efficiency—the devotion to efficiency. But these chaps were not much account, really. They were
no colonists; their administration was merely a squeeze, and nothing more, I
suspect. They were conquerors, and for that you want only brute force—
nothing to boast of, when you have it, since your strength is just an accident
arising from the weakness of others. They grabbed what they could get for the
sake of what was to be got. It was just robbery with violence, aggravated murder

4. A Roman galley with three banks of oars.
5. Name used by the Romans to refer to the
three regions of what is now France.
6. The members of a legion, a unit of Roman
infantrymen.
7. An instrument resembling an accordion,
with a bellows and buttons on either end:
hence, not rigid at all.

8. Wine from a famous wine-making district
in southern Italy.
9. Once a major Roman port on the Adriatic
Sea.
1. Siddhartha Gautama, founder of Buddhism, is traditionally portrayed seated cross-
legged on a lotus flower.

on a great scale, and men going at it blind—as is very proper for those who tackle a darkness. The conquest of the earth, which mostly means the taking it away from those who have a different complexion or slightly flatter noses than ourselves, is not a pretty thing when you look into it too much. What redeems it is the idea only. An idea at the back of it; not a sentimental pretence but an idea; and an unselfish belief in the idea—something you can set up, and bow down before, and offer a sacrifice to. . . ."

He broke off. Flames glided in the river, small green flames, red flames, white flames, pursuing, overtaking, joining, crossing each other—then separating slowly or hastily. The traffic of the great city went on in the deepening night upon the sleepless river. We looked on, waiting patiently—there was nothing else to do till the end of the flood; but it was only after a long silence, when he said, in a hesitating voice, "I suppose you fellows remember I did once turn fresh-water sailor for a bit," that we knew we were fated, before the ebb began to run,[2] to hear about one of Marlow's inconclusive experiences.

"I don't want to bother you much with what happened to me personally," he began, showing in this remark the weakness of many tellers of tales who seem so often unaware of what their audience would best like to hear; "yet to understand the effect of it on me you ought to know how I got out there, what I saw, how I went up that river to the place where I first met the poor chap. It was the farthest point of navigation and the culminating point of my experience. It seemed somehow to throw a kind of light on everything about me—and into my thoughts. It was sombre enough too—and pitiful—not extraordinary in any way—not very clear either. No, not very clear. And yet it seemed to throw a kind of light.

"I had then, as you remember, just returned to London after a lot of Indian Ocean, Pacific, China Seas—a regular dose of the East—six years or so, and I was loafing about, hindering you fellows in your work and invading your homes, just as though I had got a heavenly mission to civilise you. It was very fine for a time, but after a bit I did get tired of resting. Then I began to look for a ship—I should think the hardest work on earth. But the ships wouldn't even look at me. And I got tired of that game too.

"Now when I was a little chap I had a passion for maps. I would look for hours at South America, or Africa, or Australia, and lose myself in all the glories of exploration. At that time there were many blank spaces[3] on the earth, and when I saw one that looked particularly inviting on a map (but they all look that) I would put my finger on it and say, When I grow up I will go there. The North Pole was one of these places, I remember. Well, I haven't been there yet, and shall not try now. The glamour's off. Other places were scattered about the Equator, and in every sort of latitude all over the two hemispheres. I have been in some of them, and . . . well, we won't talk about that. But there was one yet—the biggest, the most blank, so to speak—that I had a hankering after.

"True, by this time it was not a blank space any more. It had got filled since my boyhood with rivers and lakes and names. It had ceased to be a blank space of delightful mystery—a white patch for a boy to dream gloriously over. It had become a place of darkness. But there was in it one river especially, a mighty

---

2. "Flood" and "ebb": the rise and fall of the tide in the river.

3. I.e., regions unexplored by Europeans at the time and hence left blank on European maps.

big river,[4] that you could see on the map, resembling an immense snake uncoiled, with its head in the sea, its body at rest curving afar over a vast country, and its tail lost in the depths of the land. And as I looked at the map of it in a shop-window, it fascinated me as a snake would a bird—a silly little bird. Then I remembered there was a big concern, a Company for trade on that river. Dash it all! I thought to myself, they can't trade without using some kind of craft on that lot of fresh water—steamboats![5] Why shouldn't I try to get charge of one? I went on along Fleet Street,[6] but could not shake off the idea. The snake had charmed me.

"You understand it was a Continental concern, that Trading Society;[7] but I have a lot of relations living on the Continent, because it's cheap and not so nasty as it looks, they say.

"I am sorry to own I began to worry them. This was already a fresh departure for me. I was not used to get things that way, you know. I always went my own road and on my own legs where I had a mind to go. I wouldn't have believed it of myself; but, then—you see—I felt somehow I must get there by hook or by crook. So I worried them. The men said, 'My dear fellow,' and did nothing. Then—would you believe it?—I tried the women. I, Charlie Marlow, set the women to work—to get a job. Heavens! Well, you see, the notion drove me. I had an aunt, a dear enthusiastic soul. She wrote: 'It will be delightful. I am ready to do anything, anything for you. It is a glorious idea. I know the wife of a very high personage in the Administration, and also a man who has lots of influence with,' etc. etc. She was determined to make no end of fuss to get me appointed skipper of a river steamboat, if such was my fancy.

"I got my appointment—of course; and I got it very quick. It appears the Company had received news that one of their captains had been killed in a scuffle with the natives. This was my chance, and it made me the more anxious to go. It was only months and months afterwards, when I made the attempt to recover what was left of the body, that I heard the original quarrel arose from a misunderstanding about some hens. Yes, two black hens. Fresleven—that was the fellow's name, a Dane—thought himself wronged somehow in the bargain, so he went ashore and started to hammer the chief of the village with a stick. Oh, it didn't surprise me in the least to hear this, and at the same time to be told that Fresleven was the gentlest, quietest creature that ever walked on two legs. No doubt he was; but he had been a couple of years already out there engaged in the noble cause, you know, and he probably felt the need at last of asserting his self-respect in some way. Therefore he whacked the old nigger mercilessly, while a big crowd of his people watched him, thunderstruck, till some man—I was told the chief's son—in desperation at hearing the old chap yell, made a tentative jab with a spear at the white man—and of course it went quite easy between the shoulder-blades. Then the whole population cleared into the forest, expecting all kinds of calamities to happen, while, on the other hand, the steamer Fresleven commanded left also in a bad panic, in charge of

4. The Congo River.
5. Flat-bottomed steamboats were essential for navigating the shallow waters of the Congo.
6. A major street in central London, famous as a publishing center.

7. The trading company—specifically, a Belgian company that operated ships on the Congo River in the protectorate of King Leopold II of Belgium.

the engineer, I believe. Afterwards nobody seemed to trouble much about Fresleven's remains, till I got out and stepped into his shoes. I couldn't let it rest, though; but when an opportunity offered at last to meet my predecessor, the grass growing through his ribs was tall enough to hide his bones. They were all there. The supernatural being had not been touched after he fell. And the village was deserted, the huts gaped black, rotting, all askew within the fallen enclosures. A calamity had come to it, sure enough. The people had vanished. Mad terror had scattered them, men, women, and children, through the bush, and they had never returned. What became of the hens I don't know either. I should think the cause of progress got them, anyhow. However, through this glorious affair I got my appontment, before I had fairly begun to hope for it.

"I flew around like mad to get ready, and before forty-eight hours I was cross-ing the Channel to show myself to my employers, and sign the contract. In a very few hours I arrived in a city that always makes me think of a whited sepul-chre.[8] Prejudice no doubt. I had no difficulty in finding the Company's offices. It was the biggest thing in the town, and everybody I met was full of it. They were going to run an overseas empire, and make no end of coin by trade.

"A narrow and deserted street in deep shadow, high houses, innumerable windows with venetian blinds, a dead silence, grass sprouting between the stones, imposing carriage archways right and left, immense double doors stand-ing ponderously ajar. I slipped through one of these cracks, went up a swept and ungarnished staircase, as arid as a desert, and opened the first door I came to. Two women, one fat and the other slim, sat on straw-bottomed chairs, knit-ting black wool.[9] The slim one got up and walked straight at me—still knitting with downcast eyes—and only just as I began to think of getting out of her way, as you would for a somnambulist, stood still, and looked up. Her dress was as plain as an umbrella-cover, and she turned round without a word and preceded me into a waiting-room. I gave my name, and looked about. Deal table in the middle, plain chairs all round the walls, on one end a large shining map, marked with all the colours of a rainbow. There was a vast amount of red—good to see at any time, because one knows that some real work is done in there, a deuce of a lot of blue, a little green, smears of orange, and, on the East Coast, a purple patch, to show where the jolly pioneers of progress drink the jolly lager-beer.[1] However, I wasn't going into any of these. I was going into the yellow. Dead in the centre. And the river was there—fascinating—deadly—like a snake. Ough! A door opened, a white-haired secretarial head, but wearing a compassionate expression, appeared, and a skinny forefinger beckoned me into

---

8. The city is based on Brussels. "Whited sep-ulchre": a biblical allusion, Matthew 23.27: "Woe unto you, scribes and Pharisees, hypo-crites! for ye are like unto whited sepulchres, which indeed appear beautiful outward, but are within full of dead men's bones, and of all uncleanness."

9. The knitters allude to at least two sources: in Charles Dickens's *Tale of Two Cities*, the villainous Madame Defarge knits the names of those she condemns to die. In Greek mythol-ogy, the Fates were usually three women spin-ning, measuring, and cutting the thread of life.

1. The map shows territories claimed by European nations in the aftermath of the Ber-lin Conference of 1884–85: red is England, Conrad's adopted nation; blue territories belonged to France; and purple, Germany. Although color schemes varied, in the map Marlow is looking at, orange presumably refers to Portugal and green to Italy, which also had holdings in Africa. Yellow stands for the Congo Free State, controlled by King Leopold II.

the sanctuary. Its light was dim, and a heavy writing desk squatted in the middle. From behind that structure came out an impression of pale plumpness in a frockcoat. The great man himself. He was five feet six, I should judge, and had his grip on the handle-end of ever so many millions. He shook hands, I fancy, murmured vaguely, was satisfied with my French. *Bon voyage.*[2]

"In about forty-five seconds I found myself again in the waiting-room with the compassionate secretary, who, full of desolation and sympathy, made me sign some document. I believe I undertook amongst other things not to disclose any trade secrets. Well, I am not going to.

"I began to feel slightly uneasy. You know I am not used to such ceremonies, and there was something ominous in the atmosphere. It was just as though I had been let into some conspiracy—I don't know—something not quite right; and I was glad to get out. In the outer room the two women knitted black wool feverishly. People were arriving, and the younger one was walking back and forth introducing them. The old one sat on her chair. Her flat cloth slippers were propped up on a foot-warmer, and a cat reposed on her lap. She wore a starched white affair on her head, had a wart on one cheek, and silver-rimmed spectacles hung on the tip of her nose. She glanced at me above the glasses. The swift and indifferent placidity of that look troubled me. Two youths with foolish and cheery countenances were being piloted over, and she threw at them the same quick glance of unconcerned wisdom. She seemed to know all about them and about me too. An eerie feeling came over me. She seemed uncanny and fateful. Often far away there I thought of these two, guarding the door of Darkness, knitting black wool as for a warm pall, one introducing, introducing continuously to the unknown, the other scrutinising the cheery and foolish faces with unconcerned old eyes. *Ave!* Old knitter of black wool. *Morituri te salutant.*[3] Not many of those she looked at ever saw her again—not half, by a long way.

"There was yet a visit to the doctor. 'A simple formality,' assured me the secretary, with an air of taking an immense part in all my sorrows. Accordingly a young chap wearing his hat over the left eyebrow, some clerk I suppose—there must have been clerks in the business, though the house was as still as a house in a city of the dead—came from somewhere upstairs, and led me forth. He was shabby and careless, with ink-stains on the sleeves of his jacket, and his cravat was large and billowy, under a chin shaped like the toe of an old boot. It was a little too early for the doctor, so I proposed a drink, and thereupon he developed a vein of joviality. As we sat over our vermuths[4] he glorified the Company's business, and by and by I expressed casually my surprise at him not going out there. He became very cool and collected all at once. 'I am not such a fool as I look, quoth Plato to his disciples,' he said sententiously, emptied his glass with great resolution, and we rose.

"The old doctor felt my pulse, evidently thinking of something else the while. 'Good, good for there,' he mumbled, and then with a certain eagerness asked me whether I would let him measure my head. Rather surprised, I said Yes, when he produced a thing like callipers and got the dimensions back and front

---

2. "Have a good trip" (French).
3. "Those who are about to die salute you" (Latin): the greeting of gladiators to the Roman emperor before beginning combat in the arena.

4. Vermuth, now known as vermouth, is wine fortified with alcohol and, usually, additional flavors.

and every way, taking notes carefully. He was an unshaven little man in a threadbare coat like a gaberdine, with his feet in slippers, and I thought him a harmless fool. 'I always ask leave, in the interests of science, to measure the crania of those going out there,'[5] he said. 'And when they come back too?' I asked. 'Oh, I never see them,' he remarked; 'and, moreover, the changes take place inside, you know.' He smiled, as if at some quiet joke. 'So you are going out there. Famous. Interesting too.' He gave me a searching glance, and made another note. 'Ever any madness in your family?' he asked, in a matter-of-fact tone. I felt very annoyed. 'Is that question in the interests of science too?' 'It would be,' he said, without taking notice of my irritation, 'interesting for science to watch the mental changes of individuals, on the spot, but . . .' 'Are you an alienist?' I interrupted. 'Every doctor should be—a little,' answered that original[6] imperturbably. 'I have a little theory which you Messieurs who go out there must help me to prove. This is my share in the advantages my country shall reap from the possession of such a magnificent dependency. The mere wealth I leave to others. Pardon my questions, but you are the first Englishman coming under my observation . . .' I hastened to assure him I was not in the least typical. 'If I were,' said I, 'I wouldn't be talking like this with you.' 'What you say is rather profound, and probably erroneous,' he said, with a laugh. 'Avoid irritation more than exposure to the sun. Adieu. How do you English say, eh? Good-bye. Ah! Good-bye. Adieu. In the tropics one must before everything keep calm.' . . . He lifted a warning forefinger. . . . 'Du calme, du calme. Adieu.'[7]

"One thing more remained to do—say good-bye to my excellent aunt. I found her triumphant. I had a cup of tea—the last decent cup of tea for many days—and in a room that most soothingly looked just as you would expect a lady's drawing-room to look, we had a long quiet chat by the fireside. In the course of these confidences it became quite plain to me I had been represented to the wife of the high dignitary, and goodness knows to how many more people besides, as an exceptional and gifted creature—a piece of good fortune for the Company—a man you don't get hold of every day. Good heavens! and I was going to take charge of a two-penny-halfpenny river-steamboat with a penny whistle attached! It appeared, however, I was also one of the Workers, with a capital—you know. Something like an emissary of light, something like a lower sort of apostle. There had been a lot of such rot let loose in print and talk just about that time,[8] and the excellent woman, living right in the rush of all that humbug, got carried off her feet. She talked about 'weaning those ignorant millions from their horrid ways,' till, upon my word, she made me quite uncomfortable. I ventured to hint that the Company was run for profit.

"'You forget, dear Charlie, that the labourer is worthy of his hire,'[9] she said brightly. It's queer how out of touch with truth women are. They live in a world of their own, and there had never been anything like it, and never can be. It is

---

5. The doctor may practice some form of phrenology, a pseudoscience holding that personality traits could be determined by the shape and size of the skull.
6. Unusual or eccentric person. "Alienist": early term for a psychiatrist.
7. "Calm, calm. Goodbye" (French).
8. Initially, Leopold II was viewed as a

philanthropist—bringing missionaries to pagans and, it was thought, using Belgian military forces to rescue the native people from homegrown slave traders.
9. The aunt quotes Luke 10.7, one of Christ's instructions to his disciples as they depart to proselytize: to make themselves welcome in the homes they visit.

too beautiful altogether, and if they were to set it up it would go to pieces before the first sunset. Some confounded fact we men have been living contentedly with ever since the day of creation would start up and knock the whole thing over.

"After this I got embraced, told to wear flannel, be sure to write often, and so on—and I left. In the street—I don't know why—a queer feeling came to me that I was an impostor. Odd thing that I, who used to clear out for any part of the world at twenty-four hours' notice, with less thought than most men give to the crossing of a street, had a moment—I won't say of hesitation, but of startled pause, before this commonplace affair. The best way I can explain it to you is by saying that, for a second or two, I felt as though, instead of going to the centre of a continent, I were about to set off for the centre of the earth.[1]

"I left in a French steamer, and she called in every blamed port they have out there, for, as far as I could see, the sole purpose of landing soldiers and custom-house officers.[2] I watched the coast. Watching a coast as it slips by the ship is like thinking about an enigma. There it is before you—smiling, frowning, inviting, grand, mean, insipid, or savage, and always mute with an air of whispering, Come and find out. This one was almost featureless, as if still in the making, with an aspect of monotonous grimness. The edge of a colossal jungle, so dark green as to be almost black, fringed with white surf, ran straight, like a ruled line, far, far away along a blue sea whose glitter was blurred by a creeping mist. The sun was fierce, the land seemed to glisten and drip with steam. Here and there greyish-whitish specks showed up clustered inside the white surf, with a flag flying above them perhaps—settlements some centuries old, and still no bigger than pin-heads on the untouched expanse of their background. We pounded along, stopped, landed soldiers; went on, landed custom-house clerks to levy toll in what looked like a God-forsaken wilderness, with a tin shed and a flag-pole lost in it; landed more soldiers—to take care of the custom-house clerks presumably. Some, I heard, got drowned in the surf; but whether they did or not, nobody seemed particularly to care. They were just flung out there, and on we went. Every day the coast looked the same, as though we had not moved; but we passed various places—trading places—with names like Gran' Bassam, Little Popo;[3] names that seemed to belong to some sordid farce acted in front of a sinister back-cloth. The idleness of a passenger, my isolation amongst all these men with whom I had no point of contact, the oily and languid sea, the uniform sombreness of the coast, seemed to keep me away from the truth of things, within the toil of a mournful and senseless delusion. The voice of the surf heard now and then was a positive pleasure, like the speech of a brother. It was something natural, that had its reason, that had a meaning. Now and then a boat from the shore gave one a momentary contact with reality. It was paddled by black fellows. You could see from afar the white of their eyeballs glistening. They shouted, sang; their bodies streamed with perspiration; they had faces like grotesque masks—these chaps; but they had bone, muscle, a wild vitality, an intense energy of movement, that was as

---

1. Jules Verne's science fiction novel *Journey to the Center of the Earth* (1864) featured characters encountering prehistoric animals of greater age in successive layers of the earth.
2. Colonial officials.

3. The former name of Aného, a coastal city in Togo, then under German control. "Gran' Bassam": Grand-Bassam, a city in Côte d'Ivoire, was then a French colony and a major seaport.

natural and true as the surf along their coast. They wanted no excuse for being there. They were a great comfort to look at. For a time I would feel I belonged still to a world of straightforward facts; but the feeling would not last long. Something would turn up to scare it away. Once, I remember, we came upon a man-of-war anchored off the coast. There wasn't even a shed there, and she was shelling the bush. It appears the French had one of their wars going on thereabouts. Her ensign dropped limp like a rag; the muzzles of the long six-inch guns stuck out all over the low hull; the greasy, slimy swell swung her up lazily and let her down, swaying her thin masts. In the empty immensity of earth, sky, and water, there she was, incomprehensible, firing into a continent. Pop, would go one of the six-inch guns; a small flame would dart and vanish, a little white smoke would disappear, a tiny projectile would give a feeble screech—and nothing happened. Nothing could happen. There was a touch of insanity in the proceeding, a sense of lugubrious drollery in the sight; and it was not dissipated by somebody on board assuring me earnestly there was a camp of natives—he called them enemies!—hidden out of sight somewhere.

"We gave her her letters (I heard the men in that lonely ship were dying of fever at the rate of three a day) and went on. We called at some more places with farcical names, where the merry dance of death and trade goes on in a still and earthy atmosphere as of an overheated catacomb; all along the formless coast bordered by dangerous surf, as if Nature herself had tried to ward off intruders; in and out of rivers, streams of death in life, whose banks were rotting into mud, whose waters, thickened into slime, invaded the contorted mangroves, that seemed to writhe at us in the extremity of an impotent despair. Nowhere did we stop long enough to get a particularised impression, but the general sense of vague and oppressive wonder grew upon me. It was like a weary pilgrimage amongst hints for nightmares.

"It was upward of thirty days before I saw the mouth of the big river. We anchored off the seat of the government.[4] But my work would not begin till some two hundred miles farther on. So as soon as I could I made a start for a place thirty miles higher up.

"I had my passage on a little sea-going steamer. Her captain was a Swede, and knowing me for a seaman, invited me on the bridge. He was a young man, lean, fair, and morose, with lanky hair and a shuffling gait. As we left the miserable little wharf, he tossed his head contemptuously at the shore. 'Been living there?' he asked. I said, 'Yes.' 'Fine lot these government chaps—are they not?' he went on, speaking English with great precision and considerable bitterness. 'It is funny what some people will do for a few francs a month. I wonder what becomes of that kind when it goes up country?' I said to him I expected to see that soon. 'So-o-o!' he exclaimed. He shuffled athwart, keeping one eye ahead vigilantly. 'Don't be too sure,' he continued. 'The other day I took up a man who hanged himself on the road. He was a Swede, too.' 'Hanged himself! Why, in God's name?' I cried. He kept on looking out watchfully. 'Who knows? The sun too much for him, or the country perhaps.'

"At last we opened a reach.[5] A rocky cliff appeared, mounds of turned-up earth by the shore, houses on a hill, others with iron roofs, amongst a waste of

4. The capital of the Congo Free State was Boma, a port at the mouth of the Congo.

5. Found an open, visible stretch of river.

excavations, or hanging to the declivity. A continuous noise of the rapids above hovered over this scene of inhabited devastation. A lot of people, mostly black and naked, moved about like ants. A jetty projected into the river. A blinding sunlight drowned all this at times in a sudden recrudescence of glare. 'There's your Company's station,' said the Swede, pointing to three wooden barrack-like structures on the rocky slope. 'I will send your things up. Four boxes did you say? So. Farewell.'

"I came upon a boiler[6] wallowing in the grass, then found a path leading up the hill. It turned aside for the boulders, and also for an undersized railway truck lying there on its back with its wheels in the air. One was off. The thing looked as dead as the carcass of some animal. I came upon more pieces of decaying machinery, a stack of rusty nails. To the left a clump of trees made a shady spot, where dark things seemed to stir feebly. I blinked, the path was steep. A horn tooted to the right, and I saw the black people run. A heavy and dull detonation shook the ground, a puff of smoke came out of the cliff, and that was all. No change appeared on the face of the rock. They were building a railway. The cliff was not in the way or anything; but this objectless blasting was all the work going on.

"A slight clinking behind me made me turn my head. Six black men advanced in a file, toiling up the path. They walked erect and slow, balancing small baskets full of earth on their heads, and the clink kept time with their footsteps. Black rags were wound round their loins, and the short ends behind waggled to and fro like tails. I could see every rib, the joints of their limbs were like knots in a rope; each had an iron collar on his neck, and all were connected together with a chain whose bights[7] swung between them, rhythmically clinking. Another report from the cliff made me think suddenly of that ship of war I had seen firing into a continent. It was the same kind of ominous voice; but these men could by no stretch of imagination be called enemies. They were called criminals, and the outraged law, like the bursting shells, had come to them, an insoluble mystery from the sea. All their meagre breasts panted together, the violently dilated nostrils quivered, the eyes stared stonily uphill. They passed me within six inches, without a glance, with that complete, deathlike indifference of unhappy savages. Behind this raw matter one of the reclaimed, the product of the new forces at work, strolled despondently, carrying a rifle by its middle. He had a uniform jacket with one button off, and seeing a white man on the path, hoisted his weapon to his shoulder with alacrity. This was simple prudence, white men being so much alike at a distance that he could not tell who I might be. He was speedily reassured, and with a large, white, rascally grin, and a glance at his charge, seemed to take me into partnership in his exalted trust. After all, I also was a part of the great cause of these high and just proceedings.

"Instead of going up, I turned and descended to the left. My idea was to let that chain-gang get out of sight before I climbed the hill. You know I am not particularly tender; I've had to strike and to fend off. I've had to resist and to attack sometimes—that's only one way of resisting—without counting the exact cost, according to the demands of such sort of life as I had blundered into. I've seen the devil of violence, and the devil of greed, and the devil of hot desire; but, by all the stars! these were strong, lusty, red-eyed devils, that

---

6. A machine for converting water into steam.   7. The dangling excess of chain.

swayed and drove men—men, I tell you. But as I stood on this hillside, I foresaw that in the blinding sunshine of that land I would become acquainted with a flabby, pretending, weak-eyed devil of a rapacious and pitiless folly. How insidious he could be, too, I was only to find out several months later and a thousand miles farther. For a moment I stood appalled, as though by a warning. Finally I descended the hill, obliquely, towards the trees I had seen.

"I avoided a vast artificial hole somebody had been digging on the slope, the purpose of which I found it impossible to divine. It wasn't a quarry or a sandpit, anyhow. It was just a hole. It might have been connected with the philanthropic desire of giving the criminals something to do. I don't know. Then I nearly fell into a very narrow ravine, almost no more than a scar in the hillside. I discovered that a lot of imported drainage-pipes for the settlement had been tumbled in there. There wasn't one that was not broken. It was a wanton smash-up. At last I got under the trees. My purpose was to stroll into the shade for a moment; but no sooner within than it seemed to me I had stepped into the gloomy circle of some Inferno.[8] The rapids were near, and an uninterrupted, uniform, headlong, rushing noise filled the mournful stillness of the grove, where not a breath stirred, not a leaf moved, with a mysterious sound—as though the tearing pace of the launched earth had suddenly become audible.

"Black shapes crouched, lay, sat between the trees, leaning against the trunks, clinging to the earth, half coming out, half effaced within the dim light, in all the attitudes of pain, abandonment, and despair. Another mine[9] on the cliff went off, followed by a slight shudder of the soil under my feet. The work was going on. The work! And this was the place where some of the helpers had withdrawn to die.

"They were dying slowly—it was very clear. They were not enemies, they were not criminals, they were nothing earthly now—nothing but black shadows of disease and starvation, lying confusedly in the greenish gloom. Brought from all the recesses of the coast in all the legality of time contracts, lost in uncongenial surroundings, fed on unfamiliar food, they sickened, became inefficient, and were then allowed to crawl away and rest.[1] These moribund shapes were free as air—and nearly as thin. I began to distinguish the gleam of eyes under the trees. Then, glancing down, I saw a face near my hand. The black bones reclined at full length with one shoulder against the tree, and slowly the eyelids rose and the sunken eyes looked up at me, enormous and vacant, a kind of blind, white flicker in the depths of the orbs, which died out slowly. The man seemed young—almost a boy—but you know with them it's hard to tell. I found nothing else to do but to offer him one of my good Swede's ship's biscuits I had in my pocket. The fingers closed slowly on it and held—there was no other movement and no other glance. He had tied a bit of white worsted[2] round his neck—Why? Where did he get it? Was it a badge—an ornament—a charm—a propitiatory act? Was there any idea at all connected with it? It looked startling round his black neck, this bit of white thread from beyond the seas.

---

8. Hell, often of fire. The term is associated with the portrayal of hell in the *Inferno*, the first section of the *Divine Comedy*, by Dante Alighieri (ca. 1265–1321).
9. Explosive charge.

1. The workers and porters who provided the infrastructure of the Congo Free State were often conscripts: overworked, underfed, and beaten, they died in enormous numbers.
2. Wool fabric.

"Near the same tree two more bundles of acute angles sat with their legs drawn up. One, with his chin propped on his knees, stared at nothing, in an intolerable and appalling manner: his brother phantom rested its forehead, as if overcome with a great weariness; and all about others were scattered in every pose of contorted collapse, as in some picture of a massacre or a pestilence. While I stood horror-struck, one of these creatures rose to his hands and knees, and went off on all-fours towards the river to drink. He lapped out of his hand, then sat up in the sunlight, crossing his shins in front of him, and after a time let his woolly head fall on his breastbone.

"I didn't want any more loitering in the shade, and I made haste towards the station. When near the buildings I met a white man, in such an unexpected elegance of get-up that in the first moment I took him for a sort of vision. I saw a high starched collar, white cuffs, a light alpaca[3] jacket, snowy trousers, a clear necktie, and varnished boots. No hat. Hair parted, brushed, oiled, under a green-lined parasol held in a big white hand. He was amazing, and had a penholder behind his ear.

"I shook hands with this miracle, and I learned he was the Company's chief accountant, and that all the book-keeping was done at this station. He had come out for a moment, he said, 'to get a breath of fresh air.' The expression sounded wonderfully odd, with its suggestion of sedentary desk-life. I wouldn't have mentioned the fellow to you at all, only it was from his lips that I first heard the name of the man who is so indissolubly connected with the memories of that time. Moreover, I respected the fellow. Yes; I respected his collars, his vast cuffs, his brushed hair. His appearance was certainly that of a hairdresser's dummy; but in the great demoralisation of the land he kept up his appearance. That's backbone. His starched collars and got-up shirt-fronts were achievements of character. He had been out nearly three years; and, later, I could not help asking him how he managed to sport such linen. He had just the faintest blush, and said modestly, 'I've been teaching one of the native women about the station. It was difficult. She had a distaste for the work.' Thus this man had verily accomplished something. And he was devoted to his books, which were in apple-pie order.

"Everything else in the station was in a muddle,—heads, things, buildings. Strings of dusty niggers with splay feet arrived and departed; a stream of manufactured goods, rubbishy cottons, beads, and brass-wire sent into the depths of darkness, and in return came a precious trickle of ivory.[4]

"I had to wait in the station for ten days—an eternity. I lived in a hut in the yard, but to be out of the chaos I would sometimes get into the accountant's office. It was built of horizontal planks, and so badly put together that, as he bent over his high desk, he was barred from neck to heels with narrow strips of sunlight. There was no need to open the big shutter to see. It was hot there too; big flies buzzed fiendishly, and did not sting, but stabbed. I sat generally on the floor, while, of faultless appearance (and even slightly scented), perching on a high stool, he wrote, he wrote. Sometimes he stood up for exercise.

---

3. An expensive fine wool that comes from a South American animal of the same name.
4. Congolese were not allowed currency, and the enormous disparity between the value of goods returning from the Congo and the value of goods being sent there eventually gave activists the first hint of the forced labor conditions that would turn public opinion against Leopold.

When a truckle-bed[5] with a sick man (some invalided agent from up country) was put in there, he exhibited a gentle annoyance. 'The groans of this sick person' he said, 'distract my attention. And without that it is extremely difficult to guard against clerical errors in this climate.'

"One day he remarked, without lifting his head, 'In the interior you will no doubt meet Mr Kurtz.' On my asking who Mr Kurtz was, he said he was a first-class agent; and seeing my disappointment at this information, he added slowly, laying down his pen, 'He is a very remarkable person.' Further questions elicited from him that Mr Kurtz was at present in charge of a trading-post, a very important one, in the true ivory-country, at 'the very bottom of there. Sends in as much ivory as all the others put together . . .' He began to write again. The sick man was too ill to groan. The flies buzzed in a great peace.

"Suddenly there was a growing murmur of voices and a great tramping of feet. A caravan had come in. A violent babble of uncouth sounds burst out on the other side of the planks. All the carriers were speaking together, and in the midst of the uproar the lamentable voice of the chief agent was heard 'giving it up' tearfully for the twentieth time that day. . . . He rose slowly. 'What a frightful row,' he said. He crossed the room gently to look at the sick man, and returning, said to me, 'He does not hear.' 'What! Dead?' I asked, startled. 'No, not yet,' he answered, with great composure. Then, alluding with a toss of the head to the tumult in the station-yard, 'When one has got to make correct entries, one comes to hate those savages—hate them to the death.' He remained thoughtful for a moment. 'When you see Mr Kurtz,' he went on, 'tell him from me that everything here'—he glanced at the desk—'is very satisfactory. I don't like to write to him—with those messengers of ours you never know who may get hold of your letter—at that Central Station.' He stared at me for a moment with his mild, bulging eyes. 'Oh, he will go far, very far,' he began again. 'He will be a somebody in the Administration before long. They, above—the Council in Europe, you know—mean him to be.'

"He turned to his work. The noise outside had ceased, and presently in going out I stopped at the door. In the steady buzz of flies the homeward-bound agent was lying flushed and insensible; the other, bent over his books, was making correct entries of perfectly correct transactions; and fifty feet below the doorstep I could see the still tree-tops of the grove of death.

"Next day I left that station at last, with a caravan of sixty men, for a two-hundred-mile tramp.

"No use telling you much about that. Paths, paths, everywhere; a stamped-in network of paths spreading over the empty land, through long grass, through burnt grass, through thickets, down and up chilly ravines, up and down stony hills ablaze with heat; and a solitude, a solitude, nobody, not a hut. The population had cleared out a long time ago. Well, if a lot of mysterious niggers armed with all kinds of fearful weapons suddenly took to travelling on the road between Deal and Gravesend,[6] catching the yokels right and left to carry heavy loads for them, I fancy every farm and cottage thereabouts would get empty very soon. Only here the dwellings were gone too. Still, I passed through several abandoned

---

5. I.e., trundle bed, a low portable bed that is on castors and that may be slid under a higher bed when not being used.

6. Deal, like Gravesend, is a coastal town in southeastern England.

villages. There's something pathetically childish in the ruins of grass walls. Day after day, with the stamp and shuffle of sixty pair of bare feet behind me, each pair under a 60-lb. load. Camp, cook, sleep, strike camp, march. Now and then a carrier dead in harness, at rest in the long grass near the path, with an empty water-gourd and his long staff lying by his side. A great silence around and above. Perhaps on some quiet night the tremor of far-off drums, sinking, swelling, a tremor vast, faint; a sound weird, appealing, suggestive, and wild—and perhaps with as profound a meaning as the sound of bells in a Christian country. Once a white man in an unbuttoned uniform, camping on the path with an armed escort of lank Zanzibaris,[7] very hospitable and festive—not to say drunk. Was looking after the upkeep of the road, he declared. Can't say I saw any road or any upkeep, unless the body of a middle-aged negro, with a bullet-hole in the forehead, upon which I absolutely stumbled three miles farther on, may be considered as a permanent improvement. I had a white companion too, not a bad chap, but rather too fleshy and with the exasperating habit of fainting on the hot hillsides, miles away from the least bit of shade and water. Annoying, you know, to hold your own coat like a parasol over a man's head while he is coming-to. I couldn't help asking him once what he meant by coming there at all. 'To make money, of course. What do you think?' he said scornfully. Then he got fever, and had to be carried in a hammock slung under a pole. As he weighed sixteen stone[8] I had no end of rows with the carriers. They jibbed, ran away, sneaked off with their loads in the night—quite a mutiny. So, one evening, I made a speech in English with gestures, not one of which was lost to the sixty pairs of eyes before me, and the next morning I started the hammock off in front all right. An hour afterwards I came upon the whole concern wrecked in a bush—man, hammock, groans, blankets, horrors. The heavy pole had skinned his poor nose. He was very anxious for me to kill somebody, but there wasn't the shadow of a carrier near. I remembered the old doctor—'It would be interesting for science to watch the mental changes of individuals, on the spot.' I felt I was becoming scientifically interesting. However, all that is to no purpose. On the fifteenth day I came in sight of the big river again, and hobbled into the Central Station. It was on a back water surrounded by scrub and forest, with a pretty border of smelly mud on one side, and on the three others enclosed by a crazy fence of rushes. A neglected gap was all the gate it had, and the first glance at the place was enough to let you see the flabby devil was running that show. White men with long staves in their hands appeared languidly from amongst the buildings, strolling up to take a look at me, and then retired out of sight somewhere. One of them, a stout, excitable chap with black moustaches, informed me with great volubility and many digressions, as soon as I told him who I was, that my steamer was at the bottom of the river. I was thunderstruck. What, how, why? Oh, it was 'all right.' The 'manager himself' was there. All quite correct. 'Everybody had behaved splendidly! splendidly!'—'You must,' he said in agitation, 'go and see the general manager at once. He is waiting!'

"I did not see the real significance of that wreck at once. I fancy I see it now, but I am not sure—not at all. Certainly the affair was too stupid—when I think

7. Mercenary soldiers from the island of Zanzibar, off the east African coast.

8. I.e., 224 pounds (1 stone equals 14 pounds).

of it—to be altogether natural. Still . . . But at the moment it presented itself simply as a confounded nuisance. The steamer was sunk. They had started two days before in a sudden hurry up the river with the manager on board, in charge of some volunteer skipper, and before they had been out three hours they tore the bottom out of her on stones, and she sank near the south bank. I asked myself what I was to do there, now my boat was lost. As a matter of fact, I had plenty to do in fishing my command out of the river. I had to set about it the very next day. That, and the repairs when I brought the pieces to the station, took some months.

"My first interview with the manager was curious. He did not ask me to sit down after my twenty-mile walk that morning. He was commonplace in complexion, in feature, in manners, and in voice. He was of middle size and of ordinary build. His eyes, of the usual blue, were perhaps remarkably cold, and he certainly could make his glance fall on one as trenchant and heavy as an axe. But even at these times the rest of his person seemed to disclaim the intention. Otherwise there was only an indefinable, faint expression of his lips, something stealthy—a smile—not a smile—I remember it, but I can't explain. It was unconscious, this smile was, though just after he had said something it got intensified for an instant. It came at the end of his speeches like a seal applied on the words to make the meaning of the commonest phrase appear absolutely inscrutable. He was a common trader, from his youth up employed in these parts—nothing more. He was obeyed, yet he inspired neither love nor fear, nor even respect. He inspired uneasiness. That was it! Uneasiness. Not a definite mistrust—just uneasiness—nothing more. You have no idea how effective such a . . . a . . . faculty can be. He had no genius for organising, for initiative, or for order even. That was evident in such things as the deplorable state of the station. He had no learning, and no intelligence. His position had come to him—why? Perhaps because he was never ill . . . He had served three terms of three years out there . . . Because triumphant health in the general rout of constitutions is a kind of power in itself. When he went home on leave he rioted on a large scale—pompously. Jack ashore[9]—with a difference—in externals only. This one could gather from his casual talk. He originated nothing, he could keep the routine going—that's all. But he was great. He was great by this little thing that it was impossible to tell what could control such a man. He never gave that secret away. Perhaps there was nothing within him. Such a suspicion made one pause—for out there there were no external checks. Once when various tropical diseases had laid low almost every 'agent' in the station, he was heard to say, 'Men who come out here should have no entrails.' He sealed the utterance with that smile of his, as though it had been a door opening into a darkness he had in his keeping. You fancied you had seen things— but the seal was on. When annoyed at meal-times by the constant quarrels of the white men about precedence, he ordered an immense round table[1] to be made, for which a special house had to be built. This was the station's messroom. Where he sat was the first place—the rest were nowhere. One felt this to be his unalterable conviction. He was neither civil nor uncivil. He was quiet.

9. The carousing of seamen ("Jack Tar") on shore leave was proverbial.
1. King Arthur, legendary ruler of England, seated his knights at a round table so that none would take precedence over any of the others.

He allowed his 'boy'—an overfed young negro from the coast—to treat the white men, under his very eyes, with provoking insolence.

"He began to speak as soon as he saw me. I had been very long on the road. He could not wait. Had to start without me. The up-river stations had to be relieved. There had been so many delays already that he did not know who was dead and who was alive, and how they got on—and so on, and so on. He paid no attention to my explanations, and, playing with a stick of sealing-wax, repeated several times that the situation was 'very grave, very grave.' There were rumours that a very important station was in jeopardy, and its chief, Mr Kurtz, was ill. Hoped it was not true. Mr Kurtz was . . . I felt weary and irritable. Hang Kurtz, I thought. I interrupted him by saying I had heard of Mr Kurtz on the coast. 'Ah! So they talk of him down there,' he murmured to himself. Then he began again, assuring me Mr Kurtz was the best agent he had, an exceptional man, of the greatest importance to the Company; therefore I could understand his anxiety. He was, he said, 'very, very uneasy.' Certainly he fidgeted on his chair a good deal, exclaimed, 'Ah, Mr Kurtz!' broke the stick of sealing-wax and seemed dumbfounded by the accident. Next thing he wanted to know 'how long it would take to' . . . I interrupted him again. Being hungry, you know, and kept on my feet too, I was getting savage. 'How can I tell?' I said, 'I haven't even seen the wreck yet—some months, no doubt.' All this talk seemed to me so futile. 'Some months,' he said. 'Well, let us say three months before we can make a start. Yes. That ought to do the affair.' I flung out of his hut (he lived all alone in a clay hut with a sort of verandah) muttering to myself my opinion of him. He was a chattering idiot. Afterwards I took it back when it was borne in upon me startlingly with what extreme nicety he had estimated the time requisite for the 'affair.'

"I went to work the next day, turning, so to speak, my back on that station. In that way only it seemed to me I could keep my hold on the redeeming facts of life. Still, one must look about sometimes; and then I saw this station, these men strolling aimlessly about in the sunshine of the yard. I asked myself sometimes what it all meant. They wandered here and there with their absurd long staves in their hands, like a lot of faithless pilgrims bewitched inside a rotten fence. The word 'ivory' rang in the air, was whispered, was sighed. You would think they were praying to it. A taint of imbecile rapacity blew through it all, like a whiff from some corpse. By Jove! I've never seen anything so unreal in my life. And outside, the silent wilderness surrounding this cleared speck on the earth struck me as something great and invincible, like evil or truth, waiting patiently for the passing away of this fantastic invasion.

"Oh, these months! Well, never mind. Various things happened. One evening a grass shed full of calico, cotton prints, beads, and I don't know what else, burst into a blaze so suddenly that you would have thought the earth had opened to let an avenging fire consume all that trash. I was smoking my pipe quietly by my dismantled steamer, and saw them all cutting capers in the light, with their arms lifted high, when the stout man with moustaches came tearing down to the river, a tin pail in his hand, assured me that everybody was 'behaving splendidly, splendidly,' dipped about a quart of water and tore back again. I noticed there was a hole in the bottom of his pail.

"I strolled up. There was no hurry. You see the thing had gone off like a box of matches. It had been hopeless from the very first. The flame had leaped high,

driven everybody back, lighted up everything—and collapsed. The shed was already a heap of embers glowing fiercely. A nigger was being beaten near by. They said he had caused the fire in some way; be that as it may, he was screeching most horribly. I saw him, later, for several days, sitting in a bit of shade looking very sick and trying to recover himself: afterwards he arose and went out—and the wilderness without a sound took him into its bosom again. As I approached the glow from the dark I found myself at the back of two men, talking. I heard the name of Kurtz pronounced, then the words, 'take advantage of this unfortunate accident.' One of the men was the manager. I wished him a good evening. 'Did you ever see anything like it—eh? it is incredible,' he said, and walked off. The other man remained. He was a first-class agent, young, gentlemanly, a bit reserved, with a forked little beard and a hooked nose. He was standoffish with the other agents, and they on their side said he was the manager's spy upon them. As to me, I had hardly ever spoken to him before. We got into talk, and by and by we strolled away from the hissing ruins. Then he asked me to his room, which was in the main building of the station. He struck a match, and I perceived that this young aristocrat had not only a silver-mounted dressing-case but also a whole candle all to himself. Just at that time the manager was the only man supposed to have any right to candles. Native mats covered the clay walls; a collection of spears, assegais,[2] shields, knives, was hung up in trophies. The business entrusted to this fellow was the making of bricks—so I had been informed; but there wasn't a fragment of a brick anywhere in the station, and he had been there more than a year—waiting. It seems he could not make bricks without something, I don't know what—straw maybe. Anyway, it could not be found there, and as it was not likely to be sent from Europe, it did not appear clear to me what he was waiting for. An act of special creation[3] perhaps. However, they were all waiting—all the sixteen or twenty pilgrims of them—for something; and upon my word it did not seem an uncongenial occupation, from the way they took it, though the only thing that ever came to them was disease—as far as I could see. They beguiled the time by backbiting and intriguing against each other in a foolish kind of way. There was an air of plotting about that station, but nothing came of it, of course. It was as unreal as everything else—as the philanthropic pretence of the whole concern, as their talk, as their government, as their show of work. The only real feeling was a desire to get appointed to a trading-post where ivory was to be had, so that they could earn percentages. They intrigued and slandered and hated each other only on that account—but as to effectually lifting a little finger—oh no. By heavens! there is something after all in the world allowing one man to steal a horse while another must not look at a halter. Steal a horse straight out. Very well. He has done it. Perhaps he can ride. But there is a way of looking at a halter that would provoke the most charitable of saints into a kick.

"I had no idea why he wanted to be sociable, but as we chatted in there it suddenly occurred to me the fellow was trying to get at something—in fact, pumping me. He alluded constantly to Europe, to the people I was supposed to know there—putting leading questions as to my acquaintances in the sepulchral city,

2. Slender hardwood javelins used as weapons.
3. The religious doctrine of "special creation" referred to a literal interpretation of Genesis in which the universe came into being by instant divine decree.

and so on. His little eyes glittered like mica[4] discs—with curiosity—though he tried to keep up a bit of superciliousness. At first I was astonished, but very soon I became awfully curious to see what he would find out from me. I couldn't possibly imagine what I had in me to make it worth his while. It was very pretty to see how he baffled himself, for in truth my body was full only of chills, and my head had nothing in it but that wretched steamboat business. It was evident he took me for a perfectly shameless prevaricator. At last he got angry, and, to conceal a movement of furious annoyance, he yawned. I rose. Then I noticed a small sketch in oils, on a panel, representing a woman, draped and blindfolded, carrying a lighted torch.[5] The background was sombre—almost black. The movement of the woman was stately, and the effect of the torchlight on the face was sinister.

"It arrested me, and he stood by civilly, holding an empty half-pint champagne bottle (medical comforts) with the candle stuck in it. To my question he said Mr Kurtz had painted this—in this very station more than a year ago—while waiting for means to go to his trading-post. 'Tell me, pray,' said I, 'who is this Mr Kurtz?'

"'The chief of the Inner Station,' he answered in a short tone, looking away. 'Much obliged,' I said, laughing. 'And you are the brickmaker of the Central Station. Every one knows that.' He was silent for a while. 'He is a prodigy,' he said at last. 'He is an emissary of pity, and science, and progress, and devil knows what else. We want,' he began to declaim suddenly, 'for the guidance of the cause entrusted to us by Europe, so to speak, higher intelligence, wide sympathies, a singleness of purpose.' 'Who says that?' I asked. 'Lots of them,' he replied. 'Some even write that; and so *he* comes here, a special being, as you ought to know.' 'Why ought I to know?' I interrupted, really surprised. He paid no attention. 'Yes. To-day he is chief of the best station, next year he will be assistant-manager, two years more and . . . but I daresay you know what he will be in two years' time. You are of the new gang—the gang of virtue. The same people who sent him specially also recommended you. Oh, don't say no. I've my own eyes to trust.' Light dawned upon me. My dear aunt's influential acquaintances were producing an unexpected effect upon that young man. I nearly burst into a laugh. 'Do you read the Company's confidential correspondence?' I asked. He hadn't a word to say. It was great fun. 'When Mr Kurtz,' I continued severely, 'is General Manager, you won't have the opportunity.'

"He blew the candle out suddenly, and we went outside. The moon had risen. Black figures strolled about listlessly, pouring water on the glow, whence proceeded a sound of hissing; steam ascended in the moonlight; the beaten nigger groaned somewhere. 'What a row the brute makes!' said the indefatigable man with the moustaches, appearing near us. 'Serve him right. Transgression—punishment—bang! Pitiless, pitiless. That's the only way. This will prevent all conflagrations for the future. I was just telling the manager . . .' He noticed my companion, and became crestfallen all at once. 'Not in bed yet,' he said, with a kind of servile heartiness; 'it's so natural. Ha! Danger—agitation.' He vanished. I went on to the river-side, and the other followed me. I heard a scathing murmur

4. A mineral silicate that separates into glittering layers.
5. Justice was traditionally portrayed as a

blindfolded woman, although usually bearing scales and a sword rather than a torch.

at my ear, 'Heap of muffs[6]—go to.' The pilgrims could be seen in knots gesticulating, discussing. Several had still their staves in their hands. I verily believe
they took these sticks to bed with them. Beyond the fence the forest stood up
spectrally in the moonlight, and through the dim stir, through the faint sounds of
that lamentable courtyard, the silence of the land went home to one's very
heart—its mystery, its greatness, the amazing reality of its concealed life. The
hurt nigger moaned feebly somewhere near by, and then fetched a deep sigh that
made me mend my pace away from there. I felt a hand introducing itself under
my arm. 'My dear sir,' said the fellow, 'I don't want to be misunderstood, and
especially by you, who will see Mr Kurtz long before I can have that pleasure. I
wouldn't like him to get a false idea of my disposition. . . .'

"I let him run on, this papier-mâché Mephistopheles,[7] and it seemed to me
that if I tried I could poke my forefinger through him, and would find nothing
inside but a little loose dirt, maybe. He, don't you see, had been planning to be
assistant-manager by and by under the present man, and I could see that the
coming of that Kurtz had upset them both not a little. He talked precipitately,
and I did not try to stop him. I had my shoulders against the wreck of my
steamer, hauled up on the slope like a carcass of some big river animal. The
smell of mud, of primeval mud, by Jove! was in my nostrils, the high stillness of
primeval forest was before my eyes; there were shiny patches on the black
creek. The moon had spread over everything a thin layer of silver—over the
rank grass, over the mud, upon the wall of matted vegetation standing higher
than the wall of a temple, over the great river I could see through a sombre gap
glittering, glittering, as it flowed broadly by without a murmur. All this was
great, expectant, mute, while the man jabbered about himself. I wondered
whether the stillness on the face of the immensity looking at us two were
meant as an appeal or as a menace. What were we who had strayed in here?
Could we handle that dumb thing, or would it handle us? I felt how big, how
confoundedly big, was that thing that couldn't talk and perhaps was deaf as
well. What was in there? I could see a little ivory coming out from there, and I
had heard Mr Kurtz was in there. I had heard enough about it too—God
knows! Yet somehow it didn't bring any image with it—no more than if I had
been told an angel or a fiend was in there. I believed it in the same way one of
you might believe there are inhabitants in the planet Mars. I knew once a
Scotch sailmaker who was certain, dead sure, there were people in Mars.[8] If
you asked him for some idea how they looked and behaved, he would get shy
and mutter something about 'walking on all-fours.' If you as much as smiled,
he would—though a man of sixty—offer to fight you. I would not have gone so
far as to fight for Kurtz, but I went for him near enough to a lie. You know I
hate, detest, and can't bear a lie, not because I am straighter than the rest of
us, but simply because it appals me. There is a taint of death, a flavour of mortality in lies—which is exactly what I hate and detest in the world—what I want
to forget. It makes me miserable and sick, like biting something rotten would

6. A "muff" is a foolish, stupid, feeble, or
incompetent person, especially in matters of
physical skill.
7. A devil, associated with the legend of Faust,
who sells his soul to Mephistopheles; in
exchange, the devil is to do his bidding on earth.

"Papier-mâché": method of constructing (e.g.,
masks, props, ornaments) using paper and glue;
suggestive of fragility, pretension, illusoriness.
8. H. G. Wells's *The War of the Worlds*, about
an invasion of Earth by aliens from Mars, was
first serialized in 1897.

do. Temperament, I suppose. Well, I went near enough to it by letting the young fool there believe anything he liked to imagine as to my influence in Europe. I became in an instant as much of a pretence as the rest of the bewitched pilgrims. This simply because I had a notion it somehow would be of help to that Kurtz whom at the time I did not see—you understand. He was just a word for me. I did not see the man in the name any more than you do. Do you see him? Do you see the story? Do you see anything? It seems to me I am trying to tell you a dream—making a vain attempt, because no relation of a dream can convey the dream-sensation, that commingling of absurdity, surprise, and bewilderment in a tremor of struggling revolt, that notion of being captured by the incredible which is of the very essence of dreams. . . ."

He was silent for a while.

". . . No, it is impossible; it is impossible to convey the life-sensation of any given epoch of one's existence—that which makes its truth, its meaning—its subtle and penetrating essence. It is impossible. We live, as we dream—alone. . . ."

He paused again as if reflecting, then added:

"Of course in this you fellows see more than I could then. You see me, whom you know. . . ."

It had become so pitch dark that we listeners could hardly see one another. For a long time already he, sitting apart, had been no more to us than a voice. There was not a word from anybody. The others might have been asleep, but I was awake. I listened, I listened on the watch for the sentence, for the word, that would give me the clue to the faint uneasiness inspired by this narrative that seemed to shape itself without human lips in the heavy night-air of the river.

". . . Yes—I let him run on," Marlow began again, "and think what he pleased about the powers that were behind me. I did! And there was nothing behind me! There was nothing but that wretched, old, mangled steamboat I was leaning against, while he talked fluently about 'the necessity for every man to get on.' 'And when one comes out here, you conceive, it is not to gaze at the moon.' Mr Kurtz was a 'universal genius,' but even a genius would find it easier to work with 'adequate tools—intelligent men.' He did not make bricks—why, there was a physical impossibility in the way—as I was well aware; and if he did secretarial work for the manager, it was because 'no sensible man rejects wantonly the confidence of his superiors.' Did I see it? I saw it. What more did I want? What I really wanted was rivets, by heaven! Rivets. To get on with the work—to stop the hole. Rivets I wanted. There were cases of them down at the coast—cases—piled up—burst—split! You kicked a loose rivet at every second step in that station yard on the hillside. Rivets had rolled into the grove of death. You could fill your pockets with rivets for the trouble of stooping down—and there wasn't one rivet to be found where it was wanted. We had plates that would do, but nothing to fasten them with. And every week the messenger, a lone negro, letter-bag on shoulder and staff in hand, left our station for the coast. And several times a week a coast caravan came in with trade goods—ghastly glazed calico that made you shudder only to look at it, glass beads value about a penny a quart, confounded spotted cotton handkerchiefs. And no rivets. Three carriers could have brought all that was wanted to set that steamboat afloat.

"He was becoming confidential now, but I fancy my unresponsive attitude must have exasperated him at last, for he judged it necessary to inform me he feared neither God nor devil, let alone any mere man. I said I could see that very well, but what I wanted was a certain quantity of rivets—and rivets were what really Mr Kurtz wanted, if he had only known it. Now letters went to the coast every week. . . . 'My dear sir,' he cried, 'I write from dictation.' I demanded rivets. There was a way—for an intelligent man. He changed his manner; became very cold, and suddenly began to talk about a hippopotamus; wondered whether sleeping on board the steamer (I stuck to my salvage night and day) I wasn't disturbed. There was an old hippo that had the bad habit of getting out on the bank and roaming at night over the station grounds. The pilgrims used to turn out in a body and empty every rifle they could lay hands on at him. Some even had sat up o' nights for him. All this energy was wasted, though. 'That animal has a charmed life,' he said; 'but you can say this only of brutes in this country. No man—you apprehend me?—no man here bears a charmed life.' He stood there for a moment in the moonlight with his delicate hooked nose set a little askew, and his mica eyes glittering without a wink, then, with a curt Good-night, he strode off. I could see he was disturbed and considerably puzzled, which made me feel more hopeful than I had been for days. It was a great comfort to turn from that chap to my influential friend, the battered, twisted, ruined, tinpot steamboat. I clambered on board. She rang under my feet like an empty Huntley & Palmer biscuit-tin[9] kicked along a gutter; she was nothing so solid in make, and rather less pretty in shape, but I had expended enough hard work on her to make me love her. No influential friend would have served me better. She had given me a chance to come out a bit—to find out what I could do. No, I don't like work. I had rather laze about and think of all the fine things that can be done. I don't like work—no man does—but I like what is in the work—the chance to find yourself. Your own reality—for yourself, not for others—what no other man can ever know. They can only see the mere show, and never can tell what it really means.

"I was not surprised to see somebody sitting aft, on the deck, with his legs dangling over the mud. You see I rather chummed with the few mechanics there were in that station, whom the other pilgrims naturally despised—on account of their imperfect manners, I suppose. This was the foreman—a boiler-maker by trade—a good worker. He was a lank, bony, yellow-faced man, with big intense eyes. His aspect was worried, and his head was as bald as the palm of my hand; but his hair in falling seemed to have stuck to his chin, and had prospered in the new locality, for his beard hung down to his waist. He was a widower with six young children (he had left them in charge of a sister of his to come out there), and the passion of his life was pigeon-flying. He was an enthusiast and a connoisseur. He would rave about pigeons. After work hours he used to sometimes come over from his hut for a talk about his children and his pigeons; at work, when he had to crawl in the mud under the bottom of the steamboat, he would tie up that beard of his in a kind of white serviette[1] he brought for the purpose. It had loops to go over his ears. In the evening he

9. Huntley & Palmer biscuits were made in Reading, England, and exported throughout the British Empire; they came in a variety of collectible tins.
1. Table napkin (French).

could be seen squatted on the bank rinsing that wrapper in the creek with great care, then spreading it solemnly on a bush to dry.

"I slapped him on the back and shouted 'We shall have rivets!' He scrambled to his feet exclaiming 'No! Rivets!' as though he couldn't believe his ears. Then in a low voice, 'You . . . eh?' I don't know why we behaved like lunatics. I put my finger to the side of my nose and nodded mysteriously. 'Good for you!' he cried, snapped his fingers above his head, lifting one foot. I tried a jig. We capered on the iron deck. A frightful clatter came out of that hulk, and the virgin forest on the other bank of the creek sent it back in a thundering roll upon the sleeping station. It must have made some of the pilgrims sit up in their hovels. A dark figure obscured the lighted doorway of the manager's hut, vanished, then, a second or so after, the doorway itself vanished too. We stopped, and the silence driven away by the stamping of our feet flowed back again from the recesses of the land. The great wall of vegetation, an exuberant and entangled mass of trunks, branches, leaves, boughs, festoons, motionless in the moonlight, was like a rioting invasion of soundless life, a rolling wave of plants, piled up, crested, ready to topple over the creek, to sweep every little man of us out of his little existence. And it moved not. A deadened burst of mighty splashes and snorts reached us from afar, as though an ichthyosaurus[2] had been taking a bath of glitter in the great river. 'After all,' said the boiler-maker in a reasonable tone, 'why shouldn't we get the rivets?' Why not, indeed! I did not know of any reason why we shouldn't. 'They'll come in three weeks,' I said confidently.

"But they didn't. Instead of rivets there came an invasion, an infliction, a visitation. It came in sections during the next three weeks, each section headed by a donkey carrying a white man in new clothes and tan shoes, bowing from that elevation right and left to the impressed pilgrims. A quarrelsome band of footsore sulky niggers trod on the heels of the donkey; a lot of tents, camp-stools, tin boxes, white cases, brown bales would be shot down in the court-yard, and the air of mystery would deepen a little over the muddle of the station. Five such instalments came, with their absurd air of disorderly flight with the loot of innumerable outfit shops and provision stores, that, one would think, they were lugging, after a raid, into the wilderness for equitable division. It was an inextricable mess of things decent in themselves but that human folly made look like the spoils of thieving.

"This devoted band called itself the Eldorado[3] Exploring Expedition, and I believe they were sworn to secrecy. Their talk, however, was the talk of sordid buccaneers: it was reckless without hardihood, greedy without audacity, and cruel without courage; there was not an atom of foresight or of serious intention in the whole batch of them, and they did not seem aware these things are wanted for the work of the world. To tear treasure out of the bowels of the land was their desire, with no more moral purpose at the back of it than there is in burglars breaking into a safe. Who paid the expenses of the noble enterprise I don't know; but the uncle of our manager was leader of that lot.

"In exterior he resembled a butcher in a poor neighbourhood, and his eyes had a look of sleepy cunning. He carried his fat paunch with ostentation on his

2. An extinct prehistoric marine reptile resembling a fish or a dolphin.
3. *El Dorado* (literally, "the gilded one," Span-ish); the mythical land of gold sought by the Spanish conquistadors in South America.

short legs, and during the time his gang infested the station spoke to no one but his nephew. You could see these two roaming about all day long with their heads close together in an everlasting confab.[4]

"I had given up worrying myself about the rivets. One's capacity for that kind of folly is more limited than you would suppose. I said Hang!—and let things slide. I had plenty of time for meditation, and now and then I would give some thought to Kurtz. I wasn't very interested in him. No. Still, I was curious to see whether this man, who had come out equipped with moral ideas of some sort, would climb to the top after all, and how he would set about his work when there."

2

"One evening as I was lying flat on the deck of my steamboat, I heard voices approaching—and there were the nephew and the uncle strolling along the bank. I laid my head on my arm again, and had nearly lost myself in a doze, when somebody said in my ear, as it were: 'I am as harmless as a little child, but I don't like to be dictated to. Am I the manager—or am I not? I was ordered to send him there. It's incredible.' . . . I became aware that the two were standing on the shore alongside the forepart of the steamboat, just below my head. I did not move; it did not occur to me to move: I was sleepy. 'It *is* unpleasant,' grunted the uncle. 'He has asked the Administration to be sent there,' said the other, 'with the idea of showing what he could do; and I was instructed accordingly. Look at the influence that man must have. Is it not frightful?' They both agreed it was frightful, then made several bizarre remarks: 'Make rain and fine weather—one man—the Council—by the nose'—bits of absurd sentences that got the better of my drowsiness, so that I had pretty near the whole of my wits about me when the uncle said, 'The climate may do away with this difficulty for you. Is he alone there?' 'Yes,' answered the manager; 'he sent his assistant down the river with a note to me in these terms: "Clear this poor devil out of the country, and don't bother sending more of that sort. I had rather be alone than have the kind of men you can dispose of with me." It was more than a year ago. Can you imagine such impudence?' 'Anything since then?' asked the other hoarsely. 'Ivory,' jerked the nephew; 'lots of it—prime sort—lots—most annoying, from him.' 'And with that?' questioned the heavy rumble. 'Invoice,' was the reply fired out, so to speak. Then silence. They had been talking about Kurtz.

"I was broad awake by this time, but, lying perfectly at ease, remained still, having no inducement to change my position. 'How did that ivory come all this way?' growled the elder man, who seemed very vexed. The other explained that it had come with a fleet of canoes in charge of an English half-caste[5] clerk Kurtz had with him; that Kurtz had apparently intended to return himself, the station being by that time bare of goods and stores, but after coming three hundred miles, had suddenly decided to go back, which he started to do alone in a small dugout with four paddlers, leaving the half-caste to continue down the river with the ivory. The two fellows there seemed astounded at anybody attempting such a thing. They were at a loss for an adequate motive. As for me, I seemed to see Kurtz for the first time. It was a distinct glimpse: the dugout, four paddling

4. Conversation.   5. Of mixed race.

savages, and the lone white man turning his back suddenly on the headquarters, on relief, on thoughts of home—perhaps; setting his face towards the depths of the wilderness, towards his empty and desolate station. I did not know the motive. Perhaps he was just simply a fine fellow who stuck to his work for its own sake. His name, you understand, had not been pronounced once. He was 'that man.' The half-caste, who, as far as I could see, had conducted a difficult trip with great prudence and pluck, was invariably alluded to as 'that scoundrel.' The 'scoundrel' had reported that the 'man' had been very ill—had recovered imperfectly. . . . The two below me moved away then a few paces, and strolled back and forth at some little distance. I heard: 'Military post—doctor—two hundred miles—quite alone now—unavoidable delays—nine months—no news—strange rumours.' They approached again, just as the manager was saying, 'No one, as far as I know, unless a species of wandering trader—a pestilential fellow, snapping ivory from the natives.' Who was it they were talking about now? I gathered in snatches that this was some man supposed to be in Kurtz's district, and of whom the manager did not approve. 'We will not be free from unfair competition till one of these fellows is hanged for an example,' he said. 'Certainly,' grunted the other; 'get him hanged! Why not? Anything—anything can be done in this country. That's what I say; nobody here, you understand, *here*, can endanger your position. And why? You stand the climate—you outlast them all. The danger is in Europe; but there before I left I took care to—' They moved off and whispered, then their voices rose again. 'The extraordinary series of delays is not my fault. I did my possible.' The fat man sighed, 'Very sad.' 'And the pestiferous absurdity of his talk,' continued the other; 'he bothered me enough when he was here. "Each station should be like a beacon on the road towards better things, a centre for trade of course, but also for humanising, improving, instructing." Conceive you[6]—that ass! And he wants to be manager! No, it's—' Here he got choked by excessive indignation, and I lifted my head the least bit. I was surprised to see how near they were—right under me. I could have spat upon their hats. They were looking on the ground, absorbed in thought. The manager was switching his leg with a slender twig: his sagacious relative lifted his head. 'You have been well since you came out this time?' he asked. The other gave a start. 'Who? I? Oh! Like a charm—like a charm. But the rest—oh, my goodness! All sick. They die so quick, too, that I haven't the time to send them out of the country—it's incredible!' 'H'm. Just so,' grunted the uncle. 'Ah! my boy, trust to this—I say, trust to this.' I saw him extend his short flipper of an arm for a gesture that took in the forest, the creek, the mud, the river—seemed to beckon with a dishonouring flourish before the sunlit face of the land a treacherous appeal to the lurking death, to the hidden evil, to the profound darkness of its heart. It was so startling that I leaped to my feet and looked back at the edge of the forest, as though I had expected an answer of some sort to that black display of confidence. You know the foolish notions that come to one sometimes. The high stillness confronted these two figures with its ominous patience, waiting for the passing away of a fantastic invasion.

"They swore aloud together—out of sheer fright, I believe—then, pretending not to know anything of my existence, turned back to the station. The sun was

6. "Just imagine." This phrase, like "I did my possible" (I did the best I could), above, and others throughout the novel, is a literal translation of the French spoken by Belgian traders.

low; and leaning forward side by side, they seemed to be tugging painfully uphill their two ridiculous shadows of unequal length, that trailed behind them slowly over the tall grass without bending a single blade.

"In a few days the Eldorado Expedition went into the patient wilderness, that closed upon it as the sea closes over a diver. Long afterwards the news came that all the donkeys were dead. I know nothing as to the fate of the less valuable animals.[7] They, no doubt, like the rest of us, found what they deserved. I did not inquire. I was then rather excited at the prospect of meeting Kurtz very soon. When I say very soon I mean it comparatively. It was just two months from the day we left the creek when we came to the bank below Kurtz's station.

"Going up that river was like travelling back to the earliest beginnings of the world, when vegetation rioted on the earth and the big trees were kings. An empty stream, a great silence, an impenetrable forest. The air was warm, thick, heavy, sluggish. There was no joy in the brilliance of sunshine. The long stretches of the waterway ran on, deserted, into the gloom of overshadowed distances. On silvery sandbanks hippos and alligators sunned themselves side by side. The broadening waters flowed through a mob of wooded islands; you lost your way on that river as you would in a desert, and butted all day long against shoals, trying to find the channel, till you thought yourself bewitched and cut off for ever from everything you had known once—somewhere—far away—in another existence perhaps. There were moments when one's past came back to one, as it will sometimes when you have not a moment to spare to yourself; but it came in the shape of an unrestful and noisy dream, remembered with wonder amongst the overwhelming realities of this strange world of plants, and water, and silence. And this stillness of life did not in the least resemble a peace. It was the stillness of an implacable force brooding over an inscrutable intention. It looked at you with a vengeful aspect. I got used to it afterwards; I did not see it any more; I had no time. I had to keep guessing at the channel; I had to discern, mostly by inspiration, the signs of hidden banks; I watched for sunken stones; I was learning to clap my teeth smartly before my heart flew out, when I shaved by a fluke some infernal sly old snag[8] that would have ripped the life out of the tin-pot steamboat and drowned all the pilgrims; I had to keep a look-out for the signs of dead wood we could cut up in the night for next day's steaming. When you have to attend to things of that sort, to the mere incidents of the surface, the reality—the reality, I tell you—fades. The inner truth is hidden—luckily, luckily. But I felt it all the same; I felt often its mysterious stillness watching me at my monkey tricks, just as it watches you fellows performing on your respective tight-ropes for—what is it? half a crown[9] a tumble—"

"Try to be civil, Marlow," growled a voice, and I knew there was at least one listener awake besides myself.

"I beg your pardon. I forgot the heartache which makes up the rest of the price. And indeed what does the price matter, if the trick be well done? You do your tricks very well. And I didn't do badly either, since I managed not to sink that steamboat on my first trip. It's a wonder to me yet. Imagine a blindfolded

---

7. I.e., humans.
8. A large branch or tree trunk embedded in the river bottom with one end pointing up.
9. British denomination of coin, equal to 2

shillings and 6 pence, or an eighth of a pound. Not much money: at the time, the value of a London cab fare or a generous tip.

man set to drive a van over a bad road. I sweated and shivered over that business considerably, I can tell you. After all, for a seaman, to scrape the bottom of the thing that's supposed to float all the time under his care is the unpardonable sin. No one may know of it, but you never forget the thump—eh? A blow on the very heart. You remember it, you dream of it, you wake up at night and think of it—years after—and go hot and cold all over. I don't pretend to say that steamboat floated all the time. More than once she had to wade for a bit, with twenty cannibals splashing around and pushing. We had enlisted some of these chaps on the way for a crew. Fine fellows—cannibals—in their place. They were men one could work with, and I am grateful to them. And, after all, they did not eat each other before my face: they had brought along a provision of hippo-meat which went rotten, and made the mystery of the wilderness stink in my nostrils. Phoo! I can sniff it now. I had the manager on board and three or four pilgrims with their staves—all complete. Sometimes we came upon a station close by the bank, clinging to the skirts of the unknown, and the white men rushing out of a tumble-down hovel, with great gestures of joy and surprise and welcome, seemed very strange—had the appearance of being held there captive by a spell. The word 'ivory' would ring in the air for a while—and on we went again into the silence, along empty reaches, round the still bends, between the high walls of our winding way, reverberating in hollow claps the ponderous beat of the stern-wheel.[1] Trees, trees, millions of trees, massive, immense, running up high; and at their foot, hugging the bank against the stream, crept the little begrimed steamboat, like a sluggish beetle crawling on the floor of a lofty portico. It made you feel very small, very lost, and yet it was not altogether depressing, that feeling. After all, if you were small, the grimy beetle crawled on—which was just what you wanted it to do. Where the pilgrims imagined it crawled to I don't know. To some place where they expected to get something, I bet! For me it crawled towards Kurtz—exclusively; but when the steam-pipes started leaking we crawled very slow. The reaches opened before us and closed behind, as if the forest had stepped leisurely across the water to bar the way for our return. We penetrated deeper and deeper into the heart of darkness. It was very quiet there. At night sometimes the roll of drums behind the curtain of trees would run up the river and remain sustained faintly, as if hovering in the air high over our heads, till the first break of day. Whether it meant war, peace, or prayer we could not tell. The dawns were heralded by the descent of a chill stillness; the woodcutters slept, their fires burned low; the snapping of a twig would make you start. We were wanderers on a prehistoric earth, on an earth that wore the aspect of an unknown planet. We could have fancied ourselves the first of men taking possession of an accursed inheritance, to be subdued at the cost of profound anguish and of excessive toil. But suddenly, as we struggled round a bend, there would be a glimpse of rush walls, of peaked grass-roofs, a burst of yells, a whirl of black limbs, a mass of hands clapping, of feet stamping, of bodies swaying, of eyes rolling, under the droop of heavy and motionless foliage. The steamer toiled along slowly on the edge of a black and incomprehensible frenzy. The prehistoric man was cursing us, praying to us, welcoming us—who could tell? We were cut off from the

---

1. The paddle wheel at the rear of the boat; the main source of propulsion on a steamboat.

comprehension of our surroundings; we glided past like phantoms, wondering and secretly appalled, as sane men would be before an enthusiastic outbreak in a madhouse. We could not understand because we were too far and could not remember, because we were travelling in the night of first ages, of those ages that are gone, leaving hardly a sign—and no memories.

"The earth seemed unearthly. We are accustomed to look upon the shackled form of a conquered monster, but there—there you could look at a thing monstrous and free. It was unearthly, and the men were—No, they were not inhuman. Well, you know, that was the worst of it—this suspicion of their not being inhuman. It would come slowly to one. They howled and leaped, and spun, and made horrid faces; but what thrilled you was just the thought of their humanity—like yours—the thought of your remote kinship with this wild and passionate uproar. Ugly. Yes, it was ugly enough; but if you were man enough you would admit to yourself that there was in you just the faintest trace of a response to the terrible frankness of that noise, a dim suspicion of there being a meaning in it which you—you so remote from the night of first ages—could comprehend. And why not? The mind of man is capable of anything—because everything is in it, all the past as well as all the future. What was there after all? Joy, fear, sorrow, devotion, valour, rage—who can tell?—but truth—truth stripped of its cloak of time. Let the fool gape and shudder—the man knows, and can look on without a wink. But he must at least be as much of a man as these on the shore. He must meet that truth with his own true stuff—with his own inborn strength. Principles? Principles won't do. Acquisitions, clothes, pretty rags—rags that would fly off at the first good shake. No; you want a deliberate belief. An appeal to me in this fiendish row—is there? Very well; I hear; I admit, but I have a voice too, and for good or evil mine is the speech that cannot be silenced. Of course, a fool, what with sheer fright and fine sentiments, is always safe. Who's that grunting? You wonder I didn't go ashore for a howl and a dance? Well, no—I didn't. Fine sentiments, you say? Fine sentiments be hanged! I had no time. I had to mess about with white-lead[2] and strips of woollen blanket helping to put bandages on those leaky steam-pipes—I tell you. I had to watch the steering, and circumvent those snags, and get the tin-pot along by hook or by crook. There was surface-truth enough in these things to save a wiser man. And between whiles I had to look after the savage who was fireman. He was an improved specimen; he could fire up a vertical boiler.[3] He was there below me, and, upon my word, to look at him was as edifying as seeing a dog in a parody of breeches and a feather hat, walking on his hind legs. A few months of training had done for that really fine chap. He squinted at the steam-gauge and at the water-gauge with an evident effort of intrepidity—and he had filed teeth too, the poor devil, and the wool of his pate shaved into queer patterns, and three ornamental scars on each of his cheeks. He ought to have been clapping his hands and stamping his feet on the bank, instead of which he was hard at work, a thrall to strange witchcraft, full of improving knowledge. He was useful because he had been instructed; and what he knew was this—that should the water in that transparent thing disappear, the evil spirit inside the boiler would get angry through the greatness of

2. Lead compound often used in white paint 3. A simple and easily fired narrow boiler.
for caulking seams and waterproofing timber.

his thirst, and take a terrible vengeance. So he sweated and fired up and watched the glass fearfully (with an impromptu charm, made of rags, tied to his arm, and a piece of polished bone, as big as a watch, stuck flatways through his lower lip), while the wooded banks slipped past us slowly, the short noise was left behind, the interminable miles of silence—and we crept on, towards Kurtz. But the snags were thick, the water was treacherous and shallow, the boiler seemed indeed to have a sulky devil in it, and thus neither that fireman nor I had any time to peer into our creepy thoughts.

"Some fifty miles below the Inner Station we came upon a hut of reeds, an inclined and melancholy pole, with the unrecognisable tatters of what had been a flag of some sort flying from it, and a neatly stacked wood-pile. This was unexpected. We came to the bank, and on the stack of firewood found a flat piece of board with some faded pencil-writing on it. When deciphered it said: 'Wood for you. Hurry up. Approach cautiously.' There was a signature, but it was illegible—not Kurtz—a much longer word. Hurry up. Where? Up the river? 'Approach cautiously.' We had not done so. But the warning could not have been meant for the place where it could be only found after approach. Something was wrong above. But what—and how much? That was the question. We commented adversely upon the imbecility of that telegraphic style.[4] The bush around said nothing, and would not let us look very far, either. A torn curtain of red twill hung in the doorway of the hut, and flapped sadly in our faces. The dwelling was dismantled; but we could see a white man had lived there not very long ago. There remained a rude table—a plank on two posts; a heap of rubbish reposed in a dark corner, and by the door I picked up a book. It had lost its covers, and the pages had been thumbed into a state of extremely dirty softness; but the back had been lovingly stitched afresh with white cotton thread, which looked clean yet. It was an extraordinary find. Its title was, *An Inquiry into some Points of Seamanship*, by a man Towser, Towson—some such name—Master in His Majesty's Navy.[5] The matter looked dreary reading enough, with illustrative diagrams and repulsive tables of figures, and the copy was sixty years old. I handled this amazing antiquity with the greatest possible tenderness, lest it should dissolve in my hands. Within, Towson or Towser was inquiring earnestly into the breaking strain of ships' chains and tackle, and other such matters. Not a very enthralling book; but at the first glance you could see there a singleness of intention, an honest concern for the right way of going to work, which made these humble pages, thought out so many years ago, luminous with another than a professional light. The simple old sailor, with his talk of chains and purchases,[6] made me forget the jungle and the pilgrims in a delicious sensation of having come upon something unmistakably real. Such a book being there was wonderful enough; but still more astounding were the notes pencilled in the margin, and plainly referring to the text. I couldn't believe my eyes! They were in cipher! Yes, it looked like cipher. Fancy a man lugging with him a book of that description into this nowhere and studying it—and making notes—in cipher at that! It was an extravagant mystery.

4. Using as few words as possible, as in a telegram.
5. I.e., the British Navy.
6. Nautical terms. "Chains": contrivances for fastening ropes supporting the mast to the deck and the sides of a ship. "Purchases": devices for applying or increasing force: pulleys, windlasses, etc.

"I had been dimly aware for some time of a worrying noise, and when I lifted my eyes I saw the wood-pile was gone, and the manager, aided by all the pilgrims, was shouting at me from the river-side. I slipped the book into my pocket. I assure you to leave off reading was like tearing myself away from the shelter of an old an solid friendship.

"I started the lame engine ahead. 'It must be this miserable trader—this intruder,' exclaimed the manager, looking back malevolently at the place we had left. 'He must be English,' I said. 'It will not save him from getting into trouble if he is not careful,' muttered the manager darkly. I observed with assumed innocence that no man was safe from trouble in this world.

"The current was more rapid now, the steamer seemed at her last gasp, the stern-wheel flopped languidly, and I caught myself listening on tiptoe for the next beat of the float,[7] for in sober truth I expected the wretched thing to give up every moment. It was like watching the last flickers of a life. But still we crawled. Sometimes I would pick out a tree a little way head to measure our progress towards Kurtz by, but I lost it invariably before we got abreast. To keep the eyes so long on one thing was too much for human patience. The manager displayed a beautiful resignation. I fretted and fumed and took to arguing with myself whether or no I would talk openly with Kurtz; but before I could come to any conclusion it occurred to me that my speech or my silence, indeed any action of mine, would be a mere futility. What did it matter what any one knew or ignored? What did it matter who was manager? One gets sometimes such a flash of insight. The essentials of this affair lay deep under the surface, beyond my reach, and beyond my power of meddling.

"Towards the evening of the second day we judged ourselves about eight miles from Kurtz's station. I wanted to push on; but the manager looked grave, and told me the navigation up there was so dangerous that it would be advisable, the sun being very low already, to wait where we were till next morning. Moreover, he pointed out that if the warning to approach cautiously were to be followed, we must approach in daylight—not at dusk, or in the dark. This was sensible enough. Eight miles meant nearly three hours' steaming for us, and I could also see suspicious ripples at the upper end of the reach. Nevertheless, I was annoyed beyond expression at the delay, and most unreasonably too, since one night more could not matter much after so many months. As we had plenty of wood, and caution was the word, I brought up in the middle of the stream. The reach was narrow, straight, with high sides like a railway cutting. The dusk came gliding into it long before the sun had set. The current ran smooth and swift, but a dumb immobility sat on the banks. The living trees, lashed together by the creepers and every living bush of the undergrowth, might have been changed into stone, even to the slenderest twig, to the lightest leaf. It was not sleep—it seemed unnatural, like a state of trance. Not the faintest sound of any kind could be heard. You looked on amazed, and began to suspect yourself of being deaf—then the night came suddenly, and struck you blind as well. About three in the morning some large fish leaped, and the loud splash made me jump as though a gun had been fired. When the sun rose there was a white fog, very warm and clammy, and more blinding than the night. It did not shift or drive; it was just there, standing all round you like something

7. The sound of the paddle ("paddle float") as it hits the water.

solid. At eight or nine, perhaps, it lifted as a shutter lifts. We had a glimpse of the towering multitude of trees, of the immense matted jungle, with the blazing little ball of the sun hanging over it—all perfectly still—and then the white shutter came down again, smoothly, as if sliding in greased grooves. I ordered the chain, which we had begun to heave in, to be paid out again. Before it stopped running with a muffled rattle, a cry, a very loud cry, as of infinite desolation, soared slowly in the opaque air. It ceased. A complaining clamour, modulated in savage discords, filled our ears. The sheer unexpectedness of it made my hair stir under my cap. I don't know how it struck the others: to me it seemed as though the mist itself had screamed, so suddenly, and apparently from all sides at once, did this tumultuous and mournful uproar arise. It culminated in a hurried outbreak of almost intolerably excessive shrieking, which stopped short, leaving us stiffened in a variety of silly attitudes, and obstinately listening to the nearly as appalling and excessive silence. 'Good God! What is the meaning—?' stammered at my elbow one of the pilgrims—a little fat man, with sandy hair and red whiskers, who wore side-spring boots, and pink pyjamas tucked into his socks. Two others remained open-mouthed a whole minute, then dashed into the little cabin, to rush out incontinently and stand darting scared glances, with Winchesters[8] at 'ready' in their hands. What we could see was just the steamer we were on, her outlines blurred as though she had been on the point of dissolving, and a misty strip of water, perhaps two feet broad, around her—and that was all. The rest of the world was nowhere, as far as our eyes and ears were concerned. Just nowhere. Gone, disappeared; swept off without leaving a whisper or a shadow behind.

"I went forward, and ordered the chain to be hauled in short, so as to be ready to trip the anchor and move the steamboat at once if necessary. 'Will they attack?' whispered an awed voice. 'We will all be butchered in this fog,' murmured another. The faces twitched with the strain, the hands trembled slightly, the eyes forgot to wink. It was very curious to see the contrast of expressions of the white men and of the black fellows of our crew, who were as much strangers to that part of the river as we, though their homes were only eight hundred miles away. The whites, of course greatly discomposed, had besides a curious look of being painfully shocked by such an outrageous row. The others had an alert, naturally interested expression; but their faces were essentially quiet, even those of the one or two who grinned as they hauled at the chain. Several exchanged short, grunting phrases, which seemed to settle the matter to their satisfaction. Their headman, a young, broad-chested black, severely draped in dark-blue fringed cloths, with fierce nostrils and his hair all done up artfully in oily ringlets, stood near me. 'Aha!' I said, just for good fellowship's sake. 'Catch 'im,' he snapped, with a bloodshot widening of his eyes and a flash of sharp teeth—'catch 'im. Give 'im to us.' 'To you, eh?' I asked; 'what would you do with them?' 'Eat 'im!' he said curtly, and, leaning his elbow on the rail, looked out into the fog in a dignified and profoundly pensive attitude. I would no doubt have been properly horrified, had it not occurred to me that he and his chaps must be very hungry: that they must have been growing increasingly hungry for at least this month past. They had been engaged for six months (I don't think a

8. Lever-action repeating rifles.

single one of them had any clear idea of time, as we at the end of countless ages have. They still belonged to the beginnings of time—had no inherited experience to teach them, as it were), and of course, as long as there was a piece of paper written over in accordance with some farcical law or other made down the river, it didn't enter anybody's head to trouble how they would live. Certainly they had brought with them some rotten hippo-meat, which couldn't have lasted very long, anyway, even if the pilgrims hadn't, in the midst of a shocking hullabaloo, thrown a considerable quantity of it overboard. It looked like a high-handed proceeding; but it was really a case of legitimate self-defence. You can't breathe dead hippo waking, sleeping, and eating, and at the same time keep your precarious grip on existence. Besides that, they had given them every week three pieces of brass wire, each about nine inches long; and the theory was they were to buy their provisions with that currency in river-side villages. You can see how *that* worked. There were either no villages, or the people were hostile, or the director, who like the rest of us fed out of tins, with an occasional old he-goat thrown in, didn't want to stop the steamer for some more or less recondite reasons. So, unless they swallowed the wire itself, or made loops of it to snare the fishes with, I don't see what good their extravagant salary could be to them. I must say it was paid with a regularity worthy of a large and honourable trading company. For the rest, the only thing to eat—though it didn't look eatable in the least—I saw in their possession was a few lumps of some stuff like half-cooked dough, of a dirty lavender colour, they kept wrapped in leaves, and now and then swallowed a piece of, but so small that it seemed done more for the look of the thing than for any serious purpose of sustenance. Why in the name of all the gnawing devils of hunger they didn't go for us—they were thirty to five—and have a good tuck-in for once, amazes me now when I think of it. They were big powerful men, with not much capacity to weigh the consequences, with courage, with strength, even yet, though their skins were no longer glossy and their muscles no longer hard. And I saw that something restraining, one of those human secrets that baffle probability, had come into play there. I looked at them with a swift quickening of interest—not because it occurred to me I might be eaten by them before very long, though I own to you that just then I perceived—in a new light, as it were—how unwholesome the pilgrims looked, and I hoped, yes, I positively hoped, that my aspect was not so—what shall I say?—so—unappetising: a touch of fantastic vanity which fitted well with the dream-sensation that pervaded all my days at that time. Perhaps I had a little fever too. One can't live with one's finger everlastingly on one's pulse. I had often 'a little fever,' or a little touch of other things—the playful paw-strokes of the wilderness, the preliminary trifling before the more serious onslaught which came in due course. Yes; I looked at them as you would on any human being, with a curiosity of their impulses, motives, capacities, weaknesses, when brought to the test of an inexorable physical necessity. Restraint! What possible restraint? Was it superstition, disgust, patience, fear—or some kind of primitive honour? No fear can stand up to hunger, no patience can wear it out, disgust simply does not exist where hunger is; and as to superstition, beliefs, and what you may call principles, they are less than chaff in a breeze. Don't you know the devilry of lingering starvation, its exasperating torment, its black thoughts, its sombre and brooding ferocity? Well, I do. It takes a man all his inborn strength to fight hunger properly. It's really easier to face bereavement, dishonour, and the perdition of one's soul—than this kind of prolonged hunger. Sad, but true. And these chaps too had no earthly reason for any kind of scruple. Restraint! I would just as soon have expected restraint from a hyena prowling amongst the corpses of a battlefield. But there was the fact facing me—the fact dazzling, to be seen, like the foam on the depths of the sea, like a ripple on an unfathomable enigma, a mystery greater—when I thought of it—than the curious, inexplicable note of desperate grief in this savage clamour that had swept by us on the river-bank, behind the blind whiteness of the fog.

"Two pilgrims were quarrelling in hurried whispers as to which bank. 'Left.' 'No, no; how can you? Right, right, of course.' 'It is very serious,' said the manager's voice behind me; 'I would be desolated if anything should happen to Mr. Kurtz before we came up.' I looked at him, and had not the slightest doubt he was sincere. He was just the kind of man who would wish to preserve appearances. That was his restraint. But when he muttered something about going on at once, I did not even take the trouble to answer him. I knew, and he knew, that it was impossible. Were we to let go our hold of the bottom, we would be absolutely in the air—in space. We wouldn't be able to tell where we were going to—whether up or down stream, or across—till we fetched against one bank or the other—and then we wouldn't know at first which it was. Of course I made no move. I had no mind for a smashup. You couldn't imagine a more deadly place for a shipwreck. Whether drowned at once or not, we were sure to perish speedily in one way or another. 'I authorise you to take all the risks,' he said, after a short silence. 'I refuse to take any,' I said shortly; which was just the answer he expected, though its tone might have surprised him. 'Well, I must defer to your judgment. You are captain,' he said, with marked civility. I turned my shoulder to him in sign of my appreciation, and looked into the fog. How long would it last? It was the most hopeless look-out. The approach to this Kurtz grubbing for ivory in the wretched bush was beset by as many dangers as though he had been an enchanted princess sleeping in a fabulous castle. 'Will they attack, do you think?' asked the manager, in a confidential tone.

"I did not think they would attack, for several obvious reasons. The thick fog was one. If they left the bank in their canoes they would get lost in it, as we would be if we attempted to move. Still, I had also judged the jungle of both banks quite impenetrable—and yet eyes were in it, eyes that had seen us. The river-side bushes were certainly very thick; but the undergrowth behind was evidently penetrable. However, during the short lift I had seen no canoes anywhere in the reach—certainly not abreast of the steamer. But what made the idea of attack inconceivable to me was the nature of the noise—of the cries we had heard. They had not the fierce character boding of immediate hostile intention. Unexpected, wild, and violent as they had been, they had given me an irresistible impression of sorrow. The glimpse of the steamboat had for some reason filled those savages with unrestrained grief. The danger, if any, I expounded, was from our proximity to a great human passion let loose. Even extreme grief may ultimately vent itself in violence—but more generally takes the form of apathy. . . .

"You should have seen the pilgrims stare! They had no heart to grin, or even to revile me; but I believe they thought me gone mad—with fright, maybe. I delivered a regular lecture. My dear boys, it was no good bothering. Keep a look-out? Well, you may guess I watched the fog for the signs of lifting as a cat watches a mouse; but for anything else our eyes were of no more use to us than if we had been buried miles deep in a heap of cottonwool. It felt like it too—choking, warm, stifling. Besides, all I said, though it sounded extravagant, was absolutely true to fact. What we afterwards alluded to as an attack was really an attempt at repulse. The action was very far from being aggressive—it was not even defensive, in the usual sense: it was undertaken under the stress of desperation, and in its essence was purely protective.

"It developed itself, I should say, two hours after the fog lifted, and its commencement was at a spot, roughly speaking, about a mile and a half below Kurtz's station. We had just floundered and flopped round a bend, when I saw an islet, a mere grassy hummock of bright green, in the middle of the stream. It was the only thing of the kind; but as we opened the reach more, I perceived it was the head of a long sandbank, or rather of a chain of shallow patches stretching down the middle of the river. They were discoloured, just awash, and the whole lot was seen just under the water, exactly as a man's backbone is seen running down the middle of his back under the skin. Now, as far as I did see, I could go to the right or to the left of this. I didn't know either channel, of course. The banks looked pretty well alike, the depth appeared the same; but as I had been informed the station was on the west side, I naturally headed for the western passage.

"No sooner had we fairly entered it than I became aware it was much narrower than I had supposed. To the left of us there was the long uninterrupted shoal, and to the right a high steep bank heavily overgrown with bushes. Above the bush the trees stood in serried ranks. The twigs overhung the current thickly, and from distance to distance a large limb of some tree projected rigidly over the stream. It was then well on in the afternoon, the face of the forest was gloomy, and a broad strip of shadow had already fallen on the water. In this shadow we steamed up—very slowly, as you may imagine. I sheered her well inshore—the water being deepest near the bank, as the sounding-pole[9] informed me.

"One of my hungry and forbearing friends was sounding in the bows just below me. This steamboat was exactly like a decked scow.[1] On the deck there were two little teak-wood houses, with doors and windows. The boiler was in the fore-end, and the machinery right astern. Over the whole there was a light roof, supported on stanchions. The funnel projected through that roof, and in front of the funnel a small cabin built of light planks served for a pilot-house. It contained a couch, two camp-stools, a loaded Martini-Henry[2] leaning in one corner, a tiny table, and the steering-wheel. It had a wide door in front and a broad shutter at each side. All these were always thrown open, of course. I spent my days perched up there on the extreme fore-end of that roof, before the door. At night I slept, or tried to, on the couch. An athletic black belonging to some coast tribe, and educated by my poor predecessor, was the helmsman. He sported a pair of brass earrings, wore a blue cloth wrapper from the waist to the

---

9. A pole with measurements, stuck in the water until it hits bottom, to determine the depth of a shallow body of water. "Sheered her well inshore": i.e., steered so as to be going upriver while close to the bank.

1. A large, flat-bottomed boat for cargo; in this case, with the addition of a deck.
2. A lever-action rifle taking an especially powerful charge; standard British service weapon of the time.

ankles, and thought all the world of himself. He was the most unstable kind of fool I had ever seen. He steered with no end of a swagger while you were by; but if he lost sight of you, he became instantly the prey of an abject funk, and would let that cripple of a steamboat get the upper hand of him in a minute.

"I was looking down at the sounding-pole, and feeling much annoyed to see at each try a little more of it stick out of that river, when I saw my poleman give up the business suddenly, and stretch himself flat on the deck, without even taking the trouble to haul his pole in. He kept hold on it though, and it trailed in the water. At the same time the fireman, whom I could also see below me, sat down abruptly before his furnace and ducked his head. I was amazed. Then I had to look at the river mighty quick, because there was a snag in the fairway. Sticks, little sticks, were flying about—thick; they were whizzing before my nose, dropping below me, striking behind me against my pilot-house. All this time the river, the shore, the woods, were very quiet—perfectly quiet. I could only hear the heavy splashing thump of the stern-wheel and the patter of these things. We cleared the snag clumsily. Arrows, by Jove! We were being shot at! I stepped in quickly to close the shutter on the land-side. That fool-helmsman, his hands on the spokes, was lifting his knees high, stamping his feet, champing his mouth, like a reined-in horse. Confound him! And we were staggering within ten feet of the bank. I had to lean right out to swing the heavy shutter, and I saw a face amongst the leaves on the level with my own, looking at me very fierce and steady; and then suddenly, as though a veil had been removed from my eyes, I made out, deep in the tangled gloom, naked breasts, arms, legs, glaring eyes— the bush was swarming with human limbs in movement, glistening, of bronze colour. The twigs shook, swayed, and rustled, the arrows flew out of them, and then the shutter came to. 'Steer her straight,' I said to the helmsman. He held his head rigid, face forward; but his eyes rolled, he kept on lifting and setting down his feet gently, his mouth foamed a little. 'Keep quiet!' I said in a fury. I might just as well have ordered a tree not to sway in the wind. I darted out. Below me there was a great scuffle of feet on the iron deck; confused exclamations; a voice screamed, 'Can you turn back?' I caught sight of a V-shaped ripple on the water ahead. What? Another snag! A fusillade[3] burst out under my feet. The pilgrims had opened with their Winchesters, and were simply squirting lead into that bush. A deuce of a lot of smoke came up and drove slowly forward. I swore at it. Now I couldn't see the ripple or the snag either. I stood in the door-way, peering, and the arrows came in swarms. They might have been poisoned, but they looked as though they wouldn't kill a cat. The bush began to howl. Our wood-cutters raised a warlike whoop; the report of a rifle just at my back deafened me. I glanced over my shoulder, and the pilot-house was yet full of noise and smoke when I made a dash at the wheel. The fool-nigger had dropped everything, to throw the shutter open and let off that Martini-Henry. He stood before the wide opening, glaring, and I yelled at him to come back, while I straightened the sudden twist out of that steamboat. There was no room to turn even if I had wanted to, the snag was somewhere very near ahead in that confounded smoke, there was no time to lose, so I just crowded her into the bank— right into the bank, where I knew the water was deep.

3. The simultaneous discharge of many firearms.

"We tore slowly along the overhanging bushes in a whirl of broken twigs and flying leaves. The fusillade below stopped short, as I had foreseen it would when the squirts got empty. I threw my head back to a glinting whizz that traversed the pilot-house, in at one shutter-hole and out at the other. Looking past that mad helmsman, who was shaking the empty rifle and yelling at the shore, I saw vague forms of men running bent double, leaping, gliding, distinct, incomplete, evanescent. Something big appeared in the air before the shutter, the rifle went overboard, and the man stepped back swiftly, looked at me over his shoulder in an extraordinary, profound, familiar manner, and fell upon my feet. The side of his head hit the wheel twice, and the end of what appeared a long cane clattered round and knocked over a little camp-stool. It looked as though after wrenching that thing from somebody ashore he had lost his balance in the effort. The thin smoke had blown away, we were clear of the snag, and looking ahead I could see that in another hundred yards or so I would be free to sheer off, away from the bank; but my feet felt so very warm and wet that I had to look down. The man had rolled on his back and stared straight up at me; both his hands clutched that cane. It was the shaft of a spear that, either thrown or lunged through the opening, had caught him in the side just below the ribs; the blade had gone in out of sight, after making a frightful gash; my shoes were full; a pool of blood lay very still, gleaming dark-red under the wheel; his eyes shone with an amazing lustre. The fusillade burst out again. He looked at me anxiously, gripping the spear like something precious, with an air of being afraid I would try to take it away from him. I had to make an effort to free my eyes from his gaze and attend to the steering. With one hand I felt above my head for the line of the steam whistle, and jerked out screech after screech hurriedly. The tumult of angry and warlike yells was checked instantly, and then from the depths of the woods went out such a tremulous and prolonged wail of mournful fear and utter despair as may be imagined to follow the flight of the last hope from the earth. There was a great commotion in the bush; the shower of arrows stopped, a few dropping shots rang out sharply—then silence, in which the languid beat of the stern-wheel came plainly to my ears. I put the helm hard a-starboard at the moment when the pilgrim in pink pyjamas, very hot and agitated, appeared in the doorway. 'The manager sends me—' he began in an official tone, and stopped short. 'Good God!' he said, glaring at the wounded man.

"We two whites stood over him, and his lustrous and inquiring glance enveloped us both. I declare it looked as though he would presently put to us some question in an understandable language; but he died without uttering a sound, without moving a limb, without twitching a muscle. Only in the very last moment, as though in response to some sign we could not see, to some whisper we could not hear, he frowned heavily, and that frown gave to his black death-mask an inconceivably sombre, brooding, and menacing expression. The lustre of inquiring glance faded swiftly into vacant glassiness. 'Can you steer?' I asked the agent eagerly. He looked very dubious; but I made a grab at his arm, and he understood at once I meant him to steer whether or no. To tell you the truth, I was morbidly anxious to change my shoes and socks. 'He is dead,' murmured the fellow, immensely impressed. 'No doubt about it,' said I, tugging like mad at the shoelaces. 'And by the way, I suppose Mr Kurtz is dead as well by this time.'

"For the moment that was the dominant thought. There was a sense of extreme disappointment, as though I had found out I had been striving after something altogether without a substance. I couldn't have been more disgusted if I had travelled all this way for the sole purpose of talking with Mr Kurtz. Talking with . . . I flung one shoe overboard, and became aware that that was exactly what I had been looking forward to—a talk with Kurtz. I made the strange discovery that I had never imagined him as doing, you know, but as discoursing. I didn't say to myself, 'Now I will never see him,' or 'Now I will never shake him by the hand,' but, 'Now I will never hear him.' The man presented himself as a voice. Not of course that I did not connect him with some sort of action. Hadn't I been told in all the tones of jealousy and admiration that he had collected, bartered, swindled, or stolen more ivory than all the other agents together? That was not the point. The point was in his being a gifted creature, and that of all his gifts the one that stood out pre-eminently, that carried with it a sense of real presence, was his ability to talk, his words— the gift of expression, the bewildering, the illuminating, the most exalted and the most contemptible, the pulsating stream of light, or the deceitful flow from the heart of an impenetrable darkness.

"The other shoe went flying unto the devil-god of that river. I thought, By Jove! it's all over. We are too late; he has vanished—the gift has vanished, by means of some spear, arrow, or club. I will never hear that chap speak after all—and my sorrow had a startling extravagance of emotion, even such as I had noticed in the howling sorrow of these savages in the bush. I couldn't have felt more of lonely desolation somehow, had I been robbed of a belief or had missed my destiny in life. . . . Why do you sigh in this beastly way, somebody? Absurd? Well, absurd. Good Lord! mustn't a man ever—Here, give me some tobacco." . . .

There was a pause of profound stillness, then a match flared, and Marlow's lean face appeared, worn, hollow, with downward folds and dropped eyelids, with an aspect of concentrated attention; and as he took vigorous draws at his pipe, it seemed to retreat and advance out of the night in the regular flicker of the tiny flame. The match went out.

"Absurd!" he cried. "This is the worst of trying to tell . . . Here you all are, each moored with two good addresses, like a hulk with two anchors, a butcher round one corner, a policeman round another, excellent appetites, and temperature normal—you hear—normal from year's end to year's end. And you say, Absurd! Absurd be—exploded! Absurd! My dear boys, what can you expect from a man who out of sheer nervousness had just flung overboard a pair of new shoes? Now I think of it, it is amazing I did not shed tears. I am, upon the whole, proud of my fortitude. I was cut to the quick at the idea of having lost the inestimable privilege of listening to the gifted Kurtz. Of course I was wrong. The privilege was waiting for me. Oh yes, I heard more than enough. And I was right, too. A voice. He was very little more than a voice. And I heard—him— it—this voice—other voices—all of them were so little more than voices—and the memory of that time itself lingers around me, impalpable, like a dying vibration of one immense jabber, silly, atrocious, sordid, savage, or simply mean, without any kind of sense. Voices, voices—even the girl herself—now—"

He was silent for a long time.

"I laid the ghost of his gifts at last with a lie," he began suddenly. "Girl! What? Did I mention a girl? Oh, she is out of it—completely. They—the women I mean—are out of it—should be out of it. We must help them to stay in that beautiful world of their own, lest ours gets worse. Oh, she had to be out of it. You should have heard the disinterred body of Mr Kurtz saying, 'My Intended.' You would have perceived directly then how completely she was out of it. And the lofty frontal bone of Mr Kurtz! They say the hair goes on growing sometimes, but this—ah—specimen was impressively bald. The wilderness had patted him on the head, and, behold, it was like a ball—an ivory ball; it had caressed him, and—lo!—he had withered; it had taken him, loved him, embraced him, got into his veins, consumed his flesh, and sealed his soul to its own by the inconceivable ceremonies of some devilish initiation. He was its spoiled and pampered favourite. Ivory? I should think so. Heaps of it, stacks of it. The old mud shanty was bursting with it. You would think there was not a single tusk left either above or below the ground in the whole country. 'Mostly fossil,' the manager had remarked disparagingly. It was no more fossil than I am; but they call it fossil when it is dug up. It appears these niggers do bury the tusks sometimes—but evidently they couldn't bury this parcel deep enough to save the gifted Mr Kurtz from his fate. We filled the steamboat with it, and had to pile a lot on the deck. Thus he could see and enjoy as long as he could see, because the appreciation of this favour had remained with him to the last. You should have heard him say, 'My ivory.' Oh yes, I heard him. 'My Intended, my ivory, my station, my river, my—' everything belonged to him. It made me hold my breath in expectation of hearing the wilderness burst into a prodigious peal of laughter that would shake the fixed stars in their places. Everything belonged to him—but that was a trifle. The thing was to know what he belonged to, how many powers of darkness claimed him for their own. That was the reflection that made you creepy all over. It was impossible—it was not good for one either—trying to imagine. He had taken a high seat amongst the devils of the land—I mean literally. You can't understand. How could you?—with solid pavement under your feet, surrounded by kind neighbours ready to cheer you or to fall on you, stepping delicately between the butcher and the policeman, in the holy terror of scandal and gallows and lunatic asylums—how can you imagine what particular region of the first ages a man's untrammelled feet may take him into by the way of solitude—utter solitude without a policeman—by the way of silence—utter silence, where no warning voice of a kind neighbour can be heard whispering of public opinion? These little things make all the great difference. When they are gone you must fall back upon your own innate strength, upon your own capacity for faithfulness. Of course you may be too much of a fool to go wrong—too dull even to know you are being assaulted by the powers of darkness. I take it, no fool ever made a bargain for his soul with the devil: the fool is too much of a fool, or the devil too much of a devil—I don't know which. Or you may be such a thunderingly exalted creature as to be altogether deaf and blind to anything but heavenly sights and sounds. Then the earth for you is only a standing place—and whether to be like this is your loss or your gain I won't pretend to say. But most of us are neither one nor the other. The earth for us is a place to live in, where we must put up with sights, with sounds, with smells, too, by Jove!—breathe dead hippo, so to speak, and not be contaminated. And there, don't you see? your strength comes in, the faith in your ability for the digging of unostentatious holes to bury the stuff in—your power of devotion, not to yourself, but to an obscure, back-breaking business. And that's difficult enough. Mind, I am not trying to excuse or even explain—I am trying to account to myself for—for—Mr Kurtz—for the shade of Mr Kurtz. This initiated wraith[4] from the back of Nowhere honoured me with its amazing confidence before it vanished altogether. This was because it could speak English to me. The original Kurtz had been educated partly in England, and—as he was good enough to say himself—his sympathies were in the right place. His mother was half-English, his father was half-French. All Europe contributed to the making of Kurtz; and by and by I learned that, most appropriately, the International Society for the Suppression of Savage Customs[5] had entrusted him with the making of a report, for its future guidance. And he had written it too. I've seen it. I've read it. It was eloquent, vibrating with eloquence, but too high-strung, I think. Seventeen pages of close writing he had found time for! But this must have been before his—let us say—nerves went wrong, and caused him to preside at certain midnight dances ending with unspeakable rites, which—as far as I reluctantly gathered from what I heard at various times—were offered up to him—do you understand?—to Mr Kurtz himself. But it was a beautiful piece of writing. The opening paragraph, however, in the light of later information, strikes me now as ominous. He began with the argument that we whites, from the point of development we had arrived at, 'must necessarily appear to them [savages] in the nature of supernatural beings—we approach them with the might as of a deity,' and so on, and so on. 'By the simple exercise of our will we can exert a power for good practically unbounded,' etc. etc. From that point he soared and took me with him. The peroration was magnificent, though difficult to remember, you know. It gave me the notion of an exotic Immensity ruled by an august Benevolence. It made me tingle with enthusiasm. This was the unbounded power of eloquence—of words—of burning noble words. There were no practical hints to interrupt the magic current of phrases, unless a kind of note at the foot of the last page, scrawled evidently much later, in an unsteady hand, may be regarded as the exposition of a method. It was very simple, and at the end of that moving appeal to every altruistic sentiment it blazed at you, luminous and terrifying, like a flash of lightning in a serene sky: 'Exterminate all the brutes!' The curious part was that he had apparently forgotten all about that valuable postscriptum, because, later on, when he in a sense came to himself, he repeatedly entreated me to take good care of 'my pamphlet' (he called it), as it was sure to have in the future a good influence upon his career. I had full information about all these things, and, besides, as it turned out, I was to have the care of his memory. I've done enough for it to give me the indisputable right to lay it, if I choose, for an everlasting rest in the dust-bin of progress, amongst all the sweepings and, figuratively speaking, all the dead cats of civilisation. But then, you see, I can't choose. He won't be forgotten. Whatever he was, he was not common. He had the power to charm or frighten rudimentary souls into an aggravated witchdance in his honour; he could also fill the small souls of the pilgrims with bitter misgivings: he had one devoted friend at least, and he had conquered one soul in the world that was neither rudimentary nor tainted with

4. Either the spectral or immaterial appearance of a living being, often viewed as a portent of that person's death, or simply a ghost.
5. This society is fictional, but in 1889–90 the international Anti-Slavery Conference at Brussels in effect granted Leopold control of the Congo trade, ostensibly in return for his help in eliminating African slavers.

self-seeking. No; I can't forget him, though I am not prepared to affirm the fellow was exactly worth the life we lost in getting to him. I missed my late helmsman awfully—I missed him even while his body was still lying in the pilot-house. Perhaps you will think it passing strange this regret for a savage who was no more account than a grain of sand in a black Sahara. Well, don't you see, he had done something, he had steered; for months I had him at my back—a help—an instrument. It was a kind of partnership. He steered for me—I had to look after him, I worried about his deficiencies, and thus a subtle bond had been created, of which I only became aware when it was suddenly broken. And the intimate profundity of that look he gave me when he received his hurt remains to this day in my memory—like a claim of distant kinship affirmed in a supreme moment.

"Poor fool! If he had only left that shutter alone. He had no restraint, no restraint—just like Kurtz—a tree swayed by the wind. As soon as I had put on a dry pair of slippers, I dragged him out, after first jerking the spear out of his side, which operation I confess I performed with my eyes shut tight. His heels leaped together over the little doorstep; his shoulders were pressed to my breast; I hugged him from behind desperately. Oh! he was heavy, heavy; heavier than any man on earth, I should imagine. Then without more ado I tipped him overboard. The current snatched him as though he had been a wisp of grass, and I saw the body roll over twice before I lost sight of it for ever. All the pilgrims and the manager were then congregated on the awning-deck about the pilot-house, chattering at each other like a flock of excited magpies, and there was a scandalised murmur at my heartless promptitude. What they wanted to keep that body hanging about for I can't guess. Embalm it, maybe. But I had also heard another, and a very ominous, murmur on the deck below. My friends the wood-cutters were likewise scandalised, and with a better show of reason—though I admit that the reason itself was quite inadmissible. Oh, quite! I had made up my mind that if my late helmsman was to be eaten, the fishes alone should have him. He had been a very second-rate helmsman while alive, but now he was dead he might have become a first-class temptation, and possibly cause some startling trouble. Besides, I was anxious to take the wheel, the man in pink pyjamas showing himself a hopeless duffer at the business.

"This I did directly the simple funeral was over. We were going half-speed, keeping right in the middle of the stream, and I listened to the talk about me. They had given up Kurtz, they had given up the station; Kurtz was dead, and the station had been burnt—and so on—and so on. The red-haired pilgrim was beside himself with the thought that at least this poor Kurtz had been properly revenged. 'Say! We must have made a glorious slaughter of them in the bush. Eh? What do you think? Say?' He positively danced, the bloodthirsty little gingery beggar.[6] And he had nearly fainted when he saw the wounded man! I could not help saying, 'You made a glorious lot of smoke, anyhow.' I had seen, from the way the tops of the bushes rustled and flew, that almost all the shots had gone too high. You can't hit anything unless you take aim and fire from the shoulder; but these chaps fired from the hip with their eyes shut. The retreat, I maintained—and I was right—was caused by the screeching of the steam-whistle. Upon this they forgot Kurtz, and began to howl at me with indignant protests.

6. Red-haired rascal (British slang).

"The manager stood by the wheel murmuring confidentially about the necessity of getting well away down the river before dark at all events, when I saw in the distance a clearing on the river-side and the outlines of some sort of building. 'What's this?' I asked. He clapped his hands in wonder. 'The station!' he cried. I edged in at once, still going half-speed.

"Through my glasses I saw the slope of a hill interspersed with rare trees and perfectly free from undergrowth. A long decaying building on the summit was half buried in the high grass; the large holes in the peaked roof gaped black from afar; the jungle and the woods made a background. There was no enclosure or fence of any kind; but there had been one apparently, for near the house half a dozen slim posts remained in a row, roughly trimmed, and with their upper ends ornamented with round carved balls. The rails, or whatever there had been between, had disappeared. Of course the forest surrounded all that. The river-bank was clear, and on the water side I saw a white man under a hat like a cart-wheel beckoning persistently with his whole arm. Examining the edge of the forest above and below, I was almost certain I could see movements—human forms gliding here and there. I steamed past prudently, then stopped the engines and let her drift down. The man on the shore began to shout, urging us to land. 'We have been attacked,' screamed the manager. 'I know—I know. It's all right,' yelled back the other, as cheerful as you please. 'Come along. It's all right. I am glad.'

"His aspect reminded me of something I had seen—something funny I had seen somewhere. As I manœuvred to get alongside, I was asking myself, 'What does this fellow look like?' Suddenly I got it. He looked like a harlequin. His clothes had been made of some stuff that was brown holland[7] probably, but it was covered with patches all over, with bright patches, blue, red, and yellow—patches on the back, patches on the front, patches on elbows, on knees; coloured binding round his jacket, scarlet edging at the bottom of his trousers; and the sunshine made him look extremely gay and wonderfully neat withal, because you could see how beautifully all this patching had been done. A beardless, boyish face, very fair, no features to speak of, nose peeling, little blue eyes, smiles and frowns chasing each other over that open countenance like sunshine and shadow on a wind-swept plain. 'Look out, captain!' he cried; 'there's a snag lodged in here last night.' What! Another snag? I confess I swore shamefully. I had nearly holed my cripple, to finish off that charming trip. The harlequin on the bank turned his little pug nose up to me. 'You English?' he asked, all smiles. 'Are you?' I shouted from the wheel. The smiles vanished, and he shook his head as if sorry for my disappointment. Then he brightened up. 'Never mind!' he cried encouragingly. 'Are we in time?' I asked. 'He is up there,' he replied, with a toss of the head up the hill, and becoming gloomy all of a sudden. His face was like the autumn sky, overcast one moment and bright the next.

"When the manager, escorted by the pilgrims, all of them armed to the teeth, had gone to the house, this chap came on board. 'I say, I don't like this. These natives are in the bush,' I said. He assured me earnestly it was all right. 'They are simple people,' he added; 'well, I am glad you came. It took me all my time to keep them off.' 'But you said it was all right,' I cried. 'Oh, they meant no

---

7. Unbleached linen fabric. "Harlequin": a traditional clown figure known by his multicolored costume.

harm,' he said; and as I stared he corrected himself, 'Not exactly.' Then viva-ciously, 'My faith, your pilot-house wants a clean up!' In the next breath he advised me to keep enough steam on the boiler to blow the whistle in case of any trouble. 'One good screech will do more for you than all your rifles. They are simple people,' he repeated. He rattled away at such a rate he quite over-whelmed me. He seemed to be trying to make up for lots of silence, and actu-ally hinted, laughing, that such was the case. 'Don't you talk with Mr Kurtz?' I said. 'You don't talk with that man—you listen to him,' he exclaimed with severe exaltation. 'But now—' He waved his arm, and in the twinkling of an eye was in the uttermost depths of despondency. In a moment he came up again with a jump, possessed himself of both my hands, shook them continuously, while he gabbled: 'Brother sailor . . . honour . . . pleasure . . . delight . . . intro-duce myself . . . Russian . . . son of an arch-priest . . . Government of Tam-bov[8] . . . What? Tobacco! English tobacco; the excellent English tobacco! Now, that's brotherly. Smoke? Where's a sailor that does not smoke?'

"The pipe soothed him, and gradually I made out he had run away from school, had gone to sea in a Russian ship; ran away again; served some time in English ships; was now reconciled with the arch-priest. He made a point of that. 'But when one is young one must see things, gather experience, ideas; enlarge the mind.' 'Here!' I interrupted. 'You can never tell! Here I met Mr Kurtz,' he said, youthfully solemn and reproachful. I held my tongue after that. It appears he had persuaded a Dutch trading-house on the coast to fit him out with stores and goods, and had started for the interior with a light heart, and no more idea of what would happen to him than a baby. He had been wandering about that river for nearly two years alone, cut off from everybody and every-thing. 'I am not so young as I look. I am twenty-five,' he said. 'At first old Van Shuyten would tell me to go to the devil,' he narrated with keen enjoyment; 'but I stuck to him, and talked and talked, till at last he got afraid I would talk the hind-leg off his favourite dog, so he gave me some cheap things and a few guns, and told me he hoped he would never see my face again. Good old Dutchman, Van Shuyten. I sent him one small lot of ivory a year ago, so that he can't call me a little thief when I get back. I hope he got it. And for the rest I don't care. I had some wood stacked for you. That was my old house. Did you see?'

"I gave him Towson's book. He made as though he would kiss me, but restrained himself. 'The only book I had left, and I thought I had lost it,' he said, looking at it ecstatically. 'So many accidents happen to a man going about alone, you know. Canoes get upset sometimes—and sometimes you've got to clear out so quick when the people get angry.' He thumbed the pages. 'You made notes in Russian?' I asked. He nodded. 'I thought they were written in cipher,' I said. He laughed, then became serious. 'I had lots of trouble to keep these people off,' he said. 'Did they want to kill you?' I asked. 'Oh no!' he cried, and checked himself. 'Why did they attack us?' I pursued. He hesitated, then said shamefacedly, 'They don't want him to go.' 'Don't they?' I said curiously. He nodded a nod full of mystery and wisdom. 'I tell you,' he cried, 'this man has enlarged my mind.' He opened his arms wide, staring at me with his little blue eyes that were perfectly round."

---

8. A province in Russia, south of Moscow, a cultural center.

3

"I looked at him, lost in astonishment. There he was before me, in motley,[9] as though he had absconded from a troupe of mimes, enthusiastic, fabulous. His very existence was improbable, inexplicable, and altogether bewildering. He was an insoluble problem. It was inconceivable how he had existed, how he had succeeded in getting so far, how he had managed to remain—why he did not instantly disappear. 'I went a little farther,' he said, 'then still a little farther—till I had gone so far that I don't know how I'll ever get back. Never mind. Plenty time. I can manage. You take Kurtz away quick—quick—I tell you.' The glamour of youth enveloped his particoloured rags, his destitution, his loneliness, the essential desolation of his futile wanderings. For months— for years—his life hadn't been worth a day's purchase; and there he was gallantly, thoughtlessly alive, to all appearance indestructible solely by the virtue of his few years and of his unreflecting audacity. I was seduced into something like admiration—like envy. Glamour urged him on, glamour kept him unscathed. He surely wanted nothing from the wilderness but space to breathe in and to push on through. His need was to exist, and to move onwards at the greatest possible risk, and with a maximum of privation. If the absolutely pure, uncalculating, unpractical spirit of adventure had ever ruled a human being, it ruled this be-patched youth. I almost envied him the possession of this modest and clear flame. It seemed to have consumed all thought of self so completely, that, even while he was talking to you, you forgot that it was he—the man before your eyes—who had gone through these things. I did not envy him his devotion to Kurtz, though. He had not meditated over it. It came to him, and he accepted it with a sort of eager fatalism. I must say that to me it appeared about the most dangerous thing in every way he had come upon so far.

"They had come together unavoidably, like two ships becalmed near each other, and lay rubbing sides at last. I suppose Kurtz wanted an audience, because on a certain occasion, when encamped in the forest, they had talked all night, or more probably Kurtz had talked. 'We talked of everything,' he said, quite transported at the recollection. 'I forgot there was such a thing as sleep. The night did not seem to last an hour. Everything! Everything! . . . Of love too.' 'Ah, he talked to you of love!' I said, much amused. 'It isn't what you think,' he cried, almost passionately. 'It was in general. He made me see things—things.'

"He threw his arms up. We were on deck at the time, and the head-man of my wood-cutters, lounging near by, turned upon him his heavy and glittering eyes. I looked around, and I don't know why, but I assure you that never, never before, did this land, this river, this jungle, the very arch of this blazing sky, appear to me so hopeless and so dark, so impenetrable to human thought, so pitiless to human weakness. 'And, ever since, you have been with him, of course?' I said.

"On the contrary. It appears their intercourse had been very much broken by various causes. He had, as he informed me proudly, managed to nurse Kurtz through two illnesses (he alluded to it as you would to some risky feat), but as a rule Kurtz wandered alone, far in the depths of the forest. 'Very often coming to this station, I had to wait days and days before he would turn up,' he said. 'Ah, it was worth waiting for!—sometimes.' 'What was he doing? exploring or what?'

9. Like a jester, who wore a distinctive multicolored costume.

I asked. 'Oh yes, of course'; he had discovered lots of villages, a lake too—he did not know exactly in what direction; it was dangerous to inquire too much—but mostly his expeditions had been for ivory. 'But he had no goods to trade with by that time,' I objected. 'There's a good lot of cartridges left even yet,' he answered, looking away. 'To speak plainly, he raided the country,'[1] I said. He nodded. 'Not alone, surely!' He muttered something about the villages round that lake. 'Kurtz got the tribe to follow him, did he?' I suggested. He fidgeted a little. 'They adored[2] him,' he said. The tone of these words was so extraordinary that I looked at him searchingly. It was curious to see his mingled eagerness and reluctance to speak of Kurtz. The man filled his life, occupied his thoughts, swayed his emotions. 'What can you expect?' he burst out; 'he came to them with thunder and lightning, you know—and they had never seen anything like it—and very terrible. He could be very terrible. You can't judge Mr Kurtz as you would an ordinary man. No, no, no! Now—just to give you an idea—I don't mind telling you, he wanted to shoot me too one day—but I don't judge him.' 'Shoot you!' I cried. 'What for?' 'Well, I had a small lot of ivory the chief of that village near my house gave me. You see I used to shoot game for them. Well, he wanted it, and wouldn't hear reason. He declared he would shoot me unless I gave him the ivory and then cleared out of the country, because he could do so, and had a fancy for it, and there was nothing on earth to prevent him killing whom he jolly well pleased. And it was true too. I gave him the ivory. What did I care! But I didn't clear out. No, no. I couldn't leave him. I had to be careful, of course, till we got friendly again for a time. He had his second illness then. Afterwards I had to keep out of the way; but I didn't mind. He was living for the most part in those villages on the lake. When he came down to the river, some-times he would take to me, and sometimes it was better for me to be careful. This man suffered too much. He hated all this, and somehow he couldn't get away. When I had a chance I begged him to try and leave while there was time; I offered to go back with him. And he would say yes, and then he would remain; go off on another ivory hunt; disappear for weeks; forget himself amongst these people—forget himself—you know.' 'Why! he's mad,' I said. He protested indig-nantly. Mr Kurtz couldn't be mad. If I had heard him talk, only two days ago, I wouldn't dare hint at such a thing. . . . I had taken up my binoculars while we talked, and was looking at the shore, sweeping the limit of the forest at each side and at the back of the house. The consciousness of there being people in that bush, so silent, so quiet—as silent and quiet as the ruined house on the hill—made me uneasy. There was no sign on the face of nature of this amazing tale that was not so much told as suggested to me in desolate exclamations, completed by shrugs, in interrupted phrases, in hints ending in deep sighs. The woods were unmoved, like a mask—heavy, like the closed door of a prison— they looked with their air of hidden knowledge, of patient expectation, of unap-proachable silence. The Russian was explaining to me that it was only lately that Mr Kurtz had come down to the river, bringing along with him all the fighting men of that lake tribe. He had been absent for several months—getting himself adored, I suppose—and had come down unexpectedly, with the intention to all appearance of making a raid either across the river or down stream. Evidently

---

1. Raids for ivory were a common practice, with little or no attempt to compensate natives for the stolen goods.
2. Literally, worshipped as a deity.

the appetite for more ivory had got the better of the—what shall I say?—less material aspirations. However, he had got much worse suddenly. 'I heard he was lying helpless, and so I came up—took my chance,' said the Russian. 'Oh, he is bad, very bad.' I directed my glass to the house. There were no signs of life, but there was the ruined roof, the long mud wall peeping above the grass, with three little square window-holes, no two of the same size; all this brought within reach of my hand, as it were. And then I made a brusque movement, and one of the remaining posts of that vanished fence leaped up in the field of my glass. You remember I told you I had been struck at the distance by certain attempts at ornamentation, rather remarkable in the ruinous aspect of the place. Now I had suddenly a nearer view, and its first result was to make me throw my head back as if before a blow. Then I went carefully from post to post with my glass, and I saw my mistake. These round knobs were not ornamental but symbolic; they were expressive and puzzling, striking and disturbing—food for thought and also for the vultures if there had been any looking down from the sky; but at all events for such ants as were industrious enough to ascend the pole. They would have been even more impressive, those heads on the stakes, if their faces had not been turned to the house. Only one, the first I had made out, was facing my way. I was not so shocked as you may think. The start back I had given was really nothing but a movement of surprise. I had expected to see a knob of wood there, you know. I returned deliberately to the first I had seen—and there it was, black, dried, sunken, with closed eyelids—a head that seemed to sleep at the top of that pole, and, with the shrunken dry lips showing a narrow white line of the teeth, was smiling too, smiling continuously at some endless and jocose dream of that eternal slumber.

"I am not disclosing any trade secrets. In fact the manager said afterwards that Mr Kurtz's methods[3] had ruined the district. I have no opinion on that point, but I want you clearly to understand that there was nothing exactly profitable in these heads being there. They only show that Mr Kurtz lacked restraint in the gratification of his various lusts, that there was something wanting in him—some small matter which, when the pressing need arose, could not be found under his magnificent eloquence. Whether he knew of this deficiency himself I can't say. I think the knowledge came to him at last—only at the very last. But the wilderness had found him out early, and had taken on him a terrible vengeance for the fantastic invasion. I think it had whispered to him things about himself which he did not know, things of which he had no conception till he took counsel with this great solitude—and the whisper had proved irresistibly fascinating. It echoed loudly within him because he was hollow at the core. . . . I put down the glass, and the head that had appeared near enough to be spoken to seemed at once to have leaped away from me into inaccessible distance.

"The admirer of Mr Kurtz was a bit crestfallen. In a hurried, indistinct voice he began to assure me he had not dared to take these—say, symbols—down. He was not afraid of the natives; they would not stir till Mr Kurtz gave the word. His ascendancy was extraordinary. The camps of these people surrounded the place, and the chiefs came every day to see him. They would

3. Perhaps an allusion to *Hamlet*, where Polonius comments on Hamlet's apparent insanity, "Though this be madness, yet there is method in 't."

crawl . . . 'I don't want to know anything of the ceremonies used when approaching Mr Kurtz,' I shouted. Curious, this feeling that came over me that such details would be more intolerable than those heads drying on the stakes under Mr Kurtz's windows. After all, that was only a savage sight, while I seemed at one bound to have been transported into some lightless region of subtle horrors, where pure, uncomplicated savagery was a positive relief, being something that had a right to exist—obviously—in the sunshine. The young man looked at me with surprise. I suppose it did not occur to him that Mr Kurtz was no idol of mine. He forgot I hadn't heard any of these splendid monologues on, what was it? on love, justice, conduct of life—or what not. If it had come to crawling before Mr Kurtz, he crawled as much as the veriest savage of them all. I had no idea of the conditions, he said: these heads were the heads of rebels. I shocked him excessively by laughing. Rebels! What would be the next definition I was to hear? There had been enemies, criminals, workers—and these were rebels. Those rebellious heads looked very subdued to me on their sticks. 'You don't know how such a life tries a man like Kurtz,' cried Kurtz's last disciple. 'Well, and you?' I said. 'I! I! I am a simple man. I have no great thoughts. I want nothing from anybody. How can you compare me to . . .?' His feelings were too much for speech, and suddenly he broke down. 'I don't understand,' he groaned. 'I've been doing my best to keep him alive, and that's enough. I had no hand in all this. I have no abilities. There hasn't been a drop of medicine or a mouthful of invalid food for months here. He was shamefully abandoned. A man like this, with such ideas. Shamefully! Shamefully! I—I—haven't slept for the last ten nights. . . .'

"His voice lost itself in the calm of the evening. The long shadows of the forest had slipped down hill while we talked, had gone far beyond the ruined hovel, beyond the symbolic row of stakes. All this was in the gloom, while we down there were yet in the sunshine, and the stretch of the river abreast of the clearing glittered in a still and dazzling splendour, with a murky and overshadowed bend above and below. Not a living soul was seen on the shore. The bushes did not rustle.

"Suddenly round the corner of the house a group of men appeared, as though they had come up from the ground. They waded waist-deep in the grass, in a compact body, bearing an improvised stretcher in their midst. Instantly, in the emptiness of the landscape, a cry arose whose shrillness pierced the still air like a sharp arrow flying straight to the very heart of the land; and, as if by enchantment, streams of human beings—of naked human beings—with spears in their hands, with bows, with shields, with wild glances and savage movements, were poured into the clearing by the darkfaced and pensive forest. The bushes shook, the grass swayed for a time, and then everything stood still in attentive immobility.

"'Now, if he does not say the right thing to them we are all done for,' said the Russian at my elbow. The knot of men with the stretcher had stopped too, halfway to the steamer, as if petrified. I saw the man on the stretcher sit up, lank and with an uplifted arm, above the shoulders of the bearers. 'Let us hope that the man who can talk so well of love in general will find some particular reason to spare us this time,' I said. I resented bitterly the absurd danger of our situation, as if to be at the mercy of that atrocious phantom had been a dishonouring necessity. I could not hear a sound, but through my glasses I saw the thin

arm extended commandingly, the lower jaw moving, the eyes of that apparition shining darkly far in its bony head that nodded with grotesque jerks. Kurtz—Kurtz—that means 'short' in German—don't it? Well, the name was as true as everything else in his life—and death. He looked at least seven feet long. His covering had fallen off, and his body emerged from it pitiful and appalling as from a winding-sheet. I could see the cage of his ribs all astir, the bones of his arm waving. It was as though an animated image of death carved out of old ivory had been shaking its hand with menaces at a motionless crowd of men made of dark and glittering bronze. I saw him open his mouth wide—it gave him a weirdly voracious aspect, as though he had wanted to swallow all the air, all the earth, all the men before him. A deep voice reached me faintly. He must have been shouting. He fell back suddenly. The stretcher shook as the bearers staggered forward again, and almost at the same time I noticed that the crowd of savages was vanishing without any perceptible movement of retreat, as if the forest that had ejected these beings so suddenly had drawn them in again as the breath is drawn in a long aspiration.

"Some of the pilgrims behind the stretcher carried his arms—two shotguns, a heavy rifle, and a light revolver-carbine[4]—the thunderbolts of that pitiful Jupiter.[5] The manager bent over him murmuring as he walked beside his head. They laid him down in one of the little cabins—just a room for a bedplace and a camp-stool or two, you know. We had brought his belated correspondence, and a lot of torn envelopes and open letters littered his bed. His hand roamed feebly amongst these papers. I was struck by the fire of his eyes and the composed languor of his expression. It was not so much the exhaustion of disease. He did not seem in pain. This shadow looked satiated and calm, as though for the moment it had had its fill of all the emotions.

"He rustled one of the letters, and looking straight in my face said, 'I am glad.' Somebody had been writing to him about me. These special recommendations were turning up again. The volume of tone he emitted without effort, almost without the trouble of moving his lips, amazed me. A voice! a voice! It was grave, profound, vibrating, while the man did not seem capable of a whisper. However, he had enough strength in him—factitious[6] no doubt—to very nearly make an end of us, as you shall hear directly.

"The manager appeared silently in the doorway; I stepped out at once and he drew the curtain after me. The Russian, eyed curiously by the pilgrims, was staring at the shore. I followed the direction of his glance.

"Dark human shapes could be made out in the distance, flitting indistinctly against the gloomy border of the forest, and near the river two bronze figures, leaning on tall spears, stood in the sunlight under fantastic head-dresses of spotted skins, warlike and still in statuesque repose. And from right to left along the lighted shore moved a wild and gorgeous apparition of a woman.

"She walked with measured steps, draped in striped and fringed cloths, treading the earth proudly, with a slight jingle and flash of barbarous ornaments. She carried her head high; her hair was done in the shape of a helmet; she had brass leggings to the knee,[7] brass wire gauntlets to the elbow, a crimson spot on her

---

4. A rifle with a revolving clip.
5. The Roman god of the sky, ruler over the other gods.

6. Not natural; got up for a particular purpose; artificial.
7. From the ankle to the knee.

tawny cheek, innumerable necklaces of glass beads on her neck; bizarre things, charms, gifts of witch-men, that hung about her, glittered and trembled at every step. She must have had the value of several elephant tusks upon her. She was savage and superb, wild-eyed and magnificent; there was something ominous and stately in her deliberate progress. And in the hush that had fallen suddenly upon the whole sorrowful land, the immense wilderness, the colossal body of the fecund and mysterious life seemed to look at her, pensive, as though it had been looking at the image of its own tenebrous[8] and passionate soul.

"She came abreast of the steamer, stood still, and faced us. Her long shadow fell to the water's edge. Her face had a tragic and fierce aspect of wild sorrow and of dumb pain mingled with the fear of some struggling, half-shaped resolve. She stood looking at us without a stir, and like the wilderness itself, with an air of brooding over an inscrutable purpose. A whole minute passed, and then she made a step forward. There was a low jingle, a glint of yellow metal, a sway of fringed draperies, and she stopped as if her heart had failed her. The young fellow by my side growled. The pilgrims murmured at my back. She looked at us all as if her life had depended upon the unswerving steadiness of her glance. Suddenly she opened her bared arms and threw them up rigid above her head, as though in an uncontrollable desire to touch the sky, and at the same time the swift shadows darted out on the earth, swept around on the river, gathering the steamer into a shadowy embrace. A formidable silence hung over the scene.

"She turned away slowly, walked on, following the bank, and passed into the bushes to the left. Once only her eyes gleamed back at us in the dusk of the thickets before she disappeared.

"'If she had offered to come aboard I really think I would have tried to shoot her,' said the man of patches nervously. 'I had been risking my life every day for the last fortnight to keep her out of the house. She got in one day and kicked up a row about those miserable rags I picked up in the storeroom to mend my clothes with. I wasn't decent. At least it must have been that, for she talked like a fury to Kurtz for an hour, pointing at me now and then. I don't understand the dialect of this tribe. Luckily for me, I fancy Kurtz felt too ill that day to care, or there would have been mischief. I don't understand. . . . No—it's too much for me. Ah, well, it's all over now.'

"At this moment I heard Kurtz's deep voice behind the curtain: 'Save me!—save the ivory, you mean. Don't tell me. Save *me*! Why, I've had to save you. You are interrupting my plans now. Sick! Sick! Not so sick as you would like to believe. Never mind. I'll carry my ideas out yet—I will return. I'll show you what can be done. You with your little peddling notions—you are interfering with me. I will return. I . . .'

"The manager came out. He did me the honour to take me under the arm and lead me aside. 'He is very low, very low,' he said. He considered it necessary to sigh, but neglected to be consistently sorrowful. 'We have done all we could for him—haven't we? But there is no disguising the fact, Mr Kurtz has done more harm than good to the Company. He did not see the time was not ripe for vigorous action. Cautiously, cautiously—that's my principle. We must be cautious yet. The district is closed to us for a time. Deplorable! Upon the whole, the trade will suffer. I don't deny there is a remarkable quantity of ivory—mostly

8. Full of darkness or shadows; obscure; gloomy.

fossil. We must save it, at all events—but look how precarious the position is— and why? Because the method is unsound.' 'Do you,' said I, looking at the shore, 'call it "unsound method"?' 'Without doubt,' he exclaimed hotly, 'Don't you?' . . . 'No method at all,' I murmured after a while. 'Exactly,' he exulted. 'I anticipated this. Shows a complete want of judgment. It is my duty to point it out in the proper quarter.' 'Oh,' said I, 'that fellow—what's his name?—the brickmaker, will make a readable report for you.' He appeared confounded for a moment. It seemed to me I had never breathed an atmosphere so vile, and I turned mentally to Kurtz for relief—positively for relief. 'Nevertheless, I think Mr Kurtz is a remarkable man,' I said with emphasis. He started, dropped on me a cold heavy glance, said very quietly, 'He *was*,' and turned his back on me. My hour of favour was over; I found myself lumped along with Kurtz as a partisan of methods for which the time was not ripe: I was unsound! Ah! but it was something to have at least a choice of nightmares.

"I had turned to the wilderness really, not to Mr Kurtz, who, I was ready to admit, was as good as buried. And for a moment it seemed to me as if I also were buried in a vast grave full of unspeakable secrets. I felt an intolerable weight oppressing my breast, the smell of the damp earth, the unseen presence of victorious corruption, the darkness of an impenetrable night. . . . The Russian tapped me on the shoulder. I heard him mumbling and stammering something about 'brother seaman—couldn't conceal—knowledge of matters that would affect Mr Kurtz's reputation.' I waited. For him evidently Mr Kurtz was not in his grave; I suspect that for him Mr Kurtz was one of the immortals. 'Well!' said I at last, 'speak out. As it happens, I am Mr Kurtz's friend—in a way.'

"He stated with a good deal of formality that had we not been 'of the same profession,' he would have kept the matter to himself without regard to consequences. He suspected 'there was an active ill-will towards him on the part of these white men that—' 'You are right,' I said, remembering a certain conversation I had overheard. 'The manager thinks you ought to be hanged.' He showed a concern at this intelligence which amused me at first. 'I had better get out of the way quietly,' he said earnestly. 'I can do no more for Kurtz now, and they would soon find some excuse. What's to stop them? There's a military post three hundred miles from here.' 'Well, upon my word,' said I, 'perhaps you had better go if you have any friends amongst the savages near by.' 'Plenty,' he said. 'They are simple people—and I want nothing, you know.' He stood biting his lip, then: 'I don't want any harm to happen to these whites here, but of course I was thinking of Mr Kurtz's reputation—but you are a brother seaman and—' 'All right,' said I, after a time. 'Mr Kurtz's reputation is safe with me.' I did not know how truly I spoke.

"He informed me, lowering his voice, that it was Kurtz who had ordered the attack to be made on the steamer. 'He hated sometimes the idea of being taken away—and then again . . . But I don't understand these matters. I am a simple man. He thought it would scare you away—that you would give it up, thinking him dead. I could not stop him. Oh, I had an awful time of it this last month.' 'Very well,' I said. 'He is all right now.' 'Ye-e-es,' he muttered, not very convinced apparently. 'Thanks,' said I; 'I shall keep my eyes open.' 'But quiet—eh?' he urged anxiously. 'It would be awful for his reputation if anybody here—' I promised a complete discretion with great gravity. 'I have a canoe and three black fellows waiting not very far. I am off. Could you give me a few Martini-Henry cartridges?' I could, and did, with proper secrecy. He helped himself, with a wink at me, to a handful of my tobacco. 'Between sailors—you know—good English tobacco.' At the door of the pilot-house he turned round—'I say, haven't you a pair of shoes you could spare?' He raised one leg. 'Look.' The soles were tied with knotted strings sandal-wise under his bare feet. I rooted out an old pair, at which he looked with admiration before tucking it under his left arm. One of his pockets (bright red) was bulging with cartridges, from the other (dark blue) peeped 'Towson's Inquiry,' etc. etc. He seemed to think himself excellently well equipped for a renewed encounter with the wilderness. 'Ah! I'll never, never meet such a man again. You ought to have heard him recite poetry—his own too it was, he told me. Poetry!' He rolled his eyes at the recollection of these delights. 'Oh, he enlarged my mind!' 'Good-bye,' said I. He shook hands and vanished in the night. Sometimes I ask myself whether I had ever really seen him—whether it was possible to meet such a phenomenon! . . .

"When I woke up shortly after midnight his warning came to my mind with its hint of danger that seemed, in the starred darkness, real enough to make me get up for the purpose of having a look round. On the hill a big fire burned, illuminating fitfully a crooked corner of the station-house. One of the agents with a picket of a few of our blacks, armed for the purpose, was keeping guard over the ivory; but deep within the forest, red gleams that wavered, that seemed to sink and rise from the ground amongst confused columnar shapes of intense blackness, showed the exact position of the camp where Mr Kurtz's adorers were keeping their uneasy vigil. The monotonous beating of a big drum filled the air with muffled shocks and a lingering vibration. A steady droning sound of many men chanting each to himself some weird incantation came out from the black, flat wall of the woods as the humming of bees comes out of a hive, and had a strange narcotic effect upon my half-awake senses. I believe I dozed off leaning over the rail, till an abrupt burst of yells, an overwhelming outbreak of a pent-up and mysterious frenzy, woke me up in a bewildered wonder. It was cut short all at once, and the low droning went on with an effect of audible and soothing silence. I glanced casually into the little cabin. A light was burning within, but Mr Kurtz was not there.

"I think I would have raised an outcry if I had believed my eyes. But I didn't believe them at first—the thing seemed so impossible. The fact is I was completely unnerved by a sheer blank fright, pure abstract terror, unconnected with any distinct shape of physical danger. What made this emotion so overpowering was—how shall I define it?—the moral shock I received, as if something altogether monstrous, intolerable to thought and odious to the soul, had been thrust upon me unexpectedly. This lasted of course the merest fraction of a second, and then the usual sense of commonplace, deadly danger, the possibility of a sudden onslaught and massacre, or something of the kind, which I saw impending, was positively welcome and composing. It pacified me, in fact, so much, that I did not raise an alarm.

"There was an agent buttoned up inside an ulster[9] and sleeping on a chair on deck within three feet of me. The yells had not awakened him; he snored very slightly; I left him to his slumbers and leaped ashore. I did not betray Mr Kurtz—it was ordered I should never betray him—it was written I should be loyal to the

9. A long, loose overcoat, often with a belt.

nightmare of my choice. I was anxious to deal with this shadow by myself alone—and to this day I don't know why I was so jealous of sharing with any one the peculiar blackness of that experience.

"As soon as I got on the bank I saw a trail—a broad trail through the grass. I remember the exultation with which I said to myself, 'He can't walk—he is crawling on all-fours—I've got him.' The grass was wet with dew. I strode rapidly with clenched fists. I fancy I had some vague notion of falling upon him and giving him a drubbing. I don't know. I had some imbecile thoughts. The knitting old woman with the cat obtruded herself upon my memory as a most improper person to be sitting at the other end of such an affair. I saw a row of pilgrims squirting lead in the air out of Winchesters held to the hip. I thought I would never get back to the steamer, and imagined myself living alone and unarmed in the woods to an advanced age. Such silly things—you know. And I remember I confounded the beat of the drum with the beating of my heart, and was pleased at its calm regularity.

"I kept to the track though—then stopped to listen. The night was very clear; a dark blue space, sparkling with dew and starlight, in which black things stood very still. I thought I could see a kind of motion ahead of me. I was strangely cocksure of everything that night. I actually left the track and ran in a wide semicircle (I verily believe chuckling to myself) so as to get in front of that stir, of that motion I had seen—if indeed I had seen anything. I was circumventing Kurtz as though it had been a boyish game.

"I came upon him, and, if he had not heard me coming, I would have fallen over him too, but he got up in time. He rose, unsteady, long, pale, indistinct, like a vapour exhaled by the earth, and swayed slightly, misty and silent before me; while at my back the fires loomed between the trees, and the murmur of many voices issued from the forest. I had cut him off cleverly; but when actually confronting him I seemed to come to my senses, I saw the danger in its right proportion. It was by no means over yet. Suppose he began to shout? Though he could hardly stand, there was still plenty of vigour in his voice. 'Go away—hide yourself,' he said, in that profound tone. It was very awful. I glanced back. We were within thirty yards of the nearest fire. A black figure stood up, strode on long black legs, waving long black arms, across the glow. It had horns—antelope horns, I think—on its head. Some sorcerer, some witchman no doubt: it looked fiend-like enough. 'Do you know what you are doing?' I whispered. 'Perfectly,' he answered, raising his voice for that single word: it sounded to me far off and yet loud, like a hail through a speaking-trumpet. If he makes a row we are lost, I thought to myself. This clearly was not a case for fisticuffs, even apart from the very natural aversion I had to beat that Shadow—this wandering and tormented thing. 'You will be lost,' I said—'utterly lost.' One gets sometimes such a flash of inspiration, you know. I did say the right thing, though indeed he could not have been more irretrievably lost than he was at this very moment, when the foundations of our intimacy were being laid—to endure—to endure—even to the end—even beyond.

"'I had immense plans,' he muttered irresolutely. 'Yes,' said I; 'but if you try to shout I'll smash your head with—' There was not a stick or a stone near. 'I will throttle you for good,' I corrected myself. 'I was on the threshold of great things,' he pleaded, in a voice of longing, with a wistfulness of tone that made my blood run cold. 'And now for this stupid scoundrel—' 'Your success in

Europe is assured in any case,' I affirmed steadily. I did not want to have the throttling of him, you understand—and indeed it would have been very little use for any practical purpose. I tried to break the spell—the heavy, mute spell of the wilderness—that seemed to draw him to its pitiless breast by the awakening of forgotten and brutal instincts, by the memory of gratified and monstrous passions. This alone, I was convinced, had driven him out to the edge of the forest, to the bush, towards the gleam of fires, the throb of drums, the drone of weird incantations; this alone had beguiled his unlawful soul beyond the bounds of permitted aspirations. And, don't you see, the terror of the position was not in being knocked on the head—though I had a very lively sense of that danger too—but in this, that I had to deal with a being to whom I could not appeal in the name of anything high or low. I had, even like the niggers, to invoke him—himself—his own exalted and incredible degradation. There was nothing either above or below him, and I knew it. He had kicked himself loose of the earth. Confound the man! he had kicked the very earth to pieces. He was alone, and I before him did not know whether I stood on the ground or floated in the air. I've been telling you what we said—repeating the phrases we pronounced—but what's the good? They were common everyday words—the familiar, vague sounds exchanged on every waking day of life. But what of that? They had behind them, to my mind, the terrific suggestiveness of words heard in dreams, of phrases spoken in nightmares. Soul! If anybody had ever struggled with a soul, I am the man. And I wasn't arguing with a lunatic either. Believe me or not, his intelligence was perfectly clear—concentrated, it is true, upon himself with horrible intensity, yet clear; and therein was my only chance—barring, of course, the killing him there and then, which wasn't so good, on account of unavoidable noise. But his soul was mad. Being alone in the wilderness, it had looked within itself, and, by heavens! I tell you, it had gone mad. I had—for my sins, I suppose, to go through the ordeal of looking into it myself. No eloquence could have been so withering to one's belief in mankind as his final burst of sincerity. He struggled with himself too. I saw it—I heard it. I saw the inconceivable mystery of a soul that knew no restraint, no faith, and no fear, yet struggling blindly with itself. I kept my head pretty well; but when I had him at last stretched on the couch, I wiped my forehead, while my legs shook under me as though I had carried half a ton on my back down that hill. And yet I had only supported him, his bony arm clasped round my neck—and he was not much heavier than a child.

"When next day we left at noon, the crowd, of whose presence behind the curtain of trees I had been acutely conscious all the time, flowed out of the woods again, filled the clearing, covered the slope with a mass of naked, breathing, quivering, bronze bodies. I steamed up a bit, then swung downstream, and two thousand eyes followed the evolutions of the splashing, thumping, fierce river-demon beating the water with its terrible tail and breathing black smoke into the air. In front of the first rank, along the river, three men, plastered with bright red earth from head to foot, strutted to and fro restlessly. When we came abreast again, they faced the river, stamped their feet, nodded their horned heads, swayed their scarlet bodies; they shook towards the fierce river-demon a bunch of black feathers, a mangy skin with a pendent tail—something that looked like a dried gourd; they shouted periodically together strings of amazing words that resembled no sounds of human language; and the deep murmurs of the crowd, interrupted suddenly, were like the responses of some satanic litany.

"We had carried Kurtz into the pilot-house: there was more air there. Lying on the couch, he stared through the open shutter. There was an eddy in the mass of human bodies, and the woman with helmeted head and tawny cheeks rushed out to the very brink of the stream. She put out her hands, shouted something, and all that wild mob took up the shout in a roaring chorus of articulated, rapid, breathless utterance.

"'Do you understand this?' I asked.

"He kept on looking out past me with fiery, longing eyes, with a mingled expression of wistfulness and hate. He made no answer, but I saw a smile, a smile of indefinable meaning, appear on his colourless lips that a moment after twitched convulsively. 'Do I not?' he said slowly, gasping, as if the words had been torn out of him by a supernatural power.

"I pulled the string of the whistle, and I did this because I saw the pilgrims on deck getting out their rifles with an air of anticipating a jolly lark. At the sudden screech there was a movement of abject terror through that wedged mass of bodies. 'Don't! don't you frighten them away,' cried someone on deck disconsolately. I pulled the string time after time. They broke and ran, they leaped, they crouched, they swerved, they dodged the flying terror of the sound. The three red chaps had fallen flat, face down on the shore, as though they had been shot dead. Only the barbarous and superb woman did not so much as flinch, and stretched tragically her bare arms after us over the sombre and glittering river.

"And then that imbecile crowd down on the deck started their little fun, and I could see nothing more for smoke.

"The brown current ran swiftly out of the heart of darkness, bearing us down towards the sea with twice the speed of our upward progress; and Kurtz's life was running swiftly too, ebbing, ebbing out of his heart into the sea of inexorable time. The manager was very placid, he had no vital anxieties now, he took us both in with a comprehensive and satisfied glance: the 'affair' had come off as well as could be wished. I saw the time approaching when I would be left alone of the party of 'unsound method.' The pilgrims looked upon me with disfavour. I was, so to speak, numbered with the dead. It is strange how I accepted this unforeseen partnership, this choice of nightmares forced upon me in the tenebrous land invaded by these mean and greedy phantoms.

"Kurtz discoursed. A voice! a voice! It rang deep to the very last. It survived his strength to hide in the magnificent folds of eloquence the barren darkness of his heart. Oh, he struggled! he struggled! The wastes of his weary brain were haunted by shadowy images now—images of wealth and fame revolving obsequiously round his unextinguishable gift of noble and lofty expression. My Intended, my station, my career, my ideas—these were the subjects for the occasional utterances of elevated sentiments. The shade of the original Kurtz frequented the bedside of the hollow sham, whose fate it was to be buried presently in the mould of primeval earth. But both the diabolic love and the unearthly hate of the mysteries it had penetrated fought for the possession of that soul satiated with primitive emotions, avid of lying fame, of sham distinction, of all the appearances of success and power.

"Sometimes he was contemptibly childish. He desired to have kings meet him at railway stations on his return from some ghastly Nowhere, where he intended to accomplish great things. 'You show them you have in you something that is really profitable, and then there will be no limits to the recognition of your ability,' he would say. 'Of course you must take care of the motives—right motives—always.' The long reaches that were like one and the same reach, monotonous bends that were exactly alike, slipped past the steamer with their multitude of secular[1] trees looking patiently after this grimy fragment of another world, the forerunner of change, of conquest, of trade, of massacres, of blessings. I looked ahead—piloting. 'Close the shutter,' said Kurtz suddenly one day; 'I can't bear to look at this.' I did so. There was a silence. 'Oh, but I will wring your heart yet!' he cried at the invisible wilderness.

"We broke down—as I had expected—and had to lie up for repairs at the head of an island. This delay was the first thing that shook Kurtz's confidence. One morning he gave me a packet of papers and a photograph—the lot tied together with a shoe-string. 'Keep this for me,' he said. 'This noxious fool' (meaning the manager) 'is capable of prying into my boxes when I am not looking.' In the afternoon I saw him. He was lying on his back with closed eyes, and I withdrew quietly, but I heard him mutter, 'Live rightly, die, die . . .' I listened. There was nothing more. Was he rehearsing some speech in his sleep, or was it a fragment of a phrase from some newspaper article? He had been writing for the papers and meant to do so again, 'for the furthering of my ideas. It's a duty.'

"His was an impenetrable darkness. I looked at him as you peer down at a man who is lying at the bottom of a precipice where the sun never shines. But I had not much time to give him, because I was helping the engine-driver to take to pieces the leaky cylinders, to straighten a bent connecting-rod, and in other such matters. I lived in an infernal mess of rust, filings, nuts, bolts, spanners, hammers, ratchet-drills—things I abominate, because I don't get on with them. I tended the little forge we fortunately had aboard; I toiled wearily in a wretched scrap-heap—unless I had the shakes too bad to stand.

"One evening coming in with a candle I was startled to hear him say a little tremulously, 'I am lying here in the dark waiting for death.' The light was within a foot of his eyes. I forced myself to murmur, 'Oh, nonsense!' and stood over him as if transfixed.

"Anything approaching the change that came over his features I have never seen before, and hope never to see again. Oh, I wasn't touched. I was fascinated. It was as though a veil had been rent. I saw on that ivory face the expression of sombre pride, of ruthless power, of craven terror—of an intense and hopeless despair. Did he live his life again in every detail of desire, temptation, and surrender during that supreme moment of complete knowledge? He cried in a whisper at some image, at some vision—he cried out twice, a cry that was no more than a breath:

"'The horror! The horror!'

"I blew the candle out and left the cabin. The pilgrims were dining in the mess-room, and I took my place opposite the manager, who lifted his eyes to give me a questioning glance, which I successfully ignored. He leaned back,

1. Centuries old (from *séculaire*, French).

serene, with that peculiar smile of his sealing the unexpressed depths of his meanness. A continuous shower of small flies streamed upon the lamp, upon the cloth, upon our hands and faces. Suddenly the manager's boy put his insolent black head in the doorway, and said in a tone of scathing contempt:

"'Mistah Kurtz—he dead.'

"All the pilgrims rushed out to see. I remained, and went on with my dinner. I believe I was considered brutally callous. However, I did not eat much. There was a lamp in there—light, don't you know—and outside it was so beastly, beastly dark. I went no more near the remarkable man who had pronounced a judgement upon the adventures of his soul on this earth. The voice was gone. What else had been there? But I am of course aware that next day the pilgrims buried something in a muddy hole.

"And then they very nearly buried me.

"However, as you see, I did not go to join Kurtz there and then. I did not. I remained to dream the nightmare out to the end, and to show my loyalty to Kurtz once more. Destiny. My destiny! Droll thing life is—that mysterious arrangement of merciless logic for a futile purpose. The most you can hope from it is some knowledge of yourself—that comes too late—a crop of unextinguishable regrets. I have wrestled with death. It is the most unexciting contest you can imagine. It takes place in an impalpable greyness, with nothing underfoot, with nothing around, without spectators, without clamour, without glory, without the great desire of victory, without the great fear of defeat, in a sickly atmosphere of tepid scepticism, without much belief in your own right, and still less in that of your adversary. If such is the form of ultimate wisdom, then life is a greater riddle than some of us think it to be. I was within a hair's-breadth of the last opportunity for pronouncement, and I found with humiliation that probably I would have nothing to say. This is the reason why I affirm that Kurtz was a remarkable man. He had something to say. He said it. Since I had peeped over the edge myself, I understand better the meaning of his stare, that could not see the flame of the candle, but was wide enough to embrace the whole universe, piercing enough to penetrate all the hearts that beat in the darkness. He had summed up—he had judged. 'The horror!' He was a remarkable man. After all, this was the expression of some sort of belief; it had candour, it had conviction, it had a vibrating note of revolt in its whisper, it had the appalling face of a glimpsed truth—the strange commingling of desire and hate. And it is not my own extremity I remember best—a vision of greyness without form filled with physical pain, and a careless contempt for the evanescence of all things—even of this pain itself. No! It is his extremity that I seem to have lived through. True, he had made that last stride, he had stepped over the edge, while I had been permitted to draw back my hesitating foot. And perhaps in this is the whole difference; perhaps all the wisdom, and all truth, and all sincerity, are just compressed into that inappreciable moment of time in which we step over the threshold of the invisible. Perhaps! I like to think my summing-up would not have been a word of careless contempt. Better his cry—much better. It was an affirmation, a moral victory paid for by innumerable defeats, by abominable terrors, by abominable satisfactions. But it was a victory! That is why I have remained loyal to Kurtz to the last, and even beyond, when a long time after I heard once more, not his own voice, but the echo of his magnificent eloquence thrown to me from a soul as translucently pure as a cliff of crystal.

"No, they did not bury me, though there is a period of time which I remember mistily, with a shuddering wonder, like a passage through some inconceivable world that had no hope in it and no desire. I found myself back in the sepulchral city resenting the sight of people hurrying through the streets to filch a little money from each other, to devour their infamous cookery, to gulp their unwholesome beer, to dream their insignificant and silly dreams. They trespassed upon my thoughts. They were intruders whose knowledge of life was to me an irritating pretence, because I felt so sure they could not possibly know the things I knew. Their bearing, which was simply the bearing of commonplace individuals going about their business in the assurance of perfect safety, was offensive to me like the outrageous flauntings of folly in the face of a danger it is unable to comprehend. I had no particular desire to enlighten them, but I had some difficulty in restraining myself from laughing in their faces, so full of stupid importance. I daresay I was not very well at that time. I tottered about the streets—there were various affairs to settle—grinning bitterly at perfectly respectable persons. I admit my behaviour was inexcusable, but then my temperature was seldom normal in these days. My dear aunt's endeavours to 'nurse up my strength' seemed altogether beside the mark. It was not my strength that wanted nursing, it was my imagination that wanted soothing. I kept the bundle of papers given me by Kurtz, not knowing exactly what to do with it. His mother had died lately, watched over, as I was told, by his Intended. A clean-shaven man, with an official manner and wearing gold-rimmed spectacles, called on me one day and made inquiries, at first circuitous, afterwards suavely pressing, about what he was pleased to denominate certain 'documents.' I was not surprised, because I had had two rows with the manager on the subject out there. I had refused to give up the smallest scrap out of that package, and I took the same attitude with the spectacled man. He became darkly menacing at last, and with much heat argued that the Company had the right to every bit of information about its 'territories.' And, said he, 'Mr Kurtz's knowledge of unexplored regions must have been necessarily extensive and peculiar—owing to his great abilities and to the deplorable circumstances in which he had been placed: therefore—' I assured him Mr Kurtz's knowledge, however extensive, did not bear upon the problems of commerce or administration. He invoked then the name of science. 'It would be an incalculable loss if,' etc. etc. I offered him the report on the 'Suppression of Savage Customs,' with the postscriptum torn off. He took it up eagerly, but ended by sniffing at it with an air of contempt. 'This is not what we had a right to expect,' he remarked. 'Expect nothing else,' I said. 'There are only private letters.' He withdrew upon some threat of legal proceedings, and I saw him no more; but another fellow, calling himself Kurtz's cousin, appeared two days later, and was anxious to hear all the details about his dear relative's last moments. Incidentally he gave me to understand that Kurtz had been essentially a great musician. 'There was the making of an immense success,' said the man, who was an organist, I believe, with lank grey hair flowing over a greasy coat-collar. I had no reason to doubt his statement; and to this day I am unable to say what was Kurtz's profession, whether he ever had any—which was the greatest of his talents. I had taken him for a painter who wrote for the papers, or else for a journalist who could paint—but even the cousin (who took snuff during the interview) could not tell me what he had been—exactly. He was a universal genius—on that point I agreed with the old chap, who thereupon blew his nose noisily into a large cotton handkerchief and withdrew in senile agitation, bearing off some family letters and memoranda without importance. Ultimately a journalist anxious to know something of the fate of his 'dear colleague' turned up. This visitor informed me Kurtz's proper sphere ought to have been politics 'on the popular side.' He had furry straight eyebrows, bristly hair cropped short, an eyeglass on a broad ribbon, and, becoming expansive, confessed his opinion that Kurtz really couldn't write a bit—'but heavens! how that man could talk! He electrified large meetings. He had faith—don't you see?—he had the faith. He could get himself to believe anything—anything. He would have been a splendid leader of an extreme party.' 'What party?' I asked. 'Any party,' answered the other. 'He was an—an—extremist.' Did I not think so? I assented. Did I know, he asked, with a sudden flash of curiosity, 'what it was that had induced him to go out there?' 'Yes,' said I, and forthwith handed him the famous Report for publication, if he thought fit. He glanced through it hurriedly, mumbling all the time, judged 'it would do,' and took himself off with this plunder.

"Thus I was left at last with a slim packet of letters and the girl's portrait. She struck me as beautiful—I mean she had a beautiful expression. I know that the sunlight can be made to lie too, yet one felt that no manipulation of light and pose could have conveyed the delicate shade of truthfulness upon those features. She seemed ready to listen without mental reservation, without suspicion, without a thought for herself. I concluded I would go and give her back her portrait and those letters myself. Curiosity? Yes; and also some other feeling perhaps. All that had been Kurtz's had passed out of my hands: his soul, his body, his station, his plans, his ivory, his career. There remained only his memory and his Intended—and I wanted to give that up too to the past, in a way—to surrender personally all that remained of him with me to that oblivion which is the last word of our common fate. I don't defend myself. I had no clear perception of what it was I really wanted. Perhaps it was an impulse of unconscious loyalty, or the fulfilment of one of those ironic necessities that lurk in the facts of human existence. I don't know. I can't tell. But I went.

"I thought his memory was like the other memories of the dead that accumulate in every man's life—a vague impress on the brain of shadows that had fallen on it in their swift and final passage; but before the high and ponderous door, between the tall houses of a street as still and decorous as a well-kept alley in a cemetery, I had a vision of him on the stretcher, opening his mouth voraciously, as if to devour all the earth with all its mankind. He lived then before me; he lived as much as he had ever lived—a shadow insatiable of splendid appearances, of frightful realities; a shadow darker than the shadow of the night, and draped nobly in the folds of a gorgeous eloquence. The vision seemed to enter the house with me—the stretcher, the phantom-bearers, the wild crowd of obedient worshippers, the gloom of the forests, the glitter of the reach between the murky bends, the beat of the drum, regular and muffled like the beating of a heart—the heart of a conquering darkness. It was a moment of triumph for the wilderness, an invading and vengeful rush which, it seemed to me, I would have to keep back alone for the salvation of another soul. And the memory of what I had heard him say afar there, with the horned shapes stirring at my back, in the glow of fires, within the patient woods, those broken phrases came back to me, were heard again in their ominous and terrifying simplicity. I remembered his abject pleading, his abject threats, the colossal scale of his vile desires, the meanness, the torment, the tempestuous anguish of his soul. And later on I seemed to see his collected languid manner, when he said one day, 'This lot of ivory now is really mine. The Company did not pay for it. I collected it myself at a very great personal risk. I am afraid they will try to claim it as theirs though. H'm. It is a difficult case. What do you think I ought to do— resist? Eh? I want no more than justice.' . . . He wanted no more than justice— no more than justice. I rang the bell before a mahogany door on the first floor, and while I waited he seemed to stare at me out of the glossy panel—stare with that wide and immense stare embracing, condemning, loathing all the universe. I seemed to hear the whispered cry, 'The horror! The horror!'

"The dusk was falling. I had to wait in a lofty drawing room with three long windows from floor to ceiling that were like three luminous and bedraped columns. The bent gilt legs and backs of the furniture shone in indistinct curves. The tall marble fireplace had a cold and monumental whiteness. A grand piano stood massively in a corner; with dark gleams on the flat surfaces like a sombre and polished sarcophagus. A high door opened—closed. I rose.

"She came forward, all in black, with a pale head, floating towards me in the dusk. She was in mourning. It was more than a year since his death, more than a year since the news came; she seemed as though she would remember and mourn for ever. She took both my hands in hers and murmured, 'I had heard you were coming.' I noticed she was not very young—I mean not girlish. She had a mature capacity for fidelity, for belief, for suffering. The room seemed to have grown darker, as if all the sad light of the cloudy evening had taken refuge on her forehead. This fair hair, this pale visage, this pure brow, seemed surrounded by an ashy halo from which the dark eyes looked out at me. Their glance was guileless, profound, confident, and trustful. She carried her sorrowful head as though she were proud of that sorrow, as though she would say, I—I alone know how to mourn for him as he deserves. But while we were still shaking hands, such a look of awful desolation came upon her face that I perceived she was one of those creatures that are not the playthings of Time. For her he had died only yesterday. And, by Jove! the impression was so powerful that for me too he seemed to have died only yesterday—nay, this very minute. I saw her and him in the same instant of time—his death and her sorrow—I saw her sorrow in the very moment of his death. Do you understand? I saw them together—I heard them together. She had said, with a deep catch of the breath, 'I have survived'; while my strained ears seemed to hear distinctly, mingled with her tone of despairing regret, the summing-up whisper of his eternal condemnation. I asked myself what I was doing there, with a sensation of panic in my heart as though I had blundered into a place of cruel and absurd mysteries not fit for a human being to behold. She motioned me to a chair. We sat down. I laid the packet gently on the little table, and she put her hand over it. . . . 'You knew him well,' she murmured, after a moment of mourning silence.

"'Intimacy grows quickly out there,' I said. 'I knew him as well as it is possible for one man to know another.'

"'And you admired him,' she said. 'It was impossible to know him and not to admire him. Was it?'

"'He was a remarkable man,' I said unsteadily. Then before the appealing fixity of her gaze, that seemed to watch for more words on my lips, I went on, 'It was impossible not to—'

"'Love him,' she finished eagerly, silencing me into an appalled dumbness. 'How true! how true! But when you think that no one knew him so well as I! I had all his noble confidence. I knew him best.'

"'You knew him best,' I repeated. And perhaps she did. But with every word spoken the room was growing darker, and only her forehead, smooth and white, remained illumined by the unextinguishable light of belief and love.

"'You were his friend,' she went on. 'His friend,' she repeated, a little louder. 'You must have been, if he had given you this, and sent you to me. I feel I can speak to you—and oh! I must speak. I want you—you who have heard his last words—to know I have been worthy of him. . . . It is not pride. . . . Yes! I am proud to know I understood him better than any one on earth—he told me so himself. And since his mother died I have had no one—no one—to—to—'

"I listened. The darkness deepened. I was not even sure whether he had given me the right bundle. I rather suspect he wanted me to take care of another batch of his papers which, after his death, I saw the manager examining under the lamp. And the girl talked, easing her pain in the certitude of my sympathy; she talked as thirsty men drink. I had heard that her engagement with Kurtz had been disapproved by her people. He wasn't rich enough or something. And indeed I don't know whether he had not been a pauper all his life. He had given me some reason to infer that it was his impatience of comparative poverty that drove him out there.

"'. . . Who was not his friend who had heard him speak once?' she was saying. 'He drew men towards him by what was best in them.' She looked at me with intensity. 'It is the gift of the great,' she went on, and the sound of her low voice seemed to have the accompaniment of all the other sounds, full of mystery, desolation, and sorrow, I had ever heard—the ripple of the river, the soughing[2] of the trees swayed by the wind, the murmurs of the crowds, the faint ring of incomprehensible words cried from afar, the whisper of a voice speaking from beyond the threshold of an eternal darkness. 'But you have heard him! You know!' she cried.

"'Yes, I know,' I said with something like despair in my heart, but bowing my head before the faith that was in her, before that great and saving illusion that shone with an unearthly glow in the darkness, in the triumphant darkness from which I could not have defended her—from which I could not even defend myself.

"'What a loss to me—to us!'—she corrected herself with beautiful generosity; then added in a murmur, 'To the world.' By the last gleams of twilight I could see the glitter of her eyes, full of tears—of tears that would not fall.

"'I have been very happy—very fortunate—very proud,' she went on. 'Too fortunate. Too happy for a little while. And now I am unhappy for—for life.'

"She stood up; her fair hair seemed to catch all the remaining light in a glimmer of gold. I rose too.

"'And of all this,' she went on mournfully, 'of all his promise, and of all his greatness, of his generous mind, of his noble heart, nothing remains—nothing but a memory. You and I—'

2. A rushing or murmuring sound.

"'We shall always remember him,' I said hastily.

"'No!' she cried. 'It is impossible that all this should be lost—that such a life should be sacrificed to leave nothing—but sorrow. You know what vast plans he had. I knew of them too—I could not perhaps understand—but others knew of them. Something must remain. His words, at least, have not died.'

"'His words will remain,' I said.

"'And his example,' she whispered to herself. 'Men looked up to him—his goodness shone in every act. His example—'

"'True,' I said; 'his example too. Yes, his example. I forgot that.'

"'But I do not. I cannot—I cannot believe—not yet. I cannot believe that I shall never see him again, that nobody will see him again, never, never, never.'

"She put out her arms as if after a retreating figure, stretching them back and with clasped pale hands across the fading and narrow sheen of the window. Never see him! I saw him clearly enough then. I shall see this eloquent phantom as long as I live, and I shall see her too, a tragic and familiar Shade, resembling in this gesture another one, tragic also, and bedecked with powerless charms, stretching bare brown arms over the glitter of the infernal stream, the stream of darkness. She said suddenly very low, 'He died as he lived.'

"'His end,' said I, with dull anger stirring in me, 'was in every way worthy of his life.'

"'And I was not with him,' she murmured. My anger subsided before a feeling of infinite pity.

"'Everything that could be done—' I mumbled.

"'Ah, but I believed in him more than any one on earth—more than his own mother, more than—himself. He needed me! Me! I would have treasured every sigh, every word, every sign, every glance.'

"I felt like a chill grip on my chest. 'Don't,' I said, in a muffled voice.

"'Forgive me. I—I—have mourned so long in silence—in silence. . . . You were with him—to the last? I think of his loneliness. Nobody near to understand him as I would have understood. Perhaps no one to hear. . . .'

"'To the very end,' I said shakily. 'I heard his very last words. . . .' I stopped in a fright.

"'Repeat them,' she murmured in a heart-broken tone. 'I want—I want—something—something—to—to live with.'

"I was on the point of crying at her, 'Don't you hear them?' The dusk was repeating them in a persistent whisper all around us, in a whisper that seemed to swell menacingly like the first whisper of a rising wind. 'The horror! The horror!'

"'His last word—to live with,' she insisted. 'Don't you understand I loved him—I loved him—I loved him!'

"I pulled myself together and spoke slowly.

"'The last word he pronounced was—your name.'

"I heard a light sigh and then my heart stood still, stopped dead short by an exulting and terrible cry, by the cry of inconceivable triumph and of unspeakable pain. 'I knew it—I was sure!'. . . . She knew. She was sure. I heard her weeping; she had hidden her face in her hands. It seemed to me that the house would collapse before I could escape, that the heavens would fall upon my head. But nothing happened. The heavens do not fall for such a trifle. Would they have fallen, I wonder, if I had rendered Kurtz that justice which was his due? Hadn't he said he wanted only justice? But I couldn't. I could not tell her. It would have been too dark—too dark altogether. . . ."

Marlow ceased, and sat apart, indistinct and silent, in the pose of a meditating Buddha. Nobody moved for a time. "We have lost the first of the ebb," said the Director suddenly. I raised my head. The offing was barred by a black bank of clouds, and the tranquil waterway leading to the uttermost ends of the earth flowed sombre under an overcast sky—seemed to lead into the heart of an immense darkness.

1899

THOMAS MANN
1875–1955

The greatest German novelist of the twentieth century, Thomas Mann also became an international figure to whom people looked for statements on art, modern society, and the human condition. Carrying on the nineteenth-century tradition of psychological realism, Mann took as his subject the cultural and spiritual crises of Europe at the turn of the century. His career spanned a time of great change, including the upheaval of two world wars and the disintegration of an entire society. Whereas other modern novelists such as **James Joyce**, **William Faulkner**, and **Virginia Woolf** stressed innovative language and style, Mann wrote in a more traditional, realistic style about the universal human conflicts between art and life, sensuality and intellect, individual and social will. Yet in his struggle with themes like time, subjectivity, and homosexuality, he too participated in the modernist movement that transformed the literature of the twentieth century.

Mann was born on June 6, 1875, in Lübeck, a historic seaport and commercial city in northern Germany. His father was a grain merchant and head of the family firm; his mother, who came from a German-Brazilian family, was known for her beauty and musical talent. The contrast between Nordic and Latin that plays such a large part in Mann's work began in his consciousness of his own heritage. Mann became acquainted with mortality early on: his father died when he was sixteen, and later both his sister and his son committed suicide. Although Thomas failed two years in school, he viewed the failure as liberating, since it relieved him of his parents' high expectations. He graduated from high school in 1894. Joining his family in Munich, where they had moved after his father's death, he worked as an unpaid apprentice in a fire insurance business, but was more interested in university lectures in history, political economy, and art. He decided against a business career after his first published story, *Fallen* (1896), received praise from the noted poet Richard Dehmel. He lived and wrote for two years in Italy before returning to Munich for a stint as manuscript reader for the satiric weekly *Simplicissimus*. In 1905 he married Katia Pringsheim, with whom he had six children. Yet as a young man he had experienced homosexual attractions, which continued throughout his life and became a recurring theme in his fiction. He recorded these attractions privately in his diary but never acted on them; he commented that "I would never have wanted to go to bed even with the Belvedere Apollo."

His first major work, *Buddenbrooks* (1901), describes the decline of a prosperous German family through four generations and is to some extent based on the history of the Mann family business. Nonetheless, the elements of autobiography are quickly absorbed into the universal themes of the inner decay of the German burgher ("bourgeois," or middle-class) tradition and its growing isolation from other segments of society—a decline paralleled in the portrait of a developing artistic sensitivity and its relation to death. Throughout his writings before and during the First World War, Mann established himself as an important spokesman for modern Germany. He argued with his brother Heinrich about politics; Heinrich was a passionate liberal, but Thomas defined freedom as "a moral, spiritual idea" and said that "for political freedom I've absolutely no interest." The political crises after the First World War shook Mann, however, and the subsequent rise of the Nazis changed his views. He rejected his early conservatism and defense of an authoritarian nationalist government (*Reflections of a Non-Political Man*, 1918) in favor of ardent support for democracy and liberal humanism.

One of the first signs of this new attitude was Mann's most famous novel, *The Magic Mountain* (1924), a bildungsroman (a novel of the protagonist's education and development) that uses the isolation of a mountaintop tuberculosis sanatorium to gain perspective on the philosophic issues of twentieth-century Europe. *The Magic Mountain* was immensely popular, and in 1929 its author received the Nobel Prize. As his international stature grew, Mann spoke out against the Nazis; his wife, Katia, came from a Jewish family, and when Hitler rose to power in 1933, the Manns went into voluntary exile in neutral Switzerland. Stung by Mann's criticism, the Nazis revoked his citizenship. Moving to the United States in 1938, he wrote and lectured against Nazism, and in 1944 he became an American citizen. After the Second World War, Mann refused to live in Germany, arguing that the country had not expiated its crimes. He became an active advocate for the cause of peace; criticized by the House Un-American Activities Committee for his support of allegedly Communist peace organizations, Mann left the United States for Switzerland in 1952.

Mann's later works deal with the conflicts and interrelations between society and inspired individuals whose spiritual, intellectual, or artistic gifts set them apart. *Joseph and His Brothers* (1933–45) is a tetralogy that reimagines the biblical tale of Joseph, who, abandoned for dead by his brothers, survives and comes to power in Egypt. *Doctor Faustus* (1947), which Mann called "the novel of my epoch, dressed up in the story of a highly precarious and sinful artistic life," portrays the composer Adrian Leverkühn as a modern Faust who personifies the temptation and corruption of contemporary Germany. Well after the war, when Mann had moved to Zurich, he published a final, comic picture of the artist figure as a confidence man who uses his skill and ironic insight to manipulate society (*The Confessions of Felix Krull*, 1954). Mann's last work before his death, on August 12, 1955, the *Confessions* recapitulates his familiar themes, but in a lighthearted parody of the traditional bildungsroman that is a far cry from the moral seriousness of earlier tales.

Many of Mann's themes derive from the nineteenth-century German aesthetic tradition in which he grew up. The philosophers Schopenhauer and Nietzsche and the composer Wagner had the most influence on his work: Arthur Schopenhauer (1788–1860) for his vision of the artist's suffering and development; Friedrich Nietzsche (1844–1900) for his portrait of the diseased artist overcoming chaos and decay to produce, through discipline and will, works that justify existence; and Richard Wagner (1813–1883) for embodying the complete artist who controlled all aspects of his work: music, lyrics, the very staging of his operas. Mann's well-known use of the verbal leitmotif is also borrowed from Wagner, whose operas are notable for the recurrent musical theme (the leitmotif) associated with a particular person, thing, action, or state of being. In Mann's literary adaptation, evocative phrases, repeated almost without change, link memories throughout the text and establish a cumulative emotional resonance. Inside the tradition of realistic narration, Mann creates a highly organized literary structure with subtly interrelated themes and images that build up rich associations of ideas: in his own words, an "epic prose composition . . . understood by me as spiritual thematic pattern, as a musical complex of associations." At the same time, Mann's works cultivate objectivity, distance, and irony, and no character—including the narrator—is immune from the author's critical eye. Indeed, it is in his tendency to treat realist techniques with irony that Mann most reveals himself as a modern, unable to accept narrative convention at face value.

DEATH IN VENICE

The work presented here, *Death in Venice*, is Mann's most famous novella, published in 1912, shortly after the author's vacation in Venice and two years before the First World War. Its sense of impending doom involves the cultural disintegration of the "European soul" (soon to be expressed in the war), which has its symbol in the corruption and death of the writer Gustav von Aschenbach during an epidemic. The story portrays a loss of psychological balance, a sickness of the artistic soul to match that of plague-ridden Venice masking its true condition before unsuspecting tourists. Erotic and artistic themes mingle as the respected Aschenbach, escaping a lifetime of laborious creation and self-discipline, allows himself to be swept away by the classical beauty of a young boy until he becomes a grotesque figure, dyeing his hair and rouging his cheeks in a vain attempt to appear young. Aschenbach's fatal obsession with Tadzio casts light on the artist's whole career.

Aschenbach has laboriously repressed emotions and spontaneity to achieve the disciplined, classical style of a master—and also to earn fame. Plagued by nervous exhaustion at the beginning of the story, he reacts to the sight of a foreign traveler with a "sudden, strange expansion of his inner space" and starts dreaming of exotic, dangerous landscapes. From the tropical swampland and tigers of the Ganges delta to the mountains of a later dream's Dionysiac revels, these visionary landscapes become a metaphor for all the subterranean impulses he has rejected in himself and for his art. Enigmatic figures guide Aschenbach's adventure of the emotions: the traveler, the grotesque old man on the boat, the gondolier, the street singer, and Tadzio himself, interpreted as a godlike figure out of Greek myth. Indeed, allusions to ancient myth and literature multiply rapidly as Aschenbach falls under Tadzio's spell and begins to rationalize his fascination as the artist's pursuit of divine beauty. Turning to Plato's *Phaedrus*, a dialogue that combines themes of love with the search for absolute beauty and truth, Aschenbach sketches his own "Platonic" argument as a meditation on the dual nature of the artist. "Who can untangle the riddle of the artist's essence and character?" asks the narrator. *Death in Venice* is a crystallization of Mann's work at its best, displaying the penetrating detail of his social and psychological realism, the power of his tightly interwoven symbolic structure, and the tragic force of his artist-hero's crisis.

Death in Venice[1]

CHAPTER I

On a spring afternoon in 19—,[2] a year that for months glowered threateningly over our continent, Gustav Aschenbach—or von[3] Aschenbach, as he had been known officially since his fiftieth birthday—set off alone from his dwelling in Prinzregentenstrasse[4] in Munich on a rather long walk. He had been overstrained by the difficult and dangerous morning's work, which just now required particular discretion, caution, penetration, and precision of will: even after his midday meal the writer had not been able to halt the running on of the productive machinery within him, that "motus animi continuus" which Cicero[5] claims is the essence of eloquence, nor had he been able to obtain the relaxing slumber so necessary to him once a day to relieve the increasing demands on his resources. Thus, he sought the open air right after tea, hoping that fresh air and exercise would restore him and help him to have a profitable evening.

It was early May, and after weeks of cold, wet weather a premature summer had set in. The Englischer Garten,[6] although only beginning to come into leaf, was as muggy as in August and at the end near the city was full of vehicles and people out for a stroll. Increasingly quiet paths led Aschenbach toward Aumeister,[7] where he spent a moment surveying the lively crowd in the beer garden, next to which several hackneys and carriages were lingering; but then as the sun went down he took a route homeward outside the park over the open fields and, since he felt tired and thunder clouds now threatened over Föhring,[8] he waited at the North Cemetery stop for the tram that would take him directly back into the city.

1. Translated by and some notes adapted from Clayton Koelb.
2. In 1911, when the story was written, the "Moroccan crisis" was precipitated when a German gunboat appeared off the coast of Agadir, prompting negotiations between France and Germany over their respective national interests. A series of similar diplomatic crises led to the outbreak of World War 1 in 1914.
3. From or of. "Von" appears only in the names of nobility. Aschenbach was made an honorary nobleman on his fiftieth birthday.
4. A street in Munich that forms the southern boundary of the Englischer Garten (English Garden). Mann lived in various apartments in this neighborhood.
5. Marcus Tullius Cicero (106–43 B.C.E.), Roman orator. "Motus animi continuus": the continuous motion of the spirit (Latin, attributed to Cicero).
6. The English Garden, a 900-acre public park with diverse attractions that extended from the city to the water meadows of the Isar River.
7. A beer garden in the northern section.
8. A district in Munich.

As it happened he found the tram stop and the surrounding area deserted. Neither on the paved Ungererstrasse, whose streetcar-tracks stretched in glistening solitude toward Schwabing, nor on the Föhringer Chaussee[9] was there a vehicle to be seen, nothing stirred behind the fences of the stonemasons' shops, where the crosses, headstones, and monuments for sale formed a second, untenanted graveyard, and the Byzantine architecture of the mortuary chapel across the way lay silent in the glow of the departing day. Its facade was decorated with Greek crosses and hieratic paintings in soft colors; in addition it displayed symmetrically arranged scriptural quotations in gold letters, such as, "They are entering the house of God," or, "May the eternal light shine upon them." Waiting, he found a few moments' solemn diversion in reading these formulations and letting his mind's eye bask in their radiant mysticism, when, returning from his reveries, he noticed a man in the portico, above the two apocalyptic beasts guarding the front steps. The man's not altogether ordinary appearance took his thoughts in a completely different direction.

It was not clear whether the man had emerged from the chapel through the bronze door or had climbed the steps up to the entry from the outside without being noticed. Aschenbach, without entering too deeply into the question, inclined to the first assumption. Moderately tall, thin, clean-shaven, and strikingly snub-nosed, the man belonged to the red-haired type and possessed a redhead's milky and freckled complexion. He was clearly not of Bavarian stock, and in any case the wide and straight-brimmed straw hat that covered his head lent him the appearance of a foreigner, of a traveler from afar. To be sure, he also wore the familiar native rucksack strapped to his shoulders and a yellowish Norfolk suit[1] apparently of loden cloth. He had a gray mackintosh over his left forearm, which he held supported against his side, and in his right hand he held a stick with an iron tip, which he propped obliquely against the ground, leaning his hip against its handle and crossing his ankles. With his head held up, so that his Adam's apple protruded nakedly from the thin neck that emerged from his loose sport shirt, he gazed intently into the distance with colorless, red-lashed eyes, between which stood two stark vertical furrows that went rather oddly with his short, turned-up nose. It may be that his elevated and elevating location had something to do with it, but his posture conveyed an impression of imperious surveillance, fortitude, even wildness. His lips seemed insufficient, perhaps because he was squinting, blinded, toward the setting sun or maybe because he was afflicted by a facial deformity—in any case they were retracted to such an extent that his teeth, revealed as far as the gums, menacingly displayed their entire white length.

It is entirely possible that Aschenbach had been somewhat indiscreet in his half-distracted, half-inquisitive survey of the stranger, for he suddenly realized that his gaze was being returned, and indeed returned so belligerently, so directly eye to eye, with such a clear intent to bring matters to a head and force the other to avert his eyes, that Aschenbach, with an awkward sense of embarrassment, turned away and began to walk along the fence, intending for the time being to pay no more attention to the fellow. In a moment he had forgotten about him. But perhaps the man had the look of the traveler about him, or

9. A street. Ungererstrasse is a street that borders the North Cemetery. Schwabing is another district in Munich.

1. A belted suit.

perhaps because he exercised some physical or spiritual influence, Aschenbach's imagination was set working. He felt a sudden, strange expansion of his inner space, a rambling unrest, a youthful thirst for faraway places, a feeling so intense, so new—or rather so long unused and forgotten—that he stood rooted to the spot, his hands behind his back and his gaze to the ground, pondering the essence and direction of his emotion.

It was wanderlust and nothing more, but it was an overwhelming wanderlust that rose to a passion and even to a delusion. His desire acquired vision, and his imagination, not yet calmed down from the morning's work, created its own version of the manifold marvels and terrors of the earth, all of them at once now seeking to take shape within him. He saw, saw a landscape, a tropical swamp under a vaporous sky, moist, luxuriant, and monstrous, a sort of primitive wilderness of islands, morasses, and alluvial estuaries; saw hairy palm trunks rise up near and far out of rank fern brakes, out of thick, swollen, wildly blooming vegetation; saw wondrously formless trees sink their aerial roots into the earth through stagnant, green-shadowed pools, where exotic birds, their shoulders high and their bills shaped weirdly, stood motionless in the shallows looking askance amidst floating flowers that were white as milk and big as platters; saw the eyes of a lurking tiger sparkle between the gnarled stems of a bamboo thicket; and felt his heart pound with horror and mysterious desire. Then the vision faded, and with a shake of his head Aschenbach resumed his promenade along the fences bordering the headstone-makers' yard.

He had regarded travel, at least since he had commanded the financial resources to enjoy the advantages of global transportation at will, as nothing more than a measure he had to take for his health, no matter how much it went against his inclination. Too much taken up with the tasks that his problematic self and the European soul posed for him, too burdened with the obligation of productivity, too averse to distraction to be a success as a lover of the world's motley show, he had quite contented himself with the view of the earth's surface anyone could get without stirring very far from home. He had never even been tempted to leave Europe. Especially now that his life was slowly waning, now that his artist's fear of never getting finished—his concern that the sands might run out of the glass before he had done his utmost and given his all—could no longer be dismissed as pure fancy, his external existence had confined itself almost exclusively to the lovely city that had become his home and to the rustic country house he had built in the mountains where he spent the rainy summers.

Besides, even this impulse that had come over him so suddenly and so late in life was quickly moderated and set right by reason and a self-discipline practiced since early youth. He had intended to keep at the work to which he now devoted his life until he reached a certain point and then move out to the country. The thought of sauntering about the world, of thereby being seduced away from months of work, seemed all too frivolous, too contrary to plan, and ultimately impermissible. And yet he knew all too well why this temptation had assailed him so unexpectedly. He had to admit it to himself: it was the urge to escape that was behind this yearning for the far away and the new, this desire for release, freedom, and forgetfulness. It was the urge to get away from his work, from the daily scene of an inflexible, cold, and passionate service. Of course he loved this service and almost loved the enervating struggle, renewed each day, between his stubborn, proud, so-often-tested will and his growing lassitude, about which no one could be allowed to know and which the product of his toil could not be permitted to reveal in any way, by any sign of failure or of negligence. Yet it seemed reasonable not to overbend the bow and not to stifle obstinately the outbreak of such a vital need. He thought about his work, thought about the place where once again, today as yesterday, he had been forced to abandon it, a passage that would submit, it seemed, neither to patient care nor to surprise attack. He considered it again, sought once more to break through or untangle the logjam, then broke off the effort with a shudder of repugnance. The passage presented no extraordinary difficulty; what disabled him was the malaise of scrupulousness confronting him in the guise of an insatiable perfectionism. Even as a young man, to be sure, he had considered perfectionism the basis and most intimate essence of his talent, and for its sake he had curbed and cooled his emotions, because he knew that emotion inclines one to satisfaction with a comfortable approximation, a half of perfection. Was his enslaved sensitivity now avenging itself by leaving him, refusing to advance his project and give wings to his art, taking with it all his joy, all his delight in form and expression? It was not that he was producing bad work—that at least was the advantage of his advanced years; he felt every moment comfortably secure in his mastery. But, though the nation honored it, he himself was not pleased with his mastery, and indeed it seemed to him that his work lacked those earmarks of a fiery, playful fancy that, stemming from joy, gave more joy to his appreciative audience than did any inner content or weighty excellence. He was fearful of the summer in the country, all alone in the little house with the maid who prepared his meals and the servant who waited on him at table, fearful too of the familiar mountaintops and mountainsides that once more would surround him in his discontented, slow progress. And so what he needed was a respite, a kind of spur-of-the-moment existence, a way to waste some time, foreign air and an infusion of new blood, to make the summer bearable and productive. Travel it would be then—it was all right with him. Not too far, though, not quite all the way to the tigers. One night in a sleeping car and a siesta for three or maybe four weeks in some fashionable vacation spot in the charming south . . .

Such were his thoughts as the noise of the electric tram approached along the Ungererstrasse, and he decided as he got on to devote this evening to studying maps and time tables. Once aboard it occurred to him to look around for the man in the straw hat, his comrade in this excursion that had been, in spite of all, so consequential. But he could get no clear idea of the man's whereabouts; neither his previous location, nor the next stop, nor the tram car itself revealed any signs of his presence.

CHAPTER 2

Gustav Aschenbach, the author of the clear and vigorous prose epic on the life of Frederick the Great;[2] the patient artist who wove together with enduring diligence the novelistic tapestry *Maia*,[3] a work rich in characters and eminently

---

2. King Frederick II (1712–1786) started Prussia on its rise to domination of Germany and made his court a prominent European cultural center.

3. In Hinduism, the illusory appearance of the world concealing a higher spiritual reality.

successful in gathering together many human destinies under the shadow of a single idea; the creator of that powerful story bearing the title "A Man of Misery," which had earned the gratitude of an entire young generation by showing it the possibility for a moral resolution that passed through and beyond the deepest knowledge; the author, finally (and this completes the short list of his mature works), of the passionate treatment of the topic "Art and Intellect,"[4] an essay whose power of organization and antithetical eloquence had prompted serious observers to rank it alongside Schiller's "On Naïve and Sentimental Poetry";[5] Gustav Aschenbach, then, was born the son of a career civil servant in the justice ministry in L., a district capital in the province of Silesia. His ancestors had been officers, judges, and government functionaries, men who had led upright lives of austere decency devoted to the service of king and country. A more ardent spirituality had expressed itself once among them in the person of a preacher; more impetuous and sensuous blood had entered the family line in the previous generation through the writer's mother, the daughter of a Bohemian music director. It was from her that he had in his features the traits of a foreign race. The marriage of sober conscientiousness devoted to service with darker, more fiery impulses engendered an artist and indeed this very special artist.

Since his entire being was bent on fame, he emerged early on as, perhaps not exactly precocious, but nonetheless, thanks to the decisiveness and peculiar terseness of his style, surprisingly mature and ready to go before the public. He was practically still in high school when he made a name for himself. Ten years later he learned how to keep up appearances, to manage his fame from his writing desk, to produce gracious and significant sentences for his necessarily brief letters (for many demands are made on such a successful and reliable man). By the age of forty, exhausted by the tortures and vicissitudes of his real work, he had to deal with a daily flood of mail bearing stamps from countries in every corner of the globe.

Tending neither to the banal nor to the eccentric, his talent was such as to win for his stories both the acceptance of the general public and an admiring, challenging interest from a more discerning audience. Thus he found himself even as a young man obliged in every way to achieve and indeed to achieve extraordinary things. He had therefore never known sloth, never known the carefree, laissez-faire attitude of youth. When he got sick in Vienna around the age of thirty-five, a canny observer remarked about him to friends, "You see, Aschenbach has always lived like this"—and the speaker closed the fingers of his left hand into a fist—"never like this"—and he let his open hand dangle comfortably from the arm of the chair. How right he was! And the morally courageous aspect of it was that, possessing anything but a naturally robust constitution, he was not so much born for constant exertion as he was called to it.

Medical concerns had prevented him from attending school as a child and compelled the employment of private instruction at home. He had grown up alone and without companions, and yet he must have realized early on that he belonged to a tribe in which talent was not so much a rarity as was the bodily

---

4. Frederick, Maia, A Man of Misery, and Art and Intellect are titles of projects Mann had worked on and abandoned.

5. An influential essay by the German Romantic writer Friedrich Schiller (1759–1805).

frame talent needs to find its fulfillment, a tribe known for giving their best early in life but not for longevity. His watchword, however, was "Endure," and he saw in his novel about Frederick the Great precisely the apotheosis of this commandment, which seemed to him the essence of a selflessly active virtue. He harbored, moreover, a keen desire to live to a ripe old age, for he had long believed that an artistic career could be called truly great, encompassing, indeed truly worthy of honor only if the artist were allotted sufficient years to be fruitful in his own way at all stages of human life.

Since he thus bore the burdens of his talent on slender shoulders and wished to carry those burdens far, he was in great need of discipline. Fortunately for him discipline was his heritage at birth from his paternal side. At forty, at fifty, even at an age when others squander and stray, content to put their great plans aside for the time being, he started his day at an early hour by dousing his chest and back with cold water. Then, placing two tall wax candles in silver candlesticks at the head of his manuscript, he would spend two or three fervently conscientious morning hours sacrificing on the altar of art the powers he had assembled during his sleep. It was forgivable—indeed it even indicated the victory of his moral force—that uninformed readers mistook the Maia-world or the epic scroll on which unrolled Frederick's heroic life for the products of single sustained bursts of energy, whereas they actually grew into grandeur layer by layer, out of small daily doses of work and countless individual flashes of inspiration. These works were thoroughly excellent in every detail solely because their creator had endured for years under the pressure of a single project, bringing to bear a tenacity and perseverance similar to that which had conquered his home province,[6] and because he had devoted only his freshest and worthiest hours to actual composition.

If a work of the intellect is to have an immediate, broad, and deep effect, there must be a mysterious affinity, a correspondence between the personal fate of its originator and the more general fate of his contemporaries. People do not know why they accord fame to a particular work. Far from being experts, they suppose they see in it a hundred virtues that would justify their interest; but the real reason for their approval is something imponderable—it is sympathy. Aschenbach had actually stated forthrightly, though in a relatively inconspicuous passage, that nearly everyone achieving greatness did so under the banner of "Despite"—despite grief and suffering, despite poverty, destitution, infirmity, affliction, passion, and a thousand obstacles. But this was more than an observation, it was the fruit of experience; no, it was the very formula for his life and his fame, the key to his work. Was it any wonder, then, that it was also the basis for the moral disposition and outward demeanor of his most original fictional characters?

Early on an observant critic had described the new type of hero that this writer preferred, a figure returning over and over again in manifold variation: it was based on the concept of "an intellectual and youthful manliness which grits its teeth in proud modesty and calmly endures the swords and spears as they pass through its body." It was a nice description, ingenious and precise, despite its seemingly excessive emphasis on passivity. For meeting one's fate

6. As a result of the Seven Years' War (1759–63), Frederick the Great wrested Silesia from Austria. Today, most of Silesia has become a region in southwestern Poland.

with dignity, grace under pressure of pain, is not simply a matter of sufferance; it is an active achievement, a positive triumph, and the figure of St. Sebastian[7] is thus the most beautiful image, if not of art in general, then surely of the art under discussion here. Having looked at the characters in Aschenbach's narrated world, having seen the elegant self-discipline that managed right up to the last moment to hide from the eyes of the world the undermining process, the biological decline, taking place within; having seen the yellow, physically handicapped ugliness that nonetheless managed to kindle its smoldering ardor into a pure flame, managed even to catapult itself to mastery in the realm of beauty; or having seen the pale impotence that pulls out of the glowing depths of the spirit enough power to force a whole frivolous people to fall at the feet of the cross, at the feet of that very impotence; or the lovable charm that survives even the empty and rigorous service of pure form; or the false, dangerous life of the born deceiver, with the quick enervation of its longing and with its artfulness—having seen all these human destinies and many more besides, it was easy enough to doubt that there could be any other sort of heroism than that of weakness. In any case, what kind of heroism was more appropriate to the times than this? Gustav Aschenbach was the poet of all those who work on the edge of exhaustion, of the overburdened, worn down moralists of achievement who nonetheless still stand tall, those who, stunted in growth and short of means, use ecstatic feats of will and clever management to extract from themselves at least for a period of time the effects of greatness. Their names are legion, and they are the heroes of the age. And all of them recognized themselves in his work; they saw themselves justified, exalted, their praises sung. And they were grateful; they heralded his name.

He had been once as young and rough as the times and, seduced by them, had made public blunders and mistakes, had made himself vulnerable, had committed errors against tact and good sense in word and deed. But he had won the dignity toward which, in his opinion, every great talent feels an inborn urge and spur. One could say in fact that his entire development had been a conscious and defiant rise to dignity, beyond any twinge of doubt and of irony that might have stood in his way.

Pleasing the great mass of middle-class readers depends mainly on offering vividly depicted, intellectually undemanding characterizations, but passionately uncompromising youth is smitten only with what is problematic; and Aschenbach had been as problematic and uncompromising as any young man can be. He had pandered to the intellect, exhausted the soil of knowledge, milled flour from his seed corn, revealed secrets, put talent under suspicion, betrayed art. Indeed, while his portrayals entertained, elevated, invigorated the blissfully credulous among his readers, as a youthful artist it was his cynical observations on the questionable nature of art and of the artist's calling that had kept the twenty-year-old element fascinated.

But it seems that nothing so quickly or so thoroughly blunts a high-minded and capable spirit as the sharp and bitter charm of knowledge; and it is certain that the melancholy, scrupulous thoroughness characteristic of the young seems shallow in comparison with the solemn decision of masterful maturity to dis-

---

7. A 3rd-century Roman martyr whose arrow-pierced body was a popular subject for Renaissance painters.

avow knowledge, to reject it, to move beyond it with head held high, to forestall the least possibility that it could cripple, dishearten, or dishonor his will, his capacity for action and feeling, or even his passion. How else could one interpret the famous story "A Man of Misery" save as an outbreak of disgust at the indecent psychologism then current? This disgust was embodied in the figure of that soft and foolish semi-villain who, out of weakness, viciousness, and moral impotence, buys a black-market destiny for himself by driving his wife into the arms of a beardless boy, who imagines profundity can justify committing the basest acts. The weight of the words with which the writer of that work reviled the vile announced a decisive turn away from all moral skepticism, from all sympathy with the abyss, a rejection of the laxity inherent in the supposedly compassionate maxim that to understand everything is to forgive everything. What was coming into play here—or rather, what was already in full swing—was that "miracle of ingenuousness reborn" about which there was explicit discussion, not without a certain mysterious emphasis, in one of the author's dialogues published only slightly later. Strange relationships! Was it an intellectual consequence of this "rebirth," of this new dignity and rigor, that just then readers began to notice an almost excessive increase in his sense of beauty, a noble purity, simplicity, and sense of proportion that henceforth gave his works such a palpable, one might say deliberately classical and masterful quality? But moral determination that goes beyond knowledge, beyond analytic and inhibiting perception—would that not also be a reduction, a moral simplification of the world and of the human soul and therefore also a growing potential for what is evil, forbidden, and morally unacceptable? And does form not have two faces? Is it not moral and amoral at the same time—moral insofar as form is the product and expression of discipline, but amoral and indeed immoral insofar as it harbors within itself by nature a certain moral indifference and indeed is essentially bent on forcing the moral realm to stoop under its proud and absolute scepter?

That is as may be. Since human development is human destiny, how could a life led in public, accompanied by the accolades and confidence of thousands, develop as does one led without the glory and the obligations of fame? Only those committed to eternal bohemianism would be bored and inclined to ridicule when a great talent emerges from its libertine chrysalis, accustoms itself to recognizing emphatically the dignity of the spirit, takes on the courtly airs of solitude, a solitude full of unassisted, defiantly independent suffering and struggle, and ultimately achieves power and honor in the public sphere. And how much playfulness, defiance, and indulgence there is in the way talent develops! A kind of official, educative element began in time to appear in Aschenbach's productions. His style in later years dispensed with the sheer audacity, the subtle and innovative shadings of his younger days, and moved toward the paradigmatic, the polished and traditional, the conservative and formal, even formulaic. Like Louis XIV[8]—as report would have it—the aging writer banished from his vocabulary every base expression. About this time it came to pass that the educational authorities began using selected passages from his works in their prescribed textbooks.[9] He seemed to sense the inner

8. King of France (1638–1715), the "great monarch" of the French classical period.
9. I.e., he received national recognition in the highly centralized German educational system.

appropriateness of it, and he did not refuse when a German prince, newly ascended to the throne, bestowed on the author of *Frederick*, on his fiftieth birthday, a nonhereditary title.

Relatively early on, after a few years of moving about, a few tries at living here and there, he chose Munich as his permanent residence and lived there in bourgeois respectability such as comes to intellectuals sometimes, in exceptional cases. His marriage to a girl from a learned family, entered upon when still a young man, was terminated after only a short term of happiness by her death. A daughter, already married, remained to him. He never had a son.

Gustav Aschenbach was a man of slightly less than middle height, dark-haired and clean shaven. His head seemed a little too big for a body that was almost dainty. His hair, combed back, receding at the top, still very full at the temples, though quite gray, framed a high, furrowed, and almost embossed-looking brow. The gold frame of his rimless glasses cut into the bridge of his full, nobly curved nose. His mouth was large, sometimes relaxed and full, sometimes thin and tense; his cheeks were lean and hollow, and his well-proportioned chin was marked by a slight cleft. Important destinies seemed to have played themselves out on this long-suffering face, which he often held tilted somewhat to one side. And yet it was art alone, not a difficult and troubled life, that had taken over the task of chiseling these features. Behind this brow was born the scintillating repartee between Voltaire and King Frederick on the subject of war; these eyes, looking tiredly but piercingly through the glasses, had seen the bloody inferno of the field hospitals during the Seven Years' War.[1] Indeed, even on the personal level art provides an intensified version of life. Art offers a deeper happiness, but it consumes one more quickly. It engraves upon the faces of its servants the traces of imaginary, mental adventures and over the long term, even given an external existence of cloistered quietude, engenders in them a nervous sensitivity, an over-refinement, a weariness and an inquisitiveness such as are scarcely ever produced by a life full of extravagant passions and pleasures.

CHAPTER 3

Several obligations of both a practical and a literary nature forced the eager traveler to remain in Munich for about two weeks after his walk in the park. Finally he gave instructions for his country house to be prepared for his moving in within a month's time and, on a day sometime between the middle and end of May, he took the night train to Trieste, where he remained only twenty-four hours and where he boarded the boat to Pola[2] on the morning of the next day.

What he sought was someplace foreign, someplace isolated, but someplace nonetheless easy to get to. He thus took up residence on an Adriatic island, a destination that had been highly spoken of in recent years and lay not far from the Istrian coast. It was populated by locals dressed in colorful rags who spoke

1. A global war (1756–63) fought in Europe, North America, and India between European powers. François-Marie Arouet de Voltaire (1694–1778), French writer and philosopher, was a guest at the court of Frederick the Great from 1750 until 1753, when he found it wise to leave after a disagreement.
2. Trieste (in Italy) and Pola (or Pula, in Croatia) are major ports at the head of the Adriatic Sea. Until 1919 they were Austrian possessions.

in wildly exotic accents, and the landscape was graced by rugged cliffs on the coast facing the open sea. But the rain and oppressive air, the provincial, exclusively Austrian clientele at the hotel, and the lack of the peaceful, intimate relation with the sea that only a soft sandy beach can offer—these things irritated him, denied him a sense of having found the place he was looking for; he was troubled by a pressure within him pushing in a direction he could not quite grasp; he studied ship schedules, he sought about for something; and suddenly the surprising but obvious destination came to him. If you wanted to reach in a single night someplace incomparable, someplace as out of the ordinary as a fairy tale, where did you go? The answer was clear. What was he doing here? He had gone astray. It was over there that he had wanted to go all along. He did not hesitate a moment in remedying his error and gave notice of his departure. A week and a half after his arrival on the island a swift motorboat carried him and his baggage through the early morning mist across the water to the military port, where he landed only long enough to find the gangway leading him onto the damp deck of a ship that was already getting up steam for a trip to Venice.[3]

It was an aged vessel, long past its prime, sooty, and gloomy, sailing under the Italian flag. In a cavernous, artificially lit cabin in the ship's interior—to which Aschenbach had been conducted with smirking politeness by a hunchbacked, scruffy sailor the moment he embarked—sat a goateed man behind a desk. With his hat cocked over his brow and a cigarette butt hanging from the corner of his mouth, his facial features were reminiscent of an old time ringmaster. He took down the passengers' personal information and doled out tickets with the grimacing, easy demeanor of the professional. "To Venice!" He repeated Aschenbach's request, stretching his arm to dip his pen in the congealed remains at the bottom of his slightly tilted inkwell. "To Venice, first class! There, sir, you're all taken care of." He inscribed great letters like crane's feet on a piece of paper, poured blue sand out of a box onto them, poured it back into an earthenware bowl, folded the paper with his yellow, bony fingers, and resumed writing. "What a fine choice for your destination!" he babbled in the meantime. "Ah, Venice, a wonderful city! A city that is irresistible to cultured people both for its history and for its modern charm!" The smooth swiftness of his movements and the empty chatter with which he accompanied them had an anesthetic and diversionary effect, as if he were concerned that the traveler should change his mind about his decision to go to Venice. He hastily took the money and dropped the change on the stained cloth covering the table with the practiced swiftness of a croupier.[4] "Enjoy yourself, sir!" he said with a theatrical bow. "It is an honor to be of service to you. . . . Next, please!" he cried with his arm raised, acting as if he were still doing a brisk business, though in fact there was no one else there to do business with. Aschenbach returned above deck.

With one arm resting on the rail, he observed the passengers on board and the idle crowd loitering on the pier to watch the ship depart. The second-class

3. An ancient city whose network of bridges and canals links 118 islands in the Gulf of Venice. The Republic of Venice was headed by a doge (duke) and was a cultural, commercial, and political center in Europe from the 14th century.
4. Attendant at a gambling table who handles bets and money.

passengers, both men and women, crouched on the forward deck using boxes and bundles as seats. A group of young people, apparently employees of businesses in Pola, who had banded together in great excitement for an excursion to Italy, formed the social set of the first upper deck. They made no little fuss over themselves and their plans, chattered, laughed, and took complacent enjoyment in their own continual gesturing. Leaning over the railing they called out in fluent and mocking phrases to various friends going about their business, briefcases under their arms, along the dockside street below, while the latter in turn made mock-threatening gestures with their walking sticks at the celebrants above. One of the merrymakers, wearing a bright yellow, overly fashionable summer suit, red tie, and a panama hat with a cockily turned-up brim, outdid all the others in his screeching gaiety. But scarcely had Aschenbach gotten a closer look at him when he realized with something like horror that this youth was not genuine. He was old, no doubt about it. There were wrinkles around his eyes and mouth. The faint carmine of his cheeks was rouge; the brown hair beneath the colorfully banded hat was a wig; his neck was shrunken and sinewy; his clipped mustache and goatee were dyed; the full, yellowish set of teeth he exposed when he laughed was a cheap set of dentures; and his hands, bedecked with signet rings on both forefingers, were those of an old man. With a shudder Aschenbach watched him and his interaction with his friends. Did they not know, had they not noticed that he was old, that he had no right to wear their foppish and colorful clothes, had no right to pretend to be one of their own? They apparently tolerated him in their midst as a matter of course, out of habit, and treated him as an equal, answering in kind without reluctance when he teasingly poked one of them in the ribs. But how could this be? Aschenbach covered his brow with his hand and closed his eyes, which were feeling inflamed from not getting enough sleep. It seemed to him that things were starting to take a turn away from the ordinary, as if a dreamy estrangement, a bizarre distortion of the world were setting in and would spread if he did not put a stop to it by shading his eyes a bit and taking another look around him. Just at this moment he experienced a sensation of motion and, looking up with an unreasoning terror, realized that the heavy and gloomy hulk of the ship was slowly parting company with the stone pier. The engines ran alternately forward and reverse, and inch by inch the band of oily, iridescent water between the pier and the hull of the ship widened. After a set of cumbersome maneuvers the steamer managed to point its bowsprit toward the open sea. Aschenbach went over to the starboard side, where the hunchback had set up a deck chair for him and a steward dressed in a stained tailcoat offered him service.

The sky was gray and the wind was moist. The harbor and the island were left behind, and soon all sight of land vanished beyond the misty horizon. Flakes of coal soot saturated with moisture fell on the scrubbed, never drying deck. No more than an hour later a canvas canopy was put up, since it had started to rain.

Wrapped in his cloak, a book on his lap, the traveler rested, and the hours passed by unnoticed. It stopped raining; the linen canopy was removed. The horizon was unobstructed. Beneath the overcast dome of the sky the immense disk of the desolate sea stretched into the distance all around. But in empty, undivided space our sense of time fails us, and we lose ourselves in the immeasurable. Strange and shadowy figures—the old fop, the goat-beard from below deck—invaded Aschenbach's mind as he rested. They gestured obscurely and spoke the confused speech of dreams. He fell asleep.

At noon they called him to lunch down in the corridorlike dining hall onto which opened the doors of all the sleeping quarters and in which stood a long table. He dined at one end, while at the other the business employees from Pola, including the old fop, had been carousing since ten o'clock with the jolly captain. The meal was wretched and he soon got up. He felt an urgent need to get out, to look at the sky, to see if it might not be brightening over Venice.

It had never occurred to him that anything else could happen, for the city had always received him in shining glory. But the sky and the sea remained overcast and leaden. From time to time a misty rain fell, and he came to the realization that he would approach a very different Venice by sea than the one he had previously reached by land. He stood by the foremast, gazing into the distance, awaiting the sight of land. He remembered the melancholy, enthusiastic poet of long ago who had furnished his dreams with the domes and bell towers rising from these waters. He softly repeated to himself some of those verses in which the awe, joy, and sadness of a former time had taken stately shape[5] and, easily moved by sensations thus already formed, looked into his earnest and weary heart to see if some new enthusiasm or entanglement, some late adventure of feeling might be in store for him, the idle traveler.

Then the flat coastline emerged on the right; the sea became populated with fishing boats; the barrier island with its beach appeared. The steamer soon left the island behind to the left, slipping at reduced speed through the narrow harbor named after it.[6] They came to a full stop in the lagoon in view of rows of colorfully wretched dwellings and awaited the arrival of the launch belonging to the health service.

An hour passed before it appeared. One had arrived and yet had not arrived; there was no great hurry and yet one felt driven by impatience. The young people from Pola had come up on deck, apparently yielding to a patriotic attraction to the military trumpet calls resounding across the water from the public garden. Full of excitement and Asti, they shouted cheers at the *bersaglieri*[7] conducting drills over there. It was disgusting, however, to see the state into which the made-up old coot's false fellowship with the young people had brought him. His aged brain had not been able to put up the same resistance to the wine as the younger and more vigorous heads, and he was wretchedly drunk. His vision blurred; a cigarette dangled from his shaking fingers; he stood swaying tipsily in place, pulled to and fro by intoxication, barely able to maintain his balance. Since he would have fallen over at the first step, he dared not move from the spot. Yet he maintained a woeful bravado, buttonholing everyone who came near; he stammered, blinked, giggled, raised his beringed, wrinkled forefinger in fatuous banter, and ran the tip of his tongue around the corners of his mouth in an obscenely suggestive manner. Aschenbach watched

---

5. The lines are probably from *Sonnets on Venice* (1825) by the German classical poet August Graf Platen (1796–1835): "My eye left the high seas behind / as the temples of [the architect Andrea] Palladio rose from the waters."

6. Both the barrier island and the harbor are called Lido. The island is the site of a famous resort.

7. Elite Italian troops. "Asti": or asti spumante, a sweet, sparkling Italian wine.

him from under a darkened brow and was once again seized by a feeling of giddiness, as if the world were displaying a slight but uncontrollable tendency to distort, to take on a bizarre and sneering aspect. It was a feeling, to be sure, that conditions prevented him from indulging, for just then the engine began anew its pounding, and the ship, interrupted so close to its destination, resumed its course through the canal of San Marco.[8]

Once more, then, it lay before him, that most astounding of landing places, that dazzling grouping of fantastic buildings that the republic presented to the awed gaze of approaching mariners: the airy splendor of the palace and the Bridge of Sighs; the pillars on the water's edge bearing the lion and the saint; the showy projecting flank of the fairy tale cathedral; the view toward the gate and the great clock.[9] It occurred to him as he raised his eyes that to arrive in Venice by land, at the railway station, was like entering a palace by a back door; that one ought not to approach this most improbable of cities save as he now did, by ship, over the high seas.

The engine stopped, gondolas swarmed about, the gangway was lowered, customs officials boarded and haughtily went about their duties; disembarkation could begin. Aschenbach let it be known that he desired a gondola to take him and his luggage over to the landing where he could get one of the little steamboats that ran between the city and the Lido; for it was his intention to take up residence by the sea. His wishes met with acquiescence; a call went down with his request to the water's surface where the gondoliers were quarreling with each other in dialect. He was still prevented from disembarking; his trunk presented problems; only with considerable difficulty could it be pulled and tugged down the ladderlike gangway. He therefore found himself unable for several moments to escape from the importunities of the ghastly old impostor, who, driven by some dark drunken impulse, was determined to bid elaborate farewell to the foreign traveler. "We wish you the happiest of stays," he bleated, bowing and scraping. "Keeping a fond memory of us! Au revoir, excusez, and bonjour,[1] your excellency!" He drooled, he batted his eyes, he licked the corners of his mouth, and the dyed goatee on his elderly chin bristled. "Our compliments," he babbled, two fingertips at his mouth, "our compliments to your beloved, your dearly beloved, your lovely beloved . . ." And suddenly his uppers fell out of his jaw onto his lower lip. Aschenbach took his chance to escape. "Your beloved, your sweet beloved . . ." He heard the cooing, hollow, obstructed sounds behind his back as he descended the gangway, clutching at the rope handrail as he went.

Who would not need to fight off a fleeting shiver, a secret aversion and anxiety, at the prospect of boarding a Venetian gondola for the first time or after a long absence? This strange conveyance, surviving unchanged since legendary times and painted the particular sort of black[2] ordinarily reserved for coffins, makes

---

8. Saint Mark's Canal, named for the patron saint of Venice.

9. A large clock tower built in the late 15th century. "Bridge of Sighs": condemned prisoners walked over this bridge when proceeding to prison from the ducal palace. "Pillars": one is surmounted by a statue of St. Theodore stepping on a crocodile; the second, by a winged lion, emblem of St. Mark. "Cathedral": the Church of St. Mark.

1. "Goodbye, excuse me, and good-day" (French).

2. Legend explains the gondolas' traditional black through an ancient law forbidding ostentation.

one think of silent, criminal adventures in a darkness full of splashing sounds; makes one think even more of death itself, of biers and gloomy funerals, and of that final, silent journey. And has anyone noticed that the seat of one of these boats, this armchair painted coffin-black and upholstered in dull black cloth, is one of the softest, most luxurious, most sleep-inducing seats in the world? Aschenbach certainly realized this as he sat down at the gondolier's feet, opposite his luggage lying in a copious pile in the bow. The oarsmen were still quarreling in a rough, incomprehensible language punctuated by threatening gestures. The peculiar quiet of this city of water, however, seemed to soften their voices, to disembody them, to disperse them over the sea. It was warm here in the harbor. Stroked by the mild breath of the sirocco,[3] leaning back into the cushions as the yielding element carried him, the traveler closed his eyes in the pleasure of indulging in an indolence both unaccustomed and sweet. The trip will be short, he thought; if only it could last forever! The gondola rocked softly, and he felt himself slip away from the crowded ship and the clamoring voices.

How quiet, ever more quiet it grew around him! Nothing could be heard but the splashing of the oar, the hollow slap of the waves against the gondola's prow, rising rigid and black above the water with its halberdlike beak—and then a third thing, a voice, a whisper. It was the murmur of the gondolier, who was talking to himself through his clenched teeth in fits and starts, emitting sounds that were squeezed out of him by the labor of his arms. Aschenbach looked up and realized with some astonishment that the lagoon was widening about him and that he was traveling in the direction of the open sea. It seemed, then, that he ought not to rest quite so peacefully but instead make sure his wishes were carried out.

"I told you to take me to the steamer landing," he said with a half turn toward the stern. The murmur ceased. He received no answer.

"I told you to take me to the steamer landing!" he repeated, turning around completely and looking up into the face of the gondolier, whose figure, perched on the high deck and silhouetted against the dun sky, towered behind him. The man had a disagreeable, indeed brutal-looking appearance; he wore a blue sailor suit belted with a yellow sash, and a shapeless straw hat that was beginning to come unraveled and was tilted rakishly on his head. His facial features and the blond, curly mustache under his short, turned-up nose marked him as clearly not of Italian stock. Although rather slender of build, so that one would not have thought him particularly well suited to his profession, he plied his oar with great energy, putting his whole body into every stroke. Several times he pulled his lips back with the strain, baring his white teeth. His reddish eyebrows puckered, he looked out over his passenger's head and replied in a decisive, almost curt tone of voice: "You are going to the Lido."

Aschenbach responded, "Indeed. But I took the gondola only to get over to San Marco. I want to use the vaporetto."[4]

"You cannot use the vaporetto, sir."

"And why not?"

"Because the vaporetto does not accept luggage."

---

3. A hot wind originating in the Sahara, which becomes humid as it picks up moisture over the Mediterranean.

4. Little steamboat (Italian); used for public transport.

He was right about that; Aschenbach remembered. He said nothing. But the gruff, presumptuous manner of the man, so unlike the normal way of treating foreigners in this country, was not to be endured. He said, "That is my business. Perhaps I intend to put my luggage in storage. You will kindly turn back."

There was silence. The oar splashed, the waves slapped dully against the bow. And the murmuring and whispering began anew: the gondolier was talking to himself through his clenched teeth.

What to do? Alone at sea with this strangely insubordinate, uncannily resolute person, the traveler saw no way to enforce his wishes. And anyway, if he could just avoid getting angry, what a lovely rest he could have! Had he not wished the trip could last longer, could last forever? The smartest thing to do was to let matters take their course; more important, it was also the most pleasant thing to do. A magic circle of indolence seemed to surround the place where he sat, this low armchair upholstered in black, so gently rocked by the rowing of the autocratic gondolier behind him. The idea that he might have fallen into the hands of a criminal rambled about dreamily in Aschenbach's mind, but it was incapable of rousing his thoughts to active resistance. More annoying was the possibility that all this was simply a device by which to extort money from him. A sense of duty or of pride, the memory, as it were, that one must prevent such things, induced him once more to pull himself together. He asked, "What do you want for the trip?"

And the gondolier, looking out over him, answered, "You will pay."

It was clear what reply was necessary here. Aschenbach said mechanically, "I will pay nothing, absolutely nothing, if you take me where I do not want to go."

"You want to go to the Lido."

"But not with you."

"I row you well."

True enough, thought Aschenbach, and relaxed. True enough, you row me well. Even if you are just after my money, even if you send me to the house of Aides[5] with a stroke of your oar from behind, you will have rowed me well.

But no such thing occurred. In fact, some company even happened by in the form of a boat filled with musicians, both men and women, who waylaid the gondola, sailing obtrusively right alongside. They sang to the accompaniment of guitars and mandolins and filled the quiet air over the lagoon with the strains of their mercenary tourist lyrics. Aschenbach threw some money in the hat they held out to him, whereupon they fell silent and sailed off. The murmur of the gondolier became perceptible once again as he talked to himself in fits and starts.

And so they arrived, bobbing in the wake of a steamer sailing back to the city. Two municipal officials walked up and down along the landing, their hands behind their backs and their faces turned to the lagoon. Aschenbach stepped from the gondola onto the dock assisted by one of those old men who seemed on hand, armed with a boathook, at every pier in Venice. Since he had no small coins with him, he crossed over to the hotel next to the steamer wharf to get

---

5. A Greek spelling of "Hades," the ruler of the world of the dead in Greek and Roman mythology. The newly dead entered the underworld by paying a coin to the boatman, Charon, who then ferried them across the river Styx.

change with which to pay the boatman an appropriate fee. His needs met in the lobby, he returned to find his baggage stowed on a cart on the dock. Gondola and gondolier had disappeared.

"He took off," said the old man with the boathook. "A bad man he was, sir, a man without a license. He's the only gondolier who doesn't have a license. The others telephoned over. He saw that we were on the lookout for him, so he took off."

Aschenbach shrugged his shoulders.

"You had a free ride, sir," the old man said, holding out his hat. Aschenbach threw some coins in it. He gave instructions that his luggage be taken to the Hotel des Bains[6] and then followed the cart along the boulevard of white blossoms, lined on both sides by taverns, shops, and boarding houses, that runs straight across the island to the beach.

He entered the spacious hotel from behind, from the garden terrace, and crossed the great lobby to reach the vestibule where the office was. Since he had a reservation, he was received with officious courtesy. A manager, a quiet, flatteringly polite little man with a black mustache and a French-style frock coat, accompanied him in the elevator to the third floor and showed him to his room. It was a pleasant place, furnished in cherry wood, decorated with highly fragrant flowers, and offering a view of the open sea through a set of tall windows. After the manager had withdrawn and while his luggage was being brought up and put in place in his room, he went up to one of the windows and looked out on the beach. It was nearly deserted in the afternoon lull, and the ocean, at high tide and bereft of sunshine, was sending long, low waves against the shore in a peaceful rhythm.

A lonely, quiet person has observations and experiences that are at once both more indistinct and more penetrating than those of one more gregarious; his thoughts are weightier, stranger, and never without a tinge of sadness. Images and perceptions that others might shrug off with a glance, a laugh, or a brief conversation occupy him unduly, become profound in his silence, become significant, become experience, adventure, emotion. Loneliness fosters that which is original, daringly and bewilderingly beautiful, poetic. But loneliness also fosters that which is perverse, incongruous, absurd, forbidden. Thus the events of the journey that brought him here—the ghastly old fop with his drivel about a beloved, the outlaw gondolier who was cheated of his reward—continued to trouble the traveler's mind. Though they did not appear contrary to reason, did not really give cause for second thoughts, the paradox was that they were nonetheless fundamentally and essentially odd, or so it seemed to him, and therefore troubling precisely because of this paradox. In the meantime his eyes greeted the sea, and he felt joy in knowing Venice to be in such comfortable proximity. He turned away at last, went to wash his face, gave some instructions to the maid with regard to completing arrangements to insure his comfort, and then put himself in the hands of the green-uniformed elevator operator, who took him down to the ground floor.

He took his tea on the terrace facing the sea, then went down to the shore and walked along the boardwalk for a good distance toward the Hotel Excelsior. When he got back it seemed about time to change for dinner. He did so

---

6. Hotel of the Baths (French, literal trans.); a famous seaside hotel.

slowly and precisely, the way he did everything, because he was used to working as he got dressed. Still, he found himself in the lobby a bit on the early side
for dinner. There he found many of the hotel's guests gathered, unfamiliar
with and affecting indifference to each other, sharing only the wait for the dinner bell. He picked up a newspaper from a table, sat down in a leather chair,
and looked over the assembled company. It differed from that of his previous
sojourn in a way that pleased him.

A broad horizon, tolerant and comprehensive, opened up before him. All the
great languages of Europe melded together in subdued tones. Evening dress,
the universal uniform of cultured society, provided a decorous external unity
to the variety of humanity assembled here. There was the dry, long face of an
American, a Russian extended family, English ladies, German children with
French nannies. The Slavic component seemed to predominate. Polish was
being spoken nearby.

It came from a group of adolescents and young adults gathered around a little wicker table under the supervision of a governess or companion. There
were three young girls who looked to be fifteen to seventeen years old and a
long-haired boy of maybe fourteen. Aschenbach noted with astonishment that
the boy was perfectly beautiful. His face, pale and gracefully reserved, was
framed by honey-colored curls. He had a straight nose and a lovely mouth and
wore an expression of exquisite, divine solemnity. It was a face reminiscent of
Greek statues from the noblest period of antiquity; it combined perfection of
form with a unique personal charm that caused the onlooker to doubt ever
having met with anything in nature or in art that could match its perfection.
One could not help noticing, furthermore, that widely differing views on childrearing had evidently directed the dress and general treatment of the siblings.
The three girls, the eldest of whom was for all intents an adult, were got up in a
way that was almost disfiguringly chaste and austere. Every grace of figure was
suppressed and obscured by their uniformly habitlike half-length dresses, sober
and slate-gray in color, tailored as if to be deliberately unflattering, relieved by
no decoration save white, turned-down collars. Their smooth hair, combed
tightly against their heads, made their faces appear nunnishly vacant and
expressionless. It could only be a mother who was in charge here, one who
never once considered applying to the boy the severity of upbringing that
seemed required of her when it came to the girls. Softness and tenderness were
the obvious conditions of the boy's existence. No one had yet been so bold as
to take the scissors to his lovely hair, which curled about his brows, over his
ears, and even further down the back of his neck—as it does on the statue of
the "Boy Pulling a Thorn from his Foot."[7] His English sailor suit had puffy
sleeves that narrowed at the cuff to embrace snugly the delicate wrists of his
still childlike yet delicate hands. The suit made his slim figure seem somehow
opulent and pampered with all its decoration, its bow, braidwork, and embroidery. He sat so that the observer saw him in profile. His feet were clad in black
patent leather and arranged one in front of the other; one elbow was propped
on the arm of his wicker chair with his cheek resting on his closed hand; his
demeanor was one of careless refinement, quite without the almost submissive

7. A bronze Greco-Roman statue admired for the graceful pose and handsome appearance of
the boy it depicts.

stiffness that seemed to be the norm for his sisters. Was he in poor health? Perhaps, for the skin of his face was white as ivory and stood out in sharp contrast to the darker gold of the surrounding curls. Or was he simply a coddled favorite, the object of a biased and capricious affection? Aschenbach was inclined to suppose the latter. There is inborn in every artistic disposition an indulgent and treacherous tendency to accept injustice when it produces beauty and to respond with complicity and even admiration when the aristocrats of this world get preferential treatment.

A waiter went about and announced in English that dinner was ready. Most of the company gradually disappeared through the glass door into the dining room. Latecomers passed by, arriving from the vestibule or from the elevators. Dinner was beginning to be served inside, but the young Poles still lingered by their wicker table. Aschenbach, comfortably seated in his deep armchair, his eyes captivated by the beautiful vision before him, waited with them.

The governess, a short, corpulent, rather unladylike woman with a red face, finally gave the sign to get up. With her brows raised she pushed back her chair and bowed as a tall lady, dressed in gray and white and richly bejeweled with pearls, entered the lobby. The demeanor of this woman was cool and measured; the arrangement of her lightly powdered hair and the cut of her clothes displayed the taste for simplicity favored by those who regard piety as an essential component of good breeding. She could have been the wife of a highly placed German official. Her jewelry was the only thing about her appearance that suggested fabulous luxury; it was priceless, consisting of earrings and a very long, triple strand of softly shimmering pearls, each as big as a cherry.

The boy and the girls had risen quickly. They bent to kiss their mother's hand while she, with a restrained smile on her well-preserved but slightly tired and rather pointy-nosed face, looked across the tops of their heads at the governess, to whom she directed a few words in French. Then she walked to the glass door. The young ones followed her, the girls in the order of their ages, behind them the governess, the boy last of all. For some reason he turned around before crossing the threshold. Since there was no one else left in the lobby, his strangely misty gray eyes met those of Aschenbach, who was sunk deep in contemplation of the departing group, his newspaper on his knees.

What he had seen was, to be sure, in none of its particulars remarkable. They did not go in to dinner before their mother; they had waited for her, greeted her respectfully when she came, and then observed perfectly normal manners going into the dining room. It was just that it had all happened so deliberately, with such a sense of discipline, responsibility, and self-respect, that Aschenbach felt strangely moved. He lingered a few moments more, then went along into the dining room himself. He was shown to his table, which, he noted with a brief twinge of regret, was very far away from that of the Polish family.

Tired but nonetheless mentally stimulated, he entertained himself during the tedious meal with abstract, even transcendent matters. He pondered the mysterious combination of regularity and individuality that is necessary to produce human beauty; proceeded then to the general problem of form and of art; and ultimately concluded that his thoughts and discoveries resembled those inspirations that come in dreams: they seem wonderful at the time, but in the sober light of day they show up as utterly shallow and useless. After dinner he spent some time smoking, sitting, and wandering about in the park, which was fragrant in the evening air. He went to bed early and passed the night in a sleep uninterruptedly deep but frequently enlivened by all sorts of dreams.

The next day the weather had gotten no better. There was a steady wind off the land. Under a pale overcast sky the sea lay in a dull calm, almost as if it had shriveled up, with a soberingly contracted horizon; it had receded so far from the beach that it uncovered several rows of long sandbars. When Aschenbach opened his window, he thought he could detect the stagnant smell of the lagoon.

He was beset by ill humor. He was already having thoughts of leaving. Once years ago, after several lovely weeks here in springtime, just such weather had been visited upon him and had made him feel so poorly that he had had to take flight from Venice like a fugitive. Was he not feeling once again the onset of the feverish listlessness he had felt then, the throbbing of his temples, the heaviness in his eyelids? To change his vacation spot yet again would be a nuisance; but if the wind did not shift soon, he simply could not remain here. He did not unpack everything, just in case. He ate at nine in the special breakfast room between the lobby and the dining room.

In this room prevailed the solemn stillness that great hotels aspire to. The waiters went about on tip-toe. The clink of the tea service and a half-whispered word were all one could hear. Aschenbach noticed the Polish girls and their governess at a table in the corner diagonally across from the door, two tables away. They sat very straight, their ash-blond hair newly smoothed down flat, their eyes red. They wore starched blue linen dresses with little white turned-down collars and cuffs, and they passed a jar of preserves to each other. They had almost finished their breakfast. The boy was not there.

Aschenbach smiled. Well, little Phaeacian, he thought. It seems you, and not they, have the privilege of sleeping to your heart's content. Suddenly cheered, he recited to himself the line:

"Changes of dress, warm baths, and downy beds."[8]

He ate his breakfast at a leisurely pace, received some mail that had been forwarded—delivered personally by the doorman, who entered the room with his braided hat in hand—and opened a few letters while he smoked a cigarette. Thus it happened that he was present for the entrance of the late sleeper they were waiting for over there in the corner.

He came through the glass door and traversed the silent room diagonally over to the table where his sisters sat. His carriage was extraordinarily graceful, not only in the way he held his torso but also in the way he moved his knees and set one white-shod foot in front of the other. He moved lightly, in a manner both gentle and proud, made more lovely still by the childlike bashfulness with which he twice lifted and lowered his eyelids as he went by, turning his face out toward the room. Smiling, he murmured a word in his soft, indistinct speech and took his place, showing his full profile to the observer. The latter was once more, and now especially, struck with amazement, indeed even alarm, at the truly godlike beauty possessed by this mortal child. Today the boy wore a lightweight sailor suit of blue and white striped cotton with a red silk bow on the chest, finished at

8. A reference to Homer's *Odyssey* 8.249. The Phaeacians were a peaceful, happy people who showed hospitality to the shipwrecked Odysseus.

the neck with a simple white upright collar. And above this collar, which did not even fit in very elegantly with the character of the costume, rose up that blossom, his face, a sight unforgettably charming. It was the face of Eros, with the yellowish glaze of Parian marble,[9] with delicate and serious brows, the temples and ears richly and rectangularly framed by soft, dusky curls.

Fine, very fine, thought Aschenbach with that professional, cool air of appraisal artists sometimes use to cover their delight, their enthusiasm when they encounter a masterpiece. He thought further: Really, if the sea and the sand were not waiting for me, I would stay here as long as you stay. With that, however, he departed, walking past the attentive employees through the lobby, down the terrace steps, and straight across the wooden walkway to the hotel's private beach. There he let a barefoot old man in linen pants, sailor shirt, and straw hat who managed affairs on the beach show him to his rented beach cabana and arrange a table and chair on its sandy, wooden platform. Then he made himself comfortable in his beach chair, which he had pulled through the pale yellow sand closer to the sea.

The beach scene, this view of a carefree society engaged in purely sensual enjoyment on the edge of the watery element, entertained and cheered him as it always did. The gray, smooth ocean was already full of wading children, swimmers, and colorful figures lying on the sandbars with their arms crossed behind their heads. Others were rowing about in little flat-bottomed boats painted red and blue, capsizing to gales of laughter. People sat on the platforms of the cabanas, arranged in a long neat row along the beach, as if they were little verandas. In front of them people played games, lounged lazily, visited and chatted, some dressed in elegant morning clothes and others enjoying the nakedness sanctioned by the bold and easy freedom of the place. Down on the moist, hard sand there were a few individuals strolling about in white beach robes or in loose, brightly colored bathing dresses. To the right some children had built an elaborate sand castle and bedecked it with little flags in the colors of every country. Vendors of mussels, cakes, and fruit knelt and spread their wares before them. On the left, a Russian family was encamped in front of one of the cabanas that were set at a right angle between the others and the sea, thus closing that end of the beach. The family included men with beards and huge teeth; languid women past their prime; a young lady from a Baltic country, sitting at an easel and painting the ocean to the accompaniment of cries of frustration; two affable, ugly children; and an old maid in a babushka, displaying the affectionately servile demeanor of a slave. They resided there in grateful enjoyment, called out endlessly the names of their unruly, giddy children, exchanged pleasantries at surprising length in their few words of Italian with the jocular old man from whom they bought candy, kissed each other on the cheeks, and cared not a whit for anyone who might witness their scene of shared humanity.

Well, then, I will stay, thought Aschenbach. Where could things be better? His hands folded in his lap, he let his eyes roam the ocean's distances, let his gaze slip out of focus, grow hazy, blur in the uniform distances, mistiness of empty space. He loved the sea from the depth of his being: first of all because

9. White marble from the island of Paros was especially prized by sculptors in antiquity. Eros was the Greek god of love.

a hardworking artist needs his rest from the demanding variety of phenomena he works with and longs to take refuge in the bosom of simplicity and enormity; and, second, because he harbors an affinity for the undivided, the immeasurable, the eternal, the void. It was a forbidden affinity, directly contrary to his calling, and seductive precisely for that reason. To rest in the arms of perfection is what all those who struggle for excellence long to do; and is the void not a form of perfection? But while he was thus dreaming away toward the depths of emptiness, the horizontal line of the sea's edge was crossed by a human figure. When he had retrieved his gaze from the boundless realms and refocused his eyes, he saw it was the lovely boy who, coming from the left, was passing before him across the sand. He went barefoot, ready to go in wading, his slim legs bare from the knees down. He walked slowly but with a light, proud step, as if he were used to going about without shoes, and looked around at the row of cabanas that closed the end of the beach. The Russian family was still there, gratefully leading its harmonious existence, but no sooner had he laid eyes on them than a storm cloud of angry contempt crossed his face. His brow darkened, his lips began to curl, and from one side of his mouth emerged a bitter grimace that gouged a furrow in his cheek. He frowned so deeply that his eyes seemed pressed inward and sunken, seemed to speak dark and evil volumes of hatred from their depths. He looked down at the ground, cast one more threatening glance backward, and then, shrugging his shoulders as if to discard something and get away from it, he left his enemies behind.

A sort of delicacy or fright, something like a mixture of respect and shame, caused Aschenbach to turn away as if he had not seen anything; for it is repugnant to a chance witness, if he is a serious person, to make use of his observations, even to himself. But Aschenbach felt cheered and shaken at the same time—that is, happiness overwhelmed him. This childish fanaticism directed against the most harmless, good-natured target imaginable put into a human perspective something that otherwise seemed divinely indeterminate. It transformed a precious creation of nature that had before been no more than a feast for the eyes into a worthy object of deeper sympathy. It endowed the figure of the youngster, who had already shone with significance because of his beauty, with an aura that allowed him to be taken seriously beyond his years.

Still turned away, Aschenbach listened to the boy's voice, his clear, somewhat weak voice, by means of which he was trying to hail from afar his playmates at work on the sand castle. They answered him, calling again and again his name or an affectionate variation on his name. Aschenbach listened with a certain curiosity, unable to distinguish anything more than two melodious syllables—something like Adgio or more frequently Adgiu, with a drawn-out *u* at the end of the cry. The sound made him glad, it seemed to him that its harmony suited its object, and he repeated it softly to himself as he turned back with satisfaction to his letters and papers.

With his small traveling briefcase on his knees, he took his fountain pen and began to attend to various matters of correspondence. But after a mere quarter of an hour he was feeling regret that he should thus take leave in spirit and miss out on this, the most charming set of circumstances he knew of, for the sake of an activity he carried on with indifference. He cast his writing materials aside and turned his attention back to the sea; and not long after, distracted by the voices of the youngsters at the sand castle, he turned his head to the right and let it rest comfortably on the back of his chair, where he could once more observe the comings and goings of the exquisite Adgio.

His first glance found him; the red bow on his breast could not be missed. He was engaged with some others in setting up an old board as a bridge over the moat around the sand castle, calling out advice on proper procedure and nodding his head. There were about ten companions with him, boys and girls, most of an age with him but a few younger, chattering in a confusion of tongues—Polish, French, and even some Balkan languages. But it was his name that most often resounded through it all. He was evidently popular, sought after, admired. One companion, likewise a Pole, a sturdy boy called something like Yashu, who wore a belted linen suit and had black hair slicked down with pomade, seemed to be his closest friend and vassal. With the work on the sand castle finished for the time being, they went off together along the beach, arms about each other, and the one called Yashu gave his beautiful partner a kiss.

Aschenbach was tempted to shake his finger at him. "Let me give you a piece of advice, Kritobulos," he thought and smiled to himself. "Take a year's journey. You will need at least that much time for your recovery."[1] And then he breakfasted on large, fully ripe strawberries that he obtained from a peddler. It had gotten very warm, although the sun had not managed to pierce the layer of mist that covered the sky. Lassitude seized his spirit, while his senses enjoyed the enormous, lulling entertainment afforded by the quiet sea. The task of puzzling out what name it was that sounded like Adgio struck the serious man as a fitting, entirely satisfying occupation. With the help of a few Polish memories he determined that it was probably Tadzio he had heard, the nickname for Tadeusz. It was pronounced Tadziu in the form used for direct address.

Tadzio was taking a swim. Aschenbach, who had lost sight of him for a moment, spotted his head and then his arm, which rose as it stroked. He was very far out; the water apparently stayed shallow for a long way. But already his family seemed to be getting concerned about him, already women's voices were calling to him from the cabanas, shouting out once more this name that ruled over the beach almost like a watchword and that possessed something both sweet and wild in its soft consonants and drawnout cry of *uuu* at the end. "Tadziu! Tadziu!" He turned back; he ran through the sea with his head thrown back, beating the resisting water into a foam with his legs. The sight of this lively adolescent figure, seductive and chaste, lovely as a tender young god, emerging from the depths of the sky and the sea with dripping locks and escaping the clutches of the elements—it all gave rise to mythic images. It was a sight belonging to poetic legends from the beginning of time that tell of the origins of form and of the birth of the gods. Aschenbach listened with his eyes closed to this mythic song reverberating within him, and once again he thought about how good it was here and how he wanted to stay.

Later on Tadzio lay on the sand, resting from his swim, wrapped in a white beach towel that was drawn up under his right shoulder, his head resting on his bare arm. Even when Aschenbach refrained from looking at him, instead reading a few pages in his book, he almost never forgot who was lying nearby or forgot that it would cost him only a slight turn of his head to the right to bring

---

1. Recalling Socrates' advice to Kritobulos when the latter kissed Alcibiades' handsome son (Xenophon's *Memorabilia* 1.3).

the adorable sight back into view. It almost seemed to him that he was sitting here with the express purpose of keeping watch over the resting boy. Busy as he might be with his own affairs, he maintained his vigilant care for the noble human figure not far away on his right. A paternal kindness, an emotional attachment filled and moved his heart, the attachment that someone who produces beauty at the cost of intellectual self-sacrifice feels toward someone who naturally possesses beauty.

After midday he left the beach, returned to the hotel, and took the elevator up to his room. There he spent a considerable length of time in front of the mirror looking at his gray hair and his severe, tired face. At the same time he thought about his fame and about the fact that many people recognized him on the street and looked at him with respect, all on account of those graceful, unerringly accurate words of his. He called the roll of the long list of successes his talent had brought him, as many as he could think of, and even recalled his elevation to the nobility. He then retired to the dining room for lunch and ate at his little table. As he was entering the elevator when the meal was over, a throng of young people likewise coming from lunch crowded him to the back of the swaying little chamber. Tadzio was among them. He stood very close by, so close in fact that for the first time Aschenbach had the opportunity to view him not from a distance like a picture but minutely, scrutinizing every detail of his human form. Someone was talking to the boy, and while he was answering with his indescribably sweet smile they reached the second floor, where he got off, backing out, his eyes cast down. Beauty breeds modesty, Aschenbach thought and gave urgent consideration as to why. He had had occasion to notice, however, that Tadzio's teeth were not a very pleasing sight. They were rather jagged and pale and had no luster of health but rather a peculiar brittle transparency such as one sometimes sees in anemics. He is very sensitive, he is sickly, thought Aschenbach. He will probably not live long. And he refrained from trying to account for the feeling of satisfaction and reassurance that accompanied this thought.

He passed a couple of hours in his room and in the afternoon took the vaporetto across the stagnant-smelling lagoon to Venice. He got off at San Marco, took tea in the piazza,[2] and then, following his habitual routine in Venice, set off on a walk through the streets. It was this walk, however, that initiated a complete reversal of his mood and his plans.

The air in the little streets was odiously oppressive, so thick that the smells surging out of the dwellings, shops, and restaurants, a suffocating vapor of oil, perfume, and more, all hung about and failed to disperse. Cigarette smoke hovered in place and only slowly disappeared. The press of people in the small spaces annoyed rather than entertained him as he walked. The longer he went on, the more it became a torture. He was overwhelmed by that horrible condition produced by the sea air in combination with the sirocco, a state of both nervousness and debility at once. He began to sweat uncomfortably. His eyes ceased to function, his breathing was labored, he felt feverish, the blood pounded in his head. He fled from the crowded shop-lined streets across bridges into the poor quarter. There beggars molested him, and the evil emanations from the canals hindered his breathing. In a quiet piazza, one of those forgotten, seemingly enchanted little places in the interior of the city, he rested

2. A famous public square in front of the church, lined by restaurants and cafés.

on the edge of a well, dried his forehead, and reached the conclusion that he would have to leave Venice.

For the second time, and this time definitively, it became clear that this city in this weather was particularly harmful to his health. To remain stubbornly in place obviously went against all reason, and the prospect of a change in the direction of the wind was highly uncertain. A quick decision had to be made. To return home this soon was out of the question. Neither his summer nor his winter quarters were prepared for his arrival. But this was not the only place with beaches on the ocean, and those other places did not have the noxious extra of the lagoon and its fever-inducing vapors. He recalled a little beach resort not far from Trieste that had been enthusiastically recommended to him. Why not go there and, indeed, without delay, so that yet another change of location would still be worthwhile? He declared himself resolved and stood up. At the next gondola stop he boarded a boat to take him to San Marco through the dim labyrinth of canals, under graceful marble balconies flanked by stone lions, around corners of slippery masonry, past mournful palace facades affixed with business insignia[3] reflected in the garbage-strewn water. He had trouble getting to his destination, since the gondolier was in league with lace and glass factories and made constant efforts to induce him to stop at them to sightsee and buy; and so whenever the bizarre journey through Venice began to weave its magic, the mercenary lust for booty afflicting this sunken queen of cities[4] did what it could to bring the enchanted spirit back to unpleasant reality.

Upon returning to the hotel he did not even wait for dinner but went right to the office and declared that unforeseen circumstances compelled him to depart the next morning. With many expressions of regret the staff acknowledged the payment of his bill. He dined and then passed the mild evening reading magazines in a rocking chair on the rear terrace. Before going to bed he did all his packing for the morning's departure.

He did not sleep especially well, as the impending move made him restless. When he opened the windows the next morning the sky was still overcast, but the air seemed fresher and . . . he already started to have second thoughts. Had he been hasty or wrong to give notice thus? Was it a result of his sick and unreliable condition? If he had just put it off a bit, if he had just made an attempt to get used to the Venetian air or to hold out for an improvement in the weather instead of losing heart so quickly! Then, instead of this hustle and bustle, he would have a morning on the beach like the one yesterday to look forward to. Too late. Now he would have to go ahead with it, to wish today what he wished for yesterday. He got dressed and at eight o'clock took the elevator down to breakfast on the ground floor.

The breakfast room was still empty when he entered. A number of individual guests arrived while he sat waiting for his order. With his teacup at his lips he watched the Polish girls and their attendant come in. Severe and morning-fresh, eyes still red, they proceeded to their table in the corner by the window. Immediately thereafter the doorman approached him with hat in hand to tell him it was time to leave. The car was ready, he said, to take him and some other travelers to the Hotel Excelsior, and from there a motor boat would convey

---

3. Once-stately Renaissance homes that now house businesses.

4. A major sea power by the 15th century, Venice was called Queen of the Seas.

them through the company's private canal to the railroad station. Time was pressing, he said. Aschenbach found it not at all pressing. There was more than an hour until the departure of his train. He was annoyed at the habitual hotel practice of packing departing guests off earlier than necessary and informed the doorman that he wanted to finish his breakfast in peace. The man withdrew hesitatingly only to show up again five minutes later. The car simply could not wait longer, he said. Very well, let it go and take his trunks with it, Aschenbach replied with annoyance. As for himself, he preferred to take the public steamer at the proper time and asked that they let him take care of his own arrangements. The employee bowed. Aschenbach, happy to have fended off this nuisance, finished his meal without haste and even had the waiter bring him a newspaper. Time had become short indeed when at last he got up to leave. And it just so happened that at that very moment Tadzio came in through the glass door.

He crossed the path of the departing traveler on his way to his family's table. He lowered his eyes modestly before the gray-haired, high-browed gentleman, only to raise them again immediately in his own charming way, displaying their soft fullness to him. Then he was past. Adieu, Tadzio, thought Aschenbach. I saw you for such a short time. And enunciating his thought as it occurred to him, contrary to his every habit, he added under his breath the words: "Blessings on you." He then made his departure, dispensed tips, received a parting greeting from the quiet little manager in the French frock coat, and left the hotel on foot, as he had arrived. Followed by a servant with his hand luggage, he traversed the island along the boulevard, white with flowers, that led to the steamer landing. He arrived, he took his seat—and what followed was a journey of pain and sorrow through the uttermost depths of regret.

It was the familiar trip across the lagoon, past San Marco, up the Grand Canal. Aschenbach sat on the curved bench in the bow, his arm resting on the railing, his hand shading his eyes. They left the public gardens behind them; the Piazzetta once more revealed its princely splendor, and soon it too was left behind. Then came the great line of palaces, and as the waterway turned there appeared the magnificent marble arch of the Rialto.[5] The traveler looked, and his heart was torn. He breathed the atmosphere of the city, this slightly stagnant smell of sea and of swamp from which he had felt so strongly compelled to flee, breathed it now deeply, in tenderly painful draughts. Was it possible that he had not known, had not considered how desperately he was attached to all this? What this morning had been a partial regret, a slight doubt as to the rightness of his decision, now became affliction, genuine pain, a suffering in his soul so bitter that it brought tears to his eyes more than once. He told himself he could not possibly have foreseen such a reaction. What was so hard to take, actually sometimes down-right impossible to endure, was the thought that he would never see Venice again, that this was a parting forever. Since it had become evident for the second time that the city made him sick, since for the second time he had been forced to run head over heels away, he would have to regard it henceforth as an impossible destination, forbidden to him, something he simply was not up to, something it would be pointless for him to try for again. Yes, he felt that, should he go away now, shame and spite would certainly

---

5. A famous, highly arched bridge over the Grand Canal.

prevent him from ever seeing the beloved city again, now that it had twice forced him to admit physical defeat. This conflict between the inclination of his soul and the capacity of his body seemed to the aging traveler suddenly so weighty and so important, his physical defeat so ignominious, so much to be resisted at all cost, that he could no longer grasp the ease with which he had reached the decision yesterday, without serious struggle, to acquiesce.

Meanwhile, the steamer was approaching the railway station, and his pain and helplessness were rising to the level of total disorientation. His tortured mind found the thought of departure impossible, the thought of return no less so. In such a state of acute inner strife he entered the station. It was already very late, he had not a moment to lose if he was to catch his train. He wanted to, and he did not want to. But time was pressing, it goaded him onward; he made haste to obtain his ticket and looked about in the bustle of the station for the hotel employee stationed here. This person appeared and announced that the large trunk was already checked and on its way. Already on its way? Yes indeed—to Como.[6] To Como? After a frantic exchange, after angry questions and embarrassed answers, the fact emerged that the trunk had been put together with the baggage of other, unknown travelers in the luggage office at the Hotel Excelsior and sent off in precisely the wrong direction.

Aschenbach had difficulty maintaining the facial expression expected under such circumstances. An adventurous joy, an unbelievable cheerfulness seized his breast from within like a spasm. The hotel employee sped off to see if he could retrieve the trunk and returned, as one might have expected, with no success whatever. Only then did Aschenbach declare that he did not wish to travel without his luggage and that he had decided to return and await the recovery of the trunk at the Hotel des Bains. Was the company boat still here at the station? The man assured him it was waiting right at the door. With an impressive display of Italian cajolery he persuaded the agent to take back Aschenbach's ticket. He swore he would telegraph ahead, that no effort would be spared to get the trunk back with all due speed, and . . . thus came to pass something very odd indeed. The traveler, not twenty minutes after his arrival at the station, found himself once again on the Grand Canal on his way back to the Lido.

What a wondrous, incredible, embarrassing, odd and dreamlike adventure! Thanks to a sudden reversal of destiny, he was to see once again, within the very hour, places that he had thought in deepest melancholy he was leaving forever. The speedy little vessel shot toward its destination, foam flying before its bow, maneuvering with droll agility between gondolas and steamers, while its single passenger hid beneath a mask of annoyed resignation the anxious excitement of a boy playing hooky. Still from time to time his frame was shaken with laughter over this mischance, which he told himself could not have worked out better for the luckiest person in the world. Explanations would have to be made, amazed faces confronted, but then—so he told himself—all would be well again, a great disaster averted, a terrible error made right, and everything he thought he had left behind would be open to him once more, would be his to enjoy at his leisure. . . . And by the way, was it just the rapid movement of the boat, or could it really be that he felt a strong breeze off the ocean to complete his bliss?

6. A large lake and resort area in northwest Italy.

The waves slapped against the concrete walls of the narrow canal that cut through the island to the Hotel Excelsior. A motor bus was waiting there for the returning traveler and conveyed him alongside the curling waves down the straight road to the Hotel des Bains. The little manager with the mustache and the cutaway frock coat came down the broad flight of steps to meet him.

With quiet cajolery the manager expressed his regret over the incident, declared it extremely embarrassing for himself personally and for the establishment, but expressed his emphatic approval of Aschenbach's decision to wait here for the return of his luggage. To be sure, his room was already taken, but another, by no means worse, stood ready. "Pas de chance, monsieur,"[7] said the elevator man with a smile as they glided upwards. And so the fugitive was billeted once again, and in a room that matched almost exactly his previous one in orientation and furnishings.

Tired, numb from the whirl of this strange morning, he distributed the contents of his small suitcase in his room and then sank down in an armchair by the open window. The sea had taken on a light green coloration, the air seemed thinner and purer, the beach with its cabanas and boats seemed more colorful, although the sky was still gray. Aschenbach looked out, his hands folded in his lap, content to be here once more, but shaking his head in reproach at his own fickle mood, his lack of knowledge of his own desires. He sat thus for perhaps an hour, resting and thoughtlessly dreaming. At noon he spied Tadzio, dressed in his striped linen suit with red bow, returning from the shore through the beach barrier and along the wooden walkway to the hotel. Aschenbach recognized him at once from his high vantage point even before he got a good look at him, and he was just about to form a thought something like: Look, Tadzio, you too have returned! But at that very moment he felt the casual greeting collapse and fall silent before the truth of his heart. He felt the excitement in his blood, the joy and pain in his soul, and recognized that it was because of Tadzio that his departure had been so difficult.

He sat quite still, quite unseen in his elevated location and looked into himself. His features were active; his brows rose; an alert, curious, witty smile crossed his lips. Then he raised his head and with both his arms, which were hanging limp over the arms of his chair, he made a slow circling and lifting movement that turned his palms forward, as if to signify an opening and extending of his embrace. It was a gesture of readiness, of welcome, and of relaxed acceptance.

CHAPTER 4

The god with fiery cheeks[8] now, naked, directed his horses, four-abreast, fire-breathing, day by day through the chambers of heaven, and his yellow curls fluttered along with the blast of the east wind. A silky-white sheen lay on the Pontos,[9] its broad stretches undulating languidly. The sands burned. Under the silvery shimmering blue of the ether there were rustcolored canvas awnings spread out in front of the beach cabanas, and one passed the morning hours in

---

7. "No luck, sir" (French).
8. Helios, Greek god of the sun (later equated with Apollo).

9. The sea (Greek, literal trans.); a figurative reference to the Adriatic Sea.

the sharply framed patch of shade they offered. But the evening was also delightful, when the plants in the park wafted balsamic perfumes, the stars above paced out their circuits, and the murmur of the nightshrouded sea, softly penetrating, cast a spell on the soul. Such an evening bore the joyful promise of another festive day of loosely ordered leisure, bejeweled with countless, thickly strewn possibilities of happy accidents.

The guest, whom accommodating mischance kept here, was far from disposed to see in the return of his belongings a reason to depart once more. He had been obliged to get along without a few things for a couple of days and to appear at meals in the great dining room wearing his traveling clothes. Then, when the errant baggage was finally set down once more in his room, he unpacked thoroughly and filled closets and drawers with his things, determined for the time being to stay indefinitely, happy to be able to pass the morning's hours on the beach in his silk suit and to present himself once more at his little table at dinner time wearing proper evening attire.

The benevolent regularity of this existence had at once drawn him into its power; the soft and splendid calm of this lifestyle had him quickly ensnared. What a fine place to stay, indeed, combining the charms of a refined southern beach resort with the cozy proximity of the wondrous, wonder-filled city! Aschenbach was no lover of pleasure. Whenever and wherever it seemed proper to celebrate, to take a rest, to take a few days off, he soon had to get back—it was especially so in his younger days—anxiously and reluctantly back to the affliction of his high calling, the sacred, sober service of his day-to-day life. This place alone enchanted him, relaxed his will, made him happy. Sometimes in the morning, under the canopy of his beach cabana, dreaming away across the blue of the southern sea, or sometimes as well on a balmy night, leaning back under the great starry sky on the cushions of a gondola taking him back home to the Lido from the Piazza San Marco, where he had tarried long—and the bright lights and the melting sounds of the serenade were left behind—he remembered his country home in the mountains, the site of his summertime struggles, where the clouds drifted through the garden, where in the evening fearful thunderstorms extinguished the lights in the house and the revens he fed soared to the tops of the spruce trees. Then it might seem to him that he had been transported to the land of Elysium[1] at the far ends of the earth, where a life of ease is bestowed upon mortals, where there is no snow, no winter, no storms or streaming rain, but rather always the cooling breath rising from Okeanos,[2] where the days run out in blissful leisure, trouble-free, struggle-free, dedicated only to the sun and its revels.

Aschenbach saw the boy Tadzio often, indeed almost continually; limited space and a regular schedule common to all the guests made it inevitable that the lovely boy was in his vicinity nearly all day, with brief interruptions. He saw, he met him everywhere: in the hotel's public places, on the cooling boat trips to the city and back, in the ostentation of the piazza itself; and often too in the streets and byways a chance encounter would take place. Chiefly, however, it was the mornings on the beach that offered him with delightful regularity an

1. Located at the western edge of the Earth, a pleasant otherworld for those heroes favored by the gods.

2. According to Greek mythology, a river encircling the world.

extended opportunity to study and worship the charming apparition. Yes, it was this narrow and constrained happiness, this regularly recurring good fortune that filled him with contentment and joy in life, that made his stay all the more dear to him and caused one sunny day after another to fall so agreeably in line.

He got up early, as he otherwise did under the relentless pressure of work, and was one of the first on the beach when the sun was still mild and the sea lay white in the glare of morning dreams. He gave a friendly greeting to the guard at the beach barrier, said a familiar hello to the barefoot old man who got his place ready, spreading the brown awning and arranging the cabana furniture on the platform, and settled in. Three hours or four were then his in which, as the sun rose to its zenith and grew fearsome in strength and the sea turned a deeper and deeper blue, he could watch Tadzio.

He would see him coming from the left along the edge of the sea, would see him from the back as he appeared from between the cabanas, or sometimes would suddenly discover, not without a happy shudder, that he had missed his arrival and that he was already there, already in the blue and white bathing suit that was now his only article of attire on the beach, that he was already up to his usual doings in sand and sun—his charmingly trivial, lazily irregular life that was both recreation and rest, filled with lounging, wading, digging, catching, resting, and swimming, watched over by the women on the platform who called to him, making his name resound with their high voices: "Tadziu! Tadziu!" He would come running to them gesturing excitedly and telling them what he had done, showing them what he had found or caught: mussels and sea horses, jelly fish, crabs that ran off going sideways. Aschenbach understood not a single word he said, and though it may have been the most ordinary thing in the world it was all a vague harmony to his ear. Thus, foreignness raised the boy's speech to the level of music, a wanton sun poured unstinting splendor over him, and the sublime perspectives of the sea always formed the background and aura that set off his appearance.

Soon the observer knew every line and pose of this noble body that displayed itself so freely; he exulted in greeting anew every beauty, familiar though it had become, and his admiration, the discreet arousal of his senses, knew no end. They called the boy to pay his compliments to a guest who was attending the ladies at the cabana; he came running, still wet from the sea; he tossed his curls, and as he held out his hand he stood on one foot while holding the other up on tiptoe. His body was gracefully poised in the midst of a charming turning motion, while his face showed an embarrassed amiability, a desire to please that came from an aristocratic sense of duty. Sometimes he would lie stretched out with his beach towel wrapped about his chest, his delicately chiseled arm propped in the sand, his chin in the hollow of his hand. The one called Yashu sat crouching by him, playing up to him, and nothing could have been more enchanting than the smiling eyes and lips with which the object of this flattery looked upon his inferior, his vassal. Or he would stand at the edge of the sea, alone, separated from his friends, very near Aschenbach, erect, his hands clasped behind his neck, slowly rocking on the balls of his feet and dreaming off into the blue yonder, while little waves that rolled in bathed his toes. His honey-colored hair clung in circles to his temples and his neck; the sun made the down shine on his upper back; the subtle definition of the ribs and the symmetry of his chest stood out through the tight-fitting material covering his torso; his armpits were still as smooth as those of a statue, the hollows behind his knees shone likewise, and the blue veins showing through made his body seem to be made of translucent material. What discipline, what precision of thought was expressed in the stretch of this youthfully perfect body! But was not the rigorous and pure will that had been darkly active in bringing this divine form into the clear light of day entirely familiar to the artist in him? Was this same will not active in him, too, when he, full of sober passion, freed a slender form from the marble mass of language,[3] a form he had seen with his spiritual eye and that he presented to mortal men as image and mirror of spiritual beauty?

Image and mirror! His eyes embraced the noble figure there on the edge of the blue, and in a transport of delight he thought his gaze was grasping beauty itself, the pure form of divine thought, the universal and pure perfection that lives in the spirit and which here, graceful and lovely, presented itself for worship in the form of a human likeness and exemplar. Such was his intoxication; the aging artist welcomed the experience without reluctance, even greedily. His intellect was in labor, his educated mind set in motion. His memory dredged up ancient images passed on to him in the days of his youth, thoughts not until now touched by the spark of his personal involvement. Was it not written that the sun turns our attention from intellectual to sensuous matters?[4] It was said that the sun numbs and enchants our reason and memory to such an extent that the soul in its pleasure forgets its ordinary condition; its amazed admiration remains fixed on the loveliest of sun-drenched objects. Indeed, only with the help of a body can the soul rise to the contemplation of still higher things. Amor[5] truly did as mathematicians have always done by assisting slow-learning children with concrete pictures of pure forms: so, too, did the god like to make use of the figure and coloration of human youth in order to make the spiritual visible to us, furnishing it with the reflected glory of beauty and thus making of it a tool of memory, so that seeing it we might then be set aflame with pain and hope.

Those, at any rate, were the thoughts of the impassioned onlooker. He was capable of sustaining just such a high pitch of emotion. He spun himself a charming tapestry out of the roar of the sea and the glare of the sun. He saw the ancient plane tree not far from the walls of Athens,[6] that sacred, shadowy place filled with the scent of willow blossoms, decorated with holy images and votive offerings in honor of the nymphs and of Achelous.[7] The stream flowed in crystal clarity over smooth pebbles past the foot of the wide-branched tree. The crickets sang. Two figures reclined on the grass that gently sloped so that you could lie with your head held up; they were sheltered here from the heat of the day—an older man and a younger, one ugly and one handsome, wisdom at the

---

3. The Italian artist Michelangelo Buonarroti (1475–1564) explained that he created his statues by carving away the marble block until the figure within was set free.
4. In section 764E of the *Erotikos* (Dialogue on love) by the Greek essayist Plutarch (46–120).
5. The god of love (Latin).
6. A reference to the scene and some of the

arguments in Plato's dialogue *Phaedrus*. Plato's school, or Academy, was located in a grove of plane trees outside Athens; in the dialogue, the young student Phaedrus tells Socrates of Lysias's speech on love, and Socrates responds with two speeches of his own.
7. A brook or small river in ancient Athens, here personified as a god.

side of charm. Amidst polite banter and wooing wit Socrates taught Phaedrus about longing and virtue. He spoke to him of the searing terror that the sensitive man experiences when his eye lights on an image of eternal beauty; spoke to him of the appetites of the impious, bad man who cannot conceive of beauty when he sees beauty's image and is incapable of reverence; spoke of the holy fear that overcomes a noble heart when a godlike face or a perfect body appears before him—how he then trembles and is beside himself and scarcely dares turn his eyes upon the sight and honors him who has beauty, indeed would even sacrifice to him as to a holy image, if he did not fear looking foolish in the eyes of others. For beauty, my dear Phaedrus, beauty alone is both worthy of love and visible at the same time; beauty, mark me well, is the only form of spirit that our senses can both grasp and endure. For what should become of us if divinity itself, or reason and virtue and truth were to appear directly to our senses? Would we not be overcome and consumed in the flames of love, as Semele[8] was at the sight of Zeus? Thus beauty is the sensitive man's way to the spirit—just the way, just the means, little Phaedrus. . . . And then he said the subtlest thing of all, crafty wooer that he was: he said that the lover was more divine than the beloved, because the god was in the former and not in the latter—perhaps the tenderest, most mocking thought that ever was thought, a thought alive with all the guile and the most secret bliss of love's longing.

A writer's chief joy is that thought can become all feeling, that feeling can become all thought. The lonely author possessed and commanded at this moment just such a vibrant thought, such a precise feeling: namely, that nature herself would shiver with delight were intellect to bow in homage before beauty. He suddenly wanted to write. They say, to be sure, that Eros loves idleness; the god was made to engage in no other activity. But at this moment of crisis the excitement of the love-struck traveler drove him to productivity, and the occasion was almost a matter of indifference. The intellectual world had been challenged to profess its views on a certain great and burning problem of culture and of taste, and the challenge had reached him. The problem was well known to him, was part of his experience; the desire to illuminate it with the splendor of his eloquence was suddenly irresistible. And what is more, he wanted to work here in the presence of Tadzio, to use the boy's physical frame as the model for his writing, to let his style follow the lines of that body that seemed to him divine, to carry his beauty into the realm of intellect as once the eagle carried the Trojan shepherd into the ethereal heavens.[9] Never had his pleasure in the word seemed sweeter to him, never had he known so surely that Eros dwelt in the word as now in the dangerous and delightful hours he spent at his rough table under the awning. There with his idol's image in full view, the music of his voice resounding in his ear, he formed his little essay after the image of Tadzio's beauty—composed that page-and-a-half of choice prose that soon would amaze many a reader with its purity, nobility, and surging depth of feeling. It is surely for the best that the world knows only the lovely work and not also its origins, not the conditions under which it came into being; for

8. The mortal mother of Zeus's son Dionysus. She perished in flames when the king of the gods appeared (at her request) in his divine glory.

9. The Trojan prince Ganymede was tending flocks when Zeus, in the form of an eagle, carried him off to Olympus where he became Zeus's lover and the cupbearer to the gods.

knowledge of the origins from which flowed the artist's inspiration would surely often confuse the world, repel it, and thus vitiate the effects of excellence. Strange hours! Strangely enervating effort! Strangely fertile intercourse between a mind and a body! When Aschenbach folded up his work and left the beach, he felt exhausted, even unhinged, as if his conscience were indicting him after a debauch.

The next morning as he was about to leave the hotel he chanced to notice from the steps that Tadzio was already on his way to the shore, alone; he was just approaching the beach barrier. He felt first a suggestion, then a compulsion: the wish, the simple thought that he might make use of the opportunity to strike up a casual, cheerful acquaintanceship with this boy who unwittingly had caused such a stir in his mind and heart, speak with him and enjoy his answer and his gaze. The lovely lad sauntered along; he could be easily caught up with; Aschenbach quickened his steps. He reached him on the walkway behind the cabanas, was about to put his hand on his head or on his shoulder, was about to let some word pass his lips, some friendly French phrase. But then he felt his heart beating like a hammer, perhaps only because of his rapid walk, so that he was short of breath and could only have spoken in a trembling gasp. He hesitated, tried to master himself, then suddenly feared he had been walking too long right behind the handsome boy, feared he might notice, might turn around with an inquiring look. He took one more run at him, but then he gave up, renounced his goal, and hung his head as he went by.

Too late! he thought at that moment. Too late! But was it really too late? This step he had failed to take might very possibly have led to something good, to something easy and happy, to a salutary return to reality. But it may have been that the aging traveler did not wish to return to reality, that he was too much in love with his own intoxication. Who can untangle the riddle of the artist's essence and character? Who can understand the deep instinctive fusion of discipline and a desire for licentiousness upon which that character is based? For it is licentiousness to be unable to wish for a salutary return to reality. Aschenbach was no longer inclined to self-criticism. The taste, the intellectual constitution that came with his years, his self-esteem, maturity, and the simplicity of age made him disinclined to analyze the grounds for his behavior or to decide whether it was conscience or debauchery and weakness that caused him not to carry out his plan. He was confused; he feared that someone, if only the custodian on the beach, might have observed his accelerated gait and his defeat; he feared very much looking foolish. And all the while he made fun of himself, of his comically solemn anxiety. "We've been quite confounded," he thought, "and now we're as crestfallen as a gamecock that lets its wings droop during a fight.[1] It must surely be the god himself who thus destroys our courage at the very sight of loveliness, who crushes our proud spirit so deeply in the dust. . . ." His thoughts roamed playfully: he was far too arrogant to be fearful of a mere emotion.

He had already ceased to pay much attention to the extent of time he was allowing himself for his holiday; the thought of returning home did not even cross his mind. He had an ample amount of money sent to him by mail. His

---

1. From the Greek tragedian Phrynichus (512–476 B.C.E.), quoted in Plutarch's *Erotikos* (762E).

sole source of concern was the possible departure of the Polish family, but he had privately obtained information, thanks to casual inquiries at the hotel barber shop, that the Polish party had arrived only very shortly before he did. The sun tanned his face and hands, the bracing salt air stimulated his emotions. Just as he ordinarily used up all the resources he gathered from sleep, nourishment, or nature on literary work, so now he expended each contribution that sun, leisure, and sea air made to his daily increase in strength in a generous, extravagant burst of enthusiasm and sentiment.

He slept fitfully; the exquisitely uniform days were separated by short nights full of happy restlessness. To be sure he retired early, for at nine o'clock, when Tadzio had left the scene, the day was over as far as he was concerned. At the first glimmer of dawn, however, a softly penetrating pang of alarm awakened him, as his heart remembered its great adventure. No longer able to endure the pillow, he arose, wrapped himself in a light robe against the morning chill, and positioned himself at the open window to await the sunrise. This wonderful occurrence filled his sleep-blessed soul with reverence. Heaven, earth, and sea still lay in the ghostly, glassy pallor of dawn; a fading star still floated in the insubstantial distance. Then a breath of wind arose, a winged message from unapproachable abodes announcing that Eos was arising from the side of her spouse. There became visible on the furthest boundary between sea and sky that first sweet blush of red that reveals creation assuming perceptible form. The goddess was approaching, she who seduced young men, she who had stolen Kleitos and Kephalos and enjoyed the love of handsome Orion in defiance of all the envious Olympians.[2] A strewing of roses began there on the edge of the world, where all shone and blossomed in unspeakable purity. Childlike clouds, transfigured and luminous, hovered like attending Cupids in the rosy bluish fragrance. Purple light fell on the sea, then washed forward in waves. Golden spears shot up from below to the heights of the heavens, and the brilliance began to burn. Silently, with divine ascendancy, glow and heat and blazing flames spun upwards, as the brother-god's sacred chargers, hooves beating, mounted the heavens. The lonely, wakeful watcher sat bathed in the splendor of the god's rays; he closed his eyes and let the glory kiss his eyelids. With a confused, wondering smile on his lips he recognized feelings from long ago, early, exquisite afflictions of the heart that had withered in the severe service that his life had become and now returned so strangely transformed. He meditated, he dreamed. Slowly his lips formed a name, and still smiling, his face turned upward, his hands folded in his lap, he fell asleep once more in his armchair.

The whole day that had thus began in fiery celebration was strangely heightened and mythically transformed. Where did that breath of air come from, the one that suddenly played about his temples and ears so softly and significantly like a whisper from a higher realm? White feathery clouds stood in scattered flocks in the heavens like grazing herds that the gods tend. A stronger wind blew up; Poseidon's[3] steeds reared and ran, and the bulls obedient to the god with the

---

2. Eos, the Greek goddess of dawn, was known for seducing handsome young men, including Kleitos and Kephalos. When she took the hunter Orion for her lover, Artemis, the jealous goddess of the hunt, killed him with her arrows.

3. God of the sea and brother of Zeus in Greek mythology, associated with the horse and the bull.

blue-green locks lowered their horns and bellowed as they charged. But amid the boulders on the distant beach the waves hopped up like leaping goats. A magical world, sacred and animated by the spirit of Pan,[4] surrounded the beguiled traveler, and his heart dreamed tender fables. Often, as the sun set behind Venice, he would sit on a bench in the park to watch Tadzio, dressed in white with a colorful sash, delight in playing ball on the smooth, rolled gravel; and it was as if he were watching Hyacinthos, who had to die because two gods loved him.[5] Indeed he felt the painful envy Zephyros felt toward his rival in love, the god who abandoned his oracle, his bow, and his cithara to spend all his time playing with the beautiful boy. He saw the discus, directed by cruel jealousy, strike the lovely head; he too, turned pale as he received the stricken body; and the flower that sprang from that sweet blood bore the inscription of his unending lament. . . .

There is nothing stranger or more precarious than the relationship between people who know each other only by sight, who meet and watch each other every day, even every hour, yet are compelled by convention or their own whim to maintain the appearance of indifference and unfamiliarity, to avoid any word or greeting. There arises between them a certain restlessness and frustrated curiosity, the hysteria of an unsatisfied, unnaturally suppressed urge for acquaintanceship and mutual exchange, and in point of fact also a kind of tense respect. For people tend to love and honor other people so long as they are not in a position to pass judgment on them; and longing is the result of insufficient knowledge.

Some sort of relationship or acquaintance necessarily had to develop between Aschenbach and the young Tadzio, and with a pang of joy the older man was able to ascertain that his involvement and attentions were not altogether unrequited. For example, what impelled the lovely boy no longer to use the boardwalk behind the cabanas when he appeared on the beach in the morning but instead to saunter by toward his family's cabana on the front path, through the sand, past Aschenbach's customary spot, sometimes unnecessarily close by him, almost touching his table, his chair? Did Aschenbach's superior emotional energy exercise such an attraction, such a fascination on the tender, unreflecting object of those emotions? The writer waited daily for Tadzio's appearance; sometimes he would act as if he were busy when this event took place and let the lovely one pass by without seeming to notice. Sometimes, though, he would look up, and their eyes would meet. Both of them were gravely serious when it happened. In the refined and respectable bearing of the older man nothing betrayed his inner tumult; but in Tadzio's eyes there was the hint of an inquiry, of a thoughtful question. A hesitation became visible in his gait, he looked at the ground, he looked up again in his charming way, and when he was past there seemed to be something in his demeanor saying that only his good breeding prevented him from turning around.

One evening, however, something quite different happened. The Polish children and their governess were missing at the main meal in the large dining

---

4. A Greek demigod, half man and half goat, associated with fertility and sexuality.
5. Apollo and Zephyr, god of the west wind, both loved the youth Hyacinthos. When Apollo accidentally killed him in a discus game—

Zephyr blew the discus off course—a flower marked with the Greek syllables "ai ai" ("alas!") sprang from the boy's blood. Apollo is an archer and musician as well as the god of the Delphic oracle.

room. Aschenbach had taken note of it with alarm. Concerned about their absence, he was strolling in front of the hotel at the bottom of the terrace after dinner, dressed in his evening clothes and a straw hat, when he suddenly saw appear in the light of the arc lamps the nunlike sisters and their attendant, with Tadzio four steps behind. They were apparently returning from the steamer landing after having taken their meal for some reason in the city. It must have been cool on the water: Tadzio wore a dark blue sailor's coat with gold buttons and a sailor's hat to go with it. The sun and sea air had not browned him. His skin was the same marble-like yellow color it had been from the beginning. But today he seemed paler than usual, whether because of the cool temperature or because of the pallid moonglow cast by the lamps. His even brows showed in starker contrast, his eyes darkened to an even deeper tone. He was more beautiful than words could ever tell, and Aschenbach felt as he often had before the painful truth that words are capable only of praising physical beauty, not of rendering it visible.

He had not been expecting the exquisite apparition: it had come on unhoped for. He had not had time to fortify himself in a peaceful, respectable demeanor. Joy, surprise, and admiration might have been clearly displayed in the gaze that met that of the one he had so missed—and in that very second, it came to pass that Tadzio smiled. He smiled at Aschenbach, smiled eloquently, intimately, charmingly, and without disguise, with lips that began to open only as he smiled. It was the smile of Narcissus[6] leaning over the mirroring water, that deep, beguiled, unresisting smile that comes as he extends his arm toward the reflection of his own beauty—a very slightly distorted smile, distorted by the hopelessness of his desire to kiss the lovely lips of his shadow—a coquettish smile, curious and faintly pained, infatuated and infatuating.

He who had been the recipient of this smile rushed away with it as if it were a gift heavy with destiny. He was so thoroughly shaken that he was forced to flee the light of the terrace and the front garden and to seek with a hasty tread the darkness of the park in the rear. Strangely indignant and tender exhortations broke forth from him: "You must not smile so! Listen, no one is allowed to smile that way at anyone!" He threw himself on a bench; he breathed in the nocturnal fragrance of the plants, beside himself. Leaning back with his arms hanging at his sides, overpowered and shivering uncontrollably, he whispered the eternal formula of longing—impossible under these conditions, absurd, reviled, ridiculous, and yet holy and venerable even under these conditions—"I love you!"

CHAPTER 5

In the fourth week of his stay on the Lido Gustav Aschenbach made a number of disturbing discoveries regarding events in the outside world. In the first place it seemed to him that as the season progressed toward its height the number of guests at the hotel declined rather than increased. In particular it

---

6. A beautiful Greek youth who fell in love with his own image in a pool and drowned trying to reach it. "Tadzio's smile is Narcissus', who sees his own reflection—he sees it in the face of another / he sees his beauty in its effects. Coquettishness and tenderness are also in this smile" [Mann's note].

seemed that the German language ceased to be heard around him: lately his ear could detect only foreign sounds in the dining room and on the beach. He had taken to visiting the barbershop frequently, and in a conversation there one day he heard something that startled him. The barber had mentioned a German family that had just left after staying only a short time; then he added by way of flattering small talk, "But you're staying, sir, aren't you. You're not afraid of the disease." Aschenbach looked at him. "The disease?" he repeated. The man broke off his chatter, acted busy, ignored the question. When Aschenbach pressed the issue, he explained that he knew nothing and tried to change the subject with a stream of embarrassed eloquence.

That was at noon. In the afternoon Aschenbach sailed across to Venice in a dead calm and under a burning sun. He was driven by his mania to pursue the Polish children, whom he had seen making for the steamer landing along with their attendant. He did not find his idol at San Marco. But at tea, sitting at his round wrought-iron table on the shady side of the piazza, he suddenly smelled a peculiar aroma in the air, one that he now felt had been lurking at the edge of his consciousness for several days without his becoming fully aware of it. It was a medicinally sweet smell that put in mind thoughts of misery and wounds and ominous cleanliness. After a few moments' reflection he recognized it; then he finished his snack and left the piazza on the side opposite the cathedral. The odor became stronger in the narrow streets. At the street corners there were affixed printed posters in which the city fathers warned the population about certain illnesses of the gastric system that could be expected under these atmospheric conditions, advising that they should not eat oysters and mussels or use the water in the canals. The euphemistic nature of the announcement was obvious. Groups of local people stood together silently on the bridges and in the piazzas, and the foreign traveler stood among them, sniffing and musing.

There was a shopkeeper leaning in the doorway of his little vaulted quarters among coral necklaces and imitation amethyst trinkets, and Aschenbach asked him for some information about the ominous odor. The man took his measure with a heavy-lidded stare and then hastily put on a cheerful expression. "A precautionary measure, sir," he answered with many a gesture. "A police regulation that we must accept. The weather is oppressive, the sirocco is not conductive to good health. In short, you understand—perhaps they're being too careful. . . ." Aschenbach thanked him and went on. Even on the steamer that took him back to the Lido he could now detect the odor of disinfectant.

Once back at the hotel he went directly to the lobby to have a look at the newspapers. In the ones in foreign languages he found nothing. The German papers mentioned rumors, cited highly varying figures, quoted official denials, and offered doubts about their veracity. This explained the departure of the German and Austrian element. The citizens of other nations apparently knew nothing, suspected nothing, and were not yet concerned. "Best to keep quiet," thought Aschenbach anxiously, as he threw the papers back on the table. "Best to keep it under wraps." But at the same time his heart filled with a feeling of satisfaction over this adventure in which the outside world was becoming involved. For passion, like crime, does not sit well with the sure order and even course of everyday life; it welcomes every loosening of the social fabric, every confusion and affliction visited upon the world, for passion sees in such disorder a vague hope of finding an advantage for itself. Thus Aschenbach felt a dark satisfaction over the official cover-up of events in the dirty alleys of Venice. This heinous secret belonging to the city fused and became one with his own innermost secret, which he was likewise intent upon keeping. For the lovesick traveler had no concern other than that Tadzio might depart, and he recognized, not without a certain horror, that he would not know how to go on living were that to happen.

Recently he had not contented himself with allowing chance and the daily routine to determine his opportunities to see and be near the lovely lad; he pursued him, he lay in wait for him. On Sundays, for example, the Polish family never went to the beach. He guessed that they went to mass at San Marco. He followed speedily, entered the golden twilight of the sanctuary from the heat of the piazza, and found him, the one he had missed so, bent over a priedieu[7] taking part in the holy service. He stood in the background on the fissured mosaic floor, in the midst of a kneeling, murmuring crowd of people who kept crossing themselves, and felt the condensed grandeur of the oriental temple weigh voluptuously on his senses. Up in front the priest moved about, conducted his ritual, and chanted away, while incense billowed up and enshrouded the feeble flames of the altar candles. Mixed in with the sweet, heavy, ceremonial fragrance seemed to be another: the smell of the diseased city. But through all the haze and glitter Aschenbach saw how the lovely one up in front turned his head, looked for him, and found him.

When at last the crowd streamed out of the open portals into the shining piazza with its flocks of pigeons, the infatuated lover hid in the vestibule where he lay in wait, staking out his quarry. He saw the Polish family leave the church, saw the children take leave of their mother with great ceremony, saw her make for the Piazzetta on her way home. He ascertained that the lovely one, his cloisterly sisters, and the governess were on their way off to the right, through the clock tower gate, and into the Merceria,[8] and after giving them a reasonable head start he followed. He followed like a thief as they strolled through Venice. He had to stop when they lingered somewhere, had to flee into restaurants or courtyards to avoid them when they turned back. He lost them, got hot and tired as he searched for them over bridges and in dirty cul-de-sacs, and suffered long moments of mortal pain when he saw them coming toward him in a narrow passage where no escape was possible. And yet one cannot really say he suffered. He was intoxicated in head and heart, and his steps followed the instructions of the demon whose pleasure it is to crush under foot human reason and dignity.[9]

At some point or other Tadzio and his party would take a gondola, and Aschenbach, remaining hidden behind a portico or a fountain while they got in, did likewise shortly after they pulled away from the bank. He spoke quickly and in subdued tones to the gondolier, instructing him that a generous tip was in store for him if he would follow that gondola just now rounding the corner—but not too close, as unobtrusively as possible. Sweat trickled over his body as the gondolier, with the roguish willingness of a procurer, assured him in the

---

7. Pray God (French, literal trans.); a low bench on which to kneel during prayers, with a raised shelf for elbows or book.
8. Commercial district north of the Piazza San Marco.
9. Dionysus, originally an Eastern fertility god, worshipped with wild dances in ecstatic rites.

same lowered tones that he would get service, that he would get conscientious service.

He leaned back in the soft black cushions and glided and rocked in pursuit of the other black, beak-prowed bark, to which his passion held him fastened as if by a chain. Sometimes he lost sight of it, and at those times he would feel worried and restless. But his boatman seemed entirely familiar with such assignments and always knew just how to bring the object of his desire back into view by means of clever maneuvers and quick passages and shortcuts. The air was still, and it smelled. The sun burned heavily through a haze that gave the sky the color of slate. Water gurgled against wood and stone. The cry of the gondolier, half warning and half greeting, received distant answer from out of the silent labyrinth as if by mysterious arrangement. Umbels of flowers hung down over crumbling walls from small gardens on higher ground. They were white and purple and smelled like almonds. Moorish window casings showed their forms in the haze. The marble steps of a church descended into the waters; a beggar crouching there and asserting his misery held out his hat and showed the whites of his eyes as if he were blind; a dealer in antiques stood before his cavelike shop and with fawning gestures invited the passerby to stop, hoping for a chance to swindle him. That was Venice, that coquettish, dubious beauty of a city, half fairy tale and half tourist trap, in whose noisome air the fine arts once thrived luxuriantly and where musicians were inspired to create sounds that cradle the listener and seductively rock him to sleep. To the traveler in the midst of his adventure it seemed as if his eyes were drinking in just this luxury, as if his ears were wooed by just such melodies. He remembered, too, that the city was sick and was keeping its secret out of pure greed, and he cast an even more licentious leer toward the gondola floating in the distance before him.

Entangled and besotted as he was, he no longer wished for anything else than to pursue the beloved object that inflamed him, to dream about him when he was absent and to speak amorous phrases, after the manner of lovers, to his mere shadow. His solitary life, the foreign locale, and his late but deep transport of ecstasy encouraged and persuaded him to allow himself the most bewildering transgressions without timidity or embarrassment. That is how it happened that on his return from Venice late in the evening he had stopped on the second floor of the hotel in front of the lovely one's door, leaned his brow against the hinge in complete intoxication, unable for a protracted period to drag himself away, heedless of the danger of being caught in such an outrageous position.

Still, there were moments when he paused and half came to his senses. How has this come to pass? he wondered in alarm. How did I come to this? Like everyone who has achieved something thanks to his natural talents, he had an aristocratic interest in his family background. At times when his life brought him recognition and success he would think about his ancestors and try to reassure himself that they would approve, that they would be pleased, that they would have had to admire him. Even here and now he thought about them, entangled as he was in such an illicit experience, seized by such exotic emotional aberrations. He thought about their rigorous self-possession, their manly respectability, and he smiled a melancholy smile. What would they say? But then what would they have said about his whole life, a life that had so diverged, one might say degenerated, from theirs, a life under the spell of art that he himself had mocked in the precocity of his youth, this life that yet so fundamentally resembled theirs? He too had done his service, he too had practiced a strict discipline; he too had been a soldier and a man of war, like many of them. For art was a war, a grinding battle that one was just no longer up to fighting for very long these days. It was a life of self-control and a life lived in despite, a harsh, steadfast, abstemious existence that he had made the symbol of a tender and timely heroism. He had every right to call it manly, call it courageous, and he wondered if the love-god who had taken possession of him might be particularly inclined and partial somehow to those who lived such a life. Had not that very god enjoyed the highest respect among the bravest nations of the earth? Did they not say that it was because of their courage that he had flourished in their cities? Numerous war heroes of ages past had willingly borne the yoke imposed by the god, for a humiliation imposed by the god did not count. Acts that would have been denounced as signs of cowardice when done in other circumstances and for other ends—prostrations, oaths, urgent pleas, and fawning behavior—none redounded to the shame of the lover, but rather he more likely reaped praise for them.[1]

Such was the infatuated thinker's train of thought; thus he sought to offer himself support; thus he attempted to preserve his dignity. But at the same time he stubbornly kept on the track of the dirty doings in the city's interior, that adventure of the outside world that darkly joined together with his heart's adventure and nourished his passion with vague, lawless hopes. Obsessed with finding out the latest and most reliable news about the status and progress of the disease, he went to the city's coffee houses and leafed through the German newspapers, which had long since disappeared from the table in the hotel lobby. He read alternating assertions and denials. The number of illnesses and deaths might be as high as twenty, forty, even a hundred or more; but then in the next article or next issue any outbreak of the epidemic, if not categorically denied, would be reported as limited to a few isolated cases brought in by foreigners. There were periodic doubts, warnings, and protests against the dangerous game being played by the Italian authorities. Reliable information was simply not available.

The solitary guest was nonetheless conscious of having a special claim on his share in the secret. Though he was excluded, he took a bizarre pleasure in pressing knowledgeable people with insidious questions and forcing those who were part of the conspiracy of silence to utter explicit lies. At breakfast one day in the main dining room, for example, he engaged the manager in conversation. This unobtrusive little person in his French frock coat was going about between the tables greeting everyone and supervising the help. He made a brief stop at Aschenbach's table, too, for a casual chat. Now then why, the guest just happened to ask very casually, why in the world had they been disinfecting Venice for all this time? "It's a police matter," the toady answered, "a measure intended to stop in due and timely fashion any and all unwholesome conditions, any disturbance of the public health that might come about owing to the brooding heat of this exceptionally warm weather." "The police are to be com-

1. A reference to the Athenian code of love as described by Pausanias in Plato's *Symposium*, sections 182d–e and 183b.

mended," replied Aschenbach. After the exchange of a few more meteorological observations the manager took his leave.

On that very same day, in the evening after dinner, it happened that a little band of street singers from the city performed in the hotel's front garden. They stood, two men and two women, next to the iron lamppost of an arc light and raised their faces, shining in the white illumination, toward the great terrace, where the guests were enjoying this traditional popular entertainment while drinking coffee and cooling beverages. Hotel employees—elevator boys, waiters, and office personnel—stood by listening at the entrances to the lobby. The Russian family, zealous and precise in taking their pleasure, had wicker chairs moved down into the garden so as to be nearer the performers. There they sat in a semi-circle, in their characteristically grateful attitude. Behind the ladies and gentlemen stood the old slave woman in her turbanlike headdress.

The low-life virtuosos were extracting sounds from a mandolin, a guitar, a harmonica, and a squeaky violin. Interspersed among the instrumental numbers were vocals in which the younger of the women blended her sharp, quavering voice with the sweet falsetto of the tenor in a love duet full of yearning. But the chief talent and real leader of the group was clearly the other man, the guitar player, who sang a kind of buffo[2] baritone while he played. Though his voice was weak, he was a gifted mime and projected remarkable comic energy. Often he would move away from the group, his great instrument under his arm, and advance toward the terrace with many a flourish. The audience rewarded his antics with rousing laughter. The Russians in particular, ensconced in their orchestra seats, displayed particular delight over all this southern vivacity and encouraged him with applause and cheers to ever bolder and more brazen behavior.

Aschenbach sat at the balustrade, cooling his lips from time to time with a mixture of pomegranate[3] juice and soda that sparkled ruby-red in his glass. His nerves greedily consumed the piping sounds, the vulgar, pining melodies; for passion numbs good taste and succumbs in all seriousness to enticements that a sober spirit would receive with humor or even reject scornfully. His features, reacting to the antics of the buffoon, had become fixed in a rigid and almost painful smile. He sat in an apparently relaxed attitude, and all the while he was internally tense and sharply attentive, for Tadzio stood no more than six paces away, leaning against the stone railing.

He stood there in the white belted suit that he sometimes wore to dinner, a figure of inevitable and innate grace, his left forearm on the railing, his ankles crossed, his right hand supported on his hip. He wore an expression that was not quite a smile but more an air of distant curiosity or polite receptivity as he looked down toward the street musicians. Sometimes he straightened up and, with a lovely movement of both arms that lifted his chest, he would pull his white blouse down through his leather belt. Occasionally, though—as the aging observer noted with triumph and even with horror, his reason staggering— Tadzio would turn his head to look across his left shoulder in the direction of *the one* who loved him, sometimes with deliberate hesitation, sometimes with

2. Comic.
3. A tropical fruit with many seeds, associated in Greek mythology both with Persephone,

the queen of Hades, and with the world of the dead.

sudden swiftness as if to catch him unawares. Their eyes never met, for an ignominious caution forced the errant lover to keep his gaze fearfully in check. The women guarding Tadzio were sitting in the back of the terrace, and things had reached the point that the smitten traveler had to take care lest his behavior should become noticeable and he fall under suspicion. Indeed his blood had nearly frozen on a number of occasions when he had been compelled to notice on the beach, in the hotel lobby, or in the Piazza San Marco that Tadzio was called away from his vicinity, that they were intent on keeping the boy away from him. He felt horribly insulted, and his pride flinched from unfamiliar tortures that his conscience prevented him from dismissing.

In the meantime the guitar player had begun singing a solo to his own accompaniment, a popular ditty in many verses that was quite the hit just then all over Italy. He was adept at performing it in a highly histrionic manner, and his band joined in the refrain each time, both with their voices and all their instruments. He was of a lean build, and even his face was thin to the point of emaciation. He stood there on the gravel in an attitude of impertinent bravura, apart from his fellow performers, his shabby felt hat so far back on his head that a roll of red hair surged forth from beneath the brim, and as he thumped the guitar strings, he hurled his buffooneries toward the terrace above in an insistent recitative. The veins on his brow swelled in response to his exertions. He seemed not to be of Venetian stock, more likely a member of the race of Neapolitan comics, half pimp, half actor, brutal and daring, dangerous and entertaining. The lyrics of his song were as banal as could be, but in his mouth they acquired an ambiguous, vaguely offensive quality because of his facial expressions and his gestures, his suggestive winks and his manner of letting his tongue play lasciviously at the corner of his mouth. His strikingly large Adam's apple protruded nakedly from his scrawny neck, which emerged from the soft collar of a sport shirt worn in incongruous combination with more formal city clothes. His pale, snubnosed face was beardless and did not permit an easy reckoning of his age; it seemed ravaged by grimaces and by vice. The two defiant, imperious, even wild-looking furrows that stood between his reddish eyebrows went rather oddly with the grin on his mobile lips. What particularly drew the attention of the lonely spectator, however, was his observation that this questionable figure seemed to carry with it its own questionable atmosphere. For every time the refrain began again the singer would commence a grotesque circular march, clowning and shaking the hands of his audience; every time his path would bring him directly underneath Aschenbach's spot, and every time that happened there wafted up to the terrace from his clothes and from his body a choking stench of carbolic acid.[4]

His song finished, he began collecting money. He started with the Russians, who produced a generous offering, and then ascended the steps. As bold as he had been during the performance, just so obsequious was he now. Bowing and scraping, he slithered about between the tables, a smile of crafty submissiveness laying bare his large teeth, and all the while the two furrows between his red eyebrows stood forth menacingly. The guests surveyed with curiosity and some revulsion this strange being who was gathering in his livelihood. They threw coins in his hat from a distance and were careful not to touch him. The

4. A chemical used as a disinfectant.

elimination of the physical separation between the performer and his respectable audience always tends to produce a certain embarrassment, no matter how pleasurable the performance. The singer felt it and sought to excuse himself by acting servile. He came up to Aschenbach, and with him came the smell, though no one else in the vicinity seemed concerned about it.

"Listen," the lonely traveler said in lowered tones, almost mechanically. "They are disinfecting Venice. Why?" The jester answered hoarsely: "Because of the police. That, sir, is the procedure when it gets hot like this and when the sirocco comes. The sirocco is oppressive. It's not conducive to good health. . . ." He spoke as if he were amazed that anyone could ask such questions, and he demonstrated by pushing with his open palm just how oppressive the sirocco was. "So there is no disease in Venice?" Aschenbach asked very quietly through his closed teeth. The tense muscles in the comedian's face produced a grimace of comic perplexity. "A disease? What sort of disease? Is the sirocco a disease? Do you suppose our police force is a disease? You like to make fun, don't you? A disease! Why on earth? Some preventive measures, you understand. A police regulation to minimize the effects of the oppressive weather . . . ," he gesticulated. "Very well," Aschenbach said once again, briefly and quietly, and he dropped an indecently large coin into the hat. Then he indicated with a look that the man should go. He obeyed with a grin and a bow. But even before he reached the steps two hotel employees intercepted him and, putting their faces very close to his, cross-examined him in whispers. He shrugged, he protested, he swore that he had been circumspect. You could tell. Dismissed, he returned to the garden and, after making a few arrangements with his group by the light of the arc lamp, he stepped forward to offer one parting song.

It was a song the solitary traveler could not remember ever having heard before, an impudent Italian hit in an incomprehensible dialect embellished with a laughing refrain in which the whole group regularly joined, fortissimo. The refrain had neither words nor instrumental accompaniment; nothing was left but a certain rhythmically structured but still very natural-sounding laughter, which the soloist in particular was capable of producing with great talent and deceptive realism. Having reestablished a proper artistic distance between himself and his audience, he had regained all his former impudence. His artfully artificial laughter, directed impertinently up to the terrace, was the laughter of scorn. Even before the part of the song with actual lyrics had come to a close, one could see him begin to battle an irresistible itch. He would hiccup, his voice would catch, he would put his hand up to his mouth, he would twist his shoulders, and at the proper moment the unruly laughter would break forth, exploding in a hoot, but with such realism that it was infectious. It spread among the listeners so that even on the terrace an unfounded mirth set in, feeding on nothing but itself. This appeared only to double the singer's exuberance. He bent his knees, slapped his thighs, held his sides, fairly split with laughter; but he was no longer laughing, he was howling. He pointed his finger upwards, as if to say that there could be nothing funnier than the laughing audience up there, and soon everyone in the garden and on the veranda was laughing, including the waiters, elevator boys, and servants lingering in the doorways.

Aschenbach no longer reclined in his chair; he sat upright as if trying to defend himself or to flee. But the laughter, the rising smell of hospital sanitation, and the nearness of the lovely boy—all blended to cast a dreamy spell about him that held his mind and his senses in an unbreakable, inescapable embrace. In the general confusion of the moment he made so bold as to cast a glance at Tadzio, and when he did so he was granted the opportunity to see that the lovely lad answered his gaze with a seriousness equal to his own. It was as if the boy were regulating his behavior and attitude according to that of the man, as if the general mood of gaiety had no power over the boy so long as the man kept apart from it. This childlike and meaningful docility was so disarming, so overwhelming, that the gray-haired traveler could only with difficulty refrain from hiding his face in his hands. It had also seemed to him that Tadzio's habit of straightening up and taking a deep sighing breath suggested an obstruction in his breathing. "He is sickly; he will probably not live long," he thought once again with that sobriety that sometimes frees itself in some strange manner from intoxication and longing. Ingenuous solicitude mixed with a dissolute satisfaction filled his heart.

The Venetian singers had meanwhile finished their number and left, accompanied by applause. Their leader did not fail to adorn even his departure with jests. He bowed and scraped and blew kisses so that everyone laughed, which made him redouble his efforts. When his fellow performers were already gone, he pretended to back hard into a lamppost at full speed, then crept toward the gate bent over in mock pain. There at last he cast off the mask of the comic loser, unbent or rather snapped up straight, stuck his tongue out impudently at the guests on the terrace, and slipped into the darkness. The audience dispersed; Tadzio was already long gone from his place at the balustrade. But the lonely traveler remained sitting for a long time at his little table, nursing his pomegranate drink much to the annoyance of the waiters. The night progressed; time crumbled away. Many years ago in his parents' house there had been an hourglass. He suddenly could see the fragile and portentous little device once more, as though it were standing right in front of him. The rust-colored fine sand ran silently through the glass neck, and as it began to run out of the upper vessel a rapid little vortex formed.

In the afternoon of the very next day the obstinate visitor took a further step in his probing of the outside world, and this time he met with all possible success. What he did was to enter the English travel agency in the Piazza San Marco and, having changed some money at the cash register and having assumed the demeanor of a diffident foreigner, he directed his fateful question to the clerk who was taking care of him. The clerk was a wool-clad Briton, still young, his hair parted in the middle and eyes set close together, possessed of that steady, trustworthy bearing that stands out as so foreign and so remarkable among the roguishly nimble southerners. He began: "No cause for concern, sir. A measure of no serious importance. Such regulations are frequently imposed to ward off the ill effects of the heat and the sirocco. . . . " But when he raised his blue eyes he met the foreigner's gaze. It was a tired and rather sad gaze, and it was directed with an air of mild contempt toward his lips. The Englishman blushed. "That is," he continued in a low voice, somewhat discomfited, "the official explanation, which they see fit to stick to hereabouts. I can tell you, though, that there's a good deal more to it." And then, in his candid and comfortable language, he told the truth.

For some years now Asiatic cholera had shown an increasing tendency to spread and roam. The pestilence originated in the warm swamps of the Ganges delta,[5] rising on the foul-smelling air of that lushly uninhabitable primeval world, that wilderness of islands avoided by humankind where tigers lurk in bamboo thickets. It had raged persistently and with unusual ferocity throughout Hindustan; then it had spread eastwards to China and westwards to Afghanistan and Persia; and, following the great caravan routes, it had brought its horrors as far as Astrakhan and even Moscow. But while Europe was shaking in fear lest the specter should progress by land from Russia westward, it had emerged simultaneously in several Mediterranean port cities, having been carried in on Syrian merchant ships. It had raised its grisly head in Toulon and Malaga, shown its grim mask several times in Palermo and Naples, and seemed now firmly ensconced throughout Calabria and Apulia.[6] The northern half of the peninsula had so far been spared. On a single day in mid-May of this year, however, the terrible vibrioid[7] bacteria had been found on two emaciated, blackening corpses, that of a ship's hand and that of a woman who sold vegetables. These cases were hushed up. A week later, though, there were ten more, twenty more, thirty more, not localized but spread through various parts of the city. A man from the Austrian hinterlands who had come for a pleasant holiday of a few days in Venice died upon returning to his home town, exhibiting unmistakable symptoms. Thus it was that the first rumors of the affliction visited upon the city on the lagoon appeared in German newspapers. In response the Venetian authorities promulgated the assertion that matters of health had never been better in the city. They also immediately instituted the most urgent measures to counter the disease. But apparently the food supply—vegetables, meat, and milk—had been infected, for death, though denied and hushed up, devoured its way through the narrow streets. The early arrival of summer's heat made a lukewarm broth of the water in the canals and thus made conditions for the disease's spread particularly favorable. It almost seemed as though the pestilence had been reinvigorated, as if the tenacity and fecundity of its microscopic agitators had been redoubled. Cures were rare; out of a hundred infected eighty died, and in a particularly gruesome fashion, for the evil raged here with extreme ferocity. Often it took on its most dangerous form, commonly known as the "dry type." In such cases the body is unable to rid itself of the massive amounts of water secreted by the blood-vessels. In a few hours' time the patient dries up and suffocates, his blood as viscous as pitch, crying out hoarsely in his convulsions. It sometimes happened that a few lucky ones suffered only a mild discomfort followed by a loss of consciousness from which they would never again, or only rarely, awaken. At the beginning of June the quarantine wards of the Ospedale Civico quietly filled up, space became scarce in both of the orphanages, and a horrifyingly brisk traffic clogged the routes between the docks at the Fondamenta Nuove[8] and San Michele, the cemetery island. But the fear of adverse consequences to the city, concern for the newly opened exhibit of paintings in the public gardens, for the losses that the hotels, businesses, and the whole tourist industry would suffer in case of a panic or a

5. In India.
6. Regions in southern Italy. Astrakhan, Toulon, Málaga, Palermo, and Naples are seaports in Russia, France, Spain, Sicily, and southern Italy, respectively.

7. Belonging to a class of comma-shaped bacteria.
8. New footings (Italian, literal trans.); the new piers. "Ospedale Civico": city hospital.

boycott—these matters proved weightier in the city than the love of truth or respect for international agreements. They prompted the authorities stubbornly to maintain their policy of concealment and denial. The highest medical official in Venice, a man of considerable attainments, had angrily resigned his post and was surreptitiously replaced by a more pliable individual. The citizenry knew all about it, and the combination of corruption in high places with the prevailing uncertainty, the state of emergency in which the city was placed when death was striking all about, caused a certain demoralization of the lower levels of society. It encouraged those antisocial forces that shun the light, and they manifested themselves as immoderate, shameless, and increasingly criminal behavior. Contrary to the norm, one saw many drunks at evening time; people said that gangs of rogues made the streets unsafe at night; muggings and even murders multiplied. Already on two occasions it had come to light that alleged victims of the plague had in fact been robbed of their lives by their own relatives who administered poison. Prostitution and lasciviousness took on brazen and extravagant forms never before seen here and thought to be at home only in the southern parts of the country and in the seraglios of the orient.

The Englishman explained the salient points of these developments. "You would do well," he concluded, "to depart today rather than tomorrow. The imposition of a quarantine cannot be more than a few days off." "Thank you," said Aschenbach and left the agency.

The piazza was sunless and sultry. Unsuspecting foreigners sat in the sidewalk cafes or stood in front of the cathedral completely covered with pigeons. They watched as the swarming birds beat their wings and jostled each other for their chance to pick at the kernels of corn offered to them in an open palm. In feverish excitement, triumphant in his possession of the truth, but with a taste of gall in his mouth and a fantastic horror in his heart, the lonely traveler paced back and forth over the flagstones of the magnificent plaza. He considered doing the decent thing, the thing that would cleanse him. Tonight after dinner he could go up to the lady with the pearls and speak to her. He planned exactly what he would say: "Permit me, Madame, stranger though I may be, to be of service to you with a piece of advice, a word of warning concerning a matter that has been withheld from you by self-serving people. Depart at once, taking Tadzio and your daughters with you. There is an epidemic in Venice." He could then lay his hand in farewell on the head of that instrument of a scornful deity, turn away, and flee this swamp. But at the same time he sensed that he was infinitely far from seriously wanting to take such a step. It would bring him back to his senses, would make him himself again; but when one is beside oneself there is nothing more abhorrent than returning to one's senses. He remembered a white building decorated with inscriptions that gleamed in the evening light, inscriptions in whose radiant mysticism his mind's eye had become lost. He remembered too that strange figure of the wanderer who had awakened in the aging man a young man's longing to roam in faraway and exotic places. The thought of returning home, of returning to prudence and sobriety, toil and mastery, was so repugnant to him that his face broke out in an expression of physical disgust. "Let them keep quiet," he whispered vehemently. And: "I will keep quiet!" The consciousness of his guilty complicity intoxicated him, just as small amounts of wine will intoxicate a weary brain. The image of the afflicted and ravaged city hovered chaotically in his imagination, incited in him inconceivable hopes, beyond all reason, monstrously sweet. How could that tender happiness he had dreamed of a moment earlier compare with these expectations? What value did art and virtue hold for him when he could have chaos? He held his peace and stayed.

That night he had a terrifying dream—if indeed one can call "dream" an experience that was both physical and mental, one that visited him in the depths of his sleep, in complete isolation as well as sensuous immediacy, but yet such that he did not see himself as physically and spatially present apart from its action. Instead, its setting was in his soul itself, and its events burst in upon him from outside, violently crushing his resistance, his deep, intellectual resistance, passing through easily and leaving his whole being, the culmination of a lifetime of effort, ravaged and annihilated.

It began with fear, fear and desire and a horrified curiosity about what was to come. Night ruled, and his senses were attentive; for from afar there approached a tumult, a turmoil, a mixture of noises: rattling, clarion calls and muffled thunder, shrill cheering on top of it all, and a certain howl with a drawn-out *uuu* sound at the end. All this was accompanied and drowned out by the gruesomely sweet tones of a flute playing a cooing, recklessly persistent tune that penetrated to the very bowels, where it cast a shameless enchantment. But there was a phrase, darkly familiar, that named what was coming: *"The stranger god!"*[9] A smoky glow welled up, and he recognized a mountain landscape like the one around his summer house. And in the fragmented light he could see people, animals, a swarm, a roaring mob, all rolling and plunging and whirling down from the forested heights, past tree-trunks and great moss-covered fragments of rock, overflowing the slope with their bodies, flames, tumult, and reeling circular dance. Women, stumbling over the fur skirts that hung too long from their belts, moaned, threw their heads back, shook their tambourines on high, brandished naked daggers and torches that threw off sparks, held serpents with flickering tongues by the middle of their bodies, or cried out, lifting their breasts in both hands. Men with horns on their brows, girdled with hides, their own skins shaggy, bent their necks and raised their arms and thighs, clashed brazen cymbals and beat furiously on drums, while smooth-skinned boys used garlanded staves to prod their goats, clinging to the horns so they could be dragged along, shouting with joy, when the goats sprang. And the ecstatic band howled the cry with soft consonants in the middle and a drawn-out *uuu* sound on the end, a cry that was sweet and wild at the same time, like none ever heard before: here it rang in the air like the bellowing of stags in rut; and there many voices echoed it back in anarchic triumph, using it to goad each other to dance and shake their limbs, never letting it fall silent. But it was all suffused and dominated by the deep, beckoning melody of the flute. Was it not also beckoning him, the resisting dreamer, with shameless persistence to the festival, to its excesses, and to its ultimate sacrifice? Great was his loathing, great his fear, sincere his resolve to defend his own against the foreign invader, the enemy of self-controlled and dignified intellect. But the noise and the howling, multiplied by the echoing mountainsides, grew, gained the upper hand, swelled to a madness that swept everything along with it. Fumes oppressed the senses: the acrid

9. Dionysus (also Bacchus), whose cult was brought to Greece from Thrace and Phrygia. The dream describes the orgiastic rites of his worship.

scent of the goats, the emanation of panting human bodies, a whiff as of stagnant water—and another smell perceptible through it all, a familiar reek of wounds and raging sickness. His heart pounded with the rhythm of the drum beats, his mind whirled, rage took hold of him and blinded him, he was overcome by a numbing lust, and his soul longed to join in the reeling dance of the god. Their obscene symbol,[1] gigantic, wooden, was uncovered and raised on high, and they howled out their watchword all the more licentiously. With foam on their lips they raved; they stimulated each other with lewd gestures and fondling hands; laughing and wheezing, they pierced each other's flesh with their pointed staves and then licked the bleeding limbs. Now among them, now a part of them, the dreamer belonged to the stranger god. Yes, they were he, and he was they, when they threw themselves on the animals, tearing and killing, devouring steaming gobbets of flesh, when on the trampled moss-covered ground there began an unfettered rite of copulation in sacrifice to the god. His soul tasted the lewdness and frenzy of surrender.

The afflicted dreamer awoke unnerved, shattered, a powerless victim of the demon. He no longer shunned the observant glances of people about him; he no longer cared if he was making himself a target of their suspicions. And in any case they were all departing, fleeing the sickness. Many cabanas now stood empty, the population of the dining room was seriously depleted, and in the city one only rarely saw a foreigner. The truth seemed to have leaked out, and in spite of the stubborn conniving of those with vested interests at stake, panic could no longer be averted. The lady with the pearls nonetheless remained with her family, perhaps because the rumors did not reach her or perhaps because she was too proud and fearless to succumb to them. Tadzio remained, and to Aschenbach, blind to all but his own concerns, it seemed at times that death and departure might very well remove all the distracting human life around them and leave him alone with the lovely one on this island. Indeed, in the mornings on the beach when his gaze would rest heavily, irresponsibly, fixedly on the object of his desire; or at the close of day when he would take up his shameful pursuit of the boy through narrow streets where loathsome death did its hushed-up business; then everything monstrous seemed to him to have a prosperous future, the moral law to have none.

He wished, like any other lover, to please his beloved and felt a bitter concern that it would not be possible. He added youthfully cheerful touches to his dress, took to using jewelry and perfume. Several times a day he took lengthy care getting dressed and then came down to the dining room all bedecked, excited and expectant. His aging body disgusted him when he looked at the sweet youth with whom he was smitten; the sight of his gray hair and his sharp facial features overwhelmed him with shame and hopelessness. He felt a need to restore and revive his body. He visited the barbershop more and more frequently.

Leaning back in the chair under the protective cloth, letting the manicured hands of the chattering barber care for him, he confronted the tortured gaze of his image in the mirror.

"Gray," he said with his mouth twisted.

"A bit," the man replied. "It's all because of a slight neglect, an indifference to externals—quite understandable in the case of important people, but still

1. The phallus.

not altogether praiseworthy, all the less so since just such people ought not to harbor prejudices in matters of the natural and the artificial. If certain people were to extend the moral qualms they have about the cosmetic arts to their teeth, as logic compels, they would give no little offense. And anyway, we're only as old we feel in our hearts and minds. Gray hair can in certain circumstances give more of a false impression than the dye that some would scorn. In your case, sir, you have a right to your natural hair color. Will you allow me to give you back what is rightfully yours?"

"How?" Aschenbach inquired.

So the glib barber washed his customer's hair with two liquids, one clear and one dark, and it turned as black as it had been in youth. Then he rolled it with the curling iron into soft waves, stepped back and admired his handiwork.

"All that's left," he said, "is to freshen up the complexion a bit."

He went about, with ever renewed solicitude, moving from one task to another the way a person does who can never finish anything and is never satisfied. Aschenbach, resting comfortably, was in any case quite incapable of fending him off. Actually he was rather excited about what was happening, watching in the mirror as his brows took on a more decisive and symmetrical arch and his eyes grew in width and brilliance with the addition of a little shadow on the lids. A little further down he could see his skin, previously brown and leathery, perk up with a light application of delicate carmine rouge, his lips, pale and bloodless only a moment a ago, swell like raspberries, the furrows in his cheeks and mouth, the wrinkles around his eyes give way to a dab of cream and the glow of youth. His heart pounded as he saw in the mirror a young man in full bloom. The cosmetic artist finally pronounced himself satisfied and thanked the object of his ministrations with fawning politeness, the way such people do. "A minor repair job," he said as he put a final touch to Aschenbach's appearance. "Now, sir, you can go and fall in love without second thoughts." The beguiled lover went out, happy as in a dream, yet confused and timid. His tie was red, and his broad-brimmed straw hat was encircled by a band of many colors.

A tepid breeze had come up; it rained only seldom and then not hard, but the air was humid, thick, and full of the stench of decay. Rustling, rushing, and flapping sounds filled his ears. He burned with fever beneath his makeup, and it seemed to him that the air was filled with vile, evil windspirits, impure winged sea creatures who raked over, gnawed over, and defiled with garbage the meals of their victim.[2] For the sultry weather ruined one's appetite, and one could not suppress the idea that all the food was poisoned with infection.

Trailing the lovely boy one afternoon, Aschenbach had penetrated deep into the maze in the heart of the diseased city. He had lost his sense of direction, for the little streets, canals, bridges, and piazzas in the labyrinth all looked alike. He could no longer even tell east from west, since his only concern had been not to lose sight of the figure he pursued so ardently. He was compelled to a disgraceful sort of discretion that involved clinging to walls and seeking protection behind the backs of passersby, and so he did not for some time become conscious of the

---

2. "Harpies: hideously thin, they flew swiftly in, fell with insatiable greed on whatever food was there, ate without being satisfied, and *befouled* whatever they left with their filth" [Mann's note]. See Virgil's *Aeneid* 3.210–62.

fatigue, the exhaustion which a high pitch of emotion and continual tension had inflicted on his body and spirit. Tadzio walked behind the rest of his family. In these narrow streets he would generally let the governess and the nunlike sisters go first, while he sauntered along by himself, occasionally turning his head to assure himself with a quick glance of his extraordinary dawn-gray eyes over his shoulder that his lover was still following. He saw him, and he did not betray him. Intoxicated by this discovery, lured onward by those eyes, tied to the apron string of his own passion, the lovesick traveler stole forth in pursuit of his unseemly hope—but ultimately found himself disappointed. The Polish family had gone across a tightly arched bridge, and the height of the arch had hidden them from their pursuer. When he was at last able to cross, he could no longer find them. He searched for them in three directions—straight ahead and to both sides along the narrow, dirty landing—but in vain. He finally had to give up, too debilitated and unnerved to go on.

His head was burning hot, his body was sticky with sweat, the scruff of his neck was tingling, an unbearable thirst assaulted him, and he looked about for immediate refreshment of any sort. In front of a small greengrocer's shop he bought some fruit, strawberries that were overripe and soft, and he ate them while he walked. A little piazza that was quite deserted and seemed enchanted opened out before him. He recognized it, for it was here that weeks ago he had made his thwarted plan to flee the city. He collapsed on the steps of the well in the very middle of the plaza and rested his head on the stone rim. It was quiet, grass grew between the paving stones, refuse lay strewn about. Among the weathered buildings of varying heights around the periphery was one that looked rather palatial. It had Gothic-arched windows, now gaping emptily, and little balconies decorated with lions. On the ground floor of another there was a pharmacy. Warm gusts of wind from time to time carried the smell of carbolic acid.

He sat there, the master, the artist who had attained to dignity, the author of the "Man of Misery," that exemplary work which had with clarity of form renounced bohemianism and the gloomy murky depths, had condemned sympathy for the abyss, reviled the vile. There he sat, the great success who had overcome knowledge and outgrown every sort of irony, who had accustomed himself to the obligations imposed by the confidence of his large audience. There he sat, the author whose greatness had been officially recognized and whose name bore the title of nobility, the author whose style children were encouraged to emulate—sat there with his eyes shut, though from time to time a mocking and embarrassed look would slip sidelong out from underneath his lids, only to conceal itself again swiftly; and his slack, cosmetically enhanced lips formed occasional words that emerged out of the strange dream-logic engendered in his half-dozing brain.[3]

"For beauty, Phaedrus—mark me well—only beauty is both divine and visible at the same time, and thus it is the way of the senses, the way of the artist, little Phaedrus, to the spirit. But do you suppose, my dear boy, that anyone could ever attain to wisdom and genuine manly honor by taking a path to the spirit that leads through the senses? Or do you rather suppose (I leave the deci-

---

3. Aschenbach adopts the role of Socrates in Plato's *Phaedrus* to examine the role of the artist. Although the Platonic dialogue briefly contrasts inspired art with mere technical perfection, it is chiefly concerned with moral choices and absolute beauty.

sion entirely up to you) that this is a dangerously delightful path, really a path of error and sin that necessarily leads astray? For you must know that we poets cannot walk the path of beauty without Eros joining our company and even making himself our leader; indeed, heroes though we may be after our own fashion, disciplined warriors though we may be, still we are as women, for passion is our exaltation, and our longing must ever be for love. That is our bliss and our shame. Do you see, then, that we poets can be neither wise nor honorable, that we necessarily go astray, that we necessarily remain dissolute adventurers of emotion? The masterly demeanor of our style is a lie and a folly, our fame and our honor a sham, the confidence accorded us by our public utterly ridiculous, the education of the populace and of the young by means of art a risky enterprise that ought not to be allowed. For how can a person succeed in educating others who has an inborn, irremediable, and natural affinity for the abyss? We may well deny it and achieve a certain dignity, but wherever we may turn that affinity abides. Let us say we renounce analytical knowledge; for knowledge, Phaedrus, has neither dignity nor discipline; it is knowing, understanding, forgiving, formless and unrestrained; it has sympathy for the abyss; it *is* the abyss. Let us therefore resolutely reject it, and henceforth our efforts will be directed only toward beauty, that is to say toward simplicity, grandeur, and a new discipline, toward reborn ingenuousness and toward form. But form and ingenuousness, Phaedrus, lead to intoxication and to desire, might lead the noble soul to horrible emotional outrages that his own lovely discipline would reject as infamous, lead him to the abyss. Yes, they too lead to the abyss. They lead us poets there, I say, because we are capable not of resolution but only of dissolution. And now I shall depart, Phaedrus; but you stay here until you can no longer see me, and then you depart as well."

A few days afterwards Gustav von Aschenbach left the hotel at a later hour than usual, since he was feeling unwell. He was struggling with certain attacks of dizziness that were only partly physical and were accompanied by a powerfully escalating sense of anxiety and indecision, a feeling of having no prospects and no way out. He was not at all sure whether these feelings concerned the outside world or his own existence. He noticed in the lobby a great pile of luggage prepared for departure, and when he asked the doorman who was leaving, he received for an answer the aristocratic Polish name he had in his heart been expecting to hear all along. He took it in with no change in the expression on his ravaged face, briefly raising his head as people do to acknowledge casually the receipt of a piece of information they do not need, and asked, "When?" The answer came: "After lunch." He nodded and went to the beach.

It was dreary there. Rippling tremors crossed from near to far on the wide, flat stretch of water between the beach and the first extended sandbar. Where so recently there had been color, life, and joy, it was now almost deserted, and an autumnal mood prevailed, a feeling that the season was past its prime. The sand was no longer kept clean. A camera with no photographer to operate it stood on its tripod at the edge of the sea, a black cloth that covered it fluttering with a snapping noise in a wind that now blew colder.

Tadzio and three or four playmates that still remained were active in front of his family's cabana to Aschenbach's right; and, resting in his beach chair approximately halfway between the ocean and the row of cabanas, with a blanket over his legs, Aschenbach watched him once more. Their play was unsupervised, since the women must have been busy with preparations for their departure. The game seemed to have no rules and quickly degenerated. The sturdy boy with the belted suit and the black, slicked-down hair who was called Yashu, angered and blinded by sand thrown in his face, forced Tadzio into a wrestling match, which ended swiftly with the defeat of the weaker, lovely boy. It seemed as if in the last moments before leave-taking the subservient feelings of the underling turned to vindictive cruelty as he sought to take revenge for a long period of slavery. The winner would not release his defeated opponent but instead kneeled on his back and pushed his face in the sand, persisting for so long that Tadzio, already out of breath from the fight, seemed in danger of suffocating. He made spasmodic attempts to shake off his oppressor, lay still for whole moments, then tried again with no more than a twitch. Horrified, Aschenbach wanted to spring to the rescue, but then the bully finally released his victim. Tadzio was very pale; he got up halfway and sat motionless for several minutes supported on one arm, his hair disheveled and his eyes darkening. Then he rose to his feet and slowly walked away. They called to him, cheerfully at first but then with pleading timidity. He paid no attention. The black-haired boy, apparently instantly regretting his transgression, caught up with him and tried to make up. A jerk of a lovely shoulder put him off. Tadzio crossed diagonally down to the water. He was barefoot and wore his striped linen suit with the red bow.

He lingered at the edge of the sea with his head hung down, drawing figures in the wet sand with his toe. Then he went into the shallows, which at their deepest point did not wet his knees, strode through them, and progressed idly to the sandbar. Upon reaching it he stood for a moment, his face turned to the open sea, then began to walk slowly to the left along the narrow stretch of uncovered ground. Separated from the mainland by the broad expanse of water, separated from his mates by a proud mood, he strode forth, a highly remote and isolated apparition with wind-blown hair, wandering about out there in the sea, in the wind, on the edge of the misty boundlessness. Once more he stopped to gaze outward. Suddenly, as if prompted by a memory or an impulse, he rotated his upper body in a lovely turn out of its basic posture, his hand resting on his hip, and looked over his shoulder toward the shore. The observer sat there as he had sat once before, when for the first time he had met the gaze of those dawn-gray eyes cast back at him from that threshold. His head, resting on the back of the chair, had slowly followed the movements of the one who was striding about out there; now his head rose as if returning the gaze, then sank on his chest so that his eyes looked out from beneath. His face took on the slack, intimately absorbed expression of deep sleep. It seemed to him, though, as if the pale and charming psychagogue[4] out there were smiling at him, beckoning to him; as if, lifting his hand from his hip, he were pointing outwards, hovering before him in an immensity full of promise. And, as so often before, he arose to follow him.

Minutes passed before anyone rushed to the aid of the man who had collapsed to one side in his chair. They carried him to his room. And later that same day a respectfully shaken world received the news of his death.

1912

4. Leader of souls to the underworld (Greek); a title of the god Hermes.

MARCEL PROUST

1871–1922

Marcel Proust's influence on twentieth-century literature is unequaled by that of any other writer, except **James Joyce**. Known primarily as a minor essayist until the age of forty, Proust devoted the last decade of his life to a massive sequence—*In Search of Lost Time (À la recherche du temps perdu*, 1913–27), also known in English as *Remembrance of Things Past*—that transformed the way writers and readers think about the novel as a form. It is a monumental construction coordinated down to its smallest part not by the progress of a traditional plot but by the narrator's intuition and "involuntary memory," and all external events are presented through the prism of the narrator's experience.

Proust was born on July 10, 1871, the older of two sons in a wealthy middle-class Parisian family. His father was a well-known doctor and professor of medicine, a Catholic from a small town outside Paris. His mother, a sensitive, scrupulous, and highly educated woman to whom Marcel was devoted, came from an urban Jewish family. When he was nine, Proust fell ill with severe asthma; thereafter, he spent his childhood holidays at a seaside resort in Normandy that became the model for the fictional Balbec, the setting for a portion of *In Search of Lost Time*. His asthma interfered with his favorite pastimes: walking in the country and smelling the flowering hawthorns near his aunt's home in Illiers (the fictional Combray, where the novel's protagonist grows up). In spite of his illness, which limited what he could do, Marcel graduated with honors from the Lycée Condorcet in Paris in 1889. He

then did a year's military service at Orléans, which provided more material for his later novel. He went on to attend law school briefly and graduated with a degree in philosophy from the Sorbonne. As a student, Proust met many young writers and composers, and he frequented the salons of the wealthy bourgeoisie and the aristocracy of the Faubourg Saint-Germain (an elegant area of Paris), from which he drew much of the material for his portraits of society. He wrote for symbolist magazines, such as *Le Banquet* and *La Revue blanche*, and published a collection of essays, poems, and stories in an elegant book, *Pleasures and Days* (1896), but his work received relatively little attention from readers or critics. In 1899 (with his mother's help, since he knew little English), he began to translate the English social and art critic John Ruskin. He did not need to work, since his parents supported him, but he did briefly have a volunteer position at one of France's national libraries; after a few days' work, he went on permanent sick leave.

Proust is known as the author of one novel: the enormous, seven-volume exploration of time and consciousness called *In Search of Lost Time*. As early as 1895, he embarked on a shorter novel that traced the same themes and autobiographical awareness as his masterwork would, but *Jean Santeuil* (published posthumously in 1952) never found a coherent structure for its numerous episodes, and Proust abandoned it in 1899. Themes, ideas, and some episodes from the earlier novel were absorbed into *In Search of Lost Time*; the major difference (aside from length) between the two works is simply the highly sophisticated and subtle structure that Proust devised for the later one.

Proust's parents both died in 1905. The following year, his asthma worsening, he moved into a cork-lined, fumigated room in Paris, where he stayed until forced to move in 1919. From 1907 to 1914, he spent summers in the seacoast town of Cabourg (another source of material for the fictional Balbec), but when in Paris he emerged rarely from his apartment and then only late at night for dinners with friends. Proust was, he later said, "from the medical point of view, many different things, though in fact no one has ever known exactly what. But I am above all, and indisputably, an asthmatic." In an effort to control his symptoms, which he believed were exacerbated by drafts, sunlight, smells, noises, and digestive discomfort, he developed a number of rituals. For example, he ate only once a day, ordering in from high-end restaurants. He slept during the daylight hours, rising around eight in the evening and working through the night. He insisted that everything that touched his skin—bathwater, changes of clothes—had to be just his temperature, so his housekeeper kept extra shirts and long underwear in the oven.

While considering what to write next, Proust improved his style by creating a series of pastiches of great French writers. In 1909 he conceived the structure of his novel as a whole and wrote its first and last chapters together. A first draft was finished by September 1912, but Proust had difficulty finding a publisher and finally published the first volume, *Swann's Way* (*Du côte de chez Swann*), at his own expense, in 1913. Though this volume was a success, the First World War delayed publication of subsequent volumes, and Proust began the painstaking revision and enlargement of the whole manuscript (from fifteen hundred to four thousand pages,

and three to seven parts) that was to occupy him until his death. He continually added material, even as his health deteriorated, often pasting strips onto earlier pages of the manuscript so that he could present a more detailed account of a particular incident or memory. *Within a Budding Grove* (*À l'ombre des jeunes filles en fleurs,* or "In the shadow of young girls in flower") won the prestigious Goncourt Prize in 1919, and *The Guermantes Way* (*Le Côté de Guermantes*) followed, in 1920–21. The last volume published in Proust's lifetime was *Sodom and Gomorrah* (*Sodome et Gomorrhe II,* 1922), and the remaining volumes—*The Captive* (*La Prisonnière,* 1923), *The Fugitive* (*Albertine disparue,* or "Albertine disappeared," 1925), and *Time Regained* (*Le Temps retrouvé,* 1927)—were released posthumously from manuscripts on which he had been working.

Throughout 1922, Proust's symptoms, particularly nausea, vomiting, and occasional delirium, grew more and more perilous. On November 18, after an especially bad week, his housekeeper, already alarmed by his deterioration, noticed the normally untidy Proust "pulling up the sheet and picking up the papers strewn over the bed." "I'd never been at a deathbed before," she later wrote, "but in our village I'd heard people say that dying men gather things." By that afternoon three doctors, including the patient's brother, Robert Proust, had determined that he had only a few hours to live. Proust died before nightfall. A man who had always looked eerily young, he preserved enough of a glow in death to allow friends and colleagues to visit the bedroom over the weekend to pay their respects. When the writer Jean Cocteau visited, he remarked on the tall stacks of notebooks near the bed: "That pile of paper on his left was still alive, like watches ticking on the wrists of dead soldiers." Proust had achieved fame and was buried with military honors as a knight of the French Legion of Honor.

The selection presented here, from "Combray," is the first section of the first volume of *In Search of Lost Time*. Written almost completely in the first person and based on events in the author's life (although by no means purely autobiographical), the novel is famous both for its evocation of the closed world of Parisian society at the turn of the century and as a meditation on time. Proust was homosexual, and homosexuality eventually became a major theme in his writing. He once told another gay French writer, André Gide, that in a novel or short story one could say whatever one wanted about sexuality as long as the words were those of a fictional character: "never say I." Although the first-person pronoun appears on most pages of his novel, homosexuality is attributed to many characters but never to the narrator; likewise, in a novel with a number of Jewish characters, the narrator does not share Proust's religious heritage. Indeed, Proust took the events of his life and the traits of people he knew and rearranged them, combining them into fictional composites.

When *Swann's Way* appeared, in 1913, it was immediately seen as a new kind of fiction. Unlike nineteenth-century novels such as **Flaubert**'s **Madame Bovary,** *In Search of Lost Time* has no clear and continuous plotline building to a denouement, nor (until the final volume, published in 1927) could the reader detect a consistent development of the central character, Marcel. Proust's plot acquires purpose only gradually, through the interconnection of several themes. Likewise, the characters, Marcel included, are not sketched in fully from the beginning, but rather are revealed piece by piece, evolving within the distinctive perspectives of individual chapters. Only at the end does the narrator recognize the meaning and value of what has preceded, and

when he retells his story, he does so not from an omniscient, explanatory point of view but as the reliving and gradual assessment of Marcel's lifelong experience. Most of the novel sets forth a roughly chronological sequence of events, yet its opening pages swing through recollections of times and places before settling on the narrator's childhood in Combray. The second section, *Swann in Love (Un Amour de Swann)*, recounts the story of the title character in the third person. Thus the novel proceeds by apparently discontinuous blocks of recollection, bound together by the central consciousness of the narrator. This was always Proust's plan: he insisted that, from the beginning, he had in mind a fixed structure and a goal for the novel in its entirety that would reach down to the "solidity of the smallest parts." Still, his substantial revisions and expansion of the first draft enriched the existing structure; and as he was writing, history intruded: he moved the location of the fictional Combary to the front lines in order to include the war.

The overall theme of the novel is suggested by the translation of its title: "In Search of Lost Time." The narrator, "Marcel," who suggests but is not identical to the author, is an old man, weakened by a long illness, who puzzles over the events of his past, trying to find in them a significant pattern. He begins with his childhood, orderly and comfortable in the security of accepted manners and ideals in the family home at Combray. In succeeding volumes Marcel goes out into the world, experiences love and disappointment, discovers the disparity between idealized images of places and their crude, sometimes banal reality, and is increasingly overcome by disillusionment with himself and with society.

In the short ending chapter, things suddenly come into focus as Marcel reaches an understanding of the role of time. Abruptly reliving a childhood experience when he sees a familiar book and recognizing the ravages of time in the aged and enfeebled figures of his old friends, Marcel faces the approach of death with a sense of existential continuity and realizes that his vocation as an artist lies in giving form to this buried existence. Apparently lost, the past is still alive within us, a part of our being, and memory can recapture it to give coherence and depth to present identity. By the end of the last volume, *Time Regained,* Marcel has not yet begun to write, but paradoxically the book that he plans to write is already there: Proust's *In Search of Lost Time.*

"Swann's Way" is one of the two directions in which Marcel's family took walks from their home in Combray, toward Tansonville, home of Charles Swann, and is associated with various scenes and anecdotes of love and private life. The longer walk toward the estate of the Guermantes (*The Guermantes Way*), a fictional family of the highest aristocracy appearing frequently in the novel, evokes an aura of high society and French history, a more public sphere. Fictional people and places mingle throughout with the real; here, names that are not annotated are Proust's inventions. The narrator of "Combray" is Marcel as an old man, and the French verb tense used in his recollections (here and throughout all but the final volume) is appropriately the imperfect, a tense of uncompleted action ("I used to . . . I would ask myself"). The famous first sentence points to a period in the narrator's life that is both private and somehow universal: "For a long time, I went to bed early." He would often wake up unsure where he was, what year it was, and even who he was. Proust then presents a kaleidoscopic vision of the many bedrooms where his narrator will sleep during the course of the novel, thus plunging the reader into the fictional world and demonstrating the instability of time and space.

The first chapter of "Combray" introduces the work's themes and methods, rather like the overture of an opera. All but one of the main characters appear or are mentioned, and the patterns of future encounters are set. Marcel, waiting anxiously for his beloved mother's response to a note sent down to her during dinner, suffers the same agony of separation as does Swann in his love for the promiscuous Odette, or the older Marcel himself for Albertine. The strange world of half-sleep, half-waking with which the novel begins prefigures later awakenings of memory. Long passages of intricate introspection, and sudden shifts of time and space, introduce us to the style and point of view of the rest of the book.

The selection ends with Proust's most famous image, summing up for many readers the world, the style, and the process of discovery of the author's vision. Nibbling at a madeleine (a small, rich cookielike pastry) that he has dipped in lime-blossom tea, Marcel suddenly has an overwhelming feeling of happiness. He soon associates this tantalizing, puzzling phenomenon with the memory of earlier times when he sipped tea with his aunt Leonie. He realizes that there is something valuable about such passive, spontaneous, and sensuous memory, quite different from the abstract operations of reason. Although the Marcel of "Combray" does not yet know it, he will pursue the elusive significance of this moment of happiness until, in *Time Regained,* he can, as a complete artist, bring it to the surface and link past and present in a fuller and richer vision.

Proust's novel has a unique architectural design that integrates large blocks of material: themes, situations, places, and events recur and are transformed across time. His long sentences and mammoth paragraphs reflect the slow, careful progression of thought among the changing objects of its perception. The ending paragraph of the "overture" is composed of two long sentences that encompass a wide range of meditative detail as the narrator not only recalls his childhood world—the old gray house, garden, public square and country roads, Swann's park, the river, the villagers, and indeed the whole town of Combray—but simultaneously compares the sudden recollection of the house to a stage set, and the unfolding village itself to the twists and turns of a Japanese paper flower expanding inside a bowl of water: here, inside the narrator's cup of lime-blossom tea. Characters are remembered in shifting settings and perspectives, creating a "multiple self" that is free to change and still remain the same.

Swann's Way[1]

Part 1. Combray

I

For a long time, I went to bed early. Sometimes, my candle scarcely out, my eyes would close so quickly that I did not have time to say to myself: "I'm falling asleep." And, half an hour later, the thought that it was time to try to sleep would wake me; I wanted to put down the book I thought I still had in my hands and blow out my light; I had not ceased while sleeping to form reflections on what I had just read, but these reflections had taken a rather peculiar turn; it seemed to me that I myself was what the book was talking about: a church, a quartet, the rivalry between François I and Charles V.[2] This belief lived on for a few seconds after my waking; it did not shock my reason but lay heavy like scales on my eyes and kept them from realizing that the candlestick was no longer lit. Then it began to grow unintelligible to me, as after metempsychosis do the thoughts of an earlier existence; the subject of the book detached itself from me, I was free to apply myself to it or not; immediately I recovered my sight and I was amazed to find a darkness around me soft and restful for the eyes, but perhaps even more so for my mind, to which it appeared a thing without cause, incomprehensible, a thing truly dark. I would ask myself what time it might be; I could hear the whistling of the trains which, remote or nearby, like the singing of a bird in a forest, plotting the distances, described to me the extent of the deserted countryside where the traveler hastens toward the nearest station; and the little road he is following will be engraved on his memory by the excitement he owes to new places, to unaccustomed activities, to the recent conversation and the farewells under the unfamiliar lamp that follow him still through the silence of the night, to the imminent sweetness of his return.

I would rest my cheeks tenderly against the lovely cheeks of the pillow, which, full and fresh, are like the cheeks of our childhood. I would strike a match to look at my watch. Nearly midnight. This is the hour when the invalid

1. Translated by Lydia Davis.
2. Francis I (1496–1567), king of France, and Charles V (1500–1558), Holy Roman emperor and king of Spain, fought four wars over the empire's expansion in Europe.

who has been obliged to go off on a journey and has had to sleep in an unfamiliar hotel, wakened by an attack, is cheered to see a ray of light under the door. How fortunate, it's already morning! In a moment the servants will be up, he will be able to ring, someone will come help him. The hope of being relieved gives him the courage to suffer. In fact he thought he heard footsteps; the steps approach, then recede. And the ray of light that was under his door has disappeared. It is midnight; they have just turned off the gas; the last servant has gone and he will have to suffer the whole night through without remedy.

I would go back to sleep, and would sometimes afterward wake again for brief moments only, long enough to hear the organic creak of the woodwork, open my eyes and stare at the kaleidoscope of the darkness, savor in a momentary glimmer of consciousness the sleep into which were plunged the furniture, the room, that whole of which I was only a small part and whose insensibility I would soon return to share. Or else while sleeping I had effortlessly returned to a period of my early life that had ended forever, rediscovered one of my childish terrors such as my great-uncle pulling me by my curls, a terror dispelled on the day—the dawn for me of a new era—when they were cut off. I had forgotten that event during my sleep, I recovered its memory as soon as I managed to wake myself up to escape the hands of my great-uncle, but as a precautionary measure I would completely surround my head with my pillow before returning to the world of dreams.

Sometimes, as Eve was born from one of Adam's ribs, a woman was born during my sleep from a cramped position of my thigh. Formed from the pleasure I was on the point of enjoying, she, I imagined, was the one offering it to me. My body, which felt in hers my own warmth, would try to find itself inside her, I would wake up. The rest of humanity seemed very remote compared with this woman I had left scarcely a few moments before; my cheek was still warm from her kiss, my body aching from the weight of hers. If, as sometimes happened, she had the features of a woman I had known in life, I would devote myself entirely to this end: to finding her again, like those who go off on a journey to see a longed-for city with their own eyes and imagine that one can enjoy in reality the charm of a dream. Little by little the memory of her would fade, I had forgotten the girl of my dream.

A sleeping man holds in a circle around him the sequence of the hours, the order of the years and worlds. He consults them instinctively as he wakes and reads in a second the point on the earth he occupies, the time that has elapsed before his waking; but their ranks can be mixed up, broken. If toward morning, after a bout of insomnia, sleep overcomes him as he is reading, in a position quite different from the one in which he usually sleeps, his raised arm alone is enough to stop the sun and make it retreat,[3] and, in the first minute of his waking, he will no longer know what time it is, he will think he has only just gone to bed. If he dozes off in a position still more displaced and divergent, after dinner sitting in an armchair for instance, then the confusion among the disordered worlds will be complete, the magic armchair will send him traveling at top speed through time and space, and, at the moment of opening his eyelids, he will believe he went to bed several months earlier in another country. But it was enough if, in my own bed, my sleep was deep and allowed my mind to relax

---

3. If his uplifted arm prevents him from seeing the sunlight, he will think it is still night.

entirely; then it would let go of the map of the place where I had fallen asleep and, when I woke in the middle of the night, since I did not know where I was, I did not even understand in the first moment who I was; I had only, in its original simplicity, the sense of existence as it may quiver in the depths of an animal; I was more destitute than a cave dweller; but then the memory—not yet of the place where I was, but of several of those where I had lived and where I might have been—would come to me like help from on high to pull me out of the void from which I could not have got out on my own; I crossed centuries of civilization in one second, and the image confusedly glimpsed of oil lamps, then of wingcollar shirts, gradually recomposed my self's original features.

Perhaps the immobility of the things around us is imposed on them by our certainty that they are themselves and not anything else, by the immobility of our mind confronting them. However that may be, when I woke thus, my mind restlessly attempting, without success, to discover where I was, everything revolved around me in the darkness, things, countries, years. My body, too benumbed to move, would try to locate, according to the form of its fatigue, the position of its limbs so as to deduce from this the direction of the wall, the placement of the furniture, so as to reconstruct and name the dwelling in which it found itself. Its memory, the memory of its ribs, its knees, its shoulders, offered in succession several of the rooms where it had slept, while around it the invisible walls, changing place according to the shape of the imagined room, spun through the shadows. And even before my mind, hesitating on the thresholds of times and shapes, had identified the house by reassembling the circumstances, it—my body—would recall the kind of bed in each one, the location of the doors, the angle at which the light came in through the windows, the existence of a hallway, along with the thought I had had as I fell asleep and that I had recovered upon waking. My stiffened side, trying to guess its orientation, would imagine, for instance, that it lay facing the wall in a big canopied bed and immediately I would say to myself: "Why, I went to sleep in the end even though Mama didn't come to say goodnight to me," I was in the country in the home of my grandfather, dead for many years; and my body, the side on which I was resting, faithful guardians of a past my mind ought never to have forgotten, recalled to me the flame of the night-light of Bohemian glass, in the shape of an urn, which hung from the ceiling by little chains, the mantelpiece of Siena marble,[4] in my bedroom at Combray, at my grandparents' house, in faraway days which at this moment I imagined were present without picturing them to myself exactly and which I would see more clearly in a little while when I was fully awake.

Then the memory of a new position would reappear; the wall would slip away in another direction: I was in my room at Mme. de Saint-Loup's,[5] in the country; good Lord! It's ten o'clock or even later, they will have finished dinner! I must have overslept during the nap I take every evening when I come back from my walk with Mme. de Saint-Loup, before putting on my evening clothes. For many years have passed since Combray, where, however late we returned,

4. Marble from central Italy, mottled and reddish in color. "Bohemian glass": likely to have been ornately engraved. Bohemia (now part of the Czech Republic) was a major center of the glass industry.
5. Charles Swann's daughter, Gilberte, who has married Robert de Saint-Loup, a nephew of the Guermantes.

it was the sunset's red reflections I saw in the panes of my window. It is another sort of life one leads at Tansonville, at Mme. de Saint-Loup's, another sort of pleasure I take in going out only at night, in following by moonlight those lanes where I used to play in the sun; and the room where I fell asleep instead of dressing for dinner—from far off I can see it, as we come back, pierced by the flares of the lamp, a lone beacon in the night.

These revolving, confused evocations never lasted for more than a few seconds; often, in my brief uncertainty about where I was, I did not distinguish the various suppositions of which it was composed any better than we isolate, when we see a horse run, the successive positions shown to us by a kinetoscope.[6] But I had seen sometimes one, sometimes another, of the bedrooms I had inhabited in my life, and in the end I would recall them all in the long reveries that followed my waking: winter bedrooms in which, as soon as you are in bed, you bury your head in a nest braided of the most disparate things: a corner of the pillow, the top of the covers, a bit of shawl, the side of the bed and an issue of the *Débats roses*,[7] which you end by cementing together using the birds' technique of pressing down on it indefinitely; where in icy weather the pleasure you enjoy is the feeling that you are separated from the outdoors (like the sea swallow which makes its nest deep in an underground passage in the warmth of the earth) and where, since the fire is kept burning all night in the fireplace, you sleep in a great cloak of warm, smoky air, shot with the glimmers from the logs breaking into flame again, a sort of immaterial alcove, a warm cave dug out of the heart of the room itself, a zone of heat with shifting thermal contours, aerated by drafts which cool your face and come from the corners, from the parts close to the window or far from the hearth, and which have grown cold again: summer bedrooms where you delight in becoming one with the soft night, where the moonlight leaning against the half-open shutters casts its enchanted ladder to the foot of the bed, where you sleep almost in the open air, like a titmouse rocked by the breeze on the tip of a ray of light; sometimes the Louis XVI[8] bedroom, so cheerful that even on the first night I had not been too unhappy there and where the slender columns that lightly supported the ceiling stood aside with such grace to show and reserve the place where the bed was; at other times, the small bedroom with the very high ceiling, hollowed out in the form of a pyramid two stories high and partly paneled in mahogany, where from the first second I had been mentally poisoned by the unfamiliar odor of the vetiver,[9] convinced of the hostility of the violet curtains and the insolent indifference of the clock chattering loudly as though I were not there; where a strange and pitiless quadrangular cheval glass, barring obliquely one of the corners of the room, carved from deep inside the soft fullness of my usual field of vision a site for itself which I had not expected; where my mind, struggling for hours to dislodge itself, to stretch upward so as to assume the exact shape of the room and succeed in filling its gigantic funnel to the very top, had suffered many hard nights, while I lay stretched out in my bed, my eyes lifted, my ear anxious, my nostril

6. An early moving-picture machine that showed photographs in rapid succession, giving the illusion of motion.
7. The evening edition of the daily newspaper *Le Journal des Débats*.

8. Furnished in late 18th-century style, named for the French king of the time and marked by great elegance.
9. The aromatic root of a tropical grass packaged as a moth repellent.

restive, my heart pounding, until habit had changed the color of the curtains, silenced the clock, taught pity to the cruel oblique mirror, concealed, if not driven out completely, the smell of the vetiver and appreciably diminished the apparent height of the ceiling. Habit! That skillful but very slow housekeeper who begins by letting our mind suffer for weeks in a temporary arrangement; but whom we are nevertheless truly happy to discover, for without habit our mind, reduced to no more than its own resources, would be powerless to make a lodging habitable.

Certainly I was now wide-awake, my body had veered around one last time and the good angel of certainty had brought everything around me to a standstill, laid me down under my covers, in my bedroom, and put approximately where they belonged in the darkness my chest of drawers, my desk, my fireplace, the window onto the street and the two doors. But even though I knew I was not in any of the houses of which my ignorance upon waking had instantly, if not presented me with the distinct picture, at least made me believe the presence possible, my memory had been stirred; generally I would not try to go back to sleep right away; I would spend the greater part of the night remembering our life in the old days, in Combray at my great-aunt's house, in Balbec,[1] in Paris, in Doncières, in Venice, elsewhere still, remembering the places, the people I had known there, what I had seen of them, what I had been told about them.

At Combray, every day, in the late afternoon, long before the moment when I would have to go to bed and stay there, without sleeping, far away from my mother and grandmother, my bedroom again became the fixed and painful focus of my preoccupations. They had indeed hit upon the idea, to distract me on the evenings when they found me looking too unhappy, of giving me a magic lantern,[2] which, while awaiting the dinner hour, they would set on top of my lamp; and, after the fashion of the first architects and master glaziers of the Gothic age, it replaced the opacity of the walls with impalpable iridescences, supernatural multicolored apparitions, where legends were depicted as in a wavering, momentary stained-glass window. But my sadness was only increased by this since the mere change in lighting destroyed the familiarity which my bedroom had acquired for me and which, except for the torment of going to bed, had made it tolerable to me. Now I no longer recognized it and I was uneasy there, as in a room in some hotel or "chalet" to which I had come for the first time straight from the railway train.

Moving at the jerky pace of his horse, and filled with a hideous design, Golo[3] would come out of the small triangular forest that velveted the hillside with dark green and advance jolting toward the castle of poor Geneviève de Brabant. This castle was cut off along a curved line that was actually the edge of one of the glass ovals arranged in the frame which you slipped between the grooves of the lantern. It was only a section of castle and it had a moor in front of it where Geneviève stood dreaming, wearing a blue belt. The castle and the moor were yellow, and I had not had to wait to see them to find out their color

1. The narrator's room at the fictional seaside resort of Balbec, a setting in the later novel *Within a Budding Grove*.
2. A kind of slide projector.

3. Villain of a 5th-century legend. He falsely accuses Geneviève de Brabant of adultery. Brabant was a principality in what is now Belgium.

since, before the glasses of the frame did so, the bronze sonority of the name Brabant had shown it to me clearly. Golo would stop for a moment to listen sadly to the patter read out loud by my great-aunt,[4] which he seemed to understand perfectly, modifying his posture, with a meekness that did not exclude a certain majesty, to conform to the directions of the text; then he moved off at the same jerky pace. And nothing could stop his slow ride. If the lantern was moved, I could make out Golo's horse continuing to advance over the window curtains, swelling out with their folds, descending into their fissures. The body of Golo himself, in its essence as supernatural as that of his steed, accommodated every material obstacle, every hindersome object that he encountered by taking it as his skeleton and absorbing it into himself, even the doorknob he immediately adapted to and floated invincibly over with his red robe or his pale face as noble and as melancholy as ever, but revealing no disturbance at this transvertebration.

Certainly I found some charm in these brilliant projections, which seemed to emanate from a Merovingian[5] past and send out around me such ancient reflections of history. But I cannot express the uneasiness caused in me by this intrusion of mystery and beauty into a room I had at last filled with myself to the point of paying no more attention to the room than to that self. The anesthetizing influence of habit having ceased, I would begin to have thoughts, and feelings, and they are such sad things. That doorknob of my room, which differed for me from all other doorknobs in the world in that it seemed to open of its own accord, without my having to turn it, so unconscious had its handling become for me, was now serving as an astral body[6] for Golo. And as soon as they rang for dinner, I hastened to run to the dining room where the big hanging lamp, ignorant of Golo and Bluebeard,[7] and well acquainted with my family and beef casserole, shed the same light as on every other evening; and to fall into the arms of Mama, whom Geneviève de Brabant's misfortunes made all the dearer to me, while Golo's crimes drove me to examine my own conscience more scrupulously.

After dinner, alas, I soon had to leave Mama, who stayed there talking with the others, in the garden if the weather was fine, in the little drawing room to which everyone withdrew if the weather was bad. Everyone, except my grandmother, who felt that "it's a pity to shut oneself indoors in the country", and who had endless arguments with my father on days when it rained too heavily, because he sent me to read in my room instead of having me stay outdoors. "That's no way to make him strong and active," she would say sadly, "especially that boy, who so needs to build up his endurance and willpower." My father would shrug his shoulders and study the barometer, for he liked meteorology, while my mother, making no noise so as not to disturb him, watched him with a tender respect, but not so intently as to try to penetrate the mystery of his superior qualities. But as for my grandmother, in all weathers, even in a downpour when Françoise had rushed the precious wicker armchairs indoors so that

4. Marcel's great-aunt is reading the story to him as they wait for dinner.
5. The first dynasty of French kings (ca. 500–751).
6. Spiritual counterpart of the physical body. According to the doctrine of Theosophy (a

spiritualist movement originating in 1875), the astral body survives the death of the physical body.
7. The legendary wife murderer, presumably shown on another set of slides.

they would not get wet, we would see her in the empty, rain-lashed garden, pushing back her disordered gray locks so that her forehead could more freely drink in the salubriousness of the wind and rain. She would say: "At last, one can breathe!" and would roam the soaked paths—too symmetrically aligned for her liking by the new gardener, who lacked all feeling for nature and whom my father had been asking since morning if the weather would clear—with her jerky, enthusiastic little step, regulated by the various emotions excited in her soul by the intoxication of the storm, the power of good health, the stupidity of my upbringing, and the symmetry of the gardens, rather than by the desire, quite unknown to her, to spare her plum-colored skirt the spots of mud under which it would disappear up to a height that was always, for her maid, a source of despair and a problem.

When these garden walks of my grandmother's took place after dinner, one thing had the power to make her come inside again: this was—at one of the periodic intervals when her circular itinerary brought her back, like an insect, in front of the lights of the little drawing room where the liqueurs were set out on the card table—if my great-aunt called out to her: "Bathilde! Come and stop your husband from drinking cognac!" To tease her, in fact (she had brought into my father's family so different a mentality that everyone poked fun at her and tormented her), since liqueurs were forbidden to my grandfather, my great-aunt would make him drink a few drops. My poor grandmother would come in, fervently beg her husband not to taste the cognac; he would become angry, drink his mouthful despite her, and my grandmother would go off again, sad, discouraged, yet smiling, for she was so humble at heart and so gentle that her tenderness for others, and the lack of fuss she made over her own person and her sufferings, came together in her gaze in a smile in which, unlike what one sees in the faces of so many people, there was irony only for herself, and for all of us a sort of kiss from her eyes, which could not see those she cherished without caressing them passionately with her gaze. This torture which my great-aunt inflicted on her, the spectacle of my grandmother's vain entreaties and of her weakness, defeated in advance, trying uselessly to take the liqueur glass away from my grandfather, were the kinds of things which you later become so accustomed to seeing that you smile as you contemplate them and take the part of the persecutor resolutely and gaily enough to persuade yourself privately that no persecution is involved; at that time they filled me with such horror that I would have liked to hit my great-aunt. But as soon as I heard: "Bathilde, come and stop your husband from drinking cognac!," already a man in my cowardice, I did what we all do, once we are grown up, when confronted with sufferings and injustices: I did not want to see them; I went up to sob at the very top of the house next to the schoolroom,[8] under the roofs, in a little room that smelled of orris root[9] and was also perfumed by a wild black-currant bush which had sprouted outside between the stones of the wall and extended a branch of flowers through the half-open window. Intended for a more specialized and more vulgar use, this room, from which during the day you could see all the way to the keep[1] of Roussainville-le-Pin, for a long time served me as a refuge, no

---

8. A room in the house dedicated to the children's schoolwork.
9. A powder then used as a room deodorizer.

1. The best-fortified tower of a medieval castle. "Vulgar use": it was used as a toilet.

doubt because it was the only one I was permitted to lock, for all those occupations of mine that demanded an inviolable solitude: reading, reverie, tears, and sensuous pleasure. Alas! I did not know that, much more than her husband's little deviations from his regimen, it was my weak will, my delicate health, the uncertainty they cast on my future that so sadly preoccupied my grandmother in the course of those incessant perambulations, afternoon and evening, when we would see, as it passed and then passed again, lifted slantwise toward the sky, her beautiful face with its brown furrowed cheeks, which with age had become almost mauve like the plowed fields in autumn, crossed, if she was going out, by a veil half raised, while upon them, brought there by the cold or some sad thought, an involuntary tear was always drying.

My sole consolation, when I went upstairs for the night, was that Mama would come and kiss me once I was in bed. But this goodnight lasted so short a time, she went down again so soon, that the moment when I heard her coming up, then the soft sound of her garden dress of blue muslin, hung with little cords of plaited straw, passing along the hallway with its double doors, was for me a painful one. It heralded the moment that was to follow it, when she had left me, when she had gone down again. So that I came to wish that this goodnight I loved so much would take place as late as possible, so as to prolong the time of respite in which Mama had not yet come. Sometimes when, after kissing me, she opened the door to go, I wanted to call her back, to say "kiss me one more time," but I knew that immediately her face would look vexed, because the concession she was making to my sadness and agitation by coming up to kiss me, by bringing me this kiss of peace, irritated my father, who found these rituals absurd, and she would have liked to try to induce me to lose the need for it, the habit of it, far indeed from allowing me to acquire that of asking her, when she was already on the doorstep, for one kiss more. And to see her vexed destroyed all the calm she had brought me a moment before, when she had bent her loving face down over my bed and held it out to me like a host[2] for a communion of peace from which my lips would draw her real presence and the power to fall asleep. But those evenings, when Mama stayed so short a time in my room, were still sweet compared to the ones when there was company for dinner and when, because of that, she did not come up to say goodnight to me. That company was usually limited to M. Swann, who, apart from a few acquaintances passing through, was almost the only person who came to our house at Combray, sometimes for a neighborly dinner (more rarely after that unfortunate marriage of his, because my parents did not want to receive his wife), sometimes after dinner, unexpectedly. On those evenings when, as we sat in front of the house under the large chestnut tree, around the iron table, we heard at the far end of the garden, not the copious high-pitched bell that drenched, that deafened in passing with its ferruginous,[3] icy, inexhaustible noise any person in the household who set it off by coming in "without ringing," but the shy, oval, golden double tinkling of the little visitors' bell, everyone would immediately wonder: "A visitor—now who can that be?" but we knew very well it could only be M. Swann; my great-aunt speaking loudly, to set an example, in a tone of voice that she strained to make natural, said not to whisper that way; that nothing is more disagreeable for a visitor just coming

2. Communion wafer.   3. Ironlike.

in who is led to think that people are saying things he should not hear; and they would send as a scout my grandmother, who was always glad to have a pretext for taking one more walk around the garden and who would profit from it by surreptitiously pulling up a few rose stakes on the way so as to make the roses look a little more natural, like a mother who runs her hand through her son's hair to fluff it up after the barber has flattened it too much.

We would all remain hanging on the news my grandmother was going to bring us of the enemy, as though there had been a great number of possible assailants to choose among, and soon afterward my grandfather would say: "I recognize Swann's voice." In fact one could recognize him only by his voice, it was difficult to make out his face, his aquiline nose, his green eyes under a high forehead framed by blond, almost red hair, cut Bressant-style,[4] because we kept as little light as possible in the garden so as not to attract mosquitoes, and I would go off, as though not going for that reason, to say that the syrups should be brought out; my grandmother placed a great deal of importance, considering it more amiable, on the idea that they should not seem anything exceptional, and for visitors only. M. Swann, though much younger, was very attached to my grandfather, who had been one of the closest friends of his father, an excellent man but peculiar, in whom, apparently, a trifle was sometimes enough to interrupt the ardor of his feelings, to change the course of his thinking. Several times a year I would hear my grandfather at the table telling anecdotes, always the same ones, about the behavior of old M. Swann upon the death of his wife, over whom he had watched day and night. My grandfather, who had not seen him for a long time, had rushed to his side at the estate the Swanns owned in the vicinity of Combray and, so that he would not be present at the coffining, managed to entice him for a while, all in tears, out of the death chamber. They walked a short way in the park, where there was a little sunshine. Suddenly M. Swann, taking my grandfather by the arm, cried out: "Oh, my old friend, what a joy it is to be walking here together in such fine weather! Don't you think it's pretty, all these trees, these hawthorns! And my pond—which you've never congratulated me on! You look as sad as an old nightcap. Feel that little breeze? Oh, say what you like, life has something to offer despite everything, my dear Amédée!" Suddenly the memory of his dead wife came back to him and, no doubt feeling it would be too complicated to try to understand how he could have yielded to an impulse of happiness at such a time, he confined himself, in a habitual gesture of his whenever a difficult question came into his mind, to passing his hand over his forehead, wiping his eyes and the lenses of his lorgnon. Yet he could not be consoled for the death of his wife, but, during the two years he survived her, would say to my grandfather: "It's odd, I think of my poor wife often, but I can't think of her for long at a time." "Often, but only a little at a time, like poor old Swann," had become one of my grandfather's favorite phrases, which he uttered apropos of the most different sorts of things. I would have thought Swann's father was a monster, if my grandfather, whom I considered a better judge and whose pronouncement, forming a legal precedent for me, often allowed me later to dismiss offenses I might have been inclined to condemn, had not exclaimed: "What! He had a heart of gold!"

---

4. Crew cut in front and longer in back: a hair style popularized by the actor Jean-Baptiste Bressant (1815–1886).

For many years, even though, especially before his marriage, the younger M. Swann often came to see them at Combray, my great-aunt and my grandparents did not suspect that he had entirely ceased to live in the kind of society his family had frequented and that, under the sort of incognito which this name Swann gave him among us, they were harboring—with the perfect innocence of honest innkeepers who have under their roof, without knowing it, some celebrated highwayman—one of the most elegant members of the Jockey Club, a favorite friend of the Comte de Paris and the Prince of Wales, one of the men most sought after by the high society of the Faubourg Saint-Germain.[5]

Our ignorance of this brilliant social life that Swann led was obviously due in part to the reserve and discretion of his character, but also to the fact that bourgeois people in those days formed for themselves a rather Hindu notion of society and considered it to be made up of closed castes, in which each person, from birth, found himself placed in the station which his family occupied and from which nothing, except the accidents of an exceptional career or an unhoped-for marriage, could withdraw him in order to move him into a higher caste. M. Swann, the father, was a stockbroker; "Swann the son" would find he belonged for his entire life to a caste in which fortunes varied, as in a tax bracket, between such and such fixed incomes. One knew which had been his father's associations, one therefore knew which were his own, with which people he was "in a position" to consort. If he knew others, these were bachelor acquaintances on whom old friends of the family, such as my relatives, would close their eyes all the more benignly because he continued, after losing his parents, to come faithfully to see us; but we would have been ready to wager that these people he saw, who were unknown to us, were the sort he would not have dared greet had he encountered them when he was with us. If you were determined to assign Swann a social coefficient that was his alone, among the other sons of stockbrokers in a position equal to that of his parents, this coefficient would have been a little lower for him because, very simple in his manner and with a long-standing "craze" for antiques and painting, he now lived and amassed his collections in an old town house which my grandmother dreamed of visiting, but which was situated on the quai d'Orléans,[6] a part of town where my great-aunt felt it was ignominious to live. "But are you a connoisseur? I ask for your own sake, because you're likely to let the dealers unload some awful daubs on you," my great-aunt would say to him; in fact she did not assume he had any competence and even from an intellectual point of view had no great opinion of a man who in conversation avoided serious subjects and showed a most prosaic preciseness not only when he gave us cooking recipes, entering into the smallest details, but even when my grandmother's sisters talked about artistic subjects. Challenged by them to give his opinion, to express his admiration for a painting, he would maintain an almost ungracious silence and then, on the other hand, redeem himself if he could provide, about the museum in which it was to be found, about the

5. A fashionable area of Paris on the left bank of the Seine; many of the French aristocracy lived there. "Jockey Club": an exclusive men's club devoted to horse racing, opera, and other diversions. Louis-Philippe-Albert d'Orléans, comte de Paris (1838–1894), was the heir apparent to the French throne, should the monarchy ever be restored; the Prince of Wales became, in 1901, King Edward VII of England.
6. A beautiful though less fashionable section in the heart of Paris, along the Seine.

date at which it had been painted, a pertinent piece of information. But usually he would content himself with trying to entertain us by telling a new story each time about something that had just happened to him involving people selected from among those we knew, the Combray pharmacist, our cook, our coachman. Certainly these tales made my great-aunt laugh, but she could not distinguish clearly if this was because of the absurd role Swann always assigned himself or because of the wit he showed in telling them: "You are quite a character, Monsieur Swann!" Being the only rather vulgar person in our family, she took care to point out to strangers, when they were talking about Swann, that, had he wanted to, he could have lived on the boulevard Haussmann or the avenue de l'Opéra, that he was the son of M. Swann, who must have left four or five million,[7] but that this was his whim. One that she felt moreover must be so amusing to others that in Paris, when M. Swann came on New Year's Day to bring her her bag of marrons glacés,[8] she never failed, if there was company, to say to him: "Well, Monsieur Swann! Do you still live next door to the wine warehouse, so as to be sure of not missing the train when you go to Lyon?"[9] And she would look out of the corner of her eye, over her lorgnon, at the other visitors.

But if anyone had told my great-aunt that this same Swann, who, as the son of old M. Swann, was perfectly "qualified" to be received by all the "best of the bourgeoisie," by the most respected notaries or lawyers of Paris (a hereditary privilege he seemed to make little use of), had, as though in secret, quite a different life; that on leaving our house, in Paris, after telling us he was going home to bed, he retraced his steps as soon as he had turned the corner and went to a certain drawing room that no eye of any broker or broker's associate would ever contemplate, this would have seemed to my aunt as extraordinary as might to a better-educated lady the thought of being personally on close terms with Aristaeus[1] and learning that, after having a chat with her, he would go deep into the heart of the realms of Thetis, into an empire hidden from mortal eyes, where Virgil shows him being received with open arms; or—to be content with an image that had more chance of occurring to her, for she had seen it painted on our petits-fours plates at Combray—of having had as a dinner guest Ali Baba,[2] who, as soon as he knows he is alone, will enter the cave dazzling with unsuspected treasure.

One day when he had come to see us in Paris after dinner apologizing for being in evening clothes, Françoise having said, after he left, that she had learned from the coachman that he had dined "at the home of a princess," "Yes, a princess of the demimonde!"[3] my aunt had responded, shrugging her shoulders without raising her eyes from her knitting, with serene irony.

---

7. I.e., francs—nearly $1 million in the currency of the day, about $19 million in 2011. (The franc has since been replaced by the euro.) "Boulevard Haussmann" and "avenue de l'Opéra": large modern avenues where the wealthy bourgeoisie liked to live.
8. Candied chestnuts, a traditional Parisian New Year's gift.
9. The wine warehouse was close to the Gare de Lyon, the terminal from which trains left for the industrial city of Lyon and other desti-

nations in southeastern France.
1. Son of the Greek god Apollo. In Virgil's *Fourth Georgic*, Aristacus seeks help from the sea nymph Thetis.
2. Hero of an *Arabian Nights* tale, a poor youth who discovers a robbers' cave filled with treasure.
3. Literally, "half-world" (French): women of questionable reputation, not quite members of society.

Thus, my great-aunt was cavalier in her treatment of him. Since she believed he must be flattered by our invitations, she found it quite natural that he never came to see us in the summertime without having in his hand a basket of peaches or raspberries from his garden and that from each of his trips to Italy he would bring me back photographs of masterpieces.

They did not hesitate to send him off in search of it when they needed a recipe for gribiche sauce[4] or pineapple salad for large dinners to which they had not invited him, believing he did not have sufficient prestige for one to be able to serve him up to acquaintances who were coming for the first time. If the conversation turned to the princes of the House of France:[5] "people you and I will never know, will we, and we can manage quite well without that, can't we," my great-aunt would say to Swann, who had, perhaps, a letter from Twickenham[6] in his pocket; she had him push the piano around and turn the pages on the evenings when my grandmother's sister sang, handling this creature, who was elsewhere so sought after, with the naive roughness of a child who plays with a collector's curio no more carefully than with some object of little value. No doubt the Swann who was known at the same time to so many clubmen was quite different from the one created by my great-aunt, when in the evening, in the little garden at Combray, after the two hesitant rings of the bell had sounded, she injected and invigorated with all that she knew about the Swann family the dark and uncertain figure who emerged, followed by my grandmother, from a background of shadows, and whom we recognized by his voice. But even with respect to the most insignificant things in life, none of us constitutes a material whole, identical for everyone, which a person has only to go look up as though we were a book of specifications or a last testament; our social personality is a creation of the minds of others. Even the very simple act that we call "seeing a person we know" is in part an intellectual one. We fill the physical appearance of the individual we see with all the notions we have about him, and of the total picture that we form for ourselves, these notions certainly occupy the greater part. In the end they swell his cheeks so perfectly, follow the line of his nose in an adherence so exact, they do so well at nuancing the sonority of his voice as though the latter were only a transparent envelope that each time we see this face and hear this voice, it is these notions that we encounter again, that we hear. No doubt, in the Swann they had formed for themselves, my family had failed out of ignorance to include a host of details from his life in the fashionable world that caused other people, when they were in his presence, to see refinements rule his face and stop at his aquiline nose as though at their natural frontier; but they had also been able to garner in this face disaffected of its prestige, vacant and spacious, in the depths of these depreciated eyes, the vague, sweet residue—half memory, half forgetfulness— of the idle hours spent together after our weekly dinners, around the card table or in the garden, during our life of good country neighborliness. The corporeal

4. A seasoned mayonnaise that includes chopped hard-boiled eggs.
5. The French royal family, headed by the comte de Paris. The political climate was anti-royalist, and all claimants to the French throne and their heirs were banished from France by law in 1886.
6. Fashionable London suburb. The French royal family had a house there, which was, for some time, the residence of the exiled comte de Paris.

envelope of our friend had been so well stuffed with all this, as well as with a few memories relating to his parents, that this particular Swann had become a complete and living being, and I have the impression of leaving one person to go to another distinct from him, when, in my memory, I pass from the Swann I knew later with accuracy to that first Swann—to that first Swann in whom I rediscover the charming mistakes of my youth and who in fact resembles less the other Swann than he resembles the other people I knew at the time, as though one's life were like a museum in which all the portraits from one period have a family look about them, a single tonality—to that first Swann abounding in leisure, fragrant with the smell of the tall chestnut tree, the baskets of raspberries, and a sprig of tarragon.

Yet one day when my grandmother had gone to ask a favor from a lady she had known at the Sacré-Coeur[7] (and with whom, because of our notion of the castes, she had not wished to remain in close contact despite a reciprocal congeniality), this lady, the Marquise de Villeparisis of the famous de Bouillon family, had said to her: "I believe you know M. Swann very well; he is a great friend of my nephew and niece, the des Laumes."[8] My grandmother had returned from her visit full of enthusiasm for the house, which overlooked some gardens and in which Mme. de Villeparisis had advised her to rent a flat, and also for a waistcoat maker and his daughter, who kept a shop in the courtyard where she had gone to ask them to put a stitch in her skirt, which she had torn in the stairwell. My grandmother had found these people wonderful, she declared that the girl was a gem and the waistcoat maker was most distinguished, the finest man she had ever seen. Because for her, distinction was something absolutely independent of social position. She went into ecstasies over an answer the waistcoat maker had given her, saying to Mama: "Sévigné[9] couldn't have said it any better!" and, in contrast, of a nephew of Mme. de Villeparisis whom she had met at the house: "Oh, my dear daughter, how common he is!"

Now the remark about Swann had had the effect, not of raising him in my great-aunt's estimation, but of lowering Mme. de Villeparisis. It seemed that the respect which, on my grandmother's faith, we accorded Mme. de Villeparisis created a duty on her part to do nothing that would make her less worthy, a duty in which she had failed by learning of Swann's existence, by permitting relatives of hers to associate with him. "What! She knows Swann? A person you claim is a relation of the Maréchal de MacMahon?"[1] My family's opinion regarding Swann's associations seemed confirmed later by his marriage to a woman of the worst social station, practically a cocotte, whom, what was more, he never attempted to introduce, continuing to come to our house alone, though less and less, but from whom they believed they could judge—assuming

---

7. A convent school in Paris, attended by daughters of the aristocracy and the wealthy bourgeoisie.
8. A fictional family, like the Guermantes. Proust strengthens the apparent reality of the Guermantes family, including the marquise de Villeparis, by relating them to the historical house of Bouillon, a famous aristocratic family that could trace its descent from the Middle Ages.
9. The marquise de Sévigné (1626–1696), known for her lively style in letters that described contemporary events and the life of the aristocracy.
1. Marshal of France (1808–1893), elected president of the French Republic in 1873.

it was there that he had found her—the social circle, unknown to them, that he habitually frequented.

But one time, my grandfather read in a newspaper that M. Swann was one of the most faithful guests at the Sunday lunches given by the Duc de X . . ., whose father and uncle had been the most prominent statesmen in the reign of Louis-Philippe.[2] Now, my grandfather was interested in all the little facts that could help him enter imaginatively into the private lives of men like Molé, the Duc Pasquier, the Duc de Broglie.[3] He was delighted to learn that Swann associated with people who had known them. My great-aunt, however, interpreted this news in a sense unfavorable to Swann: anyone who chose his associations outside the caste into which he had been born, outside his social "class," suffered in her eyes a regrettable lowering of his social position. It seemed to her that he gave up forthwith the fruit of all the good relations with well-placed people so honorably preserved and stored away for their children by foresightful families (my great-aunt had even stopped seeing the son of a lawyer we knew because he had married royalty and was therefore in her opinion demoted from the respected rank of lawyer's son to that of one of those adventurers, former valets or stableboys, on whom they say that queens sometimes bestowed their favors). She disapproved of my grandfather's plan to question Swann, the next evening he was to come to dinner, about these friends of his we had discovered. At the same time my grandmother's two sisters, old maids who shared her nobility of character, but not her sort of mind, declared that they could not understand what pleasure their brother-in-law could find in talking about such foolishness. They were women of lofty aspirations, who for that very reason were incapable of taking an interest in what is known as tittle-tattle, even if it had some historic interest, and more generally in anything that was not directly connected to an aesthetic or moral subject. The disinterestedness of their minds was such, with respect to all that, closely or distantly, seemed connected with worldly matters, that their sense of hearing—having finally understood its temporary uselessness when the conversation at dinner assumed a tone that was frivolous or merely pedestrian without these two old spinsters being able to lead it back to the subjects dear to them—would suspend the functioning of its receptive organs and allow them to begin to atrophy. If my grandfather needed to attract the two sisters' attention at such times, he had to resort to those bodily signals used by alienists with certain lunatics suffering from distraction: striking a glass repeatedly with the blade of a knife while speaking to them sharply and looking them suddenly in the eye, violent methods which these psychiatrists often bring with them into their ordinary relations with healthy people, either from professional habit or because they believe everyone is a little crazy.

They were more interested when, the day before Swann was to come to dinner, and had personally sent them a case of Asti wine, my aunt, holding a copy

2. King of France from 1830 to 1848, father of the comte de Paris.
3. Achille-Charles-Léon-Victor, duc de Broglie (1785–1870) had a busy public career that ended in 1851. Louis-Mathieu, comte Molé (1781–1855) held various cabinet positions before becoming premier of France in 1836. Duc Etienne-Denis Pasquier (1767–1862) also held important public positions up to 1837. All three were active during the reign of Louis-Philippe.

of the *Figaro*[4] in which next to the title of a painting in an exhibition of Corot,[5] these words appeared: "From the collection of M. Charles Swann," said: "Did you see this? Swann is 'front page news' in the *Figaro*." "But I've always told you he had a great deal of taste," said my grandmother. "Of course you would! Anything so long as your opinion is not the same as *ours*," answered my great-aunt, who, knowing that my grandmother was never of the same opinion as she, and not being quite sure that she herself was the one we always declared was right, wanted to extract from us a general condemnation of my grandmother's convictions against which she was trying to force us into solidarity with her own. But we remained silent. When my grandmother's sisters expressed their intention of speaking to Swann about this mention in the *Figaro*, my great-aunt advised them against it. Whenever she saw in others an advantage, however small, that she did not have, she persuaded herself that it was not an advantage but a detriment and she pitied them so as not to have to envy them. "I believe you would not be pleasing him at all; I am quite sure I would find it very unpleasant to see my name printed boldly like that in the newspaper, and I would not be at all gratified if someone spoke to me about it." But she did not persist in trying to convince my grandmother's sisters; for they in their horror of vulgarity had made such a fine art of concealing a personal allusion beneath ingenious circumlocutions that it often went unnoticed even by the person to whom it was addressed. As for my mother, she thought only of trying to persuade my father to agree to talk to Swann not about his wife but about his daughter, whom he adored and because of whom it was said he had finally entered into this marriage. "You might just say a word to him; just ask how she is: It must be so hard for him." But my father would become annoyed: "No, no; you have the most absurd ideas. It would be ridiculous."

But the only one of us for whom Swann's arrival became the object of a painful preoccupation was I. This was because on the evenings when strangers, or merely M. Swann, were present, Mama did not come up to my room. I had dinner before everyone else and afterward I came and sat at the table, until eight o'clock when it was understood that I had to go upstairs; the precious and fragile kiss that Mama usually entrusted to me in my bed when I was going to sleep I would have to convey from the dining room to my bedroom and protect during the whole time I undressed, so that its sweetness would not shatter, so that its volatile essence would not disperse and evaporate, and on precisely those evenings when I needed to receive it with more care, I had to take it, I had to snatch it brusquely, publicly, without even having the time and the freedom of mind necessary to bring to what I was doing the attention of those individuals controlled by some mania, who do their utmost not to think of anything else while they are shutting a door, so as to be able, when the morbid uncertainty returns to them, to confront it victoriously with the memory of the moment when they did shut the door. We were all in the garden when the two hesitant rings of the little bell sounded. We knew it was Swann; even so we all looked at one another questioningly and my grandmother was sent on reconnaissance. "Remember to thank him intelligibly for the wine, you know how delicious it is and the case is enormous," my grandfather exhorted his two sisters-in-law. "Don't start whispering,"

4. A leading Parisian newspaper. "Asti": an Italian white wine.

5. Jean-Baptiste-Camille Corot (1796–1875), a popular French landscape painter.

said my great-aunt. "How comfortable would you feel arriving at a house where everyone is speaking so quietly!" "Ah! Here's M. Swann. Let's ask him if he thinks the weather will be good tomorrow," said my father. My mother thought that one word from her would wipe out all the pain that we in our family might have caused Swann since his marriage. She found an opportunity to take him aside. But I followed her; I could not bring myself to part from her by even one step while thinking that very soon I would have to leave her in the dining room and that I would have to go up to my room without having the consolation I had on the other evenings, that she would come kiss me. "Now, M. Swann," she said to him, "do tell me about your daughter; I'm sure she already has a taste for beautiful things like her papa." "Here, come and sit with the rest of us on the veranda," said my grandfather, coming up to them. My mother was obliged to stop, but she derived from this very constraint one more delicate thought, like good poets forced by the tyranny of rhyme to find their most beautiful lines: "We can talk about her again when we're by ourselves," she said softly to Swann. "Only a mother is capable of understanding you. I'm sure her own mother would agree with me." We all sat down around the iron table. I would have preferred not to think about the hours of anguish I was going to endure that evening alone in my room without being able to go to sleep; I tried to persuade myself they were not at all important, since I would have forgotten them by tomorrow morning, and to fix my mind on ideas of the future that should have led me as though across a bridge beyond the imminent abyss that frightened me so. But my mind, strained by my preoccupation, convex like the glance which I shot at my mother, would not allow itself to be penetrated by any foreign impressions. Thoughts certainly entered it, but only on condition that they left outside every element of beauty or simply of playfulness that could have moved or distracted me. Just as a patient, by means of an anesthetic, can watch with complete lucidity the operation being performed on him, but without feeling anything, I could recite to myself some lines that I loved or observe the efforts my grandfather made to talk to Swann about the Duc d'Audiffret-Pasquier,[6] without the former making me feel any emotion, the latter any hilarity. Those efforts were fruitless. Scarcely had my grandfather asked Swann a question relating to that orator than one of my grandmother's sisters, in whose ears the question was resonating like a profound but untimely silence that should be broken for the sake of politeness, would address the other: "Just imagine, Céline,[7] I've met a young Swedish governess who has been telling me about cooperatives in the Scandinavian countries; the details are most interesting. We really must have her here for dinner one evening." "Certainly!" answered her sister Flora, "but I haven't been wasting my time either. At M. Vinteuil's I met a learned old man who knows Maubant[8] very well, and Maubant has explained to him in the greatest detail how he creates his parts. It's most interesting. He's a neighbor of M. Vinteuil's, I had no idea; and he's very nice." "M. Vinteuil isn't the only one who has nice neighbors," exclaimed my aunt Céline in a voice amplified by her shyness and given an artificial tone by her premeditation, while casting at Swann what she called a mean-

---

6. The duc d'Audiffret-Pasquier (1823–1905) was president of the Chamber of Peers during the reign of Louis-Philippe.
7. A misprint—as the context makes clear, it is Céline who speaks and Flora who responds.
8. Henri-Polydore Maubant (1823–1902), an actor at the Comédie Française. "Vinteuil": a fictitious composer.

ingful look. At the same time my aunt Flora, who had understood that this phrase was Céline's way of thanking Swann for the Asti, was also looking at Swann with an expression that combined congratulation and irony, either simply to emphasize her sister's witticism, or because she envied Swann for having inspired it, or because she could not help making fun of him since she thought he was being put on the spot. "I think we can manage to persuade the old gentleman to come for dinner," continued Flora; "when you get him started on Maubant or Mme. Materna,[9] he talks for hours without stopping." "That must be delightful," sighed my grandfather, in whose mind, unfortunately, nature had as completely failed to include the possibility of taking a passionate interest in Swedish cooperatives or the creation of Maubant's parts as it had forgotten to furnish those of my grandmother's sisters with the little grain of salt one must add oneself, in order to find some savor in it, to a story about the private life of Molé or the Comte de Paris. "Now, then," said Swann to my grandfather, "what I'm going to say has more to do than it might appear with what you were asking me, because in certain respects things haven't changed enormously. This morning I was rereading something in Saint-Simon[1] that would have amused you. It's in the volume about his mission to Spain; it's not one of the best, hardly more than a journal, but at least it's a marvelously well written one, which already makes it rather fundamentally different from the deadly boring journals we think we have to read every morning and evening." "I don't agree, there are days when reading the papers seems to me very pleasant indeed . . ." my aunt Flora interrupted, to show that she had read the sentence about Swann's Corot in Le Figaro. "When they talk about things or people that interest us!" said my aunt Céline, going one better. "I don't deny it," answered Swann with surprise. "What I fault the newspapers for is that day after day they draw our attention to insignificant things whereas only three or four times in our lives do we read a book in which there is something really essential. Since we tear the band off the newspaper so feverishly every morning, they ought to change things and put into the newspaper, oh, I don't know, perhaps . . . Pascal's *Pensées*![2] (He isolated this word with an ironic emphasis so as not to seem pedantic.) "And then, in the gilt-edged volume that we open only once in ten years," he added, showing the disdain for worldly matters affected by certain worldly men, "we would read that the Queen of Greece has gone to Cannes or that the Princesse de Léon has given a costume ball. This way, the proper proportions would be reestablished." But, feeling sorry he had gone so far as to speak even lightly of serious things: "What a lofty conversation we're having," he said ironically; "I don't know why we're climbing to such 'heights' "—and turning to my grandfather: "Well, Saint-Simon describes how Maulévrier[3] had the audacity to offer to shake hands with Saint-Simon's sons.

9. Amalie Materna (1845–1918), Austrian soprano who took part in the premiere of Wagner's *Ring* cycle at Bayreuth in 1876.
1. The memoirs of the duc de Saint-Simon (1675–1755) describe court life and intrigue during the reigns of Louis XIV and Louis XV. He was sent to Spain in 1721 to arrange the marriage of Louis XV to the daughter of the king of Spain.
2. The *Thoughts* of the religious philosopher

Blaise Pascal (1623–1662) are comments on the human condition and one of the major works of French classicism.
3. Jean-Baptiste-Louis Andrault, marquis de Maulévrier-Langeron (1677–1754), the French ambassador to Spain. Saint-Simon considered him of inferior birth and would not let his own children shake Maulévrier's hand (*Memoirs*, vol. 39).

You know, this is the same Maulévrier of whom he says: 'Never did I see in that thick bottle anything but ill-humor, vulgarity, and foolishness.'" "Thick or not, I know some bottles in which there is something quite different," said Flora vivaciously, determined that she too should thank Swann, because the gift of Asti was addressed to both of them. Céline laughed. Swann, disconcerted, went on: "'I cannot say whether it was ignorance or a trap,' wrote Saint-Simon. 'He tried to shake hands with my children. I noticed it in time to prevent him.'" My grandfather was already in ecstasies over "ignorance or a trap," but Mlle. Céline, in whom the name of Saint-Simon—a literary man—had prevented the complete anesthesia of her auditory faculties, was already growing indignant: "What? You admire that? Well, that's a fine thing! But what can it mean; isn't one man as good as the next? What difference does it make whether he's a duke or a coachman, if he's intelligent and good-hearted? Your Saint-Simon had a fine way of raising his children, if he didn't teach them to offer their hands to all decent people. Why, it's quite abominable. And you dare to quote that?" And my grandfather, terribly upset and sensing how impossible it would be, in the face of this obstruction, to try to get Swann to tell the stories that would have amused him, said quietly to Mama: "Now remind me of the line you taught me that comforts me so much at times like this. Oh, yes! 'What virtues, Lord, Thou makest us abhor!'[4] Oh, how good that is!"

I did not take my eyes off my mother, I knew that when we were at the table, they would not let me stay during the entire dinner and that, in order not to annoy my father, Mama would not let me kiss her several times in front of the guests as though we were in my room. And so I promised myself that in the dining room, as they were beginning dinner and I felt the hour approaching, I would do everything I could do alone in advance of this kiss which would be so brief and furtive, choose with my eyes the place on her cheek that I would kiss, prepare my thoughts so as to be able, by means of this mental beginning of the kiss, to devote the whole of the minute Mama would grant me to feeling her cheek against my lips, as a painter who can obtain only short sittings prepares his palette and, guided by his notes, does in advance from memory everything for which he could if necessary manage without the presence of the model. But now before the dinner bell rang my grandfather had the unwitting brutality to say: "The boy looks tired, he ought to go up to bed. We're dining late tonight anyway." And my father, who was not as scrupulous as my grandmother and my mother about honoring treaties, said: "Yes, go on now, up to bed with you." I tried to kiss Mama, at that moment we heard the dinner bell. "No, really, leave your mother alone, you've already said goodnight to each other as it is, these demonstrations are ridiculous. Go on now, upstairs!" And I had to leave without my viaticum;[5] I had to climb each step of the staircase, as the popular expression has it, "against my heart,"[6] climbing against my heart which wanted to go back to my mother because she had not, by kissing me, given it license to go with me. That detested staircase which I always entered with such gloom exhaled an odor of varnish that had in some sense absorbed, fixated, the particular sort of sorrow I felt every eve-

4. Adaptation of a line from *Pompey's Death* (III.4), a tragedy by the French classical dramatist Pierre Corneille (1606–1684).
5. The communion wafer and wine given to the dying in Catholic rites.
6. The literal translation of a common phrase meaning "reluctantly" (French).

ning and made it perhaps even crueler to my sensibility because, when it took that olfactory form, my intelligence could no longer share in it. When we are asleep and a raging toothache is as yet perceived by us only in the form of a girl whom we attempt two hundred times to pull out of the water or a line by Molière[7] that we repeat to ourselves incessantly, it is a great relief to wake up so that our intelligence can divest the idea of raging toothache of its disguise of heroism or cadence. It was the opposite of this relief that I experienced when my sorrow at going up to my room entered me in a manner infinitely swifter, almost instantaneous, at once insidious and abrupt, through the inhalation—far more toxic than the intellectual penetration—of the smell of varnish peculiar to that staircase. Once in my room, I had to stop up all the exits, close the shutters, dig my own grave by undoing my covers, put on the shroud of my nightshirt. But before burying myself in the iron bed which they had added to the room because I was too hot in the summer under the rep curtains of the big bed, I had a fit of rebelliousness, I wanted to attempt the ruse of a condemned man. I wrote to my mother begging her to come upstairs for something serious that I could not tell her in my letter. My fear was that Françoise, my aunt's cook who was charged with looking after me when I was at Combray, would refuse to convey my note. I suspected that, for her, delivering a message to my mother when there was company would seem as impossible as for a porter to hand a letter to an actor while he was onstage. With respect to things that could or could not be done she possessed a code at once imperious, extensive, subtle, and intransigent about distinctions that were impalpable or otiose (which made it resemble those ancient laws which, alongside such fierce prescriptions as the massacre of children at the breast, forbid one with an exaggerated delicacy to boil a kid in its mother's milk, or to eat the sinew from an animal's thigh).[8] This code, to judge from her sudden obstinacy when she did not wish to do certain errands that we gave her, seemed to have anticipated social complexities and worldly refinements that nothing in Françoise's associations or her life as a village domestic could have suggested to her; and we had to say to ourselves that in her there was a very old French past, noble and ill understood, as in those manufacturing towns where elegant old houses testify that there was once a court life, and where the employees of a factory for chemical products work surrounded by delicate sculptures representing the miracle of Saint Théophile or the four sons of Aymon.[9] In this particular case, the article of the code which made it unlikely that except in case of fire Françoise would go bother Mama in the presence of M. Swann for so small a personage as myself simply betokened the respect she professed not only for the family—as for the dead, for priests, and for kings—but also for the visitor to whom one was offering one's hospitality, a respect that would perhaps have touched me in a book but that always irritated me on her lips, because of the solemn and tender tones she adopted in speaking of it, and especially so this evening when the sacred character she conferred on the dinner might have the effect of making her refuse to disturb its ceremonial. But to give myself a better

7. Jean-Baptiste Poquelin Molière (1622–1673), French classical dramatist.
8. References to the strict dietary laws of Deuteronomy 14.21 and Genesis 31.32, respectively.

9. The four sons of Aymon, heroic knights who together rode the magic horse Bayard. "Théophile": a cleric who was saved from damnation by the Virgin Mary after he repented for having signed a pact with the devil.

chance, I did not hesitate to lie and tell her that it was not in the least I who had wanted to write to Mama, but that it was Mama who, as she said goodnight to me, had exhorted me not to forget to send her an answer concerning something she had asked me to look for; and she would certainly be very annoyed if this note was not delivered to her. I think Françoise did not believe me, for, like those primitive men whose senses were so much more powerful than ours, she could immediately discern, from signs imperceptible to us, any truth that we wanted to hide from her; she looked at the envelope for five minutes as if the examination of the paper and the appearance of the writing would inform her about the nature of the contents or tell her which article of her code she ought to apply. Then she went out with an air of resignation that seemed to signify: "If it isn't a misfortune for parents to have a child like that!" She came back after a moment to tell me that they were still only at the ice stage, that it was impossible for the butler to deliver the letter right away in front of everyone, but that, when the mouth-rinsing bowls[1] were put round, they would find a way to hand it to Mama. Instantly my anxiety subsided; it was now no longer, as it had been only a moment ago, until tomorrow that I had left my mother, since my little note, no doubt annoying her (and doubly because this stratagem would make me ridiculous in Swann's eyes), would at least allow me, invisible and enraptured, to enter the same room as she, would whisper about me in her ear; since that forbidden, hostile dining room, where, just a moment before, the ice itself—the "*granité*"[2]— and the rinsing bowls seemed to me to contain pleasures noxious and mortally sad because Mama was enjoying them far away from me, was opening itself to me and, like a fruit that has turned sweet and bursts its skin, was about to propel, to project, all the way to my intoxicated heart, Mama's attention as she read my lines. Now I was no longer separated from her; the barriers were down, an exquisite thread joined us. And that was not all: Mama would probably come!

I thought Swann would surely have laughed at the anguish I had just suffered if he had read my letter and guessed its purpose; yet, on the contrary, as I learned later, a similar anguish[3] was the torment of long years of his life and no one, perhaps, could have understood me as well as he; in his case, the anguish that comes from feeling that the person you love is in a place of amusement where you are not, where you cannot join her, came to him through love, to which it is in some sense predestined, by which it will be hoarded, appropriated; but when, as in my case, this anguish enters us before love has made its appearance in our life, it drifts as it waits for it, vague and free, without a particular assignment, at the service of one feeling one day, of another the next, sometimes of filial tenderness or affection for a friend. And the joy with which I served my first apprenticeship when Françoise came back to tell me my letter would be delivered Swann too had known well, that deceptive joy given to us by some friend, some relative of the woman we love when, arriving at the house or theater where she is, for some dance, gala evening, or premiere at which he is going to see her, this friend notices us wandering outside, desperately awaiting some opportunity to communicate with her. He recognizes us, speaks to us familiarly, asks us what we are doing there. And when we invent the story that

1. Bowls with warm water for rinsing were passed around at the end of the meal.
2. A sherbetlike ice served as a separate course or after dinner.
3. I.e., his unhappy love for Odette de Crécy, described later in *Swann in Love*.

we have something urgent to say to his relative or friend, he assures us that nothing could be simpler, leads us into the hall, and promises to send her to us in five minutes. How we love him, as at that moment I loved Françoise—the well-intentioned intermediary who with a single word has just made tolerable, human, and almost propitious the unimaginable, infernal festivity into the thick of which we had been imagining that hostile, perverse, and exquisite vortices of pleasure were carrying away from us and inspiring with derisive laughter the woman we love! If we are to judge by him, the relative who has come up to us and is himself also one of the initiates in the cruel mysteries, the other guests at the party cannot have anything very demoniacal about them. Those inaccessible and excruciating hours during which she was about to enjoy unknown pleasures—now, through an unexpected breach, we are entering them; now, one of the moments which, in succession, would have composed those hours, a moment as real as the others, perhaps even more important to us, because our mistress is more involved in it, we can picture to ourselves, we possess it, we are taking part in it, we have created it, almost: the moment in which he will tell her we are here, downstairs. And no doubt the other moments of the party would not have been essentially very different from this one, would not have had anything more delectable about them that should make us suffer so, since the kind friend has said to us: "Why, she'll be delighted to come down! It'll be much nicer for her to chat with you than to be bored up there." Alas! Swann had learned by experience that the good intentions of a third person have no power over a woman who is annoyed to find herself pursued even into a party by someone she does not love. Often, the friend comes back down alone.

My mother did not come, and with no consideration for my pride (which was invested in her not denying the story that she was supposed to have asked me to let her know the results of some search) asked Françoise to say these words to me: "There is no answer," words I have so often since then heard the doormen in grand hotels or the footmen in bawdy houses bring back to some poor girl who exclaims in surprise: "What, he said nothing? Why, that's impossible! Did you really give him my note? All right, I'll go on waiting." And—just as she invariably assures him she does not need the extra gas jet which the doorman wants to light for her, and remains there, hearing nothing further but the few remarks about the weather exchanged by the doorman and a lackey whom he sends off suddenly, when he notices the time, to put a customer's drink on ice—having declined Françoise's offer to make me some tea or to stay with me, I let her return to the servant's hall, I went to bed and closed my eyes, trying not to hear the voices of my family, who were having their coffee in the garden. But after a few seconds, I became aware that, by writing that note to Mama, by approaching, at the risk of angering her, so close to her that I thought I could touch the moment when I would see her again, I had shut off from myself the possibility of falling asleep without seeing her again, and the beating of my heart grew more painful each minute because I was increasing my agitation by telling myself to be calm, to accept my misfortune. Suddenly my anxiety subsided, a happiness invaded me as when a powerful medicine begins to take effect and our pain vanishes: I had just formed the resolution not to continue trying to fall asleep without seeing Mama again, to kiss her at all costs even though it was with the certainty of being on bad terms with her for a long time after, when she came up to bed. The calm that came with the end of my distress filled me with an extraordinary joy, quite as much as did my expectation, my thirst for and my fear of danger. I opened the window noiselessly and sat down on the foot of my bed; I hardly moved so that I would not be heard from below. Outdoors, too, things seemed frozen in silent attention so as not to disturb the moonlight which, duplicating and distancing each thing by extending its shadow before it, denser and more concrete than itself, had at once thinned and enlarged the landscape like a map that had been folded and was now opened out. What needed to move, some foliage of the chestnut tree, moved. But its quivering, minute, complete, executed even in its slightest nuances and ultimate refinements, did not spill over onto the rest, did not merge with it, remained circumscribed. Exposed against this silence, which absorbed nothing of them, the most distant noises, those that must have come from gardens that lay at the other end of town, could be perceived detailed with such "finish" that they seemed to owe this effect of remoteness only to their pianissimo, like those muted motifs so well executed by the orchestra of the Conservatoire[4] that, although you do not lose a single note, you nonetheless think you are hearing them far away from the concert hall and all the old subscribers—my grandmother's sisters too, when Swann had given them his seats—strained their ears as if they were listening to the distant advances of an army on the march that had not yet turned the corner of the rue de Trévise.[5]

I knew that the situation I was now placing myself in was the one that could provoke the gravest consequences of all for me, coming from my parents, much graver in truth than a stranger would have supposed, the sort he would have believed could be produced only by truly shameful misdeeds. But in my upbringing, the order of misdeeds was not the same as in that of other children, and I had become accustomed to placing before all the rest (because there were probably no others from which I needed to be more carefully protected) those whose common characteristic I now understand was that you lapse into them by yielding to a nervous impulse. But at the time no one uttered these words, no one revealed this cause, which might have made me believe I was excusable for succumbing to them or even perhaps incapable of resisting them. But I recognized them clearly from the anguish that preceded them as well as from the rigor of the punishment that followed them; and I knew that the one I had just committed was in the same family as others for which I had been severely punished, though infinitely graver. When I went and placed myself in my mother's path at the moment she was going up to bed, and when she saw that I had stayed up to say goodnight to her again in the hallway, they would not let me continue to live at home, they would send me away to school the next day, that much was certain. Well! Even if I had had to throw myself out of the window five minutes later, I still preferred this. What I wanted now was Mama, to say goodnight to her, I had gone too far along the road that led to the fulfillment of that desire to be able to turn back now.

I heard the footsteps of my family, who were seeing Swann out; and when the bell on the gate told me he had left, I went to the window. Mama was asking my father if he had thought the lobster was good and if M. Swann had had more coffee-and-pistachio ice. "I found it quite ordinary," said my mother; "I think

4. The national music conservatory (academy) in Paris.   5. A street in Combray.

next time we'll have to try another flavor." "I can't tell you how changed I find Swann," said my great-aunt, "he has aged so!" My great-aunt was so used to seeing Swann always as the same adolescent that she was surprised to find him suddenly not as young as the age she continued to attribute to him. And my family was also beginning to feel that in him this aging was abnormal, excessive, shameful, and more deserved by the unmarried, by all those for whom it seems that the great day that has no tomorrow is longer than for others, because for them it is empty and the moments in it add up from morning on without then being divided among children. "I think he has no end of worries with that wretched wife of his who is living with a certain Monsieur de Charlus,[6] as all of Combray knows. It's the talk of the town." My mother pointed out that in spite of this he had been looking much less sad for some time now. "He also doesn't make that gesture of his as often, so like his father, of wiping his eyes and running his hand across his forehead. I myself think that in his heart of hearts he no longer loves that woman." "Why, naturally he doesn't love her anymore," answered my grandfather. "I received a letter from him about it a long time ago, by now, a letter with which I hastened not to comply and which leaves no doubt about his feelings, at least his feelings of love, for his wife. Well now! You see, you didn't thank him for the Asti," added my grandfather, turning to his two sisters-in-law. "What? We didn't thank him? I think, just between you and me, that I put it quite delicately," answered my aunt Flora. "Yes, you managed it very well: quite admirable," said my aunt Céline. "But you were very good too." "Yes, I was rather proud of my remark about kind neighbors." "What? Is that what you call thanking him?" exclaimed my grandfather. "I certainly heard that, but devil take me if I thought it was directed at Swann. You can be sure he never noticed." "But see here, Swann isn't stupid, I'm sure he appreciated it. After all, I couldn't tell him how many bottles there were and what the wine cost!" My father and mother were left alone there, and sat down for a moment; then my father said: "Well, shall we go up to bed?" "If you like, my dear, even though I'm not the least bit sleepy; yet it couldn't be that perfectly harmless coffee ice that's keeping me so wide-awake; but I can see a light in the servants' hall, and since poor Françoise has waited up for me, I'll go and ask her to unhook my bodice while you're getting undressed." And my mother opened the latticed door that led from the vestibule to the staircase. Soon, I heard her coming upstairs to close her window. I went without a sound into the hallway; my heart was beating so hard I had trouble walking, but at least it was no longer pounding from anxiety, but from terror and joy. I saw the light cast in the stairwell by Mama's candle. Then I saw Mama herself; I threw myself forward. In the first second, she looked at me with astonishment, not understanding what could have happened. Then an expression of anger came over her face, she did not say a single word to me, and indeed for much less than this they would go several days without speaking to me. If Mama had said one word to me, it would have been an admission that they could talk to me again and in any case it would perhaps have seemed to me even more terrible, as a sign that, given the gravity of the punishment that was going to be prepared for me, silence, and estrangement, would have been childish. A word would have been like the calm with which you answer a servant when you have just decided to dismiss him;

6. The brother of the duc de Guermantes.

the kiss you give a son you are sending off to enlist, whereas you would have refused it if you were simply going to be annoyed with him for a few days. But she heard my father coming up from the dressing room where he had gone to undress and, to avoid the scene he would make over me, she said to me in a voice choked with anger: "Run, run, so at least your father won't see you waiting like this as if you were out of your mind!" But I repeated to her: "Come say goodnight to me," terrified as I saw the gleam from my father's candle already rising up the wall, but also using his approach as a means of blackmail and hoping that Mama, to avoid my father's finding me there still if she continued to refuse, would say: "Go back to your room, I'll come." It was too late, my father was there in front of us. Involuntarily, though no one heard, I murmured these words: "I'm done for!"

It was not so. My father was constantly refusing me permission for things that had been authorized in the more generous covenants granted by my mother and grandmother because he did not bother about "principles" and for him there was no "rule of law."[7] For a completely contingent reason, or even for no reason at all, he would at the last minute deny me a certain walk that was so customary, so consecrated that to deprive me of it was a violation, or, as he had done once again this evening, long before the ritual hour he would say to me: "Go on now, up to bed, no arguments!" But also, because he had no principles (in my grandmother's sense), he was not strictly speaking intransigent. He looked at me for a moment with an expression of surprise and annoyance, then as soon as Mama had explained to him with a few embarrassed words what had happened, he said to her: "Go along with him, then. You were just saying you didn't feel very sleepy, stay in his room for a little while, I don't need anything." "But my dear," answered my mother timidly, "whether I'm sleepy or not doesn't change anything, we can't let the child get into the habit . . ." "But it isn't a question of habit," said my father, shrugging his shoulders, "you can see the boy is upset, he seems very sad; look, we're not executioners! You'll end by making him ill, and that won't do us much good! There are two beds in his room; go tell Françoise to prepare the big one for you and sleep there with him tonight. Now then, goodnight, I'm not as high-strung as the two of you, I'm going to bed."

It was impossible to thank my father; he would have been irritated by what he called mawkishness. I stood there not daring to move; he was still there in front of us, tall in his white nightshirt, under the pink and violet Indian cashmere shawl that he tied around his head now that he had attacks of neuralgia, with the gesture of Abraham in the engraving after Benozzo Gozzoli[8] that M. Swann had given me, as he told Sarah she must leave Issac's side. This was many years ago. The staircase wall on which I saw the rising glimmer of his candle has long since ceased to exist. In me, too, many things have been destroyed that I thought were bound to last forever and new ones have formed that have given birth to new sorrows and joys which I could not have foreseen then, just as the old ones have become difficult for me to understand. It was a very long time ago, too, that my father ceased to be able to say to Mama: "Go

---

7. Natural law, supposed to govern international and public relations. Marcel sees his relationship with his mother and grandmother as a social contract; his father, who does not respect

the rules, becomes the unpredictable tyrant.
8. Florentine painter (1420–1497) whose frescoes at Pisa contain scenes from the life of the biblical patriarch Abraham.

with the boy." The possibility of such hours will never be reborn for me. But for a little while now, I have begun to hear again very clearly, if I take care to listen, the sobs that I was strong enough to contain in front of my father and that broke out only when I found myself alone again with Mama. They have never really stopped; and it is only because life is now becoming quieter around me that I can hear them again, like those convent bells covered so well by the clamor of the town during the day that one would think they had ceased altogether but which begin sounding again in the silence of the evening.

Mama spent that night in my room; when I had just committed such a misdeed that I expected to have to leave the house, my parents granted me more than I could ever have won from them as a reward for any good deed. Even at the moment when it manifested itself through this pardon, my father's conduct toward me retained that arbitrary and undeserved quality that characterized it and was due to the fact that it generally resulted from fortuitous convenience rather than a premeditated plan. It may even be that what I called his severity, when he sent me to bed, deserved that name less than my mother's or my grandmother's, for his nature, in certain respects more different from mine than theirs was, had probably kept him from discovering until now how very unhappy I was every evening, something my mother and my grandmother knew well; but they loved me enough not to consent to spare me my suffering, they wanted to teach me to master it in order to reduce my nervous sensitivity and strengthen my will. As for my father, whose affection for me was of another sort, I do not know if he would have been courageous enough for that: the one time he realized that I was upset, he had said to my mother: "Go and comfort him." Mama stayed in my room that night and, as though not to allow any remorse to spoil those hours which were so different from what I had had any right to expect, when Françoise, realizing that something extraordinary was happening when she saw Mama sitting next to me, holding my hand and letting me cry without scolding me, asked her: "Why, madame, now what's wrong with Monsieur that he's crying so?" Mama answered her: "Why, even he doesn't know, Françoise, he's in a state; prepare the big bed for me quickly and then go on up to bed yourself." And so, for the first time, my sadness was regarded no longer as a punishable offense but as an involuntary ailment that had just been officially recognized, a nervous condition for which I was not responsible; I had the relief of no longer having to mingle qualms of conscience with the bitterness of my tears, I could cry without sin. I was also not a little proud, with respect to Françoise, of this turnabout in human affairs which, an hour after Mama had refused to come up to my room and had sent the disdainful answer that I should go to sleep, raised me to the dignity of a grown-up and brought me suddenly to a sort of puberty of grief, of emancipation from tears. I ought to have been happy: I was not. It seemed to me that my mother had just made me a first concession which must have been painful to her, that this was a first abdication on her part from the ideal she had conceived for me, and that for the first time she, who was so courageous, had to confess herself beaten. It seemed to me that, if I had just gained a victory, it was over her, that I had succeeded, as illness, affliction, or age might have done, in relaxing her will, in weakening her judgment, and that this evening was the beginning of a new era, would remain as a sad date. If I had dared, now, I would have said to Mama: "No, I don't want you to do this, don't sleep here." But I was aware of the practical wisdom, the realism as it would be called now, which in her tempered my grandmother's ardently idealistic nature, and I knew that, now that the harm was done, she would prefer to let me at least enjoy the soothing pleasure of it and not disturb my father. To be sure, my mother's lovely face still shone with youth that evening when she so gently held my hands and tried to stop my tears; but it seemed to me that this was precisely what should not have been, her anger would have saddened me less than this new gentleness which my childhood had not known before; it seemed to me that with an impious and secret hand I had just traced in her soul a first wrinkle and caused a first white hair to appear. At the thought of this my sobs redoubled, and then I saw that Mama, who never let herself give way to any emotion with me, was suddenly overcome by my own and was trying to suppress a desire to cry. When she saw that I had noticed, she said to me with a smile: "There now, my little chick, my little canary, he's going to make his mama as silly as himself if this continues. Look, since you're not sleepy and your mama isn't either, let's not go on upsetting each other, let's do something, let's get one of your books." But I had none there. "Would you enjoy it less if I took out the books your grandmother will be giving you on your saint's day? Think about it carefully: you mustn't be disappointed not to have anything the day after tomorrow." On the contrary, I was delighted, and Mama went to get a packet of books, of which I could not distinguish, through the paper in which they were wrapped, more than their shape, short and thick, but which, in this first guise, though summary and veiled, already eclipsed the box of colors from New Year's Day and the silkworms from last year. They were *La Mare au Diable, François le Champi, La Petite Fadette*, and *Les Maîtres Sonneurs*.[9] My grandmother, as I learned afterward, had first chosen the poems of Musset, a volume of Rousseau, and *Indiana*;[1] for though she judged frivolous reading to be as unhealthy as sweets and pastries, it did not occur to her that a great breath of genius might have a more dangerous and less invigorating influence on the mind even of a child than would the open air and the sea breeze on his body. But as my father had nearly called her mad when he learned which books she wanted to give me, she had returned to the bookstore, in Jouy-le-Vicomte herself, so that I would not risk not having my present (it was a burning-hot day and she had come home so indisposed that the doctor had warned my mother not to let her tire herself out that way again) and she had resorted to the four pastoral novels of George Sand. "My dear daughter," she said to Mama, "I could not bring myself to give the boy something badly written."

In fact, she could never resign herself to buying anything from which one could not derive an intellectual profit, and especially that which beautiful things afford us by teaching us to seek our pleasure elsewhere than in the satisfactions of material comfort and vanity. Even when she had to make someone a present of the kind called "useful," when she had to give an armchair, silverware, a

9. *The Devil's Pool, François the Foundling Discovered in the Fields, Little Fadette*, and *The Master Bellringers,* all novels of idealized country life by the French woman writer George Sand (1806–1876).
1. The works of Alfred de Musset (1810–1857) and Jean-Jacques Rousseau (1712–1778), often romantic and sometimes confessional, and George Sand's *Indiana* (1832), a novel of free love, would be thought unsuitable reading for a young child.

walking stick, she looked for "old" ones, as though, now that long desuetude had effaced their character of usefulness, they would appear more disposed to tell us about the life of people of other times than to serve the needs of our own life. She would have liked me to have in my room photographs of the most beautiful monuments or landscapes. But at the moment of buying them, and even though the thing represented had an aesthetic value, she would find that vulgarity and utility too quickly resumed their places in that mechanical mode of representation, the photograph. She would try to use cunning and, if not to eliminate commercial banality entirely, at least to reduce it, to substitute for the greater part of it more art, to introduce into it in a sense several "layers" of art: instead of photographs of Chartres Cathedral, the Fountains of Saint-Cloud, or Mount Vesuvius, she would make inquiries of Swann as to whether some great painter had not depicted them, and preferred to give me photographs of Char-tres Cathedral by Corot, of the Fountains of Saint-Cloud by Hubert Robert, of Mount Vesuvius by Turner,[2] which made one further degree of art. But if the photographer had been removed from the representation of the masterpiece or of nature and replaced by a great artist, he still reclaimed his rights to reproduce that very interpretation. Having deferred vulgarity as far as possible, my grand-mother would try to move it back still further. She would ask Swann if the work had not been engraved, preferring, whenever possible, old engravings that also had an interest beyond themselves, such as those that represent a masterpiece in a state in which we can no longer see it today (like the engraving by Morghen of Leonardo's *Last Supper* before its deterioration).[3] It must be said that the results of this interpretation of the art of gift giving were not always brilliant. The idea I formed of Venice from a drawing by Titian[4] that is supposed to have the lagoon in the background was certainly far less accurate than the one I would have derived from simple photographs. We could no longer keep count, at home, when my great-aunt wanted to draw up an indictment against my grandmother, of the armchairs she had presented to young couples engaged to be married or old married couples which, at the first attempt to make use of them, had immediately collapsed under the weight of one of the recipients. But my grandmother would have believed it petty to be overly concerned about the solidity of a piece of wood in which one could still distinguish a small flower, a smile, sometimes a lovely invention from the past. Even what might, in these pieces of furniture, answer a need, since it did so in a manner to which we are no longer accustomed, charmed her like the old ways of speaking in which we see a metaphor that is obliterated, in our modern language, by the abrasion of habit. Now, in fact, the pastoral novels of George Sand that she was giving me for my saint's day were, like an old piece of furniture, full of expressions that had fallen into disuse and turned figurative again, the sort you no longer find anywhere but in the country. And my grandmother had bought them in prefer-ence to others just as she would sooner have rented an estate on which there

2. All photographs of paintings: the cathedral at Chartres, painted in 1830 by Corot; the foun-tains in the old park at Saint-Cloud, outside Paris, painted by Hubert Robert (1733–1809); and Vesuvius, a famous volcano near Naples, painted by J. M. W. Turner (1775–1851).
3. Leonardo da Vinci's *Last Supper* was the subject of a famous engraving by Raphael Mor-ghen (1758–1833). The paints in the original fresco had deteriorated rapidly, and a major restoration took place only in the 19th century.
4. Tiziano Vecellio (1488?–1576), Renais-sance painter of the Venetian school.

was a Gothic dovecote or another of those old things that exercise such a happy influence on the mind by filling it with longing for impossible voyages through time.

Mama sat down by my bed; she had picked up *François le Champi*, whose reddish cover and incomprehensible title[5] gave it, in my eyes, a distinct personality and a mysterious attraction. I had not yet read a real novel. I had heard people say that George Sand was an exemplary novelist. This already predisposed me to imagine something indefinable and delicious in *François le Champi*. Narrative devices intended to arouse curiosity or emotion, certain modes of expression that make one uneasy or melancholy, and that a reader with some education will recognize as common to many novels, appeared to me—who considered a new book not as a thing having many counterparts, but as a unique person, having no reason for existing but in itself—simply as a disturbing emanation of *François le Champi*'s peculiar essence. Behind those events so ordinary, those things so common, those words so current, I sensed a strange sort of intonation, accentuation. The action began; it seemed to me all the more obscure because in those days, when I read, I often daydreamed, for entire pages, of something quite different. And in addition to the lacunae that this distraction left in the story, there was the fact, when Mama was the one reading aloud to me, that she skipped all the love scenes. Thus, all the bizarre changes that take place in the respective attitudes of the miller's wife and the child and that can be explained only by the progress of a nascent love seemed to me marked by a profound mystery whose source I readily imagined must be in that strange and sweet name "Champi," which gave the child, who bore it without my knowing why, its vivid, charming purplish color. If my mother was an unfaithful reader she was also, in the case of books in which she found the inflection of true feeling, a wonderful reader for the respect and simplicity of her interpretation, the beauty and gentleness of the sound of her voice. Even in real life, when it was people and not works of art which moved her to compassion or admiration, it was touching to see with what deference she removed from her voice, from her motions, from her words, any spark of gaiety that might hurt some mother who had once lost a child, any recollection of a saint's day or birthday that might remind some old man of his advanced age, any remark about housekeeping that might seem tedious to some young scholar. In the same way, when she was reading George Sand's prose, which always breathes that goodness, that moral distinction which Mama had learned from my grandmother to consider superior to all else in life, and which I was to teach her only much later not to consider superior to all else in books too, taking care to banish from her voice any pettiness, any affectation which might have prevented it from receiving that powerful torrent, she imparted all the natural tenderness, all the ample sweetness they demanded to those sentences which seemed written for her voice and which remained, so to speak, entirely within the register of her sensibility. She found, to attack them in the necessary tone, the warm inflection that preexists them and that dictated them, but that the words do not indicate; with this inflection she softened as she went along any crudeness in the tenses of the verbs, gave the imperfect and the past historic the sweetness that lies in goodness, the melancholy that lies in tenderness, directed the sentence that was ending toward the one that was about to begin, sometimes

5. *Champi* ("foundling") is an old French word that the child Marcel would not have known.

hurrying, sometimes slowing down the pace of the syllables so as to bring them, though their quantities were different, into one uniform rhythm, she breathed into this very common prose a sort of continuous emotional life.

My remorse was quieted, I gave in to the sweetness of that night in which I had my mother close to me. I knew that such a night could not be repeated; that the greatest desire I had in the world, to keep my mother in my room during those sad hours of darkness, was too contrary to the necessities of life and the wishes of others for its fulfillment, granted this night, to be anything other than artificial and exceptional. Tomorrow my anxieties would reawaken and Mama would not stay here. But when my anxieties were soothed, I no longer understood them; and then tomorrow night was still far away; I told myself I would have time to think of what to do, even though that time could not bring me any access of power, since these things did not depend on my will and seemed more avoidable to me only because of the interval that still separated them from me.

So it was that, for a long time, when, awakened at night, I remembered Combray again, I saw nothing of it but this sort of luminous panel, cut out among indistinct shadows, like those panels which the glow of a Bengal light[6] or some electric projection will cut out and illuminate in a building whose other parts remain plunged in darkness: at the rather broad base, the small parlor, the dining room, the opening of the dark path by which M. Swann, the unconscious author of my sufferings, would arrive, the front hall where I would head toward the first step of the staircase, so painful to climb, that formed, by itself, the very narrow trunk of this irregular pyramid; and, at the top, my bedroom with the little hallway and its glass-paned door for Mama's entrance; in a word, always seen at the same hour, isolated from everything that might surround it, standing out alone against the darkness, the bare minimum of scenery (such as one sees prescribed at the beginnings of the old plays for performances in the provinces) needed for the drama of my undressing; as though Combray had consisted only of two floors connected by a slender staircase and as though it had always been seven o'clock in the evening there. The fact is, I could have answered anyone who asked me that Combray also included other things and existed at other times of day. But since what I recalled would have been supplied to me only by my voluntary memory, the memory of the intelligence, and since the information it gives about the past preserves nothing of the past itself, I would never have had any desire to think about the rest of Combray. It was all really quite dead for me.

Dead forever? Possibly.

There is a great deal of chance in all this, and a second sort of chance event, that of our own death, often does not allow us to wait long for the favors of the first.

I find the Celtic belief very reasonable, that the souls of those we have lost are held captive in some inferior creature, in an animal, in a plant, in some inanimate object, effectively lost to us until the day, which for many never comes, when we happen to pass close to the tree, come into possession of the object that is their prison.[7] Then they quiver, they call out to us, and as soon as

---

6. A steady, blue-colored firework often used for signals.

7. A belief attributed to Druids, the priests of the ancient Celtic peoples.

we have recognized them, the spell is broken. Delivered by us, they have overcome death and they return to live with us.

It is the same with our past. It is a waste of effort for us to try to summon it, all the exertions of our intelligence are useless. The past is hidden outside the realm of our intelligence and beyond its reach, in some material object (in the sensation that this material object would give us) which we do not suspect. It depends on chance whether we encounter this object before we die, or do not encounter it.

For many years, already, everything about Combray that was not the theater and drama of my bedtime had ceased to exist for me, when one day in winter, as I returned home, my mother, seeing that I was cold, suggested that, contrary to my habit, I have a little tea. I refused at first and then, I do not know why, changed my mind. She sent for one of those squat, plump cakes called *petites madeleines* that look as though they have been molded in the grooved valve of a scallop shell. And soon, mechanically, oppressed by the gloomy day and the prospect of another sad day to follow, I carried to my lips a spoonful of the tea in which I had let soften a bit of madeleine. But at the very instant when the mouthful of tea mixed with cake crumbs touched my palate, I quivered, attentive to the extraordinary thing that was happening inside me. A delicious pleasure had invaded me, isolated me, without my having any notion as to its cause. It had immediately rendered the vicissitudes of life unimportant to me, its disasters innocuous, its brevity illusory, acting in the same way that love acts, by filling me with a precious essence: or rather this essence was not merely inside me, it was me. I had ceased to feel mediocre, contingent, mortal. Where could it have come to me from—this powerful joy? I sensed that it was connected to the taste of the tea and the cake, but that it went infinitely far beyond it, could not be of the same nature. Where did it come from? What did it mean? How could I grasp it? I drink a second mouthful, in which I find nothing more than in the first, a third that gives me a little less than the second. It is time for me to stop, the virtue of the drink seems to be diminishing. Clearly, the truth I am seeking is not in the drink, but in me. The drink has awoken it in me, but does not know this truth, and can do no more than repeat indefinitely, with less and less force, this same testimony which I do not know how to interpret and which I want at least to be able to ask of it again and find again, intact, available to me, soon, for a decisive clarification. I put down the cup and turn to my mind. It is up to my mind to find the truth. But how? Such grave uncertainty, whenever the mind feels overtaken by itself; when it, the seeker, is also the obscure country where it must seek and where all its baggage will be nothing to it. Seek? Not only that: create. It is face-to-face with something that does not yet exist and that only it can accomplish, then bring into its light.

And I begin asking myself again what it could be, this unknown state which brought with it no logical proof, but only the evidence of its felicity, its reality, and in whose presence the other states of consciousness faded away. I want to try to make it reappear. I return in my thoughts to the moment when I took the first spoonful of tea. I find the same state again, without any new clarity. I ask my mind to make another effort, to bring back once more the sensation that is slipping away. And, so that nothing may interrupt the thrust with which it will try to grasp it again, I clear away every obstacle, every foreign idea, I protect my ears and my attention from the noises in the next room. But feeling my mind grow tired without succeeding, I now compel it to accept the very distraction I was denying it, to think of something else, to recover its strength before a supreme attempt. Then for a second time I create an empty space before it, I confront it again with the still recent taste of that first mouthful, and I feel something quiver in me, shift, try to rise, something that seems to have been unanchored at a great depth; I do not know what it is, but it comes up slowly; I feel the resistance and I hear the murmur of the distances traversed.

Undoubtedly what is palpitating thus, deep inside me, must be the image, the visual memory which is attached to this taste and is trying to follow it to me. But it is struggling too far away, too confusedly; I can just barely perceive the neutral glimmer in which the elusive eddying of stirred-up colors is blended; but I cannot distinguish the form, cannot ask it, as the one possible interpreter, to translate for me the evidence of its contemporary, its inseparable companion, the taste, ask it to tell me what particular circumstance is involved, what period of the past.

Will it reach the clear surface of my consciousness—this memory, this old moment which the attraction of an identical moment has come from so far to invite, to move, to raise up from the deepest part of me? I don't know. Now I no longer feel anything, it has stopped, gone back down perhaps; who knows if it will ever rise up from its darkness again? Ten times I must begin again, lean down toward it. And each time, the laziness that deters us from every difficult task, every work of importance, has counseled me to leave it, to drink my tea and think only about my worries of today, my desires for tomorrow, upon which I may ruminate effortlessly.

And suddenly the memory appeared. That taste was the taste of the little piece of madeleine which on Sunday mornings at Combray (because that day I did not go out before it was time for Mass), when I went to say good morning to her in her bedroom, my aunt Léonie would give me after dipping it in her infusion of tea or lime blossom. The sight of the little madeleine had not reminded me of anything before I tasted it; perhaps because I had often seen them since, without eating them, on the shelves of the pastry shops, and their image had therefore left those days of Combray and attached itself to others more recent; perhaps because of these recollections abandoned so long outside my memory, nothing survived, everything had come apart; the forms and the form, too, of the little shell made of cake, so fatly sensual within its severe and pious pleating—had been destroyed, or, still half asleep, had lost the force of expansion that would have allowed them to rejoin my consciousness. But, when nothing subsists of an old past, after the death of people, after the destruction of things, alone, frailer but more enduring, more immaterial, more persistent, more faithful, smell and taste still remain for a long time, like souls, remembering, waiting, hoping, upon the ruins of all the rest, bearing without giving way, on their almost impalpable droplet, the immense edifice of memory.

And as soon as I had recognized the taste of the piece of madeleine dipped in lime-blossom tea that my aunt used to give me (though I did not yet know and had to put off to much later discovering why this memory made me so happy), immediately the old gray house on the street, where her bedroom was, came like a stage set to attach itself to the little wing opening onto the garden that had been built for my parents behind it (that truncated section which was all I had seen before then); and with the house the town, from morning to night and in all weathers, the Square, where they sent me before lunch, the streets where I went on errands, the paths we took if the weather was fine. And as in that game in which the Japanese amuse themselves by filling a porcelain bowl with water and steeping in it little pieces of paper until then undifferentiated which, the moment they are immersed in it, stretch and bend, take color and distinctive shape, turn into flowers, houses, human figures, firm and recognizable, so now all the flowers in our garden and in M. Swann's park, and the water lilies on the Vivonne,[8] and the good people of the village and their little dwellings and the church and all of Combray and its surroundings, all of this, acquiring form and solidity, emerged, town and gardens alike, from my cup of tea.

1913

8. The local river.

JAMES JOYCE
1882–1941

More than any other writer of the twentieth century, James Joyce shaped modern literature. His experiments with narrative form helped to define the major literary movements of the century, from modernism to postmodernism. By developing methods of tracing individual consciousness, Joyce, along with **Marcel Proust** and **Virginia Woolf**, helped us to understand the functioning of the human mind. Equally capable of realistic portrayal of urban life in Dublin and playful deformations of the English language, Joyce expanded the possibilities of the novel—as a record of intimate human experiences, as a massive encyclopedia of human culture, and as a funhouse mirror that shows the world a transformed image of itself.

Joyce left Ireland as a young man but made his native country the subject of all his works. Born in Dublin on February 2, 1882, to May Murray and John Stanislaus Joyce, he was given the impressive name James Augustine Aloysius Joyce; he was the eldest surviving child of what would soon be a large family (ten children plus three who died in infancy). His father held a well-paid and undemanding post in the civil service, and the family was comfortable until 1891, when his job was eliminated. John received a small pension and declined to take up more demanding work elsewhere. The Joyce family moved steadily down the social and economic scale, and life became difficult under the improvident guidance of a man whom Joyce later portrayed as "a drinker, a good fellow, a storyteller, somebody's secretary, something in a distillery, a tax-gatherer, a bankrupt, and at present a praiser of his own past."

Joyce attended the well-known Catholic preparatory school of Clongowes

Wood College from the ages of six to nine, leaving when his family could no longer afford the tuition. Two years later, he was admitted as a scholarship student to Belvedere College in Dublin. Both were Jesuit schools and provided a rigorous Catholic training against which Joyce violently rebelled but which he never forgot. In Belvedere College, shaken by a dramatic hell-fire sermon shortly after his first experience with sex, he even seriously considered becoming a priest; in the end, the life of the senses and his sense of vocation as an artist won out. After graduating from Belvedere in 1898, Joyce entered another Catholic institution—University College, Dublin—where he rejected Irish tradition and looked abroad for new values. Teaching himself Norwegian in order to read **Henrik Ibsen** in the original, he criticized the writers of the Irish Literary Renaissance as provincial and showed no interest in joining their ranks. His first published piece was an essay on Ibsen, to which the great playwright responded in a brief note of thanks. Like the hero of his autobiographical novel, *A Portrait of the Artist as a Young Man* (1916), Stephen Dedalus, Joyce decided (in 1902) to escape the stifling conventions of his native country and leave for the Continent.

This trip did not last long. He studied medicine briefly, then for six months supported himself in Paris by giving English lessons, but when his mother became seriously ill, he was called home. After her death, he taught school for a time in Dublin and then returned to the Continent with Nora Barnacle, a country woman from western Ireland with whom he had two children and whom he married (after twenty-seven years of cohabitation) in 1931. The young couple moved to Trieste, where Joyce taught English in a Berlitz school and started writing both the short stories collected as *Dubliners* (1914) and an early version, partially published as *Stephen Hero* in 1944, of *A Portrait of the Artist as a Young Man*. He also wrote some mostly forgettable poetry and a play, *Exiles* (1918), that he had trouble getting produced. The couple remained poor for much of Joyce's life and relied on grants from the British government and gifts from wealthy patrons to allow Joyce to complete his literary projects. Joyce made a few brief business trips to Dublin, but, after 1912, never returned to the city.

When the First World War broke out, the Joyces moved to neutral Zurich, then after the war to Paris, where Joyce completed his most famous work, *Ulysses* (1922). In Paris he briefly met the other great novelist of the day, Marcel Proust, but claimed never to have read his work. He did, however, attend Proust's funeral. By now, Joyce was a celebrity and developed a circle of literary friends who supported and publicized his work. Throughout his life Joyce was a heavy drinker, and his conversation was legendary. His eyesight deteriorated as he devoted himself to the project he called *Work in Progress* (completed as *Finnegans Wake* in 1939). He sometimes relied on others, including the young Irish writer **Samuel Beckett**, to take dictation. These years were blighted by the mental illness of Joyce's daughter, Lucia, who ended up institutionalized for most of her life. The Joyces remained in Paris until the German occupation during the Second World War, when Joyce and his wife returned to Zurich, where Joyce died in 1941 after an operation for a perforated ulcer.

From *Dubliners* to *Ulysses* and *Finnegans Wake*, Joyce developed ways of exploring the lives and dreams of characters, including his youthful self, from the parochial Dublin society he had fled. Each of the major works presents innovative literary approaches that were to have a substantial impact on later writers. *A Portrait of the Artist as a Young Man* introduced into English the technique of stream of consciousness, as a means of capturing thoughts and emotions. Because it suggests the seemingly arbitrary manner in which thoughts and feelings often arise and then dissipate, stream-of-conscious writing may sound illogical or confusing; nevertheless it can indeed be convincing, since it gives the reader apparent access to the workings of a character's mind. The author's aim in employing the technique is to achieve a deeper understanding of human experience by displaying subconscious associations along with conscious thoughts. *Portrait* is based on Joyce's life until 1902, but the novel is clearly not a conventional autobiography and the reader recognizes in the first pages a radical experiment in fictional language. The novel's sophisticated symbolism and stress on dramatic dialogue hint at the radical break with narrative tradition that Joyce was preparing in *Ulysses*.

While introducing a host of stylistic devices to English, including an expanded form of stream of consciousness, a complex set of mythic parallels, and a series of literary parodies, *Ulysses* also provided one of the most celebrated instances of modern literary censorship. Its serial publication in the New York *Little Review* (from 1918 to 1920) was halted by the U.S. Post Office after a complaint, from the New York Society for the Prevention of Vice, that the work was obscene. The novel was outlawed and all available copies were actually burned in England and in America, until a 1933 decision by Judge Woolsey in federal district court lifted the ban in the United States. Although Joyce's descriptions have lost none of their pungency, it is hard to imagine a reader who would not be struck by another element—the density and mythic scope of this complex, symbolic, and linguistically innovative novel. Openly referring to an ancient predecessor, the *Odyssey* of Homer ("Ulysses" is the Latin name for the hero

Odysseus), *Ulysses* structures numerous episodes to suggest parallels with the Greek epic, and transforms the twenty-year Homeric journey home into the daylong wanderings through Dublin of an unheroic advertising man, Leopold Bloom, and a rebellious young teacher and writer from *Portrait*, Stephen Dedalus. **T. S. Eliot** saw Joyce's use of ancient myth to explore modern life as "a way of controlling, of ordering, of giving a shape and significance to the immense panorama of futility and anarchy which is contemporary history." The first half of *Ulysses* uses stream-of-consciousness technique to explore Bloom's and Stephen's thoughts through the course of the day. By the second half of the novel, however, a number of intrusive and parodic narrators intervene in the action; Joyce's games with language and representation in this section were prime influences on postmodernism.

After the publication of *Ulysses*, Joyce spent the next seventeen years writing an even more complex work: *Finnegans Wake* (1939). Despite the title, a reference to a balled in which the bricklayer Tim Finnegan is brought back to life at his wake when somebody spills whiskey on him, the novel is the multivoiced, multidimensional dream of Humphrey Chimpden Earwicker. *Finnegans Wake* expands on the encyclopedic series of literary and cultural references underlying *Ulysses*, in language that has been even more radically broken apart and reassembled than that of *Ulysses*. Digressing exuberantly in all directions at once, with complex puns and hybrid words that mix languages, *Finnegans Wake* is—in spite of its cosmic symbolism—a game of language and reference by an artist "hoppy on akkant of his joyicity."

"THE DEAD"

These influential literary experiments had their roots in Joyce's command of more traditional narrative technique.

"The Dead," presented here, was the last and greatest story in Joyce's first published volume, *Dubliners*. The collection as a whole sketches aspects of life in the Irish capital as Joyce knew it, in which the parochialism, piety, and repressive conventions of life are shown stifling artistic and psychological development. Whether it is the young boy who arrives too late at the fair in "Araby," the poor-aunt laundress of "Clay," or the frustrated writer Gabriel Conroy of "The Dead," the characters in *Dubliners* dream of a better life against a dismal, impoverishing background whose cumulative effect is of despair. The style of *Dubliners* is more realistic than in Joyce's later fiction, but he already employs a structure of symbolic meanings and revelatory moments he called "epiphanies." Joyce wrote to his publisher that the collection would be "a chapter of the moral history of my country," and he further explained that he had chosen Dublin because it was the "centre of paralysis" in Ireland—a city of blunted hopes and lost dreams: desperately poor, with large slums and more people than jobs, it stagnated in political, religious, and cultural divisions that color the lives of the characters in the stories. The book is arranged, Joyce noted, in an order that represents four aspects of life in the city: "childhood, adolescence, maturity and public life." Individual stories focus on one or a few characters, who may dream of a better life but are eventually frustrated by, or sink voluntarily back into, their shabby reality. Stories often end with a moment of special insight (epiphany), evident to the reader but not always to the protagonist, that puts events into sharp and illuminating perspective.

Several aspects of "The Dead" recall—and transmute—elements in Joyce's life. As in other stories, the neighborhood setting is familiar from his youth. The real-life models for Miss Kate and Miss Julia were indeed music teachers. Mr. Bartell D'Arcy evokes a contemporary tenor who performed under a similar name. The figure of Gabriel Conroy—who writes reviews for local journals, dislikes Irish nationalism, and prefers European culture—physically resembles Joyce—a lesser Joyce who might never have had the courage to leave home for Europe. The tale that Gretta tells Gabriel at the end of the story echoes Nora's experience.

"The Dead" is divided into three parts, chronicling the stages of the Misses Morkan's party and also the stages by which Gabriel Conroy moves from the rather pompous, insecure, and externally oriented figure of the beginning to a man who has been forced to reassess himself and human relationships at the end. The party is an annual dinner dance that takes place after the New Year, probably on January 6, the Catholic Feast of the Epiphany (which many have connected with Gabriel's personal epiphany at the end of the story). A jovial occasion, it brings together friends and acquaintances for an evening of music, dancing, sumptuous food, and a formal after-dinner speech that Gabriel delivers. The undercurrents are not always harmonious, however, for small anxieties and personal frictions crop up that both create a realistic picture and suggest tensions in contemporary Irish society: nationalism, religion, poverty, and class differences. Gabriel has a position to maintain, and he is determined to live up to his responsibilities: he is at once cultured speaker and intellectual, carver and master of ceremonies, and the man whom the Misses Morkan expect to take care of occasional problems like alcoholic guests. He is a complex character, both a writer of real imagination and a narcissistic figure who is so used to focusing on himself that he has drawn apart from other people.

Joyce's method in "The Dead" relies heavily on free indirect discourse, the presentation of a character's thoughts (without quotation marks) by the narrator. Joyce drew this style partly from **Flaubert**—in *Portrait*, Stephen Dedalus quotes Flaubert's idea of the artist who "like the God of the creation, remains within or behind or beyond or above his handiwork, invisible, refined out of existence, indifferent, paring his fingernails." Joyce's later development of stream of consciousness would allow the character's thoughts to be presented directly to the reader, sometimes without the intervention of a narrator, but in "The Dead" the narrator unobtrusively filters Gabriel's thoughts for us, allowing us to sympathize with Gabriel in his insecurity but also inviting us to judge him in his complacency.

The Dead

Lily, the caretaker's daughter, was literally run off her feet. Hardly had she brought one gentleman into the little pantry behind the office on the ground floor and helped him off with his overcoat than the wheezy hall-door bell clanged again and she had to scamper along the bare hallway to let in another guest. It was well for her she had not to attend to the ladies also. But Miss Kate and Miss Julia had thought of that and had converted the bathroom upstairs into a ladies' dressing-room. Miss Kate and Miss Julia were there, gossiping and laughing and fussing, walking after each other to the head of the stairs, peering down over the banisters and calling down to Lily to ask her who had come.

It was always a great affair, the Misses Morkan's annual dance. Everybody who knew them came to it, members of the family, old friends of the family, the members of Julia's choir, any of Kate's pupils that were grown up enough and even some of Mary Jane's pupils too. Never once had it fallen flat. For years and years it had gone off in splendid style as long as anyone could remember; ever since Kate and Julia, after the death of their brother Pat, had left the house in Stoney Batter and taken Mary Jane, their only niece, to live with them in the dark gaunt house on Usher's Island,[1] the upper part of which they had rented from Mr. Fulham, the cornfactor[2] on the ground floor. That was a good thirty years ago if it was a day. Mary Jane, who was then a little girl in short clothes, was now the main prop of the household for she had the organ[3] in Haddington Road. She had been through the Academy[4] and gave a pupils' concert every year in the upper room of the Antient Concert Rooms. Many of her pupils belonged to better-class families on the Kingstown and Dalkey line.[5] Old as they were, her aunts also did their share. Julia, though she was quite grey, was still the leading soprano in Adam and Eve's, and Kate, being too feeble to go about much, gave music lessons to beginners on the old square[6] piano in the back room. Lily, the caretaker's daughter, did housemaid's work for them. Though their life was modest they believed in eating well; the best of everything: diamond-bone sirloins,

1. Not an island, but an area in western Dublin on the south bank of the River Liffey. Stoney Batter is a street of small shops and a few houses in Dublin.
2. Dealer in grain.
3. I.e., earned money by playing the organ at church.
4. The Royal Academy of Music.
5. Railway to a fashionable section of Dublin.
6. I.e., upright. "Adam and Eve's": popular name (taken from a nearby inn) for a Dublin Catholic church.

three-shilling tea and the best bottled stout.[7] But Lily seldom made a mistake in the orders so that she got on well with her three mistresses. They were fussy, that was all. But the only thing they would not stand was back answers.

Of course they had good reason to be fussy on such a night. And then it was long after ten o'clock and yet there was no sign of Gabriel and his wife. Besides they were dreadfully afraid that Freddy Malins might turn up screwed.[8] They would not wish for worlds that any of Mary Jane's pupils should see him under the influence; and when he was like that it was sometimes very hard to manage him. Freddy Malins always came late but they wondered what could be keeping Gabriel: and that was what brought them every two minutes to the banisters to ask Lily had Gabriel or Freddy come.

—O, Mr. Conroy, said Lily to Gabriel when she opened the door for him, Miss Kate and Miss Julia thought you were never coming. Good-night, Mrs. Conroy.

—I'll engage they did, said Gabriel, but they forgot that my wife here takes three mortal hours to dress herself.

He stood on the mat, scraping the snow from his goloshes, while Lily led his wife to the foot of the stairs and called out:

—Miss Kate, here's Mrs. Conroy.

Kate and Julia came toddling down the dark stairs at once. Both of them kissed Gabriel's wife, said she must be perished alive and asked was Gabriel with her.

—Here I am as right as the mail,[9] Aunt Kate! Go on up. I'll follow, called out Gabriel from the dark.

He continued scraping his feet vigorously while the three women went upstairs, laughing, to the ladies' dressing-room. A light fringe of snow lay like a cape on the shoulders of his overcoat and like toecaps on the toes of his goloshes: and, as the buttons of his overcoat slipped with a squeaking noise through the snow-stiffened frieze, a cold fragrant air from out-of-doors escaped from crevices and folds.

—Is it snowing again, Mr. Conroy? asked Lily.

She had preceded him into the pantry to help him off with his overcoat. Gabriel smiled at the three syllables she had given his surname and glanced at her. She was a slim, growing girl, pale in complexion and with hay-coloured hair. The gas in the pantry made her look still paler. Gabriel had known her when she was a child and used to sit on the lowest step nursing a rag doll.

—Yes, Lily, he answered, and I think we're in for a night of it.

He looked up at the pantry ceiling, which was shaking with the stamping and shuffling of feet on the floor above, listened for a moment to the piano and then glanced at the girl, who was folding his overcoat carefully at the end of a shelf.

—Tell me, Lily, he said in a friendly tone, do you still go to school?

—O no, sir, she answered. I'm done schooling this year and more.

—O, then, said Gabriel gaily, I suppose we'll be going to your wedding one of these fine days with your young man, eh?

The girl glanced back at him over her shoulder and said with great bitterness:

—The men that is now is only all palaver[1] and what they can get out of you.

---

7. Strong beer.
8. Drunk.

9. Reliable as mail delivery.
1. Fancy talk.

Gabriel coloured as if he felt he had made a mistake and, without looking at her, kicked off his goloshes and flicked actively with his muffler at his patent-leather shoes.

He was a stout tallish young man. The high colour of his cheeks pushed upwards even to his forehead where it scattered itself in a few formless patches of pale red; and on his hairless face there scintillated restlessly the polished lenses and the bright gilt rims of the glasses which screened his delicate and restless eyes. His glossy black hair was parted in the middle and brushed in a long curve behind his ears where it curled slightly beneath the groove left by his hat.

When he had flicked lustre into his shoes he stood up and pulled his waistcoat down more tightly on his plump body. Then he took a coin rapidly from his pocket.

—O Lily, he said, thrusting it into her hands, it's Christmastime, isn't it? Just . . . here's a little. . . .

He walked rapidly towards the door.

—O no, sir! cried the girl, following him. Really, sir, I wouldn't take it.

—Christmas-time! Christmas-time! said Gabriel, almost trotting to the stairs and waving his hand to her in deprecation.

The girl, seeing that he had gained the stairs, called out after him:

—Well, thank you, sir.

He waited outside the drawing-room door until the waltz should finish, listening to the skirts that swept against it and to the shuffling of feet. He was still discomposed by the girl's bitter and sudden retort. It had cast a gloom over him which he tried to dispel by arranging his cuffs and the bows of his tie. Then he took from his waistcoat pocket a little paper and glanced at the headings he had made for his speech. He was undecided about the lines from Robert Browning[2] for he feared they would be above the heads of his hearers. Some quotation that they could recognise from Shakespeare or from the Melodies[3] would be better. The indelicate clacking of the men's heels and the shuffling of their soles reminded him that their grade of culture differed from his. He would only make himself ridiculous by quoting poetry to them which they could not understand. They would think that he was airing his superior education. He would fail with them just as he had failed with the girl in the pantry. He had taken up a wrong tone. His whole speech was a mistake from first to last, an utter failure.

Just then his aunts and his wife came out of the ladies' dressing-room. His aunts were two small plainly dressed old women. Aunt Julia was an inch or so the taller. Her hair, drawn low over the tops of her ears, was grey; and grey also, with darker shadows, was her large flaccid face. Though she was stout in build and stood erect her slow eyes and parted lips gave her the appearance of a woman who did not know where she was or where she was going. Aunt Kate was more vivacious. Her face, healthier than her sister's, was all puckers and creases, like a shrivelled red apple, and her hair, braided in the same old-fashioned way, had not lost its ripe nut colour.

They both kissed Gabriel frankly. He was their favourite nephew, the son of their dead elder sister, Ellen, who had married T. J. Conroy of the Port and Docks.[4]

---

2. English poet (1812–1889) who had a contemporary reputation for obscurity.
3. Thomas Moore's (1779–1852) immensely popular *Irish Melodies*, a collection of poems with many set to old Irish melodies.
4. The Dublin Port and Docks Board, which regulated customs and shipping.

—Gretta tells me you're not going to take a cab back to Monkstown[5] tonight, Gabriel, said Aunt Kate.

—No, said Gabriel, turning to his wife, we had quite enough of that last year, hadn't we? Don't you remember, Aunt Kate, what a cold Gretta got out of it? Cab windows rattling all the way, and the east wind blowing in after we passed Merrion.[6] Very jolly it was. Gretta caught a dreadful cold.

Aunt Kate frowned severely and nodded her head at every word.

—Quite right, Gabriel, quite right, she said. You can't be too careful.

—But as for Gretta there, said Gabriel, she'd walk home in the snow if she were let.

Mrs. Conroy laughed.

—Don't mind him, Aunt Kate, she said. He's really an awful bother, what with green shades for Tom's eyes at night and making him do the dumb-bells, and forcing Eva to eat the stirabout.[7] The poor child! And she simply hates the sight of it! . . . O, but you'll never guess what he makes me wear now!

She broke out into a peal of laughter and glanced at her husband, whose admiring and happy eyes had been wandering from her dress to her face and hair. The two aunts laughed heartily too, for Gabriel's solicitude was a standing joke with them.

—Goloshes! said Mrs. Conroy. That's the latest. Whenever it's wet underfoot I must put on my goloshes. To-night even he wanted me to put them on, but I wouldn't. The next thing he'll buy me will be a diving suit.

Gabriel laughed nervously and patted his tie reassuringly while Aunt Kate nearly doubled herself, so heartily did she enjoy the joke. The smile soon faded from Aunt Julia's face and her mirthless eyes were directed towards her nephew's face. After a pause she asked:

—And what are goloshes, Gabriel?

—Goloshes, Julia! exclaimed her sister. Goodness me, don't you know what goloshes are? You wear them over your . . . over your boots, Gretta, isn't it?

—Yes, said Mrs. Conroy. Guttapercha[8] things. We both have a pair now. Gabriel says everyone wears them on the continent.

—O, on the continent, murmured Aunt Julia, nodding her head slowly.

Gabriel knitted his brows and said, as if he were slightly angered:

—It's nothing very wonderful but Gretta thinks it very funny because she says the word reminds her of Christy Minstrels.[9]

—But tell me, Gabriel, said Aunt Kate, with brisk tact. Of course, you've seen about the room. Gretta was saying . . .

—O, the room is all right, replied Gabriel. I've taken one in the Gresham.[1]

—To be sure, said Aunt Kate, by far the best thing to do. And the children, Gretta, you're not anxious about them?

—O, for one night, said Mrs. Conroy. Besides, Bessie will look after them.

—To be sure, said Aunt Kate again. What a comfort it is to have a girl like that, one you can depend on! There's that Lily, I'm sure I don't know what has come over her lately. She's not the girl she was at all.

5. Well-to-do suburb of Dublin.
6. Village on Dublin Bay.
7. Porridge.
8. A rubberlike substance.

9. "Goloshes" sounds like "golly shoes," which reminds Gretta of the Christy Minstrels, a popular blackface minstrel show.
1. Fashionable hotel in central Dublin.

Gabriel was about to ask his aunt some questions on this point but she broke off suddenly to gaze after her sister who had wandered down the stairs and was craning her neck over the banisters.

—Now, I ask you, she said, almost testily, where is Julia going? Julia! Julia! Where are you going?

Julia, who had gone halfway down one flight, came back and announced blandly:

—Here's Freddy.

At the same moment a clapping of hands and a final flourish of the pianist told that the waltz had ended. The drawing-room door was opened from within and some couples came out. Aunt Kate drew Gabriel aside hurriedly and whispered into his ear:

—Slip down, Gabriel, like a good fellow and see if he's all right, and don't let him up if he's screwed. I'm sure he's screwed. I'm sure he is.

Gabriel went to the stairs and listened over the banisters. He could hear two persons talking in the pantry. Then he recognised Freddy Malins' laugh. He went down the stairs noisily.

—It's such a relief, said Aunt Kate to Mrs. Conroy, that Gabriel is here. I always feel easier in my mind when he's here. . . . Julia, there's Miss Daly and Miss Power will take some refreshment. Thanks for your beautiful waltz, Miss Daly. It made lovely time.

A tall wizen-faced man, with a stiff grizzled moustache and swarthy skin, who was passing out with his partner said:

—And may we have some refreshment, too, Miss Morkan?

—Julia, said Aunt Kate summarily, and here's Mr. Browne and Miss Furlong. Take them in, Julia, with Miss Daly and Miss Power.

—I'm the man for the ladies, said Mr. Browne, pursing his lips until his moustache bristled and smiling in all his wrinkles. You know, Miss Morkan, the reason they are so fond of me is—

He did not finish his sentence, but, seeing that Aunt Kate was out of earshot, at once led the three young ladies into the back room. The middle of the room was occupied by two square tables placed end to end, and on these Aunt Julia and the caretaker were straightening and smoothing a large cloth. On the sideboard were arrayed dishes and plates, and glasses and bundles of knives and forks and spoons. The top of the closed square piano served also as a sideboard for viands and sweets. At a smaller sideboard in one corner two young men were standing, drinking hop-bitters.[2]

Mr. Browne led his charges thither and invited them all, in jest, to some ladies' punch, hot, strong and sweet. As they said they never took anything strong he opened three bottles of lemonade for them. Then he asked one of the young men to move aside, and, taking hold of the decanter, filled out for himself a goodly measure of whiskey. The young men eyed him respectfully while he took a trial sip.

—God help me, he said, smiling, it's the doctor's orders.

His wizened face broke into a broader smile, and the three young ladies laughed in musical echo to his pleasantry, swaying their bodies to and fro, with nervous jerks of their shoulders. The boldest said:

2. Unfermented beer.

—O, now, Mr. Browne, I'm sure the doctor never ordered anything of the kind.

Mr. Browne took another sip of his whiskey and said, with sidling mimicry:

—Well, you see, I'm like the famous Mrs. Cassidy, who is reported to have said: *Now, Mary Grimes, if I don't take it, make me take it, for I feel I want it.*

His hot face had leaned forward a little too confidentially and he had assumed a very low Dublin accent so that the young ladies, with one instinct, received his speech in silence. Miss Furlong, who was one of Mary Jane's pupils, asked Miss Daly what was the name of the pretty waltz she had played; and Mr. Browne, seeing that he was ignored, turned promptly to the two young men who were more appreciative.

A red-faced young woman, dressed in pansy,[3] came into the room, excitedly clapping her hands and crying:

—Quadrilles![4] Quadrilles!

Close on her heels came Aunt Kate, crying:

—Two gentlemen and three ladies, Mary Jane!

—O, here's Mr. Bergin and Mr. Kerrigan, said Mary Jane. Mr. Kerrigan, will you take Miss Power? Miss Furlong, may I get you a partner, Mr. Bergin. O, that'll just do now.

—Three ladies, Mary Jane, said Aunt Kate.

The two young gentlemen asked the ladies if they might have the pleasure, and Mary Jane turned to Miss Daly.

—O, Miss Daly, you're really awfully good, after playing for the last two dances, but really we're so short of ladies to-night.

—I don't mind in the least, Miss Morkan.

—But I've a nice partner for you, Mr. Bartell D'Arcy, the tenor. I'll get him to sing later on. All Dublin is raving about him.

—Lovely voice, lovely voice! said Aunt Kate.

As the piano had twice begun the prelude to the first figure Mary Jane led her recruits quickly from the room. They had hardly gone when Aunt Julia wandered slowly into the room, looking behind her at something.

—What is the matter, Julia? asked Aunt Kate anxiously. Who is it?

Julia, who was carrying in a column of table-napkins turned to her sister and said, simply, as if the question had surprised her:

—It's only Freddy, Kate, and Gabriel with him.

In fact right behind her Gabriel could be seen piloting Freddy Malins across the landing. The latter, a young man of forty, was of Gabriel's size and build, with very round shoulders. His face was fleshy and pallid, touched with colour only at the thick hanging lobes of his ears and at the wide wings of his nose. He had coarse features, a blunt nose, a convex and receding brow, tumid and protruded lips. His heavy-lidded eyes and the disorder of his scanty hair made him look sleepy. He was laughing heartily in a high key at a story which he had been telling Gabriel on the stairs and at the same time rubbing the knuckles of his left fist backwards and forwards into his left eye.

—Good-evening, Freddy, said Aunt Julia.

---

3. Violet.   4. An intricate square dance for four couples.

Freddy Malins bade the Misses Morkan good-evening in what seemed an offhand fashion by reason of the habitual catch in his voice and then, seeing that Mr. Browne was grinning at him from the sideboard, crossed the room on rather shaky legs and began to repeat in an undertone the story he had just told to Gabriel.

—He's not so bad, is he? said Aunt Kate to Gabriel.

Gabriel's brows were dark but he raised them quickly and answered:

—O no, hardly noticeable.

—Now, isn't he a terrible fellow! she said. And his poor mother made him take the pledge on New Year's Eve. But come on, Gabriel, into the drawing-room.

Before leaving the room with Gabriel she signalled to Mr. Browne by frowning and shaking her forefinger in warning to and fro. Mr. Browne nodded in answer and, when she had gone, said to Freddy Malins:

—Now, then, Teddy, I'm going to fill you out a good glass of lemonade just to buck you up.

Freddy Malins, who was nearing the climax of his story, waved the offer aside impatiently but Mr. Browne, having first called Freddy Malins' attention to a disarray in his dress,[5] filled out and handed him a full glass of lemonade. Freddy Malins' left hand accepted the glass mechanically, his right hand being engaged in the mechanical readjustment of his dress. Mr. Browne, whose face was once more wrinkling with mirth, poured out for himself a glass of whisky while Freddy Malins exploded, before he had well reached the climax of his story, in a kink of high-pitched bronchitic laughter and, setting down his untasted and overflowing glass, began to rub the knuckles of his left fist backwards and forwards into his left eye, repeating words of his last phrase as well as his fit of laughter would allow him.

Gabriel could not listen while Mary Jane was playing her Academy piece, full of runs and difficult passages, to the hushed drawing-room. He liked music but the piece she was playing had no melody for him and he doubted whether it had any melody for the other listeners, though they had begged Mary Jane to play something. Four young men, who had come from the refreshment-room to stand in the doorway at the sound of the piano, had gone away quietly in couples after a few minutes. The only persons who seemed to follow the music were Mary Jane herself, her hands racing along the key-board or lifted from it at the pauses like those of a priestess in momentary imprecation, and Aunt Kate standing at her elbow to turn the page.

Gabriel's eyes, irritated by the floor, which glittered with beeswax under the heavy chandelier, wandered to the wall above the piano. A picture of the balcony scene in *Romeo and Juliet* hung there and beside it was a picture of the two murdered princes[6] in the Tower which Aunt Julia had worked in red, blue and brown wools when she was a girl. Probably in the school they had gone to as girls that kind of work had been taught, for one year his mother had worked for him as a birthday present a waistcoat of purple tabinet,[7] with little foxes'

---

5. That his fly was open.
6. According to Shakespeare's *Richard III*, the young heirs to the British throne were murdered in the Tower of London by order of

their uncle, King Richard III. *Balcony scene*: Shakespeare's *Romeo and Juliet* 2.2.
7. A damasklike fabric.

heads upon it, lined with brown satin and having round mulberry buttons. It was strange that his mother had had no musical talent though Aunt Kate used to call her the brains carrier of the Morkan family. Both she and Julia had always seemed a little proud of their serious and matronly sister. Her photograph stood before the pierglass.[8] She held an open book on her knees and was pointing out something in it to Constantine who, dressed in a man-o'-war suit,[9] lay at her feet. It was she who had chosen the names for her sons for she was very sensible of the dignity of family life. Thanks to her, Constantine was now senior curate in Balbriggan and, thanks to her, Gabriel himself had taken his degree in the Royal University. A shadow passed over his face as he remembered her sullen opposition to his marriage. Some slighting phrases she had used still rankled in his memory; she had once spoken of Gretta as being country cute[1] and that was not true of Gretta at all. It was Gretta who had nursed her during all her last long illness in their house at Monkstown.

He knew that Mary Jane must be near the end of her piece for she was playing again the opening melody with runs of scales after every bar and while he waited for the end the resentment died down in his heart. The piece ended with a trill of octaves in the treble and a final deep octave in the bass. Great applause greeted Mary Jane as, blushing and rolling up her music nervously, she escaped from the room. The most vigorous clapping came from the four young men in the doorway who had gone away to the refreshment-room at the beginning of the piece but had come back when the piano had stopped.

Lancers were arranged. Gabriel found himself partnered with Miss Ivors. She was a frank-mannered talkative young lady, with a freckled face and prominent brown eyes. She did not wear a low-cut bodice and the large brooch which was fixed in the front of her collar bore on it an Irish device.

When they had taken their places she said abruptly:

—I have a crow to pluck[2] with you.

—With me? said Gabriel.

She nodded her head gravely.

—What is it? asked Gabriel, smiling at her solemn manner.

—Who is G. C.? answered Miss Ivors, turning her eyes upon him.

Gabriel coloured and was about to knit his brows, as if he did not understand, when she said bluntly:

—O, innocent Amy! I have found out that you write for *The Daily Express*.[3] Now, aren't you ashamed of yourself?

—Why should I be ashamed of myself? asked Gabriel, blinking his eyes and trying to smile.

—Well, I'm ashamed of you, said Miss Ivors frankly. To say you'd write for a rag like that. I didn't think you were a West Briton.[4]

A look of perplexity appeared on Gabriel's face. It was true that he wrote a literary column every Wednesday in *The Daily Express*, for which he was paid fifteen shillings. But that did not make him a West Briton surely. The books he received for review were almost more welcome than the paltry cheque. He

8. A large mirror.
9. A sailor suit.
1. Unintelligent (not acute).
2. A bone to pick; an argument.

3. Conservative Dublin newspaper opposed to Irish independence.
4. An Irishman who supports union with Britain (an insult).

loved to feel the covers and turn over the pages of newly printed books. Nearly every day when his teaching in the college was ended he used to wander down the quays to the second-hand booksellers, to Hickey's on Bachelor's Walk, to Webb's or Massey's on Aston's Quay, or to O'Clohissey's in the by-street. He did not know how to meet her charge. He wanted to say that literature was above politics. But they were friends of many years' standing and their careers had been parallel, first at the University and then as teachers: he could not risk a grandiose phrase with her. He continued blinking his eyes and trying to smile and murmured lamely that he saw nothing political in writing reviews of books.

When their turn to cross[5] had come he was still perplexed and inattentive. Miss Ivors promptly took his hand in a warm grasp and said in a soft friendly tone:

—Of course, I was only joking. Come, we cross now.

When they were together again she spoke of the University question,[6] and Gabriel felt more at ease. A friend of hers had shown her his review of Browning's poems. That was how she had found out the secret: but she liked the review immensely. Then she said suddenly:

—O, Mr. Conroy, will you come for an excursion to the Aran Isles[7] this summer? We're going to stay there a whole month. It will be splendid out in the Atlantic. You ought to come. Mr. Clancy is coming, and Mr. Kilkelly and Kathleen Kearney. It would be splendid for Gretta too if she'd come. She's from Connacht,[8] isn't she?

—Her people are, said Gabriel shortly.

—But you will come, won't you? said Miss Ivors, laying her warm hand eagerly on his arm.

—The fact is, said Gabriel, I have already arranged to go—

—Go where? asked Miss Ivors.

—Well, you know, every year I go for a cycling tour with some fellows and so—

—But where? asked Miss Ivors.

—Well, we usually go to France or Belgium or perhaps Germany, said Gabriel awkwardly.

—And why do you go to France and Belgium, said Miss Ivors, instead of visiting your own land?

—Well, said Gabriel, it's partly to keep in touch with the languages and partly for a change.

—And haven't you your own language to keep in touch with—Irish? asked Miss Ivors.

—Well, said Gabriel, if it comes to that, you know, Irish is not my language.

Their neighbours had turned to listen to the cross-examination. Gabriel glanced right and left nervously and tried to keep his good humour under the ordeal which was making a blush invade his forehead.

5. A step in the square dance.
6. Controversy over the establishment of Irish Catholic universities to rival the dominant Protestant tradition of Oxford and Cambridge in England, and Trinity College in Dublin.

7. Off the west coast of Ireland, idealized by the nationalists as an example of unspoiled Irish culture and language.
8. The westernmost province of Ireland.

—And haven't you your own land to visit, continued Miss Ivors, that you know nothing of, your own people, and your own country?

—O, to tell you the truth, retorted Gabriel suddenly, I'm sick of my own country, sick of it!

—Why? asked Miss Ivors.

Gabriel did not answer for his retort had heated him.

—Why? repeated Miss Ivors.

They had to go visiting together[9] and, as he had not answered her, Miss Ivors said warmly:

—Of course, you've no answer.

Gabriel tried to cover his agitation by taking part in the dance with great energy. He avoided her eyes for he had seen a sour expression on her face. But when they met in the long chain[1] he was surprised to feel his hand firmly pressed. She looked at him from under her brows for a moment quizzically until he smiled. Then, just as the chain was about to start again, she stood on tiptoe and whispered into his ear:

—West Briton!

When the lancers were over Gabriel went away to a remote corner of the room where Freddy Malins' mother was sitting. She was a stout feeble old woman with white hair. Her voice had a catch in it like her son's and she stuttered slightly. She had been told that Freddy had come and that he was nearly all right. Gabriel asked her whether she had had a good crossing. She lived with her married daughter in Glasgow and came to Dublin on a visit once a year. She answered placidly that she had had a beautiful crossing and that the captain had been most attentive to her. She spoke also of the beautiful house her daughter kept in Glasgow, and of all the nice friends they had there. While her tongue rambled on Gabriel tried to banish from his mind all memory of the unpleasant incident with Miss Ivors. Of course the girl or woman, or whatever she was, was an enthusiast but there was a time for all things. Perhaps he ought not to have answered her like that. But she had no right to call him a West Briton before people, even in joke. She had tried to make him ridiculous before people, heckling him and staring at him with her rabbit's eyes.

He saw his wife making her way towards him through the waltzing couples. When she reached him she said into his ear:

—Gabriel, Aunt Kate wants to know won't you carve the goose as usual. Miss Daly will carve the ham and I'll do the pudding.

—All right, said Gabriel.

—She's sending in the younger ones first as soon as this waltz is over so that we'll have the table to ourselves.

—Were you dancing? asked Gabriel.

—Of course I was. Didn't you see me? What words had you with Molly Ivors?

—No words. Why? Did she say so?

—Something like that. I'm trying to get that Mr. D'Arcy to sing. He's full of conceit, I think.

---

9. A square-dance step.   1. Another square-dance step.

—There were no words, said Gabriel moodily, only she wanted me to go for a trip to the west of Ireland and I said I wouldn't.

His wife clasped her hands excitedly and gave a little jump.

—O, do go, Gabriel, she cried. I'd love to see Galway again.

—You can go if you like, said Gabriel coldly.

She looked at him for a moment, then turned to Mrs. Malins and said:

—There's a nice husband for you, Mrs. Malins.

While she was threading her way back across the room Mrs. Malins, without adverting to the interruption, went on to tell Gabriel what beautiful places there were in Scotland and beautiful scenery. Her son-in-law brought them every year to the lakes and they used to go fishing. Her son-in-law was a splendid fisher. One day he caught a fish, a beautiful big big fish, and the man in the hotel boiled it for their dinner.

Gabriel hardly heard what she said. Now that supper was coming near he began to think again about his speech and about the quotation. When he saw Freddy Malins coming across the room to visit his mother Gabriel left the chair free for him and retired into the embrasure of the window. The room had already cleared and from the back room came the clatter of plates and knives. Those who still remained in the drawing-room seemed tired of dancing and were conversing quietly in little groups. Gabriel's warm trembling fingers tapped the cold pane of the window. How cool it must be outside! How pleasant it would be to walk out alone, first along by the river and then through the park! The snow would be lying on the branches of the trees and forming a bright cap on the top of the Wellington Monument.[2] How much more pleasant it would be there than at the supper-table!

He ran over the headings of his speech: Irish hospitality, sad memories, the Three Graces, Paris,[3] the quotation from Browning. He repeated to himself a phrase he had written in his review: *One feels that one is listening to a thought-tormented music.* Miss Ivors had praised the review. Was she sincere? Had she really any life of her own behind all her propagandism? There had never been any ill-feeling between them until that night. It unnerved him to think that she would be at the supper-table, looking up at him while he spoke with her critical quizzing eyes. Perhaps she would not be sorry to see him fail in his speech. An idea came into his mind and gave him courage. He would say, alluding to Aunt Kate and Aunt Julia: *Ladies and Gentlemen, the generation which is now on the wane among us may have had its faults but for my part I think it had certain qualities of hospitality, of humour, of humanity, which the new and very serious and hypereducated generation that is growing up around us seems to me to lack.* Very good: that was one for Miss Ivors. What did he care that his aunts were only two ignorant old women?

A murmur in the room attracted his attention. Mr. Browne was advancing from the door, gallantly escorting Aunt Julia, who leaned upon his arm, smiling and hanging her head. An irregular musketry of applause escorted her also as

2. A tall obelisk in Phoenix Park, celebrating the duke of Wellington (1769–1852), an Anglo-Irish statesman and general, who served as British prime minister and commander-in-chief of the army.

3. The Trojan prince of Homer's *Iliad*. "Three Graces": daughters of Zeus and Eurynome in Greek mythology; they embodied (and bestowed) charm.

far as the piano and then, as Mary Jane seated herself on the stool, and Aunt Julia, no longer smiling, half turned so as to pitch her voice fairly into the room, gradually ceased. Gabriel recognized the prelude. It was that of an old song of Aunt Julia's—*Arrayed for the Bridal*.[4] Her voice, strong and clear in tone, attacked with great spirit the runs which embellish the air and though she sang very rapidly she did not miss even the smallest of the grace notes. To follow the voice, without looking at the singer's face, was to feel and share the excitement of swift and secure flight. Gabriel applauded loudly with all the others at the close of the song and loud applause was borne in from the invisible supper-table. It sounded so genuine that a little colour struggled into Aunt Julia's face as she bent to replace in the music-stand the old leather-bound song-book that had her initials on the cover. Freddy Malins, who had listened with his head perched sideways to hear her better, was still applauding when everyone else had ceased and talking animatedly to his mother who nodded her head gravely and slowly in acquiescence. At last, when he could clap no more, he stood up suddenly and hurried across the room to Aunt Julia whose hand he seized and held in both his hands, shaking it when words failed him or the catch in his voice proved too much for him.

—I was just telling my mother, he said, I never heard you sing so well, never. No, I never heard your voice so good as it is to-night. Now! Would you believe that now? That's the truth. Upon my word and honour that's the truth. I never heard your voice sound so fresh and so . . . so clear and fresh, never.

Aunt Julia smiled broadly and murmured something about compliments as she released her hand from his grasp. Mr. Browne extended his open hand towards her and said to those who were near him in the manner of a showman introducing a prodigy to an audience:

—Miss Julia Morkan, my latest discovery!

—He was laughing very heartily at this himself when Freddy Malins turned to him and said:

—Well, Browne, if you're serious you might make a worse discovery. All I can say is I never heard her sing half so well as long as I am coming here. And that's the honest truth.

—Neither did I, said Mr. Browne. I think her voice has greatly improved.

Aunt Julia shrugged her shoulders and said with meek pride:

—Thirty years ago I hadn't a bad voice as voices go.

—I often told Julia, said Aunt Kate emphatically, that she was simply thrown away in that choir. But she never would be said by me.

She turned as if to appeal to the good sense of the others against a refractory child while Aunt Julia gazed in front of her, a vague smile of reminiscence playing on her face.

—No, continued Aunt Kate, she wouldn't be said or led by anyone, slaving there in that choir night and day, night and day. Six o'clock on Christmas morning! And all for what?

—Well, isn't it for the honour of God, Aunt Kate? asked Mary Jane, twisting round on the piano-stool and smiling.

Aunt Kate turned fiercely on her niece and said:

4. An English lyric by George Linley; from the first act of Vincenzo Bellini's 1835 opera *I Puritani* (The Puritans).

—I know all about the honour of God, Mary Jane, but I think it's not at all honourable for the pope to turn out the women out of the choirs that have slaved there all their lives and put little whipper-snappers of boys over their heads.[5] I suppose it is for the good of the Church if the pope does it. But it's not just, Mary Jane, and it's not right.

She had worked herself into a passion and would have continued in defence of her sister for it was a sore subject with her but Mary Jane, seeing that all the dancers had come back, intervened pacifically:

—Now, Aunt Kate, you're giving scandal to Mr. Browne who is of the other persuasion.

Aunt Kate turned to Mr. Browne, who was grinning at this allusion to his religion, and said hastily:

—O, I don't question the pope's being right. I'm only a stupid old woman and I wouldn't presume to do such a thing. But there's such a thing as common everyday politeness and gratitude. And if I were in Julia's place I'd tell that Father Healy straight up to his face . . . .

—And besides, Aunt Kate, said Mary Jane, we really are all hungry and when we are hungry we are all very quarrelsome.

—And when we are thirsty we are also quarrelsome, added Mr. Browne.

—So that we had better go to supper, said Mary Jane, and finish the discussion afterwards.

On the landing outside the drawing-room Gabriel found his wife and Mary Jane trying to persuade Miss Ivors to stay for supper. But Miss Ivors, who had put on her hat and was buttoning her cloak, would not stay. She did not feel in the least hungry and she had already overstayed her time.

—But only for ten minutes, Molly, said Mrs. Conroy. That won't delay you.

—To take a pick itself, said Mary Jane, after all your dancing.

—I really couldn't, said Miss Ivors.

—I am afraid you didn't enjoy yourself at all, said Mary Jane hopelessly.

—Ever so much, I assure you, said Miss Ivors, but you really must let me run off now.

—But how can you get home? asked Mrs. Conroy.

—O, it's only two steps up the quay.

Gabriel hesitated a moment and said:

—If you will allow me, Miss Ivors, I'll see you home if you really are obliged to go.

But Miss Ivors broke away from them.

—I won't hear of it, she cried. For goodness sake go in to your suppers and don't mind me. I'm quite well able to take care of myself.

—Well, you're the comical girl, Molly, said Mrs. Conroy frankly.

—*Beannacht libh*,[6] cried Miss Ivors, with a laugh, as she ran down the staircase.

Mary Jane gazed after her, a moody puzzled expression on her face, while Mrs. Conroy leaned over the banisters to listen for the hall-door. Gabriel asked himself was he the cause of her abrupt departure. But she did not seem to be in ill humour: she had gone away laughing. He stared blankly down the staircase.

---

5. In 1903, Pope Pius X decreed that all church singers be male.   6. Farewell: blessings on you (Irish).

At that moment Aunt Kate came toddling out of the supper-room, almost wringing her hands in despair.

—Where is Gabriel? she cried. Where on earth is Gabriel? There's everyone waiting in there, stage to let, and nobody to carve the goose!

—Here I am, Aunt Kate! cried Gabriel, with sudden animation, ready to carve a flock of geese, if necessary.

A fat brown goose lay at one end of the table and at the other end, on a bed of creased paper strewn with sprigs of parsley, lay a great ham, stripped of its outer skin and peppered over with crust crumbs, a neat paper frill round its shin and beside this was a round of spiced beef. Between these rival ends ran parallel lines of side-dishes: two little minsters[7] of jelly, red and yellow; a shallow dish full of blocks of blancmange and red jam, a large green leaf-shaped dish with a stalk-shaped handle, on which lay bunches of purple raisins and peeled almonds, a companion dish on which lay a solid rectangle of Smyrna figs, a dish of custard topped with grated nutmeg, a small bowl full of chocolates and sweets wrapped in gold and silver papers and a glass vase in which stood some tall celery stalks. In the center of the table there stood, as sentries to a fruit-stand which upheld a pyramid of oranges and American apples, two squat old-fashioned decanters of cut glass, one containing port and the other dark sherry. On the closed square piano a pudding in a huge yellow dish lay in waiting and behind it were three squads of bottles of stout and ale and minerals,[8] drawn up according to the colours of their uniforms, the first two black, with brown and red labels, the third and smallest squad white, with transverse green sashes.

Gabriel took his seat boldly at the head of the table and, having looked to the edge of the carver, plunged his fork firmly into the goose. He felt quite at ease now for he was an expert carver and liked nothing better than to find himself at the head of a well-laden table.

—Miss Furlong, what shall I send you? he asked. A wing or a slice of the breast?

—Just a small slice of the breast.

—Miss Higgins, what for you?

—O, anything at all, Mr. Conroy.

While Gabriel and Miss Daly exchanged plates of goose and plates of ham and spiced beef Lily went from guest to guest with a dish of hot floury potatoes wrapped in a white napkin. This was Mary Jane's idea and she had also suggested apple sauce for the goose but Aunt Kate had said that plain roast goose without apple sauce had always been good enough for her and she hoped she might never eat worse. Mary Jane waited on her pupils and saw that they got the best slices and Aunt Kate and Aunt Julia opened and carried across from the piano bottles of stout and ale for the gentlemen and bottles of minerals for the ladies. There was a great deal of confusion and laughter and noise, the noise of orders and counter-orders, of knives and forks, of corks and glass-stoppers. Gabriel began to carve second helpings as soon as he had finished the first round without serving himself. Everyone protested loudly so that he compromised by taking a long draught of stout for he had found the carving hot

7. Confectioneries shaped to look like cathedrals.

8. Carbonated drinks.

work. Mary Jane settled down quietly to her supper but Aunt Kate and Aunt Julia were still toddling round the table, walking on each other's heels, getting in each other's way and giving each other unheeded orders. Mr. Browne begged of them to sit down and eat their suppers and so did Gabriel but they said there was time enough so that, at last, Freddy Malins stood up and, capturing Aunt Kate, plumped her down on her chair amid general laughter.

When everyone had been well served Gabriel said, smiling:

—Now, if anyone wants a little more of what vulgar people call stuffing let him or her speak.

A chorus of voices invited him to begin his own supper and Lily came forward with three potatoes which she had reserved for him.

—Very well, said Gabriel amiably, as he took another preparatory draught, kindly forget my existence, ladies and gentlemen, for a few minutes.

He sat to his supper and took no part in the conversation with which the table covered Lily's removal of the plates. The subject of talk was the opera company which was then at the Theatre Royal. Mr. Bartell D'Arcy, the tenor, a dark-complexioned young man with a smart moustache, praised very highly the leading contralto of the company but Miss Furlong thought she had a rather vulgar style of production. Freddy Malins said there was a negro chieftain[9] singing in the second part of the Gaiety pantomime who had one of the finest tenor voices he had ever heard.

—Have you heard him? he asked Mr. Bartell D'Arcy across the table.

—No, answered Mr. Bartell D'Arcy carelessly.

—Because, Freddy Malins explained, now I'd be curious to hear your opinion of him. I think he has a grand voice.

—It takes Teddy to find out the really good things, said Mr. Browne familiarly to the table.

—And why couldn't he have a voice too? asked Freddy Malins sharply. Is it because he's only a black?

Nobody answered this question and Mary Jane led the table back to the legitimate opera. One of her pupils had given her a pass for *Mignon*.[1] Of course it was very fine, she said, but it made her think of poor Georgina Burns. Mr. Browne could go back farther still, to the old Italian companies that used to come to Dublin—Tietjens, Ilma de Murzka, Campanini, the great Trebelli, Giuglini, Ravelli, Aramburo.[2] Those were the days, he said, when there was something like singing to be heard in Dublin. He told too of how the top gallery of the old Royal used to be packed night after night, of how one night an Italian tenor had sung five encores to *Let Me Like a Soldier Fall*,[3] introducing a high C every time, and of how the gallery boys would sometimes in their enthusiasm unyoke the horses from the carriage of some great *prima donna* and pull her themselves through the streets to her hotel. Why did they never play the grand old operas now, he asked, *Dinorah, Lucrezia Borgia?*[4] Because they could not get the voices to sing them: that was why.

---

9. Actually, a blackface performer.
1. Popular French opera (1866) by Ambroise Thomas.
2. Famous opera singers.

3. From William V. Wallace's romantic light opera *Maritana* (1845).
4. Operas by Giacomo Meyerbeer (1859) and Gaetano Donizetti (1833), respectively.

—O, well, said Mr. Bartell D'Arcy, I presume there are as good singers today as there were then.

—Where are they? asked Mr. Browne defiantly.

—In London, Paris, Milan, said Mr. Bartell D'Arcy warmly. I suppose Caruso,[5] for example, is quite as good, if not better than any of the men you have mentioned.

—Maybe so, said Mr. Browne. But I may tell you I doubt it strongly.

—O, I'd give anything to hear Caruso sing, said Mary Jane.

—For me, said Aunt Kate, who had been picking a bone, there was only one tenor. To please me, I mean. But I suppose none of you ever heard of him.

—Who was he, Miss Morkan? asked Mr. Bartell D'Arcy politely.

—His name, said Aunt Kate, was Parkinson. I heard him when he was in his prime and I think he had then the purest tenor voice that was ever put into a man's throat.

—Strange, said Mr. Bartell D'Arcy. I never even heard of him.

—Yes, yes, Miss Morkan is right, said Mr. Browne. I remember hearing of old Parkinson but he's too far back for me.

—A beautiful pure sweet mellow English tenor, said Aunt Kate with enthusiasm.

Gabriel having finished, the huge pudding was transferred to the table. The clatter of forks and spoons began again. Gabriel's wife served out spoonfuls of the pudding and passed the plates down the table. Midway down they were held up by Mary Jane, who replenished them with raspberry or orange jelly or with blancmange and jam. The pudding was of Aunt Julia's making and she received praises for it from all quarters. She herself said that it was not quite brown enough.

—Well, I hope, Miss Morkan, said Mr. Browne, that I'm brown enough for you because, you know, I'm all brown.

All the gentlemen, except Gabriel, ate some of the pudding out of compliment to Aunt Julia. As Gabriel never ate sweets the celery had been left for him. Freddy Malins also took a stalk of celery and ate it with his pudding. He had been told that celery was a capital thing for the blood and he was just then under doctor's care. Mrs. Malins, who had been silent all through the supper, said that her son was going down to Mount Melleray[6] in a week or so. The table then spoke of Mount Melleray, how bracing the air was down there, how hospitable the monks were and how they never asked for a penny-piece from their guests.

—And do you mean to say, asked Mr. Browne incredulously, that a chap can go down there and put up there as if it were a hotel and live on the fat of the land and then come away without paying a farthing?

—O, most people give some donation to the monastery when they leave, said Mary Jane.

—I wish we had an institution like that in our Church, said Mr. Browne candidly.

He was astonished to hear that the monks never spoke, got up at two in the morning and slept in their coffins.[7] He asked what they did it for.

5. Enrico Caruso (1873–1921).
6. A Trappist abbey whose hospitality included the treatment of wealthy alcoholics.
7. The coffin story is a popular fiction.

1864 | JAMES JOYCE

—That's the rule of the order, said Aunt Kate firmly.

—Yes, but why? asked Mr. Browne.

Aunt Kate repeated that it was the rule, that was all. Mr. Browne still seemed not to understand. Freddy Malins explained to him, as best he could, that the monks were trying to make up for the sins committed by all the sinners in the outside world. The explanation was not very clear for Mr. Browne grinned and said:

—I like that idea very much but wouldn't a comfortable spring bed do them as well as a coffin?

—The coffin, said Mary Jane, is to remind them of their last end.

As the subject had grown lugubrious it was buried in a silence of the table during which Mrs. Malins could be heard saying to her neighbour in an indistinct undertone:

—They are very good men, the monks, very pious men.

The raisins and almonds and figs and apples and oranges and chocolates and sweets were now passed about the table and Aunt Julia invited all the guests to have either port or sherry. At first Mr. Bartell D'Arcy refused to take either but one of his neighbours nudged him and whispered something to him upon which he allowed his glass to be filled. Gradually as the last glasses were being filled the conversation ceased. A pause followed, broken only by the noise of the wine and by unsettlings of chairs. The Misses Morkan, all three, looked down at the tablecloth. Someone coughed once or twice and then a few gentlemen patted the table gently as a signal for silence. The silence came and Gabriel pushed back his chair and stood up.

The patting at once grew louder in encouragement and then ceased altogether. Gabriel leaned his ten trembling fingers on the tablecloth and smiled nervously at the company. Meeting a row of upturned faces he raised his eyes to the chandelier. The piano was playing a waltz tune and he could hear the skirts sweeping against the drawing-room door. People, perhaps, were standing in the snow on the quay outside, gazing up at the lighted windows and listening to the waltz music. The air was pure there. In the distance lay the park where the trees were weighted with snow. The Wellington Monument wore a gleaming cap of snow that flashed westward over the white field of Fifteen Acres.[8]

He began:

—Ladies and Gentlemen.

—It has fallen to my lot this evening, as in years past, to perform a very pleasing task but a task for which I am afraid my poor powers as a speaker are all too inadequate.

—No, no! said Mr. Browne.

—But, however that may be, I can only ask you to-night to take the will for the deed and to lend me your attention for a few moments while I endeavour to express to you in words what my feelings are on this occasion.

—Ladies and Gentlemen. It is not the first time that we have gathered together under this hospitable roof, around this hospitable board. It is not the first time that we have been the recipients—or perhaps, I had better say, the victims—of the hospitality of certain good ladies.

---

8. A section of Phoenix Park used for British military reviews.

He made a circle in the air with his arm and paused. Everyone laughed or smiled at Aunt Kate and Aunt Julia and Mary Jane who all turned crimson with pleasure. Gabriel went on more boldly:

—I feel more strongly with every recurring year that our country has no tradition which does it so much honour and which it should guard so jealously as that of its hospitality. It is a tradition that is unique as far as my experience goes (and I have visited not a few places abroad) among the modern nations. Some would say, perhaps, that with us it is rather a failing than anything to be boasted of. But granted even that, it is, to my mind, a princely failing, and one that I trust will long be cultivated among us. Of one thing, at least, I am sure. As long as this one roof shelters the good ladies aforesaid—and I wish from my heart it may do so for many and many a long year to come—the tradition of genuine warm-hearted courteous Irish hospitality, which our forefathers have handed down to us and which we in turn must hand down to our descendants, is still alive among us.

A hearty murmur of assent ran around the table. It shot through Gabriel's mind that Miss Ivors was not there and that she had gone away discourteously: and he said with confidence in himself:

—Ladies and Gentlemen.

—A new generation is growing up in our midst, a generation actuated by new ideas and new principles. It is serious and enthusiastic for these new ideas and its enthusiasm, even when it is misdirected, is, I believe, in the main sincere. But we are living in a skeptical and, if I may use the phrase, a thought-tormented age: and sometimes I fear that this new generation, educated or hypereducated as it is, will lack those qualities of humanity, of hospitality, of kindly humour which belonged to an older day. Listening tonight to the names of all those great singers of the past it seemed to me, I must confess, that we were living in a less spacious age. Those days might, without exaggeration, be called spacious days: and if they are gone beyond recall let us hope, at least, that in gatherings such as this we shall still speak of them with pride and affection, still cherish in our hearts the memory of those dead and gone great ones whose fame the world will not willingly let die.

—Hear, hear! said Mr. Browne loudly.

—But yet, continued Gabriel, his voice falling into a softer inflection, there are always in gatherings such as this sadder thoughts that will recur to our minds: thoughts of the past, of youth, of changes, of absent faces that we miss here tonight. Our path through life is strewn with many such sad memories: and were we to brood upon them always we could not find the heart to go on bravely with our work among the living. We have all of us living duties and living affections which claim, and rightly claim, our strenuous endeavours.

—Therefore, I will not linger on the past. I will not let any gloomy moralising intrude upon us here to-night. Here we are gathered together for a brief moment from the bustle and rush of our everyday routine. We are met here as friends, in the spirit of good-fellowship, as colleagues, also to a certain extent, in the true spirit of *camaraderie*, and as the guests of—what shall I call them?—the Three Graces of the Dublin musical world.

The table burst into applause and laughter at this sally. Aunt Julia vainly asked each of her neighbours in turn to tell her what Gabriel had said.

—He says we are the Three Graces, Aunt Julia, said Mary Jane.

Aunt Julia did not understand but she looked up, smiling, at Gabriel, who continued in the same vein:

—Ladies and Gentlemen.

—I will not attempt to play to-night the part that Paris played on another occasion.[9] I will not attempt to choose between them. The task would be an invidious one and one beyond my poor powers. For when I view them in turn, whether it be our chief hostess herself, whose good heart, whose too good heart, has become a byword with all who know her, or her sister, who seems to be gifted with perennial youth and whose singing must have been a surprise and a revelation to us all to-night, or, last but not least, when I consider our youngest hostess, talented, cheerful, hard-working and the best of nieces, I confess, Ladies and Gentlemen, that I do not know to which of them I should award the prize.

Gabriel glanced down at his aunts and, seeing the large smile on Aunt Julia's face and the tears which had risen to Aunt Kate's eyes, hastened to his close. He raised his glass of port gallantly, while every member of the company fingered a glass expectantly, and said loudly:

—Let us toast them all three together. Let us drink to their health, wealth, long life, happiness and prosperity and may they long continue to hold the proud and self-won position which they hold in their profession and the position of honour and affection which they hold in our hearts.

All the guests stood up, glass in hand, and, turning towards the three seated ladies, sang in unison, with Mr. Browne as leader:

> *For they are jolly gay fellows,*
> *For they are jolly gay fellows,*
> *For they are jolly gay fellows,*
> *Which nobody can deny.*

Aunt Kate was making frank use of her handkerchief and even Aunt Julia seemed moved. Freddy Malins beat time with his pudding-fork and the singers turned towards one another, as if in melodious conference, while they sang, with emphasis:

> *Unless he tells a lie,*
> *Unless he tells a lie,*

Then, turning once more towards their hostesses, they sang:

> *For they are jolly gay fellows,*
> *For they are jolly gay fellows,*
> *For they are jolly gay fellows,*
> *Which nobody can deny.*

The acclamation which followed was taken up beyond the door of the supper-room by many of the other guests and renewed time after time, Freddy Malins acting as officer with his fork on high.

---

9. Paris was required to judge a beauty contest between the Greek goddesses Hera, Athena, and Aphrodite; see p. 1858, n. 3.

The piercing morning air came into the hall where they were standing so that Aunt Kate said:

—Close the door, somebody. Mrs. Malins will get her death of cold.

—Browne is out there, Aunt Kate, said Mary Jane.

—Browne is everywhere, said Aunt Kate, lowering her voice.

Mary Jane laughed at her tone.

—Really, she said archly, he is very attentive.

—He has been laid on here like the gas, said Aunt Kate in the same tone, all during the Christmas.

She laughed herself this time good-humouredly and then added quickly:

—But tell him to come in, Mary Jane, and close the door. I hope to goodness he didn't hear me.

At that moment the hall-door was opened and Mr. Browne came in from the doorstep, laughing as if his heart would break. He was dressed in a long green overcoat with mock astrakhan cuffs and collar and wore on his head an oval fur cap. He pointed down the snow-covered quay from where the sound of shrill prolonged whistling was borne in.

—Teddy will have all the cabs in Dublin out, he said.

Gabriel advanced from the little pantry behind the office, struggling into his overcoat and, looking round the hall, said:

—Gretta not down yet?

—She's getting on her things, Gabriel, said Aunt Kate.

—Who's playing up there? asked Gabriel.

—Nobody. They're all gone.

—O no, Aunt Kate, said Mary Jane. Bartell D'Arcy and Miss O'Callaghan aren't gone yet.

—Someone is strumming at the piano, anyhow, said Gabriel.

Mary Jane glanced at Gabriel and Mr. Browne and said with a shiver:

—It makes me feel cold to look at you two gentlemen muffled up like that. I wouldn't like to face your journey home at this hour.

—I'd like nothing better this minute, said Mr. Browne stoutly, than a rattling fine walk in the country or a fast drive with a good spanking goer between the shafts.

—We used to have a very good horse and trap at home, said Aunt Julia sadly.

—The never-to-be-forgotten Johnny, said Mary Jane, laughing.

Aunt Kate and Gabriel laughed too.

—Why, what was wonderful about Johnny? asked Mr. Browne.

—The late lamented Patrick Morkan, our grandfather, that is, explained Gabriel, commonly known in his later years as the old gentleman, was a glue-boiler.

—O, now, Gabriel, said Aunt Kate, laughing, he had a starch mill.

—Well, glue or starch, said Gabriel, the old gentleman had a horse by the name of Johnny. And Johnny used to work in the old gentleman's mill, walking round and round in order to drive the mill. That was all very well; but now comes the tragic part about Johnny. One fine day the old gentleman thought he'd like to drive out with the quality to a military review in the park.

—The Lord have mercy on his soul, said Aunt Kate compassionately.

—Amen, said Gabriel. So the old gentleman, as I said, harnessed Johnny and put on his very best tall hat and his very best stock collar and drove out in grand style from his ancestral mansion somewhere near Back Lane,[1] I think.

Everyone laughed, even Mrs. Malins, at Gabriel's manner and Aunt Kate said:

—O now, Gabriel, he didn't live in Back Lane, really. Only the mill was there.

—Out from the mansion of his forefathers, continued Gabriel, he drove with Johnny. And everything went on beautifully until Johnny came in sight of King Billy's[2] statue: and whether he fell in love with the horse King Billy sits on or whether he thought he was back again in the mill, anyhow he began to walk round the statue.

Gabriel paced in a circle round the hall in his goloshes amid the laughter of the others.

—Round and round he went, said Gabriel, and the old gentleman, who was a very pompous old gentleman, was highly indignant. *Go on, sir! What do you mean, sir? Johnny! Johnny! Most extraordinary conduct! Can't understand the horse!*

The peals of laughter which followed Gabriel's imitation of the incident were interrupted by a resounding knock at the hall-door. Mary Jane ran to open it and let in Freddy Malins. Freddy Malins, with his hat well back on his head and his shoulders humped with cold, was puffing and steaming after his exertions.

—I could only get one cab, he said.

—O, we'll find another along the quay, said Gabriel.

—Yes, said Aunt Kate. Better not keep Mrs. Malins standing in the draught.

Mrs. Malins was helped down the front steps by her son and Mr. Browne and, after many manœuvres, hoisted into the cab. Freddy Malins clambered in after her and spent a long time settling her on the seat, Mr. Browne helping him with advice. At last she was settled comfortably and Freddy Malins invited Mr. Browne into the cab. There was a good deal of confused talk, and then Mr. Browne got into the cab. The cabman settled his rug over his knees, and bent down for the address. The confusion grew greater and the cabman was directed differently by Freddy Malins and Mr. Browne, each of whom had his head out through a window of the cab. The difficulty was to know where to drop Mr. Browne along the route and Aunt Kate, Aunt Julia and Mary Jane helped the discussion from the doorstep with cross-directions and contradictions and abundance of laughter. As for Freddy Malins he was speechless with laughter. He popped his head in and out of the window every moment, to the great danger of his hat, and told his mother how the discussion was progressing till at last Mr. Browne shouted to the bewildered cabman above the din of everybody's laughter:

—Do you know Trinity College?

—Yes, sir, said the cabman.

—Well, drive bang up against Trinity College gates, said Mr. Browne, and then we'll tell you where to go. You understand now?

1. A shabby street in a run-down area of Dublin.
2. William III, king of England from 1689 to 1702, defeated the Irish nationalists at the Battle of the Boyne.

—Yes, sir, said the cabman.

—Make like a bird for Trinity College.

—Right, sir, cried the cabman.

The horse was whipped up and the cab rattled off along the quay amid a chorus of laughter and adieus.

Gabriel had not gone to the door with the others. He was in a dark part of the hall gazing up the staircase. A woman was standing near the top of the first flight, in the shadow also. He could not see her face but he could see the terracotta and salmonpink panels of her skirt which the shadow made appear black and white. It was his wife. She was leaning on the banisters, listening to something. Gabriel was surprised at her stillness and strained his ear to listen also. But he could hear little save the noise of laughter and dispute on the front steps, a few chords struck on the piano and a few notes of a man's voice singing.

He stood still in the gloom of the hall, trying to catch the air that the voice was singing and gazing up at his wife. There was grace and mystery in her attitude as if she were a symbol of something. He asked himself what is a woman standing on the stairs in the shadow, listening to distant music, a symbol of. If he were a painter he would paint her in that attitude. Her blue felt hat would show off the bronze of her hair against the darkness and the dark panels of her skirt would show off the light ones. *Distant Music* he would call the picture if he were a painter.

The hall-door was closed; and Aunt Kate, Aunt Julia and Mary Jane came down the hall, still laughing.

—Well, isn't Freddy terrible? said Mary Jane. He's really terrible.

Gabriel said nothing but pointed up the stairs towards where his wife was standing. Now that the hall-door was closed the voice and the piano could be heard more clearly. Gabriel held up his hand for them to be silent. The song seemed to be in the old Irish tonality[3] and the singer seemed uncertain both of his words and of his voice. The voice, made plaintive by distance and by the singer's hoarseness, faintly illuminated the cadence of the air with words expressing grief:

> *O, the rain falls on my heavy locks*
> *And the dew wets my skin,*
> *My babe lies cold*[4] . . .

—O, exclaimed Mary Jane. It's Bartell D'Arcy singing and he wouldn't sing all the night. O, I'll get him to sing a song before he goes.

—O do, Mary Jane, said Aunt Kate.

Mary Jane brushed past the others and ran to the staircase but before she reached it the singing stopped and the piano was closed abruptly.

—O, what a pity! she cried. Is he coming down, Gretta?

Gabriel heard his wife answer yes and saw her come down towards them. A few steps behind her were Mr. Bartell D'Arcy and Miss O'Callaghan.

---

3. Based on five (and later seven) tones rather than the modern eight-tone scale.
4. From "The Lass of Aughrim," a ballad about a peasant girl seduced by a lord; when she brings her baby to the castle door, the lord's mother imitates his voice and sends her away. Mother and child are drowned at sea, and the repentant lord curses his mother.

—O, Mr. D'Arcy, cried Mary Jane, it's downright mean of you to break off like that when we were all in raptures listening to you.

—I have been at him all the evening, said Miss O'Callaghan, and Mrs. Conroy too and he told us he had a dreadful cold and couldn't sing.

—O, Mr. D'Arcy, said Aunt Kate, now that was a great fib to tell.

—Can't you see that I'm as hoarse as a crow? said Mr. D'Arcy roughly.

He went into the pantry hastily and put on his overcoat. The others, taken aback by his rude speech, could find nothing to say. Aunt Kate wrinkled her brows and made signs to the others to drop the subject. Mr. D'Arcy stood swathing his neck carefully and frowning.

—It's the weather, said Aunt Julia, after a pause.

—Yes, everybody has colds, said Aunt Kate readily, everybody.

—They say, said Mary Jane, we haven't had snow like it for thirty years; and I read this morning in the newspapers that the snow is general all over Ireland.

—I love the look of snow, said Aunt Julia sadly.

—So do I, said Miss O'Callaghan. I think Christmas is never really Christmas unless we have the snow on the ground.

—But poor Mr. D'Arcy doesn't like the snow, said Aunt Kate, smiling.

Mr. D'Arcy came from the pantry, fully swathed and buttoned, and in a repentant tone told them the history of his cold. Everyone gave him advice and said it was a great pity and urged him to be very careful of his throat in the night air. Gabriel watched his wife who did not join in the conversation. She was standing right under the dusty fanlight and the flame of the gas lit up the rich bronze of her hair which he had seen her drying at the fire a few days before. She was in the same attitude and seemed unaware of the talk about her. At last she turned towards them and Gabriel saw that there was colour on her cheeks and that her eyes were shining. A sudden tide of joy went leaping out of his heart.

—Mr. D'Arcy, she said, what is the name of that song you were singing?

—It's called *The Lass of Aughrim*, said Mr. D'Arcy, but I couldn't remember it properly. Why? Do you know it?

—*The Lass of Aughrim*, she repeated. I couldn't think of the name.

—It's a very nice air, said Mary Jane. I'm sorry you were not in voice to-night.

—Now, Mary Jane, said Aunt Kate, don't annoy Mr. D'Arcy. I won't have him annoyed.

Seeing that all were ready to start she shepherded them to the door where good-night was said:

—Well, good-night, Aunt Kate, and thanks for the pleasant evening.

—Good-night, Gabriel. Good-night, Gretta!

—Good-night, Aunt Kate, and thanks ever so much. Good-night, Aunt Julia.

—O, good-night, Gretta, I didn't see you.

—Good-night, Mr. D'Arcy. Good-night, Miss O'Callaghan.

—Good-night, Miss Morkan.

—Good-night, again.

—Good-night, all. Safe home.

—Good-night. Good-night.

The morning was still dark. A dull yellow light brooded over the houses and the river; and the sky seemed to be descending. It was slushy underfoot; and only streaks and patches of snow lay on the roofs, on the parapets of the quay and on the area railings. The lamps were still burning redly in the murky air and, across the river, the palace of the Four Courts[5] stood out menacingly against the heavy sky.

She was walking on before him with Mr. Bartell D'Arcy, her shoes in a brown parcel tucked under one arm and her hands holding her skirt up from the slush. She had no longer any grace of attitude but Gabriel's eyes were still bright with happiness. The blood went bounding along his veins; and the thoughts went rioting through his brain, proud, joyful, tender, valorous.

She was walking on before him so lightly and so erect that he longed to run after her noiselessly, catch her by the shoulders and say something foolish and affectionate into her ear. She seemed to him so frail that he longed to defend her against something and then to be alone with her. Moments of their secret life together burst like stars upon his memory. A heliotrope envelope was lying beside his breakfast-cup and he was caressing it with his hand. Birds were twittering in the ivy and the sunny web of the curtain was shimmering along the floor: he could not eat for happiness. They were standing on the crowded platform and he was placing a ticket inside the warm palm of her glove. He was standing with her in the cold, looking in through a grated window at a man making bottles in a roaring furnace. It was very cold. Her face, fragrant in the cold air, was quite close to his; and suddenly she called out to the man at the furnace:

—Is the fire hot, sir?

But the man could not hear her with the noise of the furnace. It was just as well. He might have answered rudely.

A wave of yet more tender joy escaped from his heart and went coursing in warm flood along his arteries. Like the tender fires of stars moments of their life together, that no one knew of or would ever know of, broke upon and illumined his memory. He longed to recall to her those moments, to make her forget the years of their dull existence together and remember only their moments of ecstasy. For the years, he felt, had not quenched his soul or hers. Their children, his writing, her household cares had not quenched all their souls' tender fire. In one letter that he had written to her then he had said: *Why is it that words like these seem to me so dull and cold? Is it because there is no word tender enough to be your name?*

Like distant music these words that he had written years before were borne towards him from the past. He longed to be alone with her. When the others had gone away, when he and she were in their room in the hotel, then they would be alone together. He would call her softly:

—Gretta!

Perhaps she would not hear at once: she would be undressing. Then something in his voice would strike her. She would turn and look at him.

At the corner of Winetavern Street they met a cab. He was glad of its rattling noise as it saved him from conversation. She was looking out of the window and seemed tired. The others spoke only a few words, pointing out some building or street. The horse galloped along wearily under the murky morning sky, dragging his old rattling box after his heels, and Gabriel was again in a cab with her, galloping to catch the boat, galloping to their honeymoon.

5. The Irish law courts building.

As the cab drove across O'Connell Bridge Miss O'Callaghan said:

—They say you never cross O'Connell Bridge without seeing a white horse.

—I see a white man this time, said Gabriel.

—Where? asked Mr. Bartell D'Arcy.

Gabriel pointed to the statue,[6] on which lay patches of snow. Then he nodded familiarly to it and waved his hand.

—Good-night, Dan, he said gaily.

When the cab drew up before the hotel Gabriel jumped out and, in spite of Mr. Bartell D'Arcy's protest, paid the driver. He gave the man a shilling over his fare. The man saluted and said:

—A prosperous New Year to you, sir.

—The same to you, said Gabriel cordially.

She leaned for a moment on his arm in getting out of the cab and while standing at the curbstone, bidding the others good-night. She leaned lightly on his arm, as lightly as when she had danced with him a few hours before. He had felt proud and happy then, happy that she was his, proud of her grace and wifely carriage. But now, after the kindling again of so many memories, the first touch of her body, musical and strange and perfumed, sent through him a keen pang of lust. Under cover of her silence he pressed her arm closely to his side; and, as they stood at the hotel door, he felt that they had escaped from their lives and duties, escaped from home and friends and run away together with wild and radiant hearts to a new adventure.

An old man was dozing in a great hooded chair in the hall. He lit a candle in the office and went before them to the stairs. They followed him in silence, their feet falling in soft thuds on the thickly carpeted stairs. She mounted the stairs behind the porter, her head bowed in the ascent, her frail shoulders curved as with a burden, her skirt girt tightly about her. He could have flung his arms about her hips and held her still for his arms were trembling with desire to seize her and only the stress of his nails against the palms of his hands held the wild impulse of his body in check. The porter halted on the stairs to settle his guttering candle. They halted too on the steps below him. In the silence Gabriel could hear the falling of the molten wax into the tray and the thumping of his own heart against his ribs.

The porter led them along a corridor and opened a door. Then he set his unstable candle down on a toilet-table and asked at what hour they were to be called in the morning.

—Eight, said Gabriel.

The porter pointed to the tap of the electric-light and began a muttered apology but Gabriel cut him short.

—We don't want any light. We have light enough from the street. And I say, he added, pointing to the candle, you might remove that handsome article, like a good man.

The porter took up his candle again, but slowly for he was surprised by such a novel idea. Then he mumbled good-night and went out. Gabriel shot the lock to.

6. Of Daniel O'Connell (1775–1847), called "The Liberator" by the Irish independence movement.

A ghostly light from the street lamp lay in a long shaft from one window to the door. Gabriel threw his overcoat and hat on a couch and crossed the room towards the window. He looked down into the street in order that his emotion might calm a little. Then he turned and leaned against a chest of drawers with his back to the light. She had taken off her hat and cloak and was standing before a large swinging mirror, unhooking her waist.[7] Gabriel paused for a few moments, watching her, and then said:

—Gretta!

She turned away from the mirror slowly and walked along the shaft of light towards him. Her face looked so serious and weary that the words would not pass Gabriel's lips. No, it was not the moment yet.

—You looked tired, he said.

—I am a little, she answered.

—You don't feel ill or weak?

—No, tired: that's all.

She went on to the window and stood there, looking out. Gabriel waited again and then, fearing that diffidence was about to conquer him, he said abruptly:

—By the way, Gretta!

—What is it?

—You know that poor fellow Malins? he said quickly.

—Yes. What about him?

—Well, poor fellow, he's a decent sort of chap after all, continued Gabriel in a false voice. He gave me back that sovereign I lent him and I didn't expect it really. It's a pity he wouldn't keep away from that Browne, because he's not a bad fellow at heart.

He was trembling now with annoyance. Why did she seem so abstracted? He did not know how he could begin. Was she annoyed, too, about something? If she would only turn to him or come to him of her own accord! To take her as she was would be brutal. No, he must see some ardour in her eyes first. He longed to be master of her strange mood.

—When did you lend him the pound? she asked, after a pause.

Gabriel strove to restrain himself from breaking out into brutal language about the sottish Malins and his pound. He longed to cry to her from his soul, to crush her body against his, to overmaster her. But he said:

—O, at Christmas, when he opened that little Christmas-card shop in Henry Street.

He was in such a fever of rage and desire that he did not hear her come from the window. She stood before him for an instant, looking at him strangely. Then, suddenly raising herself on tiptoe and resting her hands lightly on his shoulders, she kissed him.

—You are a very generous person, Gabriel, she said.

Gabriel, trembling with delight at her sudden kiss and at the quaintness of her phrase, put his hands on her hair and began smoothing it back, scarcely touching it with his fingers. The washing had made it fine and brilliant. His heart was brimming over with happiness. Just when he was wishing for it she had come to him of her own accord. Perhaps her thoughts had been running

7. I.e., loosening her waistband.

with his. Perhaps she had felt the impetuous desire that was in him and then the yielding mood had come upon her. Now that she had fallen to him so easily he wondered why he had been so diffident.

He stood, holding her head between his hands. Then, slipping one arm swiftly about her body and drawing her towards him, he said softly:

—Gretta dear, what are you thinking about?

She did not answer nor yield wholly to his arm. He said again, softly:

—Tell me what it is, Gretta. I think I know what is the matter. Do I know?

She did not answer at once. Then she said in an outburst of tears:

—O, I am thinking about that song, *The Lass of Aughrim*.

She broke loose from him and ran to the bed and, throwing her arms across the bed-rail, hid her face. Gabriel stood stock-still for a moment in astonishment and then followed her. As he passed in the way of the cheval-glass he caught sight of himself in full length, his broad, well-filled shirt-front, the face whose expression always puzzled him when he saw it in a mirror and his glimmering gilt-rimmed eyeglasses. He halted a few paces from her and said:

—What about the song? Why does that make you cry?

She raised her head from her arms and dried her eyes with the back of her hand like a child. A kinder note than he had intended went into his voice.

—Why, Gretta? he asked.

—I am thinking about a person long ago who used to sing that song.

—And who was the person long ago? asked Gabriel, smiling.

—It was a person I used to know in Galway when I was living with my grandmother, she said.

The smile passed away from Gabriel's face. A dull anger began to gather again at the back of his mind and the dull fires of his lust began to glow angrily in his veins.

—Someone you were in love with? he asked ironically.

—It was a young boy I used to know, she answered, named Michael Furey. He used to sing that song, *The Lass of Aughrim*. He was very delicate.

Gabriel was silent. He did not wish her to think that he was interested in this delicate boy.

—I can see him so plainly, she said after a moment. Such eyes as he had: big dark eyes! And such an expression in them—an expression!

—O then, you were in love with him? said Gabriel.

—I used to go out walking with him,[8] she said, when I was in Galway. A thought flew across Gabriel's mind.

—Perhaps that was why you wanted to go to Galway with that Ivors girl? he said coldly.

She looked at him and asked in surprise:

—What for?

Her eyes made Gabriel feel awkward. He shrugged his shoulders and said:

—How do I know? To see him perhaps.

She looked away from him along the shaft of light towards the window in silence.

—He is dead, she said at length. He died when he was only seventeen. Isn't it a terrible thing to die so young as that?

8. I.e., she dated him.

—What was he? asked Gabriel, still ironically.

—He was in the gasworks,[9] she said.

Gabriel felt humiliated by the failure of his irony and by the evocation of this figure from the dead, a boy in the gasworks. While he had been full of memories of their secret life together, full of tenderness and joy and desire, she had been comparing him in her mind with another. A shameful consciousness of his own person assailed him. He saw himself as a ludicrous figure, acting as a pennyboy[1] for his aunts, a nervous well-meaning sentimentalist, orating to vulgarians and idealising his own clownish lusts, the pitiable fatuous fellow he had caught a glimpse of in the mirror. Instinctively he turned his back more to the light lest she might see the shame that burned upon his forehead.

He tried to keep up his tone of cold interrogation but his voice when he spoke was humble and indifferent.

—I suppose you were in love with this Michael Furey, Gretta, he said.

—I was great[2] with him at that time, she said.

Her voice was veiled and sad. Gabriel, feeling now how vain it would be to try to lead her whither he had purposed, caressed one of her hands and said, also sadly:

—And what did he die of so young, Gretta? Consumption, was it?

—I think he died for me, she answered.

A vague terror seized Gabriel at this answer as if, at that hour when he had hoped to triumph, some impalpable and vindictive being was coming against him, gathering forces against him in its vague world. But he shook himself free of it with an effort of reason and continued to caress her hand. He did not question her again for he felt that she would tell him of herself. Her hand was warm and moist: it did not respond to his touch but he continued to caress it just as he had caressed her first letter to him that spring morning.

—It was in the winter, she said, about the beginning of the winter when I was going to leave my grandmother's and come up here to the convent. And he was ill at the time in his lodgings in Galway and wouldn't be let out and his people in Oughterard[3] were written to. He was in decline, they said, or something like that. I never knew rightly.

She paused for a moment and sighed.

—Poor fellow, she said. He was very fond of me and he was such a gentle boy. We used to go out together, walking, you know, Gabriel, like the way they do in the country. He was going to study singing only for his health. He had a very good voice, poor Michael Furey.

—Well; and then? asked Gabriel.

—And then when it came to the time for me to leave Galway and come up to the convent he was much worse and I wouldn't be let see him so I wrote a letter saying I was going up to Dublin and would be back in the summer and hoping he would be better then.

She paused for a moment to get her voice under control and then went on:

—Then the night before I left I was in my grandmother's house in Nun's Island,[4] packing up, and I heard gravel thrown up against the window. The

9. A utilities plant that manufactured coal gas. Working there was an unhealthy occupation.

1. Errand boy.

2. Close friends.

3. A small village in western Ireland.

4. An island in the western city of Galway, on which is located the Convent of Poor Clares.

window was so wet I couldn't see so I ran downstairs as I was and slipped out the back into the garden and there was the poor fellow at the end of the garden, shivering.

—And did you not tell him to go back? asked Gabriel.

—I implored of him to go home at once and told him he would get his death in the rain. But he said he did not want to live. I can see his eyes as well as well! He was standing at the end of the wall where there was a tree.

—And did he go home? asked Gabriel.

—Yes, he went home. And when I was only a week in the convent he died and he was buried in Oughterard where his people came from. O, the day I heard that, that he was dead!

She stopped, choking with sobs, and, overcome by emotion, flung herself face downward on the bed, sobbing in the quilt. Gabriel held her hand for a moment longer, irresolutely, and then, shy of intruding on her grief, let it fall gently and walked quietly to the window.

She was fast asleep.

Gabriel, leaning on his elbow, looked for a few moments unresentfully on her tangled hair and half-open mouth, listening to her deep-drawn breath. So she had that romance in her life: a man had died for her sake. It hardly pained him now to think how poor a part he, her husband, had played in her life. He watched her while she slept as though he and she had never lived together as man and wife. His curious eyes rested long upon her face and on her hair: and, as he thought of what she must have been then, in that time of her first girlish beauty, a strange friendly pity for her entered his soul. He did not like to say even to himself that her face was no longer beautiful but he knew that it was no longer the face for which Michael Furey had braved death.

Perhaps she had not told him all the story. His eyes moved to the chair over which she had thrown some of her clothes. A petticoat string dangled to the floor. One boot stood upright, its limp upper fallen down: the fellow of it lay upon its side. He wondered at his riot of emotions of an hour before. From what had it proceeded? From his aunt's supper, from his own foolish speech, from the wine and dancing, the merrymaking when saying goodnight in the hall, the pleasure of the walk along the river in the snow. Poor Aunt Julia! She, too, would soon be a shade with the shade of Patrick Morkan and his horse. He had caught that haggard look upon her face for a moment when she was singing *Arrayed for the Bridal*. Soon, perhaps, he would be sitting in that same drawing-room, dressed in black, his silk hat on his knees. The blinds would be drawn down and Aunt Kate would be sitting beside him, crying and blowing her nose and telling him how Julia had died. He would cast about in his mind for some words that might console her, and would find only lame and useless ones. Yes, yes: that would happen very soon.

The air of the room chilled his shoulders. He stretched himself cautiously along under the sheets and lay down beside his wife. One by one they were all becoming shades. Better pass boldly into that other world, in the full glory of some passion, than fade and wither dismally with age. He thought of how she who lay beside him had locked in her heart for so many years that image of her lover's eyes when he had told her that he did not wish to live.

Generous tears filled Gabriel's eyes. He had never felt like that himself towards any woman but he knew that such a feeling must be love. The tears gathered more thickly in his eyes and in the partial darkness he imagined he saw the form of a young man standing under a dripping tree. Other forms were near. His soul had approached that region where dwell the vast hosts of the dead. He was conscious of, but could not apprehend, their wayward and flickering existence. His own identity was fading out into a grey impalpable world: the solid world itself which these dead had one time reared and lived in was dissolving and dwindling.

A few light taps upon the pane made him turn to the window. It had begun to snow again. He watched sleepily the flakes, silver and dark, falling obliquely against the lamplight. The time had come for him to set out on his journey westward. Yes, the newspapers were right: snow was general all over Ireland. It was falling on every part of the dark central plain, on the treeless hills, falling softly upon the Bog of Allen and, farther westward, softly falling into the dark mutinous Shannon[5] waves. It was falling, too, upon every part of the lonely churchyard on the hill where Michael Furey lay buried. It lay thickly drifted on the crooked crosses and headstones, on the spears of the little gate, on the barren thorns. His soul swooned slowly as he heard the snow falling faintly through the universe and faintly falling, like the descent of their last end, upon all the living and the dead.

1914

5. An estuary of the Shannon River, west-southwest of Dublin. The Bog of Allen is southwest of Dublin.

FRANZ KAFKA

1883–1924

Franz Kafka's stories and novels contain such nightmarish scenarios that the word *Kafkaesque* has been coined to describe the most unpleasant and bizarre aspects of modern life, especially when it comes to bureaucracy. Despite the bleakness of the world he depicted, Kafka was in fact a highly amusing writer who, when reading his work to friends, would sometimes leave them laughing out loud. A master of dark humor and an artist of unique vision, Kafka captures perfectly the anxiety and absurdity of contemporary urban society.

Born in Prague, a majority Catholic, Czech-speaking city in the Austro-Hungarian Empire, to a nonobservant Jewish, German-speaking family, Kafka trained as a lawyer and went to work for an insurance company, while living at home with his parents. He began writing in his twenties and published his first short prose works in 1908. Around the same time, he developed a renewed interest in Judaism, which he had mostly ignored as a child. Although he was an attractive and popular person—in this respect not much like his character Gregor Samsa—he was never quite satisfied with his relationships with women or with his family. He was engaged three times, twice to the same woman, and broke off all three engagements. Kafka had a difficult relationship with his father, a self-made man who could not take his son's writing seriously. Having learned from friends about the psychoanalytic theories of Sigmund Freud, Kafka recognized the oedipal tension in aspects of his family life and expressed uneasiness with authority, especially parental authority, in his fiction. He also kept extensive diaries about his dissatisfaction with his personal and work life and, in his late thirties, wrote a long letter to his father harshly criticizing his upbringing.

Most of Kafka's writing published during his life consisted of short stories, parables, and two novellas, including *The Metamorphosis*, the selection here, which were released in six slim volumes. Kafka did not believe himself to be a successful author, although he had won a prestigious literary award, the Fontane Prize of the City of Berlin, for one of his early stories, "The Stoker." He wrote three long novels, *The Trial, The Castle*, and *Amerika*, but completed none of them. In despair, he asked his friend and executor, Max Brod, to have them all burned at his death. Brod disobeyed Kafka's instructions and, instead, had the three novels published posthumously. Apparently reflecting the guilt their author experienced over his relations with women, and his failure to get married, the three novels are haunted by regret and a sense of culpability, although the source of the characters' disquiet can never be identified with certainty.

Unlike some of his characters—resentful employees of large bureaucracies—Kafka was a successful senior executive who handled an array of business matters. Nonetheless, he was unhappy with his day job and blamed the hours he spent at work for his inability to complete the novels: in his mind, he was a failure both in life and in art. After developing tuberculosis

in his mid-thirties, Kafka quit his job, at age thirty-nine, in 1922. He published a number of stories, collected in *The Hunger Artist*, and traveled extensively, spending a year in Berlin; but as his health deteriorated, he eventually moved to a sanatorium outside Vienna, where he died. Once Brod released the novels and unfinished stories, the author's fame quickly grew. During the Great Depression and the political crises of the 1930s, Kafka became popular in the English-speaking world. Readers viewed his work as demonstrating the anxiety and isolation of modern life, particularly the problem of living in alienation from God, a major theme of existentialist philosophers after World War II. More recently, however, critics have emphasized Kafka's humor and the social contexts of his work, including his experiences in his native Prague.

Until the middle of the nineteenth century, Jews had been excluded from most aspects of Austro-Hungarian society. Kafka and his family felt a strong affinity for the emperor, who represented for them German high culture and whose family had emancipated the Jews. The old city of Prague, with its narrow streets, crowded apartment houses, Gothic cathedral, and huge medieval castle, was cosmopolitan for a small town. After 1918, Czechoslovakia became an independent republic, and Czech replaced German as the official language. Kafka was able to adapt—he knew Czech well—and in fact was one of the few "German" business executives who were retained after Czech independence. And yet he felt himself to be an outsider—a German-speaking Jew among Czech-speaking Christians. This feeling was no doubt reinforced by a resurgent anti-Semitism that coincided with the rise of Czech nationalism and that threatened the Jews' relatively recent emancipation. (Kafka didn't live to see the final confirmation of his sense of alienation and isolation, but his three sisters would later die in Nazi concentration camps.) In his thirties, Kafka studied Hebrew and Yiddish and became interested in the Yiddish theater; the Jewish Enlightenment of his friend Martin Buber (Austrian philosopher, 1878–1965); Jewish folklore; and the philosophical writings of Søren Kierkegaard (1813–1855). Kafka's work seldom discusses Judaism directly, but the sense of exclusion and persecution that underlies much of his writing may spring in part from his experience of anti-Semitism; certainly his interest in interpretation and the nature of language owes much to his understanding of Jewish thought.

THE METAMORPHOSIS

Written in 1912 and published in 1915, *The Metamorphosis*, Kafka's longest work published in his lifetime, was, as well, his most famous work released before his death. It is a consummate narrative: from the moment Gregor Samsa wakes up to find himself transformed into a "monstrous cockroach," the reader asks, "What happens next?" Although the events seem dreamlike, the narrator assures us "it was no dream," no nightmarish fantasy in which Gregor temporarily identified himself with other downtrodden vermin of society. Instead, this grotesque transformation is permanent, a single, unshakable fact that renders almost comic his family's calculations and attempts to adjust. Indeed, the events of the story are described in great detail, often with an emphasis on the kind of concrete, vivid imagery that plays a prominent role in dreams and in Freud's interpretations of them: the father's fist, the bug's blood, the sister's violin playing.

When the novella begins, Gregor seems to be simply a man in a bug suit, but as the tale progresses, his thinking becomes increasingly buglike, and he loses touch with the people around him. A major theme of the work is the meaning of humanity, and Gregor experiences a sense of exclusion from what Kafka calls the "human circle." As the author relays the protagonist's thoughts, the reader gets the impression that Gregor considers himself to be put upon: he has taken a job he dislikes in order to pay off his parents' debt. Yet even before his transformation, he felt that his family misunderstood him. Once he becomes a bug, he loses the power of speech: although he continues to think, he cannot express his thoughts. Thus, when he turns into a despised species, the lack of communication Gregor perceived as a man becomes an actuality.

"The terror of art," said Kafka in a conversation about *The Metamorphosis*, is that "the dream reveals the reality." This dream, which in the novella becomes Gregor's reality, sheds light on the intolerable nature of his former existence. Another aspect of his professional life is its mechanical rigidity, personal rivalries, and threatening suspicion of any deviation from the norm. Gregor himself is part of this world, as he shows when he fawns on the chief clerk and tries to manipulate him by criticizing their boss.

More disturbing is the transformation that takes place in Gregor's family, where the expected love and support turns into shamed acceptance and animal resentment now that Gregor has let the family down. Mother and sister are ineffectual, and their sympathy is slowly replaced by disgust. Gregor father quickly reassumes his position of authority and beats the vermin back into his room: first with the newspaper and chief clerk's cane, and later with a barrage of apples from the family table. Gregor eventually becomes an "it" for whom the family feels no affection. Even before his transformation, Gregor seems to have lost all purpose in life except earning money to repay his parents' debts.

These frustrated desires contribute to the central conflict: whether Gregor can ever emerge from his bedroom and become part of the family again. The slapstick-like comedy of Gregor's attempts to use his insect body underlines the sense of exclusion and broadens the novella's appeal. Perhaps everyone has, occasionally, felt like an outsider, but Gregor's metamorphosis makes him an alien of a literal sort. His attitude at times reflects the sullenness of an unhappy teenager; at other times, he seems more like a terminal patient who fears placing an undue burden on his family. The theme of transformation goes back to Ovid's *Metamorphoses*, in which frustrated sexual desire often plays a role in turning people into plants or animals. The dark humor and uncanniness of Kafka's work links it to fantastic works by authors such as Edgar Allan Poe (American, 1809–1849) and Heinrich Wilhelm Kleist (German, 1771–1811) and to the analysis of the psyche conducted, during Kafka's lifetime, by Sigmund Freud. Without directly blaming Gregor, Kafka sometimes seems to hint that his transformation results in part from the protagonist's desire to escape from human interaction.

Kafka exposes both the pathos and the humor of the situation, and for this reason the story retains its attraction today. He has been recognized as an important influence by a range of modern writers, including **Samuel Beckett**, Harold Pinter (English playwright, 1930–2008), and many Latin Americans—among them, **Jorge Luis Borges** and **Gabriel García Márquez**. Kafka was one of the great storytellers of modern life, capable of showing the emptiness that can lie at the heart even of a busy life in a crowded city apartment.

The Metamorphosis[1]

I

When Gregor Samsa woke one morning from troubled dreams, he found himself transformed right there in his bed into some sort of monstrous insect. He was lying on his back—which was hard, like a carapace—and when he raised his head a little he saw his curved brown belly segmented by rigid arches atop which the blanket, already slipping, was just barely managing to cling. His many legs, pitifully thin compared to the rest of him, waved helplessly before his eyes.

"What in the world has happened to me?" he thought. It was no dream. His room, a proper human room, if admittedly rather too small, lay peacefully between the four familiar walls. Above the table, where an unpacked collection of cloth samples was arranged (Samsa was a traveling salesman), hung the picture he had recently clipped from a glossy magazine and placed in an attractive gilt frame. This picture showed a lady in a fur hat and fur boa sitting very straight, holding out to the viewer a heavy fur muff in which her entire forearm had vanished.

Gregor's gaze then shifted to the window, where the bleak weather—raindrops could be heard striking the metal sill—made him feel quite melancholy. "What if I just go back to sleep for a little while and forget all this foolishness," he

1. Translated by Susan Bernofsky.

thought, but this proved utterly impossible, for it was his habit to sleep on his right side, and in his present state he was unable to assume this position. No matter how forcefully he thrust himself onto his side, he kept rolling back. Perhaps a hundred times he attempted it, closing his eyes so as not to have to see those struggling legs, and relented only when he began to feel a faint dull ache in his side, unlike anything he'd ever felt before.

"Good Lord," he thought, "what an exhausting profession I've chosen. Day in and day out on the road. Work like this is far more unsettling than business conducted at home, and then I have the agony of traveling itself to contend with: worrying about train connections, the irregular, unpalatable meals, and human intercourse that is constantly changing, never developing the least constancy or warmth. Devil take it all!" He felt a faint itch high up on his belly; still on his back, he laboriously edged himself over to the bedpost so he could raise his head more easily; identified the site of the itch: a cluster of tiny white dots he was unable to judge; and wanted to probe the spot with a leg, but drew it back again at once, for the touch sent cold shivers rippling through him.

He slid back into his earlier position. "All this early rising," he thought, "it's enough to make one soft in the head. Human beings need their sleep. Other traveling salesmen live like harem girls. When I go back to the boardinghouse, for example, to copy out the morning's commissions: why, these gentlemen may still be sitting at breakfast. I'd like to see my boss's face if I tried that some time; he'd can me on the spot. Although who knows, maybe that would be the best thing for me. If I didn't have to hold back for my parents' sake, I'd have given notice long ago—I'd have marched right up to him and given him a piece of my mind. He'd have fallen right off his desk! And what an odd custom that is: perching high up atop one's elevated desk and from this considerable height addressing one's employee down below, especially as the latter is obliged to stand quite close because his boss is hard of hearing. Well, all hope is not yet lost; as soon as I've saved up enough money to pay back what my parents owe him—another five or six years ought to be enough—I'll most definitely do just that. This will be the great parting of ways. For the time being, though, I've got to get up, my train leaves at five."

And he glanced over at the alarm clock ticking away atop the wardrobe. "Heavenly Father!" he thought. It was half past six, and the clock's hands kept shifting calmly forward, in fact the half-hour had already passed, it was getting on toward six forty-five. Could the alarm have failed to ring? Even from the bed one could see it was properly set for four o'clock; it must have rung. Yes, but was it possible to sleep tranquilly through this furniture-shaking racket? Well, his sleep hadn't been exactly tranquil, but no doubt that's why it had been so sound. But what should he do now? The next train was at seven o'clock; to catch it, he would have to rush like a madman, and his sample case wasn't even packed yet, and he himself felt far from agile or alert. And even if he managed to catch this train, his boss was certain to unleash a thunderstorm of invective upon his head, for the clerk who met the five o'clock train had no doubt long since reported Gregor's absence. This clerk was the boss's underling, a creature devoid of backbone and wit. What if he called in sick? But that would be mortifying and also suspicious, since Gregor had never once been ill in all his five years of service. No doubt his boss would come calling with the company doctor, would reproach Gregor's parents for their son's laziness, silencing all objections by referring them to this doctor, in whose opinion there existed only healthy individuals unwilling to work. And would the doctor be so terribly wrong in this instance? Aside from a mild drowsiness that was certainly super-fluous after so many hours of sleep, Gregor felt perfectly fine; in fact, he was ravenous.

While he was considering these matters with the greatest possible speed, yet still without managing to make up his mind to leave the bed (the clock was just striking a quarter to seven), a timid knock came at the door at the head of his bed. "Gregor," the voice called—it was his mother—"it's a quarter to seven. Didn't you want to catch your train?" That gentle voice! Gregor flinched when he heard his own in response: it was unmistakably his old voice, but now it had been infiltrated as if from below by a tortured peeping sound that was impos-sible to suppress—leaving each word intact, comprehensible, but only for an instant before so completely annihilating it as it continued to reverberate that a person could not tell for sure whether his ears were deceiving him. Gregor had meant to give a proper response explaining everything, but under the cir-cumstances he limited himself to saying, "Yes, thank you, Mother, I'm just getting up." Because of the wooden door, the change in Gregor's voice appeared not to be noticeable from the other side, for his mother was reassured by his response and shuffled off. But their brief conversation had alerted the other family members that Gregor was unexpectedly still at home, and already his father was knocking at one of the room's side doors, softly, but with his fist: "Gregor, Gregor," he called. "What's the matter?" And after a short while he repeated his question in a deeper register: "Gregor! Gregor!" Meanwhile, at the other side door came his sister's faint lament: "Gregor? Are you unwell? Do you need anything?" "Just a second," Gregor answered in both directions at once, making an effort, by enunciating as clearly as possible and inserting long pauses between the individual words, to remove anything conspicuous from his voice. And in fact his father returned to his breakfast, but his sister whis-pered: "Gregor, open the door, I implore you." But Gregor had no intention of opening the door; he praised the cautious habit he had acquired while travel-ing of locking all his doors at night, even at home.

First he would get up calmly and undisturbed, he would get dressed and above all have breakfast, and only then would he consider his next steps, for all these supine contemplations, he suddenly realized, would yield no useful results. He recalled often having felt mild aches and pains in bed, caused per-haps by lying in an awkward position, and this pain had then proven to be a figment of his imagination the moment he got up; he was curious to see how this morning's imaginings would gradually fade. The change in his voice was nothing more than the harbinger of a proper head cold, an occupational hazard among traveling salesmen; this he doubted not in the least.

It was simple enough to rid himself of the blanket; he needed only puff him-self up a bit, and it fell right off. But the rest proved difficult, not least because he was so exceedingly wide. He would have needed arms and hands to prop himself up; but instead all he had were these many little legs, variously in motion, that he was unable to master. If he tried to bend one leg, it would be the first to straighten; and when he finally succeeded in getting one leg to do his bidding, all the others went flailing about in an unnerving frenzy. "Enough of this lying about uselessly in bed," Gregor said to himself.

At first he tried to maneuver the lower part of his body out of the bed, but this lower part—which, by the way, he had not yet seen and couldn't properly imagine—proved too unwieldy; it all went so slowly; and when at last, half-mad with impatience, he propelled himself recklessly forward with all his strength, it was in the wrong direction, and he slammed against the lower bedpost; the throbbing pain he felt instructed him that for now at least the lower part of his body was perhaps the most sensitive.

So he decided to try leading instead with his upper body and carefully twisted his head toward the edge of the bed. This was easily accomplished, and in the end, despite his width and weight, the mass of his body slowly followed the turning of his head. But once his head was dangling in midair outside the bed, he was afraid to keep shifting forward in this manner, since if eventually he had to let himself fall in this position, it would be practically a miracle if his head escaped injury. And right now he had to keep his wits about him at all costs, even if it meant staying where he was.

But when, sighing after redoubled efforts, he found himself lying there as before, watching his little legs engaged in their struggles, perhaps more flailingly this time, and seeing no possible way to bring calm or order to this chaos, he told himself once more that he could not possibly remain lying here any longer and that the most sensible thing would be to sacrifice anything and everything as long as there remained even the tiniest hope of liberating himself from the bed. Simultaneously, though, he continued to remind himself that calm consideration—indeed, the calmest consideration—was far preferable to resolutions seized on in despair. At such moments he fixed his eyes as sharply as possible on the window, but regrettably the view of the morning fog, which veiled even the far side of the narrow street, offered little by way of optimism and good spirits. "Seven o'clock already," he said to himself as the clock struck once more, "already seven and still such dense fog." And for a little while he lay there quietly, his breathing shallow, in the expectation, perhaps, that this perfect silence might possibly restore the real and ordinary state of things.

Then he said to himself: "Before it strikes a quarter past seven, I must absolutely have gotten myself completely out of bed. Besides, by then someone will have come from the office to inquire after me, as the office opens before seven." And he now set himself to rocking his body out of the bed as evenly as possible along his entire length. If he allowed himself to fall from the bed like this, his head—which he intended to lift up cleanly as he fell—would in all likelihood remain uninjured. His back seemed to be hard; surely it would sustain no damage as he fell to the rug. His greatest concern was what to do about the loud crash that would clearly result, no doubt calling forth not terror perhaps but certainly alarm behind each door. Nonetheless it would have to be ventured.

By the time Gregor was already protruding halfway out of bed—this new method was more a game than a struggle, all he had to do was keep rocking sideways a little at a time—it occurred to him how simple things would be if only someone came to assist him. Two strong individuals—he was thinking of his father and the maidservant—would suffice; all they'd have to do was slip their arms beneath his curved back to scoop him out of bed, then crouch down with their burden and wait patiently for him to flip himself over onto the floor, where he hoped those tiny legs of his would take on some meaning. But even aside from the fact that the doors were locked, should he really call for help? Despite his distress, he couldn't help smiling at the thought.

Already he'd reached the point where the vigorous rocking motion was making it almost impossible for him to keep his balance, and soon he would have to make up his mind and take the plunge, for a quarter after seven was only five minutes away—when the front doorbell rang. "It's someone from the office," he said to himself and nearly froze while his little legs went on scrabbling all the more frenetically. For a moment all was still. "They won't answer," Gregor said to himself, caught up in some deluded hope. But then of course, as always, the maid strode resolutely to the door and opened it.

Gregor needed only hear the visitor's first words of greeting to know who it was: the general manager himself. Why oh why was Gregor condemned to serve in a firm where even the most negligible falling short was enough to arouse the greatest possible suspicion? Was every last one of the firm's employees a scoundrel, was there not a single loyal, devoted soul among them who would be driven mad by pangs of conscience should he fail to make the best possible use of even just a few morning hours for his employer's benefit, such that his guilt would render him virtually incapable of rising from his bed? Would it really not have sufficed to send an apprentice to inquire—if indeed such inquiries were necessary at all—did the general manager have to come in person, and was it necessary to demonstrate to the entire innocent family that the investigation of this suspicious matter could be entrusted only to the general manager's sharp intellect? And more because of the agitation aroused in Gregor by this train of thought than because of some proper resolution on his part, he swung himself out of bed with all his might. There was a loud thud, you couldn't really call it a crash. The rug cushioned the impact a little, and since his back was more elastic than he'd thought, the resulting sound was muffled and not so obvious. But he hadn't managed to hold his head up carefully enough and had bumped it; he turned it this way and that, pressing it against the rug in his vexation and pain.

"Something just fell in there," the general manager now said in the room on the left. Gregor tried to imagine whether anything like what he was now experiencing could ever befall the general manager; the possibility must certainly be admitted. But as if brusquely dismissing the question, the manager now took a few purposeful steps in the next room, making his patent leather boots creak. From the room on the right came the whisper of Gregor's sister informing him: "Gregor, the general manager is here." "I know," Gregor murmured; but he didn't dare raise his voice high enough for his sister to hear.

"Gregor," his father now said from the room on the left, "the general manager has come to inquire why you failed to depart by the early train. We don't know what to tell him. Besides, he'd like to have a word with you in person. So please open the door. I'm sure he'll be kind enough not to take offense at the untidiness of your room." "Good morning, Herr Samsa," the general manager now cried out in a friendly tone. "He isn't well," Gregor's mother said to the general manager while his father was still having his say beside the door, "not well at all, take my word for it, sir. Why else would Gregor miss his train! The office is the only thing that boy ever thinks of. It really bothers me that he never goes out in the evening; he's been back in the city an entire week now, but he's spent every last evening at home. He just sits at the table with us, quietly reading the newspaper, or else studies the timetables. Even just doing woodworking projects seems to entertain him. For example, he carved a little picture frame over two or three evenings with his fretsaw; you'll be amazed how pretty it is; it's hanging there in his room; you'll see it in a minute when Gregor opens the door. Oh, and I'm so glad you paid us a visit, sir; on our own we'd never have managed to persuade Gregor to open up; he's so stubborn; and surely he isn't well, even though he denied it this morning." "Be . . . right . . . there," Gregor said, not moving, so as not to miss a single word of their conversation. "No other explanation, madam, is conceivable to me," the general manager said. "Let us hope it is nothing grave. Though on the other hand I would note that, as businessmen—fortunately or unfortunately, as one will—we are very often obliged to suppress indispositions out of consideration for the firm." "So are you ready to let the general manager in?" Gregor's impatient father asked, knocking again at the door. "No," Gregor responded. In the left-hand room horrified silence, while in the room on the right Gregor's sister began to sob.

Why didn't his sister go to join the others? She must have just gotten out of bed and not yet begun to dress. And why was she crying? Because he wasn't getting up and opening his door to the general manager, because he was in danger of losing his position, and because his boss would then start hounding his parents once more over their ancient debt? For the time being, all such worries were assuredly unnecessary. Gregor was still here, and abandoning his family was the farthest thing from his thoughts. At the moment, to be sure, he was lying on the rug, and no one familiar with his current state would seriously expect him to let the general manager in. But surely he wouldn't be sent packing just like that because of so trivial an act of discourtesy, for which it would be simple enough to find an appropriate excuse later on. And it seemed to Gregor it would be far more sensible to just leave him in peace rather than disturbing him with all this weeping and cajoling. But the others were distressed by the uncertainty of it all; their behavior was understandable.

"Herr Samsa," the general manager now called out, raising his voice. "What has come over you? You barricade yourself in your room, you reply to queries only with yes and no, you cause your parents onerous, unnecessary worries, and you are neglecting—let me permit myself to note—your professional responsibilities in a truly unprecedented manner. I speak here in the name of your parents as well as your employer and in all seriousness must ask you for a clear and immediate explanation. I am astonished, utterly astonished. I have always known you as a calm, sensible person, and now it seems you've begun to permit yourself the most whimsical extravagances. To be sure, the boss did suggest one possible explanation for your absence this morning—it concerns the cash payments recently entrusted to your care—and truthfully, I all but gave him my word of honor that this explanation could not be correct. But confronted here with your incomprehensible obstinacy, I find myself losing any desire I might have had to come to your defense. And your position is anything but secure. It was originally my intention to discuss all this with you in a private conversation, but since you have compelled me to waste my time here in vain, I do not know why your esteemed parents should not hear of it as well. In short: your productivity of late has been highly unsatisfactory; admittedly this is not the best season for drumming up business, we do acknowledge this; but a season in which no business at all is drummed up is something that does not, and indeed may not exist, Herr Samsa."

"But sir," Gregor cried out, beside himself and forgetting all else in his agitation, "I shall open the door at once, this very instant. A slight indisposition, a fit of dizziness prevented me from getting up. Even now I'm still in bed. But already I am feeling very much refreshed. Here, I'm getting up. Just a moment's patience! It's a bit more difficult than I thought. But already I'm feeling quite fine. How odd, the way such a thing can suddenly come over one. Yesterday evening I felt perfectly well, my parents can attest to this, or rather: I did in fact feel a mild foreboding yesterday evening already. Surely it was noticeable to anyone looking at me. Why didn't I send word to the office? But we always just assume we'll be able to overcome these illnesses without staying home. Sir! Do be gentle with my parents. The allegations you make are unfounded, and no one has ever mentioned anything of the sort to me. Perhaps you haven't yet looked over the most recent commissions I sent in. In any case, I'll be back on the road in time for the eight o'clock train; these additional hours of rest have fortified me. Please do not allow me to detain you any longer, sir; I shall be at the office myself in no time; do be so good as to say I'm on my way and give my regards to the boss."

And while Gregor was hastily blurting out all of this, scarcely knowing what he said, he edged closer to the wardrobe with minimal effort, no doubt thanks to the practice he had already acquired while still in bed, and now he did his best to haul himself upright. Indeed, he really did want to open the door, to show himself and speak with the general manager; he was eager to learn what the others, who were so anxious to see him, would say when they finally laid eyes on him. If they recoiled in horror, Gregor could surrender all responsibility and rest easy. But if they accepted it all calmly, that meant he too had no reason to get himself worked up, and if he hurried, he could still make it to the station by eight. At first he couldn't get a grip on the wardrobe's smooth surface, but finally he gave a great heave and found himself standing upright; he no longer paid any heed to the pain in his lower body, ache as it might. Now he let himself drop against the back of a nearby chair, clinging to its edges with his little legs. And having thus attained control over himself, he fell silent, for now he could listen to the general manager.

"Did you understand a single word?" the manager was asking Gregor's parents. "Surely he isn't trying to make fools of us?" "For heaven's sake," Gregor's mother cried, already weeping, "he might be gravely ill, and here we are tormenting him. Grete! Grete!" she cried out. "Mother?" Gregor's sister called from the other side. They were communicating with one another through Gregor's room. "You must go for the doctor at once. Gregor is ill. Quick, fetch the doctor. Did you hear him speaking just now?" "That was an animal's voice," the general manager said, speaking in noticeably subdued tones compared to the cries of Gregor's mother. "Anna! Anna!" the father shouted into the kitchen through the vestibule, clapping his hands. "Run and fetch a locksmith, hurry!" And already the two girls were racing through the vestibule, their skirts rustling (how had Gregor's sister possibly gotten dressed so quickly?), and flung open the front door. There was no sound of the door closing again; no doubt they had left it standing open, as one sees with apartments in which a great calamity has occurred.

But Gregor was far less troubled now. Even though the others were no longer able to understand his words—though they had seemed to him clear enough, clearer than in the past, perhaps because his ear had grown accustomed to their sound—they were now convinced that things were not right with him and were prepared to offer help. The confidence and conviction with which these first arrangements had been made comforted him. He felt drawn once more into the circle of humankind and was expecting both the doctor and the locksmith—without properly differentiating between the two—to perform magnificent, astounding feats. So as to have as intelligible a voice as possible for the crucial discussions that lay ahead, he cleared his throat a little, making an effort to do this as discreetly as possible, since even this sound might differ from human throat-clearing, which he no longer trusted himself to judge. In the next room, meanwhile, all was quiet. Perhaps his parents sat whispering at the table with the general manager, or perhaps all of them were leaning against the door, listening.

Gregor slowly pushed himself over to the door using the armchair, then let go and allowed himself to fall against the door, propping himself upright—the pads of his little legs turned out to be slightly sticky—and there he rested briefly from his exertions. Then he set about turning the key in the lock using his mouth. Unfortunately it seemed he had no real teeth—so how was he supposed to grasp the key?—but his jaws turned out to be surprisingly strong; and with their help he actually succeeded in causing the key to move, paying no heed to the fact that he was no doubt injuring himself in the process, for a brown fluid ran out of his mouth and down the key, dripping onto the floor. "Listen to that," the general manager said in the next room, "he's turning the key in the lock." Gregor found these words most encouraging; but all of them should have been cheering him on, including his father and mother: "Come on, Gregor!" they should have shouted, "just keep at it, keep working on that lock!" And now, imagining all of them following his efforts with great suspense, he bit down on the key uncomprehendingly, with all the force he could muster. With each revolution of the key, he danced about the lock, holding himself upright using only his mouth and, as needed, either clinging to the key or using the entire weight of his body to press it down. The brighter sound of the lock finally springing open positively revived him. Sighing in relief, he said to himself: "I guess I didn't need the locksmith after all," and he laid his head upon the handle of the door to press it open.

But he remained hidden from view as the door swung toward him, even after it was wide open. To be seen, he had to work his way slowly around one of the wings of the double door, a delicate operation if he wanted to avoid plopping down awkwardly on his back before he'd even entered the room. He was still occupied with this difficult maneuver and had no leisure to attend to anything else when he heard the general manager utter a loud "Oh!"—it sounded like wind howling—and now he saw him too, saw how the general manager, who was standing closest to the door, pressed his hand to his open mouth, slowly retreating, as though being driven back by an invisible, steady force. Gregor's mother—who despite the general manager's presence stood with her hair still undone from the night, wildly bristling—first looked over at his father, her hands clasped, then took two steps in Gregor's direction before falling down in the midst of all her billowing skirts, her face vanishing completely where it sank to her bosom. Gregor's father clenched his fist with a hostile grimace, as if he intended to thrust Gregor back into his room, then glanced uncertainly about the living room, shaded his eyes with his hands, and wept until his mighty chest shook.

Gregor did not enter the room at all, instead he leaned from the inside against the wing of the door that was bolted fast, so that only half his body and the head inclined sideways above it could be seen as he peered across at the others. Meanwhile it had grown much lighter out; on the far side of the street, a section of the infinitely long, dark gray building opposite—a hospital—came into view with its regular windows punched into the facade; rain was still falling, but only in large drops that were separately visible and seemed to have been hurled one by one to the ground. An inordinate number of breakfast dishes crowded the table, for Gregor's father considered breakfast the most important meal of the day and would drag it out for hours reading various newspapers. Straight ahead, on the opposite wall, hung a photograph of Gregor from his time in the military, showing him as a second lieutenant whose carefree smile as he rested his hand on his dagger commanded respect for his bearing and his uniform. The door to the vestibule was open, and since the front door was open as well, one could see all the way out to the landing and the head of the stairs leading down.

"Well," Gregor said, quite conscious of the fact that he was the only one who had retained his composure, "I shall get dressed at once, pack up my samples and be on my way. As for the rest of you, are you prepared to let me do so? You can see, sir"—he said, addressing the general manager—"I am not obstinate, nor a shirker; traveling is burdensome, but without it I could not live. Where are you going now, sir? To the office? Yes? Will you report all these things truthfully? A person can be incapable of working at the moment, but this is precisely the right time to recall his earlier accomplishments and consider that he will later, once the hindrance has been overcome, work all the more industriously and with greater focus. I am so dreadfully indebted to the boss, surely you're aware of this. On the other hand, I have my parents and sister to think of. Truly I'm in a bind, but I shall work my way out of it. Don't make things more difficult for me than they already are. Take my side at the office! No one loves us drummers, I know. Everyone thinks the salesmen rake in a king's ransom while enjoying life's pleasures. And there's never any particular cause to reconsider this prejudice. But you, sir, have a far better grasp of the general circumstances than the rest of the staff, better even—if I may speak confidentially—than the boss himself, who in his role as businessman can easily err in his opinion to an employee's disadvantage. And you no doubt know quite well that a drummer, who spends almost the entire year away from the office, can easily become the victim of gossip, happenstance and groundless complaints against which he cannot possibly defend himself, as he usually never even learns of them, or only when he has completed one of his journeys, exhausted, and then back at home is forced to observe the dire physical effects of causes that can no longer be identified. Please, sir, do not leave without saying something to show you agree with me at least to some small extent!"

But the general manager had already turned away as soon as Gregor began to speak, and merely glanced back at him over a hunched shoulder, his mouth contorted. And during Gregor's speech he did not stand still for a moment but instead continued to retreat—not letting Gregor out of his sight—in the direction of the door, but only gradually, as though it were secretly prohibited to exit this room. Already he was in the vestibule, and to judge by the abrupt motion with which he withdrew his foot from the living room for the last time, one might have supposed he'd just burned it. Having reached the vestibule, however, he stretched out his right hand, gesturing broadly in the direction of the stairs, as if some all but supernatural salvation awaited him there.

Gregor realized he could not possibly allow the general manager to depart in his present frame of mind if his own position at the firm was not to be put in the gravest jeopardy. His parents didn't fully comprehend his situation: over these long years they had formed the conviction that Gregor was provided for in this office for life, and besides they were so preoccupied with their present worries that they were bereft of all foresight. But Gregor had this foresight. The general manager would have to be detained, reasoned with, convinced and finally won over; after all, Gregor's future and that of his family depended on it. If only his sister were here! She was clever; she had already begun to weep while Gregor was still lying quietly on his back. And surely the general manager, ever the ladies' man, would have let himself be assuaged by her; she would have closed the front door of the apartment and talked him out of his fear in the vestibule. But his sister was not there, so Gregor himself would have to act. And without stopping to consider that he was not yet familiar with his current abilities with respect to locomotion, nor even taking into account the fact that this last speech of his had quite possibly—indeed probably—eluded comprehension, he let go of the door; forced his way through the opening; meant to walk over to where the general manager, already out on the landing, was foolishly clutching at the banister with both hands; but right away, groping in vain for something to catch hold of, he fell with a faint shriek upon his many little legs. No sooner had this occurred when he felt—for the first time all morning—a sense of physical well-being; his legs had solid ground beneath them; they obeyed his will perfectly, as he noted to his delight; they even strove to bear him wherever he wished; and already it seemed to him he would soon be delivered from all his sufferings. But as he lay there on the floor directly in front of his mother and not far from her, swaying with mobility held in check, she suddenly leapt up—rapt as she had appeared within her own contemplations— leapt high up into the air, her arms thrust wide, fingers spread, crying out: "Help me, for God's sake, help!" her head cocked at an angle, as if to see Gregor better, but then, contradicting this, she senselessly retreated; but she had forgotten the table set for breakfast just behind her; sat down hurriedly upon it as soon as she reached it, as if absentmindedly; and didn't seem to notice that the big overturned coffeepot beside her was pouring a thick stream of coffee on the rug.

"Mother, Mother," Gregor said softly, gazing up at her. For a moment he had forgotten all about the general manager; on the other hand, he could not restrain himself, when he beheld this flowing coffee, from snapping his jaws several times. At this, the mother gave another shriek and fled from the table into the arms of Gregor's father as he rushed to her aid. But Gregor had no time for his parents now; the general manger was already on the stairs; his chin propped on the banister, he looked back on the scene one last time. Gregor was just preparing to dash after him to be sure of catching up with him; but the manager must have sensed something, for he leapt down several steps at once and vanished; and the cry of horror he gave as he fled resounded through the stairwell. Unfortunately the manager's flight now appeared to utterly discombobulate Gregor's father, who up till then had been relatively composed, for instead of running after the manager himself or at least not hindering Gregor in his own pursuit, he seized the manager's walking stick in one hand—it had been left lying on an armchair along with his overcoat and hat—with the other took up a large newspaper from the table, and set about driving Gregor back into his room with a great stamping of feet, brandishing both newspaper and stick. All Gregor's entreaties were in vain, nor were they even understood, for as submissively as he might swivel his head, his father only stamped his feet all the more ferociously. Across the room, his mother had flung open a window despite the chilly weather, and, leaning out, she pressed her face into her hands far outside the window frame. Between street and stairwell, a powerful draft arose, the window curtains flew into the air, the newspapers on the table rustled, and a few pages scudded across the floor. Inexorably Gregor's father drove him backward, uttering hissing sounds like a wild man. But Gregor had no practice at all in reverse locomotion, and his progress was very slow. If only he'd been permitted to turn around, he'd have been back in his room at once, but he was afraid of provoking his father's fury with this time-consuming maneuver, and at any moment a fatal blow from the stick in his father's hand might come crashing down on his back or head. In the end, though, he had no alternative: horrified, he realized he was incapable of controlling his direction; and so he began, with constant anxious glances back at his father, to turn around as quickly as he could, which in fact was rather slowly. Perhaps his father discerned his good intentions, for he did not hinder him in this operation but instead even guided his rotation here and there from a distance, using the tip of his stick. If only his father were not making that unbearable hissing noise! It made Gregor lose his head completely. He had already turned almost all the way around when—still with this hissing in his ear—he became confused and started turning back in the wrong direction. But when finally he succeeded in positioning his head in front of the doorway, it turned out that his body was too wide to fit through the opening. And of course in his father's current state it could not possibly have occurred to him to open the door's other wing to create an adequate passage. He was fixated on the notion that Gregor must disappear into his room as quickly as possible. Never would he have tolerated the complicated preparations necessary for Gregor to prop himself up so as possibly to pass through the door in an upright position. Instead, as though there were no obstacle at all, he now drove Gregor before him, raising a great din: what Gregor heard at his back no longer resembled the voice of merely a single father; it was do or die, and Gregor thrust himself—come what would—into the doorway. One side of his body tilted up, rising at an angle as he pressed forward, scraping his one flank raw and leaving ugly stains behind on the white door, and soon he was wedged tight, unable to move on his own; on one side, his little legs dangled trembling in midair, while on the other they were crushed painfully beneath him—then his father administered a powerful shove from behind, a genuinely liberating thrust that sent him flying, bleeding profusely, into the far reaches of his room. The door was banged shut with the stick, and then at last all was still.

II

Only as dusk was falling did Gregor wake from his heavy, faintlike sleep. He probably wouldn't have slept much longer even without a disturbance, for he felt sufficiently rested and restored, but it seemed to him he had been woken by a fleeting step and the careful shutting of the door to the vestibule. The pallid gleam of the electric streetlamps touched the ceiling here and there and the upper edges of the furniture, but down where Gregor lay, all was dark. Slowly, groping awkwardly with his feelers, which he was only now learning to appreciate, he dragged himself toward the door, wanting to see what had happened. His left side felt like one long unpleasantly contracting scar, and he was forced to limp outright on his two rows of legs. One of these diminutive legs, incidentally, had suffered grievous injuries in the course of the morning's events—it was almost miraculous only one had been injured—and now trailed lifelessly behind him.

Not until he reached the door did he realize what in fact had lured him there: it was the smell of something edible. There stood a bowl filled with sweet milk in which little pieces of white bread were floating. He almost laughed with delight, for his hunger was now even more powerful than in the morning, and right away he dunked his head in the milk almost up to his eyes. But he quickly drew it out again in disappointment; it wasn't just that eating was difficult thanks to his tender left side—and he couldn't eat at all without his entire body becoming gaspingly involved—but beyond that: even though milk had always been his favorite drink, which is no doubt why his sister had brought him some, now it didn't taste good to him at all, indeed it was almost with revulsion that he turned away from the bowl and crept back to the center of the room.

In the living room, as Gregor saw through the crack, the gas had been lit, but while usually at this hour his father liked to read aloud from the afternoon paper to Gregor's mother and sometimes his sister as well in a dramatic voice, now there was not a sound to be heard. Well, perhaps this customary reading aloud that his sister had often told and written him about had recently fallen out of practice. But even in the other rooms everything was so still, even though the apartment was surely not empty. "What a quiet life my family has been leading," Gregor said to himself, and as he gazed fixedly into the darkness before him, he felt great pride at having been able to give his parents and sister a life like this in such a beautiful apartment. But what if all this tranquility, all this prosperity and contentment were now coming to a horrific end? So as not to get lost in such contemplations, Gregor set himself in motion, crawling back and forth across the room.

Once in the course of this long evening one of the side doors was opened a tiny crack and then quickly shut again, and once the other one; someone must have felt an urge to enter and then been overcome by misgivings. Gregor now stationed himself just in front of the living room door, determined to somehow coax the hesitant visitor inside or at least find out who it was; but the door did not open again, and Gregor waited in vain. Before, when all the doors were locked, everyone kept trying to come in, and now that he had opened the one door and the others had apparently been opened during the day, no one came, and the keys were sticking in their locks from the outside.

It was late at night by the time the light in the living room went out, and now it was easy to ascertain that Gregor's parents and sister had remained awake all this time, for all three of them could clearly be heard departing on tiptoe. Now it was unlikely anyone would come into Gregor's room before morning; so he had plenty of time to ponder how best to reorder his life. But this high open room in which he was forced to lie flat on the floor distressed him, without his being able to determine the cause—after all, it was his room, which he had been living in for five years now—and with a half-unconscious motion, and not without a twinge of shame, he scurried beneath the settee, where even though his back was a bit cramped and he could no longer raise his head, he at once felt right at home, his only regret being that his body was too wide across to be accommodated entirely beneath this piece of furniture.

Here he remained the entire night, which he spent by turns dozing—though he was woken again and again by his hunger—and mulling over his worries and indistinct hopes, which however all led to the conclusion that, for the time being, he should behave calmly and, by employing patience and the utmost consideration, assist his family in enduring the inconveniences his current state inevitably forced him to impose on them.

Early the next morning already, so early it was almost still night, Gregor had the opportunity to test the strength of these resolutions he had made, for from the vestibule his sister, almost completely clothed, opened his door, and cast an anxious glance into the room. She didn't immediately spot him, but when she noticed him beneath the settee—well, goodness, he had to be somewhere, it's not as if he might have flown away—the sight so alarmed her that, unable to control herself, she slammed the door from the outside. But as if regretting this conduct, she opened it again at once and came in, walking on tiptoe as though she were entering the room of a gravely ill patient or even a stranger. Gregor, having slid his head to just beneath the edge of the settee, observed her. Would she see that he had left the milk standing, and not because of an absence of hunger, and would she bring him some other food more to his liking? If she failed to do so of her own accord, he would sooner starve than call this to her attention, though in fact he felt a nearly monstrous urge to scoot out from beneath the settee, throw himself at his sister's feet, and beg her for something good to eat. But his sister immediately remarked with surprise that the bowl was still full, with just a little of its milk spilled on the floor around it, and she picked it up right away—not with her bare hands, to be sure, but with a rag—and carried it out of the room. Gregor was exceptionally curious to see what she would bring in its stead and mulled over various possibilities. But never would he have been able to predict what his sister in her kindness actually did. To gauge his tastes, she brought him an entire assortment of foodstuffs, all spread out on an old newspaper. There were old, half-rotten vegetables; bones from the family supper the night before caked in a congealed white sauce; a few raisins and almonds; a piece of cheese Gregor had declared inedible two days before; a dry piece of bread; a slice of buttered bread; and a slice of bread with butter and salt. In addition, she placed beside this feast the bowl that apparently had been reserved for Gregor once and for all; it was now filled with water. And out of delicacy, since she knew Gregor would not eat in front of her, she quickly withdrew and even turned the key in the lock so that Gregor would understand he could make himself comfortable. Gregor's little legs whirred as he now went to take his meal. His wounds, incidentally, seemed to have healed entirely in the meantime, for he no longer felt the least impairment; this was astonishing, for more than a month ago he had cut his finger just a tiny bit with a knife, and this wound had still been painful enough just the day before yesterday. "Might I be less fastidious than before?" he thought, already sucking greedily at the cheese, to which he'd found himself immediately, inexorably drawn, more than to any of the other items. Quickly, his eyes shedding tears of gratification, he devoured in swift succession: the cheese, the vegetables, and the sauce; the fresh food, by contrast, did not taste good to him, in fact he could not even stand the smell of it and so dragged the things he wished to eat a little to one side. He had long since finished everything and was just lying indolently where he was when his sister slowly turned the key in the lock as a signal for him to withdraw. At once he gave a start, though he'd been on the point of nodding off, and he hurried back under the settee. But it cost him a great deal of willpower to remain there even for the short period of time his sister spent in the room, for the hearty meal he'd enjoyed had caused his abdomen to swell, and he could scarcely breathe in his confinement. In between little attacks of suffocation, he peered out with slightly bulging eyes as his sister, oblivious, used a broom to sweep up not only the remains of his meal but also the food he hadn't even touched, as if these items too were no longer fit for consumption, then she hastily dumped everything in a bucket that she covered with a wooden lid before carrying it all out of the room again. She had scarcely turned her back when Gregor hauled himself out from under the settee, stretching and puffing up his body.

This was how Gregor now received his food each day, once in the morning, when his parents and the maid were still asleep, and the second time after everyone had eaten lunch, for his parents would always nap a little afterward, and his sister would send the maid out on some errand or other. Surely they didn't want Gregor to starve either, but perhaps it would have been too much for them to experience his meals through more than hearsay, or perhaps his sister wanted to spare them even this modest sorrow, for Lord knows they were suffering enough.

Gregor never learned on what pretext the doctor and locksmith had been sent away that first morning, for since he himself could not be understood, it occurred to no one, not even his sister, that he could understand the others, so when his sister came to his room, he had to be content merely with hearing the sighs she heaved now and then and her words of supplication addressed to the saints. Only later, when she had started to grow accustomed to all of this— though of course it was impossible to become fully accustomed to circumstances like these—would Gregor sometimes catch a remark that was meant in a friendly way or could be interpreted as such. "He tucked right in today," she would say when Gregor had found the food she left him particularly tasty, while in the opposite case, which gradually began to occur more and more often, she was in the habit of saying almost mournfully: "This time he didn't touch a thing."

But while no news reached Gregor directly, he sometimes was able to overhear this and that from the rooms to either side of his, and whenever he heard voices, he would immediately run over to the door in question and press his entire body against it. Especially in the early days there was rarely a conversation that did not somehow, if only indirectly, refer to him. For two days, every meal-time was spent deliberating how the family should now comport itself; but even between meals this same discussion continued, for at least two members of the household were present at all times, since apparently no one wanted to remain at home alone, and of course leaving the apartment unattended was out of the question. What's more, the maid had fallen on her knees before Gregor's mother that very first day—it was not entirely clear what and how much she knew of what had occurred—begging to be released from the family's service, and when she took her leave a quarter of an hour later, she tearfully thanked them for dismissing her, as though this were the greatest benefaction she had experienced at their hands, and without anyone asking this of her, she swore a solemn oath never to reveal anything at all to anyone.

Now Gregor's sister was forced to do the cooking in concert with his mother; to be sure, not much effort was involved, as no one did much eating. Again and again Gregor would hear one of them pressing the others to eat—always in vain, and never with any other response than "Thank you, I've had all I want," or similar words. Perhaps they didn't drink anything either. Often Gregor's sister would ask her father if he wouldn't like a beer, affectionately offering to fetch it herself, and when he did not respond, she would say, wishing to relieve him of all scruples, that she could send the porter's wife for it as well, but then the father would utter a great "No," and no one spoke of it any longer.

Already in the course of the first day, Gregor's father explained the family's finances and prospects not only to Gregor's mother but to his sister as well. Now and then he would get up from the table and, from his small Wertheim safe, which he had salvaged when his business collapsed five years before, extract some receipt or memorandum book. One could hear him opening the complicated lock and then bolting it shut again after removing the desired item. These explanations on his father's part included the first bits of heartening news Gregor had heard since his captivity began. He had been under the impression that his father had retained nothing at all of his former firm's holdings, or at least his father had never said anything to the contrary, and admittedly Gregor himself had never asked him about this. At the time, his only concern had been to do everything in his power to let the family forget, as quickly as possible, the mercantile catastrophe that had plunged all of them into a state of utter hopelessness. And so he had set to work with particular zeal and risen almost overnight from petty clerk to saleman, in which capacity of course he had a quite different earning potential, and his professional accomplishments, in the form of commissions, were immediately transformed into cash that could be plunked down on the table at home, before the eyes of his astonished, delighted family. Those had been lovely times, and never since had they been repeated, at least not with such glory, although Gregor later earned so much money that he was in a position to cover the expenses for the entire family, which is what he did. All had grown accustomed to this arrangement, not just the family but Gregor as well: they gratefully accepted the money, and he was happy to provide it, but the exchange no longer felt particularly warm. Only Gregor's sister had remained close to him all this time, and it was his secret plan to send her off to study at the Conservatory next year (unlike Gregor, she dearly loved music and could play the violin quite movingly), despite the considerable costs this would no doubt entail, money that could surely be brought in by other means. Often during the brief periods of time Gregor spent in town, the Conservatory would come up in his conversations with his sister, but only ever as a lovely dream whose realization was unthinkable, and their parents did not like to hear it mentioned even in this innocuous way; but Gregor was thinking the matter over with great determination and intended to make a formal announcement on Christmas Eve.

Thoughts like these, utterly futile in his current state, passed through his head as he stood pressed against the door, eavesdropping. Sometimes general exhaustion made it impossible for him to go on listening, and he would carelessly let his head bang against the door, but then he would immediately hold his head still again, for even the faint sound this produced had been heard in the next room, causing everyone to fall silent. "I wonder what he's getting up to now," his father would say after a while, apparently facing the door, and only then would the interrupted conversation resume.

Gregor now learned, and learned quite well (his father tended to repeat himself in his explanations, in part because it had been so long since he'd last concerned himself with such matters, in part because Gregor's mother did not always understand everything the first time), that despite all their misfortunes, a small nest egg—really only a tiny one—still remained to them from before, and had even grown a little thanks to the untouched interest that had accumulated meanwhile. In addition, the money Gregor had brought home each month—he only ever kept a few gulden for himself—had not yet been entirely used up and had grown into a small capital. Behind his door, Gregor nodded eagerly, delighted at this unexpected prudence and thrift. To be sure, he might have used this surplus to pay off more of his father's debts with his boss, and the day on which he would have been able to divest himself of his post would no longer have been nearly so far off, but as things stood, his father's arrangements were no doubt for the best.

Now this money was by no means sufficient to allow the family to live off the interest or anything of that sort; it might possibly have been enough to sustain the family for a year, two at most, but that's all there was. So in fact it was the kind of sum one really shouldn't touch, one to be set aside in case of emergency; the money to live on would have to be earned. Gregor's father was admittedly in good health, but he was old and hadn't worked in a full five years, and in any case he was supposed to avoid overexerting himself; in those five years—the first holiday in his strenuous and yet unsuccessful life—he had put on a lot of weight and now lumbered as he walked. And was Gregor's old mother now supposed to hold down a job, despite her asthma and the fact that it was already an exertion for her to cross from one end of the apartment to the other, for which reason she spent every second day gasping for breath on the sofa beside the open window? And was his sister to go out working, this child of seventeen whose lifestyle no one would begrudge her: dressing nicely, sleeping late, helping out around the house, taking part in a few modest entertainments, and above all, playing the violin? Whenever the family came to speak of the necessity of someone earning money, Gregor would let go of the door and throw himself down upon the cool leather sofa beside it, burning with shame and sorrow.

Often he would lie there the entire long night, not sleeping for a moment, just scrabbling for hours against the leather. Or, not shunning the great effort it cost him to push an armchair over to the window, he would climb up the sill and, propped in the armchair, lean against the window, apparently lost in some sort of reverie of how liberating he'd always found it to gaze outside. For in truth he saw even the objects that were quite near at hand less and less clearly as the days progressed; the hospital across the way whose all too constant sight he had earlier reviled was now no longer even visible to him, and if he had not known perfectly well that he was a resident of Charlottenstrasse, a quiet but perfectly urban street, he might have imagined he was gazing out his window onto a desert in which the gray sky and the gray earth were indistinguishably conjoined. His attentive sister only had to see the armchair standing beside the window twice before she started pushing it back to its place there each time she tidied his room; indeed she even began leaving the window's inner sash open.

If only Gregor had been able to speak to his sister and thank her for all she was compelled to do for him, he would have found her ministrations easier to bear; as it was, he suffered beneath them. His sister, to be sure, did all she could to obscure the awkwardness of the situation, and the more time passed, the better she succeeded, of course, but Gregor came to see it all more and more clearly. Even the way she made her entrance jangled his nerves. The moment she came in, without even pausing to shut the door—although she always took such pains to shield the others from the sight of Gregor's room—she would race straightaway to the window and fling it open with hasty hands as though she were on the point of suffocating, then remain standing there, however cold it might be, gulping in the air. All this racing and racket was inflicted on Gregor twice a day; he would be trembling beneath the settee, painfully aware that she would no doubt have willingly spared him this disruption if it were possible for her to endure being in the same room as Gregor with the window closed.

Once—it must have been a month since Gregor's metamorphosis, so there was no particular call for his sister to be startled by his appearance—she came into his room a little earlier than usual and discovered him, motionless and propped upright as if for horrific effect, gazing out the window. Gregor would not have found it surprising if she had chosen not to enter, since his position prevented her from opening the window right away, but she didn't just not enter: she started in alarm and shut the door; a stranger might have thought Gregor had been lying in wait, meaning to bite her. Gregor naturally went and hid himself away beneath the settee, but he had to wait there until noon before his sister returned, and she seemed far more agitated than usual. From this he understood that his appearance was still unbearable to her and would remain so, and that she no doubt had to struggle to force herself not to run away at the sight of even the small part of his body that protruded from beneath the settee. In order to spare her even this sight, one day he carried the bedsheet over to the settee on his back—this labor cost him four hours—and arranged it in such a way that he was now completely covered, so that his sister would not be able to see him even if she bent down. If she considered the sheet unnecessary, she could have removed it, since it was clear enough that it could not possibly be considered a pleasure for Gregor to shut himself off so completely, but she left the sheet where it was, and Gregor even thought he glimpsed a grateful look when at one point he carefully lifted the sheet just a little with his head to see how his sister liked the new arrangement.

During the first fortnight, Gregor's parents could not bring themselves to enter his room, and often he heard them expressing their heartfelt appreciation of his sister's labors, whereas earlier they had often been annoyed with her, since she had seemed to them a rather useless girl. But now both of them, father and mother alike, would often be waiting just outside Gregor's door while his sister tidied up his room, and as soon as she emerged, she had to give a full report on what things looked like in the room, what Gregor had eaten, how he had behaved this time, and whether perhaps any modest improvement could be seen. His mother, incidentally, had wanted to visit him relatively soon, but his father and sister held her back, appealing at first to her sense of reason as Gregor listened attentively, wholeheartedly approving. Later, though, she had to be held back by force, and when she then cried out: "Let me go to Gregor, he is my unhappy son! Can't you understand that I must go to him?" then Gregor thought it would perhaps be good for his mother to visit him, not every day of course, but perhaps once a week; after all, she had a far better grasp of things than his sister, who despite her courage was still a child and, when it came right down to it, had perhaps only taken on this difficult task out of childish frivolity.

Gregor's wish to see his mother was soon fulfilled. During the day, Gregor avoided showing himself at the window, if only out of consideration for his parents, but there wasn't much crawling he could do in the few square meters of space the floor provided, lying still was already difficult for him to endure during the night, eating had soon ceased to give him even the slightest pleasure, and so to divert himself he took up the habit of crawling back and forth across the walls and ceiling. He particularly liked hanging from the ceiling high above the room; it was completely different from lying on the floor; one could breathe more freely there; a gentle swaying motion rocked the body; and in the almost happy absentmindedness Gregor experienced, it might happen, to his own astonishment, that he would let go and crash to the floor. But now, of course, he had his body far better under control than before, and even as great a fall as this did him no harm. His sister immediately noticed the new entertainment Gregor had devised for himself—his peregrinations left behind sticky trails here and there—and she got it into her head to make it possible for Gregor to range as widely as possible by removing the furniture that impeded his movement, above all the wardrobe and desk. But she wasn't able to do so on her own; she didn't dare ask her father for help; the maid most certainly would not have helped her, for this girl of sixteen or so, though she had courageously remained in the household after the departure of the former cook, had at the same time requested the privilege of keeping the kitchen locked at all times and only opening the door upon particular request; and so the sister had no choice but to summon her mother one day when her father was out. The mother arrived with exclamations of feverish joy but fell silent at the door to Gregor's room. At first, of course, Gregor's sister checked to confirm that all in the room was as it should be; only then did she allow her mother to enter. With the utmost haste, Gregor had tugged the sheet down lower and in looser folds so that it really did look as if a bedsheet just happened to have been tossed over the settee. He also refrained from peering out from beneath the sheet this time; for the moment, he would resign himself to not seeing his mother and just be glad she had come. "It's all right, come in, you won't see him," Gregor's sister said, apparently leading her mother by the hand. Gregor now heard the sounds of these two weak women grappling with this in fact quite heavy old wardrobe, with his sister laying claim to the bulk of the work, not listening to the admonitions of her mother, who was afraid she would overtax herself. It took a very long time. After perhaps a quarter of an hour's labor, Gregor's mother said they should leave the wardrobe where it was after all; in the first place, it was too heavy—they would not finish before Gregor's father came home, and by leaving the wardrobe in the middle of the room, they would prevent Gregor from moving around at all—and secondly, it wasn't even clear they were doing him a favor by taking away the furniture. To her, it seemed the opposite was true: the sight of the empty wall positively oppressed her heart; and why should Gregor not experience this same sentiment, since after all he was long accustomed to having this furniture around him—wouldn't he feel abandoned in an emptied-out room? "And is it not as if," his mother concluded in a low voice—in fact, she had been whispering all along, as though she wished to avoid letting Gregor, whose exact whereabouts she did not know, hear so much as the sound of her voice, for she was convinced he could not understand her words—"and is it not as if by removing the furniture we would be showing that we are giving up all hope of a cure and are ruthlessly abandoning him to his own devices? I think it would be best if we try to keep the room in precisely the same state it was in before, so that when Gregor returns to us he will find everything unchanged, which will make it that much easier for him to forget all that has happened in the meantime."

Hearing his mother's words, Gregor realized that the absence of all direct human address, combined with the monotony of life in his family's midst, must have muddled his understanding over the course of these two months, for he could not otherwise explain to himself how he could seriously have wished to have his room emptied out. Did he really want to have this warm room, cozily appointed with inherited furniture, transformed into a cave or den—in which, to be sure, he would be able to crawl about unhindered in every direction, but at the price of simultaneously swiftly and completely forgetting his human past? He was already on the verge of forgetting, and only his mother's voice, which he had gone so long now without hearing, had shaken him awake. Nothing should be removed; everything must remain; he was unwilling to forego the good influence this furniture had upon his condition; and if the furniture got in the way of his practicing this mindless crawling about, this was by no means to his detriment, in fact, it was a great advantage.

Unfortunately his sister was of a different opinion; she had developed the habit—not entirely without cause, to be sure—of presenting herself as the holder of particular expertise when discussing Gregor with her parents, and so now too her mother's council was reason enough for her to insist on the removal not only of the wardrobe and desk, as she had originally been intending, but of every last bit of the room's furnishings, with the exception of the indispensable settee. Naturally, it was not simply childish defiance and the hard-won self-assurance she had so unexpectedly acquired in recent weeks that dictated this demand; she had, in fact, observed that Gregor needed a great deal of space to crawl around in, while as far as anyone could see, he made no use whatever of the furniture. But perhaps the fanciful imagination of a girl of her age played a role as well, a sensibility always seeking its own gratification, and one which Grete now allowed to persuade her to render Gregor's situation even more horrific than before, so as to be able to do even more for him than she had hitherto. For a room in which Gregor held sole dominion over empty walls was a place where no one other than Grete would ever dare to set foot.

And so she held fast to her resolve despite the protests of her mother, who appeared troubled to the point of indecision even by the room in its present state; she soon fell silent and helped Gregor's sister remove the wardrobe as best she could. Well, the wardrobe was something Gregor could do without if need be, but the desk would certainly have to stay. And no sooner had the women left the room with the cabinet, groaning as they pressed against its weight, than Gregor poked out his head from beneath the settee to see how he might, cautiously and as considerately as possible, intervene. But unfortunately his mother was the first to return while Grete was still in the next room, clasping the wardrobe in her arms and tipping it back and forth on her own—without, of course, moving it from the spot. But Gregor's mother was unaccustomed to his appearance, it might have made her ill to catch a glimpse of him, and so Gregor in alarm withdrew as fast as he could to the far end of the settee, but it was too late to prevent the front edge of the bedsheet from stirring a little. This was enough to attract his mother's notice. Startled, she froze for a moment, then went back to where Grete was.

Although Gregor kept telling himself that nothing extraordinary was happening, just a few sticks of furniture being shifted about, he was soon forced to admit that all this coming and going on the part of the women, their little exclamations, the furniture scraping against the floor, had the combined effect of a tumultuous hubbub intensifying all around him, and no matter how tightly he drew his head and legs in and pressed his body against the floor, he soon was forced to consider that he would not be able to endure this much longer. They were clearing out his room; taking from him all that was dear to him; they had already borne away the cabinet in which lay his fretsaw and other tools; and now they were prying loose the desk that had dug itself firmly into the floorboards, this desk at which he had written his homework assignments as a student at the commercial academy, and as a secondary and even primary school pupil—truly there was no time left to explore the good intentions of these two women, whose existence, by the way, he had almost forgotten, for their exhaustion was now making them labor in silence, and one heard only their heavy footsteps.

And so he burst out of hiding—the women in the next room were just leaning on the desk to catch their breath—changing direction four times as he raced about, for he really didn't know what to save first, but then his eyes lit on the picture of the lady clad all in furs, conspicuous now on the otherwise empty wall, and quickly he made his way up to it and pressed himself against the glass, which adhered to him, pleasantly cool against his hot belly. At least this picture, which Gregor's body now covered up completely, was absolutely certain not to be taken away from him. He swiveled his head toward the living room door to observe the women as they returned.

They hadn't permitted themselves much rest at all and were already on their way back; Grete had slung one arm about her mother and was nearly carrying her. "So what should we take next?" Grete said, looking around. Then her eyes met those of Gregor where he clung to the wall. It was no doubt only because of her mother's presence that she kept her composure; bowing her face toward her mother to prevent her from looking around, she said—hastily and trembling, to be sure—"Let's go back to the living room for a moment, shall we?" Grete's intentions were perfectly clear to Gregor: she meant to bring their mother to safety and then chase him from the wall. Well, let her try! He sat there on his picture and would not give it up. He'd sooner leap right in her face.

But Grete's words succeeded in unsettling her mother even more: taking one step to the side, she saw the huge brown blotch on the flowered wallpaper, and before she was even able to realize that what she saw there was Gregor, she cried out in a hoarse, shrieking voice, "Oh God, oh God!" and fell back upon the settee, her arms spread wide as though she were giving up everything, and lay there without moving. "Gregor!" his sister shouted, raising her fist with a threatening glower. It was the first time she had addressed him directly since his metamorphosis. She ran into the next room to fetch some sort of essence that could be used to awaken her mother from her faint; Gregor wanted to help as well—there would be time enough to save the picture later—but he stuck fast to the glass and had to tear himself away by force; he too then ran into the next room as if he might offer his sister advice of some sort, like in the old days; but then could only stand idly behind her as she rummaged among various little bottles, and scared her out of her wits when she turned around; one bottle flew to the floor and shattered; a shard of glass scratched Gregor's face, and some sort of corrosive medicine engulfed him; without further delay, Grete took up as many bottles as she could hold and ran with them to her mother, slamming the door behind her with her foot. Gregor was now cut off from his mother, who was possibly on the brink of death, for which he himself was to blame; he could not open the door if he didn't want to drive away his sister, who had to stay there with his mother; there was nothing for him to do but wait; and tormented by his worries and self-reproach, he began to crawl about, crawling over everything, walls, furniture, the ceiling, and finally in his despair, as the entire room began to spin around him, he fell smack in the middle of the big table.

A short while passed. Gregor lay there, spent, and around him all was still, possibly a good sign. Then the bell rang. The maid was naturally locked up in her kitchen and so Grete had to open the door. Their father was back. "What happened?" were his first words; the look on Grete's face had no doubt revealed all. Grete's voice as she responded was muffled, apparently she was pressing her face against his chest: "Mother fainted, but she's better already. Gregor has broken out." "That's just what I expected," the father said. "I kept telling you, but you women refused to listen." To Gregor it was clear his father had misinterpreted Grete's all too brief pronouncement to assume him guilty of some act of violence. So it behooved Gregor to try to pacify his father, as he was lacking both the time and means to enlighten him. With this in mind, he fled to the door of his room and pressed himself against it, so that the moment his father came into the living room from the vestibule he would see that Gregor had every intention of returning at once to his room, that it was unnecessary to drive him back inside, and that one had merely to open the door, and he would disappear at once.

But his father was in no mood to take note of subtleties. "Ah!" he exclaimed upon entering, in a tone of voice suggesting he was at once furious and glad. Gregor pulled his head back from the door and turned it toward his father. He had truly not expected to see his father looking as he looked now standing before him; though to be sure the novelty of crawling about had distracted him recently from paying as much attention as before to the goings-on in the rest of the apartment, and really he ought to have been prepared to find a changed set of circumstances. Even so, even so: was this still his father? The same man who used to lie wearily entombed in his bed when Gregor set off on a business trip; who would greet him on the evening of his return sitting in an armchair in his nightshirt; who, incapable of rising, would merely raise his arms to signify his delight, and on the rare walks they still shared, a few Sundays each year and on major holidays, would trudge between Gregor and his mother, who themselves were already walking rather slowly, moving even a bit slower than they, bundled up in his old overcoat, always with his gingerly advancing cane and almost invariably coming to a halt and collecting his companions around him whenever he had something to say? Now he was standing properly erect; dressed in a smart blue uniform with gold buttons of the sort worn by porters in banking establishments; above the jacket's tall, stiff collar his powerful double chin unfurled; beneath bushy eyebrows, his black eyes peered out acutely and attentively; his once disheveled white hair had been painstakingly combed and parted until it gleamed. He tossed his cap, to which a gold mono-gram was affixed, probably that of a bank, across the entire room in a wide arc to land on the settee, then advanced grim-faced upon Gregor with the tips of his long uniform jacket flung back and his hands in his trouser pockets. He himself probably had no idea what he intended to do; at any rate, he raised up each foot unusually high, and Gregor marveled at the gigantic dimensions of his boot-soles. But he did not lose any time over them, having learned on the very first day of his new life that his father considered only the utmost severity appropriate for him. And so he fled from his father, hesitating whenever his father stopped short, and then rushing forward again as soon as he stirred. They circled the room several times in this manner without anything decisive occurring, and indeed, given the slow speed at which this interaction was tak-ing place, without its even having the appearance of a chase. For this reason Gregor remained at floor level for the time being, especially as he feared his father might consider it particular wickedness on his part if he were to take refuge on the walls or ceiling. To be sure, he was forced to realize he would not be able to keep up even this pace for long, since each time his father took a step, he himself had to execute any number of motions. A shortness of breath began to set in—even in his earlier life his lungs had been none too reliable. As he now lurched along, reserving all his strength for this continued flight, his eyes barely open (and not thinking, in his stupefaction, that there might be other ways of saving himself than running across the floor, indeed he had almost forgotten he also had the walls at his disposal, though here, to be sure, they were obstructed by delicately carved furniture full of jagged, pointy edges), all at once something flew to the rug beside him, casually flung, and rolled across his path. It was an apple; and already a second one came flying after it; in horror, Gregor stopped in his tracks; there was no point continuing to run now that his father had decided to bombard him. He had filled his pockets from the fruit bowl on the sideboard and now was tossing apple after apple in Gregor's direction, for the moment not even bothering to take particular aim. The petite red apples rolled around the floor as if electrified, knocking into each other. One lightly lobbed apple grazed Gregor's back and slid off again harmlessly. But it was immediately followed by another one that embedded itself in his back. Gregor tried to drag himself forward, as if this sudden shocking pain might vanish with a change of place; but he felt nailed to the spot and collapsed there, his legs splaying out, all his senses in a state of utter bewilderment. He caught only a last glimpse of the door to his room flying open, his shrieking sister, and his mother running out of the room before her wearing only a chemise, for his sister had undressed the unconscious woman to let her breathe more freely, then he saw his mother rush to his father's side, her unfastened skirts slipping one by one from about her waist as she ran, saw her stumble across these skirts as she threw herself at his father and, embracing him, in perfect union with him—but now Gregor's vision began to fail him—she clasped her hands at the back of his father's head and pleaded with him to spare Gregor's life.

III

The grievous wound Gregor had received, which plagued him for over a month—the apple remained lodged there in his flesh, a visible memento, since no one dared to remove it—seemed to have reminded even his father that Gregor, despite his current lamentable, repulsive form, was a member of the family who should not be treated like an enemy, for family duty dictated that the others swallow down the disgust he aroused in them and show him tolerance, only tolerance.

And even though this wound cost Gregor some of his mobility, probably for good, and for the time being he required many, many minutes to hobble across his room like an old invalid—crawling up the walls was out of the question now—he was compensated for this worsening of his condition by what seemed to him a perfectly adequate substitute: as evening approached, the door to the living room, on which he would start keeping a sharp eye an hour or two beforehand, would now always be opened so as to permit him, lying in his own dark room and invisible from the living room, to watch the entire family sitting at the brightly lit table and listen to their conversations now, as it were, in an officially sanctioned capacity and thus quite differently than before.

To be sure, these were no longer the animated conversations of earlier times that Gregor used to think back on with a certain longing from various cramped hotel rooms when it was time to throw himself, exhausted, into the damp bedding. Now everything was fairly quiet. Gregor's father would fall asleep in his armchair soon after supper; his mother and sister would admonish one another to silence; his mother, bent far over beneath the light, would be sewing ladies' underthings for a dress shop; his sister, who had taken a job as a salesgirl, was studying stenography and French in the evenings so as possibly to move to a better position later on. Sometimes Gregor's father would wake up and, as if unaware he had been sleeping, would say to Gregor's mother: "How long you've been sewing again today!" and then go right back to sleep, which would prompt Gregor's mother and sister to exchange weary smiles.

In a peculiar form of stubbornness, Gregor's father refused to take off his porter's uniform even at home; and while his nightshirt hung uselessly on its hook, he would slumber where he sat, fully clothed, as though he remained ready for service at all times and even here was awaiting his supervisor's call. As a result, his uniform, which had not been new to start with, soon forfeited much of its cleanliness, despite the care lavished on it by mother and sister, and Gregor would sometimes gaze for an entire evening at this stain-covered jacket resplendent with gold buttons, always highly polished, in which the old man slept in considerable discomfort but nonetheless soundly.

The moment the clock struck ten, Gregor's mother would attempt to rouse his father with a few hushed words and then persuade him to go to bed, for he would get no proper sleep sitting here, and sleep was something Gregor's father—who had to report for duty at six in the morning—desperately needed. But in keeping with the stubbornness that had taken hold of him when he started working as a porter, he always insisted on continuing to sit there at the table, even though he kept falling asleep, and then it was only with the greatest effort that he could be persuaded to exchange armchair for bed. Gregor's mother and sister could persist in their little admonishments as doggedly as they liked; for a quarter of an hour, he would just shake his head slowly, his eyes closed, without getting up. Gregor's mother would pluck at his sleeve, whispering cajoling words in his ear, and his sister would set aside her studies to come to her mother's aid, but all to no avail. Gregor's father only settled deeper into his armchair. Only when the women gripped him beneath the arms would he open his eyes, looking by turns at mother and sister and saying: "What sort of life is this? Is this the peace and quiet of my old age?" Then, supported by the two women, he would rise, laboriously, as though he himself were receiving the brunt of this burden, and allow the women to escort him to the doorway, where he would shoo them away and continue on his own, while Gregor's mother hastily threw down her sewing and his sister her pen so they could run after him to offer further assistance. The household was ever further reduced; the maid was now let go after all; a bony giant of a charwoman with white hair flapping about her head came by in the morning and evening to perform the heaviest labors; everything else was handled by Gregor's mother along with all her sewing. It even came to pass that several pieces of jewelry that had been in the family—jewels Gregor's mother and sister had delighted in wearing at entertainments and festivities—were sold, as Gregor would learn in the evening when the price each piece had brought would be discussed. But their greatest lament was always that they were unable to leave this apartment, which was far too large for their current circumstances, since no one could imagine how Gregor might be moved. But Gregor understood that it was not only out of consideration for him that a move was being ruled out, since he could easily enough have been transported in a crate of appropriate size with a few air holes; the main thing keeping the family from moving to a new apartment was their complete sense of hopelessness and the thought that they had been struck with a misfortune such as no one else in their entire circle of relations and friends had ever experienced. They were fulfilling to the utmost the demands the world makes on the poor: Gregor's father fetched breakfast for the petty employees at the bank, his mother sacrificed herself for the underclothes of strangers, his sister ran back and forth behind the shop counter at her customers' behest, but this was all the strength they had. And the wound in Gregor's back would begin to ache anew when mother and sister, having brought his father to bed, would now return and, leaving their work where it lay, huddle close beside one another pressing their cheeks together; when Gregor's mother, gesturing toward his room, would say: "Shut the door now, Grete"; and when Gregor was left in the dark again while next door the two women intermingled their tears or else sat there tearless, staring down at the table.

Gregor spent his nights and days almost entirely without sleeping. Sometimes he thought about taking the family's affairs in hand again, just as he used to, the next time his door was opened; once more his boss and the general manager would appear before his mind's eye after all this time, the clerks and apprentices, the dull-witted hired man, two or three friends from other firms, a chambermaid from a provincial hotel (a sweet, fleeting specter), the shopgirl from a haberdashery whom he had courted earnestly but too slowly—all of these now appeared to him, interspersed with strangers or people already forgotten, but instead of coming to his aid and that of his family, every last one of them was unapproachable, and he was glad when they disappeared. At other times he would be not at all in a frame of mind to look after his family; instead he was filled with rage at how poorly he was attended to, and although he could not imagine anything he would have liked to eat, he plotted how he might gain access to the pantry so as to help himself to what—despite his total absence of hunger—was his due. Without bothering to consider how she might give Gregor particular pleasure, his sister would quickly thrust some randomly chosen foodstuff into his room with her foot on her way to work in the morning or at midday, only to sweep it out again at night with a quick swipe of the broom, paying no heed if the food had been only barely nibbled at or—as was most often the case now—not touched at all. Setting Gregor's room to rights, a task she now saved for the evenings, could not possibly have been done any more perfunctorily. Great streaks of dirt extended across the walls, with balls of dust and rubbish lying scattered about. At first when Gregor's sister came into his room he would position himself in corners particularly indicative of this problem—to reproach her, as it were, by his presence there. But he could just as well have spent entire weeks sitting there without any improvement on his sister's part; after all, she saw the dirt as plainly as he did, but had made up her mind to leave it be. At the same time, with a sensitivity that was new in her, one that had now taken hold of the family as a whole, she was on her guard to make sure the task of tidying Gregor's room was reserved for her. Once Gregor's mother had subjected his room to a thorough scrubbing, which she accomplished only after using up several buckets of water—admittedly, all this moisture was itself an affront to Gregor, who lay stretched out, bitter and immobile, upon the settee—but his mother did not escape punishment. For no sooner had his sister remarked the change in Gregor's room that evening than she ran into the living room, grievously insulted, and ignoring her mother's imploringly raised hands, set to weeping so violently that her parents—naturally her father was startled out of his chair—at first stood by helpless and astonished; until they too began to stir; on the right, Gregor's father reproached his mother for not having left the cleaning of Gregor's room to his sister; while on the left he shouted at Gregor's sister, threatening that she would never again be permitted to clean Gregor's room; while his mother attempted to drag his father, now so agitated he hardly recognized himself, into the bedroom; Gregor's sister, shaking with sobs, pummeled the table with her tiny fists; and Gregor hissed loudly in fury because it had occurred to no one to shut the door of his room to spare him this sight and commotion.

But even if Gregor's sister, who was exhausted by her professional work, had wearied of caring for Gregor as she'd previously done, there was absolutely no need for his mother to fill her shoes, and Gregor needn't have suffered neglect. For now the charwoman was here. This old widow—who had seen and survived the worst in her long life with the help of her sturdy bones—felt no particular repugnance toward Gregor. Without being at all inquisitive, she had once chanced to open the door to his room and, seeing Gregor, who had begun to run back and forth although no one was chasing him, she stood there staring in astonishment, her hands clasped across her lap. Ever since, she never failed to open the door a crack for a moment every morning and evening to look in on him. At the beginning she would call him over to her, saying things that were probably intended to sound friendly, like "Hey, over here, you old dung beetle!" or "Just look at the old dung beetle!" Thus addressed, Gregor gave no reply but instead remained where he was, immobile, as if the door had never been opened. If only this charwoman, instead of being allowed to disturb him uselessly at whim, had been given instructions to clean his room daily! Once, early in the morning—a heavy rain, perhaps already a portent of the coming spring, was beating against the windowpanes—Gregor became so infuriated when the charwoman started up again with her quips that he turned on her as if to attack, if admittedly slowly and decrepitly. But instead of being frightened, the charwoman just picked up a chair that was standing beside the door and held it high in the air; and as she stood there, her mouth gaping wide, her intention was clear: not to close her mouth again until the chair in her hand had come crashing down upon Gregor's back. "Aha, so that's as far as it goes?" she asked as Gregor turned around again, and she placed the chair calmly back in its corner.

Gregor now ate almost nothing at all. Only if he happened by chance to wander past the food that had been prepared for him might he playfully take a bite of something into his mouth, where he would hold it for hours and then usually spit it out again later. At first he thought it was his sorrow at the state of his room that prevented him from eating, but in fact he had resigned himself very quickly to the changes there. Everyone had gotten into the habit of using his room to store things they had no space for in other parts of the apartment, and now there were many such things here, since one room of the apartment had been rented out to three lodgers. These solemn gentlemen—all three of them were bearded, as Gregor once noted, peering through the crack of the door— were scrupulously intent on having everything tidy, not just in their room but also, since they were now paying rent here, in the entire household, particularly the kitchen. They could not bear the presence of unnecessary, let alone dirty items. Moreover, they had brought most of their own furnishings with them. For this reason, many things had become superfluous, things that could not be sold but were still too valuable to throw out. All of this found its way into Gregor's room. As did the ash box and the garbage pail from the kitchen. The charwoman, always in a great hurry, would simply fling any unserviceable item into Gregor's room; mercifully, Gregor generally saw only the object in question and the hand that held it. The charwoman may have intended at some point, when she had occasion or a free minute, to come collect these items, or else throw all of them out at once, but as it was they remained wherever they first landed, except when Gregor made his way through the refuse, stirring it around—at first out of necessity, since there was no room left for him to crawl about, but later with ever-increasing pleasure, though after these wanderings, which left him mortally exhausted and sad, he would spend hours without moving.

Since the lodgers sometimes also took their supper at home in the shared living room, the living room door remained shut on some evenings, but Gregor was happy to forgo having the door open; in fact, even when it was open, he sometimes failed to take advantage of it and instead, unbeknownst to his family, would remain lying in the darkest corner of his room. Once, however, the charwoman had left the door to the living room slightly ajar, and ajar it remained even when the lodgers came in that evening and struck a light. They sat down at the head of the table, where in earlier times Gregor had sat with his father and mother, unfolded the napkins and took up their knives and forks. At once Gregor's mother appeared in the doorway with a serving dish filled with meat, and right behind her came his sister bearing a plate piled high with potatoes. A heavy vapor rose from the steaming food. The lodgers bent over the dishes that had been placed before them, as though wishing to inspect them before beginning their meal, and in fact the one who sat in the middle and appeared to be an authority figure to the other two cut off a piece of meat right there on the platter to check whether it was tender enough and didn't have to be sent back to the kitchen. He was satisfied, and Gregor's mother and sister, who had been watching nervously, now smiled with relief.

The family members themselves ate in the kitchen. Nonetheless Gregor's father visited the living room on his way to the kitchen and with a single bow, cap in hand, took a tour around the table. The lodgers all rose from their seats and mumbled into their beards. Left alone again, they ate in almost perfect silence. It struck Gregor as peculiar that amid all the various sounds of this meal, one could also make out their champing teeth, as if to demonstrate to Gregor that a person needs teeth to eat and that even the most splendid jaws, if toothless, can accomplish nothing at all. "I'm hungry," Gregor said sorrowfully to himself, "but not for these things. Just look how these lodgers take their nourishment while I am wasting away!"

On this very evening—Gregor couldn't remember having heard the violin once in all this time—the sound of it was heard coming from the kitchen. The lodgers had already finished their evening meal, the one in the middle had pulled out a newspaper, giving each of the others a page, and now the three of them were reading, leaning back in their chairs and smoking. When the violin began to play, their interest was piqued, they got up from their chairs and tiptoed over to the doorway leading to the vestibule, where they stood in a tight cluster. The sounds of this activity must have traveled to the kitchen, for Gregor's father now called out: "Are the gentlemen disturbed by this playing? It can be silenced at once." "On the contrary," said the one in the middle, "would the young lady care to join us and play here in the living room, where it is much more comfortable and pleasant?" "Why, of course," Gregor's father exclaimed, as though he were the violinist. The gentlemen went back into the room and waited. Soon Gregor's father arrived with the music stand, his mother with the sheet music and his sister with the violin. His sister calmly prepared to play; his parents, who never rented out rooms in earlier days and therefore were treating these lodgers with exaggerated deference, did not even dare to sit in their own armchairs; his father leaned against the door, his right hand tucked between two buttons of his closed livery jacket; his mother, meanwhile, was offered an armchair by one of the lodgers, and since she left the chair where he had happened to place it, she sat off to one side in a corner.

Gregor's sister began to play; on either side, his father and mother attentively followed each movement of her hands. Attracted by her playing, Gregor had ventured a bit further than usual and was already sticking his head into the living room. It scarcely surprised him that he had become so inconsiderate of the others; earlier on, his considerateness had been a source of pride. And he had all the more reason to keep himself hidden away now: thanks to the dust that lay everywhere in his room and would swirl up at the slightest motion, he too was covered in dust; he dragged around threads, hair and food scraps clinging to his back and sides; his general indifference was far too great now for him to keep up with a habit he'd once practiced several times a day: flipping over so as to scrub his back against the rug. And despite his condition, he did not hesitate now to continue his advance a little way out onto the immaculate floor of the living room.

To be sure, no one paid him the slightest heed. The family was completely absorbed in the violin playing; the lodgers, on the other hand, having at first positioned themselves, hands in their trouser pockets, much too close behind his sister's music stand, so that they could all look at the sheet music, which surely must have distracted her, soon withdrew to the window, conversing in an undertone, and remained there, anxiously observed by Gregor's father. It appeared more than clear they had been disappointed in their expectation of hearing beautiful or entertaining violin music and now, tired of the whole performance, were continuing to tolerate this disturbance of their peace only out of politeness. Particularly the way in which all of them were blowing the smoke of their cigars high into the air from their noses and mouths suggested extreme agitation. And yet his sister's playing was so lovely. Her face was tilted to one side; searchingly, sadly, her eyes followed the lines of notes. Gregor crept a bit farther forward and ducked his head down close to the floor so as perhaps to catch her eye. Was he a beast, that music so moved him? He felt as if he were being shown the way to that unknown nourishment he craved. He was determined to creep all the way up to his sister, to pluck at her skirt and in this way indicate to her that she should come to his room with her violin, for no one here was rewarding her playing as he meant to reward her. He would not allow her to leave his room ever again, at least as long as he was alive; his horrific figure would, for the first time ever, be useful to him; he would be at all the doors of his room at once, growling at his attackers; but his sister should remain with him not by force but of her own free will; she should sit beside him on the settee, bend down, the better to hear, and he would confess to her that he'd had the firm intention of sending her to the Conservatory and that if the disaster had not disrupted his plans, he would have made a general announcement last Christmas—Christmas had passed now, hadn't it?—without letting himself be swayed by objections of any sort. After this declaration, his sister would be moved to the point of tears, and Gregor would raise himself to the height of her armpit and kiss her throat, which, now that she went to the office every day, she wore free of ribbon or collar.

"Herr Samsa!" the gentleman in the middle shouted at Gregor's father, and without wasting a single word, pointed his finger at Gregor, who was slowly advancing. The violin fell silent, the middle lodger at first just smiled and shook his head, turning toward his friends, then looked again at Gregor. Gregor's father apparently found the task of driving Gregor back into his room less urgent than that of calming the lodgers, despite the fact that they did not appear particularly worked up and seemed to be finding Gregor more entertaining than the music. He hurried over to them and tried with outspread arms to herd them back into their room, at the same time using his body to shield Gregor from their view. And now they did in fact become a little angry, though it was no longer clear whether this was on account of Gregor's father's behavior or the realization dawning on them that without their knowledge they had been sharing their home with a roommate of this sort. They demanded explanations of Gregor's father; now it was their turn to throw their arms into the air; they plucked uneasily at their beards and only slowly withdrew in the direction of their room. Meanwhile Gregor's sister, who had been standing there at a loss since her playing had been so abruptly interrupted—she still held violin and bow in her carelessly dangling hands, looking over at the notes as though she were continuing to play—all at once pulled herself together, laid her instrument in the lap of her mother, who still sat there in her armchair, her lungs heaving as she fought for breath, and ran into the next room, toward which the lodgers were now moving somewhat more quickly as Gregor's father urged them on. One saw how, beneath his sister's practiced hands, the beds' blankets and pillows flew into the air and into orderliness. Even before the lodgers reached the room, she had finished making up the beds and slipped out. Gregor's father appeared to be once more so firmly in the grip of his own stubbornness that he forgot the basic respect that, after all, he owed his tenants. He kept up his pressing and urging until, already standing in the doorway, the middle lodger thunderously stamped his foot, causing Gregor's father to stop short. "I hereby declare," he said, raising his hand and seeking out Gregor's mother and sister too as he glanced about, "that in consideration of the reprehensible circumstances prevailing in this apartment and family"—and here he spit on the floor without forethought—"I give notice on my room effective immediately. It goes without saying that I will not pay a penny for the days I have spent here; on the contrary, I shall consider whether or not to pursue you with—please believe me—easily justifiable claims." He fell silent and went on looking straight before him expectantly. And indeed his two friends at once chimed in with the words, "We too give notice effective immediately." Hereupon he seized the door handle and with a great crash slammed the door.

Gregor's father staggered to his armchair with groping hands and let himself fall into it; it looked as though he was stretching out for his customary evening nap, but the violent nodding of his anchorless head showed that he was absolutely not sleeping. Gregor had gone on lying quietly on the spot where the lodgers had espied him. His disappointment at the failure of his plan and perhaps also the weakness caused by starvation rendered him incapable of moving. With a certain definitiveness he sensed, terrified, that everything was about to collapse all around him, and so he waited. Not even the violin startled him when it fell from his mother's lap beneath her trembling fingers, giving off a note that echoed in the air.

"Dear parents," his sister said, striking the table by way of preamble, "things cannot go on like this. Even if you two perhaps do not realize it, I most certainly do. I am unwilling to utter my brother's name before this creature, and therefore will say only: we have to try to get rid of it. We have done everything humanly possible to care for it and show it tolerance, I don't think anyone would reproach us on this account."

"She is right a thousand times over," Gregor's father murmured under his breath. His mother, still incapable of breathing freely, began to cough dully into her lifted hand, a lunatic expression in her eyes.

Gregor's sister hurried over to her mother and held her forehead. Her words seemed to have given her father an idea, for he now sat up straight, playing with his uniform cap between the plates left behind on the table from the lodgers' supper and glancing over from time to time at a quiet Gregor.

"We have to try to get rid of it," his sister said, addressing her words exclusively to Gregor's father this time, for his mother was coughing too hard to hear anything. "It'll be the death of you two, I can see it now. When people have to work as hard as all of us having been doing, it just isn't possible to endure these endless torments at home. I cannot bear it anymore either." And she burst into sobs, weeping so forcefully that her tears flowed down upon her mother's face, from which the girl wiped them with a mechanical gesture.

"Child," her father said sympathetically and with noticeable compassion, "but what can we do?"

Gregor's sister just shrugged her shoulders as a sign of the helplessness that had come over her while she was weeping, in contrast to the confidence she'd displayed a moment before.

"If he understood us," Gregor's father said, half-questioning; his sister, still caught up in her weeping, shook one hand vehemently as a sign of how unthinkable she found this.

"If he understood us," his father repeated, closing his eyes to absorb her conviction that this was utterly out of the question, "then it might be possible to come to an agreement with him. But as things stand—"

"It has to go," Gregor's sister cried out, "that's the only way, Father. You just have to try to let go of the notion that this thing is Gregor. The real disaster is that we believed this for so long. But how could it be Gregor? If it were Gregor, it would have realized a long time ago that it just isn't possible for human beings to live beside such a creature, and it would have gone away on its own. We still would have been lacking a brother but we would have been able to go on living and honoring his memory. But now we have this beast tormenting us; it drives away our lodgers and apparently intends to take over the entire apartment and have us sleep in the gutter. Just look, Father," she suddenly shrieked, "he's starting again!" And in a fright that Gregor found bewildering, she now went so far as to leave her mother behind, launching herself from her chair as if she would rather sacrifice her mother than remain in Gregor's proximity, and ran to take cover behind her father who, agitated by the way she was carrying on, rose from his own chair and half-raised his arms as if to shield her.

But Gregor was far from wanting to frighten anyone, above all his sister. All he'd done was start to turn around to make his way back to his room, and admittedly this operation would have been hard not to notice, since in his current injured state he was obliged to use his head to help with this difficult maneuver; he kept raising it up and then thumping it against the floor. Pausing, he glanced around. His good intentions seemed to have been recognized; it had been only a momentary fright. Now all of them gazed at him sadly and in silence. His mother lay in her armchair, her extended legs pressed together, barely able to keep her eyes open in her exhaustion; his father and sister sat side by side, and his sister had draped one hand across her father's neck.

"Perhaps I'll be allowed to turn around now," Gregor thought and resumed his labors. He could not entirely suppress the wheezing this exertion produced, and now and then he had to rest. Otherwise no one was harassing him, he had been left to attend to matters on his own. When he had completed this rotation, he immediately made straight for the door to his room. He was astonished at how great a distance separated him from his destination, and he didn't understand how, weak as he was, he had been able to traverse the same distance just a little while before almost without noticing. Steadfastly concentrating only on crawling as quickly as possible, he scarcely paid any heed to the fact that not a word, not a cry came from his family to disturb him. Only when he was already in the doorway did he turn his head—not all the way around, as he felt his neck growing stiff, but even so he was able to see that all was unchanged behind him, except that his sister had risen to her feet. The last thing he saw was a glimpse of his mother, who had now fallen entirely asleep.

No sooner was he in his room again than the door was hastily pressed shut, locked and bolted. The sudden commotion at his back gave him such a frightful start that his little legs gave way beneath him. It was his sister who had hurried thus. She had already been standing there upright and waiting, then pounced so lightfootedly Gregor didn't hear her approach, and she cried out, "Finally!" to her parents as she turned the key in the lock.

"And now?" Gregor wondered, looking around in the dark. He soon made the discovery that he was no longer capable of moving at all. He wasn't surprised at this; on the contrary, it struck him as unnatural that he had actually until now been able to support himself on those thin little legs. As for the rest, he felt relatively at ease. Admittedly his entire body was racked with pain, but it seemed to him as if it was gradually becoming weaker and weaker and in the end would fade away altogether. Already he could scarcely feel the rotting apple in his back, nor the inflamed area surrounding it, both now enveloped in soft dust. He thought back on his family with tenderness and love. His opinion that he must by all means disappear was possibly even more emphatic than that of his sister. He remained in this state of empty, peaceful reflection until the clocktower struck the third hour of morning. He watched as everything began to lighten outside his window. Then his head sank all the way to the floor without volition and from his nostrils his last breath faintly streamed.

When the charwoman arrived early the next morning, slamming the doors so loudly in her strength and haste—often as she'd been asked to avoid this—that sleep was out of the question anywhere in the apartment after her arrival, her usual cursory visit to Gregor's room revealed at first nothing out of the ordinary. She thought he was lying there so motionless on purpose, feigning indignation; she considered him perfectly capable of rational thought. Since she happened to be holding the long broom in her hand, she tried tickling Gregor with it from the doorway. When even this had no effect, she grew vexed and began to poke Gregor a little, and only when she had actually shifted him from the spot where he lay with no resistance at all were her suspicions roused. When soon thereafter the facts of the matter became clear to her, she gawked in surprise, gave a low whistle, then without further delay flung open the door of the bedroom and in a loud voice shouted into the darkness: "Come have a look, it's gone and croaked—just lying there, dead as a doornail!"

The Samsa couple shot upright in their marital bed and first had to struggle to recover from their shock at the charwoman's conduct before they were able to grasp her words. But then Herr and Frau Samsa hurriedly got out of bed, one on either side, Herr Samsa threw the blanket about his shoulders while Frau Samsa emerged wearing only her nightdress; in this state, they entered Gregor's room. Meanwhile the door to the living room, where Grete had been sleeping since the lodgers' arrival, had opened as well; she was fully dressed, as though she had not slept at all, as even the pallor of her cheeks seemed to prove. "Dead?" Frau Samsa asked, looking questioningly up at the charwoman, although she herself was free to investigate and, indeed, could see how things stood even without investigation. "I should say so," the charwoman said, and by way of proof, pushed Gregor's corpse quite some way to the side with her broom. Frau Samsa made a gesture as though she wanted to hold back the broom but didn't. "Well," Herr Samsa said, "now we can thank God." He crossed himself, and the three women followed his example. Grete, who did not take her eyes off the corpse for a moment, said: "Just look how skinny he was. He went such a long time without eating anything at all. All the food that went into his room would come out again just as before." And indeed Gregor's body was completely flat and dry, which hadn't really been noticeable until now when he was no longer raised up on those little legs and nothing else remained to divert the gaze.

"Grete, come sit with us for a bit," Frau Samsa said with a melancholy smile, and Grete, glancing back at the corpse, followed her parents into their bedroom. The charwoman shut the door and opened the window wide. Despite the early morning, the crisp air was already tempered by a certain mildness: after all, it was already the end of March.

The three lodgers now emerged from their room and looked about in astonishment for their breakfast; they had been forgotten. "Where's breakfast?" the one in the middle asked the charwoman peevishly. But she just put a finger to her lips and then quickly, without a word, beckoned the lodgers into Gregor's room. They did as she bade them and with their hands in the pockets of their slightly threadbare little jackets, they surrounded Gregor's corpse in the room that had meanwhile become quite bright.

Then the bedroom door opened, and Herr Samsa appeared wearing his livery, with his wife on one arm, his daughter on the other. All three looked as if they'd been weeping; Grete kept pressing her face against her father's arm.

"Leave my home at once!" Herr Samsa said, pointing at the door without letting go of the womenfolk. "What do you mean?" the gentleman in the middle inquired, dumbfounded, and gave a saccharine smile. The two others held their hands at their backs and kept rubbing them together uninterruptedly, as if in gleeful expectation of a fight that was certain to be decided in their favor. "I mean exactly what I say," Herr Samsa replied, now advancing on the lodger flanked by his two companions. The lodger just stood there at first, looking at the ground, as if things were just rearranging themselves in his head into a new order. "So we'll be leaving," he said then, looking up at Herr Samsa as if this new humility that had suddenly come over him required him to petition for the approval of even this decision. Herr Samsa merely nodded curtly in his direction a few times, wide-eyed. At this, the gentleman did, in fact, make haste to stride back out to the vestibule, where his two friends had been listening attentively for some moments, their hands at rest, and now they practically hopped and skipped in their hurry to follow, as if worried Herr Samsa might somehow precede them into the vestibule, cutting off their line of communication with their leader.

In the vestibule, all three of them took their hats from the coat rack, withdrew their walking sticks from the cane stand, made a silent bow and left the apartment. Displaying what soon proved to be an utterly unfounded mistrustfulness, Herr Samsa stepped out onto the landing with the two women; leaning against the banister, they watched as the three gentlemen descended the long staircase, moving slowly but at a steady pace and disappearing on each floor at a certain bend of the stairwell only to appear again a few moments later; the farther down they went, the more the Samsa family's interest in them faded, and when a butcher's apprentice came toward and then passed them on his way up, proudly bearing his tray upon his head, Herr Samsa and the women abandoned the banister, and all of them returned, seemingly relieved, to their apartment.

They decided to spend the day resting and go out for a stroll; they had not only earned this respite from their work, but were desperately in need of it. And so they all sat down at the table and wrote three letters of excuse: Herr Samsa to his supervisor, Frau Samsa to her employer, and Grete to her superior. While they were writing, the charwoman came in to say she was leaving, as her morning's work was completed. The three scribes at first merely nodded without looking up, and only when the charwoman failed to go on her way did they glance up in annoyance. "Well?" Herr Samsa asked. The charwoman stood smiling in the doorway as if she had some splendid good fortune to announce to the family but would not do so until she was properly questioned. The nearly vertical little ostrich feathers on her hat, which had annoyed Herr Samsa for as long as she had been in the family's service, bobbed gently in all directions. "So what is it you want?" she was asked now by Frau Samsa, the member of the family for whom the charwoman still had the most respect. "Well," the charwoman replied, her own good-natured laughter making it impossible at first for her to go on speaking, "there's no need for you to go worrying about how to get rid of that mess in there. It's already taken care of."

Frau Samsa and Grete bent down over their letters as if they meant to go on writing; Herr Samsa, who saw that the charwoman was about to start describing everything in detail, summarily silenced her with an outstretched hand. And since she was not permitted to say what she wished, she suddenly remembered the great hurry she was in, and so with an insulted air she cried, "So long, everyone," turned wildly on her heel, and with the most excruciating slamming of doors left the apartment.

"Tonight she'll be let go," Herr Samsa said, but received an answer neither from his wife nor his daughter, for the charwoman seemed to have disturbed the equanimity they had only just attained. They rose from their seats, went to the window, and remained there with their arms about each other. Herr Samsa turned in his chair to look at them and observed them quietly for a little while. Then he cried out: "So come here already. Let these old matters rest. And show a little consideration for me as well." At once the women obeyed, hurried over to him, caressed him and quickly finished their letters.

Then all three of them left the apartment together, something they had not done for months, and took the electric tram all the way to the open countryside at the edge of town. The car in which they sat all alone was entirely suffused with warm sunlight. Cozily leaning back in their seats, they discussed their future prospects, and on closer investigation it appeared that these prospects were not bad at all, for all three of their positions—something they had never before properly discussed—were in fact quite advantageous and above all offered promising opportunities for advancement. The greatest immediate improvement in their situation, of course, would be easily achieved by moving to a new apartment; they now wished to take a smaller and cheaper but more convenient and above all more practical flat than their current one, which had been picked out for them by Gregor. As they were conversing in this way, Herr and Frau Samsa were struck almost as one while observing their daughter, who was growing ever more vivacious, by the thought that despite all the torments that had made her cheeks grow pale, she had recently blossomed into a beautiful, voluptuous girl. Growing quieter now and communicating with one another almost unconsciously by an exchange of glances, they thought about how it would soon be time to find her a good husband. And when they arrived at their destination, it seemed to them almost a confirmation of their new dreams and good intentions when their daughter swiftly sprang to her feet and stretched her young body.

LUIGI PIRANDELLO

1867–1936

"Who am I?" and "What is real?" are the persistent questions that underlie Luigi Pirandello's novels, short stories, and plays. Sometimes in a playful mood, sometimes more anxiously, Pirandello toys with these questions but refuses to answer them definitively. In fact, the term *Pirandellismo*, or "Pirandellism"—coined from the author's name—has come to stand in for the idea that there are as many truths as there are points of view. Yet Pirandello treats such weighty philosophical issues with a combination of humor and pathos that makes them highly entertaining.

Pirandello's great fame came late in life, as a result of his experimental dramas, but he had been an active writer for decades. Born in Girgenti (now Agrigento), Sicily, on June 28, 1867, Pirandello was the son of a sulfur merchant who intended his son to follow him into business. Pirandello preferred language and literature. After studying in Palermo and at the University of Rome, he traveled to the University of Bonn, where he received a doctorate in romance philology with a dissertation on the dialect of his hometown. Soon after completing his doctorate, Pirandello agreed to an arranged marriage with the daughter of a rich sulfur merchant, although he had never met her. They lived for ten years in Rome, where he wrote poetry and short stories, until the collapse of the sulfur mines destroyed the fortunes of both families, and he was suddenly forced to earn a living. To add to his misfortune, his wife developed a jealous paranoia that lasted until her death, in 1918.

Pirandello's early work included short stories and novellas written under the influence of the narrative style *verismo* (realism or naturalism) that he found exemplified in the work of the Sicilian writer Giovanni Verga (1840–1922). Pirandello wrote hundreds of stories of all lengths. He is recognized—in his clarity, realism, and psychological acuteness (often including a taste for the grotesque)—as an Italian master of the story form. His anthology of 1922, *A Year's Worth of Stories*, remains hugely popular in Italy. Not until he was in his fifties, however, did Pirandello write the more experimental plays, such as *Six Characters in Search of an Author* (1921) and *Henry IV* (1922), which established him as a major dramatist.

Despite the intellectualism of his plays, in politics Pirandello favored the irrational appeal of a strong leader. He was drawn toward the Fascist dictator Benito Mussolini and supported his regime at key moments—for example, in the wake of the murder by Fascists of a Socialist member of Parliament, Giacomo Matteotti. As Pirandello's fame spread, he directed his own company (the Teatro d'Arte di Roma) with support from Mussolini's government and toured Europe with his plays. In 1934 he received the Nobel Prize for Literature. His later plays, featuring fantastic and grotesque elements, did not achieve the wide popularity of their predecessors.

Pirandello's plays turn the trappings of the theater itself—the stage, the producer, the author, the actors—into the material for comedy and invention. In their manipulation of ambiguous appearances and tragicomic effects, these plays foreshadow the absurdist theater of **Samuel Beckett** and others. Above all, they insist that "real" life is that which changes from moment to moment, exhibiting a fluidity that renders difficult and perhaps impossible any single formulation of either character or situation. Pirandello's playful treatment of the theatrical enterprise has been dubbed "metatheater," or theater about theater.

SIX CHARACTERS IN SEARCH OF AN AUTHOR

Six Characters in Search of an Author, the selection below, combines the elements of "metatheater" in an extraordinary self-reflexive style. At the beginning of the play, the Stage Hand's interrupted hammering suggests that the audience has chanced on a rehearsal—of still another play by Pirandello—instead of coming to an actual performance. Concurrently, Pirandello's stage dialogue pokes fun at his reputation for obscurity. Just as the Actors are apparently set to rehearse *The Rules of the Game*, six unexpected persons come down the aisle seeking the Producer: they are Characters from an unwritten novel who demand to be given dramatic existence. The play *Six Characters* is continually in the process of being composed: composed as the interwoven double plot we see on stage, composed by the Prompter writing a script in shorthand for the Actors to reproduce, and composed as the inner drama of the Characters finally achieves its rightful existence as a work of art.

The play's initial absurdity emerges when the six fictional Characters arrive with their claim to be "truer and more real" than the "real" Actors who seek to impersonate them. (Of course, to the audience all the figures onstage are equally real.) Each Character represents a particular identity created by the author. Pirandello later had the Characters wear masks to distinguish them from the Actors—not the conventional masks of ancient Greek drama or of the Japanese *Noh* theater that identify the characters' roles, nor the cere-monial masks, representing spirits in African ritual, that temporarily invest the wearer with the spirit's identity and authority. Instead, they are a theatrical device, a symbol and visual reminder of each Character's unchanging being. The six Characters are incapable of developing outside their roles and are condemned, in their search for existence, painfully to reenact their essential roles.

Conversely, the fictional Characters have more stable personalities than "real" people, including the Actors, who are still "nobody," incomplete, open to change and misinterpretation. Characters can claim to be "somebody" because their natures have been decided once and for all. Yet further complications attend this contrast between fictional characters and real actors: for instance, the Characters feel the urge to play their own roles and are disturbed at the prospect of having Actors represent them incorrectly. All human beings, indicates Pirandello, whether fictional or real, are subject to misunderstanding. We even misunderstand ourselves when we think we are the same person in all situations. "We always have the illusion of being the same person for everybody," says the Father, "but it's not true!"

Pirandello does not hold his audience's attention simply by uttering grand philosophical truths, however. *Six Characters* hums with suspense and discovery, from the moment that the Characters interrupt the rehearsal with its complaining Actors and Stage Manager. The story that the Characters tell about themselves hints of melodrama and family scandal, like headlines from a sensationalist newspaper, that attracts the viewer's interest. Indeed, Pirandello plays with the risqué element by focusing on the characters' repeated attempts to portray one florid scene. Eventually, the pathos of this play within the play comes to overwhelm the more philosophical metatheatrical frame.

Six Characters in Search of an Author underwent an interesting evolution to become the play that we see today. First performed in Rome in 1921, where its unsettling plot and characters already scandalized a traditionalist audience, it was reshaped in more radical form after the remarkable performance produced by Georges Pitoëff in 1923. Pirandello, who came to Paris wary of Pitoëff's innovations (for instance, he had the Characters arrive in a green-lit stage elevator), was soon convinced that the Russian director's stagecraft enhanced the original text. Pitoëff used his knowledge of technical effects to accentuate the relationship of appearance and reality: he extended the stage with several steps leading down to the auditorium (a break in the conventional "fourth wall" concept, in which the actors on stage proceed as if unaware of the audience, that Pirandello was quick to exploit); he underscored the play within a play with rehearsal effects, showing the Stage Hand hammering and the Director arranging suitable props and lighting; he emphasized the division between Characters and Actors by separating the groups on stage and dressing all the Characters (except the Little Girl) in black. Pirandello welcomed these changes and expanded on many of them. To distinguish the Characters even further from the Actors, he proposed contrasting clothing in addition to masks,

black for the former and pale for the latter. Most striking, however, is his transformation of Pitoëff's steps into an actual bridge between the world of the stage and the auditorium, a strategy that allows the Actors (and Characters) to come and go in the "real world" of the audience.

In breaking down comfortable illusions of compartmentalized, stable reality, Pirandello revolutionized European stage techniques. In place of the nineteenth century's "well-made play"—with its neatly constructed plot that boxes real life into a conventional beginning, middle, and end, and its safely inaccessible characters on the other side of the footlights—he offers unpredictable plots and ambiguous roles. It is not easy to know the truth about others, he suggests, or to make oneself known behind the "mask" that each of us wears.

Readers might enjoy testing the continued liveliness of Pirandello's dialogue by rehearsing their own selection of scenes—or perhaps by relocating them in a contemporary setting. According to the director Robert Brustein, whose 1988 production of *Six Characters in Search of an Author* set the action in New York and replaced Madame Pace with a pimp, "Pirandello both encourages and stimulates a pluralism in theater because there can be dozens, hundreds, thousands of productions of *Six Characters*, and every one of them is going to be different."

Six Characters in Search of an Author[1]

A Comedy in the Making

The Characters	The Company
FATHER	THE PRODUCER
MOTHER	THE STAGE STAFF
STEPDAUGHTER	THE ACTORS
SON	
LITTLE BOY	
LITTLE GIRL	
MADAME PACE	

Act 1

When the audience enters, the curtain is already up and the stage is just as it would be during the day. There is no set; it is empty, in almost total darkness. This is so that from the beginning the audience will have the feeling of being present, not at a performance of a properly rehearsed play, but at a performance of a play that happens spontaneously. Two small sets of steps, one on the right and one on the left, lead up to the stage from the auditorium. On the stage, the top is off the PROMPTER's *box and is lying next to it. Downstage, there is a small table and a chair with arms for the* PRODUCER: *it is turned with its back to the audience.*

Also downstage there are two small tables, one a little bigger than the other, and several chairs, ready for the rehearsal if needed. There are more chairs scattered on both left and right for the ACTORS *to one side at the back and nearly hidden is a piano.*

When the houselights go down the STAGE HAND *comes on through the back door. He is in blue overalls and carries a tool bag. He brings some pieces of wood on, comes to the front, kneels down and starts to nail them together.*

The STAGE MANAGER *rushes on from the wings.*

STAGE MANAGER   Hey! What are you doing?

STAGE HAND   What do you think I'm doing? I'm banging nails in.

STAGE MANAGER   Now? [*He looks at his watch.*] It's half-past ten already. The Producer will be here in a moment to rehearse.

STAGE HAND   I've got to do my work some time, you know.

STAGE MANAGER   Right—but not now.

STAGE HAND   When?

STAGE MANAGER   When the rehearsal's finished. Come on, get all this out of the way and let me set for the second act of *The Rules of the Game.*[2]

[*The* STAGE HAND *picks up his tools and wood and goes off, grumbling and muttering. The* ACTORS *of the company come in through the door, men and women, first one then another, then two together and so on: there will be*

1. Translated by John Linstrum. In the Italian editions, Pirandello notes that he did not divide the play into formal acts or scenes. The translator has marked the divisions for clarity, however, according to the stage directions.
2. *Il giuoco delle parti,* written in 1918. The hero, Leone Gala, pretends to ignore his wife, Silia's, infidelity until the end, when he takes revenge by tricking her lover, Guido Venanzi, into taking his place in a fatal duel she had engineered to get rid of her husband.

nine or ten, enough for the parts for the rehearsal of a play by Pirandello, The Rules of the Game, *today's rehearsal. They come in, say their "Good-mornings" to the* STAGE MANAGER *and each other. Some go off to the dressing-rooms; others, among them the* PROMPTER *with the text rolled up under his arm, scatter about the stage waiting for the* PRODUCER *to start the rehearsal. Meanwhile, sitting or standing in groups, they chat together; some smoke, one complains about his part, another one loudly reads something from "The Stage." It would be as well if the* ACTORS *and* ACTRESSES *were dressed in colourful clothes, and this first scene should be improvised naturally and vivaciously. After a while somebody might sit down at the piano and play a song; the younger* ACTORS *and* ACTRESSES *start dancing.*]

STAGE MANAGER [*Clapping his hands to call their attention.*]   Come on, every-body! Quiet please. The Producer's here.
   [*The piano and the dancing both stop. The* ACTORS *turn to look out into the theatre and through the door at the back comes the* PRODUCER; *he walks down the gangway between the seats and, calling "Good-morning" to the* ACTORS, *climbs up one of the sets of stairs onto the stage. The* SECRETARY *gives him the post, a few magazines, a script. The* ACTORS *move to one side of the stage.*]

PRODUCER   Any letters?

SECRETARY   No. That's all the post there is. [*Giving him the script.*]

PRODUCER   Put it in the office. [*Then looking round and turning to the* STAGE MANAGER.] I can't see a thing here. Let's have some lights please.

STAGE MANAGER   Right. [*Calling.*] Workers please!
   [*In a few seconds the side of the stage where the* ACTORS *are standing is bril-liantly lit with white light. The* PROMPTER *has gone into his box and spread out his script.*]

PRODUCER   Good. [*Clapping hands.*] Well then, let's get started. Anybody missing?

STAGE MANAGER [*Heavily ironic.*]   Our leading lady.

PRODUCER   Not again! [*Looking at his watch.*] We're ten minutes late already. Send her a note to come and see me. It might teach her to be on time for rehearsals. [*Almost before he has finished, the* LEADING ACTRESS's *voice is heard from the auditorium.*]

LEADING ACTRESS   Morning everybody. Sorry I'm late. [*She is very expensively dressed and is carrying a lap-dog. She comes down the aisle and goes up on to the stage.*]

PRODUCER   You're determined to keep us waiting, aren't you?

LEADING ACTRESS   I'm sorry. I just couldn't find a taxi anywhere. But you haven't started yet and I'm not on at the opening anyhow. [*Calling the* STAGE MANAGER, *she gives him the dog.*] Put him in my dressing-room for me will you?

PRODUCER   And she's even brought her lap-dog with her! As if we haven't enough lap-dogs here already. [*Clapping his hands and turning to the* PROMPTER.] Right then, the second act of The Rules of the Game. [*Sits in his arm-chair.*] Quiet please! Who's on?
   [*The* ACTORS *clear from the front of the stage and sit to one side, except for three who are ready to start the scene—and the* LEADING ACTRESS. *She has ignored the* PRODUCER *and is sitting at one of the little tables.*]

PRODUCER   Are you in this scene, then?

LEADING ACTRESS   No—I've just told you.

PRODUCER [*Annoyed*.]   Then get off, for God's sake. [*The* LEADING ACTRESS *goes and sits with the others. To the* PROMPTER.] Come on then, let's get going.

PROMPTER [*Reading his script*.]   "The house of Leone Gala. A peculiar room, both dining-room and study."

PRODUCER [*To the* STAGE MANAGER.]   We'll use the red set.

STAGE MANAGER [*Making a note*.]   The red set—right.

PROMPTER [*Still reading*.]   "The table is laid and there is a desk with books and papers. Bookcases full of books and china cabinets full of valuable china. An exit at the back leads to Leone's bedroom. An exit to the left leads to the kitchen. The main entrance is on the right."

PRODUCER   Right. Listen carefully everybody: there, the main entrance, there, the kitchen. [*To the* LEADING ACTOR *who plays Socrates.*[3]] Your entrances and exits will be from there. [*To the* STAGE MANAGER.] We'll have the French windows there and put the curtains on them.

STAGE MANAGER [*Making a note*.]   Right.

PROMPTER [*Reading*.]   "Scene One. Leone Gala, Guido Venanzi, and Filippo, who is called Socrates." [*To* PRODUCER.] Have I to read the directions as well?

PRODUCER   Yes, you have! I've told you a hundred times.

PROMPTER [*Reading*.]   "When the curtain rises, Leone Gala, in a cook's hat and apron, is beating an egg in a dish with a little wooden spoon. Filippo is beating another and he is dressed as a cook too. Guido Venanzi is sitting listening."

LEADING ACTOR   Look, do I really have to wear a cook's hat?

PRODUCER [*Annoyed by the question*.]   I expect so! That's what it says in the script. [*Pointing to the script*.]

LEADING ACTOR   If you ask me it's ridiculous.

PRODUCER [*Leaping to his feet furiously*.]   Ridiculous? It's ridiculous, is it? What do you expect me to do if nobody writes good plays any more[4] and we're reduced to putting on plays by Pirandello? And if you can understand them you must be very clever. He writes them on purpose so nobody enjoys them, neither actors nor critics nor audience. [*The* ACTORS *laugh. Then crosses to* LEADING ACTOR *and shouts at him*.] A cook's hat and you beat eggs. But don't run away with the idea that that's all you are doing—beating eggs. You must be joking! You have to be symbolic of the shells of the eggs you are beating. [*The* ACTORS *laugh again and start making ironical comments to each other*.] Be quiet! Listen carefully while I explain. [*Turns back to* LEADING ACTOR.] Yes, the shells, because they are symbolic of the empty form of reason, without its content, blind instinct! You are reason and your wife is instinct: you are playing a game where you have been given parts and in which you are not just yourself but the puppet of yourself.[5] Do you see?

---

3. Nickname given to Gala's servant, Philip, in *The Rules of the Game*, the play they are rehearsing.

4. The producer refers to the realistic, tightly constructed plays (often French) that were internationally popular in the late 19th century and a staple of Italian theaters at the beginning of the 20th.

5. Leone Gala is a rationalist and an aesthete—the opposite of his impulsive, passionate wife, Silia. By masking his feelings and constantly playing the role of gourmet cook, he chooses his own role and thus becomes his own "puppet."

LEADING ACTOR [*Spreading his hands.*]   Me? No.

PRODUCER [*Going back to his chair.*]   Neither do I! Come on, let's get going; you wait till you see the end! You haven't seen anything yet! [*Confidentially.*] By the way, I should turn almost to face the audience if I were you, about three-quarters face. Well, what with the obscure dialogue and the audience not being able to hear you properly in any case, the whole lot'll go to hell. [*Clapping hands again.*] Come on. Let's get going!

PROMPTER   Excuse me, can I put the top back on the prompt-box? There's a bit of a draught.

PRODUCER   Yes, yes, of course. Get on with it.

[*The* STAGE DOORKEEPER, *in a braided cap, has come into the auditorium, and he comes all the way down the aisle to the stage to tell the* PRODUCER *the* SIX CHARACTERS *have come, who, having come in after him, look about them a little puzzled and dismayed. Every effort must be made to create the effect that the* SIX CHARACTERS *are very different from the* ACTORS *of the company. The placings of the two groups, indicated in the directions, once the* CHARACTERS *are on the stage, will help this: so will using different coloured lights. But the most effective idea is to use masks for the* CHARACTERS, *masks specially made of a material that will not go limp with perspiration and light enough not to worry the actors who wear them: they should be made so that the eyes, the nose and the mouth are all free. This is the way to bring out the deep significance of the play. The* CHARACTERS *should not appear as ghosts, but as created realities, timeless creations of the imagination, and so more real and consistent than the changeable realities of the* ACTORS. *The masks are designed to give the impression of figures constructed by art, each one fixed forever in its own fundamental emotion; that is, Remorse for the* FATHER, *Revenge for the* STEP-DAUGHTER, *Scorn for the* SON, *Sorrow for the* MOTHER. *Her mask should have wax tears in the corners of the eyes and down the cheeks like the sculptured or painted weeping Madonna in a church. Her dress should be of a plain material, in stiff folds, looking almost as if it were carved and not of an ordinary material you can buy in a shop and have made up by a dressmaker.*

The FATHER *is about fifty: his reddish hair is thinning at the temples, but he is not bald: he has a full moustache that almost covers his young-looking mouth, which often opens in an uncertain and empty smile. He is pale, with a high forehead: he has blue oval eyes, clear and sharp: he is dressed in light trousers and a dark jacket: his voice is sometimes rich, at other times harsh and loud.*

The MOTHER *appears crushed by an intolerable weight of shame and humiliation. She is wearing a thick black veil and is dressed simply in black; when she raises her veil she shows a face like wax, but not suffering, with her eyes turned down humbly.*

The STEPDAUGHTER, *who is eighteen years old, is defiant, even insolent. She is very beautiful, dressed in mourning as well, but with striking elegance. She is scornful of the timid, suffering, dejected air of her young brother, a grubby* LITTLE BOY *of fourteen, also dressed in black; she is full of a warm tenderness, on the other hand, for the* LITTLE SISTER (GIRL), *a girl of about four, dressed in white with a black silk sash round her waist.*

The SON *is twenty-two, tall, almost frozen in an air of scorn for the* FATHER *and indifference to the* MOTHER: *he is wearing a mauve overcoat and a long green scarf round his neck.*]

DOORMAN   Excuse me, sir.

PRODUCER [*Angrily.*]   What the hell is it now?

DOORMAN   There are some people here—they say they want to see you, sir.

> [*The* PRODUCER *and the* ACTORS *are astonished and turn to look out into the auditorium.*]

PRODUCER   But I'm rehearsing! You know perfectly well that no-one's allowed in during rehearsals. [*Turning to face out front.*] Who are you? What do you want?

FATHER [*Coming forward, followed by the others, to the foot of one of the sets of steps.*]   We're looking for an author.

PRODUCER [*Angry and astonished.*]   An author? Which author?

FATHER   Any author will do, sir.

PRODUCER   But there isn't an author here because we're not rehearsing a new play.

STEPDAUGHTER [*Excitedly as she rushes up the steps.*]   That's better still, better still! We can be your new play.

ACTORS [*Lively comments and laughter from the* ACTORS.]   Oh, listen to that, etc.

FATHER [*Going up on the stage after the* STEPDAUGHTER.]   Maybe, but if there isn't an author here . . . [*To the* PRODUCER.] Unless you'd like to be . . .

> [*Hand in hand, the* MOTHER *and the* LITTLE GIRL, *followed by the* LITTLE BOY, *go up on the stage and wait. The* SON *stays sullenly behind.*]

PRODUCER   Is this some kind of joke?

FATHER   Now, how can you think that? On the contrary, we are bringing you a story of anguish.

STEPDAUGHTER   We might make your fortune for you!

PRODUCER   Do me a favour, will you? Go away. We haven't time to waste on idiots.

FATHER [*Hurt but answering gently.*]   You know very well, as a man of the theatre, that life is full of all sorts of odd things which have no need at all to pretend to be real because they are actually true.

PRODUCER   What the devil are you talking about?

FATHER   What I'm saying is that you really must be mad to do things the opposite way round: to create situations that obviously aren't true and try to make them seem to be really happening. But then I suppose that sort of madness is the only reason for your profession.

> [*The* ACTORS *are indignant.*]

PRODUCER [*Getting up and glaring at him.*]   Oh, yes? So ours is a profession of madmen, is it?

FATHER   Well, if you try to make something look true when it obviously isn't, especially if you're not forced to do it, but do it for a game . . . Isn't it your job to give life on the stage to imaginary people?

PRODUCER [*Quickly answering him and speaking for the* ACTORS *who are growing more indignant.*]   I should like you to know, sir, that the actor's profession is one of great distinction. Even if nowadays the new writers only give us dull plays to act and puppets to present instead of men, I'd have you know that it is our boast that we have given life, here on this stage, to immortal works.

> [*The* ACTORS, *satisfied, agree with and applaud the* PRODUCER].

FATHER [*Cutting in and following hard on his argument.*]   There! You see? Good! You've given life! You've created living beings with more genuine life than people have who breathe and wear clothes! Less real, perhaps, but nearer the truth. We are both saying the same thing.

[*The* ACTORS *look at each other, astonished.*]

PRODUCER   But just a moment! You said before . . .

FATHER   I'm sorry, but I said that before, about acting for fun, because you shouted at us and said you'd no time to waste on idiots, but you must know better than anyone that Nature uses human imagination to lift her work of creation to even higher levels.

PRODUCER   All right then: but where does all this get us?

FATHER   Nowhere. I want to try to show that one can be thrust into life in many ways, in many forms: as a tree or a stone, as water or a butterfly—or as a woman. It might even be as a character in a play.

PRODUCER   [*Ironic, pretending to be annoyed.*]   And you, and these other people here, were thrust into life, as you put it, as characters in a play?

FATHER   Exactly! And alive, as you can see.

[*The* PRODUCER *and the* ACTORS *burst into laughter as if at a joke.*]

FATHER   I'm sorry you laugh like that, because we carry in us, as I said before, a story of terrible anguish as you can guess from this woman dressed in black.

> [*Saying this, he offers his hand to the* MOTHER *and helps her up the last steps and, holding her still by the hand, leads her with a sense of tragic solemnity across the stage which is suddenly lit by a fantastic light.*
>
> *The* LITTLE GIRL *and the* (LITTLE) BOY *follow the* MOTHER: *then the* SON *comes up and stands to one side in the background: then the* STEP-DAUGHTER *follows and leans against the proscenium arch: the* ACTORS *are astonished at first, but then, full of admiration for the "entrance," they burst into applause—just as if it were a performance specially for them.*]

PRODUCER   [*At first astonished and then indignant.*]   My God! Be quiet all of you. [*Turns to the* CHARACTERS.] And you lot get out! Clear off! [*Turns to the* STAGE MANAGER.] Jesus! Get them out of here.

STAGE MANAGER   [*Comes forward but stops short as if held back by something strange.*]   Go on out! Get out!

FATHER   [*To* PRODUCER.]   Oh no, please, you see, we . . .

PRODUCER   [*Shouting.*]   We came here to work, you know.

LEADING ACTOR   We really can't be messed about like this.

FATHER   [*Resolutely, coming forward.*]   I'm astonished! Why don't you believe me? Perhaps you are not used to seeing the characters created by an author spring into life up here on the stage face to face with each other. Perhaps it's because we're not in a script? [*He points to the* PROMPTER'S *box.*]

STEPDAUGHTER   [*Coming down to the* PRODUCER, *smiling and persuasive.*]   Believe me, sir, we really are six of the most fascinating characters. But we've been neglected.

FATHER   Yes, that's right, we've been neglected. In the sense that the author who created us, living in his mind, wouldn't or couldn't make us live in a written play for the world of art.[6] And that really is a crime sir, because whoever has the luck to be born a character can laugh even at death.

---

6. In the 1925 preface to *Six Characters*, Pirandello explains that these characters came to him first as characters for a novel that he later abandoned. Haunted by their half-realized personalities, he decided to use the situation in a play.

Because a character will never die! A man will die, a writer, the instrument of creation: but what he has created will never die! And to be able to live for ever you don't need to have extraordinary gifts or be able to do miracles. Who was Sancho Panza? Who was Prospero?[7] But they will live for ever because—living seeds—they had the luck to find a fruitful soil, an imagination which knew how to grow them and feed them, so that they will live for ever.

PRODUCER   This is all very well! But what do you want here?

FATHER   We want to live, sir.

PRODUCER [*Ironically.*]   For ever!

FATHER   No, no: only for a few moments—in you.

AN ACTOR   Listen to that!

LEADING ACTRESS   They want to live in us!

YOUNG ACTOR [*Pointing to the* STEPDAUGHTER.]   I don't mind . . . so long as I get her.

FATHER   Listen, listen: the play is all ready to be put together and if you and your actors would like to, we can work it out now between us.

PRODUCER [*Annoyed.*]   But what exactly do you want to do? We don't make up plays like that here! We present comedies and tragedies here.

FATHER   That's right, we know that of course. That's why we've come.

PRODUCER   And where's the script?

FATHER   It's in us, sir. [*The* ACTORS *laugh.*] The play is in us: we are the play and we are impatient to show it to you: the passion inside us is driving us on.

STEPDAUGHTER [*Scornfully, with the tantalising charm of deliberate impudence.*]   My passion, if only you knew! My passion for him! [*She points at the* FATHER *and suggests that she is going to embrace him: but stops and bursts into a screeching laugh.*]

FATHER [*With sudden anger.*]   You keep out of this for the moment! And stop laughing like that!

STEPDAUGHTER   Really? Then with your permission, ladies and gentlemen; even though it's only two months since I became an orphan, just watch how I can sing and dance.

[*The* ACTORS, *especially the younger, seem strangely attracted to her while she sings and dances and they edge closer and reach out their hands to catch hold of her.*[8] *She eludes them, and when the* ACTORS *applaud her and the* PRODUCER *speaks sharply to her she stays still quite removed from them all.*]

FIRST ACTOR   Very good! etc.

PRODUCER [*Angrily.*]   Be quiet! Do you think this is a nightclub? [*Turns to* FATHER *and asks with some concern.*] Is she a bit mad?

FATHER   Mad? Oh no—it's worse than that.

STEPDAUGHTER [*Suddenly running to the* PRODUCER.]   Yes. It's worse, much worse! Listen please! Let's put this play on at once, because you'll see that

---

7. The magician and exiled duke of Milan in Shakespeare's *The Tempest.* Sancho Panza was Don Quixote's servant in Cervantes' novel *Don Quixote* (1605–15).

8. Pirandello uses a contemporary popular song, "Chu-Chin-Chow" from the Ziegfeld Follies of 1917, for the Stepdaughter to display her talents.

at a particular point I—when this darling little girl here—[*Taking the* LITTLE GIRL *by the hand from next to the* MOTHER *and crossing with her to the* PRODUCER.] Isn't she pretty? [*Takes her in her arms.*] Darling! Darling! [*Puts her down again and adds, moved very deeply but almost without wanting to.*] Well, this lovely little girl here, when God suddenly takes her from this poor Mother: and this little idiot here [*Turning to the* LITTLE BOY *and seizing him roughly by the sleeve.*] does the most stupid thing, like the half-wit he is,— then you will see me run away! Yes, you'll see me rush away! But not yet, not yet! Because, after all the intimate things there have been between him and me [*In the direction of the* FATHER, *with a horrible vulgar wink.*] I can't stay with them any longer, to watch the insult to this mother through that supercilious cretin over there. [*Pointing to the* SON.] Look at him! Look at him! Condescending, stand-offish, because he's the legitimate son, him! Full of contempt for me, for the boy and for the little girl: because we are bastards. Do you understand? Bastards. [*Running to the* MOTHER *and embracing her.*] And this poor mother—she—who is the mother of all of us—he doesn't want to recognise her as his own mother—and he looks down on her, he does, as if she were only the mother of the three of us who are bastards—the traitor. [*She says all this quickly, with great excitement, and after having raised her voice on the word "bastards" she speaks quietly, half-spitting the word "traitor."*]

MOTHER [*With deep anguish to the* PRODUCER.]   Sir, in the name of these two little ones, I beg you . . . [*Feels herself grow faint and sways.*] Oh, my God.

FATHER [*Rushing to support her with almost all the* ACTORS *bewildered and concerned.*]   Get a chair someone . . . quick, get a chair for this poor widow.

[*One of the* ACTORS *offers a chair: the others press urgently around. The* MOTHER, *seated now, tries to stop the* FATHER *lifting her veil.*]

ACTORS   Is it real? Has she really fainted? etc.

FATHER   Look at her, everybody, look at her.

MOTHER   No, for God's sake, stop it.

FATHER   Let them look?

MOTHER [*Lifting her hands and covering her face, desperately.*]   Oh, please, I beg you, stop him from doing what he is trying to do; it's hateful.

PRODUCER [*Overwhelmed, astounded.*]   It's no use, I don't understand this any more. [*To the* FATHER.] Is this woman your wife?

FATHER [*At once.*]   That's right, she is my wife.

PRODUCER   How is she a widow, then, if you're still alive?

[*The* ACTORS *are bewildered too and find relief in a loud laugh.*]

FATHER [*Wounded, with rising resentment.*]   Don't laugh! Please don't laugh like that! That's just the point, that's her own drama. You see, she had another man. Another man who ought to be here.

MOTHER   No, no! [*Crying out.*]

STEPDAUGHTER   Luckily for him he died. Two months ago, as I told you: we are in mourning for him, as you can see.

FATHER   Yes, he's dead: but that's not the reason he isn't here. He isn't here because—well just look at her, please, and you'll understand at once—hers is not a passionate drama of the love of two men, because she was incapable of love, she could feel nothing—except, perhaps a little gratitude (but not to me, to him). She's not a woman; she's a mother. And her drama—and, believe me, it's a powerful one—her drama is focused completely on these four children of the two men she had.

MOTHER   I had them? How dare you say that I had them, as if I wanted them myself? It was him, sir! He forced the other man on me. He made me go away with him!

STEPDAUGHTER [*Leaping up, indignantly.*]   It isn't true!

MOTHER [*Bewildered.*]   How isn't it true?

STEPDAUGHTER   It isn't true, it just isn't true.

MOTHER   What do you know about it?

STEPDAUGHTER   It isn't true. [*To the* PRODUCER.] Don't believe it! Do you know why she said that? She said it because of him, over there. [*Pointing to the* SON.] She tortures herself, she exhausts herself with worry and all because of the indifference of that son of hers. She wants to make him believe that she abandoned him when he was two years old because the Father made her do it.

MOTHER [*Passionately.*]   He did! He made me! God's my witness. [*To the* PRODUCER.] Ask him if it isn't true. [*Pointing to the* FATHER.] Make him tell our son it's true. [*Turning to the* STEPDAUGHTER.] You don't know anything about it.

STEPDAUGHTER   I know that when my father was alive you were always happy and contented. You can't deny it.

MOTHER   No, I can't deny it.

STEPDAUGHTER   He was always full of love and care for you. [*Turning to the* LITTLE BOY *with anger.*] Isn't it true? Admit it. Why don't you say something, you little idiot?

MOTHER   Leave the poor boy alone! Why do you want to make me appear ungrateful? You're my daughter. I don't in the least want to offend your father's memory. I've already told him that it wasn't my fault or even to please myself that I left his house and my son.

FATHER   It's quite true. It was my fault.

LEADING ACTOR [*To other actors.*]   Look at this. What a show!

LEADING ACTRESS   And we're the audience.

YOUNG ACTOR   For a change.

PRODUCER [*Beginning to be very interested.*]   Let's listen to them! Quiet! Listen!

[*He goes down the steps into the auditorium and stands there as if to get an idea of what the scene will look like from the audience's viewpoint.*]

SON [*Without moving, coldly, quietly, ironically.*]   Yes, listen to his little scrap of philosophy. He's going to tell you all about the Daemon of Experiment.

FATHER   You're a cynical idiot, and I've told you so a hundred times. [*To the* PRODUCER *who is now in the stalls.*] He sneers at me because of this expression I've found to defend myself.

SON   Words, words.

FATHER   Yes words, words! When we're faced by something we don't understand, by a sense of evil that seems as if it's going to swallow us, don't we all find comfort in a word that tells us nothing but that calms us?

STEPDAUGHTER   And dulls your sense of remorse, too. That more than anything.

FATHER   Remorse? No, that's not true. It'd take more than words to dull the sense of remorse in me.

STEPDAUGHTER   It's taken a little money too, just a little money. The money that he was going to offer as payment, gentlemen.

[*The* ACTORS *are horrified.*]

SON [*Contemptuously to his stepsister.*]   That's a filthy trick.

STEPDAUGHTER   A filthy trick? There it was in a pale blue envelope on the little mahogany table in the room behind the shop at Madame Pace's. You know Madame Pace, don't you? One of those Madames who sell "Robes et Manteaux" so that they can attract poor girls like me from decent families into their workroom.[9]

SON   And she's bought the right to tyrannise over the whole lot of us with that money—with what he was going to pay her: and luckily—now listen carefully—he had no reason to pay it to her.

STEPDAUGHTER   But it was close!

MOTHER [*Rising up angrily.*]   Shame on you, daughter! Shame!

STEPDAUGHTER   Shame? Not shame, revenge! I'm desperate, desperate to live that scene! The room . . . over here the showcase of coats, there the divan, there the mirror, and the screen, and over there in front of the window, that little mahogany table with the pale blue envelope and the money in it. I can see it all quite clearly. I could pick it up! But you should turn your faces away, gentlemen: because I'm nearly naked! I'm not blushing any longer—I leave that to him. [*Pointing at the* FATHER.] But I tell you he was very pale, very pale then. [*To the* PRODUCER.] Believe me.

PRODUCER   I don't understand any more.

FATHER   I'm not surprised when you're attacked like that! Why don't you put your foot down and let me have my say before you believe all these horrible slanders she's so viciously telling about me.

STEPDAUGHTER   We don't want to hear any of your long winded fairy-stories.

FATHER   I'm not going to tell any fairy-stories! I want to explain things to him.

STEPDAUGHTER   I'm sure you do. Oh, yes! In your own special way.

[*The* PRODUCER *comes back up on stage to take control.*]

FATHER   But isn't that the cause of all the trouble? Words! We all have a world of things inside ourselves and each one of us has his own private world. How can we understand each other if the words I use have the sense and the value that I expect them to have, but whoever is listening to me inevitably thinks that those same words have a different sense and value, because of the private world he has inside himself too. We think we understand each other: but we never do. Look! All my pity, all my compassion for this woman [*Pointing to the* MOTHER.] she sees as ferocious cruelty.

MOTHER   But he turned me out of the house!

FATHER   There, do you hear? I turned her out! She really believed that I had turned her out.

MOTHER   You know how to talk. I don't . . . But believe me, sir, [*Turning to the* PRODUCER.] after he married me . . . I can't think why! I was a poor, simple woman.

FATHER   But that was the reason! I married you for your simplicity, that's what I loved in you, believing—[*He stops because she is making gestures of*

9. The implication is that Madame Pace (Italian for "peace") runs a call-girl operation under the guise of selling fashionable "dresses and coats."

contradiction. Then, seeing the impossibility of making her understand, he throws his arms wide in a gesture of desperation and turns back to the PRODUCER.] No, do you see? She says no! It's terrifying, sir, believe me, terrifying, her deafness, her mental deafness. [*He taps his forehead.*] Affection for her children, oh yes. But deaf, mentally deaf, deaf, sir, to the point of desperation.

STEPDAUGHTER   Yes, but make him tell you what good all his cleverness has brought us.

FATHER   If only we could see in advance all the harm that can come from the good we think we are doing.

> [*The* LEADING ACTRESS, *who has been growing angry watching the* LEADING ACTOR *flirting with the* STEPDAUGHTER, *comes forward and snaps at the* PRODUCER.]

LEADING ACTRESS   Excuse me, are we going to go on with our rehearsal?

PRODUCER   Yes, of course. But I want to listen to this first.

YOUNG ACTOR   It's such a new idea.

YOUNG ACTRESS   It's fascinating.

LEADING ACTRESS   For those who are interested. [*She looks meaningfully at the* LEADING ACTOR.]

PRODUCER [*To the* FATHER.]   Look here, you must explain yourself more clearly. [*He sits down.*]

FATHER   Listen then. You see, there was a rather poor fellow working for me as my assistant and secretary, very loyal: he understood her in everything. [*Pointing to the* MOTHER.] But without a hint of deceit, you must believe that: he was good and simple, like her: neither of them was capable even of thinking anything wrong, let alone doing it.

STEPDAUGHTER   So instead he thought of it for them and did it too!

FATHER   It's not true! What I did was for their good—oh yes and mine too, I admit it! The time had come when I couldn't say a word to either of them without there immediately flashing between them a sympathetic look: each one caught the other's eye for advice, about how to take what I had said, how not to make me angry. Well, that was enough, as I'm sure you'll understand, to put me in a bad temper all the time, in a state of intolerable exasperation.

PRODUCER   Then why didn't you sack this secretary of yours?

FATHER   Right! In the end I did sack him! But then I had to watch this poor woman wandering about in the house on her own, forlorn, like a stray animal you take in out of pity.

MOTHER   It's quite true.

FATHER [*Suddenly, turning to her, as if to stop her.*]   And what about the boy? Is that true as well?

MOTHER   But first he tore my son from me, sir.

FATHER   But not out of cruelty! It was so that he could grow up healthy and strong, in touch with the earth.

STEPDAUGHTER [*Pointing to the* SON *jeeringly.*]   And look at the result!

FATHER [*Quickly.*]   And is it my fault, too, that he's grown up like this? I took him to a nurse in the country, a peasant, because his mother didn't seem strong enough to me, although she is from a humble family herself. In fact that was what made me marry her. Perhaps it was superstitious of me; but what was I to do? I've always had this dreadful longing for a kind of sound moral healthiness.

[*The* STEPDAUGHTER *breaks out again into noisy laughter*.]

Make her stop that! It's unbearable.

PRODUCER   Stop it will you? Let me listen, for God's sake.

[*When the* PRODUCER *has spoken to her, she resumes her previous position . . . absorbed and distant, a half-smile on her lips. The* PRODUCER *comes down into the auditorium again to see how it looks from there*.]

FATHER   I couldn't bear the sight of this woman near me. [*Pointing to the* MOTHER.] Not so much because of the annoyance she caused me, you see, or even the feeling of being stifled, being suffocated that I got from her, as for the sorrow, the painful sorrow that I felt for her.

MOTHER   And he sent me away.

FATHER   With everything you needed, to the other man, to set her free from me.

MOTHER   And to set yourself free!

FATHER   Oh, yes, I admit it. And what terrible things came out of it. But I did it for the best, and more for her than for me: I swear it! [*Folds his arms: then turns suddenly to the* MOTHER.] I never lost sight of you did I? Until that fellow, without my knowing it, suddenly took you off to another town one day. He was idiotically suspicious of my interest in them, a genuine interest, I assure you, without any ulterior motive at all. I watched the new little family growing up round her with unbelievable tenderness, she'll confirm that. [*He points to the* STEPDAUGHTER.]

STEPDAUGHTER   Oh yes, I can indeed. I was a pretty little girl, you know, with plaits down to my shoulders and my little frilly knickers showing under my dress—so pretty—he used to watch me coming out of school. He came to see how I was maturing.

FATHER   That's shameful! It's monstrous.

STEPDAUGHTER   No it isn't! Why do you say it is?

FATHER   It's monstrous! Monstrous. [*He turns excitely to the* PRODUCER *and goes on in explanation*.] After she'd gone away [*Pointing to the* MOTHER.] my house seemed empty. She'd been like a weight on my spirit but she'd filled the house with her presence. Alone in the empty rooms I wandered about like a lost soul. This boy here, [*Indicating the* SON.] growing up away from home—whenever he came back to the home—I don't know—but he didn't seem to be mine any more. We needed the mother between us, to link us together, and so he grew up by himself, apart, with no connection to me either through intellect or love. And then—it must seem odd, but it's true—first I was curious about and then strongly attracted to the little family that had come about because of what I'd done. And the thought of them began to fill all the emptiness that I felt around me. I needed, I really needed to believe that she was happy, wrapped up in the simple cares of her life, lucky because she was better off away from the complicated torments of a soul like mine. And to prove it, I used to watch that child coming out of school.

STEPDAUGHTER   Listen to him! He used to follow me along the street; he used to smile at me and when we came near the house he'd wave his hand—like this! I watched him, wide-eyed, puzzled. I didn't know who he was. I told my mother about him and she knew at once who it must be. [MOTHER *nods*

agreement.] At first, she didn't let me go to school again, at any rate for a few days. But when I did go back, I saw him standing near the door again—looking ridiculous—with a brown paper bag in his hand. He came close and petted me: then he opened the bag and took out a beautiful straw hat with a hoop of rosebuds round it—for me!

PRODUCER All this is off the point, you know.

SON [*Contemptuously.*] Yes . . . literature, literature.

FATHER What do you mean, literature? This is real life: real passions.

PRODUCER That may be! But you can't put it on the stage just like that.

FATHER That's right you can't. Because all this is only leading up to the main action. I'm not suggesting that this part should be put on the stage. In any case, you can see for yourself, [*Pointing at the* STEPDAUGHTER.] she isn't a pretty little girl any longer with plaits down to her shoulders.

STEPDAUGHTER —and with frilly knickers showing under her frock.

FATHER The drama begins now: and it's new and complex.

STEPDAUGHTER [*Coming forward, fierce and brooding.*] As soon as my father died . . .

FATHER [*Quickly, not giving her time to speak.*] They were so miserable. They came back here, but I didn't know about it because of the Mother's stubbornness. [*Pointing to the* MOTHER.] She can't really write you know; but she could have got her daughter to write, or the boy, or tell me that they needed help.

MOTHER But tell me, sir, how could I have known how he felt?

FATHER And hasn't that always been your fault? You've never known anything about how I felt.

MOTHER After all the years away from him and after all that had happened.

FATHER And was it my fault if that fellow took you so far away? [*Turning back to the* PRODUCER.] Suddenly, overnight, I tell you, he'd found a job away from here without my knowing anything about it: I couldn't possibly trace them; and then, naturally I suppose, my interest in them grew less over the years. The drama broke out, unexpected and violent, when they came back: when I was driven in misery by the needs of my flesh, still alive with desire . . . and it is misery, you know, unspeakable misery for the man who lives alone and who detests sordid, casual affairs; not old enough to do without women, but not young enough to be able to go and look for one without shame! Misery? Is that what I called it. It's horrible, it's revolting, because there isn't a woman who will give her love to him any more. And when he realises this, he should do without . . . It's easy to say though. Each of us, face to face with other men, is clothed with some sort of dignity, but we know only too well all the unspeakable things that go on in the heart. We surrender, we give in to temptation: but afterwards we rise up out of it very quickly, in a desperate hurry to rebuild our dignity, whole and firm as if it were a gravestone that would cover every sign and memory of our shame, and hide it from even our own eyes. Everyone's like that, only some of us haven't the courage to talk about it.

STEPDAUGHTER But they've all got the courage to do it!

FATHER Yes! But only in secret! That's why it takes more courage to talk about it! Because if a man does talk about it—what happens then?—everybody says he's a cynic. And it's simply not true; he's just like everybody

else; only better perhaps, because he's not afraid to use his intelligence to point out the blushing shame of human bestiality, that man, the beast, shuts his eyes to, trying to pretend it doesn't exist. And what about woman—what is she like? She looks at you invitingly, teasingly. You take her in your arms. But as soon as she feels your arms round her she closes her eyes. It's the sign of her mission, the sign by which she says to a man, "Blind yourself— I'm blind!"

STEPDAUGHTER   And when she doesn't close her eyes any more? What then? When she doesn't feel the need to hide from herself any more, to shut her eyes and hide her own shame. When she can see instead, dispassionately and dry-eyed this blushing shame of a man who has blinded himself, who is without love. What then? Oh, then what disgust, what utter disgust she feels for all these intellectual complications, for all this philosophy that points to the bestiality of man and then tries to defend him, to excuse him . . . I can't listen to him, sir. Because when a man says he needs to "simplify" life like this—reducing it to bestiality—and throws away every human scrap of innocent desire, genuine feeling, idealism, duty, modesty, shame, then there's nothing more contemptible and nauseating than his remorse—crocodile tears!

PRODUCER   Let's get to the point, let's get to the point. This is all chat.

FATHER   Right then! But a fact is like a sack—it won't stand up if it's empty. To make it stand up, first you have to put in it all the reasons and feelings that caused it in the first place. I couldn't possibly have known that when that fellow died they'd come back here, that they were desperately poor and that the Mother had gone out to work as a dressmaker, nor that she'd gone to work for Madame Pace, of all people.

STEPDAUGHTER   She's a very high-class dressmaker—you must understand that. She apparently has only high-class customers, but she has arranged things carefully so that these high-class customers in fact serve her—they give her a respectable front . . . without spoiling things for the other ladies at the shop who are not quite so high-class at all.

MOTHER   Believe me, sir, the idea never entered my head that the old hag gave me work because she had an eye on my daughter . . .

STEPDAUGHTER   Poor Mummy! Do you know what that woman would do when I took back the work that my mother had been doing? She would point out how the dress had been ruined by giving it to my mother to sew: she bargained, she grumbled. So, you see, I paid for it, while this poor woman here thought she was sacrificing herself for me and these two children, sew- ing dresses all night for Madame Pace.

[The ACTORS make gestures and noises of disgust.]

PRODUCER [Quickly.]   And there one day, you met . . .

STEPDAUGHTER [Pointing at the FATHER.]   Yes, him. Oh, he was an old cus- tomer of hers! What a scene that's going to be, superb!

FATHER   With her, the mother, arriving—

STEPDAUGHTER [Quickly, viciously.]   —Almost in time!

FATHER [Crying out.]   —No, just in time, just in time! Because, luckily, I found out who she was in time. And I took them all back to my house, sir. Can you imagine the situation now, for the two of us living in the same house? She, just as you see her here; and I, not able to look her in the face.

STEPDAUGHTER   It's so absurd! Do you think it's possible for me, sir, after what happened at Madame Pace's, to pretend that I'm a modest little miss, well brought up and virtuous just so that I can fit in with his damned pretensions to a "sound moral healthiness"?

FATHER   This is the real drama for me; the belief that we all, you see, think of ourselves as one single person: but it's not true: each of us is several different people, and all these people live inside us. With one person we seem like this and with another we seem very different. But we always have the illusion of being the same person for everybody and of always being the same person in everything we do. But it's not true! It's not true! We find this out for ourselves very clearly when by some terrible chance we're suddenly stopped in the middle of doing something and we're left dangling there, suspended. We realise then, that every part of us was not involved in what we'd been doing and that it would be a dreadful injustice of other people to judge us only by this one action as we dangle there, hanging in chains, fixed for all eternity, as if the whole of one's personality were summed up in that single, interrupted action. Now do you understand this girl's treachery? She accidentally found me somewhere I shouldn't have been, doing something I shouldn't have been doing! She discovered a part of me that shouldn't have existed for her: and now she wants to fix on me a reality that I should never have had to assume for her: it came from a single brief and shameful moment in my life. This is what hurts me most of all. And you'll see that the play will make a tremendous impact from this idea of mine. But then, there's the position of the others. His . . . [*Pointing to the* SON.]

SON [*Shrugging his shoulders scornfully.*]   Leave me out of it. I don't come into this.

FATHER   Why don't you come into this?

SON   I don't come into it and I don't want to come into it, because you know perfectly well that I wasn't intended to be mixed up with you lot.

STEPDAUGHTER   We're vulgar, common people, you see! He's a fine gentleman. But you've probably noticed that every now and then I look at him contemptuously, and when I do, he lowers his eyes—he knows the harm he's done me.

SON [*Not looking at her.*]   I have?

STEPDAUGHTER   Yes, you. It's your fault, dearie, that I went on the streets! Your fault! [*Movement of horror from the* ACTORS.] Did you or didn't you, with your attitude, deny us—I won't say the intimacy of your home—but that simple hospitality that makes guests feel comfortable? We were intruders who had come to invade the country of your "legitimacy"! [*Turning to the* PRODUCER.] I'd like you to have seen some of the little scenes that went on between him and me, sir. He says that I tyrannised over everyone. But don't you see? It was because of the way he treated us. He called it "vile" that I should insist on the right we had to move into his house with my mother— and she's his mother too. And I went into the house as its mistress.

SON [*Slowly coming forward.*]   They're really enjoying themselves, aren't they, sir? It's easy when they all gang up against me. But try to imagine what happened: one fine day, there is a son sitting quietly at home and he sees arrive as bold as brass, a young woman like this, who cheekily asks for his father, and heaven knows what business she has with him. Then he sees her come back with the same brazen look in her eye accompanied by that little girl there: and he sees her treat his father—without knowing why—in a most ambiguous and insolent way—asking him for money in a tone that leads one to suppose he really ought to give it, because he is obliged to do so.

FATHER   But I was obliged to do so: I owed it to your mother.

SON   And how was I to know that? When had I ever seen her before? When had I ever heard her mentioned? Then one day I see her come in with her, [*Pointing at the* STEPDAUGHTER.] that boy and that little girl: they say to me, "Oh, didn't you know? This is your mother, too." Little by little I began to understand, mostly from her attitude. [*Points to* STEPDAUGHTER.] Why they'd come to live in the house so suddenly. I can't and I won't say what I feel, and what I think. I wouldn't even like to confess it to myself. So I can't take any active part in this. Believe me, sir, I am a character who has not been fully developed dramatically, and I feel uncomfortable, most uncomfortable, in their company. So please leave me out of it.

FATHER   What! But it's precisely because you feel like this . . .

SON   [*Violently exasperated.*]   How do you know what I feel?

FATHER   All right! I admit it! But isn't that a situation in itself? This withdrawing of yourself, it's cruel to me and to your mother: when she came back to the house, seeing you almost for the first time, not recognising you, but knowing that you're her own son . . . [*Turning to point out the* MOTHER *to the* PRODUCER.] There, look at her: she's weeping.

STEPDAUGHTER   [*Angrily, stamping her foot.*]   Like the fool she is!

FATHER   [*Quickly pointing at the* STEPDAUGHTER *to the* PRODUCER.]   She can't stand that young man, you know. [*Turning and referring to the* SON.] He says that he doesn't come into it, but he's really the pivot of the action! Look here at this little boy, who clings to his mother all the time, frightened, humiliated. And it's because of him over there! Perhaps this little boy's problem is the worst of all: he feels an outsider, more than the others do; he feels so mortified, so humiliated just being in the house,—because it's charity, you see. [*Quietly.*] He's like his father: timid; he doesn't say anything . . .

PRODUCER   It's not a good idea at all, using him: you don't know what a nuisance children are on the stage.

FATHER   He won't need to be on the stage for long. Nor will the little girl— she's the first to go.

PRODUCER   That's good! Yes. I tell you all this interests me—it interests me very much. I'm sure we've the material here for a good play.

STEPDAUGHTER   [*Trying to push herself in.*]   With a character like me you have!

FATHER [*Driving her off, wanting to hear what the* PRODUCER *has decided.*]   You stay out of it!

PRODUCER   [*Going on, ignoring the interruption.*]   It's new, yes.

FATHER   Oh, it's absolutely new!

PRODUCER   You've got a nerve, though, haven't you, coming here and throwing it at me like this?

FATHER   I'm sure you understand. Born as we are for the *stage* . . .

PRODUCER   Are you amateur actors?

FATHER   No! I say we are born for the stage because . . .

PRODUCER   Come on now! You're an old hand at this, at acting!

FATHER   No I'm not. I only act, as everyone does, the part in life that he's chosen for himself, or that others have chosen for him. And you can see that sometimes my own passion gets a bit out of hand, a bit theatrical, as it does with all of us.

PRODUCER   Maybe, maybe . . . But you do see, don't you, that without an author . . . I could give you someone's address . . .

FATHER   Oh no! Look here! You do it.

PRODUCER   Me? What are you talking about?

FATHER   Yes, you. Why not?

PRODUCER   Because I've never written anything!

FATHER   Well, why not start now, if you don't mind my suggesting it? There's nothing to it. Everybody's doing it. And your job is even easier, because we're here, all of us, alive before you.

PRODUCER   That's not enough.

FATHER   Why isn't it enough? When you've seen us live our drama . . .

PRODUCER   Perhaps so. But we'll still need someone to write it.

FATHER   Only to write it down, perhaps, while it happens in front of him— live—scene by scene. It'll be enough to sketch it out simply first and then run through it.

PRODUCER [*Coming back up, tempted by the idea.*]   Do you know I'm almost tempted . . . just for fun . . . it might work.

FATHER   Of course it will. You'll see what wonderful scenes will come right out of it! I could tell you what they will be!

PRODUCER   You tempt me . . . you tempt me! We'll give it a chance. Come with me to the office. [*Turning to the* ACTORS.] Take a break: but don't go far away. Be back in a quarter of an hour or twenty minutes. [*To the* FATHER.] Let's see, let's try it out. Something extraordinary might come out of this.

FATHER   Of course it will! Don't you think it'd be better if the others came too? [*Indicating the other* CHARACTERS.]

PRODUCER   Yes, come on, come on. [*Going, then turning to speak to the* ACTORS.] Don't forget: don't be late: back in a quarter of an hour.

   [*The* PRODUCER *and the* SIX CHARACTERS *cross the stage and go. The* ACTORS *look at each other in astonishment.*]

LEADING ACTOR   Is he serious? What's he going to do?

YOUNG ACTOR   I think he's gone round the bend.

ANOTHER ACTOR   Does he expect to make up a play in five minutes?

YOUNG ACTOR   Yes, like the old actors in the commedia dell'arte![1]

LEADING ACTRESS   Well if he thinks I'm going to appear in that sort of nonsense . . .

YOUNG ACTOR   Nor me!

FOURTH ACTOR   I should like to know who they are.

THIRD ACTOR   Who do you think? They're probably escaped lunatics—or crooks.

YOUNG ACTOR   And is he taking them seriously?

YOUNG ACTRESS   It's vanity. The vanity of seeing himself as an author.

---

1. A form of popular theater beginning in 16th-century Italy; the actors improvised dialogue according to basic comic or dramatic plots and in response to the audience's reaction.

LEADING ACTOR   I've never heard of such a thing! If the theatre, ladies and gentlemen, is reduced to this . . .

FIFTH ACTOR   I'm enjoying it!

THIRD ACTOR   Really! We shall have to wait and see what happens next I suppose.

[*Talking, they leave the stage. Some go out through the back door, some to the dressing-rooms.*
The curtain stays up.
The interval lasts twenty minutes.]

Act 2

The theatre warning-bell sounds to call the audience back. From the dressing-rooms, the door at the back and even from the auditorium, the ACTORS, *the* STAGE MANAGER, *the* STAGE HANDS, *the* PROMPTER, *the* PROPERTY MAN *and the* PRODUCER, *accompanied by the* SIX CHARACTERS *all come back on to the stage.*
The house lights go out and the stage lights come on again.

PRODUCER   Come on, everybody! Are we all here? Quiet now! Listen! Let's get started! Stage manager?

STAGE MANAGER   Yes, I'm here.

PRODUCER   Give me that little parlour setting, will you? A couple of plain flats and a door flat will do. Hurry up with it!

[*The* STAGE MANAGER *runs off to order someone to do this immediately and at the same time the* PRODUCER *is making arrangements with the* PROPERTY MAN, *the* PROMPTER, *and the* ACTORS: *the two flats and the door flat are painted in pink and gold stripes.*]

PRODUCER [*To* PROPERTY MAN.]   Go see if we have a sofa in stock.

PROPERTY MAN   Yes, there's that green one.

STEPDAUGHTER   No, no, not a green one! It was yellow, yellow velvet with flowers on it: it was enormous! And so comfortable!

PROPERTY MAN   We haven't got one like that.

PRODUCER   It doesn't matter! Give me whatever there is.

STEPDAUGHTER   What do you mean, it doesn't matter? It was Mme. Pace's famous sofa.

PRODUCER   It's only for a rehearsal! Please, don't interfere. [*To the* STAGE MANAGER.] Oh, and see if there's a shop window, will you—preferably a long, low one.

STEPDAUGHTER   And a little table, a little mahogany table for the blue envelope.

STAGE MANAGER [*To the* PRODUCER.]   There's that little gold one.

PRODUCER   That'll do—bring it.

FATHER   A mirror!

STEPDAUGHTER   And a screen! A screen, please, or I won't be able to manage, will I?

STAGE MANAGER   All right. We've lots of big screens, don't you worry.

PRODUCER [*To* STEPDAUGHTER.]   Then don't you want some coat-hangers and some clothes racks?

STEPDAUGHTER   Yes, lots of them, lots of them.

PRODUCER [*To the* STAGE MANAGER.]   See how many there are and have them brought up.

STAGE MANAGER   Right, I'll see to it.

[*The* STAGE MANAGER *goes off to do it: and while the* PRODUCER *is talking to the* PROMPTER, *the* CHARACTERS *and the* ACTORS, *the* STAGE MANAGER *is telling the* SCENE SHIFTERS *where to set up the furniture they have brought.*]

PRODUCER [*To the* PROMPTER.]   Now you, go sit down, will you? Look, this is an outline of the play, act by act. [*He hands him several sheets of paper.*] But you'll need to be on your toes.

PROMPTER   Shorthand?

PRODUCER [*Pleasantly surprised.*]   Oh, good! You know shorthand?

PROMPTER   I don't know much about prompting, but I do know about shorthand.

PRODUCER   Thank God for that anyway! [*He turns to a* STAGE HAND.] Go fetch me some paper from my office—lots of it—as much as you can find!

[*The* STAGE HAND *goes running off and then comes back shortly with a bundle of paper that he gives to the* PROMPTER.]

PRODUCER [*Crossing to the* PROMPTER.]   Follow the scenes, one after another, as they are played and try to get the lines down . . . at least the most important ones. [*Then turning to the* ACTORS.] Get out of the way everybody! Here, go over to the prompt side [*Pointing to stage left.*] and pay attention.

LEADING ACTRESS   But, excuse me, we . . .

PRODUCER [*Anticipating her.*]   You won't be expected to improvise, don't worry!

LEADING ACTOR   Then what are we expected to do?

PRODUCER   Nothing! Just go over there, listen and watch. You'll all be given your parts later written out. Right now we're going to rehearse, as well as we can. And they will be doing the rehearsal. [*He points to the* CHARACTERS.]

FATHER [*Rather bewildered, as if he had fallen from the clouds into the middle of the confusion on the stage.*]   We are? Excuse me, but what do you mean, a rehearsal?

PRODUCER   I mean a rehearsal—a rehearsal for the benefit of the actors. [*Pointing to the* ACTORS.]

FATHER   But if we are the characters . . .

PRODUCER   That's right, you're "the characters": but characters don't act here, my dear chap. It's actors who act here. The characters are there in the script—[*Pointing to the* PROMPTER.] that's when there is a script.

FATHER   That's the point! Since there isn't one and you have the luck to have the characters alive in front of you . . .

PRODUCER   Great! You want to do everything yourselves, do you? To act your own play, to produce your own play!

FATHER   Well yes, just as we are.

PRODUCER   That would be an experience for us, I can tell you!

LEADING ACTOR   And what about us? What would we be doing then?

PRODUCER   Don't tell me you think you know how to act! Don't make me laugh! [*The* ACTORS *in fact laugh.*] There you are, you see, you've made them laugh. [*Then remembering.*] But let's get back to the point! We need to cast the play. Well, that's easy: it almost casts itself. [*To the* SECOND ACTRESS.] You, the mother. [*To the* FATHER.] You'll need to give her a name.

FATHER Amalia.

PRODUCER But that's the real name of your wife isn't it? We can't use her real name.

FATHER But why not? That is her name . . . But perhaps if this lady is to play the part . . . [*Indicating the* ACTRESS *vaguely with a wave of his hand.*] I don't know what to say . . . I'm already starting to . . . how can I explain it . . . to sound false, my own words sound like someone else's.

PRODUCER Now don't worry yourself about it, don't worry about it at all. We'll work out the right tone of voice. As for the name, if you want it to be Amalia, then Amalia it shall be: or we can find another. For the moment we'll refer to the characters like this: [*To the* YOUNG ACTOR, *the juvenile lead.*] you are The Son. [*To the* LEADING ACTRESS.] You, of course, are The Stepdaughter.

STEPDAUGHTER [*Excitedly.*] What did you say? That woman is me? [*Bursts into laughter.*]

PRODUCER [*Angrily.*] What are you laughing at?

LEADING ACTRESS [*Indignantly.*] Nobody has ever dared to laugh at me before! Either you treat me with respect or I'm walking out! [*Starting to go.*]

STEPDAUGHTER I'm sorry. I wasn't really laughing at you.

PRODUCER [*To the* STEPDAUGHTER.] You should feel proud to be played by . . .

LEADING ACTRESS [*Quickly, scornfully.*] . . . that woman!

STEPDAUGHTER But I wasn't thinking about her, honestly. I was thinking about me: I can't see myself in you at all . . . you're not a bit like me!

FATHER Yes, that's right: you see, our meaning . . .

PRODUCER What are you talking about, "our meaning"? Do you think you have exclusive rights to what you represent? Do you think it can only exist inside you? Not a bit of it!

FATHER What? Don't we even have our own meaning?

PRODUCER Not a bit of it! Whatever you mean is only material here, to which the actors give form and body, voice and gesture, and who, through their art, have given expression to much better material than what you have to offer: yours is really very trivial and if it stands up on the stage, the credit, believe me, will all be due to my actors.

FATHER I don't dare to contradict you. But you for your part, must believe me—it doesn't seem trivial to us. We are suffering terribly now, with these bodies, these faces . . .

PRODUCER [*Interrupting impatiently.*] Yes, well, the make-up will change that, make-up will change that, at least as far as the faces are concerned.

FATHER Yes, but the voices, the gestures . . .

PRODUCER That's enough! You can't come on the stage here as yourselves. It is our actors who will represent you here: and let that be the end of it!

FATHER I understand that. But now I think I see why our author who saw us alive as we are here now, didn't want to put us on the stage. I don't want to offend your actors. God forbid that I should! But I think that if I saw myself represented . . . by I don't know whom . . .

LEADING ACTOR [*Rising majestically and coming forward, followed by a laughing group of* YOUNG ACTRESSES.] By me, if you don't object.

FATHER [*Respectfully, smoothly.*] I shall be honoured, sir. [*He bows.*] But I think, that no matter how hard this gentleman works with all his will and all his art to identify himself with me . . . [*He stops, confused.*]

LEADING ACTOR   Yes, go on.

FATHER   Well, I was saying the performance he will give, even if he is made up to look like me . . . I mean with the difference in our appearance . . . [*All the* ACTORS *laugh.*] it will be difficult for it to be a performance of me as I really am. It will be more like—well, not just because of his figure—it will be more an interpretation of what I am, what he believes me to be, and not how I know myself to be. And it seems to me that this should be taken into account by those who are going to comment on us.

PRODUCER   So you are already worrying about what the critics will say, are you? And I'm still waiting to get this thing started! The critics can say what they like: and we'll worry about putting on the play. If we can! [*Stepping out of the group and looking around.*] Come on, come on! Is the scene set for us yet? [*To the* ACTORS *and* CHARACTERS.] Out of the way! Let's have a look at it. [*Climbing down off the stage.*] Don't let's waste any more time. [*To the* STEPDAUGHTER.] Does it look all right to you?

SON   What! That? I don't recognise it at all.

PRODUCER   Good God! Did you expect us to reconstruct the room at the back of Mme. Pace's shop here on the stage? [*To the* FATHER.] Did you say the room had flowered wallpaper?

FATHER   White, yes.

PRODUCER   Well it's not white: it's striped. That sort of thing doesn't matter at all! As for the furniture, it looks to me as if we have nearly everything we need. Move that little table a bit further downstage. [*A* STAGE HAND *does it. To the* PROPERTY MAN.] Go and fetch an envelope, pale blue if you can find one, and give it to that gentleman there. [*Pointing to the* FATHER.]

STAGE HAND   An envelope for letters?

PRODUCER }
FATHER   } Yes, an envelope for letters!

STAGE HAND   Right. [*He goes off.*]

PRODUCER   Now then, come on! The first scene is the young lady's. [*The* LEADING ACTRESS *comes to the centre.*] No, no, not yet. I said the young lady's. [*He points to the* STEPDAUGHTER.] You stay there and watch.

STEPDAUGHTER [*Adding quickly.*]   . . . how I bring it to life.

LEADING ACTRESS [*Resenting this.*]   I shall know how to bring it to life, don't you worry, when I am allowed to.

PRODUCER [*His head in his hands.*]   Ladies, please, no more arguments! Now then. The first scene is between the young lady and Mme. Pace. Oh! [*Worried, turning round and looking out into the auditorium.*] Where is Mme. Pace?

FATHER   She isn't here with us.

PRODUCER   So what do we do now?

FATHER   But she is real. She's real too!

PRODUCER   All right. So where is she?

FATHER   May I deal with this? [*Turns to the* ACTRESSES.] Would each of you ladies be kind enough to lend me a hat, a coat, a scarf or something?

ACTRESSES [*Some are surprised or amused.*]   What? My scarf? A coat? What's he want my hat for? What are you wanting to do with them? [*All the* ACTRESSES *are laughing.*]

FATHER   Oh, nothing much, just hang them up here on the racks for a minute or two. Perhaps someone would be kind enough to lend me a coat?

ACTORS   Just a coat? Come on, more! The man must be mad.

AN ACTRESS   What for? Only my coat?

FATHER   Yes, to hang up here, just for a moment. I'm very grateful to you. Do you mind?

ACTRESSES [*Taking off various hats, coats, scarves, laughing and going to hang them on the racks.*]   Why not? Here you are. I really think it's crazy. Is it to dress the set?

FATHER   Yes, exactly. It's to dress the set.

PRODUCER   Would you mind telling me what you are doing?

FATHER   Yes, of course: perhaps, if we dress the set better, she will be drawn by the articles of her trade and, who knows, she may even come to join us . . . [*He invites them to watch the door at the back of the set.*] Look! Look!

[*The door at the back opens and* MME. PACE *takes a few steps downstage: she is a gross old harridan wearing a ludicrous carroty-coloured wig with a single red rose stuck in at one side, Spanish fashion: garishly made-up: in a vulgar but stylish red silk dress, holding an ostrich-feather fan in one hand and a cigarette between two fingers in the other. At the sight of this apparition, the* ACTORS *and the* PRODUCER *immediately jump off the stage with cries of fear, leaping down into the auditorium and up the aisles. The* STEP-DAUGHTER, *however, runs across to* MME. PACE, *and greets her respectfully, as if she were the mistress.*]

STEPDAUGHTER [*Running across to her.*]   Here she is! Here she is!

FATHER [*Smiling broadly.*]   It's her! What did I tell you? Here she is!

PRODUCER [*Recovering from his shock, indignantly.*]   What sort of trick is this?

LEADING ACTOR [*Almost at the same time as the others.*]   What the hell is happening?

JUVENILE LEAD   Where on earth did they get that extra from?

YOUNG ACTRESS   They were keeping her hidden!

LEADING ACTRESS   It's a game, a conjuring trick!

FATHER   Wait a minute! Why do you want to spoil a miracle by being factual? Can't you see this is a miracle of reality, that is born, brought to life, lured here, reproduced, just for the sake of this scene, with more right to be alive here than you have? Perhaps it has more truth than you have yourselves. Which actress can improve on Mme. Pace there? Well? That is the real Mme. Pace. You must admit that the actress who plays her will be less true than she is herself—and there she is in person! Look! My daughter recognised her straight away and went to meet her. Now watch—just watch this scene.

[*Hesitantly, the* PRODUCER *and the* ACTORS *move back to their original places on the stage.*

But the scene between the STEPDAUGHTER *and* MME. PACE *had already begun while the* ACTORS *were protesting and the* FATHER *explaining: it is being played under their breaths, very quietly, very naturally, in a way that is obviously impossible on stage. So when the* ACTORS' *attention is recalled by the* FATHER *they turn and see that* MME. PACE *has just put her hand under the* STEPDAUGHTER's *chin to make her lift her head up: they also hear her speak in a way that is unintelligible to them. They watch and listen hard for a few moments, then they start to make fun of them.*]

PRODUCER   Well?

LEADING ACTOR   What's she saying?

LEADING ACTRESS   Can't hear a thing!

JUVENILE LEAD   Louder! Speak up!

STEPDAUGHTER [*Leaving* MME. PACE *who has an astonishing smile on her face, and coming down to the* ACTORS.]   Louder? What do you mean, "Louder"? What we're talking about you can't talk about loudly. I could shout about it a moment ago to embarrass him [*Pointing to the* FATHER.] to shame him and to get my own back on him! But it's a different matter for Mme. Pace. It would mean prison for her.

PRODUCER   What the hell are you on about? Here in the theatre you have to make yourself heard! Don't you see that? We can't hear you even from here, and we're on the stage with you! Imagine what it would be like with an audience out front! You need to make the scene go! And after all, you would speak normally to each other when you're alone, and you will be, because we shan't be here anyway. I mean we're only here because it's a rehearsal. So just imagine that there you are in the room at the back of the shop, and there's no one to hear you.

[*The* STEPDAUGHTER, *with a knowing smile, wags her finger and her head rather elegantly, as if to say no.*]

PRODUCER   Why not?

STEPDAUGHTER [*Mysteriously, whispering loudly.*]   Because there is someone who will hear if she speaks normally. [*Pointing to* MME. PACE.]

PRODUCER [*Anxiously.*]   You're not going to make someone else appear are you?

[*The* ACTORS *get ready to dive off the stage again.*]

FATHER   No, no. She means me. I ought to be over there, waiting behind the door: and Mme. Pace knows I'm there, so excuse me will you: I'll go there now so that I shall be ready for my entrance.

[*He goes towards the back of the stage.*]

PRODUCER [*Stopping him.*]   No, no wait a minute! You must remember the stage conventions! Before you can go on to that part . . .

STEPDAUGHTER [*Interrupts him.*]   Oh yes, let's get on with that part. Now! Now! I'm dying to do that scene. If he wants to go through it now, I'm ready!

PRODUCER [*Shouting.*]   But before that we must have, clearly stated, the scene between you and her. [*Pointing to* MME. PACE.] Do you see?

STEPDAUGHTER   Oh God! She's only told me what you already know, that my mother's needlework is badly done again, the dress is spoilt and that I shall have to be patient if I want her to go on helping us out of our mess.

MME. PACE [*Coming forward, with a great air of importance.*]   Ah, yes, sir, for that I do not wish to make a profit, to make advantage.

PRODUCER [*Half frightened.*]   What? Does she really speak like that? [*All the* ACTORS *burst out laughing.*]

STEPDAUGHTER [*Laughing too.*]   Yes, she speaks like that, half in Spanish, in the silliest way imaginable!

MME. PACE   Ah it is not good manners that you laugh at me when I make myself to speak, as I can, English, señor.

PRODUCER   No, no, you're right! Speak like that, please speak like that, madam. It'll be marvelous. Couldn't be better! It'll add a little touch of comedy to a rather crude situation. Speak like that! It'll be great!

STEPDAUGHTER   Great! Why not? When you hear a proposition made in that sort of accent, it'll almost seem like a joke, won't it? Perhaps you'll want to laugh when you hear that there's an "old señor"[2] who wants to "amuse himself with me"—isn't that right, Madame?

MME. PACE   Not so old . . . but not quite young, no? But if he is not to your taste . . . he is, how you say, discreet!

[*The* MOTHER *leaps up, to the astonishment and dismay of the* ACTORS *who had not been paying any attention to her, so that when she shouts out they are startled and then smilingly restrain her: however she has already snatched off* MME. PACE's *wig and flung it on the floor.*]

MOTHER   You witch! Witch! Murderess! Oh, my daughter!

STEPDAUGHTER [*Running across and taking hold of the* MOTHER.]   No! No! Mother! Please!

FATHER [*Running across to her as well.*]   Calm yourself, calm yourself! Come and sit down.

MOTHER   Get her away from here!

STEPDAUGHTER [*To the* PRODUCER *who has also crossed to her.*]   My mother can't bear to be in the same place with her.

FATHER [*Also speaking quietly to the* PRODUCER.]   They can't possibly be in the same place! That's why she wasn't with us when we first came, do you see! If they meet, everything's given away from the very beginning.

PRODUCER   It's not important, that's not important! This is only a first run-through at the moment! It's all useful stuff, even if it is confused. I'll sort it all out later. [*Turning to the* MOTHER *and taking her to sit down on her chair.*] Come on, my dear, take it easy; take it easy: come and sit down again.

STEPDAUGHTER   Go on, Mme. Pace.

MME. PACE [*Offended.*]   Oh no, thank-you! I no longer do nothing here with your mother present.

STEPDAUGHTER   Get on with it, bring in this "old señor" who wants to "amuse himself with me"! [*Turning majestically to the others.*] You see, this next scene has got to be played out—we must do it now. [*To* MME. PACE.] Oh, you can go!

MME. PACE   Ah, I go, I go—I go! Most probably! I go!

[*She leaves banging her wig back into place, glaring furiously at the* ACTORS *who applaud her exit, laughing loudly.*]

STEPDAUGHTER [*To the* FATHER.]   Now you come on! No, you don't need to go off again! Come back! Pretend you've just come in! Look, I'm standing here with my eyes on the ground, modestly—well, come on, speak up! Use that special sort of voice, like somebody who has just come in. "Good afternoon, my dear."

PRODUCER [*Off the stage by now.*]   Look here, who's the director here, you or me? [*To the* FATHER *who looks uncertain and bewildered.*] Go on, do as she says: go upstage—no, no don't bother to make an entrance. Then come down stage again.

[*The* FATHER *does as he is told, half mesmerised. He is very pale but already involved in the reality of his re-created life, smiles as he draws near the back of the stage, almost as if he genuinely is not aware of the drama that is about to sweep over him. The* ACTORS *are immediately intent on the scene that is beginning now.*]

2. Old gentleman.

The Scene

FATHER [*Coming forward with a new note in his voice.*]   Good afternoon, my dear.

STEPDAUGHTER [*Her head down trying to hide her fright.*]   Good afternoon.

FATHER [*Studying her a little under the brim of her hat which partly hides her face from him and seeing that she is very young, he exclaims to himself a little complacently and a little guardedly because of the danger of being compromised in a risky adventure.*]   Ah . . . but . . . tell me, this won't be the first time, will it? The first time you've been here?

STEPDAUGHTER   No, sir.

FATHER   You've been here before? [*And after the* STEPDAUGHTER *has nodded an answer.*] More than once? [*He waits for her reply: tries again to look at her under the brim of her hat: smiles: then says.*] Well then . . . it shouldn't be too . . . May I take off your hat?

STEPDAUGHTER [*Quickly, to stop him, unable to conceal her shudder of fear and disgust.*]   No, don't! I'll do it!

[*She takes it off unsteadily.*

The MOTHER *watches the scene intently with the* SON *and the two smaller children who cling close to her all the time: they make a group on one side of the stage opposite the* ACTORS: *She follows the words and actions of the* FATHER *and the* STEPDAUGHTER *in this scene with a variety of expressions on her face—sadness, dismay, anxiety, horror: sometimes she turns her face away and sobs.*]

MOTHER   Oh God! Oh God!

FATHER [*He stops as if turned to stone by the sobbing: then he goes on in the same tone of voice.*]   Here, give it to me. I'll hang it up for you. [*He takes the hat in his hand.*] But such a pretty, dear little head like yours should have a much smarter hat than this! Would you like to help me choose one, then, from these hats of Madame's hanging up here? Would you?

YOUNG ACTRESS [*Interrupting.*]   Be careful! Those are our hats!

PRODUCER [*Quickly and angrily.*]   For God's sake, shut up! Don't try to be funny! We're rehearsing! [*Turns back to the* STEPDAUGHTER.] Please go on, will you, from where you were interrupted.

STEPDAUGHTER [*Going on.*]   No, thank you, sir.

FATHER   Oh, don't say no to me please! Say you'll have one—to please me. Isn't this a pretty one—look! And then it will please Madame too, you know. She's put them out here on purpose, of course.

STEPDAUGHTER   No, look, I could never wear it.

FATHER   Are you thinking of what they would say at home when you went in wearing a new hat? Goodness me! Don't you know what to do? Shall I tell you what to say at home?

STEPDAUGHTER [*Furiously, nearly exploding.*]   That's not why! I couldn't wear it because . . . as you can see: you should have noticed it before. [*Indicating her black dress.*]

FATHER   You're in mourning! Oh, forgive me. You're right, I see that now. Please forgive me. Believe me, I'm really very sorry.

STEPDAUGHTER [*Gathering all her strength and making herself overcome her contempt and revulsion.*]   That's enough. Don't go on, that's enough. I ought to be thanking you and not letting you blame yourself and get upset. Don't think any more about what I told you, please. And I should do the same. [*Forcing herself to smile and adding.*] I should try to forget that I'm dressed like this.

PRODUCER [*Interrupting, turning to the* PROMPTER *in the box and jumping up on the stage again.*]   Hold it, hold it! Don't put that last line down, leave it out. [*Turning to the* FATHER *and the* STEPDAUGHTER.] It's going well! It's going well! [*Then to the* FATHER *alone.*] Then we'll put in there the bit that we talked about. [*To the* ACTORS.] That scene with the hats is good, isn't it?

STEPDAUGHTER   But the best bit is coming now! Why can't we get on with it?

PRODUCER   Just be patient, wait a minute. [*Turning and moving across to the* ACTORS.] Of course, it'll all have to be made a lot more light-hearted.

LEADING ACTOR   We shall have to play it a lot quicker, I think.

LEADING ACTRESS   Of course: there's nothing particularly difficult in it. [*To the* LEADING ACTOR.] Shall we run through it now?

LEADING ACTOR   Yes right . . . Shall we take it from my entrance? [*He goes to his position behind the door upstage.*]

PRODUCER [*To the* LEADING ACTRESS.]   Now then, listen, imagine the scene between you and Mme. Pace is finished. I'll write it up myself properly later on. You ought to be over here I think—[*She goes the opposite way.*] Where are you going now?

LEADING ACTRESS   Just a minute, I want to get my hat—[*She crosses to take her hat from the stand.*]

PRODUCER   Right, good, ready now? You are standing here with your head down.

STEPDAUGHTER [*Very amused.*]   But she's not dressed in black!

LEADING ACTRESS   Oh, but I shall be, and I'll look a lot better than you do, darling.

PRODUCER [*To the* STEPDAUGHTER.]   Shut up, will you! Go over there and watch! You might learn something! [*Clapping his hands.*] Right! Come on! Quiet please! Take it from his entrance.

> [*He climbs off stage so that he can see better. The door opens at the back of the set and the* LEADING ACTOR *enters with the lively, knowing air of an ageing roué.[3] The playing of the following scene by the* ACTORS *must seem from the very beginning to be something quite different from the earlier scene, but without having the faintest air of parody in it.*
>
> Naturally the STEPDAUGHTER *and the* FATHER *unable to see themselves in the* LEADING ACTOR *and* LEADING ACTRESS, *hearing their words said by them, express their reactions in different ways, by gestures, or smiles or obvious protests so that we are aware of their suffering, their astonishment, their disbelief.*
>
> The PROMPTER's *voice is heard clearly between every line in the scene, telling the* ACTORS *what to say next.*]

LEADING ACTOR   Good afternoon, my dear.

FATHER [*Immediately, unable to restrain himself.*]   Oh, no!

> [*The* STEPDAUGHTER, *watching the* LEADING ACTOR *enter this way, bursts into laughter.*]

---

3. Dissipated lover.

PRODUCER [*Furious.*]   Shut up, for God's sake! And don't you dare laugh like that! We're never going to get anywhere at this rate.

STEPDAUGHTER [*Coming to the front.*]   I'm sorry, I can't help it! The lady stands exactly where you told her to stand and she never moved. But if it were me and I heard someone say good afternoon to me in that way and with a voice like that I should burst out laughing—so I did.

FATHER [*Coming down a little too.*]   Yes, she's right, the whole manner, the voice . . .

PRODUCER   To hell with the manner and the voice! Get out of the way, will you, and let me watch the rehearsal!

LEADING ACTOR [*Coming down stage.*]   If I have to play an old man who has come to a knocking shop—

PRODUCER   Take no notice, ignore them. Go on please! It's going well, it's going well! [*He waits for the* ACTOR *to begin again.*] Right, again!

LEADING ACTOR   Good afternoon, my dear.

LEADING ACTRESS   Good afternoon.

LEADING ACTOR [*Copying the gestures of the* FATHER, *looking under the brim of the hat, but expressing distinctly the two emotions, first, complacent satisfaction and then anxiety.*]   Ah! But tell me . . . this won't be the first time I hope.

FATHER [*Instinctively correcting him.*]   Not "I hope"—"will it," "will it."

PRODUCER   Say "will it"—and it's a question.

LEADING ACTOR [*Glaring at the* PROMPTER.]   I distinctly heard him say "I hope."

PRODUCER   So what? It's all the same, "I hope" or "isn't it." It doesn't make any difference. Carry on, carry on. But perhaps it should still be a little bit lighter; I'll show you—watch me! [*He climbs up on the stage again, and going back to the entrance, he does it himself.*] Good afternoon, my dear.

LEADING ACTRESS   Good afternoon.

PRODUCER   Ah, tell me . . . [*He turns to the* LEADING ACTOR *to make sure that he has seen the way he has demonstrated of looking under the brim of the hat.*] You see—surprise . . . anxiety and self-satisfaction. [*Then, starting again, he turns to the* LEADING ACTRESS.] This won't be the first time, will it? The first time you've been here? [*Again turns to the* LEADING ACTOR *questioningly.*] Right? [*To the* LEADING ACTRESS.] And then she says, "No, sir." [*Again to* LEADING ACTOR.] See what I mean? More subtlety. [*And he climbs off the stage.*]

LEADING ACTRESS   No, sir.

LEADING ACTOR   You've been here before? More than once?

PRODUCER   No, no, no! Wait for it, wait for it. Let her answer first. "You've been here before?"

> [*The* LEADING ACTRESS *lifts her head a little, her eyes closed in pain and disgust, and when the* PRODUCER *says "Now" she nods her head twice.*]

STEPDAUGHTER [*Involuntarily.*]   Oh, my God! [*And she immediately claps her hand over her mouth to stifle her laughter.*]

PRODUCER   What now?

STEPDAUGHTER [*Quickly.*]   Nothing, nothing!

PRODUCER [*To* LEADING ACTOR.]   Come on, then, now it's you.

LEADING ACTOR   More than once? Well then, it shouldn't be too . . . May I take off your hat?

[*The* LEADING ACTOR *says this last line in such a way and adds to it such a gesture that the* STEPDAUGHTER, *even with her hand over her mouth trying to stop herself laughing, can't prevent a noisy burst of laughter.*]

LEADING ACTRESS [*Indignantly turning.*] I'm not staying any longer to be laughed at by that woman!

LEADING ACTOR Nor am I! That's the end—no more!

PRODUCER [*To* STEPDAUGHTER, *shouting.*] Once and for all, will you shut up! Shut up!

STEPDAUGHTER Yes, I'm sorry . . . I'm sorry.

PRODUCER You're an ill-mannered little bitch! That's what you are! And you've gone too far this time!

FATHER [*Trying to interrupt.*] Yes, you're right, she went too far, but please forgive her . . .

PRODUCER [*Jumping on the stage.*] Why should I forgive her? Her behaviour is intolerable!

FATHER Yes, it is, but the scene made such a peculiar impact on us . . .

PRODUCER Peculiar? What do you mean peculiar? Why peculiar?

FATHER I'm full of admiration for your actors, for this gentleman [*To the* LEADING ACTOR.] and this lady. [*To the* LEADING ACTRESS.] But, you see, well . . . they're not us!

PRODUCER Right! They're not! They're actors!

FATHER That's just the point—they're actors. And they are acting our parts very well, both of them. But that's what's different. However much they want to be the same as us, they're not.

PRODUCER But why aren't they? What is it now?

FATHER It's something to do with . . . being themselves, I suppose, not being us.

PRODUCER Well we can't do anything about that! I've told you already. You can't play the parts yourselves.

FATHER Yes, I know, I know . . .

PRODUCER Right then. That's enough of that. [*Turning back to the* ACTORS.] We'll rehearse this later on our own, as we usually do. It's always a bad idea to have rehearsals with authors there! They're never satisfied. [*Turns back to the* FATHER *and the* STEPDAUGHTER.] Come on, let's get on with it; and let's see if it's possible to do it without laughing.

STEPDAUGHTER I won't laugh any more, I won't really. My best bit's coming up now, you wait and see!

PRODUCER Right: when you say "Don't think any more about what I told you, please. And I should do the same." [*Turning to the* FATHER.] Then you come in immediately with the line "I understand, ah yes, I understand" and then you ask . . .

STEPDAUGHTER [*Interrupting.*] Ask what? What does he ask?

PRODUCER Why you're in mourning.

STEPDAUGHTER No! No! That's not right! Look: when I said that I should try not to think about the way I was dressed, do you know what he said? "Well then, let's take it off, we'll take it off at once, shall we, your little black dress."

PRODUCER   That's great! That'll be wonderful! That'll bring the house down!

STEPDAUGHTER   But it's the truth!

PRODUCER   The truth! Do me a favour will you? This is the theatre you know! Truth's all very well up to a point but . . .

STEPDAUGHTER   What do you want to do then?

PRODUCER   You'll see! You'll see! Leave it all to me.

STEPDAUGHTER   No. No I won't. I know what you want to do! Out of my feeling of revulsion, out of all the vile and sordid reasons why I am what I am, you want to make a sugary little sentimental romance. You want him to ask me why I'm in mourning and you want me to reply with the tears running down my face that it is only two months since my father died. No. No. I won't have it! He must say to me what he really did say. "Well then, let's take it off, we'll take it off at once, shall we, your little black dress." And I, with my heart still grieving for my father's death only two months before, I went behind there, do you see? Behind that screen and with my fingers trembling with shame and loathing I took off the dress, unfastened my bra . . .

PRODUCER [His head in his hands.]   For God's sake! What are you saying!

STEPDAUGHTER [Shouting excitedly.]   The truth! I'm telling you the truth!

PRODUCER   All right then. Now listen to me. I'm not denying it's the truth. Right. And believe me I understand your horror, but you must see that we can't really put a scene like that on the stage.

STEPDAUGHTER   You can't? Then thanks very much. I'm not stopping here.

PRODUCER   No, listen . . .

STEPDAUGHTER   No, I'm going. I'm not stopping. The pair of you have worked it all out together, haven't you, what to put in the scene. Well, thank you very much! I understand everything now! He wants to get to the scene where he can talk about his spiritual torments but I want to show you my drama! Mine!

PRODUCER [Shaking with anger.]   Now we're getting to the real truth of it, aren't we? Your drama—yours! But it's not only yours, you know. It's drama for the other people as well! For him [Pointing to the FATHER.] and for your mother! You can't have one character coming on like you're doing, trampling over the others, taking over the play. Everything needs to be balanced and in harmony so that we can show what has to be shown! I know perfectly well that we've all got a life inside us and that we all want to parade it in front of other people. But that's the difficulty, how to present only the bits that are necessary in relation to the other characters: and in the small amount we show, to hint at all the rest of the inner life of the character! I agree, it would be so much simpler, if each character, in a soliloquy or in a lecture could pour out to the audience what's bubbling away inside him. But that's not the way we work. [In an indulgent, placating tone.] You must restrain yourself, you see. And believe me, it's in your own interests: because you could so easily make a bad impression, with all this uncontrollable anger, this disgust and exasperation. That seems a bit odd, if you don't mind my saying so, when you've admitted that you'd been with other men at Mme. Pace's and more than once.

STEPDAUGHTER I suppose that's true. But you know, all the other men were all him as far as I was concerned.

PRODUCER [*Not understanding*.] Uum—? What? What are you talking about?

STEPDAUGHTER If someone falls into evil ways, isn't the responsibility for all the evil which follows to be laid at the door of the person who caused the first mistake? And in my case, it's him, from before I was even born. Look at him: see if it isn't true.

PRODUCER Right then! What about the weight of remorse he's carrying? Isn't that important? Then, give him the chance to show it to us.

STEPDAUGHTER But how? How on earth can he show all his long-suffering remorse, all his moral torments as he calls them, if you don't let him show his horror when he finds me in his arms one fine day, after he had asked me to take my dress off, a black dress for my father who had just died: and he finds that I'm the child he used to go and watch as she came out of school, me, a woman now, and a woman he could buy. [*She says these last words in a voice trembling with emotion*.]

   [*The* MOTHER, *hearing her say this, is overcome and at first gives way to stifled sobs: but then she bursts out into uncontrollable crying. Everyone is deeply moved. There is a long pause*.]

STEPDAUGHTER [*As soon as the* MOTHER *has quietened herself she goes on, firmly and thoughtfully*.] At the moment we are here on our own and the public doesn't know about us. But tomorrow you will present us and our story in whatever way you choose, I suppose. But wouldn't you like to see the real drama? Wouldn't you like to see it explode into life, as it really did?

PRODUCER Of course, nothing I'd like better, then I can use as much of it as possible.

STEPDAUGHTER Then persuade my mother to leave.

MOTHER [*Rising and her quiet weeping changing to a loud cry*.] No! No! Don't let her! Don't let her do it!

PRODUCER But they're only doing it for me to watch—only for me, do you see?

MOTHER I can't bear it, I can't bear it!

PRODUCER But if it's already happened, I can't see what's the objection.

MOTHER No! It's happening now, as well: it's happening all the time. I'm not acting my suffering! Can't you understand that? I'm alive and here now but I can never forget that terrible moment of agony, that repeats itself endlessly and vividly in my mind. And these two little children here, you've never heard them speak have you? That's because they don't speak any more, not now. They just cling to me all the time: they help to keep my grief alive, but they don't really exist for themselves any more, not for themselves. And she [*Indicating the* STEPDAUGHTER.] . . . she has gone away, left me completely, she's lost to me, lost . . . you see her here for one reason only: to keep perpetually before me, always real, the anguish and the torment I've suffered on her account.

FATHER The eternal moment, as I told you, sir. She is here [*Indicating the* STEPDAUGHTER.] to keep me too in that moment, trapped for all eternity, chained and suspended in that one fleeting shameful moment of my life. She can't give up her role and you cannot rescue me from it.

PRODUCER   But I'm not saying that we won't present that bit. Not at all! It will be the climax of the first act, when she [*He points to the* MOTHER.] surprises you.

FATHER   That's right, because that is the moment when I am sentenced: all our suffering should reach a climax in her cry. [*Again indicating the* MOTHER.]

STEPDAUGHTER   I can still hear it ringing in my ears! It was that cry that sent me mad! You can have me played just as you like: it doesn't matter! Dressed, too, if you want, so long as I can have at least an arm—only an arm—bare, because, you see, as I was standing like this [*She moves across to the* FATHER *and leans her head on his chest.*] with my head like this and my arms round his neck, I saw a vein, here in my arm, throbbing: and then it was almost as if that throbbing vein filled me with a shivering fear, and I shut my eyes tightly like this, like this and buried my head in his chest. [*Turning to the* MOTHER.] Scream, Mummy, scream. [*She buries her head in the* FATHER's *chest, and with her shoulders raised as if to try not to hear the scream, she speaks with a voice tense with suffering.*] Scream, as you screamed then!

MOTHER   [*Coming forward to pull them apart.*]   No! She's my daughter! My daughter! [*Tearing her from him.*] You brute, you animal, she's my daughter! Can't you see she's my daughter?

PRODUCER   [*Retreating as far as the footlights while the* ACTORS *are full of dismay.*]   Marvellous! Yes, that's great! And then curtain, curtain!

FATHER   [*Running downstage to him, excitedly.*]   That's it, that's it! Because it really was like that!

PRODUCER   [*Full of admiration and enthusiasm.*]   Yes, yes, that's got to be the curtain line! Curtain! Curtain!

[*At the repeated calls of the* PRODUCER, *the* STAGE MANAGER *lowers the curtain, leaving on the apron in front, the* PRODUCER *and the* FATHER.]

PRODUCER   [*Looking up to heaven with his arms raised.*]   The idiots! I didn't mean now! The bloody idiots—dropping it in on us like that! [*To the* FATHER, *and lifting up a corner of the curtain.*] That's marvellous! Really marvellous! A terrific effect! We'll end the act like that! It's the best tag line I've heard for ages. What a First Act ending! I couldn't have done better if I'd written it myself!

[*They go through the curtain together.*]

Act 3

When the curtain goes up we see that the STAGE MANAGER *and* STAGE HANDS *have struck the first scene and have set another, a small garden fountain.*

From one side of the stage the ACTORS *come on and from the other the* CHAR-ACTERS. *The* PRODUCER *is standing in the middle of the stage with his hand over his mouth, thinking.*

PRODUCER [*After a short pause, shrugging his shoulders.*]   Well, then: let's get on to the second act! Leave it all to me, and everything will work out properly.

STEPDAUGHTER   This is where we go to live at his house [*Pointing to the* FATHER.] In spite of the objections of him over there. [*Pointing to the* SON.]

PRODUCER [*Getting impatient.*]   All right, all right! But leave it all to me, will you?

STEPDAUGHTER   Provided that you make it clear that he objected!

MOTHER [*From the corner, shaking her head.*]   That doesn't matter. The worse it was for us, the more he suffered from remorse.

PRODUCER [*Impatiently.*]   I know, I know! I'll take it all into account. Don't worry!

MOTHER [*Pleading.*]   To set my mind at rest, sir, please do make sure it's clear that I tried all I could—

STEPDAUGHTER [*Interrupting her scornfully and going on.*]   —to pacify me, to persuade me that this despicable creature wasn't worth making trouble about! [*To the* PRODUCER.] Go on, set her mind at rest, because it's true, she tried very hard. I'm having a whale of a time now! You can see, can't you, that the meeker she was and the more she tried to worm her way into his heart, the more lofty and distant he became! How's that for a dramatic situation!

PRODUCER   Do you think that we can actually begin the Second Act?

STEPDAUGHTER   I won't say another word! But you'll see that it won't be possible to play everything in the garden, like you want to do.

PRODUCER   Why not?

STEPDAUGHTER [*Pointing to the* SON.]   Because to start with, he stays shut up in his room in the house all the time! And then all the scenes for this poor little devil of a boy happen in the house. I've told you once.

PRODUCER   Yes, I know that! But on the other hand we can't put up a notice to tell the audience where the scene is taking place, or change the set three or four times in each Act.

LEADING ACTOR   That's what they used to do in the good old days.

PRODUCER   Yes, when the audience was about as bright as that little girl over there!

LEADING ACTRESS   And it makes it easier to create an illusion.

FATHER [*Leaping up.*]   An illusion? For pity's sake don't talk about illusions! Don't use that word, it's especially hurtful to us!

PRODUCER [*Astonished.*]   And why, for God's sake?

FATHER   It's so hurtful, so cruel! You ought to have realised that!

PRODUCER   What else should we call it? That's what we do here—create an illusion for the audience . . .

LEADING ACTOR   With our performance . . .

PRODUCER   A perfect illusion of reality!

FATHER   Yes, I know that, I understand. But on the other hand, perhaps you don't understand us yet. I'm sorry! But you see, for you and for your actors what goes on here on the stage is, quite rightly, well, it's only a game.

LEADING ACTRESS [*Interrupting indignantly.*]   A game! How dare you! We're not children! What happens here is serious!

FATHER   I'm not saying that it isn't serious. And I mean, really, not just a game but an art, that tries, as you've just said, to create the perfect illusion of reality.

PRODUCER   That's right!

FATHER   Now try to imagine that we, as you see us here, [*He indicates himself and the other* CHARACTERS.] that we have no other reality outside this illusion.

PRODUCER [*Astonished and looking at the* ACTORS *with the same sense of bewilderment as they feel themselves.*]   What the hell are you talking about now?

FATHER [*After a short pause as he looks at them, with a faint smile.*]   Isn't it obvious? What other reality is there for us? What for you is an illusion you create, for us is our only reality. [*Brief pause. He moves towards the* PRODUCER *and goes on.*] But it's not only true for us, it's true for others as well, you know. Just think about it. [*He looks intently into the* PRODUCER's *eyes.*] Do you really know who you are? [*He stands pointing at the* PRODUCER.]

PRODUCER [*A little disturbed but with a half smile.*]   What? Who I am? I am me!

FATHER   What if I told you that that wasn't true: what if I told you that you were me?

PRODUCER   I would tell you that you were mad!

[*The* ACTORS *laugh.*]

FATHER   That's right, laugh! Because everything here is a game! [*To the* PRODUCER.] And yet you object when I say that it is only for a game that the gentleman there [*Pointing to the* LEADING ACTOR.] who is "himself" has to be "me," who, on the contrary, am "myself." You see, I've caught you in a trap.

[*The* ACTORS *start to laugh.*]

PRODUCER   Not again! We've heard all about this a little while ago.

FATHER   No, no. I didn't really want to talk about this. I'd like you to forget about your game. [*Looking at the* LEADING ACTRESS *as if to anticipate what she will say.*] I'm sorry—your artistry! Your art!—that you usually pursue here with your actors; and I am going to ask you again in all seriousness, who are you?

PRODUCER [*Turning with a mixture of amazement and annoyance, to the* ACTORS.]   Of all the bloody nerve! A fellow who claims he is only a character comes and asks me who I am!

FATHER [*With dignity but without annoyance.*]   A character, my dear sir, can always ask a man who he is, because a character really has a life of his own, a life full of his own specific qualities, and because of these he is always "someone." While a man—I'm not speaking about you personally, of course, but man in general—well, he can be an absolute "nobody."

PRODUCER   All right, all right! Well, since you've asked me, I'm the Director, the Producer—I'm in charge! Do you understand?

FATHER [*Half smiling, but gently and politely.*]   I'm only asking to try to find out if you really see yourself now in the same way that you saw yourself, for instance, once upon a time in the past, with all the illusions you had then, with everything inside and outside yourself as it seemed then—and not only seemed, but really was! Well then, look back on those illusions, those ideas that you don't have any more, on all those things that no longer seem the same to you. Don't you feel that not only this stage is falling away from under your feet but so is the earth itself, and that all these realities of today are going to seem tomorrow as if they had been an illusion?

PRODUCER   So? What does that prove?

FATHER   Oh, nothing much. I only want to make you see that if we [*Pointing to himself and the other* CHARACTERS.] have no other reality outside our own illusion, perhaps you ought to distrust your own sense of reality: because whatever is a reality today, whatever you touch and believe in and that seems real for you today, is going to be—like the reality of yesterday—an illusion tomorrow.

PRODUCER   [*Deciding to make fun of him.*]   Very good! So now you're saying that you as well as this play you're going to show me here, are more real than I am?

FATHER   [*Very seriously.*]   There's no doubt about that at all.

PRODUCER   Is that so?

FATHER   I thought you'd realised that from the beginning.

PRODUCER   More real than I am?

FATHER   If your reality can change between today and tomorrow—

PRODUCER   But everybody knows that it can change, don't they? It's always changing! Just like everybody else's!

FATHER   [*Crying out.*]   But ours doesn't change! Do you see? That's the difference! Ours doesn't change, it can't change, it can never be different, never, because it is already determined, like this, for ever, that's what's so terrible! We are an eternal reality. That should make you shudder to come near us.

PRODUCER   [*Jumping up, suddenly struck by an idea, and standing directly in front of the* FATHER.]   Then I should like to know when anyone saw a character step out of his part and make a speech like you've done, proposing things, explaining things. Tell me when, will you? I've never seen it before.

FATHER   You've never seen it because an author usually hides all the difficulties of creating. When the characters are alive, really alive and standing in front of their author, he has only to follow their words, the actions that they suggest to him: and he must want them to be what they want to be: and it's his bad luck if he doesn't do what they want! When a character is born he immediately assumes such an independence even of his own author that everyone can imagine him in scores of situations that his author hadn't even thought of putting him in, and he sometimes acquires a meaning that his author never dreamed of giving him.

PRODUCER   Of course I know all that.

FATHER   Well, then. Why are you surprised by us? Imagine what a disaster it is for a character to be born in the imagination of an author who then refuses to give him life in a written script. Tell me if a character, left like this, suspended, created but without a final life, isn't right to do what we are doing now, here in front of you. We spent such a long time, such a very long time, believe me, urging our author, persuading him, first me, then her, [*Pointing to the* STEPDAUGHTER.] then this poor Mother . . .

STEPDAUGHTER   [*Coming down the stage as if in a dream.*]   It's true, I would go, would go and tempt him, time after time, in his gloomy study just as it was growing dark, when he was sitting quietly in an armchair not even bothering to switch a light on but leaving the shadows to fill the room: the shadows were swarming with us, we had come to tempt him. [*As if she could see herself there in the study and is annoyed by the presence of the* ACTORS.] Go away will you! Leave us alone! Mother there, with that son of hers—me with the little girl—that poor little kid always on his own—and then me with him [*Pointing to the* FATHER.] and then at last, just me, on my own, all on my own, in the shadows. [*She turns quickly as if she wants to cling on to the vision she has of herself, in the shadows.*] Ah, what scenes, what scenes we suggested to him! What a life I could have had! I tempted him more than the others!

FATHER   Oh yes, you did! And it was probably all your fault that he did nothing about it! You were so insistent, you made too many demands.

STEPDAUGHTER   But he wanted me to be like that! [*She comes closer to the* PRODUCER *to speak to him in confidence.*] I think it's more likely that he felt discouraged about the theatre and even despised it because the public only wants to see . . .

PRODUCER   Let's go on, for God's sake, let's go on. Come to the point will you?

STEPDAUGHTER   I'm sorry, but if you ask me, we've got too much happening already, just with our entry into his house. [*Pointing to the* FATHER.] You said that we couldn't put up a notice or change the set every five minutes.

PRODUCER   Right! Of course we can't! We must combine things, group them together in one continuous flowing action: not the way you've been wanting, first of all seeing your little brother come home from school and wander about the house like a lost soul, hiding behind the doors and brooding on some plan or other that would—what did you say it would do?

STEPDAUGHTER   Wither him . . . shrivel him up completely.

PRODUCER   That's good! That's a good expression. And then you "can see it there in his eyes, getting stronger all the time"—isn't that what you said?

STEPDAUGHTER   Yes, that's right. Look at him! [*Pointing to him as he stands next to his* MOTHER.]

PRODUCER   Yes, great! And then, at the same time, you want to show the little girl playing in the garden, all innocence. One in the house and the other in the garden—we can't do it, don't you see that?

STEPDAUGHTER   Yes, playing in the sun, so happy! It's the only pleasure I have left, her happiness, her delight in playing in the garden: away from the misery, the squalor of that sordid flat where all four of us slept and where she slept with me—with me! Just think of it! My vile, contaminated body close to hers, with her little arms wrapped tightly round my neck, so lovingly, so innocently. In the garden, wherever she saw me, she would run and take my hand. She never wanted to show me the big flowers, she would run about looking for the "little weeny" ones, so that she could show them to me; she was so happy, so thrilled! [*As she says this, tortured by the memory, she breaks out into a long desperate cry, dropping her head on her arms that rest on a little table. Everybody is very affected by her. The* PRODUCER *comes to her almost paternally and speaks to her in a soothing voice.*]

PRODUCER   We'll have the garden scene, we'll have it, don't worry: and you'll see, you'll be very pleased with what we do! We'll play all the scenes in the garden! [*He calls out to a* STAGE HAND *by name.*] Hey . . . , let down a few bits of tree, will you? A couple of cypresses will do, in front of the fountain. [*Someone drops in the two cypresses and a* STAGE HAND *secures them with a couple of braces and weights.*]

PRODUCER [*To the* STEPDAUGHTER.]   That'll do for now, won't it? It'll just give us an idea. [*Calling out to a* STAGE HAND *by name again.*] Hey, . . . give me something for the sky will you?

STAGE HAND   What's that?

PRODUCER   Something for the sky! A small cloth to come in behind the fountain. [*A white cloth is dropped from the flies.*] Not white! I asked for a sky! Never mind: leave it! I'll do something with it. [*Calling out.*] Hey lights! Kill everything will you? Give me a bit of moonlight—the blues in the batten and a blue spot on the cloth . . . [*They do.*] That's it! That'll do! [*Now on the scene there is the light he asked for, a mysterious blue light that makes the* ACTORS *speak and move as if in the garden in the evening under a moon. To the* STEP- DAUGHTER.] Look here now: the little boy can come out here in the garden and hide among the trees instead of hiding behind the doors in the house. But it's going to be difficult to find a little girl to play the scene with you where she shows you the flowers. [*Turning to the* LITTLE BOY.] Come on, come on, son, come across here. Let's see what it'll look like. [*But the* (LITTLE) BOY *doesn't move.*] Come on will you, come on. [*Then he pulls him forward and tries to make him hold his head up, but every time it falls down again on his chest.*] There's something very odd about this lad . . . What's wrong with him? My God, he'll have to say something sometime! [*He comes over to him again, puts his hand on his shoulder and pushes him between the trees.*] Come a bit nearer: let's have a look. Can you hide a bit more? That's it. Now pop your head out and look round. [*He moves away to look at the effect and as the* BOY *does what he has been told to do, the* ACTORS *watch impressed and a little disturbed.*] Ahh, that's good, very good . . . [*He turns to the* STEPDAUGHTER.] How about having the little girl, surprised to see him there, run across. Wouldn't that make him say something?

STEPDAUGHTER [*Getting up.*]   It's no use hoping he'll speak, not as long as that creature's there. [*Pointing to the* SON.] You'll have to get him out of the way first.

SON [*Moving determinedly to one of the sets of steps leading off the stage.*]   With pleasure! I'll go now! Nothing will please me better!

PRODUCER [*Stopping him immediately.*]   Hey, no! Where are you going? Hang on!

[*The* MOTHER *gets up, anxious at the idea that he is really going and instinctively raising her arms as if to hold him back, but without moving from where she is.*]

SON [*At the footlights, to the* PRODUCER *who is restraining him there.*]   There's no reason why I should be here! Let me go will you? Let me go!

PRODUCER   What do you mean there's no reason for you to be here?

STEPDAUGHTER [*Calmly, ironically.*]   Don't bother to stop him. He won't go!

FATHER   You have to play that terrible scene in the garden with your mother.

SON [*Quickly, angry and determined.*]   I'm not going to play anything! I've said that all along! [*To the* PRODUCER.] Let me go will you?

STEPDAUGHTER [*Crossing to the* PRODUCER.]   It's all right. Let him go. [*She moves the* PRODUCER's *hand from the* SON. *Then she turns to the* SON *and says.*] Well, go on then! Off you go!

[*The* SON *stays near the steps but as if pulled by some strange force he is quite unable to go down them: then to the astonishment and even the dismay of the* ACTORS, *he moves along the front of the stage towards the other set of steps down into the auditorium: but having got there, he again stays near and doesn't actually go down them. The* STEPDAUGHTER *who has watched him scornfully but very intently, bursts into laughter.*]

STEPDAUGHTER   He can't, you see? He can't! He's got to stay here! He must. He's chained to us for ever! No, I'm the one who goes, when what must happen does happen, and I run away, because I hate him, because I can't bear the sight of him any longer. Do you think it's possible for him to run away? He has to stay here with that wonderful father of his and his mother there. She doesn't think she has any other son but him. [*She turns to the* MOTHER.] Come on, come on, Mummy, come on! [*Turning back to the* PRODUCER *to point her out to him.*] Look, she's going to try to stop him . . . [*To the* MOTHER, *half compelling her, as if by some magic power.*] Come on, come on. [*Then to the* PRODUCER *again.*] Imagine how she must feel at showing her affection for him in front of your actors! But her longing to be near him is so strong that—look! She's going to go through that scene with him again! [*The* MOTHER *has now actually come close to the* SON *as the* STEPDAUGHTER *says the last line: she gestures to show that she agrees to go on.*]

SON [*Quickly.*]   But I'm not! I'm not! If I can't get away then I suppose I shall have to stay here; but I repeat that I will not have any part in it.

FATHER [*To the* PRODUCER, *excitedly.*]   You must make him!

SON   Nobody's going to make me do anything!

FATHER   I'll make you!

STEPDAUGHTER   Wait! Just a minute! Before that, the little girl has to go to the fountain. [*She turns to take the* LITTLE GIRL, *drops on her knees in front of her and takes her face between her hands.*]   My poor little darling, those beautiful eyes, they look so bewildered. You're wondering where you are, aren't you? Well, we're on a stage, my darling! What's a stage? Well, it's a place where you pretend to be serious. They put on plays here. And now we're going to put on a play. Seriously! Oh, yes! Even you . . . [*She hugs her tightly and rocks her gently for a moment.*] Oh, my little one, my little darling, what a terrible play it is for you! What horrible things have been planned for you! The garden, the fountain . . . Oh, yes, it's only a pretend fountain, that's right. That's part of the game, my pretty darling: everything is pretends here. Perhaps you'll like a pretends fountain better than a real one: you can play here then. But it's only a game for the others; not for you, I'm afraid, it's real for you, my darling, and your game is in a real fountain, a big beautiful green fountain with bamboos casting shadows, looking at your own reflection, with lots of baby ducks paddling about, shattering the reflections. You want to stroke one! [*With a scream that electrifies and terrifies everybody.*] No, Rosetta, no! Your mummy isn't watching you, she's over there with that self-ish bastard! Oh, God, I feel as if all the devils in hell were tearing me apart inside . . . And you . . . [*Leaving the* LITTLE GIRL *and turning to the* LITTLE BOY *in the usual way.*] What are you doing here, hanging about like a beggar? It'll be your fault too, if that little girl drowns; you're always like this, as if I wasn't paying the price for getting all of you into this house. [*Shaking his arm to make him take his hand out of his pocket.*] What have you got there? What are you hiding? Take it out, take your hand out! [*She drags his hand out of his pocket and to everyone's horror he is holding a revolver. She looks at him for a moment, almost with satisfaction: then she says, grimly.*] Where on earth did you get that? [*The* (LITTLE) BOY, *looking frightened, with his eyes wide and empty, doesn't answer.*] You idiot, if I'd been you, instead of killing myself, I'd have killed one of those two: either or both, the father and the son. [*She pushes him toward the cypress trees where he then stands watching: then she takes the* LITTLE GIRL *and helps her to climb in to the fountain, making her lie so that she is hidden: after that she kneels down and puts her head and arms on the rim of the fountain.*]

PRODUCER   That's good! It's good! [*Turning to the* STEPDAUGHTER.] And at the same time . . .

SON [*Scornfully.*]   What do you mean, at the same time? There was nothing at the same time! There wasn't any scene between her and me. [*Pointing to the* MOTHER.] She'll tell you the same thing herself, she'll tell you what happened.

[*The* SECOND ACTRESS *and the* JUVENILE LEAD *have left the group of* ACTORS *and have come to stand nearer the* MOTHER *and the* SON *as if to study them so as to play their parts.*]

MOTHER   Yes, it's true. I'd gone to his room . . .

SON   Room, do you hear? Not the garden!

PRODUCER   It's not important! We've got to reorganize the events anyway. I've told you that already.

SON [*Glaring at the* JUVENILE LEAD *and the* SECOND ACTRESS.]   What do you want?

JUVENILE LEAD   Nothing. I'm just watching.

SON [*Turning to the* SECOND ACTRESS]   You as well! Getting ready to play her part are you? [*Pointing to the* MOTHER.]

PRODUCER   That's it. And I think you should be grateful—they're paying you a lot of attention.

SON   Oh, yes, thank you! But haven't you realised yet that you'll never be able to do this play? There's nothing of us inside you and you actors are only looking at us from the outside. Do you think we could go on living with a mirror held up in front of us that didn't only freeze our reflection for ever, but froze us in a reflection that laughed back at us with an expression that we didn't even recognize as our own?

FATHER   That's right! That's right!

PRODUCER [*To* JUVENILE LEAD *and* SECOND ACTRESS.]   Okay. Go back to the others.

SON   It's quite useless. I'm not prepared to do anything.

PRODUCER Oh, shut up, will you, and let me listen to your mother. [*To the MOTHER.*] Well, you'd gone to his room, you said.

MOTHER Yes, to his room. I couldn't bear it any longer. I wanted to empty my heart to him, tell him about all the agony that was crushing me. But as soon as he saw me come in . . .

SON Nothing happened. I got away! I wasn't going to get involved. I never have been involved. Do you understand?

MOTHER It's true! That's right!

PRODUCER But we must make up the scene between you, then. It's vital!

MOTHER I'm ready to do it! If only I had the chance to talk to him for a moment, to pour out all my troubles to him.

FATHER [*Going to the SON and speaking violently.*] You'll do it! For your Mother! For your Mother!

SON [*More than ever determined.*] I'm doing nothing!

FATHER [*Taking hold of his coat collar and shaking him.*] For God's sake, do as I tell you! Do as I tell you! Do you hear what she's saying? Haven't you any feelings for her?

SON [*Taking hold of his FATHER.*] No I haven't! I haven't! Let that be the end of it!

[*There is a general uproar. The MOTHER frightened out of her wits, tries to get between them and separate them.*]

MOTHER Please stop it! Please!

FATHER [*Hanging on*] Do as I tell you! Do as I tell you!

SON [*Wrestling with him and finally throwing him to the ground near the steps. Everyone is horrified.*] What's come over you? Why are you so frantic? Do you want to parade our disgrace in front of everybody? Well, I'm having nothing to do with it! Nothing! And I'm doing what our author wanted as well—he never wanted to put us on the stage.

PRODUCER Then why the hell did you come here?

SON [*Pointing to the FATHER.*] He wanted to, I didn't.

PRODUCER But you're here now, aren't you?

SON He was the one who wanted to come and he dragged all of us here with him and agreed with you in there about what to put in the play; and that meant not only what had really happened, as if that wasn't bad enough, but what hadn't happened as well.

PRODUCER All right, then, you tell me what happened. You tell me! Did you rush out of your room without saying anything?

SON [*After a moment's hesitation.*] Without saying anything. I didn't want to make a scene.

PRODUCER [*Needling him.*] What then? What did you do then?

SON [*He is now the centre of everyone's agonised attention and he crosses the stage.*] Nothing . . . I went across the garden . . . [*He breaks off gloomy and absorbed.*]

PRODUCER [*Urging him to say more, impressed by his reluctance to speak.*] Well? What then? You crossed the garden?

SON [*Exasperated, putting his face into the crook of his arm.*] Why do you want me to talk about it? It's horrible! [*The MOTHER is trembling with stifled sobs and looking towards the fountain.*]

PRODUCER [*Quietly, seeing where she is looking and turning to the* SON *with growing apprehension.*] The little girl?

SON [*Looking straight in front, out to the audience.*] There, in the fountain . . .

FATHER [*On the floor still, pointing with pity at the* MOTHER.] She was trailing after him!

PRODUCER [*To the* son, *anxiously.*] What did you do then?

SON [*Still looking out front and speaking slowly.*] I dashed across. I was going to jump in and pull her out . . . But something else caught my eye: I saw something behind the tree that made my blood run cold: the little boy, he was standing there with a mad look in his eyes: he was standing looking into the fountain at his little sister, floating there, drowned.

[*The* STEPDAUGHTER *is still bent at the fountain hiding the* LITTLE GIRL, *and she sobs pathetically, her sobs sounding like an echo. There is a pause.*]

SON [*Continued.*] I made a move towards him: but then . . .

[*From behind the trees where the* LITTLE BOX *is standing there is the sound of a shot.*]

MOTHER [*With a terrible cry she runs along with the* SON *and all the* ACTORS *in the midst of a great general confusion.*] My son! My son! [*And then from out of the confusion and crying her voice comes out.*] Help! Help me!

PRODUCER [*Amidst the shouting he tries to clear a space whilst the* LITTLE BOX *is carried by his feet and shoulders behind the white skycloth.*] Is he wounded? Really wounded?

[*Everybody except the* PRODUCER *and the* FATHER *who is still on the floor by the steps, has gone behind the skycloth and stays there talking anxiously. Then independently the* ACTORS *start to come back into view.*]

LEADING ACTRESS [*Coming from the right, very upset.*] He's dead! The poor boy! He's dead! What a terrible thing!

LEADING ACTOR [*Coming back from the left and smiling.*] What do you mean, dead? It's all make-believe. It's a sham! He's not dead. Don't you believe it!

OTHER ACTORS FROM THE RIGHT Make-believe? It's real! Real! He's dead!

OTHER ACTORS FROM THE LEFT No, he isn't. He's pretending! It's all make-believe.

FATHER [*Running off and shouting at them as he goes.*] What do you mean, make-believe? It's real! It's real, ladies and gentlemen! It's reality! [*And with desperation on his face he too goes behind the skycloth.*]

PRODUCER [*Not caring any more.*] Make-believe?! Reality?! Oh, go to hell the lot of you! Lights! Lights! Lights!

[*At once all the stage and auditorium is flooded with light. The* PRODUCER *heaves a sigh of relief as if he has been relieved of a terrible weight and they all look at each other in distress and with uncertainty.*]

PRODUCER God! I've never known anything like this! And we've lost a whole day's work! [*He looks at the clock.*] Get off with you, all of you! We can't do anything now! It's too late to start a rehearsal. [*When the* ACTORS *have gone, he calls out.*] Hey, lights! Kill everything! [*As soon as he has said this, all the lights go out completely and leave him in the pitch dark.*] For God's sake!! You might have left the workers![4] I can't see where I'm going!

4. Working lights.

VIRGINIA WOOLF
1882–1941

Virginia Woolf was one of the great modern novelists, on par with James Joyce, Marcel Proust, and Thomas Mann. Woolf is known for her precise evocations of states of mind—or of mind and body, since she refused to separate the two. She was an ardent feminist who explored—directly in her essays and indirectly in her novels and short stories—the situation of women in society, the construction of gender identity, and the predicament of the woman writer.

Born Adeline Virginia Stephen on January 25, 1882, she was one of the four children of the eminent Victorian editor and historian Leslie Stephen and his wife, Julia, both of whom also had children from earlier marriages. The family actively pursued intellectual and artistic interests, and Julia was admired and sketched by some of the most famous Pre-Raphaelite artists. Following the customs of the day, only the sons, Adrian and Thoby, were sent to boarding school and university; Virginia and her sister, Vanessa (the painter Vanessa Bell), were instructed at home by their parents and depended for further education on their father's immense library. Woolf bitterly resented this unequal treatment and the systematic discouragement of women's intellectual development that it implied.

After her mother's death in 1895, Woolf was expected to take over the supervision of the household, which she did until her father's death in 1904.

[Suddenly, behind the skycloth, as if because of a bad connection, a green light comes up to throw on the cloth a huge sharp shadow of the CHARAC-TERS, but without the LITTLE BOY and the LITTLE GIRL. The PRODUCER, seeing this, jumps off the stage, terrified. At the same time the flood of light on them is switched off and the stage is again bathed in the same blue light as before. Slowly the SON comes on from the right, followed by the MOTHER with her arms raised towards him. Then from the left, the FATHER enters.
They come together in the middle of the stage and stand there as if trans-fixed. Finally from the left the STEPDAUGHTER comes on and moves towards the steps at the front: on the top step she pauses for a moment to look back at the other three and then bursts out in a raucous laugh, dashes down the steps and turns to look at the three figures still on the stage. Then she runs out of the auditorium and we can still hear her manic laughter out into the foyer and beyond.
After a pause the curtain falls slowly.]

1921

She worried that women in literary families like hers were expected to write memoirs of their fathers or to edit their correspondence. Woolf did in fact write a memoir of her father, but she later noted that if he had not died when she was relatively young, she never would have become an author. Of fragile physical health after an attack of whooping cough when she was six, Woolf suffered psychological breakdowns after the death of each parent and was frequently hospitalized, especially after a number of suicide attempts. During her lifetime Woolf consulted at least twelve doctors and, consequently, experienced first-hand the developments in medicine for treating the mentally ill, from the Victorian era to the shell shock of the First World War.

Woolf moved to central London with her sister and brother Adrian after their father's death and took a house in the Bloomsbury district. It was a time of shifting social and cultural mores, of which Woolf later claimed: "on or about December, 1910, human character changed." She and her sister, though unmarried, lived with several men (some of them openly homosexual), challenging the social conventions that respectable unmarried women were expected to follow. She and her friends soon became the focus of what was later called the Bloomsbury Group, a gathering of writers, artists, and intellectuals impatient with conservative Edwardian society who met regularly to discuss ideas and to promote a freer view of culture. It was an eclectic group and included the novelist E. M. Forster, the historian Lytton Strachey, the economist John Maynard Keynes, and the art critics Clive Bell (who married Vanessa) and Roger Fry (who introduced the group to the work of French painters Édouard Manet and Paul Cézanne).

Woolf was not yet writing fiction but contributed reviews to the *Times Literary Supplement*, taught literature and composition at Morley College (an institution with a volunteer faculty that pro-vided educational opportunities for workers), and participated in the adult suffrage movement and a feminist group. In 1912 she married Leonard Woolf, who encouraged her to write and with whom she founded the Hogarth Press in 1917. One of the most respected of the small literary presses, it published works by such major authors as T. S. Eliot, Katherine Mansfield, Strachey, Forster, Maxim Gorky, and John Middleton Murry, as well as Woolf's own novels and translations of Sigmund Freud's most significant output. Over the next two decades she produced her best-known work while coping with frequent bouts of physical and mental illness. Already depressed during World War II and exhausted after the completion of her final novel, *Between the Acts* (1941), Woolf sensed the approach of a serious attack of psychosis and the confinement it would entail: in such situations, she was obliged to "rest" and forbidden to read or write. In March 1941 she drowned herself in a river close to her Sussex home.

Woolf is admired for her poetic evocations of the way we think and feel. Like Proust and Joyce, she brings to life the concrete, sensuous details of everyday experience; like them, she explores the structures of consciousness. Championing modern fiction as an alternative to the realism of the preceding generation, she proposed a more subjective and, therefore, more accurate account of experience. Her focus was not so much on the object under observation as on the observers' perception of it: "Let us record the atoms as they fall upon the mind in the order in which they fall, let us trace the pattern, however disconnected and incoherent in appearance, which sight or incident scores upon the consciousness." Such writing, undertaken with a woman's creative vision, would open avenues for literature. Although she was dismayed by what she saw as Joyce's vulgarity, she recognized him as one of the few living writers who achieved the successful rendering of stream of consciousness.

Woolf's writing has been compared with modern painting in its emphasis on the abstract arrangement of perspectives to suggest networks of meaning. After two relatively traditional novels, she developed a more flexible approach that manipulated fictional structure. The unfolding plot gave way to an organization by juxtaposed points of view; the experience of "real," or chronological, time was partially displaced by a mind ranging ambiguously among its memories; and an intricate pattern of symbolic themes connected otherwise unrelated characters. These techniques made unfamiliar demands on the reader's ability to synthesize and re-create a complete picture. In *Jacob's Room* (1922), an understanding of the hero must be assembled from a series of partial points of view. In *The Waves* (1931), the multiple perspectives of several characters soliloquizing on their relationship to the dead Percival are broken by ten interludes that together construct an additional, interacting perspective as they describe the passage of a single day from dawn to dusk. Woolf's novels may expand or telescope the passage of time: *Mrs. Dalloway* (1925) seems to focus on Clarissa Dalloway's preparations for a party that evening, but at the same time calls up—at different times, and according to different contexts—her entire life, from childhood to her present age of fifty. Woolf also concerned herself with the question of women's equality with men in marriage, and she brilliantly evoked the inequality in her parents' marriage in her novel *To the Lighthouse* (1927).

A ROOM OF ONE'S OWN

One of Woolf's major themes is society's different attitudes toward men and toward women. The work presented here, *A Room of One's Own*

(1929), examines the history of literature written by women and offers an impassioned plea that women writers be given conditions equal to those available for men: specifically, the privacy of a room in which to write and economic independence. (At the time Woolf wrote, it was unusual for women to have money of their own or to be able to devote themselves to a career.) *A Room of One's Own* does not conform to any fixed form. At once lecture and essay, autobiography and fiction, it originated in a pair of lectures on women and fiction that the author gave at Newnham and Girton Colleges (for women) at Cambridge University in 1928. Woolf warns her audience that, instead of defining either women or fiction, she will use "all the liberties and licenses of a novelist" to approach the matter obliquely and leave her auditors to sort out the truth from the "lies [that] will flow from my lips." She will, she claims, retrace the days (that is, the narrator's days) preceding her visit, and lay bare the thought processes leading up to the lecture itself.

The lecture (or, in its written form, Chapter 1), continues as a meditative ramble through various parts of Oxbridge (an informal verbal linking of *Oxford* and *Cambridge* universities) and London. It includes the famous, and apparently true, anecdote in which Woolf is warned off the university lawn and forbidden entrance to the library because she is a woman, as well as a vivid description of the differences between the food and the living quarters for women and those for men at Oxbridge. By the end of her visit, frustrated, furious, and puzzled, she decides that the subject needs research—and London's British Museum, at least, is open to all.

In Chapter 2 the narrator heads for the British Museum to locate a comprehensive definition of femininity. To her surprise and mounting anger, she discovers that the thousands of books on the subject written by men all define women as inferior animals, useful but somewhat alien in nature. Moreover, those very definitions have become prescriptions for generations of young women who learn to see themselves and their place in life accordingly. Raised in poverty and dependence, such women have neither the material means nor the self-confidence to write seriously or to become anything other than the Victorian "Angel of the House." What they require, asserts the narrator, is the self-sufficiency brought by an annual income of five hundred pounds. (Woolf had recently inherited such a sum.)

Chapter 3 pursues similar themes, adding to the five hundred pounds the need for "a room of one's own" and the privacy necessary to follow out an idea. Moving to history, and focusing on the Elizabethan Age, after a discouraging inspection of the well-known *History of England*, by George Macaulay Trevelyan (1876–1962), Woolf evokes the career of the "terribly gifted" Judith Shakespeare, William's imaginary sister (his actual sister was named Joan). Judith has the same literary and dramatic ambitions as her brother, and she too finds her way to London, but she is blocked at each turn by her identity as a woman. Woolf does not belittle William Shakespeare with this con-trast; instead, her narrator remarks meaningfully that his work reveals an "incandescent, unimpeded mind."

The bleak portrayals in these chapters are lightened by satirical wit and humor, often conveyed by calculated historical distortion. Woolf uses her novelist's license to subvert and criticize the patriarchal message she describes. The Reading Room of the British Museum, august repository of masculine knowledge about women, is seen as a (bald-foreheaded) dome crowned with the names of famous men. The narrator's scholarly-seeming list of feminine characteristics is not only amusingly biased but contradictory and incoherent; it implies that the "masculine" passion for lists and documentation is not the best way to learn about human nature. Professor von X.'s portrait is an open caricature linked to suggestions that his scientific disdain hides repressed fear and anger. *A Room of One's Own* is still famous for its vivid, scathing, and occasionally humorous portrayal of women as objects of male definition and disapproval. Its model of a feminine literary history and its hypothesis of a separate feminine consciousness and manner of writing had substantial influence on writers and literary theory in the latter half of the twentieth century.

From *A Room of One's Own*[1]

CHAPTER I

But, you may say, we asked you to speak about women and fiction—what has that got to do with a room of one's own? I will try to explain. When you asked me to speak about women and fiction I sat down on the banks of a river and began to wonder what the words meant. They might mean simply a few remarks about Fanny Burney; a few more about Jane Austen; a tribute to the Brontës and a

1. This essay is based upon two papers read to the Arts Society at Newnham and the Odtaa at Girton in October 1928. The papers were too long to be read in full, and have since been altered and expanded [Woolf's note]. Newnham and Girton are women's colleges at Cambridge University, and Odtaa ("One damn thing after another") is the acronym of a literary society. Woolf's talk was entitled *Women and Fiction.*

sketch of Haworth Parsonage under snow; some witticisms if possible about Miss Mitford; a respectful allusion to George Eliot; a reference to Mrs. Gaskell[2] and one would have done. But at second sight the words seemed not so simple. The title women and fiction might mean, and you may have meant it to mean, women and what they are like; or it might mean women and the fiction that they write; or it might mean women and the fiction that is written about them; or it might mean that somehow all three are inextricably mixed together and you want me to consider them in that light. But when I began to consider the subject in this last way, which seemed the most interesting, I soon saw that it had one fatal drawback. I should never be able to come to a conclusion. I should never be able to fulfil what is, I understand, the first duty of a lecturer—to hand you after an hour's discourse a nugget of pure truth to wrap up between the pages of your notebooks and keep on the mantelpiece for ever. All I could do was to offer you an opinion upon one minor point—a woman must have money and a room of her own if she is to write fiction; and that, as you will see, leaves the great problem of the true nature of woman and the true nature of fiction unsolved. I have shirked the duty of coming to a conclusion upon these two questions—women and fiction remain, so far as I am concerned, unsolved problems. But in order to make some amends I am going to do what I can to show you how I arrived at this opinion about the room and the money. I am going to develop in your presence as fully and freely as I can the train of thought which led me to think this. Perhaps if I lay bare the ideas, the prejudices, that lie behind this statement you will find that they have some bearing upon women and some upon fiction. At any rate, when a subject is highly controversial—and any question about sex is that—one cannot hope to tell the truth. One can only show how one came to hold whatever opinion one does hold. One can only give one's audience the chance of drawing their own conclusions as they observe the limitations, the prejudices, the idiosyncrasies of the speaker. Fiction here is likely to contain more truth than fact. Therefore I propose, making use of all the liberties and licences of a novelist, to tell you the story of the two days that preceded my coming here—how, bowed down by the weight of the subject which you have laid upon my shoulders, I pondered it, and made it work in and out of my daily life. I need not say that what I am about to describe has no existence; Oxbridge[3] is an invention; so is Fernham; "I" is only a convenient term for somebody who has no real being. Lies will flow from my lips, but there may perhaps be some truth mixed up with them; it is for you to seek out this truth and to decide whether any part of it is worth keeping. If not, you will of course throw the whole of it into the wastepaper basket and forget all about it.

Here then was I (call me Mary Beton, Mary Seton, Mary Carmichael or by any name you please—it is not a matter of any importance) sitting on the banks of a river a week or two ago in fine October weather, lost in thought. That collar

2. English novelist Elizabeth Gaskell (1810–1865) was the author of *Cranford* (1853). British writers: Fanny (Frances) Burney (1752–1840), author of *Evelina* (1778); Jane Austen (1775–1817), author of *Pride and Prejudice* (1813); the three Brontë sisters, who were raised in the Yorkshire parsonage of Haworth—Charlotte (1816–1855), author of *Jane Eyre* (1847); Emily (1818–1848), author of *Wuther-ing Heights* (1847); and Anne (1820–1849), author of *Agnes Grey* (1847); Mary Russell Mit-ford (1787–1855), author of the blank-verse tragedy *Rienzi* (1828); George Eliot (pen name of Mary Ann Evans, 1819–1880), author of *Middlemarch* (1871–72).

3. A fictional university combining the names of Oxford and Cambridge.

I have spoken of, women and fiction, the need of coming to some conclusion on a subject that raises all sorts of prejudices and passions, bowed my head to the ground. To the right and left bushes of some sort, golden and crimson, glowed with the colour, even it seemed burnt with the heat, of fire. On the further bank the willows wept in perpetual lamentation, their hair about their shoulders. The river reflected whatever it chose of sky and bridge and burning tree, and when the undergraduate had oared his boat through the reflections they had closed again, completely, as if he had never been. There one might have sat the clock round lost in thought. Thought—to call it by a prouder name than it deserved—had let its line down into the stream. It swayed, minute after minute, hither and thither among the reflections and the weeds, letting the water lift it and sink it, until—you know the little tug—the sudden conglomeration of an idea at the end of one's line; and then the cautious hauling of it in, and the careful laying of it out? Alas, laid on the grass how small, how insignificant this thought of mine looked; the sort of fish that a good fisherman puts back into the water so that it may grow fatter and be one day worth cooking and eating. I will not trouble you with that thought now, though if you look carefully you may find it for yourselves in the course of what I am going to say.

But however small it was, it had, nevertheless, the mysterious property of its kind—put back into the mind, it became at once very exciting, and important; and as it darted and sank, and flashed hither and thither, set up such a wash and tumult of ideas that it was impossible to sit still. It was thus that I found myself walking with extreme rapidity across a grass plot. Instantly a man's figure rose to intercept me. Nor did I at first understand that the gesticulations of a curious-looking object, in a cut-away coat and evening shirt, were aimed at me. His face expressed horror and indignation. Instinct rather than reason came to my help; he was a Beadle;[4] I was a woman. This was the turf; there was the path. Only the Fellows and Scholars are allowed here; the gravel is the place for me. Such thoughts were the work of a moment. As I regained the path the arms of the Beadle sank, his face assumed its usual repose, and though turf is better walking than gravel, no very great harm was done. The only charge I could bring against the Fellows and Scholars of whatever the college might happen to be was that in protection of their turf, which has been rolled for 300 years in succession, they had sent my little fish into hiding.

What idea it had been that had sent me so audaciously trespassing I could not now remember. The spirit of peace descended like a cloud from heaven, for if the spirit of peace dwells anywhere, it is in the courts and quadrangles of Oxbridge on a fine October morning. Strolling through those colleges past those ancient halls the roughness of the present seemed smoothed away; the body seemed contained in a miraculous glass cabinet through which no sound could penetrate, and the mind, freed from any contact with facts (unless one trespassed on the turf again), was at liberty to settle down upon whatever meditation was in harmony with the moment. As chance would have it, some stray memory of some old essay about revisiting Oxbridge in the long vacation brought Charles Lamb to mind—Saint Charles, said Thackeray,[5] putting a letter of Lamb's to his forehead. Indeed,

---

4. A lower-ranked university officer, assistant to authority.

5. I.e., William Makepeace Thackeray (1811–1863), whose novels include *Vanity Fair* (1847–1848) and *The History of Henry Esmond,* *Esq.* (1852). *Charles Lamb* (1775–1834): English essayist and letter writer, author of *Essays of Elia* (1823), which contains *Oxford in the Vacation,* mentioned in Woolf's text.

among all the dead (I give you my thoughts as they came to me), Lamb is one of the most congenial; one to whom one would have liked to say, Tell me then how you wrote your essays? For his essays are superior even to Max Beerbohm's,[6] I thought, with all their perfection, because of that wild flash of imagination, that lightning crack of genius in the middle of them which leaves them flawed and imperfect, but starred with poetry. Lamb then came to Oxbridge perhaps a hundred years ago. Certainly he wrote an essay—the name escapes me—about the manuscript of one of Milton's poems which he saw here. It was *Lycidas* perhaps, and Lamb wrote how it shocked him to think it possible that any word in *Lycidas* could have been different from what it is. To think of Milton changing the words in that poem seemed to him a sort of sacrilege. This led me to remember what I could of *Lycidas* and to amuse myself with guessing which word it could have been that Milton had altered, and why. It then occurred to me that the very manuscript itself which Lamb had looked at was only a few hundred yards away, so that one could follow Lamb's footsteps across the quadrangle to that famous library[7] where the treasure is kept. Moreover, I recollected, as I put this plan into execution, it is in this famous library that the manuscript of Thackeray's *Esmond* is also preserved. The critics often say that *Esmond* is Thackeray's most perfect novel. But the affectation of the style, with its imitation of the eighteenth century, hampers one, so far as I remember; unless indeed the eighteenth-century style was natural to Thackeray—a fact that one might prove by looking at the manuscript and seeing whether the alterations were for the benefit of the style or of the sense. But then one would have to decide what is style and what is meaning, a question which—but here I was actually at the door which leads into the library itself. I must have opened it, for instantly there issued, like a guardian angel barring the way with a flutter of black gown instead of white wings, a deprecating, silvery, kindly gentleman, who regretted in a low voice as he waved me back that ladies are only admitted to the library if accompanied by a Fellow of the College or furnished with a letter of introduction.

That a famous library has been cursed by a woman is a matter of complete indifference to a famous library. Venerable and calm, with all its treasures safe locked within its breast, it sleeps complacently and will, so far as I am concerned, so sleep for ever. Never will I wake those echoes, never will I ask for that hospitality again, I vowed as I descended the steps in anger. Still an hour remained before luncheon, and what was one to do? Stroll on the meadows? sit by the river? Certainly it was a lovely autumn morning; the leaves were fluttering red to the ground; there was no great hardship in doing either. But the sound of music reached my ear. Some service or celebration was going forward. The organ complained magnificently as I passed the chapel door. Even the sorrow of Christianity sounded in that serene air more like the recollection of sorrow than sorrow itself; even the groanings of the ancient organ seemed lapped in peace. I had no wish to enter had I the right, and this time the verger might have stopped me; demanding perhaps my baptismal certificate, or a letter of introduction from the Dean. But the outside of these magnificent buildings is often as beautiful as the inside. Moreover, it was amusing enough to watch the congregation assembling, coming in and going out again, busying themselves at the door of the chapel like bees at the mouth of a hive.

6. English caricaturist and writer (1872–1956).

7. Trinity College Library, in Cambridge, designed by Sir Christopher Wren and built from 1676 to 1684.

Many were in cap and gown; some had tufts of fur on their shoulders; others were wheeled in bath-chairs; others, though not past middle age, seemed creased and crushed into shapes so singular that one was reminded of those giant crabs and crayfish who heave with difficulty across the sand of an aquarium. As I leant against the wall the University indeed seemed a sanctuary in which are preserved rare types which would soon be obsolete if left to fight for existence on the pavement of the Strand.[8] Old stories of old deans and old dons came back to mind, but before I had summoned up courage to whistle—it used to be said that at the sound of a whistle old Professor —— instantly broke into a gallop—the venerable congregation had gone inside. The outside of the chapel remained. As you know, its high domes and pinnacles can be seen, like a sailing-ship always voyaging never arriving, lit up at night and visible for miles, far away across the hills. Once, presumably, this quadrangle with its smooth lawns, its massive buildings, and the chapel itself was marsh too, where the grasses waved and the swine rooted. Teams of horses and oxen, I thought, must have hauled the stone in wagons from far countries, and then with infinite labour the grey blocks in whose shade I was now standing were poised in order one on top of another, and then the painters brought their glass for the windows, and the masons were busy for centuries[9] up on that roof with putty and cement, spade and trowel. Every Saturday somebody must have poured gold and silver out of a leathern purse into their ancient fists, for they had their beer and skittles presumably of an evening. An unending stream of gold and silver, I thought, must have flowed into this court perpetually to keep the stones coming and the masons working; to level, to ditch, to dig and to drain. But it was then the age of faith, and money was poured liberally to set these stones on a deep foundation, and when the stones were raised, still more money was poured in from the coffers of kings and queens and great nobles to ensure that hymns should be sung here and scholars taught. Lands were granted; tithes were paid. And when the age of faith was over and the age of reason had come, still the same flow of gold and silver went on; fellowships were founded; lectureships endowed; only the gold and silver flowed now, not from the coffers of the king, but from the chests of merchants and manufacturers, from the purses of men who had made, say, a fortune from industry, and returned, in their wills, a bounteous share of it to endow more chairs, more lectureships, more fellowships in the university where they had learnt their craft. Hence the libraries and laboratories; the observatories; the splendid equipment of costly and delicate instruments which now stands on glass shelves, where centuries ago the grasses waved and the swine rooted. Certainly, as I strolled round the court, the foundation of gold and silver seemed deep enough; the pavement laid solidly over the wild grasses. Men with trays on their heads went busily from staircase to staircase. Gaudy blossoms flowered in window-boxes. The strains of the gramophone blared out from the rooms within. It was impossible not to reflect—the reflection whatever it may have been was cut short. The clock struck. It was time to find one's way to luncheon.

It is a curious fact that novelists have a way of making us believe that luncheon parties are invariably memorable for something very witty that was said, or for

8. One of the busiest streets in London, the main artery between the city and the West End.

9. Just over one century; King's College Chapel at Cambridge was built from 1446 to 1547. The college guidebook attributes its superb craftsmanship to the work of four master masons: Reginald Ely, John Wolrich, Simon Clerk, and John Wastell.

something very wise that was done. But they seldom spare a word for what was eaten. It is part of the novelist's convention not to mention soup and salmon and ducklings, as if soup and salmon and ducklings were of no importance whatsoever, as if nobody ever smoked a cigar or drank a glass of wine. Here, however, I shall take the liberty to defy that convention and to tell you that the lunch on this occasion began with soles, sunk in a deep dish, over which the college cook had spread a counterpane of the whitest cream, save that it was branded here and there with brown spots like the spots on the flanks of a doe. After that came the partridges, but if this suggests a couple of bald, brown birds on a plate you are mistaken. The partridges, many and various, came with all their retinue of sauces and salads, the sharp and the sweet, each in its order; their potatoes, thin as coins but not so hard; their sprouts, foliated as rosebuds but more succulent. And no sooner had the roast and its retinue been done with than the silent serving-man, the Beadle himself perhaps in a milder manifestation, set before us, wreathed in napkins, a confection which rose all sugar from the waves. To call it pudding and so relate it to rice and tapioca would be an insult. Meanwhile the wineglasses had flushed yellow and flushed crimson; had been emptied; had been filled. And thus by degrees was lit, halfway down the spine, which is the seat of the soul, not that hard little electric light which we call brilliance, as it pops in and out upon our lips, but the more profound, subtle and subterranean glow, which is the rich yellow flame of rational intercourse. No need to hurry. No need to sparkle. No need to be anybody but oneself. We are all going to heaven and Vandyck[1] is of the company—in other words, how good life seemed, how sweet its rewards, how trivial this grudge or that grievance, how admirable friendship and the society of one's kind, as, lighting a good cigarette, one sunk among the cushions in the window-seat.

If by good luck there had been an ash-tray handy, if one had not knocked the ash out of the window in default, if things had been a little different from what they were, one would not have seen, presumably, a cat without a tail. The sight of that abrupt and truncated animal padding softly across the quadrangle changed by some fluke of the subconscious intelligence the emotional light for me. It was as if some one had let fall a shade. Perhaps the excellent hock was relinquishing its hold. Certainly, as I watched the Manx cat pause in the middle of the lawn as if it too questioned the universe, something seemed lacking, something seemed different. But what was lacking, what was different, I asked myself, listening to the talk. And to answer that question I had to think myself out of the room, back into the past, before the war indeed, and to set before my eyes the model of another luncheon party held in rooms not very far distant from these; but different. Everything was different. Meanwhile the talk went on among the guests, who were many and young, some of this sex, some of that; it went on swimmingly, it went on agreeably, freely, amusingly. And as it went on I set it against the background of that other talk, and as I matched the two together I had no doubt that one was the descendant, the legitimate heir of the other. Nothing was changed; nothing was different save only—here I listened with all my ears not entirely to what was being said, but to the murmur or current behind it. Yes, that was it—the change was there. Before the war at a luncheon party like this people

1. The Flemish portrait painter Sir Anthony Van Dyck (1599–1641), who was appointed court painter by Charles 1 of England in 1632 and painted many portraits of the royal family and the nobility.

would have said precisely the same things but they would have sounded different, because in those days they were accompanied by a sort of humming noise, not articulate, but musical, exciting, which changed the value of the words themselves. Could one set that humming noise to words? Perhaps with the help of the poets one could. A book lay beside me and, opening it, I turned casually enough to Tennyson.[2] And here I found Tennyson was singing:

There has fallen a splendid tear
From the passion-flower at the gate.
She is coming, my dove, my dear;
She is coming, my life, my fate;
The red rose cries, "She is near, she is near";
And the white rose weeps, "She is late";
The larkspur listens, "I hear, I hear";
And the lily whispers, "I wait."

Was that what men hummed at luncheon parties before the war? And the women?

My heart is like a singing bird
Whose nest is in a water'd shoot;
My heart is like an apple tree
Whose boughs are bent with thick-set fruit;
My heart is like a rainbow shell
That paddles in a halcyon sea;
My heart is gladder than all these
Because my love is come to me.[3]

Was that what women hummed at luncheon parties before the war?

There was something so ludicrous in thinking of people humming such things even under their breath at luncheon parties before the war that I burst out laughing, and had to explain my laughter by pointing at the Manx cat, who did look a little absurd, poor beast, without a tail, in the middle of the lawn. Was he really born so, or had he lost his tail in an accident? The tailless cat, though some are said to exist in the Isle of Man, is rarer than one thinks. It is a queer animal, quaint rather than beautiful. It is strange what a difference a tail makes—you know the sort of things one says as a lunch party breaks up and people are finding their coats and hats.

This one, thanks to the hospitality of the host, had lasted far into the afternoon. The beautiful October day was fading and the leaves were falling from the trees in the avenue as I walked through it. Gate after gate seemed to close with gentle finality behind me. Innumerable beadles were fitting innumerable keys into well-oiled locks; the treasure-house was being made secure for another night. After the avenue one comes out upon a road—I forget its name—which leads you, if you take the right turning, along to Fernham. But there was plenty of time. Dinner was not till half-past seven. One could almost do without dinner after such a luncheon. It is strange how a scrap of poetry

2. Alfred, Lord Tennyson (1809–1892); a passage from his long poem *Maud* (1855) follows.

3. The first stanza of "A Birthday," a short poem by Christina Rossetti (1830–1894).

works in the mind and makes the legs move in time to it along the road. Those words—

> *There has fallen a splendid tear*
> *From the passion-flower at the gate.*
> *She is coming, my dove, my dear—*

sang in my blood as I stepped quickly along towards Headingley.⁴ And then, switching off into the other measure, I sang, where the waters are churned up by the weir:

> *My heart is like a singing bird*
> *Whose nest is in a water'd shoot;*
> *My heart is like an apple tree . . .*

What poets, I cried aloud, as one does in the dusk, what poets they were!

In a sort of jealousy, I suppose, for our own age, silly and absurd though these comparisons are, I went on to wonder if honestly one could name two living poets now as great as Tennyson and Christina Rossetti were then. Obviously it is impossible, I thought, looking into those foaming waters, to compare them. The very reason why the poetry excites one to such abandonment, such rapture, is that it celebrates some feeling that one used to have (at luncheon parties before the war perhaps), so that one responds easily, familiarly, without troubling to check the feeling, or to compare it with any that one has now. But the living poets express a feeling that is actually being made and torn out of us at the moment. One does not recognize it in the first place; often one fears it; one watches it with keenness and compares it jealously and suspiciously with the old feeling that one knew. Hence the difficulty of modern poetry; and it is because of this difficulty that one cannot remember more than two consecutive lines of any good modern poet. For this reason—that my memory failed me—the argument flagged for want of material. But why, I continued, moving on towards Headingley, have we stopped humming under our breath at luncheon parties? Why has Alfred ceased to sing

> *She is coming, my dove, my dear?*

Why has Christina ceased to respond

> *My heart is gladder than all these*
> *Because my love is come to me?*

Shall we lay the blame on the war? When the guns fired in August 1914, did the faces of men and women show so plain in each other's eyes that romance was killed? Certainly it was a shock (to women in particular with their illusions about education, and so on) to see the faces of our rulers in the light of the shell-fire. So ugly they looked—German, English, French—so stupid. But lay the blame where one will, on whom one will, the illusion which inspired Tennyson and Christina Rossetti to sing so passionately about the coming of their

4. In Leeds (Yorkshire).

loves is far rarer now than then. One has only to read, to look, to listen, to remember. But why say "blame"? Why, if it was an illusion, not praise the catastrophe, whatever it was, that destroyed illusion and put truth in its place? For truth . . . those dots mark the spot where, in search of truth, I missed the turning up to Fernham. Yes indeed, which was truth and which was illusion, I asked myself. What was the truth about these houses, for example, dim and festive now with their red windows in the dusk, but raw and red and squalid, with their sweets and their boot-laces, at nine o'clock in the morning? And the willows and the river and the gardens that run down to the river, vague now with the mist stealing over them, but gold and red in the sunlight—which was the truth, which was the illusion about them? I spare you the twists and turns of my cogitations, for no conclusion was found on the road to Headingley, and I ask you to suppose that I soon found out my mistake about the turning and retraced my steps to Fernham.

As I have said already that it was an October day, I dare not forfeit your respect and imperil the fair name of fiction by changing the season and describing lilacs hanging over garden walls, crocuses, tulips and other flowers of spring. Fiction must stick to facts, and the truer the facts the better the fiction—so we are told. Therefore it was still autumn and the leaves were still yellow and falling, if anything, a little faster than before, because it was now evening (seven twenty-three to be precise) and a breeze (from the southwest to be exact) had risen. But for all that there was something odd at work:

My heart is like a singing bird
Whose nest is in a water'd shoot;
My heart is like an apple tree
Whose boughs are bent with thick-set fruit—

perhaps the words of Christina Rossetti were partly responsible for the folly of the fancy—it was nothing of course but a fancy—that the lilac was shaking its flowers over the garden walls, and the brimstone butterflies were scudding hither and thither, and the dust of the pollen was in the air. A wind blew, from what quarter I know not, but it lifted the half-grown leaves so that there was a flash of silver grey in the air. It was the time between the lights when colours undergo their intensification and purples and golds burn in window-panes like the beat of an excitable heart; when for some reason the beauty of the world revealed and yet soon to perish (here I pushed into the garden, for, unwisely, the door was left open and no beadles seemed about), the beauty of the world which is so soon to perish, has two edges, one of laughter, one of anguish, cutting the heart asunder. The gardens of Fernham lay before me in the spring twilight, wild and open, and in the long grass, sprinkled and carelessly flung, were daffodils and bluebells, not orderly perhaps at the best of times, and now wind-blown and waving as they tugged at their roots. The windows of the building, curved like ships' windows among generous waves of red brick, changed from lemon to silver under the flight of the quick spring clouds. Somebody was in a hammock, somebody, but in this light they were phantoms only, half guessed, half seen, raced across the grass—would no one stop her?—and then on the terrace, as if popping out to breathe the air, to glance at the garden, came a bent figure, formidable yet humble, with her great forehead and her shabby dress—could it be the famous scholar, could it be J——H——herself?[5] All was dim, yet intense too, as if the scarf which the dusk had flung over the garden were torn asunder by star or sword—the flash of some terrible reality leaping, as its way is, out of the heart of the spring. For youth——

Here was my soup. Dinner was being served in the great dining-hall. Far from being spring it was in fact an evening in October. Everybody was assembled in the big dining-room. Dinner was ready. Here was the soup. It was a plain gravy soup. There was nothing to stir the fancy in that. One could have seen through the transparent liquid any pattern that there might have been on the plate itself. But there was no pattern. The plate was plain. Next came beef with its attendant greens and potatoes—a homely trinity, suggesting the rumps of cattle in a muddy market, and sprouts curled and yellowed at the edge, and bargaining and cheapening, and women with string bags on Monday morning. There was no reason to complain of human nature's daily food, seeing that the supply was sufficient and coal-miners doubtless were sitting down to less. Prunes and custard followed. And if any one complains that prunes, even when mitigated by custard, are an uncharitable vegetable (fruit they are not), stringy as a miser's heart and exuding a fluid such as might run in misers' veins who have denied themselves wine and warmth for eighty years and yet not given to the poor, he should reflect that there are people whose charity embraces even the prune. Biscuits and cheese came next, and here the water-jug was liberally passed round, for it is the nature of biscuits to be dry, and these were biscuits to the core. That was all. The meal was over. Everybody scraped their chairs back; the swing-doors swung violently to and fro; soon the hall was emptied of every sign of food and made ready no doubt for breakfast next morning. Down corridors and up staircases the youth of England went banging and singing. And was it for a guest, a stranger (for I had no more right here in Fernham than in Trinity or Somerville or Girton or Newnham or Christchurch), to say, "The dinner was not good," or to say (we were now, Mary Seton and I, in her sitting-room), "Could we not have dined up here alone?" for if I had said anything of the kind I should have been prying and searching into the secret economies of a house which to the stranger wears so fine a front of gaiety and courage. No, one could say nothing of the sort. Indeed, conversation for a moment flagged. The human frame being what it is, heart, body and brain all mixed together, and not contained in separate compartments as they will be no doubt in another million years, a good dinner is of great importance to good talk. One cannot think well, love well, sleep well, if one has not dined well. The lamp in the spine does not light on beef and prunes. We are all probably going to heaven, and Vandyck is, we hope, to meet us round the next corner—that is the dubious and qualifying state of mind that beef and prunes at the end of the day's work breed between them. Happily my friend, who taught science, had a cupboard where there was a squat bottle and little glasses—(but there should have been sole and partridge to begin with)—so that we were able to draw up to the fire and repair some of the damages of the day's living. In a minute or so

5. Jane Harrison (1850–1928), English classical scholar, fellow, and lecturer at Newnham College, and author of *Prolegomena to the Study of Greek Religion* (1903) and *Ancient Art and Ritual* (1913).

we were slipping freely in and out among all those objects of curiosity and interest which form in the mind in the absence of a particular person, and are naturally to be discussed on coming together again—how somebody has married, another has not; one thinks this, another that; one has improved out of all knowledge, the other most amazingly gone to the bad—with all those speculations upon human nature and the character of the amazing world we live in which spring naturally from such beginnings. While these things were being said, however, I became shamefacedly aware of a current setting in of its own accord and carrying everything forward to an end of its own. One might be talking of Spain or Portugal, of book or racehorse, but the real interest of whatever was said was none of those things, but a scene of masons on a high roof some five centuries ago. Kings and nobles brought treasure in huge sacks and poured it under the earth. This scene was for ever coming alive in my mind and placing itself by another of lean cows and a muddy market and withered greens and the stringy hearts of old men—these two pictures, disjointed and disconnected and nonsensical as they were, were for ever coming together and combating each other and had me entirely at their mercy. The best course, unless the whole talk was to be distorted, was to expose what was in my mind to the air, when with good luck it would fade and crumble like the head of the dead king when they opened the coffin at Windsor.[6] Briefly, then, I told Miss Seton about the masons who had been all those years on the roof of the chapel, and about the kings and queens and nobles bearing sacks of gold and silver on their shoulders, which they shovelled into the earth; and then how the great financial magnates of our own time came and laid cheques and bonds, I suppose, where the others had laid ingots and rough lumps of gold. All that lies beneath the colleges down there, I said; but this college, where we are now sitting, what lies beneath its gallant red brick and the wild unkempt grasses of the garden? What force is behind the plain china off which we dined, and (here it popped out of my mouth before I could stop it) the beef, the custard and the prunes?

Well, said Mary Seton, about the year 1860—Oh, but you know the story, she said, bored, I suppose, by the recital. And she told me—rooms were hired. Committees met. Envelopes were addressed. Circulars were drawn up. Meetings were held; letters were read out; so-and-so has promised so much; on the contrary, Mr. —— won't give a penny. The Saturday Review has been very rude. How can we raise a fund to pay for offices? Shall we hold a bazaar? Can't we find a pretty girl to sit in the front row? Let us look up what John Stuart Mill said on the subject. Can any one persuade the editor of the —— to print a letter? Can we get Lady —— to sign it? Lady —— is out of town. That was the way it was done, presumably, sixty years ago, and it was a prodigious effort, and a great deal of time was spent on it. And it was only after a long struggle and with the utmost difficulty that they got thirty thousand pounds together.[7] So obviously we cannot have wine and partridges and servants carrying tin dishes

6. At the royal residence of Windsor Castle, nine English kings are buried in two chapels serving as royal mausoleums.

7. "We are told that we ought to ask for £30,000 at least. . . . It is not a large sum, considering that there is to be but one college of this sort for Great Britain, Ireland and the Colonies, and considering how easy it is to raise immense sums for boys' schools. But considering how few people really wish women to be educated, it is a good deal."—Lady Stephen, *Life of Miss Emily Davies* [Woolf's note].

on their heads," she said. "We cannot have sofas and separate rooms. "The amenities," she said, quoting from some book or other, "will have to wait."[8]

At the thought of all those women working year after year and finding it hard to get two thousand pounds together, and as much as they could do to get thirty thousand pounds, we burst out in scorn at the reprehensible poverty of our sex. What had our mothers been doing then that they had no wealth to leave us? Powdering their noses? Looking in at shop windows? Flaunting in the sun at Monte Carlo? There were some photographs on the mantel-piece. Mary's mother—if that was her picture—may have been a wastrel in her spare time (she had thirteen children by a minister of the church), but if so her gay and dissipated life had left too few traces of its pleasures on her face. She was a homely body; an old lady in a plaid shawl which was fastened by a large cameo; and she sat in a basket-chair, encouraging a spaniel to look at the camera, with the amused, yet strained expression of one who is sure that the dog will move directly the bulb is pressed. Now if she had gone into business; had become a manufacturer of artificial silk or a magnate on the Stock Exchange; if she had left two or three hundred thousand pounds to Fernham, we could have been sitting at our ease tonight and the subject of our talk might have been archaeology, botany, anthropology, physics, the nature of the atom, mathematics, astronomy, relativity, geography. If only Mrs Seton and her mother and her mother before her had learnt the great art of making money and had left their money, like their fathers and their grandfathers before them, to found fellowships and lectureships and prizes and scholarships appropriated to the use of their own sex, we might have dined very tolerably up here alone off a bird and a bottle of wine; we might have looked forward without undue confidence to a pleasant and honourable lifetime spent in the shelter of one of the liberally endowed professions. We might have been exploring or writing; mooning about the venerable places of the earth, sitting contemplative on the steps of the Parthenon, or going at ten to an office and coming home comfortably at half-past four to write a little poetry. Only, if Mrs Seton and her like had gone into business at the age of fifteen, there would have been—that was the snag in the argument—no Mary. What, I asked, did Mary think of that? There between the curtains was the October night, calm and lovely, with a star or two caught in the yellowing trees. Was she ready to resign her share of it and her memories (for they had been a happy family, though a large one) of games and quarrels up in Scotland, which she is never tired of praising for the fineness of its air and the quality of its cakes, in order that Fernham might have been endowed with fifty thousand pounds or so by a stroke of the pen? For, to endow a college would necessitate the suppression of families altogether. Making a fortune and bearing thirteen children—no human being could stand it. Consider the facts, we said. First there are nine months before the baby is born. Then the baby is born. Then there are three or four months spent in feeding the baby. After the baby is fed there are certainly five years spent in playing with the baby. You cannot, it seems, let children run about the streets. People who have seen them running wild in Russia say that the sight is not a pleasant one. People say, too, that human nature takes its shape in the years between one and five. If Mrs Seton, I said, had been making money, what sort of memories would you have had of games and quarrels? What would you have known of Scotland, and its fine air and cakes and all the rest of it? But it is use-less to ask these questions, because you would never have come into existence at all. Moreover, it is equally useless to ask what might have happened if Mrs Seton and her mother and her mother before her had amassed great wealth and laid it under the foundations of college and library, because, in the first place, to earn money was impossible for them, and in the second, had it been possible, the law denied them the right to possess what money they earned. It is only for the last forty-eight years that Mrs Seton has had a penny of her own. For all the centuries before that it would have been her husband's property—a thought which, perhaps, may have had its share in keeping Mrs Seton and her mothers off the Stock Exchange. Every penny I earn, they may have said, will be taken from me and disposed of according to my husband's wisdom—perhaps to found a scholarship or to endow a fellowship in Balliol or Kings,[9] so that to earn money, even if I could earn money, is not a matter that interests me very greatly. I had better leave it to my husband.

At any rate, whether or not the blame rested on the old lady who was looking at the spaniel, there could be no doubt that for some reason or other our moth-ers had mismanaged their affairs very gravely. Not a penny could be spared for "amenities"; for partridges and wine, beadles and turf, books and cigars, librar-ies and leisure. To raise bare walls out of the bare earth was the utmost they could do.

So we talked standing at the window and looking, as so many thousands look every night, down on the domes and towers of the famous city beneath us. It was very beautiful, very mysterious in the autumn moonlight. The old stone looked very white and venerable. One thought of all the books that were assembled down there; of the pictures of old prelates and worthies hanging in the panelled rooms; of the painted windows that would be throwing strange globes and crescents on the pavement; of the tablets and memorials and inscriptions; of the fountains and the grass; of the quiet rooms looking across the quiet quadrangles. And (pardon me the thought) I thought, too, of the admirable smoke and drink and the deep armchairs and the pleasant carpets: of the urbanity, the geniality, the dignity which are the offspring of luxury and privacy and space. Certainly our mothers had not provided us with anything comparable to all this—our mothers who found it difficult to scrape together thirty thousand pounds, our mothers who bore thirteen children to ministers of religion at St Andrews.[1]

So I went back to my inn, and as I walked through the dark streets I pon-dered this and that, as one does at the end of the day's work. I pondered why it was that Mrs Seton had no money to leave us; and what effect poverty has on the mind; and what effect wealth has on the mind; and I thought of the queer old gentlemen I had seen that morning with tufts of fur upon their shoulders; and I remembered how if one whistled one of them ran; and I thought of the organ booming in the chapel and of the shut doors of the library; and I thought

1. Probably St. Andrew's in Holborn, an old London church rebuilt under the famous architect Sir Christopher Wren during 1683–1695.

9. I.e., King's College, Cambridge; "Balliol": Balliol College, Oxford.

how unpleasant it is to be locked out; and I thought how it is worse perhaps to be locked in; and, thinking of the safety and prosperity of the one sex and of the poverty and insecurity of the other and of the effect of tradition and of the lack of tradition upon the mind of a writer, I thought at last that it was time to roll up the crumpled skin of the day, with its arguments and its impressions and its anger and its laughter, and cast it into the hedge. A thousand stars were flashing across the blue wastes of the sky. One seemed alone with an inscrutable society. All human beings were laid asleep—prone, horizontal, dumb. Nobody seemed stirring in the streets of Oxbridge. Even the door of the hotel sprang open at the touch of an invisible hand—not a boots was sitting up to light me to bed, it was so late.

CHAPTER 2

The scene, if I may ask you to follow me, was now changed. The leaves were still falling, but in London now, not Oxbridge; and I must ask you to imagine a room, like many thousands, with a window looking across people's hats and vans and motor-cars to other windows, and on the table inside the room a blank sheet of paper on which was written in large letters WOMEN AND FICTION, but no more. The inevitable sequel to lunching and dining at Oxbridge seemed, unfortunately, to be a visit to the British Museum. One must strain off what was personal and accidental in all these impressions and so reach the pure fluid, the essential oil of truth. For that visit to Oxbridge and the luncheon and the dinner had started a swarm of questions. Why did men drink wine and women water? Why was one sex so prosperous and the other so poor? What effect has poverty on fiction? What conditions are necessary for the creation of works of art?—a thousand questions at once suggested themselves. But one needed answers, not questions; and an answer was only to be had by consulting the learned and the unprejudiced, who have removed themselves above the strife of tongue and the confusion of body and issued the result of their reasoning and research in books which are to be found in the British Museum. If truth is not to be found on the shelves of the British Museum, where, I asked myself, picking up a notebook and a pencil, is truth?

Thus provided, thus confident and enquiring, I set out in the pursuit of truth. The day, though not actually wet, was dismal, and the streets in the neighborhood of the Museum were full of open coal-holes, down which sacks were showering; four-wheeled cabs were drawing up and depositing on the pavement corded boxes containing, presumably, the entire wardrobe of some Swiss or Italian family seeking fortune or refuge or some other desirable commodity which is to be found in the boarding-houses of Bloomsbury[2] in the winter. The usual hoarse-voiced men paraded the streets with plants on barrows. Some shouted; others sang. London was like a workshop. London was like a machine. We were all being shot backwards and forwards on this plain foundation to make some pattern. The British Museum was another department of the factory. The swing-doors swung open; and there one stood under the vast dome, as if one were a thought in the huge bald forehead which is so

---

2. A residential and academic borough in London, site of the British Museum and various educational institutions.

splendidly encircled by a band of famous names.[3] One went to the counter; one took a slip of paper; one opened a volume of the catalogue, and . . . . . the five dots here indicate five separate minutes of stupefaction, wonder and bewilderment. Have you any notion how many books are written about women in the course of one year? Have you any notion how many are written by men? Are you aware that you are, perhaps, the most discussed animal in the universe? Here had I come with a notebook and a pencil proposing to spend a morning reading, supposing that at the end of the morning I should have transferred the truth to my notebook. But I should need to be a herd of elephants, I thought, and a wilderness of spiders, desperately referring to the animals that are reputed longest lived and most multitudinously eyed, to cope with all this. I should need claws of steel and beak of brass even to penetrate the husk. How shall I ever find the grains of truth embedded in all this mass of paper, I asked myself, and in despair began running my eye up and down the long list of titles. Even the names of the books gave me food for thought. Sex and its nature might well attract doctors and biologists; but what was surprising and difficult of explanation was the fact that sex—woman, that is to say—also attracts agreeable essayists, light-fingered novelists, young men who have taken the M.A. degree; men who have taken no degree; men who have no apparent qualification save that they are not women. Some of these books were, on the face of it, frivolous and facetious; but many, on the other hand, were serious and prophetic, moral and hortatory. Merely to read the titles suggested innumerable schoolmasters, innumerable clergymen mounting their platforms and pulpits and holding forth with a loquacity which far exceeded the hour usually allotted to such discourse on this one subject. It was a most strange phenomenon; and apparently—here I consulted the letter M—one confined to male sex. Women do not write books about men—a fact that I could not help welcoming with relief, for if I had first to read all that men have written about women, then all that women have written about men, the aloe that flowers once in a hundred years would flower twice before I could set pen to paper. So, making a perfectly arbitrary choice of a dozen volumes or so, I sent my slips of paper to lie in the wire tray, and waited in my stall, among the other seekers for the essential oil of truth.

What could be the reason, then, of this curious disparity, I wondered, drawing cart-wheels on the slips of paper provided by the British taxpayer for other purposes. Why are women, judging from this catalogue, so much more interesting to men than men are to women? A very curious fact it seemed, and my mind wandered to picture the lives of men who spend their time in writing books about women; whether they were old or young, married or unmarried, red-nosed or humpbacked—anyhow, it was flattering, vaguely, to feel oneself the object of such attention, provided that it was not entirely bestowed by the crippled and the infirm—so I pondered until all such frivolous thoughts were ended by an avalanche of books sliding down on to the desk in front of me. Now the trouble began. The student who has been trained in research at Oxbridge has no doubt some method of shepherding his question past all dis-

---

3. The names of famous men, including Chaucer, Spenser, Shakespeare, Milton, Pope, Wordsworth, Byron, Carlyle, and Tennyson, are painted in a circle around the dome of the Reading Room at the British Museum.

tractions till it runs into its answer as a sheep runs into its pen. The student by my side, for instance, who was copying assiduously from a scientific manual was, I felt sure, extracting pure nuggets of the essential ore every ten minutes or so. His little grunts of satisfaction indicated so much. But if, unfortunately, one has had no training in a university, the question far from being shepherded to its pen flies like a frightened flock hither and thither, helter-skelter, pursued by a whole pack of hounds. Professors, schoolmasters, sociologists, clergymen, novelists, essayists, journalists, men who had no qualification save that they were not women, chased my simple and single question—Why are women poor?—until it became fifty questions; until the fifty questions leapt frantically into mid-stream and were carried away. Every page in my notebook was scribbled over with notes. To show the state of mind I was in, I will read you a few of them, explaining that the page was headed quite simply, WOMEN AND POVERTY, in block letters; but what followed was something like this:

Condition in Middle Ages of,
Habits in the Fiji Islands of,
Worshipped as goddesses by,
Weaker in moral sense than,
Idealism of,
Greater conscientiousness of,
South Sea Islanders, age of puberty among,
Attractiveness of,
Offered as sacrifice to,
Small size of brain of,
Profounder sub-consciousness of,
Less hair on the body of,
Mental, moral and physical inferiority of,
Love of children of,
Greater length of life of,
Weaker muscles of,
Strength of affections of,
Vanity of,
Higher education of,
Shakespeare's opinion of,
Lord Birkenhead's opinion of,
Dean Inge's opinion of,
La Bruyère's opinion of,
Dr. Johnson's opinion of,
Mr. Oscar Browning's[4] *opinion of, . . .*

---

4. A schoolmaster and later fellow of King's College, Cambridge (1837–1923); anecdotes about his strong opinions (see p. 1990) were published in a 1927 biography. The first earl of Birkenhead, F. E. Smith (1872–1930), a conservative politician who opposed women's suffrage and praised the domestic "true functions of womanhood." William Ralph Inge (1860–1954), dean of St. Paul's Cathedral in London and a religious writer. Jean de La Bruyère (1645–1696), French moralist and author of satirical *Characters* (1688), imitating the Greek writer Theophrastus. Samuel Johnson (1709–1784), author of moral essays and of the famous *A Dictionary of the English Language* (1747).

Here I drew breath and added, indeed, in the margin, Why does Samuel But-ler[5] say, "Wise men never say what they think of women"? Wise men never say anything else apparently. But, I continued, leaning back in my chair and look-ing at the vast dome in which I was a single but by now somewhat harassed thought, what is so unfortunate is that wise men never think the same thing about women. Here is Pope:[6]

> Most women have no character at all.

And here is La Bruyère:

> Les femmes sont extrêmes; elles sont meilleures ou pires que les hommes—[7]

a direct contradiction by keen observers who were contemporary. Are they capable of education or incapable? Napoleon thought them incapable.[8] Dr. Johnson thought the opposite.[9] Have they souls or have they not souls? Some savages say they have none. Others, on the contrary, maintain that women are half divine and worship them on that account.[1] Some sages hold that they are shallower in the brain; others that they are deeper in the consciousness. Goethe honoured them; Mussolini[2] despises them. Wherever one looked men thought about women and thought differently. It was impossible to make head or tail of it all, I decided, glancing with envy at the reader next door who was making the neatest abstracts, headed often with an A or a B or a C, while my own notebook rioted with the wildest scribble of contradictory jottings. It was distressing, it was bewildering, it was humiliating. Truth had run through my fingers. Every drop had escaped.

I could not possibly go home, I reflected, and add as a serious contribution to the study of women and fiction that women have less hair on their bodies than men, or that the age of puberty among the South Sea Islanders[3] is nine— or is it ninety?—even the handwriting had become in its distraction indeci-

---

5. Satirical author (1835–1902) who wrote *Erewhon* (1872) and *The Way of All Flesh* (1903); his *Notebooks* are the source of this statement.
6. Alexander Pope (1688–1744), translator of Homer and author of *An Essay on Man* (1733–34) and the satirical *The Rape of the Lock* (1712–14).
7. Women are extreme; they are better or worse than men (French).
8. Napoleon wrote: "What we ask of education is not that girls should think, but that they should believe. The weakness of women's brains, the instability of their ideas, the place they will fill in society, their need for perpetual resignation, and for an easy and generous type of charity—all this can only be met by religion" (notes written on May 15, 1807, concerning the establishment of a girl's school at Écouen).
9. "'Men know that women are an overmatch for them, and therefore they choose the weakest or the most ignorant. If they did not think so, they never could be afraid of women knowing as much as themselves.'. . . In justice to the sex, I think it but candid to acknowledge that, in a subsequent conversation, he told me that he was serious in what he said."—BOSWELL, *The Journal of a Tour to the Hebrides* [Woolf's note].
1. "The ancient Germans believed that there was something holy in women, and accordingly consulted them as oracles."—FRAZER, *Golden Bough* [Woolf's note].
2. Benito Mussolini (1883–1945), Fascist dictator of Italy between 1922 and 1943. Johann Wolfgang von Goethe (1749–1832), German author of *Faust*. "The eternal feminine draws us along" is the last line of *Faust*, Part 2.
3. The native peoples of the islands in the south-central Pacific Ocean were the subject of several anthropological studies in the early 20th century, including Margaret Mead's widely read *Coming of Age in Samoa* (1928).

pherable. It was disgraceful to have nothing more weighty or respectable to show after a whole morning's work. And if I could not grasp the truth about W. (as for brevity's sake I had come to call her) in the past, why bother about W. in the future? It seemed pure waste of time to consult all those gentlemen who specialise in woman and her effect on whatever it may be—politics, children, wages, morality—numerous and learned as they are. One might as well leave their books unopened.

But while I pondered I had unconsciously, in my listlessness, in my desperation, been drawing a picture where I should, like my neighbour, have been writing a conclusion. I had been drawing a face, a figure. It was the face and the figure of Professor von X. engaged in writing his monumental work entitled *The Mental, Moral, and Physical Inferiority of the Female Sex*.[4] He was not in my picture a man attractive to women. He was heavily built; he had a great jowl; to balance that he had very small eyes; he was very red in the face. His expression suggested that he was labouring under some emotion that made him jab his pen on the paper as if he were killing some noxious insect as he wrote, but even when he had killed it that did not satisfy him; he must go on killing it; and even so, some cause for anger and irritation remained. Could it be his wife, I asked, looking at my picture. Was she in love with a cavalry officer? Was the cavalry officer slim and elegant and dressed in astrachan?[5] Had he been laughed at, to adopt the Freudian theory, in his cradle by a pretty girl? For even in his cradle the professor, I thought, could not have been an attractive child. Whatever the reason, the professor was made to look very angry and very ugly in my sketch, as he wrote his great book upon the mental, moral and physical inferiority of women. Drawing pictures was an idle way of finishing an unprofitable morning's work. Yet it is in our idleness, in our dreams, that the submerged truth sometimes comes to the top. A very elementary exercise in psychology, not to be dignified by the name of psycho-analysis, showed me, on looking at my notebook, that the sketch of the angry professor had been made in anger. Anger had snatched my pencil while I dreamt. But what was anger doing there? Interest, confusion, amusement, boredom—all these emotions I could trace and name as they succeeded each other throughout the morning. Had anger, the black snake, been lurking among them? Yes, said the sketch, anger had. It referred me unmistakably to the one book, to the one phrase, which had roused the demon; it was the professor's statement about the mental, moral and physical inferiority of women. My heart had leapt. My cheeks had burnt. I had flushed with anger. There was nothing specially remarkable, however foolish, in that. One does not like to be told that one is naturally the inferior of a little man—I looked at the student next me— who breathes hard, wears a ready-made tie, and has not shaved this fortnight. One has certain foolish vanities. It is only human nature, I reflected, and began drawing cart-wheels and circles over the angry professor's face till he looked like a burning bush or a flaming comet—anyhow, an apparition without human semblance or significance. The professor was nothing now but a faggot burning on the top of Hampstead Heath.[6] Soon my own anger was explained and done with;

---

4. A fictional portrait, probably based on Otto Weininger's *Sex and Character* (1906), that distinguished between male (productive and moral) and female (negative and amoral) characteristics.

5. Curly lambskin.

6. A public open space in the village of Hampstead, in London. "Faggot": a bundle of sticks.

but curiosity remained. How explain the anger of the professors? Why were they angry? For when it came to analysing the impression left by these books there was always an element of heat. This heat took many forms; it showed itself in satire, in sentiment, in curiosity, in reprobation. But there was another element which was often present and could not immediately be identified. Anger, I called it. But it was anger that had gone underground and mixed itself with all kinds of other emotions. To judge from its odd effects, it was anger disguised and complex, not anger simple and open.

Whatever the reason, all these books,[7] I thought, surveying the pile on the desk, are worthless for my purposes. They were worthless scientifically, that is to say, though humanly they were full of instruction, interest, boredom, and very queer facts about the habits of the Fiji Islanders. They had been written in the red light of emotion and not in the white light of truth. Therefore they must be returned to the central desk and restored each to his own cell in the enormous honeycomb. All that I had retrieved from that morning's work had been the one fact of anger. The professors—I lumped them together thus—were angry. But why, I asked myself, having returned the books, why, I repeated, standing under the colonnade among the pigeons and the prehistoric canoes, why are they angry? And, asking myself this question, I strolled off to find a place for luncheon. What is the real nature of what I call for the moment their anger? I asked. Here was a puzzle that would last all the time that it takes to be served with food in a small restaurant somewhere near the British Museum. Some previous luncher had left the lunch edition of the evening paper on a chair, and, waiting to be served, I began idly reading the headlines. A ribbon of very large letters ran across the page. Somebody had made a big score in South Africa. Lesser ribbons announced that Sir Austen Chamberlain was at Geneva.[8] A meat axe with human hair on it had been found in a cellar. Mr. Justice —— commented in the Divorce Courts upon the Shamelessness of Women. Sprinkled about the paper were other pieces of news. A film actress had been lowered from a peak in California and hung suspended in mid-air. The weather was going to be foggy. The most transient visitor to this planet, I thought, who picked up this paper could not fail to be aware, even from this scattered testimony, that England is under the rule of a patriarchy. Nobody in their senses could fail to detect the dominance of the professor. His was the power and the money and the influence. He was the proprietor of the paper and its editor and sub-editor. He was the Foreign Secretary and the Judge. He was the cricketer; he owned the race-horses and the yachts. He was the director of the company that pays two hundred per cent to its shareholders. He left millions to charities and colleges that were ruled by himself. He suspended the film actress in mid-air. He will decide if the hair on the meat axe is human; he it is who will acquit or convict the murderer, and hang him, or let him go free. With the exception of the fog he seemed to control everything. Yet he was angry. I knew that he was angry by this token. When I read what he wrote about women I thought, not of what he was saying, but of himself. When an arguer argues dispassionately he

---

7. E.g., *Fijian Society, or the Sociology and Psychology of the Fijians* (1921), by Reverend W. Deane, principal of a teachers' training college in Ndávuilévu, Fiji; and *The Hill Tribes of Fiji* (1922), by A. B. Brewster, a colonial functionary, mixed facts with interpretation. Reverend Deane remarks that "the amount of sexual immorality and promiscuous intercourse during the past forty years is appalling." Fiji is an island in the South Pacific (see n. 3, p. 355).
8. The site of the League of Nations. Chamberlain was the British foreign secretary between 1924 and 1929.

thinks only of the argument; and the reader cannot help thinking of the argument too. If he had written dispassionately about women, had used indisputable proofs to establish his argument and had shown no trace of wishing that the result should be one thing rather than another, one would not have been angry either. One would have accepted the fact, as one accepts the fact that a pea is green or a canary yellow. So be it, I should have said. But I had been angry because he was angry. Yet it seemed absurd, I thought, turning over the evening paper, that a man with all this power should be angry. Or is anger, I wondered, somehow, the famil-iar, the attendant sprite on power? Rich people, for example, are often angry because they suspect that the poor want to seize their wealth. The professors, or patriarchs, as it might be more accurate to call them, might be angry for that rea-son partly, but partly for one that lies a little less obviously on the surface. Possi-bly they were not "angry" at all; often, indeed, they were admiring, devoted, exemplary in the relations of private life. Possibly when the professor insisted a little too emphatically upon the inferiority of women, he was concerned not with their inferiority, but with his own superiority. That was what he was protecting rather hot-headedly and with too much emphasis, because it was a jewel to him of the rarest price. Life for both sexes—and I looked at them, shouldering their way along the pavement—is arduous, difficult, a perpetual struggle. It calls for gigan-tic courage and strength. More than anything, perhaps, creatures of illusion as we are, it calls for confidence in oneself. Without self-confidence we are as babes in the cradle. And how can we generate this imponderable quality, which is yet so invaluable, most quickly? By thinking that other people are inferior to oneself. By feeling that one has some innate superiority—it may be wealth, or rank, a straight nose, or the portrait of a grandfather by Romney[9]—for there is no end to the pathetic devices of the human imagination—over other people. Hence the enor-mous importance to a patriarch who has to conquer, who has to rule, of feeling that great numbers of people, half the human race indeed, are by nature inferior to himself. It must indeed be one of the chief sources of his power. But let me turn the light of this observation on to real life, I thought. Does it help to explain some of those psychological puzzles that one notes in the margin of daily life? Does it explain my astonishment the other day when Z, most humane, most mod-est of men, taking up some book by Rebecca West[1] and reading a passage in it, exclaimed, "The arrant feminist! She says that men are snobs!" The exclamation, to me so surprising—for why was Miss West an arrant feminist for making a pos-sibly true if uncomplimentary statement about the other sex?—was not merely the cry of wounded vanity; it was a protest against some infringement of his power to believe in himself. Women have served all these centuries as looking-glasses possessing the magic and delicious power of reflecting the figure of man at twice its natural size. Without that power probably the earth would still be swamp and jungle. The glories of all our wars would be unknown. We should still be scratch-ing the outlines of deer on the remains of mutton bones and bartering flints for sheepskins or whatever simple ornament took our unsophisticated taste. Super-men[2] and Fingers of Destiny would never have existed. The Czar and the Kaiser

9. George Romney (1734–1802), portrait painter of 18th-century British society.
1. Pseudonym of Cicely Isabel Andrews (1892–1983), British novelist and journalist.
2. Fascist politicians, such as Adolf Hitler (1889–1945) in Germany and Mussolini (1883–1945) in Italy, rationalized their aggres-sive policies by exploiting and distorting Friedrich Nietzsche's (1844–1900) concept of the *Übermensch*, or superior being (in *Thus Spake Zarathustra*, 1883–85).

would never have worn their crowns or lost them. Whatever may be their use in civilized societies, mirrors are essential to all violent and heroic action. That is why Napoleon and Mussolini both insist so emphatically upon the inferiority of women, for if they were not inferior, they would cease to enlarge. That serves to explain in part the necessity that women so often are to men. And it serves to explain how restless they are under her criticism; how impossible it is for her to say to them this book is bad, this picture is feeble, or whatever it may be, without giving far more pain and rousing far more anger than a man would do who gave the same criticism. For if she begins to tell the truth, the figure in the looking-glass shrinks; his fitness for life is diminished. How is he to go on giving judgment, civilising natives, making laws, writing books, dressing up and speechifying at banquets, unless he can see himself at breakfast and at dinner at least twice the size he really is? So I reflected, crumbling my bread and stirring my coffee and now and again looking at the people in the street. The looking-glass vision is of supreme importance because it charges the vitality; it stimulates the nervous system. Take it away and man may die, like the drug fiend deprived of his cocaine. Under the spell of that illusion, I thought, looking out of the window, half the people on the pavement are striding to work. They put on their hats and coats in the morning under its agreeable rays. They start the day confident, braced, believing themselves desired at Miss Smith's tea party; they say to themselves as they go into the room, I am the superior of half the people here, and it is thus that they speak with that self-confidence, that self-assurance, which have had such profound consequences in public life and lead to such curious notes in the margin of the private mind.

But these contributions to the dangerous and fascinating subject of the psychology of the other sex—it is one, I hope, that you will investigate when you have five hundred a year of your own—were interrupted by the necessity of paying the bill. It came to five shillings and ninepence. I gave the waiter a ten-shilling note and he went to bring me change. There was another ten-shilling note in my purse; I noticed it, because it is a fact that still takes my breath away—the power of my purse to breed ten-shilling notes automatically. I open it and there they are. Society gives me chicken and coffee, bed and lodging, in return for a certain number of pieces of paper which were left me by an aunt, for no other reason than that I share her name.

My aunt, Mary Beton, I must tell you, died by a fall from her horse when she was riding out to take the air in Bombay. The news of my legacy reached me one night about the same time that the act was passed that gave votes to women.[3] A solicitor's letter fell into the post-box and when I opened it I found that she had left me five hundred pounds[4] a year for ever. Of the two—the vote and the money—the money, I own, seemed infinitely the more important. Before that I had made my living by cadging odd jobs from newspapers, by reporting a donkey show here or a wedding there; I had earned a few pounds by addressing envelopes, reading to old ladies, making artificial flowers, teaching the alphabet to

3. Women were given the vote in 1918; the voting age for women was lowered from thirty to twenty-one in 1928.
4. Roughly $30,000 today, calculating inflation and exchange rates between the pound and the dollar in 1918 and 2011. Such calculations are never perfectly reliable, however, since the relative cost of specific items (such as bread or rent) varies.

small children in a kindergarten. Such were the chief occupations that were open to women before 1918. I need not, I am afraid, describe in any detail the hardness of the work, for you know perhaps women who have done it; nor the difficulty of living on the money when it was earned, for you may have tried. But what still remains with me as a worse infliction than either was the poison of fear and bitterness which those days bred in me. To begin with, always to be doing work that one did not wish to do, and to do it like a slave, flattering and fawning, not always necessarily perhaps, but it seemed necessary and the stakes were too great to run risks; and then the thought of that one gift which it was death to hide[5]—a small one but dear to the possessor—perishing and with it myself, my soul—all this became like a rust eating away the bloom of the spring, destroying the tree at its heart. However, as I say, my aunt died; and whenever I change a ten-shilling note a little of that rust and corrosion is rubbed off; fear and bitterness go. Indeed, I thought, slipping the silver into my purse, it is remarkable, remembering the bitterness of those days, what a change of temper a fixed income will bring about. No force in the world can take from me my five hundred pounds. Food, house and clothing are mine for ever. Therefore not merely do effort and labour cease, but also hatred and bitterness. I need not hate any man; he cannot hurt me. I need not flatter any man; he has nothing to give me. So imperceptibly I found myself adopting a new attitude towards the other half of the human race. It was absurd to blame any class or any sex, as a whole. Great bodies of people are never responsible for what they do. They are driven by instincts which are not within their control. They too, the patriarchs, the professors, had endless difficulties, terrible drawbacks to contend with. Their education had been in some ways as faulty as my own. It had bred in them defects as great. True, they had money and power, but only at the cost of harbouring in their breasts an eagle, a vulture, for ever tearing the liver out and plucking at the lungs—the instinct for possession, the rage for acquisition which drives them to desire other people's fields and goods perpetually; to make frontiers and flags; battleships and poison gas; to offer up their own lives and their children's lives. Walk through the Admiralty Arch[6] (I had reached that monument), or any other avenue given up to trophies and cannon, and reflect upon the kind of glory celebrated there. Or watch in the spring sunshine the stockbroker and the great barrister going indoors to make money and more money and more money when it is a fact that five hundred pounds a year will keep one alive in the sunshine. These are unpleasant instincts to harbour, I reflected. They are bred of the conditions of life; of the lack of civilisation, I thought, looking at the statue of the Duke of Cambridge,[7] and in particular at the feathers in his cocked hat, with a fixity that they have scarcely ever received before. And, as I realised these drawbacks, by degrees fear and bitterness modified themselves into pity and toleration; and then in a year or two, pity and toleration went, and the greatest release of all came, which is freedom to think of things in themselves. That building, for example, do I like it or not? Is that picture beautiful or not? Is that in my opinion a good book or a bad? Indeed my aunt's legacy

5. From "When I Consider How My Light Is Spent" by John Milton (1608–1673): "And that one talent which is death to hide, / Lodged with me useless."
6. A triple arch in Trafalgar Square (London) at the entrance to the Mall, erected in 1910.
7. An equestrian statue of the second duke of Cambridge (1819–1904), cousin of Queen Victoria, in the full dress uniform of a field marshal.

unveiled the sky to me, and substituted for the large and imposing figure of a gentleman, which Milton recommended for my perpetual adoration, a view of the open sky.

So thinking, so speculating, I found my way back to my house by the river. Lamps were being lit and an indescribable change had come over London since the morning hour. It was as if the great machine after labouring all day had made with our help a few yards of something very exciting and beautiful—a fiery fabric flashing with red eyes, a tawny monster roaring with hot breath. Even the wind seemed flung like a flag as it lashed the houses and rattled the hoardings.

In my little street, however, domesticity prevailed. The house painter was descending his ladder; the nursemaid was wheeling the perambulator carefully in and out back to nursery tea; the coal-heaver was folding his empty sacks on top of each other; the woman who keeps the green-grocer's shop was adding up the day's takings with her hands in red mittens. But so engrossed was I with the problem you have laid upon my shoulders that I could not see even these usual sights without referring them to one centre. I thought how much harder it is now than it must have been even a century ago to say which of these employments is the higher, the more necessary. Is it better to be a coal-heaver or a nursemaid; is the charwoman who has brought up eight children of less value to the world than the barrister who has made a hundred thousand pounds? It is useless to ask such questions; for nobody can answer them. Not only do the comparative values of charwoman and lawyers rise and fall from decade to decade, but we have no rods with which to measure them even as they are at the moment. I had been foolish to ask my professor to furnish me with "indisputable proofs" of this or that in his argument about women. Even if one could state the value of any one gift at the moment, those values will change; in a century's time very possibly they will have changed completely. Moreover, in a hundred years, I thought, reaching my own doorstep, women will have ceased to be the protected sex. Logically they will take part in all the activities and exertions that were once denied them. The nursemaid will heave coal. The shop-woman will drive an engine. All assumptions founded on the facts observed when women were the protected sex will have disappeared—as, for example (here a squad of soldiers marched down the street), that women and clergymen and gardeners live longer than other people. Remove that protection, expose them to the same exertions and activities, make them soldiers and sailors and engine-drivers and dock labourers, and will not women die off so much younger, so much quicker, than men that one will say, "I saw a woman today," as one used to say, "I saw an aero-plane." Anything may happen when womanhood has ceased to be a protected occupation, I thought, opening the door. But what bearing has all this upon the subject of my paper, Women and Fiction? I asked, going indoors.

CHAPTER 3

It was disappointing not to have brought back in the evening some important statement, some authentic fact. Women are poorer than men because—this or that. Perhaps now it would be better to give up seeking for the truth, and receiving on one's head an avalanche of opinion hot as lava, discoloured as dish-water. It would be better to draw the curtains; to shut out distractions; to light the lamp; to narrow the enquiry and to ask the historian, who records not opinions but facts, to describe under what conditions women lived, not throughout the ages, but in England, say in the time of Elizabeth.[8]

For it is a perennial puzzle why no woman wrote a word of that extraordinary literature when every other man, it seemed, was capable of song or sonnet. What were the conditions in which women lived, I asked myself; for fiction, imaginative work that is, is not dropped like a pebble upon the ground, as science may be; fiction is like a spider's web, attached ever so lightly perhaps, but still attached to life at all four corners. Often the attachment is scarcely perceptible; Shakespeare's plays, for instance, seem to hang there complete by themselves. But when the web is pulled askew, hooked up at the edge, torn in the middle, one remembers that these webs are not spun in mid-air by incorporeal creatures, but are the work of suffering human beings, and are attached to grossly material things, like health and money and the houses we live in.

I went, therefore, to the shelf where the histories stand and took down one of the latest, Professor Trevelyan's *History of England*.[9] Once more I looked up Women, found "position of," and turned to the pages indicated. "Wife-beating," I read, "was a recognised right of man, and was practised without shame by high as well as low. . . . Similarly," the historian goes on, "the daughter who refused to marry the gentleman of her parents' choice was liable to be locked up, beaten and flung about the room, without any shock being inflicted on public opinion. Marriage was not an affair of personal affection, but of family avarice, particularly in the 'chivalrous' upper classes. . . . Betrothal often took place while one or both of the parties was in the cradle, and marriage when they were scarcely out of the nurses' charge." That was about 1470, soon after Chaucer's[1] time. The next reference to the position of women is some two hundred years later, in the time of the Stuarts.[2] "It was still the exception for women of the upper and middle class to choose their own husbands, and when the husband had been assigned, he was lord and master, so far at least as law and custom could make him. Yet even so," Professor Trevelyan concludes, "neither Shakespeare's women nor those of authentic seventeenth-century memoirs, like the Verneys and the Hutchinsons,[3] seem wanting in personality and character." Certainly, if we consider it, Cleopatra must have had a way with her; Lady Macbeth,[4] one would suppose, had a will of her own; Rosalind, one might conclude, was an attractive girl. Professor Trevelyan is speaking no more than the truth when he remarks that Shakespeare's women do not seem wanting in personality and character. Not being a historian, one might go even further and say that women have burnt like beacons in all the works of all the poets from the beginning of time—Clytemnestra, Antigone, Cleopatra, Lady

8. Queen of England from 1558 to 1603.
9. Published in London in 1926. References are to pages 260–61 and, later, to pages 436–37.
1. Geoffrey Chaucer (1340?–1400), author of *The Canterbury Tales* (1390–1400).
2. The British royal house from 1603 to 1714 (except for the Commonwealth interregnum of 1649–60).

3. F. P. Verney compiled *The Memoirs of the Verney Family during the Seventeenth Century* (1892–1899), and Lucy Hutchinson recounted her husband's life in *Memoirs of the Life of Colonel Hutchinson* (1806).
4. Heroine of Shakespeare's *Macbeth*. Cleopatra (69–30 B.C.E.), queen of Egypt and heroine of Shakespeare's *Antony and Cleopatra*.

Macbeth, Phèdre, Cressida, Rosalind, Desdemona, the Duchess of Malfi,[5] among the dramatists; then among the prose writers: Millamant, Clarissa, larissa, Becky Sharp, Anna Karenina, Emma Bovary, Madame de Guermantes[6]— the names flock to mind, nor do they recall women "lacking in personality and character." Indeed, if woman had no existence save in the fiction written by men, one would imagine her a person of the utmost importance; very various; heroic and mean; splendid and sordid; infinitely beautiful and hideous in the extreme; as great as a man, some think even greater.[7] But this is woman in fiction. In fact, as Professor Trevelyan points out, she was locked up, beaten and flung about the room.

A very queer, composite being thus emerges. Imaginatively she is of the highest importance; practically she is completely insignificant. She pervades poetry from cover to cover; she is all but absent from history. She dominates the lives of kings and conquerors in fiction; in fact she was the slave of any boy whose parents forced a ring upon her finger. Some of the most inspired words, some of the most profound thoughts in literature fall from her lips; in real life she could hardly read, could scarcely spell, and was the property of her husband.

It was certainly an odd monster that one made up by reading the historians first and the poets afterwards—a worm winged like an eagle; the spirit of life and beauty in a kitchen chopping up suet. But these monsters, however amusing to the imagination, have no existence in fact. What one must do to bring her to life was to think poetically and prosaically at one and the same moment, thus keeping in touch with fact—that she is Mrs. Martin, aged thirty-six, dressed in blue, wearing a black hat and brown shoes; but not losing sight of fiction either—that she is a vessel in which all sorts of spirits and forces are coursing and flashing perpetually. The moment, however, that one tries this method with the Elizabethan woman, one branch of illumination fails; one is held up by the scarcity of facts. One knows nothing detailed, nothing perfectly

---

5. Doomed heroine of John Webster's *The Duchess of Malfi* (ca. 1613). Clytemnestra is the heroine of Aeschylus's *Agamemnon* (458 B.C.E.). Antigone is the eponymous heroine of a 442 B.C.E. play by Sophocles. Phèdre is the heroine of Jean Racine's *Phèdre* (1677). Cressida, Rosalind, and Desdemona are heroines of Shakespeare's *Troilus and Cressida*, *As You Like It*, and *Othello*, respectively.
6. A character in Marcel Proust's *Remembrance of Things Past* (*The Guermantes Way*, 1920–21). Millamant is the heroine of William Congreve's satirical comedy *The Way of the World* (1700). Clarissa is the eponymous heroine of Samuel Richardson's seven-volume epistolary novel (1747–48). Becky Sharp appears in William Thackeray's *Vanity Fair* (1847–48). Anna Karenina is the title character in a Leo Tolstoy novel (1875–77). Emma Bovary is the heroine of Gustave Flaubert's *Madame Bovary* (1856).
7. "It remains a strange and almost inexplicable fact that in Athena's city, where women were kept in almost Oriental suppression as

odalisques or drudges, the stage should yet have produced figures like Clytemnestra and Cassandra, Atossa and Antigone, Phèdre and Medea, and all the other heroines who dominate play after play of the 'misogynist' Euripides. But the paradox of this world where in real life a respectable woman could hardly show her face alone in the street, and yet on the stage woman equals or surpasses man, has never been satisfactorily explained. In modern tragedy the same predominance exists. At all events, a very cursory survey of Shakespeare's work (similarly with Webster, though not with Marlowe or Jonson) suffices to reveal how this dominance, this initiative of women, persists from Rosalind to Lady Macbeth. So too in Racine; six of his tragedies bear their heroines' names; and what male characters of his shall we set against Hermione and Andromaque, Bérénice and Roxane, Phèdre and Athalie? So again with Ibsen; what men shall we match with Solveig and Nora, Hedda and Hilda Wangel and Rebecca West?"—F. L. LUCAS, *Tragedy*, pp. 114–15 [Woolf's note].

true and substantial about her. History scarcely mentions her. And I turned to Professor Trevelyan again to see what history meant to him. I found by looking at his chapter headings that it meant—

"The Manor Court and the Methods of Open-field Agriculture . . . The Cistercians and Sheep-farming . . . The Crusades . . . The University . . . The House of Commons . . . The Hundred Years' War . . . The Wars of the Roses . . . The Renaissance Scholars . . . The Dissolution of the Monasteries . . . Agrarian and Religious Strife . . . The Origin of English Sea-power . . . The Armada . . ." and so on. Occasionally an individual woman is mentioned, an Elizabeth, or a Mary; a queen or a great lady. But by no possible means could middle-class women with nothing but brains and character at their command have taken part in any one of the great movements which, brought together, constitute the historian's view of the past. Nor shall we find her in any collection of anecdotes. Aubrey[8] hardly mentions her. She never writes her own life and scarcely keeps a diary; there are only a handful of her letters in existence. She left no plays or poems by which we can judge her. What one wants, I thought—and why does not some brilliant student at Newnham or Girton[9] supply it?—is a mass of information; at what age did she marry; how many children had she as a rule; what was her house like; had she a room to herself; did she do the cooking; would she be likely to have a servant? All these facts lie somewhere, presumably, in parish registers and account books; the life of the average Elizabethan woman must be scattered about somewhere, could one collect it and make a book of it. It would be ambitious beyond my daring, I thought, looking about the shelves for books that were not there, to suggest to the students of those famous colleges that they should re-write history, though I own that it often seems a little queer as it is, unreal, lop-sided; but why should they not add a supplement to history? calling it, of course, by some inconspicuous name so that women might figure there without impropriety? For one often catches a glimpse of them in the lives of the great, whisking away into the background, concealing, I sometimes think, a wink, a laugh, perhaps a tear. And, after all, we have lives enough of Jane Austen; it scarcely seems necessary to consider again the influence of the tragedies of Joanna Baillie[1] upon the poetry of Edgar Allan Poe; as for myself, I should not mind if the homes and haunts of Mary Russell Mitford were closed to the public for a century at least. But what I find deplorable, I continued, looking about the bookshelves again, is that nothing is known about women before the eighteenth century. I have no model in my mind to turn about this way and that. Here am I asking why women did not write poetry in the Elizabethan age, and I am not sure how they were educated; whether they were taught to write; whether they had sitting-rooms to themselves; how many women had children before they were twenty-one; what, in short, they did from eight in the morning till eight at night. They had no money evidently; according to Professor Trevelyan they were married whether they liked it or not before they were out of the nursery, at fifteen or sixteen very likely. It would have been extremely odd, even upon this showing, had one of them suddenly written the plays of Shakespeare,

8. John Aubrey (1626–1697), author of *Brief Lives*, which includes sketches of his famous contemporaries.
9. Woolf delivered her lectures at Newnham and Girton Colleges for women, part of Cambridge University since 1880 and 1873, respectively.
1. Joanna Baillie (1762–1851) was a poet and dramatist whose *Plays on the Passions* (1798–1812) were famous in her day.

I concluded, and I thought of that old gentleman, who is dead now, but was a bishop, I think, who declared that it was impossible for any woman, past, present, or to come, to have the genius of Shakespeare. He wrote to the papers about it. He also told a lady who applied to him for information that cats do not as a matter of fact go to heaven, though they have, he added, souls of a sort. How much thinking those old gentlemen used to save one! How the borders of ignorance shrank back at their approach! Cats do not go to heaven. Women cannot write the plays of Shakespeare.

Be that as it may, I could not help thinking, as I looked at the works of Shakespeare on the shelf, that the bishop was right at least in this; it would have been impossible, completely and entirely, for any woman to have written the plays of Shakespeare in the age of Shakespeare. Let me imagine, since facts are so hard to come by, what would have happened had Shakespeare had a wonderfully gifted sister, called Judith,[2] let us say. Shakespeare himself went, very probably— his mother was an heiress—to the grammar school, where he may have learnt Latin—Ovid, Virgil and Horace[3]—and the elements of grammar and logic. He was, it is well known, a wild boy who poached rabbits, perhaps shot a deer, and had, rather sooner than he should have done, to marry a woman in the neighbourhood, who bore him a child rather quicker than was right. That escapade sent him to seek his fortune in London. He had, it seemed, a taste for the theatre; he began by holding horses at the stage door. Very soon he got work in the theatre, became a successful actor, and lived at the hub of the universe, meeting everybody, knowing everybody, practising his art on the boards, exercising his wits in the streets, and even getting access to the palace of the queen. Meanwhile his extraordinarily gifted sister, let us suppose, remained at home. She was as adventurous, as imaginative, as agog to see the world as he was. But she was not sent to school. She had no chance of learning grammar and logic, let alone of reading Horace and Virgil. She picked up a book now and then, one of her brother's perhaps, and read a few pages. But then her parents came in and told her to mend the stockings or mind the stew and not moon about with books and papers. They would have spoken sharply but kindly, for they were substantial people who knew the conditions of life for a woman and loved their daughter—indeed, more likely than not she was the apple of her father's eye. Perhaps she scribbled some pages up in an apple loft on the sly, but was careful to hide them or set fire to them. Soon, however, before she was out of her teens, she was to be betrothed to the son of a neighbouring wool-stapler.[4] She cried out that marriage was hateful to her, and for that she was severely beaten by her father. Then he ceased to scold her. He begged her instead not to hurt him, not to shame him in this matter of her marriage. He would give her a chain of beads or a fine petticoat, he said; and there were tears in his eyes. How could she disobey him? How could she break his heart? The force of her own gift alone drove her to it. She made up a small parcel of her belongings, let herself down by a rope one summer's night and took the road to London. She was not seventeen. The birds that sang in the hedge were not more musical than

---

2. The name of Shakespeare's younger daughter.
3. Roman authors. Publius Ovidius Naso (43 B.C.E.–17 C.E.), author of the *Metamorphoses*. Publius Vergilius Maro (70–19 B.C.E.),

author of the *Aeneid*. Quintus Horatius Flaccus (65–8 B.C.E.), author of *Odes* and satires.
4. A dealer in woolen goods, which were a "staple" or established type of merchandise.

she was. She had the quickest fancy, a gift like her brother's, for the tune of words. Like him, she had a taste for the theatre. She stood at the stage door; she wanted to act, she said. Men laughed in her face. The manager—a fat, loose-lipped man—guffawed. He bellowed something about poodles dancing and women acting—no woman, he said, could possibly be an actress. He hinted—you can imagine what. She could get no training in her craft. Could she even seek her dinner in a tavern or roam the streets at midnight? Yet her genius was for fiction and lusted to feed abundantly upon the lives of men and women and the study of their ways. At last—for she was very young, oddly like Shakespeare the poet in her face, with the same grey eyes and rounded brows—at last Nick Greene[5] the actor-manager took pity on her; she found herself with child by that gentleman and so—who shall measure the heat and violence of the poet's heart when caught and tangled in a woman's body?—killed herself one winter's night and lies buried at some cross-roads where the omnibuses now stop outside the Elephant and Castle.[6]

That, more or less, is how the story would run, I think, if a woman in Shakespeare's day had had Shakespeare's genius. But for my part, I agree with the deceased bishop, if such he was—it is unthinkable that any woman in Shakespeare's day should have had Shakespeare's genius. For genius like Shakespeare's is not born among labouring, uneducated, servile people. It was not born in England among the Saxons and the Britons. It is not born today among the working classes. How, then, could it have been born among women whose work began, according to Professor Trevelyan, almost before they were out of the nursery, who were forced to it by their parents and held to it by all the power of law and custom? Yet genius of a sort must have existed among women as it must have existed among the working classes. Now and again an Emily Brontë or a Robert Burns[7] blazes out and proves its presence. But certainly it never got itself on to paper. When, however, one reads of a witch being ducked, of a woman possessed by devils, of a wise woman selling herbs, or even of a very remarkable man who had a mother, then I think we are on the track of a lost novelist, a suppressed poet, of some mute and inglorious[8] Jane Austen, some Emily Brontë who dashed her brains out on the moor or mopped and mowed about the highways crazed with the torture that her gift had put her to. Indeed, I would venture to guess that Anon, who wrote so many poems without signing them, was often a woman. It was a woman Edward Fitzgerald,[9] I think, suggested who made the ballads and the folk-songs, crooning them to her children, beguiling her spinning with them, or the length of the winter's night.

This may be true or it may be false—who can say?—but what is true in it, so it seemed to me, reviewing the story of Shakespeare's sister as I had made it, is that any woman born with a great gift in the sixteenth century would certainly have gone crazed, shot herself, or ended her days in some lonely cottage outside the village, half witch, half wizard, feared and mocked at. For it needs little

5. A fictional character based on Shakespeare's contemporary Robert Greene (1558–1592) and appearing in Woolf's *Orlando*.
6. A popular London pub. "Cross-roads": suicides were commonly buried at crossroads.
7. Scottish poet (1759–1796).

8. A reference to Thomas Gray's line in *Elegy Written in a Country Churchyard* (1751): "Some mute inglorious Milton here may rest."
9. British author (1809–1883), known for his translation from the Persian of *The Rubáiyát of Omar Khayyám* (1859).

skill in psychology to be sure that a highly gifted girl who had tried to use her gift for poetry would have been so thwarted and hindered by other people, so tortured and pulled asunder by her own contrary instincts, that she must have lost her health and sanity to a certainty. No girl could have walked to London and stood at a stage door and forced her way into the presence of actor-managers without doing herself a violence and suffering an anguish which may have been irrational—for chastity may be a fetish invented by certain societies for unknown reasons—but were none the less inevitable. Chastity had then, it has even now, a religious importance in a woman's life, and has so wrapped itself round with nerves and instincts that to cut it free and bring it to the light of day demands courage of the rarest. To have lived a free life in London in the sixteenth century would have meant for a woman who was poet and playwright a nervous stress and dilemma which might well have killed her. Had she survived, whatever she had written would have been twisted and deformed, issuing from a strained and morbid imagination. And undoubtedly, I thought, looking at the shelf where there are no plays by women, her work would have gone unsigned. That refuge she would have sought certainly. It was the relic of the sense of chastity that dictated anonymity to women even so late as the nineteenth century. Currer Bell, George Eliot, George Sand,[1] all the victims of inner strife as their writings prove, sought ineffectively to veil themselves by using the name of a man. Thus they did homage to the convention, which if not implanted by the other sex was liberally encouraged by them (the chief glory of a woman is not to be talked of, said Pericles,[2] himself a much-talked-of man), that publicity in women is detestable. Anonymity runs in their blood. The desire to be veiled still possesses them. They are not even now as concerned about the health of their fame as men are, and, speaking generally, will pass a tombstone or a signpost without feeling an irresistible desire to cut their names on it, as Alf, Bert or Chas. must do in obedience to their instinct, which murmurs if it sees a fine woman go by, or even a dog, Ce chien est à moi.[3] And, of course, it may not be a dog, I thought, remembering Parliament Square, the Sièges Allée[4] and other avenues; it may be a piece of land or a man with curly black hair. It is one of the great advantages of being a woman that one can pass even a very fine negress without wishing to make an Englishwoman of her.

That woman, then, who was born with a gift of poetry in the sixteenth century, was an unhappy woman, a woman at strife against herself. All the conditions of her life, all her own instincts, were hostile to the state of mind which is needed to set free whatever is in the brain. But what is the state of mind that is most propitious to the act of creation, I asked. Can one come by any notion of the state that furthers and makes possible that strange activity? Here I opened the volume containing the Tragedies of Shakespeare. What was Shakespeare's state of mind, for instance, when he wrote *Lear* and *Antony and Cleopatra*? It was

---

1. Pseudonyms of Charlotte Brontë, Mary Ann Evans (1819–1880), and Lucile-Aurore Dupin (1804–1876), author of *Lélia* (1833), respectively.

2. From the Greek leader Pericles' funeral oration (431 B.C.E.). as reported in Thucydides' history of the Peloponnesian War (2.35–46).

3. This dog is mine (French); from the philoso-

pher Blaise Pascal's *Thoughts* (1657–58). He uses an anecdote about poor children to illustrate a universal impulse to assert property claims.

4. An avenue in Berlin containing statues of Hohenzollern rulers. Parliament Square is in London next to the Houses of Parliament and Westminster Abbey.

certainly the state of mind most favourable to poetry that there has ever existed. But Shakespeare himself said nothing about it. We only know casually and by chance that he "never blotted a line."[5] Nothing indeed was ever said by the artist himself about his state of mind until the eighteenth century perhaps. Rousseau[6] perhaps began it. At any rate, by the nineteenth century self-consciousness had developed so far that it was the habit for men of letters to describe their minds in confessions and autobiographies. Their lives also were written, and their letters were printed after their deaths. Thus, though we do not know what Shakespeare went through when he wrote *Lear*, we do know what Carlyle went through when he wrote the *French Revolution*; what Flaubert went through when he wrote *Madame Bovary*; what Keats[7] was going through when he tried to write poetry against the coming of death and the indifference of the world.

And one gathers from this enormous modern literature of confession and self-analysis that to write a work of genius is almost always a feat of prodigious difficulty. Everything is against the likelihood that it will come from the writer's mind whole and entire. Generally material circumstances are against it. Dogs will bark; people will interrupt; money must be made; health will break down. Further, accentuating all these difficulties and making them harder to bear is the world's notorious indifference. It does not ask people to write poems and novels and histories; it does not need them. It does not care whether Flaubert finds the right word or whether Carlyle scrupulously verifies this or that fact. Naturally, it will not pay for what it does not want. And so the writer, Keats, Flaubert, Carlyle, suffers, especially in the creative years of youth, every form of distraction and discouragement. A curse, a cry of agony, rises from those books of analysis and confession. "Mighty poets in their misery dead"[8]—that is the burden of their song. If anything comes through in spite of all this, it is a miracle, and probably no book is born entire and uncrippled as it was conceived.

But for women, I thought, looking at the empty shelves, these difficulties were infinitely more formidable. In the first place, to have a room of her own, let alone a quiet room or a sound-proof room, was out of the question, unless her parents were exceptionally rich or very noble, even up to the beginning of the nineteenth century. Since her pin money, which depended on the good will of her father, was only enough to keep her clothed, she was debarred from such alleviations as came even to Keats or Tennyson or Carlyle, all poor men, from a walking tour, a little journey to France, from the separate lodging which, even if it were miserable enough, sheltered them from the claims and tyrannies of their families. Such material difficulties were formidable; but much worse were the immaterial. The indifference of the world which Keats and Flaubert and other men of genius have found so hard to bear was in her case not indifference but hostility. The world did not say to her as it said to them, Write if you choose; it makes no difference to me. The world said with a guffaw, Write? What's the good of your writing? Here the psychologists of Newnham and Girton might come to our help, I thought, looking again at the blank spaces on the shelves. For surely it is

---

5. Ben Jonson's (1572–1637) description of Shakespeare.

6. Jean-Jacques Rousseau (1712–1778), French author of the *Confessions* (1781).

7. John Keats (1795–1821), British poet.

Thomas Carlyle (1795–1881), essayist and historian, translator of Goethe and author of *The French Revolution* (1837).

8. From Wordsworth's "Resolution and Independence" (1807).

time that the effect of discouragement upon the mind of the artist should be measured, as I have seen a dairy company measure the effect of ordinary milk and Grade A milk upon the body of the rat. They set two rats in cages side by side, and of the two one was furtive, timid and small, and the other was glossy, bold and big. Now what food do we feed women as artists upon? I asked, remembering, I suppose, that dinner of prunes and custard. To answer that question I had only to open the evening paper and to read that Lord Birkenhead is of opinion—but really I am not going to trouble to copy out Lord Birkenhead's opinion upon the writing of women. What Dean Inge says I will leave in peace. The Harley Street specialist may be allowed to rouse the echoes of Harley Street[9] with his vociferations without raising a hair on my head. I will quote, however, Mr. Oscar Browning, because Mr. Oscar Browning was a great figure in Cambridge at one time, and used to examine the students at Girton and Newnham. Mr. Oscar Browning was wont to declare "that the impression left on his mind, after looking over any set of examination papers, was that, irrespective of the marks he might give, the best woman was intellectually the inferior of the worst man." After saying that Mr. Browning went back to his rooms—and it is this sequel that endears him and makes him a human figure of some bulk and majesty—he went back to his rooms and found a stable-boy lying on the sofa—"a mere skeleton, his cheeks were cavernous and sallow, his teeth were black, and he did not appear to have the full use of his limbs. . . .'That's Arthur' [said Mr. Browning]. 'He's a dear boy really and most high-minded.'" The two pictures always seem to me to complete each other. And happily in this age of biography the two pictures often do complete each other, so that we are able to interpret the opinions of great men not only by what they say, but by what they do.

But though this is possible now, such opinions coming from the lips of important people must have been formidable enough even fifty years ago. Let us suppose that a father from the highest motives did not wish his daughter to leave home and become writer, painter or scholar. "See what Mr. Oscar Browning says," he would say; and there was not only Mr. Oscar Browning; there was the *Saturday Review*; there was Mr. Greg[1]—the "essentials of a woman's being," said Mr. Greg emphatically, "are that *they are supported by, and they minister to, men*"—there was an enormous body of masculine opinion to the effect that nothing could be expected of women intellectually. Even if her father did not read out loud these opinions, any girl could read them for herself; and the reading, even in the nineteenth century, must have lowered her vitality, and told profoundly upon her work. There would always have been that assertion—you cannot do this, you are incapable of doing that—to protest against, to overcome. Probably for a novelist this germ is no longer of much effect; for there have been women novelists of merit. But for painters it must still have some sting in it; and for musicians, I imagine, is even now active and poisonous in the extreme. The woman composer stands where the actress stood in the time of Shakespeare. Nick Greene, I thought, remembering the story I had made about Shakespeare's sister, said that a woman acting put him in mind of a dog dancing. Johnson repeated the phrase two hundred years later of women

9. A London street known for its many prominent physicians.
1. William Rathbone Greg (1809–1891),
cited from a *Saturday Review* essay entitled
"Why Are Women Redundant" (1873).

preaching. And here, I said, opening a book about music, we have the very words used again in this year of grace, 1928, of women who try to write music. "Of Mlle. Germaine Tailleferre one can only repeat Dr. Johnson's dictum concerning a woman preacher, transposed into terms of music. 'Sir, a woman's composing is like a dog's walking on his hind legs. It is not done well, but you are surprised to find it done at all.' "[2] So accurately does history repeat itself.

Thus, I concluded, shutting Mr. Oscar Browning's life and pushing away the rest, it is fairly evident that even in the nineteenth century a woman was not encouraged to be an artist. On the contrary, she was snubbed, slapped, lectured and exhorted. Her mind must have been strained and her vitality lowered by the need of opposing this, of disproving that. For here again we come within range of that very interesting and obscure masculine complex which has had so much influence upon the woman's movement; that deep-seated desire, not so much that *she* shall be inferior as that *he* shall be superior, which plants him wherever one looks, not only in front of the arts, but barring the way to politics too, even when the risk to himself seems infinitesimal and the suppliant humble and devoted. Even Lady Bessborough,[3] I remembered, with all her passion for politics, must humbly bow herself and write to Lord Granville Leveson-Gower: ". . . notwithstanding all my violence in politics and talking so much on that subject, I perfectly agree with you that no woman has any business to meddle with that or any other serious business, farther than giving her opinion (if she is ask'd)." And so she goes on to spend her enthusiasm where it meets with no obstacle whatsoever upon that immensely important subject, Lord Granville's maiden speech in the House of Commons. The spectacle is certainly a strange one, I thought. The history of men's opposition to women's emancipation is more interesting perhaps than the story of that emancipation itself. An amusing book might be made of it if some young student at Girton or Newnham would collect examples and deduce a theory—but she would need thick gloves on her hands, and bars to protect her of solid gold.

But what is amusing now, I recollected, shutting Lady Bessborough, had to be taken in desperate earnest once. Opinions that one now pastes in a book labelled cock-a-doodle-dum and keeps for reading to select audiences on summer nights once drew tears, I can assure you. Among your grandmothers and great-grandmothers there were many that wept their eyes out. Florence Nightingale shrieked aloud in her agony.[4] Moreover, it is all very well for you, who have got yourselves to college and enjoy sitting-rooms—or is it only bed-sitting-rooms?—of your own to say that genius should disregard such opinions; that genius should be above caring what is said of it. Unfortunately, it is precisely the men or women of genius who mind most what is said of them. Remember Keats. Remember the words he had cut on his tombstone.[5] Think of Tennyson;

2. *A Survey of Contemporary Music,* Cecil Gray, p. 246 [Woolf's note]. The statement is originally found in James Boswell's *Life of Johnson* (1791).
3. Henrietta, Countess of Bessborough (1761–1821), who corresponded with Lord Granville George Leveson-Gower (1815–1891), British foreign secretary in William Gladstone's administrations and after him the leader of the Liberal Party.
4. See *Cassandra,* by Florence Nightingale, printed in *The Cause,* by R. Strachey [Woolf's note]. Nightingale (1820–1910) was an English nurse and founder of nursing as a profession for women.
5. "Here lies one whose name was writ in water."

think—but I need hardly multiply instances of the undeniable, if very, unfortunate, fact that it is the nature of the artist to mind excessively what is said about him. Literature is strewn with the wreckage of men who have minded beyond reason the opinions of others.

And this susceptibility of theirs is doubly unfortunate, I thought, returning again to my original enquiry into what state of mind is most propitious for creative work, because the mind of an artist, in order to achieve the prodigious effort of freeing whole and entire the work that is in him, must be incandescent, like Shakespeare's mind, I conjectured, looking at the book which lay open at *Antony and Cleopatra*. There must be no obstacle in it, no foreign matter unconsumed.

For though we say that we know nothing about Shakespeare's state of mind, even as we say that, we are saying something about Shakespeare's state of mind. The reason perhaps why we know so little of Shakespeare—compared with Donne or Ben Jonson or Milton—is that his grudges and spites and antipathies are hidden from us. We are not held up by some "revelation" which reminds us of the writer. All desire to protest, to preach, to proclaim an injury, to pay off a score, to make the world the witness of some hardship or grievance was fired out of him and consumed. Therefore his poetry flows from him free and unimpeded. If ever a human being got his work expressed completely, it was Shakespeare. If ever a mind was incandescent, unimpeded, I thought, turning again to the bookcase, it was Shakespeare's mind.

1929

WILLIAM FAULKNER
1897–1962

Chronicler of the American South, William Faulkner gained an international reputation for his vivid imagination and innovative use of language. His account of the historical change between the Old and the New South transcends regional issues or the mythical community of Yoknapatawpha, Mississippi, where most of his work is situated; it came to influence writers in societies undergoing transition in Europe, Latin America, and China. Although his canvas is a single region, Faulkner encompasses broad themes: the clash of generations and ways of life, racial and family tragedies, and, in almost archetypal terms, the opposition of good and evil.

William Cuthbert Falkner was born on September 25, 1897, in New Albany, Mississippi, to a prosperous family with many ties to Southern history; their prosperity, however, was on the wane. The eldest of four sons, Faulkner (he adopted this spelling as a young man) was named for a great-grandfather who commanded a Confederate regiment in the Civil War, built railroads, and wrote novels. When asked as a child, "What do you want to be when you grow up?" William would reply, "I want to be a writer like my great-granddaddy." Faulkner's father worked for the family railroad enterprise until it was sold in 1902, afterward moving the family to Oxford and eventually becoming business manager of the University of Mississippi. The writer's close acquaintance with Southern customs and attitudes, his experience as the descendant of a once-prosperous and influential family, and his attachment to Lafayette County and the town of Oxford (Yoknapatawpha County and Jefferson in the novels) helped shape themes and setting in his fiction.

Young Faulkner read widely in his grandfather's library and borrowed books from an older friend, Philip Stone. Leaving high school after two years to work as a bookkeeper in his grandfather's bank, he continued reading and discussing literature with Stone, who encouraged his writing and introduced him to novels of the nineteenth-century French realist writer Honoré de Balzac (1799–1850). In his own novels, Faulkner would transform the Balzacian tradition of the human comedy—the novel as a panorama of society—by giving it a vocabulary drawn from the American South and a renewed place in literary history.

In the last six months of the First World War, Faulkner trained in Canada as a fighter pilot—then a common way of getting more quickly into combat—but the hostilities ended before he actually flew any missions; he returned to Oxford to enroll at the university as a special student (all the while claiming to have been shot down over France). By this time, Faulkner was known as a heavy drinker and teller of tall tales. Leaving the university in 1920 to work in a New York bookstore, he returned in 1921 and became postmaster for three years at the university. During this period he wrote poetry and seems to have been influenced by the French symbolists: his first published poem, *L'Après-midi d'un faune*, takes its title from **Stéphane Mallarmé**; he also admired the poetry of **T. S. Eliot**. Faulkner's first book, a collection of lyrics called *The Marble Faun*, appeared in 1924.

In 1925 the young writer spent six months in New Orleans, where he was attracted to a literary group associated with *The Double Dealer*, a magazine in which his poems, essays, and prose sketches appeared. The group's chief figure was Sherwood Anderson, author of a series of regional stories published as *Winesburg, Ohio* (1919), who encouraged Faulkner to make fictional use of his Southern background and who recommended Faulkner's first novel to his New York publisher. After completing *Soldier's Pay* (1926), Faulkner took a freighter to Europe, bicycling and hiking through Italy and France and living for a short while in Paris. At the end of the year, he returned to Mississippi, where he wrote his second novel, *Mosquitoes* (1927), a satire on the New Orleans group.

Taking up Anderson's earlier suggestion, Faulkner embarked on the regional "Yoknapatawpha" (*yok-na-pa-taw'-pha*) series with *Sartoris* (1929), an account of the return home, marriage, and death of a wounded First World War veteran, Bayard Sartoris. In *The Sound and the Fury* (1929), Faulkner experimented with the stream-of-consciousness technique pioneered by other modernists. Adapting **James Joyce**'s methods, Faulkner developed distinct literary styles, from brief fragments to the elaborate, lengthy sentences that have become famous as "Faulknerian," to represent the minds of the various characters. Both *Sartoris* and *The Sound and the Fury* were rejected several times before being published, and Faulkner supported himself, in the late 1920s, by working at odd jobs (on a shrimp trawler, in a lumber mill and a power plant, and as a carpenter, painter, and paperhanger) and then, between 1930 and 1932, from the sale of thirty short stories. One of his major experimental novels, *As I Lay Dying* (1930), was written in six weeks during his night shifts at the power plant. In 1929, Faulkner married Estelle Oldham Franklin, with whom he had one child, Jill, in 1933 (an earlier daughter died in infancy in 1931). Around this time he purchased an antebellum mansion, which he called Rowan Oak, that allowed him to establish a life akin to that of an impoverished Southern gentleman, a status he had known years before when his family lost the railroad.

Irritated at how hard it was to find publishers for his serious or experimental works, the novelist set out to write a best seller—and succeeded. *Sanctuary* (1931), a novel of the Deep South that described the rape and prostitution of a schoolgirl as well as murder, perjury, and the lynching of an innocent man, was made into a movie (*The Story of Temple Drake*, 1933) and brought its author invitations to work on movie scripts for a variety of Hollywood studios. From 1932 to 1955, Faulkner added to his income by working as a film doctor, revising and collaborating on scripts for films such as *To Have and Have Not* and *The Big Sleep*. In Hollywood the movie star Clark Gable once asked him what modern books to read. Faulkner suggested his own works. When Gable asked, "Do you write?" Faulkner replied, "Yes, Mr. Gable. What do you do?"

Although his works continued to receive critical praise, Faulkner had no commercial successes after *Sanctuary*. In 1945, when he was, according to the French writer and philosopher Jean-Paul Sartre, the idol of young French readers, most of his novels were out of print. It took an anthology, *The Portable Faulkner* (1946), to reintroduce the author to a wider audience. In 1950 he won the Nobel Prize for Literature; five years later he received the Pulitzer Prize and the National Book Award for *A Fable* (1954). He used the Nobel Prize money to establish the William Faulkner Foundation to assist Latin American writers and to award educational scholarships to Mississippi blacks. His fantastic, sometimes allegorical depictions of events influenced the development of "magical realism" in Latin America, while his forthright treatment of race relations inspired African American writers, including **James Baldwin** and **Toni Morrison**. In later years, Faulkner supported civil rights for African Americans but aroused controversy by suggesting that they "go slow, now." He died of a heart attack in Oxford, Mississippi, on July 6, 1962.

In setting many of his works in Yoknapatawpha County, Faulkner created a fictional world, with characters who reappear from novel to novel. Here imaginary families such as the Sartorises, Compsons, Sutpens, McCaslins, and Snopeses rise to prosperity or descend into weakness, degradation, and death. Individual characters may believe they have control of their lives but they work out destinies that are already half-shaped by family tradition and invisible community pressures. Caught in close, often incestuous relationships, they make their way in a world in which the values, traditions, and privileges of the old plantation society are yielding to those of an emerging mercantile class. A network of dynasties illustrates the picture of a changing society: the decaying and impoverished Compson family (*The Sound and the Fury*); two generations of Sutpens rising to great wealth and dying in madness and isolation (*Absalom, Absalom!*, 1936); and the McCaslin family, with its history of incest, miscegenation, and guilt (*Go Down, Moses*, 1942). *Light in August* (1932) shows the force of history and family tradition by having the central character, Joe Christmas, engage in a catastrophic struggle with his heritage without even knowing what it is.

"The past is never dead. It's not even past," wrote Faulkner: his characters constantly struggle with the ambiguous legacies of history, family, and their personal traumas.

These are violent works, and the murders, lynchings, and bestialities that appear in them account for Faulkner's early reputation, in the United States, as a lurid local writer. European critics, however, especially the French, who recognized his ability as early as 1931, were quick to identify mythic overtones and classical, even biblical prototypes in these tales of twisted family relationships. Faulkner himself described his approach as follows: "There's always a moment in experience—a thought—an incident—that's there. Then all I do is work up to that moment. I figure what must have happened before to lead people to that particular moment, and I work away from it, finding out how people act after the moment."

The stories paired here are early versions of material alluded to and incorporated into *The Hamlet* (1940), which tells of the rise of Flem Snopes (the unnamed brother in "Barn Burning"). These stories exhibit the range of Faulkner's art: "Spotted Horses" (1931), one of Faulkner's first portrayals of the Snopes family, is a comic tall tale about Flem's trickery of his community, while "Barn Burning" (1938) unearths Snopes family history through its presentation of Abner Snopes's dehumanized menace. "Barn Burning" appears here first because it is set earlier. The viciously grasping ambitious "Snopes family" rises and falls over the course of three novels (*The Hamlet*, 1940, which includes adapted versions of "Barn Burning" and "Spotted Horses"; *The Town*, 1957; and *The Mansion*, 1959). Both Flem Snopes and his victims are socially and geographically distant from the wealthy Compsons, Sartorises, and Sutpens, whose lives take them to the center of Jefferson; the residents of Frenchman's Bend are rural, white, and poor, like the Bundren family of *As I Lay Dying*, whose trip to town to bury their mother becomes an arduous journey fit for a novel. Just as the Sartoris family represents Southern aristocratic tradition in all its romanticism and humanity, the Snopeses originate as the shiftless "poor whites" and come to embody the cold, calculating, exploitative side of human nature that is working its way to the fore in an industrializing, commercially oriented age. Although, when described separately, members of the Snopes family take on individuality and human traits (generally perverse), together they turn into "Snopesism," a vision of evil that is openly diabolical. In Faulkner's view of the eternal battle between good and evil, "There is always someone that will never stop trying to cope with Snopes, that will never stop trying to get rid of Snopes."

These stories connect a local, isolated setting, with its colloquialisms and dialect speech, with grandiose convictions about human nature and society, often expressed in Latinate rhetoric. In "Barn Burning," Abner Snopes, father of Flem (unnamed in this story) and Colonel Sartoris Snopes, is a personification of inhuman, two-dimensional evil: "without face or depth—a shape black, flat, and bloodless as though cut from tin . . . , the voice harsh like tin and without heat like tin." His human qualities are purely destructive: a ferocious independence and a conviction of his own rectitude, linked to deep jealousy and rage against others' prosperity or authority; a vicious paranoia that creates opportunities for revenge; an arsonist's love for the destructive element of fire that speaks to "some deep mainspring" of his being. Young Colonel Sartoris Snopes is torn between two loyalties, as his name implies. To the psychological realism of individual portraits, and the conflict between father and son, Faulkner adds a struggle between right and wrong—two sides inextricably related to each other and, at the end, both left with an unknown future.

The picture of pure destruction that plays such a significant role in "Barn Burning" returns in comic vein in "Spotted Horses," as the animals bursting out of their pen run wild over the countryside and defy their new owners' best attempts to catch them. Literally an unbridled force of nature (spotted horses are often demonic in folklore), they upset the normal order of things. V. K. Ratliff, the sewing-machine agent who narrates the story, cannot help admire the craftiness with which Snopes manipulates events for his own profit, although Ratliff opposes everything that Snopes stands for and tries to shame him into returning some of his ill-gotten money. For this comedy has somber overtones as well: For some members of the community, the consequences of the action are severe. The farce ends with bitter irony, showing the hopelessness of its defeated characters against the legalistic precision and economic forces Flem represents.

Barn Burning

The store in which the Justice of the Peace's court was sitting smelled of cheese. The boy, crouched on his nail keg at the back of the crowded room, knew he smelled cheese, and more: from where he sat he could see the ranked shelves close-packed with the solid, squat, dynamic shapes of tin cans whose labels his stomach read, not from the lettering which meant nothing to his mind but from the scarlet devils and the silver curve of fish—this, the cheese which he knew he smelled and the hermetic[1] meat which his intestines believed he smelled coming in intermittent gusts momentary and brief between the other constant one, the smell and sense just a little of fear because mostly of despair and grief, the old fierce pull of blood. He could not see the table where the Justice sat and before which his father and his father's enemy (*our enemy* he thought in that despair; *ourn! mine and hisn both! He's my father!*) stood, but he could hear them, the two of them that is, because his father had said no word yet:

"But what proof have you, Mr. Harris?"

"I told you. The hog got into my corn. I caught it up and sent it back to him. He had no fence that would hold it. I told him so, warned him. The next time I put the hog in my pen. When he came to get it I gave him enough wire to patch up his pen. The next time I put the hog up and kept it. I rode down to his house and saw the wire I gave him still rolled on to the spool in his yard. I told him he could have the hog when he paid me a dollar pound fee. That evening a nigger came with the dollar and got the hog. He was a strange nigger. He said, 'He say to tell you wood and hay kin burn.' I said, 'What?' 'That whut he say to tell you,' the nigger said. 'Wood and hay kin burn.' That night my barn burned. I got the stock out but I lost the barn."

"Where is the nigger? Have you got him?"

"He was a strange nigger, I tell you. I don't know what became of him."

"But that's not proof. Don't you see that's not proof?"

1. Canned in tins whose labels display scarlet devils and the silver curve of fish.

"Get that boy up here. He knows." For a moment the boy thought too that the man meant his older brother until Harris said, "Not him. The little one. The boy," and, crouching, small for his age, small and wiry like his father, in patched and faded jeans even too small for him, with straight, uncombed, brown hair and eyes gray and wild as storm scud, he saw the men between himself and the table part and become a lane of grim faces, at the end of which he saw the Justice, a shabby, collarless, graying man in spectacles, beckoning him. He felt no floor under his bare feet; he seemed to walk beneath the palpable weight of the grim turning faces. His father, stiff in his black Sunday coat donned not for the trial but for the moving, did not even look at him. *He aims for me to lie*, he thought, again with that frantic grief and despair. *And I will have to do hit*.

"What's your name, boy?" the Justice said.

"Colonel Sartoris Snopes,"[2] the boy whispered.

"Hey?" the Justice said. "Talk louder. Colonel Sartoris? I reckon anybody named for Colonel Sartoris in this country can't help but tell the truth, can they?" The boy said nothing. *Enemy! Enemy!* he thought; for a moment he could not even see, could not see that the Justice's face was kindly nor discern that his voice was troubled when he spoke to the man named Harris: "Do you want me to question this boy?" But he could hear, and during those subsequent long seconds while there was absolutely no sound in the crowded little room save that of quiet and intent breathing it was as if he had swung outward at the end of a grape vine, over a ravine, and at the top of the swing had been caught in a prolonged instant of mesmerized gravity, weightless in time.

"No!" Harris said violently, explosively. "Damnation! Send him out of here!" Now time, the fluid world, rushed beneath him again, the voices coming to him again through the smell of cheese and sealed meat, the fear and despair and the old grief of blood:

"This case is closed. I can't find against you, Snopes, but I can give you advice. Leave this country and don't come back to it."

His father spoke for the first time, his voice cold and harsh, level, without emphasis: "I aim to. I don't figure to stay in a country among people who . . ." he said something unprintable and vile, addressed to no one.

"That'll do," the Justice said. "Take your wagon and get out of this country before dark. Case dismissed."

His father turned, and he followed the stiff black coat, the wiry figure walking a little stiffly from where a Confederate provost's man's[3] musket ball had taken him in the heel on a stolen horse thirty years ago, followed the two backs now, since his older brother had appeared from somewhere in the crowd, no taller than the father but thicker, chewing tobacco steadily, between the two lines of grim-faced men and out of the store and across the worn gallery and down the sagging steps and among the dogs and half-grown boys in the mild May dust, where as he passed a voice hissed:

"Barn burner!"

Again he could not see, whirling; there was a face in a red haze, moonlike, bigger than the full moon, the owner of it half again his size, he leaping in the

2. The Snopes boy is named for Colonel [John] Sartoris, legendary founder of the aris-

tocratic Sartoris family.
3. Military policeman.

red haze toward the face, feeling no blow, feeling no shock when his head struck the earth, scrabbling up and leaping again, feeling no blow this time either and tasting no blood, scrabbling up to see the other boy in full flight and himself already leaping into pursuit as his father's hand jerked him back, the harsh, cold voice speaking above him: "Go get in the wagon."

It stood in a grove of locusts and mulberries across the road. His two hulking sisters in their Sunday dresses and his mother and her sister in calico and sun-bonnets were already in it, sitting on and among the sorry residue of the dozen and more movings which even the boy could remember—the battered stove, the broken beds and chairs, the clock inlaid with mother-of-pearl, which would not run, stopped at some fourteen minutes past two o'clock of a dead and for-gotten day and time, which had been his mother's dowry. She was crying, though when she saw him she drew her sleeve across her face and began to descend from the wagon. "Get back," the father said.

"He's hurt. I got to get some water and wash his . . ."

"Get back in the wagon," his father said. He got in too, over the tailgate. His father mounted to the seat where the older brother already sat and struck the gaunt mules two savage blows with the peeled willow, but without heat. It was not even sadistic; it was exactly that same quality which in later years would cause his descendants to over-run the engine before putting a motor car into motion, striking and reining back in the same movement. The wagon went on, the store with its quiet crowd of grimly watching men dropped behind; a curve in the road hid it. *Forever* he thought. *Maybe he's done satisfied now, now that he has* . . . stopping himself, not to say it aloud even to himself. His mother's hand touched his shoulder.

"Does hit hurt?" she said.

"Naw," he said. "Hit don't hurt. Lemme be."

"Can't you wipe some of the blood off before hit dries?"

"I'll wash to-night," he said. "Lemme be, I tell you."

The wagon went on. He did not know where they were going. None of them ever did or ever asked, because it was always somewhere, always a house of sorts waiting for them a day or two days or even three days away. Likely his father had already arranged to make a crop on another farm before he . . . Again he had to stop himself. He (the father) always did. There was something about his wolflike independence and even courage when the advantage was at least neutral which impressed strangers, as if they got from his latent ravening ferocity not so much a sense of dependability as a feeling that his ferocious conviction in the rightness of his own actions would be of advantage to all whose interest lay with his.

That night they camped, in a grove of oaks and beeches where a spring ran. The nights were still cool and they had a fire against it, of a rail lifted from a nearby fence and cut into lengths—a small fire, neat, niggard almost, a shrewd fire; such fires were his father's habit and custom always, even in freezing weather. Older, the boy might have remarked this and wondered why not a big one; why should not a man who had not only seen the waste and extravagance of war, but who had in his blood an inherent voracious prodigality with mate-rial not his own, have burned everything in sight? Then he might have gone a step farther and thought that that was the reason: that niggard blaze was the living fruit of nights passed during those four years in the woods hiding from all men, blue or gray,[4] with his strings of horses (captured horses, he called them). And older still, he might have divined the true reason: that the element of fire spoke to some deep mainspring of his father's being, as the element of steel or of powder spoke to other men, as the one weapon for the preservation of integrity, else breath were not worth the breathing, and hence to be regarded with respect and used with discretion.

But he did not think this now and he had seen those same niggard blazes all his life. He merely ate his supper beside it and was already half asleep over his iron plate when his father called him, and once more he followed the stiff back, the stiff and ruthless limp, up the slope and on to the starlit road where, turning, he could see his father against the stars but without face or depth—a shape black, flat, and bloodless as though cut from tin in the iron folds of the frockcoat which had not been made for him, the voice harsh like tin and without heat like tin:

"You were fixing to tell them. You would have told him." He didn't answer. His father struck him with the flat of his hand on the side of the head, hard but without heat, exactly as he had struck the two mules at the store, exactly as he would strike either of them with any stick in order to kill a horse fly, his voice still without heat or anger: "You're getting to be a man. You got to learn. You got to learn to stick to your own blood or you ain't going to have any blood to stick to you. Do you think either of them, any man there this morning, would? Don't you know all they wanted was a chance to get at me because they knew I had them beat? Eh?" Later, twenty years later, he was to tell himself, "If I had said they wanted only truth, justice, he would have hit me again." But now he said nothing. He was not crying. He just stood there. "Answer me," his father said.

"Yes," he whispered. His father turned.

"Get on to bed. We'll be there to-morrow."

To-morrow they were there. In the early afternoon the wagon stopped before a paintless two-room house identical almost with the dozen others it had stopped before even in the boy's ten years, and again, as on the other dozen occasions, his mother and aunt got down and began to unload the wagon, although his two sisters and his father and brother had not moved.

"Likely hit ain't fitten for hawgs," one of the sisters said.

"Nevertheless, fit it will and you'll hog it and like it," his father said. "Get out of them chairs and help your Ma unload."

The two sisters got down, big, bovine, in a flutter of cheap ribbons; one of them drew from the jumbled wagon bed a battered lantern, the other a worn broom. His father handed the reins to the older son and began to climb stiffly over the wheel. "When they get unloaded, take the team to the barn and feed them." Then he said, and at first the boy thought he was still speaking to his brother: "Come with me."

"Me?" he said.

"Yes," his father said. "You."

"Abner," his mother said. His father paused and looked back—the harsh level stare beneath the shaggy, graying, irascible brows.

4. In the Civil War (1861–65), Union soldiers wore blue and Confederate soldiers gray uniforms.

"I reckon I'll have a word with the man that aims to begin to-morrow owning me body and soul for the next eight months."

They went back up the road. A week ago—or before last night, that is—he would have asked where they were going, but not now. His father had struck him before last night but never before had he paused afterward to explain why; it was as if the blow and the following calm, outrageous voice still rang, repercussed, divulging nothing to him save the terrible handicap of being young, the light weight of his few years, just heavy enough to prevent his soaring free of the world as it seemed to be ordered but not heavy enough to keep him footed solid in it, to resist it and try to change the course of its events.

Presently he could see the grove of oaks and cedars and the other flowering trees and shrubs where the house would be, though not the house yet. They walked beside a fence massed with honeysuckle and Cherokee roses[5] and came to a gate swinging open between two brick pillars, and now, beyond a sweep of drive, he saw the house for the first time and at that instant he forgot his father and the terror and despair both, and even when he remembered his father again (who had not stopped) the terror and despair did not return. Because, for all the twelve movings, they had sojourned until now in a poor country, a land of small farms and fields and houses, and he had never seen a house like this before. *Hit's big as a courthouse* he thought quietly, with a surge of peace and joy whose reason he could not have thought into words, being too young for that: *They are safe from him. People whose lives are a part of this peace and dignity are beyond his touch, he no more to them than a buzzing wasp: capable of stinging for a little moment but that's all; the spell of this peace and dignity rendering even the barns and stable and cribs which belong to it impervious to the puny flames he might contrive* . . . this, the peace and joy, ebbing for an instant as he looked again at the stiff black back, the stiff and implacable limp of the figure which was not dwarfed by the house, for the reason that it had never looked big anywhere and which now, against the serene columned backdrop, had more than ever that impervious quality of something cut ruthlessly from tin, depthless, as though, sidewise to the sun, it would cast no shadow. Watching him, the boy remarked the absolutely undeviating course which his father held and saw the stiff foot come squarely down in a pile of fresh droppings where a horse had stood in the drive and which his father could have avoided by a simple change of stride. But it ebbed only for a moment, though he could not have thought this into words either, walking on in the spell of the house, which he could even want but without envy, without sorrow, certainly never with that ravening and jealous rage which unknown to him walked in the ironlike black coat before him: *Maybe he will feel it too. Maybe it will even change him now from what maybe he couldn't help but be.*

They crossed the portico. Now he could hear his father's stiff foot as it came down on the boards with clocklike finality, a sound out of all proportion to the displacement of the body it bore and which was not dwarfed either by the white door before it, as though it had attained to a sort of vicious and ravening minimum not to be dwarfed by anything—the flat, wide, black hat, the formal coat of broadcloth which had once been black but which had now that friction-glazed greenish cast of the bodies of old house flies, the lifted sleeve which was too large,

5. An evergreen climbing rose with white flowers.

the lifted hand like a curled claw. The door opened so promptly that the boy knew the Negro must have been watching them all the time, an old man with neat grizzled hair, in a linen jacket, who stood barring the door with his body, saying, "Wipe you foots, white man, fo you come in here. Major ain't home nohow."

"Get out of my way, nigger," his father said, without heat too, flinging the door back and the Negro also and entering, his hat still on his head. And now the boy saw the prints of the stiff foot on the doorjamb and saw them appear on the pale rug behind the machinelike deliberation of the foot which seemed to bear (or transmit) twice the weight which the body compassed. The Negro was shouting "Miss Lula! Miss Lula!"[6] somewhere behind them, then the boy, deluged as though by a warm wave by a suave turn of carpeted stair and a pendant glitter of chandeliers and a mute gleam of gold frames, heard the swift feet and saw her too, a lady—perhaps he had never seen her like before either—in a gray, smooth gown with lace at the throat and an apron tied at the waist and the sleeves turned back, wiping cake or biscuit dough from her hands with a towel as she came up the hall, looking not at his father at all but at the tracks on the blond rug with an expression of incredulous amazement.

"I tried," the Negro cried. "I tole him to . . ."

"Will you please go away?" she said in a shaking voice. "Major de Spain is not at home. Will you please go away?"

His father had not spoken again. He did not speak again. He did not even look at her. He just stood stiff in the center of the rug, in his hat, the shaggy iron-gray brows twitching slightly above the pebble-colored eyes as he appeared to examine the house with brief deliberation. Then with the same deliberation he turned; the boy watched him pivot on the good leg and saw the stiff foot drag round the arc of the turning, leaving a final long and fading smear. His father never looked at it, he never once looked down at the rug. The Negro held the door. It closed behind them, upon the hysteric and indistinguishable woman-wail. His father stopped at the top of the steps and scraped his boot clean on the edge of it. At the gate he stopped again. He stood for a moment, planted stiffly on the stiff foot, looking back at the house. "Pretty and white, ain't it?" he said. "That's sweat. Nigger sweat. Maybe it ain't white enough yet to suit him. Maybe he wants to mix some white sweat with it."

Two hours later the boy was chopping wood behind the house within which his mother and aunt and the two sisters (the mother and aunt, not the two girls, he knew that; even at this distance and muffled by walls the flat loud voices of the two girls emanated an incorrigible idle inertia) were setting up the stove to prepare a meal, when he heard the hooves and saw the linen-clad man on a fine sorrel mare, whom he recognized even before he saw the rolled rug in front of the Negro youth following on a fat bay carriage horse—a suffused, angry face vanishing, still at full gallop, beyond the corner of the house where his father and brother were sitting in the two tilted chairs; and a moment later, almost before he could have put the axe down, he heard the hooves again and watched the sorrel mare go back out of the yard, already galloping again. Then his father began to shout one of the sisters' names, who presently emerged backward from the kitchen door dragging the rolled rug along the ground by one end while the other sister walked behind it.

6. "Miss" is a traditional southern form of respectful address used also for married women.

"If you ain't going to tote, go on and set up the wash pot," the first said.

"You, Sarty!" the second shouted. "Set up the wash pot!" His father appeared at the door, framed against that shabbiness, as he had been against that other bland perfection, impervious to either, the mother's anxious face at his shoulder.

"Go on," the father said. "Pick it up." The two sisters stooped, broad, lethargic; stooping, they presented an incredible expanse of pale cloth and a flutter of tawdry ribbons.

"If I thought enough of a rug to have to git hit all the way from France I wouldn't keep hit where folks coming in would have to tromp on hit," the first said. They raised the rug.

"Abner," the mother said. "Let me do it."

"You go back and git dinner," his father said. "I'll tend to this."

From the woodpile through the rest of the afternoon the boy watched them, the rug spread flat in the dust beside the bubbling wash-pot, the two sisters stooping over it with that profound and lethargic reluctance, while the father stood over them in turn, implacable and grim, driving them though never raising his voice again. He could smell the harsh homemade lye[7] they were using; he saw his mother come to the door once and look toward them with an expression not anxious now but very like despair; he saw his father turn, and he fell to with the axe and saw from the corner of his eye his father raise from the ground a flattish fragment of field stone and examine it and return to the pot, and this time his mother actually spoke: "Abner. Abner. Please don't. Please, Abner."

Then he was done too. It was dusk; the whippoorwills had already begun. He could smell coffee from the room where they would presently eat the cold food remaining from the mid-afternoon meal, though when he entered the house he realized they were having coffee again probably because there was a fire on the hearth, before which the rug now lay spread over the backs of the two chairs. The tracks of his father's foot were gone. Where they had been were now long, water-cloudy scoriations resembling the sporadic course of a lilliputian[8] mowing machine.

It still hung there while they ate the cold food and then went to bed, scattered without order or claim up and down the two rooms, his mother in one bed, where his father would later lie, the older brother in the other, himself, the aunt, and the two sisters on pallets on the floor. But his father was not in bed yet. The last thing the boy remembered was the depthless, harsh silhouette of the hat and coat bending over the rug and it seemed to him that he had not even closed his eyes when the silhouette was standing over him, the fire almost dead behind it, the stiff foot prodding him awake. "Catch up the mule," his father said.

When he returned with the mule his father was standing in the black door, the rolled rug over his shoulder. "Ain't you going to ride?" he said.

"No. Give me your foot."

He bent his knee into his father's hand, the wiry, surprising power flowed smoothly, rising, he rising with it, on to the mule's bare back (they had owned

7. A caustic cleanser made from leaching ashes, certain to damage any delicate material.
8. Miniature, after the tiny inhabitants of Lil-
liput described in Jonathan Swift's *Gulliver's Travels* (1726).

a saddle once; the boy could remember it though not when or where) and with the same effortlessness his father swung the rug up in front of him. Now in the starlight they retraced the afternoon's path, up the dusty road rife with honey-suckle, through the gate and up the black tunnel of the drive to the lightless house, where he sat on the mule and felt the rough warp of the rug drag across his thighs and vanish.

"Don't you want me to help?" he whispered. His father did not answer and now he heard again that stiff foot striking the hollow portico with that wooden and clocklike deliberation, that outrageous overstatement of the weight it carried. The rug, hunched, not flung (the boy could tell that even in the darkness) from his father's shoulder struck the angle of wall and floor with a sound unbelievably loud, thunderous, then the foot again, unhurried and enormous; a light came on in the house and the boy sat, tense, breathing steadily and quietly and just a little fast, though the foot itself did not increase its beat at all, descending the steps now; now the boy could see him.

"Don't you want to ride now?" he whispered. "We kin both ride now," the light within the house altering now, flaring up and sinking. *He's coming down the stairs now*, he thought. He had already ridden the mule up beside the horse block; presently his father was up behind him and he doubled the reins over and slashed the mule across the neck, but before the animal could begin to trot the hard, thin arm came round him, the hard, knotted hand jerking the mule back to a walk.

In the first red rays of the sun they were in the lot, putting plow gear on the mules. This time the sorrel mare was in the lot before he heard it at all, the rider collarless and even bareheaded, trembling, speaking in a shaking voice as the woman in the house had done, his father merely looking up once before stooping again to the hame he was buckling, so that the man on the mare spoke to his stooping back:

"You must realize you have ruined that rug. Wasn't there anybody here, any of your women . . . ." he ceased, shaking, the boy watching him, the older brother leaning now in the stable door, chewing, blinking slowly and steadily at nothing apparently. "It cost a hundred dollars. But you never had a hundred dollars. You never will. So I'm going to charge you twenty bushels of corn against your crop. I'll add it in your contract and when you come to the commissary you can sign it. That won't keep Mrs. de Spain quiet but maybe it will teach you to wipe your feet off before you enter her house again."

Then he was gone. The boy looked at his father, who still had not spoken or even looked up again, who was now adjusting the logger-head in the hame.

"Pap," he said. His father looked at him—the inscrutable face, the shaggy brows beneath which the gray eyes glinted coldly. Suddenly the boy went toward him, fast, stopping as suddenly. "You done the best you could!" he cried. "If he wanted hit done different why didn't he wait and tell you how? He won't git no twenty bushels! He won't git none! We'll gether hit and hide hit! I kin watch . . ."

"Did you put the cutter back in that straight stock like I told you?"

"No, sir," he said.

"Then go do it."

That was Wednesday. During the rest of that week he worked steadily, at what was within his scope and some which was beyond it, with an industry that did not need to be driven nor even commanded twice; he had this from his mother, with the difference that some at least of what he did he liked to do, such as splitting wood with the half-size axe which his mother and aunt had earned, or saved money somehow, to present him with at Christmas. In company with the two older women (and on one afternoon, even one of the sisters), he built pens for the shoat and the cow which were a part of his father's contract with the landlord, and one afternoon, his father being absent, gone somewhere on one of the mules, he went to the field.

They were running a middle buster[9] now, his brother holding the plow straight while he handled the reins, and walking beside the straining mule, the rich black soil shearing cool and damp against his bare ankles, he thought *Maybe this is the end of it. Maybe even that twenty bushels that seems hard to have to pay for just a rug will be a cheap price for him to stop forever and always from being what he used to be*; thinking, dreaming now, so that his brother had to speak sharply to him to mind the mule: *Maybe he even won't collect the twenty bushels. Maybe it will all add up and balance and vanish—corn, rug, fire; the terror and grief, the being pulled two ways like between two teams of horses—gone, done with for ever and ever.*

Then it was Saturday; he looked up from beneath the mule he was harnessing and saw his father in the black coat and hat. "Not that," his father said. "The wagon gear." And then, two hours later, sitting in the wagon bed behind his father and brother on the seat, the wagon accomplished a final curve, and he saw the weathered paintless store with its tattered tobacco- and patent-medicine posters and the tethered wagons and saddle animals below the gallery. He mounted the gnawed steps behind his father and brother, and there again was the lane of quiet, watching faces for the three of them to walk through. He saw the man in spectacles sitting at the plank table and he did not need to be told this was a Justice of the Peace; he sent one glare of fierce, exultant, partisan defiance at the man in collar and cravat now, whom he had seen but twice before in his life, and that on a galloping horse, who now wore on his face an expression not of rage but of amazed unbelief which the boy could not have known was at the incredible circumstance of being used by one of his own tenants, and came and stood against his father and cried at the Justice: "He ain't done it! He ain't burnt . . . ."

"Go back to the wagon," his father said.

"Burnt?" the Justice said. "Do I understand this rug was burned too?"

"Does anybody here claim it was?" his father said. "Go back to the wagon." But he did not, he merely retreated to the rear of the room, crowded as that other had been, but not to sit down this time, instead, to stand pressing among the motionless bodies, listening to the voices:

"And you claim twenty bushels of corn is too high for the damage you did to the rug?"

"He brought the rug to me and said he wanted the tracks washed out of it. I washed the tracks out and took the rug back to him."

"But you didn't carry the rug back to him in the same condition it was in before you made the tracks on it."

9. A double moldboard plow that throws a ridge of earth both ways.

His father did not answer, and now for perhaps half a minute there was no sound at all save that of breathing, the faint, steady suspiration of complete and intent listening.

"You decline to answer that, Mr. Snopes?" Again his father did not answer. "I'm going to find against you, Mr. Snopes. I'm going to find that you were responsible for the injury to Major de Spain's rug and hold you liable for it. But twenty bushels of corn seems a little high for a man in your circumstances to have to pay. Major de Spain claims it cost a hundred dollars. October corn will be worth about fifty cents. I figure that if Major de Spain can stand a ninety-five dollar loss on something he paid cash for, you can stand a five-dollar loss you haven't earned yet. I hold you in damages to Major de Spain to the amount of ten bushels of corn over and above your contract with him, to be paid to him out of your crop at gathering time. Court adjourned."

It had taken no time hardly, the morning was but half begun. He thought they would return home and perhaps back to the field, since they were late, far behind all other farmers. But instead his father passed on behind the wagon, merely indicating with his hand for the older brother to follow with it, and crossed the road toward the blacksmith shop opposite, pressing on after his father, overtaking him, speaking, whispering up at the harsh, calm face beneath the weathered hat: "He won't git no ten bushels neither. He won't git one. We'll . . ." until his father glanced for an instant down at him, the face absolutely calm, the grizzled eyebrows tangled above the cold eyes, the voice almost pleasant, almost gentle:

"You think so? Well, we'll wait till October anyway."

The matter of the wagon—the setting of a spoke or two and the tightening of the tires—did not take long either, the business of the tires accomplished by driving the wagon into the spring branch behind the shop and letting it stand there, the mules nuzzling into the water from time to time, and the boy on the seat with the idle reins, looking up the slope and through the sooty tunnel of the shed where the slow hammer rang and where his father sat on an upended cypress bolt, easily, either talking or listening, still sitting there when the boy brought the dripping wagon up out of the branch and halted it before the door.

"Take them on to the shade and hitch," his father said. He did so and returned. His father and the smith and a third man squatting on his heels inside the door were talking, about crops and animals; the boy, squatting too in the ammoniac dust and hoof-parings and scales of rust, heard his father tell a long and unhurried story out of the time before the birth of the older brother even when he had been a professional horsetrader. And then his father came up beside him where he stood before a tattered last year's circus poster on the other side of the store, gazing rapt and quiet at the scarlet horses, the incredible poisings and convolutions of tulle and tights and the painted leers of comedians, and said, "It's time to eat."

But not at home. Squatting beside his brother against the front wall, he watched his father emerge from the store and produce from a paper sack a segment of cheese and divide it carefully and deliberately into three with his pocket knife and produce crackers from the same sack. They all three squatted on the gallery and ate, slowly, without talking; then in the store again, they drank from a tin dipper tepid water smelling of the cedar bucket and of living beech trees. And still they did not go home. It was a horse lot this time, a tall rail fence upon and along which men stood and sat and out of which one by one horses were led, to be walked and trotted and then cantered back and forth along the road while the slow swapping and buying went on and the sun began to slant westward, they—the three of them—watching and listening, the older brother with his muddy eyes and his steady, inevitable tobacco, the father commenting now and then on certain of the animals, to no one in particular.

It was after sundown when they reached home. They ate supper by lamplight, then, sitting on the doorstep, the boy watched the night fully accomplish, listening to the whippoorwills and the frogs, when he heard his mother's voice: "Abner! No! No! Oh, God. Oh, God. Abner!" and he rose, whirled, and saw the altered light through the door where a candle stub now burned in a bottle neck on the table and his father, still in the hat and coat, at once formal and burlesque as though dressed carefully for some shabby and ceremonial violence, emptying the reservoir of the lamp back into the five-gallon kerosene can from which it had been filled, while the mother tugged at his arm until he shifted the lamp to the other hand and flung her back, not savagely or viciously, just hard, into the wall, her hands flung out against the wall for balance, her mouth open and in her face the same quality of hopeless despair as had been in her voice. Then his father saw him standing in the door.

"Go to the barn and get that can of oil we were oiling the wagon with," he said. The boy did not move. Then he could speak.

"What . . ." he cried. "What are you . . ."

"Go get that oil," his father said. "Go."

Then he was moving, running, outside the house, toward the stable: this the old habit, the old blood which he had not been permitted to choose for himself, which had been bequeathed him willy nilly and which had run for so long (and who knew where, battening on what of outrage and savagery and lust) before it came to him. *I could keep on,* he thought. *I could run on and on and never look back, never need to see his face again. Only I can't I can't,* the rusted can in his hand now, the liquid sploshing in it as he ran back to the house and into it, into the sound of his mother's weeping in the next room, and handed the can to his father.

"Ain't you going to even send a nigger?" he cried. "At least you sent a nigger before!"

This time his father didn't strike him. The hand came even faster than the blow had, the same hand which had set the can on the table with almost excruciating care flashing from the can toward him too quick for him to follow it, gripping him by the back of his shirt and on to tiptoe before he had seen it quit the can, the face stooping at him in breathless and frozen ferocity, the cold, dead voice speaking over him to the older brother, who leaned against the table, chewing with that steady, curious, sidewise motion of cows:

"Empty the can into the big one and go on. I'll catch up with you."

"Better tie him up to the bedpost," the brother said.

"Do like I told you," the father said. Then the boy was moving, his bunched shirt and the hard, bony hand between his shoulder-blades, his toes just touching the floor, across the room and into the other one, past the sisters sitting with spread heavy thighs in the two chairs over the cold hearth, and to where his mother and aunt sat side by side on the bed, the aunt's arms about his mother's shoulders.

"Hold him," the father said. The aunt made a startled movement. "Not you," the father said. "Lennie. Take hold of him. You'll hold him better than that. If he gets loose don't you know what he is going to do? He will go up yonder." He jerked his head toward the road. "Maybe I'd better tie him."

"I'll hold him," his mother whispered.

"See you do then." Then his father was gone, the stiff foot heavy and measured upon the boards, ceasing at last.

Then he began to struggle. His mother caught him in both arms, he jerking and wrenching at them. He would be stronger in the end, he knew that. But he had no time to wait for it. "Lemme go!" he cried. "I don't want to have to hit you!"

"Let him go!" the aunt said. "If he don't go, before God, I am going up there myself!"

"Don't you see I can't?" his mother cried. "Sarty! Sarty! No! No! Help me, Lizzie!"

Then he was free. His aunt grasped at him but it was too late. He whirled, running, his mother stumbled forward on to her knees behind him, crying to the nearer sister: "Catch him, Net! Catch him!" But that was too late too, the sister (the sisters were twins, born at the same time, yet either of them now gave the impression of being, encompassing as much living meat and volume and weight as any other two of the family) not yet having begun to rise from the chair, her head, face, alone merely turned, presenting to him in the flying instant an astonishing expanse of young female features untroubled by any surprise even, wearing only an expression of bovine interest. Then he was out of the room, out of the house, in the mild dust of the starlit road and the heavy rifeness of honeysuckle, the pale ribbon unspooling with terrific slowness under his running feet, reaching the gate at last and turning in, running, his heart and lungs drumming, on up the drive toward the lighted house, the lighted door. He did not knock, he burst in, sobbing for breath, incapable for the moment of speech; he saw the astonished face of the Negro in the linen jacket without knowing when the Negro had appeared.

"De Spain!" he cried, panted. "Where's . . ." then he saw the white man too emerging from a white door down the hall. "Barn!" he cried. "Barn!"

"What?" the white man said. "Barn?"

"Yes!" the boy cried. "Barn!"

"Catch him!" the white man shouted.

But it was too late this time too. The Negro grasped his shirt, but the entire sleeve, rotten with washing, carried away, and he was out that door too and in the drive again, and had actually never ceased to run even while he was screaming into the white man's face.

Behind him the white man was shouting, "My horse! Fetch my horse!" and he thought for an instant of cutting across the park and climbing the fence into the road, but he did not know the park nor how high the vine-massed fence might be and he dared not risk it. So he ran on down the drive, blood and breath roaring; presently he was in the road again though he could not see it. He could not hear either: the galloping mare was almost upon him before he heard her, and even then he held his course, as if the very urgency of his wild grief and need must in a moment more find his wings, waiting until the ultimate instant to hurl himself aside and into the weed-choked roadside ditch as the horse thundered past and on, for an instant in furious silhouette against the stars, the tranquil early summer night sky which, even before the shape of the horse and rider vanished, stained abruptly and violently upward: a long, swirling roar incredible and soundless, blotting the stars, and he springing up and into the road again, running again, knowing it was too late yet still running even after he heard the shot and, an instant later, two shots, pausing now without knowing he had ceased to run, crying "Pap! Pap!", running again before he knew he had begun to run, stumbling, tripping over something and scrabbling up again without ceasing to run, looking backward over his shoulder at the glare as he got up, running on among the invisible trees, panting, sobbing, "Father! Father!"

At midnight he was sitting on the crest of a hill. He did not know it was midnight and he did not know how far he had come. But there was no glare behind him now and he sat now, his back toward what he had called home for four days anyhow, his face toward the dark woods which he would enter when breath was strong again, small, shaking steadily in the chill darkness, hugging himself into the remainder of his thin, rotten shirt, the grief and despair now no longer terror and fear but just grief and despair. *Father. My father*, he thought. "He was brave!" he cried suddenly, aloud but not loud, no more than a whisper: "He was! He was in the war! He was in Colonel Sartoris' cav'ry!" not knowing that his father had gone to that war a private in the fine old European sense, wearing no uniform, admitting the authority of and giving fidelity to no man or army or flag, going to war as Malbrouck[1] himself did: for booty—it meant nothing and less than nothing to him if it were enemy booty or his own.

The slow constellations wheeled on. It would be dawn and then sun-up after a while and he would be hungry. But that would be to-morrow and now he was only cold, and walking would cure that. His breathing was easier now and he decided to get up and go on, and then he found that he had been asleep because he knew it was almost dawn, the night almost over. He could tell that from the whippoorwills. They were everywhere now among the dark trees below him, constant and inflectioned and ceaseless, so that, as the instant for giving over to the day birds drew nearer and nearer, there was no interval at all between them. He got up. He was a little stiff, but walking would cure that too as it would the cold, and soon there would be the sun. He went on down the hill, toward the dark woods within which the liquid silver voices of the birds called unceasing—the rapid and urgent beating of the urgent and quiring heart of the late spring night. He did not look back.

1938

---

1. The Duke of Marlborough (1650–1722), an English general whose name became distorted as Malbrouch and Malbrouck in Eng- lish and French popular songs celebrating his exploits.

Spotted Horses

I

Yes, sir. Flem Snopes[1] has filled that whole country full of spotted horses. You can hear folks running them all day and all night, whooping and hollering, and the horses running back and forth across them little wooden bridges ever now and then kind of like thunder. Here I was this morning pretty near halfway to town, with the team ambling along and me setting in the buckboard about half asleep, when all of a sudden something come swurging up outen the bushes and jumped the road clean, without touching hoof to it. It flew right over my team, big as a billboard and flying through the air like a hawk. It taken me thirty minutes to stop my team and untangle the harness and the buckboard and hitch them up again.

That Flem Snopes. I be dog[2] if he ain't a case, now. One morning about ten years ago, the boys was just getting settled down on Varner's porch for a little talk and tobacco, when here come Flem out from behind the counter, with his coat off and his hair all parted like he might have been clerking for Varner for ten years already. Folks all knowed him; it was a big family of them about five miles down the bottom. That year, at least. Sharecropping. They never stayed on any place over a year. Then they would move on to another place, with the chap or maybe the twins of that year's litter. It was a regular nest of them. But Flem. The rest of them stayed tenant farmers, moving ever year, but here come Flem one day, walking out from behind Jody Varner's counter like he owned it. And he wasn't there but a year or two before folks knowed that, if him and Jody was both still in that store in ten years more, it would be Jody clerking for Flem Snopes. Why, that fellow could make a nickel where it wasn't but four cents to begin with. He skun me in two trades, myself, and the fellow that can do that, I just hope he'll get rich before I do; that's all.

All right. So here Flem was, clerking at Varner's, making a nickel here and there and not telling nobody about it. No, sir. Folks never knowed when Flem got the better of somebody lessen the fellow he beat told it. He'd just set there in the store-chair, chewing his tobacco and keeping his own business to hisself, until about a week later we'd find out it was somebody else's business he was keeping to hisself—provided the fellow he trimmed was mad enough to tell it. That's Flem.

We give him ten years to own everything Jody Varner had. But he never waited no ten years. I reckon you-all know that gal of Uncle Billy Varner's, the youngest one; Eula. Jody's sister. Ever Sunday ever yellow-wheeled buggy and curried riding horse in that country would be hitched to Bill Varner's fence, and the young bucks setting on the porch, swarming around Eula like bees around a honey pot. One of these here kind of big, soft-looking gals that could giggle richer than plowed newground. Wouldn't none of them leave before the others, and so they would set there on the porch until time to go home, with some of them with nine and ten miles to ride and then get up tomorrow and go back to the field. So they would all leave together and they would ride in a clump down to the creek ford and hitch them curried horses and yellow-wheeled

---

1. The now older brother from "Barn Burning."   2. "I'll be darned."

buggies and get out and fight one another. Then they would get in the buggies again and go on home.

Well, one day about a year ago, one of them yellow-wheeled buggies and one of them curried saddle-horses quit this country. We heard they was heading for Texas. The next day Uncle Billy and Eula and Flem come into town in Uncle Bill's surrey, and when they come back, Flem and Eula was married. And on the next day we heard that two more of them yellow-wheeled buggies had left the country. They mought have gone to Texas, too. It's a big place.

Anyway, about a month after the wedding, Flem and Eula went to Texas, too. They was gone pretty near a year. Then one day last month, Eula come back, with a baby. We figgered up, and we decided that it was as well-growed a three-months-old baby as we ever see. It can already pull up on a chair. I reckon Texas makes big men quick, being a big place. Anyway, if it keeps on like it started, it'll be chewing tobacco and voting time it's eight years old.

And so last Friday here come Flem himself. He was on a wagon with another fellow. The other fellow had one of these two-gallon hats and a ivory-handled pistol and a box of gingersnaps sticking out of his hind pocket, and tied to the tailgate of the wagon was about two dozen of them Texas ponies, hitched to one another with barbed wire. They was colored like parrots and they was quiet as doves, and ere[3] a one of them would kill you quick as a rattlesnake. Nere a one of them had two eyes the same color, and nere a one of them had ever see a bridle, I reckon; and when that Texas man got down offen the wagon and walked up to them to show how gentle they was, one of them cut his vest clean offen him, same as with a razor.

Flem had done already disappeared; he had went on to see his wife, I reckon, and to see if that ere baby had done gone on to the field to help Uncle Billy plow, maybe. It was the Texas man that taken the horses on to Mrs. Little-john's lot. He had a little trouble at first, when they come to the gate, because they hadn't never see a fence before, and when he finally got them in and taken a pair of wire cutters and unhitched them and got them into the barn and poured some shell corn into the trough, they durn night tore down the barn. I reckon they thought that shell corn was bugs, maybe. So he left them in the lot and he announced that the auction would begin at sunup tomorrow.

That night we was setting on Mrs. Littlejohn's porch. You-all mind the moon was nigh full that night, and we would watch them spotted varmints swirling along the fence and back and forth across the lot same as minnows in a pond. And then now and then they would all kind of huddle up against the barn and rest themselves by biting and kicking one another. We would hear a squeal, and then a set of hoofs would go Bam! against the barn, like a pistol. It sounded just like a fellow with a pistol, in a nest of cattymounts,[4] taking his time.

II

It wasn't ere a man knowed yet if Flem owned them things or not. They just knowed one thing: that they wasn't never going to know for sho if Flem did or not, or if maybe he didn't just get on that wagon at the edge of town, for the ride or not.

---

3. Any.   4. Catamounts, wildcats.

Even Eck Snopes didn't know, Flem's own cousin. But wasn't nobody surprised at that. We knowed that Flem would skin Eck quick as he would ere a one of us.

They was there by sunup next morning, some of them come twelve and sixteen miles, with seed-money tied up in tobacco sacks in their overalls, standing along the fence, when the Texas man come out of Mrs. Littlejohn's after breakfast and clumb onto the gate post with that ere white pistol butt sticking outen his hind pocket. He taken a new box of gingersnaps outen his pocket and bit the end offen it like a cigar and spit out the paper, and said the auction was open. And still they was coming up in wagons and a horse-and-mule-back and hitching the teams across the road and coming to the fence. Flem wasn't nowhere in sight.

But he couldn't get them started. He begun to work on Eck, because Eck holp him last night to get them into the barn and feed them that shell corn. Eck got out just in time. He come outen that barn like a chip of the crest on a busted dam of water, and clumb into the wagon just in time.

He was working on Eck when Henry Armstid come up in his wagon. Eck was saying he was skeered to bid on one of them, because he might get it, and the Texas man says, "Them ponies? Them little horses?" He clumb down offen the gate post and went toward the horses. They broke and run, and him following them, kind of chirping to them, with his hand out like he was fixing to catch a fly, until he got three or four of them cornered. Then he jumped into them, and then we couldn't see nothing for a while because of the dust. It was a big cloud of it, and them blare-eyed, spotted things swoaring outen it twenty foot to a jump, in forty directions without counting up. Then the dust settled and there they was, that Texas man and the horse. He had its head twisted clean around like a owl's head. Its legs was braced and it was trembling like a new bride and groaning like a saw mill, and him holding its head wrung clean around on its neck so it was snuffing sky. "Look it over," he says, with his heels dug too and that white pistol sticking outen his pocket and his neck swole up like a spreading adder's until you could just tell what he was saying, cussing the horse and talking to us all at once: "Look him over, the fiddle-headed son of fourteen fathers. Try him, buy him; you will get the best—" Then it was all dust again, and we couldn't see nothing but spotted hide and mane, and that ere Texas man's boot-heels like a couple of walnuts on two strings, and after a while that two-gallon hat come sailing out like a fat old hen crossing a fence.

When the dust settled again, he was just getting outen the far fence corner, brushing himself off. He come and got his hat and brushed it off and come and clumb onto the gate post again. He was breathing hard. He taken the gingersnap box outen his pocket and et one, breathing hard. The hammerhead horse was still running round and round the lot like a merry-go-round at a fair. That was when Henry Armstid come shoving up to the gate in them patched overalls and one of them dangle-armed shirts of hisn. Hadn't nobody noticed him until then. We was all watching the Texas man and the horses. Even Mrs. Littlejohn; she had done come out and built a fire under the washpot in her back yard, and she would stand at the fence a while and then go back into the house and come out again with a armful of wash and stand at the fence again. Well, here come Henry shoving up, and then we see Mrs. Armstid right behind him, in that ere faded wrapper and sunbonnet and them tennis shoes. "Git on back to that wagon," Henry says.

"Henry," she says.

"Here, boys," the Texas man says; "make room for missus to git up and see. Come on, Henry," he says; "here's your chance to buy that saddle-horse missus has been wanting. What about ten dollars, Henry?"

"Henry," Mrs. Armstid says. She put her hand on Henry's arm. Henry knocked her hand down.

"Git on back to that wagon, like I told you," he says.

Mrs. Armstid never moved. She stood behind Henry, with her hands rolled into her dress, not looking at nothing. "He hain't no more despair[5] than to buy one of them things," she says. "And us not five dollars ahead of the porehouse, he hain't no more despair." It was the truth, too. They ain't never made more than a bare living offen that place of theirs, and them with four chaps and the very clothes they wears she earns by weaving by the firelight at night while Henry's asleep.

"Shut your mouth and git on back to that wagon," Henry says. "Do you want I taken a wagon stake to you here in the big road?"

Well, that Texas man taken one look at her. Then he begun on Eck again, like Henry wasn't even there. But Eck was skeered. "I can git me a snapping turtle or a water moccasin for nothing. I ain't going to buy none."

So the Texas man said he would give Eck a horse. "To start the auction, and because you help me last night. If you'll start the bidding on the next horse," he says, "I'll give you that fiddle-head horse."

I wish you could have seen them, standing there with their seed-money in their pockets, watching that Texas man give Eck Snopes a live horse, all fixed to call him a fool if he taken it or not. Finally Eck says he'll take it. "Only I just starts the bidding," he says. "I don't have to buy the next one lessen I ain't over-topped." The Texas man said all right, and Eck bid a dollar on the next one, with Henry Armstid standing there with his mouth already open, watching Eck and the Texas man like a mad dog or something. "A dollar," Eck says.

The Texas man looked at Eck. His mouth was already open too, like he had started to say something and what he was going to say had up and died on him. "A dollar?" he says. "One dollar? You mean, *one* dollar, Eck?"

"Durn it," Eck says; "Two dollars, then."

Well, sir, I wish you could a seen that Texas man. He taken out that ginger-snap box and held it up and looked into it, careful, like it might have been a diamond ring in it, or a spider. Then he throwed it away and wiped his face with a bandanna. "Well," he says. "Well. Two dollars. Two dollars. Is your pulse all right, Eck?" he says. "Do you have ager-sweats[6] at night, maybe?" he says. "Well," he says, "I got to take it. But are you boys going to stand there and see Eck get two horses at a dollar a head?"

That done it. I be dog if he wasn't nigh as smart as Flem Snopes. He hadn't no more than got the words outen his mouth before here was Henry Armstid, waving his hand. "Three dollars," Henry says. Mrs. Armstid tried to hold him again. He knocked her hand off, shoving up to the gate post.

"Mister," Mrs. Armstid says, "we got chaps in the house and not corn to feed the stock. We got five dollars I earned my chaps a-weaving after dark, and him snoring in the bed. And he hain't no more despair."

---

5. To spare.

6. Ague; chills and fever with sweating.

"Henry bids three dollars," the Texas man says. "Raise him a dollar, Eck, and the horse is yours."

"Henry," Mrs. Armstid says.

"Raise him, Eck," the Texas man says.

"Four dollars," Eck says.

"Five dollars," Henry says, shaking his fist. He shoved up right under the gate post. Mrs. Armstid was looking at the Texas man too.

"Mister," she says, "if you take that five dollars I earned my chaps a-weaving for one of them things, it'll be a curse onto you and yourn during all the time of man."

But it wasn't no stopping Henry. He had shoved up, waving his first at the Texas man. He opened it; the money was in nickels and quarters, and one dollar bill that looked like a cow's cud. "Five dollars," he says. "And the man that raises it'll have to beat my head off, or I'll beat hisn."

"All right," the Texas man says. "Five dollars is bid. But don't you shake your hand at me."

III

It taken till nigh sundown before the last one was sold. He got them hotted up once and the bidding got up to seven dollars and a quarter, but most of them went around three or four dollars, him setting on the gate post and picking the horses out one at a time by mouthword, and Mrs. Littlejohn pumping up and down at the tub and stopping and coming to the fence for a while and going back to the tub again. She had done got done too, and the wash was hung on the line in the back yard, and we could smell supper cooking. Finally they was all sold; he swapped the last two and the wagon for a buckboard.

We was all kind of tired, but Henry Armstid looked more like a mad dog than ever. When he bought, Mrs. Armstid had went back to the wagon, setting in it behind them two rabbit-sized, bone-pore mules, and the wagon itself looking like it would fall all to pieces soon as the mules moved. Henry hadn't even waited to pull it outen the road; it was still in the middle of the road and her setting in it, not looking at nothing, ever since this morning.

Henry was right up against the gate. He went up to the Texas man. "I bought a horse and I paid cash," Henry says. "And yet you expect me to stand around here until they are all sold before I can get my horse. I'm going to take my horse outen that lot."

The Texas man looked at Henry. He talked like he might have been asking for a cup of coffee at the table. "Take your horse," he says.

Then Henry quit looking at the Texas man. He begun to swallow, holding onto the gate. "Ain't you going to help me?" he says.

"It ain't my horse," the Texas man says.

Henry never looked at the Texas man again, he never looked at nobody. "Who'll help me catch my horse?" he says. Never nobody said nothing. "Bring the plowline," Henry says. Mrs. Armstid got outen the wagon and brought the plowline. The Texas man got down offen the post. The woman made to pass him, carrying the rope.

"Don't you go in there, missus," the Texas man says.

Henry opened the gate. He didn't look back. "Come on here," he says.

"Don't you go in there, missus," the Texas man says.

Mrs. Armstid wasn't looking at nobody, neither, with her hands across her middle, holding the rope. "I reckon I better," she says. Her and Henry went into the lot. The horses broke and run. Henry and Mrs. Armstid followed.

"Get him into the corner," Henry says. They got Henry's horse cornered finally, and Henry taken the rope, but Mrs. Armstid let the horse get out. They hemmed it up again, but Mrs. Armstid let it get out again, and Henry turned and hit her with the rope. "Why didn't you head him back?" Henry says. He hit her again. "Why didn't you?" It was about that time I looked around and see Flem Snopes standing there.

It was the Texas man that done something. He moved fast for a big man. He caught the rope before Henry could hit the third time, and Henry whirled and made like he would jump at the Texas man. But he never jumped. The Texas man went and taken Henry's arm and led him outen the lot. Mrs. Armstid come behind them and the Texas man taken some money outen his pocket and he give it into Mrs. Armstid's hand. "Get him into the wagon and take him on home," the Texas man says, like he might have been telling them he enjoyed his supper.

Then here comes Flem. "What's that for, Buck?" Flem says.

"Thinks he bought one of them ponies," the Texas man says. "Get him on away, missus."

But Henry wouldn't go. "Give him back that money," he says. "I bought that horse and I aim to have him if I have to shoot him."

And there was Flem, standing there with his hands in his pockets, chewing, like he had just happened to be passing.

"You take your money and I take my horse," Henry says. "Give it back to him," he says to Mrs. Armstid.

"You don't own no horse of mine," the Texas man says. "Get him on home, missus."

Then Henry seen Flem. "You got something to do with these horses," he says. "I bought one. Here's the money for it." He taken the bill outen Mrs. Armstid's hand. He offered it to Flem. "I bought one. Ask him. Here. Here's the money," he says, giving the bill to Flem.

When Flem taken the money, the Texas man dropped the rope he had snatched outen Henry's hand. He had done sent Eck Snopes's boy up to the store for another box of gingersnaps, and he taken the box of gingersnaps, and he taken the box outen his pocket and looked into it. It was empty and he dropped it on the ground. "Mr. Snopes will have your money for you tomorrow," he says to Mrs. Armstid. "You can get it from him tomorrow. He don't own no horse. You get him into the wagon and get him on home." Mrs. Armstid went back to the wagon and got in. "Where's that ere buckboard I bought?" the Texas man says. It was after sundown then. And then Mrs. Littlejohn come out on the porch and rung the supper bell.

IV

I come on in and et supper. Mrs. Littlejohn would bring in a pan of bread or something, then she would go out to the porch a minute and come back and tell us. The Texas man had hitched his team to the buckboard he had swapped them last two horses for, and him and Flem had gone, and then she told that the rest of them that never had ropes had went back to the store with I. O. Snopes to get some ropes, and wasn't nobody at the gate but Henry Armstid, and Mrs. Armstid setting in the wagon in the road, and Eck Snopes and that boy of hisn. "I don't care how many of them fool men gets killed by them things," Mrs. Littlejohn says, "but I ain't going to let Eck Snopes take that boy into that lot again." So she went down to the gate, but she come back without the boy or Eck neither.

"It ain't no need to worry about that boy," I says. "He's charmed." He was right behind Eck last night when Eck went to help feed them. The whole drove of them jumped clean over that boy's head and never touched him. It was Eck that touched him. Eck snatched him into the wagon and taken a rope and frailed the tar outen him.

So I had done et and went to my room and was undressing, long as I had a long trip to make next day; I was trying to sell a machine[7] to Mrs. Bundren up past Whiteleaf; when Henry Armstid opened that gate and went in by hisself. They couldn't make him wait for the balance of them to get back with their ropes. Eck Snopes said he tried to make Henry wait, but Henry wouldn't do it. Eck said Henry walked right up to them and that when they broke, they run clean over Henry like a hay-mow breaking down. Eck said he snatched that boy of hisn out of the way just in time and that them things went through that gate like a creek flood and into the wagons and teams hitched side the road, busting wagon tongues and snapping harness like it was fishing line, with Mrs. Armstid still setting in their wagon in the middle of it like something carved outen wood. Then they scattered, wild horses and tame mules with pieces of harness and single trees dangling offen them, both ways up and down the road.

"There goes ourn, paw!" Eck says his boy said. "There it goes, into Mrs. Little-john's house." Eck says it run right up the steps and into the house like a boarder late for supper. I reckon so. Anyway, I was in my room, in my underclothes, with one sock on and one sock in my hand, leaning out the window when the commotion busted out, when I heard something run into the melodeon[8] in the hall; it sounded like a railroad engine. Then the door to my room come sailing in like when you throw a tin bucket top into the wind and I looked over my shoulder and see something that looked like a fourteen-foot pinwheel a-blaring its eyes at me. It had to blare them fast, because I was already done jumped out the window.

I reckon it was anxious, too. I reckon it hadn't never seen barbed wire or shell corn before, but I know it hadn't never seen underclothes before, or maybe it was a sewing-machine agent it hadn't never seen. Anyway, it swirled and turned to run back up the hall and outen the house, when it met Eck Snopes and that boy just coming in, carrying a rope. It swirled again and run down the hall and out the back door just in time to meet Mrs. Littlejohn. She had just gathered up the clothes she had washed, and she was coming onto the back porch with a armful of washing on one hand and a scrubbing board in the other, when the horse skidded up to her, trying to stop and swirl again. It never taken Mrs. Littlejohn no time a-tall.

"Git outen here, you son," she says. She hit it across the face with the scrubbing board; that ere scrubbing board split as neat as ere a axe could have done it,

7. The narrator, V. K. Ratliff, is a traveling salesman who sells sewing machines.
8. A small keyboard organ.

and when the horse swirled to run back up the hall, she hit it again with what was left of the scrubbing board, not on the head this time. "And stay out," she says.

Eck and that boy was halfway down the hall by this time. I reckon that horse looked like a pinwheel to Eck too. "Git to hell outen here, Ad!" Eck says. Only there wasn't time. Eck dropped flat on his face, but the boy never moved. The boy was about a yard tall maybe, in overhalls just like Eck's; that horse swoared over his head without touching a hair. I saw that, because I was just coming back up the front steps, still carrying that ere sock and still in my underclothes, when the horse come onto the porch again. It taken one look at me and swirled again and run to the end of the porch and jumped the banisters and the lot fence like a hen-hawk and lit in the lot running and went out the gate again and jumped eight or ten upside-down wagons and went on down the road. It was a full moon then. Mrs. Armstid was still setting in the wagon like she had done been carved outen wood and left there and forgot.

That horse. It ain't never missed a lick. It was going about forty miles a hour when it come to the bridge over the creek. It would have had a clear road, but it so happened that Vernon Tull was already using the bridge when it got there. He was coming back from town; he hadn't heard about the auction; him and his wife and three daughters and Mrs. Tull's aunt, all setting in chairs in the wagon bed, and all asleep, including the mules. They waked up when the horse hit the bridge one time, but Tull said the first he knew was when the mules tried to turn the wagon around in the middle of the bridge and he seen that spotted varmint run right twixt the mules and run up the wagon tongue like a squirrel. He said he just had time to hit it across the face with his whip-stock, because about that time the mules turned the wagon around on that ere one-way bridge and that horse clumb across one of the mules and jumped down onto the bridge again and went on, with Vernon standing up in the wagon and kicking at it.

Tull said the mules turned in the harness and clumb back into the wagon too, with Tull trying to beat them out again, with the reins wrapped around his wrist. After that he says all he seen was over-turned chairs and womenfolks' legs and white drawers shining in the moonlight, and his mules and that spotted horse going on up the road like a ghost.

The mules jerked Tull outen the wagon and drug him a spell on the bridge before the reins broke. They thought at first that he was dead, and while they was kneeling around him, picking the bridge splinters outen him, here comes Eck and that boy, still carrying the rope. They was running and breathing a little hard. "Where'd he go?" Eck says.

V

I went back and got my pants and shirt and shoes on just in time to go and help get Henry Armstid outen the trash in the lot. I be dog if he didn't look like he was dead, with his head hanging back and his teeth showing in the moonlight, and a little rim of white under his eyelids. He could still hear them horses, here and there; hadn't none of them got more than four-five miles away yet, not knowing the country, I reckon. So we could hear them and folks yelling now and then: "Whooey. Head him!"

We toted Henry into Mrs. Littlejohn's. She was in the hall; she hadn't put down the armful of clothes. She taken one look at us, and she laid down the busted scrubbing board and taken up the lamp and opened a empty door. "Bring him in here," she says.

We toted him in and laid him on the bed. Mrs. Littlejohn set the lamp on the dresser, still carrying the clothes. "I'll declare, you men," she says. Our shadows was way up the wall, tiptoeing too; we could hear ourselves breathing. "Better get his wife," Mrs. Littlejohn says. She went out, carrying the clothes.

"I reckon we had," Quick says. "Go get her, somebody."

"Whyn't you go?" Winterbottom says.

"Let Ernest git her," Durley says. "He lives neighbors with them."

Ernest went to fetch her. I be dog if Henry didn't look like he was dead. Mrs. Littlejohn come back, with a kettle and some towels. She went to work on Henry, and then Mrs. Armstid and Ernest come in. Mrs. Armstid come to the foot of the bed and stood there, with her hands rolled into her apron, watching what Mrs. Littlejohn was doing, I reckon.

"You men get outen the way," Mrs. Littlejohn says. "Git outside," she says. "See if you can't find something else to play with that will kill some more of you."

"Is he dead?" Winterbottom says.

"It ain't your fault if he ain't," Mrs. Littlejohn says. "Go tell Will Varner to come up here. I reckon a man ain't so different from a mule, come long come short. Except maybe a mule's got more sense."

We went to get Uncle Billy. It was a full moon. We could hear them, now and then, four mile away: "Whooey. Head him." The country was full of them, one on ever wooden bridge in the land, running across it like thunder: "Whooey. There he goes. Head him."

We hadn't got far before Henry begun to scream. I reckon Mrs. Littlejohn's water had brung him to: anyway, he wasn't dead. We went on to Uncle Billy's. The house was dark. We called to him, and after a while the window opened and Uncle Billy put his head out, peart as a peckerwood,[9] listening. "Are they still trying to catch them durn rabbits?" he says.

He come down, with his britches on over his nightshirt, and his suspenders dangling, carrying his horse-doctoring grip. "Yes, sir," he says, cocking his head like a woodpecker; "they're still a-trying."

We could hear Henry before we reached Mrs. Littlejohn's. He was going Ah-Ah-Ah. We stopped in the yard. Uncle Billy went on in. We could hear Henry. We stood in the yard, hearing them on the bridges, this-a-way and that: "Whooey. Whooey."

"Eck Snopes ought to caught hisn," Ernest says.

"Looks like he ought," Winterbottom said.

Henry was going Ah-Ah-Ah steady in the house; then he begun to scream. "Uncle Billy's started," Quick says. We looked into the hall. We could see the light where the door was. Then Mrs. Littlejohn come out.

"Will needs some help," she says. "You, Ernest. You'll do." Ernest went into the house.

"Hear them?" Quick said. "That one was on Four Mile bridge." We could hear them; it sounded like thunder a long way off; it didn't last long:

"Whooey."

9. Pert as a woodpecker.

We could hear Henry: "Ah-Ah-Ah-Ah-Ah."

"They are both started now," Winterbottom says. "Ernest too."

That was early in the night. Which was a good thing, because it taken a long night for folks to chase them things right and for Henry to lay there and holler, being as Uncle Billy never had none of this here chloryfoam to set Henry's leg with. So it was considerate in Flem to get them started early. And what do you reckon Flem's comment was?

That's right. Nothing. Because he wasn't there. Hadn't nobody see him since that Texas man left.

VI

That was Saturday night. I reckon Mrs. Armstid got home about daylight, to see about the chaps. I don't know where they thought her and Henry was. But lucky the oldest one was a gal, about twelve, big enough to take care of the little ones. Which she did for the next two days. Mrs. Armstid would nurse Henry all night and work in the kitchen for hern and Henry's keep, and in the afternoon she would drive home (it was about four miles) to see to the chaps. She would cook up a pot of victuals and leave it on the stove, and the gal would bar the house and keep the little ones quiet. I would hear Mrs. Littlejohn and Mrs. Armstid talking in the kitchen. "How are the chaps making out?" Mrs. Littlejohn says.

"All right," Mrs. Armstid says.

"Don't they git skeered at night?" Mrs. Littlejohn says.

"Ina May bars the door when I leave," Mrs. Armstid says. "She's got the axe in bed with her. I reckon she can make out."

I reckon they did. And I reckon Mrs. Armstid was waiting for Flem to come back to town; hadn't nobody seen him until this morning; to get her money the Texas man said Flem was keeping for her. Sho. I reckon she was.

Anyway, I heard Mrs. Armstid and Mrs. Littlejohn talking in the kitchen this morning while I was eating breakfast. Mrs. Littlejohn had just told Mrs. Armstid that Flem was in town. "You can ask him for that five dollars," Mrs. Littlejohn says.

"You reckon he'll give it to me?" Mrs. Armstid says.

Mrs. Littlejohn was washing dishes, washing them like a man, like they was made out of iron. "No," she says. "But asking him won't do no hurt. It might shame him. I don't reckon it will, but it might."

"If he wouldn't give it back, it ain't no use to ask," Mrs. Armstid says.

"Suit yourself," Mrs. Littlejohn says. "It's your money."

I could hear the dishes.

"Do you reckon he might give it back to me?" Mrs. Armstid says. "That Texas man said he would. He said I could get it from Mr. Snopes later."

"Then go and ask him for it," Mrs. Littlejohn says.

I could hear the dishes.

"He won't give it back to me," Mrs. Armstid says.

"All right," Mrs. Littlejohn says. "Don't ask him for it, then."

I could hear the dishes; Mrs. Armstid was helping. "You don't reckon he would, do you?" she says. Mrs. Littlejohn never said nothing. It sounded like she was throwing the dishes at one another. "Maybe I better go and talk to Henry about it," Mrs. Armstid says.

"I would," Mrs. Littlejohn says. I be dog if it didn't sound like she had two plates in her hands, beating them together. "Then Henry can buy another five-dollar horse with it. Maybe he'll buy one next time that will out and out kill him. If I thought that, I'd give you back the money, myself."

"I reckon I better talk to him first," Mrs. Armstid said. Then it sounded like Mrs. Littlejohn taken up all the dishes and throwed them at the cookstove, and I come away.

That was this morning. I had been up to Bundren's and back, and I thought that things would have kind of settled down. So after breakfast, I went up to the store. And there was Flem, setting in the store chair and whittling, like he might not have ever moved since he come to clerk for Jody Varner. I. O. was leaning in the door, in his shirt sleeves and with his hair parted too, same as Flem was before he turned the clerking job over to I. O. It's a funny thing about them Snopes: they all looks alike, yet there ain't ere a two of them that claims brothers. They're always just cousins, like Flem and Eck and Flem and I. O. Eck was there too, squatting against the wall, him and that boy, eating cheese and crackers outen a sack; they told me that Eck hadn't been home a-tall. And that Lon Quick hadn't got back to town, even. He followed his horse clean down to Samson's Bridge, with a wagon and a camp outfit. Eck finally caught one of hisn. It run into a blind lane at Freeman's and Eck and the boy taken and tied their rope across the end of the lane, about three foot high. The horse come to the end of the lane and whirled and run back without ever stopping. Eck says it never seen the rope a-tall. He says it looked just like one of these here Christmas pinwheels. "Didn't it try to run again?" I says.

"No," Eck says, eating a bit of cheese often his knife blade. "Just kicked some."

"Kicked some?" I says.

"It broke its neck," Eck says.

Well, they was squatting there, about six of them, talking, talking at Flem; never nobody knowed yet if Flem had ere a interest in them horses or not. So finally I come right out and asked him. "Flem's done skun all of us so much," I says, "that we're proud of him. Come on, Flem," I says, "how much did you and that Texas man make offen them horses? You can tell us. Ain't nobody here but Eck that bought one of them; the others ain't got back to town yet, and Eck's your own cousin; he'll be proud to hear, too. How much did you-all make?"

They was all whittling, not looking at Flem, making like they was studying. But you could a heard a pin drop. And I. O. He had been rubbing his back up and down on the door, but he stopped now, watching Flem like a pointing dog. Flem finished cutting the sliver offen his stick. He spit across the porch, into the road. "'Twarn't none of my horses," he says.

I. O. cackled, like a hen, slapping his legs with both hands. "You boys might just as well quit trying to get ahead of Flem," he said.

Well, about that time I see Mrs. Armstid come outen Mrs. Littlejohn's gate, coming up the road. I never said nothing. I says, "Well, if a man can't take care of himself in a trade, he can't blame the man that trims him."

Flem never said nothing, trimming at the stick. He hadn't seen Mrs. Armstid. "Yes, sir," I says. "A fellow like Henry Armstid ain't got nobody but hisself to blame."

"Course he ain't," I. O. says. He ain't seen her, neither. "Henry Armstid's a born fool. Always is been. If Flem hadn't a got his money, somebody else would."

We looked at Flem. He never moved. Mrs. Armstid come on up the road.

"That's right," I says. "But, come to think of it, Henry never bought no horse." We looked at Flem; you could a heard a match drop. "That Texas man told her to get that five dollars back from Flem next day. I reckon Flem's done already taken that money to Mrs. Littlejohn's and give it to Mrs. Armstid."

We watched Flem. I. O. quit rubbing his back against the door again. After a while Flem raised his head and spit across the porch, into the dust. I. O. cackled, just like a hen. "Ain't he a beating fellow, now?" I. O. says.

Mrs. Armstid was getting closer, so I kept on talking, watching to see if Flem would look up and see her. But he never looked up. I went on talking about Tull, about how he was going to sue Flem, and Flem setting there, whittling his stick, not saying nothing else after he said they wasn't none of his horses.

Then I. O. happened to look around. He seen Mrs. Armstid. "Psssst!" he says. Flem looked up. "Here she comes!" I. O. says. "Go out the back. I'll tell her you done went in to town today."

But Flem never moved. He just set there, whittling, and we watched Mrs. Armstid come up onto the porch, in that ere faded sunbonnet and wrapper and them tennis shoes that made a kind of hissing noise on the porch. She come onto the porch and stopped, her hands rolled into her dress in front, not looking at nothing.

"He said Saturday," she says, "that he wouldn't sell Henry no horse. He said I could get the money from you."

Flem looked up. The knife never stopped. It went on trimming off a sliver same as if he was watching it. "He taken that money off with him when he left," Flem says.

Mrs. Armstid never looked at nothing. We never looked at her, neither, except the boy of Eck's. He had a half-et cracker in his hand, watching her, chewing.

"He said Henry hadn't bought no horse," Mrs. Armstid says. "He said for me to get the money from you today."

"I reckon he forgot about it," Flem said. "He taken that money off with him Saturday." He whittled again. I. O. kept on rubbing his back, slow. He licked his lips. After a while the woman looked up the road, where it went on up the hill, toward the graveyard. She looked up that way for a while, with that boy of Eck's watching her and I. O. rubbing his back slow against the door. Then she turned back toward the steps.

"I reckon it's time to get dinner started," she says.

"How's Henry this morning, Mrs. Armstid?" Winterbottom says.

She looked at Winterbottom; she almost stopped. "He's resting, I thank you kindly," she says.

Flem got up, outen the chair, putting his knife away. He spit across the porch. "Wait a minute, Mrs. Armstid," he says. She stopped again. She didn't look at him. Flem went on into the store, with I. O. done quit rubbing his back now, with his head craned after Flem, and Mrs. Armstid standing there with her hands rolled into her dress, not looking at nothing. A wagon come up the road and passes; it was Freeman, on the way to town. Then Flem come out again, with I. O. still watching him. Flem had one of these little striped sacks of Jody Varner's candy; I bet he still owes Jody that nickel, too. He put the sack into Mrs. Armstid's hand, like he would have put it into a hollow stump. He spit again across the porch. "A little sweetening for the chaps," he says.

"You're right kind," Mrs. Armstid says. She held the sack of candy in her hand, not looking at nothing. Eck's boy was watching the sack, the half-et cracker in his hand; he wasn't chewing now. He watched Mrs. Armstid roll the sack into her apron. "I reckon I better get on back and help with dinner," she says. She turned and went back across the porch. Flem set down in the chair again and opened his knife. He spit across the porch again, past Mrs. Armstid where she hadn't went down the steps yet. Then she went on, in that ere sun-bonnet and wrapper all the same color, back down the road toward Mrs. Little-john's. You couldn't see her dress move, like a natural woman walking. She looked like a old snag[1] still standing up and moving along on a high water. We watched her turn in at Mrs. Littlejohn's and go outen sight. Flem was whit-tling. I. O. begun to rub his back on the door. Then he begun to cackle, just like a durn hen.

"You boys might just as well quit trying," I. O. says. "You can't git ahead of Flem. You can't touch him. Ain't he a sight, now?"

I be dog if he ain't. If I had brung a herd of wild cattymounts into town and sold them to my neighbors and kinfolks, they would have lynched me. Yes, sir.

1931

1. Drifting tree.

BERTOLT BRECHT
1898–1956

Bertolt Brecht wrote several plays that became modern classics; per-haps just as important, he introduced a radical concept of theater that would have a profound impact on contempo-rary playwrights and producers. Dis-satisfied with the traditional notion, derived from Aristotle's *Poetics*, that drama should draw its spectators into sympathy for the characters, Brecht proposed the idea of the "Epic The-ater," which would alienate the audi-ence from the action of the play, making the familiar appear strange. Inspired by Marxist theory, Brecht hoped that his spectators would be more critical than traditional theater audiences—would not just enjoy a play but think critically about it and then take steps to transform the society from which the drama had sprung.

Eugen Berthold Brecht was born in the medieval town of Augsburg, Bavaria, on February 10, 1898. His father was a respected citizen, director of a paper mill, and a Catholic. His mother, the daughter of a civil servant from the Black Forest region, was a Protestant who raised young Berthold in her faith. (The spelling *Bertolt* was adopted later.) Brecht attended local schools until 1917, when he enrolled in Munich

University to study natural science and medicine. He continued his studies while acting as drama critic for an Augsburg newspaper and writing plays: *Drums in the Night* (1918) won the Kleist Prize in 1922. Toward the end of the First World War, Brecht was mobilized for a year as an orderly in a military hospital, and he pursued medical studies in Munich until 1921. Several years later he married Helene Weigel, an actress and director who worked closely with him and for whom he wrote many leading roles.

Moving to Berlin in 1924, Brecht worked briefly with the directors Max Reinhardt and Erwin Piscator but was chiefly interested in writing: he was especially concerned with the plight of ordinary men and women, buffeted by social and economic forces beyond their control until they lose both identity and humanity. After Brecht became a fervent Marxist in the mid-1920s, he felt even more strongly that he had a moral and artistic duty to encourage the audience to remedy social ills. *The Threepenny Opera* (1928), a work sung in ballads, was written with composer Kurt Weill (1900–1950) and modeled on John Gay's *The Beggar's Opera* (1728). It satirizes capitalist society from the point of view of outcasts and romanticizes thieves. It is probably Brecht's most popular play, largely because of Weill's music, including the song of the gangster Macheath, "Mack the Knife," which became an American standard when it was recorded by Louis Armstrong, Frank Sinatra, and others. Moreover, Brecht wrote a number of "teaching" plays intended to set forth Communist doctrine and instruct German workers in the meaning of social revolution. The lesson is particularly harsh in *The Measures Taken* (1930), which describes the necessary execution of a young party member who has broken discipline by helping the local poor, thus postponing the revolution. Such drama, however doctrinally pure, was not likely to win adherents to the cause, and the Communist press in Berlin and Moscow condemned the teaching plays as unattractive and "intellectualist."

Brecht's desire to create an activist theater embodying a Marxist view of art put him at odds with the rise of Hitler's National Socialism. He fled Germany for Denmark in 1933, before the Nazis could include him in their purge of left-wing intellectuals; in 1935 he was deprived of his German citizenship. Brecht would flee several more times as the Nazi invasions expanded throughout Europe: in 1939 to Sweden, in 1940 to Finland, and in 1941 to the United States, where he joined a colony of German expatriates in Santa Monica, California, working for the film industry. This was the period of some of his greatest plays. *The Life of Galileo* (1938–39) attacks society for suppressing the Italian astronomer's discovery, in the seventeenth century, that the Earth revolves around the sun (the traditional belief was in the opposite phenomenon), but the drama also condemns the scientist for not insisting on the truth. *Mother Courage and Her Children* (1939) portrays an avaricious peddler who doggedly pursues the profits to be made from war even though her three children are victims of it. *The Good Woman of Setzuan* (1938–40) shows how an instinctively generous person can survive only by putting on a mask of hardness and calculation. In *The Caucasian Chalk Circle* (1944–45), an adaptation of the story of the Judgment of Solomon, the child is given to the servant girl rather than to the governor's wife (the implied comparison is between those who do the work of society and those who merely profit from their possessions). Brecht arranged for the translation of his work into English, and *Galileo*, with Charles Laughton in the title role, was produced in 1947. That same year Brecht was questioned by the House Un-American Activities Committee as part of a wide-ranging inquiry into possible Communist activity in the entertainment business. No charges were filed against Brecht, but he left for Europe the day after being brought before the committee.

After leaving the United States, Brecht worked for a year in Zurich before going to Berlin with his wife to stage *Mother Courage*. The East Berlin government offered the couple positions as directors of their own troupe, the Berliner Ensemble, and Brecht—who had just finished a theoretical treatise, *A Little Organon for the Theater* (1949)—turned his attention to the professional role of director. (Throughout his life, Brecht had often collaborated with other authors, notably Elisabeth Hauptmann, who was also his mistress.) Although the East Berliners subsidized Brecht's work and advertised his presence as a tribute to their economic system, Brecht was forced to defend some of his plays against charges of political unorthodoxy and indeed to revise them. After 1934 the Communist Party generally advocated "socialist realism," an approach to the humanities in which the goal was to offer simple messages and to foster identification with revolutionary heroes. Brecht's mind was too keen and questioning, too attracted by irony and paradox, for him to provide simplistic dramas or to have a comfortable relation with authority, either on the right or on the left. After settling in East Berlin, he wrote no major plays but only minor propaganda pieces and adaptations of classical works such as **Molière**'s *Don Juan*, Shakespeare's *Coriolanus*, and Sophocles' *Antigone*. As an additional measure of protection, he took out Austrian citizenship through his wife's nationality. Brecht died in Berlin on August 14, 1956.

The epic theater movement, born in the 1920s, suited Brecht's needs, and through his plays, theoretical writings, and dramatic productions, he developed its basic ideas into one of the most powerful theatrical styles of the twentieth century. Brecht rejected the aesthetic of naturalness and psychological credibility that created an illusion of reality on the stage. Like **Luigi Pirandello**, Brecht believed that the stage should break through the closed world that playwrights such as the Norwegian **Henrik Ibsen** (1828–1906) and the Russian **Anton Chekhov** (1860–1904) had established as a dramatic convention: audiences were to look at the action from outside, as if the play were a slice of life going on behind the invisible "fourth wall." Unlike Pirandello, however, Brecht did not stress the anguish of individuals lacking self-awareness; his focus was on social responsibility and the community at large. For Brecht the audience must not be allowed to indulge in passive empathy or in the subjective whirlpool of existential identity crises. His characters are to be seen as members of society, and his audience should be educated and moved to action.

The epic theater derives its name from a famous essay, *On Epic and Dramatic Poetry* (1797), by **Johann Wolfgang von Goethe** and Friedrich Schiller, who described *dramatic* poetry as pulling the audience into emotional identification, in contrast to *epic* poetry, which, distanced in the time, place, and nature of the action, can be absorbed in calm contemplation. The idea of an epic theater is a paradox: how can a play engage an audience that is held at a distance? Brecht's solution was to employ "estrangement effects" to encourage spectators to think critically about what is taking place. Here Brecht echoed the work of the revolutionary Soviet director Vsevolod Meyerhold, whose antirealistic use of masks, pantomime, posters and film projections, song interludes, and direct address to the audience was well known to German audiences in the 1920s. He also drew on the tradition of vaudeville theater. Despite Brecht's intentions and frequent revisions, however, the characters and situations of his plays remain emotionally engrossing, especially in his best-known works, such as *The Good Woman of Setzuan*. As for the estrangement effects themselves, they have become standard production techniques in contemporary theater.

Brecht's concept of epic theater encompasses dramatic structure, stage setting, music, and performance. Episodes may be performed independently as self-contained dramatic parables, rather than tied to a developing plot. Songs break dramatic action and yet crystallize themes. Sometimes a narrator comments on the action. The estrangement effects are heightened by setting most of the plays in distant times or faraway lands, such as China in *The Good Woman of Setzuan*.

Events on stage may be announced beforehand by signs or accompanied by projected images during the action. Place-names printed on signs are suspended over the actors, and footlights and stage machinery are displayed. Masks identify wicked people; soldiers' faces are chalked white to suggest a stylized fear. Songs that interrupt the dramatic action are addressed directly to the audience, sometimes heralded by a sign. In addition, actors should "demonstrate" their parts instead of being submerged in them. At rehearsals Brecht often asked actors to speak their parts in the third person instead of the first. Such artificiality makes it difficult for the audience to identify unself-consciously with the characters on stage; instead spectators maintain, ideally, the impartiality of a jury.

The Good Woman of Setzuan, printed here, was written between 1938 and 1940, with the collaboration of Margarete Steffin and Ruth Berlau, and with music by Paul Dessau. Painfully drafted while Brecht, his family, Steffin, and Berlau sought refuge in Scandinavia from the Nazis, the play is stamped with disillusionment with a world in which it is impossible to be good and survive. The "good woman," Shen Te, must save herself from a swarm of parasites and opportunists. The split that develops stands for the broader gulf between the intimate sphere in which moral action is possible and the social world in which one must struggle for survival. The play's setting in China was probably suggested by a 1935 visit to Moscow, where Brecht was impressed by the highly stylized performances of the Chinese actor Mei Lan-fang. (He also admired Japanese Noh and Kabuki theater.)

Shen Te's story reflects a larger thematic concern: the state of the universe or, more mundanely, whether the world is so corrupt that drastic intervention is needed. Her situation arises from a good deed that has counterparts in world mythologies and also in the Bible: hospitality offered to disguised divine messengers, who reward the giver accordingly. Three Chinese gods visiting Earth in search of good people give Shen Te, a penniless prostitute, a thousand silver dollars in recompense for being the only person in Setzuan to provide them with lodging. Brecht borrows from the Old Testament story of Sodom and Gomorrah, in which God sends angels down to find ten good people in the debauched city of Sodom so that it may be saved from destruction. But these modern gods are comic and certainly ineffectual. Wearing old-fashioned clothes and dusty shoes, they have been delegated by bureaucratic Resolution on high (whose terms they debate); they ignore inconvenient questions and merely repeat the inapplicable regulations; and they are terrified of complications that would disturb the status quo. Their refusal to be involved reinforces Brecht's underlying thesis that "good" and "evil" are not divine entities but rather social issues, and that the way to reform a corrupt world is for people to unite in action focused on the common good.

The Good Woman of Setzuan[1]

CHARACTERS

WONG, *a water seller*

THREE GODS

SHEN TE, *a prostitute, later a shopkeeper*

MRS. SHIN, *former owner of Shen Te's shop*

A *family of eight* (HUSBAND, WIFE, BROTHER, SISTER-IN-LAW, GRANDFATHER, NEPHEW, NIECE, BOY)

An UNEMPLOYED MAN

A CARPENTER

MRS. MI TZU, *Shen Te's landlady*

MR. SHUI TA

YANG SUN, *an unemployed pilot, later a factory manager*

An OLD WHORE

A POLICEMAN

An OLD MAN

An OLD WOMAN, *his wife*

MR. SHU FU, *a barber*

MRS. YANG, *mother of Yang Sun*

GENTLEMEN, VOICES, PRIEST, WAITER, *children (three), etc.*

Prologue

At the gates of the half-Westernized city of Setzuan. Evening. WONG *the water seller*[2] *introduces himself to the audience.*

WONG   I sell water here in the city of Setzuan. It isn't easy. When water is scarce, I have long distances to go in search of it, and when it is plentiful, I have no income. But in our part of the world there is nothing unusual about poverty. Many people think only the gods can save the situation. And I hear from a cattle merchant—who travels a lot—that some of the highest gods are on their way here at this very moment. Informed sources have it that heaven is quite disturbed at all the complaining.[3] I've been coming out here to the city gates for three days now to bid these gods welcome. I want to be the first to greet them. What about those fellows over there? No, no, they *work*. And that one there has ink on his fingers, he's no god, he must be a clerk from the cement factory. *Those* two are another story. They look as though they'd like to beat you. But gods don't need to beat you, do they? [THREE GODS *appear.*] What about those three? Old-fashioned clothes—dust on their feet—they *must* be gods! [*He throws himself at their feet.*] Do with me what you will, illustrious ones!

FIRST GOD   [*With an ear trumpet.*] Ah! [*He is pleased.*] So we were expected?

WONG [*Giving them water.*]   Oh, yes. And I *knew* you'd come.

FIRST GOD   We need somewhere to stay the night. You know of a place?

WONG   The whole town is at your service, illustrious ones! What sort of a place would you like?

[*The* GODS *eye each other.*]

---

1. Translated by Eric Bentley. Setzuan is a province in China; the play's setting is both the capital of Setzuan and, according to a later statement in the play, a generalized location: "wherever man is exploited by man."

2. Water peddlers were common in ancient China.

3. Heaven, in Chinese philosophy, was identical with absolute and transcendental order.

FIRST GOD   Just try the first house you come to, my son.

WONG   That would be Mr. Fo's place.

FIRST GOD   Mr. Fo.

WONG   One moment! [*He knocks at the first house.*]

VOICE FROM MR. FO'S.   No!

[WONG *returns a little nervously.*]

WONG   It's too bad. Mr. Fo isn't in. And his servants don't dare do a thing without his consent. He'll have a fit when he finds out who they turned away, won't he?

FIRST GOD [*Smiling.*]   He will, won't he?

WONG   One moment! The next house is Mr. Cheng's. Won't he be thrilled!

FIRST GOD   Mr. Cheng.

[WONG *knocks.*]

VOICE FROM MR. CHENG'S   Keep your gods. We have our own troubles!

WONG [*Back with the* GODS.]   Mr. Cheng is very sorry, but he has a houseful of relations. I think some of them are a bad lot, and naturally, he wouldn't like you to see them.

THIRD GOD   Are we so terrible?

WONG   Well, only with bad people, of course. Everyone knows the province of Kwan is always having floods.

SECOND GOD   Really? How's that?

WONG   Why, because they're so irreligious.

SECOND GOD   Rubbish. It's because they neglected the dam.

FIRST GOD [*To* SECOND.]   Sh! [*To* WONG.] You're still in hopes, aren't you, my son?

WONG   Certainly. All Setzuan is competing for the honor! What happened up to now is pure coincidence. I'll be back. [*He walks away, but then stands undecided.*]

SECOND GOD   What did I tell you?

THIRD GOD   It *could* be pure coincidence.

SECOND GOD   The same coincidence in Shun, Kwan, and Setzuan? People just aren't religious any more, let's face the fact. Our mission has failed!

FIRST GOD   Oh come, we might run into a good person any minute.

THIRD GOD   How did the resolution read? [*Unrolling a scroll and reading from it.*] "The world can stay as it is if enough people are found [*At the word "found" he unrolls it a little more*] living lives worthy of human beings." Good people, that is. Well, what about this water seller himself? *He's* good, or I'm very much mistaken.

SECOND GOD   You're very much mistaken. When he gave us a drink, I had the impression there was something odd about the cup. Well, look! [*He shows the cup to the* FIRST GOD.]

FIRST GOD   A false bottom!

SECOND GOD   The man is a swindler.

FIRST GOD   Very well, count *him* out. That's one man among millions. And as a matter of fact, we only need one on *our* side. These atheists are saying, "The world must be changed because no one can *be* good and *stay* good." No one, eh? I say: let us find one—just one—and we have those fellows where we want them!

THIRD GOD [*To* WONG.] Water seller, is it so hard to find a place to stay?

WONG Nothing could be easier. It's just me. I don't go about it right.

THIRD GOD Really?

[*He returns to the others. A* GENTLEMAN *passes by.*]

WONG Oh dear, they're catching on. [*He accosts the* GENTLEMAN.] Excuse the intrusion, dear sir, but three gods have just turned up. Three of the very highest. They need a place for the night. Seize this rare opportunity—to have real gods as your guests!

GENTLEMAN [*laughing*]. A new way of finding free rooms for a gang of crooks. [*Exit* GENTLEMAN.]

WONG [*shouting at him.*] Godless rascal! Have you no religion, gentlemen of Setzuan? [*Pause*]. Patience, illustrious ones! [*Pause.*] There's only one person left. Shen Te, the prostitute. She *can't* say no. [*Calls up to a window.*] Shen Te!

[SHEN TE *opens the shutters and looks out.*]

WONG Shen Te, it's Wong. *They're* here, and nobody wants them. Will you take them?

SHEN TE Oh, no, Wong, I'm expecting a gentleman.

WONG Can't you forget about him for tonight?

SHEN TE The rent has to be paid by tomorrow or I'll be out on the street.

WONG This is no time for calculation, Shen Te.

SHEN TE Stomachs rumble even on the Emperor's birthday, Wong.

WONG Setzuan is one big dung hill!

SHEN TE Oh, very well! I'll hide till my gentleman has come and gone. Then I'll take them. [*She disappears.*]

WONG They mustn't see her gentleman or they'll know what she is.

FIRST GOD [*Who hasn't heard any of this.*] I think it's hopeless.

[*They approach* WONG.]

WONG [*Jumping, as he finds them behind him*]. A room has been found, illustrious ones! [*He wipes sweat off his brow.*]

SECOND GOD Oh, good.

THIRD GOD Let's see it.

WONG [*Nervously.*] Just a minute. It has to be tidied up a bit.

THIRD GOD Then we'll sit down here and wait.

WONG [*Still more nervous.*] No, no! [*Holding himself back.*] Too much traffic, you know.

THIRD GOD [*With a smile.*] Of course, if you *want* us to move.

[*They retire a little. They sit on a doorstep.* WONG *sits on the ground.*]

WONG [*After a deep breath.*] You'll be staying with a single girl—the finest human being in Setzuan!

THIRD GOD That's nice.

WONG [*To the audience.*] They gave me such a look when I picked up my cup just now.

THIRD GOD You're worn out, Wong.

WONG A little, maybe.

FIRST GOD Do people here have a hard time of it?

WONG The good ones do.

FIRST GOD What about yourself!

WONG   You mean I'm not good. That's true. And I don't have an easy time either!
  [*During this dialogue, a* GENTLEMAN *has turned up in front of Shen Te's House, and has whistled several times. Each time* WONG *has given a start.*]
THIRD GOD [*To* WONG, *softly.*]   Psst! I think he's gone now.
WONG [*Confused and surprised.*]   Ye-e-es.
  [*The* GENTLEMAN *has left now, and* SHEN TE *has come down to the street.*]
SHEN TE [*softly.*]   Wong!
  [*Getting no answer, she goes off down the street.* WONG *arrives just too late, forgetting his carrying pole.*]
WONG [*Softly.*]   Shen Te! Shen Te! [*To himself.*] So she's gone off to earn the rent. Oh dear, I can't go to the gods *again* with no room to offer them. Having failed in the service of the gods, I shall run to my den in the sewer pipe down by the river and hide from their sight!
  [*He rushes off.* SHEN TE *returns, looking for him, but finding the* GODS. *She stops in confusion.*]
SHEN TE   You are the illustrious ones? My name is Shen Te. It would please me very much if my simple room could be of use to you.
THIRD GOD   Where is the water seller, Miss . . . Shen Te?
SHEN TE   I missed him, somehow.
FIRST GOD   Oh, he probably thought you weren't coming, and was afraid of telling us.
THIRD GOD [*Picking up the carrying pole.*]   We'll leave this with you. He'll be needing it.
  [*Led by* SHEN TE, *they go into the house. It grows dark, then light. Dawn. Again escorted by* SHEN TE, *who leads them through the half-light with a little lamp, the* GODS *take their leave.*]
FIRST GOD   Thank you, thank you, dear Shen Te, for your elegant hospitality! We shall not forget! And give our thanks to the water seller—he showed us a good human being.
SHEN TE   Oh, *I'm* not good. Let me tell you something: when Wong asked me to put you up, I hesitated.
FIRST GOD   It's all right to hesitate if you then go ahead! And in giving us that room you did much more than you knew. You proved that good people still exist, a point that has been disputed of late—even in heaven. Farewell!
SECOND GOD   Farewell!
THIRD GOD   Farewell!
SHEN TE   Stop, illustrious ones! I'm not sure you're right. I'd like to be good, it's true, but there's the rent to pay. And that's not all: I sell myself for a living. Even so I can't make ends meet, there's too much competition. I'd like to honor my father and mother and speak nothing but the truth and not covet my neighbor's house. I should love to stay with one man. But how? How is it done? Even breaking a few of your commandments,[4] I can hardly manage.
FIRST GOD [*Clearing his throat.*]   These thoughts are but, um, the misgivings of an unusually good woman!
THIRD GOD   Good-bye, Shen Te! Give our regards to the water seller!

---

4. An allusion to the Decalogue of the Old Testament and specifically to Commandments 4, 6, 8, 9, and 10 (Exodus 20).

SECOND GOD   And above all: be good! Farewell!

FIRST GOD   Farewell!

THIRD GOD   Farewell!

[*They start to wave good-bye.*]

SHEN TE   But everything is so expensive, I don't feel sure I can do it!

SECOND GOD   That's not in our sphere. We never meddle with economics.

THIRD GOD   One moment. [*They stop.*] Isn't it true she might do better if she had more money?

SECOND GOD   Come, come! How could we ever account for it Up Above?

FIRST GOD   Oh, there are ways. [*They put their heads together and confer in dumb show. To* SHEN TE, *with embarrassment.*] As you say you can't pay your rent, well, um, we're not paupers, so of course we *insist* on paying for our room. [*Awkwardly thrusting money into her hands.*] There! [*Quickly.*] But don't tell anyone! The incident is open to misinterpretation.

SECOND GOD   It certainly is!

FIRST GOD [*Defensively.*]   But there's no law against it! It was never decreed that a god mustn't pay hotel bills!

[*The* GODS *leave.*]

1

A small tobacco shop. The shop is not as yet completely furnished and hasn't started doing business.

SHEN TE [*To the audience.*]   It's three days now since the gods left. When they said they wanted to pay for the room, I looked down at my hand, and there was more than a thousand silver dollars![5] I bought a tobacco shop with the money, and moved in yesterday. I don't own the building, of course, but I can pay the rent, and I hope to do a lot of good here. Beginning with Mrs. Shin, who's just coming across the square with her pot. She had the shop before me, and yesterday she dropped in to ask for rice for her children. [*Enter* MRS. SHIN. *Both women bow.*] How do you do, Mrs. Shin.

MRS. SHIN   How do you do, Miss Shen Te. You like your new home?

SHEN TE   Indeed, yes. Did your children have a good night?

MRS. SHIN   In that hovel? The youngest is coughing already.

SHEN TE   Oh, dear!

MRS. SHIN   You're going to learn a thing or two in these slums.

SHEN TE   Slums? That's not what you said when you sold me the shop!

MRS. SHIN   Now don't start nagging! Robbing me and my innocent children of their home and then calling it a slum! That's the limit!

[*She weeps.*]

SHEN TE [*Tactfully.*]   I'll get your rice.

MRS. SHIN   And a little cash while you're at it.

SHEN TE   I'm afraid I haven't sold anything yet.

MRS. SHIN [*Screeching.*]   I've got to have it. Strip the clothes from my back and then cut my throat, will you? I know what I'll do: I'll dump my children on your doorstep! [*She snatches the pot out of* SHEN TE's *hands.*]

---

5. Either official Chinese silver dollars (yuan) or coins from one of the foreign currencies in circulation.

SHEN TE   Please don't be angry. You'll spill the rice.

[*Enter an elderly* HUSBAND *and* WIFE *with their shabbily dressed* NEPHEW.]

WIFE   Shen Te, dear! You've come into money, they tell me. And we haven't a roof over our heads! A tobacco shop. We had one too. But it's gone. Could we spend the night here, do you think?

NEPHEW [*Appraising the shop.*]   Not bad!

WIFE   He's our nephew. We're inseparable!

MRS. SHIN   And who are these . . . ladies and gentlemen?

SHEN TE   They put me up when I first came in from the country. [*To the audience.*] Of course, when my small purse was empty, they put me out on the street, and they may be afraid I'll do the same to them [*To the newcomers, kindly.*] Come in, and welcome, though I've only one little room for you— it's behind the shop.

HUSBAND   That'll do. Don't worry.

WIFE [*Bringing* SHEN TE *some tea.*]   We'll stay over here, so we won't be in your way. Did you make it a tobacco shop in memory of your first real home? We can certainly give you a hint or two! That's one reason we came.

MRS SHIN [*To* SHEN TE.]   Very nice! As long as you have a few customers too!

HUSBAND   Sh! A customer!

[*Enter an* UNEMPLOYED MAN, *in rags.*]

UNEMPLOYED MAN   Excuse me. I'm unemployed.

[MRS. SHIN *laughs.*]

SHEN TE   Can I help you?

UNEMPLOYED MAN   Have you any damaged cigarettes? I thought there might be some damage when you're unpacking.

WIFE   What nerve, begging for tobacco! [*Rhetorically.*] Why don't they ask for bread?

UNEMPLOYED MAN   Bread is expensive. One cigarette butt and I'll be a new man.

SHEN TE [*Giving him cigarettes.*]   That's very important—to be a new man. You'll be my first customer and bring me luck.

[*The* UNEMPLOYED MAN *quickly lights a cigarette, inhales, and goes off, coughing.*]

WIFE   Was that right, Shen Te, dear?

MRS. SHIN   If this is the opening of a shop, you can hold the closing at the end of the week.

HUSBAND   I bet he had money on him.

SHEN TE   Oh, no, he said he hadn't!

NEPHEW   How d'you know he wasn't lying?

SHEN TE [*Angrily.*]   How do you know he was?

WIFE [*Wagging her head.*]   You're too good, Shen Te, dear. If you're going to keep this shop, you'll have to learn to say no.

HUSBAND   Tell them the place isn't yours to dispose of. Belongs to . . . some relative who insists on all accounts being strictly in order . . .

MRS. SHIN   That's right! What do you think you are—a philanthropist?

SHEN TE [*Laughing.*]   Very well, suppose I ask you for my rice back, Mrs. Shin?

WIFE [*Combatively, at* MRS. SHIN.]   So that's *her* rice?

[*Enter the* CARPENTER, *a small man.*]

MRS. SHIN [*Who, at the sight of him, starts to hurry away.*] See you tomorrow, Miss Shen Te! [*Exit* MRS. SHIN.]

CARPENTER Mrs. Shin, it's you I want!

WIFE [*To* SHEN TE.] Has she some claim on you?

SHEN TE She's hungry. That's a claim.

CARPENTER Are you the new tenant? And filling up the shelves already? Well, they're not yours till they're paid for, ma'am. I'm the carpenter, so I should know.

SHEN TE I took the shop "furnishings included."

CARPENTER You're in league with that Mrs. Shin, of course. All right. I demand my hundred silver dollars.

SHEN TE I'm afraid I haven't got a hundred silver dollars.

CARPENTER Then you'll find it. Or I'll have you arrested.

WIFE [*Whispering to* SHEN TE.] That relative: make it a cousin.

SHEN TE Can't it wait till next month?

CARPENTER No!

SHEN TE Be a little patient, Mr. Carpenter, I can't settle all claims at once.

CARPENTER Who's patient with me? [*He grabs a shelf from the wall.*] Pay up—or I take the shelves back!

WIFE Shen Te! Dear! Why don't you let your . . . cousin settle this affair? [*To* CARPENTER.] Put your claim in writing. Shen Te's cousin will see you get paid.

CARPENTER [*Derisively.*] Cousin, eh?

HUSBAND Cousin, yes.

CARPENTER I know these cousins!

NEPHEW Don't be silly. He's a personal friend of mine.

HUSBAND What a man! Sharp as a razor!

CARPENTER All right. I'll put my claim in writing. [*Puts shelf on floor, sits on it, writes out bill.*]

WIFE [*To* SHEN TE.] He'd tear the dress off your back to get his shelves. Never recognize a claim! That's my motto.

SHEN TE He's done a job, and wants something in return. It's shameful that I can't give it to him. What will the gods say?

HUSBAND You did your bit when you took *us* in.

[*Enter the* BROTHER, *limping, and the* SISTER-IN-LAW, *pregnant.*]

BROTHER [*To* HUSBAND *and* WIFE.] So this is where you're hiding out! There's family feeling for you! Leaving us on the corner!

WIFE [*Embarrassed, to* SHEN TE.] It's my brother and his wife. [*To them.*] Now stop grumbling, and sit quietly in that corner. [*To* SHEN TE.] It can't be helped. She's in her fifth month.

SHEN TE Oh yes. Welcome!

WIFE [*To the couple.*] Say thank you. [*They mutter something.*] The cups are there. [*To* SHEN TE.] Lucky you bought this shop when you did!

SHEN TE [*Laughing and bringing tea.*] Lucky indeed!

[*Enter* MRS. MI TZU, *the landlady.*]

MRS. MI TZU Miss Shen Te? I am Mrs. Mi Tzu, your landlady. I hope our relationship will be a happy one. I like to think I give my tenants modern, personalized service. Here is your lease. [*To the others, as* SHEN TE *reads the lease.*] There's nothing like the opening of a little shop, is there? A moment of true beauty! [*She is looking around.*] Not very much on the shelves, of course. But everything in the gods' good time! Where are your references, Miss Shen Te?

SHEN TE   Do I *have* to have references?

MRS. MI TZU   After all, I haven't a notion who you are!

HUSBAND   Oh, *we'd* be glad to vouch for Miss Shen Te! We'd go through fire for her!

MRS. MI TZU   And who may *you* be?

HUSBAND [*Stammering.*]   Ma Fu, tobacco dealer.

MRS. MI TZU   Where is your shop, Mr. . . . . Ma Fu?

HUSBAND   Well, um, I haven't got a shop—I've just sold it.

MRS. MI TZU   I see. [*To* SHEN TE.] Is there no one else that knows you?

WIFE [*Whispering to* SHEN TE.]   Your cousin! Your cousin!

MRS. MI TZU   This is a respectable house, Miss Shen Te. I never sign a lease without certain assurances.

SHEN TE [*Slowly, her eyes downcast.*]   I have . . . a cousin.

MRS. MI TZU   On the square? Let's go over and see him. What does he do?

SHEN TE [*As before.*]   He lives . . . in another city.

WIFE [*Prompting.*]   Didn't you say he was in Shung?

SHEN TE   That's right. Shung.

HUSBAND [*Prompting.*]   I had his name on the tip of my tongue, Mr. . . .

SHEN TE [*With an effort.*]   Mr. . . . . Shui . . . Ta.

HUSBAND   That's it! Tall, skinny fellow!

SHEN TE   Shui Ta!

NEPHEW [*To* CARPENTER.]   *You* were in touch with him, weren't you? About the shelves?

CARPENTER [*Surlily.*]   Give him this bill. [*He hands it over.*] I'll be back in the morning. [*Exit* CARPENTER.]

NEPHEW [*Calling after him, but with his eyes on* MRS. MI TZU.]   Don't worry! Mr. Shui Ta pays on the nail!

MRS. MI TZU [*Looking closely at* SHEN TE.]   I'll be happy to make his acquaintance, Miss Shen Te. [*Exit* MRS. MI TZU.]
        [*Pause.*]

WIFE   By tomorrow morning she'll know more about you than you do yourself.

SISTER-IN-LAW [*To* NEPHEW.]   This thing isn't built to last.
        [*Enter* GRANDFATHER.]

WIFE   It's Grandfather! [*To* SHEN TE.] Such a good old soul!
        [*The* BOY *enters.*]

BOY [*Over his shoulder.*]   Here they are!

WIFE   And the boy, how he's grown! But he always could eat enough for ten.
        [*Enter the* NIECE.]

WIFE [*To* SHEN TE.]   Our little niece from the country. There are more of us now than in your time. The less we had, the more there were of us; the more there were of us, the less we had. Give me the key. We must protect ourselves from unwanted guests. [*She takes the key and locks the door.*] Just make yourself at home. I'll light the little lamp.

NEPHEW [*A big joke.*]   I hope her cousin doesn't drop in tonight! The strict Mr. Shui Ta!
        [SISTER-IN-LAW *laughs.*]

BROTHER [*Reaching for a cigarette.*]   One cigarette more or less . . .

HUSBAND   One cigarette more or less.

[*They pile into the cigarettes. The* BROTHER *hands a jug of wine round.*]

NEPHEW   Mr. Shui Ta'll pay for it!

GRANDFATHER   [*Gravely, to* SHEN TE.] How do you do?

[SHEN TE, *a little taken aback by the belatedness of the greeting, bows. She has the carpenter's bill in one hand, the landlady's lease in the other.*]

WIFE   How about a bit of a song? To keep Shen Te's spirits up?

NEPHEW   Good idea. Grandfather: you start!

SONG OF THE SMOKE

GRANDFATHER
> I used to think (before old age beset me)
>   That brains could fill the pantry of the poor.
> But where did all my cerebration get me?
>   I'm just as hungry as I was before.
>   So what's the use?
>   See the smoke float free
>   Into ever colder coldness!
>   It's the same with me.[6]

HUSBAND
> The straight and narrow path leads to disaster
> And so the crooked path I tried to tread.
> That got me to disaster even faster.
> (They say we shall be happy when we're dead.)
>   So what's the use?
>   See the smoke float free
>   Into ever colder coldness!
>   It's the same with me

NIECE
> You older people, full of expectation,
>   At any moment now you'll walk the plank!
> The future's for the younger generation!
>   Yes, even if that future is a blank.
>   So what's the use?
>   See the smoke float free
>   Into ever colder coldness!
>   It's the same with me.

NEPHEW [*To the* BROTHER.]   Where'd you get that wine?

SISTER-IN-LAW [*Answering for the* BROTHER.]   He pawned the sack of tobacco.

HUSBAND [*Stepping in.*]   What? That tobacco was all we had to fall back on! You pig!

BROTHER   *You'd* call a man a pig because your wife was frigid! Did you refuse to drink it?

[*They fight. The shelves fall over.*]

SHEN TE [*Imploringly.*]   Oh don't! Don't break everything! Take it, take it all, but don't destroy a gift from the gods!

---

6. The refrain in this song is taken from a poem Brecht wrote in the 1920s entitled "The Song of the Opium Den."

WIFE [*Disparagingly.*] This shop isn't big enough. I should never have mentioned it to Uncle and the others. When *they* arrive, it's going to be disgustingly overcrowded.

SISTER-IN-LAW   And did you hear our gracious hostess? She cools off quick!

[*Voices outside. Knocking at the door.*]

UNCLE'S VOICE   Open the door!

WIFE   Uncle? Is that you, Uncle?

UNCLE'S VOICE   Certainly, it's me. Auntie says to tell you she'll have the children here in ten minutes.

WIFE [*To* SHEN TE.]   I'll have to let him in.

SHEN TE [*Who scarcely hears her.*]

> The little lifeboat is swiftly sent down
> Too many men too greedily
> Hold on to it as they drown.

1a

WONG'S *den in a sewer pipe.*

WONG [*Crouching there.*]   All quiet! It's four days now since I left the city. The gods passed this way on the second day. I heard their steps on the bridge over there. They must be a long way off by this time, so I'm safe. [*Breathing a sigh of relief, he curls up and goes to sleep. In his dream the pipe becomes transparent, and the* GODS *appear. Raising an arm, as if in self-defense.*] I know, I know, illustrious ones! I found no one to give you a room—not in all Setzuan! There, it's out. Please continue on your way!

FIRST GOD [*Mildly.*]   But you did find someone. Someone who took us in for the night, watched over us in our sleep, and in the early morning lighted us down to the street with a lamp.

WONG   It was . . . Shen Te that took you in?

THIRD GOD   Who else?

WONG   And I ran away! "She isn't coming," I thought, "she just can't afford it."

GODS [*Singing.*]

> O you feeble, well-intentioned, and yet feeble chap
> Where there's need the fellow thinks there is no goodness!
> When there's danger he thinks courage starts to ebb away!
> Some people only see the seamy side!
> What hasty judgment! What premature desperation!

WONG   I'm *very* ashamed, illustrious ones.

FIRST GOD   Do us a favor, water seller. Go back to Setzuan. Find Shen Te, and give us a report on her. We hear that she's come into a little money. Show interest in her goodness—for no one can be good for long if goodness is not in demand. Meanwhile we shall continue the search, and find other good people. After which, the idle chatter about the impossibility of goodness will stop!

[*The* GODS *vanish.*]

2

A knocking.

WIFE   Shen Te! Someone at the door. Where is she anyway?

NEPHEW   She must be getting the breakfast. Mr. Shui Ta will pay for it.
[*The* WIFE *laughs and shuffles to the door. Enter Mr.* SHUI TA *and the* CARPENTER.]

WIFE   Who is it?

SHUI TA   I am Miss Shen Te's cousin.

WIFE   What??

SHUI TA   My name is Shui Ta.

WIFE   Her cousin?

NEPHEW   Her cousin?

NIECE   But that was a joke. She hasn't got a cousin.

HUSBAND   So early in the morning?

BROTHER   What's all the noise?

SISTER-IN-LAW   This fellow says he's her cousin.

BROTHER   Tell him to prove it.

NEPHEW   Right. If you're Shen Te's cousin, prove it by getting the breakfast.

SHUI TA [*Whose regime begins as he puts out the lamp to save oil; loudly, to all present, asleep or awake.*]   Would you all please get dressed! Customers will be coming! I wish to open my shop!

HUSBAND   *Your* shop? Doesn't it belong to our good friend Shen Te?
[SHUI TA *shakes his head.*]

SISTER-IN-LAW   So we've been cheated. Where *is* the little liar?

SHUI TA   Miss Shen Te has been delayed. She wishes me to tell you there will be nothing she can do—now I am here.

WIFE [*Bowled over.*]   I thought she was good!

NEPHEW   Do you have to believe *him*?

HUSBAND   I don't.

NEPHEW   Then do something.

HUSBAND   Certainly! I'll send out a search party at once. You, you, you, and you, go out and look for Shen Te. [*As the* GRANDFATHER *rises and makes for the door*] Not you, Grandfather, you and I will hold the fort.

SHUI TA   You won't find Miss Shen Te. She has suspended her hospitable activity for an unlimited period. There are too many of you. She asked me to say: this is a tobacco shop, not a gold mine.

HUSBAND   Shen Te never said a thing like that. Boy, food! There's a bakery on the corner. Stuff your shirt full when they're not looking!

SISTER-IN-LAW   Don't overlook the raspberry tarts.

HUSBAND   And don't let the policeman see you.
[*The* BOY *leaves.*]

SHUI TA   Don't you depend on this shop now? Then why give it a bad name by stealing from the bakery?

NEPHEW   Don't listen to him. Let's find Shen Te. She'll give him a piece of her mind.

SISTER-IN-LAW   Don't forget to leave us some breakfast.
[BROTHER, SISTER-IN-LAW *and* NEPHEW *leave.*]

SHUI TA [*To the* CARPENTER.] You see, Mr. Carpenter, nothing has changed since the poet, eleven hundred years ago, penned these lines:

> A governor was asked what was needed
> To save the freezing people in the city.
> He replied:
> "A blanket ten thousand feet long
> To cover the city and all its suburbs."[7]

[*He starts to tidy up the shop.*]

CARPENTER Your cousin owes me money. I've got witnesses. For the shelves.

SHUI TA Yes, I have your bill. [*He takes it out of his pocket.*] Isn't a hundred silver dollars rather a lot?

CARPENTER No deductions! I have a wife and children.

SHUI TA How many children?

CARPENTER Three.

SHUI TA I'll make you an offer. Twenty silver dollars.

[*The* HUSBAND *laughs.*]

CARPENTER You're crazy. Those shelves are real walnut.

SHUI TA Very well, take them away.

CARPENTER What?

SHUI TA They cost too much. Please take them away.

WIFE Not bad! [*And she, too, is laughing.*]

CARPENTER [*A little bewildered.*] Call Shen Te, someone! [*To* SHUI TA.] She's good!

SHUI TA Certainly. She's ruined.

CARPENTER [*Provoked into taking some of the shelves.*] All right, you can keep your tobacco on the floor.

SHUI TA [*to the* HUSBAND.] Help him with the shelves.

HUSBAND [*Grins and carries one shelf over to the door where the* CARPENTER *now is.*] Good-bye, shelves!

CARPENTER [*To the* HUSBAND.] You dog! You want my family to starve?

SHUI TA I repeat my offer. I have no desire to keep my tobacco on the floor. Twenty silver dollars.

CARPENTER [*With desperate aggressiveness.*] One hundred!

[SHUI TA *shows indifference, looks through the window. The* HUSBAND *picks up several shelves.*]

CARPENTER [*To* HUSBAND.] You needn't smash them against the doorpost, you idiot! [*To* SHUI TA.] These shelves were made to measure. They're no use anywhere else!

SHUI TA Precisely.

[*The* WIFE *squeals with pleasure.*]

CARPENTER [*Giving up, sullenly.*] Take the shelves. Pay what you want to pay.

SHUI TA [*Smoothly.*] Twenty silver dollars.

[*He places two large coins on the table. The* CARPENTER *picks them up.*]

HUSBAND [*Brings the shelves back in.*] And quite enough too!

CARPENTER [*Slinking off.*] Quite enough to get drunk on.

---

7. Reference to a poem, "The Big Rug," by the classical Chinese poet Po Chü-i (772–846 C.E.).

HUSBAND [*Happily.*] Well, we got rid of *him*!

WIFE [*Weeping with fun, gives a rendition of the dialogue just spoken.*] "Real walnut," says he. "Very well, take them away," says his lordship. "I have three children," says he. "Twenty silver dollars," says his lordship. "They're no use anywhere else," says he. "Pre-cisely," said his lordship! [*She dissolves into shrieks of merriment.*]

SHUI TA And now: go!

HUSBAND What's that?

SHUI TA You're thieves, parasites. I'm giving you this chance. Go!

HUSBAND [*Summoning all his ancestral dignity.*] That sort deserves no answer. Besides, one should never shout on an empty stomach.

WIFE Where's that boy?

SHUI TA Exactly. The boy. I want no stolen goods in this shop. [*Very loudly.*] I strongly advise you to leave! [*But they remain seated, noses in the air. Quietly.*] As you wish. [SHUI TA *goes to the door. A* POLICEMAN *appears.* SHUI TA *bows.*] I am addressing the officer in charge of this precinct?

POLICEMAN That's right, Mr., um, what was the name, sir?

SHUI TA Mr. Shui Ta.

POLICEMAN Yes, of course, sir.

[*They exchange a smile.*]

SHUI TA Nice weather we're having.

POLICEMAN A little on the warm side, sir.

SHUI TA Oh, a little on the warm side.

HUSBAND [*Whispering to the* WIFE.] If he keeps it up till the boy's back, we're done for. [*Tries to signal* SHUI TA.]

SHUI TA [*Ignoring the signal.*] Weather, of course, is one thing indoors, another out on the dusty street!

POLICEMAN Oh, quite another, sir!

WIFE [*To the* HUSBAND.] It's all right as long as he's standing in the doorway— the boy will see him.

SHUI TA Step inside for a moment! It's quite cool indoors. My cousin and I have just opened the place. And we attach the greatest importance to being on good terms with the, um, authorities.

POLICEMAN [*Entering.*] Thank you, Mr. Shui Ta. It *is* cool!

HUSBAND [*Whispering to the* WIFE.] And now the boy *won't* see him.

SHUI TA [*Showing* HUSBAND *and* WIFE *to the* POLICEMAN.] Visitors, I think my cousin knows them. They were just leaving.

HUSBAND [*Defeated.*] Ye-e-es, we were . . . just leaving.

SHUI TA I'll tell my cousin you couldn't wait.

[*Noise from the street. Shouts of* "Stop, Thief!"]

POLICEMAN What's that?

[*The* BOY *is in the doorway with cakes and buns and rolls spilling out of his shirt. The* WIFE *signals desperately to him to leave. He gets the idea.*]

POLICEMAN No, you don't. [*He grabs the* BOY *by the collar.*] Where's all this from?

BOY [*Vaguely pointing.*] Down the street.

POLICEMAN [*Grimly.*] So that's it. [*Prepares to arrest the* BOY.]

WIFE [*Stepping in.*] And *we* knew nothing about it. [*To the* BOY.] Nasty little thief!

POLICEMAN [*Dryly.*]   Can you clarify the situation, Mr. Shui Ta?
> [SHUI TA *is silent.*]

POLICEMAN [*Who understands silence.*]   Aha. You're all coming with me—to the station.

SHUI TA   I can hardly say how sorry I am that *my* establishment . . .

WIFE   Oh, he saw the boy leave not ten minutes ago!

SHUI TA   And to conceal the theft asked a policeman in?

POLICEMAN   Don't listen to her, Mr. Shui Ta, I'll be happy to relieve you of their presence one and all! [*To all three.*] Out!
> [*He drives them before him.*]

GRANDFATHER [*Leaving last, gravely.*]   Good morning!

POLICEMAN   Good morning!
> [SHUI TA, *left alone, continues to tidy up.* MRS. MI TZU *breezes in.*]

MRS. MI TZU   *You're* her cousin, are you? Then have the goodness to explain what all this means—police dragging people from a respectable house! By what right does your Miss Shen Te turn my property into a house of assignation?—Well, as you see, I know all!

SHUI TA   Yes. My cousin has the worst possible reputation: that of being poor.

MRS. MI TZU   No sentimental rubbish, Mr. Shui Ta. Your cousin was a common . . .

SHUI TA   Pauper. Let's use the uglier word.

MRS. MI TZU   I'm speaking of her conduct, not her earnings. But there must have *been* earnings, or how did she buy all this? Several elderly gentlemen took care of it, I suppose. I repeat: this is a respectable house! I have tenants who prefer not to live under the same roof with such a person.

SHUI TA [*Quietly.*]   How much do you want?

MRS. MI TZU [*He is ahead of her now.*]   I beg your pardon.

SHUI TA   To reassure yourself. To reassure your tenants. How much will it cost?

MRS. MI TZU   You're a cool customer.

SHUI TA [*Picking up the lease.*]   The rent is high. [*He reads on.*] I assume it's payable by the month?

MRS. MI TZU   Not in her case.

SHUI TA [*Looking up.*]   What?

MRS. MI TZU   Six months' rent payable in advance. Two hundred silver dollars.

SHUI TA   Six . . . ! Sheer usury! And where am I to find it?

MRS. MI TZU   You should have thought of that before.

SHUI TA   Have you no heart, Mrs. Mi Tzu? It's true Shen Te acted foolishly, being kind to all those people, but she'll improve with time. I'll see to it she does. She'll work her fingers to the bone to pay her rent, and all the time be as quiet as a mouse, as humble as a fly.

MRS. MI TZU   Her social background . . .

SHUI TA   Out of the depths! She came out of the depths! And before she'll go back there, she'll work, sacrifice, shrink from nothing. . . . Such a tenant is worth her weight in gold, Mrs. Mi Tzu.

MRS. MI TZU   It's silver we were talking about, Mr. Shui Ta. Two hundred silver dollars or . . .
> [*Enter the* POLICEMAN.]

POLICEMAN   Am I intruding, Mr. Shui Ta?

MRS. MI TZU   This tobacco shop is well known to the police, I see.

POLICEMAN   Mr. Shui Ta has done us a service, Mrs. Mi Tzu. I am here to present our official felicitations!

MRS. MI TZU   That means less than nothing to me, sir. Mr. Shui Ta, all I can say is: I hope your cousin will find my terms acceptable. Good day, gentlemen. [*Exit.*]

SHUI TA   Good day, ma'am.

[*Pause.*]

POLICEMAN   Mrs. Mi Tzu a bit of a stumbling block, sir?

SHUI TA   She wants six months' rent in advance.

POLICEMAN   And you haven't got it, eh? [SHUI TA *is silent.*] But surely you can get it, sir? A man like you?

SHUI TA   What about a woman like Shen Te?

POLICEMAN   You're not staying, sir?

SHUI TA   No, and I won't be back. Do you smoke?

POLICEMAN   [*Taking two cigars, and placing them both in his pocket.*]   Thank you, sir—I see your point, Miss Shen Te—let's mince no words—Miss Shen Te lived by selling herself. "What else could she have done?" you ask. "How else was she to pay the rent?" True. But the fact remains, Mr. Shui Ta, it is not respectable. Why not? A very deep question. But, in the first place, love—love isn't bought and sold like cigars, Mr. Shui Ta. In the second place, it isn't respectable to go waltzing off with someone that's paying his way, so to speak—it must be for love! Thirdly and lastly, as the proverb has it: not for a handful of rice but for love! [*Pause. He is thinking hard.*] "Well," you may say, "and what good is all this wisdom if the milk's already spilt?" Miss Shen Te is what she is. Is *where* she is. We have to face the fact that if she doesn't get hold of six months' rent pronto, she'll be back on the streets. The question then as I see it—everything in this world is a matter of opinion—the question as I see it is: *how* is she to get hold of this rent? How? Mr. Shui Ta: I don't know. [*Pause.*] I take that back, sir. It's just come to me. A husband. We must find her a husband!

[*Enter a little* OLD WOMAN.]

OLD WOMAN   A good cheap cigar for my husband, we'll have been married forty years tomorrow and we're having a little celebration.

SHUI TA   Forty years? And you still want to celebrate?

OLD WOMAN   As much as we can afford to. We have the carpet shop across the square. We'll be good neighbors, I hope?

SHUI TA   I hope so too.

POLICEMAN   [*Who keeps making discoveries.*]   Mr. Shui Ta, you know what we need? We need capital. And how do we acquire capital? We get married.

SHUI TA   [*To* OLD WOMAN.]   I'm afraid I've been pestering this gentleman with my personal worries.

POLICEMAN   [*Lyrically.*]   We can't pay six months' rent, so what do we do? We marry money.

SHUI TA   That might not be easy.

POLICEMAN   Oh, I don't know. She's a good match. Has a nice, growing business. [*To the* OLD WOMAN.] What do you think?

OLD WOMAN   [*Undecided.*]   Well—

POLICEMAN   Should she put an ad in the paper?

OLD WOMAN [*Not eager to commit herself.*]   Well, if *she* agrees—

POLICEMAN   I'll write it for her. *You* lend us a hand, and *we* write an ad for you! [*He chuckles away to himself, takes out his notebook, wets the stump of a pencil between his lips, and writes away.*]

SHUI TA [*Slowly.*]   Not a bad idea.

POLICEMAN   "What . . . *respectable* . . . man . . . with small capital . . . widower . . . not excluded . . . desires . . . marriage . . . into flourishing . . . tobacco shop?" And now let's add: "Am . . . pretty . . ." No! . . . "Prepossessing appearance."

SHUI TA   If you don't think that's an exaggeration?

OLD WOMAN   Oh, not a bit. I've seen her.

> [*The* POLICEMAN *tears the page out of his notebook, and hands it over to* SHUI TA.]

SHUI TA [*With horror in his voice.*]   How much luck we need to keep our heads above water! How many ideas! How many friends! [*To the* POLICEMAN.] Thank you, sir, I think I see my way clear.

3

Evening in the municipal park. Noise of a plane overhead. YANG SUN, *a young man in rags, is following the plane with his eyes: one can tell that the machine is describing a curve above the park.* YANG SUN *then takes a rope out of his pocket, looking anxiously about him as he does so. He moves toward a large willow. Enter two prostitutes, one old, the other the* NIECE *whom we have already met.*

NIECE   Hello. Coming with me?

YANG SUN [*Taken aback.*]   If you'd like to buy me a dinner.

OLD WHORE   Buy you a dinner! [*To the* NIECE.] Oh, we know him—it's the unemployed pilot. Waste no time on him!

NIECE   But he's the only man left in the park. And it's going to rain.

OLD WHORE   Oh, how do you know?

> [*And they pass by.* YANG SUN *again looks about him, again takes his rope, and this time throws it round a branch of the willow tree. Again he is interrupted. It is the two prostitutes returning—and in such a hurry they don't notice him.*]

NIECE   It's going to pour!

> [*Enter* SHEN TE.]

OLD WHORE   There's that *gorgon* Shen Te! That *drove* your family out into the cold!

NIECE   It wasn't her. It was that cousin of hers. She offered to pay for the cakes. I've nothing against her.

OLD WHORE   I have, though. [*So that* SHEN TE *can hear.*] Now where could the little lady be off to? She may be rich now but that won't stop her snatching our young men, will it?

SHEN TE   I'm going to the tearoom by the pond.

NIECE   Is it true what they say? You're marrying a widower—with three children?

SHEN TE   Yes. I'm just going to see him.

YANG SUN [*His patience at breaking point.*] Move on there! This is a park, not a whorehouse!

OLD WHORE Shut your mouth!

[*But the two prostitutes leave.*]

YANG SUN Even in the farthest corner of the park, even when it's raining, you can't get rid of them! [*He spits.*]

SHEN TE [*Overhearing this.*] And what right have you to scold them? [*But at this point she sees the rope.*] Oh!

YANG SUN Well, what are you staring at?

SHEN TE That rope. What is it for?

YANG SUN Think! Think! I haven't a penny. Even if I had, I wouldn't spend it on you. I'd buy a drink of water.

[*The rain starts.*]

SHEN TE [*Still looking at the rope.*] What is the rope for? You mustn't!

YANG SUN What's it to you? Clear out!

SHEN TE [*Irrelevantly.*] It's raining.

YANG SUN Well, don't try to come under this tree.

SHEN TE Oh, no. [*She stays in the rain.*]

YANG SUN Now go away. [*Pause.*] For one thing, I don't like your looks, you're bowlegged.

SHEN TE [*Indignantly.*] That's not true!

YANG SUN Well, don't show 'em to me. Look, it's raining. You better come under this tree.

[*Slowly, she takes shelter under the tree.*]

SHEN TE Why did you want to do it?

YANG SUN You really want to know? [*Pause.*] To get rid of you! [*Pause.*] You know what a flyer is?

SHEN TE Oh yes, I've met a lot of pilots. At the tearoom.

YANG SUN You call *them* flyers? Think they know what a machine is? Just 'cause they have leather helmets? They gave the airfield director a bribe, that's the way *those* fellows got up in the air! Try one of them out sometime. "Go up to two thousand feet," tell him, "then let it fall, then pick it up again with a flick of the wrist at the last moment." Know what he'll say to that? "It's not in my contract." Then again, there's the landing problem. It's like landing on your own backside. It's no different, planes are human. Those fools don't understand. [*Pause.*] And I'm the biggest fool for reading the book on flying in the Peking school and skipping the page where it says: "We've got enough flyers and we don't need you." I'm a mail pilot with no mail. You understand that?

SHEN TE [*Shyly.*] Yes, I do.

YANG SUN No, you don't. You'd never understand that.

SHEN TE When we were little we had a crane with a broken wing. He made friends with us and was very good-natured about our jokes. He would strut along behind us and call out to stop us going too fast for him. But every spring and autumn when the cranes flew over the villages in great swarms, he got quite restless. [*Pause.*] I understand that.

[*She bursts out crying.*]

YANG SUN Don't!

SHEN TE [*Quieting down.*]   No.

YANG SUN   It's bad for the complexion.

SHEN TE [*Sniffing.*]   I've stopped.

> [*She dries her tears on her big sleeve. Leaning against the tree, but not looking at her, he reaches for her face.*]

YANG SUN   You can't even wipe your own face. [*He is wiping it for her with his handkerchief. Pause.*]

SHEN TE [*Still sobbing.*]   I don't know *anything*!

YANG SUN   You interrupted me! What for?

SHEN TE   It's such a rainy day. You only wanted to do . . . . *that* because it's such a rainy day. [*To the audience.*]

> In our country
> The evenings should never be somber
> High bridges over rivers
> The gray hour between night and morning
> And the long, long winter:
> Such things are dangerous
> For, with all the misery,
> A very little is enough
> And men throw away an unbearable life.

> [*Pause.*]

YANG SUN   Talk about yourself for a change.

SHEN TE   What about me? I have a shop.

YANG SUN [*Incredulous.*]   You have a shop, have you? Never thought of walking the streets?

SHEN TE   I did walk the streets. Now I have a shop.

YANG SUN [*Ironically.*]   A gift of the gods, I suppose!

SHEN TE   How did you know?

YANG SUN [*Even more ironical.*]   One fine evening the gods turned up saying: here's some money!

SHEN TE [*Quickly.*]   One fine morning.

YANG SUN [*Fed up.*]   This isn't much of an entertainment.

> [*Pause.*]

SHEN TE   I can play the zither a little. [*Pause.*] And I can mimic men. [*Pause.*] I got the shop, so the first thing I did was to give my zither away. I can be as stupid as a fish now, I said to myself, and it won't matter.

> I'm rich now, I said
> I walk alone, I sleep alone
> For a whole year, I said
> I'll have nothing to do with a man.

YANG SUN   And now you're marrying one! The one at the tearoom by the pond?

> [SHEN TE *is silent.*]

YANG SUN   What do you know about love?

SHEN TE   Everything.

YANG SUN   Nothing. [*Pause.*] Or d'you just mean you enjoyed it?

SHEN TE   No.

YANG SUN   [*Again without turning to look at her, he strokes her cheek with his hand.*] You like that?

SHEN TE   Yes.

YANG SUN [*Breaking off.*]   You're easily satisfied, I must say. [*Pause.*] What a
    town!

SHEN TE   You have no friends?

YANG SUN [*Defensively.*]   Yes, I have! [*Change of tone.*] But they don't want to
    hear I'm still unemployed. "What?" they ask. "Is there still water in the sea?"
    You have friends?

SHEN TE [*Hesitating.*]   Just a . . . cousin.

YANG SUN   Watch him carefully.

SHEN TE   He only came once. Then he went away. He won't be back. [YANG SUN
    is looking away.] But to be without hope, they say, is to be without goodness!
        [*Pause.*]

YANG SUN   Go on talking. A voice is a voice.

SHEN TE   Once, when I was a little girl, I fell, with a load of brushwood. An
    old man picked me up. He gave me a penny too. Isn't it funny how people
    who don't have very much like to give some of it away? They must like to
    show what they can do, and how could they show it better than by being
    kind? Being wicked is just like being clumsy. When we sing a song, or build
    a machine, or plant some rice, we're being kind. You're kind.

YANG SUN   You make it sound easy.

SHEN TE   Oh, no. [*Little pause.*] Oh! A drop of rain!

YANG SUN   Where'd you feel it?

SHEN TE   Between the eyes.

YANG SUN   Near the right eye? Or the left?

SHEN TE   Near the left eye.

YANG SUN   Oh, good. [*He is getting sleepy.*] So you're through with men, eh?

SHEN TE [*With a smile.*]   But I'm not bowlegged.

YANG SUN   Perhaps not.

SHEN TE   Definitely not.
        [*Pause.*]

YANG SUN   [*Leaning wearily against the willow.*]   I haven't had a drop to drink
    all day, I haven't eaten anything for two days. I couldn't love you if I tried.
        [*Pause.*]

SHEN TE   I like it in the rain.
        [*Enter* WONG *the water seller, singing.*]

THE SONG OF THE WATER SELLER IN THE RAIN

"Buy my water," I am yelling
And my fury restraining
For no water I'm selling
'Cause it's raining, 'cause it's raining!
    I keep yelling: "Buy my water!"
    But no one's buying
    Athirst and dying
    And drinking and paying!
    Buy water!
    Buy water, you dogs!

Nice to dream of lovely weather!
Think of all the consternation

Were there no precipitation
Half a dozen years together!
　　Can't you hear them shrieking: "Water!"
　　Pretending they adore me?
　　They all would go down on their knees before me!
　　Down on your knees!
　　Go down on your knees, you dogs!

What are lawns and hedges thinking?
What are fields and forests saying?
　　"At the cloud's breast we are drinking!
　　And we've no idea who's paying!"
　　　　I keep yelling: "Buy my water!"
　　　　But no one's buying
　　　　Athirst and dying
　　　　And drinking and paying!
　　　　Buy water!
　　　　Buy water, you dogs!

[*The rain has stopped now.* SHEN TE *sees* WONG *and runs toward him.*]

SHEN TE　Wong! You're back! Your carrying pole's at the shop.

WONG　Oh, thank you, Shen Te. And how is life treating *you*?

SHEN TE　I've just met a brave and clever man. And I want to buy him a cup
of your water.

WONG [*Bitterly.*]　Throw back your head and open your mouth and you'll have
all the water you need—

SHEN TE [*Tenderly.*]
　　I want *your* water, Wong
　　The water that has tired you so
　　The water that you carried all this way
　　The water that is hard to sell because it's been raining.
I need it for the young man over there—he's a flyer!
　　A flyer is a bold man:
　　Braving the storms
　　In company with the clouds
　　He crosses the heavens
　　And brings to friends in faraway lands
　　The friendly mail!

[*She pays* WONG, *and runs over to* YANG SUN *with the cup. But* YANG SUN *is
fast asleep.*]

SHEN TE [*Calling to* WONG, *with a laugh.*]　He's fallen asleep! Despair and rain
and I have worn him out!

3a

WONG's *den. The sewer pipe is transparent, and the* GODS *again appear to*
WONG *in a dream.*

WONG [*Radiant*]　I've seen her, illustrious ones! And she hasn't changed!

FIRST GOD　That's good to hear.

WONG   She loves someone.

FIRST GOD   Let's hope the experience gives her the strength to stay good!

WONG   It does. She's doing good deeds all the time.

FIRST GOD   Ah? What sort? What sort of good deeds, Wong?

WONG   Well, she has a kind word for everybody.

FIRST GOD [*Eagerly.*]   And then?

WONG   Hardly anyone leaves her shop without tobacco in his pocket—even if he can't pay for it.

FIRST GOD   Not bad at all. Next?

WONG   She's putting up a family of eight.

FIRST GOD [*Gleefully, to the* SECOND GOD.]   Eight! [*To* WONG.] And that's not all, of course!

WONG   She bought a cup of water from me even though it was raining.

FIRST GOD   Yes, yes, yes, all these smaller good deeds!

WONG   Even they run into money. A little tobacco shop doesn't make so much.

FIRST GOD [*Sententiously.*]   A prudent gardener works miracles on the smallest plot.

WONG   She hands out rice every morning. That eats up half her earnings.

FIRST GOD [*A little disappointed.*]   Well, as a beginning . . .

WONG   They call her the Angel of the Slums—whatever the carpenter may say!

FIRST GOD   What's this? A carpenter speaks ill of her?

WONG   Oh, he only says her shelves weren't paid for in full.

SECOND GOD [*Who has a bad cold and can't pronounce his n's and m's.*]   What's this? Not paying a carpenter? Why was that?

WONG   I suppose she didn't have the money.

SECOND GOD [*Severely.*]   One pays what one owes, that's in our book of rules! First the letter of the law, then the spirit.

WONG   But it wasn't Shen Te, illustrious ones, it was her cousin. She called *him* in to help.

SECOND GOD   Then her cousin must never darken her threshold again!

WONG   Very well, illustrious ones! But in fairness to Shen Te, let me say that her cousin is a businessman.

FIRST GOD   Perhaps we should inquire what is customary? I find business quite unintelligible. But everybody's doing it. Business! Did the Seven Good Kings do business? Did Kung the Just[8] sell fish?

SECOND GOD   In any case, such a thing must not occur again!

   [*The* GODS *start to leave.*]

THIRD GOD   Forgive us for taking this tone with you, Wong, we haven't been getting enough sleep. The rich recommend us to the poor, and the poor tell us they haven't enough room.

SECOND GOD   Feeble, feeble, the best of them!

FIRST GOD   No great deeds! No heroic daring!

THIRD GOD   On such a *small* scale!

SECOND GOD   Sincere, yes, but what is actually *achieved*?

   [*One can no longer hear them.*]

---

8. The philosopher Confucius (551–479 B.C.E.). "Seven Good Kings": legendary wise kings who personified the old order and traditional values.

WONG [*Calling after them.*]   I've thought of something, illustrious ones: Perhaps you shouldn't ask—too—much—all—at—once!

4

The square in front of Shen Te's tobacco shop. Besides Shen Te's place, two other shops are seen: the carpet shop and a barber's. Morning. Outside Shen Te's the GRANDFATHER, *the* SISTER-IN-LAW, *the* UNEMPLOYED MAN, *and* MRS. SHIN *stand waiting.*

SISTER-IN-LAW   She's been out all night again.

MRS. SHIN   No sooner did we get rid of that crazy cousin of hers than Shen Te herself starts carrying on! Maybe she does give us an ounce of rice now and then, but can you depend on her? Can you depend on her?
[*Loud voices from the barber's.*]

VOICE OF SHU FU   What are you doing in my shop? Get out—at once!

VOICE OF WONG   But sir. They all let me sell . . .
[WONG *comes staggering out of the barber's shop pursued by Mr.* SHU FU, *the barber, a fat man carrying a heavy curling iron.*]

SHU FU   Get out, I said! Pestering my customers with your slimy old water! Get out! Take your cup!
[*He holds out the cup.* WONG *reaches out for it. Mr.* SHU FU *strikes his hand with the curling iron, which is hot.* WONG *howls.*]

SHU FU   You had it coming my man!
[*Puffing, he returns to his shop. The* UNEMPLOYED MAN *picks up the cup and gives it to* WONG.]

UNEMPLOYED MAN   You can report that to the police.

WONG   My hand! It's smashed up!

UNEMPLOYED MAN   Any bones broken?

WONG   I can't move my fingers.

UNEMPLOYED MAN   Sit down. I'll put some water on it.
[WONG *sits.*]

MRS. SHIN   The water won't cost you anything.

SISTER-IN-LAW   You might have got a bandage from Miss Shen Te till she took to staying out all night. It's a scandal.

MRS. SHIN [*Despondently.*]   If you ask me, she's forgotten we ever existed!
[*Enter* SHEN TE *down the street, with a dish of rice.*]

SHEN TE [*To the audience.*]   How wonderful to see Setzuan in the early morning! I always used to stay in bed with my dirty blanket over my head afraid to wake up. This morning I saw the newspapers being delivered by little boys, the streets being washed by strong men, and fresh vegetables coming in from the country on ox carts. It's a long walk from where Yang Sun lives, but I feel lighter at every step. They say you walk on air when you're in love, but it's even better walking on the rough earth, on the hard cement. In the early morning, the old city looks like a great heap of rubbish! Nice, though, with all its little lights. And the sky, so pink, so transparent, before the dust comes and muddies it! What a lot you miss if you never see your city rising from its slumbers like an honest old craftsman pumping his lungs full of air and reaching for his tools, as the poet says! [*Cheerfully, to her waiting guests.*] Good morning, everyone, here's your rice! [*Distributing the rice, she comes *upon* WONG.] Good morning, Wong, I'm quite lightheaded today. On my way over, I looked at myself in all the shop windows. I'd love to be beautiful.

[*She slips into the carpet shop.* Mr. SHU FU *has just emerged from his shop.*]

SHU FU [*To the audience.*] It surprises me how beautiful Miss Shen Te is looking today! I never gave her a passing thought before. But now I've been gazing upon her comely form for exactly three minutes! I begin to suspect I am in love with her. She is overpoweringly attractive! [*Crossly, to* WONG.] Be off with you rascal!

[*He returns to his shop.* SHEN TE *comes back out of the carpet shop with the* OLD MAN, *its proprietor, and his wife—whom we have already met—the* OLD WOMAN. SHEN TE *is wearing a shawl. The* OLD MAN *is holding up a looking glass for her.*]

OLD WOMAN Isn't it lovely? We'll give you a reduction because there's a little hole in it.

SHEN TE [*Looking at another shawl on the old woman's arm.*] The other one's nice too.

OLD WOMAN [*Smiling.*] Too bad there's no hole in that!

SHEN TE That's right. My shop doesn't make very much.

OLD WOMAN And your deeds eat it all up! Be more careful, my dear . . .

SHEN TE [*Trying on the shawl with the hole.*] Just now, I'm lightheaded! Does the color suit me?

OLD WOMAN You'd better ask a man.

SHEN TE [*To the* OLD MAN.] Does the color suit me?

OLD MAN You'd better ask your young friend.

SHEN TE I'd like to have your opinion.

OLD MAN It suits you very well. But wear it this way: the dull side out.

[SHEN TE *pays up.*]

OLD WOMAN If you decide you don't like it, you can exchange it. [*She pulls* SHEN TE *to one side.*] Has he got money?

SHEN TE [*With a laugh*] Yang Sun? Oh, no.

OLD WOMAN Then how're you going to pay your rent?

SHEN TE I'd forgotten about that.

OLD WOMAN And next Monday is the first of the month! Miss Shen Te, I've got something to say to you. After we [*Indicating her husband.*] got to know you, we had our doubts about that marriage ad. We thought it would be better if you'd let *us* help you. Out of our savings. We reckon we could lend you two hundred silver dollars. We don't need anything in writing—you could pledge us your tobacco stock.

SHEN TE You're prepared to lend money to a person like me?

OLD WOMAN It's folks like you that need it. We'd think twice about lending anything to your cousin.

OLD MAN [*Coming up.*] All settled, my dear?

SHEN TE I wish the gods could have heard what your wife was just saying, Mr. Ma. They're looking for good people who're happy—and helping me makes you happy because you know it was love that got me into difficulties!

[*The old couple smile knowingly at each other.*]

OLD MAN And here's the money, Miss Shen Te.

[*He hands her an envelope.* SHEN TE *takes it. She bows. They bow back. They return to their shop.*]

SHEN TE [*Holding up her envelope.*] Look, Wong, here's six months' rent! Don't you believe in miracles now? And how do you like my new shawl?

WONG For the young fellow I saw you with in the park?

[SHEN TE *nods.*]

MRS. SHIN Never mind all that. It's time you took a look at this hand!

SHEN TE Have you hurt your hand?

MRS. SHIN That barber smashed it with his hot curling iron. Right in front of our eyes.

SHEN TE [*Shocked at herself.*] And I never noticed! We must get you to a doctor this minute or who knows what will happen?

UNEMPLOYED MAN It's not a doctor he should see, it's a judge. He can ask for compensation. The barber's filthy rich.

WONG You think I have a chance?

MRS. SHIN [*With relish.*] If it's really good and smashed. But is it?

WONG I think so. It's very swollen. Could I get a pension?

MRS. SHIN You'd need a witness.

WONG Well, you all saw it. You could all testify.

[*He looks round. The* UNEMPLOYED MAN, *the* GRANDFATHER, *and the* SISTER-IN-LAW *are all sitting against the wall of the shop eating rice. Their concentration on eating is complete.*]

SHEN TE [*To* MRS. SHIN.] You saw it yourself.

MRS. SHIN I want nothing to do with the police. It's against my principles.

SHEN TE [*To* SISTER-IN-LAW.] What about you?

SISTER-IN-LAW Me? I wasn't looking.

SHEN TE [*To the* GRANDFATHER, *coaxingly.*] Grandfather, *you'll* testify, won't you?

SISTER-IN-LAW And a lot of good that will do. He's simple-minded.

SHEN TE [*To the* UNEMPLOYED MAN.] You seem to be the only witness left.

UNEMPLOYED MAN My testimony would only hurt him. I've been picked up twice for begging.

SHEN TE

Your brother is assaulted, and you shut your eyes?
He is hit, cries out in pain, and you are silent?
The beast prowls, chooses and seizes his victim, and you say:
"Because we showed no displeasure, he has spared us."

If no one present will be a witness, I will. I'll say *I* saw it.

MRS. SHIN [*Solemnly.*] The name for that is perjury.

WONG I don't know if I can accept that. Though maybe I'll have to. [*Looking at his hand.*] Is it swollen enough, do you think? The swelling's not going down.

UNEMPLOYED MAN No, no, the swelling's holding up well.

WONG Yes. It's *more* swollen if anything. Maybe my wrist is broken after all. I'd better see a judge at once.

[*Holding his hand very carefully, and fixing his eyes on it, he runs off.* MRS. SHIN *goes quickly into the barber's shop.*]

UNEMPLOYED MAN [*Seeing her.*] She is getting on the right side of Mr. Shu Fu.

SISTER-IN-LAW You and I can't change the world, Shen Te.

SHEN TE Go away! Go away all of you! [*The* UNEMPLOYED MAN, *the* SISTER-IN-LAW, *and the* GRANDFATHER *stalk off, eating and sulking. To the audience.*]

They've stopped answering
They stay put

They do as they're told
They don't care
Nothing can make them look up
But the smell of food.

[*Enter* MRS. YANG, *Yang Sun's mother, out of breath.*]

MRS. YANG   Miss Shen Te. My son has told me everything. I am Mrs. Yang, Sun's mother. Just think. He's got an offer. Of a job as a pilot. A letter has just come. From the director of the airfield in Peking!

SHEN TE   So he can fly again! Isn't that wonderful!

MRS. YANG [*Less breathlessly all the time.*]   They won't give him the job for nothing. They want five hundred silver dollars.

SHEN TE   We can't let money stand in his way, Mrs. Yang!

MRS. YANG   If only you could help him out!

SHEN TE   I have the shop. I can try! [*She embraces* MRS. YANG.] I happen to have two hundred with me now. Take it. [*She gives her the old couple's money.*] It was a loan but they said I could repay it with my tobacco stock.

MRS. YANG   And they were calling Sun the Dead Pilot of Setzuan! A friend in need!

SHEN TE   We must find another three hundred.

MRS. YANG   How?

SHEN TE   Let me think. [*Slowly.*] I know someone who can help. I didn't want to call on his services again, he's hard and cunning. But a flyer must fly. And I'll make this the last time.

[*Distant sound of a plane.*]

MRS. YANG   If the man you mentioned can do it . . . Oh, look, there's the morning mail plane, heading for Peking!

SHEN TE   The pilot can see us, let's wave!

[*They wave. The noise of the engine is louder.*]

MRS. YANG   You know that pilot up there?

SHEN TE   Wave, Mrs. Yang! I know the pilot who will be up there. He gave up hope. But he'll do it now. One man to raise himself above the misery, above us all. [*To the audience.*]

Yang Sun, my lover:
Braving the storms
In company with the clouds
Crossing the heavens
And bringing to friends in faraway lands
The friendly mail!

4a

In front of the inner curtain. Enter SHEN TE, *carrying* SHUI TA's *mask. She sings.*

THE SONG OF DEFENSELESSNESS

In our country
A useful man needs luck
Only if he finds strong backers
Can he prove himself useful.
The good can't defend themselves and
Even the gods are defenseless.

Oh, why don't the gods have their own ammunition
And launch against badness their own expedition
Enthroning the good and preventing sedition
And bringing the world to a peaceful condition?

Oh, why don't the gods do the buying and selling
Injustice forbidding, starvation dispelling
Give bread to each city and joy to each dwelling?
Oh, why don't the gods do the buying and selling?

[*She puts on Shui Ta's mask and sings in his voice.*]

You can only help one of your luckless brothers
By trampling down a dozen others.

Why is it the gods do not feel indignation
And come down in fury to end exploitation
Defeat all defeat and forbid desperation
Refusing to tolerate such toleration?

Why is it?

5

SHEN TE's *tobacco shop. Behind the counter, Mr.* SHUI TA, *reading the paper.* MRS.
SHIN *is cleaning up. She talks and he takes no notice.*

MRS. SHIN   And when certain rumors get about, what *happens* to a little place
like this? It goes to pot. *I* know. So, if you want my advice, Mr. Shui Ta, find
out just what has been going on between Miss Shen Te and that Yang Sun
from Yellow Street. And remember: a certain interest in Miss Shen Te has
been expressed by the barber next door, a man with twelve houses and only
one wife,[9] who, for that matter, is likely to drop off at any time. A certain
interest has been expressed. He was even inquiring about her means and, if
that doesn't prove a man is getting serious, what would?
　　[*Still getting no response, she leaves with her bucket.*]
YANG SUN'S VOICE   Is that Miss Shen Te's tobacco shop?
MRS. SHIN'S VOICE   Yes, it is, but it's Mr. Shui Ta who's here today.
　　[SHUI TA *runs to the mirror with the short, light steps of* SHEN TE, *and is just
　　about to start primping, when he realizes his mistake, and turns away, with
　　a short laugh. Enter* YANG SUN. MRS. SHIN *enters behind him and slips into
　　the back room to eavesdrop.*]
YANG SUN   I am Yang Sun. [SHUI TA *bows.*] Is Shen Te in?
SHUI TA   No.
YANG SUN   I guess you know our relationship? [*He is inspecting the stock.*]
Quite a place! And I thought she was just talking big. I'll be flying again, all
right. [*He takes a cigar, solicits and receives a light from* SHUI TA.] You think
we can squeeze the other three hundred out of the tobacco stock?

9. Ancient Chinese law permitted a man to have more than one wife.

SHUI TA   May I ask if it is your intention to sell at once?

YANG SUN   It was decent of her to come out with the two hundred but they aren't much use with the other three hundred still missing.

SHUI TA   Shen Te was overhasty promising so much. She might have to sell the shop itself to raise it. Haste, they say, is the wind that blows the house down.

YANG SUN   Oh, she isn't a girl to keep a man waiting. For one thing or the other, if you take my meaning.

SHUI TA   I take your meaning

YANG SUN [*Leering.*]   Uh, huh.

SHUI TA   Would you explain what the five hundred silver dollars are for?

YANG SUN   Want to sound me out? Very well. The director of the Peking airfield is a friend of mine from flying school. I give him five hundred: he gets me the job.

SHUI TA   The price is high.

YANG SUN   Not as these things go. He'll have to fire one of the present pilots— for negligence. Only the man he has in mind isn't negligent. Not easy, you understand. You needn't mention that part of it to Shen Te.

SHUI TA [*Looking intently at* YANG SUN.]   Mr. Yang Sun, you are asking my cousin to give up her possessions, leave her friends, and place her entire fate in your hands. I presume you intend to marry her?

YANG SUN   I'd be prepared to.

[*Slight pause.*]

SHUI TA   Those two hundred silver dollars would pay the rent here for six months. If you were Shen Te wouldn't you be tempted to continue in business?

YANG SUN   What? Can you imagine Yang Sun the flyer behind a counter? [*In an oily voice.*] "A strong cigar or a mild one, worthy sir?" Not in this century!

SHUI TA   My cousin wishes to follow the promptings of her heart, and, from her own point of view, she may even have what is called the right to love. Accordingly, she has commissioned me to help you to this post. There is nothing here that I am not empowered to turn immediately into cash. Mrs. Mi Tzu, the landlady, will advise me about the sale.

[*Enter* MRS. MI TZU.]

MRS. MI TZU   Good morning, Mr. Shui Ta, you wish to see me about the rent? As you know it falls due the day after tomorrow.

SHUI TA   Circumstances have changed, Mrs. Mi Tzu: my cousin is getting married. Her future husband here, Mr. Yang Sun, will be taking her to Peking. I am interested in selling the tobacco stock.

MRS. MI TZU   How much are you asking, Mr. Shui Ta?

YANG SUN   Three hundred sil—

SHUI TA   Five hundred silver dollars.

MRS. MI TZU   How much did she pay for it, Mr. Shui Ta?

SHUI TA   A thousand. And very little has been sold.

MRS. MI TZU   She was robbed. But I'll make you a special offer if you'll promise to be out by the day after tomorrow. Three hundred silver dollars.

YANG SUN [*Shrugging.*]   Take it, man, take it.

SHUI TA   It is not enough.

YANG SUN   Why not? Why not? Certainly, it's enough.

SHUI TA   Five hundred silver dollars.

YANG SUN   But why? We only need three!

SHUI TA [*To* MRS. MI TZU.]   Excuse me. [*Takes* YANG SUN *on one side.*] The tobacco stock is pledged to the old couple who gave my cousin the two hundred.

YANG SUN   Is it in writing?

SHUI TA   No.

YANG SUN [*To* MRS. MI TZU.]   Three hundred will do.

MRS. MI TZU   Of course, I need an assurance that Miss Shen Te is not in debt.

YANG SUN   Mr. Shui Ta?

SHUI TA   She is not in debt.

YANG SUN   When can you let us have the money?

MRS. MI TZU   The day after tomorrow. And remember: I'm doing this because I have a soft spot in my heart for young lovers! [*Exit.*]

YANG SUN [*Calling after her.*]   Boxes, jars and sacks—three hundred for the lot and the pain's over! [*To* SHUI TA.] Where else can we raise money by the day after tomorrow?

SHUI TA   Nowhere. Haven't you enough for the trip and the first few weeks?

YANG SUN   Oh, certainly.

SHUI TA   How much, exactly.

YANG SUN   Oh, I'll dig it up, even if I have to steal it.

SHUI TA   I see.

YANG SUN   Well, don't fall off the roof. I'll get to Peking somehow.

SHUI TA   Two people can't travel for nothing.

YANG SUN [*Not giving* SHUI TA *a chance to answer.*]   I'm leaving *her* behind. No millstones round *my* neck!

SHUI TA   Oh.

YANG SUN   Don't look at me like that!

SHUI TA   How precisely is my cousin to live?

YANG SUN   Oh, you'll think of something.

SHUI TA   A small request, Mr. Yang Sun. Leave the two hundred silver dollars here until you can show me two tickets for Peking.

YANG SUN   You learn to mind your own business, Mr. Shui Ta.

SHUI TA   I'm afraid Miss Shen Te may not wish to sell the shop when she discovers that . . .

YANG SUN   You don't know women. She'll want to. Even then.

SHUI TA [*A slight outburst.*]   She is a human being, sir! And not devoid of common sense!

YANG SUN   Shen Te is a woman: she *is* devoid of common sense. I only have to lay my hand on her shoulder, and church bells ring.

SHUI TA [*With difficulty.*]   Mr. Yang Sun!

YANG SUN   Mr. Shui Whatever-it-is!

SHUI TA   My cousin is devoted to you . . . because . . .

YANG SUN   Because I have my hands on her breasts. Give me a cigar. [*He takes one for himself, stuffs a few more in his pocket, then changes his mind and takes the whole box.*] Tell her I'll marry her, then bring me the three hundred. Or let her bring it. One or the other. [*Exit.*]

MRS. SHIN [*Sticking her head out of the back room.*] Well, he has your cousin under his thumb, and doesn't care if all Yellow Street knows it!

SHUI TA [*Crying out.*] I've lost my shop! And he doesn't love me! [*He runs berserk through the room, repeating these lines incoherently. Then stops suddenly, and addresses* MRS. SHIN.] Mrs. Shin, you grew up in the gutter, like me. Are we lacking in hardness? I doubt it. If you steal a penny from me, I'll take you by the throat till you spit it out! You'd do the same to me. The times are bad, this city is hell, but we're like ants, we keep coming, up and up the walls, however smooth! Till bad luck comes. Being in love, for instance. One weakness is enough, and love is the deadliest.

MRS. SHIN [*Emerging from the back room.*] You should have a little talk with Mr. Shu Fu, the barber. He's a real gentleman and just the thing for your cousin. [*She runs off.*]

SHUI TA

> A caress becomes a stranglehold
> A sigh of love turns to a cry of fear
> Why are there vultures circling in the air?
> A girl is going to meet her lover.

[SHUI TA *sits down and Mr.* SHU FU *enters with* MRS. SHIN.]

SHUI TA Mr. Shu Fu?

SHU FU Mr. Shui Ta.

[*They both bow.*]

SHUI TA I am told that you have expressed a certain interest in my cousin Shen Te. Let me set aside all propriety and confess: she is at this moment in grave danger.

SHU FU Oh, dear!

SHUI TA She has lost her shop, Mr. Shu Fu.

SHU FU The charm of Miss Shen Te, Mr. Shui Ta, derives from the goodness, not of her shop, but of her heart. Men call her the Angel of the Slums.

SHUI TA Yet her goodness has cost her two hundred silver dollars in a single day: we must put a stop to it.

SHU FU Permit me to differ, Mr. Shui Ta. Let us, rather, open wide the gates to such goodness! Every morning, with pleasure tinged by affection, I watch her charitable ministrations. For they are hungry, and she giveth them to eat! Four of them, to be precise. Why only four? I ask. Why not four hundred?[1] I hear she has been seeking shelter for the homeless. What about my humble cabins behind the cattle run? They are at her disposal. And so forth. And so on. Mr. Shui Ta, do you think Miss Shen Te could be persuaded to listen to certain ideas of mine? Ideas like these?

SHUI TA Mr. Shu Fu, she would be honored.

[*Enter* WONG *and the* POLICEMAN. *Mr.* SHU FU *turns abruptly away and studies the shelves.*]

WONG Is Miss Shen Te here?

SHUI TA No.

WONG I am Wong the water seller. You are Mr. Shui Ta?

SHUI TA I am.

---

1. An allusion to the biblical miracle of loaves and fishes, when Christ fed five thousand people (Matthew 14.13–21).

WONG   I am a friend of Shen Te's.

SHUI TA   An intimate friend, I hear.

WONG [*To the* POLICEMAN.]   You see? [*To* SHUI TA.] It's because of my hand.

POLICEMAN   He hurt his hand, sir, that's a fact.

SHUI TA [*Quickly.*]   You need a sling, I see. [*He takes a shawl from the back room, and throws it to* WONG.]

WONG   But that's her new shawl!

SHUI TA   She has no more use for it.

WONG   But she bought it to please someone!

SHUI TA   It happens to be no longer necessary.

WONG [*Making the sling.*]   She is my only witness.

POLICEMAN   Mr. Shui Ta, your cousin is supposed to have seen the barber hit the water seller with a curling iron.

SHUI TA   I'm afraid my cousin was not present at the time.

WONG   But she was, sir! Just ask her! Isn't she in?

SHUI TA [*Gravely.*]   Mr. Wong, my cousin has her own troubles. You wouldn't wish her to add to them by committing perjury?

WONG   But it was she that told me to go to the judge!

SHUI TA   Was the judge supposed to heal your hand?

      [*Mr.* SHU FU *turns quickly around.* SHUI TA *bows to* SHU FU, *and vice versa.*]

WONG [*Taking the sling off, and putting it back.*]   I see how it is.

POLICEMAN   Well, I'll be on my way. [*To* WONG.] And you be careful. If Mr. Shu Fu wasn't a man who tempers justice with mercy, as the saying is, you'd be in jail for libel. Be off with you!

      [*Exit* WONG *followed by* POLICEMAN.]

SHUI TA   Profound apologies, Mr. Shu Fu.

SHU FU   Not at all, Mr. Shui Ta. [*Pointing to the shawl.*] The episode is over?

SHUI TA   It may take her time to recover. There are some fresh wounds.

SHU FU   We shall be discreet. Delicate. A short vacation could be arranged . . .

SHUI TA   First of course, you and she would have to talk things over.

SHU FU   At a small supper in a small, but high-class, restaurant.

SHUI TA   I'll go and find her. [*Exit into back room.*]

MRS. SHIN [*Sticking her head in again.*]   Time for congratulations, Mr. Shu Fu?

SHU FU   Ah, Mrs. Shin! Please inform Miss Shen Te's guests they may take shelter in the cabins behind the cattle run!

      [MRS. SHIN *nods, grinning.*]

SHU FU [*To the audience.*]   Well? What do you think of me, ladies and gentlemen? What could a man do more? Could he be less selfish? More farsighted? A small supper in a small but . . . Does that bring rather vulgar and clumsy thoughts into your mind? Ts, ts, ts. Nothing of the sort will occur. She won't even be touched. Not even accidentally while passing the salt. An exchange of ideas only. Over the flowers on the table—white chrysanthemums, by the way [*He writes down a note of this.*]—yes, over the white chrysanthemums, two young souls will . . . shall I say "find each other"? We shall NOT exploit the misfortune of others. Understanding? Yes. An offer of assistance? Certainly. But quietly. Almost inaudibly. Perhaps with a single glance. A glance that could also—mean more.

MRS. SHIN [*Coming forward.*]   Everything under control, Mr. Shu Fu?

SHU FU Oh, Mrs. Shin, what do you know about this worthless rascal Yang Sun?

MRS. SHIN Why, he's the most worthless rascal . . .

SHU FU Is he really? You're sure? [*As she opens her mouth.*] From now on, he doesn't exist! Can't be found anywhere!

[*Enter* YANG SUN.]

YANG SUN What's been going on here?

MRS. SHIN Shall I call Mr. Shui Ta, Mr. Shu Fu? He wouldn't want strangers in here!

SHU FU Mr. Shui Ta is in conference with Miss Shen Te. Not to be disturbed!

YANG SUN Shen Te here? I didn't see her come in. What kind of conference?

SHU FU [*Not letting him enter the back room.*] Patience, dear sir! And if by chance I have an inkling who you are, pray take note that Miss Shen Te and I are about to announce our engagement.

YANG SUN What?

MRS. SHIN You didn't expect that, did you?

[YANG SUN *is trying to push past the barber into the back room when* SHEN TE *comes out.*]

SHU FU My dear Shen Te, ten thousand apologies! Perhaps you . . .

YANG SUN What is it, Shen Te? Have you gone crazy?

SHEN TE [*Breathless.*] My cousin and Mr. Shu Fu have come to an understanding. They wish me to hear Mr. Shu Fu's plans for helping the poor.

YANG SUN Your cousin wants to part us.

SHEN TE Yes.

YANG SUN And you've agreed to it?

SHEN TE Yes.

YANG SUN They told you I was bad. [SHEN TE *is silent.*] And suppose I am. Does that make me need you less? I'm low, Shen Te, I have no money, I don't do the right thing but at least I put up a fight! [*He is near her now, and speaks in an undertone.*] Have you no eyes? Look at him. Have you forgotten already?

SHEN TE No.

YANG SUN How it was raining?

SHEN TE No.

YANG SUN How you cut me down from the willow tree? Bought me water? Promised me money to fly with?

SHEN TE [*Shakily.*] Yang Sun, what do you want?

YANG SUN I want you to come with me.

SHEN TE [*In a small voice.*] Forgive me, Mr. Shu Fu, I want to go with Mr. Yang Sun.

YANG SUN We're lovers, you know. Give me the key to the shop. [SHEN TE *takes the key from around her neck.* YANG SUN *puts it on the counter. To* MRS. SHIN.] Leave it under the mat when you're through. Let's go, Shen Te.

SHU FU But this is rape! Mr. Shui Ta!!

YANG SUN [*To* SHEN TE.] Tell him not to shout.

SHEN TE Please don't shout for my cousin, Mr. Shu Fu. He doesn't agree with me, I know, but he's wrong. [*To the audience.*]

I want to go with the man I love
I don't want to count the cost

> I don't want to consider if it's wise
> I don't want to know if he loves me
> I want to go with the man I love.

YANG SUN   That's the spirit.
    [*And the couple leave.*]

5a

In front of the inner curtain. SHEN TE *in her wedding clothes, on the way to her wedding.*

SHEN TE   Something terrible has happened. As I left the shop with Yang Sun, I found the old carpet dealer's wife waiting on the street, trembling all over. She told me her husband had taken to his bed—sick with all the worry and excitement over the two hundred silver dollars they lent me. She said it would be best if I gave it back now. Of course, I had to say I would. She said she couldn't quite trust my cousin Shui Ta or even my fiancé, Yang Sun. There were tears in her eyes. With my emotions in an uproar, I threw myself into Yang Sun's arms, I couldn't resist him. The things he'd said to Shui Ta had taught Shen Te nothing. Sinking into his arms, I said to myself:

> To let no one perish, not even oneself
> To fill everyone with happiness, even oneself
> Is so good

How could I have forgotten those two old people? Yang Sun swept me away like a small hurricane. But he's not a bad man, and he loves me. He'd rather work in the cement factory than owe his flying to a crime. Though, of course, flying *is* a great passion with Sun. Now, on the way to my wedding, I waver between fear and joy.

6

The "private dining room" on the upper floor of a cheap restaurant in a poor section of town. With SHEN TE: *the* GRANDFATHER, *the* SISTER-IN-LAW, THE NIECE, MRS. SHIN, *the* UNEMPLOYED MAN. *In a corner, alone, a* PRIEST.[2] *A* WAITER *pouring wine. Downstage,* YANG SUN *talking to his mother. He wears a dinner jacket.*

YANG SUN   Bad news, Mamma. She came right out and told me she can't sell the shop for me. Some idiot is bringing a claim because he lent her the two hundred she gave you.
MRS. YANG   What did you say? Of course, you can't marry her now.
YANG SUN   It's no use saying anything to *her*. I've sent for her cousin, Mr. Shui Ta. He said there was nothing in writing.
MRS. YANG   Good idea. I'll go out and look for him. Keep an eye on things.
    [*Exit* MRS. YANG. SHEN TE *has been pouring wine.*]
SHEN TE [*To the audience, pitcher in hand.*]   I wasn't mistaken in him. He's bearing up well. Though it must have been an awful blow—giving up flying. I do love him so. [*Calling across the room to him.*] Sun, you haven't drunk a toast with the bride!

2. A Buddhist monk or priest.

YANG SUN   What do we drink to?

SHEN TE   Why, to the future!

YANG SUN   When the bridegroom's dinner jacket won't be a hired one!

SHEN TE   But when the bride's dress will still get rained on sometimes!

YANG SUN   To everything we ever wished for!

SHEN TE   May all our dreams come true!

　　　　　[*They drink.*]

YANG SUN [*With loud conviviality.*]   And now, friends, before the wedding gets under way, I have to ask the bride a few questions. I've no idea what kind of a wife she'll make, and it worries me. [*Wheeling on* SHEN TE.] For example. Can you make five cups of tea with three tea leaves?

SHEN TE   No.

YANG SUN   So I won't be getting very much tea. Can you sleep on a straw mattress the size of that book? [*He points to the large volume the* PRIEST *is reading.*]

SHEN TE   The two of us?

YANG SUN   The one of you.

SHEN TE   In that case, no.

YANG SUN   What a wife! I'm shocked!

　　　　　[*While the audience is laughing, his mother returns. With a shrug of her shoulders, she tells* SUN *the expected guest hasn't arrived. The* PRIEST *shuts the book with a bang, and makes for the door.*]

MRS. YANG   Where are *you* off to? It's only a matter of minutes.

PRIEST [*Watch in hand.*]   Time goes on, Mrs. Yang, and I've another wedding to attend to. Also a funeral.

MRS. YANG [*Irately.*]   D'you think we planned it this way? I was hoping to manage with one pitcher of wine, and we've run through two already. [*Points to empty pitcher. Loudly.*] My dear Shen Te, I don't know where your cousin can be keeping himself!

SHEN TE   My cousin?!

MRS. YANG   Certainly. I'm old-fashioned enough to think such a close relative should attend the wedding.

SHEN TE   Oh, Sun, is it the three hundred silver dollars?

YANG SUN [*Not looking her in the eye.*]   Are you deaf? Mother says she's old-fashioned. And I say I'm considerate. We'll wait another fifteen minutes.

HUSBAND   Another fifteen minutes.

MRS. YANG [*Addressing the company.*]   Now you all know, don't you, that my son is getting a job as a mail pilot?

SISTER-IN-LAW   In Peking, too, isn't it?

MRS. YANG   In Peking, too! The two of us are moving to Peking!

SHEN TE   Sun, tell your mother Peking is out of the question now.

YANG SUN   Your cousin'll tell her. If he agrees. I don't agree.

SHEN TE [*Amazed, and dismayed.*]   Sun!

YANG SUN   I hate this godforsaken Setzuan. What people! Know what they look like when I half close my eyes? Horses! Whinnying, fretting, stamping, screwing their necks up! [*Loudly.*] And what is it the thunder says? They are su-per-flu-ous! [*He hammers out the syllables.*] They've run their last race! They can go trample themselves to death! [*Pause.*] I've got to get out of here.

SHEN TE   But I've promised the money to the old couple.

YANG SUN   And since you always do the wrong thing, it's lucky your cousin's coming. Have another drink.

SHEN TE [*Quietly.*]   My cousin can't be coming.

YANG SUN   How d'you mean?

SHEN TE   My cousin can't be where I am.

YANG SUN   Quite a conundrum!

SHEN TE [*Desperately.*]   Sun, I'm the one that loves you. Not my cousin. He was thinking of the job in Peking when he promised you the old couple's money—

YANG SUN   Right. And that's why he's bringing the three hundred silver dollars. Here—to my wedding.

SHEN TE   He is not bringing the three hundred silver dollars.

YANG SUN   Huh? What makes you think that?

SHEN TE [*Looking into his eyes.*]   He says you only bought one ticket to Peking. [*Short pause.*]

YANG SUN   That was yesterday. [*He pulls two tickets part way out of his inside pocket, making her look under his coat.*] Two tickets. I don't want Mother to know. She'll get left behind. I sold her furniture to buy these tickets, so you see . . .

SHEN TE   But what's to become of the old couple?

YANG SUN   What's to become of me? Have another drink. Or do you believe in moderation? If I drink, I fly again. And if you drink, you may learn to understand me.

SHEN TE   You want to fly. But I can't help you.

YANG SUN   "Here's a plane, my darling—but it's only got one wing!"
     [*The* WAITER *enters.*]

WAITER   Mrs. Yang!

MRS. YANG   Yes?

WAITER   Another pitcher of wine, ma'am?

MRS. YANG   We have enough, thanks. Drinking makes me sweat.

WAITER   Would you mind paying, ma'am?

MRS. YANG [*To everyone.*]   Just be patient a few moments longer, everyone, Mr. Shui Ta is on his way over! [*To the* WAITER.] Don't be a spoilsport.

WAITER   I can't let you leave till you've paid your bill, ma'am.

MRS. YANG   But they know me here!

WAITER   That's just it.

PRIEST [*Ponderously getting up.*]   I humbly take my leave. [*And he does.*]

MRS. YANG [*To the others, desperately.*]   Stay where you are, everybody! The priest says he'll be back in two minutes!

YANG SUN   It's no good, Mamma. Ladies and gentlemen, Mr. Shui Ta still hasn't arrived and the priest has gone home. We won't detain you any longer.
     [*They are leaving now.*]

GRANDFATHER [*In the doorway, having forgotten to put his glass down.*]   To the bride! [*He drinks, puts down the glass, and follows the others.*]
     [*Pause.*]

SHEN TE   Shall I go too?

YANG SUN   You? Aren't you the bride? Isn't this your wedding? [*He drags her across the room, tearing her wedding dress.*] If we can wait, you can wait. Mother calls me her falcon. She wants to see me in the clouds. But I think it may be St. Nevercome's Day before she'll go to the door and see my plane thunder by. [*Pause. He pretends the guests are still present.*] Why such a lull in the conversation, ladies and gentlemen? Don't you like it here? The ceremony is only slightly postponed—because an important guest is expected at any moment. Also because the bride doesn't know what love is. While we're waiting, the bridegroom will sing a little song. [*He does so.*]

THE SONG OF ST. NEVERCOME'S DAY

On a certain day, as is generally known,
  One and all will be shouting: Hooray, hooray!
For the beggar maid's son has a solid-gold throne
  And the day is St. Nevercome's Day
On St. Nevercome's, Nevercome's, Nevercome's Day
  He'll sit on his solid-gold throne

Oh, hooray, hooray! That day goodness will pay!
  That day badness will cost you your head!
And merit and money will smile and be funny
  While exchanging salt and bread
On St. Nevercome's Nevercome's, Nevercome's Day
  While exchanging salt and bread

And the grass, oh, the grass will look down at the sky
  And the pebbles will roll up the stream
And all men will be good without batting an eye
  They will make of our earth a dream
On St. Nevercome's Nevercome's, Nevercome's Day
  They will make of our earth a dream

And as for me, that's the day I shall be
  A flyer and one of the best
Unemployed man, you will have work to do
  Washerwoman, you'll get your rest
On St. Nevercome's, Nevercome's, Nevercome's Day
  Washerwoman, you'll get your rest

MRS. YANG It looks like he's not coming.
  [*The three of them sit looking at the door.*]

6a

WONG's *den. The sewer pipe is again transparent and again the* GODS *appear to* WONG *in a dream.*

WONG   I'm so glad you've come, illustrious ones. It's Shen Te. She's in great trouble from following the rule about loving thy neighbor. Perhaps she's *too* good for this world!
FIRST GOD   Nonsense! You are eaten up by lice and doubts!
WONG   Forgive me, illustrious one, I only meant you might deign to intervene.
FIRST GOD   Out of the question! My colleague here intervened in some squabble or other only yesterday. [*He points to the* THIRD GOD, *who has a black eye.*] The results are before us!

WONG   She had to call on her cousin again. But not even he could help. I'm afraid the shop is done for.

THIRD GOD [*A little concerned.*]   Perhaps we should help after all?

FIRST GOD   The gods help those that help themselves.

WONG   What if we *can't* help ourselves, illustrious ones?
        [*Slight pause.*]

SECOND GOD   Try, anyway! Suffering ennobles!

FIRST GOD   Our faith in Shen Te is unshaken!

THIRD GOD   We certainly haven't found any *other* good people. You can see where we spend our nights from the straw on our clothes.

WONG   You might help her find her way by—

FIRST GOD   The good man finds his own way here below!

SECOND GOD   The good woman too.

FIRST GOD   The heavier the burden, the greater her strength!

THIRD GOD   We're only onlookers, you know.

FIRST GOD   And everything will be all right in the end, O ye of little faith!
        [*They are gradually disappearing through these last lines.*]

7

The yard behind SHEN TE's *shop. A few articles of furniture on a cart.* SHEN TE *and* MRS. SHIN *are taking the washing off the line.*

MRS. SHIN   If you ask me, you should fight tooth and nail to keep the shop.

SHEN TE   How can I? I have to sell the tobacco to pay back the two hundred silver dollars today.

MRS. SHIN   No husband, no tobacco, no house and home! What are you going to live on?

SHEN TE   I can work. I can sort tobacco.

MRS. SHIN   Hey, look, Mr. Shui Ta's trousers! He must have left here stark naked!

SHEN TE   Oh, he may have another pair, Mrs. Shin.

MRS. SHIN   But if he's gone for good as you say, why has he left his pants behind?

SHEN TE   Maybe he's thrown them away.

MRS. SHIN   Can I take them?

SHEN TE   Oh, no.
        [*Enter Mr.* SHU FU, *running.*]

SHU FU   Not a word! Total silence! I know all. You have sacrificed your own love and happiness so as not to hurt a dear old couple who had put their trust in you! Not in vain does this district—for all its malevolent tongues—call you the Angel of the Slums! That young man couldn't rise to your level, so you left him. And now, when I see you closing up the little shop, that veritable haven of rest for the multitude, well, I cannot, I cannot let it pass. Morning after morning I have stood watching in the doorway not unmoved—while you graciously handed out rice to the wretched. Is that never to happen again? Is the good woman of Setzuan to disappear? If only you would allow *me* to assist you! Now don't say anything! No assurances, no exclamations of gratitude! [*He has taken out his checkbook.*] Here! A blank check. [*He places it on the cart.*] Just my signature. Fill it out as you wish. Any sum in the world. I herewith retire from the scene, quietly, unobtrusively, making no claims, on tiptoe, full of veneration, absolutely selflessly . . . [*He has gone.*]

MRS. SHIN Well! You're saved. There's always some idiot of a man. . . . Now hurry! Put down a thousand silver dollars and let me fly to the bank before he comes to his senses.

SHEN TE I can pay you for the washing without any check.

MRS. SHIN What? You're not going to cash it just because you might have to marry him? Are you crazy? Men like him *want* to be led by the nose! Are you still thinking of that flyer? All Yellow Street knows how he treated you!

SHEN TE

When I heard his cunning laugh, I was afraid
But when I saw the holes in his shoes, I loved him dearly.

MRS. SHIN Defending that good-for-nothing after all that's happened!

SHEN TE [*Staggering as she holds some of the washing.*] Oh!

MRS. SHIN [*Taking the washing from her, dryly.*] So you feel dizzy when you stretch and bend? There couldn't be a little visitor on the way? If that's it, you can forget Mr. Shu Fu's blank check: it wasn't meant for a christening present!

[*She goes to the back with a basket.* SHEN TE's *eyes follow* MRS. SHIN *for a moment. Then she looks down at her own body, feels her stomach, and a great joy comes into her eyes.*]

SHEN TE O joy! A new human being is on the way. The world awaits him. In the cities the people say: he's got to be reckoned with, this new human being! [*She imagines a little boy to be present, and introduces him to the audience.*] This is my son, the well-known flyer!

Say: Welcome
To the conqueror of unknown mountains and unreachable regions
Who brings us our mail across the impassable deserts!

[*She leads him up and down by the hand.*]

Take a look at the world, my son. That's a tree. Tree, yes. Say: "Hello, tree!" And bow. Like this. [*She bows.*] Now you know each other. And, look, here comes the water seller. He's a friend, give him your hand. A cup of fresh water for my little son, please. Yes, it *is* a warm day. [*Handing the cup.*] Oh dear, a policeman, we'll have to make a circle round *him.* Perhaps we can pick a few cherries over there in the rich Mr. Pung's garden. But we mustn't be seen. You want cherries? Just like children with fathers. No, no, you can't go straight at them like that. Don't pull. We must learn to be reasonable. Well, have it your own way. [*She has let him make for the cherries.*] Can you reach? Where to put them? Your mouth is the best place. [*She tries one herself.*] Mmm, they're good. But the policeman, we must run! [*They run.*] Yes, back to the street. Calm now, so no one will notice us. [*Walking the street with her child, she sings.*]

Once a plum—'twas in Japan—
Made a conquest of a man
But the man's turn soon did come
For he gobbled up the plum

[*Enter* WONG, *with a child by the hand. He coughs.*]

SHEN TE Wong!

WONG It's about the carpenter, Shen Te. He's lost his shop, and he's been drinking. His children are on the streets. This is one. Can you help?

SHEN TE [*To the child.*]   Come here, little man. [*Takes him down to the foot-lights. To the audience.*]
>   You there! A man is asking you for shelter!
>   A man of tomorrow says: what about today?
>   His friend the conqueror, whom you know,
>   Is his advocate!

[*To* WONG.] He can live in Mr. Shu Fu's cabins. I may have to go there myself. I'm going to have a baby. That's a secret—don't tell Yang Sun—we'd only be in his way. Can you find the carpenter for me?

WONG   I knew you'd think of something. [*To the child.*] Good-bye, son, I'm going for your father.

SHEN TE   What about your hand, Wong? I wanted to help, but my cousin . . .

WONG   Oh, I can get along with one hand, don't worry. [*He shows how he can handle his pole with his left hand alone.*]

SHEN TE   But your right hand! Look, take this cart, sell everything that's on it, and go to the doctor with the money . . .

WONG   She's still good. But first I'll bring the carpenter. I'll pick up the cart when I get back [*Exit* WONG.]

SHEN TE [*To the child.*]   Sit down over here, son, till your father comes.
>   [*The child sits crosslegged on the ground. Enter the* HUSBAND *and* WIFE, *each dragging a large, full sack.*]

WIFE [*Furtively.*]   You're alone, Shen Te, dear?
>   [SHEN TE *nods. The* WIFE *beckons to the* NEPHEW *offstage. He comes on with another sack.*]

WIFE   Your cousin's away? [SHEN TE *nods.*] He's not coming back?

SHEN TE   No. I'm giving up the shop.

WIFE   That's why we're here. We want to know if we can leave these things in your new home. Will you do us this favor?

SHEN TE   Why, yes, I'd be glad to.

HUSBAND [*Cryptically.*]   And if anyone asks about them, say they're yours.

SHEN TE   Would anyone ask?

WIFE [*With a glance back at her husband.*]   Oh, someone might. The police, for instance. They don't seem to like us. Where can we put it?

SHEN TE   Well, I'd rather not get in any more trouble . . .

WIFE   Listen to her! The good woman of Setzuan!
>   [SHEN TE *is silent.*]

HUSBAND   There's enough tobacco in those sacks to give us a new start in life. We could have our own tobacco factory!

SHEN TE [*Slowly.*]   You'll have to put them in the back room.
>   [*The sacks are taken offstage, while the child is alone. Shyly glancing about him, he goes to the garbage can, starts playing with the contents, and eating some of the scraps. The others return.*]

WIFE   We're counting on you, Shen Te!

SHEN TE   Yes. [*She sees the child and is shocked.*]

HUSBAND   We'll see you in Mr. Shu Fu's cabins.

NEPHEW   The day after tomorrow.

SHEN TE   Yes. Now, go. Go! I'm not feeling well.
>   [*Exeunt all three, virtually pushed off.*]
>   He is eating the refuse in the garbage can!
>   Only look at his little gray mouth!

[*Pause. Music.*]

> As this is the world *my* son will enter
> I will study to defend him.
> To be good to you, my son,
> I shall be a tigress to all others
> If I have to.
> And I shall have to.

[*She starts to go*]

> One more time, then. I hope really the last.

[*Exit* SHEN TE, *taking* SHUI TA'S *trousers*. MRS. SHIN *enters and watches her with marked interest. Enter the* SISTER-IN-LAW *and the* GRANDFATHER.]

SISTER-IN-LAW   So it's true, the shop has closed down. And the furniture's in the back yard. It's the end of the road!

MRS. SHIN [*Pompously.*]   The fruit of high living, selfishness, and sensuality! Down the primrose path to Mr. Shu Fu's cabins—with you!

SISTER-IN-LAW   Cabins? Rat holes! He gave them to us because his soap supplies only went moldy there!

[*Enter the* UNEMPLOYED MAN.]

UNEMPLOYED MAN   Shen Te is moving?

SISTER-IN-LAW   Yes, she was sneaking away.

MRS. SHIN   She's ashamed of herself, and no wonder!

UNEMPLOYED MAN   Tell her to call Mr. Shui Ta or she's done for this time!

[*Enter* WONG *and* CARPENTER, *the latter with a child on each hand*.]

CARPENTER   So we'll have a roof over our heads for a change!

MRS. SHIN   Roof? Whose roof?

CARPENTER   Mr. Shu Fu's cabins. And we have little Feng to thank for it. [*Feng, we find, is the name of the child already there; his father now takes him. To the other two.*] Bow to your little brother, you two!

[*The* CARPENTER *and the two new arrivals bow to Feng. Enter* SHUI TA.]

UNEMPLOYED MAN   Sst! Mr. Shui Ta!

[*Pause.*]

SHUI TA   And what is this crowd here for, may I ask?

WONG   How do you do, Mr. Shui Ta. This is the carpenter. Miss Shen Te promised him space in Mr. Shu Fu's cabins.

SHUI TA   That will not be possible.

CARPENTER   We can't go there after all?

SHUI TA   All the space is needed for other purposes.

SISTER-IN-LAW   You mean we have to get out? But we've got nowhere to go.

SHUI TA   Miss Shen Te finds it possible to provide employment. If the proposition interests you, you may stay in the cabins.

SISTER-IN-LAW [*With distaste.*]   You mean *work*? Work for Miss Shen Te?

SHUI TA   Making tobacco, yes. There are three bales here already. Would you like to get them?

SISTER-IN-LAW [*Trying to bluster.*]   We have our own tobacco! We were in the tobacco business before you were born!

SHUI TA [*To the* CARPENTER *and the* UNEMPLOYED MAN.]   You *don't* have your own tobacco. What about you?

[*The* CARPENTER *and the* UNEMPLOYED MAN *get the point, and go for the sacks. Enter* MRS. MI TZU.]

MRS. MI TZU   Mr. Shui Ta? I've brought you your three hundred silver dollars.

SHUI TA   I'll sign your lease instead. I've decided not to sell.

MRS. MI TZU   What? You don't need the money for that flyer?

SHUI TA   No.

MRS. MI TZU   And you can pay six months' rent?

SHUI TA [*Takes the barber's blank check from the cart and fills it out.*]   Here is a check for ten thousand silver dollars. On Mr. Shu Fu's account. Look. [*He shows her the signature on the check.*] Your six months' rent will be in your hands by seven this evening. And now, if you'll excuse me.

MRS. MI TZU   So it's Mr. Shu Fu now. The flyer has been given his walking papers. These modern girls! In my day they'd have said she was flighty. That poor, deserted Mr. Yang Sun!

[*Exit* MRS. MI TZU. *The* CARPENTER *and the* UNEMPLOYED MAN *drag the three sacks back on the stage.*]

CARPENTER [*To* SHUI TA.]   I don't know why I'm doing this for you.

SHUI TA   Perhaps your children want to eat, Mr. Carpenter.

SISTER-IN-LAW [*Catching sight of the sacks.*]   Was my brother-in-law here?

MRS. SHIN   Yes, he was.

SISTER-IN-LAW   I thought as much. I know those sacks! That's our tobacco!

SHUI TA   Really? I thought it came from my back room! Shall we consult the police on the point?

SISTER-IN-LAW [*Defeated.*]   No.

SHUI TA   Perhaps you will show me the way to Mr. Shu Fu's cabins?

[*Taking Feng by the hand,* SHUI TA *goes off, followed by the* CARPENTER *and his two older children, the* SISTER-IN-LAW, *the* GRANDFATHER, *and the* UNEMPLOYED MAN. *Each of the last three drags a sack. Enter* OLD MAN *and* OLD WOMAN.]

MRS. SHIN   A pair of pants—missing from the clothes line one minute—and next minute on the honorable backside of Mr. Shui Ta.

OLD WOMAN   We thought Miss Shen Te was here.

MRS. SHIN [*Preoccupied.*]   Well, she's not.

OLD MAN   There was something she was going to give us.

WONG   She was going to help me too. [*Looking at his hand.*] It'll be too late soon. But she'll be back. This cousin has never stayed long.

MRS. SHIN [*Approaching a conclusion.*]   No, he hasn't, has he?

7a

The Sewer Pipe: WONG *asleep. In his dream, he tells the* GODS *his fears. The* GODS *seem tired from all their travels. They stop for a moment and look over their shoulders at the water seller.*

WONG   Illustrious ones. I've been having a bad dream. Our beloved Shen Te was in great distress in the rushes down by the river—the spot where the bodies of suicides are washed up. She kept staggering and holding her head down as if she was carrying something and it was dragging her down into the mud. When I called out to her, she said she had to take your Book of

Rules[3] to the other side, and not get it wet, or the ink would all come off. You had talked to her about the virtues, you know, the time she gave you shelter in Setzuan.

THIRD GOD   Well, but what do you suggest, my dear Wong?

WONG   Maybe a little relaxation of the rules, Benevolent One, in view of the bad times.

THIRD GOD   As for instance?

WONG   Well, um, good-will, for instance, might do instead of love?

THIRD GOD   I'm afraid that would create new problems.

WONG   Or, instead of justice, good sportsmanship?

THIRD GOD   That would only mean more work.

WONG   Instead of honor, outward propriety?

THIRD GOD   Still more work! No, no! The rules will have to stand, my dear Wong!

[*Wearily shaking their heads, all three journey on.*]

8

SHUI TA's *tobacco factory in* SHU FU's *cabins. Huddled together behind bars, several families, mostly women and children. Among these people the* SISTER-IN-LAW, *the* GRANDFATHER, *the* CARPENTER, *and his three children. Enter* MRS. YANG *followed by* YANG SUN.

MRS. YANG   [*To the audience.*]   There's something I just *have* to tell you: strength and wisdom are wonderful things. The strong and wise Mr. Shui Ta has transformed my son from a dissipated good-for-nothing into a model citizen. As you may have heard, Mr. Shui Ta opened a small tobacco factory near the cattle runs. It flourished. Three months ago—I shall never forget it—I asked for an appointment, and Mr. Shui Ta agree to see us—me and my son. I can see him now as he came through the door to meet us. . . .

[*Enter* SHUI TA, *from a door.*]

SHUI TA   What can I do for you, Mrs. Yang?

MRS. YANG   This morning the police came to the house. We find you've brought an action for breach of promise of marriage. In the name of Shen Te. You also claim that Sun came by two hundred silver dollars by improper means.

SHUI TA   That is correct.

MRS. YANG   Mr. Shui Ta, the money's all gone. When the Peking job didn't materialize, he ran through it all in three days. I know he's a good-for-nothing. He sold my furniture. He was moving to Peking without me. Miss Shen Te thought highly of him at one time.

SHUI TA   What do *you* say, Mr. Yang Sun?

YANG SUN   The money's gone.

SHUI TA   [*To* MRS. YANG.]   Mrs. Yang, in consideration of my cousin's incomprehensible weakness for your son, I am prepared to give him another

3. Reference to neo-Confucianist commentators' rigid and prescriptive interpretation of Confucius's *Analects*, especially regarding the role of women.

chance. He can have a job—here. The two hundred silver dollars will be taken out of his wages.

YANG SUN   So it's the factory or jail?

SHUI TA   Take your choice.

YANG SUN   May I speak with Shen Te?

SHUI TA   You may not.

[Pause.]

YANG SUN [Sullenly.]   Show me where to go.

MRS. YANG   Mr. Shui Ta, you are kindness itself: the gods will reward you! [To YANG SUN.] And honest work will make a man of you, my boy. [YANG SUN follows SHUI TA into the factory. MRS. YANG comes down again to the footlights.] Actually, honest work didn't agree with him—at first. And he got no opportunity to distinguish himself till—in the third week—when the wages were being paid . . .

[SHUI TA has a bag of money. Standing next to his foreman—the former UNEMPLOYED MAN—he counts out the wages. It is YANG SUN's turn.]

UNEMPLOYED MAN [Reading.]   Carpenter, six silver dollars. Yang Sun, six silver dollars.

YANG SUN [Quietly.]   Excuse me, sir. I don't think it can be more than five. May I see? [He takes the foreman's list.] It says six working days. But that's a mistake, sir. I took a day off for court business. And I won't take what I haven't earned, however miserable the pay is!

UNEMPLOYED MAN   Yang Sun. Five silver dollars. [To SHUI TA.] A rare case, Mr. Shui Ta!

SHUI TA   How is it the book says six when it should say five?

UNEMPLOYED MAN   I must've made a mistake, Mr. Shui Ta. [With a look at YANG SUN.] It won't happen again.

SHUI TA [Taking YANG SUN aside.]   You don't hold back, do you? You give your all to the firm. You're even honest. Do the foreman's mistakes always favor the workers?

YANG SUN   He does have . . . friends.

SHUI TA   Thank you. May I offer you any little recompense?

YANG SUN   Give me a trial period of one week, and I'll prove my intelligence is worth more to you than my strength.

MRS. YANG [Still down at the footlights.]   Fighting words, fighting words! That evening, I said to Sun: "If you're a flyer, then fly, my falcon! Rise in the world!" And he got to be foreman. Yes, in Mr. Shui Ta's tobacco factory, he worked real miracles.

[We see YANG SUN with his legs apart standing behind the workers, who are handing along a basket of raw tobacco above their heads.]

YANG SUN   Faster! Faster! You, there, d'you think you can just stand around, now you're not foreman any more? It'll be your job to lead us in song. Sing!

[UNEMPLOYED MAN starts singing. The others join in the refrain.]

SONG OF THE EIGHTH ELEPHANT

Chang had seven elephants—all much the same—
But then there was Little Brother
The seven, they were wild, Little Brother, he was tame

And to guard them Chang chose Little Brother
Run faster!
Mr. Chang has a forest park
Which must be cleared before tonight
And already it's growing dark!

When the seven elephants cleared that forest park
Mr. Chang rode high on Little Brother
While the seven toiled and moiled till dark
On his big behind sat Little Brother
Dig faster!
Mr. Chang has a forest park
Which must be cleared before tonight
And already it's growing dark!

And the seven elephants worked many an hour
Till none of them could work another
Old Chang, he looked sour, on the seven he did glower
But gave a pound of rice to Little Brother
What was that?
Mr. Chang has a forest park
Which must be cleared before tonight
And already it's growing dark!

And the seven elephants hadn't any tusks
The one that had the tusks was Little Brother
Seven are no match for one, if the one has a gun!
How old Chang did laugh at Little Brother!
Keep on digging!
Mr. Chang has a forest park
Which must be cleared before tonight
And already it's growing dark!

[*Smoking a cigar,* SHUI TA *strolls by.* YANG SUN, *laughing, has joined in the refrain of the third stanza and speeded up the tempo of the last stanza by clapping his hands.*]

MRS. YANG   And that's why I say: strength and wisdom are wonderful things. It took the strong and wise Mr. Shui Ta to bring out the best in Yang Sun. A real superior man is like a bell. If you ring it, it rings, and if you don't, it don't, as the saying is.[4]

9

SHEN TE's *shop, now an office with club chairs and fine carpets. It is raining.* SHUI TA, *now fat, is just dismissing the* OLD MAN *and* OLD WOMAN. MRS. SHIN, *in obviously new clothes, looks on, smirking.*

SHUI TA   No! I cannot tell you when we expect her back.

4. A saying by the Chinese philosopher Mo-tzu (470–391 B.C.E.).

OLD WOMAN   The two hundred silver dollars came today. In an envelope. There was no letter, but it must be from Shen Te. We want to write and thank her. May we have her address?

SHUI TA   I'm afraid I haven't got it.

OLD MAN [*Pulling Old Woman's sleeve.*]   Let's be going.

OLD WOMAN   She's got to come back some time!

[*They move off, uncertainly, worried.* SHUI TA *bows.*]

MRS. SHIN   They lost the carpet shop because they couldn't pay their taxes. The money arrived too late.

SHUI TA   They could have come to me.

MRS. SHIN   People don't like coming to you.

SHUI TA [*Sits suddenly, one hand to his head.*]   I'm dizzy.

MRS. SHIN   After all, you *are* in your seventh month. But old Mrs. Shin will be there in your hour of trial! [*She cackles feebly.*]

SHUI TA [*In a stifled voice.*]   Can I count on that?

MRS. SHIN   We all have our price, and mine won't be too high for the great Mr. Shui Ta! [*She opens* SHUI TA'S *collar.*]

SHUI TA   It's for the child's sake. All of this.

MRS. SHIN   "All for the child," of course.

SHUI TA   I'm so fat. People must notice.

MRS. SHIN   Oh no, they think it's 'cause you're rich.

SHUI TA [*More feelingly.*]   What will happen to the child?

MRS. SHIN   You ask that nine times a day. Why, it'll have the best that money can buy!

SHUI TA   He must never see Shui Ta.

MRS. SHIN   Oh, no. Always Shen Te.

SHUI TA   What about the neighbors? There are rumors, aren't there?

MRS. SHIN   As long as Mr. Shu Fu doesn't find out, there's nothing to worry about. Drink this.

[*Enter* YANG SUN *in a smart business suit, and carrying a businessman's briefcase.* SHUI TA *is more or less in* MRS. SHIN'S *arms.*]

YANG SUN [*Surprised.*]   I guess I'm in the way.

SHUI TA [*Ignoring this, rises with an effort.*]   Till tomorrow, Mrs. Shin.

[MRS. SHIN *leaves with a smile, putting on her new gloves.*]

YANG SUN   Gloves now! She couldn't be fleecing you? And since when did *you* have a private life? [*Taking a paper from the briefcase.*] You haven't been at your best lately, and things are getting out of hand. The police want to close us down. They say that at the most they can only permit twice the lawful number of workers.

SHUI TA [*Evasively.*]   The cabins are quite good enough.

YANG SUN   For the workers maybe, not for the tobacco. They're too damp. We must take over some of Mrs. Mi Tzu's buildings.

SHUI TA   Her price is double what I can pay.

YANG SUN   Not unconditionally. If she has me to stroke her knees she'll come down.

SHUI TA   I'll never agree to that.

YANG SUN   What's wrong? Is it the rain? You get so irritable whenever it rains.

SHUI TA   Never! I will never . . .

YANG SUN   Mrs. Mi Tzu'll be here in five minutes. *You* fix it. And Shu Fu will be with her. . . . What's all that noise?

> [*During the above dialogue,* WONG *is heard offstage, calling:* "The good Shen Te, where *is* she? Which of you has seen Shen Te, good people? Where is Shen Te?" *A knock. Enter* WONG.]

WONG   Mr. Shui Ta, I've come to ask when Miss Shen Te will be back, it's six months now. . . . There are rumors. People say something's happened to her.

SHUI TA   I'm busy. Come back next week.

WONG [*Excited.*]   In the morning there was always rice on her doorstep—for the needy. It's been there again lately!

SHUI TA   And what do people conclude from this?

WONG   That Shen Te is still in Setzuan! She's been . . . [*He breaks off.*]

SHUI TA   She's been what? Mr. Wong, if you're Shen Te's friend, talk a little less about her, that's my advice to you.

WONG   I don't want your advice! Before she disappeared, Miss Shen Te told me something very important—she's pregnant!

YANG SUN   What? What was that?

SHUI TA [*Quickly.*]   The man is lying.

WONG   A good woman isn't so easily forgotten, Mr. Shui Ta.

> [*He leaves.* SHUI TA *goes quickly into the back room.*]

YANG SUN [*To the audience.*]   Shen Te pregnant? So that's why. Her cousin sent her away, so I wouldn't get wind of it. I have a son, a Yang appears on the scene, and what happens? Mother and child vanish into thin air! That scoundrel, that unspeakable . . . [*The sound of sobbing is heard from the back room.*] What was that? Someone sobbing? Who was it? Mr. Shui Ta the Tobacco King doesn't weep his heart out. And where does the rice come from that's on the doorstep in the morning? [SHUI TA *returns. He goes to the door and looks out into the rain.*] Where is she?

SHUI TA   Sh! It's nine o'clock. But the rain's so heavy, you can't hear a thing.

YANG SUN   What do you want to hear?

SHUI TA   The mail plane.

YANG SUN   What?!

SHUI TA   I've been told *you* wanted to fly at one time. Is that all forgotten?

YANG SUN   Flying mail is night work. I prefer the daytime. And the firm is very dear to me—after all it belongs to my ex-fiancée, even if she's not around. And she's not, is she?

SHUI TA   What do you mean by that?

YANG SUN   Oh, well, let's say I haven't altogether—lost interest.

SHUI TA   My cousin might like to know that.

YANG SUN   I might not be indifferent—if I found she was being kept under lock and key.

SHUI TA   By whom?

YANG SUN   By you.

SHUI TA   What could you do about it?

YANG SUN   I could submit for discussion—my position in the firm.

SHUI TA   You are now my manager. In return for a more . . . appropriate position, you might agree to drop the inquiry into your ex-fiancée's whereabouts?

YANG SUN   I might.

SHUI TA   What position *would* be more appropriate?

YANG SUN   The one at the top.

SHUI TA   My own? [*Silence.*] And if I preferred to throw you out on your neck?

YANG SUN   I'd come back on my feet. With suitable escort.

SHUI TA   The police?

YANG SUN   The police.

SHUI TA   And when the police found no one?

YANG SUN   I might ask them not to overlook the back room. [*Ending the pretense.*] In short, Mr. Shui Ta, my interest in this young woman has not been officially terminated. I should like to see more of her. [*Into* SHUI TA'S *face.*] Besides, she's pregnant and needs a friend. [*He moves to the door.*] I shall talk about it with the water seller.

> [*Exit.* SHUI TA *is rigid for a moment, then he quickly goes into the back room. He returns with* SHEN TE'S *belongings: underwear, etc. He takes a long look at the shawl of the previous scene. He then wraps the things in a bundle, which, upon hearing a noise, he hides under the table. Enter* MRS. MI TZU *and Mr.* SHU FU. *They put away their umbrellas and galoshes.*]

MRS. MI TZU   I thought your manager was here, Mr. Shui Ta. He combines charm with business in a way that can only be to the advantage of all of us.

SHU FU   You sent for us, Mr. Shui Ta?

SHUI TA   The factory is in trouble.

SHU FU   It always is.

SHUI TA   The police are threatening to close us down unless I can show that the extension of our facilities is imminent.

SHU FU   Mr. Shui Ta, I'm sick and tired of your constantly expanding projects. I place cabins at your cousin's disposal; you make a factory of them. I hand your cousin a check; you present it. Your cousin disappears; you find the cabins too small and start talking of yet more—

SHUI TA   Mr. Shu Fu, I'm authorized to inform you that Miss Shen Te's return is now imminent.

SHU FU   Imminent? It's becoming his favorite word.

MRS. MI TZU   Yes, what does it mean?

SHUI TA   Mrs. Mi Tzu, I can pay you exactly half what you asked for your buildings. Are you ready to inform the police that I am taking them over?

MRS. MI TZU   Certainly, if I can take over your manager.

SHU FU   What?

MRS. MI TZU   He's so efficient.

SHUI TA   I'm afraid I need Mr. Yang Sun.

MRS. MI TZU   So do I.

SHUI TA   He will call on you tomorrow.

SHU FU   So much the better. With Shen Te likely to turn up at any moment, the presence of that young man is hardly in good taste.

SHUI TA   So we have reached a settlement. In what was once the good Shen Te's little shop we are laying the foundations for the great Mr. Shui Ta's twelve magnificent super tobacco markets. You will bear in mind that though they call me the Tobacco King of Setzuan, it is my cousin's interests that have been served . . .

VOICES [*Off.*]   The police, the police! Going to the tobacco shop! Something must have happened!

[*Enter* YANG SUN, WONG, *and the* POLICEMAN.]

POLICEMAN   Quiet there, quiet, quiet! [*They quiet down.*] I'm sorry, Mr. Shui Ta, but there's a report that you've been depriving Miss Shen Te of her freedom. Not that I believe all I hear, but the whole city's in an uproar.

SHUI TA   That's a lie.

POLICEMAN   Mr. Yang Sun has testified that he heard someone sobbing in the back room.

SHU FU   Mrs. Mi Tzu and myself will testify that no one here has been sobbing.

MRS. MI TZU   We have been quietly smoking our cigars.

POLICEMAN   Mr. Shui Ta, I'm afraid I shall have to take a look at that room. [*He does so. The room is empty.*] No one there, of course, sir.

YANG SUN   But I heard sobbing. What's that?

[*He finds the clothes.*]

WONG   Those are Shen Te's things. [*To crowd.*] Shen Te's clothes are here!

VOICES [*Off, in sequence.*]   Shen Te's clothes!
—They've been found under the table!
—Body of murdered girl still missing!
—Tobacco King suspected!

POLICEMAN   Mr. Shui Ta, unless you can tell us where the girl is, I'll have to ask you to come along.

SHUI TA   I do not know.

POLICEMAN   I can't say how sorry I am, Mr. Shui Ta. [*He shows him the door.*]

SHUI TA   Everything will be cleared up in no time. There are still judges in Setzuan.

YANG SUN   I heard sobbing!

9a

WONG's *den. For the last time, the* GODS *appear to the water seller in his dream. They have changed and show signs of a long journey, extreme fatigue, and plenty of mishaps. The* FIRST *no longer has a hat; the* THIRD *has lost a leg; all three are barefoot.*

WONG   Illustrious ones, at last you're here. Shen Te's been gone for months and today her cousin's been arrested. They think he murdered her to get the shop. But I had a dream and in this dream Shen Te said her cousin was keeping her prisoner. You must find her for us, illustrious ones!

FIRST GOD   We've found very few good people anywhere, and even they didn't keep it up. Shen Te is still the only one that stayed good.

SECOND GOD   If she *has* stayed good.

WONG   Certainly she has. But she's vanished.

FIRST GOD   That's the last straw. All is lost!

SECOND GOD   A little moderation, dear colleague!

FIRST GOD [*Plaintively.*]   What's the good of moderation now? If she can't be found, we'll have to resign! The world is a terrible place! Nothing but misery, vulgarity, and waste! Even the countryside isn't what it used to be. The trees are getting their heads chopped off by telephone wires, and there's such a noise from all the gunfire, and I can't stand those heavy clouds of smoke, and—

THIRD GOD   The place is absolutely unlivable! Good intentions bring people to the brink of the abyss, and good deeds push them over the edge. I'm afraid our book of rules is destined for the scrap heap—

SECOND GOD   It's people! They're a worthless lot!

THIRD GOD   The world is too cold!

SECOND GOD   It's people! They're too weak!

FIRST GOD   Dignity, dear colleagues, dignity! Never despair! As for this world, didn't we agree that we only have to find one human being who can stand the place? Well, we found her. True, we lost her again. We must find her again, that's all! And at once!

[*They disappear.*]

10

Courtroom. Groups: SHU FU *and* MRS. MI TZU; YANG SUN *and* MRS. YANG; WONG, *the* CARPENTER, *the* GRANDFATHER, *the* NIECE, *the* OLD MAN, *the* OLD WOMAN; MRS. SHIN, *the* POLICEMAN; *the* UNEMPLOYED MAN, *the* SISTER-IN-LAW.

OLD MAN   So much power isn't good for one man.

UNEMPLOYED MAN   And he's going to open twelve super tobacco markets!

WIFE   One of the judges is a friend of Mr. Shu Fu's.

SISTER-IN-LAW   Another one accepted a present from Mr. Shui Ta only last night. A great fat goose.

OLD WOMAN [*To* WONG]   And Shen Te is nowhere to be found.

WONG   Only the gods will ever know the truth.

POLICEMAN   Order in the court! My lords the judges!

[*Enter the* THREE GODS *in judges' robes. We overhear their conversation as they pass along the footlights to their bench.*]

THIRD GOD   We'll never get away with it, our certificates were so badly forged.

SECOND GOD   My predecessor's "sudden indigestion" will certainly cause comment.

FIRST GOD   But he *had* just eaten a whole goose.

UNEMPLOYED MAN   Look at that! *New* judges.

WONG   New judges. And what good ones!

[*The* THIRD GOD *hears this, and turns to smile at* WONG. *The* GODS *sit. The* FIRST GOD *beats on the bench with his gavel. The* POLICEMAN *brings in* SHUI TA, *who walks with lordly steps. He is whistled[5] at.*]

POLICEMAN [*To* SHUI TA.]   Be prepared for a surprise. The judges have been changed.

[SHUI TA *turns quickly round, looks at them, and staggers.*]

NIECE   What's the matter now?

WIFE   The great Tobacco King nearly fainted.

5. Hissed.

HUSBAND   Yes, as soon as he saw the new judges.

WONG   Does *he* know who they are?

[SHUI TA *picks himself up, and the proceedings open.*]

FIRST GOD   Defendant Shui Ta, you are accused of doing away with your cousin Shen Te in order to take possession of her business. Do you plead guilty or not guilty?

SHUI TA   Not guilty, my lord.

FIRST GOD [*Thumbing through the documents of the case.*]   The first witness is the policeman. I shall ask him to tell us something of the respective reputations of Miss Shen Te and Mr. Shui Ta.

POLICEMAN   Miss Shen Te was a young lady who aimed to please, my lord. She liked to live and let live, as the saying goes. Mr. Shui Ta, on the other hand, is a man of principle. Though the generosity of Miss Shen Te forced him at times to abandon half measures, unlike the girl he was always on the side of the law, my lord. One time, he even unmasked a gang of thieves to whom his too trustful cousin had given shelter. The evidence, in short, my lord, proves that Mr. Shui Ta was *incapable* of the crime of which he stands accused!

FIRST GOD   I see. And are there others who could testify along, shall we say, the same lines?

[SHU FU *rises.*]

POLICEMAN [*Whispering to* GODS.]   Mr. Shu Fu—a very important person.

FIRST GOD [*Inviting him to speak.*]   Mr. Shu Fu!

SHU FU   Mr. Shui Ta is a businessman, my lord. Need I say more?

FIRST GOD   Yes.

SHU FU   Very well, I will. He is Vice President of the Council of Commerce and is about to be elected a Justice of the Peace. [*He returns to his seat.* MRS. MI TZU *rises.*]

WONG   Elected! *He* gave him the job!

[*With a gesture the* FIRST GOD *asks who* MRS. MI TZU *is.*]

POLICEMAN   Another very important person. Mrs. Mi Tzu.

FIRST GOD [*Inviting her to speak.*]   Mrs. Mi Tzu!

MRS. MI TZU   My lord, as Chairman of the Committee on Social Work, I wish to call attention to just a couple of eloquent facts: Mr. Shui Ta not only has erected a model factory with model housing in our city, he is a regular contributor to our home for the disabled. [*She returns to her seat.*]

POLICEMAN [*Whispering.*]   And she's a great friend of the judge that ate the goose!

FIRST GOD [*To the* POLICEMAN.]   Oh, thank you. What next? [*To the Court, genially.*]   Oh, yes. We should find out if any of the evidence is less favorable to the defendant.

[WONG, *the* CARPENTER, *the* OLD MAN, *the* OLD WOMAN, *the* UNEMPLOYED MAN, *the* SISTER-IN-LAW, *and the* NIECE *come forward.*]

POLICEMAN [*Whispering.*]   Just the riffraff, my lord.

FIRST GOD [*Addressing the "riffraff."*]   Well, um, riffraff—do you know anything of the defendant, Mr. Shui Ta?

WONG   Too much, my lord.

UNEMPLOYED MAN   What don't we know, my lord.

CARPENTER   He ruined us.

SISTER-IN-LAW He's a cheat.

NIECE Liar.

WIFE Thief.

BOY Blackmailer.

BROTHER Murderer.

FIRST GOD Thank you. We should now let the defendant state his point of view.

SHUI TA I only came on the scene when Shen Te was in danger of losing what I had understood was a gift from the gods. Because I did the filthy jobs which someone had to do, they hate me. My activities were restricted to the minimum, my lord.

SISTER-IN-LAW He had us arrested!

SHUI TA Certainly. You stole from the bakery!

SISTER-IN-LAW Such concern for the bakery! You didn't want the shop for yourself, I suppose!

SHUI TA I didn't want the shop overrun with parasites.

SISTER-IN-LAW We had nowhere else to go.

SHUI TA There were too many of you.

WONG What about this old couple: Were *they* parasites?

OLD MAN We lost our shop because of you!

OLD WOMAN And we gave your cousin money!

SHUI TA My cousin's fiancé was a flyer. The money had to go to *him*.

WONG Did you care whether he flew or not? Did you care whether she married him or not? You wanted her to marry someone else! [*He points to* SHU FU.]

SHUI TA The flyer unexpectedly turned out to be a scoundrel.

YANG SUN [*Jumping up.*] Which was the reason you made him your manager?

SHUI TA Later on he improved.

WONG And when he improved, you sold him to her? [*He points out* MRS. MI TZU.]

SHUI TA She wouldn't let me have her premises unless she had him to stroke her knees!

MRS. MI TZU What? The man's a pathological liar. [*To him.*] Don't mention my property to me as long as you live! Murderer! [*She rustles off, in high dudgeon.*]

YANG SUN [*Pushing in.*] My lord, I wish to speak for the defendant.

SISTER-IN-LAW Naturally. He's your employer.

UNEMPLOYED MAN And the worst slave driver in the country.

MRS. YANG That's a lie! My lord, Mr. Shui Ta is a great man. He . . .

YANG SUN He's this and he's that, but he is not a murderer, my lord. Just fifteen minutes before his arrest I heard Shen Te's voice in his own back room.

FIRST GOD Oh? Tell us more!

YANG SUN I heard sobbing, my lord!

FIRST GOD But lots of women sob, we've been finding.

YANG SUN Could I fail to recognize her voice?

SHU FU No, you made her sob so often yourself, young man!

YANG SUN   Yes. But I also made her happy. Till he [*Pointing at* SHUI TA.] decided to sell her to you!

SHUI TA   Because you didn't love her.

WONG   Oh, no: it was for the money, my lord!

SHUI TA   And what was the money for, my lord? For the poor! And for Shen Te so she could go on being good!

WONG   For the poor? That he sent to his sweatshops? And why didn't you let Shen Te be good when you signed the big check?

SHUI TA   For the child's sake, my lord.

CARPENTER   What about *my* children? What did he do about them?
    [SHUI TA *is silent.*]

WONG   The shop was to be a fountain of goodness. That was the gods' idea. You came and spoiled it!

SHUI TA   If I hadn't, it would have run dry!

MRS. SHIN   There's a lot in that, my lord.

WONG   What have you done with the good Shen Te, bad man? She *was* good, my lords, she was, I swear it! [*He raises his hand in an oath.*]

THIRD GOD   What's happened to your hand, water seller?

WONG [*Pointing to* SHUI TA.]   It's all his fault, my lord, *she* was going to send me to a doctor—[*To* SHUI TA.] You were her worst enemy!

SHUI TA   I was her only friend!

WONG   Where is she then? Tell us where your good friend is!
    [*The excitement of this exchange has run through the whole crowd.*]

ALL   Yes, where is she? Where is Shen Te? [*Etc.*]

SHUI TA   Shen Te . . . had to go.

WONG   Where? Where to?

SHUI TA   I cannot tell you! I cannot tell you!

ALL   Why? Why did she have to go away? [*Etc.*]

WONG [*Into the din with the first words, but talking on beyond the others.*]   Why not, why not? Why did she have to go away?

SHUI TA [*Shouting.*]   Because you'd all have torn her to shreds, that's why! My lords, I have a request. Clear the court! When only the judges remain, I will make a confession.

ALL [*Except* WONG, *who is silent, struck by the new turn of events.*]   So he's guilty? He's confessing! [*Etc.*]

FIRST GOD [*Using the gavel.*]   Clear the court!

POLICEMAN   Clear the court!

WONG   Mr. Shui Ta has met his match this time.

MRS. SHIN [*With a gesture toward the judges.*]   You're in for a little surprise.
    [*The court is cleared. Silence.*]

SHUI TA   Illustrious ones!
    [*The* GODS *look at each other, not quite believing their ears.*]

SHUI TA   Yes, I recognize you!

SECOND GOD [*Taking matters in hand, sternly.*]   What have you done with our good woman of Setzuan?

SHUI TA   I have a terrible confession to make: I am she! [*He takes off his mask, and tears away his clothes.* SHEN TE *stands there.*]

SECOND GOD   Shen Te!

SHEN TE   Shen Te, yes. Shui Ta *and* Shen Te. Both.

> Your injunction
> To be good and yet to live
> Was a thunderbolt:
> It has torn me in two
> I can't tell how it was
> But to be good to others
> And myself at the same time
> I could not do it
> Your world is not an easy one, illustrious ones!
> When we extend our hand to a beggar, he tears it off for us
> When we help the lost, we are lost ourselves
> And so
> Since not to eat is to die
> Who can long refuse to be bad?
> As I lay prostrate beneath the weight of good intentions
> Ruin stared me in the face
> It was when I was unjust that I ate good meat
> And hobnobbed with the mighty
> Why?
> Why are bad deeds rewarded?
> Good ones punished?
> I enjoyed giving
> I truly wished to be the Angel of the Slums
> But washed by a foster-mother in the water of the gutter
> I developed a sharp eye
> The time came when pity was a thorn in my side
> And, later, when kind words turned to ashes in my mouth
> And anger took over
> I became a wolf
> Find me guilty, then, illustrious ones,
> But know:
> All that I have done I did
> To help my neighbor
> To love my lover
> And to keep my little one from want
> For your great, godly deeds, I was too poor, too small.

[*Pause.*]

FIRST GOD [*Shocked.*]   Don't go on making yourself miserable, Shen Te! We're overjoyed to have found you!

SHEN TE   I'm telling you I'm the bad man who committed all those crimes!

FIRST GOD [*Using—or failing to use—his ear trumpet.*]   The good woman who did all those good deeds?

SHEN TE   Yes, but the bad man too!

FIRST GOD [*As if something had dawned.*]   Unfortunate coincidences! Heartless neighbors!

THIRD GOD [*Shouting in his ear.*]   But how is she to continue?

FIRST GOD   Continue? Well, she's a strong, healthy girl . . .

SECOND GOD   You didn't hear what she said!

FIRST GOD   I heard every word! She is confused, that's all! [*He begins to bluster.*] And what about this book of rules—we can't renounce our rules, can we? [*More quietly.*] Should the world be changed? How? By whom? The world should *not* be changed! [*At a sign from him, the lights turn pink, and music plays.*]

> And now the hour of parting is at hand.
> Dost thou behold, Shen Te, yon fleecy cloud?
> It is our chariot. At a sign from me
> 'Twill come and take us back from whence we came
> Above the azure vault and silver stars. . . .

SHEN TE   No! Don't go, illustrious ones!

FIRST GOD

> Our cloud has landed now in yonder field
> From which it will transport us back to heaven.
> Farewell, Shen Te, let not thy courage fail thee. . . .

[*Exeunt* GODS.]

SHEN TE   What about the old couple? They've lost their shop! What about the water seller and his hand? And I've got to defend myself against the barber, because I don't love him! And against Sun, because I do love him! How? How?

[SHEN TE's *eyes follow the* GODS *as they are imagined to step into a cloud, which rises and moves forward over the orchestra and up beyond the balcony.*]

FIRST GOD [*From on high.*]   We have faith in you, Shen Te!

SHEN TE   There'll be a child. And he'll have to be fed. I can't stay here. Where shall I go?

FIRST GOD   Continue to be good, good woman of Setzuan!

SHEN TE   I need my bad cousin!

FIRST GOD   But not very often!

SHEN TE   Once a week at least!

FIRST GOD   Once a month will be quite enough!

SHEN TE [*Shrieking.*]   No, no! Help!

[*But the cloud continues to recede as the* GODS *sing.*]

VALEDICTORY HYMN

> What rapture, oh, it is to know
>   A good thing when you see it
> And having seen a good thing, oh,
>   What rapture 'tis to flee it
>
> Be good, sweet maid of Setzuan
>   Let Shui Ta be clever
> Departing, we forget the man
>   Remember your endeavor
>
> Because through all the length of days
>   Her goodness faileth never
> Sing hallelujah! Make Shen Te's
>   Good name live on forever!

SHEN TE   Help!

Epilogue

You're thinking, aren't you, that this is no right
Conclusion to the play you've seen tonight?
After a tale, exotic, fabulous,
A nasty ending was slipped up on us.
We feel deflated too. We too are nettled
To see the curtain down and nothing settled.
How could a better ending be arranged?
Could one change people? Can the world be changed?
Would new gods do the trick? Will atheism?
Moral rearmament? Materialism?
It is for you to find a way, my friends,
To help good men arrive at happy ends.
You write the happy ending to the play!
There must, there must, there's got to be a way!

1941

JORGE LUIS BORGES
1899–1986

In the briefest of short stories, Jorge Luis Borges created convincing fictional worlds: alternate universes that obey their own laws of time and causation and shed light on the peculiarities of our own world. Borges's favorite symbol of these imaginary settings was the labyrinth, and readers the world over have enjoyed being lost in the mazes Borges built from his thought experiments. To read one of Borges's stories is to enter a new reality, imagined with great concreteness as an extension of our own world yet bearing distinctive features of the universes of fantasy and science fiction.

Born in Buenos Aires, Argentina, on August 24, 1899, Borges grew up in a large house whose library and garden were to form an essential part of his imagination. His father, who was half-English, was an unsuccessful lawyer with philosophical and literary interests; he spent much of his son's childhood working on a novel that he eventually published in middle age. Borges's mother also had literary ambitions; she translated works by **William Faulkner**, **Franz Kafka**, and D. H. Lawrence into Spanish. Her family, which the young Borges idealized, included Argentine patriots who had fought for independence from Spain and in the civil wars of the nineteenth century. At home Borges spoke English with his father, his paternal grandmother, and his tutor. He read widely in English as well as Spanish; his first publication was a Spanish translation of a children's story by Oscar Wilde, which a Buenos Aires newspaper published when he was only nine years old. Later he would translate works by **Walt Whitman**, **James Joyce**, and others. He remained close to his mother all his life and lived with her until her death, when she was ninety-nine and he was seventy-five.

Borges's father suffered from eye troubles and traveled to Europe with his family in 1914 for an operation. The family was caught in Geneva at the outbreak of World War I. Borges attended secondary school in Switzerland, learning French, German, and Latin. After the war the family moved to Spain, where he associated with a group of young experimental poets known as the Ultraists. When he returned to his homeland in 1921, Borges founded the Argentinian Ultraists, and befriended and collaborated with other intellectuals and artists, including the philosopher Macedonio Fernandez and a younger writer, Adolfo Bioy Casares.

Around the time of his father's death, in 1938, Borges got his first job, as a librarian in a small municipal library. His workplace served as the basis for one of the first, and most famous, of his stories, partly inspired by Kafka, "The Library of Babel." Taking the format of an academic essay, it tells of an endless library whose mazelike, interlocking galleries contain not only all books ever written but all possible combinations of letters. Although the library is infinite, the books, many of them meaningless, are shelved at random and therefore useless.

Early in the twentieth century, Argentina was among the wealthiest Latin American countries, but it suffered during the Great Depression and the years of Juan Perón's military dictatorship that followed. Borges openly opposed the Perón regime and its Fascist tendencies, making his political views plain in his speeches and nonliterary writings, some of which circulated privately and were not published until after his death. His attitude did not go unnoticed. When Perón became president in 1946, his government removed Borges from the librarian's post that he had

held since 1938 and offered him a job as a chicken inspector. Borges refused the position and instead began teaching English and North American literature at the University of Buenos Aires. Having inherited weak eyes from his father, Borges suffered from increasingly poor vision in middle age; despite undergoing eight operations, he was forced eventually to dictate his work and to rely on his prodigious memory.

After the fall of Perón's regime in 1955, Borges was given the prestigious post of director of the National Library—in the same year that he became almost totally blind. When Perón's party returned to power, Borges opposed him, eventually supporting the military coup that overthrew the Peronists in 1976. His failure to recognize the autocratic character of the military government was a misjudgment that tarnished his image in his final years. Until his death, Borges lived in his beloved Buenos Aires, the city he had celebrated in his first volume of poetry.

The Garden of Forking Paths (1941), his first major collection, introduced Borges to a wider public as an idealist writer whose short stories subordinate character, scene, plot, and narration to a central concept, which is often a philosophical premise. Borges uses these ideas not didactically but as the starting point of fantastic elaborations that entertain and perplex readers—much like a challenging game or puzzle. In the immense labyrinth, or "garden of forking paths," that is Borges's world, images of mazes and infinite mirroring, of cyclical repetition and recall, leave the reader in a sort of hall of mirrors, unsure of what is reality and what is illusion. In *Borges and I* the author commented on the parallel existence of two Borgeses: the one who exists in his work (the one his readers know) and the warm, living identity felt by the man who sets pen to paper. "Little by little, I am giving over everything to him. . . . I do not know which one of us has written this page." Borges elaborated this notion by spinning out fictional identities and alternate realities. Disdaining the "psychological fakery" of realistic novels (the "draggy novel of characters"), he preferred art that calls attention to its own artificiality. He wrote many of his stories in the style of encyclopedia entries or historical essays, as in "The Garden of Forking Paths." Borges was fond, too, of detective stories (and wrote several of them), in which the search for an elusive explanation, the pursuit of intricately planted clues, matters more than the characters' recognizability. The author contrives an art of puzzles and discovery.

"The Garden of Forking Paths," the selection below, begins as a simple spy story purporting to reveal the hidden truth about a German bombing raid during World War I. Borges alludes to documented facts: the geographic setting of the town of Albert and the Ancre River; a famous Chinese novel that serves as Ts'ui Pên's proposed model; the *History of the World War (1914–1918)* published by B. H. Liddell Hart in 1934. Official history is undermined on the first page, however, both by the recently discovered confession of Dr. Yu Tsun and by his editor's suspiciously defensive footnote, which calls into question the work we are about to read. Although Borges presents the story as a historical document, he warns his readers that it contains interpretive traps. In fact, the story is far from

simple—it is a complex labyrinth in which the reader may easily be misled.

Borges executes his detective story with the carefully planted clues traditional to the genre, such as the need to convey the name of a bombing target and the presence of a single bullet in a revolver. Yet halfway through, what started as a conventional spy story takes on bizarre spatial and temporal dimensions. Coincidences—those chance relationships that might well have had different outcomes—introduce the idea of forking paths, or choice between two routes, for history. By inventing an ancient Chinese text modeled on a labyrinth, Borges portrays the universe as a series of alternative versions of experience. An infinite number of worlds opens up—but only one is embodied in this particular story: Yu Tsun faces a dilemma that places his personal loyalties at odds with his military duty. Both the personal and the philosophical ramifications of this choice are at the center of Borges's story.

Just as the "forking paths" present alternative versions of experience, so too has Borges's reputation and influence led in various directions. Perceived by outsiders as a major Argentine writer and a forerunner of the magical realism of successive Latin American generations, he is seen by many Latin Americans as a primarily European writer, a precursor to postmodernism. A favorite of literary intellectuals, he has influenced the development of science fiction. In the labyrinth of contemporary literature, Borges's fictions open up many paths for later writers.

The Garden of Forking Paths[1]

On page 22 of Liddell Hart's *History of World War I* you will read that an attack against the Serre-Montauban line by thirteen British divisions (supported by 1,400 artillery pieces), planned for the 24th of July, 1916, had to be postponed until the morning of the 29th. The torrential rains, Captain Liddell Hart comments, caused this delay, an insignificant one, to be sure.

The following statement, dictated, reread and signed by Dr. Yu Tsun, former professor of English at the *Hochschule* at Tsingtao,[2] throws an unsuspected light over the whole affair. The first two pages of the document are missing.

". . . and I hung up the receiver. Immediately afterwards, I recognized the voice that had answered in German. It was that of Captain Richard Madden. Madden's presence in Viktor Runeberg's apartment meant the end of our anxieties and—but this seemed, *or should have seemed*, very secondary to me—also the end of our lives. It meant that Runeberg had been arrested or murdered.[3] Before the sun set on that day, I would encounter the same fate. Madden was implacable. Or rather, he was obliged to be so. An Irishman at the service of England, a man accused of laxity and perhaps of treason, how could he fail to seize and be thankful for such a miraculous opportunity: the discovery, capture, maybe even the death of two agents of the German Reich?[4] I went up to my room; absurdly I locked the door and threw myself on my back on the narrow iron cot. Through the window I saw the familiar roofs and the cloud-shaded six o'clock sun. It seemed incredible to me that that day without premonitions or symbols should be the one of my inexorable death. In spite of my dead father, in spite of having been a child in a symmetrical garden of Hai Feng, was I—now—going to die? Then I reflected that everything happens to a man precisely, precisely *now*. Centuries of centuries and only in the present do things happen; countless men in the air, on the face of the earth and the sea, and all that really is happening is happening to me . . . The almost intolerable recollection of Madden's horselike face banished these wanderings. In the midst of my hatred and terror (it means nothing to me now to speak of terror, now that I have mocked Richard Madden, now that my throat yearns for the noose) it occurred to me that that tumultuous and doubtless happy warrior did not suspect that I possessed the Secret. The name of the exact location of the new British artillery park on the River Ancre. A bird streaked across the gray sky and blindly I translated it into an airplane and that airplane into many (against the French sky) annihilating the artillery station with vertical bombs. If only my mouth, before a bullet shattered it, could cry out that secret name so it could be heard in Germany . . . My human voice was very weak. How might I make it carry to the ear of the Chief? To the ear of that sick and hateful man who knew nothing of Runeberg and me save that we were in Stafford shire[5]

1. Translated by Donald A. Yates.
2. Or Ch'ing-tao; a major port in east China, part of territory leased to (and developed by) Germany in 1898. "Hochschule": university (German).
3. "A hypothesis both hateful and odd. The Prussian spy Hans Rabener, alias Viktor Runeberg, attacked with drawn automatic the bearer of the warrant for his arrest, Captain Richard Madden. The latter, in self-defense, inflicted the wound which brought about Runeberg's death [Editor's note]." This entire note is by Borges as "Editor."
4. Empire (German).
5. County in west-central England.

and who was waiting in vain for our report in his arid office in Berlin, endlessly examining newspapers . . . I said out loud: *I must flee*. I sat up noiselessly, in a useless perfection of silence, as if Madden were already lying in wait for me. Something—perhaps the mere vain ostentation of proving my resources were nil—made me look through my pockets. I found what I knew I would find. The American watch, the nickel chain and the square coin, the key ring with the incriminating useless keys to Runeberg's apartment, the notebook, a letter which I resolved to destroy immediately (and which I did not destroy), a crown, two shillings and a few pence, the red and blue pencil, the handkerchief, the revolver with one bullet. Absurdly, I took it in my hand and weighed it in order to inspire courage within myself. Vaguely I thought that a pistol report can be heard at a great distance. In ten minutes my plan was perfected. The telephone book listed the name of the only person capable of transmitting the message; he lived in a suburb of Fenton,[6] less than a half hour's train ride away.

I am a cowardly man. I say it now, now that I have carried to its end a plan whose perilous nature no one can deny. I know its execution was terrible. I didn't do it for Germany, no. I care nothing for a barbarous country which imposed upon me the abjection of being a spy. Besides, I know of a man from England—a modest man—who for me is no less great than Goethe.[7] I talked with him for scarcely an hour, but during that hour he was Goethe . . . I did it because I sensed that the Chief somehow feared people of my race—for the innumerable ancestors who merge within me. I wanted to prove to him that a yellow man could save his armies. Besides, I had to flee from Captain Madden. His hands and his voice could call at my door at any moment. I dressed silently, bade farewell to myself in the mirror, went downstairs, scrutinized the peaceful street and went out. The station was not far from my home, but I judged it wise to take a cab. I argued that in this way I ran less risk of being recognized; the fact is that in the deserted street I felt myself visible and vulnerable, infinitely so. I remember that I told the cab driver to stop a short distance before the main entrance. I got out with voluntary, almost painful slowness; I was going to the village of Ashgrove but I bought a ticket for a more distant station. The train left within a very few minutes, at eight-fifty. I hurried; the next one would leave at nine-thirty. There was hardly a soul on the platform. I went through the coaches; I remember a few farmers, a woman dressed in mourning, a young boy who was reading with fervor the *Annals* of Tacitus,[8] a wounded and happy soldier. The coaches jerked forward at last. A man whom I recognized ran in vain to the end of the platform. It was Captain Richard Madden. Shattered, trembling, I shrank into the far corner of the seat, away from the dreaded window.

From this broken state I passed into an almost abject felicity. I told myself that the duel had already begun and that I had won the first encounter by frustrating, even if for forty minutes, even if by a stroke of fate, the attack of my

---

6. In Lincolnshire, a county in east England.
7. Johann Wolfgang von Goethe (1749–1832), German poet, novelist, and dramatist; author of *Faust*; often taken as representing the peak of German cultural achievement.

8. Cornelius Tacitus (55–117). Roman historian whose *Annals* give a vivid picture of the decadence and corruption of the Roman Empire under Tiberius, Claudius, and Nero.

adversary. I argued that this slightest of victories foreshadowed a total victory. I argued (no less fallaciously) that my cowardly felicity proved that I was a man capable of carrying out the adventure successfully. From this weakness I took strength that did not abandon me. I foresee that man will resign himself each day to more atrocious undertakings; soon there will be no one but warriors and brigands; I give them this counsel: *The author of an atrocious undertaking ought to imagine that he has already accomplished it, ought to impose upon himself a future as irrevocable as the past.* Thus I proceeded as my eyes of a man already dead registered the elapsing of that day, which was perhaps the last, and the diffusion of the night. The train ran gently along, amid ash trees. It stopped, almost in the middle of the fields. No one announced the name of the station. "Ashgrove?" I asked a few lads on the platform. "Ashgrove," they replied. I got off.

A lamp enlightened the platform but the faces of the boys were in shadow. One questioned me, "Are you going to Dr. Stephen Albert's house?" Without waiting for my answer, another said, "The house is a long way from here, but you won't get lost if you take this road to the left and at every crossroads turn again to your left." I tossed them a coin (my last), descended a few stone steps and started down the solitary road. It went downhill, slowly. It was of elemental earth; overhead the branches were tangled; the low, full moon seemed to accompany me.

For an instant, I thought that Richard Madden in some way had penetrated my desperate plan. Very quickly, I understood that that was impossible. The instructions to turn always to the left reminded me that such was the common procedure for discovering the central point of certain labyrinths. I have some understanding of labyrinths: not for nothing am I the great grandson of that Ts'ui Pên who was governor of Yunnan and who renounced worldly power in order to write a novel that might be even more populous than the *Hung Lu Meng*[9] and to construct a labyrinth in which all men would become lost. Thirteen years he dedicated to these heterogeneous tasks, but the hand of a stranger murdered him—and his novel was incoherent and no one found the labyrinth. Beneath English trees I meditated on that lost maze: I imagined it inviolate and perfect at the secret crest of a mountain; I imagined it erased by rice fields or beneath the water; I imagined it infinite, no longer composed of octagonal kiosks and returning paths, but of rivers and provinces and kingdoms . . . I thought of a labyrinth of labyrinths, of one sinuous spreading labyrinth that would encompass the past and the future and in some way involve the stars. Absorbed in these illusory images, I forgot my destiny of one pursued. I felt myself to be, for an unknown period of time, an abstract perceiver of the world. The vague, living countryside, the moon, the remains of the day worked on me, as well as the slope of the road which eliminated any possibility of weariness. The afternoon was intimate, infinite. The road descended and forked among the now confused meadows. A high-pitched, almost syllabic music approached and receded in the shifting of the wind, dimmed by leaves and distance. I thought that a man can be an enemy of other men, of the moments of other

9. *The Dream of the Red Chamber* (1791) by Ts'ao Hsüeh-ch'in; the most famous Chinese novel, a love story and panorama of Chinese family life involving more than 430 characters.

men, but not of a country: not of fireflies, words, gardens, streams of water, sunsets. Thus I arrived before a tall, rusty gate. Between the iron bars I made out a poplar grove and a pavilion. I understood suddenly two things, the first trivial, the second almost unbelievable: the music came from the pavilion, and the music was Chinese. For precisely that reason I had openly accepted it without paying it any heed. I do not remember whether there was a bell or whether I knocked with my hand. The sparkling of the music continued.

From the rear of the house within a lantern approached: a lantern that the trees sometimes striped and sometimes eclipsed, a paper lantern that had the form of a drum and the color of the moon. A tall man bore it. I didn't see his face for the light blinded me. He opened the door and said slowly, in my own language: "I see that the pious Hsi P'êng persists in correcting my solitude. You no doubt wish to see the garden?"

I recognized the name of one of our consuls and I replied, disconcerted, "The garden?"

"The garden of forking paths."

Something stirred in my memory and I uttered with incomprehensible certainty, "The garden of my ancestor Ts'ui Pên."

"Your ancestor? Your illustrious ancestor? Come in."

The damp path zigzagged like those of my childhood. We came to a library of Eastern and Western books. I recognized bound in yellow silk several volumes of the Lost Encyclopedia, edited by the Third Emperor of the Luminous Dynasty but never printed.[1] The record on the phonograph revolved next to a bronze phoenix. I also recall a *famille rose*[2] vase and another, many centuries older, of that shade of blue which our craftsmen copied from the potters of Persia . . .

Stephen Albert observed me with a smile. He was, as I have said, very tall, sharp-featured, with gray eyes and a gray beard. He told me that he had been a missionary in Tientsin "before aspiring to become a Sinologist."

We sat down—I on a long, low divan, he with his back to the window and a tall circular clock. I calculated that my pursuer, Richard Madden, could not arrive for at least an hour. My irrevocable determination could wait.

"An astounding fate, that of Ts'ui Pên," Stephen Albert said. "Governor of his native province, learned in astronomy, in astrology and in the tireless interpretation of the canonical books, chess player, famous poet and calligrapher— he abandoned all this in order to compose a book and a maze. He renounced the pleasures of both tyranny and justice, of his populous couch, of his banquets and even of erudition—all to close himself up for thirteen years in the Pavilion of the Limpid Solitude. When he died, his heirs found nothing save chaotic manuscripts. His family, as you may be aware, wished to condemn them to the fire; but his executor—a Taoist or Buddhist monk—insisted on their publication."

---

1. The Yung-lo emperor of the Ming ("bright") Dynasty commissioned a massive encyclopedia between 1403 and 1408. A single copy of the 11,095 manuscript volumes was made in the mid-1500s; the original was later destroyed, and only 370 volumes of the copy remain today.

2. Pink family (French); refers to a Chinese decorative enamel ranging in color from an opaque pink to purplish rose. *Famille rose* pottery was at its best during the reign of Yung Chên (1723–35).

"We descendants of Ts'ui Pên," I replied, "continue to curse that monk. Their publication was senseless. The book is an indeterminate heap of contradictory drafts. I examined it once: in the third chapter the hero dies, in the fourth he is alive. As for the other undertaking of Ts'ui Pên, his labyrinth . . ."

"Here is Ts'ui Pên's labyrinth," he said, indicating a tall lacquered desk.

"An ivory labyrinth!" I exclaimed. "A minimum labyrinth."

"A labyrinth of symbols," he corrected. "An invisible labyrinth of time. To me, a barbarous Englishman, has been entrusted the revelation of this diaphanous mystery. After more than a hundred years, the details are irretrievable; but it is not hard to conjecture what happened. Ts'ui Pên must have said once: *I am withdrawing to write a book*. And another time: *I am withdrawing to construct a labyrinth*. Every one imagined two works; to no one did it occur that the book and the maze were one and the same thing. The Pavilion of the Limpid Solitude stood in the center of a garden that was perhaps intricate; that circumstance could have suggested to the heirs a physical labyrinth. Ts'ui Pên died; no one in the vast territories that were his came upon the labyrinth; the confusion of the novel suggested to me that *it* was the maze. Two circumstances gave me the correct solution of the problem. One: the curious legend that Ts'ui Pên had planned to create a labyrinth which would be strictly infinite. The other: a fragment of a letter I discovered."

Albert rose. He turned his back on me for a moment; he opened a drawer of the black and gold desk. He faced me and in his hands he held a sheet of paper that had once been crimson, but was now pink and tenuous and cross-sectioned. The fame of Ts'ui Pên as a calligrapher had been justly won. I read, uncomprehendingly and with fervor, these words written with a minute brush by a man of my blood: *I leave to the various futures (not to all) my garden of forking paths*. Wordlessly, I returned the sheet. Albert continued:

"Before unearthing this letter, I had questioned myself about the ways in which a book can be infinite. I could think of nothing other than a cyclic volume, a circular one. A book whose last page was identical with the first, a book which had the possibility of continuing indefinitely. I remembered too that night which is at the middle of the Thousand and One Nights when Scheherazade[3] (through a magical oversight of the copyist) begins to relate word for word the story of the Thousand and One Nights, establishing the risk of coming once again to the night when she must repeat it, and thus on to infinity. I imagined as well a Platonic, hereditary work, transmitted from father to son, in which each new individual adds a chapter or corrects with pious care the pages of his elders. These conjectures diverted me; but none seemed to correspond, not even remotely, to the contradictory chapters of Ts'ui Pên. In the midst of this perplexity, I received from Oxford the manuscript you have examined. I lingered, naturally, on the sentence: *I leave to the various futures (not to all) my garden of forking paths*. Almost instantly, I understood: 'The garden of forking paths' was the chaotic novel; the phrase 'the various futures (not to all)' suggested to me the forking in time, not in

---

3. The narrator of the collection also known as the *Arabian Nights*, a thousand and one tales supposedly told by Scheherazade to her husband, Shahrayar, king of Samarkand, to postpone her execution.

space. A broad rereading of the work confirmed the theory. In all fictional works, each time a man is confronted with several alternatives, he chooses one and eliminates the others; in the fiction of Ts'ui Pên, he chooses—simultaneously—all of them. *He creates*, in this way, diverse futures, diverse times which themselves also proliferate and fork. Here, then, is the explanation of the novel's contradictions. Fang, let us say, has a secret; a stranger calls at his door; Fang resolves to kill him. Naturally, there are several possible outcomes: Fang can kill the intruder, the intruder can kill Fang, they both can escape, they both can die, and so forth. In the work of Ts'ui Pên, all possible outcomes occur; each one is the point of departure for other forkings. Sometimes, the paths of this labyrinth converge: for example, you arrive at this house, but in one of the possible pasts you are my enemy, in another, my friend. If you will resign yourself to my incurable pronunciation, we shall read a few pages."

His face, within the vivid circle of the lamplight, was unquestionably that of an old man, but with something unalterable about it, even immortal. He read with slow precision two versions of the same epic chapter. In the first, an army marches to a battle across a lonely mountain; the horror of the rocks and shadows makes the men undervalue their lives and they gain an easy victory. In the second, the same army traverses a palace where a great festival is taking place; the resplendent battle seems to them a continuation of the celebration and they win the victory. I listened with proper veneration to these ancient narratives, perhaps less admirable in themselves than the fact that they had been created by my blood and were being restored to me by a man of a remote empire, in the course of a desperate adventure, on a Western isle. I remember the last words, repeated in each version like a secret commandment: *Thus fought the heroes, tranquil their admirable hearts, violent their swords, resigned to kill and to die.*

From that moment on, I felt about me and within my dark body an invisible, intangible swarming. Not the swarming of the divergent, parallel and finally coalescent armies, but a more inaccessible, more intimate agitation that they in some manner prefigured. Stephen Albert continued:

"I don't believe that your illustrious ancestor played idly with these variations. I don't consider it credible that he would sacrifice thirteen years to the infinite execution of a rhetorical experiment. In your country, the novel is a subsidiary form of literature; in Ts'ui Pên's time it was a despicable form. Ts'ui Pên was a brilliant novelist, but he was also a man of letters who doubtless did not consider himself a mere novelist. The testimony of his contemporaries proclaims—and his life fully confirms—his metaphysical and mystical interests. Philosophic controversy usurps a good part of the novel. I know that of all problems, none disturbed him so greatly nor worked upon him so much as the abysmal problem of time. Now then, the latter is the only problem that does not figure in the pages of the *Garden*. He does not even use the word that signifies *time*. How do you explain this voluntary omission?"

I proposed several solutions—all unsatisfactory. We discussed them. Finally, Stephen Albert said to me:

"In a riddle whose answer is chess, what is the only prohibited word?"

I thought a moment and replied, "The word *chess*."

"Precisely," said Albert. "*The Garden of Forking Paths* is an enormous riddle, or parable, whose theme is time; this recondite cause prohibits its mention. To omit a word always, to resort to inept metaphors and obvious periphrases, is perhaps the most emphatic way of stressing it. That is the tortuous method preferred, in each of the meanderings of his indefatigable novel, by the oblique Ts'ui Pên. I have compared hundreds of manuscripts, I have corrected the errors that the negligence of the copyists has introduced, I have guessed the plan of this chaos, I have re-established—I believe I have re-established—the primordial organization, I have translated the entire work: it is clear to me that not once does he employ the word 'time.' The explanation is obvious: *The Garden of Forking Paths* is an incomplete, but not false, image of the universe as Ts'ui Pên conceived it. In contrast to Newton and Schopenhauer,[4] your ancestor did not believe in a uniform, absolute time. He believed in an infinite series of times, in a growing, dizzying net of divergent, convergent and parallel times. This network of times which approached one another, forked, broke off, or were unaware of one another for centuries, embraces *all* possibilities of time. We do not exist in the majority of these times; in some you exist, and not I; in others I, and not you; in others, both of us. In the present one, which a favorable fate has granted me, you have arrived at my house; in another, while crossing the garden, you found me dead; in still another, I utter these same words, but I am a mistake, a ghost."

"In every one," I pronounced, not without a tremble to my voice, "I am grateful to you and revere you for your re-creation of the garden of Ts'ui Pên."

"Not in all," he murmured with a smile. "Time forks perpetually toward innumerable futures. In one of them I am your enemy."

Once again I felt the swarming sensation of which I have spoken. It seemed to me that the humid garden that surrounded the house was infinitely saturated with invisible persons. Those persons were Albert and I, secret, busy and multiform in other dimensions of time. I raised my eyes and the tenuous nightmare dissolved. In the yellow and black garden there was only one man; but this man was as strong as a statue . . . this man was approaching along the path and he was Captain Richard Madden.

"The future already exists," I replied, "but I am your friend. Could I see the letter again?"

Albert rose. Standing tall, he opened the drawer of the tall desk; for the moment his back was to me. I had readied the revolver. I fired with extreme caution. Albert fell uncomplainingly, immediately. I swear his death was instantaneous—a lightning stroke.

The rest is unreal, insignificant. Madden broke in, arrested me. I have been condemned to the gallows. I have won out abominably; I have communicated to Berlin the secret name of the city they must attack. They bombed it yesterday; I read it in the same papers that offered to England the mystery of the

4. German philosopher (1788–1860), whose concept of will proceeded from a concept of the self as enduring through time. In *Seven Conversations with Jorge Luis Borges*, Borges also comments on Schopenhauer's interest in the "oneiric [dreamlike] essence of life." Newton (1642–1727), English mathematician and philosopher best known for his formulation of laws of gravitation and motion.

learned Sinologist Stephen Albert who was murdered by a stranger, one Yu Tsun. The Chief had deciphered this mystery. He knew my problem was to indicate (through the uproar of the war) the city called Albert, and that I had found no other means to do so than to kill a man of that name. He does not know (no one can know) my innumerable contrition and weariness.

For Victoria Ocampo

1941

MODERN POETRY

Modern poets often proclaimed their break with nineteenth-century precursors, notably the Romantics and the symbolists. Romanticism had aspired, according to the English poet **William Wordsworth**, to speak in the "real language of men," but a century later, Romantic reveries about natural beauty or the soul had become, in the eyes of the modernists, just another set of poetic clichés. Wordsworth had also claimed that "all good poetry is the spontaneous overflow of powerful feelings"; the modernists were more skeptical of emotion. They sought, instead, precision and clarity; in place of self-expression, they emphasized the construction of the literary work. Correspondingly, they turned away from ballads and narrative poetry and toward compressed lyrics that often used language in a shocking or an unfamiliar way, far from the everyday language that Wordsworth had praised.

Some modernists likewise saw the late nineteenth-century symbolism of the French poets **Charles Baudelaire** and **Stéphane Mallarmé** as merely an overwrought kind of Romanticism in which personal vision counted for more than precision and formal innovation. In fact, however, many modernists drew on the symbolist inheritance in their attempts to transform verse. One area of continuity was the role of images and symbols. **William Butler Yeats** and **Constantine Cavafy**, who were already writing poetry during the heyday of symbolism, stress the power of what Yeats called "masterful images"—striking visual creations hermetic or esoteric enough to require challenging acts of interpretation on the reader's part. Both poets found inspiration in the storehouse of images associated with myth and legend to create complex personal mythologies that enriched their poems, even for the reader who might be unaware of the poet's private associations.

Rainer Maria Rilke and **T. S. Eliot** likewise incorporated elements of ancient myth in their poetry, but they were less comfortable with symbolist subjectivity; their aim was to achieve impersonal objectivity. Rilke became known in particular for his "object poems," in which precise observation yields indirect commentary on human society. Eliot used complex metrical play and surprising rhymes to revitalize the resources of English verse. (A parallel movement in Russia, Acmeism, influenced the young **Anna Akhmatova**.) Eliot frequently alluded to or quoted other writers, creating layers of voices or registers that collide uneasily in the poems and keep the reader on edge. Yeats, who (like Cavafy in Greek and Rilke in German) generally relied on traditional stanza forms, used meter to achieve a high formality while evoking the rhythms of spoken English. Both English-language poets were substantially influenced by Ezra Pound, who, in arguing against adherence to the most widely used metrical pattern, iambic pentameter, asserted that poets should "compose in the sequence of the musical phrase, not the sequence of a metronome."

Although the modernists often undertook long poems, these works were seldom narrative epics but, rather, fragmentary collections of lyrics, like Eliot's *The Waste Land* (1922) and *Four Quartets* (1943) or Akhmatova's *Requiem* (1963). Eliot argued that "our civilization comprehends great variety and complexity, and this variety and complexity, playing upon a refined sensibility, must produce various and complex results. The poet must become more and more comprehensive, more allusive, more indirect, in order to force, to dislocate if necessary, language to his meaning." While many poets undertook the dislocation of language through play with traditional forms, rhymes, and meters, the literary avant-gardes—especially the advocates of surrealism—launched a fundamental attack on traditional poetry. Led by André Breton and inspired by Sigmund Freud and Karl Marx, the surrealists tapped into the unconscious and undermined the repressive tendencies of Western society. Many of them, moreover, hoped to transform society through a Communist revolution. In different ways, **Aimé Césaire**, **Pablo Neruda**, and **Octavio Paz** were all influenced by surrealism's quest for political, erotic, and spiritual liberation. To varying degrees they embraced free verse, long and loose poetic lines, and the startling juxtaposition of images. That the three came from the developing or colonized world, and spent formative periods in Paris, helps to explain their openness to the surrealist revolution against traditional poetry.

The more politically oriented poets, notably Neruda, often found themselves balancing their interest in literary experiment with a desire to write in a direct, unadorned style that could attract a wide readership. Although **Federico García Lorca** befriended the early surrealists and shared their experimental attitude in his plays, his elegy **"Lament for Ignacio Sánchez Mejías"** (1935) is in many respects a more traditional poem than anything produced by the avant-gardes. His use of repetition and rhetorical techniques intended to move an audience shares something with the work of his friend Neruda, who would later memorialize Lorca himself in **"I'm Explaining a Few Things"** (1937).

Modernist poetry, particularly as exemplified by Eliot's *The Waste Land* and championed in his essays, has been rejected by some critics as elitist. It can certainly be challenging, inviting the reader to engage with untested literary forms and to respond to unexpected meaning. Whether cryptic like some of Yeats's symbols or direct like Neruda's odes, intricate like Rilke's poetry or explosive like Césaire's free verse, the poetry of the early twentieth century reinvents and reinvigorates language for an age in which words can all too easily lose their meanings and traditional forms their power to structure experience. The selection of modernist poetry that follows suggests the variety and complexity of this rich period in literary history, a period whose implications are still being worked out by poets and readers today.

CONSTANTINE CAVAFY

1863–1933

A private poet who circulated his work in folders to relatives and friends and never offered a book for sale, Constantine Cavafy became, almost in spite of himself, the most influential Greek poet of the twentieth century when a posthumous edition of 154 short poems was published in 1935. His precisely worded, obliquely evocative portraits of historical figures, displayed with their poignant desires and personal tragedies, subtly link the past and the present. The present-day world is present, too: glimpses of contemporary Alexandria spark the recall of erotic memories, and forgotten landscapes resurge with complex emotional and intellectual associations.

Cavafy was born in 1863 to Greek parents living in Alexandria, Egypt. The export-import firm of Cavafy Brothers had once been wealthy, but its fortunes declined and Constantine's father died in 1870. Two years later, Cavafy's mother took the family to England, where the boy's parents had lived in the 1850s and where she hoped they would prosper again. Unfortunately, the boy's two older brothers were inexperienced in business affairs; the rest of their funds vanished, obliging them to return to Alexandria, where they lived in straitened circumstances. During the poet's seven years in England, however, he became bilingual and read widely in English literature. In 1882, Cavafy's mother returned to her father's house outside Constantinople with Cavafy and his two brothers. They remained there for three years, during which time Cavafy discovered his ho-mosexuality and had his first love affair. The young writer—who was now fluent in English, Greek, and French—began to write poems in the three languages. In 1885 the family returned to Alexandria where Cavafy settled for the rest of his life, living with his mother until 1899 and, after her death, sharing quarters with his unmarried brothers. Although he became the greatest of modern Greek poets, he did not visit Greece itself until he was almost fifty.

Cavafy continued to write poetry and essays while working for an Alexandrian newspaper and for the Egyptian Stock Exchange before receiving the position he would hold from then on: special clerk in the Irrigation Service of the Ministry of Public Works. Although Cavafy shared his poetry with friends and relatives, he seems to have had no interest in seeking a wider audience. He had several pamphlets printed privately—an initial booklet of fourteen poems in 1904, enlarged with seven more in 1910—but otherwise restricted himself to folders of poems given to a few readers. In his later years, his reputation spread internationally through the efforts of the British novelist E. M. Forster, who met Cavafy during the First World War in Alexandria and remained a friend for the next twenty years. Cavafy's poem "Ithaka" was published in **T. S. Eliot**'s journal *Criterion*; occasionally, European visitors to Alexandria came to meet its author. He was reportedly a sociable person and a fascinating conversationalist, but he kept to himself and his circle of friends. Forster described him as a Greek gentleman with a straw hat standing "at a slight angle to the universe," and he was virtually unknown in Greece when he died in 1933.

Cavafy's poetry draws his readers into an astonishingly real personal world, establishing a common bond between them and fictional characters in an immense variety of circumstances. The sense of participation comes not merely from the recognition of familiar emotional situations but also from Cavafy's ironic and philosophical perspective that makes subtle demands on the reader's imagination. Cavafy observed that his works could be divided into three broad categories—historical, philosophical, and erotic—and he arranged his folders of poetry in thematic as well as chronological order. It is easy to see how a primary division could be made: of the poems printed here, "Kaisarion" (1918) is historical; "The Next Table" (1919) is erotic; and "Ithaka" (1911) is philosophical. But isn't such compartmentalizing too simple? The young Kaisarion is "good-looking and sensitive," with a "dreamy, an appealing beauty"; "The Next Table" involves memory, self-deception, and a portrait of aging as much as the act of love; and "Ithaka" would not exist without its basis in historical legend. The primary categories are not only broad but (as Cavafy undoubtedly knew) they overlap and leave room for others, whether political allusion ("When the Watchman Saw the Light," 1900), psychological portrait ("The City," 1910, "A Sculptor from Tyana," 1911), or devotion to art ("A Craftsman of Wine Bowls," 1921),

or philosophical evocation of memory ("Evening," 1917).

In these poems history exists on several levels. It is not the better-known Homeric and Periclean ages of Greek history, but rather the Hellenistic period and the Byzantine Empire, whose tangled politics, sophisticated art, social decadence, and vulnerability to invasion have their analogue in twentieth-century Alexandria. Cavafy's Alexandria is a modern metropolis with a glorious past, and the poet searches history for dramatic anecdotes that reveal the texture of life in that turbulent earlier age. It is not merely the murdered Kaisarion—son of Caesar and Cleopatra—who interests him, but John Kantakuzinos, a minor, impoverished ruler forced to decorate his crown with glass jewels; King Dimitrios, who in 288 B.C.E. disguised himself in simple clothes to escape capture after being deserted by his soldiers; and the scheming Anna Komnina, furious at seeing the Byzantine throne slip out of her hands in 1137. Ancient Greece appears primarily as a reference point in the distant past: the home of heroes like Patroklos or the god Hermes, who are both subjects for the vain sculptor of Tyana; of gods who fleetingly appear in the streets of Alexandria or the landscape of Ionia; or of Odysseus, whose epic voyage becomes a lesson that you can't go home again. From whatever era, Cavafy's precisely rendered narratives invite readers to enter, for a moment, the world of his poetic imagination and to draw their own connections to contemporary life.

When the Watchman Saw the Light[1]

Winter and summer the watchman sat on the roof
of the palace of the sons of Atreus and looked out. Now he tells
the joyful news. He saw a fire flare in the distance.[2]
And he is glad, and his labor is over as well.
It is hard work night and day,   5
in heat or cold, to look far off
to Arachnaion[3] for a fire. Now the desired
omen has appeared. When happiness
arrives it brings a lesser joy
than expected.[4] Clearly,   10
we've gained this much: we are saved from hopes
and expectations. Many things will happen
to the Atreus dynasty. One doesn't have to be wise
to surmise this now that the watchman
has seen the light. So, no exaggeration.   15
The light is good, and those that will come are good.
Their words and deeds are also good.
And we hope all will go well. But
Argos can manage without the Atreus family.
Great houses are not eternal.   20
Of course, many will have much to say.
We'll listen. But we won't be fooled
by the Indispensable, the Only, the Great.
Some other indispensable, only, and great
is always instantly found.   25

1900

---

1. All poems in this selection are translated by Aliki Barnstone. This poem was written in 1900 and was not published during the poet's lifetime. The title, a reference to the prologue of Aeschylus's play *Agamemnon*, a speech given by the watchman who is waiting for the signal that announces the king's return to Argos, is a reminder of the hereditary curse on the family: King Atreus was Agamemnon's father, and Atreus himself was supposed to have revenged himself on his brother Thyestes by serving his children to him for dinner.

2. A chain of bonfires that stretched from Troy to Greece had been prepared as a way of announcing the long-awaited return of Agamemnon's ship from the Trojan War.
3. A mountain in the Epidauros (Argeia) region of Greece.
4. A general statement but also a reminder that Agamemnon is coming home to his death at the hands of his wife, Queen Clytemnestra. Just as in Aeschylus's play, the watchman knows that all is not well at home.

Waiting for the Barbarians[1]

—What are we waiting for, gathered in the agora?[2]

    The barbarians are arriving today.

—Why is nothing happening in the Senate?
Why do the Senators sit making no laws?

    Because the barbarians are arriving today.   5
    What laws can the Senators make now?
    When the barbarians come, they will make laws.
—Why did our emperor wake up so early,
and, in the city's grandest gate, sit in state
on his throne, wearing his crown?   10

    Because the barbarians are arriving today,
    and the emperor is waiting to receive
    their leader. In fact, he prepared
    a parchment to give them, where
    he wrote down many titles and names.   15

—Why did our two consuls and the praetors[3]
come out today in their crimson embroidered togas;
why did they don bracelets with so many amethysts
and rings resplendent with glittering emeralds;
why do they hold precious staffs today,   20
beautifully wrought in silver and gold?

    Because the barbarians are arriving today,
    and such things dazzle barbarians.

—Why don't the worthy orators come as usual
to deliver their speeches and say their piece?   25

    Because the barbarians are arriving today
    and they are bored by eloquence and harangues.

—Why should this anxiety and confusion
suddenly begin. (How serious faces have become.)

---

1. Written in 1898; published in 1904. The setting appears to be ancient Rome during the decadence of the empire, when the city was sacked by the Visigoth leader Alaric in 410 C.E. Cavafy has specified that there is no precise reference, however, noting that the barbarians are only a symbol and that "the emperor, the senators and the orators are not necessarily Roman."

2. A large public area, containing temples, shops, and buildings; in Rome, the equivalent would be the forum, which also contained the Senate building.

3. Judicial officers in Rome who held preliminary hearings before cases were assigned to a judge. "Consuls": the two chief administrative officers of the state who presided over the Senate. They were elected by the people under the republic but named by the emperor during the empire.

Why have the streets and squares emptied so quickly,   30
and why has everyone returned home so pensive?

Because night's fallen and the barbarians have not arrived.
And some people came from the border
and they say the barbarians no longer exist.

Now what will become of us without barbarians?   35
Those people were some kind of solution.

1904

The City[1]

You said, "I'll go to another land, I'll go to another sea.
I'll find a city better than this one.
My every effort is a written indictment,
and my heart—like someone dead—is buried.
How long will my mind remain in this decaying state.   5
Wherever I cast my eyes, wherever I look,
I see my life in black ruins here,
where I spent so many years, and ruined and wasted them."

You will not find new lands, you will not find other seas.
The city will follow you. You will roam   10
the same streets. And you will grow old in the same neighborhood,
and your hair will turn white in the same houses.
You will always arrive in this city. Don't hope for elsewhere—
there is no ship for you, there is no road.
As you have wasted your life here,   15
in this small corner, so you have ruined it on the whole earth.

1910

A Sculptor from Tyana[1]

As you may have heard, I'm not a beginner.
Quite a lot of stone has taken shape in my hands.
In my homeland, Tyana, I am well known,
and here senators have commissioned
many statues from me.   5
                    Let me show you
a few right now. Observe this Rhea,[2]

---

1. Written in 1894 under the title "Once More in the Same City" and listed under "Prisons." It was published with the current title in 1910.
1. First written in June 1893, entitled "A

Sculptor's Studio"; published in 1911. Tyana was a city in Cappadocia, a district in Asia Minor, but the scene—in Rome—is imaginary.
2. Daughter of heaven and earth, and mother of the gods on Olympus.

inspiring reverence, full of fortitude, wholly archaic.
Observe Pompey. Marius,
Paulus Aemilius, Scipio Africanus.[3]
Likenesses faithful as I could make them.   10
Patroklos (I'll retouch him a bit).
Near the yellowish marble—
those pieces over there—is Kaisarion.[4]

For some time now I've been working on
a Poseidon.[5] I'm particularly studying   15
his horses, how to form them.
They must be made so light
to show clearly that their bodies, their feet
don't tread on earth, only gallop on water.
But look, here is my work I love most,   20
made with feeling and greatest care.
With him, on a warm summer day,
when my mind was rising to the ideal,
he came to me in a dream, this young Hermes.[6]

                                                          1911

Ithaka[1]

As you set out on the journey to Ithaka,
wish that the way be long,
full of adventures, full of knowledge.
Don't be afraid of Laistrygonians, the Cyclops,
angry Poseidon,[2] you'll never find them on your way   5
if your thought stays exalted, if a rare
emotion touches your spirit and body.
You won't meet the Laistrygonians
and the Cyclops and wild Poseidon,

---

3. Scipio Africanus the Younger (185–129 B.C.E.) led the army that destroyed Carthage in 146 B.C.E. "Pompey": Gnaeus Pompeius Magnus (106–48 B.C.E.), Roman general and statesman who fled to Egypt after being defeated by Julius Caesar, was assassinated by King Ptolemy. Gaius Marius (157–86 B.C.E.), a popular general, was elected consul seven times. Lucius Aemilius Paulus (228–160 B.C.E.) was a Roman consul whose army was disastrously defeated by Hannibal at the Battle of Cannae (216 B.C.E.).
4. Or Caesarion ("Little Caesar," 47–30 B.C.E.), the son of Cleopatra and Julius Caesar. Co-ruler of Egypt with his mother, he was killed by Octavian (the future emperor Augustus Caesar) for political reasons after her death. "Patroklos": Achilles' friend in Homer's Iliad, killed in battle.
5. Greek god of the sea.
6. Son of Zeus and messenger of the gods, often depicted as a nude youth bearing a herald's wand, or caduceus.
1. Ithaka is Odysseus's island kingdom and the destination of his homeward journey after the Trojan War. An early, different version of this poem was entitled "Second Odyssey."
2. Greek god of the sea. Odysseus encounters both the Laistrygonians (fierce rock-throwing cannibal giants in Odyssey 10) and the Cyclops (one-eyed cannibal giant in Odyssey 9) on his voyage home.

if you don't bear them along in your soul,   10
if your soul doesn't raise them before you.

Wish that the way be long.
May there be many summer mornings
when with such pleasure, such joy
you enter ports seen for the first time;   15
may you stop in Phoenician emporia[3]
to buy fine merchandise,
mother-of-pearl and coral, amber and ebony,
and every kind of sensual perfume,
buy abundant sensual perfumes, as many as you can.   20
Travel to many Egyptian cities
to learn and learn from their scholars.
Always keep Ithaka in your mind.
Arriving there is your destination.
But don't hurry the journey at all.   25
Better if it lasts many years,
and you moor on the island when you are old,
rich with all you have gained along the way,
not expecting Ithaka to make you rich.

Ithaka gave you the beautiful journey.   30
Without her you would not have set out on your way.
She has no more to give you.

And if you find her poor, Ithaka did not betray you.
With all your wisdom, all your experience,
you understand by now what Ithakas mean.   35

                                                                    1911

Evening[1]

Anyway, they would not have lasted long. So the experience
of the years shows me. But Fate came
somewhat hastily and stopped them.
The good life was short.
But how strong the perfumes were,   5
how divine the beds where we lay,
to what pleasure we gave our bodies.

An echo of the days of pleasure,
an echo of the days came close to me,

---

3. The Phoenicians (from Phoenicia, in modern Syria and Lebanon) were famous merchants and sailors who established trade routes throughout the Mediterranean.

1. Published in 1917; written in 1916 as "Alexandrian" (a reference to the city of Alexandria, Egypt).

something of our youth's fire, something of the two of us.   10
In my hands was a letter I picked up again,
and I read it again and again until the light was gone.

I went out on the balcony, melancholy—
I went out to change my thoughts, at least to see
a little of the beloved city,   15
a little of the activity in the streets and the stores.

1917

Kaisarion[1]

In part to verify an era,
in part to pass the time,
last night I chose a collection
of Ptolemaic epigraphs to read.
The extravagant praise and flattery   5
was the same for everybody. All are splendid,
glorious, powerful, and altruistic;
every undertaking very wise.
If you talk about the women of that generation, they, too,
all the Berenikis and Kleopatras,[2] were marvelous.   10

When I succeeded in verifying the era,
I would have put the book down if a small
and unimportant note about King Kaisarion
did not immediately attract my attention.

Ah, here you came with your ambiguous   15
charm. In history only a few
lines about you exist,
and so I created you more freely in my mind.
I created you handsome and sensitive.
My art gives your face   20
a dreamy, amiable beauty.

And I imagine you so fully
that late last night as my light
went out—I let it go out on purpose—
I imagined you came in my room,   25
it seemed to me you stood as before, as you would have
in the vanquished Alexandria,
pale and tired, ideal in your sorrow,

1. Kaisarion or Caesarion ("Little Caesar," 47–30 B.C.E.) was the son of Cleopatra and Julius Caesar.
2. Kleopatra or Cleopatra (69–30 B.C.E.) was queen of Egypt and mother of Kaisarion. Bere-

niki or Berenice (ca. 273–221 B.C.E.), the sister of Ptolemy III Euergetes (ca. 284–221 B.C.E.), married Antiochus II, king of Syria and, after his death, would have married the emperor Titus if the Romans had not objected.

still hoping they might show you compassion,
the vicious ones—who whispered, "too many Caesars."[3]   30

1918

The Next Table

He[1] must be barely twenty-three years old.
And yet I am sure almost as many
years ago, I enjoyed this same body.

It isn't merely an erotic flush.
I've only been in the casino[2] a little while   5
and haven't even had time to drink a lot.
I enjoyed this same body.

And even if I don't recall where—one lapse of memory means nothing.

Ah, now, there, now that he sits at the next table,
I know each way he moves—and under his clothes,   10
naked, are the loved limbs I see again.

1919

A Craftsman of Wine Bowls[1]

On this wine bowl   made of pure silver
that was made   for the home of Irakleidis[2]
where good taste   prevails supreme—
look, here are elegant flowers   and streams and thyme,
and in the center I have placed   a beautiful young man   5
naked, erotic;   he still dangles one of his calves
in the water.—   Oh, memory, I prayed
to find you my best   helper, so I might make
the face of the young man   I loved, as it was.
It turned out to be   a vast difficulty   10
because almost fifteen years   have passed since the day
he fell, a soldier   in the defeat of Magnesia.[3]

1921

3. The teenage Kaisarion was killed because, as the son of Julius Caesar and Cleopatra, he represented a political threat to the future emperor Augustus (then Octavian). The reason for his execution was given in a sentence modeled on a line from Homer's *Iliad* (2.204): "It is not a good thing to have too many Caesars."
1. The language of the Greek original does not reveal the gender of the person seated at the next table, but this calculated ambiguity is not possible in English translation.
2. Casinos were respectable places of entertainment.
1. Printed in 1921; written in 1903 and twice revised.
2. Treasurer of Antiochus IV Epiphanes (ruled 175–163 B.C.E.).
3. In 190 B.C.E. at the battle of Magnesia, the Romans defeated Antiochus III the Great, the father of Antiochus IV.

WILLIAM BUTLER YEATS

1865–1939

The twentieth century's greatest English-language poet, William Butler Yeats became a major voice of modern, independent Ireland. His captivating imagery and his fusion of history and vision continue to stir readers around the world, and many of his poetic phrases have entered the language. Yeats created a private mythology that helped him come to terms with personal and cultural pain and allowed him to explain—as symptoms of Western civilization's declining spiral—the plight of Irish society and the chaos in Europe in the period surrounding the First World War.

The eldest of four children born to John Butler and Susan Pollexfen Yeats, William came from a middle-class Protestant family. His father, a cosmopolitan Irishman who had turned from law to painting and whose inherited fortune had mostly evaporated, gave his son an unconventional education at home. J. B. Yeats was an argumentative religious skeptic who alternately terrorized his son and fostered the boy's interest in poetry and the visual arts, inspiring rebellion against scientific rationalism and belief in the superiority of art. His mother's ties to her home in County Sligo, where Yeats spent many summers and school holidays with his wealthy grandparents, introduced him to the beauties of the Irish countryside and to the folklore and supernatural legends that appear throughout his work. Living alternately in Ireland and England for much of his youth, Yeats became part of literary society in both countries and—though an Irish nationalist—rejected any narrowly patriotic point of view. Before he turned fully to literature in 1886, Yeats attended art school and had planned to become an artist. (His brother Jack became a well-known painter.) Yeats's early works show the influence of the Pre-Raphaelite school in art and in literature. Pre-Raphaelitism called for a return to the sensuous representation and concrete details found in Italian painting before Raphael (1483–1520); Pre-Raphaelite poetry evoked a realm of luminous supernatural beauty in allusive, erotic imagery. Yeats combined the Pre-Raphaelite fascination with the medieval with his exploration of Irish legend: in 1889 he published an archaically styled poem describing a traveler in fairyland ("The Wanderings of Oisin") that established his reputation and won the praise of the designer and writer William Morris. The musical style of Yeats's Pre-Raphaelite period is evident in one of his most popular poems, "The Lake Isle of Innisfree" (1890), with its hidden "bee-loud glade" where "peace comes dropping slow" and evening, after the "purple glow" of noon, is "full of the linnet's wings."

In 1887, Yeats's family moved to London, where the writer pursued his interest in mystical philosophy by studying theosophy under its Russian interpreter, Madame Blavatsky. She claimed mystical knowledge from Tibetan monks and preached the doctrine of the Universal Oversoul, individual spiritual evolution through cycles of reincarnation, and the world as a conflict of opposing forces. Yeats was taken with the grandeur of her cosmology, although he inconveniently wished to test it by experiment and analysis and, in 1890, was expelled from the Theosophical

Society. He found a more congenial literary model in the works of **William Blake**, which he coedited in 1893 with F. J. Ellis. The appeal that mysticism had for Yeats later waned but never disappeared; traces may be seen in the introduction he wrote in 1913 for *Gitanjali*, a collection of poems by the Indian author Rabindranath Tagore, the preeminent figure in modern Bengali literature.

Several anthologies of Irish folk and fairy tales and a book describing Irish traditions (*The Celtic Twilight*, 1893) demonstrated a corresponding interest in Irish national identity. In 1896 he had met Lady Augusta Gregory, a nationalist who invited him to spend summers at Coole Park, her country house in Galway, and who worked closely with him (and later J. M. Synge) in founding the Irish National Theater (later the Abbey Theater). Along with other participants in the Irish literary renaissance, Yeats aimed to create "a national literature that made Ireland beautiful in the memory . . . freed from provincialism by an exacting criticism." To this end, he wrote *Cathleen ni Houlihan* (1902), a play in which the title character personified Ireland; it became immensely popular with the nationalists. Yeats also established literary societies, promoted and reviewed Irish books, and lectured and wrote about the need for Irish community. Gradually Yeats became embittered by the barriers he believed nationalism was erecting around the free expression of Irish culture. He was outraged at the attacks on Synge's *Playboy of the Western World* (1907) for its supposed derogatory picture of Irish culture, and he commented scathingly in *Poems Written in Discouragement* (1913; reprinted in *Responsibilities*, 1914) on the inability of the middle class to appreciate art or literature.

Except for summers at Coole Park, Yeats in his middle age was spending more time in England than in Ireland. He began *Autobiographies* in 1914 and wrote symbolic plays intended for small audiences on the model of the Japanese Noh theater. His works of this period display a change in tone—a precision and epigrammatic quality that reflects partly his disappointment with Irish nationalism and partly the tastes in poetry promulgated by his friend Ezra Pound and by **T. S. Eliot**. Although Yeats had claimed in a poem just before the First World War that "Romantic Ireland's dead and gone," he found himself drawn again to politics as a subject for poetry and as an arena for action. Shocked by the aftermath of the Easter 1916 uprising against British rule, when sixteen leaders were shot for treason, Yeats wrote that, through their sacrifice, "a terrible beauty is born." The revolutionary figures whom Yeats had known in life took their place in a mythic framework within which he interpreted human history. In the subsequent Anglo-Irish War (1919–21) and Irish Civil War (1922–23), great violence, as Yeats had prophesied, attended the birth of the Irish nation-state. In the Irish Free State, Yeats became a senator from 1922 to 1928, Nobel Prize laureate in 1924, and a "sixty-year-old smiling public man," in the words of "Among School Children" (1926). Much of his best poetry was still to come.

Yeats's marriage in 1917 to Georgie Hyde-Lees provided him with much-needed stability. Intrigued by his wife's experiments with automatic writing (jotting down whatever comes to mind, without correction or rational intent), he viewed them as glimpses into a cosmic order; he gradually evolved his interpretation into a symbolic scheme. He explained the system in *A Vision* (1926): the wheel of history takes 26,000 years to turn; and inside the wheel, civilizations evolve in roughly 2,000-year gyres, spirals expanding outward until they collapse at the onset of a new gyre, which reverses the direction of the old. Within the system human personalities fall into various types, and both gyres and types relate to the phases of the moon. Yeats's later poems in *The Tower* (1928), *The Winding Stair* (1933), and *Last Poems* (1939) are set in the context of this system. His enthusiasms for mythical systems sometimes led him astray, notably when he flirted with the Irish Blue Shirts, a para-Fascist movement in the 1930s. Throughout his life, he affected an aristocratic disdain for the rough-and-tumble of democratic politics; by the end of his life, he had abandoned practical politics and devoted himself to the reality of personal experience inside a mystic view of history. The final poem in his posthumous *Last Poems*, "Politics," suggests that events in Russia, Italy, and Spain (communism, Fascism, and the impending Second World War) held less interest for the poet than a girl standing nearby: "maybe what they say is true / Of war and war's alarms / But O that I were young again / And held her in my arms."

For many readers Yeats's "masterful images" (in the words of another late poem, "The Circus Animals' Desertion," 1939) define his work. From his early use of symbols as metaphors for personal emotions, to the cosmology of his last work, Yeats created a poetry whose power derives from the interweaving of sharp-edged images. Symbols such as the Tower, Byzantium, Helen of Troy, the sun and the moon, birds of prey, the blind man, and the fool recur frequently and draw their meaning not from connections established inside the poem (as is true for the French symbolists) but from an underlying myth based on occult tradition, Irish folklore, history, and Yeats's private experience. Even readers unacquainted with his mythic system will respond to images that express a situa-

tion or state of mind—for example, golden Byzantium for intellect, art, wisdom—all that "body" cannot supply.

The nine poems included here cover the range of Yeats's career, which embraced several styles. A poem from his early, Pre-Raphaelite period, "When You Are Old" (1895), pleads his love for the beautiful actress and Irish nationalist Maud Gonne, whom he met in 1889 and who repeatedly refused to marry him. From the love poems of his youth to those of his old age, when in "The Circus Animals' Desertion" he describes Gonne as prey to fanaticism and hate, Yeats again and again examines his feelings for this woman, who for him personified love, beauty, and nationalism along with hope, frustration, and despair.

In middle age, when Yeats adopted a more political tone, he did so with an element of meditative distance. When he celebrates the abortive nationalist uprisings in "Easter 1916" (1916), it is from a universal, aesthetic point of view: "A terrible beauty is born" in the self-sacrifice that leads even a "drunken, vainglorious lout" (Major John MacBride, Maud Gonne's husband) to be "transformed utterly" by martyrdom. Yeats recognized that the Easter Rebellion, led by radicals whose politics and violence he disapproved, had altered not just the political situation in Ireland but its spiritual state as well.

His early poetry made substantial use of public, straightforward symbols, such as the rose for Ireland. Later on, Yeats employed symbols in a more indirect, allusive way. For example, in "The Second Coming" (1921), the "gyre," or spiral unfolding of history, is represented by the falcon's spiral flight. The sphinxlike beast slouching blank-eyed toward Bethlehem is an enigmatic but terrifying image. Yeats believed that contemporary society was witnessing a transformation similar to that of the fall of Troy or the birth of Christ: "twenty centuries of stony sleep" since Christ's birth are again to be "vexed to nightmare by a rocking cradle," the poem declares; he asks what sort of savior or Antichrist will announce the impending age. This poem demonstrates how Yeats, a master of English meter and rhyme, evolved a loose poetic line with only hints of rhyme. The fourteen lines of the second stanza can be read as an unconventional sonnet.

In form a more conventional sonnet, "Leda and the Swan" (1924) is an erotic retelling of a mythical rape. But it also foreshadows the Trojan War—brute force mirroring brute force. Yeats called the poem's subject "a violent annunciation": as the event that conceives Helen of Troy, Zeus's transformation into a swan and rape of Leda embodies a moment of world-historical change. Once again Yeats draws parallels between the upheavals of history and the catastrophic events of ancient narratives. The poem combines the Shakespearean sonnet in its first two quatrains (the eight lines rhyming *ababcdcd*) with the Petrarchan form in the sestet (the final six lines rhyming *defdef*).

In the two poems on the legendary city of Byzantium, "Sailing to Byzantium" (1926) and "Byzantium" (1930), Yeats admires an artistic civilization that "could answer all my questions" but that was, in fact, only a moment in history. Byzantine art, with its stylized perspectives and mosaics assembled from colored bits of stone, represents the opposite of the tendency of Western art to imitate nature, and it provides a kind of escape for the poet. The idea in "Sailing to Byzantium" of an inhuman, metallic, abstract beauty that art separates "out of nature" expresses a mystic, symbolist quest for an invulnerable world distinct from the ravages of time. This world is to be found in an idealized Byzantium, where the poet's body will be transmuted into artifice. By the time of the second of these

poems, the possibility of achieving such a separation seems problematic: the speaker recognizes, on the one hand, that artistic images remain close to the living, suffering world—"the dolphin's mire and blood"—and, on the other hand, that such images have a life independent of the people who would merge with them—"Those images that yet / Fresh images beget."

At the close of "Among School Children," the sixty-year-old "public man" compensates for the passing of youth by dreaming of pure "Presences" that never fade. This poem, like "Sailing to Byzantium" and "The Circus Animals' Desertion," is written in a complex, courtly stanza form, ottava rima (eight lines rhyming *ababababcc*), which Yeats often uses for philosophical reflection. He often adopts, as well, the persona of the old man for whom the perspectives of age, idealized beauty, and history are ways to keep human agony at a distance. In "Lapis Lazuli," the tragic figures of history transcend their roles by the calm "gaiety" with which they accept their fate: the ancient Chinamen carved in the blue stone climb toward a vantage point where they can gaze, without concern, upon the world's tragedies: "Their eyes mid many wrinkles, their eyes, / Their ancient, glittering eyes, are gay."

Yet the world is still there, tragedies still abound, and Yeats's poetry remains aware of the physical and emotional roots from which the words spring. Whatever the wished-for distance, his poems are full of passionate feelings, erotic desire and disappointment, delight in beauty, horror at civil war and anarchy, dismay at degradation and change. By the time of his death, on January 28, 1939, Yeats had rejected his Byzantine identity as the golden songbird and sought out "the brutality, the ill breeding, the barbarism of truth." In "The Circus Animals' Desertion," Yeats describes his former themes as so many performing creatures on display. Yeats's poetry, which draws its initial power from the formal mastery of images and verbal rhythm, resonates in the reader's mind for its attempt to come to terms with reality, to grasp and make sense of human experience in the language of art.

When You Are Old[1]

When you are old and gray and full of sleep,
And nodding by the fire, take down this book,
And slowly read, and dream of the soft look
Your eyes had once, and of their shadows deep;

How many loved your moments of glad grace,   5
And loved your beauty with love false or true,
But one man loved the pilgrim soul in you,
And loved the sorrows of your changing face;

And bending down beside the glowing bars,
Murmur, a little sadly, how Love fled   10
And paced upon the mountains overhead
And hid his face amid a crowd of stars.

1895

Easter 1916[1]

I have met them at close of day
Coming with vivid faces
From counter or desk among grey
Eighteenth-century houses.
I have passed with a nod of the head   5
Or polite meaningless words,
Or have lingered awhile and said
Polite meaningless words,
And thought before I had done
Of a mocking tale or a gibe   10
To please a companion
Around the fire at the club,
Being certain that they and I
But lived where motley is worn:
All changed, changed utterly: 15
A terrible beauty is born.

1. An adaptation of a love sonnet by the French Renaissance poet Pierre de Ronsard (1524–1585), which begins similarly ("Quand vous serez bien vieille") but ends by asking the beloved to "pluck the roses of life today."

1. On Easter Sunday 1916, Irish nationalists began an unsuccessful rebellion against British rule, which lasted throughout the week and ended in the surrender and execution of its leaders.

That woman's[2] days were spent
In ignorant good-will,
Her nights in argument
Until her voice grew shrill.   20
What voice more sweet than hers
When, young and beautiful,
She rode to harriers?
This man had kept a school
And rode our wingèd horse;   25
This other his helper and friend[3]
Was coming into his force;
He might have won fame in the end,
So sensitive his nature seemed,
So daring and sweet his thought.   30
This other man[4] I had dreamed
A drunken, vainglorious lout.
He had done most bitter wrong
To some who are near my heart,
Yet I number him in the song;   35
He, too, has resigned his part
In the casual comedy;
He, too, has been changed in his turn,
Transformed utterly:
A terrible beauty is born.   40

Hearts with one purpose alone
Through summer and winter seem
Enchanted to a stone
To trouble the living stream.
The horse that comes from the road,   45
The rider, the birds that range
From cloud to tumbling cloud,
Minute by minute they change;
A shadow of cloud on the stream
Changes minute by minute;   50
A horse-hoof slides on the brim,
And a horse plashes within it;
The long-legged moor-hens dive,
And hens to moor-cocks call;
Minute by minute they live: 55
The stone's in the midst of all.

Too long a sacrifice
Can make a stone of the heart.

2. Constance Gore-Booth (1868–1927), later Countess Markiewicz, an ardent nationalist.
3. Patrick Pearse (1879–1916) and his friend Thomas MacDonagh (1878–1916), both schoolmasters and leaders of the rebellion and both executed by the British. As a Gaelic poet, Pearse symbolically rode the winged horse of the Muses, Pegasus.
4. Major John MacBride (1865–1916), who had married and separated from Maud Gonne (1866–1953), Yeats's great love.

O when may it suffice?
That is Heaven's part, our part   60
To murmur name upon name,
As a mother names her child
When sleep at last has come
On limbs that had run wild.
What is it but nightfall?   65
No, no, not night but death;
Was it needless death after all?
For England may keep faith
For all that is done and said.
We know their dream; enough   70
To know they dreamed and are dead;
And what if excess of love
Bewildered them till they died?
I write it out in a verse—
MacDonagh and MacBride   75
And Connolly[5] and Pearse
Now and in time to be,
Wherever green is worn,
Are changed, changed utterly:
A terrible beauty is born.   80

                                                                1916

The Second Coming[1]

Turning and turning in the widening gyre[2]
The falcon cannot hear the falconer;
Things fall apart; the centre cannot hold;
Mere anarchy is loosed upon the world,
The blood-dimmed tide is loosed, and everywhere   5
The ceremony of innocence is drowned;
The best lack all conviction, while the worst
Are full of passionate intensity.

Surely some revelation is at hand;
Surely the Second Coming is at hand.   10
The Second Coming! Hardly are those words out
When a vast image out of *Spiritus Mundi*[3]

5. James Connolly (1870–1916), labor leader and nationalist executed by the British.
1. The Second Coming of Christ, believed by Christians to herald the end of the world, is transformed here into the prediction of a birth initiating an era and terminating the two-thousand-year cycle of Christianity.

2. The cone pattern of the falcon's flight and of historical cycles, in Yeats's vision.
3. World-soul (Latin) or, as *Anima Mundi* in Yeats's *Per Amica Silentia Lunae*, a "great memory" containing archetypal images; recalls C. G. Jung's collective unconscious.

Troubles my sight: somewhere in sands of the desert
A shape with lion body and the head of a man
A gaze blank and pitiless as the sun,   15
Is moving its slow thighs, while all about it
Reel shadows of the indignant desert birds.
The darkness drops again; but now I know
That twenty centuries of stony sleep
Were vexed to nightmare by a rocking cradle,   20
And what rough beast, its hour come round at last,
Slouches towards Bethlehem to be born?

                                                                    1921

Leda and the Swan[1]

A sudden blow: the great wings beating still
Above the staggering girl, her thighs caressed
By the dark webs, her nape caught in his bill,
He holds her helpless breast upon his breast.

How can those terrified vague fingers push   5
The feathered glory from her loosening thighs?
And how can body, laid in that white rush,
But feel the strange heart beating where it lies?

A shudder in the loins engenders there
The broken wall, the burning roof and tower   10
And Agamemnon dead.[2]
                              Being so caught up,
So mastered by the brute blood of the air,
Did she put on his knowledge with his power
Before the indifferent beak could let her drop?

                                                                    1924

---

1. Zeus, ruler of the Greek gods, took the form of a swan to rape the mortal Leda; she gave birth to Helen of Troy, whose beauty caused the Trojan War.
2. The ruins of Troy and the death of Agamem-non, the Greek leader, whose sacrifice of his daughter Iphigenia to win the gods' favor caused his wife, Clytemnestra (also a daughter of Leda), to assassinate him on his return.

Sailing to Byzantium[1]

1

That is no country for old men. The young
In one another's arms, birds in the trees
—Those dying generations—at their song,
The salmon-falls, the mackerel-crowded seas,
Fish, flesh, or fowl, commend all summer long   5
Whatever is begotten, born, and dies.
Caught in the sensual music all neglect
Monuments of unageing intellect.

2

An aged man is but a paltry thing,
A tattered coat upon a stick, unless   10
Soul clap its hands and sing, and louder sing
For every tatter in its mortal dress,
Nor is there singing school but studying
Monuments of its own magnificence;
And therefore I have sailed the seas and come   15
To the holy city of Byzantium.

3

O sages standing in God's holy fire
As in the gold mosaic of a wall,
Come from the holy fire, perne in a gyre,[2]
And be the singing-masters of my soul.   20
Consume my heart away; sick with desire
And fastened to a dying animal
It knows not what it is; and gather me
Into the artifice of eternity.

4

Once out of nature I shall never take   25
My bodily form from any natural thing,
But such a form as Grecian goldsmiths make
Of hammered gold and gold enamelling
To keep a drowsy Emperor awake;
Or set upon a golden bough to sing   30
To lords and ladies of Byzantium
Of what is past, or passing, or to come.

1926

---

1. The ancient name for modern Istanbul, the capital of the Eastern Roman Empire, which represented for Yeats (who had seen Byzantine mosaics in Italy) a highly stylized and perfectly integrated artistic world where "religious, aesthetic, and practical life were one."
2. I.e., come spinning down in a spiral. "Perne": a spool or bobbin. "Gyre": the cone pattern of the falcon's flight and of historical cycles, in Yeats's vision.

Among School Children

1

I walk through the long schoolroom questioning;
A kind old nun in a white hood replies;
The children learn to cipher and to sing,
To study reading-books and history,
To cut and sew, be neat in everything   5
In the best modern way—the children's eyes
In momentary wonder stare upon
A sixty-year-old smiling public man.[1]

2

I dream of a Ledaean[2] body, bent
Above a sinking fire, a tale that she   10
Told of a harsh reproof, or trivial event
That changed some childish day to tragedy—
Told, and it seemed that our two natures blent
Into a sphere from youthful sympathy,
Or else, to alter Plato's parable,   15
Into the yolk and white of the one shell.[3]

3

And thinking of that fit of grief or rage
I look upon one child or t'other there
And wonder if she stood so at that age—
For even daughters of the swan can share   20
Something of every paddler's heritage—
And had that color upon cheek or hair,
And thereupon my heart is driven wild:
She stands before me as a living child.

4

Her present image floats into the mind—   25
Did Quattrocento finger fashion it
Hollow of cheek[4] as though it drank the wind
And took a mess of shadows for its meat?
And I though never of Ledaean kind
Had pretty plumage once—enough of that,   30
Better to smile on all that smile, and show
There is a comfortable kind of old scarecrow.

1. Yeats was elected senator of the Irish Free State in 1922.
2. Beautiful as Leda or as her daughter, Helen of Troy.
3. In Plato's *Symposium*, Socrates explains love by telling how the gods split human beings into two halves—like halves of an egg—so that each half seeks its opposite throughout life. Yeats compares the two parts to the yolk and white of an egg.
4. Italian painters of the 15th century (the Quattrocento), such as Botticelli (1444–1510), were known for their delicate figures.

5

What youthful mother, a shape upon her lap
Honey of generation had betrayed,
And that must sleep, shriek, struggle to escape   35
As recollection or the drug decide,[5]
Would think her son, did she but see that shape
With sixty or more winters on its head,
A compensation for the pang of his birth,
Or the uncertainty of his setting forth?   40

6

Plato thought nature but a spume that plays
Upon a ghostly paradigm of things;
Solider Aristotle played the taws
Upon the bottom of a king of kings;
World-famous golden-thighed Pythagoras[6]   45
Fingered upon a fiddle-stick or strings
What a star sang and careless Muses heard:
Old clothes upon old sticks to scare a bird.

7

Both nuns and mothers worship images,
But those the candles light are not as those   50
That animate a mother's reveries,
But keep a marble or a bronze repose.
And yet they too break hearts—O Presences
That passion, piety, or affection knows,
And that all heavenly glory symbolize—   55
O self-born mockers of man's enterprise;

8

Labor is blossoming or dancing where
The body is not bruised to pleasure soul,
Nor beauty born out of its own despair,
Nor blear-eyed wisdom out of midnight oil.   60
O chestnut tree, great-rooted blossomer,
Are you the leaf, the blossom, or the bole?
O body swayed to music, O brightening glance,
How can we know the dancer from the dance?

1926

5. Yeats's note to this poem recalls the Greek
scholar Porphyry (ca. 234–305), who associates
"honey" with "the pleasure arising from copulation" that engenders children; the poet further
describes honey as a drug that destroys the
child's "'recollection' of pre-natal freedom."
6. Greek philosophers. Plato (427–337 B.C.E.)
believed that nature was a series of illusionistic
reflections or appearances cast by abstract

"forms" that were the true realities. Aristotle
(384–322 B.C.E.), more pragmatic, was Alexander the Great's tutor and spanked him with
the "taws" (leather straps). Pythagoras (582–
407 B.C.E.), a demigod to his disciples and
thought to have a golden thigh bone, pondered
the relationship between music, mathematics,
and the stars.

Byzantium[1]

The unpurged images of day recede;
The Emperor's drunken soldiery are abed;
Night resonance recedes, night-walkers' song
After great cathedral gong;
A starlit or a moonlit dome[2] disdains   5
All that man is,
All mere complexities,
The fury and the mire of human veins.

Before me floats an image, man or shade,
Shade more than man, more image than a shade;   10
For Hades' bobbin bound in mummy-cloth
May unwind the winding path;[3]
A mouth that has no moisture and no breath
Breathless mouths may summon;
I hail the superhuman;   15
I call it death-in-life and life-in-death.

Miracle, bird or golden handiwork,
More miracle than bird or handiwork,
Planted on the starlit golden bough,
Can like the cocks of Hades crow,[4]   20
Or, by the moon embittered, scorn aloud
In glory of changeless metal
Common bird or petal
And all complexities of mire or blood.

At midnight on the Emperor's pavement flit   25
Flames that no faggot feeds, nor steel has lit,
Nor storm disturbs, flames begotten of flame,
Where blood-begotten spirits come
And all complexities of fury leave,
Dying into a dance,   30
An agony of trance,
An agony of flame that cannot singe a sleeve.

Astraddle on the dolphin's[5] mire and blood,
Spirit after spirit! The smithies break the flood,

1. The holy city of "Sailing to Byzantium" (p. 526), seen here as it resists and transforms the blood and mire of human life into its own transcendent world of art.
2. According to Yeats's system in *A Vision* (1925), the first "starlit" phase in which the moon does not shine and the fifteenth, opposing phase of the full moon represent complete objectivity (potential being) and complete subjectivity (the achievement of complete beauty). In between these absolute phases lie the evolving "mere complexities" of human life.

3. Unwinding the spool of fate that leads from mortal death to the superhuman. "Hades": the realm of the dead in Greek mythology.
4. To mark the transition from death to the dawn of new life.
5. A dolphin rescued the famous singer Arion by carrying him on his back over the sea. Dolphins were associated with Apollo, Greek god of music and prophecy, and in ancient art they are often shown escorting the souls of the dead to the Isles of the Blessed. Here, the dolphin is also flesh and blood, a part of life.

The golden smithies of the Emperor!   35
Marbles of the dancing floor
Break bitter furies of complexity,
Those images that yet
Fresh images beget,
That dolphin-torn, that gong-tormented sea.   40

                                                            1930

Lapis Lazuli[1]

For Harry Clifton

I have heard that hysterical women say
They are sick of the palette and fiddle-bow,
Of poets that are always gay,
For everybody knows or else should know
That if nothing drastic is done   5
Aeroplane and Zeppelin will come out,
Pitch like King Billy[2] bomb-balls in
Until the town lie beaten flat.
All perform their tragic play,
There struts Hamlet, there is Lear,   10
That's Ophelia, that Cordelia;[3]
Yet they, should the last scene be there,
The great stage curtain about to drop,
If worthy their prominent part in the play,
Do not break up their lines to weep.   15
They know that Hamlet and Lear are gay;
Gaiety transfiguring all that dread.
All men have aimed at, found and lost;
Black out; Heaven blazing into the head:[4]
Tragedy wrought to its uttermost.   20
Though Hamlet rambles and Lear rages,
And all the drop-scenes drop at once
Upon a hundred thousand stages,
It cannot grow by an inch or an ounce.

On their own feet they came, or on shipboard,   25
Camel-back, horse-back, ass-back, mule-back,

1. A deep blue semiprecious stone. One of Yeats's letters (to Dorothy Wellesley, July 6, 1935) describes a Chinese carving in lapis lazuli that depicts an ascetic and pupil about to climb a mountain: "Ascetic, pupil, hard stone, eternal theme of the sensual east . . . the east has its solutions always and therefore knows nothing of tragedy."
2. A linkage of past and present. According to an Irish ballad, King William III of England "threw his bomb-balls in" and set fire to the tents of the deposed James II at the Battle of the Boyne in 1690. Also a reference to Kaiser Wilhelm II (King William II) of Germany, who sent zeppelins to bomb London during World War I. "Zeppelin": a long, cylindrical airship, supported by internal gas chambers.
3. Tragic figures in Shakespeare's plays.
4. The loss of rational consciousness making way for the blaze of inner revelation or "mad" tragic vision. Also suggests the final curtain and an air raid curfew.

Old civilisations put to the sword.
Then they and their wisdom went to rack:
No handiwork of Callimachus[5]
Who handled marble as if it were bronze,   30
Made draperies that seemed to rise
When sea-wind swept the corner, stands;
His long lamp-chimney shaped like the stem
Of a slender palm, stood but a day;
All things fall and are built again,   35
And those that build them again are gay.
Two Chinamen, behind them a third,
Are carved in Lapis Lazuli,
Over them flies a long-legged bird,[6]
A symbol of longevity;   40
The third, doubtless a serving-man,
Carries a musical instrument.

Every discoloration of the stone,
Every accidental crack or dent,
Seems a water-course or an avalanche,   45
Or lofty slope where it still snows
Though doubtless plum or cherry-branch
Sweetens the little half-way house
Those Chinamen climb towards, and I
Delight to imagine them seated there;   50
There, on the mountain and the sky,
On all the tragic scene they stare.
One asks for mournful melodies;
Accomplished fingers begin to play.
Their eyes mid many wrinkles, their eyes,   55
Their ancient, glittering eyes, are gay.

                                                    1938

The Circus Animals' Desertion

I

I sought a theme and sought for it in vain,
I sought it daily for six weeks or so.
Maybe at last, being but a broken man,
I must be satisfied with my heart, although
Winter and summer till old age began   5
My circus animals were all on show,
Those stilted boys, that burnished chariot,
Lion and woman[1] and the Lord knows what.

---

5. Athenian sculptor (5th century B.C.E.), famous for a gold lamp in the Erechtheum (temple on the Acropolis) and for using drill lines in marble to give the effect of flowing drapery.

6. A crane.
1. Yeats enumerates images and themes from his earlier work; here, the sphinx of "The Double Vision of Michael Robartes."

2

What can I but enumerate old themes?
First that sea-rider Oisin led by the nose   10
Through three enchanted islands, allegorical dreams,[2]
Vain gaiety, vain battle, vain repose,
Themes of the embittered heart, or so it seems,
That might adorn old songs or courtly shows;
But what cared I that set him on to ride,   15
I, starved for the bosom of his faery bride?

And then a counter-truth filled out its play,
The Countess Cathleen[3] was the name I gave it;
She, pity-crazed, had given her soul away,
But masterful Heaven had intervened to save it.   20
I thought my dear must her own soul destroy,
So did fanaticism and hate enslave it,
And this brought forth a dream and soon enough
This dream itself had all my thought and love.

And when the Fool and Blind Man stole the bread   25
Cuchulain[4] fought the ungovernable sea;
Heart-mysteries there, and yet when all is said
It was the dream itself enchanted me:
Character isolated by a deed
To engross the present and dominate memory.   30
Players and painted stage took all my love,
And not those things that they were emblems of.

3

Those masterful images because complete
Grew in pure mind, but out of what began?
A mound of refuse or the sweepings of a street,   35
Old kettles, old bottles, and a broken can,
Old iron, old bones, old rags, that raving slut
Who keeps the till. Now that my ladder's gone,
I must lie down where all the ladders start,
In the foul rag-and-bone shop of the heart.   40

1939

2. In "The Wanderings of Oisin" (1889), an early poem in which Yeats describes a legendary Irish hero who wandered in fairyland for 150 years.
3. A play (1892), dedicated to Maud Gonne, in which the countess is saved by heaven after having sold her soul to the devil in exchange for food for the poor. The figure of Cathleen comes up frequently in Yeats's work and is often taken as a personification of nationalist Ireland.
4. A legendary Irish hero. Yeats is referring to the play On Baile's Strand (1904).

RAINER MARIA RILKE
1875–1926

In his intensely personal quest to understand the "great mysteries" of the universe, Rilke asks questions that we ordinarily think of as religious. Whether his gaze turns toward earth, which he describes with extraordinary clarity and affection, or toward a higher realm whose enigmas remain to be deciphered, he seeks a comprehensive vision of cosmic unity. Rilke's sharply focused yet visionary lyricism made him the best-known and most influential German poet of the twentieth century.

Born in Prague on December 4, 1875, to German-speaking parents who separated when he was nine, Rilke had an unhappy childhood. His mother dressed him as a girl to compensate for the earlier loss of a baby daughter; as a teenager he was sent to military academies, where he was lonely and miserable. After a year in business school, he worked in his uncle's law firm and studied at the University of Prague. His heart was already set on a literary career, however, and between his work and his studies, he stole enough time to publish two books of poetry and write plays, stories, and reviews. In 1897 he moved to Munich and fell in love with the married psychoanalyst Lou Andreas-Salomé, who would be an influence on him throughout his life. Accompanying Andreas-Salomé and her husband to Russia in 1899, Rilke met **Leo Tolstoy** and Boris Pasternak and—swayed by Russian mysticism and the Russian landscape—wrote some of his first successful poems. Rilke met his future wife, the sculptor Clara Westhoff, when the two were living in the artists' colony Worpswede, in northern Germany; they soon separated, and Rilke moved to Paris to begin a book on the sculptor Rodin. In Paris the German poet encountered an unexpected kind of literary and artistic inspiration. In Rodin, who became his friend, Rilke found a dedication to the technical demands of his craft; an intense concentration on visible, tangible objects; and, above all, a belief in art as an essentially religious activity. Rilke was also struck by the poetry of **Charles Baudelaire**. Although he wrote in distress to Lou Andreas-Salomé, complaining of nightmares and a sense of failure, it is at this time (and with her encouragement) that Rilke launched his major work. The anguished, semiautobiographical spiritual confessions of *The Notebook of Malte Laurids Brigge* (1910) date from this period, as do *New Poems* (1907–08), in which the writer develops a symbolic vision focused on objects.

When a patron, Princess Marie von Thurn und Taxis-Hohenlohe, proposed that he stay by himself in her castle at Duino, near Trieste, during the winter of 1911–12, Rilke found the quiet and isolation that he needed as a writer. Walking on the rocks above the sea and puzzling over his answer to a bothersome business letter, Rilke seemed to hear in the roar of the wind the first lines of an elegy: "Who, if I cried out, would hear me among the angels' / hierarchies?" By February he had written two elegies, and when he left Duino Castle in May, he had conceived the cycle and written fragments of four other elegies, which would eventually be published in the sequence of ten poems called the *Duino Elegies* (1923). (An elegy is a mournful lyric poem, usually a lament for loss.) Drafted into the German army during the First World War, Rilke spent his days drawing precise vertical and horizontal lines on paper for the War Archives Office in Vienna. Released from military service in 1916, he produced few poems and feared that he would never be able to complete the Duino sequence. In 1922, however, a friend's purchase of the tiny Château de Muzot in Switzerland gave him a peaceful place to retire to and write. Not only did he complete the *Duino Elegies* in Muzot; he also wrote—as a memorial for the young daughter of a friend—a two-part sequence of fifty-five sonnets, *Sonnets to Orpheus* (1922). Affirming the essential unity of life and death, Rilke closed his two complementary sequences ("the little rust-colored sail of the Sonnets and the Elegies' gigantic white canvas") and wrote little—chiefly poems in French—over the next few years. Increasingly ill with leukemia, he died on December 29, 1926, as the result of an infection after pricking himself on roses he cut for a friend in his garden.

The five selections from *New Poems* (1907–08) printed here demonstrate Rilke's visual imagination of his "thing-poems" (*Dinggedichte*). *New Poems* emphasizes physical reality, the absolute otherness and "thing-like" nature of what is observed—be it fountain, panther, flower, human being, or the "Archaic Torso of Apollo." A letter to Andreas-Salomé describes the poet's sense that ancient art objects take on a peculiar luster once they are detached from history and are seen as "things" in and for themselves: "No subject matter is attached to

them, no irrelevant voice interrupts the silence of their concentrated reality . . . no history casts a shadow over their naked clarity—: they *are*. That is all . . . one day one of them reveals itself to you, and shines like a first star." Such "things" are not dead or inanimate but supremely alive, filled with a strange vitality before the poet's glance: the charged sexuality of the marble torso, the caged panther padding around his prison, and the metamorphosis of the Spanish dancer. Faced with a physical presence that transcends words, the viewer is challenged on an existential level. The "archaic torso of Apollo" is not a living being but an ancient Greek sculpture on display in the Louvre Museum in Paris. This headless marble is truly a "thing": a lifeless, even defaced chunk of stone. Yet such is the perfection of its luminous sensuality—derived, the speaker suggests, from the brilliant gaze of its missing head and "ripening" eyes—that it seems alive, and an inner radiance bursts starlike from the marble. The torso puts to shame the observer's puny existence, demanding: "You must change your life."

In his poetry Rilke is haunted by the incompleteness of human experience and by the passage of time. His response is to turn to art to draw objects into a "human" world, infusing them with ideas, emotions, and value. The poet's role, according to Rilke, is to observe with renewed sensitivity "this fleeting world, which in some strange way / keeps calling to us," and to bear witness, by means of language, to the transfiguration of its materiality through human emotions.

From NEW POEMS[1]

Archaic Torso of Apollo[2]

We cannot know his legendary head[3]
with eyes like ripening fruit. And yet his torso
is still suffused with brilliance from inside,
like a lamp, in which his gaze, now turned to low,

gleams in all its power. Otherwise   5
the curved breast could not dazzle you so, nor could
a smile run through the placid hips and thighs
to that dark center where procreation flared.

Otherwise this stone would seem defaced
beneath the translucent cascade of the shoulders   10
and would not glisten like a wild beast's fur:

would not, from all the borders of itself,
burst like a star: for here there is no place
that does not see you. You must change your life.

1908

The Panther

In the Jardin des Plantes,[1] *Paris*

His vision, from the constantly passing bars,
has grown so weary that it cannot hold
anything else. It seems to him there are
a thousand bars; and behind the bars, no world.

As he paces in cramped circles, over and over,   5
the movement of his powerful soft strides
is like a ritual dance around a center
in which a mighty will stands paralyzed.

---

1. All selections are translated by Stephen Mitchell.
2. The first poem in the second volume of Rilke's *New Poems* (1908), which were dedicated "to my good friend, Auguste Rodin" (the French sculptor, 1840–1917, whose secretary Rilke was for a brief period and on whom he wrote two monographs, in 1903 and 1907). The poem itself was inspired by an ancient Greek statue discovered at Miletus (a Greek colony on the coast of Asia Minor) that was called simply the *Torso of a Youth from Miletus;* since the god Apollo was an ideal of youthful male beauty, his name was often associated with such statues.
3. In a torso, the head and limbs are missing.
1. A zoo in Paris. Rilke also admired, at Rodin's studio, the plaster cast of an ancient statue of a panther.

Only at times, the curtain of the pupils
lifts, quietly—. An image enters in,   10
rushes down through the tensed, arrested muscles,
plunges into the heart and is gone.

                                                              1907

The Swan

This laboring through what is still undone,
as though, legs bound, we hobbled along the way,
is like the awkward walking of the swan.

And dying—to let go, no longer feel
the solid ground we stand on every day—   5
is like his anxious letting himself fall

into the water, which receives him gently
and which, as though with reverence and joy,
draws back past him in streams on either side;
while, infinitely silent and aware,   10
in his full majesty and ever more
indifferent, he condescends to glide.

                                                              1907

Spanish Dancer[1]

As on all its sides a kitchen-match darts white
flickering tongues before it bursts into flame:
with the audience around her, quickened, hot,
her dance begins to flicker in the dark room.

And all at once it is completely fire.   5

One upward glance and she ignites her hair
and, whirling faster and faster, fans her dress
into passionate flames, till it becomes a furnace
from which, like startled rattlesnakes, the long
naked arms uncoil, aroused and clicking.[2]   10

And then: as if the fire were too tight
around her body, she takes and flings it out
haughtily, with an imperious gesture,

1. The dance described is the flamenco (from   rhythmic clicking of castanets (worn on the
flamear, "to flame").   fingers).
2. The dancer accompanies herself with the

and watches: it lies raging on the floor,
still blazing up, and the flames refuse to die—. 15
Till, moving with total confidence and a sweet
exultant smile, she looks up finally
and stamps it out with powerful small feet.

1907

T. S. ELIOT
1888–1965

Thomas Stearns Eliot had a unique role in defining modernist taste and style. As a poet and as a literary critic, he rejected the narrative, moralizing, frequently "noble" style of late Victorian poetry, instead employing highly focused, startling images and an elliptical, ironic voice that has had enormous impact on modern poetry throughout the world. Readers in far-flung regions who know nothing of Eliot's other works are likely to be familiar with *The Waste Land* (1922), a literary-historical landmark representing the cultural crisis in Europe after the First World War. Although Eliot did not consider himself a generational icon, his challenging, quirky, memorable poetry is indissolubly linked with the spiritual and intellectual crises of modernism.

Two countries, England and the United States, claim Eliot as part of their national literature. Although Eliot was born in St. Louis, the Eliots were a distinguished New England family; Eliot's grandfather had gone west to found Washington University in St. Louis. Eliot attended Harvard (where his father's cousin was president of the university) for his undergraduate and graduate education. There he found literary models that would feed his work in future years: the poetry of Dante and John Donne, and the plays of Elizabethan and Jacobean dramatists. In 1908, Eliot read Arthur Symons's *The Symbolist Movement in Literature* and became acquainted with the French Symbolist poets, whose richly allusive images—and highly self-conscious, ironic, and craftsmanlike technique—he would adopt as his own. He began writing poetry while still in college and published his first major work, "The Love Song of J. Alfred Prufrock," in *Poetry* magazine in 1915.

At twenty-two he left for Europe to study at Oxford and the Sorbonne; the outbreak of the First World War prevented him from returning to Harvard, where he intended to continue graduate study in philosophy. Nonetheless, he completed a doctoral dissertation on the philosopher F. H. Bradley, whose examination of private consciousness became a theme of Eliot's later essays and poems. Settling in England, Eliot married, taught briefly, and worked for several years in the foreign department of Lloyd's Bank. Unhappy in his marriage and under pressure in his job at the bank, Eliot suffered from writer's block and then had a breakdown soon after the First World War. He wrote most of *The Waste Land* (1922) while recovering in a sanatorium in Lausanne, Switzerland. It was immediately hailed as one of the most important poems of the modernist movement and an expression of the postwar sense of social crisis. Already well known for his essays, collected in *The Sacred Wood* (1920), and his editorial work for the literary journals *The Egoist* and *The Criterion*, Eliot left Lloyd's for a position with the publishing firm Faber & Faber.

Raised an American Unitarian, Eliot joined the Church of England in 1927 and became a naturalized British subject the same year. He continued to write poetry, and also turned to drama, composing a verse play on the death of the English St. Thomas à Becket (*Murder in the Cathedral*, 1935) as well as more conventional stage plays, *The Family Reunion* (1939), which recasts the Orestes story from Greek tragedy, and *The Cocktail Party* (1949), a drawing-room comedy that explores the search for salvation. During this time, Eliot became increasingly conservative in his political attitudes; the anti-Semitic remarks in his speeches and poems from this period have tarnished his reputation. By the time he received the Nobel Prize for Literature, in 1948, however, Eliot was recognized as a major contemporary writer in English. For such an influential poet, his output was relatively small; but in addition to writing some of the greatest verse of the twentieth century and essays that shaped literary opinion, he nurtured many younger writers as a director at Faber & Faber. Despite his social, political, and religious conservatism, Eliot ushered in the revolution in literary form known as modernism.

The selection here includes three of Eliot's major poems from different phases of his career. "The Love Song of J. Alfred Prufrock," begun while Eliot was in college and published in 1915, displays the evocative yet confounding images, abrupt shifts in focus, and combination of human sympathy and ironic wit that would attract and puzzle readers of his later works. Clearly Prufrock's dramatic monologue aims to startle readers—by bidding them, in the opening lines, to imagine the evening spread out "like a patient etherised upon a table," and by shifting focus abruptly among metaphysical questions, drawing-room chatter, imaginary landscapes, and literary and biblical allusions. Tones of high seriousness jar against banal and even singsong speech: "I grow old . . . I grow old . . . / I shall wear the bottoms of my trousers rolled." The stanzas of "Prufrock" are individual scenes, each with a stylistic coherence (for example, the third stanza's yellow fog as a cat). Together, they create a symbolic landscape that unfolds in the narrator's mind as a combination of factual observation and subjective feelings. In its discontinuity, its precise yet evocative imagery, its mixture of romantic and everyday reference, and its formal and conversational speech, as well as in the complex and ironic self-consciousness of its very unheroic hero, "The Love Song of J. Alfred Prufrock" anticipates the modernist traits typical of Eliot's larger corpus. Also anticipating Eliot's later work are the theme of spiritual void and the disoriented protagonist helpless to cope with a crisis that is as much the face of modern Western culture as of his personal tragedy.

Eliot dedicated *The Waste Land* (1922), the next selection, to his friend, fellow poet, and editor Ezra Pound, with a quotation from Dante that praises the "better craftsman." Quotations from, or allusions to, a vast range of sources—including Shakespeare, Dante, **Charles Baudelaire**, Richard Wagner, Ovid, St. Augustine, Buddhist sermons, folk songs, and the anthropologists Jessie Weston and James Frazer—punctuate this lengthy work, to which Eliot added explanatory notes when it appeared in book form. A poem that depicts society in a time of cultural and spiritual crisis, *The Waste Land* juxtaposes images of the fragmentation of modern experience, on the one hand, and references (some in foreign languages) to a more stable heritage, on the other. The classical prophet Tiresias is contrasted to the contemporary charlatan Madame Sosostris; the celebrated lovers Antony and Cleopatra, to a real estate agent's clerk who mechanically seduces a bored typist at the end of her workday; Buddhist sermons and the religious visions of St. Augustine, to a sterile world of rock and dust where "one can neither stand nor lie nor sit." Throughout the poem runs a series of oblique allusions to the legend of a knight passing trials in a Chapel Perilous and healing a Fisher King by asking the right questions about the Holy Grail and the Holy Lance. The implication is that the modern wasteland might be redeemed if its inhabitants learned to answer (or perhaps to ask) the appropriate questions. These and other references that Eliot integrates into the poem constitute, the speaker says, "fragments I have shored against my ruins"—pieces of a puzzle whose resolution might bring "shantih," or the peace that passeth understanding but that remains enigmatically out of reach, as the poem's final lines in a mosaic of foreign languages suggest.

The groundbreaking technical innovation in *The Waste Land* is the deliberate use of fragmentation and discontinuity. Eliot pointedly refused to provide transitional passages or narrative thread, relying on the reader to construct a pattern whose implications would make sense as a whole. The writer's approach represents a direct attack on the conventional experience of the written word; the poem undercuts readers' expectations of linearity by inserting unexplained literary references, sudden shifts

in scene or perspective, interpolations of foreign language, and changes of verbal register from lofty diction to slang. Eliot's refusal to fulfill traditional expectations serves several functions: it contributes to the poem's picture of cultural disintegration; it allows Eliot to exploit the Symbolist or allusive powers of language, since the diction rather than the narrative content must carry the burden of meaning; and by drawing attention to itself as a technique, it exemplifies modernist self-reflexive, or self-conscious, style.

As its title suggests, *Four Quartets*, from which the last selection, "Little Gidding," is taken, is divided into parts much like the movements of a musical quartet. Each part has five sections, within which themes are introduced, developed, and resolved. Each part bears the title of a place: "Little Gidding" is the name of a village in Huntingdonshire, England, that was home to a seventeenth-century Anglican Catholic religious community. In Eliot's day only a chapel (rebuilt after the English Civil Wars) remained. All of the quartets use varying forms of free verse, ranging from intense, short lyrics to— for the first time in Eliot's poetry— continuous narrative passages of the kind the poet once disdained. Throughout, the speaker ponders the relationship between historical transformation and eternal order.

"Little Gidding" incorporates Eliot's experiences, in the Second World War, as a watchman checking for fires during bombing raids; the chapel in the village serves as the point of departure for a meditation on what strife and change mean in a universe that the mind strives to structure, always imperfectly, by the timeless truths of religion. The quartet opens with a section that is itself divided into three movements: the season of "midwinter spring," with the sun blazing on ice; the chapel as the goal of pilgrimage in any season; and the chapel as a place that prayer has so consecrated that within its locus, the dead may communicate with the living. The lyrics that open the second section mourn the chapel's present decay by the four elements of earth, air, fire, and water, and progress to an imaginary conversation between the speaker (wandering after the last bomb and before the all-clear signal) and an anonymous "dead master." The mood is pessimistic, and the dead master (a "compound ghost" who contains aspects of Eliot, the Virgil of Dante's *Divine Comedy*, and **W. B. Yeats**) prophesies, for the speaker, a bitter old age full of remorse and impotent rage at human folly. (Their conversation suggests a comparison with Dante's *Inferno*, for it echoes the triple-line stanzaic form of *The Divine Comedy* and recalls the Italian poet's encounter with his former master, Brunetto Latini, in Hell [*Inferno* 15.22–124].) Yet the poem's final movement points toward a resolution that takes place out of time. The third section's opening rhetoric of logical persuasion ("There are three conditions") introduces the notion that memory expands our perspectives and enables us to transcend the narrow commitments of history and civil war (both private and public). The fourth section's intense lyrics propose that the flames of the annunciatory dove (or bomb) may represent purgation as well as destruction. In the final section, as the afternoon fades, the speaker ends his meditation on time and eternity by asserting his faith in a condition of mind and spirit that combines both *now* and *always*—a transcendental vision that is both a "condition of complete simplicity" and "crowned knot of fire."

The poem's conclusion is thus a religious one, moving from the agony of history to an eternal, purifying flame, perhaps recalling a similar mystic vision of all-penetrating light that closes Dante's *Paradiso*. It may seem paradoxical that the poet whom posterity knows best for expressing the dilemma of modern consciousness and for developing a poetic style appropriate to a specifically twentieth-century experience should resolve that experience in a metaphor of transcendence. Yet from his earliest work, Eliot was preoccupied with the spiritual implications of mundane reality. His yoking of the concrete with transcendental vision defines the range and depth of his modernist style.

Eliot's early essays on literature and literary history helped to bring about a different understanding of poetry, which afterward was no longer seen as the expression of personal feeeling but as a carefully made aesthetic object. Yet much of Eliot's impact was not merely formal but spiritual and philosophical. The search for meaning that pervades his work created a lasting picture of the barrenness of modern culture and of the search for alternatives. But while many later poets rejected Eliot's religious beliefs, they found inspiration in his expression of the dilemmas facing an anxious and infinitely vulnerable modern soul.

The Love Song of J. Alfred Prufrock

S'io credessi che mia risposta fosse
a persona che mai tornasse al mondo,
questa fiamma staria senza più scosse.
Ma per ciò che giammai di questo fondo
non tornò vivo alcun, s'i'odo il vero,
senza tema d'infamia ti rispondo.[1]

Let us go then, you and I,
When the evening is spread out against the sky
Like a patient etherised upon a table;
Let us go, through certain half-deserted streets,
The muttering retreats   5
Of restless nights in one-night cheap hotels
And sawdust restaurants with oyster-shells:
Streets that follow like a tedious argument
Of insidious intent
To lead you to an overwhelming question . . .   10
Oh, do not ask, "What is it?"
Let us go and make our visit.

    In the room the women come and go
Talking of Michelangelo.[2]

    The yellow fog that rubs its back upon the window-panes,   15
The yellow smoke that rubs its muzzle on the window-panes
Licked its tongue into the corners of the evening,
Lingered upon the pools that stand in drains,
Let fall upon its back the soot that falls from chimneys,
Slipped by the terrace, made a sudden leap,   20
And seeing that it was a soft October night,
Curled once about the house, and fell asleep.

    And indeed there will be time[3]
For the yellow smoke that slides along the street,
Rubbing its back upon the window-panes;   25
There will be time, there will be time
To prepare a face to meet the faces that you meet;
There will be time to murder and create,
And time for all the works and days of hands[4]

1. From Dante's *Inferno* 27.61–66, in which the false counselor Guido da Montefeltro, enveloped in flame, explains that he would never reveal his past if he thought the traveler could report it: "If I thought my reply were meant for one / who ever could return into the world, / this flame would stir no more; and yet, since none— / if what I hear is true—ever returned / alive from this abyss, then without fear / of facing infamy, I answer you."
2. Michelangelo Buonarroti (1475–1564),

famous Italian Renaissance sculptor, painter, architect, and poet; here, merely a topic of fashionable conversation.
3. Echo of a love poem by Andrew Marvell (1621–1678), *To His Coy Mistress*: "Had we but world enough and time."
4. An implied contrast with the more productive agricultural labor of hands in the *Works and Days* of the Greek poet Hesiod (8th century B.C.E.).

That lift and drop a question on your plate; 30
Time for you and time for me,
And time yet for a hundred indecisions,
And for a hundred visions and revisions,
Before the taking of a toast and tea.

    In the room the women come and go 35
Talking of Michelangelo.

    And indeed there will be time
To wonder, "Do I dare?" and, "Do I dare?"
Time to turn back and descend the stair,
With a bald spot in the middle of my hair— 40
(They will say: "How his hair is growing thin!")
My morning coat, my collar mounting firmly to the chin,
My necktie rich and modest, but asserted by a simple pin—
(They will say: "But how his arms and legs are thin!")
Do I dare 45
Disturb the universe?
In a minute there is time
For decisions and revisions which a minute will reverse.

    For I have known them all already, known them all—
Have known the evenings, mornings, afternoons, 50
I have measured out my life with coffee spoons;
I know the voices dying with a dying fall[5]
Beneath the music from a farther room.
    So how should I presume?

    And I have known the eyes already, known them all— 55
The eyes that fix you in a formulated phrase,
And when I am formulated, sprawling on a pin,
When I am pinned and wriggling on the wall,
Then how should I begin
To spit out all the butt-ends of my days and ways? 60
    And how should I presume?

    And I have known the arms already, known them all—
Arms that are braceleted and white and bare
(But in the lamplight, downed with light brown hair!)
Is it perfume from a dress 65
That makes me so digress?
Arms that lie along a table, or wrap about a shawl.
    And should I then presume?
    And how should I begin?

*   *   *

5. Recalls Duke Orsino's description of a musical phrase in Shakespeare's *Twelfth Night* (1.1.4):
"It has a dying fall."

Shall I say, I have gone at dusk through narrow streets   70
And watched the smoke that rises from the pipes
Of lonely men in shirt-sleeves, leaning out of windows? . . .

I should have been a pair of ragged claws
Scuttling across the floors of silent seas.

. . .

And the afternoon, the evening, sleeps so peacefully!   75
Smoothed by long fingers,
Asleep . . . tired . . . or it malingers,
Stretched on the floor, here beside you and me.
Should I, after tea and cakes and ices,
Have the strength to force the moment to its crisis?   80
But though I have wept and fasted, wept and prayed,
Though I have seen my head (grown slightly bald) brought in
        upon a platter,
I am no prophet[6]—and here's no great matter;
I have seen the moment of my greatness flicker,
And I have seen the eternal Footman hold my coat, and snicker,   85
And in short, I was afraid.

And would it have been worth it, after all,
After the cups, the marmalade, the tea,
Among the porcelain, among some talk of you and me,
Would it have been worth while,   90
To have bitten off the matter with a smile,
To have squeezed the universe into a ball
To roll it toward some overwhelming question,[7]
To say: "I am Lazarus, come from the dead,[8]
Come back to tell you all, I shall tell you all"—   95
If one, settling a pillow by her head,
        Should say: "That is not what I meant at all.
        That is not it, at all."

And would it have been worth it, after all,
Would it have been worth while,   100
After the sunsets and the dooryards and the sprinkled streets,
After the novels, after the teacups, after the skirts that trail along
        the floor—
And this, and so much more?—
It is impossible to say just what I mean!
But as if a magic lantern[9] threw the nerves in patterns on a screen: 105
Would it have been worth while
If one, settling a pillow or throwing off a shawl,

6. Salome obtained the head of the prophet John the Baptist on a platter as a reward for dancing before the tetrarch Herod (Matthew 14.3–11).
7. Another echo of Marvell's "To His Coy Mistress," when the lover suggests rolling "all our

strength and all / our sweetness up into one ball" to send against the "iron gates of life."
8. The story of Lazarus, raised from the dead, is told in John 11.1–44.
9. A slide projector.

And turning toward the window, should say:
    "That is not it at all,
    That is not what I meant, at all."   110

                    •   •   •

        No! I am not Prince Hamlet, nor was meant to be;
Am an attendant lord, one that will do
To swell a progress,[1] start a scene or two,
Advise the prince; no doubt, an easy tool,
Deferential, glad to be of use,   115
Politic, cautious, and meticulous;
Full of high sentence, but a bit obtuse;
At times, indeed, almost ridiculous—
Almost, at times, the Fool.

        I grow old . . . I grow old . . .   120
I shall wear the bottoms of my trousers rolled.

        Shall I part my hair behind? Do I dare to eat a peach?
I shall wear white flannel trousers, and walk upon the beach.
I have heard the mermaids singing, each to each.

I do not think that they will sing to me.   125

        I have seen them riding seaward on the waves
Combing the white hair of the waves blown back
When the wind blows the water white and black.

        We have lingered in the chambers of the sea
By sea-girls wreathed with seaweed red and brown   130
Till human voices wake us, and we drown.

                                                        1915

The Waste Land[1]

"Nam Sibyllam quidem Cumis ego ipse oculis meis vidi in ampulla
pendere, et cum illi pueri dicerent: Σίβυλλα τί θέλεισ; respondebat
illa: αποθανεῖν θέλω."[2]

1. A procession of attendants accompanying a
king or nobleman across the stage, as in Elizabethan drama.
1. Eliot provided footnotes for *The Waste
Land* when it was first published in book form;
these notes are included here. A general note
at the beginning referred readers to the religious symbolism described in Jessie L.
Weston's study of the Grail legend, *From Ritual to Romance* (1920), and to fertility myths
and vegetation ceremonies (especially those

involving Adonis, Attis, and Osiris) as described
in the *The Golden Bough* (1890–1918) by the
anthropologist Sir James Frazer.
2. Lines from Petronius's *Satyricon* (ca. 60 C.E.)
describing the Sibyl, a prophetess shriveled
with age and suspended in a bottle. "For indeed
I myself have seen with my own eyes the Sibyl
at Cumae, hanging in a bottle, and when those
boys would say to her: 'Sibyl, what do you
want?' she would reply: 'I want to die.'"

For Ezra Pound
il miglior fabbro.[3]

1. The Burial of the Dead[4]

April is the cruellest month, breeding
Lilacs out of the dead land, mixing
Memory and desire, stirring
Dull roots with spring rain.
Winter kept us warm, covering   5
Earth in forgetful snow, feeding
A little life with dried tubers.
Summer surprised us, coming over the Starnbergersee[5]
With a shower of rain; we stopped in the colonnade,
And went on in sunlight, into the Hofgarten,[6]   10
And drank coffee, and talked for an hour.
Bin gar keine Russin, stamm' aus Litauen, echt deutsch.[7]
And when we were children, staying at the arch-duke's,
My cousin's, he took me out on a sled,
And I was frightened. He said, Marie,   15
Marie, hold on tight. And down we went.[8]
In the mountains, there you feel free.
I read, much of the night, and go south in the winter.

What are the roots that clutch, what branches grow
Out of this stony rubbish? Son of man,[9]   20
You cannot say, or guess, for you know only
A heap of broken images, where the sun beats,
And the dead tree gives no shelter, the cricket no relief,[1]
And the dry stone no sound of water. Only
There is shadow under this red rock,   25
(Come in under the shadow of this red rock),
And I will show you something different from either
Your shadow at morning striding behind you
Or your shadow at evening rising to meet you;
I will show you fear in a handful of dust.   30
            Frisch weht der Wind
            Der Heimat zu

---

3. The dedication to Pound, who suggested cuts and changes in the first manuscript of *The Waste Land*, borrows words used by Guido Guinizelli to describe his predecessor, the Provençal poet Arnaut Daniel, in Dante's *Purgatorio* (26.117): he is "the better craftsman."
4. From the burial service of the Anglican Church.
5. A lake near Munich.
6. A public park.
7. "I am certainly no Russian, I come from Lithuania and am pure German." German set-

tlers in Lithuania considered themselves superior to the Baltic natives.
8. Lines 8–16 recall *My Past*, the memoirs of Countess Marie Larisch.
9. "Cf. Ezekiel II, i" [Eliot's note]. The passage reads "Son of man, stand upon thy feet, and I will speak unto thee."
1. "Cf. Ecclesiastes XII, v" [Eliot's note]. "Also when they shall be afraid of that which is high, and fears shall be in the way, . . . the grasshopper shall be a burden, and desire shall fail."

Mein Irisch Kind,
Wo weilest du?[2]
"You gave me hyacinths first a year ago;   35
"They called me the hyacinth girl."
—Yet when we came back, late, from the hyacinth garden,
Your arms full, and your hair wet, I could not
Speak, and my eyes failed, I was neither
Living nor dead, and I knew nothing,   40
Looking into the heart of light, the silence.
Oed' und leer das Meer.[3]

    Madame Sosostris,[4] famous clairvoyante,
Had a bad cold, nevertheless
Is known to be the wisest woman in Europe,   45
With a wicked pack of cards.[5] Here, said she,
Is your card, the drowned Phoenician Sailor,
(Those are pearls that were his eyes.[6] Look!)
Here is Belladonna, the Lady of the Rocks,
The lady of situations.   50
Here is the man with three staves, and here the Wheel,
And here is the one-eyed merchant, and this card,
Which is blank, is something he carries on his back,
Which I am forbidden to see. I do not find
The Hanged Man. Fear death by water.   55
I see crowds of people, walking round in a ring.
Thank you. If you see dear Mrs. Equitone,
Tell her I bring the horoscope myself:
One must be so careful these days.

---

2. "V. *Tristan und Isolde*, I, verses 5–8" [Eliot's note]. A sailor in Richard Wagner's opera sings, "The wind blows fresh / Towards the homeland / My Irish child / Where are you waiting?" (German)
3. "Id. III, verse 24" [Eliot's note]. "Barren and empty is the sea" (German) is the erroneous report the dying Tristan hears as he waits for Isolde's ship in the third act of Wagner's opera.
4. A fortune-teller with an assumed Egyptian name, possibly suggested by a similar figure in a novel by Aldous Huxley (*Crome Yellow*, 1921).
5. "I am not familiar with the exact constitution of the Tarot pack of cards, from which I have obviously departed to suit my own convenience. The Hanged Man, a member of the traditional pack, fits my purpose in two ways: because he is associated in my mind with the Hanged God of Frazer, and because I associate him with the hooded figure in the passage of the disciples to Emmaus in Part V. The Phoenician Sailor and the Merchant appear later; also the 'crowds of people,' and Death by Water is executed in Part IV. The Man with

Three Staves (an authentic member of the Tarot pack) I associate, quite arbitrarily, with the Fisher King himself" [Eliot's note]. Tarot cards are used for telling fortunes; the four suits (cup, lance, sword, and coin) are life symbols related to the Grail legend; and, as Eliot suggests, various figures on the cards are associated with different characters and situations in *The Waste Land*. For example, the "drowned Phoenician Sailor" (line 47) recurs in the merchant from Smyrna (III) and Phlebas the Phoenician (IV). "Belladonna" (line 49)—a poison, hallucinogen, medicine, and cosmetic (in Italian, "beautiful lady"); also an echo of Leonardo da Vinci's painting of the Virgin, *Madonna of the Rocks*—heralds the neurotic society woman amid her jewels and perfumes (II). "The Wheel" (line 51) is the wheel of fortune. "The Hanged Man" (line 55) becomes the sacrificed fertility god whose death ensures resurrection and new life for his people.
6. A line from Ariel's song in Shakespeare's *The Tempest* (1.2.398), which describes the transformation of a drowned man.

Unreal City,[7]   60
Under the brown fog of a winter dawn,
A crowd flowed over London Bridge, so many,
I had not thought death had undone so many.[8]
Sighs, short and infrequent, were exhaled,[9]
And each man fixed his eyes before his feet.   65
Flowed up the hill and down King William Street,
To where Saint Mary Woolnoth kept the hours
With a dead sound on the final stroke of nine.[1]
There I saw one I knew, and stopped him, crying: "Stetson!
"You who were with me in the ships at Mylae![2]   70
"That corpse you planted last year in your garden,
"Has it begun to sprout? Will it bloom this year?
"Or has the sudden frost disturbed its bed?
"Oh keep the Dog far hence, that's friend to men,[3]
"Or with his nails he'll dig it up again!   75
"You! hypocrite lecteur!—mon semblable,—mon frère!"[4]

II. A Game of Chess[5]

The Chair she sat in, like a burnished throne,[6]
Glowed on the marble, where the glass

7. "Cf. Baudelaire: 'Fourmillante cité, cité pleine de rêves, / Où le spectre en plein jour raccroche le passant'" [Eliot's note]. "Swarming city, city full of dreams, / Where the specter in broad daylight accosts the passerby"; a description of Paris from "The Seven Old Men" in *The Flowers of Evil* (1857).

8. "Cf. *Inferno* III, 55–57: 'si lunga tratta / di gente, ch'io non avrei mai creduto / che morte tanta n' avesse disfatta'" [Eliot's note]. "Behind that banner trailed so long a file / of people—I should never have believed / that death could have unmade so many souls"; not only is Dante amazed at the number of people who have died but he is also describing a crowd of people who were neither good nor bad—non-entities denied even the entrance to hell.

9. "Cf. *Inferno* IV, 25–27: 'Quivi, secondo che per ascoltare, / non avea pianto, ma' che di sospiri, / che l'aura eterna facevan tremare'" [Eliot's note]. "Here, so far as I could tell by listening, there was no weeping but so many sighs that they caused the everlasting air to tremble"; the first circle of hell, or limbo, contained the souls of virtuous people who lived before Christ or had not been baptized.

1. "A phenomenon which I have often noticed" [Eliot's note]. The church is in the financial district of London, where King William Street is also located.

2. An "average" modern name (with business associations) linked to the ancient battle of Mylae (260 B.C.E.), where Rome was victorious over its commercial rival, Carthage.

3. "Cf. the Dirge in Webster's *White Devil*" [Eliot's note]. The dirge, or song of lamentation, sung by Cornelia in John Webster's play (1625), asks to "keep the wolf far thence, that's foe to men," so that the wolf's nails may not dig up the bodies of her murdered relatives. Eliot's reversal of dog for wolf, and friend for foe, domesticates the grotesque scene; it may also foreshadow rebirth since (according to Weston's book), the rise of the Dog Star, Sirius, announced the flooding of the Nile and the consequent return of fertility to Egyptian soil.

4. "V. Baudelaire, Preface to *Fleurs du Mal*" [Eliot's note]. Baudelaire's poem preface, titled "To the Reader," ended "Hypocritical reader!—my likeness!—my brother!" The poet challenges the reader to recognize that both are caught up in the worst sin of all—the moral wasteland of *ennui* ("boredom") as lack of will, the refusal to care one way or the other.

5. Reference to a play, *A Game of Chess* (1627) by Thomas Middleton (1580–1627); see n. 5, p. 2131. Part II juxtaposes two scenes of modern sterility: an initial setting of wealthy boredom, neurosis, and lack of communication, and a pub scene in which similar concerns of appearance, sexual attraction, and thwarted childbirth are brought out more visibly, and in more vulgar language.

6. "Cf. *Antony and Cleopatra*, II, ii, l.190" [Eliot's note]. A paler version of Cleopatra's splendor as she met her future lover, Antony: "The barge she sat in, like a burnished throne, / Burned on the water."

Held up by standards wrought with fruited vines
From which a golden Cupidon peeped out   80
(Another hid his eyes behind his wing)
Doubled the flames of sevenbranched candelabra
Reflecting light upon the table as
The glitter of her jewels rose to meet it,
From satin cases poured in rich profusion.   85
In vials of ivory and coloured glass
Unstoppered, lurked her strange synthetic perfumes,
Unguent, powdered, or liquid—troubled, confused
And drowned the sense in odours; stirred by the air
That freshened from the window, these ascended   90
In fattening the prolonged candle-flames,
Flung their smoke into the laquearia,[7]
Stirring the pattern on the coffered ceiling.
Huge sea-wood fed with copper
Burned green and orange, framed by the coloured stone,   95
In which sad light a carvèd dolphin swam.
Above the antique mantel was displayed
As though a window gave upon the sylvan scene[8]
The change of Philomel,[9] by the barbarous king
So rudely forced; yet there the nightingale[1]   100
Filled all the desert with inviolable voice
And still she cried, and still the world pursues,
"Jug Jug"[2] to dirty ears.
And other withered stumps of time
Were told upon the walls; staring forms   105
Leaned out, leaning, hushing the room enclosed.
Footsteps shuffled on the stair.
Under the firelight, under the brush, her hair
Spread out in fiery points
Glowed into words, then would be savagely still.   110

   'My nerves are bad to-night. Yes, bad. Stay with me.
'Speak to me. Why do you never speak. Speak.
   'What are you thinking of? What thinking? What?
'I never know what you are thinking. Think.'

   I think we are in rats' alley[3]   115
Where the dead men lost their bones.

---

7. "Laquearia. V. *Aeneid*, 1, 726: dependent lychni laquearibus aureis incensi, et noctem flammis funalia vincunt" [Eliot's note]. "Glowing lamps hang from the gold-paneled ceiling, and the torches conquer night with their flames"; the banquet setting of another classical love scene, in which Dido is inspired with a fatal passion for Aeneas.
8. "Sylvan scene. V. Milton, *Paradise Lost*, IV, 140" [Eliot's note]. Eden as first seen by Satan.
9. "V. Ovid, *Metamorphoses*, VI, Philomela"

[Eliot's note]. Philomela was raped by her brother-in-law, King Tereus, who cut out her tongue so that she could not tell her sister, Procne. Later Procne is changed into a swallow and Philomela into a nightingale to save them from the king's rage after they have revenged themselves by killing his son.
1. "Cf. Part III, 1.204" [Eliot's note].
2. Represents the nightingale's song in Elizabethan poetry.
3. "Cf. Part III, 1.195" [Eliot's note].

'What is that noise?'

The wind under the door.[4]

'What is that noise now? What is the wind doing?'

Nothing again nothing.   120

'Do

'You know nothing? Do you see nothing? Do you remember

'Nothing?'

      I remember

Those are pearls that were his eyes.   125

'Are you alive, or not? Is there nothing in your head?'

But

O O O O that Shakespeherian Rag—

It's so elegant

So intelligent   130

'What shall I do now? What shall I do?'

'I shall rush out as I am, and walk the street

'With my hair down, so. What shall we do to-morrow?

'What shall we ever do?'

The hot water at ten.   135

And if it rains, a closed car at four.

And we shall play a game of chess,[5]

Pressing lidless eyes and waiting for a knock upon the door.

    When Lil's husband got demobbed,[6] I said—

I didn't mince my words, I said to her myself,   140

HURRY UP PLEASE ITS TIME[7]

Now Albert's coming back, make yourself a bit smart.

He'll want to know what you done with that money he gave you

To get yourself some teeth. He did, I was there.

You have them all out, Lil, and get a nice set,   145

He said, I swear, I can't bear to look at you.

And no more can't I, I said, and think of poor Albert,

He's been in the army four years, he wants a good time,

And if you don't give it him, there's others will, I said.

Oh is there, she said. Something o' that, I said.   150

Then I'll know who to thank, she said, and give me a straight look.

HURRY UP PLEASE ITS TIME

If you don't like it you can get on with it, I said.

Others can pick and choose if you can't.

But if Albert makes off, it won't be for lack of telling.   155

You ought to be ashamed, I said, to look so antique.

(And her only thirty-one.)

I can't help it, she said, pulling a long face,

---

4. "Cf. Webster: 'Is the wind in that door still?'" [Eliot's note]. From *The Devil's Law Case* (1623), 3.2.162, with the implied meaning "is there still breath in him?"

5. "Cf. the game of chess in Middleton's *Women Beware Women*" [Eliot's note]. In this scene, a woman is seduced in a series of stra-

tegic steps that parallel the moves of a chess game, which is occupying her mother-in-law at the same time.

6. Demobilized, discharged from the army.

7. The British bartender's warning that the pub is about to close.

It's them pills I took, to bring it off, she said.
(She's had five already, and nearly died of young George.)
The chemist[8] said it would be all right, but I've never been the same.
You are a proper fool, I said.
Well, if Albert won't leave you alone, there it is, I said,
What you get married for if you don't want children?
HURRY UP PLEASE ITS TIME
Well, that Sunday Albert was home, they had a hot gammon,[9]
And they asked me in to dinner, to get the beauty of it hot—
HURRY UP PLEASE ITS TIME
HURRY UP PLEASE ITS TIME
Goonight Bill. Goonight Lou. Goonight May. Goonight.
Ta ta. Goonight. Goonight.
Good night, ladies, good night, sweet ladies, good night, good night.[1]

160

165

170

III. The Fire Sermon[2]

The river's tent is broken: the last fingers of leaf
Clutch and sink into the wet bank. The wind
Crosses the brown land, unheard. The nymphs are departed.
Sweet Thames, run softly, till I end my song.[3]
The river bears no empty bottles, sandwich papers,
Silk handkerchiefs, cardboard boxes, cigarette ends
Or other testimony of summer nights. The nymphs are departed.
And their friends, the loitering heirs of city directors;
Departed, have left no addresses.
By the waters of Leman I sat down and wept[4] . . .
Sweet Thames, run softly till I end my song,
Sweet Thames, run softly, for I speak not loud or long.
But at my back in a cold blast I hear[5]
The rattle of the bones, and chuckle spread from ear to ear.

175

180

185

A rat crept softly through the vegetation
Dragging its slimy belly on the bank
While I was fishing in the dull canal
On a winter evening round behind the gashouse

190

---

8. The druggist, who gave her pills to cause a miscarriage.
9. Ham.
1. The popular song for a party's end ("Good Night, Ladies") shifts into Ophelia's last words in *Hamlet* (4.5.72) as she goes off to drown herself.
2. Reference to the Buddha's Fire Sermon (see n. 2, p. 555), in which he denounced the fiery lusts and passions of earthly experience. "All things are on fire . . . with the fire of passion . . . of hatred . . . of infatuation." Part III describes the degeneration of even these passions in the sterile decadence of the modern Waste Land.

3. "V. Spenser, *Prothalamion*" [Eliot's note]. The line is the refrain of a marriage song by the Elizabethan poet Edmund Spenser (1552?–1599) and evokes a river of unpolluted pastoral beauty.
4. In Psalms 137.1, the exiled Hebrews sit by the rivers of Babylon and weep for their lost homeland. "Waters of Leman": Lake Geneva (where Eliot wrote much of *The Waste Land*). A "leman" is a mistress or lover.
5. Distorted echo of Andrew Marvell's (1621–1678) poem "To His Coy Mistress." "But at my back I always hear / Time's wingèd chariot hurrying near."

Musing upon the king my brother's wreck
And on the king my father's death before him.[6]
White bodies naked on the low damp ground
And bones cast in a little low dry garret,
Rattled by the rat's foot only, year to year.   195
But at my back from time to time I hear[7]
The sound of horns and motors, which shall bring[8]
Sweeney to Mrs. Porter in the spring.
O the moon shone bright on Mrs. Porter[9]
And on her daughter   200
They wash their feet in soda water
Et O ces voix d'enfants, chantant dans la coupole![1]

Twit twit twit
Jug jug jug jug jug jug
So rudely forc'd.   205
Tereu[2]

Unreal City
Under the brown fog of a winter noon
Mr. Eugenides, the Smyrna merchant
Unshaven, with a pocket full of currants   210
C.i.f. London: documents at sight,[3]
Asked me in demotic French
To luncheon at the Cannon Street Hotel
Followed by a weekend at the Metropole.[4]

At the violet hour, when the eyes and back   215
Turn upward from the desk, when the human engine waits
Like a taxi throbbing waiting,

---

6. "Cf. *The Tempest* I.ii" [Eliot's note]. Ferdinand, the king's son, believing his father drowned and mourning his death, hears in the air a song containing the line that Eliot quotes earlier at lines 48 and 125.

7. "Cf. Marvell, 'To His Coy Mistress'" [Eliot's note].

8. "Cf. Day, *Parliament of Bees*: 'When of the sudden, listening, you shall hear, / A noise of horns and hunting, which shall bring / Actaeon to Diana in the spring, / Where all shall see her naked skin'" [Eliot's note]. The young hunter Actaeon was changed into a stag, hunted down, and killed when he came upon the goddess Diana bathing. Sweeney is in no such danger from his visit to Mrs. Porter.

9. "I do not know the origin of the ballad from which these lines are taken: it was reported to me from Sydney, Australia" [Eliot's note]. A song popular among Allied troops during World War I. One version continues lines 199–201 as follows: "And so they oughter / To keep them clean."

1. "V. Verlaine, *Parsifal*" [Eliot's note]. "And O these children's voices, singing in the dome!" (French); the last lines of a sonnet by Paul Verlaine (1844–1896), which ambiguously celebrates the Grail hero's chaste restraint. In Richard Wagner's opera, Parsifal's feet are washed to purify him before entering the presence of the Grail.

2. Tereus, who raped Philomela (see line 99); also the nightingale's song.

3. "The currants were quoted at a price 'carriage and insurance free to London'; and the Bill of Lading etc. were to be handed to the buyer upon payment of the sight draft" [Eliot's note].

4. Smyrna is an ancient Phoenician seaport, and early Smyrna merchants spread the Eastern fertility cults. In contrast, their descendant Mr. Eugenides ("Well-born") invites the poet to lunch in a large commercial hotel and a weekend at a seaside resort in Brighton.

I Tiresias,[5] though blind, throbbing between two lives,
Old man with wrinkled female breasts, can see
At the violet hour, the evening hour that strives   220
Homeward, and brings the sailor home from sea,[6]
The typist home at teatime, clears her breakfast, lights
Her stove, and lays out food in tins.
Out of the window perilously spread
Her drying combinations touched by the sun's last rays,   225
On the divan are piled (at night her bed)
Stockings, slippers, camisoles, and stays.
I Tiresias, old man with wrinkled dugs
Perceived the scene, and foretold the rest—
I too awaited the expected guest.   230
He, the young man carbuncular, arrives,
A small house agent's clerk, with one bold stare,
One of the low on whom assurance sits
As a silk hat on a Bradford[7] millionaire.
The time is now propitious, as he guesses,   235
The meal is ended, she is bored and tired,
Endeavours to engage her in caresses
Which still are unreproved, if undesired.
Flushed and decided, he assaults at once;
Exploring hands encounter no defence;   240
His vanity requires no response,
And makes a welcome of indifference.
(And I Tiresias have foresuffered all
Enacted on this same divan or bed;
I who have sat by Thebes below the wall   245
And walked among the lowest of the dead.)[8]
Bestows one final patronising kiss,
And gropes his way, finding the stairs unlit . . .

She turns and looks a moment in the glass,
Hardly aware of her departed lover;   250
Her brain allows one half-formed thought to pass:
'Well now that's done: and I'm glad it's over.'

---

5. "Tiresias, although a mere spectator and not indeed a 'character,' is yet the most important personage in the poem, uniting all the rest. Just as the one-eyed merchant, seller of currants, melts into the Phoenician Sailor, and the latter is not wholly distinct from Ferdinand Prince of Naples, so all the women are one woman, and the two sexes meet in Tiresias. What Tiresias *sees*, in fact, is the substance of the poem. The whole passage from Ovid is one of great anthropological interest" [Eliot's note]. The passage then quoted from Ovid's *Metamorphoses* (3.320–38) describes how Tiresias spent seven years of his life as a woman and thus experienced love from the point of view of both sexes. Blinded by Juno, he was recompensed by Jove with the gift of prophecy.

6. "This may or may not appear as exact as Sappho's lines, but I had in mind the 'longshore' or 'dory' fisherman, who returns at nightfall" [Eliot's note]. The Greek poet Sappho's poem describes how the evening star brings home those whom dawn has sent abroad; there is also an echo of Robert Louis Stevenson's (1850–1894) *Requiem* 1.221: "Home is the sailor, home from the sea."

7. A manufacturing town in Yorkshire that prospered greatly during World War I.

8. Tiresias prophesied in the marketplace at Thebes for many years before dying and continuing to prophesy in Hades.

When lovely woman stoops to folly and[9]
Paces about her room again, alone,
She smoothes her hair with automatic hand,　　　　255
And puts a record on the gramophone.

'This music crept by me upon the waters'[1]
And along the Strand, up Queen Victoria Street.
O City city,[2] I can sometimes hear
Beside a public bar in Lower Thames Street,　　　　260
The pleasant whining of a mandoline
And a clatter and a chatter from within
Where fishmen lounge at noon: where the walls
Of Magnus Martyr[3] hold
Inexplicable splendour of Ionian white and gold.　　　　265

　　　　The river sweats[4]
　　　　Oil and tar
　　　　The barges drift
　　　　With the turning tide
　　　　Red sails　　　　270
　　　　Wide
　　　　To leeward, swing on the heavy spar.
　　　　The barges wash
　　　　Drifting logs
　　　　Down Greenwich reach　　　　275
　　　　Past the Isle of Dogs.[5]
　　　　　　　　Weialala leia
　　　　　　　　Wallala leialala

　　　　Elizabeth and Leicester[6]
　　　　Beating oars　　　　280

9. "V. Goldsmith, the song in *The Vicar of Wakefield*" [Eliot's note]. "When lovely woman stoops to folly / And finds too late that men betray / What charm can soothe her melancholy, / What art can wash her guilt away?" Oliver Goldsmith (ca. 1730–1774), *The Vicar of Wakefield* (1766).
1. "V. *The Tempest*, as above" [Eliot's note, referring to line 191]. Spoken by Ferdinand as he hears Ariel sing of his father's transformation by the sea, his eyes turning to pearls, his bones to coral, and everything else he formerly was into "something rich and strange."
2. A double invocation: the city of London and the City as London's central financial district (see lines 60 and 207). See also lines 375–76, the great cities of Western civilization.
3. "The interior of St. Magnus Martyr is to my mind one of the finest among Wren's interiors. See *The Proposed Demolition of Nineteen City Churches*: (P. S. King & Son, Ltd)" [Eliot's note]. The architect was Christopher Wren (1632–1723), and the church is located just below Lon-

don Bridge on Lower Thames Street.
4. "The Song of the (three) Thames-daughters begins here. From line 292 to 306 inclusive they speak in turn. V. *Götterdämmerung* III.i.: the Rhine-daughters" [Eliot's note]. In Wagner's opera *The Twilight of the Gods* (1876), the three Rhine-maidens mourn the loss of their gold, which gave the river its sparkling beauty; lines 277–78 here echo the Rhine-maidens' refrain.
5. A peninsula opposite Greenwich on the Thames.
6. "V. Froude, *Elizabeth*, vol. I, ch. iv, letter of De Quadra to Philip of Spain: 'In the afternoon we were in a barge, watching the games on the river. (The queen) was alone with Lord Robert and myself on the poop, when they began to talk nonsense, and went so far that Lord Robert at last said, as I was on the spot there was no reason why they should not be married if the queen pleased" [Eliot's note]. Sir Robert Dudley (1532–1588), the earl of Leicester, was a favorite of Queen Elizabeth and at one point hoped to marry her.

The stern was formed
A gilded shell
Red and gold
The brisk swell
Rippled both shores   285
Southwest wind
Carried down stream
The peal of bells
White towers
            Weialala leia   290
            Wallala leialala

'Trams and dusty trees.
Highbury bore me. Richmond and Kew
Undid me.[7] By Richmond I raised my knees
Supine on the floor of a narrow canoe.'   295
'My feet are at Moorgate,[8] and my heart
Under my feet. After the event
He wept. He promised "a new start."
I made no comment. What should I resent?'

'On Margate Sands.[9]   300
I can connect
Nothing with nothing.
The broken fingernails of dirty hands.
My people humble people who expect
Nothing.'   305
            la la

To Carthage then I came[1]

Burning burning burning burning[2]
O Lord Thou pluckest me out[3]
O Lord Thou pluckest   310

burning

---

7. "Cf. *Purgatorio*, V, 133: 'Ricorditi di me, che son la Pia; / Siena mi fe', disfecemi Maremma'" [Eliot's note]. La Pia, in Purgatory, recalls her seduction: "Remember me, who am La Pia. / Siena made me, Maremma undid me." Eliot's parody substitutes Highbury (a London suburb) and Richmond and Kew, popular excursion points on the Thames.
8. A London slum.
9. A seaside resort on the Thames.
1. "V. St. Augustine's *Confessions*: 'to Carthage then I came, where a cauldron of unholy loves sang all about mine ears'" [Eliot's note]. The youthful Augustine is described. Carthage is also the scene of Dido's faithful love for Aeneas, referred to in line 92.

2. "The complete text of the Buddha's Fire Sermon (which corresponds in importance to the Sermon on the Mount) from which these words are taken, will be found translated in the late Henry Clarke Warren's *Buddhism in Translation* (Harvard Oriental Studies). Mr. Warren was one of the great pioneers of Buddhist studies in the Occident" [Eliot's note]. The Sermon on the Mount is in Matthew 5–7.
3. "From St. Augustine's *Confessions* again. The collocation of these two representatives of eastern and western asceticism, as the culmination of this part of the poem is not an accident" [Eliot's note]. See also Zechariah 3.2, where the high priest Joshua is described as a "brand plucked out of the fire."

IV. Death by Water

Phlebas the Phoenician, a fortnight dead,
Forgot the cry of gulls, and the deep sea swell
And the profit and loss.
                              A current under sea   315
Picked his bones in whispers. As he rose and fell
He passed the stages of his age and youth
Entering the whirlpool.
                              Gentile or Jew
O you who turn the wheel and look to windward,   320
Consider Phlebas, who was once handsome and tall as you.

V. What the Thunder Said[4]

After the torchlight red on sweaty faces
After the frosty silence in the gardens
After the agony in stony places
The shouting and the crying   325
Prison and palace and reverberation
Of thunder of spring over distant mountains
He who was living is now dead[5]
We who were living are now dying
With a little patience   330

Here is no water but only rock
Rock and no water and the sandy road
The road winding above among the mountains
Which are mountains of rock without water
If there were water we should stop and drink   335
Amongst the rock one cannot stop or think
Sweat is dry and feet are in the sand
If there were only water amongst the rock
Dead mountain mouth of carious teeth that cannot spit
Here one can neither stand nor lie nor sit   340
There is not even silence in the mountains
But dry sterile thunder without rain
There is not even solitude in the mountains
But red sullen faces sneer and snarl
From doors of mudcracked houses   345
                              If there were water

   And no rock
   If there were rock

---

4. "In the first part of Part V three themes are employed: the journey to Emmaus, the approach to the Chapel Perilous (see Miss Weston's book) and the present decay of eastern Europe" [Eliot's note]. On their journey to Emmaus (Luke 24.13–34), Jesus's disciples were joined by a stranger who later revealed himself to be the crucified and resurrected Christ. The *thunder* of the title is a divine voice in the Hindu *Upanishads* (see n. 3, p. 2139).

5. Allusions to stages in Christ's Passion: the betrayal, prayer in the garden of Gethsemane, imprisonment, trial, crucifixion, and burial. Despair reigns, for this is death before the Resurrection.

And also water
And water
A spring
A pool among the rock
If there were the sound of water only
Not the cicada[6]
And dry grass singing
But sound of water over a rock
Where the hermit-thrush[7] sings in the pine trees
Drip drop drip drop drop drop drop
But there is no water

    Who is the third who walks always beside you?
When I count, there are only you and I together[8]
But when I look ahead up the white road
There is always another one walking beside you
Gliding wrapt in a brown mantle, hooded
I do not know whether a man or a woman
—But who is that on the other side of you?

    What is that sound high in the air[9]
Murmur of maternal lamentation
Who are those hooded hordes swarming
Over endless plains, stumbling in cracked earth
Ringed by the flat horizon only
What is the city over the mountains
Cracks and reforms and bursts in the violet air
Falling towers
Jerusalem Athens Alexandria
Vienna London
Unreal

    A woman drew her long black hair out tight
And fiddled whisper music on those strings
And bats with baby faces in the violet light
Whistled, and beat their wings
And crawled head downward down a blackened wall
And upside down in air were towers
Tolling reminiscent bells, that kept the hours
And voices singing out of empty cisterns and exhausted wells.

350

355

360

365

370

375

380

385

6. Grasshopper or cricket; see line 23.
7. "The hermit-thrush which I have heard in Quebec Province. . . . Its 'water-dripping song' is justly celebrated" [Eliot's note].
8. "The following lines were stimulated by the account of one of the Antarctic expeditions (I forget which, but I think one of Shackleton's): it was related that the party of explorers, at the extremity of their strength, had the constant delusion that there was *one more member* than could actually be counted" [Eliot's note]. See also n. 4, p. 2137.

9. Eliot's note to lines 367–77 refers to Hermann Hesse's *Blick ins Chaos* (Glimpse into Chaos) and a passage that reads, translated, "Already half of Europe, already at least half of Eastern Europe is on the way to Chaos, drives drunk in holy madness on the edge of the abyss and sings at the same time, sings drunk and hymn-like, as Dimitri Karamazov sang [in Dostoevsky's *The Brothers Karamazov*]. The offended bourgeois laughs at the songs; the saint and the seer hear them with tears."

In this decayed hole among the mountains
In the faint moonlight, the grass is singing
Over the tumbled graves, about the chapel
There is the empty chapel, only the wind's home.
It has no windows, and the door swings,   390
Dry bones can harm no one.
Only a cock stood on the rooftree
Co co rico co co rico[1]
In a flash of lightning. Then a damp gust
Bringing rain   395

    Ganga was sunken, and the limp leaves
Waited for rain, while the black clouds
Gathered far distant, over Himavant.[2]
The jungle crouched, humped in silence.
Then spoke the thunder   400
DA
Datta: what have we given?[3]
My friend, blood shaking my heart
The awful daring of a moment's surrender
Which an age of prudence can never retract   405
By this, and this only, we have existed
Which is not to be found in our obituaries
Or in memories draped by the beneficent spider[4]
Or under seals broken by the lean solicitor
In our empty rooms   410
DA
Dayadhvam:[5] I have heard the key
Turn in the door once and turn once only
We think of the key, each in his prison
Thinking of the key, each confirms a prison   415
Only at nightfall, aethereal rumours

---

1. European version of the cock's crow: *cock-a-doodle-doo*. The cock crowed in Matthew 26.34 and 74, after Peter had denied Jesus three times.
2. A mountain in the Himalayas. "Ganga": the river Ganges in India.
3. "'Datta, dayadhvam, damyata' (Give, sympathise, control). The fable of the meaning of the Thunder is found in the *Brihadaranyaka*—Upanishad 5,1" [Eliot's note]. In the fable, the word *DA*, spoken by the supreme being Prajapati, is interpreted as *Datta* ("to give alms"), *Dayadhvam* ("to sympathize or have compassion"), and *Damyata* ("to have self-control") by gods, human beings, and demons respectively. The conclusion is that when the thunder booms DA DA DA, Prajapati is commanding that all three virtues be practiced simultaneously.
4. "Cf. Webster, *The White Devil*, V, vi: '. . . they'll remarry / Ere the worm pierce your winding-sheet, ere the spider / Make a thin curtain for your epitaphs'" [Eliot's note].

5. Eliot's note on the command "to sympathize" or reach outside the self, cites two descriptions of helpless isolation. The first comes from Dante's *Inferno* 33.46: as Ugolino, imprisoned in a tower with his children to die of starvation, says, "And I heard below the door of the horrible tower being locked up." The second is a modern description by the English philosopher F. H. Bradley (1846–1924) of the inevitably self-enclosed or private nature of consciousness: "My external sensations are no less private to myself than are my thoughts or my feelings. In either case my experience falls within my own circle, a circle closed on the outside; and, with all its elements alike, every sphere is opaque to the others which surround it. . . . In brief, regarded as an existence which appears in a soul, the whole world for each is peculiar and private to that soul" (*Appearance and Reality*).

Revive for a moment a broken Coriolanus[6]
D<small>A</small>
Damyata: The boat responded
Gaily, to the hand expert with sail and oar   420
The sea was calm, your heart would have responded
Gaily, when invited, beating obedient
To controlling hands
                            I sat upon the shore
Fishing,[7] with the arid plain behind me   425
Shall I at least set my lands in order?
London Bridge is falling down falling down falling down

Poi s'ascose nel foco che gli affina[8]
Quando fiam uti chelidon[9]—O swallow swallow
Le Prince d'Aquitaine à la tour abolie[1]   430
These fragments I have shored against my ruins
Why then Ile fit you. Hieronymo's mad againe.[2]
Datta. Dayadhvam. Damyata.
        Shantih   shantih   shantih[3]

                                      1922

From Four Quartets

Little Gidding[1]

Midwinter spring is its own season
Sempiternal though sodden towards sundown,
Suspended in time, between pole and tropic.

6. A proud Roman patrician who was exiled and led an army against his homeland. In Shakespeare's play, both his grandeur and his downfall come from a desire to be ruled only by himself.

7. "V. Weston: *From Ritual to Romance*; chapter on the Fisher King" [Eliot's note].

8. Eliot's note quotes a passage in the *Purgatorio* in which Arnaut Daniel (see n. 3, p. 545) asks Dante to remember his pain. The line cited here, "then he hid himself in the fire which refines them" (*Purgatorio* 26.148), shows Daniel departing in fire which—in Purgatory—exists as a purifying rather than a destructive element.

9. "V. *Pervigilium Veneris*. Cf. Philomela in Parts II and III" [Eliot's note]. "When shall I be as a swallow?" A line from the *Vigil of Venus*, an anonymous late Latin poem, that asks for the gift of song; here associated with Philomela as a swallow, not the nightingale of lines 99–103 and 203–06.

1. "V. Gerard de Nerval, Sonnet *El Desdi-*

chado" [Eliot's note]. The Spanish title means "The Disinherited One," and the sonnet is a monologue describing the speaker as a melancholy, ill-starred dreamer: "the Prince of Aquitaine in his ruined tower." Another line recalls the scene at the end of "The Love Song of J. Alfred Prufrock" (p. 2126): "I dreamed in the grotto where sirens swim."

2. "V. Kyd's *Spanish Tragedy*" [Eliot's note]. Thomas Kyd's revenge play (1594) is subtitled *Hieronymo's Mad Againe*. The protagonist "fits" his son's murderers into appropriate roles in a court entertainment so that they may all be killed.

3. "Shantih. Repeated as here, a formal ending to an Upanishad. 'The Peace which passeth understanding' is our equivalent to this word" [Eliot's note]. The *Upanishads* comment on the sacred Hindu scriptures, the *Vedas*.

1. A village in Huntingdonshire that housed a religious community in the 17th century. Eliot visited the (rebuilt) chapel on a midwinter day.

When the short day is brightest, with frost and fire,
The brief sun flames the ice, on pond and ditches,   5
In windless cold that is the heart's heat,
Reflecting in a watery mirror
A glare that is blindness in the early afternoon.
And glow more intense than blaze of branch, or brazier,
Stirs the dumb spirit: no wind, but pentecostal fire[2]   10
In the dark time of the year. Between melting and freezing
The soul's sap quivers. There is no earth smell
Or smell of living thing. This is the spring time
But not in time's covenant. Now the hedgerow
Is blanched for an hour with transitory blossom   15
Of snow, a bloom more sudden
Than that of summer, neither budding nor fading,
Not in the scheme of generation.
Where is the summer, the unimaginable
Zero summer?   20

     If you came this way,
Taking the route you would be likely to take
From the place you would be likely to come from,
If you came this way in may time,[3] you would find the hedges
White again, in May, with voluptuary sweetness.   25
It would be the same at the end of the journey,
If you came at night like a broken king,[4]
If you came by day not knowing what you came for,
It would be the same, when you leave the rough road
And turn behind the pig-sty to the dull façade   30
And the tombstone. And what you thought you came for
Is only a shell, a husk of meaning
From which the purpose breaks only when it is fulfilled
If at all. Either you had no purpose
Or the purpose is beyond the end you figured   35
And is altered in fulfilment. There are other places
Which also are the world's end, some at the sea jaws,
Or over a dark lake, in a desert or a city—
But this is the nearest, in place and time,
Now and in England.   40

     If you came this way,
Taking any route, starting from anywhere,
At any time or at any season,
It would always be the same: you would have to put off
Sense and notion. You are not here to verify,   45
Instruct yourself, or inform curiosity
Or carry report. You are here to kneel

---

2. On the Pentecost day after Christ's resurrection, the apostles saw "cloven tongues like as of fire" (Acts 2.3) and were "filled with the Holy Ghost" (Acts 2.4).
3. When the May (Hawthorne) is in bloom.

4. Charles I, king of England (1600–1649), visited the religious community several times and went there secretly after his final defeat in the English Civil War.

Where prayer has been valid. And prayer is more
Than an order of words, the conscious occupation
Of the praying mind, or the sound of the voice praying.   50
And what the dead had no speech for, when living,
They can tell you, being dead: the communication
Of the dead is tongued with fire beyond the language of the living.
Here, the intersection of the timeless moment
Is England and nowhere. Never and always.   55

II

Ash on an old man's sleeve
Is all the ash the burnt roses leave.
Dust in the air suspended
Marks the place where a story ended.
Dust inbreathed was a house—   60
The wall, the wainscot and the mouse.
The death of hope and despair,
  This is the death of air.[5]

There are flood and drouth
Over the eyes and in the mouth,   65
Dead water and dead sand
Contending for the upper hand.
The parched eviscerate soil
Gapes at the vanity of toil,
Laughs without mirth.   70
  This is the death of earth.

Water and fire succeed
The town, the pasture and the weed.
Water and fire deride
The sacrifice that we denied.   75
Water and fire shall rot
The marred foundations we forgot,
Of sanctuary and choir.
  This is the death of water and fire.

In the uncertain hour before the morning[6]   80
  Near the ending of interminable night
  At the recurrent end of the unending
After the dark dove[7] with the flickering tongue
  Had passed below the horizon of his homing
  While the dead leaves still rattled on like tin   85

---

5. Allusion to "Fire lives in the death of air," a phrase from the pre-Socratic philosopher Heraclitus (535–475 B.C.E.) describing how one element (here, fire) lives at the expense of another (here, air).
6. The narrative passage from here to the end of Part II is written in tercets, a form that recalls Dante's use of *terza rima* (triple rhyme) in The

Divine Comedy. Eliot later commented that this section was "the nearest equivalent to a canto of the *Inferno* or *Purgatorio*" that he could create.
7. A play on the emblem of the Holy Spirit that descended to the apostles at Pentecost and on the then-current German slang for bomb, *Taube* ("dove").

Over the asphalt where no other sound was
    Between three districts whence the smoke arose
    I met one walking, loitering and hurried
As if blown towards me like the metal leaves
    Before the urban dawn wind unresisting.   90
    And as I fixed upon the down-turned face
That pointed scrutiny with which we challenge
    The first-met stranger in the waning dusk
    I caught the sudden look of some dead master
Whom I had known, forgotten, half recalled   95
    Both one and many; in the brown baked features
    The eyes of a familiar compound ghost
Both intimate and unidentifiable.
    So I assumed a double part,[8] and cried
    And heard another's voice cry: 'What! are *you* here?'   100
Although we were not. I was still the same,
    Knowing myself yet being someone other—
    And he a face still forming; yet the words sufficed
To compel the recognition they preceded.
    And so, compliant to the common wind,   105
    Too strange to each other for misunderstanding,
In concord at this intersection time
    Of meeting nowhere, no before and after,
    We trod the pavement in a dead patrol.
I said: 'The wonder that I feel is easy,   110
    Yet ease is cause of wonder. Therefore speak:
    I may not comprehend, may not remember.'
And he: 'I am not eager to rehearse
    My thought and theory which you have forgotten.
    These things have served their purpose: let them be.   115
So with your own, and pray they be forgiven
    By others, as I pray you to forgive
    Both bad and good. Last season's fruit is eaten
And the fullfed beast shall kick the empty pail.
    For last year's words belong to last year's language   120
    And next year's words await another voice.
But, as the passage now presents no hindrance
    To the spirit unappeased and peregrine
    Between two worlds become much like each other,
So I find words I never thought to speak   125
    In streets I never thought I should revisit
    When I left my body on a distant shore.
Since our concern was speech, and speech impelled us
    To purify the dialect of the tribe[9]
    And urge the mind to aftersight and foresight,   130

---

8. The role of questioner of souls (after Dante in *The Divine Comedy*) and the role of one interrogating himself.
9. In his epitaph-sonnet for Edgar Allan Poe, "The Tomb of Edgar Poe," the French poet Stéphane Mallarmé (1842–1898) defines the poet's role as purifying speech by using ordinary language (*the dialect of the tribe*) in a more precise and yet complex way, creating a new structure of interlocking or multiple meanings (see lines 221–24).

Let me disclose the gifts reserved for age
   To set a crown upon your lifetime's effort.
   First, the cold friction of expiring sense
Without enchantment, offering no promise
   But bitter tastelessness of shadow fruit   135
   As body and soul begin to fall asunder.
Second, the conscious impotence of rage
   At human folly, and the laceration
   Of laughter at what ceases to amuse.
And last, the rending pain of re-enactment   140
   Of all that you have done, and been; the shame
   Of motives late revealed, and the awareness
Of things ill done and done to others' harm
   Which once you took for exercise of virtue.
   Then fools' approval stings, and honour stains.   145
From wrong to wrong the exasperated spirit
   Proceeds, unless restored by that refining fire
   Where you must move in measure, like a dancer.'[1]
The day was breaking. In the disfigured street
   He left me, with a kind of valediction,   150
   And faded on the blowing of the horn.[2]

III

There are three conditions which often look alike
Yet differ completely, flourish in the same hedgerow:
Attachment to self and to things and to persons; detachment
From self and from things and from persons; and, growing between
   them, indifference   155
Which resembles the others as death resembles life,
Being between two lives—unflowering, between
The live and the dead nettle. This is the use of memory:
For liberation—not less of love but expanding
Of love beyond desire, and so liberation   160
From the future as well as the past. Thus, love of a country
Begins as attachment to our own field of action
And comes to find that action of little importance
Though never indifferent. History may be servitude,
History may be freedom. See, now they vanish,   165
The faces and places, with the self which, as it could, loved them,
To become renewed, transfigured, in another pattern.

Sin is Behovely,[3] but
All shall be well, and

---

1. In Dante's *Purgatorio* (26.148), fire is seen as a purgative or refining element, and characters are enveloped in flames that move in accord with their bodies.
2. The horn that marks the all-clear signal after an air raid; also the disappearance of Hamlet's father's ghost (*Hamlet* 1.2.157): "It faded on the crowing of the cock."
3. Inevitable. Lines 168–70 repeat the consoling words of Dame Julian of Norwich, a 14th-century English mystic: "Sin is behovabil, but all shall be well and all manner of thing shall be well."

All manner of thing shall be well.   170
If I think, again, of this place,
And of people, not wholly commendable,
Of no immediate kin or kindness,
But some of peculiar genius,
All touched by a common genius,   175
United in the strife which divided them;
If I think of a king at nightfall,
Of three men, and more, on the scaffold[4]
And a few who died forgotten
In other places, here and abroad,   180
And of one who died blind and quiet,[5]
Why should we celebrate
These dead men more than the dying?
It is not to ring the bell backward
Nor is it an incantation   185
To summon the spectre of a Rose.
We cannot revive old factions[6]
We cannot restore old policies
Or follow an antique drum.
These men, and those who opposed them   190
And those whom they opposed
Accept the constitution of silence
And are folded in a single party.
Whatever we inherit from the fortunate
We have taken from the defeated   195
What they had to leave us—a symbol:
A symbol perfected in death.
And all shall be well and
All manner of thing shall be well
By the purification of the motive   200
In the ground of our beseeching.

IV

The dove descending breaks the air
With flame of incandescent terror
Of which the tongues declare
The one discharge from sin and error.
The only hope, or else despair   205
    Lies in the choice of pyre or pyre—
    To be redeemed from fire by fire.

---

4. Charles I and his chief advisers were executed on the scaffold after the English Civil War.
5. The poet John Milton (1608–1674), who supported Parliament and the Commonwealth in the English Civil War.
6. Alluding to the factionalisms of history exemplified here in the Wars of the Roses (1555–85), when Yorkists, whose badge was the white rose, fought Lancastrians, whose badge was a red rose, for the English throne. The struggle ended in the strong centralized monarchy of the Tudors, whose Tudor Rose "in-folded" (cf. line 259) the other two. There is also allusion to the discovery, beyond history, of the vast rose of pure light seen by Dante in the *Paradiso* (30.112 ff), evoked in line 261.

Who then devised the torment? Love.
Love is the unfamiliar Name
Behind the hands that wove
The intolerable shirt of flame[7]
Which human power cannot remove.
  We only live, only suspire
    Consumed by either fire or fire.   215

V

What we call the beginning is often the end
And to make an end is to make a beginning.
The end is where we start from. And every phrase
And sentence that is right (where every word is at home,
Taking its place to support the others,   220
The word neither diffident nor ostentatious,
An easy commerce of the old and the new,
The common word exact without vulgarity,
The formal word precise but not pedantic,
The complete consort[8] dancing together)   225
Every phrase and every sentence is an end and a beginning,
Every poem an epitaph. And any action
Is a step to the block, to the fire, down the sea's throat
Or to an illegible stone: and that is where we start.
We die with the dying: 230
See, they depart, and we go with them.
We are born with the dead:
See, they return, and bring us with them.
The moment of the rose and the moment of the yew-tree
Are of equal duration. A people without history   235
Is not redeemed from time, for history is a pattern
Of timeless moments. So, while the light fails
On a winter's afternoon, in a secluded chapel
History is now and England.

With the drawing of this Love and the voice of this Calling[9]   240
We shall not cease from exploration
And the end of all our exploring
Will be to arrive where we started
And know the place for the first time.
Through the unknown, remembered gate   245
When the last of earth left to discover
Is that which was the beginning;
At the source of the longest river
The voice of the hidden waterfall

---

7. The shirt, poisoned with the blood of Nessus the centaur, that Deianeira (unknowingly) gave her husband, Hercules, to strengthen his love for her. Instead, the shirt so burned Hercules' flesh that he chose death on a funeral pyre to escape the agony.
8. Both "harmony" and "company."
9. Line from *The Cloud of Unknowing*, a 14th-century book of Christian mysticism.

And the children in the apple-tree   250
Not known, because not looked for
But heard, half-heard, in the stillness
Between two waves of the sea.
Quick now, here, now, always[1]—
A condition of complete simplicity   255
(Costing not less than everything)
And all shall be well and
All manner of thing shall be well
When the tongues of flame are in-folded
Into the crowned knot of fire   260
And the fire and the rose are one.

                                                   1942, 1943

1. This same line occurs toward the end of "Burnt Norton," the first of the *Four Quartets*, where it also follows voices of children hidden in foliage; there is a suggestion of sudden insight gained in a moment of passive openness to illumination.

ANNA AKHMATOVA
1889–1966

One of the great Russian poets of the twentieth century, Anna Akhmatova expresses herself in an intensely personal, poetic voice, whether as lover, wife, and mother or as a national poet commemorating the mute agony of millions. From the subjective romantic lyrics of her earliest work to the communal mourning of *Requiem*, she conveys universal themes in terms of individual experience, and historical events through the filter of fear, love, hope, and pain. Yet what most distinguishes her work is the way these basic emotions arise from the historical traumas of Akhmatova's native land.

Born Anna Andreevna Gorenko, in a suburb of the Black Sea port of Odessa, she was the daughter of a maritime engineer and an independent woman of revolutionary sympathies. She took the pen name Akhmatova (accented on the second syllable) from her maternal great-grandmother, who was of Tatar descent. Anna attended the local school at Tsarskoe Selo, near St. Petersburg, but completed her degree in Kiev. In 1907 she briefly studied law at the Kiev College for Women before moving to St. Petersburg to study literature. In Tsarskoe Selo, Akhmatova met Nikolai Gumilyov, whom she married in 1910. Gumilyov helped organize the Poets Guild, which became the core of a small new literary movement. Acmeism rejected the romantic, quasireligious aims of Russian symbolism and valued clarity, concreteness, and closeness to the things of this earth. The Symbolist–Acmeist debate went on inside a lively literary and social life, while the three main figures of the movement—Akhmatova, Gumilyov, and Osip Mandelstam—gained a reputation as important poets.

Although Akhmatova and Gumilyov divorced, his arrest and execution for counterrevolutionary activities in 1921 put her status into question. After 1922 she was no longer allowed to publish and was forced into the withdrawal from public activity that Russians call "internal emigration." Officially forgotten, she was not forgotten in fact; in the schools, students who would never hear her name mentioned in class copied out her poems by hand and circulated them secretly. Relying for her living on a meager, irregular pension, Akhmatova prepared essays on the life and works of the Russian author Aleksandr Pushkin (1799–1837) and wrote poems that would not appear until much later. Stalin's "Great Purge" of 1935–38 sent millions of people to prison camps and made the 1930s a time of terror and uncertainty for everyone.

Akhmatova's friend Osip Mandelstam was exiled to Voronezh in 1934 and then sent to a prison camp in 1938, where he died that year. In 1935 her partner, the art critic Nikolai Punin, was arrested briefly and her son Lev Gumilyov, then twenty-three, was imprisoned, an event that inspired the first poems of the cycle that would become *Requiem*. Lev was ultimately imprisoned for a total of fourteen years as the government sought a way to punish his mother for what it perceived as her disloyalty to the regime. Composing *Requiem* was a risky act carried out over several years, and Akhmatova and her friend Lidia Chukovskaya memorized the stanzas in order to preserve the poem in the absence of written copy.

During the Second World War, Akhmatova's interest in larger musical forms motivated her to develop cycles of poems instead of her accustomed individual lyrics. She also began work on *Poem Without a Hero*, a long, complex verse narrative in three parts that sums up many of her earlier themes: love, death, creativity, the unity of European culture, and the suffering of her people. The poet was allowed a partial return to public life, addressing women on the radio during the siege of Leningrad (St. Petersburg) in 1941 and writing patriotic lyrics such as the famous *Courage* (published in *Pravda* in 1942), which rallied the Russian people to defend their homeland (and their national language) from enslavement. Her son was briefly released to serve in the military before being imprisoned again after the war.

Despite her patriotic activities, Akhmatova was subject to vicious official attacks after the war. Because she was considered too independent and cosmopolitan to be tolerated by the authorities, Akhmatova's books were suppressed: they did not fit the government-approved model of literature: they were too "individualistic" and were not "socially useful." After the death of Joseph Stalin, in 1953, however, her collected poems—including poems of the war years and unknown texts written during the periods of enforced silence—brought the range of her work to public attention. *Requiem* was first published "without her consent" in Munich in 1963 (not until 1987 was the complete text published in the Soviet Union). Her death, in 1966, signaled the end of an era in modern Russian poetry, for she was the last of the famous "quartet" that also included Mandelstam, Tsvetaeva, and Boris Pasternak.

Requiem (1940), presented here, is a lyrical cycle, a series of poems written on a theme, but it is also a short epic narrative. The story it tells is acutely personal, even autobiographical, but like an epic it transcends personal significance and describes (as in *The Song of Roland*) a moment in the history of a nation. Akhmatova, who had seen her husband and son arrested and her friends die in prison camps, was only one of millions who had suffered similar losses in the purges of the 1930s. "Instead of a Preface," "Dedication," and two epilogues to *Requiem* constitute a framework examining this image of a common fate, while the core group of numbered poems develops a subjective picture and stages an individual drama. The "Dedication" and "Prologue" establish the context for the poem as a whole: the mass arrests in the 1930s after the assassination on December 1, 1934, of Sergei Kirov, the top Communist Party official in Leningrad. In the inner poems, Akhmatova blends her individual personal losses—husband, son, and friends—to create a single focus: the figure of a mother grieving for her condemned son. The speaker identifies herself with the crowd of women with whom she waited for seventeen months outside the Kresty ("Crosses") prison in Leningrad; at dawn each day they would all arrive, hoping to be allowed to pass their loved ones a parcel or a letter, and fearing that the prisoners would be sentenced to death or exile to the prison camps of Siberia. Instead of experiencing a natural life—one in which "for someone the sunset luxuriates"—these women and the prisoners are forced into a suspended, uncertain existence where all values are inverted and the city itself has become merely the setting for its prisons.

The "I" of the speaker throughout remains anonymous, in spite of the fact that Akhmatova describes her personal emotions in the central poems; her identity is that of a sorrowing mother, and she is distinguished from her fellow sufferers only by the poetic gift that makes her the "exhausted mouth, / Through which a hundred million scream." *Requiem* is at once both public and private: a picture of

individual grief linked to the country's disaster, and a vision of community suffering that extends beyond contemporary national tragedy into medieval Russian history and Greek mythology. The poem consistently figures the martyrdom of the Soviet people in religious terms, from the recurrent mention of crosses and Crucifixion to the culminating image of maternal suffering in Mary, the mother of Christ.

With the numbered poems, Akhmatova recounts the growing anguish of a mother as her son is arrested and sentenced to death. The speaker has described her partner's arrest at dawn, in the midst of the family. Her son is arrested later, and in the rest of the poem she relives her numb incomprehension as she struggles against the increasing likelihood that he will be condemned to death. After the sentence is passed, the mother can speak of his execution only in oblique terms, by shifting the image of death onto the plane of the Crucifixion and God's will. It is a tragedy that cannot be comprehended or beheld directly, just as, she suggests, at the Crucifixion "No one glanced and no one would have dared" to look at the grieving Mary.

In the two epilogues, the grieving speaker returns from religious transcendence to Earth and current history. Here she takes on a composite identity, seeing herself not as an isolated sufferer but as the women whose fate she has shared. It is their memory she perpetuates by writing *Requiem*, and it is in their memory that she herself lives on. No longer the victim of purely personal tragedy, she has become a bronze statue commemorating a community of suffering—a figure shaped by circumstances into a monument of public and private grief.

Requiem[1]

1935–1940

No, not under the vault of alien skies,[2]
And not under the shelter of alien wings—
I was with my people then,
There, where my people, unfortunately, were.

1961

Instead of a Preface

In the terrible years of the Yezhov terror,[3] I spent seventeen months in the prison lines of Leningrad. Once, someone "recognized" me. Then a woman with bluish lips standing behind me, who, of course, had never heard me called by name before, woke up from the stupor to which every one had succumbed and whispered in my ear (everyone spoke in whispers there):

"Can you describe this?"

And I answered: "Yes, I can."

Then something that looked like a smile passed over what had once been her face.

April 1, 1957
Leningrad[4]

Dedication

Mountains bow down to this grief,
Mighty rivers cease to flow,
But the prison gates hold firm,
And behind them are the "prisoners' burrows"
And mortal woe.   5
For someone a fresh breeze blows,
For someone the sunset luxuriates—
We[5] wouldn't know, we are those who everywhere
Hear only the rasp of the hateful key
And the soldiers' heavy tread.   10
We rose as if for an early service,
Trudged through the savaged capital
And met there, more lifeless than the dead;
The sun is lower and the Neva[6] mistier,
But hope keeps singing from afar.   15

---

1. Translated by Judith Hemschemeyer.
2. A phrase borrowed from *Message to Siberia* by the Russian poet Aleksandr Pushkin (1799–1837).
3. In 1937–38, mass arrests were carried out by the secret police, headed by Nikolai Yezhov.
4. The prose preface was written after her son had been released from prison and it was possible to think of editing the poem for publication.
5. The women waiting in line before the prison gates.
6. The large river that flows through St. Petersburg.

The verdict . . . And her tears gush forth,
Already she is cut off from the rest,
As if they painfully wrenched life from her heart,
As if they brutally knocked her flat,
But she goes on . . . Staggering . . . Alone . . .   20
Where now are my chance friends
Of those two diabolical years?
What do they imagine is in Siberia's storms,[7]
What appears to them dimly in the circle of the moon?
I am sending my farewell greeting to them.   25

March 1940

Prologue

That was when the ones who smiled
Were the dead, glad to be at rest.
And like a useless appendage, Leningrad
Swung from its prisons.
And when, senseless from torment,   5
Regiments of convicts marched,
And the short songs of farewell
Were sung by locomotive whistles.
The stars of death stood above us
And innocent Russia writhed   10
Under bloody boots
And under the tires of the Black Marias.[8]

I

They led you away at dawn,
I followed you, like a mourner,
In the dark front room the children were crying,[9]
By the icon shelf the candle was dying.
On your lips was the icon's chill.[1]   5
The deathly sweat on your brow . . . Unforgettable!—
I will be like the wives of the Streltsy,[2]
Howling under the Kremlin towers.

1935

---

7. Victims of the purges who were not executed were condemned to prison camps in
Siberia. Their wives were allowed to accompany them into exile, although they had to live
in towns at a distance from the camps.
8. Police cars for conveying those arrested.
9. Akhmatova's third husband, the art historian
Nikolai Punin, was arrested at dawn while the
children (his daughter and her cousin) cried.

1. The icon—a small religious painting—was
set on a shelf before which a candle was kept
lit. Punin had kissed the icon before being
taken away.
2. Elite troops organized by Ivan the Terrible
around 1550. They rebelled and were executed
by Peter the Great in 1698. Pleading in vain,
their wives and mothers saw the men killed
under the towers of the Kremlin.

II

Quietly flows the quiet Don,[3]
Yellow moon slips into a home.

He slips in with cap askew,
He sees a shadow, yellow moon.

This woman is ill,   5
This woman is alone,
Husband in the grave,[4] son in prison,
Say a prayer for me.

III

No, it is not I, it is somebody else who is suffering.
I would not have been able to bear what happened,
Let them shroud it in black,
And let them carry off the lanterns . . .

                                                    Night.   5

1940

IV

You should have been shown, you mocker,
Minion of all your friends,
Gay little sinner of Tsarskoye Selo,[5]
What would happen in your life—
How three-hundredth in line, with a parcel,   5
You would stand by the Kresty prison,

Your tempestuous tears
Burning through the New Year's ice.
Over there the prison poplar bends,
And there's no sound—and over there how many   10
Innocent lives are ending now . . .

V

For seventeen months I've been crying out,
Calling you home.
I flung myself at the hangman's[6] feet,
You are my son and my horror.
Everything is confused forever,   5
And it's not clear to me

3. The great Russian river, often celebrated in folk songs. This poem is modeled on a simple, rhythmic, short folk song known as a *chastuska*.
4. Akhmatova's first husband, the poet Nikolai Gumilyov, was shot in 1921.

5. Akhmatova recalls her early, carefree, and privileged life in Tsarskoe Selo, outside St. Petersburg.
6. Stalin's. Akhmatova wrote a letter to him pleading for the release of her son.

Who is a beast now, who is a man,
And how long before the execution.
And there are only dusty flowers,
And the chinking of the censer, and tracks   10
From somewhere to nowhere.
And staring me straight in the eyes,
And threatening impending death,
Is an enormous star.[7]

1939

VI

The light weeks will take flight,
I won't comprehend what happened.
Just as the white nights[8]
Stared at you, dear son, in prison

So they are staring again,   5
With the burning eyes of a hawk,
Talking about your lofty cross,
And about death.

1939

VII

THE SENTENCE

And the stone word fell
On my still-living breast.
Never mind, I was ready.
I will manage somehow.

Today I have so much to do: 5
I must kill memory once and for all,
I must turn my soul to stone,
I must learn to live again—

Unless . . . Summer's ardent rustling
Is like a festival outside my window.   10
For a long time I've foreseen this
Brilliant day, deserted house.

June 22, 1939[9]
Fountain House

---

7. The *star*, the *censer*, the foliage, and the confusion between beast and man recall apocalyptic passages in the Book of Revelation (8.5, 7, 10–11 and 9.7–10).
8. In St. Petersburg, because it is so far north, the nights around the summer solstice are never totally dark.
9. The date that her son was sentenced to labor camp.

VIII

TO DEATH

You will come in any case—so why not now?
I am waiting for you—I can't stand much more.
I've put out the light and opened the door
For you, so simple and miraculous.
So come in any form you please,   5
Burst in as a gas shell
Or, like a gangster, steal in with a length of pipe,
Or poison me with typhus fumes.
Or be that fairy tale you've dreamed up,[1]
So sickeningly familiar to everyone—   10
In which I glimpse the top of a pale blue cap[2]
And the house attendant white with fear.
Now it doesn't matter anymore. The Yenisey[3] swirls,
The North Star shines.
And the final horror dims   15
The blue luster of beloved eyes.

August 19, 1939
Fountain House

IX

Now madness half shadows
My soul with its wing,
And makes it drunk with fiery wine
And beckons toward the black ravine.

And I've finally realized   5
That I must give in,
Overhearing myself
Raving as if it were somebody else.

And it does not allow me to take
Anything of mine with me   10
(No matter how I plead with it,
No matter how I supplicate):

Not the terrible eyes of my son—
Suffering turned to stone,
Not the day of the terror,   15
Not the hour I met with him in prison,

Not the sweet coolness of his hands,
Not the trembling shadow of the lindens,

---

1. A denunciation to the police for imaginary crimes, common during the purges as people hastened to protect themselves by accusing their neighbors.

2. The NKVD (secret police) wore blue caps.
3. A river in Siberia along which there were many prison camps.

Not the far-off, fragile sound—
Of the final words of consolation.   20

May 4, 1940
Fountain House

X

CRUCIFIXION

"Do not weep for Me, Mother,
I am in the grave."

1

A choir of angels sang the praises of that momentous hour,
And the heavens dissolved in fire.
To his Father He said: "Why hast Thou forsaken me!"[4]
And to his Mother: "Oh, do not weep for Me . . ."[5]

1940
Fountain House

2

Mary Magdalene beat her breast and sobbed,
The beloved disciple[6] turned to stone,
But where the silent Mother stood, there
No one glanced and no one would have dared.

1943
Tashkent

Epilogue I

I learned how faces fall,
How terror darts from under eyelids,
How suffering traces lines
Of stiff cuneiform on cheeks,
How locks of ashen-blonde or black   5
Turn silver suddenly,
Smiles fade on submissive lips
And fear trembles in a dry laugh.
And I pray not for myself alone,
But for all those who stood there with me   10
In cruel cold, and in July's heat,
At that blind, red wall.

---

4. Jesus' last words from the Cross (Matthew 27.46).
5. These words and the epigraph refer to a line from the Russian Orthodox prayer sung at services on Easter Saturday: "Weep not for Me, Mother, when you look upon the grave." Jesus is comforting Mary with the promise of his resurrection.
6. The apostle John.

Epilogue II

Once more the day of remembrance[7] draws near.
I see, I hear, I feel you:

The one they almost had to drag at the end,
And the one who tramps her native land no more,

And the one who, tossing her beautiful head,   5
Said: "Coming here's like coming home."

I'd like to name them all by name,
But the list[8] has been confiscated and is nowhere to be found.

I have woven a wide mantle for them
From their meager, overheard words.   10

I will remember them always and everywhere,
I will never forget them no matter what comes.

And if they gag my exhausted mouth
Through which a hundred million scream,

Then may the people remember me   15
On the eve of my remembrance day.

And if ever in this country
They decide to erect a monument to me,

I consent to that honor
Under these conditions—that it stand   20

Neither by the sea, where I was born:
My last tie with the sea is broken,

Nor in the tsar's garden near the cherished pine stump,[9]
Where an inconsolable shade[1] looks for me,

But here, where I stood for three hundred hours,   25
And where they never unbolted the doors for me.

This, lest in blissful death
I forget the rumbling of the Black Marias,

---

7. In the Russian Orthodox Church, a memorial service is held on the anniversary of a death.
8. Of prisoners.
9. The gardens and park surrounding the summer palace in Tsarskoe Selo. Akhmatova writes elsewhere of the stump of a favorite

tree in the gardens and of the poet Pushkin, whom she describes as walking in the park.
1. A ghost; probably the restless spirit of Akhmatova's executed husband, Gumilyov, who had courted her in Tsarskoe Selo.

Forget how that detested door slammed shut
And an old woman howled like a wounded animal.   30

And may the melting snow stream like tears
From my motionless lids of bronze,

And a prison dove coo in the distance,
And the ships of the Neva sail calmly on.

March 1940

1963

FEDERICO GARCÍA LORCA
1898–1936

The poet and playwright Federico García Lorca, the best known writer of modern Spain and perhaps the greatest Spanish author since Cervantes, wrote poignantly about death and would himself suffer an early and infamous death. A member of the "Generation of 1927" who sought to revive the grandeur of Spanish poetry, Lorca is known for the striking imagery and lyric musicality of his work, which was both classical and modern, traditional and innovative, difficult and popular, regional and universal. The poetry and plays that began as personal statements took on larger significance, first as the expression of tragic conflicts in Spanish culture and then as poignant laments for humanity—especially the plight of those who are deprived, by society or simply by death, of the fulfillment that could have been theirs.

Lorca (despite the Spanish practice of using both paternal and maternal names—correctly, "García Lorca"—the author is generally called "Lorca") was born on June 5, 1898, in the small village of Fuentevaqueros, near the Andalusian city of Granada. He studied law at the University of Granada but left in 1919 for Madrid, where he entered the Residencia de Estudiantes, a college that provided a cosmopolitan education for Spanish youth. Madrid, the capital of Spain, was the center of intellectual and artistic ferment, and the Residencia attracted those who would become the most influential writers and artists of their generation (including the artist Salvador Dalí and the film director Luis Buñuel). Lorca also came under the influence of **Vicente Huidobro**'s ultraist movement. Although he lived at the Residencia almost continuously until 1928, he never seriously pursued a degree but spent his time reading, writing, improvising music and poetry with his friends, and producing his first plays.

Lorca's early poems celebrate his home province of Andalusia, a region known for its mixture of Arab and Spanish culture and for a tradition of wandering Gypsy singers who improvised, to guitar accompaniment, rhythmic laments of love and death, often with repetitive refrains such as that in the *Lament for Ignacio Sánchez Mejías*. Impelled by an emotional crisis, Lorca left Spain for New York in 1929 and there wrote a series of poems later published as *Poet in New York* (1940). Along with the familiar themes of doomed love and death is Lorca's tentative exploration of his homosexuality, which he could not reveal in conservative Spanish society and which, in this and later works, announced itself only with hesitation and anxiety. He traveled to Argentina, where he befriended the Chilean poet **Pablo Neruda**. From 1930 to his death, Lorca was active in the theater both as a writer and as a director of a traveling theatrical group (La Barraca) subsidized by the Spanish Republic. After a series of farces that mixed romantically tragic and comic themes, he presented the tragedies for which he is best known: *Blood Wedding* (1933) and *Yerma* (1934). All of Lorca's theater work rejects the conventionally realistic nineteenth-century drama, employing an openly poetic form that suggests musical patterns, with choruses, songs, and stylized movement.

Lorca published his *Lament for Ignacio Sánchez Mejías* in 1935. This long poem commemorates the death of a good friend, a famous toreador who was gored by a bull on August 11, 1934, and died two days later. Lorca's *Lament* celebrates both his friend and the value of human grace and courage in a world in which death is inevitable.

Lorca's *Lament*, cast as an elegy (a poem that mourns a death), recalls one of the most famous poems of Spanish literature: the *Verses on the Death of His Father*, by the medieval poet Jorge Manrique (1440–1479). Yet there is a fundamental difference between the two: while Manrique's elegy stresses religious themes and the prospect of eternal life, Lorca—in grim contrast—rejects such consolation and insists that his friend's death is permanent.

The four parts of the *Lament* incorporate diverse forms and perspectives, all working together to suggest a progression from the report of death in the first line—"At five in the afternoon"—to the close, where the dead man's nobility and elegance survive in "a sad breeze through the olive trees." The insistent refrain colors the first section, "Cogida and Death," with its throbbing return to the moment of death. The scene in the arena wavers between objective reporting—the boy with the shroud, the coffin on wheels—and the shared agony of the bull's bellowing and wounds burning like suns. In the second section, the speaker refuses to accept his friend's death ("I will not see it!") and requests that images of whiteness cover up the spilled blood; he imagines Ignacio climbing steps in pursuit of a mystic meeting with his true self and instead, bewildered, encountering his broken body. After paying his friend tribute, the speaker admits what he cannot force himself to envision: the finality of decay as moss and grass invade the bullfighter's buried skull.

At the end of section 3, the speaker accepts physical death ("even the sea dies!") but signals in the rhythmic free verse of the final section that his poetry will preserve a vision of his noble countryman against complete obliteration. In life, Sánchez Mejías was known to his friends for "the signal maturity of your understanding. / Of your appetite for death and the taste of its mouth." These qualities survive in memory. Echoing the pride with which the Latin poet Horace claimed to perpetuate his subjects in a "monument of lasting bronze," Lorca sings of his friend "for posterity" and captures, in his poem, the death and life of Sánchez Mejías.

On August 16, 1936, shortly after the outbreak of the Spanish Civil War, when right-wing troops led by General Francisco Franco, with support from the Catholic Church, attacked the young Spanish Republic, and almost precisely two years after the death of Sánchez Mejías, Lorca was dragged from a friend's house by a squadron of Franco's Fascist guards; three days later he was killed. Unlike that of his friend Ignacio, his body was never recovered. Lorca's murder, commemorated in Pablo Neruda's poem "**I'm Explaining a Few Things**," outraged the European and American literary and artistic community; it seemed to symbolize the mindless destruction of humane values that loomed with the approach of World War II.

Lament for Ignacio Sánchez Mejías[1]

1. Cogida[2] and Death

At five in the afternoon.
It was exactly five in the afternoon.
A boy brought the white sheet
at five in the afternoon.
A frail of lime[3] ready prepared   5
at five in the afternoon.
The rest was death, and death alone
at five in the afternoon.

The wind carried away the cottonwool[4]
at five in the afternoon.   10
And the oxide scattered crystal and nickel
at five in the afternoon.
Now the dove and the leopard[5] wrestle
at five in the afternoon.
And a thigh with a desolate horn   15
at five in the afternoon.
The bass-string struck up
at five in the afternoon.
Arsenic bells[6] and smoke
at five in the afternoon.   20
Groups of silence in the corners
at five in the afternoon.
And the bull alone with a high heart!
At five in the afternoon.
When the sweat of snow was coming   25

---

1. Translated by Stephen Spender and J. L. Gili.
2. Harvesting (Spanish, literal trans.); the toss when the bull catches the bullfighter.
3. A disinfectant that was sprinkled on the body after death. "Frail": a basket.
4. To stop the blood; the beginning of a series of medicinal, chemical, and inhuman images that emphasize the presence of death.
5. Traditional symbols for peace and violence; they wrestle with one another as the bullfighter's thigh struggles with the bull's horn.
6. Bells are rung to announce a death. The "bass-string" of the guitar strums a lament.

at five in the afternoon.
when the bull ring was covered in iodine[7]
at five in the afternoon.
death laid eggs in the wound
at five in the afternoon.   30
At five in the afternoon.
Exactly at five o'clock in the afternoon.

A coffin on wheels is his bed
at five in the afternoon.
Bones and flutes resound in his ears[8]   35
at five in the afternoon.
Now the bull was bellowing through his forehead
at five in the afternoon.
The room[9] was iridescent with agony
at five in the afternoon.   40
In the distance the gangrene now comes
at five in the afternoon.
Horn of the lily through green[1] groins
at five in the afternoon.
The wounds were burning like suns   45
at five in the afternoon,
and the crowd was breaking the windows[2]
at five in the afternoon.
At five in the afternoon.
Ah, that fatal five in the afternoon!   50
It was five by all the clocks!
It was five in the shade of the afternoon!

2. The Spilled Blood

I will not see it!

Tell the moon to come
for I do not want to see the blood
of Ignacio on the sand.
I will not see it!

The moon wide open.
Horse of still clouds,
and the grey bull ring of dreams   60
with willows in the barreras.[3]
I will not see it!

---

7. A blood-colored disinfectant for wounds.
8. A suggestion of the medieval dance of
death.
9. The room adjoining the arena where wounded
bullfighters are taken for treatment.
1. Gangrene turns flesh a greenish color.
"Lily": the shape of the wound resembles this

flower.
2. A Spanish idiom for the crowd's loud roar.
3. The barriers around the ring within which
the fight takes place and over which a fighter
may escape the bull's charge. "Willows": symbols of mourning.

Let my memory kindle![4]
Warn the jasmines[5]
of such minute whiteness!
I will not see it!

The cow of the ancient world
passed her sad tongue
over a snout of blood
spilled on the sand,
and the bulls of Guisando,[6]   70
partly death and partly stone,
bellowed like two centuries
sated with treading the earth.
No.
I do not want to see it!   75
I will not see it!

Ignacio goes up the tiers[7]
with all his death on his shoulders.
He sought for the dawn
but the dawn was no more.
He seeks for his confident profile
and the dream bewilders him.
He sought for his beautiful body
and encountered his opened blood.   85
Do not ask me to see it!
I do not want to hear it spurt
each time with less strength:
that spurt that illuminates
the tiers of seats, and spills   90
over the corduroy and the leather
of a thirsty multitude.
Who shouts that I should come near!
Do not ask me to see it!

His eyes did not close   95
when he saw the horns near,
but the terrible mothers
lifted their heads.[8]
And across the ranches,[9]
an air of secret voices rose,   100
shouting to celestial bulls,
herdsmen of pale mist.

4. My memory burns within me (literal trans.).
5. The poet calls on (*warn* as "notify") the small white jasmine flowers to come and cover the blood.
6. Carved stone bulls from the Celtic past, a tourist attraction in the province of Madrid.
7. An imaginary scene in which the bullfighter mounts the stairs of the arena.
8. The three Fates traditionally raised their heads when the thread of life was cut.
9. Fighting bulls are raised on the ranches of Lorca's home province of Andalusia.

There was no prince in Seville[1]
who could compare with him,
nor sword like his sword
nor heart so true.   105
Like a river of lions
was his marvellous strength,
and like a marble torso
his firm drawn moderation.
The air of Andalusian Rome   110
gilded his head[2]
where his smile was a spikenard[3]
of wit and intelligence.
What a great torero[4] in the ring!
What a good peasant in the sierra![5]   115
How gentle with the sheaves!
How hard with the spurs!
How tender with the dew!
How dazzling in the fiesta!
How tremendous with the final   120
banderillas[6] of darkness!

But now he sleeps without end.
Now the moss and the grass
open with sure fingers
the flower of his skull.   125
And now his blood comes out singing;
singing along marshes and meadows,
sliding on frozen horns,
faltering soulless in the mist,
stumbling over a thousand hoofs   130
like a long, dark, sad tongue,
to form a pool of agony
close to the starry Guadalquivir.[7]
Oh, white wall of Spain!
Oh, black bull of sorrow!   135
Oh, hard blood of Ignacio!
Oh, nightingale of his veins!
No.
I will not see it!
No chalice can contain it,   140
no swallows[8] can drink it,

---

1. Leading city of Andalusia.
2. The image suggests a statue from Roman times, when Andalusia was part of the Roman Empire.
3. A small, white, fragrant flower common in Andalusia; by extension, the bullfighter's white teeth.
4. Bullfighter.
5. Mountainous country. Sánchez Mejías is seen as a good *serrano* or "man of the hills."
6. The multicolored short spears that are thrust into the bull's shoulders to provoke him to attack.
7. A great river that passes through all the major cities of Andalusia. The singing stream of the bullfighter's blood suggests both the river and a nightingale.
8. According to a Spanish legend of the Crucifixion, swallows—a symbol of innocence—drank the blood of Christ on the Cross. The "chalice" refers to the legend of the Holy Grail, said to have held Christ's blood after the Crucifixion. The poet is seeking ways of concealing the dead man's blood.

no frost of light can cool it,
nor song nor deluge of white lilies,
no glass can cover it with silver.   145
No.
I will not see it!

3. *The Laid Out Body*[9]

Stone is a forehead where dreams grieve
without curving waters and frozen cypresses.
Stone is a shoulder on which to bear Time   150
with trees formed of tears and ribbons and planets.[1]

I have seen grey showers move towards the waves
raising their tender riddled arms,
to avoid being caught by the lying stone
which loosens their limbs without soaking their blood.   155

For stone gathers seed and clouds,
skeleton larks and wolves of penumbra:
but yields not sounds nor crystals nor fire,
only bull rings and bull rings and more bull rings without walls.

Now Ignacio the well born lies on the stone.   160
All is finished. What is happening? Contemplate his face:
death has covered him with pale sulphur
and has placed on him the head of a dark minotaur.[2]

All is finished. The rain penetrates his mouth.
The air, as if mad, leaves his sunken chest,   165
and Love, soaked through with tears of snow,
warms itself on the peak of the herd.[3]

What are they saying? A stenching silence settles down.
We are here with a body laid out which fades away,
with a pure shape which had nightingales
and we see it being filled with depthless holes.   170

Who creases the shroud? What he says is not true![4]
Nobody sings here, nobody weeps in the corner,
nobody pricks the spurs, nor terrifies the serpent.
Here I want nothing else but the round eyes   175
to see this body without a chance of rest.

9. Present body (literal trans.); the Spanish
expression for a funeral wake, when the body
is laid out for public mourning. The title contrasts with that of the next section: *Absent Soul*.
1. Traditional funeral imagery carved on
gravestones.
2. A monster from Greek myth: half man, half
bull.
3. Of the ranch (literal trans).
4. The speaker criticizes the conventional
pieties voiced by someone standing close to
the shrouded body; he prefers a clear-eyed,
realistic view of death.

Here I want to see those men of hard voice.
Those that break horses and dominate rivers;
those men of sonorous skeleton who sing
with a mouth full of sun and flint.   180

Here I want to see them. Before the stone.
Before this body with broken reins.
I want to know from them the way out
for this captain strapped down by death.

I want them to show me a lament like a river   185
which will have sweet mists and deep shores,
to take the body of Ignacio where it loses itself
without hearing the double panting of the bulls.

Loses itself in the round bull ring of the moon
which feigns in its youth a sad quiet bull: 190
loses itself in the night without song of fishes
and in the white thicket of frozen smoke.

I don't want them to cover his face with handkerchiefs
that he may get used to the death he carries.
Go, Ignacio; feel not the hot bellowing.   195
Sleep, fly, rest: even the sea dies!

4. Absent Soul

The bull does not know you, nor the fig tree,
nor the horses, nor the ants in your own house.
The child and the afternoon do not know you
because you have died for ever.   200

The back of the stone does not know you,
nor the black satin in which you crumble.
Your silent memory does not know you
because you have died for ever.

The autumn will come with small white snails,[5]   205
misty grapes and with clustered hills,
but no one will look into your eyes
because you have died for ever.

Because you have died for ever,
like all the death of the Earth,   210
like all the dead who are forgotten
in a heap of lifeless dogs.[6]

---

5. Horns in the shape of conch shells; the
shepherds' horns that sound in the hills each
fall as the sheep are driven to new pastures.

6. Dogs as an image for undignified, inferior
creatures.

Nobody knows you. No. But I sing of you.
For posterity I sing of your profile and grace.
Of the signal maturity of your understanding.   215
Of your appetite for death and the taste of its mouth.
Of the sadness of your once valiant gaiety.

It will be a long time, if ever, before there is born
an Andalusian so true, so rich in adventure.
I sing of his elegance with words that groan,   220
and I remember a sad breeze through the olive trees.

1935

PABLO NERUDA
1904–1973

The son of a railroad worker and a schoolteacher, with both Spanish and Indian ancestry, the Nobel Prize winner Pablo Neruda became Latin America's most important twentieth-century poet, as well as an advocate for social justice and a leading cultural figure on the Communist left. He wrote in a variety of styles (lyrical, polemic, objective, and prophetic) on an array of subjects (love, daily life, the natural world, political oppression), evoking the most elemental levels of human emotion and experience. In the second half of his life, moved especially by the Spanish Civil War, Neruda adopted the role of public poet, putting his writing at the service of the people.

The writer was born Neftalí Ricardo Reyes y Basoalto, on July 12, 1904, in the small town of Parral, in southern Chile. His mother died a month after his birth. Two years later his father moved to Temuco, where he remarried and where Neruda had his early schooling. Temuco was a frontier town, and the boy's father, who disapproved of aesthetic pursuits, did not encourage his love of literature. Neruda was fortunate to find a mentor in the poet Gabriela Mistral, the principal of the girls' school at Temuco, who would herself win the Nobel Prize in Literature in 1945. To encourage the young writer, Mistral loaned him books. He began publishing his poetry at age thirteen. Seeking a pen name that would not be tied to the provinces, he chose the surname of a Czech writer, Jan Neruda, and the given name Pablo, which some critics have associated with Saint Paul the apostle.

After working and studying in poverty in Chile's capital, Santiago, from 1921 to 1927, Neruda was appointed the nation's consul to Rangoon, Burma (now Myanmar). He would serve in Ceylon (now Sri Lanka), Java (in Indonesia), and Singapore, and then, after 1933, in Buenos Aires, Barcelona, Madrid, Paris, and Mexico City. During his residence in Spain, Neruda, influenced by his friends the poets

Federico García Lorca, Rafael Alberti, and Miguel Hernández, assumed a more activist political stance. In 1936, civil war broke out in Spain between the Republic and the forces of General Francisco Franco. Franco's Fascist guards dragged Neruda's friend Lorca out of a friend's house; he was presumably shot, but his body was never recovered. (Neruda recalls the event in the poem "I'm Explaining a Few Things.") From that point on, Neruda would be a public poet, dedicating his voice to social issues rather than to private feelings and addressing a larger community.

Neruda returned to Chile in 1943, and, within two years, was elected to the Senate, as a representative of the Communist Party. When he criticized Chile's president in a speech on the Senate floor, Neruda's house was attacked, the government ordered his arrest, and he was forced to flee the country. Though he was celebrated internationally, with official honors from Latin America, the Soviet Union, Europe, India, and China, Neruda nonetheless could not return to Chile until 1952. He retained his close association with the Communist Party and even wrote a poem in praise of the Soviet dictator Joseph Stalin.

In 1970, Neruda ran for president of Chile as the Communist candidate, but he withdrew in favor of the Socialist Salvador Allende, who won the election and appointed Neruda ambassador to Paris. In 1971, Neruda received the Nobel Prize for Literature; the following year he returned to his home in Isla Negra, gravely ill with cancer. The news at home was not good: political tensions were mounting, and Neruda watched television coverage of the rising unrest. On September 11, 1973, President Allende was assassinated in a military coup led by General Augusto Pinochet. Neruda died twelve days later. It was at Neruda's funeral that the first public demonstration against Pinochet's military government took place—a fitting tribute to Chile's national poet and representative of the people.

The selections presented here begin with Neruda's beautiful and popular early love poem "Tonight I Can Write . . ." (1924), which makes use of couplets, repetition, and chiasmus (rhetorical inversion) to explore the speaker's evolving consciousness of a love affair. While maintaining the lyrical and personal tone of his earlier poetry, "Walking Around" demonstrates Neruda's turn toward public subject matter—here expressed not in the political terms of his later work but as a description of urban life and the sufferings of the poor. In "I'm Explaining a Few Things" (1936), however, Neruda engages explicitly with politics, and his repeated exhortation, "Come and see the blood in the streets!" illustrates the speaker's intention to address his audience directly and to dedicate his voice to public issues rather than private feelings.

Canto General (1950) celebrates both Latin American identity and humanity at large. It also recreates the continent's history—anchored, for Neruda, especially after a spiritual experience he had in 1943, in the lost Inca city of Macchu Picchu, in Peru. (The usual spelling is "Machu Picchu," but Neruda uses "Macchu" throughout.) On climbing to the city's stone ruins in October of that year, the poet had an almost mystical vision showing the past linked with natural forces and the progress of humanity—a vision he described two years later in the crucial second canto of *Canto General: The Heights of Macchu Picchu*, published as a separate poem in 1946 and only later integrated into the larger work. Its twelve sections (also called cantos) are divided into two broad movements that express several philosophical attitudes and represent a turning point in the poet's thought. Throughout the first five cantos, the speaker struggles with a sense of loss and alienation; but, starting with Canto VI, as he depicts his ascent to Macchu Picchu, he comes to an understanding of a suffering human community that now gives meaning to his hitherto solitary existence. The portion printed here, the second half of *The Heights of Macchu Picchu*, begins with the speaker's invocation of the abandoned city, after climbing to its perch on a precipice in the Andes. He addresses the city as a "mother of stone"—the mother of the Latin American people— and bears witness to a lost civilization. Canto IX consists of a sequence of extraordinary metaphors that portray the city in fused images of nature and daily life—images of the passage of time and of intuited connections that transcend chronology. In Cantos X through XII, the speaker imagines the experience of the people who interest him most: the laborers who built Macchu Picchu and knew

hunger and fatigue. Though they are long dead, he senses their voices and memories entering his flesh and blood, as both he and they are reborn in a unity of the people.

The final work here, "Ode to the Tomato" (1954), shows Neruda shifting his poetic style once again, employing an unadorned expression to focus on everyday subject matter. His *Elemental Odes* (1954) examines such ordinary topics as fire, rain, bread, clothes, bees, and tomatoes. The new simplicity stemmed from Neruda's commitment to his role as public poet; he felt a responsibility to write for a broader audience, he said, including those who were just learning to read. "We must go back to what is simply human," he said; the joyous "Ode to the Tomato" responds to this need.

Tonight I Can Write . . .[1]

Tonight I can write the saddest lines.

Write, for example, 'The night is shattered
and the blue stars shiver in the distance.'

The night wind revolves in the sky and sings.

Tonight I can write the saddest lines.   5
I loved her, and sometimes she loved me too.

Through nights like this one I held her in my arms.
I kissed her again and again under the endless sky.

She loved me, sometimes I loved her too.
How could one not have loved her great still eyes.   10

Tonight I can write the saddest lines.
To think that I do not have her. To feel that I have lost her.

To hear the immense night, still more immense without her.
And the verse falls to the soul like dew to the pasture.

1. Translated by W. S. Merwin.

What does it matter that my love could not keep her. 15
The night is shattered and she is not with me.

This is all. In the distance someone is singing. In the distance.
My soul is not satisfied that it has lost her.

My sight searches for her as though to go to her.
My heart looks for her, and she is not with me. 20

The same night whitening the same trees.
We, of that time, are no longer the same.

I no longer love her, that's certain, but how I loved her.
My voice tried to find the wind to touch her hearing.

Another's. She will be another's. Like my kisses before. 25
Her voice. Her bright body. Her infinite eyes.

I no longer love her, that's certain, but maybe I love her.
Love is so short, forgetting is so long.

Because through nights like this one I held her in my arms
my soul is not satisfied that it has lost her. 30

Though this be the last pain that she makes me suffer
and these the last verses that I write for her.

1924

Walking Around[1]

It happens that I am tired of being a man.
It happens that I go into the tailor's shops and the movies
all shrivelled up, impenetrable, like a felt swan
navigating on a water of origin and ash.

The smell of barber shops makes me sob out loud. 5
I want nothing but the repose either of stones or of wool,
I want to see no more establishments, no more gardens,
nor merchandise, nor glasses, nor elevators.

It happens that I am tired of my feet and my nails
and my hair and my shadow. 10
It happens that I am tired of being a man.

Just the same it would be delicious
to scare a notary with a cut lily
or knock a nun stone dead with one blow of an ear.

1. Translated by W. S. Merwin.

It would be beautiful   15
to go through the streets with a green knife
shouting until I died of cold.

I do not want to go on being a root in the dark,
hesitating, stretched out, shivering with dreams,
downwards, in the wet tripe of the earth,   20
soaking it up and thinking, eating every day.

I do not want to be the inheritor of so many misfortunes.
I do not want to continue as a root and as a tomb,
as a solitary tunnel, as a cellar full of corpses,
stiff with cold, dying with pain.   25

For this reason Monday burns like oil
at the sight of me arriving with my jail-face,
and it howls in passing like a wounded wheel,
and its footsteps towards nightfall are filled with hot blood.

And it shoves me along to certain corners, to certain damp houses,   30
to hospitals where the bones come out of the windows,
to certain cobblers' shops smelling of vinegar,
to streets horrendous as crevices.

There are birds the colour of sulphur, and horrible intestines
hanging from the doors of the houses which I hate,   35
there are forgotten sets of teeth in a coffee-pot,
there are mirrors
which should have wept with shame and horror,
there are umbrellas all over the place, and poisons, and navels.

I stride along with calm, with eyes, with shoes,   40
with fury, with forgetfulness,
I pass, I cross offices and stores full of orthopaedic appliances,
and courtyards hung with clothes on wires,
underpants, towels and shirts which weep
slow dirty tears.   45

1933

I'm Explaining a Few Things[1]

You are going to ask: and where are the lilacs?
and the poppy-petalled metaphysics?
and the rain repeatedly spattering
its words and drilling them full
of apertures and birds?   5

1. Translated by Nathaniel Tarn.

I'll tell you all the news.

I lived in a suburb,
a suburb of Madrid,[2] with bells,
and clocks, and trees.

From there you could look out   10
over Castile's[3] dry face:
a leather ocean.
              My house was called
the house of flowers, because in every cranny
geraniums burst: it was
a good-looking house   15
with its dogs and children.
                    Remember, Raúl?
Eh, Rafael?
              Federico,[4] do you remember
from under the ground
my balconies on which
the light of June drowned flowers in your mouth?
                              Brother, my brother!   20
Everything
loud with big voices, the salt of merchandises,
pile-ups of palpitating bread,
the stalls of my suburb of Argüelles with its statue
like a drained inkwell in a swirl of hake:[5]   25
oil flowed into spoons,
a deep baying
of feet and hands swelled in the streets,
metres, litres, the sharp
measure of life,
              stacked-up fish,   30
the texture of roofs with a cold sun in which
the weather vane falters,
the fine, frenzied ivory of potatoes,
wave on wave of tomatoes rolling down to the sea.

And one morning all that was burning,   35
one morning the bonfires
leapt out of the earth
devouring human beings—
and from then on fire,
gunpowder from then on,   40
and from then on blood.
Bandits with planes and Moors,

2. The capital of Spain.
3. Spain.
4. I.e., the poet Federico García Lorca, who was
murdered by the Fascists on August 19, 1936.

"Rafael": his friend, the poet Rafael Alberti.
5. A fish similar to the cod. "Argüelles": a busy
shopping area in Madrid, near the university.

bandits with finger-rings and duchesses,
bandits with black friars[6] spattering blessings
came through the sky to kill children   45
and the blood of children ran through the streets
without fuss, like children's blood.

Jackals that the jackals would despise,
stones that the dry thistle would bite on and spit out,
vipers that the vipers would abominate!   50

Face to face with you I have seen the blood
of Spain tower like a tide
to drown you in one wave
of pride and knives!

Treacherous   55
generals:
see my dead house,
look at broken Spain:
from every house burning metal flows
instead of flowers,   60
from every socket of Spain
Spain emerges
and from every dead child a rifle with eyes,
and from every crime bullets are born
which will one day find   65
the bull's eye of your hearts.

And you will ask: why doesn't his poetry
speak of dreams and leaves
and the great volcanoes of his native land?

Come and see the blood in the streets.   70
Come and see
the blood in the streets.
Come and see the blood
in the streets!

                                                                1936

---

6. "Finger-rings," "duchesses," "friars" imply a collusion of the wealthy, the aristocracy, and the Church to suppress the people. "Bandits": Neruda lists categories of invaders. "Moors": probably an analogy between the early Muslim invaders of Spain and German and Italian pilots who bombed the village of Guernica in April 1937.

General Song (Canto General)[1]

From *Canto II. The Heights of Macchu Picchu*[2]

VI

And so I scaled the ladder of the earth
amid the atrocious maze of lost jungles
up to you, Macchu Picchu.
High citadel of terraced stones,
at long last the dwelling of him whom the earth   5
did not conceal in its slumbering vestments.
In you, as in two parallel lines,
the cradle of lightning and man
was rocked in a wind of thorns.

Mother of stone, sea spray of the condors.   10

Towering reef of the human dawn.

Spade lost in the primal sand.

This was the dwelling, this is the site:
here the full kernels of corn rose
and fell again like red hailstones.   15
Here the golden fiber emerged from the vicuña[3]
to clothe love, tombs, mothers,
the king, prayers, warriors.

Here man's feet rested at night
beside the eagle's feet, in the high gory   20
retreats, and at dawn
they trod the rarefied mist with feet of thunder
and touched lands and stones
until they recognized them in the night or in death.

I behold vestments and hands,   25
the vestige of water in the sonorous void,
the wall tempered by the touch of a face
that beheld with my eyes the earthen lamps,
that oiled with my hands the vanished
wood: because everything—clothing, skin, vessels,   30
words, wine, bread—
is gone, fallen to earth.

---

1. Translated by Jack Schmitt.
2. Ancient city of the Incas, situated on a remote precipice in the Andes mountains of Peru; the city escaped the Spanish invaders and was rediscovered in 1911. The Inca empire flourished in the 14th century and was destroyed by Francisco Pizarro in 1532.
3. A llama-like animal, found in the Andes, that has a fine soft fleece.

And the air flowed with orange-blossom
fingers over all the sleeping:
a thousand years of air, months, weeks of air,   35
of blue wind, of iron cordillera,[4]
like gentle hurricanes of footsteps
polishing the solitary precinct of stone.

VII

O remains of a single abyss, shadows of one gorge—
the deep one—the real, most searing death
attained the scale
of your magnitude,
and from the quarried stones,   5
from the spires,
from the terraced aqueducts
you tumbled as in autumn
to a single death.
Today the empty air no longer weeps,   10
no longer knows your feet of clay,
has now forgotten your pitchers that filtered the sky
when the lightning's knives emptied it,
and the powerful tree was eaten away
by the mist and felled by the wind.   15
It sustained a hand that fell suddenly
from the heights to the end of time.
You are no more, spider hands, fragile
filaments, spun web:
all that you were has fallen: customs, frayed   20
syllables, masks of dazzling light.
But a permanence of stone and word:
the citadel was raised like a chalice in the hands
of all, the living, the dead, the silent, sustained
by so much death, a wall, from so much life a stroke   25
of stone petals: the permanent rose, the dwelling:
this Andean reef of glacial colonies.

When the clay-colored hand
turned to clay, when the little eyelids closed,
filled with rough walls, brimming with castles,   30
and when the entire man was trapped in his hole,
exactitude remained hoisted aloft:
this high site of the human dawn:
the highest vessel that has contained silence:
a life of stone after so many lives.   35

---

4. Mountain range.

VIII

Rise up with me, American[5] love.

Kiss the secret stones with me.
The torrential silver of the Urubamba[6]
makes the pollen fly to its yellow cup.
It spans the void of the grapevine,   5
the petrous plant, the hard wreath
upon the silence of the highland casket.
Come, minuscule life, between the wings
of the earth, while—crystal and cold, pounded air
extracting assailed emeralds—   10
O, wild water, you run down from the snow.

Love, love, even the abrupt night,
from the sonorous Andean flint
to the dawn's red knees,
contemplates the snow's blind child.   15

O, sonorous threaded Wilkamayu,
when you beat your lineal thunder
to a white froth, like wounded snow,
when your precipitous storm
sings and batters, awakening the sky,   20
what language do you bring to the ear recently
wrenched from your Andean froth?

Who seized the cold's lightning
and left it shackled in the heights,
dispersed in its glacial tears,   25
smitten in its swift swords,
hammering its embattled stamens,
borne on its warrior's bed,
startled in its rocky end?

What are your tormented sparks saying?   30
Did your secret insurgent lightning
once journey charged with words?
Who keeps on shattering frozen syllables,
black languages, golden banners,
deep mouths, muffled cries,   35
in your slender arterial waters?

Who keeps on cutting floral eyelids
that come to gaze from the earth?
Who hurls down the dead clusters
that fell in your cascade hands   40

5. For Neruda (and for many Latin Americans), *America* refers to Latin America; North
America is called "Saxon America."

6. The river flowing through the valley below
Macchu Picchu, called Wilkamayu by the
Indians.

to strip the night stripped
in the coal of geology?

Who flings the branch down from its bonds?
Who once again entombs farewells?

Love, love, never touch the brink   45
or worship the sunken head:
let time attain its stature
in its salon of shattered headsprings,
and, between the swift water and the walls,
gather the air from the gorge,   50
the parallel sheets of the wind,
the cordilleras' blind canal,
the harsh greeting of the dew,
and, rise up, flower by flower, through the dense growth,
treading the hurtling serpent.   55

In the steep zone—forest and stone,
mist of green stars, radiant jungle—
Mantur explodes like a blinding lake
or a new layer of silence.

Come to my very heart, to my dawn,   60
up to the crowned solitudes.
The dead kingdom is still alive.

And over the Sundial the sanguinary shadow
of the condor[7] crosses like a black ship.

IX

Sidereal eagle, vineyard of mist.
Lost bastion, blind scimitar.
Spangled waistband, solemn bread.
Torrential stairway, immense eyelid.
Triangular tunic, stone pollen.   5
Granite lamp, stone bread.
Mineral serpent, stone rose.
Entombed ship, stone headspring.
Moonhorse, stone light.
Equinoctial square, stone vapor.   10
Ultimate geometry, stone book.
Tympanum fashioned amid the squalls.
Madrepore[8] of sunken time.

7. The heights of Macchu Picchu and the smaller Huayna Picchu were said to form the shape of a condor, a large vulturelike bird seen as the messenger of humanity. "Sundial": the *intihuatana*, or "hitching post of the sun," a large altar carved directly out of the granite; its shape and position served to predict the date of the winter solstice and other periods of importance to agriculture.
8. Coral.

Rampart tempered by fingers.
Ceiling assailed by feathers.   15
Mirror bouquets, stormy foundations.
Thrones toppled by the vine.
Regime of the enraged claw.
Hurricane sustained on the slopes.
Immobile cataract of turquoise.   20
Patriarchal bell of the sleeping.
Hitching ring of the tamed snows.
Iron recumbent upon its statues.
Inaccessible dark tempest.
Puma hands, bloodstained rock.   25
Towering sombrero, snowy dispute.
Night raised on fingers and roots.
Window of the mists, hardened dove.
Nocturnal plant, statue of thunder.
Essential cordillera, searoof.   30
Architecture of lost eagles.
Skyrope, heavenly bee.
Bloody level, man-made star.
Mineral bubble, quartz moon.
Andean serpent, brow of amaranth.[9]   35
Cupola of silence, pure land.
Seabride, tree of cathedrals.
Cluster of salt, black-winged cherry tree.
Snow-capped teeth, cold thunderbolt.
Scored moon, menacing stone.   40
Headdresses of the cold, action of the air.
Volcano of hands, obscure cataract.
Silver wave, pointer of time.

X

Stone upon stone, and man, where was he?
Air upon air, and man, where was he?
Time upon time, and man, where was he?
Were you too a broken shard
of inconclusive man, of empty raptor,   5
who on the streets today, on the trails,
on the dead autumn leaves, keeps
tearing away at the heart right up to the grave?
Poor hand, foot, poor life . . .
Did the days of light   10
unraveled in you, like raindrops
on the banners of a feast day,
give petal by petal of their dark food
to the empty mouth?
                  Hunger, coral of mankind,
hunger, secret plant, woodcutters' stump,   15

9. An annual plant with flowers and highly nutritious edible seeds.

hunger, did the edge of your reef rise up
to these high suspended towers?

I want to know, salt of the roads,
show me the spoon—architecture, let me
scratch at the stamens of stone with a little stick,   20
ascend the rungs of the air up to the void,
scrape the innards until I touch mankind.

Macchu Picchu, did you put
stone upon stone and, at the base, tatters?
Coal upon coal and, at the bottom, tears?   25
Fire in gold and, within it, the trembling
drop of red blood?
Bring me back the slave that you buried!
Shake from the earth the hard bread
of the poor wretch, show me   30
the slave's clothing and his window.
Tell me how he slept when he lived.
Tell me if his sleep was
harsh, gaping, like a black chasm
worn by fatigue upon the wall.   35
The wall, the wall! If upon his sleep
each layer of stone weighed down, and if he fell beneath it
as beneath a moon, with his dream!
Ancient America, sunken bride,
your fingers too,   40
on leaving the jungle for the high void of the gods,
beneath the nuptial standards of light and decorum,
mingling with the thunder of drums and spears,
your fingers, your fingers too,
which the abstract rose, the cold line, and   45
the crimson breast of the new grain transferred
to the fabric of radiant substance, to the hard cavities—
did you, entombed America, did you too store in the depths
of your bitter intestine, like an eagle, hunger?

XI

Through the hazy splendor,
through the stone night, let me plunge my hand,
and let the aged heart of the forsaken beat in me
like a bird captive for a thousand years!
Let me forget, today, this joy, which is greater than the sea,   5
because man is greater than the sea and its islands,
and we must fall into him as into a well to emerge from the bottom
with a bouquet of secret water and sunken truths.
Let me forget, great stone, the powerful proportion,
the transcendent measure, the honeycombed stones,   10
and from the square let me today run
my hand over the hypotenuse of rough blood and sackcloth.

When, like a horseshoe of red elytra,[1] the frenzied condor
beats my temples in the order of its flight,
and the hurricane of cruel feathers sweeps the somber dust   15
from the diagonal steps, I do not see the swift brute,
I do not see the blind cycle of its claws,
I see the man of old, the servant, asleep in the fields,
I see a body, a thousand bodies, a man, a thousand women,
black with rain and night, beneath the black squall,   20
with the heavy stone of the statue:
Juan Stonecutter, son of Wiracocha[2]
Juan Coldeater, son of a green star,
Juan Barefoot, grandson of turquoise,
rise up to be born with me, my brother.   25

XII

Rise up to be born with me, my brother.

Give me your hand from the deep
zone of your disseminated sorrow.
You'll not return from the bottom of the rocks.
You'll not return from subterranean time.   5
Your stiff voice will not return.
Your drilled eyes will not return.
Behold me from the depths of the earth,
laborer, weaver, silent herdsman:
tamer of the tutelary guanacos:[3]   10
mason of the defied scaffold:
bearer of the Andean tears:
jeweler with your fingers crushed:
tiller trembling in the seed:
potter spilt in your clay: 15
bring to the cup of this new life, brothers,
all your timeless buried sorrows.
Show me your blood and your furrow,
tell me: I was punished here,
because the jewel did not shine or the earth   20
did not surrender the gemstone or kernel on time:
show me the stone on which you fell
and the wood on which you were crucified,
strike the old flintstones,
the old lamps, the whips sticking   25
throughout the centuries to your wounds
and the war clubs glistening red.
I've come to speak through your dead mouths.
Throughout the earth join all
the silent scattered lips   30

1. An insect's wing cases.
2. Inca rain god who taught the arts of civilization to humanity.

3. Reddish-brown grazing animals related to
the llama.

and from the depths speak to me all night long,
as if I were anchored with you,
tell me everything, chain by chain,
link by link, and step by step,
sharpen the knives that you've kept,   35
put them in my breast and in my hand,
like a river of yellow lightning,
like a river of buried jaguars,
and let me weep hours, days, years,
blind ages, stellar centuries.   40

Give me silence, water, hope.

Give me struggle, iron, volcanoes.

Cling to my body like magnets.

Hasten to my veins and to my mouth.

Speak through my words and my blood.   45

1950

Ode to the Tomato[1]

The street
drowns in tomatoes:
noon,
summer,
light   5
breaks
in two
tomato
halves,
and the streets   10
run
with juice.
In December[2]
the tomato
cuts loose,   15
invades
kitchens,
takes over lunches,
settles
at rest   20
on sideboards,

1. Translated by Nathaniel Tarn.   2. Summer in Chile.

with the glasses,
butter dishes,
blue salt-cellars.
It has   25
its own radiance,
a goodly majesty.
Too bad we must
assassinate:
a knife   30
plunges
into its living pulp,
red
viscera,
a fresh,   35
deep,
inexhaustible
sun
floods the salads
of Chile,   40
beds cheerfully
with the blonde onion,
and to celebrate
oil
the filial essence   45
of the olive tree
lets itself fall
over its gaping hemispheres,
the pimento
adds   50
its fragrance,
salt its magnetism—
we have the day's
wedding:
parsley   55
flaunts
its little flags,
potatoes
thump to a boil,
the roasts   60
beat
down the door
with their aromas:
it's time!
let's go!   65
and upon
the table,
belted by summer,
tomatoes,
stars of the earth,   70
stars multiplied
and fertile

show off
their convolutions,
canals   75
and plenitudes
and the abundance
boneless,
without husk,
or scale or thorn,   80
grant us
the festival
of ardent colour
and all-embracing freshness.

1954

OCTAVIO PAZ

1914–1998

A leading Mexican writer of the twentieth century, the Nobel Prize winner Octavio Paz drew on ancient myth to characterize urban life in his native land and around the world. A poet, cultural critic, diplomat, and public intellectual, Paz applied the experimental forms of Latin American and European modernism to the challenge of expressing contemporary Mexican identity.

Paz was born during the chaotic years of the Mexican Revolution. His father, a journalist and lawyer, supported the revolutionary Emiliano Zapata and was exiled from Mexico after Zapata's death in 1919. Although Paz lived briefly with his father in Los Angeles, he grew up mostly in the suburban Mexico City home of his paternal grandfather, a liberal intellectual whose library included great works of Spanish classical literature and Latin American modernism. Paz started writing poetry in his teens and soon became involved

in the literary journal *Contemporáneos*, which published translations of many French- and English-language modernists. He particularly admired the poetry of **Stéphane Mallarmé** and **T. S. Eliot**'s *The Waste Land.* Paz studied law at college before dropping out to teach at a school for peasant children in the Yucatán peninsula.

Inspired by the ideals of social justice espoused by the revolution, Paz became active in international left-wing politics. In 1937, during the Spanish Civil War, he attended the second International Congress of Anti-Fascist Writers in Spain as the guest of the Chilean poet **Pablo Neruda**, whose work Paz admired. "For me," he wrote, "Neruda was the great destructor-creator of Hispanic poetry." Like Neruda, Paz entered his country's diplomatic service, first representing Mexico as a cultural attaché in Paris from 1946 to 1951. He had long been interested in surrealism and became friendly with the movement's founder, **André Breton**. Later he would represent Mexico in Geneva, New York, and India, where he developed an interest in Buddhism and Hinduism.

The writer's most famous work on Mexican history and culture, *The Labyrinth of Solitude* (1950), emphasized the condition of solitude and despair that affected Mexicans but was in some sense universal: "our situation of alienation is that of the majority of people." He saw the Mexican as by nature reserved, enclosed, and isolated. At this time, Paz still acknowledges the legacy of the Mexican Revolution in bringing individuals together as a community. He became disillusioned with Mexican politics and resigned his post as ambassador to India in 1968, however, in protest against the Mexican government massacre of student demonstrators. Paz returned to Mexico City and wrote a series of poems later collected as *Vuelta* (*Return*), which was also the title of a journal he edited from 1975 until his death. In 1990 he celebrated the end of communism in Eastern Europe by hosting a conference of leading writers and intellectuals from East and West in Mexico City. That same year the Nobel committee honored him for his "impassioned writing with wide horizons, characterized by sensuous intelligence and humanistic integrity."

The works selected here span the later stages of Paz's career, when he was at the height of his poetic powers. They combine intense lyricism with a surrealist-inspired fascination with the irrational and the unconscious. Surrealism, Buddhism, and Hinduism seemed to Paz to offer alternatives to the rationalism of traditional European culture. "Surrealism was not merely an esthetic, poetic and philosophical doctrine," he once said. "It was a vital attitude. A negation of the contemporary world and at the same time an attempt to substitute other values for those of democratic bourgeois society: eroticism, poetry, imagination, liberty, spiritual adventure, vision." Paz's long poem "I Speak of the City" (1976) evokes elements of the Mexican capital, New York City, London, and Rome and draws on the tradition of free verse from **Walt Whitman** and T. S. Eliot through the surrealists. Another late poem, specifically about New York, "Central Park" (1987) was inspired by a painting by the Belgian artist Pierre Alechinsky and contains the repeated warning (in English in the original) "Don't cross Central Park at night." "Small Variation" (1987), written when the poet was in his seventies, recollects the sorrow of Gilgamesh in the ancient epic and echoes other, later laments to create a moving meditation on human mortality. Throughout these lyrical and imaginative works, Paz uses rhythmic, loose poetic forms, in the tradition of free verse, to present a haunting vision of urban life that is in touch with the deeper, subterranean forces of the human spirit.

I Speak of the City[1]

for Eliot Weinberger

a novelty today, tomorrow a ruin from the past, buried and resurrected every day,

   lived together in streets, plazas, buses, taxis, movie houses, theaters,
bars, hotels, pigeon coops and catacombs,

   the enormous city that fits in a room three yards square, and endless as   5
a galaxy,

   the city that dreams us all, that all of us build and unbuild and rebuild
as we dream,

   the city we all dream, that restlessly changes while we dream it,

   the city that wakes every hundred years and looks at itself in the mir-   10
ror of a word and doesn't recognize itself and goes back to sleep,

   the city that sprouts from the eyelids of the woman who sleeps at my
side, and is transformed,

   with its monuments and statues, its histories and legends,

   into a fountain made of countless eyes, and each eye reflects the same   15
landscape, frozen in time,

   before schools and prisons, alphabets and numbers, the altar and the
law:

   the river that is four rivers, the orchard, the tree, the Female and Male,
dressed in wind—   20

   to go back, go back, to be clay again, to bathe in that light, to sleep
under those votive lights,

   to float on the waters of time like the flaming maple leaf the current
drags along,

   to go back—are we asleep or awake?—we are, we are nothing more,   25
day breaks, it's early,

   we are in the city, we cannot leave except to fall into another city,
different yet identical,

   I speak of the immense city, that daily reality composed of two words:
the others,   30

   and in every one of them there is an I clipped from a we, an I adrift,

   I speak of the city built by the dead, inhabited by their stern ghosts,
ruled by their despotic memory,

   the city I talk to when I talk to nobody, the city that dictates these
insomniac words,   35

   I speak of towers, bridges, tunnels, hangars, wonders and disasters,

   the abstract State and its concrete police, the schoolteachers, jailers,
preachers,

   the shops that have everything, where we spend everything, and it all
turns to smoke,   40

   the markets with their pyramids of fruit, the turn of the seasons, the
sides of beef hanging from the hooks, the hills of spices and the towers of
bottles and preserves,

   all of the flavors and colors, all the smells and all the stuff, the tide of
voices—water, metal, wood, clay—the bustle, the haggling and conniv-   45
ing as old as time,

---

1. Translated by Eliot Weinberger, a frequent translator of Paz's work to whom the poem is
dedicated.

I speak of the buildings of stone and marble, of cement, glass and steel, of the people in the lobbies and doorways, of the elevators that rise and fall like the mercury in thermometers,

of the banks and their boards of directors, of factories and their man- 50
agers, of the workers and their incestuous machines,

I speak of the timeless parade of prostitution through streets long as desire and boredom,

of the coming and going of cars, mirrors of our anxieties, business, passions (why? toward what? for what?), 55

of the hospitals that are always full, and where we always die alone,

I speak of the half-light of certain churches and the flickering candles at the altars,

the timid voices with which the desolate talk to saints and virgins in a passionate, failing language, 60

I speak of dinner under a squinting light at a limping table with chipped plates,

of the innocent tribes that camp in the empty lots with their women and children, their animals and their ghosts,

of the rats in the sewers and the brave sparrows that nest in the wires, 65
in the cornices and the martyred trees,

of the contemplative cats and their libertine novels in the light of the moon, cruel goddess of the rooftops,

of the stray dogs that are our Franciscans and *bhikkus*,[2] the dogs that scratch up the bones of the sun, 70

I speak of the anchorite and the libertarian brotherhood, of the secret plots of law enforcers and of bands of thieves,

of the conspiracies of levelers and the Society of Friends of Crime, of the Suicide Club, and of Jack the Ripper,[3]

of the Friend of the People, sharpener of the guillotine, of Caesar, De- 75
light of Humankind,[4]

I speak of the paralytic slum, the cracked wall, the dry fountain, the graffitied statue,

I speak of garbage heaps the size of mountains, and of melancholy sunlight filtered by the smog, 80

of broken glass and the desert of scrap iron, of last night's crime, and of the banquet of the immortal Trimalchio,[5]

of the moon in the television antennas, and a butterfly on a filthy jar,

I speak of dawns like a flight of herons on the lake, and the sun of transparent wings that lands on the rock foliage of the churches, and the 85
twittering of light on the glass stalks of the palaces,

2. Buddhist monks. "Franciscans": Catholic monks.
3. Famous serial killer in 19th-century London whose identity was never discovered. The Society of Friends of Crime is a fictional organization invented by the Marquis de Sade (1740–1814). The Suicide Club was a similar organization invented by the Scottish novelist Robert Louis Stevenson (1850–1894). All three references concern urban criminality.

4. An epithet of the Roman emperor Titus (39–81). Caesar was a title associated with several Roman emperors. The French revolutionary Jean-Paul Marat said that the king should be "a friend of the people." These references concern the power of a strong leader to control the mob.
5. Character in *The Satyricon* by Petronius, famous for throwing ostentatious dinners of many courses.

I speak of certain afternoons in early fall, waterfalls of immaterial gold, the transformation of this world, when everything loses its body, everything is held in suspense,

and the light thinks, and each one of us feels himself thought by that reflec- 90
tive light, and for one long moment time dissolves, we are air once more,

I speak of the summer, of the slow night that grows on the horizon like a mountain of smoke, and bit by bit it crumbles, falling over us like a wave,

the elements are reconciled, night has stretched out, and its body is a powerful river of sudden sleep, we rock in the waves of its breathing, the 95
hour is tangible, we can touch it like a fruit,

they have lit the lights, and the avenues burn with the brilliancy of desire, in the parks electric light breaks through the branches and falls over us like a green and phosphorescent mist that illuminates but does not wet us, the trees murmur, they tell us something, 100

there are streets in the half-light that are a smiling insinuation, we don't know where they lead, perhaps to the ferry for the lost islands,

I speak of the stars over the high terraces and the indecipherable sentences they write on the stone of the sky,

I speak of the sudden downpour that lashes the windowpanes and 105
bends the trees, that lasted twenty-five minutes and now, up above, there are blue slits and streams of light, steam rises from the asphalt, the cars glisten, there are puddles where ships of reflections sail,

I speak of nomadic clouds, and of a thin music that lights a room on the fifth floor, and a murmur of laughter in the middle of the night like 110
water that flows far-off through roots and grasses,

I speak of the longed-for encounter with that unexpected form with which the unknown is made flesh, and revealed to each of us:

eyes that are the night half-open and the day that wakes, the sea stretching out and the flame that speaks, powerful breasts: lunar tide, 115

lips that say sesame, and time opens, and the little room becomes a garden of change, air and fire entwine, earth and water mingle,

or the arrival of that moment there, on the other side that is really here, where the key locks and time ceases to flow:

the moment of until now, the last of the gasps, the moaning, the an- 120
guish, the soul loses its body and crashes through a hole in the floor, falling in itself, and time has run aground, and we walk through an endless corridor, panting in the sand,

is that music coming closer or receding, are those pale lights just lit or going out? space is singing, time has vanished: it is the gasp, it is the glance 125
that slips through the blank wall, it is the wall that stays silent, the wall,

I speak of our public history, and of our secret history, yours and mine,

I speak of the forest of stone, the desert of the prophets, the ant-heap of souls, the congregation of tribes, the house of mirrors, the labyrinth of echoes, 135

I speak of the great murmur that comes from the depths of time, the incoherent whisper of nations uniting or splitting apart, the wheeling of multitudes and their weapons like boulders hurling down, the dull sound of bones falling into the pit of history,

I speak of the city, shepherd of the centuries, mother that gives birth 140
to us and devours us, that creates us and forgets.

1976

Small Variation[1]

Like music come back to life—
who brings it from over there, from the other side,
who conducts it through the spirals
of the mind's ear?—
like the vanished   5
moment that returns
and is again the same
presence erasing itself,
the syllables unearthed
make sound without sound: 10
and at the hour of our death, amen.[2]

In the school chapel
I spoke them many times
without conviction. Now I hear them
spoken by a voice without lips,   15
a sound of sand sifting away,
while in my skull the hours toll
and time takes another turn around my night.
I am not the first man on earth—
I tell myself in the manner of Epictetus[3]—   20
who is going to die.
And as I say this
the world breaks down in my blood.

                                                               The sorrow
of Gilgamesh[4] when he returned   25
from the land without twilight
is my sorrow. On our shadowy earth
each man is Adam:
                                  with him the world begins,[5]
with him it ends.   30
                         Between after and before—
brackets of stone—
for an instant that will never return I shall be
the first man and I shall be the last.
And as I say it, the instant—   35
bodiless, weightless—
opens under my feet
and closes over me and is pure time.

                                                                                        1987

1. Translated by Mark Strand.
2. Final line of the Lord's Prayer.
3. Greek stoic philosopher who counseled acceptance of fate, including mortality.
4. Protagonist of the Mesopotamian *Epic of Gilgamesh*, who visits the underworld where the dead dwell.
5. Adam was punished with mortality for his disobedience (Genesis 2.17).

Central Park[1]

Green and black thickets, bare spots,
leafy river knotting into itself:
it runs motionless through the leaden buildings
and there, where light turns to doubt
and stone wants to be shadow, it vanishes.   5
Don't cross Central Park at night.[2]

Day falls, night flares up,
Alechinsky draws a magnetic rectangle,
a trap of lines, a corral of ink:
inside there is a fallen beast,   10
two eyes and a twisting rage.
Don't cross Central Park at night.

There are no exits or entrances,
enclosed in a ring of light
the grass beast sleeps with eyes open,   15
the moon exhumes razors,
the water in the shadows has become green fire.
Don't cross Central Park at night.

There are no entrances but everyone,
in the middle of a phrase dangling from the telephone,   20
from the top of the fountain of silence or laughter,
from the glass cage of the eye that watches us,
everyone, all of us are falling in the mirror.
Don't cross Central Park at night.

The mirror is made of stone and the stone now is shadow,   25
there are two eyes the color of anger,
a ring of cold, a belt of blood,
there is a wind that scatters the reflections
of Alice, dismembered in the pond.
Don't cross Central Park at night.   30

Open your eyes: now you are inside yourself,
you sail in a boat of monosyllables
across the mirror-pond, you disembark
at the Cobra dock: it is a yellow taxi
that carries you to the land of flames   35
across Central Park at night.

1987

---

1. Translated by Eliot Weinberger. The poem
was inspired by a painting by Belgian artist
Pierre Alechinsky entitled *Central Park* (1965).

2. This line is in English in the Spanish version of the poem.

MANIFESTOS

The manifesto is one of the most distinctive genres of the twentieth century. Artists—painters, writers, composers, and other creative people—had always thought deeply about, and sometimes openly declared the principles of, their work, but in the twentieth century they devoted more time and attention to doing so than ever before. Individual artists and, more often, groups hammered out declarations with which they hoped to outdo their predecessors and rivals. Soon hundreds and even thousands of manifestos started to appear in newspapers, as leaflets, or as performance pieces declaimed loudly at gatherings large and small, announcing the birth of movements or "-isms." Some artists rejected these shrill pronouncements and recommended that their colleagues just get on with their work. But even detractors had to admit that they were living in an age of manifestos.

Manifestos came to dominate literature and the arts, but they originated in the world of politics. Inspired by political assertions such as the **Declaration of Independence** in the United States and the **Declaration of the Rights of Man and of the Citizen** in France, disenfranchised groups sought to articulate their demands and visions. In 1848, Karl Marx and Friedrich Engels penned the document that was, finally, to give specific meaning to the word: the *Manifesto of the Communist Party*. By the early twentieth century, the *Communist Manifesto*, as it came to be known, was a revolutionary best seller, a text that had set out to change the world and had already partly succeeded.

Both the notoriety and the success of Marx and Engels's text inspired artists to continue writing manifestos whose goal was to revolutionize literature and other forms of creative work. The Chinese Communist Chen Duxiu, for example, praised the European experience of political revolution and sought to translate it into a literary revolution through his manifesto. The Italian **F. T. Marinetti**, who had been a Socialist before he made common cause with the Fascist Benito Mussolini, gained an unsavory reputation for the dozens of manifestos he wrote. He also changed their form. Whereas Marx and Engels had devoted a significant part of their manifesto to historical analysis, Marinetti condensed the genre to highlight a series of short, numbered declarations and demands. "Precision and clarity," he said, were the main features of the manifesto, but he forgot to include the third one: aggression. Yet not all writers of the genre employed an assertive style. **André Breton** wrote long, meandering manifestos, whereas the Dadaists liked to poke fun at the form even as they used it to great effect. Still others, such as the Chilean **Vicente Huidobro**, fused the making of manifestos with the writing of poetry.

World War II and the period of reconstruction that followed dampened the revolutionary ambitions of artists, but in the 1960s and 1970s a wave of both political and artistic proclamations emerged. The **Black Panther Party** harkened back to the Declaration of Independence in voicing their demands,

---

Cabaret Voltaire, 1916, by Marcel Janco. The raunchy birthplace of the radical Dada movement in Zurich.

and **Valerie Solanas** presented the more extreme fringe of feminism with her **SCUM Manifesto** (the acronym stands for Society for Cutting Up Men). Meanwhile, the Caribbean **Frantz Fanon** had written one of the crucial documents in the struggle for independence from colonialism, *The Wretched of the Earth*. Even though manifestos do not dominate contemporary literature, they continue to be written in large numbers, by groups and individuals alike.

KARL MARX AND FRIEDRICH ENGELS

The Manifesto of the Communist Party was penned by two unlikely collaborators. Karl Marx (1818–1883), born in Germany but living in Paris and Brussels, brought his training in philosophy, in particular his study of G. W. F. Hegel, to bear on the document. Friedrich Engels (1820–1895), who had moved from Germany to England to work for his father's textile business in Manchester, contributed his firsthand knowledge of the conditions of workers. Together, the two exiles were charged with writing the manifesto of the newly formed Communist League. The timing was good. All across Europe, monarchies and empires were entrenched, fortifying their positions. But they also watched jealously for any sign of new revolutionary groups threatening the status quo. Word had gone around of a new revolutionary movement sowing discontent, but no one knew anything specific about it. It was nothing but a rumor, difficult to pin down. "There is a specter haunting Europe," Marx and Engels wrote in their famous first sentence, a specter called communism. It was time to replace the specter, the rumor, with the real thing. The secret society needed to become visible, public—manifest. For this purpose, the authors sketched a history of humankind, written with breathless energy, leading up to the present. They also introduced a new agent of history, the proletariat, dispossessed workers utterly dependent on the owners of factories. And they predicted that this new agent was going to revolutionize society. *The Manifesto*'s publication coincided with revolutionary fervor spreading across Europe in 1848, but it did not have a significant impact on this movement. But slowly, over the next decades, it was translated into more and more languages and started its triumphal rise. By the early twentieth century, it had become the most important revolutionary text, one that all subsequent manifestos would use, update, or modify. Marx and Engels had changed history. In the process, they had also created a new type of revolutionary genre, the manifesto, that was soon used by different groups, including artists, hoping to introduce radical change to their work. The era of manifestos had begun.

From Manifesto of the Communist Party[1]

I.

Bourgeois and Proletarians[2]

The history of all hitherto existing society is the history of class struggles.

Freeman and slave, patrician and plebeian, lord and serf, guild-master[3] and journeyman, in a word, oppressor and oppressed, stood in constant opposition to one another, carried on an uninterrupted, now hidden, now open fight, a fight that each time ended, either in a revolutionary re-constitution of society at large, or in the common ruin of the contending classes.

In the earlier epochs of history, we find almost everywhere a complicated arrangement of society into various orders, a manifold gradation of social rank. In ancient Rome we have patricians, knights, plebeians, slaves; in the Middle Ages, feudal lords, vassals, guild-masters, journeymen, apprentices, serfs; in almost all of these classes, again, subordinate gradations.

The modern bourgeois society that has sprouted from the ruins of feudal society has not done away with clash antagonisms. It has but established new classes, new conditions of oppression, new forms of struggle in place of the old ones.

Our epoch, the epoch of the bourgeoisie, possesses, however, this distinctive feature: it has simplified the class antagonisms: Society as a whole is more and more splitting up into two great hostile camps, into two great classes directly facing each other: Bourgeoisie and Proletariat.

From the serfs of the Middle Ages sprang the chartered burghers of the earliest towns. From these burgesses the first elements of the bourgeoisie[4] were developed.

The discovery of America, the rounding of the Cape, opened up fresh ground for the rising bourgeoisie. The East-Indian and Chinese markets, the colonization of America, trade with the colonies, the increase in the means of exchange and in commodities generally, gave to commerce, to navigation, to industry, an impulse never before known, and thereby, to the revolutionary element in the tottering feudal society, a rapid development.

The feudal system of industry, under which industrial production was monopolized by closed guilds, now no longer sufficed for the growing wants of the new markets. The manufacturing system took its place. The guild-masters were pushed on one side by the manufacturing middle class; division of labor between the different corporate guilds vanished in the face of division of labor in each single workshop.

Meantime the markets kept ever growing, the demand ever rising. Even manufacture no longer sufficed. Thereupon, steam and machinery revolutionized industrial production. The place of manufacture was taken by the giant,

---

1. First published in German in 1848. This text is taken from the English edition, published in 1888 and edited by Engels.
2. By bourgeoisie is meant the class of modern capitalists, owners of the means of social production and employers of wage-labor. By proletariat, the class of modern wage-laborers who, having no means of production of their own, are reduced to selling their labor-power in order to live [Engels's note].
3. Guild-master, that is, a full member of a guild, a master within, not a head of a guild [Engels's note].
4. The words *burghers, burgesses,* and *bourgeoisie* all stem from the same root meaning "city." Marx focuses on urban society.

Modern Industry, the place of the industrial middle class, by industrial millionaires, the leaders of whole industrial armies, the modern bourgeois.

Modern industry has established the world-market, for which the discovery of America paved the way. This market has given an immense development to commerce, to navigation, to communication by land. This development has, in its turn, reacted on the extension of industry, and in proportion as industry, commerce, navigation, railways extended, in the same proportion the bourgeoisie developed, increased its capital, and pushed into the background every class handed down from the Middle Ages.

We see, therefore, how the modern bourgeoisie is itself the product of a long course of development, of a series of revolutions in the modes of production and of exchange.

Each step in the development of the bourgeoisie was accompanied by a corresponding political advance of that class. An oppressed class under the sway of the feudal nobility, an armed and self-governing association in the medieval commune, here independent urban republic (as in Italy and Germany), there taxable "third estate" of the monarchy (as in France), afterwards, in the period of manufacture proper, serving either the semi-feudal or the absolute monarchy as a counterpoise against the nobility, and, in fact, corner-stone of the great monarchies in general, the bourgeoisie has at last, since the establishment of Modern Industry and of the world-market, conquered for itself, in the modern representative State, exclusive political sway. The executive of the modern State is but a committee for managing the common affairs of the whole bourgeoisie.

The bourgeoisie, historically, has played a most revolutionary part.

The bourgeoisie, wherever it has got the upper hand, has put an end to all feudal, patriarchal, idyllic relations. It has pitilessly torn asunder the motley feudal ties that bound man to his "natural superiors," and has left remaining no other nexus between man and man than naked self-interest, than callous "cash payment." It has drowned the most heavenly ecstasies of religious fervor, of chivalrous enthusiasm, of philistine sentimentalism, in the icy water of egotistical calculation. It has resolved personal worth into exchange value, and in place of the numberless indefeasible chartered freedoms, has set up that single, unconscionable freedom—Free Trade. In one word, for exploitation, veiled by religious and political illusions, it has substituted naked, shameless, direct, brutal exploitation.

The bourgeoisie has stripped of its halo every occupation hitherto honored and looked up to with reverent awe. It has converted the physician, the lawyer, the priest, the poet, the man of science, into its paid wage-laborers.

The bourgeoisie has torn away from the family its sentimental veil, and has reduced the family relation to a mere money relation.

The bourgeoisie has disclosed how it came to pass that the brutal display of vigor in the Middle Ages, which Reactionists[5] so much admire, found its fitting complement in the most slothful indolence. It has been the first to show what man's activity can bring about. It has accomplished wonders far surpassing Egyptian pyramids, Roman aqueducts, and Gothic cathedrals; it has conducted expeditions that put in the shade all former Exoduses of nations and crusades.

The bourgeoisie cannot exist without constantly revolutionizing the instruments of production, and thereby the relations of production, and with them the

---

5. Reactionaries.

whole relations of society. Conservation of the old modes of production in unaltered form, was, on the contrary, the first condition of existence for all earlier industrial classes. Constant revolutionizing of production, uninterrupted disturbance of all social conditions, everlasting uncertainty and agitation distinguish the bourgeois epoch from all earlier ones. All fixed, fast-frozen relations, with their train of ancient and venerable prejudices and opinions, are swept away, all new-formed ones become antiquated before they can ossify. All that is solid melts into air,[6] all that is holy is profaned, and man is at last compelled to face with sober senses, his real conditions of life, and his relations with his kind.

The need of a constantly expanding market for its products chases the bourgeoisie over the whole surface of the globe. It must nestle everywhere, settle everywhere, establish connections everywhere.

The bourgeoisie has through its exploitation of the world-market given a cosmopolitan character to production and consumption in every country. To the great chagrin of Reactionists, it has drawn from under the feet of industry the national ground on which it stood. All old-established national industries have been destroyed or are daily being destroyed. They are dislodged by new industries, whose introduction becomes a life and death question for all civilized nations, by industries that no longer work up indigenous raw material, but raw material drawn from the remotest zones; industries whose products are consumed, not only at home, but in every quarter of the globe. In place of the old wants, satisfied by the productions of the country, we find new wants, requiring for their satisfaction the products of distant lands and climes. In place of the old local and national seclusion and self-sufficiency, we have intercourse in every direction, universal inter-dependence of nations. And as in material, so also in intellectual production. The intellectual creations of individual nations become common property. National one-sidedness and narrow-mindedness become more and more impossible, and from the numerous national and local literatures, there arises a world literature.

The bourgeoisie, by the rapid improvement of all instruments of production, by the immensely facilitated means of communication, draws all, even the most barbarian, nations into civilization. The cheap prices of its commodities are the heavy artillery with which it batters down all Chinese walls,[7] with which it forces the barbarians' intensely obstinate hatred of foreigners to capitulate. It compels all nations, on pain of extinction, to adopt the bourgeois mode of production; it compels them to introduce what it calls civilization into their midst, i.e., to become bourgeois themselves. In one word, it creates a world after its own image.

The bourgeoisie has subjected the country to the rule of the towns. It has created enormous cities, has greatly increased the urban population as compared with the rural, and has thus rescued a considerable part of the population from the idiocy of rural life. Just as it has made the country dependent on the towns, so it has made barbarian and semi-barbarian countries dependent on the civilized ones, nations of peasants on nations of bourgeois, the East on the West.

6. See Prospero's lines in Shakespeare's *The Tempest* 4.1, "These our actors / (as I foretold you) were all spirits, and / are melted into air."

7. A reference to the first Opium War (1839–1842), in which England forced China to accept trade with Western countries.

The bourgeoisie keeps more and more doing away with the scattered state of the population, of the means of production, and of property. It has agglomerated population, centralized means of production, and has concentrated property in a few hands. The necessary consequence of this was political centralization. Independent, or but loosely connected provinces, with separate interests, laws, governments and systems of taxation, became lumped together into one nation, with one government, one code of laws, one national class-interest, one frontier and one customs-tariff.

The bourgeoisie, during its rule of scarce one hundred years, has created more massive and more colossal productive forces than have all preceding generations together. Subjection of Nature's forces to man, machinery, application of chemistry to industry and agriculture, steam-navigation, railways, electric telegraphs, clearing of whole continents for cultivation, canalisation of rivers, whole populations conjured out of the ground—what earlier century had even a presentiment that such productive forces slumbered in the lap of social labor?

We see then: the means of production and of exchange, on whose foundation the bourgeoisie built itself up, were generated in feudal society. At a certain stage in the development of these means of production and of exchange, the conditions under which feudal society produced and exchanged, the feudal organization of agriculture and manufacturing industry, in one word, the feudal relations of property became no longer compatible with the already developed productive forces; they became so many fetters. They had to be burst asunder; they were burst asunder.

Into their place stepped free competition, accompanied by a social and political constitution adapted to it, and by the economical and political sway of the bourgeois class.

A similar movement is going on before our own eyes. Modern bourgeois society with its relations of production, of exchange and of property, a society that has conjured up such gigantic means of production and of exchange, is like the sorcerer, who is no longer able to control the powers of the nether world whom he has called up by his spells. For many a decade past the history of industry and commerce is but the history of the revolt of modern productive forces against modern conditions of production, against the property relations that are the conditions for the existence of the bourgeoisie and of its rule. It is enough to mention the commercial crises that by their periodical return put on its trial, each time more threateningly, the existence of the entire bourgeois society. In these crises a great part not only of the existing products, but also of the previously created productive forces, are periodically destroyed. In these crises there breaks out an epidemic that, in all earlier epochs, would have seemed an absurdity—the epidemic of over-production. Society suddenly finds itself put back into a state of momentary barbarism; it appears as if a famine, a universal war of devastation had cut off the supply of every means of subsistence; industry and commerce seem to be destroyed; and why? Because there is too much civilisation, too much means of subsistence, too much industry, too much commerce. The productive forces at the disposal of society no longer tend to further the development of the conditions of bourgeois property; on the contrary, they have become too powerful for these conditions, by which they are fettered, and so soon as they overcome these fetters, they bring disorder into the whole of bourgeois society, endanger the existence of bourgeois property. The conditions of bourgeois society are too narrow to comprise the wealth created by them. And how does the bourgeoisie get over these crises? On the one hand by enforced destruction of a mass of productive forces; on the other, by the conquest of new markets, and by the more thorough exploitation of the old ones. That is to say, by paving the way for more extensive and more destructive crises, and by diminishing the means whereby crises are prevented.

The weapons with which the bourgeoisie felled feudalism to the ground are now turned against the bourgeoisie itself.

But not only has the bourgeoisie forged the weapons that bring death to itself; it has also called into existence the men who are to wield those weapons—the modern working class—the proletarians.

In proportion as the bourgeoisie, *i.e.*, capital, is developed, in the same proportion is the proletariat, the modern working class, developed—a class of laborers, who live only so long as they find work, and who find work only so long as their labor increases capital. These laborers, who must sell themselves piece-meal, are a commodity, like every other article of commerce, and are consequently exposed to all the vicissitudes of competition, to all the fluctuations of the market.

Owing to the extensive use of machinery and to division of labor, the work of the proletarians has lost all individual character, and consequently, all charm for the workman. He becomes an appendage of the machine, and it is only the most simple, most monotonous, and most easily acquired knack, that is required of him. Hence, the cost of production of a workman is restricted, almost entirely, to the means of subsistence that he requires for his maintenance, and for the propagation of his race. But the price of a commodity, and therefore also of labor, is equal to its cost of production. In proportion, therefore, as the repulsiveness of the work increases, the wage decreases. Nay more, in proportion as the use of machinery and division of labor increases, in the same proportion the burden of toil also increases, whether by prolongation of the working hours, by increase of the work exacted in a given time or by increased speed of the machinery, etc.

Modern industry has converted the little workshop of the patriarchal master into the great factory of the industrial capitalist. Masses of laborers, crowded into the factory, are organized like soldiers. As privates of the industrial army they are placed under the command of a perfect hierarchy of officers and sergeants. Not only are they slaves of the bourgeois class, and of the bourgeois State; they are daily and hourly enslaved by the machine, by the over-looker, and, above all, by the individual bourgeois manufacturer himself. The more openly this despotism proclaims gain to be its end and aim, the more petty, the more hateful and the more embittering it is.

The less the skill and exertion of strength implied in manual labor, in other words, the more modern industry becomes developed, the more is the labor of men superseded by that of women. Differences of age and sex have no longer any distinctive social validity for the working class. All are instruments of labor, more or less expensive to use, according to their age and sex.

No sooner is the exploitation of the laborer by the manufacturer, so far, at an end, that he receives his wages in cash, than he is set upon by the other portions of the bourgeoisie, the landlord, the shopkeeper, the pawnbroker, etc.

The lower strata of the middle class—the small tradespeople, shopkeepers, and retired tradesmen generally, the handicraftsmen and peasants—all these sink gradually into the proletariat, partly because their diminutive capital does not suffice for the scale on which Modern Industry is carried on, and is swamped in the competition with the large capitalists, partly because their specialized skill is rendered worthless by new methods of production. Thus the proletariat is recruited from all classes of the population.

The proletariat goes through various stages of development. With its birth begins its struggle with the bourgeoisie. At first the contest is carried on by individual laborers, then by the workpeople of a factory, then by the operatives of one trade, in one locality, against the individual bourgeois who directly exploits them. They direct their attacks not against the bourgeois conditions of production, but against the instruments of production themselves; they destroy imported wares that compete with their labor, they smash to pieces machinery, they set factories ablaze, they seek to restore by force the vanished status of the workman of the Middle Ages.

At this stage the laborers still form an incoherent mass scattered over the whole country, and broken up by their mutual competition. If anywhere they unite to form more compact bodies, this is not yet the consequence of their own active union, but of the union of the bourgeoisie, which class, in order to attain its own political ends, is compelled to set the whole proletariat in motion, and is moreover yet, for a time, able to do so. At this stage, therefore, the proletarians do not fight their enemies, but the enemies of their enemies, the remnants of absolute monarchy, the landowners, the non-industrial bourgeois, the petty bourgeoisie. Thus the whole historical movement is concentrated in the hands of the bourgeoisie; every victory so obtained is a victory for the bourgeoisie.

But with the development of industry the proletariat not only increases in number; it becomes concentrated in greater masses, its strength grows, and it feels that strength more. The various interests and conditions of life within the ranks of the proletariat are more and more equalized, in proportion as machinery obliterates all distinctions of labor, and nearly everywhere reduces wages to the same low level. The growing competition among the bourgeois, and the resulting commercial crises, make the wages of the workers ever more fluctuating. The unceasing improvement of machinery, ever more rapidly developing, makes their livelihood more and more precarious; the collisions between individual workmen and individual bourgeois take more and more the character of collisions between two classes. Thereupon the workers begin to form combinations (Trades Unions) against the bourgeois; they club together in order to keep up the rate of wages; they found permanent associations in order to make provision beforehand for these occasional revolts. Here and there the contest breaks out into riots.

Now and then the workers are victorious, but only for a time. The real fruit of their battles lies, not in the immediate result, but in the ever-expanding union of the workers. This union is helped on by the improved means of communication that are created by modern industry and that place the workers of different localities in contact with one another. It was just this contact that was needed to centralise the numerous local struggles, all of the same character, into one national struggle between classes. But every class struggle is a political struggle. And that union, to attain which the burghers of the Middle Ages, with their miserable highways, required centuries, the modern proletarians, thanks to railways, achieve in a few years.

This organization of the proletarians into a class, and consequently into a political party, is continually being upset again by the competition between the workers themselves. But it ever rises up again, stronger, firmer, mightier. It compels legislative recognition of particular interests of the workers, by taking advantage of the divisions among the bourgeoisie itself. Thus the ten-hours' bill in England was carried.[8]

Altogether collisions between the classes of the old society further, in many ways, the course of development of the proletariat. The bourgeoisie finds itself involved in a constant battle. At first with the aristocracy; later on, with those portions of the bourgeoisie itself, whose interests have become antagonistic to the progress of industry; at all times, with the bourgeoisie of foreign countries. In all these battles it sees itself compelled to appeal to the proletariat, to ask for its help, and thus, to drag it into the political arena. The bourgeoisie itself, therefore, supplies the proletariat with its own elements of political and general education, in other words, it furnishes the proletariat with weapons for fighting the bourgeoisie.

Further, as we have already seen, entire sections of the ruling classes are, by the advance of industry, precipitated into the proletariat, or are at least threatened in their conditions of existence. These also supply the proletariat with fresh elements of enlightenment and progress.

Finally, in times when the class struggle nears the decisive hour, the process of dissolution going on within the ruling class, in fact within the whole range of society, assumes such a violent, glaring character, that a small section of the ruling class cuts itself adrift, and joins the revolutionary class, the class that holds the future in its hands. Just as, therefore, at an earlier period, a section of the nobility went over to the bourgeoisie, so now a portion of the bourgeoisie goes over to the proletariat, and in particular, a portion of the bourgeois ideologists, who have raised themselves to the level of comprehending theoretically the historical movement as a whole.

Of all the classes that stand face to face with the bourgeoisie today, the proletariat alone is a really revolutionary class. The other classes decay and finally disappear in the face of Modern Industry; the proletariat is its special and essential product.

The lower middle class, the small manufacturer, the shopkeeper, the artisan, the peasant, all these fight against the bourgeoisie, to save from extinction their existence as fractions of the middle class. They are therefore not revolutionary, but conservative. Nay more, they are reactionary, for they try to roll back the wheel of history. If by chance they are revolutionary, they are so only in view of their impending transfer into the proletariat, they thus defend not their present, but their future interests, they desert their own standpoint to place themselves at that of the proletariat.

The "dangerous class," the social scum, that passively rotting mass thrown off by the lowest layers of old society, may, here and there, be swept into the movement by a proletarian revolution; its conditions of life, however, prepare it far more for the part of a bribed tool of reactionary intrigue.

In the conditions of the proletariat, those of old society at large are already virtually swamped. The proletarian is without property; his relation to his wife and children has no longer anything in common with the bourgeois family-relations;

8. In 1847, after fierce opposition, a bill was passed in Parliament that limited the time a minor could work to ten hours a day. Minors were defined as persons under eighteen, but far younger children worked in the factories.

modern industrial labour, modern subjection to capital, the same in England as in France, in America as in Germany, has stripped him of every trace of national character. Law, morality, religion, are to him so many bourgeois prejudices, behind which lurk in ambush just as many bourgeois interests.

All the preceding classes that got the upper hand, sought to fortify their already acquired status by subjecting society at large to their conditions of appropriation. The proletarians cannot become masters of the productive forces of society, except by abolishing their own previous mode of appropriation, and thereby also every other previous mode of appropriation. They have nothing of their own to secure and to fortify; their mission is to destroy all previous securities for, and insurances of, individual property.

All previous historical movements were movements of minorities, or in the interests of minorities. The proletarian movement is the self-conscious, independent movement of the immense majority, in the interests of the immense majority. The proletariat, the lowest stratum of our present society, cannot stir, cannot raise itself up, without the whole superincumbent strata of official society being sprung into the air.

Though not in substance, yet in form, the struggle of the proletariat with the bourgeoisie is at first a national struggle. The proletariat of each country must, of course, first of all settle matters with its own bourgeoisie.

In depicting the most general phases of the development of the proletariat, we traced the more or less veiled civil war, raging within existing society, up to the point where that war breaks out into open revolution, and where the violent overthrow of the bourgeoisie lays the foundation for the sway of the proletariat.

Hitherto, every form of society has been based, as we have already seen, on the antagonism of oppressing and oppressed classes. But in order to oppress a class, certain conditions must be assured to it under which it can, at least, continue its slavish existence. The serf, in the period of serfdom, raised himself to membership in the commune, just as the petty bourgeois, under the yoke of feudal absolutism, managed to develop into a bourgeois. The modern laborer, on the contrary, instead of rising with the progress of industry, sinks deeper and deeper below the conditions of existence of his own class. He becomes a pauper, and pauperism develops more rapidly than population and wealth. And here it becomes evident, that the bourgeoisie is unfit any longer to be the ruling class in society, and to impose its conditions of existence upon society as an over-riding law. It is unfit to rule because it is incompetent to assure an existence to its slave within his slavery, because it cannot help letting him sink into such a state, that it has to feed him, instead of being fed by him. Society can no longer live under this bourgeoisie, in other words, its existence is no longer compatible with society.

The essential condition for the existence, and for the sway of the bourgeois class, is the formation and augmentation of capital; the condition for capital is wage-labor. Wage-labor rests exclusively on competition between the laborers. The advance of industry, whose involuntary promoter is the bourgeoisie, replaces the isolation of the laborers, due to competition, by their revolutionary combination, due to association. The development of Modern Industry, therefore, cuts from under its feet the very foundation on which the bourgeoisie produces and appropriates products. What the bourgeoisie, therefore, produces, above all, is its own grave-diggers. Its fall and the victory of the proletariat are equally inevitable.

F. T. MARINETTI

The Italian Filippo Tommaso Mari-netti (1876–1944) began as a sym-bolist poet and Socialist believer before he broke with socialism by agitating for Italy's entry into World War I. By that time, he had started a movement named futurism. Advertised through manifestos, futurism quickly became the paradigm for an avant-garde effort whose primary purpose was to attack what was inherited and to celebrate what was new. Museums, repositories of previ-ous generations' achievements, were the chief target of futurist critique, together with Italy's beautiful old cities such as Venice. In fact, Marinetti carried numerous copies of one of his manifes-tos up the clock tower in Piazza San Marco, in Venice, and let them rain down on tourists and inhabitants alike. The writer did not set his eyes on mod-ernizing just Italy, however. Dubbed "the caffeine of Europe," he traveled around, seeking to promote his cause. While Marinetti managed to turn futurism into a household word in art circles and beyond, he failed to turn the movement into an official Fascist art. Mussolini tolerated Marinetti as a fellow Fascist, but he nevertheless kept both him and his movement at arm's length.

The Foundation and Manifesto of Futurism[1]

My friends and I had stayed up all night, sitting beneath the lamps of a mosque, whose star-studded, filigreed brass domes resembled our souls, all aglow with the concentrated brilliance of an electric heart. For many hours, we'd been trailing our age-old indolence back and forth over richly adorned, oriental carpets, debating at the uttermost boundaries of logic and filling up masses of paper with our frenetic writings.

Immense pride filled our hearts, for we felt that at that hour we alone were vigilant and unbending, like magnificent beacons or guards in forward positions, facing an army of hostile stars, which watched us closely from their celestial encampments. Alone we were, with the stokers working feverishly at the infernal fires of great liners; alone with the black specters that rake through the red-hot bellies of locomotives, hurtling along at breakneck speed; alone with the floun-dering drunks, with the uncertain beating of our wings, along the city walls.

Suddenly we were startled by the terrifying clatter of huge, double-decker trams jolting by, all ablaze with different-colored lights, as if they were villages in festive celebration, which the River Po,[2] in full spate, suddenly shakes and uproots to sweep them away down to the sea, over the falls and through the whirlpools of a mighty flood.

Then the silence became more somber. Yet even while we were listening to the tedious, mumbled prayers of an ancient canal and the creaking bones of dilapidated palaces on their tiresome stretches of soggy lawn, we caught the sudden roar of ravening motorcars, right there beneath our windows.

1. Translated by Doug Thompson.
2. Marinetti was living in Milan, not far from the Po River, to which the city is connected by the Naviglio Canal.

"Come on! Let's go!" I said. "Come on, my lads, let's get out of here! At long last, all the myths and mystical ideals are behind us. We're about to witness the birth of a Centaur[3] and soon we shall witness the flight of the very first Angels! . . . We shall have to shake the gates of life itself to test their locks and hinges! . . . Let's be off! See there, the Earth's very first dawn! Nothing can equal the splendor of the sun's red sword slicing through our millennial darkness, for the very first time!"

We approached the three panting beasts to stroke their burning breasts, full of loving admiration. I stretched myself out on my car like a corpse on its bier, but immediately I was revived as the steering wheel, like a guillotine blade, menaced my belly.

A furious gust of madness tore us out of ourselves and hurled us along roads as deep and plunging as the beds of torrents. Every now and then a feeble light, flickering behind some windowpane, made us mistrust the calculations of our all-too-fallible eyes. I cried out: "The scent, nothing but the scent! That's all an animal needs!"

And we, like young lions, chased after Death, whose black pelt was dotted with pale crosses, as he sped away across the vast, violet-tinted sky, vital and throbbing.

And yet we had no idealized Lover whose sublime being rose up into the skies; no cruel Queen to whom we might offer up our corpses, contorted like Byzantine rings! Nothing at all worth dying for, other than the desire to divest ourselves finally of the courage that weighed us down!

But we sped on, squashing beneath our scorching tires the snarling guard dogs at the doorsteps of their houses, like crumpled collars under a hot iron. Death, tamed by this time, went past me at each bend, only to offer me his willing paw; and sometimes he would lie down, his teeth grinding, eyeing me with his soft, gentle look from every puddle in the road.

"Let's leave wisdom behind as if it were some hideous shell, and cast ourselves, like fruit, flushed with pride, into the immense, twisting jaws of the wind! . . . Let's become food for the Unknown, not out of desperation, but simply to fill up the deep wells of the Absurd to the very brim!"

I had hardly got these words out of my mouth when I swung the car right around sharply, with all the crazy irrationality of a dog trying to bite its own tail. Then suddenly a pair of cyclists came toward me, gesticulating that I was on the wrong side, dithering about in front of me like two different lines of thought, both persuasive but for all that, quite contradictory. Their stupid uncertainty was in my way . . . How ridiculous! What a nuisance! . . . I braked hard and to my disgust the wheels left the ground and I flew into a ditch . . .

O mother of a ditch, brimful with muddy water! Fine repair shop of a ditch! How I relished your strength-giving sludge that reminded me so much of the saintly black breast of my Sudanese nurse . . . When I got myself up—soaked, filthy, foul-smelling rag that I was—from beneath my overturned car, I had a wonderful sense of my heart being pierced by the red-hot sword of joy!

A crowd of fishermen, with their lines, and some gouty old naturalists were already milling around this wondrous spectacle. Patiently, meticulously, they set up tall trestles and laid out huge iron-mesh nets to fish out my car, as if it were a great shark that had been washed up and stranded. Slowly the car's

---

3. Half-horse, half-human (as the automobile with driver is half-machine, half-human).

frame emerged, leaving its heavy, sober bodywork at the bottom of the ditch as well as its soft, comfortable upholstery, as though they were merely scales.

They thought it was dead, that gorgeous shark of mine, but a caress was all it needed to revive it, and there it was, back from the dead, darting along with its powerful fins!

So, with my face covered in repair-shop grime—a fine mixture of metallic flakes, profuse sweat, and pale-blue soot—with my arms all bruised and bandaged, yet quite undaunted, I dictated our foremost desires to all men on Earth who are truly alive:

THE FUTURIST MANIFESTO

1. We want to sing about the love of danger, about the use of energy and recklessness as common, daily practice.
2. Courage, boldness, and rebellion will be essential elements in our poetry.
3. Up to now, literature has extolled a contemplative stillness, rapture, and reverie. We intend to glorify aggressive action, a restive wakefulness, life at the double, the slap and the punching fist.
4. We believe that this wonderful world has been further enriched by a new beauty, the beauty of speed. A racing car, its bonnet decked out with exhaust pipes like serpents with galvanic breath . . . a roaring motorcar, which seems to race on like machine-gun fire, is more beautiful than the Winged Victory of Samothrace.[4]
5. We wish to sing the praises of the man behind the steering wheel, whose sleek shaft traverses the Earth, which itself is hurtling at breakneck speed along the racetrack of its orbit.
6. The poet will have to do all in his power, passionately, flamboyantly, and with generosity of spirit, to increase the delirious fervor of the primordial elements.
7. There is no longer any beauty except the struggle. Any work of art that lacks a sense of aggression can never be a masterpiece. Poetry must be thought of as a violent assault upon the forces of the unknown with the intention of making them prostrate themselves at the feet of mankind.
8. We stand upon the furthest promontory of the ages! . . . Why should we be looking back over our shoulders, if what we desire is to smash down the mysterious doors of the Impossible? Time and Space died yesterday. We are already living in the realms of the Absolute, for we have already created infinite, omnipresent speed.
9. We wish to glorify war—the sole cleanser of the world—militarism, patriotism, the destructive act of the libertarian, beautiful ideas worth dying for, and scorn for women.
10. We wish to destroy museums, libraries, academies of any sort, and fight against moralism, feminism, and every kind of materialistic, self-serving cowardice.
11. We shall sing of the great multitudes who are roused up by work, by pleasure, or by rebellion; of the many-hued, many-voiced tides of revolution in our modern capitals; of the pulsating, nightly ardor of arsenals and shipyards,

---

4. A famous Hellenistic sculpture (2nd century B.C.E.) from the Greek island of Samothrace; now housed in the Louvre Museum, Paris.

ablaze with their violent electric moons; of railway stations, voraciously devouring smoke-belching serpents; of workshops hanging from the clouds by their twisted threads of smoke; of bridges which, like giant gymnasts, bestride the rivers, flashing in the sunlight like gleaming knives; of intrepid steamships that sniff out the horizon; of broad-breasted locomotives, champing on their wheels like enormous steel horses, bridled with pipes; and of the lissome flight of the airplane, whose propeller flutters like a flag in the wind, seeming to applaud, like a crowd excited.

It is from Italy that we hurl at the whole world this utterly violent, inflammatory manifesto of ours, with which today we are founding "Futurism," because we wish to free our country from the stinking canker of its professors, archaeologists, tour guides, and antiquarians.

For far too long has Italy been a marketplace for junk dealers. We want to free our country from the endless number of museums that everywhere cover her like countless graveyards. Museums, graveyards! . . . They're the same thing, really, because of their grim profusion of corpses that no one remembers. Museums. They're just public flophouses, where things sleep on forever, alongside other loathsome or nameless things! Museums: ridiculous abattoirs for painters and sculptors, who are furiously stabbing one another to death with colors and lines, all along the walls where they vie for space.

Sure, people may go there on pilgrimage about once a year, just as they do to the cemetery on All Souls Day—I'll grant you that! And yes, once a year a wreath of flowers is laid at the feet of the *Gioconda*[5]—I'll grant you that too! But what I won't allow is that all our miseries, our fragile courage, or our sickly anxieties get marched daily around these museums. Why should we want to poison ourselves? Why should we want to rot?

What on earth is there to be discovered in an old painting other than the labored contortions of the artist, trying to break down the insuperable barriers which prevent him from giving full expression to his artistic dream? . . . Admiring an old painting is just like pouring our purest feelings into a funerary urn, instead of projecting them far and wide, in violent outbursts of creation and of action.

Do you really want to waste all your best energies in this unending, futile veneration for the past, from which you emerge fatally exhausted, diminished, trampled down?

Make no mistake, I'm convinced that for an artist to go every day to museums and libraries and academies (the cemeteries of wasted effort, calvaries of crucified dreams, records of impulses cut short! . . .) is every bit as harmful as the prolonged overprotectiveness of parents for certain young people who get carried away by their talent and ambition. For those who are dying anyway, for the invalids, for the prisoners—who cares? The admirable past may be a balm to their worries, since for them the future is a closed book . . . but we, the powerful young Futurists, don't want to have anything to do with it, the past!

So let them come, the happy-go-lucky fire raisers with their blackened fingers! Here they come! Here they are! . . . . Come on then! Set fire to the library shelves! . . . Divert the canals so they can flood the museums! . . . Oh, what a

---

5. The Italian name for *Mona Lisa*, the famous painting by Leonardo da Vinci (1452–1519).

pleasure it is to see those revered old canvases, washed out and tattered, drifting away in the water! . . . Grab your picks and your axes and your hammers and then demolish, pitilessly demolish, all venerated cities!

The oldest among us are thirty; so we have at least ten years in which to complete our task. When we reach forty, other, younger, and more courageous men will very likely toss us into the trash can, like useless manuscripts. And that's what we want!

Our successors will rise up against us, from far away, from every part of the world, dancing on the winged cadenzas[6] of their first songs, flexing their hooked, predatory claws, sniffing like dogs at the doors of our academies, at the delicious scent of our decaying minds, already destined for the catacombs of libraries.

But we won't be there . . . Eventually, they will find us, on a winter's night, in a humble shed, far away in the country, with an incessant rain drumming upon it, and they'll see us huddling anxiously together beside our airplanes, warming our hands around the flickering flames of our present-day books, which burn away beneath our images as they are taking flight.

They will rant and rave around us, gasping in outrage and fury, and then—frustrated by our proud, unwavering boldness—they will hurl themselves upon us to kill us, driven by a hatred made all the more implacable because their hearts overflow with love and admiration for us.

Strong, healthy Injustice will flash dazzlingly in their eyes. Art, indeed, can be nothing but violence, cruelty, and injustice.

The oldest among us are only thirty. And yet we have squandered fortunes, a thousand fortunes of strength, love, daring, cleverness, and of naked willpower. We have tossed them aside impatiently, in anger, without thinking of the cost, without a moment's hesitation, without ever resting, gasping for breath . . . Just look at us! We're not exhausted yet! Our hearts feel no weariness, for they feed on fire, on hatred and on speed! . . . Does that surprise you? . . . That's logical enough, I suppose, as you don't even remember having lived! Standing tall on the roof of the world, yet again we fling our challenge at the stars!

Do you have any objections? . . . All right! Sure, we know what they are . . . We have understood! . . . Our sharp, duplicitous intelligence tells us that we are the sum total and the extension of our forebears.—Well, maybe! . . . Be that as it may! . . . But what does it matter? We want nothing to do with it! . . . Woe betide anybody whom we catch repeating these infamous words of ours.

Look around you!

Standing tall on the roof of the world, yet once again, we hurl our defiance at the stars! . . .

1909

---

6. The close of a musical phrase.

TRISTAN TZARA

Born in Romania, Tristan Tzara (1896–1963) made his first contribution to the avant-garde in Zurich, Switzerland, during World War I, where a group of international pacifists had fled to escape the war. There they started the Cabaret Voltaire, a nightclub with a stage, presenting an array of outré artworks, performances, and concerts as well as manifestos announcing a movement called Dadaism. Much less programmatic than futurism, Dadaism was sure only of what it was *against*, not what it was *for*; the Dadaists could not even agree on the meaning of the word *Dada*. After the war Tzara moved to Paris, still the center of the art world, and founded the Paris branch of Dada. As was so often the case, one movement begot the next, and out of Dadaism emerged surrealism, whose chief advocate was **André Breton**. But Tzara could never accept the leadership of Breton and split off, continuing his pranks and activities as well as his involvement in various leftist causes throughout his life.

From Dada Manifesto 1918

DADAIST DISGUST[1]

Every product of disgust capable of becoming a negation of the family is *dada*; the whole being protesting in its destructive force with clenched fists: **DADA**; knowledge of all the means rejected up to this point by the timid sex of easy compromise and sociability: DADA; abolition of logic, dance of all those impotent to create: **DADA**; of all hierarchy and social equation installed for the preservation of values by our valets: DADA; each and every object, feelings and obscurities, apparitions and the precise shock of parallel lines, can be means for the combat: DADA; abolition of memory: **DADA**; abolition of archeology: *DADA*; abolition of the prophets: *DADA*; abolition of the future: DADA; an absolute indisputable belief in each god immediate product of spontaneity: **DADA**; elegant and unprejudicial leap from one harmony to the other sphere; trajectory of a word tossed like a sonorous cry of phonograph record; respecting all individualities in their momentary madness: serious, fearful, timid, ardent, vigorous, determined, enthusiastic; stripping its chapel of every useless awkward accessory; spitting out like a luminous waterfall any unpleasant or amorous thought, or coddling it—with the lively satisfaction of knowing that it doesn't matter—with the same intensity in the bush of his soul, free of insects for the aristocrats, and gilded with archangels' bodies. Freedom: *DADA DADA DADA*, shrieking of contracted pains, intertwining of contraries and of all contradictions, grotesqueries, nonsequiturs: LIFE.

1. Translated from the French by Mary Ann Caws. This is the last section of Tzara's "Dada Manifesto 1918."

ANDRÉ BRETON

André Breton (1896–1966) can be credited with turning surrealism into one of the most successful avant-garde movements, whose influence can still be felt today. Although he didn't invent the word *surrealism*, Breton developed the notion of incongruity and fantasy as the basis of creativity and turned it into a distinct cultural movement. Jealously guarding his leadership over the group, he would expel rivals when necessary. Briefly allied with the French Communist Party, surrealism remained a movement of the left even though its most lasting ambitions could not be reduced to party politics. Rather, its great task was to explore the world behind humdrum reality and human reason. To this purpose,

Breton drew on Freud's theory of the unconscious as a resource for producing literature through "automatic writing," a technique of composition seeking to evade conscious planning. His most widely read work is his novel *Nadja* (1928), in which he sought to capture the effects of a chance encounter in the street. Breton laid down the principles of his art in his "First Manifesto of Surrealism" (1924), but this complex text is more than just a declaration of principles: a meandering and allusive composition, it is itself an example of surrealist art. Although Breton was a writer, surrealism's most lasting impact would be on photography, cinema, painting, and, later, advertising.

Manifesto of Surrealism[1]

So strong is the belief in life, in what is most fragile in life—*real* life, I mean—that in the end this belief is lost. Man, that inveterate dreamer, daily more discontent with his destiny, has trouble assessing the objects he has been led to use, objects that his nonchalance has brought his way, or that he has earned through his own efforts, almost always through his own efforts, for he has agreed to work, at least he has not refused to try his luck (or what he calls his luck!). At this point he feels extremely modest: he knows what women he has had, what silly affairs he has been involved in; he is unimpressed by his wealth or poverty, in this respect he is still a newborn babe and, as for the approval of his conscience, I confess that he does very nicely without it. If he still retains a certain lucidity, all he can do is turn back toward his childhood which, however his guides and mentors may have botched it, still strikes him as somehow charming. There, the absence of any known restrictions allows him the perspective of several lives lived at once; this illusion becomes firmly rooted within him; now he is only interested in the fleeting, the extreme facility of everything. Children set off each day without a worry in the world. Everything is near at hand, the worst material conditions are fine. The woods are white or black, one will never sleep.

But it is true that we would not dare venture so far, it is not merely a question of distance. Threat is piled upon threat, one yields, abandons a portion of

1. Translated by Richard Seaver and Helen Lane.

the terrain to be conquered. This imagination which knows no bounds is henceforth allowed to be exercised only in strict accordance with the laws of an arbitrary utility; it is incapable of assuming this inferior role for very long and, in the vicinity of the twentieth year, generally prefers to abandon man to his lusterless fate.

Though he may later try to pull himself together upon occasion, having felt that he is losing by slow degrees all reason for living, incapable as he has become of being able to rise to some exceptional situation such as love, he will hardly succeed. This is because he henceforth belongs body and soul to an imperative practical necessity which demands his constant attention. None of his gestures will be expansive, none of his ideas generous or far-reaching. In his mind's eye, events real or imagined will be seen only as they relate to a welter of similar events, events in which he has not participated, *abortive* events. What am I saying: he will judge them in relationship to one of these events whose consequences are more reassuring than the others. On no account will he view them as his salvation.

Beloved imagination, what I most like in you is your unsparing quality.

The mere word "freedom" is the only one that still excites me. I deem it capable of indefinitely sustaining the old human fanaticism. It doubtless satisfies my only legitimate aspiration. Among all the many misfortunes to which we are heir, it is only fair to admit that we are allowed the greatest degree of freedom of thought. It is up to us not to misuse it. To reduce the imagination to a state of slavery—even though it would mean the elimination of what is commonly called happiness—is to betray all sense of absolute justice within oneself. Imagination alone offers me some intimation of what *can be*, and this is enough to remove to some slight degree the terrible injunction; enough, too, to allow me to devote myself to it without fear of making a mistake (as though it were possible to make a bigger mistake). Where does it begin to turn bad, and where does the mind's stability cease? For the mind, is the possibility of erring not rather the contingency of good?

There remains madness, "the madness that one locks up," as it has aptly been described. That madness or another. . . . We all know, in fact, that the insane owe their incarceration to a tiny number of legally reprehensible acts and that, were it not for these acts their freedom (or what we see as their freedom) would not be threatened. I am willing to admit that they are, to some degree, victims of their imagination, in that it induces them not to pay attention to certain rules—outside of which the species feels itself threatened—which we are all supposed to know and respect. But their profound indifference to the way in which we judge them, and even to the various punishments meted out to them, allows us to suppose that they derive a great deal of comfort and consolation from their imagination, that they enjoy their madness sufficiently to endure the thought that its validity does not extend beyond themselves. And, indeed, hallucinations, illusions, etc., are not a source of trifling pleasure. The best controlled sensuality partakes of it, and I know that there are many evenings when I would gladly tame that pretty hand which, during the last pages of Taine's *L'Intelligence*,[2] indulges in some curious misdeeds. I could spend my whole life prying loose the secrets of the insane. These

2. An 1870 work by French historian and critic Hippolyte Taine (1828–1893).

people are honest to a fault, and their naiveté has no peer but my own. Christopher Columbus should have set out to discover America with a boatload of madmen. And note how this madness has taken shape, and endured.

*   *   *

We are still living under the reign of logic: this, of course, is what I have been driving at. But in this day and age logical methods are applicable only to solving problems of secondary interest. The absolute rationalism that is still in vogue allows us to consider only facts relating directly to our experience. Logical ends, on the contrary, escape us. It is pointless to add that experience itself has found itself increasingly circumscribed. It paces back and forth in a cage from which it is more and more difficult to make it emerge. It too leans for support on what is most immediately expedient, and it is protected by the sentinels of common sense. Under the pretense of civilization and progress, we have managed to banish from the mind everything that may rightly or wrongly be termed superstition, or fancy; forbidden is any kind of search for truth which is not in conformance with accepted practices. It was, apparently, by pure chance that a part of our mental world which we pretended not to be concerned with any longer—and, in my opinion by far the most important part—has been brought back to light. For this we must give thanks to the discoveries of Sigmund Freud.[3] On the basis of these discoveries a current of opinion is finally forming by means of which the human explorer will be able to carry his investigations much further, authorized as he will henceforth be not to confine himself solely to the most summary realities. The imagination is perhaps on the point of reasserting itself, of reclaiming its rights. If the depths of our mind contain within it strange forces capable of augmenting those on the surface, or of waging a victorious battle against them, there is every reason to seize them—first to seize them, then, if need be, to submit them to the control of our reason. The analysts themselves have everything to gain by it. But it is worth noting that no means has been designated a priori for carrying out this undertaking, that until further notice it can be construed to be the province of poets as well as scholars, and that its success is not dependent upon the more or less capricious paths that will be followed.

Freud very rightly brought his critical faculties to bear upon the dream. It is, in fact, inadmissible that this considerable portion of psychic activity (since, at least from man's birth until his death, thought offers no solution of continuity, the sum of the moments of dream, from the point of view of time, and taking into consideration only the time of pure dreaming, that is the dreams of sleep, is not inferior to the sum of the moments of reality, or, to be more precisely limiting, the moments of waking) has still today been so grossly neglected. I have always been amazed at the way an ordinary observer lends so much more credence and attaches so much more importance to waking events than to those occurring in dreams. It is because man, when he ceases to sleep, is above all the plaything of his memory, and in its normal state memory takes pleasure in weakly retracing for him the circumstances of the dream, in stripping it of any real importance, and in dismissing the only *determinant* from the point where he thinks he has

3. Founder of psychoanalysis (1856–1939).

left it a few hours before: this firm hope, this concern. He is under the impression of continuing something that is worthwhile. Thus the dream finds itself reduced to a mere parenthesis, as is the night. And, like the night, dreams generally contribute little to furthering our understanding. This curious state of affairs seems to me to call for certain reflections.

* * *

From the moment when it is subjected to a methodical examination, when, by means yet to be determined, we succeed in recording the contents of dreams in their entirety (and that presupposes a discipline of memory spanning generations; but let us nonetheless begin by noting the most salient facts), when its graph will expand with unparalleled volume and regularity, we may hope that the mysteries which really are not will give way to the great Mystery. I believe in the future resolution of these two states, dream and reality, which are seemingly so contradictory, into a kind of absolute reality, a *surreality*,[4] if one may so speak. It is in quest of this surreality that I am going, certain not to find it but too unmindful of my death not to calculate to some slight degree the joys of its possession.

A story is told according to which Saint-Pol-Roux,[5] in times gone by, used to have a notice posted on the door of his manor house in Camaret, every evening before he went to sleep, which read: THE POET IS WORKING.

A great deal more could be said, but in passing I merely wanted to touch upon a subject which in itself would require a very long and much more detailed discussion; I shall come back to it. At this juncture, my intention was merely to mark a point by noting the *hate of the marvelous* which rages in certain men, this absurdity beneath which they try to bury it. Let us not mince words: the marvelous is always beautiful, anything marvelous is beautiful, in fact only the marvelous is beautiful.

* * *

Completely occupied as I still was with Freud at that time, and familiar as I was with his methods of examination which I had had some slight occasion to use on some patients during the war, I resolved to obtain from myself what we were trying to obtain from them, namely, a monologue spoken as rapidly as possible without any intervention on the part of the critical faculties, a monologue consequently unencumbered by the slightest inhibition and which was, as closely as possible, akin to *spoken thought*. It had seemed to me, and still does—the way in which the phrase about the man cut in two had come to me[6] is an indication of it—that the speed of thought is no greater than the speed of speech, and that thought does not necessarily defy language, nor even the fast-moving pen. It was in this frame of mind that Philippe Soupault[7]—to whom I had confided these initial conclusions—and I decided to blacken some paper, with a praiseworthy disdain for what might result from a literary point of view. The ease of execution did the rest. By the end of the first day we were able to read to ourselves some fifty or so pages obtained in this manner, and begin to compare our results. All in all, Soupault's pages and mine proved to be remark-

4. I.e., something beyond or above reality.
5. French symbolist poet (1861–1940).
6. A phrase mentioned in an earlier section of

the manifesto.
7. Dadaist and, later, surrealist poet (1897–1990).

ably similar: the same overconstruction, shortcomings of a similar nature, but also, on both our parts, the illusion of an extraordinary verve, a great deal of emotion, a considerable choice of images of a quality such that we would not have been capable of preparing a single one in longhand, a very special picturesque quality and, here and there, a strong comical effect. The only difference between our two texts seemed to me to derive essentially from our respective tempers, Soupault's being less static than mine, and, if he does not mind my offering this one slight criticism, from the fact that he had made the error of putting a few words by way of titles at the top of certain pages, I suppose in a spirit of mystification. On the other hand, I must give credit where credit is due and say that he constantly and vigorously opposed any effort to retouch or correct, however slightly, any passage of this kind which seemed to me unfortunate. In this he was, to be sure, absolutely right.[8] It is, in fact, difficult to appreciate fairly the various elements present; one may even go so far as to say that it is impossible to appreciate them at a first reading. To you who write, these elements are, on the surface, *as strange to you as they are to anyone else*, and naturally you are wary of them. Poetically speaking, what strikes you about them above all is their *extreme degree of immediate absurdity*, the quality of this absurdity, upon closer scrutiny, being to give way to everything admissible, everything legitimate in the world: the disclosure of a certain number of properties and of facts no less objective, in the final analysis, than the others.

In homage to Guillaume Apollinaire,[9] who had just died and who, on several occasions, seemed to us to have followed a discipline of this kind, without however having sacrificed to it any mediocre literary means, Soupault and I baptized the new mode of pure expression which we had at our disposal and which we wished to pass on to our friends, by the name of SURREALISM. I believe that there is no point today in dwelling any further on this word and that the meaning we gave it initially has generally prevailed over its Apollinarian sense. To be even fairer, we could probably have taken over the word SUPERNATURALISM employed by Gérard de Nerval in his dedication to the *Filles de feu*.[1] It appears, in fact, that Nerval possessed to a tee the spirit with which we claim a kinship, Apollinaire having possessed, on the contrary, naught but *the letter*, still imperfect, of Surrealism, having shown himself powerless to give a valid theoretical idea of it. Here are two passages by Nerval which seem to me to be extremely significant in this respect:

> I am going to explain to you, my dear Dumas,[2] the phenomenon of which you have spoken a short while ago. There are, as you know, certain storytellers who cannot invent without identifying with the characters their imagination has

8. I believe more and more in the infallibility of my thought with respect to myself, and this is too fair. Nonetheless, with this *thought-writing*, where one is at the mercy of the first outside distraction, 'ebullitions' can occur. It would be inexcusable for us to pretend otherwise. By definition, thought is strong, and incapable of catching itself in error. The blame for these obvious weaknesses must be placed on suggestions that come to it from without. [Breton's note].

9. Poet and playwright (1880–1918) who coined the term *surrealism*.
1. "And also by Thomas Carlyle in *Sartor Resartus* ([Book III] Chapter VIII, 'Natural Supernaturalism'), 1833–34." [Breton's note]. "*Filles de feu*": Girls of Fire by Gérard de Nerval, French Romantic poet (1808–1855). Carlyle (1795–1881) was a Scottish essayist.
2. Alexandre Dumas (1802–1870), French novelist, author of *The Three Musketeers*.

dreamt up. You may recall how convincingly our old friend Nodier[3] used to tell how it had been his misfortune during the Revolution to be guillotined; one became so completely convinced of what he was saying that one began to wonder how he had managed to have his head glued back on.

. . . And since you have been indiscreet enough to quote one of the sonnets composed in this SUPERNATURALISTIC dream-state, as the Germans would call it, you will have to hear them all. You will find them at the end of the volume. They are hardly any more obscure than Hegel's metaphysics or Swedenborg's MEMORA-BILIA, and would lose their charm if they were explained, if such were possible; at least admit the worth of the expression.[4] . . .

Those who might dispute our right to employ the term SURREALISM in the very special sense that we understand it are being extremely dishonest, for there can be no doubt that this word had no currency before we came along. Therefore, I am defining it once and for all:

SURREALISM, *n.* Psychic automatism in its pure state, by which one proposes to express—verbally, by means of the written word, or in any other manner—the actual functioning of thought. Dictated by thought, in the absence of any control exercised by reason, exempt from any aesthetic or moral concern.

ENCYCLOPEDIA. *Philosophy.* Surrealism is based on the belief in the superior reality of certain forms of previously neglected associations, in the omnipotence of dream, in the disinterested play of thought. It tends to ruin once and for all all other psychic mechanisms and to substitute itself for them in solving all the principal problems of life. The following have performed acts of ABSO-LUTE SURREALISM: Messrs. Aragon, Baron, Boiffard, Breton, Carrive, Crevel, Delteil, Desnos, Eluard, Gérard, Limbour, Malkine, Morise, Naville, Noll, Péret, Picon, Soupault, Vitrac.[5]

They seem to be, up to the present time, the only ones, and there would be no ambiguity about it were it not for the case of Isidore Ducasse[6] about whom I lack information. And, of course, if one is to judge them only superficially by their results, a good number of poets could pass for Surrealists, beginning with Dante and, in his finer moments, Shakespeare.[7] *In the course of the various attempts I have made to reduce what is, by breach of trust, called genius, I have found nothing which in the final analysis can be attributed to any other method than that.*

3. Charles Nodier (1780–1844), French short-story writer.
4. "See also *L'idéoréalisme* by Saint-Pol-Roux" [Breton's note]. *L'idéoréalisme* translates into English as "ideorealism." Georg Wilhelm Friedrich Hegel (1770–1831) was a German idealist philosopher. Emanuel Swedenborg (1688–1772) was a mystical Swedish philosopher and religious leader.

5. Friends of Breton's who enlisted in the surrealist movement.
6. Also known as the Comte de Lautréamont (1846–1870); Uruguayan-born French poet, obscure during his lifetime, who was championed by the surrealists.
7. Breton here invokes two acknowledged geniuses as forerunners of surrealism.

Young's *Nights*[8] are Surrealist from one end to the other; unfortunately it is a priest who is speaking, a bad priest no doubt, but a priest nonetheless.

Swift[9] is Surrealist in malice,
Sade[1] is Surrealist in sadism.
Chateaubriand[2] is Surrealist in exoticism.
Constant[3] is Surrealist in politics.
Hugo[4] is Surrealist when he isn't stupid.
Desbordes-Valmore[5] is Surrealist in love.
Bertrand[6] is Surrealist in the past.
Rabbe[7] is Surrealist in death.
Poe[8] is Surrealist in adventure.
Baudelaire[9] is Surrealist in morality.
Rimbaud is Surrealist in the way he lived, and elsewhere.[1]
Mallarmé is Surrealist when he is confiding.[2]
Jarry is Surrealist in absinthe.[3]
Nouveau is Surrealist in the kiss.[4]
Saint-Pol-Roux[5] is Surrealist in his use of symbols.
Fargue[6] is Surrealist in the atmosphere.
Vaché[7] is Surrealist in me.
Reverdy[8] is Surrealist at home.
Saint-Jean-Perse[9] is Surrealist at a distance.
Roussel[1] is Surrealist as a storyteller.
Etc.

1924

8. *Night Thoughts*, a poem by Edward Young (1681–1765).
9. Jonathan Swift (1667–1745), Irish satirist and author of *Gulliver's Travels*.
1. The Marquis de Sade (1740–1814), French aristocrat and author of libertine works.
2. François-Auguste-René de Chateaubriand (1768–1848), French Romantic writer with an interest in the East.
3. Benjamin Constant (1767–1830), liberal political theorist.
4. Victor Hugo (1802–1885), French Romantic poet and novelist.
5. Marceline Desbordes-Valmore (1786–1859), French poet and actress.
6. Aloysius Bertrand (1807–1841), French prose poet.
7. Alphonse Rabbe (1784–1829), author of *Album of a Pessimist*, who died from a drug overdose.
8. Edgar Allan Poe (1809–1849), American Romantic writer whose macabre tales were much admired by French modernists.
9. Charles Baudelaire (1821–1867), French Romantic poet who inspired modernism and

who was charged with obscenity; he also translated Poe's works into French.
1. Arthur Rimbaud (1854–1891), French poet infamous for his decadent lifestyle.
2. Stéphane Mallarmé (1842–1898), French symbolist poet.
3. Alfred Jarry (1873–1907), avant-garde playwright who was addicted to absinthe, a strong alcoholic drink popular in 19th-century France.
4. Germain Nouveau (1851–1920), French symbolist poet, author of *The Kiss*.
5. Saint-Pol-Roux (Paul-Pierre Roux) (1861–1940), French Symbolist poet.
6. Léon-Paul Fargue (1876–1947), French symbolist poet.
7. Jacques Vaché (1895–1919), Breton's close friend, had died of an opium overdose.
8. Pierre Reverdy (1889–1960), surrealist poet.
9. St. John Perse (1887–1975), French poet who would win the Nobel Prize for Literature in 1960.
1. Raymond Roussel (1877–1933), experimental French writer.

VICENTE HUIDOBRO

A Chilean by birth, Vicente Huidobro (1893–1948) lived in Argentina, as well as in Madrid and Paris, where he joined the international avant-garde assembled there. He coined the term *creationism*, the title of his 1925 manifesto offered as the selection here, for the movement hailing the expressive powers of the poet. Huidobro's most influential work is a long poem, *Altazor*, in which he captured, through a modern form, the essence of the world in which he lived. Despite his allegiance to creationism, he collaborated with Dadaists and surrealists, demonstrating how fluid the relation between these various movements could be. Even some of his manifestos are playful texts that seem to take lightly the task of defining the distinctive features of a new movement. While he remained attracted to Paris, the center of the avant-garde, Huidobro sought to introduce a contemporary sensibility to Latin America.

Creationism[1]

Creationism is not a school of thought I want to impose on anyone. Creationism is a general aesthetic theory that I began to elaborate around 1912 and of which you can find the gropings and the first steps in my books and in my articles, well before my first trip to Paris.

In number 5 of the Chilean review *Young Muse*, I said:

> The reign of literature is over. The twentieth century will witness the birth of the reign of poetry in the true sense of the word; this will be creation, as the Greeks called it, although they never came to realize their definition.

Later, towards 1913 or 1914, I repeated almost the same thing in a little interview which appeared in the magazine *Ideals*, at the head of my poems. Also in my book *In Passing*, which appeared in December, 1913, I said that the only thing which should interest poets is "the act of creation" and I emphasized this first and foremost, counter to prevailing commentaries and in direct defiance of the universal temptation to set poetry *round and about*. The thing created versus the thing sung.

In my poem *Adam*, which I wrote on vacation in 1914, and which was published in 1916, you will find in the preface these phrases from Emerson[2] concerning the constitution of the poem:

> A living thought, like the spirit of an animal or a plant, has its own architecture, and embellishes nature with something new.

1. Translated from Spanish by Gilbert Alter-Gilbert.

2. Ralph Waldo Emerson (1803–1882), American essayist and poet.

But where the theory was fully exposed was at the Atheneum in Buenos Aires during a lecture I gave in June of 1916. It was there that I was baptized a "creationist" for having said during my lecture that the first condition of a poet is to create, the second to create, and the third, to create.

I recall that the Argentine professor José Ingenieros,[3] who attended the function, told me at a dinner to which he had invited me and a few friends after the lecture:

> Your dream of a poetry invented in all respects by poets, seems to me unrealizable, though you have expounded it quite clearly and even in a scientific fashion.

This is nearly the same reservation expressed by certain philosophers in Germany and everywhere else I have explicated the same theories. "It's beautiful, but unrealizable."

And why should it be unrealizable?

I will reiterate here the statements with which I finished my lecture to the attendees of the Convention for Philosophic and Scientific Studies presided over by Doctor Allendy,[4] at Paris, in January of 1922:

> If man has subjugated the three realms of nature—the mineral realm, the vegetable realm and the animal realm—why should it be impossible for him to add to them the worldly realms: his own realm, the realm of his creations?

He has already invented an altogether new fauna which walks, which flies, which swims, which fills the earth, the air, and the oceans, with its frantic footsteps and wailings and groanings.

Those things which are true of the mechanical realm are equally true of poetry. I will tell you what I mean by the created poem. It's a poem in which each constituent part and everything together presents a new fact, independent of the external world and detached from all reality other than itself, because it takes its place in the world as a particular phenomenon separate and apart from other phenomena.

This poem is a thing which cannot exist elsewhere than in the head of the poet. It isn't beautiful out of nostalgia, it isn't beautiful because we recall some things seen which were beautiful, nor because it describes beautiful things that we have the possibility of seeing. It is beautiful in itself and it doesn't admit of terms of comparison. It cannot be conceived anywhere but in a book.

There is nothing resembling it in the external world. It renders real that which doesn't exist; that is to say, it makes its own reality. It creates the marvelous and gives it a life of its own. It creates extraordinary situations which could never exist in truth and on account of that, they must exist in the poem, if they are to exist anywhere.

3. Argentine philosopher (1877–1925).
4. René Allendy, French doctor and psychoanalyst (1889–1942).

As soon as I say "The bird perched on a rainbow," I present to you a new phenomenon, a thing which you have never seen, which you will never see, even though you may very much wish you could.

A poet must say those things which without him would never be said.

Created poems acquire cosmogonic proportions; they give you unstintingly the true sublime, the sublime which so many texts have misrepresented and of which we have been provided with so many unconvincing examples. For this isn't the provocatively alluring and grandiose sublime. It's a sublime without pretention, without terror, without the ambition to crush the reader or grind him flat. It's a sublime you can put in your pocket.

The creationist poem is comprised of created images, created situations, created concepts; it neither lacks nor dispenses with a single element of traditional poetry, only here those elements are all invented without the least concern for what is real, nor for any truth anterior to the act of their realization.

Therefore, when I write:

> The ocean defeats itself
> Ruffled by the wind of whistling fishermen

I am presenting a created description; when I say: "The ingots of the storm," I present to you a purely created image and when I tell you: "she was so beautiful that she couldn't speak" or "a hatful of night," I present to you a created concept.

I find in the work of Tristan Tzara[5] some admirable poems which come very close to the strictest conception of Creationism. Although with him creation generally is more formal than fundamental. But the man who wrote the following lines is, beyond a shadow of a doubt, a poet:

> IN PORCELAIN, thought the song, I am tired—the song of queens breaks the tree of nourishment like a lamp.

> I WEEP wanting to rise higher than the jet of water snaking skyward because terrestrial gravity no longer exists in school or in the brain.

> > When the fish rows
> > through the lakes discourse
> > when it runs the gamut
> > ladies step out for a stroll.

* * *

I want to state firmly today that which I stated ten years ago at the Atheneum in Buenos Aires: "Not a single poem has ever been made in this world; all that has transpired adds up to a few vague attempts at making a poem. Poetry is just now being born around our globe. And its birth will be an event which will turn

---

5. Romanian-French founder of Dadaism (1896–1963).

people upside down like the strongest earthquake." I ask myself sometimes if it won't pass unperceived.

Therefore, having well established this framework, it should be understood that each time I speak of the poet I employ the word only as a reference point, and I stretch this word like a rubber band in order to loop it around and bundle together those who are closest in approximating the importance I have assigned him.

At the time of the review *Nord-Sud*, of which I was one of the founders, we all branched from more or less the same tree of research, but at bottom some were far removed from others.

Whereas others made crescent-shaped fanlights, I made square horizons. And there's the difference expressed in two words. All fanlights are crescent-shaped, so poetry remains bound by realism. Horizons, on the other hand, aren't square, so the author presents here a thing he has created.[6]

This is how I explained my title *Square Horizon* in a letter to my friend the critic Thomas Chazal at the time the book was published:

> Square horizon. A new fact invented by me, which would not exist without me. In the little ball of this title, esteemed friend, is rolled up my entire aesthetic; an aesthetic with which you have been familiar for quite some while.

This title explains the entire basis for my poetic theory. It has, condensed in it, the essence of my principles.

1. Humanize things. All that intersects the poet's organism must absorb as much of his warmth as possible. Here something vast, something as enormous as the horizon, is humanized, made intimate and filial, by the adjective "square." Infinity settles in the nest of our heart.
2. The vague should become precise. In closing the windows of our soul, that which could escape and become fluffy and gaseous, stays bottled up and solidifies.
3. The abstract should become concrete and the concrete abstract. That is to say, a perfect equilibrium should obtain between the two, because if the abstract keeps stretching you further towards the abstract, it will come apart in your hands, and sift through your fingers. The concrete, if made still more concrete, can perhaps serve you some wine to drink or furnish your parlor, but it can never furnish your soul.
4. That which is too poetic to be created, becomes a creation when its customary meaning is changed, because if the horizon is poetic in itself, if it is poetry in life, with the qualifier "square," it becomes poetry in art. From dead poetry living poetry comes into being.

---

6. "The poet of crescent-shaped fanlights and I occupy opposite poles, in the same sense spoken of by Picasso in his journal *Comedy* when he writes: 'I, a born painter? On the contrary, I am the anti-painter par excellence; I am but a humble poet'" [Huidobro's note]; the reference is to Pablo Picasso, Spanish painter (1881–1973).

These few explicatory words concerning my conception of poetry, from the first page of the aforementioned book, will tell you what it was I wanted to do with these poems. I said:

> To create a poem is to borrow from life its motifs and transform them so as to lend them new and independent life.

> Nothing anecdotal or descriptive. Emotion should emerge strictly in concert with the virtue of creativity alone.

> Make a poem the way nature makes a tree.

This was exactly what was at the base of my conception of poetry before I ever arrived in Paris—the act of pure creation that you will find, like a veritable obsession, running everywhere through my work from 1912 onwards. This remains my conception of poetry today. The poem created, in all respects, as an all-new object.

I feel compelled once again to repeat that axiom I set forth in my lecture at the Atheneum in Madrid in 1921 and later in Paris during my lecture at the Sorbonne, in summarizing my aesthetic principles: "Art is one thing and nature another. I love Art very much and I very much love Nature. If you accept the representations that a man makes of Nature, that proves that you love neither Nature nor Art."

In two words and in conclusion: Creationists have been the *first poets* to exalt to the station of art the poem invented in all respects by its author.

Here in these pages on Creationism has been outlined my poetic testament. I bequeath it to the poets of tomorrow, to those who will be the first animals in this new species, the poet; of this new species which is going to be born, I believe, soon. There are signs in the heavens.

The near-poets of today are very interesting, but their interest doesn't interest me.

The wind bends my flute towards what is to come.

FRANTZ FANON

Psychiatrist, revolutionary, and supporter of the Algerian struggle for independence from France, Frantz Fanon (1925–1961) also dedicated himself to a larger battle: to free the minds of the dispossessed—"the wretched of the earth"—from the psychological bonds left by decades of colonialism. Born on the French Caribbean island of Martinique, he had seen the effects of those bonds with his own eyes. Fanon moved to Paris to study medicine and associated with other members of the black diaspora at a time when Négritude (black consciousness) was being widely discussed. He then worked as a psychiatrist in Algeria and Tunisia during the region's tumul-tuous struggles for independence. *The Wretched of the Earth*, which takes its title from the first line of *The International*, the French socialist song, is Fanon's last book, published months before his death of leukemia. It captures the destructive imprint of colonial rule not just on the bodies but also on the minds of the colonized. Advertised by its American publisher as a "handbook of revolution," it argues that only an independent, national culture can heal the wounds of colonial oppression. Blending political and psychological insight, *The Wretched of the Earth* became a foundational document for anticolonial struggles in Algeria and all over the third world.

The Wretched of the Earth[1]

From *On National Culture*

Each generation must out of relative obscurity discover its mission, fulfill it, or betray it. In underdeveloped countries the preceding generations have both resisted the work or erosion carried by colonialism and also helped on the maturing of the struggles of today. We must rid ourselves of the habit, now that we are in the thick of the fight, of minimizing the action of our fathers or of feigning incomprehension when considering their silence and passivity. They fought as well as they could, with the arms that they possessed then; and if the echoes of their struggle have not resounded in the international arena, we must realize that the reason for this silence lies less in their lack of heroism than in the fundamentally different international situation of our time. It needed more than one native to say "We've had enough"; more than one peasant rising crushed, more than one demonstration put down before we could today hold our own, certain in our victory. As for we who have decided to break the back of colonialism, our historic mission is to sanction all revolts, all desperate actions, all those abortive attempts drowned in rivers of blood.

In this chapter we shall analyze the problem, which is felt to be fundamental, of the legitimacy of the claims of a nation. It must be recognized that the political party which mobilizes the people hardly touches on this problem of legitimacy. The political parties start from living reality and it is in the name of

1. Translated by Constance Farrington; published in 1961.

this reality, in the name of the stark facts which weigh down the present and the future of men and women, that they fix their line of action. The political party may well speak in moving terms of the nation, but what it is concerned with is that the people who are listening understand the need to take part in the fight if, quite simply, they wish to continue to exist.

* * *

Inside the political parties, and most often in offshoots from these parties, cultured individuals of the colonized race make their appearance. For these individuals, the demand for a national culture and the affirmation of the existence of such a culture represent a special battlefield. While the politicians situate their action in actual present-day events, men of culture take their stand in the field of history. Confronted with the native intellectual who decides to make an aggressive response to the colonialist theory of pre-colonial barbarism, colonialism will react only slightly, and still less because the ideas developed by the young colonized intelligentsia are widely professed by specialists in the mother country. It is in fact a commonplace to state that for several decades large numbers of research workers have, in the main, rehabilitated the African, Mexican, and Peruvian civilizations. The passion with which native intellectuals defend the existence of their national culture may be a source of amazement; but those who condemn this exaggerated passion are strangely apt to forget that their own psyche and their own selves are conveniently sheltered behind a French or German culture which has given full proof of its existence and which is uncontested.

I am ready to concede that on the plane of factual being the past existence of an Aztec civilization does not change anything very much in the diet of the Mexican peasant of today. I admit that all the proofs of a wonderful Songhai civilization[2] will not change the fact that today the Songhais are underfed and illiterate, thrown between sky and water with empty heads and empty eyes. But it has been remarked several times that this passionate search for a national culture which existed before the colonial era finds its legitimate reason in the anxiety shared by native intellectuals to shrink away from that Western culture in which they all risk being swamped. Because they realize they are in danger of losing their lives and thus becoming lost to their people, these men, hotheaded and with anger in their hearts, relentlessly determine to renew contact once more with the oldest and most pre-colonial springs of life of their people.

Let us go further. Perhaps this passionate research and this anger are kept up or at least directed by the secret hope of discovering beyond the misery of today, beyond self-contempt, resignation, and abjuration, some very beautiful and splendid era whose existence rehabilitates us both in regard to ourselves and in regard to others. I have said that I have decided to go further. Perhaps unconsciously, the native intellectuals, since they could not stand wonderstruck before the history of today's barbarity, decided to back further and to delve deeper down; and, let us make no mistake, it was with the greatest delight that they discovered that there was nothing to be ashamed of in the past, but rather dignity, glory, and solemnity. The claim to a national culture in the past does not only rehabilitate that nation and serve as a justification for

2. A great trading empire, based in central Mali, that flourished in the fifteenth and sixteenth centuries.

the hope of a future national culture. In the sphere of psycho-affective equilibrium it is responsible for an important change in the native. Perhaps we have not sufficiently demonstrated that colonialism is not simply content to impose its rule upon the present and the future of a dominated country. Colonialism is not satisfied merely with holding a people in its grip and emptying the native's brain of all form and content. By a kind of perverted logic, it turns to the past of the oppressed people, and distorts, disfigures, and destroys it. This work of devaluing pre-colonial history takes on a dialectical significance today.

When we consider the efforts made to carry out the cultural estrangement so characteristic of the colonial epoch, we realize that nothing has been left to chance and that the total result looked for by colonial domination was indeed to convince the natives that colonialism came to lighten their darkness. The effect consciously sought by colonialism was to drive into the natives' heads the idea that if the settlers were to leave, they would at once fall back into barbarism, degradation, and bestiality.

On the unconscious plane, colonialism therefore did not seek to be considered by the native as a gentle, loving mother who protects her child from a hostile environment, but rather as a mother who unceasingly restrains her fundamentally perverse offspring from managing to commit suicide and from giving free rein to its evil instincts. The colonial mother protects her child from itself, from its ego, and from its physiology, its biology, and its own unhappiness which is its very essence.

In such a situation the claims of the native intellectual are not a luxury but a necessity in any coherent program. The native intellectual who takes up arms to defend his nation's legitimacy and who wants to bring proofs to bear out that legitimacy, who is willing to strip himself naked to study the history of his body, is obliged to dissect the heart of his people.

Such an examination is not specifically national. The native intellectual who decides to give battle to colonial lies fights on the field of the whole continent. The past is given back its value. Culture, extracted from the past to be displayed in all its splendor, is not necessarily that of his own country. Colonialism, which has not bothered to put too fine a point on its efforts, has never ceased to maintain that the Negro is a savage; and for the colonist, the Negro was neither an Angolan nor a Nigerian, for he simply spoke of "the Negro." For colonialism, this vast continent was the haunt of savages, a country riddled with superstitions and fanaticism, destined for contempt, weighed down by the curse of God, a country of cannibals—in short, the Negro's country. Colonialism's condemnation is continental in its scope. The contention by colonialism that the darkest night of humanity lay over pre-colonial history concerns the whole of the African continent. The efforts of the native to rehabilitate himself and to escape from the claws of colonialism are logically inscribed from the same point of view as that of colonialism. The native intellectual who has gone far beyond the domains of Western culture and who has got it into his head to proclaim the existence of another culture never does so in the name of Angola or of Dahomey. The culture which is affirmed is African culture. The Negro, never so much a Negro as since he has been dominated by the whites, when he decides to prove that he has a culture and to behave like a cultured person, comes to realize that history points out a well-defined path to him: he must demonstrate that a Negro culture exists.

And it is only too true that those who are most responsible for this racialization of thought, or at least for the first movement toward that thought, are and remain those Europeans who have never ceased to set up white culture to fill the gap left by the absence of other cultures. Colonialism did not dream of wasting its time in denying the existence of one national culture after another. Therefore the reply of the colonized peoples will be straight away continental in its breadth. In Africa, the native literature of the last twenty years is not a national literature but a Negro literature. The concept of negritude, for example, was the emotional if not the logical antithesis of that insult which the white man flung at humanity.

* * *

BLACK PANTHER PARTY

Founded in the mid-1960s in Oakland, California, the Black Panther Party represents the radical wing of the civil rights movement. Disappointed with the ethos of nonviolent resistance advocated by civil rights activists such as Martin Luther King Jr., the Black Panthers vowed to defend themselves against police brutality as well as political and social disenfranchisement. Demanding basic rights, such as freedom to determine the fate of the black community and full employment, the Panthers espoused Socialist doctrines to better the lot of African Americans. Their famous ten-point manifesto (1966) details the movement's demands in clear and hard-hitting phrases. Most remarkable, however, is the tenth point in their list of beliefs, which reprints, verbatim, the opening of the **Declaration of Independence**. The significance of the words is clear: the Black Panthers saw parallels between their insistence on human rights and that of the founders of the Republic, as stated in the document from the American Revolution.

Black Panther Platform

What we want
1. We want freedom. We want power to determine the destiny of our black community.
2. We want full employment for our people.
3. We want an end to the robbery by the white man of our black community.
4. We want decent housing, fit for shelter of human beings.
5. We want education for our people that exposes the true nature of this decadent American society. We want education that teaches us our true history and our role in the present day society.

6. We want all black men to be exempt from military service.
7. We want an immediate end to *police brutality* and *murder* of black people.
8. We want freedom for all black men held in federal, state, county, and city prisons and jails.
9. We want all black people when brought to trial to be tried in court by a jury of their peer group or people from their black communities as defined by the constitution of the United States.
10. We want land, bread, housing, education, clothing, justice and peace.

What we believe

1. We believe that black people will not be free until we are able to determine our destiny.
2. We believe that the federal government is responsible and obligated to give every man employment or a guaranteed income. We believe that if the white American businessmen will not give full employment, then the means of production should be taken from the businessmen and placed in the community so that the people of the community can organize and employ all of its people and give a high standard of living.
3. We believe that this racist government has robbed us and now we are demanding the overdue debt of forty acres and two mules.[1] Forty acres and two mules was promised 100 years ago as retribution for slave labor and mass murder of black people. We will accept the payment in currency which will be distributed to our many communities. The Germans murdered 6,000,000 Jews. The American racist has taken part in the slaughter of over 50,000,000 black people; therefore, we feel that this is a modest demand that we make.
4. We believe that if the white landlords will not give decent housing to our black community, then the housing and the land should be made into cooperatives so that our community, with government aid, can build and make decent housing for its people.
5. We believe in an educational system that will give to our people a knowledge of self. If a man does not have knowledge of himself and his position in society and the world, then he has little chance to relate to anything else.
6. We believe that black people should not be forced to fight in the military service to defend a racist government that does not protect us. We will not fight and kill other people of color in the world who, like black people, are being victimized by the white racist government of America. We will protect ourselves from the force and violence of the racist police and the racist military, by whatever means necessary.
7. We believe we can end police brutality in our black community by organizing black *self defense* groups that are dedicated to defending our black community from racist police oppression and brutality. The second amendment of the constitution of the United States gives us a right to bear arms. We therefore believe that all black people should arm themselves for *self defense*.
8. *We believe that all black people should be released from the many jails and prisons because they have not received a fair and impartial trial.*

---

1. Promised in 1865 to freed slaves who had served in the Union Army during the American Civil War.

9. We believe that the courts should follow the United States constitution so that black people will receive fair trials. The 14th Amendment of the U.S. Constitution gives a man a right to be tried by his peer group.[2] A peer is a person from a similar economic, social, religious, geographical, environmental, historical and racial background. To do this the court will be forced to select a jury from the black community from which the black defendant came. We have been, and are being tried by all white juries that have no understanding of the 'average reasoning man' of the black community.

10. When in the course of human events, it becomes necessary for one people to dissolve the political bonds which have connected them with another, and to assume among the powers of the earth the separate and equal station to which the laws of nature and nature's god entitle them, a decent respect to the opinions of mankind requires that they should declare the causes which impel them to separation. We hold these truths to be self-evident, that all men are created equal, that they are endowed by their creator with certain inalienable rights, that among these are life, liberty and the pursuit of happiness. That to secure these rights, governments are instituted among men, deriving their just power from the consent of the governed—that whenever any form of government becomes destructive of these ends, it is the right of people to alter or to abolish it, and to institute new government, laying its foundations on such principles and organizing its powers in such form as to them shall seem most likely to effect their safety and happiness. Prudence, indeed, will dictate that governments long established should not be changed for light and transient causes; and accordingly all experience hath shewn, that mankind are more disposed to suffer while evils are sufferable, than to right themselves by abolishing the forms to which they are accustomed. But when a long train of abuses and usurpations, pursuing invariably the same object, evinces a design to reduce them under absolute despotism, it is their right, it is their duty, to throw off such government, and to provide new guards for their future security.[3]

2. Amendment to the U.S. Constitution, adopted in 1868, to confer citizenship rights on African Americans; it guarantees all citizens equal protection under the law and due process, including, by extension, the right to trial by jury, as established by the Sixth Amendment, adopted in 1791.
3. The final paragraph is a verbatim transcription of the Preamble to the U.S. Declaration of Independence (1776).

VALERIE SOLANAS

Valerie Solanas (1936–1988) is known not so much for her writings as for the attempted assassination of Andy Warhol (1928?–1987), a Pop Art icon. Solanas accused Warhol of losing her play, *Up Your Ass*, which she had given him for review. Warhol survived, and Solanas remained on the fringe of New York's bohemian Greenwich Village, whose appetite for radical causes she captured in her SCUM Manifesto (1968). The founding document of the Society for Cutting Up Men, of which she was the only member, this text is an outrageous provocation advocating the killing of all males and the creation of a female-only society. Littered with images of violence, it captures in an extreme form the spirit of 1960s radicalism.

SCUM Manifesto[1]

Life in this society being, at best, an utter bore and no aspect of society being at all relevant to women, there remains to civic-minded, responsible, thrill-seeking females only to overthrow the government, eliminate the money system, institute complete automation and destroy the male sex.

It is now technically possible to reproduce without the aid of males (or, for that matter, females) and to produce only females. We must begin immediately to do so. The male is a biological accident: the y (male) gene is an incomplete x (female) gene, that is, has an incomplete set of chromosomes. In other words, the male is an incomplete female, a walking abortion, aborted at the gene stage. To be male is to be deficient, emotionally limited; maleness is a deficiency disease and males are emotional cripples.

The male is completely egocentric, trapped inside himself, incapable of empathizing or identifying with others, of love, friendship, affection or tenderness. He is a completely isolated unit, incapable of rapport with anyone. His responses are entirely visceral, not cerebral; his intelligence is a mere tool in the service of his drives and needs; he is incapable of mental passion, mental interaction; he can't relate to anything other than his own physical sensations. He is a half dead, unresponsive lump, incapable of giving or receiving pleasure or happiness; consequently, he is at best an utter bore, an inoffensive blob, since only those capable of absorption in others can be charming. He is trapped in a twilight zone halfway between humans and apes, and is far worse off than the apes because, unlike the apes, he is capable of a large array of negative feelings—hate, jealousy, contempt, disgust, guilt, shame, doubt—and, moreover he is *aware* of what he is and isn't.

* * *

Why produce even females? Why should there be future generations? What is their purpose? When aging and death are eliminated, why continue to reproduce?

1. *SCUM* stands for Society for Cutting Up Men.

Even if they are not eliminated, why reproduce? Why should we care what happens when we're dead? Why should we care that there is no younger generation to succeed us?

Eventually the natural course of events, of social evolution, will lead to total female control of the world and, subsequently, to the cessation of the production of males and, ultimately, to the cessation of the production of females.

But SCUM is impatient; SCUM is not consoled by the thought that future generations will thrive; SCUM wants to grab some swinging living for itself. And, if a large majority of women were SCUM, they could acquire complete control of this country within a few weeks simply by withdrawing from the labor force, thereby paralyzing the entire nation. Additional measures, any one of which would be sufficient to completely disrupt the economy and everything else, would be for women to declare themselves off the money system, stop buying, just loot and simply refuse to obey all laws they don't care to obey. The police force, National Guard, Army, Navy and Marines combined couldn't squelch a rebellion of over half the population, particularly when it's made up of people they are utterly helpless without.

If all women simply left men, refused to have anything to do with any of them—ever, all men, the government, and the national economy would collapse completely. Even without leaving men, women who are aware of the extent of their superiority to and power over men, could acquire complete control over everything within a few weeks, could effect a total submission of males to females. In a sane society the male would trot along obediently after the female. The male is docile and easily led, easily subjected to the domination of any female who cares to dominate him. The male, in fact, wants desperately to be led by females, wants Mama in charge, wants to abandon himself to her care. But this is not a sane society, and most women are not even dimly aware of where they're at in relation to men.

The conflict, therefore, is not between females and males, but between SCUM—dominant, secure, self-confident, nasty, violent, selfish, independent, proud, thrill-seeking, free-wheeling, arrogant females, who consider themselves fit to rule the universe, who have free-wheeled to the limits of this "society" and are ready to wheel on to something far beyond what it has to offer—and nice, passive, accepting, "cultivated", polite, dignified, subdued, dependent, scared, mindless, insecure, approval-seeking Daddy's Girls, who can't cope with the unknown, who want to continue to wallow in the sewer that is, at least, familiar, who want to hang back with the apes, who feel secure only with Big Daddy standing by, with a big, strong man to lean on and with a fat, hairy face in the White House, who are too cowardly to face up to the hideous reality of what a man is, what Daddy is, who have cast their lot with the swine, who have adapted themselves to animalism, feel superficially comfortable with it and know no other way of "life", who have reduced their minds, thoughts and sights to the male level, who, lacking sense, imagination and wit can have value only in a male "society", who can have a place in the sun, or, rather, in the slime, only as soothers, ego boosters, relaxers and breeders, who are dismissed as inconsequents by other females, who project their deficiencies, their maleness, onto all females and see the female as a worm.

But SCUM is too impatient to hope and wait for the de-brainwashing of millions of assholes. Why should the swinging females continue to plod dismally along with the dull male ones? Why should the fates of the groovy and the creepy be intertwined? Why should the active and imaginative consult the passive and dull on social policy? Why should the independent be confined to the sewer along with the dependent who need Daddy to cling to?

A small handful of SCUM can take over the country within a year by systematically fucking up the system, selectively destroying property, and murder:

SCUM will become members of the unwork force, the fuck-up force; they will get jobs of various kinds and unwork. For example, SCUM salesgirls will not charge for merchandise; SCUM telephone operators will not charge for calls; SCUM office and factory workers, in addition to fucking up their work, will secretly destroy equipment. SCUM will unwork at a job until fired, then get a new job to unwork at.

SCUM will forcibly relieve bus drivers, cab drivers and subway token sellers of their jobs and run busses and cabs and dispense free tokens to the public.

SCUM will destroy all useless and harmful objects—cars, store windows, "Great Art", etc.

Eventually SCUM will take over the airwaves—radio and T.V. networks—by forcibly relieving of their jobs all radio and T.V. employees who would impede SCUM's entry into the broadcasting studios.

SCUM will couple-bust—barge into mixed (male-female) couples, wherever they are, and bust them up.

* * *

The sick, irrational men, those who attempt to defend themselves against their disgustingness, when they see SCUM barreling down on them, will cling in terror to Big Mama with her Big Bouncy Boobies, but Boobies won't protect them against SCUM; Big Mama will be clinging to Big Daddy, who will be in the corner shitting in his forceful, dynamic pants. Men who are rational, however, won't kick or struggle or raise a distressing fuss, but will just sit back, relax, enjoy the show and ride the waves to their demise.

V

Postwar and Postcolonial Literature, 1945–1968

I n the middle of the twentieth century, the two superpowers, the United States and the Soviet Union, having emerged from the bloody, or "hot," wars of the previous decades, found themselves locked in a Cold War: their most powerful weapons, though fired only in tests, would be capable of annihilating the planet. The two sides—the North Atlantic Treaty Organization, representing Western Europe and North America, and the Warsaw Pact, uniting the military forces of Soviet-dominated Eastern Europe—divided most of the globe into spheres of influence. By 1949, with the success of the Communist Revolution in China, led by Mao Zedong, almost half of the world's population lived under communism. The competing blocs, as they were called, understood that if either one launched a nuclear attack, the enemy would retaliate, an unstable balance known as "mutually assured destruction" (producing an ironic acronym).

To avoid planetary disaster, the two sides fought wars by proxy, notably in Korea (1950–53) and Vietnam (1955–75). Within the Communist world, the purges and mass imprisonments initiated by the Soviet dictator Joseph Stalin were selectively repudiated, after Stalin's death in 1953, by his successor,

The Algerian writer Albert Camus (1913–1960), on the balcony of his Paris publisher's office in 1955.

Nikita Khrushchev. It was during this period of de-Stalinization that the works of the dissident **Alexander Solzhenitsyn** were briefly allowed to be published. The bloody suppression of the Hungarian revolt against communism in 1956, however, showed the limits of de-Stalinization. Stalin's techniques spread, moreover, to Mao's China. The forced collectivization of the Great Leap Forward (1958–59) led to a famine that caused an estimated twenty million deaths, while the Cultural Revolution, which began in 1966 and lasted until Mao's death in 1976, attacked intellectuals and the middle classes, resulting in the destruction of most of the country's functioning institutions.

While the Communist world was undergoing radical transformations, the colonial powers of Western Europe, facing pressure from nationalist movements among their subject peoples, began to relinquish direct political control of their colonies. The process of decolonization, often accompanied by conflicts over redrawn borders, became a major topic for a generation of writers who, though born in the formerly colonized nations, were likely to have been educated in Europe and who sought to give voice to the concerns of their recently independent nations. The initial stages of postcolonial development were frequently marked by internal conflicts, civil wars, and dictatorships, and by jockeying to align newly independent nations with either the United States or the Soviet Union (or to find an alternative, "nonaligned" path). It was also in these years, however, that the basis was laid for the prosperity of what was then known as the "third world" (in contrast to the liberal capitalist democracies of the developed first world and the rapidly industrializing second world of Communist regimes). In particular, the Green Revolution of the 1960s and 1970s improved agricultural methods in the developing world

and made it possible to feed a rapidly expanding population, while smallpox was eliminated and other serious illnesses, such as tuberculosis, malaria, and plague, were brought under control. Still, in the poorer countries of Africa and South Asia, it was common for as much as half the population to live in poverty.

In Western Europe, the postwar period saw rapid rebuilding and further industrialization, even as thinkers and writers struggled to comprehend the enormity of the Holocaust. The young Polish journalist **Tadeusz Borowski** shocked his compatriots with his account of life in the Nazi concentration camps, while the Romanian-born Jew **Paul Celan**, writing in German, turned his experiences in the camps into austere and beautiful poetry. In the wake of the Nazi occupation of France (1940–44), the theme of choice became critical to a generation of authors who had had to decide between allegiance to the collaborationist Vichy state or to the Resistance movement. The philosophy of existentialism, derived by Jean-Paul Sartre from the writings of the German philosophers Friedrich Nietzsche and Martin Heidegger, emphasized the role of free choice in human life. Glimpses of existentialism occur in the bleak humor of Samuel Beckett's apocalyptic *Endgame*. Like Beckett, **Albert Camus** had worked for the Resistance. He develops the theme of choice in his account of a schoolteacher's experiences in Algeria in "**The Guest**." In different ways, these writers turned to a stripped-down literary style—either direct and realistic, like Camus and Borowski, or elusive and minimalist, like Celan and Beckett—and thus away from the exuberant modernism of the earlier part of the century.

Partly because it had been incorporated into the French state (unlike

British colonies, which tended to be governed locally), Algeria became one of the bloodiest colonial battlefields until its eventual independence in 1962. Elsewhere, decolonization occurred more rapidly. In the immediate aftermath of the war, faced with nationalist pressures in the colonies and with the moral bankruptcy of any claims to racial superiority, many colonial powers began granting independence. At midnight on August 14, 1947, Britain divided its territorial possessions in South Asia into two states, India and Pakistan. The partition took place along religious (or "communal") lines between Hindus and Muslims, but there remained many Muslims in India and Hindus in Pakistan. During the weeks before and after independence, large populations were transferred and an untold number were killed in communal violence—the subject of **Salman Rushdie**'s *Midnight's Children*. The following year, under a United Nations mandate, Britain left most of its former territories in Palestine in the hands of the new Jewish state, Israel. Its Arab neighbors attacked the new country and, during a series of short wars from 1948 to 1968, Israel expanded its national boundaries, at the same time occupying territories inhabited by Arab Palestinians.

Elsewhere in the Middle East and North Africa, a series of military coups created dictatorships, sometimes focused on the Pan-Arabist movement for Muslim unity, at other times oriented more toward socialism. Sub-Saharan Africa also experienced a series of civil wars and dictatorships, as well as ongoing minority rule by the white settler communities in South Africa and Rhodesia, which **Doris Lessing** describes. Despite Africa's hardships, it developed a remarkable literature, typically in the languages of the former colonial powers, represented here by **Chinua Achebe, Ngugi Wa Thiong'o, Wole Soyinka, and Bessie Head**. Although they sometimes took inspiration from the celebration of African identity typical of the earlier French-speaking writers of the Négritude movement, these anglophone authors typically explore village life as it has been transformed by contact with Europeans and then by the process of establishing independence.

In the United States, too, racial segregation and the disenfranchisement of African Americans were challenged in the civil rights movement, whose landmarks included the Supreme Court decision *Brown v. Board of Education* of 1954, which ended public school segregation, and the Civil Rights Acts of 1964, which banned segregation in public accommodations and outlawed discriminatory voter registration. **James Baldwin** explores the challenges that African Americans faced in the North during and after the Second World War.

With the increasing globalization of literature and the media, writers frequently adapted certain genres, especially the short story and the novel but drama and lyric poetry as well, to local conditions. For example, authors might use the language of a traditional literature to produce a colloquial, contemporary short story. In other cases, writers transformed a historically European genre by introducing elements of local customs and storytelling techniques (examples include magic realism in Latin America; the postcolonial African novel). More broadly, the encounters between indigenous societies and widely accepted literary forms caused writers to rethink the defining characteristics of their homeland; many authors valued hybrid qualities that tended to dismantle claims to cultural uniqueness or homogeneity.

Much of the writing of the postwar period engages in the movement toward "neorealism"—a return to political and social issues, in contrast to the interiority and linguistic inventiveness of the modernists. While sometimes drawing on modernist techniques such as the representation of individual consciousness and intense irony, the realists tended to use the chronological plot, omniscient narrator, and objective description typical of nineteenth-century European works. Such preferences apply equally to postcolonial writers eager to portray the history of their nations and to Western authors grappling with social issues such as civil rights, immigration, and gender relations. There are some notable exceptions, however, to the reinvigorated realism of postwar literature. Many politically oriented writers, such as Solzhenitsyn, wove allegory into their seeming realism, sometimes conveying hidden political messages in apparently straightforward narratives, at other times using allegory openly as a way of commenting on current events. At the same time, writers of all nationalities continued to use language wittily, finding expressiveness in the sounds and unexpected meanings of words.

The most intense linguistic playfulness can be found in the works of **Vladimir Nabokov, Jorge Luis Borges, Julio Cortázar**, and (albeit in a minor key) Samuel Beckett. They are among the writers who introduced many of the characteristics associated with postmodernism, although the term itself became widespread only in the later decades of the twentieth century. Like the modernists before them, they called attention to their use of language and choice of literary form. They differ from the earlier group in their sense of the limits of literature's ability to find meaning in the world; an acute consciousness of the instability of language and of its potential to carry multiple meanings; and a particular concern with the boundary between fiction and reality— what is sometimes called "metafiction" or "metatheater." Although they did not think of themselves as postmodernists, these authors were conscious of succeeding the modernists **Proust, Joyce, Woolf**, and **Kafka**, and of seeking the possibilities for literary experiment even if they no longer believed that such efforts could reveal the ultimate meaningfulness of life.

LÉOPOLD SÉDAR SENGHOR

1906–2001

Léopold Sédar Senghor was a poet, a founder of the Négritude movement, and the first president of independent Senegal. His poetry takes as its central subject the encounter between Africa and Europe. The harsh circumstances of the encounter on both the personal and social levels, the conflict between two races and their conceptions of life, provide the background to his intense exploration of the historical and moral implications of the African and black experience in modern times.

Senghor was born in Joal, a small fishing village in the Sine-Saloum basin in west-central Senegal, then a colony of France. His father, a Serer (the dominant ethnic group of his native region), was a prosperous and influential merchant. His mother was a Peul, one of a pastoral and nomadic people found all over the northern savannah belt of western Africa. This double ethnic ancestry was later to assume a larger meaning for Senghor. As he says in *Prayer of the Senegalese Soldiers*: "I grew up in the heartland of Africa, at the crossroads / Of castes and races and roads." An award-winning student, Senghor originally intended to become a Catholic priest, but he decided instead to continue his education in France, where he attended the prestigious École Normale Supérieure. As the first African student to pass the highly competitive examination for the *agrégation*, he was qualified to pursue a career in the French educational system. He held various teaching positions in France until the outbreak of the Second World War, in 1939, when he was drafted as an officer into the French army. Sen-

ghor served on the northern front, where he was taken prisoner by the Germans in 1940. Two years later, released on medical grounds but confined to Paris, he resumed teaching and in 1944 was appointed professor of African languages at the École Nationale de la France d'Outre-Mer.

Throughout this eventful period, Senghor was writing poetry, inspired by the French symbolists and surrealists and by Marxist theory. From the beginning of his sojourn in France, Senghor found himself at the center of a group of African and Caribbean students and intellectuals who had been influenced by radical currents in Western thought, especially Marxism, and by the militant literature of black American writers associated with the Harlem Renaissance. This group included a fellow student, **Aimé Césaire**, with whom Senghor struck up an important friendship. It was through their collaboration that the Négritude (or "blackness") movement developed, with its challenge of the colonial order and its passionate concern for the rehabilitation of Africa and the black race. After the war Senghor was active in the effort to launch a cultural journal, *Présence Africaine*, a vehicle for African and black self-affirmation. Senghor also published the historic *Anthologie de la nouvelle poésie nègre et malgache* (1948), which may be said to have launched Négritude as a movement, largely because of the impact of the prefatory essay, "Orphée noir" ("Black Orpheus"), by the eminent French philosopher Jean-Paul Sartre. Sartre provided both a critical review of black poetry and a philosophical exposition of the concept of Négritude. As

Senghor imagined it, Négritude put forth African culture as the source of strengths from which Europe could benefit. In arguing that Africans could teach each other and Europeans about their homeland, rather than merely being beneficiaries of European civilization, Senghor was reacting against his experience of the French colonial educational system.

Meanwhile, with his election in 1946 to the French Constituent Assembly as deputy for Senegal, Senghor had launched his political career, which was to be distinguished by service as an advocate for Africa in the French Parliament and would culminate in his election to the presidency of Senegal at its independence in 1960. Politics and literature thus ran more or less parallel in his career, as complementary aspects of a life devoted to the African cause.

Although he was a controversial figure in African literary and intellectual circles, Senghor was widely respected as both poet and statesman. When he voluntarily gave up the presidency of Senegal in 1980 to return to private life, he left behind an outstanding contribution to the political and social development of Africa and to the continent's cultural and intellectual renaissance. His election to the French Academy in 1983—the first black African to attain this honor—came as a fitting recognition of one of the foremost modern writers in the French language.

The selections from Senghor's poetry printed here represent the range of his career. "Letter to a Poet" (1945), addressed to Aimé Césaire, appeared in Senghor's first volume, *Chants d'ombre* (1945), a kind of mental diary of his experience of cultural exile in Europe. Although the volume came out at the end of the Second World War, many of the poems were composed before the conflict started. The

long, loose verses draw on the cadences of the Bible; although the original French makes use of rhyme, the effect is of free verse. Césaire had by this time returned to his home in Martinique, and Senghor wrote this poem as a letter of praise to his intellectual companion. The next three poems, all from the first volume, draw on Senghor's nostalgia for his homeland. "Night in Sine" (1945) is a love poem addressed to a woman, but the love expressed is also for Africa itself. Likewise, "Black Woman" (1945) celebrates the beauty of an idealized woman who is at once mother, lover, and symbol of a continent. "Prayer to the Masks" (1945) focuses on an element in traditional African religion. While these masks had become a symbol of European fascination with the supposedly primitive (especially after Pablo Picasso used them as the basis for some of his cubist paintings), Senghor understands the faces, in their starkness, as speaking for his ancestors. Here he addresses the challenge of reimagining the relations between Europe and Africa.

Senghor's second collection of poems, *Hosties noires* (*Black Hosts*, 1948), includes many of his wartime poems. "Letter to a Prisoner" (1942) addressed to a friend from Senghor's time in a German prisoner-of-war camp, recalls their homeland in Africa and despairs of the bleached and sterile quality of life in wartime Paris. Through their references to the war, the poems in this volume provide commentary on public events and a judgment on the passions that impelled them. The colonial protest and the critique of Europe are intertwined—a point that the title of the volume conveys, suggesting the sacrifice of Africans to the blind fury of the European war. The association also carries religious overtones: that of the collective passion of the black race, conferring on it the nobility of suffering.

Between 1949 and 1960, Senghor's energies were absorbed by politics and his campaign, through a stream of essays and lectures in France and other parts of Europe, as well as in Africa, for the rehabilitation of the continent and its peoples. In 1956, Senghor's collection *Ethiopiques* represented a new direction in his poetry, one less overtly related to the colonial experience. "The Kaya-Magan" (1956), from this collection, celebrates a legendary African ruler and the bounty of the continent, without reference to European colonialism. From the same volume, "To New York" (1956) begins by admiring the metropolis and associating it with African American jazz, but quickly turns to contrasting the barrenness and artificiality of New York with the authenticity of the African countryside. The speaker finds a sort of synthesis in imagining the "black blood" of Harlem transforming New York and making it more organic and closer to God, imagined here as a jazz saxophonist.

Senghor's later poetry confirms his standing as a lyric poet, as he pursues a deeper exploration of the poetic self and develops a more complex attitude toward the world. The interplay between the elegiac and the lyrical that runs as an undercurrent in the early poems receives, in the later work, an expanded frame of reference. The final two poems in the selection here were published in the collection *Nocturnes* (1961) after Senghor became president of Senegal. "Songs for Signare" (1961) belongs to the pastoral tradition, observing the simple lives of herdsmen, but transfers this tradition from Greece and Western Europe to central Africa. "Elegy of the Circumcised" (1961) celebrates adolescent circumcision as a male rite of passage. Throughout Senghor's later works, the tensions of public life are balanced against the comforts of love, the deaths of individuals and civilizations, and the assurance of rebirth in the stream of life. In his early volumes Senghor portrays an individual predicament as part of a collective historical plight; in the later poetry his vision embraces a wider range of experience. Africa appears in poetic terms, becoming an image of both the racial homeland and humanity's appropriate relation to the universe.

Letter to a Poet[1]

to Aimé Césaire

To my Brother *aimé*,[2] beloved friend, my bluntly fraternal greetings!
Black sea gulls like seafaring boatmen have brought me a taste
Of your tidings mixed with spices and the noisy fragrance of
　　Southern Rivers[3]
And Islands.[4] They showed your influence, your distinguished brow,
The flower of your delicate lips. They are now your disciples,　　　　5
A hive of silence, proud as peacocks. You keep their breathless zeal
From fading until moonrise. Is it your perfume of exotic fruits,
Or your wake of light in the fullness of day?
O, the many plum-skin women in the harem of your mind!

---

1. All selections translated by Melvin Dixon.
2. Beloved (French). The poem pays homage to fellow poet Aimé Césaire.
3. Senghor plays here on the poetic resonance of the French administrative term (*Rivières du Sud*) for the area comprising the former French empire in west and central Africa.
4. The Caribbean, where Césaire was born.

Still charming beyond the years, embers aglow under the ash 10
Of your eyelids, is the music we stretched our hands
And hearts to so long ago. Have you forgotten your nobility?
Your talent to praise the Ancestors, the Princes,
And the Gods, neither flower nor drops of dew?[5]
You were to offer the Spirits the virgin fruits of your garden 15
—You ate only the newly harvested millet blossom
And stole not a petal to sweeten your mouth.
At the bottom of the well of my memory, I touch your face
And draw water to refresh my long regret.
You recline royally, elbow on a cushion of clear hillside, 20
Your bed presses the earth, easing the toil of wetland drums
Beating the rhythm of your song, and your verse
Is the breath of the night and the distant sea.
You praised the Ancestors and the legitimate princes.
For your rhyme and counterpoint you scooped a star from the
     heavens. 25
At your bare feet poor men threw down a mat of their year's wages,
And women their amber[6] hearts and soul-wrenching dance.

My friend, my friend—Oh, you will come back, come back!
I shall await you under the mahogany tree,[7] the message
Already sent to the woodcutter's boss. You will come back 30
For the feast of first fruits[8] when the soft night
In the sloping sun rises steaming from the rooftops
And athletes,[9] befitting your arrival,
Parade their youthfulness, adorned like the beloved.

                                                        1945

Night in Sine[1]

Woman, place your soothing hands upon my brow,
Your hands softer than fur.
Above us balance the palm trees, barely rustling
In the night breeze. Not even a lullaby.
Let the rhythmic silence cradle us. 5
Listen to its song. Hear the beat of our dark blood,
Hear the deep pulse of Africa in the mist of lost villages.

Now sets the weary moon upon its slack seabed
Now the bursts of laughter quiet down, and even the storyteller
Nods his head like a child on his mother's back 10

---

5. The conventions of Western lyricism are contrasted with the more pressing social themes of the black poet.
6. A translucent stone, with a brownish yellow hue.
7. Of royal significance.

8. The harvest festival.
9. Wrestlers, the traditional sporting heroes of Senegal.
1. A river in Senegal. The Serer, Senghor's ethnic group, inhabit the basin formed by the confluence of Sine and Saloum.

The dancers' feet grow heavy, and heavy, too,
Come the alternating voices of singers.

Now the stars appear and the Night dreams
Learning on that hill of clouds, dressed in its long, milky pagne.[2]
The roofs of the huts shine tenderly. What are they saying   15
So secretly to the stars? Inside, the fire dies out
In the closeness of sour and sweet smells.

Woman, light the clear-oil lamp. Let the Ancestors
Speak around us as parents do when the children are in bed.
Let us listen to the voices of the Elissa[3] Elders. Exiled like us   20
They did not want to die, or lose the flow of their semen in the sands.
Let me hear, a gleam of friendly souls visits the smoke-filled hut,
My head upon your breast as warm as tasty *dang*[4] steaming from the fire,
Let me breathe the odor of our Dead, let me gather
And speak with their living voices, let me learn to live   25
Before plunging deeper than the diver[5]
Into the great depths of sleep.

1945

Black Woman

Naked woman, black woman
Dressed in your color[1] that is life, in your form that is beauty!
I grew up in your shadow. The softness of your hands
Shielded my eyes, and now at the height of Summer and Noon,
From the crest of a charred hilltop I discover you, Promised Land[2]   5
And your beauty strikes my heart like an eagle's lightning flash.

Naked woman, dark woman
Ripe fruit with firm flesh, dark raptures of black wine,
Mouth that gives music to my mouth
Savanna of clear horizons, savanna quivering to the fervent caress   10
Of the East Wind,[3] sculptured tom-tom, stretched drumskin
Moaning under the hands of the conqueror
Your deep contralto voice[4] is the spiritual song of the Beloved.

---

2. Printed cloth (French African); here the Milky Way, with which the moon appears to be robed.
3. A village in Guinea Bissau, south of Senegal, where Senghor's ancestors are buried.
4. A cereal meal.
5. The setting moon.
1. A reference to the green vegetation of the African landscape, to which the black woman is assimilated.

2. The analogy with the Israelites in the Old Testament of the Bible confers a religious note on this poem.
3. The Harmattan, a dry, sharp wind that blows from the Sahara, northeast of Senegal, between November and April.
4. An allusion to the vocal register of Marian Anderson (1897–1993), an African American singer famous for her rendering of Negro spirituals.

Naked woman, dark woman
Oil no breeze can ripple, oil soothing the thighs 15
Of athletes and the thighs of the princes of Mali[5]
Gazelle with celestial limbs, pearls are stars
Upon the night of your skin. Delight of the mind's riddles,
The reflections of red gold from your shimmering skin
In the shade of your hair, my despair 20
Lightens in the close suns of your eyes.

Naked woman, black woman
I sing your passing beauty and fix it for all Eternity
before jealous Fate reduces you to ashes to nourish the roots of life.

1945

Prayer to the Masks

Masks![1] O Masks!
Black mask, red mask, you white-and-black masks
Masks of the four cardinal points where the Spirit blows
I greet you in silence!
And you, not the least of all, Ancestor with the lion head.[2] 5
You keep this place safe from women's laughter
And any wry, profane smiles[3]
You exude the immortal air where I inhale
The breath of my Fathers.
Masks with faces without masks, stripped of every dimple 10
And every wrinkle
You created this portrait, my face leaning
On an altar of blank paper[4]
And in your image, listen to me!
The Africa of empires is dying—it is the agony 15
Of a sorrowful princess
And Europe, too, tied to us at the navel.
Fix your steady eyes on your oppressed children
Who give their lives like the poor man his last garment.
Let us answer "present" at the rebirth of the World 20
As white flour cannot rise without the leaven.[5]
Who else will teach rhythm to the world
Deadened by machines and cannons?

---

5. The ancient empire of the West African savanna.
1. Representatives of the spirits of the ancestors. In African belief, the ancestors inhabit the immaterial world beyond the visible, from there offering protection to their living descendants.
2. The animal totem of Senghor's family. His father bore the Serer name Diogoye ("Lion"). A totem is an animal or plant that is closely associated with a family, sometimes consid-

ered to be a member of the family.
3. Ancestral masks are usually kept in an enclosure, a sacred place forbidden to women and uninitiated males. There is also a suggestion here that Senghor will protect them from the patronizing gaze of white people.
4. An ironic reference to Senghor's Western education.
5. An ingredient (for example, yeast) in baked goods that make them rise; also a biblical image.

Who will sound the shout of joy at daybreak to wake orphans and the dead?
Tell me, who will bring back the memory of life   25
To the man of gutted hopes?
They call us men of cotton, coffee, and oil
They call us men of death.
But we are men of dance, whose feet get stronger
As we pound upon firm ground.[6]   30

1945

Letter to a Prisoner

Ngom! Champion of Tyâné![1]

It is I who greet you, I your village neighbor, your heart's neighbor.
I send you my white[2] greeting like the dawn's white cry,
Over the barbed wires of hate and stupidity,
And I call you by your name and your honor.   5
My greetings to Tamsir Dargui Ndyâye, who lives off parchments[3]
That give him a subtle tongue and long thin fingers,[4]
To Samba Dyouma, the poet, whose voice is the color of flame[5]
And whose forehead bears the signs of his destiny,
To Nyaoutt Mbodye and to Koli Ngom, your namesake   10
And to all those who, at the hour when the great arms
Are sad like branches beaten by the sun, huddle at night
Shivering around the dish of friendship.

I write you from the solitude of my precious—and closely guarded—
Residence of my black skin. Fortunate are my friends   15
Who know nothing of the icy walls and the brightly lit
Apartments that sterilize every seed on the ancestors' masks
And even the memories of love.
You know nothing of the good white bread, milk, and salt,
Or those substantial dishes that do not nourish,   20
That separate the refined from the boulevard crowds,
Sleepwalkers who have renounced their human identity
Chameleons[6] deaf to change, and their shame locks you
In your cage of solitude.
You know nothing of restaurants and swimming pools   25
Forbidden to noble black blood

6. A reference to Antaeus, who in Greek mythology drew strength by touching the earth with his feet.
1. A Serer female name. The direct address with which the poem opens is a convention of oral poetry. Ngom, a comrade in the German prisoner-of-war camp, is addressed by his praise name as a champion wrestler, whose exploits in the arena bring honor to his beloved, Tyâné. In the poem, Senghor shares his experience of wartime Paris, to which he has returned after his release from the camp,
with the Africans whom he left behind.
2. Wan, melancholic.
3. Implies intellectual and spiritual nourishment. "Tamsir": a title for a learned man, equivalent to "doctor."
4. Of the ascetic man of letters.
5. A reference to Dyouma's golden voice and the passionate content of his lyrics. Oral poets sang or declaimed their compositions.
6. A reference to those French people who collaborated with the German forces of the Occupation.

And Science and Humanity erecting their police lines
At the borders of negritude.[7]
Must I shout louder? Tell me, can you hear me?
I no longer recognize white men, my brothers,   30
Like this evening at the cinema, so lost were they
Beyond the void made around my skin.[8]

I write to you because my books are white like boredom,
Like misery, like death.
Make room for me around the pot so I can take my place   35
Again, still warm.
Let our hands touch as they reach into the steaming
Rice of friendship. Let the old Serer words
Pass from mouth to mouth like a pipe among friends.
Let Dargui share his succulent fruits,[9] the hay   40
Of every smelly drought! And you, serve us your wise words
As huge as the navel[1] of prodigious Africa.
Which singer this evening will summon the Ancestors around us,
Gathering like a peaceful herd of beasts of the bush?
Who will nestle our dreams under the eyelids of the stars?   45

Ngom! Answer me by the new-moon mail.
At the turn in the road, I shall meet your naked, hesitant words.
Like the fledgling emerging from his cage
Your words are put together so naively; and the learned may mock them,
But they bring me back to the surreal   50
And their milk gushes on my face.
I await your letter at the hour when morning lays death low.
I shall receive it piously like the morning ablution,
Like the dew of dawn.

                                                                Paris, June 1942

To New York

(for jazz orchestra and trumpet solo)

I

New York! At first I was bewildered by your beauty,
Those huge, long-legged, golden girls.
So shy, at first, before your blue metallic eyes and icy smile,
So shy. And full of despair at the end of skyscraper streets
Raising my owl eyes at the eclipse of the sun.   5
Your light is sulphurous against the pale towers

7. Here, a collective term for the black race, in its historical circumstance the world over.
8. A rare report of Senghor's personal experience of racial discrimination.
9. Of his mind, which is well stocked with learning and wisdom.
1. Many African children have large navels. Senghor turns this into a mark of natural strength.

Whose heads strike lightning into the sky,
Skyscrapers defying storms with their steel shoulders
And weathered skin of stone.
But two weeks on the naked sidewalks of Manhattan— 10
At the end of the third week the fever
Overtakes you with a jaguar's leap
Two weeks without well water or pasture all birds of the air
Fall suddenly dead under the high, sooty terraces.
No laugh from a growing child, his hand in my cool hand. 15
No mother's breast, but nylon legs. Legs and breasts
Without smell or sweat. No tender word, and no lips,
Only artificial hearts paid for in cold cash
And not one book offering wisdom.
The painter's palette yields only coral crystals. 20
Sleepless nights, O nights of Manhattan!
Stirring with delusions while car horns blare the empty hours
And murky streams carry away hygenic loving
Like rivers overflowing with the corpses of babies.

II

Now is the time for signs and reckoning, New York! 25
Now is the time of manna and hyssop.[1]
You have only to listen to God's trombones,[2] to your heart
Beating to the rhythm of blood, your blood.
I saw Harlem teeming with sounds and ritual colors
And outrageous smells— 30
At teatime in the home of the drugstore-deliveryman
I saw the festival of Night begin at the retreat of day.
And I proclaim Night more truthful than the day.
It is the pure hour when God brings forth
Life immemorial in the streets, 35
All the amphibious elements shining like suns.
Harlem, Harlem! Now I've seen Harlem, Harlem!
A green breeze of corn rising from the pavements
Plowed by the Dan[3] dancers' bare feet,
Hips rippling like silk and spearhead breasts, 40
Ballets of water lilies and fabulous masks
And mangoes of love rolling from the low houses
To the feet of police horses.
And along sidewalks I saw streams of white rum
And streams of black milk in the blue haze of cigars. 45
And at night I saw cotton flowers snow down
From the sky and the angels' wings and sorcerers' plumes.
Listen, New York! O listen to your bass male voice,

1. An aromatic herb with religious associations. "Manna": the food that came down
miraculously from Heaven to feed the Israelites when they were wandering in the desert
after leaving Egypt.
2. The title of a book of sermons by James
Weldon Johnson, written in the idiom of black
preachers. The work has become a classic of
African American literature.
3. An ethnic group in Ivory Coast, reputed for
the vigor of its dances. These lines establish a
racial and cultural connection between Africa
and black America.

Your vibrant oboe voice, the muted anguish of your tears
Falling in great clots of blood,   50
Listen to the distant beating of your nocturnal heart,
The tom-tom's rhythm and blood, tom-tom blood and tom-tom.

III

New York! I say New York, let black blood flow into your blood.
Let it wash the rust from your steel joints, like an oil of life
Let it give your bridges the curve of hips and supple vines.   55
Now the ancient age returns, unity is restored,
The reconciliation of Lion and Bull and Tree[4]
Idea links to action, the ear to the heart, sign to meaning.
See your rivers stirring with musk alligators[5]
And sea cows[6] with mirage eyes. No need to invent the Sirens.   60
Just open your eyes to the April rainbow
And your ears, especially your ears, to God
Who in one burst of saxophone laughter
Created heaven and earth in six days,
And on the seventh slept a deep Negro sleep.   65

                                                                        1956

Songs for Signare[1]

(for flutes[2])

A *hand of light*[3] caressed my dark eyelids and your smile rose
Over the mists floating monotonously on my Congo.[4]
My heart has echoed the virgin song of the dawn birds
As my blood used to beat to the white song of sap in my branching arms.
See the bush flower and the star in my hair   5
And the bandana on the brow of the herdsman athlete.[5]
I will take up the flute and play a rhythm for the peace
Of the herds and sitting all day in the shade of your lashes,
Close to the Fimla Springs[6] I shall graze faithfully the golden
Lowings[7] of your herds. For this morning a hand of light   10
Caressed my dark eyelids, and all day long
My heart has echoed the virgin song of the birds.

                                                                        1961

4. Symbolic of suffering, from the Christian cross. "Lion": a symbol of the black race. "Bull": a symbol of the white race.
5. Held in Serer mythology to conserve the memory of the past.
6. Or manatees, credited by the Serer with being able to see into the future.
1. The name of the woman addressed is also the French word for a mixed-race woman of Portuguese and African descent.
2. Associated with shepherds in the pastoral tradition.
3. That is, of the beloved. This is a love poem based on the Western pastoral convention.
4. A river in central Africa that flows through dense tropical landscape; here, an image of the poet's state of mind.
5. The poet himself.
6. The source of a stream in Sine-Saloum.
7. This association of the sound of the cattle with color is an example of synaesthesia.

Elegy of the Circumcised[1]

Childhood Night,[2] blue Night, gold Night, O Moon!
How often have I invoked you, O Night! while weeping by the road,
Feeling the pain of adulthood. Loneliness! and its dunes all around.
One night during childhood it was a night as black as pitch.
Our backs were bent with fear at the lion's roar,[3] and the shifting   5
Silence in the night bent the tall grass. Branches caught fire
And you were fired with hope! and my pale memory of the Sun
Barely reassured my innocence. I had to die.[4]
I laid my hands on my neck like the virgin who shivers in the throes
Of death. I had to die to the beauty of the song—all things drift   10
Along the thread of death. Look at twilight on the turtledoves' breast,
When blue ringdoves coo and dream sea gulls fly
With their plaintive cries.

Let us die and dance elbow to elbow in a braided garland[5]
May our clothes not impede our steps, but let the gift   15
Of the betrothed girl glow like sparks under the clouds.
Woi![6] The drum furrows the holy silence.
Let us dance, the song whipping the blood, and let the rhythm
Chase away the agony that grabs us by the throat.
Life keeps death away.   20
Let us dance to the refrain of agony, may the night of sex[7]
Rise above our ignorance, above our innocence.
Ah! To die to childhood, let the poem die, the syntax disintegrate,
And all the unimportant words become spoiled.
The rhythm's weight is sufficient, no need for cement words   25
To build the city of tomorrow on rock.
May the Sun rise up from the sea of shadows
Blood![8] The waves are the color of dawn.

But God, I have wailed too much—how many times?
—The transparent childhood nights.   30
The Male-Noon is the time of Spirits, when all form
Gets rid of its flesh, like trees in Europe under the winter sun.
See, the bones are abstract, they obey only the measures
Of the ruler, the compass, the sextant.
Like sand, life slips freely from man's fingers,   35
And snowflakes imprison the water's life,

1. The circumcision rite is the essential element in the initiation ceremony that marks the formal passage of the adolescent to adult status. The ceremony involves the confinement of candidates in the bush for a long period, during which they undergo a series of tests and receive instruction in the history and customs of the land. At the end of this period, on a designated night, they are circumcised one after the other.
2. The night of the circumcision.
3. Simulated, as part of the initiation cere-
mony, and intended to develop the virtue of courage in the boys.
4. Initiation is the symbolic death of the child who is reborn an adult.
5. The triumphant dance of the initiates after the ceremony.
6. A chant.
7. Initiation also purifies the adolescent, in preparation for sexuality in its creative function.
8. That shed at circumcision, heralding a new birth.

The water snake[9] glides through the vain hands of the reeds.
Lovely Nights, friendly Nights, childhood Nights
Along the salt flats and in the woods, nights throbbing
With presences and with eyelids, full of wings and breaths   40
And living silence, now tell me how many times
Have I cried for you in the bloom of my age?

The poem withers in the midday sun and feeds upon the evening dew,
The tom-tom beats the rhythm of sap in the smell of ripe fruit.
Master of the Initiates,[1] I know I need your knowledge
　　to understand   45
The cipher of things, to be aware of my duties as father and *lamarque*,[2]
To measure exactly the scope of my responsibilities, to distribute
The harvest without forgetting any worker or orphan.
The song is not just a charm, it feeds the woolly heads of my flock.
The poem is a snake-bird,[3] the dawn marriage of shadow and light   50
It soars like the Phoenix![4] It sings with wings spread
Over the slaughter of words.

                                                                           1961

9. A symbol of wisdom and durability.
1. An elder who supervises the ceremony.
2. A word coined by Senghor from the Wolof *lam* and the Greek *archos*, both meaning "landowner." The line refers to the civic and moral obligations taught to the initiates.
3. Or plumed serpent, which is endowed with

visionary powers. This creature is found in the mythology of many cultures.
4. A mythical bird that is supposed to rise from its own ashes, thus a symbol of regeneration. Like the bird, poetry embodies the force of renewal in nature.

JULIO CORTÁZAR
1914–1984

Known for his vivid sense of fantasy and his ability to portray alternative realities, Julio Cortázar was considered one of the leading figures of the Latin American "Boom" of the 1960s and 1970s—a period of great creativity and productivity—although by then he had left his native Argentina to live and work in Paris. His friend and mentor, **Jorge Luis Borges**, declared, "No one can retell the plot of a Cortázar story; each one consists of determined words

in a determined order. If we try to summarize them, we realize that something precious has been lost." The compounded sense of perfect, shimmering order and underlying mystery pervades Cortázar's work.

Cortázar's parents, wealthy Argentines, were visiting Belgium on business in August 1914 when Germany invaded the country at the outbreak of the First World War. Three weeks later, Cortázar was born in Brussels. The

Cortázar family (like the Borges family) spent most of the war in neutral Switzerland. In 1918 the family returned to Argentina; but Cortázar's father soon abandoned the family, and the young boy was raised by his mother and a house full of female relatives in a suburb of Buenos Aires. A sickly child, Julio spent much of his youth reading science fiction and fantasy novels, with a particular interest in Jules Verne and other French writers. He expressed his writerly aspirations early, claiming to have completed his first novel at the age of nine. Cortázar trained as a teacher and taught high school in several small towns near Buenos Aires. He opposed the rise of the dictator Juan Perón, and in 1944 was even briefly imprisoned for political activities while teaching French at the University of Cuyo.

During his teaching years, Cortázar wrote in a variety of genres: poetry, short stories, plays, and essays. He published several essays and a collection of poems, *Presencia*, under the pseudonym Julio Denis. Later he would repudiate these early works, explaining that when he wrote them, he did not yet know what he really wanted to say. Only after 1945 did he begin publishing stories in his own name. The first of these, "House Taken Over," appeared in 1946 in a magazine under the editorship of Borges, who helped to launch Cortázar's career. The two writers share important affinities as inventors of imaginary worlds, but Borges is the more intellectual of the two, Cortázar the more playful, although his is a playfulness with a dark side. Cortázar's stories of the postwar period, which he often based on his nightmares, frequently concern themselves with imaginary beasts; he collected them in 1951 under the title *Bestiario* (*Bestiary*). That same year Cortázar emigrated to Paris, where he lived until his death. While there, he wrote his best-known novel, *Hopscotch* (1963), which can be read either sequentially (chapters 1–155) or by hopping through the chapters according to a series of patterns that the author provides. Sometimes called an "anti-novel," *Hopscotch* is an example of experimental fiction and is considered postmodernist because of the liberties it takes with narrative order. Cortázar also translated, into Spanish, Daniel Defoe's *Robinson Crusoe* and many short stories by Edgar Allan Poe, whose influence is evident throughout Cortázar's work. He remained politically engaged throughout his life, opposing human rights abuses by right-wing Latin American dictators, supporting the Communist government of Fidel Castro in Cuba, and even giving royalties from his work to the Sandinistas in Nicaragua, a Socialist organization.

The story selected here, "House Taken Over" (1946), was based on a dream. Cortázar later recalled the origin of the story, "which I dreamed with all the details which figure in the text and which I wrote upon jumping out of bed, still enveloped in the horrible nausea of its ending." The use Cortázar made of this dream owes something to surrealism and its rejection of rational thought in favor of responses arising from the unconscious. A tale that starts out representing everyday life in dreamlike simplicity soon takes on shivering distortions of a nightmare. The story begins with the peaceful lives of a middle-aged brother and sister who live in a large house in Buenos Aires; little information about them is provided, except that their family has lived in this house for generations. Although a suggestion of incest lingers in the idea of a "quiet, simple marriage of sister and brother," their existence seems straightforward until the strange events of the middle of the story. The siblings accept their sudden change of circumstance serenely, but it remains puzzling, even uncanny, for the reader: who are the "they" who have taken over the house?

Critics have analyzed the story as a commentary on life under the authoritarian regime of Perón, or as a critique of the backwardness and conservatism of postwar Argentine society. Written as it was near the end of the Second World War, "House Taken Over" may also refer to the occupation of Europe by the Nazis—an event that would have had special interest for Cortázar, who was born in German-occupied Belgium more than thirty years earlier. Yet while Cortázar's stories seem open to reading as allegories (coded statements about political events), they tend to remain evasive and ambiguous, to resist efforts at final interpretation. In this respect, the story resembles **Franz Kafka's** *The Metamorphosis*. Whatever its political or biographical implications, "House Taken Over" is haunting in its suggestion of forces beyond the grasp of rationality or even description. Cortázar complained that readers wanted his works to be less obscure and hermetic, more directly involved in political life; yet his genius lies precisely in creating those disturbing images and events that register historical conflicts so uneasily and obscurely.

House Taken Over[1]

We liked the house because, apart from its being old and spacious (in a day when old houses go down for a profitable auction of their construction materials), it kept the memories of great-grandparents, our paternal grandfather, our parents and the whole of childhood.

Irene and I got used to staying in the house by ourselves, which was crazy, eight people could have lived in that place and not have gotten in each other's way. We rose at seven in the morning and got the cleaning done, and about eleven I left Irene to finish off whatever rooms and went to the kitchen. We lunched at noon precisely; then there was nothing left to do but a few dirty plates. It was pleasant to take lunch and commune with the great hollow, silent house, and it was enough for us just to keep it clean. We ended up thinking, at times, that that was what had kept us from marrying. Irene turned down two suitors for no particular reason, and María Esther went and died on me before we could manage to get engaged. We were easing into our forties with the unvoiced concept that the quiet, simple marriage of sister and brother was the indispensable end to a line established in this house by our grandparents. We would die here someday, obscure and distant cousins would inherit the place, have it torn down, sell the bricks and get rich on the building plot; or more justly and better yet, we would topple it ourselves before it was too late.

Irene never bothered anyone. Once the morning housework was finished, she spent the rest of the day on the sofa in her bedroom, knitting. I couldn't tell you why she knitted so much; I think women knit when they discover that it's a fat excuse to do nothing at all. But Irene was not like that, she always knitted necessities, sweaters for winter, socks for me, handy morning robes and bedjackets for herself. Sometimes she would do a jacket, then unravel it the next moment because there was something that didn't please her; it was

1. Translated from Spanish by Paul Blackburn.

pleasant to see a pile of tangled wool in her knitting basket fighting a losing battle for a few hours to retain its shape. Saturdays I went downtown to buy wool; Irene had faith in my good taste, was pleased with the colors and never a skein had to be returned. I took advantage of these trips to make the rounds of the bookstores, uselessly asking if they had anything new in French literature. Nothing worthwhile had arrived in Argentina since 1939.[2]

But it's the house I want to talk about, the house and Irene, I'm not very important. I wonder what Irene would have done without her knitting. One can reread a book, but once a pullover is finished you can't do it over again, it's some kind of disgrace. One day I found that the drawer at the bottom of the chiffonier, replete with mothballs, was filled with shawls, white, green, lilac. Stacked amid a great smell of camphor—it was like a shop; I didn't have the nerve to ask her what she planned to do with them. We didn't have to earn our living, there was plenty coming in from the farms each month, even piling up. But Irene was only interested in the knitting and showed a wonderful dexterity, and for me the hours slipped away watching her, her hands like silver sea-urchins, needles flashing, and one or two knitting baskets on the floor, the balls of yarn jumping about. It was lovely.

How not to remember the layout of that house. The dining room, a living room with tapestries, the library and three large bedrooms in the section most recessed, the one that faced toward Rodríguez Peña.[3] Only a corridor with its massive oak door separated that part from the front wing, where there was a bath, the kitchen, our bedrooms and the hall. One entered the house through a vestibule with enameled tiles, and a wrought-iron grated door opened onto the living room. You had to come in through the vestibule and open the gate to go into the living room; the doors to our bedrooms were on either side of this, and opposite it was the corridor leading to the back section; going down the passage, one swung open the oak door beyond which was the other part of the house; or just before the door, one could turn to the left and go down a narrower passageway which led to the kitchen and the bath. When the door was open, you became aware of the size of the house; when it was closed, you had the impression of an apartment, like the ones they build today, with barely enough room to move around in. Irene and I always lived in this part of the house and hardly ever went beyond the oak door except to do the cleaning. Incredible how much dust collected on the furniture. It may be Buenos Aires is a clean city, but she owes it to her population and nothing else. There's too much dust in the air, the slightest breeze and it's back on the marble console tops and in the diamond patterns of the tooled-leather desk set. It's a lot of work to get it off with a feather duster; the motes rise and hang in the air, and settle again a minute later on the pianos and the furniture.

I'll always have a clear memory of it because it happened so simply and without fuss. Irene was knitting in her bedroom, it was eight at night, and I suddenly decided to put the water up for *mate*.[4] I went down the corridor as far as the

2. The outbreak of World War II, in 1939, prevented books from being exported from Europe.

3. Street in Buenos Aires.
4. A popular Argentine herbal tea made from the leaf *yerba mate*, a type of holly.

oak door, which was ajar, then turned into the hall toward the kitchen, when I heard something in the library or the dining room. The sound came through muted and indistinct, a chair being knocked over onto the carpet or the muffled buzzing of a conversation. At the same time or a second later, I heard it at the end of the passage which led from those two rooms toward the door. I hurled myself against the door before it was too late and shut it, leaned on it with the weight of my body; luckily, the key was on our side; moreover, I ran the great bolt into place, just to be safe.

I went down to the kitchen, heated the kettle, and when I got back with the tray of *mate*, I told Irene:

"I had to shut the door to the passage. They've taken over the back part."

She let her knitting fall and looked at me with her tired, serious eyes.

"You're sure?"

I nodded.

"In that case," she said, picking up her needles again, "we'll have to live on this side."

I sipped at the *mate* very carefully, but she took her time starting her work again. I remember it was a grey vest she was knitting. I liked that vest.

The first few days were painful, since we'd both left so many things in the part that had been taken over. My collection of French literature, for example, was still in the library. Irene had left several folios of stationery and a pair of slippers that she used a lot in the winter. I missed my briar pipe, and Irene, I think, regretted the loss of an ancient bottle of Hesperidin.[5] It happened repeatedly (but only in the first few days) that we would close some drawer or cabinet and look at one another sadly.

"It's not here."

One thing more among the many lost on the other side of the house.

But there were advantages, too. The cleaning was so much simplified that, even when we got up late, nine thirty for instance, by eleven we were sitting around with our arms folded. Irene got into the habit of coming to the kitchen with me to help get lunch. We thought about it and decided on this: while I prepared the lunch, Irene would cook up dishes that could be eaten cold in the evening. We were happy with the arrangement because it was always such a bother to have to leave our bedrooms in the evening and start to cook. Now we made do with the table in Irene's room and platters of cold supper.

Since it left her more time for knitting, Irene was content. I was a little lost without my books, but so as not to inflict myself on my sister, I set about reordering papa's stamp collection; that killed some time. We amused ourselves sufficiently, each with his own thing, almost always getting together in Irene's bedroom, which was the more comfortable. Every once in a while, Irene might say:

"Look at this pattern I just figured out, doesn't it look like clover?"

After a bit it was I, pushing a small square of paper in front of her so that she could see the excellence of some stamp or another from Eupen-et-Malmédy.[6]

5. A citrus-flavored Argentine aperitif. "Briar": a common wood used in making smoking pipes.
6. A region ceded by Germany to Belgium at the end of World War I, then reannexed to Germany during World War II; well-known among stamp collectors because a variety of stamps were issued there by the Belgian and German governments during the wars.

We were fine, and little by little we stopped thinking. You can live without thinking.

(Whenever Irene talked in her sleep, I woke up immediately and stayed awake. I never could get used to this voice from a statue or a parrot, a voice that came out of the dreams, not from a throat. Irene said that in my sleep I flailed about enormously and shook the blankets off. We had the living room between us, but at night you could hear everything in the house. We heard each other breathing, coughing, could even feel each other reaching for the light switch when, as happened frequently, neither of us could fall asleep.

Aside from our nocturnal rumblings, everything was quiet in the house. During the day there were the household sounds, the metallic click of knitting needles, the rustle of stamp-album pages turning. The oak door was massive, I think I said that. In the kitchen or the bath, which adjoined the part that was taken over, we managed to talk loudly, or Irene sang lullabies. In a kitchen there's always too much noise, the plates and glasses, for there to be interruptions from other sounds. We seldom allowed ourselves silence there, but when we went back to our rooms or to the living room, then the house grew quiet, half-lit, we ended by stepping around more slowly so as not to disturb one another. I think it was because of this that I woke up irremediably and at once when Irene began to talk in her sleep.)

Except for the consequences, it's nearly a matter of repeating the same scene over again. I was thirsty that night, and before we went to sleep, I told Irene that I was going to the kitchen for a glass of water. From the door of the bedroom (she was knitting) I heard the noise in the kitchen; if not the kitchen, then the bath, the passage off at that angle dulled the sound. Irene noticed how brusquely I had paused, and came up beside me without a word. We stood listening to the noises, growing more and more sure that they were on our side of the oak door, if not the kitchen then the bath, or in the hall itself at the turn, almost next to us.

We didn't wait to look at one another. I took Irene's arm and forced her to run with me to the wrought-iron door, not waiting to look back. You could hear the noises, still muffled but louder, just behind us. I slammed the grating and we stopped in the vestibule. Now there was nothing to be heard.

"They've taken over our section," Irene said. The knitting had reeled off from her hands and the yarn ran back toward the door and disappeared under it. When she saw that the balls of yarn were on the other side, she dropped the knitting without looking at it.

"Did you have time to bring anything?" I asked hopelessly.

"No, nothing."

We had what we had on. I remembered fifteen thousand pesos[7] in the wardrobe in my bedroom. Too late now.

I still had my wrist watch on and saw that it was 11 P.M. I took Irene around the waist (I think she was crying) and that was how we went into the street. Before we left, I felt terrible; I locked the front door up tight and tossed the key down the sewer. It wouldn't do to have some poor devil decide to go in and rob the house, at that hour and with the house taken over.

1946

7. About $3,500 at the time (worth about $40,000 in 2011).

TADEUSZ BOROWSKI

1922–1951

Incarcerated in the extermination camps of Auschwitz-Birkenau, Daut-mergen, and Dachau-Allach between the ages of twenty and twenty-two, a tormented suicide by gas at twenty-eight, Tadeusz Borowski wrote stories of life in the camps that have made him the foremost writer of what is called the "literature of atrocity." His fiction is still read for its powerful evocation of the death camps, for its analysis of human relationships under pressure, and for its agonizing portrayal of individuals forced to choose between physical or spiritual survival.

Tadeusz Borowski was born on November 12, 1922, to Polish Catholic parents in Żytomierz, a Soviet-controlled city with Polish, Ukrainian, Jewish, and Russian residents. When he was three years old, his father was sent to a labor camp in Siberia as a suspected dissident. Four years later, his mother was deported as well, and Tadeusz was separated from his twelve-year-old brother. Tadeusz was raised by an aunt and educated in a Soviet school until a prisoner exchange in 1932 brought his father home; his mother's release in 1934 reunited the family. Money was scarce, however, and the boy was sent away to a Franciscan boarding school where he could be educated inexpensively. Later he commented that he had never had a family life: "Either my father was sitting in Murmansk or my mother was in Siberia, or I was in a boarding school, on my own, or in a camp." The Second World War began when he was sixteen, and—since the Nazis did not permit higher education for Poles—Borowski continued his studies at Warsaw University via illegal underground classes. Unlike his fellow students, he refused to join political groups and did not become involved in the Resistance; he wanted merely to write poetry and continue his literary studies. Polish publications were illegal, however, and his first poetry collection, *Wherever the Earth* (1942)—run off in 165 copies on a clandestine mimeograph machine—was enough to condemn him. *Wherever the Earth* prefigures the bleak perspective of the concentration camp stories: prophesying the end of the human race, it sees the world as a gigantic labor camp and the sky as a "low, steel lid" or "a factory ceiling" (an oppressive image that he may have adapted from **Baudelaire's "Spleen LXXXI"**). In late February 1943, Borowski and his fiancée, Maria Rundo, were arrested; they were sent to Auschwitz two months later. In the meantime, Borowski was able to see, from his cell window, both the Jewish uprising in the Warsaw ghetto and the ghetto's fiery destruction by Nazi soldiers.

On arriving in Auschwitz, Borowski was put to hard labor with the other prisoners. After a bout with pneumonia, he survived by taking a position as an orderly in the Auschwitz hospital—which was not just a clinic but a place where doctors used prisoners as experimental subjects. Rundo had been sent to the women's barracks at the same camp, and he wrote daily letters that were smuggled to her. He got to see her when he was sent to the women's camp to pick up the corpses of infants, and later when he was assigned to repair roofs in the women's camp. Borowski wrote about his camp experiences immediately after the war, when he was living in Munich with two other former Auschwitz prisoners, Janusz Nel Siedlecki and Krystyn Olszewski. The three men were transferred from Dachau-Allach to the Freimann repatriation camp, outside Munich, which they soon left when the Polish artist and publisher Anatol Girs located them and found them jobs. Sharing an apartment in Munich, they published their slightly fictionalized memoirs, including Borowski's "This Way for the Gas, Ladies and Gentlemen," in the 1946 collection *We Were in Auschwitz*. On his return to Poland, Borowski's searing talent was recognized and he became a prominent writer. He married Maria Rundo and was courted by Poland's Stalinist government. At the government's urging, he wrote journalism and weekly stories that followed communist political lines and employed a newly strident tone. The Cold War had begun, and Borowski was persuaded that he had joined a popular revolution that would prevent more horrors like Auschwitz. He went so far as to do intelligence work in Berlin for the Polish secret police in 1949. The revelation of Soviet prison camps, however, as well as the spectacle of political purges in Poland, gradually disillusioned him: once more, he was part of a concentration-camp system and complicit with the oppressors. Although he and his wife had a newborn daughter, he committed suicide by gas on July 1, 1951.

Narrated in an impersonal tone by one of the prisoners, "This Way for the Gas, Ladies and Gentlemen" describes the extermination camp of Birkenau, the largest of three concentration camps at Auschwitz (Polish: *Oświęcim*), an enclosed world of hierarchical authority and desperate struggles to survive. Food, shoes, shirts, underwear: this vital currency of the camp is obtained when prisoners are stripped of their belongings as they arrive in railway cattle cars. The story follows the narrator's first trip to the railroad station with the labor battalion "Canada." The trip will salvage goods from a train bringing fifteen thousand Polish Jews, former inhabitants of the cities Sosnowiec and Będzin. By the end of the day, most of the travelers will be burning in the crematorium, and the camp will live for a few more days on the loot from "a good, rich transport."

Borowski suggests from the beginning the systematic dehumanization of the camps: prisoners are equated with lice, and they mill around by the naked thousands in blocked-off sections. The same gas is used in exterminating lice and humans—who will later be equated with sick horses (the converted stables retain their old signs), lumber and concrete trucked in from the railroad station, and insects whose jaws work away at moldy pieces of bread. Constantly supervised, subject to arbitrary rules and punishment, malnourished and pushed to exhaustion, their identities reduced to numerals tattooed on their arms, the prisoners live in the shadow of a hierarchical authority that is to be both feared and placated. Paradoxically, their common vulnerability leads to alienation and rage at their fellow victims rather than at the executioners. The Nazis have foreseen everything, explains the narrator's friend Henri, including the fact that weakness needs to vent itself on the weaker. The only way to cope is to distance oneself from what is happening, to become a cog in the machine so that one does not actually experience the events—to suspend, for the moment, one's humanity.

The story's brutal realism and matter-of-fact tone convey as no passionate oratory could the mind-numbing horror of a situation in which systematic slaughter was the background for everyday life. The narrator, Tadeusz, is modeled partly on Borowski, but he is also a composite figure; he has become another part of the concentration-camp system, a survivor. He has a job in the system; assists the Kapos, or senior prisoners who organize the camp; and carries a burden of guilt that his adopted impersonal attitude cannot quite suppress. Borowski's stories shocked their postwar audience with their uncompromising honesty: here were no saintly victims and demonic executioners, but rather human beings— human beings—going about the business of extermination or, reduced to near-animal level, cooperating in the destruction of themselves and others. It is a picture that sorely tests any belief in civilization, common humanity, or divine providence; Borowski's bleak outlook questions everything and does not pretend to offer encouragement.

The narrator's dispassionate tone, as he describes senseless cruelty and mass murder, individual scenes of desperation, or the eccentric emotions of people about to die, continues to shock many readers. Borowski is certainly describing a world of antiheroes, those who survive by accommodating themselves to things as they are and avoiding acts of heroism. Borowski wrote this story after the Nazi defeat, but for its duration the picture is one of a spiritual desolation that not only illustrates a shameful moment in modern history but raises questions about what it means to be civilized, or even human.

This Way for the Gas, Ladies and Gentlemen[1]

All of us[2] walk around naked. The delousing is finally over, and our striped suits are back from the tanks of Cyclone B[3] solution, an efficient killer of lice in clothing and of men in gas chambers. Only the inmates in the blocks cut off from ours by the 'Spanish goats'[4] still have nothing to wear. But all the same, all of us walk around naked: the heat is unbearable. The camp has been sealed off tight. Not a single prisoner, not one solitary louse, can sneak through the gate. The labour Kommandos have stopped working. All day, thousands of naked men shuffle up and down the roads, cluster around the squares, or lie against the walls and on top of the roofs. We have been sleeping on plain boards, since our mattresses and blankets are still being disinfected. From the rear blockhouses we have a view of the F.K.L.—*Frauen Konzentration Lager*;[5] there too the delousing is in full swing. Twenty-eight thousand women have been stripped naked and driven out of the barracks. Now they swarm around the large yard between the blockhouses.

The heat rises, the hours are endless. We are without even our usual diversion: the wide roads leading to the crematoria are empty. For several days now, no new transports have come in. Part of 'Canada'[6] has been liquidated and detailed to a labour Kommando—one of the very toughest—at Harmenz.[7] For there exists in the camp a special brand of justice based on envy: when the rich

1. Translated by Barbara Vedder.
2. Inmates in Auschwitz 11, or Birkenau, the largest of the Nazi extermination camps, established in October 1941 near the town of Birkenau, Poland. Its death toll is usually estimated between 1 million and 2.5 million people.
3. Gas used in extermination camps.
4. Crossed wooden beams wrapped in barbed wire.

5. Women's concentration camp (German).
6. The name given to the camp stores (as well as prisoners working there) where valuables and clothing taken from prisoners were sorted for dispatch to Germany. Like the nation of Canada, the store symbolized wealth and prosperity to the camp inmates.
7. One of the subcamps outside Birkenau itself.

and mighty fall, their friends see to it that they fall to the very bottom. And Canada, our Canada, which smells not of maple forests but of French perfume, has amassed great fortunes in diamonds and currency from all over Europe.

Several of us sit on the top bunk, our legs dangling over the edge. We slice the neat loaves of crisp, crunchy bread. It is a bit coarse to the taste, the kind that stays fresh for days. Sent all the way from Warsaw[8]—only a week ago my mother held this white loaf in her hands . . . dear Lord, dear Lord . . .

We unwrap the bacon, the onion, we open a can of evaporated milk. Henri, the fat Frenchman, dreams aloud of the French wine brought by the transports from Strasbourg, Paris, Marseille[9] . . . Sweat streams down his body.

'Listen, *mon ami*,[1] next time we go up on the loading ramp, I'll bring you real champagne. You haven't tried it before, eh?'

'No. But you'll never be able to smuggle it through the gate, so stop teasing. Why not try and "organize" some shoes for me instead—you know, the perforated kind, with a double sole,[2] and what about that shirt you promised me long ago?'

'*Patience, patience.* When the new transports come, I'll bring all you want. We'll be going on the ramp again!'

'And what if there aren't any more "cremo"[3] transports?' I say spitefully. 'Can't you see how much easier life is becoming around here: no limit on packages, no more beatings? You even write letters home . . . One hears all kind of talk, and, dammit, they'll run out of people!'

'Stop talking nonsense.' Henri's serious fat face moves rhythmically, his mouth is full of sardines. We have been friends for a long time, but I do not even know his last name. 'Stop talking nonsense,' he repeats, swallowing with effort. 'They can't run out of people, or we'll starve to death in this blasted camp. All of us live on what they bring.'

'All? We have our packages . . .'

'Sure, you and your friend, and ten other friends of yours. Some of you Poles get packages. But what about us, and the Jews, and the Russkis? And what if we had no food, no "organization" from the transports, do you think you'd be eating those packages of yours in peace? We wouldn't let you!'

'You would, you'd starve to death like the Greeks. Around here, whoever has grub, has power.'

'Anyway, you have enough, we have enough, so why argue?'

Right, why argue? They have enough, I have enough, we eat together and we sleep on the same bunks. Henri slices the bread, he makes a tomato salad. It tastes good with the commissary mustard.

Below us, naked, sweat-drenched men crowd the narrow barracks aisles or lie packed in eights and tens in the lower bunks. Their nude, withered bodies stink of sweat and excrement; their cheeks are hollow. Directly beneath me, in the bottom bunk, lies a rabbi. He has covered his head[4] with a piece of rag torn

---

8. Capital of Poland; most of its Jewish residents were executed by the Nazis.
9. A large French port on the Mediterranean Sea. Strasbourg is a city in northeast France.
1. My friend (French).

2. A Hungarian style.
3. The crematorium.
4. Jews are expected to keep their heads covered while at prayer.

off a blanket and reads from a Hebrew prayer book (there is no shortage of this type of literature at the camp), wailing loudly, monotonously.

'Can't somebody shut him up? He's been raving as if he'd caught God himself by the feet.'

'I don't feel like moving. Let him rave. They'll take him to the oven that much sooner.'

'Religion is the opium of the people,'[5] Henri, who is a Communist and a *rentier*,[6] says sententiously. 'If they didn't believe in God and eternal life, they'd have smashed the crematoria long ago.'

'Why haven't you done it then?'

The question is rhetorical; the Frenchman ignores it.

'Idiot,' he says simply, and stuffs a tomato in his mouth.

Just as we finish our snack, there is a sudden commotion at the door. The Muslims[7] scurry in fright to the safety of their bunks, a messenger runs into the Block Elder's shack. The Elder,[8] his face solemn, steps out at once.

'Canada! *Antreten!*'[9] But fast! There's a transport coming!'

'Great God!' yells Henri, jumping off the bunk. He swallows the rest of his tomato, snatches his coat, screams '*Raus*'[1] at the men below, and in a flash is at the door. We can hear a scramble in the other bunks. Canada is leaving for the ramp.

'Henri, the shoes!' I call after him.

'*Keine Angst!*'[2] he shouts back, already outside.

I proceed to put away the food. I tie a piece of rope around the suitcase where the onions and the tomatoes from my father's garden in Warsaw mingle with Portuguese sardines, bacon from Lublin (that's from my brother), and authentic sweetmeats from Salonica.[3] I tie it all up, pull on my trousers, and slide off the bunk.

'*Platz!*'[4] I yell, pushing my way through the Greeks. They step aside. At the door I bump into Henri.

'*Was ist los?*'[5]

'Want to come with us on the ramp?'

'Sure, why not?'

'Come along then, grab your coat! We're short of a few men. I've already told the Kapo,' and he shoves me out of the barracks door.

We line up. Someone has marked down our numbers, someone up ahead yells, 'March, march,' and now we are running towards the gate, accompanied by the shouts of a multilingual throng that is already being pushed back to the barracks. Not everybody is lucky enough to be going on the ramp . . . We have almost reached the gate. *Links, zwei, drei, vier! Mützen ab!*[6] Erect, arms stretched stiffly along our hips, we march past the gate briskly, smartly, almost

---

5. A quotation from the German political philosopher Karl Marx (1818–1883).
6. Someone with unearned income, a stockholder (French).
7. Camp nickname for people who had given up, considered the camp pariahs.
8. A Kapo, or senior prisoner in charge of a group of prisoners.

9. Report (German).
1. Outside (German).
2. Don't panic (German).
3. Major port city in northeast Greece. Lublin is a city in eastern Poland.
4. Make room (German).
5. What's the matter? (German).
6. Left, two, three, four! Caps off! (German).

gracefully. A sleepy S.S.[7] man with a large pad in his hand checks us off, waving us ahead in groups of five.

'Hundert!'[8] he calls after we have all passed.

'Stimmt!'[9] comes a hoarse answer from out front.

We march fast, almost at a run. There are guards all around, young men with automatics. We pass camp II B, then some deserted barracks and a clump of unfamiliar green—apple and pear trees. We cross the circle of watchtowers and, running, burst on to the highway. We have arrived. Just a few more yards. There, surrounded by trees, is the ramp.

A cheerful little station, very much like any other provincial railway stop: a small square framed by tall chestnuts and paved with yellow gravel. Not far off, beside the road, squats a tiny wooden shed, uglier and more flimsy than the ugliest and flimsiest railway shack; farther along lie stacks of old rails, heaps of wooden beams, barracks parts, bricks, paving stones. This is where they load freight for Birkenau: supplies for the construction of the camp, and people for the gas chambers. Trucks drive around, load up lumber, cement, people—a regular daily routine.

And now the guards are being posted along the rails, across the beams, in the green shade of the Silesian chestnuts,[1] to form a tight circle around the ramp. They wipe the sweat from their faces and sip out of their canteens. It is unbearably hot; the sun stands motionless at its zenith.

'Fall out!'

We sit down in the narrow streaks of shade along the stacked rails. The hungry Greeks (several of them managed to come along, God only knows how) rummage underneath the rails. One of them finds some pieces of mildewed bread, another a few half-rotten sardines. They eat.

'Schweinedreck,'[2] spits a young, tall guard with corn-coloured hair and dreamy blue eyes. 'For God's sake, any minute you'll have so much food to stuff down your guts, you'll bust!' He adjusts his gun, wipes his face with a handkerchief.

'Hey you, fatso!' His boot lightly touches Henri's shoulder. 'Pass mal auf,[3] want a drink?'

'Sure, but I haven't got any marks,' replies the Frenchman with a professional air.

'Schade, too bad.'

'Come, come, Herr[4] Posten, isn't my word good enough any more? Haven't we done business before? How much?'

'One hundred. Gemacht?'[5]

'Gemacht.'

---

7. Abbreviation for *Schutzstaffel* (Protective Echelon, German), the Nazi police system that began as Hitler's private guard and grew, by 1939, to a 250,000-member military and political organization that administered all state security functions. The SS was divided into numerous bureaucratic units, one of which, the Death's Head Battalions, managed the concentration camps. Selected for physical perfection and (Aryan) racial purity, SS members wore black or gray-green uniforms decorated with silver insignia.

8. A hundred! (German).
9. Right! (German).
1. Probably local chestnuts. Silesia, in central Europe, was partitioned among Poland, Czechoslovakia, and Germany after World War I; Germany occupied Polish Silesia in 1939.
2. Dirty pigs (German).
3. See here (German).
4. Mister (German).
5. Done? (German).

We drink the water, lukewarm and tasteless. It will be paid for by the people who have not yet arrived.

'Now you be careful,' says Henri, turning to me. He tosses away the empty bottle. It strikes the rails and bursts into tiny fragments. 'Don't take any money, they might be checking. Anyway, who the hell needs money? You've got enough to eat. Don't take suits, either, or they'll think you're planning to escape. Just get a shirt, silk only, with a collar. And a vest. And if you find something to drink, don't bother calling me. I know how to shift for myself, but you watch your step or they'll let you have it.'

'Do they beat you up here?'

'Naturally. You've got to have eyes in your ass. *Arschaugen.*'[6]

Around us sit the Greeks, their jaws working greedily, like huge human insects. They munch on stale lumps of bread. They are restless, wondering what will happen next. The sight of the large beams and the stacks of rails has them worried. They dislike carrying heavy loads.

'*Was wir arbeiten?*'[7] they ask.

'*Niks. Transport kommen, alles Krematorium, compris?*'[8]

'*Alles verstehen,*' they answer in crematorium Esperanto.[9] All is well—they will not have to move the heavy rails or carry the beams.

In the meantime, the ramp has become increasingly alive with activity, increasingly noisy. The crews are being divided into those who will open and unload the arriving cattle cars and those who will be posted by the wooden steps. They receive instructions on how to proceed most efficiently. Motor cycles drive up, delivering S.S. officers, bemedalled, glittering with brass, beefy men with highly polished boots and shiny, brutal faces. Some have brought their briefcases, others hold thin, flexible whips. This gives them an air of military readiness and agility. They walk in and out of the commissary—for the miserable little shack by the road serves as their commissary, where in the summertime they drink mineral water, Sudetenquelle,[1] and where in winter they can warm up with a glass of hot wine. They greet each other in the state-approved way, raising an arm Roman fashion, then shake hands cordially, exchange warm smiles, discuss mail from home, their children, their families. Some stroll majestically on the ramp. The silver squares on their collars glitter, the gravel crunches under their boots, their bamboo whips snap impatiently.

We lie against the rails in the narrow streaks of shade, breathe unevenly, occasionally exchange a few words in our various tongues, and gaze listlessly at the majestic men in green uniforms, at the green trees, and at the church steeple of a distant village.

'The transport is coming,' somebody says. We spring to our feet, all eyes turn in one direction. Around the bend, one after another, the cattle cars begin rolling in. The train backs into the station, a conductor leans out, waves his hand, blows a whistle. The locomotive whistles back with a shrieking noise, puffs, the

---

6. Eyes on your ass (German; literal trans.).
7. What are we working on? (German).
8. Nothing. Transport coming, everything crematorium, understood? (German; *compris* is French).
9. An artificial language, created in 1887 by L. L. Zamenhof, to simplify communication

between nationalities. "*Alles verstehen*": Everything understood.
1. Water from the Sudetenland or Sudeten Mountains; a narrow strip of land on the northern and western borders of the Czech Republic. The Sudeten was annexed by Hitler in 1938.

train rolls slowly alongside the ramp. In the tiny barred windows appear pale, wilted, exhausted human faces, terror-stricken women with tangled hair, unshaven men. They gaze at the station in silence. And then, suddenly, there is a stir inside the cars and a pounding against the wooden boards.

'Water! Air!'—weary, desperate cries.

Heads push through the windows, mouths gasp frantically for air. They draw a few breaths, then disappear; others come in their place, then also disappear. The cries and moans grow louder.

A man in a green uniform covered with more glitter than any of the others jerks his head impatiently, his lips twist in annoyance. He inhales deeply, then with a rapid gesture throws his cigarette away and signals to the guard. The guard removes the automatic from his shoulder, aims, sends a series of shots along the train. All is quiet now. Meanwhile, the trucks have arrived, steps are being drawn up, and the Canada men stand ready at their posts by the train doors. The S.S. officer with the briefcase raises his hand.

'Whoever takes gold, or anything at all besides food, will be shot for stealing Reich property. Understand? *Verstanden?*'

'*Jawohl!*'[2] we answer eagerly.

'*Also los!*[3] Begin!'

The bolts crack, the doors fall open. A wave of fresh air rushes inside the train. People . . . inhumanly crammed, buried under incredible heaps of luggage, suitcases, trunks, packages, crates, bundles of every description (everything that had been their past and was to start their future). Monstrously squeezed together, they have fainted from heat, suffocated, crushed one another. Now they push towards the opened doors, breathing like fish cast out on the sand.

'Attention! Out, and take your luggage with you! Take out everything. Pile all your stuff near the exits. Yes, your coats too. It is summer. March to the left. Understand?'

'Sir, what's going to happen to us?' They jump from the train on to the gravel, anxious, worn-out.

'Where are you people from?'

'Sosnowiec-Będzin.[4] Sir, what's going to happen to us?' They repeat the question stubbornly, gazing into our tired eyes.

'I don't know. I don't understand Polish.'

It is the camp law: people going to their death must be deceived to the very end. This is the only permissible form of charity. The heat is tremendous. The sun hangs directly over our heads, the white, hot sky quivers, the air vibrates, an occasional breeze feels like a sizzling blast from a furnace. Our lips are parched, the mouth fills with the salty taste of blood, the body is weak and heavy from lying in the sun. Water!

A huge, multicoloured wave of people loaded down with luggage pours from the train like a blind, mad river trying to find a new bed. But before they have a chance to recover, before they can draw a breath of fresh air and look at the

---

2. Yes! (German). "*Verstanden*": understand? (German).
3. Then get going! (German).
4. Two cities in Katowice province (southern Poland). Będzin was also the site of a concentration camp, and more than ten thousand of its inhabitants were exterminated.

sky, bundles are snatched from their hands, coats ripped off their backs, their purses and umbrellas taken away.

'But please, sir, it's for the sun, I cannot . . .'

'*Verboten!*'[5] one of us barks through clenched teeth. There is an S.S. man standing behind your back, calm, efficient, watchful.

'*Meine Herrschaften*,[6] this way, ladies and gentlemen, try not to throw your things around, please. Show some goodwill,' he says courteously, his restless hands playing with the slender whip.

'Of course, of course,' they answer as they pass, and now they walk alongside the train somewhat more cheerfully. A woman reaches down quickly to pick up her handbag. The whip flies, the woman screams, stumbles, and falls under the feet of the surging crowd. Behind her, a child cries in a thin little voice 'Mamele!'—a very small girl with tangled black curls.

The heaps grow. Suitcases, bundles, blankets, coats, handbags that open as they fall, spilling coins, gold, watches; mountains of bread pile up at the exits, heaps of marmalade, jams, masses of meat, sausages; sugar spills on the gravel. Trucks, loaded with people, start up with a deafening roar and drive off amidst the wailing and screaming of the women separated from their children, and the stupefied silence of the men left behind. They are the ones who had been ordered to step to the right—the healthy and the young who will go to the camp. In the end, they too will not escape death, but first they must work.

Trucks leave and return, without interruption, as on a monstrous conveyor belt. A Red Cross van drives back and forth, back and forth, incessantly: it transports the gas that will kill these people. The enormous cross on the hood, red as blood, seems to dissolve in the sun.

The Canada men at the trucks cannot stop for a single moment, even to catch their breath. They shove the people up the steps, pack them in tightly, sixty per truck, more or less. Near by stands a young, cleanshaven 'gentleman', an S.S. officer with a notebook in his hand. For each departing truck he enters a mark; sixteen gone means one thousand people, more or less. The gentleman is calm, precise. No truck can leave without a signal from him, or a mark in his notebook: *Ordnung muss sein*.[7] The marks swell into thousands, the thousands into whole transports, which afterwards we shall simply call 'from Salonica', 'from Strasbourg', 'from Rotterdam'.[8] This one will be called 'Sosnowiec-Będzin'. The new prisoners from Sosnowiec-Będzin will receive serial numbers 131–2— thousand, of course, though afterwards we shall simply say 131–2, for short.

The transports swell into weeks, months, years. When the war is over, they will count up the marks in their notebooks—all four and a half million of them. The bloodiest battle of the war, the greatest victory of the strong, united Germany. *Ein Reich, ein Volk, ein Führer*[9]—and four crematoria.

The train has been emptied. A thin, pock-marked S.S. man peers inside, shakes his head in disgust and motions to our group, pointing his finger at the door.

'*Rein.*[1] Clean it up!'

---

5. Forbidden (German).
6. Gentlemen (German).
7. Order in everything (German).
8. Large port city in the Netherlands.

9. One State, One People, One Leader! (the slogan of Nazi Germany).
1. Clean (German).

We climb inside. In the corners amid human excrement and abandoned wrist-watches lie squashed, trampled infants, naked little monsters with enormous heads and bloated bellies. We carry them out like chickens, holding several in each hand.

'Don't take them to the trucks, pass them on to the women,' says the S.S. man, lighting a cigarette. His cigarette lighter is not working properly; he examines it carefully.

'Take them, for God's sake!' I explode as the women rush from me in horror, covering their eyes.

The name of God sounds strangely pointless, since the women and the infants will go on the trucks, every one of them without exception. We all know what this means, and we look at each other with hate and horror.

'What, you don't want to take them?' asks the pockmarked S.S. man with a note of surprise and reproach in his voice, and reaches for his revolver.

'You mustn't shoot, I'll carry them.' A tall, grey-haired woman takes the little corpses out of my hands and for an instant gazes straight into my eyes.

'My poor boy,' she whispers and smiles at me. Then she walks away, staggering along the path. I lean against the side of the train. I am terribly tired. Someone pulls at my sleeve.

'*En avant*,[2] to the rails, come on!'

I look up, but the face swims before my eyes, dissolves, huge and transparent, melts into the motionless trees and the sea of people . . . I blink rapidly: Henri.

'Listen, Henri, are we good people?'

'That's stupid. Why do you ask?'

'You see, my friend, you see, I don't know why, but I am furious, simply furious with these people—furious because I must be here because of them. I feel no pity. I am not sorry they're going to the gas chamber. Damn them all! I could throw myself at them, beat them with my fists. It must be pathological, I just can't understand . . .'

'Ah, on the contrary, it is natural, predictable, calculated. The ramp exhausts you, you rebel—and the easiest way to relieve your hate is to turn against someone weaker. Why, I'd even call it healthy. It's simple logic, *compris*?' He props himself up comfortably against the heap of rails. 'Look at the Greeks, they know how to make the best of it! They stuff their bellies with anything they find. One of them has just devoured a full jar of marmalade.'

'Pigs! Tomorrow half of them will die of the shits.'

'Pigs? You've been hungry.'

'Pigs!' I repeat furiously. I close my eyes. The air is filled with ghastly cries, the earth trembles beneath me, I can feel sticky moisture on my eyelids. My throat is completely dry.

The morbid procession streams on and on—trucks growl like mad dogs. I shut my eyes tight, but I can still see corpses dragged from the train, trampled infants, cripples piled on top of the dead, wave after wave . . . freight cars roll in, the heaps of clothing, suitcases and bundles grow, people climb out, look at the sun, take a few breaths, beg for water, get into the trucks, drive away. And again freight cars roll in, again people . . . The scenes become confused in my

2. Forward (French).

mind—I am not sure if all of this is actually happening, or if I am dreaming. There is a humming inside my head; I feel that I must vomit.

Henri tugs at my arm.

'Don't sleep, we're off to load up the loot.'

All the people are gone. In the distance, the last few trucks roll along the road in clouds of dust, the train has left, several S.S. officers promenade up and down the ramp. The silver glitters on their collars. Their boots shine, their red, beefy faces shine. Among them there is a woman—only now I realize she has been here all along—withered, flat-chested, bony, her thin, colourless hair pulled back and tied in a 'Nordic'[3] knot; her hands are in the pockets of her wide skirt. With a rat-like, resolute smile glued on her thin lips she sniffs around the corners of the ramp. She detests feminine beauty with the hatred of a woman who is herself repulsive, and knows it. Yes, I have seen her many times before and I know her well: she is the commandant of the F.K.L. She has come to look over the new crop of women, for some of them, instead of going on the trucks, will go on foot—to the concentration camp. There our boys, the barbers from Zauna,[4] will shave their heads and will have a good laugh at their 'outside world' modesty.

We proceed to load the loot. We lift huge trunks, heave them on to the trucks. There they are arranged in stacks, packed tightly. Occasionally somebody slashes one open with a knife, for pleasure or in search of vodka and perfume. One of the crates falls open; suits, shirts, books drop out on the ground . . . I pick up a small, heavy package. I unwrap it—gold, about two handfuls, bracelets, rings, brooches, diamonds . . .

'*Gib hier*,'[5] an S.S. man says calmly, holding up his briefcase already full of gold and colourful foreign currency. He locks the case, hands it to an officer, takes another, an empty one, and stands by the next truck, waiting. The gold will go to the Reich.[6]

It is hot, terribly hot. Our throats are dry, each word hurts. Anything for a sip of water! Faster, faster, so that it is over, so that we may rest. At last we are done, all the trucks have gone. Now we swiftly clean up the remaining dirt: there must be 'no trace left of the *Schweinerei*'. But just as the last truck disappears behind the trees and we walk, finally, to rest in the shade, a shrill whistle sounds around the bend. Slowly, terribly slowly, a train rolls in, the engine whistles back with a deafening shriek. Again weary, pale faces at the windows, flat as though cut out of paper, with huge, feverishly burning eyes. Already trucks are pulling up, already the composed gentleman with the notebook is at his post, and the S.S. men emerge from the commissary carrying briefcases for the gold and money. We unseal the train doors.

It is impossible to control oneself any longer. Brutally we tear suitcases from their hands, impatiently pull off their coats. Go on, go on, vanish! They go, they vanish. Men, women, children. Some of them know.

Here is a woman—she walks quickly, but tries to appear calm. A small child with a pink cherub's face runs after her and, unable to keep up, stretches out his little arms and cries: 'Mama! Mama!'

3. A northern (especially Scandinavian) style encouraged by the Nazis to establish an image of Teutonic racial purity.
4. The "sauna" barracks, in front of Canada, where prisoners were bathed, shaved, and deloused.
5. Give it to me (German).
6. The German state.

'Pick up your child, woman!'

'It's not mine, sir, not mine!' she shouts hysterically and runs on, covering her face with her hands. She wants to hide, she wants to reach those who will not ride the trucks, those who will go on foot, those who will stay alive. She is young, healthy, good-looking, she wants to live.

But the child runs after her, wailing loudly: 'Mama, mama, don't leave me!'

'It's not mine, not mine, no!'

Andrei, a sailor from Sevastopol,[7] grabs hold of her. His eyes are glassy from vodka and the heat. With one powerful blow he knocks her off her feet, then, as she falls, takes her by the hair and pulls her up again. His face twitches with rage.

'Ah, you bloody Jewess! So you're running from your own child! I'll show you, you whore!' His huge hand chokes her, he lifts her in the air and heaves her on to the truck like a heavy sack of grain.

'Here! And take this with you, bitch!' and he throws the child at her feet.

'Gut gemacht, good work. That's the way to deal with degenerate mothers,' says the S.S. man standing at the foot of the truck. 'Gut, gut, Russki.'[8]

'Shut your mouth,' growls Andrei through clenched teeth, and walks away. From under a pile of rags he pulls out a canteen, unscrews the cork, takes a few deep swallows, passes it to me. The strong vodka burns the throat. My head swims, my legs are shaky, again I feel like throwing up.

And suddenly, above the teeming crowd pushing forward like a river driven by an unseen power, a girl appears. She descends lightly from the train, hops on to the gravel, looks around inquiringly, as if somewhat surprised. Her soft, blonde hair has fallen on her shoulders in a torrent, she throws it back impatiently. With a natural gesture she runs her hands down her blouse, casually straightens her skirt. She stands like this for an instant, gazing at the crowd, then turns and with a gliding look examines our faces, as though searching for someone. Unknowingly, I continue to stare at her, until our eyes meet.

'Listen, tell me, where are they taking us?'

I look at her without saying a word. Here, standing before me, is a girl, a girl with enchanting blonde hair, with beautiful breasts, wearing a little cotton blouse, a girl with a wise, mature look in her eyes. Here she stands, gazing straight into my face, waiting. And over there is the gas chamber: communal death, disgusting and ugly. And over in the other direction is the concentration camp: the shaved head, the heavy Soviet trousers in sweltering heat, the sickening, stale odour of dirty, damp female bodies, the animal hunger, the inhuman labour, and later the same gas chamber, only an even more hideous, more terrible death . . .

Why did she bring it? I think to myself, noticing a lovely gold watch on her delicate wrist. They'll take it away from her anyway.

'Listen, tell me,' she repeats.

I remain silent. Her lips tighten.

'I know,' she says with a shade of proud contempt in her voice, tossing her head. She walks off resolutely in the direction of the trucks. Someone tries to

---

7. A Soviet (now, Ukrainian) port on the Black Sea.

8. Good, good, Russky (German). "Gut gemacht": well done (German).

stop her; she boldly pushes him aside and runs up the steps. In the distance I can only catch a glimpse of her blonde hair flying in the breeze.

I go back inside the train; I carry out dead infants; I unload luggage. I touch corpses, but I cannot overcome the mounting, uncontrollable terror. I try to escape from the corpses, but they are everywhere: lined up on the gravel, on the cement edge of the ramp, inside the cattle cars. Babies, hideous naked women, men twisted by convulsions. I run off as far as I can go, but immediately a whip slashes across my back. Out of the corner of my eye I see an S.S. man, swearing profusely. I stagger forward and run, lose myself in the Canada group. Now, at last, I can once more rest against the stack of rails. The sun has leaned low over the horizon and illuminates the ramp with a reddish glow; the shadows of the trees have become elongated, ghostlike. In the silence that settles over nature at this time of day, the human cries seem to rise all the way to the sky.

Only from this distance does one have a full view of the inferno on the teeming ramp. I see a pair of human beings who have fallen to the ground locked in a last desperate embrace. The man has dug his fingers into the woman's flesh and has caught her clothing with his teeth. She screams hysterically, swears, cries, until at last a large boot comes down over her throat and she is silent. They are pulled apart and dragged like cattle to the truck. I see four Canada men lugging a corpse: a huge, swollen female corpse. Cursing, dripping wet from the strain, they kick out of their way some stray children who have been running all over the ramp, howling like dogs. The men pick them up by the collars, heads, arms, and toss them inside the trucks, on top of the heaps. The four men have trouble lifting the fat corpse on to the car, they call others for help, and all together they hoist up the mound of meat. Big, swollen, puffed-up corpses are being collected from all over the ramp; on top of them are piled the invalids, the smothered, the sick, the unconscious. The heap seethes, howls, groans. The driver starts the motor, the truck begins rolling.

'Halt! Halt!' an S.S. man yells after them. 'Stop, damn you.'

They are dragging to the truck an old man wearing tails and a band around his arm. His head knocks against the gravel and pavement; he moans and wails in an uninterrupted monotone: 'Ich will mit dem Herrn Kommandanten sprechen[9]— I wish to speak with the commandant . . .' With senile stubbornness he keeps repeating these words all the way. Thrown on the truck, trampled by others, choked, he still wails: 'Ich will mit dem . . .'

'Look here, old man!' a young S.S. man calls, laughing jovially. 'In half an hour you'll be talking with the top commandant! Only don't forget to greet him with a Heil Hitler!'

Several other men are carrying a small girl with only one leg. They hold her by the arms and the one leg. Tears are running down her face and she whispers faintly: 'Sir, it hurts, it hurts . . .' They throw her on the truck on top of the corpses. She will burn alive along with them.

The evening has come, cool and clear. The stars are out. We lie against the rails. It is incredibly quiet. Anaemic bulbs hang from the top of the high lampposts; beyond the circle of light stretches an impenetrable darkness. Just one

9. I want to speak with the commandant (German).

step, and a man could vanish for ever. But the guards are watching, their automatics ready.

'Did you get the shoes?' asks Henri.

'No.'

'Why?'

'My God, man, I am finished, absolutely finished!'

'So soon? After only two transports? Just look at me, I . . . since Christmas, at least a million people have passed through my hands. The worst of all are the transports from around Paris—one is always bumping into friends.'

'And what do you say to them?'

'That first they will have a bath, and later we'll meet at the camp. What would you say?'

I do not answer. We drink coffee with vodka; somebody opens a tin of cocoa and mixes it with sugar. We scoop it up by the handful, the cocoa sticks to the lips. Again coffee, again vodka.

'Henri, what are we waiting for?'

'There'll be another transport.'

'I'm not going to unload it! I can't take any more.'

'So, it's got you down? Canada is nice, eh?' Henri grins indulgently and disappears into the darkness. In a moment he is back again.

'All right. Just sit here quietly and don't let an S.S. man see you. I'll try to find you your shoes.'

'Just leave me alone. Never mind the shoes.' I want to sleep. It is very late.

Another whistle, another transport. Freight cars emerge out of the darkness, pass under the lamp-posts, and again vanish in the night. The ramp is small, but the circle of lights is smaller. The unloading will have to be done gradually. Somewhere the trucks are growling. They back up against the steps, black, ghostlike, their searchlights flash across the trees. *Wasser! Luft!*[1] The same all over again, like a late showing of the same film: a volley of shots, the train falls silent. Only this time a little girl pushes herself halfway through the small window and, losing her balance, falls out on to the gravel. Stunned, she lies still for a moment, then stands up and begins walking around in a circle, faster and faster, waving her rigid arms in the air, breathing loudly and spasmodically, whining in a faint voice. Her mind has given way in the inferno inside the train. The whining is hard on the nerves: an S.S. man approaches calmly, his heavy boot strikes between her shoulders. She falls. Holding her down with his foot, he draws his revolver, fires once, then again. She remains face down, kicking the gravel with her feet, until she stiffens. They proceed to unseal the train.

I am back on the ramp, standing by the doors. A warm, sickening smell gushes from inside. The mountain of people filling the car almost halfway up to the ceiling is motionless, horribly tangled, but still steaming.

'*Ausladen!*[2] comes the command. An S.S. man steps out from the darkness. Across his chest hangs a portable searchlight. He throws a stream of light inside.

'Why are you standing about like sheep? Start unloading!' His whip flies and falls across our backs. I seize a corpse by the hand; the fingers close tightly

---

1. Water! Air! (German).   2. Unload! (German).

around mine. I pull back with a shriek and stagger away. My heart pounds, jumps up to my throat. I can no longer control the nausea. Hunched under the train I begin to vomit. Then, like a drunk, I weave over to the stack of rails.

I lie against the cool, kind metal and dream about returning to the camp, about my bunk, on which there is no mattress, about sleep among comrades who are not going to the gas tonight. Suddenly I see the camp as a haven of peace. It is true, others may be dying, but one is somehow still alive, one has enough food, enough strength to work . . .

The lights on the ramp flicker with a spectral glow, the wave of people—feverish, agitated, stupefied people—flows on and on, endlessly. They think that now they will have to face a new life in the camp, and they prepare themselves emotionally for the hard struggle ahead. They do not know that in just a few moments they will die, that the gold, money, and diamonds which they have so prudently hidden in their clothing and on their bodies are now useless to them. Experienced professionals will probe into every recess of their flesh, will pull the gold from under the tongue and the diamonds from the uterus and the colon. They will rip out gold teeth. In tightly sealed crates they will ship them to Berlin.[3]

The S.S. men's black figures move about, dignified, businesslike. The gentleman with the notebook puts down his final marks, rounds out the figures: fifteen thousand.

Many, very many, trucks have been driven to the crematoria today.

It is almost over. The dead are being cleared off the ramp and piled into the last truck. The Canada men, weighed down under a load of bread, marmalade and sugar, and smelling of perfume and fresh linen, line up to go. For several days the entire camp will live off this transport. For several days the entire camp will talk about 'Sosnowiec-Będzin'. 'Sosnowiec-Będzin' was a good, rich transport.

The stars are already beginning to pale as we walk back to the camp. The sky grows translucent and opens high above our heads—it is getting light.

Great columns of smoke rise from the crematoria and merge up above into a huge black river which very slowly floats across the sky over Birkenau and disappears beyond the forests in the direction of Trzebinia.[4] The 'Sosnowiec-Będzin' transport is already burning.

We pass a heavily armed S.S. detachment on its way to change guard. The men march briskly, in step, shoulder to shoulder, one mass, one will.

'*Und morgen die ganze Welt* . . .'[5] they sing at the top of their lungs.

'*Rechts ran!*[6] To the right march!' snaps a command from up front. We move out of their way.

1946

---

3. The capital of Germany.
4. A town west of Auschwitz, near Krakow.
5. And tomorrow the whole world (German): the last line of the Nazi song "The Rotten

Bones Are Shaking," written by Hans Baumann. The previous line reads "for today Germany belongs to us."
6. To the right, get going! (German).

ALAIN ROBBE-GRILLET

1922–2008

Known as a proponent of the *antinovel* or *new novel*, Alain Robbe-Grillet was one of the most influential postmodernist writers of the mid-twentieth century. Rejecting linear plots, he wrote ambiguous, circular detective stories where erotic and violent crimes *seem* to have been committed. He may refuse to portray a consistently developing character, but his minute descriptions of objects and gestures impel the reader to imagine an underlying psychology and to speculate on the meaning of the observer's repetition and distortion of details.

Robbe-Grillet was born in Brittany, in northwestern France, to a family of scientists and engineers. His early training was not at all literary: in 1939 and 1941 the future writer took baccalaureate degrees in mathematics and natural science, and in 1946 (his career interrupted by forced labor in a German factory) a further degree from the National Agronomy Institute. His second published novel, *The Voyeur*, was controversially awarded the Critics' Prize in 1955; the jury was split between those who believed that it was not a novel at all (and was immoral and insane to boot) and those who admired its formal innovations. Mathias, the voyeur of the title, is a traveling watch salesman who may or may not have murdered a young girl during a sales trip to an island.

With the controversy over *The Voyeur*, Robbe-Grillet and his new mode of writing became the focus of critical debate in France. In *Objective Literature*, the influential critic Roland Barthes proposed that Robbe-Grillet had discovered a truer "neutral" writing by focusing on objects instead of repeating traditional socially inspired interpretations of reality. In 1955 Robbe-Grillet began a series of articles on modern literature, which he collected in 1963 as *For a New Novel*. The term *new novel* became popular, and although not all those described as "new novelists" wrote in the same way, they all rejected the traditional novel's assumption of a core of meaning—with a logically developing plot and psychologically consistent characters—that claimed to reflect a similar core of meaning in reality. In 1959 he temporarily abandoned novels to experiment with films, writing the script for *Last Year at Marienbad* (1961, filmed by Alain Resnais) and writing and directing *The Immortal One* (1963). Films, like novels, allowed Robbe-Grillet to manipulate visions of reality as he insistently focused on surfaces and shapes, presented different versions of the same scene, composed a sound track that contradicted or commented on photographed action and—in later works—challenged his own imagination by including unexpected incidents that occurred on location.

Robbe-Grillet was admired as a master of formal experimentation but also criticized for the quarantined atmosphere and obsessive sadism of his work. Women, for example, are repeatedly victimized, and terror and death are constant themes in Robbe-Grillet's work. Uncomfortable, perhaps, with such criticism, he justified sadistic fantasies in his work partly as reflecting popular themes in a correspondingly sadistic and dehumanized world and partly as the therapeutic expression of his own obsessions. Therapeutic or not, there is no mistaking the basic images of Robbe-Grillet's world or the disturbing angles from which they are presented. *The Secret Room*, reprinted here from *Snapshots* (1962), arranges in an artistic homage to the Symbolist painter Gustave Moreau (1826–1898) many of Robbe-Grillet's most obsessive images: a spreading bloodstain, a young woman stretched out erotically in chains and stabbed under the left breast, an ascending staircase, different points of view directed down on the victim, a mysterious anonymous criminal, and even a figure eight of smoke coiling upward from the incense burner. The scene is bound to shock for its overt sadism, for its aesthetic and amoral appreciation of the visual elements of human sacrifice, and for the erotic pleasure it suggests in female victimization. It would not be appropriate to ignore or repress this response, for the subject matter is not neutral or intended as such. Robbe-Grillet has presented an additional challenge, however, by insisting on the stylized *unreality* of the scene. It is a bizarre and disturbing tableau, made to unsettle readers who try to reconcile its various aspects: its manipulation of stereotypes of the victimized woman, the horror of the helpless sacrifice, and an alienated perspective that suggests sadistic impersonality but at the same time is attributed to art.

The Secret Room[1]

To Gustave Moreau[2]

The first thing to be seen is a red stain, of a deep, dark, shiny red, with almost black shadows. It is in the form of an irregular rosette, sharply outlined, extending in several directions in wide outflows of unequal length, dividing and dwindling afterward into single sinuous streaks. The whole stands out against a smooth, pale surface, round in shape, at once dull and pearly, a hemisphere joined by gentle curves to an expanse of the same pale color—white darkened by the shadowy quality of the place: a dungeon, a sunken room, or a cathedral—glowing with a diffused brilliance in the semidarkness.

Farther back, the space is filled with the cylindrical trunks of columns, repeated with progressive vagueness in their retreat toward the beginning of a vast stone stairway, turning slightly as it rises, growing narrower and narrower as it approaches the high vaults where it disappears.

The whole setting is empty, stairway and colonnades. Alone, in the foreground, the stretched-out body gleams feebly, marked with the red stain—a white body whose full, supple flesh can be sensed, fragile, no doubt, and vulnerable. Alongside the bloody hemisphere another identical round form, this one intact, is seen at almost the same angle of view; but the haloed point at its summit, of darker tint, is in this case quite recognizable, whereas the other one is entirely destroyed, or at least covered by the wound.

In the background, near the top of the stairway, a black silhouette is seen fleeing, a man wrapped in a long, floating cape, ascending the last steps with-

1. Translated by Bruce Morrissette.
2. French Symbolist painter (1826–1898) known for exotic, luminous scenes with subtly erotic and morbid overtones, such as *The Death of Darius* and *Dance of Salome*.

out turning around, his deed accomplished. A thin smoke rises in twisting scrolls from a sort of incense burner placed on a high stand of ironwork with a silvery glint. Nearby lies the milkwhite body, with wide streaks of blood running from the left breast, along the flank and on the hip.

It is a fully rounded woman's body, but not heavy, completely nude, lying on its back, the bust raised up somewhat by thick cushions thrown down on the floor, which is covered with Oriental rugs. The waist is very narrow, the neck long and thin, curved to one side, the head thrown back into a darker area where, even so, the facial features may be discerned, the partly opened mouth, the wide-staring eyes, shining with a fixed brilliance, and the mass of long, black hair spread out in a complicated wavy disorder over a heavily folded cloth, of velvet perhaps, on which also rest the arm and shoulder.

It is a uniformly colored velvet of dark purple, or which seems so in this lighting. But purple, brown, blue also seem to dominate in the colors of the cushions—only a small portion of which is hidden beneath the velvet cloth, and which protrude noticeably, lower down, beneath the bust and waist—as well as in the Oriental patterns of the rugs on the floor. Farther on, these same colors are picked up again in the stone of the paving and the columns, and vaulted archways, the stairs, and the less discernible surfaces that disappear into the farthest reaches of the room.

The dimensions of this room are difficult to determine exactly; the body of the young sacrificial victim seems at first glance to occupy a substantial portion of it, but the vast size of the stairway leading down to it would imply rather that this is not the whole room, whose considerable space must in reality extend all around, right and left, as it does toward the faraway browns and blues among the columns standing in line, in every direction, perhaps toward other sofas, thick carpets, piles of cushions and fabrics, other tortured bodies, other incense burners.

It is also difficult to say where the light comes from. No clue, on the columns or on the floor, suggests the direction of the rays. Nor is any window or torch visible. The milkwhite body itself seems to light the scene, with its full breasts, the curve of its thighs, the rounded belly, the full buttocks, the stretched-out legs, widely spread, and the black tuft of the exposed sex, provocative, proffered, useless now.

The man has already moved several steps back. He is now on the first steps of the stairs, ready to go up. The bottom steps are wide and deep, like the steps leading up to some great building, a temple or theater; they grow smaller as they ascend, and at the same time describe a wide, helical curve, so gradually that the stairway has not yet made a half-turn by the time it disappears near the top of the vaults, reduced then to a steep, narrow flight of steps without handrail, vaguely outlined, moreover, in the thickening darkness beyond.

But the man does not look in this direction, where his movement nonetheless carries him; his left foot on the second step and his right foot already touching the third, with his knee bent, he has turned around to look at the spectacle for one last time. The long, floating cape thrown hastily over his shoulders, clasped in one hand at his waist, has been whirled around by the rapid circular motion that has just caused his head and chest to turn in the opposite direction, and a corner of the cloth remains suspended in the air as if blown by a gust of wind; this corner, twisting around upon itself in the form of a loose S, reveals the red silk lining with its gold embroidery.

The man's features are impassive, but tense, as if in expectation—or perhaps fear—of some sudden event, or surveying with one last glance the total immobility of the scene. Though he is looking backward, his whole body is turned slightly forward, as if he were continuing up the stairs. His right arm—not the one holding the edge of the cape—is bent sharply toward the left, toward a point in space where the balustrade should be, if this stairway had one, an interrupted gesture, almost incomprehensible, unless it arose from an instinctive movement to grasp the absent support.

As to the direction of his glance, it is certainly aimed at the body of the victim lying on the cushions, its extended members stretched out in the form of a cross, its bust raised up, its head thrown back. But the face is perhaps hidden from the man's eyes by one of the columns, standing at the foot of the stairs. The young woman's right hand touches the floor just at the foot of this column. The fragile wrist is encircled by an iron bracelet. The arm is almost in darkness, only the hand receiving enough light to make the thin, outspread fingers clearly visible against the circular protrusion at the base of the stone column. A black metal chain running around the column passes through a ring affixed to the bracelet, binding the wrist tightly to the column.

At the top of the arm a rounded shoulder, raised up by the cushions, also stands out well lighted, as well as the neck, the throat, and the other shoulder, the armpit with its soft hair, the left arm likewise pulled back with its wrist bound in the same manner to the base of another column, in the extreme foreground; here the iron bracelet and the chain are fully displayed, represented with perfect clarity down to the slightest details.

The same is true, still in the foreground but at the other side, for a similar chain, but not quite as thick, wound directly around the ankle, running twice around the column and terminating in a heavy iron embedded in the floor. About a yard farther back, or perhaps slightly farther, the right foot is identically chained. But it is the left foot, and its chain, that are the most minutely depicted.

The foot is small, delicate, finely modeled. In several places the chain has broken the skin, causing noticeable if not extensive depressions in the flesh. The chain links are oval, thick, the size of an eye. The ring in the floor resembles those used to attach horses; it lies almost touching the stone pavement to which it is riveted by a massive iron peg. A few inches away is the edge of a rug; it is grossly wrinkled at this point, doubtless as a result of the convulsive, but necessarily very restricted, movements of the victim attempting to struggle.

The man is still standing about a yard away, half leaning over her. He looks at her face, seen upside down, her dark eyes made larger by their surrounding eyeshadow, her mouth wide open as if screaming. The man's posture allows his face to be seen only in a vague profile, but one senses in it a violent exaltation, despite the rigid attitude, the silence, the immobility. His back is slightly arched. His left hand, the only one visible, holds up at some distance from the body a piece of cloth, some dark-colored piece of clothing, which drags on the carpet, and which must be the long cape with its gold-embroidered lining.

This immense silhouette hides most of the bare flesh over which the red stain, spreading from the globe of the breast, runs in long rivulets that branch out, growing narrower, upon the pale background of the bust and the flank.

One thread has reached the armpit and runs in an almost straight, thin line along the arm; others have run down toward the waist and traced out, along one side of the belly, the hip, the top of the thigh, a more random network already starting to congeal. Three or four tiny veins have reached the hollow between the legs, meeting in a sinuous line, touching the point of the V formed by the outspread legs, and disappearing into the black tuft.

Look, now the flesh is still intact: the black tuft and the white belly, the soft curve of the hips, the narrow waist, and, higher up, the pearly breasts rising and falling in time with the rapid breathing, whose rhythm grows more accelerated. The man, close to her, one knee on the floor, leans farther over. The head, with its long, curly hair, which alone is free to move somewhat, turns from side to side, struggling; finally the woman's mouth twists open, while the flesh is torn open, the blood spurts out over the tender skin, stretched tight, the carefully shadowed eyes grow abnormally large, the mouth opens wider, the head twists violently, one last time, from right to left, then more gently, to fall back finally and become still, amid the mass of black hair spread out on the velvet.

Afterward, the whole setting is empty, the enormous room with its purple shadows and its stone columns proliferating in all directions, the monumental staircase with no handrail that twists upward, growing narrower and vaguer as it rises into the darkness, toward the top of the vaults where it disappears.

Near the body, whose wound has stiffened, whose brilliance is already growing dim, the thin smoke from the incense burner traces complicated scrolls in the still air: first a coil turned horizontally to the left, which then straightens out and rises slightly, then returns to the axis of its point of origin, which it crosses as it moves to the right, then turns back in the first direction, only to wind back again, thus forming an irregular sinusoidal[3] curve, more and more flattened out, and rising, vertically, toward the top of the canvas.

---

3. S-shaped.

ITALO CALVINO

1923–1985

Italo Calvino is a marvelously entertaining storyteller whose tales, read by young and old, bring a lightness and fanciful imagination to everyday life—even though that "every day" may take place on the moon, among the first invertebrates or in a world where space and time obey unique laws. Whether writing novels and short stories or openly retelling fables, he is at once simple and complex, humorous and profound. For Calvino, the art of literature offers a complement to science: art helps us explore possibilities that can be conceived only by the imagination, and it shows us how to break free of old habits of thought.

Calvino was born in a town near Havana, Cuba, in 1923, to Mario and Eva Calvino, Italian citizens who had lived in Cuba for many years. Both parents were botanists, and they returned to the family farm in San Remo (a picturesque town on the north Italian coast) two years after Italo's birth. Calvino's father joined the science faculty at the University of Turin, and his parents conducted plant experiments on the farm. Their interest in science and their independent frame of mind contributed to young Calvino's own outlook and to his ironic perspective. It was a difficult period for freethinkers: the Fascists were in power, and Benito Mussolini was dictator of Italy from 1922 until his fall in 1943. Mussolini's militarist nationalism was the order of the day, and Calvino—like others his age—was required to join a Fascist youth group. Calvino felt isolated from his peers, and when he was drafted into the national army in 1943, he deserted and joined a Resistance group. In 1944,

he joined the Communist Party, which he left in 1957 after the Soviet invasion of Hungary the previous year.

Calvino's wartime experiences formed the basis for his first novel, *The Path to the Nest of Spiders* (1947). The publishing firm Einaudi gave him a job in which he met many leading authors, although he later regretted that "For fifteen years . . . I devoted much more time to other people's books than to my own." Nonetheless, he continued to write and publish prolifically. He wrote fantastic historical novels and hundreds of short fables and science fiction tales. In many of his works, the unreal atmosphere of dream, folktale, and fable enables the writer to comment indirectly on human tendencies and the ills of modern urban society.

In 1964, Calvino married the Argentinian translator Judith Esther (Chichita) Singer and moved to Paris, where he lived until he returned to Rome in 1980. Under the influence of French structuralism and postmodernism, Calvino's later work became dense and intricately layered. For example, in *The Castle of Crossed Destinies* (1969–73), a variation on Boccaccio's *Decameron*, the gathered storytellers cannot speak and must represent their tales through a dwindling deck of tarot cards, whose images are also reproduced in the margins of the novel. Calvino's work shares much in common with such philosophical fabulists as **Franz Kafka, Vladimir Nabokov**, and **Jorge Luis Borges**.

Invisible Cities (1972), which some consider Calvino's best work, is structured as an imaginary dialogue between the thirteenth-century Venetian explorer Marco Polo and the Mongol emperor Kublai Khan. According to Marco Polo's *Travels,* he remained for seventeen years in China and was sent on several occasions to bring back news of distant regions. In this imaginary account, the Khan has also asked Polo to report on the various cities throughout the realm, and the traveler brings back exemplary objects ("a helmet, a seashell, a coconut, a fan") on the basis of which he delivers his reports. Kublai Khan soon recognizes that the cities (all fifty-five of them) are imaginary and that Marco Polo's travels are equally unreal. In the meantime, the individual reports have established themselves as brilliantly ambiguous prose poems, both real and unreal, which lead the Khan to ponder the "invisible order that sustains cities" and ultimately to question reality.

Calvino's fantastic works raise implicitly the same questions about human identity that are found in the major European moralists: they ask what it means to be human, how we ought to live, and what our relationship is to the universe. These questions are raised, however, as images, as imaginary sequences of "what if," whose logic is pursued extensively—

even mathematically—to its ironic conclusion. The underlying question in his close observation of the minutiae of everyday life is, What does it all mean?

Invisible Cities pursues this question, stated more and more openly by the Khan as the reports proceed. Like all nine chapters, Chapter 8 is framed by a brief dialogue between Marco Polo and Kublai Khan. The Khan, who has sent Polo to report on the farthest reaches of his empire, is eager to gain the knowledge that will mean mastery of his dominions. The sequence of his questions and the richly evocative reports delivered in answer take on the character of a chess game, whether the board be the tiles on which Polo spreads out his samples, a traditional chessboard, or a briefly glimpsed metaphysical plane. Throughout, the Khan seeks to discern a pattern of relationships that will let him grasp the game (and his empire), while Marco Polo's "essential landscapes," at once concretely real and bafflingly fabulous, refuse to be contained within a system. Moving deeper into understanding the game's principles, the Khan encounters only a checkmate—but one that carries with it the promise of another beginning.

Invisible Cities[1]

CHAPTER 8

From the foot of the Great Khan's[2] throne a majolica pavement extended. Marco Polo, mute informant,[3] spread out on it the samples of the wares he had brought back from his journeys to the ends of the empire: a helmet, a seashell, a coconut, a fan. Arranging the objects in a certain order on the black and white tiles, and occasionally shifting them with studied moves, the ambassador tried to depict for

1. Translated by William Weaver. Published in 1972.
2. I.e., Kublai Khan (1215–1294), grandson of Genghis Khan, emperor of China (which he had conquered as a Mongol general) and ruler of the Mongolian dominions, which stretched from Mongolia to southern Russia and Persia. He welcomed foreign travelers and their information.

3. Initially, Marco Polo, who did not know either Chinese or Tartar, communicated with the Khan "with gestures, leaps, cries of wonder and of horror . . . or with objects he took from his knapsacks—ostrich plumes, peashooters, quartzes—which he arranged in front of him like chessmen" (Chapter 1).

the monarch's eyes the vicissitudes of his travels, the conditions of the empire, the prerogatives of the distant provincial seats.

Kublai was a keen chess player; following Marco's movements, he observed that certain pieces implied or excluded the vicinity of other pieces and were shifted along certain lines. Ignoring the objects' variety of form, he could grasp the system of arranging one with respect to the others on the majolica floor. He thought: "If each city is like a game of chess, the day when I have learned the rules, I shall finally possess my empire, even if I shall never succeed in knowing all the cities it contains."

Actually, it was useless for Marco's speeches to employ all this bric-a-brac: a chessboard would have sufficed, with its specific pieces. To each piece, in turn, they could give an appropriate meaning: a knight could stand for a real horseman, or for a procession of coaches, an army on the march, an equestrian monument: a queen could be a lady looking down from her balcony, a fountain, a church with a pointed dome, a quince tree.

Returning from his last mission, Marco Polo found the Khan awaiting him, seated at a chessboard. With a gesture he invited the Venetian[4] to sit opposite him and describe, with the help only of the chessmen, the cities he had visited. Marco did not lose heart. The Great Khan's chessmen were huge pieces of polished ivory: arranging on the board looming rooks and sulky knights, assembling swarms of pawns, drawing straight or oblique avenues like a queen's progress, Marco recreated the perspectives and the spaces of black and white cities on moonlit nights.

Contemplating these essential landscapes, Kublai reflected on the invisible order that sustains cities, on the rules that decreed how they rise, take shape and prosper, adapting themselves to the seasons, and then how they sadden and fall in ruins. At times he thought he was on the verge of discovering a coherent, harmonious system underlying the infinite deformities and discords, but no model could stand up to the comparison with the game of chess. Perhaps, instead of racking one's brain to suggest with the ivory pieces' scant help visions which were anyway destined to oblivion, it would suffice to play a game according to the rules, and to consider each successive state of the board as one of the countless forms that the system of forms assembles and destroys.

Now Kublai Khan no longer had to send Marco Polo on distant expeditions: he kept him playing endless games of chess. Knowledge of the empire was hidden in the pattern drawn by the angular shifts of the knight, by the diagonal passages opened by the bishop's incursions, by the lumbering, cautious tread of the king and the humble pawn, by the inexorable ups and downs of every game.

The Great Khan tried to concentrate on the game: but now it was the game's purpose that eluded him. Each game ends in a gain or a loss: but of what? What were the true stakes? At checkmate, beneath the foot of the king, knocked aside by the winner's hand, a black or a white square remains. By disembodying his conquests to reduce them to the essential, Kublai had arrived at the extreme operation: the definitive conquest, of which the empire's multiform treasures were only illusory envelopes. It was reduced to a square of planed wood: nothingness. . . .

---

4. The Polos were a family of Venetian merchants who traveled throughout the Middle East and Asia.

Cities & Names 5[5]

Irene is the city visible when you lean out from the edge of the plateau at the hour when the lights come on, and in the limpid air, the pink of the settlement can be discerned spread out in the distance below: where the windows are more concentrated, where it thins out in dimly lighted alleys, where it collects the shadows of gardens, where it raises towers with signal fires; and if the evening is misty, a hazy glow swells like a milky sponge at the foot of the gulleys.

Travelers on the plateau, shepherds shifting their flocks, bird-catchers watching their nets, hermits gathering greens: all look down and speak of Irene. At times the wind brings a music of bass drums and trumpets, the bang of firecrackers in the light-display of a festival; at times the rattle of guns, the explosion of a powder magazine in the sky yellow with the fires of civil war. Those who look down from the heights conjecture about what is happening in the city; they wonder if it would be pleasant or unpleasant to be in Irene that evening. Not that they have any intention of going there (in any case the roads winding down to the valley are bad), but Irene is a magnet for the eyes and thoughts of those who stay up above.

At this point Kublai Khan expects Marco to speak of Irene as it is seen from within. But Marco cannot do this: he has not succeeded in discovering which is the city that those of the plateau call Irene. For that matter, it is of slight importance: if you saw it, standing in its midst, it would be a different city; Irene is a name for a city in the distance, and if you approach, it changes.

For those who pass it without entering, the city is one thing; it is another for those who are trapped by it and never leave. There is the city where you arrive for the first time; and there is another city which you leave never to return. Each deserves a different name; perhaps I have already spoken of Irene under other names; perhaps I have spoken only of Irene.

Cities & the Dead 4

What makes Argia different from other cities is that it has earth instead of air. The streets are completely filled with dirt, clay packs the rooms to the ceiling, on every stair another stairway is set in negative, over the roofs of the houses hang layers of rocky terrain like skies with clouds. We do not know if the inhabitants can move about the city, widening the worm tunnels and the crevices where roots twist: the dampness destroys people's bodies and they have scant strength; everyone is better off remaining still, prone; anyway, it is dark.

From up here, nothing of Argia can be seen; some say, "It's down below there," and we can only believe them. The place is deserted. At night, putting your ear to the ground, you can sometimes hear a door slam.

Cities & the Sky 3

Those who arrive at Thekla can see little of the city, beyond the plank fences, the sackcloth screens, the scaffoldings, the metal armatures, the wooden catwalks

---

5. The five section titles in Chapter 8 are selected from eleven thematic titles appearing throughout the different chapters: the others are "Cities & Memory," "Cities & Desire," "Cities & Signs," "Thin Cities," "Trading Cities," and "Cities & Eyes."

hanging from ropes or supported by sawhorses, the ladders, the trestles. If you ask, "Why is Thekla's construction taking such a long time?" the inhabitants continue hoisting sacks, lowering leaded strings, moving long brushes up and down, as they answer, "So that its destruction cannot begin." And if asked whether they fear that, once the scaffoldings are removed, the city may begin to crumble and fall to pieces, they add hastily, in a whisper, "Not only the city."

If, dissatisfied with the answers, someone puts his eye to a crack in a fence, he sees cranes pulling up other cranes, scaffoldings that embrace other scaffoldings, beams that prop up other beams. "What meaning does your construction have?" he asks. "What is the aim of a city under construction unless it is a city? Where is the plan you are following, the blueprint?"

"We will show it to you as soon as the working day is over; we cannot interrupt our work now," they answer.

Work stops at sunset. Darkness falls over the building site. The sky is filled with stars. "There is the blueprint," they say.

Continuous Cities 2

If on arriving at Trude I had not read the city's name written in big letters, I would have thought I was landing at the same airport from which I had taken off. The suburbs they drove me through were no different from the others, with the same little greenish and yellowish houses. Following the same signs we swung around the same flower beds in the same squares. The downtown streets displayed goods, packages, signs that had not changed at all. This was the first time I had come to Trude, but I already knew the hotel where I happened to be lodged; I had already heard and spoken my dialogues with the buyers and sellers of hardware; I had ended other days identically, looking through the same goblets at the same swaying navels.

Why come to Trude? I asked myself. And I already wanted to leave.

"You can resume your flight whenever you like," they said to me, "but you will arrive at another Trude, absolutely the same, detail by detail. The world is covered by a sole Trude which does not begin and does not end. Only the name of the airport changes."

Hidden Cities 1

In Olinda, if you go out with a magnifying glass and hunt carefully, you may find somewhere a point no bigger than the head of a pin which, if you look at it slightly enlarged, reveals within itself the roofs, the antennas, the skylights, the gardens, the pools, the streamers across the streets, the kiosks in the squares, the horse-racing track. That point does not remain there: a year later you will find it the size of half a lemon, then as large as a mushroom, then a soup plate. And then it becomes a full-size city, enclosed within the earlier city: a new city that forces its way ahead in the earlier city and presses it toward the outside.

Olinda is certainly not the only city that grows in concentric circles, like tree trunks which each year add one more ring. But in other cities there remains, in the center, the old narrow girdle of the walls from which the withered spires rise, the towers, the tiled roofs, the domes, while the new quarters sprawl around them like a loosened belt. Not Olinda: the old walls expand bearing the old quarters with them, enlarged, but maintaining their proportions on a broader horizon at the edges of the city; they surround the slightly newer quarters, which also grew up on the margins and became thinner to make room for still more recent ones pressing from inside; and so, on and on, to the heart of the city, a totally new Olinda which, in its reduced dimensions retains the features and the flow of lymph of the first Olinda and of all the Olindas that have blossomed one from the other; and within this innermost circle there are already blossoming—though it is hard to discern them—the next Olinda and those that will grow after it.

. . . The Great Khan tried to concentrate on the game: but now it was the game's reason that eluded him. The end of every game is a gain or a loss: but of what? What were the real stakes? At checkmate, beneath the foot of the king, knocked aside by the winner's hand, nothingness remains: a black square, or a white one. By disembodying his conquests to reduce them to the essential, Kublai had arrived at the extreme operation: the definitive conquest, of which the empire's multiform treasures were only illusory envelopes; it was reduced to a square of planed wood.

Then Marco Polo spoke: "Your chessboard, sire, is inlaid with two woods: ebony and maple. The square on which your enlightened gaze is fixed was cut from the ring of a trunk that grew in a year of drought: you see how its fibers are arranged? Here a barely hinted knot can be made out: a bud tried to burgeon on a premature spring day, but the night's frost forced it to desist."

Until then the Great Khan had not realized that the foreigner knew how to express himself fluently in his language, but it was not this fluency that amazed him.

"Here is a thicker pore: perhaps it was a larvum's nest; not a woodworm, because, once born, it would have begun to dig, but a caterpillar that gnawed the leaves and was the cause of the tree's being chosen for chopping down . . . This edge was scored by the wood carver with his gouge so that it would adhere to the next square, more protruding. . . ."

The quantity of things that could be read in a little piece of smooth and empty wood overwhelmed Kublai; Polo was already talking about ebony forests, about rafts laden with logs that come down the rivers, of docks, of women at the windows. . . .

PAUL CELAN

1920–1970

A survivor of the Holocaust, Paul Celan wrote spare, hauntingly beautiful lyric poems about suffering and loss. The critic Theodor Adorno famously noted that "to write a poem after Auschwitz is barbaric." Yet Celan, who lost both parents in Nazi prison camps and who himself spent much of the Second World War in a forced labor camp, managed to write poetry that spoke directly about the unspeakable.

Born Paul Antschel in Czernowitz, Romania, Celan came from a religious Jewish family. (Celan is an anagram of the Romanian spelling of his last name, Ancel.) He was raised speaking German, and his mother passed on to him her love of German literature, while his father transmitted his Zionism and concern with the Jewish tradition. Czernowitz was linguistically and ethnically diverse, and Celan quickly learned Yiddish and Romanian, as well as Hebrew; later in life, he learned French, Russian, Ukranian, and English as well.

In 1938, Celan enrolled in a premedical program in Paris, where he was exposed to avant-garde literary movements such as surrealism; he had recently begun writing poetry. Returning home in the summer of 1939, he was trapped in Czernowitz by the outbreak of the Second World War. Under the Hitler-Stalin pact, the Soviet Union occupied Czernowitz in 1940. Distressed by harsh Soviet rule, Celan abandoned his youthful support of communism. After the Nazi invasion of the Soviet Union in the summer of 1941, the Germans took control of Czernowitz, and the Jews of the city were attacked and confined to a ghetto by the Nazi SS (abbreviation for the German word *Schutzstaffel*, the elite security organization) and by Romanian soldiers. Celan was given the task of clearing trash and destroying Russian books. On June 27, 1942, while Celan was away from the house, the Germans seized his parents and deported them to Nazi prison camps in the Ukraine. His father died of typhus later that year, and his mother was shot when she was no longer capable of working. Celan spent the next year and a half in labor camps in German-allied Romania, where, though conditions were severe, he was at less risk of being killed. He continued to write poetry. After the Soviet Red Army reoccupied eastern Romania and the full horror of the concentration camps came to be known, Celan, now released from his prison camp, wrote "Deathfugue," one of the first and most moving poems about the camps, published first in Romanian translation in 1947, then in German in 1952.

Near the end of the war, Celan left Czernowitz for Bucharest, where he worked translating literature, including some of **Franz Kafka**'s parables, into Romanian. For the remainder of his life, he was active as a translator of much modern French, Russian, and English poetry (and also Shakespeare) into German. Celan fled Bucharest in 1947, just before the Soviet takeover, and was smuggled with his poems over the border to Vienna. From there he went on to Paris and the prestigious École Normale Supérieure, where he received his degree and then taught German literature. He visited Germany occasionally, receiving the premier German literary award, the Büchner Prize, in 1960 and later meeting the existential philosopher

Martin Heidegger, whose work had inspired Celan despite the German's support of the Nazi regime. In 1969, Celan visited Israel for the first time.

During the 1960s, however, Celan suffered periods of increasing paranoia, the result of his concerns about anti-Semitism and of false accusations of plagiarism that continually dogged him. He briefly entered a psychiatric clinic in 1965, and remained under psychiatric treatment for the following five years. On April 20, 1970, Celan committed suicide by jumping off a bridge into the Seine, in Paris.

The poems printed here represent the range of Celan's career. They show his use of a restrained and difficult language to bear witness to the horrors suffered by his parents and other victims of the Holocaust. "Deathfugue," his first published poem and eventually his most famous, originally appeared in Romanian translation as "Tangoul Mortii" (Tango of Death). That title refers to the dance music that an SS commander forced prisoners to play during marches and executions at the Janowska camp in L'vov, Ukraine. The poem contrasts the golden hair of the commander's beloved Margareta (a typically German name) with the dark hair of the Jewish Shulamith, a prisoner in the camp. Her hair is described as "ashen," recalling the crematoria where the bodies of concentration camp victims were often burned. Celan re-creates the musical quality of the tango or fugue—two very different musical forms both characterized by rhythmic repetition—in his repetition of short, rhythmic phrases. The fragmentation and absence of punctuation suggest a breakdown of the moral order. The translator, John Felstiner, has left some of the poem in German to give the sense of its original language. Of the German language and why he continued to write in it, Celan once said, "Only in the mother tongue can one speak one's own truth. In a foreign tongue the poet lies."

Many of Celan's early poems have an elegiac tone, grieving for the dead of the Holocaust and the war. Written in the final years of the war, "Aspen Tree" (published in 1948) is a simpler, more direct poem than "Deathfugue." It laments the death of the poet's mother by addressing inanimate objects (the tree, the dandelion, the cloud, the star, the door) that remind him of her absence. "Corona" (1949), a response to a poem by **Rainer Maria Rilke**, tells of two lovers who realize that their love is haunted by the losses in wartime but who also believe that human decency will eventually reassert itself—that "It's time the stone consented to bloom." "Shibboleth" (1955), named after a biblical password, alludes to two incidents in the rise of Nazism and Fascism—the suppression of the Viennese Socialists in 1934 and the Spanish Civil War (1936–1939). While stating Celan's allegiance to the political left, the poem creates a powerful image of the exile who has no homeland but cries out into "homeland strangeness."

Later in life, Celan wrote poems that were less political and often more explicitly religious. The title "Tenebrae" (1959), or "darkness" in Latin, refers to the Crucifixion. Drawing on both the Old and the New Testaments, the poem uses the language of the Psalms and the Lamentations of Jeremiah to commemorate the suffering of victims in the Holocaust, which is likened to Christ's suffering on the cross. Although the poem's speakers ("we") insistently address the Lord, they seem to sense his absence. Indeed, since they are presumably Jewish, they may be praying to a God who is not their own. "Near are we," they cry, but the Lord is nowhere near and appears to have abandoned his people. "Zurich, at the Stork" (1963) recalls Celan's debate with an older poet, Nelly Sachs, about God's existence. Though deeply concerned with Jewish religious teaching, Celan never believed in God in a straightforward sense. And yet, in keeping with certain forms of Jewish mysticism, he believed in God as an absence, to which he prays in "Psalm" (1963).

During the last years of his life, Celan's poetry became increasingly difficult and hermetic. Two brief poems from this period, "You were" (1968) and "World to be stuttered after" (1968), combine the political and religious themes of his earlier works with a more intimate despair. The condensation of the lyrics in these years resembles a darker version of the late work of **Samuel Beckett**, whom Celan never met but of whom he said, late in life, "That's probably the only man here [in Paris] I could have an understanding with." Like Beckett, Celan responded to the calamities and horrors of his time with a restrained, minimalist art that spoke the truth about the unnamable.

Deathfugue[1]

Black milk of daybreak we drink it at evening
we drink it at midday and morning we drink it at night
we drink and we drink
we shovel a grave in the air where you won't lie too cramped
A man lives in the house he plays with his vipers he writes   5
he writes when it grows dark to Deutschland[2] your golden hair
    Margareta[3]
he writes it and steps out of doors and the stars are all sparkling he
    whistles his hounds to stay close
he whistles his Jews into rows has them shovel a grave in the ground
he commands us play up for the dance[4]

Black milk of daybreak we drink you at night   10
we drink you at morning and midday we drink you at evening
we drink and we drink
A man lives in the house he plays with his vipers he writes
he writes when it grows dark to Deutschland your golden hair
    Margareta
Your ashen hair Shulamith[5] we shovel a grave in the air
    where you won't lie too cramped   15

He shouts dig this earth deeper you lot there you others sing up and play
he grabs for the rod in his belt he swings it his eyes are so blue
stick your spades deeper you lot there you others play on for the dancing

Black milk of daybreak we drink you at night
we drink you at midday and morning we drink you at evening   20
we drink and we drink

---

1. All selections translated from German by John Felstiner.
2. Germany (German).
3. A typically German name.

4. Concentration camp commanders are reported to have forced prisoners to play dance tunes, sometimes while graves were being dug.
5. A typically Jewish name.

a man lives in the house your goldenes Haar[6] Margareta
your aschenes Haar[7] Shulamith he plays with his vipers

He shouts play death more sweetly this Death is a master from
   Deutschland
he shouts scrape your strings darker you'll rise up as smoke to the sky[8]
you'll then have a grave in the clouds where you won't lie too cramped

Black milk of daybreak we drink you at night   25
we drink you at midday Death is a master aus Deutschland
we drink you at evening and morning we drink and we drink
this Death is ein Meister aus Deutschland his eye it is blue
he shoots you with shot made of lead shoots you level and true
a man lives in the house your goldenes Haar Margarete   30
he looses his hounds on us grants us a grave in the air
he plays with his vipers and daydreams der Tod ist ein Meister aus
   Deutschland[9]

dein goldenes Haar Margarete
dein aschenes Haar Sulamith

                                        1947

Aspen Tree

Aspen tree, your leaves glance white into the dark.
My mother's hair never turned white.

Dandelion, so green is the Ukraine.[1]
My fair-haired mother did not come home.

Rain cloud, do you linger at the well?   5
My soft-voiced mother weeps for all.

Rounded star, you coil the golden loop.
My mother's heart was hurt by lead.

Oaken door, who hove you off your hinge?
My gentle mother cannot return.   10

                                        1948

6. Golden hair (German). The translator has left some phrases in the original.
7. Ashen hair (German).
8. Murdered prisoners were burned in crematoria.

9. Death is a Master from Germany (German).
1. Many concentration camps were located in Ukraine; Celan's mother died in one of these.

Corona

Autumn nibbles its leaf from my hand: we are friends.
We shell time from the nuts and teach it to walk:
time returns into its shell.

In the mirror is Sunday,
in the dream comes sleeping,   5
the mouth speaks true.

My eye goes down to my lover's loins:
we gaze at each other,
we speak dark things,
we love one another like poppy and memory,   10
we slumber like wine in the seashells,
like the sea in the moon's blood-jet.

We stand at the window embracing, they watch from the street:
it's time people knew!
It's time the stone consented to bloom,   15
a heart beat for unrest.
It's time it came time.

It is time.

1949

Shibboleth[1]

Together with my stones
wept large
behind the bars,

they dragged me
to the midst of the market,   5
to where
the flag unfurls that I
swore no kind of oath to.

Flute,
double flute of night: 10
think of the dark
twin reddenings
in Vienna and Madrid.[2]

---

1. A password in the Bible (Judges 12). The Ephraimites, who could not pronounce the word, were put to death by their opponents, the Gileadites.
2. Refers to the destruction of Viennese socialism (1934), to the unification of Austria with Nazi Germany (1938), and to the Fascist defeat of the Republic in the Spanish Civil War (1936–39).

Set your flag at half mast,
memory.   15
At half mast
today and for ever.

Heart:
make yourself known even here,
here in the midst of the market.   20
Cry out the shibboleth
into your homeland strangeness:
February. No pasaran.[3]

Einhorn:[4]
you know of the stones,   25
you know of the waters,
come,
I'll lead you away
to the voices
of Estremadura.[5]   30

1955

Tenebrae[1]

Near are we, Lord,
near and graspable.

Grasped already, Lord,
clawed into each other, as if
each of our bodies were
your body, Lord.   5

Pray, Lord,
pray to us,
we are near.

Wind-skewed we went there,
went there to bend   10
over pit and crater.

Went to the water-trough, Lord.
It was blood, it was
what you shed, Lord.   15

It shined.

---

3. "They shall not pass" (Spanish). An international leftist slogan during and after the Spanish Civil War.
4. Erich Einhorn, a friend of Celan's.
5. A region in western Spain where some of

the earliest battles of the Civil War were fought.
1. "Darkness" (Latin), with special reference to the Crucifixion.

It cast your image into our eyes, Lord.
Eyes and mouth stand so open and void, Lord.
We have drunk, Lord.
The blood and the image that was in the blood, Lord.   20

Pray, Lord.
We are near.

1959

Zurich, at the Stork[1]

For Nelly Sachs

Our talk was of Too Much, of
Too Little. Of Thou
and Yet-Thou, of
clouding through brightness, of
Jewishness, of   5
your God.

Of
that.
On the day of an ascension, the
Minster stood over there, it came   10
with some gold across the water.

Our talk was of your God, I spoke
against him, I let the heart
I had
hope: 15
for
his highest, death-rattled, his
wrangling word—

Your eye looked at me, looked away,
your mouth   20
spoke toward the eye, I heard:

We
really don't know, you know,
we
really don't know   25
what
counts.

1963 ·

---

1. A hotel where Celan had a theological conversation with his friend the poet Nelly Sachs
(1891–1970).

Psalm

No one kneads us again out of earth and clay,[1]
no one incants our dust.
No one.

Blessèd art thou, No One.
In thy sight would   5
we bloom.
In thy
spite.

A Nothing
we were, are now, and ever   10
shall be, blooming:
the Nothing-, the
No-One's-Rose.

With
our pistil soul-bright,
our stamen heaven-waste,   15
our corona red
from the purpleword we sang
over, O over
the thorn.[2]   20

                                                                1963

You were

You were my death:
you I could hold
while everything slipped from me.

                                                                1968

World to be stuttered after

World to be stuttered after,
which I'll have been
a guest, a name
sweated down from the wall
where a wound licks up high.   5

                                                                1968

1. In Genesis 2.7 God creates Adam out of the "dust of the ground." Adam's name in Hebrew resembles the Hebrew word for clay.
2. Recalling the crown of thorns Jesus is made to wear on the way to the Crucifixion (Matthew 27.29). When God banishes Adam from Eden, he says that the ground will bring forth thorns for Adam, rather than food (Genesis 3.18).

DORIS LESSING

1919–2013

Conflicts between cultures, between values within a culture, and even between elements of a personality, are fundamental themes in Doris Lessing's work—as is the struggle to integrate these entities into a higher, unified order. The recipient of the 2007 Nobel Prize in Literature, Lessing spent her life in the midst of such conflicts. A witness to harsh colonial policies toward native subjects in Rhodesia as well as to the sexual and feminist revolutions in Europe, she used her writing to interrogate both the psychology of the self and the larger relations between the personal and the political.

Lessing was born Doris May Tayler in October 1919 in Persia (now Iran). Her parents were British: her mother was a nurse, and her father a clerk in the Imperial Bank of Persia who had been crippled in World War I; his horrific memories of combat would seep into his daughter's recollections of childhood. In 1925 the family moved to the British colony of Rhodesia (now Zimbabwe), where the colonial government was offering economic incentives to encourage the immigration of white settlers. For ten shillings an acre, the family bought three thousand acres of farmland in Mashonaland, a section of Southern Rhodesia that once had been the home of the Matabele tribe but from which the government had evicted most of the native population. The farm never prospered. Lessing attended a convent school until she was fourteen, but she considered herself largely self-educated, from her avid reading of the classics of European and American literature. Above all, she loved the nineteenth-century novel; realists such as Stendhal,

Tolstoy, and Dostoevsky impressed her, she later said, with "the warmth, the compassion, the humanity, the love of people" that gave impetus and passion to their social criticism. Gradually Lessing became aware of the racial injustice in Southern Rhodesia, and of the fact that she was, as she later put it, "a member of the white minority pitted against a black majority that was abominably treated and still is."

Social awareness is a defining theme of her early work, especially her first novel, *The Grass Is Singing* (1949), and the collection *African Stories* (1964). Arguing that "literature should be committed" to political issues, Lessing was herself politically active in Rhodesia, as well as a member of the British Communist Party from 1952 until 1956, the year of the Soviet intervention in Hungary. Her activism and socially oriented writing made their mark, and in 1956 she was declared a prohibited alien in both Southern Rhodesia and South Africa.

While still in Rhodesia, Lessing worked in several office jobs in Salisbury and made two unsuccessful marriages. (Lessing is the name of her second husband.) In 1949 she moved to England with the son from her second marriage and took a gamble on a literary career: "I was working in a lawyer's office at the time, and I remember walking in and saying to my boss, 'I'm giving up my job and writing a novel.' He very properly laughed, and I indignantly walked home and wrote *The Grass Is Singing*." The novel was a surprising and immediate success, and she was able, from that point, to make a profession of writing. Her next project was the five-volume series, *Children of Violence* (1952–69): the portrait of an era, after the form of the nineteenth-century bildungsroman, or "education novel," *Children of Violence* follows the life of a symbolically named heroine, Martha Quest, while exploring social and moral issues including race relations, the conflict between autonomy and socialization, and the hopes and frustrations of political idealism.

Lessing's most famous novel, *The Golden Notebook* (1962), makes a sharp break with the linear narrative style that *Children of Violence* shares with the bildungsroman tradition. In this work, too, a female protagonist (Anna Wulf) struggles to build a unified identity from the multiple, fragmented elements that constitute her personality; yet the exploratory process by which she pursues this goal takes her story beyond the confines of chronological narrative. Although the book is framed by a conventional short novel called *Free Women*, the governing structure is a series of different-colored notebooks that Anna uses to record the distinct versions of her experience: black for Africa, red for politics, yellow for a fictionalized rendering of herself as a character named Ella, and blue for a factual diary. By analyzing her life from these varying perspectives, Anna learns to understand and reconcile her contradictions—to write, ultimately, the "Golden Notebook," which is "all of me in one book."

During the 1970s and early 1980s, Lessing embarked on a series of science-fiction novels, which she termed "inner-space fiction," extending her interest in psychology and consciousness into speculative and quasi-mystical regions of the imagination. She then shifted to realistic stories that carry a sharp satiric or symbolic twist, such as *The Good Terrorist* (1985), a satire in which a group of naive British terrorists try to make a homey atmosphere in an empty house in London while carrying out bombing raids. She also published collections of essays and interviews that address politics, life, and art in a nonfiction voice. In presenting Lessing with the Nobel Prize in 2007, the committee praised her as an epic poet of "the female experience, who with scepticism, fire and visionary power has subjected a divided civilisation to scrutiny."

"The Old Chief Mshlanga" is one of Lessing's earliest African stories, written during the period, from 1950 to 1958, when she wrote most of her fiction set on that continent. The collection in which the story first appeared, *This Was the Old Chief's Country* (1951), together with *The Grass Is Singing* and *Five* (1953), a group of novellas set in Africa, established Lessing as an important interpreter of the colonial experience in contemporary Africa. The long act of dispossession that underlies "The Old Chief Mshlanga" began with the economic infiltration of the country by white settlers, under the leadership of the Chartered Company, a private firm that ruled the land under a British charter. Company policies soon formalized segregation by dividing land into tracts categorized as "alienated" (owned by white settlers) or "unalienated" (occupied by natives). The Land Apportionment Act of 1930 confirmed this arrangement by dividing the territory into areas called Native and European. In the story the figure of the Old Chief bridges the earlier dispensation, an era fifty years before, when his people owned the country, and the new, when they can be forcibly relocated to a Reserve after disagreeing with a white settler. Yet the Old Chief is not the protagonist here: significantly, his story comes into the foreground only some distance in, when it intrudes on the consciousness of a young white girl. The "vein of richness" that his tribe represents makes itself known only gradually. By the narrative's end, the tribe has disappeared altogether; the girl visits their village to find it disintegrating into the landscape.

Yet in spite of her remark that "there was nothing there," the girl's intimate description of the lush landscape shows that her encounter, however brief, with its former inhabitants has opened her eyes to an African presence that initially she had not been able to see. Nonetheless, the gain is one-sided: even her altered perceptions can bring her no closer to the members of the tribe, only throw light on the ground they occupied. For the Old Chief, there is no advantage: he and his people have disappeared into a symbolic essence, a "richness" that the settlers derive from the land they take over. Lessing's observant young girl has been changed by her encounter with the Old Chief, but the awakening is a bleak one that endows her with a sense of loss and responsibility.

The Old Chief Mshlanga

They were good, the years of ranging the bush over her father's farm which, like every white farm, was largely unused, broken only occasionally by small patches of cultivation. In between, nothing but trees, the long sparse grass, thorn and cactus and gully, grass and outcrop and thorn. And a jutting piece of rock which had been thrust up from the warm soil of Africa unimaginable eras of time ago, washed into hollows and whorls by sun and wind that had travelled so many thousands of miles of space and bush, would hold the weight of a small girl whose eyes were sightless for anything but a pale willowed river, a pale gleaming castle—a small girl singing: "Out flew the web and floated wide, the mirror cracked from side to side . . ."[1]

Pushing her way through the green aisles of the mealie[2] stalks, the leaves arching like cathedrals veined with sunlight far overhead, with the packed red earth underfoot, a fine lace of red starred witchweed would summon up a black bent figure croaking premonitions: the Northern witch, bred of cold Northern forests, would stand before her among the mealie fields, and it was the mealie fields that faded and fled, leaving her among the gnarled roots of an oak, snow falling thick and soft and white, the woodcutter's fire glowing red welcome through crowding tree trunks.

A white child, opening its eyes curiously on a sun-suffused landscape, a gaunt and violent landscape, might be supposed to accept it as her own, to make the msasa trees and the thorn trees as familiars, to feel her blood running free and responsive to the swing of the seasons.

This child could not see a msasa tree,[3] or the thorn, for what they were. Her books held tales of alien fairies, her rivers ran slow and peaceful, and she knew the shape of the leaves of an ash or an oak, the names of the little creatures that lived in English streams, when the words "the veld"[4] meant strangeness, though she could remember nothing else.

1. The child is reciting lines 114–15 of Tennyson's "The Lady of Shalott."
2. Maize; corn.
3. A large tree of central Africa, notable for the vivid colorings (pink through copper) of its spring foliage and for the fragrance of its white flowers.
4. Unenclosed country, open grassland.

Because of this, for many years, it was the veld that seemed unreal; the sun was a foreign sun, and the wind spoke a strange language.

The black people on the farm were as remote as the trees and the rocks. They were an amorphous black mass, mingling and thinning and massing like tadpoles, faceless, who existed merely to serve, to say "Yes, Baas,"[5] take their money and go. They changed season by season, moving from one farm to the next, according to their outlandish needs, which one did not have to understand, coming from perhaps hundreds of miles north or east, passing on after a few months—where? Perhaps even as far away as the fabled gold mines of Johannesburg,[6] where the pay was so much better than the few shillings a month and the double handful of mealie meal twice a day which they earned in that part of Africa.

The child was taught to take them for granted: the servants in the house would come running a hundred yards to pick up a book if she dropped it. She was called "Nkosikaas"—Chieftainess, even by the black children her own age.

Later, when the farm grew too small to hold her curiosity, she carried a gun in the crook of her arm and wandered miles a day, from vlei to vlei, from *kopje*[7] to *kopje*, accompanied by two dogs: the dogs and the gun were an armour against fear. Because of them she never felt fear.

If a native came into sight along the kaffir[8] paths half a mile away, the dogs would flush him up a tree as if he were a bird. If he expostulated (in his uncouth language which was by itself ridiculous) that was cheek. If one was in a good mood, it could be a matter for laughter. Otherwise one passed on, hardly glancing at the angry man in the tree.

On the rare occasions when white children met together they could amuse themselves by hailing a passing native in order to make a buffoon of him; they could set the dogs on him and watch him run; they could tease a small black child as if he were a puppy—save that they would not throw stones and sticks at a dog without a sense of guilt.

Later still, certain questions presented themselves in the child's mind; and because the answers were not easy to accept, they were silenced by an even greater arrogance of manner.

It was even impossible to think of the black people who worked about the house as friends, for if she talked to one of them, her mother would come running anxiously: "Come away; you mustn't talk to natives."

It was this instilled consciousness of danger, of something unpleasant, that made it easy to laugh out loud, crudely, if a servant made a mistake in his English or if he failed to understand an order—there is a certain kind of laughter that is fear, afraid of itself.

---

5. Boss.
6. The largest city in the Union (now Republic) of South Africa.

7. A small hill (Afrikaans). "Vlei": a shallow pool or swamp (Afrikaans).
8. A black African; usually used disparagingly.

One evening, when I was about fourteen, I was walking down the side of a mealie field that had been newly ploughed, so that the great red clods showed fresh and tumbling to the vlei beyond, like a choppy red sea; it was that hushed and listening hour, when the birds send long sad calls from tree to tree, and all the colours of earth and sky and leaf are deep and golden. I had my rifle in the curve of my arm, and the dogs were at my heels.

In front of me, perhaps a couple of hundred yards away, a group of three Africans came into sight around the side of a big antheap. I whistled the dogs close in to my skirts and let the gun swing in my hand, and advanced, waiting for them to move aside, off the path, in respect for my passing. But they came on steadily, and the dogs looked up at me for the command to chase. I was angry. It was "cheek"[9] for a native not to stand off a path, the moment he caught sight of you.

In front walked an old man, stooping his weight on to a stick, his hair grizzled white, a dark red blanket slung over his shoulders like a cloak. Behind him came two young men, carrying bundles of pots, assegais,[1] hatchets.

The group was not a usual one. They were not natives seeking work. These had an air of dignity, of quietly following their own purpose. It was the dignity that checked my tongue. I walked quietly on, talking softly to the growling dogs, till I was ten paces away. Then the old man stopped, drawing his blanket close.

"Morning, Nkosikaas," he said, using the customary greeting for any time of the day.

"Good morning," I said. "Where are you going?" My voice was a little truculent.

The old man spoke in his own language, then one of the young men stepped forward politely and said in careful English: "My Chief travels to see his brothers beyond the river."

A Chief! I thought, understanding the pride that made the old man stand before me like an equal—more than an equal, for he showed courtesy, and I showed none.

The old man spoke again, wearing dignity like an inherited garment, still standing ten paces off, flanked by his entourage, not looking at me (that would have been rude) but directing his eyes somewhere over my head at the trees.

"You are the little Nkosikaas from the farm of Baas Jordan?"

"That's right," I said.

"Perhaps your father does not remember," said the interpreter for the old man, "but there was an affair with some goats. I remember seeing you when you were . . ." The young man held his hand at knee level and smiled.

We all smiled.

"What is your name?" I asked.

"This is Chief Mshlanga," said the young man.

"I will tell my father that I met you," I said.

The old man said: "My greetings to your father, little Nkosikaas."

"Good morning," I said politely, finding the politeness difficult, from lack of use.

"Morning, little Nkosikaas," said the old man, and stood aside to let me pass.

9. Impudence. 1. Spears.

I went by, my gun hanging awkwardly, the dogs sniffing and growling, cheated of their favourite game of chasing natives like animals.

Not long afterwards I read in an old explorer's book the phrase: "Chief Mshlanga's country." It went like this: "Our destination was Chief Mshlanga's country, to the north of the river; and it was our desire to ask his permission to prospect for gold in his territory."

The phrase "ask his permission" was so extraordinary to a white child, brought up to consider all natives as things to use, that it revived those questions, which could not be suppressed: they fermented slowly in my mind.

On another occasion one of those old prospectors who still move over Africa looking for neglected reefs, with their hammers and tents, and pans for sifting gold from crushed rock, came to the farm and, in talking of the old days, used that phrase again: "This was the Old Chief's country," he said. "It stretched from those mountains over there way back to the river, hundreds of miles of country." That was his name for our district: "The Old Chief's Country"; he did not use our name for it—a new phrase which held no implication of usurped ownership.

As I read more books about the time when this part of Africa was opened up, not much more than fifty years before, I found Old Chief Mshlanga had been a famous man, known to all the explorers and prospectors. But then he had been young; or maybe it was his father or uncle they spoke of—I never found out.

During that year I met him several times in the part of the farm that was traversed by natives moving over the country. I learned that the path up the side of the big red field where the birds sang was the recognized highway for migrants. Perhaps I even haunted it in the hope of meeting him: being greeted by him, the exchange of courtesies, seemed to answer the questions that troubled me.

Soon I carried a gun in a different spirit; I used it for shooting food and not to give me confidence. And now the dogs learned better manners. When I saw a native approaching, we offered and took greetings; and slowly that other landscape in my mind faded, and my feet struck directly on the African soil, and I saw the shapes of tree and hill clearly, and the black people moved back, as it were, out of my life: it was as if I stood aside to watch a slow intimate dance of landscape and men, a very old dance, whose steps I could not learn.

But I thought: this is my heritage, too; I was bred here; it is my country as well as the black man's country; and there is plenty of room for all of us, without elbowing each other off the pavements and roads.

It seemed it was only necessary to let free that respect I felt when I was talking with old Chief Mshlanga, to let both black and white people meet gently, with tolerance for each other's differences: it seemed quite easy.

Then, one day, something new happened. Working in our house as servants were always three natives: cook, houseboy, garden boy. They used to change as the farm natives changed: staying for a few months, then moving on to a new job, or back home to their kraals.[2] They were thought of as "good" or "bad" natives; which meant: how did they behave as servants? Were they lazy, efficient, obedient, or disrespectful? If the family felt good-humoured, the phrase

2. Native villages: collections of huts surrounding a central space.

was: "What can you expect from raw black savages?" If we were angry, we said: "These damned niggers, we would be much better off without them."

One day, a white policeman was on his rounds of the district, and he said laughingly: "Did you know you have an important man in your kitchen?"

"What!" exclaimed my mother sharply. "What do you mean?"

"A Chief's son." The policeman seemed amused. "He'll boss the tribe when the old man dies."

"He'd better not put on a Chief's son act with me," said my mother.

When the policeman left, we looked with different eyes at our cook: he was a good worker, but he drank too much at week-ends—that was how we knew him.

He was a tall youth, with very black skin, like black polished metal, his tightly growing black hair parted white man's fashion at one side, with a metal comb from the store stuck into it; very polite, very distant, very quick to obey an order. Now that it had been pointed out, we said: "Of course, you can see. Blood always tells."

My mother became strict with him now she knew about his birth and prospects. Sometimes, when she lost her temper, she would say: "You aren't the Chief yet, you know." And he would answer her very quietly, his eyes on the ground: "Yes, Nkosikaas."

One afternoon he asked for a whole day off, instead of the customary half-day, to go home next Sunday.

"How can you go home in one day?"

"It will take me half an hour on my bicycle," he explained.

I watched the direction he took; and the next day I went off to look for this kraal; I understood he must be Chief Mshlanga's successor: there was no other kraal near enough our farm.

Beyond our boundaries on that side the country was new to me. I followed unfamiliar paths past *kopjes* that till now had been part of the jagged horizon, hazed with distance. This was Government land, which had never been cultivated by white men; at first I could not understand why it was that it appeared, in merely crossing the boundary, I had entered a completely fresh type of landscape. It was a wide green valley, where a small river sparkled, and vivid water-birds darted over the rushes. The grass was thick and soft to my calves, the trees stood tall and shapely.

I was used to our farm, whose hundreds of acres of harsh eroded soil bore trees that had been cut for the mine furnaces and had grown thin and twisted, where the cattle had dragged the grass flat, leaving innumerable criss-crossing trails that deepened each season into gullies, under the force of the rains.

This country had been left untouched, save for prospectors whose picks had struck a few sparks from the surface of the rocks as they wandered by; and for migrant natives whose passing had left, perhaps, a charred patch on the trunk of a tree where their evening fire had nestled.

It was very silent: a hot morning with pigeons cooing throatily, the midday shadows lying dense and thick with clear yellow spaces of sunlight between and in all that wide green park-like valley, not a human soul but myself.

I was listening to the quick regular tapping of a woodpecker when slowly a chill feeling seemed to grow up from the small of my back to my shoulders, in a constricting spasm like a shudder, and at the roots of my hair a tingling sensation began and ran down over the surface of my flesh, leaving me goose-fleshed and cold, though I was damp with sweat. Fever? I thought; then uneasily, turned to look over my shoulder; and realized suddenly that this was fear. It was extraordinary, even humiliating. It was a new fear. For all the years I had walked by myself over this country I had never known a moment's uneasiness; in the beginning because I had been supported by a gun and the dogs, then because I had learnt an easy friendliness for the Africans I might encounter.

I had read of this feeling, how the bigness and silence of Africa, under the ancient sun, grows dense and takes shape in the mind, till even the birds seem to call menacingly, and a deadly spirit comes out of the trees and the rocks. You move warily, as if your very passing disturbs something old and evil, something dark and big and angry that might suddenly rear and strike from behind. You look at groves of entwined trees, and picture the animals that might be lurking there; you look at the river running slowly, dropping from level to level through the vlei, spreading into pools where at night the bucks come to drink, and the crocodiles rise and drag them by their soft noses into underwater caves. Fear possessed me. I found I was turning round and round, because of that shapeless menace behind me that might reach out and take me; I kept glancing at the files of *kopjes* which, seen from a different angle, seemed to change with every step so that even known landmarks, like a big mountain that had sentinelled my world since I first became conscious of it, showed an unfamiliar sunlit valley among its foothills. I did not know where I was. I was lost. Panic seized me. I found I was spinning round and round, staring anxiously at this tree and that, peering up at the sun which appeared to have moved into an eastern slant, shedding the sad yellow light of sunset. Hours must have passed! I looked at my watch and found that this state of meaningless terror had lasted perhaps ten minutes.

The point was that it was meaningless. I was not ten miles from home: I had only to take my way back along the valley to find myself at the fence; away among the foothills of the *kopjes* gleamed the roof of a neighbour's house, and a couple of hours' walking would reach it. This was the sort of fear that contracts the flesh of a dog at night and sets him howling at the full moon. It had nothing to do with what I thought or felt; and I was more disturbed by the fact that I could become its victim than of the physical sensation itself: I walked steadily on, quietened, in a divided mind, watching my own pricking nerves and apprehensive glances from side to side with a disgusted amusement. Deliberately I set myself to think of this village I was seeking, and what I should do when I entered it—if I could find it, which was doubtful, since I was walking aimlessly and it might be anywhere in the hundreds of thousands of acres of bush that stretched about me. With my mind on that village, I realized that a new sensation was added to the fear: loneliness. Now such a terror of isolation invaded me that I could hardly walk; and if it were not that I came over the crest of a small rise and saw a village below me, I should have turned and gone home. It was a cluster of thatched huts in a clearing among trees. There were neat patches of mealies and pumpkins and millet, and cattle grazed under some trees at a distance. Fowls scratched among the huts, dogs lay sleeping on the grass, and goats friezed a *kopje* that jutted up beyond a tributary of the river lying like an enclosing arm around the village.

As I came close I saw the huts were lovingly decorated with patterns of yellow and red and ochre mud on the walls; and the thatch was tied in place with plaits of straw.

This was not at all like our farm compound, a dirty and neglected place, a temporary home for migrants who had no roots in it.

And now I did not know what to do next. I called a small black boy, who was sitting on a lot playing a stringed gourd, quite naked except for the strings of blue beads round his neck, and said: "Tell the Chief I am here." The child stuck his thumb in his mouth and stared shyly back at me.

For minutes I shifted my feet on the edge of what seemed a deserted village, till at last the child scuttled off, and then some women came. They were draped in bright cloths, with brass glinting in their ears and on their arms. They also stared, silently; then turned to chatter among themselves.

I said again: "Can I see Chief Mshlanga?" I saw they caught the name; they did not understand what I wanted. I did not understand myself.

At last I walked through them and came past the huts and saw a clearing under a big shady tree, where a dozen old men sat crosslegged on the ground, talking. Chief Mshlanga was leaning back against the tree, holding a gourd in his hand, from which he had been drinking. When he saw me, not a muscle of his face moved, and I could see he was not pleased: perhaps he was afflicted with my own shyness, due to being unable to find the right forms of courtesy for the occasion. To meet me, on our own farm, was one thing; but I should not have come here. What had I expected? I could not join them socially: the thing was unheard of. Bad enough that I, a white girl, should be walking the veld alone as a white man might: and in this part of the bush where only Government officials had the right to move.

Again I stood, smiling foolishly, while behind me stood the groups of brightly clad, chattering women, their faces alert with curiosity and interest, and in front of me sat the old men, with old lined faces, their eyes guarded, aloof. It was a village of ancients and children and women. Even the two young men who kneeled beside the Chief were not those I had seen with him previously: the young men were all away working on the white men's farms and mines, and the Chief must depend on relatives who were temporarily on holiday for his attendants.

"The small white Nkosikaas is far from home," remarked the old man at last.

"Yes," I agreed, "it is far." I wanted to say: "I have come to pay you a friendly visit, Chief Mshlanga." I could not say it. I might now be feeling an urgent helpless desire to get to know these men and women as people, to be accepted by them as a friend, but the truth was I had set out in a spirit of curiosity: I had wanted to see the village that one day our cook, the reserved and obedient young man who got drunk on Sundays, would one day rule over.

"The child of Nkosi Jordan is welcome," said Chief Mshlanga.

"Thank you," I said, and could think of nothing more to say. There was a silence, while the flies rose and began to buzz around my head; and the wind shook a little in the thick green tree that spread its branches over the old men.

"Good morning," I said at last. "I have to return now to my home."

"Morning, little Nkosikaas," said Chief Mshlanga.

I walked away from the indifferent village, over the rise past the staring amber-eyed goats, down through the tall stately trees into the great rich green valley where the river meandered and the pigeons cooed tales of plenty and the woodpecker tapped softly.

The fear had gone; the loneliness had set into stiff-necked stoicism; there was now a queer hostility in the landscape, a cold, hard, sullen indomitability that walked with me, as strong as a wall, as intangible as smoke; it seemed to say to me: you walk here as a destroyer. I went slowly homewards, with an empty heart: I had learned that if one cannot call a country to heel like a dog, neither can one dismiss the past with a smile in an easy gush of feeling, saying: I could not help it, I am also a victim.

I only saw Chief Mshlanga once again.

One night my father's big red land was trampled down by small sharp hooves, and it was discovered that the culprits were goats from Chief Mshalanga's kraal. This had happened once before, years ago.

My father confiscated all the goats. Then he sent a message to the old Chief that if he wanted them he would have to pay for the damage.

He arrived at our house at the time of sunset one evening, looking very old and bent now, walking stiffly under his regally-draped blanket, leaning on a big stick. My father sat himself down in his big chair below the steps of the house; the old man squatted carefully on the ground before him, flanked by his two young men.

The palaver was long and painful, because of the bad English of the young man who interpreted, and because my father could not speak dialect, but only kitchen kaffir.

From my father's point of view, at least two hundred pounds' worth of damage had been done to the crop. He knew he could not get the money from the old man. He felt he was entitled to keep the goats. As for the old Chief, he kept repeating angrily: "Twenty goats! My people cannot lose twenty goats! We are not rich, like the Nkosi Jordan, to lose twenty goats at once."

My father did not think of himself as rich, but rather as very poor. He spoke quickly and angrily in return, saying that the damage done meant a great deal to him, and that he was entitled to the goats.

At last it grew so heated that the cook, the Chief's son, was called from the kitchen to be interpreter, and now my father spoke fluently in English, and our cook translated rapidly so that the old man could understand how very angry my father was. The young man spoke without emotion, in a mechanical way, his eyes lowered, but showing how he felt his position by a hostile uncomfortable set of the shoulders.

It was now in the late sunset, the sky a welter of colours, the birds singing their last songs, and the cattle, lowing peacefully, moving past us towards their sheds for the night. It was the hour when Africa is most beautiful; and here was this pathetic, ugly scene, doing no one any good.

At last my father stated finally: "I'm not going to argue about it. I am keeping the goats."

The old Chief flashed back in his own language: "That means that my people will go hungry when the dry season comes."

"Go to the police, then," said my father, and looked triumphant.

There was, of course, no more to be said.

The old man sat silent, his head bent, his hands dangling helplessly over his withered knees. Then he rose, the young men helping him, and he stood facing my father. He spoke once again, very stiffly; and turned away and went home to his village.

"What did he say?" asked my father of the young man, who laughed uncomfortably and would not meet his eyes.

"What did he say?" insisted my father.

Our cook stood straight and silent, his brows knotted together. Then he spoke. "My father says: All this land, this land you call yours, is his land, and belongs to our people."

Having made this statement, he walked off into the bush after his father, and we did not see him again.

Our next cook was a migrant from Nyasaland, with no expectations of greatness.

Next time the policeman came on his rounds he was told this story. He remarked: "That kraal has no right to be there; it should have been moved long ago. I don't know why no one has done anything about it. I'll have a chat with the Native Commissioner next week. I'm going over for tennis on Sunday, anyway."

Some time later we heard that Chief Mshlanga and his people had been moved two hundred miles east, to a proper Native Reserve; the Government land was going to be opened up for white settlement soon.

I went to see the village again, about a year afterwards. There was nothing there. Mounds of red mud, where the huts had been, had long swathes of rotting thatch over them, veined with the red galleries of the white ants. The pumpkin vines rioted everywhere, over the bushes, up the lower branches of trees so that the great golden balls rolled underfoot and dangled overhead: it was a festival of pumpkins. The bushes were crowding up, the new grass sprang vivid green.

The settler lucky enough to be allotted the lush warm valley (if he chose to cultivate this particular section) would find, suddenly, in the middle of a mealie field, the plants were growing fifteen feet tall, the weight of the cobs dragging at the stalks, and wonder what unsuspected vein of richness he had struck.

1951

JAMES BALDWIN
1924–1987

A leading African American novelist, James Baldwin was one of the great prose stylists of the twentieth century. He is best known for his remarkable essays that, in poetic rhetoric drawing on both the classics of English literature and the tones of biblical prophecy, combine personal reflection with a wider view of social justice. An icon of the civil rights movement, Baldwin nonetheless felt considerably alienated both from black culture and from white liberal society. He lived much of his life abroad but continually affirmed his American identity as a "native son."

Baldwin grew up in his "father's house"—that is, in the Harlem home of his stepfather, David Baldwin, a preacher whom his mother married when James was two. David Baldwin, a preacher in small black churches, reacted with suspicion when a white teacher, Orilla Miller, took James to plays, including Orson Welles's all-black production of Shakespeare's *Macbeth*. (The elder Baldwin did not approve of theater.) David Baldwin's mother, who had been born in slavery, lived with the family in Harlem. Although his acquaintance with secular literature strained his relationship to the church, James remained affiliated with various churches over the years and preached sermons as a young man.

As the United States mobilized for the Second World War, Baldwin found a job in a defense plant in New Jersey— and hated both the job and the place, where he had his first serious experiences of racial discrimination. When his stepfather died, in 1943, he was expected to move back home and take care of his mother and siblings. Instead, Baldwin moved to Greenwich Village,

in lower Manhattan, to pursue his career as a writer. Here he met older writers, including Richard Wright. "Writing was an act of love," Baldwin would later say, "an attempt to be loved." While living in the Village, he became aware of his homosexuality.

After the war Baldwin left New York for Paris, following in the paths of a generation of famous American writers before him. Of this self-imposed expatriation, he later wrote, "In my own case, I think my exile saved my life." In the years that followed, Baldwin wrote and then suffered writer's block; he was arrested on a false charge of theft; he tried to commit suicide; and he succeeded in finishing *Go Tell It on the Mountain* (1953), his first published novel, an autobiographical story of a deeply religious young man who ultimately leaves the church. For the rest of his life, Baldwin divided his time between New York, Paris, Switzerland, and Turkey. Amid constant interpersonal turmoil (and additional suicide attempts), his literary career was now on the rise: in 1955, *Notes of a Native Son*, a collection of essays that cemented his public voice, was released; a year later, *Giovanni's Room*, a novel about a white American in Paris struggling with his homosexuality, appeared. Despite difficulties in finding a publisher, the work increased Baldwin's fame. Encouraged by the rise of the civil rights movement, he renewed his political engagement; with *The Fire Next Time* (1963), in which he commented on race and American history, he became an international figure.

Like other leading African Americans of the civil rights era, Baldwin was unhappy with the radicalization of movements with which he had been associated. Although he had known the Black Nationalist leader Malcolm X and met Elijah Muhammad of the Nation of Islam, their successors in such groups as the Black Panthers tended to think of Baldwin as a darling of white liberals who was more concerned with cosmopolitan life in Paris than with the plight of ordinary African Americans. Baldwin's generally optimistic, liberal views led him to exhort his readers to work together for change: "If we—and now I mean the relatively conscious whites and the relatively conscious blacks, who must, like lovers, insist on, or create, the consciousness of the others—do not falter in our duty now, we may be able, handful that we are, to end the racial nightmare, and achieve our country, and change the history of the world." In his later years, Baldwin's primary home was a farmhouse in Saint-Paul-de-Vence, a town in southern France, but he continued traveling in the United States, writing essays, and teaching in several colleges. He died in Saint-Paul in 1987.

Baldwin begins "Notes of a Native Son," the essay printed here, with the conjunction of two profound events in his personal life: the death of his father (actually his stepfather) and the birth of his father's youngest child. These personal rites of passage are, however, quickly placed in the context of broader social and political events—namely, the race riots that shook Detroit in June 1943. The protests, in which nearly three dozen people died, were a shocking episode in a series of conflicts between blacks and whites in the wake of the Great Migration between the two world wars. African Americans were leaving the segregated South in search of greater freedom, and work, in northern industrial cities, where they were not always welcomed. Baldwin's father had likewise moved to New York from New Orleans not long before the boy's birth, and Baldwin describes the racial tensions of wartime New York and New Jersey. The juxtaposition of experiences of great personal significance with momentous public events becomes a central issue in the essay.

While it offers a profound meditation on a relationship between a son and a father who was both physically and mentally ill, the essay explains how both men's encounters with racial discrimination contributed to the conflicts in their private lives. Baldwin represents the relationship, and his evolving consciousness of his place in the family and in American society, with subtlety and nuance. Baldwin's style—direct but meditative, confessional but aware of the broader context—gives this classic work its status as one of the most memorable personal meditations published in the twentieth century.

Notes of a Native Son[1]

On the 29th of July, in 1943, my father died. On the same day, a few hours later, his last child was born. Over a month before this, while all our energies were concentrated in waiting for these events, there had been, in Detroit, one of the bloodiest race riots of the century.[2] A few hours after my father's funeral, while he lay in state in the undertaker's chapel, a race riot broke out in Harlem. On the morning of the 3rd of August, we drove my father to the graveyard through a wilderness of smashed plate glass.

1. The title alludes to Richard Wright's novel *Native Son* (1940).
2. Three days of rioting in June 1943, in which 25 African Americans and 9 whites were killed.

The day of my father's funeral had also been my nineteenth birthday. As we drove him to the graveyard, the spoils of injustice, anarchy, discontent, and hatred were all around us. It seemed to me that God himself had devised, to mark my father's end, the most sustained and brutally dissonant of codas. And it seemed to me, too, that the violence which rose all about us as my father left the world had been devised as a corrective for the pride of his eldest son. I had declined to believe in that apocalypse which had been central to my father's vision; very well, life seemed to be saying, here is something that will certainly pass for an apocalypse until the real thing comes along. I had inclined to be contemptuous of my father for the conditions of his life, for the conditions of our lives. When his life had ended I began to wonder about that life and also, in a new way, to be apprehensive about my own.

I had not known my father very well. We had got on badly, partly because we shared, in our different fashions, the vice of stubborn pride. When he was dead I realized that I had hardly ever spoken to him. When he had been dead a long time I began to wish I had. It seems to be typical of life in America, where opportunities, real and fancied, are thicker than anywhere else on the globe, that the second generation has no time to talk to the first. No one, including my father, seems to have known exactly how old he was, but his mother had been born during slavery. He was of the first generation of free men. He, along with thousands of other Negroes, came North after 1919 and I was part of that generation which had never seen the landscape of what Negroes sometimes call the Old Country.[3]

He had been born in New Orleans and had been a quite young man there during the time that Louis Armstrong,[4] a boy, was running errands for the dives and honky-tonks of what was always presented to me as one of the most wicked of cities—to this day, whenever I think of New Orleans, I also helplessly think of Sodom and Gomorrah.[5] My father never mentioned Louis Armstrong, except to forbid us to play his records; but there was a picture of him on our wall for a long time. One of my father's strong-willed female relatives had placed it there and forbade my father to take it down. He never did, but he eventually maneuvered her out of the house and when, some years later, she was in trouble and near death, he refused to do anything to help her.

He was, I think, very handsome. I gather this from photographs and from my own memories of him, dressed in his Sunday best and on his way to preach a sermon somewhere, when I was little. Handsome, proud, and ingrown, "like a toe-nail," somebody said. But he looked to me, as I grew older, like pictures I had seen of African tribal chieftains: he really should have been naked, with war-paint on and barbaric mementos, standing among spears. He could be chilling in the pulpit and indescribably cruel in his personal life and he was certainly the most bitter man I have ever met; yet it must be said that there was something else in him, buried in him, which lent him his tremendous power and, even, a rather crushing charm. It had something to do with his blackness,

3. The South. Over a million African Americans left the South for the Midwest and the Northeast after the First World War (1914–18).

4. Armstrong (1901–1971), jazz trumpeter, cornetist, and singer.

5. Biblical cities destroyed by God for their wickedness. See Genesis 18–19.

I think—he was very black—with his blackness and his beauty, and with the fact that he knew that he was black but did not know that he was beautiful. He claimed to be proud of his blackness but it had also been the cause of much humiliation and it had fixed bleak boundaries to his life. He was not a young man when we were growing up and he had already suffered many kinds of ruin; in his outrageously demanding and protective way he loved his children, who were black like him and menaced, like him; and all these things sometimes showed in his face when he tried, never to my knowledge with any success, to establish contact with any of us. When he took one of his children on his knee to play, the child always became fretful and began to cry; when he tried to help one of us with our homework the absolutely unabating tension which emanated from him caused our minds and our tongues to become paralyzed, so that he, scarcely knowing why, flew into a rage and the child, not knowing why, was punished. If it ever entered his head to bring a surprise home for his children, it was, almost unfailingly, the wrong surprise and even the big watermelons he often brought home on his back in the summertime led to the most appalling scenes. I do not remember, in all those years, that one of his children was ever glad to see him come home. From what I was able to gather of his early life, it seemed that this inability to establish contact with other people had always marked him and had been one of the things which had driven him out of New Orleans. There was something in him, therefore, groping and tentative, which was never expressed and which was buried with him. One saw it most clearly when he was facing new people and hoping to impress them. But he never did, not for long. We went from church to smaller and more improbable church, he found himself in less and less demand as a minister, and by the time he died none of his friends had come to see him for a long time. He had lived and died in an intolerable bitterness of spirit and it frightened me, as we drove him to the graveyard through those unquiet, ruined streets, to see how powerful and overflowing this bitterness could be and to realize that this bitterness now was mine.

When he died I had been away from home for a little over a year. In that year I had had time to become aware of the meaning of all my father's bitter warnings, had discovered the secret of his proudly pursed lips and rigid carriage: I had discovered the weight of white people in the world. I saw that this had been for my ancestors and now would be for me an awful thing to live with and that the bitterness which had helped to kill my father could also kill me.

He had been ill a long time—in the mind, as we now realized, reliving instances of his fantastic intransigence in the new light of his affliction and endeavoring to feel a sorrow for him which never, quite, came true. We had not known that he was being eaten up by paranoia, and the discovery that his cruelty, to our bodies and our minds, had been one of the symptoms of his illness was not, then, enough to enable us to forgive him. The younger children felt, quite simply, relief that he would not be coming home anymore. My mother's observation that it was he, after all, who had kept them alive all these years meant nothing because the problems of keeping children alive are not real for children. The older children felt, with my father gone, that they could invite their friends to the house without fear that their friends would be insulted or, as had sometimes happened with me, being told that their friends were in league with the devil and intended to rob our family of everything we owned. (I didn't fail to wonder, and it made me hate him, what on earth we owned that anybody else would want.)

His illness was beyond all hope of healing before anyone realized that he was ill. He had always been so strange and had lived, like a prophet, in such unimaginably close communion with the Lord that his long silences which were punctuated by moans and hallelujahs and snatches of old songs while he sat at the living-room window never seemed odd to us. It was not until he refused to eat because, he said, his family was trying to poison him that my mother was forced to accept as a fact what had, until then, been only an unwilling suspicion. When he was committed, it was discovered that he had tuberculosis and, as it turned out, the disease of his mind allowed the disease of his body to destroy him. For the doctors could not force him to eat, either, and, though he was fed intravenously, it was clear from the beginning that there was no hope for him.

In my mind's eye I could see him, sitting at the window, locked up in his terrors; hating and fearing every living soul including his children who had betrayed him, too, by reaching towards the world which had despised him. There were nine of us. I began to wonder what it could have felt like for such a man to have had nine children whom he could barely feed. He used to make little jokes about our poverty, which never, of course, seemed very funny to us; they could not have seemed very funny to him, either, or else our all too feeble response to them would never have caused such rages. He spent great energy and achieved, to our chagrin, no small amount of success in keeping us away from the people who surrounded us, people who had all-night rent parties[6] to which we listened when we should have been sleeping, people who cursed and drank and flashed razor blades on Lenox Avenue.[7] He could not understand why, if they had so much energy to spare, they could not use it to make their lives better. He treated almost everybody on our block with a most uncharitable asperity and neither they, nor, of course, their children were slow to reciprocate.

The only white people who came to our house were welfare workers and bill collectors. It was almost always my mother who dealt with them, for my father's temper, which was at the mercy of his pride, was never to be trusted. It was clear that he felt their very presence in his home to be a violation: this was conveyed by his carriage, almost ludicrously stiff, and by his voice, harsh and vindictively polite. When I was around nine or ten I wrote a play which was directed by a young, white schoolteacher, a woman, who then took an interest in me, and gave me books to read and, in order to corroborate my theatrical bent, decided to take me to see what she somewhat tactlessly referred to as "real" plays. Theater-going was forbidden in our house, but, with the really cruel intuitiveness of a child, I suspected that the color of this woman's skin would carry the day for me. When, at school, she suggested taking me to the theater, I did not, as I might have done if she had been a Negro, find a way of discouraging her, but agreed that she should pick me up at my house one evening. I then, very cleverly, left all the rest to my mother, who suggested to my

6. Parties at which money was collected from the guests to help cover tenants' rent; normally, the parties included hired bands; during Prohibition (1920–33), bootlegged alcohol was served.
7. Major north–south thoroughfare in Harlem.

father, as I knew she would, that it would not be very nice to let such a kind woman make the trip for nothing. Also, since it was a schoolteacher, I imagine that my mother countered the idea of sin with the idea of "education," which word, even with my father, carried a kind of bitter weight.

Before the teacher came my father took me aside to ask *why* she was coming, what *interest* she could possibly have in our house, in a boy like me. I said I didn't know but I, too, suggested that it had something to do with education. And I understood that my father was waiting for me to say something—I didn't quite know what; perhaps that I wanted his protection against this teacher and her "education." I said none of these things and the teacher came and we went out. It was clear, during the brief interview in our living room, that my father was agreeing very much against his will and that he would have refused permission if he had dared. The fact that he did not dare caused me to despise him: I had no way of knowing that he was facing in that living room a wholly unprecedented and frightening situation.

Later, when my father had been laid off from his job, this woman became very important to us. She was really a very sweet and generous woman and went to a great deal of trouble to be of help to us, particularly during one awful winter. My mother called her by the highest name she knew: she said she was a "christian." My father could scarcely disagree but during the four or five years of our relatively close association he never trusted her and was always trying to surprise in her open, Midwestern face the genuine, cunningly hidden, and hideous motivation. In later years, particularly when it began to be clear that this "education" of mine was going to lead me to perdition, he became more explicit and warned me that my white friends in high school were not really my friends and that I would see, when I was older, how white people would do anything to keep a Negro down. Some of them could be nice, he admitted, but none of them were to be trusted and most of them were not even nice. The best thing was to have as little to do with them as possible. I did not feel this way and I was certain, in my innocence, that I never would.

But the year which preceded my father's death had made a great change in my life. I had been living in New Jersey, working in defense plants, working and living among southerners, white and black. I knew about the south, of course, and about how southerners treated Negroes and how they expected them to behave, but it had never entered my mind that anyone would look at me and expect *me* to behave that way. I learned in New Jersey that to be a Negro meant, precisely, that one was never looked at but was simply at the mercy of the reflexes the color of one's skin caused in other people. I acted in New Jersey as I had always acted, that is as though I thought a great deal of myself—I had to *act* that way— with results that were, simply, unbelievable. I had scarcely arrived before I had earned the enmity, which was extraordinarily ingenious, of all my superiors and nearly all my co-workers. In the beginning, to make matters worse, I simply did not know what was happening. I did not know what I had done, and I shortly began to wonder what *anyone* could possibly do, to bring about such unanimous, active, and unbearably vocal hostility. I knew about jim-crow[8] but I had never experienced it. I went to the same self-service restaurant three times and

8. System of laws and customs enforcing segregation of blacks and whites in southern states; some aspects of Jim Crow were also in force in northern states, including New Jersey.

stood with all the Princeton boys before the counter, waiting for a hamburger and coffee; it was always an extraordinarily long time before anything was set before me; but it was not until the fourth visit that I learned that, in fact, nothing had ever been set before me: I had simply picked something up. Negroes were not served there, I was told, and they had been waiting for me to realize that I was always the only Negro present. Once I was told this, I determined to go there all the time. But now they were ready for me and, though some dreadful scenes were subsequently enacted in that restaurant, I never ate there again.

It was the same story all over New Jersey, in bars, bowling alleys, diners, places to live. I was always being forced to leave, silently, or with mutual imprecations. I very shortly became notorious and children giggled behind me when I passed and their elders whispered or shouted—they really believed that I was mad. And it did begin to work on my mind, of course; I began to be afraid to go anywhere and to compensate for this I went places to which I really should not have gone and where, God knows, I had no desire to be. My reputation in town naturally enhanced my reputation at work and my working day became one long series of acrobatics designed to keep me out of trouble. I cannot say that these acrobatics succeeded. It began to seem that the machinery of the organization I worked for was turning over, day and night, with but one aim: to eject me. I was fired once, and contrived, with the aid of a friend from New York, to get back on the payroll; was fired again, and bounced back again. It took a while to fire me for the third time, but the third time took. There were no loopholes anywhere. There was not even any way of getting back inside the gates.

That year in New Jersey lives in my mind as though it were the year during which, having an unsuspected predilection for it, I first contracted some dread, chronic disease, the unfailing symptom of which is a kind of blind fever, a pounding in the skull and fire in the bowels. Once this disease is contracted, one can never be really carefree again, for the fever, without an instant's warning, can recur at any moment. It can wreck more important things than race relations. There is not a Negro alive who does not have this rage in his blood—one has the choice, merely, of living with it consciously or surrendering to it. As for me, this fever has recurred in me, and does, and will until the day I die.

My last night in New Jersey, a white friend from New York took me to the nearest big town, Trenton, to go to the movies and have a few drinks. As it turned out, he also saved me from, at the very least, a violent whipping. Almost every detail of that night stands out very clearly in my memory. I even remember the name of the movie we saw because its title impressed me as being so patly ironical. It was a movie about the German occupation of France, starring Maureen O'Hara and Charles Laughton and called *This Land Is Mine*. I remember the name of the diner we walked into when the movie ended: it was the "American Diner." When we walked in the counterman asked what we wanted and I remember answering with the casual sharpness which had become my habit: "We want a hamburger and a cup of coffee, what do you think we want?" I do not know why, after a year of such rebuffs, I so completely failed to anticipate his answer, which was, of course, "We don't serve Negroes here." This reply failed to discompose me, at least for the moment. I made some sardonic comment about the name of the diner and we walked out into the streets.

This was the time of what was called the "brown-out," when the lights in all American cities were very dim. When we re-entered the streets something happened to me which had the force of an optical illusion, or a nightmare. The streets were very crowded and I was facing north. People were moving in every direction but it seemed to me, in that instant, that all of the people I could see, and many more than that, were moving toward me, against me, and that everyone was white. I remember how their faces gleamed. And I felt, like a physical sensation, a *click* at the nape of my neck as though some interior string connecting my head to my body had been cut. I began to walk. I heard my friend call after me, but I ignored him. Heaven only knows what was going on in his mind, but he had the good sense not to touch me—I don't know what would have happened if he had—and to keep me in sight. I don't know what was going on in my mind, either; I certainly had no conscious plan. I wanted to do something to crush these white faces, which were crushing me. I walked for perhaps a block or two until I came to an enormous, glittering, and fashionable restaurant in which I knew not even the intercession of the Virgin would cause me to be served. I pushed through the doors and took the first vacant seat I saw, at a table for two, and waited.

I do not know how long I waited and I rather wonder, until today, what I could possibly have looked like. Whatever I looked like, I frightened the waitress who shortly appeared, and the moment she appeared all of my fury flowed towards her. I hated her for her white face, and for her great, astounded, frightened eyes. I felt that if she found a black man so frightening I would make her fright worth-while.

She did not ask me what I wanted, but repeated, as though she had learned it somewhere, "We don't serve Negroes here." She did not say it with the blunt, derisive hostility to which I had grown so accustomed, but, rather, with a note of apology in her voice, and fear. This made me colder and more murderous than ever. I felt I had to do something with my hands. I wanted her to come close enough for me to get her neck between my hands.

So I pretended not to have understood her, hoping to draw her closer. And she did step a very short step closer, with her pencil poised incongruously over her pad, and repeated the formula: ". . . don't serve Negroes here."

Somehow, with the repetition of that phrase, which was already ringing in my head like a thousand bells of a nightmare, I realized that she would never come any closer and that I would have to strike from a distance. There was nothing on the table but an ordinary watermug half full of water, and I picked this up and hurled it with all my strength at her. She ducked and it missed her and shattered against the mirror behind the bar. And, with that sound, my frozen blood abruptly thawed, I returned from wherever I had been, I *saw*, for the first time, the restaurant, the people with their mouths open, already, as it seemed to me, rising as one man, and I realized what I had done, and where I was, and I was frightened. I rose and began running for the door. A round, potbellied man grabbed me by the nape of the neck just as I reached the doors and began to beat me about the face. I kicked him and got loose and ran into the streets. My friend whispered, "*Run!*" and I ran.

My friend stayed outside the restaurant long enough to misdirect my pursuers and the police, who arrived, he told me, at once. I do not know what I said to him when he came to my room that night. I could not have said much. I felt, in the oddest, most awful way, that I had somehow betrayed him. I lived it over and over and over again, the way one relives an automobile accident after it has happened and one finds oneself alone and safe. I could not get over two facts, both equally difficult for the imagination to grasp, and one was that I could have been murdered. But the other was that I had been ready to commit murder. I saw nothing very clearly but I did see this: that my life, my *real* life, was in danger, and not from anything other people might do but from the hatred I carried in my own heart.

II

I had returned home around the second week in June—in great haste because it seemed that my father's death and my mother's confinement were both but a matter of hours. In the case of my mother, it soon became clear that she had simply made a miscalculation. This had always been her tendency and I don't believe that a single one of us arrived in the world, or has since arrived anywhere else, on time. But none of us dawdled so intolerably about the business of being born as did my baby sister. We sometimes amused ourselves, during those endless, stifling weeks, by picturing the baby sitting within in the safe, warm dark, bitterly regretting the necessity of becoming a part of our chaos and stubbornly putting it off as long as possible. I understood her perfectly and congratulated her on showing such good sense so soon. Death, however, sat as purposefully at my father's bedside as life stirred within my mother's womb and it was harder to understand why he so lingered in that long shadow. It seemed that he had bent, and for a long time, too, all of his energies towards dying. Now death was ready for him but my father held back.

All of Harlem, indeed, seemed to be infected by waiting. I had never before known it to be so violently still. Racial tensions throughout this country were exacerbated during the early years of the war,[9] partly because the labor market brought together hundreds of thousands of ill-prepared people and partly because Negro soldiers, regardless of where they were born, received their military training in the south. What happened in defense plants and army camps had repercussions, naturally, in every Negro ghetto. The situation in Harlem had grown bad enough for clergymen, policemen, educators, politicians, and social workers to assert in one breath that there was no "crime wave" and to offer, in the very next breath, suggestions as to how to combat it. These suggestions always seemed to involve playgrounds, despite the fact that racial skirmishes were occurring in the playgrounds, too. Playground or not, crime wave or not, the Harlem police force had been augmented in March, and the unrest grew—perhaps, in fact, partly as a result of the ghetto's instinctive hatred of policemen. Perhaps the most revealing news item, out of the steady parade of reports of muggings, stabbings, shootings, assaults, gang wars, and accusations of police brutality, is the item concerning six Negro girls who set upon a white girl in the subway because, as they all too accurately put it, she was stepping on their toes. Indeed she was, all over the nation.

I had never before been so aware of policemen, on foot, on horseback, on corners, everywhere, always two by two. Nor had I ever been so aware of small

9. The Second World War (1939–45), which the United States entered on December 8, 1941.

knots of people. They were on stoops and on corners and in doorways, and what was striking about them, I think, was that they did not seem to be talking. Never, when I passed these groups, did the usual sound of a curse or a laugh ring out and neither did there seem to be any hum of gossip. There was certainly, on the other hand, occurring between them communication extraordinarily intense. Another thing that was striking was the unexpected diversity of the people who made up these groups. Usually, for example, one would see a group of sharpies standing on the street corner, jiving the passing chicks;[1] or a group of older men, usually, for some reason, in the vicinity of a barber shop, discussing baseball scores, or the numbers,[2] or making rather chilling observations about women they had known. Women, in a general way, tended to be seen less often together—unless they were church women, or very young girls, or prostitutes met together for an unprofessional instant. But that summer I saw the strangest combinations: large, respectable, churchly matrons standing on the stoops or the corners with their hair tied up, together with a girl in sleazy satin whose face bore the marks of gin and the razor, or heavy-set, abrupt, no-nonsense older men, in company with the most disreputable and fanatical "race" men,[3] or these same "race" men with the sharpies, or these sharpies with the churchly women. Seventh Day Adventists and Methodists and Spiritualists seemed to be hobnobbing with Holyrollers[4] and they were all, alike, entangled with the most flagrant disbelievers; something heavy in their stance seemed to indicate that they had all, incredibly, seen a common vision, and on each face there seemed to be the same strange, bitter shadow.

The churchly women and the matter-of-fact, no-nonsense men had children in the Army. The sleazy girls they talked to had lovers there, the sharpies and the "race" men had friends and brothers there. It would have demanded an unquestioning patriotism, happily as uncommon in this country as it is undesirable, for these people not to have been disturbed by the bitter letters they received, by the newspaper stories they read, not to have been enraged by the posters, then to be found all over New York, which described the Japanese as "yellow-bellied Japs." It was only the "race" men, to be sure, who spoke ceaselessly of being revenged—how this vengeance was to be exacted was not clear— for the indignities and dangers suffered by Negro boys in uniform; but everybody felt a directionless, hopeless bitterness, as well as that panic which can scarcely be suppressed when one knows that a human being one loves is beyond one's reach, and in danger. This helplessness and this gnawing uneasiness does something, at length, to even the toughest mind. Perhaps the best way to sum all this up is to say that the people I knew felt, mainly, a peculiar kind of relief when they knew that their boys were being shipped out of the south, to do battle overseas. It was, perhaps, like feeling that the most dangerous part of a dangerous journey had been passed and that now, even if death should come, it would come with honor and without the complicity of their countrymen. Such a death would be, in short, a fact with which one could hope to live.

It was on the 28th of July, which I believe was a Wednesday, that I visited my father for the first time during his illness and for the last time in his life. The

---

1. Talking nonsense with the girls passing by. "Sharpies": tricksters or con men.
2. An illegal lottery.
3. Men who emphasized the importance of

African American pride and mutual support.
4. Pentecostalists, who emphasized prophecy, healing, and speaking in tongues.

moment I saw him I knew why I had put off this visit so long. I had told my mother that I did not want to see him because I hated him. But this was not true. It was only that I *had* hated him and I wanted to hold on to this hatred. I did not want to look on him as a ruin: it was not a ruin I had hated. I imagine that one of the reasons people cling to their hates so stubbornly is because they sense, once hate is gone, that they will be forced to deal with pain.

We traveled out to him, his older sister and myself, to what seemed to be the very end of a very Long Island. It was hot and dusty and we wrangled, my aunt and I, all the way out, over the fact that I had recently begun to smoke and, as she said, to give myself airs. But I knew that she wrangled with me because she could not bear to face the fact of her brother's dying. Neither could I endure the reality of her despair, her unstated bafflement as to what had happened to her brother's life, and her own. So we wrangled and I smoked and from time to time she fell into a heavy reverie. Covertly, I watched her face, which was the face of an old woman; it had fallen in, the eyes were sunken and lightless; soon she would be dying, too.

In my childhood—it had not been so long ago—I had thought her beautiful. She had been quick-witted and quick-moving and very generous with all the children and each of her visits had been an event. At one time one of my brothers and myself had thought of running away to live with her. Now she could no longer produce out of her handbag some unexpected and yet familiar delight. She made me feel pity and revulsion and fear. It was awful to realize that she no longer caused me to feel affection. The closer we came to the hospital the more querulous she became and at the same time, naturally, grew more dependent on me. Between pity and guilt and fear I began to feel that there was another me trapped in my skull like a jack-in-the-box who might escape my control at any moment and fill the air with screaming.

She began to cry the moment we entered the room and she saw him lying there, all shriveled and still, like a little black monkey. The great, gleaming apparatus which fed him and would have compelled him to be still even if he had been able to move brought to mind, not beneficence, but torture; the tubes entering his arm made me think of pictures I had seen when a child, of Gulliver,[5] tied down by the pygmies on that island. My aunt wept and wept, there was a whistling sound in my father's throat; nothing was said; he could not speak. I wanted to take his hand, to say something. But I do not know what I could have said, even if he could have heard me. He was not really in that room with us, he had at last really embarked on his journey; and though my aunt told me that he said he was going to meet Jesus, I did not hear anything except that whistling in his throat. The doctor came back and we left, into that unbearable train again, and home. In the morning came the telegram saying that he was dead. Then the house was suddenly full of relatives, friends, hysteria, and confusion and I quickly left my mother and the children to the care of those impressive women, who, in Negro communities at least, automatically appear at times of bereavement armed with lotions, proverbs, and patience, *and an ability to cook.* I went downtown. By the time I returned, later the same day, my mother had been carried to the hospital and the baby had been born.

---

5. The hero of *Gulliver's Travels* (1726) by the English-Irish writer Jonathan Swift (1667–1745); Gulliver is washed ashore on Lilliput, an island inhabited by tiny people who tie him down with cords while he is sleeping.

III

For my father's funeral I had nothing black to wear and this posed a nagging problem all day long. It was one of those problems, simple, or impossible of solution, to which the mind insanely clings in order to avoid the mind's real trouble. I spent most of that day at the downtown apartment of a girl I knew, celebrating my birthday with whiskey and wondering what to wear that night. When planning a birthday celebration one naturally does not expect that it will be up against competition from a funeral and this girl had anticipated taking me out that night, for a big dinner and a night club afterwards. Sometime during the course of that long day we decided that we would go out anyway, when my father's funeral service was over. I imagine *I* decided it, since, as the funeral hour approached, it became clearer and clearer to me that I would not know what to do with myself when it was over. The girl, stifling her very lively concern as to the possible effects of the whiskey on one of my father's chief mourners, concentrated on being conciliatory and practically helpful. She found a black shirt for me somewhere and ironed it and, dressed in the darkest pants and jacket I owned, and slightly drunk, I made my way to my father's funeral.

The chapel was full, but not packed, and very quiet. There were, mainly, my father's relatives, and his children, and here and there I saw faces I had not seen since childhood, the faces of my father's one-time friends. They were very dark and solemn now, seeming somehow to suggest that they had known all along that something like this would happen. Chief among the mourners was my aunt, who had quarreled with my father all his life; by which I do not mean to suggest that her mourning was insincere or that she had not loved him. I suppose that she was one of the few people in the world who had, and their incessant quarreling proved precisely the strength of the tie that bound them. The only other person in the world, as far as I knew, whose relationship to my father rivaled my aunt's in depth was my mother, who was not there.

It seemed to me, of course, that it was a very long funeral. But it was, if anything, a rather shorter funeral than most, nor, since there were no overwhelming, uncontrollable expressions of grief, could it be called—if I dare to use the word—successful. The minister who preached my father's funeral sermon was one of the few my father had still been seeing as he neared his end. He presented to us in his sermon a man whom none of us had ever seen—a man thoughtful, patient, and forbearing, a Christian inspiration to all who knew him, and a model for his children. And no doubt the children, in their disturbed and guilty state, were almost ready to believe this; he had been remote enough to be anything and, anyway, the shock of the incontrovertible, that it was really our father lying up there in that casket, prepared the mind for anything. His sister moaned and this grief-stricken moaning was taken as corroboration. The other faces held a dark, non-committal thoughtfulness. This was not the man they had known, but they had scarcely expected to be confronted with *him*; this was, in a sense deeper than questions of fact, the man they had not known, and the man they had not known may have been the real one. The real man, whoever he had been, had suffered and now he was dead: this was all that was sure and all that mattered now. Every man in the chapel hoped that when his hour came he, too, would be eulogized, which is to say forgiven, and that all of his lapses, greeds, errors, and strayings from the truth would be invested with coherence and looked upon with charity. This was perhaps the last thing human beings could give each other and it was what they demanded, after all, of the Lord. Only the Lord saw the midnight tears, only He was present when one of His children, moaning and wringing hands, paced up and down the room. When one slapped one's child in anger the recoil in the heart reverberated through heaven and became part of the pain of the universe. And when the children were hungry and sullen and distrustful and one watched them, daily, growing wilder, and further away, and running headlong into danger, it was the Lord who knew what the charged heart endured as the strap was laid to the backside; the Lord alone who knew what one *would* have said if one had had, like the Lord, the gift of the living word. It was the Lord who knew of the impossibility every parent in that room faced: how to prepare the child for the day when the child would be despised and how to *create* in the child—by what means?—a stronger antidote to this poison than one had found for oneself. The avenues, side streets, bars, billiard halls, hospitals, police stations, and even the playgrounds of Harlem—not to mention the houses of correction, the jails, and the morgue—testified to the potency of the poison while remaining silent as to the efficacy of whatever antidote, irresistibly raising the question of whether or not such an antidote existed; raising, which was worse, the question of whether or not an antidote was desirable; perhaps poison should be fought with poison. With these several schisms in the mind and with more terrors in the heart than could be named, it was better not to judge the man who had gone down under an impossible burden. It was better to remember: *Thou knowest this man's fall; but thou knowest not his wrassling.*[6]

While the preacher talked and I watched the children—years of changing their diapers, scrubbing them, slapping them, taking them to school, and scolding them had had the perhaps inevitable result of making me love them, though I am not sure I knew this then—my mind was busily breaking out with a rash of disconnected impressions. Snatches of popular songs, indecent jokes, bits of books I had read, movie sequences, faces, voices, political issues—I thought I was going mad; all these impressions suspended, as it were, in the solution of the faint nausea produced in me by the heat and liquor. For a moment I had the impression that my alcoholic breath, inefficiently disguised with chewing gum, filled the entire chapel. Then someone began singing one of my father's favorite songs and, abruptly, I was with him, sitting on his knee, in the hot, enormous, crowded church which was the first church we attended. It was the Abyssinia Baptist Church on 138th Street.[7] We had not gone there long. With this image, a host of others came. I had forgotten, in the rage of my growing up, how proud my father had been of me when I was little. Apparently, I had had a voice and my father had liked to show me off before the members of the church. I had forgotten what he had looked like when he was pleased but now I remembered that he had always been grinning with pleasure when my solos ended. I even remembered certain expressions on his face when he teased my mother—had he loved her? I would never know. And when had it all

6. From the English author John Donne (1572–1631), *Biathanatos* (1608), a defense of suicide. "Wrassling": wrestling.

7. A famous African American church in Harlem.

begun to change? For now it seemed that he had not always been cruel. I remembered being taken for a haircut and scraping my knee on the footrest of the barber's chair and I remembered my father's face as he soothed my crying and applied the stinging iodine. Then I remembered our fights, fights which had been of the worst possible kind because my technique had been silence.

I remembered the one time in all our life together when we had really spoken to each other.

It was on a Sunday and it must have been shortly before I left home. We were walking, just the two of us, in our usual silence, to or from church. I was in high school and had been doing a lot of writing and I was, at about this time, the editor of the high school magazine. But I had also been a Young Minister and had been preaching from the pulpit. Lately, I had been taking fewer engagements and preached as rarely as possible. It was said in the church, quite truthfully, that I was "cooling off."

My father asked me abruptly, "You'd rather write than preach, wouldn't you?"

I was astonished at his question—because it was a real question. I answered, "Yes."

That was all we said. It was awful to remember that that was all we had *ever* said.

The casket now was opened and the mourners were being led up the aisle to look for the last time on the deceased. The assumption was that the family was too overcome with grief to be allowed to make this journey alone and I watched while my aunt was led to the casket and, muffled in black, and shaking, led back to her seat. I disapproved of forcing the children to look on their dead father, considering that the shock of his death, or, more truthfully, the shock of death as a reality, was already a little more than a child could bear, but my judgment in this matter had been overruled and there they were, bewildered and frightened and very small, being led, one by one, to the casket. But there is also something very gallant about children at such moments. It has something to do with their silence and gravity and with the fact that one cannot help them. Their legs, somehow, seem *exposed*, so that it is at once incredible and terribly clear that their legs are all they have to hold them up.

I had not wanted to go to the casket myself and I certainly had not wished to be led there, but there was no way of avoiding either of these forms. One of the deacons led me up and I looked on my father's face. I cannot say that it looked like him at all. His blackness had been equivocated by powder and there was no suggestion in that casket of what his power had or could have been. He was simply an old man dead, and it was hard to believe that he had ever given anyone either joy or pain. Yet, his life filled that room. Further up the avenue his wife was holding his newborn child. Life and death so close together, and love and hatred, and right and wrong, said something to me which I did not want to hear concerning man, concerning the life of man.

After the funeral, while I was downtown desperately celebrating my birthday, a Negro soldier, in the lobby of the Hotel Braddock,[8] got into a fight with a white policeman over a Negro girl. Negro girls, white policemen, in or out of uniform, and Negro males—in or out of uniform—were part of the furniture of

8. Hotel at Eighth Avenue and 126th Street in Harlem.

the lobby of the Hotel Braddock and this was certainly not the first time such an incident had occurred. It was destined, however, to receive an unprecedented publicity, for the fight between the policeman and the soldier ended with the shooting of the soldier. Rumor, flowing immediately to the streets outside, stated that the soldier had been shot in the back, an instantaneous and revealing invention, and that the soldier had died protecting a Negro woman. The facts were somewhat different—for example, the soldier had not been shot in the back, and was not dead, and the girl seems to have been as dubious a symbol of womanhood as her white counterpart in Georgia usually is,[9] but no one was interested in the facts. They preferred the invention because this invention expressed and corroborated their hates and fears so perfectly. It is just as well to remember that people are always doing this. Perhaps many of those legends, including Christianity, to which the world clings began their conquest of the world with just some such concerted surrender to distortion. The effect, in Harlem, of this particular legend was like the effect of a lit match in a tin of gasoline. The mob gathered before the doors of the Hotel Braddock simply began to swell and to spread in every direction, and Harlem exploded.

The mob did not cross the ghetto lines. It would have been easy, for example, to have gone over Morningside Park on the west side or to have crossed the Grand Central railroad tracks at 125th Street on the east side, to wreak havoc in white neighborhoods. The mob seems to have been mainly interested in something more potent and real than the white face, that is, in white power, and the principal damage done during the riot of the summer of 1943 was to white business establishments in Harlem. It might have been a far bloodier story, of course, if, at the hour the riot began, these establishments had still been open. From the Hotel Braddock the mob fanned out, east and west along 125th Street, and for the entire length of Lenox, Seventh, and Eighth avenues. Along each of these avenues, and along each major side street—116th, 125th, 135th, and so on—bars, stores, pawnshops, restaurants, even little luncheonettes had been smashed open and entered and looted—looted, it might be added, with more haste than efficiency. The shelves really looked as though a bomb had struck them. Cans of beans and soup and dog food, along with toilet paper, corn flakes, sardines and milk tumbled every which way, and abandoned cash registers and cases of beer leaned crazily out of the splintered windows and were strewn along the avenues. Sheets, blankets, and clothing of every description formed a kind of path, as though people had dropped them while running. I truly had not realized that Harlem *had* so many stores until I saw them all smashed open; the first time the word *wealth* ever entered my mind in relation to Harlem was when I saw it scattered in the streets. But one's first, incongruous impression of plenty was countered immediately by an impression of waste. None of this was doing anybody any good. It would have been better to have left the plate glass as it had been and the goods lying in the stores.

It would have been better, but it would also have been intolerable, for Harlem had needed something to smash. To smash something is the ghetto's chronic need. Most of the time it is the members of the ghetto who smash each other, and themselves. But as long as the ghetto walls are standing there will

---

9. Baldwin here refers to the origins of many lynchings in the South: allegations that black men had insulted white women.

always come a moment when these outlets do not work. That summer, for example, it was not enough to get into a fight on Lenox Avenue, or curse out one's cronies in the barber shops. If ever, indeed, the violence which fills Harlem's churches, pool halls, and bars erupts outward in a more direct fashion, Harlem and its citizens are likely to vanish in an apocalyptic flood. That this is not likely to happen is due to a great many reasons, most hidden and powerful among them the Negro's real relation to the white American. This relation prohibits, simply, anything as uncomplicated and satisfactory as pure hatred. In order really to hate white people, one has to blot so much out of the mind—and the heart—that this hatred itself becomes an exhausting and self-destructive pose. But this does not mean, on the other hand, that love comes easily: the white world is too powerful, too complacent, too ready with gratuitous humiliation, and, above all, too ignorant and too innocent for that. One is absolutely forced to make perpetual qualifications and one's own reactions are always canceling each other out. It is this, really, which has driven so many people mad, both white and black. One is always in the position of having to decide between amputation and gangrene. Amputation is swift but time may prove that the amputation was not necessary—or one may delay the amputation too long. Gangrene is slow, but it is impossible to be sure that one is reading one's symptoms right. The idea of going through life as a cripple is more than one can bear, and equally unbearable is the risk of swelling up slowly, in agony, with poison. And the trouble, finally, is that the risks are real even if the choices do not exist.

"But as for me and my house," my father had said, "we will serve the Lord." I wondered, as we drove him to his resting place, what this line had meant for him. I had heard him preach it many times. I had preached it once myself, proudly giving it an interpretation different from my father's. Now the whole thing came back to me, as though my father and I were on our way to Sunday school and I were memorizing the golden text: *And if it seem evil unto you to serve the Lord, choose you this day whom you will serve; whether the gods which your fathers served that were on the other side of the flood, or the gods of the Amorites, in whose land ye dwell: but as for me and my house, we will serve the Lord.*[1] I suspected in these familiar lines a meaning which had never been there for me before. All of my father's texts and songs, which I had decided were meaningless, were arranged before me at his death like empty bottles, waiting to hold the meaning which life would give them for me. This was his legacy: nothing is ever escaped. That bleakly memorable morning I hated the unbelievable streets and the Negroes and whites who had, equally, made them that way. But I knew that it was folly, as my father would have said, this bitterness was folly. It was necessary to hold on to the things that mattered. The dead man mattered, the new life mattered; blackness and whiteness did not matter; to believe that they did was to acquiesce in one's own destruction. Hatred, which could destroy so much, never failed to destroy the man who hated and this was an immutable law.

It began to seem that one would have to hold in the mind forever two ideas which seemed to be in opposition. The first idea was acceptance, the acceptance, totally without rancor, of life as it is, and men as they are: in the light of

1. Joshua 24.15.

this idea, it goes without saying that injustice is a commonplace. But this did not mean that one could be complacent, for the second idea was of equal power: that one must never, in one's own life, accept these injustices as commonplace but must fight them with all one's strength. This fight begins, however, in the heart and it now had been laid to my charge to keep my own heart free of hatred and despair. This intimation made my heart heavy and, now that my father was irrecoverable, I wished that he had been beside me so that I could have searched his face for the answers which only the future would give me now.

1955

ALBERT CAMUS
1913–1960

From his childhood among the most disadvantaged in Algiers to his later roles as journalist, Resistance fighter in World War II, iconic literary figure, and winner of the Nobel Prize in Literature, in 1957, Albert Camus was intensely aware of the basic levels of human existence and of the struggles of the poor and the oppressed. "I can understand only in human terms," he said. "I understand the things I touch, things that offer me resistance." He describes the raw experience of life that human beings share, the humble but ineradicable bond between them. Camus kept a sympathetic yet critical eye on the tensions of his day: observing the Soviet Union from afar, and the bloody battles for Algerian independence up-close, led him to examine the way people can respond to oppressive systems without themselves becoming oppressors.

Camus was born on November 7, 1913, into a "world of poverty and light" in Mondavi, Algeria, then a colony of France. He was the second son in a poor family of mixed Alsatian and Spanish descent, and his father died in an early battle of the First World War. Camus's mother was illiterate; an untreated childhood illness had left her deaf and with a speech impediment. The two boys lived together with their mother, uncle, and grandmother in a two-room apartment in the working-class section of the capital city, Algiers. Camus and his brother, Lucien, were raised by their strict grandmother while their mother worked as a cleaning woman to support the family. Images of the Mediterranean landscape, with the sensual appeal of sea and blazing sun, recur throughout his work, as does a profound compassion for those who—like his mother—labor unrecognized and in silence.

A passionate athlete as well as a scholarship recipient, Camus completed his secondary education and enrolled as a philosophy student at the University of Algiers before contracting, at seventeen, the tuberculosis that corroded his health and made him aware of the body's vulnerability to disease and death. Camus eventually finished his degree, but in the meantime his illness had provided a metaphor for the personal and natural events that oppose and limit human fulfillment and happiness: elements he was later to term the "plague," which infects bodies, minds, cities, and society. (*The Plague* is the title of his second novel.)

Camus lived and worked as a journalist and essayist. Then, as later, however, his work extended well beyond journalism. He founded a collective theater, Le Théâtre du Travail (The Labor Theater), for which he wrote and adapted a number of plays. The theater fascinated Camus, possibly because it involved groups of people and spontaneous interaction between actors and audience. Sponsored by the Communist Party, the Labor Theater was designed for the working people, with performances on the docks in Algiers. Like many intellectuals of his day, Camus joined the Communist Party, but he withdrew after a year to protest its opposition to Algerian nationalism. He eventually left the Labor Theater too and, with a group of young Algerians associated with the publishing house Charlot, organized the politically independent Team Theater (Théâtre de l'Équipe). In 1940 he moved to France after his political commentary, including a famous report on administrative mismanagement during a famine among the Berbers (tribal peoples in North Africa), so outraged the Algerian government that his newspaper was suspended and he himself refused a work permit.

Soon after leaving Algeria, Camus published his first and most famous novel, *The Stranger* (1942), the play *Caligula* (1944), and a lengthy essay defining his concept of the "absurd" hero, *The Myth of Sisyphus* (1942). During World War II, Camus worked in Paris as a reader for the publishing firm of Gallimard, a post that he kept until his death, in 1960. At the same time, he took part in the French Resistance and helped edit the underground journal *Combat*. His friendship with the existentialist philosopher Jean-

Paul Sartre began in 1944; after the war he and Sartre were internationally known as uncompromising analysts of the modern conscience. Camus's second novel, *The Plague* (1947), portrays an epidemic in a quarantined city, Oran, Algeria, to symbolize the spread of evil during World War II ("the feeling of suffocation from which we all suffered, and the atmosphere of threat and exile") and to show the struggle against physical and spiritual death in its many forms. He continued, as well, to write plays (*Cross Purposes*, 1944; *The Just Assassins*, 1949). Not content to express his views symbolically in fiction, Camus also spoke out in philosophical essays and political statements. His independent mind and rejection of doctrinaire positions brought him attacks from both the left and the right.

Unlike many intellectuals of his day, Camus did not place a higher value on ideology than on its practical effects: when word emerged about Stalinist labor camps, for instance, he criticized the Soviets rather than defend the Communist ideal, as many of his friends did. Camus's open anti-Communism led to a spectacular break with Sartre, whose magazine, *Les Temps Modernes* (Modern Times), condemned Camus's book-length essay *The Rebel* (1951); the personal and public dispute between the old friends may have been unavoidable. In the bitter struggle over Algeria, Camus supported the claims of French colonists, including his own family, and therefore opposed Algerian independence, while at the same time attacking the violence of the French colonial regime. Camus did not live to witness the end of the Algerian conflict, which led to independence in 1962. After being awarded the Nobel Prize in 1957, he died in a car accident in 1960. His death at the height of his powers contributed to his posthumous fame as an analyst of the tragic elements of the human condition.

Camus is often linked with Sartre as an existentialist writer, and indeed—as novelist, playwright, and essayist—he is widely known for his analysis of two issues fundamental to existentialism: its distinctive assessment of the human condition and its search for authentic beliefs and values. Yet Camus rejected doctrinaire labels, and Sartre himself suggested that Camus was better placed in the tradition of French moralist writers, such as Michel de Montaigne and René Pascal, who observed human behavior within an implied ethical context that had its own standards of good and evil.

A consummate artist as well as a moralist, Camus was well aware of both the opportunities and the illusions of his craft. When he received the Nobel Prize, his acceptance speech emphasized the artificial but necessary "human" order that art imposes on the chaos of immediate experience. Artists are important as *creators*, because they shape a human perspective, allow understanding in human terms, and therefore provide a basis for action. By stressing the gap between art and reality, Camus provides a link between two poles of human understanding. His works juxtapose realistic detail and a philosophical, almost mythical dimension. The symbolism of his titles, from *The Stranger* to the last collection of stories, *Exile and the Kingdom* (1957), indicates the status of outsider, and the feeling of alienation in the world, while suggesting a search for the realm of human solidarity and agency.

The two terms around which Camus's thinking and writing revolve are the nouns *the absurd* and *revolt*. Camus's wartime output established his reputation as a philosopher of the absurd: the impossibility of "making sense" of a world that has no discernible sense. How to live in such an enviroment nevertheless becomes the main object of his philosophical and literary work. *Revolt*, for Camus, is more ethical than political, a rejection of the conventional and the inauthentic, but also an embrace of a shared humanity. Because the impulse to rebel is a basis for social tolerance and has no patience for master plans that prescribe patterns of thought or action, *revolt* actually opposes revolutionary nihilism.

In the story presented here, "The Guest" (1957), taken from *Exile and the Kingdom*, Camus returns to the landscape of his native Algeria. The colonial context is crucial in this story, not only to explain the real threat of guerrilla reprisal (Camus may be recalling the actual killing of rural schoolteachers in 1954) but to establish the dimensions of a political situation in which the government, police, educational system, and economic welfare of Algeria are all controlled by France. As in the works of **Doris Lessing**, **Chinua Achebe**, and **Wole Soyinka**, the colonial (or newly postcolonial) setting generates a charged atmosphere. The beginning of the story illustrates how French colonial education emphasizes French rather than local concerns: the schoolteacher's geography lesson outlines the four main rivers of France. The Arab is led along like an animal behind the gendarme Balducci, who rides a horse (here too, Camus may be recalling a humiliation reported two decades before and used as a way to inspire Algerian nationalists). Within this specific context, however, Camus concentrates on wider issues: freedom, brotherhood, responsibility, and the ambiguity of actions along with the inevitability of choice.

The remote desert landscape establishes a complete physical and moral isolation for the story's events. "No one, in this desert, . . . mattered," and the schoolteacher and his guest must each decide, independently, what to do. When Balducci invades Daru's monastic solitude and tells him that he must deliver the Arab to prison, Daru is outraged to be given involvement in, and indeed responsibility for, another's fate. Cursing both the system that tries to force him into complicity and the Arab who has not had enough sense to get away, Daru tries, in every way possible, to avoid taking a stand. Yet he finds himself confronted with the essential human demand for hospitality, which creates burdens and links between guest and host. The choice that Daru must make leads to a further necessary choice by the Arab prisoner.

As possible titles for this story, Camus considered "Cain" and "The Law" before settling on "The Guest": the title word, *l'hôte*, means both "guest" and "host" in French. Joined in their fundamental humanity, both guest and host are obliged to shoulder the ambiguous, and potentially fatal, burden of freedom.

The Guest[1]

The schoolmaster was watching the two men climb toward him. One was on horseback, the other on foot. They had not yet tackled the abrupt rise leading to the schoolhouse built on the hillside. They were toiling onward, making slow progress in the snow, among the stones, on the vast expanse of the high, deserted plateau. From time to time the horse stumbled. Without hearing anything yet, he could see the breath issuing from the horse's nostrils. One of the men, at least, knew the region. They were following the trail although it had disappeared days ago under a layer of dirty white snow. The schoolmaster calculated that it would take them half an hour to get onto the hill. It was cold; he went back into the school to get a sweater.

He crossed the empty, frigid classroom. On the blackboard the four rivers of France,[2] drawn with four different colored chalks, had been flowing toward their estuaries for the past three days. Snow had suddenly fallen in mid-October after eight months of drought without the transition of rain, and the twenty pupils, more or less, who lived in the villages scattered over the plateau had stopped coming. With fair weather they would return. Daru now heated only the single room that was his lodging, adjoining the classroom and giving also onto the plateau to the east. Like the class windows, his window looked to the south too. On that side the school was a few kilometers from the point where the plateau began to slope toward the south. In clear weather could be seen the purple mass of the mountain range where the gap opened onto the desert.

Somewhat warmed, Daru returned to the window from which he had first seen the two men. They were no longer visible. Hence they must have tackled the rise. The sky was not so dark, for the snow had stopped falling during the night. The morning had opened with a dirty light which had scarcely become brighter as the ceiling of clouds lifted. At two in the afternoon it seemed as if the day were merely beginning. But still this was better than those three days when the thick snow was falling amidst unbroken darkness with little gusts of wind that rattled the double door of the classroom. Then Daru had spent long hours in his room, leaving it only to go to the shed and feed the chickens or get some coal. Fortunately the delivery truck from Tadjid, the nearest village to the north, had brought his supplies two days before the blizzard. It would return in forty-eight hours.

1. Translated by Justin O'Brien.
2. The Seine, Loire, Rhone, and Gironde rivers. French geography was taught in the French colonies.

Besides, he had enough to resist a siege, for the little room was cluttered with bags of wheat that the administration left as a stock to distribute to those of his pupils whose families had suffered from the drought. Actually they had all been victims because they were all poor. Every day Daru would distribute a ration to the children. They had missed it, he knew, during these bad days. Possibly one of the fathers or big brothers would come this afternoon and he could supply them with grain. It was just a matter of carrying them over to the next harvest. Now shiploads of wheat were arriving from France and the worst was over. But it would be hard to forget that poverty, that army of ragged ghosts wandering in the sunlight, the plateaus burned to a cinder month after month, the earth shriveled up little by little, literally scorched, every stone bursting into dust under one's foot. The sheep had died then by thousands and even a few men, here and there, sometimes without anyone's knowing.

In contrast with such poverty, he who lived almost like a monk in his remote schoolhouse, nonetheless satisfied with the little he had and with the rough life, had felt like a lord with his whitewashed walls, his narrow couch, his unpainted shelves, his well, and his weekly provision of water and food. And suddenly this snow, without warning, without the foretaste of rain. This is the way the region was, cruel to live in, even without men—who didn't help matters either. But Daru had been born here. Everywhere else, he felt exiled.

He stepped out onto the terrace in front of the schoolhouse. The two men were now halfway up the slope. He recognized the horseman as Balducci, the old gendarme he had known for a long time. Balducci was holding on the end of a rope an Arab who was walking behind him with hands bound and head lowered. The gendarme waved a greeting to which Daru did not reply, lost as he was in contemplation of the Arab dressed in a faded blue jellaba, his feet in sandals but covered with socks of heavy raw wool, his head surmounted by a narrow, short *chèche*.[3] They were approaching. Balducci was holding back his horse in order not to hurt the Arab, and the group was advancing slowly.

Within earshot, Balducci shouted: "One hour to do the three kilometers from El Ameur!" Daru did not answer. Short and square in his thick sweater, he watched them climb. Not once had the Arab raised his head. "Hello," said Daru when they got up onto the terrace. "Come in and warm up." Balducci painfully got down from his horse without letting go the rope. From under his bristling mustache he smiled at the schoolmaster. His little dark eyes, deep-set under a tanned forehead, and his mouth surrounded with wrinkles made him look attentive and studious. Daru took the bridle, led the horse to the shed, and came back to the two men, who were now waiting for him in the school. He led them into his room. "I am going to heat up the classroom," he said. "We'll be more comfortable there." When he entered the room again, Balducci was on the couch. He had undone the rope tying him to the Arab, who had squatted near the stove. His hands still bound, the *chèche* pushed back on his head, he was looking toward the window. At first Daru noticed only his huge lips, fat, smooth, almost Negroid; yet his nose was straight, his eyes were dark and full of fever. The *chèche* revealed an obstinate forehead and, under the weathered skin now rather discolored by the cold, the whole face had a restless

---

3. Scarf; here, wound as a turban around the head. "Jellaba": a long hooded robe worn by Arabs in North Africa.

and rebellious look that struck Daru when the Arab, turning his face toward him, looked him straight in the eyes. "Go into the other room," said the schoolmaster, "and I'll make you some mint tea." "Thanks," Balducci said. "What a chore! How I long for retirement." And addressing his prisoner in Arabic: "Come on, you." The Arab got up and, slowly, holding his bound wrists in front of him, went into the classroom.

With the tea, Daru brought a chair. But Balducci was already enthroned on the nearest pupil's desk and the Arab had squatted against the teacher's platform facing the stove, which stood between the desk and the window. When he held out the glass of tea to the prisoner, Daru hesitated at the sight of his bound hands. "He might perhaps be untied." "Sure," said Balducci. "That was for the trip." He started to get to his feet. But Daru, setting the glass on the floor, had knelt beside the Arab. Without saying anything, the Arab watched him with his feverish eyes. Once his hands were free, he rubbed his swollen wrists against each other, took the glass of tea, and sucked up the burning liquid in swift little sips.

"Good," said Daru. "And where are you headed?"

Balducci withdrew his mustache from the tea. "Here, son."

"Odd pupils! And you're spending the night?"

"No. I'm going back to El Ameur. And you will deliver this fellow to Tinguit. He is expected at police headquarters."

Balducci was looking at Daru with a friendly little smile.

"What's this story?" asked the schoolmaster. "Are you pulling my leg?"

"No, son. Those are the orders."

"The orders? I'm not . . ." Daru hesitated, not wanting to hurt the old Corsican.[4] "I mean, that's not my job."

"What! What's the meaning of that? In wartime people do all kinds of jobs."

"Then I'll wait for the declaration of war!"

Balducci nodded.

"O.K. But the orders exist and they concern you too. Things are brewing, it appears. There is talk of a forthcoming revolt. We are mobilized, in a way."

Daru still had his obstinate look.

"Listen, son," Balducci said. "I like you and you must understand. There's only a dozen of us at El Ameur to patrol throughout the whole territory of a small department[5] and I must get back in a hurry. I was told to hand this guy over to you and return without delay. He couldn't be kept there. His village was beginning to stir; they wanted to take him back. You must take him to Tinguit tomorrow before the day is over. Twenty kilometers shouldn't faze a husky fellow like you. After that, all will be over. You'll come back to your pupils and your comfortable life."

Behind the wall the horse could be heard snorting and pawing the earth. Daru was looking out the window. Decidedly, the weather was clearing and the light was increasing over the snowy plateau. When all the snow was melted, the sun would take over again and once more would burn the fields of stone. For days, still, the unchanging sky would shed its dry light on the solitary expanse where nothing had any connection with man.

4. Balducci is a native of Corsica, a French island north of Sardinia.

5. French administrative and territorial division; like a county.

"After all," he said, turning around toward Balducci, "what did he do?" And, before the gendarme had opened his mouth, he asked: "Does he speak French?"

"No, not a word. We had been looking for him for a month, but they were hiding him. He killed his cousin."

"Is he against us?"[6]

"I don't think so. But you can never be sure."

"Why did he kill?"

"A family squabble, I think. One owed the other grain, it seems. It's not at all clear. In short, he killed his cousin with a billhook. You know, like a sheep, *kreezk!*"

Balducci made the gesture of drawing a blade across his throat and the Arab, his attention attracted, watched him with a sort of anxiety. Daru felt a sudden wrath against the man, against all men with their rotten spite, their tireless hates, their blood lust.

But the kettle was singing on the stove. He served Balducci more tea, hesitated, then served the Arab again, who, a second time, drank avidly. His raised arms made the jellaba fall open and the schoolmaster saw his thin, muscular chest.

"Thanks, kid," Balducci said. "And now, I'm off."

He got up and went toward the Arab, taking a small rope from his pocket.

"What are you doing?" Daru asked dryly.

Balducci, disconcerted, showed him the rope.

"Don't bother."

The old gendarme hesitated. "It's up to you. Of course, you are armed?"

"I have my shotgun."

"Where?"

"In the trunk."

"You ought to have it near your bed."

"Why? I have nothing to fear."

"You're crazy, son. If there's an uprising, no one is safe, we're all in the same boat."

"I'll defend myself. I'll have time to see them coming."

Balducci began to laugh, then suddenly the mustache covered the white teeth.

"You'll have time? O.K. That's just what I was saying. You have always been a little cracked. That's why I like you, my son was like that."

At the same time he took out his revolver and put it on the desk.

"Keep it; I don't need two weapons from here to El Ameur."

The revolver shone against the black paint of the table. When the gendarme turned toward him, the schoolmaster caught the smell of leather and horseflesh.

"Listen, Balducci," Daru said suddenly, "every bit of this disgusts me, and first of all your fellow here. But I won't hand him over. Fight, yes, if I have to. But not that."

The old gendarme stood in front of him and looked at him severely.

"You're being a fool," he said slowly. "I don't like it either. You don't get used to putting a rope on a man even after years of it, and you're even ashamed— yes, ashamed. But you can't let them have their way."

6. I.e., against the French colonial government.

"I won't hand him over," Daru said again.

"It's an order, son, and I repeat it."

"That's right. Repeat to them what I've said to you: I won't hand him over."

Balducci made a visible effort to reflect. He looked at the Arab and at Daru. At last he decided.

"No, I won't tell them anything. If you want to drop us, go ahead; I'll not denounce you. I have an order to deliver the prisoner and I'm doing so. And now you'll just sign this paper for me."

"There's no need. I'll not deny that you left him with me."

"Don't be mean with me. I know you'll tell the truth. You're from hereabouts and you are a man. But you must sign, that's the rule."

Daru opened his drawer, took out a little square bottle of purple ink, the red wooden penholder with the "sergeant-major" pen he used for making models of penmanship, and signed. The gendarme carefully folded the paper and put it into his wallet. Then he moved toward the door.

"I'll see you off," Daru said.

"No," said Balducci. "There's no use being polite. You insulted me."

He looked at the Arab, motionless in the same spot, sniffed peevishly, and turned away toward the door. "Good-by, son," he said. The door shut behind him. Balducci appeared suddenly outside the window and then disappeared. His footsteps were muffled by the snow. The horse stirred on the other side of the wall and several chickens fluttered in fright. A moment later Balducci reappeared outside the window leading the horse by the bridle. He walked toward the little rise without turning around and disappeared from sight with the horse following him. A big stone could be heard bouncing down. Daru walked back toward the prisoner, who, without stirring, never took his eyes off him. "Wait," the schoolmaster said in Arabic and went toward the bedroom. As he was going through the door, he had a second thought, went to the desk, took the revolver, and stuck it in his pocket. Then, without looking back, he went into his room.

For some time he lay on his couch watching the sky gradually close over, listening to the silence. It was this silence that had seemed painful to him during the first days here, after the war. He had requested a post in the little town at the base of the foothills separating the upper plateaus from the desert. There, rocky walls, green and black to the north, pink and lavender to the south, marked the frontier of eternal summer. He had been named to a post farther north, on the plateau itself. In the beginning, the solitude and the silence had been hard for him on these wastelands peopled only by stones. Occasionally, furrows suggested cultivation, but they had been dug to uncover a certain kind of stone good for building. The only plowing here was to harvest rocks. Elsewhere a thin layer of soil accumulated in the hollows would be scraped out to enrich paltry village gardens. This is the way it was: bare rock covered three quarters of the region. Towns sprang up, flourished, then disappeared; men came by, loved one another or fought bitterly, then died. No one in this desert, neither he nor his guest, mattered. And yet, outside this desert neither of them, Daru knew, could have really lived.

When he got up, no noise came from the classroom. He was amazed at the unmixed joy he derived from the mere thought that the Arab might have fled and that he would be alone with no decision to make. But the prisoner was there. He had merely stretched out between the stove and the desk. With eyes open, he was staring at the ceiling. In that position, his thick lips were particularly noticeable, giving him a pouting look. "Come," said Daru. The Arab got up and followed him. In the bedroom, the schoolmaster pointed to a chair near the table under the window. The Arab sat down without taking his eyes off Daru.

"Are you hungry?"

"Yes," the prisoner said.

Daru set the table for two. He took flour and oil, shaped a cake in a frying-pan, and lighted the little stove that functioned on bottled gas. While the cake was cooking, he went out to the shed to get cheese, eggs, dates, and condensed milk. When the cake was done he set it on the window sill to cool, heated some condensed milk diluted with water, and beat up the eggs into an omelette. In one of his motions he knocked against the revolver stuck in his right pocket. He set the bowl down, went into the classroom, and put the revolver in his desk drawer. When he came back to the room, night was falling. He put on the light and served the Arab. "Eat," he said. The Arab took a piece of the cake, lifted it eagerly to his mouth, and stopped short.

"And you?" he asked.

"After you. I'll eat too."

The thick lips opened slightly. The Arab hesitated, then bit into the cake determinedly.

The meal over, the Arab looked at the schoolmaster. "Are you the judge?"

"No, I'm simply keeping you until tomorrow."

"Why do you eat with me?"

"I'm hungry."

The Arab fell silent. Daru got up and went out. He brought back a folding bed from the shed, set it up between the table and the stove, perpendicular to his own bed. From a large suitcase which, upright in a corner, served as a shelf for papers, he took two blankets and arranged them on the camp bed. Then he stopped, felt useless, and sat down on his bed. There was nothing more to do or to get ready. He had to look at this man. He looked at him, therefore, trying to imagine his face bursting with rage. He couldn't do so. He could see nothing but the dark yet shining eyes and the animal mouth.

"Why did you kill him?" he asked in a voice whose hostile tone surprised him.

The Arab looked away.

"He ran away. I ran after him."

He raised his eyes to Daru again and they were full of a sort of woeful interrogation. "Now what will they do to me?"

"Are you afraid?"

He stiffened, turning his eyes away.

"Are you sorry?"

The Arab stared at him openmouthed. Obviously he did not understand. Daru's annoyance was growing. At the same time he felt awkward and self-conscious with his big body wedged between the two beds.

"Lie down there," he said impatiently. "That's your bed."

The Arab didn't move. He called to Daru:

"Tell me!"

The schoolmaster looked at him.

"Is the gendarme coming back tomorrow?"

"I don't know."

"Are you coming with us?"

"I don't know. Why?"

The prisoner got up and stretched out on top of the blankets, his feet toward the window. The light from the electric bulb shone straight into his eyes and he closed them at once.

"Why?" Daru repeated, standing beside the bed.

The Arab opened his eyes under the blinding light and looked at him, trying not to blink.

"Come with us," he said.

In the middle of the night, Daru was still not asleep. He had gone to bed after undressing completely; he generally slept naked. But when he suddenly realized that he had nothing on, he hesitated. He felt vulnerable and the temptation came to him to put his clothes back on. Then he shrugged his shoulders; after all, he wasn't a child and, if need be, he could break his adversary in two. From his bed he could observe him, lying on his back, still motionless with his eyes closed under the harsh light. When Daru turned out the light, the darkness seemed to coagulate all of a sudden. Little by little, the night came back to life in the window where the starless sky was stirring gently. The schoolmaster soon made out the body lying at his feet. The Arab still did not move, but his eyes seemed open. A faint wind was prowling around the schoolhouse. Perhaps it would drive away the clouds and the sun would reappear.

During the night the wind increased. The hens fluttered a little and then were silent. The Arab turned over on his side with his back to Daru, who thought he heard him moan. Then he listened for his guest's breathing, become heavier and more regular. He listened to that breath so close to him and mused without being able to go to sleep. In this room where he had been sleeping alone for a year, this presence bothered him. But it bothered him also by imposing on him a sort of brotherhood he knew well but refused to accept in the present circumstances. Men who share the same rooms, soldiers or prisoners, develop a strange alliance as if, having cast off their armor with their clothing, they fraternized every evening, over and above their differences, in the ancient community of dream and fatigue. But Daru shook himself; he didn't like such musings, and it was essential to sleep.

A little later, however, when the Arab stirred slightly, the schoolmaster was still not asleep. When the prisoner made a second move, he stiffened, on the alert. The Arab was lifting himself slowly on his arms with almost the motion of a sleepwalker. Seated upright in bed, he waited motionless without turning his head toward Daru, as if he were listening attentively. Daru did not stir; it had just occurred to him that the revolver was still in the drawer of his desk. It was better to act at once. Yet he continued to observe the prisoner, who, with the same slithery motion, put his feet on the ground, waited again, then began to stand up slowly. Daru was about to call out to him when the Arab began to walk, in a quite natural but extraordinarily silent way. He was heading toward the door at the end of the room that opened into the shed. He lifted the latch with precaution and went out, pushing the door behind him but without shutting it. Daru had not stirred. "He is running away," he merely thought. "Good riddance!" Yet he listened attentively. The hens were not fluttering; the guest must be on the plateau. A faint sound of water reached him, and he didn't know what it was until the Arab again stood framed in the doorway, closed the door carefully, and came back to bed without a sound. Then Daru turned his back on him and fell asleep. Still later he seemed, from the depths of his sleep, to hear furtive steps around the schoolhouse. "I'm dreaming! I'm dreaming!" he repeated to himself. And he went on sleeping.

When he awoke, the sky was clear; the loose window let in a cold, pure air. The Arab was asleep, hunched up under the blankets now, his mouth open, utterly relaxed. But when Daru shook him, he started dreadfully, staring at Daru with wild eyes as if he had never seen him and such a frightened expression that the schoolmaster stepped back. "Don't be afraid. It's me. You must eat." The Arab nodded his head and said yes. Calm had returned to his face, but his expression was vacant and listless.

The coffee was ready. They drank it seated together on the folding bed as they munched their pieces of the cake. Then Daru led the Arab under the shed and showed him the faucet where he washed. He went back into the room, folded the blankets and the bed, made his own bed and put the room in order. Then he went through the classroom and out onto the terrace. The sun was already rising in the blue sky; a soft, bright light was bathing the deserted plateau. On the ridge the snow was melting in spots. The stones were about to reappear. Crouched on the edge of the plateau, the schoolmaster looked at the deserted expanse. He thought of Balducci. He had hurt him, for he had sent him off in a way as if he didn't want to be associated with him. He could still hear the gendarme's farewell and, without knowing why, he felt strangely empty and vulnerable. At that moment, from the other side of the schoolhouse, the prisoner coughed. Daru listened to him almost despite himself and then, furious, threw a pebble that whistled through the air before sinking into the snow. That man's stupid crime revolted him, but to hand him over was contrary to honor. Merely thinking of it made him smart with humiliation. And he cursed at one and the same time his own people who had sent him this Arab and the Arab too who had dared to kill and not managed to get away. Daru got up, walked in a circle on the terrace, waited motionless, and then went back into the schoolhouse.

The Arab, leaning over the cement floor of the shed, was washing his teeth with two fingers. Daru looked at him and said: "Come." He went back into the room ahead of the prisoner. He slipped a hunting-jacket on over his sweater and put on walking-shoes. Standing, he waited until the Arab had put on his *chèche* and sandals. They went into the classroom and the schoolmaster pointed to the exit, saying: "Go ahead." The fellow didn't budge. "I'm coming," said Daru. The Arab went out. Daru went back into the room and made a package of pieces of rusk, dates, and sugar. In the classroom, before going out, he hesitated a second in front of his desk, then crossed the threshold and locked the door. "That's the way," he said. He started toward the east, followed by the prisoner. But, a short distance from the schoolhouse, he thought he heard a slight sound behind them. He retraced his steps and examined the surroundings of the house, there was no one there. The Arab watched him without seeming to understand. "Come on," said Daru.

They walked for an hour and rested beside a sharp peak of limestone. The snow was melting faster and faster and the sun was drinking up the puddles at once, rapidly cleaning the plateau, which gradually dried and vibrated like the air itself. When they resumed walking, the ground rang under their feet. From time to time a bird rent the space in front of them with a joyful cry. Daru breathed in deeply the fresh morning light. He felt a sort of rapture before the vast familiar expanse, now almost entirely yellow under its dome of blue sky. They walked an hour more, descending toward the south. They reached a level height made up of crumbly rocks. From there on, the plateau sloped down, eastward, toward a low plain where there were a few spindly trees and, to the south, toward outcroppings of rock that gave the landscape a chaotic look.

Daru surveyed the two directions. There was nothing but the sky on the horizon. Not a man could be seen. He turned toward the Arab, who was looking at him blankly. Daru held out the package to him. "Take it," he said. "There are dates, bread, and sugar. You can hold out for two days. Here are a thousand francs too." The Arab took the package and the money but kept his full hands at chest level as if he didn't know what to do with what was being given him. "Now look," the schoolmaster said as he pointed in the direction of the east, "there's the way to Tinguit. You have a two-hour walk. At Tinguit you'll find the administration and the police. They are expecting you." The Arab looked toward the east, still holding the package and the money against his chest. Daru took his elbow and turned him rather roughly toward the south. At the foot of the height on which they stood could be seen a faint path. "That's the trail across the plateau. In a day's walk from here you'll find pasturelands and the first nomads. They'll take you in and shelter you according to their law." The Arab had now turned toward Daru and a sort of panic was visible in his expression. "Listen," he said. Daru shook his head: "No, be quiet. Now I'm leaving you." He turned his back on him, took two long steps in the direction of the school, looked hesitantly at the motionless Arab, and started off again. For a few minutes he heard nothing but his own step resounding on the cold ground and did not turn his head. A moment later, however, he turned around. The Arab was still there on the edge of the hill, his arms hanging now, and he was looking at the schoolmaster. Daru felt something rise in his throat. But he swore with impatience, waved vaguely, and started off again. He had already gone some distance when he again stopped and looked. There was no longer anyone on the hill.

Daru hesitated. The sun was now rather high in the sky and was beginning to beat down on his head. The schoolmaster retraced his steps, at first somewhat uncertainly, then with decision. When he reached the little hill, he was bathed in sweat. He climbed it as fast as he could and stopped, out of breath, at the top. The rock-fields to the south stood out sharply against the blue sky, but on the plain to the east a steamy heat was already rising. And in that slight haze, Daru, with heavy heart, made out the Arab walking slowly on the road to prison.

A little later, standing before the window of the classroom, the schoolmaster was watching the clear light bathing the whole surface of the plateau, but he hardly saw it. Behind him on the blackboard, among the winding French rivers, sprawled the clumsily chalked-up words he had just read: "You handed over our brother. You will pay for this." Daru looked at the sky, the plateau, and, beyond, the invisible lands stretching all the way to the sea. In this vast landscape he had loved so much, he was alone.

1957

SAMUEL BECKETT

1906–1989

At once among the grimmest and funniest of modern writers, Samuel Beckett offers in his novels and plays a stark, spare representation of the human condition in its "absurd" emptiness. Beckett's world is haunted by an absence of meaning at the core, yet the absence of meaning becomes the occasion for puns, parodies, and clowning. Filling the void with desperate stagecraft and patter, Beckett's characters live out a hopeless attempt to find or to create meaning for themselves. Often they spend their lives waiting for an explanation that never comes; and yet Beckett makes this predicament a source of intense black humor.

Born near Dublin on April 13, 1906 (Good Friday), to a well-to-do Protestant family, Beckett was educated in Ireland and received a bachelor's degree from Trinity College in 1927. He then taught English for two years at the École Normale Supérieure in Paris, where he met **James Joyce** and was influenced by the older novelist's exuberant and punning use of language. Beckett wrote an essay on the early stages of Joyce's *Finnegans Wake* and later helped in the French translation of some portions of the book. In 1930, Beckett entered a competition for a poem on the subject of time and won first prize with a ninety-eight-line (and seventeen-footnote) dramatic monologue, *Whoroscope*; the poem's speaker is the seventeenth-century French philosopher René Descartes, whose ideas about the dualism between mind and body became an obsession of Beckett's literary work. Beckett returned to Trinity College, where he took a master's degree in 1931, published an essay on **Marcel Proust**, and

briefly taught French. In 1937, after living in England, France, and Germany, Beckett made Paris his permanent home. During the Second World War, Beckett worked for the French Resistance, helping to collate intelligence reports from occupied France. Nearly discovered by the Nazis, he fled south to Roussillon, where he remained for the rest of the war. On a visit to his mother in Dublin after the war, Beckett experienced a revelation, seemingly connected with the concept of nothingness, that he recalled (in his characteristically elliptical way) in the later play *Krapp's Last Tape* (1958). In the scene the main character listens to a tape of his own voice recollecting an earlier vision:

> Spiritually a year of profound gloom and indigence until that memorable night in March, at the end of the jetty, in the howling wind, never to be forgotten, when suddenly I saw the whole thing. The vision, at last. . . . What I suddenly saw then was this, that the belief I had been going on all my life, namely—. . . that the dark I have always struggled to keep under is in reality my most . . .

Before this belief can be revealed, however, Krapp switches off the tape and winds it forward, so that the audience never learns the content of the revelation. Beckett later told his biographer that the missing words were "precious ally." Certainly, in the years after the war, Beckett made darkness his ally.

Although two highly amusing early novels, *Murphy* (1938) and *Watt* (published in 1953), were written in English, during the war Beckett turned to French as his preferred language for composition. In the years after the war, he wrote almost exclusively in French and only later translated the texts (often with substantial changes) into English. He explained his choice of language for creating his works: "in French it is easier to write without style"—without the native speaker's temptation to elegance and virtuoso display. Comparing the French and English versions of Beckett's works often suggests such a contrast, with the French text closer to basic grammatical forms and therefore possessing a harsher, starker focus. Indeed, Beckett claimed to care little about the formalities of language. "Grammar and Style," he wrote: "To me they seem to have become as irrelevant as a Victorian bathing suit or the imperturbability of a true gentleman. A mask. Let us hope the time will come . . . when language is most efficiently used where it is most efficiently misused." He sought a way to achieve a language of darkness, a language suitable to the postwar world in which old proprieties should be discarded in favor of a more austere, less artificial reality. Yet, as if against his will, he infused these dark and minimalist works with the wit and eloquence of his personal idiom. He later compared himself to his old friend Joyce: "The more Joyce knew the more he could. He's tending toward omniscience and omnipotence as an artist. I'm working with impotence, ignorance." The movement toward reductionism and minimalism helped to define postwar literature.

Beckett's first works in the spare style were a trilogy of novels, completed in 1949: *Molloy* (published in 1951), *Malone Dies* (1951), and *The Unnamable* (1953). The narrative perspective moves from a series of related monologues (in which a number of narrators, all of whose names begin with "M," come increasingly to resemble one another) to the ramblings, at the end, of

an "unnamable" speaker who seems to represent them all. The reader can never be sure who is speaking, whether what the narrator is saying is true in the fictional world, or what the relationships among the various narrators might be. Beckett's early fiction received admiring attention from the philosopher Jean-Paul Sartre, among others, but Beckett's true fame came suddenly with the production of his first play, *Waiting for Godot* (published in 1952), first in French (1953), then in English (1955). The play's popularity showed that absurdist theater—with its empty, repetitive dialogue, its grotesquely bare yet evidently symbolic settings, and its refusal to build to a dramatic climax—could have meaning even for audiences accustomed to theatrical realism and logical plots. The audiences encountered two clownlike tramps, Vladimir and Estragon (Didi and Gogo), talking, quarreling, falling down, contemplating suicide, and generally filling up time with conversation that ranges from vaudeville patter to metaphysical speculation as they wait under a tree for "Godot," who never comes. Instead, the two are joined by another grotesque pair: the rich Pozzo and his brutally abused servant, Lucky, whom he leads around by a rope tied to the neck. As the first act comes to an end, Vladimir and Estragon agree to give up waiting, to leave; yet as the curtain falls, they stay where they were. A plot summary of the second act would be virtually identical with a summary of the first. As one critic put it, in *Waiting for Godot*, "nothing happens, twice." The popular interpretation of "Godot" as a diminutive for "God," and of the play as a statement of existential anguish at the inexplicable human condition, is scarcely defused by Beckett's caution that "If by Godot I had meant God, I would have said God." Yet identifying Godot is less important than identifying the wretched plight on stage as symbolically our own, and identifying *with* the characters as they express the anxious, often repugnant, but also comic picture of human relationships in an absurd universe. Both *Waiting for Godot* and *Endgame* draw on the full resources of modern theater while stripping the elements of traditional theater—plot, character, setting, dialogue—to a minimum.

After the popular success of *Waiting for Godot*, Beckett wrote *Endgame* (French version performed 1957; English, 1958) and a series of stage plays and brief pieces for the radio. The stage plays have the same bare yet striking settings: *Krapp's Last Tape* presents an old man sitting at a table with his tape recorder, recalling a love affair thirty years past; *Happy Days* (1961) portrays a married couple, with the wife chattering ceaselessly about her possessions, although she is buried in dirt up to her waist in the first act and up to her neck in the second. When he received the Nobel Prize for Literature in 1969, Beckett's wife declared the prize a "catastrophe" and another friend advised him to go into hiding—he was now a world-famous author, much sought after by admirers. In later years he wrote a number of shorter plays and novels, moving in the direction he had identified as distinguishing him from Joyce: toward minimalism, ignorance, and impotence. An unidentified voice in one of his final novellas, *Worstward Ho* (1983), says, "Fail again. Fail better." Beckett continued to produce successful works about failure for the rest of his long life. He died in a nursing home at the age of 83. The Nobel Prize conferred recognition on Beckett as the purest exponent of the twentieth century's chief philosophical dilemma: the notion of the "absurd," or the contradiction between human attempts to discover meaning in life and the simultaneous conviction that no "meaning" exists that we have not created ourselves.

Endgame, the play printed here, often called Beckett's major achievement, is a prime example of this dilemma. When the curtain rises on *Endgame*, the world seems to awaken from sleep. The sheets draping the furniture and central character are taken off, and Hamm sets himself in motion like an actor or a chess pawn: "Me . . . to play." Yet we are also near the story's end, for, as the title implies, nothing new will happen. An "endgame" is the final phase of a chess game, the stage at which the end is predictably in sight although the play must still be completed. Throughout, the theme of "end," "finish," "no more" resounds, even while Hamm notes the passage of time: "Something is taking its course." But time does not lead anywhere; it is either past or present and always barren. The past exists as Nagg's and Nell's memories, as Hamm's story, which may or may not describe Clov's entry into the home, and as a period when Clov once loved Hamm. The present shows four characters dwindling away, alone in a dead world, caught between bleak visions of hell and dreams of life reborn. In one of the biblical echoes that permeate the play, Hamm and Clov repeatedly evoke the final words of the crucified Jesus in the Gospel according to John: "It is finished." But this is not a biblical morality play, and *Endgame* describes a world not of divine creation but of self-creation. It is even possible that Hamm is composing and directing the entire performance: he is a storyteller and playwright with "asides" and "last soliloquy" whose "dialogue" keeps Clov onstage against his will, who (when looking out the window onto a clearly flourishing world) can see only dust and ashes, or a magician presiding over an imaginary kingdom who concludes a personal narrative and hopeless prayer with Prospero's line from Shakespeare's *The Tempest* (4.1.148): "Our revels now are ended." Or perhaps Hamm is simply the only character who is aware of his or her life *as* a performance, without other meaning. (As Shakespeare's passage continues later, "We are such stuff / As dreams are made on, and our little life / Is rounded with a sleep.") By the end of the play, the situation has changed little: it just becomes barer, as Hamm discards his stick, whistle, and dog, "reckoning closed and story ended." Yet as Hamm covers his face after this line, Clov is still waiting to depart rather than actually departing. It is not impossible that the play will resume in precisely the same terms tomorrow.

Like *Waiting for Godot*, *Endgame* has been given a number of interpretations. Some refer to Beckett's love of wordplay: Hamm as Hamm-actor, Hammlet, Hammer. The setting of a boxlike room with two windows is seen as a skull, the seat of consciousness, or (emphasizing the bloody handkerchief and the reference to fontanelles—the soft spot in the skull of a newborn) as a womb. The characters' isolation in a dead world after an unnamed catastrophe (which may be Hamm's fault) suggests the world after atomic holocaust. Or, for those who recall Beckett's fascination with the apathetic figure of Belacqua waiting, in the Purgatory of Dante's *Divine Comedy*, for his punishment to begin, *Endgame* evokes an image of pre-Purgatorial consciousness. The ash cans in which Hamm has "bottled" his parents, and the general cruelty between characters, may represent the dustbin of modern Western civilized values (while they also offer a sort of slapstick humor). Hamm and Clov represent the uneasy adjustment of soul and body, the class struggle of rich and poor, or the master-slave relationship in all senses (including the slave's acceptance of victimization). Clearly Beckett has created a structure that accommodates all these readings while authorizing none. He himself said to the director Alan Schneider that he was less interested in symbolism than in describing a "local situation," an interaction of four characters in a given set of circumstances, and that the audience's interpretation was its own responsibility.

Beckett both authorized and denied these interpretations. He pruned down an earlier, more anecdotal two-act play to achieve *Endgame*'s skeletal plot and almost anonymous characters, and in doing so, created a structure that immediately elicits the reader's instinct to "fill in the blanks." His puns and allusions point to a further meaning that *may* be contained in the implied reference but may also be part of an infinite regress of meaning—expressing the "absurd" itself. Working against too heavy an insistence on symbolic meanings is the fact that the play is funny—especially when performed on stage. The characters popping out of ash cans; the jerky, repetitive motions with which Clov carries out his master's commands; and the often obscene vaudeville patter accompanied by appropriate gestures—all provide a comic perspective that keeps *Endgame* from sinking into tragic despair. The intellectual distance offered by comedy is entirely in keeping with the more somber side of the play, which rejects pathos and constantly drags its characters' escapist fancies down to the minimal facts of survival: food, shelter, sleep, painkiller. Thus it is possible to say that *Endgame* describes—but only among many other things—what it is like to be alive, declining toward death in a world without meaning.

Endgame[1]

For Roger Blin

CHARACTERS

NAGG
NELL
HAMM
CLOV

Bare interior.
Gray light.
Left and right back, high up, two small windows, curtains drawn.
Front right, a door. Hanging near door, its face to wall, a picture.
Front left, touching each other, covered with an old sheet, two ashbins.
Center, in an armchair on castors, covered with an old sheet, HAMM.
Motionless by the door, his eyes fixed on HAMM, CLOV. *Very red face.*
Brief tableau.

[CLOV *goes and stands under window left. Stiff, staggering walk. He looks up at window left. He turns and looks at window right. He goes and stands under window right. He looks up at window right. He turns and looks at window left. He goes out, comes back immediately with a small step-ladder, carries it over and sets it down under window left, gets up on it, draws back curtain. He gets down, takes six steps (for example) towards window right, goes back for ladder, carries it over and sets it down under window right, gets up on it, draws back curtain. He gets down, takes three steps towards window right, goes back for ladder, carries it over and sets it down under window left, gets up on it, looks out of window. Brief laugh. He gets down, takes one step towards window right, goes back for ladder, carries it over and sets it down under window right, gets up on it, looks out of window. Brief laugh. He gets down, goes with ladder towards ashbins, halts, turns, carries back ladder and sets it down under window right, goes to ashbins, removes sheet covering them, folds it over his arm. He raises one lid, stoops and looks into bin. Brief laugh. He closes lid. Same with other bin. He goes to* HAMM, *removes sheet covering him, folds it over his arm. In a dressing-gown, a stiff toque[2] on his head, a large blood-stained handkerchief over his face, a whistle hanging from his neck, a rug over his knees, thick socks on his feet,* HAMM *seems to be asleep.* CLOV *looks him over. Brief laugh. He goes to door, halts, turns towards auditorium.*]

CLOV [*Fixed gaze, tonelessly.*]   Finished, it's finished, nearly finished, it must be nearly finished. [*Pause.*] Grain upon grain, one by one, and one day, suddenly, there's a heap, a little heap, the impossible heap. [*Pause.*] I can't be punished any more. [*Pause.*] I'll go now to my kitchen, ten feet by ten feet by ten feet, and wait for him to whistle me. [*Pause.*] Nice dimensions, nice proportions, I'll lean on the table, and look at the wall, and wait for him to whistle me.

    [*He remains a moment motionless, then goes out. He comes back immediately, goes to window right, takes up the ladder and carries it out. Pause.*

---

1. Translated by the author.
2. A fitted cloth hat with little or no brim, sometimes indicating official status, as with a judge's toque.

HAMM *stirs. He yawns under the handkerchief. He removes the handker-chief from his face. Very red face. Black glasses.*]

HAMM   Me— [*He yawns.*] —to play[3] [*He holds the handkerchief spread out before him.*] Old Stancher![4] [*He takes off his glasses, wipes his eyes, his face, the glasses, puts them on again, folds the handkerchief and puts it back neatly in the breast-pocket of his dressing-gown. He clears his throat, joins the tips of his fingers.*] Can there be misery— [*He yawns.*] —loftier than mine? No doubt. Formerly. But now? [*Pause.*] My father? [*Pause.*] My mother? [*Pause.*] My . . . dog? [*Pause.*] Oh I am willing to believe they suffer as much as such creatures can suffer. But does that mean their sufferings equal mine? No doubt. [*Pause.*] No, all is a— [*He yawns.*] —bsolute, [*Proudly.*] the bigger a man is the fuller he is. [*Pause. Gloomily.*] And the emptier. [*He sniffs.*] Clov! [*Pause.*] No, alone. [*Pause.*] What dreams! Those forests! [*Pause.*] Enough, it's time it ended, in the shelter too. [*Pause.*] And yet I hesitate, I hesitate to . . . to end. Yes, there it is, it's time it ended and yet I hesitate to— [*He yawns.*] —to end. [*Yawns.*] God, I'm tired, I'd be better off in bed. [*He whis-tles. Enter* CLOV *immediately. He halts beside the chair.*] You pollute the air! [*Pause.*] Get me ready, I'm going to bed.

CLOV   I've just got you up.

HAMM   And what of it?

CLOV   I can't be getting you up and putting you to bed every five minutes, I have things to do. [*Pause.*]

HAMM   Did you ever see my eyes?

CLOV   No.

HAMM   Did you never have the curiosity, while I was sleeping, to take off my glasses and look at my eyes?

CLOV   Pulling back the lids? [*Pause.*] No.

HAMM   One of these days I'll show them to you. [*Pause.*] It seems they've gone all white. [*Pause.*] What time is it?

CLOV   The same as usual.

HAMM   [*Gesture towards window right.*]   Have you looked?

CLOV   Yes.

HAMM   Well?

CLOV   Zero.

HAMM   It'd need to rain.

CLOV   It won't rain. [*Pause.*]

HAMM   Apart from that, how do you feel?

CLOV   I don't complain.

HAMM   You feel normal?

CLOV   [*Irritably.*]   I tell you I don't complain.

HAMM   I feel a little queer. [*Pause.*] Clov!

CLOV   Yes.

HAMM   Have you not had enough?

CLOV   Yes! [*Pause.*] Of what?

---

3. Hamm announces that it is his move at the beginning of *Endgame*: the comparison is with a game of chess, of which the "endgame" is the final stage.

4. The handkerchief that stanches his blood.

HAMM   Of this . . . this . . . thing.

CLOV   I always had. [*Pause.*] Not you?

HAMM [*Gloomily.*]   Then there's no reason for it to change.

CLOV   It may end. [*Pause.*] All life long the same questions, the same answers.

HAMM   Get me ready. [CLOV *does not move.*] Go and get the sheet. [CLOV *does not move.*] Clov!

CLOV   Yes.

HAMM   I'll give you nothing more to eat.

CLOV   Then we'll die.

HAMM   I'll give you just enough to keep you from dying. You'll be hungry all the time.

CLOV   Then we won't die. [*Pause.*] I'll go and get the sheet. [*He goes towards the door.*]

HAMM   No! [CLOV *halts.*] I'll give you one biscuit per day. [*Pause.*] One and a half. [*Pause.*] Why do you stay with me?

CLOV   Why do you keep me?

HAMM   There's no one else.

CLOV   There's nowhere else. [*Pause.*]

HAMM   You're leaving me all the same.

CLOV   I'm trying.

HAMM   You don't love me.

CLOV   No.

HAMM   You loved me once.

CLOV   Once!

HAMM   I've made you suffer too much. [*Pause.*] Haven't I?

CLOV   It's not that.

HAMM [*Shocked.*]   I haven't made you suffer too much?

CLOV   Yes!

HAMM [*Relieved.*]   Ah you gave me a fright! [*Pause. Coldly.*] Forgive me. [*Pause. Louder.*] I said, Forgive me.

CLOV   I heard you. [*Pause.*] Have you bled?

HAMM   Less. [*Pause.*] Is it not time for my pain-killer?

CLOV   No. [*Pause.*]

HAMM   How are your eyes?

CLOV   Bad.

HAMM   How are your legs?

CLOV   BAD.

HAMM   But you can move.

CLOV   Yes.

HAMM [*Violently.*]   Then move! [CLOV *goes to back wall, leans against it with his forehead and hands.*] Where are you?

CLOV   Here.

HAMM   Come back! [CLOV *returns to his place beside the chair.*] Where are you?

CLOV   Here.

HAMM   Why don't you kill me?

CLOV   I don't know the combination of the cupboard. [*Pause.*]

HAMM   Go and get two bicycle-wheels.

CLOV   There are no more bicycle-wheels.

HAMM   What have you done with your bicycle?

CLOV   I never had a bicycle.

HAMM   The thing is impossible.

CLOV   When there were still bicycles I wept to have one. I crawled at your feet. You told me to go to hell. Now there are none.

HAMM   And your rounds? When you inspected my paupers. Always on foot?

CLOV   Sometimes on horse. [*The lid of one of the bins lifts and the hands of* NAGG *appear, gripping the rim. Then his head emerges. Nightcap. Very white face.* NAGG *yawns, then listens.*] I'll leave you, I have things to do.

HAMM   In your kitchen?

CLOV   Yes.

HAMM   Outside of here it's death. [*Pause.*] All right, be off. [*Exit* CLOV. *Pause.*] We're getting on.

NAGG   Me pap![5]

HAMM   Accursed progenitor!

NAGG   Me pap!

HAMM   The old folks at home! No decency left! Guzzle, guzzle, that's all they think of. [*He whistles. Enter* CLOV. *He halts beside the chair.*] Well! I thought you were leaving me.

CLOV   Oh not just yet, not just yet.

NAGG   Me pap!

HAMM   Give him his pap.

CLOV   There's no more pap.

HAMM   [*To* NAGG.]   Do you hear that? There's no more pap. You'll never get any more pap.

NAGG   I want me pap!

HAMM   Give him a biscuit. [*Exit* CLOV.] Accursed fornicator! How are your stumps?

NAGG   Never mind me stumps.

[*Enter* CLOV *with biscuit.*]

CLOV   I'm back again, with the biscuit. [*He gives biscuit to* NAGG *who fingers it, sniffs it.*]

NAGG   [*Plaintively.*] What is it?

CLOV   Spratt's medium.[6]

NAGG [*As before.*]   It's hard! I can't!

HAMM   Bottle him!

[CLOV *pushes* NAGG *back into the bin, closes the lid.*]

CLOV [*Returning to his place beside the chair.*]   If age but knew!

HAMM   Sit on him!

CLOV   I can't sit.

HAMM   True. And I can't stand.

CLOV   So it is.

HAMM   Every man his speciality. [*Pause.*] No phone calls? [*Pause.*] Don't we laugh?

5. Food, mush.
6. A common plain cookie.

CLOV [*After reflection.*]   I don't feel like it.

HAMM [*After reflection.*]   Nor I. [*Pause.*] Clov!

CLOV   Yes.

HAMM   Nature has forgotten us.

CLOV   There's no more nature.

HAMM   No more nature! You exaggerate.

CLOV   In the vicinity.

HAMM   But we breathe, we change! We lose our hair, our teeth! Our bloom! Our ideals!

CLOV   Then she hasn't forgotten us.

HAMM   But you say there is none.

CLOV [*Sadly.*]   No one that ever lived ever thought so crooked as we.

HAMM   We do what we can.

CLOV   We shouldn't. [*Pause.*]

HAMM   You're a bit of all right, aren't you?[7]

CLOV   A smithereen.[8] [*Pause.*]

HAMM   This is slow work. [*Pause.*] Is it not time for my pain-killer?

CLOV   No. [*Pause.*] I'll leave you, I have things to do.

HAMM   In your kitchen?

CLOV   Yes.

HAMM   What, I'd like to know.

CLOV   I look at the wall.

HAMM   The wall! And what do you see on your wall? Mene, mene?[9] Naked bodies?

CLOV   I see my light dying.

HAMM   Your light dying! Listen to that! Well, it can die just as well here, *your* light. Take a look at me and then come back and tell me what you think of *your* light. [*Pause.*]

CLOV   You shouldn't speak to me like that. [*Pause.*]

HAMM [*Coldly.*]   Forgive me. [*Pause. Louder.*] I said, Forgive me.

CLOV   I heard you.

[*The lid of* NAGG's *bin lifts. His hands appear, gripping the rim. Then his head emerges. In his mouth the biscuit. He listens.*]

HAMM   Did your seeds come up?

CLOV   No.

HAMM   Did you scratch round them to see if they had sprouted?

CLOV   They haven't sprouted.

HAMM   Perhaps it's still too early.

CLOV   If they were going to sprout they would have sprouted. [*Violently.*] They'll never sprout!

[*Pause.* NAGG *takes biscuit in his hand.*]

HAMM   This is not much fun. [*Pause.*] But that's always the way at the end of the day, isn't it, Clov?

CLOV   Always.

---

7. You're pretty good, aren't you? (British slang).
8. A tiny bit.
9. From Daniel 5.25: "Mene, mene, tekel, upharsin"; words written by a divine hand on the wall during the feast of Belshazzar, king of Babylon. They predict doom and tell the king "Thou art weighed in the balances, and art found wanting" (Daniel 5.27).

HAMM It's the end of the day like any other day, isn't it, Clov?
CLOV Looks like it. [*Pause.*]
HAMM [*Anguished.*] What's happening, what's happening?
CLOV Something is taking its course. [*Pause.*]
HAMM All right, be off. [*He leans back in his chair, remains motionless.* CLOV *does not move, heaves a great groaning sigh.* HAMM *sits up.*] I thought I told you to be off.
CLOV I'm trying. [*He goes to door, halts.*] Ever since I was whelped.
      [*Exit* CLOV.]
HAMM We're getting on.
      [*He leans back in his chair, remains motionless.* NAGG *knocks on the lid of the other bin. Pause. He knocks harder. The lid lifts and the hands of* NELL *appear, gripping the rim. Then her head emerges. Lace cap. Very white face.*]
NELL What is it, my pet? [*Pause.*] Time for love?
NAGG Were you asleep?
NELL Oh no!
NAGG Kiss me.
NELL We can't.
NAGG Try.
      [*Their heads strain towards each other, fail to meet, fall apart again.*]
NELL Why this farce, day after day? [*Pause.*]
NAGG I've lost me tooth.
NELL When?
NAGG I had it yesterday.
NELL [*Elegiac.*] Ah yesterday!
      [*They turn painfully towards each other.*]
NAGG Can you see me?
NELL Hardly. And you?
NAGG What?
NELL Can you see me?
NAGG Hardly.
NELL So much the better, so much the better.
NAGG Don't say that. [*Pause.*] Our sight has failed.
NELL Yes.
      [*Pause. They turn away from each other.*]
NAGG Can you hear me?
NELL Yes. And you?
NAGG Yes. [*Pause.*] Our hearing hasn't failed.
NELL Our what?
NAGG Our hearing.
NELL No. [*Pause.*] Have you anything else to say to me?
NAGG Do you remember—
NELL No.
NAGG When we crashed on our tandem[1] and lost our shanks.
      [*They laugh heartily.*]
NELL It was in the Ardennes.
      [*They laugh less heartily.*]

___
1. A bicycle built for two.

NAGG   On the road to Sedan.[2] [*They laugh still less heartily.*] Are you cold?

NELL   Yes, perished. And you?

NAGG [*Pause.*]   I'm freezing. [*Pause.*] Do you want to go in?

NELL   Yes.

NAGG   Then go in. [NELL *does not move.*] Why don't you go in?

NELL   I don't know. [*Pause.*]

NAGG   Has he changed your sawdust?

NELL   It isn't sawdust. [*Pause. Wearily.*] Can you not be a little accurate, Nagg?

NAGG   Your sand then. It's not important.

NELL   It is important. [*Pause.*]

NAGG   It was sawdust once.

NELL   Once!

NAGG   And now it's sand. [*Pause.*] From the shore. [*Pause. Impatiently.*] Now it's sand he fetches from the shore.

NELL   Now it's sand.

NAGG   Has he changed yours?

NELL   No.

NAGG   Nor mine. [*Pause.*] I won't have it! [*Pause. Holding up the biscuit.*] Do you want a bit?

NELL   No. [*Pause.*] Of what?

NAGG   Biscuit. I've kept you half. [*He looks at the biscuit. Proudly.*] Three quarters. For you. Here. [*He proffers the biscuit.*] No? [*Pause.*] Do you not feel well?

HAMM [*Wearily.*]   Quiet, quiet, you're keeping me awake. [*Pause.*] Talk softer. [*Pause.*] If I could sleep I might make love. I'd go into the woods. My eyes would see . . . the sky, the earth. I'd run, they wouldn't catch me. [*Pause.*] Nature! [*Pause.*] There's something dripping in my head. [*Pause.*] A heart, a heart in my head. [*Pause.*]

NAGG [*Soft.*]   Do you hear him? A heart in his head! [*He chuckles cautiously.*]

NELL   One mustn't laugh at those things, Nagg. Why must you always laugh at them?

NAGG   Not so loud!

NELL [*Without lowering her voice.*]   Nothing is funnier than unhappiness, I grant you that. But—

NAGG [*Shocked.*]   Oh!

NELL   Yes, yes, it's the most comical thing in the world. And we laugh, we laugh, with a will, in the beginning. But it's always the same thing. Yes, it's like the funny story we have heard too often, we still find it funny, but we don't laugh any more. [*Pause.*] Have you anything else to say to me?

NAGG   No.

NELL   Are you quite sure? [*Pause.*] Then I'll leave you.

NAGG   Do you not want your biscuit? [*Pause.*] I'll keep it for you. [*Pause.*] I thought you were going to leave me.

NELL   I am going to leave you.

NAGG   Could you give me a scratch before you go?

---

2. Town in northern France where the French were defeated in the Franco-Prussian War (1870). Ardennes is a forest in northern France, the scene of bitter fighting in both world wars.

NELL No. [*Pause.*] Where?

NAGG In the back.

NELL No. [*Pause.*] Rub yourself against the rim.

NAGG It's lower down. In the hollow.

NELL What hollow?

NAGG The hollow! [*Pause.*] Could you not? [*Pause.*] Yesterday you scratched me there.

NELL [*Elegiac.*] Ah yesterday!

NAGG Could you not? [*Pause.*] Would you like me to scratch you? [*Pause.*] Are you crying again?

NELL I was trying. [*Pause.*]

HAMM Perhaps it's a little vein. [*Pause.*]

NAGG What was that he said?

NELL Perhaps it's a little vein.

NAGG What does that mean? [*Pause.*] That means nothing. [*Pause.*] Will I tell you the story of the tailor?

NELL No. [*Pause.*] What for?

NAGG To cheer you up.

NELL It's not funny.

NAGG It always made you laugh. [*Pause.*] The first time I thought you'd die.

NELL It was on Lake Como.[3] [*Pause.*] One April afternoon. [*Pause.*] Can you believe it?

NAGG What?

NELL That we once went out rowing on Lake Como. [*Pause.*] One April afternoon.

NAGG We had got engaged the day before.

NELL Engaged!

NAGG You were in such fits that we capsized. By rights we should have been drowned.

NELL It was because I felt happy.

NAGG [*Indignant.*] It was not, it was not, it was my story and nothing else. Happy! Don't you laugh at it still? Every time I tell it. Happy!

NELL It was deep, deep. And you could see down to the bottom. So white. So clean.

NAGG Let me tell it again. [*Raconteur's voice.*] An Englishman, needing a pair of striped trousers in a hurry for the New Year festivities, goes to his tailor who takes his measurements. [*Tailor's voice.*] "That's the lot, come back in four days, I'll have it ready." Good. Four days later. [*Tailor's voice.*] "So sorry, come back in a week, I've made a mess of the seat." Good, that's all right, a neat seat can be very ticklish. A week later. [*Tailor's voice.*] "Frightfully sorry, come back in ten days. I've made a hash of the crotch." Good, can't be helped, a snug crotch is always a teaser. Ten days later. [*Tailor's voice.*] "Dreadfully sorry, come back in a fortnight, I've made a balls of the fly." Good, at a pinch, a smart fly is a stiff proposition. [*Pause. Normal voice.*] I never told it worse. [*Pause. Gloomy.*] I tell this story worse and worse. [*Pause. Raconteur's voice.*] Well, to make it short, the bluebells are

---

3. A large lake and tourist resort in northern Italy, near the Swiss border.

blowing and he ballockses[4] the buttonholes. [*Customer's voice.*] "God damn you to hell, Sir, no, it's indecent, there are limits! In six days, do you hear me, six days, God made the world. Yes Sir, no less Sir, the WORLD! And you are not bloody well capable of making me a pair of trousers in three months!" [*Tailor's voice, scandalized.*] "But my dear Sir, my dear Sir, look— [*Disdainful gesture, disgustedly.*] —at the world— [*Pause.*] and look— [*Loving gesture, proudly.*] —at my TROUSERS!"

> [*Pause. He looks at* NELL *who has remained impassive, her eyes unseeing, breaks into a high forced laugh, cuts it short, pokes his head towards* NELL, *launches his laugh again.*]

HAMM   Silence!

> [NAGG *starts, cuts short his laugh.*]

NELL   You could see down to the bottom.

HAMM [*Exasperated.*]   Have you not finished? Will you never finish? [*With sudden fury.*] Will this never finish? [NAGG *disappears into his bin, closes the lid behind him.* NELL *does not move. Frenziedly.*] My kingdom for a nightman![5] [*He whistles. Enter* CLOV.] Clear away this muck! Chuck it in the sea!

> [CLOV *goes to bins, halts.*]

NELL   So white.

HAMM   What? What's she blathering about?

> [CLOV *stoops, takes* NELL's *hand, feels her pulse.*]

NELL [*To* CLOV.]   Desert!

> [CLOV *lets go her hand, pushes her back in the bin, closes the lid.*]

CLOV [*Returning to his place beside the chair.*]   She has no pulse.

HAMM   What was she drivelling about?

CLOV   She told me to go away, into the desert.

HAMM   Damn busybody! Is that all?

CLOV   No.

HAMM   What else?

CLOV   I didn't understand.

HAMM   Have you bottled her?

CLOV   Yes.

HAMM   Are they both bottled?

CLOV   Yes.

HAMM   Screw down the lids. [CLOV *goes towards door.*] Time enough. [CLOV *halts.*] My anger subsides, I'd like to pee.

CLOV [*With alacrity.*]   I'll go and get the catheter. [*He goes towards door.*]

HAMM   Time enough. [CLOV *halts.*] Give me my pain-killer.

CLOV   It's too soon. [*Pause.*] It's too soon on top of your tonic, it wouldn't act.

HAMM   In the morning they brace you up and in the evening they calm you down. Unless it's the other way round. [*Pause.*] That old doctor, he's dead naturally?

CLOV   He wasn't old.

HAMM   But he's dead?

---

4. "Bollixes," botches.
5. Parody of Shakespeare's *Richard III*, where the defeated king seeks a horse to escape from the battlefield: "A horse! a horse! My kingdom for a horse!" (5.4.7).

CLOV Naturally. [*Pause.*] *You* ask *me* that? [*Pause.*]

HAMM Take me for a little turn. [CLOV *goes behind the chair and pushes it forward.*] Not too fast! [CLOV *pushes chair.*] Right round the world! [CLOV *pushes chair.*] Hug the walls, then back to the center again. [CLOV *pushes chair.*] I was right in the center, wasn't I?

CLOV [*Pushing.*] Yes.

HAMM We'd need a proper wheel-chair. With big wheels. Bicycle wheels! [*Pause.*] Are you hugging?

CLOV [*Pushing.*] Yes.

HAMM [*Groping for wall.*] It's a lie! Why do you lie to me?

CLOV [*Bearing closer to wall.*] There! There!

HAMM Stop! [CLOV *stops chair close to back wall.* HAMM *lays his hand against wall.*] Old wall! [*Pause.*] Beyond is the . . . other hell. [*Pause. Violently.*] Closer! Closer! Up against!

CLOV Take away your hand. [HAMM *withdraws his hand.* CLOV *rams chair against wall.*] There!

[HAMM *leans towards wall, applies his ear to it.*]

HAMM Do you hear? [*He strikes the wall with his knuckles.*] Do you hear? Hollow bricks! [*He strikes again.*] All that's hollow! [*Pause. He straightens up. Violently.*] That's enough. Back!

CLOV We haven't done the round.

HAMM Back to my place! [CLOV *pushes chair back to center.*] Is that my place?

CLOV Yes, that's your place.

HAMM Am I right in the center?

CLOV I'll measure it.

HAMM More or less! More or less!

CLOV [*Moving chair slightly.*] There!

HAMM I'm more or less in the center?

CLOV I'd say so.

HAMM You'd say so! Put me right in the center!

CLOV I'll go and get the tape.

HAMM Roughly! Roughly! [CLOV *moves chair slightly.*] Bang in the center!

CLOV There! [*Pause.*]

HAMM I feel a little too far to the left. [CLOV *moves chair slightly.*] Now I feel a little too far to the right. [CLOV *moves chair slightly.*] I feel a little too far forward. [CLOV *moves chair slightly.*] Now I feel a little too far back. [CLOV *moves chair slightly.*] Don't stay there, [*i.e., behind the chair*] you give me the shivers.

[CLOV *returns to his place beside the chair.*]

CLOV If I could kill him I'd die happy. [*Pause.*]

HAMM What's the weather like?

CLOV As usual.

HAMM Look at the earth.

CLOV I've looked.

HAMM With the glass?

CLOV No need of the glass.

HAMM Look at it with the glass.

CLOV I'll go and get the glass.

[*Exit* CLOV.]

HAMM   No need of the glass!

[*Enter* CLOV *with telescope.*]

CLOV   I'm back again, with the glass. [*He goes to window right, looks up at it.*] I need the steps.

HAMM   Why? Have you shrunk? [*Exit* CLOV *with telescope.*] I don't like that, I don't like that.

[*Enter* CLOV *with ladder, but without telescope.*]

CLOV   I'm back again, with the steps. [*He sets down ladder under window right, gets up on it, realizes he has not the telescope, gets down.*] I need the glass. [*He goes towards door.*]

HAMM [*Violently.*]   But you have the glass!

CLOV [*Halting, violently.*]   No, I haven't the glass!

[*Exit* CLOV.]

HAMM   This is deadly.

[*Enter* CLOV *with telescope. He goes towards ladder.*]

CLOV   Things are livening up. [*He gets up on ladder, raises the telescope, lets it fall.*] I did it on purpose. [*He gets down, picks up the telescope, turns it on auditorium.*] I see . . . a multitude . . . in transports . . . of joy.[6] [*Pause.*] That's what I call a magnifier. [*He lowers the telescope, turns towards* HAMM.] Well? Don't we laugh?

HAMM [*After reflection.*]   I don't.

CLOV [*After reflection.*]   Nor I. [*He gets up on ladder, turns the telescope on the without.*] Let's see. [*He looks, moving the telescope.*] Zero . . . [*he looks*] . . . zero . . . [*he looks*] . . . and zero.

HAMM   Nothing stirs. All is—

CLOV   Zer—

HAMM [*Violently.*]   Wait till you're spoke to! [*Normal voice.*] All is . . . all is . . . all is what? [*Violently.*] All is what?

CLOV   What all is? In a word? Is that what you want to know? Just a moment. [*He turns the telescope on the without, looks, lowers the telescope, turns towards* HAMM.] Corpsed. [*Pause.*] Well? Content?

HAMM   Look at the sea.

CLOV   It's the same.

HAMM   Look at the ocean!

[CLOV *gets down, takes a few steps towards window left, goes back for ladder, carries it over and sets it down under window left, gets up on it, turns the telescope on the without, looks at length. He starts, lowers the telescope, examines it, turns it again on the without.*]

CLOV   Never seen anything like that!

HAMM [*Anxious.*]   What? A sail? A fin? Smoke?

CLOV [*Looking.*]   The light is sunk.

HAMM [*Relieved.*]   Pah! We all knew that.

CLOV [*Looking.*]   There was a bit left.

HAMM   The base.

CLOV [*Looking.*]   Yes.

HAMM   And now?

---

6. Echo of Revelation 7.9–10: "After this I beheld, and, lo, a great multitude, which . . . cried with a loud voice, saying, Salvation."

CLOV [*Looking.*]   All gone.

HAMM   No gulls?

CLOV [*Looking.*]   Gulls!

HAMM   And the horizon? Nothing on the horizon?

CLOV [*Lowering the telescope, turning towards* HAMM, *exasperated.*]   What in God's name could there be on the horizon? [*Pause.*]

HAMM   The waves, how are the waves?

CLOV   The waves? [*He turns the telescope on the waves.*] Lead.

HAMM   And the sun?

CLOV [*Looking.*]   Zero.

HAMM   But it should be sinking. Look again.

CLOV [*Looking.*]   Damn the sun.

HAMM   Is it night already then?

CLOV [*Looking.*]   No.

HAMM   Then what is it?

CLOV [*Looking.*]   Gray. [*Lowering the telescope, turning towards* HAMM, *louder.*] Gray! [*Pause. Still louder.*] GRRAY! [*Pause. He gets down, approaches* HAMM *from behind, whispers in his ear.*]

HAMM [*Starting.*]   Gray! Did I hear you say gray?

CLOV   Light black. From pole to pole.

HAMM   You exaggerate. [*Pause.*] Don't stay there, you give me the shivers.
      [CLOV *returns to his place beside the chair.*]

CLOV   Why this farce, day after day?

HAMM   Routine. One never knows. [*Pause.*] Last night I saw inside my breast. There was a big sore.

CLOV   Pah! You saw your heart.

HAMM   No, it was living. [*Pause. Anguished.*] Clov!

CLOV   Yes.

HAMM   What's happening?

CLOV   Something is taking its course. [*Pause.*]

HAMM   Clov!

CLOV [*Impatiently.*]   What is it?

HAMM   We're not beginning to . . . to . . . mean something?

CLOV   Mean something! You and I, mean something! [*Brief laugh.*] Ah that's a good one!

HAMM   I wonder. [*Pause.*] Imagine if a rational being came back to earth, wouldn't he be liable to get ideas into his head if he observed us long enough. [*Voice of rational being.*] Ah, good, now I see what it is, yes, now I understand what they're at! [CLOV *starts, drops the telescope and begins to scratch his belly with both hands. Normal voice.*] And without going so far as that, we ourselves . . . [*With emotion.*] . . . we ourselves . . . at certain moments . . . [*Vehemently.*] To think perhaps it won't all have been for nothing!

CLOV [*Anguished, scratching himself.*]   I have a flea!

HAMM   A flea! Are there still fleas?

CLOV   On me there's one. [*Scratching.*] Unless it's a crablouse.

HAMM [*Very perturbed.*]   But humanity might start from there all over again! Catch him, for the love of God!

CLOV   I'll go and get the powder.
      [*Exit* CLOV.]

HAMM   A flea! This is awful! What a day!
   [*Enter* CLOV *with a sprinkling-tin.*]
CLOV   I'm back again, with the insecticide.
HAMM   Let him have it!
   [CLOV *loosens the top of his trousers, pulls it forward and shakes powder
   into the aperture. He stoops, looks, waits, starts, frenziedly shakes more
   powder, stoops, looks, waits.*]
CLOV   The bastard!
HAMM   Did you get him?
CLOV   Looks like it. [*He drops the tin and adjusts his trousers.*] Unless he's lay-
   ing doggo.
HAMM   Laying! Lying you mean. Unless he's *lying* doggo.
CLOV   Ah? One says lying? One doesn't say laying?
HAMM   Use your head, can't you. If he was laying we'd be bitched.
CLOV   Ah. [*Pause.*] What about that pee?
HAMM   I'm having it.
CLOV   Ah that's the spirit, that's the spirit! [*Pause.*]
HAMM [*With ardour.*]   Let's go from here, the two of us! South! You can make
   a raft and the currents will carry us away, far away, to other . . . mammals!
CLOV   God forbid!
HAMM   Alone, I'll embark alone! Get working on that raft immediately. Tomor-
   row I'll be gone for ever.
CLOV [*Hastening towards door.*]   I'll start straight away.
HAMM   Wait! [CLOV *halts.*] Will there be sharks, do you think?
CLOV   Sharks? I don't know. If there are there will be. [*He goes towards
   door.*]
HAMM   Wait! [CLOV *halts.*] Is it not yet time for my pain-killer?
CLOV [*Violently.*]   No! [*He goes towards door.*]
HAMM   Wait! [CLOV *halts.*] How are your eyes?
CLOV   Bad.
HAMM   But you can see.
CLOV   All I want.
HAMM   How are your legs?
CLOV   Bad.
HAMM   But you can walk.
CLOV   I come . . . and go.
HAMM   In my house. [*Pause. With prophetic relish.*] One day you'll be blind,
   like me. You'll be sitting there, a speck in the void, in the dark, for ever, like
   me. [*Pause.*] One day you'll say to yourself, I'm tired, I'll sit down, and you'll
   go and sit down. Then you'll say, I'm hungry, I'll get up and get something
   to eat. But you won't get up. You'll say, I shouldn't have sat down, but since
   I have I'll sit on a little longer, then I'll get up and get something to eat. But
   you won't get up and you won't get anything to eat. [*Pause.*] You'll look at
   the wall awhile, then you'll say, I'll close my eyes, perhaps have a little sleep,
   after that I'll feel better, and you'll close them. And when you open them
   again there'll be no wall any more. [*Pause.*] Infinite emptiness will be all
   around you, all the resurrected dead of all the ages wouldn't fill it, and there
   you'll be like a little bit of grit in the middle of the steppe. [*Pause.*] Yes, one
   day you'll know what it is, you'll be like me, except that you won't have anyone

with you, because you won't have had pity on anyone and because there won't be anyone left to have pity on. [*Pause.*]

CLOV   It's not certain. [*Pause.*] And there's one thing you forget.

HAMM   Ah?

CLOV   I can't sit down.

HAMM   [*Impatiently.*]   Well you'll lie down then, what the hell! Or you'll come to a standstill, simply stop and stand still, the way you are now. One day you'll say, I'm tired, I'll stop. What does the attitude matter? [*Pause.*]

CLOV   So you all want me to leave you.

HAMM   Naturally.

CLOV   Then I'll leave you.

HAMM   You can't leave us.

CLOV   Then I won't leave you. [*Pause.*]

HAMM   Why don't you finish us? [*Pause.*] I'll tell you the combination of the cupboard if you promise to finish me.

CLOV   I couldn't finish you.

HAMM   Then you won't finish me. [*Pause.*]

CLOV   I'll leave you, I have things to do.

HAMM   Do you remember when you came here?

CLOV   No. Too small, you told me.

HAMM   Do you remember your father?

CLOV   [*Wearily.*]   Same answer. [*Pause.*] You've asked me these questions millions of times.

HAMM   I love the old questions. [*With fervor.*] Ah the old questions, the old answers, there's nothing like them! [*Pause.*] It was I was a father to you.

CLOV   Yes. [*He looks at* HAMM *fixedly.*] You were that to me.

HAMM   My house a home for you.

CLOV   Yes. [*He looks about him.*] This was that for me.

HAMM   [*Proudly.*]   But for me, [*Gesture towards himself.*] no father. But for Hamm, [*Gesture towards surroundings.*] no home. [*Pause.*]

CLOV   I'll leave you.

HAMM   Did you ever think of one thing?

CLOV   Never.

HAMM   That here we're down in a hole. [*Pause.*] But beyond the hills? Eh? Perhaps it's still green. Eh? [*Pause.*] Flora! Pomona! [*Ecstatically.*] Ceres![7] [*Pause.*] Perhaps you won't need to go very far.

CLOV   I can't go very far. [*Pause.*] I'll leave you.

HAMM   Is my dog ready?

CLOV   He lacks a leg.

HAMM   Is he silky?

CLOV   He's a kind of Pomeranian.

HAMM   Go and get him.

CLOV   He lacks a leg.

HAMM   Go and get him! [*Exit* CLOV.] We're getting on.

[*Enter* CLOV *holding by one of its three legs a black toy dog.*]

CLOV   Your dogs are here. [*He hands the dog to* HAMM *who feels it, fondles it.*]

HAMM   He's white, isn't he?

7. In Roman mythology, the goddesses of flowers, fruits, and fertility.

CLOV   Nearly.

HAMM   What do you mean, nearly? Is he white or isn't he?

CLOV   He isn't. [*Pause.*]

HAMM   You've forgotten the sex.

CLOV [*Vexed.*]   But he isn't finished. The sex goes on at the end. [*Pause.*]

HAMM   You haven't put on his ribbon.

CLOV [*Angrily.*]   But he isn't finished, I tell you! First you finish your dog and
   then you put on his ribbon! [*Pause.*]

HAMM   Can he stand?

CLOV   I don't know.

HAMM   Try. [*He hands the dog to* CLOV *who places it on the ground.*] Well?

CLOV   Wait! [*He squats down and tries to get the dog to stand on its three legs,
   fails, lets it go. The dog falls on its side.*]

HAMM [*Impatiently.*]   Well?

CLOV   He's standing.

HAMM [*Groping for the dog.*]   Where? Where is he?
      [CLOV *holds up the dog in a standing position.*]

CLOV   There. [*He takes* HAMM's *hand and guides it towards the dog's head.*]

HAMM [*His hand on the dog's head.*]   Is he gazing at me?

CLOV   Yes.

HAMM [*Proudly.*]   As if he were asking me to take him for a walk?

CLOV   If you like.

HAMM [*As before.*]   Or as if he were begging me for a bone. [*He withdraws his
   hand.*] Leave him like that, standing there imploring me.
      [CLOV *straightens up. The dog falls on its side.*]

CLOV   I'll leave you.

HAMM   Have you had your visions?

CLOV   Less.

HAMM   Is Mother Pegg's light on?

CLOV   Light! How could anyone's light be on?

HAMM   Extinguished!

CLOV   Naturally it's extinguished. If it's not on it's extinguished.

HAMM   No, I mean Mother Pegg.

CLOV   But naturally she's extinguished! [*Pause.*] What's the matter with you
   today?

HAMM   I'm taking my course. [*Pause.*] Is she buried?

CLOV   Buried! Who would have buried her?

HAMM   You.

CLOV   Me! Haven't I enough to do without burying people?

HAMM   But you'll bury me.

CLOV   No I won't bury you. [*Pause.*]

HAMM   She was bonny once, like a flower of the field. [*With reminiscent leer.*]
   And a great one for the men!

CLOV   We too were bonny—once. It's a rare thing not to have been bonny—
   once. [*Pause.*]

HAMM   Go and get the gaff.[8]
      [CLOV *goes to door, halts.*]

---

8. A long stick with a hook, usually for catching fish.

CLOV   Do this, do that, and I do it. I never refuse. Why?

HAMM   You're not able to.

CLOV   Soon I won't do it any more.

HAMM   You won't be able to any more. [*Exit* CLOV.] Ah the creatures, the creatures, everything has to be explained to them.

> [*Enter* CLOV *with gaff.*]

CLOV   Here's your gaff. Stick it up. [*He gives the gaff to* HAMM *who, wielding it like a puntpole, tries to move his chair.*]

HAMM   Did I move?

CLOV   No.

> [HAMM *throws down the gaff.*]

HAMM   Go and get the oilcan.

CLOV   What for?

HAMM   To oil the castors.

CLOV   I oiled them yesterday.

HAMM   Yesterday! What does that mean? Yesterday!

CLOV [*Violently.*]   That means that bloody awful day, long ago, before this bloody awful day. I use the words you taught me. If they don't mean anything any more, teach me others. Or let me be silent. [*Pause.*]

HAMM   I once knew a madman who thought the end of the world had come. He was a painter—and engraver. I had a great fondness for him. I used to go and see him, in the asylum. I'd take him by the hand and drag him to the window. Look! There! All that rising corn! And there! Look! The sails of the herring fleet! All that loveliness! [*Pause.*] He'd snatch away his hand and go back into his corner. Appalled. All he had seen was ashes. [*Pause.*] He alone had been spared. [*Pause.*] Forgotten. [*Pause.*] It appears the case is . . . was not so . . . so unusual.

CLOV   A madman! When was that?

HAMM   Oh way back, way back, you weren't in the land of the living.

CLOV   God be with the days!

> [*Pause.* HAMM *raises his toque.*]

HAMM   I had a great fondness for him. [*Pause. He puts on his toque again.*] He was a painter—and engraver.

CLOV   There are so many terrible things.

HAMM   No, no, there are not so many now. [*Pause.*] Clov!

CLOV   Yes.

HAMM   Do you not think this has gone on long enough?

CLOV   Yes! [*Pause.*] What?

HAMM   This . . . this . . . thing.

CLOV   I've always thought so. [*Pause.*] You not?

HAMM [*Gloomily.*]   Then it's a day like any other day.

CLOV   As long as it lasts. [*Pause.*] All life long the same inanities.

HAMM   I can't leave you.

CLOV   I know. And you can't follow me. [*Pause.*]

HAMM   If you leave me how shall I know?

CLOV [*Briskly.*]   Well you simply whistle me and if I don't come running it means I've left you. [*Pause.*]

HAMM   You won't come and kiss me goodbye?

CLOV   Oh I shouldn't think so. [*Pause.*]

HAMM   But you might be merely dead in your kitchen.

CLOV   The result would be the same.

HAMM   Yes, but how would I know, if you were merely dead in your kitchen?

CLOV   Well . . . sooner or later I'd start to stink.

HAMM   You stink already. The whole place stinks of corpses.

CLOV   The whole universe.

HAMM   [*Angrily.*]   To hell with the universe. [*Pause.*] Think of something.

CLOV   What?

HAMM   An idea, have an idea. [*Angrily.*] A bright idea!

CLOV   Ah good. [*He starts pacing to and fro, his eyes fixed on the ground, his hands behind his back. He halts.*] The pains in my legs! It's unbelievable! Soon I won't be able to think any more.

HAMM   You won't be able to leave me. [CLOV *resumes his pacing.*] What are you doing?

CLOV   Having an idea. [*He paces.*] Ah! [*He halts.*]

HAMM   What a brain! [*Pause.*] Well?

CLOV   Wait! [*He meditates. Not very convinced.*] Yes . . . [*Pause. More convinced.*] Yes! [*He raises his head.*] I have it! I set the alarm. [*Pause.*]

HAMM   This is perhaps not one of my bright days, but frankly—

CLOV   You whistle me. I don't come. The alarm rings. I'm gone. It doesn't ring. I'm dead. [*Pause.*]

HAMM   Is it working? [*Pause. Impatiently.*] The alarm, is it working?

CLOV   Why wouldn't it be working?

HAMM   Because it's worked too much.

CLOV   But it's hardly worked at all.

HAMM   [*Angrily.*]   Then because it's worked too little!

CLOV   I'll go and see. [*Exit* CLOV. *Brief ring of alarm off. Enter* CLOV *with alarm-clock. He holds it against* HAMM's *ear and releases alarm. They listen to it ringing to the end. Pause.*] Fit to wake the dead! Did you hear it?

HAMM   Vaguely.

CLOV   The end is terrific!

HAMM   I prefer the middle. [*Pause.*] Is it not time for my pain-killer?

CLOV   No! [*He goes to door, turns.*] I'll leave you.

HAMM   It's time for my story. Do you want to listen to my story.

CLOV   No.

HAMM   Ask my father if he wants to listen to my story.

[CLOV *goes to bins, raises the lid of* NAGG's, *stoops, looks into it. Pause. He straightens up.*]

CLOV   He's asleep.

HAMM   Wake him.

[CLOV *stoops, wakes* NAGG *with the alarm. Unintelligible words.* CLOV *straightens up.*]

CLOV   He doesn't want to listen to your story.

HAMM   I'll give him a bon-bon.

[CLOV *stoops. As before.*]

CLOV   He wants a sugar-plum.

HAMM   He'll get a sugar-plum.

[CLOV *stoops. As before.*]

CLOV   It's a deal. [*He goes towards door.* NAGG's *hands appear, gripping the rim. Then the head emerges.* CLOV *reaches door, turns.*] Do you believe in the life to come?

HAMM   Mine was always that. [*Exit* CLOV.] Got him that time!

NAGG   I'm listening.

HAMM   Scoundrel! Why did you engender me?

NAGG   I didn't know.

HAMM   What? What didn't you know?

NAGG   That it'd be you. [*Pause.*] You'll give me a sugar-plum?

HAMM   After the audition.

NAGG   You swear?

HAMM   Yes.

NAGG   On what?

HAMM   My honor.
        [*Pause. They laugh heartily.*]

NAGG   Two.

HAMM   One.

NAGG   One for me and one for—

HAMM   One! Silence! [*Pause.*] Where was I? [*Pause. Gloomily.*] It's finished,
we're finished. [*Pause.*] Nearly finished. [*Pause.*] There'll be no more speech.
[*Pause.*] Something dripping in my head, ever since the fontanelles. [*Stifled
hilarity of* NAGG.] Splash, splash, always on the same spot. [*Pause.*] Perhaps
it's a little vein. [*Pause.*] A little artery. [*Pause. More animated.*] Enough of
that, it's story time, where was I? [*Pause. Narrative tone.*] The man came
crawling towards me, on his belly. Pale, wonderfully pale and thin, he seemed
on the point of— [*Pause. Normal tone.*] No, I've done that bit. [*Pause. Narrative tone.*] I calmly filled my pipe—the meerschaum, lit it with . . . let us say
a vesta, drew a few puffs. Aah! [*Pause.*] Well, what is it *you* want? [*Pause.*]
It was an extraordinarily bitter day, I remember, zero by the thermometer.
But considering it was Christmas Eve there was nothing . . . extra-ordinary
about that. Seasonable weather, for once in a way. [*Pause.*] Well, what ill
wind blows you my way? He raised his face to me, black with mingled dirt
and tears. [*Pause. Normal tone.*] That should do it. [*Narrative tone.*] No, no,
don't look at me, don't look at me. He dropped his eyes and mumbled something, apologies I presume. [*Pause.*] I'm a busy man, you know, the final
touches, before the festivities, you know what it is. [*Pause. Forcibly.*] Come
on now, what is the object of this invasion? [*Pause.*] It was a glorious bright
day, I remember, fifty by the heliometer,[9] but already the sun was sinking
down into the . . . down among the dead. [*Normal tone.*] Nicely put, that.
[*Narrative tone.*] Come on now, come on, present your petition and let
me resume my labors. [*Pause. Normal tone.*] There's English for you. Ah
well . . . [*Narrative tone.*] It was then he took the plunge. It's my little one,
he said. Tsstss, a little one, that's bad. My little boy, he said, as if the sex
mattered. Where did he come from? He named the hole. A good half-day,
on horse. What are you insinuating? That the place is still inhabited? No no,
not a soul, except himself and the child—assuming he existed. Good. I
enquired about the situation at Kov, beyond the gulf. Not a sinner. Good.
And you expect me to believe you have left your little one back there, all
alone, and alive into the bargain? Come now! [*Pause.*] It was a howling wild

---

9. Literally, a "sun meter." Ordinarily, a telescope used to measure distances between celestial
bodies.

day, I remember, a hundred by the anemometer.[1] The wind was tearing up the dead pines and sweeping them . . . away. [*Pause. Normal tone.*] A bit feeble, that. [*Narrative tone.*] Come on, man, speak up, what is you want from me, I have to put up my holly. [*Pause.*] Well to make it short it finally transpired that what he wanted from me was . . . bread for his brat? Bread? But I have no bread, it doesn't agree with me. Good. Then perhaps a little corn? [*Pause. Normal tone.*] That should do it. [*Narrative tone.*] Corn, yes, I have corn, it's true, in my granaries. But use your head. I give you some corn, a pound, a pound and a half, you bring it back to your child and you make him—if he's still alive—a nice pot of porridge, [NAGG *reacts.*] a nice pot and a half of porridge, full of nourishment. Good. The colors come back into his little cheeks—perhaps. And then? [*Pause.*] I lost patience. [*Violently.*] Use your head, can't you, use your head, you're on earth, there's no cure for that! [*Pause.*] It was an exceedingly dry day, I remember, zero by the hygrometer.[2] Ideal weather, for my lumbago. [*Pause. Violently.*] But what in God's name do you imagine? That the earth will awake in spring? That the rivers and seas will run with fish again? That there's manna in heaven still for imbeciles like you? [*Pause.*] Gradually I cooled down, sufficiently at least to ask him how long he had taken on the way. Three whole days. Good. In what condition he had left the child. Deep in sleep. [*Forcibly.*] But deep in what sleep, deep in what sleep already? [*Pause.*] Well to make it short I finally offered to take him into my service. He had touched a chord. And then I imagined already that I wasn't much longer for this world. [*He laughs. Pause.*] Well? [*Pause.*] Well? Here if you were careful you might die a nice natural death, in peace and comfort. [*Pause.*] Well? [*Pause.*] In the end he asked me would I consent to take in the child as well—if he were still alive. [*Pause.*] It was the moment I was waiting for. [*Pause.*] Would I consent to take in the child . . . [*Pause.*] I can see him still, down on his knees, his hands flat on the ground, glaring at me with his mad eyes, in defiance of my wishes. [*Pause. Normal tone.*] I'll soon have finished with this story. [*Pause.*] Unless I bring in other characters. [*Pause.*] But where would I find them? [*Pause.*] Where would I look for them? [*Pause. He whistles. Enter* CLOV.] Let us pray to God.

NAGG   Me sugar-plum!

CLOV   There's a rat in the kitchen!

HAMM   A rat! Are there still rats?

CLOV   In the kitchen there's one.

HAMM   And you haven't exterminated him?

CLOV   Half. You disturbed us.

HAMM   He can't get away?

CLOV   No.

HAMM   You'll finish him later. Let us pray to God.

CLOV   Again!

NAGG   Me sugar-plum!

HAMM   God first! [*Pause.*] Are you right?

CLOV [*Resigned.*]   Off we go.

1. A wind meter.
2. A moisture meter.

HAMM [*To* NAGG.]   And you?

NAGG [*Clasping his hands, closing his eyes, in a gabble.*]   Our Father which art—

HAMM   Silence! In silence! Where are your manners? [*Pause.*] Off we go. [*Attitudes of prayer. Silence. Abandoning his attitude, discouraged.*] Well?

CLOV [*Abandoning his attitude.*]   What a hope! And you?

HAMM   Sweet damn all! [*To* NAGG.] And you?

NAGG   Wait! [*Pause. Abandoning his attitude.*] Nothing doing!

HAMM   The bastard! He doesn't exist!

CLOV   Not yet.

NAGG   Me sugar-plum!

HAMM   There are no more sugar-plums! [*Pause.*]

NAGG   It's natural. After all I'm your father. It's true if it hadn't been me it would have been someone else. But that's no excuse. [*Pause.*] Turkish Delight,[3] for example, which no longer exists, we all know that, there is nothing in the world I love more. And one day I'll ask you for some, in return for a kindness, and you'll promise it to me. One must live with the times. [*Pause.*] Whom did you call when you were a tiny boy, and were frightened, in the dark? Your mother? No. Me. We let you cry. Then we moved you out of earshot, so that we might sleep in peace. [*Pause.*] I was asleep, as happy as a king, and you woke me up to have me listen to you. It wasn't indispensable, you didn't really need to have me listen to you. [*Pause.*] I hope the day will come when you'll really need to have me listen to you, and need to hear my voice, any voice. [*Pause.*] Yes, I hope I'll live till then, to hear you calling me like when you were a tiny boy, and were frightened, in the dark, and I was your only hope. [*Pause.* NAGG *knocks on lid of* NELL's *bin. Pause.*] Nell! [*Pause. He knocks louder. Pause. Louder.*] Nell! [*Pause.* NAGG *sinks back into his bin, closes the lid behind him. Pause.*]

HAMM   Our revels now are ended.[4] [*He gropes for the dog.*] The dog's gone.

CLOV   He's not a real dog, he can't go.

HAMM [*Groping.*]   He's not there.

CLOV   He's lain down.

HAMM   Give him up to me. [CLOV *picks up the dog and gives it to* HAMM. HAMM *holds it in his arms. Pause.* HAMM *throws away the dog.*] Dirty brute! [CLOV *begins to pick up the objects lying on the ground.*] What are you doing?

CLOV   Putting things in order. [*He straightens up. Fervently.*] I'm going to clear everything away! [*He starts picking up again.*]

HAMM   Order!

CLOV [*Straightening up.*]   I love order. It's my dream. A world where all would be silent and still and each thing in its last place, under the last dust. [*He starts picking up again.*]

HAMM [*Exasperated.*]   What in God's name do you think you are doing?

CLOV [*Straightening up.*]   I'm doing my best to create a little order.

HAMM   Drop it!
          [CLOV *drops the objects he has picked up.*]

CLOV   After all, there or elsewhere. [*He goes towards door.*]

---

3. A sticky sweet candy.
4. Lines spoken by Prospero in Shakespeare's *The Tempest* 4.1.148.

HAMM [*Irritably.*]   What's wrong with your feet?

CLOV   My feet?

HAMM   Tramp! Tramp!

CLOV   I must have put on my boots.

HAMM   Your slippers were hurting you? [*Pause.*]

CLOV   I'll leave you.

HAMM   No!

CLOV   What is there to keep me here?

HAMM   The dialogue. [*Pause.*] I've got on with my story. [*Pause.*] I've got on with it well. [*Pause. Irritably.*] Ask me where I've got to.

CLOV   Oh, by the way, your story?

HAMM [*Surprised.*]   What story?

CLOV   The one you've been telling yourself all your days.

HAMM   Ah you mean my chronicle?

CLOV   That's the one. [*Pause.*]

HAMM [*Angrily.*]   Keep going, can't you, keep going!

CLOV   You've got on with it, I hope.

HAMM [*Modestly.*]   Oh not very far, not very far. [*He sighs.*] There are days like that, one isn't inspired. [*Pause.*] Nothing you can do about it, just wait for it to come. [*Pause.*] No forcing, no forcing, it's fatal. [*Pause.*] I've got on with it a little all the same. [*Pause.*] Technique, you know. [*Pause. Irritably.*] I say I've got on with it a little all the same.

CLOV [*Admiringly.*]   Well I never! In spite of everything you were able to get on with it!

HAMM [*Modestly.*]   Oh not very far, you know, not very far, but nevertheless, better than nothing.

CLOV   Better than nothing! Is it possible?

HAMM   I'll tell you how it goes. He comes crawling on his belly—

CLOV   Who?

HAMM   What?

CLOV   Who do you mean, he?

HAMM   Who do I mean! Yet another.

CLOV   Ah him! I wasn't sure.

HAMM   Crawling on his belly, whining for bread for his brat. He's offered a job as gardener. Before— [CLOV *bursts out laughing.*] What is there so funny about that?

CLOV   A job as gardener!

HAMM   Is that what tickles you?

CLOV   It must be that.

HAMM   It wouldn't be the bread?

CLOV   Or the brat. [*Pause.*]

HAMM   The whole thing is comical, I grant you that. What about having a good guffaw the two of us together?

CLOV [*After reflection.*]   I couldn't guffaw again today.

HAMM [*After reflection.*]   Nor I. [*Pause.*] I continue then. Before accepting with gratitude he asks if he may have his little boy with him.

CLOV   What age?

HAMM   Oh tiny.

CLOV   He would have climbed the trees.

HAMM   All the little odd jobs.

CLOV   And then he would have grown up.

HAMM   Very likely. [*Pause.*]

CLOV   Keep going, can't you, keep going!

HAMM   That's all. I stopped there. [*Pause.*]

CLOV   Do you see how it goes on.

HAMM   More or less.

CLOV   Will it not soon be the end?

HAMM   I'm afraid it will.

CLOV   Pah! You'll make up another.

HAMM   I don't know. [*Pause.*] I feel rather drained. [*Pause.*] The prolonged creative effort. [*Pause.*] If I could drag myself down to the sea! I'd make a pillow of sand for my head and the tide would come.

CLOV   There's no more tide. [*Pause.*]

HAMM   Go and see is she dead.
      [CLOV *goes to bins, raises the lid of* NELL's, *stoops, looks into it. Pause.*]

CLOV   Looks like it.
      [*He closes the lid, straightens up.* HAMM *raises his toque. Pause. He puts it on again.*]

HAMM   [*With his hand to his toque.*]   And Nagg?
      [CLOV *raises lid of* NAGG's *bin, stoops, looks into it. Pause.*]

CLOV   Doesn't look like it. [*He closes the lid, straightens up.*]

HAMM   [*Letting go his toque.*]   What's he doing? [CLOV *raises lid of* NAGG's *bin, stoops, looks into it. Pause.*]

CLOV   He's crying. [*He closes lid, straightens up.*]

HAMM   Then he's living. [*Pause.*] Did you ever have an instant of happiness?

CLOV   Not to my knowledge. [*Pause.*]

HAMM   Bring me under the window. [CLOV *goes towards chair.*] I want to feel the light on my face. [CLOV *pushes chair.*] Do you remember, in the beginning, when you took me for a turn? You used to hold the chair too high. At every step you nearly tipped me out. [*With senile quaver.*] Ah great fun, we had, the two of us, great fun. [*Gloomily.*] And then we got into the way of it. [CLOV *stops the chair under window right.*] There already? [*Pause. He tilts back his head.*] Is it light?

CLOV   It isn't dark.

HAMM   [*Angrily.*]   I'm asking you is it light.

CLOV   Yes. [*Pause.*]

HAMM   The curtain isn't closed?

CLOV   No.

HAMM   What window is it?

CLOV   The earth.

HAMM   I knew it! [*Angrily.*] But there's no light there! The other! [CLOV *stops the chair under window left.* HAMM *tilts back his head.*] That's what I call light! [*Pause.*] Feels like a ray of sunshine. [*Pause.*] No?

CLOV   No.

HAMM   It isn't a ray of sunshine I feel on my face?

CLOV   No. [*Pause.*]

HAMM   Am I very white? [*Pause. Angrily.*] I'm asking you am I very white!

CLOV   Not more so than usual. [*Pause.*]

HAMM   Open the window.

CLOV   What for?

HAMM   I want to hear the sea.

CLOV   You wouldn't hear it.

HAMM   Even if you opened the window?

CLOV   No.

HAMM   Then it's not worth while opening it?

CLOV   No.

HAMM   [*Violently.*]   Then open it! [CLOV *gets up on the ladder, opens the window. Pause.*] Have you opened it?

CLOV   Yes. [*Pause.*]

HAMM   You swear you've opened it?

CLOV   Yes. [*Pause.*]

HAMM   Well . . . ! [*Pause.*] It must be very calm. [*Pause. Violently.*] I'm asking you is it very calm!

CLOV   Yes.

HAMM   It's because there are no more navigators. [*Pause.*] You haven't much conversation all of a sudden. Do you not feel well?

CLOV   I'm cold.

HAMM   What month are we? [*Pause.*] Close the window, we're going back. [CLOV *closes the window, gets down, pushes the chair back to its place, remains standing behind it, head bowed.*] Don't stay there, you give me the shivers! [CLOV *returns to his place beside the chair.*] Father! [*Pause. Louder.*] Father! [*Pause.*] Go and see did he hear me.

   [CLOV *goes to* NAGG'*s bin, raises the lid, stoops. Unintelligible words.* CLOV *straightens up.*]

CLOV   Yes.

HAMM   Both times?

   [CLOV *stoops. As before.*]

CLOV   Once only.

HAMM   The first time or the second?

   [CLOV *stoops. As before.*]

CLOV   He doesn't know.

HAMM   It must have been the second.

CLOV   We'll never know. [*He closes lid.*]

HAMM   Is he still crying?

CLOV   No.

HAMM   The dead go fast. [*Pause.*] What's he doing?

CLOV   Sucking his biscuit.

HAMM   Life goes on. [CLOV *returns to his place beside the chair.*] Give me a rug. I'm freezing.

CLOV   There are no more rugs. [*Pause.*]

HAMM   Kiss me. [*Pause.*] Will you not kiss me?

CLOV   No.

HAMM   On the forehead.

CLOV   I won't kiss you anywhere. [*Pause.*]

HAMM [*Holding out his hand.*]   Give me your hand at least. [*Pause.*] Will you not give me your hand?

CLOV   I won't touch you. [*Pause.*]

HAMM   Give me the dog. [CLOV *looks round for the dog.*] No!
CLOV   Do you not want your dog?
HAMM   No.
CLOV   Then I'll leave you.
HAMM   [*Head bowed, absently.*]   That's right.
            [CLOV *goes to door, turns.*]
CLOV   If I don't kill that rat he'll die.
HAMM   [*As before.*]   That's right. [*Exit* CLOV. *Pause.*] Me to play. [*He takes out his handkerchief, unfolds it, holds it spread out before him.*] We're getting on. [*Pause.*] You weep, and weep, for nothing, so as not to laugh, and little by little . . . you begin to grieve. [*He folds the handkerchief, puts it back in his pocket, raises his head.*] All those I might have helped. [*Pause.*] Helped! [*Pause.*] Saved. [*Pause.*] Saved! [*Pause.*] The place was crawling with them! [*Pause. Violently.*] Use your head, can't you, use your head, you're on earth, there's no cure for that! [*Pause.*] Get out of here and love one another! Lick your neighbor as yourself![5] [*Pause. Calmer.*] When it wasn't bread they wanted it was crumpets. [*Pause. Violently.*] Out of my sight and back to your petting parties! [*Pause.*] All that, all that! [*Pause.*] Not even a real dog! [*Calmer.*] The end is in the beginning and yet you go on. [*Pause.*] Perhaps I could go on with my story, end it and begin another. [*Pause.*] Perhaps I could throw myself out on the floor. [*He pushes himself painfully off his seat, falls back again.*] Dig my nails into the cracks and drag myself forward with my fingers. [*Pause.*] It will be the end and there I'll be, wondering what can have brought it on and wondering what can have . . . [*He hesitates.*] . . . why it was so long coming. [*Pause.*] There I'll be, in the old shelter, alone against the silence and . . . [*He hesitates.*] . . . the stillness. If I can hold my peace, and sit quiet, it will be all over with sound, and motion, all over and done with. [*Pause.*] I'll have called my father and I'll have called my . . . [*He hesitates.*] . . . my son. And even twice, or three times, in case they shouldn't have heard me, the first time, or the second. [*Pause.*] I'll say to myself, He'll come back. [*Pause.*] And then? [*Pause.*] And then? [*Pause.*] He couldn't, he has gone too far. [*Pause.*] And then? [*Pause. Very agitated.*] All kinds of fantasies! That I'm being watched! A rat! Steps! Breath held and then . . . [*He breathes out.*] Then babble, babble, words, like the solitary child who turns himself into children, two, three, so as to be together, and whisper together, in the dark. [*Pause.*] Moment upon moment, pattering down, like the millet grains of . . . [*He hesitates.*] . . . that old Greek,[6] and all life long you wait for that to mount up to a life. [*Pause. He opens his mouth to continue, renounces.*] Ah let's get it over! [*He whistles. Enter* CLOV *with alarm-clock. He halts beside the chair.*] What? Neither gone nor dead?
CLOV   In spirit only.
HAMM   Which?

---

5. Parody of Jesus' words in the Bible: "Thou shalt love thy neighbor as thyself" (Matthew 19.19).
6. Zeno of Elea, a Greek philosopher active around 450 B.C., known for logical paradoxes that reduce to absurdity various attempts to define *Being.* Aristotle reports that Zeno's paradox on sound questioned: If a grain of millet falling makes no sound, how can a bushel of grains make any sound? (Aristotle's *Physics* 5.250a.19).

CLOV   Both.

HAMM   Gone from me you'd be dead.

CLOV   And vice versa.

HAMM   Outside of here it's death! [*Pause.*] And the rat?

CLOV   He's got away.

HAMM   He can't go far. [*Pause. Anxious.*] Eh?

CLOV   He doesn't need to go far. [*Pause.*]

HAMM   Is it not time for my pain-killer?

CLOV   Yes.

HAMM   Ah! At last! Give it to me! Quick! [*Pause.*]

CLOV   There's no more pain-killer. [*Pause.*]

HAMM [*Appalled.*]   Good . . . ! [*Pause.*] No more pain-killer!

CLOV   No more pain-killer. You'll never get any more pain-killer. [*Pause.*]

HAMM   But the little round box. It was full!

CLOV   Yes. But now it's empty.
        [*Pause.* CLOV *starts to move about the room. He is looking for a place to put down the alarm-clock.*]

HAMM [*Soft.*]   What'll I do? [*Pause. In a scream.*] What'll I do? [CLOV *sees the picture, takes it down, stands it on the floor with its face to the wall, hangs up the alarm-clock in its place.*] What are you doing?

CLOV   Winding up.

HAMM   Look at the earth.

CLOV   Again!

HAMM   Since it's calling to you.

CLOV   Is your throat sore? [*Pause.*] Would you like a lozenge? [*Pause.*] No. [*Pause.*] Pity. [*He goes, humming, towards window right, halts before it, looks up at it.*]

HAMM   Don't sing.

CLOV [*Turning towards* HAMM.]   One hasn't the right to sing any more?

HAMM   No.

CLOV   Then how can it end?

HAMM   You want it to end?

CLOV   I want to sing.

HAMM   I can't prevent you.
        [*Pause.* CLOV *turns towards window right.*]

CLOV   What did I do with that steps? [*He looks around for ladder.*] You didn't see that steps? [*He sees it.*] Ah, about time. [*He goes towards window left.*] Sometimes I wonder if I'm in my right mind. Then it passes over and I'm as lucid as before. [*He gets up on ladder, looks out of window.*] Christ, she's under water! [*He looks.*] How can that be? [*He pokes forward his head, his hand above his eyes.*] It hasn't rained. [*He wipes the pane, looks. Pause.*] Ah what a fool I am! I'm on the wrong side! [*He gets down, takes a few steps towards window right.*] Under water! [*He goes back for ladder.*] What a fool I am! [*He carries ladder towards window right.*] Sometimes I wonder if I'm in my right senses. Then it passes off and I'm as intelligent as ever. [*He sets down ladder under window right, gets up on it, looks out of window. He turns towards* HAMM.] Any particular sector you fancy? Or merely the whole thing?

HAMM   Whole thing.

CLOV   The general effect? Just a moment. [*He looks out of window. Pause.*]

HAMM   Clov.

CLOV [*Absorbed.*]   Mmm.

HAMM   Do you know what it is?

CLOV [*As before.*]   Mmm.

HAMM   I was never there. [*Pause.*] Clov!

CLOV [*Turning towards* HAMM, *exasperated.*]   What is it?

HAMM   I was never there.

CLOV   Lucky for you. [*He looks out of window.*]

HAMM   Absent, always. It all happened without me. I don't know what's happened. [*Pause.*] Do you know what's happened? [*Pause.*] Clov!

CLOV [*Turning towards* HAMM, *exasperated.*]   Do you want me to look at this muckheap, yes or no?

HAMM   Answer me first.

CLOV   What?

HAMM   Do you know what's happened?

CLOV   When? Where?

HAMM [*Violently.*]   When! What's happened? Use your head, can't you! What has happened?

CLOV   What for Christ's sake does it matter? [*He looks out of window.*]

HAMM   I don't know.

[*Pause.* CLOV *turns towards* HAMM.]

CLOV [*Harshly.*]   When old Mother Pegg asked you for oil for her lamp and you told her to get out to hell, you knew what was happening then, no? [*Pause.*] You know what she died of, Mother Pegg? Of darkness.

HAMM [*Feebly.*]   I hadn't any.

CLOV [*As before.*]   Yes, you had. [*Pause.*]

HAMM   Have you the glass?

CLOV   No, it's clear enough as it is.

HAMM   Go and get it.

[*Pause.* CLOV *casts up his eyes, brandishes his fists. He loses balance, clutches on to the ladder. He starts to get down, halts.*]

CLOV   There's one thing I'll never understand. [*He gets down.*] Why I always obey you. Can you explain that to me?

HAMM   No. . . . Perhaps it's compassion. [*Pause.*] A kind of great compassion. [*Pause.*] Oh you won't find it easy, you won't find it easy.

[*Pause.* CLOV *begins to move about the room in search of the telescope.*]

CLOV   I'm tired of our goings on, very tired. [*He searches.*] You're not sitting on it? [*He moves the chair, looks at the place where it stood, resumes his search.*]

HAMM [*Anguished.*]   Don't leave me there! [*Angrily* CLOV *restores the chair to its place.*] Am I right in the center?

CLOV   You'd need a microscope to find this— [*He sees the telescope.*] Ah, about time. [*He picks up the telescope, gets up on the ladder, turns the telescope on the without.*]

HAMM   Give me the dog.

CLOV [*Looking.*]   Quiet!

HAMM [*Angrily.*]   Give me the dog!

[CLOV *drops the telescope, clasps his hands to his head. Pause. He gets down precipitately, looks for the dogs, sees it, picks it up, hastens towards* HAMM *and strikes him violently on the head with the dog.*]

CLOV There's your dog for you!

   [*The dog falls to the ground. Pause.*]

HAMM He hit me!

CLOV You drive me mad, I'm mad!

HAMM If you must hit me, hit me with the axe. [*Pause.*] Or with the gaff, hit
me with the gaff. Not with the dog. With the gaff. Or with the axe.

   [CLOV *picks up the dog and gives it to* HAMM *who takes it in his arms.*]

CLOV [*Imploringly.*] Let's stop playing!

HAMM Never! [*Pause.*] Put me in my coffin.

CLOV There are no more coffins.

HAMM Then let it end! [CLOV *goes towards ladder.*] With a bang! [CLOV *gets up
on ladder, gets down again, looks for telescope, sees it, picks it up, gets up ladder,
raises telescope.*] Of darkness! And me? Did anyone ever have pity on me?

CLOV [*Lowering the telescope, turning towards* HAMM.] What? [*Pause.*] Is it
me you're referring to?

HAMM [*Angrily.*] An aside, ape! Did you never hear an aside before? [*Pause.*]
I'm warming up for my last soliloquy.

CLOV I warn you. I'm going to look at this filth since it's an order. But it's the
last time. [*He turns the telescope on the without.*] Let's see. [*He moves the
telescope.*] Nothing . . . nothing . . . good . . . good . . . nothing . . . goo—
[*He starts, lowers the telescope, examines it, turns it again on the without.
Pause.*] Bad luck to it!

HAMM More complications! [CLOV *gets down.*] Not an underplot, I trust.

   [CLOV *moves ladder nearer window, gets up on it, turns telescope on the
without.*]

CLOV [*Dismayed.*] Looks like a small boy!

HAMM [*Sarcastic.*] A small . . . boy!

CLOV I'll go and see. [*He gets down, drops the telescope, goes towards door,
turns.*] I'll take the gaff. [*He looks for the gaff, sees it, picks it up, hastens
towards door.*]

HAMM No! [CLOV *halts.*]

CLOV No? A potential procreator?

HAMM If he exists he'll die there or he'll come here. And if he doesn't . . .
[*Pause.*]

CLOV You don't believe me? You think I'm inventing? [*Pause.*]

HAMM It's the end, Clov, we've come to the end. I don't need you any more.
[*Pause.*]

CLOV Lucky for you. [*He goes towards door.*]

HAMM Leave me the gaff.

   [CLOV *gives him the gaff, goes towards door, halts, looks at alarm-clock,
takes it down, looks round for a better place to put it, goes to bins, puts it
on lid of* NAGG's *bin. Pause.*]

CLOV I'll leave you. [*He goes towards door.*]

HAMM Before you go . . . [CLOV *halts near door.*] . . . say something.

CLOV There is nothing to say.

HAMM A few words . . . to ponder . . . in my heart.

CLOV Your heart!

HAMM Yes. [*Pause. Forcibly.*] Yes! [*Pause.*] With the rest, in the end, the
shadows, the murmurs, all the trouble, to end up with. [*Pause.*] Clov. . . .

He never spoke to me. Then, in the end, before he went, without my having asked him, he spoke to me. He said . . .

CLOV [*Despairingly.*] Ah . . . !

HAMM Something . . . from your heart.

CLOV My heart!

HAMM A few words . . . from your heart. [*Pause.*]

CLOV [*Fixed gaze, tonelessly, towards auditorium.*] They said to me, That's love, yes, yes, not a doubt, now you see how—

HAMM Articulate!

CLOV [*As before.*] How easy it is. They said to me, That's friendship, yes, yes, no question, you've found it. They said to me, Here's the place, stop, raise your head and look at all that beauty. That order! They said to me. Come now, you're not a brute beast, think upon these things and you'll see how all becomes clear. And simple! They said to me, What skilled attention they get, all these dying of their wounds.

HAMM Enough!

CLOV [*As before.*] I say to myself—sometimes, Clov, you must learn to suffer better than that if you want them to weary of punishing you—one day. I say to myself—sometimes, Clov, you must be there better than that if you want them to let you go—one day. But I feel too old, and too far, to form new habits. Good, it'll never end, I'll never go. [*Pause.*] Then one day, suddenly, it ends, it changes, I don't understand, it dies, or it's me, I don't understand, that either. I ask the words that remain—sleeping, waking, morning, evening. They have nothing to say. [*Pause.*] I open the door of the cell and go. I am so bowed I only see my feet, if I open my eyes, and between my legs a little trail of black dust. I say to myself that the earth is extinguished, though I never saw it lit. [*Pause.*] It's easy going. [*Pause.*] When I fall I'll weep for happiness. [*Pause. He goes towards door.*]

HAMM Clov! [CLOV *halts, without turning.*] Nothing. [CLOV *moves on.*] Clov!
[CLOV *halts, without turning.*]

CLOV This is what we call making an exit.

HAMM I'm obliged to you, Clov. For your services.

CLOV [*Turning, sharply.*] Ah pardon, it's I am obliged to you.

HAMM It's we are obliged to each other. [*Pause.* CLOV *goes towards door.*] One thing more. [CLOV *halts.*] A last favor. [*Exit* CLOV.] Cover me with the sheet. [*Long pause.*] No? Good. [*Pause.*] Me to play. [*Pause. Wearily.*] Old endgame lost of old, play and lose and have done with losing. [*Pause. More animated.*] Let me see. [*Pause.*] Ah yes! [*He tries to move the chair, using the gaff as before. Enter* CLOV, *dressed for the road. Panama hat, tweed coat, raincoat over his arm, umbrella, bag. He halts by the door and stands there, impassive and motionless, his eyes fixed on* HAMM, *till the end.* HAMM *gives up.*] Good. [*Pause.*] Discard. [*He throws away the gaff, makes to throw away the dog, thinks better of it.*] Take it easy. [*Pause.*] And now? [*Pause.*] Raise hat. [*He raises his toque.*] Peace to our . . . arses. [*Pause.*] And put on again. [*He puts on his toque.*] Deuce. [*Pause. He takes off his glasses.*] Wipe. [*He takes out his handkerchief and, without unfolding it, wipes his glasses.*] And put on again. [*He puts on his glasses, puts back the handkerchief in his pocket.*] We're coming. A few more squirms like that and I'll call. [*Pause.*] A little poetry. [*Pause.*] You prayed— [*Pause. He corrects himself.*] You CRIED for night; it comes— [*Pause. He corrects himself.*] It FALLS: now cry in darkness. [*He repeats, chanting.*] You cried for night; it falls: now cry in darkness.[7] [*Pause.*] Nicely put, that. [*Pause.*] And now? [*Pause.*] Moments for nothing, now as always, time was never and time is over, reckoning closed and story ended. [*Pause. Narrative tone.*] If he could have his child with him. . . . [*Pause.*] It was the moment I was waiting for. [*Pause.*] You don't want to abandon him? You want him to bloom while you are withering? Be there to solace your last million last moments? [*Pause.*] He doesn't realize, all he knows is hunger, and cold, and death to crown it all. But you! You ought to know what the earth is like, nowadays. Oh I put him before his responsibilities! [*Pause. Normal tone.*] Well, there we are, there I am, that's enough. [*He raises the whistle to his lips, hesitates, drops it. Pause.*] Yes, truly! [*He whistles. Pause. Louder. Pause.*] Good. [*Pause.*] Father! [*Pause. Louder.*] Father! [*Pause.*] Good. [*Pause.*] We're coming. [*Pause.*] And to end up with? [*Pause.*] Discard. [*He throws away the dog. He tears the whistle from his neck.*] With my compliments. [*He throws whistle towards auditorium. Pause. He sniffs. Soft.*] Clov! [*Long pause.*] No? Good. [*He takes out the handkerchief.*] Since that's the way we're playing it . . . [*He unfolds handkerchief.*] . . . let's play it that way . . . [*He unfolds.*] . . . and speak no more about it . . . [*He finishes unfolding.*] . . . speak no more. [*He holds handkerchief spread out before him.*] Old stancher! [*Pause.*] You . . . remain.

> [*Pause. He covers his face with handkerchief, lowers his arms to armrests, remains motionless.*]
>
> [*Brief tableau.*]

Curtain

1957

7. Parody of a line from the poem *Meditation*, by Baudelaire: "You were calling for evening; it falls; here it is."

VLADIMIR NABOKOV

1899–1977

Exiled first from revolutionary Russia and then from Nazi-dominated Western Europe, Vladimir Nabokov became one of the great literary explorers of the contemporary United States. An urbane European modernist, in middle age he traveled throughout his adoptive country, maintaining an ironic detachment from postwar American society even as he developed an intimate familiarity with American English. His extraordinary, playful use of the language to describe the culture from an outsider's point of view made him one of the most famous and controversial novelists of the twentieth century.

Born in St. Petersburg to a wealthy, aristocratic family, Nabokov grew up speaking Russian, English, and French; he later recalled with nostalgia the extraordinary family estate where he spent much of his childhood (he inherited the nearby estate of his uncle at age 17, only to lose it to the Russian Revolution the following year). His father, also named Vladimir, a prominent liberal politician, became a minister in the provisional government after the February 1917 Revolution. When the Communists came to power later that year in the October Revolution, the Nabokovs fled Moscow. They lived at first in non-Communist Russia, but once it was clear that the Communists would maintain power, the family moved to London, then to Berlin. In 1922, while attending a political conference, Nabokov's father was killed by right-wing assassins. A gunman had attacked another Russian exile speaking at the conference. While Nabokov's father tried to wrestle the gun away from him, he was shot by an accomplice of the first killer. The younger Nabokov remained haunted by his father's death, which would surface in disguised form in many of his novels.

After completing his studies at Cambridge University, Nabokov joined his family in Berlin and supported himself as a language teacher and tennis and boxing coach while beginning to publish his writing. He had written poetry and plays but gained most attention for his first nine novels, written in Russian, usually featuring Russian émigrés, as well as some of Nabokov's later obsessions, such as unreliable narrators, young girls, and chess problems. One of his major themes, like that of such modernists as **Marcel Proust**, was the mystery of consciousness and memory. Although widely recognized as a leading young novelist, Nabokov could reach only a small audience of Russian émigrés, since his works could not be published in his homeland.

Nabokov married Véra Slonim, a Russian-Jewish exile, and after the Nazis took power in Germany, the family, now impoverished, moved to Paris. Shortly before the Nazis conquered France, in 1940, the Nabokovs managed to escape yet again, this time to the United States, where Nabokov taught at Standard University, Wellesley College, and later Cornell University. In addition to teaching Russian and comparative literature, Nabokov, an avid collector of butterflies, served for a time as curator of lepidoptery at Harvard University's Museum of Comparative Zoology. Having become an American citizen, Nabokov took lengthy summer road trips with his wife to collect butterflies and thus became familiar with the postwar highways and motels of the United States, while gaining glimpses of many small college towns.

Although Nabokov had previously translated some of his Russian novels into French and English, only in 1938 did he begin writing fiction in English. His first novel in his adopted language, *The Real Life of Sebastian Knight* (1941), takes the form of a highly subjective biography of a fictional Russian-born English novelist, written by his disturbed half brother, V. Like some of the works of his contemporary **Jorge Luis Borges**, the novel both draws on modernist themes and prefigures postmodernism by playing with the line between fiction and nonfiction, biography and novel. Nabokov has also often been compared with **Samuel Beckett**, another bilingual émigré novelist dedicated to wordplay and meditations on the status of fiction. This "metafictional" tendency is present, too, in *Lolita* (1955), which brought Nabokov his initial commercial success. Narrated in the first person by Humbert Humbert, who is, like Nabokov, a witty and urbane language professor but, unlike Nabokov, a child molester, the novel was controversial from the first. By creating an unreliable narrator, Nabokov challenges his readers to disentangle the pleasure they may take in Humbert's wit from the horror of Humbert's evil. Nabokov does not make it easy to separate one from the other.

Because of fear of censorship, the novel was originally published in Paris, but even in the less repressive French society, the work was banned for a brief period. In 1958, the novel was finally released in the United States, to great acclaim, huge sales, and frequent expressions of moral disapproval. The financial success of *Lolita* (and the 1962 film version, directed by Stanley Kubrick) allowed Nabokov to retire from academia and return to Europe. He took up residence in Switzerland, where he remained for the rest of his life, continuing to write in English. A major contributor to modern American literature, he had spent only two of his eight decades in the United States.

Nabokov considered "The Vane Sisters" (1959), presented here, his best story. It is a detective story of an unusual kind. What makes it unusual is the fact that the narrator himself does not quite understand the story he is telling; in this respect, he is an extreme form of the unreliable narrator. Though capable of witty observations about the Vane sisters and his friends, he is blinded by his arrogance. He believes himself to be supremely observant, "one big eyeball rolling in the world's socket," but in fact he misses the clues that the Vane sisters have left for him. One of the first hints that his visible world is in fact full of signs is the icicle shaped like an exclamation mark at the beginning of the story. In an explanatory letter to his editor at *The New Yorker* (who had rejected the story), Nabokov described the narrator, apparently so like the author, as "a somewhat obtuse scholar and a rather callous observer of the superficial planes of life." The reader's task, he suggested, was to see further than the narrator. Indeed, throughout his fiction, Nabokov encourages readers to seek signs and hints that the characters themselves may ignore. Although the surface of the story seems to depict the external world realistically—the narrator spots every visual detail of the scenes he observes— the story's plot suggests that this surface actually contains a complex set of indicators intended to lead, or mislead, the narrator and the reader. As Nabokov also explained to his editor, the reader is meant to discover the clues left by the author because "by means of various allusions to trick-reading I have arranged matters so that the reader almost automatically slips into this discovery, especially because of the abrupt change in *style*." Some readers dislike such trickiness, but the pleasure of discovery repays the reader who is attentive to Nabokov's clues.

The Vane Sisters

I

I might never have heard of Cynthia's death, had I not run, that night, into D., whom I had also lost track of for the last four years or so; and I might never have run into D. had I not got involved in a series of trivial investigations.

The day, a compunctious Sunday after a week of blizzards, had been part jewel, part mud. In the midst of my usual afternoon stroll through the small hilly town attached to the girls' college where I taught French literature, I had stopped to watch a family of brilliant icicles drip-dripping from the eaves of a frame house. So clear-cut were their pointed shadows on the white boards behind them that I was sure the shadows of the falling drops should be visible too. But they were not. The roof jutted too far out, perhaps, or the angle of vision was faulty, or, again, I did not chance to be watching the right icicle when the right drop fell. There was a rhythm, an alternation in the dripping that I found as teasing as a coin trick. It led me to inspect the corners of several house blocks, and this brought me to Kelly Road, and right to the house where D. used to live when he was instructor here. And as I looked up at the eaves of the adjacent garage with its full display of transparent stalactites backed by their blue silhouettes, I was rewarded at last, upon choosing one, by the sight of what might be described as the dot of an exclamation mark leaving its ordinary position to glide down very fast—a jot faster than the thaw-drop it raced. This twinned twinkle was delightful but not completely satisfying; or rather it only sharpened my appetite for other tidbits of light and shade, and I walked on in a state of raw awareness that seemed to transform the whole of my being into one big eyeball rolling in the world's socket.

Through peacocked lashes I saw the dazzling diamond reflection of the low sun on the round back of a parked automobile. To all kinds of things a vivid pictorial sense had been restored by the sponge of the thaw. Water in overlapping festoons flowed down one sloping street and turned gracefully into another. With ever so slight a note of meretricious appeal, narrow passages between buildings revealed treasures of brick and purple. I remarked for the first time the humble fluting—last echoes of grooves on the shafts of columns—ornamenting a garbage can, and I also saw the rippling upon its lid—circles diverging from a fantastically ancient center. Erect, dark-headed shapes of dead snow (left by the blades of a bulldozer last Friday) were lined up like rudimentary penguins along the curbs, above the brilliant vibration of live gutters.

I walked up, and I walked down, and I walked straight into a delicately dying sky, and finally the sequence of observed and observant things brought me, at my usual eating time, to a street so distant from my usual eating place that I decided to try a restaurant which stood on the fringe of the town. Night had fallen without sound or ceremony when I came out again. The lean ghost, the elongated umbra[1] cast by a parking meter upon some damp snow, had a strange ruddy tinge; this I made out to be due to the tawny red light of the restaurant sign above the sidewalk; and it was then—as I loitered there, wondering rather wearily if in the course of my return tramp I might be lucky enough to find the

1. Shadow.

same in neon blue—it was then that a car crunched to a standstill near me and D. got out of it with an exclamation of feigned pleasure.

He was passing, on his way from Albany to Boston, through the town he had dwelt in before, and more than once in my life have I felt that stab of vicarious emotion followed by a rush of personal irritation against travelers who seem to feel nothing at all upon revisiting spots that ought to harass them at every step with wailing and writhing memories. He ushered me back into the bar that I had just left, and after the usual exchange of buoyant platitudes came the inevitable vacuum which he filled with the random words: "Say, I never thought there was anything wrong with Cynthia Vane's heart. My lawyer tells me she died last week."

2

He was still young, still brash, still shifty, still married to the gentle, exquisitely pretty woman who had never learned or suspected anything about his disastrous affair with Cynthia's hysterical young sister, who in her turn had known nothing of the interview I had had with Cynthia when she suddenly summoned me to Boston to make me swear I would talk to D. and get him "kicked out" if he did not stop seeing Sybil at once—or did not divorce his wife (whom incidentally she visualized through the prism of Sybil's wild talk as a termagant and a fright). I had cornered him immediately. He had said there was nothing to worry about—had made up his mind, anyway, to give up his college job and move with his wife to Albany, where he would work in his father's firm; and the whole matter, which had threatened to become one of those hopelessly entangled situations that drag on for years, with peripheral sets of well-meaning friends endlessly discussing it in universal secrecy—and even founding, among themselves, new intimacies upon its alien woes—came to an abrupt end.

I remember sitting next day at my raised desk in the large classroom where a midyear examination in French Lit. was being held on the eve of Sybil's suicide. She came in on high heels, with a suitcase, dumped it in a corner where several other bags were stacked, with a single shrug slipped her fur coat off her thin shoulders, folded it on her bag, and with two or three other girls stopped before my desk to ask when I would mail them their grades. It would take me a week, beginning from tomorrow, I said, to read the stuff. I also remember wondering whether D. had already informed her of his decision—and I felt acutely unhappy about my dutiful little student as during 150 minutes my gaze kept reverting to her, so childishly slight in close-fitting gray, and kept observing that carefully waved dark hair, that small, small-flowered hat with a little hyaline veil as worn that season, and under it her small face broken into a cubist pattern by scars due to a skin disease, pathetically masked by a sunlamp tan that hardened her features, whose charm was further impaired by her having painted everything that could be painted, so that the pale gums of her teeth between cherry-red chapped lips and the diluted blue ink of her eyes under darkened lids were the only visible openings into her beauty.

Next day, having arranged the ugly copybooks alphabetically, I plunged into their chaos of scripts and came prematurely to Valevsky and Vane, whose books I had somehow misplaced. The first was dressed up for the occasion in a semblance of legibility, but Sybil's work displayed her usual combination of several demon hands. She had begun in very pale, very hard pencil which had conspicuously embossed the black verso,[2] but had produced little of permanent value on the upper side of the page. Happily the tip soon broke, and Sybil continued in another, darker lead, gradually lapsing into the blurred thickness of what looked almost like charcoal, to which, by sucking the blunt point, she had contributed some traces of lipstick. Her work, although even poorer than I had expected, bore all the signs of a kind of desperate conscientiousness, with underscores, transposes, unnecessary footnotes, as if she were intent upon rounding up things in the most respectable manner possible. Then she had borrowed Mary Valevsky's fountain pen and added: "*Cette examain est finie ainsi que ma vie. Adieu, jeunes filles!*[3] Please, *Monsieur le Professeur*, contact *ma soeur*[4] and tell her that Death was not better than D minus, but definitely better than Life minus D."

I lost no time in ringing up Cynthia, who told me it was all over—had been all over since eight in the morning—and asked me to bring her the note, and when I did, beamed through her tears with proud admiration for the whimsical use ("Just like her!") Sybil had made of an examination in French literature. In no time she "fixed" two highballs, while never parting with Sybil's notebook— by now splashed with soda water and tears—and went on studying the death message, whereupon I was impelled to point out to her the grammatical mistakes in it and to explain the way "girl" is translated in American colleges lest students innocently bandy around the French equivalent of "wench," or worse.[5] These rather tasteless trivialities pleased Cynthia hugely as she rose, with gasps, above the heaving surface of her grief. And then, holding that limp notebook as if it were a kind of passport to a casual Elysium (where pencil points do not snap and a dreamy young beauty with an impeccable complexion winds a lock of her hair on a dreamy forefinger, as she meditates over some celestial test), Cynthia led me upstairs to a chilly little bedroom, just to show me, as if I were the police or a sympathetic Irish neighbor, two empty pill bottles and the tumbled bed from which a tender, inessential body, that D. must have known down to its last velvet detail, had been already removed.

3

It was four or five months after her sister's death that I began seeing Cynthia fairly often. By the time I had come to New York for some vocational research in the Public Library she had also moved to that city, where for some odd reason (in vague connection, I presume, with artistic motives) she had taken what people, immune to gooseflesh, term a "cold water" flat,[6] down in the scale of the city's transverse streets. What attracted me was neither her ways, which I thought repulsively vivacious, nor her looks, which other men thought striking. She had wide-spaced eyes very much like her sister's, of a frank, frightened blue with dark points in a radial arrangement. The interval between her thick black eyebrows was always shiny, and shiny too were the fleshy volutes of her nostrils. The coarse texture of her epiderm looked almost masculine, and, in

---

2. Reverse side of a sheet of paper.
3. This exam is done, like my life. Goodbye, girls (misspelled French).
4. My sister (French). "Monsieur le Professeur":

Professor (French).
5. *Jeune fille* (French for girl) could be used in American slang to refer to a prostitute.
6. An inexpensive, possibly illegal apartment.

the stark lamplight of her studio, you could see the pores of her thirty-two-year-old face fairly gaping at you like something in an aquarium. She used cosmetics with as much zest as her little sister had, but with an additional slovenliness that would result in her big front teeth getting some of the rouge. She was handsomely dark, wore a not too tasteless mixture of fairly smart heterogeneous things, and had a so-called good figure; but all of her was curiously frowzy, after a way I obscurely associated with left-wing enthusiasms in politics and "advanced" banalities in art, although, actually, she cared for neither. Her coily hairdo, on a part-and-bun basis, might have looked feral and bizarre had it not been thoroughly domesticated by its own soft unkemptness at the vulnerable nape. Her fingernails were gaudily painted, but badly bitten and not clean. Her lovers were a silent young photographer with a sudden laugh and two older men, brothers, who owned a small printing establishment across the street. I wondered at their tastes whenever I glimpsed, with a secret shudder, the higgledy-piggledy striation of black hairs that showed all along her pale shins through the nylon of her stockings with the scientific distinctness of a preparation flattened under glass; or when I felt, at her every movement, the dullish, stalish, not particularly conspicuous but all-pervading and depressing emanation that her seldom bathed flesh spread from under weary perfumes and creams.

Her father had gambled away the greater part of a comfortable fortune, and her mother's first husband had been of Slav origin, but otherwise Cynthia Vane belonged to a good, respectable family. For aught we know, it may have gone back to kings and soothsayers in the mists of ultimate islands. Transferred to a newer world, to a landscape of doomed, splendid deciduous trees, her ancestry presented, in one of its first phases, a white churchful of farmers against a black thunderhead, and then an imposing array of townsmen engaged in mercantile pursuits, as well as a number of learned men, such as Dr. Jonathan Vane, the gaunt bore (1780–1839), who perished in the conflagration of the steamer *Lexington* to become later an habitué of Cynthia's tilting table.[7] I have always wished to stand genealogy on its head, and here I have an opportunity to do so, for it is the last scion, Cynthia, and Cynthia alone, who will remain of any importance in the Vane dynasty. I am alluding of course to her artistic gift, to her delightful, gay, but not very popular paintings, which the friends of her friends bought at long intervals—and I dearly should like to know where they went after her death, those honest and poetical pictures that illumined her living room—the wonderfully detailed images of metallic things, and my favorite, *Seen Through a Windshield*—a windshield partly covered with rime,[8] with a brilliant trickle (from an imaginary car roof) across its transparent part and, through it all, the sapphire flame of the sky and a green-and-white fir tree.

4

Cynthia had a feeling that her dead sister was not altogether pleased with her—had discovered by now that she and I had conspired to break her romance; and so, in order to disarm her shade, Cynthia reverted to a rather primitive type

---

7. I.e., she attempted to contact his spirit through séances, where one proof of contact with the supernatural was an unexplained tilting or movement of a table.

8. Hard ice.

of sacrificial offering (tinged, however, with something of Sybil's humor), and began to send to D.'s business address, at deliberately unfixed dates, such trifles as snapshots of Sybil's tomb in a poor light; cuttings of her own hair which was indistinguishable from Sybil's; a New England sectional map with an inked-in cross, midway between two chaste towns, to mark the spot where D. and Sybil had stopped on October the twenty-third, in broad daylight, at a lenient motel, in a pink and brown forest; and, twice, a stuffed skunk.

Being as a conversationalist more voluble than explicit, she never could describe in full the theory of intervenient auras[9] that she had somehow evolved. Fundamentally there was nothing particularly new about her private creed since it presupposed a fairly conventional hereafter, a silent solarium of immortal souls (spliced with mortal antecedents) whose main recreation consisted of periodical hoverings over the dear quick.[1] The interesting point was a curious practical twist that Cynthia gave to her tame metaphysics. She was sure that her existence was influenced by all sorts of dead friends each of whom took turns in directing her fate much as if she were a stray kitten which a schoolgirl in passing gathers up, and presses to her cheek, and carefully puts down again, near some suburban hedge—to be stroked presently by another transient hand or carried off to a world of doors by some hospitable lady.

For a few hours, or for several days in a row, and sometimes recurrently, in an irregular series, for months or years, anything that happened to Cynthia, after a given person had died, would be, she said, in the manner and mood of that person. The event might be extraordinary, changing the course of one's life; or it might be a string of minute incidents just sufficiently clear to stand out in relief against one's usual day and then shading off into still vaguer trivia as the aura gradually faded. The influence might be good or bad; the main thing was that its source could be identified. It was like walking through a person's soul, she said. I tried to argue that she might not always be able to determine the exact source since not everybody has a recognizable soul; that there are anonymous letters and Christmas presents which anybody might send; that, in fact, what Cynthia called "a usual day" might be itself a weak solution of mixed auras or simply the routine shift of a humdrum guardian angel. And what about God? Did or did not people who would resent any omnipotent dictator on earth look forward to one in heaven? And wars? What a dreadful idea—dead soldiers still fighting with living ones, or phantom armies trying to get at each other through the lives of crippled old men.

But Cynthia was above generalities as she was beyond logic. "Ah, that's Paul," she would say when the soup spitefully boiled over, or: "I guess good Betty Brown is dead" when she won a beautiful and very welcome vacuum cleaner in a charity lottery. And, with Jamesian[2] meanderings that exasperated my French mind, she would go back to a time when Betty and Paul had not yet departed, and tell me of the showers of well-meant, but odd and quite unacceptable, bounties—beginning with an old purse that contained a check for three dollars which she picked up in the street and, of course, returned (to the aforesaid Betty Brown—this is where she first comes in—a decrepit colored

---

9. Spiritual energy fields that intervene in the material world.
1. Living.

2. I.e., in the style of the American novelist Henry James (1843–1916).

woman hardly able to walk), and ending with an insulting proposal from an old beau of hers (this is where Paul comes in) to paint "straight" pictures of his house and family for a reasonable remuneration—all of which followed upon the demise of a certain Mrs. Page, a kindly but petty old party who had pestered her with bits of matter-of-fact advice since Cynthia had been a child.

Sybil's personality, she said, had a rainbow edge as if a little out of focus. She said that had I known Sybil better I would have at once understood how Sybil-like was the aura of minor events which, in spells, had suffused her, Cynthia's, existence after Sybil's suicide. Ever since they had lost their mother they had intended to give up their Boston home and move to New York, where Cynthia's paintings, they thought, would have a chance to be more widely admired; but the old home had clung to them with all its plush tentacles. Dead Sybil, however, had proceeded to separate the house from its view—a thing that affects fatally the sense of home. Right across the narrow street a building project had come into loud, ugly, scaffolded life. A pair of familiar poplars died that spring, turning to blond skeletons. Workmen came and broke up the warm-colored lovely old sidewalk that had a special violet sheen on wet April days and had echoed so memorably to the morning footsteps of museum-bound Mr. Lever, who upon retiring from business at sixty had devoted a full quarter of a century exclusively to the study of snails.

Speaking of old men, one should add that sometimes these posthumous auspices and interventions were in the nature of parody. Cynthia had been on friendly terms with an eccentric librarian called Porlock[3] who in the last years of his dusty life had been engaged in examining old books for miraculous misprints such as the substitution of *l* for the second *h* in the word "hither." Contrary to Cynthia, he cared nothing for the thrill of obscure predictions; all he sought was the freak itself, the chance that mimics choice, the flaw that looks like a flower; and Cynthia, a much more perverse amateur of misshapen or illicitly connected words, puns, logogriphs,[4] and so on, had helped the poor crank to pursue a quest that in the light of the example she cited struck me as statistically insane. Anyway, she said, on the third day after his death she was reading a magazine and had just come across a quotation from an imperishable poem (that she, with other gullible readers, believed to have been really composed in a dream) when it dawned upon her that "Alph" was a prophetic sequence of the initial letters of Anna Livia Plurabelle[5] (another sacred river running through, or rather around, yet another fake dream), while the additional *h* modestly stood, as a private signpost, for the word that had so hypnotized Mr. Porlock. And I wish I could recollect that novel or short story (by some contemporary writer, I believe) in which, unknown to its author, the first letters of the words in its last paragraph formed, as deciphered by Cynthia, a message from his dead mother.

3. An allusion to Samuel Taylor Coleridge's poem "Kubla Khan" (1797). Coleridge claimed that the poem came to him in a dream that was interrupted by a visitor from the town of Porlock.

4. A word puzzle, such as an anagram.

5. An allusion to James Joyce's novel *Finnegans Wake* (1939). Anna Livia Plurabelle is a character based on the River Liffey in Dublin. Alph is the name of a river mentioned in Coleridge's "Kubla Khan." The name Alph contains the initials of Anna Livia Plurabelle plus the letter *h*, which the narrator interprets as standing for Hitler (the word that interested the librarian Porlock).

5

I am sorry to say that not content with these ingenious fancies Cynthia showed a ridiculous fondness for spiritualism. I refused to accompany her to sittings in which paid mediums took part: I knew too much about that from other sources. I did consent, however, to attend little farces rigged up by Cynthia and her two poker-faced gentlemen friends of the printing shop. They were podgy, polite, and rather eerie old fellows, but I satisfied myself that they possessed considerable wit and culture. We sat down at a light little table, and crackling tremors started almost as soon as we laid our fingertips upon it. I was treated to an assortment of ghosts that rapped out their reports most readily though refusing to elucidate anything that I did not quite catch. Oscar Wilde came in and in rapid garbled French, with the usual anglicisms, obscurely accused Cynthia's dead parents of what appeared in my jottings as *"plagiatisme."*[6] A brisk spirit contributed the unsolicited information that he, John Moore, and his brother Bill had been coal miners in Colorado and had perished in an avalanche at "Crested Beauty" in January 1883. Frederic Myers,[7] an old hand at the game, hammered out a piece of verse (oddly resembling Cynthia's own fugitive productions) which in part reads in my notes:

> What is this—a conjuror's rabbit,
> Or a flawy but genuine gleam—
> Which can check the perilous habit
> And dispel the dolorous dream?

Finally, with a great crash and all kinds of shudderings and jiglike movements on the part of the table, Leo Tolstoy[8] visited our little group and, when asked to identify himself by specific traits of terrene habitation, launched upon a complex description of what seemed to be some Russian type of architectural woodwork ("figures on boards—man, horse, cock, man, horse, cock"), all of which was difficult to take down, hard to understand, and impossible to verify.

I attended two or three other sittings which were even sillier but I must confess that I preferred the childish entertainment they afforded and the cider we drank (Podgy and Pudgy were teetotalers) to Cynthia's awful house parties.

She gave them at the Wheelers' nice flat next door—the sort of arrangement dear to her centrifugal nature, but then, of course, her own living room always looked like a dirty old palette. Following a barbaric, unhygienic, and adulterous custom, the guests' coats, still warm on the inside, were carried by quiet, baldish Bob Wheeler into the sanctity of a tidy bedroom and heaped on the conjugal bed. It was also he who poured out the drinks, which were passed around by the young photographer while Cynthia and Mrs. Wheeler took care of the canapés.

A late arrival had the impression of lots of loud people unnecessarily grouped within a smoke-blue space between two mirrors gorged with reflections. Because,

---

6. Plagiarism (French). The narrator has accidentally written *t* for *r*. "Oscar Wilde": Irish writer (1854–1900).
7. Frederic Myers (1843–1901), British philosopher and noted researcher into spiritualism, the belief in supernatural powers and the possi-

bility of communication with the dead. "Crested Butte": The Colorado site in mining country was subject to frequent avalanches, including a notably destructive one in March 1884.
8. Leo Tolstoy (1828–1910), Russian novelist and moralist, known for his mystical beliefs.

CLOV   The result would be the same.

HAMM   Yes, but how would I know, if you were merely dead in your kitchen?

CLOV   Well . . . sooner or later I'd start to stink.

HAMM   You stink already. The whole place stinks of corpses.

CLOV   The whole universe.

HAMM   [*Angrily.*]   To hell with the universe. [*Pause.*] Think of something.

CLOV   What?

HAMM   An idea, have an idea. [*Angrily.*] A bright idea!

CLOV   Ah good. [*He starts pacing to and fro, his eyes fixed on the ground, his hands behind his back. He halts.*] The pains in my legs! It's unbelievable! Soon I won't be able to think any more.

HAMM   You won't be able to leave me. [CLOV *resumes his pacing.*] What are you doing?

CLOV   Having an idea. [*He paces.*] Ah! [*He halts.*]

HAMM   What a brain! [*Pause.*] Well?

CLOV   Wait! [*He meditates. Not very convinced.*] Yes . . . [*Pause. More convinced.*] Yes! [*He raises his head.*] I have it! I set the alarm. [*Pause.*]

HAMM   This is perhaps not one of my bright days, but frankly—

CLOV   You whistle me. I don't come. The alarm rings. I'm gone. It doesn't ring. I'm dead. [*Pause.*]

HAMM   Is it working? [*Pause. Impatiently.*] The alarm, is it working?

CLOV   Why wouldn't it be working?

HAMM   Because it's worked too much.

CLOV   But it's hardly worked at all.

HAMM   [*Angrily.*]   Then because it's worked too little!

CLOV   I'll go and see. [*Exit* CLOV. *Brief ring of alarm off. Enter* CLOV *with alarm-clock. He holds it against* HAMM's *ear and releases alarm. They listen to it ringing to the end. Pause.*] Fit to wake the dead! Did you hear it?

HAMM   Vaguely.

CLOV   The end is terrific!

HAMM   I prefer the middle. [*Pause.*] Is it not time for my pain-killer?

CLOV   No! [*He goes to door, turns.*] I'll leave you.

HAMM   It's time for my story. Do you want to listen to my story.

CLOV   No.

HAMM   Ask my father if he wants to listen to my story.

[CLOV *goes to bins, raises the lid of* NAGG's, *stoops, looks into it. Pause. He straightens up.*]

CLOV   He's asleep.

HAMM   Wake him.

[CLOV *stoops, wakes* NAGG *with the alarm. Unintelligible words.* CLOV *straightens up.*]

CLOV   He doesn't want to listen to your story.

HAMM   I'll give him a bon-bon.

[CLOV *stoops. As before.*]

CLOV   He wants a sugar-plum.

HAMM   He'll get a sugar-plum.

[CLOV *stoops. As before.*]

CLOV   It's a deal. [*He goes towards door.* NAGG's *hands appear, gripping the rim. Then the head emerges.* CLOV *reaches door, turns.*] Do you believe in the life to come?

HAMM   Mine was always that. [*Exit* CLOV.] Got him that time!
NAGG   I'm listening.
HAMM   Scoundrel! Why did you engender me?
NAGG   I didn't know.
HAMM   What? What didn't you know?
NAGG   That it'd be you. [*Pause.*] You'll give me a sugar-plum?
HAMM   After the audition.
NAGG   You swear?
HAMM   Yes.
NAGG   On what?
HAMM   My honor.
        [*Pause. They laugh heartily.*]
NAGG   Two.
HAMM   One.
NAGG   One for me and one for—
HAMM   One! Silence! [*Pause.*] Where was I? [*Pause. Gloomily.*] It's finished,
    we're finished. [*Pause.*] Nearly finished. [*Pause.*] There'll be no more speech.
    [*Pause.*] Something dripping in my head, ever since the fontanelles. [*Stifled
    hilarity of* NAGG.] Splash, splash, always on the same spot. [*Pause.*] Perhaps
    it's a little vein. [*Pause.*] A little artery. [*Pause. More animated.*] Enough of
    that, it's story time, where was I? [*Pause. Narrative tone.*] The man came
    crawling towards me, on his belly. Pale, wonderfully pale and thin, he seemed
    on the point of— [*Pause. Normal tone.*] No, I've done that bit. [*Pause. Nar-
    rative tone.*] I calmly filled my pipe—the meerschaum, lit it with . . . let us say
    a vesta, drew a few puffs. Aah! [*Pause.*] Well, what is it *you* want? [*Pause.*]
    It was an extraordinarily bitter day, I remember, zero by the thermometer.
    But considering it was Christmas Eve there was nothing . . . extra-ordinary
    about that. Seasonable weather, for once in a way. [*Pause.*] Well, what ill
    wind blows you my way? He raised his face to me, black with mingled dirt
    and tears. [*Pause. Normal tone.*] That should do it. [*Narrative tone.*] No, no,
    don't look at me, don't look at me. He dropped his eyes and mumbled some-
    thing, apologies I presume. [*Pause.*] I'm a busy man, you know, the final
    touches, before the festivities, you know what it is. [*Pause. Forcibly.*] Come
    on now, what is the object of this invasion? [*Pause.*] It was a glorious bright
    day, I remember, fifty by the heliometer,[9] but already the sun was sinking
    down into the . . . down among the dead. [*Normal tone.*] Nicely put, that.
    [*Narrative tone.*] Come on now, come on, present your petition and let
    me resume my labors. [*Pause. Normal tone.*] There's English for you. Ah
    well . . . [*Narrative tone.*] It was then he took the plunge. It's my little one,
    he said. Tsstss, a little one, that's bad. My little boy, he said, as if the sex
    mattered. Where did he come from? He named the hole. A good half-day,
    on horse. What are you insinuating? That the place is still inhabited? No no,
    not a soul, except himself and the child—assuming he existed. Good. I
    enquired about the situation at Kov, beyond the gulf. Not a sinner. Good.
    And you expect me to believe you have left your little one back there, all
    alone, and alive into the bargain? Come now! [*Pause.*] It was a howling wild

---

9. Literally, a "sun meter." Ordinarily, a telescope used to measure distances between celestial
bodies.

uniform type of delicate adolescent in bleak Epworth or Tedworth, radiating the same disturbances as in old Peru; solemn Victorian orgies with roses falling and accordions floating to the strains of sacred music; professional impostors regurgitating moist cheesecloth; Mr. Duncan, a lady medium's dignified husband, who, when asked if he would submit to a search, excused himself on the ground of soiled underwear; old Alfred Russel Wallace, the naive naturalist, refusing to believe that the white form with bare feet and unperforated earlobes before him, at a private pandemonium in Boston, could be prim Miss Cook whom he had just seen asleep, in her curtained corner, all dressed in black, wearing laced-up boots and earrings; two other investigators, small, puny, but reasonably intelligent and active men, closely clinging with arms and legs about Eusapia, a large, plump elderly female reeking of garlic, who still managed to fool them; and the skeptical and embarrassed magician, instructed by charming young Margery's "control" not to get lost in the bathrobe's lining but to follow up the left stocking until he reached the bare thigh—upon the warm skin of which he felt a "teleplastic" mass that appeared to the touch uncommonly like cold, uncooked liver.

7

I was appealing to flesh, and the corruption of flesh, to refute and defeat the possible persistence of discarnate[6] life. Alas, these conjurations only enhanced my fear of Cynthia's phantom. Atavistic peace came with dawn, and when I slipped into sleep the sun through the tawny window shades penetrated a dream that somehow was full of Cynthia.

This was disappointing. Secure in the fortress of daylight, I said to myself that I had expected more. She, a painter of glass-bright minutiae—and now so vague! I lay in bed, thinking my dream over and listening to the sparrows outside: Who knows, if recorded and then run backward, those bird sounds might not become human speech, voiced words, just as the latter become a twitter when reversed? I set myself to reread my dream—backward, diagonally, up, down—trying hard to unravel something Cynthia-like in it, something strange and suggestive that must be there.

I could isolate, consciously, little. Everything seemed blurred, yellow-clouded, yielding nothing tangible. Her inept acrostics, maudlin evasions, theopathies[7]—every recollection formed ripples of mysterious meaning. Everything seemed yellowly blurred, illusive, lost.

1959

---

6. Disembodied.
7. Spiritual emotions resulting from the contemplation of God. The first letter of each word in this paragraph spells out a message. Nabokov claimed that "by means of various allusions to trick-reading I have arranged matters so that the reader almost automatically slips into this discovery, especially because of the abrupt change in *style*."

CLARICE LISPECTOR

1920–1977

Reaching for an apple in the dark, claims Brazilian modernist Clarice Lispector, demonstrates the limits of our knowledge: we know that the object is an apple, but little more. Its color and ripeness remain shrouded in obscurity—tantalizingly *there* and *not there* at the same time. The characters in Lispector's novels and short stories live in the constant awareness of this kind of mystery; theirs is a plane of immediate experience and bodily sensations that has little to do with the orderly, daylight world of our shared rationality, where everything has been named and placed within a cognitive or social system. A pivotal figure in modern Brazilian literature, Lispector deploys a simple vocabulary but an unusual syntax; she makes extended use of interior monologues to evoke the immediacy of subjective consciousness.

Lispector was born in December 1920 in Tchetchelik, a small town in Ukraine, as her parents—Russian Jews who had been the victims of pogroms—made the long journey to a new home in Brazil. Upon their arrival, they changed their infant daughter's name from Chaya to Clarice. They settled in Recife, the capital of the northeastern state of Pernambuco, where Lispector received her early schooling, but later moved to Rio de Janeiro. There, Lispector entered law school and became the first woman reporter at the major newspaper *A Noite*. Her first novel, *Close to the Savage Heart*, published in 1943 (the title derives from a line in **James Joyce**'s *A Portrait of the Artist as a Young Man*), won her the Graça Aranha Prize and a reputation as an innovative young Brazilian writer.

Over the next fifteen years, she traveled widely with her husband, a diplomat she married when they were both in law school. They lived in Italy, Switzerland, England, and the United States. Lispector published some further fiction but spent much of her time in Washington, D.C., between 1952 and 1960, writing detailed notes that she would later incorporate into her fiction. Returning to Rio after separating from her husband, she made use of notes she had written during the previous eight years to compose her best-known short-story collection, *Family Ties* (1960), from which the selection here is taken. The collection won the prestigious Jabuti Prize, the foremost literary award in Brazil. Lispector published novels, short stories, chronicles (nonfiction pieces), and children's tales during the remaining years before her death from cancer in 1977.

Lispector is best known as a writer of intense, tightly structured short stories that portray the external world through a character's innermost thoughts and feelings and that emphasize sensuous perception to attain intuitive knowledge beyond words. She has often been compared, in this respect, with **Virginia Woolf**. Lispector's special contribution to literary modernism may lie in her ability to draw connections between bodily sensations, the limits of language, and the mysteries of existence—and to make these connections the unifying structure of her work. Her fluid, lyrical style has been called "feminine writing," because it explores the relationship of immediate bodily experience to language.

The work presented here, "The Daydreams of a Drunk Woman" (1960) is a disturbing tale. The title disposes of the protagonist in a few words: she is an alcoholic, and she imagines things. (The *rapariga* [young woman] of the original title suggests, in Brazilian Portuguese, that she may be promiscuous and possibly of poor immigrant stock.) The narrative's course confirms these descriptions: it begins with the protagonist in bed at home, possibly already drunk, and goes on to show her flying into alcoholic rages and bouts of self-pity. Yet the story reveals deeper possibilities in this woman. Oblique details and brilliant imagery suggest other dimensions to her life: the reasons for her misery and repressed rage, the choices that she has made while seeking security and protection, and the social conditions that foster such pitiable circumstances. From the beginning, when she stares at her reflection in a triple mirror and sees "the intersected breasts of several women," her identity appears fragmented, her self-image either in shards or swollen and unreachable. As she congratulates herself repeatedly on being "protected like everyone who had attained a position in life," and viciously criticizes a more stylish woman she sees in the restaurant, it gradually becomes clearer that she has arrived at her position, and escaped poverty, by exploiting her body to marry a man she neither loves nor respects. While filling in a devastatingly detailed picture of this abject modern figure in her day-to-day delusions, unhappiness, and destructive relationships, Lispector's prose evokes the existential dilemma that the young woman feels and half understands.

The Daydreams of a Drunk Woman[1]

It seemed to her that the trolley cars were about to cross through the room as they caused her reflected image to tremble. She was combing her hair at her leisure in front of the dressing table with its three mirrors, and her strong white arms shivered in the coolness of the evening. Her eyes did not look away as the mirrors trembled, sometimes dark, sometimes luminous. Outside, from a window above, something heavy and hollow fell to the ground. Had her husband and the little ones been at home, the idea would already have occurred to her that they were to blame. Her eyes did not take themselves off her image, her comb worked pensively, and her open dressing gown revealed in the mirrors the intersected breasts of several women.

"Evening News" shouted the newsboy to the mild breeze in Riachuelo Street,[2] and something trembled as if foretold. She threw her comb down on the dressing table and sang dreamily: "Who saw the little spar-row . . . it passed by the window . . . and flew beyond Minho!"[3]—but, suddenly becoming irritated, she shut up abruptly like a fan.

She lay down and fanned herself impatiently with a newspaper that rustled in the room. She clutched the bedsheet, inhaling its odor as she crushed its starched embroidery with her red-lacquered nails. Then, almost smiling, she started to fan herself once more. Oh my!—she sighed as she began to smile. She beheld the picture of her bright smile, the smile of a woman who was still

---

1. Translated by Giovanni Pontiero.
2. A street in Rio de Janeiro that intersects with Mem de Sá Street. Riachuelo is the name of a large department store; Mem de Sá was a
16th-century Portuguese governor-general of Brazil and the founder of Rio de Janeiro.
3. A river in northwest Portugal.

young, and she continued to smile to herself, closing her eyes and fanning herself still more vigorously. Oh my!—she would come fluttering in from the street like a butterfly.

"Hey there! Guess who came to see me today?" she mused as a feasible and interesting topic of conversation. "No idea, tell me," those eyes asked her with a gallant smile, those sad eyes set in one of those pale faces that make one feel so uncomfortable. "Maria Quiteria, my dear!" she replied coquettishly with her hand on her hip. "And who, might we ask, would she be?" they insisted gallantly, but now without any expression. "You!" she broke off, slightly annoyed. How boring!

Oh what a succulent room! Here she was, fanning herself in Brazil. The sun, trapped in the blinds, shimmered on the wall like the strings of a guitar. Riachuelo Street shook under the gasping weight of the trolley cars which came from Mem de Sá Street. Curious and impatient, she listened to the vibrations of the china cabinet in the drawing room. Impatiently she rolled over to lie face downward, and, sensuously stretching the toes of her dainty feet, she awaited her next thought with open eyes. "Whosoever found, searched," she said to herself in the form of a rhymed refrain, which always ended up by sounding like some maxim. Until eventually she fell asleep with her mouth wide open, her saliva staining the pillow.

She only woke up when her husband came into the room the moment he returned from work. She did not want to eat any dinner nor to abandon her dreams, and she went back to sleep: let him content himself with the leftovers from lunch.

And now that the kids were at the country house of their aunts in Jacarepaguá,[4] she took advantage of their absence in order to begin the day as she pleased: restless and frivolous in her bed . . . one of those whims perhaps. Her husband appeared before her, having already dressed, and she did not even know what he had prepared for his breakfast. She avoided examining his suit to see whether it needed brushing . . . little did she care if this was his day for attending to his business in the city. But when he bent over to kiss her, her capriciousness crackled like a dry leaf.

"Don't paw me!"

"What the devil's the matter with you?" the man asked her in amazement, as he immediately set about attempting some more effective caress.

Obstinate, she would not have known what to reply, and she felt so touchy and aloof that she did not even know where to find a suitable reply. She suddenly lost her temper. "Go to hell! . . . prowling round me like some old tomcat."

He seemed to think more clearly and said, firmly, "You're ill, my girl."

She accepted his remark, surprised, and vaguely flattered.

She remained in bed the whole day long listening to the silence of the house without the scurrying of the kids, without her husband who would have his meals in the city today. Her anger was tenuous and ardent. She only got up to go to the bathroom, from which she returned haughty and offended.

The morning turned into a long enormous afternoon, which then turned into a shallow night, which innocently dawned throughout the entire house.

She was still in bed, peaceful and casual. She was in love. . . . She was anticipating her love for the man whom she would love one day. Who knows, this

4. A quiet neighborhood in Rio de Janeiro with a beach where families would gather to picnic.

sometimes happened, and without any guilt or injury for either partner. Lying in bed thinking and thinking, and almost laughing as one does over some gossip. Thinking and thinking. About what? As if she knew. So she just stayed there.

The next minute she would get up, angry. But in the weakness of that first instant she felt dizzy and fragile in the room which swam round and round until she managed to grope her way back to bed, amazed that it might be true. "Hey, girl, don't you go getting sick on me!" she muttered suspiciously. She raised her hand to her forehead to see if there was any fever.

That night, until she fell asleep, her mind became more and more delirious—for how many minutes?—until she flopped over, fast asleep, to snore beside her husband.

She awoke late, the potatoes waiting to be peeled, the kids expected home that same evening from their visit to the country. "God, I've lost my self-respect, I have! My day for washing and darning socks. . . . What a lazy bitch you've turned out to be!" she scolded herself, inquisitive and pleased . . . shopping to be done, fish to remember, already so late on a hectic sunny morning.

But on Saturday night they went to the tavern in Tiradentes Square[5] at the invitation of a rich businessman, she with her new dress which didn't have any fancy trimmings but was made of good material, a dress that would last her a lifetime. On Saturday night, drunk in Tiradentes Square, inebriated but with her husband at her side to give her support, and being very polite in front of the other man who was so much more refined and rich—striving to make conversation, for she was no provincial ninny and she had already experienced life in the capital. But so drunk that she could no longer stand.

And if her husband was not drunk it was only because he did not want to show disrespect for the businessman, and, full of solicitude and humility, he left the swaggering to the other fellow. His manner suited such an elegant occasion, but it gave her such an urge to laugh! She despised him beyond words! She looked at her husband stuffed into his new suit and found him so ridiculous . . . so drunk that she could no longer stand, but without losing her self-respect as a woman. And the green wine[6] from her native Portugal slowly being drained from her glass.

When she got drunk, as if she had eaten a heavy Sunday lunch, all things which by their true nature are separate from each other—the smell of oil on the one hand, of a male on the other; the soup tureen on the one hand, the waiter on the other—became strangely linked by their true nature and the whole thing was nothing short of disgraceful . . . shocking!

And if her eyes appeared brilliant and cold, if her movements faltered clumsily until she succeeded in reaching the toothpick holder, beneath the surface she really felt so far quite at ease . . . there was that full cloud to transport her without effort. Her puffy lips, her teeth white, and her body swollen with wine. And the vanity of feeling drunk, making her show such disdain for everything, making her feel swollen and rotund like a large cow.

Naturally she talked, since she lacked neither the ability to converse nor topics to discuss. But the words that a woman uttered when drunk were like being

---

5. A square in Rio de Janeiro named after the Brazilian revolutionary patriot; he was executed by the Portuguese in 1792.

6. *Vinho Verde*, literally "green wine," is a soft wine produced in Portugal and often drunk cold before meals.

pregnant—mere words on her lips which had nothing to do with the secret core that seemed like a pregnancy. God, how queer she felt! Saturday night, her every-day soul lost, and how satisfying to lose it, and to remind her of former days, only her small, ill-kempt hands—and here she was now with her elbows resting on the white and red checked tablecloth like a gambling table, deeply launched upon a degrading and revolting existence. And what about her laughter? . . . this outburst of laughter which mysteriously emerged from her full white throat, in response to the polite manners of the businessman, an outburst of laughter coming from the depths of that sleep, and from the depths of that security of someone who has a body. Her white flesh was as sweet as lobster, the legs of a live lobster wriggling slowly in the air . . . that urge to be sick in order to plunge that sweetness into something really awful . . . and that perversity of someone who has a body.

She talked and listened with curiosity to what she herself was about to reply to the well-to-do businessman who had so kindly invited them out to dinner and paid for their meal. Intrigued and amazed, she heard what she was on the point of replying, and what she might say in her present state would serve as an augury for the future. She was no longer a lobster, but a harsher sign—that of the scorpion. After all, she had been born in November.

A beacon that sweeps through the dawn while one is asleep, such was her drunkenness which floated slowly through the air.

At the same time, she was conscious of such feelings! Such feelings! When she gazed upon that picture which was so beautifully painted in the restaurant, she was immediately overcome by an artistic sensibility. No one would get it out of her head that she had really been born for greater things. She had always been one for works of art.

But such sensibility! And not merely excited by the picture of grapes and pears and dead fish with shining scales. Her sensibility irritated her without causing her pain, like a broken fingernail. And if she wanted, she could allow herself the luxury of becoming even more sensitive, she could go still further, because she was protected by a situation, protected like everyone who had attained a position in life. Like someone saved from misfortune. I'm so miserable, dear God! If she wished, she could even pour more wine into her glass, and, protected by the position which she had attained in life, become even more drunk just so long as she did not lose her self-respect. And so, even more drunk, she peered round the room, and how she despised the barren people in that restaurant. Not a real man among them. How sad it really all seemed. How she despised the barren people in that restaurant, while she was plump and heavy and generous to the full. And everything in the restaurant seemed so remote, the one thing distant from the other, as if the one might never be able to converse with the other. Each existing for itself, and God existing there for everyone.

Her eyes once more settled on that female whom she had instantly detested the moment she had entered the room. Upon arriving, she had spotted her seated at a table accompanied by a man and all dolled up in a hat and jewelry, glittering like a false coin, all coy and refined. What a fine hat she was wearing! . . . Bet you anything she isn't even married for all that pious look on her face . . . and that fine hat stuck on her head. A fat lot of good her hypocrisy would do her, and she had better watch out in case her airs and graces proved her undoing! The more sanctimonious they were, the bigger frauds they turned out to be. And as for the waiter, he was a great nitwit, serving her, full of gestures and finesse, while the sallow man with her pretended not to notice. And that pious ninny so pleased with herself in that hat and so modest about her slim waistline, and I'll bet she couldn't even bear her man a child. All right, it was none of her business, but from the moment she arrived she felt the urge to give that blonde prude of a woman playing the grand lady in her hat a few good slaps on the face. She didn't even have any shape, and she was flat-chested. And no doubt, for all her fine hats, she was nothing more than a fishwife trying to pass herself off as a duchess.

Oh, how humiliated she felt at having come to the bar without a hat, and her head now felt bare. And that madam with her affectations, playing the refined lady! I know what you need, my beauty, you and your sallow boy friend! And if you think I envy you with your flat chest, let me assure you that I don't give a damn for you and your hats. Shameless sluts like you are only asking for a good hard slap on the face.

In her holy rage, she stretched out a shaky hand and reached for a toothpick.

But finally, the difficulty of arriving home disappeared; she now bestirred herself amidst the familiar reality of her room, now seated on the edge of the bed, a slipper dangling from one foot.

And, as she had half closed her blurred eyes, everything took on the appearance of flesh, the foot of the bed, the window, the suit her husband had thrown off, and everything became rather painful. Meanwhile, she was becoming larger, more unsteady, swollen and gigantic. If only she could get closer to herself, she would find she was even larger. Each of her arms could be explored by someone who didn't even recognize that they were dealing with an arm, and someone could plunge into each eye and swim around without knowing that it was an eye. And all around her everything was a bit painful. Things of the flesh stricken by nervous twinges. The chilly air had caught her as she had come out of the restaurant.

She was sitting up in bed, resigned and sceptical. And this was nothing yet, God only knew—she was perfectly aware that this was nothing yet. At this moment things were happening to her that would only hurt later and in earnest. When restored to her normal size, her anesthetized body would start to wake up, throbbing, and she would begin to pay for those big meals and drinks. Then, since this would really end up by happening, I might as well open my eyes right now (which she did) and then everything looked smaller and clearer, without her feeling any pain. Everything, deep down, was the same, only smaller and more familiar. She was sitting quite upright in bed, her stomach so full, absorbed and resigned, with the delicacy of one who sits waiting until her partner awakens. "You gorge yourself and I pay the piper," she said sadly, looking at the dainty white toes of her feet. She looked around her, patient and obedient. Ah, words, nothing but words, the objects in the room lined up in the order of words, to form those confused and irksome phrases that he who knows how will read. Boredom . . . such awful boredom. . . . How sickening! How very annoying! When all is said and done, heaven help me— God knows best. What was one to do? How can I describe this thing inside me? Anyhow, God knows best. And to think that she had enjoyed herself so much last night . . . and to think of how nice it all was—a restaurant to her liking— and how she had been seated elegantly at table. At table! The world would exclaim. But she made no reply, drawing herself erect with a bad-tempered click of her tongue . . . irritated . . . "Don't come to me with your endearments" . . . disenchanted, resigned, satiated, married, content, vaguely nauseated.

It was at this moment that she became deaf: one of her senses was missing. She clapped the palm of her hand over her ear, which only made things worse . . . suddenly filling her eardrum with the whirr of an elevator . . . life suddenly becoming loud and magnified in its smallest movements. One of two things: either she was deaf or hearing all too well. She reacted against this new suggestion with a sensation of spite and annoyance, with a sigh of resigned satiety. "Drop dead," she said gently . . . defeated.

"And when in the restaurant . . ." she suddenly recalled when she had been in the restaurant her husband's protector had pressed his foot against hers beneath the table, and above the table his face was watching her. By coincidence or intentionally? The rascal. A fellow, to be frank, who was not unattractive. She shrugged her shoulders.

And when above the roundness of her low-cut dress—right in the middle of Tiradentes Square! she thought, shaking her head incredulously—that fly had settled on her bare bosom. What cheek!

Certain things were good because they were almost nauseating . . . the noise like that of an elevator in her blood, while her husband lay snoring at her side . . . her chubby little children sleeping in the other room, the little villains. Ah, what's wrong with me! she wondered desperately. Have I eaten too much? Heavens above! What *is* wrong with me?

It was unhappiness.

Her toes playing with her slipper . . . the floor not too clean at that spot. "What a slovenly, lazy bitch you've become."

Not tomorrow, because her legs would not be too steady, but the day after tomorrow that house of hers would be a sight worth seeing: she would give it a scouring with soap and water which would get rid of all the dirt! "You mark my words," she threatened in her rage. Ah, she was feeling so well, so strong, as if she still had milk in those firm breasts. When her husband's friend saw her so pretty and plump he had immediately felt respect for her. And when she started to get embarrassed she did not know which way to look. Such misery! What was one to do? Seated on the edge of the bed, blinking in resignation. How well one could see the moon on these summer nights. She leaned over slightly, indifferent and resigned. The moon! How clearly one could see it. The moon high and yellow gliding through the sky, poor thing. Gliding, gliding . . . high up, high up. The moon! Then her vulgarity exploded in a sudden outburst of affection; "you slut," she cried out, laughing.

1960

CHINUA ACHEBE

1930–2013

The best-known African writer today is the Nigerian Chinua Achebe, whose first novel, *Things Fall Apart*, exploded the colonialist image of Africans as childlike people living in a primitive society. Achebe's novels, stories, poetry, and essays made him a respected and prophetic figure in Africa and the West. In Western countries, where he traveled, taught, and lectured widely, he is admired as a major writer who gave a new direction to the English-language novel. Achebe helped to create the African postcolonial novel with its themes and characters; he also developed a complex narrative voice that questions cultural assumptions with a subtle irony and compassion born from bicultural experience.

Achebe was born in Ogidi, an Igbo-speaking town of Eastern Nigeria, on November 16, 1930. He was the fifth of six children in the family of Isaiah Okafor Achebe, a teacher for the Church Missionary Society, and his wife, Janet. Achebe's parents christened him Albert after Prince Albert, husband of Queen Victoria. Two cultures coexisted in Ogidi: on the one hand, African social customs and traditional religion; on the other, British colonial authority and Christianity. Instead of being torn between the two, Achebe found himself curious about both ways of life and fascinated with the dual perspective that came from living "at the crossroads of cultures."

He attended church schools in Ogidi, *where instruction* was carried out in English. Achebe read the various books in his father's library, most of them primers or church related, but he also listened eagerly to his mother and sister when they told traditional Igbo stories. Entering a prestigious secondary school in Umuahia, he immediately took advantage of its well-stocked library. Achebe later recalled that when he read books about Africa, he tended to identify with the white narrators rather than the black inhabitants: "I did not see myself as an African in those books. I took sides with the white men against the savages." After graduating in 1948, Achebe entered University College, Ibadan, on a scholarship to study medicine. In the following year he changed to a program in liberal arts that combined English, history, and religious studies. Research in the last two fields deepened his knowledge of Nigerian history and culture; the assigned literary texts, however, brought into sharp focus the distorted image of African culture offered by British colonial literature. Reading Joyce Cary's *Mister Johnson* (1939), a novel recommended for its depiction of life in Nigeria, he was shocked to find Nigerians described as violent savages with passionate instincts and simple minds: "and so I thought if this was famous, then perhaps someone ought to try and look at this from the inside." While at the university, Achebe rejected his British name in favor of his indigenous name Chinua, which abbreviates *Chinualumogu*, or "My spirit come fight for me."

Achebe began writing while at the university, contributing articles and sketches to several campus papers and publishing four stories in the *University Herald*, a magazine whose editor he became in his third year. His first novel, *Things Fall Apart* (1958), was a conscious attempt to counteract the distortions of English literature about Africa by describing the richness and complexity of traditional African society before the colonial and missionary invasion. It was important, Achebe said, to "teach my readers that their past—with all its imperfections— was not one long night of savagery from which the first Europeans acting on God's behalf delivered them." The novel was recognized immediately as an extraordinary work of literature in English. It also became the first classic work of modern African fiction, translated into nine languages, and Achebe became, for many readers and writers, the teacher of a whole generation. His later novels continue to examine the individual and cultural dilemmas of Nigerian society, although their background varies from the traditional religious society of *Arrow of God* (1964) to thinly disguised accounts of contemporary political strife.

Achebe worked as a radio journalist for the Nigerian Broadcasting Service, ultimately rising to the position of director of external services in charge of the Voice of Nigeria. The radio position was more than a merely administrative post, for Achebe and his colleagues were creating a sense of shared national identity through the broadcasting of national news and information about Nigerian culture. Since the end of the Second World War, Nigeria had been torn by intellectual and political rivalries that overlaid the common struggle for independence (achieved in 1960). The three major ethnolinguistic groups—Yoruba, Hausa-Fulani, and Igbo—were increasingly locked in economic and political competition at the same time they were fighting to erase the vestiges of British colonial rule. These problems eventually boiled over in the Nigerian Civil War (1967–70).

It is hard to overestimate the influence of Nigerian politics on Achebe's life after 1966. In January a military coup d'état led by young Igbo officers overthrew the government; six months later a second coup led by non-Igbo officers took power. Ethnic strife intensified: thousands of Igbos were killed and driven out of the north. Soldiers were sent to find Achebe in Lagos; his wife and young children fled by boat to Eastern Nigeria, where after a dangerous and roundabout journey, Achebe joined them, taking up the post of senior research fellow at the University of Nigeria, Nsukka. In May 1967 the eastern region, mainly populated by Igbo-speakers, seceded as the new nation of Biafra. From then until the defeat of Biafra in January 1970, a bloody civil war was waged with high civilian casualties and widespread starvation. Achebe traveled in Europe, North America, and Africa to win support for Biafra, proclaiming that "no government, black or white, has the right to stigmatize and destroy groups of its own citizens without undermining the basis of its own existence." A group of his poems about the war won the Commonwealth Poetry Prize in 1972, the same year that he published a volume of short stories, *Girls at War*, and left Nigeria to take up a three-year position at the University of Massachusetts at Amherst. Returning to Nsukka as professor of literature in 1976, Achebe continued to participate in his country's political life. Badly hurt in a car accident in 1990, Achebe slowly recovered and returned to writing and teaching at Bard College in Annandale-on-Hudson, New York, where he stayed for most of the following two decades moving on to teach at Brown University in Providence, Rhode Island. Among many other novels and memoirs, he published the essay collection *Education of a British Protected Child* (2009).

Achebe was convinced of the writer's social responsibility, and he drew frequent contrasts between the European "art for art's sake" tradition and the African belief in the indivisibility of art and society. His favorite example is the Owerri Igbo custom of *mbari*, a communal art project in which villagers selected by the priest of the earth goddess Ala live in a forest clearing for a year or more, working under the direction of master artists to prepare a temple of images in the goddess's honor. This creative communal enterprise and its culminating festival are diametrically opposed, Achebe wrote, to the European custom of secluding art objects in museums or private collections. Instead, *mbari* celebrates art as a cultural process, affirming that "art belongs to all and is a 'function' of society." Achebe's own practice as novelist, poet, essayist, founder and editor of two journals, lecturer, and active representative of African letters exemplified this commitment to the community.

"Chike's School Days" (1960), published in the year of Nigerian independence, tells the story of a child with a dual inheritance like Achebe's own. Like Achebe himself, the boy has three names: the Christian John, the familiar Chike, and the more formal African name Obiajulu, meaning "the mind at last is at rest." Yet if Chike is the answer to his parents' prayers for a son, he is also about to enter a transformative experience in a Christian school, where he will master the English language. Achebe's literary language is an English skillfully blended with Igbo vocabulary, proverbs, images, and speech patterns to create a voice embodying the linguistic pluralism of modern African experience. By including Standard English, Igbo, and pidgin in different contexts, Achebe demonstrates the existence of a diverse society that is otherwise concealed behind language barriers. He thereby acknowledges that his primary African audience is composed of younger, schooled readers who are relatively fluent in English, readers like Chike. Chike's story, however, focuses less on the school days of the title than on his background. Chike's education turns out to be the product of his paternal grandmother's conversion to Christianity, and of his father's marriage (following his own new Christian convictions) to an outcaste woman, an *Osu* (a member of the traditional Igbo slave caste). Thus a seemingly simple tale about a boy going to school turns out to be a story of historical change as it affects three generations. Chike's love of English, while it separates him from his neighbors, suggests the potential for a love of literature. Elsewhere, Achebe wrote that literature is important because it liberates the human imagination; it "begins as an adventure in self-discovery and ends in wisdom and human conscience."

Chike's School Days

Sarah's last child was a boy, and his birth brought great joy to the house of his father, Amos. The child received three names at his baptism—John, Chike, Obiajulu. The last name means "the mind at last is at rest."[1] Anyone hearing this name knew at once that its owner was either an only child or an only son. Chike was an only son. His parents had had five daughters before him.

Like his sisters Chike was brought up "in the ways of the white man," which meant the opposite of traditional. Amos had many years before bought a tiny bell with which he summoned his family to prayers and hymn-singing first

---

1. In the Igbo or Ibo language.

thing in the morning and last thing at night. This was one of the ways of the white man. Sarah taught her children not to eat in their neighbours' houses because "they offered their food to idols." And thus she set herself against the age-old custom which regarded children as the common responsibility of all so that, no matter what the relationship between parents, their children played together and shared their food.

One day a neighbour offered a piece of yam to Chike, who was only four years old. The boy shook his head haughtily and said, "We don't eat heathen food." The neighbour was full of rage, but she controlled herself and only muttered under her breath that even an *Osu*[2] was full of pride nowadays, thanks to the white man.

And she was right. In the past an *Osu* could not raise his shaggy head in the presence of the free-born. He was a slave to one of the many gods of the clan. He was a thing set apart, not to be venerated but to be despised and almost spat on. He could not marry a free-born, and he could not take any of the titles of his clan. When he died, he was buried by his kind in the Bad Bush.

Now all that had changed, or had begun to change. So that an *Osu* child could even look down his nose at a free-born, and talk about heathen food! The white man had indeed accomplished many things.

Chike's father was not originally an *Osu*, but had gone and married an *Osu* woman in the name of Christianity. It was unheard of for a man to make himself *Osu* in that way, with his eyes wide open. But then Amos was nothing if not mad. The new religion had gone to his head. It was like palm-wine. Some people drank it and remained sensible. Others lost every sense in their stomach.

The only person who supported Amos in his mad marriage venture was Mr. Brown, the white missionary, who lived in a thatch-roofed, red-earth-walled parsonage and was highly respected by the people, not because of his sermons, but because of a dispensary he ran in one of his rooms. Amos had emerged from Mr. Brown's parsonage greatly fortified. A few days later he told his widowed mother, who had recently been converted to Christianity and had taken the name of Elizabeth. The shock nearly killed her. When she recovered, she went down on her knees and begged Amos not to do this thing. But he would not hear; his ears had been nailed up. At last, in desperation, Elizabeth went to consult the diviner.

This diviner was a man of great power and wisdom. As he sat on the floor of his hut beating a tortoise shell, a coating of white chalk round his eyes, he saw not only the present, but also what had been and what was to be. He was called "the man of the four eyes." As soon as old Elizabeth appeared, he cast his stringed cowries[3] and told her what she had come to see him about. "Your son has joined the white man's religion. And you too in your old age when you should know better. And do you wonder that he is stricken with insanity? Those who gather ant-infested faggots must be prepared for the visit of lizards." He cast his cowries a number of times and wrote with a finger on a bowl of sand, and all the while his *nwifulu*,[4] a talking calabash, chatted to itself.

2. An untouchable, the lowest caste in the Igbo class system.
3. Snail shells used as currency and, here, in fortune-telling.
4. A pipe made of a gourd.

"Shut up!" he roared, and it immediately held its peace. The diviner then muttered a few incantations and rattled off a breathless reel of proverbs that followed one another like the cowries in his magic string.

At last he pronounced the cure. The ancestors were angry and must be appeased with a goat. Old Elizabeth performed the rites, but her son remained insane and married an *Osu* girl whose name was Sarah. Old Elizabeth renounced her new religion and returned to the faith of her people.

We have wandered from our main story. But it is important to know how Chike's father became an *Osu*, because even today when everything is upside down, such a story is very rare. But now to return to Chike who refused heathen food at the tender age of four years, or maybe five.

Two years later he went to the village school. His right hand could now reach across his head to his left ear, which proved that he was old enough to tackle the mysteries of the white man's learning. He was very happy about his new slate and pencil, and especially about his school uniform of white shirt and brown khaki shorts. But as the first day of the new term approached, his young mind dwelt on the many stories about teachers and their canes. And he remembered the song his elder sisters sang, a song that had a somewhat disquieting refrain:

> *Onye nkuzi ewelu itali piagbusie umuaka.*[5]

One of the ways an emphasis is laid in Ibo is by exaggeration, so that the teacher in the refrain might not actually have flogged the children to death. But there was no doubt he did flog them. And Chike thought very much about it.

Being so young, Chike was sent to what was called the "religious class" where they sang, and sometimes danced, the catechism. He loved the sound of words and he loved rhythm. During the catechism lesson the class formed a ring to dance the teacher's question. "Who was Caesar?"[6] he might ask, and the song would burst forth with much stamping of feet.

> *Siza bu eze Rome*
> *Onye nachi enu uwa dum.*[7]

It did not matter to their dancing that in the twentieth century Caesar was no longer ruler of the whole world.

And sometimes they even sang in English. Chike was very fond of "Ten Green Bottles." They had been taught the words but they only remembered the first and the last lines. The middle was hummed and hie-ed and mumbled:

> *Ten grin botr angin on dar war,*
> *Ten grin botr angin on dar war,*
> *Hm hm hm hm hm*
> *Hm, hm hm hm hm hm,*
> *An ten grin botr angin on dar war.*[8]

---

5. "The teacher took a whip and flogged the pupils mercilessly" (Ibo).
6. Julius Caesar (100–44 B.C.E.), Roman general and political leader whose near-monopoly on power in the late days of the Roman Republic led to the creation of the Roman Empire.

7. "Caesar was the chief of Rome, / the ruler of the whole world" (Ibo).
8. A British children's song, "Ten green bottles hanging on the wall," as pronounced by African children who are learning English.

In this way the first year passed. Chike was promoted to the "Infant School," where work of a more serious nature was undertaken.

We need not follow him through the Infant School. It would make a full story in itself. But it was no different from the story of other children. In the Primary School, however, his individual character began to show. He developed a strong hatred for arithmetic. But he loved stories and songs. And he liked particularly the sound of English words, even when they conveyed no meaning at all. Some of them simply filled him with elation. "Periwinkle" was such a word. He had now forgotten how he learned it or exactly what it was. He had a vague private meaning for it and it was something to do with fairyland. "Constellation" was another.

Chike's teacher was fond of long words. He was said to be a very learned man. His favourite pastime was copying out jaw-breaking words from his *Chambers' Etymological Dictionary*. Only the other day he had raised applause from his class by demolishing a boy's excuse for lateness with unanswerable erudition. He had said: "Procrastination is a lazy man's apology." The teacher's erudition showed itself in every subject he taught. His nature study lessons were memorable. Chike would always remember the lesson on the methods of seed dispersal. According to teacher, there were five methods: by man, by animals, by water, by wind, and by explosive mechanism. Even those pupils who forgot all the other methods remembered "explosive mechanism."

Chike was naturally impressed by teacher's explosive vocabulary. But the fairyland quality which words had for him was of a different kind. The first sentences in his *New Method Reader* were simple enough and yet they filled him with a vague exultation: "Once there was a wizard. He lived in Africa. He went to China to get a lamp." Chike read it over and over again at home and then made a song of it. It was a meaningless song. "Periwinkles" got into it, and also "Damascus." But it was like a window through which he saw in the distance a strange, magical new world. And he was happy.

1960

CARLOS FUENTES
1928–2012

One of the first Mexican novelists to achieve international success, Carlos Fuentes helped to ignite the Latin American "Boom," or literary flowering, of the 1960s. Combining meditations on Mexican history with modern literary techniques, Fuentes became a leading novelist and public intellectual in his home country. His worldwide reputation rests on his experimental fiction, a precursor to postmodernism.

Born in Panama City, Fuentes was the son of a Mexican diplomat. With his parents, he lived in several Latin American capitals (Montevideo, Uruguay; Rio de Janeiro, Brazil; Santiago,

Chile; and Buenos Aires, Argentina)—and, from 1934 to 1940, in Washington, D.C., where he acquired an admiration for the liberal politics of Franklin Delano Roosevelt and the New Deal. In Washington, Fuentes learned about Mexico's relationship with its superpower neighbor. At the age of ten, while attending a film about the Texan Sam Houston, Fuentes says, "During the attack on the Alamo, I couldn't restrain my patriotism. I jumped on the seat, screaming, 'Viva Mexico—death to the gringo,'" using a generally unflattering term to refer to Mexico's neighbors to the north. His father hustled him out of the theater. As an adult, Fuentes often criticized U.S. policy in Latin America and was once prevented from entering the United States because of suspected Communist ties; but he remained relatively friendly toward the country where he had spent much of his childhood, and later in life he taught at some American universities.

When he was a teenager, Fuentes and his family returned to Mexico City. Although he wanted to become a writer, he also worked in foreign affairs, for the United Nations and the International Labor Organization. Fuentes's first novel was the immensely successful *Where the Air Is Clear* (1958). Its hero is Mexico City itself, with its dramatic mixture of Spanish, indigenous, and mestizo cultures. Fuentes's novels draw on the techniques of modernism, such as stream-of-consciousness narration, to portray the inner lives of characters. After achieving fame as a novelist, he would serve briefly as Mexican ambassador to France.

In the novella presented here, *Aura* (1962), Fuentes makes use of second-person narration. By addressing the main character, Felipe Montero, as "you"—as if Montero were a reader—Fuentes draws his actual readers into the story, plunging them into the life of an unemployed Mexican intellectual. The unsettling quality is heightened by the advertisement Montero reads in the newspaper, on the first page of the story, which appears to have been written specifically for him. Montero seems closely identified with the author of the story, too. Like Fuentes, who wrote a panoramic overview of Latin American history, *The Buried Mirror* (1992), Montero is knowledgeable about history and fluent in French.

Montero journeys to the old center of Mexico City, which has fallen into disrepair, and mysteriously finds his way into a luxurious but faded apartment. There he is met by an old woman who seems to know all about him and who addresses him in French. As he learns what tasks the lady wants him to perform, the protagonist becomes fascinated by the role of her late, legendary husband in Mexican history and by the unreal beauty of her young niece, Aura. Like many uncanny stories (notably those of Henry James, whom Fuentes admires), *Aura* leaves us in suspense about which of the events may be real or imagined, natural or supernatural.

Fuentes recalls the origins of the story in his vision of a young woman in a certain light in a mirror-filled room in Paris:

> In this almost instantaneous succession, the girl I remembered when she was fourteen years old and who was now twenty suffered the same changes as the light coming through the windowpanes: that threshold between the parlour and the bedroom became the lintel between all the ages of this girl: the light that had been struggling against the clouds also fought against her flesh, took it, sketched it, granted her a shadow of years, sculpted a death in her eyes, tore the smile from her lips, waned through her hair with the floating melancholy of madness.

The next day, Fuentes sat down in a café to write *Aura*.

Aura[1]

Man hunts and struggles.
Woman intrigues and dreams;
she is the mother of fantasy,
the mother of the gods.
She has second sight,
the wings that enable her to fly
to the infinite of
desire and the imagination . . .
The gods are like men:
they are born and they die
on a woman's breast . . .

—JULES MICHELET[2]

I

You're reading the advertisement: an offer like this isn't made every day. You read it and reread it. It seems to be addressed to you and nobody else. You don't even notice when the ash from your cigarette falls into the cup of tea you ordered in this cheap, dirty café. You read it again. "Wanted, young historian, conscientious, neat. Perfect knowledge colloquial French." Youth . . . knowledge of French, preferably after living in France for a while . . . "Four thousand pesos a month, all meals, comfortable bedroom-study." All that's missing is your name. The advertisement should have two more words, in bigger, blacker type: Felipe Montero. Wanted, Felipe Montero, formerly on scholarship at the Sorbonne, historian full of useless facts, accustomed to digging among yellowed documents, part-time teacher in private schools, nine hundred pesos a month. But if you read that, you'd be suspicious, and take it as a joke. "Address, Donceles 815."[3] No telephone. Come in person.

You leave a tip, reach for your brief case, get up. You wonder if another young historian, in the same situation you are, has seen the same advertisement, has got ahead of you and taken the job already. You walk down to the corner, trying to forget this idea. As you wait for the bus, you run over the dates you must have on the tip of your tongue so that your sleepy pupils will respect you. The bus is coming now, and you're staring at the tips of your black shoes. You've got to be prepared. You put your hand in your pocket, search among the coins, and finally take out thirty centavos. You've got to be prepared. You grab the handrail— the bus slows down but doesn't stop—and jump aboard. Then you shove your way forward, pay the driver the thirty centavos,[4] squeeze yourself in among the passengers already standing in the aisle, hang onto the over-head rail, press your brief case tighter under your left arm, and automatically put your left hand over the back pocket where you keep your billfold.

This day is just like any other day, and you don't remember the advertisement until the next morning, when you sit down in the same café and order

---

1. Translated from Spanish by Lysander Kemp.
2. French historian (1798–1874). The quotation is from Satanism and Witchcraft (1862).
3. In downtown Mexico City.
4. A few cents.

breakfast and open your newspaper. You come to the advertising section and there it is again: *young historian*. The job is still open. You reread the advertisement, lingering over the final words: four thousand pesos.

It's surprising to know that anyone lives on Donceles Street. You always thought that nobody lived in the old center of the city. You walk slowly, trying to pick out the number 815 in that conglomeration of old colonial mansions, all of them converted into repair shops, jewelry shops, shoe stores, drugstores. The numbers have been changed, painted over, confused. A 13 next to a 200. An old plaque reading 47 over a scrawl in blurred charcoal: *Now 924*. You look up at the second stories. Up there, everything is the same as it was. The jukeboxes don't disturb them. The mercury streetlights don't shine in. The cheap merchandise on sale along the street doesn't have any effect on that upper level; on the baroque harmony of the carved stones; on the battered stone saints with pigeons clustering on their shoulders; on the latticed balconies, the copper gutters, the sandstone gargoyles; on the greenish curtains that darken the long windows; on that window from which someone draws back when you look at it. You gaze at the fanciful vines carved over the doorway, then lower your eyes to the peeling wall and discover 815, *formerly 69.*

You rap vainly with the knocker, that copper head of a dog, so worn and smooth that it resembles the head of a canine foetus in a museum of natural science. It seems as if the dog is grinning at you and you let go of the cold metal. The door opens at the first light push of your fingers, but before going in you give a last look over your shoulder, frowning at the long line of stalled cars that growl, honk, and belch out the unhealthy fumes of their impatience. You try to retain some single image of that indifferent outside world.

You close the door behind you and peer into the darkness of a roofed alleyway. It must be a patio of some sort, because you can smell the mold, the dampness of the plants, the rotting roots, the thick drowsy aroma. There isn't any light to guide you, and you're searching in your coat pocket for the box of matches when a sharp, thin voice tells you, from a distance: "No, it isn't necessary. Please. Walk thirteen steps forward and you'll come to a stairway at your right. Come up, please. There are twenty-two steps. Count them."

Thirteen. To the right. Twenty-two.

The dank smell of the plants is all around you as you count out your steps, first on the paving-stones, then on the creaking wood, spongy from the dampness. You count to twenty-two in a low voice and then stop, with the matchbox in your hand, and the brief case under your arm. You knock on a door that smells of old pine. There isn't any knocker. Finally you push it open. Now you can feel a carpet under your feet, a thin carpet, badly laid. It makes you trip and almost fall. Then you notice the grayish filtered light that reveals some of the humps.

"Señora," you say, because you seem to remember a woman's voice. "Señora . . ."

"Now turn to the left. The first door. Please be so kind."

You push the door open: you don't expect any of them to be latched, you know they all open at a push. The scattered lights are braided in your eyelashes, as if you were seeing them through a silken net. All you can make out are the dozens of flickering lights. At last you can see that they're votive lights, all set on brackets or hung between unevenly-spaced panels. They cast a faint glow on the silver objects, the crystal flasks, the gilt-framed mirrors. Then you see the bed in the shadows beyond, and the feeble movement of a hand that seems to be beckoning to you.

But you can't see her face until you turn your back on that galaxy of religious lights. You stumble to the foot of the bed, and have to go around it in order to get to the head of it. A tiny figure is almost lost in its immensity. When you reach out your hand, you don't touch another hand, you touch the ears and thick fur of a creature that's chewing silently and steadily, looking up at you with its glowing red eyes. You smile and stroke the rabbit that's crouched beside her hand. Finally you shake hands, and her cold fingers remain for a long while in your sweating palm.

"I'm Felipe Montero. I read your advertisement."

"Yes, I know. I'm sorry, there aren't any chairs."

"That's all right. Don't worry about it."

"Good. Please let me see your profile. No, I can't see it well enough. Turn toward the light. That's right. Excellent."

"I read your advertisement . . ."

"Yes, of course. Do you think you're qualified? *Avez-vous fait des études?*"

"*A Paris, madame.*"

"*Ah, oui, ça me fait plaisir, toujours, toujours, d'entendre . . . oui . . . vous savez . . . on était tellement habitué . . . et après . . .*"[5]

You move aside so that the light from the candles and the reflections from the silver and crystal show you the silk coif that must cover a head of very white hair, and that frames a face so old it's almost childlike. Her whole body is covered by the sheets and the feather pillows and the high, tightly buttoned white collar, all except for her arms, which are wrapped in a shawl, and her pallid hands resting on her stomach. You can only stare at her face until a movement of the rabbit lets you glance furtively at the crusts and bits of bread scattered on the worn-out red silk of the pillows.

"I'll come directly to the point. I don't have many years ahead of me, Señor Montero, and therefore I decided to break a lifelong rule and place an advertisement in the newspaper."

"Yes, that's why I'm here."

"Of course. So you accept."

"Well, I'd like to know a little more."

"Yes. You're wondering."

She sees you glance at the night table, the different-colored bottles, the glasses, the aluminium spoons, the row of pillboxes, the other glasses—all stained with whitish liquids—on the floor within reach of her hand. Then you notice that the bed is hardly raised above the level of the floor. Suddenly the rabbit jumps down and disappears in the shadows.

"I can offer you four thousand pesos."

"Yes, that's what the advertisement said today."

"Ah, then it came out."

"Yes, it came out."

5. "Have you studied?"
  "In Paris, Madame."
  "Ah, yes, it always, always pleases me to
hear . . . yes . . . you know . . . we were so
accustomed to it . . . and afterwards . . ."
(French).

"It has to do with the memoirs of my husband, General Llorente. They must be put in order before I die. I want them to be published. I decided that a short time ago."

"But the General himself? Wouldn't he be able to . . ."

"He died sixty years ago, Señor. They're his unfinished memoirs. They have to be completed before I die."

"But . . ."

"I can tell you everything. You'll learn to write in my husband's own style. You'll only have to arrange and read his manuscripts to become fascinated by his style . . . his clarity . . . his . . ."

"Yes, I understand."

"Saga, Saga. Where are you? *Ici*, Saga!"

"Who?"

"My companion."

"The rabbit?"

"Yes. She'll come back."

When you raise your eyes, which you've been keeping lowered, her lips are closed but you can hear her words again—"She'll come back"—as if the old lady were pronouncing them at that instant. Her lips remain still. You look in back of you and you're almost blinded by the gleam from the religious objects. When you look at her again you see that her eyes have opened very wide, and that they're clear, liquid, enormous, almost the same colour as the yellowish whites around them, so that only the black dots of the pupils mar that clarity. It's lost a moment later in the heavy folds of her lowered eyelids, as if she wanted to protect that glance which is now hiding at the back of its dry cave.

"Then you'll stay here. Your room is upstairs. It's sunny there."

"It might be better if I didn't trouble you, Señora. I can go on living where I am and work on the manuscripts there."

"My conditions are that you have to live here. There isn't much time left."

"I don't know if . . ."

"Aura . . ."

The old woman moves for the first time since you entered her room. As she reaches out her hand again, you sense that agitated breathing beside you, and another hand reaches out to touch the Señora's fingers. You look around and a girl is standing there, a girl whose whole body you can't see because she's standing so close to you and her arrival was so unexpected, without the slightest sound—not even those sounds that can't be heard but are real anyway because they're remembered immediately afterwards, because in spite of everything they're louder than the silence that accompanies them.

"I told you she'd come back."

"Who?"

"Aura. My companion. My niece."

"Good afternoon."

The girl nods and at the same instant the old lady imitates her gesture.

"This is Señor Montero. He's going to live with us."

You move a few steps so that the light from the candles won't blind you. The girl keeps her eyes closed, her hands at her sides. She doesn't look at you at first, then little by little she opens her eyes as if she were afraid of the light. Finally you can see that those eyes are sea green and that they surge, break to foam, grow calm again, then surge again like a wave. You look into them and tell yourself it isn't true, because they're beautiful green eyes just like all the beautiful green eyes you've ever known. But you can't deceive yourself: those eyes do surge, do change, as if offering you a landscape that only you can see and desire.

"Yes. I'm going to live with you."

2

The old woman laughs sharply and tells you that she is grateful for your kindness and that the girl will show you to your room. You're thinking about the salary of four thousand pesos, and how the work should be pleasant because you like these jobs of careful research that don't include physical effort or going from one place to another or meeting people you don't want to meet. You're thinking about this as you follow her out of the room, and you discover that you've got to follow her with your ears instead of your eyes: you follow the rustle of her skirt, the rustle of taffeta, and you're anxious now to look into her eyes again. You climb the stairs behind that sound in the darkness, and you're still unused to the obscurity. You remember it must be about six in the afternoon, and the flood of light surprises you when Aura opens the door to your bedroom—another door without a latch—and steps aside to tell you: "This is your room. We'll expect you for supper in an hour."

She moves away with the same faint rustle of taffeta, and you weren't able to see her face again.

You close the door and look up at the skylight that serves as a roof. You smile when you find that the evening light is blinding compared with the darkness in the rest of the house, and smile again when you try out the mattress on the gilded metal bed. Then you glance around the room: a red wool rug, olive and gold wallpaper, an easy chair covered in red velvet, an old walnut desk with a green leather top, an old Argand lamp with its soft glow for your nights of research, and a bookshelf over the desk in reach of your hand. You walk over to the other door, and on pushing it open you discover an outmoded bathroom: a four-legged bathtub with little flowers painted on the porcelain, a blue hand basin, an old-fashioned toilet. You look at yourself in the large oval mirror on the door of the wardrobe—it's also walnut—in the bathroom hallway. You move your heavy eyebrows and wide thick lips, and your breath fogs the mirror. You close your black eyes, and when you open them again the mirror has cleared. You stop holding your breath and run your hand through your dark, limp hair; you touch your fine profile, your lean cheeks; and when your breath hides your face again you're repeating her name: "Aura."

After smoking two cigarettes while lying on the bed, you get up, put on your jacket, and comb your hair. You push the door open and try to remember the route you followed coming up. You'd like to leave the door open so that the lamplight could guide you, but that's impossible because the springs close it behind you. You could enjoy playing with that door, swinging it back and forth. You don't do it. You could take the lamp down with you. You don't do it. This house will always be in darkness, and you've got to learn it and relearn it by touch. You grope your way like a blind man, with your arms stretched out wide, feeling your way along the wall, and by accident you turn on the light-switch.

You stop and blink in the bright middle of that long, empty hall. At the end of it you can see the bannister and the spiral staircase.

You count the stairs as you go down: another custom you've got to learn in Señora Llorente's house. You take a step backward when you see the reddish eyes of the rabbit, which turns its back on you and goes hopping away.

You don't have time to stop in the lower hallway because Aura is waiting for you at a half-open stained-glass door, with a candelabra in her hand. You walk toward her, smiling, but you stop when you hear the painful yowling of a number of cats—yes, you stop to listen, next to Aura, to be sure that they're cats—and then follow her to the parlor.

"It's the cats," Aura tells you. "There are lots of rats in this part of the city."

You go through the parlor: furniture upholstered in faded silk; glass-fronted cabinets containing porcelain figurines, musical clocks, medals, glass balls; carpets with Persian designs; pictures of rustic scenes; green velvet curtains. Aura is dressed in green.

"Is your room comfortable?"

"Yes. But I have to get my things from the place where . . ."

"It won't be necessary. The servant has already gone for them."

"You shouldn't have bothered."

You follow her into the dining room. She places the candelabra in the middle of the table. The room feels damp and cold. The four walls are paneled in dark wood carved in Gothic style, with fretwork arches and large rosettes. The cats have stopped yowling. When you sit down, you notice that four places have been set. There are two large, covered plates and an old, grimy bottle.

Aura lifts the cover from one of the plates. You breathe in the pungent odour of the liver and onions she serves you, then you pick up the old bottle and fill the cut-glass goblets with that thick red liquid. Out of curiosity you try to read the label on the wine bottle, but the grime has obscured it. Aura serves you some whole broiled tomatoes from the other plate.

"Excuse me," you say, looking at the two extra places, the two empty chairs, "but are you expecting someone else?"

Aura goes on serving the tomatoes. "No. Señora Consuelo feels a little ill tonight. She won't be joining us."

"Señora Consuelo? Your aunt?"

"Yes. She'd like you to go in and see her after supper."

You eat in silence. You drink that thick wine, occasionally shifting your glance so that Aura won't catch you in the hypnotized stare that you can't control. You'd like to fix the girl's features in your mind. Every time you look away you forget them again, and an irresistible urge forces you to look at her once more. As usual, she has her eyes lowered. While you're searching for the pack of cigarettes in your coat pocket, you run across that big key, and remember, and say to Aura: "Ah! I forgot that one of the drawers in my desk is locked. I've got my papers in it."

And she murmurs: "Then you want to go out?" She says it as a reproach.

You feel confused, and reach out your hand to her with the key dangling from one finger.

"It isn't important. The servant can go for them tomorrow."

But she avoids touching your hand, keeping her own hands on her lap. Finally she looks up, and once again you question your senses, blaming the wine for your bewilderment, for the dizziness brought on by those shining, clear green eyes, and you stand up after Aura does, running your hand over the wooden back of the Gothic chair, without daring to touch her bare shoulder or her motionless head.

You make an effort to control yourself, diverting your attention away from her by listening to the imperceptible movement of a door behind you—it must lead to the kitchen—or by separating the two different elements that make up the room: the compact circle of light around the candelabra, illuminating the table and one carved wall, and the larger circle of darkness surrounding it. Finally you have the courage to go up to her, take her hand, open it, and place your key-ring in her smooth palm as a token.

She closes her hand, looks up at you, and murmurs, "Thank you." Then she rises and walks quickly out of the room.

You sit down in Aura's chair, stretch your legs, and light a cigarette, feeling a pleasure you've never felt before, one that you knew was part of you but that only now you're experiencing fully, setting it free, bringing it out because this time you know it'll be answered and won't be lost . . . And Señora Consuelo is waiting for you, as Aura said. She's waiting for you after supper . . .

You leave the dining room, and with the candelabra in your hand you walk through the parlour and the hallway. The first door you come to is the old lady's. You rap on it with your knuckles, but there isn't any answer. You knock again. Then you push the door open because she's waiting for you. You enter cautiously, murmuring: "Señora . . . Señora . . ."

She doesn't hear you, for she's kneeling in front of that wall of religious objects, with her head resting on her clenched fists. You see her from a distance: she's kneeling there in her coarse woollen nightgown with her head sunk into her narrow shoulders; she's thin, even emaciated, like a medieval sculpture; her legs are like two sticks, and they're inflamed with erysipelas.[6] While you're thinking of the continual rubbing of that rough wool against her skin, she suddenly raises her fists and strikes feebly at the air, as if she were doing battle against the images you can make out as you tiptoe closer: Christ, the Virgin, St. Sebastian, St. Lucia, the Archangel Michael,[7] and the grinning demons in an old print, the only happy figures in that iconography of sorrow and wrath, happy because they're jabbing their pitchforks into the flesh of the damned, pouring cauldrons of boiling water on them, violating the women, getting drunk, enjoying all the liberties forbidden to the saints. You approach that central image, which is surrounded by the tears of Our Lady of Sorrows, the blood of Our Crucified Lord, the delight of Lucifer, the anger of the Archangel, the viscera preserved in bottles of alcohol, the silver heart: Señora Consuelo, kneeling, threatens them with her fists, stammering the words you can hear as you move even closer: "Come, City of God! Gabriel, sound your trumpet! Ah, how long the world takes to die!"[8]

She beats her breast until she collapses in front of the images and candles in a spasm of coughing. You raise her by the elbow, and as you gently help her to

6. Acute skin infection.
7. Catholic religious images.
8. The Archangel Gabriel will sound his trum-pet to announce the return of the Messiah and the end of the world.

the bed you're surprised at her smallness: she's almost a little girl, bent over almost double. You realize that without your assistance she would have had to get back to bed on her hands and knees. You help her into that wide bed with its bread crumbs and old feather pillows, and cover her up, and wait until her breathing is back to normal, while the involuntary tears run down her parchment cheeks.

"Excuse me . . . excuse me, Señor Montero. Old ladies have nothing left but . . . the pleasure of devotion . . . Give me my handkerchief, please."

"Señorita Aura told me . . ."

"Yes, of course. I don't want to lose any time. We should . . . we should begin working as soon as possible. Thank you."

"You should try to rest."

"Thank you . . . Here . . ."

The old lady raises her hand to her collar, unbuttons it, and lowers her head to remove the frayed purple ribbon that she hands to you. It's heavy because there's a copper key hanging from it.

"Over in that corner . . . Open that trunk and bring me the papers at the right, on top of the others . . . They're tied with a yellow ribbon."

"I can't see very well . . ."

"Ah, yes . . . it's just that I'm so accustomed to the darkness. To my right . . . Keep going till you come to the trunk. They've walled us in, Señor Montero. They've built up all around us and blocked off the light. They've tried to force me to sell, but I'll die first. This house is full of memories for us. They won't take me out of here till I'm dead! Yes, that's it. Thank you. You can begin reading this part. I will give you the others later. Goodnight, Señor Montero. Thank you. Look, the candelabra has gone out. Light it outside the door, please. No, no, you can keep the key. I trust you."

"Señora, there's a rat's nest in the corner."

"Rats? I never go over there."

"You should bring the cats in here."

"The cats? What cats? Goodnight. I'm going to sleep. I'm very tired."

"Goodnight."

3

That same evening you read those yellow papers written in mustard-coloured ink, some of them with holes where a careless ash had fallen, others heavily fly-specked. General Llorente's French doesn't have the merits his wife attributed to it. You tell yourself you can make considerable improvements in the style, can tighten up his rambling account of past events: his childhood on a hacienda in Oaxaca, his military studies in France, his friendship with the duc de Morny and the intimates of Napoleon III, his return to Mexico on the staff of Maximilian, the imperial ceremonies and gatherings, the battles, the defeat in 1867, his exile in France.[9] Nothing that hasn't been described before. As you

9. Maximilian I (1832–1867) ruled Mexico from 1864 to 1867 with the support of French Emperor Napoleon III (1808–1873). Maximil-ian was executed by the Republican forces of Benito Juárez (1806–1872).

undress you think of the old lady's distorted notions, the value she attributes to these memoirs. You smile as you get into bed, thinking of the four thousand pesos.

You sleep soundly until a flood of light wakes you up at six in the morning: that glass roof doesn't have any curtain. You bury your head under the pillow and try to go back to sleep. Ten minutes later you give it up and walk into the bathroom, where you find all your things neatly arranged on a table and your few clothes hanging in the wardrobe. Just as you finish shaving the early morning silence is broken by that painful, desperate yowling.

You try to find out where it's coming from: you open the door to the hallway, but you can't hear anything from there: those cries are coming from up above, from the skylight. You jump up on the chair, from the chair onto the desk, and by supporting yourself on the bookshelf you can reach the skylight. You open one of the windows and pull yourself up to look out at that side garden, that square of yew trees and brambles where five, six, seven cats—you can't count them, can't hold yourself up there for more than a second—are all twined together, all writhing in flames and giving off a dense smoke that reeks of burnt fur. As you get down again you wonder if you really saw it: perhaps you only imagined it from those dreadful cries that continue, grow less, and finally stop.

You put on your shirt, brush off your shoes with a piece of paper, and listen to the sound of a bell that seems to run through the passageways of the house until it arrives at your door. You look out into the hallway. Aura is walking along it with a bell in her hand. She turns her head to look at you and tells you that breakfast is ready. You try to detain her but she goes down the spiral staircase, still ringing that black-painted bell as if she were trying to wake up a whole asylum, a whole boarding–school.

You follow her in your shirt-sleeves, but when you reach the downstairs hallway you can't find her. The door of the old lady's bedroom opens behind you and you see a hand that reaches out from behind the partly-opened door, sets a chamberpot in the hallway and disappears again, closing the door.

In the dining room your breakfast is already on the table, but this time only one place has been set. You eat quickly, return to the hallway, and knock at Señora Consuelo's door. Her sharp, weak voice tells you to come in. Nothing has changed: the perpetual shadows, the glow of the votive lights and the silver objects.

"Good morning, Señor Montero. Did you sleep well?"

"Yes. I read till quite late."

The old lady waves her hand as if in a gesture of dismissal. "No, no, no. Don't give me your opinion. Work on those pages and when you've finished I'll give you the others."

"Very well. Señora, would I be able to go into the garden?"

"What garden, Señor Montero?"

"The one that's outside my room."

"This house doesn't have any garden. We lost our garden when they built up all around us."

"I think I could work better outdoors."

"This house has only got that dark patio where you came in. My niece is growing some shade plants there. But that's all."

"It's all right, Señora."

"I'd like to rest during the day. But come to see me tonight."

"Very well, Señora."

You spend all morning working on the papers, copying out the passages you intend to keep, rewriting the ones you think are especially bad, smoking one cigarette after another and reflecting that you ought to space your work so that the job lasts as long as possible. If you can manage to save at least twelve thousand pesos, you can spend a year on nothing but your own work, which you've postponed and almost forgotten. Your great, inclusive work on the Spanish discoveries and conquests in the New World. A work that sums up all the scattered chronicles, makes them intelligible, and discovers the resemblances among all the undertakings and adventures of Spain's Golden Age, and all the human prototypes and major accomplishments of the Renaissance. You end up by putting aside the General's tedious pages and starting to compile the dates and summaries of your own work. Time passes and you don't look at your watch until you hear the bell again. Then you put on your coat and go down to the dining room.

Aura is already seated. This time Señora Llorente is at the head of the table, wrapped in her shawl and nightgown and coif, hunching over her plate. But the fourth place has also been set. You note it in passing. It doesn't bother you any more. If the price of your future creative liberty is to put up with all the manias of this old woman, you can pay it easily. As you watch her eating her soup you try to figure out her age. There's a time after which it's impossible to detect the passing of the years, and Señora Consuelo crossed that frontier a long time ago. The General hasn't mentioned her in what you've already read of the memoirs. But if the General was 42 at the time of the French invasion, and died in 1901, forty years later, he must have died at the age of 82. He must have married the Señora after the defeat at Querétaro[1] and his exile. But she would only have been a girl at that time . . .

The dates escape you because now the Señora is talking in that thin, sharp voice of hers, that bird-like chirping. She's talking to Aura and you listen to her as you eat, hearing her long list of complaints, pains, suspected illnesses, more complaints about the cost of medicines, the dampness of the house and so forth. You'd like to break in on this domestic conversation to ask about the servant who went for your things yesterday, the servant you've never even glimpsed and who never waits on table. You're going to ask about him but you're suddenly surprised to realize that up to this moment Aura hasn't said a word and is eating with a sort of mechanical fatality, as if she were waiting for some outside impulse before picking up her knife and fork, cutting a piece of liver—yes, it's liver again, apparently the favorite dish in this house—and carrying it to her mouth. You glance quickly from the aunt to the niece, but at that moment the Señora becomes motionless, and at the same moment Aura puts her knife on her plate and also becomes motionless, and you remember that the Señora put down her knife only a fraction of a second earlier.

There are several minutes of silence: you finish eating while they sit there rigid as statues, watching you. At last the Señora says, "I'm very tired. I ought not to eat at the table. Come, Aura, help me to my room."

1. One of Maximilian's final battles (1867).

The Señora tries to hold your attention: she looks directly at you so that you'll keep looking at her, although what she's saying is aimed at Aura. You have to make an effort in order to evade that look, which once again is wide, clear, and yellowish, free of the veils and wrinkles that usually obscure it. Then you look at Aura, who is staring fixedly at nothing and silently moving her lips. She gets up with a motion like those you associate with dreaming, takes the arm of the bent old lady, and slowly helps her from the dining room.

Alone now, you help yourself to the coffee that has been there since the beginning of the meal, the cold coffee you sip as you wrinkle your brow and ask yourself if the Señora doesn't have some secret power over her niece: if the girl, your beautiful Aura in her green dress, isn't kept in this dark old house against her will. But it would be so easy for her to escape while the Señora was asleep in her shadowy room. You tell yourself that her hold over the girl must be terrible. And you consider the way out that occurs to your imagination: perhaps Aura is waiting for you to release her from the chains in which the perverse, insane old lady, for some unknown reason, has bound her. You remember Aura as she was a few moments ago, spiritless, hypnotized by her terror, incapable of speaking in front of the tyrant, moving her lips in silence as if she were silently begging you to set her free; so enslaved that she imitated every gesture of the Señora, as if she were permitted to do only what the Señora did.

You rebel against this tyranny. You walk toward the other door, the one at the foot of the staircase, the one next to the old lady's room: that's where Aura must live, because there's no other room in the house. You push the door open and go in. This room is dark also, with whitewashed walls, and the only decoration is an enormous black Christ. At the left there's a door that must lead into the widow's bedroom. You go up to it on tiptoe, put your hands against it, then decide not to open it: you should talk with Aura alone.

And if Aura wants your help she'll come to your room. You go up there for a while, forgetting the yellowed manuscripts and your own notebooks, thinking only about the beauty of your Aura. And the more you think about her, the more you make her yours, not only because of her beauty and your desire, but also because you want to set her free: you've found a moral basis for your desire, and you feel innocent and self-satisfied. When you hear the bell again you don't go down to supper because you can't bear another scene like the one at the middle of the day. Perhaps Aura will realize it, and come up to look for you after supper.

You force yourself to go on working on the papers. When you're bored with them you undress slowly, get into bed, and fall asleep at once, and for the first time in years you dream, dream of only one thing, of a fleshless hand that comes toward you with a bell, screaming that you should go away, everyone should go away; and when that face with its empty eye-sockets comes close to yours, you wake up with a muffled cry, sweating, and feel those gentle hands caressing your face, those lips murmuring in a low voice, consoling you and asking you for affection. You reach out your hands to find that other body, that naked body with a key dangling from its neck, and when you recognize the key you recognize the woman who is lying over you, kissing you, kissing your whole body. You can't see her in the black of the starless night, but you can smell the fragrance of the patio plants in her hair, can feel her smooth, eager body in your arms; you kiss her again and don't ask her to speak.

When you free yourself, exhausted, from her embrace, you hear her first whisper: "You're my husband." You agree. She tells you it's daybreak, then leaves you, saying that she'll wait for you that night in her room. You agree again, and then fall asleep, relieved, unburdened, emptied of desire, still feeling the touch of Aura's body, her trembling, her surrender.

It's hard for you to wake up. There are several knocks on the door, and at last you get out of bed, groaning and still half asleep. Aura, on the other side of the door, tells you not to open it: she says that Señora Consuelo wants to talk with you, is waiting for you in her room.

Ten minutes later you enter the widow's sanctuary. She's propped up against the pillows, motionless, her eyes hidden by those drooping, wrinkled, dead-white lids; you notice the puffy wrinkles under her eyes, the utter weariness of her skin.

Without opening her eyes she asks you, "Did you bring the key to the trunk?"

"Yes, I think so . . . Yes, here it is."

"You can read the second part. It's in the same place. It's tied with a blue ribbon."

You go over to the trunk, this time with a certain disgust: the rats are swarming around it, peering at you with their glittering eyes from the cracks in the rotted floorboards, galloping toward the holes in the rotted walls. You open the trunk and take out the second batch of papers, then return to the foot of the bed. Señora Consuelo is petting her white rabbit. A sort of croaking laugh emerges from her buttoned-up throat, and she asks you, "Do you like animals?"

"No, not especially. Perhaps because I've never had any."

"They're good friends. Good companions. Above all when you're old and lonely."

"Yes, they must be."

"They're always themselves, Señor Montero. They don't have any pretensions."

"What did you say his name is?"

"The rabbit? She's Saga. She's very intelligent. She follows her instincts. She's natural and free."

"I thought it was a male rabbit."

"Oh? Then you still can't tell the difference."

"Well, the important thing is that you don't feel all alone."

"They want us to be alone, Señor Montero, because they tell us that solitude is the only way to achieve saintliness. They forget that in solitude the temptation is even greater."

"I don't understand, Señora."

"Ah, it's better that you don't. Get back to work now, please."

You turn your back on her, walk to the door, leave her room. In the hallway you clench your teeth. Why don't you have courage enough to tell her that you love the girl? Why don't you go back and tell her, once and for all, that you're planning to take Aura away with you when you finish the job? You approach the door again and start pushing it open, still uncertain, and through the crack you see Señora Consuelo standing up, erect, transformed, with a military tunic in her arms: a blue tunic with gold buttons, red epaulettes, bright medals with crowned eagles—a tunic the old lady bites ferociously, kisses tenderly, drapes over her shoulders as she performs a few teetering dance steps. You close the door.

"She was fifteen years old when I met her," you read in the second part of the memoirs. *"Elle avait quinze ans lorsque je l'ai connue et, si j'ose le dire, ce sont ses yeux verts qui ont fait ma perdition."*[2] Consuelo's green eyes, Consuelo who was only fifteen in 1867, when General Llorente married her and took her with him into exile in Paris. *"Ma jeune poupée,"* he wrote in a moment of inspiration, *"ma jeune poupée aux yeux verts; je t'ai comblée d'amour."*[3] He described the house they lived in, the outings, the dances, the carriages, the world of the Second Empire, but all in a dull enough way. *"J'ai même supporté ta haine des chats, moi qu'aimais tellement les jolies bêtes . . ."*[4] One day he found her torturing a cat: she had it clasped between her legs, with her crinoline skirt pulled up, and he didn't know how to attract her attention because it seemed to him that *"tu faisais ca d'une façon si innocent, par pur enfantillage,"*[5] and in fact it excited him so much that if you can believe what he wrote, he made love to her that night with extraordinary passion, *"parce que tu m'avais dit que torturer les chats était ta manière à toi de rendre notre amour favorable, par un sacrifice symbolique . . ."*[6] You've figured it up: Señora Consuelo must be 109. Her husband died fifty-nine years ago. *"Tu sais si bien t'habiller, ma douce Consuelo, toujours drappé dans de velours verts, verts comme tes yeux. Je pense que tu seras toujours belle, même dans cent ans . . ."*[7] Always dressed in green. Always beautiful, even after a hundred years. *"Tu es si fière de ta beauté; que ne ferais-tu pas pour rester toujours jeune?"*[8]

4

Now you know why Aura is living in this house: to perpetuate the illusion of youth and beauty in that poor, crazed old lady. Aura, kept here like a mirror, like one more icon on that votive wall with its clustered offerings, preserved hearts, imagined saints and demons.

You put the manuscript aside and go downstairs, suspecting there's only one place Aura could be in the morning—the place that greedy old woman has assigned to her.

Yes, you find her in the kitchen, at the moment she's beheading a kid; the vapour that rises from the open throat, the smell of spilt blood, the animal's glazed eyes, all give you nausea. Aura is wearing a ragged, blood-stained dress and her hair is dishevelled; she looks at you without recognition and goes on with her butchering.

2. "She was fifteen when I met her and, if I dare say so, her green eyes were my perdition" (French).
3. "My young doll . . . my young doll with green eyes; I filled you with love."
4. "I even endured your hatred of cats, I who so loved the pretty beasts."
5. "You did that in such an innocent way, from pure childishness."

6. "Because you told me that torturing the cats was your own way of making our love favorable, by a symbolic sacrifice . . ."
7. "You know how to dress so well, my sweet Consuelo, always draped in green velvet, green like your eyes. I think that you will always be beautiful, even in a hundred years . . ."
8. "You are so proud of your beauty; what would you not do to stay young forever?"

You leave the kitchen: this time you'll really speak to the old lady, really throw her greed and tyranny in her face. When you push open the door she's standing behind the veil of lights, performing a ritual with the empty air, one hand stretched out and clenched, as if holding something up, and the other clasped around an invisible object, striking again and again at the same place. Then she wipes her hands against her breast, sighs, and starts cutting the air again, as if—yes, you can see it clearly—as if she were skinning an animal . . .

You run through the hallway, the parlour, the dining room, to where Aura is slowly skinning the kid, absorbed in her work, heedless of your entrance or your words, looking at you as if you were made of air.

You climb up to your room, go in, and brace yourself against the door as if you were afraid someone would follow you: panting, sweating, victim of your horror, of your certainty. If something or someone should try to enter, you wouldn't be able to resist, you'd move away from the door, you'd let it happen. Frantically you drag the armchair over to that latchless door, push the bed up against it, then fall onto the bed, exhausted, drained of your willpower, with your eyes closed and your arms wrapped around your pillow—the pillow that isn't yours. Nothing is yours.

You fall into a stupor, into the depths of a dream that's your only escape, your only means of saying No to insanity. "She's crazy, she's crazy," you repeat again and again to make yourself sleepy, and you can see her again as she skins the imaginary kid with an imaginary knife. "She's crazy, she's crazy . . ."

in the depths of the dark abyss, in your silent dream with its mouths opening in silence, you see her coming toward you from the blackness of the abyss, you see her crawling toward you.

in silence,

moving her fleshless hand, coming toward you until her face touches yours and you see the old lady's bloody gums, her toothless gums, and you scream and she goes away again, moving her hand, sowing the abyss with the yellow teeth she carries in her blood-stained apron:

your scream is an echo of Aura's, she's standing in front of you in your dream, and she's screaming because someone's hands have ripped her green taffeta skirt in two, and then

she turns her head toward you

with the torn folds of the skirt in her hands, turns toward you and laughs silently, with the old lady's teeth superimposed on her own, while her legs, her naked legs, shatter into bits and fly toward the abyss . . .

There's a knock at the door, then the sound of the bell, the supper bell. Your head aches so much that you can't make out the hands on the clock, but you know it must be late: above your head you can see the night clouds beyond the skylight. You get up painfully, dazed and hungry. You hold the glass pitcher under the tap, wait for the water to run, fill the pitcher, then pour it into the basin. You wash your face, brush your teeth with your worn toothbrush that's clogged with greenish paste, dampen your hair—you don't notice you're doing all this in the wrong order—and comb it meticulously in front of the oval mirror on the walnut wardrobe. Then you tie your tie, put on your jacket and go down to the empty dining room, where only one place has been set—yours.

Beside your plate, under your napkin, there's an object you start caressing with your fingers: a clumsy little rag doll, filled with a powder that trickles from its badly-sewn shoulder; its face is drawn with India ink, and its body is naked, sketched with a few brush strokes. You eat the cold supper—liver, tomatoes, wine—with your right hand while holding the doll in your left.

You eat mechanically, without noticing at first your own hypnotized attitude, but later you glimpse a reason for your oppressive sleep, your nightmare, and finally identify your sleep-walking movements with those of Aura and the old lady. You're suddenly disgusted by that horrible little doll, in which you begin to suspect a secret illness, a contagion. You let it fall to the floor. You wipe your lips with the napkin, look at your watch, and remember that Aura is waiting for you in her room.

You go cautiously up to Señora Consuelo's door, but there isn't a sound from within. You look at your watch again: it's barely nine o'clock. You decide to feel your way down to that dark, roofed patio you haven't been in since you came through it, without seeing anything, on the day you arrived here.

You touch the damp, mossy walls, breathe the perfumed air, and try to isolate the different elements you're breathing, to recognize the heavy, sumptuous aromas that surround you. The flicker of your match lights up the narrow, empty patio, where various plants are growing on each side in the loose, reddish earth. You can make out the tall, leafy forms that cast their shadows on the walls in the light of the match. But it burns down, singeing your fingers, and you have to light another one to finish seeing the flowers, fruits and plants you remember reading about in old chronicles, the forgotten herbs that are growing here so fragrantly and drowsily: the long, broad, downy leaves of the henbane; the twining stems with flowers that are yellow outside, red inside; the pointed, heart-shaped leaves of the nightshade; the ash-colored down of the grape-mullein with its clustered flowers; the bushy gatheridge with its white blossoms; the bella-donna. They come to life in the flare of your match, swaying gently with their shadows, while you recall the uses of these herbs that dilate the pupils, alleviate pain, reduce the pangs of childbirth, bring consolation, weaken the will, induce a voluptuous calm.

You're all alone with the perfumes when the third match burns out. You go up to the hallway slowly, listen again at Señora Consuelo's door, then tiptoe on to Aura's. You push it open without knocking and go into the bare room, where a circle of light reveals the bed, the huge Mexican crucifix, and the woman who comes toward you when the door is closed. Aura is dressed in green, in a green taffeta robe from which, as she approaches, her moonpale thighs reveal themselves. The woman, you repeat as she comes close, the woman, not the girl of yesterday: the girl of yesterday—you touch Aura's fingers, her waist—couldn't have been more than twenty; the woman of today—you caress her loose black hair, her pallid cheeks—seems to be forty. Between yesterday and today, something about her green eyes has turned hard; the red of her lips has strayed beyond their former outlines, as if she wanted to fix them in a happy grimace, a troubled smile; as if, like that plant in the patio, her smile combined the taste of honey and the taste of gall. You don't have time to think of anything more.

"Sit down on the bed, Felipe."

"Yes."

"We're going to play. You don't have to do anything. Let me do everything myself."

Sitting on the bed, you try to make out the source of that diffuse, opaline light that hardly lets you distinguish the objects in the room, and the presence of Aura, from the golden atmosphere that surrounds them. She sees you looking up, trying to find where it comes from. You can tell from her voice that she's kneeling down in front of you.

"The sky is neither high nor low. It's over us and under us at the same time."

She takes off your shoes and socks and caresses your bare feet.

You feel the warm water that bathes the soles of your feet, while she washes them with a heavy cloth, now and then casting furtive glances at that Christ carved from black wood. Then she dries your feet, takes you by the hand, fastens a few violets in her loose hair, and begins to hum a melody, a waltz, to which you dance with her, held by the murmur of her voice, gliding around to the slow, solemn rhythm she's setting, very different from the light movements of her hands, which unbutton your shirt, caress your chest, reach around to your back and grasp it. You also murmur that wordless song, that melody rising naturally from your throat: you glide around together, each time closer to the bed, until you muffle the song with your hungry kisses on Aura's mouth, until you stop the dance with your crushing kisses on her shoulders and breasts.

You're holding the empty robe in your hands. Aura, squatting on the bed, places an object against her closed thighs, caressing it, summoning you with her hand. She caresses that thin wafer, breaks it against her thighs, oblivious of the crumbs that roll down her hips: she offers you half of the wafer and you take it, place it in your mouth at the same time she does, and swallow it with difficulty. Then you fall on Aura's naked body, you fall on her naked arms, which are stretched out from one side of the bed to the other like the arms of the crucifix hanging on the wall, the black Christ with that scarlet silk wrapped around his thighs, his spread knees, his wounded side, his crown of thorns set on a tangled black wig with silver spangles. Aura opens up like an altar.

You murmur her name in her ear. You feel the woman's full arms against your back. You hear her warm voice in your ear: "Will you love me forever?"

"Forever, Aura. I'll love you forever."

"Forever? Do you swear it?"

"I swear it."

"Even though I grow old? Even though I lose my beauty? Even though my hair turns white?"

"Forever, my love, forever."

"Even if I die, Felipe? Will you love me forever, even if I die?"

"Forever, forever. I swear it. Nothing can separate us."

"Come, Felipe, come . . ."

When you wake up, you reach out to touch Aura's shoulder, but you touch only the still-warm pillow and the white sheet that covers you.

You murmur her name.

You open your eyes and see her standing at the foot of the bed, smiling but not looking at you. She walks slowly toward the corner of the room, sits down on the floor, places her arms on the knees that emerge from the darkness you can't peer into, and strokes the wrinkled hand that comes forward from the lessening darkness: she's sitting at the feet of the old lady, of Señora Consuelo, who is seated in an armchair you hadn't noticed earlier: Señora Consuelo smiles at you, nodding her head, smiling at you along with Aura, who moves her head in rhythm with the old lady's: they both smile at you, thanking you. You lie back, without any will, thinking that the old lady has been in the room all the time;

you remember her movements, her voice, her dance,
though you keep telling yourself she wasn't there.

The two of them get up at the same moment, Consuelo from the chair, Aura from the floor. Turning their backs on you, they walk slowly toward the door that leads to the widow's bedroom, enter that room where the lights are forever trembling in front of the images, close the door behind them, and leave you to sleep in Aura's bed.

<h1 style="text-align:center">5</h1>

Your sleep is heavy and unsatisfying. In your dreams you had already felt the same vague melancholy, the weight on your diaphragm, the sadness that won't stop oppressing your imagination. Although you're sleeping in Aura's room, you're sleeping all alone, far from the body you believe you've possessed.

When you wake up, you look for another presence in the room, and realize it's not Aura who disturbs you but rather the double presence of something that was engendered during the night. You put your hands on your forehead, trying to calm your disordered senses: that dull melancholy is hinting to you in a low voice, the voice of memory and premonition, that you're seeking your other half, that the sterile conception last night engendered your own double.

And you stop thinking, because there are things even stronger than the imagination: the habits that force you to get up, look for a bathroom off this room without finding one, go out into the hallway rubbing your eyelids, climb the stairs tasting the thick bitterness of your tongue, enter your own room feeling the rough bristles on your chin, turn on the bath taps and then slide into the warm water, letting yourself relax into forgetfulness.

But while you're drying yourself, you remember the old lady and the girl as they smiled at you before leaving the room arm in arm; you recall that whenever they're together they always do the same things: they embrace, smile, eat, speak, enter, leave, at the same time, as if one were imitating the other, as if the will of one depended on the existence of the other . . . You cut yourself lightly on one cheek as you think of these things while you shave; you make an effort to get control of yourself. When you finish shaving you count the objects in your traveling case, the bottles and tubes which the servant you've never seen brought over from your boarding house: you murmur the names of these objects, touch them, read the contents and instructions, pronounce the names of the manufacturers, keeping to these objects in order to forget that other one, the one without a name, without a label, without any rational consistency. What is Aura expecting of you? you ask yourself, closing the traveling case. What does she want, what does she want?

In answer you hear the dull rhythm of her bell in the corridor telling you breakfast is ready. You walk to the door without your shirt on. When you open it you find Aura there: it must be Aura because you see the green taffeta she always wears, though her face is covered with a green veil. You take her by the wrist, that slender wrist which trembles at your touch . . .

"Breakfast is ready," she says, in the faintest voice you've ever heard.

"Aura, let's stop pretending."

"Pretending?"

"Tell me if Señora Consuelo keeps you from leaving, from living your own life. Why did she have to be there when you and I . . . Please tell me you'll go with me when . . ."

"Go away? Where?"

"Out of this house. Out into the world, to live together. You shouldn't feel bound to your aunt forever . . . Why all this devotion? Do you love her that much?"

"Love her?"

"Yes. Why do you have to sacrifice yourself this way?"

"Love her? She loves me. She sacrifices herself for me."

"But she's an old woman, almost a corpse. You can't . . ."

"She has more life than I do. Yes, she's old and repulsive . . . Felipe, I don't want to become . . . to be like her . . . another . . ."

"She's trying to bury you alive. You've got to be reborn, Aura."

"You have to die before you can be reborn . . . No, you don't understand. Forget about it, Felipe. Just have faith in me."

"If you'd only explain."

"Just have faith in me. She's going to be out today for the whole day."

"She?"

"Yes, the other."

"She's going out? But she never . . ."

"Yes, sometimes she does. She makes a great effort and goes out. She's going out today. For all day. You and I could . . ."

"Go away?"

"If you want to."

"Well . . . perhaps not yet. I'm under contract. But as soon as I can finish the work, then . . ."

"Ah, yes. But she's going to be out all day. We could do something."

"What?"

"I'll wait for you this evening in my aunt's bedroom. I'll wait for you as always."

She turns away, ringing her bell like the lepers who use a bell to announce their approach, telling the unwary: "Out of the way, out of the way." You put on your shirt and coat and follow the sound of the bell calling you to the dining room. In the parlour the widow Llorente comes toward you, bent over, leaning on a knobby cane; she's dressed in an old white gown with a stained and tattered gauze veil. She goes by without looking at you, blowing her nose into a handkerchief, blowing her nose and spitting. She murmurs, "I won't be at home today, Señor Montero. I have complete confidence in your work. Please keep at it. My husband's memoirs must be published."

She goes away, stepping across the carpets with her tiny feet, which are like those of an antique doll, and supporting herself with her cane, spitting and sneezing as if she wanted to clear something from her congested lungs. It's only by an effort of the will that you keep yourself from following her with your eyes, despite the curiosity you feel at seeing the yellowed bridal gown she's taken from the bottom of that old trunk in her bedroom.

You scarcely touch the cold coffee that's waiting for you in the dining room. You sit for an hour in the tall, arch-back chair, smoking, waiting for the sounds you never hear, until finally you're sure the old lady has left the house and can't catch you at what you're going to do. For the last hour you've had the key to the trunk clutched in your hand, and now you get up and silently walk through the parlor into the hallway, where you wait for another fifteen minutes—your watch tells you how long—with your ear against Señora Consuelo's door. Then you slowly push it open until you can make out, beyond the spider's web of candles, the empty bed on which her rabbit is gnawing at a carrot: the bed that's always littered with scraps of bread, and that you touch gingerly as if you thought the old lady might be hidden among the rumples of the sheets. You walk over to the corner where the trunk is, stepping on the tail of one of those rats; it squeals, escapes from your foot, and scampers off to warn the others. You fit the copper key into the rusted padlock, remove the padlock, and then raise the lid, hearing the creak of the old, stiff hinges. You take out the third portion of the memoirs—it's tied with a red ribbon—and under it you discover those photographs, those old, brittle dog-eared photographs. You pick them up without looking at them, clutch the whole treasure to your breast, and hurry up of the room without closing the trunk, forgetting the hunger of the rats. You close the door, lean against the wall in the hallway till you catch your breath, then climb the stairs to your room.

Up there you read the new pages, the continuation, the events of an agonized century. In his florid language General Llorente describes the personality of Eugenia de Montijo, pays his respects to Napoleon the Little, summons up his most martial rhetoric to proclaim the Franco-Prussian War, fills whole pages with his sorrow at the defeat, harangues all men of honor about the Republican monster, sees a ray of hope in General Boulanger, sighs for Mexico, believes that in the Dreyfus affairs the honor—always that word "honor"—of the army has asserted itself again.[9]

The brittle pages crumble at your touch: you don't respect them now, you're only looking for a reappearance of the woman with green eyes. "I know why you weep at times, Consuelo. I have not been able to give you children, although you are so radiant with life . . ." And later: "Consuelo, you should not tempt God. We must reconcile ourselves. Is not my affection enough? I know that you love me; I feel it. I am not asking you for resignation, because that would offend you. I am only asking you to see, in the great love which you say you have for me, something sufficient, something that can fill both of us, without the need of turning to sick imaginings . . ." On another page: "I told Consuelo that those medicines were utterly useless. She insists on growing her own herbs in the garden. She says she is not deceiving herself. The herbs are not to strengthen the body, but rather the soul." Later: "I found her in a delirium, embracing the pillow. She cried, 'Yes, yes, yes, I've done it, I've re-created

---

9. General Llorente reflects on the course of later 19th-century history. The Empress Eugenia de Montijo was the wife of Napoleon III (the "Little" because less great than Napoleon I). The Franco-Prussian War (1870–71) ended in the defeat of France and the fall of the empire. General Boulanger staged a failed coup against the new French Third Republic in 1888. Alfred Dreyfus, a French army captain, was falsely accused of treason, leading to a series of trials and social upheaval; the General's views on all these matters are reactionary.

her! I can invoke her, I can give her life with my own life!' It was necessary to call the doctor. He told me he could not quiet her, because the truth was that she was under the effects of narcotics, not of stimulants." And finally: "Early this morning I found her walking barefooted through the hallways. I wanted to stop her. She went by without looking at me, but her words were directed to me. 'Don't stop me,' she said. 'I'm going toward my youth, and my youth is coming toward me. It's coming in, it's in the garden, it's come back . . .' Consuelo, my poor Consuelo! Even the devil was an angel once."

There isn't any more. The memoirs of General Llorente end with that sentence: *"Consuelo, le démon aussi était un ange, avant . . ."*[1]

And after the last page, the portraits. The portrait of an elderly gentleman in a military uniform, an old photograph with these words in one corner: *"Moulin, Photographe, 35 Boulevard Haussmann"* and the date *"1894."*[2] Then the photograph of Aura, of Aura with her green eyes, her black hair gathered in ringlets, leaning against a Doric column with a painted landscape in the background: the landscape of a Lorelei in the Rhine. Her dress is buttoned up to the collar, there's a handkerchief in her hand, she's wearing a bustle: Aura, and the date *"1876"* in white ink, and on the back of the daguerreotype, in spidery handwriting: *"Fait pour notre dixième anniversaire de mariage,"*[3] and a signature in the same hand, *"Consuelo Llorente."* In the third photograph you see both Aura and the old gentleman, but this time they're dressed in outdoor clothes, sitting on a bench in a garden. The photograph has become a little blurred: Aura doesn't look as young as she did in the other picture, but it's she, it's he, it's . . . it's you. You stare and stare at the photographs, then hold them up to the skylight. You cover General Llorente's beard with your finger, and imagine him with black hair, and you discover only yourself: blurred, lost, forgotten, but you, you, you.

Your head is spinning, overcome by the rhythms of that distant waltz, by the odor of damp, fragrant plants: you fall exhausted on the bed, touching your cheeks, your eyes, your nose, as if you were afraid that some invisible hand had ripped off the mask you've been wearing for twenty-seven years, the cardboard features that hid your true face, your real appearance, the appearance you once had but then forgot. You bury your face in the pillow, trying to keep the wind of the past from tearing away your own features, because you don't want to lose them. You lie there with your face in the pillow, waiting for what has to come, for what you can't prevent. You don't look at your watch again, that useless object tediously measuring time in accordance with human vanity, those little hands marking out the long hours that were invented to disguise the real passage of time, which races with a mortal and insolent swiftness no clock could ever measure. A life, a century, fifty years: you can't imagine those lying measurements any longer, you can't hold that bodiless dust within your hands.

When you look up from the pillow you find you're in darkness. Night has fallen.

Night has fallen. Beyond the skylight the swift black clouds are hiding the moon, which tries to free itself, to reveal its pale, round, smiling face. It

1. "Consuelo, the demon was also an angel, before . . ." (French).
2. The picture was taken by the photographer Moulin in Paris.
3. "Taken on our tenth wedding anniversary."

escapes for only a moment, then the clouds hide it again. You haven't got any hope left. You don't even look at your watch. You hurry down the stairs, out of that prison cell with its old papers and faded daguerreotypes, and stop at the door of Señora Consuelo's room, and listen to your own voice, muted and transformed after all those hours of silence: "Aura . . ."

Again: "Aura . . ."

You enter the room. The votive lights have gone out. You remember that the old lady has been away all day: without her faithful attention the candles have all burned up. You grope forward in the darkness to the bed.

And again: "Aura . . ."

You hear a faint rustle of taffeta, and the breathing that keeps time with your own. You reach out your hand to touch Aura's green robe.

"No. Don't touch me. Lie down at my side."

You find the edge of the bed, swing up your legs, and remain there stretched out and motionless. You can't help feeling a shiver of fear: "She might come back any minute."

"She won't come back."

"Ever?"

"I'm exhausted. She's already exhausted. I've never been able to keep her with me for more than three days."

"Aura . . ."

You want to put your hand on Aura's breasts. She turns her back: you can tell by the difference in her voice.

"No . . . Don't touch me . . ."

"Aura . . . I love you."

"Yes. You love me. You told me yesterday that you'd always love me."

"I'll always love you, always. I need your kisses, your body . . ."

"Kiss my face. Only my face."

You bring your lips close to the head that's lying next to yours. You stroke Aura's long black hair. You grasp that fragile woman by the shoulders, ignoring her sharp complaint. You tear off her taffeta robe, embrace her, feel her small and lost and naked in your arms, despite her moaning resistance, her feeble protests, kissing her face without thinking, without distinguishing, and you're touching her withered breasts when a ray of moonlight shines in and surprises you, shines in through a chink in the wall that the rats have chewed open, an eye that lets in a beam of silvery moonlight. It falls on Aura's eroded face, as brittle and yellowed as the memoirs, as creased with wrinkles as the photographs. You stop kissing those fleshless lips, those toothless gums: the ray of moonlight shows you the naked body of the old lady, of Señora Consuelo, limp, spent, tiny, ancient, trembling because you touch her. You love her, you too have come back . . .

You plunge your face, your open eyes, into Consuelo's silver-white hair, and you'll embrace her again when the clouds cover the moon, when you're both hidden again, when the memory of youth, of youth re-embodied, rules the darkness.

"She'll come back, Felipe. We'll bring her back together. Let me recover my strength and I'll bring her back . . ."

1962

ALEXANDER SOLZHENITSYN
1918–2008

Like his great predecessors **Tolstoy** and **Dostoevsky**, Alexander Solzhenitsyn was both a popular writer and a prophetic voice of moral conscience during the last decades of Soviet dictatorship. Solzhenitsyn used the techniques of nineteenth-century realism to explore a distinctively twentieth-century society. Imprisoned by the Stalinist regime, then later expelled from the Soviet Union and stripped of his citizenship, Solzhenitsyn criticized both the political oppression of the East and the materialism of the West, while proclaiming the virtues of an older, religious way of life.

He was born Alexander Isayevich Solzhenitsyn on December 11, 1918, a little more than a year after the Russian Revolution, in Kislovodsk, in the northern Caucasus. His father had died six months earlier, and his mother supported the family in Rostov-on-Don by working as a typist. They were extremely poor, and—although Solzhenitsyn would have preferred studying literature in Moscow—he was obliged, on graduation from high school, to enroll in the local Department of Mathematics at Rostov University. The choice, he later said, was a lucky one, for his double degree in mathematics and physics allowed him to spend four years of his prison-camp sentence in a relatively privileged *sharashka*, or research institute, instead of at hard manual labor. Unlike other writers (such as **Anna Akhmatova** and Boris Pasternak) who had known life before the revolution, Solzhenitsyn grew up a committed Communist, supporting the regime even during the catastrophic famine of 1933, but during the Second World War he became disillusioned with the Soviet leadership.

Soon after graduating from the university, Solzhenitsyn was put in charge of an artillery reconnaissance battery at the front; he served for almost four years before his sudden arrest in February 1945. The military censor had found passages in his letters to a friend that showed him to be—even under a pseudonym—disrespectful of the Soviet dictator Joseph Stalin, and Solzhenitsyn was sentenced to eight years in the prison camps. He worked at first as a mathematician in research institutes staffed by prisoners but in 1950 was taken to a new kind of camp for political prisoners, where he worked as a manual laborer. The hardships he endured there became the material for his most memorable writing, which combined autobiography, fiction, and historical events.

After his sentence was over, an administrative order sent him into permanent exile in southern Kazakhstan, a republic in Central Asia that was then a part of the Soviet Union. Solzhenitsyn spent the years of exile teaching physics and mathematics in a rural school and writing prose in secret. A cancerous tumor that had developed in his first labor camp grew worse, and in 1954 the author received treatment in a clinic in Tashkent (events recalled in the novel *Cancer Ward*, published in 1968). Solzhenitsyn remained in internal exile during the first phases of de-Stalinization, after the dictator's death in 1953, but was rehabilitated in 1957. He moved to Ryazan, in European Russia, where he continued to teach, while secretly writing fiction. The novella *Matryona's Home* and the novel *One Day in the Life of Ivan Denisovich* were composed during this period.

At the age of forty-two, Solzhenitsyn had written a great deal but published nothing. In 1961, however, it looked as though the climate of political censorship might change. Soviet Premier Nikita Khrushchev publicly attacked the "cult of personality" and hero worship that had surrounded Stalin, and the poet and editor Alexander Tvardovsky called on writers to portray "truth," not the idealized picture of Soviet society that Stalin had preferred. Solzhenitsyn was encouraged to submit *One Day in the Life of Ivan Denisovich*, an account of a bricklayer in a Russian concentration camp, beset, from morning to night, by hunger, cold, and brutally demanding work. The novel appeared, with Khrushchev's approval, in the November 1962 issue of Tvardovsky's journal *Novy Mir* (*The New World*) and seemed to announce a more relaxed era in Soviet culture—never before had the prison camps been openly discussed. Solzhenitsyn's matter-of-fact narration of the prisoners' day-to-day struggle to survive and retain their humanity shocked readers in Russia and in the West. In January 1963, Tvardovsky issued *Matryona's Home* and another novella, *An Incident at Krechetovka Station*, but—with the exception of two short stories and an article on style—Solzhenitsyn would not be allowed to publish anything more in his native land for more than twenty-five years. Even the highly praised *One Day in the Life of Ivan Denisovich* was removed from candidacy for the Lenin Prize in 1963.

Khrushchev himself was forced into retirement in October 1964, and the temporary loosening of censorship came to an end. The only means of publishing officially unacceptable works was to convey them to a Western publishing house or to circulate copies of typewritten manuscripts in *samizdat* ("self-publishing") form. Solzhenitsyn made arrangements to have his works, including the novels *Cancer Ward* and *The First Circle*, published in the West, in 1968. Within a year he was expelled from the official Writer's Union; in 1970 he was awarded the Nobel Prize in Literature, which he accepted in absentia because he was afraid that he would not be permitted to reenter the Soviet Union once he left. He continued work on his masterpiece, *The Gulag Archipelago* (1973–75), a three-volume, seven-section account of Stalin's widespread prison camp system, in which up to sixty million people suffered. Solzhenitsyn described the horror of these camps in quasi-anecdotal form, using personal experience, oral testimony, excerpts of documents, written eyewitness reports, and a massive collection of evidence accumulated inside *An Attempt at Artistic Investigation* (the subtitle). In the book there is a tension between the bare facts that Solzhenitsyn transmits and the spiritual interpretation of history into which they are made to fit. The author is overtly present, commenting, guessing intuitively from context when particular facts are missing, and stressing, in his own voice, the theme that has pervaded all his work: the purification of the soul through suffering. Solzhenitsyn tried to keep the work in progress a secret, but the KGB (the Soviet secret police) found a copy of the manuscript as a result of their interrogation of Solzhenitsyn's typist, who subsequently committed suicide. After the publication abroad of the first volume, Solzhenitsyn was arrested and expelled from the country. He went first to Zurich, then to the United States, where he lived in seclusion on a farm in Vermont.

The expulsion remained in effect until 1990, when the president of the Soviet Union, Mikhail S. Gorbachev, offered to restore Solzhenitsyn's citizenship as part of the rehabilitation of artists and writers disgraced during previous regimes. Solzhenitsyn did not accept the offer, though, and refused a prize awarded by the Russian Republic for *The Gulag Archipelago*—noting that the book was not widely available in the Soviet Union and that the "phenomenon of the Gulag" had not been overcome. In September 1991 the old charge of treason was officially dropped, and the writer returned to Russia in May 1994 to widespread public acclaim. The novelist expected, and was expected, to be a prominent voice in contemporary Russian society—for a while, he even had a television program. His moral strictures and nostalgia for a simpler past, however, proved alien to a post-Soviet society intent on prosperity. His massive series of historical novels about the Russian Revolution, *The Red Wheel*, on which he spent some thirty years, was poorly received. Disillusioned by post-Communist Russia, he increasingly supported authoritarian figures, including the Russian President Vladimir Putin.

Since Solzhenitsyn was such a dedicated anti-Communist and anti-Marxist, many Westerners jumped to the conclusion—incorrectly, as it turned out—that he supported the capitalist, democratic system. Instead, he looked back to an earlier, more nationalist and spiritual authoritarianism represented for him by the image of Holy Russia: "For a thousand years Russia lived with an authoritarian order . . . that authoritarian order possessed a strong moral foundation . . . Christian Orthodoxy." In a speech given at Harvard in 1978, "A World Split Apart," he criticized Western democracy's "herd instinct" and "need to accommodate mass standards," its emphasis on "well-being" and "constant desire to have still more things," its "spiritual exhaustion" in which "mediocrity triumphs under the guise of democratic restraints." He returned to the theme of purification by suffering that permeates his fiction: "We have been through a spiritual training far in advance of Western experience. The complex and deadly crush of life has produced stronger, deeper, and more interesting personalities than those generated by standardized Western well-being."

One of those strong, deep personalities is surely Matryona in *Matryona's Home*, the novella reprinted here. The story, which is probably modeled on the old Russian literary form of the saint's life, is a testimony to Matryona's absolute simplicity, her refusal to possess anything more than the necessities (she will not raise a pig to kill for food), her willingness to help others without promise of reward. The narrator, like Solzhenitsyn an ex-convict and mathematics teacher, has buried himself deep in the country to avoid signs of modern Soviet society and to find—if it still exists—an image of the Old Russia. The town of Talnovo itself is tainted not just by the *kolkhoz* (collective farm) system, which ceases to consider Matryona part of the collective as soon as she becomes ill, but by the laziness, selfishness, and predatory greed of its inhabitants. Although Matryona's life has been filled with disappointment and deprivation, and she remains an outsider in a materialist society that despises her lack of acquisitive instinct, she seems to live in a dimension of spiritual contentment and love that is unknown to those around her. Only the narrator, who has learned to value essential qualities from his experience in the concentration camps, is able finally to recognize her as "the righteous one" (Genesis 18.23–33), one of those whose spiritual merit seems alien to modern society yet is needed to save society from divine retribution.

Matryona's Home[1]

I

A hundred and fifteen miles from Moscow trains were still slowing down to a crawl a good six months after it happened. Passengers stood glued to the windows or went out to stand by the doors. Was the line under repair, or what? Would the train be late?

It was all right. Past the crossing the train picked up speed again and the passengers went back to their seats.

Only the engine drivers knew what it was all about.

The engine drivers and I.

In the summer of 1953 I was coming back from the hot and dusty desert, just following my nose—so long as it led me back to European Russia. Nobody waited or wanted me at my particular place, because I was a little matter of ten years overdue. I just wanted to get to the central belt, away from the great heat, close to the leafy muttering of forests. I wanted to efface myself, to lose myself in deepest Russia . . . if it was still anywhere to be found.

A year earlier I should have been lucky to get a job carrying a hod this side of the Urals.[2] They wouldn't have taken me as an electrician on a decent construction job. And I had an itch to teach. Those who knew told me that it was a waste of money buying a ticket, that I should have a journey for nothing.

But things were beginning to move.[3] When I went up the stairs of the N——— Regional Education Department and asked for the Personnel Section, I was surprised to find Personnel sitting behind a glass partition, like in a chemist's shop, instead of the usual black leather-padded door. I went timidly up to the window, bowed, and asked, "Please, do you need any mathematicians somewhere where the trains don't run? I should like to settle there for good."

They passed every dot and comma in my documents through a fine comb, went from one room to another, made telephone calls. It was something out of the ordinary for them too—people always wanted the towns, the bigger the better. And lo and behold, they found just the place for me—Vysokoe Polye. The very sound of it gladdened my heart.

Vysokoe Polye[4] did not belie its name. It stood on rising ground, with gentle hollows and other little hills around it. It was enclosed by an unbroken ring of forest. There was a pool behind a weir. Just the place where I wouldn't mind living and dying. I spent a long time sitting on a stump in a coppice and wishing with all my heart that I didn't need breakfast and dinner every day but could just stay here and listen to the branches brushing against the roof in the night, with not a wireless anywhere to be heard and the whole world silent.

Alas, nobody baked bread in Vysokoe Polye. There was nothing edible on sale. The whole village lugged its victuals in sacks from the big town.

---

1. Translated by H. T. Willetts.
2. Mountain chain separating European Russia from (Asiatic) Siberia.
3. Stalin's death, on March 5, 1953, brought a gradual relaxation of the Soviet state's repressive policies.
4. High meadow.

I went back to the Personnel Section and raised my voice in prayer at the little window. At first they wouldn't even talk to me. But then they started going from one room to another, made a telephone call, scratched with their pens, and stamped on my orders the word "Torfoprodukt."

Torfoprodukt? Turgenev[5] never knew that you can put words like that together in Russian.

On the station building at Torfoprodukt, an antiquated temporary hut of gray wood, hung a stern notice, BOARD TRAINS ONLY FROM THE PASSENGERS' HALL. A further message had been scratched on the boards with a nail, *And Without Tickets*. And by the booking office, with the same melancholy wit, somebody had carved for all time the words, *No Tickets*. It was only later that I fully appreciated the meaning of these addenda. Getting to Torfoprodukt was easy. But not getting away.

Here too, deep and trackless forests had once stood and were still standing after the Revolution. Then they were chopped down by the peat cutters and the neighboring kolkhoz.[6] Its chairman, Shashkov, had razed quite a few hectares of timber and sold it at a good profit down in the Odessa region.

The workers' settlement sprawled untidily among the peat bogs—monotonous shacks from the thirties, and little houses with carved façades and glass verandas, put up in the fifties. But inside these houses I could see no partitions reaching up to the ceilings, so there was no hope of renting a room with four real walls.

Over the settlement hung smoke from the factory chimney. Little locomotives ran this way and that along narrow-gauge railway lines, giving out more thick smoke and piercing whistles, pulling loads of dirty brown peat in slabs and briquettes. I could safely assume that in the evening a loudspeaker would be crying its heart out over the door of the club and there would be drunks roaming the streets and, sooner or later, sticking knives in each other.

This was what my dream about a quiet corner of Russia had brought me to—when I could have stayed where I was and lived in an adobe hut looking out on the desert, with a fresh breeze at night and only the starry dome of the sky overhead.

I couldn't sleep on the station bench, and as soon as it started getting light I went for another stroll round the settlement. This time I saw a tiny marketplace. Only one woman stood there at that early hour, selling milk, and I took a bottle and started drinking it on the spot.

I was struck by the way she talked. Instead of a normal speaking voice, she used an ingratiating singsong, and her words were the ones I was longing to hear when I left Asia for this place.

"Drink, and God bless you. You must be a stranger round here?"

"And where are you from?" I asked, feeling more cheerful.

I learnt that the peat workings weren't the only thing, that over the railway lines there was a hill, and over the hill a village, that this village was Talnovo, and it had been there ages ago, when the "gipsy woman" lived in the big house and the wild woods stood all round. And farther on there was a whole countryside full of villages—Chaslitsy, Ovintsy, Spudni, Shevertni, Shestimirovo, deeper

5. A master of Russian prose style (1818–1883), best known for the novel *Fathers and Sons* (1861) and for a series of sympathetic sketches of peasant life published as *A Sportsman's Sketches* (1882). "Torfoprodukt": peat product; a new word made by combining two words of Germanic origin: *torf* ("peat") and *produkt*.
6. Collective farm.

and deeper into the woods, farther and farther from the railway, up towards the lakes.

The names were like a soothing breeze to me. They held a promise of backwoods Russia. I asked my new acquaintance to take me to Talnovo after the market was over and find a house for me to lodge in.

It appeared that I was a lodger worth having: in addition to my rent, the school offered a truckload of peat for the winter to whoever took me. The woman's ingratiating smile gave way to a thoughtful frown. She had no room herself, because she and her husband were "keeping" her aged mother, so she took me first to one lot of relatives then to another. But there wasn't a separate room to be had and both places were crowded and noisy.

We had come to a dammed-up stream that was short of water and had a little bridge over it. No other place in all the village took my fancy as this did: there were two or three willows, a lopsided house, ducks swimming on the pond, geese shaking themselves as they stepped out of the water.

"Well, perhaps we might just call on Matryona," said my guide, who was getting tired of me by now. "Only it isn't so neat and cozy-like in her house, neglects things she does. She's unwell."

Matryona's house stood quite near by. Its row of four windows looked out on the cold backs, the two slopes of the roof were covered with shingles, and a little attic window was decorated in the old Russian style. But the shingles were rotting, the beam ends of the house and the once mighty gates had turned gray with age, and there were gaps in the little shelter over the gate.

The small gate was fastened, but instead of knocking my companion just put her hand under and turned the catch, a simple device to prevent animals from straying. The yard was not covered, but there was a lot under the roof of the house. As you went through the outer door a short flight of steps rose to a roomy landing, which was open, to the roof high overhead. To the left, other steps led up to the top room, which was a separate structure with no stove, and yet another flight led down to the basement. To the right lay the house proper, with its attic and its cellar.

It had been built a long time ago, built sturdily, to house a big family, and now one lonely woman of nearly sixty lived in it.

When I went into the cottage she was lying on the Russian stove[7] under a heap of those indeterminate dingy rags which are so precious to a working man or woman.

The spacious room, and especially the big part near the windows, was full of rubber plants in pots and tubs standing on stools and benches. They peopled the householder's loneliness like a speechless but living crowd. They had been allowed to run wild, and they took up all the scanty light on the north side. In what was left of the light, and half-hidden by the stovepipe, the mistress of the house looked yellow and weak. You could see from her clouded eyes that illness had drained all the strength out of her.

While we talked she lay on the stove face downward, without a pillow, her head toward the door, and I stood looking up at her. She showed no pleasure at getting a lodger, just complained about the wicked disease she had. She was just getting over an attack: it didn't come upon her every month, but when it

---

7. A large stove built of masonry, used for both heating and cooking.

did, "It hangs on two or three days so as I shan't manage to get up and wait on you. I've room and to spare, you can live here if you like."

Then she went over the list of other housewives with whom I should be quieter and cozier and wanted me to make the round of them. But I had already seen that I was destined to settle in this dimly lit house with the tarnished mirror, in which you couldn't see yourself, and the two garish posters (one advertising books, the other about the harvest), bought for a ruble each to brighten up the walls.

Matryona Vasilyevna made me go off round the village again, and when I called on her the second time she kept trying to put me off, "We're not clever, we can't cook, I don't know how we shall suit. . . ." But this time she was on her feet when I got there, and I thought I saw a glimmer of pleasure in her eyes to see me back. We reached an agreement about the rent and the load of peat which the school would deliver.

Later on I found out that, year in year out, it was a long time since Matryona Vasilyevna had earned a single ruble. She didn't get a pension. Her relatives gave her very little help. In the kolkhoz she had worked not for money but for credits; the marks recording her labor days in her well-thumbed workbook.

So I moved in with Matryona Vasilyevna. We didn't divide the room. Her bed was in the corner between the door and the stove, and I unfolded my camp bed by one window and pushed Matryona's beloved rubber plants out of the light to make room for a little table by another. The village had electric light, laid on back in the twenties, from Shatury. The newspapers were writing about "Ilyich's little lamps," but the peasants talked wide-eyed about "Tsar Light."[8]

Some of the better-off people in the village might not have thought Matryona's house much of a home, but it kept us snug enough that autumn and winter. The roof still held the rain out, and the freezing winds could not blow the warmth of the stove away all at once, though it was cold by morning, especially when the wind blew on the shabby side.

In addition to Matryona and myself, a cat, some mice, and some cockroaches lived in the house.

The cat was no longer young, and was gammy-legged as well. Matryona had taken her in out of pity, and she had stayed. She walked on all four feet but with a heavy limp: one of her feet was sore and she favored it. When she jumped from the stove she didn't land with the soft sound a cat usually makes, but with a heavy thud as three of her feet struck the floor at once—such a heavy thud that until I got used to it, it gave me a start. This was because she stuck three feet out together to save the fourth.

It wasn't because the cat couldn't deal with them that there were mice in the cottage: she would pounce into the corner like lightning and come back with a mouse between her teeth. But the mice were usually out of reach because somebody, back in the good old days, had stuck embossed wallpaper of a greenish color on Matryona's walls, and not just one layer of it but five. The layers held together all right, but in many places the whole lot had come away from the wall, giving the room a sort of inner skin. Between the timber of the

---

8. The newspapers reflect the new order. "Ilyich": i.e., Vladimir Ilyich Lenin (1870–1924), leader of the 1917 Russian Revolution and first head of the new state. The peasants still think in terms of the emperor (*Tsar*, or czar).

walls and the skin of wallpaper the mice had made themselves runs where they impudently scampered about, running at times right up to the ceiling. The cat followed their scamperings with angry eyes, but couldn't get at them.

Sometimes the cat ate cockroaches as well, but they made her sick. The only thing the cockroaches respected was the partition which screened the mouth of the Russian stove and the kitchen from the best part of the room.

They did not creep into the best room. But the kitchen at night swarmed with them, and if I went in late in the evening for a drink of water and switched on the light the whole floor, the big bench, and even the wall would be one rustling brown mass. From time to time I brought home some borax from the school laboratory and we mixed it with dough to poison them. There would be fewer cockroaches for a while, but Matryona was afraid that we might poison the cat as well. We stopped putting down poison and the cockroaches multiplied anew.

At night, when Matryona was already asleep and I was working at my table, the occasional rapid scamper of mice behind the wallpaper would be drowned in the sustained and ceaseless rustling of cockroaches behind the screen, like the sound of the sea in the distance. But I got used to it because there was nothing evil in it, nothing dishonest. Rustling was life to them.

I even got used to the crude beauty on the poster, forever reaching out from the wall to offer me Belinsky, Panferov,[9] and a pile of other books—but never saying a word. I got used to everything in Matryona's cottage.

Matryona got up at four or five o'clock in the morning. Her wall clock was twenty-seven years old and had been bought in the village shop. It was always fast, but Matryona didn't worry about that—just as long as it didn't lose and make her late in the morning. She switched on the light behind the kitchen screen and moving quietly, considerately, doing her best not to make a noise, she lit the stove, went to milk the goat (all the livestock she had was this one dirty-white goat with twisted horns), fetched water and boiled it in three iron pots: one for me, one for herself, and one for the goat. She fetched potatoes from the cellar, picking out the littlest for the goat, little ones for herself and egg-sized ones for me. There were no big ones, because her garden was sandy, had not been manured since the war, and she always planted with potatoes, potatoes, and potatoes again, so that it wouldn't grow big ones.

I scarcely heard her about her morning tasks. I slept late, woke up in the wintry daylight, stretched a bit, and stuck my head out from under my blanket and my sheepskin. These, together with the prisoner's jerkin round my legs and a sack stuffed with straw underneath me, kept me warm in bed even on nights when the cold wind rattled our wobbly windows from the north. When I heard the discreet noises on the other side of the screen I spoke to her, slowly and deliberately:

"Good morning, Matryona Vasilyevna!"

And every time the same good-natured words came to me from behind the screen. They began with a warm, throaty gurgle, the sort of sound grandmothers make in fairy tales.

"M-m-m . . . same to you too!"

And after a little while, "Your breakfast's ready for you now."

---

9. Fedor Ivanovich Panferov (1896–1960), socialist-realist writer popular in the 1920s, best known for his novel *The Iron Flood*. Vis- sarion Grigoryevich Belinsky (1811–1848), Russian literary critic who emphasized social and political ideas.

She didn't announce what was for breakfast, but it was easy to guess: taters in their jackets or tatty soup (as everybody in the village called it), or barley gruel (no other grain could be bought in Torfoprodukt that year, and even the barley you had to fight for, because it was the cheapest and people bought it up by the sack to fatten their pigs on it). It wasn't always salted as it should be, it was often slightly burnt, it furred the palate and the gums, and it gave me heartburn.

But Matryona wasn't to blame: there was no butter in Torfoprodukt either, margarine was desperately short, and only mixed cooking fat was plentiful, and when I got to know it, I saw that the Russian stove was not convenient for cooking: the cook cannot see the pots and they are not heated evenly all round. I suppose the stove came down to our ancestors from the Stone Age, because you can stoke it up once before daylight, and food and water, mash and swill will keep warm in it all day long. And it keeps you warm while you sleep.

I ate everything that was cooked for me without demur, patiently putting aside anything uncalled-for that I came across: a hair, a bit of peat, a cockroach's leg. I hadn't the heart to find fault with Matryona. After all, she had warned me herself.

"We aren't clever, we can't cook—I don't know how we shall suit. . . ."

"Thank you," I said quite sincerely.

"What for? For what is your own?" she answered, disarming me with a radiant smile. And, with a guileless look of her faded blue eyes, she would ask, "And what shall I cook you for just now?"

For just now meant for supper. I ate twice a day, like at the front. What could I order for just now? It would have to be one of the same old things, taters or tater soup.

I resigned myself to it, because I had learned by now not to look for the meaning of life in food. More important to me was the smile on her roundish face, which I tried in vain to catch when at last I had earned enough to buy a camera. As soon as she saw the cold eye of the lens upon her, Matryona assumed a strained or else an exaggeratedly severe expression.

Just once I did manage to get a snap of her looking through the window into the street and smiling at something.

Matryona had a lot of worries that winter. Her neighbors put it into her head to try and get a pension. She was all alone in the world, and when she began to be seriously ill she had been dismissed from the kolkhoz as well. Injustices had piled up, one on top of another. She was ill, but was not regarded as a disabled person. She had worked for a quarter of a century in the kolkhoz, but it was a kolkhoz and not a factory, so she was not entitled to a pension for herself. She could only try and get one for her husband, for the loss of her breadwinner. But she had had no husband for twelve years now, not since the beginning of the war, and it wasn't easy to obtain all the particulars from different places about his length of service and how much he had earned. What a bother it was getting those forms through! Getting somebody to certify that he'd earned, say, three hundred rubles a month; that she lived alone and nobody helped her; what year she was born in. Then all this had to be taken to the Pension Office. And taken somewhere else to get all the mistakes corrected. And taken back again. Then you had to find out whether they would give you a pension.

To make it all more difficult the Pension Office was twelve miles east of Talnovo, the Rural Council Offices six miles to the west, the Factory District

Council an hour's walk to the north. They made her run around from office to office for two months on end, to get an *i* dotted or a *t* crossed. Every trip took a day. She goes down to the Rural District Council—and the secretary isn't there today. Secretaries of rural councils often aren't here today. So come again tomorrow. Tomorrow the secretary is in, but he hasn't got his rubber stamp. So come again the next day. And the day after that back she goes yet again, because all her papers are pinned together and some cockeyed clerk has signed the wrong one.

"They shove me around, Ignatich," she used to complain to me after these fruitless excursions. "Worn out with it I am."

But she soon brightened up. I found that she had a sure means of putting herself in a good humor. She worked. She would grab a shovel and go off to pull potatoes. Or she would tuck a sack under her arm and go after peat. Or take a wicker basket and look for berries deep in the woods. When she'd been bending her back to bushes instead of office desks for a while, and her shoulders were aching from a heavy load, Matryona would come back cheerful, at peace with the world and smiling her nice smile.

"I'm on to a good thing now, Ignatich. I know where to go for it (peat she meant), a lovely place it is."

"But surely my peat is enough, Matryona Vasilyevna? There's a whole truck-load of it."

"Pooh! Your peat! As much again, and then as much again, that might be enough. When the winter gets really stiff and the wind's battling at the windows, it blows the heat out of the house faster than you can make the stove up. Last year we got heaps and heaps of it. I'd have had three loads in by now. But they're out to catch us. They've summoned one woman from our village already."

That's how it was. The frightening breath of winter was already in the air. There were forests all round, and no fuel to be had anywhere. Excavators roared away in the bogs, but there was no peat on sale to the villagers. It was delivered, free, to the bosses and to the people round the bosses, and teachers, doctors, and workers got a load each. The people of Talnovo were not supposed to get any peat, and they weren't supposed to ask about it. The chairman of the kolkhoz walked about the village looking people in the eye while he gave his orders or stood chatting and talked about anything you liked except fuel. He was stocked up. Who said anything about winter coming?

So just as in the old days they used to steal the squire's wood, now they pinched peat from the trust. The women went in parties of five or ten so that they would be less frightened. They went in the daytime. The peat cut during the summer had been stacked up all over the place to dry. That's the good thing about peat, it can't be carted off as soon as it's cut. It lies around drying till autumn, or, if the roads are bad, till the snow starts falling. This was when the women used to come and take it. They could get six peats in a sack if it was damp, or ten if it was dry. A sackful weighed about half a hundred-weight and it sometimes had to be carried over two miles. This was enough to make the stove up once. There were two hundred days in the winter. The Russian stove had to be lit in the mornings, and the "Dutch"[1] stove in the evenings.

---

1. Not a real tiled Dutch stove, but a cheap small stove (probably made from an oil barrel) that provided heat with less fuel than a big Russian stove.

"Why beat about the bush?" said Matryona angrily to someone invisible. "Since there've been no more horses, what you can't have around yourself you haven't got. My back never heals up. Winter you're pulling sledges, summer it's bundles on your back, it's God's truth I'm telling you."

The women went more than once in a day. On good days Matryona brought six sacks home. She piled my peat up where it could be seen and hid her own under the passageway, boarding up the hole every night.

"If they don't just happen to think of it, the devils will never find it in their born days," said Matryona smiling and wiping the sweat from her brow.

What could the peat trust do? Its establishment didn't run to a watchman for every bog. I suppose they had to show a rich haul in their returns, and then write off so much for crumbling, so much washed away by the rain. Sometimes they would take it into their heads to put out patrols and try to catch the women as they came into the village. The women would drop their sacks and scatter. Or somebody would inform and there would be a house-to-house search. They would draw up a report on the stolen peat and threaten a court action. The women would stop fetching it for a while, but the approach of winter drove them out with sledges in the middle of the night.

When I had seen a little more of Matryona I noticed that, apart from cooking and looking after the house, she had quite a lot of other jobs to do every day. She kept all her jobs, and the proper times for them, in her head and always knew when she woke up in the morning how her day would be occupied. Apart from fetching peat and stumps which the tractors unearthed in the bogs, apart from the cranberries which she put to soak in big jars for the winter ("Give your teeth an edge, Ignatich," she used to say when she offered me some), apart from digging potatoes and all the coming and going to do with her pension, she had to get hay from somewhere for her one and only dirty-white goat.

"Why don't you keep a cow, Matryona?"

Matryona stood there in her grubby apron, by the opening in the kitchen screen, facing my table, and explained to me.

"Oh, Ignatich, there's enough milk from the goat for me. And if I started keeping a cow she'd eat me out of house and home in no time. You can't cut the grass by the railway track, because it belongs to the railway, and you can't cut any in the woods, because it belongs to the foresters, and they won't let me have any at the kolkhoz because I'm not a member any more, they reckon. And those who are members have to work there every day till the white flies swarm and make their own hay when there's snow on the ground—what's the good of grass like that? In the old days they used to be sweating to get the hay in at midsummer, between the end of June and the end of July, while the grass was sweet and juicy."

So it meant a lot of work for Matryona to gather enough hay for one skinny little goat. She took her sickle and a sack and went off early in the morning to places where she knew there was grass growing—round the edges of fields, on the roadside, on hummocks in the bog. When she had stuffed her sack with heavy fresh grass she dragged it home and spread it out in her yard to dry. From a sackful of grass she got one forkload of dry hay.

The farm had a new chairman, sent down from the town not long ago, and the first thing he did was to cut down the garden plots for those who were not fit to work. He left Matryona a third of an acre of sand—when there was over a thousand square yards just lying idle on the other side of the fence. Yet when they were short of working hands, when the women dug in their heels and wouldn't budge, the chairman's wife would come to see Matryona. She was from the town as well, a determined woman whose short gray coat and intimidating glare gave her a somewhat military appearance. She walked into the house without so much as a good morning and looked sternly at Matryona. Matryona was uneasy.

"Well now, Comrade Vasilyevna," said the chairman's wife, drawing out her words. "You will have to help the kolkhoz! You will have to go and help cart manure out tomorrow!"

A little smile of forgiveness wrinkled Matryona's face—as though she understood the embarrassment which the chairman's wife must feel at not being able to pay her for her work.

"Well—er," she droned. "I'm not well, of course, and I'm not attached to you any more . . . ," then she hurried to correct herself, "What time should I come then?"

"And bring your own fork!" the chairman's wife instructed her. Her stiff skirt crackled as she walked away.

"Think of that!" grumbled Matryona as the door closed. "Bring your own fork! They've got neither forks nor shovels at the kolkhoz. And I don't have a man who'll put a handle on for me!"

She went on thinking about it out loud all evening.

"What's the good of talking, Ignatich. I must help, of course. Only the way they work it's all a waste of time—don't know whether they're coming or going. The women stand propped up on their shovels and waiting for the factory whistle to blow twelve o'clock. Or else they get on to adding up who's earned what and who's turned up for work and who hasn't. Now what I call work, there isn't a sound out of anybody, only—oh dear, dear—dinner time's soon rolled round—what, getting dark already."

In the morning she went off with her fork.

But it wasn't just the kolkhoz—any distant relative, or just a neighbor, could come to Matryona of an evening and say, "Come and give me a hand tomorrow, Matryona. We'll finish pulling the potatoes."

Matryona couldn't say no. She gave up what she should be doing next and went to help her neighbor, and when she came back she would say without a trace of envy, "Ah, you should see the size of her potatoes, Ignatich! It was a joy to dig them up. I didn't want to leave the allotment, God's truth I didn't."

Needless to say, not a garden could be plowed without Matryona's help. The women of Talnovo had got it neatly worked out that it was a longer and harder job for one woman to dig her garden with a spade than for six of them to put themselves in harness and plow six gardens. So they sent for Matryona to help them.

"Well—did you pay her?" I asked sometimes.

"She won't take money. You have to try and hide it on her when she's not looking."

Matryona had yet another troublesome chore when her turn came to feed the herdsmen. One of them was a hefty deaf mute, the other a boy who was never without a cigaret in his drooling mouth. Matryona's turn came round only every six weeks, but it put her to great expense. She went to the shop to buy canned fish and was lavish with sugar and butter, things she never ate herself. It seems that the housewives showed off in this way, trying to outdo one another in feeding the herdsmen.

"You've got to be careful with tailors and herdsmen," Matryona explained. "They'll spread your name all round the village if something doesn't suit them."

And every now and then attacks of serious illness broke in on this life that was already crammed with troubles. Matryona would be off her feet for a day or two, lying flat out on the stove. She didn't complain and didn't groan, but she hardly stirred either. On these days Masha, Matryona's closest friend from her earliest years, would come to look after the goat and light the stove. Matryona herself ate nothing, drank nothing, asked for nothing. To call in the doctor from the clinic at the settlement would have seemed strange in Talnovo and would have given the neighbors something to talk about—what does she think she is, a lady? They did call her in once, and she arrived in a real temper and told Matryona to come down to the clinic when she was on her feet again. Matryona went, although she didn't really want to; they took specimens and sent them off to the district hospital—and that's the last anybody heard about it. Matryona was partly to blame herself.

But there was work waiting to be done, and Matryona soon started getting up again, moving slowly at first and then as briskly as ever.

"You never saw me in the old days, Ignatich. I'd lift any sack you liked, I didn't think a hundredweight was too heavy. My father-in-law used to say, 'Matryona, you'll break your back.' And my brother-in-law didn't have to come and help me lift on the cart. Our horse was a warhorse, a big strong one."

"What do you mean, a warhorse?"

"They took ours for the war and gave us this one instead—he'd been wounded. But he turned out a bit spirited. Once he bolted with the sledge right into the lake, the men folk hopped out of the way, but I grabbed the bridle, as true as I'm here, and stopped him. Full of oats that horse was. They liked to feed their horses well in our village. If a horse feels his oats he doesn't know what heavy means."

But Matryona was a long way from being fearless. She was afraid of fire, afraid of "the lightning," and most of all she was for some reason afraid of trains.

"When I had to go to Cherusti,[2] the train came up from Nechaevka way with its great big eyes popping out and the rails humming away—put me in a regular fever. My knees started knocking. God's truth I'm telling you!" Matryona raised her shoulders as though she surprised herself.

"Maybe it's because they won't give people tickets, Matryona Vasilyevna?"

"At the window? They try to shove only first-class tickets on to you. And the train was starting to move. We dashed about all over the place, 'Give us tickets for pity's sake.'"

"The men folk had climbed on top of the carriages. Then we found a door that wasn't locked and shoved straight in without tickets—and all the carriages

---

2. About 100 miles east of Moscow and some 250 miles northwest of Nechaevka.

were empty, they were all empty, you could stretch out on the seat if you wanted to. Why they wouldn't give us tickets, the hardhearted parasites, I don't know. . . ."

Still, before winter came, Matryona's affairs were in a better state than ever before. They started paying her at last a pension of eighty rubles. Besides this she got just over one hundred from the school and me.

Some of her neighbors began to be envious.

"Hm! Matryona can live forever now! If she had any more money, she wouldn't know what to do with it at her age."

Matryona had some new felt boots made. She bought a new jerkin. And she had an overcoat made out of the worn-out railwayman's greatcoat given to her by the engine driver from Cherusti who had married Kira, her foster daughter. The hump-backed village tailor put a padded lining under the cloth and it made a marvelous coat, such as Matryona had never worn before in all her sixty years.

In the middle of winter Matryona sewed two hundred rubles into the lining of this coat for her funeral. This made her quite cheerful.

"Now my mind's a bit easier, Ignatich."

December went by, January went by—and in those two months Matryona's illness held off. She started going over to Masha's house more often in the evening, to sit chewing sunflower seeds with her. She herself didn't invite guests in the evening out of consideration for my work. Once, on the feast of the Epiphany, I came back from school and found a party going on and was introduced to Matryona's three sisters, who called her "nan-nan" or "nanny" because she was the oldest. Until then not much had been heard of the sisters in our cottage—perhaps they were afraid that Matryona might ask them for help.

But one ominous event cast a shadow on the holiday for Matryona. She went to the church three miles away for the blessing of the water and put her pot down among the others. When the blessing was over, the women went rushing and jostling to get their pots back again. There were a lot of women in front of Matryona and when she got there her pot was missing, and no other vessel had been left behind. The pot had vanished as though the devil had run off with it.

Matryona went round the worshipers asking them, "Have any of you girls accidentally mistook somebody else's holy water? In a pot?"

Nobody owned up. There had been some boys there, and boys got up to mischief sometimes. Matryona came home sad.

No one could say that Matryona was a devout believer. If anything, she was a heathen, and her strongest beliefs were superstitious: you mustn't go into the garden on the fast of St. John or there would be no harvest next year. A blizzard meant that somebody had hanged himself. If you pinched your foot in the door, you could expect a guest. All the time I lived with her I didn't once see her say her prayers or even cross herself. But, whatever job she was doing, she began with a "God bless us," and she never failed to say "God bless you," when I set out for school. Perhaps she did say her prayers, but on the quiet, either because she was shy or because she didn't want to embarrass me. There were icons[3] on

---

3. Religious images or portraits, usually painted on wood. A small lamp was set in front of the icons to illuminate them.

the walls. Ordinary days they were left in darkness, but for the vigil of a great feast, or on the morning of a holiday, Matryona would light the little lamp.

She had fewer sins on her conscience than her gammy-legged cat. The cat did kill mice.

Now that her life was running more smoothly, Matryona started listening more carefully to my radio. (I had, of course, installed a speaker, or as Matryona called it, a peeker.)[4]

When they announced on the radio that some new machine had been invented, I heard Matryona grumbling out in the kitchen, "New ones all the time, nothing but new ones. People don't want to work with the old ones any more, where are we going to store them all?"

There was a program about the seeding of clouds from airplanes. Matryona, listening up on the stove, shook her head, "Oh, dear, dear, dear, they'll do away with one of the two—summer or winter."

Once Shalyapin[5] was singing Russian folk songs. Matryona stood listening for a long time before she gave her emphatic verdict, "Queer singing, not our sort of singing."

"You can't mean that, Matryona Vasilyevna—just listen to him."

She listened a bit longer and pursed her lips, "No, it's wrong. It isn't our sort of tune, and he's tricky with his voice."

She made up for this another time. They were broadcasting some of Glinka's[6] songs. After half a dozen of these drawing-room ballads, Matryona suddenly came from behind the screen clutching her apron, with a flush on her face and a film of tears over her dim eyes.

"That's our sort of singing," she said in a whisper.

2

So Matryona and I got used to each other and took each other for granted. She never pestered me with questions about myself. I don't know whether she was lacking in normal female curiosity or just tactful, but she never once asked if I had been married. All the Talnovo women kept at her to find out about me. Her answer was, "You want to know—you ask him. All I know is he's from distant parts."

And when I got round to telling her that I had spent a lot of time in prison, she said nothing but just nodded, as though she had already suspected it.

And I thought of Matryona only as the helpless old woman she was now and didn't try to rake up her past, didn't even suspect that there was anything to be found there.

I knew that Matryona had got married before the Revolution and had come to live in the house I now shared with her, and she had gone "to the stove"

4. The translator is imitating Solzhenitsyn's wordplay. In the original, the narrator calls the speaker *razvedka* ("scout," literal trans: a military term); Matryona calls it *rozetka* (an electric plug).
5. Feodor Ivanovich Shalyapin (or Chaliapin, 1873–1938), Russian operatic bass with an international reputation as a great singer and

actor; he included popular Russian music in his song recitals.
6. Mikhail Ivanovich Glinka (1804–1857), Russian composer who was instrumental in developing a "Russian" style of music, including the two operas *A Life for the Czar* and *Ruslan and Ludmila*.

immediately. (She had no mother-in-law and no older sister-in-law, so it was her job to put the pots in the oven on the very first morning of her married life.) I knew that she had had six children and that they had all died very young, so that there were never two of them alive at once. Then there was a sort of foster daughter, Kira. Matryona's husband had not come back from the last war. She received no notification of his death. Men from the village who had served in the same company said that he might have been taken prisoner, or he might have been killed and his body not found. In the eight years that had gone by since the war Matryona had decided that he was not alive. It was a good thing that she thought so. If he was still alive he was probably in Brazil or Australia and married again. The village of Talnovo and the Russian language would be fading from his memory.

One day when I got back from school, I found a guest in the house. A tall, dark man, with his hat on his lap, was sitting on a chair which Matryona had moved up to the Dutch stove in the middle of the room. His face was completely surrounded by bushy black hair with hardly a trace of gray in it. His thick black moustache ran into his full black beard, so that his mouth could hardly be seen. Black side-whiskers merged with the black locks which hung down from his crown, leaving only the tips of his ears visible; his broad black eyebrows met in a wide double span. But the front of his head as far as the crown was a spacious bald dome. His whole appearance made an impression of wisdom and dignity. He sat squarely on his chair, with his hands folded on his stick, and his stick resting vertically on the floor, in an attitude of patient expectation, and he obviously hadn't much to say to Matryona, who was busy behind the screen.

When I came in, he eased his majestic head round toward me and suddenly addressed me, "Schoolmaster, I can't see you very well. My son goes to your school. Grigoryev, Antoshka."

There was no need for him to say any more. However strongly inclined I felt to help this worthy old man, I knew and dismissed in advance all the pointless things he was going to say. Antoshka Grigoryev was a plump, red-faced lad in 8-D who looked like a cat that's swallowed the cream. He seemed to think that he came to school for a rest and sat at his desk with a lazy smile on his face. Needless to say, he never did his homework. But the worst of it was that he had been put up into the next class from year to year because our district, and indeed the whole region and the neighboring region were famous for the high percentage of passes they obtained; the school had to make an effort to keep its record up. So Antoshka had got it clear in his mind that however much the teachers threatened him they would promote him in the end, and there was no need for him to learn anything. He just laughed at us. There he sat in the eighth class, and he hadn't even mastered his decimals and didn't know one triangle from another. In the first two terms of the school year I had kept him firmly below the passing line and the same treatment awaited him in the third.

But now this half-blind old man, who should have been Antoshka's grandfather rather than his father, had come to humble himself before me—how could I tell him that the school had been deceiving him for years, and that I couldn't go on deceiving him, because I didn't want to ruin the whole class, to become a liar and a fake, to start despising my work and my profession.

For the time being I patiently explained that his son had been very slack, that he told lies at school and at home, that his record book must be checked frequently, and that we must both take him severely in hand.

"Severe as you like, Schoolmaster," he assured me, "I beat him every week now. And I've got a heavy hand."

While we were talking I remembered that Matryona had once interceded for Antoshka Grigoryev, but I hadn't asked what relation of hers he was and I had refused to do what she wanted. Matryona was standing in the kitchen doorway like a mute suppliant on this occasion too. When Faddey Mironovich left, saying that he would call on me to see how things were going, I asked her, "I can't make out what relation this Antoshka is to you, Matryona Vasilyevna."

"My brother-in-law's son," said Matryona shortly, and went out to milk the goat.

When I'd worked it out, I realized that this determined old man with the black hair was the brother of the missing husband.

The long evening went by, and Matryona didn't bring up the subject again. But late at night, when I had stopped thinking about the old man and was working in a silence broken only by the rustling of the cockroaches and the heavy tick of the wall-clock, Matryona suddenly spoke from her dark corner, "You know, Ignatich, I nearly married him once."

I had forgotten that Matryona was in the room. I hadn't heard a sound from her—and suddenly her voice came out of the darkness, as agitated as if the old man were still trying to win her.

I could see that Matryona had been thinking about nothing else all evening.

She got up from her wretched rag bed and walked slowly toward me, as though she were following her own words. I sat back in my chair and caught my first glimpse of a quite different Matryona.

There was no overhead light in our big room with its forest of rubber plants. The table lamp cast a ring of light round my exercise books, and when I tore my eyes from it the rest of the room seemed to be half-dark and faintly tinged with pink. I thought I could see the same pinkish glow in her usually sallow cheeks.

"He was the first one who came courting me, before Efim did—he was his brother—the older one—I was nineteen and Faddey was twenty-three. They lived in this very same house. Their house it was. Their father built it."

I looked round the room automatically. Instead of the old gray house rotting under the faded green skin of wallpaper where the mice had their playground, I suddenly saw new timbers, freshly trimmed, not yet discolored, and caught the cheerful smell of pine tar.

"Well, and what happened then?"

"That summer we went to sit in the woods together," she whispered. "There used to be a woods where the stable yard is now. They chopped it down. I was just going to marry him, Ignatich. Then the German war started. They took Faddey into the army."

She let fall these few words—and suddenly the blue and white and yellow July of the year 1914 burst into flower before my eyes: the sky still peaceful, the floating clouds, the people sweating to get the ripe corn in. I imagined them side by side, the black-haired Hercules with a scythe over his shoulder, and the red-faced girl clasping a sheaf. And there was singing out under the open sky, such songs as nobody can sing nowadays, with all the machines in the fields.

"He went to the war—and vanished. For three years I kept to myself and waited. Never a sign of life did he give."

Matryona's round face looked out at me from an elderly threadbare head-scarf. As she stood there in the gentle reflected light from my lamp, her face seemed to lose its slovenly workday wrinkles, and she was a scared young girl again with a frightening decision to make.

Yes . . . I could see it. The trees shed their leaves, the snow fell and melted. They plowed and sowed and reaped again. Again the trees shed their leaves, and the snow fell. There was a revolution. Then another revolution.[7] And the whole world was turned upside down.

"Their mother died and Efim came to court me. 'You wanted to come to our house,' he says, 'so come.' He was a year younger than me, Efim was. It's a saying with us—sensible girls get married after Michaelmas, and silly ones at midsummer. They were shorthanded. I got married. . . . The wedding was on St. Peter's day, and then about St. Nicholas' day[8] in the winter he came back—Faddey, I mean, from being a prisoner in Hungary."

Matryona covered her eyes.

I said nothing.

She turned toward the door as though somebody were standing there. "He stood there at the door. What a scream I let out! I wanted to throw myself at his feet! . . . but I couldn't. 'If it wasn't my own brother,' he says, 'I'd take my ax to the both of you.'"

I shuddered. Matryona's despair, or her terror, conjured up a vivid picture of him standing in the dark doorway and raising his ax to her.

But she quieted down and went on with her story in a sing-song voice, leaning on a chairback, "Oh dear, dear me, the poor dear man! There were so many girls in the village—but he wouldn't marry. I'll look for one with the same name as you, a second Matryona, he said. And that's what he did—fetched himself a Matryona from Lipovka. They built themselves a house of their own and they're still living in it. You pass their place every day on your way to school."

So that was it. I realized that I had seen the other Matryona quite often. I didn't like her. She was always coming to my Matryona to complain about her husband—he beat her, he was stingy, he was working her to death. She would weep and weep, and her voice always had a tearful note in it. As it turned out, my Matryona had nothing to regret, with Faddey beating his Matryona every day of his life and being so tightfisted.

"Mine never beat me once," said Matryona of Efim. "He'd pitch into another man in the street, but me he never hit once. Well, there was one time—I quarreled with my sister-in-law and he cracked me on the forehead with a spoon. I jumped up from the table and shouted at them, 'Hope it sticks in your gullets, you idle lot of beggars, hope you choke!' I said. And off I went into the woods. He never touched me any more."

7. The February and the October revolutions (1917).
8. December 19 (December 6, old style).

"Michaelmas": October 12 (September 29, old style). "St. Peter's Day": probably July 12 (June 29, old style), Sts. Peter and Paul's Day.

Faddey didn't seem to have any cause for regret either. The other Matryona had borne him six children (my Antoshka was one of them, the littlest, the runt) and they had all lived, whereas the children of Matryona and Efim had died, every one of them, before they reached the age of three months, without any illness.

"One daughter, Elena, was born and was alive when they washed her, and then she died right after. . . . My wedding was on St. Peter's day, and it was St. Peter's day I buried my sixth, Alexander."

The whole village decided that there was a curse on Matryona.

Matryona still nodded emphatic belief when she talked about it. "There was a *course*[9] on me. They took me to a woman who used to be a nun to get cured, she set me off coughing and waited for the *course* to jump out of me like a frog. Only nothing jumped out."

And the years had run by like running water. In 1941 they didn't take Faddey into the army because of his poor sight, but they took Efim. And what had happened to the elder brother in the First World War happened to the younger in the Second—he vanished without a trace. Only he never came back at all. The once noisy cottage was deserted, it grew old and rotten, and Matryona, all alone in the world, grew old in it.

So she begged from the other Matryona, the cruelly beaten Matryona, a child of her womb (or was it a drop of Faddey's blood?), the youngest daughter, Kira.

For ten years she brought the girl up in her own house, in place of the children who had not lived. Then, not long before I arrived, she had married her off to a young engine driver from Cherusti. The only help she got from anywhere came in dribs and drabs from Cherusti: a bit of sugar from time to time, or some of the fat when they killed a pig.

Sick and suffering, and feeling that death was not far off, Matryona had made known her will: the top room, which was a separate frame joined by tie beams to the rest of the house, should go to Kira when she died.[1] She said nothing about the house itself. Her three sisters had their eyes on it too.

That evening Matryona opened her heart to me. And, as often happens, no sooner were the hidden springs of her life revealed to me than I saw them in motion.

Kira arrived from Cherusti. Old Faddey was very worried. To get and keep a plot of land in Cherusti the young couple had to put up some sort of building. Matryona's top room would do very well. There was nothing else they could put up, because there was no timber to be had anywhere. It wasn't Kira herself so much, and it wasn't her husband, but old Faddey who was consumed with eagerness for them to get their hands on the plot at Cherusti.

He became a frequent visitor, laying down the law to Matryona and insisting that she should hand over the top room right away, before she died. On these occasions I saw a different Faddey. He was no longer an old man propped up by a stick, whom a push or a harsh word would bowl over. Although he was slightly bent by backache, he was still a fine figure; in his sixties he had kept the vigorous black hair of a young man; he was hot and urgent.

---

9. *Curse/course* reflects wordplay in the Russian original, where a similar misuse of language indicates Matryona's lack of formal education.

1. Lumber was scarce and valuable, and old houses were well built. Moving houses or sections of houses is still common in the country.

Matryona had not slept for two nights. It wasn't easy for her to make up her mind. She didn't grudge them the top room, which was standing there idle, any more than she ever grudged her labor or her belongings. And the top room was willed to Kira in any case. But the thought of breaking up the roof she had lived under for forty years was torture to her. Even I, a mere lodger, found it painful to think of them stripping away boards and wrenching out beams. For Matryona it was the end of everything.

But the people who were so insistent knew that she would let them break up her house before she died.

So Faddey and his sons and sons-in-law came along one February morning, the blows of five axes were heard and boards creaked and cracked as they were wrenched out. Faddey's eyes twinkled busily. Although his back wasn't quite straight yet, he scrambled nimbly up under the rafters and bustled about down below, shouting at his assistants. He and his father had built this house when he was a lad, a long time ago. The top room had been put up for him, the oldest son, to move into with his bride. And now he was furiously taking it apart, board by board, to carry it out of somebody else's yard.

After numbering the beam ends and the ceiling boards, they dismantled the top room and the storeroom underneath it. The living room and what was left of the landing they boarded up with a thin wall of deal. They did nothing about the cracks in the wall. It was plain to see that they were wreckers, not builders, and that they did not expect Matryona to be living there very long.

While the men were busy wrecking, the women were getting the drink ready for moving day—vodka would cost too much. Kira brought forty pounds of sugar from the Moscow region, and Matryona carried the sugar and some bottles to the distiller under cover of night.

The timbers were carried out and stacked in front of the gates, and the engine-driver son-in-law went off to Cherusti for the tractor.

But the very same day a blizzard, or "a blower," as Matryona once called it, began. It howled and whirled for two days and nights and buried the road under enormous drifts. Then, no sooner had they made the road passable and a couple of trucks had gone by, than it got suddenly warmer. Within a day everything was thawing out, damp mist hung in the air and rivulets gurgled as they burrowed into the snow, and you could get stuck up to the top of your jackboots.

Two weeks passed before the tractor could get at the dismantled top room. All this time Matryona went around like someone lost. What particularly upset her was that her three sisters came, with one voice called her a fool for giving the top room away, said they didn't want to see her any more, and went off. At about the same time the lame cat strayed and was seen no more. It was just one thing after another. This was another blow to Matryona.

At last the frost got a grip on the slushy road. A sunny day came along, and everybody felt more cheerful. Matryona had had a lucky dream the night before. In the morning she heard that I wanted to take a photograph of some-body at an old-fashioned handloom. (There were looms still standing in two cottages in the village; they wove coarse rugs on them.) She smiled shyly and said, "You just wait a day or two, Ignatich, I'll just send off the top room there and I'll put my loom up, I've still got it, you know, and then you can snap me. Honest to God!"

She was obviously attracted by the idea of posing in an old-fashioned setting. The red frosty sun tinged the window of the curtailed passageway with a faint pink, and this reflected light warmed Matryona's face. People who are at ease with their consciences always have nice faces.

Coming back from school before dusk I saw some movement near our house. A big new tractor-drawn sledge was already fully loaded, and there was no room for a lot of the timbers, so old Faddey's family and the helpers they had called in had nearly finished knocking together another homemade sledge. They were all working like madmen, in the frenzy that comes upon people when there is a smell of good money in the air or when they are looking forward to some treat. They were shouting at one another and arguing.

They could not agree on whether the sledges should be hauled separately or both together. One of Faddey's sons (the lame one) and the engine-driver son-in-law reasoned that the sledges couldn't both be taken at once because the tractor wouldn't be able to pull them. The man in charge of the tractor, a hefty fat-faced fellow who was very sure of himself, said hoarsely that he knew best, he was the driver, and he would take both at once. His motives were obvious: according to the agreement, the engine driver was paying him for the removal of the upper room, not for the number of trips he had to make. He could never have made two trips in a night—twenty-five kilometers each way, and one return journey. And by morning he had to get the tractor back in the garage from which he had sneaked it out for this job on the side.

Old Faddey was impatient to get the top room moved that day, and at a nod from him his lads gave in. To the stout sledge in front they hitched the one they had knocked together in such a hurry.

Matryona was running about among the men, fussing and helping them to heave the beams on the sledge. Suddenly I noticed that she was wearing my jacket and had dirtied the sleeves on the frozen mud round the beams. I was annoyed and told her so. That jacket held memories for me: it had kept me warm in the bad years.

This was the first time that I was ever angry with Matryona Vasilyevna.

Matryona was taken aback. "Oh dear, dear me," she said. "My poor head. I picked it up in a rush, you see, and never thought about it being yours. I'm sorry, Ignatich."

And she took it off and hung it up to dry.

The loading was finished, and all the men who had been working, about ten of them, clattered past my table and dived under the curtain into the kitchen. I could hear the muffled rattle of glasses and, from time to time, the clink of a bottle, the voices got louder and louder, the boasting more reckless. The biggest braggart was the tractor driver. The stink of hooch floated in to me. But they didn't go on drinking long. It was getting dark and they had to hurry. They began to leave. The tractor driver came out first, looking pleased with himself and fierce. The engine-driver son-in-law, Faddey's lame son, and one of his nephews were going to Cherusti. The others went off home. Faddey was flourishing his stick, trying to overtake somebody and put him right about something. The lame son paused at my table to light up and suddenly started telling me how he loved Aunt Matryona, and that he had got married not long ago, and his wife had just had a son. Then they shouted for him and he went out. The tractor set up a roar outside.

After all the others had gone, Matryona dashed out from behind the screen. She looked after them, anxiously shaking her head. She had put on her jacket and her headscarf. As she was going through the door, she said to me, "Why ever couldn't they hire two? If one tractor had cracked up, the other would have pulled them. What'll happen now, God only knows!"

She ran out after the others.

After the boozing and the arguments and all the coming and going, it was quieter than ever in the deserted cottage, and very chilly because the door had been opened so many times. I got into my jacket and sat down to mark exercise books. The noise of the tractor died away in the distance.

An hour went by. And another. And a third. Matryona still hadn't come back, but I wasn't surprised. When she had seen the sledge off, she must have gone round to her friend Masha.

Another hour went by. And yet another. Darkness, and with it a deep silence had descended on the village. I couldn't understand at the time why it was so quiet. Later, I found out that it was because all evening not a single train had gone along the line five hundred yards from the house. No sound was coming from my radio, and I noticed that the mice were wilder than ever. Their scampering and scratching and squeaking behind the wallpaper was getting noisier and more defiant all the time.

I woke up. It was one o'clock in the morning, and Matryona still hadn't come home.

Suddenly I heard several people talking loudly. They were still a long way off, but something told me that they were coming to our house. And sure enough, I heard soon afterward a heavy knock at the gate. A commanding voice, strange to me, yelled out an order to open up. I went out into the pitch darkness with a torch. The whole village was asleep, there was no light in the windows, and the snow had started melting in the last week so that it gave no reflected light. I turned the catch and let them in. Four men in greatcoats went on toward the house. It's a very unpleasant thing to be visited at night by noisy people in greatcoats.

When we got into the light though, I saw that two of them were wearing railway uniforms. The older of the two, a fat man with the same sort of face as the tractor driver, asked, "Where's the woman of the house?"

"I don't know."

"This is the place the tractor with a sledge came from?"

"This is it."

"Had they been drinking before they left?"

All four of them were looking around, screwing up their eyes in the dim light from the table lamp. I realized that they had either made an arrest or wanted to make one.

"What's happened then?"

"Answer the question!"

"But . . . ."

"Were they drunk when they went?"

"Were they drinking here?"

Had there been a murder? Or hadn't they been able to move the top room? The men in greatcoats had me off balance. But one thing was certain: Matryona could do time for making hooch.

I stepped back to stand between them and the kitchen door. "I honestly didn't notice. I didn't see anything." (I really hadn't seen anything—only heard.) I made what was supposed to be a helpless gesture, drawing attention to the state of the cottage: a table lamp shining peacefully on books and exercises, a crowd of frightened rubber plants, the austere couch of a recluse, not a sign of debauchery.

They had already seen for themselves, to their annoyance, that there had been no drinking in that room. They turned to leave, telling each other this wasn't where the drinking had been then, but it would be a good thing to put in that it was. I saw them out and tried to discover what had happened. It was only at the gate that one of them growled. "They've all been cut to bits. Can't find all the pieces."

"That's a detail. The nine o'clock express nearly went off the rails. That would have been something." And they walked briskly away.

I went back to the hut in a daze. Who were "they"? What did "all of them" mean? And where was Matryona?

I moved the curtain aside and went into the kitchen. The stink of hooch rose and hit me. It was a deserted battlefield: a huddle of stools and benches, empty bottles lying around, one bottle half-full, glasses, the remains of pickled herring, onion, and sliced fat pork.

Everything was deathly still. Just cockroaches creeping unperturbed about the field of battle.

They had said something about the nine o'clock express. Why? Perhaps I should have shown them all this? I began to wonder whether I had done right. But what a damnable way to behave—keeping their explanations for official persons only.

Suddenly the small gate creaked. I hurried out on to the landing. "Matryona Vasilyevna?"

The yard door opened, and Matryona's friend Masha came in, swaying and wringing her hands. "Matryona—our Matryona, Ignatich—"

I sat her down, and through her tears she told me the story.

The approach to the crossing was a steep rise. There was no barrier. The tractor and the first sledge went over, but the towrope broke and the second sledge, the homemade one, got stuck on the crossing and started falling apart— the wood Faddey had given them to make the second sledge was no good. They towed the first sledge out of the way and went back for the second. They were fixing the towrope—the tractor driver and Faddey's lame son, and Matryona (heaven knows what brought her there) were with them, between the tractor and the sledge. What help did she think she could be to the men? She was forever meddling in men's work. Hadn't a bolting horse nearly tipped her into the lake once, through a hole in the ice? Why did she have to go to the damned crossing? She had handed over the top room and owed nothing to anybody. The engine driver kept a lookout in case the train from Cherusti rushed up on them. Its headlamps would be visible a long way off. But two engines coupled *together* came from the other direction, from our station, backing without lights. Why they were without lights nobody knows. When an engine is backing, coal dust blows into the driver's eyes from the tender and he can't see very well. The two engines flew into them and crushed the three people between the tractor and the sledge to pulp. The tractor was wrecked, the sledge was matchwood, the rails were buckled, and both engines turned over.

"But how was it they didn't hear the engines coming?"

"The tractor engine was making such a din."

"What about the bodies?"

"They won't let anybody in. They've roped them off."

"What was that somebody was telling me about the express?"

"The nine o'clock express goes through our station at a good clip and on to the crossing. But the two drivers weren't hurt when their engines crashed, they jumped out and ran back along the line waving their hands, and they managed to stop the train. The nephew was hurt by a beam as well. He's hiding at Klavka's now so that they won't know he was at the crossing. If they find out they'll drag him in as a witness. . . .'Don't know lies up, and do know gets tied up.' Kira's husband didn't get a scratch. He tried to hang himself, they had to cut him down. It's all because of me, he says, my aunty's killed and my brother. Now he's gone and given himself up. But the madhouse is where he'll be going, not prison. Oh, Matryona, my dearest Matryona. . . ."

Matryona was gone. Someone close to me had been killed. And on her last day I had scolded her for wearing my jacket.

The lovingly drawn red and yellow woman in the book advertisement smiled happily on.

Old Masha sat there weeping a little longer. Then she got up to go. And suddenly she asked me, "Ignatich, you remember, Matryona had a gray shawl. She meant it to go to my Tanya when she died, didn't she?"

She looked at me hopefully in the half-darkness—surely I hadn't forgotten?

No, I remembered. "She said so, yes."

"Well, listen, maybe you could let me take it with me now. The family will be swarming in tomorrow and I'll never get it then." And she gave me another hopeful, imploring look. She had been Matryona's friend for half a century, the only one in the village who truly loved her.

No doubt she was right.

"Of course—take it."

She opened the chest, took out the shawl, tucked it under her coat, and went out.

The mice had gone mad. They were running furiously up and down the walls, and you could almost see the green wallpaper rippling and rolling over their backs.

In the morning I had to go to school. The time was three o'clock. The only thing to do was to lock up and go to bed.

Lock up, because Matryona would not be coming.

I lay down, leaving the light on. The mice were squeaking, almost moaning, racing and running. My mind was weary and wandering, and I couldn't rid myself of an uneasy feeling that an invisible Matryona was flitting about and saying good-bye to her home.

And suddenly I imagined Faddey standing there, young and black-haired, in the dark patch by the door, with his ax uplifted. "If it wasn't my own brother, I'd chop the both of you to bits."

The threat had lain around for forty years, like an old broad sword in a corner, and in the end it had struck its blow.

3

When it was light the women went to the crossing and brought back all that was left of Matryona on a hand sledge with a dirty sack over it. They threw off the sack to wash her. There was just a mess . . . no feet, only half a body, no left hand. One woman said, "The Lord has left her her right hand. She'll be able to say her prayers where she's going."

Then the whole crowd of rubber plants were carried out of the cottage— these plants that Matryona had loved so much that once when smoke woke her up in the night she didn't rush to save her house but to tip the plants onto the floor in case they were suffocated. The women swept the floor clean. They hung a wide towel of old homespun over Matryona's dim mirror. They took down the jolly posters. They moved my table out of the way. Under the icons, near the windows, they stood a rough unadorned coffin on a row of stools.

In the coffin lay Matryona. Her body, mangled and lifeless, was covered with a clean sheet. Her head was swathed in a white kerchief. Her face was almost undamaged, peaceful, more alive than dead.

The villagers came to pay their last respects. The women even brought their small children to take a look at the dead. And if anyone raised a lament, all the women, even those who had looked in out of idle curiosity, always joined in, wailing where they stood by the door or the wall, as though they were providing a choral accompaniment. The men stood stiff and silent with their caps off.

The formal lamentation had to be performed by the women of Matryona's family. I observed that the lament followed a coldly calculated, age-old ritual. The more distant relatives went up to the coffin for a short while and made low wailing noises over it. Those who considered themselves closer kin to the dead woman began their lament in the doorway and when they got as far as the coffin, bowed down and roared out their grief right in the face of the departed. Every lamenter made up her own melody. And expressed her own thoughts and feelings.

I realized that a lament for the dead is not just a lament, but a kind of politics. Matryona's three sisters swooped, took possession of the cottage, the goat, and the stove, locked up the chest, ripped the two hundred rubles for the funeral out of the coat lining, and drummed it into everybody who came that only they were near relatives. Their lament over the coffin went like this, "*Oh, nanny, nanny! Oh nan-nan!* All we had in the world was you! You could have lived in peace and quiet, you could. And we should always have been kind and loving to you. Now your top room's been the death of you. Finished you off, it has, the cursed thing! Oh, why did you have to take it down? Why didn't you listen to us?"

Thus the sisters' laments were indictments of Matryona's husband's family: they shouldn't have made her take the top room down. (There was an underlying meaning, too: you've taken the top room, all right, but we won't let you have the house itself!)

Matryona's husband's family, her sisters-in-law, Efim and Faddey's sisters, and the various nieces lamented like this, "*Oh poor auntie, poor auntie!* Why didn't you take better care of yourself! Now they're angry with us for sure. Our own dear Matryona you were, and it's your own fault! The top room is nothing to do with it. Oh why did you go where death was waiting for you? Nobody

asked you to go there. And what a way to die! Oh why didn't you listen to us?"
(Their answer to the others showed through these laments: we are not to
blame for her death, and the house we'll talk about later.)

But the "second" Matryona, a coarse, broad-faced woman, the substitute
Matryona whom Faddey had married so long ago for the sake of her name, got
out of step with family policy, wailing and sobbing over the coffin in her simplicity, "*Oh my poor dear sister!* You won't be angry with me, will you now? Oh-
oh-oh! How we used to talk and talk, you and me! Forgive a poor miserable
woman! You've gone to be with your dear mother, and you'll come for me some
day, for sure! Oh-oh-oh-oh! . . ."

At every "oh-oh-oh" it was as though she were giving up the ghost. She
writhed and gasped, with her breast against the side of the coffin. When her
lament went beyond the ritual prescription, the women, as though acknowledging its success, all started saying, "Come away now, come away."

Matryona came away, but back she went again, sobbing with even greater
abandon. Then an ancient woman came out of a corner, put her hand on
Matryona's shoulder, and said, "There are two riddles in this world: how I was
born, I don't remember, how I shall die, I don't know."

And Matryona fell silent at once, and all the others were silent, so that there
was an unbroken hush.

But the old woman herself, who was much older than all the other old
women there and didn't seem to belong to Matryona at all, after a while started
wailing, "Oh, my poor sick Matryona! Oh my poor Vasilyevna! Oh what a weary
thing it is to be seeing you into your grave!"

There was one who didn't follow the ritual, but wept straight-forwardly, in
the fashion of our age, which has had plenty of practice at it. This was Matryona's unfortunate foster daughter, Kira, from Cherusti, for whom the top room
had been taken down and moved. Her ringlets were pitifully out of curl. Her
eyes looked red and bloodshot. She didn't notice that her headscarf was slipping off out in the frosty air and that her arm hadn't found the sleeve of her
coat. She walked in a stupor from her foster mother's coffin in one house to
her brother's in another. They were afraid she would lose her mind, because
her husband had to go on trial as well.

It looked as if her husband was doubly at fault: not only had he been moving
the top room, but as an engine driver, he knew the regulations about unprotected crossings and should have gone down to the station to warn them about
the tractor. There were a thousand people on the Urals express that night,
peacefully sleeping in the upper and lower berths of their dimly lit carriages,
and all those lives were nearly cut short. All because of a few greedy people,
wanting to get their hands on a plot of land, or not wanting to make a second
trip with a tractor.

All because of the top room, which had been under a curse ever since Faddey's hands had started itching to take it down.

The tractor driver was already beyond human justice. And the railway authorities were also at fault, both because a busy crossing was unguarded and because
the coupled engines were traveling without lights. That was why they had tried
at first to blame it all on the drink, and then to keep the case out of court.

The rails and the track were so twisted and torn that for three days, while the
coffins were still in the house, no trains ran—they were diverted onto another

line. All Friday, Saturday, and Sunday, from the end of the investigation until the funeral, the work of repairing the line went on day and night. The repair gang was frozen, and they made fires to warm themselves and to light their work at night, using the boards and beams from the second sledge, which were there for the taking, scattered around the crossing.

The first sledge just stood there, undamaged and still loaded, a little way beyond the crossing.

One sledge, tantalizingly ready to be towed away, and the other perhaps still to be plucked from the flames—that was what harrowed the soul of black-bearded Faddey all day Friday and all day Saturday. His daughter was going out of her mind, his son-in-law had a criminal charge hanging over him, in his own house lay the son he had killed, and along the street the woman he had killed and whom he had once loved. But Faddey stood by the coffins, clutching his beard, only for a short time, and went away again. His high forehead was clouded by painful thoughts, but what he was thinking about was how to save the timbers of the top room from the flames and from Matryona's scheming sisters.

Going over the people of Talnovo in my mind, I realized that Faddey was not the only one like that.

Property, the people's property, or my property, is strangely called our "goods." If you lose your goods, people think you disgrace yourself and make yourself look foolish.

Faddey dashed about, never stopping to sit down, from the settlement to the station, from one official to another, there he stood with his bent back, leaning heavily on his stick, and begged them all to take pity on an old man and give him permission to recover the top room.

Somebody gave permission. And Faddey gathered together his surviving sons, sons-in-law, and nephews, got horses from the kolkhoz and from the other side of the wrecked crossing, by a roundabout way that led through three villages, brought the remnants of the top room home to his yard. He finished the job in the early hours of Sunday morning.

On Sunday afternoon they were buried. The two coffins met in the middle of the village, and the relatives argued about which of them should go first. Then they put them side by side on an open sledge, the aunt and the nephew, and carried the dead over the damp snow, with a gloomy February sky above, to the churchyard two villages away. There was an unkind wind, so the priest and the deacon waited inside the church and didn't come out to Talnovo to meet them.

A crowd of people walked slowly behind the coffins, singing in chorus. Outside the village they fell back.

When Sunday came the women were still fussing around the house. An old woman mumbled psalms by the coffin, Matryona's sisters flitted about, popping things into the oven, and the air round the mouth of the stove trembled with the heat of red-hot peats, those Matryona had carried in a sack from a distant bog. They were making unappetizing pies with poor flour.

When the funeral was over and it was already getting on toward evening, they gathered for the wake. Tables were put together to make a long one, which hid the place where the coffin had stood in the morning. To start with they all stood round the table, and an old man, the husband of a sister-in-law, said the Lord's Prayer. Then they poured everybody a little honey and warm water,[2] just enough to cover the bottom of the bowl. We spooned it up without bread or anything, in memory of the dead. Then we ate something and drank vodka and the conversation became more animated. Before the jelly they all stood up and sang "Eternal remembrance" (they explained to me that it had to be sung before the jelly). There was more drinking. By now they were talking louder than ever, and not about Matryona at all. The sister-in-law's husband started boasting, "Did you notice, brother Christians, that they took the funeral service slowly today? That's because Father Mikhail noticed me. He knows I know the service. Other times, it's saints defend us, homeward wend us, and that's all."

At last the supper was over. They all rose again. They sang "Worthy Is She." Then again, with a triple repetition of "Eternal Remembrance."[3] But the voices were hoarse and out of tune, their faces drunken, and nobody put any feeling into this "eternal memory."

Then most of the guests went away, and only the near relatives were left. They pulled out their cigarets and lit up, there were jokes and laughter. There was some mention of Matryona's husband and his disappearance. The sister-in-law's husband, striking himself on the chest, assured me and the cobbler who was married to one of Matryona's sisters, "He was dead, Efim was dead! What could stop him coming back if he wasn't? If I knew they were going to hang me when I got to the old place, I'd come back just the same!"

The cobbler nodded in agreement. He was a deserter and had never left the old place. All through the war he was hiding in his mother's cellar.

The stern and silent old woman who was more ancient than all the ancients was staying the night and sat high up on the stove. She looked down in mute disapproval on the indecently animated youngsters of fifty and sixty.

But the unhappy foster daughter, who had grown up within these walls, went away behind the kitchen screen to cry.

Faddey didn't come to Matryona's wake—perhaps because he was holding a wake for his son. But twice in the next few days he walked angrily into the house for discussions with Matryona's sisters and the deserting cobbler.

The argument was about the house. Should it go to one of the sisters or to the foster daughter? They were on the verge of taking it to court, but they made peace because they realized that the court would hand over the house to neither side, but to the Rural District Council. A bargain was struck. One sister took the goat, the cobbler and his wife got the house, and to make up Faddey's share, since he had "nursed every bit of timber here in his arms," in addition to the top room which had already been carried away, they let him have the shed which had housed the goat and the whole of the inner fence between the yard and the garden.

Once again the insatiable old man got the better of sickness and pain and became young and active. Once again he gathered together his surviving sons

2. Traditionally Russians have *kutiia*, a wheat pudding with honey and almonds, at funerals and memorial gatherings; the villagers are too poor to have the main ingredients and their honey and water are symbolic of the *kutiia*.

3. Dirges, religious hymns sung to honor the dead. The village still follows religious rituals in time of crisis and does not use the civil ceremony proposed by the Soviet government.

and sons-in-law, they dismantled the shed and the fence, he hauled the timbers himself, sledge by sledge, and only toward the end did he have Antoshka of 8-D, who didn't slack this time, to help him.

They boarded Matryona's house up till the spring, and I moved in with one of her sisters-in-law, not far away. This sister-in-law on several occasions came out with some recollection of Matryona and made me see the dead woman in a new light. "Efim didn't love her. He used to say, 'I like to dress in an educated way, but she dresses any old way, like they do in the country.' Well then, he thinks, if she doesn't want anything, he might as well drink whatever's to spare. One time I went with him to the town to work, and he got himself a madam there and never wanted to come back to Matryona."

Everything she said about Matryona was disapproving. She was slovenly, she made no effort to get a few things about her. She wasn't the saving kind. She didn't even keep a pig, because she didn't like fattening them up for some reason. And the silly woman helped other people without pay. (What brought Matryona to mind this time was that the garden needed plowing, and she couldn't find enough helpers to pull the plow.)

Matryona's sister-in-law admitted that she was warmhearted and straightforward, but pitied and despised her for it.

It was only then, after these disapproving comments from her sister-in-law, that a true likeness of Matryona formed before my eyes, and I understood her as I never had when I lived side by side with her.

Of course! Every house in the village kept a pig. But she didn't. What can be easier than fattening a greedy piglet that cares for nothing in the world but food! You warm his swill three times a day, you live for him—then you cut his throat and you have some fat.

But she had none.

She made no effort to get things round her. She didn't struggle and strain to buy things and then care for them more than life itself.

She didn't go all out after fine clothes. Clothes, that beautify what is ugly and evil.

She was misunderstood and abandoned even by her husband. She had lost six children, but not her sociable ways. She was a stranger to her sisters and sisters-in-law, a ridiculous creature who stupidly worked for others without pay. She didn't accumulate property against the day she died. A dirty-white goat, a gammy-legged cat, some rubber plants. . . .

We had all lived side by side with her and had never understood that she was the righteous one without whom, as the proverb says, no village can stand.[4]

Nor any city.

Nor our whole land.

1963

---

4. See Genesis 18.23–33, the story of Sodom.

ALICE MUNRO

born 1931

"I don't take up a story and follow it as if it were a road, taking me somewhere, with views and neat diversions along the way," writes Alice Munro in her essay "What Is Real?" "I go into it and move back and forth and settle here and there, and stay in it for a while." This description of Munro as a reader applies equally to Munro as a writer. Her stories join the familiar with the enigmatic. Whether focused on fox farming, high school dances, chance sexual encounters, marriage and divorce, or discovery and self-discovery, Munro's vision typically centers on the lives of girls and women and on their introspective responses to the world around them. The author is less concerned with getting "somewhere" than with pausing "here and there" to reveal the mystery and complexity of apparently simple, day-to-day realities.

Born Alice Anne Laidlaw in the Scots-Irish community of Wingham, Ontario, Munro began writing stories in her teens—tales of romance and adventure far removed from her rural Canadian home. Her parents struggled to make ends meet—fox farming during the Depression, selling wares door to door, raising turkeys—but no venture was successful enough to lift the family out of poverty. In 1949, Munro enrolled at the University of Western Ontario, entering the journalism program and contributing short stories to *Folio*, the school's literary magazine. A classmate later recalled seeing the magazine's editor, on reading the first manuscript Munro sent in, a piece of short fiction titled "Dimensions of a Shadow," thundering down the corridor with pages aflutter: "You've got to read this. You've got to read this." Soon afterward Munro changed her major to English: "I was corralled by the English professors," she later explained.

Leaving school in 1951 to marry James Munro and moving with him to Vancouver, British Columbia, Munro honed her storytelling skills while managing a bookshop there and raising three daughters. When, in 1968, the short-story collection *Dance of the Happy Shades* introduced her to the reading public, the response was overwhelming. Praised by critics, recipient of the prestigious Governor General's Award for fiction (the first of three), she had found a place for herself in the world of professional writers. In 1972, Munro published *Lives of Girls and Women*, a novel composed of a series of linked stories. Munro's first marriage ended in divorce in 1976, after which she remarried and moved to the central Canadian town of Clinton, Ontario. Since then, she has published a dozen other collections of short fiction. She continues to receive awards, including the 2009 Man Booker International Prize for lifetime achievement. Munro is also the recipient of the 2013 Nobel Prize in Literature.

Because life in rural Canada figures prominently in Munro's writing, some critics have labeled her a "regionalist." Her characters often inhabit small fictional towns similar to the Wingham of her youth, and the area of "Walker Brothers Cowboy" recalls just such a region in southwestern Ontario. Yet the worlds of human relationships these stories create are more expansive than the term *regionalist* implies—indeed, they have a universal quality. In this,

Munro resembles **James Joyce** in *Dubliners*; **William Faulkner** bringing to life his mythic Yoknapatawpha County; and writers of the modern American South with whom Munro registers a marked affinity: Flannery O'Connor, Eudora Welty, Carson McCullers, and Walker Percy. Like them, Munro focuses on interconnected lives in small communities and on the puzzles and revelations of growing up. Munro's characters often hide their identities from themselves and from one another, but they seek, at the same time, to be unmasked, discovered, and more fully human. Describing her fondness for the short-story form, Munro says: "I like looking at people's eyes over a number of years, without continuity. Like catching them in snapshots. And I like the way people relate, or don't relate, to the people they were earlier."

Like Munro's later work, the story presented here, "Walker Brothers Cowboy" (1968) catches a snapshot of the relationship between a character's present and past lives. The story also illustrates the way the writer manipulates the boundaries between autobiography and fiction, basing her stories in personal experience but radically changing historical facts. Thus there actually was a Nora who loved dancing and clothes with flowered prints; and Nora did give a dance lesson to the nine-year-old Alice Laidlaw, whose father was a traveling salesman; and Alice was impressed by Nora's vitality and joy. The romantic nostalgia that is crucial to "Walker Brothers Cowboy," however, is fiction. Using memory, introspection, and a supreme gift for adapting reality to her

end, Munro the storyteller creates characters who struggle to understand and accept the vicissitudes of human relationships and, correspondingly, of life itself.

One of Munro's first and best-known stories, "Walker Brothers Cowboy" reveals the mixture of realistic observation and overtones of mystery that permeate her work. The small towns with their cracking sidewalks, the isolated farmhouses, the pricks of sunlight that blink through a straw hat: such details not only confirm the reality of these scenes; they establish an atmosphere of awareness and discovery that will be important later on in the story. Here, two children accompany their father, a door-to-door salesman, on a sales trip around the back country roads of southwestern Ontario. The narrator, a solitary young girl, reports the day's events in a matter-of-fact tone, sketching, in the process, a picture of the family and its everyday existence. Their disappointed, plaintive, somewhat snobbish mother strives to maintain appearances and cannot resign herself to having come down in the world; their father copes cheerfully, telling the children stories as they walk by the lake, or making up funny songs as they drive from place to place; the narrator and her younger brother, usually required to stay in their yard, find the sales trip a chance for adventure. It is a settled existence, with small frictions and disappointments but no surprises. An unscheduled trip to Nora's home, however, opens up other dimensions and changes the landscape, once so familiar and ordinary, of the narrator's life.

Walker Brothers Cowboy[1]

After supper my father says, "Want to go down and see if the Lake's still there?" We leave my mother sewing under the dining-room light, making clothes for me against the opening of school. She has ripped up for this purpose an old suit and an old plaid wool dress of hers, and she has to cut and match very cleverly and also make me stand and turn for endless fittings, sweaty, itching from the hot wool, ungrateful. We leave my brother in bed in the little screened porch at the end of the front veranda, and sometimes he kneels on his bed and presses his face against the screen and calls mournfully, "Bring me an ice-cream cone!" but I call back, "You will be asleep," and do not even turn my head.

Then my father and I walk gradually down a long, shabby sort of street, with Silverwoods Ice Cream signs standing on the sidewalk, outside tiny, lighted stores. This is in Tuppertown, an old town on Lake Huron,[2] an old grain port. The street is shaded, in some places, by maple trees whose roots have cracked and heaved the sidewalk and spread out like crocodiles into the bare yards. People are sitting out, men in shirtsleeves and undershirts and women in aprons—not people we know but if anybody looks ready to nod and say, "Warm night," my father will nod too and say something the same. Children are still playing. I don't know them either because my mother keeps my brother and me in our own yard, saying he is too young to leave it and I have to mind him. I am not so sad to watch their evening games because the games themselves are ragged, dissolving. Children, of their own will, draw apart, separate into islands of two or one under the heavy trees, occupying themselves in such solitary ways as I do all day, planting pebbles in the dirt or writing in it with a stick.

Presently we leave these yards and houses behind; we pass a factory with boarded-up windows, a lumberyard whose high wooden gates are locked for the night. Then the town falls away in a defeated jumble of sheds and small junkyards, the sidewalk gives up and we are walking on a sandy path with burdocks, plantains, humble nameless weeds all around. We enter a vacant lot, a kind of park really, for it is kept clear of junk and there is one bench with a slat missing on the back, a place to sit and look at the water. Which is generally gray in the evening, under a lightly overcast sky, no sunsets, the horizon dim. A very quiet, washing noise on the stones of the beach. Further along, towards the main part of town, there is a stretch of sand, a water slide, floats bobbing around the safe swimming area, a lifeguard's rickety throne. Also a long dark-green building, like a roofed veranda, called the Pavilion, full of farmers and their wives, in stiff good clothes, on Sundays. That is the part of the town we used to know when we lived at Dungannon and came here three or four times a summer, to the Lake. That, and the docks where we would go and look at the grain boats, ancient, rusty, wallowing, making us wonder how they got past the breakwater let alone to Fort William.

1. A door-to-door salesman for a Canadian company that is probably modeled on the still-operating Watkins Products firm.
2. One of the Great Lakes, bordering on Ontario (Canada) and eastern Michigan. Place-names are both real and invented. Real places mentioned in the story include Sunshine, a small town close to Munro's childhood home in Wingham; Dungannon, a small town close to Goderich; Fort William, which merged with Port Arthur in 1970 to become the city of Thunder Bay; and Brantford, a city in south-eastern Ontario. Other place names, like Tuppertown, Turnaround, and Boylesbridge, are adapted or fictitious.

Tramps hang around the docks and occasionally on these evenings wander up the dwindling beach and climb the shifting, precarious path boys have made, hanging on to dry bushes, and say something to my father which, being frightened of tramps, I am too alarmed to catch. My father says he is a bit hard up himself. "I'll roll you a cigarette if it's any use to you," he says, and he shakes tobacco out carefully on one of the thin butterfly papers, flicks it with his tongue, seals it and hands it to the tramp, who takes it and walks away. My father also rolls and lights and smokes one cigarette of his own.

He tells me how the Great Lakes came to be. All where Lake Huron is now, he says, used to be flat land, a wide flat plain. Then came the ice, creeping down from the North, pushing deep into the low places. Like *that*—and he shows me his hand with his spread fingers pressing the rock-hard ground where we are sitting. His fingers make hardly any impression at all and he says, "Well, the old ice cap had a lot more power behind it than this hand has." And then the ice went back, shrank back towards the North Pole where it came from, and left its fingers of ice in the deep places it had gouged, and ice turned to lakes and there they were today. They were *new*, as time went. I try to see that plain before me, dinosaurs walking on it, but I am not able even to imagine the shore of the Lake when the Indians were there, before Tuppertown. The tiny share we have of time appalls me, though my father seems to regard it with tranquillity. Even my father, who sometimes seems to me to have been at home in the world as long as it has lasted, has really lived on this earth only a little longer than I have, in terms of all the time there has been to live in. He has not known a time, any more than I, when automobiles and electric lights did not at least exist. He was not alive when this century started. I will be barely alive—old, old—when it ends. I do not like to think of it. I wish the Lake to be always just a lake, with the safe-swimming floats marking it, and the breakwater and the lights of Tuppertown.

My father has a job, selling for Walker Brothers. This is a firm that sells almost entirely in the country, the back country. Sunshine, Boylesbridge, Turnaround—that is all his territory. Not Dungannon where we used to live, Dungannon is too near town and my mother is grateful for that. He sells cough medicine, iron tonic, corn plasters, laxatives, pills for female disorders, mouthwash, shampoo, liniment, salves, lemon and orange and raspberry concentrate for making refreshing drinks, vanilla, food coloring, black and green tea, ginger, cloves, and other spices, rat poison. He has a song about it, with these two lines:

> And have all liniments and oils,
> For everything from corns to boils. . . .

Not a very funny song, in my mother's opinion. A peddler's song, and that is what he is, a peddler knocking at backwoods kitchens. Up until last winter we had our own business, a fox farm. My father raised silver foxes and sold their pelts to the people who make them into capes and coats and muffs. Prices *fell*, my father hung on hoping they would get better next year, and they fell again, and he hung on one more year and one more and finally it was not possible to hang on anymore, we owed everything to the feed company. I have heard my mother explain this, several times, to Mrs. Oliphant, who is the only neighbor she talks to. (Mrs. Oliphant also has come down in the world, being a schoolteacher who married the janitor.) We poured all we had into it, my mother says, and we came out with nothing. Many people could say the same thing, these days, but my mother has no time for the national calamity, only ours. Fate has flung us onto a street of poor people (it does not matter that we were poor before; that was a different sort of poverty), and the only way to take this, as she sees it, is with dignity, with bitterness, with no reconciliation. No bathroom with a claw-footed tub and a flush toilet is going to comfort her, nor water on tap and side-walks past the house and milk in bottles, not even the two movie theatres and the Venus Restaurant and Woolworths so marvellous it has live birds singing in its fan-cooled corners and fish as tiny as fingernails, as bright as moons, swim-ming in its green tanks. My mother does not care.

In the afternoons she often walks to Simon's Grocery and takes me with her to help carry things. She wears a good dress, navy blue with little flowers, sheer, worn over a navy-blue slip. Also a summer hat of white straw, pushed down on the side of the head, and white shoes I have just whitened on a news-paper on the back steps. I have my hair freshly done in long damp curls which the dry air will fortunately soon loosen, a stiff large hair ribbon on top of my head. This is entirely different from going out after supper with my father. We have not walked past two houses before I feel we have become objects of uni-versal ridicule. Even the dirty words chalked on the sidewalk are laughing at us. My mother does not seem to notice. She walks serenely like a lady shop-ping, like a *lady* shopping, past the housewives in loose beltless dresses torn under the arms. With me her creation, wretched curls and flaunting hair bow, scrubbed knees and white socks—all I do not want to be. I loathe even my name when she says it in public, in a voice so high, proud, and ringing, delib-erately different from the voice of any other mother on the street.

My mother will sometimes carry home, for a treat, a brick of ice cream—pale Neapolitan; and because we have no refrigerator in our house we wake my brother and eat it at once in the dining room, always darkened by the wall of the house next door. I spoon it up tenderly, leaving the chocolate till last, hoping to have some still to eat when my brother's dish is empty. My mother tries then to imitate the conversations we used to have at Dungannon, going back to our earliest, most leisurely days before my brother was born, when she would give me a little tea and a lot of milk in a cup like hers and we would sit out on the step facing the pump, the lilac tree, the fox pens beyond. She is not able to keep from mentioning those days. "Do you remember when we put you in your sled and Major pulled you?" (Major our dog, that we had to leave with neighbors when we moved.) "Do you remember your sandbox outside the kitchen window?" I pretend to remember far less than I do, wary of being trapped into sympathy or any unwanted emotion.

My mother has headaches. She often has to lie down. She lies on my broth-er's narrow bed in the little screened porch, shaded by heavy branches. "I look up at that tree and I think I am at home," she says.

"What you need," my father tells her, "is some fresh air and a drive in the country." He means for her to go with him, on his Walker Brothers route.

That is not my mother's idea of a drive in the country.

"Can I come?"

"Your mother might want you for trying on clothes."

"I'm beyond sewing this afternoon," my mother says.

"I'll take her then. Take both of them, give you a rest."

What is there about us that people need to be given a rest from? Never mind. I am glad enough to find my brother and make him go to the toilet and get us both into the car, our knees unscrubbed, my hair unringleted. My father brings from the house his two heavy brown suitcases, full of bottles, and sets them on the back seat. He wears a white shirt, brilliant in the sunlight, a tie, light trousers belonging to his summer suit (his other suit is black, for funerals, and belonged to my uncle before he died), and a creamy straw hat. His salesman's outfit, with pencils clipped in the shirt pocket. He goes back once again, probably to say goodbye to my mother, to ask her if she is sure she doesn't want to come, and hear her say, "No. No thanks, I'm better just to lie here with my eyes closed." Then we are backing out of the driveway with the rising hope of adventure, just the little hope that takes you over the bump into the street, the hot air starting to move, turning into a breeze, the houses growing less and less familiar as we follow the shortcut my father knows, the quick way out of town. Yet what is there waiting for us all afternoon but hot hours in stricken farmyards, perhaps a stop at a country store and three ice-cream cones or bottles of pop, and my father singing? The one he made up about himself has a title— "The Walker Brothers Cowboy"—and it starts out like this:

> Old Ned Fields, he now is dead,
> So I am ridin' the route instead. . . .

Who is Ned Fields? The man he has replaced, surely, and if so he really is dead; yet my father's voice is mournful-jolly, making his death some kind of nonsense, a comic calamity. "Wisht I was back on the Rio Grande,[3] plungin' through the dusky sand." My father sings most of the time while driving the car. Even now, heading out of town, crossing the bridge and taking the sharp turn onto the highway, he is humming something, mumbling a bit of a song to himself, just tuning up, really, getting ready to improvise, for out along the highway we pass the Baptist Camp, the Vacation Bible Camp, and he lets loose:

> Where are the Baptists, where are the Baptists,
>   where are all the Baptists today?
> They're down in the water, in Lake Huron water,
>   with their sins all a-gittin' washed away.

My brother takes this for straight truth and gets up on his knees trying to see down to the Lake. "I don't see any Baptists," he says accusingly. "Neither do I, son," says my father. "I told you, they're down in the Lake."

No roads paved when we left the highway. We have to roll up the windows because of dust. The land is flat, scorched, empty. Bush lots at the back of the farms hold shade, black pine-shade like pools nobody can ever get to. We bump up a long lane and at the end of it what could look more unwelcoming, more deserted than the tall unpainted farmhouse with grass growing uncut right up to the front door, green blinds down, and a door upstairs opening on nothing but air? Many houses have this door, and I have never yet been able to find out why. I ask my father and he says they are for walking in your sleep. *What*? Well, if you happen to be walking in your sleep and you want to step

3. A large river that begins in Colorado and flows south, becoming the border between Mexico and the United States.

outside. I am offended, seeing too late that he is joking, as usual, but my brother says sturdily, "If they did that they would break their necks."

The 1930s. How much this kind of farmhouse, this kind of afternoon seem to me to belong to that one decade in time, just as my father's hat does, his bright flared tie, our car with its wide running board (an Essex, and long past its prime). Cars somewhat like it, many older, none dustier, sit in the farmyards. Some are past running and have their doors pulled off, their seats removed for use on porches. No living things to be seen, chickens or cattle. Except dogs. There are dogs lying in any kind of shade they can find, dreaming, their lean sides rising and sinking rapidly. They get up when my father opens the car door, he has to speak to them. "Nice boy, there's a boy, nice old boy." They quiet down, go back to their shade. He should know how to quiet animals, he has held desperate foxes with tongs around their necks. One gentling voice for the dogs and another, rousing, cheerful, for calling at doors. "Hello there, missus, it's the Walker Brothers man and what are you out of today?" A door opens, he disappears. Forbidden to follow, forbidden even to leave the car, we can just wait and wonder what he says. Sometimes trying to make my mother laugh, he pretends to be himself in a farm kitchen, spreading out his sample case. "Now then, missus, are you troubled with parasitic life? Your children's scalps, I mean. All those crawly little things we're too polite to mention that show up on the heads of the best of families? Soap alone is useless, kerosene is not too nice a perfume, but I have here—" Or else, "Believe me, sitting and driving all day the way I do I *know* the value of these fine pills. Natural relief. A problem common to old folks too, once their days of activity are over—How about you, Grandma?" He would wave the imaginary box of pills under my mother's nose and she would laugh finally, unwillingly. "He doesn't say that really, does he?" I said, and she said no of course not, he was too much of a gentleman.

One yard after another, then, the old cars, the pumps, dogs, views of gray barns and falling-down sheds and unturning windmills. The men, if they are working in the fields, are not in any fields that we can see. The children are far away, following dry creek beds or looking for blackberries, or else they are hidden in the house, spying at us through cracks in the blinds. The car seat has grown slick with our sweat. I dare my brother to sound the horn, wanting to do it myself but not wanting to get the blame. He knows better. We play I Spy, but it is hard to find many colors. Gray for the barns and sheds and toilets and houses, brown for the yard and fields, black or brown for the dogs. The rusting cars show rainbow patches, in which I strain to pick out purple or green; likewise I peer at doors for shreds of old peeling paint, maroon or yellow. We can't play with letters, which would be better, because my brother is too young to spell. The game disintegrates anyway. He claims my colors are not fair, and wants extra turns.

In one house no door opens, though the car is in the yard. My father knocks and whistles, calls, "Hullo there! Walker Brothers man!" but there is not a stir of reply anywhere. This house has no porch, just a bare, slanting slab of cement on which my father stands. He turns around, searching the barnyard, the barn whose mow must be empty because you can see the sky through it, and finally he bends to pick up his suitcases. Just then a window is opened upstairs, a white pot appears on the sill, is tilted over and its contents splash down the outside wall. The window is not directly above my father's head, so only a stray splash would catch him. He picks up his suitcases with no particular hurry and walks, no longer whistling, to the car. "Do you know what that was?" I say to my brother. "*Pee*." He laughs and laughs.

My father rolls and lights a cigarette before he starts the car. The window has been slammed down, the blind drawn, we never did see a hand or face. "Pee, pee," sings my brother ecstatically. "Somebody dumped down pee!" "Just don't tell your mother that," my father says. "She isn't liable to see the joke." "Is it in your song?" my brother wants to know. My father says no but he will see what he can do to work it in.

I notice in a little while that we are not turning in any more lanes, though it does not seem to me that we are headed home. "Is this the way to Sunshine?" I ask my father, and he answers, "No, ma'am, it's not." "Are we still in your territory?" He shakes his head. "We're going *fast*," my brother says approvingly, and in fact we are bouncing along through dry puddle-holes so that all the bottles in the suitcases clink together and gurgle promisingly.

Another lane, a house, also unpainted, dried to silver in the sun.

"I thought we were out of your territory."

"We are."

"Then what are we going in here for?"

"You'll see."

In front of the house a short, sturdy woman is picking up washing, which had been spread on the grass to bleach and dry. When the car stops she stares at it hard for a moment, bends to pick up a couple more towels to add to the bundle under her arm, comes across to us and says in a flat voice, neither welcoming nor unfriendly, "Have you lost your way?"

My father takes his time getting out of the car. "I don't think so," he says. "I'm the Walker Brothers man."

"George Golley is our Walker Brothers man," the woman says, "and he was out here no more than a week ago. Oh, my Lord God," she says harshly, "it's you."

"It was, the last time I looked in the mirror," my father says.

The woman gathers all the towels in front of her and holds on to them tightly, pushing them against her stomach as if it hurt. "Of all the people I never thought to see. And telling me you were the Walker Brothers man."

"I'm sorry if you were looking forward to George Golley," my father says humbly.

"And look at me, I was prepared to clean the henhouse. You'll think that's just an excuse but it's true. I don't go round looking like this every day." She is wearing a farmer's straw hat, through which pricks of sunlight penetrate and float on her face, a loose, dirty print smock, and canvas shoes. "Who are those in the car, Ben? They're not yours?"

"Well, I hope and believe they are," my father says, and tells our names and ages. "Come on, you can get out. This is Nora, Miss Cronin. Nora, you better tell me, is it still Miss, or have you got a husband hiding in the woodshed?"

"If I had a husband that's not where I'd keep him, Ben," she says, and they both laugh, her laugh abrupt and somewhat angry. "You'll think I got no manners, as well as being dressed like a tramp," she says. "Come on in out of the sun. It's cool in the house."

We go across the yard ("Excuse me taking you in this way but I don't think the front door has been opened since Papa's funeral, I'm afraid the hinges might drop off"), up the porch steps, into the kitchen, which really is cool, high-ceil-inged, the blinds of course down, a simple, clean, threadbare room with waxed worn linoleum, potted geraniums, drinking-pail and dipper, a round table with scrubbed oilcloth. In spite of the cleanness, the wiped and swept surfaces, there is a faint sour smell—maybe of the dishrag or the tin dipper or the oilcloth, or the old lady, because there is one, sitting in an easy chair under the clock shelf. She turns her head slightly in our direction and says, "Nora? Is that company?"

"Blind," says Nora in a quick explaining voice to my father. Then, "You won't guess who it is, Momma. Hear his voice."

My father goes to the front of her chair and bends and says hopefully, "After-noon, Mrs. Cronin."

"Ben Jordan," says the old lady with no surprise. "You haven't been to see us in the longest time. Have you been out of the country?"

My father and Nora look at each other.

"He's married, Momma," says Nora cheerfully and aggressively. "Married and got two children and here they are." She pulls us forward, makes each of us touch the old lady's dry, cool hand while she says our names in turn. Blind! This is the first blind person I have ever seen close up. Her eyes are closed, the eyelids sunk away down, showing no shape of the eyeball, just hollows. From one hollow comes a drop of silver liquid, a medicine, or a miraculous tear.

"Let me get into a decent dress," Nora says. "Talk to Momma. It's a treat for her. We hardly ever see company, do we, Momma?"

"Not many makes it out this road," says the old lady placidly. "And the ones that used to be around here, our old neighbors, some of them have pulled out."

"True everywhere," my father says.

"Where's your wife then?"

"Home. She's not too fond of the hot weather, makes her feel poorly."

"Well." This is a habit of country people, old people, to say "well," meaning, "Is that so?" with a little extra politeness and concern.

Nora's dress, when she appears again—stepping heavily on Cuban heels down the stairs in the hall—is flowered more lavishly than anything my mother owns, green and yellow on brown, some sort of floating sheer crêpe, leaving her arms bare. Her arms are heavy, and every bit of her skin you can see is covered with little dark freckles like measles. Her hair is short, black, coarse and curly, her teeth very white and strong. "It's the first time I knew there was such a thing as green poppies," my father says, looking at her dress.

"You would be surprised all the things you never knew," says Nora, sending a smell of cologne far and wide when she moves and displaying a change of voice to go with the dress, something more sociable and youthful. "They're not pop-pies anyway, they're just flowers. You go and pump me some good cold water and I'll make these children a drink." She gets down from the cupboard a bot-tle of Walker Brothers Orange syrup.

"You telling me you were the Walker Brothers man!"

"It's the truth, Nora. You go and look at my sample cases in the car if you don't believe me. I got the territory directly south of here."

"Walker Brothers? Is that a fact? You selling for Walker Brothers?"

"Yes, ma'am."

"We always heard you were raising foxes over Dungannon way."

"That's what I was doing, but I kind of run out of luck in that business."

"So where're you living? How long've you been out selling?"

"We moved into Tuppertown. I been at it, oh, two, three months. It keeps the wolf from the door. Keeps him as far away as the back fence."

Nora laughs. "Well, I guess you count yourself lucky to have the work. Isabel's husband in Brantford, he was out of work the longest time. I thought if he didn't find something soon I was going to have them all land in here to feed, and I tell you I was hardly looking forward to it. It's all I can manage with me and Momma."

"Isabel married," my father says. "Muriel married too?"

"No, she's teaching school out West. She hasn't been home for five years. I guess she finds something better to do with her holidays. I would if I was her." She gets some snapshots out of the table drawer and starts showing him. "That's Isabel's oldest boy, starting school. That's the baby sitting in her carriage. Isabel and her husband. Muriel. That's her roommate with her. That's a fellow she used to go around with, and his car. He was working in a bank out there. That's her school, it has eight rooms. She teaches Grade Five." My father shakes his head. "I can't think of her any way but when she was going to school, so shy I used to pick her up on the road—I'd be on my way to see you—and she would not say one word, not even to agree it was a nice day."

"She's got over that."

"Who are you talking about?" says the old lady.

"Muriel. I said she's got over being shy."

"She was here last summer."

"No, Momma, that was Isabel. Isabel and her family were here last summer. Muriel's out West."

"I meant Isabel."

Shortly after this the old lady falls asleep, her head on the side, her mouth open. "Excuse her manners," Nora says. "It's old age." She fixes an afghan over her mother and says we can all go into the front room where our talking won't disturb her.

"You two," my father says. "Do you want to go outside and amuse yourselves?"

Amuse ourselves how? Anyway, I want to stay. The front room is more interesting than the kitchen, though barer. There is a gramophone and a pump organ and a picture on the wall of Mary, Jesus' mother—I know that much—in shades of bright blue and pink with a spiked band of light around her head. I know that such pictures are found only in the homes of Roman Catholics and so Nora must be one. We have never known any Roman Catholics at all well, never well enough to visit in their houses. I think of what my grandmother and my Aunt Tena, over in Dungannon, used to always say to indicate that somebody was a Catholic. *So-and-so digs with the wrong foot,* they would say. *She digs with the wrong foot.* That was what they would say about Nora.[4]

Nora takes a bottle, half full, out of the top of the organ and pours some of what is in it into the two glasses that she and my father have emptied of the orange drink.

"Keep it in case of sickness?" my father says.

"Not on your life," says Nora. "I'm never sick. I just keep it because I keep it. One bottle does me a fair time, though, because I don't care for drinking alone.

---

4. Protestant-Catholic feuds were transplanted to southern Ontario by Irish settlers.

Here's luck!" She and my father drink and I know what it is. Whisky. One of the things my mother has told me in our talks together is that my father never drinks whisky. But I see he does. He drinks whisky and he talks of people whose names I have never heard before. But after a while he turns to a familiar incident. He tells about the chamberpot that was emptied out the window. "Picture me there," he says, "hollering my heartiest. *Oh, lady, it's your Walker Brothers man, anybody home?*" He does himself hollering, grinning absurdly, waiting, looking up in pleased expectation, and then—oh, ducking, covering his head with his arms, looking as if he begged for mercy (when he never did anything like that, I was watching), and Nora laughs, almost as hard as my brother did at the time.

"That isn't true! That's not a word true!"

"Oh, indeed it is, ma'am. We have our heroes in the ranks of Walker Brothers. I'm glad you think it's funny," he says sombrely.

I ask him shyly, "Sing the song."

"What song? Have you turned into a singer on top of everything else?"

Embarrassed, my father says, "Oh, just this song I made up while I was driving around, it gives me something to do, making up rhymes."

But after some urging he does sing it, looking at Nora with a droll, apologetic expression, and she laughs so much that in places he has to stop and wait for her to get over laughing so he can go on, because she makes him laugh too. Then he does various parts of his salesman's spiel. Nora when she laughs squeezes her large bosom under her folded arms. "You're crazy," she says. "That's all you are." She sees my brother peering into the gramophone and she jumps up and goes over to him. "Here's us sitting enjoying ourselves and not giving you a thought, isn't it terrible?" she says. "You want me to put a record on, don't you? You want to hear a nice record? Can you dance? I bet your sister can, can't she?"

I say no. "A big girl like you and so good-looking and can't dance!" says Nora. "It's high time you learned. I bet you'd make a lovely dancer. Here, I'm going to put on a piece I used to dance to and even your daddy did, in his dancing days. You didn't know your daddy was a dancer, did you? Well, he is a talented man, your daddy!"

She puts down the lid and takes hold of me unexpectedly around the waist, picks up my other hand, and starts making me go backwards. "This is the way, now, this is how they dance. Follow me. This foot, see. One and one-two. One and one-two. That's fine, that's lovely, don't look at your feet! Follow me, that's right, see how easy? You're going to be a lovely dancer! One and one-two. One and one-two. Ben, see your daughter dancing!" *Whispering while you cuddle near me, Whispering so no one can hear me . . .*[5]

Round and round the linoleum, me proud, intent, Nora laughing and moving with great buoyancy, wrapping me in her strange gaiety, her smell of whisky, cologne, and sweat. Under the arms her dress is damp, and little drops form along her upper lip, hang in the soft black hairs at the corners of her mouth. She whirls me around in front of my father—causing me to stumble, for I am by no means so swift a pupil as she pretends—and lets me go, breathless.

"Dance with me, Ben."

---

5. From the popular song "Whispering," words and music by John Schonberger, Vincent Rose, and Richard Coburn. The original 1920 recording by Paul Whiteman's band was one of the first records to sell a million copies.

"I'm the world's worst dancer, Nora, and you know it."

"I certainly never thought so."

"You would now."

She stands in front of him, arms hanging loose and hopeful, her breasts, which a moment ago embarrassed me with their warmth and bulk, rising and falling under her loose flowered dress, her face shining with the exercise, and delight.

"Ben."

My father drops his head and says quietly, "Not me, Nora."

So she can only go and take the record off. "I can drink alone but I can't dance alone," she says. "Unless I am a whole lot crazier than I think I am."

"Nora," says my father, smiling. "You're not crazy."

"Stay for supper."

"Oh, no. We couldn't put you to the trouble."

"It's no trouble. I'd be glad of it."

"And their mother would worry. She'd think I'd turned us over in a ditch."

"Oh, well. Yes."

"We've taken a lot of your time now."

"Time," says Nora bitterly. "Will you come by ever again?"

"I will if I can," says my father.

"Bring the children. Bring your wife."

"Yes, I will," says my father. "I will if I can."

When she follows us to the car he says, "You come to see us too, Nora. We're right on Grove Street, left-hand side going in, that's north, and two doors this side—east—of Baker Street."

Nora does not repeat these directions. She stands close to the car in her soft, brilliant dress. She touches the fender, making an unintelligible mark in the dust there.

On the way home my father does not buy any ice cream or pop, but he does go into a country store and get a package of licorice, which he shares with us. She digs with the wrong foot, I think, and the words seem sad to me as never before, dark, perverse. My father does not say anything to me about not mentioning things at home, but I know, just from the thoughtfulness, the pause when he passes the licorice, that there are things not to be mentioned. The whisky, maybe the dancing. No worry about my brother, he does not notice enough. At most he might remember the blind lady, the picture of Mary.

"Sing," my brother commands my father, but my father says gravely, "I don't know, I seem to be fresh out of songs. You watch the road and let me know if you see any rabbits."

So my father drives and my brother watches the road for rabbits and I feel my father's life flowing back from our car in the last of the afternoon, darkening and turning strange, like a landscape that has an enchantment on it, making it kindly, ordinary and familiar while you are looking at it, but changing it, once your back is turned, into something you will never know, with all kinds of weathers, and distances you cannot imagine.

When we get closer to Tuppertown the sky becomes gently overcast, as always, nearly always, on summer evenings by the Lake.

1968

VI

Global and Local
in Contemporary
World
Literature

Certain years in world history stand out in the blaze of a revolution that transforms world politics: 1789 for the French Revolution, 1848 for a series of European revolutions, 1917 for the Russian Revolution. More recently, 1968, a year of student rebellion in Prague, Paris, Mexico City, and elsewhere, seemed at the time to be such a milestone. Challenges to traditional authority shook the 1960s. The subsequent changes to Western culture have shaped all that came after—especially in literature, where the intimate relations among men and women and the tensions between public responsibility and private desire play a central role. Meanwhile, the vision of a post-Communist world that was glimpsed in Prague in the spring of 1968 found its realization in the dismantling of Communist regimes in Eastern Europe in 1989 and the dissolution of the Soviet Union in 1991. The crushing of the Prague Spring led immediately to a period of pessimism and "normalization" (that is, a return to repressive practices) that restricted social movements. The only successful effort to thwart normalization

Celebration of New Year's Eve, 1990, at the Berlin Wall.

was the Polish trade union Solidarity, which, however, was trampled by the imposition of martial law in 1981.

In the West, especially in the United States, the focus of protest was the Vietnam War—a conflict the Americans had taken over from the French—in which over half a million (mostly drafted) Americans had failed to defeat a guerrilla insurgency. Communist North Vietnam, backed by the Soviet Union (and for a time by China), eventually reached Saigon, the capital of South Vietnam, in 1975, and unified the country the following year. There were a number of other minor proxy wars between the superpowers during the 1970s and 1980s, but this was the period of détente, or relaxation of hostility, when the Soviet premier Leonid Brezhnev and American presidents including Richard Nixon and Jimmy Carter sought to defuse Cold War tensions and signed a number of treaties on arms control and human rights. Détente, eclipsed by the Soviet invasion of Afghanistan in 1979, was followed by a period of rearmament under President Ronald Reagan, which culminated,

surprisingly, in the disarmament agreement with Russian premier Mikhail Gorbachev at Reykjavik, Iceland, in 1986. Seeking to transform the moribund economy and society he had inherited from his Communist predecessors, Gorbachev introduced the principles of glasnost (or openness) and perestroika (or restructuring), intending to make the Soviet system more flexible and accountable. In the end, however, the restructuring went much further than Gorbachev had intended, resulting in the demise of the Communist Party and the dissolution of both the Warsaw Pact military alliance and the Soviet Union itself.

If 1968 marks the high point of the protest movements that would transform contemporary society, 1989 is an equally memorable year, during which the nations of Eastern Europe rebelled against—and finally overthrew—Communist regimes, and the Wall that had separated East and West Berlin fell. Also in 1989, the first steps were taken to dismantle the system of apartheid, or racial segregation and white minority rule in South Africa (white minority rule had ended in

Young men in Ho Chi Minh City (formerly Saigon, the capital of South Vietnam), in 1975, after "Liberation Day."

Zimbabwe, formerly Rhodesia, in 1980). That same year thousands of Chinese students mounted an unsuccessful rebellion against the Communist government of the People's Republic of China; this brief uprising ended with a massacre in Tiananmen Square, in Beijing, the historic center of Chinese politics.

During the 1990s, as the Soviet Union disintegrated and as China moved closer to a capitalist economy, many hoped that humanity's bloodiest century would end with something like the accomplishment of world peace that had been such a bright dream at its beginning. The dictatorships of Latin America, supported by the United States as a bulwark against communism, gave way to democratically elected governments. Peace agreements in Northern Ireland and between Israel and Palestine seemed to confirm such promises. Another date, September 11, 2001, undermined such hopes: on that day, terrorists claiming to act in the name of Islam hijacked four airplanes and flew into the World Trade Center, in New York, and the Pentagon, near Washington, D.C. (one of the planes was forced, by the passengers, to crash in a remote field in Pennsylvania). The wars of the twenty-first century, which began in the aftermath of the terrorist attacks, have chilled the hope that ours would be a uniquely peaceful age. Likewise, the expectation that industrialization would lead inevitably to a more secular world has proved mistaken. Communal violence continues in India, and the Arab-Israeli conflict and Islamic fundamentalism have intensified during the first decades of the twenty-first century, while in much of the world outside Europe, religion is resurgent.

During the past half century or so, even if dreams of world peace have often appeared illusory, great improvement in the living standards of much of the world's still-expanding population has occurred. Four-fifths of the global popu-

Supporters of antiapartheid activist Nelson Mandela gather outside the Victor Verster prison in Cape Town, South Africa, demanding his freedom. After twenty-seven years of confinement, Mandela was finally released in 1990. In 1994 he became South Africa's first black president.

lation now benefits from the fruits of industrialization, even as one-fifth remains in poverty. The years since World War II have been an era of globalization in investment, knowledge, politics, and culture. The information revolution, made possible first by satellite television and then by ever-more-sophisticated computers and the Internet, has unified distant parts of the globe more rapidly than did the telegraph and telephone at the beginning of the twentieth century. Today, a world connected by telecommunications responds more quickly than ever before to news about politics, markets, and even sporting events. It is also a world of increased migration, in which the movements of people from poorer to richer nations have created immense cultural hybridity while sometimes producing tensions in the host countries.

ARCTIC OCEAN

Spitsbergen (Nor.)

Greenland (Den.)

Iceland

NORTH AMERICA

Canada

NORTH ATLANTIC OCEAN

Chicago

New York

United States of America

Los Angeles

Mexico

Mexico City

Cuba

Jamaica

Belize
Guatemala
El Salvador
Honduras
Nicaragua
Costa Rica
Panama

Haiti Dominican Rep.
VIRGIN IS. (Br. & U.S.)
Antigua
Martinique (Fr.)
St. Lucia

Venezuela

Trinidad & Tobago

Guyana
Surinam
French Guiana

GALAPAGOS IS.
(Ecuador)

Colombia

Ecuador

Equator

Peru

Brazil

Bolivia

Paraguay

Rio de Janeiro

SOUTH AMERICA

SOUTH PACIFIC OCEAN

Chile

Santiago

Argentina

Uruguay

Buenos Aires

SOUTH ATLANTIC OCEAN

FALKLAND IS.
(Br.)

Northern Ireland
Ireland
Dublin
United Kingdom
London

Norway
Sweden
Finland

Leningrad (St. Pete

Moscow

Union

E

Denmark
Netherlands
Belgium
Paris
France

East
Berlin
Germany
Prague
Vienna
Austria
Venice
Italy
Rome

Poland
Warsaw
Czechoslovakia
Hungary
Romania
Yugoslavia
Bulgaria
Albania Greece

Istanbul
Turkey

Syria
Iraq

Portugal
Spain
Madrid

Morocco

W. Sahara

Mauritania

Algeria

Mediterranean Sea

Tunisia

Libya

Alexandria
Cairo
Egypt

Beirut
Israel Lebanon
Jerusalem
Jordan

Saudi Ar

Bah

AFRICA

Mali

Niger

Chad

Sudan

Eritrea

Somal

Senegal
Gambia
Guinea-Bissau
Guinea
Sierra
Leone
Liberia
Ivory
Coast
Ghana
Togo
Benin

Burkina
Faso

Nigeria

Ibadan

Cameroon

Central African Rep.

Ethiopia

Equatorial Guinea
Gabon
Congo

Zaire

Uganda Kenya
Rwanda Nairobi
Burundi

Tanzania

SEY

Angola

Zambia

Malawi

Mozambique

Namibia

Botswana

Zimbabwe

Johannesburg
Swaziland
South Africa
Lesotho

MILES

0   1200   2400   3600   4800

AT THE EQUATOR

KILOMETERS

0   2400   4800

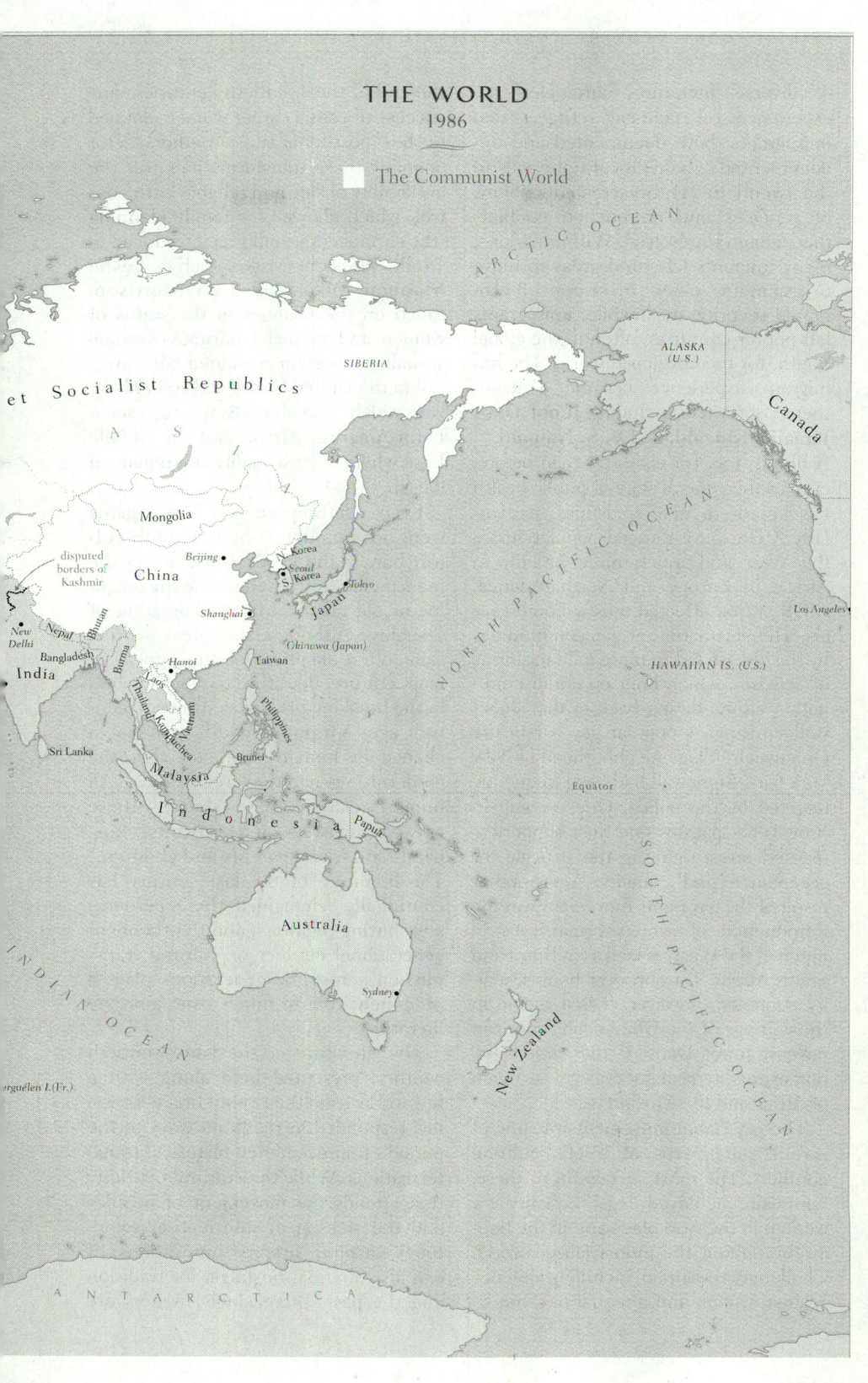

THE WORLD
1986

■ The Communist World

ARCTIC OCEAN

ALASKA
(U.S.)

Canada

SIBERIA

et Socialist Republics

A S I A

Mongolia

disputed
borders of
Kashmir

China

Beijing

Korea

Seoul
S. Korea

Japan

Tokyo

Shanghai

Okinawa (Japan)

New
Delhi

Nepal   Bhutan

Bangladesh

India   Burma   Hanoi   Taiwan

Laos

Thailand Kampuchea

Philippines

Sri Lanka

Brunei

Malaysia

Indonesia   Papua

NORTH PACIFIC OCEAN

Los Angeles

HAWAIIAN IS. (U.S.)

Equator

SOUTH PACIFIC OCEAN

Australia

INDIAN OCEAN

Sydney

New Zealand

erguélen I.(Fr.)

ANTARCTICA

A diverse literature chronicles the experiences of political refugees and immigrants, both documented and undocumented. The political upheavals of the twentieth century created millions of refugees and entrenched conflicts that remain unresolved. Within nations, many migrants left rural areas to move to expanding cities. In search of economic security, meanwhile, immigrants left poorer countries, often in the global South, for the developed world. The immigrant experience became a major theme of writers including **Junot Díaz**, **Jamaica Kincaid**, and **V. S. Naipaul**.

Illness, too, travels faster than before; even as the general state of public health has improved, new epidemics, particularly AIDS, have ravaged populations in the West and much more broadly in Africa. In Europe and North America, AIDS at first affected mostly homosexuals. The decimation of gay communities by the disease led to more militant forms of activism, which built on antidiscrimination efforts dating back to the Stonewall uprising. A popular gay bar in the Greenwich Village neighborhood of New York City, Stonewall had been frequently targeted by the police. One evening in June 1969, patrons and their supporters resisted arrest, igniting the struggle for acceptance and equality. Yet another result of the gay rights movement was the introduction of same-sex marriages in much of the West, as well as in Brazil and South Africa. Tension over homosexuality remained, however: it is a theme in the writings of the Dominican American novelist Junot Díaz. At the same time, homosexuality remained illegal in much of Africa and the Muslim world.

The gay rights movement was one of several outgrowths of 1960s cultural conflicts. The most successful of these, feminism, achieved legal equality for women in the workplace and in the family throughout the industrialized world. Challenges remained, including violence against women and unequal pay, but by the end of the twentieth century, many successful young career women claimed to be "post-feminist." Another factor enabling these transformations was the availability of safe and reliable birth control, which allowed for family planning (the contraceptive pill was introduced in 1960). Works by writers such as **Leslie Marmon Silko,** and **Toni Morrison,** touch on the changes in the status of women and in social norms governing sexuality. Abortion remained controversial in the United States and Ireland but was widely available elsewhere, except Latin America, Africa, and the Middle East, where homosexuality also remained illegal.

Even relatively conservative regions were not untouched by the youth culture born in the 1960s, broadcast by the mass media, and emphasizing the breaking of old taboos and the liberation of sexuality. Although the great writers were often skeptical of the appeal of mass culture, literature too participated in the breaking of taboos. Almost a century ago, **Virginia Woolf** spoke of a change in human character that the modernist generation registered: "All human relations have shifted—those between masters and servants, husbands and wives, parents and children." The literature of the last century has continually reimagined these perpetually shifting relations, and the theme of generational conflict or cultural transmission across the generations plays a prominent role in much contemporary literature.

The literature of the late twentieth century, presented here along with a few works from the twenty-first century, has responded in manifold ways to the period's unprecedented historical transformations. While the cultural hybridity that attends the movement of peoples and the sharing of information sometimes inspires literary innovations, it can also sharpen nostalgia for tradition and the past. Increasingly, writers are conscious of having an audience beyond their nation or region and even beyond their language. Writers with a global readership may feel both responsibility for representing their own people to the world and the need to accommodate their style of writing to the demands of the international marketplace. Indeed, Nobel Prize winners such as V. S. Naipaul and **J. M. Coetzee** have often been accused in their homelands of speaking primarily to an international audience. Writers thus find themselves striving to defend and honor the spirit and culture of historically marginalized groups while reaching out to a more elite international audience.

As in the immediate postwar period, many writers seeking to address the need for social change and the elimination of political inequality turn to traditional literary realism or to political allegory. A literary movement emerging in the 1960s, magic realism draws both on the realist tradition of the historical novel and on the inspiration of modernists such as **Franz Kafka**, who depicted his nightmarish worlds in lifelike detail. In various ways, Latin American novelists including **Gabriel García Marquéz**, **Carlos Fuentes**, and **Isabel Allende**, and the Indian-born **Salman Rushdie**, combine realistic historical narration with fanciful folktales in which individuals and societies seem to be transformed by distinctly nonrealistic events—a character who can fly, perhaps, or a mystical link among people born on the night of Indian independence. The juxtaposition emphasizes the coexistence of modern notions of causality and traditional, prescientific belief in the unexplainable and thus has had its greatest impact in zones of uneven economic development, where educated writers have incorporated the folk wisdom of their rural, sometimes illiterate communities. Toni Morrison has made effective use of such techniques in her writings on African American life. Like the magic realists, Morrison is sometimes described as a postmodernist. In common with an earlier generation inspired by the modernists (Borges, **Nabokov**, **Beckett**), postmodernists often question the boundary between fiction and history. While treating historical events, such writers as **Roberto Bolaño** and J. M. Coetzee may call attention to the fictionality of their reconstruction of those events—encouraging the reader to keep in mind that stories are the creations of writers who may, by the very act of narration, distort historical reality. These authors tend to present an oblique account of atrocities, whether involving colonization, genocide, or political repression. Both in magic realism and in postmodernism, stories may seem whimsical or fantastical even when they are playing for deadly serious stakes.

The twenty-first century began with reminders of the interconnectedness of a global society linked by industrial capitalism and communications technology but divided by religion and politics. While war, terrorism, and poverty are events that divide us, the greatest world literature suggests, as it always has, what unites us.

DEREK WALCOTT

born 1930

A cosmopolitan poet from a small Caribbean island, a West Indian of mixed African and European ancestry, Derek Walcott depicts the hybridity of Caribbean culture while drawing on the traditions of English literature. In contemplating the violent uprising in Kenya against British colonialism, he wrote in an early poem, "A Far Cry from Africa" (1956), of his dual inheritance: "I who am poisoned with the blood of both / Where shall I turn, divided to the vein?" Yet if he treats his mixed blood as poison, he also makes it a source of strength in his verse, which draws on the rhythms and idioms of Caribbean speech to enliven what he called, in the same poem, "the English tongue I love."

Derek Walcott was born, along with his twin brother, Roderick, on January 23, 1930, in Castries, the capital of the island of St. Lucia, then a British colony. (It had been occupied alternately by the French and the British since the seventeenth century and would not gain its independence from Britain until 1979.) Shortly after their first birthday, the boys' father, who was a government functionary and a talented artist, suddenly died, and the two boys were brought up by their mother, a schoolteacher who later became headmistress of the Methodist elementary school where they began their education. Both inherited their father's creative gift, Derek primarily in language, Roderick in the pictorial arts, and they remained intellectual and artistic companions until Roderick's death, in 1999. Their mother provided an environment in which their talents could be nurtured, an essential factor in Walcott's development as a poet.

Walcott acquired, early on, a sense of his singularity from the fact that he was of mixed ancestry in a predominantly black society (both his grandfathers were white, his grandmothers black). He was also a Protestant and member of the educated middle class in a peasant, Catholic community. Moreover, although he was brought up to speak Standard English as his first language, his exposure to the local French creole reinforced his sense of his ambiguous relation to the communal life around him. Far from unsettling Walcott, these factors of personal history became a source of strength and fascination. He began to write poetry in high school and published his first works as a teenager.

After high school education at St. Mary's College, Walcott studied at the University of West Indies in Jamaica, where he came to understand the Caribbean as a region unified by a common experience and a common historical legacy. His literary studies familiarized him with the great works of Western literature and particularly with the modern English poets **T. S. Eliot, W. B. Yeats**, and W. H. Auden. After his graduation, in 1953, Walcott taught school for a while in Kingston, while doing occasional work in journalism, before moving to Port of Spain, Trinidad, where he became a feature writer for a major local newspaper, the *Sunday Guardian*. In 1957, he was awarded a Rockefeller Fellowship to study theater at New York University. His encounter with the problems of race during his American sojourn gave further definition to his self-awareness as a West Indian; the experience confirmed for him the inescapable connection between race and history with which black people in the New World have to contend. On his return two years later to

Port of Spain, he founded the Trinidad Theatre Workshop, to which he devoted his energies for nearly two decades. He was eager to bring the technical knowledge associated with the theater and stagecraft to the West Indies. He became well-known for his plays before he gained an international following for his poetry, which gained an international audience after the publication of his collection *In a Green Night* (1962) in England. Alienated by the Black Power revolts of the 1970s in Trinidad, Walcott resigned from the Trinidad Theatre Workshop and, after winning a MacArthur Fellowship ("genius" grant) in 1981, began teaching regularly at Boston University. Since then, he has divided his time between the United States and St. Lucia. He was awarded the Nobel Prize for Literature in 1992.

The poems selected here range from one Walcott wrote as a teenager to his mature masterpiece, *Omeros*. His early poems are marked by a striking eloquence of diction and a rich tapestry of imagery. "As John to Patmos" (1947), written when Walcott was only seventeen, already announces Walcott's poetic vocation: "To praise lovelong, the living and the brown dead." Here, as in later works, Walcott draws a parallel between St. Lucia and the Greek islands, specifically Patmos, where John the Divine was said to have written the Book of Revelation. In poems such as "Ruins of a Great House" (1956), Walcott assumes the weight of English literary tradition by translating its references and resources into a poetic register determined by his Caribbean experience and sensibility. Here, he recognizes the oppression of English colonizers, as he draws on the writings of Thomas Browne, William Blake, and John Donne to provide an alternative English heritage.

The next few poems, from *The Castaway* (1965), showing Walcott in his maturity as a poet, celebrate the role of the heroic or creative individual in the shaping of history. In poems such as "The Almond Trees," Walcott understands the poet as a type of castaway, the node of consciousness in the larger community but who will seldom be heeded by that community. "Crusoe's Journal" lends a poetic grandeur to such a figure, the lonely and bold adventurer who assumes the burden of pathfinder, creating a reality—and, indeed, a new world—out of the unpromising materials at hand. In "Verandah," he imagines himself in conversation with the English colonizers to whom he feels connected by his English grandfather.

Walcott turned to the subject of the Caribbean in relation to the Americas in his poem "Elegy," written in the year of student rebellion, 1968. In "The Sea Is History," he places his native region in the even broader sweep of biblical history. The context of this interrogation emerges more fully in poems from *The Fortunate Traveller* (1981), where Walcott's perception of the racial divide between the affluent North and the impoverished South dictates the ironic posture indicated by the volume title. In "North and South," Walcott evokes North America in its quotidian ordinariness but against a background of a violent history. "Sea Cranes" develops this theme more explicitly, and it is given its ultimate shape in Walcott's masterpiece, *Omeros* (1990).

All Walcott's poetry flows into *Omeros*, which is best grasped as the imaginative summation of human history as seen from his Caribbean perspective. Its retrospective vision assumes an emotional value for the poet for whom, as he says, "Art is History's nostalgia." In an expansive recollection of his previous themes, *Omeros* sums up the West Indian experience through the adventures of Achille, a humble St. Lucian fisherman, whose travels take him to the points of compass of the West Indian consciousness. Homer's great epics, the *Iliad* and the *Odyssey*, serve as explicit references for the work, and the figure of Homer himself, in his modern Greek rendering of "Omeros," is evoked in a key passage of the poem in which he is represented as the quintessential exile. Moreover, Walcott's use of the blind poet in the character of Seven Seas, modeled on Demodokos in Homer's *Odyssey*, reinforces the importance of this Greek frame of reference. The poem employs some of the standard tropes of the classical epic, such as descent into the underworld and conflict and contest.

Despite these connections, *Omeros* is not a mere rehash of Homer. Although the poem contains stretches of narration, they do not build up to a dramatic progression of events such as we find in the conventional epic. The rivalry between Achille and another local fisherman, Hector, over Helen (who is hardly idealized in the poem and remains, for all her beauty, an ordinary village woman) is presented as part of a strictly local history that features other characters such as the white settler couple, Major Plunkett and his wife, Maud, as well as minor characters who move in and out of the narrative. Thus the poem does not develop a linear plot, but represents, rather, a vast kaleidoscope, a series of episodes that are woven around its protagonist. Achilles' descent into the underworld recounted in Chapter VIII, for example, renders the sea as the graveyard of history and the site of the turbulent history of the Caribbean. This plunge into a violent past has an obvious connection with the poet's recollection, in Chapter XXXV, of the Native Americans' experience and condition, the pathos of a "tribal sorrow" that originates in the tragic confrontation with the white race.

Walcott's exploration of the African element in Caribbean life, dramatized in Chapter XXV in the dream sequence, takes Achille back to the ancestral homeland. The theme of collective memory and its relation to identity is developed in the dialogue between Achille and his mythic progenitor, Afolabe. *Omeros* reconnects with Africa by emphasizing the continuing tie of the West Indians to the continent of their forbears yet helps its West Indian audience take cultural repossession of their island home. *Omeros* registers both the Afro-Caribbean quest for an established sense of place and of community and, at the same time, the compulsion to move toward the wider horizon of world literature.

As John to Patmos

As John to Patmos,[1] among the rocks and the blue, live air, hounded
His heart to peace, as here surrounded
By the strewn-silver on waves, the wood's crude hair, the rounded
Breasts of the milky bays,[2] palms, flocks, the green and dead

Leaves, the sun's brass coin on my cheek, where   5
Canoes brace the sun's strength, as John, in that bleak air,
So am I welcomed richer by these blue scapes, Greek there,[3]
So I shall voyage no more from home; may I speak here.

1. The Evangelist John the Divine's name is associated with the Greek island of Patmos, where he was banished for several years and wrote the Book of Revelation.
2. Low hills (in French patois, *mornes*) rising on the gently sloping landscape against the background of the sea, a feature of many of the smaller Caribbean islands.
3. Walcott establishes a parallel between Patmos and the poet's own island home of St. Lucia.

This island is heaven—away from the dustblown blood of cities;
See the curve of bay, watch the straggling flower, pretty is   10
The wing'd sound of trees, the sparse-powdered[4] sky, when lit is
The night. For beauty has surrounded
Its black children, and freed them of homeless ditties.[5]

As John to Patmos, in each love-leaping air,
O slave, soldier, worker under red trees sleeping,[6] hear   15
What I swear now, as John did:
To praise lovelong, the living and the brown dead.[7]

                                                                        1947

Ruins of a Great House[1]

> though our longest sun sets at right declensions and
> makes but winter arches, it cannot be long before we
> lie down in darkness, and have our light in ashes . . .
>
> —BROWNE, *Urn Burial*[2]

Stones only, the disjecta membra[3] of this Great House,
Whose moth-like girls are mixed with candledust,
Remain to file the lizard's dragonish claws.[4]
The mouths of those gate cherubs[5] shriek with stain;
Axle and coach wheel silted under the muck   5
Of cattle droppings
                    Three crows[6] flap for the trees
And settle, creaking the eucalyptus boughs.
A smell of dead limes quickens in the nose
The leprosy of empire[7]   10
                    "Farewell, green fields,
                    Farewell, ye happy groves!"[8]
Marble like Greece, like Faulkner's South in stone,[9]
Deciduous[1] beauty prospered and is gone,
But where the lawn breaks in a rash of trees   15

4. Almost cloudless.
5. I.e., Negro spirituals, songs of exile.
6. The poet's self-dedication addressed to his fellow countrymen.
7. The total "organic" community.
1. The principal building around which life in the slave plantation revolved. As in the American South, many of the great houses in the Caribbean were constructed on a grand scale, modeled on classical Greek architectural style (cf. line 13).
2. Thomas Browne (1605–1682) was an English physician and essayist, best known for his book *Religio Medici*. The epigram here is taken from *Urn Burial* (1658), a work that dwells on the passing of time and on human mortality.

3. Disjointed limbs (Latin).
4. The dragon is often represented as a great lizard.
5. Gates that display little angels with chubby cheeks and wings.
6. Birds of ill omen.
7. Slavery as moral blight.
8. The quotation is from Blake's poem "Night."
9. William Faulkner (1897–1962), considered by many to be the greatest writer of the American South.
1. Said of trees that shed their leaves in the winter. The idea here is that the splendor of the great house and the lifestyle associated with it seemed destined to last forever.

A spade below dead leaves will ring the bone
Of some dead animal or human thing
Fallen from evil days, from evil times.

It seems that the original crops were limes
Grown in the silt that clogs the river's skirt;   20
The imperious rakes[2] are gone, their bright girls gone,
The river flows, obliterating hurt.[3]
I climbed a wall with the grille ironwork
Of exiled craftsmen protecting that great house
From guilt,[4] perhaps, but not from the worm's rent[5]   25
Nor from the padded cavalry of the mouse.
And when a wind shook in the limes I heard
What Kipling[6] heard, the death of a great empire, the abuse
Of ignorance by Bible and by sword.[7]

A green lawn, broken by low walls of stone,   30
Dipped to the rivulet, and pacing, I thought next
Of men like Hawkins, Walter Raleigh, Drake,[8]
Ancestral murderers and poets, more perplexed
In memory now by every ulcerous crime.
The world's green age then was a rotting lime   35
Whose stench became the charnel galleon's text.
The rot remains with us, the men are gone.
But, as dead ash is lifted in a wind
That fans the blackening ember of the mind,
My eyes burned from the ashen prose of Donne.[9]   40

Ablaze with rage I thought,
Some slave is rotting in this manorial lake,
But still the coal of my compassion fought
That Albion[1] too was once
A colony like ours, "part of the continent, piece of the main,"   45
Nook-shotten, rook o'erblown, deranged

2. Young men in the slave-owning community who lived wild and riotous lives.
3. Symbolizing the impersonal flow of time.
4. Presumably of slavery.
5. I.e., inevitable decay and death, a tribute to time.
6. Rudyard Kipling (1865–1936), English writer born in India. He is often remembered for the slogan he coined, "the white man's burden," to justify European colonial domination of nonwhite races.
7. The two means by which native populations were conquered.
8. Significant figures of English imperial history. John Hawkins was a noted early slaver; Walter Raleigh was a favorite of Queen Elizabeth I of England, who knighted him for his

exploration in America on behalf of the crown; Francis Drake was knighted for his daring acts of piracy against Spanish merchant ships.
9. John Donne (1572–1631) was dean of St. Paul's Cathedral in London and the leading figure among the Renaissance English poets known as "the Metaphysicals." The reference here is to Donne's sermons, specifically Meditation 17, which contains the sentence "Ask not for whom the bell tolls, it tolls for thee," a reminder of human mortality—hence, "ashen prose." The quotations in lines 45 and 51 are from the same sermon; they express the theme of our common humanity, summed up by the famous phrase "No Man is an island" that occurs elsewhere in the sermon.
1. Poetic name for England.

By foaming channels and the vain expense
Of bitter faction
          All in compassion ends
So differently from what the heart arranged: 50
"as well as if a manor of thy friend's . . ."

                          1956

The Almond Trees[1]

There's nothing here
this early;
cold sand
cold churning ocean, the Atlantic,
no visible history,[2]   5

except this stand
of twisted, coppery, sea-almond trees[3]
their shining postures surely
bent as metal, and one

foam-haired, salt-grizzled fisherman,   10
his mongrel growling, whirling on the stick
he pitches him; its spinning rays
'no visible history'
until their lengthened shapes amaze the sun.

By noon,   15
this further shore of Africa[4] is strewn
with the forked limbs of girls toasting their flesh
in scarves, sunglasses, Pompeian bikinis,[5]

brown daphnes,[6] laurels, they'll all have
like their originals, their sacred grove,   20

1. The tropical almond (also known as the Indian almond) is a tree that bears a fleshy fruit with a kernel that has some resemblance to the temperate variety. It denotes here a sense of place, the poet's rootedness in the resilience and enduring quality of his people.
2. I.e., one marked by monuments and a sense of achievement. This negative view of the Caribbean was first put forward by the English historian James Anthony Froude (1818–1894) and later echoed by the Caribbean novelist V. S. Naipaul (born 1932). The reprise of the phrase as a quotation eight lines further draws attention to these sources.
3. The trees have assimilated to the fauna and flora as elements of a common landscape of experience. The idea, restated in line 33, governs the poem's theme and imagery.
4. The Caribbean as an extension of Africa in terms of climate, natural environment, ethnic composition, and, ultimately, forms of cultural expression.
5. The scantily clad girls evoke the liberal lifestyle for which the ancient Roman city of Pompeii was famous. Pompeii was destroyed in 63 by volcanic lava from the eruption of the Mount Vesuvius.
6. The immediate reference is to the laurel tree. It also refers to the Greek myth of the nymph Daphne, who was turned into a laurel while fleeing from Apollo.

this frieze
of twisted, coppery, sea-almond trees.

The fierce acetylene[7] air
has singed
their writhing trunks with rust, the same   25
hues as a foundered, peeling barge.
It'll sear a pale skin copper with its flame.

The sand's white-hot ash underheel,
but their aged limbs have got their brazen sheen
from fire. Their bodies fiercely shine!   30
They're cured,
they endured their furnace.[8]

Aged trees and oiled limbs share a common colour!

Welded in one flame,
huddling naked, stripped of their name,   35
for Greek or Roman tags,[9] they were lashed
raw by wind, washed
out with salt and fire-dried,
bitterly nourished where their branches died,

their leaves' broad dialect[1] a coarse,   40
enduring sound
they shared together.

Not as some running hamadryad's[2] cries
rooted, broke slowly into leaf
her nipples peaking to smooth, wooden boles   45

Their grief[3]
howls seaward through charred, ravaged holes.

One sunburnt body now acknowledges
that past and its own metamorphosis
as, moving from the sun, she kneels to spread   50
her wrap within the beat arms of this grove
that grieves in silence,[4] like parental love.[5]

1965

---

7. A gas-fired flame used to soften metal.
8. I.e., the furnace of history. The black
people are represented as having gone through
a trial by fire, becoming tempered like steel.
9. Slaves were often given classical names by
their owners.
1. The language and expressive culture of a

new, distinctive community that has emerged
from a common history.
2. A nymph who lives in a tree.
3. The pathos of the slave experience.
4. I.e., that grieves not so much in resignation
as in forgiveness.
5. A love marked by tolerance and understanding.

Crusoe's Journal

I looked now upon the world as a thing remote, which I
had nothing to do with, no expectation from, and, indeed,
no desires about. In a word, I had nothing indeed
to do with it, nor was ever like to have; so I thought
it looked as we may perhaps look upon it hereafter,
viz., as a place I had lived in but was come out
of it; and well might I say, as Father Abraham
to Dives, "Between me and thee is a great gulf fixed."

—ROBINSON CRUSOE[1]

Once we have driven past Mundo Nuevo[2] trace
    safely to this beach house
perched between ocean and green, churning forest
    the intellect appraises
objects surely, even the bare necessities   5
    of style are turned to use,
like those plain iron tools he salvages
    from shipwreck,[3] hewing a prose
as odorous as raw wood to the adze;[4]
    out of such timbers   10
came our first book, our profane Genesis[5]
    whose Adam speaks that prose
which, blessing some sea-rock, startles itself
    with poetry's surprise,
in a green world, one without metaphors;   15
    like Christofer[6] he bears
in speech mnemonic[7] as a missionary's
    the Word to savages,
its shape an earthen, water-bearing vessel's
    whose sprinkling alters us   20
into good Fridays[8] who recite His praise,
    parroting our master's
style and voice, we make his language ours,
    converted cannibals
we learn with him to eat the flesh of Christ[9]   25

1. The epigraph from Daniel Defoe's (1660–1731) novel captures the Western frame of mind, a rational approach that establishes a rigorous separation between consciousness and the world of experience.
2. A route in Trinidad that leads to the house that Walcott is describing.
3. Apart from the reference to the Crusoe story, this is also a metaphor for the historical experience of slavery.
4. Sharp tool like a small ax used for carving wood.
5. The first book of the Judeo-Christian Bible containing the story of the world's creation and of Adam, the first man who was entrusted by God to name the objects of the world.
6. I.e., Christopher Columbus (1451–1506), acknowledged as the first European to encounter the New World.
7. Aiding memory.
8. Defoe's hero, Robinson Crusoe, gave the name Friday to the indigenous man he captured and made his manservant on the island. Note the punning allusion to the Christian observation of the Crucifixion of Christ.
9. In the Catholic doctrine of transubstantiation, the bread eaten at the Sacrament of Communion was deemed to be the body of Christ.

All shapes, all objects multiplied from his,
   our ocean's Proteus,[1]
in childhood, his derelict's old age
    was like a god's. (Now pass
in memory, in serene parenthesis,   30
    the cliff-deep leeward coast
of my own island filing past the noise
    of stuttering canvas,[2]
some noon-struck village, Choiseul, Canaries,[3]
    crouched crocodile canoes,   35
a savage settlement from Henty's novels,
    Marryat or R.L.S.[4]
with one boy signalling at the sea's edge,
    though what he cried is lost.)
So time, that makes us objects, multiplies   40
   our natural loneliness.

For the hermetic skill,[5] that from earth's clays
    shapes something without use,
and, separate from itself, lives somewhere else,[6]
    sharing with every beach   45
a longing for those gulls that cloud the cays[7]
    with raw, mimetic cries,
never surrenders wholly, for it knows
    it needs another's praise
like hoar, half-cracked Ben Gunn,[8] until it cries   50
    at last, "O happy desert!"
and learns again the self-creating peace
    of islands. So from this house
that faces nothing but the sea, his journals
    assume a household use;   55
we learn to shape from them, where nothing was
    the language of a race,[9]
and since the intellect demands its mask
    that sun-cracked, bearded face[1]
provides us with the wish to dramatize   60
    ourselves at nature's cost,

1. The Greek sea god who had the power of changing into various forms.
2. The Caribbean landscape envisioned as a work of art.
3. Villages in St. Lucia.
4. The works of Henty, Marryat, and R.L.S. were staples of colonial education throughout the former British Empire. George Alfred Henty (1832–1902) was a prolific writer of children's stories; Frederick Marryat (1792–1848) was an officer of the British navy who wrote a series of sea novels, of which the best known is *Mr. Midshipman Easy*; Robert Louis Stevenson (1850–1894) is renowned for his classic novel of adventure *Treasure Island*.

5. Poetry, which is sometimes regarded as a form of prophecy or divination. As an art form, it has no practical purpose ("without use") since its aesthetic significance is an end in itself.
6. In another dimension.
7. Inlets into the sea.
8. A character in Stevenson's *Treasure Island*. He had been marooned on the island and was found by the party of treasure seekers.
9. Like Crusoe, the inhabitants of the Caribbean have created a new culture out of the debris of their historical experience.
1. The physical outward aspect expressive of an inward attitude of stern resolution.

to attempt a beard, to squint through the sea-haze,
    posing as naturalists,
drunks, castaways, beachcombers, all of us
    yearn for those fantasies   65
of innocence,[2] for our faith's arrested phase
    when the clear voice
startled itself saying "water, heaven, Christ,"
    hoarding such heresies[3] as
God's loneliness moves in His smallest creatures.   70

                                      1965

Verandah

[for Ronald Bryden][1]

Grey apparitions[2] at verandah ends
like smoke,[3] divisible, but one
your age is ashes, its coherence gone,

Planters[4] whose tears were marketable gum,[5] whose voices
scratch the twilight like dried fronds   5
edged with reflection,

Colonels, hard as the commonwealth's greenheart,
middlemen, usurers whose art
kept an empire in the red,[6]

Upholders of Victoria's china seas[7]
lapping embossed around a drinking mug,   10
bully-boy roarers[8] of the empire club,

To the tarantara of the bugler, the sunset furled
round the last post,
the "flamingo colours"[9] of a fading world,

2. As of Eden, of new beginnings.
3. The pantheism given expression in the final line.

1. As literary editor of the Royal Shakespeare Company, he commissioned Walcott's *The Joker of Seville.*
2. Ghosts of the imperial past.
3. Insubstantial.
4. The term for white settlers in the West Indies who owned sugar plantations worked by slaves.
5. A pun on "medicinible gum" from Shakespeare's *Othello,* 5.2.360.

6. An allusion to the violent repression of colonized populations by the various imperial agents mentioned in the stanza.
7. Possibly an allusion to the attempt by the British to annex China and to the Opium Wars of 1839–1842 that resulted. "Victoria": queen of England from 1837 to 1901.
8. Pun on bullroarers, indigenous instruments that make a frightening sound.
9. The pageantry of empire exemplified by the ceremonial lowering of the flag at sunset to the sound of the bugle, a ritual that, ironically, anticipates the decline of empire ("fading world").

A ghost steps from you, my grandfather's ghost![1]
Uprooted from some rainy English shire,   15
you sought your Roman

End in suicide by fire.[2]
Your mixed son gathered your charred blackened bones
in a child's coffin.

And buried them himself on a strange coast.   20
Sire,
why do I raise you up? Because

Your house has voices, your burnt house
shrills with unguessed, lovely inheritors,[3]
your genealogical roof tree, fallen, survives,   25
like seasoned timber through green, little lives.

I ripen towards your twilight, sir, that dream
where I am singed in that sea-crossing, steam
towards that vaporous world, whose souls,

Like pressured trees, brought diamonds out of coals.[4]   30
The sparks pitched from your burning house are stars.
I am the man my father loved and was.

I climb the stair
and stretch a darkening hand to greet those friends[5]
who share with you the last inheritance   35
of earth, our shrine and pardoner,

grey, ghostly loungers at verandah ends.

                                                         1965

Elegy[1]

Our hammock swung between Americas,[2]
we miss you, Liberty. Che's

---

1. The poet is of English ancestry on his
father's side.
2. In contrast to the Roman habit of falling
on one's sword.
3. The black and mulatto children are the
unlikely continuators of the white grandfather's ancestral line, which they rejuvenate
("green, little lives," line 26).
4. Of the same chemical composition and
evolving into diamonds under intense pressure
over time.

5. Portraits of those who have passed away
and now form part of the general life of the
earth ("our shrine," line 36).
1. Since the date of composition at the end of
the poem indicates that it was written shortly
after the assassination of Robert Kennedy in
1968, the poem can be taken as an elegy to
him, even though he is not mentioned in it.
2. A reference to the Caribbean, which is
between North and South America.

bullet-riddled body falls,[3]
and those who cried, the Republic must first die
to be reborn, are dead,   5
the freeborn citizen's ballot in the head.[4]
Still, everybody wants to go to bed
with Miss America.[5] And, if there's no bread,
let them eat cherry pie,[6]

But the old choice of running, howling, wounded   10
wolf-deep in her woods,
while the white papers snow on
genocide is gone;
no face can hide
its public, private pain,   15
wincing, already statued.[7]

Some splintered arrowhead lodged in her brain
sets the black singer howling in his bear trap,
shines young eyes with the brightness of the mad,
tires the old with her residual sadness;   20
and yearly lilacs in her dooryards bloom,[8]
and the cherry orchard's surf
blinds Washington[9] and whispers
to the assassin in his furnished room[1]
of an ideal America, whose flickering screens   25
show, in slow herds, the ghosts of the Cheyennes[2]
scuffling across the staked and wired plains
with whispering, rag-bound feet,

while the farm couple framed in their Gothic door[3]
like Calvin's saints,[4] waspish, pragmatic, poor,   30

---

3. Ernesto (Che) Guevara (1928–1967) was a companion of Fidel Castro who was killed by government forces in Colombia, where he had gone to lead a revolutionary movement.
4. The bullet rather than the ballot as a political weapon; a commentary on the peculiar strain of violence in American life.
5. The winner of the popular annual beauty pageant, she is considered the ideal American beauty. Walcott uses the pageant as a symbol of popular culture in the United States.
6. Ironic echo, in pointedly American terms, of the French queen Marie Antoinette's celebrated phrase "Let them eat cake" in response to the clamor that arose from the populace for bread during the French Revolution. The expression has since been taken as a reflection of the insensitiveness of the privileged to the plight of the poor.
7. Open to public gaze.
8. An allusion to the opening lines of the famous elegy by Walt Whitman (1819–1892)

to U.S. president Abraham Lincoln (1809–1865), assassinated shortly after the end of the Civil War.
9. A reference to the white flowers of the cherry orchards in Washington, D.C., which burst into bloom early in the spring.
1. Suggesting the assassin is untroubled by his crime.
2. A Native American nation that was forced to migrate from Minnesota to the Platte River.
3. A reference to *American Gothic* (1930), a painting by Iowa Regionalist Grant Wood (1892–1942) that shows in sharp, cold detail a severe-looking farm couple standing in front of their barn, she looking slightly sideways at him, he looking directly at the viewer.
4. Puritans, followers of John Calvin (1509–1564), the Protestant reformer whose doctrine of predestination is considered by other Christian sects too rigid and dogmatic. The passage relies for its meaning on this view of the doctrine.

gripping the devil's pitchfork
stare rigidly towards the immortal wheat.

6 June 1968   1968

The Sea Is History

Where are your monuments, your battles, martyrs?
Where is your tribal memory? Sirs,
in that gray vault. The sea. The sea
has locked them up. The sea is History.

First, there was the heaving oil,   5
heavy as chaos;
then, like a light at the end of a tunnel,

the lantern of a caravel,
and that was Genesis.
Then there were the packed cries,   10
the shit, the moaning:

Exodus.[1]
Bone soldered by coral to bone,
mosaics
mantled by the benediction of the shark's shadow,   15
that was the Ark of the Covenant.[2]
Then came from the plucked wires
of sunlight on the sea floor

the plangent[3] harps of the Babylonian bondage,[4]
as the white cowries[5] clustered like manacles   20
on the drowned women,

and those were the ivory bracelets
of the Song of Solomon,[6]
but the ocean kept turning blank pages

looking for History.   25
Then came the men with eyes heavy as anchors
who sank without tombs,

1. Into exile in the New World, as opposed to the exodus of the Jews, under the leadership of Moses, out of bondage in Egypt.
2. Noah, whose ark survived the Flood, was given the rainbow as a sign of assurance that the earth would never again be destroyed by water.
3. Pouring out in waves of sound.
4. Which occurred between the fall of Jerusalem in 586 B.C. and the restoration of worship there by the decree of Cyrus the Great in 538 B.C.
5. Seashells that used to serve as currency in pre-colonial West Africa. They were also used in divination.
6. A book in the Old Testament that is a collection of love poems; it is generally thought to be an allegory of God's love for Israel.

brigands who barbecued cattle,
leaving their charred ribs like palm leaves on the shore,
then the foaming, rabid maw   30

of the tidal wave swallowing Port Royal,[7]
and that was Jonah,[8]
but where is your Renaissance?

Sir, it is locked in them sea sands
out there past the reef's moiling shelf,[9]   35
where the men-o'-war floated down;

strop[1] on these goggles, I'll guide you there myself.
It's all subtle and submarine,
through colonnades of coral,

past the gothic windows of sea fans   40
to where the crusty grouper,[2] onyx[3]-eyed,
blinks, weighted by its jewels, like a bald queen;

and these groined caves with barnacles
pitted like stone
are our cathedrals,   45

and the furnace before the hurricanes:
Gomorrah.[4] Bones ground by windmills
into marl[5] and cornmeal,

and that was Lamentations[6]—
that was just Lamentations,   50
it was not History;

then came, like scum on the river's drying lip,
the brown reeds of villages
mantling[7] and congealing into towns,

and at evening, the midges[8] choirs,   55
and above them, the spires
lancing the side of God[9]

7. The former capital of Jamaica, destroyed in 1692 by an earthquake, during which most of the city sank into the sea.
8. In the Old Testament, the man who lived in the belly of a whale for three days and nights before being disgorged alive.
9. "Shelf" here suggests the continental shelf, *the relatively shallow stretch of coastal land* ending in a sharp dip to the deep seabed. "Moiling": turbulent.
1. Strap (dialect).
2. A species of fish.
3. A highly valued gem, usually jet black.

4. A city often associated with Sodom, both synonymous with sin.
5. Finely ground sand.
6. Songs in the Old Testament by the prophet Jeremiah, lamenting the fall of Jerusalem.
7. A reference to Shakespeare's *The Tempest*, where "mantling" apparently describes the scummy covering of the shore.
8. Small insects, chirping in chorus.
9. An allusion to the Roman soldier's piercing the side of the crucified Jesus to ascertain whether he was dead or not (see "His son set" in the following line).

as His son set, and that was the New Testament.

Then came the white sisters clapping
to the waves' progress,   60
and that was Emancipation[1]—

jubilation, O jubilation—
vanishing swiftly
as the sea's lace dries in the sun,

but that was not History,
that was only faith,   65
and then each rock broke into its own nation;[2]

then came the synod of flies,
then came the secretarial heron,
then came the bullfrog bellowing for a vote,   70

fireflies with bright ideas
and bats like jetting ambassadors
and the mantis,[3] like khaki police,

and the furred caterpillars of judges[4]
examining each case closely,   75
and then in the dark ears of ferns

and in the salt chuckle of rocks
with their sea pools, there was the sound
like a rumor without any echo

of History, really beginning.   80

1979

North and South

Now, at the rising of Venus[1]—the steady star
that survives translation, if one can call this lamp
the planet that pierces us over indigo islands—
despite the critical sand flies, I accept my function
as a colonial upstart at the end of an empire,   5
a single, circling, homeless satellite.
I can listen to its guttural death rattle in the shoal

1. Which, in the British West Indies, occurred
in 1834.
2. A reference to the breakup of the West
Indian Federation in 1962. The next two stanzas describe the ensuing confusion in the
political life of the West Indies.
3. The characteristic posture of the praying

mantis is generally interpreted as a demonstration of hypocrisy.
4. A reference to the dress of judges in formal
sessions.
1. The morning star, the brightest in the solar
system.

of the legions' withdrawing roar, from the raj,[2]
from the Reich,[3] and see the full moon again
like a white flag rising over Fort Charlotte,[4]   10
and sunset slowly collapsing like the flag.[5]

It's good that everything's gone, except their language,[6]
which is everything. And it may be a childish revenge
at the presumption of empires to hear the worm
gnawing their solemn columns into coral,   15
to snorkel over Atlantis,[7] to see, through a mask,
Sidon up to its windows in sand, Tyre, Alexandria,[8]
with their wavering seaweed spires through a glass-bottom boat,
and to buy porous fragments of the Parthenon[9]
from a fisherman in Tobago,[1] but the fear exists,   20
Delenda est Carthago[2] on the rose horizon,[3]

and the side streets of Manhattan are sown with salt,[4]
as those in the North all wait for that white glare
of the white rose of inferno,[5] all the world's capitals.
Here, in Manhattan, I lead a tight life   25
and a cold one, my soles stiffen with ice
even through woollen socks; in the fenced back yard,
trees with clenched teeth endure the wind of February,
and I have some friends under its iron ground.
Even when spring comes with its rain of nails,   30
with its soiled ice oozing into black puddles,
the world will be one season older but no wiser.

Fragments of paper swirl round the bronze general
of Sheridan Square,[6] syllables of Nordic tongues
(as an Obeah priestess[7] sprinkles flour on the doorstep   35
to ward off evil, so Carthage was sown with salt);
the flakes are falling like a common language
on my nose and lips, and rime forms on the mouth

---

2. Term for British rule in India.
3. German word for "empire," associated with Adolf Hitler's Third Reich and his ambitions for the German people to rule over the rest of the world.
4. On the West Indian island of St. Vincent.
5. The flag is lowered at sunset.
6. I.e., English, valued by the poet as a positive inheritance of British colonial rule.
7. In Greek mythology, a fabled island situated in the Atlantic Ocean off the southwestern coast of Spain.
8. Great centers of ancient civilization.
9. The temple of Athena built in the 5th century B.C.E. on the summit of the Acropolis in Athens.
1. An English-speaking Caribbean island federated with Trinidad, just to its north.

2. "Carthage must be destroyed," words attributed to the Roman Senator Marcus Porcius Cato (234–149 B.C.E.), who was so obsessed with the threat of this African state to Rome that he used the phrase to conclude every speech he gave in the Roman Senate.
3. Homeric epithet for dawn.
4. The salt is used to melt the snow in winter, but there is a suggestion of sterility.
5. A species of the begonia flower that comes into full bloom in the spring.
6. The statue of General Philip Sheridan in Christopher Park, in Greenwich Village, New York, not far from the square named after him. Sheridan (1831–1888) was a Union general during the Civil War (see line 41) and later became commander in chief of the U.S. Army.
7. African-derived religion in the West Indies.

of a shivering exile from his African province;
a blizzard of moths whirls around the extinguished lamp   40
of the Union general, sugary insects crunched underfoot.

You move along dark afternoons where death
entered a taxi and sat next to a friend,
or passed another a razor, or whispered "Pardon"
in a check-clothed restaurant behind her cough—   45
I am thinking of an exile farther than any country.
And, in this heart of darkness,[8] I cannot believe
they are now talking over palings by the doddering
banana fences,[9] or that seas can be warm.

How far I am from those cacophonous seaports   50
built round the single exclamation of one statue
of Victoria Regina![1] There vultures shift on the roof
of the red iron market, whose patois[2]
is brittle as slate, a gray stone flecked with quartz.
I prefer the salt freshness of that ignorance,   55
as language crusts and blackens on the pots
of this cooked culture, coming from a raw one;
and these days in bookstores I stand paralyzed

by the rows of shelves along whose wooden branches
the free-verse nightingales are trilling "Read me! Read me!"   60
in various metres of asthmatic pain;
or I shiver before the bellowing behemoths
with the snow still falling in white words on Eighth Street,
those burly minds that barrelled through contradictions
like a boar through bracken, or an old tarpon[3]   65
bristling with broken hooks, or an old stag
spanielled[4] by critics to a crag at twilight,

the exclamation of its antlers like a hat rack
on which they hang their theses. I am tired of words,
and literature is an old couch stuffed with fleas,   70
of culture stuffed in the taxidermist's hides.
I think of Europe as a gutter of autumn leaves
choked like the thoughts in an old woman's throat.
But she was home to some consul in snow-white ducks[5]

8. An image of Africa used in Joseph Conrad's
novel of the same name. It implies alienation
in a foreign land and applies here to the poet's
despondent mood in New York in winter.
9. These separate the homesteads in the
poet's native island. He feels so removed from
its human atmosphere and landscape—its
warmth—that it now seems to him unimaginable.
1. Queen Victoria, proclaimed empress of
India in 1877, came to embody the British
empire during her long reign.

2. A French term for a local dialect. It refers
here to the form of French pidgin spoken in
St. Lucia.
3. A large fish found in the warm waters of
the Caribbean. Since it is difficult to catch, it
is considered a rare prize among game fishermen and women.
4. The critics are like spaniels, fawning and
obsequious.
5. Trousers of light white flannel worn by
colonial officers in the tropics.

doing out his service in the African provinces,   75
who wrote letters like this one home and feared malaria
as I mistrust the dark snow, who saw the lances of rain

marching like a Roman legion over the fens.
So, once again, when life has turned into exile,
and nothing consoles, not books, work, music, or a woman,   80
and I am tired of trampling the brown grass,
whose name I don't know, down an alley of stone,
and I must turn back to the road, its winter traffic,
and others sure in the dark of their direction,
I lie under a blanket on a cold couch,   85
feeling the flu in my bones like a lantern.

Under the blue sky of winter in Virginia
the brick chimneys flute white smoke through skeletal lindens,[6]
as a spaniel churns up a pyre of blood-rusted leaves;[7]
there is no memorial here to their Treblinka[8]—   90
as a van delivers from the ovens loaves
as warm as flesh, its brakes jaggedly screech
like the square wheel of a swastika.[9] The mania
of history veils even the clearest air,
the sickly-sweet taste of ash, of something burning.   95

And when one encounters the slow coil of an accent,[1]
reflexes step aside as if for a snake,
with the paranoid anxiety of the victim.
The ghosts of white-robed horsemen[2] float through the trees,
the galloping hysterical abhorrence of my race—   100
like any child of the Diaspora,[3] I remember this
even as the flakes whiten Sheridan's shoulders,
and I remember once looking at my aunt's face,
the wintry blue eyes, the rusty hair, and thinking

maybe we are part Jewish, and felt a vein   105
run through this earth and clench itself like a fist
around an ancient root, and wanted the privilege
to be yet another of the races they fear and hate
instead of one of the haters and the afraid.
Above the spiny woods, dun[4] grass, skeletal trees,   110

---

6. Also known as basswood, this tree has romantic associations.
7. Note the grim associations of the imagery.
8. A Nazi concentration camp in Poland where many people—especially Jews—perished. The five lines that follow develop the theme of the Holocaust introduced by this reference.
9. Symbol of the Nazis in the form of a Greek cross, the end of its arms extended at right angles all going in the same direction.

1. That is, the Southern accent, which sets off a cautious reflex in the poet due to its association with hatred for black people.
2. Members of the Ku Klux Klan. They would terrorize black people by, among other things, lynching them by hanging them on trees.
3. An ethnic or national community separated from its original homeland.
4. Light brown in color.

the chimney serenely fluting something from Schubert[5]—
like the wraith of smoke that comes from someone burning—
veins the air with an outcry that I cannot help.

The winter branches are mined with buds,
the fields of March will detonate the crocus,[6]   115
the olive[7] battalions of the summer woods
will shout orders back to the wind. To the soldier's mind
the season's passage round the pole is martial,
the massacres of autumn sheeted in snow, as
winter turns white as a veterans hospital.   120
Something quivers in the blood beyond control—
something deeper than our transient fevers.

But in Virginia's woods there is also an old man
dressed like a tramp in an old Union greatcoat,
walking to the music of rustling leaves, and when   125
I collect my change from a small-town pharmacy,
the cashier's fingertips still wince from my hand
as if it would singe hers—well, yes, *je suis un singe*,[8]
I am one of that tribe of frenetic or melancholy
primates who made your music[9] for many more moons   130
than all the silver quarters in the till.

                                                                   1981

Sea Cranes[1]

"Only in a world where there are cranes and horses,"
wrote Robert Graves,[2] "can poetry survive."
Or adept goats on crags. Epic
follows the plough, metre the ring of the anvil;
prophecy divines the figurations of storks,[3] and awe   5
the arc of the stallion's neck.[4]

The flame has left the charred wick of the cypress;
the light will catch these islands in their turn.[5]

---

5. Franz Schubert (1797–1828) was a German
Romantic composer. Overseers at the Nazi
death camps often played classical music while
Jews were gassed and their bodies cremated.
6. The crocus puts out its white flowers in
late winter and very early spring.
7. Here, a reference to the olive drab uniforms worn by the U.S. Army.
8. "I am a monkey" (French).
9. Of poetry, nobler than the ring of coins in
the shopkeeper's till.
1. Tall wading birds with white plumage and
long legs.

2. Graves (1895–1985), an English writer who
first gained attention as a poet, also wrote an
autobiography, nonfiction, essays, and a series
of historical novels based in antiquity. He is the
author of the two-volume *The Greek Myths*, in
which he not only retells the tales of the Greek
gods and heroes, but reinterprets them.
3. Ancient diviners claimed to be able to read
the future from the entrails of birds.
4. Apart from its beauty, the stallion is a symbol of elemental force.
5. The islands destined for glory.

Magnificent frigates inaugurate the dusk
that flashes through the whisking tails of horses,   10
the stony fields they graze.
From the hammered anvil of the promontory
the spray settles in stars.[6]

Generous ocean,[7] turn the wanderer
from his salt sheets, the prodigal   15
drawn to the deep troughs of the swine-black porpoise.[8]

Wrench his heart's wheel and set his forehead here.[9]

                                                                    1981

OMEROS

From Book One

From *Chapter I*

II

Achille looked up at the hole[1] the laurel had left.
He saw the hole silently healing with the foam
of a cloud like a breaker. Then he saw the swift[2]

crossing the cloud-surf, a small thing, far from its home,
confused by the waves of blue hills. A thorn vine gripped   5
his heel. He tugged it free. Around him, other ships

were shaping from the saw. With his cutlass he made
a swift sign of the cross, his thumb touching his lips
while the height rang with axes. He swayed back the blade,

and hacked the limbs from the dead god,[3] knot after knot,   10
wrenching the severed veins from the trunk as he prayed:
"Tree! You can be a canoe! Or else you cannot!"

The bearded elders endured the decimation
of their tribe without uttering a syllable
of the language they had uttered as one nation,[4]   15

---

6. The sea spray linking earth and sky.
7. In the sense of being large, copious, and
bountiful.
8. A small, gregarious toothed whale with
black skin and white underbelly.
9. That is, facing homeward.
1. The opening stanza describes the ritual felling of a laurel tree from which a dugout canoe

is to be made. This refers to the hole in the
ground where the tree had stood. The section
that follows describes the making of the canoe.
2. A small, plainly colored bird, related to the
swallow, that serves as a guide to the wandering hero.
3. The laurel tree, venerated as nature.
4. The flora as part of the total living environment.

the speech taught their saplings: from the towering babble
of the cedar to green vowels of *bois-campêche*.
The *bois-flot* held its tongue with the *laurier-cannelle*,[5]

the red-skinned logwood endured the thorns in its flesh,
while the Aruacs' patois[6] crackled in the smell   20
of a resinous bonfire that turned the leaves brown

with curling tongues, then ash, and their language was lost.
Like barbarians striding columns they have brought down,
the fishermen shouted. The gods were down at last.

Like pygmies they hacked the trunks of wrinkled giants   25
for paddles and oars. They were working with the same
concentration as an army of fire-ants.[7]

But vexed by the smoke for defaming their forest,
blow-darts of mosquitoes kept needling Achille's trunk.
He frotted white rum on both forearms that, at least,   30

those that he flattened to asterisks would die drunk.
They went for his eyes. They circled them with attacks
that made him weep blindly. Then the host retreated

to high bamboo like the archers of Aruacs
running from the muskets of cracking logs,[8] routed   35
by the fire's banner and the remorseless axe

hacking the branches. The men bound the big logs first
with new hemp[9] and, like ants, trundled them to a cliff
to plunge through tall nettles.[1] The logs gathered that thirst

for the sea which their own vined bodies were born with.   40
Now the trunks in eagerness to become canoes
ploughed into breakers of bushes, making raw holes

of boulders, feeling not death inside them, but use—
to roof the sea, to be hulls. Then, on the beach, coals[2]
were set in their hollows that were chipped with an adze.   45

A flat-bed truck had carried their rope-bound bodies.
The charcoals, smouldering, cored the dugouts for days
till heat widened the wood enough for ribbed gunwales.[3]

---

5. *Bois-campêche, bois-flot, laurier-cannelle*:
French for logwood, timber, and laurel,
respectively.
6. Dialect. "Aruacs": the original inhabitants
of the Caribbean; also Arawaks.
7. Omnivorous ants with powerful stingers in
their tails.
8. Log houses from which white men shot at
the Aruacs.
9. The vine is excellent for making ropes.
1. A plant that stings.
2. They are used to fire the hollowed-out logs.
3. That is, the heat expanded the wood so
that metal strips could be inserted to reinforce
the sides of the boat.

Under his tapping chisel Achille felt their hollows
exhaling to touch the sea, lunging towards the haze   50
of bird-printed islets, the beaks of their parted bows.

Then everything fit. The pirogues[4] crouched on the sand
like hounds with sprigs in their teeth. The priest
sprinkled them with a bell, then he made the swift's sign.[5]

When he smiled at Achille's canoe, *In God We Troust,*[6]   55
Achille said: "Leave it! Is God' spelling and mine."
After Mass one sunrise the canoes entered the troughs[7]

of the surpliced[8] shallows, and their nodding prows
agreed with the waves to forget their lives as trees;
one would serve Hector and another, Achilles.   60

From *Chapter VIII*

I

In the islet's museum there is a twisted
wine-bottle, crusted with fool's gold[1] from the iron-
cold depth below the redoubt. It has been listed

variously by experts; one, that a galleon
blown by a hurricane out of Cartagena,[2]   5
this far east, had bled a trail of gold bullion

and wine from its hold (a view held by many a
diver lowering himself); the other was nonsense
and far too simple: that the gold-crusted bottle

came from a flagship in the Battle of the Saints,[3]   10
but the glass was so crusted it was hard to tell.
Still, the myth widened its rings every century:[4]

that the *Ville de Paris*[5] sank there, not a galleon
crammed with imperial coin, and for her sentry,
an octopus-cyclops,[6] its one eye like the moon.   15

---

4. French for dugout canoes.
5. The swift's wings are shaped like a cross.
6. The boat's name. The phrase "In God We Trust" is found on American money.
7. Sea channels.
8. The canoes make a lacelike pattern on the water, resembling the surplice worn by Catholic priests at Mass.
1. Pyrite or, by extension, any pyritic material that resembles gold.
2. I.e., Cartagena, a seaport on the northwest coast of Colombia.
3. Naval battle fought off the coast of Martin-

ique on April 12, 1782, between the French fleet commanded by Admiral de Grasset and a British fleet under Admiral Sir George Bridges Rodney. The French were routed, their fleet annihilated.
4. Like rings on a tree as it ages.
5. The flagship of the French fleet.
6. Here Walcott conflates an octopus—a mollusk that has eight arms, each with two rows of suckers—with Greek mythology's Cyclops, a one-eyed giant who, in Homer's *Odyssey*, holds Odysseus and his men captive until they escape by blinding him.

Deep as a diver's faith but never discovered,
their trust in the relic converted the village,
who came to believe that circling frigates hovered

over the relic, that gulls attacked them in rage.
They kept their faith when the experts' ended in doubt.   20
The galleon's shadow rode over the ruled page

where Achille, rough weather coming, counted his debt
by the wick of his kerosene lamp; the dark ship
divided his dreams, while the moon's octopus eye

climbed from the palms that lifted their tentacles' shape.   25
It glared like a shilling.[7] Everything was money.
Money will change her, he thought. Is this bad living

that make her come wicked. He had mocked the belief
in a wrecked ship out there. Now he began diving
in a small shallop[8] beyond the line of the reef,   30

with spear-gun[9] and lobster-pot.[1] He had to make sure
no sail would surprise him, feathering the oars back
without clicking the oarlocks. He fed the anchor

carefully overside. He tied the cinder-block
to one heel with a slip-knot[2] for faster descent,   35
then slipped the waterproof bag around his shoulders

for a money-pouch. She go get every red cent,
he swore, crossing himself as he dived. Wedged in boulders
down there was salvation and change. The concrete, tied

to his heel, pulled him down faster than a lead-   40
weighted, canvas-bound carcass, the stone heart inside
his chest added its poundage. What if love was dead

inside her already? What good lay in pouring
silver coins on a belly that had warmed him once?
This weighed him down even more, so he kept falling   45

for fathoms towards his fortune: moidores, doubloons,[3]
while the slow-curling fingers of weeds kept calling;
he felt the cold of the drowned entering his loins.

---

7. An English coin worth one-twentieth of a pound. Its use was discontinued when Britain adopted the decimal currency in 1969.
8. A small boat (from French *chaloupe*).
9. A gun that has a forked end on which fish are speared.

1. A basket for trapping lobsters.
2. A knot that moves along the rope on which it is tied.
3. These are Portuguese and Spanish gold coins, respectively.

II

Why was he down here, from their coral palaces.
pope-headed turtles asked him, waving their paddles[4]
crusted with rings, nudged by curious porpoises   50

with black friendly skins. Why? asked the glass sea-horses,[5]
curling like questions. What on earth had he come for,
when he had a good life up there? The sea-mosses[6]

shook their beards angrily, like submarine cedars,   55
while he trod the dark water. Wasn't love worth more
than the coins of light pouring from the galleon's doors?

In the corals' bone kingdom his skin calcifies.[7]
In that wavering garden huge fans on hinges
swayed, while fingers of seaweed pocketed the eyes[8]   60

of coins with the profiles of Iberian kings;[9]
here the sea-floor was mud, not corrugating sand
that showed you its ribs; here, the mutating fishes

had goggling eye-bulbs; in that world without sound,
they sucked the white coral, draining it like leeches,   65
and what looked like boulders sprung the pincers of crabs.

This was not a world meant for the living, he thought.
The dead didn't need money, like him, but perhaps
they hated surrendering things their hands had brought.

The shreds of the ocean's floor passed him from corpses   70
that had perished in the crossing, their hair like weeds,
their bones were long coral fingers, bubbles of eyes

watched him, a brain-coral[1] gurgled their words,
and every bubble englobed a biography,
no less than the wine-bottle's mouth, but for Achille,   75

treading the mulch floor of the Caribbean Sea,
no coins were enough to repay its deep evil.
The ransom of centuries shone through the mossy doors

4. The turtles propel themselves using their
flippers as paddles.
5. Small bony fishes that have a horse-shaped
head and the body of a fish with a curved tail
(hence "curling like questions").
6. Any of certain frondlike red algae that look
like moss (and hence "shook their beards").

7. Hardens.
8. Here, covered completely.
9. Relating to Iberia, the peninsula made up
of Spain and Portugal.
1. A reef coral with its surface covered by
ridges and furrows.

that the moon-blind Cyclops counted, every tendril
raked in the guineas[2] it tested with its soft jaws.   80
Light paved the ceiling with silver with every swell.

Then he saw the galleon. Her swaying cabin-doors
fanned vaults of silvery mackerel. He caught the glint
of their coin-packed scales,[3] then the tentacle-shadows

whose motion was a miser's harvesting his mint.   85
He loosened the block[4] and shot up. Next day, her stealth
increased, her tentacles calling, until the wreck

vanished with all hope of Helen. Once more the whelk[5]
was his coin, his bank the sea-conch's.[6] Now, every day
he was clear-headed as the sea, wrenching lace fans   90

from the forbidden reef, or tailing a sting-ray[7]
floating like a crucifix when it sensed his lance,
and saving the conch-shells he himself had drowned.

And though he lost faith[8] in any fictional ship,
an anchor still forked his brow whenever he frowned,   95
for she was a spectre now, in her ribbed shape,

he did not know where she was. She'd never be found.
He thought of the white skulls rolling out there like dice
rolled by the hand of the swell, their luck was like his;

he saw drowned Portuguese captains, their coral eyes   100
entered by minnows,[9] as he hauled the lobster-pot,
bearded with moss, in the cold shade of the redoubt.[1]

From Book Three

Chapter XXV

I

Mangroves,[1] their ankles in water, walked with the canoe.
The swift, racing its browner shadow, screeched, then veered
into a dark inlet. It was the last sound Achille knew

---

2. English coins, supposedly struck from gold
from the Guinea coast in West Africa.
3. The fishes' scales are like silver coins.
4. Concrete (referred to in lines 39–42).
5. A large marine snail with a spiral shell.
6. A large spiral-shelled marine mollusk. Its
shell resonates when blown into; runaway slaves
often sent messages to each other this way.

7. A ray with a flat body and whiplike tail with
spines near its base capable of inflicting severe
wounds.
8. See line 16, above.
9. Tiny fish.
1. A small, usually temporary fort.
1. Tropical trees that grow in lagoons and
waterways.

from the other world. He feathered the paddle,[2] steered
away from the groping mangroves, whose muddy shelves   5
slipped warted crocodiles,[3] slitting the pods of their eyes;

then the horned river-horses[4] rolling over themselves
could capsize the keel. It was like the African movies
he had yelped at in childhood. The endless river unreeled

those images that flickered into real mirages: 10
naked mangroves walking beside him, knotted logs
wriggling into the water, the wet, yawning boulders

of oven-mouthed hippopotami. A skeletal[5] warrior
stood up straight in the stern and guided his shoulders,
clamped his neck in cold iron,[6] and altered the oar.   15

Achille wanted to scream, he wanted the brown water
to harden into a road, but the river widened ahead
and closed behind him. He heard screeching laughter

in a swaying tree, as monkeys swung from the rafter
of their tree-house, and the bared sound rotted the sky   20
like their teeth. For hours the river gave the same show

for nothing, the canoe's mouth muttered its lie.
The deepest terror was the mud. The mud with no shadow
like the clear sand. Then the river coiled into a bend.

He saw the first signs of men, tall sapling fishing-stakes;   25
he came into his own beginning and his end,
for the swiftness of a second is all that memory takes.

Now the strange, inimical river surrenders its stealth
to the sunlight. And a light inside him wakes,[7]
skipping centuries, ocean and river, and Time itself.   30

And God said to Achille, "Look, I giving you permission
to come home. Is I send the sea-swift as a pilot,
the swift whose wings is the sign of my crucifixion.

And thou shalt have no God should in case you forgot
my commandments." And Achille felt the homesick shame   35
and pain of his Africa. His heart and his bare head

2. Turned the oar so that it was horizontal when lifted from the water at the end of a stroke. This reduces air resistance.
3. The skin of the crocodiles seems to be covered with hardened protuberances.
4. I.e., hippopotami.

5. Here, ghostly, which is appropriate to the character of the passage as a dream sequence.
6. Reminiscent of the chains with which slaves were bound.
7. I.e., awakens ancestral memory.

were bursting as he tried to remember the name
of the river- and the tree-god in which he steered,
whose hollow body carried him to the settlement ahead.

II

He remembered this sunburnt river with its spindly   40
stakes and the peaked huts platformed above the spindles
where thin, naked figures as he rowed past looked unkindly

or kindly in their silence. The silence an old fence kindles
in a boy's heart. They walked with his homecoming
canoe past bonfires in a scorched clearing near the edge   45

of the soft-lipped shallows whose noise hurt his drumming
heart as the pirogue slid its raw, painted wedge
towards the crazed sticks of a vine-fastened pier.

The river was sloughing[8] its old skin like a snake
in wrinkling sunshine; the sun resumed its empire   50
over this branch of the Congo; the prow found its stake

in the river and nuzzled it the way that a piglet
finds its favourite dug[9] in the sweet-grunting sow,
and now each cheek ran with its own clear rivulet

of tears, as Achille, weeping, fastened the bow   55
of the dugout, wiped his eyes with one dry palm,
and felt a hard hand help him up the shaking pier.

Half of me was with him. One half with the midshipman
by a Dutch canal.[1] But now, neither was happier
or unhappier than the other. An old man put an arm   60

around Achille, and the crowd, chattering, followed both.
They touched his trousers, his undershirt, their hands
scrabbling[2] the texture, as a kitten does with cloth,

till they stood before an open hut. The sun stands
with expectant silence. The river stops talking,   65
the way silence sometimes suddenly turns off a market.

The wind squatted low in the grass. A man kept walking
steadily towards him, and he knew by that walk it
was himself in his father, the white teeth, the widening hands.

---

8. Shedding.
9. The nipple of a pig from which the young
suck milk.
1. Spoken in the author's own voice, this passage expresses the split in Walcott's heritage—
half African, half Dutch.
2. Scraping.

III

He sought his own features in those of their life-giver, 70
and saw two worlds mirrored there: the hair was surf
curling round a sea-rock, the forehead a frowning river,

as they swirled in the estuary of a bewildered love,
and Time stood between them. The only interpreter
of their lips' joined babble, the river with the foam, 75

and the chuckles of water under the sticks of the pier,
where the tribe stood like sticks themselves, reversed
by reflection.[3] Then they walked up to the settlement,

and it seemed, as they chattered, everything was rehearsed
for ages before this. He could predict the intent 80
of his father's gestures; he was moving with the dead.

Women paused at their work, then smiled at the warrior
returning from his battle with smoke,[4] from the kingdom
where he had been captured, they cried and were happy.

Then the fishermen sat near a large tree under whose dome 85
stones sat in a circle. His father said:
                              "Afo-la-be,"[5]
touching his own heart.
                    "In the place you have come from

what do they call you?"
                              Time translates. 90
                                    Tapping his chest,

the son answers:
                    "Achille." The tribe rustles, "Achille."
Then, like cedars at sunrise, the mutterings settle.

AFOLABE

Achille. What does the name mean? I have forgotten the one 95
that I gave you. But it was, it seems, many years ago.
What does it mean?

ACHILLE

                    Well, I too have forgotten.

Everything was forgotten. You also. I do not know.
The deaf sea has changed around every name that you gave 100
us; trees, men, we yearn for a sound that is missing.

3. Mirrored upside down in the river.   5. A Yoruba name meaning "born with honor."
4. Of an ordeal, in the dim past.

AFOLABE

A name means something.[6] The qualities desired in a son,
and even a girl-child; so even the shadows who called
you expected one virtue, since every name is a blessing,

since I am remembering the hope I had for you as a child.   105
Unless the sound means nothing. Then you would be nothing.
Did they think you were nothing in that other kingdom?[7]

ACHILLE

I do not know what the name means. It means something,
maybe. What's the difference? In the world I come from
we accept the sounds we were given. Men, trees, water.   110

AFOLABE

And therefore, Achille, if I pointed and I said, There
is the name of that man, that tree, and this father,
would every sound be a shadow that crossed your ear,

without the shape of a man or a tree? What would it be?
(And just as branches sway in the dusk from their fear   115
of amnesia,[8] of oblivion, the tribe began to grieve.)

ACHILLE

What would it be? I can only tell you what I believe,
or had to believe. It was prediction, and memory,
to bear myself back, to be carried here by a swift,

or the shadow of a swift making its cross on water,   120
with the same sign I was blessed with[9] with the gift
of this sound whose meaning I still do not care to know.

AFOLABE

No man loses his shadow except it is in the night,
and even then his shadow is hidden, not lost. At the glow
of sunrise, he stands on his own in that light.   125

When he walks down to the river with the other fishermen
his shadow stretches in the morning, and yawns, but you,
if you're content with not knowing what our names mean,

---

6. African names always have a meaning of
great social significance.
7. I.e., the New World.

8. Loss of memory.
9. Baptized as a Christian, with possibly a
pun on the French blessé, "wounded."

then I am not Afolabe, your father, and you look through
my body as the light looks through a leaf. I am not here   130
or a shadow. And you, nameless son, are only the ghost

of a name. Why did I never miss you until you returned?
Why haven't I missed you, my son, until you were lost?
Are you the smoke from a fire that never burned?

There was no answer to this, as in life.[1] Achille nodded,   135
the tears glazing his eyes, where the past was reflected
as well as the future. The white foam lowered its head.

From *Chapter XXVI*

I

In a language as brown[1] and leisurely as the river,
they muttered about a future Achille already knew
but which he could not reveal even to his breath-giver

or in the council of elders. But he learned to chew
in the ritual of the kola nut,[2] drain gourds of palm-wine,[3]   5
to listen to the moan of the tribe's triumphal sorrow

in a white-eyed storyteller[4] to a balaphon's whine,[5]
who perished in what battle, who was swift with the arrow,
who mated with a crocodile,[6] who entered a river-horse

and lived in its belly, who was the thunder's favourite,   10
who the serpent-god[7] conducted miles off his course
for some blasphemous offence and how he would pay for it

by forgetting his parents, his tribe, and his own spirit
for an albino god,[8] and how that warrior was scarred
for innumerable moons so badly that he would disinherit   15

himself. And every night the seed-eyed, tree-wrinkled[9] bard,
the crooked tree who carried the genealogical leaves[1]
of the tribe in his cave-throated moaning,

1. Which is filled with unresolved questions.
1. Muddy, alluvial, and therefore fertile.
2. The bitter, caffeine-laden seed of the kola
tree; it is chewed on ceremonial occasions.
3. The natural sap of the tropical palm, which,
when drawn, ferments and becomes alcoholic.
4. The bard, or griot, whose function was to preserve the community's history (see lines 16–20).
5. An African instrument with flat wooden
keys like the xylophone that is played to accompany the griot's narrative.
6. In myths, heroes were often said to descend
from mixed parentage of humans and animals;
in other instances, certain animals are held to
be ancestors or relatives of members of the
tribe and thus function as their totem.
7. The cult of the serpent is central to many
African religions and to their derivatives in the
New World.
8. Lacking in pigment, white, and therefore
an alien god.
9. Gaunt, like an old tree.
1. I.e., the leaves of the family tree.

traced the interlacing branches of their river-rooted lives
as intricately as the mangrove roots. Until morning   20
he sang, till the river was the only one to hear it.

Achille did not go down to the fishing stakes one dawn,
but left the hut door open, the hut he had been given
for himself and any woman he chose as his companion,

and he climbed a track of huge yams, to find that heaven   25
of soaring trees, that sacred circle of clear ground
where the gods assembled. He stood in the clearing

and recited the gods' names. The trees within hearing
ignored his incantation. He heard only the cool sound
of the river. He saw a tree-hole, raw in the uprooted ground.[2]   30

*   *   *

III

He walked the ribbed sand under the flat keels of whales,
under the translucent belly of the snaking current,
the tiny shadows of tankers passed over him like snails

as he breathed water, a walking fish in its element.
He floated in stride, his own shadow over his eyes   35
like a grazing shark, through vast meadows of coral,

over barnacled[3] cannons whose hulks sprouted anemones[4]
like Philoctete's shin; he walked for three hundred years
in the silken wake like a ribbon of the galleons,

their bubbles fading like the transparent men-o'-wars   40
with their lilac dangling tendrils, bursting like aeons,[5]
like phosphorous galaxies; he saw the huge cemeteries

of bone and the huge crossbows of the rusted anchors,
and groves of coral with hands as massive as trees
like calcified ferns and the greening gold ingots of bars   45

whose value had outlasted that of the privateers.[6]
Then, one afternoon, the ocean lowered and clarified
its ceiling, its emerald net, and after three centuries

2. See n. 1, p. 2469.
3. A barnacle is a type of marine crustacean with feathery appendages for gathering food; as adults, they affix themselves permanently to objects.
4. A reference to sea anemones, marine coel-enterates whose form, bright colors, and clusters of tentacles resemble flowers.
5. Vast stretches of time.
6. Armed ships and their crew commissioned by governments to attack enemy ships on the open sea.

of walking, he thought he could hear the distant quarrel
of breaker with shore; then his head broke clear,[7] and
his neck; then he could see his own shadow in the coral

grove, ribbed and rippling with light on the clear sand,
as his fins spread their toes, and he saw the leaf
of his own canoe far out, the life he had left behind

and the white line of surf around low Barrel of Beef[8]
with its dead lantern. The salt glare left him blind
for a minute, then the shoreline returned in relief.[9]

He woke to the sound of sunlight scratching at the door
of the hut, and he smelt not salt but the sluggish odour
of river. Fingers of light rethatched the roof's straw.

On the day of his feast they wore the same plantain trash
like Philoctete at Christmas. A bannered mitre[1]
of bamboo was placed on his head, a calabash

mask, and skirts that made him both woman and fighter.
That was how they danced at home, to fifes and tambours,
the same berries round their necks and the small mirrors

flashing from their stuffed breasts. One of the warriors
mounted on stilts walked like lightning over the thatch
of the peaked village. Achille saw the same dances

that the mitred warriors did with their bamboo stick
as they scuttered around him, lifting, dipping their lances
like divining rods turning the earth to music,

the same chac-chac and ra-ra,[2] the drumming the same,
and the chant of the seed-eyed prophet to the same
response from the blurring ankles. The same, the same.[3]

50

55

60

65

70

75

7. As he resurfaced.
8. A rocky site off the coast of St. Lucia, a prominent landmark on the island.
9. In the double sense of being sharply outlined and of bringing a sense of relief.
1. A ritual headdress, but more usually applied to the liturgical headdress worn by bishops and abbots.
2. Dance forms in the Caribbean. "Ra-ra" is derived from a Yoruba genre of chanted poetry.
3. Walcott registers the protagonist's recognition of his cultural connection of Africa.

From Book Four

From *Chapter XXXV*

I

"Somewhere over there," said my guide, "the Trail of Tears
started." I leant towards the crystalline creek. Pines
shaded it. Then I made myself hear the water's

language around the rocks in its clear-running lines
and its small shelving falls with their eddies, "Choctaws," 5
"Creeks," "Choctaws,"[1] and I thought of the Greek revival

carried past the names of towns with columned porches,
and how Greek it was, the necessary evil
of slavery, in the catalogue of Georgia's

marble past, the Jeffersonian ideal[2] in 10
plantations with its Hectors and Achilleses,
its foam in the dogwood's spray, past towns named Helen,

Athens, Sparta, Troy. The slave shacks, the rolling peace
of the wave-rolling meadows, oak, pine, and pecan,
and a creek like this one. From the window I saw 15

the bundles of women moving in ragged bands
like those on the wharf,[3] headed for Oklahoma;
then I saw Seven Seas,[4] a rattle in his hands.

A huge thunderhead[5] was unclenching its bruised fist
over the county. Shadows escaped through the pines 20
and the pecan groves and hounds[6] were closing in fast

deep into Georgia, where history happens
to be the baying echoes of brutality,
and terror in the oaks along red country roads,

or the gibbet[7] branches of a silk-cotton tree 25
from which Afolabes hung like bats. Hooded clouds[8]
guarded the town squares with their calendar churches,

1. Native American nations expelled from their original homes and forced to march to reservations in Oklahoma (see line 17).
2. "Life, liberty and the pursuit of happiness," belied by the institution of slavery.
3. Captured Africans waiting to be shipped to America. This passage establishes a parallel between the fate of Native Americans and that of African slaves.
4. A blind poet and singer in St. Lucia who features prominently in Walcott's play *The*

Odyssey, a stage adaptation of Homer's epic.
5. A large mass of dark cumulus clouds presaging a thunderstorm.
6. Dogs were used to recapture runaway slaves; they were also set upon black protesters during the civil rights movement.
7. Gallows. The reference here is to the lynching in the Deep South of blacks, usually by hanging.
8. The Ku Klux Klan.

whose white, peaked belfries asserted that pastoral
of brooks with leisurely accents. On their verges,
like islands reflected on windscreens, Negro shacks   30

moved like a running wound, like the rusty anchor
that scabbed Philoctete's shin,[9] I imagined the backs
moving through the foam of pods, one arm for an oar,

one for the gunny sack.[1] Brown streams tinkled in chains.
Bridges arched their spines. Led into their green pasture,[2]   35
horses sagely grazed or galloped the plantations.

II

"Life is so fragile. It trembles like the aspens.[3]
All its shadows are seasonal, including pain.
In drizzling dusk the rain enters the lindens

with its white lances, then lindens enclose the rain.   40
So that day isn't far when they will say, 'Indians
bowed under those branches, which tribe is not certain.'

Nor am I certain I lived. I breathed what the farm
exhaled. Its soils, its seasons. The swayed goldenrod,
the corn where summer hid me, pollen on my arm,   45

sweat tickling my armpits. The Plains were fierce as God
and wide as His mind. I enjoyed diminishing,
I exalted in insignificance after

the alleys of Boston, in the unfinishing
chores of the farm, alone. Once, from the barn's rafter   50
a swift or a swallow shot out, taking with it

my son's brown, whirring soul,[4] and I knew that its aim
was heaven. More and more we learn to do without
those we still love. With my father it was the same.

The bounty of God pursued me over the Plains   55
of the Dakotas, the pheasants, the quick-volleyed
arrows of finches; smoke bound me to the Indians

from morning to sunset when I have watched its veiled
rising, because I am a widow, barbarous
and sun-cured in the face, I loved them ever since   60

---

9. The companion of Achille in his Caribbean
home and, like him, a fisherman.
1. A bag made from coarse, heavy material.
2. Conveying an impression of blessed peace,
but deceptive.
3. A type of poplar tree whose leaves flutter in

the slightest breeze. The speaker here is Catherine Weldon, a historical figure that Walcott
has woven into the poem.
4. Perhaps a reference to an aspect of Native
American beliefs.

I worked as a hand in Colonel Cody's[5] circus,
under a great canvas larger than all their tents,
when they were paid to ride round in howling circles,

with a dime for their glory, and boys screamed in fright
at the galloping braves. Now the aspens enclosed   65
the lances of rain, and the wet leaves shake with light."

*   *   *

From Book Six

From *Chapter LII*

II

Provinces, Protectorates, Colonies, Dominions,
Governors-General, black Knights, ostrich-plumed[1] Viceroys,
deserts, jungles, hill-stations, all an empire's zones,

lay spilled from a small tea-chest; felt-footed houseboys
on fern-soft verandahs, hearty Toby-jugged[2] Chiefs   5
of Police, Girl-Guide Commissioners, Secretaries,

poppies on cenotaphs,[3] green-spined Remembrance wreaths,
cornets, kettledrums, gum-chewing dromedaries[4]
under Lawrence,[5] parasols, palm-striped pavilions,

dhows[6] and feluccas,[7] native-draped paddle-ferries   10
on tea-brown rivers, statue-rehearsing lions,
sandstorms seaming their eyes, horizontal monsoons,

rank odour of a sea-chest, mimosa memories
touched by a finger, lead soldiers, clopping Dragoons.[8]
Breadfruit hands on a wall. The statues close their eyes.   15

Mosquito nets, palm-fronds, scrolled Royal Carriages,
dacoits,[9] gun-bearers,[1] snarling apes on Gibraltar,[2]
sermons to sweat-soaked kerchiefs, the Rock of Ages[3]

---

5. I.e., William F. Cody, also called Buffalo
Bill (1846–1917), who founded a circus and a
traveling show that featured Native Americans
in various humiliating roles. "A dime for their
glory" (line 64) is an ironic comment on this.
1. The ceremonial uniform of British colonial
governors was topped by a cap with ostrich
feathers.
2. A Toby jug is a small vessel—a mug, for
instance—shaped like a fat man wearing a
cocked hat.
3. Flowers atop tombs or monuments.
4. Camels, which constantly chew their cud.
5. A reference to T. E. Lawrence (1888–
1935), also known as Lawrence of Arabia, who

served as liaison officer between the British
forces and Arab guerrillas fighting against
Turkish rule during the First World War.
6. Arab sailboats.
7. Small, fast sailing vessels common to the
Mediterranean. They are equipped with both
masts and oars.
8. Heavily armed cavalry unit.
9. A gang of robbers of (Hindi).
1. Armored vehicles.
2. A reference to the Barbary macaques that
live in Gibraltar, a British enclave at the southern tip of Spain, long a tourist attraction.
3. A well-known Judeo-Christian hymn.

pumped by a Zouave[4] band, lilies light the altar,
soldiers and doxies[5] by a splashing esplanade,   20
waves turning their sheet music, the yellowing teeth

of the parlour piano, *Airs from Erin*[6] played
to the whistling kettle, and on the teapot's head
the cozy's bearskin shako,[7] biscuits break with grief,

gold-braid laburnums,[8] lilac whiff of lavender,
columned poplars marching to Mafeking's relief.[9]   25
Naughty seaside cards, the sepia surrender

of Gordon[1] on the mantel, the steps of Khartoum,
The World's Classics[2] condensed, Clive[3] as brown as India
bathers in Benares,[4] an empire in costume.

His will be done, O Maud, His kingdom come,   30
as the sunflower turns,[5] and the white eyes widen
in the ebony faces, the sloe-eyes, the bent smoke

where a pig totters across a village midden[6]
over the sunset's shambles, Rangoon to Malta,[7]
the regimental button of the evening star.   35

Solace of laudanum, menstrual cramps, the runnings,
tinkles in the jordan, at dusk the zebra shade
of louvres on the quilt, the maps spread their warnings

and the tribal odour of the second chambermaid.
And every fortnight, ten sharp on Sunday mornings,   40
shouts and wheeling patterns from our Cadet Brigade.[8]

---

4. The Zouaves were Algerian infantry units in the French and American Confederate armies.
5. Prostitutes.
6. Ireland.
7. The tea cozy, a cushioned cover draped over a teapot to keep the contents warm, resembles a *shako,* a stiff military hat with a high crown, in this case made from bearskin.
8. A shrub with bright yellow flowers (i.e., "gold-braid").
9. A town in South Africa relieved by British forces after a long siege by Afrikaners during the Boer War.
1. Charles Gordon (1833–1885), British governor-general in the Sudan who was killed on the steps of his residence at Khartoum during an uprising by the local population.
2. A famous collection of great literature published by Oxford University Press.

3. Robert Clive (1725–1774), an agent of the East India Company considered to have secured India for the British by thwarting the French and by defeating the local Bengali ruler at the Battle of Plassey in 1757.
4. Holy Hindu city situated on the northern bank of the Ganges in India and associated with Buddha.
5. Fragment of an Irish song beginning "Believe me if all those endearing young charms."
6. Rubbish heap.
7. Rangoon is a city in Myanmar (formerly Burma), a former British colony; Malta, an island in the Mediterranean off the Italian coast, was also a British colony.
8. A company of schoolboys selected and groomed to be future officers in the colonial army.

All spilt from a tea-chest, a studded souvenir,
props for an opera, Victoria Regina,[9]
for a bolster-plump Queen the pillbox sentries stamp,

piss, straw and saddle-soap, heaume[1] and crimson feather,   45
post-red double-deckers,[2] spit-and-polished leather,
and iron dolphins leaping round an Embankment[3] lamp.

* * *

From Book Seven

From *Chapter LXIV*

I

I sang[1] of quiet Achille, Afolabe's son,
who never ascended in an elevator,
who had no passport, since the horizon needs none,

never begged nor borrowed, was nobody's waiter,
whose end, when it comes, will be a death by water   5
(which is not for this book, which will remain unknown

and unread by him). I sang the only slaughter
that brought him delight, and that from necessity—
of fish, sang the channels of his back[2] in the sun.

I sang our wide country, the Caribbean Sea.   10
Who hated shoes, whose soles were as cracked as a stone,
who was gentle with ropes, who had one suit alone,

whom no man dared insult and who insulted no one,
whose grin was a white breaker cresting, but whose frown
was a growing thunderhead, whose fist of iron   15

would do me a greater honour if it held on
to my casket's oarlocks[3] than mine lifting his own
when both anchors are lowered in the one island,

but now the idyll dies, the goblet is broken,
and rainwater trickles down the brown cheek of a jar   20
from the clay of Choiseul. So much left unspoken

9. I.e., Queen Victoria (Latin): the insignia of
Queen Victoria on English coins.
1. Helmet worn by armored men in the Middle Ages.
2. London buses.
3. Area in London where the Houses of Parliament and the main government offices are
located.

1. The invocation, usually placed at the beginning of an epic poem, is here put at the end
and expressed in the past tense.
2. The ripples of muscles, denoting strength.
The human frame represented as a furrowed
landscape.
3. At the poet's own funeral.

by my chirping nib![4] And my earth-door lies ajar.
I lie wrapped in a flour-sack sail. The clods thud
on my rope-lowered canoe. Rasping shovels scrape

a dry rain of dirt on its hold, but turn your head   25
when the sea-almond rattles or the rust-leaved grape
from the shells of my unpharaonic pyramid[5]

towards paper shredded by the wind and scattered
like white gulls that separate their names from the foam
and nod to a fisherman[6] with his khaki dog   30

that the skitters from the wave-crash, then frown at his form
for one swift second. In its earth-trough, my pirogue
with its brass-handled oarlocks is sailing. Not from

but with them, with Hector, with Maud[7] in the rhythm
of her beds[8] trowelled over, with a swirling log   35
lifting its mossed head from the swell; let the deep hymn

of the Caribbean continue my epilogue;
may waves remove their shawls as my mourners walk home
to their rusted villages, good shoes in one hand,

passing a boy who walked through the ignorant foam,   40
and saw a sail going out or else coming in,
and watched asterisks of rain[9] puckering the sand.

* * *

1990

---

4. The point of a pen dipped in ink often makes a rasping noise on the paper.
5. Modest, without the monumental grandeur of Egypt's pyramids.
6. I.e., Philoctete.
7. The wife of an English colonial officer, Major Plunkett, whose adventures, intertwined with the life of the St. Lucians, are narrated in earlier passages of the poem. "Hector": rival of Achille who was killed in a car accident.
8. A reference to the flowerbeds tended by Maud. The image evokes her final resting place in the earth.
9. Which is life-giving.

SEAMUS HEANEY

1939–2013

Having reached his maturity as a poet during the sectarian violence known as the Troubles in his native Northern Ireland, Seamus Heaney developed a keen awareness of the poet's relationship to history and conflict. A student of the Irish language and of Anglo-Saxon (Old English), he has drawn on the resources of both in reinventing modern English poetry. His verse, alive to historical resonances, explores the ethical commitments of the poet in a world of enduring conflicts.

Born to a Catholic family on a farm in County Derry, Northern Ireland, Heaney was the eldest of nine children. He attended the nearby Anahorish School and then St. Columb's College, a Catholic boarding school in Derry, Northern Ireland's second city, before enrolling in Queen's University, Belfast, where he studied English language and literature. In addition to Anglo-Saxon, he learned Irish and Latin. After briefly teaching middle school, Heaney returned to Queen's in 1966 as an instructor in English literature. In the same year, his first major volume of poems, *Death of a Naturalist,* was released. During the following several years, as tensions heightened in Northern Ireland, Heaney addressed political concerns in his poetry, although often in an indirect fashion that was sometimes criticized for its lack of explicit commitment. In 1972, in a move that was seen at the time as indicating sympathies with the Nationalist cause (unification with the Republic of Ireland), Heaney moved to Dublin. He taught college there for several years, then, as his reputation as a poet grew, began an association with Harvard University, where he would teach part-time for a quarter of a century. He also taught at Oxford University. In 1995, he received the Nobel Prize for Literature.

The late 1960s were a period of intense violence in Northern Ireland, a majority Protestant region that had remained part of the United Kingdom when the rest of Ireland gained its independence. Some members of the substantial Catholic population of Northern Ireland supported the illegal Irish Republican Army, which used violence to promote unification with the Irish Republic (the "Nationalist" position). Catholics often faced hostility and discrimination from Protestant groups, notably the paramilitary Ulster Volunteer Force, that favored continued union with Britain (the "Unionists"). British police and military forces were generally perceived as supporting the Unionists, particularly in the Bloody Sunday massacre of 1972, when thirteen unarmed Catholic protesters were killed by British army forces. The cycle of violence by the IRA, the UVF, and British forces continued until the Good Friday agreement of 1998, which ushered in a period of disarmament and power sharing by Nationalist and Unionist politicians.

The Northern Irish landscape of Heaney's youth plays a central role in his poetry. Regularly placed by Heaney at the beginning of collections of his poetry, "Digging" (1964) announces his poetic vocation by comparing the poet's pen to the shovels wielded by Heaney's father and grandfather, both farmers, and also to a gun. Heaney the poet will use a pen to make his mark. Although not following a strict form, the poem generally has four heavy accents per line and caesuras (pauses in the middle of a line); its rhythm and use of alliteration and assonance (repetition of vowel sounds) echo those of Old English poetry. Heaney is interested in the sounds of words, and many of his poems draw on the significance and pronunciation of place-names. "Anahorish" (1972), or "place of clear waters," was the name of a rural area where he attended elementary school. The poem suggests those clear waters and the wells of Anahorish as sources of inspiration; it also hints at a darker landscape of barrows (burial mounds) and dunghills—creativity arises not just from water but from earth, which contains the refuse of earlier generations. In "Broagh" (1972), the very sound of the place-name (meaning "riverbank") suggests some hidden personal, as well as communal, knowledge.

"The Tollund Man" (1972) is one of the first of Heaney's poems about the bog people, an ancient folk, related to the Irish, whose bodies were preserved in the wetlands of Jutland, Denmark. In this poem and in "Punishment" (1975), the speaker contemplates the bodies of victims of sacrificial slaughter in the Iron Age society, hinting that such primitive violence is not all that different from the Troubles of Northern Ireland. A more personal poem about that violence, "The Strand at Lough Beg" (1979), is an elegy for the poet's cousin Colum McCartney, a victim of sectarian conflict. Recollecting Dante's visits with the dead in *The Inferno* and *Purgatorio,* Heaney here imagines himself in conversation with his cousin's ghost. He would later criticize the poem, however, for having "whitewashed ugliness."

"The Guttural Muse" (1979), also a personal poem, this time about age and youth, was written in the poet's fortieth year. A later work, "The Haw Lantern" (1987), an unrhymed sonnet in free verse, marks Heaney's movement toward abstract symbolism. The lantern (which burns the small berries of the hawthorn tree) recollects the lamp of Diogenes, who sought for one just man; the speaker wonders whether he himself meets the criterion. While the "small people" referred to in the poem's opening lines may be the Northern Irish, the symbolism is not simply local. Here, more explicitly than elsewhere, Heaney raises the question of the poet's responsibility not only to speak the truth but to work for justice. And yet the poem has a mystical side: the writing of poetry itself may be the test referred to in the final lines.

Heaney is attentive to the formal qualities of his verse, whether in the loose blank verse (unrhymed iambic pentameter) of "The Strand at Lough Beg" or in his characteristic short quatrains (four-line stanzas). Although seldom making use of rhyme, these quatrains recall ballad forms associated with folk tradition, while in other poems (like "The Tollund Man" and "Punishment") they create a melancholy, meditative mood. Heaney frequently uses words of Anglo-Saxon origin, which he seems to associate with the land. Preferring relatively formal poetry rather than experimental verse, Heaney drew heavily on the literary tradition, including Dante, **T. S. Eliot**, and the medieval *Beowulf,* which he translated into modern English. His work is distinguished by its concreteness and descriptive precision.

Digging

Between my finger and my thumb
The squat pen rests; snug as a gun.

Under my window, a clean rasping sound
When the spade sinks into gravelly ground:
My father, digging. I look down   5

Till his straining rump among the flowerbeds
Bends low, comes up twenty years away
Stooping in rhythm through potato drills
Where he was digging.

The coarse boot nestled on the lug, the shaft   10
Against the inside knee was levered firmly.
He rooted out tall tops, buried the bright edge deep
To scatter new potatoes that we picked,
Loving their cool hardness in our hands.

By God, the old man could handle a spade.   15
Just like his old man.

My grandfather cut more turf in a day
Than any other man on Toner's bog.[1]
Once I carried him milk in a bottle
Corked sloppily with paper. He straightened up   20
To drink it, then fell to right away
Nicking and slicing neatly, heaving sods
Over his shoulder, going down and down
For the good turf. Digging.

The cold smell of potato mould, the squelch and slap   25
Of soggy peat, the curt cuts of an edge
Through living roots awaken in my head.
But I've no spade to follow men like them.

Between my finger and my thumb
The squat pen rests.   30
I'll dig with it.

1964

Anahorish[1]

My 'place of clear water',
the first hill in the world
where springs washed into
the shiny grass

---

1. The bog belongs to a man named Toner.
The speaker's father cuts turf as fuel for a fire.

1. The place-name means "place of clear water";
Heaney attended elementary school there.

and darkened cobbles
in the bed of the lane.
Anahorish, soft gradient
of consonant, vowel-meadow,

after-image of lamps
swung through the yards
on winter evenings.
With pails and barrows

those mound-dwellers
go waist-deep in mist
to break the light ice
at wells and dunghills.

5

10

15

1972

Broagh[1]

Riverbank, the long rigs[2]
ending in broad docken[3]
and a canopied pad
down to the ford.

The garden mould[4]
bruised easily, the shower
gathering in your heelmark
was the black *O*

in *Broagh*,
its low tattoo[5]
among the windy boortrees[6]
and rhubarb-blades

ended almost
suddenly, like that last
gh the strangers found
difficult to manage.

5

10

15

1972

---

1. The place-name means "riverbank."
2. Strips of cultivated land.
3. A green weedy plant.

4. Rich earth suitable for a garden.
5. Drumbeat.
6. Trees forming a bower.

The Tollund Man[1]

I

Some day I will go to Aarhus[2]
To see his peat-brown head,
The mild pods of his eyelids,
His pointed skin cap.

In the flat country nearby   5
Where they dug him out,
His last gruel of winter seeds
Caked in his stomach,

Naked except for
The cap, noose and girdle,   10
I will stand a long time.
Bridegroom to the goddess,

She tightened her torc[3] on him
And opened her fen,
Those dark juices working   15
Him to a saint's kept body,

Trove of the turf-cutters'
Honeycombed workings.
Now his stained face
Reposes at Aarhus.   20

II

I could risk blasphemy,
Consecrate the cauldron bog
Our holy ground and pray
Him to make germinate

The scattered, ambushed   5
Flesh of labourers,
Stockinged corpses
Laid out in the farmyards,

Tell-tale skin and teeth
Flecking the sleepers   10
Of four young brothers,[4] trailed
For miles along the lines.

---

1. The corpse of a man killed in the 4th century B.C.E, probably a sacrificial victim, preserved in a bog in Jutland, Denmark. Heaney had seen photographs of the Tollund Man and associated Denmark's bogs with those of Northern Ireland.
2. A town in Jutland (the Tollund Man is actually displayed in nearby Silkeborg).
3. An ancient style of metal necklace.
4. The speaker compares the Tollund Man to four Irish nationalist brothers killed by the Protestant Ulster Constabulary Force (forerunner of the Ulster Volunteer Force), in the early 1920s, in Northern Ireland.

III

Something of his sad freedom
As he rode the tumbril
Should come to me, driving,   15
Saying the names

Tollund, Grauballe, Nebelgard,[5]
Watching the pointing hands
Of country people,
Not knowing their tongue.   20

Out there in Jutland
In the old man-killing parishes
I will feel lost,
Unhappy and at home.

1972

Punishment[1]

I can feel the tug
of the halter at the nape
of her neck, the wind
on her naked front.

It blows her nipples
to amber beads,   5
it shakes the frail rigging
of her ribs.

I can see her drowned
body in the bog,   10
the weighing stone,
the floating rods and boughs.

Under which at first
she was a barked sapling
that is dug up   15
oak-bone, brain-firkin:[2]

her shaved head
like a stubble of black corn,
her blindfold a soiled bandage,
her noose a ring   20

to store
the memories of love.

---

5. Other places in Jutland where bog bodies had been found.

1. The speaker contemplates the body, pre-served in a bog, of a young woman in ancient Scandinavia, drowned for adultery.

2. Refers to a head covering on the dead body.

Little adulteress,
before they punished you

you were flaxen-haired,
undernourished, and your
tar-black face was beautiful.
My poor scapegoat,

I almost love you
but would have cast, I know,
the stones of silence.
I am the artful voyeur

of your brain's exposed
and darkened combs,
your muscles' webbing
and all your numbered bones:

I who have stood dumb
when your betraying sisters,
cauled in tar,
wept by the railings,

who would connive
in civilized outrage
yet understand the exact
and tribal, intimate revenge.

25

30

35

40

1975

The Strand at Lough Beg[1]

in memory of Colum McCartney

All round this little island, on the strand
Far down below there, where the breakers strive,
Grow the tall rushes from the oozy sand
                              —DANTE, *Purgatorio, I, 100–3*[2]

Leaving the white glow of filling stations
And a few lonely streetlamps among fields
You climbed the hills towards Newtownhamilton
Past the Fews Forest, out beneath the stars—
Along that road, a high, bare pilgrim's track
Where Sweeney[3] fled before the bloodied heads,

5

---

1. I.e., the shore of a lake in Northern Ireland.
Colum McCartney was a cousin of Heaney's,
killed in sectarian violence.
2. Dante writes of the shores of the island on
which stands the mountain of Purgatory, where

the souls of the dead undergo punishment as
they await admission to Paradise.
3. A legendary pagan Irish king who kills a
Christian monk and goes mad.

Goat-beards and dogs' eyes in a demon pack
Blazing out of the ground, snapping and squealing.
What blazed ahead of you? A faked roadblock?
The red lamp swung, the sudden brakes and stalling   10
Engine, voices, heads hooded and the cold-nosed gun?
Or in your driving mirror, tailing headlights
That pulled out suddenly and flagged you down
Where you weren't known and far from what you knew:
The lowland clays and waters of Lough Beg,   15
Church Island's spire, its soft treeline of yew.

There you once heard guns fired behind the house
Long before rising time, when duck shooters
Haunted the marigolds and bulrushes,
But still were scared to find spent cartridges,   20
Acrid, brassy, genital, ejected,
On your way across the strand to fetch the cows.
For you and yours and yours and mine fought shy,
Spoke an old language of conspirators
And could not crack the whip or seize the day: 25
Big-voiced scullions, herders, feelers round
Haycocks and hindquarters, talkers in byres,[4]
Slow arbitrators of the burial ground.

Across that strand of yours the cattle graze
Up to their bellies in an early mist   30
And now they turn their unbewildered gaze
To where we work our way through squeaking sedge
Drowning in dew. Like a dull blade with its edge
Honed bright, Lough Beg half-shines under the haze.
I turn because the sweeping of your feet   35
Has stopped behind me, to find you on your knees
With blood and roadside muck in your hair and eyes,
Then kneel in front of you in brimming grass
And gather up cold handfuls of the dew
To wash you, cousin. I dab you clean with moss   40
Fine as the drizzle out of a low cloud.
I lift you under the arms and lay you flat.
With rushes that shoot green again, I plait
Green scapulars[5] to wear over your shroud.

1979

---

4. Cow-sheds. "Haycocks": haystacks.
5. Patches of cloth indicating religious devotion, hung from the shoulders.

The Guttural Muse

Late summer, and at midnight
I smelt the heat of the day:
At my window over the hotel car park
I breathed the muddied night airs off the lake
And watched a young crowd leave the discotheque.   5

Their voices rose up thick and comforting
As oily bubbles the feeding tench sent up
That evening at dusk—the slimy tench
Once called the 'doctor fish' because his slime
Was said to heal the wounds of fish that touched it.   10

A girl in a white dress
Was being courted out among the cars:
As her voice swarmed and puddled into laughs
I felt like some old pike all badged with sores
Wanting to swim in touch with soft-mouthed life.   15

1979

The Haw Lantern[1]

The wintry haw is burning out of season,
crab of the thorn, a small light for small people,
wanting no more from them but that they keep
the wick of self-respect from dying out,
not having to blind them with illumination.   5

But sometimes when your breath plumes in the frost
it takes the roaming shape of Diogenes[2]
with his lantern, seeking one just man;
so you end up scrutinized from behind the haw
he holds up at eye-level on its twig,   10
and you flinch before its bonded pith and stone,
its blood-prick that you wish would test and clear you,
its pecked-at ripeness that scans you, then moves on.

1987

---

1. A lantern burning berries from the hawthorn tree.

2. Diogenes the Cynic (ca. 412–323 B.C.E.)
sought one just man.

INGEBORG BACHMANN

1926–1973

Ingeborg Bachmann's reputation as one of the most significant postwar writers in the German language is almost overshadowed by her reputation as an interpreter of women's experience and a critic of fascism. Her powerful intellect and gift for precise description fused with a lyric tendency and strong ethical concerns to create a remarkable body of work that has been translated into twenty-two languages and continues to influence contemporary writers.

The oldest of three children, Bachmann was born on June 25, 1926, in Klagenfurt, a city in southern Austria close to the border with Italy and present-day Slovenia. Bachmann's experience of political borders was sharpened when the Nazis marched into Klagenfurt in 1938. She was twelve years old, and that moment, she said, marked the end of her childhood. Attending schools in Klagenfurt throughout the war, she graduated in 1944 and studied briefly in Innsbruck and Graz before entering the University of Vienna in 1946.

Bachmann's first story, "The Ferryboat," was published in 1946, and other stories as well as her first poems appeared over the next few years. While earning recognition as a creative writer, she also pursued a Ph.D. in philosophy. In the years after earning her doctorate, Bachmann traveled to Paris and London, gave poetry readings, held a series of jobs ranging from scriptwriter to newspaper correspondent, and began to write in different genres. She was best known as a poet and won awards and renown at an early age.

Bachmann's work took a sharp turn in the 1960s, so that critics have often spoken of the "two Bachmanns," the first aiming at formal beauty and the second a socially and politically engaged writer of prose who once proclaimed: "I no longer try to make each sentence a work of art. The only thing that matters is what needs to be said." Her turn from poetry to prose corresponded to a renewed commitment to feminism. Bachmann was preoccupied throughout her career with fascism, and her analysis of fascism underpinned her feminism. Fascism must begin somewhere, she said, before it becomes a political movement and an agent of mass destruction. She located the principles of fascism—the oppression of the weak and a sadistic desire for dominance and control—uncomfortably close to home, in the subordination of women by men. "Fascism is the first thing in the relationship between a man and a woman," she declared in an interview.

In response to this understanding of feminism, Bachmann envisaged a novel cycle, *Ways of Death*, that would illuminate women's experience through the linked stories of individual figures appearing and reappearing in major or minor roles. While she did not complete that cycle, she did publish her masterpiece, *Malina* (1971), a challenging modernist work that includes a variety of forms and techniques: fairy tale, letters, dream sequences, dramatic dialogue, and finally the inexplicable disappearance of the narrator from a story that previously depended on her. Bachmann was still working on *Ways of Death* when she died from injuries suffered during a fire in her apartment in Rome on October 17, 1973.

The Barking (1972) chronicles an episode from her unfinished novel *The Franza Case*, part of the cycle *Ways of Death*. The major figure is Frau Jordan, now old and in failing health, who is befriended by her daughter-in-law Franziska. In a series of conversations, the topic of which is invariably Frau Jordan's son, the brilliant psychiatrist, Leo, the two women inadvertently bring to light his real selfishness and cruelty. Old Frau Jordan is unable to admit her fear and dislike of Leo and has lived a devoted lie all her life.

Franziska, in contrast, becomes more critical of Leo's behavior even though she also cannot bring herself to blame him openly. Her relationship with Leo disintegrates during the course of the story, although we are never told exactly why. There is no indication here of the systematic attempt to drive Franziska mad that is explicitly described in other portions of *The Franza Case,* but what

we are shown in *The Barking* is the picture of a homophobic, control-obsessed man who displays a mentality allied with fascism.

Much of the story's strength lies in its subtly *indirect* depiction and simultaneous analysis of this mentality. Leo is described obliquely, through the eyes of his dependent mother and wife. He instills fear in them and controls their lives, but this control also depends on their willingness to obliterate their own personalities to appease him. Bachmann leaves open the possibility of other modes of being: Frau Jordan's truly maternal relationship with another child, Kiki; Franziska's care for her mother-in-law; even Franziska's brother's generosity in paying Frau Jordan's taxi bills. The fate of the story's two main characters, however, illustrates Bachmann's bleak view of oppressive power relationships between men and women.

The Barking[1]

Old Frau Jordan had been called "old Frau Jordan" for the past three decades because there had been first one and now another young Frau Jordan, and although she did live in Hietzing,[2] she had only a one-room apartment in a dilapidated villa, with a tiny kitchen and no more than half a tub in the bathroom. From her distinguished son Leo, the professor, she received 1,000 schillings[3] per month, and somehow she managed to make do, although those 1,000 schillings had depreciated so much over the last twenty years that she was just barely able to pay an older woman, a certain Frau Agnes, who "looked in" on her twice a week, to tidy up a little, just "the bare minimum." She even saved some of the money for birthday and Christmas presents for her son and grandson from her son's first marriage, whom the first young wife sent over punctually every Christmas to pick up his present. Leo on the other hand was too busy to notice, and since he had become famous and his local prestige had blossomed into international renown, he was busier than ever. Things only changed when the latest young Frau Jordan began to visit the old woman as often as she could, a really nice, likable girl, as the old woman soon admitted to herself, but at each visit she said only: But Franziska, it's not right, you

---

1. Translated by Mary Fran Gilbert.
2. A suburb west of Vienna, Austria. "Frau":

Mrs. (German).
3. The basic Austrian unit of currency.

shouldn't come so often, it's such a waste. You two surely have enough expenses as it is, but Leo is just such a good son!

Franziska always brought something with her, delicacies and sherry, some pastries, because she had guessed that the old woman liked to take a sip now and then and, moreover, attached great importance to having something in the house "for the company." After all, Leo might drop by, and he mustn't notice how much she was missing and that all day long she wondered how to allocate her money and how much she could put aside for presents. Her apartment was meticulously clean, but gave off a faint "old-woman" smell which she was not aware of and which put Leo Jordan to flight, apart from the fact that he had no time to lose and no idea what to talk about with his eighty-five-year-old mother. Sometimes, seldom, he had been amused—that much Franziska knew— namely, when he was having a relationship with a married woman, because then old Frau Jordan had gone without sleep and made strange, convoluted allusions, trembling for his safety: she believed that the married men whose wives Leo Jordan was living with were dangerous and jealous and bloodthirsty, and she wasn't able to calm down until he married Franziska, who did not have a jealous husband lurking in the bushes but was young and cheerful, an orphan, admittedly not from an educated family, but at least with a brother who had gone to college. Families of the educated classes and educated men in general carried great weight with Frau Jordan, although she didn't do much socializing; she only heard about things. But her son had the right to marry into an educated family. The old woman and Franziska talked almost exclusively about Leo, because he was the only productive topic the two of them had, and Franziska was shown the photo album over and over again, Leo in a stroller, Leo at the beach, and Leo through the years, taking hikes, pasting stamps in his collection, and so on until his military service.

The Leo she came to know through the old woman was a completely different Leo from the man she had married, and when the two women sat drinking their sherry the old woman would say: He was a complicated child, a strange boy, actually you could tell all along that he was destined for great things.

For a while Franziska was happy to hear these assertions, that Leo was so good to his mother and had always done everything conceivable to help her, but then she noticed that something was wrong, and with dismay she realized—the old woman was afraid of her son. It began with the old woman saying, sometimes hastily and parenthetically (she believed it to be a clever tactic that Franziska would never see through because she was blinded by admiration for her husband): But please don't mention a word of it to Leo, you know how concerned he is, it might upset him, whatever you do, please don't tell him that something is wrong with my knee, it's such a little thing, he might get upset about it.

Although Franziska had since learned that Leo never got upset at all, certainly not because of his mother, and only listened to her reports with half an ear, she suppressed this first realization. Unfortunately she had already told him about the knee but swore to the old woman she wouldn't say a word. Leo had reacted with annoyance and then, to placate her, had explained that he really couldn't drive out to Hietzing because of such a trifle. Just tell her—he rattled off some medical terminology—she should buy this and that and do and walk as little as possible. Franziska bought the medication without further comment and claimed in Hietzing that she had secretly spoken with one of her husband's assistants without mentioning any names and that he had given her this advice, although she was at a loss as to how to keep the old woman in bed without the help of a nurse. But she no longer had enough courage to approach Leo about it, because a nurse cost money, and now she was caught in the middle. On the one hand Frau Jordan didn't want anything to do with it, and on the other Leo Jordan—albeit for completely different reasons—simply didn't want to hear about it. When Frau Jordan's knee was swollen, Franziska lied to her husband several times; she drove quickly to Hietzing, allegedly to the hairdresser's, and straightened up the little apartment, bringing all sorts of things with her. She purchased a radio but was uneasy afterward: Leo was bound to notice the expenditure, so she quickly transferred the money back and broke into the meager savings she had set aside for some sort of emergency which would hopefully never arise and could only be a minor emergency at any rate. She and her brother had divided what little remained after the death of their entire family, with the exception of a cottage in southern Carinthia[4] which was slowly falling into disrepair. In the end she called a general practitioner in the neighborhood and asked him to treat the old woman for a while, paying him out of her own savings. More importantly, she didn't dare reveal to the doctor who she was and who the old woman was, because that would only have hurt Leo's reputation, and protecting Leo's reputation was also in Franziska's best interest. But the old woman thought much more selflessly: there was no way she could ask her famous son to go so far as to come and take a look at her knee. She had used a cane before on occasion, but after this knee problem she really needed it, so Franziska sometimes drove her to town. Shopping with the old woman was a somewhat laborious undertaking: once she had only needed a comb, but there were no combs like the ones "in her day," and although the old woman was polite, standing in the store with erect dignity, she annoyed the little saleswoman by eyeing the price tags suspiciously, unable to refrain from telling Franziska in a clearly audible whisper that the prices here were outrageous, they'd better go somewhere else. The saleswoman, who was in no position to judge how important buying this comb was to the old woman, replied rudely that they wouldn't find this comb cheaper anywhere in town. Franziska launched into embarrassed negotiations with the mother, took the comb the old woman wanted but looked on as costing a fortune and quickly paid for it, saying: Just consider it a Christmas present from us, a present in advance. Prices have really gone up horrendously everywhere. The old woman didn't say a word, she sensed her defeat, but still, if prices really were so outrageous—a comb like this used to cost two schillings and nowadays it cost sixty—well then there wasn't much left for her to understand in this world.

After a while the topic "the good son" had been exhausted and Franziska repeatedly steered the conversation to the old woman herself, because the only thing she knew was that Leo's father had died young of a heart attack or stroke, quite suddenly, on a staircase, and that must have been a long time ago, because if you stopped to figure it out this woman had been a widow for almost half a century. First she had worked for years to raise her only child, and then she was suddenly an old woman nobody cared about anymore. She never spoke

4. A southwestern province of Austria.

about her marriage, only in connection with Leo who had had a very difficult life, without a father, and she was so preoccupied with Leo that she failed to see the parallel to Franziska, who had lost both her parents when she was young. Her son was the only one who could have had a difficult time, and then it turned out that it hadn't been so bad after all, because a distant cousin had paid for his education, a certain Johannes about whom Franziska had heard very little, merely a few derogatory, critical references to some eternal—now aging—loafer who was swimming in money and supposedly led a life of idleness with all its ridiculous affectations. He dabbled a little in art, collected Chinese lacquerware, and was just another one of those freeloaders found in every family. Franziska knew also that he was homosexual, but she was really amazed how someone like Leo, whose very profession obliged him to uphold a neutral and scientific attitude toward homosexuality and phenomena of a quite different magnitude, could go on and on about this cousin as though he had somehow, through his own negligence, fallen prey to works of art, homosexuality, and an inheritance to boot, but at that time Franziska still admired her husband too much to be more than irritated and hurt. With relief she heard from the old woman, in discussing those hard times, that Leo was infinitely grateful and had been a big help to this Johannes, who was then in the throes of a number of personal crises—which were better left untold. The old woman hesitated and then added, because she was, after all, sitting opposite the wife of a psychiatrist: I think you should know that Johannes is sexual.

Franziska controlled herself and suppressed a laugh, it was surely the most daring revelation the old woman had roused herself to in years, but with Franziska she was opening up more and more. She told her how Leo had often given Johannes advice, naturally free of charge, but Johannes was a hopeless case, and if a person didn't have the willpower to change it was understandable that he would be at his wits' end, and from what she heard, Johannes just kept on with it, the same as always. Franziska carefully translated this naive story into reality and understood even less why Leo talked about this cousin in such a disparaging and malicious way. At that time the obvious reason escaped her, namely, that Leo was reluctant to be reminded of his mother and his former wives and lovers who were nothing to him but a conspiracy of creditors from whom he could escape only by belittling them to himself and others. His tirades about his first wife were similar: she had been the epitome of everything diabolical, unappreciative and spiteful, traits that had not been revealed in depth until the divorce when her aristocratic father had hired a lawyer for her to secure some of the money for the child, money she'd given him when he was a young doctor and hard times had struck again. It was an alarmingly large sum to Franziska but, as she was told, one could expect nothing less from the "baroness," as Leo ironically called her, because the family had always treated him like an upstart, without having the slighest idea who was dwelling in their midst. It amused him to note that the "baroness" had never remarried and lived in total seclusion. After him she hadn't been able to find another fool—young and gullible and poor, as he had been—who would have married such a deserving Fräulein. She had understood nothing about his work, absolutely nothing, and although she behaved fairly in respect to the agreement about their son, sending him for regular visits and teaching him to respect his father, she obviously did it for no other reason than to prove to the world how generous she was.

The brilliant doctor's rise to fame along the thorny path of suffering had already become Franziska's religion at that time, and again and again she reproached herself with the image of him making his way, against indescribable odds and despite the obstacle that dreadful marriage posed, all the way to the top. And the cross he was forced to bear because of his mother, the financial and moral burden, was no light one for him, but that at least Franziska could take off his shoulders. Although it otherwise might not have occurred to her to spend her free hours with an old woman the time became something special when she thought of Leo: a helping hand, evidence of her love for him, allowing him to devote his undivided attention to his work.

Leo was just too good to her, he told her that she was overdoing it, the way she took care of his mother, a telephone call now and again would have sufficed. For the past few years the old woman had had a telephone which she feared more than loved: she didn't like to talk on the phone and always shouted into the mouthpiece and couldn't hear what the other party said, and besides that, the phone was too expensive, but of course Franziska wasn't to mention that to Leo. Once the old woman—prompted by Franziska and a second glass of sherry—did in fact begin to talk about the old days, the very old days, and it turned out that she wasn't from an educated family, her father had knit gloves and socks in a small factory in Lower Austria and she had been the oldest of eight children, but then she'd had a wonderful time when she took up employment with a Greek family, immensely rich people with a little boy, the most beautiful child she had ever laid eyes on, and she was his nursemaid. Being a nursemaid was a really good job, nothing degrading about it, and the Greek's young wife had had servants aplenty, oh yes, she'd had a real stroke of luck, such a good position had been hard to find back then. The child's name was Kiki, at least everyone had called him Kiki. When the old woman began talking about Kiki more and more frequently, remembering every detail—what Kiki had said, how cute and affectionate he was, the walks they'd taken together— her eyes lit up as they never did when she spoke of her own child. Kiki had simply been a little angel, never naughty, she stressed, never naughty at all, and the separation must have been terrible, they hadn't told Kiki that the Fräulein was leaving, and she had cried all night long, and once, years later, she had tried to find out what had become of the family. First she'd heard that they were traveling, then that they were back in Greece, and now she had no idea whatsoever what had happened to Kiki, who must be over sixty by now, yes, over sixty she said pensively, and she had been forced to leave because the Greek family had planned their first major trip and couldn't take her along, and when they left the young wife had given her a wonderful present. The old woman stood up and rummaged in a jewelry box, then showed her the brooch from Kiki's mother, it was the real thing, with diamonds, but she still asked herself today if they hadn't let her go because the wife had noticed that Kiki was more attached to her than to his own mother, she could understand that all right, but it had been the hardest blow of all, and she had never completely recovered from it. Franziska regarded the brooch thoughtfully; perhaps it really was quite valuable, she didn't know much about jewelry, but she was beginning to realize something else: this Kiki must have meant more to the old woman than Leo. She often hesitated to talk about Leo's childhood, or she began only to break off in fright saying abruptly: It was just childish nonsense, you know boys are so hard to raise, he didn't do it on purpose, he was just having such a bad time and it was all I could do to make ends meet. But you get everything back a hundredfold when a child has grown up and made his own way and become so famous, he takes after his father more than me, you know.

Franziska carefully handed back the brooch, and once again the old woman started in fear. Please Franziska, don't mention a word of this to Leo, it could annoy him. I have my plans, you know, if I get sick I could sell it so that I won't become even more of a burden to him. Franziska embraced the old woman with a hug that was both timid and fierce. Don't ever do that, promise me you'll never sell this brooch. You're not a burden to us at all!

On the way home she made one detour after the other, in a state of inner turmoil, this poor woman shouldn't sell her brooch while she and Leo spent money freely, went on trips, entertained. She kept debating what she should say to Leo, but a first, faint alarm sounded inside her, because even though the old woman had her quirks and exaggerated things, she must be right about something, and so in the end she didn't say a word about it at home and only reported cheerfully that his mother was doing very well. But before they left for a conference in London she arranged a contract with a garage which ran a private taxi service, made a downpayment, and said to the old woman: An idea has occurred to us, because you shouldn't walk too far by yourself. Just call a taxi when you want to go out, it hardly costs a thing, it's just a favor from an old patient, but don't say anything about it, especially not to Leo, you know how he is, he doesn't like it when you thank him and everything, and you just ride to town when you need something, and have the taxi wait, but always have Herr Pineider take you, the young one. He doesn't know that his father was one of Leo's patients though, that comes under professional secrecy, you know, I was just there and talked to him, and you have to promise me, for Leo's sake, that you'll take the taxi, it would ease our minds. In the beginning, the old woman made little use of the taxi, and Franziska scolded her for it when she returned from England; her leg had worsened and the old woman had naturally done all her shopping on foot, once even going so far as to take the streetcar into town because one could hardly get anything in Hietzing, and Franziska said firmly, as if to a stubborn child: This is definitely not to happen again.

They exhausted one topic after another: Kiki, the life of a young nursemaid in Vienna before the First World War and before her marriage, and sometimes it was only Franziska who talked, especially when she had just returned from a trip with Leo, a brilliant talk he'd delivered at the conference, and that he had given her this offprint for his mother. The old woman labored through the title with an effort: "The Significance of Endogenous and Exogenous Factors in Connection with the Occurrence of Paranoid and Depressive Psychoses in Former Concentration Camp Inmates and Refugees." Franziska assured her it was merely the groundwork for a much larger study he was working on, and he was even letting her help him with it. It would probably become the most significant and the first really important book in the field. A work of incalculable impact.

The old woman was strangely mute, surely she didn't understand the implications of these studies, maybe nothing at all of what her son was doing. Then she said, surprisingly: I hope he won't make too many enemies with it, here in Vienna, and then there's that other thing . . .

Franziska grew agitated: But that's exactly the point, that would be a very good thing, it's a provocation, too, and Leo isn't afraid of anyone, for him it's the only thing that counts, that has a purpose far beyond its scientific significance.

Yes, of course, the old woman said quickly, and he knows how to defend himself, and if you're famous you always have enemies. I was just thinking about Johannes, but that's so long ago now. Did you know that he was in a concentration camp for a year and a half before the war ended? Franziska was surprised, she hadn't known, but she failed to see the connection. The old woman didn't want to say any more but then continued: It meant a certain amount of danger for Leo, having a relative who, well, you know what I mean. Yes, of course, said Franziska, still somewhat confused; sometimes the old woman had such a roundabout way of saying things without really saying them, and she couldn't make head or tail of it, although suddenly she was bursting with pride that a member of Leo's family had been through something so terrible and that Leo, in his tactful, modest way, had never said anything about it to her, not even about the danger he must have faced as a young doctor. That afternoon the old woman didn't want to go on talking; she merely asked disjointedly: Do you hear it, too?

What?

The dogs, the old woman said. There were never so many dogs in Hietzing, I've heard them barking again, and they bark at night, too. Frau Schönthal next door has a poodle now. It doesn't bark much though, it's such a nice dog, I see her almost every day when I go shopping, but we only say hello, her husband doesn't have much of an education.

Franziska drove home as quickly as she could; this time she wanted to ask Leo if there was anything to the fact that his mother had suddenly begun talking about dogs, if it was an alarming symptom, maybe it had something to do with her age. She had also noticed that the old woman had been upset once about ten schillings which had been lying on the table and then disappeared when Frau Agnes left, all this excitement about ten missing schillings, certainly she had only imagined it anyway, weren't those all signs of the process of aging? It couldn't possibly have been the cleaning woman, she was what people in certain circles—that is, in better circles—called a "God-fearing" woman who came more out of pity than for the money, which she didn't need anyway—she did it as a favor and nothing more. And old Frau Jordan's pitiful presents—an ancient, threadbare purse or some other useless paraphernalia—would hardly have induced Frau Agnes to come; she had realized long ago that she had nothing to expect from the old woman or from her son, and she knew nothing of Franziska's enthusiastic plans for improving the situation; Franziska had chided the old woman as though she were a child, because she didn't want to lose this valuable help over a bout of senile obstinacy and an unfounded suspicion.

More and more often she found the old woman at the window when she arrived, and they no longer sat together when Franziska came to drink sherry and nibble on pastries. The business with the dogs continued, although at the same time her hearing problem grew worse, and Franziska was at a loss. Something had to be done, and Leo, whom she bothered with none of this, was not going to avoid devoting some attention to his mother one of these days. Only then things started becoming complicated between Leo and herself, and she discovered that he had so intimidated her that she was afraid of him. But at least once, in a fit of her old courage, she overcame her inexplicable fear and suggested at dinner: Why don't we invite your mother to come and stay with us, we have enough room, and then our Rosi could always be with her and you would never have to worry, besides, she's so quiet and undemanding, she would never disturb you, and certainly not me, I'm suggesting it for your sake because I know how much you worry. Leo was in a good mood that evening and secretly happy about something. She didn't realize what it was but had decided to make use of the opportunity, and he answered, laughing: What an idea, you have no feel for the situation, my dear, you can't uproot an elderly person after a while, it would only depress her and she needs her freedom, she's a strong woman who has lived alone for decades. You don't know her the way I do, she would die of fright here, just from the kind of people who come over. She'd probably debate for hours on end whether to use the bathroom, out of fear that one of us just might want to use it. Come on, my little Franziska, please don't make such a face, I think your impulse is touching and admirable, but that wonderful idea of yours would be the death of her. Believe me, it's just that I happen to know more about these things.

But this business with the dogs . . . ? Franziska began to stutter, she hadn't wanted to talk about it and would gladly have immediately taken back what she'd said. She was no longer capable of putting her apprehension into words.

What, her husband asked in a completely different tone of voice, she doesn't still want a mutt, does she? I don't understand, Franziska answered. Why should she—you don't mean she wants to have a dog, do you?

Of course I do, and I'm more than glad that this childish interlude has blown over so quickly, at her age she just couldn't handle a dog, she should take care of herself, that's more important to me, a dog is such a nuisance, she has no idea what they would mean, with her advancing senility. She never said anything about it, Franziska replied half-heartedly, I don't think she wants a dog. I wanted to say something entirely different, but it's not important, sorry. Would you like a cognac, are you going to work later, should I type anything for you?

At her next visit Franziska didn't know how to persuade the old woman, who was always on the alert, to give her answers she needed to know. She approached the subject in a roundabout way, remarking casually: Incidentally, I saw Frau Schönthal's dog today, really a cute dog, I like poodles a lot, actually all animals, because I grew up in the country, you know, we always had dogs, I mean my grandparents and everyone in the village, and cats, too, of course. Wouldn't it be good for you to have a dog or a cat, now that you have trouble reading. I mean, certainly that kind of thing passes, but I for one would absolutely love to have a dog. But you know, in the city it's just a bother and not really fair to the dog, but here in Hietzing, where it can frisk around in the yard and you can go for walks . . .

The old woman exclaimed in agitation: A dog, no, no, I don't want a dog! Franziska realized she had done something wrong, but felt at the same time that she hadn't offended the old woman as she might have had she suggested a parrot or canaries: it must have been something else entirely that had put her in such a state of agitation. After a while the old woman said very quietly: Nuri was a really nice dog, and I got along well with him, that was, let me think, it must have been five years ago, but then I had to give him away, to a home or a place where they resell them. Leo doesn't like dogs. No, what am I saying, it was different, there was something in that dog I can't really understand, he couldn't stand Leo, he always jumped at him and barked madly whenever Leo made the slightest move toward the door, and then once he almost bit him, and Leo was so indignant, of course that's understandable, when a dog is that wild, but he was never like that otherwise, not even with strangers, and then naturally I gave him away. I couldn't let Leo be barked at and bitten by Nuri, no, that would have been too much, Leo should be able to feel at home when he visits me and not have to get angry about some poorly trained dog.

Franziska thought that, although there was no longer a dog who jumped at him and disliked him, Leo came seldom enough as it was, and even less often since Franziska came instead. How long had it been anyway since his last visit? Once the three of them had gone for a short ride along the Weinstrasse and into the Helenenthal and lunched at an inn with his mother; otherwise Franziska always came alone.

Be sure not to say anything to Leo, though, that business with Nuri really hurt his feelings, he's very sensitive, you know, and to this day I can't forgive myself for being so selfish as to want to have Nuri, but old people are very selfish, dear Franziska, you can't understand that yet, you're still so young and good, but when you're very old you get all these selfish desires, and you can't just let yourself give in to them. What would have become of me if Leo hadn't taken care of me, his father died all of a sudden like that and there was no time to make any arrangements, and there wasn't any money, either, my husband was a little careless, no, not a spendthrift, but he had a hard time of it and didn't have much of a knack with money, Leo doesn't take after him in that respect. In those days I could still work, the boy was a reason to keep going, and I was still young, but what would I do nowadays? My one fear has always been having to go to an old people's home, but Leo would never stand for that, and if I didn't have this apartment I'd have to go to some home, and I guess a dog isn't worth all that. Franziska listened to her, clenched up inside, and she said to herself: So that's it, that's it, she gave her dog away for his sake. And she asked herself: What kind of people are we?—because she was incapable of thinking: What kind of a man is my husband!—we're just so cruel, and she thinks she's selfish, and all the time we have everything we want! In order to hide her tears she quickly unpacked a small package from Meinl, little things, and acted as though she hadn't understood. Oh, by the way, I'm so scatterbrained today, I've only brought you the tea and coffee and a little smoked salmon and Russian salad. Actually it doesn't go together all that well, but I was really flustered at the store because Leo is leaving and one of the manuscripts isn't finished yet. But he'll give you a call tonight, and he'll be back in a week anyway.

He needs a break, the old woman said, see to it that he gets one if you can, you two haven't had any vacation at all yet this year. Franziska said brightly: That's a good idea, I'll convince him some way or another, I just need to think of a strategy, but thanks a lot, that's really a good piece of advice, he's constantly overworked, you know, and at some point I have to make him slow down.

What Franziska did not know was that this was her last visit to the old woman and she no longer needed the strategy, because other things came to pass, events of such hurricane force that she almost forgot the old woman and a great many other things as well.

In her fear, the old woman didn't ask her son on the phone why Franziska had stopped coming. She was worried, but her son sounded cheerful and unconcerned, and once he even came over and stayed for twenty minutes. He didn't touch the pastries, he didn't finish the sherry and he didn't talk about Franziska, but he did talk quite a bit about himself, and that made her ecstatic because it had been such a long time since he had spoken about himself. So he was leaving on vacation now, he needed a break, but the word "Mexico" gave the old woman a mild shock, wasn't that the place where they had scorpions and revolutions and savages and earthquakes, but he laughed reassuringly, kissed her and promised to write. He sent a few postcards, which she read religiously. Franziska hadn't added her regards. Once Franziska called her from Carinthia. Really, the money these young people throw out the window! Franziska had only called to ask if everything was okay. Then they talked about Leo, but the old woman kept shouting at the most inappropriate times: It's getting too expensive, child, but Franziska kept talking, yes, she had finally succeeded, he was finally taking a break, and she had had to go to her brother's, there was something to settle here, that was why she hadn't been able to accompany Leo. Family matters in Carinthia. Because of the house. Then the old woman received a strange envelope with a few lines from Franziska. She didn't say anything, just sent her regards and wrote that she would like her to have this photo she had taken herself, the photograph was of Leo, apparently on the Semmering Pass,[5] laughing in a snowy landscape in front of a large hotel. The old woman decided not to say anything to Leo; he wouldn't have asked her anyway. She hid the photograph under the brooch in her jewelry box.

She could no longer read books and was bored by the radio; newspapers were all she wanted, and Frau Agnes got them for her. It took her hours to decipher them, she read the obituaries and always felt a certain satisfaction when someone younger than herself had passed away. Well, look at that, Professor Haderer too, he could hardly have been more than seventy. Frau Schönthal's mother had died, too, of cancer, she wasn't even sixty-five. The old woman stiffly offered her condolences in the grocery store and didn't even look at the poodle, and then she went home and stood at the window. She slept more than old people are said to sleep, but she often awoke, only to hear the dogs again. She was startled whenever the cleaning woman came: since Franziska's visits had ended, it bothered her when anyone came over, and she had the impression that she was changing. Now she actually was frightened of suddenly collapsing in the street or losing control of herself when she had to go to town for something, and so she obediently called young Herr Pineider, who drove her around. And she became accustomed to this small precaution for her own safety. She completely lost her sense of time, and when Leo once came by to see her, deeply tanned, she no longer knew if he was returning from Mexico or when he had been there at all. But she was careful not to ask, and gathered from something he said that he had just arrived from Ischia,[6] back from a trip to Italy. Confused, she said: Good, good. That was good for you. And while he was telling her something the dogs began to bark, several of them, all at once, very near, and she was so completely encircled by the barking and a very gentle, gentle terror that she was no longer afraid of her son. The fear of an entire lifetime suddenly left her.

When he said on his way out: Next time I'll bring Elfi over, you have to meet her one of these days! she had no idea what he was talking about. Wasn't he married to Franziska anymore, how long had it been, how many wives was that

---

5. In the Alps in southern Austria, known as a tourist resort and center for winter sports.

6. An island vacation spot north of the Bay of Naples.

now anyway, she could no longer remember how long he had lived with Franziska and when, and she said: Go ahead and bring her over. Fine. Whatever is best for you. The barking was so close now that for an instant she was certain that Nuri was with her again and would jump at him and bark. She wished he would finally leave, she wanted to be alone. She thanked him out of habit, just in case, and he asked in astonishment: Whatever for? Now I really did go and forget to bring you my book after all. A phenomenal success. I'll have it sent.

Well then, thank you so much my child. Send it over, but unfortunately your dumb old mother can hardly read anymore and doesn't understand much anyway.

She let him embrace her and found herself alone again surrounded by the barking. It came from every garden and house in Hietzing, an invasion of the beasts had begun, the dogs came closer, barking to her, and she stood erect, as always, no longer dreaming of the time with Kiki and the Greeks, no longer thinking of the day when the last ten schillings had disappeared and Leo had lied to her. Instead she redoubled her efforts to hide things better, wishing she could throw them away, especially the brooch and the photograph, so that Leo wouldn't find anything after she died. But she couldn't think of a good hiding place, maybe the bucket with the scraps, but she trusted Frau Agnes less and less, too, because she would have had to give her the rubbish, and she suspected that the woman would rummage through it and find the brooch. Once she said, a little too harshly: At least you could give the bones and the leftovers to the dogs.

The cleaning woman looked at her in amazement and asked: What dogs? To the dogs, of course, insisted the old woman in an imperious tone, I want the dogs to have them!

She was a suspicious looking creature, a thief. She probably took the bones home with her.

To the dogs, I said. Can't you understand me, are you deaf or something? No wonder, at your age.

Then the barking diminished, and she thought: someone has chased the dogs off or given them away, because now it was no longer that same powerful, recurrent, barking. The fainter the barking, the more adamant she became: she was only biding her time until the louder barking resumed. One had to be able to wait, and she could wait. All at once it was no longer a barking sound, although there was no doubt it came from the dogs in the neighborhood. It wasn't a growling either, just now and again the great, wild, triumphant howling of a single dog, then a whimpering, the faint barking of all the others fading into the distance.

One day nearly two years after the death of his sister Franziska, Dr. Martin Ranner received a bill from a company by the name of Pineider for taxi services listed separately by date, for which Frau Franziska Jordan had made a downpayment and signed a contract. But because only very few trips had been made while Franziska was alive and the majority after her death he called the company for an explanation of this mysterious bill. Although the explanation actually explained very little, he had no desire to call his former brother-in-law or ever see him again, so he paid the fares, in installments, for a woman he had never known and never had anything to do with. He came to the conclusion that the old Frau Jordan must have passed away some time ago; the company had let several months go by since her last trip, perhaps out of reverence, before asserting its claims.

GABRIEL GARCÍA MÁRQUEZ

born 1928

The best-known novelist of the Latin American "Boom" of the 1960s and 1970s, Gabriel García Márquez embodies, in his work, the mixture of fantasy and actuality known as "magic realism." Again and again García Márquez returns to certain themes: the contrast between dreamlike experiences and everyday reality; the enchanted or inexplicable aspect of fictional creation; and the solitude of individuals in societies that can never quite incorporate them. His fiction, which contains mythic dimensions that are often rooted in local folklore, reimagines regional tales to explore broader social and psychological conflicts. Even those works based in historical fact transform the characters and events into a fictional universe with its own set of laws.

García Márquez was born on March 6, 1928, in the small town of Aracataca, in the "banana zone" of Colombia. The first of twelve children, he was raised by his maternal grandparents until 1936, when his grandfather died. As an adult, he would attribute his love of fantasy to his grandmother, who told him fantastical tales whenever she wanted to shush his incessant questions. His grandfather, meanwhile, passed on a marked interest in politics, having fought on the Liberal side of a civil war early in the century. After receiving his undergraduate degree as a scholarship student at the National Colegio in Zipaquirá, García Márquez studied law at the University of Bogotá in 1947. It was there, he later claimed, that he read **Kafka's The Metamorphosis**, in a Spanish translation by **Jorge Luis Borges**. "Shit," he said to himself after reading the first sentence, "that's just the way my grandmother talked!" The next day he wrote "The Third Resignation," the Kafkaesque tale of a man in his coffin who continued to grow (and retain consciousness) for seventeen years after his death. It was the first of his works to be published. García Márquez found in Kafka the mobile balance of nonrealistic events and realistic detail that—combined with his grandmother's quixotic stories and his grandfather's political concerns—would become the genre known as magic realism. In this mode the narrator treats the subjective beliefs and experiences of the characters, often derived from folklore and supernatural beliefs, as if they were real, even when (to a scientifically minded observer) they seem impossible. Some of García Márquez's early novels also reflected the influence of **William Faulkner,** whom he later described as "my master"—in particular, Faulkner's representation of subjective experience through stream-of-consciousness technique and the southern writer's depiction of an underdeveloped geographical region beset by a long history of conflict.

In 1950, García Márquez abandoned his legal studies for journalism. As a correspondent for various Latin American newspapers, he traveled to Paris and later to Eastern Europe, Venezuela, Cuba, and New York. After writing several novels, short stories, and film scripts, he gained international fame for his novel *One Hundred Years of Solitude*. Published in 1967, it chronicles the rise and fall of the fortunes of the Buendía family in a mythical town called Macondo (based on the author's hometown of Aracataca). A global best seller, it was soon translated into multiple languages and received prizes in Italy and France. When it was published in English, in 1970, American critics praised it as one of the best books of the year, and it has since become a monument of world literature.

The author's later work was preoccupied with contemporary events, especially the prevalence of dictatorship in Latin American societies. As García Márquez continued to publish successful novels, he also became an advocate for social justice, speaking out for revolutionary governments in Latin America and organizing assistance for political prisoners. There were even rumors of a plot, backed by the Colombian government, to assassinate García Márquez because of his antigovernment activities; in 1981 he sought asylum in Mexico. He lives partly in Mexico City and spends time in Colombia and Europe as well.

The story printed here, "Death Constant Beyond Love" (1970), dates from the author's later, more politically active period. It has a political background, although its protagonist, Senator Onésimo Sánchez, appears chiefly through the lens of his struggles with the existential problem of death. García Márquez presents an essentially satirical portrait of Sánchez, a corrupt politician who accepts bribes and stays in power by helping the local property owners avoid reform. His electoral train is a traveling circus with carnival wagons, fireworks, a ready-made audience of hired Indians, and a cardboard village with imitation brick houses and a painted ocean liner to represent the (shallow) promise of prosperity. Among the citizenry, Sánchez uses carefully placed gifts to encourage support and a feeling of dependence.

Yet the spectacle of the senator's campaign for office, and even the sordid background of poverty and corruption that enables it, fade into insignificance before the broader themes of life and death. Forty-two, happily married, and in full control, as a powerful politician in mid-career, of the lives of himself and others, he is made suddenly to feel—when told that he will be dead "forever" by next Christmas—helpless, vulnerable, and alone. Theoretically he knows that death is inevitable and that the course of nature cannot be defeated. He has read Marcus Aurelius (121–180 C.E.) and refers to the Stoic philosopher's *Meditations*, which criticizes the delusions of those "who have tenaciously stuck to life" and recommends the cheerful acceptance of natural order, including death.

In this crisis the senator is reduced to basic, instinctual existence, drawing him deeper into García Márquez's recurrent themes of solitude, love, and death. The beautiful Laura provides an opportunity for him to submerge his fear of death in erotic passion. This choice means scandal and the destruction of his political career, but by now Onésimo Sánchez has felt the emptiness of his earlier activities—and has given them up for the hopeless struggle to cheat death. "Death Constant Beyond Love" reverses the ambitious claim of a famous sonnet by the Spanish Golden Age writer Quevedo (1580–1645), according to which there is "Love Constant Beyond Death." Such love is an illusion, for it is death, beyond everything else, that awaits us.

Gabriel García Márquez received the Nobel Prize in Literature in 1982. In his acceptance speech he drew connections between his novels and the sufferings of the peoples of Latin America through dictatorship and civil war. Voicing hope for an end to the nuclear arms race, the writer spoke of a "new and sweeping utopia of life, where no one will be able to decide for others how they die, where love will prove true and happiness be possible, and where the races condemned to one hundred years of solitude will have, at last and forever, a second opportunity on earth."

Death Constant Beyond Love[1]

Senator Onésimo Sánchez had six months and eleven days to go before his death when he found the woman of his life. He met her in Rosal del Virrey,[2] an illusory village which by night was the furtive wharf for smugglers' ships, and on the other hand, in broad daylight looked like the most useless inlet on the desert, facing a sea that was arid and without direction and so far from everything no one would have suspected that someone capable of changing the destiny of anyone lived there. Even its name was a kind of joke, because the only rose in that village was being worn by Senator Onésimo Sánchez himself on the same afternoon when he met Laura Farina.

It was an unavoidable stop in the electoral campaign he made every four years. The carnival wagons had arrived in the morning. Then came the trucks with the rented Indians[3] who were carried into the towns in order to enlarge the crowds at public ceremonies. A short time before eleven o'clock, along with the music and rockets and jeeps of the retinue, the ministerial automobile, the color of strawberry soda, arrived. Senator Onésimo Sánchez was placid and weatherless inside the air-conditioned car, but as soon as he opened the door he was shaken by a gust of fire and his shirt of pure silk was soaked in a kind of light-colored soup and he felt many years older and more alone than ever. In real life he had just turned forty-two, had been graduated from Göttingen[4] with honors as a metallurgical engineer, and was an avid reader, although without much reward, of badly translated Latin classics. He was married to a radiant German woman who had given him five children and they were all happy in their home, he the happiest of all until they told him, three months before, that he would be dead forever by next Christmas.

While the preparations for the public rally were being completed, the senator managed to have an hour alone in the house they had set aside for him to rest in. Before he lay down he put in a glass of drinking water the rose he had kept alive all across the desert, lunched on the diet cereals that he took with him so as to avoid the repeated portions of fried goat that were waiting for him during the rest of the day, and he took several analgesic pills before the time prescribed so that he would have the remedy ahead of the pain. Then he put the electric fan close to the hammock and stretched out naked for fifteen minutes in the shadow of the rose, making a great effort at mental distraction so as not to think about death while he dozed. Except for the doctors, no one knew that he had been sentenced to a fixed term, for he had decided to endure his secret all alone, with no change in his life, not because of pride but out of shame.[5]

He felt in full control of his will when he appeared in public again at three in the afternoon, rested and clean, wearing a pair of coarse linen slacks and a floral shirt, and with his soul sustained by the anti-pain pills. Nevertheless, the erosion of death was much more pernicious than he had supposed, for as he

---

1. Translated by Gregory Rabassa.
2. The Rosebush of the Viceroy (governor).
3. People descended from the original inhabitants of the continent; generally poorer and less privileged than those descended from Spanish or Portuguese colonists.

4. A well-known German university.
5. "Death is such as generation is, a mystery of nature . . . altogether not a thing of which any man should be ashamed" (Marcus Aurelius, *Meditations* 4.5).

went up onto the platform he felt a strange disdain for those who were fighting for the good luck to shake his hand, and he didn't feel sorry as he had at other times for the groups of barefoot Indians who could scarcely bear the hot saltpeter coals of the sterile little square. He silenced the applause with a wave of his hand, almost with rage, and he began to speak without gestures, his eyes fixed on the sea, which was sighing with heat. His measured, deep voice had the quality of calm water, but the speech that had been memorized and ground out so many times had not occurred to him in the nature of telling the truth, but, rather, as the opposite of a fatalistic pronouncement by Marcus Aurelius in the fourth book of his *Meditations*.

"We are here for the purpose of defeating nature," he began, against all his convictions. "We will no longer be foundlings in our own country, orphans of God in a realm of thirst and bad climate, exiles in our own land. We will be different people, ladies and gentlemen, we will be a great and happy people."

There was a pattern to his circus. As he spoke his aides threw clusters of paper birds into the air and the artificial creatures took on life, flew about the platform of planks, and went out to sea. At the same time, other men took some prop trees with felt leaves out of the wagons and planted them in the saltpeter soil behind the crowd. They finished by setting up a cardboard façade with make-believe houses of red brick that had glass windows, and with it they covered the miserable real-life shacks.

The senator prolonged his speech with two quotations in Latin in order to give the farce more time. He promised rainmaking machines, portable breeders for table animals, the oils of happiness which would make vegetables grow in the saltpeter and clumps of pansies in the window boxes. When he saw that his fictional world was all set up, he pointed to it. "That's the way it will be for us, ladies and gentlemen," he shouted. "Look! That's the way it will be for us."

The audience turned around. An ocean liner made of painted paper was passing behind the houses and it was taller than the tallest houses in the artificial city. Only the senator himself noticed that since it had been set up and taken down and carried from one place to another the superimposed cardboard town had been eaten away by the terrible climate and that it was almost as poor and dusty as Rosal del Virrey.

For the first time in twelve years, Nelson Farina didn't go to greet the senator. He listened to the speech from his hammock amidst the remains of his siesta, under the cool bower of a house of unplaned boards which he had built with the same pharmacist's hands with which he had drawn and quartered his first wife. He had escaped from Devil's Island[6] and appeared in Rosal del Virrey on a ship loaded with innocent macaws, with a beautiful and blasphemous black woman he had found in Paramaribo[7] and by whom he had a daughter. The woman died of natural causes a short while later and she didn't suffer the fate of the other, whose pieces had fertilized her own cauliflower patch, but was buried whole and with her Dutch name in the local cemetery. The daughter had inherited her color and her figure along with her father's yellow and astonished eyes, and he had good reason to imagine that he was rearing the most beautiful woman in the world.

6. A former French penal colony off the coast of French Guiana in northern South America.

7. Capital of Suriname (formerly Dutch Guiana) and a large port.

Ever since he had met Senator Onésimo Sánchez during his first electoral campaign, Nelson Farina had begged for his help in getting a false identity card which would place him beyond the reach of the law. The senator, in a friendly but firm way, had refused. Nelson Farina never gave up, and for several years, every time he found the chance, he would repeat his request with a different recourse. But this time he stayed in his hammock, condemned to rot alive in that burning den of buccaneers. When he heard the final applause, he lifted his head, and looking over the boards of the fence, he saw the back side of the farce: the props for the buildings, the framework of the trees, the hidden illusionists who were pushing the ocean liner along. He spat without rancor.

"*Merde*," he said. "*C'est le Blacamán de la politique.*"[8]

After the speech, as was customary, the senator took a walk through the streets of the town in the midst of the music and the rockets and was besieged by the townspeople, who told him their troubles. The senator listened to them good-naturedly and he always found some way to console everybody without having to do them any difficult favors. A woman up on the roof of a house with her six youngest children managed to make herself heard over the uproar and the fireworks.

"I'm not asking for much, Senator," she said. "Just a donkey to haul water from Hanged Man's Well."

The senator noticed the six thin children. "What became of your husband?" he asked.

"He went to find his fortune on the island of Aruba,"[9] the woman answered good-humoredly, "and what he found was a foreign woman, the kind that put diamonds on their teeth."

The answer brought on a roar of laughter.

"All right," the senator decided, "you'll get your donkey."

A short while later an aide of his brought a good pack donkey to the woman's house and on the rump it had a campaign slogan written in indelible paint so that no one would ever forget that it was a gift from the senator.

Along the short stretch of street he made other, smaller gestures, and he even gave a spoonful of medicine to a sick man who had had his bed brought to the door of his house so he could see him pass. At the last corner, through the boards of the fence, he saw Nelson Farina in his hammock, looking ashen and gloomy, but nonetheless the senator greeted him, with no show of affection.

"Hello, how are you?"

Nelson Farina turned in his hammock and soaked him in the sad amber of his look.

"*Moi, vous savez,*"[1] he said.

His daughter came out into the yard when she heard the greeting. She was wearing a cheap, faded Guajiro Indian[2] robe, her head was decorated with

---

8. Shit. He's the Blacamán of politics (French). Blacamán is a charlatan and huckster who appears in several stories, including *Blacamán the Good, Vendor of Miracles.*

9. Off the coast of Venezuela, famous as a tourist resort.

1. "Oh well, as for me, you know" (French).

2. Inhabitant of the rural Guajira Peninsula of northern Colombia. The figure of Laura Farina is thus connected with the rustic poor, with earthy reality (*farina* means "flour"), and with erotic inspiration. (*Laura* was the beloved celebrated by the Italian Renaissance poet Francis Petrarch, 1304–1374.)

colored bows, and her face was painted as protection against the sun, but even in that state of disrepair it was possible to imagine that there had never been another so beautiful in the whole world. The senator was left breathless. "I'll be damned!" he breathed in surprise. "The Lord does the craziest things!"

That night Nelson Farina dressed his daughter up in her best clothes and sent her to the senator. Two guards armed with rifles who were nodding from the heat in the borrowed house ordered her to wait on the only chair in the vestibule.

The senator was in the next room meeting with the important people of Rosal del Virrey, whom he had gathered together in order to sing for them the truths he had left out of his speeches. They looked so much like all the ones he always met in all the towns in the desert that even the senator himself was sick and tired of that perpetual nightly session. His shirt was soaked with sweat and he was trying to dry it on his body with the hot breeze from an electric fan that was buzzing like a horse fly in the heavy heat of the room.

"We, of course, can't eat paper birds," he said. "You and I know that the day there are trees and flowers in this heap of goat dung, the day there are shad instead of worms in the water holes, that day neither you nor I will have anything to do here, do I make myself clear?"

No one answered. While he was speaking, the senator had torn a sheet off the calendar and fashioned a paper butterfly out of it with his hands. He tossed it with no particular aim into the air current coming from the fan and the butterfly flew about the room and then went out through the half-open door. The senator went on speaking with a control aided by the complicity of death.

"Therefore," he said, "I don't have to repeat to you what you already know too well: that my reelection is a better piece of business for you than it is for me, because I'm fed up with stagnant water and Indian sweat, while you people, on the other hand, make your living from it."

Laura Farina saw the paper butterfly come out. Only she saw it because the guards in the vestibule had fallen asleep on the steps, hugging their rifles. After a few turns, the large lithographed butterfly unfolded completely, flattened against the wall, and remained stuck there. Laura Farina tried to pull it off with her nails. One of the guards, who woke up with the applause from the next room, noticed her vain attempt.

"It won't come off," he said sleepily. "It's painted on the wall."

Laura Farina sat down again when the men began to come out of the meeting. The senator stood in the doorway of the room with his hand on the latch, and he only noticed Laura Farina when the vestibule was empty.

"What are you doing here?"

"*C'est de la part de mon père,*"[3] she said.

The senator understood. He scrutinized the sleeping guards, then he scrutinized Laura Farina, whose unusual beauty was even more demanding than his pain, and he resolved then that death had made his decision for him.

"Come in," he told her.

Laura Farina was struck dumb standing in the doorway to the room: thousands of bank notes were floating in the air, flapping like the butterfly. But the

---

3. "My father sent me" (French).

senator turned off the fan and the bills were left without air and alighted on the objects in the room.

"You see," he said, smiling, "even shit can fly."

Laura Farina sat down on a schoolboy's stool. Her skin was smooth and firm, with the same color and the same solar density as crude oil, her hair was the mane of a young mare, and her huge eyes were brighter than the light. The senator followed the thread of her look and finally found the rose, which had been tarnished by the saltpeter.

"It's a rose," he said.

"Yes," she said with a trace of perplexity. "I learned what they were in Riohacha."[4]

The senator sat down on an army cot, talking about roses as he unbuttoned his shirt. On the side where he imagined his heart to be inside his chest he had a corsair's tattoo of a heart pierced by an arrow. He threw the soaked shirt to the floor and asked Laura Farina to help him off with his boots.

She knelt down facing the cot. The senator continued to scrutinize her, thoughtfully, and while he was untying the laces he wondered which one of them would end up with the bad luck of that encounter.

"You're just a child," he said.

"Don't you believe it," she said. "I'll be nineteen in April."

The senator became interested.

"What day?"

"The eleventh," she said.

The senator felt better. "We're both Aries,"[5] he said. And smiling, he added: "It's the sign of solitude."

Laura Farina wasn't paying attention because she didn't know what to do with the boots. The senator, for his part, didn't know what to do with Laura Farina, because he wasn't used to sudden love affairs and, besides, he knew that the one at hand had its origins in indignity. Just to have some time to think, he held Laura Farina tightly between his knees, embraced her about the waist, and lay down on his back on the cot. Then he realized that she was naked under her dress, for her body gave off the dark fragrance of an animal of the woods, but her heart was frightened and her skin disturbed by a glacial sweat.

"No one loves us," he sighed.

Laura Farina tried to say something, but there was only enough air for her to breathe. He laid her down beside him to help her, he put out the light and the room was in the shadow of the rose. She abandoned herself to the mercies of her fate. The senator caressed her slowly, seeking her with his hand, barely touching her, but where he expected to find her, he came across something iron that was in the way.

"What have you got there?"

"A padlock,"[6] she said.

"What in hell!" the senator said furiously and asked what he knew only too well. "Where's the key?"

---

4. A port on the Guajira Peninsula.
5. Sign in the zodiac; people born between March 21 and April 19 are said to be under the sign of Aries.
6. She is wearing a chastity belt, a medieval device worn by women to prevent sexual intercourse.

Laura Farina gave a breath of relief.

"My papa has it," she answered. "He told me to tell you to send one of your people to get it and to send along with him a written promise that you'll straighten out his situation."

The senator grew tense. "Frog[7] bastard," he murmured indignantly. Then he closed his eyes in order to relax and he met himself in the darkness. *Remember,* he remembered, *that whether it's you or someone else, it won't be long before you'll be dead and it won't be long before your name won't even be left.*[8]

He waited for the shudder to pass.

"Tell me one thing," he asked then. "What have you heard about me?"

"Do you want the honest-to-God truth?"

"The honest-to-God truth."

"Well," Laura Farina ventured, "they say you're worse than the rest because you're different."

The senator didn't get upset. He remained silent for a long time with his eyes closed, and when he opened them again he seemed to have returned from his most hidden instincts.

"Oh, what the hell," he decided. "Tell your son of a bitch of a father that I'll straighten out his situation."

"If you want, I can go get the key myself," Laura Farina said.

The senator held her back.

"Forget about the key," he said, "and sleep awhile with me. It's good to be with someone when you're so alone."

Then she laid his head on her shoulder with her eyes fixed on the rose. The senator held her about the waist, sank his face into woods-animal armpit, and gave in to terror. Six months and eleven days later he would die in that same position, debased and repudiated because of the public scandal with Laura Farina and weeping with rage at dying without her.

1970

7. Epithet for "French."
8. A direct translation of a sentence from Marcus Aurelius's *Meditations* (4.6).

V. S. NAIPAUL

born 1932

Trinidadian Nobel laureate V. S. Naipaul has traveled widely to document the lives of the poor and downtrodden, in essays and novels set on five continents. Of Indian descent, raised in multicultural Trinidad, and educated in England, Naipaul was one of the first writers to gain international prominence for representing the postcolonial world, but he has often riled critics and intellectuals with his controversial views. He has, for example, been critical of postcolonial governments and cultures and displayed an almost nostalgic attitude toward colonial times. His rejection of any political ideology has helped give his observations of the contemporary world their intensity and precision.

Vidiadhar Surajprasad Naipaul was born to Hindu parents on August 17, 1932, in the small town of Chaguanas, Trinidad. For the first six years of his life, Naipaul lived in the "Lion's Den," a house run with an iron fist by his grandmother and filled with her daughters, sons-in-law, and grandchildren. His father, Seepersad, who would serve as the model for Mr. Biswas in Naipaul's most famous novel, *A House for Mr. Biswas* (1961), was a struggling journalist for the Trinidad *Guardian* and occasional writer of poetry and short stories; he encouraged his son's literary ambitions until his death, in 1953. Depressive and resentful of the domineering influence of his wife and his mother-in-law, Seepersad was a distant but loved figure in Naipaul's early life.

A scholarship student at the elite Queen's Royal College, Naipaul, desperate to escape Trinidad, won one of four scholarships for the entire island in 1949 and left for Oxford the next year, never to see his father again. While at Oxford, Naipaul struggled to publish his work and occasionally felt homesick, even attempting suicide at one point. He met Patricia Hale, an Oxford undergraduate, whom he married in 1955. The two remained unhappily married until Hale's death, in 1996. Naipaul's infidelities and abuses were many and public.

After leaving Oxford and failing to find employment in the civil service or journalism, Naipaul began work, in 1954, as a broadcaster for the BBC's *Caribbean Voices*, reviewing novels and interviewing writers. Later he regularly reviewed books for the *New Statesman*. His first novel, *The Mystic Masseur* (1957), was indebted to his father's

comic short stories. His second, more mature novel, *Miguel Street* (1959), written on a BBC typewriter, was a critical success and was soon followed by *A House for Mr. Biswas,* the first of Naipaul's many masterpieces.

Naipaul's work has often been compared with that of **Joseph Conrad,** and many of his novels and travel books deal with the political and psychological implications of exile, colonization, and violence. *A Bend in the River* (1979), in fact, revisits the Congo almost a century after Conrad's experiences there. Naipaul won acclaim as one of the century's greatest travel writers, with books on the West Indies (*The Middle Passage,* 1962), India (*An Area of Darkness,* 1964), and Africa (*A Congo Diary,* 1980). In addition, the writer often used observations gleaned in his travels as the basis for his fiction. His withering criticism of contemporary Islamic movements in Pakistan in *Among the Believers* (1981) brought him notoriety, as has his ambivalent attitude toward Trinidad. He famously said of the country, "I was born there, yes. I thought it was a great mistake." While traveling the world, he has had his permanent home in Britain. In 2001 he was awarded the Nobel Prize for Literature.

Despite his sometimes controversial attitudes toward formerly colonized peoples, and particularly toward those of African descent, Naipaul has been one of the most sympathetic chroniclers of postcolonial life and of migration. In the short story presented here, "One Out of Many" (1971), his setting, unusually for him, is the United States. The title refers to the motto on the Great Seal of the United States, *E pluribus unum,* which originally referred to the union of the states in a federal system. Today, however, the phrase suggests the ideal that, made up of many cultures and races, the United States forms a unified society. In the context of the story, the phrase also reflects the fact that the main character,

Santosh, is just one of many immigrants to the United States.

Santosh leaves his wife and children in the hills of India and arrives in Washington, D.C., as servant to an Indian diplomat, only to discover that his unofficial status and low pay seriously restrict his options. Santosh undergoes a number of comic embarrassments as he accustoms himself to the American way of life. Missing his friends and family at home, he meets a sympathetic Indian restaurant owner and several African Americans, whom he describes as *hubshi*, a somewhat demeaning Hindi term for a person of African descent. Santosh has arrived at a time of racial tension, the late 1960s, and feels threatened by riots in Washington (after the assassination of Martin Luther King, Jr., in April 1968). Yet he gradually comes to accept his life in his new country.

Naipaul, who once said that modernism had "bypassed" him, achieves his sympathetic portrait of Santosh's situation by means of a precise realism. As the well-rounded first-person narrator tells his story, it is the vivid rendering of his experiences and emotions that gives the work its power.

One Out of Many[1]

I am now an American citizen and I live in Washington, capital of the world. Many people, both here and in India, will feel that I have done well. But.

I was so happy in Bombay. I was respected, I had a certain position. I worked for an important man. The highest in the land came to our bachelor chambers and enjoyed my food and showered compliments on me. I also had my friends. We met in the evenings on the pavement below the gallery of our chambers. Some of us, like the tailor's bearer and myself, were domestics who lived in the street. The others were people who came to that bit of pavement to sleep. Respectable people; we didn't encourage riff-raff.

In the evenings it was cool. There were few passers-by and, apart from an occasional double-decker bus or taxi, little traffic. The pavement was swept and sprinkled, bedding brought out from daytime hiding-places, little oil-lamps lit. While the folk upstairs chattered and laughed, on the pavement we read newspapers, played cards, told stories and smoked. The clay pipe passed from friend to friend; we became drowsy. Except of course during the monsoon, I preferred to sleep on the pavement with my friends, although in our chambers a whole cupboard below the staircase was reserved for my personal use.

It was good after a healthy night in the open to rise before the sun and before the sweepers came. Sometimes I saw the street lights go off. Bedding was rolled up; no one spoke much; and soon my friends were hurrying in silent competition to secluded lanes and alleys and open lots to relieve themselves. I was spared this competition; in our chambers I had facilities.

Afterwards for half an hour or so I was free simply to stroll. I liked walking beside the Arabian Sea, waiting for the sun to come up. Then the city and the ocean gleamed like gold. Alas for those morning walks, that sudden ocean dazzle, the moist salt breeze on my face, the flap of my shirt, that first cup of hot sweet tea from a stall, the taste of the first leaf-cigarette.

1. Refers to the Latin motto of the United States, *E pluribus unum.*

Observe the workings of fate. The respect and security I enjoyed were due to the importance of my employer. It was this very importance which now all at once destroyed the pattern of my life.

My employer was seconded by his firm to Government service and was posted to Washington. I was happy for his sake but frightened for mine. He was to be away for some years and there was nobody in Bombay he could second me to. Soon, therefore, I was to be out of a job and out of the chambers. For many years I had considered my life as settled. I had served my apprenticeship, known my hard times. I didn't feel I could start again. I despaired. Was there a job for me in Bombay? I saw myself having to return to my village in the hills, to my wife and children there, not just for a holiday but for good. I saw myself again becoming a porter during the tourist season, racing after the buses as they arrived at the station and shouting with forty or fifty others for luggage. Indian luggage, not this lightweight American stuff! Heavy metal trunks!

I could have cried. It was no longer the sort of life for which I was fitted. I had grown soft in Bombay and I was no longer young. I had acquired possessions, I was used to the privacy of my cupboard. I had become a city man, used to certain comforts.

My employer said, "Washington is not Bombay, Santosh. Washington is expensive. Even if I was able to raise your fare, you wouldn't be able to live over there in anything like your present style."

But to be barefoot in the hills, after Bombay! The shock, the disgrace! I couldn't face my friends. I stopped sleeping on the pavement and spent as much of my free time as possible in my cupboard among my possessions, as among things which were soon to be taken from me.

My employer said, "Santosh, my heart bleeds for you."

I said, "Sahib,[2] if I look a little concerned it is only because I worry about you. You have always been fussy, and I don't see how you will manage in Washington."

"It won't be easy. But it's the principle. Does the representative of a poor country like ours travel about with his cook? Will that create a good impression?"

"You will always do what is right, sahib."

He went silent.

After some days he said, "There's not only the expense, Santosh. There's the question of foreign exchange. Our rupee[3] isn't what it was."

"I understand, sahib. Duty is duty."

A fortnight later, when I had almost given up hope, he said, "Santosh, I have consulted Government. You will accompany me. Government has sanctioned, will arrange accommodation. But no expenses. You will get your passport and your P form. But I want you to think, Santosh. Washington is not Bombay."

I went down to the pavement that night with my bedding.

I said, blowing down my shirt, "Bombay gets hotter and hotter."

"Do you know what you are doing?" the tailor's bearer said. "Will the Americans smoke with you? Will they sit and talk with you in the evenings? Will they hold you by the hand and walk with you beside the ocean?"

It pleased me that he was jealous. My last days in Bombay were very happy.

2. Master (Hindi).
3. Indian unit of currency, worth about ten cents at the time of the story.

I packed my employer's two suitcases and bundled up my own belongings in lengths of old cotton. At the airport they made a fuss about my bundles. They said they couldn't accept them as luggage for the hold because they didn't like the responsibility. So when the time came I had to climb up to the aircraft with all my bundles. The girl at the top, who was smiling at everybody else, stopped smiling when she saw me. She made me go right to the back of the plane, far from my employer. Most of the seats there were empty, though, and I was able to spread my bundles around and, well, it was comfortable.

It was bright and hot outside, cool inside. The plane started, rose up in the air, and Bombay and the ocean tilted this way and that. It was very nice. When we settled down I looked around for people like myself, but I could see no one among the Indians or the foreigners who looked like a domestic. Worse, they were all dressed as though they were going to a wedding and, brother, I soon saw it wasn't they who were conspicuous. I was in my ordinary Bombay clothes, the loose long-tailed shirt, the wide-waisted pants held up with a piece of string. Perfectly respectable domestic's wear, neither dirty nor clean, and in Bombay no one would have looked. But now on the plane I felt heads turning whenever I stood up.

I was anxious. I slipped off my shoes, tight even without the laces, and drew my feet up. That made me feel better. I made myself a little betel-nut mixture[4] and that made me feel better still. Half the pleasure of betel, though, is the spitting; and it was only when I had worked up a good mouthful that I saw I had a problem. The airline girl saw too. That girl didn't like me at all. She spoke roughly to me. My mouth was full, my cheeks were bursting, and I couldn't say anything. I could only look at her. She went and called a man in uniform and he came and stood over me. I put my shoes back on and swallowed the betel juice. It made me feel quite ill.

The girl and the man, the two of them, pushed a little trolley of drinks down the aisle. The girl didn't look at me but the man said, "You want a drink, chum?" He wasn't a bad fellow. I pointed at random to a bottle. It was a kind of soda drink, nice and sharp at first but then not so nice. I was worrying about it when the girl said, "Five shillings sterling or sixty cents U.S." That took me by surprise. I had no money, only a few rupees. The girl stamped, and I thought she was going to hit me with her pad when I stood up to show her who my employer was.

Presently my employer came down the aisle. He didn't look very well. He said, without stopping, "Champagne, Santosh? Already we are overdoing?" He went on to the lavatory. When he passed back he said, "Foreign exchange, Santosh! Foreign exchange!" That was all. Poor fellow, he was suffering too.

The journey became miserable for me. Soon, with the wine I had drunk, the betel juice, the movement and the noise of the aeroplane, I was vomiting all over my bundles, and I didn't care what the girl said or did. Later there were more urgent and terrible needs. I felt I would choke in the tiny, hissing room at the back. I had a shock when I saw my face in the mirror. In the fluorescent light it was the colour of a corpse. My eyes were strained, the sharp air hurt my nose and seemed to get into my brain. I climbed up on the lavatory seat and squatted. I lost control of myself. As quickly as I could I ran back out into the

---

4. A popular, mildly narcotic substance like chewing tobacco, normally chewed and spat out.

comparative openness of the cabin and hoped no one had noticed. The lights were dim now; some people had taken off their jackets and were sleeping. I hoped the plane would crash.

The girl woke me up. She was almost screaming. "It's you, isn't it? Isn't it?"

I thought she was going to tear the shirt off me. I pulled back and leaned hard on the window. She burst into tears and nearly tripped on her sari as she ran up the aisle to get the man in uniform.

Nightmare. And all I knew was that somewhere at the end, after the airports and the crowded lounges where everybody was dressed up, after all those take-offs and touchdowns, was the city of Washington. I wanted the journey to end but I couldn't say I wanted to arrive at Washington. I was already a little scared of that city, to tell the truth. I wanted only to be off the plane and to be in the open again, to stand on the ground and breathe and to try to understand what time of day it was.

At last we arrived. I was in a daze. The burden of those bundles! There were more closed rooms and electric lights. There were questions from officials.

"Is he diplomatic?"

"He's only a domestic," my employer said.

"Is that his luggage? What's in that pocket?"

I was ashamed.

"Santosh," my employer said.

I pulled out the little packets of pepper and salt, the sweets, the envelopes with scented napkins, the toy tubes of mustard. Airline trinkets. I had been collecting them throughout the journey, seizing a handful, whatever my condition, every time I passed the galley.

"He's a cook," my employer said.

"Does he always travel with his condiments?"

"Santosh, Santosh," my employer said in the car afterwards, "in Bombay it didn't matter what you did. Over here you represent your country. I must say I cannot understand why your behaviour has already gone so much out of character."

"I am sorry, sahib."

"Look at it like this, Santosh. Over here you don't only represent your country, you represent me."

For the people of Washington it was late afternoon or early evening, I couldn't say which. The time and the light didn't match, as they did in Bombay. Of that drive I remember green fields, wide roads, many motor cars travelling fast, making a steady hiss, hiss, which wasn't at all like our Bombay traffic noise. I remember big buildings and wide parks; many bazaar areas; then smaller houses without fences and with gardens like bush, with the *hubshi*[5] standing about or sitting down, more usually sitting down, everywhere. Especially I remember the *hubshi*. I had heard about them in stories and had seen one or two in Bombay. But I had never dreamt that this wild race existed in such numbers in Washington and were permitted to roam the streets so freely. O father, what was this place I had come to?

I wanted, I say, to be in the open, to breathe, to come to myself, to reflect. But there was to be no openness for me that evening. From the aeroplane to

5. Mildly derogatory term for a person of African descent (Hindi).

the airport building to the motor car to the apartment block to the elevator to the corridor to the apartment itself, I was forever enclosed, forever in the hissing, hissing sound of air-conditioners.

I was too dazed to take stock of the apartment. I saw it as only another halting place. My employer went to bed at once, completely exhausted, poor fellow. I looked around for my room. I couldn't find it and gave up. Aching for the Bombay ways, I spread my bedding in the carpeted corridor just outside our apartment door. The corridor was long: doors, doors. The illuminated ceiling was decorated with stars of different sizes; the colours were grey and blue and gold. Below that imitation sky I felt like a prisoner.

Waking, looking up at the ceiling, I thought just for a second that I had fallen asleep on the pavement below the gallery of our Bombay chambers. Then I realized my loss. I couldn't tell how much time had passed or whether it was night or day. The only clue was that newspapers now lay outside some doors. It disturbed me to think that while I had been sleeping, alone and defenceless, I had been observed by a stranger and perhaps by more than one stranger.

I tried the apartment door and found I had locked myself out. I didn't want to disturb my employer. I thought I would get out into the open, go for a walk. I remembered where the elevator was. I got in and pressed the button. The elevator dropped fast and silently and it was like being in the aeroplane again. When the elevator stopped and the blue metal door slid open I saw plain concrete corridors and blank walls. The noise of machinery was very loud. I knew I was in the basement and the main floor was not far above me. But I no longer wanted to try; I gave up ideas of the open air. I thought I would just go back up to the apartment. But I hadn't noted the number and didn't even know what floor we were on. My courage flowed out of me. I sat on the floor of the elevator and felt the tears come to my eyes. Almost without noise the elevator door closed, and I found I was being taken up silently at great speed.

The elevator stopped and the door opened. It was my employer, his hair uncombed, yesterday's dirty shirt partly unbuttoned. He looked frightened.

"Santosh, where have you been at this hour of morning? Without your shoes."

I could have embraced him. He hurried me back past the newspapers to our apartment and I took the bedding inside. The wide window showed the early morning sky, the big city; we were high up, way above the trees.

I said, "I couldn't find my room."

"Government sanctioned," my employer said. "Are you sure you've looked?"

We looked together. One little corridor led past the bathroom to his bedroom; another, shorter corridor led to the big room and the kitchen. There was nothing else.

"Government sanctioned," my employer said, moving about the kitchen and opening cupboard doors. "Separate entrance, shelving. I have the correspondence." He opened another door and looked inside. "Santosh, do you think it is possible that this is what Government meant?"

The cupboard he had opened was as high as the rest of the apartment and as wide as the kitchen, about six feet. It was about three feet deep. It had two doors. One door opened into the kitchen; another door, directly opposite, opened into the corridor.

"Separate entrance," my employer said. "Shelving, electric light, power point, fitted carpet."

"This must be my room, sahib."

"Santosh, some enemy in Government has done this to me."

"Oh no, sahib. You mustn't say that. Besides, it is very big. I will be able to make myself very comfortable. It is much bigger than my little cubby-hole in the chambers. And it has a nice flat ceiling. I wouldn't hit my head."

"You don't understand, Santosh. Bombay is Bombay. Here if we start living in cupboards we give the wrong impression. They will think we all live in cupboards in Bombay."

"O sahib, but they can just look at me and see I am dirt."

"You are very good, Santosh. But these people are malicious. Still, if you are happy, then I am happy."

"I am very happy, sahib."

And after all the upset, I was. It was nice to crawl in that evening, spread my bedding and feel protected and hidden. I slept very well.

In the morning my employer said, "We must talk about money, Santosh. Your salary is one hundred rupees a month. But Washington isn't Bombay. Everything is a little bit more expensive here, and I am going to give you a Dearness Allowance. As from today you are getting one hundred and fifty rupees."

"Sahib."

"And I'm giving you a fortnight's pay in advance. In foreign exchange. Seventy-five rupees. Ten cents to the rupee, seven hundred and fifty cents. Seven fifty U.S. Here, Santosh. This afternoon you go out and have a little walk and enjoy. But be careful. We are not among friends, remember."

So at last, rested, with money in my pocket, I went out in the open. And of course the city wasn't a quarter as frightening as I had thought. The buildings weren't particularly big, not all the streets were busy, and there were many lovely trees. A lot of the *hubshi* were about, very wild-looking some of them, with dark glasses and their hair frizzed out, but it seemed that if you didn't trouble them they didn't attack you.

I was looking for a café or a tea-stall where perhaps domestics congregated. But I saw no domestics, and I was chased away from the place I did eventually go into. The girl said, after I had been waiting some time, "Can't you read? We don't serve hippies or bare feet here."

O father! I had come out without my shoes. But what a country, I thought, walking briskly away, where people are never allowed to dress normally but must forever wear their very best! Why must they wear out shoes and fine clothes for no purpose? What occasion are they honouring? What waste, what presumption! Who do they think is noticing them all the time?

And even while these thoughts were in my head I found I had come to a roundabout with trees and a fountain where—and it was like a fulfilment in a dream, not easy to believe—there were many people who looked like my own people. I tightened the string around my loose pants, held down my flapping shirt and ran through the traffic to the green circle.

Some of the *hubshi* were there, playing musical instruments and looking quite happy in their way. There were some Americans sitting about on the grass and the fountain and the kerb. Many of them were in rough, friendly-looking

clothes; some were without shoes; and I felt I had been over hasty in condemning the entire race. But it wasn't these people who had attracted me to the
circle. It was the dancers. The men were bearded, bare-footed and in saffron
robes, and the girls were in saris and canvas shoes that looked like our own
Bata shoes. They were shaking little cymbals and chanting and lifting their
heads up and down and going round in a circle, making a lot of dust. It was a
little bit like a Red Indian dance in a cowboy movie, but they were chanting
Sanskrit words in praise of Lord Krishna.[6]

I was very pleased. But then a disturbing thought came to me. It might have
been because of the half-caste appearance of the dancers; it might have been
their bad Sanskrit pronunciation and their accent. I thought that these people
were now strangers, but that perhaps once upon a time they had been like me.
Perhaps, as in some story, they had been brought here among the *hubshi* as
captives a long time ago and had become a lost people, like our own wandering
gipsy folk, and had forgotten who they were. When I thought that, I lost my
pleasure in the dancing; and I felt for the dancers the sort of distaste we feel
when we are faced with something that should be kin but turns out not to be,
turns out to be degraded, like a deformed man, or like a leper, who from a distance looks whole.

I didn't stay. Not far from the circle I saw a café which appeared to be serving bare feet. I went in, had a coffee and a nice piece of cake and bought a
pack of cigarettes; matches they gave me free with the cigarettes. It was all
right, but then the bare feet began looking at me, and one bearded fellow came
and sniffed loudly at me and smiled and spoke some sort of gibberish, and then
some others of the bare feet came and sniffed at me. They weren't unfriendly,
but I didn't appreciate the behaviour; and it was a little frightening to find,
when I left the place, that two or three of them appeared to be following me.
They weren't unfriendly, but I didn't want to take any chances. I passed a cinema; I went in. It was something I wanted to do anyway. In Bombay I used to
go once a week.

And that was all right. The movie had already started. It was in English, not
too easy for me to follow, and it gave me time to think. It was only there, in the
darkness, that I thought about the money I had been spending. The prices had
seemed to me very reasonable, like Bombay prices. Three for the movie ticket,
one fifty in the café, with tip. But I had been thinking in rupees and paying in
dollars. In less than an hour I had spent nine days' pay.

I couldn't watch the movie after that. I went out and began to make my way
back to the apartment block. Many more of the *hubshi* were about now and I
saw that where they congregated the pavement was wet, and dangerous with
broken glass and bottles. I couldn't think of cooking when I got back to the
apartment. I couldn't bear to look at the view. I spread my bedding in the cupboard, lay down in the darkness and waited for my employer to return.

When he did I said, "Sahib, I want to go home."

"Santosh, I've paid five thousand rupees to bring you here. If I send you back
now, you will have to work for six or seven years without salary to pay me back."

6. Hindu deity, also worshipped by the Hare
Krishnas, mostly white American Hindus sometimes viewed as a cult, who wear traditional
Indian clothes and chant the names of Krishna
in Sanskrit, a classical Indian language.

I burst into tears.

"My poor Santosh, something has happened. Tell me what has happened."

"Sahib, I've spent more than half the advance you gave me this morning. I went out and had a coffee and cake and then I went to a movie."

His eyes went small and twinkly behind his glasses. He bit the inside of his top lip, scraped at his moustache with his lower teeth, and he said, "You see, you see. I told you it was expensive."

I understood I was a prisoner. I accepted this and adjusted. I learned to live within the apartment, and I was even calm.

My employer was a man of taste and he soon had the apartment looking like something in a magazine, with books and Indian paintings and Indian fabrics and pieces of sculpture and bronze statues of our gods. I was careful to take no delight in it. It was of course very pretty, especially with the view. But the view remained foreign and I never felt that the apartment was real, like the shabby old Bombay chambers with the cane chairs, or that it had anything to do with me.

When people came to dinner I did my duty. At the appropriate time I would bid the company goodnight, close off the kitchen behind its folding screen and pretend I was leaving the apartment. Then I would lie down quietly in my cupboard and smoke. I was free to go out; I had my separate entrance. But I didn't like being out of the apartment. I didn't even like going down to the laundry room in the basement.

Once or twice a week I went to the supermarket on our street. I always had to walk past groups of *hubshi* men and children. I tried not to look, but it was hard. They sat on the pavement, on steps and in the bush around their redbrick houses, some of which had boarded-up windows. They appeared to be very much a people of the open air, with little to do; even in the mornings some of the men were drunk.

Scattered among the *hubshi* houses were others just as old but with gas-lamps that burned night and day in the entrance. These were the houses of the Americans. I seldom saw these people; they didn't spend much time on the street. The lighted gas-lamp was the American way of saying that though a house looked old outside it was nice and new inside. I also felt that it was like a warning to the *hubshi* to keep off.

Outside the supermarket there was always a policeman with a gun. Inside, there were always a couple of *hubshi* guards with truncheons, and, behind the cashiers, some old *hubshi* beggar men in rags. There were also many young *hubshi* boys, small but muscular, waiting to carry parcels, as once in the hills I had waited to carry Indian tourists' luggage.

These trips to the supermarket were my only outings, and I was always glad to get back to the apartment. The work there was light. I watched a lot of television and my English improved. I grew to like certain commercials very much. It was in these commercials I saw the Americans whom in real life I so seldom saw and knew only by their gas-lamps. Up there in the apartment, with a view of the white domes and towers and greenery of the famous city, I entered the homes of the Americans and saw them cleaning those homes. I saw them cleaning floors and dishes. I saw them buying clothes and cleaning clothes, buying motor cars and cleaning motor cars. I saw them cleaning, cleaning.

The effect of all this television on me was curious. If by some chance I saw an American on the street I tried to fit him or her into the commercials; and I felt I had caught the person in an interval between his television duties. So to some extent Americans have remained to me, as people not quite real, as people temporarily absent from television.

Sometimes a *hubshi* came on the screen, not to talk of *hubshi* things, but to do a little cleaning of his own. That wasn't the same. He was too different from the *hubshi* I saw on the street and I knew he was an actor. I knew that his television duties were only make-believe and that he would soon have to return to the street.

One day at the supermarket, when the *hubshi* girl took my money, she sniffed and said, "You always smell sweet, baby."

She was friendly, and I was at last able to clear up that mystery, of my smell. It was the poor country weed I smoked. It was a peasant taste of which I was slightly ashamed, to tell the truth; but the cashier was encouraging. As it happened, I had brought a quantity of the weed with me from Bombay in one of my bundles, together with a hundred razor blades, believing both weed and blades to be purely Indian things. I made an offering to the girl. In return she taught me a few words of English. "Me black and beautiful" was the first thing she taught me. Then she pointed to the policeman with the gun outside and taught me: "He pig."

My English lessons were taken a stage further by the *hubshi* maid who worked for someone on our floor in the apartment block. She too was attracted by my smell, but I soon began to feel that she was also attracted by my smallness and strangeness. She herself was a big woman, broad in the face, with high cheeks and bold eyes and lips that were full but not pendulous. Her largeness disturbed me; I found it better to concentrate on her face. She misunderstood; there were times when she frolicked with me in a violent way. I didn't like it, because I couldn't fight her off as well as I would have liked and because in spite of myself I was fascinated by her appearance. Her smell mixed with the perfumes she used could have made me forget myself.

She was always coming into the apartment. She disturbed me while I was watching the Americans on television. I feared the smell she left behind. Sweat, perfume, my own weed: the smells lay thick in the room, and I prayed to the bronze gods my employer had installed as living-room ornaments that I would not be dishonoured. Dishonoured, I say; and I know that this might seem strange to people over here, who have permitted the *hubshi* to settle among them in such large numbers and must therefore esteem them in certain ways. But in our country we frankly do not care for the *hubshi*. It is written in our books, both holy and not so holy, that it is indecent and wrong for a man of our blood to embrace the *hubshi* woman. To be dishonoured in this life, to be born a cat or a monkey or a *hubshi* in the next!

But I was falling. Was it idleness and solitude? I was found attractive: I wanted to know why. I began to go to the bathroom of the apartment simply to study my face in the mirror. I cannot easily believe it myself now, but in Bombay a week or a month could pass without my looking in the mirror; and then it wasn't to consider my looks but to check whether the barber had cut off too much hair or whether a pimple was about to burst. Slowly I made a discovery.

My face was handsome. I had never thought of myself in this way. I had thought of myself as unnoticeable, with features that served as identification alone.

The discovery of my good looks brought its strains. I became obsessed with my appearance, with a wish to see myself. It was like an illness. I would be watching television, for instance, and I would be surprised by the thought: are you as handsome as that man? I would have to get up and go to the bathroom and look in the mirror.

I thought back to the time when these matters hadn't interested me, and I saw how ragged I must have looked, on the aeroplane, in the airport, in that café for bare feet, with the rough and dirty clothes I wore, without doubt or question, as clothes befitting a servant. I was choked with shame. I saw, too, how good people in Washington had been, to have seen me in rags and yet to have taken me for a man.

I was glad I had a place to hide. I had thought of myself as a prisoner. Now I was glad I had so little of Washington to cope with: the apartment, my cupboard, the television set, my employer, the walk to the supermarket, the *hubshi* woman. And one day I found I no longer knew whether I wanted to go back to Bombay. Up there, in the apartment, I no longer knew what I wanted to do.

I became more careful of my appearance. There wasn't much I could do. I bought laces for my old black shoes, socks, a belt. Then some money came my way. I had understood that the weed I smoked was of value to the *hubshi* and the bare feet; I disposed of what I had, disadvantageously as I now know, through the *hubshi* girl at the supermarket. I got just under two hundred dollars. Then, as anxiously as I had got rid of my weed, I went out and bought some clothes.

I still have the things I bought that morning. A green hat, a green suit. The suit was always too big for me. Ignorance, inexperience; but I also remember the feeling of presumption. The salesman wanted to talk, to do his job. I didn't want to listen. I took the first suit he showed me and went into the cubicle and changed. I couldn't think about size and fit. When I considered all that cloth and all that tailoring I was proposing to adorn my simple body with, that body that needed so little, I felt I was asking to be destroyed. I changed back quickly, went out of the cubicle and said I would take the green suit. The salesman began to talk; I cut him short; I asked for a hat. When I got back to the apartment I felt quite weak and had to lie down for a while in my cupboard.

I never hung the suit up. Even in the shop, even while counting out the precious dollars, I had known it was a mistake. I kept the suit folded in the box with all its pieces of tissue paper. Three or four times I put it on and walked about the apartment and sat down on chairs and lit cigarettes and crossed my legs, practising. But I couldn't bring myself to wear the suit out of doors. Later I wore the pants, but never the jacket. I never bought another suit; I soon began wearing the sort of clothes I wear today, pants with some sort of zippered jacket.

Once I had had no secrets from my employer; it was so much simpler not to have secrets. But some instinct told me now it would be better not to let him know about the green suit or the few dollars I had, just as instinct had already told me I should keep my growing knowledge of English to myself.

Once my employer had been to me only a presence. I used to tell him then that beside him I was as dirt. It was only a way of talking, one of the courtesies of our language, but it had something of truth. I meant that he was the man who adventured in the world for me, that I experienced the world through him, that I was content to be a small part of his presence. I was content, sleeping on the Bombay pavement with my friends, to hear the talk of my employer and his guests upstairs. I was more than content, late at night, to be identified among the sleepers and greeted by some of those guests before they drove away.

Now I found that, without wishing it, I was ceasing to see myself as part of my employer's presence, and beginning at the same time to see him as an outsider might see him, as perhaps the people who came to dinner in the apartment saw him. I saw that he was a man of my own age, around thirty-five; it astonished me that I hadn't noticed this before. I saw that he was plump, in need of exercise, that he moved with short, fussy steps; a man with glasses, thinning hair, and that habit, during conversation, of scraping at his moustache with his teeth and nibbling at the inside of his top lip; a man who was frequently anxious, took pains over his work, was subjected at his own table to unkind remarks by his office colleagues; a man who looked as uneasy in Washington as I felt, who acted as cautiously as I had learned to act.

I remember an American who came to dinner. He looked at the pieces of sculpture in the apartment and said he had himself brought back a whole head from one of our ancient temples; he had got the guide to hack it off.

I could see that my employer was offended. He said, "But that's illegal."

"That's why I had to give the guide two dollars. If I had a bottle of whisky he would have pulled down the whole temple for me."

My employer's face went blank. He continued to do his duties as host but he was unhappy throughout the dinner. I grieved for him.

Afterwards he knocked on my cupboard. I knew he wanted to talk. I was in my underclothes but I didn't feel underdressed, with the American gone. I stood in the door of my cupboard; my employer paced up and down the small kitchen; the apartment felt sad.

"Did you hear that person, Santosh?"

I pretended I hadn't understood, and when he explained I tried to console him. I said, "Sahib, but we know these people are Franks and barbarians."

"They are malicious people, Santosh. They think that because we are a poor country we are all the same. They think an official in Government is just the same as some poor guide scraping together a few rupees to keep body and soul together, poor fellow."

I saw that he had taken the insult only in a personal way, and I was disappointed. I thought he had been thinking of the temple.

A few days later I had my adventure. The *hubshi* woman came in, moving among my employer's ornaments like a bull. I was greatly provoked. The smell was too much; so was the sight of her armpits. I fell. She dragged me down on the couch, on the saffron spread which was one of my employer's nicest pieces of Punjabi folk-weaving. I saw the moment, helplessly, as one of dishonour. I saw her as Kali, goddess of death and destruction, coal-black, with a red tongue and white eyeballs and many powerful arms. I expected her to be wild and fierce; but she added insult to injury by being very playful, as though, because I was small and strange, the act was not real. She laughed all the time. I would have liked to withdraw, but the act took over and completed itself. And then I felt dreadful.

I wanted to be forgiven, I wanted to be cleansed, I wanted her to go. Nothing frightened me more than the way she had ceased to be a visitor in the apartment and behaved as though she possessed it. I looked at the sculpture and the fabrics and thought of my poor employer, suffering in his office somewhere.

I bathed and bathed afterwards. The smell would not leave me. I fancied that the woman's oil was still on that poor part of my poor body. It occurred to me to rub it down with half a lemon. Penance and cleansing; but it didn't hurt as much as I expected, and I extended the penance by rolling about naked on the floor of the bathroom and the sitting-room and howling. At last the tears came, real tears, and I was comforted.

It was cool in the apartment; the air-conditioning always hummed; but I could see that it was hot outside, like one of our own summer days in the hills. The urge came upon me to dress as I might have done in my village on a religious occasion. In one of my bundles I had a dhoti-length of new cotton, a gift from the tailor's bearer that I had never used. I draped this around my waist and between my legs, lit incense sticks, sat down crosslegged on the floor and tried to meditate and become still. Soon I began to feel hungry. That made me happy; I decided to fast.

Unexpectedly my employer came in. I didn't mind being caught in the attitude and garb of prayer; it could have been so much worse. But I wasn't expecting him till late afternoon.

"Santosh, what has happened?"

Pride got the better of me. I said, "Sahib, it is what I do from time to time."

But I didn't find merit in his eyes. He was far too agitated to notice me properly. He took off his lightweight fawn jacket, dropped it on the saffron spread, went to the refrigerator and drank two tumblers of orange juice, one after the other. Then he looked out at the view, scraping at his moustache.

"Oh, my poor Santosh, what are we doing in this place? Why do we have to come here?"

I looked with him. I saw nothing unusual. The wide window showed the colours of the hot day: the pale-blue sky, the white, almost colourless, domes of famous buildings rising out of dead-green foliage; the untidy roofs of apartment blocks where on Saturday and Sunday mornings people sunbathed; and, below, the fronts and backs of houses on the tree-lined street down which I walked to the supermarket.

My employer turned off the air-conditioning and all noise was absent from the room. An instant later I began to hear the noises outside: sirens far and near. When my employer slid the window open the roar of the disturbed city rushed into the room. He closed the window and there was near-silence again. Not far from the supermarket I saw black smoke, uncurling, rising, swiftly turning colourless. This was not the smoke which some of the apartment blocks gave off all day. This was the smoke of a real fire.

"The *hubshi* have gone wild, Santosh. They are burning down Washington."[7]

I didn't mind at all. Indeed, in my mood of prayer and repentance, the news was even welcome. And it was with a feeling of release that I watched and heard

7. Refers to riots in 1968 after the assassination of the civil rights leader Martin Luther King, Jr.

the city burn that afternoon and watched it burn that night. I watched it burn again and again on television; and I watched it burn in the morning. It burned like a famous city and I didn't want it to stop burning. I wanted the fire to spread and spread and I wanted everything in the city, even the apartment block, even the apartment, even myself, to be destroyed and consumed. I wanted escape to be impossible; I wanted the very idea of escape to become absurd. At every sign that the burning was going to stop I felt disappointed and let down.

For four days my employer and I stayed in the apartment and watched the city burn. The television continued to show us what we could see and what, whenever we slid the window back, we could hear. Then it was over. The view from our window hadn't changed. The famous buildings stood; the trees remained. But for the first time since I had understood that I was a prisoner I found that I wanted to be out of the apartment and in the streets.

The destruction lay beyond the supermarket. I had never gone into this part of the city before, and it was strange to walk in those long wide streets for the first time, to see trees and houses and shops and advertisements, everything like a real city, and then to see that every signboard on every shop was burnt or stained with smoke, that the shops themselves were black and broken, that flames had burst through some of the upper windows and scorched the red bricks. For mile after mile it was like that. There were *hubshi* groups about, and at first when I passed them I pretended to be busy, minding my own business, not at all interested in the ruins. But they smiled at me and I found I was smiling back. Happiness was on the faces of the *hubshi*. They were like people amazed they could do so much, that so much lay in their power. They were like people on holiday. I shared their exhilaration.

The idea of escape was a simple one, but it hadn't occurred to me before. When I adjusted to my imprisonment I had wanted only to get away from Washington and to return to Bombay. But then I had become confused. I had looked in the mirror and seen myself, and I knew it wasn't possible for me to return to Bombay to the sort of job I had had and the life I had lived. I couldn't easily become part of someone else's presence again. Those evening chats on the pavement, those morning walks: happy times, but they were like the happy times of childhood: I didn't want them to return.

I had taken, after the fire, to going for long walks in the city. And one day, when I wasn't even thinking of escape, when I was just enjoying the sights and my new freedom of movement, I found myself in one of those leafy streets where private houses had been turned into business premises. I saw a fellow countryman superintending the raising of a signboard on his gallery. The signboard told me that the building was a restaurant, and I assumed that the man in charge was the owner. He looked worried and slightly ashamed, and he smiled at me. This was unusual, because the Indians I had seen on the streets of Washington pretended they hadn't seen me; they made me feel that they didn't like the competition of my presence or didn't want me to start asking them difficult questions.

I complimented the worried man on his signboard and wished him good luck in his business. He was a small man of about fifty and he was wearing a double-breasted suit with old-fashioned wide lapels. He had dark hollows below his eyes and he looked as though he had recently lost a little weight. I could see that in our country he had been a man of some standing, not quite the sort of person who would go into the restaurant business. I felt at one with him. He invited me in to look around, asked my name and gave his. It was Priya.

Just past the gallery was the loveliest and richest room I had ever seen. The wallpaper was like velvet; I wanted to pass my hand over it. The brass lamps that hung from the ceiling were in a lovely cut-out pattern and the bulbs were of many colours. Priya looked with me, and the hollows under his eyes grew darker, as though my admiration was increasing his worry at his extravagance. The restaurant hadn't yet opened for customers and on a shelf in one corner I saw Priya's collection of good-luck objects: a brass plate with a heap of uncooked rice, for prosperity; a little copybook and a little diary pencil, for good luck with the accounts; a little clay lamp, for general good luck.

"What do you think, Santosh? You think it will be all right?"

"It is bound to be all right, Priya."

"But I have enemies, you know, Santosh. The Indian restaurant people are not going to appreciate me. All mine, you know, Santosh. Cash paid. No mortgage or anything like that. I don't believe in mortgages. Cash or nothing."

I understood him to mean that he had tried to get a mortgage and failed, and was anxious about money.

"But what are you doing here, Santosh? You used to be in Government or something?"

"You could say that, Priya."

"Like me. They have a saying here. If you can't beat them, join them. I joined them. They are still beating me." He sighed and spread his arms on the top of the red wall-seat. "Ah, Santosh, why do we do it? Why don't we renounce and go and meditate on the riverbank?" He waved about the room. "The yemblems[8] of the world, Santosh. Just yemblems."

I didn't know the English word he used, but I understood its meaning; and for a moment it was like being back in Bombay, exchanging stories and philosophies with the tailor's bearer and others in the evening.

"But I am forgetting, Santosh. You will have some tea or coffee or something?"

I shook my head from side to side to indicate that I was agreeable, and he called out in a strange harsh language to someone behind the kitchen door.

"Yes, Santosh. Yem-*blems*!" And he sighed and slapped the red seat hard.

A man came out from the kitchen with a tray. At first he looked like a fellow countryman, but in a second I could tell he was a stranger.

"You are right," Priya said, when the stranger went back to the kitchen. "He is not of Bharat.[9] He is a Mexican. But what can I do? You get fellow countrymen, you fix up their papers and everything, green card and everything. And then? Then they run away. Run-run-runaway. Crooks this side, crooks that side, I can't tell you. Listen, Santosh. I was in cloth business before. Buy for fifty rupees that side, sell for fifty dollars this side. Easy. But then. Caftan, everybody wants caftan. Caftan-aftan, I say, I will settle your caftan. I buy one thousand, Santosh. Delays India-side, of course. They come one year later.

8. I.e., emblems.   9. India (Hindi).

Nobody wants caftan then. We're not organized, Santosh. We don't do enough consumer research. That's what the fellows at the embassy tell me. But if I do consumer research, when will I do my business? The trouble, you know, Santosh, is that this shopkeeping is not in my blood. The damn thing goes *against* my blood. When I was in cloth business I used to hide sometimes for shame when a customer came in. Sometimes I used to pretend I was a shopper myself. Consumer research! These people make us dance, Santosh. You and I, we will renounce. We will go together and walk beside Potomac[1] and meditate."

I loved his talk. I hadn't heard anything so sweet and philosophical since the Bombay days. I said, "Priya, I will cook for you, if you want a cook."

"I feel I've known you a long time, Santosh. I feel you are like a member of my own family. I will give you a place to sleep, a little food to eat and a little pocket money, as much as I can afford."

I said, "Show me the place to sleep."

He led me out of the pretty room and up a carpeted staircase. I was expecting the carpet and the new paint to stop somewhere, but it was nice and new all the way. We entered a room that was like a smaller version of my employer's apartment.

"Built-in cupboards and everything, you see, Santosh."

I went to the cupboard. It had a folding door that opened outward. I said, "Priya, it is too small. There is room on the shelf for my belongings. But I don't see how I can spread my bedding inside here. It is far too narrow."

He giggled nervously. "Santosh, you are a joker. I feel that we are of the same family already."

Then it came to me that I was being offered the whole room. I was stunned.

Priya looked stunned too. He sat down on the edge of the soft bed. The dark hollows under his eyes were almost black and he looked very small in his double-breasted jacket. "This is how they make us dance over here, Santosh. You say staff quarters and they say staff quarters. This is what they mean."

For some seconds we sat silently, I fearful, he gloomy, meditating on the ways of this new world.

Someone called from downstairs, "Priya!"

His gloom gone, smiling in advance, winking at me, Priya called back in an accent of the country, "Hi, Bab!"

I followed him down.

"Priya," the American said, "I've brought over the menus."

He was a tall man in a leather jacket, with jeans that rode up above thick white socks and big rubber-soled shoes. He looked like someone about to run in a race. The menus were enormous; on the cover there was a drawing of a fat man with a moustache and a plumed turban, something like the man in the airline advertisements.

"They look great, Bab."

"I like them myself. But what's that, Priya? What's that shelf doing there?"

Moving like the front part of a horse, Bab walked to the shelf with the rice and the brass plate and the little clay lamp. It was only then that I saw that the shelf was very roughly made.

---

1. River in Washington, D.C.

Priya looked penitent and it was clear he had put the shelf up himself. It was also clear he didn't intend to take it down.

"Well, it's yours," Bab said. "I suppose we had to have a touch of the East somewhere. Now, Priya—"

"Money-money-money, is it?" Priya said, racing the words together as though he was making a joke to amuse a child. "But, Bab, how can *you* ask *me* for money? Anybody hearing you would believe that this restaurant is mine. But this restaurant isn't mine, Bab. This restaurant is yours."

It was only one of our courtesies, but it puzzled Bab and he allowed himself to be led to other matters.

I saw that, for all his talk of renunciation and business failure, and for all his jumpiness, Priya was able to cope with Washington. I admired this strength in him as much as I admired the richness of his talk. I didn't know how much to believe of his stories, but I liked having to guess about him. I liked having to play with his words in my mind. I liked the mystery of the man. The mystery came from his solidity. I knew where I was with him. After the apartment and the green suit and the *hubshi* woman and the city burning for four days, to be with Priya was to feel safe. For the first time since I had come to Washington I felt safe.

I can't say that I moved in. I simply stayed. I didn't want to go back to the apartment even to collect my belongings. I was afraid that something might happen to keep me a prisoner there. My employer might turn up and demand his five thousand rupees. The *hubshi* woman might claim me for her own; I might be condemned to a life among the *hubshi*. And it wasn't as if I was leaving behind anything of value in the apartment. The green suit I was even happy to forget. But.

Priya paid me forty dollars a week. After what I was getting, three dollars and seventy-five cents, it seemed a lot; and it was more than enough for my needs. I didn't have much temptation to spend, to tell the truth. I knew that my old employer and the *hubshi* woman would be wondering about me in their respective ways and I thought I should keep off the streets for a while. That was no hardship; it was what I was used to in Washington. Besides, my days at the restaurant were pretty full; for the first time in my life I had little leisure.

The restaurant was a success from the start, and Priya was fussy. He was always bursting into the kitchen with one of those big menus in his hand, saying in English, "Prestige job, Santosh, prestige." I didn't mind. I liked to feel I had to do things perfectly; I felt I was earning my freedom. Though I was in hiding, and though I worked every day until midnight, I felt I was much more in charge of myself than I had ever been.

Many of our waiters were Mexicans, but when we put turbans on them they could pass. They came and went, like the Indian staff. I didn't get on with these people. They were frightened and jealous of one another and very treacherous. Their talk amid the biryanis and the pillaus was all of papers and green cards. They were always about to get green cards or they had been cheated out of green cards or they had just got green cards. At first I didn't know what they were talking about. When I understood I was more than depressed.

I understood that because I had escaped from my employer I had made myself illegal in America. At any moment I could be denounced, seized, jailed, deported, disgraced. It was a complication. I had no green card; I didn't know how to set about getting one; and there was no one I could talk to.

I felt burdened by my secrets. Once I had none; now I had so many. I couldn't tell Priya I had no green card. I couldn't tell him I had broken faith with my old employer and dishonoured myself with a *hubshi* woman and lived in fear of retribution. I couldn't tell him that I was afraid to leave the restaurant and that nowadays when I saw an Indian I hid from him as anxiously as the Indian hid from me. I would have felt foolish to confess. With Priya, right from the start, I had pretended to be strong; and I wanted it to remain like that. Instead, when we talked now, and he grew philosophical, I tried to find bigger causes for being sad. My mind fastened on to these causes, and the effect of this was that my sadness became like a sickness of the soul.

It was worse than being in the apartment, because now the responsibility was mine and mine alone. I had decided to be free, to act for myself. It pained me to think of the exhilaration I had felt during the days of the fire; and I felt mocked when I remembered that in the early days of my escape I had thought I was in charge of myself.

The year turned. The snow came and melted. I was more afraid than ever of going out. The sickness was bigger than all the causes. I saw the future as a hole into which I was dropping. Sometimes at night when I awakened my body would burn and I would feel the hot perspiration break all over.

I leaned on Priya. He was my only hope, my only link with what was real. He went out; he brought back stories. He went out especially to eat in the restaurants of our competitors.

He said, "Santosh, I never believed that running a restaurant was a way to God. But it is true. I eat like a scientist. Every day I eat like a scientist. I feel I have already renounced."

This was Priya. This was how his talk ensnared me and gave me the bigger causes that steadily weakened me. I became more and more detached from the men in the kitchen. When they spoke of their green cards and the jobs they were about to get I felt like asking them: Why? Why?

And every day the mirror told its own tale. Without exercise, with the sickening of my heart and my mind, I was losing my looks. My face had become pudgy and sallow and full of spots; it was becoming ugly. I could have cried for that, discovering my good looks only to lose them. It was like a punishment for my presumption, the punishment I had feared when I bought the green suit.

Priya said, "Santosh, you must get some exercise. You are not looking well. Your eyes are getting like mine. What are you pining for? Are you pining for Bombay or your family in the hills?"

But now, even in my mind, I was a stranger in those places.

Priya said one Sunday morning, "Santosh, I am going to take you to see a Hindi movie today. All the Indians of Washington will be there, domestics and everybody else."

I was very frightened. I didn't want to go and I couldn't tell him why. He insisted. My heart began to beat fast as soon as I got into the car. Soon there were no more houses with gas-lamps in the entrance, just those long wide burnt-out *hubshi* streets, now with fresh leaves on the trees, heaps of rubble on bulldozed, fenced-in lots, boarded-up shop windows, and old smoke-stained signboards announcing what was no longer true. Cars raced along the wide roads; there was life only on the roads. I thought I would vomit with fear.

I said, "Take me back, *sahib.*"

I had used the wrong word. Once I had used the word a hundred times a day. But then I had considered myself a small part of my employer's presence, and the word was not servile; it was more like a name, like a reassuring sound, part of my employer's dignity and therefore part of mine. But Priya's dignity could never be mine; that was not our relationship. Priya I had always called Priya; it was his wish, the American way, man to man. With Priya the word was servile. And he responded to the word. He did as I asked; he drove me back to the restaurant. I never called him by his name again.

I was good-looking; I had lost my looks. I was a free man; I had lost my freedom.

One of the Mexican waiters came into the kitchen late one evening and said, "There is a man outside who wants to see the chef."

No one had made this request before, and Priya was at once agitated. "Is he an American? Some enemy has sent him here. Sanitary-anitary, health-ealth, they can inspect my kitchens at any time."

"He is an Indian," the Mexican said.

I was alarmed. I thought it was my old employer; that quiet approach was like him. Priya thought it was a rival. Though Priya regularly ate in the restaurants of his rivals he thought it unfair when they came to eat in his. We both went to the door and peeked through the glass window into the dimly lit dining-room.

"Do you know that person, Santosh?"

"Yes, sahib."

It wasn't my old employer. It was one of his Bombay friends, a big man in Government, whom I had often served in the chambers. He was by himself and seemed to have just arrived in Washington. He had a new Bombay haircut, very close, and a stiff dark suit, Bombay tailoring. His shirt looked blue, but in the dim multi-coloured light of the dining-room everything white looked blue. He didn't look unhappy with what he had eaten. Both his elbows were on the curry-spotted tablecloth and he was picking his teeth, half closing his eyes and hiding his mouth with his cupped left hand.

"I don't like him," Priya said. "Still, big man in Government and so on. You must go to him, Santosh."

But I couldn't go.

"Put on your apron, Santosh. And that chef's cap. Prestige. You must go, Santosh."

Priya went out to the dining-room and I heard him say in English that I was coming.

I ran up to my room, put some oil on my hair, combed my hair, put on my best pants and shirt and my shining shoes. It was so, as a man about town rather than as a cook, I went to the dining-room.

The man from Bombay was as astonished as Priya. We exchanged the old courtesies, and I waited. But, to my relief, there seemed little more to say. No difficult questions were put to me; I was grateful to the man from Bombay for his tact. I avoided talk as much as possible. I smiled. The man from Bombay smiled back. Priya smiled uneasily at both of us. So for a while we were, smiling in the dim blue-red light and waiting.

The man from Bombay said to Priya, "Brother, I just have a few words to say to my old friend Santosh."

Priya didn't like it, but he left us.

I waited for those words. But they were not the words I feared. The man from Bombay didn't speak of my old employer. We continued to exchange courtesies. Yes, I was well and he was well and everybody else we knew was well; and I was doing well and he was doing well. That was all. Then, secretively, the man from Bombay gave me a dollar. A dollar, ten rupees, an enormous tip for Bombay. But, from him, much more than a tip: an act of graciousness, part of the sweetness of the old days. Once it would have meant so much to me. Now it meant so little. I was saddened and embarrassed. And I had been anticipating hostility!

Priya was waiting behind the kitchen door. His little face was tight and serious, and I knew he had seen the money pass. Now, quickly, he read my own face, and without saying anything to me he hurried out into the dining-room.

I heard him say in English to the man from Bombay, "Santosh is a good fellow. He's got his own room with bath and everything. I am giving him a hundred dollars a week from next week. A thousand rupees a week. This is a first-class establishment."

A thousand chips a week! I was staggered. It was much more than any man in Government got, and I was sure the man from Bombay was also staggered, and perhaps regretting his good gesture and that precious dollar of foreign exchange.

"Santosh," Priya said, when the restaurant closed that evening, "that man was an enemy. I knew it from the moment I saw him. And because he was an enemy I did something very bad, Santosh."

"Sahib."

"I lied, Santosh. To protect you. I told him, Santosh, that I was going to give you seventy-five dollars a week after Christmas."

"Sahib."

"And now I have to make that lie true. But, Santosh, you know that is money we can't afford. I don't have to tell you about overheads and things like that. Santosh, I will give you sixty."

I said, "Sahib, I couldn't stay on for less than a hundred and twenty-five."

Priya's eyes went shiny and the hollows below his eyes darkened. He giggled and pressed out his lips. At the end of that week I got a hundred dollars. And Priya, good man that he was, bore me no grudge.

Now here was a victory. It was only after it happened that I realized how badly I had needed such a victory, how far, gaining my freedom, I had begun to accept death not as the end but as the goal. I revived. Or rather, my senses revived. But in this city what was there to feed my senses? There were no walks to be taken, no idle conversations with understanding friends. I could buy new clothes. But then? Would I just look at myself in the mirror? Would I go walking, inviting passers-by to look at me and my clothes? No, the whole business of clothes and dressing up only threw me back into myself.

There was a Swiss or German woman in the cake-shop some doors away, and there was a Filipino woman in the kitchen. They were neither of them attractive, to tell the truth. The Swiss or German could have broken my back with a slap, and the Filipino, though young, was remarkably like one of our older hill women. Still, I felt I owed something to the senses, and I thought I might frolic with these women. But then I was frightened of the responsibility. Goodness, I had learned that a woman is not just a roll and a frolic but a big creature weighing a hundred-and-so-many pounds who is going to be around afterwards.

So the moment of victory passed, without celebration. And it was strange, I thought, that sorrow lasts and can make a man look forward to death, but the mood of victory fills a moment and then is over. When my moment of victory was over I discovered below it, as if waiting for me, all my old sickness and fears: fear of my illegality, my former employer, my presumption, the *hubshi* woman. I saw then that the victory I had was not something I had worked for, but luck; and that luck was only fate's cheating, giving an illusion of power.

But that illusion lingered, and I became restless. I decided to act, to challenge fate. I decided I would no longer stay in my room and hide. I began to go out walking in the afternoons. I gained courage; every afternoon I walked a little farther. It became my ambition to walk to that green circle with the fountain where, on my first day out in Washington, I had come upon those people in Hindu costumes, like domestics abandoned a long time ago, singing their Sanskrit gibberish and doing their strange Red Indian dance. And one day I got there.

One day I crossed the road to the circle and sat down on a bench. The *hubshi* were there, and the bare feet, and the dancers in saris and the saffron robes. It was mid-afternoon, very hot, and no one was active. I remembered how magical and inexplicable that circle had seemed to me the first time I saw it. Now it seemed so ordinary and tired: the roads, the motor cars, the shops, the trees, the careful policemen: so much part of the waste and futility that was our world. There was no longer a mystery. I felt I knew where everybody had come from and where those cars were going. But I also felt that everybody there felt like me, and that was soothing. I took to going to the circle every day after the lunch rush and sitting until it was time to go back to Priya's for the dinners.

Late one afternoon, among the dancers and the musicians, the *hubshi* and the bare feet, the singers and the police, I saw her. The *hubshi* woman. And again I wondered at her size; my memory had not exaggerated. I decided to stay where I was. She saw me and smiled. Then, as if remembering anger, she gave me a look of great hatred; and again I saw her as Kali, many-armed, goddess of death and destruction. She looked hard at my face; she considered my clothes. I thought: is it for this I bought these clothes? She got up. She was very big and her tight pants made her much more appalling. She moved towards me. I got up and ran. I ran across the road and then, not looking back, hurried by devious ways to the restaurant.

Priya was doing his accounts. He always looked older when he was doing his accounts, not worried, just older, like a man to whom life could bring no further surprises. I envied him.

"Santosh, some friend brought a parcel for you."

It was a big parcel wrapped in brown paper. He handed it to me, and I thought how calm he was, with his bills and pieces of paper, and the pen with which he made his neat figures, and the book in which he would write every day until that book was exhausted and he would begin a new one.

I took the parcel up to my room and opened it. Inside there was a cardboard box; and inside that, still in its tissue paper, was the green suit.

I felt a hole in my stomach. I couldn't think. I was glad I had to go down almost immediately to the kitchen, glad to be busy until midnight. But then I had to go up to my room again, and I was alone. I hadn't escaped; I had never been free. I had been abandoned. I was like nothing; I had made myself nothing. And I couldn't turn back.

In the morning Priya said, "You don't look very well, Santosh."

His concern weakened me further. He was the only man I could talk to and I didn't know what I could say to him. I felt tears coming to my eyes. At that moment I would have liked the whole world to be reduced to tears. I said, "Sahib, I cannot stay with you any longer."

They were just words, part of my mood, part of my wish for tears and relief. But Priya didn't soften. He didn't even look surprised. "Where will you go, Santosh?"

How could I answer his serious question?

"Will it be different where you go?"

He had freed himself of me. I could no longer think of tears. I said, "Sahib, I have enemies."

He giggled. "You are a joker, Santosh. How can a man like yourself have enemies? There would be no profit in it. *I* have enemies. It is part of your happiness and part of the equity of the world that you cannot have enemies. That's why you can run-run-runaway." He smiled and made the running gesture with his extended palm.

So, at last, I told him my story. I told him about my old employer and my escape and the green suit. He made me feel I was telling him nothing he hadn't already known. I told him about the *hubshi* woman. I was hoping for some rebuke. A rebuke would have meant that he was concerned for my honour, that I could lean on him, that rescue was possible.

But he said, "Santosh, you have no problems. Marry the *hubshi*. That will automatically make you a citizen. Then you will be a free man."

It wasn't what I was expecting. He was asking me to be alone forever. I said, "Sahib, I have a wife and children in the hills at home."

"But this is your home, Santosh. Wife and children in the hills, that is very nice and that is always there. But that is over. You have to do what is best for you here. You are alone here. *Hubshi-ubshi*, nobody worries about that here, if that is your choice. This isn't Bombay. Nobody looks at you when you walk down the street. Nobody cares what you do."

He was right. I was a free man; I could do anything I wanted. I could, if it were possible for me to turn back, go to the apartment and beg my old employer for forgiveness. I could, if it were possible for me to become again what I once was, go to the police and say, "I am an illegal immigrant here. Please deport me to Bombay." I could run away, hang myself, surrender, confess, hide. It didn't matter what I did, because I was alone. And I didn't know what I wanted to do. It was like the time when I felt my senses revive and I wanted to go out and enjoy and I found there was nothing to enjoy.

To be empty is not to be sad. To be empty is to be calm. It is to renounce. Priya said no more to me; he was always busy in the mornings. I left him and went up to my room. It was still a bare room, still like a room that in half an hour could be someone else's. I had never thought of it as mine. I was frightened of its spotless painted walls and had been careful to keep them spotless. For just such a moment.

I tried to think of the particular moment in my life, the particular action, that had brought me to that room. Was it the moment with the *hubshi* woman, or was it when the American came to dinner and insulted my employer? Was it the moment of my escape, my sight of Priya in the gallery, or was it when I looked in the mirror and bought the green suit? Or was it much earlier, in that other life, in Bombay, in the hills? I could find no one moment; every moment seemed important. An endless chain of action had brought me to that room. It was frightening; it was burdensome. It was not a time for new decisions. It was time to call a halt.

I lay on the bed watching the ceiling, watching the sky. The door was pushed open. It was Priya.

"My goodness, Santosh! How long have you been here? You have been so quiet I forgot about you."

He looked about the room. He went into the bathroom and came out again.

"Are you all right, Santosh?"

He sat on the edge of the bed and the longer he stayed the more I realized how glad I was to see him. There was this: when I tried to think of him rushing into the room I couldn't place it in time; it seemed to have occurred only in my mind. He sat with me. Time became real again. I felt a great love for him. Soon I could have laughed at his agitation. And later, indeed, we laughed together.

I said, "Sahib, you must excuse me this morning. I want to go for a walk. I will come back about tea time."

He looked hard at me, and we both knew I had spoken truly.

"Yes, yes, Santosh. You go for a good long walk. Make yourself hungry with walking. You will feel much better."

Walking, through streets that were now so simple to me, I thought how nice it would be if the people in Hindu costumes in the circle were real. Then I might have joined them. We would have taken to the road; at midday we would have halted in the shade of big trees; in the late afternoon the sinking sun would have turned the dust clouds to gold; and every evening at some village there would have been welcome, water, food, a fire in the night. But that was a dream of another life. I had watched the people in the circle long enough to know that they were of their city; that their television life awaited them; that their renunciation was not like mine. No television life awaited me. It didn't matter. In this city I was alone and it didn't matter what I did.

As magical as the circle with the fountain the apartment block had once been to me. Now I saw that it was plain, not very tall, and faced with small white tiles. A glass door; four tiled steps down; the desk to the right, letters and keys in the pigeonholes; a carpet to the left, upholstered chairs, a low table with paper flowers in the vase; the blue door of the swift, silent elevator. I saw the simplicity of all these things. I knew the floor I wanted. In the corridor, with its illuminated star-decorated ceiling, an imitation sky, the colours were blue, grey and gold. I knew the door I wanted. I knocked.

The *hubshi* woman opened. I saw the apartment where she worked. I had never seen it before and was expecting something like my old employer's apartment, which was on the same floor. Instead, for the first time, I saw something arranged for a television life.

I thought she might have been angry. She looked only puzzled. I was grateful for that.

I said to her in English, "Will you marry me?"

And there, it was done.

"It is for the best, Santosh," Priya said, giving me tea when I got back to the restaurant. "You will be a free man. A citizen. You will have the whole world before you."

I was pleased that he was pleased.

So I am now a citizen, my presence is legal, and I live in Washington. I am still with Priya. We do not talk together as much as we did. The restaurant is one world, the parks and green streets of Washington are another, and every evening some of these streets take me to a third. Burnt-out brick houses, broken fences, overgrown gardens; in a levelled lot between the high brick walls of two houses, a sort of artistic children's playground which the *hubshi* children never use; and then the dark house in which I now live.

Its smells are strange, everything in it is strange. But my strength in this house is that I am a stranger. I have closed my mind and heart to the English language, to newspapers and radio and television, to the pictures of *hubshi* runners and boxers and musicians on the wall. I do not want to understand or learn any more.

I am a simple man who decided to act and see for himself, and it is as though I have had several lives. I do not wish to add to these. Some afternoons I walk to the circle with the fountain. I see the dancers but they are separated from me as by glass. Once, when there were rumours of new burnings, someone scrawled in white paint on the pavement outside my house: *Soul Brother.*[2] I understand the words; but I feel, brother to what or to whom? I was once part of the flow, never thinking of myself as a presence. Then I looked in the mirror and decided to be free. All that my freedom has brought me is the knowledge that I have a face and have a body, that I must feed this body and clothe this body for a certain number of years. Then it will be over.

1971

---

2. An African American man or friend to African Americans, here indicating that Santosh's house should not be vandalized.

LESLIE MARMON SILKO

born 1948

Novelist, poet, memoirist, and writer of short fiction, Leslie Marmon Silko can comfortably alternate between prose and poetry within the confines of a single work, in a manner reminiscent of traditional Native American storytellers. For all its seriousness and lyricism, Silko's work is marked by a touch of irreverence. Well acquainted with the proverbial trickster Coyote, Silko has demonstrated her own wit and versatility as a narrator of Coyote tales. But storytelling is a game with serious ends. "I will tell you something about stories," warns an unnamed voice in one of her novels: "They aren't just entertainment. Don't be fooled."

Silko was born in Albuquerque but grew up in Laguna Pueblo, New Mexico. "I am of mixed-breed ancestry," she has written, "but what I know is Laguna. This place I am from is everything I am as a writer and human being." A Keresan-speaking district, Laguna Pueblo is an old Native community that whites first joined in the mid-nineteenth century when two government employees from Ohio, Walter and Robert Marmon, arrived as surveyors and set down roots. The brothers wrote a constitution for Laguna modeled after the U.S. Constitution; each served a term as governor of the pueblo, an office that no non-Native had held before. They also married Laguna women: Robert Marmon is the great-grandfather of Leslie Marmon Silko. Silko attended Laguna Day School until fifth grade, when she was transferred to Manzano Day School, a small private academy in Albuquerque. Between 1964 and 1969, she studied English at the University of New Mexico, married while still in college, and gave birth to the older of her two sons, Cazimir Silko. During these years she published her first story, "Tony's Story," a provocative tale of witchery.

Following graduation, Silko stayed on at the university and taught courses in creative writing and oral literature. She studied for a time in the university's American Indian Law Program, with the intention of working in the legal area of Native land claims. In 1971, however, a National Endowment for the Arts Discovery Grant changed Silko's mind about law school, and she quit to devote herself to writing. Seven of her stories, including "Yellow Woman," were published in 1974 in a collection edited by Kenneth Rosen—*The Man to Send Rain Clouds: Contemporary Stories by American Indians*. The novel *Ceremony*, her first large-scale work, appeared in 1977. An enormously complex novel that appeared just after the Vietnam War, *Ceremony* follows a Second World War veteran of mixed ancestry through his struggle for healing. Widely hailed, the novel propelled its author to the front of the growing ranks of indigenous writers in the United States. On the strength of *Ceremony*, Silko was awarded a MacArthur Fellowship (known as the "genius grant") in 1981.

Although much of Silko's work emphasizes the healing of conflicts—between white and Native Americans, between the human and natural worlds, between warring aspects of the self—some of her novels also reveal a more aggressive and despairing tone. Such a novel is *Almanac of the Dead* (1991), which turns a merciless eye on an America that drugs, prostitution, torture, organized crime, and forms of sexual violence have corrupted and deformed. On the map that opens the book read the stern lines: "The Indian Wars have never ended in the Americas. Native Americans acknowledge no borders; they seek nothing less than the return of all tribal lands." Formerly a professor at the University of Arizona, Silko continues to live and write in Tucson.

The story presented here, "Yellow Woman," is one of Silko's shortest and earliest pieces, but it occupies a still-growing place in the canon of short fiction. Often reprinted, it became the subject of a volume of critical essays published in 1993. In traditional Laguna lore, Yellow Woman is either the heroine or a minor character in a wide range of tales. In her earliest incarnations, she might possibly have been a corn spirit—occasionally, Yellow Woman is named together with her three sisters, Blue Woman, Red Woman, and White Woman, thus completing the four colors of corn—but in Laguna lore she eventually became a kind of Everywoman. A traditional Laguna prayer song, recited at the naming ceremony for a newborn daughter, begins, "Yellow Woman is born, Yellow Woman is born." In narrative lore Yellow Woman most frequently appears in tales of abduction, where she is said to have been captured by a strange man at a stream while she is fetching water. Her captor, who carries her off to another world, is sometimes a kachina, or ancestral spirit; and when at last she returns to her home, she is imbued with power that proves of value for her people. In Silko's version of the tale, traditional elements remain constantly in the foreground. Yet whether the central figures in the story are human or supernatural remains unclear; the story's ambiguity is the source of its fascination. Thus Silko draws on Native tradition to make a major contribution to contemporary American fiction.

Yellow Woman

My thigh clung to his with dampness, and I watched the sun rising up through the tamaracks and willows. The small brown water birds came to the river and hopped across the mud, leaving brown scratches in the alkali-white crust. They bathed in the river silently. I could hear the water, almost at our feet where the narrow fast channel bubbled and washed green ragged moss and fern leaves. I looked at him beside me, rolled in the red blanket on the white river sand. I cleaned the sand out of the cracks between my toes, squinting because the sun was above the willow trees. I looked at him for the last time, sleeping on the white river sand.

I felt hungry and followed the river south the way we had come the afternoon before, following our footprints that were already blurred by lizard tracks and bug trails. The horses were still lying down, and the black one whinnied when he saw me but he did not get up—maybe it was because the corral was made out of thick cedar branches and the horses had not yet felt the sun like I had. I tried to look beyond the pale red mesas to the pueblo. I knew it was there, even if I could not see it, on the sandrock hill above the river, the same river that moved past me now and had reflected the moon last night.

The horse felt warm underneath me. He shook his head and pawed the sand. The bay whinnied and leaned against the gate trying to follow, and I remembered him asleep in the red blanket beside the river. I slid off the horse and tied him close to the other horse, I walked north with the river again, and the white sand broke loose in footprints over footprints.

"Wake up."

He moved in the blanket and turned his face to me with his eyes still closed. I knelt down to touch him.

"I'm leaving."

He smiled now, eyes still closed. "You are coming with me, remember?" He sat up now with his bare dark chest and belly in the sun.

"Where?"

"To my place."

"And will I come back?"

He pulled his pants on. I walked away from him, feeling him behind me and smelling the willows.

"Yellow Woman," he said.

I turned to face him. "Who are you?" I asked.

He laughed and knelt on the low, sandy bank, washing his face in the river. "Last night you guessed my name, and you knew why I had come."

I stared past him at the shallow moving water and tried to remember the night, but I could only see the moon in the water and remember his warmth around me.

"But I only said that you were him and that I was Yellow Woman—I'm not really her—I have my own name and I come from the pueblo on the other side of the mesa. Your name is Silva and you are a stranger I met by the river yesterday afternoon."

He laughed softly. "What happened yesterday has nothing to do with what you will do today, Yellow Woman."

"I know—that's what I'm saying—the old stories about the ka'tsina[1] spirit and Yellow Woman can't mean us."

My old grandpa liked to tell those stories best. There is one about Badger and Coyote who went hunting and were gone all day, and when the sun was going down they found a house. There was a girl living there alone, and she had light hair and eyes and she told them that they could sleep with her. Coyote wanted to be with her all night so he sent Badger into a prairie-dog hole, telling him he thought he saw something in it. As soon as Badger crawled in, Coyote blocked up the entrance with rocks and hurried back to Yellow Woman.

"Come here," he said gently.

He touched my neck and I moved close to him to feel his breathing and to hear his heart. I was wondering if Yellow Woman had known who she was—if she knew that she would become part of the stories. Maybe she'd had another name that her husband and relatives called her so that only the ka'tsina from the north and the storytellers would know her as Yellow Woman. But I didn't go on; I felt him all around me, pushing me down into the white river sand.

Yellow Woman went away with the spirit from the north and lived with him and his relatives. She was gone for a long time, but then one day she came back and she brought twin boys.

"Do you know the story?"

1. Kachina, an ancestral spirit.

"What story?" He smiled and pulled me close to him as he said this. I was afraid lying there on the red blanket. All I could know was the way he felt, warm, damp, his body beside me. This is the way it happens in the stories, I was thinking, with no thought beyond the moment she meets the ka'tsina spirit and they go.

"I don't have to go. What they tell in stories was real only then, back in time immemorial, like they say."

He stood up and pointed at my clothes tangled in the blanket. "Let's go," he said.

I walked beside him, breathing hard because he walked fast, his hand around my wrist. I had stopped trying to pull away from him, because his hand felt cool and the sun was high, drying the river bed into alkali. I will see someone, eventually I will see someone, and then I will be certain that he is only a man—some man from nearby—and I will be sure that I am not Yellow Woman. Because she is from out of time past and I live now and I've been to school and there are highways and pickup trucks that Yellow Woman never saw.

It was an easy ride north on horseback. I watched the change from the cottonwood trees along the river to the junipers that brushed past us in the foothills, and finally there were only piñons, and when I looked up at the rim of the mountain plateau I could see pine trees growing on the edge. Once I stopped to look down, but the pale sandstone had disappeared and the river was gone and the dark lava hills were all around. He touched my hand, not speaking, but always singing softly a mountain song and looking into my eyes.

I felt hungry and wondered what they were doing at home now—my mother, my grandmother, my husband, and the baby. Cooking breakfast, saying, "Where did she go?—maybe kidnapped." And Al going to the tribal police with the details: "She went walking along the river."

The house was made with black lava rock and red mud. It was high above the spreading miles of arroyos and long mesas. I smelled a mountain smell of pitch and buck brush. I stood there beside the black horse, looking down on the small, dim country we had passed, and I shivered.

"Yellow Woman, come inside where it's warm."

He lit a fire in the stove. It was an old stove with a round belly and an enamel coffeepot on top. There was only the stove, some faded Navajo blankets, and a bedroll and cardboard box. The floor was made of smooth adobe plaster, and there was one small window facing east. He pointed at the box.

"There's some potatoes and the frying pan." He sat on the floor with his arms around his knees pulling them close to his chest and he watched me fry the potatoes. I didn't mind him watching me because he was always watching me—he had been watching me since I came upon him sitting on the river bank trimming leaves from a willow twig with his knife. We ate from the pan and he wiped the grease from his fingers on his Levi's.

"Have you brought women here before?" He smiled and kept chewing, so I said, "Do you always use the same tricks?"

"What tricks?" He looked at me like he didn't understand.

"The story about being a ka'tsina from the mountains. The story about Yellow Woman."

Silva was silent; his face was calm.

"I don't believe it. Those stories couldn't happen now," I said.

He shook his head and said softly, "But someday they will talk about us, and they will say, 'Those two lived long ago when things like that happened.' "

He stood up and went out. I ate the rest of the potatoes and thought about things—about the noise the stove was making and the sound of the mountain wind outside. I remembered yesterday and the day before, and then I went outside.

I walked past the corral to the edge where the narrow trail cut through the black rim rock. I was standing in the sky with nothing around me but the wind that came down from the blue mountain peak behind me. I could see faint mountain images in the distance miles across the vast spread of mesas and valleys and plains. I wondered who was over there to feel the mountain wind on those sheer blue edges—who walks on the pine needles in those blue mountains.

"Can you see the pueblo?" Silva was standing behind me.

I shook my head. "We're too far away."

"From here I can see the world." He stepped out on the edge. "The Navajo reservation begins over there." He pointed to the east. "The Pueblo boundaries are over here." He looked below us to the south, where the narrow trail seemed to come from. "The Texans have their ranches over there, starting with that valley, the Concho Valley. The Mexicans run some cattle over there too."

"Do you ever work for them?"

"I steal from them," Silva answered. The sun was dropping behind us and the shadows were filling the land below. I turned away from the edge that dropped forever into the valleys below.

"I'm cold," I said, "I'm going inside." I started wondering about this man who could speak the Pueblo language so well but who lived on a mountain and rustled cattle. I decided that this man Silva must be Navajo, because Pueblo men didn't do things like that.

"You must be a Navajo."

Silva shook his head gently. "Little Yellow Woman," he said, "you never give up, do you? I have told you who I am. The Navajo people know me, too." He knelt down and unrolled the bedroll and spread the extra blankets out on a piece of canvas. The sun was down, and the only light in the house came from outside—the dim orange light from sundown.

I stood there and waited for him to crawl under the blankets.

"What are you waiting for?" he said, and I lay down beside him. He undressed me slowly like the night before beside the river—kissing my face gently and running his hands up and down my belly and legs. He took off my pants and then he laughed.

"Why are you laughing?"

"You are breathing so hard."

I pulled away from him and turned my back to him.

He pulled me around and pinned me down with his arms and chest. "You don't understand, do you, little Yellow Woman? You will do what I want."

And again he was all around me with his skin slippery against mine, and I was afraid because I understood that his strength could hurt me. I lay underneath him and I knew that he could destroy me. But later, while he slept beside me, I touched his face and I had a feeling—the kind of feeling for him that overcame me that morning along the river. I kissed him on the forehead and he reached out for me.

When I woke up in the morning he was gone. It gave me a strange feeling because for a long time I sat there on the blankets and looked around the little house for some object of his—some proof that he had been there or maybe that he was coming back. Only the blankets and the cardboard box remained. The .30-30 that had been leaning in the corner was gone, and so was the knife I had used the night before. He was gone, and I had my chance to go now. But first I had to eat, because I knew it would be a long walk home.

I found some dried apricots in the cardboard box, and I sat down on a rock at the edge of the plateau rim. There was no wind and the sun warmed me. I was surrounded by silence. I drowsed with apricots in my mouth, and I didn't believe that there were highways or railroads or cattle to steal.

When I woke up, I stared down at my feet in the black mountain dirt. Little black ants were swarming over the pine needles around my foot. They must have smelled the apricots. I thought about my family far below me. They would be wondering about me, because this had never happened to me before. The tribal police would file a report. But if old Grandpa weren't dead he would tell them what happened—he would laugh and say, "Stolen by a ka'tsina, a mountain spirit. She'll come home—they usually do." There are enough of them to handle things. My mother and grandmother will raise the baby like they raised me. Al will find someone else, and they will go on like before, except that there will be a story about the day I disappeared while I was walking along the river. Silva had come for me; he said he had. I did not decide to go. I just went. Moonflowers blossom in the sand hills before dawn, just as I followed him. That's what I was thinking as I wandered along the trail through the pine trees.

It was noon when I got back. When I saw the stone house I remembered that I had meant to go home. But that didn't seem important any more, maybe because there were little blue flowers growing in the meadow behind the stone house and the gray squirrels were playing in the pines next to the house. The horses were standing in the corral, and there was a beef carcass hanging on the shady side of a big pine in front of the house. Flies buzzed around the clotted blood that hung from the carcass. Silva was washing his hands in a bucket full of water. He must have heard me coming because he spoke to me without turning to face me.

"I've been waiting for you."

"I went walking in the big pine trees."

I looked into the bucket full of bloody water with brown-and-white animal hairs floating in it. Silva stood there letting his hand drip, examining me intently.

"Are you coming with me?"

"Where?" I asked him.

"To sell the meat in Marquez."

"If you're sure it's O.K."

"I wouldn't ask you if it wasn't," he answered.

He sloshed the water around in the bucket before he dumped it out and set the bucket upside down near the door. I followed him to the corral and watched him saddle the horses. Even beside the horses he looked tall, and I asked him again if he wasn't Navajo. He didn't say anything; he just shook his head and kept cinching up the saddle.

"But Navajos are tall."

"Get on the horse," he said, "and let's go."

The last thing he did before we started down the steep trail was to grab the .30-30 from the corner. He slid the rifle into the scabbard that hung from his saddle.

"Do they ever try to catch you?" I asked.

"They don't know who I am."

"Then why did you bring the rifle?"

"Because we are going to Marquez where the Mexicans live."

The trail leveled out on a narrow ridge that was steep on both sides like an animal spine. On one side I could see where the trail went around the rocky gray hills and disappeared into the southeast where the pale sandrock mesas stood in the distance near my home. On the other side was a trail that went west, and as I looked far into the distance I thought I saw the little town. But Silva said no, that I was looking in the wrong place, that I just thought I saw houses. After that I quit looking off into the distance; it was hot and the wildflowers were closing up their deep-yellow petals. Only the waxy cactus flowers bloomed in the bright sun, and I saw every color that a cactus blossom can be; the white ones and the red ones were still buds, but the purple and the yellow were blossoms, open full and the most beautiful of all.

Silva saw him before I did. The white man was riding a big gray horse, coming up the trail towards us. He was traveling fast and the gray horse's feet sent rocks rolling off the trail into the dry tumbleweeds. Silva motioned for me to stop and we watched the white man. He didn't see us right away, but finally his horse whinnied at our horses and he stopped. He looked at us briefly before he lapped the gray horse across the three hundred yards that separated us. He stopped his horse in front of Silva, and his young fat face was shadowed by the brim of his hat. He didn't look mad, but his small, pale eyes moved from the blood-soaked gunny sacks hanging from my saddle to Silva's face and then back to my face.

"Where did you get the fresh meat?" the white man asked.

"I've been hunting," Silva said, and when he shifted his weight in the saddle the leather creaked.

"The hell you have, Indian. You've been rustling cattle. We've been looking for the thief for a long time."

The rancher was fat, and sweat began to soak through his white cowboy shirt and the wet cloth stuck to the thick rolls of belly fat. He almost seemed to be panting from the exertion of talking, and he smelled rancid, maybe because Silva scared him.

Silva turned to me and smiled. "Go back up the mountain, Yellow Woman."

The white man got angry when he heard Silva speak in a language he couldn't understand. "Don't try anything, Indian. Just keep riding to Marquez. We'll call the state police from there."

The rancher must have been unarmed because he was very frightened and if he had a gun he would have pulled it out then. I turned my horse around and the rancher yelled, "Stop!" I looked at Silva for an instant and there was

2548 | LESLIE MARMON SILKO

something ancient and dark—something I could feel in my stomach—in his eyes, and when I glanced at his hand I saw his finger on the trigger of the .30-30 that was still in the saddle scabbard. I slapped my horse across the flank and the sacks of raw meat swung against my knees as the horse leaped up the trail. It was hard to keep my balance, and once I thought I felt the saddle slipping backward; it was because of this that I could not look back.

I didn't stop until I reached the ridge where the trail forked. The horse was breathing deep gasps and there was a dark film of sweat on its neck. I looked down in the direction I had come from, but I couldn't see the place. I waited. The wind came up and pushed warm air past me. I looked up at the sky, pale blue and full of thin clouds and fading vapor trails left by jets.

I think four shots were fired—I remember hearing four hollow explosions that reminded me of deer hunting. There could have been more shots after that, but I couldn't have heard them because my horse was running again and the loose rocks were making too much noise as they scattered around his feet.

Horses have a hard time running downhill, but I went that way instead of uphill to the mountain because I thought it was safer. I felt better with the horse running southeast past the round gray hills that were covered with cedar trees and black lava rock. When I got to the plain in the distance I could see the dark green patches of tamaracks that grew along the river; and beyond the river I could see the beginning of the pale sandrock mesas. I stopped the horse and looked back to see if anyone was coming; then I got off the horse and turned the horse around, wondering if it would go back to its corral under the pines on the mountain. It looked back at me for a moment and then plucked a mouthful of green tumbleweeds before it trotted back up the trail with its ears pointed forward, carrying its head daintily to one side to avoid stepping on the dragging reins. When the horse disappeared over the last hill, the gunny sacks full of meat were still swinging and bouncing.

I walked toward the river on a wood-hauler's road that I knew would eventually lead to the paved road. I was thinking about waiting beside the road for someone to drive by, but by the time I got to the pavement I had decided it wasn't very far to walk if I followed the river back the way Silva and I had come.

The river water tasted good, and I sat in the shade under a cluster of silvery willows. I thought about Silva, and I felt sad at leaving him; still, there was something strange about him, and I tried to figure it out all the way back home.

I came back to the place on the river bank where he had been sitting the first time I saw him. The green willow leaves that he had trimmed from the branch were still lying there, wilted in the sand. I saw the leaves and I wanted to go back to him—to kiss him and to touch him—but the mountains were too far away now. And I told myself, because I believe it, he will come back sometime and be waiting again by the river.

I followed the path up from the river into the village. The sun was getting low, and I could smell supper cooking when I got to the screen door of my house. I could hear their voices inside—my mother was telling my grandmother how to fix the Jell-O and my husband, Al, was playing with the baby. I decided to tell them that some Navajo had kidnaped me, but I was sorry that old Grandpa wasn't alive to hear my story because it was the Yellow Woman stories he liked to tell best.

1974

NGUGI WA THIONG'O

born 1938

As the first successful English-language novelist from East Africa, Ngugi Wa Thiong'o made the surprising decision in middle age to stop writing in English. Believing that Africans should use their native tongues, he began writing in Kikuyu, a language spoken by about six million Kenyans (a quarter of the country's population). At the same time, Ngugi's politics became more radical and he turned from the experimental style of his early fiction to a form of socialist realism and satire in his Kikuyu works. Imprisoned for his criticisms of the Kenyan regime in the late 1970s, Ngugi some became a symbol of the resistance of African writers to the abuse of state power.

Born James Ngugi in 1938 in British-ruled Kenya, the author lived as a youth through the Mau Mau uprising, in which the Mau Mau (a primarily Kikuyu group) rebelled against British laws that gave land to white settlers and forced Africans to work the land for little compensation. His stepbrother was killed in the rebellion; his mother was tortured. The uprising lasted for a decade, until 1963, when Kenya gained its independence. By this time, Ngugi had graduated from Makerere University College in Kampala, the capital of Uganda, and had his first play, *The Black Hermit* (1962), produced by the Uganda National Theatre. Like many African authors of his generation, Ngugi found early inspiration in the modern classics of Western literature, including the works of **Joseph Conrad.** For a brief period he became a Christian.

Shortly after Kenyan independence, Ngugi enrolled at the University of Leeds in England, where he completed three novels. While in England, he became interested in the radical theorists Karl Marx and Frantz Fanon; he would later visit the Soviet Union. In 1967 he was appointed the first African faculty member in the English Department of University College, Nairobi, rising to head of the department within a few years. In the 1970s the author decided to leave behind the name James Ngugi and the English language as his primary vehicle for creative expression. His first experiments with writing in Kikuyu began at this time, although he continued to publish some English-language fiction.

A turning point came in 1977, as he released his first novel in a decade, *Petals of Blood*. His last in English and his most explicitly political novel to date, it focused on Marxist analysis of relations among social classes rather than on the nationalist questions that had concerned the author earlier. In the same year, a play in Kikuyu, *I Will Marry When I Want*, had great success with its criticism of capitalism and Christianity. Its indirect attacks on government policies drew the attention of Daniel arap Moi, then vice president, who ordered Ngugi detained. He was imprisoned for almost a year; during this time Moi became president of Kenya, and when Ngugi was released, he was refused employment as a professor and eventually reimprisoned. His time in confinement led to his being declared a Prisoner of Conscience by Amnesty International; in 1978 an open letter calling for his release was published, signed by many Western authors. While in prison, Ngugi composed the first full-length novel written in Kikuyu, *Devil on the Cross* (1980), using prison toilet paper as stationery.

Shortly after his release, he left Kenya to live in London, and did not return until 2004, after Moi's departure from office.

Ngugi has continued his career as a novelist and a playwright, a journalist and a teacher, and an essayist and a postcolonial theorist. He has argued for the importance of writing in native languages rather than in English and has maintained his Socialist ideological commitments, although he currently lives in the United States, where he is a professor of English and Comparative Literature at the University of California, Irvine.

Like **Chinua Achebe**, Ngugi explores the disastrous consequences for Africans of contact with the British. In the English-language work from the earliest years of his career, Ngugi wrote historical fiction about colonial rule in Kenya. By the middle years of his career, he turned his eye to independent Kenya and his writings became increasingly satirical and critical of Kenyan society and government. In the story included here, "Wedding at the Cross" (1975), Ngugi shows the effects of the previous decades of Kenyan history on a particular married couple and thus chronicles the compromises made by the Westernized middle classes in the pursuit of prosperity. He said of the collection in which it appears, *Secret Lives* (1975), his only collection of stories in English, that it contained his "creative autobiography over the last twelve years," that is, the years since independence.

Christianity plays an ambiguous role in Ngugi's works. On the one hand, it is an antimaterialist religion that exalts the poor; on the other hand, it is the religion of the colonizers and thus potentially a vehicle for social advancement. The story begins with the rebellious and charismatic Wariuki seeking to marry Miriamu, the daughter of a wealthy grocer in the years of colonial rule. Miriamu's father, a Christian who gets along well with the British authorities, opposes the match because of Wariuki's poverty. The young couple elopes, and the initial tone of the story is positive, even romantic. As the narrator relates the history of their marriage, however, it becomes clear that Wariuki's personality has suffered from his rejection by Miriamu's father. He fights for the British during the Second World War, becomes a Christian, and takes an English name, but even as he gains in prosperity, his resentment of Miriamu's father remains. As independence comes and Wariuki benefits from the discriminatory policies of the Kenyan government against his employers (South Asian Kenyans who were expelled from the country in the late 1960s), Miriamu discovers a more authentic, but unofficial, Christianity, the Religion of Sorrows. The conflict between their two views of Christianity leads to the crisis of "Wedding at the Cross." Ngugi's subtle rendering of the tensions between official Christianity and popular religion adds depth to his memorable portrayal of postcolonial African society.

Wedding at the Cross

Everyone said of them: what a nice family; he, the successful timber merchant; and she, the obedient wife who did her duty to God, husband and family. Wariuki and his wife Miriamu were a shining example of what cooperation between man and wife united in love and devotion could achieve: he tall, correct, even a little stiff, but wealthy; she, small, quiet, unobtrusive, a diminishing shadow beside her giant of a husband.

He had married her when he was without a cent buried anywhere, not even for the rainiest day, for he was then only a milk clerk in a settler farm earning thirty shillings a month—a fortune in those days, true, but drinking most of it by the first of the next month. He was young; he did not care; dreams of material possessions and power little troubled him. Of course he joined the other workers in collective protests and demands, he would even compose letters for them; from one or two farms he had been dismissed as a dangerous and subversive character. But his heart was really elsewhere, in his favourite sports and acts. He would proudly ride his Raleigh Bicycle[1] around, whistling certain lines from old records remembered, yodelling in imitation of Jim Rogers,[2] and occasionally demonstrating his skill on the machine to an enthusiastic audience in Molo township. He would stand on the bicycle balancing with the left leg, arms stretched about to fly, or he would simply pedal backwards to the delight of many children. It was an old machine, but decorated in loud colours of red, green and blue with several Wariuki home-manufactured headlamps and reflectors and with a warning scrawled on a signboard mounted at the back seat: Overtake Me, Graveyard Ahead. From a conjurer on a bicycle, he would move to other roles. See the actor now mimicking his white bosses, satirizing their way of talking and walking and also their mannerisms and attitudes to black workers. Even those Africans who sought favours from the whites were not spared. He would vary his acts with dancing, good dancer too, and his mwomboko steps, with the left trouser leg deliberately split along the seam to an inch above the knee, always attracted approving eyes and sighs from maids in the crowd.

That's how he first captured Miriamu's heart.

On every Sunday afternoon she would seize any opportunity to go to the shopping square where she would eagerly join the host of worshippers. Her heart would then rise and fall with his triumphs and narrow escapes, or simply pound in rhythm with his dancing hips. Miriamu's family was miles better off than most squatters in the Rift Valley. Her father, Douglas Jones, owned several groceries and tea-rooms around the town. A God-fearing couple he and his wife were: they went to church on Sundays, they said their prayers first thing in the morning, last thing in the evening and of course before every meal. They were looked on with favour by the white farmers around; the District Officer would often stop by for a casual greeting. Theirs then was a good Christian home and hence they objected to their daughter marrying into sin, misery and poverty: what could she possibly see in that Murebi, Murebi bii-u? They told her not to attend those heathen Sunday scenes of idleness and idol worship. But Miriamu had an independent spirit, though it had since childhood been schooled into inactivity by Sunday sermons—thou shalt obey thy father and mother and those that rule over us—and a proper upbringing with rules straight out of the Rt. Reverend Clive Schomberg's classic: *British Manners for Africans*.[3] Now Wariuki with his Raleigh bicycle, his milkman's tunes, his baggy trousers and dance which gave freedom to the body, was the light that beckoned her from the sterile world of Douglas Jones to a neon-lit city in a far

1. A British make of bicycle.
2. American country singer Jimmie Rodgers (1897–1933), known for his yodeling.
3. A work encouraging Africans to imitate a British lifestyle.

horizon. Part of her was suspicious of the heavy glow, she was even slightly revolted by his dirt and patched up trousers, but she followed him, and was surprised at her firmness. Douglas Jones relented a little: he loved his daughter and only desired the best for her. He did not want her to marry one of those useless half-educated upstarts, who disturbed the ordered life, peace and prosperity on European farms. Such men, as the Bwana District Officer[4] often told him, would only end in jails: they were motivated by greed and wanted to cheat the simple-hearted and illiterate workers about the evils of white settlers and missionaries. Wariuki looked the dangerous type in every way.

He summoned Wariuki, 'Our would-be-son-in-law', to his presence. He wanted to find the young man's true weight in silver and gold. And Wariuki, with knees weakened a little, for he, like most workers, was a little awed by men of that Christian and propertied class, carefully mended his left trouser leg, combed and brushed his hair and went there. They made him stand at the door, without offering him a chair, and surveyed him up and down. Wariuki, bewildered, looked alternately to Miriamu and to the wall for possible deliverance. And then when he finally got a chair, he would not look at the parents and the dignitaries invited to sit in judgement but fixed his eyes to the wall. But he was aware of their naked gaze and condemnation. Douglas Jones, though, was a model of Christian graciousness: tea for our—well—our son—well—this young man here. What work? Milk clerk? Ahh, well, well—no man was born with wealth—wealth was in the limbs you know and you, you are so young—salary? Thirty shillings a month?[5] Well, well, others had climbed up from worse and deeper pits: true wealth came from the Lord on high, you know. And Wariuki was truly grateful for these words and even dared a glance and a smile at old Douglas Jones. What he saw in those eyes made him quickly turn to the wall and wait for the execution. The manner of the execution was not rough: but the cold steel cut deep and clean. Why did Wariuki want to marry when he was so young? Well, well, as you like—the youth today—so different from our time. And who 'are we' to tell what youth ought to do? We do not object to the wedding: but we as Christians have a responsibility. I say it again: we do not object to this union. But it must take place at the cross. A church wedding, Wariuki, costs money. Maintaining a wife also costs money. Is that not so? You nod your head? Good. It is nice to see a young man with sense these days. All that I now want, and that is why I have called in my counsellor friends, is to see your savings account. Young man, can you show these elders your post office book?

Wariuki was crushed. He now looked at the bemused eyes of the elders present. He then fixed them on Miriamu's mother, as if in appeal. Only he was not seeing her. Away from the teats and rich udder of the cows, away from his bicycle and the crowd of rich admirers, away from the anonymous security of bars and tea-shops, he did not know how to act. He was a hunted animal, now cornered: and the hunters, panting with anticipation, were enjoying every moment of that kill. A buzz in his head, a blurring vision, and he heard the still gracious voice of Douglas Jones trailing into something about not signing his daughter to a life of misery and drudgery. Desperately Wariuki looked to the door and to the open space.

---

4. Highest-ranking British officer in a locality.
5. About $5 in the period of the story, or around $60 today.

Escape at last: and he breathed with relief. Although he was trembling a little, he was glad to be in a familiar world, his own world. But he looked at it slightly differently, almost as if he had been wounded and could not any more enjoy what he saw. Miriamu followed him there: for a moment he felt a temporary victory over Douglas Jones. They ran away and he got a job with Ciana Timber Merchants in Ilmorog forest. The two lived in a shack of a room to which he escaped from the daily curses of his Indian[6] employers. Wariuki learnt how to endure the insults. He sang with the movement of the saw: kneeling down under the log, the other man standing on it, he would make up words and stories about the log and the forest, sometimes ending on a tragic note when he came to the fatal marriage between the saw and the forest. This somehow would lighten his heart so that he did not mind the falling saw-dust. Came his turn to stand on top of the log and he would experience a malicious power as he sawed through it, gingerly walking backwards step by step and now singing of Demi na Mathathi[7] who, long ago, cleared woods and forests more dense than Ilmorog.

And Miriamu the erstwhile daughter of Douglas Jones would hear his voice rising above the whispering or uproarious wind and her heart rose and fell with it. This, this, dear Lord, was so different from the mournful church hymns of her father's compound, so, so, different and she felt good inside. On Saturdays and Sundays he took her to dances in the wood. On their way home from the dances and the songs, they would look for a suitable spot on the grass and make love. For Miriamu these were nights of happiness and wonder as the thorny pine leaves painfully but pleasantly pricked her buttocks even as she moaned under him, calling out to her mother and imaginary sisters for help when he plunged into her.

And Wariuki too was happy. It always seemed to him a miracle that he, a boy from the streets and without a father (he had died while carrying guns and food for the British in their expeditions against the Germans in Tanganyika[8] in the first European World War), had secured the affections of a girl from that class. But he was never the old Wariuki. Often he would go over his life beginning with his work picking pyrethrum[9] flowers for others under a scorching sun or icy cold winds in Limuru, to his recent job as a milk clerk in Molo:[1] his reminiscences would abruptly end with that interview with Douglas Jones and his counsellors. He would never forget that interview: he was never to forget the cackling throaty laughter as Douglas Jones and his friends tried to diminish his manhood and selfworth in front of Miriamu and her mother.

Never. He would show them. He would yet laugh in their faces.

But soon a restless note crept into his singing: bitterness of an unfulfilled hope and promise. His voice became rugged like the voice-teeth of the saw and he tore through the air with the same greedy malice. He gave up his job with the Ciana Merchants and took Miriamu all the way to Limuru. He dumped Miriamu with his aged mother and he disappeared from their lives. They heard of him in Nairobi, Mombasa, Nakuru, Kisumu and even Kampala.[2] Rumours

---

6. Indians often worked in Africa as merchants.
7. Mythical Kikuyu (Kenyan) giants.
8. Modern Tanzania, south of Kenya.
9. A relative of the chrysanthemum.

1. A town in western Kenya; Limuru is a town in central Kenya.
2. The capital of Uganda; the other towns listed are in various regions of Kenya.

reached them: that he was in prison, that he had even married a Muganda girl.[3] Miriamu waited: she remembered her moments of pained pleasure under Ilmorog woods, ferns and grass and endured the empty bed and the bite of Limuru cold in June and July. Her parents had disowned her and anyway she would not want to go back. The seedling he had planted in her warmed her. Eventually the child arrived and this together with the simple friendship of her mother-in-law consoled her. Came more rumours: whitemen were gathering arms for a war amongst themselves, and black men, sons of the soil, were being drafted to aid in the slaughter. Could this be true? Then Wariuki returned from his travels and she noticed the change in her man. He was now of few words: where was the singing and the whistling of old tunes remembered? He stayed a week. Then he said: I am going to war. Miriamu could not understand: why this change? Why this wanderlust[4]? But she waited and worked on the land.

Wariuki had the one obsession: to erase the memory of that interview, to lay for ever the ghost of those contemptuous eyes. He fought in Egypt, Palestine, Burma and in Madagascar.[5] He did not think much about the war, he did not question what it meant for black people, he just wanted it to end quickly so that he might resume his quest. Why, he might even go home with a little loot from the war. This would give him the start in life he had looked for, without success, in towns all over Colonial Kenya. A lucrative job even: the British had promised them jobs and money-rewards once the wicked Germans were routed. After the war he was back in Limuru, a little emaciated in body but hardened in resolve.

For a few weeks after his return, Miriamu detected a little flicker of the old fires and held him close to herself. He made a few jokes about the war, and sang a few soldiers' songs to his son. He made love to her and another seed was planted. He again tried to get a job. He heard of a workers' strike in a Limuru shoe factory. All the workers were summarily dismissed. Wariuki and others flooded the gates to offer their sweat for silver. The striking workers tried to picket the new hands, whom they branded traitors to the cause, but helmeted police were called to the scene, baton charged the old workers away from the fenced compound and escorted the new ones into the factory. But Wariuki was not among them. Was he born into bad luck? He was back in the streets of Nairobi joining the crowd of the unemployed recently returned from the War. No jobs no money-rewards: the 'good' British and the 'wicked' Germans were shaking hands with smiles. But questions as to why black people were not employed did not trouble him: when young men gathered in Pumwani, Kari-okor, Shauri Moyo[6] and other places to ask questions he did not join them: they reminded him of his old association and flirtation with farm workers before the war: those efforts had come to nought: even these ones would come to nought: he was in any case ashamed of that past: he thought that if he had been less of a loafer and more enterprising he would never have been so humil-iated in front of Miriamu and her mother. The young men's talk of proces-sions, petitions and pistols, their talk of gunning the whites out of the country,

---

3. From a Ugandan ethnic group.
4. Desire for travel (German).
5. Theaters of action in the Second World
War (1939–45).
6. Neighborhoods of Nairobi, Kenya.

seemed too remote from his ambition and quest. He had to strike out on his own for moneyland. On arrival, he would turn round and confront old Douglas Jones and contemptuously flaunt success before his face. With the years the memory of that humiliation in the hands of the rich became so sharp and fresh that it often hurt him into sleepless nights. He did not think of the whites and the Indians as the real owners of property, commerce and land. He only saw the picture of Douglas Jones in his grey woollen suit, his waistcoat, his hat and his walking stick of a folded umbrella. What was the secret of that man's success? What? What? He attempted odd jobs here and there: he even tried his hand at trading in the hawk market at Bahati.[7] He would buy pencils and handkerchiefs from the Indian Bazaar and sell them at a retail price that ensured him a bit of profit. Was this his true vocation?

But before he could find an answer to his question, the Mau Mau war of national liberation broke out. A lot of workers, employed and unemployed, were swept off the streets of Nairobi into concentration camps. Somehow he escaped the net and was once again back in Limuru. He was angry. Not with the whites, not with the Indians, all of whom he saw as permanent features of the land like the mountains and the valleys, but with his own people. Why should they upset the peace? Why should they upset the stability just when he had started gathering a few cents from his trade? He now believed, albeit without much conviction, the lies told by the British about imminent prosperity and widening opportunities for blacks. For about a year he remained aloof from the turmoil around: he was only committed to his one consuming passion. Then he drifted into the hands of the colonial regime and cooperated. This way he avoided concentration camps and the forest. Soon his choice of sides started bearing fruit: he was excited about the prospects for its ripening. While other people's strips of land were being taken by the colonialists, his piece, although small, was left intact. In fact, during land consolidation forced on women and old men while their husbands and sons were decaying in detention or resisting in the forest, he, along with other active collaborators, secured additional land. Wariuki was not a cruel man: he just wanted this nightmare over so that he might resume his trade. For even in the midst of battle the image of D. Jones never really left him: the humiliation ached: he nursed it like one nurses a toothache with one's tongue, and felt that a day would come when he would stand up to that image.

Jomo Kenyatta[8] returned home from Maralal. Wariuki was a little frightened, his spirits were dampened: what would happen to his kind at the gathering of the braves to celebrate victory? Alas, where were the Whites he had thought of as permanent features of the landscape? But with independence approaching, Wariuki had his first real reward: the retreating colonialists gave him a loan: he bought a motor-propelled saw and set up as a Timber Merchant.

For a time after Independence, Wariuki feared for his life and business as the sons of the soil streamed back from detention camps and from the forests: he expected a retribution, but people were tired. They had no room in their hearts for vengeance at the victorious end of a just struggle. So Wariuki

---

7. A neighborhood in Nairobi.
8. Leader of the independence movement and

later prime minister and president of Kenya (ca. 1894–1978).

prospered undisturbed: he had, after all, a fair start over those who had really fought for Uhuru.[9]

He joined the Church in gratitude. The Lord had spared him: he dragged Miriamu into it, and together they became exemplary Church-goers.

But Miriamu prayed a different prayer, she wanted her man back. Her two sons were struggling their way through Siriana Secondary School. For this she thanked the Lord. But she still wanted her real Wariuki back. During the Emergency[1] she had often cautioned him against excessive cruelty. It pained her that his singing, his dancing and his easy laughter had ended. His eyes were hard and set and this frightened her.

Now in Church he started singing again. Not the tunes that had once captured her soul, but the mournful hymns she knew so well; how sweet the name of Jesus sounds in a believer's ears. He became a pillar of the Church Choir. He often beat the drum which, after Independence, had been introduced into the church as a concession to African culture. He attended classes in baptism and great was the day he cast away Wariuki and became Dodge W. Livingstone, Jr. Thereafter he sat in the front bench. As his business improved, he gradually worked his way to the holy aisle. A new Church elder.

Other things brightened. His parents-in-law still lived in Molo, though their fortunes had declined. They had not yet forgiven him. But with his eminence, they sent out feelers: would their daughter pay them a visit? Miriamu would not hear of it. But Dodge W. Livingstone was furious: where was her Christian forgiveness? He was insistent. She gave in. He was glad. But that gesture, by itself, could not erase the memory of his humiliation. His vengeance would still come.

Though his base was at Limuru, he travelled to various parts of the country. So he got to know news concerning his line of business. It was the year of the Asian exodus.[2] Ciana Merchants were not Kenya Citizens. Their licence would be withdrawn. They quickly offered Livingstone partnership on a fifty-fifty share basis. Praise the Lord and raise high his name. Truly God never ate Ugali.[3] Within a year he had accumulated enough to qualify for a loan to buy one of the huge farms in Limuru previously owned by whites. He was now a big timber merchant: they made him a senior elder of the church.

Miriamu still waited for her Wariuki in vain. But she was a model wife. People praised her Christian and wifely meekness. She was devout in her own way and prayed to the Lord to rescue her from the dreams of the past. She never put on airs. She even refused to wear shoes. Every morning, she would wake early, take her Kiondo, and go to the farm where she would work in the tea estate alongside the workers. And she never forgot her old strip of land in the Old Reserve. Sometimes she made lunch and tea for the workers. This infuriated her husband: why, oh why did she choose to humiliate him before these people? Why would she not conduct herself like a Christian lady? After all, had she not come from a Christian home? Need she dirty her hands now, he asked her, and with labourers too? On clothes, she gave in: she put on shoes

9. Independence (Swahili).
1. State of emergency during the anticolonial Mau Mau uprising of the 1950s.
2. In 1968–69, under pressure from a nation-

alist Kenyan government, South Asian residents of Kenya fled the country.
3. A type of porridge.

and a white hat especially when going to Church. But work was in her bones and this she would not surrender. She enjoyed the touch of the soil: she enjoyed the free and open conversation with the workers.

They liked her. But they resented her husband. Livingstone thought them a lazy lot: why would they not work as hard as he himself had done? Which employer's wife had ever brought him food in a shamba[4]? Miriamu was spoiling them and he told her so. Occasionally he would look at their sullen faces: he would then remember the days of the Emergency or earlier when he received insults from Ciana employers. But gradually he learnt to silence these unsettling moments in prayer and devotion. He was aware of their silent hatred but thought this a natural envy of the idle and the poor for the rich.

Their faces brightened only in Miriamu's presence. They would abandon their guarded selves and joke and laugh and sing. They gradually let her into their inner lives. They were members of a secret sect that believed that Christ suffered and died for the poor. They called theirs *The Religion of Sorrows*.[5] When her husband was on his business tours, she would attend some of their services. A strange band of men and women: they sang songs they themselves had created and used drums, guitars, jingles and tambourines, producing a throbbing powerful rhythm that made her want to dance with happiness. Indeed they themselves danced around, waving hands in the air, their faces radiating warmth and assurance, until they reached a state of possession and heightened awareness. Then they would speak in tongues strange and beautiful. They seemed united in a common labour and faith: this was what most impressed Miriamu. Something would stir in her, some dormant wings would beat with power inside her, and she would go home trembling in expectation. She would wait for her husband and she felt sure that together they could rescue something from a shattered past. But when he came back from his tours, he was still Dodge W. Livingstone, Jr., senior church elder, and a prosperous farmer and timber merchant. She once more became the model wife listening to her husband as he talked business and arithmetic for the day: what contracts he had won, what money he had won and lost, and tomorrow's prospects. On Sunday man and wife would go to church as usual: same joyless hymns, same prayers from set books; same regular visits to brothers and sisters in Christ; the inevitable tea-parties and charity auctions to which Livingstone was a conspicuous contributor. What a nice family everyone said in admiration and respect: he, the successful farmer and timber merchant; and she, the obedient wife who did her duty to God and husband.

One day he came home early. His face was bright—not wrinkled with the usual cares and worries. His eyes beamed with pleasure. Miriamu's heart gave a gentle leap, could this be true? Was the warrior back? She could see him trying to suppress his excitement. But the next moment her heart fell again. He had said it. His father-in-law, Douglas Jones, had invited him, had begged him to visit them at Molo. He whipped out the letter and started reading it aloud. Then he knelt down and praised the Lord, for his mercy and tender understanding. Miriamu could hardly join in the Amen. Lord, Lord, what has hardened my heart so, she prayed and sincerely desired to see the light.

---

4. Vegetable garden (Kikuyu).
5. Christianity has frequently been called a "religion of sorrow" because of its emphasis on sin and suffering (although it also emphasizes redemption).

The day of reunion drew near. His knees were becoming weak. He could not hide his triumph. He reviewed his life and saw in it the guiding finger of God. He the boy from the gutter, a mere milk clerk . . . but he did not want to recall the ridiculous young man who wore patched-up trousers and clowned on a bicycle. Could that have been he, making himself the laughing stock of the whole town? He went to Benbros and secured a new Mercedes Benz 220S. This would make people look at him differently. On the day in question, he himself wore a worsted woollen suit, a waistcoat, and carried a folded umbrella. He talked Miriamu into going in an appropriate dress bought from Nairobi Drapers in Government Road.[6] His own mother had been surprised into a frock and shoe-wearing lady. His two sons in their school uniform spoke nothing but English. (They affected to find it difficult speaking Kikuyu,[7] they made so many mistakes.) A nice family, and they drove to Molo. The old man met them. He had aged, with silver hair covering his head, but he was still strong in body. Jones fell on his knees; Livingstone fell on his knees. They prayed and then embraced in tears. Our son, our son. And my grandchildren too. The past was drowned in tears and prayers. But for Miriamu, the past was vivid in the mind.

Livingstone, after the initial jubilations, found that the memories of that interview rankled a little. Not that he was angry with Jones: the old man had been right, of course. He could not imagine himself giving his own daughter to such a ragamuffin of an upstart clerk. Still he wanted that interview erased from memory forever. And suddenly, and again he saw in that revelation the hand of God, he knew the answer. He trembled a little. Why had he not thought of it earlier? He had a long intimate conversation with his father-in-law and then made the proposal. Wedding at the cross. A renewal of the old. Douglas Jones immediately consented. His son had become a true believer. But Miriamu could not see any sense in the scheme. She was ageing. And the Lord had blessed her with two sons. Where was the sin in that? Again they all fell on her. A proper wedding at the cross of Jesus would make their lives complete. Her resistance was broken. They all praised the Lord. God worked in mysterious ways, his wonders to perform.[8]

The few weeks before the eventful day were the happiest in the life of Livingstone. He savoured every second. Even anxieties and difficulties gave him pleasure. That this day would come: a wedding at the cross. A wedding at the cross, at the cross where he had found the Lord. He was young again. He bounced in health and a sense of well-being. The day he would exchange rings at the cross would erase unsettling memories of yesterday. Cards were printed and immediately despatched. Cars and buses were lined up. He dragged Miriamu to Nairobi. They went from shop to shop all over the city: Kenyatta Avenue, Muindi Bingu Streets, Bazaar, Government Road, Kimathi Street, and back again to Kenyatta Avenue. Eventually he bought her a snow-white long-sleeved satin dress, a veil, white gloves, white shoes and stockings and of course plastic roses. He consulted Rev. Clive Schomberg's still modern classic on good manners for Africans and he hardly departed from the rules and instructions in the matrimonial section. Dodge W. Livingstone, Jr. did not want to make a mistake.

---

6. An expensive commercial area in Nairobi.
7. The language of the Kikuyu ethnic group, to which Ngugi belongs.

8. Paraphrase of a hymn by William Cowper (1731–1800), "Light Shining Out of Darkness."

Miriamu did not send or give invitation cards to anybody. She daily prayed that God would give her the strength to go through the whole affair. She wished that the day would come and vanish as in a dream. A week before the day, she was driven all the way back to her parents. She was a mother of two; she was no longer the young girl who once eloped; she simply felt ridiculous pretending that she was a virgin maid at her father's house. But she submitted almost as if she were driven by a power stronger than man. Maybe she was wrong, she thought. Maybe everybody else was right. Why then should she ruin the happiness of many? For even the church was very happy. He, a successful timber merchant, would set a good example to others. And many women had come to congratulate her on her present luck in such a husband. They wanted to share in her happiness. Some wept.

The day itself was bright. She could see some of the rolling fields in Molo: the view brought painful memories of her childhood. She tried to be cheerful. But attempts at smiling only brought out tears: What of the years of waiting? What of the years of hope? Her face-wrinkled father was a sight to see: a dark suit with tails, a waist jacket, top hat and all. She inclined her head to one side, in shame. She prayed for yet more strength: she hardly recognized anybody as she was led towards the holy aisle. Not even her fellow workers, members of the *Religion of Sorrows*, who waited in a group among the crowd outside.

But for Livingstone this was the supreme moment. Sweeter than vengeance. All his life he had slaved for this hour. Now it had come. He had specially dressed for the occasion: a dark suit, tails, top hat and a beaming smile at any dignitary he happened to recognize, mostly MPs,[9] priests and businessmen. The church, Livingstone had time to note, was packed with very important people. Workers and not so important people sat outside. Members of the *Religion of Sorrows* wore red wine-coloured dresses and had with them their guitars, drums and tambourines. The bridegroom as he passed gave them a rather sharp glance. But only for a second. He was really happy.

Miriamu now stood before the cross: her head was hidden in the white veil. Her heart pounded. She saw in her mind's eye a grandmother pretending to be a bride with a retinue of aged bridesmaids. The Charade. The Charade. And she thought: there were ten virgins when the bridegroom came. And five of them were wise—and five of them were foolish—Lord, Lord that this cup would soon be over—over me, and before I be a slave . . .[1] and the priest was saying: 'Dodge W. Livingstone, Jr., do you accept this woman for a wife in sickness and health until death do you part?' Livingstone's answer was a clear and loud yes. It was now her turn; . . . Lord that this cup . . . this cup . . . over meeeee. . . . 'Do you Miriamu accept this man for a husband. . . . She tried to answer. Saliva blocked her throat . . . five virgins . . . five virgins . . . came bridegroom . . . groom . . . and the Church was now silent in fearful expectation.

Suddenly, from outside the Church, the silence was broken. People turned their eyes to the door. But the adherents of the *Religion of Sorrows* seemed unaware of the consternation on people's faces. Maybe they thought the cere-*mony was over*. Maybe they were seized by the spirit. They beat their drums,

9. Members of Parliament.
1. Miriamu is thinking of the parable of the wise and foolish virgins in Matthew 25; the fool-ish virgins seek oil to light their lamps and thus miss the opportunity to meet the bridegroom.

they beat their tambourines, they plucked their guitars all in a jazzy bouncing unison. Church stewards rushed out to stop them, ssh, ssh, the wedding ceremony was not yet over—but they were way beyond hearing. Their voices and faces were raised to the sky, their feet were rocking the earth.

For the first time Miriamu raised her head. She remembered vaguely that she had not even invited her friends. How had they come to Molo? A spasm of guilt. But only for a time. It did not matter. Not now. The vision had come back . . . At the cross, at the cross where I found the Lord . . . she saw Wariuki standing before her even as he used to be in Molo. He rode a bicycle: he was playing his tricks before a huge crowd of respectful worshippers . . . At the cross, at the cross where I found the Lord . . . he was doing it for her . . . he had singled only her out of the thrilling throng . . . of this she was certain . . . came the dancing and she was even more certain of his love . . . He was doing it for her. Lord, I have been loved once . . . once . . . I have been loved, Lord . . . And those moments in Ilmorog forest and woods were part of her: what a moaning, oh, Lord what a moaning . . . and the drums and the tambourines were now moaning in her dancing heart. She was truly Miriamu. She felt so powerful and strong and raised her head even more proudly; . . . and the priest was almost shouting: 'Do you Miriamu . . .' The crowd waited. She looked at Livingstone, she looked at her father, and she could not see any difference between them. Her voice came in a loud whisper: 'No.'

A current went right through the church. Had they heard the correct answer? And the priest was almost hysterical: 'Do you Miriamu . . .' Again the silence made even more silent by the singing outside. She lifted the veil and held the audience with her eyes. 'No, I cannot . . . I cannot marry Livingstone . . . because . . . because . . . I have been married before. I am married to . . . to . . . Wariuki . . . and he is dead.'

Livingstone became truly a stone. Her father wept. Her mother wept. They all thought her a little crazed. And they blamed the whole thing on these breakaway churches that really worshipped the devil. No properly trained priest, etc. . . . etc. . . . And the men and women outside went on singing and dancing to the beat of drums and tambourines, their faces and voices raised to the sky.

1975

WOLE SOYINKA
born 1934

A political activist as well as a playwright, Wole Soyinka portrays modern Africa in transition, capturing the transformations in life, sensibility, and thought that have taken place as Western modernity impinges on indigenous customs. But Soyinka shows, as well, the tensions within the Yoruba world, its own struggle for modernity. To move beyond a simple division between Western and Yoruba traditions, Soyinka draws on both Yoruba and Greek myths, weaving them into a poetic system. It is perhaps his reliance on this frame of reference that has allowed Soyinka to turn the violence of British colonialism into the material for compelling novels and plays, which combine satire and myth with a meditation on the most fundamental human and historical conflicts of the twentieth century.

Soyinka's sense of Africa as a divided culture owes much to his personal background. He was born on July 13, 1934, in Abeokuta, western Nigeria, the second child in a family that had ties to the traditional Yoruba ruling class as well as to the educated elite that arose from Christian missionary activity; his father was a Christian clergyman. Soyinka has written extensively about his childhood and the growth of the Yoruba intelligentsia, whose nationalist aspirations and modernizing zeal have been largely responsible for the making of present-day Nigeria.

Soyinka began his education at the parsonage school at Aké, where his father was headmaster. He later attended Government College, an elite English-style boarding school at Ibadan, some sixty miles north of his native city. After two years at the newly founded University College, Ibadan, Soyinka entered the University of Leeds, in England, to study English literature; he had a particular interest in Shakespeare. After graduating, Soyinka evaluated new plays for the Royal Court Theatre in London, an influential institution that produced innovative works by **Samuel Beckett**, John Osborne, and Arnold Wesker. Soyinka was also influenced by the verse drama of **T. S. Eliot** and the "theatre of ideas" of George Bernard Shaw and **Bertolt Brecht**. From these sources and his knowledge of Yoruba culture, the writer developed a type of performance that combines dialogue in verse and prose with mime and song, a version of the "total theater" that has intrigued modernist and postmodernist playwrights elsewhere in the West. Soyinka's first plays were performed at the University Arts Theatre at Ibadan, where he returned in 1960 (the year of Nigerian independence) with the intention of researching traditional West African drama. He later taught at the universities of Ife and Lagos.

In writing plays for his recently independent nation, Soyinka was motivated by his conception of the creative artist as one who must serve as a public agent of moral insight and renewal. He thus incorporated Yoruba folktales, performance styles, and even religious practices into his English-language dramas. Soyinka founded the Orisun Theatre, a semiprofessional company that he trained and directed in a wide range of plays. His own works were already appearing in print, helping to establish his reputation beyond Nigeria. His first novel, *The Interpreters* (1965), portrayed a group of young Nigerian intellectuals seeking to give purpose to their lives and to chart a moral course for their society.

During these turbulent postindependence years, Soyinka became involved in Nigerian politics. Arrested in 1965 for broadcasting a message critical of rigged elections and accused of storming a government radio station, Soyinka was acquitted at his trial for lack of evidence. Civil war broke out in Nigeria in 1967, and Soyinka was arrested again for his efforts at reconciliation with the rebel regime of Biafra; he was held without trial until October 1969. His prison experience gave urgency to his moral concerns. As he writes in *The Man Died* (1972), a moving account of his detention and a searing indictment of the military regime, "The man dies in all who keep silent in the face of tyranny." These years of crisis and war account for the somber mood that runs through Soyinka's subsequent plays. In 1971, the author went into exile, living mostly in England until it was safe to return home to Nigeria, where he continued his teaching and writing. Awarded the Nobel Prize for Literature in 1986, he devoted his acceptance speech to condemning apartheid, the system of racial segregation and minority rule in South Africa. During the 1990s he was sentenced to death in absentia under the government of dictator Sani Abacha; again he went into exile. Soyinka has remained a prominent critic of dictatorships in Nigeria and elsewhere in Africa; in the years following the terrorist attacks of September 11, 2001, he has spoken against both Islamic fundamentalism and racial profiling. Since his homeland's return to democracy, in 1999, Soyinka has divided his time between Nigeria and the United States, where he has held a number of professorships.

Death and the King's Horseman (1975) is based on an actual event: a British colonial officer's intervention to prevent the ritual suicide, following the death of the king of Oyo, of his "horseman," a minor chief whose privileges were conditional on his accompanying the king to the afterworld. The officer does not realize the dire consequences his intervention will have for the village and, most important, for the King's Horseman's son, who is also the officer's protégé. In depicting historical figures, Soyinka shifts the focus from the story's symbolic and ethnographic interest to the concrete response of human beings to death.

The opening scene offers a view of Yoruba society. The market setting, with its fusion of economic, social, and religious life, projects the people's belief system in festive tones. Elesin, the King's Horseman destined to die, prepares to accept his burden joyously. Although the opening scene seems to display the original coherence of the Yoruba world, it hints at its latent tensions. Essential for this effect is the presence of the oral tradition, for much of the language the characters exchange, especially that between Elesin and his praise singer, derives from familiar forms of oral poetry, proverbs, and lineage praise names (*oriki orile*) that situate the individual within a network of social relations and obligations.

The intensity of this scene contrasts with the deliberate flatness of the second, when the ignorance of the British colonial officers becomes the object of satire and, in fact, the British colonial system is depicted as offensive and violent. Pilkings, the colonial official, for example, wears traditional Yoruba dress, which is reserved for specific ritual uses, as costume for a masked ball. When he learns of the impending suicide of the King's Horseman and seeks to prevent it, the colonial and indigenous worlds collide. Yet Soyinka insists that the play should not be reduced to a simple conflict between two cultures. And indeed, the play spends considerable energy bridging this gulf: for instance, Soyinka shows that both cultures have a tradition of honorable suicide and that both have rituals involving masked dancing.

Mediating figures such as Mrs. Pilkings and Olunde, the son of the King's Horseman, offer more nuanced perspectives on the central conflict, which nevertheless cannot yield to an easy solution. This impasse reflects the challenges of Soyinka's attempt to negotiate, in his work, the competing claims of Yoruba tradition and Western theater, as he seeks to help shape a Nigerian culture that would draw on native traditions without barricading them from the wider world.

The different forms of ceremony, ritual, and dance that make up this complex play are mirrored and reinforced by its unusual language and poetry. Certain Yoruba songs are rendered in poetic English. The idiom of the non-British characters is informed by the syntax, expressions, proverbs, and metaphors of Yoruba. The result is a multilayered English that draws on the Yoruba world, its flora, fauna, social structure, and cosmology, for comparison and insight. The play contrasts and intermingles languages, cultures, characters, and forms of theater and performance.

Such juxtaposing is perhaps the most important innovation of *Death and the King's Horseman*. The play certainly shows the violence that occurs at a moment of contact between British and Yoruba ways of life. By revealing the tensions within each society, however, Soyinka avoids blaming the conflicts arising under colonialism on each side's ignorance, and often intolerance, of the other. Yoruba culture, for Soyinka, is never simple, authentic, or monolithic. Rather, for Soyinka, it has itself undergone a process of modernization; it therefore is compatible with the international, cosmopolitan world represented by the son of the King's Horseman. At the same time, Soyinka points to the traditionalist, even ritualistic, aspects of British life. This way, both the Yoruba people and the British are divided between tradition and modernization—even if Soyinka never lets us forget that it was the British who sought to interrupt and dismiss Yoruba traditions, not the other way around.

Death and the King's Horseman is Soyinka's masterpiece. In it the verbal resourcefulness and mastery of theatrical effects evident in his earlier plays unite to produce a work whose evocative power ensures its appeal as both a model of connection to an indigenous tradition and an exploration of a universal human dilemma.

Death and the King's Horseman

Cast

PRAISE-SINGER	BRIDE
ELESIN, *Horseman of the King*	H. R. H. THE PRINCE
IYALOJA, *"Mother" of the market*	THE RESIDENT
SIMON PILKINGS, *District Officer*	AIDE-DE-CAMP
JANE PILKINGS, *his wife*	OLUNDE, *eldest son of Elesin*
SERJEANT AMUSA	DRUMMERS, WOMEN, YOUNG GIRLS,
JOSEPH, *houseboy to the Pilkingses*	DANCERS *at the Ball*

Scene One

A passage through a market in its closing stages. The stalls are being emptied, mats folded. A few WOMEN *pass through on their way home, loaded with baskets. On a cloth-stand, bolts of cloth are taken down, display pieces folded and piled on a tray.*

ELESIN OBA *enters along a passage before the market, pursued by his* DRUMMERS *and* PRAISE-SINGERS. *He is a man of enormous vitality, speaks, dances and sings with that infectious enjoyment of life which accompanies all his actions.*

PRAISE-SINGER: Elesin o! Elesin Oba! Howu![1] What tryst is this the cockerel goes to keep with such haste that he must leave his tail behind?

ELESIN: [*Slows down a bit, laughing.*] A tryst where the cockerel needs no adornment.

PRAISE-SINGER: O-oh, you hear that my companions? That's the way the world goes. Because the man approaches a brand new bride he forgets the long faithful mother of his children.

ELESIN: When the horse sniffs the stable does he not strain at the bridle? The market is the long-suffering home of my spirit and the women are packing up to go. That Esu[2]-harrassed day slipped into the stewpot while we feasted. We ate it up with the rest of the meat. I have neglected my women.

PRAISE-SINGER: We know all that. Still it's no reason for shedding your tail on this day of all days. I know the women will cover you in damask and *alari*[3] but when the wind blows cold from behind, that's when the fowl knows his true friends.

ELESIN: Olohun-iyo![4]

PRAISE-SINGER: Are you sure there will be one like me on the other side?

ELESIN: Olohun-iyo!

PRAISE-SINGER: Far be it for me to belittle the dwellers of that place but, a man is either born to his art or he isn't. And I don't know for certain that you'll meet my father, so who is going to sing these deeds in accents that will pierce the deafness of the ancient ones. I have prepared my going— just tell me: Olohun-iyo, I need you on this journey and I shall be behind you.

ELESIN: You're like a jealous wife. Stay close to me, but only on this side. My fame, my honour are legacies to the living; stay behind and let the world sip its honey from your lips.

PRAISE-SINGER: Your name will be like the sweet berry a child places under his tongue to sweeten the passage of food. The world will never spit it out.

ELESIN: Come then. This market is my roost. When I come among the women I am a chicken with a hundred mothers. I become a monarch whose palace is built with tenderness and beauty.

PRAISE-SINGER: They love to spoil you but beware. The hands of women also weaken the unwary.

ELESIN: This night I'll lay my head upon their lap and go to sleep. This night I'll touch feet with their feet in a dance that is no longer of this earth. But the smell of their flesh, their sweat, the smell of indigo[5] on their cloth, this is the last air I wish to breathe as I go to meet my great forebears.

PRAISE-SINGER: In their time the world was never tilted from its groove, it shall not be in yours.

---

1. An exclamation of surprise.
2. The god of fate in the Yoruba pantheon: also a trickster figure.
3. A rich woven cloth, brightly coloured

[Author's note].
4. "Sweet voice": affectionate nickname for the praise-singer.
5. A deep blue dye.

ELESIN: The gods have said No.

PRAISE-SINGER: In their time the great wars came and went, the little wars came and went; the white slavers came and went, they took away the heart of our race, they bore away the mind and muscle of our race. The city fell and was rebuilt; the city fell and our people trudged through mountain and forest to find a new home but Elesin Oba do you hear me?

ELESIN: I hear your voice Olohun-iyo.

PRAISE-SINGER: Our world was never wrenched from its true course.

ELESIN: The gods have said No.

PRAISE-SINGER: There is only one home to the life of a river-mussel; there is only one home to the life of a tortoise; there is only one shell to the soul of man; there is only one world to the spirit of our race. If that world leaves its course and smashes on boulders of the great void, whose world will give us shelter?

ELESIN: It did not in the time of my forebears, it shall not in mine.

PRAISE-SINGER: The cockerel must not be seen without his feathers.

ELESIN: Nor will the Not-I bird be much longer without his nest.

PRAISE-SINGER: [*Stopped in his lyric stride.*] The Not-I bird, Elesin?

ELESIN: I said, the Not-I bird.

PRAISE-SINGER: All respect to our elders but, is there really such a bird?

ELESIN: What! Could it be that he failed to knock on your door?

PRAISE-SINGER: [*Smiling.*] Elesin's riddles are not merely the nut in the kernel that breaks human teeth; he also buries the kernel in hot embers and dares a man's fingers to draw it out.

ELESIN: I am sure he called on you, Olohun-iyo. Did you hide in the loft and push out the servant to tell him you were out?

> [ELESIN *executes a brief, half-taunting dance. The* DRUMMER *moves in and draws a rhythm out of his steps.* ELESIN *dances towards the market-place as he chants the story of the Not-I bird, his voice changing dexterously to mimic his characters. He performs like a born raconteur,[6] infecting his retinue with his humour and energy. More* WOMEN *arrive during his recital, including* IYALOJA.]

> Death came calling
> Who does not know his rasp of reeds?
> A twilight whisper in the leaves before
> The great araba[7] falls? Did you hear it?
> Not I! swears the farmer. He snaps
> His fingers round his head,[8] abandons
> A hard-worn harvest and begins
> A rapid dialogue with his legs.
>
> "Not I," shouts the fearless hunter, "but—
> It's getting dark, and this night-lamp
> Has leaked out all its oil. I think
> It's best to go home and resume my hunt
> Another day." But now he pauses, suddenly
> Lets out a wail: "Oh foolish mouth, calling

---

6. A storyteller.

7. A tall and majestic tropical tree.

8. The gesture for warding off evil.

Down a curse on your own head! Your lamp
Has leaked out all its oil, has it?"
Forwards or backwards now he dare not move.
To search for leaves and make etutu[9]
On that spot? Or race home to the safety
Of his hearth? Ten market-days have passed
My friends, and still he's rooted there
Rigid as the plinth of Orayan[1]

The mouth of the courtesan barely
Opened wide enough to take a ha'penny *robo*[2]
When she wailed: "Not I." All dressed she was
To call upon my friend the Chief Tax Officer.
But now she sends her go between instead:
"Tell him I'm ill: my period[3] has come suddenly
But not—I hope—my time."

Why is the pupil crying?
His hapless head was made to taste
The knuckles of my friend the Mallam:[4]
"If you were then reciting the Koran
Would you have ears for idle noises
Darkening the trees, you child of ill omen?"
He shuts down school before its time
Runs home and rings himself with amulets.
And take my good kinsman Ifawomi.[5]
His hands were like a carver's, strong
And true. I saw them
Tremble like wet wings of a fowl.
One day he cast his time-smoothed opele[6]
Across the divination board. And all because
The suppliant looked him in the eye and asked,
"Did you hear that whisper in the leaves?"
"Not I," was his reply; "perhaps I'm growing deaf—
Good-day." And Ifa spoke no more that day
The priest locked fast his doors,
Sealed up his leaking roof—but wait!
This sudden care was not for Fawomi
But for Osenyin,[7] a courier-bird of Ifa's
Heart of wisdom. I did not know a kite
Was hovering in the sky
And Ifa now a twittering chicken in
The brood of Fawomi the Mother Hen.[8]

---

9. Rites of propitiation, often involving a sacrifice.
1. The mythical founder of Ife, the sacred city of the Yoruba people. "Plinth": a tall stone column planted into the earth at Ife, reputed to have been the staff of Oranyan.
2. A delicacy made from crushed melon seeds, fried in tiny balls [Author's note].
3. That is, she is menstruating.
4. A teacher in a koranic school.
5. A name (later shortened to Fawomi) that

designates a devotee of Ifa, the god of divination, referred to further in the passage.
6. A string of beads used in Ifa divination [Author's note].
7. The tutelary deity of Yoruba traditional healers.
8. That is, reduced in status, humiliated. Even a god as powerful as Ifa can be cowed by death.

> Ah, but I must not forget my evening
> Courier from the abundant palm, whose groan
> Became Not I, as he constipated down
> A wayside bush. He wonders if Elegbara[9]
> Has tricked his buttocks to discharge
> Against a sacred grove. Hear him
> Mutter spells to ward off penalties
> For an abomination he did not intend.
> If any here
> Stumbles on a gourd of wine, fermenting
> Near the road, and nearby hears a stream
> Of spells issuing from a crouching form.
> Brother to a *sigidi*,[1] bring home my wine,
> Tell my tapper I have ejected
> Fear from home and farm. Assure him,
> All is well.

PRAISE-SINGER: In your time we do not doubt the peace of farmstead and
home, the peace of road and hearth, we do not doubt the peace of the forest.

ELESIN: There was fear in the forest too.
> Not-I was lately heard even in the lair
> Of beasts. The hyena cackled loud. Not I,
> The civet twitched his fiery tail and glared:
> Not I. Not-I became the answering name
> Of the restless bird,[2] that little one
> Whom Death found nesting in the leaves
> When whisper of his coming ran
> Before him on the wind. Not-I
> Has long abandoned home. This same dawn
> I heard him twitter in the gods' abode.
> Ah, companions of this living world
> What a thing this is, that even those
> We call immortal
> Should fear to die.

IYALOJA: But you, husband of multitudes?

ELESIN: I, when that Not-I bird perched
> Upon my roof, bade him seek his nest again.
> Safe, without care or fear. I unrolled
> My welcome mat for him to see. Not-I
> Flew happily away, you'll hear his voice
> No more in this lifetime—You all know
> What I am.

PRAISE-SINGER: That rock which turns its open lodes
> Into the path of lightning. A gay
> Thoroughbred whose stride disdains
> To falter though an adder[3] reared
> Suddenly in his path.

---

9. Another name for Esu.
1. A malevolent spirit.
2. Most likely the canary, which, when caged,

is constantly making short, rapid movements.
3. Or puff-adder, an extremely poisonous
snake.

ELESIN: My rein is loosened.
I am master of my Fate. When the hour comes
Watch me dance along the narrowing path
Glazed by the soles of my great precursors.
My soul is eager. I shall not turn aside.

WOMEN: You will not delay?

ELESIN: Where the storm pleases, and when, it directs
The giants of the forest. When friendship summons
Is when the true comrade goes.

WOMEN: Nothing will hold you back?

ELESIN: Nothing. What! Has no one told you yet
I go to keep my friend and master company.
Who says the mouth does not believe in
"No, I have chewed all that before?" I say I have.
The world is not a constant honey-pot.
Where I found little I made do with little,
Where there was plenty I gorged myself.
My master's hands and mine have always
Dipped together and, home or sacred feast,
The bowl was beaten bronze, the meats
So succulent our teeth accused us of neglect.
We shared the choicest of the season's
Harvest of yams. How my friend would read
Desire in my eyes before I knew the cause—
However rare, however precious, it was mine.

WOMEN: The town, the very land was yours.

ELESIN: The world was mine. Our joint hands
Raised housepots[4] of trust that withstood
The siege of envy and the termites of time.
But the twilight hour brings bats and rodents—
Shall I yield them cause to foul the rafters?

PRAISE-SINGER: Elesin Oba! Are you not that man who
Looked out of doors that stormy day
The god of luck[5] limped by, drenched
To the very lice that held
His rags together? You took pity upon
His sores and wished him fortune.
Fortune was footloose this dawn, he replied,
Till you trapped him in a heartfelt wish
That now returns to you. Elesin Oba!
I say you are that man who
Chanced upon the calabash of honour
You thought it was palm wine[6] and
Drained its contents to the final drop.

4. Used for storing the household's water.

5. Esu, who is represented as lame.

6. The sweet sap of the palm oil tree, which ferments naturally to become a potent drink. "Calabash": container made from the fruit of a vine.

ELESIN: Life has an end. A life that will outlive
Fame and friendship begs another name.
What elder takes his tongue to his plate,
Licks it clean of every crumb?[7] He will encounter
Silence when he calls on children to fulfill
The smallest errand! Life is honour.
It ends when honour ends.

WOMEN: We know you for a man of honour.

ELESIN: Stop! Enough of that!

WOMEN: [*Puzzled, they whisper among themselves, turning mostly to* IYALOJA.]
What is it? Did we say something to give offence? Have we slighted him in
some way?

ELESIN: Enough of that sound I say. Let me hear no more in that vein. I've
heard enough.

IYALOJA: We must have said something wrong. [*Comes forward a little*.] Elesin Oba, we ask forgiveness before you speak.

ELESIN: I am bitterly offended.

IYALOJA: Our unworthiness has betrayed us. All we can do is ask your forgiveness. Correct us like a kind father.

ELESIN: This day of all days . . .

IYALOJA: It does not bear thinking. If we offend you now we have mortified
the gods. We offend heaven itself. Father of us all, tell us where we went
astray. [*She kneels, the other* WOMEN *follow*.]

ELESIN: Are you not ashamed? Even a tear-veiled
Eye preserves its function of sight.
Because my mind was raised to horizons
Even the boldest man lowers his gaze
In thinking of, must my body here
Be taken for a vagrant's?

IYALOJA: Horseman of the King, I am more baffled than ever.

PRAISE-SINGER: The strictest father unbends his brow when the child is
penitent, Elesin. When time is short, we do not spend it prolonging the
riddle. Their shoulders are bowed with the weight of fear lest they have
marred your day beyond repair. Speak now in plain words and let us pursue
the ailment to the home of remedies.

ELESIN: Words are cheap. "We know you for
A man of honour." Well tell me, is this how
A man of honour should be seen?
Are these not the same clothes in which
I came among you a full half-hour ago?

[*He roars with laughter and the* WOMEN, *relieved, rise and rush into stalls
to fetch rich clothes*.]

WOMEN: The gods are kind. A fault soon remedied is soon forgiven. Elesin Oba,
even as we match our words with deed, let your heart forgive us completely.

ELESIN: You who are breath and giver of my being
How shall I dare refuse you forgiveness
Even if the offence was real.

7. Elders are expected to deny themselves for the young.

IYALOJA:	[*Dancing round him. Sings.*]
	He forgives us. He forgives us.
	What a fearful thing it is when
	The voyager sets forth
	But a curse remains behind.
WOMEN:	For a while we truly feared
	Our hands had wrenched the world adrift
	In emptiness.
IYALOJA:	Richly, richly, robe him richly
	The cloth of honour is alari
	Sanyan[8] is the band of friendship
	Boa-skin makes slippers of esteem.
WOMEN:	For a while we truly feared
	Our hands had wrenched the world adrift
	In emptiness.
PRAISE-SINGER:	He who must, must voyage forth
	The world will not roll backwards
	It is he who must, with one
	Great gesture overtake the world.
WOMEN:	For a while we truly feared
	Our hands had wrenched the world
	In emptiness.
PRAISE-SINGER:	The gourd[9] you bear is not for shirking.
	The gourd is not for setting down
	At the first crossroad or wayside grove.
	Only one river may know its contents.
WOMEN:	We shall all meet at the great market
	We shall all meet at the great market
	He who goes early takes the best bargains
	But we shall meet, and resume our banter.

[ELESIN *stands resplendent in rich clothes, cap, shawl, etc. His sash is of a bright red alari cloth. The* WOMEN *dance round him. Suddenly, his attention is caught by an object off-stage.*]

ELESIN:	The world I know is good.
WOMEN:	We know you'll leave it so.
ELESIN:	The world I know is the bounty
	Of hives after bees have swarmed.
	No goodness teems with such open hands
	Even in the dreams of deities.
WOMEN:	And we know you'll leave it so.
ELESIN:	I was born to keep it so. A hive
	Is never known to wander. An anthill
	Does not desert its roots. We cannot see
	The still great womb of the world—
	No man beholds his mother's womb—
	Yet who denies it's there? Coiled

---

8. Richly decorated woven cloth.   9. Used for carrying water.

	To the navel of the world is that
	Endless cord that links us all
	To the great origin. If I lose my way
	The trailing cord will bring me to the roots.
WOMEN:	The world is in your hands.

[*The earlier distraction, a beautiful young girl, comes along the passage through which* ELESIN *first made his entry.*]

ELESIN:	I embrace it. And let me tell you, women—
	I like this farewell that the world designed,
	Unless my eyes deceive me, unless
	We are already parted, the world and I,
	And all that breeds desire is lodged
	Among our tireless ancestors. Tell me friends,
	Am I still earthed in that beloved market
	Of my youth? Or could it be my will
	Has outleapt the conscious act and I have come
	Among the great departed?

PRAISE-SINGER: Elesin Oba why do your eyes roll like a bush-rat who sees his fate like his father's spirit, mirrored in the eye of a snake? And all those questions! You're standing on the same earth you've always stood upon. This voice you hear is mine, Oluhun-iyo, not that of an acolyte in heaven.

ELESIN:	How can that be? In all my life
	As Horseman of the King, the juiciest
	Fruit on every tree was mine. I saw,
	I touched, I wooed, rarely was the answer No.
	The honour of my place, the veneration I
	Received in the eye of man or woman
	Prospered my suit and
	Played havoc with my sleeping hours.
	And they tell me my eyes were a hawk
	In perpetual hunger. Split an iroko tree[1]
	In two, hide a woman's beauty in its heartwood
	And seal it up again—Elesin, journeying by,
	Would make his camp beside that tree
	Of all the shades in the forest.

PRAISE-SINGER: Who would deny your reputation, snake-on-the-loose in dark passages of the market! Bed-bug who wages war on the mat and receives the thanks of the vanquished! When caught with his bride's own sister he protested—but I was only prostrating myself to her as becomes a grateful in-law. Hunter who carries his powder-horn on the hips and fires crouching or standing! Warrior who never makes that excuse of the whining coward—but how can I go to battle without my trousers?—trouserless or shirtless it's all one to him. Oka[2]-rearing-from-a-camouflage-of-leaves, before he strikes the victim is already prone! Once they told me, Howu, a stallion does not feed on the grass beneath him; he replied, true, but surely he can roll on it!

---

1. A tropical hardwood tree: it is a large tree with abundant foliage.

2. The python, a huge snake that swallows its victims whole.

WOMEN: Ba-a-a-ba O![3]

PRAISE-SINGER: Ah, but listen yet. You know there is the leaf-nibbling grub
and there is the cola-chewing beetle; the leaf-nibbling grub lives on the leaf,
the cola-chewing beetle lives in the colanut. Don't we know what our man
feeds on when we find him cocooned in a woman's wrapper?

ELESIN: Enough, enough, you all have cause
          To know me well. But, if you say this earth
          Is still the same as gave birth to those songs,
          Tell me who was that goddess through whose lips
          I saw the ivory pebbles of Oya's[4] river-bed.
          Iyaloja, who is she? I saw her enter
          Your stall; all your daughters I know well.
          No, not even Ogun[5]-of-the-farm toiling
          Dawn till dusk on his tuber patch
          Not even Ogun with the finest hoe he ever
          Forged at the anvil could have shaped
          That rise of buttocks, not though he had
          The richest earth between his fingers.
          Her wrapper was no disguise
          For thighs whose ripples shamed the river's
          Coils around the hills of Ilesi.[6] Her eyes
          Were new-laid eggs glowing in the dark.
          Her skin . . .

IYALOJA: Elesin Oba . . .

ELESIN: What! Where do you all say I am?

IYALOJA: Still among the living.

ELESIN: And that radiance which so suddenly
                 Lit up this market I could boast
                 I knew so well?

IYALOJA: Has one step already in her husband's home. She is betrothed.

ELESIN: [Irritated.] Why do you tell me that?
          [IYALOJA falls silent. The WOMEN shuffle uneasily.]

IYALOJA: Not because we dare give you offence Elesin. Today is your day and
the whole world is yours. Still, even those who leave town to make a new
dwelling elsewhere like to be remembered by what they leave behind.

ELESIN: Who does not seek to be remembered?
          Memory is Master of Death, the chink
          In his armour of conceit. I shall leave
          That which makes my going the sheerest
          Dream of an afternoon. Should voyagers
          Not travel light? Let the considerate traveller
          Shed, of his excessive load, all
          That may benefit the living.

WOMEN: [Relieved.] Ah Elesin Oba, we knew you for a man of honour.

ELESIN: Then honour me. I deserve a bed of honour to lie upon.

---

3. A form of salute to an elder male.
4. A Yoruba goddess said to live in the River
Niger.

5. The Yoruba god of iron and of war (equivalent in some ways to Mars).
6. A town.

IYALOJA: The best is yours. We know you for a man of honour. You are not
one who eats and leaves nothing on his plate for children. Did you not say
it yourself? Not one who blights the happiness of others for a moment's
pleasure.

ELESIN: Who speaks of pleasure? O women, listen!
Pleasure palls. Our acts should have meaning.
The sap of the plantain[7] never dries.
You have seen the young shoot swelling
Even as the parent stalk begins to wither.
Women, let my going be likened to
The twilight hour of the plantain.

WOMEN: What does he mean Iyaloja? This language is the language of our
elders, we do not fully grasp it.

IYALOJA: I dare not understand you yet Elesin.

ELESIN: All you who stand before the spirit that dares
The opening of the last door of passage,
Dare to rid my going of regrets! My wish
Transcends the blotting out of thought
In one mere moment's tremor of the senses.
Do me credit. And do me honour.
I am girded for the route beyond
Burdens of waste and longing.
Then let me travel light. Let
Seed that will not serve the stomach
On the way remain behind. Let it take root
In the earth of my choice, in this earth
I leave behind.

IYALOJA: [*Turns to* WOMEN.] The voice I hear is already touched by the waiting
fingers of our departed. I dare not refuse.

WOMAN: But Iyaloja . . .

IYALOJA: The matter is no longer in our hands.

WOMAN: But she is betrothed to your own son. Tell him.

IYALOJA: My son's wish is mine. I did the asking for him, the loss can be remedied. But who will remedy the blight of closed hands on the day when all
should be openness and light? Tell him, you say! You wish that I burden him
with knowledge that will sour his wish and lay regrets on the last moments
of his mind. You pray to him who is your intercessor to the world—don't set
this world adrift in your own time; would you rather it was my hand whose
sacrilege wrenched it loose?

WOMAN: Not many men will brave the curse of a dispossessed husband.

IYALOJA: Only the curses of the departed are to be feared. The claims of one
whose foot is on the threshold of their abode surpasses even the claims of
blood. It is impiety even to place hindrances in their ways.

ELESIN: What do my mothers[8] say? Shall I step
Burdened into the unknown?

---

7. A plant related to the banana. It constantly   8. Here, a term of affection.
regenerates itself from its young shoots ("suckers").

IYALOJA: Not we, but the very earth says No. The sap in the plantain does not dry. Let grain that will not feed the voyager at his passage drop here and take root as he steps beyond this earth and us. Oh you who fill the home from hearth to threshold with the voices of children, you who now bestride the hidden gulf and pause to draw the right foot across and into the resting-home of the great forebears, it is good that your loins be drained into the earth we know, that your last strength be ploughed back into the womb that gave you being.

PRAISE-SINGER: Iyaloja, mother of multitudes in the teeming market of the world, how your wisdom transfigures you!

IYALOJA: [*Smiling broadly, completely reconciled.*] Elesin, even at the narrow end of the passage I know you will look back and sigh a last regret for the flesh that flashed past your spirit in flight. You always had a restless eye. Your choice has my blessing. [*To the* WOMEN.] Take the good news to our daughter and make her ready. [*Some* WOMEN *go off.*]

ELESIN: Your eyes were clouded at first.

IYALOJA: Not for long. It is those who stand at the gateway of the great change to whose cry we must pay heed. And then, think of this—it makes the mind tremble. The fruit of such a union is rare. It will be neither of this world nor of the next. Nor of the one behind us. As if the timelessness of the ancestor world and the unborn have joined spirits to wring an issue of the elusive being of passage . . . Elesin!

ELESIN: I am here. What is it?

IYALOJA: Did you hear all I said just now?

ELESIN: Yes.

IYALOJA: The living must eat and drink. When the moment comes, don't turn the food to rodents' droppings in their mouth. Don't let them taste the ashes of the world when they step out at dawn to breathe the morning dew.

ELESIN: This doubt is unworthy of you Iyaloja.

IYALOJA: Eating the awusa nut is not so difficult as drinking water afterwards.[9]

ELESIN: The waters of the bitter stream are honey to a man
Whose tongue has savoured all.

IYALOJA: No one knows when the ants desert their home; they leave the mound intact. The swallow is never seen to peck holes in its nest when it is time to move with the season. There are always throngs of humanity behind the leave-taker. The rain should not come through the roof for them, the wind must not blow through the walls at night.

ELESIN: I refuse to take offence.

IYALOJA: You wish to travel light. Well, the earth is yours. But be sure the seed you leave in it attracts no curse.

ELESIN: You really mistake my person Iyaloja.

IYALOJA: I said nothing. Now we must go prepare your bridal chamber. Then these same hands will lay your shrouds.

ELESIN: [*Exasperated.*] Must you be so blunt? [*Recovers.*] Well, weave your shrouds, but let the fingers of my bride seal my eyelids with earth and wash my body.

---

9. The awasa nut eaten alone has a pleasant taste, but it turns bitter in the mouth if water is drunk just after.

IYALOJA: Prepare yourself Elesin.

[*She gets up to leave. At that moment the* WOMEN *return, leading the* BRIDE. ELESIN'*s face glows with pleasure. He flicks the sleeves of his agbada*[1] *with renewed confidence and steps forward to meet the group. As the girl kneels before* IYALOJA, *lights fade out on the scene.*]

Scene Two

The verandah of the District Officer's bungalow. A tango is playing from an old hand-cranked gramophone and, glimpsed through the wide windows and doors which open onto the forestage verandah, are the shapes of SIMON PILKINGS *and his wife,* JANE, *tangoing in and out of shadows in the living room. They are wearing what is immediately apparent as some form of fancy-dress. The dance goes on for some moments and then the figure of a "Native Administration"* POLICEMAN *emerges and climbs up the steps onto the verandah. He peeps through and observes the dancing couple, reacting with what is obviously a long-standing bewilderment. He stiffens suddenly, his expression changes to one of disbelief and horror. In his excitement he upsets a flower-pot and attracts the attention of the couple. They stop dancing.*

PILKINGS: Is there anyone out there?

JANE: I'll turn off the gramophone.

PILKINGS: [*Approaching the verandah.*] I'm sure I heard something fall over. [*The* CONSTABLE *retreats slowly, open-mouthed as* PILKINGS *approaches the verandah.*] Oh it's you Amusa. Why didn't you just knock instead of knocking things over?

AMUSA: [*Stammers badly and points a shaky finger at his dress.*] Mista Pirinkin . . . Mista Pirinkin . . .

PILKINGS: What is the matter with you?

JANE: [*Emerging.*] Who is it dear? Oh, Amusa . . .

PILKINGS: Yes it's Amusa, and acting most strangely.

AMUSA: [*His attention now transferred to* MRS. PILKINGS.] Mammadam[2] . . . you too!

PILKINGS: What the hell is the matter with you man!

JANE: Your costume darling. Our fancy dress.

PILKINGS: Oh hell, I'd forgotten all about that. [*Lifts the face mask over his head showing his face. His wife follows suit.*]

JANE: I think you've shocked his big pagan heart bless him.

PILKINGS: Nonsense, he's a Moslem. Come on Amusa, you don't believe in all that nonsense do you? I thought you were a good Moslem.

AMUSA: Mista Pirinkin, I beg you sir, what you think you do with that dress? It belong to dead cult, not for human being.

PILKINGS: Oh Amusa, what a let down you are. I swear by you at the club you know—thank God for Amusa, he doesn't believe in any mumbo-jumbo. And now look at you!

AMUSA: Mista Pirinkin, I beg you, take it off. Is not good for man like you to touch that cloth.

---

1. A long flowing robe.

2. A confused stammer of the word "madam."

PILKINGS: Well, I've got it on. And what's more Jane and I have bet on it we're taking first prize at the ball. Now, if you can just pull yourself together and tell me what you wanted to see me about . . .

AMUSA: Sir, I cannot talk this matter to you in that dress. I no fit.

PILKINGS: What's that rubbish again?

JANE: He is dead earnest too Simon. I think you'll have to handle this delicately.

PILKINGS: Delicately my . . . ! Look here Amusa, I think this little joke has gone far enough hm? Let's have some sense. You seem to forget that you are a police officer in the service of His Majesty's Government. I order you to report your business at once or face disciplinary action.

AMUSA: Sir, it is a matter of death. How can man talk against death to person in uniform of death? Is like talking against government to person in uniform of police. Please sir, I go and come back.

PILKINGS: [*Roars.*] Now! [AMUSA *switches his gaze to the ceiling suddenly, remains mute.*]

JANE: Oh Amusa, what is there to be scared of in the costume? You saw it confiscated last month from those *egungun*³ men who were creating trouble in town. You helped arrest the cult leaders yourself—if the juju⁴ didn't harm you at the time how could it possibly harm you now? And merely by looking at it?

AMUSA: [*Without looking down.*] Madam, I arrest the ringleaders who make trouble but me I no touch *egungun*. That *egungun* inself,⁵ I no touch. And I no abuse 'am. I arrest ringleader but I treat *egungun* with respect.

PILKINGS: It's hopeless. We'll merely end up missing the best part of the ball. When they get this way there is nothing you can do. It's simply hammering against a brick wall. Write your report or whatever it is on that pad Amusa and take yourself out of here. Come on Jane. We only upset his delicate sensibilities by remaining here.

> [AMUSA *waits for them to leave, then writes in the notebook, somewhat laboriously. Drumming from the direction of the town wells up.* AMUSA *listens, makes a movement as if he wants to recall* PILKINGS *but changes his mind. Completes his note and goes. A few moments later* PILKINGS *emerges, picks up the pad and reads.*]

Jane!

JANE: [*From the bedroom.*] Coming darling. Nearly ready.

PILKINGS: Never mind being ready, just listen to this.

JANE: What is it?

PILKINGS: Amusa's report. Listen. "I have to report that it come to my information that one prominent chief, namely, the Elesin Oba, is to commit death tonight as a result of native custom. Because this is criminal offence I await further instruction at charge office. Sergeant Amusa."

> [JANE *comes out onto the verandah while he is reading.*]

JANE: Did I hear you say commit death?

PILKINGS: Obviously he means murder.

JANE: You mean a ritual murder?

---

3. Ancestral masks.   5. Itself (pidgin English).
4. Charms and the occult power they possess.

PILKINGS: Must be. You think you've stamped it all out but it's always lurking under the surface somewhere.

JANE: Oh. Does it mean we are not getting to the ball at all?

PILKINGS: No-o. I'll have the man arrested. Everyone remotely involved. In any case there may be nothing to it. Just rumours.

JANE: Really? I thought you found Amusa's rumours generally reliable.

PILKINGS: That's true enough. But who knows what may have been giving him the scare lately. Look at his conduct tonight.

JANE: [Laughing.] You have to admit he had his own peculiar logic. [Deepens her voice.] How can man talk against death to person in uniform of death? [Laughs.] Anyway, you can't go into the police station dressed like that.

PILKINGS: I'll send Joseph with instructions. Damn it, what a confounded nuisance!

JANE: But don't you think you should talk first to the man, Simon?

PILKINGS: Do you want to go to the ball or not?

JANE: Darling, why are you getting rattled? I was only trying to be intelligent. It seems hardly fair just to lock up a man—and a chief at that—simply on the er . . . what is the legal word again? uncorroborated word of a sergeant.

PILKINGS: Well, that's easily decided. Joseph!

JOSEPH: [From within.] Yes master.

PILKINGS: You're quite right of course, I am getting rattled. Probably the effect of those bloody drums. Do you hear how they go on and on?

JANE: I wondered when you'd notice. Do you suppose it has something to do with this affair?

PILKINGS: Who knows? They always find an excuse for making a noise . . . [Thoughtfully.] Even so . . .

JANE: Yes Simon?

PILKINGS: It's different Jane. I don't think I've heard this particular—sound—before. Something unsettling about it.

JANE: I thought all bush drumming sounded the same.

PILKINGS: Don't tease me now Jane. This may be serious.

JANE: I'm sorry. [Gets up and throws her arms around his neck. Kisses him. The houseboy enters, retreats and knocks.]

PILKINGS: [Wearily.] Oh, come in Joseph! I don't know where you pick up all these elephantine notions of tact. Come over here.

JOSEPH: Sir?

PILKINGS: Joseph, are you a Christian or not?

JOSEPH: Yessir.

PILKINGS: Does seeing me in this outfit bother you?

JOSEPH: No sir, it has no power.

PILKINGS: Thank God for some sanity at last. Now Joseph, answer me on the honour of a Christian—what is supposed to be going on in town tonight?

JOSEPH: Tonight sir? You mean the chief who is going to kill himself?

PILKINGS: What?

JANE: What do you mean, kill himself?

PILKINGS: You do mean he is going to kill somebody don't you?

JOSEPH: No master. He will not kill anybody and no one will kill him. He will simply die.

JANE: But why Joseph?

JOSEPH: It is native law and custom. The King die last month. Tonight is his burial. But before they can bury him, the Elesin must die so as to accompany him to heaven.

PILKINGS: I seem to be fated to clash more often with that man than with any of the other chiefs.

JOSEPH: He is the King's Chief Horseman.

PILKINGS: [*In a resigned way.*] I know.

JANE: Simon, what's the matter?

PILKINGS: It would have to be him!

JANE: Who is he?

PILKINGS: Don't you remember? He's that chief with whom I had a scrap some three or four years ago. I helped his son get to a medical school in England, remember? He fought tooth and nail to prevent it.

JANE: Oh now I remember. He was that very sensitive young man. What was his name again?

PILKINGS: Olunde.[6] Haven't replied to his last letter come to think of it. The old pagan wanted him to stay and carry on some family tradition or the other. Honestly I couldn't understand the fuss he made. I literally had to help the boy escape from close confinement and load him onto the next boat. A most intelligent boy, really bright.

JANE: I rather thought he was much too sensitive you know. The kind of person you feel should be a poet munching rose petals in Bloomsbury.[7]

PILKINGS: Well, he's going to make a first-class doctor. His mind is set on that. And as long as he wants my help he is welcome to it.

JANE: [*After a pause.*] Simon.

PILKINGS: Yes?

JANE: This boy, he was the eldest son wasn't he?

PILKINGS: I'm not sure. Who could tell with that old ram?

JANE: Do you know, Joseph?

JOSEPH: Oh yes madam. He was the eldest son. That's why Elesin cursed master good and proper. The eldest son is not supposed to travel away from the land.

JANE: [*Giggling.*] Is that true Simon? Did he really curse you good and proper?

PILKINGS: By all accounts I should be dead by now.

JOSEPH: Oh no, master is white man. And good Christian. Black man juju can't touch master.

JANE: If he was his eldest, it means that he would be the Elesin to the next king. It's a family thing isn't it Joseph?

JOSEPH: Yes madam. And if this Elesin had died before the King, his eldest son must take his place.

JANE: That would explain why the old chief was so mad you took the boy away.

PILKINGS: Well it makes me all the more happy I did.

---

6. "My lord or deliverer has come"; a contraction of Olumide.

7. An area in central London associated with a brilliant group of writers in the years between the world wars; Virginia Woolf was the principal figure among them.

JANE: I wonder if he knew.

PILKINGS: Who? Oh, you mean Olunde?

JANE: Yes. Was that why he was so determined to get away? I wouldn't stay if I knew I was trapped in such a horrible custom.

PILKINGS: [*Thoughtfully.*] No, I don't think he knew. At least he gave no indication. But you couldn't really tell with him. He was rather close you know, quite unlike most of them. Didn't give much away, not even to me.

JANE: Aren't they all rather close, Simon?

PILKINGS: These natives here? Good gracious. They'll open their mouths and yap with you about their family secrets before you can stop them. Only the other day . . .

JANE: But Simon, do they really give anything away? I mean, anything that really counts. This affair for instance, we didn't know they still practised that custom did we?

PILKINGS: Ye-e-es, I suppose you're right there. Sly, devious bastards.

JOSEPH: [*Stiffly.*] Can I go now master? I have to clean the kitchen.

PILKINGS: What? Oh, you can go. Forgot you were still here.

[JOSEPH goes.]

JANE: Simon, you really must watch your language. Bastard isn't just a simple swear-word in these parts, you know.

PILKINGS: Look, just when did you become a social anthropologist, that's what I'd like to know.

JANE: I'm not claiming to know anything. I just happen to have overheard quarrels among the servants. That's how I know they consider it a smear.

PILKINGS: I thought the extended family system took care of all that. Elastic family, no bastards.

JANE: [*Shrugs.*] Have it your own way.

[*Awkward silence. The drumming increases in volume.* JANE *gets up suddenly, restless.*]

That drumming Simon, do you think it might really be connected with this ritual? It's been going on all evening.

PILKINGS: Let's ask our native guide. Joseph! Just a minute Joseph. [JOSEPH *re-enters.*] What's the drumming about?

JOSEPH: I don't know master.

PILKINGS: What do you mean you don't know? It's only two years since your conversion. Don't tell me all that holy water nonsense also wiped out your tribal memory.

JOSEPH: [*Visibly shocked.*] Master!

JANE: Now you've done it.

PILKINGS: What have I done now?

JANE: Never mind. Listen Joseph, just tell me this. Is that drumming connected with dying or anything of that nature?

JOSEPH: Madam, this is what I am trying to say: I am not sure. It sounds like the death of a great chief and then, it sounds like the wedding of a great chief. It really mix me up.

PILKINGS: Oh get back to the kitchen. A fat lot of help you are.

JOSEPH: Yes master. [*Goes.*]

JANE: Simon . . .

PILKINGS: All right, all right. I'm in no mood for preaching.

JANE: It isn't my preaching you have to worry about, it's the preaching of the missionaries who preceded you here. When they make converts they really convert them. Calling holy water nonsense to our Joseph is really like insulting the Virgin Mary before a Roman Catholic. He's going to hand in his notice tomorrow you mark my word.

PILKINGS: Now you're being ridiculous.

JANE: Am I? What are you willing to bet that tomorrow we are going to be without a steward-boy? Did you see his face?

PILKINGS: I am more concerned about whether or not we will be one native chief short by tomorrow. Christ! Just listen to those drums. [*He strides up and down, undecided.*]

JANE: [*Getting up.*] I'll change and make up some supper.

PILKINGS: What's that?

JANE: Simon, it's obvious we have to miss this ball.

PILKINGS: Nonsense. It's the first bit of real fun the European club has managed to organise for over a year, I'm damned if I'm going to miss it. And it is a rather special occasion. Doesn't happen every day.

JANE: You know this business has to be stopped Simon. And you are the only man who can do it.

PILKINGS: I don't have to stop anything. If they want to throw themselves off the top of a cliff or poison themselves for the sake of some barbaric custom what is that to me? If it were ritual murder or something like that I'd be duty-bound to do something. I can't keep an eye on all the potential suicides in this province. And as for that man—believe me it's good riddance.

JANE: [*Laughs.*] I know you better than that Simon. You are going to have to do something to stop it—after you've finished blustering.

PILKINGS: [*Shouts after her.*] And suppose after all it's only a wedding? I'd look a proper fool if I interrupted a chief on his honeymoon, wouldn't I? [*Resumes his angry stride, slows down.*] Ah well, who can tell what those chiefs actually do on their honeymoon anyway? [*He takes up the pad and scribbles rapidly on it.*] Joseph! Joseph! Joseph! [*Some moments later* JOSEPH *puts in a sulky appearance.*] Did you hear me call you? Why the hell didn't you answer?

JOSEPH: I didn't hear master.

PILKINGS: You didn't hear me! How come you are here then?

JOSEPH: [*Stubbornly.*] I didn't hear master.

PILKINGS: [*Controls himself with an effort.*] We'll talk about it in the morning. I want you to take this note directly to Sergeant Amusa. You'll find him at the charge office. Get on your bicycle and race there with it. I expect you back in twenty minutes exactly. Twenty minutes, is that clear?

JOSEPH: Yes master [*Going.*]

PILKINGS: Oh er . . . Joseph.

JOSEPH: Yes master?

PILKINGS: [*Between gritted teeth.*] Er . . . forget what I said just now. The holy water is not nonsense. *I* was talking nonsense.

JOSEPH: Yes master [*Goes.*]

JANE: [*Pokes her head round the door.*] Have you found him?

PILKINGS: Found who?

JANE: Joseph. Weren't you shouting for him?

PILKINGS: Oh yes, he turned up finally.

JANE: You sounded desperate. What was it all about?

PILKINGS: Oh nothing. I just wanted to apologise to him. Assure him that the holy water isn't really nonsense.

JANE: Oh? And how did he take it?

PILKINGS: Who the hell gives a damn! I had a sudden vision of our Very Reverend Macfarlane[8] drafting another letter of complaint to the Resident about my unchristian language towards his parishioners.

JANE: Oh I think he's given up on you by now.

PILKINGS: Don't be too sure. And anyway, I wanted to make sure Joseph didn't "lose" my note on the way. He looked sufficiently full of the holy crusade to do some such thing.

JANE: If you've finished exaggerating, come and have something to eat.

PILKINGS: No, put it all away. We can still get to the ball.

JANE: Simon . . .

PILKINGS: Get your costume back on. Nothing to worry about. I've instructed Amusa to arrest the man and lock him up.

JANE: But that station is hardly secure Simon. He'll soon get his friends to help him escape.

PILKINGS: A-ah, that's where I have out-thought you. I'm not having him put in the station cell. Amusa will bring him right here and lock him up in my study. And he'll stay with him till we get back. No one will dare come here to incite him to anything.

JANE: How clever of you darling. I'll get ready.

PILKINGS: Hey.

JANE: Yes darling.

PILKINGS: I have a surprise for you. I was going to keep it until we actually got to the ball.

JANE: What is it?

PILKINGS: You know the Prince is on a tour of the colonies don't you? Well, he docked in the capital only this morning but he is already at the Residency. He is going to grace the ball with his presence later tonight.

JANE: Simon! Not really.

PILKINGS: Yes he is. He's been invited to give away the prizes and he has agreed. You must admit old Engleton is the best Club Secretary we ever had. Quick off the mark that lad.

JANE: But how thrilling.

PILKINGS: The other provincials are going to be damned envious.

JANE: I wonder what he'll come as.

PILKINGS: Oh I don't know. As a coat-of-arms perhaps. Anyway it won't be anything to touch this.

JANE: Well that's lucky. If we are to be presented I won't have to start looking for a pair of gloves. It's all sewn on.[9]

---

8. Irish priests were predominant in Catholic missionary activity in Nigeria.

9. The masquerade costume is designed to cover the entire body of the wearer, to conceal his or her identity.

PILKINGS: [*Laughing.*] Quite right. Trust a woman to think of that. Come on,
let's get going.

JANE: [*Rushing off.*] Won't be a second. [*Stops.*] Now I see why you've been
so edgy all evening. I thought you weren't handling this affair with your
usual brilliance—to begin with, that is.

PILKINGS: [*His mood is much improved.*] Shut up woman and get your things
on.

JANE: All right boss, coming.

> [PILKINGS *suddenly begins to hum the tango to which they were dancing
> before. Starts to execute a few practice steps. Lights fade.*]

Scene Three

*A swelling, agitated hum of women's voices rises immediately in the background.
The lights come on and we see the frontage of a converted cloth stall in the market.
The floor leading up to the entrance is covered in rich velvets and woven cloth. The*
WOMEN *come on stage, borne backwards by the determined progress of Sergeant*
AMUSA *and his two* CONSTABLES *who already have their batons out and use them as
a pressure against the* WOMEN. *At the edge of the cloth-covered floor however the*
WOMEN *take a determined stand and block all further progress of the* MEN. *They
begin to tease them mercilessly.*

AMUSA: I am tell you women for last time to commot my road.[1] I am here on
official business.

WOMAN: Official business you white man's eunuch? Official business is taking place where you want to go and it's a business you wouldn't understand.

WOMAN: [*Makes a quick tug at the* CONSTABLE's *baton.*] That doesn't fool anyone you know. It's the one you carry under your government knickers that
counts. [*She bends low as if to peep under the baggy shorts. The embarrassed*
CONSTABLE *quickly puts his knees together. The* WOMEN *roar.*]

WOMAN: You mean there is nothing there at all?

WOMAN: Oh there was something. You know that handbell which the whiteman uses to summon his servants . . . ?

AMUSA: [*He manages to preserve some dignity throughout.*] I hope you women
know that interfering with officer in execution of his duty is criminal
offence.

WOMAN: Interfere? He says we're interfering with him. You foolish man we're
telling you there's nothing to interfere with.

AMUSA: I am order you now to clear the road.

WOMAN: What road? The one your father built?

WOMAN: You are a policeman not so? Then you know what they call trespassing in court. Or—[*pointing to the cloth-lined steps*]—do you think that kind
of road is built for every kind of feet.

WOMAN: Go back and tell the white man who sent you to come himself.

AMUSA: If I go I will come back with reinforcement. And we will all return
carrying weapons.

---

1. Get out of my way.

WOMAN: Oh, now I understand. Before they can put on those knickers the white man first cuts off their weapons.

WOMAN: What a cheek! You mean you come here to show power to women and you don't even have a weapon.

AMUSA: [*Shouting above the laughter.*] For the last time I warn you women to clear the road.

WOMAN: To where?

AMUSA: To that hut. I know he dey dere.

WOMAN: Who?

AMUSA: The chief who call himself Elesin Oba.

WOMAN: You ignorant man. It is not he who calls himself Elesin Oba, it is his blood that says it. As it called out to his father before him and will to his son after him. And that is in spite of everything your white man can do.

WOMAN: Is it not the same ocean that washes this land and the white man's land? Tell your white man he can hide our son away as long as he likes. When the time comes for him, the same ocean will bring him back.

AMUSA: The government say dat kin' ting[2] must stop.

WOMAN: Who will stop it? You? Tonight our husband and father will prove himself greater than the laws of strangers.

AMUSA: I tell you nobody go prove anything tonight or anytime. Is ignorant and criminal to prove dat kin' prove.

IYALOJA: [*Entering from the hut. She is accompanied by a group of young girls who have been attending the* BRIDE.] What is it Amusa? Why do you come here to disturb the happiness of others.

AMUSA: Madame Iyaloja, I glad you come. You know me, I no like trouble but duty is duty. I am here to arrest Elesin for criminal intent. Tell these women to stop obstructing me in the performance of my duty.

IYALOJA: And you? What gives you the right to obstruct our leader of men in the performance of his duty.

AMUSA: What kin' duty be dat one Iyaloja.

IYALOJA: What kin' duty? What kin' duty does a man have to his new bride?

AMUSA: [*Bewildered, looks at the women and at the entrance to the hut.*] Iyaloja, is it wedding you call dis kin' ting?

IYALOJA: You have wives haven't you? Whatever the white man has done to you he hasn't stopped you having wives. And if he has, at least he is married. If you don't know what a marriage is, go and ask him to tell you.

AMUSA: This no to wedding.[3]

IYALOJA: And ask him at the same time what he would have done if anyone had come to disturb him on his wedding night.

AMUSA: Iyaloja, I say dis no to wedding.

IYALOJA: You want to look inside the bridal chamber? You want to see for yourself how a man cuts the virgin knot?

AMUSA: Madam . . .

WOMAN: Perhaps his wives are still waiting for him to learn.

AMUSA: Iyaloja, make you tell dese women make den no insult me again. If I hear dat kin' insult once more . . .

2. That kind of thing.　　　　　3. This is not a wedding.

GIRL: [*Pushing her way through.*] You will do what?

GIRL: He's out of his mind. It's our mothers you're talking to, do you know that? Not to any illiterate villager you can bully and terrorise. How dare you intrude here anyway?

GIRL: What a cheek, what impertinence!

GIRL: You've treated them too gently. Now let them see what it is to tamper with the mothers of this market.

GIRL: Your betters dare not enter the market when the women say no!

GIRL: Haven't you learnt that yet, you jester in khaki and starch?

IYALOJA: Daughters . . .

GIRL: No no Iyaloja, leave us to deal with him. He no longer knows his mother, we'll teach him.

    [*With a sudden movement they snatch the batons of the two* CONSTABLES. *They begin to hem them in.*]

GIRL: What next? We have your batons? What next? What are you going to do?

    [*With equally swift movements they knock off their hats.*]

GIRL: Move if you dare. We have your hats, what will you do about it? Didn't the white man teach you to take off your hats before women?

IYALOJA: It's a wedding night. It's a night of joy for us. Peace . . .

GIRL: Not for him. Who asked him here?

GIRL: Does he dare go to the Residency without an invitation?

GIRL: Not even where the servants eat the left-overs.

GIRLS: [*In turn. In an "English" accent.*] Well well it's Mister Amusa. Were you invited? [*Play acting to one another. The older* WOMEN *encourage them with their titters.*]

—Your invitation card please?

—Who are you? Have we been introduced?

—And who did you say you were?

—Sorry, I didn't quite catch your name.

—May I take your hat?

—If you insist. May I take yours? [*Exchanging the* POLICEMEN's *hats.*]

—How very kind of you.

—Not at all. Won't you sit down?

—After you.

—Oh no.

—I insist.

—You're most gracious.

—And how do you find the place?

—The natives are all right.

—Friendly?

—Tractable.

—Not a teeny-weeny bit restless?

—Well, a teeny-weeny bit restless.

—One might, even say, difficult?

—Indeed one might be tempted to say, difficult.

—But you do manage to cope?

—Yes indeed I do. I have a rather faithful ox called Amusa.

—He's loyal?

—Absolutely.

—Lay down his life for you what?

—Without a moment's thought.

—Had one like that once. Trust him with my life.

—Mostly of course they are liars.

—Never known a native to tell the truth.

—Does it get rather close around here?

—It's mild for this time of the year.

—But the rains may still come.

—They are late this year aren't they?

—They are keeping African time.[4]

—Ha ha ha ha

—Ha ha ha ha

—The humidity is what gets me.

—It used to be whisky

—Ha ha ha ha

—Ha ha ha ha

—What's your handicap old chap?

—Is there racing by golly?

—Splendid golf course, you'll like it.

—I'm beginning to like it already.

—And a European club, exclusive.

—You've kept the flag flying.

—We do our best for the old country.

—It's a pleasure to serve.

—Another whisky old chap?

—You are indeed too too kind.

—Not at all sir. Where is that boy? [*With a sudden bellow.*] Sergeant!

AMUSA: [*Snaps to attention.*] Yessir!

[*The* WOMEN *collapse with laughter.*]

GIRL: Take your men out of here.

AMUSA: [*Realising the trick, he rages from loss of face.*] I'm give you warning . . .

GIRL: All right then. Off with his knickers! [*They surge slowly forward.*]

IYALOJA: Daughters, please.

AMUSA: [*Squaring himself for defence.*] The first woman wey touch me . . .

IYALOJA: My children, I beg of you . . .

GIRL: Then tell him to leave this market. This is the home of our mothers. We don't want the eater of white left-overs at the feast their hands have prepared.

IYALOJA: You heard them Amusa. You had better go.

GIRL: Now!

AMUSA: [*Commencing his retreat.*] We dey go now, but make you no say we no warn you.[5]

GIRLS: Now!

---

4. A standard colonial prejudice was that Africans lack a sense of time.

5. Don't say that we didn't warn you.

GIRL: Before we read the riot act—you should know all about that.

AMUSA: Make we go. [*They depart, more precipitately.*]

[*The* WOMEN *strike their palms across in the gesture of wonder.*]

WOMEN: Do they teach you all that at school?

WOMAN: And to think I nearly kept Apinke[6] away from the place.

WOMAN: Did you hear them? Did you see how they mimicked the white man?

WOMAN: The voices exactly. Hey, there are wonders in this world!

IYALOJA: Well, our elders have said it: Dada[7] may be weak, but he has a younger sibling who is truly fearless.

WOMAN: The next time the white man shows his face in this market I will set Wuraola[8] on his tail.

[*A* WOMAN *bursts into song and dance of euphoria—"Tani l'awa o l'ogbeja? Kayi! A l'ogbeja. Omo Kekere l'ogbeja."[9] The rest of the* WOMEN *join in, some placing the* GIRLS *on their back like infants, others dancing round them. The dance becomes general, mounting in excitement.* ELESIN *appears, in wrapper only. In his hands a white velvet cloth folded loosely as if it held some delicate object. He cries out.*]

ELESIN: Oh you mothers of beautiful brides! [*The dancing stops. They turn and see him, and the object in his hands.* IYALOJA *approaches and gently takes the cloth from him.*] Take it. It is no mere virgin stain, but the union of life and the seeds of passage. My vital flow, the last from this flesh is intermingled with the promise of future life. All is prepared. Listen! [*A steady drum beat from the distance.*] Yes. It is nearly time. The King's dog has been killed. The King's favourite horse is about to follow his master. My brother chiefs know their task and perform it well. [*He listens again.*]

[*The* BRIDE *emerges, stands shyly by the door. He turns to her.*]

Our marriage is not yet wholly fulfilled. When earth and passage wed, the consummation is complete only when there are grains of earth on the eyelids of passage. Stay by me till then. My faithful drummers, do me your last service. This is where I have chosen to do my leave-taking, in this heart of life, this hive which contains the swarm of the world in its small compass. This is where I have known love and laughter away from the palace. Even the richest food cloys when eaten days on end; in the market, nothing ever cloys. Listen. [*They listen to the drums.*] They have begun to seek out the heart of the King's favourite horse. Soon it will ride in its bolt of raffia[1] with the dog at its feet. Together they will ride on the shoulders of the King's grooms through the pulse centres of the town. They know it is here I shall await them. I have told them. [*His eyes appear to cloud. He passes his hand over them as if to clear his sight. He gives a faint smile.*] It promises well; just then I felt my spirit's eagerness. The kite makes for wide spaces and the wind creeps up behind its tail; can the kite say less than—thank you, the quicker the better? But wait a while my spirit. Wait. Wait for the coming of

---

6. "One Who Is Equally Cherished by All"; the name of one of the girls.

7. A child born with tangled hair.

8. "Dear as Gold"; a woman's name.

9. Who says we haven't a defender? Silence!

We have our defenders. Little children are our champions [Author's translation].

1. The stem of this shrub is used for the decorative skirt worn in many African dances.

the courier of the King. Do you know friends, the horse is born to this one destiny, to bear the burden that is man upon its back. Except for this night, this night alone when the spotless stallion will ride in triumph on the back of man. In the time of my father I witnessed the strange sight. Perhaps tonight also I shall see it for the last time. If they arrive before the drums beat for me, I shall tell him to let the Alafin[2] know I follow swiftly. If they come after the drums have sounded, why then, all is well for I have gone ahead. Our spirits shall fall in step along the great passage. [*He listens to the drums. He seems again to be falling into a state of semi-hypnosis; his eyes scan the sky but it is in a kind of daze. His voice is a little breathless.*] The moon has fed, a glow from its full stomach fills the sky and air, but I cannot tell where is that gateway through which I must pass. My faithful friends, let our feet touch together this last time, lead me into the other market with sounds that cover my skin with down yet make my limbs strike earth like a thoroughbred. Dear mothers, let me dance into the passage even as I have lived beneath your roofs. [*He comes down progressively among them. They make way for him, the drummers playing. His dance is one of solemn, regal motions, each gesture of the body is made with a solemn finality. The* WOMEN *join him, their steps a somewhat more fluid version of his. Beneath the* PRAISE-SINGER's *exhortations the* WOMEN *dirge "Ale le le, awo mi lo."*]

PRAISE-SINGER:	Elesin Alafin, can you hear my voice?
ELESIN:	Faintly, my friend, faintly.
PRAISE-SINGER:	Elesin Alafin, can you hear my call?
ELESIN:	Faintly my king, faintly.
PRAISE-SINGER:	Is your memory sound Elesin?
	Shall my voice be a blade of grass and
	Tickle the armpit of the past?
ELESIN:	My memory needs no prodding but
	What do you wish to say to me?
PRAISE-SINGER:	Only what has been spoken. Only what concerns
	The dying wish of the father of all.
ELESIN:	It is buried like seed-yam in my mind
	This is the season of quick rains, the harvest
	Is this moment due for gathering.
PRAISE-SINGER:	If you cannot come, I said, swear
	You'll tell my favourite horse. I shall
	Ride on through the gates alone.
ELESIN:	Elesin's message will be read
	Only when his loyal heart no longer beats.
PRAISE-SINGER:	If you cannot come Elesin, tell my dog.
	I cannot stay the keeper too long
	At the gate.
ELESIN:	A dog does not outrun the hand
	That feeds it meat. A horse that throws its rider
	Slows down to a stop. Elesin Alafin
	Trusts no beasts with messages between
	A king and his companion.

2. "Owner of the Palace" (literal trans.); the title of the king of Oyo.

PRAISE-SINGER:	If you get lost my dog will track The hidden path to me.
ELESIN:	The seven-way crossroads confuses Only the stranger. The Horseman of the King Was born in the recesses of the house.
PRAISE-SINGER:	I know the wickedness of men. If there is Weight on the loose end of your sash, such weight As no mere man can shift; if your sash is earthed By evil minds who mean to part us at the last . . .
ELESIN:	My sash is of the deep purple *alari*; It is no tethering-rope. The elephant Trails no tethering-rope; that king Is not yet crowned who will peg an elephant— Not even you my friend and King.
PRAISE-SINGER:	And yet this fear will not depart from me The darkness of this new abode is deep— Will your human eyes suffice?
ELESIN:	In a night which falls before our eyes However deep, we do not miss our way.
PRAISE-SINGER:	Shall I now not acknowledge I have stood Where wonders met their end? The elephant deserves Better than that we say "I have caught A glimpse of something."[3] If we see the tamer Of the forest let us say plainly, we have seen An elephant.
ELESIN:	[*His voice is drowsy.*] I have freed myself of earth and now It's getting dark. Strange voices guide my feet.
PRAISE-SINGER:	The river is never so high that the eyes Of a fish are covered. The night is not so dark That the albino fails to find his way.[4] A child Returning homewards craves no leading by the hand. Gracefully does the mask[5] regain his grove at the end of the day . . . Gracefully. Gracefully does the mask dance Homeward at the end of the day, gracefully . . .

[ELESIN'*s trance appears to be deepening, his steps heavier.*]

IYALOJA:	It is the death of war that kills the valiant, Death of water is how the swimmer goes It is the death of markets that kills the trader And death of indecision takes the idle away The trade of the cutlass blunts its edge And the beautiful die the death of beauty. It takes an Elesin to die the death of death . . . Only Elesin . . . dies the unknowable death of death . . .

---

3. A Yoruba saying, meaning that an outstanding person or deed must be granted
proper recognition.

4. Many albinos have poor eyesight.
5. Of the *egungun* masquerade.

Gracefully, gracefully does the horseman regain
The stables at the end of day, gracefully . . .

PRAISE-SINGER: How shall I tell what my eyes have seen? The Horseman gallops on before the courier, how shall I tell what my eyes have seen? He says a dog may be confused by new scents of beings he never dreamt of, so he must precede the dog to heaven. He says a horse may stumble on strange boulders and be lamed, so he races on before the horse to heaven. It is best, he says, to trust no messenger who may falter at the outer gate, oh how shall I tell what my ears have heard? But do you hear me still Elesin, do you hear your faithful one?

[ELESIN *in his motions appears to feel for a direction of sound, subtly, but he only sinks deeper into his trance dance.*]

Elesin Alafin, I no longer sense your flesh. The drums are changing now but you have gone far ahead of the world. It is not yet noon in heaven; let those who claim it is begin their own journey home. So why must you rush like an impatient bride: why do you race to desert your Olohun-iyo?

[ELESIN *is now sunk fully deep in his trance, there is no longer sign of any awareness of his surroundings.*]

Does the deep voice of *gbedu*[6] cover you then, like the passage of royal elephants? Those drums that brook no rivals, have they blocked the passage to your ears that my voice passes into wind, a mere leaf floating in the night? Is your flesh lightened Elesin, is that lump of earth I slid between your slippers to keep you longer slowly sifting from your feet? Are the drums on the other side now tuning skin to skin with ours in *osugbo*?[7] Are there sounds there I cannot hear, do footsteps surround you which pound the earth like *gbedu*, roll like thunder round the dome of the world? Is the darkness gathering in your head Elesin? Is there now a streak of light at the end of the passage, a light I dare not look upon? Does it reveal whose voices we often heard, whose touches we often felt, whose wisdoms come suddenly into the mind when the wisest have shaken their heads and murmured: It cannot be done? Elesin Alafin, don't think I do not know why your lips are heavy, why your limbs are drowsy as palm oil in the cold of harmattan.[8] I would call you back but when the elephant heads for the jungle, the tail is too small a handhold for the hunter that would pull him back. The sun that heads for the sea no longer heeds the prayers of the farmer. When the river begins to taste the salt of the ocean, we no longer know what deity to call on, the river-god or Olokun.[9] No arrow flies back to the string, the child does not return through the same passage that gave it birth. Elesin Oba, can you hear me at all? Your eyelids are glazed like a courtesan's, is it that you see the dark groom and master of life? And will you see my father? Will you tell him that I stayed with you to the last? Will my voice ring in your ears awhile, will you remember Olohun-iyo even if the music on the other side surpasses his mortal craft? But will they know you over there? Have they eyes to gauge

---

6. Drums. Their deep resonance is caused by the hardwood from which they are made.
7. The secret executive cult of the Yoruba; its meeting place [Author's note].
8. A sharp, dry wind from the Sahara that blows over western Africa in December. The wind brings dust and noticeably cools the air. Palm oil congeals in cold weather and is thus said to sleep. Compare the American "slow as molasses in January."
9. Goddess of the sea.

your worth, have they the heart to love you, will they know what thorough-bred prances towards them in caparisons[1] of honour? If they do not Elesin, if any there cuts your yam with a small knife, or pours you wine in a small calabash, turn back and return to welcoming hands. If the world were not greater than the wishes of Olohun-iyo, I would not let you go . . . .

[*He appears to break down.* ELESIN *dances on, completely in a trance. The dirge wells up louder and stronger.* ELESIN'S *dance does not lose its elasticity but his gestures become, if possible, even more weighty. Lights fade slowly on the scene.*]

Scene Four

A Masque. The front side of the stage is part of a wide corridor around the great hall of the Residency extending beyond vision into the rear and wings. It is redolent of the tawdry decadence of a far-flung but key imperial frontier. The COUPLES *in a variety of fancy-dress are ranged around the walls, gazing in the same direction. The guest-of-honour is about to make an appearance. A portion of the local police brass band with its white* CONDUCTOR *is just visible. At last, the entrance of* ROYALTY. *The band plays "Rule Britannia," badly, beginning long before he is visible. The couples bow and curtsey as he passes by them. Both he and his companions are dressed in seventeenth century European costume. Following behind are the* RESIDENT *and his* PARTNER *similarly attired. As they gain the end of the hall where the orchestra dais begins the music comes to an end. The* PRINCE *bows to the guests. The* BAND *strikes up a Viennese waltz and the* PRINCE *formally opens the floor. Several bars later the* RESIDENT *and his companion follow suit. Others follow in appropriate pecking order. The orchestra's waltz rendition is not of the highest musical standard.*

Some time later the PRINCE *dances again into view and is settled into a corner by the* RESIDENT *who then proceeds to select* COUPLES *as they dance past for introduction, sometimes threading his way through the dancers to tap the lucky* COUPLE *on the shoulder. Desperate efforts from many to ensure that they are recognised in spite of perhaps, their costume. The ritual of introductions soon takes in* PILKINGS *and his* WIFE. *The* PRINCE *is quite fascinated by their costume and they demonstrate the adaptations they have made to it, pulling down the mask to demonstrate how the egungun normally appears, then showing the various press-button controls they have innovated for the face flaps, the sleeves, etc. They demonstrate the dance steps and the guttural sounds made by the egungun, harrass other dancers in the hall,* MRS. PILKINGS *playing the "restrainer"[2] to* PILKINGS' *manic darts. Everyone is highly entertained, the Royal Party especially who lead the applause.*

At this point a liveried FOOTMAN *comes in with a note on a salver and is intercepted almost absent-mindedly by the* RESIDENT *who takes the note and reads it. After polite coughs he succeeds in excusing the* PILKINGS *from the* PRINCE *and takes them aside. The* PRINCE *considerately offers the* RESIDENT'S WIFE *his hand and dancing is resumed.*

On their way out the RESIDENT *gives an order to his* AIDE-DE-CAMP. *They come into the side corridor where the* RESIDENT *hands the note to* PILKINGS.

---

1. Rich ceremonial cloth draped over the saddle of a horse.
2. Masqueraders sometimes become possessed and go berserk; ropes are, therefore, tied to their waists and held by "restrainers."

RESIDENT: As you see it says "emergency" on the outside. I took the liberty of opening it because His Highness was obviously enjoying the entertainment. I didn't want to interrupt unless really necessary.

PILKINGS: Yes, yes of course, sir.

RESIDENT: Is it really as bad as it says? What's it all about?

PILKINGS: Some strange custom they have, sir. It seems because the King is dead some important chief has to commit suicide.

RESIDENT: The King? Isn't it the same one who died nearly a month ago?

PILKINGS: Yes, sir.

RESIDENT: Haven't they buried him yet?

PILKINGS: They take their time about these things, sir. The pre-burial ceremonies last nearly thirty days. It seems tonight is the final night.

RESIDENT: But what has it got to do with the market women? Why are they rioting? We've waived that troublesome tax haven't we?

PILKINGS: We don't quite know that they are exactly rioting yet, sir. Sergeant Amusa is sometimes prone to exaggerations.

RESIDENT: He sounds desperate enough. That comes out even in his rather quaint grammar. Where is the man anyway? I asked my aide-de-camp to bring him here.

PILKINGS: They are probably looking in the wrong verandah. I'll fetch him myself.

RESIDENT: No no you stay here. Let your wife go and look for them. Do you mind my dear . . . ?

JANE: Certainly not, your Excellency. [*Goes.*]

RESIDENT: You should have kept me informed, Pilkings. You realise how disastrous it would have been if things had erupted while His Highness was here.

PILKINGS: I wasn't aware of the whole business until tonight, sir.

RESIDENT: Nose to the ground Pilkings, nose to the ground. If we all let these little things slip past us where would the empire be eh? Tell me that. Where would we all be?

PILKINGS: [*Low voice.*] Sleeping peacefully at home I bet.

RESIDENT: What did you say, Pilkings?

PILKINGS: It won't happen again, sir.

RESIDENT: It mustn't, Pilkings. It mustn't. Where is that damned sergeant? I ought to get back to His Highness as quickly as possible and offer him some plausible explanation for my rather abrupt conduct. Can you think of one, Pilkings?

PILKINGS: You could tell him the truth, sir.

RESIDENT: I could? No no no no Pilkings, that would never do. What! Go and tell him there is a riot just two miles away from him? This is supposed to be a secure colony of His Majesty, Pilkings.

PILKINGS: Yes, sir.

RESIDENT: Ah, there they are. No, these are not our native police. Are these the ring-leaders of the riot?

PILKINGS: Sir, these are my police officers.

RESIDENT: Oh, I beg your pardon officers. You do look a little . . . I say, isn't there something missing in their uniform? I think they used to have some rather colourful sashes. If I remember rightly I recommended them myself in my young days in the service. A bit of colour always appeals to the natives, yes, I remember putting that in my report. Well well well, where are we? Make your report man.

PILKINGS: [*Moves close to* AMUSA, *between his teeth.*] And let's have no more superstitious nonsense from you Amusa or I'll throw you in the guardroom for a month and feed you pork![3]

RESIDENT: What's that? What has pork to do with it?

PILKINGS: Sir, I was just warning him to be brief. I'm sure you are most anxious to hear his report.

RESIDENT: Yes yes yes of course. Come on man, speak up. Hey, didn't we give them some colourful fez[4] hats with all those wavy things, yes, pink tassells . . .

PILKINGS: Sir, I think if he was permitted to make his report we might find that he lost his hat in the riot.

RESIDENT: Ah yes indeed. I'd better tell His Highness that. Lost his hat in the riot, ha ha. He'll probably say well, as long as he didn't lose his head. [*Chuckles to himself.*] Don't forget to send me a report first thing in the morning young Pilkings.

PILKINGS: No, sir.

RESIDENT: And whatever you do, don't let things get out of hand. Keep a cool head and—nose to the ground Pilkings. [*Wanders off in the general direction of the hall.*]

PILKINGS: Yes, sir.

AIDE-DE-CAMP: Would you be needing me, sir?

PILKINGS: No thanks, Bob. I think His Excellency's need of you is greater than ours.

AIDE-DE-CAMP: We have a detachment of soldiers from the capital, sir. They accompanied His Highness up here.

PILKINGS: I doubt if it will come to that but, thanks, I'll bear it in mind. Oh, could you send an orderly with my cloak.

AIDE-DE-CAMP: Very good, sir. [*Goes.*]

PILKINGS: Now, sergeant.

AMUSA: Sir . . . [*Makes an effort, stops dead. Eyes to the ceiling.*]

PILKINGS: Oh, not again.

AMUSA: I cannot against death to dead cult. This dress get power of dead.

PILKINGS: All right, let's go. You are relieved of all further duty Amusa. Report to me first thing in the morning.

JANE: Shall I come, Simon?

PILKINGS: No, there's no need for that. If I can get back later I will. Otherwise get Bob to bring you home.

JANE: Be careful Simon . . . I mean, be clever.

PILKINGS: Sure I will. You two, come with me. [*As he turns to go, the clock in the Residency begins to chime.* PILKINGS *looks at his watch then turns, horror-stricken, to stare at his wife. The same thought clearly occurs to her. He swallows hard. An* ORDERLY *brings his cloak.*] It's midnight. I had no idea it was that late.

---

3. Muslims are prohibited from eating pork.
4. Red caps worn by African officials in the colonial service.

JANE: But surely . . . they don't count the hours the way we do. The moon, or something . . .

PILKINGS: I am . . . not so sure.

[*He turns and breaks into a sudden run. The two* CONSTABLES *follow, also at a run.* AMUSA, *who has kept his eyes on the ceiling throughout waits until the last of the footsteps has faded out of hearing. He salutes suddenly, but without once looking in the direction of the* WOMAN.]

AMUSA: Goodnight, madam.

JANE: Oh. [*She hesitates.*] Amusa . . . [*He goes off without seeming to have heard.*] Poor Simon . . . [*A figure emerges from the shadows, a young black* MAN *dressed in a sober western suit. He peeps into the hall, trying to make out the figures of the dancers.*]

Who is that?

OLUNDE: [*Emerges into the light.*] I didn't mean to startle you madam. I am looking for the District Officer.

JANE: Wait a minute . . . don't I know you? Yes, you are Olunde, the young man who . . .

OLUNDE: Mrs. Pilkings! How fortunate. I came here to look for your husband.

JANE: Olunde! Let's look at you. What a fine young man you've become. Grand but solemn. Good God, when did you return? Simon never said a word. But you do look well Olunde. Really!

OLUNDE: You are . . . well, you look quite well yourself Mrs. Pilkings. From what little I can see of you.

JANE: Oh, this. It's caused quite a stir I assure you, and not all of it very pleasant. You are not shocked I hope?

OLUNDE: Why should I be? But don't you find it rather hot in there? Your skin must find it difficult to breathe.

JANE: Well, it is a little hot I must confess, but it's all in a good cause.

OLUNDE: What cause Mrs. Pilkings?

JANE: All this. The ball. And His Highness being here in person and all that.

OLUNDE: [*Mildly.*] And that is the good cause for which you desecrate an ancestral mask?

JANE: Oh, so you are shocked after all. How disappointing.

OLUNDE: No I am not shocked, Mrs. Pilkings. You forget that I have now spent four years among your people. I discovered that you have no respect for what you do not understand.

JANE: Oh. So you've returned with a chip on your shoulder. That's a pity Olunde. I am sorry.

[*An uncomfortable silence follows.*]

I take it then that you did not find your stay in England altogether edifying.

OLUNDE: I don't say that. I found your people quite admirable in many ways, their conduct and courage in this war[5] for instance.

JANE: Ah yes, the war. Here of course it is all rather remote. From time to time we have a black-out drill just to remind us that there is a war on. And the rare convoy passes through on its way somewhere or on manoeuvres.

5. That is, World War II.

Mind you there is the occasional bit of excitement like that ship that was blown up in the harbour.[6]

OLUNDE: Here? Do you mean through enemy action?

JANE: Oh no, the war hasn't come that close. The captain did it himself. I don't quite understand it really. Simon tried to explain. The ship had to be blown up because it had become dangerous to the other ships, even to the city itself. Hundreds of the coastal population would have died.

OLUNDE: Maybe it was loaded with ammunition and had caught fire. Or some of those lethal gases they've been experimenting on.

JANE: Something like that. The captain blew himself up with it. Deliberately. Simon said someone had to remain on board to light the fuse.

OLUNDE: It must have been a very short fuse.

JANE: [Shrugs.] I don't know much about it. Only that there was no other way to save lives. No time to devise anything else. The captain took the decision and carried it out.

OLUNDE: Yes . . . I quite believe it. I met men like that in England.

JANE: Oh just look at me! Fancy welcoming you back with such morbid news. Stale too. It was at least six months ago.

OLUNDE: I don't find it morbid at all. I find it rather inspiring. It is an affirmative commentary on life.

JANE: What is?

OLUNDE: That captain's self-sacrifice.

JANE: Nonsense. Life should never be thrown deliberately away.

OLUNDE: And the innocent people around the harbour?

JANE: Oh, how does one know? The whole thing was probably exaggerated anyway.

OLUNDE: That was a risk the captain couldn't take. But please Mrs. Pilkings, do you think you could find your husband for me? I have to talk to him.

JANE: Simon? [As she recollects for the first time the full significance of OLUNDE's presence.] Simon is . . . there is a little problem in town. He was sent for. But . . . when did you arrive? Does Simon know you're here?

OLUNDE: [Suddenly earnest.] I need your help Mrs. Pilkings. I've always found you somewhat more understanding than your husband. Please find him for me and when you do, you must help me talk to him.

JANE: I'm afraid I don't quite . . . follow you. Have you seen my husband already?

OLUNDE: I went to your house. Your houseboy told me you were here. [He smiles.] He even told me how I would recognise you and Mr. Pilkings.

JANE: Then you must know what my husband is trying to do for you.

OLUNDE: For me?

JANE: For you. For your people. And to think he didn't even know you were coming back! But how do you happen to be here? Only this evening we were talking about you. We thought you were still four thousand miles away.

OLUNDE: I was sent a cable.

JANE: A cable? Who did? Simon? The business of your father didn't begin till tonight.

6. A reference to an incident that occurred in Lagos, the capital of Nigeria, in 1944.

OLUNDE: A relation sent it weeks ago, and it said nothing about my father. All it said was, Our King is dead. But I knew I had to return home at once so as to bury my father. I understood that.

JANE: Well, thank God you don't have to go through that agony. Simon is going to stop it.

OLUNDE: That's why I want to see him. He's wasting his time. And since he has been so helpful to me I don't want him to incur the enmity of our people. Especially over nothing.

JANE: [*Sits down open mouthed.*] You . . . you Olunde!

OLUNDE: Mrs. Pilkings, I came home to bury my father. As soon as I heard the news I booked my passage home. In fact we were fortunate. We travelled in the same convoy as your Prince, so we had excellent protection.

JANE: But you don't think your father is also entitled to whatever protection is available to him?

OLUNDE: How can I make you understand? He *has* protection. No one can undertake what he does tonight without the deepest protection the mind can conceive. What can you offer him in place of his peace of mind, in place of the honour and veneration of his own people? What would you think of your Prince if he refused to accept the risk of losing his life on this voyage? This . . . showing the flag tour of colonial possessions.

JANE: I see. So it isn't just medicine you studied in England.

OLUNDE: Yet another error into which your people fall. You believe that everything which appears to make sense was learnt from you.

JANE: Not so fast Olunde. You have learnt to argue I can tell that, but I never said you made sense. However clearly you try to put it, it is still a barbaric custom. It is even worse—it's feudal! The king dies and a chieftan must be buried with him. How feudalistic can you get!

OLUNDE: [*Waves his hand towards the background. The* PRINCE *is dancing past again—to a different step—and all the guests are bowing and curtseying as he passes.*] And this? Even in the midst of a devastating war, look at that. What name would you give to that?

JANE: Therapy, British style. The preservation of sanity in the midst of chaos.

OLUNDE: Others would call it decadence. However, it doesn't really interest me. You white races know how to survive; I've seen proof of that. By all logical and natural laws this war should end with all the white races wiping out one another, wiping out their so-called civilisation for all time and reverting to a state of primitivism the like of which has so far only existed in your imagination when you thought of us. I thought all that at the beginning. Then I slowly realised that your greatest art is the art of survival. But at least have the humility to let others survive in their own way.

JANE: Through ritual suicide?

OLUNDE: Is that worse than mass suicide? Mrs. Pilkings, what do you call what those young men are sent to do by their generals in this war? Of course you have also mastered the art of calling things by names which don't remotely describe them.

JANE: You talk! You people with your long-winded, roundabout way of making conversation.

OLUNDE: Mrs. Pilkings, whatever we do, we never suggest that a thing is the opposite of what it really is. In your newsreels I heard defeats, thorough, murderous defeats described as strategic victories. No wait, it wasn't just on your newsreels. Don't forget I was attached to hospitals all the time. Hordes of your wounded passed through those wards. I spoke to them. I spent long evenings by their bedsides while they spoke terrible truths of the realities of that war. I know now how history is made.

JANE: But surely, in a war of this nature, for the morale of the nation you must expect . . .

OLUNDE: That a disaster beyond human reckoning be spoken of as a triumph? No, I mean, is there no mourning in the home of the bereaved that such blasphemy is permitted?

JANE: [After a moment's pause.] Perhaps I can understand you now. The time we picked for you was not really one for seeing us at our best.

OLUNDE: Don't think it was just the war. Before that even started I had plenty of time to study your people. I saw nothing, finally, that gave you the right to pass judgement on other peoples and their ways. Nothing at all.

JANE: [Hesitantly.] Was it the . . . colour thing? I know there is some discrimination.

OLUNDE: Don't make it so simple, Mrs. Pilkings. You make it sound as if when I left, I took nothing at all with me.

JANE: Yes . . . and to tell the truth, only this evening, Simon and I agreed that we never really knew what you left with.

OLUNDE: Neither did I. But I found out over there. I am grateful to your country for that. And I will never give it up.

JANE: Olunde, please . . . promise me something. Whatever you do, don't throw away what you have started to do. You want to be a doctor. My husband and I believe you will make an excellent one, sympathetic and competent. Don't let anything make you throw away your training.

OLUNDE: [Genuinely surprised.] Of course not. What a strange idea. I intend to return and complete my training. Once the burial of my father is over.

JANE: Oh, please . . . !

OLUNDE: Listen! Come outside. You can't hear anything against that music.

JANE: What is it?

OLUNDE: The drums. Can you hear the drums? Listen.

[The drums come over, still distant but more distinct. There is a change of rhythm, it rises to a crescendo and then, suddenly, it is cut off. After a silence, a new beat begins, slow and resonant.]

There it's all over.

JANE: You mean he's . . . .

OLUNDE: Yes, Mrs. Pilkings, my father is dead. His will power has always been enormous; I know he is dead.

JANE: [Screams.] How can you be so callous! So unfeeling! You announce your father's own death like a surgeon looking down on some strange . . . stranger's body! You're just a savage like all the rest.

AIDE-DE-CAMP: [Rushing out.] Mrs. Pilkings. Mrs. Pilkings. [She breaks down, sobbing.] Are you all right, Mrs. Pilkings?

OLUNDE: She'll be all right. [Turns to go.]

AIDE-DE-CAMP: Who are you? And who the hell asked your opinion?

OLUNDE: You're quite right, nobody. [*Going.*]

AIDE-DE-CAMP: What the hell! Did you hear me ask you who you were?

OLUNDE: I have business to attend to.

AIDE-DE-CAMP: I'll give you business in a moment you impudent nigger. Answer my question!

OLUNDE: I have a funeral to arrange. Excuse me. [*Going.*]

AIDE-DE-CAMP: I said stop! Orderly!

JANE: No, no, don't do that. I'm all right. And for heaven's sake don't act so foolishly. He's a family friend.

AIDE-DE-CAMP: Well he'd better learn to answer civil questions when he's asked them. These natives put a suit on and they get high opinions of themselves.

OLUNDE: Can I go now?

JANE: No no don't go. I must talk to you. I'm sorry about what I said.

OLUNDE: It's nothing, Mrs. Pilkings. And I'm really anxious to go. I couldn't see my father before, it's forbidden for me, his heir and successor to set eyes on him from the moment of the king's death. But now . . . I would like to touch his body while it is still warm.

JANE: You will. I promise I shan't keep you long. Only, I couldn't possibly let you go like that. Bob, please excuse us.

AIDE-DE-CAMP: If you're sure . . .

JANE: Of course I'm sure. Something happened to upset me just then, but I'm all right now. Really.

   [*The* AIDE DE CAMP *goes, somewhat reluctantly.*]

OLUNDE: I mustn't stay long.

JANE: Please, I promise not to keep you. It's just that . . . oh you saw yourself what happens to one in this place. The Resident's man thought he was being helpful, that's the way we all react. But I can't go in among that crowd just now and if I stay by myself somebody will come looking for me. Please, just say something for a few moments and then you can go. Just so I can recover myself.

OLUNDE: What do you want me to say?

JANE: Your calm acceptance for instance, can you explain that? It was so unnatural. I don't understand that at all. I feel a need to understand all I can.

OLUNDE: But you explained it yourself. My medical training perhaps. I have seen death too often. And the soldiers who returned from the front, they died on our hands all the time.

JANE: No. It has to be more than that. I feel it has to do with the many things we don't really grasp about your people. At least you can explain.

OLUNDE: All these things are part of it. And anyway, my father has been dead in my mind for nearly a month. Ever since I learnt of the King's death. I've lived with my bereavement so long now that I cannot think of him alive. On that journey on the boat, I kept my mind on my duties as the one who must perform the rites over his body. I went through it all again and again in my mind as he himself had taught me. I didn't want to do anything wrong, something which might jeopardise the welfare of my people.

JANE: But he had disowned you. When you left he swore publicly you were no longer his son.

OLUNDE: I told you, he was a man of tremendous will. Sometimes that's another way of saying stubborn. But among our people, you don't disown a child just like that. Even if I had died before him I would still be buried like his eldest son. But it's time for me to go.

JANE: Thank you. I feel calmer. Don't let me keep you from your duties.

OLUNDE: Goodnight, Mrs. Pilkings.

JANE: Welcome home.

[*She holds out her hand. As he takes it footsteps are heard approaching the drive. A short while later a woman's sobbing is also heard.*]

PILKINGS: [*Off.*] Keep them here till I get back. [*He strides into view, reacts at the sight of* OLUNDE *but turns to his wife.*] Thank goodness you're still here.

JANE: Simon, what happened?

PILKINGS: Later Jane, please. Is Bob still here?

JANE: Yes, I think so. I'm sure he must be.

PILKINGS: Try and get him out here as quickly as you can. Tell him it's urgent.

JANE: Of course. Oh Simon, you remember . . .

PILKINGS: Yes yes. I can see who it is. Get Bob out here. [*She runs off.*] At first I thought I was seeing a ghost.

OLUNDE: Mr. Pilkings, I appreciate what you tried to do. I want you to believe that. I can tell you it would have been a terrible calamity if you'd succeeded.

PILKINGS: [*Opens his mouth several times, shuts it.*] You . . . said what?

OLUNDE: A calamity for us, the entire people.

PILKINGS: [*Sighs.*] I see. Hm.

OLUNDE: And now I must go. I must see him before he turns cold.

PILKINGS: Oh ah . . . em . . . but this is a shock to see you. I mean er thinking all this while you were in England and thanking God for that.

OLUNDE: I came on the mail boat. We travelled in the Prince's convoy.

PILKINGS: Ah yes, a ah, hm . . . er well . . .

OLUNDE: Goodnight. I can see you are shocked by the whole business. But you must know by now there are things you cannot understand—or help.

PILKINGS: Yes. Just a minute. There are armed policemen that way and they have instructions to let no one pass. I suggest you wait a little. I'll er . . . give you an escort.

OLUNDE: That's very kind of you. But do you think it could be quickly arranged.

PILKINGS: Of course. In fact, yes, what I'll do is send Bob over with some men to the er . . . place. You can go with them. Here he comes now. Excuse me a minute.

AIDE-DE-CAMP: Anything wrong sir?

PILKINGS: [*Takes him to one side.*] Listen Bob, that cellar in the disused annex of the Residency, you know, where the slaves were stored before being taken down to the coast . . .

AIDE-DE-CAMP: Oh yes, we use it as a storeroom for broken furniture.

PILKINGS: But it's still got the bars on it?

AIDE-DE-CAMP: Oh yes, they are quite intact.

PILKINGS: Get the keys please. I'll explain later. And I want a strong guard over the Residency tonight.

AIDE-DE-CAMP: We have that already. The detachment from the coast . . .

PILKINGS: No, I don't want them at the gates of the Residency. I want you to deploy them at the bottom of the hill, a long way from the main hall so they can deal with any situation long before the sound carries to the house.

AIDE-DE-CAMP: Yes of course.

PILKINGS: I don't want His Highness alarmed.

AIDE-DE-CAMP: You think the riot will spread here?

PILKINGS: It's unlikely but I don't want to take a chance. I made them believe I was going to lock the man up in my house, which was what I had planned to do in the first place. They are probably assailing it by now. I took a round-about route here so I don't think there is any danger at all. At least not before dawn. Nobody is to leave the premises of course—the native employees I mean. They'll soon smell something is up and they can't keep their mouths shut.

AIDE-DE-CAMP: I'll give instructions at once.

PILKINGS: I'll take the prisoner down myself. Two policemen will stay with him throughout the night. Inside the cell.

AIDE-DE-CAMP: Right sir. [*Salutes and goes off at the double.*]

PILKINGS: Jane. Bob is coming back in a moment with a detachment. Until he gets back please stay with Olunde. [*He makes an extra warning gesture with his eyes.*]

OLUNDE: Please, Mr. Pilkings . . .

PILKINGS: I hate to be stuffy old son, but we have a crisis on our hands. It has to do with your father's affair if you must know. And it happens also at a time when we have His Highness here. I am responsible for security so you'll simply have to do as I say. I hope that's understood.
    [*Marches off quickly, in the direction from which he made his first appearance.*]

OLUNDE: What's going on? All this can't be just because he failed to stop my father killing himself.

JANE: I honestly don't know. Could it have sparked off a riot?

OLUNDE: No. If he'd succeeded that would be more likely to start the riot. Perhaps there were other factors involved. Was there a chieftancy dispute?

JANE: None that I know of.

ELESIN: [*An animal bellow from off.*] Leave me alone! Is it not enough that you have covered me in shame! White man, take your hand from my body!
    [OLUNDE *stands frozen to the spot.* JANE *understanding at last, tries to move him.*]

JANE: Let's go in. It's getting chilly out here.

PILKINGS: [*Off.*] Carry him.

ELESIN: Give me back the name you have taken away from me you ghost from the land of the nameless!

PILKINGS: Carry him! I can't have a disturbance here. Quickly! stuff up his mouth.

JANE: Oh God! Let's go in. Please Olunde.
    [OLUNDE *does not move.*]

ELESIN: Take your albino's hand from me you . . .
    [*Sounds of a struggle. His voice chokes as he is gagged.*]

OLUNDE: [*Quietly.*] That was my father's voice.

JANE: Oh you poor orphan, what have you come home to?
      [*There is a sudden explosion of rage from off-stage and powerful steps come running up the drive.*]

PILKINGS: You bloody fools, after him!
      [*Immediately* ELESIN, *in handcuffs, comes pounding in the direction of* JANE *and* OLUNDE, *followed some moments afterwards by* PILKINGS *and the* CONSTABLES. ELESIN, *confronted by the seeming statue of his son, stops dead.* OLUNDE *stares above his head into the distance. The* CONSTABLES *try to grab him.* JANE *screams at them.*]

JANE: Leave him alone! Simon, tell them to leave him alone.

PILKINGS: All right, stand aside you. [*Shrugs.*] Maybe just as well. It might help to calm him down.
      [*For several moments they hold the same position.* ELESIN *moves a step forward, almost as if he's still in doubt.*]

ELESIN: Olunde? [*He moves his head, inspecting him from side to side.*] Olunde! [*He collapses slowly at* OLUNDE's *feet.*] Oh son, don't let the sight of your father turn you blind!

OLUNDE: [*He moves for the first time since he heard his voice, brings his head slowly down to look on him.*] I have no father, eater of left-overs.
      [*He walks slowly down the way his father had run. Light fades out on* ELESIN, *sobbing into the ground.*]

Scene Five

A wide iron barred gate stretches almost the whole width of the cell in which ELESIN *is imprisoned. His wrists are encased in thick iron bracelets, chained together; he stands against the bars, looking out. Seated on the ground to one side on the outside is his recent* BRIDE, *her eyes bent perpetually to the ground. Figures of the two* GUARDS *can be seen deeper inside the cell, alert to every movement* ELESIN *makes.* PILKINGS *now in a police officer's uniform enters noiselessly, observes him a while. Then he coughs ostentatiously and approaches. Leans against the bars near a corner, his back to* ELESIN. *He is obviously trying to fall in mood with him. Some moments' silence.*

PILKINGS: You seem fascinated by the moon.

ELESIN: [*After a pause.*] Yes, ghostly one. Your twin-brother up there engages my thoughts.

PILKINGS: It is a beautiful night.

ELESIN: Is that so?

PILKINGS: The light on the leaves, the peace of the night . . .

ELESIN: The night is not at peace, District Officer.

PILKINGS: No? I would have said it was. You know, quiet . . .

ELESIN: And does quiet mean peace for you?

PILKINGS: Well, nearly the same thing. Naturally there is a subtle difference . . .

ELESIN: The night is not at peace, ghostly one. The world is not at peace. You have shattered the peace of the world for ever. There is no sleep in the world tonight.

PILKINGS: It is still a good bargain if the world should lose one night's sleep as the price of saving a man's life.

ELESIN: You did not save my life, District Officer. You destroyed it.

PILKINGS: Now come on . . .

ELESIN: And not merely my life but the lives of many. The end of the night's work is not over. Neither this year nor the next will see it. If I wished you well, I would pray that you do not stay long enough on our land to see the disaster you have brought upon us.

PILKINGS: Well, I did my duty as I saw it. I have no regrets.

ELESIN: No. The Regrets of life always come later.

[Some moments' pause.]

You are waiting for dawn, white man. I hear you saying to yourself: only so many hours until dawn and then the danger is over. All I must do is to keep him alive tonight. You don't quite understand it all but you know that tonight is when what ought to be must be brought about. I shall ease your mind even more, ghostly one. It is not an entire night but a moment of the night, and that moment is past. The moon was my messenger and guide. When it reached a certain gateway in the sky, it touched that moment for which my whole life has been spent in blessings. Even I do not know the gateway. I have stood here and scanned the sky for a glimpse of that door but, I cannot see it. Human eyes are useless for a search of this nature. But in the house of *osugbo*, those who keep watch through the spirit recognised the moment, they sent word to me through the voice of our sacred drums to prepare myself. I heard them and I shed all thoughts of earth. I began to follow the moon to the abode of the gods . . . servant of the white king, that was when you entered my chosen place of departure on feet of desecration.

PILKINGS: I'm sorry, but we all see our duty differently.

ELESIN: I no longer blame you. You stole from me my first-born, sent him to your country so you could turn him into something in your own image. Did you plan it all beforehand? There are moments when it seems part of a larger plan. He who must follow my footsteps is taken from me, sent across the ocean. Then, in my turn, I am stopped from fulfilling my destiny. Did you think it all out before, this plan to push our world from its course and sever the cord that links us to the great origin?

PILKINGS: You don't really believe that. Anyway, if that was my intention with your son, I appear to have failed.

ELESIN: You did not fail in the main, ghostly one. We know the roof covers the rafters, the cloth covers blemishes; who would have known that the white skin covered our future, preventing us from seeing the death our enemies had prepared for us. The world is set adrift and its inhabitants are lost. Around them, there is nothing but emptiness.

PILKINGS: Your son does not take so gloomy a view.

ELESIN: Are you dreaming now, white man? Were you not present at my reunion of shame? Did you not see when the world reversed itself and the father fell before his son, asking forgiveness?

PILKINGS: That was in the heat of the moment. I spoke to him and . . . if you want to know, he wishes he could cut out his tongue for uttering the words he did.

ELESIN: No. What he said must never be unsaid. The contempt of my own son rescued something of my shame at your hands. You have stopped me in my duty but I know now that I did give birth to a son. Once I mistrusted him for seeking the companionship of those my spirit knew as enemies of our race. Now I understand. One should seek to obtain the secrets of his enemies. He will avenge my shame, white one. His spirit will destroy you and yours.

PILKINGS: That kind of talk is hardly called for. If you don't want my consolation . . .

ELESIN: No white man, I do not want your consolation.

PILKINGS: As you wish. Your son anyway, sends his consolation. He asks your forgiveness. When I asked him not to despise you his reply was: I cannot judge him, and if I cannot judge him, I cannot despise him. He wants to come to you and say goodbye and to receive your blessing.

ELESIN: Goodbye? Is he returning to your land?

PILKINGS: Don't you think that's the most sensible thing for him to do? I advised him to leave at once, before dawn, and he agrees that is the right course of action.

ELESIN: Yes, it is best. And even if I did not think so, I have lost the father's place of honour. My voice is broken.

PILKINGS: Your son honours you. If he didn't he would not ask your blessing.

ELESIN: No. Even a thoroughbred is not without pity for the turf he strikes with his hoof. When is he coming?

PILKINGS: As soon as the town is a little quieter. I advised it.

ELESIN: Yes, white man, I am sure you advised it. You advise all our lives although on the authority of what gods, I do not know.

PILKINGS: [*Opens his mouth to reply, then appears to change his mind. Turns to go. Hesitates and stops again.*] Before I leave you, may I ask just one thing of you?

ELESIN: I am listening.

PILKINGS: I wish to ask you to search the quiet of your heart and tell me—do you not find great contradictions in the wisdom of your own race?

ELESIN: Make yourself clear, white one.

PILKINGS: I have lived among you long enough to learn a saying or two. One came to my mind tonight when I stepped into the market and saw what was going on. You were surrounded by those who egged you on with song and praises. I thought, are these not the same people who say: the elder grimly approaches heaven and you ask him to bear your greetings yonder; do you really think he makes the journey willingly? After that, I did not hesitate.

[*A pause.* ELESIN *sighs. Before he can speak a sound of running feet is heard.*]

JANE: [*Off.*] Simon! Simon!

PILKINGS: What on earth . . . ! [*Runs off.*]

[ELESIN *turns to his new wife, gazes on her for some moments.*]

ELESIN: My young bride, did you hear the ghostly one? You sit and sob in your silent heart but say nothing to all this. First I blamed the white man, then I blamed my gods for deserting me. Now I feel I want to blame you for the mystery of the sapping of my will. But blame is a strange peace offering for a man to bring a world he has deeply wronged, and to its innocent dwellers. Oh little mother, I have taken countless women in my life but you were more than a desire of the flesh. I needed you as the abyss across which my body must be drawn, I filled it with earth and dropped my seed in it at the moment of preparedness for my crossing. You were the final gift of the living to their emissary to the land of the ancestors, and perhaps your warmth and youth brought new insights of this world to me and turned my feet leaden on this side of the abyss. For I confess to you, daughter, my weakness came not merely from the abomination of the white man who came violently into my fading presence, there was also a weight of longing on my earth-held limbs. I would have shaken it off, already my foot had begun to lift but then, the white ghost entered and all was defiled.

[*Approaching voices of* PILKINGS *and his wife.*]

JANE: Oh Simon, you will let her in won't you?

PILKINGS: I really wish you'd stop interfering.

[*They come into view.* JANE *is in a dressing gown.* PILKINGS *is holding a note to which he refers from time to time.*]

JANE: Good gracious, I didn't initiate this. I was sleeping quietly, or trying to anyway, when the servant brought it. It's not my fault if one can't sleep undisturbed even in the Residency.

PILKINGS: He'd have done the same thing if we were sleeping at home so don't sidetrack the issue. He knows he can get round you or he wouldn't send you the petition in the first place.

JANE: Be fair Simon. After all he was thinking of your own interests. He is grateful you know, you seem to forget that. He feels he owes you something.

PILKINGS: I just wish they'd leave this man alone tonight, that's all.

JANE: Trust him Simon. He's pledged his word it will all go peacefully.

PILKINGS: Yes, and that's the other thing. I don't like being threatened.

JANE: Threatened? [*Takes the note.*] I didn't spot any threat.

PILKINGS: It's there. Veiled, but it's there. The only way to prevent serious rioting tomorrow—what a cheek!

JANE: I don't think he's threatening you Simon.

PILKINGS: He's picked up the idiom all right. Wouldn't surprise me if he's been mixing with commies or anarchists over there. The phrasing sounds too good to be true. Damn! If only the Prince hadn't picked this time for his visit.

JANE: Well, even so Simon, what have you got to lose? You don't want a riot on your hands, not with the Prince here.

PILKINGS: [*Going up to* ELESIN.] Let's see what he has to say. Chief Elesin, there is yet another person who wants to see you. As she is not a next-of-kin I don't really feel obliged to let her in. But your son sent a note with her, so it's up to you.

ELESIN: I know who that must be. So she found out your hiding place. Well, it was not difficult. My stench of shame is so strong, it requires no hunter's dog to follow it.

PILKINGS: If you don't want to see her, just say so and I'll send her packing.

ELESIN: Why should I not want to see her? Let her come. I have no more holes in my rag of shame. All is laid bare.

PILKINGS: I'll bring her in. [*Goes off.*]

JANE: [*Hesitates, then goes to* ELESIN.] Please, try and understand. Everything my husband did was for the best.

ELESIN: [*He gives her a long strange stare, as if he is trying to understand who she is.*] You are the wife of the District Officer?

JANE: Yes. My name, is Jane.

ELESIN: That is my wife sitting down there. You notice how still and silent she sits? My business is with your husband.

[PILKINGS *returns with* IYALOJA.]

PILKINGS: Here she is. Now first I want your word of honour that you will try nothing foolish.

ELESIN: Honour? White one, did you say you wanted my word of honour?

PILKINGS: I know you to be an honourable man. Give me your word of honour you will receive nothing from her.

ELESIN: But I am sure you have searched her clothing as you would never dare touch your own mother. And there are these two lizards[7] of yours who roll their eyes even when I scratch.

PILKINGS: And I shall be sitting on that tree trunk watching even how you blink. Just the same I want your word that you will not let her pass anything to you.

ELESIN: You have my honour already. It is locked up in that desk in which you will put away your report of this night's events. Even the honour of my people you have taken already; it is tied together with those papers of treachery[8] which make you masters in this land.

PILKINGS: All right. I am trying to make things easy but if you must bring in politics we'll have to do it the hard way. Madam, I want you to remain along this line and move no nearer to the cell door. Guards! [*They spring to attention.*] If she moves beyond this point, blow your whistle. Come on Jane. [*They go off.*]

IYALOJA: How boldly the lizard struts before the pigeon when it was the eagle itself he promised us he would confront.

ELESIN: I don't ask you to take pity on me Iyaloja. You have a message for me or you would not have come. Even if it is the curses of the world, I shall listen.

IYALOJA: You made so bold with the servant of the white king who took your side against death. I must tell your brother chiefs when I return how bravely you waged war against him. Especially with words.

ELESIN: I more than deserve your scorn.

IYALOJA: [*With sudden anger.*] I warned you, if you must leave a seed behind, be sure it is not tainted with the curses of the world. Who are you to open a new life when you dared not open the door to a new existence? I say who are you to make so bold? [*The* BRIDE *sobs and* IYALOJA *notices her. Her contempt noticeably increases as she turns back to* ELESIN.] Oh you self-vaunted stem of the plantain, how hollow it all proves. The pith is gone in the parent stem, so how will it prove with the new shoot? How will it go with that earth that bears it? Who are you to bring this abomination on us!

ELESIN: My powers deserted me. My charms, my spells, even my voice lacked strength when I made to summon the powers that would lead me over the last measure of earth into the land of the fleshless. You saw it, Iyaloja. You

7. That is, the guards.
8. The treaties of annexation forced by the British on African traditional rulers, who often did not understand their implications.

saw me struggle to retrieve my will from the power of the stranger whose shadow fell across the doorway and left me floundering and blundering in a maze I had never before encountered. My senses were numbed when the touch of cold iron came upon my wrists. I could do nothing to save myself.

IYALOJA: You have betrayed us. We fed you sweetmeats such as we hoped awaited you on the other side. But you said No, I must eat the world's leftovers. We said you were the hunter who brought the quarry down; to you belonged the vital portions of the game. No, you said, I am the hunter's dog and I shall eat the entrails of the game and the faeces of the hunter. We said you were the hunter returning home in triumph, a slain buffalo pressing down on his neck; you said wait, I first must turn up this cricket hole with my toes. We said yours was the doorway at which we first spy the tapper when he comes down from the tree, yours was the blessing of the twilight wine, the purl[9] that brings night spirits out of doors to steal their portion before the light of day. We said yours was the body of wine whose burden shakes the tapper like a sudden gust on his perch. You said, No, I am content to lick the dregs from each calabash when the drinkers are done. We said, the dew on earth's surface was for you to wash your feet along the slopes of honour. You said No, I shall step in the vomit of cats and the droppings of mice; I shall fight them for the left-overs of the world.

ELESIN: Enough Iyaloja, enough.

IYALOJA: We called you leader and oh, how you led us on. What we have no intention of eating should not be held to the nose.[1]

ELESIN: Enough, enough. My shame is heavy enough.

IYALOJA: Wait. I came with a burden.

ELESIN: You have more than discharged it.

IYALOJA: I wish I could pity you.

ELESIN: I need neither pity nor the pity of the world. I need understanding. Even I need to understand. You were present at my defeat. You were part of the beginnings. You brought about the renewal of my tie to earth, you helped in the binding of the cord.

IYALOJA: I gave you warning. The river which fills up before our eyes does not sweep us away in its flood.

ELESIN: What were warnings beside the moist contact of living earth between my fingers? What were warnings beside the renewal of famished embers lodged eternally in the heart of man. But even that, even if it overwhelmed one with a thousandfold temptations to linger a little while, a man could overcome it. It is when the alien hand pollutes the source of will, when a stranger's force of violence shatters the mind's calm resolution, this is when a man is made to commit the awful treachery of relief, commit in his thought the unspeakable blasphemy of seeing the hand of the gods in this alien rupture of his world. I know it was this thought that killed me, sapped my powers and turned me into an infant in the hands of unnamable strangers. I made to utter my spells anew but my tongue merely rattled in my mouth. I fingered hidden charms and the contact was damp; there was no

9. The frothy head of the palm wine. "Tapper": one who climbs to the very top of the palm tree for its wine. The profession is a highly specialized one. "Cricket hole": hunting crickets is a favorite game of Yoruba boys.
1. Considered uncouth by Yorubas.

spark left to sever the life-strings that should stretch from every fingertip. My will was squelched in the spittle of an alien race, and all because I had committed this blasphemy of thought—that there might be the hand of the gods in a stranger's intervention.

IYALOJA: Explain it how you will, I hope it brings you peace of mind. The bush rat fled his rightful cause, reached the market and set up a lamentation. "Please save me!"—are these fitting words to hear from an ancestral mask? "There's a wild beast at my heels" is not becoming language from a hunter.

ELESIN: May the world forgive me.

IYALOJA: I came with a burden I said. It approaches the gates which are so well guarded by those jackals whose spittle will from this day be on your food and drink. But first, tell me, you who were once Elesin Oba, tell me, you who know so well the cycle of the plantain: is it the parent shoot which withers to give sap to the younger or, does your wisdom see it running the other way?

ELESIN: I don't see your meaning Iyaloja?

IYALOJA: Did I ask you for a meaning? I asked a question. Whose trunk withers to give sap to the other? The parent shoot or the younger?

ELESIN: The parent.

IYALOJA: Ah. So you do know that. There are sights in this world which say different Elesin. There are some who choose to reverse the cycle of our being. Oh you emptied bark that the world once saluted for a pith-laden being, shall I tell you what the gods have claimed of you?

[In her agitation she steps beyond the line indicated by PILKINGS and the air is rent by piercing whistles. The two GUARDS also leap forward and place safe-guarding hands on ELESIN. IYALOJA stops, astonished. PILKINGS comes racing in, followed by JANE.]

PILKINGS: What is it? Did they try something?

GUARD: She stepped beyond the line.

ELESIN: [In a broken voice.] Let her alone. She meant no harm.

IYALOJA: Oh Elesin, see what you've become. Once you had no need to open your mouth in explanation because evil-smelling goats, itchy of hand and foot had lost their senses. And it was a brave man indeed who dared lay hands on you because Iyaloja stepped from one side of the earth onto another. Now look at the spectacle of your life. I grieve for you.

PILKINGS: I think you'd better leave. I doubt you have done him much good by coming here. I shall make sure you are not allowed to see him again. In any case we are moving him to a different place before dawn, so don't bother to come back.

IYALOJA: We foresaw that. Hence the burden I trudged here to lay beside your gates.

PILKINGS: What was that you said?

IYALOJA: Didn't our son explain? Ask that one. He knows what it is. At least we hope the man we once knew as Elesin remembers the lesser oaths he need not break.

PILKINGS: Do you know what she is talking about?

ELESIN: Go to the gates, ghostly one. Whatever you find there, bring it to me.

IYALOJA: Not yet. It drags behind me on the slow, weary feet of women. Slow as it is Elesin, it has long overtaken you. It rides ahead of your laggard will.

PILKINGS: What is she saying now? Christ! Must your people forever speak in riddles?

ELESIN: It will come white man, it will come. Tell your men at the gates to let it through.

PILKINGS: [*Dubiously.*] I'll have to see what it is.

IYALOJA: You will. [*Passionately.*] But this is one oath he cannot shirk. White one, you have a king here, a visitor from your land. We know of his presence here. Tell me, were he to die would you leave his spirit roaming restlessly on the surface of earth? Would you bury him here among those you consider less than human? In your land have you no ceremonies of the dead?

PILKINGS: Yes. But we don't make our chiefs commit suicide to keep him company.

IYALOJA: Child, I have not come to help your understanding. [*Points to* ELE-SIN.] This is the man whose weakened understanding holds us in bondage to you. But ask him if you wish. He knows the meaning of a king's passage; he was not born yesterday. He knows the peril to the race when our dead father, who goes as intermediary, waits and waits and knows he is betrayed. He knows when the narrow gate was opened and he knows it will not stay for laggards who drag their feet in dung and vomit, whose lips are reeking of the left-overs of lesser men. He knows he has condemned our king to wander in the void of evil with beings who are enemies of life.

PILKINGS: Yes er . . . but look here . . .

IYALOJA: What we ask is little enough. Let him release our King so he can ride on homewards alone. The messenger is on his way on the backs of women. Let him send word through the heart that is folded up within the bolt. It is the least of all his oaths, it is the easiest fulfilled.

[*The* AIDE-DE-CAMP *runs in.*]

PILKINGS: Bob?

AIDE-DE-CAMP: Sir, there's a group of women chanting up the hill.

PILKINGS: [*Rounding on* IYALOJA.] If you people want trouble . . .

JANE: Simon, I think that's what Olunde referred to in his letter.

PILKINGS: He knows damned well I can't have a crowd here! Damn it, I explained the delicacy of my position to him. I think it's about time I got him out of town. Bob, send a car and two or three soldiers to bring him in. I think the sooner he takes his leave of his father and gets out the better.

IYALOJA: Save your labour white one. If it is the father of your prisoner you want, Olunde, he who until this night we knew as Elesin's son, he comes soon himself to take his leave. He has sent the women ahead, so let them in.

[PILKINGS *remains undecided.*]

AIDE-DE-CAMP: What do we do about the invasion? We can still stop them far from here.

PILKINGS: What do they look like?

AIDE-DE-CAMP: They're not many. And they seem quite peaceful.

PILKINGS: No men?

AIDE-DE-CAMP: Mm, two or three at the most.

JANE: Honestly, Simon, I'd trust Olunde. I don't think he'll deceive you about their intentions.

PILKINGS: He'd better not. All right then, let them in Bob. Warn them to control themselves. Then hurry Olunde here. Make sure he brings his baggage because I'm not returning him into town.

AIDE-DE-CAMP: Very good, sir. [*Goes.*]

PILKINGS: [*To* IYALOJA.] I hope you understand that if anything goes wrong it will be on your head. My men have orders to shoot at the first sign of trouble.

IYALOJA: To prevent one death you will actually make other deaths? Ah, great is the wisdom of the white race. But have no fear. Your Prince will sleep peacefully. So at long last will ours. We will disturb you no further, servant of the white king. Just let Elesin fulfil his oath and we will retire home and pay homage to our King.

JANE: I believe her Simon, don't you?

PILKINGS: Maybe.

ELESIN: Have no fear ghostly one. I have a message to send my King and then you have nothing more to fear.

IYALOJA: Olunde would have done it. The chiefs asked him to speak the words but he said no, not while you lived.

ELESIN: Even from the depths to which my spirit has sunk, I find some joy that this little has been left to me.

[*The* WOMEN *enter, intoning the dirge "Ale le le" and swaying from side to side. On their shoulders is borne a longish object roughly like a cylindrical bolt, covered in cloth. They set it down on the spot where* IYALOJA *had stood earlier, and form a semi-circle round it. The* PRAISE-SINGER *and* DRUMMER *stand on the inside of the semi-circle but the drum is not used at all. The* DRUMMER *intones under the* PRAISE-SINGER's *invocations.*]

PILKINGS: [*As they enter.*] What is *that?*

IYALOJA: The burden you have made white one, but we bring it in peace.

PILKINGS: I said *what* is it?

ELESIN: White man, you must let me out. I have a duty to perform.

PILKINGS: I most certainly will not.

ELESIN: There lies the courier of my King. Let me out so I can perform what is demanded of me.

PILKINGS: You'll do what you need to do from inside there or not at all. I've gone as far as I intend to with this business.

ELESIN: The worshipper who lights a candle in your church to bear a message to his god bows his head and speaks in a whisper to the flame. Have I not seen it ghostly one? His voice does not ring out to the world. Mine are no words for anyone's ears. They are not words even for the bearers of this load. They are words I must speak secretly, even as my father whispered them in my ears and I in the ears of my first-born. I cannot shout them to the wind and the open night sky.

JANE: Simon . . .

PILKINGS: Don't interfere. Please!

IYALOJA: They have slain the favourite horse of the king and slain his dog. They have borne them from pulse to pulse centre of the land receiving prayers for their king. But the rider has chosen to stay behind. Is it too much to ask that he speak his heart to heart of the waiting courier? [PILKINGS *turns his back on her.*] So be it. Elesin Oba, you see how even the mere leavings are denied you. [*She gestures to the* PRAISE SINGER.]

PRAISE-SINGER: Elesin Oba! I call you by that name only this last time. Remember when I said, if you cannot come, tell my horse. [*Pause.*] What? I cannot hear you? I said, if you cannot come, whisper in the ears of my horse. Is your tongue severed from the roots? Elesin? I can hear no response. I said, if there are boulders you cannot climb, mount my horse's back, this spotless black stallion, he'll bring you over them. [*Pauses.*] Elesin Oba, once you had a tongue that darted like a drummer's stick. I said, if you get lost my dog will track a path to me. My memory fails me but I think you replied: My feet have found the path, Alafin.

> [*The dirge rises and falls.*]

I said at the last, if evil hands hold you back, just tell my horse there is weight on the hem of your smock. I dare not wait too long.

> [*The dirge rises and falls.*]

There lies the swiftest ever messenger of a king, so set me free with the errand of your heart. There lie the head and heart of the favourite of the gods, whisper in his ears. Oh my companion, if you had followed when you should, we would not say that the horse preceded its rider. If you had followed when it was time, we would not say the dog has raced beyond and left his master behind. If you had raised your will to cut the thread of life at the summons of the drums, we would not say your mere shadow fell across the gateway and took its owner's place at the banquet. But the hunter, laden with slain buffalo, stayed to root in the cricket's hole with his toes. What now is left? If there is a dearth of bats, the pigeon must serve us for the offering.[2] Speak the words over your shadow which must now serve in your place.

ELESIN: I cannot approach. Take off the cloth. I shall speak my message from heart to heart of silence.

IYALOJA: [*Moves forward and removes the covering.*] Your courier Elesin, cast your eyes on the favoured companion of the King.

> [*Rolled up in the mat, his head and feet showing at either end, is the body of* OLUNDE.]

There lies the honour of your household and of our race. Because he could not bear to let honour fly out of doors, he stopped it with his life. The son has proved the father Elesin, and there is nothing left in your mouth to gnash but infant gums.

PRAISE-SINGER: Elesin, we placed the reins of the world in your hands yet you watched it plunge over the edge of the bitter precipice. You sat with folded arms while evil strangers tilted the world from its course and crashed it beyond the edge of emptiness—you muttered, there is little that one man can do, you left us floundering in a blind future. Your heir has taken the burden on himself. What the end will be, we are not gods to tell. But this young shoot has poured its sap into the parent stalk, and we know this is not the way of life. Our world is tumbling in the void of strangers, Elesin.

> [ELESIN *has stood rock-still, his knuckles taut on the bars, his eyes glued to the body of his son. The stillness seizes and paralyses everyone, including* PILKINGS *who has turned to look. Suddenly* ELESIN *flings one arm round his neck, once, and with the loop of the chain, strangles himself in a swift,*

2. Sacrifice.

decisive pull. The GUARDS rush forward to stop him but they are only in time to let his body down. PILKINGS has leapt to the door at the same time and struggles with the lock. He rushes within, fumbles with the handcuffs and unlocks them, raises the body to a sitting position while he tries to give resuscitation. The WOMEN continue their dirge, unmoved by the sudden event.]

IYALOJA: Why do you strain yourself? Why do you labour at tasks for which no one, not even the man lying there would give you thanks? He is gone at last into the passage but oh, how late it all is. His son will feast on the meat and throw him bones. The passage is clogged with droppings from the King's stallion; he will arrive all stained in dung.

PILKINGS: [In a tired voice.] Was this what you wanted?

IYALOJA: No child, it is what you brought to be, you who play with strangers' lives, who even usurp the vestments of our dead, yet believe that the stain of death will not cling to you. The gods demanded only the old expired plantain but you cut down the sap-laden shoot to feed your pride. There is your board, filled to overflowing. Feast on it. [She screams at him suddenly, seeing that PILKINGS is about to close ELESIN's staring eyes.] Let him alone! However sunk he was in debt he is no pauper's carrion abandoned on the road. Since when have strangers donned clothes of indigo[3] before the bereaved cries out his loss?

[She turns to the BRIDE who has remained motionless throughout.] Child.

[The girl takes up a little earth, walks calmly into the cell and closes ELESIN's eyes. She then pours some earth over each eyelid and comes out again.]

Now forget the dead, forget even the living. Turn your mind only to the unborn.

[She goes off, accompanied by the BRIDE. The dirge rises in volume and the WOMEN continue their sway. Lights fade to a black-out.]

1975

3. Worn for mourning.

BESSIE HEAD
1937–1986

Bessie Head's works combine myth, legend, and oral tradition with realistic detail to portray the struggles of newly liberated southern Africa. Drawing on folktales, she relates them to modern African life to create a picture of contemporary society that is at once convincing and dreamlike. While suffering from mental illness and the effects of political oppression, Head managed to give voice in her writings to the people of Africa.

Born to a single mother in a South African mental asylum, Bessie Amelia Emery was adopted at birth by Nellie and George Heathcote. She grew up thinking of the Heathcotes as her parents and learned only as a teenager that she had a black father and a white mother; her mother had a history of mental illness and had been committed to the asylum when she became pregnant with a servant's child. The apartheid system of racial classification was formalized during her youth, and her adoptive parents were considered "colored" (that is, mixed race). Educated at St. Monica's Home, an Anglican mission school for colored girls, Head later taught at Clairwood Colored School. There, inspired by the teachings and writings of Mahatma Gandhi, Head developed an interest in Hinduism. "Never have I read anything that aroused my feelings like Gandhi's political statements," she later wrote. "There was a simple and astonishing clarity in the way he summarized political truths, there was an appalling tenderness and firmness in the man. I paused every now and then over his paper, almost swooning with worship because I recognized that this could only be God as man." She later worked as a court reporter in Cape Town, where she became interested in the Négritude and Pan-Africanist movements and began writing stories about social injustice. In 1960 she started a newspaper, *The Citizen*, focused on the injustices of apartheid. After marrying a fellow journalist, Harold Head, she moved to Serowe, Botswana, taking her infant son with her but leaving her husband behind in South Africa.

In Botswana, which had recently gained its independence from Britain, Head taught high school and continued writing fiction, receiving favorable reviews internationally for her first novel, *When the Rain Clouds Gather* (1969), which concerns a South African political prisoner who flees to Botswana. Around this time, Head began to suffer symptoms of bipolar disorder and schizophrenia. After denouncing the president of Botswana, Seretse Khama, as an assassin, Head was arrested by the police and confined in Lobatse Mental Hospital. As she recovered, she continued to write and in 1977 attended the University of Iowa's International Writing Program. In the next several years, she published a collection of short stories, two novels, an oral history of the village of Serowe, and *A Question of Power* (1974), a combination of fiction, autobiography, and political statement. These works often take up themes of cultural conflict similar to those in the works of her contemporary **Chinua Achebe**. Head traveled frequently to writers' conferences around the world, but after her estranged husband filed for divorce, she began to drink heavily, slipped into a coma, and died at age forty-eight. In one of her last published essays, "Why Do I Write?" she explained: "I am building a stairway to the stars. I have the authority to take the whole of mankind up there with me. That is why I write."

Head's works, many of which are set in Botswana, depict in realistic detail the lives of the downtrodden. They also have a mythic element. In "The Deep River: A Story of Ancient Tribal Migration," presented here, a traditional tale about the origins of a Botswanan ethnic group inspires a meditation on the conflicts between an imagined communal past and the pull of modern individuality, between a mythic origin in the "deep river" of the people, when individuals had no identity apart from the group, and a present defined by the sense of self and by notions of romantic love. Although Head narrates the story in a manner sympathetic to the claims of the individual, she laments the passing of what she sees as the unified traditional society. Similarly, while she quotes the opinions of old men about the events in the story, she attends to the concerns of the youngest wife, Rankwana. It is in the balance of these sympathies that Head manages to retell the old tale for a contemporary audience, both celebrating traditional culture and acknowledging its limitations.

The Deep River: A Story of Ancient Tribal Migration

Long ago, when the land was only cattle tracks and footpaths, the people lived together like a deep river. In this deep river which was unruffled by conflict or a movement forward, the people lived without faces, except for their chief, whose face was the face of all the people; that is, if their chief's name was Monemapee, then they were all the people of Monemapee. The Talaote tribe have forgotten their origins and their original language during their journey southwards—they have merged and remerged again with many other tribes—and the name, Talaote,[1] is all they have retained in memory of their history. Before a conflict ruffled their deep river, they were all the people of Monemapee, whose kingdom was somewhere in the central part of Africa.

They remembered that Monemapee ruled the tribe for many years as the hairs on his head were already saying white! by the time he died. On either side of the deep river there might be hostile tribes or great dangers, so all the people lived in one great town. The lands where they ploughed their crops were always near the town. That was done by all the tribes for their own protection, and their day-to-day lives granted them no individual faces either for they ploughed their crops, reared their children, and held their festivities according to the laws of the land.

Although the people were given their own ploughing lands, they had no authority to plough them without the chief's order. When the people left home to go to plough, the chief sent out the proclamation for the beginning of the ploughing season. When harvest time came, the chief perceived that the corn was ripe. He gathered the people together and said:

'Reap now, and come home.'

When the people brought home their crops, the chief called the thanksgiving for the harvest. Then the women of the whole town carried their corn in flat baskets, to the chief's place. Some of that corn was accepted on its arrival, but the rest was returned so that the women might soak it in their own yards. After a few days, the chief sent his special messenger to proclaim that the harvest thanksgiving corn was to be pounded. The special messenger went around the whole town and in each place where there was a little hill or mound, he climbed it and shouted:

'Listen, the corn is to be pounded!'

So the people took their sprouting corn and pounded it. After some days the special messenger came back and called out:

'The corn is to be fermented now!'

1. An ethnic group in central Botswana, originally from Zimbabwe.

A few days passed and then he called out:
  'The corn is to be cooked now!'

So throughout the whole town the beer was boiled and when it had been strained, the special messenger called out for the last time:
  'The beer is to be brought now!'

On the day on which thanksgiving was to be held, the women all followed one another in single file to the chief's place. Large vessels had been prepared at the chief's place, so that when the women came they poured the beer into them. Then there was a gathering of all the people to celebrate thanksgiving for the harvest time. All the people lived this way, like one face, under their chief. They accepted this regimental levelling down of their individual souls, but on the day of dispute or when strife and conflict and greed blew stormy winds over their deep river, the people awoke and showed their individual faces.

Now, during his lifetime Monemapee had had three wives. Of these marriages he had four sons: Sebembele by the senior wife; Ntema and Mosemme by the second junior wife; and Kgagodi by the third junior wife. There was a fifth son, Makobi, a small baby who was still suckling at his mother's breast by the time the old chief, Monemapee, died. This mother was the third junior wife, Rankwana. It was about the fifth son, Makobi, that the dispute arose. There was a secret there. Monemapee had married the third junior wife, Rankwana, late in his years. She was young and beautiful and Sebembele, the senior son, fell in love with her—but in secret. On the death of Monemapee, Sebembele, as senior son, was installed chief of the tribe and immediately made a blunder. He claimed Rankwana as his wife and exposed the secret that the fifth son, Makobi, was his own child and not that of his father.

This news was received with alarm by the people as the first ripples of trouble stirred over the even surface of the river of their lives. If both the young man and the old man were visiting the same hut, they reasoned, perhaps the old man had not died a normal death. They questioned the councillors who knew all secrets.

'Monemapee died just walking on his own feet,' they said reassuringly.

That matter settled, the next challenge came from the two junior brothers, Ntema and Mosemme. If Sebembele were claiming the child, Makobi, as his son, they said, it meant that the young child displaced them in seniority. That they could not allow. The subtle pressure exerted on Sebembele by his junior brothers and the councillors was that he should renounce Rankwana and the child and all would be well. A chief lacked nothing and there were many other women more suitable as wives. Then Sebembele made the second blunder. In a world where women were of no account, he said truthfully:

'The love between Rankwana and I is great.'

This was received with cold disapproval by the councillors.

'If we were you,' they said, 'we would look for a wife somewhere else. A ruler must not be carried away by his emotions. This matter is going to cause disputes among the people.'

They noted that on being given this advice, Sebembele became very quiet, and they left him to his own thoughts, thinking that sooner or later he would come to a decision that agreed with theirs.

In the meanwhile the people quietly split into two camps. The one camp said:

'If he loves her, let him keep her. We all know Rankwana. She is a lovely person, deserving to be the wife of a chief.'

The other camp said:

'He must be mad. A man who is influenced by a woman is no ruler. He is like one who listens to the advice of a child. This story is really bad.'

There was at first no direct challenge to the chieftaincy which Sebembele occupied. But the nature of the surprising dispute, that of his love for a woman and a child, caused it to drag on longer than time would allow. Many evils began to rear their heads like impatient hissing snakes, while Sebembele argued with his own heart or engaged in tender dialogues with his love, Rankwana.

'I don't know what I can do,' Sebembele said, torn between the demands of his position and the strain of a love affair which had been conducted in deep secrecy for many, many months. The very secrecy of the affair seemed to make it shout all the louder for public recognition. At one moment his heart would urge him to renounce the woman and child, but each time he saw Rankwana it abruptly said the opposite. He could come to no decision.

It seemed little enough that he wanted for himself—the companionship of a beautiful woman to whom life had given many other attractive gifts; she was gentle and kind and loving. As soon as Sebembele communicated to her the advice of the councillors, she bowed her head and cried a little.

'If that is what they say, my love,' she said in despair, 'I have no hope left for myself and the child. It were better if we were both dead.'

'Another husband could be chosen for you,' he suggested.

'You doubt my love for you, Sebembele,' she said. 'I would kill myself if I lose you. If you leave me, I would kill myself.'

Her words had meaning for him because he was trapped in the same kind of anguish. It was a terrible pain which seemed to paralyse his movements and thoughts. It filled his mind so completely that he could think of nothing else, day and night. It was like a sickness, this paralysis, and like all ailments it could not be concealed from sight; Sebembele carried it all around with him.

'Our hearts are saying many things about this man,' the councillors said among themselves. They were saying that he was unmanly; that he was unfit to be a ruler; that things were slipping from his hands. Those still sympathetic approached him and said:

'Why are you worrying yourself like this over a woman, Sebembele? There are no limits to the amount of wives a chief may have, but you cannot have that woman and that child.'

And he only replied with a distracted mind: 'I don't know what I can do.'

But things had been set in motion. All the people were astir over events; if a man couldn't make up his mind, other men could make it up for him.

Everything was arranged in secret and on an appointed day Rankwana and the child were forcibly removed back to her father's home. Ever since the controversy had started, her father had been harassed day and night by the councillors as an influence that could help to end it. He had been reduced to a state of agitated muttering to himself by the time she was brought before him. The plan was to set her up with a husband immediately and settle the matter. She was not yet formally married to Sebembele.

'You have put me in great difficulties, my child,' her father said, looking away from her distressed face. 'Women never know their own minds and once this has passed away and you have many children you will wonder what all the fuss was about.'

'Other women may not know their minds . . .' she began, but he stopped her with a raised hand, indicating the husband who had been chosen for her. In all the faces surrounding her there was no sympathy or help, and she quietly allowed herself to be led away to her new home.

When Sebembele arrived in his own yard after a morning of attending to the affairs of the land, he found his brothers, Ntema and Mosemme there.

'Why have you come to visit me?' he asked, with foreboding. 'You never come to visit me. It would seem that we are bitter enemies rather than brothers.'

'You have shaken the whole town with your madness over a woman,' they replied mockingly. 'She is no longer here so you don't have to say any longer "I-don't-know-what-I-can-do". But we still request that you renounce the child, Makobi, in a gathering before all the people, in order that our position is clear. You must say: "That child Makobi is the younger brother of my brothers, Ntema and Mosemme, and not the son of Sebembele who rules".'

Sebembele looked at them for a long moment. It was not hatred he felt but peace at last. His brothers were forcing him to leave the tribe.

'Tell the people that they should all gather together,' he said. 'But what I say to them is my own affair.'

The next morning the people of the whole town saw an amazing sight which stirred their hearts. They saw their ruler walk slowly and unaccompanied through the town. They saw him pause at the yard of Rankwana's father. They saw Sebembele and Rankwana's father walk to the home of her new husband where she had been secreted. They saw Rankwana and Sebembele walk together through the town. Sebembele held the child Makobi in his arms. They saw that they had a ruler who talked with deeds rather than words. They saw that the time had come for them to offer up their individual faces to the face of this ruler. But the people were still in two camps. There was a whole section of the people who did not like this face; it was too out-of-the-way and shocking; it made them very uneasy. Theirs was not a tender, compassionate, and romantic world. And yet in a way it was. The arguments in the other camp which supported Sebembele had flown thick and fast all this time, and they said:

'Ntema and Mosemme are at the bottom of all this trouble. What are they after for they have set a difficult problem before us all? We don't trust them. But why not? They have not yet had time to take anything from us. Perhaps we ought to wait until they do something really bad; at present they are only filled with indignation at the behaviour of Sebembele. But no, we don't trust them. We don't like them. It is Sebembele we love, even though he has shown himself to be a man with a weakness . . .'

That morning, Sebembele completely won over his camp with his extravagant, romantic gesture, but he lost everything else and the rulership of the kingdom of Monemapee.

When all the people had gathered at the meeting place of the town, there were not many arguments left. One by one the councillors stood up and condemned the behaviour of Sebembele. So the two brothers, Ntema and Mosemme won the day. Still working together as one voice, they stood up and asked if their senior brother had any words to say before he left with his people.

'Makobi is my child,' he said.

'Talaote,' they replied, meaning in the language then spoken by the tribe—'all right, you can go'.

And the name Talaote was all they were to retain of their identity as the people of the kingdom of Monemapee. That day, Sebembele and his people packed their belongings on the backs of their cattle and slowly began the journey southwards. They were to leave many ruins behind them and it is said that they lived, on the journey southwards, with many other tribes like the Baphaleng, Bakaa, and Batswapong until they finally settled in the land of the Bamangwato.[2] To this day there is a separate Botalaote ward in the capital village of the Bamangwato, and the people refer to themselves still as the people of Talaote. The old men there keep on giving confused and contradictory accounts of their origins, but they say they lost their place of birth over a woman. They shake their heads and say that women have always caused a lot of trouble in the world. They say that the child of their chief was named, Talaote, to commemorate their expulsion from the kingdom of Monemapee.

FOOTNOTE:
The story is an entirely romanticized and fictionalized version of the history of the Botalaote tribe. Some historical data was given to me by the old men of the tribe, but it was unreliable as their memories had tended to fail them. A re-construction was made therefore in my own imagination; I am also partly indebted to the London Missionary Society's 'Livingstone Tswana Readers', Padiso III, school textbook, for those graphic paragraphs on the harvest thanksgiving ceremony which appear in the story.

B. HEAD.

1977

2. Ethnic groups in Botswana.

SALMAN RUSHDIE
born 1947

Salman Rushdie, whose extended family lives in India as well as Pakistan, published his fourth novel, *The Satanic Verses*, in England in September 1988. On Valentine's Day 1989, Ayatollah Ruholla Khomeini, then the leader of Shi'a Muslims in Iran, issued a *fatwa*, or religious decree, urging Muslims around the world to murder Rushdie for his acts of blasphemy against Islam in writing the novel. With typical irony, Rushdie called the *fatwa* an unusually harsh "book review." The incident sparked off a global controversy about freedom of expression, modernity, and "Islam versus the West," and Rushdie had to live underground for a decade, with maximum security provided by the British secret service. For many readers ever since, the international fallout from *The Satanic Verses* has been a public measure of its literary value, and a confirmation of Rushdie's status as the world's most important living writer.

Rushdie was born into a wealthy Muslim business family in Bombay in 1947, a few weeks before the end of British colonial rule and the Partition of the subcontinent into the two new nations of India and Pakistan. After early education in the city, Rushdie attended boarding school in England and received his undergraduate and master's degrees from the University of Cambridge, where he studied Islamic history. He worked in advertising in London for several years, and wrote his first book—a science-fiction novel—on the side. With the publication of *Midnight's Children* (1980) and its immense literary and commercial success, however, Rushdie was able to turn to writing full time, contributing to periodicals throughout the anglophone world in the 1980s while producing his next two novels, *Shame* (1983) and *The Satanic Verses*.

During his retreat from public view for a dozen years after the Ayatollah Khomeini's *fatwa*, Rushdie's "normal" life was seriously interrupted—two of his first three marriages ended—but seemingly the experience did not affect his creativity. In fact, the voluminous, multifarious criticism of his work and the continued threat to his life strengthened his resolve to imagine, write, and speak his mind as freely as possible. Among his important works published during this period were *The Moor's Last Sigh* (1995), the surreal saga of an Indian family of Jewish Portuguese descent, with connections to the last Muslim ruler of Moorish Spain in the fifteenth century, and *The Ground Beneath Her Feet* (1999), a novel about a love triangle interwoven with the Greek myth of Orpheus and Eurydice. Around the end of the millennium, Rushdie eased back into public life by moving to the United States, teaching at various universities as a writer-in-residence, and reading from his work and speaking to large audiences. In the first decade of the twenty-first century, his novels—such as *Shalimar the Clown* (2005) and *The Enchantress of Florence* (2008)—and a book for children, *Luka and the Fire of Life* (2010), have not won as much acclaim as his early work. Rushdie's preeminence among his contemporaries was affirmed when the Booker Prize was awarded to *Midnight's Children* in 1981; the novel's enduring achievement was confirmed by special Booker awards, in 1993 and 2008. As a naturalized British citizen, Rushdie was knighted in 2007; toward the end of the decade, he began to spend time in London again, helping his third (former) wife to raise their son.

Rushdie has frequently described himself as a "historian of ideas," and many of his novels are "novels of ideas" rather than narratives centered on plot or character. He is not a realistic writer; he is the foremost practitioner in English of magic realism. Invented before the middle of the twentieth century by Latin American fiction writers, who popularized the genre in the 1950s and 1960s, magic realism is a mode or style in which "reality" is permeated by supernatural forces, miraculous events, larger-than-life presences, and extraordinary characters who may possess magical powers. In his works of magic realism, Rushdie creates characters, objects, and occurrences that break the rules of everyday logic and causality: a person may be present in two places at once, for example, or a human being may travel in time, or live for centuries. Rushdie's goal is to bring the reader closer to reality, which has its rational or rationally explicable features (as described by science) but is also irrational, unpredictable, and bizarre. If magic realism gives Rushdie's work its dimension of fantasy, his fascination with ideas gives it the quality of abstraction. Many of his characters are allegorical, or personifications of ideas: Saleem Sinai, the protagonist of *Midnight's Children*, for instance, is an embodiment of "the idea of India," with his large nose shaped like the country's peninsula on a map, and his physique threatening to break up into 580 million pieces, as many as India's population at the time of writing. In *The Satanic Verses*, a voice asks one of the novel's characters: "What kind of idea are you?" Unlike realistically represented characters, Rushdie's have inner conflicts not of emotions or passions but of ideas.

Rushdie builds his narratives around conflicting ideas and fantastic characters and events with wit and playfulness, and with precise attention to the sensuous details of everyday life. A significant element of his disorienting realism comes from the use of newspaper reports of current events and historical accounts. *Midnight's Children* and *Shame*, for example, draw extensively on the journalistic record on contemporary India and Pakistan, respectively; much of *The Satanic Verses*, *The Moor's Last Sigh*, and *The Enchantress of Florence* relies on readers' historical knowledge of diverse regions of the world, from Arabia in the seventh century, and Spain and Portugal between the eighth and fifteenth centuries, to Italy in the high Renaissance. These shifts in place and time stem from Rushdie's interest in large-scale flux and transformation in human societies: he is the foremost writer of our times on migration, immigrant communities, diasporas, and cultural mixing, or hybridity.

"The Perforated Sheet," the selection below, reads like a self-contained

short story but is actually an excerpt, prepared by Rushdie himself, from the first two chapters of *Midnight's Children*, with a few connecting lines not found in the novel. It introduces us to Saleem Sinai, the protagonist and narrator, and to the story of his life and origins, which constitutes the novel's Protean narrative. Saleem is born at midnight, between August 14 and 15, 1947, the moment at which India and Pakistan became separate nations; as a "child" of that historic hour, he finds that his destiny is entwined with India's fate as a nation, so that his life unfolds as a precise parallel to the country's collective history thereafter. In "The Perforated Sheet" we encounter the beginning of that story as Saleem sees it: the time, almost half a century before his birth, when his grandfather returns from Europe with a medical degree; sets up a practice in his hometown of Srinagar, Kashmir; and meets the woman who is destined to become his wife, thereby launching the cascade of events that will culminate, two generations later, in Saleem's momentous arrival.

In the novel itself, every important event in the history of the Sinai family, from Saleem's grandparents onward, is a funny, farcical echo of every major event in the history of the Indian subcontinent. Thus Saleem's birth coincides with the birth of the nation of India. And, since the twin nations of India and Pakistan (which represent the religions of Hinduism and Islam, respectively) are born at the same moment, the birth of Saleem (a Muslim boy) coincides, as well, with the birth of his hateful "nemesis," Shiva (a Hindu boy). Saleem and Shiva's lives, from infancy to adulthood, then replicate the simultaneous histories of India/Hinduism and Pakistan/Islam. This comical story is complicated by the fact that a poor Christian nurse at the hospital where Saleem and Shiva are born (to different mothers) switches the babies, as an act of impersonal class revenge on their well-to-do parents. Saleem, who grows up in the Sinai family believing that he is a Muslim, is actually the biological son of a Hindu mother, and the reverse is true of Shiva.

A further fictional complication then ensues. During the first hour after the fateful midnight of August 14–15, 1947, exactly 1,001 children are born in India and Pakistan, and all of them—including Saleem and Shiva—possess magical powers. They are, as it were, the Chosen Ones; they are all "Midnight's Children" (hence the novel's title), they can tele-pathically connect with one another, and their individual destinies are intertwined with their nations' and each other's destinies, down to the last detail. Saleem grows up with an inexplicable "buzzing" in his head, and discovers that it is the buzz of the voices of hundreds of other Midnight's Children, with whom he can communicate directly. The culmination of the narrative is that everything that happens on the Indian subcontinent after 1947 has only one objective: to destroy these gifted children. "The Perforated Sheet" is thus the beginning of a story that is at once comic and tragic, on an epic scale.

The Perforated Sheet[1]

I was born in the city of Bombay . . . once upon a time. No, that won't do, there's no getting away from the date: I was born in Doctor Narlikar's Nursing Home on August 15th, 1947.[2] And the time? The time matters, too. Well then: at night. No, it's important to be more . . . On the stroke of midnight, as a matter of fact. Clock-hands joined palms in respectful greeting as I came. Oh, spell it out, spell it out: at the precise instant of India's arrival at independence, I tumbled forth into the world. There were gasps. And, outside the window, fireworks and crowds. A few seconds later, my father broke his big toe; but his accident was a mere trifle when set beside what had befallen me in that benighted moment, because thanks to the occult tyrannies of those blandly saluting clocks I had been mysteriously handcuffed to history, my destinies indissolubly chained to those of my country. For the next three decades, there was to be no escape. Soothsayers had prophesied me, newspapers celebrated my arrival, politicos ratified my authenticity. I was left entirely without a say in the matter. I, Saleem Sinai, later variously called Snotnose, Stainface, Baldy, Sniffer, Buddha and even Piece-of-the-Moon, had become heavily embroiled in Fate—at the best of times a dangerous sort of involvement. And I couldn't even wipe my own nose at the time.

Now, however, time (having no further use for me) is running out. I will soon be thirty-one years old. Perhaps. If my crumbling, over-used body permits. But I have no hope of saving my life, nor can I count on having even a thousand nights and a night. I must work fast, faster than Scheherazade,[3] if I

1. Excerpted by the author from the first two chapters of *Midnight's Children*, with connecting material not in the original novel.
2. The date is that of India's official independence from British colonial rule.

3. Shahrazad, the narrator in the *Arabian Nights*, who, night after night, tells stories to Prince Shahrayar, the kingdom's ruler, in order to defer, perhaps indefinitely, her execution.

am to end up meaning—yes, meaning—something. I admit it: above all things, I fear absurdity.

And there are so many stories to tell, too many, such an excess of intertwined lives events miracles places rumours, so dense a commingling of the improbable and the mundane! I have been a swallower of lives; and to know me, just the one of me, you'll have to swallow the lot as well. Consumed multitudes are jostling and shoving inside me; and guided only by the memory of a large white bedsheet with a roughly circular hole some seven inches in diameter cut into the centre, clutching at the dream of that holey, mutilated square of linen, which is my talisman, my open-sesame, I must commence the business of remaking my life from the point at which it really began, some thirty-two years before anything as obvious, as *present*, as my clock-ridden crime-stained birth.

(The sheet, incidentally, is stained too, with three drops of old, faded redness. As the Quran tells us: *Recite, in the name of the Lord thy Creator, who created Man from clots of blood.*)

One Kashmiri morning in the early spring of 1915, my grandfather Aadam Aziz[4] hit his nose against a frost-hardened tussock of earth while attempting to pray. Three drops of blood plopped out of his left nostril, hardened instantly in the brittle air and lay before his eyes on the prayer-mat, transformed into rubies. Lurching back until he knelt with his head once more upright, he found that the tears which had sprung to his eyes had solidified, too; and at that moment, as he brushed diamonds contemptuously from his lashes, he resolved never again to kiss earth for any god or man. This decision, however, made a hole in him, a vacancy in a vital inner chamber, leaving him vulnerable to women and history. Unaware of this at first, despite his recently completed medical training, he stood up, rolled the prayer-mat into a thick cheroot, and holding it under his right arm surveyed the valley through clear, diamond-free eyes.

The world was new again. After a winter's gestation in its eggshell of ice, the valley had beaked its way out into the open, moist and yellow. The new grass bided its time underground: the mountains were retreating to their hill-stations for the warm season. (In the winter, when the valley shrank under the ice, the mountains closed in and snarled like angry jaws around the city on the lake.)

In those days the radio mast had not been built and the temple of Sankara Acharya, a little black blister on a khaki hill, still dominated the streets and lake of Srinagar.[5] In those days there was no army camp at the lakeside, no endless snakes of camouflaged trucks and jeeps clogged the narrow mountain roads, no soldiers hid behind the crests of the mountains past Baramulla and Gulmarg.[6] In those days travellers were not shot as spies if they took photographs of bridges, and apart from the Englishmen's houseboats on the lake, the

---

4. A Muslim name; "Aadam" is the Arabic equivalent of Adam.
5. The main city in the Valley of Kashmir, now in the northernmost state of India, Srinagar is set on Lake Dal. In the late classical period (ca. 8th to 11th centuries), Kashmir was a Hindu kingdom famous for its patron-

age of learning and the arts; Shankara Acharya (ca. 8th century) was the period's most influential Hindu philosopher and theologian.
6. Situated close to the western edge of Kashmir, Baramulla is the second-largest city in the region, after Srinagar. Gulmarg is a famous ski resort near Baramulla.

valley had hardly changed since the Mughal Empire,[7] for all its springtime renewals; but my grandfather's eyes—which were, like the rest of him, twenty-five years old—saw things differently . . . and his nose had started to itch.

To reveal the secret of my grandfather's altered vision: he had spent five years, five springs, away from home. (The tussock of earth, crucial though its presence was as it crouched under a chance wrinkle of the prayer-mat, was at bottom no more than a catalyst.) Now, returning, he saw through travelled eyes. Instead of the beauty of the tiny valley circled by giant teeth, he noticed the narrowness, the proximity of the horizon; and felt sad, to be at home and feel so utterly enclosed. He also felt—inexplicably—as though the old place resented his educated, stethoscoped return. Beneath the winter ice, it had been coldly neutral, but now there was no doubt; the years in Germany had returned him to a hostile environment. Many years later, when the hole inside him had been clogged up with hate, and he came to sacrifice himself at the shrine of the black stone god in the temple on the hill, he would try and recall his childhood springs in Paradise,[8] the way it was before travel and tussocks and army tanks messed everything up.

On the morning when the valley, gloved in a prayer-mat,[9] punched him on the nose, he had been trying, absurdly, to pretend that nothing had changed. So he had risen in the bitter cold of four-fifteen, washed himself in the pre-scribed fashion, dressed and put on his father's astrakhan cap; after which he had carried the rolled cheroot of the prayer-mat into the small lakeside garden in front of their old dark house and unrolled it over the waiting tussock. The ground felt deceptively soft under his feet and made him simultaneously uncer-tain and unwary. 'In the Name of God, the Compassionate, the Merci-ful . . .'—the exordium, spoken with hands joined before him like a book, comforted a part of him, made another, larger part feel uneasy—'. . . Praise be to Allah, Lord of the Creation . . .'[1]—but now Heidelberg invaded his head; here was Ingrid, briefly his Ingrid, her face scorning him for this Mecca-turned parroting; here, their friends Oskar and Ilse Lubin the anarchists, mocking his prayer with their anti-ideologies—'. . . The Compassionate, the Merciful. King of the Last Judgment! . . .'—Heidelberg, in which, along with medicine and politics, he learned that India—like radium—had been 'discovered' by the Europeans; even Oskar was filled with admiration for Vasco da Gama,[2] and this was what finally separated Aadam Aziz from his friends, this belief of theirs that he was somehow the invention of their ancestors—'. . . You alone we wor-ship, and to You alone we pray for help . . .'—so here he was, despite their presence in his head, attempting to re-unite himself with an earlier self which

---

7. The subcontinent's largest and wealthiest empire, the Mughal Empire lasted from 1526 to 1858. "Mughal" is a variation on "Mongol"; the Mughals were descended matrilineally from the Mongolian conqueror Genghis Khan (late 12th–early 13th centuries).
8. The Mughal emperor Jahangir (ruled 1600–25) called Kashmir "Paradise," and the epithet has been popular ever since.
9. As prescribed for Muslims, Aadam Aziz prays five times a day, kneeling on his prayer mat; his injury occurs during one of his prayers.
1. Aadam Aziz's words of prayer are from the Qur'an, and invoke Allah, the one and only true God in Islam.
2. Vasco da Gama (ca. 1460–1524), Portu-guese explorer and first European to navigate the sea route from Europe, around Africa, to India, in 1498.

ignored their influence but knew everything it ought to have known, about submission for example, about what he was doing now, as his hands, guided by old memories, fluttered upwards, thumbs pressed to ears, fingers spread, as he sank to his knees—'. . . Guide us to the straight path. The path of those whom You have favoured . . .' But it was no good, he was caught in a strange middle ground, trapped between belief and disbelief, and this was only a charade after all—'. . . Not of those who have incurred Your wrath. Nor of those who have gone astray.' My grandfather bent his forehead towards the earth. Forward he bent, and the earth, prayer-mat-covered, curved up towards him. And now it was the tussock's time. At one and the same time a rebuke from Ilse-Oskar-Ingrid-Heidelberg as well as valley-and-God, it smote him upon the point of the nose. Three drops fell. There were rubies and diamonds. And my grandfather, lurching upright, made a resolve. Stood. Rolled cheroot. Stared across the lake. And was knocked forever into that middle place, unable to worship a God in whose existence he could not wholly disbelieve. Permanent alteration: a hole.

The lake was no longer frozen over. The thaw had come rapidly, as usual; many of the small boats, the shikaras, had been caught napping, which was also normal. But while these sluggards slept on, on dry land, snoring peacefully beside their owners, the oldest boat was up at the crack as old folk often are, and was therefore the first craft to move across the unfrozen lake. Tai's shikara . . . this, too, was customary.

Watch how the old boatman,[3] Tai, makes good time through the misty water, standing stooped over at the back of his craft! How his oar, a wooden heart on a yellow stick, drives jerkily through the weeds! In these parts he's considered very odd because he rows standing up . . . among other reasons. Tai, bringing an urgent summons to Doctor Aziz, is about to set history in motion . . . while Aadam, looking down into the water, recalls what Tai taught him years ago: 'The ice is always waiting, Aadam baba,[4] just under the water's skin.' Aadam's eyes are a clear blue, the astonishing blue of mountain sky, which has a habit of dripping into the pupils of Kashmiri men; they have not forgotten how to look. They see—there! like the skeleton of a ghost, just beneath the surface of Lake Dall—the delicate tracery, the intricate crisscross of colourless lines, the cold waiting veins of the future. His German years, which have blurred so much else, haven't deprived him of the gift of seeing. Tai's gift. He looks up, sees the approaching V of Tai's boat, waves a greeting. Tai's arm rises—but this is a command. 'Wait!' My grandfather waits; and during this hiatus, as he experiences the last peace of his life, a muddy, ominous sort of peace, I had better get round to describing him.

Keeping out of my voice the natural envy of the ugly man for the strikingly impressive, I record that Doctor Aziz was a tall man. Pressed flat against a wall of his family home, he measured twenty-five bricks (a brick for each year of his life), or just over six foot two. A strong man also. His beard was thick and red—and annoyed his mother, who said only Hajis, men who had made the pilgrim-

---

3. Tai operates a ferry boat on Lake Dal in Srinagar.
4. In Hindu and Urdu, "baba" is a term of respect (for a social superior) as well as of affec-

tion (for a child, an adult, or an old person); here Tai, an old man, uses it in both senses at once.

age to Mecca, should grow red beards. His hair, however, was rather darker. His sky-eyes you know about. Ingrid had said, 'They went mad with the colours when they made your face.' But the central feature of my grandfather's anatomy was neither colour nor height, neither strength of arm nor straightness of back. There it was, reflected in the water, undulating like a mad plantain in the centre of his face . . . Aadam Aziz, waiting for Tai, watches his rippling nose. It would have dominated less dramatic faces than his easily; even on him, it is what one sees first and remembers longest. 'A cyranose,' Ilse Lubin said, and Oskar added, 'A proboscissimus.' Ingrid announced, 'You could cross a river on that nose.' (Its bridge was wide.)

My grandfather's nose: nostrils flaring, curvaceous as dancers. Between them swells the nose's triumphal arch, first up and out, then down and under, sweeping in to his upper lip with a superb and at present red-tipped flick. An easy nose to hit a tussock with. I wish to place on record my gratitude to this mighty organ—if not for it, who would ever have believed me to be truly my mother's son, my grandfather's grandson?—this colossal apparatus which was to be my birthright, too. Doctor Aziz's nose—comparable only to the trunk of the elephant-headed god Ganesh—established incontrovertibly his right to be a patriarch. It was Tai who taught him that, too. When young Aadam was barely past puberty the dilapidated boatman said, 'That's a nose to start a family on, my princeling. There'd be no mistaking whose brood they were. Mughal Emperors would have given their right hands for noses like that one. There are dynasties waiting inside it,'—and here Tai lapsed into coarseness—'like snot.'

Nobody could remember when Tai had been young. He had been plying this same boat, standing in the same hunched position, across the Dal and Nageen Lakes . . . forever. As far as anyone knew. He lived somewhere in the insanitary bowels of the old wooden-house quarter and his wife grew lotus roots and other curious vegetables on one of the many 'floating gardens' lilting on the surface of the spring and summer water. Tai himself cheerily admitted he had no idea of his age. Neither did his wife—he was, she said, already leathery when they married. His face was a sculpture of wind on water: ripples made of hide. He had two golden teeth and no others. In the town, he had few friends. Few boatmen or traders invited him to share a hookah when he floated past the shikara moorings or one of the lakes' many ramshackle, waterside provision-stores and tea-shops.

The general opinion of Tai had been voiced long ago by Aadam Aziz's father the gemstone merchant: 'His brain fell out with his teeth.' It was an impression the boatman fostered by his chatter, which was fantastic, grandiloquent and ceaseless, and as often as not addressed only to himself. Sound carries over water, and the lake people giggled at his monologues; but with undertones of awe, and even fear. Awe, because the old halfwit knew the lakes and hills better than any of his detractors; fear, because of his claim to an antiquity so immense it defied numbering, and moreover hung so lightly round his chicken's neck that it hadn't prevented him from winning a highly desirable wife and fathering four sons upon her . . . and a few more, the story went, on other lakeside wives. The young bucks at the shikara moorings were convinced he had a pile of money hidden away somewhere—a hoard, perhaps, of priceless golden teeth, rattling in a sack like walnuts. And, as a child, Aadam Aziz had loved him.

2624 | SALMAN RUSHDIE

He made his living as a simple ferryman, despite all the rumours of wealth, taking hay and goats and vegetables and wood across the lakes for cash; people, too. When he was running his taxi-service he erected a pavilion in the centre of the shikara,[5] a gay affair of flowered-patterned curtains and canopy, with cushions to match; and deodorised his boat with incense. The sight of Tai's shikara approaching, curtains flying, had always been for Doctor Aziz one of the defining images of the coming of spring. Soon the English sahibs would arrive and Tai would ferry them to the Shalimar Gardens and the King's Spring, chattering and pointy and stooped, a quirky, enduring familiar spirit of the valley.[6] A watery Caliban, rather too fond of cheap Kashmiri brandy.

The Boy Aadam, my grandfather-to-be, fell in love with the boatman Tai precisely because of the endless verbiage which made others think him cracked. It was magical talk, words pouring from him like fools' money, past his two gold teeth, laced with hiccups and brandy, soaring up to the most remote Himalayas[7] of the past, then swooping shrewdly on some present detail, Aadam's nose for instance, to vivisect its meaning like a mouse. This friendship had plunged Aadam into hot water with great regularity. (Boiling water. Literally. While his mother said. 'We'll kill that boatman's bugs if it kills you.') But still the old soliloquist would dawdle in his boat at the garden's lakeside toes and Aziz would sit at his feet until voices summoned him indoors to be lectured on Tai's filthiness and warned about the pillaging armies of germs his mother envisaged leaping from that hospitably ancient body on to her son's starched white loose-pajamas. But always Aadam returned to the water's edge to scan the mists for the ragged reprobate's hunched-up frame steering its magical boat through the enchanted waters of the morning.

'But how old are you really, Taiji?'[8] (Doctor Aziz, adult, red-bearded, slanting towards the future, remembers the day he asked the unaskable question.) For an instant, silence, noisier than a waterfall. The monologue, interrupted. Slap of oar in water. He was riding in the shikara with Tai, squatting amongst goats, on a pile of straw, in full knowledge of the stick and bathtub waiting for him at home. He had come for stories—and with one question had silenced the storyteller.

'No, tell, Taiji, how old, *truly*?' And now a brandy bottle, materialising from nowhere: cheap liquor from the folds of the great warm chugha-coat. Then a shudder, a belch, a glare. Glint of gold. And—at last!—speech. 'How old? You ask how old, you little wet-head, you nosey . . .' Tai pointed at the mountains. 'So old, nakkoo!' Aadam, the nakkoo, the nosey one, followed his pointing finger. 'I have watched the mountains being born; I have seen Emperors die. Listen. Listen, nakkoo[9] . . .'—the brandy bottle again, followed by brandy-voice, and words more intoxicating than booze—'. . . I saw that Isa, that Christ, when he came to

5. A "shikara" is a distinctive, long rowboat used on Lake Dal, similar to a British double skiff used on the Thames. It transports people and goods around Srinagar.
6. The Shalimar Gardens are the modern form of the Mughal-style rose garden first laid near Srinagar for Emperor Jahangir in 1619.
7. The western end of the Himalayas, the world's highest mountain range, wraps around the north of Kashmir.

8. In Hindi and Urdu, the main languages of northern India, the suffix "-ji" is an honorific added to names and epithets, to address elders and superiors. Aadam Aziz addresses the "lowly" boatman as "Taiji" out of respect for the latter's age.
9. "Nakkoo," literally "nosy" in Hindi and Urdu, is Tai's playful epithet for the large-nosed Aadam Aziz.

Kashmir.[1] Smile, smile, it is your history I am keeping in my head. Once it was set down in old lost books. Once I knew where there was a grave with pierced feet carved on the tombstone, which bled once a year. Even my memory is going now; but I know, although I can't read.' Illiteracy, dismissed with a flourish; literature crumbled beneath the rage of his sweeping hand. Which sweeps again to chugha-pocket,[2] to brandy bottle, to lips chapped with cold. Tai always had woman's lips. 'Nakkoo, listen, listen. I have seen plenty. Yara,[3] you should've seen that Isa when he came, beard down to his balls, bald as an egg on his head. He was old and fagged-out but he knew his manners. "You first, Taiji," he'd say, and "Please to sit"; always a respectful tongue, he never called me crackpot, never called me *tu* either. Always *aap*.[4] Polite, see? And what an appetite! Such a hunger, I would catch my ears in fright. Saint or devil, I swear he could eat a whole kid in one go. And so what? I told him, eat, fill your hole, a man comes to Kashmir to enjoy life, or to end it, or both. His work was finished. He just came up here to live it up a little.' Mesmerised by this brandied portrait of a bald, gluttonous Christ, Aziz listened, later repeating every word to the consternation of his parents, who dealt in stones and had no time for 'gas'.

'Oh, you don't believe?'—licking his sore lips with a grin, knowing it to be the reverse of the truth; 'Your attention is wandering?'—again, he knew how furiously Aziz was hanging on his words. 'Maybe the straw is pricking your behind, hey? Oh, I'm so sorry, babaji, not to provide for you silk cushions with gold brocade-work—cushions such as the Emperor Jehangir[5] sat upon! You think the Emperor Jehangir as a gardener only, no doubt,' Tai accused my grandfather, 'because he built Shalimar. Stupid! What do you know? His name meant Encompasser of the Earth. Is that a gardener's name? God knows what they teach you boys these days. Whereas I'. . . puffing up a little here . . .'I knew his precise weight, to the tola! Ask me how many maunds, how many seers! When he was happy he got heavier and in Kashmir he was heaviest of all. I used to carry his litter . . . no, no, look, you don't believe again, that big cucumber in your face is waggling like the little one in your pajamas! So, come on, come on, ask me questions! Give examination! Ask how many times the leather thongs wound round the handles of the litter—the answer is thirty-one. Ask me what was the Emperor's dying word—I tell you it was "Kashmir". He had bad breath and a good heart. Who do you think I am? Some common ignorant lying piedog? Go, get out of the boat now, your nose makes it too heavy to row; also your father is waiting to beat my gas out of you, and your mother to boil off your skin.'

Despite beating and boiling, Aadam Aziz floated with Tai in his shikara, again and again, amid goats hay flowers furniture lotus-roots, though never with the English sahibs,[6] and heard again and again the miraculous answers to that single terrifying question: 'But Taiji, how old are you, *honestly?*'

---

1. An apocryphal legend in the Muslim and Hindu worlds is that at the end of his life, as recorded in the Bible, Jesus Christ left Jerusalem, living out his last days in Kashmir.
2. "Chuga" or "choga," the Persian word for a loose, cassocklike garment for Muslim men.
3. "Yara" is the common Urdu term of endearment for friend, buddy, loved one, or close companion.
4. In Hindi and Urdu, *tu* is the intimate or familiar form of "you," whereas *aap* is the formal, respectful form of the pronoun.
5. The fourth ruler in the Mughal dynasty, on the throne from 1600 to 1625.
6. "Sahib" is the Anglicized form of the Persian *saheb*, a respectful term of address for a rich or powerful man, a ruler or administrator, or a superior; it became the common epithet for British colonial administrators in India.

From Tai, Aadam learned the secrets of the lake—where you could swim without being pulled down by weeds; the eleven varieties of water-snake; where the frogs spawned; how to cook a lotus-root; and where the three English women had drowned a few years back. 'There is a tribe of feringhee women who come to this water to drown,' Tai said. 'Sometimes they know it, sometimes they don't, but I know the minute I smell them. They hide under the water from God knows what or who—but they can't hide from me, baba!' Tai's laugh, emerging to infect Aadam—a huge, booming laugh that seemed macabre when it crashed out of that old, withered body, but which was so natural in my giant grandfather that nobody knew, in later times, that it wasn't really his. And, also from Tai, my grandfather heard about noses.

Tai tapped his left nostril. 'You know what this is, nakkoo? It's the place where the outside world meets the world inside you. If they don't get on, you feel it here. Then you rub your nose with embarrassment to make the itch go away. A nose like that, little idiot, is a great gift. I say: trust it. When it warns you, look out or you'll be finished. Follow your nose and you'll go far.' He cleared his throat; his eyes rolled away into the mountains of the past. Aziz settled back on the straw. 'I knew one officer once—in the army of that Iskandar the Great. Never mind his name. He had a vegetable just like yours hanging between his eyes. When the army halted near Gandhara,[7] he fell in love with some local floozy. At once his nose itched like crazy. He scratched it, but that was useless. He inhaled vapours from crushed boiled eucalyptus leaves. Still no good, baba! The itching sent him wild; but the damn fool dug in his heels and stayed with his little witch when the army went home. He became—what?—a stupid thing, neither this nor that, a half-and-halfer with a nagging wife and an itch in the nose, and in the end he pushed his sword into his stomach. What do you think of that?'

Doctor Aziz in 1915, whom rubies and diamonds have turned into a half-and-halfer, remembers this story as Tai enters hailing distance. His nose is itching still. He scratches, shrugs, tosses his head; and then Tai shouts.

'Ohé! Doctor Sahib! Ghani the landowner's daughter is sick.'

. . . The young Doctor has entered the throes of a most unhippocratic excitement at the boatman's cry, and shouts, 'I'm coming just now! Just let me bring my things!' The shikara's prow touches the garden's hem. Aadam is rushing indoors, prayer-mat rolled like a cheroot under one arm, blue eyes blinking in the sudden interior gloom; he has placed the cheroot on a high shelf on top of stacked copies of *Vorwärts* and Lenin's *What Is To Be Done?*[8] and other pamphlets, dusty echoes of his half-faded German life; he is pulling out, from under his bed, a second-hand leather case which his mother called his 'doctori-attaché',[9] and as he swings it and himself upwards and runs from the room, the

---

7. "Iskandar" or "Sikandar" is the Indian equivalent of "Alexander" the Great, whose army reached the subcontinent in 327 B.C.E. The farthest north Alexander went was to Gandhara, the region now around Peshawar and the Swat Valley in northwest Pakistan. When he turned back, Alexander left behind a Greek colony in Gandhara, which flourished there for several centuries as the eastern outpost of his empire.

8. Lenin's small book, first published in 1902, quickly became a classic of Socialist and Communist theory and polemics, outlining a program that culminated in the Bolshevik Revolution of 1917 in Russia.

9. "Doctori-attaché" is an Indianized term for a doctor's satchel or attache case.

word HEIDELBERG is briefly visible, burned into the leather on the bottom of the bag. A landowner's daughter is good news indeed to a doctor with a career to make, even if she is ill. No: *because* she is ill.

. . . Slap of oar in water. Plop of spittle in lake. Tai clears his throat and mutters angrily, 'A fine business. A wet-head nakkoo child goes away before he's learned one damn thing and he comes back a big doctor sahib with a big bag full of foreign machines, and he's still as silly as an owl. I swear: a too bad business.'

. . .'Big shot,' Tai is spitting into the lake, 'big bag, big shot. Pah! We haven't got enough bags at home that you must bring back that thing made of a pig's skin that makes one unclean just by looking at it? And inside, God knows what all.' Doctor Aziz, seated amongst flowery curtains and the smell of incense, has his thoughts wrenched away from the patient waiting across the lake. Tai's bitter monologue breaks into his consciousness, creating a sense of dull shock, a smell like a casualty ward overpowering the incense . . . the old man is clearly furious about something, possessed by an incomprehensible rage that appears to be directed at his erstwhile acolyte, or, more precisely and oddly, at his bag. Doctor Aziz attempts to make small talk . . .'Your wife is well? Do they still talk about your bag of golden teeth?'. . . tries to remake an old friendship; but Tai is in full flight now, a stream of invective pouring out of him. The Heidelberg bag quakes under the torrent of abuse. 'Sistersleeping pigskin bag[1] from Abroad full of foreigners' tricks. Big-shot bag. Now if a man breaks an arm that bag will not let the bone-setter bind it in leaves. Now a man must let his wife lie beside that bag and watch knives come and cut her open. A fine business, what these foreigners put in our young men's heads. I swear: it is a too-bad thing. That bag should fry in Hell with the testicles of the ungodly.'

. . .'Do you still pickle water-snakes in brandy to give you virility, Taiji? Do you still like to eat lotus-root without any spices?' Hesitant questions, brushed aside by the torrent of Tai's fury. Doctor Aziz begins to diagnose. To the ferryman, the bag represents Abroad; it is the alien thing, the invader, progress. And yes, it has indeed taken possession of the young Doctor's mind: and yes, it contains knives, and cures for cholera and malaria and smallpox; and yes, it sits between doctor and boatman, and has made them antagonists. Doctor Aziz begins to fight, against sadness, and against Tai's anger, which is beginning to infect him, to become his own, which erupts only rarely, but comes, when it does come, unheralded in a roar from his deepest places, laying waste everything in sight; and then vanishes, leaving him wondering why everyone is so upset . . . They are approaching Ghani's house. A bearer awaits the shikara, standing with clasped hands on a little wooden jetty. Aziz fixes his mind on the job in hand.

The bearer[2] holds the shikara steady as Aadam Aziz climbs out, bag in hand. And now, at last, Tai speaks directly to my grandfather. Scorn in his face, Tai asks, 'Tell me this, Doctor Sahib: have you got in that bag made of dead pigs one of those machines that foreign doctors use to smell with?' Aadam shakes his head, not understanding. Tai's voice gathers new layers of disgust. 'You know, sir, a thing like an elephant's trunk.' Aziz, seeing what he means, replies:

---

1. Muslims and Semitic people consider the pig a polluting animal; a pigskin bag is therefore a proscribed object in this context. "Sistersleep-ing" is the narrator's playful variation on the most common curse word in Hindi and Urdu.
2. Common British-Indian colonial-era term for a servant, helper, or waiter.

'A stethoscope? Naturally.' Tai pushes the shikara off from the jetty. Spits. Begins to row away. 'I knew it,' he says. 'You will use such a machine now, instead of your own big nose.'

My grandfather does not trouble to explain that a stethoscope is more like a pair of ears than a nose. He is stifling his own irritation, the resentful anger of a cast-off child; and besides, there is a patient waiting.

The house was opulent but badly lit. Ghani was a widower and the servants clearly took advantage. There were cobwebs in corners and layers of dust on ledges. They walked down a long corridor; one of the doors was ajar and through it Aziz saw a room in a state of violent disorder. This glimpse, connected with a glint of light in Ghani's dark glasses, suddenly informed Aziz that the landowner was blind. This aggravated his sense of unease . . . They halted outside a thick teak door. Ghani said, 'Wait here two moments,' and went into the room behind the door.

In later years, Doctor Aadam Aziz swore that during those two moments of solitude in the gloomy spidery corridors of the landowner's mansion he was gripped by an almost uncontrollable desire to turn and run away as fast as his legs would carry him. Unnerved by the enigma of the blind art-lover, his insides filled with tiny scrabbling insects as a result of the insidious venom of Tai's mutterings, his nostrils itching to the point of convincing him that he had somehow contracted venereal disease, he felt his feet begin slowly, as though encased in boots of lead, to turn; felt blood pounding in his temples; and was seized by so powerful a sensation of standing upon a point of no return that he very nearly wet his German woollen trousers. He began, without knowing it, to blush furiously; and at this point a woman with the biceps of a wrestler appeared, beckoning him to follow her into the room. The state of her sari[3] told him that she was a servant; but she was not servile. 'You look green as a fish,' she said. 'You young doctors. You come into a strange house and your liver turns to jelly. Come, Doctor Sahib, they are waiting for you.' Clutching his bag a fraction too tightly, he followed her through the dark teak door.

. . . Into a spacious bedchamber that was as ill-lit as the rest of the house; although here there were shafts of dusty sunlight seeping in through a fanlight high on one wall. These fusty rays illuminated a scene as remarkable as anything the Doctor had ever witnessed: a tableau of such surpassing strangeness that his feet began to twitch towards the door once again. Two more women, also built like professional wrestlers, stood stiffly in the light, each holding one corner of an enormous white bedsheet, their arms raised high above their heads so that the sheet hung between them like a curtain.[4] Mr Ghani welled up out of the murk surrounding the sunlit sheet and permitted the nonplussed Aadam to stare stupidly at the peculiar tableau for perhaps half a minute, at the end of which, and before a word had been spoken, the Doctor made a discovery:

---

3. The sari, a full-body wrap, is the most common attire for adult Hindu women.
4. Muslim women are required to be fully "veiled" in the presence of men not belonging to their families or intimate social circles. In

this part of the novel, the bedsheet serving as a "curtain" between patient and doctor becomes an elaborate, comical proxy for the traditional Muslim veil.

In the very centre of the sheet, a hole had been cut, a crude circle about seven inches in diameter.

'Close the door, ayah.' Ghani instructed the first of the lady wrestlers, and then, turning to Aziz, became confidential. 'This town contains many good-for-nothings who have on occasion tried to climb into my daughter's room. She needs,' he nodded at the three musclebound women, 'protectors.'

Aziz was still looking at the perforated sheet. Ghani said, 'All right, come on, you will examine my Naseem right now. *Pronto.*'

My grandfather peered around the room. 'But where is she, Ghani Sahib?' he blurted out finally. The lady wrestlers adopted supercilious expressions and, it seemed to him, tightened their musculatures, just in case he intended to try something fancy.

'Ah, I see your confusion,' Ghani said, his poisonous smile broadening. 'You Europe-returned chappies forget certain things. Doctor Sahib, my daughter is a decent girl, it goes without saying. She does not flaunt her body under the noses of strange men. You will understand that you cannot be permitted to see her, no, not in any circumstances; accordingly I have required her to be positioned behind that sheet. She stands there, like a good girl.'

A frantic note had crept into Doctor Aziz's voice. 'Ghani Sahib, tell me how I am to examine her without looking at her?' Ghani smiled on.

'You will kindly specify which portion of my daughter it is necessary to inspect. I will then issue her with my instructions to place the required segment against that hole which you see there. And so, in this fashion the thing may be achieved.'

'But what, in any event, does the lady complain of?'—my grandfather, despairingly. To which Mr Ghani, his eyes rising upwards in their sockets, his smile twisting into a grimace of grief, replied: 'The poor child! She has a terrible, a too dreadful stomach-ache.'

'In that case,' Doctor Aziz said with some restraint, 'will she show me her stomach, please.'

My grandfather's premonitions in the corridor were not without foundation. In the succeeding months and years, he fell under what I can only describe as the sorcerer's spell of that enormous—and as yet unstained—perforated cloth.

In those years, you see, the landowner's daughter Naseem Ghani contracted a quite extraordinary number of minor illnesses, and each time a shikara-wallah was dispatched to summon the tall young Doctor Sahib with the big nose who was making such a reputation for himself in the valley. Aadam Aziz's visits to the bedroom with the shaft of sunlight and the three lady wrestlers became weekly events; and on each occasion he was vouchsafed a glimpse, through the mutilated sheet, of a different seven-inch circle of the young woman's body. Her initial stomach-ache was succeeded by a very slightly twisted right ankle, an ingrowing toenail on the big toe of the left foot, a tiny cut on the lower left calf. 'Tetanus is a killer, Doctor Sahib,' the landowner said. 'My Naseem must not die for a scratch.' There was the matter of her stiff right knee, which the Doctor was obliged to manipulate through the hole in the sheet . . . and after a time the illnesses leapt upwards, avoiding certain unmentionable zones, and began to proliferate around her upper half. She suffered from something mysterious which her father called Finger Rot, which made the skin flake off her hands; from weakness of the wrist-bones, for which Aadam prescribed calcium tablets; and from attacks of constipation, for which he gave her a course of laxatives, since there was no question of being permitted to administer an enema. She had fevers and she also had subnormal temperatures. At these times his thermometer would be placed under her armpit and he would hum and haw about the relative inefficiency of the method. In the opposite armpit she once developed a slight case of tineachloris and he dusted her with yellow powder; after this treatment—which required him to rub the powder in, gently but firmly, although the soft secret body began to shake and quiver and he heard helpless laughter coming through the sheet, because Naseem Ghani was very ticklish—the itching went away, but Naseem soon found a new set of complaints. She waxed anaemic in the summer and bronchial in the winter. ('Her tubes are most delicate,' Ghani explained, 'like little flutes.') Far away the Great War moved from crisis to crisis, while in the cobwebbed house Doctor Aziz was also engaged in a total war against his sectioned patient's inexhaustible complaints. And, in all those war years, Naseem never repeated an illness. 'Which only shows,' Ghani told him, 'that you are a good doctor. When you cure, she is cured for good. But alas!'—he struck his forehead—'She pines for her late mother, poor baby, and her body suffers. She is a too loving child.'

So gradually Doctor Aziz came to have a picture of Naseem in his mind, a badly-fitting collage of her severally-inspected parts. This phantasm of a partitioned woman began to haunt him, and not only in his dreams. Glued together by his imagination, she accompanied him on all his rounds, she moved into the front room of his mind, so that waking and sleeping he could feel in his fingertips the softness of her ticklish skin or the perfect tiny wrists or the beauty of the ankles; he could smell her scent of lavender and chambeli; he could hear her voice and her helpless laughter of a little girl; but she was headless, because he had never seen her face.

By 1918, Aadam Aziz had come to live for his regular trips across the lake. And now his eagerness became even more intense, because it became clear that, after three years, the landowner and his daughter had become willing to lower certain barriers. Now, for the first time, Ghani said, 'A lump in the right chest. Is it worrying, Doctor? Look. Look well.' And there, framed in the hole, was a perfectly-formed and lyrically lovely . . .'I must touch it,' Aziz said, fighting with his voice. Ghani slapped him on the back. 'Touch, touch!' he cried. 'The hands of the healer! The curing touch, eh, Doctor?' And Aziz reached out a hand . . .'Forgive me for asking; but is it the lady's time of the month?' . . . Little secret smiles appearing on the faces of the lady wrestlers. Ghani, nodding affably: 'Yes. Don't be so embarrassed, old chap. We are family and doctor now.' And Aziz, 'Then don't worry. The lumps will go when the time ends.' . . . And the next time, 'A pulled muscle in the back of her thigh, Doctor Sahib. Such pain!' And there, in the sheet, weakening the eyes of Aadam Aziz, hung a superbly rounded and impossible buttock . . . And now Aziz: 'Is it permitted that . . .' Whereupon a word from Ghani; an obedient reply from behind the sheet; a drawstring pulled; and pajamas fall from the celestial rump, which swells wondrously through the hole. Aadam Aziz forces himself into a medical frame of mind . . . reaches out . . . feels. And swears to himself, in amazement, that he sees the bottom reddening in a shy, but compliant blush.

That evening, Aadam contemplated the blush. Did the magic of the sheet work on both sides of the hole? Excitedly, he envisaged his headless Naseem tingling beneath the scrutiny of his eyes, his thermometer, his stethoscope, his fingers, and trying to build a picture in her mind of *him*. She was at a disadvantage, of course, having seen nothing but his hands . . . Aadam began to hope with an illicit desperation for Naseem Ghani to develop a migraine or graze her unseen chin, so they could look each other in the face. He knew how unprofessional his feelings were; but did nothing to stifle them. There was not much he could do. They had acquired a life of their own. In short: my grandfather had fallen in love, and had come to think of the perforated sheet as something sacred and magical, because through it he had seen the things which had filled up the hole inside him which had been created when he had been hit on the nose by a tussock and insulted by the boatman Tai.

On the day the World War ended, Naseem developed the longed-for headache. Such historical coincidences have littered, and perhaps befouled, my family's existence in the world.

He hardly dared to look at what was framed in the hole in the sheet. Maybe she was hideous; perhaps that explained all this performance . . . he looked. And saw a soft face that was not at all ugly, a cushioned setting for her glittering, gemstone eyes, which were brown with flecks of gold: tiger's-eyes. Doctor Aziz's fall was complete. And Naseem burst out, 'But Doctor, my God, what a *nose!*' Ghani, angrily, 'Daughter, mind your . . .' But patient and doctor were laughing together, and Aziz was saying, 'Yes, yes, it is a remarkable specimen. They tell me there are dynasties waiting in it . . .' And he bit his tongue because he had been about to add, '. . . like snot.'

And Ghani, who had stood blindly beside the sheet for three long years, smiling and smiling and smiling, began once again to smile his secret smile, which was mirrored in the lips of the wrestlers.

1980

JAMAICA KINCAID
born 1949

Born and raised among an extended family of "poor, ordinary people," "banana and citrus-fruit farmers, fishermen, carpenters and obeah women," Jamaica Kincaid rose from humble beginnings to become a successful contemporary writer, well known for her books and magazine articles about the immigrant experience. These works often convey a sense of immediacy through Kincaid's use of first-person narration or imagined dialogue.

Born Elaine Cynthia Potter Richardson in Antigua, a small island in the Caribbean, Kincaid grew up in the island's capital city of St. Johns. Part of the British Leeward Island chain, Antigua was a colony of Britain throughout the writer's childhood and adolescence; it gained political independence in 1981 and now belongs to the British Commonwealth. Kincaid's mother was a homemaker, and her stepfather worked as a carpenter (her biological father, a taxi driver, showed no interest in his children). Though Kincaid and her brothers were raised as Methodists, her mother and grandmother also practiced obeah, West Indian voodoo. Kincaid learned from them how to protect herself against the evil eye, how to appease local spirits, how to use herbs to conjure and heal—a familiarity with the supernatural that she later incorporated into her fiction.

At school, Kincaid was a quick student, taking a special interest in history and botany. Although her family had high aspirations for her three brothers and intended them to enter the professions, because Kincaid was a girl, they placed no value on her gifts: "No one expected anything from me at all," she later said. Her teachers often treated her eagerness in the classroom as a disciplinary problem. At thirteen, when Kincaid was about to take university qualifying examinations, her stepfather fell ill, forcing her to leave school and help raise her siblings. Angry and dispirited, she withdrew into books. Later she said that her passion for reading "saved her life." The island's colonial status meant that the local libraries and bookstores carried almost exclusively British literature, mainly of the nineteenth century. The lack of access to more recent works, or to the West Indian literary canon to which Kincaid would contribute so prominent a voice, prevented her at first from seeing art as more than an escape: "I thought writing was something that people just didn't do anymore, that went out of fashion, like the bustle."

Still, she chafed against her colonial upbringing and looked for ways to enter a wider world. At the age of seventeen she accepted a job as a nanny in the United States, and for four years lived with families in the New York City borough of Manhattan and in suburban Scarsdale. She earned a general equivalency diploma and briefly attended a college in New Hampshire before deciding she was too old. Back in Manhattan, and now determined to write, she started freelancing for magazines and weekly newspapers, including the *Village Voice*. It was during this period that she changed her name. Jamaica refers to the West Indies; Kincaid, to a work by the playwright George Bernard Shaw. She explained that the alteration allowed her to evade her family, who opposed her writing, as well as her broader colonial inheritance: the new name was "a way for me to do things without being the same person who couldn't do them—the same person who had all these weights."

Kincaid's first collection of short stories, *At the Bottom of the River*, appeared in 1983. An autobiographical novel, *Annie John*, followed in 1985; her second and third novels also draw on her own and her family's experiences in Antigua. She has continued to publish books and magazine articles and has won many prestigious awards, including the 2000 French Prix Femina Etranger. In recent years the author has turned her attention to nature writing and to botanical studies of the landscape. Throughout her career, though, Kincaid has retained a strong commitment to issues of identity, colonialism, and the color line. In *A Small Place*, written following Kincaid's first visit to Antigua since her youth, she criticizes what she sees as the island's complicity in its exploitation, carried over from the colonial past.

The story selected here, "Girl" (1978), was the first piece of fiction that Kincaid published. It consists of a single, winding sentence; the speaker is a mother giving instructions to her daughter on the rules and rites of womanhood. (The daughter's replies break into the narration in two passages, both printed in italics.) The setting is Antigua, although this point is never explicitly stated and can only be inferred from the story's details. Some of the instructions refer to folk medicine and obeah; for example, the warning against throwing stones at blackbirds, which might be malicious spirits in disguise. As the speaker discusses with equal matter-of-factness such topics as keeping house, enduring a cruel husband, and aborting unwanted pregnancies, a picture emerges of the harshness of countless women's lives, not just in this setting but throughout history and across the globe. During the lecture, the mother stresses how important it is for a young woman to maintain a sense of sexual propriety: the woman warns her daughter repeatedly that she will look like a "slut" if she does not behave properly. The edict against squatting to play marbles suggests that the listener has not left childhood entirely, but the early reference to washing "your little cloths" indicates that she has reached puberty and that the time when these instructions will come into use is not far off.

Girl

Wash the white clothes on Monday and put them on the stone heap; wash the color clothes on Tuesday and put them on the clothesline to dry; don't walk barehead in the hot sun; cook pumpkin fritters in very hot sweet oil; soak your little cloths[1] right after you take them off; when buying cotton to make yourself a nice blouse, be sure that it doesn't have gum on it, because that way it won't hold up well after a wash; soak salt fish overnight before you cook it; is it true that you sing benna[2] in Sunday school?; always eat your food in such a way that it won't turn someone else's stomach; on Sundays try to walk like a lady and not like the slut you are so bent on becoming; don't sing benna in Sunday school; you mustn't speak to wharf-rat boys, not even to give directions; don't eat fruits on the street—flies will follow you; *but I don't sing benna on Sundays at all and never in Sunday school*; this is how to sew on a button; this is how to make a buttonhole for the button you have just sewed on; this is how to hem a dress when you see the hem coming down and so to prevent yourself from looking like the slut I know you are so bent on becoming; this is how you iron your father's khaki shirt so that it doesn't have a crease; this is how you iron your father's khaki pants so that they don't have a crease; this is how you grow okra—far from the house, because okra tree harbors red ants; when you are growing dasheen,[3] make sure it gets plenty of water or else it makes your throat itch when you are eating it; this is how you sweep a corner; this is how you sweep a whole house; this is how you sweep a yard; this is how you smile to someone you don't like too much; this is how you smile to someone you don't like at all; this is how you smile to someone you like completely; this is how you set a table for tea; this is how you set a table for dinner; this is how you set a table for dinner with an important guest; this is how you set a table for lunch; this is how you set a table for breakfast; this is how to behave in the presence

1. Pads for menstruation.
2. Improvised Antiguan folk song with African roots.
3. A type of taro, a root vegetable.

of men who don't know you very well, and this way they won't recognize immediately the slut I have warned you against becoming; be sure to wash every day, even if it is with your own spit; don't squat down to play marbles—you are not a boy, you know; don't pick people's flowers—you might catch something; don't throw stones at blackbirds, because it might not be a blackbird at all; this is how to make a bread pudding; this is how to make doukona;[4] this is how to make pepper pot;[5] this is how to make a good medicine for a cold; this is how to make a good medicine to throw away a child before it even becomes a child; this is how to catch a fish; this is how to throw back a fish you don't like, and that way something bad won't fall on you; this is how to bully a man; this is how a man bullies you; this is how to love a man, and if this doesn't work there are other ways, and if they don't work don't feel too bad about giving up; this is how to spit up in the air if you feel like it, and this is how to move quick so that it doesn't fall on you; this is how to make ends meet; always squeeze bread to make sure it's fresh; *but what if the baker won't let me feel the bread?*; you mean to say that after all you are really going to be the kind of woman who the baker won't let near the bread?

1978

---

4. A pudding made of plantains.   5. A spicy stew.

TONI MORRISON
born 1931

Nobel laureate Toni Morrison combines realistic depictions of African American experience with a strong sense of the past's hold on the present. She often conveys this sensitivity to the power of history by invoking magic or supernatural occurrences. The combination of techniques resembles at times the magic realism of the Latin American Boom; at other times, Morrison's concern with the border between fiction and history seems postmodernist. Her writing also addresses the role of racial and gender discrimination in contemporary society. In all her work, while drawing on the experimental fictional techniques of the early twentieth century, she maintains a close connection to African American oral and literary traditions and to everyday life in the United States.

Born Chloe Ardelia Wofford in Lorain, Ohio, Morrison took the saint's name Anthony (later shortened to Toni) as her middle name when she converted to Catholicism, at the age of twelve. Her family had participated in the Great Migration of African Americans from the South in the early decades of the century. Her father, born in Georgia, worked at miscellaneous jobs in construction and shipbuilding, while her maternal grandparents had been sharecroppers in Alabama who came to Ohio to seek a better life for their daughters. Morrison studied English at

Howard University, where she was active in student theater. Her master's thesis, at Cornell University, examined the role of suicide in the fiction of **Virginia Woolf** and **William Faulkner**; her later fictional practice made use both of the subject of violent death and of the stream-of-consciousness techniques of Woolf and Faulkner. After returning to Howard to teach, the author met and married the Jamaican architect Harold Morrison, also a faculty member; the couple would later divorce. She also began work on her first novel, *The Bluest Eye* (1970). Leaving behind her academic career, she was employed, for twenty years, as an editor at Random House, where she encouraged other African American women writers. She continued to produce novels and journalism; the works received critical praise, literary awards, and a growing audience. For her fifth novel, *Beloved* (1987), arguably her masterpiece, Morrison received the Pulitzer Prize. She has continued to write novels, essays, musical lyrics, and the libretto for an opera, and taught at Princeton University from 1989 until her retirement in 2006. In 1993, she was awarded the Nobel Prize for Literature.

Morrison's early novels focus on contemporary African American life and the impact of racism on the prospects and self-image of the young. In *The Bluest Eye,* Pecola Breedlove, a young African American girl in Morrison's hometown of Lorain, longs for blue eyes and what she imagines is the exclusively white preserve of beauty. Her family and others in the community share this false idea of attractiveness as associated with light skin, and their self-hatred leads to destructive consequences, including child molestation, incest, and insanity. With *Song of Solomon* (1977), Morrison chose a broader historical canvas, encompassing the roots of African American folk customs in the South. Here, Morrison explores the

supernatural, drawing from oral tradition such as the ghost stories her family told her as a child, to create characters who can fly or talk to the dead. The novel, which also incorporates biblical archetypes, marks an experimental turn in Morrison's writing, as she makes use of multiple perspectives. *Beloved* treats a still earlier period of African American history, the time of slavery, and does so with extensive evocation of the supernatural. Based on the true story of a runaway slave who killed her child in order to prevent the child's reenslavement, it is Morrison's most moving novel as well as one of her most experimental. Throughout her works, characters find themselves caught in patterns of violence and prejudice that threaten to destroy them, but a few manage to transcend this history and achieve a measure of freedom and self-worth.

"Recitatif" (1983), Morrison's only published short story, examines a friendship between two girls of different races. The title refers to passages of narrative or dialogue in an opera that are sung in the rhythm of ordinary speech, as opposed to the formal arias or songs. The story focuses on the dialogue between the two main characters at several junctures of life that may independently seem insignificant but that, when combined in a narrative, reveal the nature of their relationship. The narrator, Twyla, meets Roberta at "St. Bonny's," the fictional St. Bonaventure Orphanage just outside New York City. They are the only two girls there whose mothers are still alive, but neither mother is up to the task of caring for her daughter. In the course of the short story, Morrison effectively presents Twyla's childlike perspective on events at St. Bonny's and the maturation of her point of view as she grows up, has children, and looks back on half-forgotten events.

Although Twyla and Roberta have much in common, they are divided by race. Morrison later explained that she

2636 | TONI MORRISON

intended the story as "an experiment in the removal of all racial codes from a narrative about two characters of different races for whom racial identity is crucial." Twyla never specifies her own race or that of Roberta. Maggie, who works in the kitchen, is also of ambiguous race. "Until very recently," Morrison has written, "and regardless of the race of the author, the readers of virtually all of American fiction have been positioned as white." In other words, writers have tended to assume a white audience; conversely, readers, unless specifically told otherwise, have assumed that the charac-ters in fiction are white. "Recitatif" represents Morrison's effort to challenge such assumptions. Although racial conflict in society affects the girls' relationship later in life, "Recitatif" envisions the possibility of transcending racial divisions and embracing a common humanity.

This experiment in narrative ambiguity reflects Morrison's interest in the transformation of traditional narrative techniques. Inspired in part by the modernists, but equally by jazz music and African American oral tradition, Morrison has expanded the possibilities of contemporary American fiction.

Recitatif[1]

My mother danced all night and Roberta's was sick. That's why we were taken to St. Bonny's.[2] People want to put their arms around you when you tell them you were in a shelter, but it really wasn't bad. No big long room with one hundred beds like Bellevue.[3] There were four to a room, and when Roberta and me came, there was a shortage of state kids,[4] so we were the only ones assigned to 406 and could go from bed to bed if we wanted to. And we wanted to, too. We changed beds every night and for the whole four months we were there we never picked one out as our own permanent bed.

It didn't start out that way. The minute I walked in and the Big Bozo introduced us, I got sick to my stomach. It was one thing to be taken out of your own bed early in the morning—it was something else to be stuck in a strange place with a girl from a whole other race. And Mary, that's my mother, she was right. Every now and then she would stop dancing long enough to tell me something important and one of the things she said was that they never washed their hair and they smelled funny. Roberta sure did. Smell funny, I mean. So when the Big Bozo (nobody ever called her Mrs. Itkin, just like nobody every said St. Bonaventure)—when she said, "Twyla, this is Roberta. Roberta, this is Twyla. Make each other welcome." I said, "My mother won't like you putting me in here."

"Good," said Bozo. "Maybe then she'll come and take you home."

How's that for mean? If Roberta had laughed I would have killed her, but she didn't. She just walked over to the window and stood with her back to us.

"Turn around," said the Bozo. "Don't be rude. Now Twyla. Roberta. When you hear a loud buzzer, that's the call for dinner. Come down to the first floor. Any fights and no movie." And then, just to make sure we knew what we would be missing, "The Wizard of Oz."

1. A passage of narrative or dialogue in an opera sung in the rhythm of ordinary speech (French).
2. St. Bonaventure's, a fictional orphanage outside New York City.
3. A major hospital in New York City, famous for its psychiatric ward.
4. Children placed in the Catholic orphanage by the state of New York.

Roberta must have thought I meant that my mother would be mad about my being put in the shelter. Not about rooming with her, because as soon as Bozo left she came over to me and said, "Is your mother sick too?"

"No," I said. "She just likes to dance all night."

"Oh," she nodded her head and I liked the way she understood things so fast. So for the moment it didn't matter that we looked like salt and pepper standing there and that's what the other kids called us sometimes. We were eight years old and got F's all the time. Me because I couldn't remember what I read or what the teacher said. And Roberta because she couldn't read at all and didn't even listen to the teacher. She wasn't good at anything except jacks,[5] at which she was a killer: pow scoop pow scoop pow scoop.

We didn't like each other all that much at first, but nobody else wanted to play with us because we weren't real orphans with beautiful dead parents in the sky. We were dumped. Even the New York City Puerto Ricans and the upstate Indians ignored us. All kinds of kids were in there, black ones, white ones, even two Koreans. The food was good, though. At least I thought so. Roberta hated it and left whole pieces of things on her plate: Spam, Salisbury steak—even jello with fruit cocktail in it, and she didn't care if I ate what she wouldn't. Mary's idea of supper was popcorn and a can of Yoo-Hoo. Hot mashed potatoes and two weenies was like Thanksgiving for me.

It really wasn't bad, St. Bonny's. The big girls on the second floor pushed us around now and then. But that was all. They wore lipstick and eyebrow pencil and wobbled their knees while they watched TV. Fifteen, sixteen, even, some of them were. They were put-out girls, scared runaways most of them. Poor little girls who fought their uncles off but looked tough to us, and mean. God did they look mean. The staff tried to keep them separate from the younger children, but sometimes they caught us watching them in the orchard where they played radios and danced with each other. They'd light out after us and pull our hair or twist our arms. We were scared of them, Roberta and me, but neither of us wanted the other one to know it. So we got a good list of dirty names we could shout back when we ran from them through the orchard. I used to dream a lot and almost always the orchard was there. Two acres, four maybe, of these little apple trees. Hundreds of them. Empty and crooked like beggar women when I first came to St. Bonny's but fat with flowers when I left. I don't know why I dreamt about that orchard so much. Nothing really happened there. Nothing all that important, I mean. Just the big girls dancing and playing the radio. Roberta and me watching. Maggie fell down there once. The kitchen woman with legs like parentheses. And the big girls laughed at her. We should have helped her up, I know, but we were scared of those girls with lipstick and eyebrow pencil. Maggie couldn't talk. The kids said she had her tongue cut out, but I think she was just born that way: mute. She was old and sandy-colored and she worked in the kitchen. I don't know if she was nice or not. I just remember her legs like parentheses and how she rocked when she walked. She worked from early in the morning till two o'clock, and if she was late, if she had too much cleaning and didn't get out till two-fifteen or so, she'd cut through the orchard so she wouldn't miss her bus and have to wait another

5. A traditional game in which children take turns picking up small pieces of plastic between bounces of a ball.

hour. She wore this really stupid little hat—a kid's hat with ear flaps—and she wasn't much taller than we were. A really awful little hat. Even for a mute, it was dumb—dressing like a kid and never saying anything at all.

"But what about if somebody tries to kill her?" I used to wonder about that. "Or what if she wants to cry? Can she cry?"

"Sure," Roberta said. "But just tears. No sounds come out."

"She can't scream?"

"Nope. Nothing."

"Can she hear?"

"I guess."

"Let's call her," I said. And we did.

"Dummy! Dummy!" She never turned her head.

"Bow legs! Bow legs!" Nothing. She just rocked on, the chin straps of her baby-boy hat swaying from side to side. I think we were wrong. I think she could hear and didn't let on. And it shames me even now to think there was somebody in there after all who heard us call her those names and couldn't tell on us.

We got along all right, Roberta and me. Changed beds every night, got F's in civics and communication skills and gym. The Bozo was disappointed in us, she said. Out of 130 of us state cases, 90 were under twelve. Almost all were real orphans with beautiful dead parents in the sky. We were the only ones dumped and the only ones with F's in three classes including gym. So we got along—what with her leaving whole pieces of things on her plate and being nice about not asking questions.

I think it was the day before Maggie fell down that we found out our mothers were coming to visit us on the same Sunday. We had been at the shelter twenty-eight days (Roberta twenty-eight and a half) and this was their first visit with us. Our mothers would come at ten o'clock in time for chapel, then lunch with us in the teachers' lounge. I thought if my dancing mother met her sick mother it might be good for her. And Roberta thought her sick mother would get a big bang out of a dancing one. We got excited about it and curled each other's hair. After breakfast we sat on the bed watching the road from the window. Roberta's socks were still wet. She washed them the night before and put them on the radiator to dry. They hadn't, but she put them on anyway because their tops were so pretty—scalloped in pink. Each of us had a purple construction-paper basket that we had made in craft class. Mine had a yellow crayon rabbit on it. Roberta's had eggs with wiggly lines of color. Inside were cellophane grass and just the jelly beans because I'd eaten the two marshmallow eggs they gave us. The Big Bozo came herself to get us. Smiling she told us we looked very nice and to come downstairs. We were so surprised by the smile we'd never seen before, neither of us moved.

"Don't you want to see your mommies?"

I stood up first and spilled the jelly beans all over the floor. Bozo's smile disappeared while we scrambled to get the candy up off the floor and put it back in the grass.

She escorted us downstairs to the first floor, where the other girls were lining up to file into the chapel. A bunch of grown-ups stood to one side. Viewers mostly. The old biddies who wanted servants and the fags who wanted company looking for children they might want to adopt. Once in a while a grandmother. Almost never anybody young or anybody whose face wouldn't scare you in the night. Because if any of the real orphans had young relatives they wouldn't be real orphans. I saw Mary right away. She had on those green slacks I hated and hated even more now because didn't she know we were going to chapel? And that fur jacket with the pocket linings so ripped she had to pull to get her hands out of them. But her face was pretty—like always, and she smiled and waved like she was the little girl looking for her mother—not me.

I walked slowly, trying not to drop the jelly beans and hoping the paper handle would hold. I had to use my last Chiclet[6] because by the time I finished cutting everything out, all the Elmer's[7] was gone. I am left-handed and the scissors never worked for me. It didn't matter, though; I might just as well have chewed the gum. Mary dropped to her knees and grabbed me, mashing the basket, the jelly beans, and the grass into her ratty fur jacket.

"Twyla, baby. Twyla, baby!"

I could have killed her. Already I heard the big girls in the orchard the next time saying, "Twyyyyyla, baby!" But I couldn't stay mad at Mary while she was smiling and hugging me and smelling of Lady Esther dusting powder. I wanted to stay buried in her fur all day.

To tell the truth I forgot about Roberta. Mary and I got in line for the traipse into chapel and I was feeling proud because she looked so beautiful even in those ugly green slacks that made her behind stick out. A pretty mother on earth is better than a beautiful dead one in the sky even if she did leave you all alone to go dancing.

I felt a tap on my shoulder, turned, and saw Roberta smiling. I smiled back, but not too much lest somebody think this visit was the biggest thing that ever happened in my life. Then Roberta said, "Mother, I want you to meet my room-mate, Twyla. And that's Twyla's mother."

I looked up it seemed for miles. She was big. Bigger than any man and on her chest was the biggest cross I'd ever seen. I swear it was six inches long each way. And in the crook of her arm was the biggest Bible ever made.

Mary, simple-minded as ever, grinned and tried to yank her hand out of the pocket with the raggedy lining—to shake hands, I guess. Roberta's mother looked down at me and then looked down at Mary too. She didn't say anything, just grabbed Roberta with her Bible-free hand and stepped out of line, walking quickly to the rear of it. Mary was still grinning because she's not too swift when it comes to what's really going on. Then this light bulb goes off in her head and she says "That bitch!" really loud and us almost in the chapel now. Organ music whining; the Bonny Angels singing sweetly. Everybody in the world turned around to look. And Mary would have kept it up—kept calling names if I hadn't squeezed her hand as hard as I could. That helped a little, but she still twitched and crossed and uncrossed her legs all through service. Even groaned a couple of times. Why did I think she would come there and act right? Slacks. No hat like the grandmothers and viewers, and groaning all the while. When we stood for hymns she kept her mouth shut. Wouldn't even look at the words on the page. She actually reached in her purse for a mirror to check her lipstick. All I could think of was that she really needed to be killed. The sermon lasted a year, and I knew the real orphans were looking smug again.

---

6. A brand of chewing gum.   7. A brand of glue.

We were supposed to have lunch in the teachers' lounge, but Mary didn't bring anything, so we picked fur and cellophane grass off the mashed jelly beans and ate them. I could have killed her. I sneaked a look at Roberta. Her mother had brought chicken legs and ham sandwiches and oranges and a whole box of chocolate-covered grahams. Roberta drank milk from a thermos while her mother read the Bible to her.

Things are not right. The wrong food is always with the wrong people. Maybe that's why I got into waitress work later—to match up the right people with the right food. Roberta just let those chicken legs sit there, but she did bring a stack of grahams up to me later when the visit was over. I think she was sorry that her mother would not shake my mother's hand. And I liked that and I liked the fact that she didn't say a word about Mary groaning all the way through the service and not bringing any lunch.

Roberta left in May when the apple trees were heavy and white. On her last day we went to the orchard to watch the big girls smoke and dance by the radio. It didn't matter that they said, "Twyyyyyla, baby." We sat on the ground and breathed. Lady Esther.[8] Apple blossoms. I still go soft when I smell one or the other. Roberta was going home. The big cross and the big Bible was coming to get her and she seemed sort of glad and sort of not. I thought I would die in that room of four beds without her and I knew Bozo had plans to move some other dumped kid in there with me. Roberta promised to write every day, which was really sweet of her because she couldn't read a lick so how could she write anybody. I would have drawn pictures and sent them to her but she never gave me her address. Little by little she faded. Her wet socks with the pink scalloped tops and her big serious-looking eyes—that's all I could catch when I tried to bring her to mind.

I was working behind the counter at the Howard Johnson's[9] on the Thruway just before the Kingston exit. Not a bad job. Kind of a long ride from Newburgh, but okay once I got there. Mine was the second night shift—eleven to seven. Very light until a Greyhound checked in for breakfast around six-thirty. At that hour the sun was all the way clear of the hills behind the restaurant. The place looked better at night—more like shelter—but I loved it when the sun broke in, even if it did show all the cracks in the vinyl and the speckled floor looked dirty no matter what the mop boy did.

It was August and a bus crowd was just unloading. They would stand around a long while: going to the john, and looking at gifts and junk-for-sale machines, reluctant to sit down so soon. Even to eat. I was trying to fill the coffee pots and get them all situated on the electric burners when I saw her. She was sitting in a booth smoking a cigarette with two guys smothered in head and facial hair. Her own hair was so big and wild I could hardly see her face. But the eyes. I would know them anywhere. She had on a powder-blue halter and shorts outfit and earrings the size of bracelets. Talk about lipstick and eyebrow pencil. She made the big girls look like nuns. I couldn't get off the counter until seven o'clock, but I kept watching the booth in case they got up to leave before that. My replacement was on time for a change, so I counted and stacked my receipts as fast as I could and signed off. I walked over to the booth, smiling and

8. A brand of cosmetics.
9. A modestly priced restaurant and hotel chain; this branch is off the New York State Thruway near Kingston, north of New York City.

wondering if she would remember me. Or even if she wanted to remember me. Maybe she didn't want to be reminded of St. Bonny's or to have anybody know she was ever there. I know I never talked about it to anybody.

I put my hands in my apron pockets and leaned against the back of the booth facing them.

"Roberta? Roberta Fisk?"

She looked up. "Yeah?"

"Twyla."

She squinted for a second and then said, "Wow."

"Remember me?"

"Sure. Hey. Wow."

"It's been a while," I said, and gave a smile to the two hairy guys.

"Yeah. Wow. You work here?"

"Yeah," I said. "I live in Newburgh."

"Newburgh? No kidding?" She laughed then a private laugh that included the guys but only the guys, and they laughed with her. What could I do but laugh too and wonder why I was standing there with my knees showing out from under that uniform. Without looking I could see the blue and white triangle on my head, my hair shapeless in a net, my ankles thick in white oxfords. Nothing could have been less sheer than my stockings. There was this silence that came down right after I laughed. A silence it was her turn to fill up. With introductions, maybe, to her boyfriends or an invitation to sit down and have a Coke. Instead she lit a cigarette off the one she'd just finished and said, "We're on our way to the Coast. He's got an appointment with Hendrix." She gestured casually toward the boy next to her.

"Hendrix? Fantastic," I said. "Really fantastic. What's she doing now?"

Roberta coughed on her cigarette and the two guys rolled their eyes up at the ceiling.

"Hendrix. Jimi Hendrix,[1] asshole. He's only the biggest—Oh, wow. Forget it."

I was dismissed without anyone saying goodbye, so I thought I would do it for her.

"How's your mother?" I asked. Her grin cracked her whole face. She swallowed. "Fine," she said. "How's yours?"

"Pretty as a picture," I said and turned away. The backs of my knees were damp. Howard Johnson's really was a dump in the sunlight.

James is as comfortable as a house slipper. He liked my cooking and I liked his big loud family. They have lived in Newburgh all of their lives and talk about it the way people do who have always known a home. His grandmother is a porch swing[2] older than his father and when they talk about streets and avenues and buildings they call them names they no longer have. They still call the A & P[3] Rico's because it stands on property once a mom and pop store owned by Mr. Rico. And they call the new community college Town Hall because it once was. My mother-in-law puts up jelly and cucumbers and buys butter wrapped in cloth from a dairy. James and his father talk about fishing and baseball and I can see them all together on

---

1. African American rock guitarist (1942–1970).

2. I.e., even older; porch swings are proverbially old.

3. An inexpensive grocery store, originally the Great Atlantic & Pacific Tea Company.

the Hudson in a raggedy skiff. Half the population of Newburgh is on welfare now, but to my husband's family it was still some upstate paradise of a time long past. A time of ice houses and vegetable wagons, coal furnaces and children weeding gardens. When our son was born my mother-in-law gave me the crib blanket that had been hers.

But the town they remembered had changed. Something quick was in the air. Magnificent old houses, so ruined they had become shelter for squatters and rent risks, were bought and renovated. Smart IBM[4] people moved out of their suburbs back into the city and put shutters up and herb gardens in their backyards. A brochure came in the mail announcing the opening of a Food Emporium. Gourmet food it said—and listed items the rich IBM crowd would want. It was located in a new mall at the edge of town and I drove out to shop there one day—just to see. It was late in June. After the tulips were gone and the Queen Elizabeth roses were open everywhere. I trailed my cart along the aisle tossing in smoked oysters and Robert's sauce and things I knew would sit in my cupboard for years. Only when I found some Klondike ice cream bars did I feel less guilty about spending James's fireman's salary so foolishly. My father-in-law ate them with the same gusto little Joseph did.

Waiting in the check-out line I heard a voice say, "Twyla!"

The classical music piped over the aisles had affected me and the woman leaning toward me was dressed to kill. Diamonds on her hand, a smart white summer dress. "I'm Mrs. Benson," I said.

"Ho. Ho. The Big Bozo," she sang.

For a split second I didn't know what she was talking about. She had a bunch of asparagus and two cartons of fancy water.

"Roberta!"

"Right."

"For heaven's sake. Roberta."

"You look great," she said.

"So do you. Where are you? Here? In Newburgh?"

"Yes. Over in Annandale."[5]

I was opening my mouth to say more when the cashier called my attention to her empty counter.

"Meet you outside." Roberta pointed her finger and went into the express line.

I placed the groceries and kept myself from glancing around to check Roberta's progress. I remembered Howard Johnson's and looking for a chance to speak only to be greeted with a stingy "wow." But she was waiting for me and her huge hair was sleek now, smooth around a small, nicely shaped head. Shoes, dress, everything lovely and summery and rich. I was dying to know what happened to her, how she got from Jimi Hendrix to Annandale, a neighborhood full of doctors and IBM executives. Easy, I thought. Everything is so easy for them. They think they own the world.

"How long," I asked her. "How long have you been here?"

"A year. I got married to a man who lives here. And you, you're married too, right? Benson, you said."

4. International Business Machines, the leading computer company of the time, with headquarters in Armonk, New York.

5. Annandale-on-Hudson, a prosperous small town north of New York City. Nearby Newburgh is less prosperous.

"Yeah. James Benson."

"And is he nice?"

"Oh, is he nice?"

"Well, is he?" Roberta's eyes were steady as though she really meant the question and wanted an answer.

"He's wonderful, Roberta. Wonderful."

"So you're happy."

"Very."

"That's good," she said and nodded her head. "I always hoped you'd be happy. Any kids? I know you have kids."

"One. A boy. How about you?"

"Four."

"Four?"

She laughed. "Step kids. He's a widower."

"Oh."

"Got a minute? Let's have a coffee."

I thought about the Klondikes melting and the inconvenience of going all the way to my car and putting the bags in the trunk. Served me right for buying all that stuff I didn't need. Roberta was ahead of me.

"Put them in my car. It's right here."

And then I saw the dark blue limousine.

"You married a Chinaman?"

"No," she laughed. "He's the driver."

"Oh, my. If the Big Bozo could see you now."

We both giggled. Really giggled. Suddenly, in just a pulse beat, twenty years disappeared and all of it came rushing back. The big girls (whom we called gar girls—Roberta's misheard word for the evil stone faces[6] described in a civics class) there dancing in the orchard, the ploppy mashed potatoes, the double weenies, the Spam with pineapple. We went into the coffee shop holding on to one another and I tried to think why we were glad to see each other this time and not before. Once, twelve years ago, we passed like strangers. A black girl and a white girl meeting in a Howard Johnson's on the road and having nothing to say. One in a blue and white triangle waitress hat—the other on her way to see Hendrix. Now we were behaving like sisters separated for much too long. Those four short months were nothing in time. Maybe it was the thing itself. Just being there, together. Two little girls who knew what nobody else in the world knew—how not to ask questions. How to believe what had to be believed. There was politeness in that reluctance and generosity as well. Is your mother sick too? No, she dances all night. Oh—and an understanding nod.

We sat in a booth by the window and fell into recollection like veterans.

"Did you ever learn to read?"

"Watch." She picked up the menu. "Special of the day. Cream of corn soup. Entrées. Two dots and a wriggly line. Quiche. Chef salad, scallops . . ."

I was laughing and applauding when the waitress came up.

"Remember the Easter baskets?"

"And how we tried to *introduce* them?"

"Your mother with that cross like two telephone poles."

6. I.e., gargoyles.

"And yours with those tight slacks."

We laughed so loudly heads turned and made the laughter hard to suppress.

"What happened to the Jimi Hendrix date?"

Roberta made a blow-out sound with her lips.

"When he died I thought about you."

"Oh, you heard about him finally?"

"Finally. Come on, I was a small-town country waitress."

"And I was a small-town country dropout. God, were we wild. I still don't know how I got out of there alive."

"But you did."

"I did. I really did. Now I'm Mrs. Kenneth Norton."

"Sounds like a mouthful."

"It is."

"Servants and all?"

Roberta held up two fingers.

"Ow! What does he do?"

"Computers and stuff. What do I know?"

"I don't remember a hell of a lot from those days, but Lord, St. Bonny's is as clear as daylight. Remember Maggie? The day she fell down and those gar girls laughed at her?"

Roberta looked up from her salad and stared at me. "Maggie didn't fall," she said.

"Yes, she did. You remember."

"No, Twyla. They knocked her down. Those girls pushed her down and tore her clothes. In the orchard."

"I don't—that's not what happened."

"Sure it is. In the orchard. Remember how scared we were?"

"Wait a minute. I don't remember any of that."

"And Bozo was fired."

"You're crazy. She was there when I left. You left before me."

"I went back. You weren't there when they fired Bozo."

"What?"

"Twice. Once for a year when I was about ten, another for two months when I was fourteen. That's when I ran away."

"You ran away from St. Bonny's?"

"I had to. What do you want? Me dancing in that orchard?"

"Are you sure about Maggie?"

"Of course I'm sure. You've blocked it, Twyla. It happened. Those girls had behavior problems, you know."

"Didn't they, though. But why can't I remember the Maggie thing?"

"Believe me. It happened. And we were there."

"Who did you room with when you went back?" I asked her as if I would know her. The Maggie thing was troubling me.

"Creeps. They tickled themselves in the night."

My ears were itching and I wanted to go home suddenly. This was all very well but she couldn't just comb her hair, wash her face and pretend everything was hunky-dory. After the Howard Johnson's snub. And no apology. Nothing.

"Were you on dope or what that time at Howard Johnson's?" I tried to make my voice sound friendlier than I felt.

"Maybe, a little. I never did drugs much. Why?"

"I don't know, you acted sort of like you didn't want to know me then."

"Oh, Twyla, you know how it was in those days: black—white. You know how everything was."

But I didn't know. I thought it was just the opposite. Busloads of blacks and whites came into Howard Johnson's together. They roamed together then: students, musicians, lovers, protesters. You got to see everything at Howard Johnson's and blacks were very friendly with whites in those days. But sitting there with nothing on my plate but two hard tomato wedges wondering about the melting Klondikes it seemed childish remembering the slight. We went to her car, and with the help of the driver, got my stuff into my station wagon.

"We'll keep in touch this time," she said.

"Sure," I said. "Sure. Give me a call."

"I will," she said, and then just as I was sliding behind the wheel, she leaned into the window. "By the way. Your mother. Did she ever stop dancing?"

I shook my head. "No. Never."

Roberta nodded.

"And yours? Did she ever get well?"

She smiled a tiny sad smile. "No. She never did. Look, call me, okay?"

"Okay," I said, but I knew I wouldn't. Roberta had messed up my past somehow with that business about Maggie. I wouldn't forget a thing like that. Would I?

Strife came to us that fall. At least that's what the paper called it. Strife. Racial strife. The word made me think of a bird—a big shrieking bird out of 1,000,000,000 B.C. Flapping its wings and cawing. Its eye with no lid always bearing down on you. All day it screeched and at night it slept on the rooftops. It woke you in the morning and from the *Today* show to the eleven o'clock news it kept you an awful company. I couldn't figure it out from one day to the next. I knew I was supposed to feel something strong, but I didn't know what, and James wasn't any help. Joseph was on the list of kids to be transferred from the junior high school to another one at some far-out-of-the-way place and I thought it was a good thing until I heard it was a bad thing. I mean I didn't know.[7] All the schools seemed dumps to me, and the fact that one was nicer looking didn't hold much weight. But the papers were full of it and then the kids began to get jumpy. In August, mind you. Schools weren't even open yet. I thought Joseph might be frightened to go over there, but he didn't seem scared so I forgot about it, until I found myself driving along Hudson Street out there by the school they were trying to integrate and saw a line of women marching. And who do you suppose was in line, big as life, holding a sign in front of her bigger than her mother's cross? MOTHERS HAVE RIGHTS TOO! it said.

I drove on, and then changed my mind. I circled the block, slowed down, and *honked my horn.*

---

7. In the 1970s and 1980s, many municipalities, often under court order, transported students to schools distant from their neighborhoods in order to desegregate racially segregated public schools; the practice, called busing, was controversial.

Roberta looked over and when she saw me she waved. I didn't wave back, but I didn't move either. She handed her sign to another woman and came over to where I was parked.

"Hi."

"What are you doing?"

"Picketing. What's it look like?"

"What for?"

"What do you mean, 'What for?' They want to take my kids and send them out of the neighborhood. They don't want to go."

"So what if they go to another school? My boy's being bussed too, and I don't mind. Why should you?"

"It's not about us, Twyla. Me and you. It's about our kids."

"What's more *us* than that?"

"Well, it is a free country."

"Not yet, but it will be."

"What the hell does that mean? I'm not doing anything to you."

"You really think that?"

"I know it."

"I wonder what made me think you were different."

"I wonder what made me think you were different."

"Look at them," I said. "Just look. Who do they think they are? Swarming all over the place like they own it. And now they think they can decide where my child goes to school. Look at them, Roberta. They're Bozos."

Roberta turned around and looked at the women. Almost all of them were standing still now, waiting. Some were even edging toward us. Roberta looked at me out of some refrigerator behind her eyes. "No, they're not. They're just mothers."

"And what am I? Swiss cheese?"

"I used to curl your hair."

"I hated your hands in my hair."

The women were moving. Our faces looked mean to them of course and they looked as though they could not wait to throw themselves in front of a police car, or better yet, into my car and drag me away by my ankles. Now they surrounded my car and gently, gently began to rock it. I swayed back and forth like a sideways yo-yo. Automatically I reached for Roberta, like the old days in the orchard when they saw us watching them and we had to get out of there, and if one of us fell the other pulled her up and if one of us was caught the other stayed to kick and scratch, and neither would leave the other behind. My arm shot out of the car window but no receiving hand was there. Roberta was looking at me sway from side to side in the car and her face was still. My purse slid from the car seat down under the dashboard. The four policemen who had been drinking Tab in their car finally got the message and strolled over, forcing their way through the women. Quietly, firmly they spoke. "Okay, ladies. Back in line or off the streets."

Some of them went away willingly; others had to be urged away from the car doors and the hood. Roberta didn't move. She was looking steadily at me. I was fumbling to turn on the ignition, which wouldn't catch because the gear shift was still in drive. The seats of the car were a mess because the swaying had thrown my grocery coupons all over it and my purse was sprawled on the floor.

"Maybe I am different now, Twyla. But you're not. You're the same little state kid who kicked a poor old black lady when she was down on the ground. You kicked a black lady and you have the nerve to call me a bigot."

The coupons were everywhere and the guts of my purse were bunched under the dashboard. What was she saying? Black? Maggie wasn't black.

"She wasn't black," I said.

"Like hell she wasn't, and you kicked her. We both did. You kicked a black lady who couldn't even scream."

"Liar!"

"You're the liar! Why don't you just go on home and leave us alone, huh?"

She turned away and I skidded away from the curb.

The next morning I went into the garage and cut the side out of the carton our portable TV had come in. It wasn't nearly big enough, but after a while I had a decent sign: red spray-painted letters on a white background—AND SO DO CHILDREN* * * *. I meant just to go down to the school and tack it up somewhere so those cows on the picket line across the street could see it, but when I got there, some ten or so others had already assembled—protesting the cows across the street. Police permits and everything. I got in line and we strutted in time on our side while Roberta's group strutted on theirs. That first day we were all dignified, pretending the other side didn't exist. The second day there was name calling and finger gestures. But that was about all. People changed signs from time to time, but Roberta never did and neither did I. Actually my sign didn't make sense without Roberta's. "And so do children what?" one of the women on my side asked me. Have rights, I said, as though it was obvious.

Roberta didn't acknowledge my presence in any way and I got to thinking maybe she didn't know I was there. I began to pace myself in the line, jostling people one minute and lagging behind the next, so Roberta and I could reach the end of our respective lines at the same time and there would be a moment in our turn when we would face each other. Still, I couldn't tell whether she saw me and knew my sign was for her. The next day I went early before we were scheduled to assemble. I waited until she got there before I exposed my new creation. As soon as she hoisted her MOTHERS HAVE RIGHTS TOO I began to wave my new one, which said, HOW WOULD YOU KNOW? I know she saw that one, but I had gotten addicted now. My signs got crazier each day, and the women on my side decided that I was a kook. They couldn't make heads or tails out of my brilliant screaming posters.

I brought a painted sign in queenly red with huge black letters that said, IS YOUR MOTHER WELL? Roberta took her lunch break and didn't come back for the rest of the day or any day after. Two days later I stopped going too and couldn't have been missed because nobody understood my signs anyway.

It was a nasty six weeks. Classes were suspended and Joseph didn't go to anybody's school until October. The children—everybody's children—soon got bored with that extended vacation they thought was going to be so great. They looked at TV until their eyes flattened. I spent a couple of mornings tutoring my son, as the other mothers said we should. Twice I opened a text from last year that he had never turned in. Twice he yawned in my face. Other mothers organized living room sessions so the kids would keep up. None of the kids could concentrate so they drifted back to *The Price Is Right* and *The Brady Bunch*. When the school finally opened there were fights once or twice and some sirens roared through the streets every once in a while. There were a lot of photographers from Albany. And just when ABC was about to send up a news crew, the kids settled down like nothing in the world had happened. Joseph hung my HOW WOULD YOU KNOW? sign in his bedroom. I don't know what became of AND SO DO CHILDREN****. I think my father-in-law cleaned some fish on it. He was always puttering around in our garage. Each of his five children lived in Newburgh and he acted as though he had five extra homes.

I couldn't help looking for Roberta when Joseph graduated from high school, but I didn't see her. It didn't trouble me much what she had said to me in the car. I mean the kicking part. I know I didn't do that, I couldn't do that. But I was puzzled by her telling me Maggie was black. When I thought about it I actually couldn't be certain. She wasn't pitch-black, I knew, or I would have remembered that. What I remember was the kiddie hat, and the semicircle legs. I tried to reassure myself about the race thing for a long time until it dawned on me that the truth was already there, and Roberta knew it. I didn't kick her; I didn't join in with the gar girls and kick that lady, but I sure did want to. We watched and never tried to help her and never called for help. Maggie was my dancing mother. Deaf, I thought, and dumb. Nobody inside. Nobody who would hear you if you cried in the night. Nobody who could tell you anything important that you could use. Rocking, dancing, swaying as she walked. And when the gar girls pushed her down, and started rough-housing, I knew she wouldn't scream, couldn't—just like me—and I was glad about that.

We decided not to have a tree, because Christmas would be at my mother-in-law's house, so why have a tree at both places? Joseph was at SUNY New Paltz[8] and we had to economize, we said. But at the last minute, I changed my mind. Nothing could be that bad. So I rushed around town looking for a tree, something small but wide. By the time I found a place, it was snowing and very late. I dawdled like it was the most important purchase in the world and the tree man was fed up with me. Finally I chose one and had it tied onto the trunk of the car. I drove away slowly because the sand trucks were not out yet and the streets could be murder at the beginning of a snowfall. Downtown the streets were wide and rather empty except for a cluster of people coming out of the Newburgh Hotel. The one hotel in town that wasn't built out of cardboard and Plexiglas. A party, probably. The men huddled in the snow were dressed in tails and the women had on furs. Shiny things glittered from underneath their coats. It made me tired to look at them. Tired, tired, tired. On the next corner was a small diner with loops and loops of paper bells in the window. I stopped the car and went in. Just for a cup of coffee and twenty minutes of peace before I went home and tried to finish everything before Christmas Eve.

"Twyla?"

There she was. In a silvery evening gown and dark fur coat. A man and another woman were with her, the man fumbling for change to put in the cigarette machine. The woman was humming and tapping on the counter with her fingernails. They all looked a little bit drunk.

"Well. It's you."

"How are you?"

I shrugged. "Pretty good. Frazzled. Christmas and all."

"Regular?" called the woman from the counter.

"Fine," Roberta called back and then, "Wait for me in the car."

She slipped into the booth beside me. "I have to tell you something, Twyla. I made up my mind if I ever saw you again, I'd tell you."

"I'd just as soon not hear anything, Roberta. It doesn't matter now, anyway."

"No," she said. "Not about that."

"Don't be long," said the woman. She carried two regulars to go and the man peeled his cigarette pack as they left.

"It's about St. Bonny's and Maggie."

"Oh, please."

"Listen to me. I really did think she was black. I didn't make that up. I really thought so. But now I can't be sure. I just remember her as old, so old. And because she couldn't talk—well, you know, I thought she was crazy. She'd been brought up in an institution like my mother was and like I thought I would be too. And you were right. We didn't kick her. It was the gar girls. Only them. But, well, I wanted to. I really wanted them to hurt her. I said we did it, too. You and me, but that's not true. And I don't want you to carry that around. It was just that I wanted to do it so bad that day—wanting to is doing it."

Her eyes were watery from the drinks she'd had, I guess. I know it's that way with me. One glass of wine and I start bawling over the littlest thing.

"We were kids, Roberta."

"Yeah. Yeah. I know, just kids."

"Eight."

"Eight."

"And lonely."

"Scared, too."

She wiped her cheeks with the heel of her hand and smiled. "Well, that's all I wanted to say."

I nodded and couldn't think of any way to fill the silence that went from the diner past the paper bells on out into the snow. It was heavy now. I thought I'd better wait for the sand trucks before starting home.

"Thanks, Roberta."

"Sure."

"Did I tell you? My mother, she never did stop dancing."

"Yes. You told me. And mine, she never got well." Roberta lifted her hands from the tabletop and covered her face with her palms. When she took them away she really was crying. "Oh shit, Twyla. Shit, shit, shit. What the hell happened to Maggie?"

1983

ISABEL ALLENDE

born 1942

One of the best known contemporary Latin American writers, the Chilean novelist Isabel Allende brought the tradition of magic realism to bear on women's experience. Drawing on the earlier experiments by **Gabriel García Márquez** and other writers of the Latin American Boom, Allende has portrayed women's spiritual lives in the context of the political world of her childhood and youth, adding a dimension to magic realism while bringing her a wide international audience.

Born in Peru, where her father was a diplomat representing Chile, Allende returned to Chile with her mother at the age of three when her parents divorced. She lived for much of her childhood with her grandparents. Her mother's second husband, also a diplomat, later took the family to Bolivia and Beirut. As a young woman, Allende became involved in international affairs herself, working for the Food and Agriculture Organization of the United Nations, before beginning a career in journalism. In 1973 her father's cousin, Salvador Allende, the first elected Socialist president of Chile, was deposed in a coup led by General Augusto Pinochet. Historians still debate whether he killed himself or was assassinated by Pinochet's forces. In the coup's aftermath, Isabel Allende and her family left Chile for Venezuela, where she continued to work as a journalist. She has said that the departure from Chile made her a serious writer: "I don't think I would be a writer if I had stayed in Chile. I would be trapped in the chores, in the family, in the person that people expected me to be. I was not supposed to be in any way a liberated person. I was a female born in the '40s in a patriarchal family;

I was supposed to marry and make everyone around me happy." Instead, she chose a liberated, cosmopolitan lifestyle, although she would marry and have two children.

When she received news, in 1981, that her ninety-nine-year-old grandfather was dying, Allende began writing him a long letter—which developed, transformed, and expanded to become her first novel, *The House of the Spirits* (1982). This novel chronicles the experiences of a South American family haunted by spirits and torn by political events over several decades of the twentieth century. The subjects and style drew comparisons to the magic realism of García Márquez, whom Allende described as "the great writer of the century." The novel was an international success, and Allende moved to California, where she continues to live, teaching at universities throughout the United States. Her daughter died of a rare illness, porphyria, in 1992, and Allende wrote a moving personal memoir with her in mind, *Paula* (1994).

The story presented here, "And of Clay Are We Created" (1989), belongs to a stage of her career in which Allende chose a more direct, less magic, realism. The title refers to the proverb "we are all made of the same clay," which in turn refers to biblical passages (Psalms 103.14, Job 33.6, and Genesis 2–3), in which humans are said to be created of clay or earth. As God reminds Adam on his expulsion from the Garden of Eden, "dust thou art, and unto dust shalt thou return" (Gen. 3.19). In the context of the soil smothering the victims of a volcanic eruption, this passage reminds us not only of our shared humanity but of our mortality as well. The narrator is the heroine of Allende's novel *Eva Luna* (1985). The plot offers a generally straightforward account of the aftermath of a volcanic eruption, based closely on a real event, the eruption of Nevado del Ruiz, in Colombia in 1985. The one element that might represent a form of magic is the role of television and media. Technology (flight, telecommunications, labor-saving devices) has often seemed to fulfill magicians' ancient dreams of dominating the world. In this story, though, even the awe-inspiring presence of television journalism fails to reverse the effects of natural forces. The story begins with an implicit critique of the way people may experience natural disasters through the mass media: Eva Luna's longtime companion, a television reporter named Rolf Carlé, takes a helicopter to the site of an avalanche caused by volcanic activity. While he and crowds of other journalists bring broadcasting equipment to the visually exciting disaster zone, no one in the mob can locate a simple pump that would help rescue a girl trapped under fallen earth. (This character is based on a real thirteen-year-old, Omaira Sán-

chez.) The child is only one of thousands of victims, but because her plight is caught on television, she becomes famous. The camera brings the public face-to-face, in a sense, with the victims, while emphasizing the distance between its operator and the victims; over the course of the story, however, the distance starts to collapse. What began as a criticism of the media becomes personal as the story focuses on the effects of the girl's fate on Rolf Carlé, who recollects his childhood in wartime Eastern Europe. Meanwhile, as the narrator watches the events unfold on television, she is powerless to help either the girl or Rolf.

The story demonstrates a keen awareness, typical of Allende, of the plight of the poor and disenfranchised; it reveals, as well, her attention to the ethical questions posed by a media-saturated society. Magic realism, for Allende, is not so much a return to an older mode of storytelling as a way of addressing the problems of the contemporary world. Allende's works provide a feminist perspective on the complex history of twentieth-century Latin America.

And of Clay Are We Created[1]

They discovered the girl's head protruding from the mudpit, eyes wide open, calling soundlessly. She had a First Communion name, Azucena.[2] Lily. In that vast cemetery where the odor of death was already attracting vultures from far away, and where the weeping of orphans and wails of the injured filled the air, the little girl obstinately clinging to life became the symbol of the tragedy. The television cameras transmitted so often the unbearable image of the head budding like a black squash from the clay that there was no who did not recognize her and know her name. And every time we saw her on the screen, right behind her was Rolf Carlé, who had gone there on assignment, never suspecting that he would find a fragment of his past, lost thirty years before.

1. Translated from Spanish by Margaret Sayers Peden.
2. Azucena is a type of lily, known in English as the Madonna lily or white lily. "First com-

munion name": a name, often of a saint, bestowed at the time of First Communion or confirmation in the Catholic Church.

First a subterranean sob rocked the cotton fields, curling them like waves of foam. Geologists had set up their seismographs weeks before and knew that the mountain had awakened again. For some time they had predicted that the heat of the eruption could detach the eternal ice from the slopes of the volcano, but no one heeded their warnings; they sounded like the tales of frightened old women. The towns in the valley went about their daily life, deaf to the moaning of the earth, until that fateful Wednesday night in November when a prolonged roar announced the end of the world, and walls of snow broke loose, rolling in an avalanche of clay, stones, and water that descended on the villages and buried them beneath unfathomable meters of telluric[3] vomit. As soon as the survivors emerged from the paralysis of that first awful terror, they could see that houses, plazas, churches, white cotton plantations, dark coffee forests, cattle pastures—all had disappeared. Much later, after soldiers and volunteers had arrived to rescue the living and try to assess the magnitude of the cataclysm, it was calculated that beneath the mud lay more than twenty thousand human beings and an indefinite number of animals putrefying in a viscous soup. Forests and rivers had also been swept away, and there was nothing to be seen but an immense desert of mire.

When the station called before dawn, Rolf Carlé and I were together. I crawled out of bed, dazed with sleep, and went to prepare coffee while he hurriedly dressed. He stuffed his gear in the green canvas backpack he always carried, and we said goodbye, as we had so many times before. I had no presentiments. I sat in the kitchen, sipping my coffee and planning the long hours without him, sure that he would be back the next day.

He was one of the first to reach the scene, because while other reporters were fighting their way to the edges of that morass in jeeps, bicycles, or on foot, each getting there however he could, Rolf Carlé had the advantage of the television helicopter, which flew him over the avalanche. We watched on our screens the footage captured by his assistant's camera, in which he was up to his knees in muck, a microphone in his hand, in the midst of a bedlam of lost children, wounded survivors, corpses, and devastation. The story came to us in his calm voice. For years he had been a familiar figure in newscasts, reporting live at the scene of battles and catastrophes with awesome tenacity. Nothing could stop him, and I was always amazed at his equanimity in the face of danger and suffering; it seemed as if nothing could shake his fortitude or deter his curiosity. Fear seemed never to touch him, although he had confessed to me that he was not a courageous man, far from it. I believe that the lens of the camera had a strange effect on him; it was as if it transported him to a different time from which he could watch events without actually participating in them. When I knew him better, I came to realize that this fictive distance seemed to protect him from his own emotions.

Rolf Carlé was in on the story of Azucena from the beginning. He filmed the volunteers who discovered her, and the first persons who tried to reach her; his camera zoomed in on the girl, her dark face, her large desolate eyes, the plastered-down tangle of her hair. The mud was like quicksand around her, and anyone attempting to reach her was in danger of sinking. They threw a rope to her that she made no effort to grasp until they shouted to her to catch

---

3. Earthy.

it; then she pulled a hand from the mire and tried to move, but immediately sank a little deeper. Rolf threw down his knapsack and the rest of his equipment and waded into the quagmire, commenting for his assistant's microphone that it was cold and that one could begin to smell the stench of corpses.

"What's your name?" he asked the girl, and she told him her flower name. "Don't move, Azucena," Rolf Carlé directed, and kept talking to her, without a thought for what he was saying, just to distract her, while slowly he worked his way forward in mud up to his waist. The air around him seemed as murky as the mud.

It was impossible to reach her from the approach he was attempting, so he retreated and circled around where there seemed to be firmer footing. When finally he was close enough, he took the rope and tied it beneath her arms, so they could pull her out. He smiled at her with that smile that crinkles his eyes and makes him look like a little boy; he told her that everything was fine, that he was here with her now, that soon they would have her out. He signaled the others to pull, but as soon as the cord tensed, the girl screamed. They tried again, and her shoulders and arms appeared, but they could move her no farther; she was trapped. Someone suggested that her legs might be caught in the collapsed walls of her house, but she said it was not just rubble, that she was also held by the bodies of her brothers and sisters clinging to her legs.

"Don't worry, we'll get you out of here," Rolf promised. Despite the quality of the transmission, I could hear his voice break, and I loved him more than ever. Azucena looked at him, but said nothing.

During those first hours Rolf Carlé exhausted all the resources of his ingenuity to rescue her. He struggled with poles and ropes, but every tug was an intolerable torture for the imprisoned girl. It occurred to him to use one of the poles as a lever but got no result and had to abandon the idea. He talked a couple of soldiers into working with him for a while, but they had to leave because so many other victims were calling for help. The girl could not move, she barely could breathe, but she did not seem desperate, as if an ancestral resignation allowed her to accept her fate. The reporter, on the other hand, was determined to snatch her from death. Someone brought him a tire, which he placed beneath her arms like a life buoy, and then laid a plank near the hole to hold his weight and allow him to stay closer to her. As it was impossible to remove the rubble blindly, he tried once or twice to dive toward her feet, but emerged frustrated, covered with mud, and spitting gravel. He concluded that he would have to have a pump to drain the water, and radioed a request for one, but received in return a message that there was no available transport and it could not be sent until the next morning.

"We can't wait that long!" Rolf Carlé shouted, but in the pandemonium no one stopped to commiserate. Many more hours would go by before he accepted that time had stagnated and reality had been irreparably distorted.

A military doctor came to examine the girl, and observed that her heart was functioning well and that if she did not get too cold she could survive the night.

"Hang on, Azucena, we'll have the pump tomorrow," Rolf Carlé tried to console her.

"Don't leave me alone," she begged.

"No, of course I won't leave you."

Someone brought him coffee, and he helped the girl drink it, sip by sip. The warm liquid revived her and she began telling him about her small life, about her family and her school, about how things were in that little bit of world before the volcano had erupted. She was thirteen, and she had never been outside her village. Rolf Carlé, buoyed by a premature optimism, was convinced that everything would end well: the pump would arrive, they would drain the water, move the rubble, and Azucena would be transported by helicopter to a hospital where she would recover rapidly and where he could visit her and bring her gifts. He thought, She's already too old for dolls, and I don't know what would please her; maybe a dress. I don't know much about women, he concluded, amused, reflecting that although he had known many women in his lifetime, none had taught him these details. To pass the hours he began to tell Azucena about his travels and adventures as a newshound, and when he exhausted his memory, he called upon imagination, inventing things he thought might entertain her. From time to time she dozed, but he kept talking in the darkness, to assure her that he was still there and to overcome the menace of uncertainty.

That was a long night.

Many miles away, I watched Rolf Carlé and the girl on a television screen. I could not bear the wait at home, so I went to National Television, where I often spent entire nights with Rolf editing programs. There, I was near his world, and I could at least get a feeling of what he lived through during those three decisive days. I called all the important people in the city, senators, commanders of the armed forces, the North American[4] ambassador, and the president of National Petroleum, begging them for a pump to remove the silt, but obtained only vague promises. I began to ask for urgent help on radio and television, to see if there wasn't *someone* who could help us. Between calls I would run to the newsroom to monitor the satellite transmissions that periodically brought new details of the catastrophe. While reporters selected scenes with most impact for the news report, I searched for footage that featured Azucena's mudpit. The screen reduced the disaster to a single plane and accentuated the tremendous distance that separated me from Rolf Carlé; nonetheless, I was there with him. The child's every suffering hurt me as it did him; I felt his frustration, his impotence. Faced with the impossibility of communicating with him, the fantastic idea came to me that if I tried, I could reach him by force of mind and in that way give him encouragement. I concentrated until I was dizzy—a frenzied and futile activity. At times I would be overcome with compassion and burst out crying; at other times, I was so drained I felt as if I were staring through a telescope at the light of a star dead for a million years.

I watched that hell on the first morning broadcast, cadavers of people and animals awash in the current of new rivers formed overnight from the melted snow. Above the mud rose the tops of trees and the bell towers of a church where several people had taken refuge and were patiently awaiting rescue teams. Hundreds of soldiers and volunteers from the Civil Defense[5] were clawing through rubble searching for survivors, while long rows of ragged specters awaited their turn for a cup of hot broth. Radio networks announced that their

4. I.e., United States.
5. A group of trained workers prepared to respond to disasters.

phones were jammed with calls from families offering shelter to orphaned children. Drinking water was in scarce supply, along with gasoline and food. Doctors, resigned to amputating arms and legs without anesthesia, pled that at least they be sent serum and painkillers and antibiotics; most of the roads, however, were impassable, and worse were the bureaucratic obstacles that stood in the way. To top it all, the clay contaminated by decomposing bodies threatened the living with an outbreak of epidemics.

Azucena was shivering inside the tire that held her above the surface. Immobility and tension had greatly weakened her, but she was conscious and could still be heard when a microphone was held out to her. Her tone was humble, as if apologizing for all the fuss. Rolf Carlé had a growth of beard, and dark circles beneath his eyes; he looked near exhaustion. Even from that enormous distance I could sense the quality of his weariness, so different from the fatigue of other adventures. He had completely forgotten the camera; he could not look at the girl through a lens any longer. The pictures we were receiving were not his assistant's but those of other reporters who had appropriated Azucena, bestowing on her the pathetic responsibility of embodying the horror of what had happened in that place. With the first light Rolf tried again to dislodge the obstacles that held the girl in her tomb, but he had only his hands to work with; he did not dare use a tool for fear of injuring her. He fed Azucena a cup of the cornmeal mush and bananas the Army was distributing, but she immediately vomited it up. A doctor stated that she had a fever, but added that there was little he could do: antibiotics were being reserved for cases of gangrene. A priest also passed by and blessed her, hanging a medal of the Virgin around her neck. By evening a gentle, persistent drizzle began to fall.

"The sky is weeping," Azucena murmured, and she, too, began to cry.

"Don't be afraid," Rolf begged. "You have to keep your strength up and be calm. Everything will be fine. I'm with you, and I'll get you out somehow."

Reporters returned to photograph Azucena and ask her the same questions, which she no longer tried to answer. In the meanwhile, more television and movie teams arrived with spools of cable, tapes, film, videos, precision lenses, recorders, sound consoles, lights, reflecting screens, auxiliary motors, cartons of supplies, electricians, sound technicians, and cameramen: Azucena's face was beamed to millions of screens around the world. And all the while Rolf Carlé kept pleading for a pump. The improved technical facilities bore results, and National Television began receiving sharper pictures and clearer sound; the distance seemed suddenly compressed, and I had the horrible sensation that Azucena and Rolf were by my side, separated from me by impenetrable glass. I was able to follow events hour by hour; I knew everything my love did to wrest the girl from her prison and help her endure her suffering; I overheard fragments of what they said to one another and could guess the rest; I was present when she taught Rolf to pray, and when he distracted her with the stories I had told him in a thousand and one nights[6] beneath the white mosquito netting of our bed.

---

6. A reference to the collection of medieval Arabic tales, *The Thousand and One Nights*. In the collection, King Shahryar has killed a series of wives after spending a single night with each. Queen Scheherezade tells the king suspenseful stories each night, leaving the endings for the following night; her husband does not kill her because he wants to hear the endings of the stories.

When darkness came on the second day, Rolf tried to sing Azucena to sleep with old Austrian folk songs he had learned from his mother, but she was far beyond sleep. They spent most of the night talking, each in a stupor of exhaustion and hunger, and shaking with cold. That night, imperceptibly, the unyielding floodgates that had contained Rolf Carlé's past for so many years began to open, and the torrent of all that had lain hidden in the deepest and most secret layers of memory poured out, leveling before it the obstacles that had blocked his consciousness for so long. He could not tell it all to Azucena; she perhaps did not know there was a world beyond the sea or time previous to her own; she was not capable of imagining Europe in the years of the war.[7] So he could not tell her of defeat, nor of the afternoon the Russians had led them to the concentration camp to bury prisoners dead from starvation. Why should he describe to her how the naked bodies piled like a mountain of firewood resembled fragile china? How could he tell this dying child about ovens[8] and gallows? Nor did he mention the night that he had seen his mother naked, shod in stiletto-heeled red boots, sobbing with humiliation. There was much he did not tell, but in those hours he relived for the first time all the things his mind had tried to erase. Azucena had surrendered her fear to him and so, without wishing it, had obliged Rolf to confront his own. There, beside that hellhole of mud, it was impossible for Rolf to flee from himself any longer, and the visceral terror he had lived as a boy suddenly invaded him. He reverted to the years when he was the age of Azucena, and younger, and, like her, found himself trapped in a pit without escape, buried in life, his head barely above ground; he saw before his eyes the boots and legs of his father, who had removed his belt and was whipping it in the air with the never-forgotten hiss of a viper coiled to strike. Sorrow flooded through him, intact and precise, as if it had lain always in his mind, waiting. He was once again in the armoire where his father locked him to punish him for imagined misbehavior, there where for eternal hours he had crouched with his eyes closed, not to see the darkness, with his hands over his ears, to shut out the beating of his heart, trembling, huddled like a cornered animal. Wandering in the mist of his memories he found his sister Katharina, a sweet, retarded child who spent her life hiding, with the hope that her father would forget the disgrace of her having been born. With Katharina, Rolf crawled beneath the dining room table, and with her hid there under the long white tablecloth, two children forever embraced, alert to footsteps and voices. Katharina's scent melded with his own sweat, with aromas of cooking, garlic, soup, freshly baked bread, and the unexpected odor of putrescent clay. His sister's hand in his, her frightened breathing, her silk hair against his cheek, the candid gaze of her eyes. Katharina . . . Katharina materialized before him, floating on the air like a flag, clothed in the white tablecloth, now a winding sheet, and at last he could weep for her death and for the guilt of having abandoned her. He understood then that all his exploits as a reporter, the feats that had won him such recognition and fame, were merely an attempt to keep his most ancient fears at bay, a stratagem for taking refuge behind a lens to test whether reality was more tolerable from that perspective. He took excessive risks as an exercise of courage, training by day to conquer the monsters that tormented him by night! But he had come face to face with the moment of truth; he

7. The Second World War (1939–45).
8. Crematoria in which the Nazis incinerated their victims during the Second World War.

could not continue to escape his past. He *was* Azucena; he was buried in the clayey mud; his terror was not the distant emotion of an almost forgotten childhood, it was a claw sunk in his throat. In the flush of his tears he saw his mother, dressed in black and clutching her imitation-crocodile pocketbook to her bosom, just as he had last seen her on the dock when she had come to put him on the boat to South America.[9] She had not come to dry his tears, but to tell him to pick up a shovel: the war was over and now they must bury the dead.

"Don't cry. I don't hurt anymore. I'm fine," Azucena said when dawn came.

"I'm not crying for you," Rolf Carlé smiled. "I'm crying for myself. I hurt all over."

The third day in the valley of the cataclysm began with a pale light filtering through storm clouds. The President of the Republic visited the area in his tailored safari jacket to confirm that this was the worst catastrophe of the century; the country was in mourning; sister nations had offered aid; he had ordered a state of siege; the Armed Forces would be merciless, anyone caught stealing or committing other offenses would be shot on sight. He added that it was impossible to remove all the corpses or count the thousands who had disappeared; the entire valley would be declared holy ground, and bishops would come to celebrate a solemn mass for the souls of the victims. He went to the Army field tents to offer relief in the form of vague promises to crowds of the rescued, then to the improvised hospital to offer a word of encouragement to doctors and nurses worn down from so many hours of tribulations. Then he asked to be taken to see Azucena, the little girl the whole world had seen. He waved to her with a limp statesman's hand, and microphones recorded his emotional voice and paternal tone as he told her that her courage had served as an example to the nation. Rolf Carlé interrupted to ask for a pump, and the President assured him that he personally would attend to the matter. I caught a glimpse of Rolf for a few seconds kneeling beside the mudpit. On the evening news broadcast, he was still in the same position, and I, glued to the screen like a fortuneteller to her crystal ball, could tell that something fundamental had changed in him. I knew somehow that during the night his defenses had crumbled and he had given in to grief; finally he was vulnerable. The girl had touched a part of him that he himself had no access to, a part he had never shared with me. Rolf had wanted to console her, but it was Azucena who had given him consolation.

I recognized the precise moment at which Rolf gave up the fight and surrendered to the torture of watching the girl die. I was with them, three days and two nights, spying on them from the other side of life. I was there when she told him that in all her thirteen years no boy had ever loved her and that it was a pity to leave this world without knowing love. Rolf assured her that he loved her more than he could ever love anyone, more than he loved his mother, more than his sister, more than all the women who had slept in his arms, more than he loved me, his life companion, who would have given anything to be trapped in that well in her place, who would have exchanged her life for Azucena's, and I watched as he leaned down to kiss her poor forehead, consumed by a sweet, *sad emotion he could not name.* I felt how in that instant both were saved from despair, how they were freed from the clay, how they rose above the vultures and helicopters, how together they flew above the vast swamp of corruption

---

9. Many refugees fled to South America during and immediately after the Second World War.

and laments. How, finally, they were able to accept death. Rolf Carlé prayed in silence that she would die quickly, because such pain cannot be borne.

By then I had obtained a pump and was in touch with a general who had agreed to ship it the next morning on a military cargo plane. But on the night of that third day, beneath the unblinking focus of quartz lamps and the lens of a hundred cameras, Azucena gave up, her eyes locked with those of the friend who had sustained her to the end. Rolf Carlé removed the life buoy, closed her eyelids, held her to his chest for a few moments, and then let her go. She sank slowly, a flower in the mud.

You are back with me, but you are not the same man. I often accompany you to the station and we watch the videos of Azucena again; you study them intently, looking for something you could have done to save her, something you did not think of in time. Or maybe you study them to see yourself as if in a mirror, naked. Your cameras lie forgotten in a closet; you do not write or sing; you sit long hours before the window, staring at the mountains. Beside you, I wait for you to complete the voyage into yourself, for the old wounds to heal. I know that when you return from your nightmares, we shall again walk hand in hand, as before.

1989

JUNOT DÍAZ
born 1968

Pulitzer Prize–winning novelist Junot Díaz is one of the most distinctive literary voices of any Latino writing today. Díaz has a remarkable ability to create a convincing narrative by drawing on New Jersey and Hispanic slang and to combine the street talk with a high degree of linguistic inventiveness. He thus mixes high style and low, even vulgar, language to impressive effect.

An immigrant of African descent from the Dominican Republic, Díaz, at the age of six, moved with his family to Parlin, New Jersey. Of his first days in an American school, he recalls: "I showed up at school not knowing a word of English and dressed like something out of a wetback comedy. We stood out so much in this community it was remarkable." He later worked his way through college, graduating with a bachelor's degree from Rutgers University and a master of fine arts from Cornell University; he now teaches at the Massachusetts Institute of Technology.

His first novel, *The Brief Wondrous Life of Oscar Wao* (2007), describes the lives of an immigrant family as they experience poverty and persecution in the Dominican Republic under the dictatorship of Rafael Leonidas Trujillo. In this novel, and in his short stories, Díaz interweaves techniques of the magic realism of **Gabriel García Márquez** with references to North American popular culture. He also mixes Spanish and English, in a combination often called "Spanglish." While some readers may object to the presence of Spanglish, Díaz has argued, "I've almost never read an adult book where I didn't have to pick up a dictionary. . . . I want there to be an element of incomprehension. What's language without incomprehension? What's art?"

"Drown," first published in the *New Yorker* magazine in 1996, lent its title to Díaz's first book, a collection of interlocking short stories. This memorable, one-word title refers only indirectly to any events in the story; it may represent the threat of drowning in the municipal swimming pool that the characters visit at night, but more broadly it suggests that the main character is drowning in the poverty of his surroundings and in the culture to which his parents have brought him. Díaz creates a first-person narrator whose biography is similar to his own. Many of the stories in *Drown* are narrated by Yunior de las Casas, a Dominican immigrant who arrived in the United States at the age of nine. Like **James Joyce** in *Ulysses*, Díaz has based the collection partly on Homer's *Odyssey*. Yunior, like Odysseus's son Telemachus, lives alone with his unhappy mother. In Díaz's work, the mother is waiting for the boy's father to return to her from Florida, where he is living with another woman. Díaz thus places his immigrant characters in the context of the epic tradition.

In this story, the narrator (elsewhere identified as Yunior), a drug dealer, has not gone to college. His mother tells him that his old friend Beto, who is attending college (probably Rutgers), is back in the neighborhood. She wants to know why her son no longer spends time with his old friend. Yunior reveals a key fact about Beto in the third sentence of the story: "He's a pato now." Only those with a knowledge of Latino slang will understand the meaning of *pato*, and not until much later in the story does the importance of the information become apparent, when Díaz makes the meaning of the term clear. Thus Díaz develops a level of suspense and vividly evokes the minority subculture to which the narrator belongs. Later he makes extensive use of New Jersey place-names, both to ground the story in reality and to suggest the relatively limited geographic scope of the narrator's experience—while indicating, as well, the young man's command over a territory that he can call his own. Compared by a teacher to a space shuttle crashing before it goes into orbit, Yunior senses that he is going nowhere—living at home with his mother, selling drugs, occasionally shoplifting, on the verge of drowning in poverty—while his friend Beto, by going to college, may just have saved himself.

Drown

My mother tells me Beto's home, waits for me to say something, but I keep watching the TV. Only when she's in bed do I put on my jacket and swing through the neighborhood to see. He's a pato[1] now but two years ago we were friends and he would walk into the apartment without knocking, his heavy voice rousing my mother from the Spanish of her room and drawing me up from the basement, a voice that crackled and made you think of uncles or grandfathers.

We were raging then, crazy the way we stole, broke windows, the way we pissed on people's steps and then challenged them to come out and stop us. Beto was leaving for college at the end of the summer and was delirious from the thought of it—he hated everything about the neighborhood, the break-apart

---

1. Homosexual (Caribbean Spanish slang); literally, duck.

buildings, the little strips of grass, the piles of garbage around the cans, and the dump, especially the dump.

I don't know how you can do it, he said to me. I would just find me a job anywhere and go.

Yeah, I said. I wasn't like him. I had another year to go in high school, no promises elsewhere.

Days we spent in the mall or out in the parking lot playing stickball, but nights were what we waited for. The heat in the apartments was like something heavy that had come inside to die. Families arranged on their porches, the glow from their TVs washing blue against the brick. From my family apartment you could smell the pear trees that had been planted years ago, four to a court, probably to save us all from asphyxiation. Nothing moved fast, even the daylight was slow to fade, but as soon as night settled Beto and I headed down to the community center and sprang the fence into the pool. We were never alone, every kid with legs was there. We lunged from the boards and swam out of the deep end, wrestling and farting around. At around midnight abuelas, with their night hair swirled around spiky rollers, shouted at us from their apartment windows. ¡Sinvergüenzas![2] Go home!

I pass his apartment but the windows are dark; I put my ear to the busted-up door and hear only the familiar hum of the air conditioner. I haven't decided yet if I'll talk to him. I can go back to my dinner and two years will become three.

Even from four blocks off I can hear the racket from the pool—radios too—and wonder if we were ever that loud. Little has changed, not the stink of chlorine, not the bottles exploding against the lifeguard station. I hook my fingers through the plastic-coated hurricane fence. Something tells me that he will be here; I hop the fence, feeling stupid when I sprawl on the dandelions and the grass.

Nice one, somebody calls out.

Fuck me, I say. I'm not the oldest motherfucker in the place, but it's close. I take off my shirt and my shoes and then knife in. Many of the kids here are younger brothers of the people I used to go to school with. Two of them swim past, black and Latino, and they pause when they see me, recognizing the guy who sells them their shitty dope. The crackheads have their own man, Lucero, and some other guy who drives in from Paterson,[3] the only full-time commuter in the area.

The water feels good. Starting at the deep end I glide over the slick-tiled bottom without kicking up a spume or making a splash. Sometimes another swimmer churns past me, more a disturbance of water than a body. I can still go far without coming up. While everything above is loud and bright, everything below is whispers. And always the risk of coming up to find the cops stabbing their searchlights out across the water. And then everyone running, wet feet slapping against the concrete, yelling, Fuck you, officers, you puto sucios,[4] fuck you.

When I'm tired I wade through to the shallow end, past some kid who's kissing his girlfriend, watching me as though I'm going to try to cut in, and I sit

---

2. Shameless people. "Abuelas": grandmothers.
3. A town in northern New Jersey; the name Lucero, like Lucifer in English, means "morn-
ingstar."
4. Dirty faggots (Spanish slang).

near the sign that runs the pool during the day. *No Horseplay, No Running, No Defecating, No Urinating, No Expectorating*. At the bottom someone has scrawled in *No Whites, No Fat Chiks* and someone else has provided the missing *c*. I laugh. Beto hadn't known what expectorating meant though he was the one leaving for college. I told him, spitting a greener by the side of the pool.

Shit, he said. Where did you learn that?

I shrugged.

Tell me. He hated when I knew something he didn't. He put his hands on my shoulders and pushed me under. He was wearing a cross and cutoff jeans. He was stronger than me and held me down until water flooded my nose and throat. Even then I didn't tell him; he thought I didn't read, not even dictionaries.

We live alone. My mother has enough for the rent and groceries and I cover the phone bill, sometimes the cable. She's so quiet that most of the time I'm startled to find her in the apartment. I'll enter a room and she'll stir, detaching herself from the cracking plaster walls, from the stained cabinets, and fright will pass through me like a wire. She has discovered the secret to silence: pouring café[5] without a splash, walking between rooms as if gliding on a cushion of felt, crying without a sound. You have traveled to the East and learned many secret things, I've told her. You're like a shadow warrior.

And you're like a crazy, she says. Like a big crazy.

When I come in she's still awake, her hands picking clots of lint from her skirt. I put a towel down on the sofa and we watch television together. We settle on the Spanish-language news: drama for her, violence for me. Today a child has survived a seven-story fall, busting nothing but his diaper. The hysterical babysitter, about three hundred pounds of her, is head-butting the microphone.

It's a goddamn miraclevilla,[6] she cries.

My mother asks me if I found Beto. I tell her that I didn't look.

That's too bad. He was telling me that he might be starting at a school for business.

So what?

She's never understood why we don't speak anymore. I've tried to explain, all wise-like, that everything changes, but she thinks that sort of saying is only around so you can prove it wrong.

He asked me what you were doing.

What did you say?

I told him you were fine.

You should have told him I moved.

And what if he ran into you?

I'm not allowed to visit my mother?

She notices the tightening of my arms. You should be more like me and your father.

Can't you see I'm watching television?

I was angry at him, wasn't I? But now we can talk to each other.

Am I watching television here or what?

5. Coffee.
6. Mixes English "miracle" and Spanish "maravilla" (marvel).

Saturdays she asks me to take her to the mall. As a son I feel I owe her that much, even though neither of us has a car and we have to walk two miles through redneck territory to catch the M15.[7]

Before we head out she drags us through the apartment to make sure the windows are locked. She can't reach the latches so she has me test them. With the air conditioner on we never open windows but I go through the routine anyway. Putting my hand on the latch is not enough—she wants to hear it rattle. This place just isn't safe, she tells me. Lorena got lazy and look what they did to her. They punched her and kept her locked up in her place. Those morenos[8] ate all her food and even made phone calls. Phone calls!

That's why we don't have long-distance, I tell her but she shakes her head. That's not funny, she says.

She doesn't go out much, so when she does it's a big deal. She dresses up, even puts on makeup. Which is why I don't give her lip about taking her to the mall even though I usually make a fortune on Saturdays, selling to those kids going down to Belmar or out to Spruce Run.[9]

I recognize like half the kids on the bus. I keep my head buried in my cap, praying that nobody tries to score! She watches the traffic, her hands somewhere inside her purse, doesn't say a word.

When we arrive at the mall I give her fifty dollars. Buy something, I say, hating the image I have of her, picking through the sale bins, wrinkling everything. Back in the day, my father would give her a hundred dollars at the end of each summer for my new clothes and she would take nearly a week to spend it, even though it never amounted to more than a couple of t-shirts and two pairs of jeans. She folds the bills into a square. I'll see you at three, she says.

I wander through the stores, staying in sight of the cashiers so they won't have reason to follow me. The circuit I make has not changed since my looting days. Bookstore, record store, comic-book shop, Macy's. Me and Beto used to steal like mad from these places, two, three hundred dollars of shit in an outing. Our system was simple—we walked into a store with a shopping bag and came out loaded. Back then security wasn't tight. The only trick was in the exit. We stopped right at the entrance of the store and checked out some worthless piece of junk to stop people from getting suspicious. What do you think? we asked each other. Would she like it? Both of us had seen bad shoplifters at work. All grab and run, nothing smooth about them. Not us. We idled out of the stores slow, like a fat seventies car. At this, Beto was the best. He even talked to mall security, asked them for directions, his bag all loaded up, and me, standing ten feet away, shitting my pants. When he finished he smiled, swinging his shopping bag up to hit me.

You got to stop that messing around, I told him. I'm not going to jail for bullshit like that.

You don't go to jail for shoplifting. They just turn you over to your old man.

I don't know about you, but my pops hits like a motherfucker.

He laughed. You know my dad. He flexed his hands. The nigger's got arthritis.

7. A public bus.
8. Black men (Spanish).
9. A state park in central New Jersey; "Bel-

mar": a beach resort on the New Jersey shore.
1. Purchase drugs.

My mother never suspected, even when my clothes couldn't all fit in my closet, but my father wasn't that easy. He knew what things cost and knew that I didn't have a regular job.

You're going to get caught, he told me one day. Just you wait. When you do I'll show them everything you've taken and then they'll throw your stupid ass away like a bad piece of meat.

He was a charmer, my pop, a real asshole, but he was right. Nobody can stay smooth forever, especially kids like us. One day at the bookstore, we didn't even hide the drops. Four issues of the same *Playboy* for kicks, enough audio books to start our own library. No last minute juke either. The lady who stepped in front of us didn't look old, even with her white hair. Her silk shirt was half unbuttoned and a silver horn necklace sat on the freckled top of her chest. I'm sorry fellows, but I have to check your bag, she said. I kept moving, and looked back all annoyed, like she was asking us for a quarter or something. Beto got polite and stopped. No problem, he said, slamming the heavy bag into her face. She hit the cold tile with a squawk, her palms slapping the ground. There you go, Beto said.

Security found us across from the bus stop, under a Jeep Cherokee. A bus had come and gone, both of us too scared to take it, imagining a plainclothes waiting to clap the cuffs on. I remember that when the rent-a-cop tapped his nightstick against the fender and said, You little shits better come out here real slow, I started to cry. Beto didn't say a word, his face stretched out and gray, his hand squeezing mine, the bones in our fingers pressing together.

Nights I drink with Alex and Danny. The Malibou Bar is no good, just washouts and the sucias[2] we can con into joining us. We drink too much, roar at each other and make the skinny bartender move closer to the phone. On the wall hangs a cork dartboard and a Brunswick Gold Crown blocks the bathroom, its bumpers squashed, the felt pulled like old skin.

When the bar begins to shake back and forth like a rumba, I call it a night and go home, through the fields that surround the apartments. In the distance you can see the Raritan,[3] as shiny as an earthworm, the same river my homeboy goes to school on. The dump has long since shut down, and grass has spread over it like a sickly fuzz, and from where I stand, my right hand directing a colorless stream of piss downward, the landfill might be the top of a blond head, square and old.

In the mornings I run. My mother is already up, dressing for her housecleaning job. She says nothing to me, would rather point to the mangu[4] she has prepared than speak.

I run three miles easily, could have pushed a fourth if I were in the mood. I keep an eye out for the recruiter who prowls around our neighborhood in his dark K-car. We've spoken before. He was out of uniform and called me over, jovial, and I thought I was helping some white dude with directions. Would you mind if I asked you a question?

No.

Do you have a job?

---

2. Sluts (Spanish slang).
3. A major river in central New Jersey.
4. Plantain-based dish originating in the Dominican Republic.

Not right now.

Would you like one? A real career, more than you'll get around here?

I remember stepping back. Depends on what it is, I said.

Son, I know somebody who's hiring. It's the United States government.

Well. Sorry, but I ain't Army material.

That's exactly what I used to think, he said, his ten piggy fingers buried in his carpeted steering wheel. But now I have a house, a car, a gun and a wife. Discipline. Loyalty. Can you say that you have those things? Even one?

He's a southerner, red-haired, his drawl so out of place that the people around here laugh just hearing him. I take to the bushes when I see his car on the road. These days my guts feel loose and cold and I want to be away from here. He won't have to show me his Desert Eagle or flash the photos of the skinny Filipino girls sucking dick. He'll only have to smile and name the places and I'll listen.

When I reach the apartment, I lean against my door, waiting for my heart to slow, for the pain to lose its edge. I hear my mother's voice, a whisper from the kitchen. She sounds hurt or nervous, maybe both. At first I'm terrified that Beto's inside with her but then I look and see the phone cord, swinging lazily. She's talking to my father, something she knows I disapprove of. He's in Florida now, a sad guy who calls her and begs for money. He swears that if she moves down there he'll leave the woman he's living with. These are lies, I've told her, but she still calls him. His words coil inside of her, wrecking her sleep for days. She opens the refrigerator door slightly so that the whir of the compressor masks their conversation. I walk in on her and hang up the phone. That's enough, I say.

She's startled, her hand squeezing the loose folds of her neck. That was him, she says quietly.

On school days Beto and I chilled at the stop together but as soon as that bus came over the Parkwood hill I got to thinking about how I was failing gym and screwing up math and how I hated every single living teacher on the planet.

I'll see *you* in the p.m., I said.

He was already standing on line. I just stood back and grinned, my hands in my pockets. With our bus drivers you didn't have to hide. Two of them didn't give a rat fuck and the third one, the Brazilian preacher, was too busy talking Bible to notice anything but the traffic in front of him.

Being truant without a car was no easy job but I managed. I watched a lot of TV and when it got boring I trooped down to the mall or the Sayreville library, where you could watch old documentaries for free. I always came back to the neighborhood late, so the bus wouldn't pass me on Ernston[5] and nobody could yell Asshole! out the windows. Beto would usually be home or down by the swings, but other times he wouldn't be around at all. Out visiting other neighborhoods. He knew a lot of folks I didn't—a messed-up black kid from Madison Park, two brothers who were into that N.Y. club scene, who spent money on platform shoes and leather backpacks. I'd leave a message with his parents and then watch some more TV. The next day he'd be out at the bus stop, too busy smoking a cigarette to say much about the day before.

5. Ernston and Sayreville are towns in central New Jersey.

You need to learn how to walk the world, he told me. There's a lot out there.

Some nights me and the boys drive to New Brunswick.[6] A nice city, the Raritan so low and silty that you don't have to be Jesus to walk over it. We hit the Melody and the Roxy, stare at the college girls. We drink a lot and then spin out onto the dance floor. None of the chicas[7] ever dance with us, but a glance or a touch can keep us talking shit for hours.

Once the clubs close we go to the Franklin Diner, gorge ourselves on pancakes, and then, after we've smoked our pack, head home. Danny passes out in the back seat and Alex cranks the window down to keep the wind in his eyes. He's fallen asleep in the past, wrecked two cars before this one. The streets have been picked clean of students and townies and we blow through every light, red or green. At the Old Bridge Turnpike[8] we pass the fag bar, which never seems to close. Patos are all over the parking lot, drinking and talking.

Sometimes Alex will stop by the side of the road and say, Excuse me. When somebody comes over from the bar he'll point his plastic pistol at them, just to see if they'll run or shit their pants. Tonight he just puts his head out the window. Fuck you! he shouts and then settles back in his seat, laughing.

That's original, I say.

He puts his head out the window again. Eat me, then!

Yeah, Danny mumbles from the back. Eat me.

Twice. That's it.

The first time was at the end of that summer. We had just come back from the pool and were watching a porn video at his parents' apartment. His father was a nut for these tapes, ordering them from wholesalers in California and Grand Rapids. Beto used to tell me how his pop would watch them in the middle of the day, not caring a lick about his moms, who spent the time in the kitchen, taking hours to cook a pot of rice and gandules.[9] Beto would sit down with his pop and neither of them would say a word, except to laugh when somebody caught it in the eye or the face.

We were an hour into the new movie, some vaina[1] that looked like it had been filmed in the apartment next door, when he reached into my shorts. What the fuck are you doing? I asked, but he didn't stop. His hand was dry. I kept my eyes on the television, too scared to watch. I came right away, smearing the plastic sofa covers. My legs started shaking and suddenly I wanted out. He didn't say anything to me as I left, just sat there watching the screen.

The next day he called and when I heard his voice I was cool but I wouldn't go to the mall or anywhere else. My mother sensed that something was wrong and pestered me about it, but I told her to leave me the fuck alone, and my pops, who was home on a visit, stirred himself from the couch to slap me down. Mostly I stayed in the basement, terrified that I would end up abnormal, a fucking pato, but he was my best friend and back then that mattered to me

6. Town in north-central New Jersey where Rutgers University is located; the Melody and the Roxy were dance clubs on French Street in New Brunswick in the 1980s and 1990s.

7. Girls.
8. A road in north-central New Jersey.
9. Pigeon peas (Spanish).
1. Worthless item (Spanish).

more than anything. This alone got me out of the apartment and over to the pool that night. He was already there, his body pale and flabby under the water. Hey, he said. I was beginning to worry about you.

Nothing to worry about, I said.

We swam and didn't talk much and later we watched a Skytop crew pull a bikini top from a girl stupid enough to hang out alone. Give it, she said, covering herself, but these kids howled, holding it up over her head, the shiny laces flopping just out of reach. When they began to pluck at her arms, she walked away, leaving them to try the top on over their flat pecs.

He put his hand on my shoulder, my pulse a code under his palm. Let's go, he said. Unless of course you're not feeling good.

I'm feeling fine, I said.

Since his parents worked nights we pretty much owned the place until six the next morning. We sat in front of his television, in our towels, his hands bracing against my abdomen and thighs. I'll stop if you want, he said and I didn't respond. After I was done, he laid his head in my lap. I wasn't asleep or awake, but caught somewhere in between, rocked slowly back and forth the way surf holds junk against the shore, rolling it over and over. In three weeks he was leaving. Nobody can touch me, he kept saying. We'd visited the school and I'd seen how beautiful the campus was, with all the students drifting from dorm to class. I thought of how in high school our teachers loved to crowd us into their lounge every time a space shuttle took off from Florida. One teacher, whose family had two grammar schools named after it, compared us to the shuttles. A few of you are going to make it. Those are the orbiters. But the majority of you are just going to burn out. Going nowhere. He dropped his hand onto his desk. I could already see myself losing altitude, fading, the earth spread out beneath me, hard and bright.

I had my eyes closed and the television was on and when the hallway door crashed open, he jumped up and I nearly cut my dick off struggling with my shorts. It's just the neighbor, he said, laughing. He was laughing, but I was saying, Fuck this, and getting my clothes on.

I believe I see him in his father's bottomed-out Cadillac, heading towards the turnpike, but I can't be sure. He's probably back in school already. I deal close to home, trooping up and down the same dead-end street where the kids drink and smoke. These punks joke with me, pat me down for taps, sometimes too hard. Now that strip malls line Route 9,[2] a lot of folks have part-time jobs; the kids stand around smoking in their aprons, name tags dangling heavily from pockets.

When I get home, my sneakers are filthy so I take an old toothbrush to their soles, scraping the crap into the tub. My mother has thrown open the windows and propped open the door. It's cool enough, she explains. She has prepared dinner—rice and beans, fried cheese, tostones. Look what I bought, she says, showing me two blue t-shirts. They were two for one so I bought you one. Try it on.

It fits tight but I don't mind. She cranks up the television. A movie dubbed into Spanish, a classic, one that everyone knows. The actors throw themselves around, passionate, but their words are plain and deliberate. It's hard to

2. A north–south federal highway that runs through New Jersey.

imagine anybody going through life this way. I pull out the plug of bills from my pockets. She takes it from me, her fingers soothing the creases. A man who treats his plata[3] like this doesn't deserve to spend it, she says.

We watch the movie and the two hours together makes us friendly. She puts her hand on mine. Near the end of the film, just as our heroes are about to fall apart under a hail of bullets, she takes off her glasses and kneads her temples, the light of the television flickering across her face. She watches another minute and then her chin lists to her chest. Almost immediately her eyelashes begin to tremble, a quiet semaphore. She is dreaming, dreaming of Boca Raton, of strolling under the jacarandas[4] with my father. You can't be anywhere forever, was what Beto used to say, what he said to me the day I went to see him off. He handed me a gift, a book, and after he was gone I threw it away, didn't even bother to open it and read what he'd written.

I let her sleep until the end of the movie and when I wake her she shakes her head, grimacing. You better check those windows, she says. I promise her I will.

1996

---

3. Money (Spanish slang).   4. Tropical flowering plant.

ROBERTO BOLAÑO
1953–2003

Celebrated after his premature death as one of the first great novelists of the twenty-first century, Roberto Bolaño extends the Latin American tradition of combining fantasy and reality to comment on the region's tragic history. Bolaño wrote that violence appears in his works "in an accidental way, which is how violence functions everywhere." While following the lives of writers and other middle-class figures apparently unaffected by the turbulent history of their region, Bolaño reveals, almost casually, how deeply shaped their lives have in fact been by its political upheavals.

Mystery also pervades much of Bolaño's biography. Born in Chile to a truck driver and a teacher, he moved to Mexico City with his family as a teenager. After dropping out of school, Bolaño joined several friends to form a poetic movement called infrarealism, influenced by the Dadaists and vehemently opposing the hero of Mexican culture, **Octavio Paz**, for his alleged conservatism. The infrarealist manifesto declared that "the poem is a journey, and the poet is a hero who reveals heroes." True to this vision, Bolaño's later fiction would trace the journeys of many real and fictional poets.

Bolaño soon became involved in left-wing politics; he claimed to have been imprisoned while fighting against the dictatorship of Augusto Pinochet in Chile in the 1970s, although his friends later disputed his assertion. (He also claimed, in later years, to have been a longtime heroin addict, a story that his wife strenuously denied, but his death from a liver ailment that may have been hepatitis seemed to confirm it.) After further travels in Central America and Europe, Bolaño settled near Barcelona, Spain, around 1980, working for a time as a night watchman and writing poetry in his spare hours. After the birth of his son, in 1990, he switched to writing fiction, in the hope that it would provide a better living. (He was indeed able to supplement his meager income by entering minor literary contests.) Suffering from the liver disease that eventually killed him, he wrote a series of brilliant novels that drew on the tradition of Latin American fiction that intertwines fantastical phenomena with the political events of the late twentieth century. In their style, his fictions suggest the invented worlds of **Jorge Luis Borges**. "I could live under a table reading Borges," he once said, although he was not above defying the master with a boastful challenge: "My life has been infinitely more savage than Borges's." Most of his novels were published in the 1990s, but his last work, 2666, was published posthumously in 2004. Its English translation won the National Book Critics Circle award for fiction in 2008.

Bolaño's fascination with the effects of large-scale history on everyday life, as well as his frequent allusions to other writers, seem to mark him as a postmodernist, but in many respects his stories are more straightforward and less experimental than typical postmodernism. Like earlier writers of the Latin American "Boom," such as **Julio Cortázar** and **Gabriel García Márquez**, Bolaño concerns himself with politics; but rather than take sides, he tends to show his protagonists (almost all of whom are writers) making compromises with political violence in order to get by. As the novelist and critic Francisco Goldman once remarked, "the inseparable dangers of life and literature, and the relationship of life to literature, were the constant themes of Bolaño's writings and also of his life." Although the extent to which Bolaño participated in political struggle remains a mystery, there is no doubt that social and economic turmoil of the late twentieth century helped shape his fiction into a richly imagined world, very similar to—but at times a crazed glass reflecting—our own.

The story presented here, "Sensini" (1997), starts out as the chronicle of a young writer's life and his interest in the literary prizes sponsored by various Spanish towns. Drawing on Bolaño's experience, the work is set in the early 1980s, when the author was in his late twenties; like the author himself, the narrator is Chilean. The narrator, who lives near Barcelona, befriends an older, Argentine writer named Sensini, who lives with his wife and daughter in poverty in Madrid. (Sensini's character seems to be based in part on the writer Antonio di Benedetto, 1922–1986.) What begins as a simple tale of the narrator's apprenticeship and youthful literary ambitions becomes more troubling when he realizes that Sensini is looking for a substitute for his son, Gregorio, who has recently disappeared in the Argentine Dirty War (1976–83)—an extrajudicial campaign of murder and terror that the dictator Jorge Rafael Videla conducted against students, intellectuals, and opponents of his regime. Still, despite the narrator's frequent discussion of real-life Argentine authors, this is no straightforward historical account. The narrator develops a fascination with Sensini's daughter, Miranda, named after the character in Shakespeare's *The Tempest* whom the slave Caliban desires (and almost rapes). And Sensini's son, Gregorio, is named after Gregor Samsa of **Franz Kafka**'s *The Metamorphosis*, another story about complicated family relationships. Wondering whether to become an adoptive son to the writer he admires, the narrator finds himself increasingly entangled in the older man's family life, in a maze of literary allusions, and in the tragedies of Latin American political life in the 1980s.

Sensini[1]

The way in which my friendship with Sensini developed was somewhat unusual. At the time I was twenty-something and poorer than a church mouse. I was living on the outskirts of Girona,[2] in a dilapidated house that my sister and brother-in-law had left me when they moved to Mexico, and I had just lost my job as a night watchman in a Barcelona campground, a job that had exacerbated my tendency not to sleep at night. I had practically no friends and all I did was write and go for long walks, starting at seven in the evening, just after getting up, with a feeling like jet lag—an odd sensation of fragility, of being there and not there, somehow distant from my surroundings. I was living on what I had saved during the summer, and although I spent very little my savings dwindled as autumn drew on. Perhaps that was what prompted me to enter the Alcoy National Literature Competition, open to writers in Spanish, whatever their nationality or place of residence. There were three categories: for poems, stories, and essays. First I thought about trying for the poetry prize, but I felt it would be demeaning to send what I did best into the arena with the lions (or hyenas). Then I thought about the essay, but when they sent me the conditions, I discovered that it had to be about Alcoy,[3] its environs, its history, its eminent sons, its future prospects, and I couldn't face it. So I decided to go for the story prize and sent off three copies of the best one I had (not that I had many) and sat down to wait.

When the winners were announced I was working as a vendor in a handcrafts market where absolutely no one was selling anything handcrafted. I won fourth prize and ten thousand pesetas,[4] which the Alcoy Council paid with scrupulous promptitude. Shortly afterward I received the anthology, with the winning story and those of the six finalists, liberally peppered with typos. Naturally my story was better than the winner's, so I cursed the judges and told myself, Well, what can you expect? But the real surprise was coming across the name Luis Antonio Sensini,[5] the Argentinean writer, who had won third prize with a story in which the narrator went to the countryside and when he got there his son died, or went away to the country because his son had died in the city—it was hard to tell—in any case, out there in the countryside, on the bare plains, the narrator's son went on dying, that much was clear. It was a claustrophobic story, very much in Sensini's manner, set in a world where vast geographical spaces could suddenly shrink to the dimensions of a coffin, and it was better than the winning story and the one that came in second, as well as those that came in fourth, fifth, and sixth.

I don't know what moved me to ask the Alcoy Council for Sensini's address. I had read one of his novels and some of his stories in Latin American magazines. The novel was the kind of book that finds its own readers by word of mouth. Entitled *Ugarte*, it was about a series of moments in the life of Juan de Ugarte, a bureaucrat in the Viceroyalty of the Río de la Plata[6] at the end of the

1. Translated from Spanish by Chris Andrews.
2. City in northeastern Catalonia, Spain.
3. A city in Alicante province, south of Barcelona, on the Mediterranean coast of Spain.
4. Approximately $125 in the early 1980s, when the story is set (about $275 in 2011).
5. Based on the real-life Argentine writer Antonio di Benedetto (1922–1986).
6. The last Spanish-controlled government of South America before the independence of Argentina (1776–1810). Juan de Ugarte (1662–1730): actually the name of a Jesuit missionary in Mexico about a century before the Viceroyalty of the Río de la Plata.

eighteenth century. Some (mainly Spanish) critics had dismissed it as Kafka[7] in the colonies, but gradually the novel had made its way, and by the time I came across Sensini's name in the Alcoy anthology, *Ugarte* had recruited a small group of devoted readers, scattered around Latin America and Spain, most of whom knew each other, either as friends or as gratuitously bitter enemies. He had published other books, of course, in Argentina, and with Spanish publishers who had since gone broke, and he belonged to that intermediate generation of Argentinean writers, born in the twenties, after Cortázar, Bioy Casares, Sábato, and Mújica Laínez, a generation whose best-known representative (to me, back then, at any rate) was Haroldo Conti, who disappeared in one of the special camps set up by Videla and his henchmen during the dictatorship. It was a generation (although perhaps I am using the word too loosely) that hadn't come to much, but not for want of brilliance or talent: followers of Roberto Arlt,[8] journalists, teachers, and translators; in a sense they foreshadowed what was to come, in their own sad and skeptical way, which led them one by one to the abyss.

I had a soft spot for those writers. In years gone by, I had read Abelardo Castillo's plays and the stories of Daniel Moyano and Rodolfo Walsh[9] (who was killed under the dictatorship, like Conti). I read their work piecemeal, whatever I could find in Argentinean, Mexican, or Cuban magazines, or the second-hand bookshops of Mexico City: pirated anthologies of Buenos Aires writing, probably the twentieth century's best writing in Spanish. They were part of that tradition, and although, of course, they didn't have the stature of Borges or Cortázar, and were soon overtaken by Manuel Puig and Osvaldo Soriano,[1] their concise, intelligent texts were a constant source of complicit delight. Needless to say, my favorite was Sensini, and having been his fellow runner-up in a provincial literary competition—an association that I found at once flattering and profoundly depressing—encouraged me to make contact with him, to pay my respects and tell him how much his work meant to me.

The Alcoy Council sent me his address without delay—he lived in Madrid—and one night, after dinner or a light meal or just a snack, I wrote him a long letter, which rambled from *Ugarte* and the stories of his that I had read in magazines to myself, my house on the outskirts of Girona, the competition (I made fun of the winner), the political situation in Chile and in Argentina (both dictatorships were still firmly in place),[2] Walsh's stories (along with Sensini, Walsh was my other favorite in that generation), life in Spain, and life in general. To my surprise, I received a reply barely a week later. He began by thanking me for my letter; he said that the Alcoy Council had sent him the anthology,

7. Franz Kafka (1883–1924), German-Jewish-Czech author of *The Metamorphosis* (1915), in which Gregor Samsa is transformed into a giant insect.

8. Julio Cortázar (1914–1984); Adolfo Bioy Casares (1914–1999); Ernesto Sábato (1911–); Manuel Mújica Laínez (1910–1984); Haroldo Conti (1925–1976); Roberto Arlt (1900–1942): Argentine writers and critics. Jorge Rafael Videla (b. 1925), dictator of Argentina from 1976 to 1981, responsible for human rights abuses including kidnapping, extrajudi-

cial murder of political opponents, and use of concentration camps.

9. Abelardo Castillo (b. 1935); Daniel Moyano (1930–1992); Rodolfo Walsh (1927–1977): Argentine writers.

1. Jorge Luis Borges (1899–1986); Manuel Puig (1932–1990); Osvaldo Soriano (1943–1997): Argentine writers.

2. Reference to Jorge Rafael Videla's dictatorship in Argentina (1976–81) and to Augusto Pinochet's dictatorship in Chile (1973–90).

too, but that, unlike me, he hadn't found time to look at the winning story or those of the other finalists (later on, in a passing reference, he admitted that it wasn't so much a lack of time as a lack of "fortitude"), although he had just read mine and thought it well done, "a first-rate story," he said (I kept the letter), and he urged me to persevere, not, as I thought at first, to persevere with my writing, but to persevere with the competitions, as he intended to do himself, he assured me. He went on to ask me which competitions were "looming on the horizon," imploring me to notify him as soon as I heard of one. In exchange he sent me the submission guidelines for two short-story competitions, one in Plasencia and the other in Écija,[3] with prizes of 25,000 and 30,000 pesetas respectively. He had tracked these down, as I later discovered, in Madrid newspapers or magazines whose mere existence was a crime or a miracle, depending on your point of view. There was still time for me to enter both competitions, and Sensini finished his letter on a curiously enthusiastic note, as if the pair of us were on our marks for a race that, as well as being hard and meaningless, would never end. "Pen to paper now, no shirking!" he wrote.

I remember thinking, What a strange letter. I remember reading a few chapters of *Ugarte*. Around that time the traveling booksellers came to Girona to set up their stalls in the square where the movie theaters are, laying out their mostly unsaleable stock: remaindered books published by recently bankrupt companies, books printed during World War II, romance novels and wild west sagas, and collections of postcards. At one of the stalls I found a book of stories by Sensini and bought it. It was as good as new—in fact it *was* new, one of those titles that publishers sell off to the traveling salesmen when no one else can move it, when there's not a bookshop or a distributor left who's willing to take it on—and for the following week I lived and breathed Sensini. I read his letter over and over, leafed through *Ugarte*, and when I wanted a little action, something new, I turned to the stories. Although the themes and situations varied, the settings were generally rural, and the protagonists were the fabled gauchos of the pampa,[4] that is to say armed and unfortunate individuals, either loners or endowed with peculiar notions of sociability. Whereas *Ugarte* was a cold book, written with neurosurgical precision, the collection of stories was all warmth: brave and aimless characters adrift in landscapes that seemed to be gradually drawing away from the reader (and sometimes taking the reader with them).

I didn't manage to send in an entry for the Plasencia competition, but I did for the Écija one. As soon as I had mailed off the copies of my story (under the pseudonym Aloysius Acker),[5] I realized that sitting around waiting for the results could only make things worse. So I decided to look for more competitions; that way at least I'd be able to comply with Sensini's request. Over the next few days, when I went down to Girona, I spent hours looking through back copies of newspapers in search of announcements. Some papers put them in a column next to the society news; in others, they came after the crime reports and before the sports section; the most serious paper had them wedged between the weather and the obituaries. They were never with the book reviews,

3. City in the province of Seville near the Mediterranean coast of Spain; "Plasencia": city in the Extremadura region in western Spain.
4. Cowboys of the South American plains.

5. "Aloysius Acker" is the title of a poem by Martín Adán, the pseudonym of the Peruvian writer Rafael de la Fuente Benavides (1908–1985).

of course. In my search I discovered a magazine put out by the Catalonian government, which, along with advertisements for scholarships, exchanges, jobs, and postgraduate courses, published announcements of literary competitions, mostly for Catalans writing in Catalan, but there were some exceptions. I soon found three for which Sensini and I were eligible, and they were still open, so I wrote him a letter.

Like the first time, I received a reply by return mail. Sensini's letter was short. He answered some of my questions, mainly about the book of stories I had recently bought, but also included photocopies of the details for three more short-story competitions, one of which was sponsored by the National Railway Company, with a tidy sum for the winner and "50,000 pesetas per head" (as he put it) for the ten finalists: no prize for dreaming, you have to be in it to win it. I wrote back saying I didn't have enough stories for all six competitions, but most of my letter was about other things (in fact I got rather carried away): travel, lost love, Walsh, Conti, Francisco Urondo . . . I asked him about Gelman,[6] whom he was bound to have known, gave him a summary of my life story, and somehow ended up going on about the tango and labyrinths, as I always do with Argentineans (it's something Chileans are prone to).

Sensini's reply was prompt and voluble, at least as far as writing and competitions were concerned. On one sheet, recto and verso,[7] single-spaced, he set out a kind of general strategy for the pursuit of provincial literary prizes. I speak from experience, he wrote. The letter began with a blessing on prizes (whether in earnest or in jest, I have never been able to tell), those precious supplements to the writer's modest income. He referred to the sponsors—town councils and credit unions—as "those good people with their touching faith in literature" and "those disinterested and dutiful readers." He entertained no illusions, however, about the erudition of the "good people" in question, who presumably exercised their touching faith on these ephemeral anthologies (or not). He told me I must compete for as many prizes as possible, although he suggested I take the precaution of changing a story's title if I was entering it for, say, three competitions that were due to be judged around the same time. He cited the example of his story "At Dawn," a story I didn't know, which he had used to test his method, as a guinea pig is used to test the effects of a new vaccine. For the first competition, with the biggest prize, "At Dawn" was entered as "At Dawn"; for the second, he changed the title to "The Gauchos"; for the third, it was called "The Other Pampa"; and for the last, "No Regrets." Of these four competitions, it won the second and the fourth, and with the money from the prizes he was able to pay a month-and-half's rent (in Madrid the rents had gone through the roof). Of course no one realized that "The Gauchos" and "No Regrets" were the same story with different titles, although there was always the risk that one of the judges might have read the story in another contest (in Spain the peculiar occupation of judging literary prizes was obstinately monopolized by a clique of minor poets and novelists, plus former laureates). The little world of letters is terrible as well as ridiculous, he wrote. And he added that even if one's story did come before the same judge twice, the danger was minimal, since they generally didn't read the entries or only skimmed them. Furthermore, who was to say that

6. Francisco Urondo (1910–1976); Juan Gelman (b. 1930): Argentine writers.

7. Front and back.

"The Gauchos" and "No Regrets" were not two different stories whose singularity resided precisely in their respective titles? Similar, very similar even, but different. Toward the end of the letter he said that, of course, in a perfect world, he would be otherwise occupied, living and writing in Buenos Aires, for example, but the way things were, he had to earn a crust somehow (I'm not sure they say that in Argentina; we do in Chile) and, for now, the competitions were helping him get by. It's like a lesson in Spanish geography, he wrote. At the end, or maybe in a postscript, he declared: I'm going on sixty, but I feel as if I were twenty-five. At first this struck me as very sad, but when I read it for the second or third time I realized it was his way of asking me: How old are you, kid? I remember I replied immediately. I told him I was twenty-eight, three years older than him. That morning I felt not exactly happy again but more alive, as if an infusion of energy were reanimating my sense of humor and my memory.

Although I didn't follow Sensini's advice and become a full-time prize hunter, I did enter the competitions he and I had recently discovered, without any success. Sensini pulled off another double in Don Benito[8] and Écija, with a story originally called "The Sabre," renamed "Two Swords" for Écija and "The Deepest Cut" for Don Benito. And in the competition sponsored by the railways he was one of the finalists. As well as a cash sum, he won a pass that entitled him to travel free on Spanish trains for a year.

Little by little I learned more about him. He lived in a flat in Madrid with his wife and his daughter, Miranda,[9] who was seventeen years old. He had a son, from his first marriage, who had gone to ground somewhere in Latin America, or that was what he wanted to believe. The son's name was Gregorio; he was thirty-five and had worked as a journalist. Sometimes Sensini would tell me about the inquiries he was making through human rights organizations and the European Union in an attempt to determine Gregorio's whereabouts. When he got on to this subject, his prose became heavy and monotonous, as if he were trying to exorcise his ghosts by describing the bureaucratic labyrinth. I haven't lived with Gregorio, he once told me, since he was five years old, just a kid. He didn't elaborate, but I imagined a five-year-old boy and Sensini typing in a newspaper office: even then it was already too late. I also wondered about the boy's name and somehow came to the conclusion that it must have been an unconscious homage to Gregor Samsa![1] Of course I never mentioned this to Sensini. When he got on to the subject of Miranda he cheered up. Miranda was young and ready to take on the world, insatiably curious, pretty too, and kind. She looks like Gregorio, he wrote, except that (obviously) she's a girl and she has been spared what my son had to go through.

Gradually, Sensini's letters grew longer. The district where he lived in Madrid was run-down; his apartment had two bedrooms, a dining-room-cum-living-room, a kitchen, and a bathroom. At first I was surprised to discover that his place was smaller than mine; then I felt ashamed. It seemed unfair. Sensini wrote in the dining room, at night, "when the wife and the girl are asleep," and he was a heavy smoker. He earned his living doing some kind of work for a publisher (I think he edited translations) and by sending his stories out to do battle

---

8. City in the Extremadura region.
9. The name of Prospero's daughter in Shakespeare's The Tempest. The slave Caliban loves her and attempts to rape her.
1. Protagonist of The Metamorphosis (1915), by Franz Kafka.

in the provinces. Every now and then he received a royalty check for one of his many books, but most of the publishers were chronically forgetful or had gone broke. The only book that went on selling well was *Ugarte*, which had been published by a company in Barcelona. It didn't take me long to realize that he was living in poverty: not destitution, but the genteel poverty of a middle-class family fallen on hard times. His wife (her name was Carmela Zadjman, a story in itself) did freelance work for publishers and gave English, French, and Hebrew lessons, although she'd been obliged to take on cleaning jobs occasionally. The daughter was busy with her studies and would soon be going on to university. In one of my letters I asked Sensini whether Miranda wanted to be a writer too. He wrote back: No, thank God, she's going to study medicine.

One night I wrote and asked for a photo of his family. Only after putting the letter in the mail did I realize that what I really wanted was to see what Miranda looked like. A week later I received a photo, no doubt taken in the Retiro, which showed an old man and a middle-aged woman next to a tall, slim adolescent girl with straight hair and very large breasts. The old man was smiling happily, the middle-aged woman was looking at her daughter, as if saying something to her, and Miranda was facing the photographer with a serious look that I found both moving and disturbing. Sensini also sent me a photocopy of another photo, showing a young man more or less my age, with sharp features, very thin lips, prominent cheekbones and a broad forehead. He was strongly built and probably tall, and he was gazing at the camera (it was a studio photo) with a confident and perhaps slightly impatient expression. It was Gregorio Sensini, at the age of twenty-two, before he disappeared, quite a bit younger than me, in fact, but he had an air of experience that made him seem older.

The photo and the photocopy lived on my desk for a long time. I would sit there staring at them or take them to the bedroom and look at them until I fell asleep. Sensini had asked me to send a photograph of myself. I didn't have a recent one, so I decided to go to the photo booth in the station, which at the time was the only photo booth in the whole of Girona. But I didn't like the way the photos came out. I thought I looked ugly and skinny and scruffy haired. So I kept putting off sending any of them and going back to spend more money at the photo booth. Finally I chose one at random, put it in an envelope with a postcard, and sent it to him. It was a while before I received a reply. In the meantime I remember I wrote a very long, very bad poem, full of voices and faces that seemed different at first, but all belonging to Miranda Sensini, and when, in the poem, I finally realized this and could put it into words, when I could say to her, Miranda it's me, your father's friend and correspondent, she turned around and ran off in search of her brother, Gregorio Samsa, in search of Gregorio Samsa's eyes, shining at the end of a dim corridor in which the shadowy masses of Latin America's terror were shifting imperceptibly.

The reply, when it came, was long and friendly. Sensini and Carmela's verdict on my photo was positive: they thought I looked nice, like they imagined me, a bit on the skinny side maybe, but fit and well, and they liked the postcard of the Girona cathedral, which they hoped to see for themselves in the near future, as soon as they had sorted out a few financial and household problems. It was clear that they were hoping to stay at my place when they came. In return they offered to put me up whenever I wanted to go to Madrid. It's a modest apartment, and it isn't clean either, wrote Sensini, quoting a comic-strip gaucho who was famous in South America at the beginning of the seventies.[2] He didn't say anything about his literary projects. Nor did he mention any contests.

At first I thought of sending Miranda my poem, but after much hesitation and soul-searching I decided not to. I must be going mad, I thought: if I sent her that poem, there'd be no more letters from Sensini, and who could blame him? So I didn't send it. For a while I applied myself to the search for new literary prizes. In one of his letters Sensini said he was worried that he might have run his race. I misunderstood; I thought he meant he was running out of competitions to enter.

I wrote back to say they must come to Girona; he and Carmela were most welcome to stay at my house. I even spent several days cleaning, sweeping, mopping, and dusting, having convinced myself (quite unreasonably) that they might turn up at any moment, with Miranda. Since they had one free pass they'd only have to buy two tickets, and Catalonia, I stressed, was full of wonderful things to see and do. I mentioned Barcelona, Olot, the Costa Brava,[3] and talked about the happy days we could spend together. In a long reply, thanking me for my invitation, Sensini said that for the moment they couldn't leave Madrid. Unlike any of the preceding letters, this one was rather confused, although in the middle he returned to the theme of prizes (I think he had won another one) and encouraged me not to give up, to keep on trying. He also said something about the writer's trade or profession, and I had the impression that his words were meant partly for me and partly for himself, as a kind of reminder. The rest, as I said, was a muddle. When I got to the end I had the feeling that someone in his family wasn't well.

Two or three months later Sensini wrote to tell me that one of the bodies in a recently discovered mass grave was probably Gregorio's.[4] His letter was restrained. There was no outpouring of grief; all he said was that on a certain day, at a certain time, a group of forensic pathologists and officials from human rights organizations had opened a mass grave containing the bodies of more than fifty young people, etc. For the first time, I didn't want to reply in writing. I would have liked to call him, but I don't think he had a telephone, and if he did I didn't know his number. My letter was brief. I said I was sorry, and ventured to point out that they still didn't know for sure that the body was Gregorio's.

Summer came and I took a job in a hotel on the coast. In Madrid that summer there were numerous lectures, courses, and all sorts of cultural activities, but Sensini didn't participate in any of them, or if he did, it wasn't mentioned in the newspaper I was reading.

At the end of August I sent him a card. I said that maybe when the season was over I would visit him. That was all. When I got back to Girona in the middle of September, in the small pile of letters slipped under the door, I found one from Sensini dated August seventh. He had written to say good-bye. He was going back to Argentina; with the return of democracy[5] he would be safe now, so there was no point staying away any longer. And it was the only way he would be able to find out for sure what had happened to Gregorio. Carmela, of

2. An allusion to Roberto Fontanarrosa, *Inodoro Pereyra (el renegáu)* (*Stinky Pereyra, the Renegade*), a famous comic strip about the life of a gaucho.
3. A coastal region of Catalonia, Spain. Bar-

celona and Olot are cities in Catalonia.
4. The mass grave is one of many in which political enemies of Videla's regime were buried.
5. The return to democracy in Argentina took place in late 1983.

course, is returning with me, he said, but Miranda will stay. I wrote to him immediately, at the only address I had, but received no reply.

Gradually I came to accept that Sensini had gone back to Argentina for good and that, unless he wrote to me again, our correspondence had come to an end. I waited a long time for a letter from him, or so it seems to me now, looking back. The letter, of course, never came. I tried to tell myself that life in Buenos Aires must be hectic, an explosion of activity, hardly time to breathe or blink. I wrote to him again at the Madrid address, hoping that the letter would be sent on to Miranda, but a month later it was returned to me stamped "Addressee Unknown." So I gave up and let the days go by and gradually forgot about Sensini, although on my rare visits to Barcelona I would sometimes spend whole afternoons in secondhand bookshops looking for his other books, the ones I knew by their titles but was destined never to read. All I could find in the shops were old copies of *Ugarte* and the collection of stories published in Barcelona by a company that had recently gone into receivership, as if to send a message to Sensini (and to me).

A year or two later I found out that he had died. I think I read it in a newspaper, I don't know which one. Or maybe I didn't read it; maybe someone told me, but I can't remember talking around that time with anyone who knew him, so I probably did read the death notice somewhere. It was brief, as I remember it: the Argentinean writer Luis Antonio Sensini, who lived for several years in exile in Spain, had died in Buenos Aires. I think there was also a mention of *Ugarte* at the end. I don't know why, but it didn't come as a surprise. I don't know why, but it seemed logical that Sensini would go back to Buenos Aires to die.

Some time later, when the photo of Sensini, Carmela, and Miranda and the photocopied image of Gregorio were packed away with my other memories in a cardboard box that I still haven't committed to the flames for reasons I prefer not to expand upon here, there was a knock on my door. It must have been about midnight, but I was awake. It gave me a shock all the same. I knew only a few people in Girona and none of them would have turned up like that unless something out of the ordinary had happened. When I opened the door there was a woman with long hair, wearing a big black overcoat. It was Miranda Sensini, although she had changed a good deal in the years since her father had sent me the photo. Next to her was a tall young man with long blond hair and an aquiline nose. I'm Miranda Sensini, she said to me with a smile. I know, I said, and invited them in. They were on their way to Italy; after that they planned to cross the Adriatic to Greece. Since they didn't have much money they were hitchhiking. They slept in my house that night. I made them something to eat. The young man was called Sebastian Cohen, and he had been born in Argentina too, although he had lived in Madrid since he was a child. He helped me prepare the meal while Miranda looked around the house. Have you known her for long? he asked. Until a moment ago, I'd only seen her in a photo, I replied.

After dinner, I set them up in one of the rooms and said they could go to bed whenever they wanted. I thought about going to bed myself, but realized it would be hard, if not impossible, to sleep, so I gave them a while to get settled, then went downstairs and put on the television with the volume down low and sat there thinking about Sensini.

Soon I heard someone on the stairs. It was Miranda. She couldn't get to sleep either. She sat down beside me and asked for a cigarette. At first we talked about their trip, Girona (they had been in the city all day, but I didn't ask why they had come to my house so late), and the cities they were planning to visit in Italy. Then we talked about her father and her brother. According to Miranda, Sensini never got over Gregorio's death. He went back to look for him, although we all knew he was dead. Carmela too? I asked. He was the only one who hadn't accepted it, she said. I asked her how things had gone in Argentina. Same as here, same as in Madrid, said Miranda, same as everywhere. But he was well-known and loved in Argentina, I said. Same as here, she said. I got a bottle of cognac from the kitchen and offered her a drink. You're crying, she said. When I looked at her she turned away. Were you writing? she asked. No, I was watching TV. No, I mean when we arrived. Yes, I said. Stories? No, poems. Ah, said Miranda. For a long time we sat there drinking in silence, watching the black and white images on the television screen. Tell me something, I said, Why did your father choose the name Gregorio? Because of Kafka, of course, said Miranda. Gregor Samsa? Of course, she said. I thought so, I said. Then Miranda told me the story of Sensini's last months in Buenos Aires.

He was already sick when he left Madrid, against the advice of various Argentinean doctors, who never billed him and had even arranged a couple of hospital stays, paid for by the national health insurance. Returning to Buenos Aires was a painful and happy experience. In the first week he started taking steps to locate Gregorio. He wanted to go back to his job at the university, but what with bureaucracy and the inevitable jealousies and bitterness, it wasn't going to happen, so he had to make do with translating for a couple of publishing houses. Carmela, however, got a teaching position and toward the end they lived exclusively on her earnings. Each week, Sensini wrote to Miranda. He knew he didn't have long to live, she said, and sometimes it was like he was impatient, like he wanted to use up the last of his strength and get it over with. As for Gregorio, there was nothing conclusive. Some of the pathologists thought his bones might have been in the pile exhumed from the mass grave, but to be sure they would have to perform a DNA test, and the government didn't have the money or didn't really want the tests done, so they kept being postponed. Sensini also went searching for a girl who had probably been Greg's girlfriend when he was in hiding, but he couldn't find her either. Then his health deteriorated and he had to go to the hospital. He didn't even write after that, said Miranda. It had always been very important to him, writing every day, whatever else was happening. Yes, I said, that's the way he was. I asked her if he'd found any literary contests to enter in Buenos Aires. Miranda looked at me and smiled. Of course! You were the one he used to enter the competitions with; he met you through a competition. Then it struck me: the reason she had my address was simply that she had all her father's addresses, and she had only just that moment realized who I was. That's me, I said. Miranda poured me out some more cognac and said there was a year when her father used to talk about me quite a lot. I noticed she was looking at me differently. I must have annoyed him so much, I said. Annoyed him? You've got to be joking; he loved your letters. He always read them to Mom and me. I hope they were funny, I said, without much conviction. They were really funny, said Miranda, my mother even gave you guys a name. A name? Which guys? Dad and you. She called you the gunslingers or the bounty hunters, I can't remember now, something like that, or the buccaneers. I see, I said, but the real bounty hunter was your father. I just passed on some information. Yes, he was a professional, said Miranda, suddenly serious. How many prizes did he win altogether? I asked her. About fifteen, she said with an absent look. And you? So far just the one, I said. A place in the Alcoy competition, that's how I got to know your father. Did you know that Borges wrote to him once in Madrid, to say how much he liked one of his stories? No, I didn't know, I said. And Cortázar wrote about him, and Mújica Laínez too. Well, he was a very good writer, I said. Jesus! said Miranda, then she got up and went out onto the terrace as if I had said something to offend her. I let a few seconds go by, picked up the bottle of cognac, and followed her. Miranda was leaning on the balustrade, looking at the lights of Girona. You have a good view, she said. I filled her glass, then my own, and we stood there for a while looking at the moonlit city. Suddenly I realized that we were at peace, that for some mysterious reason the two of us had reached a state of peace, and that from now on, imperceptibly, things would begin to change. As if the world really was shifting. I asked her how old she was. Twenty-two, she said. I must be over thirty then, I said, and even my voice sounded different.

1997

J. M. COETZEE
born 1940

One of the most challenging of contemporary novelists, J. M. Coetzee frequently addresses moral and political issues. He does so, however, within complex fictional frameworks that present not a single ethical message but an interplay of competing views, as he hedges his authorial judgments with irony. These qualities have led Coetzee's name to be associated with postmodernism and the questioning of absolutes. Yet the ethical streak in Coetzee's work suggests that, for all his questioning of absolutes, a sense of right and wrong motivates his literary experiments, which compel our attention through their impeccably controlled style.

Born in Cape Town, South Africa, to liberal Afrikaners who opposed the system of segregation and white minority rule known as apartheid, John Maxwell Coetzee learned both Afrikaans and English as a child. He studied English literature and mathematics at the University of Cape Town before leaving for England to take up a position as a computer programmer. Bored with his work at International Business Machines, Coetzee moved to the United States and completed a doctoral degree in English at the University of Texas. There he wrote a dissertation on **Samuel Beckett**, whose spare, minimalist style and dark humor influenced Coetzee's own fiction. After teaching at the State University of New York at Buffalo, where he started his first novel, *Dusklands* (published in 1974), Coetzee was forced to leave the United States when he was denied a green card. Along with forty-five other faculty members, Coetzee had occupied a university building to protest American involvement in the Vietnam War. Coetzee returned to South Africa and took up a position at the University of Cape Town, where he remained for thirty years, witnessing the intensification of the apartheid system, its fall, and the introduction of a democracy not based on race discrimination. He earned a growing reputation from a series of spare and elegant novels, often set in bleak landscapes that recall the semidesert Karoo, where Coetzee spent many summers as a boy. His works may combine imaginary worlds with historical events or with encounters between colonizers and the colonized; they frequently make use of demented or unstable narrators. The writer has paid homage to several revered novelists, notably **Fyodor Dostoyevsky** and **Franz Kafka**, whose works explored the mind on the verge of insanity.

Coetzee often plays with the relationship between fiction and reality. His works of autobiographical fiction, *Boyhood* (1997), *Youth* (2002), and *Summertime* (2010), for example, are written in the third person, leaving open the question of whether the "John" is really an "I." *Disgrace* (1999), about a white professor accused of sexual harassment, was seen by some as a critique of the Truth and Reconciliation Commission, established by the country's first postapartheid president, Nelson Mandela, to help the nation come to terms with the crimes of the apartheid era. The novel portrays a serious crime committed by black characters, which led to accusations of racism from the ruling African National Congress. Shortly after this accusation, Coetzee moved to Australia, and in 2006 he became an Australian citizen. In 2003, he was awarded the Nobel Prize.

"The Novel in Africa" (1999) takes up the relationship between fiction and reality. The protagonist, Elizabeth Costello, is an Australian novelist who shares several characteristics with Coetzee himself (although she is older than her creator and, of course, female). Like Coetzee, she spends a great deal of time giving lectures about literature; also like the famously reclusive Coetzee, she does not relish the small talk that accompanies such assignments. In this story, while on a leisure cruise, she chooses to give a lecture titled "The Future of the Novel," even though she has little faith that the novel as a literary form has a future. Meanwhile, an old acquaintance, the fictional black African novelist Emmanuel Egudu, gives a lecture called "The Novel in Africa," in which he speaks about real African novelists, including Amos Tutuola and Ben Okri. The conflict between the two novelists seems to turn at first on literary politics, then on sexual politics, but it ultimately comes to seem more personal than political.

Elizabeth Costello was to become an alter ego for Coetzee; he later wrote several other stories about her life, including snippets of her lectures on such sensitive topics as animal rights, religion, and the Holocaust, and combined them in an unusual novel, *Elizabeth Costello: Eight Lessons* (2003). "The Novel in Africa" is the second "lesson." By putting controversial views in the mouth of his fictional heroine, Coetzee both challenges what he has criticized as the liberal consensus and creates a vivid, emotional story about a woman approaching old age. In the first lesson, "Realism," Costello discusses the way the traditional realist novel has been superseded: "We used to believe that when the text said, 'On the table stood a glass of water,' there was indeed a table, and a glass of water on it, and we had only to look in the word-mirror of the text to see them," says Costello. "But all that has ended. The word-mirror is broken, irreparably it seems." Coetzee's fiction reassembles the broken bits of the "word-mirror" to reflect a complex, multiform reality.

From Elizabeth Costello

The Novel in Africa

At a dinner party she meets X, whom she has not seen in years. Is he still teaching at the University of Queensland, she asks? No, he replies, he has retired and now works the cruise ships, travelling the world, screening old movies, talking about Bergman and Fellini to retired people! He has never regretted the move. 'The pay is good, you get to see the world, and—do you know what?—people that age actually listen to what you have to say.' He urges her to give it a try: 'You are a prominent figure, a well-known writer. The cruise line I work for will jump at the opportunity to take you on. You will be a feather in their cap. Say but the word and I'll bring it up with my friend the director.'

The proposal interests her. She was last on a ship in 1963, when she came home from England, from the mother country. Soon after that they began to retire the great ocean-going liners, one by one, and scrap them. The end of an era. She would not mind doing it again, going to sea. She would like to call at Easter Island and St Helena, where Napoleon languished.[2] She would like to visit Antarctica—not just to see with her own eyes those vast horizons, that barren waste, but to set foot on the seventh and last continent, feel what it is like to be a living, breathing creature in spaces of inhuman cold.

X is as good as his word. From the headquarters of Scandia Lines[3] in Stockholm comes a fax. In December the SS *Northern Lights* will be sailing from Christchurch on a fifteen-day cruise to the Ross Ice Shelf, and thence onward to Cape Town.[4] Might she be interested in joining the education and entertainment staff? Passengers on Scandia's cruise ships are, as the letter puts it, 'discriminating persons who take their leisure seriously'. The emphasis of the on-board programme will be on ornithology and cold-water ecology, but Scandia would be delighted if the noted writer Elizabeth Costello could find the time to offer a short course on, say, the contemporary novel. In return for which, and for making herself accessible to passengers, she will be offered an A-class berth, all expenses paid, with air connections to Christchurch and from Cape Town, and a substantial honorarium to boot.

It is an offer she cannot refuse. On the morning of 10 December she joins the ship in Christchurch harbour. Her cabin, she finds, is small but otherwise quite satisfactory; the young man who coordinates the entertainment and self-development programme is respectful; the passengers at her table at lunchtime, in the main retired people, people of her own generation, are pleasant and unostentatious.

On the list of her co-lecturers there is only one name she recognizes: Emmanuel Egudu, a writer from Nigeria. Their acquaintance goes back more years

1. Ingmar Bergman (1918–2007), Swedish filmmaker, and Federico Fellini (1920–1993), Italian filmmaker, known for their sophisticated, intellectual films.
2. The French emperor Napoleon Bonaparte (1769–1821) was exiled to Saint Helena in the South Atlantic Ocean after his defeat at the Battle of Waterloo (1815). Easter Island, in the South Pacific, is famous for its monu-

mental statues, carved before 1500 C.E.
3. An actual shipping service of the 19th century, here presumably a stand-in for Norwegian Cruise Line, a popular cruise operator.
4. The cruise will leave Christchurch, New Zealand, visit the Ross Ice Shelf in Antarctica, and end in Cape Town, South Africa, Coetzee's hometown.

than she cares to remember, to a PEN conference in Kuala Lumpur.[5] Egudu had been loud and fiery then, political; her first impression was that he was a poseur. Reading him later on, she had not changed her mind. But a poseur, she now wonders: what is that? Someone who seems to be what he is not? Which of us is what he seems to be, she seems to be? And anyway, in Africa things may be different. In Africa what one takes to be posing, what one takes to be boasting, may just be manliness. Who is she to say?

Towards men, including Egudu, she has, she notices, mellowed as she has grown older. Curious, because in other respects she has become more (she chooses the word carefully) acidulous.

She runs into Egudu at the captain's cocktail party (he has come aboard late). He is wearing a vivid green dashiki,[6] suave Italian shoes; his beard is spotted with grey, but he is still a fine figure of a man. He gives her a huge smile, enfolds her in an embrace. 'Elizabeth!' he exclaims. 'How good to see you! I had no idea! We have so much catching up to do!'

In his lexicon, it appears, catching up means talking about his own activities. He no longer spends much time in his home country, he informs her. He has become, as he puts it, 'an habitual exile, like an habitual criminal'. He has acquired American papers; he makes his living on the lecture circuit, a circuit that would appear to have expanded to encompass the cruise ships. This will be his third trip on the *Northern Lights*. Very restful, he finds it; very relaxing. Who would have guessed, he says, that a country boy from Africa would end up like this, in the lap of luxury? And he treats her again to his big smile, the special one.

I'm a country girl myself, she would like to say, but does not, though it is true, in part. *Nothing exceptional about being from the country*.

Each of the entertainment staff is expected to give a short public talk. 'Just to say who you are, where you come from,' explains the young coordinator in carefully idiomatic English. His name is Mikael; he is handsome in his tall, blond, Swedish way, but dour, too dour for her taste.

Her talk is advertised as 'The Future of the Novel', Egudu's as 'The Novel in Africa'. She is scheduled to speak on the morning of their first day out to sea; he will speak the same afternoon. In the evening comes 'The Lives of Whales', with sound recordings.

Mikael himself does the introduction. 'The famous Australian writer,' he calls her, 'author of *The House on Eccles Street*[7] and many other novels, whom we are truly privileged to have in our midst.' It vexes her to be billed once again as the author of a book from so far in the past, but there is nothing to be done about that.

'The Future of the Novel' is a talk she has given before, in fact many times before, expanded or contracted depending on the occasion. No doubt there are expanded and contracted versions of the novel in Africa and the lives of whales too. For the present occasion she has chosen the contracted version.

'The future of the novel is not a subject I am much interested in,' she begins, trying to give her auditors a jolt. 'In fact the future in general does not much

5. Capital of Malaysia. International PEN is a worldwide association of writers that promotes freedom of expression.
6. Traditional, colorful West African robe.

7. An allusion to James Joyce's *Ulysses* (1922), whose protagonist, Leopold Bloom, lives at 7 Eccles Street, Dublin.

interest me. What is the future, after all, but a structure of hopes and expectations? Its residence is in the mind; it has no reality.

'Of course, you might reply that the past is likewise a fiction. The past is history, and what is history but a story made of air that we tell ourselves? Nevertheless, there is something miraculous about the past that the future lacks. What is miraculous about the past is that we have succeeded—God knows how—in making thousands and millions of individual fictions, fictions created by individual human beings, lock well enough into one another to give us what looks like a common past, a shared story.

'The future is different. We do not possess a shared story of the future. The creation of the past seems to exhaust our collective creative energies. Compared with our fiction of the past, our fiction of the future is a sketchy, bloodless affair, as visions of heaven tend to be. Of heaven and even of hell.'

The novel, the traditional novel, she goes on to say, is an attempt to understand human fate one case at a time, to understand how it comes about that some fellow being, having started at point A and having undergone experiences B and C and D, ends up at point Z. Like history, the novel is thus an exercise in making the past coherent. Like history, it explores the respective contributions of character and circumstance to forming the present. By doing so, the novel suggests how we may explore the power of the present to produce the future. That is why we have this thing, this institution, this medium called the novel.

She is not sure, as she listens to her own voice, whether she believes any longer in what she is saying. Ideas like these must have had some grip on her when years ago she wrote them down, but after so many repetitions they have taken on a worn, unconvincing air. On the other hand, she no longer believes very strongly in belief. Things can be true, she now thinks, even if one does not believe in them, and conversely. Belief may be no more, in the end, than a source of energy, like a battery which one clips into an idea to make it run. As happens when one writes: believing whatever has to be believed in order to get the job done.

If she has trouble believing in her argument, she has even greater trouble in preventing that absence of conviction from emerging in her voice. Despite the fact that she is the noted author of, as Mikael says, *The House on Eccles Street* and other books, despite the fact that her audience is by and large of her generation and ought therefore to share with her a common past, the applause at the end lacks enthusiasm.

For Emmanuel's talk she sits inconspicuously in the back row. They have in the meantime had a good lunch; they are sailing south on what are still placid seas; there is every chance that some of the good folk in the audience—numbering, she would guess, about fifty—are going to nod off. In fact, who knows, she might nod off herself; in which case it would be best to do so unnoticed.

'You will be wondering why I have chosen as my topic the novel in Africa,' Emmanuel begins, in his effortlessly booming voice. 'What is so special about the novel in Africa? What makes it different, different enough to demand our attention today?

'Well, let us see. We all know, to begin with, that the alphabet, the idea of the alphabet, did not grow up in Africa. Many things grew up in Africa, more than you might think, but not the alphabet. The alphabet had to be brought in, first by Arabs, then again by Westerners. In Africa writing itself, to say nothing of novel-writing, is a recent affair.

'Is the novel possible without novel-writing, you may ask? Did we in Africa have a novel before our friends the colonizers appeared on our doorstep? For the time being, let me merely propose the question. Later I may return to it.

'A second remark: reading is not a typically African recreation. Music, yes; dancing, yes; eating, yes; talking, yes—lots of talking. But reading, no, and particularly not reading fat novels. Reading has always struck us Africans as a strangely solitary business. It makes us uneasy. When we Africans visit great European cities like Paris and London, we notice how people on trains take books out of their bags or their pockets and retreat into solitary worlds. Each time the book comes out it is like a sign held up. *Leave me alone, I am reading*, says the sign. *What I am reading is more interesting than you could possibly be.*

'Well, we are not like that in Africa. We do not like to cut ourselves off from other people and retreat into private worlds. Nor are we used to our neighbours retreating into private worlds. Africa is a continent where people share. Reading a book by yourself is not sharing. It is like eating alone or talking alone. It is not our way. We find it a bit crazy.'

We, we, we, she thinks. *We Africans*. It is not *our* way. She has never liked *we* in its exclusive form. Emmanuel may have grown older, he may have acquired the blessing of American papers, but he has not changed. Africanness: a special identity, a special fate.

She has visited Africa: the highlands of Kenya, Zimbabwe, the Okavango[8] swamps. She has seen Africans reading, ordinary Africans, at bus stops, in trains. They were not reading novels, admittedly, they were reading newspapers. But is a newspaper not as much an avenue to a private world as a novel?

'In the third place,' continues Egudu, 'in the great, beneficent global system under which we live today, it has been allotted to Africa to be the home of poverty. Africans have no money for luxuries. In Africa, a book must offer you a return for the money you spend on it. What do I stand to learn by reading this story, the African will ask? How will it advance me? We may deplore the attitude of the African, ladies and gentlemen, but we cannot dismiss it. We must take it seriously and try to understand it.

'We do of course make books in Africa. But the books we make are for children, teaching-books in the simplest sense. If you want to make money publishing books in Africa, you must put out books that will be prescribed for schools, that will be bought in quantity by the education system to be read and studied in the classroom. It does not pay to publish writers with serious ambitions, writers who write about adults and matters that concern adults. Such writers must look elsewhere for their salvation.

'Of course, ladies and gentlemen of the *Northern Lights*, it is not the whole picture I am giving you here today. To give you the whole picture would take all afternoon. I am giving you only a crude, hasty sketch. Of course you will find publishers in Africa, one here, one there, who will support local writers even if they will never make money. But in the broad picture, storytelling provides a livelihood neither for publishers nor for writers.

'So much for the generalities, depressing as they may be. Now let us turn our attention to ourselves, to you and to me. Here I am, you know who I am, it tells you in the programme: Emmanuel Egudu, from Nigeria, author of novels,

---

8. In southwestern Africa.

poems, plays, winner, even, of a Commonwealth Literary Award (Africa Division).[9] And here you are, wealthy folk, or at least comfortable, as you say (I am not wrong, am I?), from North America and Europe and of course let us not forget our Australasian representation, and perhaps I have even heard the odd word of Japanese whispered in the corridors, taking a cruise on this splendid ship, on your way to inspect one of the remoter corners of the globe, to check it out, perhaps to check it off your list. Here you are, after a good lunch, listening to this African fellow talk.

'Why, I imagine you asking yourselves, is this African fellow on board our ship? Why isn't he back at his desk in the land of his birth following his vocation, if he really is a writer, writing books? Why is he going on about the African novel, a subject that can be of only the most peripheral concern to us?

'The short answer, ladies and gentlemen, is that the African fellow is earning a living. In his own country, as I have tried to explain, he cannot earn a living. In his own country (I will not labour the point, I mention it only because it holds true for so many fellow African writers) he is in fact less than welcome. In his own country he is what is called a dissident intellectual, and dissident intellectuals must tread carefully, even in the new Nigeria.

'So here he is, abroad in the wide world, earning his living. Part of his living he earns by writing books that are published and read and reviewed and talked about and judged, for the most part, by foreigners. The rest of his living he earns from spin-offs of his writing. He reviews books by other writers, for example, in the press of Europe and America. He teaches in colleges in America, telling the youth of the New World about the exotic subject on which he is an expert in the same way that an elephant is an expert on elephants: the African novel. He addresses conferences; he sails on cruise ships. While so occupied, he lives in what are called temporary accommodations. All his addresses are temporary; he has no fixed abode.

'How easy do you think it is, ladies and gentlemen, for this fellow to be true to his essence as writer when there are all these strangers to please, month after month—publishers, readers, critics, students, all of them armed not only with their own ideas about what writing is or should be, what the novel is or should be, what Africa is or should be, but also about what being pleased is or should be? Do you think it is possible for this fellow to remain unaffected by all the pressure on him to please others, to be for them what they think he should be, to produce for them what they think he should produce?

'It may have escaped your attention, but I slipped in, a moment ago, a word that should have made you prick up your ears. I spoke about my essence and being true to my essence. There is much I could say about essence and its ramifications; but this is not the right occasion. Nevertheless, you must be asking yourselves, how in these anti-essential days, these days of fleeting identities that we pick up and wear and discard like clothing, can I justify speaking of my essence as an African writer?

'Around essence and essentialism, I should remind you, there is a long history of turmoil in African thought. You may have heard of the *négritude* movement of the 1940s and 1950s.[1] *Négritude*, according to the originators of the

9. An allusion to the Commonwealth Writers Prize, which awards prizes for various regions of the former British Empire.
1. A movement celebrating African heritage (French). Leading figures were Léopold Sédar Senghor (1906–2001) and Aimé Césaire (1913–2008).

movement, is the essential substratum that binds all Africans together and makes them uniquely African—not only the Africans of Africa but Africans of the great African diaspora in the New World and now in Europe.

'I want to quote some words to you from the Senegalese writer and thinker Cheikh Hamidou Kane.[2] Cheikh Hamidou was being questioned by an interviewer, a European. I am puzzled, said the interviewer, by your praise for certain writers for being truly African. In view of the fact that the writers in question write in a foreign language (specifically French) and are published and, for the most part, read in a foreign country (specifically France), can they truly be called African writers? Are they not more properly called French writers of African origin? Is language not a more important matrix than birth?

'The following is Cheikh Hamidou's reply: "The writers I speak of are truly African because they are born in Africa, they live in Africa, their sensibility is African . . . What distinguishes them lies in life experience, in sensitivities, in rhythm, in style." He goes on: "A French or English writer has thousands of years of written tradition behind him . . . We on the other hand are heirs to an oral tradition."

'There is nothing mystical in Cheikh Hamidou's response, nothing metaphysical, nothing racist. He merely gives proper weight to those intangibles of culture which, because they are not easily pinned down in words, are often passed over. The way that people live in their bodies. The way they move their hands. The way they walk. The way they smile or frown. The lilt of their speech. The way they sing. The timbre of their voices. The way they dance. The way they touch each other; how the hand lingers; the feel of the fingers. The way they make love. The way they lie after they have made love. The way they think. The way they sleep.

'We African novelists can embody these qualities in our writings (and let me remind you at this point that the word *novel*, when it entered the languages of Europe, had the vaguest of meanings: it meant the form of writing that was formless, that had no rules, that made up its own rules as it went along)—we African novelists can embody these qualities as no one else can because we have not lost touch with the body. The African novel, the true African novel, is an oral novel. On the page it is inert, only half alive; it wakes up when the voice, from deep in the body, breathes life into the words, speaks them aloud.

'The African novel is thus, I would claim, in its very being, and before the first word is written, a critique of the Western novel, which has gone so far down the road of disembodiment—think of Henry James, think of Marcel Proust[3]—that the appropriate way and indeed the only way in which to absorb it is in silence and in solitude. And I will close these remarks, ladies and gentlemen—I see my time is running out—by quoting, in support of my position and Cheikh Hamidou's, not from an African, but from a man from the snowy wastes of Canada, the great scholar of orality Paul Zumthor.[4]

'"Since the seventeenth century," writes Zumthor, "Europe has spread across the world like a cancer, at first stealthily, but for a while now at gathering pace, until today it ravages life forms, animals, plants, habitats, languages. With each day that passes several languages of the world disappear, repudiated,

2. Senegalese writer (b. 1928), author of *Ambiguous Adventure*.
3. French novelist (1871–1922) famed for his

exploration of consciousness, as was the American novelist Henry James (1843–1928).
4. Noted medievalist (1915–1995).

stifled . . . One of the symptoms of the disease has without doubt, from the beginning, been what we call literature; and literature has consolidated itself, prospered, and become what it is—one of the hugest dimensions of mankind—by denying the voice . . . The time has come to stop privileging writing . . . Perhaps great, unfortunate Africa, beggared by our political–industrial imperialism, will, because less gravely affected by writing, find itself closer to the goal than will the other continents."'

The applause when Egudu ends his talk is loud and spirited. He has spoken with force, perhaps even with passion; he has stood up for himself, for his calling, for his people; why should he not have his reward, even if what he says can have little relevance to the lives of his audience?

Nevertheless, there is something about the talk she does not like, something to do with orality and the mystique of orality. Always, she thinks, the body that is insisted on, pushed forward, and the voice, dark essence of the body, welling up from within it. *Négritude*: she had thought Emmanuel would grow out of that pseudo-philosophy. Evidently he has not. Evidently he has decided to keep it as part of his professional pitch. Well, good luck to him. There is still time, ten minutes at least, for questions. She hopes the questions will be searching, will search him out.

The first questioner is, if she is to judge by accent, from the Midwest of the United States. The first novel she ever read by an African, decades ago, says the woman, was by Amos Tutuola, she forgets the title. ('*The Palm Wine Drinkard*,'[5] suggests Egudu. 'Yes, that's it,' she replies.) She was captivated by it. She thought it was the harbinger of great things to come. So she was disappointed, terribly disappointed, to hear that Tutuola was not respected in his own country, that educated Nigerians disparaged him and considered his reputation in the West unmerited. Was this true? Was Tutuola the kind of oral novelist our lecturer had in mind? What has happened to Tutuola? Had more of his books been translated?

No, responds Egudu, Tutuola has not been translated any further, in fact he has not been translated at all, at least not into English. Why not? Because he did not need to be translated. Because he had written in English all along. 'Which is the root of the problem that the questioner raises. The language of Amos Tutuola is English, but not standard English, not the English that Nigerians of the 1950s went to school and college to learn. It is the language of a semi-educated clerk, a man with no more than elementary schooling, barely comprehensible to an outsider, fixed up for publication by British editors. Where Tutuola's writing was frankly illiterate they corrected it; what they refrained from correcting was what seemed authentically Nigerian to them, that is to say, what to their ears sounded picturesque, exotic, folkloric.

'From what I have just been saying,' Egudu continues, 'you may imagine that I too disapprove of Tutuola or the Tutuola phenomenon. Far from it. Tutuola was repudiated by so-called educated Nigerians because they were embarassed by him—embarassed that they might be lumped with him as natives who did not know how to write proper English. As for me, I am happy to be a native, a Nigerian native, a native Nigerian. In this battle I am on Tutuola's side. Tutuola is or was a gifted storyteller. I am glad you like him. Several more books penned by him were put out in England, though none, I would say, as good as *The Palm Wine Drinkard*. And, yes, he is the kind of writer I was referring to, an oral writer.

5. A novel by Nigerian writer Amos Tutuola (1920–1997).

'I have responded to you at length because the case of Tutuola is so instructive. What makes Tutuola stand out is that he did not adjust his language to the expectations—or to what he might have thought, had he been less naive, would be the expectations—of the foreigners who would read and judge him. Not knowing better, he wrote as he spoke. He therefore had to yield in a particularly helpless way to being packaged, for the West, as an African exotic.

'But, ladies and gentlemen, who among African writers is not exotic? The truth is, to the West we Africans are all exotic, when we are not simply savage. That is our fate. Even here, on this ship sailing towards the continent that ought to be the most exotic of all, and the most savage, the continent with no human standards at all, I can sense I am exotic.'

There is a ripple of laughter. Egudu smiles his big smile, engaging, to all appearances spontaneous. But she cannot believe it is a true smile, cannot believe it comes from the heart, if that is where smiles come from. If being an exotic is the fate Egudu has embraced for himself, then it is a terrible fate. She cannot believe he does not know that, know it and in his heart revolt against it. The one black face in this sea of white.

'But let me return to your question,' Egudu continues. 'You have read Tutuola, now read my countryman Ben Okri.[6] Amos Tutuola's is a very simple, very stark case. Okri's is not. Okri is an heir of Tutuola's, or they are the heirs of common ancestors. But Okri negotiates the contradictions of being himself for other people (excuse the jargon, it is just a native showing off) in a much more complex way. Read Okri. You will find the experience instructive.'

'The Novel in Africa' was intended, like all the shipboard talks, to be a light affair. Nothing on the shipboard programme is intended to be a heavy affair. Egudu, unfortunately, is threatening to be heavy. With a discreet nod, the entertainment director, the tall Swedish boy in his light blue uniform, signals from the wings; and gracefully, easily, Egudu obeys, bringing his show to an end.

The crew of the *Northern Lights* is Russian, as are the stewards. In fact, everyone but the officers and the corps of guides and managers is Russian. Music on board is furnished by a balalaika orchestra—five men, five women. The accompaniment they provide at the dinner hour is too schmaltzy for her taste; after dinner, in the ballroom, the music they play becomes livelier.

The leader of the orchestra, and occasional singer, is a blonde in her early thirties. She has a smattering of English, enough to make the announcements. 'We play piece that is calléd in Russian *My Little Dove. My Little Dove.*'[7] Her *dove* rhymes with *stove* rather than *love*. With its trills and swoops, the piece sounds Hungarian, sounds gypsy, sounds Jewish, sounds everything but Russian; but who is she, Elizabeth Costello, country girl, to say?

She is there with a couple from her table, having a drink. They are from Manchester, they inform her. They are looking forward to her course on the novel, in which they have both enrolled. The man is long-bodied, sleek, silvery: she thinks of him as a gannet. How he has made his money he does not say and she does not enquire. The woman is petite, sensual. Not at all her idea of Manchester. Steve and Shirley. She guesses they are not married.

To her relief, the conversation soon turns from her and the books she has written to the subject of ocean currents, about which Steve appears to know all

6. Nigerian novelist (b. 1959).   7. Popular Russian song of Gypsy origin.

there is to know, and to the tiny beings, tons of them to the square mile, whose life consists in being swept in serene fashion through these icy waters, eating and being eaten, multiplying and dying, ignored by history. Ecological tourists, that is what Steve and Shirley call themselves. Last year the Amazon, this year the Southern Ocean.

Egudu is standing at the entranceway, looking around. She gives a wave and he comes over. 'Join us,' she says. 'Emmanuel. Shirley. Steve.'

They compliment Emmanuel on his lecture. 'Very interesting,' says Steve. 'A completely new perspective you gave me.'

'I was thinking, as you spoke,' says Shirley more reflectively, 'I don't know your books, I'm sorry to say, but for you as a writer, as the kind of oral writer you described, maybe the printed book is not the right medium. Have you ever thought about composing straight on to tape? Why make the detour through print? Why even make a detour through writing? Speak your story direct to your listener.'

'What a clever idea!' says Emmanuel. 'It won't solve all the problems of the African writer, but it's worth thinking about.'

'Why won't it solve your problems?'

'Because, I regret to say, Africans will want more than just to sit in silence listening to a disc spinning in a little machine. That would be too much like idolatry. Africans need the living presence, the living voice.'

The living voice. There is silence as the three of them contemplate the living voice.

'Are you sure about that?' she says, interposing for the first time. 'Africans don't object to listening to the radio. A radio is a voice but not a living voice, a living presence. What you are demanding, I think, Emmanuel, is not just a voice but a performance: a living actor performing the text for you. If that is so, if that is what the African demands, then I agree, a recording cannot take its place. But the novel was never intended to be the script of a performance. From the beginning the novel has made a virtue of not depending on being performed. You can't have both live performance and cheap, handy distribution. It's the one or the other. If that is indeed what you want the novel to be—a pocket-sized block of paper that is at the same time a living being—then I agree, the novel has no future in Africa.'

'No future,' says Egudu reflectively. 'That sounds very bleak, Elizabeth. Do you have a way out to offer us?'

'A way out? It's not for me to offer you a way out. What I do have to offer is a question. Why are there so many African novelists around and yet no African novel worth speaking of? That seems to me the real question. And you yourself gave a clue to the answer in your talk. Exoticism. Exoticism and its seductions.'

'Exoticism and its seductions? You intrigue us, Elizabeth. Tell us what you mean.'

If it were only a matter of Emmanuel and herself she would, at this point, walk out. She is tired of his jeering undertone, exasperated. But before strangers, before customers, they have a front to maintain, she and he both.

'The English novel,' she says, 'is written in the first place by English people for English people. That is what makes it the English novel. The Russian novel is written by Russians for Russians. But the African novel is not written by Africans for Africans. African novelists may write about Africa, about

African experiences, but they seem to me to be glancing over their shoulder all the time they write, at the foreigners who will read them. Whether they like it or not, they have accepted the role of interpreter, interpreting Africa to their readers. Yet how can you explore a world in all its depth if at the same time you are having to explain it to outsiders? It is like a scientist trying to give full, creative attention to his investigations while at the same time explaining what he is doing to a class of ignorant students. It is too much for one person, it can't be done, not at the deepest level. That, it seems to me, is the root of your problem. Having to perform your Africanness at the same time as you write.'

'Very good, Elizabeth!' says Egudu. 'You really understand; you put it very well. The explorer as explainer.' He reaches out, pats her on the shoulder.

If we were alone, she thinks, *I would slap him.*

'If it is true that I really understand'—she is ignoring Egudu now, speaking to the couple from Manchester—'then that is only because we in Australia have been through similar trials and have come out at the other end. We finally got out of the habit of writing for strangers when a proper Australian readership grew to maturity, something that happened in the 1960s. A readership, not a writership—that already existed. We got out of the habit of writing for strangers when our market, our Australian market, decided that it could afford to support a home-grown literature. That is the lesson we can offer. That is what Africa could learn from us.'

Emmanuel is silent, though he has not lost his ironic smile.

'It's interesting to hear the two of you talk,' says Steve. 'You treat writing as a business. You identify a market and then set about supplying it. I was expecting something different.'

'Really? What were you expecting?'

'You know: where writers find their inspiration, how they dream up characters, and so forth. Sorry, pay no attention to me, I'm just an amateur.'

Inspiration. Receiving the spirit into oneself. Now that he has brought out the word he is embarrassed. There is an awkward silence.

Emmanuel speaks. 'Elizabeth and I go way back. We have had lots of disagreements in our time. That doesn't alter things between us—does it, Elizabeth? We are colleagues, fellow writers. Part of the great, worldwide writing fraternity.'

Fraternity. He is challenging her, trying to get a rise out of her before these strangers. But she is suddenly too sick of it all to take up the challenge. Not fellow writers, she thinks: fellow entertainers. Why else are we on board this expensive ship, making ourselves available, as the invitation so candidly put it, to people who bore us and whom we are beginning to bore?

He is goading her because he is restless. She knows him well enough to see that. He has had enough of the African novel, enough of her and her friends, wants something or someone new.

Their chanteuse has come to the end of her set. There is a light ripple of applause. She bows, bows a second time, takes up her balalaika. The band strikes up a Cossack dance.[8]

---

8. A folk dance from southern Russia and Ukraine.

What irritates her about Emmanuel, what she has the good sense not to bring up in front of Steve and Shirley because it will lead only to unseemliness, is the way he turns every disagreement into a personal matter. As for his beloved oral novel, on which he has built his sideline as a lecturer, she finds the idea muddled at its very core. *A novel about people who live in an oral culture*, she would like to say, *is not an oral novel. Just as a novel about women isn't a women's novel.*

In her opinion, all of Emmanuel's talk of an oral novel, a novel that has kept in touch with the human voice and hence with the human body, a novel that is not disembodied like the Western novel but speaks the body and the body's truth, is just another way of propping up the mystique of the African as the last repository of primal human energies. Emmanuel blames his Western publishers and his Western readers for driving him to exoticize Africa; but Emmanuel has a stake in exoticizing himself. Emmanuel, she happens to know, has not written a book of substance in ten years. When she first got to know him he could still honourably call himself a writer. Now he makes his living by talking. His books are there as credentials, no more. A fellow entertainer he may be; a fellow writer he is not, not any longer. He is on the lecture circuit for the money, and for other rewards too. Sex, for instance. He is dark, he is exotic, he is in touch with life's energies; if he is no longer young, at least he carries himself well, wears his years with distinction. What Swedish girl would not be a pushover?

She finishes her drink. 'I'm retiring,' she says. 'Good night, Steve, Shirley. See you tomorrow. Good night, Emmanuel.'

She wakes up in utter stillness. The clock says four thirty. The ship's engines have stopped. She glances through the porthole. There is fog outside, but through the fog she can glimpse land no more than a kilometre away. It must be Macquarie Island: she had thought they would not arrive for hours yet.

She dresses and emerges into the corridor. At the same moment the door to cabin A-230 opens and the Russian comes out, the singer. She is wearing the same outfit as last night, the port-wine blouse and wide black trousers; she carries her boots in her hand. In the unkind overhead light she looks nearer to forty than to thirty. They avert their eyes as they pass each other.

A-230 is Egudu's cabin, she knows that.

She makes her way to the upper deck. Already there are a handful of passengers, snugly dressed against the cold, leaning against the railings, peering down.

The sea beneath them is alive with what seem to be fish, large, glossy-backed black fish that bob and tumble and leap in the swell. She has never seen anything like it.

'Penguins,' says the man next to her. 'King penguins. They have come to greet us. They don't know what we are.'

'Oh,' she says. And then: 'So innocent? Are they so innocent?'

The man regards her oddly, turns back to his companion.

The Southern Ocean. Poe never laid eyes on it, Edgar Allan,[9] but criss-crossed it in his mind. Boatloads of dark islanders paddled out to meet him. They seemed ordinary folk *just like us*, but when they smiled and showed their teeth the teeth

9. American writer (1809–1849).

were not white but black. It sent a shiver down his spine, and rightly so. The seas full of things that seem like us but are not. Sea-flowers that gape and devour. Eels, each a barbed maw with a gut hanging from it. Teeth are for tearing, the tongue is for churning the swill around: that is the truth of the oral. Someone should tell Emmanuel. Only by an ingenious economy, an accident of evolution, does the organ of ingestion sometimes get to be used for song.

They will stand off Macquarie until noon, long enough for those passengers who so desire to visit the island. She has put her name down for the visiting party.

The first boat leaves after breakfast. The approach to the landing is difficult, through thick beds of kelp and across shelving rock. In the end one of the sailors has to half help her ashore, half carry her, as if she were an old old woman. The sailor has blue eyes, blond hair. Through his waterproofs she feels his youthful strength. In his arms she rides as safe as a baby. 'Thank you!' she says gratefully when he sets her down; but to him it is nothing, just a service he is paid dollars to do, no more personal than the service of a hospital nurse.

She has read about Macquarie Island! In the nineteenth century it was the hub of the penguin industry. Hundreds of thousands of penguins were clubbed to death here and flung into cast-iron steam boilers to be broken down into useful oil and useless residue. Or not clubbed to death, merely herded with sticks up a gangplank and over the edge into the seething cauldron.

Yet their twentieth-century descendants seem to have learned nothing. Still they innocently swim out to welcome visitors; still they call out greetings to them as they approach the rookeries (*Ho! Ho!* they call, for all the world like gruff little gnomes), and allow them to approach close enough to touch them, to stroke their sleek breasts.

At eleven the boats will take them back to the ship. Until then they are free to explore the island. There is an albatross colony on the hillside, they are advised; they are welcome to photograph the birds, but should not approach too closely, should not alarm them. It is breeding season.

She wanders away from the rest of the landing party, and after a while finds herself on a plateau above the coastline, crossing a vast bed of matted grass.

Suddenly, unexpectedly, there is something before her. At first she thinks it is a rock, smooth and white mottled with grey. Then she sees it is a bird, bigger than any bird she has seen before. She recognizes the long, dipping beak, the huge sternum. An albatross.

The albatross regards her steadily and, so it seems to her, with amusement. Sticking out from beneath it is a smaller version of the same long beak. The fledgling is more hostile. It opens its beak, gives a long, soundless cry of warning.

So she and the two birds remain, inspecting each other.

Before the fall, she thinks. *This is how it must have been before the fall. I could miss the boat, stay here. Ask God to take care of me.*

There is someone behind her. She turns. It is the Russian singer, dressed now in a dark green anorak with the hood down, her hair under a kerchief.

'An albatross,' she remarks to the woman, speaking softly. 'That is the English word. I don't know what they call themselves.'

The woman nods. The great bird regards them calmly, no more afraid of two than of one.

---

1. In the southwest Pacific, between New Zealand and Antarctica.

'Is Emmanuel with you?' she says.

'No. On ship.'

The woman does not seem keen to talk, but she presses on anyway. 'You are a friend of his, I know. I am too, or have been, in the past. May I ask: what do you see in him?'

It is an odd question, presumptuous in its intimacy, even rude. But it seems to her that on this island, on a visit that will never be repeated, anything can be said.

'What I see?' says the woman.

'Yes. What do you see? What do you like about him? What is the source of his charm?'

The woman shrugs. Her hair is dyed, she can now see. Forty if a day, probably with a household to support back home, one of those Russian establishments with a crippled mother and a husband who drinks too much and beats her and a lay-about son and a daughter with a shaven head and purple lipstick. A woman who can sing a little but will one of these days, sooner rather than later, be over the hill. Playing the balalaika to foreigners, singing Russian kitsch, picking up tips.

'He is free. You speak Russian? No?'

She shakes her head.

'Deutsch?'[2]

'A little.'

'Er ist freigebig. Ein guter Mann.'[3]

Freigebig, generous, spoken with the heavy g of Russian. Is Emmanuel generous? She does not know, one way or the other. Not the first word that would occur to her, though. Large, maybe. Large in his gestures.

'Aber kaum zu vertrauen,'[4] she remarks to the woman. Years since she last used the language. Is that what the two of them spoke together in bed last night: German, imperial tongue of the new Europe? *Kaum zu vertrauen*, not to be trusted.

The woman shrugs again. 'Die Zeit ist immer kurz. Man kann nicht alles haben.' There is a pause. The woman speaks again. 'Auch die Stimme. Sie macht daß man'—she searches for the word—'man schaudert.'[5]

Schaudern. Shudder. The voice makes one shudder. Probably does, when one is breast to breast with it. Between her and the Russian passes what is perhaps the beginning of a smile. As for the bird, they have been there long enough, the bird is losing interest. Only the fledgling, peering out from beneath its mother, is still wary of the intruders.

Is she jealous? How could she be? Still, hard to accept, being excluded from the game. Like being a child again, with a child's bedtime.

The voice. Her thoughts go back to Kuala Lumpur, when she was young, or nearly young, when she spent three nights in a row with Emmanuel Egudu, also young then. 'The oral poet,' she said to him teasingly. 'Show me what an oral poet can do.' And he laid her out, lay upon her, put his lips to her ears, opened them, breathed his breath into her, showed her.

1999

---

2. German (German).
3. He is generous. A good man (German).
4. But hardly to be trusted (German).

5. Time is always short. One cannot have everything . . . Also his voice. It makes one . . . one shudder (German).

Selected Bibliographies

I. The Enlightenment in Europe and the Americas

Peter Gay, *Age of Enlightenment* (1966) is the classic work on the subject. Two other good historical introductions are Dorinda Outram, *The Enlightenment* (1995; 2nd ed. 2005) and Roy Porter, *The Enlightenment* (2001). See also Porter's *Creation of the Modern World: The Untold Story of the British Enlightenment* (2001). Studies of women in the period include Carla Hesse, *The Other Enlightenment: How French Women Became Modern* (2003), Karen O'Brien, *Women and Enlightenment in Eighteenth-Century Britain* (2009), and M. Williamson, *Raising Their Voices, 1650–1750* (1990). For excellent studies of Enlightenment philosophical thinking, see F. C. Beiser, *The Sovereignty of Reason: The Defense of Rationality in the Early English Enlightenment* (1996); L. Crocker, *An Age of Crisis: Man and World in Eighteenth-Century French Thought* (1959); Knud Haakonssen, *Natural Law and Moral Philosophy: From Grotius to the Scottish Enlightenment* (1996); and Jonathan Israel, *Enlightenment Contested: Philosophy, Modernity, and the Emancipation of Man* (2006). A brilliant survey of literature, art, and history can be found in John Brewer, *The Pleasures of the Imagination: English Culture in the Eighteenth Century* (1998). Useful works for considering the literature of the period include M. Price, *To the Palace of Wisdom: Studies in Order and Energy from Dryden to Blake* (1964); L. Gossman, *French Society and Culture: Background for Eighteenth-Century Literature* (1972); S. Gearhart, *The Open Boundary of History and Fiction: A Critical Approach to the French Enlightenment* (1984); J. Sambrook, *The Eighteenth Century: The Intellectual and Cultural Context of English Literature, 1700–1789* (1986); and T. M. Kavanaugh, *Esthetics of the Moment: Literature and Art in the French Enlightenment* (1996).

Aphra Behn
Janet Todd, *The Secret Life of Aphra Behn* (1996) delves into the contradictions of Behn's biography. *Rereading Aphra Behn: History, Theory and Criticism* (1993), a collection of essays edited by Heidi Hutner, locates Behn in the larger literary culture of the Restoration. Laura Brown's *Ends of Empire: Women and Ideology in Early Eighteenth-Century English Literature* (1993) discusses *Oroonoko*, gender, and the slave trade. Recent years have seen an explosion of new work on race and colonialism in *Oroonoko*. Important essays include Srinivas Aravamudan, "Petting Oroonoko," *Tropicopolitans* (1999) and Elliott Visconsi, "A Degenerate Race: English Barbarism in Behn's *Oroonoko* and *The Widow Ranter*," *ELH* (2002). Thomas Southerne's theatrical adaptation of Behn's novella, first performed in 1695, is also available in print.

Sor Juana Inés de la Cruz
Gerard Flynn's *Sor Juana Inés de la Cruz* (1971) provides a biographical, critical, and bibliographical introduction. Octavio Paz's *Sor Juana; Or, The Traps of Faith* (1988) is a famous study by the Mexican writer and Nobel Prize winner. Other important studies include Pamela Kirk, *Sor Juana Inés de la Cruz: Religion, Art, and Feminism* (1998); Stephanie Merrim, *Early Modern Women's Writing and Sor Juana Inés de la Cruz* (1999); and Frederick Luciani, *Literary*

Self-Fashioning in Sor Juana Inés de la Cruz (2004). Feminist Perspectives on Sor Juana Inés de la Cruz (1991), ed. Stephanie Merrim, is a useful collection of essays.

Samuel Johnson

There have been many biographies of Samuel Johnson, the most famous of which is James Boswell's Life of Samuel Johnson (1791), a work of art in its own right. Boswell's account is, however, unreliable. For a more trustworthy and detailed life, see Peter Martin, Samuel Johnson: A Biography (2008). Howard D. Weinbrot has an excellent chapter on Rasselas in Aspects of Samuel Johnson: Essays on His Arts, Mind, Afterlife, and Politics (2005), as does Fred Parker, "The Skepticism of Rasselas," in The Cambridge Companion to Samuel Johnson (1997), ed. Greg Clingham. For Johnson's enduring interest in Abyssinia, see Wendy Laura Belcher, Abyssinia's Samuel Johnson: Ethiopian Thought in the Making of an English Author (2012).

Marie de La Vergne de La Fayette

Madame de Lafayette and 'La Princesse de Clèves' (1971) by Janet Raitt is a useful introduction to the author and her best-known work. The Norton Critical Edition of The Princess of Clèves (1994), ed. John D. Lyons, includes contemporary reactions to the controversial 1678 novel as well as selected critical essays. In his essay "Madame de Lafayette," French Studies 65 (2011), John Campbell reviews the contemporary relevance of her work, following his book-length study Questions of Interpretation (1996). Laurence A. Gregorio provides historical context in Order in the Court: History and Society in La Princesse de Clèves (1986). Joan de Jean analyzes Lafayette's authorial position in "Lafayette's Ellipses: The Privileges of Anonymity," PMLA 99 (1984) and places her in the history of the French novel in Tender Geographies: Women and the Origins of the Novel in France (1991).

Jean de La Fontaine

La Fontaine (1987) by Marie Sweetser is a good introduction to the author and his works. Marc Fumaroli puts the poet's biography in historical context in The Poet and the King: Jean de la Fontaine and His Century (2002). David L. Rubin dissects the Fables and surveys recent critical approaches in A Pact with Silence: Art and Thought in the Fables of Jean

de la Fontaine (1991). Maya Slater analyzes literary elements including humor, symbol, and allusion in The Craft of La Fontaine (2001).

Molière

H. Walker, Molière (1990), provides a general biographical and critical introduction to the playwright. Useful critical studies include L. Gossman, Men and Masks: A Study of Molière (1963); Jacques Guicharnaud, ed., Molière: A Collection of Critical Essays (1964); N. Gross, From Gesture to Idea: Esthetics and Ethics in Molière's Comedy (1982); J. F. Gaines, Social Structures in Molière's Theater (1984); and L. F. Norman, The Public Mirror: Molière and the Social Commerce of Depiction (1999). An excellent treatment of Molière in his historical context is W. D. Howarth, Molière: A Playwright and His Audience (1984). Harold C. Knutson, The Triumph of Wit (1988) examines Molière in relation to Shakespeare and Ben Jonson. Martin Turnell, The Classical Moment: Studies of Corneille, Molière, and Racine (1975) offers useful insight into the French dramatic tradition.

Alexander Pope

The standard edition of Pope's poetry is the eleven-volume Poems of Alexander Pope (1938–1969), ed. John Butt et al. Maynard Mack's Alexander Pope: A Life (1985) is a fascinating read, joining insightful criticism of the poetry with the poet's life. Brean Hammond's Pope Among the Satirists (2005) provides wonderful contextual material and is concise and well written. Leo Damrosch's The World of Alexander Pope (1987) includes perceptive criticism, and for a reading that focuses on the relationship between Pope's work and his disabled body, see Helen Deutsch, Resemblance and Disgrace (1996). Pope's relationship to the changing marketplace is brilliantly captured in Catherine Ingrassia's concise essay, "Money," in The Cambridge Companion to Alexander Pope (2007), ed. Pat Rogers. David Foxon's illustrated Pope and the Early Eighteenth-Century Book Trade (1991) gives a rich picture of the complex relationship between Pope and his printers, including questions of typography and design.

Jean Racine

Geoffrey Bereton's Jean Racine: A Critical Biography (1951, 1973) is a good starting point. David Maskell's Racine: A Theatrical Reading

(1991) focuses on theatrical elements and the performance history of the play. Ronald W. Tobin locates *Phedra* in the context of French classical drama in *Jean Racine Revisited* (1999), while Véronique Desnain reviews feminist criticism in *Hidden Tragedies: The Social Construction of Gender in Racine* (2002). Gregory Stephen Brown discusses the historical and political context in *A Field of Honor: Writers, Court Culture and Public Theater in French Literary Life from Racine to the Revolution* (2005).

Jonathan Swift

The most comprehensive biography is Irvin Ehrenpreis's three-volume *Swift: The Man, His Works, and the Age* (1962–1983). Joseph McMinn has a fine shorter biography called *Jonathan Swift: A Literary Life* (1991), and Victoria Glendinning gives a vivid but somewhat impressionistic picture of Swift's character in *Jonathan Swift* (1999). Paul J. Degategno and R. Jay Stubblefield have put together a usefully concise introduction to Swift's life and works in their *Critical Companion to Jonathan Swift* (2006). Gary Weiner's *Readings on Gulliver's Travels* (2000) is an excellent collection of responses to the text from Swift's time to ours, and a number of interesting essays by prominent scholars are included in Frederick N. Smith's *The Genres of Gulliver's Travels* (1990). For a look at the image of cannibalism in *A Modest Proposal*, see Ahsan Chowdhury, "Splenetic Ogres and Heroic Cannibals in Jonathan Swift's *A Modest Proposal*," *English Studies in Canada* (2008).

Voltaire

Roger Pearson has a lively biography called *Voltaire Almighty: A Life in Pursuit of Freedom* (2005). Theodore Besterman's *Voltaire* (1969) is longer and more detailed. Nicholas Cronk's collection of essays in *The Cambridge Companion to Voltaire* (2009) provides both excel-

lent readings and helpful contextual material. Haydn Mason's *Candide, Optimism Demolished* (1992) considers the ideas, the reception, and the form of the text. For a series of competing interpretations of the Eldorado section of *Candide*, see Thomas Walsh, ed., *Readings on Candide* (2001).

What Is Enlightenment?

For general introductions to Enlightenment thought, see Ernst Cassirer, *The Philosophy of the Enlightenment* (1951), trans. Fritz Koelln and James Pettegrove; Peter Gay, *The Enlightenment: The Science of Freedom* (1996); and Roy Porter, *The Enlightenment* (2001). *The Portable Enlightenment Reader* (1995), ed. Isaac Kramnick, provides a good range of short readings. Those interested in scientific developments during the period will enjoy Thomas L. Hankins, *Science and the Enlightenment* (1985). For the influence of Enlightenment thinkers on the emerging form of modern democracy, see Jonathan Yisrael, *A Revolution of the Mind* (2009). For a bleaker take on the legacy of Enlightenment power and authority, see Michel Foucault, *Discipline and Punish* (1977), trans. Alan Sheridan. Foucault also responds to Kant in his own essay, "What Is Enlightenment?" in *The Foucault Reader* (1984), ed. Paul Rabinow. Robert Darnton's *The Business of Enlightenment: A Publishing History of the Encyclopédie* (1986) tells a fascinating story about the dissemination of the encyclopedia after its initial publication. Emmanuel Chukwudi Eze has published an excellent reader called *Race and the Enlightenment* (1997). There is a lively debate among scholars concerning the relation between Enlightenment thinkers and European imperial expansion. See, for example, Uday Singh Mehta, *Liberalism and Empire* (1999); Sankar Muthu, *Enlightenment against Empire* (2003); and Jennifer Pitts, *A Turn to Empire* (2006).

II. An Age of Revolutions in Europe and the Americas

The excellent, classic resource for the industrial and political revolutions of the period is E. J. Hobsbawm, *The Age of Revolution, 1789–1848* (1962). Another fine introduction to the upheavals of the period is Charles Breunig, *Age of Revolution and Reaction, 1789–1850* (1977). For the global implications of the industrial revolution, see E. J. Hobsbawm, *Industry and Empire* (1990) and Peter N. Stearns, *The Industrial Revolution in World History* (3rd ed., 2007). Gavin Weightman tells absorbing stories about particular inventors, entrepreneurs, and industrial break-throughs in *The Industrial Revolutionaries* (2010). Good scholarly works on the French Revolution include William Doyle, *The Oxford History of the French Revolution* (2003) and Simon Schama, *Citizens* (1990). Alan Schom's *Napoleon Bonaparte: A Life* (1998) is a lively biography; see also J. Christopher Herold, *The Age of Napoleon* (2002). *Latin American Independence: An Anthology of Sources* (2010), ed. John Chasteen and Sarah C. Chambers, contains fascinating source materials; for a historical overview, see Michael Eakin, *The History of Latin America* (2007). A detailed account of the upheavals of 1848 can be found in Mike Rapport, *1848: Year of Revolution* (2009).

Anna Laetitia Barbauld

William McCarthy has written a long and exceptionally detailed scholarly biography: *Anna Letitia Barbauld: Voice of the Enlightenment* (2008). For a scholarly introduction to Barbauld's life and work, see Anne Janowitz, *Women Romantic Poets: Anna Barbauld and Mary Robinson* (2004). Janowitz also offers a specific account of Barbauld's entry into polemical debates in "Amiable and Radical Sociability: Anna Barbauld's 'Free Familiar Conversation,'" in *Romantic Sociability: Social Networks and Literary Culture in Britain, 1770–1840* (2002), ed. Gillian Russell and Clara Tuite.

Charles Baudelaire

There have been many English translations of Baudelaire's poetry, including those by the well-known poets included here. The most comprehensive collection is Walter Martin's *Charles Baudelaire: Complete Poems* (2002), which includes juvenilia and poems that have been ascribed to Baudelaire; Keith Waldrop's prose translation of *Flowers of Evil* (2006), with French and English on facing pages, is widely respected. Baudelaire's essays on painting and the other arts, including his studies of Delacroix, Poe, and Wagner, have been considered the beginning of modern criticism: see *The Painter of Modern Life and Other Essays* (1964), trans. Jonathan Mayne. The definitive biography is Claude Pichois and Jean Ziegler, *Charles Baudelaire* (1991), trans. G. Robb. The most famous essays on Baudelaire as a modern writer are Walter Benjamin's *Charles Baudelaire* (1973), trans. Harry Zohn. For useful introductions, see Lois Boe Hyslop, *Charles Baudelaire Revisited* (1992); Laurence Porter, ed., *Approaches to Teaching Baudelaire's Flowers of Evil* (2000); and Rosemary Lloyd, *Baudelaire's World* (2002). Strong readings of individual works include Barbara Johnson's classic deconstructive approach, "Poetry and Its Double: Two *Invitations au voyage*," in *The Critical Difference* (1980); Jonathan Culler's introduction to *Charles Baudelaire: The Flowers of Evil* (1993); and the collection of readings in William J. Thompson, ed., *Understanding Les Fleurs du Mal* (1997). For more on the city, see Ross Chambers, "Baudelaire's Paris," in *The Cambridge Companion to Baudelaire* (2005), ed. Rosemary Lloyd.

Andrés Bello

The best work on Andrés Bello is Julio Ramos, *Divergent Modernities* (1999), trans. John D. Blance. See also Iván Jaksić's thoughtful introduction to *The Selected Writings of Andrés Bello*, trans. Frances M. López-Morillas (1997); and Iván Jaksić, *Andrés Bello: Scholarship and Nation-Building in Nineteenth-Century Latin America* (2001). For an excellent reading of this poem as a response to Virgil, see *Bello and Bolívar: Poetry and Politics in the Spanish American Revolution* (1992).

William Blake

The standard edition of the works is David V. Erdman's *The Complete Poetry and Prose of William Blake* (rev. 1988). Peter Ackroyd's marvelously well-written biography *William Blake: A Life* (1996) is to be recommended, as is the more scholarly, detailed life by G. E. Bentley Jr., *The Stranger from Paradise* (2003). Martin K. Nurmi's *William Blake* (1976) is a helpful introduction to the man and his work. For excellent critical and contextual readings, see *The Cambridge Companion to William Blake* (2003), ed. Morris Eaves, which suggests a range of approaches to reading and teaching Blake, including serious attention to

Blake's images and processes of image making. Also helpful are Jacob Brunowski, *William Blake and the Age of Revolution* (1965); W. J. T. Mitchell, *Blake's Composite Art: A Study of the Illuminated Poetry* (1978); and Saree Makdisi, *William Blake and the Impossible History of the 1790s* (2003).

Elizabeth Barrett Browning

The Complete Works of Elizabeth Barrett Browning (2010), ed. Sandra Donaldson et al., is the only scholarly edition of her works. The standard biography is Margaret Foster's *Elizabeth Barrett Browning* (1989). The story of the Brownings' romance has been retold many times in fiction and film. A particularly appealing version is Virginia Woolf's novel *Flush*, which relates the Brownings' courtship from the perspective of her dog. Helpful critical and contextual commentary can be found in Simon Avery and Rebecca Stott, *Elizabeth Barrett Browning* (2003). For a close reading of "The Cry of the Children," see Caroline Levine, "Strategic Formalism: Toward a New Method in Cultural Studies," in *Victorian Studies* (2006).

Robert Browning

The standard edition of Browning's work is Roma King, ed., *The Complete Works of Robert Browning, with Variant Readings and Annotations*, 9 vols. (1969–1989). Clyde de L. Ryals has a clear and incisive critical biography, *The Life of Robert Browning* (1993). For superb readings of the poems, see Herbert F. Tucker, *Browning's Beginnings* (1980). Robert Langbaum's *The Poetry of Experience* (1957) provides a classic account of the dramatic monologue as a form; Alan Sinfield's *The Dramatic Monologue* (1977) is also helpful.

Anna Bunina

Wendy Rosslyn's *Anna Bunina (1774–1829) and the Origins of Women's Poetry in Russia* (1997) is a fine critical biography that includes a rich context for thinking about nineteenth-century Russian writers and audiences. Catriona Kelly's *A History of Russian Women's Writing, 1820–1992* (1998) gives a broad history of women's writing in Russia and includes a brief discussion of Bunina.

Rosalía de Castro

There is an excellent collection of Rosalía de Castro's poetry in English, with a helpful introduction, by Michael Smith, called *Selected Poems* (2007); see also *Poems* (1991), ed. Anna-Marie Aldaz, Barbara N. Gantt, and Anne C. Bromley. Kathleen Kulp-Hill has also written a good introduction to the poet's life and work: *Rosalía de Castro* (1977).

Samuel Taylor Coleridge

Princeton University Press has published a fine multivolume *Complete Works of Coleridge* (1971–2001), ed. J. C. C. Mays and Joyce Crick. For a life of Coleridge, see Richard Holmes's prize-winning two-volume biography, *Coleridge: Early Visions, 1772–1804* (1989) and *Coleridge: Darker Reflections, 1804–1834* (1998). Kelvin Everest provides an excellent reading of "Frost at Midnight" in *Coleridge's Secret Ministry* (1979). For a reading of this poem as a response to the French Revolution, see Paul Magnuson, "The Politics of 'Frost at Midnight,'" *The Wordsworth Circle* 22 (1991). An analysis of global contexts for the two other poems appears in Tim Fulford's essay "Slavery and Superstition in the Supernatural Poems," in *The Cambridge Companion to Coleridge* (2002). See also John Drew, "'Kubla Khan' and Orientalism," in *Coleridge's Visionary Languages* (1993), ed. Tim Fulford and Morton D. Paley; and Patrick J. Keane, *Coleridge's Submerged Politics* (1994).

Rubén Darío

Rubén Darío's work has been translated into English more than once, but the best version remains Lysander Kemp's *Selected Poems* (1965). Also from 1965 is Charles Watland's *Poet-Errant: A Biography of Rubén Darío*, the only book-length biography in English. It is carefully documented and reliable. Keith Ellis offers five different ways of reading Darío—biographical, sociopolitical, literary historical, formal, and structural—in *Critical Approaches to Rubén Darío* (1974), and Octavio Paz discusses Darío's work in the title essay of *The Siren and the Seashell* (1970). Cathy Login Jrade in *Rubén Darío and the Romantic Search for Unity* (1983) and Dolores Ackel Fiore in *Rubén Darío in Search of Inspiration* (1963) explore influences on Darío from ancient to contemporary times. A brief review essay by the influential scholar Roberto González Echevarría, called "Master of Modernismo," does a beautiful job of capturing Darío's importance to Spanish American literary history (*The Nation*, January 25, 2006).

Emily Dickinson

R. W. Franklin's three-volume edition of Emily Dickinson's work is carefully comprehensive and preserves as much as possible her spelling and punctuation: *The Poems of Emily Dickinson: The Variorum Edition* (1998). Franklin has also put together a more accessible, one-volume version: *The Poems of Emily Dickinson: Reading Edition* (2005) and a facsimile edition, which allows readers to see her handwritten pages (1981). The classic biography is the award-winning *Life of Emily Dickinson* (1974) by Richard B. Sewall. Alfred Habegger has added fresh material and perspectives in *My Wars Are Laid Away in Books: The Life of Emily Dickinson* (2001). The poet Adrienne Rich has a wonderful essay on Dickinson's sense of her own genius in *Critical Essays on Emily Dickinson* (1984), ed. Paul J. Ferlazzo. For critical readings, see Sharon Cameron, *Lyric Time: Dickinson and the Limits of Genre* (1979); J. Dobson, *Dickinson and the Strategies of Reticence* (1989); E. Phillips, *Emily Dickinson: Personae and Performance* (1996); Elizabeth A. Petrino, *Emily Dickinson and Her Contemporaries: Women's Verse in America, 1820–85* (1998); and Virginia Jackson, *Dickinson's Misery: A Theory of Lyric Reading* (2005). For Dickinson in context, see *The Emily Dickinson Handbook* (1998), ed. Gudrun Grabher, Roland Hagenbüchle, and Cristanne Miller; Paula Bernat Bennett, "Emily Dickinson and Her American Women Poet Peers," in *The Cambridge Companion to Emily Dickinson* (2002); and *A Historical Guide to Emily Dickinson* (2004), ed. Vivian R. Pollak.

Frederick Douglass

Douglass himself wrote three autobiographies: not only the *Narrative* but also *My Bondage and My Freedom* (1855) and *The Life and Times of Frederick Douglass, Written by Himself* (1892). For a more recent scholarly account, see William S. McFeely's *Frederick Douglass* (1991). Excellent critical and historical studies include *The Cambridge Companion to Frederick Douglass* (2009), ed. Maurice S. Lee; William L. Andrews, *To Tell a Free Story* (1986); Houston A. Baker, *Blues, Ideology, and Afro-American Literature* (1991); Audrey A. Fisch, *American Slaves in Victorian England* (2000); Dwight A. McBride, *Impossible Witnesses: Truth, Abolitionism, and Slave Testimony* (2001); and John Stauffer, *Giants: The Parallel Lives of Frederick Douglass and Abraham Lincoln* (2008). On the question of gender in the narrative, see Deborah E. McDowell, "In the First Place: Making Frederick Douglass and the Afro-American Narrative Tradition," in *Critical Essays on Frederick Douglass* (1991), ed. William L. Andrews.

Olaudah Equiano

Henry Louis Gates Jr.'s famous analysis of the "trope of the talking book" is found in his book *The Signifying Monkey: A Theory of Afro-American Literary Criticism* (1988). Angelo Costanzo's *Surprizing Narrative: Olaudah Equiano and the Beginnings of Black Autobiography* (1987) has been influential. For a consideration of Equiano's career as a public figure, see John Bugg, "The Other Interesting Narrative: Olaudah Equiano's Public Book Tour," *PMLA* 121:5 (2006). Vincent Carretta's biography, *Equiano the African: Biography of a Self-Made Man* (2005) makes the highly controversial case that Equiano was born not in Africa but in South Carolina; there is a lively debate between Carretta and Paul Lovejoy in the pages of the journal *Slavery and Abolition* 27 (2006) and 28 (2007).

Johann Wolfgang von Goethe

Nicholas Boyle's two-volume biography, *Goethe: The Poet and the Age* (1991), is the most recent and one of the most extensive, informative biographies of Goethe and his work. More compact is John R. Williams's *The Life of Goethe: A Critical Biography* (1998), which is divided by genre and thus allows for a good, concise overview of Goethe's dramatic work. A classic study of *Faust* in English is Stuart Atkins's *Goethe's Faust: A Literary Analysis* (1964), a close textual analysis of the play in the tradition of the New Critics. John R. Williams's *Goethe's* Faust (1987) is more varied in its method and includes a useful discussion of the different sources, versions, and revisions that led to the final text. Most attuned to literary form is Benjamin Bennett's *Goethe's Theory of Poetry* (1986), which discusses Goethe's use and interruption of the traditional tragic plot as well as other stylistic devices. Focusing on Goethe's theater practice is Marvin Carlson's *Goethe and the Weimar Theatre* (1978). Goethe's *Faust* has also attracted the attention of philosophers and cultural critics. An early example was the Marxist critic Georg Lukács, whose *Goethe and His Age* (1940, 1969) places Goethe within the history of political and social upheaval. This line of interpretation was later taken up by Marshall Berman, whose powerful *All That Is Solid Melts into Air* (1982) reads *Faust* alongside Marx and Engels's *Communist Manifesto,* written some fifteen years after Goethe's death, as an expression of modernist upheaval and productivity.

Nikolai Gogol
There has been no recent biography of Gogol in English, but Henri Troyat's *Gogol: The Biography of a Divided Soul* (1975) is informative. One of the best readings of *The Overcoat* is Vladimir Vladimirovich Nabokov's *Nikolai Gogol* (1961). For a nice attention to linguistic detail in the story, see Donald Fanger, *The Creation of Nikolai Gogol* (1982). *Gogol from the Twentieth Century: Eleven Essays* (1974), ed. Robert A. Maguire, brings together classic Russian essays on Gogol, including several excellent readings of *The Overcoat*. See also Victor Brombert, "Meanings and Indeterminacy in Gogol's *The Overcoat,*" *Proceedings of the American Philosophical Society* 135: 4 (1991), and Gitta Hammarberg, "Sartor Resartus: Gogol's Overcoats," *Russian Review* 67:3 (2008).

Heinrich Heine
Heine has been translated into English many times. The most comprehensive edition is Hal Draper's *The Complete Poems of Heinrich Heine* (1982). The best English-language biography is Jeffrey L. Sammons's *Heinrich Heine* (1979). Hanna Spencer provides a useful introduction to the work in *Heinrich Heine* (1982). For a series of contextualizing essays by leading Heine scholars, see Roger F. Cook, *A Companion to the Works of Heinrich Heine* (2002).

Friedrich Hölderlin
David Constantine's critical biography, *Hölderlin* (1988), does a beautiful job of reading the poems and contextualizing them in the poet's life and broader historical milieu. See also L. S. Salzberger, *Hölderlin* (1952); Adrian Del Caro, *Hölderlin: The Poetics of Being* (1991); and Theodor Adorno, "Parataxis: On Hölderlin's Late Poetry," in *Notes to Literature* (1991), trans. Sherry Nicholsen.

John Keats
Andrew Motion's *Keats* (1999) is a fine biography. William Walsh's *Introduction to Keats* (1981) is a critical biography with strong readings of the poetry. Jack Stillinger's edition of Keats's *Complete Poems* (1978) remains the standard. For a brilliant and sustained reading of the odes, see Helen Vendler, *The Odes of John Keats* (1983); see also Geoffrey Hartman's *The Fate of Reading* (1975). William Keach writes about the reception of Keats as a political member of the Cockney School in "Cockney Couplets: Keats and the Politics of Style," *Studies in Romanticism* 25 (1986); see also Jeffrey Cox, *Poetry and Politics in the Cockney School* (1998).

Giacomo Leopardi
Ottavio Casale has put together a wonderful collection of selections from Leopardi's poetry and prose, including his diary, woven together to make a critical biography: *A Leopardi Reader* (1981). The only full-length English biography of Leopardi dates from 1935 (rev. 1953): Iris Origo's *Leopardi: A Study in Solitude.* For insightful readings of the poetry, see J. H. Whitfield, *Giacomo Leopardi* (1954) and Daniela Bini, *A Fragrance from the Desert* (1983).

Stéphane Mallarmé
The fullest English edition of Mallarmé's work can be found in *Stéphane Mallarmé: Collected Poems,* trans. Henry Weinfield (1995). Rosemary Lloyd has written a strong biography, *Mallarmé: The Poet and His Circle* (1999). Roger Pearson's briefer *Stéphane Mallarmé* (2010) weaves together biography with readings of the work and thought. Malcolm Bowie's *Mallarmé and the Art of Being Difficult* (1978; repr. 2008) offers a wonderful starting point for tackling Mallarmé's poetry, inviting us to ask not, What does this poem mean? but rather, How can this poem be read fully and with enjoyment? Harold Bloom's *Stéphane Mallarmé: Modern Critical Views* (1987) brings together some of the finest, and also most sophisticated and difficult, readings of Mallarmé, including Jacques Derrida's famous philosophical reading of Mallarmé, which can also be found in *Dissemination* (1981), trans. Barbara Johnson.

José Martí
Esther Allen's *José Martí: Selected Writings* (2002) features Martí's fine prose as well as his poetry and includes a valuable essay about the poet's life, work, and reception, by renowned Latin American scholar Roberto González Echevarría. *José Martí: Major Poems,* trans. Elinor Randall (1982), ed. Philip S. Foner,

provides good translations and a helpful biographical and critical introduction.

Herman Melville

Andrew Delbanco's *Melville: His World and Work* (2005) is a well-written and comprehensive biography. Leo Marx's suggestive essay, "Parable of the Walls," is collected in *Herman Melville's Billy Budd, "Benito Cereno," Bartleby the Scrivener, and Other Tales* (1987), ed. Harold Bloom. For a wonderful reading of Bartleby as a response to Thoreau, see Michael Paul Rogin, *Subversive Genealogy: The Politics and Art of Herman Melville* (1983). Barbara Foley links the story to the worker uprisings of the 1840s in "From Wall Street to Astor Place: Historicizing Melville's 'Bartleby,'" *American Literature* (2000). Other excellent essays on the texts are collected in *Melville's Short Novels: Authoritative Texts, Contexts, Criticism* (2002), ed. Dan McCall.

Alexander Sergeyevich Pushkin

T. J. Binyon's prize-winning *Pushkin: A Biography* (2002) is lively, deeply researched, and engaging. For readings of *The Queen of Spades*, see Joseph T. Shaw, "The Conclusion of Pushkin's *Queen of Spades*," in *Studies in Russian and Polish Literature* (1962), ed. Zbigniew Folejewski; Paul Debreczeny, *The Other Pushkin: A Study of Alexander Pushkin's Prose Fiction* (1983); and J. Douglas Clayton, "*The Queen of Spades*: A Seriously Intended Joke," *Pushkin Review* 12–13 (2009–10).

Arthur Rimbaud

Graham Robb's *Rimbaud* (2000) recounts Rimbaud's tempestuous life in vivid and persuasive terms. Frederic St. Aubyn's *Arthur Rimbaud* (1988) weaves together a brief biography with readings of the poems. Other useful introductions include Cecil Arthur Hackett, *Rimbaud, a Critical Introduction* (1981) and Harold Bloom, ed., *Arthur Rimbaud* (1988). For a focus on the self in Rimbaud, see James Lawler, *Rimbaud's Theatre of the Self* (1992) and Susan Harrow, *The Material, the Real, and the Fractured Self* (2004). David Evans thinks in intriguing ways about the use of rhythm in Baudelaire, Mallarmé, and Rimbaud in *Rhythm, Illusion, and the Poetic Idea* (2004).

Romantic Poets and Their Successors

Hugh Honour's *Romanticism* (1974) offers an extremely useful brief introduction to the arts in their intellectual and political context. Michael Ferber, *A Companion to European Romanticism* (2005) provides a rich set of introductory essays to Romantic movements across genres and nations, but of course it is limited to Europe. *From Romanticism to Modernismo in Latin America* (1997), a collection of essays edited by David Foster Williams and Daniel Altamiranda, adds to the global story of the movement, though a number of the articles are in Spanish. Classic studies of British Romanticism are by M. H. Abrams, *The Mirror and the Lamp* (1971) and *Natural Supernaturalism* (1973); see also Robin Jarvis, *The Romantic Period: The Intellectual and Cultural Context of English Literature* (2004). *The Literature of German Romanticism* (2004), by Dennis F. Mahoney, provides a detailed account. An introduction to American Romanticism geared to students is Jennifer Hurley, ed., *Literary Movements and Genres: American Romanticism* (1999). For the relationship between Romantic artists and those of the avant-garde, see Renato Poggioli, *The Theory of the Avant-Garde* (1968).

Christina Rossetti

The most comprehensive edition is *The Complete Poems of Christina Rossetti* (1979–1990), ed. R. W. Crump. Jan Marsh's biography is excellent and detailed: *Christina Rossetti: A Writer's Life* (1994). Fine book-length studies include Antony Harrison, *Christina Rossetti in Context* (1988); Diane D'Amico, *Christina Rossetti: Faith, Gender, and Time* (1999); and Constance W. Hassett, *Christina Rossetti: The Patience of Style* (2006). There are rich close readings of individual Rossetti poems in Isobel Armstrong, *Victorian Poetry: Poetry, Poetics, and Politics* (1993).

Jean-Jacques Rousseau

Leo Damrosch has written an excellent, lively biography, *Jean-Jacques Rousseau: Restless Genius* (2005). For a study of Rousseau's impact, see Thomas McFarland, *Romanticism and the Heritage of Rousseau* (1995). An appealing and readable account of the relationship between Hume and Rousseau, including a meditation on the ideas of both, can be found in David Edmonds and John Eidinow, *Rousseau's Dog: Two Great Thinkers at War in the Age of Enlightenment* (2006). For classic readings of *The Confessions*, see Jean Starobinski, *Jean-Jacques Rousseau: Transparency and*

Obstruction (1988), trans. Arthur Goldhammer; Huntington Williams, *Rousseau and Romantic Autobiography* (1983); and Christopher Kelly, *Rousseau's Exemplary Life: The Confessions as Political Philosophy* (1987). One of the most important works of contemporary French philosophy is Jacques Derrida's reading of *The Confessions* in *Of Grammatology* (1976), trans. Gayatri Chakravorty Spivak. James Olney reads Rousseau as part of the history of autobiography in *Memory and Narrative: The Weave of Life-Writing* (1999). For a look at gender in Rousseau, see Linda Zerilli, *Signifying Women: Culture and Chaos in Rousseau, Burke, and Mill* (1994), and Lynda Lange, ed., *Feminist Interpretations of Jean-Jacques Rousseau* (2002). The distinguished historian Robert Darnton writes about Rousseau's reception in "Readers Respond to Rousseau" in *Jean-Jacques Rousseau: Politics, Art, and Autobiography* (2006), ed. John T. Scott.

Percy Bysshe Shelley

A comprehensive, three-volume edition of the poetry has been put together by Kelvin Everest, *The Poems of Shelley* (1989–2010); for Shelley's other influential writings, see *Shelley's Poetry and Prose* (2002), ed. Neil Fraistat and Donald Reiman. James Bieri has written a lengthy and well-researched biography, *Percy Bysshe Shelley* (2008). For readings of the poetry in the context of Shelley's politics, see Stuart Curran, "Shelley and the End(s) of Ideology," from *The Most Unfailing Herald* (1996), ed. Alan M. Weinberg and Romaine Hill; see also James Chandler, *England in 1819* (1998). Shelley's style and form have been richly treated by William Keach, *Shelley's Style* (1984) and Susan J. Wolfson, *Formal Charges: The Shaping of Poetry in British Romanticism* (1997).

Alfred, Lord Tennyson

Christopher Ricks has edited *The Poems of Tennyson* (1987). Leonee Ormond's *Alfred Tennyson: A Literary Life* (1993) is a fine biography. For excellent contextual and critical readings, see Alan Sinfield, *Alfred Tennyson* (1986), Herbert F. Tucker, *Tennyson and the Doom of Romanticism* (1988), and Isobel Armstrong, *Victorian Poetry: Poetry, Poetics, and Politics* (1993).

Paul Verlaine

Stefan Zweig's *Paul Verlaine* (1913, 1980), trans. O. F. Theis, is the classic biography.

A. E. Carter's *Verlaine* (1971) offers a general introduction to his life and work. For critical and historical studies, see Laurence M. Porter, *The Crisis of French Symbolism* (1990), and David Hillery, *Verlaine: Fixing an Image* (1988).

Walt Whitman

The standard scholarly edition of Whitman's works took many years and a number of volumes: *The Collected Writings of Walt Whitman* (1961–2004), ed. Gay Wilson Allen and Sculley Bradley. Whitman's additions and revisions are so extensive that they are difficult to capture in print. An excellent new online edition called *The Walt Whitman Archive*, ed. Kenneth M. Price and Ed Folsom, has the advantage of incorporating multiple texts, including facsimiles of original editions, poems published in periodicals, and editions of *Leaves of Grass* printed outside of the United States. The best-known scholarly biography is Gay Allen Wilson, *The Solitary Singer* (rev. 1985). Another fine biography is Jerome Loving, *Walt Whitman: The Song of Himself* (1998). David S. Reynolds has brought together a series of essays that contextualize the poet in *A Historical Guide to Walt Whitman* (2000). Ezra Greenspan's *Walt Whitman's Song of Myself: A Sourcebook and Critical Edition* (2005) brings together a rich collection of reviews and critical responses starting in the nineteenth century, and offers a good overview of the historical context for Whitman's work. For critical studies, see Mark Bauerlein, *Whitman and the American Idiom* (1991); Jimmie M. Killingsworth, *Whitman's Poetry of the Body: Sexuality, Politics, and the Text* (1989); Michael Moon, *Disseminating Whitman: Revision and Corporeality in Leaves of Grass* (1991); *Whitman East and West: New Contexts for Reading Walt Whitman* (2002), ed. Ed Folsom; and Susan Belasco, Ed Folsom, and Kenneth M. Price, eds., *Leaves of Grass: The Sesquicentennial Essays* (2007). For a valuable approach to teaching *Out of the Cradle Endlessly Rocking*, see Dennis K. Renner, "Reconciling Varied Approaches to 'Out of the Cradle Endlessly Rocking,'" in *Approaches to Teaching Whitman's "Leaves of Grass"* (1990), ed. Donald D. Kummings.

William Wordsworth

The best editions of Wordsworth's poetry are the volumes in The Cornell Wordsworth series (1974–2008), ed. Stephen Parrish. A good serious biography of the poet is Stephen Gill's *William Wordsworth: A Life* (1989); for a stunningly sensitive and intelligent reading of Wordsworth's poetry with his politics, see David Bromwich's *Disowned by Memory: Wordsworth's Poetry of the 1790s* (1998). Other fine studies include Geoffrey Hartman's *Wordsworth's Poetry* (1964), Alan Liu's *Wordsworth: A Sense of History* (1989), and Theresa M. Kelley's *Words-worth's Revisionary Aesthetics* (1988). For a study of Wordsworth's ecological consciousness, see Jonathan Bate, *Romantic Ecology* (1991) and *The Song of the Earth* (2000); for a general look at audiences of Wordsworth's historical moment, see Richard Altick's classic study, *The English Common Reader* (1957), and William St. Clair, *The Reading Nation in the Romantic Period* (2004).

III. Realism

Erich Auerbach's beautiful classic work of criticism, *Mimesis* (1946), explores a number of different attempts to capture reality in the Western tradition, including nineteenth-century realism. Pam Morris's *Realism* (2003) is a fine introduction to the concept, focusing exclusively on French and British literary examples. For a historical understanding of the rise of realism, with a special focus on the visual arts, see Linda Nochlin, *Realism* (1972). György Lukács has been one of the most influential theorists of the realist novel: see his *Theory of the Novel* (1920) and *Studies in European Realism* (1948). For the roots of British realism in eighteenth-century thought and social experience, Ian Watt's *Rise of the Novel* (1957) is a landmark study. An overview of Russian realism can be found in Dmitrij Cizevskij and Dmitrij Tschižewskij, *The History of Nineteenth-Century Russian Literature: The Age of Realism* (1974).

Anton Chekhov

Donald Rayfield's highly detailed biography *Anton Chekhov: A Life* (2000) is the most substantial in English. Also by Rayfield, *Understanding Chekhov: A Critical Study of Chekhov's Prose and Drama* (1999) brings together biography and criticism. A more popular work on Chekhov is Janet Malcolm's *Reading Chekhov* (2002), which combines travel writing, biography, and criticism in a lively and intelligent—though not scholarly—book. Dana Gioia's short essay "Anton Chekhov's 'The Lady with the Pet Dog,'" in *Eclectic Literary Review* (1998) is concise and illuminating. See also Vladimir Nabokov's wonderful essay on Chekhov in his *Lectures on Russian Literature* (1981). Three fine collections of essays offer an array of historical and critical responses to Chekhov's drama: *A Chekhov Companion* (1985), ed. Toby W. Clyman; *Critical Essays on Anton Chekhov* (1989), ed. Thomas A. Eekman; and *The Cambridge Companion to Chekhov* (2000), ed. Vera Gottlieb and Paul Allain. Jean-Louis Barrault's poetic essay "Why *The Cherry Orchard*?" explores the musical structure of the play (collected in *Anton Chek-hov's Selected Plays* [2005], ed. Laurence Senelick).

Fyodor Dostoyevsky

Written over the course of three decades, Joseph Frank's magisterial five-volume biography of Dostoyevsky is widely hailed as a great achievement (1976–2002). There is a helpfully condensed one-volume version of this, called *Dostoevsky: A Writer in His Time* (2009), ed. Mary Petrusewicz, that focuses mostly on the impact of events on the author's ideas. Mikhail Bakhtin makes his influential argument that Dostoyevsky's work is always multivoiced—"polyphonic"—in *Problems of Dostoyevsky's Poetics* (1984), trans. Caryl Emerson. The Norton Critical Edition of the text contains many useful critical commentaries, including Joseph Frank's, which considers the two parts of the text as responding to two different historical contexts, the first part concerned with the mid-1860s, the second part looking back to the idealist moment of the 1840s. This edition also includes parodies and imitations of the text by Woody Allen, Ralph Ellison, and Jean-Paul Sartre. See Fyodor

Dostoevsky, *Notes from Underground* (2000), ed. Michael Katz.

Gustave Flaubert

Frederick Brown's *Flaubert: A Biography* (2006) is rich in historical detail; Geoffrey Wall's *Flaubert: A Life* (2002) is more psychological in focus. Flaubert's *Selected Letters* (1998), ed. Geoffrey Wall, give access to the writer's feelings and opinions in a way that his literary texts deliberately do not. A valuable resource for teachers is Laurence M. Porter and Eugène F. Gray, *Approaches to Teaching Flaubert's Madame Bovary* (2005). For good critical accounts, see Victor Brombert, *The Novels of Flaubert* (1966); Lennard J. Davis, "Gustave Flaubert," in *European Writers* (1985); Michal Peled Ginsburg, *Flaubert Writing: A Study in Narrative Strategies* (1986); and Stephen Heath, *Flaubert: 'Madame Bovary'* (1992). For discussions of gender in the novel, see William C. VanderWolk, "Writing the Masculine: Gender and Creativity in *Madame Bovary*," *Romance Quarterly* (1990), and Mary Orr, *'Madame Bovary': Representations of the Masculine* (1999). Vaheed K. Ramazani has written a book-length study on Flaubert's narrative style called *The Free Indirect Mode: Flaubert and the Poetics of Irony* (1988), and Dominick LaCapra offers fascinating reading of responses to the novel in *'Madame Bovary' on Trial* (1982).

Victor Hugo

Graham Robb's excellent and well-researched *Victor Hugo: A Biography* (1997) is well worth reading. For a fine account of Hugo's style and his significance in the history of the novel, see V. Brombert, *Victor Hugo and the Visionary Novel* (1984). Adam Gopnik's introduction to Julie Rose's translation of *Les Misérables* (2009) offers helpful context and interpretation. See also L. M. Porter, "'The Great French Novel': Realistic Idealism in *Les Misérables*," in *Currencies: Fiscal Fortunes and Cultural Capital in Nineteenth-Century France* (2005), ed. S. Capitanio, et. al., and A. Metzidakis, "On Rereading French History in Hugo's *Les Misérables*," *French Review* 67 (1993).

Henrik Ibsen

Overall, the best book on Ibsen is Toril Moi's *Henrik Ibsen and the Birth of Modernism* (2006). Among the early reactions to Ibsen was George Bernard Shaw's *The Quintessence of Ibsenism* (1891), which emphasizes Ibsen's concern with pressing social and political issues, while William Archer's essays, collected by Thomas Postlewait in *William Archer on Ibsen: The Major Essays, 1889–1919* (1984), foreground Ibsen's poetic choices and techniques. Charles Lyons's compilation, *Critical Essays on Henrik Ibsen* (1987), includes landmark essays by Ibsen's modernist admirers, including James Joyce, E. M. Forster, and Georg Lukàcs. The wider cultural context of Ibsen's European success, as well as a wealth of personal detail, is captured in Michael Meyer's *Ibsen: A Biography* (1971). Michael Goldman's *Ibsen: The Dramaturgy of Fear* (1999) focuses on subtexts and psychologies. In *Ibsen and Early Modernist Theatre, 1890–1900* (1997), Kirsten Shepherd-Barr situates Ibsen in the context of theater history, and Joan Templeton's *Ibsen's Women* (2001) is the first in-depth analysis of Ibsen's construction of female characters, including Hedda Gabler. *The Cambridge Companion to Ibsen* (1994), ed. James McFarlane, provides a good introduction into recent scholarship and contemporary approaches.

Machado de Assis

There is no full-length biography of Machado in English, but Helen Caldwell's *Machado de Assis: The Brazilian Master and His Novels* (1970) interweaves details about his life with readings of the novels, and Earl E. Fitz gives an overview of both life and work in *Machado de Assis* (1989). The most famous reading of Machado's literary innovations in their social context is Roberto Schwartz, *A Master on the Periphery of Capitalism* (2001), trans. John Gledson. Helpful and informative essays on Machado can be found in *Machado de Assis: Reflections on a Brazilian Master Writer* (1999).

Guy de Maupassant

Francis Steegmuller's biography, *Maupassant: A Lion in the Path* (1949) is engaging and informative, including a list of sixty-five "fake" Maupassant stories published in the United States; Michael G. Lerner, *Maupassant* (1975) is also useful. A good introduction to Maupassant's work can be found in Michael Bettencourt, *Guy de Maupassant* (1999). Laurence A. Gregorio reads Maupassant as responding to nineteenth-century theories of evolution in *Maupassant's Fiction and the Darwinian View of Life* (2005). For studies of gender roles in the stories, see Charles J. Stivale, *The Art of Rupture* (1994), and Rachel M. Hartig, *Struggling under the Destructive Glance: Androgyny in the Novels of Guy de Maupassant* (1991). Richard Fusco's *Maupassant and the American Short Story* (1994) is an interesting and well-documented study that includes comparisons with Kate Chopin, O. Henry, and Henry James.

Orature

For excellent introductions to thinking about oral traditions, see Eric Havelock's classic *Preface to Plato* (1963); Walter J. Ong, *Orality and Literacy* (1982); Isidore Opkewho, *African Oral Literature* (1992); and Ruth Finnegan, *The Oral and Beyond* (2007). Ngugi Wa Thiong'o makes a powerful case for studying orature in order to understand African cultures in *Decolonizing the Mind* (1986). On the Grimms, see Jack David Zipes, *The Brothers Grimm* (2002) and James M. McGlathery, ed., *The Brothers Grimm and Folktale* (1988). For an intriguing study of African American folk heroes, see *From Trickster to Badman* by John W. Roberts (1989). Leonard Fox's *Hainteny* (1990) is the best English-language introduction to Malagasy wisdom poetry. James C. Faris gives a detailed description of the Navajo Night Chant in an essay called "Context and Text" in Philip G. Cohen, ed., *Texts and Textuality* (1997).

Leo Tolstoy

A. N. Wilson's *Tolstoy* (1988) is an entertaining and readable biography. Gary R. Jahn's *Tolstoy's The Death of Ivan Il'ich* (1999) contains a number of fine interpretive essays and an excellent introduction. It also includes a set of notes on connotations of phrases in the original Russian text. For other good critical essays, see R. F. Christian, *Tolstoy: A Critical Introduction* (1969); Edward Wasiolek, ed., *Critical Essays on Tolstoy* (1986); Harold Bloom, ed., *Leo Tolstoy* (1986); *Tolstoy* (1997) by John Bayley; and David Holbrook's *Tolstoy, Woman and Death* (1997). The fascinating correspondence between Tolstoy and Gandhi can be found in B. Srinivasa Murthy, ed., *Mahatma Gandhi and Leo Tolstoy: Letters* (1987).

Giovanni Verga

Alfred Alexander's *Giovanni Verga* (1972) is a good account of Verga's life and work based on a wealth of material from the family archives and includes lots of information about Verga's historical and political context. See also Giovanni Cecchetti's *Giovanni Verga* (1978), a critical guide to the author's life and work. Discussions of Verga's *verismo* can be found in D. Woolf, *The Art of Verga* (1977), and Giovanni Carsaniga, "Literary Realism in Italy," in *The Cambridge Companion to the Italian Novel* (2003), ed. Peter Bondanella and Andrea Ciccarelli.

IV. Modernity and Modernism, 1900–1945

Pericles Lewis, *The Cambridge Introduction to Modernism* (2007), offers an overview of developments in England and Europe. Ástráður Eysteinsson and Vivian Lisca, eds., *Modernism*, 2 vols. (2007) provides detailed studies of particular national contexts. Harry Levin, "What Was Modernism?" (1962, repr. in *Refractions*, 1966) is a survey of modernist writers as humanists and inheritors of the Enlightenment. Many of the original critical writings on modern literature and art are collected in Vassiliki Kolocotroni, Jane Goldman, and Olga Taxidoe, eds., *Modernism: An Anthology of Sources and Documents* (1998). Richard Gilman, *The Making of Modern Drama* (1974) treats developments in drama, while Martin Puchner, *Stage Fright: Modernism, Anti-Theatricality, and Drama* (2002) explores the modernists' ambivalence toward theater. H. H. Arnason and Elizabeth Mansfield, *History of Modern Art: Painting, Sculpture, Architecture* (6th ed., 2009, illus.) follows the evolution of the arts in the West, from the nineteenth century to the 1960s. Matei Calinescu, *Five Faces of Modernity* (1987) is an informative collection of essays on the aesthetics of modernism, avant-garde, decadence, and kitsch. Peter Gay, *Modernism: The Lure of Heresy* (2007) places the movement in historical context.

Anna Akhmatova

Eileen Feinstein, *Anna of All the Russias: A Life of Anna Akhmatova* (2007) is a good recent biography. Roberta Reeder, *Anna Akhmatova: Poet and Prophet* (1994) is thorough. David Wells, *Anna Akhmatova: Her Poetry* (1996) is a readable, well-documented study that discusses works in chronological order. Amanda Haight, *Anna Akhmatova: A Poetic Pilgrimage* (1976) and Susan Amert, *In a Shattered Mirror: The Later Poetry of Anna Akhmatova* (1992) are perceptive book-length studies. Ronald Hingley, *Nightingale Fever: Russian Poets in Revolution* (1981) discusses Akhmatova, Pasternak, Tsvetaeva, and Mandelstam in the context of Russian literary history and Soviet politics up to the early years of World War II. Anna Akhmatova, *My Half Century: Selected Prose*, ed. Ronald Meyer (1992), includes autobiographical material, correspondence, short pieces on other writers, and an essay on Akhmatova's prose.

Jorge Luis Borges

Useful biographies include James Woodall, *The Man in the Mirror of the Book: A Life of Jorge Luis Borges* (1996); James Woodall, *Borges: A Life* (1996); and Jason Wilson, *Jorge Luis Borges* (2006). George R. McMurray, *Jorge Luis Borges* (1980) and Martin S. Stabb, *Borges Revisited* (1991) are general introductions to the man and his work. Jaime Alazraki, ed., *Critical Essays on Jorge Luis Borges* (1987) assembles articles and reviews (including the 1970 *Autobiographical Essay*), four comparative essays, and a general introduction that offer valuable perspectives on Borges's writing as well as his impact on writers and critics in the United States. Edna Aizenberg, ed., *Borges and His Successors: The Borgesian Impact on Literature and the Arts* (1990) is a wide-ranging collection of essays describing Borges as the precursor of postmodern fiction and criticism. Anna Maria Barrenechea, *Borges the Labyrinth Maker* (1965) discusses the writer's intricate style, while Daniel Balderston, *Out of Context: Historical Reference and the Representation of Reality in Borges* (1993) focuses on the texts' manipulation of fictional and historical reality. Fernando Sorrentino, *Seven Conversations with Jorge Luis Borges* (1981) is a series of informal, widely ranging interviews from 1972, with a list of the topics of each conversation. Recent translations into English include *Collected Fictions*, trans. Andrew Hurley (1998) and *Selected Non-Fictions* (2000), ed. Eliot Weinberger.

Bertolt Brecht

Martin Esslin, *Brecht, the Man and His Work* (1974); John Fuegi, *Brecht and Company: Sex, Politics, and the Making of Modern Drama* (1994); and John Willett, *The Theatre of Bertolt Brecht: A Study from Eight Aspects* (1959) offer biographical and critical perspectives on the author and his work. John Willett, ed. and trans., *Brecht on Theatre: The Development of an Aesthetic* (1964) contains Brecht's essays and lectures on his theater. Ronald Hayman, *Brecht: A Biography* (1983) offers a detailed view of the playwright's life. Eric Bentley, *The Brecht Commentaries 1943–1986* (1987) presents lively essays by a friend and sometime colleague on the major plays, on Brecht's stagecraft, and on his place in modern culture. The essays in Walter Benjamin, *Understanding Brecht* (1983) provide insights, by a friend and major intellectual figure, into Brecht's work and modern thought. *The Cambridge Companion to Brecht* (1994), ed. Peter Thompson and Glendry Sacks, contains an essay on *The Good Person of Szechwan*. Fredric Jameson, *Brecht and Method* (1998) is the best book on Brecht's theory. Interesting comparative studies include Anthony Tatlow, *The Mask of Evil: Brecht's Response to the Poetry, Theatre and Thought of China and Japan* (1977).

Constantine Cavafy

Biographical information is available in Peter Bien, *Constantine Cavafy* (1964) and Robert Liddell, *Cavafy: A Critical Biography* (1974, repr. 2000), which contains a bibliography. The best full-length study in English is Edmund Keeley, *Cavafy's Alexandria* (1996). A wide-ranging collection of essays is Denise Harvey, ed., *The Mind and Art of C. P. Cavafy* (1983).

Joseph Conrad

Among the many sources of biographical information are Conrad's *The Mirror of the Sea* (1906) and *A Personal Record* (1912) and Jocelyn Baines, *Joseph Conrad: A Critical Biography* (1960). The best general biography is Zdzislaw Najder, *Joseph Conrad: A Life* (2007). Albert J. Guérard's critical study, *Conrad the Novelist* (1958), is also recommended. The best general critical study, Ian Watt's *Conrad in the Nineteenth Century* (1979), discusses Conrad's impressionist and symbolist techniques. Chinua Achebe's essay "An Image of Africa: Racism in Conrad's *Heart of Darkness*" is published in his *Hopes and Impediments* (1988). J. H. Stape, ed.,

The *Cambridge Companion to Joseph Conrad* (1996) offers a wide variety of perspectives on Conrad's work, including *Heart of Darkness*; Allan Simmons, *Heart of Darkness: A Reader's Guide* (2007) provides an introduction to the critical themes of the novella. Adam Hochschild, *King Leopold's Ghost: A Story of Greed, Terror, and Heroism in Colonial Africa* (1998) is a detailed and informative study of the Congo setting of Conrad's novella.

T. S. Eliot

Peter Ackroyd, *T. S. Eliot* (1984), and Tony Sharpe, *T. S. Eliot: A Literary Life* (1991) are brief, readable introductions to Eliot's life and works. Lyndall Gordon, *T. S. Eliot: An Imperfect Life* (1998) is a fuller biography. Several volumes of Eliot's correspondence are being published in Valerie Eliot and Hugh Haughton, ed., *The Letters of T. S. Eliot* (2009–11). The influence of Eliot's life on his poems is the subject of Ronald Schuchard, *Eliot's Dark Angel: Intersections of Life and Art* (1999). Martin Scofield, *T. S. Eliot: The Poems* (1988) offers a concise, balanced discussion of the evolution of Eliot's poetry. A fine study is Denis Donoghue, *Words Alone: The Poet T. S. Eliot* (2000). Useful general collections are Linda Wagner, ed., *T. S. Eliot: A Collection of Criticism* (1974); Ronald Bush, ed., *T. S. Eliot: The Modernist in History* (1991); A. David Moody, ed., *The Cambridge Companion to T. S. Eliot* (1995); and Harold Bloom, ed., *T. S. Eliot* (1999).

William Faulkner

Stephen B. Oates, *William Faulkner, The Man and the Artist: A Biography* (1987) is vividly written. Joseph Blotner, *Faulkner: A Biography*, 2 vols. (1974; repr. in 1 vol., 2005) is the authorized, immensely detailed account of the writer's life. Other studies include Cleanth Brooks, *William Faulkner: The Yoknapatawpha Country* (1963), a basic literary analysis and exploration of Faulkner's mythical South, with a list of his fictional characters; James B. Carothers, *William Faulkner's Short Stories* (1985), an examination of the short stories in the context of the novels; and Richard C. Moreland, ed., *A Companion to William Faulkner* (2007), a collection of recent essays.

James Joyce

Harry Levin, *James Joyce: A Critical Introduction* (1941) is an excellent, readable general introduction. The standard, detailed biography, with illustrations, is Richard Ellmann, *James Joyce* (1982). Morris Beja, *James Joyce: A Literary Life* (1992) includes recent scholarship. Derek Attridge, ed., *The Cambridge Companion to James Joyce* (1990) and Mary T. Reynolds, ed., *James Joyce: A Collection of Critical Essays* (1993) treat various aspects of the work. Daniel R. Schwarz, ed., *The Dead* (1994) is a useful short book that contains the text and contextual material, an account of *Dubliners'* history and criticism from the 1950s, and analyses by several authors using five critical perspectives. John Wyse Jackson and Bernard McGinley, eds., *Joyce's Dubliners: An Illustrated Edition with Annotations* (1995) is a fascinating, copiously illustrated and documented edition that includes allusions to other works and a capsule essay after each story. A valuable recent introduction is David Pierce, *Reading Joyce* (2008). Pierce's earlier *James Joyce's Ireland* (1992) provides contemporary photographs by Dan Harper and uses documents, photographs, and quotations to reconstruct Joyce's biography in historical context.

Franz Kafka

Kafka's life has been the subject of many studies, starting with Max Brod, *Franz Kafka: A Biography* (English trans., 1960). One of the best recent works is Nicholas Murray, *Kafka: A Biography* (2004). Readable introductions to the author's life and work include Klaus Wagenbach, *Kafka* (2003) and Louis Begley, *The Tremendous World I Have Inside My Head: Franz Kafka: A Biographical Essay* (2008). Heinz Politzer, *Franz Kafka: Parable and Paradox* (1962) is an interesting early study concerned with Kafka's symbolism. *Kafka: A Collection of Critical Essays* (1962), ed. Ronald Gray, introduces the main themes of Kafka criticism, while more recent essays, specifically on the selection here, are collected in Harold Bloom, ed., *Franz Kafka's The Metamorphosis* (1988), and Stanley Corngold, ed., *The Metamorphosis* (1996). Kafka's religious background is the subject of Sander Gilman, *Franz Kafka: The Jewish Patient* (1995), while the Czech context is discussed by Scott Spector, *Prague Territories* (2000).

Federico García Lorca

Leslie Stainton, *Lorca: A Dream of Life* (1998) is an extensive biography. Carl W. Cobb, *Federico García Lorca* (1967) is a good general biography, while Gwynne Edwards, *Lorca: Living in the Theatre* (2003) focuses on his dramatic work. Candelas Newton, *Understanding*

Federico García Lorca (1995) is a brief discussion of the work; E. Honig, *García Lorca* (1980) provides a critical introduction in literary historical context; and C. B. Morris, *Son of Andalusia: The Lyrical Landscapes of Federico García Lorca* (1997) offers a more specialized view, with illustrations. Federico Bonaddio, ed., *Companion to Federico García Lorca* (2007) is a valuable collection of essays on the poet and his work.

Thomas Mann

Hermann Kurzke, *Thomas Mann: A Biography* (2002) provides a thorough account of Mann's life. Harold Bloom, ed., *Thomas Mann* (1986), and Ritchie Robertson, ed., *The Cambridge Companion to Thomas Mann* (2001) present essays on different works and brief biographical information. Terence J. Reed, *Thomas Mann: The Uses of Tradition* (2nd ed., 1996), is an excellent, well-written general study incorporating recent material. Richard Winston, *Thomas Mann: The Making of an Artist 1875–1911* (1981), the first volume of an unfinished study, is a detailed and authoritative presentation by the translator of Mann's diaries and letters. Ellis Shookman reviews almost a century's worth of criticism in *Thomas Mann's* Death in Venice: *A Novella and Its Critics* (2003).

Modern Poetry

C. K. Stead, *The New Poetic* (1964) and David Perkins, *A History of Modern Poetry: From the 1890s to the High Modernist Mode* (1976) trace the development of modernism in English poetry. Frank Lentricchia, *Modernist Quartet* (1994) explores American modernism, with a chapter devoted to T. S. Eliot. More recent poetry is well represented in Jeffery Paine, ed., *The Poetry of Our World: An International Anthology of Contemporary Poetry* (2001).

Pablo Neruda

Pablo Neruda, *Memoirs* (1977), trans. Hardie St. Martin contains much biographical information. A good recent biography in English is Adam Feinstein, *Pablo Neruda: A Passion for Life* (2004). Manuel Duran and Margery Safir, *Earth Tones: The Poetry of Pablo Neruda* (1981) is an excellent thematic study that includes a short biography. *Pablo Neruda* (1989), ed. Harold Bloom, contains nineteen valuable essays and reminiscences by scholars, translators, and those who knew Neruda. John Felstiner, *Translating Neruda: The Way to Macchu Picchu* (1980)

describes in detail the process of translating *The Heights of Macchu Picchu* in terms of Neruda's life and perspectives. Louis Poirot, *Pablo Neruda: Absence and Presence* (1990) matches photographs of Neruda, his friends, and his homes with related passages from the poet, his wife, and friends. A recent work is *The Poetry of Pablo Neruda* (2005), trans. Ilan Stavans.

Octavio Paz

Paz discusses the development of his ideas in *Itinerary: An Intellectual Journey* (1999), trans. Jason Wilson. Wilson analyzes the Mexican writer's surrealist poetry in *Octavio Paz: A Study of His Poetics* (1979), while the essays in Harold Bloom (2002), ed., *Octavio Paz* explore a range of perspectives on his work. Nick Caistor, *Octavio Paz* (2007) provides an overview of the poet's life and works.

Luigi Pirandello

Gaspare Guidice's *Pirandello: A Biography* (1975), trans. Alastair Hamilton provides a good overview of the artist's life. The best essay on Pirandello and metatheater is by Maurizio Grande, "Pirandello and the Theatre-within-the-Theatre: Thresholds and Frames in *Cascuno a suo modo*" (in *Luigi Pirandello: Contemporary Perspectives* [1999]). Roger W. Oliver's *Dreams of Passion: The Theater of Luigi Pirandello* (1979) focuses on Pirandello's theory of humor and applies it to his best-known plays, including *Six Characters*. Ann Hallamore Caesar's *Characters and Authors in Luigi Pirandello* (1998) offers a wide-ranging discussion of Pirandello through the diversity of genres in which he worked, from novels and poetry to drama and film. Pirandello's work in the theater is captured in *Luigi Pirandello in the Theatre: A Documentary Record* (1993), ed. Susan Bassnett and Jennifer Lorch, and in A. Richard Sogliuzzo's *Luigi Pirandello, Director: The Playwright in the Theatre* (1982).

Marcel Proust

Roger Shattuck, *Proust's Way* (2001) is a general study including advice on how to read Proust. Malcolm Bowie, *Proust Among the Stars* (2000) offers a slightly more advanced starting point. George D. Painter, in *Marcel Proust: A Biography* (rev. 1996), presents a comprehensive biography. Excellent recent biographies include William C. Carter, *Marcel Proust* (2000) and Jean-Yves Tadié, *Marcel Proust* (2000). Terence Kilmartin, *A Reader's Guide to* Remembrance of Things Past (1984) is a handbook to Proust's characters, persons referred to in the text, places, and themes, all keyed to the revised translation. René Girard, *Proust: A Collection of Critical Essays* (1962); Harold Bloom, ed., *Marcel Proust's Remembrance of Things Past* (1987); and Barbara J. Bucknall, ed., *Critical Essays on Marcel Proust* (1987) are also recommended.

Rainer Maria Rilke

J. F. Hendry, *The Sacred Threshold: A Life of Rainer Maria Rilke* (1983) and Patricia Pollock Brodsky, *Rainer Maria Rilke* (1988) are brief, readable biographies with numerous citations from Rilke's letters and work. A more recent, comprehensive biography is Ralph Freedman's *Life of a Poet: Rainer Maria Rilke* (1998). Heinz F. Peters, *Rainer Maria Rilke: Masks and the Man* (1977) is a biographical and thematic study of the poet's work and influence. William H. Gass, *Reading Rilke: Reflections on the Problems of Translation* (1999) combines biography, philosophy, and commentary on specific translation problems in the *Duino Elegies*. Judith Ryan, *Rilke, Modernism and Poetic Tradition* (1999) places his work in its literary-historical context.

Virginia Woolf

Hermione Lee's biography, *Virginia Woolf* (1996) is now, and surely for a while to come, the definitive work on Woolf's life. Julia Briggs has also produced a detailed recent biography that pays close attention to the author's works and their creation, *Virginia Woolf: An Inner Life* (2005). Alison Light's study, *Mrs. Woolf and the Servants* (2007), examines Woolf's place amid the shifting social and economic issues of the era through the lens of her relationships with the domestic help. Two valuable collections of essays on Woolf's writing and her position in the modernist tradition are Patricia Clements and Isobel Grundy, eds., *Virginia Woolf: New Critical Essays* (1983) and Margaret Homans, ed., *Virginia Woolf: A Collection of Critical Essays* (1993). S. P. Rosenbaum, ed., *Virginia Woolf: Women and Fiction* (1992) transcribes and edits two draft manuscripts that are the basis for *A Room of One's Own*. Gillian Beer, *Virginia Woolf: The Common Ground* (1996) offers four useful general essays and four discussions of specific novels.

William Butler Yeats

Edward Malins presents a brief introduction with biography, illustrations, and maps in *A Preface to Yeats* (1994). Richard Ellmann, *The Identity of Yeats* (1964) is an excellent discussion of the poet's work as a whole. Norman A. Jeffares has revised his major study, *A New Commentary on the Collected Poems of W. B. Yeats* (1983); a useful reference work is Lester I. Conner, *A Yeats Dictionary: Persons and Places in the Poetry of William Butler Yeats* (1998). The most thorough and balanced biographical study is R. F. Foster, *W. B. Yeats: A Life*, 2 vols. (1997–2003). A major account of Yeats's use of poetic form is Helen Vendler, *Our Secret Discipline: Yeats and Lyric Form* (2007). Essay collections include Harold Bloom, ed., *William Butler Yeats* (1986); Richard J. Finneran, ed., *Critical Essays on W. B. Yeats* (1986); and Marjorie Howes and John Kelly, eds., *Cambridge Companion to W. B. Yeats* (2006).

V. Postwar and Postcolonial Literature, 1945–1968

Ihab and Sally Hassan, eds., *Essays in Innovation/Renovation: New Perspectives on the Humanities* (1983) explores change in Western culture in the second half of the twentieth century. Tony Judt, *Postwar: A History of Europe Since 1945* (2005) explores the historical context in Europe, while Michael Howard and William Roger Louis, eds., *The Oxford History of the Twentieth Century* (1998) includes informative essays on other parts of the world. Janheinz Jahn, *Muntu: African Culture and the Western World* (1990, orig. 1961), trans. Marjorie Grene is an influential discussion of the interface of two cultures. Anthony Appiah, *In My*

Father's House: Africa in the Philosophy of Culture (1992) explores similar issues in a postcolonial context. Marjorie Perloff, ed., *Postmodern Genres* (1989) collects essays on postmodernism in art and literature. Linda Hutcheon, *A Poetics of Postmodernism* (1988) analyzes the movement's literary forms.

Chinua Achebe

A good reference is Ezenwa Ohaeto, *Chinua Achebe: A Biography* (1997). Achebe wrote a series of memoirs of his early life, collected as *The Education of a British-Protected Child* (2009). C. L. Innes, *Chinua Achebe* (1990) is a comprehensive study of the writer's work through 1988 that emphasizes his literary techniques and Africanization of the novel. Simon Gikandi, *Reading Chinua Achebe: Language and Ideology in Fiction* (1991) is also recommended. Also of interest is *Conversations with Chinua Achebe* (1997), ed. Bernth Lindfors. Jago Morrison, *The Fiction of Chinua Achebe* (2007) is a guide to criticism that includes discussions of his short fiction.

James Baldwin

David Leeming, who served as Baldwin's personal secretary, later recollected his friend and employer in *James Baldwin: A Biography* (1995). Also recommended is James Campbell, *Talking at the Gates: A Life of James Baldwin* (1991). A collection of essays published near the end of Baldwin's life, Harold Bloom, ed., *James Baldwin: Modern Critical Views* (1986) represents a range of views by Baldwin's contemporaries. A more recent collection, Dwight A. McBride, ed., *James Baldwin Now* (1999) includes a number of essays on race and sexuality.

Samuel Beckett

Beckett's works have been collected in four volumes in the Grove Centenary Edition (2006), ed. Paul Auster. *The Letters of Samuel Beckett* (first vol., 2009) are being published in an edition by Martha Dow Fehsenfeld and Lois More Overbeck. Samuel Beckett, *Endgame: with a Revised Text* (1992), ed. S. E. Gontarski is based on productions directed or supervised by Beckett; the attached theatrical notebooks often clarify situations and settings. Arthur N. Athanason, *Endgame: The Ashbin Play* (1993) is a brief introduction; and Alexander Astro, *Understanding Samuel Beckett* (1990) discusses the complete work with interpretations emphasizing cultural and linguistic aspects. Mark S. Byron, ed., *Samuel Beckett's Endgame* (2007) collects essays on this play. Andrew Kennedy, *Samuel Beckett* (1989) provides a compact, comprehensive overview of Beckett's work, with chapters on the major plays and novels. Richard Begam, *Samuel Beckett and the End of Modernity* (1996) discusses Beckett in the context of postmodernism. Cathleen Culotta Andonian organizes *The Critical Response to Samuel Beckett* (1998) in ten sections that represent the various stages in the reception of his work. Useful biographies are Deirdre Bair, *Samuel Beckett: A Biography* (1993); Anthony Cronin, *Samuel Beckett: The Last Modernist* (1996); Lois G. Gordon, *The World of Samuel Beckett, 1906–1946* (1996); and James Knowlson, *Damned to Fame: The Life of Samuel Beckett* (1996). Hugh Kenner, *Samuel Beckett: A Critical Study* (1974) is an earlier but still valuable discussion of the writer's work. Useful essay collections are Jennifer Birkett and Kate Ince, eds., *Samuel Beckett* (2000) and Steven Connor, ed., *Waiting for Godot and Endgame—Samuel Beckett* (1992), which includes eleven essays, of which seven are wholly or partially on *Endgame*.

Tadeusz Borowski

Brief discussions of Borowski are found in Czeslaw Milosz, *The History of Polish Literature* (1969) and from a different perspective, Sidra DeKoven Ezrahi, *By Words Alone: The Holocaust in Literature* (1980), and James Hatley, *Suffering Witness: The Quandary of Responsibility after the Irreparable* (2000). Jan Kott, "Introduction," *This Way for the Gas, Ladies and Gentlemen* (1976), and Jan Walc, "When the Earth Is No Longer a Dream and Cannot Be Dreamed through to the End," *Polish Review* (1987), combine biography and literary analysis, while Czeslaw Milosz, *The Captive Mind* (1953) analyzes Borowski's later communism in relation to his generation. Selections from the poetry are available in *Selected Poems* (1990), trans. Tadeusz Pióro with Larry Rafferty. Tadeusz Drewnowski, ed., *Postal Indiscretions: The Correspondence of Tadeusz Borowski* (2007), trans. Alicia Nitecki, includes letters written to his family from Auschwitz.

Italo Calvino

Sara Maria Adler, *Calvino: The Writer as Fable-maker* (1979), is a book-length biography in English. Beno Weiss's *Understanding Italo Calvino* (1993) is a useful introductory guide to Calvino's life and writings. Discussions of *Invisible Cities* may be found in Kathryn Hume's *Calvino's Fictions: Cogito and Cosmos* (1992) and *Italo Calvino: Metamorphoses of Fantasy* (1987) by Albert Howard Carter III. See also Lulcia Re, *Calvino and the Age of Neorealism: Fables of Estrangement* (1990); I. T. Olken, *With Pleated Eye and Garnet Wing: Symmetries of Italo Calvino* (1984); and Dani Cavallaro, *The Mind of Italo Calvino* (2010).

Albert Camus

Germaine Brée, *Albert Camus* (1964) is an excellent general study. Catherine Savage Brosman, *Albert Camus* (2001) is a short introduction and biography. Herbert Lottman, *Albert Camus: A Biography* (1979) and Oliver Todd, *Albert Camus: A Life* (1997) are detailed accounts. English Showalter, *Exiles and Strangers: A Reading of Camus's* Exile and the Kingdom (1984) offers essays on the six stories in Camus's collection and separate comments on translations. For a collection of recent essays on Camus, see Edward J. Hughes, ed., *The Cambridge Companion to Camus* (2007), which contains a bibliography.

Paul Celan

A translator of Celan discusses the poet's life and the challenges that his works pose for translation in John Felstiner, *Paul Celan: Poet, Survivor, Jew* (2001). A friend of the poet and distinguished critic interprets three of his major poems in Peter Szondi, *Celan Studies* (2003). Celan has attracted much commentary from philosophers, notably Hans-Georg Gadamer, *Gadamer on Celan* (1997), ed. and trans. Richard Heinemann and Bruce Krajewski, and Philippe Lacoue-Labarthe, *Poetry as Experience*, trans. by Andrea Tarnowski (1999). Aris Fioretos, ed., *Word Traces: Readings of Paul Celan* (1994) is a valuable collection of essays.

Julio Cortázar

A useful overview is Peter Standish, *Understanding Julio Cortázar* (2001). Essays on the writer are collected in three helpful volumes in English: Harold Bloom, ed., *Julio Cortázar* (2005); Jaime Alazraki, ed., *Critical Essays on Julio Cortázar* (1999); and Carlos J. Alonso, ed., *Julio Cortázar: New Readings* (1998). His stories are discussed at greater length in Ilan Stavans, *Julio Cortázar: A Study of the Short Fiction* (1996). For further bibliography, see Sara de Mundo Lo, *Julio Cortázar: His Works and His Critics* (1985).

Carlos Fuentes

Daniel de Guzman, *Carlos Fuentes* (1972) is a brief biography. Maarten van Delden, *Carlos Fuentes, Mexico, and Modernity* (1998) explores the tension between nationalism and cosmopolitanism in Fuentes's fiction and nonfiction. Robert Brody and Charles Rossman, eds., *Carlos Fuentes, A Critical View* (1982), a collection of essays, features several notable critics of Latin American literature, writing on such topics as Fuentes's use of myth and his formal experimentation. It includes an essay on the second-person narration of *Aura*.

Doris Lessing

The most comprehensive biography is Carol Klein, *Doris Lessing* (2000). Ruth Whittaker, *Doris Lessing* (1988) is a concise, informative discussion of the writer's fiction to 1985; it includes biographical contexts and selective bibliography. Two volumes of Lessing's autobiography are published as *Under My Skin* (1995) and *Walking in the Shade* (1997). A good critical study of the novels is Roberta Rubenstein, *The Novelistic Vision of Doris Lessing* (1979). Perspectives on women and literature are the focus of Gayle Greene, *Doris Lessing: The Poetics of Change* (1994).

Clarice Lispector

The best biography is Benjamin Moser, *Why This World: A Biography of Clarice Lispector* (2008). Earl E. Fitz, *Clarice Lispector* (1985), a valuable introduction to her life and work, contains an annotated bibliography. Hélène Cixous, *Reading with Clarice Lispector* (1990), ed., trans., and intro. Verena Andermatt Conley, discusses Lispector's style with reference to three stories and three novels.

Manifestos

The best collection is Mary Ann Caws's *Manifestos: A Century of Isms* (2001). Critical studies of the genre include Janet Lyon's *Manifestoes: Provocations of the Modern* (1999), which emphasizes declarations written by women, and Martin Puchner's *Poetry of the Revolution: Marx, Manifestos, and the Avant-Gardes* (2006), which focuses on the relation between artistic manifestos and political ones.

Alice Munro

Catherine S. Ross, *Alice Munro: A Double Life* (1991) is a compact, readable biography that highlights the sources of her writing; it includes a bibliography, photographs, maps, and interview comments about Nora. E. D. Blodgett, *Alice Munro* (1988) and Coral Ann Howells, *Alice Munro* (1998) introduce the writer and her work. Robert Thacker, ed., *The Rest of the Story: Critical Essays on Alice Munro* (1999) assembles eleven essays, including a discussion of the writer's correspondence with her literary agent. Louis MacKendrick, ed., *Probable Fictions: Alice Munro's Narrative Acts* (1983) is an excellent survey of critical essays and of interviews with the author herself. Sheila Munro brings a personal perspective to *Lives of Mothers and Daughters: Growing Up with Alice Munro* (2001).

Vladimir Nabokov

A thorough scholarly biography in two volumes is Brian Boyd, *Vladimir Nabokov* (1990–1991). A shorter biography that also introduces Nabokov's works is Neil Cornwell, *Vladimir Nabokov* (1999). For more on his life, see Dmitri Nabokov and Matthew J. Bruccoli, eds., *Vladimir Nabokov: Selected Letters, 1940–1977* (1989). Nabokov's memoir, *Speak, Memory* (1966) is unforgettable, while his idiosyncratic observations on literature are collected in *Strong Opinions* (1973) and *Lectures on Literature* (1980), ed. Fredson Bowers. Valuable critical essays are collected in Julian Connolly, ed., *The Cambridge Companion to Nabokov* (2005).

Alain Robbe-Grillet

Ilona Leki, *Alain Robbe-Grillet* (1983), is a good biography and survey of Robbe-Grillet's works in historical context, discussing each work, with a last chapter on the films. Introductory essays to Alain Robbe-Grillet's, *Two Novels* (1965, 1993), trans. Richard Howard, discuss the author's descriptive strategies. Bruce Morrissette, *The Novels of Robbe-Grillet* (1975), provides a valuable critical study that takes the works and films in chronological

order. Morrissette, *Novel and Film: Essays in Two Genres* (1985), makes Robbe-Grillet the chief example in a discussion of modern cinematic vision. Ben Stoltzfus, *Alain Robbe-Grillet and the New French Novel* (1964), is an earlier introduction to Robbe-Grillet in the context of the emerging new novel form. Raylene L. Ramsay, *Robbe-Grillet and Modernity: Science, Sexuality, and Subversion* (1992), interrogates contemporary culture and the thematic of sexual violence. See also John Phillips, *Alain Robbe-Grillet* (2011).

Léopold Sédar Senghor

The selections presented here are taken from *The Collected Poetry* (1991), trans. Melvin Dixon, whose introduction is helpful. Sylvia Washington Bâ's *The Concept of Négritude in the Poetry of Léopold Sédar Senghor* (1973) provides the most comprehensive discussion of the poet's work. An essay collection, Janice Spleth, ed., *Critical Perspectives on Leopold Sedar Senghor* (1993) offers a range of views. For an account of Senghor's life and intellectual development, with incidental comments on his poetry, see Janet G. Vaillant, *Black, French and African: A Life of Léopold Sédar Senghor* (1990). A collection of essays edited by Isabelle Constant and Kahiudi C. Mabana, *Negritude: Legacy and Present Relevance* (2009) analyzes and defends the concept of Négritude.

Alexander Solzhenitsyn

Andrej Kodjak, *Alexander Solzhenitsyn* (1978) provides a biographical and critical introduction up to the writer's deportation from the Soviet Union in 1974; it includes a discussion of Russian terms. Michael Scammell's detailed *Solzhenitsyn: A Biography* (1984) is complemented by Joseph Pearce, *Solzhenitsyn: A Soul in Exile* (1999). Kathryn B. Feuer, ed., *Solzhenitsyn: A Collection of Critical Essays* (1976), and Harold Bloom, ed., *Alexander Solzhenitsyn* (2000) contain a range of essays on aspects and particular works, including *Matryona's Home*. John B. Dunlop, Richard S. Haugh, and Michael Nicholson, eds., *Solzhenitsyn in Exile: Critical Essays and Documentary Material* (1985) offers critical essays and discussions of Solzhenitsyn's reception in several countries. A collection of shorter works is available in Edward E. Ericson Jr. and Daniel J. Mahoney, eds., *The Solzhenitsyn Reader: New and Essential Writings 1946–2005* (2006).

VI. Global and Local Contemporary World Literature

Lois Parkinson Zamora and Wendy B. Faris, eds., *Magical Realism: Theory, History, Community* (1997) examines the theoretical and cultural implications of the style in Latin America and elsewhere. Nancy K. Miller, ed., *The Poetics of Gender* (1986) presents essays on various aspects of feminist criticism. Sarah Lawall, ed., *Reading World Literature: Theory, History, Practice* (1994) includes a theoretical introduction to the subject of world literature and twelve essays on specific topics. David Damrosch, *What Is World Literature?* (2003) explores a range of issues in the study of world literature, while Pascale Casanova, *The World Republic of Letters* (2004) offers a sociological view of the development of literary reputations. Accounts of crucial moments in contemporary history include Jeremi Suri, ed., *The Global Revolutions of 1968* (2007); Timothy Garton Ash, *The Magic Lantern: The Revolution of '89 Witnessed in Warsaw, Budapest, Berlin, and Prague* (1993); and Thomas L. Friedman, *The World Is Flat 3.0: A Brief History of the Twenty-First Century* (2007).

Isabel Allende

Interviews are collected in Celia Correas Zapata, *Isabel Allende: Life and Spirits* (2002) and in John Rodden, ed., *Conversations with Isabel Allende* (2004). Harold Bloom offers a critical assessment of Allende's work but collects the best early essays on her in *Isabel Allende* (2003). General introductions are available in Linda Gould Levine, *Isabel Allende* (2002), and Karen Castellucci Cox, *Isabel Allende: A Critical Companion* (2003), which contains a bibliography.

Ingeborg Bachmann

Karen R. Achberger, *Understanding Ingeborg Bachmann* (1995) is a good overview of Bachmann's work; it includes a short biography and bibliographic references. Introductions by Mark Anderson to Bachmann's *In the Storm of Roses: Selected Poems* (1986), trans. and ed. Mark Anderson, and *Three Paths to the Lake: Stories* (1989), trans. Mary Fran Gilbert, provide an excellent short overview of the writer's poetry and prose. Gudrun Brokoph-Mauch, ed., *Thunder Rumbling at My Heels: Tracing Ingeborg Bachmann* (1998) may also be consulted. Juliet Wigmore, "Ingeborg Bachmann" in Keith Bullivant, ed., *The Modern German Novel* (1987), discusses *Malina* and the *Ways of Death* cycle. Inta Ezergailis, *Women Writers— The Divided Self* (1982) has chapters on Bachmann and Doris Lessig, among others. A special issue of *Modern Austrian Literature* (1979) devoted to Austrian women writers contains several essays on Bachmann. Also see *War*

Diary: With Letters from Jack Hames (2011), ed. Hans Holler, trans. Mike Mitchell.

Roberto Bolaño

Selected short stories, including *Sensini*, appear in *Last Evenings on Earth* (2006), trans. Chris Andrews. The best overview of Bolaño's career in English is Francisco Goldman, "The Great Bolaño," *The New York Review of Books*, July 19, 2007. Bolaño discusses his life and work in his characteristically indirect way in Mónica Maristain, *Roberto Bolaño: The Last Interview & Other Conversations* (2009). Tod Thilleman and Richard Blevins, *Breathing Bolaño* (2009) contains the poet Richard Blevins's amusing meditations on Bolaño's novels and stories about poets.

J. M. Coetzee

The best, albeit unreliable, source for information on Coetzee's life is his autobiographical fiction, *Boyhood* (1997), *Youth* (2002), and *Summertime* (2010). Derek Attridge offers a rich interpretation of Coetzee's work in relation to modernism in *J. M. Coetzee and the Ethics of Reading: Literature in the Event* (2005). A more explicitly political approach to the early fiction is David Attwell, *J. M. Coetzee: South Africa and the Politics of Writing* (1993). Graham Huggan and Stephen Watson, eds., *Critical Perspectives on J. M. Coetzee* (1996), with an introduction by Nadine Gordimer, collects essays on various facets of Coetzee's work.

Junot Díaz

Díaz is interviewed in Ilan Stavans, *Conversations with Ilan Stavans* (2005). Díaz's work is discussed in Harold Augenbraum and Margarite Fernández Olmos, eds., *U.S. Latino Literature: A Critical Guide for Students and Teachers* (2000), and in Lyn Di Iorio Sandín and Richard Perez, eds., *Contemporary U.S. Latino/a Literary Criticism* (2007), which includes a bibliography.

Gabriel García Márquez

The best biography is Gerald Martin, *Gabriel García Márquez* (2008). A shorter overview is Rubén Pelayo, *Gabriel García Márquez: A Biography* (2009). García Márquez has himself published a remarkable autobiography, *Living to Tell the Tale* (2003). Regina Janes, *Gabriel García Márquez, Revolutions in Wonderland* (1981) is an excellent early study on the author in a Latin American context. Other useful introductions to the writer and his work are George P. McMurray, *Gabriel García Márquez* (1977); Robin W. Fiddian, *García Márquez* (1995); and Joan Mellen, *Gabriel García Márquez* (2000). See also Julio Ortega, ed., *Gabriel García Márquez and the Powers of Fiction* (1988), and Isabel Rodriguez-Vergara, *Haunting Demons: Critical Essays on the Works of Gabriel García Márquez* (1998). Harley D. Oberhelman, ed., *Gabriel García Márquez: A Study of the Short Fiction* (1991) includes a bibliography.

Bessie Head

Gillian Stead Eilerson presents the author's biography in *Bessie Head: Thunder Behind Her Ears, Her Life and Writing* (1995). Some of her letters are collected, with a memoir by a close friend, in Patrick Cullinan, ed., *Imaginative Trespasser: Letters Between Bessie Head and Patrick and Wendy Cullinan, 1963–1977* (2005). Craig MacKenzie provides a helpful overview of her work in *Bessie Head* (1999).

Seamus Heaney

Michael Parker, *Seamus Heaney: The Making of a Poet* (1993) combines biography with literary criticism, while the best overall critical study is Helen Vendler, *Seamus Heaney* (1998), which focuses on Heaney's intellectual and aesthetic experiments. Bernard O'Donoghue, ed., *The Cambridge Companion to Seamus Heaney* (2009) includes several essays on Heaney's relationship to other poets. A number of the poet's interviews are collected in Dennis O'Driscoll, ed., *Stepping Stones: Interviews with Seamus Heaney* (2008).

Jamaica Kincaid

Diane Simmons provides an overview of Kincaid's work, with biographical information, in *Jamaica Kincaid* (1994). Elizabeth Paravisini-Gebert, *Jamaica Kincaid: A Critical Companion* (1999) focuses on the early short stories and the first three novels. A more recent overview is Justin Edwards, *Understanding Jamaica Kincaid* (2007).

Toni Morrison

John Duvall's critical study *The Identifying Fictions of Toni Morrison: Modernist Authenticity and Postmodern Blackness* (2000) interprets the writer's novels as deeply autobiographical and presents an account of her early life. Another valuable critical study is Linden Peach, *Toni Morrison* (2000). Mark C. Connor, ed., *The Aesthetics of Toni Morrison: Speaking the Unspeakable* (2000) includes a number of excellent essays on Morrison's fiction and nonfiction. A more comprehensive overview is Justine Tally, ed., a *Cambridge Companion to Toni Morrison* (2007). Several of the author's interviews are collected in Danille K. Taylor-Guthrie, ed., *Conversations with Toni Morrison* (1994).

V. S. Naipaul

A remarkable, authorized biography is Patrick French, *The World Is What It Is* (2009). Bruce King provides an accessible introduction to Naipaul's work in *V. S. Naipaul* (1993; 2nd ed., 2003). Gillian Dooley, *V. S. Naipaul: Man and Writer* (2006) offers a sympathetic reading of the author's work in relation to his life. Naipaul's memorable correspondence with his father is collected in V. S. Naipaul, *Between Father and Son: Family Letters* (2000), ed. Gillon Aitken.

Ngugi wa Thiong'o

A good overview of Ngugi's works is David Cook and Michael Okenimkpe, *Ngugi wa Thiong'o: An Exploration of His Writings* (2nd ed., 1997). Thorough critical accounts include Simon Gikandi, *Ngugi wa Thiong'o* (2000) and Patrick Williams, *Ngugi wa Thiong'o* (1999). Oliver Lovesey provides a biography with relevant historical context in *Ngugi wa Thiong'o* (2000). The historical background is comprehensively treated in Carol Sicherman, ed., *Ngugi wa Thiong'o: The Making of a Rebel. A Source Book in Kenyan Literature and Resistance* (1990).

Salman Rushdie

Midnight's Children (1980) has been in print since its first publication. Among the many books about Rushdie and his work, particularly helpful and informative are Damian Grant, *Salman Rushdie* (1999), for an overview of much of his career; Jaina C. Sanga, *Salman Rushdie's Postcolonial Metaphors* (2001), and Sabrina Hassumani, *Salman Rushdie* (2002) for analyses of his style and major themes. Discussions of the writer's work in wider literary contexts appear in Timothy Brennan, *Salman Rushdie and the Third World* (1989), and Fawzia Afzal-Khan, *Cultural Imperialism and the Indo-English Novel* (1993). Important documentary sources include Lisa Appignanesi and Sara Maitland, *The Rushdie File* (1990); Michael R. Reder, *Conversations with Salman Rushdie* (2000); and Pradyumna S. Chauhan, *Salman Rushdie Interviews* (2001).

Leslie Marmon Silko

Gregory Salyer, *Leslie Marmon Silko* (1997) is a brief introduction to the author and her work; Brewster E. Fitz offers an updated view of the author's career in *Silko: Writing Storyteller and Medicine Woman* (2004). Helen Jaskoski, *Leslie Marmon Silko: A Study of the Short Fiction* (1998) focuses on the stories. Leslie Marmon Silko, *Sacred Water: Narratives and Pictures* (1994) is an autobiographical narrative. Melody Graulich, ed., *"Yellow Woman": Leslie Marmon Silko* (1993) collects pertinent critical essays. *Yellow Woman* and other works are treated in Louise K. Barnett and James L. Thorson, eds., *Leslie Marmon Silko: A Collection of Critical Essays* (1999). For traditional texts on Yellow Woman and other figures in Laguna mythology, the best source is Franz Boas, *Keresan Texts* (1928); the stories in Boas's volume were obtained in 1919–21 from several Laguna informants, including Leslie Silko's great-grandfather, Robert Marmon.

Wole Soyinka

For an authoritative text and extensive background readings on *Death and the King's Horseman*, consult the Norton Critical Edition of that play (2003). Derek Wright, *Wole Soyinka Revisited* (1993) provides a nuanced analysis of the dramatic oeuvre, focusing on theatrical categories, such as ritual, tragedy, and satire, that are central to an understanding of Soyinka's work. Ketu H. Katrak, *Wole Soyinka and Modern Tragedy* (1986) focuses on the author's attempt to create a Yoruba tragedy. By far the best of the critical literature on the playwright is Biodun Jeyifo, *Wole Soyinka: Politics, Poetics and Postcoloniality* (2004), which analyzes the complex relations among colonial culture, independence, and literature that mark this playwright's oeuvre. See also a collection of interviews, *Conversations with Wole Soyinka*, ed. Biodun Jeyifo (2001). The philosopher K. Anthony Appiah has devoted attention to Soyinka in his work *In My Father's House: Africa in the Philosophy of Culture* (1992). There are several useful collections of essays on Soyinka, including James Gibbs, ed., *Critical Perspectives on Wole Soyinka* (1980) and Biodun Jeyifo, ed., *Perspectives on Wole Syoinka*.

Derek Walcott

Derek Walcott, *Another Life* (1973), an autobiography in verse, traces the poet's artistic development. A full biography is Bruce King, *Derek Walcott: A Caribbean Life* (2000). Walcott's collection of essays, *What the Twilight Says* (1998), is an indispensable compendium of his social and aesthetic ideas. Robert Hamner, *Derek Walcott* (1978, rev. 1993), is a comprehensive and accessible full-length study of the writer's work; John Thieme, *Derek Walcott* (1999) is more up-to-date and provides commentaries on the key poems in Walcott's various collections and on the dramatic works. Robert Hamner, *Epic of the Dispossessed* (1997) offers a detailed discussion of *Omeros* that considers its adaptation of epic idiom to the experience and life dilemmas of the common folk. *The Art of Derek Walcott* (1991), ed. Stewart Brown, and *Critical Perspectives on Derek Walcott* (1993), ed. Robert Hamner, are collective volumes that cover Walcott's work up to the dates of their publication.

TIMELINE *for*

I. The Enlightenment in Europe and the Americas

Contexts | Texts

1600 C.E.   1610 C.E.   1620 C.E.

1637
René Descartes,
Discourse on Method

1630 C.E.   1640 C.E.   1650 C.E.

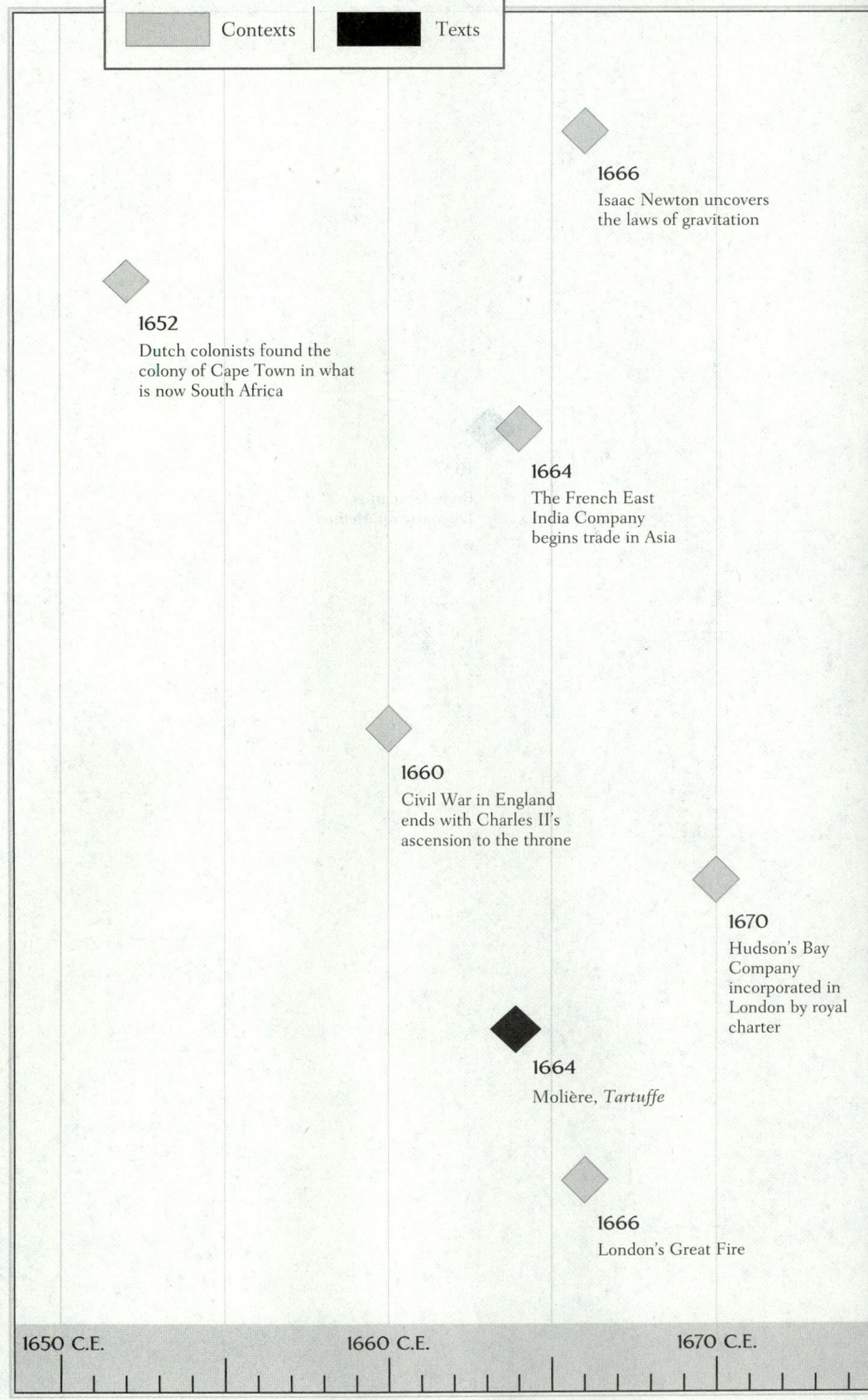

Contexts | Texts

1666
Isaac Newton uncovers
the laws of gravitation

1652
Dutch colonists found the
colony of Cape Town in what
is now South Africa

1664
The French East
India Company
begins trade in Asia

1660
Civil War in England
ends with Charles II's
ascension to the throne

1670
Hudson's Bay
Company
incorporated in
London by royal
charter

1664
Molière, *Tartuffe*

1666
London's Great Fire

1650 C.E.   1660 C.E.   1670 C.E.

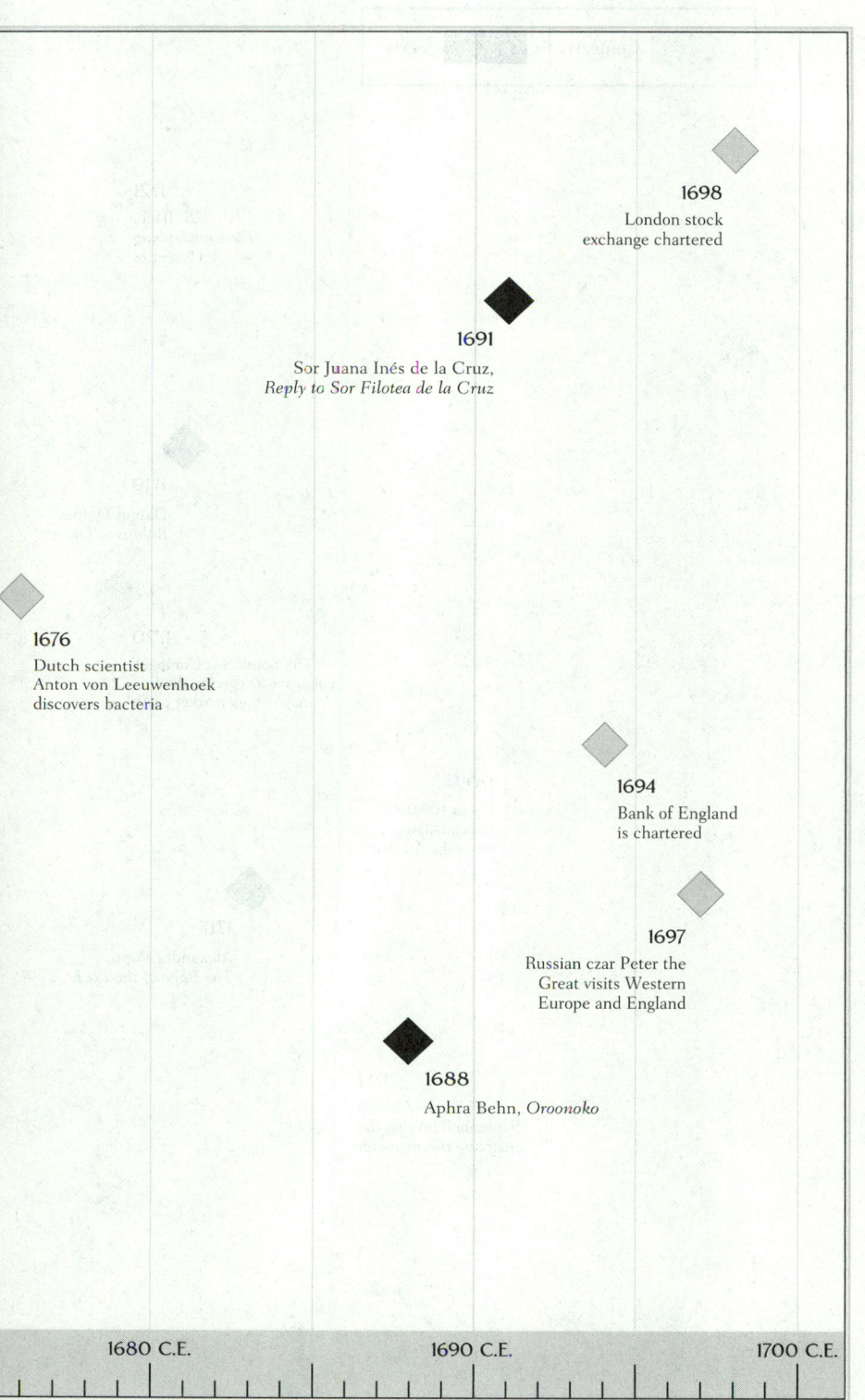

1698
London stock
exchange chartered

1691
Sor Juana Inés de la Cruz,
Reply to Sor Filotea de la Cruz

1676
Dutch scientist
Anton von Leeuwenhoek
discovers bacteria

1694
Bank of England
is chartered

1697
Russian czar Peter the
Great visits Western
Europe and England

1688
Aphra Behn, *Oroonoko*

1680 C.E.   1690 C.E.   1700 C.E.

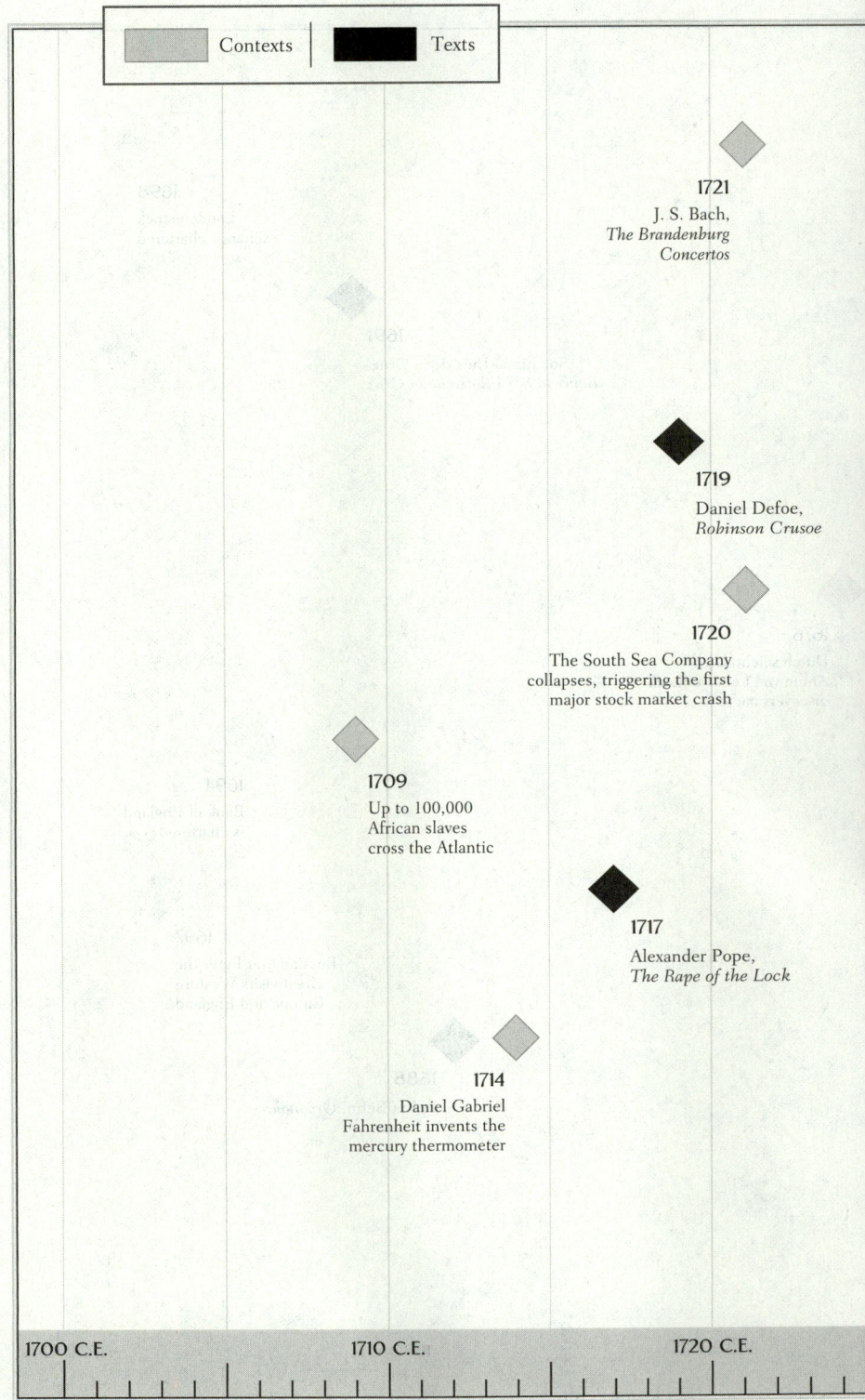

Contexts | Texts

1721
J. S. Bach,
*The Brandenburg
Concertos*

1719

Daniel Defoe,
Robinson Crusoe

1720
The South Sea Company
collapses, triggering the first
major stock market crash

1709
Up to 100,000
African slaves
cross the Atlantic

1717

Alexander Pope,
The Rape of the Lock

1714
Daniel Gabriel
Fahrenheit invents the
mercury thermometer

1700 C.E.   1710 C.E.   1720 C.E.

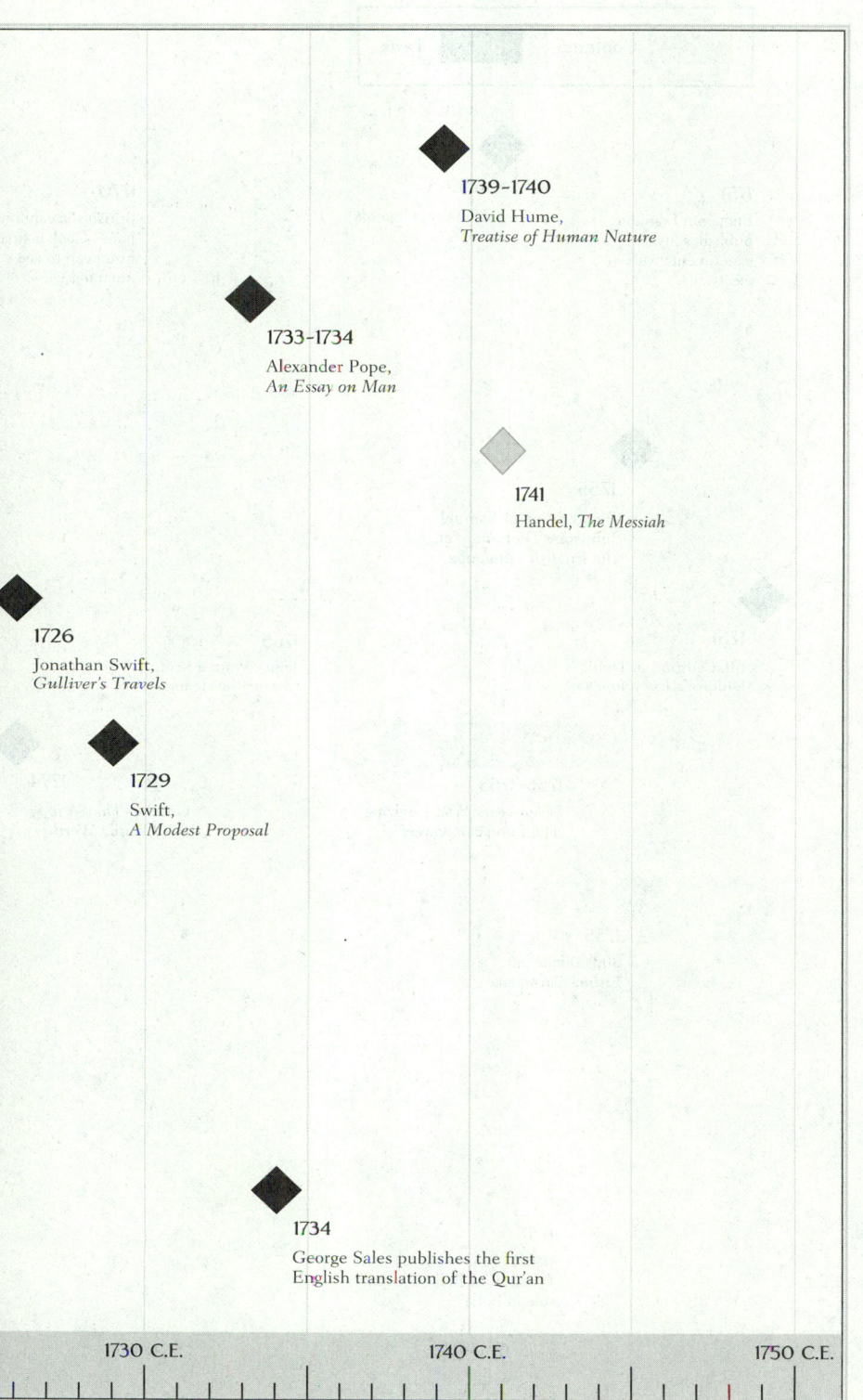

1739-1740

David Hume,
Treatise of Human Nature

1733-1734

Alexander Pope,
An Essay on Man

1741

Handel, *The Messiah*

1726

Jonathan Swift,
Gulliver's Travels

1729

Swift,
A Modest Proposal

1734

George Sales publishes the first
English translation of the Qur'an

1730 C.E.   1740 C.E.   1750 C.E.

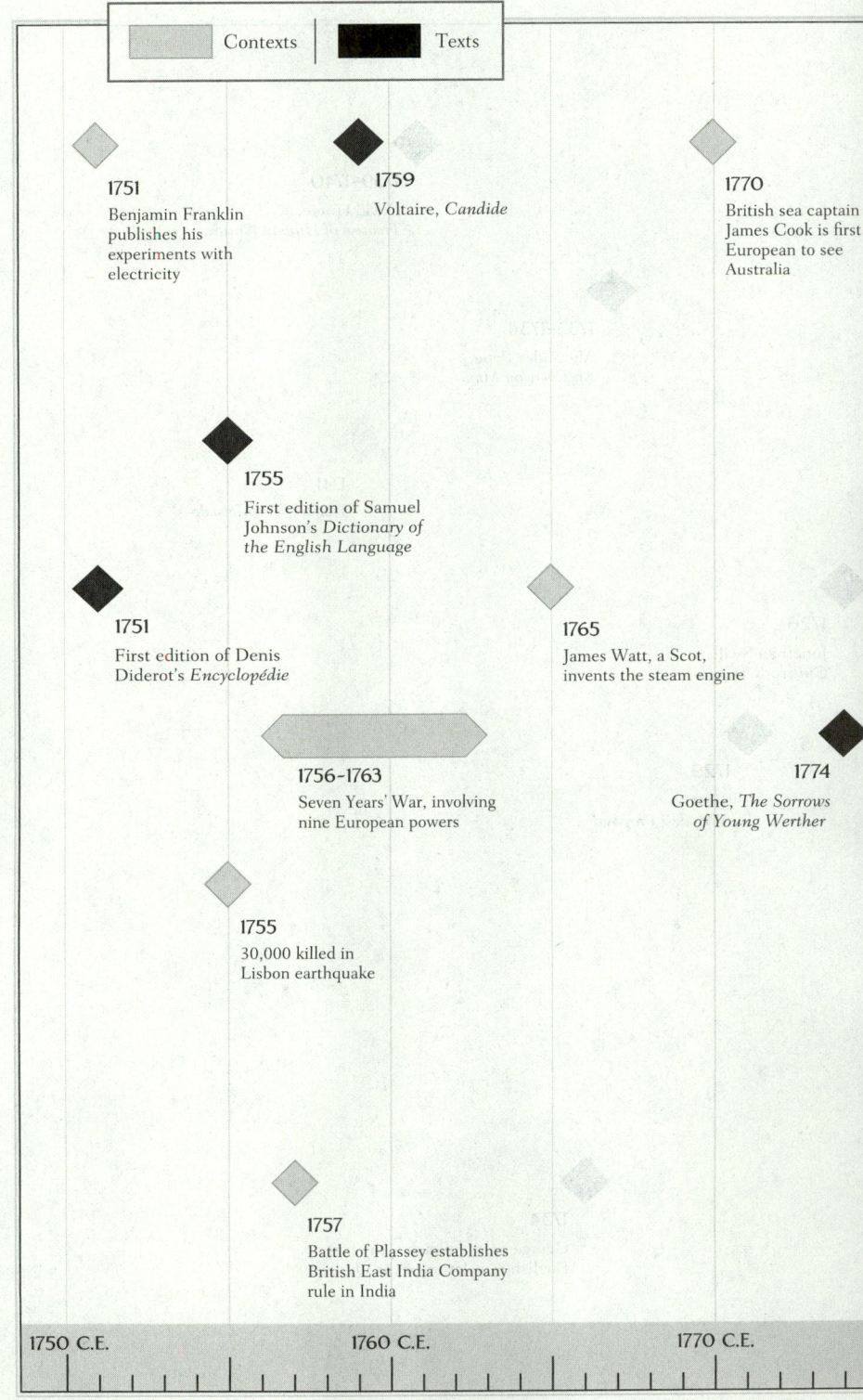

Contexts | Texts

1751
Benjamin Franklin
publishes his
experiments with
electricity

1759
Voltaire, *Candide*

1770
British sea captain
James Cook is first
European to see
Australia

1755
First edition of Samuel
Johnson's *Dictionary of
the English Language*

1751
First edition of Denis
Diderot's *Encyclopédie*

1765
James Watt, a Scot,
invents the steam engine

1756–1763
Seven Years' War, involving
nine European powers

1774
Goethe, *The Sorrows
of Young Werther*

1755
30,000 killed in
Lisbon earthquake

1757
Battle of Plassey establishes
British East India Company
rule in India

1750 C.E.   1760 C.E.   1770 C.E.

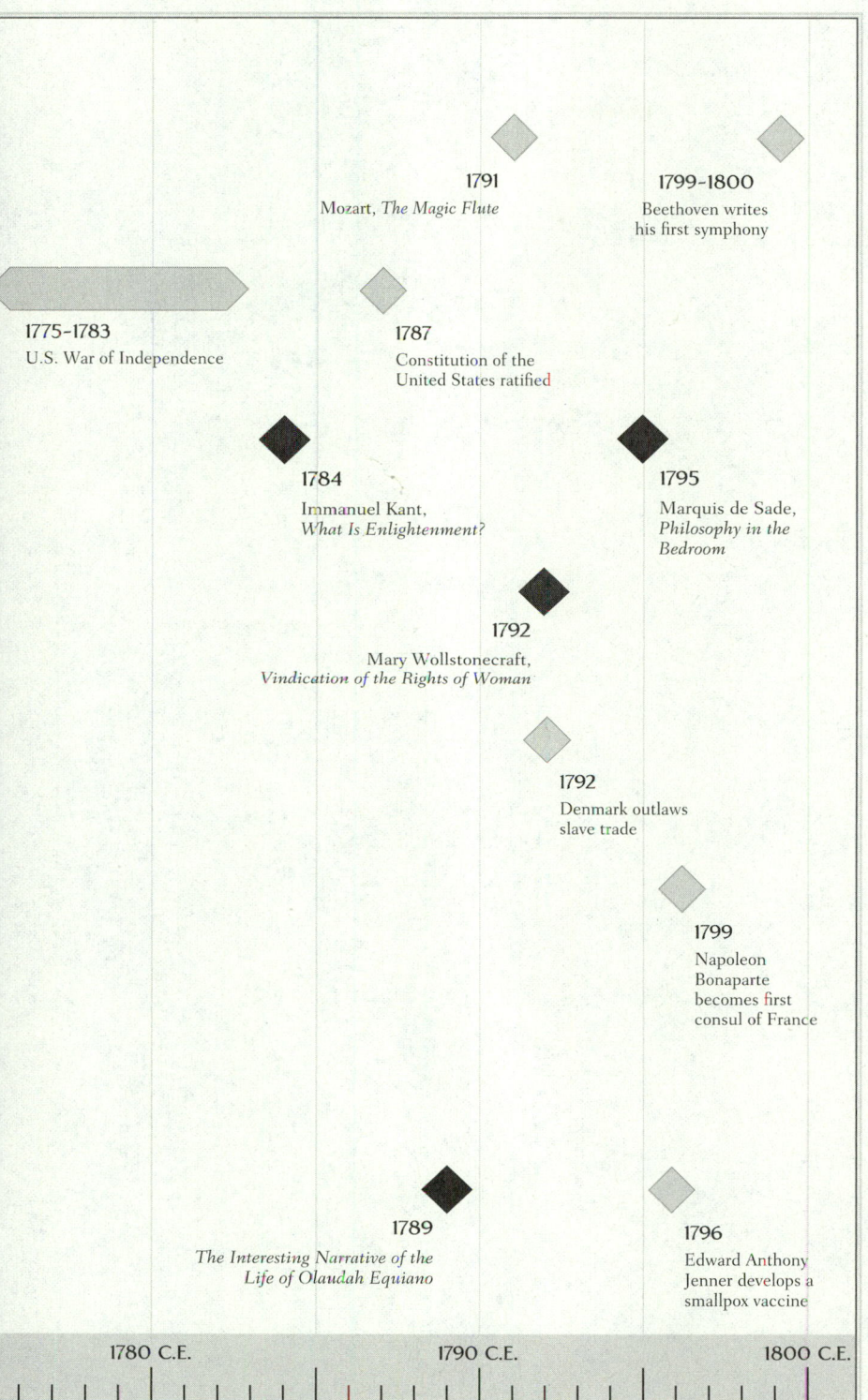

1791

Mozart, *The Magic Flute*

1799–1800

Beethoven writes
his first symphony

1775–1783

U.S. War of Independence

1787

Constitution of the
United States ratified

1784

Immanuel Kant,
What Is Enlightenment?

1795

Marquis de Sade,
*Philosophy in the
Bedroom*

1792

Mary Wollstonecraft,
Vindication of the Rights of Woman

1792

Denmark outlaws
slave trade

1799

Napoleon
Bonaparte
becomes first
consul of France

1789

*The Interesting Narrative of the
Life of Olaudah Equiano*

1796

Edward Anthony
Jenner develops a
smallpox vaccine

1780 C.E.   1790 C.E.   1800 C.E.

TIMELINE *for*

II. An Age of Revolutions in Europe and the Americas

III. Realism

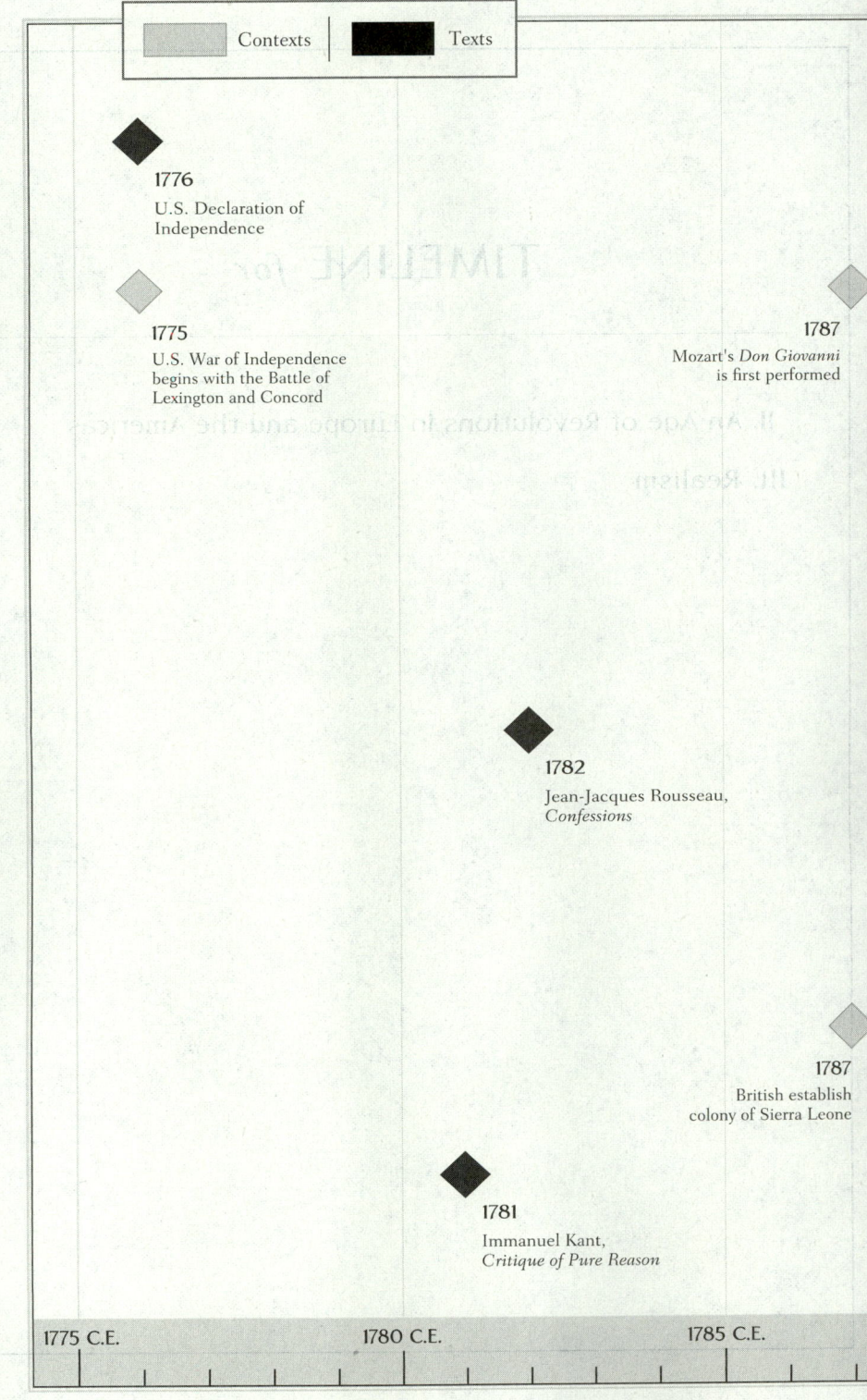

Contexts | Texts

1776
U.S. Declaration of
Independence

1775
U.S. War of Independence
begins with the Battle of
Lexington and Concord

1787
Mozart's *Don Giovanni*
is first performed

1782
Jean-Jacques Rousseau,
Confessions

1787
British establish
colony of Sierra Leone

1781
Immanuel Kant,
Critique of Pure Reason

1775 C.E.   1780 C.E.   1785 C.E.

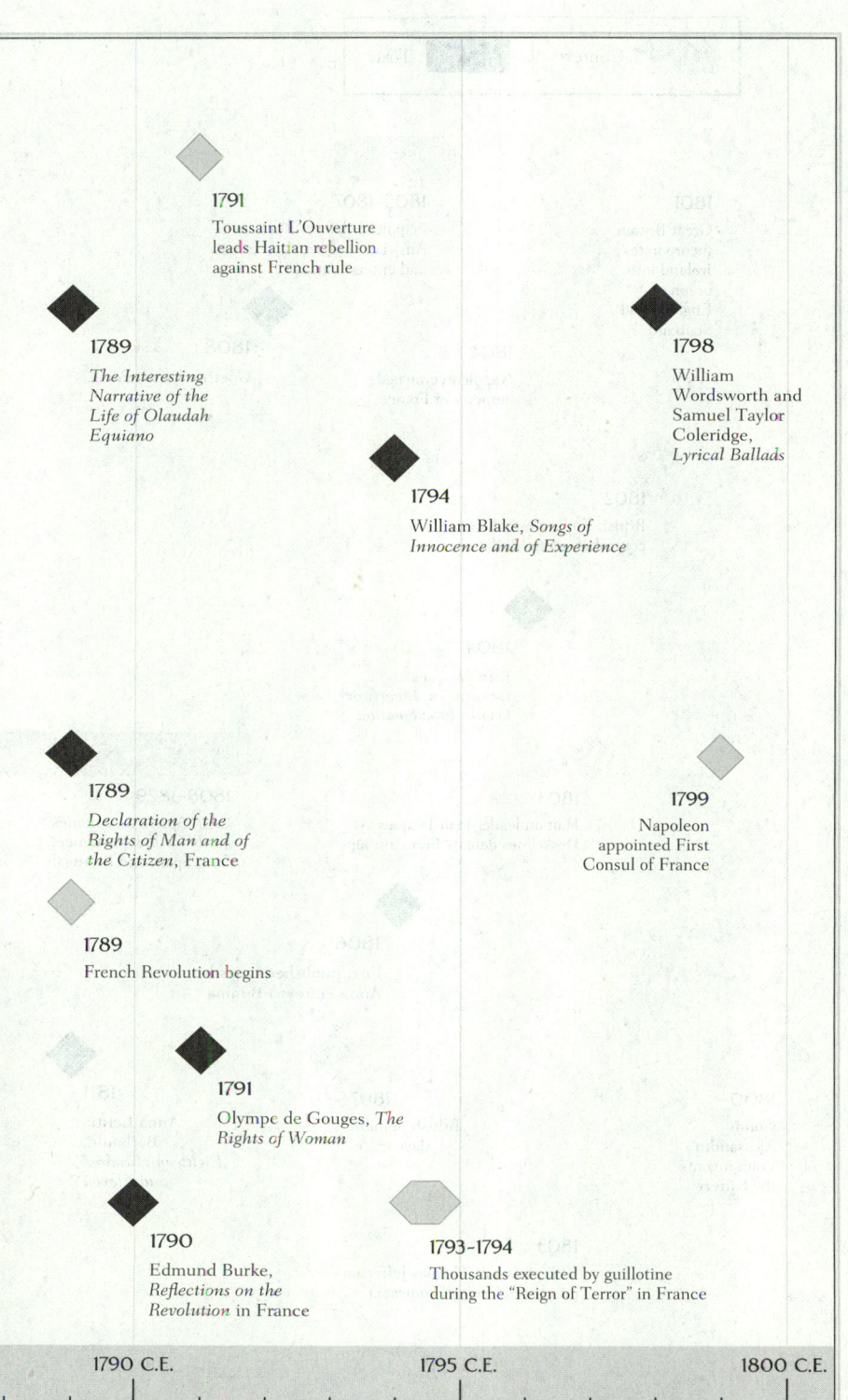

1791

Toussaint L'Ouverture leads Haitian rebellion against French rule

1789

The Interesting Narrative of the Life of Olaudah Equiano

1798

William Wordsworth and Samuel Taylor Coleridge, *Lyrical Ballads*

1794

William Blake, *Songs of Innocence and of Experience*

1789

Declaration of the Rights of Man and of the Citizen, France

1799

Napoleon appointed First Consul of France

1789

French Revolution begins

1791

Olympe de Gouges, *The Rights of Woman*

1790

Edmund Burke, *Reflections on the Revolution* in France

1793-1794

Thousands executed by guillotine during the "Reign of Terror" in France

1790 C.E.   1795 C.E.   1800 C.E.

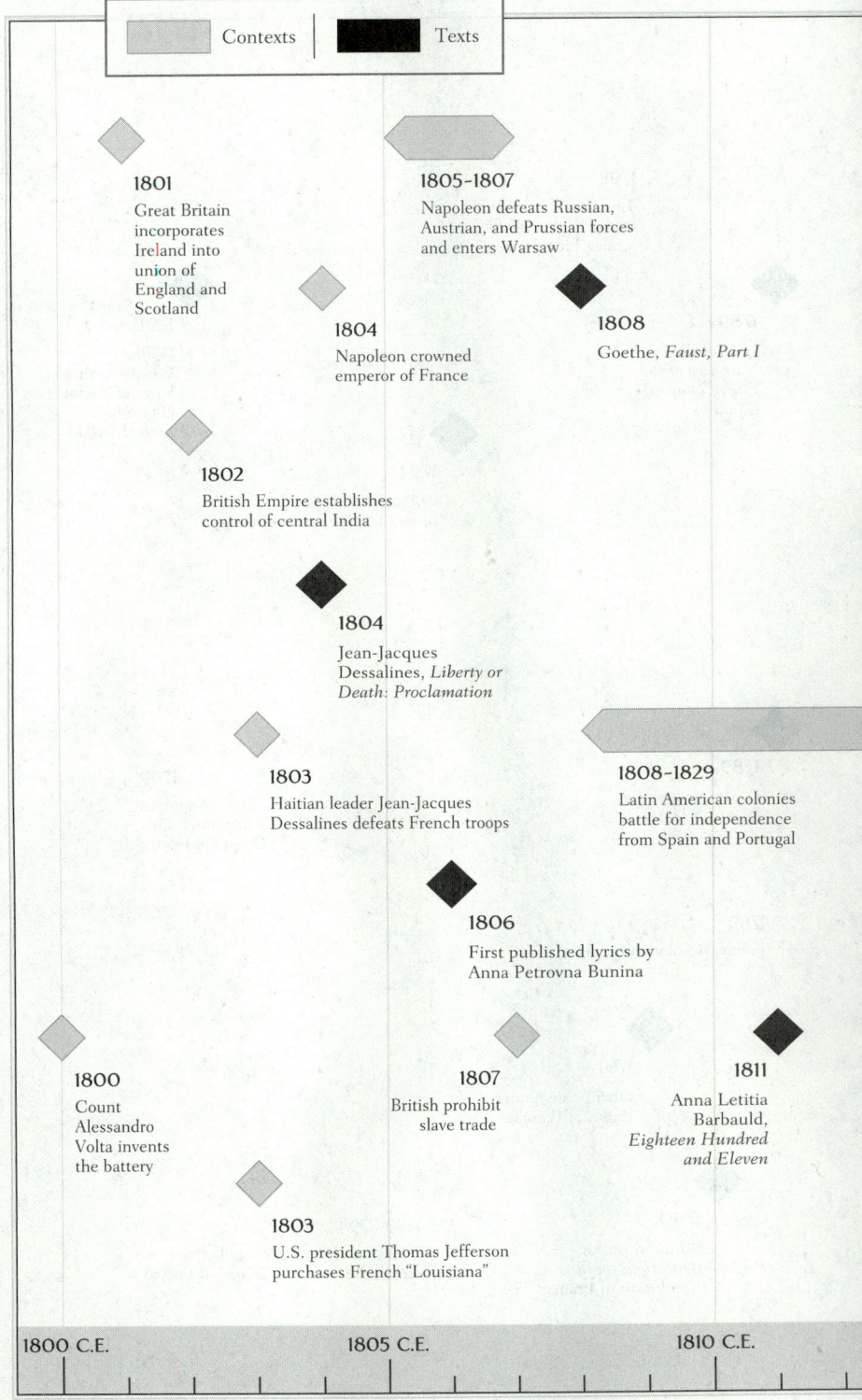

Contexts | Texts

1801
Great Britain incorporates Ireland into union of England and Scotland

1805–1807
Napoleon defeats Russian, Austrian, and Prussian forces and enters Warsaw

1804
Napoleon crowned emperor of France

1808
Goethe, *Faust, Part I*

1802
British Empire establishes control of central India

1804
Jean-Jacques Dessalines, *Liberty or Death: Proclamation*

1803
Haitian leader Jean-Jacques Dessalines defeats French troops

1808–1829
Latin American colonies battle for independence from Spain and Portugal

1806
First published lyrics by Anna Petrovna Bunina

1800
Count Alessandro Volta invents the battery

1807
British prohibit slave trade

1811
Anna Letitia Barbauld, *Eighteen Hundred and Eleven*

1803
U.S. president Thomas Jefferson purchases French "Louisiana"

1800 C.E.   1805 C.E.   1810 C.E.

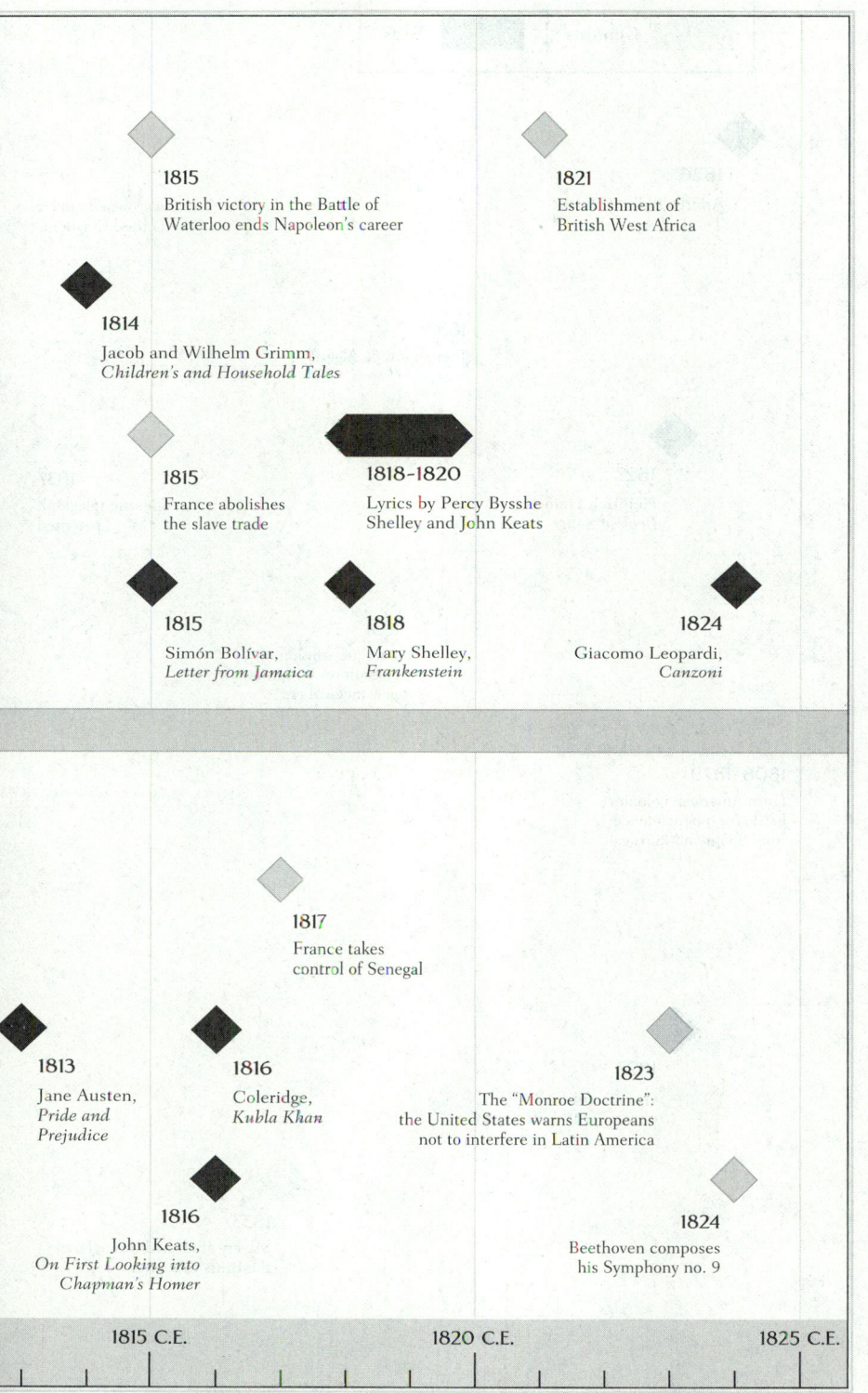

1815

British victory in the Battle of
Waterloo ends Napoleon's career

1821

Establishment of
British West Africa

1814

Jacob and Wilhelm Grimm,
Children's and Household Tales

1815

France abolishes
the slave trade

1818–1820

Lyrics by Percy Bysshe
Shelley and John Keats

1815

Simón Bolívar,
Letter from Jamaica

1818

Mary Shelley,
Frankenstein

1824

Giacomo Leopardi,
Canzoni

1817

France takes
control of Senegal

1813

Jane Austen,
*Pride and
Prejudice*

1816

Coleridge,
Kubla Khan

1823

The "Monroe Doctrine":
the United States warns Europeans
not to interfere in Latin America

1816

John Keats,
*On First Looking into
Chapman's Homer*

1824

Beethoven composes
his Symphony no. 9

1815 C.E.   **1820 C.E.**   **1825 C.E.**

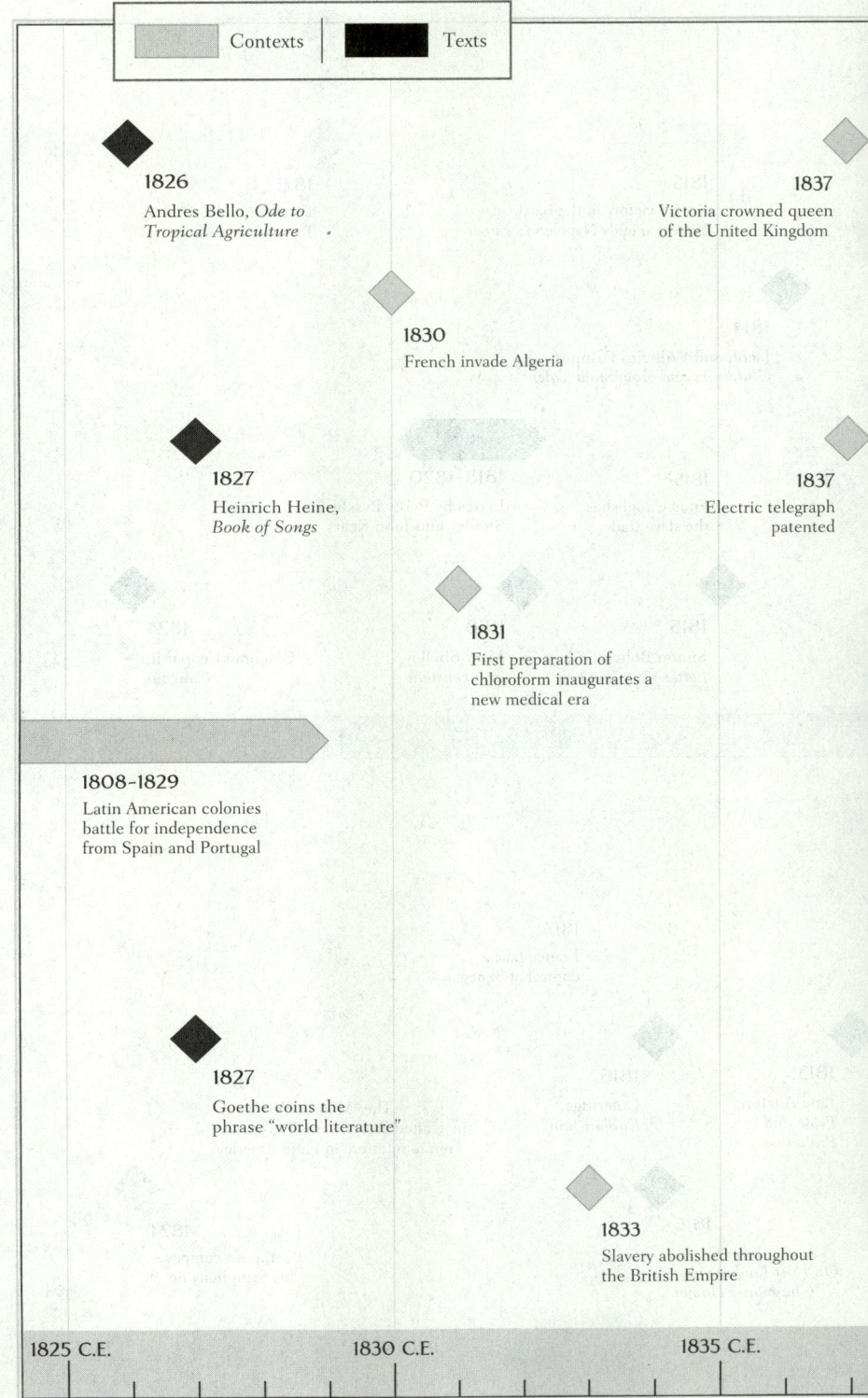

Contexts | Texts

1826
Andres Bello, *Ode to
Tropical Agriculture*

1837
Victoria crowned queen
of the United Kingdom

1830
French invade Algeria

1827
Heinrich Heine,
Book of Songs

1837
Electric telegraph
patented

1831
First preparation of
chloroform inaugurates a
new medical era

1808-1829
Latin American colonies
battle for independence
from Spain and Portugal

1827
Goethe coins the
phrase "world literature"

1833
Slavery abolished throughout
the British Empire

1825 C.E.   1830 C.E.   1835 C.E.

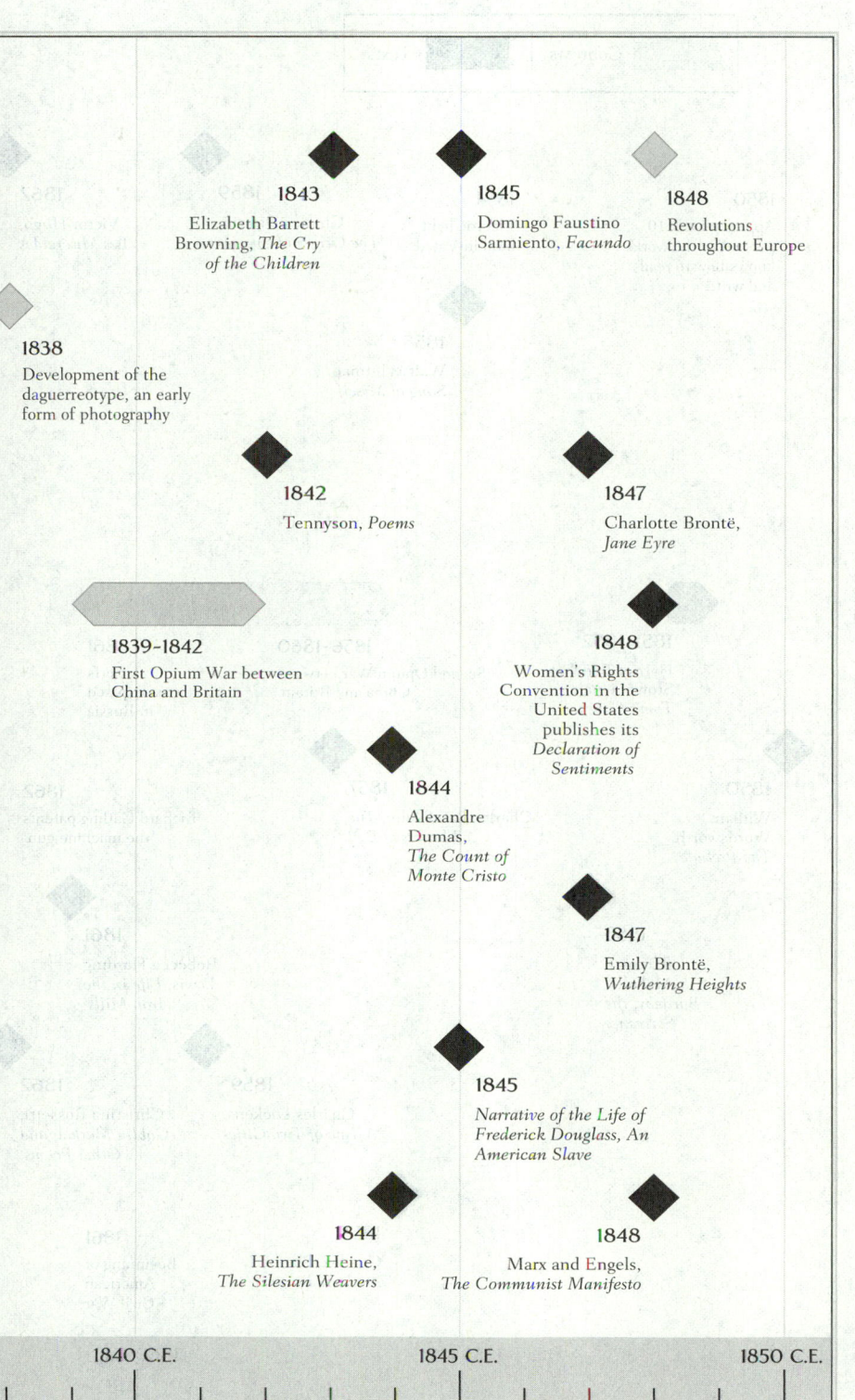

1843

Elizabeth Barrett
Browning, *The Cry
of the Children*

1845

Domingo Faustino
Sarmiento, *Facundo*

1848

Revolutions
throughout Europe

1838

Development of the
daguerreotype, an early
form of photography

1842

Tennyson, *Poems*

1847

Charlotte Brontë,
Jane Eyre

1839–1842

First Opium War between
China and Britain

1848

Women's Rights
Convention in the
United States
publishes its
*Declaration of
Sentiments*

1844

Alexandre
Dumas,
*The Count of
Monte Cristo*

1847

Emily Brontë,
Wuthering Heights

1845

*Narrative of the Life of
Frederick Douglass, An
American Slave*

1844

Heinrich Heine,
The Silesian Weavers

1848

Marx and Engels,
The Communist Manifesto

1840 C.E.   1845 C.E.   1850 C.E.

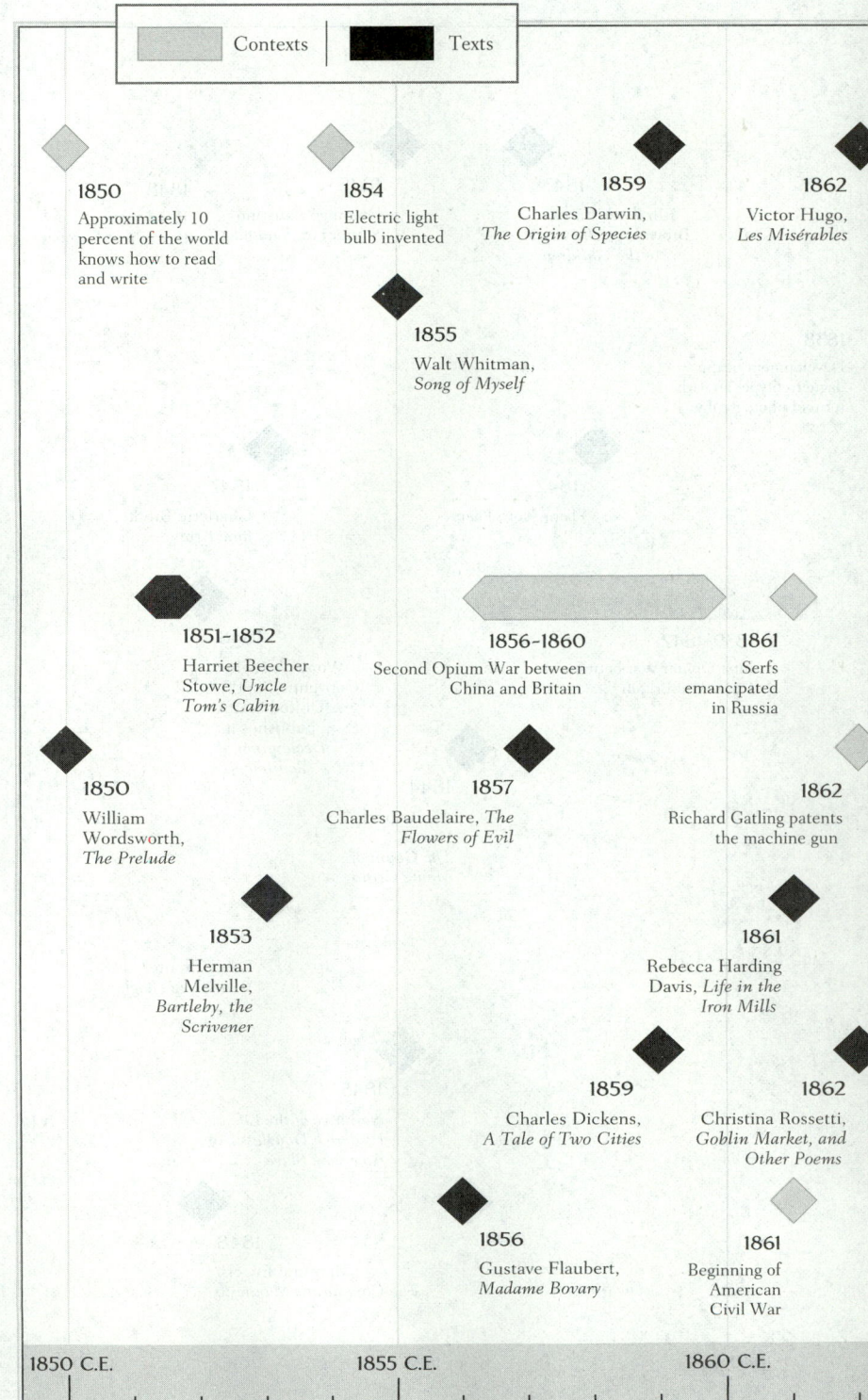

Contexts | Texts

1850

Approximately 10 percent of the world knows how to read and write

1854

Electric light bulb invented

1859

Charles Darwin, *The Origin of Species*

1862

Victor Hugo, *Les Misérables*

1855

Walt Whitman, *Song of Myself*

1851–1852

Harriet Beecher Stowe, *Uncle Tom's Cabin*

1856–1860

Second Opium War between China and Britain

1861

Serfs emancipated in Russia

1850

William Wordsworth, *The Prelude*

1857

Charles Baudelaire, *The Flowers of Evil*

1862

Richard Gatling patents the machine gun

1853

Herman Melville, *Bartleby, the Scrivener*

1861

Rebecca Harding Davis, *Life in the Iron Mills*

1859

Charles Dickens, *A Tale of Two Cities*

1862

Christina Rossetti, *Goblin Market, and Other Poems*

1856

Gustave Flaubert, *Madame Bovary*

1861

Beginning of American Civil War

1850 C.E.   1855 C.E.   1860 C.E.

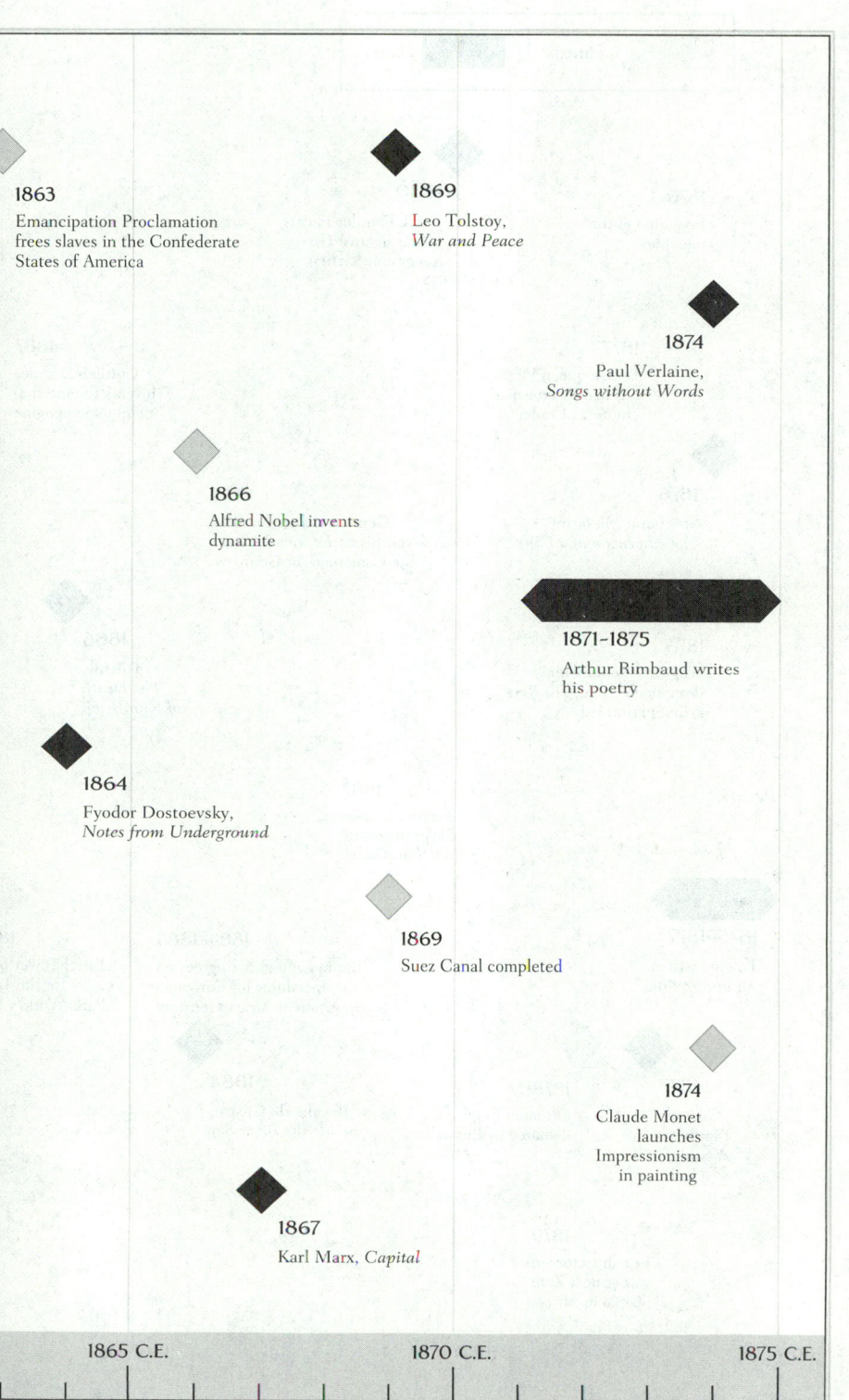

1863
Emancipation Proclamation
frees slaves in the Confederate
States of America

1869
Leo Tolstoy,
War and Peace

1874
Paul Verlaine,
Songs without Words

1866
Alfred Nobel invents
dynamite

1871–1875
Arthur Rimbaud writes
his poetry

1864
Fyodor Dostoevsky,
Notes from Underground

1869
Suez Canal completed

1874
Claude Monet
launches
Impressionism
in painting

1867
Karl Marx, *Capital*

1865 C.E.　　　　　1870 C.E.　　　　　1875 C.E.

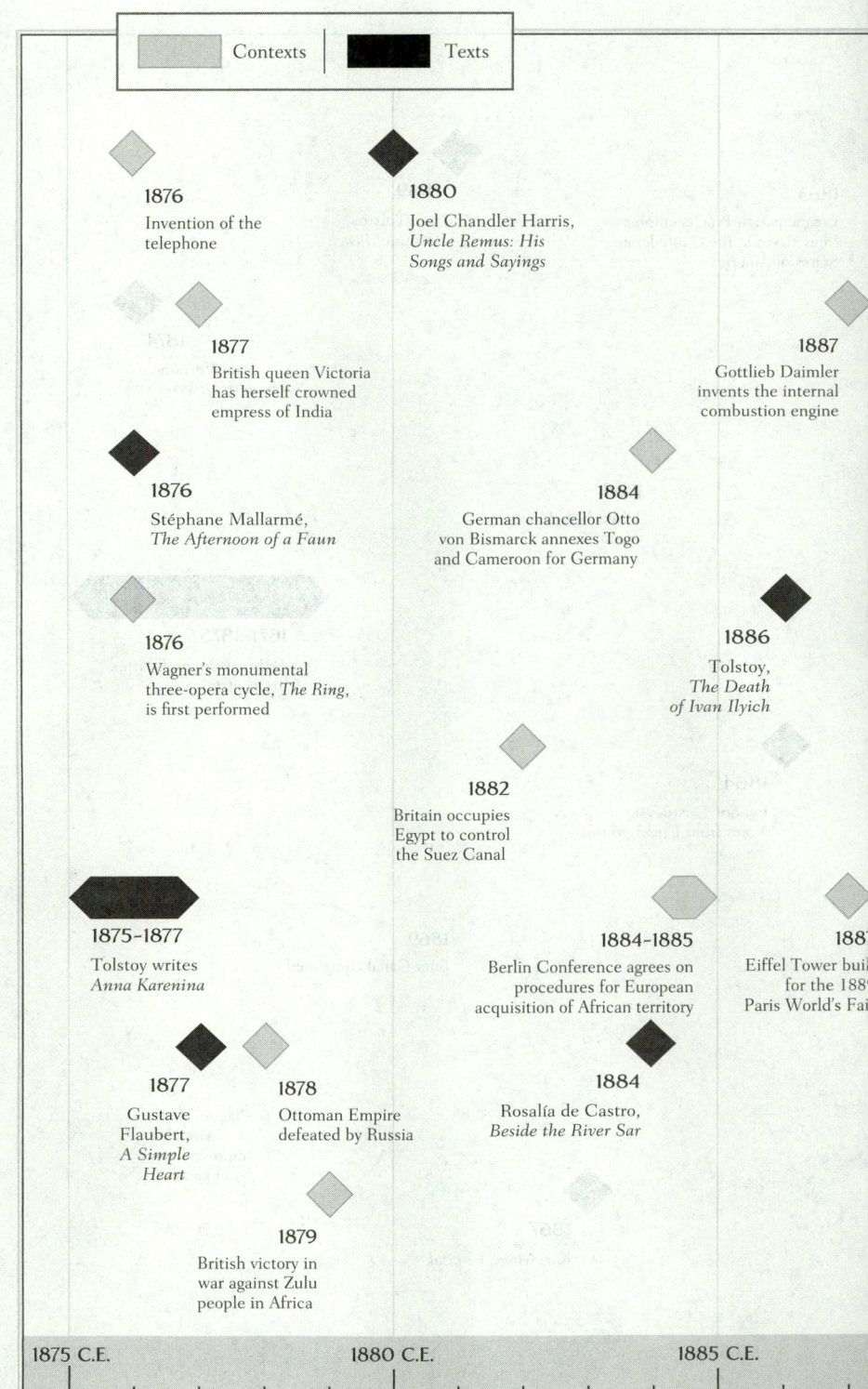

Contexts | Texts

1876
Invention of the
telephone

1880
Joel Chandler Harris,
*Uncle Remus: His
Songs and Sayings*

1877
British queen Victoria
has herself crowned
empress of India

1887
Gottlieb Daimler
invents the internal
combustion engine

1876
Stéphane Mallarmé,
The Afternoon of a Faun

1884
German chancellor Otto
von Bismarck annexes Togo
and Cameroon for Germany

1876
Wagner's monumental
three-opera cycle, *The Ring*,
is first performed

1886
Tolstoy,
*The Death
of Ivan Ilyich*

1882
Britain occupies
Egypt to control
the Suez Canal

1875–1877
Tolstoy writes
Anna Karenina

1884–1885
Berlin Conference agrees on
procedures for European
acquisition of African territory

188?
Eiffel Tower buil
for the 188?
Paris World's Fai

1877
Gustave
Flaubert,
*A Simple
Heart*

1878
Ottoman Empire
defeated by Russia

1884
Rosalía de Castro,
Beside the River Sar

1879
British victory in
war against Zulu
people in Africa

1875 C.E.   1880 C.E.   1885 C.E.

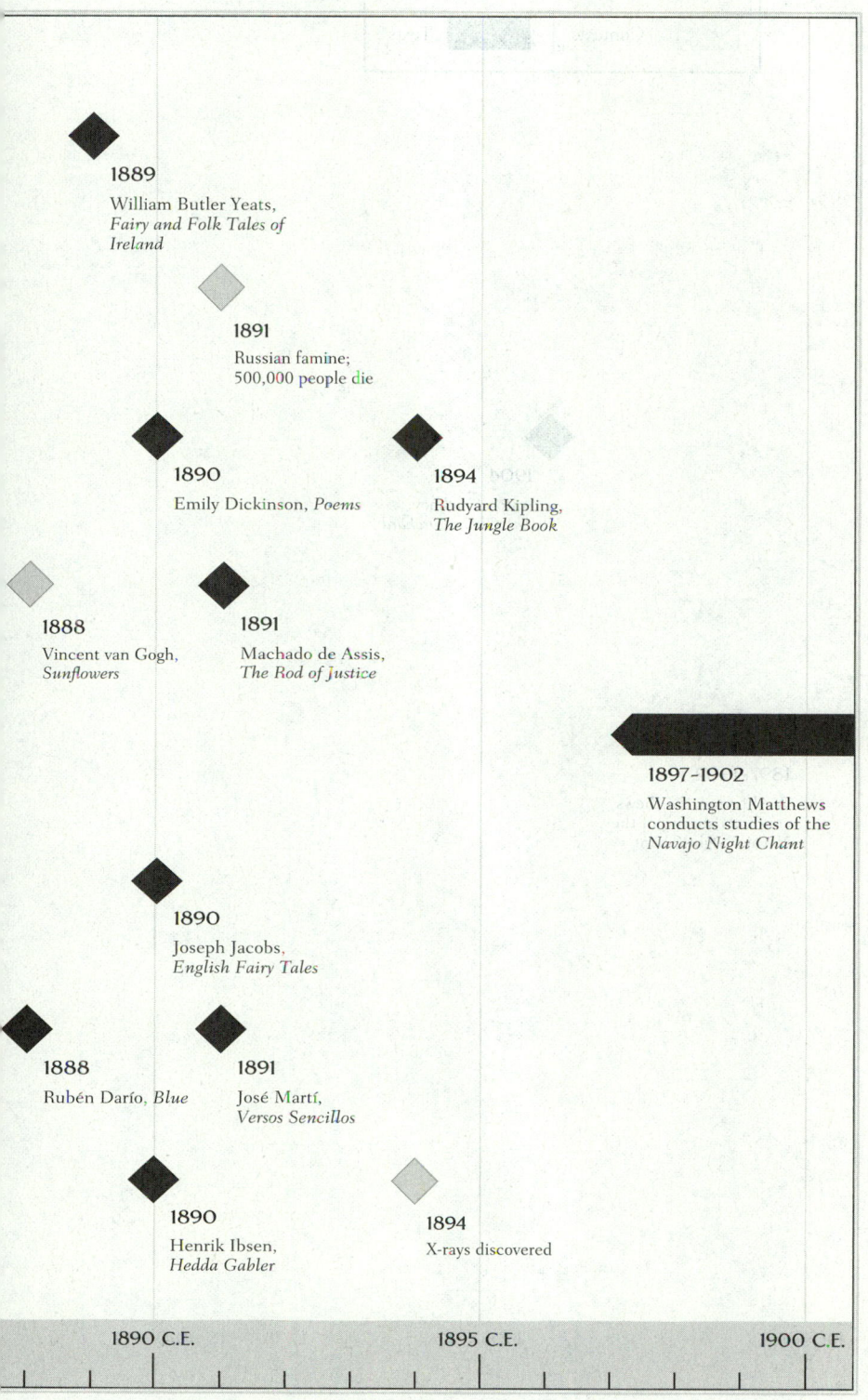

1889
William Butler Yeats,
*Fairy and Folk Tales of
Ireland*

1891
Russian famine;
500,000 people die

1890
Emily Dickinson, *Poems*

1894
Rudyard Kipling,
The Jungle Book

1888
Vincent van Gogh,
Sunflowers

1891
Machado de Assis,
The Rod of Justice

1897–1902
Washington Matthews
conducts studies of the
Navajo Night Chant

1890
Joseph Jacobs,
English Fairy Tales

1888
Rubén Darío, *Blue*

1891
José Martí,
Versos Sencillos

1890
Henrik Ibsen,
Hedda Gabler

1894
X-rays discovered

1890 C.E.   1895 C.E.   1900 C.E.

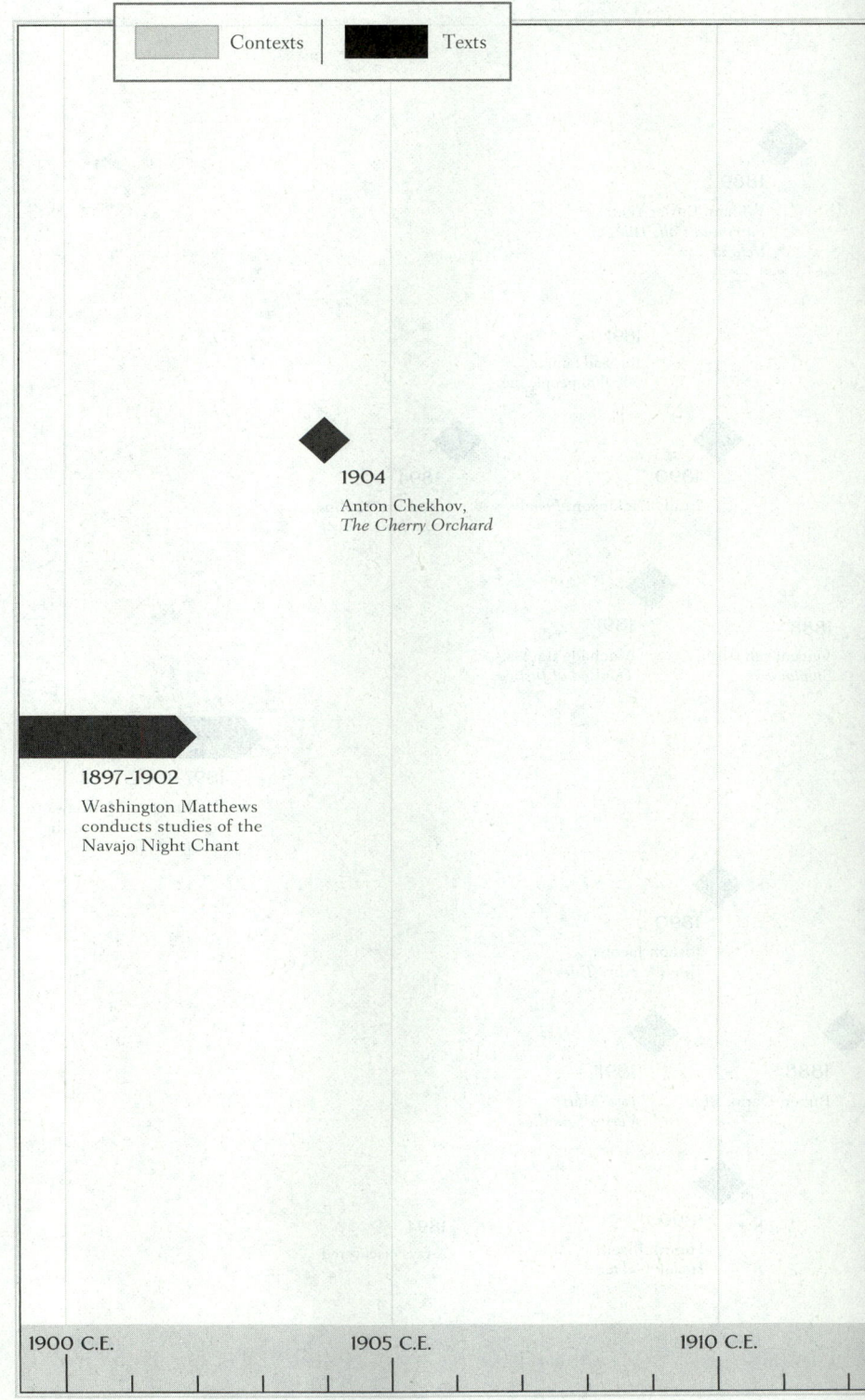

Contexts   Texts

1904
Anton Chekhov,
The Cherry Orchard

1897–1902
Washington Matthews
conducts studies of the
Navajo Night Chant

1900 C.E.   1905 C.E.   1910 C.E.

1915 C.E.   1920 C.E.   1925 C.E.

TIMELINE *for*

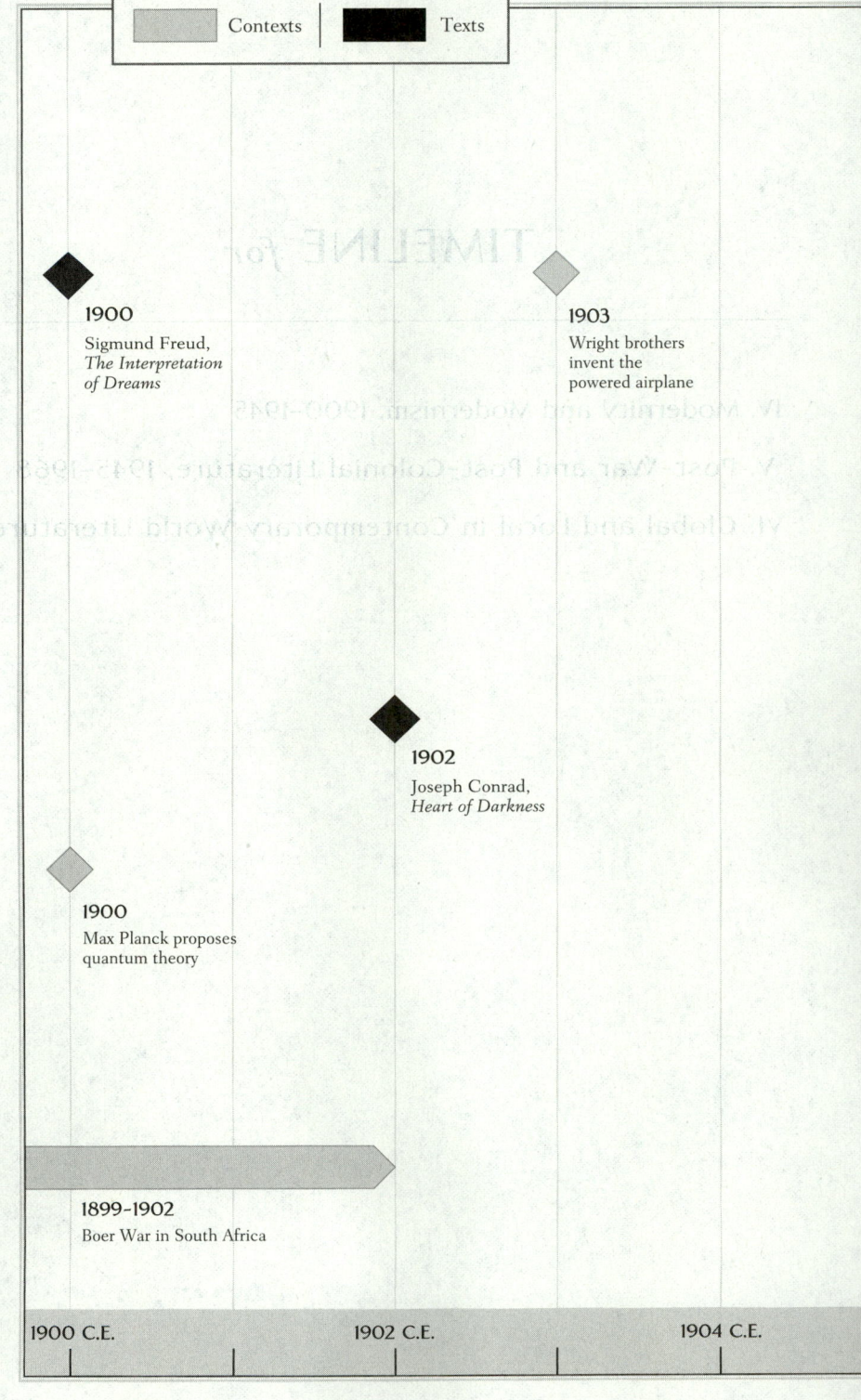

Contexts | Texts

1900
Sigmund Freud,
*The Interpretation
of Dreams*

1903
Wright brothers
invent the
powered airplane

1902
Joseph Conrad,
Heart of Darkness

1900
Max Planck proposes
quantum theory

1899–1902
Boer War in South Africa

1900 C.E.   1902 C.E.   1904 C.E.

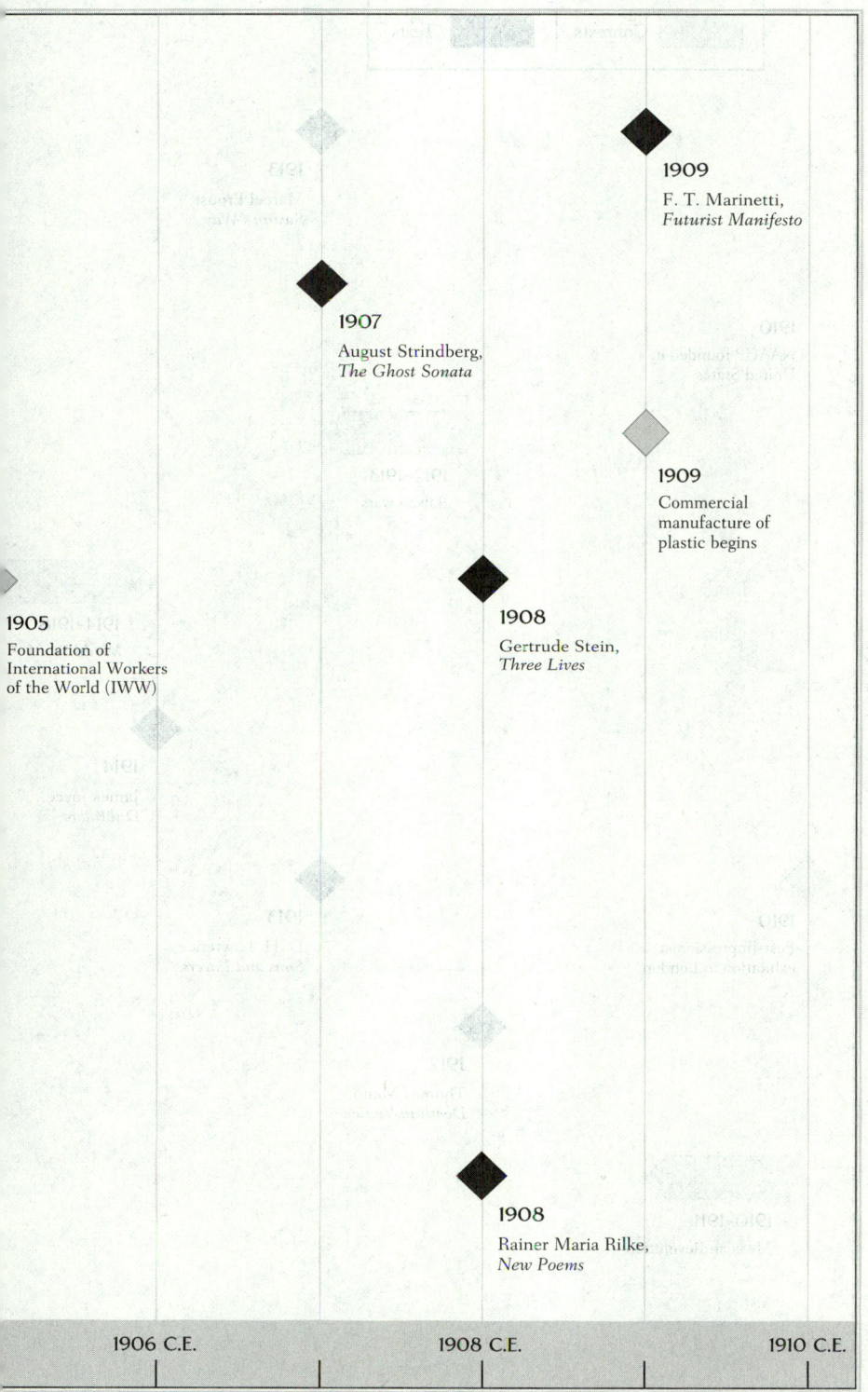

1909
F. T. Marinetti,
Futurist Manifesto

1907
August Strindberg,
The Ghost Sonata

1909
Commercial
manufacture of
plastic begins

1905
Foundation of
International Workers
of the World (IWW)

1908
Gertrude Stein,
Three Lives

1908
Rainer Maria Rilke,
New Poems

1906 C.E.   1908 C.E.   1910 C.E.

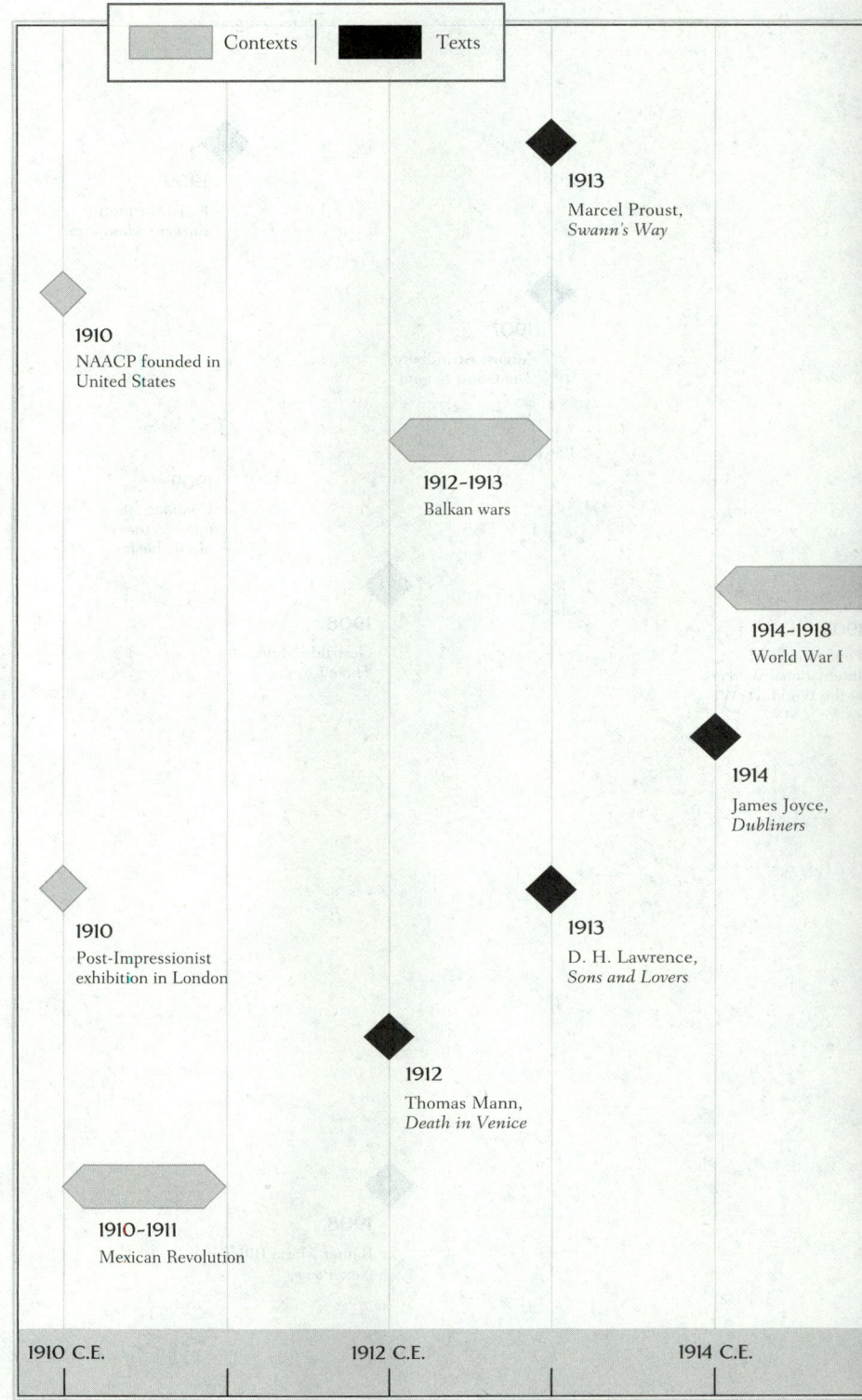

Contexts | Texts

1913
Marcel Proust,
Swann's Way

1910
NAACP founded in
United States

1912–1913
Balkan wars

1914–1918
World War I

1914
James Joyce,
Dubliners

1910
Post-Impressionist
exhibition in London

1913
D. H. Lawrence,
Sons and Lovers

1912
Thomas Mann,
Death in Venice

1910–1911
Mexican Revolution

1910 C.E.   1912 C.E.   1914 C.E.

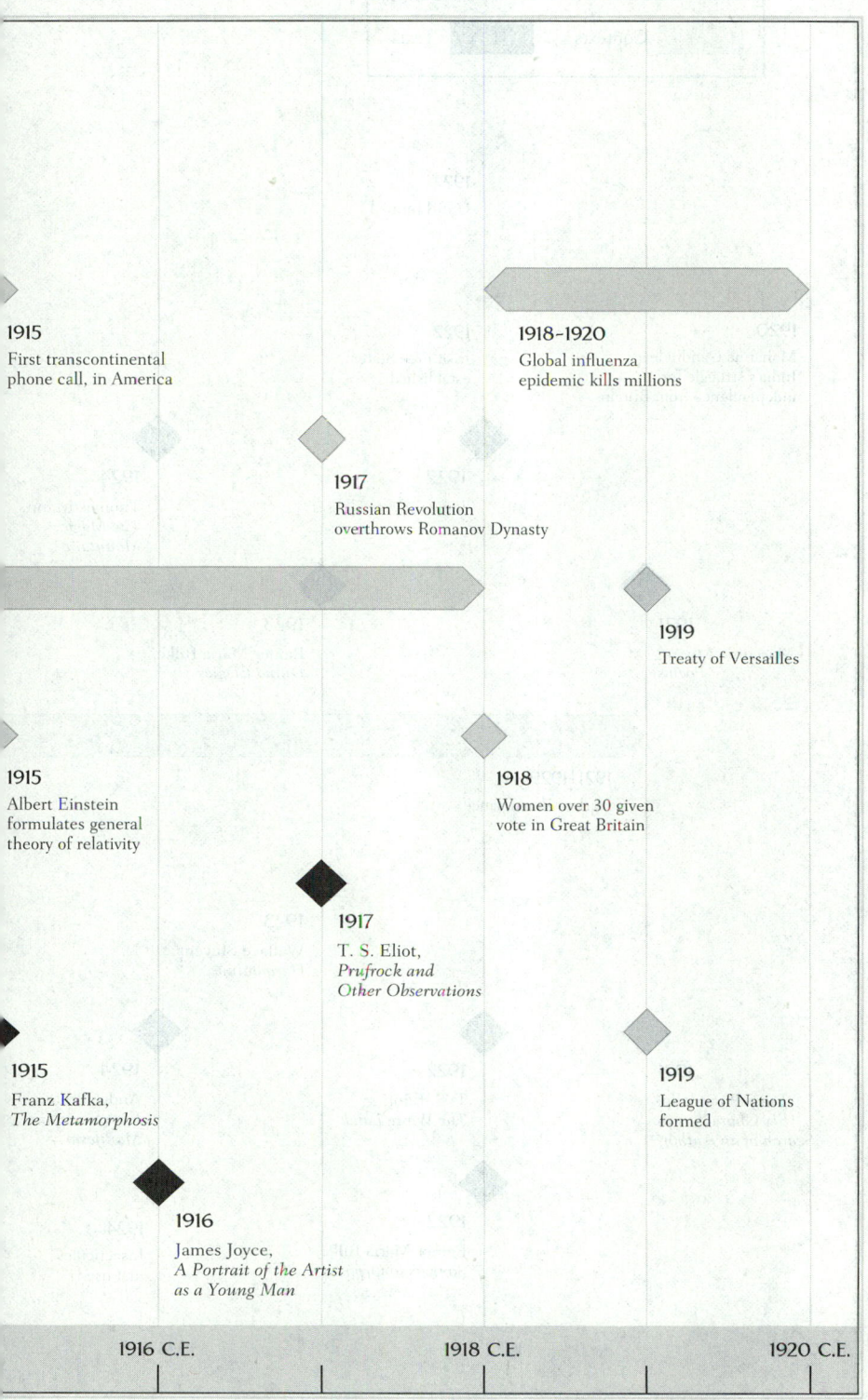

1915
First transcontinental
phone call, in America

1918–1920
Global influenza
epidemic kills millions

1917
Russian Revolution
overthrows Romanov Dynasty

1919
Treaty of Versailles

1915
Albert Einstein
formulates general
theory of relativity

1918
Women over 30 given
vote in Great Britain

1917
T. S. Eliot,
*Prufrock and
Other Observations*

1915
Franz Kafka,
The Metamorphosis

1919
League of Nations
formed

1916
James Joyce,
*A Portrait of the Artist
as a Young Man*

1916 C.E.   1918 C.E.   1920 C.E.

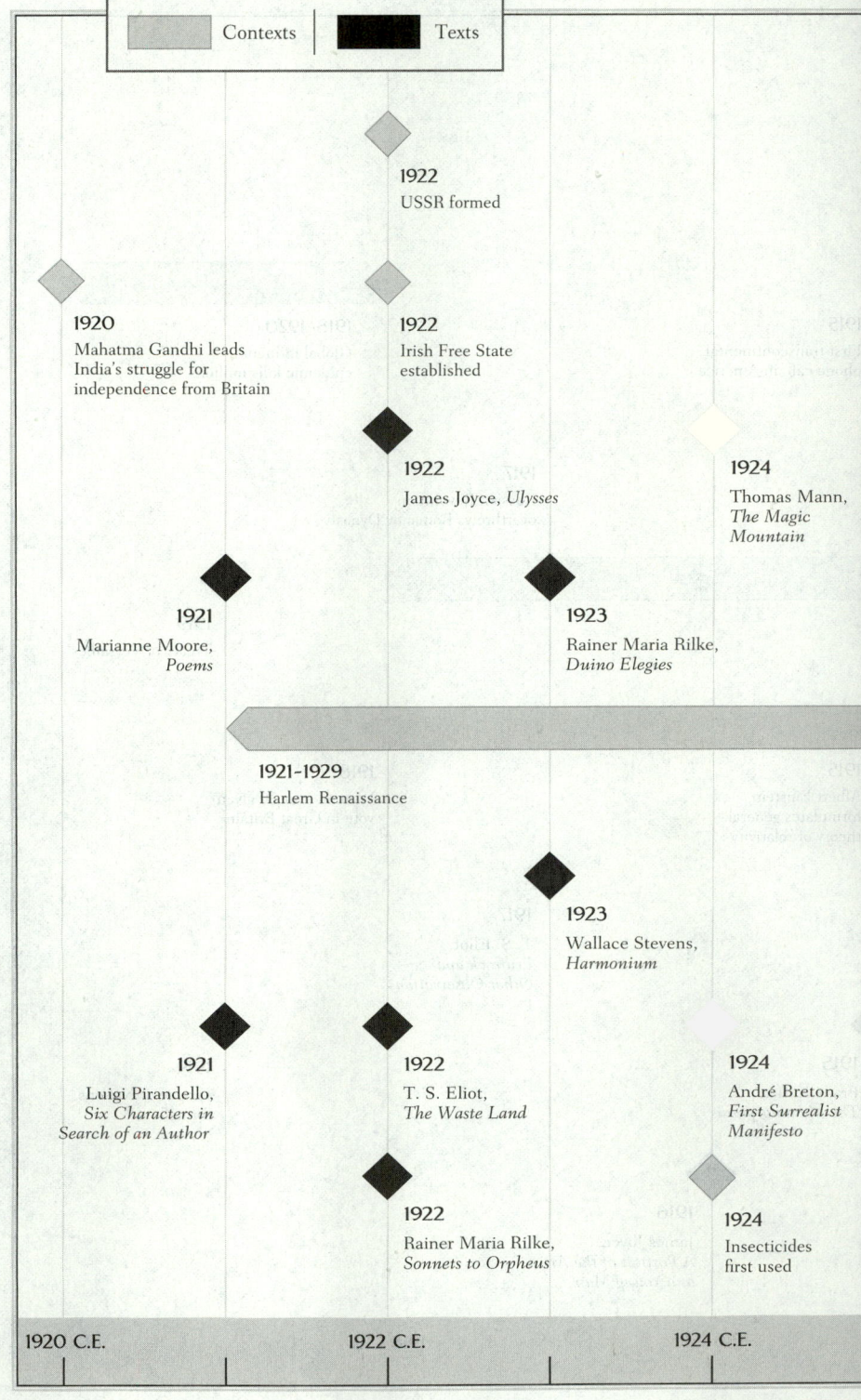

Contexts   Texts

1922
USSR formed

1920
Mahatma Gandhi leads
India's struggle for
independence from Britain

1922
Irish Free State
established

1922
James Joyce, *Ulysses*

1924
Thomas Mann,
*The Magic
Mountain*

1921
Marianne Moore,
Poems

1923
Rainer Maria Rilke,
Duino Elegies

1921–1929
Harlem Renaissance

1923
Wallace Stevens,
Harmonium

1921
Luigi Pirandello,
*Six Characters in
Search of an Author*

1922
T. S. Eliot,
The Waste Land

1924
André Breton,
*First Surrealist
Manifesto*

1922
Rainer Maria Rilke,
Sonnets to Orpheus

1924
Insecticides
first used

1920 C.E.   1922 C.E.   1924 C.E.

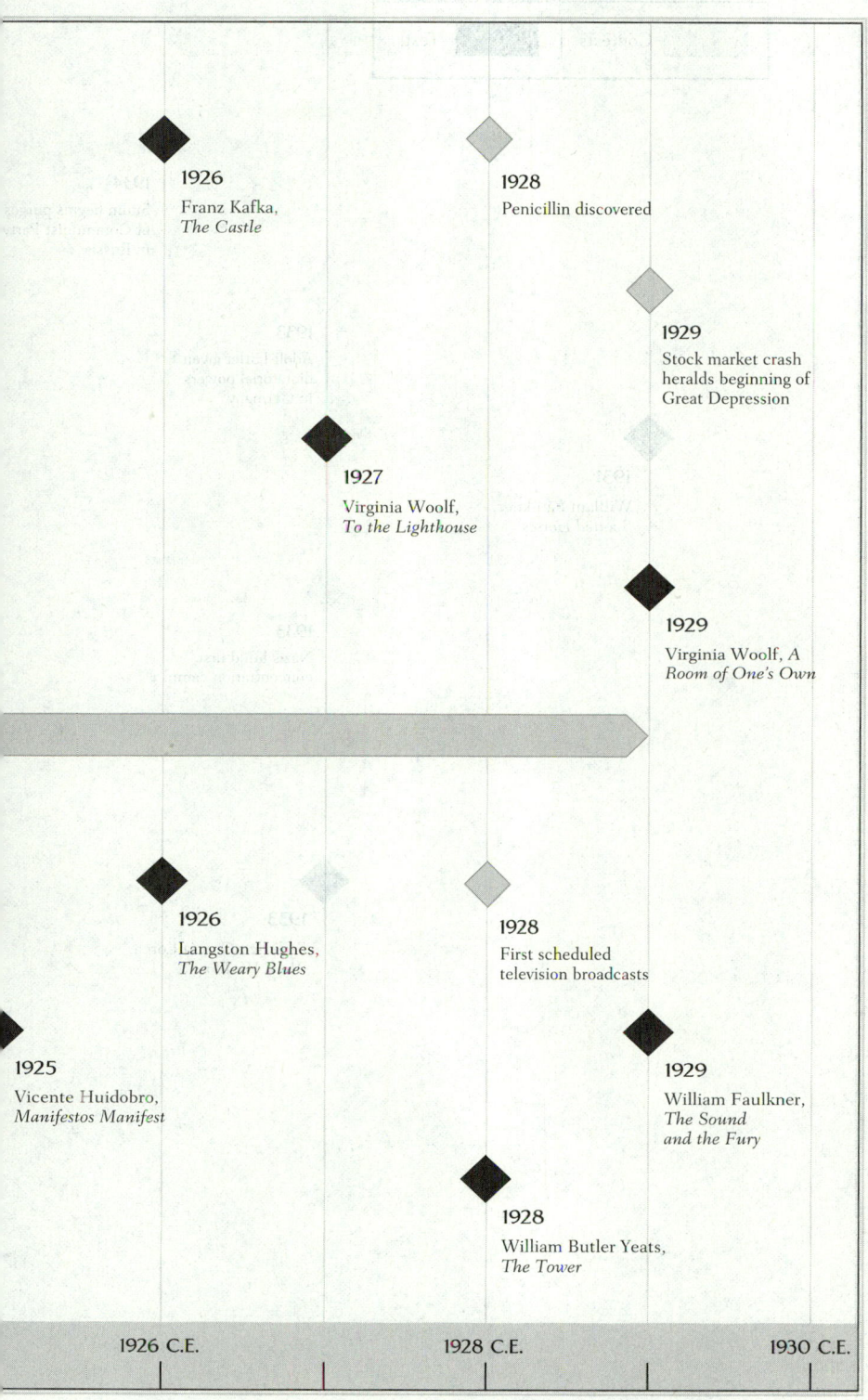

1926
Franz Kafka,
The Castle

1928
Penicillin discovered

1929
Stock market crash
heralds beginning of
Great Depression

1927
Virginia Woolf,
To the Lighthouse

1929
Virginia Woolf, *A
Room of One's Own*

1926
Langston Hughes,
The Weary Blues

1928
First scheduled
television broadcasts

1925
Vicente Huidobro,
Manifestos Manifest

1929
William Faulkner,
*The Sound
and the Fury*

1928
William Butler Yeats,
The Tower

1926 C.E.   1928 C.E.   1930 C.E.

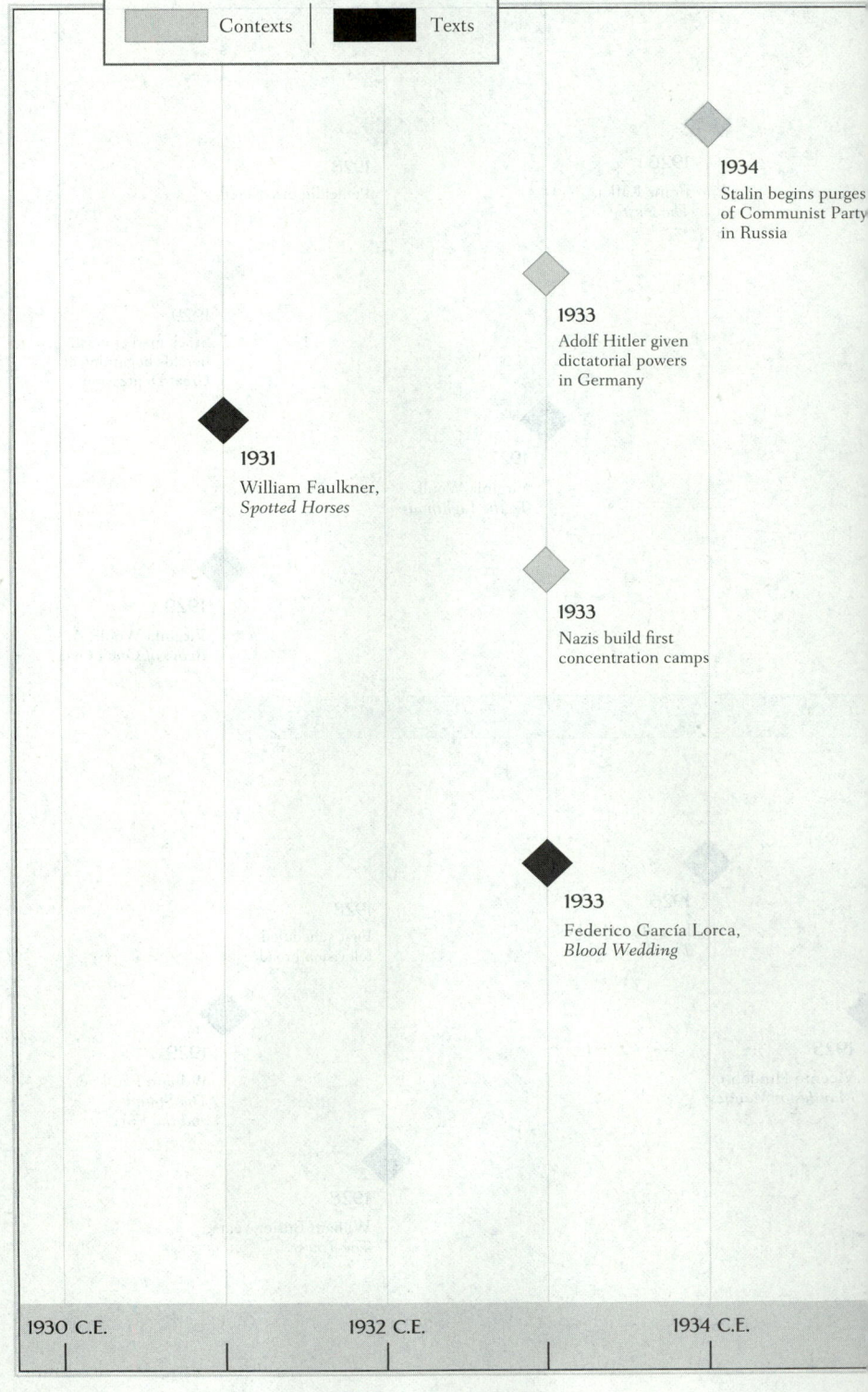

Contexts | Texts

1934
Stalin begins purges
of Communist Party
in Russia

1933
Adolf Hitler given
dictatorial powers
in Germany

1931
William Faulkner,
Spotted Horses

1933
Nazis build first
concentration camps

1933
Federico García Lorca,
Blood Wedding

1930 C.E.   1932 C.E.   1934 C.E.

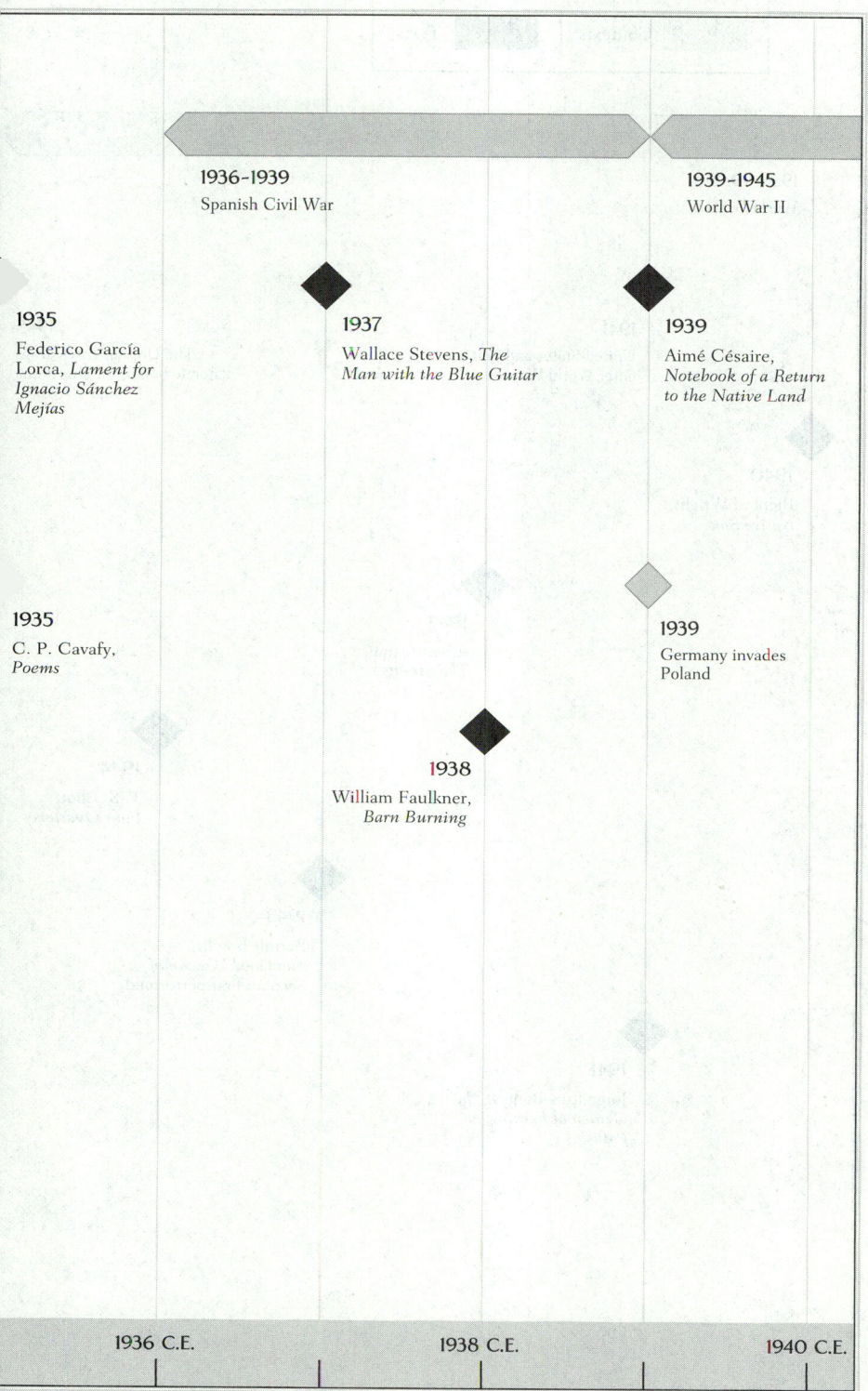

1936–1939
Spanish Civil War

1939–1945
World War II

1935
Federico García
Lorca, *Lament for
Ignacio Sánchez
Mejías*

1937
Wallace Stevens, *The
Man with the Blue Guitar*

1939
Aimé Césaire,
*Notebook of a Return
to the Native Land*

1935
C. P. Cavafy,
Poems

1939
Germany invades
Poland

1938
William Faulkner,
Barn Burning

1936 C.E.

1938 C.E.

1940 C.E.

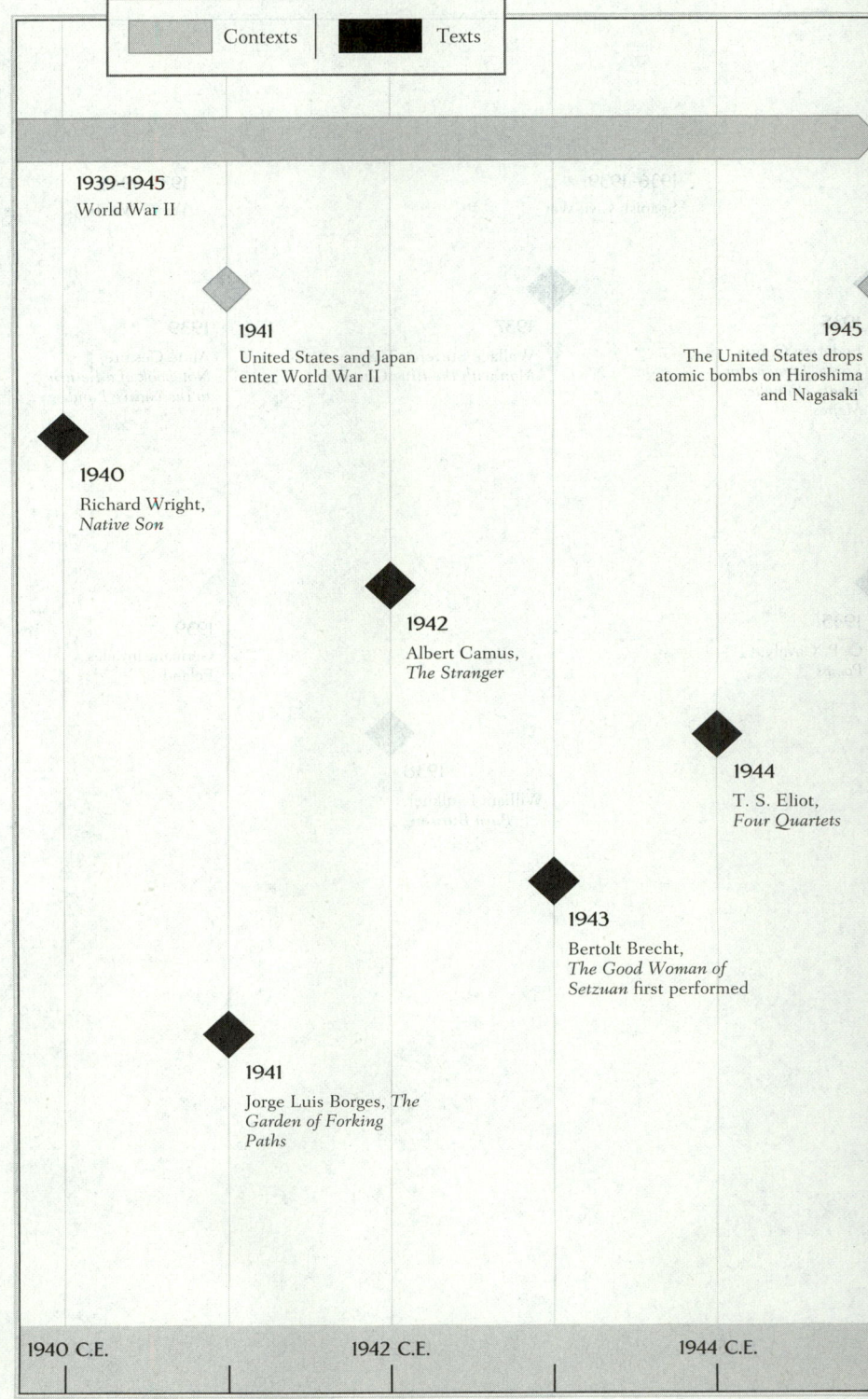

Contexts | Texts

1939–1945
World War II

1941
United States and Japan
enter World War II

1945
The United States drops
atomic bombs on Hiroshima
and Nagasaki

1940
Richard Wright,
Native Son

1942
Albert Camus,
The Stranger

1944
T. S. Eliot,
Four Quartets

1943
Bertolt Brecht,
*The Good Woman of
Setzuan* first performed

1941
Jorge Luis Borges, *The
Garden of Forking
Paths*

1940 C.E.   1942 C.E.   1944 C.E.

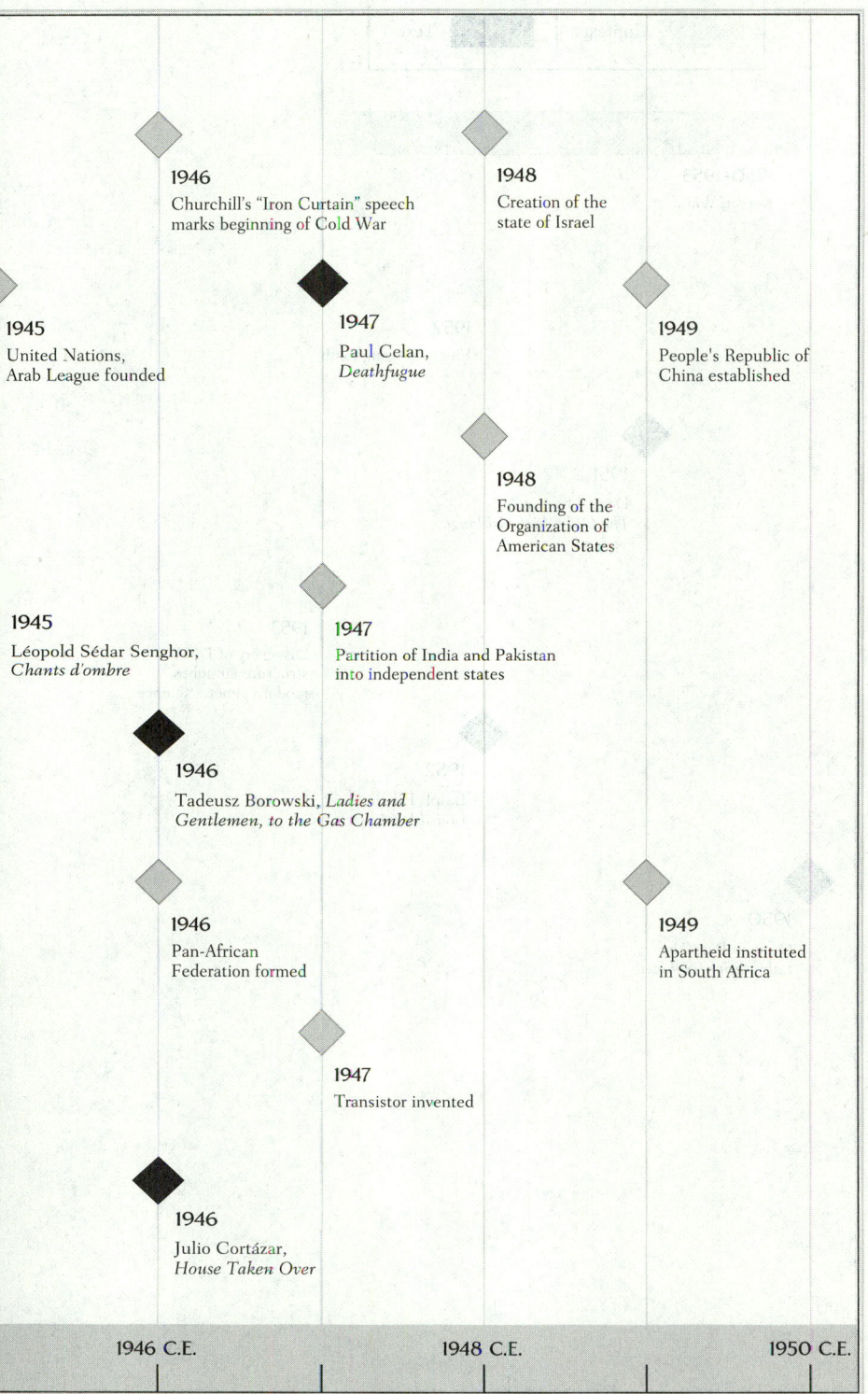

1946
Churchill's "Iron Curtain" speech
marks beginning of Cold War

1948
Creation of the
state of Israel

1945
United Nations,
Arab League founded

1947
Paul Celan,
Deathfugue

1949
People's Republic of
China established

1948
Founding of the
Organization of
American States

1945
Léopold Sédar Senghor,
Chants d'ombre

1947
Partition of India and Pakistan
into independent states

1946
Tadeusz Borowski, *Ladies and
Gentlemen, to the Gas Chamber*

1946
Pan-African
Federation formed

1949
Apartheid instituted
in South Africa

1947
Transistor invented

1946
Julio Cortázar,
House Taken Over

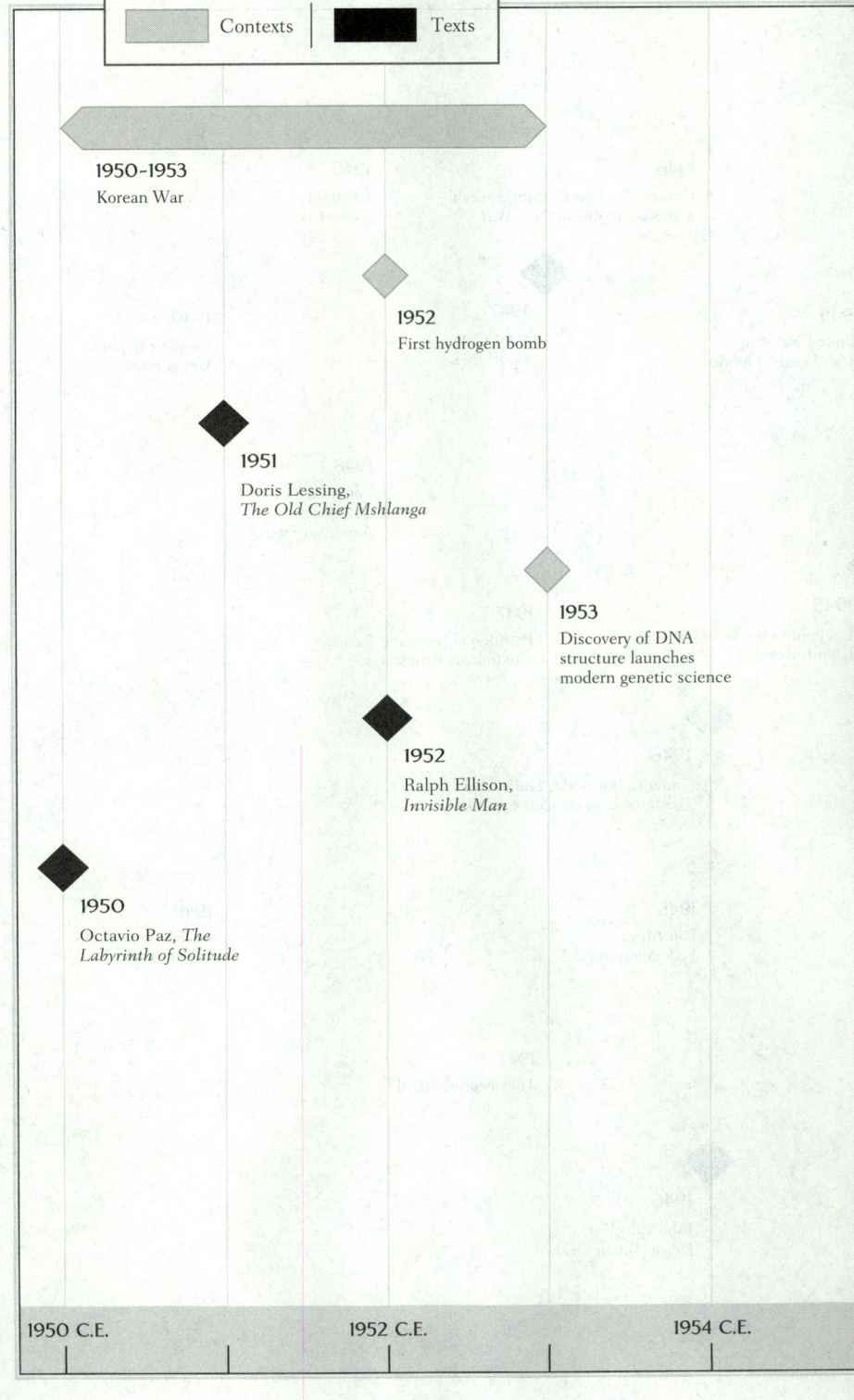

Contexts | Texts

1950-1953
Korean War

1952
First hydrogen bomb

1951
Doris Lessing,
The Old Chief Mshlanga

1953
Discovery of DNA
structure launches
modern genetic science

1952
Ralph Ellison,
Invisible Man

1950
Octavio Paz, *The
Labyrinth of Solitude*

1950 C.E.   1952 C.E.   1954 C.E.

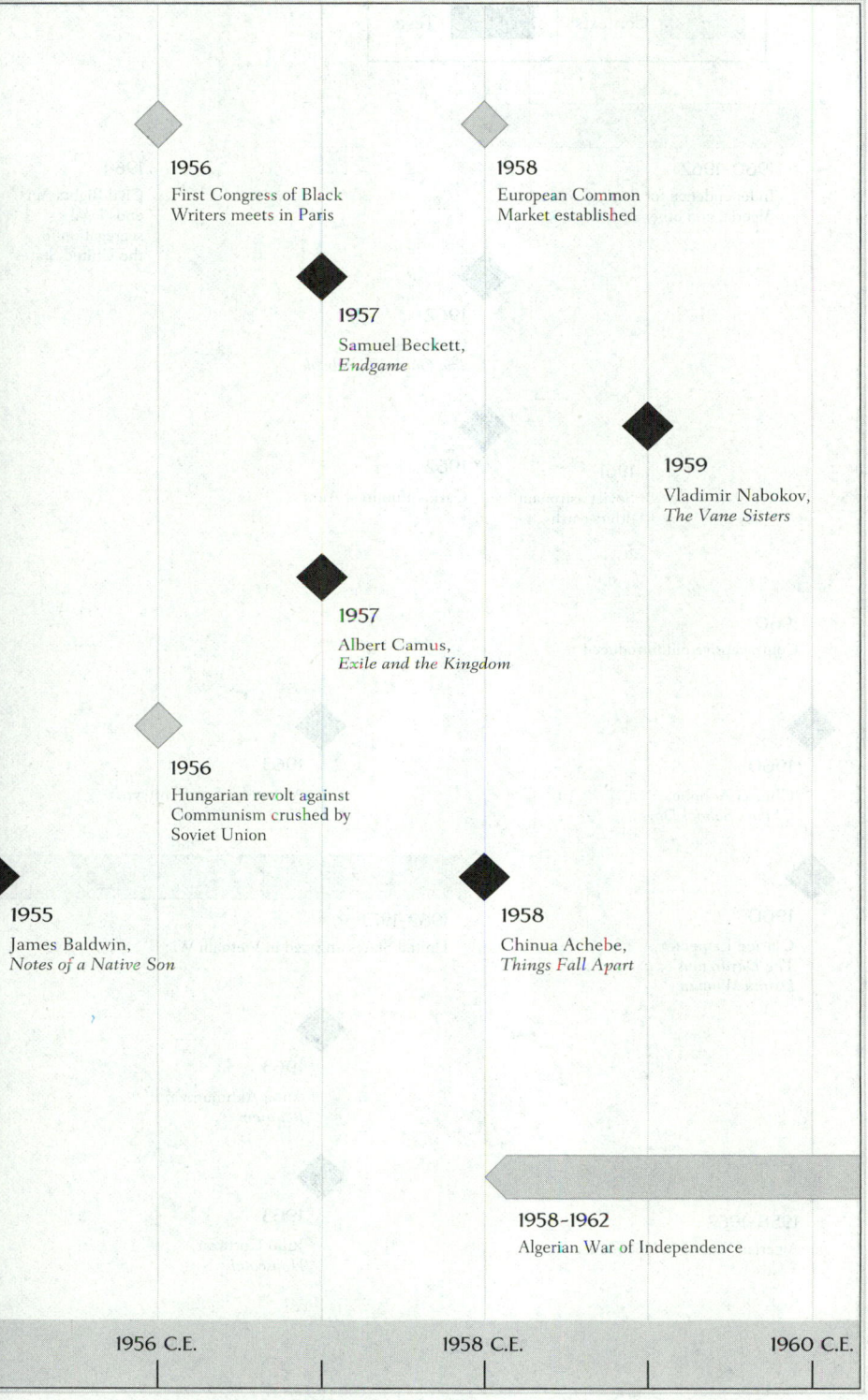

1956
First Congress of Black
Writers meets in Paris

1958
European Common
Market established

1957
Samuel Beckett,
Endgame

1959
Vladimir Nabokov,
The Vane Sisters

1957
Albert Camus,
Exile and the Kingdom

1956
Hungarian revolt against
Communism crushed by
Soviet Union

1955
James Baldwin,
Notes of a Native Son

1958
Chinua Achebe,
Things Fall Apart

1958–1962
Algerian War of Independence

1956 C.E.   1958 C.E.   1960 C.E.

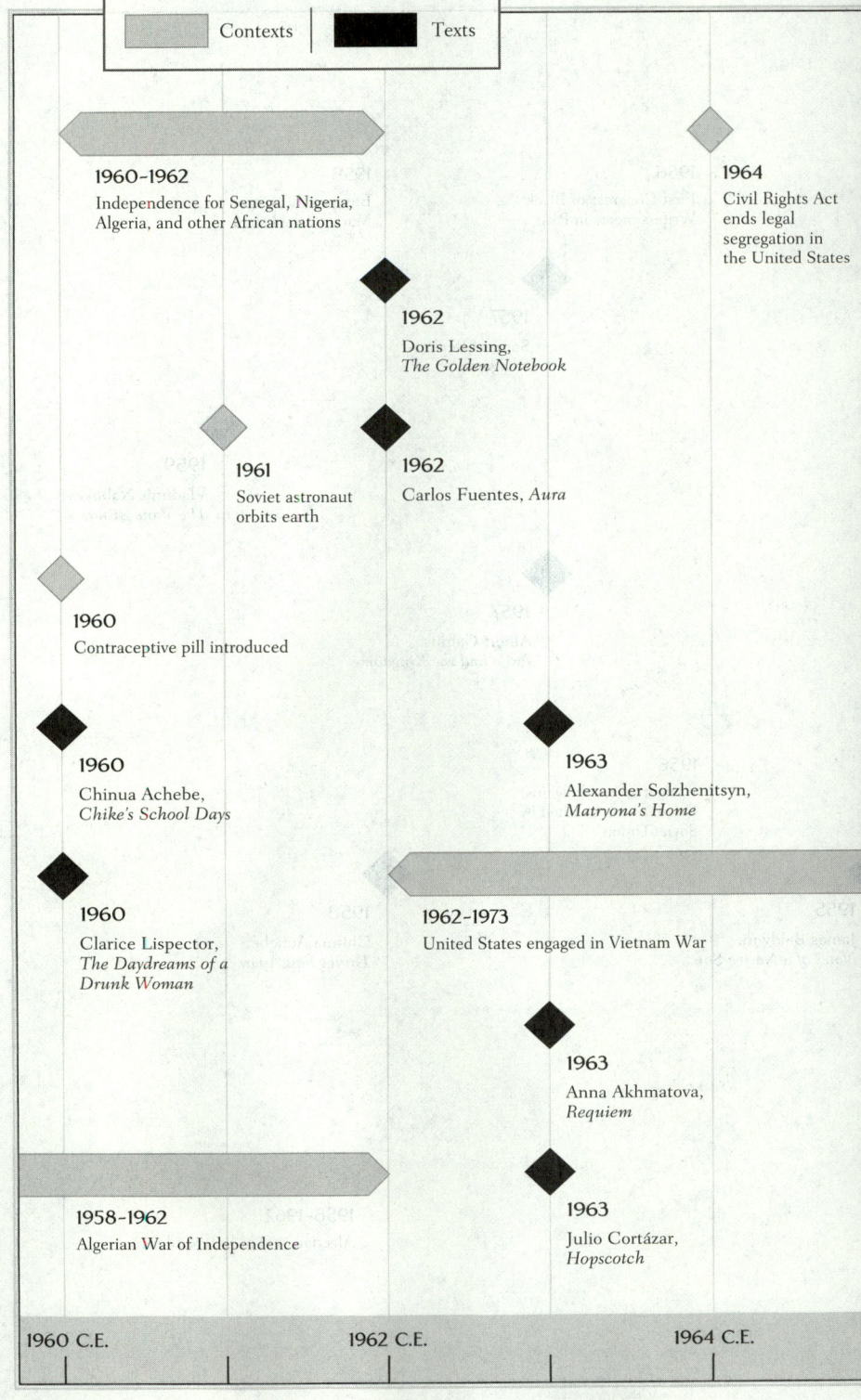

Contexts | Texts

1960–1962
Independence for Senegal, Nigeria, Algeria, and other African nations

1964
Civil Rights Act ends legal segregation in the United States

1962
Doris Lessing, *The Golden Notebook*

1961
Soviet astronaut orbits earth

1962
Carlos Fuentes, *Aura*

1960
Contraceptive pill introduced

1960
Chinua Achebe, *Chike's School Days*

1963
Alexander Solzhenitsyn, *Matryona's Home*

1960
Clarice Lispector, *The Daydreams of a Drunk Woman*

1962–1973
United States engaged in Vietnam War

1963
Anna Akhmatova, *Requiem*

1958–1962
Algerian War of Independence

1963
Julio Cortázar, *Hopscotch*

1960 C.E.   1962 C.E.   1964 C.E.

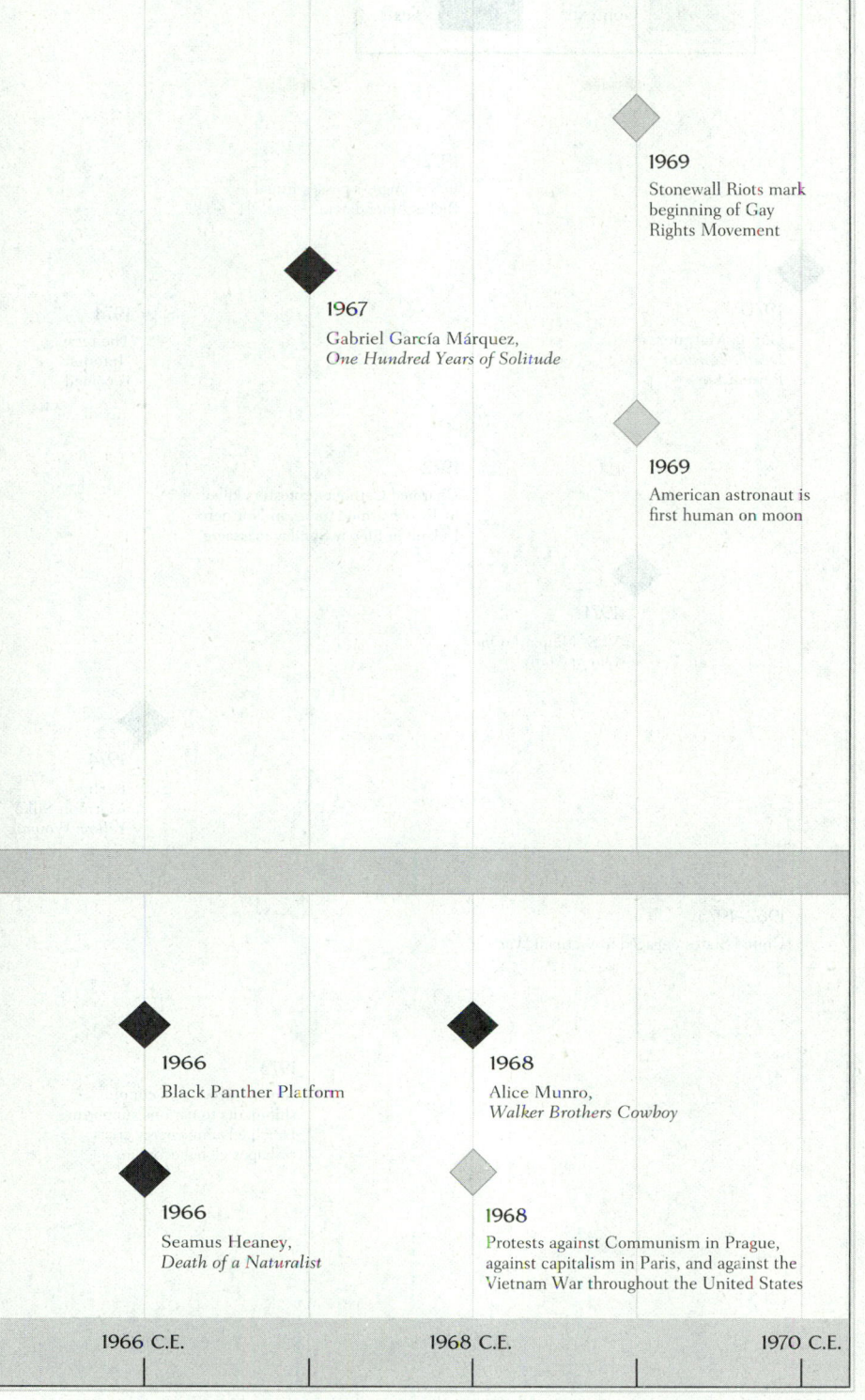

1969
Stonewall Riots mark beginning of Gay Rights Movement

1967
Gabriel García Márquez,
One Hundred Years of Solitude

1969
American astronaut is first human on moon

1966
Black Panther Platform

1968
Alice Munro,
Walker Brothers Cowboy

1966
Seamus Heaney,
Death of a Naturalist

1968
Protests against Communism in Prague, against capitalism in Paris, and against the Vietnam War throughout the United States

1966 C.E.   1968 C.E.   1970 C.E.

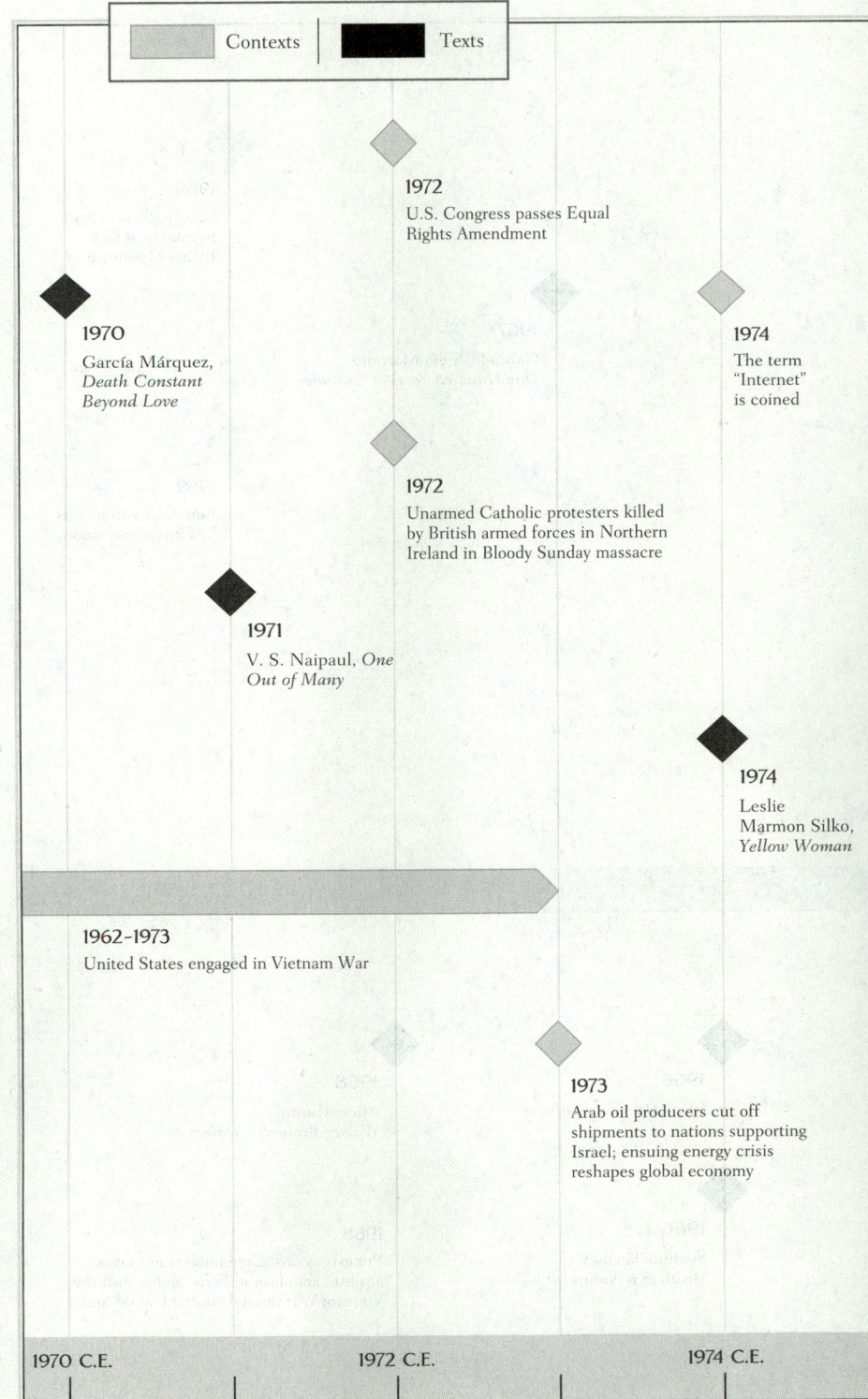

Contexts | Texts

1972
U.S. Congress passes Equal
Rights Amendment

1970
García Márquez,
*Death Constant
Beyond Love*

1974
The term
"Internet"
is coined

1972
Unarmed Catholic protesters killed
by British armed forces in Northern
Ireland in Bloody Sunday massacre

1971
V. S. Naipaul, *One
Out of Many*

1974
Leslie
Marmon Silko,
Yellow Woman

1962-1973
United States engaged in Vietnam War

1973
Arab oil producers cut off
shipments to nations supporting
Israel; ensuing energy crisis
reshapes global economy

1970 C.E.   1972 C.E.   1974 C.E.

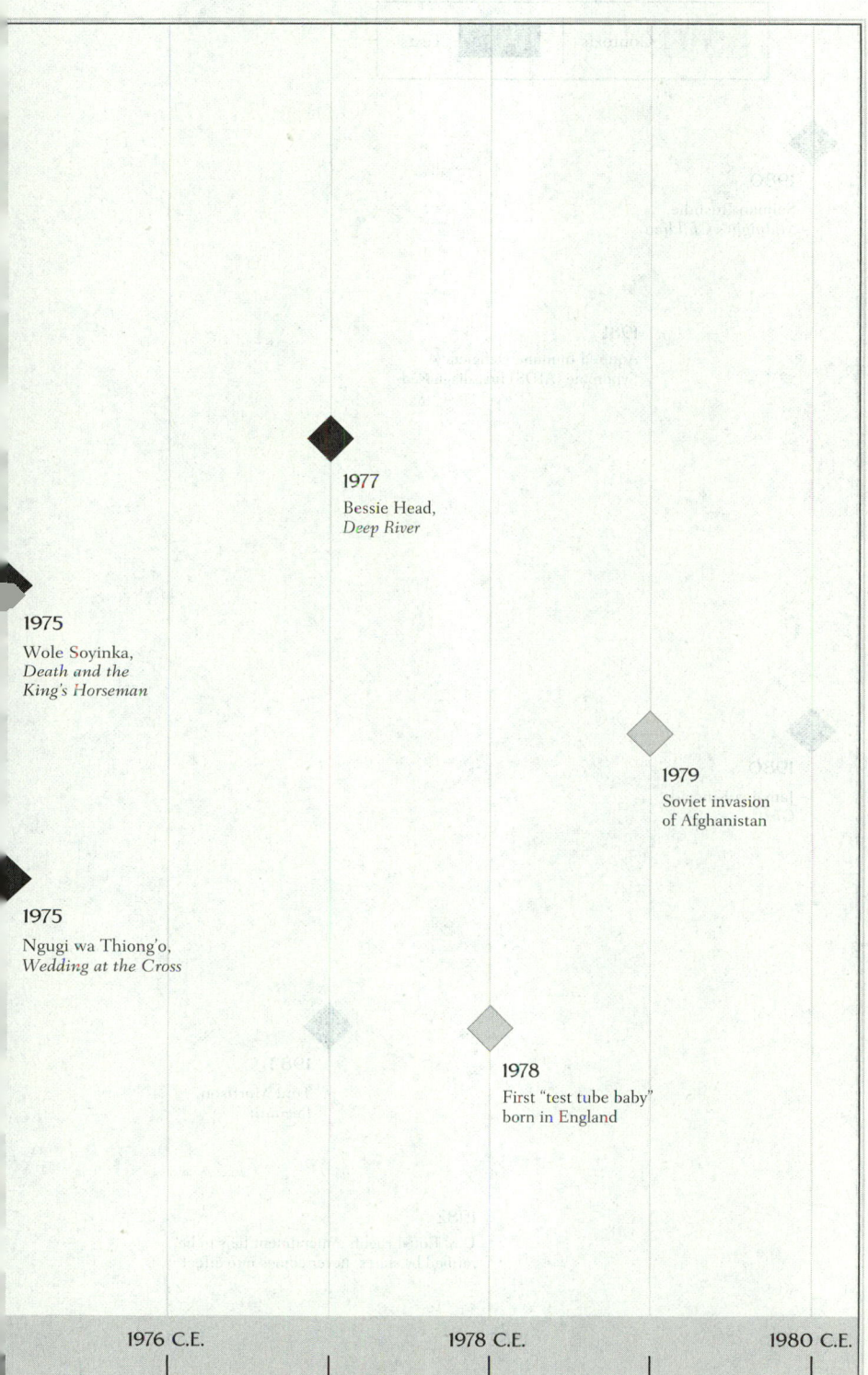

1977
Bessie Head,
Deep River

1975
Wole Soyinka,
*Death and the
King's Horseman*

1979
Soviet invasion
of Afghanistan

1975
Ngugi wa Thiong'o,
Wedding at the Cross

1978
First "test tube baby"
born in England

1976 C.E.   1978 C.E.   1980 C.E.

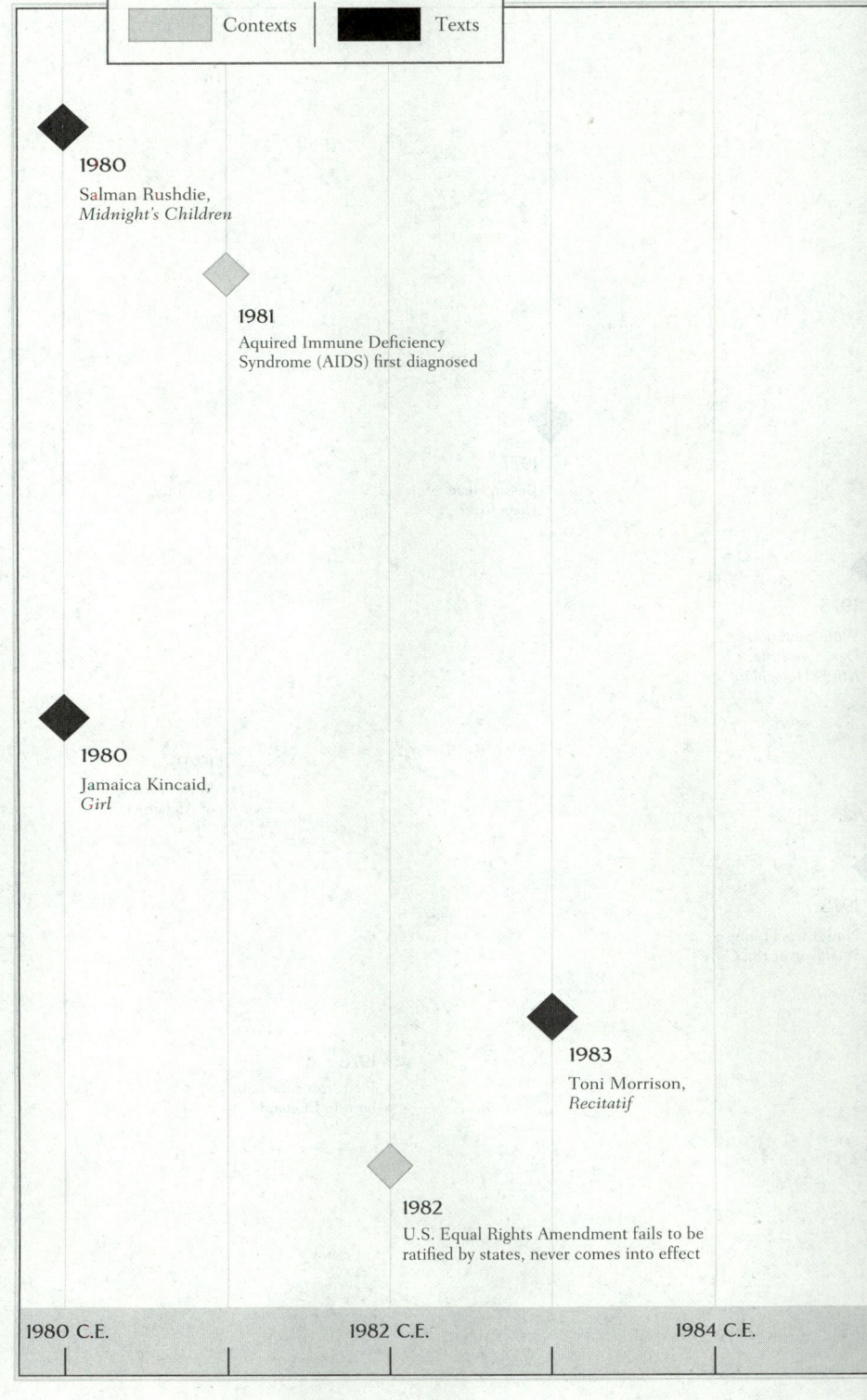

Contexts | Texts

1980
Salman Rushdie,
Midnight's Children

1981
Aquired Immune Deficiency
Syndrome (AIDS) first diagnosed

1980
Jamaica Kincaid,
Girl

1983
Toni Morrison,
Recitatif

1982
U.S. Equal Rights Amendment fails to be
ratified by states, never comes into effect

1980 C.E.   1982 C.E.   1984 C.E.

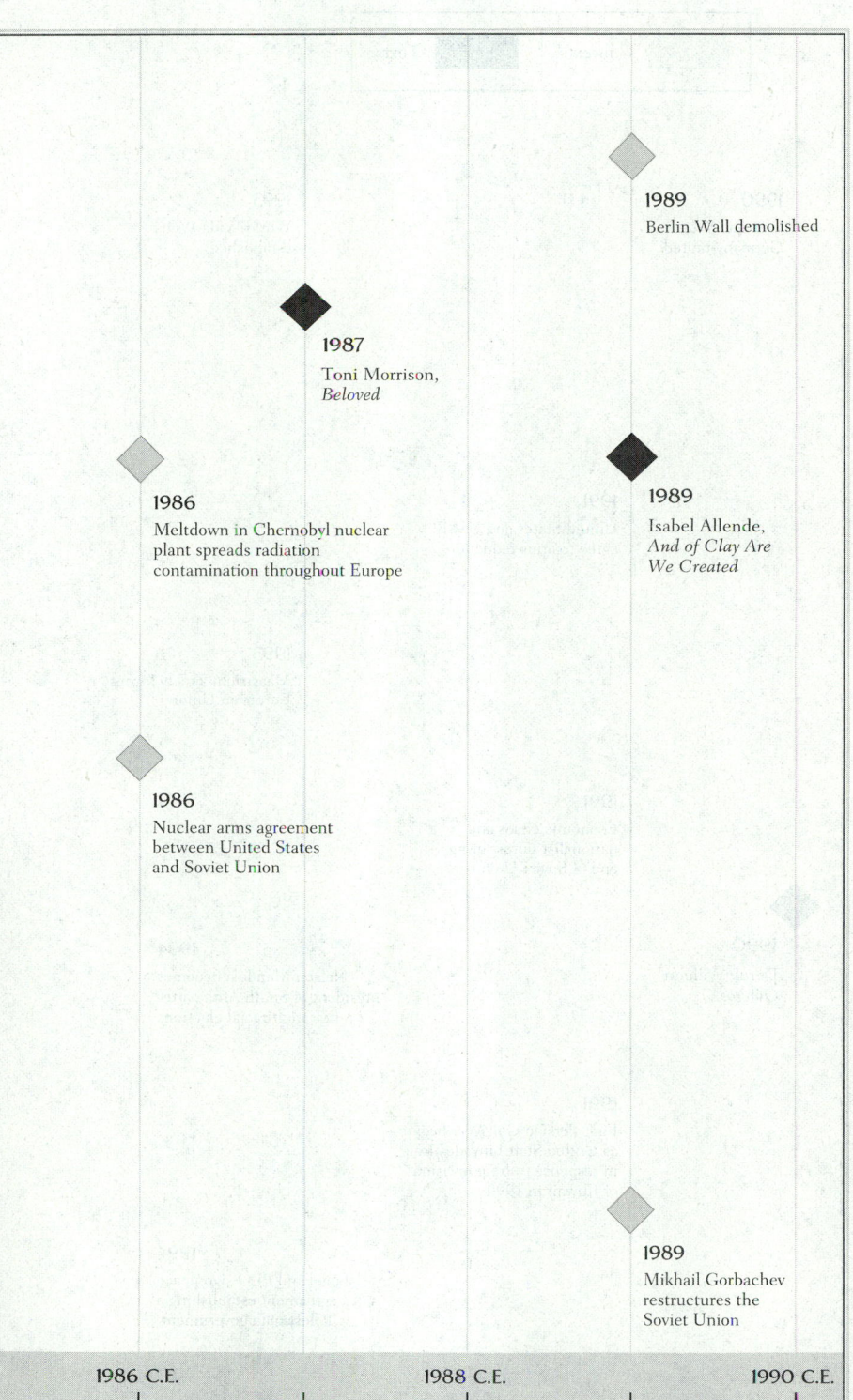

1989
Berlin Wall demolished

1987
Toni Morrison,
Beloved

1986
Meltdown in Chernobyl nuclear
plant spreads radiation
contamination throughout Europe

1989
Isabel Allende,
*And of Clay Are
We Created*

1986
Nuclear arms agreement
between United States
and Soviet Union

1989
Mikhail Gorbachev
restructures the
Soviet Union

1986 C.E.   1988 C.E.   1990 C.E.

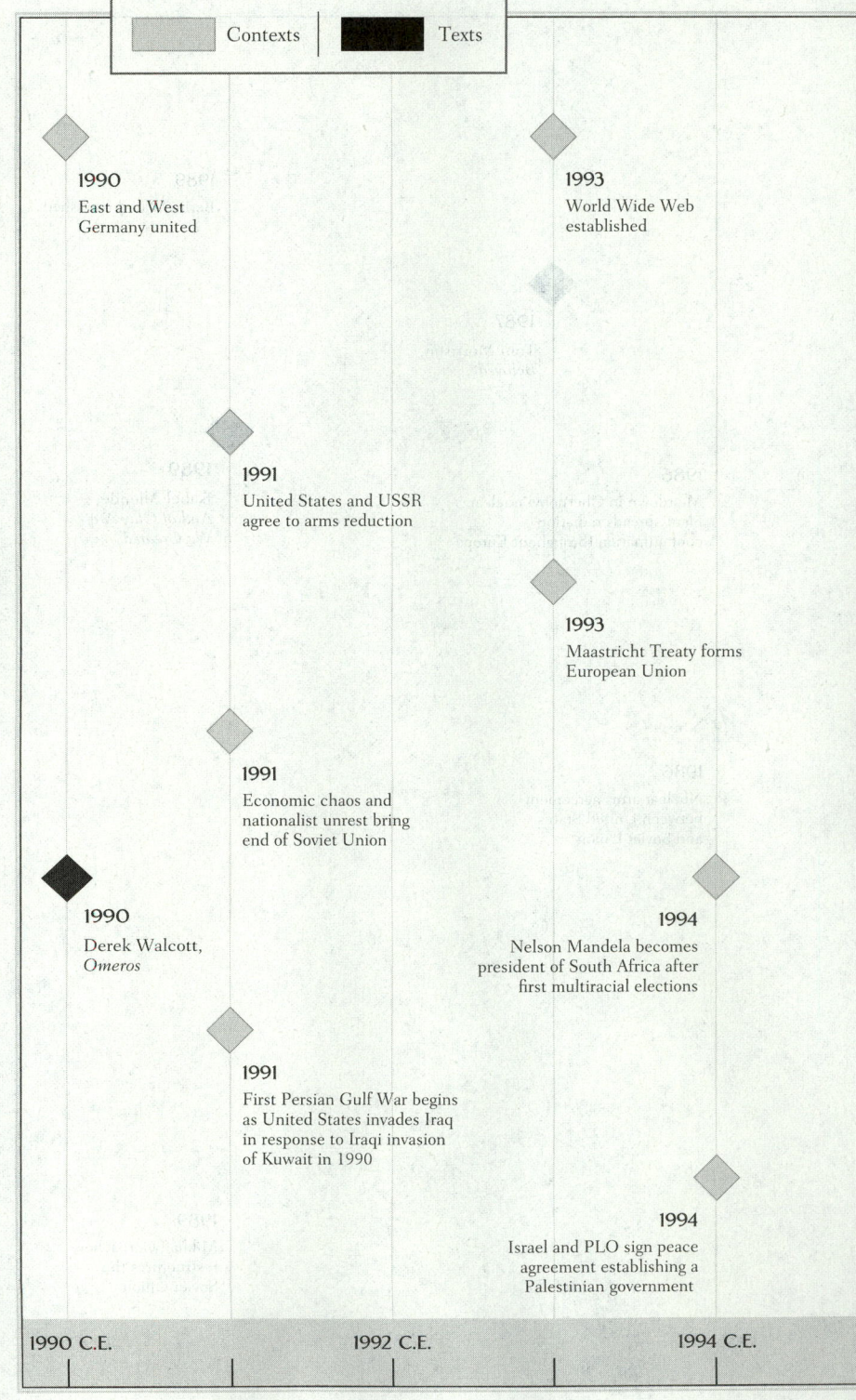

Contexts | Texts

1990
East and West
Germany united

1993
World Wide Web
established

1991
United States and USSR
agree to arms reduction

1993
Maastricht Treaty forms
European Union

1991
Economic chaos and
nationalist unrest bring
end of Soviet Union

1990
Derek Walcott,
Omeros

1994
Nelson Mandela becomes
president of South Africa after
first multiracial elections

1991
First Persian Gulf War begins
as United States invades Iraq
in response to Iraqi invasion
of Kuwait in 1990

1994
Israel and PLO sign peace
agreement establishing a
Palestinian government

1990 C.E.   1992 C.E.   1994 C.E.

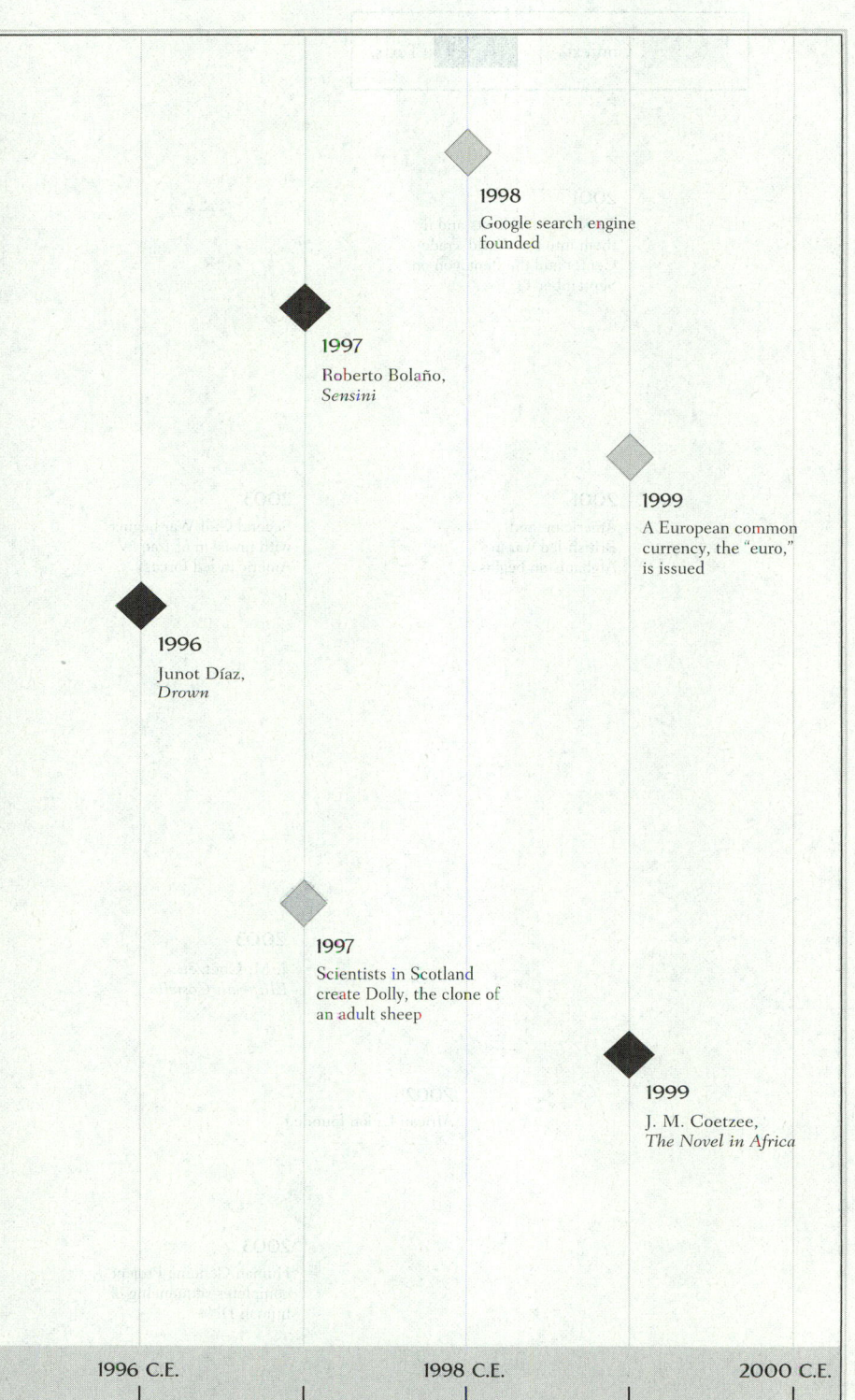

1998
Google search engine
founded

1997
Roberto Bolaño,
Sensini

1999
A European common
currency, the "euro,"
is issued

1996
Junot Díaz,
Drown

1997
Scientists in Scotland
create Dolly, the clone of
an adult sheep

1999
J. M. Coetzee,
The Novel in Africa

1996 C.E.   1998 C.E.   2000 C.E.

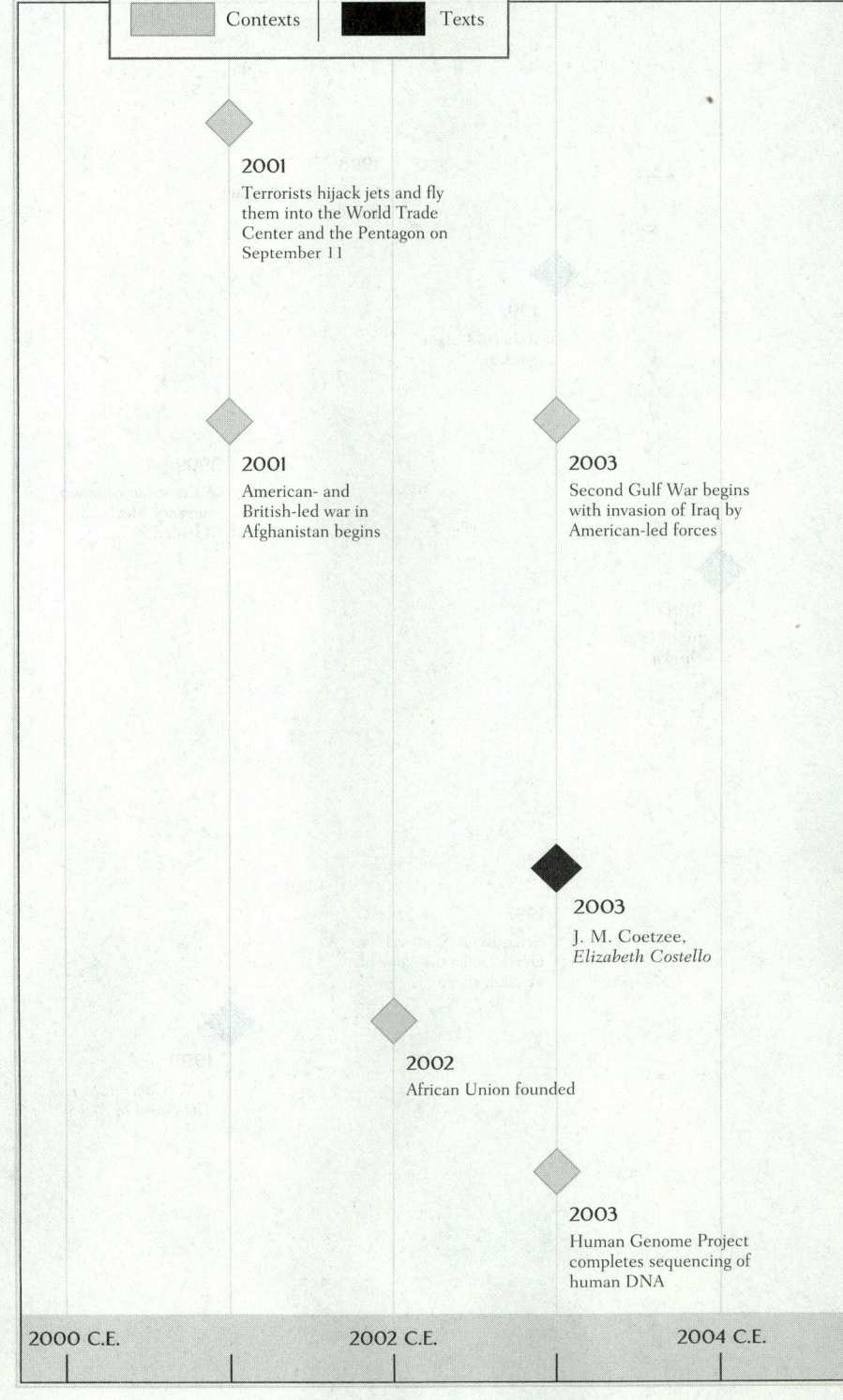

Contexts   Texts

2001
Terrorists hijack jets and fly
them into the World Trade
Center and the Pentagon on
September 11

2001
American- and
British-led war in
Afghanistan begins

2003
Second Gulf War begins
with invasion of Iraq by
American-led forces

2003
J. M. Coetzee,
Elizabeth Costello

2002
African Union founded

2003
Human Genome Project
completes sequencing of
human DNA

2000 C.E.   2002 C.E.   2004 C.E.

2008
Worldwide
financial
recession

2006 C.E.   2008 C.E.   2010 C.E.

Permissions Acknowledgments

Junot Díaz: "Drown" from DROWN, copyright © 1996 by Junot Díaz. Used by permission of Riverhead Books, an imprint of Penguin Group (USA) LLC.

Emily Dickinson: Reprinted by permission of the publishers and the Trustees of Amherst College from THE POEMS OF EMILY DICKINSON, Thomas H. Johnson, ed., Cambridge, Mass.: The Belknap Press of Harvard University Press. Copyright © 1951, 1955, 1979, 1983 by the President and Fellows of Harvard College.

Denis Diderot: From DENIS DIDEROT'S THE ENCYCLOPEDIA, SELECTIONS (1967), ed. and trans. by Stephen J. Gendzier. Reprinted by permission of the Stephen J. Gendzier.

Fyodor Dostoyevsky: NOTES FROM THE UNDERGROUND: A NORTON CRITICAL EDITION, trans. by Michael R. Katz. Copyright © 1989 by W. W. Norton & Company, Inc. Used by permission of W. W. Norton & Company, Inc.

T. S. Eliot: "The Love Song of J. Alfred Prufrock" and "The Waste Land" from COLLECTED POEMS 1909–1962. Reprinted by permission of Faber & Faber, Ltd. "Little Gidding" from FOUR QUARTETS by T. S. Eliot. Copyright © 1942 by Houghton Mifflin Harcourt Publishing Company; copyright renewed 1970 by T. S. Eliot. Reprinted by permission of Houghton Mifflin Harcourt Publishing Company, and Faber & Faber Ltd. All rights reserved.

Frantz Fanon: Excerpts from "On National Culture" from THE WRETCHED OF THE EARTH by Frantz Fanon. Copyright © 1963 by *Présence Africaine*. Used by permission of Grove/Atlantic, Inc. Any third party use of this material, outside of this publication, is prohibited.

William Faulkner: "Spotted Horses" and "Barn Burning" from THE COLLECTED SHORT STORIES OF WILLIAM FAULKNER. Copyright © 1950 by Random House, Inc. Copyright renewed 1977 by Jill Faulkner Summers. Reprinted by permission.

Gustave Flaubert: MADAME BOVARY, translated by Raymond N. MacKenzi. Copyright © 2009 Hackett Publishing Company, Inc. Reprinted by permission of Hackett Publishing Company, Inc. All rights reserved.

Carlos Fuentes: AURA, translated by Lysander Kemp. Copyright © 1965 by Carlos Fuentes. Reprinted by permission of Farrar, Straus and Giroux, LLC.

Federico García Lorca: Llanto por Ignacio Sanchez Mejias / Lament for Ignacio Sanchez Mejias copyright © Herederos de Federico García Lorca, from Obras Completas (Galaxia/Gutenberg, 1996 edition). English translation by Stephen Spender and J. L. Gili copyright © Stephen Spender, J. L. Gili and Herederos de Federico García Lorca. All rights reserved. For information regarding rights and permissions of all of Lorca's works in Spanish or in English, please contact lorca@artslaw.co.uk or William Peter Kosmas, Esq., 8 Franklin Square, London W14 9UU, England.

Gabriel García Márquez: "Death Beyond Constant Love" from INNOCENT ERENDIRA AND OTHER STORIES by Gabriel García Márquez, translated from the Spanish by Gregory Rabassa. English translation copyright © 1978 by Harper & Row, Publishers, Inc. Reprinted by permission of HarperCollins Publishers.

Guiseppi Garibaldi: "Memorandum," October 15, 1860, from PAGES FROM THE GARIBALDIAN EPIC translated by Anthony P. Campanella. We have made diligent efforts to contact the copyright holder to obtain permission to reprint this selection. If you have information that would help us, please write to W. W. Norton & Company, Inc., 500 Fifth Avenue, New York, NY 10110.

Johann Wolfgang von Goethe: From FAUST: A TRAGEDY, Part One, trans. by Martin Greenberg. Copyright © 1992 by Martin Greenberg. Revised by Martin Greenberg 2011. Used by permission of Yale University Press and the translator.

Jacob and Wilhelm Grimm: "The Three Spinners" from THE COMPLETE FAIRY TALES OF THE BROTHERS GRIMM, illustrated by Johnny Gruelle. Trans. by Jack Zipes, translation copyright © 1987 by Jack Zipes. Used by permission of Bantam Books, a division of Random House, Inc. Any third party use of this material, outside of this publication, is prohibited. Interested parties must apply directly to Random House, Inc. for permission.

Bessie Head: "The Deep River" from THE COLLECTOR OF TREASURES. Reproduced with permission of Johnson & Alcock Ltd. Copyright © 1977 by the Estate of Bessie Head.

Seamus Heaney: "Anahorish," "Broagh," "Digging," "The Haw Lantern," "Punishment," "The Guttural Muse," "The Strand at Lough Beg," and "The Tollund Man" from OPENED GROUND: SELECTED POEMS 1966–1996. Copyright © 1998 by Seamus Heaney. Reprinted by permission of Farrar, Straus and Giroux, LLC, and Faber & Faber Ltd.

Heinrich Heine: From THE COMPLETE POEMS OF HEINRICH HEINE, trans. by Hal Draper, reprinted by permission of Ernest Haberkern, director of the Center for Socialist History, Alameda CA. "To Tell the Truth," trans. by T. J. Reed and David Cram from HEINRICH HEINE (1997) is reprinted by permission of J. M. Dent, a division of the Orion Publishing Group, London.

Friedrich Hölderlin: Poems from SELECTED POEMS: FRIEDRICH HOLDERLIN [and] EDUARD MORIKE, trans. by Christopher Middleton. Copyright © 1972. Reprinted by permission of the University of Chicago Press.

Victor Hugo: From LES MISÉRABLES by Victor Hugo, translated by Julie Rose. Copyright © 2008 by Random House, Inc. Used by permission of Modern Library, a division of Random House, Inc. Any third party use of this material, outside of this publication, is prohibited. Interested parties must apply directly to Random House, Inc. for permission.

Vicente Huidobro: "Creationism" from MANIFESTOS MANIFEST, trans. from the French by Gilbert Alter-Gilbert. Copyright © 1925 by Vicente Huidobro. English translation copyright © 1999 by Gilbert Alter-Gilbert. Reprinted with the permission of the Permissions Company, Inc., on behalf of Green Integer Books, www.greeninteger.com.

Henrik Ibsen: *Hedda Gabler* from FOUR MAJOR PLAYS, Vol. 1, by Henrik Ibsen, trans. by Rick Davis and Brian Johnston. Copyright © 1995 by Rick Davis and Brian Johnston. Reprinted by permission of Smith and Kraus Publishers, Inc.

Franz Kafka: *Metamorphosis* from METAMORPHOSIS AND OTHER STORIES, trans. by Michael Hofmann, copyright © 2007 by Michael Hofmann. Used by permission of Penguin, a division of Penguin Group (USA), LLC.

Immanuel Kant: "What Is Enlightenment," trans. Lewis White Beck, rev. edition, 1990, FOUNDATIONS OF THE METAPHYSICS OF MORALS AND WHAT IS ENLIGHTENMENT, copyright © 1990. Reprinted by permission of Pearson Education, Inc., Upper Saddle River, NJ.

Jamaica Kincaid: "Girl" from AT THE BOTTOM OF THE RIVER. Copyright © 1983 by Jamaica Kincaid. Reprinted by permission of Farrar, Straus and Giroux, LLC.

Jean de La Fontaine: From LA FONTAINE: SELECTED FABLES translated by James Michie, introduction by Geoffrey Grigson. Translation copyright © 1979 James Michie. Introduction copyright © 1979 Geoffrey Grigson. "The Two Pigeons" from THE BEST OF LA FONTAINE, translated by Francis Duke. Copyright © 1965 by the Rector and Visitors of the University of Virginia. Reprinted by permission of the University of Virginia Press.

Giacomo Leopardi: Poems from A LEOPARDI READER, trans. and ed. by Ottavio M. Casale. Copyright © 1981 by the Board of Trustees of the University of Illinois. Used by permission of the Estate of Giacomo Leopardi.

Doris Lessing: "The Old Chief Mshlanga" from AFRICAN STORIES by Doris Lessing is reprinted by permission of Simon & Schuster, Inc., and Jonathan Clowes Ltd. Copyright © 1951, 1953, 1954, 1957, 1958, 1962, 1963, 1964, 1965, 1966, 1972, 1981 by Doris Lessing. All rights reserved.

Clarice Lispector: "The Daydreams of a Drunk Woman" from FAMILY TIES by Clarice Lispector, trans. by Giovanni Pontiero. Copyright © 1972. By permission of the University of Texas Press.

Stephane Mallarmé: From COLLECTED POEMS: A BILINGUAL EDITION, ed. and trans. by Henry Weinfield. Copyright © 2011 by The Regents of the University of California. Reprinted by permission of the University of California Press.

Thomas Mann: From DEATH IN VENICE: A NORTON CRITICAL EDITION, trans. by Clayton Koelb. Copyright © 1994 by W. W. Norton & Company, Inc. Used by permission of W. W. Norton & Company, Inc.

F. T. Marinetti: "Foundation and Manifesto of Futurism" from CRITICAL WRITINGS by F. T. Marinetti, edited by Günter Berghaus, translated by Doug Thompson. Copyright © 2006 by Luce Marinetti, Vittoria Marinetti Piazzoni, and Ala Marinetti Clerici. Translation, compilation, editorial work, foreword, preface, and introduction copyright © 2006 by Farrar, Straus, and Giroux, LLC. Reprinted by permission of Farrar, Straus, and Giroux, LLC.

José Martí: "Guantanamera," translated by Aviva Chomsky from THE CUBA READER, edited by Aviva Chomsky, Barry Carr, and Pamela Maria Smorkaloff, pp. 128–129. Copyright © 2003 by Duke University Press. All rights reserved. Republished by permission of the copyright holder. www.dukeupress.edu.

Molière: *Tartuffe,* trans. by Constance Congdon. Copyright © 2008 by Constance Congdon, from TARTUFFE: A NORTON CRITICAL EDITION, ed. by Constance Congdon and Virginia Scott. Used by permission of Constance Congdon.

Toni Morrison: "Recitatif," copyright © 1983 by Toni Morrison. Reprinted by permission of International Creative Management, Inc.

Alice Munro: "Walker Brothers Cowboy" from DANCE OF THE HAPPY SHADES. Originally published by McGraw-Hill Ryerson Ltd. Copyright © 1968 by Alice Munro. Reprinted by permission of William Morris Endeavor Entertainment, LLC.

Vladimir Nabokov: "The Vane Sisters" from THE STORIES OF VLADIMIR NABOKOV by Vladimir Nabokov, copyright © 1995 by Dmitri Nabokov. Used by permission of Alfred A. Knopf, a division of Random House, Inc. Any third party use of this material, outside of this publication, is prohibited. Interested parties must apply directly to Random House, Inc. for permission.

V. S. Naipaul: "One Out of Many" from IN A FREE STATE by V. S. Naipaul, copyright © 1971 by V. S. Naipaul. Used by permission of Alfred A. Knopf, a division of Random House, Inc., and Knopf Canada. Copyright © 2002 V. S. Naipaul. Any third party use of this material, outside of this publication, is prohibited. Interested parties must apply directly to Random House, Inc. for permission.

Pablo Neruda: From "General Song (Canto General)" from Canto II. "The Heights of Macchu Picchu," vi, vii, viii, ix, x, xi, xii from CANTO GENERAL: FIFTH ANNIVERSARY EDITION by Pablo Neruda, trans. by Jack Schmitt. Copyright © 1991 by the Fundacion Pablo Neruda and the Regents of the University of California. Reprinted by permission of the University of California Press. "Tonight I Can Write" and "Walking Around," trans. by W. S. Merwin, "I'm Explaining a Few Things" and "Ode to the Tomato," trans. by Nathaniel Tarn, from SELECTED POEMS, ed.

IMAGES

COLOR INSERT

Index